AN INTERMEDIATE

GREEK-ENGLISH LEXICON

FOUNDED UPON

THE SEVENTH EDITION OF

LIDDELL AND SCOTT'S

GREEK-ENGLISH LEXICON

Oxford

AT THE CLARENDON PRESS

OXFORD
UNIVERSITY PRESS

Great Clarendon Street, Oxford OX2 6DP

Oxford University Press is a department of the University of Oxford.
It furthers the University's objective of excellence in research, scholarship,
and education by publishing worldwide in

Oxford New York

Auckland Cape Town Dar es Salaam Hong Kong Karachi
Kuala Lumpur Madrid Melbourne Mexico City Nairobi
New Delhi Shanghai Taipei Toronto

With offices in

Argentina Austria Brazil Chile Czech Republic France Greece
Guatemala Hungary Italy Japan South Korea Poland Portugal
Singapore Switzerland Thailand Turkey Ukraine Vietnam

Oxford is a registered trade mark of Oxford University Press
in the UK and in certain other countries

ISBN: 978 0 19 910206 8

33
First edition 1889

Printed in India
by Gopsons Papers Ltd.

Paper used in the production of this book is a natural, recyclable product made
from wood grown in sustainable forests. The manufacturing process conforms to
the environmental regulations of the country of origin.

PREFACE.

THIS Abridgement of the Oxford Greek Lexicon has been undertaken in compliance with wishes expressed by several experienced School Masters. It is an entirely new work, and it is hoped that it will meet their requirements.

It differs from the old Abridgement, in that

1st. It is made from the last Edition (1883) of the large Lexicon.

2ndly. The matter contained in it is greatly increased. This increase has been caused by giving fuller explanations of the words, by inserting the irregular forms of Moods and Tenses more fully, by citing the leading Authorities for the different usages, and adding characteristic phrases.

With regard to the citation of Authors' names, it has been endeavoured to give the earliest authority for each usage. When the word or meaning continued in general use, an 'etc.' is added to the first authority or authorities. When the original usage seems to be continued only exceptionally, the names of the exceptional authorities have been added.

Generally speaking, words used only by late writers and scientific terms have been omitted. But from Homer downwards, to the close of Classical Attic Greek, care has been taken to insert all words. Besides these, will be found words used by Aristotle in his moral and political treatises, by Polybius and Strabo in the books generally read by students, by Plutarch in his Lives, by Lucian, by the Poets of the Anthology, and by the writers of the New Testament.

With regard to Etymology, when the word represents the Root or Primitive Form with a termination easily separable, it is printed in Capital letters, as ΓΕΜΩ, ΚΡΑΤΟΣ; when the Root and termination are not so distinctly separable, the assumed Root is added, as τύπτω (Root ΤΥΠ).

In Derived words, reference is made to the Verb or other word under which the Root is given, as νιφό-βολος (βάλλω); except that in cases where the Root can only be found in the aor. 2 or some other tense of a Defective Verb, this form and not the Verb is given, as δρόμος (δραμεῖν), ὄψις (ὄψομαι).

In Compound words, the parts of which they are made up has been marked by placing a hyphen between them, as ἀπο-βάλλω, ἀφ-ίημι, ἄ-βατος. When either part of the compound remains unaltered or only slightly altered, no reference to the simple forms has been thought necessary. And words derived from a compound already divided are left undivided, as φιλοσοφέω from φιλό-σοφος.

The Quantity of doubtful syllables is marked: when a doubtful vowel precedes another vowel, it is to be understood that the former is short, unless it is marked long.

H. G. LIDDELL.

CH. CH., OXFORD, *Oct.* 27, 1888.

= means *equal* or *equivalent to*
absol. = absolute, absolutely
acc. = accusative : acc. to = according to
Act. = Active voice
act. = active signification
Adj. = Adjective
Adv. = Adverb
Aeol. = Aeolic, in the Aeolic dialect
Aesch. = Aeschylus
Aeschin. = Aeschines
Anth. = Anthology
aor. = aorist tense
Ar. = Aristophanes
Arist. = Aristotle
Att. = Attic, in Attic Greek
Babr. = Babrius
c. = cum
c. acc. cognato = with cognate accusative, i. e. when
    the Subst. has the same or a similar signification with
    the Verb
c. gen. partit. = cum genitivo partitivo
c. gen. pers. = cum genitivo personae
cf. = confer, compare
collat. = collateral
Com. = Comic, in Comic Poets
Compar. or Comp. = Comparative
Conjunct. = Conjunction
contr. = contracted, contraction
dat. = dative
Dem. = Demosthenes
Dep. = Deponent Verb, i. e. a Verb of Middle or Passive
    form with Active sense
deriv. = derived, derivation
disyll. = disyllable
Dor. = in Doric Greek
Ep. = in Epic Greek
esp. = especially
etc. = et cetera
Eur. = Euripides
f. or fut. = future tense
fem. = feminine
fin. = finem or fine
freq. = frequent, frequently
gen. or genit. = genitive
Hdt. = Herodotus
Hes. = Hesiod
Hom. = Homer
imperat. or imper. = imperative mood
imperf. or impf. = imperfect tense
impers. = impersonal
ind. or indic. = indicative mood
inf. = infinitive mood
intr. or intrans. = intransitive
Ion. = Ionic, in the Ionic dialect
irreg. = irregular
Isocr. = Isocrates
Lat. = Latin

lengthd. = lengthened
Luc. = Lucian
Lys. = Lysias
masc. = masculine
Med., med. = medium, middle voice
metaph. = metaphorically
metri grat. = metri gratia
Mosch. = Moschus
n. pr. = nomen proprium
N. T. = New Testament
negat. = negativum
neut. = neuter
nom. = nominative
oft. = often
opp. to = opposed to
opt. or optat. = optative mood
orig. = originally
part. = participle
Pass. = Passive voice
pass. = passive signification
pecul. = peculiar
perf. or pf. = perfect tense
Pind. = Pindar
pl. or plur. = plural
Plat. = Plato
plqpf. = plusquamperfectum
Plut. = Plutarch
poët. = poetically
Polyb. = Polybius
Prep. = Preposition
pres. = present tense
q. v. = quod vide
qq. v. = quae vide
radic. = radical
regul. = regular, regularly
shortd. = shortened
signf. = signification
sing. = singular
Soph. = Sophocles
sq. = sequens
Strab. = Strabo
sub. = subaudi, subaudito
subj. = subjunctive mood
Subst. = Substantive
syll. = syllable
Theogn. = Theognis
Theophr. = Theophrastus
Thuc. = Thucydides
Trag. = Tragic, in Tragic Greek
trans. = transitive
trisyll. = trisyllable
usu. = usually
v. = vide
verb. Adj. = verbal Adjective
voc. = voce, vocem
vocat. = vocative
Xen. = Xenophon.

A.

Α, α, ἄλφα, τό, indecl., first letter of the Gr. alphabet : as Numeral, α' = εἷς and πρῶτος, but ͵α = 1000.

Changes of ᾰ: 1. Aeol., ᾰ for ε, ἄλλοτα for ἄλλοτε :—for ο, εἴκατι for εἴκοσι :—reversely ο for α, v. sub ο. 2. Dor., ᾰ for ε, ἄλλοκα for -τε :—in the body of words, ἱαρός for ἱερός. 3. Ion., ᾰ for ε, μέγαθος for μέγεθος :—reversely ε for ᾰ, v. sub ε. b. ᾰ becomes η in the num. forms, διπλήσιος, πολλαπλήσιος for διπλάσιος, πολλαπλάσιος. c. in some words, ᾰ represents η, as μεσαμβρίη for μεσημβρία, ἀμφισ-βᾰτέω for ἀμφισ-βητέω. d. ᾰ for ο, as ἀρρωδέω for ὀρρωδέω. II. changes of ᾱ: 1. η Ion. becomes ᾱ Aeol. and Dor. in the 1st decl., as πύλα, 'Ατρείδας for πύλη, 'Ατρείδης : also when α is the vowel of the root, as θνάσκω for θνήσκω (ΘΑΝ); but η for ε or ει is often retained in Aeol. and Dor., as ἠρχόμαν (ἔρχομαι), but ἀρχόμαν (ἄρχομαι). b. reversely, in Dor., αε and αι in inflexions of Verbs in άω are contr. into η, as ἐνίκη for -ᾱ, ὁρῆς for -ᾱς :—so in crasis, τῆμά for τὰ ἐμά, κἠγών for καὶ ἐγών. c. in Dor., αο and αω are contracted not into ω, but into ᾱ, v. Ω ω. 2. in Ion., η for ᾱ is characteristic, as in 1st decl., σοφίη, -ην, 'Αρισταγόρης, -ην : if the nom. ends in ᾰ, the change only takes place in gen. and dat. ἀλήθειᾰ, -ης, -η, -αν.

ἀ-, insep. Prefix in compos. : I. alpha privativum, expressing want or absence, like Lat. in-, Engl. un-, σοφός wise, ἄ-σοφος unwise : v. ἀν-. This α rarely precedes a vowel, as in ἀ-ατος, ἀ-ηθής : more often before the spir. asper, as ἀ-ήσσητος, ἀ-όρατος, ἀ-όριστος : sometimes α coalesces with the foll. vowel, as ἄκων (ἀ-έκων), ἀργός (ἀεργός) : before a vowel ἀν- is more common. Regularly, it is only compounded with nouns ; for exceptions, v. ἀβουλέω, ἀνήδομαι, ἀτίζω. II. alpha copulativum, expressing union, likeness, properly with spir. asper, as in ἄ-θροος, ἅ-πας, but with spir. lenis, ἄ-κοιτις, ἄ-λοχος, ἀ-δελφός, ἀ-τάλαντος, ἀ-κόλουθος. It is prob. akin to the Adv. ἅμα. III. alpha intensivum, said to answer to the Adv. ἄγαν, very. The existence of this α is doubtful : some words referred to it belong to α privativum, as ἀ-δάκρυτος, ἀ-θέσφατος, ἄ-ξυλος (v. sub vocc.) ; in others, as ἄ-σκιος, ἀ-τενής, ἀ-σπερχές, ἀ-σκελές, the α may be a copulativum. IV. α euphonicum, as ἀ-βληχρός, ἀ-σπαίρω, ἀ-σταφίς, ἀ-στεροπή for βληχρός, σπαίρω, σταφίς, στεροπή. [ᾰ in all these cases, except by position. But Adjs. which begin with three short syllables have ᾱ in dactylic metres, as ἀ-δάματος, ἀ-θέμιτος, ἀ-κάματος, ἀ-πάλαμος : one Adj. ἀ-θάνατος, with its derivs., has ᾰ in all metres.]

ἆ, exclamation, like Lat. and Engl. ah ! ἆ δειλέ, ἆ δειλώ, ἆ δειλοί, Hom. ; doubled, ἆ ἆ Aesch.

ἁ ἁ or ἇ ἇ, to express laughter, ha, ha, Eur., Ar.

ἁ, Dor. for Artic. ἡ. II. ἅ, Dor. for relat. Pron. ἥ. III. ᾇ, Dor. for ᾗ, dat. of ὅς.

ἀ-άατος, ον, in Il. with penult. long, (α privat., ἀάω) not to be injured, inviolable, νῦν μοι ὄμοσσον ἀάᾰτον Στυγὸς ὕδωρ, because the gods swore their most binding oaths thereby. II. ἀάᾰτος, ον, in Od. with penult. short, (α copulat., ἀάω) hurtful, perilous, aweful ; ἄεθλος ἀάᾰτος.

ἀ-ᾱγής, ές, (ἄγνυμι) unbroken, not to be broken, hard, strong, Od., Theocr.

ἄ-απτος, ον, (ἅπτομαι) not to be touched, resistless, invincible, χεῖρες ἄαπτοι Hom., Hes.

ἄασα, contr. ἆσα, aor. I of ἀάω : med. ἀᾱσάμην, ἀσάμην : pass. ἀάσθην.

ἀάσπετος, ἀάσχετος, v. ἄσπετος, ἄσχετος.

ἄᾱται, Ep. med. from ἄω (c). II. ἀᾶται, from ἀάω.

ἄ-ᾱτος, contr. ἆτος, ον, (ἄω c) insatiate, c. gen., Ἄρης ἆτος πολέμοιο Il.

ἀάω (Root ΑϜ, cf. ἄτη, αὐ-άτα), used by Hom. in aor. I act. ἄασα contr. ἆσα, med. ἀᾱσάμην contr. ἀσάμην, pass. ἀάσθην : pres. only in 3 sing. of Med. ἀᾶται :—properly to hurt, damage ; then to mislead, infatuate, of the effects of wine, sleep, divine judgments, Od. :—so in Med., Ἄτη ἣ πάντας ἀᾶται Il. II. aor. I med. and pass., to act recklessly or foolishly, ἀασάμην I was infatuated Il. ; μέγ' ἀάσθη Ib. [The quantities vary : ἄᾱσεν, ἄᾱσαν, part. ἀάσας : ἀάσάμην, ἀάσατο : ἀάσθην, ἀασθη.]

ἄβα, ἡ, Dor. for ἥβη.

ἀβακέω, f. ήσω, to be speechless, Ep. Verb only used in aor. I, οἱ δ' ἀβάκησαν πάντες Od. From

ἀ-βακής, ές, (βάζω) speechless, infantine, Sappho.

ἀ-βάκχευτος, ον, (Βακχεύω) uninitiated in the Bacchic orgies, generally, joyless, Eur.

ἄ-βᾰλε [ᾰβ], properly ἆ βάλε, expressing a wish, O that . . ! Lat. utinam, c. inf., Anth.

ἀ-βᾰρής, ές, (βάρος) without weight : not burdensome, of persons, N. T.

ἀ-βᾰσάνιστος, ον, (βασανίζω) not examined by torture, untortured ; of things, unexamined, Plut. :—Adv. -τως, without examination, Thuc.

ἀ-βᾰσίλευτος, ον, (βασιλεύω) not ruled by a king, Thuc., Xen.

ἀ-βάσκαντος, ον, (βασκαίνω) not subject to enchantment :—Adv. -τως, Anth.

ἀ-βάστακτος, ον, (βαστάζω) not to be carried, Plut.

ἄ-βᾰτος, ον, also η, ον, (βαίνω) untrodden, impassable, inaccessible, of mountains, Hdt., Soph., etc.: of a river, not fordable, Xen. 2. of holy places, not to be trodden, like ἄθικτος, Soph. : metaph. pure, chaste, ψυχή Plat. 3. of horses, not ridden, Luc. II.

act., ἄβ. πόνος a plague *that hinders walking*, i.e. gout, Luc.

'Αββᾶ, Hebr. word, *father*, N. T.

'Αβδηρίτης [ῐ], ου, ὁ, *a man of Abdera* in Thrace, proverb. of simpletons, Dem. :—Adj. **'Αβδηριτικός**, ή, όν, *like an Abderite*, i. e. *stupid*, Luc.

ἀ-βέβαιος, ον, *uncertain, unsteady; τὸ ἀβέβαιον = ἀβ?- βαιότης*, Luc.   **2.** *of persons, unstable*, Dem., etc.

ἀ-βέβηλος, ον, *not profane, inviolable*, Plut.

ἀβελτερία, ή, *silliness, stupidity, fatuity*, Plat.   From

ἀ-βέλτερος, α, ον, *good for nothing, silly, stupid, fatuous*, Ar., etc. ;—Sup. *-ώτατος*, Id.

ἀ-βίαστος, ον, (βιάζω) *unforced, without violence*, Plat.

ἄ-βιος, ον, = ἀβίωτος, Anth.   **II.** *without a living, starving*, Luc.   **III.** *of the* Ἱππημολγοί, *simple in life*, Il.

ἀ-βίοτος, ον, = ἀβίωτος, Eur.

ἀ-βίωτος, ον, *not to be lived, insupportable, ἀβ. πεποίηκε τὸν βίον* Ar.; *ἀβίωτον χρόνον βιοτεῦσαι* Eur. ; *ἀβίωτόν [ἐστι] life is intolerable*, Eur., Plat. :—Adv., *ἀβιώτως ἔχειν* to find *life intolerable*, Plut.

ἀβλάβεια, ή, *freedom from harm*, Plut.   **II.** act. *harmlessness*, Lat. *innocentia*, Cic.   From

ἀ-βλαβής, ές, (βλάβη) *without harm*, i. e.,   **I.** pass. *unharmed, unhurt, secure*, Aesch., etc.   **II.** act. *not harming, harmless, innocent*, Aesch., Plat.   **2.** *averting* or *preventing harm*, Theocr.   **3.** Adv. in Att. formularies, *ἀβλαβῶς σπονδαῖς ἐμμένειν without doing harm*, Thuc.; so the σπονδαί themselves are entitled *ἄδολοι καὶ ἀβλαβεῖς*, Id.

ἀβλαβία, ή, Ep. for ἀβλάβεια, h. Hom.

ἀ-βλέφαρος, ον, (βλέφαρον) *without eye-lids*, Anth.

ἀ-βλής, ῆτος, ὁ, ή, (βάλλω) *not thrown* or *shot, ἰὸν ἀβλῆτα an arrow not yet used*, Il.

ἄ-βλητος, ον, *not hit* by darts, Il.

ἀ-βληχής, ές, (βληχή) *without bleatings*, Anth.

ἀβληχρός, ά, όν, (α euphon., βληχρός) *weak, feeble*, Il.; *ἀβλ. θάνατος an easy death* in ripe old age, opp. to a *violent one*, Od.

ἀβληχρώδης, ες, = ἀβληχρός, *of sheep*, Babr.

ἀβοᾱτί, -ατος, Dor. for ἀβοητί, -ητος.

ἀ-βοήθητος, ον, (βοηθέω) *helpless*, Plut.

ἀ-βόητος, Dor. *-ᾱτος*, ον, (βοάω) *not loudly lamented*, Anth. :—Adv. *ἀβοᾱτί, without summons*, Pind.

ἀβός, Dor. for ἡβός.

ἀ-βόσκητος, ον, (βόσκω) *ungrazed, ὄρη* Babr.

ἀ-βουκόλητος, ον, (βουκολέω) *untended by herdsmen*: metaph. *unheeded*, Aesch.

ἀβουλέω, (α privat., βούλομαι) *to be unwilling*, Plat. (ἀβουλέω is an exception to the rule that a privat. cannot be comp. directly with Verbs ; v. ἀ-. 1.)

ἀβουλία, ή, *want of counsel, thoughtlessness*, Hdt., Soph., etc.   From

ἄ-βουλος, ον, (βουλή) *inconsiderate, ill-advised*, Soph., etc. ; *τέκνοισι ἄβουλος taking no thought for them*, Id.: Comp. *-ότερος*, Thuc. :—Adv. *-ως, inconsiderately*, Hdt. ; Sup. *ἀβουλότατα*, Id.

ἀ-βούτης, ου, ὁ, (βοῦς) *without oxen*, i. e. *poor*, Hes.

ἀ-βρῑθής, ές, (βρῖθος) *of no weight*, Eur.

ἀβρο-βάτης [ᾰ], ου, ὁ, (βαίνω) *softly* or *delicately stepping*, Aesch.

ἀβρό-βιος, ον, *living delicately, effeminate*, Plut.

ἀβρό-γοος, ον, *wailing womanishly*, Aesch.

ἀβρο-δίαιτος, ον, (δίαιτα) *living delicately*, Aesch. ; *τὸ ἀβροδίαιτον effeminacy*, Thuc.

ἀβρο-κόμης, ου, ὁ, (κόμη) *with delicate* or *luxuriant leaves, φοῖνιξ* Eur.

ἀ-βρόμιος, ον, (Βρόμιος) *without Bacchus*, Anth.

ἄ-βρομος, ον, either,   **1.** (α copul., βρέμω) *very noisy, boisterous*, or,   **2.** (α priv.) *noiseless*:—epith. of the Trojans in Il., v. αὐίαχος.

ἀβρο-πέδιλος, ον, (πέδιλον) *with soft sandals*, Anth.

ἀβρό-πηνος, ον, (πήνη) *of delicate texture*, Aesch.

ἀβρό-πλουτος, ον, *richly luxuriant*, Eur.

ἀβρός [ᾰ by nature], ά, όν, and ός, όν, (perh. from same root as ἥβη):—*delicate, graceful, beauteous, pretty*, Anacr., etc.: of things, *splendid*, Pind.—Very early the word took the notion of *over-delicate, dainty, luxurious*; hence neut. as Adv. *ἀβρὰ παθεῖν* to live *delicately*, Solon; *ἀβρὰ παρηῖδος = ἀβρὰν παρηῖδα*, Eur.; *ἀβρῶς* and *ἀβρὸν βαίνειν* to step *delicately*, Id.

ἀβροσύνη, ή, = ἀβρότης, Sappho, Eur.

ἀβροτάζω, *to miss*, c. gen., only in aor. 1 subj., *μήπως ἀβροτάξομεν* (Ep. for *-ωμεν*) *ἀλλήλοιϊν that we may not miss one another*, Il.   (From same Root with ἀμ-βροτ-εῖν, ἁμαρτ-εῖν, μ being rejected.)

ἀβρότης, ητος, ή, (ἀβρός) *delicacy, luxury*, Pind. ; *οὐκ ἐν ἀβρότητι κεῖσαι* thou art not in a position *to be fastidious*, Eur.

ἀβρό-τῑμος, ον, (τιμή) *delicate and costly*, Aesch.

ἄ-βροτος, ον and η, ον, *immortal, divine, holy, νὺξ ἀβρότη*, either *holy* Night, as a divinity, (like ἱερὸν κνέφας, ἱερὸν ἦμαρ), or *never failing* (like ἄφθιτος ἠώς), Il.; *ἔπη ἄβροτα holy hymns*, Soph.   **II.** *without men, solitary*, Aesch.

ἀβρο-χαίτης, ου, ὁ, = ἀβροκόμης, Anacreont.

ἀβρο-χίτων [ῐ], ωνος, ὁ, ή, *in soft tunic, softly clad*, Anth. :—*εὐνὰς ἀβροχίτωνας beds with soft coverings*, Aesch.

ἄ-βροχος, ον, (βρέχω) *unwetted, unmoistened*, Aeschin.: *wanting rain, waterless*, Eur.

ἀβρύνω, (ἀβρός) *to make delicate, treat delicately*, Aesch. : *to deck* or *trick out, εἰς γάμον ἀβρῦναί τινα* Anth. :—Med. or Pass. *to live delicately;* then *to wax wanton, give oneself airs*, Aesch. ; c. dat. rei, *to pride* or *plume oneself on* a thing, Eur.

Ἄβῡδος, ή, *Abydos*, the town on the Asiatic side of the Hellespont :—**Ἀβῡδόθεν**, Adv. *from Abydos*, **Ἀβῡδόθι**, *at Abydos*, Il.

ἄ-βυσσος, ον, *with no bottom, bottomless, unfathomed*, Hdt.; generally, *unfathomable, enormous*, Aesch.   **II.** ἡ ἄβυσσος, *the great deep, the abyss, bottomless pit*, N. T. (For the Root, v. βαθύς.)

ἄγ, apocop. form of ἀνά before κ, γ, χ ; v. ἀνά init.

ἀγᾶ, Dor. for ἄγη.

ἀγάασθαι, Ep. for ἄγασθαι, inf. of ἄγαμαι:—**ἀγάασθε**, for ἄγασθε, 2 pl.

ἀγάθεος, Dor. for ἠγάθεος.

ἀγαθο-ειδής, ές, (εἶδομαι) *seeming good*, Plat.

ἀγαθοεργέω, contr. *-ουργέω*, *to do good*, N. T. : and **ἀγαθοεργία**, Ion. contr. *-ουργία*, ή, *a good deed, service rendered*, Lat. *beneficium*, Hdt.   From

ἀγαθο-εργός, contr. *-ουργός*, όν, (*ἔργω) *doing good* :— οἱ Ἀγαθοεργοί, at Sparta, the five oldest and most

approved knights, who went on foreign missions for the state, Hdt.

ἀγαθοποιέω, f. ήσω, *to do good*, N. T. :—ἀγ. τινά *to do good to*, Ib. **II.** *to do well, act rightly*, Ib. : and **ἀγαθοποιΐα**, ή, *well doing*, N. T. From

ἀγαθο-ποιός, όν, (ποιέω) *doing good, beneficent.*

ἀγαθός [ἄγ], ή, όν : (deriv. uncertain) :—*good*, Lat. *bonus* : **I.** of persons, **1.** in early times, *good, gentle, noble*, in reference to birth, opp. to κακοί, πατρὸς δ᾽ εἴμ᾽ ἀγαθοῖο, θεὰ δέ με γείνατο μήτηρ Il. ; ἀγαθοὶ καὶ ἐξ ἀγαθῶν, Lat. *boni bonis prognati*, Plat. :—with this early sense was associated that of wealth and power, like Lat. *optimus quisque* in Sallust and Cicero ; esp. in the phrase καλοὶ κἀγαθοί (v. καλοκἀγαθός). **2.** *good, brave*, since these qualities were attributed to the Chiefs, Il. :—ἀγαθὸς ἐν ὑσμίνῃ, βοὴν ἀγαθός, πὺξ ἀγαθός, etc., Hom. ; ἀγ. τὰ πολέμια, τὰ πολιτικά Hdt., etc. ;—also c. dat., ἀγ. πολέμῳ Xen. ;—and, ἀγ. εἴς τι, περί τι, πρός τι Plat., etc. ; lastly, c. inf., ἀγ. μάχεσθαι, ἱππεύεσθαι, *good* at fighting, etc., Hdt. **3.** *good*, in moral sense, Plat., etc. **4.** ἀγαθοῦ δαίμονος, as a toast, 'to the good Genius,' Ar. **II.** of things, **1.** *good, serviceable*, Ἰθάκη ἀγαθὴ κουροτρόφος Od. ; ἀγ. τοῖς τοκεῦσι, τῇ πόλει Xen. ; c. gen., εἴ τι οἶδα πυρετοῦ ἀγ. *good* for fever, Id. :—ἀγαθόν [ἐστι], c. inf., *it is good* to do so and so, Hom., etc. **2.** ἀγαθόν, τό, *a good*, of persons, φίλον, ὃ μέγιστον ἀγ. εἶναί φασι Xen. ; ἐπ᾽ ἀγαθῷ τοῖς πολίταις Ar. :—τὸ ἀγαθόν or τἀγαθόν, *the good, summum bonum*, Plat., etc. :—in pl., ἀγαθά, τά, *the goods of fortune, wealth*, Hdt., etc. ; also *good qualities* of a horse, Xen. **III.** instead of the *regular* degrees of comparison, many forms are used,—Comp. ἀμείνων, ἀρείων, βελτίων, κρείσσων, λωΐων (λῴων), Ep. βέλτερος, λωΐτερος, φέρτερος ;—Sup. ἄριστος, βέλτιστος, κράτιστος, λωΐστος (λῷστος), Ep. βέλτιστος, κάρτιστος, φέρτατος, φέριστος. **IV.** the Adv. is usually εὖ : ἀγαθῶς in late writers.

ἀγαθουργέω, -ουργία, -ουργός, contr. from ἀγαθοεργ-.

ἀγαθωσύνη, ή, (ἀγαθός) *goodness, kindness*, N. T.

ἀγαίομαι, Ep. and Ion. for ἄγαμαι, only in pres. and in bad sense (cf. ἄγη II) : **1.** c. acc. rei, *to be indignant at*, Od. **2.** c. dat. pers. *to be indignant with*, Hdt.

ἀγα-κλεής, ές, voc. -κλεές : Ep. gen. ἀγακλῆος, nom. pl. ἀγακληεῖς :—shortened acc. sing. ἀγακλέᾱ ; dat. ἀγακλῆϊ, pl. ἀγακλέᾱς : cf. εὐκλεής : (κλέος) :—*very glorious, famous*, Lat. *inclytus*, Il., Pind.

ἀγα-κλειτός, ή, όν, = foreg., Hom., etc. **2.** of things, ἀγακλειτὴ ἑκατόμβη Od.

ἀγα-κλυτός, όν, = ἀγακλειτός, Lat. *inclytus*, of men, Hom., Hes. **2.** of things, Od.

ἀγα-κτιμένη, (κτίζω) poët. fem. = εὐ-κτιμένη, *well-built* or *placed*, πόλις Pind.

ἀ-γάλακτος [γᾰ], ον, (γάλα) *without milk, getting no milk*, i. e. *taken from the mother's breast*, Horace's *jam lacte depulsus*, Aesch.

ἀγαλλίᾱσις, εως, ή, *great joy, exultation*, N. T. From

ἀγαλλιάω, late form of ἀγάλλομαι, *to rejoice exceedingly*, N. T. ; aor. I ἠγαλλίᾱσα, Ib. : also as Dep. ἀγαλλιάομαι or -άζομαι : fut. -άσομαι : aor. I med. ἠγαλλιᾱσάμην and pass. ἠγαλλιάσθην, N. T.

ἀγαλλίς, ίδος, ή, *the iris* or *flag*, h. Hom.

ἈΓΑ´ΛΛΩ [ᾰ], f. ἀγαλῶ, aor. I ἤγηλα, subj. ἀγήλω, inf. ἀγῆλαι :—Pass., mostly in pres. and impf. :—*to make glorious, glorify, exalt*, c. acc. : esp. *to pay honour to a god*, ἀγ. τινὰ θυσίαισι Ar. :—*to adorn, deck*, γαμηλίους εὐνάς Eur. :—Pass. *to glory, take delight, exult in* a thing, c. dat., Hom., Att. ; absol., Hdt., etc.

ἄγαλμα, ατος, τό, (ἀγάλλω) *a glory, delight, honour*, Il., Att. ; ἀγάλματ᾽ ἀγορᾶς *mere ornaments* of the agora, Eur. **2.** *a pleasing gift*, esp. for the gods, Od. **3.** *a statue in honour of a god*, Hdt., Att. ; *an image*, as an object of worship, etc., Aesch. :—then generally, = ἀνδριάς, *any statue*, Plat. : also *a portrait, picture*, ἐξαλειφθεῖσ᾽ ὣς ἄγαλμα Eur.

ἀγαλματο-ποιός, ὁ, (ποιέω) *a maker of statues, a sculptor, statuary*, Hdt., Plat., etc.

ἈΓΑΜΑΙ [ᾰ], 2 pl. ἄγασθε Ep. ἀγάασθε, Ep. inf. ἀγάασθαι : impf. ἠγάμην :—fut. Ep. ἀγάσομαι :—aor. I ἠγασάμην, Ep. 3 sing. ἠγάσσατο or ἀγάσσατο, also in pass. form ἠγάσθην : **I.** absol. *to wonder, be astonished*, Hom. **2.** c. acc. *to admire* a person or thing, Id., Hdt. ; so in Att., ταῦτα ἀγασθείς Xen. ; c. acc. pers. et gen. rei, *to admire* one *for* a thing, Plat., Xen. **3.** c. gen. rei only, often in Com., *to wonder at*, λόγων Ar. **4.** c. acc. rei et gen. pers., οὐκ ἄγαμαι ταῦτ᾽ ἀνδρὸς I admire not this in a man, Eur. **5.** c. gen. pers., foll. by a part., *to wonder at* one's doing, ἀγ. αὐτοῦ εἰπόντος Plat. **6.** c. dat. *to be delighted with* a person or thing, Hdt., Eur., etc. **II.** in bad sense, *to feel envy, bear a grudge against* a person, c. dat., Hom. **2.** c. acc. *to be jealous* or *angry at* a thing, Hom. Cf. ἀγαίομαι.

Ἀγα-μέμνων, ονος, ὁ, (ἄγαν, μέμνων, from μένω) :—*the very steadfast*, name of the leader of the Greeks against Troy, Hom. :—Adj. **Ἀγᾰμεμνόνεος**, έα, εον, Hom. ; also -όνειος, α, ον, or -όνιος, η, ον, Pind., Aesch. : Patron. -ονίδης, ου, ὁ, Agamemnon's son, Orestes, Od.

ἀγᾰμένως, Adv. part. pres. of ἄγαμαι, *with admiration, respect* or *deference*, Plat.

ἀγᾰμία, ή, (ἄγαμος) *celibacy*, Plut. :—ἀγαμίου δίκη, ή, an action against one *for not marrying*, Plut.

ἄ-γᾰμος, ον, *unmarried, unwedded, single*, Lat. *caelebs*, Il., Trag. **II.** γάμος ἄγαμος, *a marriage that is no marriage, a fatal marriage*, Soph., Eur.

ἈΓΑΝ, Adv. *very, much, very much*, Theogn., Att., the word λίην being its equiv. in Ep. and Ion. : in bad sense, *too, too much*, Lat. *nimis*, as in the famous μηδὲν ἄγαν, *ne quid nimis*, not *too much* of any thing, Theogn., etc. [ᾰγᾰν properly, but ἄγᾱν in Anth.]

ἀγᾰνακτέω, f. ήσω, (ἄγαν) *to feel irritation* : metaph. *to be vexed*, ἀηποχεαῖ, *angry, discontented*, Ar., Plat. :— c. dat. rei, *to be vexed at* a thing, Id. ; ἐπί τινι Isocr. ; ὑπέρ τινος, διά τι Plat. **2.** *to be vexed at* or *with* a person, τινί Xen. ; πρός τινα Plut. ; κατά τινος Luc. :— c. acc. pers., ἀγ. τινὰς ἀποθνήσκοντας *to be angry at* their dying, Plat.

ἀγᾰνάκτησις, εως, ή, (ἀγανακτέω) *irritation*, of the irritation caused by teething, Plat. : metaph., ἀγανάκτησιν ἔχει the thing gives *ground for annoyance* or *displeasure*, Thuc.

ἀγᾰνακτικός, ή, όν, (ἀγανακτέω) *irritable*, Plat.

ἀγᾰνακτητός, ή, όν, verb. Adj. of ἀγανακτέω, *irritating*, Plat.

ἀγανακτικός, ή, όν, = ἀγανακτητικός, Luc.

ἀγάν-νῐφος, ον, (νίφω) much snowed on, snow-capt, Il.

ἀγᾰνο-βλέφᾰρος, ον, mild-eyed, Anth.

ἀγᾱνόρειος, ἀγανορία, Dor. for ἀγην-.

ἀγᾰνός, ή, όν, mild, gentle, kindly, of words, Hom., Pind. :—in Hom. of the shafts of Apollo and Artemis, as bringing an easy death :—Sup. ἀγανώτατος, Hes. : Adv. -νῶς, Eur. (Deriv. uncertain.)

ἀγανοφροσύνη, ή, gentleness, kindliness, Hom. From

ἀγανό-φρων, ον, gen. ονος, (φρήν) poët. Adj. gentle of mood, Hom.

ἀγάνωρ [ᾰ], Dor. for ἀγήνωρ.

ἀγάομαι, Ep. form of ἄγαμαι, only in part. ἀγώμενος, admiring, Hes.

ἀγαπάζω, Ep. form of ἀγαπάω, Dor. 3 pl. -οντι :—also in Med., Dor. impf. 'ᾱγαπάζοντο :—only in pres. and impf. :—to treat with affection, shew affection to a person, caress, c. acc., Hom. :—so in Med., Od.

ἀγαπᾱτός, όν, Dor. for ἀγαπητός.

ἀγαπάω, f. ήσω · pf. ἠγάπηκα : Ep. aor. I ἀγάπησα : (ἀγάπη) :   I. of persons, to treat with affection, to caress, love, be fond of, c. acc., Att. for ἀγαπάζω, Plat., etc. :—Pass. to be beloved, Id.   2. in N. T. to regard with brotherly love, v. ἀγάπη.   II. of things, to be well pleased or contented at or with a thing, c. dat., Dem., etc. :—also c. acc. rei, Id. :—absol. to be content, Luc. :—ἀγ. ὅτι .., εἰ .., ἐάν .., to be well pleased that . . Thuc., etc.

ἀγάπη, ή, love : esp. brotherly love, charity ; the love of God for man and of man for God, N. T.   II. in pl. a love-feast, Ib. (Deriv. uncertain.)

ἀγάπημα, ατος, τό, (ἀγαπάω) a delight, darling, Anth.

ἀγαπ-ήνωρ, ορος, ό, = ἠνορέην ἀγαπῶν, loving manliness, manly, Il.

ἀγαπητέος, α, ον, verb. Adj. of ἀγαπάω, to be loved, desired, Plat.

ἀγαπητικός, ή, όν, (ἀγαπάω) affectionate, Plut.

ἀγαπητός, ή, όν, Dor. -ᾱτός, ά, όν, verb. Adj. of ἀγαπάω, beloved, of an only son, Hom., Dem.   II. of things, worthy of love, loveable, dear, Plat., etc.   2. to be acquiesced in (as the least in a choice of evils), ἀγαπητόν [ἐστι] one must be content, εἰ .., ἐάν .., Id., Xen., etc.   III. Adv. -τῶς, cheerfully, contentedly, Plat., Dem., etc.   2. just enough to content one, only just, barely, scarcely, Plat.

ἀγάρ-ροος, ον, contr. -ρρους, ουν, (ἄγαν, ῥέω) strong-flowing, swift-flowing, Il.

ἀγάσσατο, Ep. for ἠγάσατο, 3 sing. aor. I of ἄγαμαι.

ἀγά-στονος, ον, (στένω) much groaning, howling, of waves, Od. : loud-wailing, Aesch.

ἀγαστός, όν, verb. Adj. of ἄγαμαι, deserving admiration, later form of the Hom. ἀγητός, admirable, Eur., Xen. :—Adv. -τῶς, Id.

ἀγατός, ή, όν, poët. for ἀγαστός, as θαυματός for θαυμαστός, h. Hom.

ἀ-γανός, ή, όν, (a euphon., γαίω) illustrious, noble, Hom. :—Sup. -ότατος, Od.

ἀ-γαυρός, ά, όν, (a euphon., γαῦρος) stately, proud, Hes. : superl. Adv. ἀγαυρότατα, Hdt.

ἀγγᾰρεύω, f. σω, (ἄγγαρος) to press one to serve as a courier, to press into service, N. T.

ἀγγᾰρήϊος, ό, Ion. form of ἄγγαρος, Hdt.   II. neut.

ἀγγᾰρήϊον, post-riding, the Persian system of mounted couriers, Id.

ἄγγᾰρος, ό, Persian word, a mounted courier, such as were kept ready at regular stages throughout Persia for carrying the royal despatches ; cf. ἀγγαρήϊος, and v. Xen. Cyr. 8. 6, 17.   II. as Adj., ἄγγαρον πῦρ the courier flame, said of beacon fires used for telegraphing, Aesch.

ἀγγεῖον, Ion. -ήϊον, τό, = ἄγγος, Hdt., Att.

ἀγγελία, Ion. -ίη, ή, (ἄγγελος) a message, tidings, news, Hom., Hdt., etc. ; ἀγγελίη ἐμή a report of me, concerning me, Il. ; ἀγγελίην πατρὸς φέρει ἐρχομένοιο he brings news of or about thy father's coming, Od. :— ἀγγελίην ἐλθεῖν, to go a message, i. e. on a message, like Lat. legationem obire, Il. ;—so also Ep. in gen., ἀγγελίης οἰχνέσκε went on account of a message, Ib. ; ἤλυθε σεῦ ἕνεκ' ἀγγελίης (i. e. ἀγγελίης σοῦ ἕνεκα) Ib., Hes.   2. a proclamation, command, h. Hom., etc.

ἀγγελί-αρχος, ό, = ἀρχάγγελος, Anth.

ἀγγελιᾱ-φόρος, Ion. ἀγγελιηφ-, ό, (φέρω) a messenger, Hdt. : title of the Persian minister who introduced people to the king, Id.

ἀγγελιώτης, ου, ό, = ἄγγελος, h. Hom.

ἀγγέλλω, (ἄγγελος) : Ep. and Ion. f. ἀγγελέω, Att. ἀγγελῶ : aor. I ἤγγειλα : pf. ἤγγελκα :—Med., aor. I ἠγγειλάμην :—Pass., f. ἀγγελθήσομαι : aor. I ἠγγέλθην : pf. ἤγγελμαι : aor. 2 pass. ἠγγέλην only in late Greek : —to bear a message, τινί to a person, Hom. ; c. acc. et inf. to make proclamation that, Il.   2. c. acc. rei, to announce, proclaim, report, Hom., Att.   3. c. acc. pers. to bring news of, Od. ; περί τινος Soph.   II. Med. to announce oneself, Il.   III. Pass. to be reported of, Id., etc. ; τὰ ἠγγελμένα the reports, Thuc. Hence

ἄγγελμα, ατος, τό, a message, tidings, news, Eur., Thuc., etc.

ΑΓΓΕΛΟΣ, ό, ή, a messenger, envoy, Hom., Hdt., Att.   2. generally, one that announces, of birds of augury, Il. ; Μουσῶν ἄγγελος, of a poet, Theogn. ; Διὸς ἄγγ., of the nightingale, Soph. ; c. gen. rei, ἄγγελος κακῶν ἐμῶν Id.   3. a divine messenger, an angel, N. T.

ἀγγήϊον, τό, Ion. for ἀγγεῖον.

ΑΓΓΟΣ, εος, τό, a vessel of various kinds, a jar to hold milk, etc., Hom. : a vat for the vintage, Hes. ; a vase, pitcher, pail, Hdt., Att.   II. a coffer or ark, in which children were laid, Hdt., Eur. : a chest for clothes, Soph. : a cinerary urn, Id.   III. the cell of a honey-comb, Anth.

ἀγ-γράφω, poët. for ἀνα-γράφω.

ἄγε, ἄγετε, properly imperat. of ἄγω, used as Adv. come ! come on ! well ! Lat. age ! Hom., Att.

ἀγείρω (Root ΑΓΕΡ) : impf. ἤγειρον : aor. I ἤγειρα Ep. ἄγειρα :—Med., aor. I ἠγειράμην :—Pass., aor. I ἠγέρθην : pf. ἀγήγερμαι : Ep. 3 pl. plqpf. ἀγηγέρατο :—Hom. uses a shortd. aor. 2 of med. form, but pass. sense, ἀγέροντο, inf. ἀγερέσθαι, part. ἀγρόμενος :—to bring together, gather together, c. acc., Hom., Att. :—Pass. to come together, gather, assemble, Hom. ; ἀγρόμενοι σύες herded swine, Od. ; θυμὸς ἐνὶ στήθεσσιν ἀγέρθη, ἐς φρένα θυμὸς ἀγέρθη Il.   II. of things, to get together, collect, gather, Od.; so in Med., Ib.   2. to collect by begging, Ib.   3. ὀφρύας εἰς ἓν ἀγείρειν to frown, Anth.

ἀ-γείτων, ον, gen. ονος, without neighbour, neighbour-less, Aesch.; φίλων ἀγ. with no friends as neighbours, Eur.

ἀγελᾱδόν, Dor. for ἀγελᾱηδόν.

ἀγελαῖος, α, ον, (ἀγέλη) belonging to a herd, feeding at large, Hom., Att. II. in herds or shoals, grega-rious, ἰχθύες Hdt.; ἀγελαῖα, τά, gregarious animals, Plat. 2. of the herd or multitude, i. e. common, Id., etc.

ἀγελαρχέω, f. ήσω, to lead a company, c. gen., Plut. From

ἀγελ-άρχης, ου, ὁ, (ἀγέλη, ἄρχω) the leader of a com-pany, captain, Plut., Luc.

ἀγελαστί, Adv. without laughter, Plut. From

ἀ-γέλαστος, ον, (γελάω) not laughing, grave, gloomy, sullen, h. Hom., Aesch. II. pass. not to be laughed at, not trifling, Id.

ἀγελείη, ἡ, (ἄγω, λεία) Ep. epith. of Athena, driver of spoil, forager, Il.

ἀγέλη, ἡ, (ἄγω) a herd, of horses, of oxen and kine, cf. βούνομος; of swine, Hes. II. any herd or company, Soph., Eur.; metaph., πόνων ἀγέλαι Id.

ἀγεληδόν, Adv. (ἀγέλη) in herds or companies, Il., Hdt.: —Dor. ἀγελᾱδόν, Theocr.

ἀγέληφι, Ep. dat. of ἀγέλη.

ἀγέμεν, Ep. for ἄγειν, inf. of ἄγω.

ἀγεμόνευμα, ἀγεμονεύω, ἀγεμών, Dor. for ἡγεμ-.

ἄγεν, Ep. for ἐάγησαν, 3 pl. aor. 2 pass. of ἄγνυμι. 2. Ep. for ἦγεν, 3 sing. impf. of ἄγω.

ἀ-γενεᾱλόγητος, ον, of unrecorded descent, N. T.

ἀ-γένειος, ον, (γένειον) beardless; ἀγένειόν τι εἰρηκέναι to speak like a boy, Luc.

ἀ-γένητος, ον, (γενέσθαι) unborn, uncreated, unorigin-ated, Plat. II. of things, not done, not having happened, ἀγένητον ποιεῖν, Lat. infectum reddere, Soph.

ἀ-γεννής, ές, (γέννα) of no family, low-born, Hdt., Plat., etc. II. low-minded, Hdt., Ar., etc. 2. of things, much like βάναυσος, illiberal, sordid, Plat.:— Adv. -νῶς, Eur.

ἀ-γέννητος, ον, (γεννάω) unbegotten, unborn, ἀγ. τότ' ἢ Soph. II. like ἀγεννής, low-born, Id.

ἀγέομαι, Dor. for ἡγέομαι.

ἀ-γέραστος, ον, (γέρας) without a gift of honour, un-recompensed, unrewarded, Il., Eur.

ἀγερέσθαι, Ep. aor. 2 med. inf. of ἀγείρω.

ἄγερθεν, Dor. and Ep. 3 pl. aor. 1 pass. of ἀγείρω.

ἀγέροντο, Ep. 3 pl. aor. 2 med. of ἀγείρω.

ἄγερσις, εως, ἡ, (ἀγείρω) a gathering, mustering, Hdt.

ἀγέρωχος [ᾰ], ον, poët. Adj. high-minded, lordly, Hom., etc.; in Pind. of noble actions. II. in bad sense, haughty, arrogant, insolent, Archil., Luc.: so Adv. -χως, Anth. (Deriv. uncertain.)

ἀγεσίλαος, v. ἀγησίλαος.

ἀγέ-στρατος, ὁ, ἡ, host-leading, Hes.

ἀγέτης, ἀγέτις, Dor. for ἡγ-.

ἄ-γευστος, ον, (γεύομαι) without taste of, fasting from, c. gen.; metaph., κακῶν ἄγευστος αἰών Soph.; τῶν τερπνῶν ἄγευστος Xen.

ἄγη, Dor. ἄγᾱ [ᾱγ], ἡ, (ἄγαμαι) wonder, awe, amaze-ment, Hom. II. envy, malice, Hdt.; and of the gods, jealousy, Aesch.

ἀγή, Dor. ἀγά [ᾱγ], ἡ, (ἄγνυμι) a fragment, piece, splin-ter, Aesch., Eur.

ἄγη, Ep. for ἐάγη, 3 sing. aor. 2 pass. of ἄγνυμι.

ἀγηγέρατο, Ep. 3 pl. plqpf. pass. of ἀγείρω.

ἀγηλᾰτέω, f. ήσω, (ἄγος, ἐλαύνω) to drive out a curse, i. e. an accursed or polluted person, Lat. piaculum exigere, Hdt., Soph.

ἄγημα, ατος, τό, (ἄγω) anything led, a division of an army, corps, Xen.

ἀγηνόρειος, Dor. ἀγᾱνόρ-, α, ον, = ἀγήνωρ, Aesch.: and

ἀγηνορία [ᾱ], ἡ, manliness, manhood, courage, Il. From

ἀγ-ήνωρ [ᾱ], ορος, ὁ, ἡ, (ἄγαν, ἀνήρ) poët. Adj., manly, courageous, heroic, Il.; in bad sense, headstrong, arrogant, Hom., Hes.

ἀγήοχα, pf. of ἄγω.

ἀ-γήραντος, ον, (γηράσκω) = sq., Simon., Eur.

ἀ-γήραος, ον, Att. contr. ἀγήρως, ων, acc. sing. ἀγήρων, and ἀγήρω: dual plur.: nom. ἀγήρῳ, acc. ἀγήρως, dat. ἀγήρῳς: (γῆρας):— not waxing old, undecaying, 1. of persons, Hom., Hes.; so, ἀγήρως χρόνῳ Soph. 2. of things, Il., Att.

ἀ-γήρᾱτος, ον, = ἀγήραος Eur., Xen.

ἀγήρως, ων, contr. for ἀγήραος.

ἀγησί-λᾱος [ᾱγ], ου, ὁ, leader of people, conductor of men, Aesch.; so, ἡγησίλεως, and ἀγεσίλας, α, Anth.

ἀγησί-χορος, ον, (ἀγέομαι, Dor. for ἡγ-) leading the chorus, Pind.

ἀγητήρ, ῆρος, ὁ, Dor. for ἡγητήρ.

ἀγητός, ή, όν, (ἄγαμαι) admirable, wondrous, c. acc. rei, εἶδος ἀγητός admirable in form, Il.; εἶδος ἀγητοί wonderful in form only, as a reproach, Ib.; c. dat. rei, ἀγ. χρήμασι Solon.

ἀγιάζω, later form of ἁγίζω, N. T. Hence

ἁγιασμός, οῦ, ὁ, consecration, sanctification, N. T.

ἁγίζω, f. Att. ἰῶ, (ἄγος) to hallow, dedicate, Soph.

ἁγινέω, lengthd. Ep. and Ion. for ἄγω, only in pres. and impf.: Ep. inf. ἁγινέμεναι: impf. ἡγίνεον, Ep. and Ion. ἁγίνεον or ἁγίνεσκον: f. ἁγινήσω:— to lead, bring, carry, Il., Hdt.:—Med. to cause to be brought, Id.

ἅγιος [ᾰ], α, ον, (ἄγος) devoted to the gods, sacred, holy, Lat. sacer: 1. of things, esp. temples, Hdt., Xen., etc.: τὸ ἅγιον the Temple, τὰ ἅγια τῶν ἁγίων the Holy of Holies, N. T. 2. of persons, holy, pure, Ar.:— Adv. ἁγίως, Isocr., N. T.—The word never occurs in Hom. or Trag.; ἁγνός being used instead. Hence

ἁγιότης, ητος, ἡ, = ἁγιωσύνη, N. T.

ἁγιστεία, ἡ, mostly in pl. holy rites, temple-worship, Isocr.

ἁγιστεύω, f. σω, (ἁγίζω) to perform sacred rites, Plat. 2. to live piously or chastely, Eur.

ἁγιωσύνη, ἡ, (ἅγιος) holiness, sanctity, N. T.

ἀγκάζομαι, (ἀγκάς) Dep. to lift up in the arms, Il.

ἀγκάθεν, Adv. like ἀγκάς, in the arms, Aesch. II. with bent arm, resting on the arm, Id.:—not for ἀνέ-καθεν, since ἀγκ- stands for ἀνακ-, never for ἀνεκ-.

ἀγκάλη [ᾱ], ἡ, (ἄγκος) the bent arm, Hdt., etc.; mostly in pl., ἐν ἀγκάλαις or in the arms, Aesch., Eur.; ἐν ταῖς ἀγκ. Xen.:—in sing. φέρειν ἐν τῇ ἀγκάλῃ Hdt. II. metaph. anything closely enfolding, πετραία ἀγκάλη Aesch.; πόντιαι ἀγκάλαι bights or arms of the sea, Id.; κυμάτων ἐν ἀγκάλαις Ar.

ἀγκᾰλίζομαι, Dep., = ἀγκάζομαι, to embrace, Anth. II. ἀγκαλιζόμενος in pass. sense, Aesop.

ἀγκᾰλίς, ή, in pl.= ἀγκάλαι, arms, Ep. dat. pl. ἀγκαλί-δεσσιν Il.

ἀγκάλισμα, ατος, τό, (ἀγκαλίζομαι) that which is embraced or carried in the arms, Luc.

ἄγκαλος, ό, (ἀγκάλη) an armful, bundle, h. Hom.

ἀγκάς [ἄς], Adv. in or into the arms, Hom., Theocr.

ἄγ-κειμαι, poët. for ἀνά-κειμαι.

ἀγ-κηρύσσω, poët. for ανα-κηρύσσω.

ἀγκίστριον, τό, Dim. of ἄγκιστρον, Theocr.

ἀγκιστρό-δετος, ον, with a hook, Anth.

ἄγκιστρον, τό, (ἄγκος) a fish-hook, Od., Hdt., etc. 2. the hook of a spindle, Plat.

ἀγκιστρόομαι, Pass. (ἄγκιστρον) to be furnished with barbs, Plut.

ἀγ-κλίνω, poët. for ἀνα-κλίνω.

ἀγκοίνη, ή, (ἄγκος) poët. for ἀγκάλη or ἀγκών, the bent arm, only in pl., Hom.

ἀγ-κομίζω, poët. for ἀνα-κομίζω.

ΑΓΚΟΣ, εος, τό, a bend : hence a mountain glen, dell, valley, Hom., Hdt., Eur.

ἀγ-κρεμάσας, ἀγ-κρισις, ἀγ-κρούομαι, poët. for ἀνα-κρ-.

ἀγκύλη [ῠ], ή, (ἄγκος) a loop or noose in a cord, Eur., Xen. 2. the thong of a javelin, by which it was hurled : the javelin itself, Eur. 3. a bow-string, Soph.

ἀγκύλιον, τό, Dim. of ἀγκύλη :—τὰ ἀγκύλια, the Roman ancilia, Plut.

ἀγκυλο-γλώχιν, ῑνος, of a cock, with hooked spurs, Babr.

ἀγκυλό-οδους, οντος, ὁ, ή, crook-toothed : barbed, Anth.

ἀγκυλο-μήτης, ου, ὁ, ή, (μῆτις) crooked of counsel, wily, epith. of Κρόνος, Hom. ; of Prometheus, Hes.

ἀγκῠλό-πους, ὁ, ή, gen. ποδος, with bent legs, ἀγκ. δίφρος, Rom. sella curulis, Plut.

ἀγκύλος [ῠ], η, ον, (ἄγκος) crooked, curved, of a bow, Il.: beaked, of the eagle, Pind. : of greedy fingers, hooked, Ar. II. metaph. of style, crooked, intricate, Luc.

ἀγκῠλό-τοξος, ον, (τόξον) with curved bow, Il., etc.

ἀγκυλο-χείλης, ου, ὁ, (χεῖλος) with hooked beak, ἀετός Od. ; αἰγυπιοί Il.

ἀγκυλο-χήλης, ου, ὁ, (χηλή) with crooked claws, Batr.

ἀγκῠλόω, f. ώσω, (ἀγκύλος) to crook, bend, τὴν χεῖρα :—Pass., ὄνυχας ἠγκυλωμένος with crooked claws, Ar.

ἀγκῠλωτός, ή, όν, verb. Adj. of ἀγκυλόω, of javelins, furnished with a thong (ἀγκύλη) for throwing, Eur.

ἄγκῠρα, ή, (ἄγκος) Lat. ancŏra, an anchor, first in Alcae. and Theogn., for in Hom. we hear only of εὐναί, i. e. stones used as anchors ; ἀγκύραν βάλλεσθαι, καθιέναι, μεθιέναι, ἀφιέναι to cast anchor, Pind., Hdt., etc.; so, ἐπὶ δυοῖν ἀγκύραιν ὁρμεῖν, i. e. 'to have two strings to one's bow,' Dem.; cf. ὀχέω; ἐπὶ τῆς αὐτῆς (sc. ἀγκύρας) ὁρμεῖν τοῖς πολλοῖς, i. e. 'to be in the same boat' with the many, Id.

ἀγκῠρίζω, f. Att. ιῶ, to throw by the hook-trick, i. e. by hooking your leg behind the other's knee, in wrestling, Ar.

ἀγκύριον, τό, Dim. of ἄγκυρα, Luc.

ἀγκών, ῶνος, ὁ, (ἄγκος) the bend of the arm, the elbow, Hom. 2. generally the arm, like ἀγκάλη, Pind., Soph. II. any bend, as the jutting angle of a wall, Il. : the bend or reach of a river, Hdt. ; ἕσπεροι ἀγκῶνες, in Soph., seem to be the angle of the bay of Rhoeteium.

ἀγλα-έθειρος, ον, (ἔθειρα) bright-haired, h. Hom.

ἀγλαΐα, Ion. -ίη, ή, (ἀγλαός) splendour, beauty, adorn-

ment ; ἀγλαΐηφι πεποιθώς (Ep. dat.) Il. : in bad sense, pomp, show, vanity, and in pl. vanities, Od., Eur. 2. triumph, glory, Pind., Soph. : in pl., festivities, merriment, Hes.

ἀγλαΐζω, f. Att. ιῶ : aor. 1 ἠγλάϊσα : (ἀγλαός) :—to make bright or splendid, Plut. II. Med. and Pass. to adorn oneself or be adorned with a thing, take delight in, σέ φημι ἀγλαΐεσθαι I say that thou wilt take delight in them (sc. τοῖς ἵπποις), Il. Hence

ἀγλάϊσμα, ατος, τό, an ornament, honour, Aesch., Eur.

ἀγλαό-γυιος, ον, (γυῖον) with beauteous limbs, Pind.

ἀγλαό-δενδρος, ον, (δένδρον) with beautiful trees, Pind.

ἀγλαό-δωρος, ον, (δῶρον) giving splendid gifts, h.Hom.

ἀγλαό-θυμος, ον, noble-hearted, Anth.

ἀγλαό-καρπος, ον, bearing beautiful or goodly fruit Od. : in h. Hom. of Demeter, giver of the fruits of the earth.

ἀγλαό-μορφος, ον, (μορφή) of beauteous form, Anth.

ἀγλαός, ή, όν and ός, όν, splendid, shining, bright, beautiful, Hom., Hes. II. of men, either beautiful or famous, Il. ; c. dat. rei, famous for a thing, Ib.

ἀγλαο-τρίαινης, ου, ὁ, Dor. acc. -ᾱν, (τρίαινα) god of the bright trident, Pind.

ἀγλα-ῶψ, ῶπος, ὁ, ή, bright-eyed, beaming, Soph.

ἄγλῑς, gen. ἄγλῑθος, ή :—only in pl., a head of garlic, made up of several cloves, Ar.

ἄ-γλωσσος, Att. -ττος, ον, (γλῶσσα) without tongue, of the crocodile, Arist. II. tongueless, ineloquent, Lat. elinguis, Pind., Ar. : then = βάρβαρος, Soph.

ἄγμα, ατος, τό, (ἄγνυμι) a fragment, Plut.

ἀγμός, ὁ, (ἄγνυμι) a broken cliff, crag, Eur.

ἀ-γναμπτος, ον, unbending, inflexible, Plut.

ἄ-γνᾰφος, ον, (γνάπτω) uncarded, N. T.

ἁγνεία, ή, (ἁγνεύω) purity, chastity, Soph., N. T. : in pl. purifications, Isocr.

ἅγνευμα, τό, (ἁγνεύω) chastity, Eur. From

ἁγνεύω, f. σω : pf. ἥγνευκα : (ἁγνός) :—to consider as part of purity, make it a point of religion, c. inf., ἁγνεύουσι ἔμψυχον μηδὲν κτείνειν Hdt. : absol. to be pure, Aesch. ; χεῖρας ἁγνεύει is clean in hands, Eur. : to keep oneself pure from a thing, c. gen., Dem.

ἁγνίζω, f. Att. ιῶ, (ἁγνός) to cleanse away, esp. by water, Soph. 2. to cleanse, purify, from a thing, c. gen., Eur. II. ἁγν. τὸν θανόντα to hallow the dead by fire, so that he may be received by the gods below, Soph. :—Pass., σῶμαθ' ἡγνίσθη πυρί Eur. Hence

ἅγνισμα, ατος, τό, a purification, expiation, Aesch. ; and

ἁγνιστέος, η, ον, verb. Adj., to be purified, Eur.

ἀγνοέω, Ep. ἀγνοιέω, 3 sing. subj. ἀγνοιῇσι : impf. ἠγνόουν : f. ἀγνοήσω : aor. 1 ἠγνόησα, Ep. ἠγνοίησα, also Ep. contr. 3 sing. ἀγνώσασκε : pf. ἠγνόηκα :—Pass., fut. (of med. form) ἀγνοήσομαι : aor. 1 ἠγνοήθην : pf. ἠγνόημαι : (from *ἄγνοος = ἀγνώς II) :—not to perceive or know, ἄνδρ' ἀγνοίησας' from not recognising him, Od. : mostly with negat., οὐκ ἠγνόησεν, i. e. he perceived or knew well, Il. ; μηδὲν ἀγνόει learn all, Eur.: —c. acc. to be ignorant of, Hdt., Att. ; ἀγν. περί τινος Plat. :—dependent clauses are added in part., τίς ἀγνοεῖ τὸν πόλεμον ἥξοντα ; Dem.; or with a Conjunct., οὐδεὶς ἀγνοεῖ ὅτι . . , Id. :—Pass. not to be known, Plat., etc. II. absol. to go wrong, make a false step, etc. ; ἀγνοῶν ignorantly, by mistake, Xen.

ἀγνόημα, τό, (ἀγνοέω) a fault of ignorance, error, N.T.

ἀγνοιᾱ, ἡ, (ἀγνοέω) want of perception, ignorance, Aesch., Thuc., etc.; ἣν ὑπ' ἀγνοίας ὁρᾷς, i. e. whom seeing you pretend not to know, Soph. II. = ἀγνόημα, a mistake, Dem. [In Poets sometimes ἀγνοίᾱ.]

ἀγνοιέω, Ep. for ἀγνοέω :—ἀγνοίῃσι, v. ἀγνοέω.

ἀγνό-ρῠτος, ον, (ῥέω) pure-flowing, ποταμός Aesch.

ἁγνός, ή, όν, (ἅγος) full of religious awe :— I. of places and things dedicated to gods, hallowed, holy, sacred, Od., Att. 2. of divine persons, chaste, pure, Od. II. of persons, undefiled, chaste, pure, Aesch., Eur.: c. gen. pure from a thing, Eur. 2. pure from blood, guiltless, Soph.; ἁγνὸς χεῖρας Eur. 3. in moral sense, pure, upright, Xen. :—Adv., ἁγνῶς ἔχειν to be pure, Id.

ἅγνος, ἡ, ὁ, = λύγος, a willow-like tree, vitex agnus castus, h. Hom.

ἁγνότης, ητος, ἡ, (ἁγνός) purity, chastity, N. T.

ἄγνῡμι, 3 dual ἄγνῠτον : f. ἄξω : aor. 1 ἔαξα, ἦξα, imper. ἆξον : part. ἄξας : aor. 2 ἐάγην [ᾰ mostly] :—pf. act. (in pass. sense) ἔᾱγα, Ion. ἔηγα :— to break, shiver, Hom. :—Pass. to be broken or shivered, ἄγη ξίφος Il.; ἐάγη δόρυ Ib.; πάλιν ἄγεν ὄγκοι (for ἐάγησαν) the barbs were broken backwards, Ib. ; καμπὰς πολλὰς ἀγνύμενος, of a river, with a broken, i.e. winding, course, Hdt.; ἄγνυτο ἠχῷ the sound spread around, Hes.

ἀγνωμονέω, f. ήσω, (ἀγνώμων) to act without right feeling, act unfairly, Xen., Dem. :—Pass. to be unfairly treated, ἀγνημονηθείς Plut.

ἀγνωμοσύνη, ἡ, (ἀγνώμων) want of sense, folly, Theogn.: senseless pride, arrogance, Hdt., Eur. 2. want of feeling, unkindness, unfairness, Dem. 3. in pl. misunderstandings, Xen.

ἀ-γνώμων, ον, gen. ονος, (γνώμη) ill-judging, senseless, Pind., Plat., etc. :—Adv. -όνως, senselessly, Xen. 2. headstrong, reckless, arrogant, (in Comp. -ονέστερος) Hdt.; in Sup., Xen. 3. unfeeling, unkind, hard-hearted, Soph., Xen. II. of things, senseless, brute, Soph., Aeschin.

ἀ-γνώς, ῶτος, ὁ, ἡ, (γι-γνώσκω) : I. pass. unknown, of persons, Aesch.; ἀγνὼς πατρὶ clam patre, Eur.: of things, unknown, obscure, unintelligible, Aesch., Soph.; ἀγν. δόκησις a dark suspicion, Id. 2. not known, obscure, ignoble, Eur. II. act. not knowing, ignorant, Soph. III. c. gen., where the sense fluctuates between pass. and act., ἀγνῶτες ἀλλήλων Thuc.

ἀγνωσία, ἡ, (ἀγνώς) ignorance, Eur.; διὰ τὴν ἀλλήλων ἀγν. from not knowing one another, Thuc.

ἄ-γνωστος or ἄ-γνωτος, ον, unknown, τινί; ἄγνωτον ἐς γῆν Eur.; γνωτὰ κοὐκ ἄγνωτά μοι Soph. 2. not to be known, ἄγνωστόν τινα τεύχειν Od.; ἀγνωστότατοι γλῶσσαν most unintelligible in tongue, Thuc.

ἀγ-ξηραίνω, poët. for ἀνα-ξηραίνω.

ἀγονία, ἡ, unfruitfulness, Plut. From

ἄ-γονος, ον, (γί-γνομαι) : I. pass. unborn, Il. : not yet born, Eur. II. act. not producing, unfruitful, barren ; τόκοισιν ἀγόνοις travail without issue, bringing no children to the birth, Soph., etc. 2. c. gen. not productive of, barren in a thing, Plat. III. childless, Eur.

ἄ-γοος, ον, unmourned, Aesch.

ἀγορά [ᾰγ], ᾶς, Ion. ἀγορή, ῆς, ἡ : (ἀγείρω) :—an Assembly of the People, opp. to the Council of Chiefs (βουλή), Hom. :—καθίζειν ἀγορήν to hold an assembly, opp. to λύειν ἀγ. τῷ dissolve it ; ἀγορήνδε καλέειν, κηρύσσειν, Hom. ; so, ἀγορὰν συνάγειν, συλλέγειν Xen. II. the place of Assembly, Hom. ; used not only for debating, trials, and other public purposes, but also as a market-place, like the Roman Forum, Att. ; but to lounge in the market was held to be disreputable, cf. ἀγοραῖος. III. the business of the ἀγορά, public speaking, gift of speaking, mostly in pl., Hom. IV. things sold in the ἀγορά, the market, Lat. annona ; ἀγορὰν παρασκευάζειν Thuc. V. as a mark of time, ἀγορὰ πλήθουσα or ἀγορᾶς πληθώρη, the forenoon, when the market-place was full, Hdt. ; opp. to ἀγορῆς διάλυσις, the time just after mid-day, when they went home, Id.

ἀγοράασθε [ᾰγ-], Ep. for ἠγοράασθε 2 pl. of ἀγοράομαι.

ἀγοράζω [ᾰγ], f. άσω : aor. 1 ἠγόρασα : pf. ἠγόρακα :— Med., aor. 1 ἠγορασάμην :—Pass., aor. 1 ἠγοράσθην : pf. ἠγόρασμαι (also in med. sense) :—to be in the ἀγορά, frequent it, Hdt. : to occupy the market-place, Thuc. 2. to buy in the market, buy, purchase, Ar., Xen. :—Med. to buy for oneself, Id., etc. 3. as a mark of idle fellows, to lounge in the ἀγορά, Thuc. ; cf. ἀγοραῖος.

ἀγοραῖος [ᾰγ], ον, in, of, or belonging to the ἀγορά, Hdt., Att. ; Ἑρμῆς Ἀγ. as patron of traffick, Ar. II. frequenting the market, etc. ; ἀγοραῖοι, οἱ, loungers in the market, Lat. circumforanei, subrostrani, Hdt. :— hence generally, the common sort, low fellows, Ar., Plat., etc. 2. of things, low, mean, vulgar, Ar. III. generally, proper to the ἀγορά, skilled in, suited to forensic speaking, Plut. 2. ἀγοραῖος (sc. ἡμέρα), a court-day, Strab., N. T. 3. Adv. -ως, in forensic style, Plut.

ἀγορανομικός, ή, όν, of or for the ἀγορανόμος or his office, Plat. :—used to translate Lat. aedilicius, Plut.

ἀγορά-νόμος, ὁ, (νέμω) a clerk of the market, who regulated buying and selling there, Ar. :—used to trans- late Lat. Aedilis, Plut.

ἀγοράομαι, almost wholly used in the Ep. forms, pres. ἀγοράασθε [ᾰ metri gr.] ; impf. ἠγοράασθε, ἠγορόωντο ; aor. 1, 2 sing. ἠγόρω, 3 ἀγορήσατο : (ἀγορά) :—to meet in assembly, sit in debate : then, like ἀγορεύω, to speak in the assembly, harangue, Hom. 2. to speak, utter, Il. 3. to talk with, τινι Soph.

ἀγορασ-άγένειος, ον, crasis for ἀγοράσει ἀγένειος, will lounge in the ἀγορά without a beard, Ar.

ἀγοράσδω, Dor. for ἀγοράζω.

ἀγόρασμα, ατος, τό, (ἀγοράζω) that which is bought : in pl. goods, wares, merchandise, Dem., etc.

ἀγοραστής, οῦ, ὁ, (ἀγοράζω) the slave who bought pro- visions for the house, the purveyor, Xen.

ἀγορεύω, (ἀγορά) impf. ἠγόρευον Ep. ἀγόρευον : f. -εύσω : aor. 1 ἠγόρευσα, Ep. ἀγ- : pf. ἠγόρευκα : in cor- rect Att. writers, this Verb (and its compds.) is for the most part confined to pres. and impf. ; the other tenses being borrowed (fut. ἐρῶ, pf. εἴρηκα, aor. 2 εἶπον) :— to speak in the assembly, harangue, speak, Hom. ; κακόν τι ἀγορεύειν τινὰ to speak ill of one, Od. :— of the κῆρυξ in the Ecclesia, τίς ἀγορεύειν βούλεται ; who wishes to address the people? Ar., Dem., etc. 2. μή τι φόβονδ' ἀγόρευε counsel me not to flight, Il. 3. to proclaim,

declare, mention, Hom. :—in aor. 1 med., ἀγορεύσασθαι ὡς .. *to have* it *proclaimed* that .. , Hdt., etc. : metaph., δέρμα θηρὸς ἀγ. χειρῶν ἔργον tells *a tale of* .. , Theocr.   4. Pass., of a speech, *to be spoken,* Thuc.

ἀγορή, Ep. and Ion. for ἀγορά.

ἀγορῆθεν, Adv. *from the Assembly* or *market,* Il., etc.

ἀγορήνδε, Adv. *to the Assembly* or *market,* Il.

ἀγορητής, οῦ, ὁ, (ἀγοράομαι) *a speaker, orator,* Il.

ἀγορητύς, ύος, ἡ, (ἀγοράομαι) *the gift of speaking, eloquence;* Od.

ἀγορῆφι, Adv. *in the Assembly,* Hes.

ἄγορος, ὁ, = ἀγορά, Eur.

ἀγός [ᾰ], οῦ, ὁ, (ἄγω) *a leader, chief,* Il., etc.

῎ΑΓΟΣ or ἄγος [ᾰ], εος, τό, (v. ἅζομαι) *any matter of religious awe :*   1. like Lat. *piaculum, that which requires expiation, a curse, pollution, guilt,* Hdt., Aesch., etc.   2. *the person* or *thing accursed, an abomination,* Soph., Thuc.   3. *an expiation,* Soph.   II. in good sense, = σέβας, *awe,* h. Hom.

ἀγοστός, ὁ, *the flat of the hand,* Il.   II. *the arm,* = ἀγκάλη, Theocr., Anth.

ἄγρα, Ion. ἄγρη, ἡ, (ἄγω) *a catching, hunting,* ἄγραν ἐφέπειν *to follow the chase,* Od.; ἐς ἄγρας ἰέναι Eur. : also *of fishing,* Soph.   2. *a way of catching,* Hdt.   II. *that which is taken in hunting, the booty, prey,* Hes., Trag.: *game,* Hdt. : of fish, *a draught, haul,* N. T.

ἀ-γράμματος, ον, *without learning* (γράμματα), *unlettered,* Xen., Anth.

ἄ-γραπτος, ον, (γράφω) *unwritten,* Soph.

ἀγραυλέω, f. ήσω, (ἄγραυλος) *to dwell in the field,* N. T.

ἄγρ-αυλος, ον, (ἀγρός, αὐλή) *dwelling in the field,* of shepherds, Il., Hes.; ἀγρ. ἀνήρ *a boor,* Anth.   2. of oxen, Hom., etc.   3. of things, *rural, rustic,* Eur.

ἄ-γραφος, ον, (γράφω) *unwritten,* Thuc. :—ἄγραφοι νόμοι *unwritten laws,* i. e.   1. *the laws of nature, moral law,* Dem.   2. *laws of custom, common law,* Thuc.   II. *not registered,* Id.

ἄγρει, ἀγρεῖτε, v. ἀγρέω II.

ἀγρεῖος, α, ον, (ἀγρός) *of* or *in the country,* Anth.   2. *clownish, boorish,* Ar.

ἀγρειοσύνη, ἡ, (ἀγρεῖος) *clownishness, a rude, vagrant life,* Anth.

ἀγρεῖφνα, ἡ, *a harrow, rake,* Anth.

ἀγρέμιον, τό, = ἄγρα II, Anth.

ἀγρευμα, ατος, τό, (ἀγρεύω) *that which is taken in hunting, booty, prey, spoil,* Eur.   II. *a means of catching,* Aesch. ; of *the net* thrown over Agamemnon, Id.

ἀγρεύς, έως, ὁ, (ἀγρεύω) *a hunter,* Pind., Eur.   II. of an arrow, Anth.

ἀγρευτήρ, ῆρος, ὁ, = sq., Theocr., Anth.

ἀγρευτής, οῦ, ὁ, *a hunter,* like ἀγρεύς, Soph.   II. as Adj., ἀγρ. κύνες *hounds,* Solon ; ἀγρ. κάλαμοι *a trap* of reeds, Anth. From

ἀγρεύω, f. εύσω : aor. 1 ἤγρευσα : (ἄγρα) :—*to take by hunting* or *fishing, to catch, take,* Hdt., Eur. :—also in Med., θύμαт᾽ ἠγρεύσασθ᾽ *ye caught* or *chose your victim,* Eur. :—Pass. *to be taken in the chase,* Xen.   2. metaph. *to hunt after, thirst for,* Eur. ; but ἀγρεύειν τινὰ λόγῳ *to catch* him *in* or *by his words,* N. T.

ἀγρέω, poët. form of foreg., only in pres., *to capture,*

seize, Sappho, Aesch.   II. imperat. ἄγρει, = ἄγε, *come ! come on !* Il. ; ἀγρεῖτε Od.

ἄγρη, ἡ, Ion. for ἄγρα.

ἀγριαίνω, f. ανῶ : aor. 1 ἠγρίανα : (ἄγριος) :   I. intr. *to be angered, provoked, chafed,* Plat. ; τινί *with one,* Id. :—metaph. of rivers, Plut.   II. Causal, *to make angry :* Pass. *to be angered,* Id.

ἀγριάς, άδος, ἡ, = ἀγρία, pecul. fem. of ἄγριος, *wild,* ἄμπελον ἀγριάδα Anth.

ἀγρι-έλαιος, ον, (ἐλαία) *of a wild olive,* Anth.   II. as Subst. *a wild olive,* Lat. *oleaster,* Theocr., N. T.

ἀγριο-ποιός, όν, (ποιέω) *writing wild poetry,* Ar.

ἄγριος, α, ον and ος, ον: Comp. -ώτερος; Sup. -ώτατος : (ἀγρός) :—*living in the fields,* Lat. *agrestis :*   I. of animals, *wild, savage,* αἶξ, σῦς Il.; ἵπποι, ὄνοι Hdt., etc. ; of men, Id. ; of *a countryman,* as opp. to a citizen, Mosch.   2. of trees, *wild,* Hdt., etc. ; μητρὸς ἀγρίας ἄπο made from the *wild* vine, Aesch. ; ἀγρ. ἔλαιον, Soph.   3. of countries, *wild, uncultivated,* Plat.   II. of men and animals, *having qualities incident to a wild state :*   1. in moral sense, *savage, fierce,* Lat. *ferus, ferox,* Hom., etc.   2. *wild, brutal, coarse, boorish, rude,* Hom., etc. ; ἀγριώτατα ἤθεα Hdt. ; ἐς τὸ ἀγριώτερον *to harsher measures,* Thuc.   3. of things and circumstances, *cruel, harsh,* Aesch., etc. ; νὺξ ἀγριωτέρη *more wild, stormy,* Hdt. :—ἀγρ. νόσος *a malignant disease,* Soph.   III. Adv. -ίως, *savagely,* Aesch., etc. : also ἄγρια as neut. pl., Hes., Mosch.

ἀγριότης, ητος, ἡ, (ἄγριος) *wildness, savageness,* Xen., etc.   II. in moral sense, *savageness, fierceness, cruelty,* Plat., etc.

ἀγριό-φωνος, ον, (φωνή) *with wild rough voice,* Od.

ἀγριόω, aor. 1 ἠγρίωσα : (ἄγριος) :—*to make wild* or *savage ;* τινί against one, Eur. :—Pass., impf. ἠγριούμην, aor. 1 ἠγριώθην : pf. ἠγρίωμαι :—*to grow wild* or *savage,* and in pf. *to be so,* Eur.   2. in moral sense, *to be savage, fierce,* Soph., etc.

ἀγρι-ωπός, όν, (ὤψ) *wild-looking,* Eur.

ἀγρο-βότης, ον, Dor. -ας, α, ὁ, (βόσκω) *feeding in the field, dwelling in the country,* Soph., Eur.

ἀγρο-γείτων, ονος, ὁ, *a country neighbour,* Plut.

ἀγρο-δότης, ου, ὁ, *a giver of booty* or *prey,* Anth.

ἀγρόθεν, Adv. (ἀγρός) *from the country,* Od., Eur., etc.

ἀγροικία, ἡ, *rusticity, boorishness, coarseness,* Plat. ; and

ἀγροικίζομαι, Dep. *to be rude and boorish,* Plat. From

ἄγρ-οικος, ον, *of* or *in the country,* Ar., etc.   2. of men, *dwelling in the country, a countryman, rustic,* Id. :—then, opp. to ἀστεῖος, *clownish, boorish, rude,* Id. :—the character of the ἄγροικος is described by Theophr.   II. Adv. -κως, Ar.; Comp. -οτέρως, Plat., Xen. ; but -ότερον, Plat.   2. of land, *rough, uncultivated,* Thuc.

ἀγροιώτης, ου, ὁ, = ἀγρότης I, *a countryman,* Hom., Hes., etc.   II. as Adj. *rustic,* Anth.

ἀγρόμενος, Ep. aor. 2 part. pass. of ἀγείρω.

ἀγρόνδε, Adv. (ἀγρός) *to the country,* Od.

ἀγρόνομος or -νόμος, ον, (νέμομαι) *haunting the country, rural, wild,* Od., Aesch. :—of places, Soph.   II. as Subst., *overseer of public lands,* a magistrate at Athens, Plat.

᾿ΑΓΡΟ῀Σ [ᾰ by nature], οῦ, ὁ, Lat. *AGER, a field,* in pl. *fields, lands,* Hom., etc. : in sing. *a farm,* Od.   2.

the country, opp. to the town, Ib. : ἀγρῷ or ἐπ᾽ ἀγροῦ in the country, Ib. ; κατ᾽ ἀγρούς Ib. ; ἐπ᾽ ἀγρῶν Soph.

ἀγρότερος, α, ον, poët. for ἄγριος, wild, of animals, Hom., etc. 2. of countrymen, Anth. 3. of plants, wild, Id. II. (ἄγρα) fond of the chase :—Ἀγροτέρα, the Huntress, i. e. Artemis, Il., Xen.

ἀγροτήρ [ᾰ], ῆρος, ὁ, = ἀγρότης, Eur. :—fem. ἀγρότειρα, as Adj. rustic, Id.

ἀγρότης, ου, ὁ, (ἀγρός) a country-man, rustic, Eur. II. (ἄγρα) = ἀγρευτής a hunter, Od. :—fem. ἀγρῶτις, i. e. Artemis, Anth.

ἀγρο-φύλαξ [ῠ], ὁ, a watcher of the country, Anth.

ἀγρυπνέω, f. ήσω, (ἄγρυπνος) to lie awake, be wakeful, Theogn. ; ἀγρυπνεῖν τὴν νύκτα to pass a sleepless night, Xen. 2. metaph. to be watchful, N. T.

ἀγρυπνητικός, ή, όν, (ἀγρυπνέω) wakeful, Plut.

ἀγρυπνία, Ion. -ίη, ἡ, (ἀγρυπνέω) sleeplessness, waking, watching, Plat. ; ἀγρυπνίῃσιν εἴχετο Hdt.

ἄγρ-υπνος, ον, (ἄγρυπνος) hunting after sleep, i. e. sleepless, wakeful, Plat., etc. : metaph., Ζηνὸς ἄγρ. βέλος Aesch. :—τὸ ἄγρυπνον = ἀγρυπνία, Plat. II. act. keeping awake, μέριμναι Anth.

ἀγρώσσω, only in pres., Ep. for ἀγρεύω, to catch fish, Od.

ἀγρώστης, ου, ὁ, = ἀγρότης, Subst. and Adj., Soph., Eur.

ἄγρωστις, ιδος and εως, ἡ, a grass that mules fed on, Od., Theocr.

ἀγρότης, ου, ὁ, = ἀγρότης Adj., wild, Eur.: rustic, Anth.

ἀγυιά, ἡ, a street, highway, Hom., etc. (A quasi-participial form from ἄγω, cf. ὄργυια.)

ἀγυιάτης [ᾱτ], ον, voc. -ᾱτα, ὁ, = Ἀγυιεύς, Aesch. Hence ἀγυιᾶτις, ιδος, ἡ, fem. Adj., ἀγυιάτιδες θεραπεῖαι the worship of Apollo Agyieus, Eur.

Ἀγυιεύς, έως, ὁ, (ἀγυιά) name of Apollo, guardian of the streets, Eur. 2. a pillar set up at the street door, Ar.

ἀ-γυμνασία, ἡ, (γυμνάσιον) want of training, Ar.

ἀ-γύμναστος, ον, (γυμνάζω) unexercised, untrained, Xen. 2. unpractised, τινός in a thing, Eur., Xen., etc. ; also εἴς, πρός or περί τι, Plat., etc. 3. unharrassed, Soph. II. Adv., ἀγυμνάστως ἔχειν πρός τι to be unpractised in a thing, Xen.

ἄγυρις [ᾰ], ιος, ἡ, Aeol. form of ἀγορά, a gathering, crowd, Hom.

ἀγυρμός, ὁ, = ἄγυρις, Babr.

ἀγυρτάζω, only in pres., to collect by begging, Od. From

ἀγύρτης, ου, ὁ, (ἀγείρω) a collector : esp. a begging priest of Cybelé, Anth. : then, a beggar, mountebank, vagabond, juggler, Soph., Eur.

ἀγυρτικός, ή, όν, fit for an ἀγύρτης, vagabond, Plut.

ἀγύρτρια, ἡ, fem. of ἀγυρτήρ (= ἀγύρτης), Aesch.

ἀγχι-μάχος, ον, (ἄγχι, μάχομαι) fighting hand to hand, Il., Hes. ; τὰ ἀγχ. ὅπλα arms for close fight, Xen.

ἄγχι, (ἄγχω) = ἐγγύς, Adv. of Place, near, nigh, close by, absol. or c. gen., Hom. ; Comp. ἄγχιον, ἆσσον : Sup. ἄγχιστα (v. sub ἄγχιστος).

ἀγχί-αλος, ον and η, ον, (ἅλς) near the sea, of cities, Il. ; of islands, sea-girt, Aesch., Soph.

ἀγχι-βαθής, ές, (βάθος) deep near shore, of the sea, Od.

ἀγχι-γείτων, ον, gen. ονος, neighbouring, Aesch.

ἀγχί-θεος, ον, near the gods, i. e. like the gods or dwelling with them, Od. ; later, a demigod, Luc.

ἀγχί-θυρος, ον, (θύρα) next door, Theogn., Theocr.

ἀγχί-μολος, ον, (μολεῖν) coming near, c. gen., Theocr. : —in Hom. only in neut. as Adv. near, close at hand ; so ἐξ ἀγχιμόλοιο Il.

ἀγχι-νεφής, ές, (νέφος) near the clouds, Anth.

ἀγχί-νοια, ἡ, readiness of mind, ready wit, sagacity, Plat., etc. From

ἀγχί-νοος, ον, contr. -νους, ουν, ready of wit, sagacious, shrewd, Od., Plat., etc.

ἀγχί-πλοος, ον, contr. -πλους, ουν, near by sea, ἀγχ. πόρος a short voyage, Eur.

ἀγχί-πορος, ον, passing near, always near, Anth.

ἀγχί-πτολις, εως, ὁ, ἡ, poët. for ἀγχίπολις, near the city, dwelling hard by, Aesch., Soph.

ἀγχιστεία, ἡ, (ἀγχιστεύω) nearness of kin, Plat. 2. rights of kin, of inheritance, Ar.

ἀγχιστεῖα, τά, = foreg., Soph.

ἀγχιστεύς, έως, ὁ, mostly in pl. ἀγχιστεῖς, (ἄγχιστος) closely akin, of nations, Hdt. : next of kin, Luc.

ἀγχιστεύω, f. σω, (ἄγχιστος) to be next or near, c. dat., Eur. II. to be next of kin, Isae.

ἀγχιστήρ, ῆρος, ὁ, one who brings near, the immediate author, Soph. ; and

ἀγχιστῖνος, η, ον, close together, crowded, in heaps, Hom. From

ἄγχιστος, ον, Sup. Adj., (ἄγχι) nearest, Pind., Trag. ; γένει ἄγχιστος πατρός nearest of kin to him, Eur. II. in Hom. only neut. as Adv., ἄγχιστον or ἄγχιστα, most nearly like, c. gen., Διὸς ἄγχ. next to Zeus, Aesch. ; ἄγχ. τοῦ βωμοῦ Hdt. 2. of Time, most lately, but now, most recently, Il., Hdt.

ἀγχί-στροφος, ον, (στρέφω) turning closely, quick-wheeling, of a hawk, Theogn. 2. quick-changing, sudden, Thuc. ; neut. pl. as Adv. suddenly, Hdt.

ἀγχι-τέρμων, ον, gen. ονος, (τέρμα) near the borders, neighbouring, Soph.

ἄγχ, poët. for ἀνά before γ, Aesch.

ἀγχί-τοκος, ον, (τίκτω) in the pangs of child-birth, Anth.

ἀγχόθεν, Adv. (ἀγχοῦ) from nigh at hand, Hdt.

ἀγχόθι, Adv. = ἀγχοῦ, near, c. gen., Hom. ; absol., Theocr.

ἀγχόνη, ἡ, (ἄγχω) a throttling, strangling, hanging, Trag., etc. ; ἔργα κρείσσον᾽ ἀγχόνης deeds beyond (i. e. too bad for) hanging, Soph. ; τάδ᾽ ἀγχόνης πέλας 'tis nigh as bad as hanging, Eur. :—in pl., ἐν ἀγχόναις θάνατον λαβεῖν to die by hanging, Id.

ἀγχόνιος, α, ον, (ἄγχω) fit for strangling, βρόχος Eur.

ἀγχοτάτω, Adv., Sup. of ἀγχοῦ, like ἄγχιστα, nearest, next, c. gen., Hdt. ; ἀγχ. τινός very near, i. e. very like, some one, Id. ; also τινί Id. :—οἱ ἀγχοτάτω προσήκοντες the nearest of kin, Id. :—so, ἀγχότατα ἔχειν τινός to be most like one, Id.

ἀγχότερος, α, ον, Comp. of ἀγχοῦ, nearer, c. gen., Hdt.

ἀγχοῦ, = ἄγχι, near, nigh, ἀγχοῦ δ᾽ ἱσταμένη Hom. ; c. gen., Id., Hdt.

ἄγχ-ουρος, ον, Ion. for ἄγχ-ορος, neighbouring, Anth.

ΑΓΧΩ, f. ἄγξω : aor. I ἦγξα : cf. ἀπάγχω :—to compress, press tight, esp. the throat, to strangle, throttle, choke, ἄγχε μιν ἱμὰς ὑπὸ δειρήν Il. ; τὸν Κέρβερον ἀπῆγξας ἄγχων Ar. : metaph. of creditors, Id., N. T. ; of a guilty conscience, τοῦτο ἄγχει Dem.

ἀγχ-ώμαλος, ον, (ἄγχι, ὁμαλός) nearly equal, ἀγχώμαλοι

ἐν χειροτονίᾳ Thuc.; ἀγχ. μάχη a *doubtful* battle, Id. : —neut. pl. as Adv., ἀγχώμαλα ναυμαχεῖν, Lat. *aequo Marte pugnare*, Id. Adv. -λως, Luc.

ΑΓΩ [ᾰ], impf. ἦγον, Ep. ἄγον, 3 dual ἀγέτην, Dor. ἆγον, Ion. ἄγεσκον:—fut. ἄξω, Ep. inf. ἀξέμεναι, -έμεν :— aor. 2 ἤγαγον; aor. 1 ἦξα is rare:—pf. ἦχα, redupl. ἀγήοχα:—Pass., fut. ἀχθήσομαι, also med. ἄξομαι in pass. sense : aor. 1 ἤχθην, Ion. ἄχθην: pf. ἦγμαι:

I. *to lead* or *carry*, *to convey*, *bring*, with living creatures as the object, φέρω being used of things, δῶκε δ' ἄγειν ἑτάροισι γυναῖκα, καὶ τρίποδα φέρειν Il. (v. infr. 3 ;) ἄγ. εἰς or πρὸς τόπον; poët. also c. acc. loci, 'Αχέροντος ἀκτάν Soph. b. intr. of soldiers, *to march*, Xen., etc.; so, ἄγωμεν *let us go*, N. T. c. part. ἄγων is used in gen. sense, *taking*, στῆσε δ' ἄγων, where we should use two Verbs, *took and placed*, Hom. 2. *to take with one*, ἑταίρους Id. 3. *to carry off* as captives or booty, Id., etc. :—mostly in phrase ἄγειν καὶ φέρειν *to sweep a country* of all its plunder (where φέρειν refers to *things*, ἄγειν *to men and cattle*); then c. acc. loci, φέρων καὶ ἄγων τὴν Βιθυνίδα *plundering* all Bithynia, Xen.:—in Pass., ἀγόμεθα, φερόμεθα Eur. 4. ἄγειν εἰς δίκην or δικαστήριον, ἄγ. ἐπὶ τοὺς δικαστάς *to carry one before a court of justice*, Lat. *rapere in jus*, Att.; so, simply ἄγειν, Plat. 5. *to fetch*, ἄξεθ' ὕων τὸν ἄριστον Od. : of things, *to bring in*, *import*, οἶνον νῆες ἄγουσι Il. 6. *to draw on*, *bring on*, πῆμα τόδ' ἤγαγον Οὐρανίωνες Ib.; 'Ιλίῳ φθοράν Aesch. 7. *to bear up*, φελλοὶ δ' ὣς, ἄγουσι δίκτυον Id. II. *to lead towards* a point, *lead on*, τὸν δ' ἄγε μοῖρα κακὴ θανάτοιο τέλοσδε Il.; also, c. inf., ἄγει θανεῖν *leads* to death, Id.—ὁδὸς ἄγει the road *leads*, εἰς or ἐπὶ τόπον, Soph., Plat. 2. metaph. *to lead*, as a general, Il.; ἄγ. στρατιάν, ναῦς, etc., Thuc.; ἄγ. τὴν πολιτείαν *to conduct* the government, Id. 3. *to bring up*, *train*, *educate*, Plat. III. *to draw out* in length, τεῖχος ἄγειν *to draw a line* of wall, Lat. *ducere*, Thuc.:—Pass., ἦκται ἡ διῶρυξ Hdt.; κόλπου ἀγομένου a bay *being formed*, Id. IV. *to keep in memory*, καί μευ κλέος ἦγον Ἀχαιοί Od. 2. like *agere*, *to hold*, *celebrate*, ἑορτήν, τὰ Ὀλύμπια Hdt., etc. 3. also *to hold*, *keep*, *observe*, σπονδὰς ἄγ. πρός τινας Thuc.; εἰρήνην Plat.: often c. acc., as periphrasis for a Verb, σχολὴν ἄγειν=σχολάζειν, Eur.; ἡσυχίαν ἄγ.=ἡσυχάζειν, Xen. 4. *to keep*, *maintain*, ἐλευθέραν ἦγε τὴν Ἑλλάδα Dem. 5. of Time, *to pass*, ποίας ἡμέρας δοκεῖς μ' ἄγειν; Soph. V. like ἡγέομαι, Lat. *ducere*, *to hold*, *account*, *reckon*, ἐν τιμῇ ἄγειν, ἐν οὐδεμίῃ μοίρῃ, περὶ πλείστου ἄγειν Hdt.; θεοὺς ἄγειν *to believe in* gods, Aesch.; τιμιώτερον ἄγ. τινά Thuc.: —so with Adverbs, δυσφόρως ἄγ. *to think* insufferable, Soph.; ἐντίμως ἄγειν Plat. VI. *to weigh* so much, ἄγειν μνᾶν, τριακοσίους δαρεικούς *to weigh* a mina, 300 darics, Dem., where the acc. is the weight which the thing *weighs* or *draws down*: cf. ἕλκω. VII. on ἄγε, ἄγετε, v. sub vocc.

B. Med. ἄγομαι, *to carry away for oneself*, *take with one*, χρυσόν τε καὶ ἄργυρον οἴκαδ' ἄγεσθαι Od. 2. ἄγεσθαι γυναῖκα, Lat. *uxorem ducere*, *to take to oneself* a wife, Ib. ; in full, ἄγ. γυναῖκα ἐς τὰ οἰκία Hdt.; and simply ἄγεσθαι, *to marry*, Il., etc. :—also of the father, *to bring home* a wife for his son, Od. 3. διὰ στόμα

ἄγεσθαι μῦθον *to let pass* through the mouth, i. e. *to utter*, Il. 4. ἄγεσθαί τι ἐς χεῖρας *to take* a thing into *one's* hands, and so *to undertake*, Hdt.

ἀγώ [ᾰ], crasis for ἃ ἐγώ.

ἀγωγαῖος, ον, *fit for leading by*, of a dog's leash, Anth.; and

ἀγωγεύς, έως, ὁ, *one that draws* or *drags*, Hdt. II. *a leading-rein*, *leash*, Soph., Xen. From

ἀγωγή, ἡ, (ἄγω) *a carrying away*, *carriage*, Hdt., etc.; πρὸς τὰς ἀγωγὰς χρῆσθαι ὑποζυγίοις Plat. b. intr., τὴν ἀγωγὴν ἐποιεῖτο pursued his *voyage*, Thuc.: *movement*, τοῦ ποδός Plat. 2. *a bringing to* or *in*, ὑμῶν ἡ ἐς τοὺς ὀλίγους ἀγ. your *bringing* us *before* the council, Thuc. 3. *a carrying off*, *abduction*, Aesch., Soph. II. *a leading towards* a point, *guiding*, ἵππου Xen. 2. *the leading* of an army, Plat.; ἐν ταῖς ἀγ. on *marches*, Xen. 3. *a training*, *education*, Plat., etc. :—of plants, *culture*, Theophr.

ἀγώγιμος, ον, (ἄγω) *easy to be led* or *carried*, τρισσῶν ἀμαξῶν ἀγώγιμον βάρος weight *enough to load* three wains, Eur.; τὰ ἀγώγιμα *things portable*, *wares*, Xen., etc. II. of persons, *to be carried off*, *delivered into bondage*, Dem. 2. *easily led*, *complaisant*, Plut.

ἀγώγιον, τό, (ἄγω) *the load of* a wagon, Xen.

ἀγωγός, όν, (ἄγω) *leading*, and as Subst. *a guide*, Hdt., etc.: c. gen., δύναμις ἀνθρώπων ἀγωγός power *of leading* men, Plut. II. *leading towards* a point, εἰς, πρός or ἐπί τι Plat., etc. III. *drawing forth*, *eliciting*, χοαὶ νεκρῶν ἀγωγοί Eur.; δακρύων ἀγ. Id. 2. absol. *attractive*, Plut.

ἀγών [ᾰ], crasis for ὁ ἀγών.

ἀγών [ᾰ], ῶνος, ὁ, (ἄγομαι) *a number of people brought together*, *a gathering*, *assembly*, like ἀγορά, ἵξανεν εὐρὺν ἀγῶνα, λῦτο δ' ἀγών, ἐν ἀγῶνι νεῶν Hom.: esp. *an assembly met to see games*, Id., etc. 2. *a place of contest*, *the arena*, Id., etc.; βῆτην ἐς μέσσον ἀγῶνα Il. II. *an assembly* of the Greeks at their great national games, ὁ ἐν Ὀλυμπίῃ ἀγών Hdt.; ὁ Ὀλυμπικὸς ἀγών Ar. 2. *the contest for a prize* at the games, ἀγὼν ἱππικός, γυμνικός Hdt., etc.; ἀγὼν τῶν ἀνδρῶν, in which the chorus was composed of men, opp. to τῶν παίδων, Dem., etc. :—hence, ἀγῶνα ἄγειν, καθιστάναι, τιθέναι, προτιθέναι, ποιεῖν, *to hold* or *propose a contest*; ἀγῶνα or ἐν ἀγῶνι νικᾶν, *to win one* or *at one*. III. *generally*, *any struggle*, *trial*, or *danger*, πολλοὺς ἀγῶνας ἐξιών, of Hercules, Soph.; ἀγὼν πρόκειται, c. inf., it is *hard* or *dangerous* to do a thing, Hdt.:—also, ἀγὼν περὶ τῆς ψυχῆς, περὶ μεγίστων *a struggle* for life and death, for one's highest interests, Eur. 2. *a battle*, *action*, Thuc. 3. *an action at law*, *trial*, Plat., etc. 4. metaph., οὐ λόγων ἔθ' ἀγών now is not *the time for speaking*, etc., Eur.; οὐχ ἕδρας ἀγ. 'tis no *time for sitting still*, Id.

ἀγων-άρχης, ου, ὁ, (ἄρχω) *judge of a contest*, Soph.

ἀγωνία, Ion. -ίη, ἡ, (ἀγών) *a contest*, *struggle for victory*, διὰ πάσης ἀγωνίης ἔχειν *to embrace every kind of contest*, Hdt.; πολεμίων ἀγωνία Eur.; ἐν δημοτικῇ ἀγ. Xen. 2. *gymnastic exercise*, *wrestling*, Plat., etc.: generally, *exercise*, Plut. 3. of the mind, *agony*, *anguish*, ἐν φόβῳ καὶ πολλῇ ἀγωνίᾳ Dem.

ἀγωνιάω, f. άσω [ᾰ]: aor. 1 ἠγωνίασα: pf. ἠγωνίακα: (ἀγωνία):—like ἀγωνίζομαι, *to contend eagerly*, *struggle*,

Dem., etc. **II.** *to be distressed, be in an agony,* Plat.; περί τινος Arist.; ἐπί τινι Plut.

ἀγωνίδαται, v. ἀγωνίζομαι Β.

ἀγωνίζομαι, fut. ἰοῦμαι (in pass. sense, v. infr. Β): aor. 1 ἠγωνισάμην: pf. ἠγώνισμαι (in act. sense): aor. 1 ἠγωνίσθην :—(ἀγών): **A.** as Dep. *to contend for a prize,* esp. in the public games, Hdt.; πρός τινα Plat.; τινί Id., etc.; περί τινος *about* a thing, Hdt., etc. : c. acc. cogn., ἀγ. στάδιον Id.; ἀγῶνα. περὶ τῆς ψυχῆς ἀγ. Dem. **2.** *to fight,* Hdt., Thuc.; περὶ τῶν ἁπάντων ἀγ. Id.; πρός τινα Id.: c. acc. cogn., ἣν [μάχην] ἀγωνίζεσθε Eur. **3.** *to contend for the prize on the stage,* both of the poet, Hdt., etc., and of the actor, Dem. : generally *to contend for victory,* καλῶς ἠγώνισαι Plat. **4.** of public speaking, Xen. **II.** *to contend against,* as law-term, Antipho; c. acc. cogn., ἀγ. δίκην, γραφήν *to fight a cause to the last,* Dem.; ἀγ. ψευδομαρτυριῶν (sc. γραφήν) Id.; ἀγ. ἀγῶνα Andoc., etc.; but ἀγ. φόνον *to fight against* a charge of murder, Eur. **III.** generally, *to struggle, to exert oneself,* c. inf., Thuc.; c. acc. cogn., ἃ μὲν ἠγωνίσω Dem.

B. as Pass. *to be won by a contest, to be brought to issue,* mostly in pf., πολλοὶ ἀγῶνες ἀγωνίδαται (Ion. for ἠγωνισμένοι εἰσί) Hdt.; τὰ ἠγωνισμένα the contested points, Eur., etc.; ὁ ἀγωνιζόμενος νόμος the law *under debate,* Dem.; fut. med. in pass. sense, ἀγωνιεῖται τὸ πρᾶγμα it *shall be brought to issue,* Id.

ἀγώνιος, ον, (ἀγών) *of* or *belonging to the contest,* ἄεθλος ἀγ. its prize, Pind.; of Hermes, as *president of games,* Id.; of Zeus as *decider of the contest,* Soph. ;—the ἀγώνιοι θεοί, in Aesch., etc., are prob. the gods *who presided over the great games* (Zeus, Poseidon, Apollo, Hermes). **2.** ἀγωνίῳ σχολᾷ in Soph. Aj. 195 is prob. an oxymoron, rest *full of conflict, uneasy* rest.

ἀγώνισις, ἡ, (ἀγωνίζομαι) contest *for a prize,* Thuc.

ἀγώνισμα, ατος, τό, (ἀγωνίζομαι) a contest, in pl. deeds *done in battle, brave deeds, feats,* Hdt. **2.** in sing., ἀγ. τινός a feat for him *to be proud of,* Thuc.; ξυνέσεως ἀγ. a fine stroke of wit, Id.; ἀρᾶς ἀγ. the issue of the curse, Eur. **II.** ἀγ. ποιεῖσθαί τι to make it an object *to strive for,* Hdt.; οὐ μικρὸν τὸ ἀγ. προστάττεις Luc. **III.** that *with which one contends,* a prize-essay, declamation, Plut.; τὸ παραχρῆμα Thuc.

ἀγωνισμός, ὁ, (ἀγωνίζομαι) rivalry, Thuc.

ἀγωνιστέον, verb. Adj. of ἀγωνίζομαι, one must contend, Xen., etc.

ἀγωνιστής, οῦ, ὁ, (ἀγωνίζομαι) a rival at the games, competitor, Hdt., etc. :—as Adj., ἀγ. ἵπποι *race*-horses, Plut. **2.** a debater, opponent, Plat. **II.** c. gen. one who struggles for a thing, τῆς ἀρετῆς Aeschin.

ἀγωνιστικός, ή, όν, (ἀγωνίζομαι) fit for contest or debate, Arist. **II.** of persons, contentious, eager for applause, Plat. :—Adv. -κῶς, contentiously, ἀγ. ἔχειν to be disposed to fight, Plut.

ἀγωνοθεσία, ἡ, the office of ἀγωνοθέτης, direction of games, Plut.

ἀγωνοθετέω, f. ήσω, to direct the games, exhibit them, Thuc.; ἀγ. Ὀλύμπια Anth. **2.** c. acc., ἀγ. στάσιν *to stir up* sedition, Plut. **II.** generally, *to act as judge,* decide, Dem. From

ἀγωνο-θέτης, ου, ὁ, τί-θημι) judge of the contests,

director of the games, or (later) an exhibitor of games, Hdt., Att. **2.** generally, a judge, Xen., etc.

ἀδαημονία, ἡ, ignorance or unskilfulness in doing, c. inf., Od. From

ἀ-δαήμων, ον, (*δάω) unknowing, ignorant of a thing, c. gen., Il.; κακῶν ἀδαήμονες Od.

ἀ-δαής, ές, (*δάω) = foreg., c. gen. pers., Hdt.; c. gen. rei, Id.; c. inf. unknowing how to do, Soph. : absol., Xen.

ἀ-δάητος, ον, (*δάω) unknown, Hes.

ἄ-δαιτος, ον, (δαίνυμαι) of which none might eat, Aesch.

ἄ-δακρῦς, υ, gen. υος, = ἀδάκρυτος 1, Pind., Eur. **II.** = ἀδάκρυτος 11, Id.

ἀδακρῦτί, Adv. without tears, Isocr., Plut.

ἀ-δάκρῦτος, ον, (δακρύω) without tears, i. e. **I.** act. tearless, ἀδ. καὶ ἀπήμων Il.; ἀδακρύτω ἔχειν ὄσσε Od. : —εὐνάζειν ἀδακρύτων βλεφάρων πόθον to lull the desire of her eyes so that they weep no more, Soph.; cf. ἄδερκτος. **II.** pass. unwept, unmourned, Id. **2.** costing no tears, τρόπαια Plut.

ἀδαμάντινος, η, ον, (ἀδάμας) adamantine, Aesch., etc.: —metaph. hard as adamant, σιδηροῖς καὶ ἀδαμαντίνοις λόγοις Plat.; οὐκ ἀδ. ἐντί, of a girl, Theocr. :—Adv. -νως, Plat.

ἀδἄμαντό-δετος, ον, iron-bound, Aesch.

ἀ-δάμας, αντος, ὁ, (δαμάζω) properly the untamed, unconquerable : **I.** as Subst. adamant, i.e. the hardest metal, prob. steel : metaph. of any thing unalterable, ἔπος ἐρέω ἀδάμαντι πελάσσας having fixed it firm as adamant, Orac. ap. Hdt. **2.** the diamond, Theophr. **II.** as Adj., metaph., the inflexible, of Hades, Theocr.

ἀ-δάμαστος, ον, (δαμάζω) epith. of Hades, inflexible, Il. :—later in the proper sense, untamed, unbroken, ἵππος Xen.

ἀ-δάμᾱτος, ον, = ἀδάμαστος, unconquered, Aesch., etc.; of females, unwedded, Soph. : of beasts, untaméd, v. sub πέσημα. [ἀδάμᾱτω in Theocr.]

ἀ-δάπᾱνος, ον, (δαπάνη) without expense, costing nothing, γλυκέα καδάπανα (crasis for καὶ ἀδάπανα) Ar. : —Adv. ἀδαπάνως τέρψαι φρένα Eur.

ἄδας, Ἄιδας, Dor. for ἄδης, Ἀίδης.

ἄ-δαστος, ον, (δατέομαι) undivided, Soph.

ἀδδηκότες, ἄδδην, ἀδδηφαγέω, v. ἀδέω, ἅδην, ἀδηφαγέω.

ἄδε, 3 sing. aor. 2 of ἀνδάνω.

ἀδέα, Dor. for ἡδεῖα, and also for ἡδύν : v. ἡδύς.

ἀ-δεής, Ep. ἀδειής, ές : Ep. voc. ἀδδεές : (δέος) :—without fear, fearless, εἴ περ ἀδειής τ᾿ ἐστί, of Hector, Il.; κύον ἀδδεές Ib. **2.** fearless, secure (v. ἀλεής), τὸ ἀδεές, security, Thuc.; ἀδεὲς θανάτου without fear of death, Plat.; ἀδεὲς δέος δεδιέναι to fear where no fear is, Id. **II.** causing no fear, not formidable, πρὸς ἐχθρούς Thuc. **III.** Adv. ἀδεῶς, without fear, confidently, Hdt., etc. **2.** without stint, freely, Thuc.

ἄδεια, ἡ, (ἀδεής) freedom from fear, ἀδείην διδόναι to grant an amnesty, indemnity, Hdt.; ἐν ἀδείῃ εἶναι Id.; τῶν σωμάτων ἄδειαν ποιεῖν Thuc.; ἄδειάν τινι παρασκευάζειν, παρέχειν Dem.; opp. to ἄδειαν λαμβάνειν to receive indemnity, Id.; ἀδείας τυγχάνειν Id.

ἀδειής, ές, Ep. for ἀδεής.

ἀ-δείμαντος, ον, (δειμαίνω) fearless, dauntless, Pind.,

etc. :—Adv. -τως, Aesch.   2. *where no fear is*, οἰκία Luc.

ἀδεῖν, aor. 2 inf. of ἀνδάνω.

ἄ-δειπνος, ον, (δεῖπνον) *supperless*, Xen., etc.

ἀ-δέκαστος, ον, (δεκάζω) *unbribed*, Arist. :—Comp. Adv. -ότερον Luc.

ἀ-δεκάτευτος, ον, (δεκατεύω) *not tithed, tithe-free*, Ar.

ἀδελφέα, -εή, **ἀδελφεός**, -ειός, v. ἀδελφή, ἀδελφός.

ἀδελφεο-κτόνος, ον, Ion. for ἀδελφοκτόνος.

ἀδελφή, ἡ, fem. of ἀδελφός, *a sister*, Trag., etc. ; Ion. ἀδελφεή, Hdt. ; Ep. ἀδελφείη, Anth. ; Dor. ἀδελφεά, Soph.   2. *a sister* (as a fellow Christian), N. T.

ἀδελφιδέος, contr. -οῦς, ὁ, *a brother's* or *sister's son, a nephew*, Hdt.

ἀδελφιδῆ, ἡ, Att. contr. for ἀδελφιδέη, *a brother's* or *sister's daughter, a niece*, Ar., etc.

ἀδελφίδιον, τό, Dim. of ἀδελφός, Ar.

ἀδελφο-κτόνος, ον, (κτείνω) *murdering a brother* or *sister*, Hdt. (in Ion. form ἀδελφεοκτ-), Plut.

ἀδελφός [ἄ], (a copul., δελφύς ; cf. Lat. *co-uterinus*), so that ἀδελφοί are properly *sons of the same mother* :   I. as Subst., ἀδελφός, ὁ, voc. ἄδελφε (not -φέ), Ion. ἀδελφεός, Ep. -ειός :—*a brother*, or generally, *a near kinsman*, ἀδελφοὶ *brother and sister*, like Lat. *fratres*, Eur.; ἀδελφεοὶ ἀπ' ἀμφοτέρων *brothers by both parents*, i.e. not half-brothers, Hdt.   2. *a brother* (as a fellow Christian), N. T.   II. Adj., ἀδελφός, ή, όν, *brotherly* or *sisterly*, Trag., Plat.   2. like Lat. *geminus, gemellus*, of anything *in pairs, twin*, Xen. :—then, *just like*, c. gen. or dat., ἀδελφὰ τῶνδε, ἀδελφὰ τούτοισι Soph.

ἀδελφότης, ητος, ἡ, (ἀδελφός) *the brotherhood*, N. T.

ἀ-δέξιος, ον, (δεξιά) *left-handed, awkward*, Luc.

ἀ-δερκής, ές, (δέρκομαι) *unseen, invisible*, Anth.

ἄ-δερκτος, ον, (δέρκομαι) *not seeing*, ἀδέρκτων ὀμμάτων τητώμενος *reft of thine eyes so that they see not*, Soph.; cf. ἀδάκρυτος I :—Adv. -τως, *without looking*, Id.

ἄ-δεσμος, ον, *unfettered, unbound*, ἄδ. φυλακή, Lat. *libera custodia*, our 'parole,' Thuc., etc. ; δεσμὸς ἄδεσμος *bond that is no bond*, of a wreath, Eur.

ἀ-δέσποτος, ον, (δεσπότης) *without master*, Plat., etc.

ἄ-δετος, ον, *unbound, free*, Dem.

ἀ-δευκής, ές, a word used by Hom. only in Od. as epith. of ὄλεθρος, πότμος, φῆμις, commonly expl. *not sweet, bitter, cruel* (from an old word δευκής *sweet*) ; but more prob. it means *unexpected, sudden* (from δοκ-έω).

ἀ-δέψητος, ον, (δεψέω) *untanned*, of a raw hide, Od.

ἀδέω [ἄ], (ἄω *satio*) *to be sated* (only found in two Homeric forms, aor. 1 opt. and pf. part., μὴ ξεῖνος δείπνῳ ἀδήσειε lest he *should be sated with* the repast, *feel loathing at* it ; καμάτῳ ἀδηκότες ἠδὲ καὶ ὕπνῳ *sated with* toil and sleep.

ἄδη, 3 sing. aor. 2 subj. of ἀνδάνω.

ἀ-δήϊος, contr. **ἀ-δῇος**, ον, *unassailed, unravaged*, Soph.

ἄ-δηκτος, ον, (δάκνω) *unbitten, not gnawed* or *worm-eaten*, Hes. (in Sup. ἀδηκτοτάτη) :—Adv. -τως, Plut.

ἀδηλέω, *to be in the dark about* a thing, Soph. ; and

ἀδηλία, ἡ, *uncertainty*, Anth. From

ἄ-δηλος, ον, *not seen* or *known, unknown, obscure*, Hes., Soph., Plat.   II. of things, ἄδ. θάνατοι death *by an*

unknown hand, Soph. ; ἄδ. ἔχθρα *secret* enmity, Thuc.; ῥεῖ πᾶν ἄδηλον *melts all to nothing*, Soph. ; ἄδ. τινι *unseen, unobserved by* him, Xen.   b. neut. ἄδηλόν [ἐστι] εἰ .., ὅτι .., *it is uncertain* whether .., *unknown* that .., Plat., etc.; so, ἄδηλον μή .., Id. :—absol., ἄδηλον ὄν *it being uncertain*, Thuc.; so, ἐν ἀδηλοτέρῳ εἶναι Xen.   c. ἄδηλος often agrees with the subject (like δίκαιός εἰμι), παῖδες ἄδηλοι ὁποτέρων = ἄδηλόν ἐστιν ὁποτέρων παῖδές εἰσιν Lys., etc.   III. Adv. -λως, *secretly*, Thuc., etc.; Sup. -ότατα, Id.

ἀδημονέω [ἄδ-], aor. 1 inf. ἀδημονῆσαι :—*to be sorely troubled*, ἀδημονῆσαι τὰς ψυχάς Xen.   (Deriv. uncertain.)   Hence

ἀδημονία, ἡ, *trouble, distress*, Anth., Plut.

ἄδην or **ἄδην** [ἄ], (ἄω *satio*) Adv., Lat. *satis, to one's fill*, ἔδμεναι ἄδην *to eat their fill*, Il.   2. c. gen., οἵ μιν ἄδην ἐλόωσι πολέμοιο who may drive him *to satiety* of war, Ib. ; ἄδην ἔλειξεν αἵματος *licked his fill* of blood, Aesch. ; καὶ τούτων μὲν ἄδην *enough* of this, Plat. ; c. part., ἄδην εἶχον κτείνοντες Hdt.   [ἄ, except in first place cited from Il., where it is commonly written ἄδδην.]

ἄδηος, ον, contr. for ἀδήϊος.

ἄ-δηρις, ιος, ὁ, ἡ, *without strife*, Anth.

ἀ-δήριτος, ον, (δηρίομαι) *without strife* or *battle*, Il.   II. *unconquerable*, ἀνάγκης σθένος Aesch. and εω ;

ᾅδης or **Ἅιδης**, ου, ὁ ; in Hom. also **Ἀΐδης**, αο, and εω ; Dor. **Ἀΐδας**, α : there is also a gen. **Ἀΐδι** (as if from Ἀΐς : (from a privat., ἰδεῖν) :—*Hades* or *Pluto* (cf. Πλούτων), the god of the nether world, son of Kronus and Rhea, brother to Zeus, Ζεὺς καὶ ἐγώ, τρίτατος δ' Ἀΐδης Il. ; called Ζεὺς καταχθόνιος Ib. ; εἰν or εἰς Ἀΐδαο (sc. δόμοις, δόμους) in, into *the nether world*, Hom. ; εἰν Ἀΐδος Il. ; ἐν Ἀΐδου, ἐς Ἀΐδου (sc. οἴκῳ, οἶκον) Att. :—also Ἀΐδόσδε Ib., Il.   II. as appellative, *Hades, the world below*, εἰσόκεν ἄϊδι κεύθωμαι Ib. ; ἐπὶ τὸν ᾅδην Luc. ; εἰς ἀΐδην Anth. ; ἐν τῷ ᾅδη N. T.   2. *the grave, death*, ᾅδης πόντιος death by sea, Aesch., etc. [ἀΐδης in Hom., Att. ᾅδης ; but in Trag. also ἀΐδας :—gen. ἄϊδος as an anapaest in Hom. ; gen. ἀΐδαο Id. ; gen. ἄϊδος before a vowel, Il.]

ἀδηκότες, ἀδήσειε, v. ἀδέω.

ἀδήσω, fut. of ἀνδάνω.

ἀδη-φάγος, ον, (ἄδην, φαγεῖν) *eating one's fill, gluttonous*, ἀδ. ἀνήρ, of an athlete, Theocr. ; τὴν ἀδ. νόσον this *devouring* sore, Soph.

ἀ-δήωτος, ον, (δηόω) *not ravaged*, Xen.

ἀ-διάβατος, ον, *not to be passed*, ποταμός, νάπος Xen.

ἀ-διάβλητος, ον, (διαβάλλω) *not listening to slander*, Plut.

ἀ-διάθετος, ον, (διατίθεμαι) *intestate*, Plut.

ἀ-διάκριτος, ον, *undecided*, Luc.

ἀ-διάλειπτος, ον, (διαλείπω) *unintermitting, incessant*, N. T. ; Adv. -τως, Polyb., N. T.

ἀ-διάλυτος, ον, (διαλύω) *undissolved, indissoluble*, Plat.

ἀ-δίαντος, ον, (διαίνω) *unwetted*, Simon.   II. ἀδίαντον, τό, a plant, *maiden-hair*, Theocr.

ἀ-δίαυλος, ον, *with no way back*, of Hades, Eur.

ἀ-διάφθαρτος, ον, (διαφθείρω) = ἀδιάφθορος I, Plat.

ἀ-διαφθορία, ἡ, *incorruption, uprightness*, N. T.   From

ἀ-διάφθορος, ον, (διαφθείρω) *uncorrupted*, Plat., etc.:—Adv. -ρως, Aeschin.   2. of judges and witnesses,

incorruptible, Plat., etc. : Sup. Adv. -ώτατα, Id. II. *imperishable*, Id.

ἀ-δίδακτος [ῐ], ον, *untaught, ignorant*, c. gen., ἀδ. ἐρώτων Anth. 2. *untrained*, of a chorus, Dem. II. of things, *untaught*, Plut., Luc.

ἀ-διέξοδος, ον, act. *unable to get out*, Anth.

ἀ-διερεύνητος, ον, (διερευνάω) *unquestioned*, Plut.

ἀ-διήγητος, ον, (διηγέομαι) *indescribable*, Xen., Dem.

ἀ-δίκαστος, ον, (δικάζω) *undecided*, Luc.

ἀδικείμενος, Boeot. for ἠδικημένος, pf. part. pass. of ἀδικέω.

ἀδικέω : Ion. impf. ἠδίκεον or -εῦν :—Pass., fut., in med. form ἀδικήσομαι or pass. ἀδικηθήσομαι : (ἄδικος) : —*to do wrong*, Hdt., etc.; τἀδικεῖν *wrong-doing*, Soph.; τὸ μἀδικεῖν *righteous dealing*, Aesch.; but, σχήσει τὸ μἀδικεῖν *will restrain wrong-doing*, Id.:—in legal phrase the particular case of wrong is added in part., Σωκράτης ἀδικεῖ διδάσκων Plat., Xen. :—c. acc. cogn., ἀδικίαν, ἀδίκημα, Plat., or a neut. Adj., ἀδικεῖν πολλά, μέγαλα, Id.; οὐδέν, μηδὲν ἀδ., Id. :—also, ἀδ. περί τα μυστήρια Dem. II. trans. c. acc. pers. *to do* one *wrong, to wrong, injure*, Hdt., etc. :—c. dupl. acc. *to wrong* one *in a thing*, Ar., etc.; τὰ μέγιστα ἀδ. τινά Dem.; ἀδ. τινα περί τινος Plat. :—Pass. *to be wronged*, μὴ δῆτ' ἀδικηθῶ Soph.; ἀδικεῖσθαι εἴς τι Eur. 2. *to spoil, damage*, ἀδ. γῆν Thuc.

ἀδίκημα, ατος, τό, (ἀδικέω) *a wrong done, a wrong*, Lat. *injuria*, Hdt., etc. :—c. gen. *a wrong done to* one, Dem. II. *that which is got by wrong, ill-gotten goods*, Plat.

ἀδικητέον, Verb. Adj. of ἀδικέω, *one must do wrong*, Plat.

ἀδικία, Ion. -ίη, ἡ, *wrong-doing, injustice*, Hdt., etc. II. like ἀδίκημα, *a wrong, injury*, Id., Plat.; and

ἀδίκιον, τό, *a wrong, wrong-dealing*, Hdt. II. ἀδικίου γραφή, an action *against public wrong-doers*, Plut. From

ἄ-δικος, ον, (δίκη) of persons, *wrong-doing, unrighteous, unjust*, Hes., Hdt., etc.; ἀδικώτατος Soph. :—ἀδ. εἴς τι *unjust in a thing*, ἔς τινα *towards a person*, Hdt.; περί τινα Xen.; c. inf. *so unjust as to* . . N. T. 2. ἀδ. ἵπποι *obstinate, unmanageable*, Xen. II. of things, *wrongly done, wrong, unjust*, ἔργματα Theogn., Hdt., etc.; τὸ δίκαιον καὶ τὸ ἀδ., τὰ δίκαια καὶ ἄδικα *right and wrong*, Plat. III. Adv. -κως, Solon, etc.; τοὺς ἀδ. θνήσκοντας Soph.; εἴτε δικαίως εἴτε ἀδ. *jure an injuria*, Hdt.; οὐκ ἀδ. *not without reason*, Plat.

'ΑΔΙΝΟ'Σ, ή, όν [ᾰ], *close-packed*: (v. ἀδρός):—hence, 1. *crowded, thronging*, of bees, flies, sheep, Hom.; ἀδινὰ δάκρυα *thick-falling* tears, Soph. 2. *vehement, loud*, of sounds, Il.; Σειρῆνες ἀδιναί *the loud-voiced Sirens*, Od. :—Adv. -νῶς, *frequently*, or *loudly, vehemently*, Il.; so ἀδινόν and ἀδινά as Adv., ἀδινὸν κλαίειν, μυκᾶσθαι, στοναχῆσαι Hom. : Comp. ἀδινώτερον Od.

ἀ-διόρθωτος, ον, (διορθόω) *not corrected, not set right*, Dem. :—of books, *unrevised*, Cic.; cf. διορθωτής.

ἀ-δίστακτος, ον, (διστάζω) *not doubted* :—Adv. -τως, Anth.

ἄ-διψος, ον, (δίψα) *not suffering from thirst*, Eur., etc.

ἀδμής, ῆτος, ὁ, ἡ, poët. for ἀδάματος, *untamed*, of cattle, Od. 2. of maidens, *unwedded*, Ib.

ἄ-δμητος, η, ον, poët. for ἀδάματος, in Hom. only in fem. and of cattle, *unbroken*, βοῦν ἀδμήτην, ἣν οὔ πω ὑπὸ ζυγὸν ἤγαγεν ἀνήρ Il.; ἵππον ἐξέτε' ἀδμήτην Ib. 2. like ἀδμής, *unwedded*, of maidens, h. Hom.

ἄδοι, 3 sing. aor. 2 opt. of ἀνδάνω.

ἀ-δόκητος, ον, (δοκέω) *unexpected*, Hes., Soph., etc.; τὸ ἀδ. *the unexpectedness*, Thuc. II. Adv. -τως, Id.; so ἀδόκητα as Adv., Eur.; ἀπὸ τοῦ ἀδοκήτου Thuc.

ἀ-δοκίμαστος, ον, (δοκιμάζω) *untried, unproved*, in regard to civic rights, Lys., etc.

ἀ-δόκιμος, ον, *not standing the test, spurious*, properly of coin, Plat. II. metaph. of persons, *rejected as false, disreputable, reprobate*, Eur., Xen., etc.

ἀδολεσχέω [ᾰ], f. ήσω, *to talk idly, prate*, Plat., Xen. From

ἀδο-λέσχης [ᾰ], ου, ὁ, *a garrulous fellow, idle talker*, Ar., Plat. (Prob. from ἄδην λέσχη, *talking to satiety*.)

ἀδολεσχία [ᾰ], ἡ, *garrulity, idle talk*, Ar., Plat., etc.; Theophr. wrote περὶ ἀδολεσχίας. From

ἀδό-λεσχος [ᾰ], ον = ἀδολέσχης, Anth.

ἄ-δολος, ον, *without fraud, guileless*, of treaties, σπονδαὶ ἄδ. καὶ ἀβλαβεῖς Thuc. :—Adv., often in the phrase ἀδόλως καὶ δικαίως, Lat. *sine dolo malo*, Id. II. of liquids, *unadulterated, genuine*, Aesch.; metaph. *guileless, pure*, Eur.

ἄδον, Ep. for ἔαδον, aor. 2 of ἀνδάνω.

ἀ-δόνητος, ον, (δονέω) *unshaken*, Anth.

ἀδονίς [ᾰ], ἡ, poët. for ἀηδονίς, Mosch.

ἀ-δόξαστος, ον, (δοξάζω) *not matter of opinion*, i. e. *certain*, Plat.

ἀδοξέω, f. ήσω, *to be held in no esteem, to stand in ill repute*, Eur., Dem. II. trans. *to hold in no esteem*, τινα Plut. : and

ἀδοξία, ἡ, *ill-repute, disgrace*, Thuc., Plat.; *obscurity*, Plut. From

ἄ-δοξος, ον, (δόξα) *inglorious, disreputable*, Xen., Dem.: —of persons, *obscure, ignoble*, Xen., etc. :—Adv. -ξως, Plut.

ἄδος [ᾰ], εος, τό, (ἄω *satio*) *satiety, loathing*, Il.

ἄδος, Dor. for ἧδος, for ἧδος, ἡδονή.

ἄ-δοτος, ον, *without gifts*, h. Hom.

ἄ-δουλος, ον, *unattended by slaves*, Eur.

ἀ-δούπητος, ον, (δουπέω) *noiseless*, Anth.

ἀ-δρανής, ές, (δραίνω) *inactive, powerless*, Babr., Anth. II. *intractable*, of iron, Plut.

'Αδράστεια, Ion. 'Αδρήστεια, ἡ, a name of Nemesis, Aesch. (Perhaps from *a privat.*, διδράσκω, *the Inevitable*.)

ἄ-δραστος, Ion. ἄ-δρηστος, ον, (διδράσκω) *not running away, not inclined to do so*, of slaves, Hdt.

'Αδρίας, ου, Ion. -ίης, εω, ὁ, *the Adriatic*, Hdt., etc. :— Adj. 'Αδριανός, old Att. 'Αδριηνός, ή, όν, *Adriatic*, Eur. :—also, 'Αδριακὸς ἀμφιφορεύς, i. e. *a cask of Italian wine*, Anth.

ἀδρόομαι, Pass. (ἀδρός) *to come to one's strength*, Plat.

'ΑΔΡΟ'Σ, ά, όν, in the primary sense it seems to mean *thick* : (akin to ἀδ-ινός, as κυδρός to κυδνός): I. of things, χιόνα ἀδρὴν πίπτουσαν *falling thick*, Hdt. :— *strong, great* in any way, ἀδρὸς πόλεμος Ar. II. of persons, *large, fine, well-grown*, Hdt., Plat.; of animals, Xen., Babr.; of fruit or corn, *full-grown, ripe*, Hdt.

ἀδροσύνη, ἡ, (ἀδρός) = ἀδρότης, of ears of corn, Hes.

ἁδροτής, ῆτος, ἡ, (ἁδρός) strength, Il.   II. abundance, N. T.

ἁδρόω, v. ἁδρόομαι.

ἀ-δρυάς, άδος, ἡ, (a copul., δρῦς) = Ἀμαδρυάς, Anth.

ἀδρύνω [ῡ], f. ῠνῶ, (ἁδρός) to make ripe, ripen, Xen.:— Pass. to grow ripe, ripen, of fruit or corn, Hdt., etc.

ἀδυ-βόας, -επής, Dor. for ἡδυ-βόης, ἡδυ-επής.

ἀ-δῠνᾰμία, Ion. -ίη, ἡ, (δύναμις) want of strength or power, inability, incapacity, Hdt., etc.; c. gen., ἀδ. τοῦ ἀδικεῖν for wrong-doing, Plat.   2. poverty, Xen., Dem., etc.

ἀδῠνᾰσία, ἡ, = ἀδυναμία, Hdt., etc.; c. gen., ἀδ. τοῦ λέγειν Thuc. : and

ἀδῠνᾰτέω, f. ήσω: I. of persons, to want strength, Plat., etc.; c. inf. to be unable to do, Xen.   II. of things, to be impossible, N. T. From

ἀ-δύνᾰτος [ῠ], ον,   I. of persons, unable to do a thing, c. inf., Hdt., Eur., etc.   2. absol. without strength, powerless, Hdt., Eur., etc.; οἱ ἀδύνατοι men disabled for service, incapable, Aeschin., etc.; ἀδύνατος χρήμασι poor, Thuc.; εἴς τι Plat. :—of ships, disabled, Hdt. :—τὸ ἀδ. want of strength, Plat.; τὰ ἀδ. disabilities, Dem.   II. of things, that cannot be done, impossible, Eur., Plat., etc.; ἀδύνατόν or ἀδύνατά [ἐστι], it is impossible, Hdt., etc. : τὸ ἀδ. impossibility, Id.; τολμᾶν ἀδύνατα, ἀδυνάτων ἐρᾶν Eur.

ἀδύ-πνοος, ἀδύ-πολις, Dor. for ἡδύ-.

ἀδύς, Dor. for ἡδύς.

ἄ-δῠτος, ον, (δύω) not to be entered:—hence as Subst. ἄδυτον, τό, the innermost sanctuary, Il., etc.

ᾄδω, Att. contr. for ἀείδω.

ἀδών [ᾱ], όνος, ἡ, Dor. for ἀηδών.

Ἀδων [ᾰ], ωνος, ὁ, = Ἀδωνις, Anth.

Ἀδώνια, τά, the mourning for Adonis, celebrated yearly by Greek matrons:—hence Ἀδωνιάζουσαι, αἱ, (as if from Ἀδωνιάζω, to keep the Adonia) title of the 15th Id. of Theocr.

Ἀδωνις [ᾰ], ιδος, ὁ, Adonis, favourite of Aphroditè, Sappho; ἄδωνις, crasis for ὁ Ἀδ., Theocr. :—generally, an Adonis, a darling, Luc.; Ἀδώνιδος κῆποι, quick-growing herbs grown in pots for the Adonia, Plat.

ἀ-δώρητος, ον, = ἄδωρος, h. Hom., Eur.

ἀ-δωροδόκητος, ον, = ἀδωροδόκος, Aeschin.: Adv. -τως, Dem.

ἀ-δωροδόκος, ον, incorruptible, Anth.

ἄ-δωρος, ον, (δῶρον) without gifts, taking none, incorruptible, c. gen., ἀδωρότατος χρημάτων Thuc.   II. giving no gifts, ἀδώροις ἐλαφηβολίαις by hunting from which no gifts were offered, Soph.   III. ἄδωρα δῶρα gifts that are no gifts, like βίος ἀβίωτος, Id.

ἀ-δώρητος, ον, ὁ, one who gives nothing, Hes.

ἀεθλεύω, ἀεθλέω, -ητής, Ep. and Ion. for ἀθλ-.

ἀέθλιον, Ep. and Ion. for ἄθλον, the prize of contest, Hom.   II. for ἄθλος, the contest, Od.

ἀέθλιος, ον, also α, ον, (ἄεθλον) gaining the prize, or running for it, ἵππος ἀεθλίη a race-horse, Theogn.; μῆλον ἀέθλ. the apple of discord, Anth.

ἄεθλον, τό, ἄεθλος, ὁ, Ep. and Ion. for ἄθλον, ἄθλος.

ἀεθλοσύνη, ἡ, (ἄεθλον) a contest, a struggle, Anth.

ἀεθλοφόρος, ον, Ep. and Ion. for ἀθλοφόρος.

ἀεί [ᾰ], Ep. αἰεί, αἰέν (v. sub fin.), Adv. always, for ever, Hom., etc.; often with other words of time, διαμ-

περὲς αἰεί, συνεχὲς αἰεί, ἐμμενὲς αἰεί, Id.; ἀεὶ καθ' ἡμέραν, καθ' ἡμέραν ἀεί, ἀεὶ καὶ καθ' ἡμέραν, ἀεὶ κατ' ἐνιαυτόν, ἀεὶ διὰ βίου, etc., Plat., etc.; v. εἰσαεί:—ὁ ἀεὶ χρόνος eternity, Hdt., Plat.; οἱ ἀεὶ ὄντες the immortals, Xen., etc. :—but, ὁ αἰεὶ βασιλεύων the king for the time being, Hdt.; τοῖσι τούτων αἰεὶ ἐκγόνοισι to their descendants for ever, Id.   (The Root is ΑΙϜ; cf. Lat. aev-um, aetas, i. e. aev-itas.)

ἀεί-βολος, ον, (βάλλω) continually thrown, Anth.

ἀει-γενέτης, only in Ep. form αἰει-γενέτης, ον, ὁ : (γίγνομαι):—epith. of the gods, like αἰὲν ἐόντες, everlasting, immortal, θεῶν αἰειγενετάων, θεοῖς αἰειγενέτῃσιν Il.

ἀει-γενής, ές, (γί-γνομαι) everlasting, Plat., Xen.

ἀ-ειδής, ές, (εἶδος) without form, incorporeal, Plat.

ἀει-δίνητος [ῑ], ον, (δινέω) ever-revolving, Anth.

ΑΕΙ´ΔΩ, Ion. and poët. Verb (cf. ἀείρω), Att. ᾄδω :—impf. ἤειδον, Ep. ἄειδον, Att. ᾖδον :—fut. ἀείσομαι, Att. ᾄσομαι : rarely in act. form ἀείσω ; still more rarely ᾄσω ; Dor. ᾀσεῦμαι, ᾀσῶ :—aor. 1 ἤεισα, Ep. ἄεισα [ᾰ] imper. ἄεισον, Att. ᾆσα.—Pass., Att. aor. 1 ᾔσθην, pf. ᾖσμαι :—to sing, Il., etc. :—then of any sound, to twang, of the bowstring, Od. ; to whistle, of the wind, Mosch. ; to ring, of a stone struck, Theocr.   II. trans.   1. c. acc. rei, to sing, chant, μῆνιν, παιήονα, κλέα ἀνδρῶν Hom. :—absol., ἀείδειν ἀμφί τινος to sing in one's praise, Od. :—Pass., of songs, to be sung, Hdt.; ᾆσμα καλῶς ᾀσθέν Xen.   2. c. acc. pers. to sing, praise, Att.

ἀει-ζώος, ουσα, ον, (ζάω) ever-living, φύτλη Anth.

ἀει-θᾰλής, ές, (θάλλω) ever-green, Anth.

ἀ-εικέλιος, α, ον, or ος, ον = ἀεικής, Hom., Hdt.; contr. αἰκέλιος Theogn., Eur. Adv. -ίως, Od.

ἀ-εικής, ές, (εἴκω) unseemly, shameful, ἀεικέα λοιγὸν ἀμύνειν Il.; ἀεικέα [εἵματα] Od.; δεσμὸς ἀεικής Aesch.; στολὴ Soph. ; ἀεικέστερα ἔπεα Hdt. ; οὐδὲν ἀεικὲς παρέχεσθαι to cause no inconvenience, Id. :—Adv. ἀεικῶς; Ion. -έως, Simon. ; ἀεικές as Adv., Od.   2. unseemly, shabby, μισθός, ἄποινα Il.   3. οὐδὲν ἀεικές ἐστι, c. inf., it is nothing strange that . . , Hdt., Aesch. Cf. Att. αἰκής.

ἀεικία, Ion. -ίη [ῑ], ἡ, (ἀεικής) unseemly treatment, outrage, Hom., Hdt.—Cf. Att. αἰκία.

ἀεικίζω, f. Att. ἰῶ : Ep. aor. 1 ἀείκισσα :—Med., Ep. aor. 1 ἀεικισσάμην :—Pass., Ep. aor. 1 inf. ἀεικισθήμεναι :—to treat unseemly, injure, abuse, Hom. ; οὐ γὰρ ἐγώ σ' ἔκπαγλον ἀεικιῶ I will do thee no great dishonour, Il. :—Med. in act. sense, Ib.—Cf. Att. αἰκίζω.

ἀει-λογία, ἡ, (λέγω) a continual talking :—as Att. lawterm, τὴν ἀ. προτείνεσθαι or παρέχειν to court continual inquiry into one's conduct, Dem.

ἀεί-μνηστος, ον, (μνάομαι) ever to be remembered, Trag., Thuc. Adv. -τως, Aeschin.

ἀεί-ναος, ον, = ἀέναος, q. v.

ἀεί-νηστις, ιος, ὁ, ἡ, ever-fasting, Anth.

ἀεί-νως, ων, Att. contr. for ἀέναος, v. ἀέναος.

ἀει-πάρθενος, ἡ, ever a virgin, Sapph.

ἀεί-ρῠτος, ον, ever-flowing, κρήνη Soph.

ἀείρω (Root ΑΕΡ), Ion. and poët. Verb (cf. ἀείδω), Att. αἴρω (q.v.), Aeol. ἀέρρω :— impf. ἤειρον, Ep. ἄειρον :—fut. ἀρῶ [ᾰ], contr. from ἀερῶ (not in use) :—aor. 1 ἤειρα, Ep. ἄειρα:—Med., fut. ἀροῦμαι [ᾰ] :—aor. 1 inf. ἀείρασθαι, part. -άμενος :—Pass., aor. 1 ἠέρθην, Ep. ἀέρθην, 3 pl. ἄερθεν :—pf. ἤερμαι : plqpf. Ep. 3 sing. ἄωρτο, Ion.

ἄορτο. *To lift, heave, raise up*, Hom., etc.; ἴστια στεῖλαν ἀείραντες furled the sails *by brailing them up*, Od.:—esp. *to lift for the purpose of carrying, to bear away, carry*, Il.; ἄχθος ἀείρειν, of ships of burden, Od.; μή μοι οἶνον ἄειρε *offer* me not wine, Il.   2. *to raise, levy*, λεκτὸν ἀρούμεν στόλον Aesch.   II. Med. *to lift up for oneself*, i. e. *bear off*, c. acc. rei, Il.   2. *to raise* or *stir up*, ἀείρασθαι πόλεμον *to undertake* a long war, Hdt.; βαρὺς ἀείρεσθαι *slow to undertake*, Id.   3. ἀείρασθαι τὰ ἰστία *to hoist* sail, or without ἰστία, Id.   III. Pass. *to be lifted* or *carried up*, Od.; ἀείρεσθαι εἰς . . *to rise up and go to a place*, Hdt.;—mostly of seamen, but also of land-journeys, Id.   2. *to be suspended*, πὰρ κουλεὸν αἰὲν ἄωρτο [the dagger] *hung* always by the sword-sheath, Il.   3. metaph. *to be lifted up, excited*, Soph.

ἀείς, part. of ἄημι.

ἄεισα, Ep. for ᾖεισα, aor. 1 of ἀείδω.

ἄεισμα, τό, poët. and Ion. for ᾆσμα, Hdt., etc.

ἀείσομαι, fut. of ἀείδω.

ἀει-φλεγής, ές, (φλέγω) *ever-burning*, Anth.

ἀεί-φρουρος, ον, *ever-watching*, i. e. *ever-lasting*, οἴκησις ἀείφρ., of the grave, Soph.

ἀει-φυγία, ἡ, (φυγή) *perpetual exile*, Plat.

ἀει-χρόνιος, ον, *everlasting*, Anth.

ἀεκαζόμενος, η, ον, particip. form = ἀέκων, Od.; πόλλ' ἀεκαζόμενος, Virgil's *multa reluctans*, Ib.

ἀεκήλιος, ον, = ἀεικέλιος, Il.

ἀ-έκητι, Epic Adv. *against one's will*, Hom.; c. gen.; σεῦ ἀέκητι, ἀέκητι σέθεν, Lat. *te invito*, and θεῶν ἀέκητι, ἀέκητι θεῶν, Id.

ἀ-εκούσιος, ον and α, ον: Att. contr. ἀκούσιος [ἄ], ον:—*against one's will, involuntary*, of acts, Hdt., etc.   II. of persons, only in Adv. ἀκουσίως, *involuntarily*, Thuc.

ἀ-έκων, Att. contr. ἄκων [ᾰ], ουσα, ον, *against one's will, unwilling*, of persons, ἀέκοντος ἐμεῖο Il.; πόλλ' ἀέκων, Virgil's *multa reluctans*, Ib.; ἄκοντος Διός, invito Jove, Aesch., Xen.:—Adv. ἀκόντως, *unwillingly*, Plat.   II. like ἀκούσιος, of acts, *involuntary*, ἔργα Soph.

ἀέλιος, ὁ, Dor. for ἥλιος, ἥλιος. [ᾱ, but made short by Soph. and Eur.]

ἄελλα, Ep. ἀέλλη, ης, ἡ, (εἴλω) *a stormy wind, whirl-wind, eddy*, Hom.; ἄελλαι ἀνέμων Id.   2. metaph. of any whirling motion, ὠκυδρόμοις ἀέλλαις, of an animal, Eur.; ἄστρων ὑπ' ἀέλλαισι Id.

ἀελλαῖος, α, ον, (ἄελλα) *storm-swift*, πελειάς Soph.

ἀελλάς, άδος, ἡ, = foreg., ἵπποι Soph.

ἀελλής, ὁ, (ἄελλα) *eddying*, Il.

ἀελλο-μάχος, ον, *struggling with the storm*, Anth.

ἀελλό-πος, ποδος, ὁ, ἡ, poët. for ἀελλό-πους (cf. ἀρτίπος, Οἰδίπος):—*storm-footed, storm-swift*, Il., etc.

'Αελλώ, όος contr. οῦς, ἡ, (ἄελλα) *Storm*, a Harpy, Hes.

ἀελπτέω, (ἄελπτος) *to have no hope*, only in part., ἀελπτέοντες σόον εἶναι Il.; ἀ. ὑπερβαλέεσθαι Hdt.

ἀ-ελπτής, ές, (ἔλπομαι) *unhoped for, unexpected*, Od.

ἀελπτία, ἡ, (ἄελπτος) *an unlooked for event*, ἐξ ἀελπτίης *unexpectedly*, Archil.

ἄ-ελπτος, ον, (ἔλπω) h. Hom.; ἐξ ἀέλπτου *unexpectedly*, Hdt.; so, ἐξ ἀέλπτων Soph.   2. *beyond hope, despaired of*, Solon.   II. act. *hopeless,*

desperate, h. Hom., Aesch.   III. Adv. -τως, *beyond all hope*, Lat. *insperato*, Id.:—neut. pl. as Adv., Eur.

ἀέ-ναος [ᾰ-], ον, (νάω A) also ἀεί-ναος, contr. ἀείνως (ἀέννaos is a corrupt form):—*ever-flowing*, Hes., Hdt., Trag.   2. generally, *everlasting*, ἀρετᾶς ἀέναον κλέος Simon.;—rare in Att. Prose, Xen., Plat.

ἀενάων, ουσα, ον, = foreg., Od., Hes.

ἀεξί-φυλλος, ον, (φύλλον) *nourishing leaves, leafy*, Aesch.

ἀεξί-φυτος, ον, (φυτόν) *nourishing plants*, Ἠώς Anth.

ΑΕΈΞΩ, poët. form of αὔξω (αὐξάνω), mostly in pres. and impf. without augm.: later poets have fut. ἀεξήσω, aor. 1 ἠέξησα, fut. med. ἀεξήσομαι, aor. 1 pass. ἀεξήθην. *To increase, enlarge, foster, strengthen*, μένος μέγα θυμὸς ἀέξει Il.; θυμὸν ἀέξειν Ib.; πένθος ἀ. *to cherish* woe, Od.; υἱὸν ἀ. *to rear* him *to man's estate*, Ib.; ἔργον ἀέξουσι θεοί they *bless* the work, Ib.   2. *to exalt by one's deeds, to magnify*, τὸ πλῆθος ἀέξειν Hdt.; *to magnify, exaggerate*, [ἀγγελίαν] μῦθος ἀέξει Soph.   3. ἀέξει φόνον Eur.   II. Pass. *to increase, grow*, ἀέξετο he was waxing tall, Od.; οὐ ποτ' ἀέξετο κῦμα no wave rose high, Ib.; χόλος ἐν στήθεσσιν ἀέξεται *rises high*, Il.; τόδε ἔργον ἀ. it *prospers*, Od.; ἀέξετο ἱερὸν ἦμαρ *was getting on* to noon, Il.; so, κέρδος ἀέξεται Aesch.

ἀ-εργία, Ion. -ίη [ῐ], ἡ, *a not working, idleness*, Od., Hes.—Cf. Att. ἀργία. From

ἀ-εργός, όν, (*ἔργω) *not-working, idle*, Hom., Hes., etc.;—ἀεργοὶ δόμοι *idle* houses, i. e. *where people are idle*, Theocr.—Cf. Att. ἀργός.

ἄρδην, Adv. (ἀείρω) *lifting up*, Aesch.—Cf. Att. ἄρδην.

ἀερέθομαι, see under Ion. form ᾐερ-.

ἄερθεν, Ep. for ᾐέρθησαν, 3 pl. aor. 1 pass. of ἀείρω; ἀέρθη, 3 sing. ἀερθείς part.

ἀέριος [ᾱ], ον, also α, ον: Ion. ᾐέριος, η, ον: (ἀήρ):—*in the mist* or *thick air of morning*, Eur.   II. *in the air, high in air*, Id.

ἀεροβατέω, f. ήσω, *to walk the air*, Ar., Plat.   From

ἀερο-βάτης [ᾱ], ου, ὁ, (βαίνω) *one who walks the air*, Plut.

ἀερο-δινής, ές, Ion. ᾐερ-, (δίνη) *wheeling in air*, Anth.

ἀερο-δόνητος, ον, *air-tossed, soaring*, Ar.

ἀεροδρομέω, f. ήσω, *to traverse the air*, Luc.

ἀερο-κόραξ, ἄκος, ὁ, *an air-raven*, Luc.

ἀερο-κώνωψ, ωπος, *an air-gnat*, Luc.

ἀερο-μαχία, ἡ, (μάχη) *an air-battle*, Luc.

ἀερο-μετρέω, f. ήσω, *to measure the air*: *to lose one-self in vague speculation*, Xen.

ἀερο-νηχής, ές, (νήχομαι) *floating in air*, of clouds, Ar.

ἀερό-φοιτος, ον, (φοιτάω) *roaming in air*, Aesch. ap. Ar.

ἀέρρω, Aeol. for ἀείρω.

ἀερσι-πότης, ου, ὁ, (ποτάομαι) *high-soaring*, Hes., Anth.

ἀερσι-πότητος, ον, = foreg., Hes.

ἀερσί-πους, ὁ, ἡ, *lifting the feet, brisk-trotting*, ἵπποι Il.

ἀερτάζω, lengthd. Ep. form of ἀείρω, *to lift up*:—impf. ἤερταζον Anth.

ἀερτάω, = foreg., aor. 1 ἤέρτησα, pf. pass. ᾐέρτηται, Anth.

ἄεσα, ἀέσαμεν contr. ἄσαμεν, ἄεσαν, inf. ἀέσαι, aor. 1 (from a form ἀέω, not in use) *to sleep*, Od. (Akin to ἄημι, ἄω A, ἰαύω.)

ἀεσιφροσύνη, ἡ, *silliness, folly*, Od., Hes. From

ἀεσί-φρων, ον, gen. ονος, (φρήν) *damaged in mind, wit-less, silly*, Hom., Hes. (For ἀασί-φρων, from ἀάω, φρήν.)

'ΑΕΤΟ'Σ [ᾰ], Ep. and Ion. αἰετός, οῦ, ὁ, *an eagle*, Hom., etc. :—proverb., ἀετὸς ἐν νεφέλαισι, of a thing quite out of reach, Ar.   2. *an eagle as a standard*, of the Persians, Xen.; of the Romans, Plut.   II. in architecture, *the pediment* of a temple, Ar.

ἀετο-φόρος, ὁ, (φέρω) *a standard-bearer*, Plut.

ἀετώδης [ᾰ], ες, (εἶδος) *eagle-like*, Luc.

*ἀέω, v. ἄεσα.

ἄζα, ἡ, (ἄζω) *drought* : in Od. an old shield is said to be πεπαλαγμένον ἄζῃ *coated with dry dirt or mould*.

ἀζᾰλέος, α, ον, (ἄζω) *dry, parched*, Hom.; βῶν ἀζαλέην *the dry bull's-hide*, Il.   2. metaph. *dry, harsh*, Anth.   II. act. *parching, scorching*, Σείριος Hes.

ἀζάνω, (ἄζω) *to dry, parch up*, h. Hom.

ἀζηλία, ἡ, *freedom from jealousy*, Plut.   From

ἄ-ζηλος, ον, *not subject to envy, unenviable, dreary*, Simon., Aesch., etc.   2. generally, *sorry, inconsiderable*, Plut.

ἀ-ζηλότῠπος, ον, *free from jealousy, envy*, Plut.

ἀ-ζήλωτος, ον, *not to be envied*, Plat.

ἀ-ζήμιος, ον, (ζημία) *free from further payment : without loss, scot-free*, Lat. *immunis*, Hdt., etc. :—*unpunished, not deserving punishment*, Soph., Eur.   II. act. *harmless*, of sour looks, Thuc.

ἀ-ζηχής, ές, *unceasing, excessive*, Il.; neut. as Adv., ἀζηχὲς φαγέμεν καὶ πιέμεν Od.; ὀίες ἀζ. μεμᾰκυῖαι Il. (Ep. word, perhaps an old dialectic form for ἀ-διεχής (α copulat., διέχω), v. sub ζα-.)

ἄζομαι (Root ΑΓ, v. ἄγος), Dep. only in pres. and impf.; act. only in part. ἄζοντα :—*to stand in awe of, dread*, esp. the gods and one's parents, Hom.; followed by inf., *to shrink from doing*, Id.; also ἄζομαι μὴ . . , Il.   2. absol. in part. *awe-struck*, Od., Soph.

ἄ-ζῠγος, ον, = ἄζυξ, *unwedded*, κοίτη Luc.

ἄ-ζῠμος, ον, (ζύμη) of bread, *unleavened*, ἡ ἑορτὴ τῶν ἀζύμων or τὰ ἄζυμα *the feast of unleavened bread*, N. T.

ἄ-ζυξ, ῠγος, ὁ, ἡ, τό, (ζεύγνυμι) *unyoked, unpaired, unmarried*, Eur.; of Pallas the *virgin* goddess, Id.: with a gen. added, ἄζυξ λέκτρων, γάμων, εὐνῆς, Lat. *nuptiarum expers*, Il.

ἄζω, v. sub ἄζομαι.

"ΑΖΩ, *to dry up, parch*, Hes. :—Pass., αἴγειρος ἀζομένη κεῖται the poplar lies *drying*, Il.

ἄ-ζωστος, ον, (ζώννυμι) *ungirt*, from hurry, Hes.

ἀ-ηδής, ές, (ἧδος) *unpleasant to the taste, distasteful*, of food, Plat.   2. generally, *unpleasant*, οὐδὲν οἱ ἀηδέστερον ἔσεσθαι Hdt.; in Plat. of talk, ἀηδές or οὐκ ἀηδές ἐστι.   II. of persons, *disagreeable, odious*, Id.   III. Adv. -δῶς, *unpleasantly*, Id.; ἀηδῶς ἔχειν τινί *to be on bad terms* with one, Dem.   2. *without pleasure to oneself, unwillingly*, Plat.

ἀηδία, ἡ, (ἀηδής) *unpleasantness, nauseousness*, of drugs, Hipp.   II. of persons, *odiousness*, Dem., etc.   2. *a being ill-pleased, disgust, dislike*, Plat.

ἀηδονιδεύς, έως, ὁ, (ἀηδών) *a young nightingale*, Theocr., in Ep. pl. ἀηδονιδῆες.

ἀηδόνιος, ον, *of a nightingale*, γόος, νόμος ἀ. *the nightingale's dirge*, Aesch.

ἀηδονίς, ίδος, ἡ, = ἀηδών, *a nightingale*, Eur., Theocr.; Μουσάων ἀηδονίς, of a poet, Anth.

ἀηδώ, = ἀηδών, gen. ἀηδοῦς Soph., voc. ἀηδοῖ Ar.

ἀηδών, όνος, ἡ, (ἀείδω) *the songstress*, i. e. *the nightingale*, Hes., etc.; of the daughter of Pandareüs, who was changed into a nightingale, Hom.

ἀήθεια, Ion. -ίη [ῐ], ἡ, (ἀήθης) *unaccustomedness*, Batr.; ἀήθ. τινος *inexperience of* a thing, Thuc.

ἀηθέσσω, poët. for ἀηθέω, Ep. impf. ἀηθέσσον, *to be unaccustomed to* a thing, c. gen., Il.

ἀ-ήθης, ες, (ἦθος) *unwonted, unusual*, Aesch. :—Adv. -θως, *unexpectedly*, Thuc.   II. of persons, *unused to* a thing, c. gen., Id., Dem.

ἀηθία, ἡ, = ἀήθεια, Eur.

ἄημα, τό, *a blast, gale*, Aesch., Soph.   From

ἄημι (Root FA, cf. αὔ-ω), 3 sing. ἄησι, 2 dual ἄητον, 3 pl. ἄεισι; inf. ἀῆναι, Ep. ἀήμεναι; part. ἀείς : 3 sing. impf. ἄη :—Pass., 3 sing. ἄηται, impf. ἄητο, part. ἀήμενος.   Ep. Verb, = ἄω, *to breathe hard, blow*, of winds, Hom. :—Pass. *to be beaten by the wind*, ὑόμενος καὶ ἀήμενος Od.: metaph., *to toss or wave about*, as if by the wind, δίχα θυμὸς ἄητο, i.e. *was in doubt or fear*, Il.

ἀήρ [ᾱ], ἀέρος, in Hom. ἀήρ, ἠέρος, ὁ and ἡ, (ἄημι) :—*the lower air, the air* that surrounds the earth, opp. to αἰθήρ *the upper air* (v. Il. 14. 288, where a tall pine μακροτάτη πεφυυῖα δι' ἠέρος αἰθέρ' ἵκανεν); hence *mist, gloom*, περὶ δ' ἠέρα πουλὺν ἔχευεν Il.; ἠέρα μὲν σκέδασε Ib.; cf. ἠέριος, ἠεροειδής.   2. generally, *air*, Soph., etc.; ἀέρα δέρειν (cf. Virg. *verberat auras*), N. T.

ἄησις, εως, ἡ, (ἄημι) *a blowing*, Eur.

ἀ-ήσσητος, later Att. ἀ-ήττητος, ον, (ἡσσάομαι) *unconquered*, Thuc., Dem.   2. *unconquerable*, Plat.

ἀησῠλος, for αἴσυλος, *wicked*, Il.

ἀήσῠρος, ον, (ἄημι) *light as air, small, little*, Aesch.

ἄηται, 3 sing. pres. pass. of ἄημι.

ἀήτης, ου, ὁ, (ἄημι) *a blast, gale*, Hom., etc.

ἄητο, Ep. for ἤητο, 3 sing. impf. pass. of ἄημι.

ἄητος, ον, (ἄημι?) *stormy, furious*, θάρσος ἄητον Il.

ἀ-ήττητος, ον, later Att. for ἀήσσητος.

ἀ-θάλασσωτος, Att. -ττωτος, ον, (θαλασσόω) *unused to the sea, a land-lubber*, Ar.

ἀ-θᾰλής, ές, (θάλλω) *not verdant, withered*, Plut.

ἀ-θαλπής, ές, (θάλπος) *without warmth*, Anth.

ἀ-θαμβής, ές, (θάμβος) *fearless*, Ibyc., Plut.

'Αθάνα, 'Αθᾱναι, 'Αθᾱναία, Dor. for 'Αθην-; v. 'Αθήνη.

ἀθᾰνᾰσία, ἡ, *immortality*, Plat., etc.; and

ἀθᾰνᾰτίζω, *to make immortal, to hold oneself immortal*, Hdt.   From

ἀ-θάνατος, ον, Ep. also η, ον :—*undying, immortal*, Hom., etc. :—ἀθάνατοι, οἱ, *the Immortals*, Hom., etc.; ἀθάναται ἅλιαι, i.e. the sea goddesses, Od.: Comp. -ώτερος, Plat.   2. *of immortal fame*, Tyrtae.   II. of things, *everlasting*, Od., Hdt., etc.   2. ἀθ. θρίξ *the hair on which life depended*, Aesch.   III. οἱ ἀθάνατοι *the immortals*, a body of Persian troops in which every vacancy was at once filled up, Hdt.   IV. Adv. ἀθανάτως εὕδειν Anth.   [ᾰθ- always in the Adj. and all derivs., v. Α α, fin.]

ἄ-θαπτος, ον, (θάπτω) *unburied*, Il., etc.   II. *unworthy of burial*, Anth.

'ΑΘΑ'ΡΗ [θᾰ], ἡ, *groats or meal, porridge*, Ar., etc.

ἀ-θαρσής, ές, (θάρσος) *discouraged, downhearted*, Plut.: τὸ ἀθαρσές *want of courage*, Id.   Adv. -σῶς, Id.

ἀ-θέατος, ον, *unseen, invisible*, Plut., Luc.   2. *that*

may not be seen, secret, Plut. II. act. *not seeing,*
blind to a thing, c. gen., Xen.

ἀ-θεεί, Adv. (θεός) *without the aid of God,* οὐκ ἀθεεί,
Horace's *non sine Dis,* Od.

ἀ-θείαστος, ον, (θειάζω) *uninspired,* Plut.

ἄ-θελκτος, ον, (θέλγω) *implacable,* Aesch.

ἄ-θεμις, ιτος, ὁ, ἡ, *lawless,* Pind., Eur.

ἀ-θεμίστιος, ον, (θέμις) *lawless, godless,* ἀθεμίστια εἰδώς
versed in wickedness, Od.

ἀ-θέμιστος or **ἀ-θέμιτος**, ον, (the first form prevailing
in Poetry, the latter in Prose):—*lawless, without law*
or government, of the Cyclopes, Od.; ἀθεμιστότεροι
Xen. II. of things, *lawless, unlawful,* ἀθέμιτα
ἔργα, ἀθέμιτα ἔρδειν Hdt.; ἀθ. ποιεῖν, εὐχεσθαι Xen.

ἄ-θεος, ον, *without God, denying the gods,* Plat. 2.
godless, ungodly, Trag.:—Comp. -ώτερος Lys.; Sup.
-ώτατος Xen. 3. *abandoned of the gods,* Soph. II.
Adv. -ως, *impiously,* Id.; Sup. -ώτατα, *in most un-*
holy wise, Id. Hence

ἀθεότης, ητος, ἡ, *ungodliness,* Plat.

ἀθεράπευσία, ἡ, *neglect of,* θεῶν Plat. From

ἀ-θεράπευτος, ον, *uncared for,* of animals, Xen.: τὸ
ἀθ. *neglect of one's appearance,* Luc. II. *un-*
healed, incurable, Id.

ἀθερίζω or **-ίσσω**: aor. 1 ἀθέριξα Ep. 3 sing. med. ἀθε-
ρίσσατο:—*to slight, make light of,* Lat. *nihil curare,*
c. acc. pers., Hom. (Deriv. uncertain.)

ἀ-θέρμαντος, ον, *not heated by strife* or *passion,* Aesch.

ἄ-θερμος, ον, *without heat:* τὸ ἄθερμον *want of heat,*
Plat.

ἄ-θεσμος, ον, = ἀθέσμιος, Plut.

ἀ-θέσφατος, ον, *beyond even a god's power to express:*
ineffable, aweful, ὄμβρος, θάλασσα, νύξ Hom.; *also*
marvellous in quantity, ἀθ. οἶνος, σῖτος, βόες Od.

ἀθετέω, f. ήσω, *to set aside:* ἀθ. τινα *to deny one, re-*
fuse his *request,* N. T. From

ἄ-θετος, ον, (τίθημι) *set aside:*—Adv. -τως, = ἀθέσμως,
lawlessly, despotically, Aesch.

ἀ-θεώρητος, ον, (θεωρέω) *without observation:*—Adv.
-τως, Plut.

ἄ-θηλυς, υ, *unfeminine,* Plut.

Ἀθηνᾶ, Att. for Ἀθηναίη, Ἀθήνη. Hence

Ἀθῆναι, Dor. **Ἀθᾶναι**, ῶν, αἱ, *the city of Athens,* used
in pl., because it consisted of several parts (cf. Θῆβαι,
Μυκῆναι), Hom., etc.; the sing. (like Θήβη) Od. II.
Adverbs, **Ἀθήναζε**, *to Athens,* Thuc., Xen.:—**Ἀθήνη-**
θεν, *from Athens,* Lys., etc.; poët. **Ἀθήνοθεν,** Anth.:—
Ἀθήνησιν, *at Athens,* Dem.

Ἀθήναιον, τό, ('Ἀθηνᾶ) *the temple of Athena,* Hdt.

Ἀθηναῖος, α, ον, *Athenian, of* or *from Athens,* Il., etc.

Ἀθήνη, ἡ, *Athené,* goddess of wisdom, warlike prowess,
and skill in the arts, often called Παλλὰς Ἀθήνη, also
Ἀθηναία or Παλλὰς Ἀθηναίη.—The latter name (in Att.
Ἀθηναία) was contr. into **Ἀθηνᾶ,** the Att. form: Dor.
Ἀθάνα and **Ἀθαναία** Theocr.: Aeol. **Ἀθανάα** [νᾰ],
Alcae., Theocr. II. Cf. Ἀθῆναι. (Deriv. uncertain.)

Ἀθηνιάω, (Ἀθῆναι) *to long to be at Athens,* Luc.

ἈΘΗ'Ρ, έρος, ὁ, *an ear of corn,* Hes. 2. *husks, chaff,*
Luc. II. *the point* of a weapon, Aesch., etc.

ἀ-θήρευτος, ον, (θηρεύω) *not hunted,* Xen.

ἀθηρη-λοιγός, ὁ, (ἀθήρ) *consumer of ears of corn,* of a
winnowing fan, Od.

ἄ-θηρος, ον, (θήρ) *without wild beasts* or *game,* Hdt.:
τὸ ἄθηρον *absence of game,* Plut.

ἀ-θῐγής, ές, (θιγγάνω) *untouched,* of a virgin, Anth.

ἄ-θικτος, ον, (θιγγάνω) *untouched:* c. gen. *untouched*
by a thing, Soph.; κερδῶν ἄθικτον βουλευτήριον *un-*
touched by gain, i. e. incorruptible, Aesch.; also c. dat.,
νόσοις ἀθ. Id. 2. *not to be touched, holy, sacred,*
of Delphi, Soph.; ἄθικτα *holy things,* Aesch.

ἀθλεύω, Ep. and Ion. **ἀεθλεύω,** f. -σω, (ἄθλον) *to con-*
tend for a prize, combat, wrestle, Il.; ἀθλεύων πρὸ
ἄνακτος *struggling* or *suffering* for him, Ib.

ἀθλέω, Ion. impf. ἀέθλεον: f. -ήσω: aor. 1 ἤθλησα: pf.
ἤθληκα: (ἆθλος) *commoner form of* ἀθλεύω, Λαο-
μέδοντι ἀθλήσαντες *having contended with* him, Il.;
πολλὰ περ ἀθλήσαντα *having gone through* many
struggles, Ib.: *to contend in battle,* πρός τινα Hdt.

ἄθλημα, ατος, τό, (ἀθλέω) *a contest,* Plat., etc. II.
an implement of labour, Theocr.

ἄθλησις, ἡ, (ἀθλέω) *a contest, struggle,* N. T.

ἀθλητήρ, ῆρος, ὁ, older form of ἀθλητής, Od.

ἀθλητής, contr. from ἀεθλητής, οῦ, ὁ, (ἀθλέω) *a prize-*
fighter, Lat. *athleta:* as Adj., ἀθλ. ἵππος a *race-*horse,
Lys. II. c. gen. rei, *practised in* a thing, Plat.

ἄθλιος, α, ον and ος, ον, Att. contr. from Ep. ἀέθλιος:
(ἄθλον, ἆθλον):—*gaining the prize* (this sense only
in Ep. form). II. metaph. *struggling, wretched,*
miserable (this sense only in Att. form), of persons
Aesch., etc.: Comp. -ώτερος Soph.: Sup. -ώτατος
Eur.:—also of states of life, γάμοι, βίος, τύχη Trag.:
—Adv. -ίως, *miserably,* Soph. 2. in moral sense,
pitiful, wretched, Dem. 3. without any moral sense,
wretched, sorry, θηρσὶν ἀθλία βορά Eur.:—Adv., ἀθλίως
καὶ κακῶς with *wretched success,* Dem. Hence

ἀθλιότης, ητος, ἡ, *suffering, wretchedness,* Plat., etc.

ἀθλο-θέτης, ου, ὁ, (τί-θημι) *one who awards the prize,*
the judge in the games, Plat., etc.

ἆθλον, τό, Att. contr. from Ep. and Ion. ἄεθλον, *the*
prize of contest, Hom., etc.; ἄεθλα κεῖται or πρόκειται
prizes are proposed, Hdt.; ἆθλα προφαίνειν, προτιθέναι,
τιθέναι *to propose prizes,* Xen.; ἆθλα λαμβάνειν or
φέρεσθαι *to win prizes,* Plat.; ἆθλα πολέμου, τῆς ἀρετῆς
Dem. II. = ἆθλος, *a contest,* Od.:—metaph. *a con-*
flict, struggle, Aesch., Soph.

ἆθλος, ὁ, contr. from Ep. and Ion. ἄεθλος, *a contest for*
a prize, Hom., etc.; ἄεθλος πρόκειται *a task* is set
one, Hdt.; ἄεθλον προτιθέναι *to set it,* Id.;—metaph. *a*
conflict, struggle, Aesch.

ἀθλοσύνη, ἡ, = ἆθλος, Anth.

ἀθλο-φόρος, ον, (φέρω) *bearing away the prize, vic-*
torious, ἵππος Il.; in Ion. form ἀεθλ-, Ib., Hdt.

ἄ-θολος, ον, *not turbid, clear,* Luc.

ἀ-θόλωτος, ον, (θολόω) *untroubled,* of water, Hes.

ἀ-θορύβητος, ον, (θορυβέω) *undisturbed:* τὸ ἀθ. *tran-*
quillity, Xen.

ἀ-θόρυβος, ον, *without uproar,* Plat.:—Adv. -βως, Eur.

ἆθος, Dor. for ἦθος.

ἄ-θραυστος, ον, (θραύω) *unbroken, unhurt,* Eur., etc.

ἀθρέω or **ἀθρέω:** f. ήσω: aor. 1 opt. ἀθρήσειε, inf. ἀθρῆ-
σαι:—*to look at, gaze at, observe, perceive,* Hom.,
etc. 2. absol. or with a Prep., *to look, gaze,* Il.;
δεῦρ' ἄθρησον Eur.; οὐ γὰρ ἴδοις ἂν ἀθρῶν *by observing,*
Soph. II. of the mind, *to look into* a thing, con-

sider, Id., Eur., etc. :—foll. by an interrog. or rel. clause, ταῦτ' ἄθρησον, εἰ . . consider this also, *whether* . . , Soph.; ἄθρει Plat. Hence

ἀθρητέον, verb. Adj., *one must consider*, Eur., Xen.

ἀθροίζω or **ἀθροΐζω**: f. σω: aor. 1 ἤθροισα:—Pass., aor. 1 ἠθροίσθην: pf. ἤθροισμαι: (ἀθρόος or ἀθρόος):— *to gather together*, *to muster* forces, Soph., Xen.; Τροίαν ἀθρ. *to gather* the Trojans together, Eur.; πνεῦμα ἄθροισον *collect* breath, Id. :—Med. *to gather for oneself*, *collect round one*, Id., Xen. :—Pass. *to be gathered together*, ἐς τὴν ἀγορήν Hdt.; ἀθροισθέντες *having rallied*, Thuc.; τὸ ξύμπαν ἠθροίσθη δισχίλιοι *the whole amounted collectively* to 2000, Id. **2.** in Pass. also of the mind, ἀθροίζεσθαι εἰς ἑαυτόν *to collect oneself*, Plat.; φόβος ἤθροισται *fear has gathered strength*, *arisen*, Xen. Hence

ἄθροισις, εως, ἡ, *a gathering*, *mustering*, στρατοῦ Eur.; χρημάτων Thuc.; and

ἄθροισμα, τό, *a gathering*, λαοῦ Eur.

ἀθροιστέον, verb. Adj. of ἀθροίζω, *one must collect*, Xen.

ἀ-θρός or **ἀ-θρόος**, α, ον, Att. ἄθρους, ουν: (α copulat., θρόος):—*in crowds* or *masses*, *crowded together*, mostly in pl.; πάντες ἀθρόοι Od., etc.; ἀθρόοι, of soldiers, *in close order*, Lat. conferto agmine, Hdt., Xen., etc.; also, πολλαὶ κῶμαι ἀθρόαι *close together*, Id. **II.** *taken together*, ἀθρόα πάντ' ἀπέτισεν *he paid for all at once*, Od.; ἀθρόα πόλις *the citizens as a whole*, Thuc.; τὸ ἀθρόον *their assembled* force, Xen.; ἀθρόῳ στόματι *with one voice*, Eur.; ἀθρόους κρίνειν *to condemn all by a single vote*, Plat.; κατήριπεν ἀθρόος *he fell all at once*, Theocr. **III.** *multitudinous*, δάκρυ Eur., Plat. **IV.** Comp. ἀθροώτερος Thuc., etc.; later ἀθρούστερος Plut.

ἄ-θρυπτος, ον, (θρύπτω) *not broken*, *not enervated*, Plut.; ἄθρυπτος εἰς γέλωτα *never breaking* into laughter, Id. Adv. -τως, Id.

ἀθυμέω, f. ήσω, (ἄθυμος) *to be disheartened*, *lose heart*, Aesch., etc.; τινι *at* or *for a thing*, Soph.; ἐπί τινι, εἴς τι, πρός τι, Att. Prose:—foll. by a relat. word, *to be sore afraid*, ἀθυμῶ δ' εἰ φανήσομαι Soph.; δεινῶς ἀθυμῶ μὴ βλέπων ὁ μάντις ᾖ Id. Hence

ἀθυμητέον, verb. Adj. *one must lose heart*, Xen.; and

ἀθυμία, Ion. -ίη, ἡ, *want of heart*, *faintheartedness*, Hdt., Soph., etc.; εἰς ἀθυμίαν καθιστάναι τινά Plat.; ἀθυμίαν παρέχειν τινί Xen.; ἐν ἀθυμίᾳ εἶναι Id.; ἀθυμία ἐμπίπτει τινί Id.

ἄ-θυμος, ον, *without heart*, *fainthearted*, Od., Hdt., etc.; ἄθ. εἶναι πρός τι *to have no heart* for a thing, Xen.; so Adv., ἀθύμως ἔχειν πρός τι Id. **2.** *without passion*, Plat.

ἄθυρμα, τό, (ἀθύρω) *a plaything*, *toy* : *a delight*, *joy*, Hom., etc.

ἀ-θυρόγλωττος, ον, (θύρα, γλῶττα) *one that cannot keep his mouth shut*, *a ceaseless babbler*, Eur.

ἄ-θυρος, ον, (θύρα) *without door*, Plut.

ἀθυροστομία, ἡ, = ἀθυρογλωττία, Anth. From

ἀ-θυρόστομος, ον, (θύρα, στόμα) = ἀθυρόγλωττος, *ever-babbling*, Soph.

ἄ-θυρσος, ον, *without thyrsus*, Eur.

ΑΘΥΡΩ [ῠ], only in pres. and impf., *to play*, *sport*, of children, Il., Eur.; c. acc. cogn., μοῦσαν ἀθύρων *singing sportive* songs, h. Hom. :—Med., simply, *to*

sing, Ib. **II.** c. acc., ἔργα φωτῶν ἀθ. *to play* the deeds of men, of an actor, Anth.

ἀ-θύρωτος [ῠ], ον, (θυρόω) = ἄθυρος, *never closed*, Ar.

ἄ-θυτος, ον, (θύω) *not offered*, i. e. *neglected*, ἱερὰ ἄθ., Lat. sacra inauspicata, Aeschin. **II.** act. *without sacrificing*, ἄθυτος ἀπελθεῖν Xen.

ἀθῷος, ον, (θωή) *unpunished*, *scot-free*, Eur., etc.; ἀθῴους καθιστάναι τινάς *to secure their immunity*, Dem.; ἀθῷον ἀφιέναι Id.; ἀθῷος ἀπαλλάττειν or -εσθαι *to get off scot-free*, Plat. **2.** *free from* a thing, c. gen., Ar. **3.** *unharmed by* a thing, c. gen., Dem. **II.** *not deserving punishment*, *without fault*, Id.

Ἄθῳος or **Ἄθωος**, η, ον, *of mount Athos*, Aesch.

ἀ-θώπευτος, ον, (θωπεύω) *not flattered*, *without flattery*, τῆς ἐμῆς γλώσσης *from* my tongue, Eur. **II.** act. *not flattering*, *discourteous*, Anth.

ἀ-θωράκιστος, ον, (θωρακίζω) *without breastplate*, Xen.

Ἄθως [ᾰ], ω, ὁ, acc. Ἄθων or Ἄθω : Ep. nom. Ἀθόως, όω :—*mount Athos*, Il., etc.

αἰ, Dor. and Ep. for εἰ, *if*:—αἴ κε or κεν, *if only*, *so that*, Lat. dummodo (with subj., Hom.; so Dor. αἴκα, Theocr. **II.** αἴ γάρ (with accent), Ep. for εἰ γάρ, *to express a wish*, O that! would that! Lat. utinam! with optat., Hom.; cf. αἴθε.

αἴ, Exclam. of astonishment, ha! αἴ τάλας Ar.

αἶα, ἡ, Ep. form used for γαῖα metri grat., Hom., Trag. : *never in pl.*

αἴαγμα, ατος, τό, *a wail*, Eur. From

αἰάζω, f. ξω: aor. 1 part. αἰάξας:—*to cry αἰαῖ*, *to wail*, Trag.; c. acc. *to bewail*, Aesch., Eur.

αἰαῖ, exclam. of grief, ah! Lat. vae! c. gen., αἰαῖ τόλμας Eur.; and repeated, αἰαῖ αἰαῖ μελέων ἔργων Aesch. :—later c. acc., αἰαῖ τὰν Κυθέρειαν Bion.

Αἰακίδης, ου, ὁ, son of Aeacus, Il.

αἰακτός, ή, όν, verb. Adj. of αἰάζω, *bewailed*, *lamentable*, Aesch., Ar. **II.** *wailing*, *miserable*, Aesch.

αἰανής, Ion. αἰηνής, ές, *old word*, *dreary*, *dismal*, *direful*, *horrid*, νυκτὸς αἰανῆ τέκνα, νυκτὸς αἰανῆς κύκλος, αἰανῆς νόσος Aesch., Soph., etc. **II.** *of Time*, εἰς τὸν αἰανῆ χρόνον Aesch.; and so in Adv. αἰανῶς *for ever*, Id. (The prob. deriv. is from αἰεί, *everlasting*, whence may come the notion of *never-ending*, *wearisome*, *dreary*.)

Αἴας, αντος, ὁ, Ajax, masc. pr. n., borne by two heroes, the Greater son of Telamon, the Less son of Oïleus, Hom.; voc. Αἶαν (metri grat.) Soph., elsewh. in Trag. Αἴας.

αἰβοῖ, bah! exclam. of disgust or astonishment; but αἰβοῖ, βοῖ, of laughter, Ar.

αἰγ-αγρος, ὁ and ἡ, (αἴξ, ἄγρος) *the wild goat*, Babr.

Αἰγαῖος, α, ον, Aegaean, πέλαγος Aesch.; ὄρος Αἰγ. *mount Ida*, Hes. **II.** Αἰγαῖος (sc. πόντος), ὁ, *the Aegaean*, Plat., etc.

Αἰγαίων, ωνος, ὁ, Aegaeon, the name given by men to the hundred-armed son of Uranus and Gaia, called by gods Βριάρεως, Il. **II.** *the Aegaean sea*, Eur.

αἰγάνέη, ἡ, *a hunting-spear*, *javelin*, Hom., Anth. (Perh. from αἴξ, *a goat-spear*.)

αἰγέη, v. αἴγεος.

αἴγειος, α, Ion. η, ον, Ep. for αἴγεος, (αἴξ) *of a goat* or *goats*, Lat. caprinus, αἴγειος τυρός *goats-milk* cheese, Il.; ἀσκῷ ἐν αἰγείῳ *in a goat's skin*, Ib.; αἰγείη κυνέη *a helmet* of goatskin.

Αἴγειος, α, ον, of Aegeus, Aesch.

αἴγειρος, ἡ, the poplar (cf. λεύκη), Od. (Deriv. uncertain.)

αἰγ-ελάτης [ᾰ], ου, ὁ, (ἐλαύνω) a goatherd, Plut., Anth.

αἴγεος, α, ον, = αἴγειος, Od. II. as Subst. αἰγέη (sc. δορά), ἡ, a goat's skin, Hdt.

αἰγιᾰλίτης, ου, ὁ, fem. -ῖτις, ιδος, one who haunts the shore, Anth. From

αἰγιᾰλός, ὁ, (ἀἴξ II) the sea-shore, beach, strand, Hom., Hdt.; αἰγιαλὸν ἔνδον τρέφει, i. e. he has a whole sea-beach (i. e. quantities of voting-pebbles, ψῆφοι) in his house, Ar.

αἰγί-βοσις, εως, ἡ, (αἴξ, βόσκω) a goat-pasture, Anth.

αἰγι-βότης, ου, ὁ, αἴξ, βόσκω) feeding goats, Anth.

αἰγί-βοτος, ον, (αἴξ, βόσκω) browsed by goats, Od.

αἰγίθαλλος or αἰγίθᾰλος, ὁ, the titmouse, Lat. parus, Ar.

αἰγί-κνημος, ον, (αἴξ, κνήμη) goat-shanked, Anth.

αἰγι-κορεῖς, έων, οἱ, goatherds; name of one of the four old Attic Tribes, Hdt., Eur. (If from αἴξ, κορέννυμι, the literal sense would be goat-feeders.)

αἰγί-λιψ [γῐ], ῐπος, ὁ, ἡ, (αἴξ, λείπω) destitute even of goats, hence steep, sheer, πέτρη Il.

αἴγῐλος, ἡ, (αἴξ) a herb of which goats are fond, Theocr.

Αἴγῖνα, ης, ἡ, Aegina, Il., etc.; also Αἰγιναίη (sc. νῆσος) Hdt. :—hence, Αἰγινήτης, ου, ὁ, fem. -ῆτις, ιδος, an Aeginetan, Id., etc. :—Adj. Αἰγιναῖος, α, ον, of Aegina, Thuc., etc.

αἰγῐ-νομεύς, έως, ὁ, (αἴξ, νέμω) a goatherd, Anth.

αἰγῐ-νόμος, ον, (αἴξ, νέμω) feeding goats : as Subst. a goatherd, Anth. II. αἰγίνομος (proparox.), pass. browsed by goats, βοτάνη Id.

αἰγί-οχος, ον, (ἔχω) Aegis-bearing, of Zeus, Hom.

αἰγῐ-πόδης, ου, ὁ, αἴξ, πούς) goat-footed, h. Hom.

αἰγί-πους, ποδος, ὁ, ἡ, = foreg., Hdt.

αἰγί-πῠρος, ὁ, or αἰγί-πυρον, τό, a plant of which goats were fond, perh. buckwheat, Theocr.

αἰγίς, ίδος, ἡ, (αἴξ) : I. the aegis or shield of Zeus, described in Il. 5. 738 sqq. The aegis on statues of Athena is a short cloak of goat-skin, covered with scales, set with the Gorgon's head, and fringed with snakes, v. Hdt. 4. 189. 2. a goatskin coat, Eur. II. (αἴξ II) a rushing storm, hurricane, Aesch.

αἰγλάεις, contr. αἰγλᾶς, Dor. for αἰγλήεις, Pind.

ΑΙΓΛΗ, ἡ, the light of the sun, radiance, Od. :—then simply daylight, λευκὴ αἴγλη Ib.; εἰς αἴγλαν μολεῖν, i. e. to be born, Pind. 2. any dazzling light, lustre, gleam, χαλκοῦ Il. Hence

αἰγλήεις, εσσα, εν, dazzling, radiant, lustrous, Hom.

αἰγλο-φᾰνής, ές, (φαίνομαι) radiant, Anth.

αἰγό-κερως, gen. -κερω, acc. -κερων : αἴξ, κέρας) :— goat-horned, Anth., Plut. II. as Subst. Capricorn in the Zodiac, Luc.

αἰγο-νόμος, ον, (αἴξ, νέμω) = αἰγινόμος, Anth.

αἰγ-όνυξ, υχος, ὁ, ἡ, (αἴξ, ὄνυξ) = αἰγῶνυξ, Anth.

αἰγο-πόδης, ου, ὁ, = αἰγιπόδης, Anth.

αἰγο-πρόσωπος, ον, (αἴξ, πρόσωπον) goat-faced, Hdt.

αἰγυπιός, ὁ, a vulture, Hom., etc. :—αἰγυπιός is the vulture which preys on live animals, γύψ the carrion-vulture.

Αἰγυπτιάζω, to speak Egyptian, Luc.

Αἰγυπτιακός, ή, όν, of or for the Egyptians, Plut., etc.

Αἰγύπτιος, α, ον, Egyptian, Hom., etc. [Αἰγυπτίη, Αἰγυπτίων, etc., are trisyll. in Hom.]

Αἰγυπτιστί, Adv. (as if from *Αἰγυπτίζω), in the Egyptian tongue, Hdt. II. in Egyptian fashion, craftily, Theocr.

Αἰγυπτο-γενής, ές, (γένος) of Egyptian race, Aesch.

Αἴγυπτος, ὁ, the river Nile, Od. ; called Νεῖλος first in Hes. II. ἡ, Egypt, Od. ; Αἰγυπτόνδε to Egypt, Ib.

αἰγ-ῶνυξ, ὔχος, ὁ, ἡ, αἴξ, ὄνυξ) goat-hoofed, Anth.

Ἀΐδας, Dor. for Ἀΐδης, Ἅιδης.

ΑΙΔΕΌΜΑΙ, poët. also αἴδομαι, part. αἰδόμενος ; imper. αἴδεο :—impf., Ep. 3 sing. αἴδετο, pl. αἰδέοντο Att. ᾐδοῦντο : f. αἰδέσομαι, Ep. αἰδέσσομαι : aor. 1 med. ᾐδεσάμην, Ep. imper. αἴδεσσαι : aor. 1 pass. ᾐδέσθην, Ep. 3 pl. αἴδεσθεν : pf. ᾔδεσμαι : Dep. :—to be ashamed to do a thing, c. inf., Hom., etc. ; rarely c. part., αἴδεσαι μὲν πατέρα προλείπων feel ashamed of deserting him, Soph. :—absol., αἰδεσθείς from a sense of shame, Il. 2. c. acc. pers. to stand in awe of, fear, respect, αἰδεῖο θεούς Ib., Hom., etc. ; and of things, αἴδεσσαι μέλαθρον respect the house, Il. ; ὅρκον αἰδεσθείς Soph. II. to feel regard for a person, μήδε τί μ' αἰδόμενος μήδ' ἐλεαίρων Od. Hence

αἰδέσιμος, ον, exciting shame, venerable, Luc.

αἴδεσις, ἡ, (αἰδέομαι) respect, Dem.

ἀ-ίδηλος [ῐ], Dor. -ᾱλος, ον, (*εἴδω) making unseen, annihilating, destroying, Il. :—Adv. -λως, = ὀλεθρίως, Ib. II. pass. unseen, obscure, Hes.

αἰδήμων, ον, gen. ονος, (αἰδέομαι) bashful, modest, Xen.: Sup. αἰδημονέστατος, Id. : Adv. -μόνως, Id.

ἀ-ίδης, ές, (*εἴδω) unseen, annihilated, Hes.

Ἀΐδης, ὁ, poët. for Ἅιδης ; v. ᾅδης.

ἀΐδιος [ᾱϊδ], α, ον, also, (ἀεί) everlasting, eternal, Hes. and Att. :—ἐς ἀΐδιον for ever, Thuc.

ἀ-ιδνός, ή, όν, (*εἴδω) unseen, dark, Hes. :—so ἀ-ίδνης, Poëta ap. Plut.

αἰδοῖον, τό, mostly in pl. αἰδοῖα, τά, (αἴδομαι) the genitals, pudenda, Il., etc.

αἰδοῖος, α, ον, (αἰδέομαι) of persons, regarded with reverence, august, venerable, and of women, deserving respect, tender, Hom. II. act. shamefaced, reverent, Od. :—Adv. -ως, reverently, Ib. III. Comp. αἰδοιότερος, Od. : Sup. αἰδοιέστατος, Pind.

αἴδομαι, poët. for αἰδέομαι.

Ἄϊς, Ep. gen. of an obsol. nom. Ἄϊς, v. ᾅδης.

αἰδό-φρων, ον, gen. ονος, (αἴδομαι, φρήν) respectful in mind, compassionate, Soph. ; πρός τινα Eur.

ἀϊδρείη or -ίη [ῐ], ἡ, want of knowledge, ignorance, Od., Hdt. From

ἄ-ϊδρις, ι, gen. ιος and εος, (*εἴδω) poët. Adj. unknow-ing, ignorant, Il. ; c. gen., Od., etc.

ἀ-ίδρυτος or ἀν-ίδρυτος, ον, (ἱδρύω) unsettled, vaga-bond, Ar. ; δρόμοις in vagabond courses, Eur.

Ἀϊδωνεύς, έως, later ὁ, = Ἅιδης : poets used the obl. cases Ἀϊδωνῆος, ῆι, ῆα, with ᾱ, metri grat.

αἰδώς, όος, contr. οὖς, ἡ, (αἰδέομαι) a sense of shame, shame, modesty, self-respect, Hom., etc. :—personif., Ζηνὶ σύνθακος θρόνων Αἰδώς Shame that shares his throne with Zeus, Soph. 2. regard for others, re-spect, reverence, Theogn.; τὴν ἐμὴν αἰδῶ respect for me, Aesch. II. that which causes shame, and so, 1. a shame, Il. ; as an exclam., shame ! αἰδώς, Ἀργεῖοι, κακ' ἐλέγχεα ! Ib. ; αἰδώς, ὦ Λύκιοι· ποῖ φεύγετε ; Ib. 2. = τὰ αἰδοῖα, Ib.

αἰεί, Ion. and poët. for ἀεί.

αἰει-γενέτης, ὁ, poët. for ἀειγενέτης.

αἰέλουρος, v. sub αἴλουρος.

αἰέν, poët. for ἀεί.

αἰέν-υπνος, ον, lulling in eternal sleep, of Death, Soph.

αἰετός, Ep. and Ion. for ἀετός.

αἰζηός, lengthd. αἰζήϊος, ὁ, strong, lusty, vigorous, Hom. (Deriv. uncertain.)

αἰηνής, Ion. for ἀϊανής.

αἴητος, in Il. Vulcan is πέλωρ αἴητον, = ἄητον, terrible, mighty monster.

αἰθάλη, ἡ, (αἴθω) = αἴθαλος, soot, Luc.

αἰθαλίων, ωνος, (αἴθαλος) epith. of the τέττιξ, swarthy, dusky, Theocr.

αἰθαλόεις, όεσσα, όεν, contr. αἰθαλοῦς, οῦσσα, οῦν, (αἴθαλος) smoky, sooty, Il., Theocr.; κόνις αἰθ. black ashes that are burnt out, Hom.   II. burning, Hes., Aesch.

αἴθαλος, ὁ, (αἴθω ?) soot, Eur.

αἰθαλόω, f. ώσω, to soil with soot or smoke, Eur.

αἴθε, Ep. for εἴθε, αἴθ' ὄφελες would that! Hom.; cf. αἰ.

ἄτθεος, Dor. for ἤϊθεος.

αἰθερ-εμβατέω, f. ήσω, (ἐμβαίνω) to walk in ether, Anth.

αἰθέριος, α, ον, also ος, ον, (αἰθήρ) of or in the upper air, high in air, on high, Aesch., Soph., etc.; αἰθερία ἀνέπτα flew up into the air, Eur.

αἰθερο-δρόμος, ον, (δραμεῖν) ether-skimming, Anth.

αἰθήρ, έρος, in Hom. ἡ; in Hes., Aesch., and Att. Prose ὁ; in Soph. and Eur. ὁ or ἡ: (αἴθω):—ether, the brighter purer air, the sky, above the ἀήρ (q. v.); Ζεὺς αἰθέρι ναίων Il.   II. a clime, region, Eur.

Αἰθίοψ, οπος, ὁ, Ep. al. Αἰθιοπῆες, fem. Αἰθιοπίς, ίδος: (αἴθω, ὄψ):—properly Burnt-face, i.e. an Ethiop, negro, Hom., etc.   II. Adj. Ethiopian, Hdt., etc.:— Αἰθιοπικός, ή, όν, and as Subst. Αἰθιοπία, ἡ, Id.   2. in literal sense, sun-burnt, Anth.

αἶθος, ὁ, (αἴθω) a burning heat, fire, Eur.

αἴθουσα (sc. στοά, being partic. of αἴθω), ἡ, in the Homeric house, the corridor, open in front like a veran- dah, looking E. or S. to catch the sun, whence the name; the sleeping place of travellers, Od.

αἰθ-οψ, οπος, (αἴθω, ὄψ) fiery-looking, of metal, flashing, Il., etc.; of wine, sparkling, Ib.; of smoke, mixed with flame, Od.   2. swart, dark, Anth.   II. metaph. fiery, keen, eager, Lat. ardens, Hes., Soph.

αἴθρη (not αἴθρα even in Att.), ἡ, (αἰθήρ) clear sky, fair weather, Lat. sudum, Hom.

αἰθρη-γενής, ές, (γί-γνομαι) epith. of Boreas, born in ether, sprung from ether, Il.; so αἰθρη-γενέτης, Od.

αἰθρία, Ion. -ίη, ἡ, later form of αἴθρη, Solon, etc.; αἰθρίης, Att. -ίας, in clear weather, Hdt., Ar.; ὑπὸ τῆς αἰθρίας in the open air, Lat. sub dio, Xen.   2. the clear cold air of night, Hdt. [ῑ in dactylics and ana- paestics.]

αἰθριάω, to be clear, of the sky, ὡς δ' ἠθρίασε Babr.

αἰθριο-κοιτέω, f. ήσω, (κοίτη) to sleep in open air, Theocr.

αἴθριος, ον, (αἴθρη) clear, bright, fair, of weather, h. Hom., Hdt.; epith. of Ζεύς, Theocr.

αἶθρος, ὁ, the clear chill air of morn, Od.; cf. αἰθρία.

αἴθυια, ἡ, a sea-bird, a gull or diver, Od. (Deriv. un- known.)

αἰθυκτήρ, ῆρος, ὁ, one that darts swiftly, Anth. From

αἰθύσσω, poët. aor. 1 αἴθυξα, (αἴθω) to put in rapid motion, stir up, kindle, Soph.:—Pass. to quiver, of leaves, Sappho.

ΑΙ'ΘΩ, only in pres. and impf., to light up, kindle, Hdt., Trag.   2. intr. to burn or blaze, Soph.:—in this sense the Pass. αἴθομαι is used by Hom. in part., πυρὸς μένος αἰθομένοιο Il., Od., etc.; so metaph., ἔρωτι αἴθεσθαι Xen.

αἴθων, ωνος, ὁ, ἡ, (αἴθω) fiery, burning, blazing: of metal, flashing, glittering, Hom., etc.   II. in Hom. of the horse, lion, bull, eagle,—where it is either fiery, fierce, or tawny.   2. metaph. ablaze, fiery, Aesch., Soph. [The penult. of the obl. cases may be shortd. in Poets, metri grat., αἴθονος Soph.; αἴθονα Hes.]

αἴκα [κᾰ], Dor. for εἴ κε or ἐάν, Theocr.

αἰκάλλω, only in pres. and impf., (αἰκάλος) to flatter, wheedle, fondle, c. acc., Soph., Eur.   2. absol., of a dog, to wag the tail fawningly, Babr.: (this is prob. the orig. sense).

αἴκε, αἴκεν, poët. and Dor. for ἐάν.

αἰκέλιος, ον, poët. for ἀεικέλιος.

αἶκη [ᾱ], ἡ, (ἀΐσσω) rapid flight, rush, impetus, Il.

αἰκής [ῐ], ές, poët. for ἀεικής, Adv. αἰκῶς, Il.:—in Trag., αἰκής, αἰκῶς.

αἰκία [ῐ], ἡ, Att. for the Ion. ἀεικείη (q. v.), injurious treatment, an affront, outrage, Aesch., etc.   2. in Prose mostly as law-phrase, αἰκίας δίκη an action for assault, less serious than that for ὕβρις, Plat., etc.

αἰκίζω, Att. for Ep. ἀεικίζω: I. Act. only in pres., to treat injuriously, to plague, torment, τινά Soph.; of a storm, αἰκίζων φόβην ὕλης Id.:—Pass. to be tor- mented, Aesch.   II. Dep. αἰκίζομαι: f. αἰκίσομαι, Att. -ιοῦμαι: aor. 1 med. ᾐκισάμην, pass. ᾐκίσθην: pf. ᾔκισμαι:—in same sense as Act., c. acc., Soph.; etc.; c. dupl. acc. pers. et rei, αἰκίζεσθαί τινα τὰ ἔσχατα Xen. Hence

αἴκισμα, ατος, τό, an outrage, torture, Aesch.:—in pl. mutilated corpses, Eur.

αἰκισμός, ὁ, = foreg., Dem.

ἄϊκῶς, αἰκῶς, Adv. of ἀϊκής.

αἴ-λινος, ὁ, a plaintive dirge, Trag.; (said to be from αἶ Λίνον, ah me for Linus! v. Λίνος II.)   2. Adj. αἴλινος, ον, mournful, plaintive, Eur.:—neut. pl. αἴλινα as Adv., Mosch.

αἴλουρος or αἰέλουρος, ὁ, ἡ, a cat, Hdt., Att. (Deriv. uncertain.)

αἷμα, ατος, τό, blood, Hom., etc.; in pl. streams of blood, Trag.   II. bloodshed, murder, Aesch., etc.:—ἐφ' αἵματι φεύγειν to avoid trial for murder by going into exile, Dem.; so, αἷμα φεύγειν Eur.   III. like Lat. sanguis, blood-relationship, kin, Soph., Hom., etc.; ὁ πρὸς αἵμα- τος one of the blood or race, Soph.; μητρὸς τῆς ἐμῆς ἐν αἵματι akin to her by blood, Aesch. (Deriv. uncertain.)

αἱμακτός, ή, όν, verb. Adj. of αἱμάσσω, mingled with blood, of blood, Eur.

αἱμαλέος, α, ον, (αἷμα) bloody, blood-red, Anth.

αἱμάς, άδος, ἡ, (αἷμα) a gush or stream of blood, Soph.

αἱμασιά, ή, a wall of dry stones, Lat. maceria, Od., etc. (Deriv. uncertain.)

αἱμάσσω, Att. -ττω: f. -άξω: aor. 1 ᾕμαξα:—Pass. aor. 1 ᾑμάχθην or αἱμάχθην: (αἷμα) —to make bloody stain with blood, Aesch.:—hence to smite so as to

make bloody, Soph., Eur.; so in Med., Anth.:—Pass. to welter in blood, be slain, Soph.

αἱματ-εκχυσία, ἡ, (ἐκχέω) shedding of blood, N. T.

αἱμᾱτηρός, ά, όν, also ός, όν, (αἷμα) bloody, blood-stained, murderous, Trag. II. of blood, consisting thereof, Aesch., Eur.

αἱμᾱτη-φόρος, ον, (φέρω) bringing blood, bloody, Aesch.

αἱμᾰτόεις, όεσσα, όεν, contr. αἱματοῦς, οῦσσα, οῦν, = αἱματηρός, Il. 2. blood-red or of blood, Ib. 3. bloody, murderous, Ib.

αἱμᾰτο-λοιχός, όν, (λείχω) licking blood, ἔρως αἱμ. thirst for blood, Aesch.

αἱμᾰτο-πώτης, ου, ὁ, (πίνω) a blood-drinker, Ar.

αἱμᾰτορ-ρόφος, ον, (ῥοφέω) blood-drinking, Aesch.

αἱμᾰτόρ-ρῠτος, ον, (ῥέω) blood-streaming, αἱμ. ῥανίδες a shower of blood, Eur.

αἱμᾰτο-στᾰγής, ές, (στάζω) blood-dripping, Aesch.

αἱμᾰτό-φυρτος, ον, (φύρω) blood-stained, Anth.

αἱμᾰτο-χάρμης, ου, (χαίρω) delighting in blood, Anth.

αἱμᾰτόω, f. ώσω, (αἷμα) to make bloody, stain with blood, Aesch., Eur.

αἱμᾰτ-ώδης, ες, (εἶδος) blood-red, Thuc.

αἱμᾰτ-ωπός, όν, (ὤψ) bloody to behold, Eur.

αἱμᾰτ-ωψ, ῶπος, ὁ, ἡ, = αἱματωπός, Eur.

αἱμο-βᾰφής, ές, (βάπτω) bathed in blood, Soph.

αἱμο-βόρος, ον, (βορά) blood-sucking, greedy of blood, Theocr.

αἱμό-διψος, ον, bloodthirsty, Luc.

αἱμορ-ρᾰγής, ές, (ῥήγνυμι) bleeding violently, Soph.

αἱμόρ-ραντος, ον, (ῥαίνω) blood-sprinkled, Eur.

αἱμορ-ροέω, (ῥέω) to have a αἱμόρροια.

αἱμόρροια, ἡ, a discharge of blood.

αἱμόρ-ρῠτος, ον, (ῥέω) blood-streaming, Aesch.:—poët. **αἱμό-ρυτος**, Anth.

αἱμο-στᾰγής, ές, = αἱματο-σταγής, Eur.

αἱμο-φόρυκτος, ον, (φορύσσω) defiled with blood, κρέα Od.

αἱμυλία, ἡ, (αἱμύλος) winning, wily ways, Plut.

αἱμύλιος, ον, = αἱμύλος, Od., Hes.

αἱμῠλο-μήτης, ου, ὁ, (μῆτις) of winning wiles, h. Hom.

αἱμύλος [ῠ], η, ον and ος, ον, flattering, wheedling, wily, Hes., Aesch.; τὸν αἱμυλώτατον Soph. (Deriv. unknown.)

αἱμ-ώδης, ες, (εἶδος) bloody, blood-red, Luc.

αἵμων, ονος, ὁ, = δαήμων, skilful in a thing, c. gen., αἵμονα θήρης Il. II. (αἷμα) bloody, Aesch., Eur.

αἱμ-ωπός, όν, = αἱματωπός, Anth.

αἰν-ἀρέτης, ου, ὁ, (αἰνός, ἀρετή) terribly brave, Il.

αἴνεσις, εως, ἡ, (αἰνέω) praise, N. T.

αἰνετός, ή, όν, verb. Adj. of sq., praiseworthy, Arist., Anth.

αἰνέω, impf. ᾔνουν, Ion. αἴνεον: f. αἰνήσω, Att. αἰνέσω: aor. 1 ᾔνησα, Att. ᾔνεσα, Ion. αἴνεσα: pf. ᾔνεκα:—Med., f. αἰνέσομαι:—Pass., aor. 1 ᾐνέθην: pf. ᾔνημαι. Poët. and Ion. Verb, ἐπαινέω being used in Att. Prose:— properly, to tell or speak of (cf. αἶνος), Aesch. II. commonly, to speak in praise of, praise, Lat. laudo, c. acc., Hom., Hdt. 2. to allow, recommend, Od.: c. inf. to recommend to do a thing, Aesch.; also c. part., αἰνεῖν ἰόντα to commend one's going, Id. 3. like ἀγαπάω, to be content, acquiesce, Eur.:—c. acc. rei, to be content with, acquiesce in, γάμον Pind., etc.; θῆσσαν τράπεζαν Eur. 4. to decline courteously, Hes. III. to promise or vow, τί τινι or τινὶ ποιεῖν τι Soph., Eur.

αἴνη, ἡ, = αἶνος, praise, fame, ἐν αἴνῃ ἐών Hdt.

αἴνημι, Aeol. for αἰνέω, Hes.

αἰνητός, ή, όν, = αἰνετός, Pind.

αἴνιγμα, ατος, τό, (αἰνίσσομαι) a dark saying, riddle, Aesch., etc.; ἐξ αἰνιγμάτων in riddles, Id.; δι᾽ αἰνιγμάτων Aeschin.; αἴνιγμα προβάλλειν, ξυντιθέναι to propose a riddle, Plat.; opp. to αἴνιγμα λύειν, εὑρίσκειν to solve it, Soph., etc.

αἰνιγμᾰτ-ώδης, ες, (εἶδος) riddling, dark, Aesch.

αἰνιγμός, ὁ, = αἴνιγμα, a riddle, δι᾽ αἰνιγμῶν ἐρεῖν Ar.; ἐν αἰνιγμοῖσι σημαίνειν Eur.

αἰνίζομαι, Dep., = αἰνέω, Hom.:—Act. αἰνίζω in Anth.

αἰνικτήριος, ον, known from the Adv. -ίως, in riddles, Aesch.; and

αἰνικτός, ή, όν, expressed in riddles, riddling, Soph. From

αἰνίσσομαι, Att. -ττομαι: f. ἵξομαι: aor. 1 ᾐνιξάμην:— Dep., but also as Pass., v. infr. II: (αἶνος):—to speak in riddles, Soph., Eur.; γνωρίμως αἰνίζομαι I will speak in riddles but so as to be understood, Soph.; αἰνίσσεσθαι ἔπεα to speak riddling verses, Hdt.:—c. acc. rei, to hint a thing, intimate, shadow forth, Plat. II. as Pass. to be wrapt up in riddles, only in aor. 1 ᾐνίχθην, pf. ᾔνιγμαι, Theogn., Plat., etc.

αἰνο-βίας, Ion. -βίης, ου, ὁ, (βία) awefully strong, Anth.

αἰνό-γᾰμος, ον, fatally wedded, Eur.

αἰνόθεν, (αἰνός) Adv. only in phrase αἰνόθεν αἰνῶς from horror to horror, right horribly, Il.

αἰνό-θρυπτος, ον, (θρύπτω) sadly enervated, Theocr.

αἰνο-λαμπής, ές, (λάμπω) horrid-gleaming, Aesch.

αἰνό-λεκτρος, ον, (λέκτρον) fatally wedded, Aesch.

αἰνο-λέων, οντος, ὁ, a dreadful lion, Theocr.

αἰνό-λῐνος, ον, (λίνον) unfortunate in life's thread, in allusion to the Parcae, Anth.

αἰνό-λῠκος, ὁ, a horrible wolf, Anth.

αἰνό-μορος, ον, doomed to a sad end, Hom.

αἰνο-πᾰθής, ές, (πάσχω) suffering dire ills, Od., Anth.

Αἰνό-πᾰρις, ιδος, ὁ, like Δύσπαρις, unlucky Paris, Eur.

αἰνο-πᾰτήρ, έρος, ὁ, unhappy father, Aesch.

αἶνος, ὁ, poët. and Ion. word (cf. αἰνέω): I. = μῦθος, a tale, story, Od.; αἰνεῖν αἶνον to tell a tale, Aesch., Soph.: generally, a saying, proverb, Theocr. II. = Att. ἔπαινος, praise, Hom., Trag.

αἰνός, ή, όν, poët. and Ion. word = δεινός, dread, dire, grim, terrible, Hom.; αἰνότατε Κρονίδη most dread son of Cronus, Il. II. Adv. -νῶς, terribly, i.e. strangely, exceedingly, Hom., Hdt.; also αἰνά as Adv., Il.; Sup. -ότατον, Ib.

αἰνο-τόκεια, ἡ, (τίκτω) unhappy in being a mother, Mosch.

αἰνο-τύραννος, ὁ, a dreadful tyrant, Anth.

ΑἼΝΥΜΑΙ, Dep., only in pres. and impf. without augm.: —to take, take off, take hold of, Hom.; c. gen. partit., τυρῶν αἰνυμένων taking of the cheeses, Od.

ΑἼΞ, αἰγός, ὁ, ἡ: dat. pl. αἴγεσιν:—a goat, Lat. caper, capra, Hom. 2. αἲξ ἄγριος the wild goat, the ibex, Id. II. αἶγες, old name for waves. (Prob. not from ἀΐσσω, of which the root is AΙΚ.)

ἀΐξασκε, Ion. and Ep. aor. of ἀΐσσω.

ἀΐξω, f. of ἀΐσσω.

Αἰολεύς, έως, ὁ, an Aeolian; pl. Αἰολέες, Att. Αἰολεῖς or -ῆς, Hdt., Thuc.:—Adj. Αἰολικός, ή, όν, of or like the

Aeolians, Theocr. ;—fem. **Αἰολίς, ίδος**, Hes.,etc.; poët. fem. **Αἰολῆτς**, Pind.

αἰολίζω, f. σω, (Αἰολεύς) *to speak Aeolian*, Plut.

αἰόλλω, (αἰόλος) only in pres., *to shift rapidly to and fro*, Od. :—Pass. *to shift colour*, of grapes, Hes.

αἰολο-βρόντης, ου, ὁ, (βροντή) *wielder of lightning*, Ζεύς Pind.

αἰολο-θώρηξ, ηκος, ὁ, with glancing breastplate, Il.

αἰολό-μητις, ιος, ὁ, ἡ, full of various wiles, Hes., Aesch.

αἰολο-μίτρης, ου, ὁ, (μίτρα) *with glancing* or *glittering girdle* (for it was plated with metal), Il.   II. *with variegated turban*, Theocr.

αἰολό-πωλος, ον, with quick-moving steeds, Il., Theocr.

αἰόλος, η, ον, quick-moving, Il.; αἰόλαι εὐλαί *wriggling worms*, Ib.; so of wasps and serpents, Ib.   II. *changeful of hue, gleaming, glancing*, of arms and armour, Ib.; (but here also it may be explained *moving with the body, manageable*, Lat. *habilis*) ;—also, αἰόλα νύξ *star-spangled* night, Soph.; Aesch. calls smoke flushed by fire-light αἰόλα πυρὸς κάσις; αἰόλα σάρξ *discoloured* from disease, Soph.   III. metaph., 1. *changeful, shifting, varied*, κάκα Aesch.; of sounds, ἰαχή Eur.   2. *shifty, wily, slippery*, ψεῦδος Pind. (Deriv. uncertain.)

   B. as prop. n., proparox. **Αἴολος, ου, ὁ**, lord of the winds, properly *the Rapid* or *the Changeable*, Od. [The penult. is lengthd. in the gen. Αἰόλου μεγαλήτορος, metri grat., Od.]

αἰολό-στομος, ον, (στόμα) *shifting in speech*, of an oracle, Aesch.

αἰπεινός, ή, όν, (αἰπύς) *high, lofty*, Hom.   II. metaph., 1. *precipitate, hasty*, Pind;   2. *hard to win, difficult*, Pind., Eur.

αἴπερ, Dor. for εἴπερ.

αἰπήεις, εσσα, εν, = αἰπεινός, Il.

αἰπολέω, only in pres. and impf., *to tend goats*, Theocr. : —Pass., of the flock, Aesch.

αἰπολικός, ή, όν, (αἰπόλος) *of* or *for goatherds*, Anth.

αἰπόλιον, τό, a herd of goats, Il., etc.   II. *a goat-pasture*, Anth. From

αἰ-πόλος, ὁ, a goatherd, Od., etc. (αἰ-πόλος is for αἰγο-πόλος from αἴξ, πολέω.)

αἶπος, εος, τό, (αἰπύς) *a height, a steep*, Aesch. :—πρὸς αἶπος ἔρχεσθαι, metaph. of a difficult task, Eur.

αἰπός, ή, όν, Ep. for αἰπύς, *high, lofty*, of cities, Il.; αἰπὰ ῥέεθρα streams *falling sheer down*, Ib.

αἰπυ-μήτης, ου, ὁ, (μῆτις) *with high thoughts*, Θέμιδος αἰπυμῆτα παῖ Aesch.

αἰπύ-νωτος, ον, high-backed, on a high mountain-ridge, of Dodona, Aesch.

ΑΙ'ΠΥ'Σ, εῖα, ύ, high and steep, lofty, of cities on heights, as Troy, Od.; of hills, Il.; βρόχος αἰπ. a noose *hanging straight down*, Od.   II. metaph. *sheer, utter*, αἰπὺς ὄλεθρος Hom. (death being regarded as *the plunge over a precipice*) ; so, φόνος αἰπύς Od.; also αἰπὺς χόλος *towering* wrath, Il.   2. *arduous, difficult*, Ib.

αἱρέσιμος, ον, (αἱρέω) *that can be taken*, Xen.

αἵρεσις, εως, ἡ, (αἱρέω) *a taking*, esp. of a town, Hdt., etc.; ἡ βασιλῆος αἵρ. *the taking* by the king, Id.   2. *means for taking a place*, Thuc.   II. (αἱρέομαι) *a taking for oneself, a choosing, choice*, νέμειν, προτιθέναι, προβάλλειν to give or offer *choice*, Hdt., Att.; αἵρ.

γίγνεταί τινι *a choice* is allowed one, Thuc.; αἵρεσιν λαμβάνειν to have *choice* given, Dem.   2. *choice* or *election* of magistrates, Thuc., etc.   3. *a choice, deliberate plan, purpose*, Plat., etc.   4. *a sect, school*, etc. : esp. *a religious sect*, such as the Sadducees and Pharisees, N. T.   5. *a heresy*, Eccl.

αἱρετέος, α, ον, verb. Adj. of αἱρέω, *to be taken, desirable*, Xen.   II. αἱρετέον, *one must choose*, Plat.

αἱρετίζω, f. σω, (αἱρέομαι) *to choose, select*, Babr., N. T.

αἱρετικός, ή, όν, (αἱρέομαι) *able to choose*, Plat.   2. *heretical*, N. T.

αἱρετός, ή, όν, verb. Adj. of αἱρέω, *that may be taken* or *conquered*, Hdt.; *that may be understood*, Plat.   II. (αἱρέομαι) *to be chosen, eligible*, Id., Hdt., etc.; ζοῆς πονηρᾶς θάνατος αἱρετώτερος Menand.   2. *chosen, elected*, Plat., etc.

ΑΙ'ΡΕ'Ω : impf. ᾕρεον, Ion. αἴρεον : f. αἱρήσω : pf. ᾕρηκα, Ion. ἀραίρηκα or αἴρηκα : plqpf. ἀραιρήκεε :—Med., f. αἱρήσομαι : pf. in med. sense ᾕρημαι : 3 pl. plqpf. ᾕρηντο: —Pass., f. αἱρεθήσομαι, rarely ᾑρήσομαι : aor. 1 ᾑρέθην : pf. ᾕρημαι : 3 sing. plqpf. ᾕρητο, Ion. ἀραίρητο.—From Root ΕΛ come f. ἑλῶ, aor. 1 εἷλα, only in late writers: aor. 2 εἷλον, Ion. ἕλεσκον:—Med., f. ἑλοῦμαι: aor. 2 εἱλόμην:

   A. Act. *to take with the hand, grasp*, αἱρ. τι ἐν χερσίν, μετὰ χερσίν *to take* a thing in hand, Od.; αἱρ. χερσὶ δόρυ Il.; αἱρ. τινὰ χειρός *to take* one by the hand, Ib.:—part. ἑλών is sometimes used as Adv., *by force*, Soph.   2. *to take away*, Hom.   II. *to take* by force, *to take* a city, Il., etc. ; *to overpower, kill*, Hom., etc. :—often of passions, etc., *to seize*, Id., etc. :—*to conquer* (in a race), Il.   2. *to take, catch*, as in hunting, in good sense, *to win over*, Xen., etc. :—c. part. *to catch* or *detect one doing* a thing, Soph.   3. *to win, gain*, κῦδος Il.; of the public games, Simon., etc.   4. as Att. law-term, *to convict* a person of a thing, τινά τινος Ar., etc.: also c. part., αἱρεῖν τινὰ κλέπτοντα *to convict* of theft, Id.; ᾑρῆσθαι κλοπεύς (sc. ὤν) Soph.; τοῦτ' ἔστιν ὃ ἐμὲ αἱρήσει Plat.   5. ὁ λόγος αἱρέει, Lat. *ratio evincit*, *reason proves*, Hdt.

   B. Med. *to take for oneself*, Hom., etc.; αἱρ. δόρπον, δεῖπνον *to take one's* supper, Id. :—so in most senses of Act.   II. *to choose*, Id. : *to take in preference, prefer* one thing to another, τι πρό τινος Hdt.; τι ἀντί τινος Xen.; also, τί τινος Soph.; τι μᾶλλον ἤ . ., or μᾶλλόν τινος Att. :—c. inf. *to prefer to do*, Hdt., etc.   2. αἱρεῖσθαι τά τινος or τινά *to take* another's part, *join* his *party*, Id., etc.   3. *to choose by vote, elect* to an office, Plat., etc.

   C. Pass. *to be taken*, Hdt.; but ἁλίσκομαι is used in Att. for Pass.   II. as Pass. to the med. sense, *to be chosen*, in pf. ᾕρημαι (which is also med.), Hdt., Att.

ἄ-ϊρος [ῐ], ὁ, Od. 18. 73 Ἶρος ἄϊρος *unhappy Irus*, —a play upon his name, like δῶρα ἄδωρα.

αἴρω (Ep. and poët. ἀείρω q.v.) : f. ἀρῶ [ᾰ], which must be distinguished from ἀρῶ [ᾱ], contr. from ἀερῶ, f. of ἀείρω :—aor. 1 ᾖρα, imper. ἆρον, subj. ἄρῃς, opt. ἄρειας, part. ἄρας [ᾱ] :—pf. ἦρκα : 3 pl. plqpf. ἤρκεσαν:—Med., impf. ᾐρόμην : f. ἀροῦμαι [ᾰ], poët. ἀρέομαι :—aor. 1 ἠράμην :—in Ep. poets also aor. 2 ἀρόμην [ᾰ] ; Ep. subj. ἄρηαι, ἄρηται ; opt. ἀροίμην ; inf. ἀρέσθαι ; part. ἀρόμενος :—pf. (in med. sense) ἦρμαι :—Pass., f. ἀρθήσομαι : aor. 1 ἤρθην : pf. ἦρμαι, but in med. sense, Soph. :

A. Act. *to take up, raise, lift up,* Il., etc.; αἴρειν βῆμα to step, walk, Eur.; αἴρ. σημεῖον *to hoist* a signal, Xen.:—Pass. *to mount up, ascend,* Id. **2.** *often of* armies and ships, αἴρ. τὰς ναῦς *to get* the fleet *under sail,* Thuc. :—also intr. *to get under way, start, set out,* ἄραι τῷ στρατῷ Id.;—so in Med. and Pass., Hdt., etc. **II.** *to bear, sustain,* μόρον Aesch.; ἄθλον Soph. **III.** *to raise up, exalt,* Aesch. :—of passion, *to exalt, excite,* ὑψοῦ αἴρειν θυμόν *to grow excited,* Soph.; αἴρειν θάρσος *to pluck up* courage, Eur., etc.: Pass., οὐκ ἤρθη νοῦν ἐς ἀτασθαλίην Simon. **2.** *to raise by words, to extol, exaggerate,* Eur., Dem. **IV.** *to lift and take away, to remove,* Aesch., etc. :—*to take off, kill,* N. T.

B. Med., with pf. pass. ἦρμαι (v. supr.), *to take up for oneself : to carry off, win, gain,* κλέος Il.; ἄεθλια (of horses) Ib.; κῦδος Hom. :—hence simply *to receive, get,* ἕλκος ἀρέσθαι Il.; also, δειλίαν ἀρεῖ *wilt incur* a charge of cowardice, Soph. **II.** *to take upon oneself, undergo, carry, bear,* Il., etc. **2.** *to undertake, begin,* πόλεμον Thuc., etc. ; φυγὴν ἀρέσθαι, Lat. *fugam capere,* Aesch. **III.** *to raise up,* σωτῆρά τινι Soph.: of sound, αἴρεσθαι φωνήν *to raise, lift up* one's voice, Ar.

***Ἆις,** obsol. nominat., v. ᾆδον.

Αἶσα, ἡ, like Μοῖρα, *the goddess of destiny,* Lat. *Parca,* Il. **II.** as appellat., **1.** *the decree, dispensation* of a god, Διὸς αἴσῃ, ὑπὲρ Διὸς αἶσαν Ib.; θεοῦ αἶσα Eur. :—κατ' αἶσαν *fitly, duly,* Il., etc. ; κατ' αἶσαν, οὐδ' ὑπὲρ αἶσαν Ib. **2.** *one's appointed lot, destiny,* Hom., etc. **3.** *one's share in* a thing, Od. ; ληΐδος αἶσα Ib., etc.

αἰσθάνομαι, Ion. 3 pl. opt. αἰσθανοίατο : impf. ᾐσθανόμην : f. αἰσθήσομαι : aor. 2 ᾐσθόμην : Dep. : (ἀΐω):— *to perceive, apprehend by the senses, to see, hear, feel,* Hdt., Att. **2.** *to perceive by the mind, understand, hear, learn,* often in Att. : absol., αἰσθάνει, Lat. *tenes, you are right,* Eur. :—Construct., c. gen. *to have perception of,* τῶν κακῶν Id., etc. ; also c. acc., Soph., etc. :—dependent clauses are mostly added in part. agreeing with subject, αἰσθάνομαι κάμνων Thuc. ; or agreeing with object, τυράννους ἐκπεσόντας ᾐσθόμην Aesch. Hence

αἴσθημα, ατος, τό, *perception of* a thing, κακῶν Eur.

αἴσθησις, εως, ἡ, (αἰσθάνομαι) *perception by the senses,* αἴσθ. πημάτων *perception, sense* of calamities, Eur.—The phrase αἴσθησιν ἔχειν is used **1.** of persons, αἴσθ. ἔχειν τινός, = αἰσθάνεσθαί τινος or τι, *to have a perception of* a thing, perceive it, Plat. **2.** of things, *to give a perception,* i.e. *to become perceptible,* serving as a Pass. to αἰσθάνομαι, Thuc. ; more freq. αἴσθησιν παρέχειν Id., Xen. **II.** *one of the senses,* Plat. : and in pl. *the senses,* Id. **III.** *a perception,* αἰσθήσεις θεῶν *visions* of the gods, Id. **2.** in hunting, *the scent,* Xen.

αἰσθητήριον, τό, (αἰσθάνομαι) *an organ of sense,* Arist., etc. ; τὰ αἰσθ. *the senses, faculties,* N. T.

αἰσθητικός, ή, όν, (αἰσθάνομαι) *of* or *for perception by the senses, perceptive,* Plat., etc. :—Adv. αἰσθητικῶς ἔχειν *to be quick of perception,* Arist. **II.** of things, *perceptible,* Plut.

αἰσθητός, ή, όν, and ός, όν, verb. Adj. of αἰσθάνομαι, *perceptible by the senses,* Plat.

ἀΐσθω, only in pres. and impf. (ἄημι) *to breathe out,* like

ἀποπνέω, θυμὸν ἄϊσθε *he was giving up* the ghost, Il.

αἰσιμία, ἡ, *happiness,* αἰσιμίαις πλούτου Aesch. From

αἴσιμος, ον and η, ον, (αἶσα) Lat. *fatalis, appointed by the will of the gods, destined,* αἴσιμον ἦμαρ the *fatal day, day of death,* Il., etc. ; αἴσιμόν ἐστι *'tis fated,* Ib. **II.** *agreeable to fate, meet, right,* αἴσιμα εἰπεῖν, αἴσιμα εἰδώς Od.

αἴσιος, ον and α, ον, (αἶσα) *boding well, auspicious,* Il., etc. :—Adv. -ίως, Eur.

ἄ-ῑσος, ον, = ἄνισος, *unlike, unequal,* Pind.

ἀΐσσω, (Root ΑΙΚ), contr. ᾄσσω, in later Att. ᾄττω or ᾄττω : impf. ᾔσσον, Ep. ἤϊσσον, Ion. ἀΐσσεσκον : f. ἀΐξω : aor. 1 ᾖξα; Ion. ἤϊξα, ἀΐξασκον :—Med., aor. ἀΐξασθαι : — Pass., aor. 1 ᾐχθην, Ep. ἀΐχθην. [ᾱ- in Hom.] *To move with a quick shooting motion, to shoot, dart, glance,* Lat. *impetu ferri,* Il., etc. ; so in aor. med., ἀΐξασθαι, and aor. pass. ἀϊχθῆναι Ib. ; κόμη δι' ἀέρας ᾄσσεται *floats* on the breeze, Soph. **2.** *to turn eagerly, be eager,* εἴς τι Eur. **II.** trans. *to put in motion,* Eur.

ἄ-ιστος, ον, contr. ᾆστος, (α privat., *εἴδω) not to be seen, unseen.* **II.** act. *unconscious of,* c. gen., Eur. Hence

ἀϊστόω, contr. ᾀστόω : f. ώσω : aor. 1 ᾔστωσα, contr. ᾖστ- :—Pass., aor. 1 ᾐστώθην, Ep. ἀϊστώθην :—*to make unseen, to annihilate,* Hom., etc.

ἀ-ΐστωρ, ορος, ὁ, ἡ, (α privat., εἰδέναι) *unknowing, unconscious,* Plat. ; τινός of a thing, Eur.

αἴσυλος, ον, *unseemly, evil,* Il. (Deriv. uncertain.)

αἰσυμνάω, *to rule over,* c. gen., Eur. (Deriv. uncertain.)

αἰσυμνητεία, ἡ, *an elective monarchy,* Arist.

αἰσυμνητήρ, ῆρος, ὁ, (αἰσυμνάω) *a prince,* Il.

αἰσυμνήτης, ου, ὁ, (αἰσυμνάω) *a regulator* of games, *a judge* or *umpire,* Od. : *a president, manager,* Theocr. **II.** *an elective prince,* Arist.

αἰσχίων, αἴσχιστος, Comp. and Sup. of αἰσχρός.

ΑΙ'ΣΧΟΣ, εος, τό, *shame, disgrace,* Hom., etc. :—in pl. *shameful deeds,* Od. **II.** *ugliness* or *deformity,* of mind or body, Plat., Xen.

αἰσχρήμων, ον, gen. ονος, (αἰσχρός) *shameful,* Anth.

αἰσχρο-κέρδεια, ἡ, (κέρδος) *base covetousness,* Soph.

αἰσχρο-κερδής, ές, (κέρδος) *sordidly greedy of gain,* Hdt., Eur.—Adv. -δῶς, N. T.

αἰσχρο-λογέω, f. ήσω, (λέγω) = αἰσχροεπέω, Plat. Hence

αἰσχρολογία, ἡ, *foul language, abuse,* Xen.

αἰσχρό-μητις, ιος, ὁ, ἡ, *forming base designs,* Aesch.

αἰσχρο-ποιός, όν, (ποιέω) *doing foully,* Eur.

αἰσχρο-πράγέω, f. ήσω, (πράσσω) = αἰσχρουργέω, Arist.

αἰσχρός, ά, όν and ός, όν, (αἶσχος) *causing shame, abusive,* ἔπεα Il. ; so in Adv., αἰσχροῖς ἐνένισπε Ib. **II.** opp. to καλός. **1.** of outward appearance, *ugly, ill-favoured,* of Thersites, Ib. **2.** in moral sense, *shameful, disgraceful, base, infamous,* Hdt., etc.; αἰσχρόν [ἐστι], c. inf., Il. :—τὸ αἰσχρόν, as Subst. *dishonour, disgrace,* Soph., etc.; τὸ καλὸν καὶ τὸ αἰσχρόν, Lat. *honestum et turpe, virtue and vice,* Arist. :—Adv. *shamefully,* Sup. αἴσχιστα, Trag. **3.** *awkward,* Xen. **III.** *instead of the regul.* Comp. and Sup. αἰσχρότερος, -ότατος, the forms αἰσχίων [ῑ], αἴσχιστος (formed from αἶσχος) are used. Hence

αἰσχρότης, ητος, ἡ, *ugliness, deformity,* Plat.

αἰσχυνέμεν, Ep. inf. of αἰσχύνω.

αἰσχρ-ουργία, ἡ, (*ἔργω) shameless conduct, Eur.

αἰσχύνη [ῡ], ἡ, (αἶσχος) shame done one, disgrace, dishonour, Hdt., Att.   2. a disgrace, of a person, Aesch.   II. shame for an ill deed, personified in Aesch.   2. generally, like αἰδώς, shame, the sense of shame, Soph., etc.

αἰσχυντέον, verb. Adj. of αἰσχύνομαι, one must be ashamed, Xen.

αἰσχυντηλός, ή, όν, (αἰσχύνομαι) bashful, modest, Plat.

αἰσχυντήρ, ῆρος, ὁ, (αἰσχύνω) a dishonourer, Aesch.

αἰσχυντηρός, ή, όν, = αἰσχυντηλός, Plat.

αἰσχυντικός, ή, όν, (αἰσχύνω) shameful, Arist.

αἰσχύνω [ῡ]: Ion. impf. αἰσχύνεσκε: f. –ῠνῶ, Ion.–ῠνέω: aor. 1 ἤσχῡνα :—Pass., with f. med. αἰσχῠνοῦμαι: aor. 1 ᾐσχύνθην, inf. αἰσχυνθῆναι, poët.–ήμεν: pf. ἤσχυμμαι:—to make ugly, disfigure, mar, πρόσωπον, κόμην Il.   2. in moral sense, to dishonour, tarnish, γένος πατέρων Ib., etc.   3. to dishonour a woman, Aesch., etc.   B. Pass. to be dishonoured, νέκυς ᾐσχυμμένος, of Patroclus, Il.   II. to be ashamed, feel shame, absol., Od., Hdt., etc.   2. to be ashamed at a thing, c. acc. rei, Od., etc.; also c. dat. rei, Ar., etc.; and with Preps., αἰσχ. ἐπί τινι Xen.; ἔν τινι Thuc.; ὑπέρ τινος Dem. :—c. part. to be ashamed at doing a thing, Aesch., Soph., etc. :—but c. inf. to be ashamed to do a thing, Hdt., etc.   3. c. acc. pers. to feel shame before one, Eur., etc.

ἀῑτας [ῑ], ὁ, (ἀΐω) Dor. word for a beloved youth, favourite, Theocr.: generally a lover, Anth.

αἶτε, Dor. for εἶτε.

ΑΙΤΕΏ: Ion. impf. αἴτεον: f. αἰτήσω: aor. 1 ᾔτησα : pf. ᾔτηκα; pf. pass. ᾔτημαι :—to ask, beg, Od., etc.   2. c. acc. rei, to ask for, crave, demand, Hom., etc.; ὁδὸν αἰτ. to beg one's departure, i. e. ask leave to depart, Od. :—c. acc. pers. et rei, to ask a person for a thing, Hom., etc.; δίκας αἰτ. τινὰ φόνου to demand satisfaction from one for murder, Hdt.   3. c. acc. pers. et inf. to ask one to do, Od., etc.   II. Med. to ask for oneself, to claim, Aesch., etc. :—but often used just like Act.   III. Pass.:   1. of persons, to have a thing begged of one, Hdt., Thuc.   2. of things, to be asked, τὸ αἰτεόμενον Hdt., etc. Hence

αἴτημα, ατος, τό, a request, demand, Plat., N. T.

ἀῑτης, Ion. for ἀῑτας.

αἴτησις, εως, ἡ, (αἰτέω) a request, demand, Hdt.

αἰτητέον, verb. Adj. of αἰτέω, one must ask, Xen.

αἰτητικός, ή, όν, (αἰτέω) fond of asking, c. gen., Arist.

αἰτητός, όν, verb. Adj. of αἰτέω, asked for, Soph.

αἰτία, ἡ, (αἰτέω) a charge, accusation, Lat. crimen, and then the guilt or fault implied in such accusation, Pind., Hdt. :—Phrases: αἰτίαν ἔχειν to be accused, τινὸς of a thing, Id., etc.; —reversely, αἰτία ἔχει με Id.; ἐν αἰτίᾳ εἶναι or γίγνεσθαι Xen., etc.; αἰτίαν ὑπέχειν to lie under a charge, Plat.; αἰτίαν φέρεσθαι Thuc.; αἰτίαις ἐνέχεσθαι Plat. :—opp. to these are ἐν αἰτίᾳ ἔχειν or δι' αἰτίας to hold one guilty, accuse, Hdt., Thuc., etc.; ἐν αἰτίᾳ βάλλειν Soph.; αἰτίαν νέμειν τινί Id., etc.   2. in good sense, εἰ εὖ πράξαιμεν, αἰτία θεοῦ the credit is his, Aesch.; οἱ ἔχουσι ταύτην τὴν αἰτίαν who have this as their characteristic, Plat.   3. expostulation, μὴ ἐπ' ἔχθρᾳ τὸ πλέον ἢ αἰτίᾳ Thuc.   II.

a cause, Lat. causa, Plat., etc.; dat. αἰτίᾳ, like Lat. causâ, for the sake of, κοινοῦ ἀγαθοῦ Thuc.   III. an occasion, opportunity, αἰτίαν παρέχειν Luc.   IV. the head under which a thing comes, Dem.

αἰτιάασθαι, Ep. inf. of αἰτιάομαι.

αἰτιάζομαι, (αἰτία) Pass. to be accused, Xen.

αἰτίαμα, ατος, τό, a charge, guilt imputed, λαβεῖν ἐπ' αἰτιάματί τινα Aesch.; τοιοῖσδε ἐπ' αἰτιάμασιν on such charges, Id. From

αἰτιάομαι, Ep. 3 pl. αἰτιόωνται, opt. 2 and 3 sing. αἰτιόφο, –φτο, inf. αἰτιάασθαι, impf. ᾐτιάασθε, –όωντο : —f. –άσομαι: aor. 1 ᾐτιασάμην, Ion. part. αἰτιησάμενος : pf. ᾐτίαμαι: (αἰτία):—to charge, accuse, censure, blame, c. acc. pers., τάχα κεν καὶ ἀναίτιον αἰτιόφτο Il.; αἰτ. τινά τινος to accuse of a thing, Hdt., etc. ;—c. inf., αἰτ. τινα ποιεῖν τι to accuse one of doing, Id.—in this signf., certain tenses are used in pass. sense, to be accused, aor. 1 ᾐτιάθην Thuc., Xen.; pf. ᾐτίαμαι Thuc.   2. c. acc. rei, to lay to one's charge, impute, τοῦτο αἰτ. Xen.; ταῦτα Thuc.; c. dupl. acc., τί ταῦτα τοὺς Λάκωνας αἰτιώμεθα; Ar.   II. to allege as the cause, αἰτ. τινα αἴτιον Plat.; φωνάς τε καὶ ἄλλα μυρία αἰτ. Id.; τῆς ἱερᾶς χώρας ᾐτιᾶτο εἶναι he alleged that it was part of the sacred territory, Dem.

αἰτιατέον, verb. Adj. of αἰτιάομαι, one must accuse, Xen.   II. one must allege as the cause, Plat.

αἰτίζω, Ep. form of αἰτέω, only in pres. to ask, beg, c. acc. rei, σῖτον Ib.   2. c. acc. to beg of, μνηστῆρας Ib.   3. absol. αἰτίζων βόσκειν ἣν γαστέρα to fill one's belly by begging, Ib.

αἰτιο-λογικός, ή, όν, inquiring into causes: τὸ –κόν, investigation of causes, Strab.

αἴτιος, α, ον, more rarely ος, ον, (αἰτέω) to blame, blame-worthy, culpable, Il., etc.: Comp., αἰτιώτερος more culpable, Thuc.; Sup., τοὺς αἰτιωτάτους the most guilty, Hdt.; τινος for a thing, Id.   2. as Subst., αἴτιος, ὁ, the accused, culprit, Lat. reus, Aesch., etc.; οἱ αἴτιοι τοῦ πατρός they who have sinned against my father, Id. :—c. gen. rei, οἱ αἴτ. τοῦ φόνου those guilty of murder, Id.   II. being the cause, responsible for, c. gen. rei, Hdt., etc.; c. inf., Soph.: Sup., αἰτιώτατος ναυμαχῆσαι mainly instrumental in causing the sea-fight, Thuc.   2. αἴτιον, τό, a cause, Plat., etc.

Αἰτναῖος, α, ον, of or belonging to Etna (Αἴτνη), Pind., Aesch., etc.   2. metaph. like Etna, enormous, Eur.; some explain it so when used of horses, but better Etnean, i. e. Sicilian (for the Sicilian horses were famous), Soph.

αἰφνίδιος or ἀφνίδιος, ον, (ἄφνω) unforeseen, sudden, Aesch., Thuc. :—Adv. –ίως, Id.; also –ιον, Plut.

αἰχμάεις, αἰχμάτᾱς, Dor. for αἰχμήεις, αἰχμητής.

αἰχμάζω, f. άσω, (αἰχμή) to throw the spear, Il.; ἔνδον αἰχμάζειν to play the warrior at home, Aesch.   II. to arm with the spear, ᾔχμασας χέρα Soph.

αἰχμαλωσία, ἡ, (αἰχμάλωτος) captivity : a body of captives, Diod., N. T.

αἰχμαλωτεύω, to take prisoner, N. T.; and

αἰχμαλωτικός, ή, όν, of or for a prisoner, Eur.; and

αἰχμαλωτίς, ίδος, ἡ, fem. of αἰχμάλωτος, Soph. From

αἰχμ-άλωτος, ον, taken by the spear, captive to one's spear, taken prisoner, Hdt., etc.; αἰχμάλωτον λαμβάνειν, ἄγειν to take prisoner, Xen.; αἰχμ. γίγνεσθαι

to be taken, Id.; τὰ αἰχμάλωτα *booty*, Id.   II. = αἰχμαλωτικός, δουλοσύνη αἰχμ. *such as awaits a captive*, Hdt., Aesch.

αἰχμή, ἡ, (ἀκή I, or ἀίσσω) *the point of a spear*, Lat. *cuspis*, Il., etc.   II. *a spear*, Ib., etc.; τοξουλκὸς αἰχμή, *of an arrow*, Aesch.   2. *a body of spearmen*, Pind., Eur.; cf. ἀσπίς.   3. *war, battle*, κακῶς ἡ αἰχμὴ ἑστήκεε *the war went ill*, Hdt.   III. *warlike spirit, mettle*, Pind.; so, in Aesch., γυναικὸς or γυναικεία αἰχμά seems to be a woman's *spirit*.   IV. *a sceptre*, Id.   Hence

αἰχμήεις, Dor. -άεις, εσσα, εν, *armed with the spear*, Aesch.

αἰχμητά [ἄ], ὁ, Ep. form of αἰχμητής, Il.

αἰχμητής, οῦ, Dor. -ᾱτάς, α, ὁ, (αἰχμή) *a spearman*, Hom.   II. In Pind. as Adj.,   1. *pointed*, κεραυνός.   2. *warlike*, θυμός.

αἰχμο-φόρος, ον, (φέρω) *one who trails a pike, a spearman*, Hdt.:—esp. like δορυφόρος, *of body-guards*, Id.

αἶψα, Adv. *quick, with speed, on a sudden*, Hom.

αἰψηρο-κέλευθος, ον, *swift-speeding*, of Boreas, Hes.

αἰψηρός, ά, όν, (αἶψα) *quick, speedy, in haste*, Hom.

ἈΙΩ [ἄ], only in pres. and impf. ἄιον [ἄ]:—*to perceive by the ear*, c. acc. rei, Il.; *to hear*, c. acc. rei, Il.; c. gen., Trag.:—also *to perceive by the eye, to see*, Od.   2. *to listen to, give ear to*, δίκης Hes.: *to obey*, Aesch.; cf. ἐπαΐω. [Hom. has ἄιω; but ἄιεις, ἄιων Soph.]

ἀίω, = ἄημι, *to breathe*, only in impf., ἐπεὶ φίλον ἄιον ἦτορ when *I was breathing out* my life, Il.

ἀΐων [ἄ], Dor. for ἠίων.

αἰών, ῶνος, ὁ, poët. ἡ: apocop. acc. αἰῶ (properly αἰϝών, *aevum*, v. αἰεί):—*a period of existence*:   1. *one's lifetime, life*, Hom. and Att. Poets.   2. *an age, generation*, Aesch.; ὁ μέλλων αἰών *posterity*, Dem.   3. *a long space of time, an age*, ἀπ' αἰῶνος *of old, for ages*, Hes., N. T.; τὸν δι' αἰῶνος χρόνον *for ever*, Aesch.; ἅπαντα τὸν αἰ. Lycurg.   4. *a definite space of time, an era, epoch, age, period*, ὁ αἰὼν οὗτος *this present world*, opp. to ὁ μέλλων, N. T.:—hence its usage in pl., εἰς τοὺς αἰῶνας *for ever*, Ib.

αἰώνιος, ον and α, ον, *lasting for an age* (αἰών 3), Plat.: *ever-lasting, eternal*, Id.

αἰώρα, ἡ, (ἀείρω) *a machine for suspending bodies: a noose for hanging, a halter*, Soph. (in the form ἐώρα).   II. *suspension in the air, oscillation*, Plat.

αἰωρέω, f. ήσω: aor. 1 pass. ἠωρήθην: (ἀείρω):—*to lift up, raise*, ὑγρὸν νῶτον αἰωρεῖ, of the eagle *raising* his feathers, Pind.; τοὺς ὄφεις ὑπὲρ τῆς κεφαλῆς αἰωρῶν Dem.:—cf. ἐωρέω.   2. *to hang*, Plut., Luc.   II. Pass. *to be hung, hang*, Hdt.; αἰωρουμένων τῶν ὀστῶν *being raised, lifted*, Plat.; αἷμα ᾐωρεῖτο *spouted up*, Bion.   2. *to hang suspended, float in air, hover, oscillate*, Soph., Plat.   3. metaph. *to be in suspense*, Thuc.; αἰωρεῖσθαι ἐν ἄλλοις *to depend* upon others, Plat.; αἰωρηθεὶς ὑπὲρ μεγάλων *playing for a high stake*, Hdt.   Hence

αἰώρημα, ατος, τό, *that which is hung up: a hanging cord, a halter*, Eur.

αἰωρητός, όν, verb. Adj. of αἰωρέω, *a hovering*, Anth.

ἀκά, Dor. Adv. = ἀκήν, *softly, gently*, Pind.

Ἀκᾰδήμεια or -ία [ι], ἡ, *the Academy*, a gymnasium near Athens, where Plato taught: hence Platonic philosophers were called Ἀκαδημικοί, Academics.

ἀκάθαρσία, ἡ, *uncleanness, impurity*, Dem.   From ἀ-κάθαρτος, ον,(καθαίρω) *uncleansed, unclean, impure*, Plat. :—Adv., ἀκαθάρτως ἔχειν Id.   II. *of things, not purged away*, Soph.

ἄκαινα, ης, ἡ, (ἀκίς) *a thorn, goad*, Anth.

ἀκαιρία, ἡ, (ἄκαιρος) *unfitness of times : unseasonableness*, Plat.   2. *want of opportunity*, τὴν ἀκαιρίαν τὴν ἐκείνου καιρὸν ὑμέτερον νομίσαντες Dem.

ἄ-καιρος, ον, *ill-timed, unseasonable, inopportune*, ἐς ἄκαιρα πονεῖν, Lat. *operam perdere*, Theogn.; οὐκ ἄκαιρα λέγειν Aesch.; ἀκ. προθυμία Thuc.:—Adv. -ρως, Aesch., etc.; neut. pl. as Adv., Eur.   II. *of persons, importunate*, Lat. *molestus*, Theophr.

ἀκάκης, Dor. ἀκάκας, ὁ, poët. for ἄκακος, Aesch.

ἀκάκητᾰ [ἄκᾰκ], Ep. form of ἄκακος, *guileless, gracious*, epith. of Hermes, Hom., Hes.

ἀκακία, ἡ, *guilelessness*, Dem., etc.   From ἄ-κᾰκος, ον, *unknowing of ill, guileless*, Aesch., Plat.   2. *innocent, simple*, Dem. :—Adv. -κως, Id.

ἀκάλανθίς, ίδος, ἡ, = ἀκανθίς, Ar.

ἀκάλαρ-ρείτης, ου, ὁ, (ἀκαλός, ῥέω) *soft-flowing*, of Ocean, Hom.

ἀκαλήφη, ἡ, *a nettle*, Lat. *urtīca*, Ar. (Deriv. unknown.)

ἀ-καλλής, ές, (κάλλος) *without charms*, Luc.

ἀ-καλλιέρητος, ον, *ill-omened*, ἱερά Aeschin.

ἀ-καλλώπιστος, ον, *unadorned*, Luc.

ἀ-κάλυπτος, ον, *uncovered, unveiled*, Soph.

ἀ-κᾰλῠφής, ές, = ἀκάλυπτος, Soph.

ἀκάμαντο-λόγχης, ου, ὁ, (λόγχη) *unwearied at the spear*, Pind.

ἀκάμαντο-μάχης, ου, ὁ, (μάχη) *unwearied in fight*, Pind.

ἀκάμαντό-πους, ὁ, ἡ, *untiring of foot, unwearied*, Pind.

ἀ-κάμας [ἄκᾰ], αντος, ὁ, (κάμνω) *untiring, unresting*, Il., etc.

ἀ-κάμᾰτος [κᾰ], ον and η, ον, *without sense of toil : hence — untiring, unresting*, Hom., χ. γῆ *earth that never rests from tillage*, Soph. :—neut. ἀκάματα, as Adv., Id.   [ἀκάμᾰτος, Soph.; but first syll. long in dactylics.]

ἄ-καμπτος, ον, (κάμπτω) *unbent, that will not bend, rigid*, Plat. :—metaph. *unbending, unflinching, inexorable*, Pind.; ψυχὰν ἄκαμπτος Id.; ἀκάμπτῳ μένει Aesch.; ἄκαμπτον Plut.

ἄκανθα [ἄκ], ης, ἡ, (ἀκή I) *a thorn, prickle*, Theocr., etc.   2. *a prickly plant, thistle ; in pl. thistle-down*, Od. :—also *a kind of acacia*, Hdt.   3. *the backbone or spine of animals*, Id., etc.   4. metaph., ἄκανθαι, *thorny questions*, Luc.

ἀκάνθινος, η, ον, (ἄκανθα) *of thorns*, N. T.   II. *of acacia wood*, Hdt.

ἀκανθίς, ίδος, ἡ, a bird, *the goldfinch*, or *the linnet*, Arist., Theocr.   II. as fem. Adj. *prickly*, Anth.

ἀκανθο-βάτης [ἄ], ου, ὁ, (βαίνω) *walking among thorns*, nickname of grammarians, Anth. :—fem. ἀκανθοβάτις, ιδος, Id.

ἀκανθο-λόγος, ου, ὁ, (λέγω) *gathering thorns*, nickname of quibblers, Anth.

ἄκανθος, ὁ, (ἀκή I) Lat. *acanthus, brank-ursine*, a plant imitated in Corinthian capitals, Theocr.

ἀκανθ-ώδης, ες, (εἶδος) *full of thorns, thorny,* Hdt.   2. metaph., λόγοι ἀκ. *thorny arguments,* Luc.

ἄ-καπνος, ον, *without smoke,* θυσία ἄκαπνος an offering but *no burnt offering,* Luc.; a poem is called Καλλιόπης ἄκαπνον θύος Anth.

ἀ-κάρδιος, ον, (καρδία) *wanting the heart,* Plut.

ἀ-κάρηνος, ον, (κάρηνον) *headless,* Anth.

ἀ-κᾰρής, ές, (κείρω) of hair, *too short to be cut, very short:* mostly in neut. ἀκαρές,   1. of Time, *a moment,* ἐν ἀκαρεῖ χρόνου Ar.; ἀκαρῆ διαλιπὼν (sc. χρόνον) having waited *a moment,* Id.; ἀκαρὲς ὥρας *a moment,* Plut.   2. the acc. ἀκαρῆ is used adverbially without reference to Time, οὐκ ἀκαρῆ or οὐδ' ἀκαρῆ *not a bit,* Ar.

ἀκαριαῖος, α, ον, (ἀκαρής) *momentary, brief,* Dem., etc.

ἀκαρπία, ἡ, (ἄκαρπος) *unfruitfulness, barrenness,* Aesch.

ἀ-κάρπιστος, ον, (καρπίζω) *where nothing is to be reaped, unfruitful,* of the sea, like ἀτρύγετος, Eur.

ἄ-καρπος, ον, *without fruit, barren,* Eur.   2. metaph. *fruitless, unprofitable,* Id. :—Adv. -πως, Soph.   II. act. *making barren, blasting,* Aesch.

ἀ-κάρπωτος, ον, (καρπόω) *not made fruitful, without fruit:* of an oracle, *fruitless, unfulfilled,* Aesch.; νίκας ἀκάρπωτον χάριν because of victory *which yielded no fruit,* Soph.

ἀκασκαῖος, α, ον, (*ἀκή ΙΙ) *gentle,* Aesch.

ἀ-κατάβλητος, ον, (καταβάλλω) *not to be overthrown, irrefragable,* Ar.

ἀ-κατάγνωστος, ον, (καταγιγνώσκω) *not to be condemned,* N. T.

ἀ-κατακάλυπτος, ον, (κατακαλύπτω) *uncovered,* N. T.

ἀ-κατάκρῐτος, ον, (κατακρίνω) *uncondemned,* N. T.

ἀ-κατάλλακτος, ον, (καταλλάσσω) *irreconcileable* :— Adv. -τως, ἀκ. πολεμεῖν Dem.

ἀ-κατάλῠτος, ον, (καταλύω) *indissoluble,* N. T.

ἀ-κατάπαυστος, ον, (καταπαύομαι) *that cannot cease from,* τινός N. T.

ἀ-κατάστᾰτος, ον, (καθίστημι) *unstable, unsettled,* Dem.

ἀ-κατάσχετος, ον, (κατέχω) *not to be checked* :—Adv. -τως, Plut.

ἀ-καταφρόνητος, ον, (καταφρονέω) *not to be despised, important,* Lat. *haud spernendus,* Xen., Plut., etc.

ἀ-κατάψευστος, ον, (καταψεύδομαι) *not fabulous,* Hdt.

ἀκάτιον [ᾰκ], τό, Dim. of ἄκατος, *a light boat,* Thuc., etc.   II. *a small sail,* perh. *a top-sail,* Xen., Luc.

ἄκᾰτος [ᾰκ], ἡ, rarely ὁ, *a light vessel,* Lat. *actuaria,* Hdt., etc.; cf. ἀκάτιον.   2. generally, *a ship,* Eur.

ἄ-καυστος, ον, (καίω) *unburnt,* Xen.

ἀκαχήᾰτο or -είᾰτο, Ep. for -ηντο, 3 pl. plqpf. pass. of ἀχέω.

ἀκάχημαι, pf. pass. of ἀχέω.

ἀκαχήσω, Ep. fut. of ἀχέω :—ἀκάχησα, Ep. aor. 1.

ἀκᾰχίζω [ᾰκ], (ἀχέω) only in pres. *to trouble, grieve,* τινά Od. :—Pass., μὴ λίην ἀκαχίζεο θυμῷ *be not troubled in mind,* Il.; μήτι θανὼν ἀκαχίζευ *be not grieved at death,* Od.

ἀκαχμένος, η, ον, a part. (as if from a Verb *ἄκω, v. ἀκή I), *sharpened,* of axes and swords, Hom.

ἀκάχοιτο, 3 sing. Ep. aor. 2 med. opt. of ἀχέω.

ἀκάχυντο, 3 pl. Ep. aor. 2 med. of ἀχέω.

ἀκειόμενος, Ep. part. of ἀκέομαι.

ἀ-κειρε-κόμης, Dor. -ας, ὁ, = ἀκερσεκόμης, Pind., Anth.

ἀ-κέλευστος, ον, *unbidden,* Trag., Plat.

ἀ-κέντητος, ον, (κεντέω) *needing no goad* or *spur,* Pind.

ἄ-κεντρος, ον, (κέντρον) *without sting, stingless,* Plat.

ἀκέομαι [ᾰ], Ion. imper. ἄκεο (for ἀκέεο), Ep. part. ἀκειόμενος : f. ἀκέσομαι, Ep. ἀκέσσομαι, Att. ἀκοῦμαι : aor. 1 ἠκεσάμην, Ep. imper. ἀκέσσαι: ἄκος): Dep.:   I. trans. *to heal, cure,* ἕλκος ἀκέσσαι *heal the sore,* Il.; or of part healed, βλέφαρον ἀκέσαιο Eur.; also *to heal a person,* Il.   2. *to stanch, quench,* δίψαν Ib.   3. generally, *to mend, repair,* νῆας Od.; applied to a tailor or cobbler, like Lat. *resarcire,* Luc.   4. metaph. *to repair, make amends for,* ἁμαρτάδα Hdt.; κακόν Soph. :—absol. *to make amends,* ἀλλ' ἀκεώμεθα, ἀλλ' ἀκέσασθε Hom.

ἀ-κέραιος, ον, = the poët. ἀκήρατος, *unmixed, pure in blood,* Eur.   II. *entire, unharmed, unravaged,* of cities or countries, Hdt., Thuc.; ἀκ. δύναμις an army *in full force,* Id.; ἀκ. λέχος *inviolate,* Eur.; of persons, *uncontaminated, guileless,* Id. : c. gen., ἀκέραιος κακῶν ἠθῶν *uncontaminated* by bad habits, Plat.

ἀ-κεραύνωτος, ον, (κεραυνόω) *not lightning-struck,* Luc.

ἀκέρδεια, ἡ, *want of gain, loss,* Pind. From

ἀ-κερδής, ές, (κέρδος) *without gain, bringing loss,* Soph., Plat.   II. *not greedy of gain,* Plut.

ἀκέρκιστος, ον, (κερκίζω) *unwoven,* Anth.

ἄ-κερκος, ον, *without a tail,* Arist.

ἀ-κερματία, ἡ, (κέρμα) *want of money,* Ar.

ἀ-κερσε-κόμης, ου, ὁ, (κείρω, κόμη) *with unshorn hair* (the Greek youths wore their hair long till they reached manhood), epith. of Phoebus, Il., etc.; cf. ἀκειρεκόμης.

ἀκέρωτος, ον, (κέρας) *not horned,* Anth.

ἄκεσις, εως, ἡ, (ἀκέομαι) *a healing, cure,* Hdt.

ἄκεσμα, τό, (ἀκέομαι) *a remedy, cure,* Pind., Aesch.

ἀκεστήρ, ῆρος, ὁ, (ἀκέομαι) *a healer :* metaph. as Adj., ἀκ. χαλινός the rein *that tames the steed,* Soph.

ἀκεστής, οῦ, ὁ, = ἀκεστήρ ; ἀκεσταὶ ἱματίων ῥαγέντων *menders of torn clothes,* Xen.

ἀκεστορία, ἡ, (ἀκέομαι) *the healing art,* Anth.

ἀκεστός, ή, όν, verb. Adj. of ἀκέομαι, *curable* :—metaph. *easily revived,* Il.

ἀκέστρα, ἡ, (ἀκέομαι) *a darning-needle,* Luc.

ἀκέστρια, ἡ, (ἀκέομαι) *a sempstress,* Luc.

ἀκέστωρ, ορος, ὁ, (ἀκέομαι) *a healer, saviour,* Eur.

ἀκεσ-φόρος, ον, (ἄκος, φέρω) *bringing a cure, healing,* Eur.

ἀκεσ-ώδῠνος, ον, (ἀκέομαι, ὀδύνη) *allaying pain,* Anth.

ἀ-κέφᾰλος, ον, (κεφαλή) *without head,* Hdt.   2. *without beginning,* λόγος Plat.

ἀκέων, ουσα, (v. ἀκή ΙΙ) a participial form, used as Adv. like ἀκήν, *softly, silently,* Hom.; also dual ἀκέοντε Od. —Though ἀκέουσα occurs in Hom., yet ἀκέων stands with fem., Ἀθηναίη ἀκέων ἦν Il.; and though he has dual ἀκέοντε, yet ἀκέων occurs with plur. Verbs.

ΆΚΗ, ἡ, a Subst. cited in two senses,   I. *a point,* (whence ἀκίς, ἄκων, ἀκονή, ἀκαχμένος, ἀκωκή, αἰχμή; cf. Lat. *acus, acuo, acies*).   II. *silence, calm,* (whence ἀκήν, ἀκέων, ἀκασκαῖος, ἦκα) : *a lulling, healing* (whence ἀκέομαι.

ἀ-κήδεστος, ον, (κηδέω) *uncared for, unburied,* Il. : Adv. -τως, *without due rites of burial,* or (perh.) *without care for others, recklessly, remorselessly,* Ib.

ἀ-κήδευτος, ον, (κηδεύω) *unburied,* Plut.

ἀκηδέω, f. ήσω: Ep. aor. I ἀκήδεσα: (ἀκηδής):—to take no care for, no heed of, c. gen., Il., Aesch.

ἀ-κηδής, ές, (κῆδος): I. pass. uncared for, unburied, Hom. II. act. without care or sorrow, careless, heedless, Il.

ἀκήκοα, pf. of ἀκούω.

ἀ-κήλητος, ον, (κηλέω) to be won by no charms, proof against enchantment, inexorable, Od., Soph.

ἄκημα, τό, = ἄκεσμα, a cure, relief, ὀδυνάων for pains, Il.

ἀκήν, (ἀκή II) Adv. softly, silently, Il.

ἀ-κηράσιος, ον, Ep. form of ἀκήρατος, unmixed, οἶνος Od. II. untouched, Lat. integer, ἀκ. λειμῶνες meadows not yet grazed or mown, h. Hom.; ἄνθος ἀκ. fresh, Anth.

ἀ-κήρᾱτος, ον, (κεράννυμι) unmixed, uncontaminated, undefiled, ὕδωρ Il.; ποτόν Aesch.; ὄμβρος Soph.; ἀκ. χρυσός pure gold, Hdt. II. metaph., 1. of things, untouched, unhurt, undamaged, Lat. integer, Hom.; ἀκ. κόμη unshorn hair, Eur.; ἀκ. λειμών an unmown meadow, Id., etc. 2. of persons, undefiled, Id.; c. dat., ἀκήρατος ἄλγεσι untouched by woes, Id.; c. gen., ἀκ. κακῶν without taint of ill, Id.

ἀ-κήριος (A), ον, unharmed by the Κῆρες, unharmed, Od. II. act. unharming, harmless, h. Hom., Hes.

ἀ-κήριος (B), ον, (κῆρ) without heart, i.e., I. lifeless, Il. II. heartless, spiritless, Ib.

ἀκηρότατος, a poët. Sup. of ἀκήρατος, Anth.

ἀ-κηρυκτεί and -τί, Adv. without needing a flag of truce, Thuc. From

ἀ-κήρυκτος, ον, (κηρύσσω) unannounced, unproclaimed, ἀκ. πόλεμος a sudden war, Hdt.; but also a war in which no herald was admitted, implacable, Xen., Dem.:—Adv. -τως, without needing a flag of truce, Thuc. II. not proclaimed by heralds, inglorious, Eur. III. with no tidings, not heard of, Soph.

ἀ-κήρωτος, ον, (κηρόω) unwaxed, Luc.

ἀκηχέδαται or -έαται, Ep. for ἠκάχηνται, 3 pl. pf. pass. of ἀχέω:—ἀκηχεμένος, for ἀκαχήμενος, Ep. part.

ἀ-κίβδηλος, ον, unadulterated, genuine, Plat., Luc. 2. metaph. of men, guileless, honest, Hdt.

ἀκιδνός [ἄ], ή, όν, weak, feeble, faint, Hom. always in the Comp., ἀκιδνότερος Od. (Deriv. unknown.)

ἄ-κικυς, υος, ὁ, ἡ, powerless, feeble, Od.

ἀκινάκης [ἄ], ὁ, Persian word, a short straight sword, Hdt., who declines it -εος, -εῖ, -εα; but Xen. has ἀκινάκην, ἀκινάκας as acc. sing. and pl.

ἀ-κίνδυνος, ον, without danger, free from danger, Eur., Thuc., etc. II. Adv. -νως, Eur., etc.: Comp., ἀκινδυνότερον with less danger, Plat.; Sup., ἀκινδυνότατα most free from danger, Xen.

ἀ-κίνητος, ον and η, ον, (κινέω) unmoved, motionless, of Delos, Orac.: ar. Hdt.; ἐξ ἀκινήτου ποδός without stirring a step, Soph. 2. idle, sluggish, Ar. 3. unmoved, unaltered, of laws, Thuc., etc. II. immovable, hard to move, Plat., Luc.; ἀκινήτως ἔχειν to be immovable, Plat., etc. 2. not to be stirred or touched, inviolate, Lat. non movendus, τάφος Hdt.: proverb. of sacred things, κινεῖν τὰ ἀκίνητα Id.; also τἀκίνητα φράσαι Soph. 3. of persons, not to be shaken, steadfast, stubborn, Id.

ἄ-κιος, ον, (κίς) not worm-eaten: Sup. ἀκιώτατος Hes.

ἀκῑρός, όν, prob. = ἀκιδνός, Theocr.

ἀκίς, ίδος, ἡ, (ἀκή I) a point, the barb of an arrow or hook, Plut., Anth.:—an arrow, dart, Ar. 2. metaph., πόθων ἀκίδες the stings of desire, Anth.

ἀ-κίχητος [ῑ], ον, (κιχάνω) not to be reached, unattainable, Il. II. of persons, not to be reached by prayer, inexorable, Aesch.

ἀκκίζομαι, Dep. (ἀκκώ) to affect indifference or coyness, dissemble, Plat.

ἀκκώ, ἡ, a bugbear or a silly woman. (Deriv. unknown.)

ἀκλάρωτος, Dor. for ἀκλήρωτος.

ἄ-κλαστος, ον, (κλάω) unbroken, Anth.

ἄ-κλαυτος or ἄ-κλαυστος, ον, unlamented, Hom.: (κλαίω): I. pass. unwept, φίλων by friends, Soph.; ἄκλαυτα τέκνα, i.e. children not liable to death, Eur. II. act. not weeping, tearless, Od. 2. Soph. = χαίρων, with impunity.

ἀ-κλεής, ές: gen. έος: acc. ἀκλεᾶ, Ion. ἀκλεῆ, Ep. ἀκλεέα:—Ep. ἀκλειής or ἀκληής, pl. ἀκλειεῖς or ἀκληεῖς (κλέος):—without fame, inglorious, unsung, Hom., etc. Adv. ἀκλεῶς, Hdt., Ep. ἀκλειῶς, Il., etc.: also neut. ἀκλεές as Adv., Ib.

ἀκλεία, Ion. -ίη, ἡ, (ἀκλεής) ingloriousness, Anth.

ἀ-κλειής, ές, Ep. for ἀκλεής.

ἄ-κλειστος, ον, Ion. ἄκλήϊστος, Att. ἄκληστος: (κλείω):—not closed or fastened, Eur., Thuc.

ἀκλεῶς, Adv. of ἀκλεής, q. v.

ἀκληής, Ep. for ἀκλεής.

ἄ-κληρος, ον, without lot or portion, poor, needy, Od., Xen., etc.: c. gen. without lot or share in a thing, Aesch., etc. II. unallotted, without an owner, Eur.

ἀ-κλήρωτος, ον, (κληρόω) without lot or portion in a thing, c. gen., Pind.

ἄκληστος, Att. for ἄκλειστος.

ἄ-κλητος, ον, uncalled, unbidden, Aesch., etc.

ἀ-κλῑνής, ές, (κλίνω) bending to neither side, unswerving, Plat.: steadfast, regular, Anth., etc.:—Adv. -νῶς, Ion. -νέως, Id.

ἄ-κλυστος, ον, (κλύζω) unwashed by waves, Plut., etc.; as fem., Αὐλὶν ἀκλύσταν Eur.

ἀκμάζω, f. άσω, (ἀκμή) to be in full bloom, be at one's prime or perfection, I. of persons, cities and states, Hdt., etc. 2. c. dat. to flourish or abound in a thing, πλούτῳ Id.; παρασκευῇ Thuc. 3. c. inf. to be strong enough to do, Xen. II. of things, ἀκμάζει ὁ πόλεμος, ἡ νόσος the war, the plague is at its height, Thuc.; ἀκμάζον θέρος mid-summer, Id.; of corn, to be just ripe, Id. 2. impers. ἀκμάζει, c. inf., it is high time to do, Aesch.

ἀκμαῖος, α, ον, (ἀκμή) in full bloom, at the prime, blooming, vigorous, Aesch.; ἀκμαῖος φύσιν in the prime of strength, Id. II. in time, in season, Lat. opportunus, Soph.

ἀκμή, ἡ, (ἀκή I) a point, edge: proverb., ἐπὶ ξυροῦ ἀκμῆς on the rasor's edge (v. ξυρόν); ἀμφιδέξιοι ἀκμαί the fingers of both hands, Soph.; ποδοῖν ἀκμαί the toes, Id. II. the highest point of anything, the bloom, flower, prime, of man's age, Lat. flos aetatis, ἀκμὴ ἥβης Id.; ἀκμὴ βίου Xen.; ἐν ἀκμῇ εἶναι = ἀκμάζειν, Plat.; ἀκμὴν ἔχειν, of corn, to be ripe, Soph.: also of time, ἀ. ἦρος the spring-prime, Pind.; ἀ. θέρους mid-summer, Xen.; ἀ. τῆς δόξης Thuc.; periphr. like βία, ἀκμὴ Θησειδᾶν Soph. III. like καιρός, the best,

most fitting time, Trag.; ἔργων, λόγων ἀκμή *the time* for doing, speaking, Soph.; ἀκμή ἐστι, c. inf., 'tis *high time* to do, Aesch.; ἐπ' ἀκμῆς εἶναι, c. inf., *to be on the point* of doing, Eur.; ἐπ' αὐτὴν ἥκει τὴν ἀκμήν 'tis *come* to *the critical time*, Dem.

ἀκμήν, acc. of ἀκμή, used as Adv., *just*, Xen. II. *yet, still*, Theocr., N. T.

ἀκμηνός, ή, όν, (ἀκμή) *full-grown*, Od.

ἄκμηνος, ον, *fasting*, Il.; c. gen., ἄκμηνος σίτοιο *fasting from* food, Ib. (Deriv. uncertain.)

ἀ-κμής, ῆτος, ὁ, ἡ, (κάμνω) = ἀκάμας, *untiring, unwearied*, Il., Soph.

ἄ-κμητος, ον, (κάμνω) = ἀκμής, h. Hom.

ἀκμό-θετον, τό, (ἄκμων, τί-θημι) *the anvil-block, stithy*, Hom.

ἀκμόνιον, τό, Dim. of sq., Aesop.

ἄκμων, ονος, ὁ, orig. prob. *a thunderbolt*, ἄκμων οὐρανόθεν κατιών Hes. II. *an anvil*, Hom., etc.: metaph., λόγχης ἄκμονες *very anvils* to bear blows, Aesch.

ἄκναμπτος, ἄκναπτος, ἄκναφος, = ἄγναμπτος, etc.

ἄκνηστις, ιος, ἡ, *the spine* or *backbone*, Od.

ἄ-κνῑσος, ον, (κνῖσα) *without the fat of sacrifices*, Anth.

ἀκοή, ἡ, Ep. ἀκουή, (ἀκούω) *a hearing, the sound heard*, Il. 2. *the thing heard, hearsay, report, news, tidings*, μετὰ πατρὸς ἀκουήν *in quest of tidings* of his father, Od.; ἀκοῇ ἱστορεῖν, παραλαβεῖν τι *to know by hearsay*, Hdt.; so, ἐξ ἀκοῆς λέγειν Plat. II. *the sense of hearing*, Hdt., etc. 2. *the act of hearing, hearing*, ἀκοῇ κλύειν, ἀκοαῖς δέχεσθαι, εἰς ἀκοὰς ἔρχεταί τι Soph., Eur.; δι' ἀκοῆς αἰσθάνεσθαι Plat. III. *the ear*, Sappho, Aesch.

ἀ-κοίμητος, ον, (κοιμάω) *sleepless*, of the sea, Aesch.

ἀ-κοινώνητος, ον, (κοινωνέω) *not shared with* another, c. dat., Eur. II. act. *having no share of* or *in*, c. gen., Plat.: absol. *unsocial, inhuman*, Id.

ἀ-κοίτης, ου, ὁ, (ἀ copul., κοίτη, cf. ἄλοχος) *a bedfellow, spouse, husband;* and fem. ἄκοιτις, ιος, ἡ, *a spouse, wife*, Hom., etc.

ἀκολασία, ἡ, (ἀκόλαστος) *licentiousness, intemperance*, Thuc., etc.

ἀκολασταίνω, f. ανῶ, (ἀκόλαστος) *to be licentious, intemperate*, Ar., Plat., etc.

ἀκολάστημα, ατος, τό, *an act of* ἀκολασία, Plut.

ἀ-κόλαστος, ον, (κολάζω) Lat. *non castigatus, unchastised, undisciplined, unbridled*, Hdt., Att., etc. 2. *licentious, intemperate*, opp. to σώφρων, Soph., etc.:— so in Adv., ἀκολάστως ἔχειν Plat.; Comp., ἀκολαστοτέρως ἔχειν πρός τι *to be too intemperate* in a thing, Xen.

ἄκολος, ον, ἡ, *a bit, morsel*, Od. (Deriv. uncertain.)

ἀκολουθέω, f. ήσω, (ἀκόλουθος) *to follow* one, *go after* or *with* him, c. dat. pers., Ar., etc.; also, ἀκ. μετά τινος Plat.; σύν τινι Xen.; κατόπιν τινός Ar.:—absol., Plat., etc. II. metaph. *to follow, obey*, τινι Thuc., etc.; ἀκ. τοῖς πράγμασιν *to follow* circumstances, Dem. 2. *to follow the thread* of a discourse, Plat. 3. of things, *to follow upon, be consequent upon*, τοῖς εἰρημένοις Id.

ἀκολουθητέον, verb. Adj. of ἀκολουθέω, *one must follow*, Xen., etc.

ἀκολουθία, ἡ, (ἀκολουθέω) *a following, train*, Soph., Plat. II. *a following upon, conformity with*, τοῖς πράγμασι Id.

ἀ-κόλουθος, ον, (ἀ copul., κέλευθος) *following, attending on;* as Subst. *a follower, attendant*, Lat. *pedisequus*, Ar., Thuc., etc.; οἱ ἀκόλουθοι *the camp-followers*, Xen. 2. *following after*, c. gen., Νηρήδων ἀκ. Soph. 3. *following* or *consequent upon, in conformity with*, c. gen., Ar.; also c. dat., Plat.:—absol. *agreeing with one another*, Xen., etc.:—Adv. -θως, *in accordance with*, τοῖς νόμοις Dem.

ἀ-κόλυμβος, ον, *unable to swim*, Batr., Plut.

ἀκομιστία, Ep. -ίη [ῐ], ἡ, *want of tending* or *care*, Od. From

ἀ-κόμιστος, ον, (κομίζω) *untended*.

ἄ-κομος, ον, (κόμη) *without hair, bald*, Luc.

ἀ-κόμπαστος, ον, (κομπάζω) *not boastful*, Aesch.

ἄ-κομπος, ον, *not boasting*, Aesch.

ἄ-κομψος, ον, *unadorned, boorish*, ἐγὼ δ' ἄκομψος 'rude I am *in speech*,' Eur.

ἀκονάω, f. ήσω, (ἀκόνη) *to sharpen, whet*, μαχαίρας Ar.; λόγχην Xen.:—Med., ἀκονᾶσθαι μαχαίρας *to sharpen their swords*, Id.

ἀ-κόνδυλος, ον, (κονδύλη) *without knuckles:—without blows*, Luc.

ἀκόνη [ᾰ], ἡ, (ἀκή 1) *a whetstone, hone*, Pind., etc.

ἀκονῑτί [ῑ], Adv. of ἀκόνιτος, *without the dust of the arena*, i. e. *without a struggle, without effort*, Lat. *sine pulvere*, Thuc., Xen.

ἀκονῑτικός, ή, όν, *made of aconite*, Xen. From

ἀκόνῑτον, τό, *aconite*, a poisonous plant, Theophr. (Deriv. uncertain.)

ἀ-κόνῑτος, ον, (κόνις) *without dust*.

ἀκοντί [ῑ], Adv. of ἄκων, contr. for ἀεκοντί, Plut.

ἀκοντίζω, f. Att. ιῶ, (ἄκων) *to hurl a javelin*, τινός at one, Il.; ἐπί τινι Ib.:—the weapon is put in dat., ἀκόντισε δουρί *darted with* his spear, Ib.; also in acc., ἀκόντισαν ὀξέα δοῦρα *darted* their spears, Od. 2. c. acc. pers. *to hit with a javelin*, Hdt., etc.; Pass. *to be so hit* or *wounded*, Eur., Xen. 3. *to shoot forth rays*, of the moon, Eur. II. intr. *to pierce*, εἴσω γῆς Id.

ἀκόντιον, τό, Dim. of ἄκων, h. Hom., Hdt., etc.

ἀκόντῑσις, εως, ἡ, (ἀκοντίζω) *javelin-throwing*, Xen.

ἀκόντισμα, ατος, τό, (ἀκοντίζω) *a javelin's throw*, Xen. II. *the thing thrown, a dart, javelin*, Plut.; in pl. = ἀκοντισταί, Id.

ἀκοντισμός, ὁ, = ἀκόντισις, Xen.

ἀκοντιστήρ, ῆρος, ὁ, = sq., Eur.

ἀκοντιστής, οῦ, ὁ, (ἀκοντίζω) *a darter, javelin-man*, Hom., Hdt., etc.

ἀκοντιστικός, ή, όν, (ἀκοντίζω) *skilled in throwing the javelin*, Xen.

ἀκοντιστύς, ύος, ἡ, Ion. for ἀκόντισις, *the game of throwing the javelin*, Il.

ἄ-κοπος, ον, *without weariness*, and so, I. pass. *untired*, Plat. II. act. *not wearying*, of a horse, *easy*, Xen. 2. *removing weariness, refreshing*, Plat.

ἀ-κόρεστος, ον, (κορέννυμι) Att. for ἀκόρητος, *insatiate*, Trag.; c. gen. *insatiate in* a thing, Aesch.:—in Soph. (πάντων ἀκόρεστος, *most insatiate, most shameless*), the word is either sync. for ἀκορεστότατος, or Sup. of ἀκορής = ἀκόρεστος. 2. of things, *insatiate, unceasing*, Lat. *improbus*, Trag. II. act. *not satiating*, Aesch. 2. *not liable to surfeit*, φιλία Xen.

ἀκόρετος, ον, (poët.) for ἀκόρεστος, Aesch., Soph.
ἀ-κόρητος, ον, (κορέννυμι) insatiate, unsated in or with a thing, c. gen., Il.   II. (κορέω) unswept, un-:rimmed, ungarnished, Ar.
ἄ-κορος, ον, =ἀκόρεστος: untiring, ceaseless, Lat. improbus, εἱρεσία Pind.
ΑΚΟΣ, εος, τό, a cure, relief, remedy for a thing, c. gen., Od., etc. :—absol., ἄκος εὑρεῖν Il., Soph.; ἐξευρεῖν, λαβεῖν, ποιεῖσθαι, Hdt., etc.:—by a medical metaph., ἄκος ἐντέμνειν, τέμνειν, cf. ἐντέμνω II.   2. a means of obtaining a thing, c. gen., Eur.
ἀκοσμέω, f. ήσω, (ἄκοσμος) to be disorderly, to offend, Soph., Dem., etc.
ἀ-κόσμητος, ον, (κοσμέω) unarranged, unorganised, Plat.:—Adv. -τως, Id.   2. unfurnished with, c. dat., Xen.
ἀκοσμία, ἡ, disorder, Plat.: extravagance, Eur.:—in moral sense, disorderliness, disorderly conduct, Soph. From
ἄ-κοσμος, ον, without order, disorderly, Aesch.:—in Hom. of Thersites' words, disorderly : — Adv. -μως, Hdt., etc.   II. κόσμος ἄκοσμος, a world that is no world, Anth.; also of an inappropriate ornament, Id.
ἀκοστάω or -έω, (ἀκοστή) only in aor. 1 part., ἵππος ἀκοστήσας ἐπὶ φάτνῃ a horse corn-fed at manger, a stalled horse, Il.
ἀκοστή, ἡ, barley. (Deriv. unknown.)
ἀκουάζομαι [ἄκ], Dep., only in pres., ἀκούω, to hearken or listen to, c. gen., Od.; δαιτὸς ἀκουάζεσθον ye are bidden to the feast, Il.
ἀκουή, ἡ, Ep. for ἀκοή.
ἄκουκα, Lacon. pf. of ἀκούω.
ἄ-κουρος, ον, (κοῦρος Ion. for κόρος) without male heir, Od.   II. (κουρά) unshaven, unshorn, Ar.
ἄκουσα, Ep. for ἤκουσα, aor. 1 of ἀκούω.
ἀκουσί-θεος [ἄ], ον, heard of God, Anth.
ἀκούσιος, ον, Att. contr. for ἀεκούσιος.
ἄκουσμα, ατος, τό, (ἀκούω) a thing heard, such as music, Xen.   2. a rumour, tale, Soph.
ἀκούσομαι, f. of ἀκούω.
ἀκουστέον, verb. Adj. of ἀκούω, one must hear or hearken to, c. gen. pers., Hdt., etc.; c. acc. rei, Plat.   2. ἀκουστέος, a, ον, to be hearkened to, Plat.
ἀκουστός, ή, όν, verb. Adj. of ἀκούω, heard, audible, h. Hom., Plat., etc.   II. that should be heard, Soph., Eur.
ἀκούω (Root ΑΚΟϜ) [ἄ]: Ep. impf. ἄκουον: f. ἀκούσομαι (act. form ἀκούσω only in late authors): aor. 1 ἤκουσα, Ep. ἄκουσα: pf. ἀκήκοα, Lacon. ἄκουκα: plqpf. ἠκηκόειν; old Att. ἠκηκόη, Ion. ἀκηκόειν:—Med., fut. impf. ἀκούετο: aor. 1 ἠκουόμην:—Pass., fut. ἀκουσθήσομαι: aor. 1 ἠκούσθην: pf. ἤκουσμαι.   To hear, Hom., etc. —Construct., properly, c. acc. of thing heard, gen. of pers. from whom it is heard, ταῦτα Καλυψοῦς ἤκουσα Od.; the gen. pers. may be omitted, ἀκήκοας λόγον Soph., or the acc. rei, ἄκουε τοῦ θανόντος Id.:—often however c. gen. rei, to have hearing of a thing.   2. c. gen. objecti, to hear of, hear tell of, ἀκ. πατρός Od. ; so c. acc., Ib.—so, ἀκ. περί τινος.   3. the pers. from whom the thing is heard takes a Prep., ἀκούειν τι ἀπό, ἔκ, παρά, πρός τινος, Il., Att.   II. to know by hearsay, εἴ που ἀκούεις Od.; so Plat., etc.   III. absol.

to hearken, give ear, to begin a proclamation, ἀκούετε λεῴ hear, O people.   IV. to listen to, give ear to, Il.   2. to obey, c. gen., or more rarely c. dat., Ib.   3. to hear and understand, κλύοντες οὐκ ἤκουον Aesch.   V. in pass. sense, with an Adv., to hear oneself called, be called so and so, like Lat. audire, κακῶς ἀκ. πρός τινος to be ill spoken of by one, Hdt.; εὖ, κακῶς, ἄριστα ἀκ., Lat. bene, male audire, Id., Att.   2. with a Noun, ἀκούειν κακός, καλός Soph., Plat.; κόλακες ἀκούουσι Dem.   3. c. acc. rei, ἀκ. κακά to have evil spoken of one, Ar.; φήμας κακὰς ἤκουσεν Eur.
ἄκρα, Ion. ἄκρη, ἡ, (ἄκρος) :   1. a headland, foreland, cape, Hom., etc.   2. a mountain-top, summit: used by Hom. only in the phrase κατ' ἄκρης from top to bottom, i. e. utterly, πόλιν αἱρέειν κατ' ἄκρης Hdt.; so in Att., κατ' ἄκρας utterly, Trag., Plat.   3. the citadel of a city, Lat. arx, Xen.
ἀ-κράαντος [κρᾱ], ον, Ep. form of ἄκραντος, unfulfilled, fruitless, Lat. irritus, Hom.
ἀ-κραγής, ές, ˏκράζω\ not barking, Aesch.
ἀκρ-αής, ές, (ἄκρος, ἄημι) blowing strongly, fresh-blowing, of the north and west wind, Od.; si ἀκραὲς erit, if it shall be clear weather, Cic.
ἀκραῖος, α, ον, (ἄκρα) dwelling on the heights, Eur.
ἀκραιφνής, ές, syncop. form of ἀκεραιο-φανής (ἀκέραιος, φαίνομαι˂, unmixed, pure, Eur., Ar.: metaph., πενία ἀκρ. utter poverty, Anth.   II. unharmed, entire, Lat. integer, Eur., Thuc.   2. c. gen. untouched by a thing, Soph.
ἄ-κραντος, ον, (κραίνω) like Ep. ἀκράαντος, unfulfilled, fruitless, Pind., Aesch.:—neut. pl. as Adv., in vain, Id., Eur.
ἀκρασία, ἡ, (ἄκρατος) bad mixture, ill temperature, Theophr.
ἀκράτεια, ἡ, (ἀκρᾱτής) incontinence, want of self-control, Plat. :—the later form is ἀκρασία.
ἀ-κρᾱτής, ές, (ἀ priv., κράτος) powerless, impotent, Soph.   II. c. gen. rei, not having power or command over a thing, Lat. impotens, γλώσσης Aesch.; ὀργῆς Thuc. :—also, intemperate in the use of a thing, οἴνου Xen., Arist.; περὶ τὰ πόματα Id.   2. absol. without command over oneself, incontinent, Lat. impotens sui, Id.   3. of things, immoderate, δαπάνη Anth.
ἀκρατίζομαι, f. ἰοῦμαι: Dep. ˏἄκρατος˹ :—to drink wine unmixed with water: hence, to breakfast, because this meal consisted of bread dipped in wine, Ar. Hence
ἀκράτισμα [κρᾱ], ατος, τό, a breakfast, Arist.
ἀκράτιστος [κρᾱ], ον, (ἀκρατίζομαι) having breakfasted, Theocr.
ἀκρατοποσία, Ion. ἀκρητοποσίη, ἡ, a drinking of sheer wine, Hdt. From
ἀκρᾱτο-πότης, ου, Ion. ἀκρητοπότης, εω, ὁ, (ἄκρατος, πίνω) a drinker of sheer wine, Hdt.
ἄ-κρᾱτος, Ion. ἄ-κρητος, ον: ˏκεράννυμι˹ :   1. of liquids, unmixed, sheer, of wine, Od. :—esp., οἶνος ἄκρητος wine without water, Lat. merum, Hdt.; and ἄκρατος without οἶνος˼, Ar., etc.   2. metaph., sheer, μέλαν pure black, Theophr.; ἄκρατος νύξ sheer night, Aesch.; ἀκρ. νοῦς pure intellect, Xen.   3. of conditions or states, pure, untempered, absolute, ἐλευθερία, ἡδονή Plat.; ἀκρ. ψεῦδος a sheer lie, Id. :—Adv. -τως

absolutely, Luc.　4. of persons, *intemperate, excessive, violent*, ἄκρατος ὀργήν Aesch. : so of things we feel, ἄκρ. ὀργή, ἄκρ. καῦμα, etc.　II. Comp. ἀκρατέστερος, Sup. -έστατος ˌas if from ἀκρατής᾽.

ἀκράτωρ ˌᾰ ˌ, *opos*, ὁ, = ἀκρατής I, Soph.　II. = ἀκρατής II, Plat.

ἀκράτως [ᾰ], Adv. of ἄκρατος.　II. ἀκρᾱτῶς Adv. of ἀκρᾱτής.

ἀκρά-χολος [ᾱ], ον, (ἄκρος, χόλος) *quick to anger, passionate*, Ar.　II. *in passionate distress*, Theocr.

ἀκρέμων, ονος, or ἀκρεμών, όνος, ὁ, (ἄκρος) *a branch, twig, spray*, Eur., Theocr.

ἀκρ-έσπερος, ον, ˌἄκρος II, ἑσπέρα᾽ *at eventide*, Anth.: neut. ἀκρέσπερον as Adv., Theocr.

ἀκρ-ήβης, ον, ὁ, ˌἄκρος, ἥβη᾽ *a youth in his prime*, Anth.

ἀκρ-ηβος, ον, ˌἄκρος, ἥβη᾽ *in earliest youth*, Theocr.

ἄκρητος, ἀκρητο-ποσίη, -πότης, v. sub ἀκρατ-.

ἀκρίβειᾰ [κρῐ], ἡ, ˌἀκρῑβής᾽ *exactness, minute accuracy, precision*, Thuc., etc.; with Preps. in adv. sense, δι᾽ ἀκριβείας, = ἀκριβῶς, *with minuteness* or *precision*, Plat.; so, εἰς τὴν ἀκρ., πρὸς τὴν ἀκρ. Id. :—ἡ ἀκρ. τοῦ ναυτικοῦ its *perfect condition*, Thuc.　2. *parsimony, frugality*, Plut.

ἀκρῑβής, ές, *exact, accurate, precise, made* or *done to a nicety*, Eur., etc.　II. of persons, *exact, precise, strict, consummate*, Thuc., etc. :—esp. *painfully exact, over-nice, precise, curious*, Plat. :—τὸ ἀκριβές = ἀκρίβεια, Thuc. :—Adv. -βῶς, *to a nicety, precisely*, Hdt., etc.　2. *parsimonious, frugal*, Menand. ˌDeriv. uncertain.᾽

ἀκρῑβολογέομαι, Dep. *to be exact* or *precise* in language or thought, Plat.; c. acc. rei, *to weigh accurately*, Id. From

ἀκρῑβο-λόγος, ον, *precise in argument*.

ἀκρῑβόω, f. ώσω, ˌἀκρῑβής᾽ *to make exact* or *accurate*, Eur.; ἀκρ. τᾰδε *to be perfect in* bearing these hardships, Xen. :—Pass. *to be* or *become perfect*, Ar.　2. *to investigate accurately, to understand thoroughly*, οἱ τάδ᾽ ἠκριβωκότες Eur.; τοὔνομά μου σὺ ἀκριβοῖς; *are you sure of* my name? Plat.

ἀκρῑβῶς, Adv. of ἀκρῑβής, q. v.

ἀκρῐδο-θήκη, ἡ, ˌἀκρίς᾽ *a locust-cage*, Theocr.

ἄκρις, ιος, ἡ, ˌἄκρος᾽ *a hill-top*, Od.

ἈΚΡΙ´Σ, ῖδος, ἡ, *a locust*, Il.

ἀκρῐσία, ἡ, ˌἄκριτος᾽ *want of distinctness*, Xen.

ἀκρῐτό-δακρυς, υ, *shedding floods of tears*, Anth.

ἀκρῐτό-μῡθος, ον, *recklessly* or *confusedly babbling*, Il.　II. *hard of interpretation*, Od.

ἄ-κρῐτος, ον, *undistinguishable, unarranged, disorderly*, Hom.; τύμβος ἄκριτος one *common undistinguished* grave, Il.　2. *continual, unceasing*, ἄχεα Ib.; neut. as Adv., πενθήμεναι ἄκριτον αἰεί Od. :—ὄρος ἄκρ. *a continuous* mountain-range, Anth., Babr.　II. *undecided, doubtful*, νείκεα, ἄεθλος Il.; ἀκρίτων ὄντων *while the issue* was *doubtful*, Thuc. :—Adv. ἀκρίτως, *without decisive issue*, Id.　2. *unjudged, untried*, of persons and things, ἄκριτόν τινα κτεινειν *to put to death without trial*, Lat. *indicta causa*, Hdt., etc.　III. act. *not giving a judgment*, Id. : *without judgment, ill-judged, rash*, Eur.

ἀκρῐτό-φυλλος, ον, (φύλλον) *of undistinguishable*, i.e. *closely blending, leafage*, Il.

ἀκρῐτό-φυρτος, ον, (φύρω) *undistinguishably mixed*, Aesch.

ἀκρόᾱμα, ατος, τό, (ἀκροάομαι) *anything heard with pleasure*, as *a play* or *musical piece*, Xen.

ἀκροᾱματικός, ή, όν, (ἀκροάομαι) *designed for hearing only*, Plut.

ἀκροάομαι, f. -άσομαι [ᾱ] : aor. 1 ἠκροᾱσάμην : pf. ἠκρόᾱμαι : Dep. :—*to hearken to, listen to*, c. gen. pers., acc. rei, Thuc., etc.; c. gen. rei, Id.　2. absol. *to listen*, ὁ ἀκροώμενος *a hearer, disciple*, Plat., Xen.　II. *to attend to, obey*, τινός Thuc., etc. ˌDeriv. uncertain.᾽ Hence

ἀκρόᾱσις, εως, ἡ, *a hearing* or *listening*, Thuc., etc.　2. *obedience to* another, c. gen., Id. ; and

ἀκροᾱτέον, verb. Adj., *one must listen to*, τινός Ar.

ἀκροᾱτήριον, τό, ˌἀκροάομαι᾽ *a place of audience*, N. T.　II. *an audience*, Plut.

ἀκροᾱτής, οῦ, ὁ, ˌἀκροάομαι᾽ *a hearer*, Lat. *auditor*, Thuc., etc. : *a disciple*, Arist.　II. *a lecturer*, Plut.

ἀκροᾱτικός, ή, όν, ˌἀκροάομαι᾽ *of* or *for hearing*, μισθὸς ἀκρ. *a lecturer's fee*, Luc.

ἀκρο-βᾰφής, ές, (βαφή) *tinged at the point*, Anth.

ἀκρο-βελής, ές, (βέλος) *with a point at the end*, Anth.

ἀκροβολέω, ˌἀκροβόλος᾽ *to sling*, Anth.

ἀκροβολής, ές, = ἀκροβελής, Anth.

ἀκροβολία, ἡ, ˌἀκροβόλος᾽ *a slinging, skirmishing*, App.

ἀκροβολίζομαι : aor. 1 ἠκροβολισάμην : ˌἀκροβόλος᾽ : Dep. :—*to throw from afar, to fight with missiles, to skirmish*, πρός τινα or absol., Thuc., Xen. :—metaph., ἀκρ. ἔπεσι Hdt.—The Act. in Anth. Hence

ἀκροβόλισις, εως, ἡ, *a skirmishing*, Xen., etc.; and

ἀκροβολισμός, οῦ, ὁ, = ἀκροβόλισις, Thuc., Xen.; and

ἀκροβολιστής, οῦ, ὁ, = sq., Xen.

ἀκρό-βολος, ον, (βάλλω) pass. *struck from afar*, Aesch.　II. act. ἀκροβόλος, (parox.) ὁ, *a slinger, skirmisher*.

ἀκρο-βυστία, ἡ, *the foreskin*, N. T.　II. *circumcision*, Ib. ;—and as collect. *the uncircumcision*, i. e. *the uncircumcised*, Ib. ˌDeriv. uncertain.᾽

ἀκρο-γωνιαῖος, a, ον, (γωνία) *at the extreme angle*, ἀκρ. λίθος *the corner foundation*-stone, N. T.

ἀκρό-δετος, ον, *bound at the end* or *top*, Anth.

ἀκρό-δρυα, τά, ˌδρῦς᾽ *fruit-trees*, Xen.　II. *fruits*, Arist. The sing. occurs in Anth.

ἀκρο-θῐγής, ές, (θιγγάνω) *touching on the surface, touching the lips*, Anth.

ἀκρόθινα, τά, = ἀκροθίνια, Pind.

ἀκροθῑνιάζομαι, Dep. ˌἀκροθίνια᾽ *to take of the best, pick out for oneself*, Eur.

ἀκρο-θίνιον [θῐ], τό, mostly in pl. ἀκροθίνια : (ἄκρος, θίς) :—*the topmost part of a heap, the choice part, firstfruits*, taken as an offering to the gods, Hdt., etc.

ἀκρο-κελαινιάω, (κελαινός) only in Ep. part. ἀκροκελαινιόων, *growing black on the surface*, of a swollen stream, Il.

ἀκρο-κνέφαιος, ον, (κνέφας) *at the beginning of night, in twilight*, Hes. :—so, ἀκρο-κνεφής, ές, Luc.

ἀκρό-κομος, ον, (κόμη) *with hair on the crown*, of the Thracians, who seem to have shaved all the head except the crown, Il.　II. *with leaves at the top*, Eur., Theocr.

Ἀκρο-κόρινθος, ὁ, *the citadel of Corinth*, Eur., Xen.

ἀκρό-λῐθος, ον, with the ends made of stone; ξόανον ἀκρ. a statue with the head, arms, and legs marble, the rest wood, Anth.

ἀκρο-λογέω, (λέγω) to gather at top, στάχυας Anth.

ἀκρολοφίτης [ῐ], ου, ὁ, a mountaineer, Anth. From

ἀκρό-λοφος, ον, high-crested, peaked, Anth.   II. as Subst. a mountain crest, Plut.

ἀκρο-λῠτέω, f. ήσω, (λύω) to untie at the ends, Anth.

ἀκρο-μᾰνής, ές, (μαίνομαι) on the verge of madness, Hdt.

ἀκρο-μόλιβδος, ον, leaded at the edge, of a net, Anth.

ἄκρον, ου, τό, (neut. of ἄκρος) the highest or furthest point : 1. a mountain-top, peak, Hom., etc.   2. a headland, foreland, cape, Od.   3. an end, extremity, Plat. ; ἄκρα χειρῶν the hands, Luc.   II. metaph. the highest pitch, height, Pind. ; εἰς ἄκρον exceedingly, Theocr.; τὰ ἄκρα τοῖς ἄκροις ἀποδιδόναι the highest place to the highest men, Plat. ; ἄκρα φέρεσθαι to win the prize, Theocr.   2. of persons, Ἄργεος ἄκρα the oldest rulers of Argos, Id.

ἀκρ-ονῠχί [ῐ], Adv. with the tip of the nail, Anth. From

ἀκρ-όνῠχος, ον, (ὄνυξ) = ἀκρώνυχος, Anth.

ἀκρο-νὐχος, ον, (νύξ) at night-fall, at even, Theocr.,etc.

ἀκρο-πενθής, ές, (πένθος) exceeding sad, Aesch.

ἀκρο-ποδητί or –ῑτί, Adv. (πούς) on tiptoe, Luc.

ἀκρό-πολις, poët. ἀκρό-πτολις, εως, ἡ, the upper city, i.e. the citadel, Lat. arx, Od., Hdt. :—esp. the Acropolis of Athens, which served as the treasury, Thuc.   II. metaph. of men, a tower of defence, Theogn.

ἀκρο-πόλος, ον, (πολέω) high-ranging, lofty, Hom.

ἀκρο-πόρος, ον, (πείρω) piercing with the point, Od.

ἀκρό-πρωρον, τό, (πρῷρα) the end of a ship's prow, Strab.

ἀκρό-πτερον, τό, the tip of the wing, Anth.

ἀκρό-πτολις, ἡ, poët. for ἀκρόπολις.

ἄκρος, α, ον, (ἀκή I) at the furthest point, and so either topmost = Lat. summus, or outermost = Lat. extremus : 1. highest, topmost, ἐν ἄκρῃ πόλει = ἐν ἀκροπόλει, Il. ; μέλαν ὕδωρ ἄκρον at its surface, Ib., etc.   2. outermost, ἄκρη χείρ, ἄκροι πόδες, ἄκρος ὦμος the end of the hand, ends of the feet, tip of the shoulder, Ib., Thuc. ; ἐπ' ἄκρων [δακτύλων] on tiptoe, Soph. ; ἄκροισι λαίφους κρασπέδοις with the outermost edges of the sail, i.e. under close-reefed sails, Eur.   II. of Time, it denotes completeness, ἄκρᾳ σὺν ἑσπέρᾳ when eve was fully come, Pind. ; ἄκρας νυκτός at dead of night, Soph.   III. of Degree, the highest in its kind, exceeding good, consummate, excellent : of persons, Hdt., etc. ; ἄκρος μάντις Soph. :—often with an acc. modi added, ψυχὴν οὐκ ἄκρος not strong in mind, Hdt. ; ἄκροι τὰ πολέμια, skilful in war, Id., etc. ; also c. gen. modi, οἱ ἄκροι τῆς ποιήσεως Plat. ; also, ἄκρος εἰς or περί τι Id.   IV. as Subst., v. ἄκρα, ἄκρον.   V. neut. as Adv. on the top or surface, just, ἄκρον ἐπὶ ῥηγμῖνος on the very edge of the surf, Il.   2. exceedingly, Theocr.   3. utterly, completely, Plat.

ἀκρο-σίδηρος, ον, pointed or shod with iron, Anth.

ἀκρό-σοφος, ον, high in wisdom, Pind.

ἀκρο-στόλιον, τό, (στολή) the gunwale of a ship, Plut.

ἀκρο-σφᾰλής, ές, (σφάλλω) apt to trip, unsteady, precarious, Plat.

ἀκρο-τελεύτιον, τό, the fag-end of a verse, Thuc.

ἀκροτομέω, to lop off, shave the surface, Xen.   From

ἀκρότομος, ον, (τέμνω) cut off sharp, abrupt, Polyb.

ἀκρο-φύσιον, τό, (φῦσα) the snout or pipe of a pair of bellows, Thuc.

ἀκρο-χᾰνής, ές, (χάσκω) yawning at top, Anth.

ἀκρο-χειρίζομαι, Med. to struggle at arm's length, of a kind of wrestling, in which they grasped one another's hands, without clasping the body, Plat., etc.

ἀκροχολέω, –χολία, –χολος, v. sub ἀκραχ-.

ἀκρο-χορδών, ἡ, (χορδή) a wart with a thin neck, Plut.

ἄ-κρυπτος, ον, (κρύπτω) unhidden, Eur.

ἀ-κρύσταλλος, ον, free from ice, ἡ χώρη Hdt.

ἀκρ-ωμία, ἡ, (ὦμος) the point of the shoulder ; in a horse, the withers, Xen.

ἀκρωνία, ἡ, a dub. word in Aesch., perh. = ἀκρωτηριασμός, mutilation.

ἀκρωνῠχία, ἡ, the tip of the nail : metaph. the ridge of a mountain, Xen.

ἀκρ-ώνῠχος, ον, (ἄκρος, ὄνυξ) with nails at the extremities, χειρὸς ἀκρώνυχα the tips of the fingers, Anth.

ἀκρ-ώρεια, ἡ, (ὄρος) a mountain-ridge, Xen., Theocr.

ἀκρωτηριάζω, f. σω, to cut off the extremities, mutilate, τὰς πρῴρας ἠκρωτηρίασαν cut the beaks off the prows, Hdt. :—so in Med., τὰς τριήρεις ἀκρωτηριασάμενοι Xen.; pf. pass. in med. sense, ἠκρωτηριασμένοι τὰς πατρίδας having mutilated their countries, Dem.   From

ἀκρωτήριον, τό, (ἄκρος) any prominent part, ἀκρ. τοῦ οὔρεος a mountain-peak, Hdt.   2. a cape, promontory, Id., Thuc.   II. the extremity of anything, ἀκρ. νηός a ship's beak, Hdt.   2. in pl. the extremities of the body, hands and feet, fingers and toes, Thuc., etc. ; τὰ ἀκρ. τῆς Νίκης her wings, Dem.

ἀκταίνω, only in pres. to lift up, raise, ἀκταίνειν στάσιν to raise oneself so as to stand, to stand upright, Aesch. :—so in the form ἀκταινόω, Plat. (Deriv. uncertain.)

ἀκταῖος, α, ον, (ἀκτή) on the coast, of Ionian cities, Thuc. : so, Ἀκταία (sc. γῆ), ἡ, coast-land, an old name of Attica, Id.   2. haunting the coast, βάτραχοι Babr.

ἀκτέα, ἀκτῆ, ἡ, the elder-tree, Luc. (Deriv. unknown.)

ἀ-κτέᾰνος, ον, (κτέανον) without property, poor, τίνος in a thing, Anth.

ἀ-κτένιστος, ον, (κτενίζω) uncombed, unkempt, Soph.

ἀκτέον, verb. Adj. of ἄγω, one must lead, Plat., etc. ; εἰρήνην ἀκτέον one must keep peace, Dem.   II. one must go or march, Xen.

ἀ-κτέριστος, ον, = sq., Anth.

ἀ-κτέριστος, ον, (κτερίζω) unhallowed by funeral rites, Soph.

ἀκτή (A), ἡ, a headland, foreland, promontory, shore, Od., etc. : of the banks of rivers, ἀκταὶ Σιμόεντος Aesch.; Ἀχέροντος Soph.   2. generally, coast-land, ἀκταὶ διφάσιαι of the N. and S. coasts of Asia Minor, Hdt. ; of Attica (cf. ἀκταῖος), Soph.   II. generally, any edge or strand, like the sea-coast, Lat. ora, χώματος ἀκτή of a sepulchral mound, Aesch. ; βώμιος ἀ. of an altar, Soph. (Perh. from ἄγνυμι, cf. ῥηγμίν.)

ἀκτή (B), ἡ, old word for corn or meal, Δημήτερος ἀκτή Il. ; ἀλφίτου ἀκτή Od. (Deriv. uncertain.)

ἀ-κτήμων, ον, gen. ονος, (κτῆμα) without property, poor, χρυσοῖο in gold, Il. : absol., ἀκτ. πενία Theocr.

ἄ-κτητος, ον, (κτάομαι) not worth getting, Plat.

ἀκτινηδόν, (ἀκτίς) Adv. like a ray, Luc.

ἄκτιος, ον, (ἀκτή) haunting the shore, of Pan, Theocr.

ἀκτίς [ῑ], ῖνος, ἡ, a ray, beam, of the sun, Hom. ; ἀνὰ

μέσσαν ἀκτῖνα, i. e. from the south, Soph.; ἀκτῖνες τελευτῶσαι sunset, Eur. 2. metaph. brightness, splendour, glory, Pind. II. like Lat. radius, the spoke of a wheel, Anth. (Deriv. uncertain.)

ἀκτίτης [ῑ], ου, ὁ, (ἀκτή) a dweller on the coast, Anth.

ἄ-κτῑτος, ον, (κτίζω) untilled, h. Hom.

ἄκτωρ, ορος, ὁ, (ἄγω) a leader, Aesch.

ἀ-κυβέρνητος, ον, (κυβερνάω) without steersman, Plut.

ἄκῡλος, ὁ, an acorn, the fruit of the ilex, Od.

ἀ-κύμαντος [ῡ], ον, (κυμαίνω) not washed by the waves, ψαμάθοις ἐπ᾽ ἀκυμάντοις on sands washed by no waves, i. e. on the sands of the stadium, Eur. II. waveless, calm, πέλαγος Luc.

ἄ-κῡμος, ον, (κῦμα) = ἀκύμαντος, Arist., Plut., etc.: metaph. tranquil, ἀκ. βίοτος Eur.

ἀ-κύμων [ῡ], ον, gen. ονος, (κῦμα) = ἀκύμαντος, Aesch.

ἀ-κύμων [ῡ], ον, gen. ονος, (κύεω) without fruit, barren, of women, Eur.

ἄ-κῡρος, ον, (κῦρος) without authority: I. of laws and contracts, invalid, ἄκυρον ποιεῖν, Lat. irritum facere, to set aside, and ἄκυρον γίγνεσθαι, to become of no force, to be set aside, Plat.; νόμοις ἀκύροις χρωμένη, i. e. having laws, but not enforcing them, Thuc. II. of persons, having no right or power, ἄκ. ποιεῖν τινά Xen.; c. gen., ἄκυροι πάντων γενήσεσθε Dem.

ἀ-κύρωτος, ον, verb. Adj. of κυρόω, unconfirmed, Eur.

ἀκωκή [ᾰ], ἡ, (ἀκή I) a point, Hom., etc.

ἀ-κώλῡτος, ον, (κωλύω) unhindered, Luc.: Adv. -τως, Plat.

ἀ-κωμῴδητος, ον, (κωμῳδέω) not ridiculed: Adv. -τως, Luc.

ἄκων [ᾰ], οντος, ὁ, (ἀκή I) a javelin, dart, Hom., etc.

ἄκων [ᾰ], ἄκουσα, ἆκον, Att. contr. for ἀέκων.

ἄ-κωπος, ον, (κώπη) without oars, Anth.

Ἀλᾰβάρχης, v. Ἀραβάρχης.

Ἀλᾰβαρχία [ᾰ], ἡ, the office of Ἀλαβάρχης, in Egypt, ἐξ Ἀλαβαρχίης [ῑ], Anth.

ἀλᾰβαστο-θήκη, ἡ, a case for alabaster ornaments, Dem.

ἀλάβαστος [ᾰλᾰ-], ὁ, a box or casket of alabaster, Hdt., Ar., etc.: ἀλάβαστρος is a later form in Lxx, N. T., Plut.: a neut. ἀλάβαστρον in N. T., pl. ἀλάβαστρα or -τα in Theocr. and Anth. (Prob. a foreign word.)

ἄλᾰδε [ᾰλ], Adv. of ἅλς, to or into the sea, Il., etc.; also, εἰς ἅλαδε Od.

ἀλά-δρομος [ᾰλ], ὁ, in Ar. Av. 1359,—either from ἄλλομαι, the bounding race; or from ἅλς, a race over the sea.

ἀλαζονεία, ἡ, (ἀλαζών) false pretension, imposture, quackery, Ar., Plat., etc.

ἀλαζόνευμα, ατος, τό, an imposture, piece of quackery, Ar., etc. From

ἀλαζονεύομαι, f. εύσομαι: Dep.: (ἀλαζών):—to make false pretensions, of the Sophists, Xen.

ἀλαζονικός, ή, όν, (ἀλαζών) boastful, braggart, Xen. Adv. -κῶς, Plut.

ἀλαζών [ᾰλ], όνος, ὁ, ἡ, (ἄλη) properly a vagabond: then, a false pretender, impostor, quack, of Sophists, Ar., Plat., etc. II. as Adj. swaggering, boastful, braggart, Lat. gloriosus, Hdt., Plat.

ἀλάθεια, ἀλᾱθής, Dor. for ἀλήθ-.

ἀλᾱθείς, Dor. for ἀληθείς, aor. 1 part. of ἀλάομαι.

ἀλαίνω [ᾰλ], = ἀλάομαι, to wander about, Aesch., Eur.; ἀλ. πόδα to wander on foot, Id.

ἀλακάτα, ἡ, Dor. for ἠλακάτη.

ἀλαλά, Dor. for ἀλαλή.

ἀλᾰλᾱγή, ἡ, a shouting, Soph.; and

ἀλάλαγμα, ατος, τό, = sq., Plut.; and

ἀλᾰλᾰγμός, ὁ, = ἀλαλαγή, Hdt. II. a loud noise, τυμπάνων, αὐλοῦ Eur. From

ἀλᾰλάζω, f. -άξομαι: aor. 1 ἠλάλαξα, poët. ἀλάλαξα: (formed from the cry ἀλαλαί as ἐλελίζω, ὀλολύζω from similar sounds):—to raise the war-cry, Xen.; c. acc. cogn., νίκην ἀλαλάζειν to shout the shout of victory, Soph. 2. generally, to cry or shout aloud, of Bacchus and the Bacchae, Eur. 3. rarely of a cry of pain, ἠλάλαζε δυσθνῇσκον Id. II. rarely also of other sounds than the voice, to sound loudly, clang, N. T.

ἀλᾰλαί [ᾰλ], exclam. of joy, Ar.

ἀλᾰλᾱτός, ὁ, Dor. for ἀλαλητός.

ἀλᾰλή [ᾰλᾰ], Dor. ἀλαλά, ἡ, a loud cry, Eur.:— esp. the cry with which battle was begun, hence the battle-cry, Pind. (Formed from the sound, cf. ἀλαλαί.)

ἀλάλημαι [ᾰλᾰ], pf. of ἀλάομαι, only used in pres. sense (part. ἀλαλήμενος takes the accent of pres.), to wander or roam about, like a beggar, Od.; of seamen, Ib.

ἀ-λάλητος, ον, (λαλέω) unutterable, Anth., N. T.

ἀλᾰλητός, Dor. -ᾱτός, οῦ, ὁ, (ἀλαλή) the shout of victory, Il.: war-cry, Il., Hes. 2. rarely, a cry of woe or wailing, Il. II. a loud noise, αὐλῶν Anth.

ἄλαλκε [ᾰλ], 3 sing. aor. 2 (also 2 imper.); Ep. 3 sing. subj. ἀλάλκῃσι; opt. ἀλάλκοις, -κοι, -κοιεν; inf. ἀλαλκεῖν, Ep. ἀλαλκέμεναι, -έμεν; part. ἀλαλκών:—to ward or keep off, τί τινι something from a person, Il., etc.; more rarely τί τινος Ib. (From ΑΛΚ come ἄλαλκε, ἀλκή, ἄλκαρ, ἄλκιμος, ἀλέξω: identical with ΑΡΚ (v. Α λ, IV), whence ἀρκέω, Lat. arceo, arx, arca.)

Ἀλαλκομενηΐς, ΐδος, name of Athena, prob. from ἀλαλκεῖν, the Protectress, Il.

ἀλαλκομένιος, ὁ, a Boeot. month, answering to Att. μαιμακτηριών, Plut.

ἄ-λᾰλος, ον, speechless, N. T.

ἀλαλύκτημαι [ᾰλᾰ], a pf. formed by redupl. from *ἀλυκτέω, to be sore distressed, Il.; cf. ἀλυκτάζω.

ἀ-λάμπετος, ον, (ἀ priv., λάμπω) without light, darksome, h. Hom.; of the nether world, Soph.

ἀ-λαμπής, ές, = foreg.; ἀλ. ἡλίου out of the sun's light, Soph. 2. metaph. obscure, Plut.

ἀλάομαι [ᾰλ], Ep. 3 pl. ἀλόωνται, Ep. imper. ἀλόω: impf. ἠλώμην, Ep. 3 sing. ἀλᾶτο: f. ἀλήσομαι: Ep. aor. 1 ἀλήθην, Dor. part. ἀλᾱθείς: cf. ἀλάλημαι: Pass.: (ἄλη):—to wander, stray or roam about, Hom., etc.: to wander from home, be banished, Soph.; c. acc. loci, ἀλ. γῆν to wander over the land, Id. 2. c. gen. to wander away from, cease to enjoy, εὐφροσύνας Pind.; τῆς πάροιθ᾽ εὐπραξίας Eur. II. metaph. to wander in mind, be distraught, Soph.

ἀλαός, όν, not seeing, blind, Od., Trag., etc.; ἕλκος ἀλαόν a blinding wound, i.e. blindness, Id. (Commonly regarded as a compd. of ἀ privat. and λάω video.)

ἀλαο-σκοπιά, Ion. -ιή, ἡ, (σκοπέω) a blind, i.e. useless, careless, watch, Hom., Hes.

ἀλαόω [ᾰλ], f. ώσω, (ἀλαός) to blind, ὀφθαλμοῦ of an eye, Od.

ἀλᾰπαδνός, ή, όν, (ἀλαπάζω) exhausted, powerless, feeble, Hom., Hes.; Comp. ἀλαπαδνότεροι Il.

ἀλᾰπάζω [ᾰλ], Ep. impf. ἀλάπαζον: f. άξω: Ep. aor. 1

ἀλάπαξα:—to empty, drain, exhaust, Od. ; ἀλ. πόλιν to plunder it, Il. ; and of men, to destroy, Ib. (From Root ΛΑΠ with α prefixed, cf. λαπάσσω.)

ἅλας, ατος, τό, (ἅλς) salt, N. T., Plut.

ἀλαστέω, aor. 1 part. ἀλαστήσας, (ἄλαστος) to be full of wrath, Il.

ἀλάστορος, ον, under the influence of an ἀλάστωρ: suffering cruelly, Soph.

ἄ-λαστος, Ion. ἄ-ληστος, ον, (λήθομαι) not to be forgotten, insufferable, unceasing, πένθος, ἄχος Hom. : neut. as Adv., incessantly, Od.   2. of persons, ἄλαστε accursed wretch ! Il., Soph.

ἀλάστωρ, ορος, ὁ, the Avenging Deity, destroying angel, Trag. ; ἀλ. οὑμός Soph. ; βουκόλων ἀλάστωρ the herdsmen's plague, of the Nemean lion, Id.   II. pass. he who suffers from such vengeance, an accursed wretch, Aesch., Dem. (Either from ἄλαστος, or from ἀλάομαι, he that makes to wander.)

ἀλάτας, ἀλᾱτεία, Dor. for ἀλήτης, ἀλητεία.

ἀλάτιον, τό, Dim. of ἅλας, Aesop.

ἄλατο, Dor. for ἥλατο, 3 sing. aor. 1 of ἄλλομαι.   II. ἀλᾶτο, 3 sing. impf. of ἀλάομαι.

ἀλαωτύς, ύος, ἡ, (ἀλαόω) a blinding, Od.

ἀλγεινός, ή, όν, (ἄλγος) Att. for Ep. ἀλεγεινός, giving pain, painful, grievous, Trag., Thuc. :—Adv. -νῶς, Soph., Plat.   II. rare in pass. sense, feeling pain, grievously suffering, suffering, Soph. — Cf. ἀλγίων, -ιστος.

ἀλγέω, f. ήσω, (ἄλγος) to feel bodily pain, suffer, Il., Hdt., etc.; the suffering part in acc., ἀλγ. ἧπαρ Aesch.; τὸν δάκτυλον, τὰ ὄμματα Plat.   2. to suffer hardship, Od.   II. to feel pain of mind, to grieve, be troubled or distressed, ἀλγεῖν ψυχήν, φρένα Hdt., Eur., etc. ; ἀλγ. τινι to be pained at a thing, Hdt., Soph.; ἐπί τινι Id.; διά τι Hdt.; περί τι or τινος Thuc.; c. gen., Aesch.; c. acc., ἀλγῶ μὲν ἔργα Id.; c. part., ἤλγησ' ἀκούσας Hdt.

ἀλγηδών, όνος, ἡ, (ἀλγέω) a sense of pain, pain, suffering, Hdt., Eur., etc.   II. of mind, pain, grief, Soph., Eur., etc.

ἄλγημα, ατος, τό, (ἀλγέω) pain, suffering, Soph., Eur.

ἄλγησις, εως, ἡ, (ἀλγέω) sense of pain, Soph.

ἀλγῖνόεις, εσσα, εν, (ἄλγος) painful, grievous, Hes.

ἀλγίων [ῑ], ον, ἄλγιστος, η, ον, irreg. Comp. and Sup. of ἀλγεινός, formed from ἄλγος (as καλλίων, -ιστος from κάλλος, αἰσχίων, -ιστος from αἶσχος):—more or most painful, grievous, -distressing :—of the Comp., Hom. has only neut. ἄλγιον, so much the worse, all the harder ; ἀλγίστη δαμάσασθαι (of a mule), Il. [In Hom. ἀλγῖον, but ῑ always in Att.]

ἌΛΓΟΣ, εος, τό, pain of body, Il., Soph.   2. pain of mind, grief, distress, Hom.   II. anything that causes pain, Anth.

ἀλγύνω [ῡ], Ion. 3 sing. impf. ἀλγύνεσκε: f. ὑνῶ: aor. 1 ἤλγῡνα:—Pass., with f. med. ἀλγυνοῦμαι (in pass. sense) : aor. 1 ἠλγύνθην: (ἄλγος) :—to pain, grieve, distress, τινά Aesch.; etc. :—Pass. to be grieved at a thing, τινι Soph.; ἐπί τινι Eur.; τι Soph. : c. part., εἰσιδοῦσα ἠλγύνθην Aesch.

ἀλδαίνω (Root ΑΛΔ), only in pres. and impf., except Ep. 3 sing. aor. 2 ἤλδανε :—Causal of ἀλδήσκω, to make

to grow, μέλε' ἤλδανε she filled out his limbs, Od. : to increase, multiply, ἀλδαίνειν κακά Aesch.

ἀλδήσκω, to grow, wax, Il.   II. trans. = ἀλδαίνω, Theocr.

ἀλέα (A), Ion. ἀλέη, ἡ, (ἀλέομαι) an escape, Il.; c. gen. shelter from, ὑετοῦ Hes.

ἀλέα (B), Ion. ἀλέη, ἡ, warmth, heat, Od., Ar. (Deriv. uncertain.)

ἀλεαίνω, aor. 1 ἄνα, (ἀλέα B) to warm, make warm, Arist.   II. intr. to grow warm, be warm, Ar.

ἀλέασθαι, ἀλέασθε, Ep. aor. 1 inf. and 2 pl. of ἀλέομαι: ἀλέαιτο, 3 sing. opt.

ἀλεγεινός, ή, όν, Ep. for ἀλγεινός, Hom.; c. inf., ἵπποι ἀλεγεινοὶ δαμήμεναι hard to break, Il.

ἀλεγίζω, Ep. Verb, only in pres. and impf., (ἀλέγω) to trouble oneself about a thing, to care for, in Hom. always with negat., c. gen. rei, τῶν μὲν ἄρ' οὐκ ἀλέγιζε πατήρ Il. : absol. to take heed, Ib.

ἀλεγύνω [ῡ], aor. 2 ἀλέγῡνα, (ἀλέγω) to care for, furnish, c. acc., ἄλλας δ' ἀλεγύνετε δαῖτας find your meals elsewhere ; δαῖτ' ἀλέγυνον, of invited guests ; but, δαῖτας ἔίσας ἀλ. to prepare a meal for guests, all in Od.

ἀλέγω, only in pres., to trouble oneself, have a care, mostly with negat. :   1. absol., οὐκ ἀλ. to have no care, heed not, Lat. negligo, Hom. ; κύνες οὐκ ἀλέγουσαι careless, reckless dogs, Od.; without negat., ἀλέγουσι κιούσαι are heedful in their course.   II. with a case,   1. c. gen. to care for, Od., Aesch.   2. c. acc. to heed, regard, respect, Il. :—without a negat., ὅπλα ἀλέγουσιν take care of, Od.   (Prob. from Root ΛΕΓ = LIG in Lat. re-ligio, α being euphonic.)

ἀλεεινός, ή, όν, (ἀλέα B) open to the sun, warm, hot, χώρη Hdt., Xen.

ἀλεείνω [ᾰ], Ep. Verb, only in pres. and impf. : (ἀλέα B): —to avoid, shun, c. acc., Od.; c. inf., κτεῖναι ἀλέεινε he avoided killing him, Il.

ἀλέη, Ep. for ἀλέα.

ἀλεής, ές, like ἀλεεινός, in the sun, ὕπνος Soph.

ἀλείατα, τά, (ἀλέω) wheaten flour, Od.; cf. ἄλευρον.

ἄλειμμα, ατος, τό, (ἀλείφω) anything used for anointing, unguent, fat, oil, Plat.

ἀλείπτης, ου, ὁ, (ἀλείφω) an anointer, a teacher of gymnastics, Arist. :—metaph. a teacher, Plut.

ἀλείς, εῖσα, έν, aor. 2 pass. part. of εἴλω: v. εἴλω II.

ἄλεισον [ᾰ], τό, a cup, goblet, χρύσειον Hom. (Deriv. unknown.)

ἀλείτης, ου, ὁ, (ἀλέομαι) one who flees from punishment, a culprit, a sinner, Hom.

ἄλειφα, τό, collat. form of sq., Hes., Aesch., etc.

ἄλειφαρ, ατος, τό, (ἀλείφω) anointing-oil, unguent, oil, Hom.   II. generally, anything used for smearing, pitch or resin, to seal wine-jars, Theocr.

ἀλείφω, f. -ψω: aor. 1 ἤλειψα, Ep. ἄλειψα: pf. ἀλήλιφα : —Med., f. -ψομαι: aor. 1 ἠλειψάμην, Ep. ἀλ-:—Pass., f. ἀλειφθήσομαι: aor. 1 ἠλείφθην: pf. ἀλήλιμμαι. (From Root ΛΙΠ with α prefixed, v. λίπος.) To anoint with oil, oil the skin, as was done after bathing, or before gymnastic exercises, the Act. referring to the act of another, Med. to oneself, Il.; often with λίπα added (v. λίπα):—metaph. to prepare as if for gymnastics, to stimulate, Plat., etc.   II. like ἐπαλείφω, to plaster, οὔατα ἀλεῖψαι to stop up the ears, Od.

ἄλειψις, εως, ἡ, an anointing:—a method or custom of anointing, Hdt.

ἀλεκτορίσκος, ὁ, Dim. of ἀλέκτωρ, a cockerel, Babr.

ἀλεκτορο-φωνία, ἡ, (ἀλέκτωρ, φωνή) cock-crow, i.e. the third watch of the night, Aesop., N.T.

ἄ-λεκτρος, ον, (λέκτρον) unbedded, unwedded, Soph., etc.; ἄλεκτρ᾽, ἄνυμφα γάμων ἀμιλλήματα, much like γάμος ἄγαμος, i.e. a lawless, unhallowed marriage, Id.; ἄλεκτρα, as Adv., Id.

ἀλεκτρύαινα, ἡ, a hen, Ar. From

ἀλεκτρυών [ἄ], όνος, ὁ, a cock, Theogn., etc.   II. ἡ, = ἀλεκτρύαινα, a hen, Ar. From

ἀλέκτωρ [ἄ], ορος, ὁ, = ἀλεκτρυών, a cock, Aesch., etc. (Deriv. uncertain.)

ἀλέκω [ἄ], to ward off, Anth.; v. ἄλαλκε.

ἀλέματος, ἀλεμάτως, Dor. for ἠλεμ-.

ἄλεν, aor. 2 pass. part. neut. of εἴλω.

Ἀλεξανδριστής, οῦ, ὁ, a partisan of Alexander, Plut.

ἀλέξ-ανδρος, ον, (ἀνήρ) defending men, πόλεμος Inscr. ap. Diod.   II. the usual name of Paris in Il., cf. Aesch. Ag. 61, 363.

Ἀλεξανδρ-ώδης, ες, (εἶδος) Alexander-like, Menand.

ἀλεξ-άνεμος, ον, (ἀλέξω) keeping off the wind, Od.

ἀλέξημα, ατος, τό, (ἀλέξω) a defence, remedy, Aesch.

ἀλέξησις, εως, ἡ, (ἀλέξω) a keeping off, defence, Hdt.

ἀλεξήτειρα, ἡ, fem. of sq., Anth.

ἀλεξητήρ, ῆρος, ὁ, (ἀλέξω) one who keeps off, ἀλ. μάχης a stemmer of battle, a champion, Il.

ἀλεξητήριος, α, ον, (ἀλέξω) able to keep off, of the gods, Lat. Averrunci, Aesch.; ξύλον ἀλ. a club for defence, Eur.   2. ἀλεξητήριον (sc. φάρμακον), τό, a remedy; protection, Xen.

ἀλεξήτωρ, ορος, ὁ, = ἀλεξητήρ, Soph.

ἀλεξί-άρη [ἄρ], ἡ, either (from ἀρά) she that keeps off a curse, or (from Ἄρης) she that guards from death and ruin, Hes.

ἀλεξι-βέλεμνος, ον, (βέλεμνον) keeping off darts, Anth.

ἀλεξί-κακος, ον, keeping off evil or mischief, Il.: c. gen., δίψης ἀλ. Anth.

ἀλεξί-μβροτος, ον, protecting mortals, Pind.

ἀλεξί-μορος, ον, warding off death, Soph.

ἀλεξι-φάρμἄκον, τό, an antidote, remedy, Plat.:—τινός against a thing, Id.

ἀλέξω [ἄ], Ep. inf. ἀλεξέμεναι, -έμεν: f. ἀλεξήσω: aor. 1 opt. ἀλεξήσειε:—Med., f. ἀλεξήσομαι.—Besides these tenses (formed from ἀλεξέω), we find others formed from ἀλέκω, f. ἀλέξω, med. ἀλέξομαι; aor. 1 inf. ἀλέξασθαι. (From Root ΑΛΚ, v. ἄλαλκε.)   To ward or keep off, turn away or aside; c. acc. rei, Ζεὺς τό γ᾽ ἀλεξήσειε Od.; c. acc. rei et dat. pers., Δαναοῖσιν ἀλεξήσειν κακὸν ἦμαρ will ward it off from them, Il., etc.:—then c. dat. pers. only, to assist, defend, Ib., Xen.; absol. to lend aid, Il.:—Med. to keep off from oneself, defend oneself against, c. acc., Ib.: absol. to defend oneself, Ib., Soph.   2. Med., also, to recompense, requite, τοὺς εὖ καὶ κακῶς ποιοῦντας ἀλεξόμενος Xen.

ἀλέομαι [ἄλ], contr. ἀλεῦμαι, Ep. ἀλεόμαι: impf. ἀλέοντο: aor. 1 ἠλευάμην, inf. ἀλέασθαι, ἀλεύασθαι, part. ἀλευάμενος.   (Prob. from same Root as ἀλάομαι: cf. ἀλύσκω):—Dep. to avoid, shun, c. acc. rei, ἔγχεα ἀλεώμεθα, ἠλεύατο ἔγχος, ἀλεύατο κῆρα, ἀλεώμεθα μῆνιν, τὸ κῆτος ἀλέαιτο,—all in Il.; rarely c. acc. pers., θεοὺς

ἀλέασθαι, Ib.:—c. inf. to avoid doing; ἀλεύεται (Ep. 3 sing. subj. for -ηται) ἠπεροπεύειν Od.   2. absol. to flee for one's life, flee, τὸν μὲν ἀλευάμενον τὸν δὲ κτάμενον Il.; οὔτε φυγέειν δύνατ᾽ οὔτ᾽ ἀλέασθαι Ib.

ἄλεσσα, Ep. for ἤλεσα, aor. 1 of ἀλέω.

ἀλέτης, ου, ὁ, (ἀλέω) a grinder, v. ὄνος II. 2.

ἀλετός, ὁ, (ἀλέω) a grinding, Plut.; cf. ἀλητός.

ἀλετρεύω, f. εύσω, (ἀλέω) to grind, Od.

ἀλε-τρίβανος [ἀλ, ῑ], ὁ, (ἀλέω, τρίβω) that which grinds or pounds, a pestle, Ar.

ἀλετρίς, ίδος, ἡ, (ἀλέω) a female slave who grinds corn, γυνὴ ἀλετρίς Od.

ἄλευ, poët. for ἄλευε, imp. of ἀλεύω.

ἄλευαι, Ep. aor. 1 imper. of ἀλέομαι: ἀλεύατο, Ep. 3 sing. indic.

ἄλευρον [ᾰ], τό, mostly in pl. ἄλευρα, (ἀλέω) wheaten flour, distinguished from ἄλφιτα (barley-meal), Hdt., etc.

ἀλεύω, to remove, keep away; aor. 1 imper., ἄλευσον ὕβριν Aesch.; κακὸν ἀλεύσατε Id.: absol. in pres. ἄλευ, for ἄλευε, avert the evil, Id.:—Med., ἀλεύομαι, v. ἀλέομαι.

ἀλέω [ᾰ]: impf. ἤλουν: aor. 1 ἤλεσα, Ep. ἄλεσσα: pf. ἀλήλεκα:—Pass., pf. ἀλήλεσμαι or -εμαι:—to grind, bruise, pound, Od.   (From Root ΑΛ came also ἀλήθω, ἀλείατα, ἄλευρον, ἄλως, ἀλωή.)

*ἀλέω, only used in Med. ἀλέομαι.

ἀλεωρή, Att. -ρά, ἡ, (ἀλέομαι) avoidance, escape, Il., Hdt.   2. c. gen. a means of avoiding, a defence or shelter from, δηΐων ἀνδρῶν Il.: absol. a defence, Ib., Hdt.

ἌΛΗ [ᾰ], ἡ, ceaseless wandering, Od., etc.   2. wandering of mind, distraction, Eur.   II. act., ἄλαι βροτῶν δύσορμοι, of storms such as keep men wandering without haven and rest, Aesch.; cf. ἀλάομαι.

ἀλήθειᾰ [ᾱλ], ἡ, Dor. ἀλάθεια; Ep. also ἀληθείᾱ: (ἀληθής):   I. truth: 1. truth, as opp. to a lie, παιδὸς πᾶσαν ἀλ. μυθεῖσθαι to tell the whole truth about the lad, Od.; so, χράσθαι τῇ ἀλ. Hdt.; ἡ ἀλ. περί τινος Thuc.   2. truth, reality, opp. to appearance, τῶν ἔργων ἡ ἀλ. Id.   3. adverb. usages, τῇ ἀληθείᾳ in very truth, Id.; rarely ἀληθείᾳ Plat.: ἐπ᾽ ἀληθείας in truth and reality, Dem.; μετ᾽ ἀληθείας Xen.; κατ᾽ ἀλήθειαν Arist.   II. the character of the ἀληθής, truthfulness, sincerity, frankness, candour, Hdt., etc.

ἀληθεύω, f. σω, (ἀληθής) to speak truth, Aesch., etc.; τὰς δέκα ἡμέρας ἠλήθευσε he was right about the 10 days, Xen.; ἀλ. τοὺς ἐπαίνους to prove their praises true, Luc.   II. Pass. to come true, of predictions, Xen.

ἀ-ληθής [ᾱ], Dor. ἀ-λᾱθής, ές, (ἀ priv., λήθω = λανθάνω): —unconcealed, true: I. true, opp. to ψευδής, Hom.; τὸ ἀληθές, by crasis τἀληθές, Ion. τὠληθές, and τὰ ἀληθῆ, by crasis τἀληθῆ the truth, Hdt., Att.   2. of persons, truthful, Il., Att.   3. of oracles and the like, true, coming true, Aesch., etc.   II. Adv. ἀληθῶς, Ion. -θέως, truly, Hdt., etc.; so, ὡς ἀληθῶς Eur., Plat., etc.   III. neut. as Adv., proparox. ἄληθες; itane? indeed? really? in sooth? ironically, Soph., Eur., etc.   2. τὸ ἀληθές really and truly, Lat. revera, Plat., etc.; so, τὸ ἀληθέστατον in very truth, Thuc.   Hence

ἀληθίζομαι, Dep. = ἀληθεύω, Hdt.

ἀληθῑνός, ή, όν, (ἀληθής) agreeable to truth :   1. of persons, truthful, trusty, Xen., Dem.   2. of things, true, real, Plat. ; ἐς ἀλ. ἀνδρ᾽ ἀποβῆναι to turn out a true man, Theocr. :—Adv. -νῶς, truly, really, Plat., etc.

ἀληθό-μαντις, ὁ, ἡ, prophet of truth, Aesch.

ἀληθοσύνη, ἡ, poët. for ἀλήθεια, Theogn.

ἀλήθω [ᾰ], = ἀλέω, Anth.

Ἀλήϊον πεδίον, τό, (ἄλη) the plain of wandering (over which Bellerophon wandered), in Lycia or Cilicia, Il.

ἀ-λήϊος, ον, (λήϊον) poor in lands, Il.

ἀλήλεκα, -εμαι or -εσμαι, pf. act. and pass. of ἀλέω.

ἀλήλῑφα, ἀλήλιμμαι, pf. act. and pass. of ἀλείφω.

ἄλημα [ἀλ], ατος, τό, (ἀλέω) fine meal : metaph. of a wily knave, such as Ulysses, Soph.

ἀλήμεναι, Ep. for ἀλῆναι.

ἀλήμων [ᾰ], ονος, ὁ, ἡ, (ἀλάομαι) a wanderer, rover, Od., Anth.

ἀλῆναι, aor. 2 pass. inf. of εἴλω.

ἄ-ληπτος, ον, not to be laid hold of, hard to catch, Plut. ; Comp. ἀληπτότερος less amenable, Thuc.   II. incomprehensible, Plut.

ἀλής [ᾱ], ές, (εἴλω, cf. ἀολλής) Ion. word equiv. to Att. ἀθρόος, assembled, thronged, in a mass, all at once, Lat. confertus, Hes., Hdt. ; either in pl., ὡς ἀλέες εἴησαν οἱ Ἕλληνες, or with collective nouns, ἀλὴς γενομένη πᾶσα ἡ Ἑλλάς Id.

ἄ-λαστος, ον, Ion. for ἄλαστος.

ἀλητεία, Dor. ἀλᾱτεία, ἡ, a wandering, roaming, Aesch., Eur. From

ἀλητεύω, f. σω, to wander, roam about, of beggars, Od. ; of exiles, Eur. From

ἀλήτης [ᾰ], ου, Dor. ἀλάτας, α, ὁ ; voc. ἀλῆτα, Dor. ἀλᾶτα : (ἀλάομαι) :—a wanderer, stroller, rover, vagabond, of beggars, Hom. ; of exiles, Trag. ; τὸν μακρῶν ἀλάταν πόνων one who has wandered in long labours, Soph.   2. as Adj. vagrant, roving, βίος Hdt.

ἀλητός, ὁ, poët. for ἀλετός, Babr.

ἌΛΘΟΜΑΙ, Pass. to become whole and sound, ἄλθετο χείρ (Ep. 3 sing. impf.) Il.

ἁλία, Ion. -ίη, (ἁλής) an assembly of the people, in Dor. states, answering to Att. ἐκκλησία, Hdt., etc.

ἁλιάδης [ᾰδ], ου, ὁ, (ἅλς) a seaman, Soph.

ἁλι-άετος, poët. ἁλιαίετος, ὁ, the sea-eagle, osprey, Ar.

ἁλι-αής, ές, (ἄημι) blowing seaward, Od.

ἁλι-ανθής, ές, (ἅλς, ἀνθέω) properly sea-blooming : then = ἁλιπόρφυρος, purple, Anth.

ἀ-λίαστος, ον, (λιάζομαι) unshrinking, unabating, Il. ; neut. as Adv., μηδ᾽ ἀλίαστον ὀδύρεο nor mourn incessant, Ib. ; so, φρὴν ἀλίαστος φρίσσει Eur.   II. of persons, undaunted, Il.

ἁλίβας [ᾰ-], αντος, ὁ, a dead body, corpse, Plat. (Deriv. unknown.)

ἁλίβᾰτος, ον, Dor. for ἠλίβατος.

ἁλί-βρεκτος, ον, (ἅλς, βρέχω) washed by the sea, Anth.

ἀλίγκιος [ᾰ], ον, resembling, like, Hom. ·—cf. the compd. ἐναλίγκιος. (Deriv. uncertain.)

ἁλί-δονος, ον, ἅλς, δονέω) sea-tost, Aesch.

ἁλιεία, ἡ, (ἁλιεύς) fishing, Arist.

ἁλι-ερκής, ές, (ἅλς, ἕρκος) sea-fenced, sea-girt, Pind.

ἁλιεύς, ὁ : gen. έως, Ion. ἠος and contr. ἁλιῶς : (ἅλς) :— one who has to do with the sea, and so,   1. a fisher,

Hom., etc.   2. a seaman, sailor, Od. ; with another Subst., ἐρέτας ἁλιῆας sea-faring rowers, Ib.

ἁλιευτικός, ή, όν, (ἁλιεύω) of or for fishing, Xen., Arist.; —ἡ -κή (with or without τέχνη) the art of fishing, Plat.

ἁλιεύω, f. σω, (ἅλς) to be a fisher, Plut., Luc., etc.   2. to fish, go fishing, N. T.

ἁλίζω (A) [ᾰ] : aor. 1 ἥλῐσα :—Pass., aor. 1 ἡλίσθην : Ion. part. pf. ἁλισμένος : (ἁλής) :—to gather together, to muster, military forces, Hdt. :—Pass. to meet together, assemble, Id.

ἁλίζω (B) [ᾰ], f. ίσω, (ἅλς) to salt, and Pass. to be salted, Arist., N. T.

ἁλί-ζωνος, ον, (ἅλς, ζώνη) sea-girt, Anth.

ἁλί-ζωος, ον, living on or in the sea, Anth.

ἁλίη, ἡ, Ion. for ἁλία.

ἁλι-ήρης, ες, (ἐρέσσω) sweeping the sea, κώπη Eur.

ἁλίθιος, Dor. for ἠλίθιος.

ἄ-λῐθος, ον, without stones, not stony, of land, Xen.

Ἁλικαρνασσός, Ion. -ησσός, ἡ, a Doric city of Caria, Hdt., etc. : Ἁλικαρνασσεύς, έως, Ion. -ησσεύς, έος, ὁ, a Halicarnassian, Id. :—Ἁλικαρνασσόθεν, Adv., from Halicarnassus, Luc.

ἁλικία, ἡ, Dor. for ἡλικία.

ἁλί-κλυστος, ον, (ἅλς, κλύζω) sea-washed, Soph.

ἁλίκος, α, ον, Dor. for ἡλίκος.

ἁλί-κτῠπος, ον, groaning at sea, of ships in bad weather, Soph.   2. of waves, roaring on the sea, Eur.

ἁλί-κύμων [ῠ], ον, (ἅλς, κῦμα) surrounded by waves, Anth.

ἀ-λίμενος [ῐ], ον, (λιμήν) without harbour, harbourless, Aesch., Thuc., etc.   2. metaph. without shelter, inhospitable, Eur.   Hence

ἀλῑμενότης, ἡ, want of harbours, Xen.

ἁλῐμῠρήεις, εσσα, εν, (ἅλς, μύρω) flowing into the sea, of rivers, Hom.

ἁλι-μύρης, ές, (ἅλς, μύρω) sea-flowing, of the sea, Anth.

ἀλινδέω or ἀλίνδω [ᾰ], to make to roll (but Act. only occurs in compos. with ἐξ) :—Pass. to roll in the dust (cf. ἀλινδήθρα) :—metaph. to roam about, Anth.   Hence

ἀλινδήθρα, ἡ, a sandy place for horses to roll in, Lat. volutabrum : metaph., ἀλινδήθραι ἐπῶν, i. e. words big enough for rolling places, Ar.

ἁλι-νήκτειρα, ἡ, (ἅλς, νήχω) fem. as if from *ἁλινηκτήρ, swimming in the sea, Anth.

ἁλι-νηχής, ές, (ἅλς, νήχω) swimming in the sea, Anth.

ἅλῐνος, η, ον, (ἅλς) of salt, Hdt.

ἄ-λῐνος, ον, (λίνον) without a net, ἄλ. θήρα a chase in which no net is used, Anth.

ἁλιξ, Dor. for ἧλιξ.

ἁλί-ξαντος, ον, (ἅλς, ξαίνω) worn by the sea, Anth.

ἅλιος, ὁ, Dor. for ἥλιος.

ἅλιος (A), α, ον and ος, ον, (ἅλς) of the sea, Lat. marinus, of sea-gods and nymphs, Hom., etc. ; ἄλ. ψάμαθοι the sea-sand, Od.

ἅλιος (B), α, ον, (cf. ἠλίθιος) of things, fruitless, unprofitable, vain, idle, Hom. : neut. ἅλιον as Adv., in vain, Il. ; regul. Adv. -ίως, Soph.

ἁλιο-τρεφής, ές, (τρέφω) sea-bred, φῶκαι Od.

ἁλιόω, f. ἁλιώσω : aor. 1 ἡλίωσα, Ep. ἁλίωσα : (ἅλιος B) :—to make fruitless, frustrate, disappoint, Διὸς

νόον Od.; οὐδ' ἁλίωσε βέλος nor *did he hurl* the spear *in vain*, Il.

ἀ-λῖπᾰρής, ές, *not fit for a suppliant*, Soph.

ἁλί-πεδον, τό, *a plain by the sea :*—as the plain near Piraeus was called, Xen.

ἁλί-πλαγκτος, ον, (ἅλς, πλάζομαι) *roaming the sea*, Soph., Anth.

ἁλί-πλᾰνής, ές, (ἅλς, πλανάομαι) *sea-wandering*, Anth.

ἁλιπλᾰνία, ἡ, *a wandering voyage*, Anth.

ἁλί-πληκτος, Dor. **-πλακτος**, ον, (ἅλς, πλήσσω) *sea-beaten*, Pind.

ἁλί-πλήξ, ηγος, ὁ, ἡ, = foreg., Anth.

ἁλί-πλοος, ον, contr. **-πλους**, ουν, (ἅλς, πλέω) *covered with water*, Il.   **II.** *sailing on the sea*, ναῦς Arion.

ἁλι-πόρος, ον, (ἅλς, πείρω) *through which the sea flows*, Luc.

ἁλι-πόρφυρος, ον, (ἅλς, πορφύρα) *of sea-purple, of true purple dye*, Od.

ἁλιρράγής, ές, (ἅλς, ῥήγνυμι) *against which the sea breaks*, Anth.

ἁλίρ-ραντος, ον, (ἅλς, ῥαίνω) *sea-surging*, Anth.

ἁλίρ-ρηκτος, ον, = ἁλιρραγής, Anth.

ἁλίρ-ρόθιος, ον and α, ον, (ἅλς, ῥόθος) *dashed over by the sea*, Anth.

ἁλίρ-ροθος, ον, = foreg. ἁλ. πόροι the pathways *of the raging sea*, Aesch.

ἁλίρ-ρυτος, ον, (ἅλς, ῥέω) *washed by the sea*, Anth.

ἅλις [ἄλῐς], Adv. : (ἁλής) :—*in heaps, crowds, swarms, in abundance, in plenty ;* and then, *sufficiently, enough*, Lat. *satis :*   **1.** with Verbs, ἅλις πεποίηται [μέλισσαι] Il.; περὶ δὲ Τρωαὶ ἅλις ἦσαν fly in swarms, Ib.:—also *just enough, in moderation*, like μετρίως, Eur.   **2.** attached to a Noun, χαλκόν τε χρυσόν τε ἅλις gold and silver *enough*, Od.   **3.** ἅλις (sc. ἐστι) *'tis enough*, Il.; ἦ οὐχ ἅλις, ὡς . . ; is it not *enough* that . . ? Hom.   **4.** like an Adj., ἅλις ἡ συμφορά (sc. ἐστι) Eur. :—also, ἅλις (sc. εἰμί) with a part. added, ἅλις νοσοῦσ' ἐγώ *enough* that I suffer, Soph.   **5.** c. gen. rei, *enough* of a thing, ἅλις ἔχειν τινὸς Hdt., Att.

ἁλισγέω, *to pollute* : whence ἁλίσγημα, τό, *a pollution*, N. T. (Deriv. unknown.)

ἁλίσκομαι (Root ΑΛ), a defect. Pass., the Act. being supplied by αἱρέω : impf. ἡλισκόμην :—f. ἁλώσομαι : aor. 2 ἥλων, Att. ἑάλων [ᾰ], subj. ἁλῶ, ῷς, ῷ [ᾰ], Ion. ἁλόω, ἁλώῃ [ᾰ], opt. ἁλοίην, Ep. ἁλῴην ; inf. ἁλῶναι, Ep. ἁλώμεναι ; part. ἁλούς—pf. ἥλωκα, Att. ἑάλωκα, plqpf. ἡλώκειν.   *To be taken, conquered*, of persons and places, Hom., etc.; ἁλίσκεσθαι εἰς πολεμίους *to fall into the hands of* the enemy, Plat.   **2.** *to be caught, seized*, θανάτῳ ἁλῶναι or without θανάτῳ, *to die*, Hom.; ἑάλωσαν εἰς Ἀθήνας γράμματα letters *were seized and taken* to Athens, Xen.   **3.** in good sense, *to be won, achieved, attained*, Soph., etc.   **II.** with part. *to be caught* or *detected* doing a thing, Hdt.; ἐὰν ἁλῷς τοῦτο πράττων Plat.; also with a Subst. or Adj., the part. ὤν being omitted, οὐ γὰρ δὴ φονεὺς ἁλώσομαι Soph., Ar.   **2.** as Att. law-term, *to be convicted and condemned*, Plat., Dem. :—c. gen. criminis, *to be convicted of*, ἁλῶναι ψευδομαρτυριῶν, Lys.

ἁλί-στονος, ον, (ἅλς, στένω) *sea-resounding*, Aesch.

ἁλιστός [ᾰ], ή, όν, (ἁλίζω) *salted, pickled*, Anth.

ἁλί-στρεπτος, ον, (ἅλς, στρέφω) *sea-tost*, Anth.

ἀλῑταίνω (Root ΑΛΙΤ) : aor. 2 ἥλῐτον, subj. ἀλίτω, opt. ἀλίτοιμι, part. ἀλιτών :—Med., Ep. 3 pl. aor. 2 ἀλίτοντο, subj. ἀλίτωμαι, inf. ἀλιτέσθαι : part. ἀλιτήμενος (formed as if from ἀλίτημι, cf. τιθήμενος, Ep. for τιθέμενος) :   **1.** c. acc. pers. *to sin* or *offend against* a god, Hom., Aesch.   **2.** c. acc. rei, *to transgress*, Διὸς ἐφετμάς Il.   **3.** the part. ἀλιτήμενος is used as an Adj., *sinful*, Od.

ἀλιτεῖν, aor. 2 inf. of ἀλιταίνω.

ἀλῐ-τενής, ές, (ἅλς, τείνω) *stretching along the sea, level, flat*, Plut.

ἀλῐ-τέρμων, ον, (ἅλς, τέρμα) *bounded by the sea*, Anth.

ἀλίτημα, ατος, τό, (ἀλιταίνω) *a sin, offence*, Anth.

ἀλιτήμων, ον, = sq., Il.

ἀλιτήριος, ον, (ἀλιταίνω) *sinning* or *offending against*, a god, c. gen., Ar., Thuc.   **2.** absol. *sinful, guilty*, Lys., etc.

ἀλιτηρι-ώδης, ες, (εἶδος) *abominable, accursed*, Plat.

ἀλιτηρός, όν, = ἀλιτήριος : in Soph., κὰξ ἀλιτηροῦ φρενός should prob. be κὰξ ἀλειτηρᾶς or ἐξ ἀλιτρίας.

ἀλιτό-ξενος, ον, *sinning against one's friend*, Pind.

ἀλιτο-φροσύνη, ἡ, (φρήν) *a wicked mind*, Anth.

ἀλιτραίνω, Ep. for ἀλιταίνω, *to sin, offend*, Hes., Anth.

ἀλιτρέω, (ἀλιτρός) = ἀλιταίνω, Aesch. Hence

ἀλιτρία, ἡ, *sinfulness, mischief*, Soph.

ἀλιτρός, όν, syncop. for ἀλιτηρός, *sinful, sinning ;* and as Subst., δαίμοσιν ἀλιτρός *a sinner against the gods*, Hom. : in milder sense, *a knave, rogue*, Od.

ἀλιτροσύνη, ἡ, = ἀλιτρία, Anth., etc.

ἀλι-τρῦτος, ον, (ἅλς, τρύω) *sea-beaten, sea-worn*, γέρων Theocr.; κύμβη Anth.

ἀλί-τῦπος, ον, (ἅλς, τύπτω) *sea-beaten*, ἀλ. βδρη griefs *for sea-tost corpses*, Aesch.   **2.** as Subst. *a seaman, fisherman*, Eur.

ἀλί-τῦρος, ὁ, (ἅλς) *a sort of salt-cheese*, Anth.

ἁλιφθορία, ἡ, *a disaster at sea, shipwreck*, Anth. From

ἁλι-φθόρος, ον, (ἅλς, φθείρω) *destroying on the sea :* as Subst. *a pirate*, Anth.

ἀλκαῖος, α, ον, (ἀλκή) *strong, mighty*, Eur.

ἄλκαρ, τό, (ἀλκή) only in nom. and acc., *a safeguard, defence*, c. dat., Τρώεσσιν ἄλκαρ ἔσεσθαι Il. ; c. gen. ἄλκαρ Ἀχαιῶν *defence* of the Achaeans, Ib.; but, γήραος ἄλκαρ a *defence against* old age, h. Hom.

ἀλκᾶς, Dor. for ἀλκήεις.

ἀλκή, ἡ, (ἄλαλκε) *strength* displayed in action, *prowess, courage, boldness*, ἐπιειμένος ἀλκήν clad in *prowess*, Il.; δύεσθαι ἀλκήν Ib.: in pl. *feats of strength*, Pind.   **II.** *strength to avert danger, a defence, succour*, Hom.; ἀλκή τινος *defence* or *aid against* a thing, Hes., Pind., etc.; ἐς or πρὸς ἀλκήν τρέπεσθαι to turn *and resist*, stand on one's guard, Hdt., etc.; so, ἀλκῆς μεμνῆσθαι Id.   **III.** *battle, fight*, Aesch., Eur. Hence

ἀλκήεις, εσσα, εν, *valiant, warlike*, h. Hom., Anth.

ἀλκί [ῑ], heterocl. dat. of ἀλκή (as if from ἄλξ) *might, strength*, ἀλκὶ πεποιθώς, of wild beasts, Hom.

ἀλκί-μαχος, η, ον, (μάχομαι) *bravely fighting*, Anth.

ἀλκίμος, ον and η, ον, *strong, stout*, of men and weapons, Hom.; ἀλκιμος τὰ πολεμικά Hdt.

ἀλκί-φρων, ον, gen. ονος, (φρήν) *stout-hearted*, Aesch.

ἀλκτήρ, ῆρος, ὁ, (ἄλαλκε) *a protector from* a thing, c. gen., Hom.

ἀλκυονίδες, αἱ, (with or without ἡμέραι) *the* 14 *winter*

days during which the halcyon builds its nest, and the sea is calm, the halcyon days, proverb. of undisturbed tranquillity, Ar.

ἈΛΚΥΩ'Ν, όνος, ἡ, the kingfisher, Lat. alcedo, Hom., etc. (halcyon with h is a wrong form.)

*ἄλκω, = ἀλέξω: v. ἄλαλκε.

ἀλλά, Conjunct., properly neut. pl. of ἄλλος (with changed accent), otherwise, but, stronger than δέ: I. to oppose single clauses, but, Lat. autem, the preceding clause being negat., οὐ μόνον ἅπαξ, ἀλλὰ πολλάκις Plat.; so, οὐχ (or μὴ) ὅτι, οὐχ (or μὴ) ὅπως, are followed by ἀλλά or ἀλλὰ καί . . , not only . . , but . . . 2. after a negative ἀλλά sometimes = ἀλλ' ἤ, except, but, ἔπαισεν οὔτις ἀλλ' ἐγώ Soph. II. to oppose whole sentences, but, yet, Lat. at :—used by Hom., with imperat. or subj., to remonstrate, encourage, persuade, like Lat. tandem, ἀλλ' ἴθι, ἀλλ' ἄγε, ἀλλὰ ἴωμεν, Hom. III. joined with other Particles, ἀλλ' ἄρα, or, ἀλλ' οὖν, but then, however, Hdt., etc. 2. ἀλλὰ γάρ, Lat. enimvero, but really, certainly, Att. 3. ἀλλ' ἤ in questions, Lat. an vero? ergo? Plat.: cf. ἀλλ' ἤ (suo loco).

ἀλλαγή, ἡ, (ἀλλάσσω) a change, Aesch., etc. II. exchange, barter, whether in buying or selling, Plat.

ἄλλαγμα, ατος, τό, (ἀλλάσσω) that which is given or taken in exchange: the price of a thing, Anth.

ἀλλαντοπωλέω, f. ἥσω, to deal in sausages, Ar. From

ἀλλαντο-πώλης, ου, ὁ, (πωλέω) a sausage-dealer, Ar.

ἀλλᾶς, ᾶντος, ὁ, a sausage, Ar. (Deriv. unknown.)

ἀλλάσσω, later Att. -ττω, f. ἀξω: aor. 1 ἤλλαξα: pf. ἤλλᾰχα:—Med., f. ἀλλάξομαι: aor. 1 ἠλλαξάμην:—Pass., f. ἀλλαχθήσομαι, f. 2 ἀλλᾰγήσομαι: aor. 1 ἠλλάχθην, aor. 2 ἠλλάγην [ᾰ]: pf. ἤλλαγμαι: 3 sing. plqpf. ἤλλακτο: (ἄλλος)—to make other than it is, to change, alter, Eur., Plat., etc. II. ἀλλ. τί τινος to give in exchange for, barter one thing for another, Aesch.; τι ἀντί τινος Eur.: so in Med., Thuc. 2. to repay, requite, φόνον φονεῦσιν Eur. 3. to give up, leave, quit, οὐρανίον φῶς Soph. III. to take one thing for another, κάκιον τοὐσθλοῦ Theogn.; ἀλλ. θνητὸν εἶδος to assume mortal form, Eur.:—Med., ἀλλάσσεσθαι τί τινος one thing for another, εὐδαιμονίας Hdt., etc. :—hence, to buy, τι ἀντ' ἀργυρίου Plat. IV. to interchange, alternate, σκῆπτρ' ἀλλάσσων ἔχειν to enjoy power in turn, Eur. :—Pass., ἀρεταὶ ἀλλασσόμεναι in turns, Pind.

ἀλλαχῇ, Adv. (ἄλλος) elsewhere, in another place, ἄλλος ἀλλαχῇ one here, another there, Xen.; ἄλλοτε ἀλλαχῇ now here, now there, Id.

ἀλλᾰχόθεν, Adv. from another place, Antipho.

ἀλλᾰχόθι, Adv. elsewhere, Xen.: — ἀλλᾰχόσε, Adv. elsewhither, to another place, Id.: — ἀλλᾰχοῦ, Adv. elsewhere, Soph., Xen.

ἄλλεγον, ἀλλέξαι, poët. for ἀνέλεγον, ἀναλέξαι, impf. and aor. 1 inf. of ἀναλέγω.

ἄλλῃ, Adv., properly dat. fem. of ἄλλος: I. of Place, 1. in another place, elsewhere, Hom., etc. : —c. gen. loci, ἄλλος ἄλλῃ τῆς πόλεως one in one part of the city, one in another, Thuc. 2. to another place, elsewhither, Hom., etc. II. of Manner, in another way, somehow else, otherwise, Id., etc.; ἄλλῃ γέ πῃ Plat.; ἄλλῃ πως Xen.

ἀλλ' ἤ (for ἄλλο ἤ) other than, except, but, only after

negat. words, οὐδεὶς ἀλλ' ἤ ἐκείνη no one but she, Hdt.; ἀργύριον μὲν οὐκ ἔχω ἀλλ' ἤ μικρόν τι Xen.

ἀλλ-ηγορέω, f. ἥσω, (ἄλλος, ἀγορεύω) to speak so as to imply something other than is said, to interpret allegorically, Plut. :—Pass. to be spoken allegorically, N. T. Hence

ἀλληγορία, ἡ, an allegory, i. e. description of one thing under the image of another, Cic.

ἄλ-ληκτος, ον, poët. for ἄ-ληκτος, (λήγω) unceasing, ceaseless, Od., Soph. II. implacable, Il.

ἀλληλοφᾰγία, ἡ, an eating one another, Hdt. From

ἀλληλο-φάγοι, (φαγεῖν) eating each other, Arist.

ἀλληλοφονία, Dor. ἀλλᾱλ-, ἡ, mutual slaughter, Pind. From

ἀλληλο-φόνοι, Dor. ἀλλᾱλ-, α, murdering one another, Aesch., Xen.

ἀλλήλων, gen. pl., (a nom. being impossible); dat. ἀλλήλοις, αις, οις: acc. ἀλλήλους, ας, α: dual gen. and dat. ἀλλήλοιν, Ep. ἀλλήλοιῐν, redupl. from ἄλλος, of one another, to one another, one another, Hom., etc.

ἄλλην, acc. fem. of ἄλλος, as Adv., ἄλλην καὶ ἄλλην again and again, Plat.

ἄλ-λιστος, ον, Ep. for ἄ-λιστος, (λίσσομαι) inexorable, Anth.

ἀλ-λιτάνευτος, Ep. for ἀ-λιτάνευτος, (λιτανεύω) inexorable, Anth.

ἀλλο-γενής, ές, (γένος) of another race, a stranger, N. T.

ἀλλό-γλωσσος, ον, (γλῶσσα) using a strange tongue, Hdt.

ἀλλο-γνοέω, (γι-γνώσκω) to take one for another, not know, ἀλλογνώσας (Ion. for ἀλλογνοήσας) Hdt.

ἀλλό-γνωτος, ον, mis-known, unknown, Od.

ἀλλο-δᾰπός, ή, όν, (ἄλλος, v. ποδαπός) belonging to another people or land, foreign, strange, Hom., etc.

ἀλλο-ειδής, ές, (εἶδος) or ἀλλο-ῐδής, ές, (ῐδέα) of strange appearance, neut. pl. ἀλλοειδέα (which must be ---), or ἀλλοϊδέα which must be - ∪ ∪ -, Od.

ἄλλοθ', by elision from ἄλλοθι.

ἄλλοθεν, Adv. from another place, ἄλλοθεν ἄλλος one from one place, another from another, Il., etc.; ἄλλοθεν from abroad, Od.; οὐδαμόθεν ἄλλοθεν Ib.

ἄλλοθι, Adv. elsewhere, in another place, in a strange or foreign land, Od.: c. gen., ἄλλοθι γαίης in another or strange land, Ib.; but, ἄλλοθι πάτρης elsewhere than in one's native land, i. e. away from home, Ib. II. in other ways, from other causes, Thuc., Plat.

ἀλλό-θροος, ον, Att. contr. -θρους, ουν, speaking a strange tongue, Od.; generally, foreign, strange, alien, Hdt., Trag.

ἀλλοῖος, α, ον, (ἄλλος) of another sort or kind, different, Hom.; ἀλλοῖόν τι, euphem. for κακόν τι, other than good, Hdt.:—from its comparative force, it may be foll. by ἤ . . , Id., Plat., etc.:—but an actual Comp. ἀλλοιότερος occurs in Hdt., Thuc., etc. II. Adv. -ως, otherwise, Plat.: Comp. -ότερον Xen.

ἀλλοιόω, i. ώσω, (ἀλλοῖος) to make different, to change, alter, Plat., etc. II. Pass. with f. med. -ώσομαι and pass. -ωθήσομαι :—to become different, be changed, Thuc., Xen. 2. to be changed for the worse, Id. Hence

ἀλλοίωσις, εως, ἡ, a change, alteration, Plat., etc.

ἄλλοκα, Aeol. and Dor. for ἄλλοτε.

ἀλλό-κοτος, ον, of unusual nature or form, strange, monstrous, Ar., Plat., etc. ; ἀλλ. πρᾶγμα an unwelcome business, Thuc. : c. gen., ἀλλοκότῳ γνώμᾳ τῶν πάρος with purpose utterly different from . . , Soph. Adv. -τως, Plat. (From ἄλλος, the termin. -κοτος being uncertain.)

ἄλλομαι (Root ΑΛ, Lat. SAL-io): impf. ἡλλόμην : f. ἀλοῦμαι, Dor. ἀλεῦμαι : aor. 1 ἡλάμην, part. ἀλάμενος [1st syll. long]: aor. 2 ἡλόμην, 3 sing. subj. ἅληται [ἅ], Ep. ἅλεται; opt. ἀλοίμην; inf. ἀλέσθαι; part. ἀλόμενος [ἅ] : also Ep. 2 and 3 sing. aor. 2 ἅλσο, ἅλτο, part. ἅλμενος (which have a smooth breathing). To spring, leap, bound, of living beings, Hom., etc. :—metaph. of things, ἅλτο ὀϊστός Il. ; the eye, to throb, Theocr.

ἀλλο-πρόσ-αλλος, ὁ, i. e. ἄλλοτε πρὸς ἄλλον, leaning first to one side, then to the other, of Ares, Il.; πλοῦτος Anth.

ΆΛΛΟΣ, η, ο, Lat. alius, another, one besides, ἄλλος μέν . , ἄλλος δέ . , one . , another . , Il.; ἄλλος τις or τὶς ἄλλος, any other, some other ; οὐδεὶς ἄλλος no other ; εἴ τις ἄλλος, Lat. si quis alius, any one else. 2. repeated, ἄλλος ἄλλο λέγει one man says one thing, one another, i. e. different men say different things ; ἄλλος ἄλλῃ ἐτράπετο Xen. ; λείπουσι τὸν λόφον ἄλλοι ἄλλοθεν Id. ;—v. ἀλλαχῇ. 3. ἄλλος καὶ ἄλλος, one or two ; ἄλλο καὶ ἄλλο one thing after another, Id. 4. joined with the Art., ὁ ἄλλος, the other ; in pl., οἱ ἄλλοι (Ion. ἄλλοι), all the others, the rest ; Lat. ceteri ; τὰ ἄλλα, contr. τἄλλα or τἆλλα, Lat. cetera, reliqua, not alia ;—οἵ τε ἄλλοι καὶ . . both all the others and . . , i. e. especially . . 5. with Numerals, yet, still, πέμπτος ποταμὸς ἄλλος yet a fifth river, Hdt. : with a Sup., ὀϊζυρώτατος ἄλλων most wretched of all besides, Od. II. rarely like ἀλλοῖος, of other sort, different, Il. : hence 2. sometimes just a Comp., c. gen., ἄλλα τῶν δικαίων other than just, Xen. ; followed by ἤ . . , when a negat. goes before, οὐδὲν ἄλλο, ἤ . . , nothing else than . . , Hdt., etc.

ἄλλοσε, Adv. (ἄλλος) to another place, elsewhither, Od.; ἄλλος ἄλλοσε one one way, one another, Aesch.

ἄλλ-οτε, (ἄλλος, ὅτε) at another time, at other times, ἄλλοτε . . , ἄλλοτε . . , at one time . . , at another . . , Hom.; so, ἄλλως ἄλλοτε at one time one way, at another another, Aesch. ; ἄλλοτ' ἄλλῃ, ἄλλοθι, ἄλλοσε, etc.

ἄλλο τι; anything else ? Lat. numquid aliud ? when foll. by ἤ, the sentence is interrog., ἄλλο τι ἢ πεινήσουσι ; i. e. ἄλλο τι πείσονται ἢ πεινήσουσι; will they suffer aught else but hunger ? will they not be starved ? Hdt.; —also without ἤ, ἄλλο τι ἔλεγες ; did you say anything else ? did you not say ? Plat.

ἀλλοτριο-επίσκοπος, ὁ, a busy-body in other men's matters, N. T.

ἀλλοτριο-λογέω, f. ἥσω, (λέγω) to speak of things foreign to the matter, Strab.

ἀλλοτριο-πραγμοσύνη, ἡ, (πρᾶγμα) a meddling with other people's business, Plat.

ἀλλότριος, α, ον, (ἄλλος): I. opp. to ἴδιος, of or belonging to another, Lat. alienus, Hom., etc.; ἀλλ. γυνή another man's wife, Aesch.; γναθμοῖσι γελοίων ἀλλοτρίοισιν, of the suitors, laughed with a face unlike one's own, of a forced, unnatural laugh, Od. (Horace's malis ridere alienis is different); ἀλλ. ὄμμασιν by the help of another's eyes, Soph. ; ἀλλοτριωτάτοις τοῖς σώμασιν χρῆσθαι to deal with one's body as if it absolutely belonged to another, Thuc. II. opp. to οἰκεῖος, foreign, strange, Lat. peregrinus, Hom.; often with the notion of hostile, Il. III. Adv., ἀλλοτρίως ἔχειν or διακεῖσθαι πρός τινα to be unfavourably disposed towards one, Lys. : Comp. -ιώτερον less favourably, Dem. Hence

ἀλλοτριότης, ητος, ἡ, alienation, estrangement, opp. to οἰκειότης, Plat., etc.

ἀλλοτριό-χρως, ωτος, ὁ, ἡ, changing colour, Anth.

ἀλλοτριόω, f. ώσω, (ἀλλότριος) : 1. c. gen. pers. to estrange from, τῶν σωμάτων τὴν πόλιν Thuc. 2. c. dat. pers. to make hostile to another, τὴν χώραν τοῖς πολεμίοις Xen. :— Pass. to be made an enemy, τινι Thuc. 3. in Pass. of things, to be alienated, fall into other hands, Hdt. Hence

ἀλλοτρίωσις, εως, ἡ, estrangement, τῆς ξυμμαχίας οὐχ ὁμοία ἡ ἀλλ. its estrangement, its loss, Thuc.

ἄλλου, Adv. = ἄλλοσε.

ἄλλοφος, ον, Ep. for ἄλοφος.

ἀλλο-φρονέω, f. ήσω, to think of other things, to give no heed, Od.; of one in a swoon, to be senseless, Il., Theocr. : to be seized with frenzy, Hdt. II. to be of another mind, have other views, Id.

ἀλλό-φυλος, ον, (φυλή) of another tribe, foreign, Lat. alienigena, Aesch., Thuc.; πόλεμος ἀλλ. war with foreigners, Plut.

ἀλλό-χροος, ον, contr. -χρους, ουν, (χρόα) changed in colour, Eur. :—so, ἀλλό-χρως, ωτος, ὁ, ἡ, looking strange or foreign, Id.

ἄλλυδις, Adv. (ἄλλος) Ep. for ἄλλοσε, elsewhither, ἄλλυδις ἄλλος one hither, another thither, Hom.; ἄλλυδις ἄλλῃ changes now one way, now another, Il.

ἀλλύεσκε, ἀλλύουσα [ῡ], Ep. for ἀνέλυε, ἀναλύουσα.

ἄλλως, Adv. of ἄλλος, in another way or manner, otherwise, Hom., etc. : in Att., ἄλλως πως in some other way ; ἄλλως οὐδαμῶς in no other wise ; καὶ ἄλλως and besides ; ἀρίστου καὶ ἄλλως φρονιμωτάτου Plat. 2. ἄλλως τε καί . . , both otherwise and so, . . , i. e. especially, Att., etc. II. otherwise, differently, ἄλλως εἶναι to say otherwise, i. e. to deny, Hdt. 2. in far other manner, i. e. better, Hom., etc. 3. otherwise than should be, i. e. without aim or purpose, without reason, Od., Hdt., etc. :—also fruitlessly, in vain, Il.

ἅλμα, ατος, τό, (ἅλλομαι) a spring, leap, bound, Od. ; ἅλμα πέτρας a leap or fall from the rock, Eur. ; κυνῆς ἅλμα the leap of the lot from the helmet, Soph.

ἅλμενος, Ep. aor. 2 part. of ἅλλομαι.

ἅλμη, ἡ, (ἅλς) sea-water, brine, Od., etc. : spray that has dried on the skin, Ib. : a salt incrustation on soil, Hdt. 2. the brine, i. e. the sea, Pind., Aesch.

ἁλμυρός, ά, όν, (ἅλμη) salt, briny, Od. 2. of taste, salt, brackish, Thuc., Xen. 3. metaph. bitter, distasteful, Lat. amarus, Plat., etc.; ἁλμυρὰ κλαίειν to weep bitterly, Theocr.

ἀλοάω, Ep. ἀλοιάω : Ep. 3 sing. impf. ἀλοία : f. -ήσω : aor. 1 ἠλόησα, Ep. ἠλοίησα : (ἀλέω) :—to thresh, thresh out, Plat. 2. to thresh, cudgel, beat, Il., Ar.

ἄ-λοβος, ον, with a lobe wanting, of victims' livers, Xen.

ἀ-λογέω, f. ήσω, (ἄλογος) to pay no regard to a thing,

Lat. *rationem non habere rei,* c. dat., Il. ; c. gen. *to be disregardful of,* Hdt. 2. *to be out of one's senses,* Luc. Hence

ἀλογία, Ion. -ίη, ἡ, *want of respect* or *regard,* ἀλογίην εἶχον τοῦ χρηστηρίου took *no heed of it,* Hdt. ; so, ἐν ἀλογίῃ ἔχειν or ποιεῖσθαί τι Id. 2. in Att. *want of reason, unreasonable conduct, absurdity,* Thuc., Plat.

ἀλογιστία, ἡ, *thoughtlessness, rashness,* Polyb., Plut., etc.

ἀ-λόγιστος, ον, (λογίζομαι) *unreasoning, inconsiderate, thoughtless, heedless,* Thuc., etc. : τὸ ἀλόγιστον *un-reason,* Id. :—Adv. -τως, Id., Plat., etc. II. *not to be reckoned,* Soph. : *not to be taken into account, vile,* Eur.

ἄ-λογος, ον, *without* λόγος, i.e., I. *without speech, speechless, infans,* Plat. :—Adv. ἀλόγως, Soph. 2. *unutterable,* Lat. *infandus,* Plat. II. *without reason, irrational,* Id., etc. : τὰ ἄλογα *brutes, animals,* Id., Xen.; (in modern Greek ἄλογον is *a horse*). III. *not reckoned upon, unexpected,* Thuc.

ἀλοητός, ὁ, (ἀλοάω) *a threshing,* Xen.

ἀλόθεν, Adv. (ἅλς) *from the sea,* ἐξ ἀλόθεν (showing that it is an old genit.) Il.

ἀλοιάω, Ep. for ἀλοάω.

ἀ-λοίδορος, ον, *not reviling* or *railing,* Aesch.

ἀλοιητήρ, ῆρος, ὁ, (ἀλοιάω) *a thresher, grinder,* ἀλ. ὀδόντες the grinders, Anth.

ἀλοιφή, ἡ, (ἀλείφω) *anything used for anointing, hog's-lard, grease, unguent,* Hom. II. *laying on* of unguents or paint, ἀλ. μύρων Plat.

ἀλοκίζω, f. σω, (ἄλοξ) *to trace furrows* in waxen tablets, *to write, draw* (cf. Lat. *ex-arare*), Ar.

ἀλόντε [ᾰ], aor. 2 part. dual of ἁλίσκομαι.

ἄλοξ, οκος, ἡ, = ἄὐλαξ, *a furrow :* v. αὖλαξ.

ἀλός, gen. of ἅλς.

ἄλος, Dor. for ἧλος, *a nail.*

Ἀλο-σύδνη, ἡ, (ἅλς, ὑδνέω (ΣΥΔ) *to nourish) Sea-born,* a name of Amphitrité, Od.

ἀλό-τριψ, ῐβος, ὁ, (ἅλς, τρίβω) *a pestle to pound salt,* Anth.

ἀλ-ουργής, ές, (ἅλς, *ἔργω) *wrought in the sea, sea-purple,* i.e. *genuine purple,* Plat. ; ἀλουργῆ *purple cloths,* Aesch. Hence

ἀλουργίς, ίδος, ἡ, *a purple robe,* Ar. : as Adj., ἐσθὴς ἀλουργίς Luc.

ἀλουργός, όν, = ἀλουργής, Plat.

ἀλουσία, ἡ, *a being unwashen, want of the bath,* Hdt., Eur. From

ἄ-λουτος, ον, (λούομαι) *unwashen, not using the bath,* Hdt., Eur., etc.

ἄ-λοφος, Ep. ἄλ.λοφος, ον, *without crest,* Il.

ἄ-λοχος [ᾰ], ου, ἡ, (ᾰ copul., λέχος, cf. ἀκοίτης) *a bed-fellow, spouse, wife,* Hom., Trag.

ἀλόω, Ep. for ἀλόου, ἀλῶ, imperat. of ἀλάομαι.

ἀλόωνται, Ep. 3 pl. of ἀλάομαι.

ἄλπνιστος, η, ον, Sup. Adj. (cf. ἔπ-αλπνος), *sweetest, loveliest,* Pind.

ἍΛΣ (Α), ἁλός [ᾰ], ὁ; dat. pl. ἅλασιν : Lat. SAL, *a lump of salt,* Hom. : generally, *salt,* oft. in plur., Hom., etc. ; ἁλὸς μέταλλον a *salt*-mine, Hdt., Od., etc.

ἅλς (Β), ἁλός [ᾰ], ἡ, *the sea,* Hom.

ἅλσις, εως, ἡ, (ἅλλομαι) *a leaping,* Arist.

ἅλσο, 2 sing. Ep. aor. 2 of ἅλλομαι.

ἄλσος, εος, τό, *a glade* or *grove,* Lat. *saltus,* Hom. ; *grove,* Od., Hdt., etc. (Deriv. uncertain.)

ἀλσ-ώδης, ες, (εἶδος) *like a grove,* Eur.

ἁλτικός, ή, όν, (ἅλλομαι) *good at leaping,* Xen. ; ἁλτ. ὄρχησις, of the Salii, Plut.

ἅλτο, 3 sing. Ep. aor. 2 of ἅλλομαι.

ἁλῠκίς, ίδος, ἡ, (ἅλς) *a salt spring,* Strab.

ἀλυκτάζω, (ἀλύω) only in impf., *to be in distress,* Hdt.

*ἀλυκτέω, = foreg. ; v. ἀλαλύκτημαι.

ἀλυκτο-πέδαι, αἱ, (ἀλύσσω, πέδη) *galling bonds,* Hes. ; in sing., Anth.

ἄλυξα, Ep. aor. 1 of ἀλύσκω.

ἄλυξις, εως, ἡ, (ἀλύσκω) *an escape,* Aesch.

ἀ-λύπητος, ον, (λυπέω) *not pained* or *grieved,* Soph. II. act. *not causing pain,* Id.

ἄ-λῠπος, ον, (λύπη) *without pain,* Soph., etc. ; c. gen., ἄλ. γήρως *without the pains* of age, Id. ; τὸ ἄλυπον = ἀλυπία, Plat. —Adv., ἀλύπως ζῆν to live *free from pain,* Id. II. act. *not paining, causing no pain,* Id.

ἄ-λῠρος, ον, (λύρα) *without the lyre,* ὕμνοι ἄλυροι, i.e. *wild dirges accompanied by the flute, not the lyre,* (cf. ἀφόρμικτος), Eur., etc.

ἄλυς, υος, ὁ, (ἀλύω) *listlessness, ennui,* Plut.

ἅλῠσις, εως, Ion. dat. ἁλύσι, ἡ, *a chain,* Hdt., Eur. (Deriv. uncertain.)

ἀ-λῠσῐτελής, ές, *unprofitable,* Xen. Adv. -λῶς, Id.

ἀλυσκάζω, = ἀλύσκω, only in pres. and impf., *to shun, shirk, avoid,* Hom.

ἀλυσκάνω, = ἀλύσκω, Od.

ἀλύσκω, f. ἀλύξω, med. ἀλύξομαι : aor. 1 ἤλυξα, Ep. ἄλυξα : (ἀλύω) :—*to flee from, shun, avoid, forsake,* c. acc., Hom., etc. : rarely c. gen. *to flee from,* Soph. :—absol. *to escape,* Hom.

ἀλύσσω, (ἀλύω) *to be uneasy, be in distress,* Il.

ἄ-λῠτος, ον, (λύω) *not to be loosed, indissoluble,* Hom., etc. :—*continuous, ceaseless,* κύκλος Pind.

ἀλύω or ἀλύω, (akin to ἀλάομαι) only in pres. and impf., *to wander in mind :* 1. *from grief, to be ill at ease, be distraught,* Il. : *to be beside oneself,* Hom., Soph. 2. *from perplexity, to be at a loss, not know what to do,* ἀλύει δ' ἐπὶ παντί Id.; ἀλ. λύπᾳ, ἐν πόνοις, Id. 3. *from joy or exultation, to be beside oneself,* Od., Aesch. II. *to wander* or *roam about,* Luc., Babr. [ῠ in Hom., ῡ once in Od. and in Trag.]

ἀλφάνω (Root ΑΛΦ): aor. 2 ἦλφον, opt. ἄλφοιμι :—*to bring in, yield, earn,* Hom. :—metaph., φθόνον ἀλφάνειν *to incur* envy, Eur.

ἀλφεσί-βοιος, α, ον, (ἀλφάνω, βοῦς) *bringing in oxen,* παρθένοι ἀλφεσίβοιαι maidens *whose parents receive many oxen* as presents from their suitors, i.e. *much-courted,* Il.

ἀλφηστής, οῦ, ὁ ; Ep. gen. pl. ἀλφηστάων : (ἀλφάνω) :—*working for one's daily bread, laborious, enterprising,* Od. ; esp. of *trading, seafaring* people, Ib.

ἀλφῑ́, τό, poët. abbrev. form of ἄλφιτον, h. Hom. : so κρῑ for κριθή.

ἀλφῑτ-ἀμοιβός, ὁ, *a dealer in barley-meal,* Ar.

ἄλφιτον, τό, (ἀλφός) *peeled* or *pearl-barley ;* sing. only in phrase ἀλφίτου ἀκτή, *barley*-meal, Lat. *polenta,* Hom. : in pl. ἄλφιτα, *barley-groats, barley-meal,* opp.

τὸ ἄλευρα, Hom., Att.   **II.** metaph. *one's daily bread*, Ar.; πατρῷα ἄλφ. *one's patrimony*, Id.

ἀλφῖτο-ποιΐα, ἡ, (ποιέω) *a making of barley-meal*, Xen.

ἀλφῖτο-σῑτέω, f. ήσω, (σῖτος) *to eat barley-bread*, Xen.

ἄλφοι, 3 sing. aor. 2 opt. of ἀλφάνω.

'ΑΛΦΟ'Σ, ὁ, *whiteness: white leprosy*, Hes., Plat., etc. (From same Root comes Lat. *albus*, and also ἄλφιτον, because of *the whiteness* of meal.)

ἀλωά, Dor. for ἀλωή.

'Αλωάς, άδος, ἡ, (ἀλωή) *goddess of the threshing-floor*, Theocr.

ἀλωεινός, ή, όν, (ἅλως) *of* or *for the threshing-floor*, Anth.

ἀλωή [ᾰ], Dor. ἀλωά, ή, (ἀλέω) Ep. for ἅλως, *a threshing-floor*, ἱερὰς κατ' ἀλωάς Il.; μεγάλην κατ' ἀλωήν, ἐϋκτιμένην κατ' ἀλ. Ib.   **II.** *a garden, orchard, vineyard*, v. γουνός.

ἀλώῃ, 3 sing. aor. 2 subj. of ἁλίσκομαι.   **II.** but ἀλώῃ, optat.

'Αλωΐς, ίδος, ἡ, = 'Αλωάς, Theocr.

ἀλωΐτης [ῑ], ου, ὁ, *a thresher, husbandman*, Anth.

ἀλῶναι, Ep. ἀλώμεναι, aor. 2 inf. of ἁλίσκομαι.

ἄλων, ωνος, ἡ, = ἅλως, found in the obl. cases, Arist.

ἀλωπέκειος, α, ον, Ion. -εος, η, ον, (ἀλώπηξ) *of a fox:* — ἀλωπεκέη, Att. -κῆ (sub. δορά), *a fox-skin*, Hdt., Plut.

ἀλωπεκίας, ὁ, (ἀλωπήξ) *branded with a fox*, Luc.

ἀλωπεκιδεύς, έως, ὁ, (ἀλωπήξ) *a young fox*, Ar.

ἀλωπεκίζω, f. σω, (ἀλωπήξ) *to play the fox*, Ar.

ἀλωπέκιον, τό, Dim. of ἀλώπηξ, *a little fox*, Ar.

ἀλωπεκίς, ίδος, ἡ, = κυναλώπηξ, Xen.   **II.** *a fox-skin cap*, Id.

ἀλώπηξ [ᾰ], εκος, ἡ; dat. pl. ἀλωπήκεσσι, *a fox*, Solon, Hdt., etc. (Deriv. uncertain.)

ἅλως [ᾰ], ἡ, gen. ἅλω and ἅλωος; dat. ἅλῳ; acc. ἅλω, ἅλων, ἅλωα:—pl., nom. and acc. ἅλως: (ἀλέω) :—like Ep. ἀλωή, *a threshing-floor*, Xen., etc.:—then, from its round shape,   **II.** *the disk* of the sun or moon, or of a shield, Aesch., etc.

ἁλώσιμος, ον, (ἁλίσκομαι, ἁλῶναι) *easy to take, win*, or *conquer*, Hdt., Thuc., etc.   **2.** of the mind, *easy to apprehend*, Soph.   **II.** (ἅλωσις) *of* or *for capture*, παιὰν ἁλ. a song of triumph *on taking a city*, Aesch.; βάξις ἁλ. tidings *of the capture*, Id.

ἅλωσις, εως, Ion. ιος, ἡ, (ἁλίσκομαι, ἁλῶναι) *a taking, capture, conquest, destruction*, Pind., Aesch., etc.; δαΐων ἁλ. *conquest* by the enemy, Id.: *means of conquest*, Soph.: ἁλῶναι ἰσχυρὰν ἅλωσιν *to be taken without power to escape*, Plut.   **II.** as law-term, *conviction*, Plat.

ἁλωτός, ή, όν, verb. Adj. of ἁλίσκομαι, *to be taken* or *conquered*, Thuc.   **II.** *attainable*, Soph.

ἀ-λώφητος, ον, (λωφάω) *unremitting*, Plut.

ἀλώω, Ep. for ἁλῶ, aor. 2 subj. of ἁλίσκομαι.

ἄμ, poët. for ἀνά, before a word beginning with the labials β, π, φ, μ, e.g. ἀμ βωμοῖσι, ἀμ μέσον, ἀμ πεδίον, ἀμ φυτά.

'ΑΜΑ͞ [ᾰμ], Adv., *at once, at the same time*, Hom., etc.   **II.** Prep. c. dat. *at the same time with, together with*, ἀμ' ἠοῖ at dawn, Il.; ἅμα ἕῳ, ἅμα ἕῳ γιγνομένῃ Thuc. (Cf. ὁμ-οῦ, Lat. *sim-ul*.)

ἀμᾶ or ἀμᾷ, Dor. for ἅμα.

'Αμαζών, όνος, ἡ, mostly in pl. 'Αμαζόνες, αἱ, *the Amazons*, a warlike race of women in Scythia, Il., Hdt., etc.

(Commonly derived from α priv., μαζός, from the fable that they got rid of the right breast, that it might not interfere with the use of the bow.)

'Αμαζονικός, ή, όν, *of* or *like the Amazons*, Plut.

ἀμαθαίνω, *to be untaught, stupid*, Plat. From

ἀ-μαθής, ές, (μανθάνω) *unlearned, ignorant, stupid, boorish* (v. ἀμαθία), Hdt., etc.; ἀμαθὴς τὴν ἐκείνων ἀμαθίαν *stupid with their stupidity*, Plat.; ἀμαθέστερον τῶν νόμων ὑπεροψίας παιδεύεσθαι *to be educated with too little learning to despise the laws*, Thuc. :—Adv., ἀμαθῶς ἁμαρτεῖν *to err through ignorance*, Eur.   **2.** c. gen. rei, *without knowledge* of a thing, Id.; περί τινος, πρός τι Plat.   **II.** *not heard of, unknown*, ἀμ. ἔρρει Eur. :—Adv., ἀμαθῶς χωρεῖν of events, to take *an unforeseen course*, Thuc.

ἀμαθία, ἡ, (ἀμαθής) *ignorance*, Soph., etc.; ἀμ. τινός *ignorant of* a thing, Xen.; περί τι Id.

ἄμαθος [ᾰμ], ἡ, *sandy soil*, opp. to sea-sand (ψάμαθος), Il.; in pl. *the links* or *dunes* by the sea, h. Hom.: cf. ἄμμος.

ἀμαθύνω [ῡ], (ἄμαθος) only in pres. and impf. *to level with the sand, utterly destroy*, Il., Aesch.   **2.** *to spread smooth, level*, κόνιν h. Hom.

ἀμαιμάκετος, η, ον and ος, ον, Ep. form of ἄμαχος, *irresistible*, Hom., Soph.   **2.** *strong, stubborn*, of a mast, Od.

ἀμαλδύνω [ῡ], (ἀμαλός) *to soften:* then *to destroy, efface*, Il.: *to use up, squander*, χρήματα Theocr. :— Pass., ὥς κεν τεῖχος ἀμαλδύνηται Il.; ἀμαλδυνθήσομαι Ar.   **2.** metaph. *to conceal, disguise*, h. Hom.

ἀ-μάλθακτος, ον, (μαλθάσσω) = ἀμάλακτος, Anth.

ἄμαλλα [ᾰμ], ἡ, (ἀμάω) *cut corn, a sheaf*, Soph., Plut.

ἀμαλλο-δετήρ, ῆρος, ὁ, (δέω A) *a binder of sheaves*, Il.

ἀμαλλο-δέτης, ου, ὁ, = foreg., Theocr.

ἀμαλός [ᾰμ], ή, όν, *soft, weak, feeble*, Hom., Eur. (From Root ΜΑΛ, μαλ-ακός, with α euphon.)

ἀμάμαξυς [ᾰμᾰ], ἡ, gen. vos or ύδος, *a vine trained on two poles*, Sappho, etc. (Deriv. unknown.)

ἄμ-αξα [ᾰ], Att. ἅμ-αξα, ἡ, (ἅμα, ἄγω) *a wagon, wain*, opp. to the war-chariot (ἅρμα), Lat. *plaustrum*, Hom.   **2.** c. gen. *a wagon-load of*, πετρῶν, σίτου Xen.   **II.** *the carriage of the plough*, Lat. *currus*, Hes. :—*Charles' wain* in the heavens, *the Great Bear* (ἄρκτος), Hom.   **III.** = ἀμαξιτός, Anth.

ἁμαξεύς, έως, ὁ, (ἅμαξα) *for a wagon:* βοῦς ἁ. *a draught-ox*, Plut.

ἁμαξεύω, f. σω, *to traverse with a wagon:* Pass. *to be traversed by wagon-roads*, of a country, Hdt.   **2.** metaph., ἁμαξεύειν βίοτον *to drag on a weary life*, Anth.   **II.** intr. *to be a wagoner*, Plut., Anth.

ἁμαξ-ήρης, ες, (v. -ήρης) *of* or *on a carriage*, Aesch.; ἁμ. τρίβος *a high-road*, Eur.

ἁμαξιαῖος, α, ον, (ἅμαξα) *large enough to load a wagon*, λίθος Xen., etc.

ἁμαξίς, ίδος, ἡ, Dim. of ἅμαξα, *a little wagon*, Lat. *plostellum*, Hdt., Ar.

ἁμαξίτης [ῑ], ου, ὁ, (ἅμαξα) *of* or *for a wagon*, Anth.

ἁμάξ-ῑτος, ον, Ep. and Lyr. ἀμ-, (ἅμαξα, εἶμι ibo) *traversed by wagons*, ἀμ. ὁδός *a carriage-road, high-road*, Pind., Xen.; and without ὁδός, as Subst., Il.

ἁμάξ-οικος, ον, *dwelling in a wagon*, Strab.

ἀμαξο-πηγός, ὁ, (πήγνυμι) a cartwright, Plut.
ἀμαξο-πληθής, ές, (πλῆθος) large enough to fill a wagon, like ἀμαξιαῖος, Eur.
ἀμαξ-ουργός, όν, (ἄμαξα, *ἔργω) = ἀμαξοπηγός, ἐξ ἀμαξουργοῦ λέγειν to talk cartwrights' slang, Ar.
ἄμαρ, Dor. for ἦμαρ.
ἀμάρα [ἄμᾱ], Ion. ἀμάρη, ἡ, a trench, conduit, channel, for watering meadows, Il., Theocr. (Deriv. unknown.)
ἀμάρᾰκον [ἄμᾱ], τό, and ἀμάρᾰκος, ὁ, Lat. amāracum, amāracus, Anth.
ἀμᾰράντινος, η, ον, of amaranth :—metaph. unfading, imperishable, N. T. From
ἀ-μάραντος [ἀμᾰ-], ον, (μαραίνω) unfading, undecaying, N. T. II. as Subst. amaranth, an unfading flower, Diosc.
ἁμαρτάνω. Root ΑΜΑΡΤ, f. ἁμαρτήσομαι : aor. 2 ἥμαρτον, Ep. ἥμβροτον : pf. ἡμάρτηκα :—Pass., aor. 1 ἡμαρτήθην : pf. ἡμάρτημαι : 3 sing. plqpf. ἡμάρτητο. To miss, miss the mark, c. gen., ἑκὼν ἡμάρτανε φωτός he missed the man on purpose, Il. ; ἁμ. τῆς ὁδοῦ to miss the road, Ar. ; τοῦ σκοποῦ Antipho. 2. generally, to fail of doing, fail of one's purpose, to miss one's point, fail, go wrong, Od., etc. ; c. gen., νοήματος ἥμβροτεν failed in hitting upon the thought, Ib., etc. ; ἁμ. τοῦ χρησμοῦ to mistake it, Hdt. 3. to fail of having, i. e. to be deprived of, lose, c. gen., ἁμαρτήσεσθαι ὀπωπῆς that I should lose my sight, Od. ; ἁμ. πιστῆς ἀλόχου Eur. II. to fail, do wrong, err, sin, Hom., etc.; c. dat. modi, γνώμῃ ἁμ. to err in judgment, Hdt. ; or ἐν λόγοις Id., Plat. ; with a neut. Adj., τόδε γ᾽ ἥμβροτον I erred in this, Od. ; in Prose, ἁμ. περί τι or τινος to do wrong in a matter, Plat., etc. 2. Pass., ἁμαρτάνεταί τι a sin is committed, Thuc. :—impers., ἁμαρτάνεται περί τι Plat.
ἁμαρτάς, άδος, ἡ, Ion. for ἁμαρτία, Hdt., etc.
ἁμαρτεῖν, aor. 2 inf. of ἁμαρτάνω.
ἁμ-αρτῆ or -ῇ, (ἅμα, ἀρ-αρίσκω) [ᾰμ], Adv. together, at once, Hom.
ἁμάρτημα, ατος, τό, (ἁμαρτάνω) a failure, fault, sin, Soph., Plat. 2. a bodily defect, malady, Id.
ἁμαρτητικός, ή, όν, (ἁμαρτάνω) prone to error, Arist.
ἁμαρτία, ἡ, (ἁμαρτάνω) a failure, fault, sin, Aesch., etc. ; ἁμ. τινός a fault committed by one, Id. ; ἁμ. δόξης fault of judgment, Thuc. 2. generally, guilt, sin, Plat., Arist., N. T.
ἁμαρτί-νοος, ον, (ἁμαρτάνω) erring in mind, distraught, Hes., etc.
ἁμάρτιον, τό, (ἁμάρτημα, Aesch.
ἁμαρτο-επής, ές, (ἁμαρτάνω, ἔπος) erring in words, speaking at random, Il.
ἀ-μαρτύρητος, ον, (μαρτυρέω) needing no witness, Eur.
ἀ-μάρτυρος, ον, (μάρτυς) without witness, unattested, Thuc., etc. :—Adv. -ρως, Dem.
ἁμαρτωλή, ἡ, poët. for ἁμαρτία, Theogn., etc.
ἁμαρτωλός, όν, sinful :—as Subst. a sinner, N. T.
ἀμαρυγή [Att. ὓ, Ep. ῦ], ἡ, = μαρμαρυγή, a sparkling, glancing, of the eye, h. Hom. ; of horses' feet, Ar. ; and ἀμάρυγμα, ατος, τό, a sparkle, twinkle, changing colour and light, Anth. ; quivering, of the lip, Theocr. From
ἀμᾰρύσσω (Root ΑΜΑΡΥΓ), only in pres. and impf., like μαρμαίρω, to sparkle, glance, of the eye, Hes. :—Med. of light, colour, Anth.

ἅμα-τροχάω, (τρέχω) to run together, in Ep. part. ἁματροχόων, Od.
ἅμα-τροχιά, ἡ, (τροχός) a jostling or clashing of wheels, ἁματροχιὰς ἀλεείνων Il.
ἀμαυρό-βιος, ον, living in darkness, Ar.
ἀμαυρός [ἄμ], ά, όν, 1. dimly seen, dim, faint, baffling sight, εἴδωλον ἀμ. a shadowy spectre, Od. 2. having no light, darksome, νύξ Luc. :—blind, sightless, Soph. ; so, ἀμαυρῷ κώλῳ with blind foot, said of a blind man, Id. II. metaph., 1. dim, obscure, uncertain, κληδών Aesch. ; ἐλπίς Plut. 2. obscure, unknown, Hes., Soph., Eur. 3. gloomy, troubled, φρήν Aesch. III. act. enfeebling, νοῦσος Anth. (Deriv. uncertain ; cf. ἀμυδρός.) Hence
ἀμαυρόω [ᾰμ], f. -ώσω : aor. 1 ἡμαύρωσα :—Pass., pf. ἡμαύρωμαι ; Ion. aor. 1 ἀμαυρώθην : (ἀμαυρός) :—to make dim, faint, or obscure, Xen. ; metaph. to impair, Eur., etc. :—Pass. to become dim, suffer eclipse, of the sun, Hdt. ; to disappear, Hes. Hence
ἀμαύρωσις, ατος, τό, (ἀμαυρόομαι) obscuration, Plut.
ἀμαχανία, ἀμάχανος, Dor. for ἀμηχ-.
ἀ-μαχεί or -ί, Adv. of ἄμαχος, without resistance, Thuc.
ἀ-μάχετος, ον, poët. for ἀμάχητος, Aesch.
ἀμαχητί, Adv. of sq., without battle, Il., Hdt.
ἀ-μάχητος, ον, (μάχομαι) not to be fought with, unconquerable, Soph. II. not having fought, not having been in battle, Xen.
ἀμαχί, v. ἀμαχεί.
ἀ-μᾰχος, ον, (μάχη) without battle : I. of a person, with whom no one fights, unconquered, unconquerable, invincible, Hdt., etc. ; of places, impregnable, Id. ; of things, irresistible, Pind., Aesch. II. act. not having fought, taking no part in the battle, Xen. 2. disinclined to fight, peaceful, Aesch. : not contentious, N. T.
ἀμάω [ᾰ- in Hom., ᾰ in later Poets] : impf. ἤμων : f. ἀμήσω : aor. 1 ἤμησα, Ep. ἄμησα :—Med., f. ἀμήσομαι : Ep. aor. 1 ἀμήσατο :—Pass., pf. ἤμημαι. To reap corn, absol., Il., Hes. ; metaph., ἤμησαν καλῶς they reaped abundantly, Aesch. :—so c. acc. to reap, λήϊον Od. ; σῖτον Hdt. 2. generally, to cut reeds, etc., Il., Theocr. II. in Med. to gather together, collect, as reapers gather in corn, ἀμησάμενοι [γάλα] having collected milk :—so in Act., ἀμήσας κόνιν, having scraped together earth over a corpse, Anth. (From Root ΜΑ with a euphon., cf. Lat. MET-O, to mow.)
ἀμβαίην, poët. for ἀναβαίην, aor. 2 opt. of ἀναβαίνω.
ἄμβασε, Dor. for ἀνέβησε, 3 sing. aor. 1 of ἀναβαίνω.
ἄμβᾱσις, ἀμβάτης [ᾰ], ἄμβᾱτος, poët. for ἀνάβασις, ἀναβάτης, ἀνάβατος.
ἀμ-βλήδην, Adv., poët. for ἀναβλήδην, (ἀναβάλλομαι) with sudden bursts, ἀμβλ. γοόωσα Il.
ἀμβλίσκω and ἀμβλόω : f. ἀμβλώσω : aor. 1 ἤμβλωσα : pf. ἤμβλωκα : (ἀμβλύς) :—to cause to miscarry, Soph., Plat. 2. of the woman, to miscarry, Plut.
ἀμβλύνω [ῡ], f. ῠνῶ : aor. 1 ἤμβλῠνα :—Pass., f. -υνθήσομαι : aor. 1 ἠμβλύνθην :—to blunt, take the edge off a sharp instrument, and metaph. to make dull, ὄμματος αὐγήν Anth. :—Pass. to become dull, lose its edge or force, Aesch., Thuc. From
ΆΜΒΛΎΣ, εῖα, ύ, blunt, dulled, with the edge taken off,

of a sharp instrument, Plat., etc. :—metaph. *dull, dim,* of sight, ἀμβλὺ ὁρᾶν, βλέπειν Id.; of the feelings, ἀμβλυτέρᾳ τῇ ὀργῇ with anger *less keen,* Thuc.; ἀμβλύτερον ποιεῖν τι *less vigorous,* Id. **2.** in Aesch. Eum. of Orestes, *having lost the edge* of guilt: but of persons, generally, *dull, spiritless, having lost the keenness of one's feelings,* Thuc. **II.** act. *darkening,* of a cloud, Anth. Hence

ἀμβλύτης, ητος, ἡ, *bluntness:* metaph. *dullness,* Plut.

ἀμβλυ-ωπέω, f. ήσω, (ὤψ) *to be dim-sighted,* Xen.

ἀμβλυωπία, ἡ, *dim-sightedness,* Plat.

ἀμβλυώσσω, Att. -ττω, only in pres., (ἀμβλύς) *to be dim-sighted,* Plat., etc.; ἀμβλ. πρὸς τὸ φῶς *to be blind* to it, Luc.

ἀμβλ-ωπός, όν, (ἀμβλύς, ὤψ) *bedimmed, dark,* Aesch.

ἀμβλ-ώψ, ῶπος, ὁ, ἡ, = ἀμβλωπός, Eur.

ἀμ-βόαμα, ἀμ-βοάω, poët. for ἀνα-βόαμα, ἀνα-βοάω.

ἀμ-βολά, ἡ, poët. for ἀναβολή.

ἀμβολάδην [ᾰδ], Adv., poët. for ἀναβολάδην, (ἀναβολή) *bubbling up,* Il.: metaph. *by jets, capriciously,* Anth. **II.** *like a prelude,* h. Hom., Pind.

ἀμβολάς, άδος, ἡ, for ἀναβολάς, *thrown up,* of earth, Xen.

ἀμβολι-εργός, όν, poët. for ἀναβολ- (ἀναβάλλω II, ἔργον) *putting off a work, dilatory,* Hes., Plut.

ἀμβροσία, Ion. -ίη, ἡ, (ἄμβροτος) *ambrosia* (i.e. *immortality*) the food of the gods, Hom., etc.

ἀμβρόσιος, a, ον and ος, ον, lengthd. form of ἄμβροτος, *immortal,* h. Hom.:—in Hom. night and sleep are called *ambrosial, divine,* as gifts of the gods; so of everything belonging to the gods, as their hair, robes, sandals, the fodder and the mangers of their horses.

ἀμβροτό-πωλος, ον, *with coursers of immortal strain,* Eur.

ἄ-μβροτος, ον and η, ον: (α priv., βροτός with μ inserted): —like lengthd. form ἀμβρόσιος, *immortal, divine* from Hom., Aesch. **2.** νὺξ ἄμβροτος, like ἀμβροσίη νύξ, Od.;— then of all things belonging to the gods, Hom.

ἀμβώσας, Ion. for ἀναβοήσας, aor. 1 part. of ἀναβοάω.

ἀμέ or ἄμμε, Dor. for ἡμᾶς.

ἀ-μέγαρτος, ον, (μεγαίρω) *unenviable:* **1.** *melancholy, direful,* Hom., Eur. **2.** of persons, *unhappy, miserable,* Od.

ἀ-μεθύστινος, η, ον, of *amethyst,* Luc. From

ἀ-μέθυστος, ον, (μεθύω) *not drunken,* Plut. **II.** as Subst., ἀμέθυστος, ἡ, *amethyst,* the precious stone, supposed to be *a remedy against drunkenness,* N. T.

ἀμείβοντες, οἱ, v. ἀμείβω A. II.

ἀμείβω [ᾰ]: Ep. impf. ἀμείβον: f. -ψω: aor. 1 ἤμειψα. (From Root ΜΕΙΒ or ΜΕΥ with α prefixed, cf. ἀμένομαι, Lat. MOV-eo.)

A. Act. *to change, exchange,* ἔντε' ἄμειβεν Il.; ἀμ. τί τινος, as γόνυ γουνὸς ἀμείβων *changing* one knee for the other, i.e. walking slowly, Il.:—and so, either **1.** *to give in exchange,* τεύχε' ἄμειβε χρύσεα χαλκείων *exchanged* golden armour *for* brasen, Ib.; or **2.** *to take in exchange,* πόσιν ἀντὶ σᾶς ἀμείψαι ψυχᾶς *to redeem* him at the price of thine own life, Eur. **3.** of place, *to change it,* and so *to pass, cross,* Aesch., Eur.: —then, either *to pass out of* a place, *leave* it, or *to pass into, enter* it, Hdt., Att. **4.** simply, *to change, alter,* χρῶτα one's colour, Aesch. **5.** Causal, *to make* others *change,* τεύχε' ἄμειβον Il.: *to pass on, hand on from*

one to another, Eur. **6.** like Med. 1. 3, *to repay, return,* ἀμ. χάριν Aesch. **II.** intr. in part., ἀμείβοντες, οἱ, *interchangers,* i. e. *the rafters that meet and cross each other,* Il.; ἐν ἀμείβοντι = ἀμοιβάδις, Pind. **2.** ἀμείβει καινὸν ἐκ καινῶν one new thing *comes on* after others, Eur.

B. Med. *to change one with another,* ἀμειβόμενοι *by turns, alternately,* Hom.: *to come in turn,* Eur. **2.** often of dialogue, *to answer one another,* Od.; often in part. ἀμειβόμενος, *answering, in answer,* Hom.; c. acc., ἀμ. τινα μύθῳ, μύθοις, ἐπέεσσι Id.; even, ταῦτα τοὺς φίλους ἠμείψατο Hdt. **3.** *to repay, requite,* δώροισιν ἀμ. τινα Od.; χρηστοῖσι Hdt.; also c. acc. et dat. rei, ἀμ. εὐεργεσίας χάρισιν Xen. **II.** *to get in exchange,* λῴους φρένας τῶν νῦν παρουσῶν Soph. **2.** like Act. *to change* a place, *to pass* either *out of* or *into,* Hom., etc.

ἀ-μείλικτος, ον, (μειλίσσω) *unsoftened, cruel,* Hom., Hes.

ἀ-μείλιχος, ον, (μειλίσσω) *implacable, relentless,* Il. **II.** of things, *unmitigated,* Aesch.

ἀμείνων, ον, gen. ονος, irreg. Comp. of ἀγαθός, *better, abler, stronger, braver,* Hom., etc.; v. ἀγαθός. **II.** of things, *better, fitter,* Id. **2.** ἀμεινόν [ἐστι] *'tis better,* c. inf., ἐπεὶ πείθεσθαι ἄμεινον Il., etc.; with negat., οὐ γὰρ ἄμεινον *'twere better* not, Hdt. **3.** τὰ ἀμείνω φρονέειν *to choose the better part,* Id.

ἀμείρω = ἀμέρδω, *to bereave of* a thing, c. gen., Pind.

ἄμειψις, εως, ἡ, (ἀμείβω) *exchange, interchange,* Plut. **2.** *change, succession,* Id.

ἀμέλγω [ᾰ], f. ξω, *to milk* sheep and goats; βόας Theocr.: —Med., in metaph. sense, ἀμέλγεσθαι τοὺς ξένους *to milk* them *dry,* Ar. **II.** *to draw* milk from the animals, ἀμ. γάλα Hdt.; Pass., ὄϊες ἀμελγόμεναι γάλα *having* milk *drawn from them, milch-ewes,* Il. **2.** metaph. *to squeeze out like milk, to press out,* ἐκ βοτρύων ξανθὸν ἀμέλξε γάνος Anth. **III.** *to drink,* Theocr. (From Root ΜΕΛΓ, with α prefixed, comes also ἀ-μολγεύς; cf. Lat. *MULG-eo.*)

ἀμέλει, imperat. of ἀμελέω, *never mind,* Ar., Xen.; aor. 1 ἀμέλησον Luc. **II.** as Adv. *by all means, of course,* Ar., Plat., etc.

ἀμέλεια, ἡ, (ἀμελής) *indifference, negligence,* Thuc., etc.; τινος *towards* a person, περί τινος *about* a thing, Plat.

ἀμελητία, ἡ, *want of practice,* Plat. From

ἀ-μελέτητος, ον, (μελετάω) *unpractised,* Plat., etc.

ἀμελέω [ᾰ], f. ήσω: aor. 1 ἠμέλησα, Ep. ἀμ-: pf. ἠμέληκα (ἀμελής):—*to have no care for, be neglectful of,* c. gen., Hom., Hdt., etc. **2.** absol. *to be careless, heedless, negligent,* Hes., etc.; τὸ μἀμελεῖν (crasis for μὴ ἀμελεῖν) *carefulness,* Aesch. **3.** c. acc. et part. *to overlook,* and so *to let, allow, suffer,* παῖδας θνήσκοντας ἀμελεῖ he lets them die, Eur.:—Xen. has gen. in same sense. **4.** c. inf. *to neglect* to do, Hdt., Plat. **II.** Pass. *to be slighted, overlooked,* Soph., etc.; οἱ ἠμελημένοι ἄνθρωποι Thuc.:—Adv. ἠμελημένως, *carelessly,* Xen.

ἀμελής [ᾰ], ές, (α priv., μέλει) *careless, heedless, negligent,* Ar., Xen., etc.:—Adv. -λῶς, *carelessly,* Thuc.; Comp. -έστερον, Id. **2.** c. gen. *careless of* a thing, Plat., etc.; περί τινα Isocr.:—Adv. ἀμελῶς ἔχειν *to be careless, πρός* τι or *περί* τινα Xen. **II.** pass. *uncared for, unheeded,* Id.

ἀμελητέον, verb. Adj. of ἀμελέω, one must neglect, τινός Isocr.   II. ἀμελητέος, α, ον, to be neglected, Luc.

ἀμέλητος, ον, (ἀμελέω) not to be cared for, Theogn.

ἀμελία, ἡ, poët. for ἀμέλεια, Eur.

ἀ-μέλλητος, ον, (μέλλω) not to be put off, Luc.

ἄ-μεμπτος, ον, (μέμφομαι) not to be blamed, blameless, Eur., Dem.; ἄμεμπτος χρόνου in regard of time, Aesch.   2. of things, perfect in its kind, Xen.; ἄμ. ἐκείνῃ without blame to her, Plut.: Comp. ἀμεμπτότερος, less blameworthy, Id.:—Adv. -τως, so as to merit no blame, right well, Soph., Xen.   II. act. not blaming, content, ἄμεμπτόν τινα ποιεῖσθαι Xen.:—so Adv., ἀμέμπτως δέχεσθαί τινα without censure, Id.

ἀ-μεμφής, ές, = ἄμεμπτος I, Aesch.   II. act., = ἄμεμπτος II, Plut.   Hence

ἀμεμφία, ἡ, freedom from blame, Aesch., Soph.

ἄμεναι [ᾰ], Ep. for ἄειν, pres. inf. of ἄω, to satisfy.

ἀ-μενηνός [ᾰ], όν, (μένος) powerless, fleeting, feeble, of ghosts, Od., etc.; of dreams, Ib.; of one wounded, Il.   2. of mortal men generally, h. Hom., Ar.   Hence

ἀμενηνόω, f. ώσω, to deaden the force of a thing, Il.

ἀμενής, ές, = ἀμενηνός, Eur.

ἀμέρα, Dor. for ἡμέρα.

ἀμέργω [ᾰ], f. ξω, to pluck or pull, Lat. decerpo, Sappho, Eur.:—Med. to pluck for oneself, Theocr.

ἀμέρδω [ᾰ], f. σω: aor. 1 ἤμερσα, Ep. ἄμερσα:—Med., aor. 1 part. ἀμερσάμενος:—Pass., aor. 1 ἠμέρθην: (α euphon., μείρομαι):—to deprive of, bereave of, a thing, c. gen., Hes., Od.:—Pass. to be bereft of a thing, αἰῶνος, δαιτός Hom.   2. c. acc. pers. only, to bereave of his rights, to rob, Il.; ὄσσε δ' ἄμερδεν αὐγή the glare bereft the eyes of power, blinded them, Ib.; ἔντεα καπνὸς ἀμέρδει the smoke robs the arms of lustre, tarnishes them, Od.

ἀ-μερής, ές, (μέρος) without parts, indivisible, Plat.

ἀ-μέριμνος, ον, (μέριμνα) free from care, unconcerned, Anth.   II. pass. uncared for, unheeded, Soph.   III. driving away care, Anth.

ἀμέριος, Dor. for ἡμέριος.

ἀμερό-κοιτος, Dor. for ἡμερόκοιτος.

ἄμερσα, Ep. for ἤμερσα, aor. 1 of ἀμέρδω.

ἀμές or ἁμές, Dor. for ἡμεῖς.

ἀ-μετακίνητος, ον, immovable: Adv. -τως, Arist.

ἀ-μεταμέλητος, ον, (μεταμέλομαι) not to be repented of, Plat.   II. of persons, unrepentant, Arist.

ἀ-μετανόητος, ον, not to be repented of, Luc.   II. act. unrepentant, N. T.

ἀ-μετάστατος, ον, (μεθίστημι) not to be transposed, unchangeable, unchanging, Plat.   2. not to be got rid of or put away, Id.

ἀ-μετάστρεπτος, ον, (μεταστρέφομαι) without turning about:—Adv. ἀμεταστρεπτί [ῑ] or -εί, without turning, straight forward, ἰέναι, φεύγειν Plat.

ἀ-μετάστροφος, ον, (μεταστρέφω) unalterable, Plat.

ἀ-μετάτρεπτος, ον, = foreg., Plut.

ἀμέτερος, Dor. for ἡμέτερος.

ἀ-μέτοχος, ον, (μετέχω) having no share of a thing, c. gen., Thuc.

ἀ-μέτρητος, ον and η, ον, unmeasured, immeasurable, immense, Od., etc.   2. unnumbered, countless, Eur.

ἀμετρία, ἡ, (ἄμετρος) excess, disproportion, Plat., etc.

ἀμετρό-βιος, ον, of immensely long life, Anth.

ἀμετρο-επής, ές, (ἔπος) unmeasured in words, Il.

ἀμετρο-πότης, ον, ὁ, (πίνω) drinking to excess, Anth.

ἄ-μετρος, ον, (μέτρον) without measure, immense, excessive, boundless, Plat.:—Adv. -τρως, Id.; neut. pl. ἄμετρα as Adv., Babr.   2. immoderate, in moral sense, Plat.:—Adv. -τρως, Xen., etc.

ἀμεύομαι, Aeol. for ἀμείβομαι, to conquer, Pind.

ἀμευσί-πορος, ον, with interchanging paths, Pind.

ἌΜΗ, ἡ, a shovel or mattock, Ar., Xen.

ἀμῆ, Adv. (for ἀμῇ, dat. fem. of ἀμός = τὶς), in a certain way : ἀμη-γέ-πη or -ῃ, in some way or other, Plat.

ἀμήν, Hebr. Adv. verily, of a truth, so be it, N. T.:— τὸ ἀμήν, certainly, Ib.

ἀ-μήνῑτος, ον, (μηνίω) not angry or wrathful, Hdt.; χειμὼν οὐκ ἀμήνιτος θεοῖς sent not but by the special wrath of heaven, Aesch.:—Adv. -τως, Id.

ἄμης, ητος, ὁ, a kind of milk-cake, Ar.

ἄμησα, Ep. for ἤμησα, aor. 1 of ἀμάω.

ἀμητήρ [ᾰ], ῆρος, ὁ, (ἀμάω) a reaper, Il.

ἄμητος or ἀμητός [ᾰ], ὁ, (ἀμάω) a reaping, harvesting, Il. (metaph. of slaughter).   2. harvest, harvest-time, Hes., Hdt.   II. the crop or harvest reaped, Lat. seges, Anth.

ἀ-μήτωρ, ορος, ὁ, ἡ, (μήτηρ) without mother, motherless, Hdt., Eur.   II. ἡ, unmotherly, μήτηρ ἀμήτωρ Soph.

ἀμηχανάω, = sq., Anth., in Ep. forms ἀμηχανόωσιν, -όων.

ἀμηχανέω, f. ήσω: impf. ἠμηχάνουν: (ἀμήχανος):—to be at a loss for, or in want of a thing, c. gen., Hdt.; περί τινος about a thing, Eur.; ὅπα τράπωμαι which way to turn, Aesch.   2. absol., ἀμηχανῶν βιοτεύω I live without the necessaries of life, Xen.   Hence

ἀ-μηχανής, ές, = ἀμήχανος, h. Hom. (in gen. pl. -έων).

ἀμηχανία, Ion. -ίη, ἡ, want of means, helplessness, impotence, Od., etc.; ὑπ' ἀμηχανίας Ar.   II. of things, hardship, trouble, Hes.   From

ἀ-μήχανος, Dor. ἀμάχανος, ον, (μηχανή) without means or resource, at a loss, τινος about one, Od.; ἀμ. εἴς τι awkward at a thing, Eur.:—Adv., ἀμηχάνως ἔχειν = ἀμηχανεῖν, Aesch., Eur.   2. c. inf. at a loss how to do, unable to do, Soph., Dem., etc.   II. in pass. sense,   1. impracticable, difficult, c. inf., ἀμήχανός ἐστι πιθέσθαι Il.; ὁδὸς ἀμ. εἰσελθεῖν a road hard to enter on, Xen.; ἀμήχανόν ἐστι, c. inf. 'tis impossible, Hdt., etc.:—absol., ἀμήχανα impossibilities, Aesch., etc.   2. against whom nothing can be done, irresistible, of gods, Il.:—of things, ἀμήχανα ἔργα mischief without resource or remedy, Ib., Hes., Trag.; of dreams, inexplicable, Od.   3. extraordinary, immense, Plat.; ἀμήχανον εὐδαιμονίας an extraordinary amount of happiness, Id.:—often c. acc., ἀμήχανος τὸ μέγεθος, τὸ κάλλος, τὸ πλῆθος, i. e. inconceivable in point of size, etc., Id., Xen.:—Plat. often adds the relatives οἷος, ὅσος, and ὡς, as, ἀμήχανον ὅσον χρόνον an inconceivable length of time, ἀμηχάνως ὡς εὖ extraordinarily well.

ἀ-μίαντος, ον, (μιαίνω) undefiled, Theogn.; Aesch. calls the sea simply ἡ ἀμίαντος.

ἀ-μῐγής, ές, (μίγνυμι) unmixed, pure, Arist.

ἄμιθος, Dor. for ἡμίθεος.

ἀμιθρέω, by Ep. metath. for ἀριθμέω, Theocr.

ἄ-μικτος, ον, unmingled, that will not mingle or blend, Aesch. **II.** unmixed, pure, Plat. **III.** of persons, not mingling with others (cf. μιγῆναι to have intercourse), unsociable, of Centaurs and Cyclopes, Soph., Eur. :—ἄμ. τινι having no intercourse with others, Id.; so of laws and customs, ἄμ. νόμιμα τοῖς ἄλλοις. Thuc. **2.** of places, inhospitable, Eur.

ἄμιλλα, ης, ἡ, (ἅμα) a contest for superiority, a conflict, Hdt., etc. **2.** c. gen. rei, ἰσχύος ἄμ. a trial of strength, Pind.; ποδοῖν, λόγων ἄμ. Eur.; ἀρετῆς Plat.; c. gen. objecti, ἄμ. λέκτρων a contest for marriage, Eur.; so with an Adj., ἄμ. φιλόπλουτος, πολύτεκνος a striving after wealth or children, Id.

ἀμιλλάομαι, f. -ήσομαι : aor. 1 ἡμιλλήθην, later ἡμιλλησάμην : pf. ἡμίλλημαι : (ἄμιλλα) :—Dep. to compete, vie, contend with another, Lat. aemulari, c. dat. pers., Hdt., etc.; πρός τινα Eur.; c. dat. rei, to contend in or with a thing, Hdt.; περί τινος about a thing, Luc. **2.** in pass. sense, τὸ πεζὸν πρὸς ἀλλήλους ἁμιλληθέν being matched one against another, Thuc. **II.** of a single person, to strive, struggle, ἐπί τι to a point, Xen.; πρός τι to obtain a thing, Plat. Hence

ἀμίλλημα, ατος, τό, a conflict, v. ἄλεκτρος.

ἀμιλλητήρ, ῆρος, ὁ, (ἀμιλλάομαι) a competitor in the race, v. τρόχος Β.

ἀμιμητό-βιος, ον, inimitable in one's life, Plut.

ἀ-μίμητος [ῑ], ον, (μιμέομαι) inimitable, Anth.; τινί in a thing, Plut. :—Adv. -τως, Id.

ἀμιξία, Ion. -ίη, ἡ, (ἄμικτος) of persons, want of intercourse, ἀλλήλων with one another, Thuc.; πρός τινα Luc.; ἀμιξίη χρημάτων want of money dealings, Id.

ἄμ-ιππος, ον, keeping up with horses, i. e. fleet as a horse, Soph. **II.** ἄμιπποι, οἱ, infantry mixed with cavalry, Thuc., Xen.

ἀμίς, ίδος, ἡ, a chamber-pot, Ar.

ἀμισθί [ῑ], Adv. of ἄμισθος, Eur., Dem.; χρημάτων ἀμ. without reward of money, Plut.

ἄ-μισθος, ον, without hire or pay, unhired, Aesch.

ἀ-μίσθωτος, ον, (μισθόω) bringing in no rent, Dem.

ἀ-μιτρο-χίτωνες, οἱ, epith. of Lycian, wearing no girdle (μίτρα) with their coat of mail (χιτών), Il.

ἀ-μιχθαλόεις, εσσα, εν, (μίγνυμι) epith. of Lemnos, inaccessible, inhospitable, Il.

ἄμμα, ατος, τό, (ἅπτω) anything tied or made to tie, and so, **1.** a knot, Hdt. **2.** a noose, halter, Eur. **3.** a band, Id.; ἄ. παρθενίας the maiden girdle, Anth. **4.** in pl. the wrestler's arms or hug, Plut.

ἄμμε, Aeol. for ἡμᾶς, acc. pl. of ἐγώ.

ἀμ-μεμίξεται, ἀμ-μένω, poët. for ἀναμεμίξεται, ἀναμένω.

ἄμμες, Aeol. for ἡμεῖς, nom. pl. of ἐγώ.

ἀμ-μέσον, poët. for ἀνὰ μέσον.

ἄμμι, ἄμμιν, Aeol. and Dor. for ἡμῖν, dat. pl. of ἐγώ.

ἀμ-μῖγα, ἀμ-μίγνυμι, poët. for ἀνάμιγα, ἀναμίγνυμι.

ἀμμορία, Ion. -ίη, ἡ, poët. for ἀμορία, (ἄμορος) what is not one's fate, bad fortune, Od.

ἄμ-μορος, ον, poët. for ἄ-μορος, ἄ-μοιρος, without share of a thing, c. gen., Il., Soph. :—free from, without, ὠδίνων Anth. **II.** absol. unhappy, Il.

ἄμμος or ἄμμος, ἡ, sand (v. ἄμαθος), Plat., etc. **II.** sandy ground, a racecourse, Xen.

ἀμμό-τροφος, ον, (τρέφω) growing in sand, Anth.

Ἄμμων, ωνος, ὁ, the Libyan Zeus-Ammon, Hdt., Pind.,

etc. :—fem. Adj. Ἀμμωνίς, Ἀ. ἕδρα the seat of Ammon, i. e. Libya, Eur.

ἀ-μνάμων, Dor. for ἀμνήμων.

ἀμνάς, άδος, ἡ, fem. of ἀμνός, a lamb, Theocr.

ἀμ-νάσει, ἀμ-νάσειε, Dor. 3 sing. fut. and aor. 1 opt. of ἀναμιμνήσκω.

ἀμναστέω, ἄμναστος, Dor. for -ηστέω, -ηστος.

ἀμνεῖος, α, ον, (ἀμνός) of a lamb, ἀμν. χλαῖνα a lambskin cloak, Theocr.

ἀ-μνημόνευτος, ον, unmentioned, unheeded, Eur.

ἀμνημονέω, f. ήσω : aor. 1 ἡμνημόνησα : (ἀμνήμων) :— to be unmindful, absol., Aesch., Eur. **2.** c. gen. to make no mention of, not speak of, Id., etc.; so, ἀμν. τι περί τινος Thuc.

ἀμνημοσύνη, ἡ, forgetfulness, Eur. From

ἀ-μνήμων, Dor. ἀμνάμων, ον, gen. ονος : (μνήμη) :—unmindful, forgetful, Soph., Plat.; τινός of a thing, Aesch., etc. **2.** pass. forgotten, not mentioned, Eur.

ἀμναστέω, Dor. ἀμναστέω, = ἀμνημονέω, Soph. :—Pass. to be forgotten, Thuc. Hence

ἀμναστία, ἡ, forgetfulness of wrong : an amnesty, Plut.

ἄ-μνηστος, ον, (μνάομαι) unremembered, Theocr.

ἀμνίον, τό, a bowl in which the blood of victims was caught, Od. (Deriv. uncertain.)

ἀμνίς, ίδος, ἡ, a ewe-lamb, Theocr.

ἀμνο-κῶν, ὁ, (κοέω) sheep-minded, i. e. a simpleton, Ar.

ἈΜΝΟΣ, ὁ, ἡ, a lamb, Soph., Ar.; ἀμνοὶ τοὺς τρόπους lambs in temper, Id. :—for the oblique cases, ἀρνός, ἀρνί, ἄρνα are used; v. ἀρνός.

ἀμογητί, Adv. without toil or effort, Il. From

ἀ-μόγητος, ον, (μογέω) unwearied, untiring, h. Hom.

ἀ-μοθεί, Adv. (from ἀ privat., μόθος) without quarrel, Lacon. word in Thuc.

ἀμόθεν, Ion. ἀμόθεν, Adv., (ἀμός) from some place or other, from what source soever, Od.; ἀμόθεν γέ ποθεν Plat.

ἀμοιβάδιος, α, ον, = ἀμοιβαῖος, Anth.

ἀμοιβαδίς, Adv. (ἀμοιβή) by turns, alternately, ἀμ. ἄλλοθεν ἄλλος one after another, Theocr.

ἀμοιβαῖος, ον and α (η), ον, (ἀμοιβή) giving like for like, retributive, Pind., Anth. :—Adv. -ως, in requital, Luc. **II.** interchanged, alternate, Hdt.; ἀμοιβαῖα, alternating verses, sung by two persons one in answer to the other, Plat.; ἀμοιβαίη ἀοιδή Theocr.

ἀμοιβάς, άδος, fem. of foreg., for a change of raiment, Od.

ἀμοιβή, ἡ, (ἀμείβω) a requital, recompense, compensation, return, payment, Od.; ἑκατόμβης for the hecatomb, Ib. **2.** an answer, Hdt. **II.** change, exchange, of money, Plut. **III.** alternation, κακῶν Eur.

ἀμοιβηδίς, Adv. (ἀμοιβή) alternately, in succession, Hom.

ἀμοιβός, ὁ, (ἀμείβω) one who exchanges, ἀμοιβοὶ soldiers that relieve others, Il. **II.** as Adj. in return or in exchange for a thing, c. gen., Soph.

ἀμοιρέω, to have no share in a thing, c. gen., Plut. From

ἀ-μοιρος, ον, (μοῖρα) without share in a thing, c. gen., Aesch., etc. **2.** absol. = ἄμμορος, unfortunate, Plut.

ἀμολγαῖος, α, ον, (ἀμέλγω) of milk, made with milk, or (from ἀμολγός an old word for ἀκμή), of the best flour, Hes.

ἀμολγεύς, έως, ὁ, (ἀμέλγω) a milk-pail, Lat. mulctra, Theocr., Anth.

ἀμόλγιον, τό, Dim. of ἀμολγεύς, a milk-pail, Theocr.

ἀμολγός, ὁ, a word of uncertain sense:—Hom. always joins νυκτὸς ἀμολγῷ, in the hours before daybreak, or the hours after sunset, i.e. generally, at night-time, Il. (The supposition that ἀμολγός meant milking-time (from ἀμέλγω) will not suit the sense. It is said that ἀμολγός was an old word for ἀκμή, so that νυκτὸς ἀμ. means the dead of night.)

ἀ-μόμφητος, ον, = ἀμεμφής, Aesch.

ἄ-μομφος, ον, (μομφή) blameless, Aesch.

ἀμόργῖνος, ον, made of Amorgian flax, Ar. From

ἀμοργίς, ή, fine flax from the isle of Amorgos, Ar.

ἀμορία, ή, poët. ἀμμορία, q. v.

ἄ-μορος, ον, = ἄμμορος, = ἄμοιρος, c. gen., Eur. II. absol. unlucky, wretched, Soph.

ἀμορφία, ή, unshapeliness, unsightliness, Eur. From

ἄ-μορφος, ον, (μορφή) misshapen, unsightly, Hdt., Eur.: —Sup. ἀμορφέστατος (as if from ἀμορφής), Hdt.; but regul. form -ότερος, -ότατος, Xen., Plut.

ἀμός or ἁμός [ᾰ], ή, όν, = ἡμέτερος, our, ours, Hom., etc. II. Att. = ἐμός, when a long penult. is required.

ἁμός [ᾰ], an old word equiv. to εἷς or τις, only found in the Adv. forms ἁμοῦ, ἁμῇ, ἁμοῖ, ἁμῶς, ἁμόθεν.

ἆμος, Dor. for ἦμος, as, when, Theocr.

ἄμοτος, ον, raging, savage, Theocr. II. in Hom. as Adv. ἄμοτον, insatiably, ἄμ. μεμαώς, striving incessantly; ἄμ. κλαίω I weep continually; τανύοντο they struggled restlessly forwards. (Deriv. unknown.)

ἁμοῦ, Att. ἁμοῦ, Adv. of ἁμός (= τὶς), ἁμοῦ γέ που somewhere or other, Lys.: cf. ἁμόθεν, ἁμῇ, ἁμοῖ.

ἀμουσία, ή, want of refinement, rudeness, grossness, Eur., Plat. II. want of harmony, Eur. From

ἄ-μουσος, ον, (μοῦσα) without the Muses, without taste, unrefined, inelegant, rude, gross, Eur., Ar.:—Adv. -σως, Plat. II. unmusical, Eur.; ἀμουσότεραι ᾠδαί Id.

ἀ-μοχθεί or -θί [ῐ], Adv. of ἄμοχθος, Aesch., Eur.

ἐμόχθησα, crasis for ἃ ἐμόχθησα.

ἀ-μόχθητος, ον, = sq.:—Adv. -τως, Babr.

ἄ-μοχθος, ον, free from toil and trouble, Soph.:— shrinking from toil, Theocr. 2. not tired, Xen.

ἄμ-παλος, poët. for ἀνάπαλος, Pind. II. ἄμπ-αλος, ον, Dor. for ἀμφίαλος, Theocr.

ἄμ-παυμα, ἄμ-παυσις, ἀμ-παυστήριον, ἀμ-παύω, v. ἀναπ-.

ἀμ-πεδίον, ἀμπέλαγος, should be written ἀμ πέδιον (i.e. ἀνὰ πεδίον), ἀμ πέλαγος (i.e. ἀνὰ πέλαγος).

ἀμ-πείρω, Ep. for ἀναπείρω.

ἀμπελ-άνθη, ή, = οἰνάνθη, Luc.

ἀμπελεών, ῶνος, ὁ, poët. for ἀμπελών, Theocr.

ἀμπέλινος, ον and η, ον, (ἄμπελος) of the vine, Hdt. II. of persons, given to wine, Anth.

ἀμπέλιον, τό, Dim. of ἄμπελος, Ar.

ἀμπελίς, ίδος, ή, Dim. of ἄμπελος, a vine-plant, Ar. II. the bird ἀμπελίων, Id.

ἀμπελόεις, εσσα, εν, (ἄμπελος) rich in vines, Il., etc.

ἀμπελοεργός, ὁ, = ἀμπελουργός, Anth.

ἄμπελος, ή, a vine, Lat. vitis, Od., etc. (Perh. from ἀμπί (Aeol. for ἀμφί), ἕλ-ιξ, from its clasping tendrils.)

ἀμπελουργέω, to dress vines, Theophr., Luc.

ἀμπελ-ουργός, ὁ, (*ἔργω) a vine-dresser, Ar., etc.

ἀμπελο-φύτωρ [ῠ], ορος, ὁ, (φύω) a vine-planter, Anth.

ἀμπελών, ῶνος, ὁ, (ἄμπελος) a vineyard, Aeschin., etc.

ἀμ-πέμπω, poët. for ἀναπέμπω.

ἀμ-πεπαλών, Ep. for ἀναπεπαλών, redupl. aor. 2 part. of ἀναπάλλω.

ἀμ-πετάννυμι, ἀμ-πέτομαι, poët. for ἀναπετάννυμι, ἀναπέτομαι.

ἀμπεχόνη, ή, (ἀμπέχω) a fine robe: generally, clothing, clothes, Plat., Xen.

ἀμπεχόνιον, τό, = ἀμπεχόνη, Ar., Theocr.

ἀμπ-έχω and ἀμπ-ίσχω: Ep. impf. ἄμπεχον: f. ἀμφέξω: aor. 2 ἤμπισχον:—Med. ἀμπέχομαι and ἀμπίσχομαι, with 3 pl. ἀμπισχοῦνται: impf. ἠμπειχόμην: f. ἀμφέξομαι: aor. 2 ἠμπισχόμην, part. ἀμπισχόμενος: (ἀμπί Aeol. for ἀμφί:) I. to surround, cover, Lat. cingere, c. acc., Od., Soph., etc.:—absol. σκότος ἀμπίσχων surrounding darkness, Eur. 2. to embrace, Id. II. to put round, Lat. circumdare, esp. to put on another, c. dupl. acc., Ar., etc. 2. Med. to put round oneself, to wear, χλαίνας οὐκ ἀμπισχοῦνται Id.; ἀμπισχόμενος with your cloak round you, Id.

ἀμ-πήδησε, for ἀνεπήδησε.

ἀμ-πίπτω, poët. for ἀναπίπτω.

ἀμπ-ίσχομαι, ἀμπ-ίσχω, v. ἀμπέχω.

ἀμπλακεῖν or (metri grat.) ἀπλακεῖν [ἄπλ], inf. of aor. 2 ἤμπλακον, part. ἀμπλακών: from the same Root we have pf. ἠμπλάκηκα, pass. ἠμπλάκημαι:—the pres. in use is ἀμπλακίσκω = ἁμαρτάνω. I. c. gen. to come short of, Pind., Soph. 2. to lose, be bereft of, παιδός Id.; ἀλόχου Eur. II. absol. to sin, err, do wrong, Id., etc.; ὡς τάδ᾽ ἤμπλακον when I committed these sins, Aesch. (Deriv. unknown.) Hence

ἀμπλάκημα, ατος, τό, an error, fault, offence, Aesch., etc.:—also, metri grat., ἀπλάκημα, Id.

ἀμπλάκητος, v. ἀναμπλάκητος.

ἀμπλακία, ή, = ἀμπλάκημα, Theogn., etc.

ἀμπλάκιον, τό, = ἀμπλακία, Pind.

ἀμπλακίσκειν, v. ἀμπλακεῖν.

ἀμ-πνείω, Ep. for ἀναπνέω.

ἄμ-πνευμα, ἀμ-πνοά, poët. for ἀνάπνευμα, ἀναπνοή.

ἄμ-πνυε, ἀμ-πνύνθη, ἄμ-πνῦτο, v. sub ἀναπνέω.

ἀμπτᾶσα, ἀμπταίην, ἀμπταμένος, v. sub ἀναπέτομαι.

ἀμ-πτῠχή, poët. for ἀναπτυχή.

ἀμπῠκάζω, ἄμπυξ to bind the hair with a band, Anth.

ἀμπυκτήρ, ῆρος, ὁ, (ἄμπυξ) a horse's head-band, Aesch.

ἀμπυκτήριον, τό, = ἀμπυκτήρ, Soph.

ἄμπυξ, ῠκος, ὁ or ή, (ἀμπί, Aeol. for ἀμφί) a woman's head-band, snood, Il., etc. II. anything circular, a wheel, Soph.

ἄμ-πωτις, εως, Ion. ιος, ή, for ἀνάπωτις, (ἀναπίνομαι) a being sucked back, the ebb-tide, Hdt., etc.

ἀμυγδάλινος, η, ον, of almonds, Xen. From

ἀμύγδαλος, ή, an almond-tree, Luc.

ἄμυγμα, ατος, τό, (ἀμύσσω) a scratching, tearing, Soph., Eur.

ἀμυγμός, οῦ, ὁ, = foreg., Aesch.

ἄμυδις [ῠ], = ἅμα: I. of Time, together, at the same time, Od. II. of Place, together, all together, Il.

ἀμυδρός, ά, όν, like ἀμαυρός, indistinct, dim, obscure: 1. ἀμ. γράμματα scarce legible letters,

Thuc. 2. ἀμ. πρὸς ἀλήθειαν *faint* in comparison with truth, Id.; ἀμ. ἐλπίς Plut. (Deriv. uncertain.)

ἀ-μύητος, ον, (μυέω) *uninitiated*, Plat., etc.   **II.** in Plat. Gorg. as if from μύω, = οὐ δυνάμενος μύειν, *unable to keep close, leaky.*

ἀ-μύθητος [ῡ], ον, (μυθέομαι) *unspeakable, unspeakably many* or *great*, Dem.

ἀ-μύκητος [ῡ], ον, (μυκάομαι) *where no herds low*, of places, Anth.

Ἀμύκλαι, ῶν, αἱ, a Lacon. city, famous for the worship of Apollo, Il., etc. :—Ἀμυκλαῖον, τό, *the temple of Amyclaean Apollo*, Thuc.—Adv. Ἀμύκλᾱθεν, *from Amyclae*, Pind.

Ἀμύκλαι, αἱ, a sort of shoes, made at *Amyclae*, Theocr.

Ἀμυκλαΐζω, f. σω, *to speak in the Amyclean* (i. e. *Laconian*) *dialect*, Theocr.

ἄ-μῡλος, ον, (μύλη) *not ground at the mill*, i.e. *ground by hand* :—as Subst. *a cake of fine meal*, Ar., etc.

ἀ-μύμων [ῡ], ον, gen. ονος, (μῶμος) : *blameless, noble, excellent*, used by Hom. as an honorary epithet, like our *honourable, excellency*, not implying virtue; never used of gods.   **II.** of things, Hom.

ἄμῡνα, Ep. aor. 1 of ἀμύνω.

ἀμῡνάθω [ᾰ], = ἀμύνω : but the forms assigned to it belong to an aor. 2 ἠμύναθον, (cf. διωκάθω, εἰκαθεῖν, ἐργαθεῖν, σχέθω) : the inf. therefore is ἀμυναθεῖν (not -άθειν), imper. med. ἀμυναθοῦ (not -άθου) :—*to defend, assist*, c. dat., Eur., Ar. :—*to ward off from oneself, repel*, ψόγον Aesch. : *to take vengeance on*, τινα.

Ἀμυνίας [ῡ], ου, ὁ, (ἀμύνω) masc. pr. n.   **II.** as appellat., ἣν ἀμυνίας was *on its guard*, Ar.

ἄμῡνον, Ep. for ἤμυνον, impf. of ἀμύνω.   **II.** aor. 1 imper.

ἀμυντέον, verb. Adj. of ἀμύνω, *one must assist*, c. dat. pers., Xen.; so pl. ἀμυντέα, Soph.

ἀμυντήριος, ον, (ἀμύνω) *defensive*, Plat., etc.   **II.** as Subst., ἀμυντήριον, τό, *a means of defence*, Id.

ἀμύντωρ, ορος, ὁ, *a defender, helper*, Hom.   2. *an avenger*, πατρός Eur. From

ἀμύνω [ῡ] : Ep. impf. ἄμυνον : f. ἀμῠνῶ, Ion. -ῠνέω : aor. 1 ἤμυνα, Ep. ἄμυνα [ᾰ] : for aor. 2, v. ἀμυνάθω : —Med., Ep. impf. ἠμυνόμην : f. ἀμυνοῦμαι : aor. 1 ἠμυνάμην. (From Root **MYN** with a prefixed, cf. Lat. *munio, moenia*.) *To keep off, ward off*, Hom. : **1.** c. acc. of the person or thing *to be kept off*, c. dat. of pers. *for* or *from whom* the danger *is kept off*, Δαναοῖσιν λοιγὸν ἀμύνειν *to ward off* ruin *from* the Danai, Il. :— the dat. is often omitted, λοιγὸν ἀμύνει Ib. **2.** c. dat. pers. *to defend, assist, aid, succour*, Hom., etc. **3.** c. gen. *from whom* danger *is kept off*, Τρῶας ἄμυνε νεῶν he kept the Trojans *off from* the ships, Il.; etc. **4.** absol. *to repel assaults, to aid*, Ib.; τὰ ἀμύνοντα means *of defence*, Hdt.   **II.** rarely c. acc., like Med. II, *to requite, repay*, Soph.

  B. Med. *to ward off from oneself, defend oneself against* : **1.** c. acc., Il.   **2.** c. gen. of that from which danger is warded off, *to fight for* or *in defence of*, Ib. : so, ἀμύνεσθαι περὶ πάτρης Ib.; ὑπέρ τινος Xen.   **II.** absol. *to defend oneself*, Il.   **III.** ἀμύνεσθαί τινα also *to avenge oneself on* an enemy, *to requite, repay, punish*, Soph., Thuc., etc.; also, ἀμύνεσθαί τινά τινος or ὑπέρ τινος *to punish for* a thing, Id.

ἀμύσσω, Att. -ττω : Ep. impf. ἄμυσσον : f. ξω : aor. 1 ἤμυξα :—Med., aor. 1 part. ἀμυξάμενος :—Pass., aor. 1 part. ἀμυχθέν. (From Root **MYK**, with a prefixed, cf. Lat. *muc-ro*.) *To scratch, tear, wound, lacerate, mangle*, Il., Hdt. ; also *to prick, sting*, Luc., *scratch* with both hands.   **II.** metaph., θυμὸν ἀμ. *to tear* the heart, Il., Aesch. ; φρὴν ἀμύσσεται Id.

ἀ-μυστί [ῐ], Adv. (μύω) *without closing the mouth*, i.e. *at one draught*, Luc.

ἀμυστίζω, *to drink deep*, pf. ἠμύστικα Eur. From

ἄμυστις, ιος and ιδος, ἡ, (ἀμυστί *a long draught*, Anacr., Eur., etc.   2. *deep drinking, tippling*, Id.   **II.** *a large cup*, used by the Thracians, Ar.

ἀμυχή, ἡ, (ἀμύσσω) *a scratch, skin-wound*, Dem. ; in sign of sorrow, ἀμυχὰς κοπτομένων ἀφεῖλεν Plut.

ἀμυχμός, ὁ, = ἀμυχή, Theocr.

ἀμφ-ἀγᾰπάζω, only in pres. and impf., *to embrace warmly, treat kindly, greet warmly*, Od., etc.; so in Med., Il.

ἀμφ-ἀγᾰπάω, = foreg., Hes.; aor. 1 ἀμφαγάπησα h. Hom.

ἀμφ-ἀγείρομαι, Med. *to gather round*, θεαὶ δέ μιν ἀμφαγέροντο (aor. 2) Il. : hence pres. ἀμφαγέρομαι, Theocr.

ἀμ-φάδιος [ᾰ], α, ον, poët. for ἀναφάδιος, (ἀναφαίνω) *public*, γάμος Od.   **II.** acc. fem. ἀμφαδίην as Adv., = ἀμφαδόν, Il.

ἀμ-φᾰδόν, Adv. poët. for ἀναφαδόν, (ἀναφαίνω) *publicly, openly, without disguise*, Hom.

ἄμ-φᾰδος, ον, (ἀναφαίνω) *discovered, known*, Od.

ἀμ-φαίνω, poët. for ἀναφαίνω.

ἀμφ-αΐσσομαι, Pass. *to rush on from all sides*, ἀμφὶ δέ τ' ἀΐσσονται Il.; ἀμφὶ δὲ χαῖται ὤμοις ἀΐσσοντο *floated around* his shoulders, Ib.

ἀμφ-άκης [ᾱ], ες, Dor. for ἀμφήκης.

ἀμ-φανδόν, Adv., poët. for ἀναφανδόν, Pind.

ἀμ-φανέειν, poët. for ἀναφανεῖν, fut. inf. of ἀναφαίνω.

ἀμφ-ᾰρᾰβέω, f. ήσω, *to rattle* or *ring around*, Il. :—so ἀμφᾰρᾰβίζω, Hes.

ἀμ-φᾰσίη, ἡ, Ep. for ἀ-φασία, *speechlessness*, Hom.

ἀμφ-αϋτέω, f. ήσω, *to ring around*, Il.

ἀμφ-αφάω, Ep. part. ἀμφαφόων, -όωσα : impf. ἀμφαφάασκον : Med., Ep. 3 pl. ἀμφαφόωντο, inf. ἀμφαφάασθαι :—*to touch* or *feel all round, to handle*, Hom.; so in Med., Od.   2. μαλακώτερος ἀμφαφάασθαι easier to *deal with, manage*, Il.

ἀμφ-έδρᾰμον, aor. 2 of ἀμφιτρέχω.

ἀμφ-έλικτος, ον, poët. for ἀμφιέλ-, *coiled round*, Eur.

ἀμφ-ελίσσω, poët. for ἀμφιελ-, *to wrap* or *twine round*, χέρας Eur. :—Med., Pind.

ἀμφ-έπω, poët. for ἀμφιέπω.

ἀμφ-ερέφω, *to cover up*, Anth.

ἀμφ-έρχομαι, Dep. with aor. 2 ἀμφ-ήλυθον, *to come round one, surround*, Od.

ἀμ-φέρω, poët. for ἀναφέρω.

ἀμφ-έσταν, ἀμφ-εστᾶσι, 3 pl. aor. 2 and pf. of ἀμφίστημι.

ἀμφ-έχᾰνον, aor. 2 of ἀμφιχάσκω.

ἀμφ-εχύθην [ῠ], aor. 1 pass. of ἀμφιχέω.

ἀμφ-έχυτο, 3 sing. Ep. aor. 2 pass. of ἀμφιχέω.

ἀμφ-ηγερέθομαι, Ep. for ἀμφαγείρομαι, Od.

ἀμφ-ήκης, ες, (ἀκή) *two-edged*, Il., Aesch.   **II.** metaph., γλῶττα a tongue *that will cut both ways*, i. e. maintain either right or wrong, Ar. ; of an oracle, *ambiguous*, Luc.

ἀμφ-ήλυθον, ἀμφ-ῆλθον, aor. 2 of ἀμφ-έρχομαι.

ἀμφ-ηρεφής, ές, (ἐρέφω) covered on both sides, close-covered, epith. of Apollo's quiver, Il.

ἀμφ-ήρης, ες, (v. -ήρης) fitted on both sides, well-fitted, ἀμφῆρες δόρυ, of the double rudder used in Greek ships (v. πηδάλιον), Eur. Hence

ἀμφ-ηρικός, ή, όν, rowed on both sides, worked by sculls, of a boat, Thuc.

ἀμφ-ήριστος, ον, (ἐρίζω) contested on both sides, ἀμφήριστον ἔθηκεν, i. e. made it a 'drawn' race, Il.

ἈΜΦΊ', Prep. with gen., dat., and acc.—Radic. sense, on both sides (cf. ἄμφω, Lat. ambo), whereas περί properly means all round.

A. C. GEN.: I. Causal, about, for, for the sake of a thing, ἀμφὶ γυναικός Aesch. 2. about, i. e. concerning or of a thing, ἀμφὶ φιλότητος ἀείδειν to sing about or of love, Od. II. of Place, about, around, ἀμφὶ τῆς πόλιος Hdt. B. C. DAT.: I. of Place, on both sides of, about, ἀμφὶ ὤμοις, στήθεσσι Hom.; likewise, ἀμφὶ περὶ στήθεσσι Od.:—then, just like περί, all round, κρέα ἀμφὶ ὀβελοῖς ἔπειραν they fixed the meat round, i.e. upon, the spits, Id. 2. generally, about, near, at, ἀμφὶ πύλῃσι Il. II. about, regarding, ἔρις ἀμφὶ μουσικῇ Hdt.; for the sake of, for, ἀμφ' Ἑλένῃ μάχεσθαι Il., etc. 2. like Lat. prae, ἀμφὶ τάρβει, ἀμφὶ φόβῳ, prae pavore, for very fear, Aesch., Eur. C. C. ACC.: I. of Place, about, around, mostly with a sense of motion, ἀμφὶ μιν φᾶρος βάλον Il. 2. about, near, ἀμφὶ ῥέεθρα somewhere by the banks, Ib. 3. of persons who are about one, οἱ ἀμφὶ Πρίαμον Priam and his train, Ib.; οἱ ἀμφὶ Ξέρξεα his army, Hdt.; in Att., οἱ ἀμφὶ Πρωταγόραν the school of Protagoras or Protagoras himself, Plat. 4. κλαίειν ἀμφί τινα to weep about or for one, Il. 5. εἶναι, διατρίβειν ἀμφί τι to be engaged about it, Xen. II. as a loose definition of Time, about, Pind.; ἀμφὶ Πλειάδων δύσιν Aesch.:—so of Number, Lat. circiter, ἀμφὶ τὰς δώδεκα μυριάδας about 120,000, Xen. D. WITHOUT CASE, as Adv., on both sides, about, around. 2. = ἀμφίς A. II, apart, h. Hom. E. IN COMPOS.: I. about, on both sides, as ἀμφίστομος, = δίστομος. 2. all round, on all sides, as ἀμφιλαμβάνω, ἀμφιλαφής. II. Causal, for, for the sake of, as ἀμφιμάχομαι.

ἀμφιάζω or ἀμφιέζω, aor. 1 ἠμφίασα, (ἀμφί) to clothe, τινά Plut.: metaph. of a grave, ὅστεα ἠμφίασαν Anth.

ἀμφί-αλος, ον, (ἅλς) sea-girt, of islands, Od., Soph. 2. of Corinth, between two seas, Horace's bimaris, Xen.

Ἀμφιάραος, ου, Att. Ἀμφιάρεως, ω, (a choriambus in Trag.) Amphiaraüs, the Theban seer, Aesch., etc.

ἀμφίασμα, ατος, τό, (ἀμφιάζω) a garment, Ctes., Luc.

ἀμφ-ιάχω, of a bird, to fly shrieking about, in irreg. part. pf. ἀμφιαχυῖα, Il.

ἀμφι-βαίνω, f. -βήσομαι, to go about or around, Il. 2. to bestride, Od.:—esp. to bestride a fallen friend, so as to protect him, Il.; hence of tutelary deities, to protect, Ib. II. to encompass, wrap round, c. acc., νεφέλη σκόπελον ἀμφιβέβηκε Od.: also c. dat., νέφος ἀμφιβέβηκε νηυσίν Il.:—metaph., σε πόνος φρένας ἀμφιβέβηκεν Ib., etc.

ἀμφι-βάλλω, f. -βαλῶ:—Med., Ep. fut. ἀμφιβαλεῦμαι: —to throw or put round: of clothes, to put them on a person, Lat. circumdare, c. dupl. acc. pers. et rei, ἀμφὶ δέ με χλαῖναν βάλεν Od.; also c. dat. pers., ἀμφὶ

δέ μοι ῥάκος βάλον Il.:—Med. to put round oneself, put round one, put on, Od. 2. ἀμφιβαλὼν θάλαιον having thrown a chamber over him, Ib.; ζυγὸν Ἑλλάδι ἀμφ. Aesch.:—Med., λευκὴν ἀμφιβάλλομαι τρίχα I put on, get white hair, Soph. 3. for the Med. the Act. is sometimes used, κρατερὸν μένος ἀμφιβαλόντες [ἑαυτοῖς] Il. II. to throw the arms round, to embrace, c. dat. pers., Od. III. also, c. acc. pers. to embrace, Eur.

ἀμφίβᾰσις, εως, ἡ, (ἀμφιβαίνω) a going round, encompassing, ἀμφίβασιν Τρώων = τοὺς ἀμφιβαίνοντας Τρῶας, Il.

ἀμφίβιος, ον, living a double life, i.e. both on land and in water, amphibious, Batr., Anth.

ἀμφίβλημα, ατος, τό, (ἀμφιβάλλω) something thrown round: I. an enclosure, Eur. II. a garment, cloak, Id.

ἀμφίβληστρον, τό, (ἀμφιβάλλω) anything thrown round: I. a casting-net, Hes., Hdt.:—metaph. of the garment thrown like a net over Agamemnon, Aesch. II. a fetter, bond, Id. III. of walls, encompassment of city-walls, Eur.

ἀμφι-βόητος, noised abroad, Anth.

ἀμφιβολία, Ion. -ίη, ἡ, the state of being attacked on both sides, Hdt. From

ἀμφίβολος, ον, (ἀμφιβάλλω) put round, encompassing, Eur. II. attacked on both or all sides, Aesch.; ἀμφ. εἶναι to be between two fires, Thuc. 2. act. hitting at both ends, double-pointed, Anth. III. doubtful, ambiguous, Plat., Xen., etc.; τἀγαθὰ ἐς ἀμφίβολον ἔθεντο accounted their good fortune as doubtful, Thuc.; ἐν ἀμφιβόλῳ in doubt, Luc.:—Adv., οὐκ ἀμφιβόλως Aesch.

ἀμφι-βόσκομαι, Dep. to eat all about, Luc.

ἀμφί-βουλος, ον, (βουλή) half-minded to do a thing, c. inf., Aesch.

ἀμφί-βροτος, η, ον and os, ον, covering the whole man, of a large shield, Il.

ἀμφί-βροχος, ον, (βρέχω) thoroughly soaked, Anth.

ἀμφι-βώμιος, ον, (βωμός) round the altar, Eur.

ἀμφι-γηθέω, to rejoice around or exceedingly, h. Hom.

ἀμφι-γνοέω = impf. and aor. 1 with double augm., ἠμφεγνόουν, ἠμφεγνόησα: (γι-γνώσκω):—to be doubtful about a thing, not know or understand, c. acc., Plat.; ἐπί τινος, περί τινος Id., etc.; ἠμφεγνόουν ὅ τι ἐποίουν they knew not what they were about, Xen.:—Pass., ἀμφιγνοηθείς being unknown, Id.

ἀμφι-γόητος, ον, (γοάω) bewailed all round, Anth.

Ἀμφι-γυήεις, ὁ, (γυιός) of Hephaestus, he that halts in both feet, the lame one, Il.

ἀμφί-γυος, ον, pointed at each end, double-pointed, Hom.; in Soph., of persons, armed at all points, practised combatants. (The termin. -γυος, as in ὑπό-γυος, is of uncertain sense.)

ἀμφι-δαίω, used in intr. pf. and plqpf. ἀμφιδέδηα, -ήειν, to burn or blaze around, Il.

ἀμφι-δάκνω, to bite all round: to grip close, Anth.

ἀμφι-δάκρῠτος, ον, all-tearful, Eur.

ἀμφί-δᾰσυς, εια, υ, fringed all round, of the Aegis, Il.

ἀμφι-δέαι, αἱ, (δέω A) things bound round, bracelets or anklets, Hdt.

ἀμφι-δέδρομα, pf. of ἀμφιτρέχω.

ἀμφι-δέξιος, ον, with two right hands, very dextrous,

Lat. *ambidexter*, Arist.　　**2.** like ἀμφήκης, *two-edged*, Eur.　**3.** metaph. *double-meaning, ambiguous*, Lat. *anceps*, χρηστήριον Hdt.　**4.** = ἀμφότερος, ἀμφ. ἀκμαῖς with *both* hands, Soph.; ἀμφ. πλευρόν *each* side, Id.

ἀμφι-δέρκομαι, Dep. *to look round about one*, Anth.

ἀμφί-δετος, ον, *bound* or *set all round*, Anth.

ἀμφι-δήρῑτος, ον, (δηρίομαι) *disputed*, νίκη Thuc.

ἀμφι-διαίνω, *to moisten all around*, Anth.

ἀμφι-δῑνέομαι, pf. -δεδίνημαι, Pass. *to be put round, fitted closely round*, Hom.

ἀμφι-δοκεύω, *to lie in wait for*, τινά Bion.

ἀμφι-δονέω, f. ήσω, *to agitate violently*, Theocr., Anth.

ἀμφιδοξέω, *to be doubtful* :—Pass. *to be matter for doubt*, Plut.　From

ἀμφί-δοξος, ον, (δόξα) *with doubtful mind* or *of double sense, doubtful*, Polyb., etc.

ἀμφί-δορος, ον, (δείρω) *quite flayed*, Anth.

ἀμφί-δοχμος, ον, (δοχμή) *as large as can be grasped*, λίθος Xen.; cf. χειροπληθής.

ἀμφί-δρομος, ον, (δραμεῖν) *running round, encompassing, inclosing*, Soph.

ἀμφί-δρυπτος, ον, = ἀμφίδρυφος, Anth.

ἀμφι-δρυφής, ές, (δρύπτω) *having torn both cheeks*, in grief, Il.

ἀμφίδρυφος, ον, (δρύπτω) *torn on both sides*, Il.

ἀμφί-δυμος, ον, *two-fold, double*, λιμὴν ἀμφ. Od. (The term. -δυμος recurs in δί-δυμος, τρί-δυμος.)

ἀμφι-δύω, *to put on* another :—Med. *to put on oneself*, Soph.

ἀμφιέζω, = ἀμφιάζω.

ἀμφι-έλισσα, ή, (ἑλίσσω) only in this fem. form, of ships, *rowed on both sides ;* or, rather, *swaying to and fro, rolling*.

ἀμφι-έννυμι or -ύω: f. ἀμφιέσω, Att. ἀμφιῶ: aor. 1 ἠμφίεσα:—Med., aor. ἠμφιεσάμην, Ep. 3 pl. ἀμφιέσαντο:—Pass., aor. 1 part. ἀμφιεσθείς: pf. ἠμφίεσμαι:—*to put round* or *on*, like Lat. *circumdare*, Il.: but mostly, c. dupl. acc. pers. et rei, ἐμὲ χλαῖναν ἀμφιέσασα Od. :—Pass., ἠμφιεσμένος τι *clothed in, wearing*, Ar.,etc.　**2.** c. dat. rei, ἀμφ. τινά τινι *to clothe one in* or *with a thing*, Plat.　**II.** Med. *to put round one, put on oneself*, Hom.

ἀμφι-έπω, poët. also ἀμφ-έπω: poët. impf. or aor. 2 ἀμφίεπον and ἄμφεπον :—*to go about, be all round, encompass*, Hom.　**II.** like διέπω, *to be busy about, look after*, Id.: —*to do honour* or *reverence to*, Pind.　**2.** *to tend*, Id.; *to guard, protect*, Soph., Eur.　**3.** ἀμφ. κῆδος *to court an alliance*, Lat. *ambire*, Id.　**4.** absol. in partic. *with good heed, heedfully, carefully*, Hom.　**III.** in Med. *to follow and crowd round*, Il.

ἀμφίεσμα, ατος, τό, (ἀμφιέννυμι) *a garment :* in pl. *clothes*, Plat.

ἀμφί-εσσαν, Ep. 3 pl. aor. 1 act. of ἀμφιέννυμι:—ἀμφιέσαντο, 3 pl. aor. 1 med.

ἀμφ-ιζάνω, *to sit on, settle upon*, c. dat., Il.

ἀμφί-ζευκτος, ον, (ζεύγνυμι) *joined from both sides*, Aesch.

ἀμφι-θάλασσος, Att. -ττος, ον, (θάλασσα) *with sea on both sides, sea-girt*, Pind., Xen.

ἀμφι-θαλής, ές, (θάλλω) *blooming on both sides*, of children *who have both parents alive*, Il.　**2.** *all-*

abounding, of the gods, Aesch., Ar.:—metaph. *abounding in*, c. dat., Aesch.

ἀμφι-θάλλω, pf. ἀμφιτέθηλα, *to be in full bloom*, Anth.

ἀμφι-θάλπω, *to warm on both sides* or *thoroughly*, Eur.

ἀμφι-θέατρον, τό, *a double theatre, amphitheatre.*

ἀμφί-θετος, ον, of a cup, either *that will stand on both ends*, or, *with handles on both sides*, Il.

ἀμφι-θέω, f. -θεύσομαι, *to run round about*, c. acc., Od.

ἀμφί-θηκτος, ον, *sharpened on both sides, two-edged*, Soph. :—so, ἀμφῐ-θηγής, ές, (θήγω) Anth.

ἀμφί-θρεπτος, ον, (τρέφω) *clotted round* a wound, Soph.

ἀμφί-θῠρος, ον, (θύρα) *with double entrance*, Soph.　**II.** as Subst., ἀμφίθυρον, τό, *a hall*, Theocr.

ἀμφι-κᾰλύπτω, f. ψω :　**I.** c. acc. *to cover all round, enwrap, enfold*, of garments, Il.; of a coffin, Ib.; ἀμφ. ἵππον *to receive within* the walls, Od.; of death, sleep, Ib.　**II.** ἀμφ. τί τινι *to put* a thing *round* any one *as a cover* or *shelter*, ἀμφ. σάκος τινί, νέφος τινί Ib.　**III.** after Hom., ἀμφ. τινά τινι *to surround* one *with* a thing, Batr. :—Pass., ἀμφεκαλύφθη κρᾶτα *he had* his head *covered*, Eur.

ἀμφι-κεάζω, *to cleave asunder*, Ep. aor. 1 -κεάσσα, Od.

ἀμφί-κειμαι, Pass. *to lie round*, ἐπ᾽ ἀλλήλοισιν ἀμφικείμενοι *locked in* each other's arms, Soph.; ἐπ᾽ ὀλέθρῳ ἀμφικεῖσθαι φόνον that one murder *lies close* upon another, Id.

ἀμφι-κείρω, f. -κερῶ, *to shear all round*, Anth.

ἀμφῐ-κίων [κῑ], ον, *with pillars all round*, Soph.

ἀμφί-κλαστος, ον, (κλάω) *broken all round*, Anth.

ἀμφί-κλυστος, ον, (κλύζω) *washed on both sides by the waves*, Soph.

ἀμφι-κομέω, f. ήσω, *to tend on all sides* or *carefully*, Anth.

ἀμφί-κομος, ον, (κόμη) *with hair all round*, Anth.　**2.** *thick-leafed*, Il.

ἀμφί-κρᾱνος, Ion. -κρηνος, ον, (κάρα) *two headed*, Eur.　**II.** *surrounding the head*, Anth.

ἀμφί-κρέμαμαι, Pass. *to hang round*, Pind.

ἀμφι-κρεμής, ές, (κρέμαμαι) *hanging round* or *over*, Anth.

ἀμφί-κρημνος, ον, *with cliffs all round*, Eur.

ἀμφί-κρηνος, ον, Ion. for ἀμφίκρανος.

ἀμφι-κρύπτω, f. ψω, *to cover* or *hide on every side*, τοῖον νέφος ἀμφί σε κρύπτει Eur.

ἀμφι-κτίονες, ων, οἱ, (κτίζω) *they that dwell round, next neighbours*, Hdt., Pind.

Ἀμφικτύονες, ων, οἱ, *the Amphictyons*, a Council composed of deputies chosen by the States of Greece, the *Amphictyonic League*, which met at Delphi and Anthela, Hdt., etc. (The word was orig. the same as ἀμφικτίονες.)

Ἀμφικτυονία or -εία, ἡ, *the Amphictyonic League*, Dem.

Ἀμφικτυονικός, ή, όν, *Amphictyonic, of the Amphictyons*, Dem.

Ἀμφικτυονίς, ίδος, ἡ, fem. of foreg.; Ἀμφ. (sc. πόλις) *a state in the Amphictyonic League*, Aeschin.　**II.** a name of Demeter at Anthela, *a meeting-place of the Amphictyonic Council*, Hdt.

ἀμφι-κυκλόομαι, Pass. *to encircle, surround*, Aesch.

ἀμφι-κῠλίνδω, aor. 1 -εκύλισα, *to roll around, to be pierced by* a sword, Pind.

ἀμφι-κύπελλος, ον, in Hom. ἀμφικύπελλον δέπας, *a*

double cup, i. e. one that forms a cup both at top and bottom, Il., etc.; cf. ἀμφίθετος.

ἀμφί-λᾰλος, ον, of double speech (Greek and Thracian), Ar.

ἀμφί-λᾰφής, ές, (λαμβάνω) taking in on all sides, wide-spreading, of large trees, Hdt. 2. generally, abundant, excessive, enormous, Id., etc.; γόος ἀμφ. a universal wail, Aesch. :—Adv. -φῶς, copiously, Plut. 3. of size, bulky, huge, Hdt.

ἀμφι-λᾰχαίνω, only in impf. to dig round, c. acc., Od.

ἀμφι-λέγω, f. ξω, to dispute about, τι Xen.; ἀμφ. μή.., to dispute, question that a thing is, Id.

ἀμφί-λεκτος, ον, discussed on all hands, doubtful, Aesch.: so Adv. -τως, Id. II. act. disputatious, Eur.; ἀμφ. εἶναί τινι to quarrel for a thing, Aesch.

ἀμφιλογέομαι, Dep. to dispute, περί τινος Plut.; and ἀμφιλογία, ἡ, dispute, debate, Hes., Plut. From

ἀμφί-λογος, ον, disputed, disputable, Xen.; τὰ ἀμφίλογα disputed points, Thuc.; ἀμφίλογον γίγνεταί τι πρός τινα a dispute on a point takes place with some one, Xen.; neut. pl. ἀμφίλογα as Adv., Eur. II. act. disputatious, contentious, Soph., Eur.

ἀμφί-λοφος, ον, encompassing the neck, Soph.

ἀμφι-λύκη [ῠ], νύξ, ἡ, (v. *λύκη) the morning-twilight, gray of morning, Il.

*ἀμφι-μάομαι, to wipe all round, assumed as pres. of an Ep. aor. 1 ἀμφιμάσασθε, Od.

ἀμφι-μάσχᾰλος, ον, round both arms, two-sleeved, Ar.

ἀμφι-μάτορες, Dor. for ἀμφιμήτορες.

ἀμφι-μάχητος, ον, fought for, Anth.

ἀμφι-μάχομαι [ᾰ], Dep., only in pres. and impf., to fight round : 1. c. acc. to besiege, Il. 2. c. gen. to fight for, Ib.

ἀμφι-μέλας, -μέλαινα, -μέλᾰν, black all round : φρένες ἀμφιμέλαιναι, prob. referring to the φρένες or midriff being wrapped in darkness, dark-seated.

ἀμφι-μερίζομαι, Pass. to be completely parted, Anth.

ἀμφι-μήτορες, οἱ, αἱ, (μήτηρ) brothers or sisters by different mothers, Eur.

ἀμφι-μῡκάομαι, Dep. to bellow around : metaph., δάπεδον ἀμφιμέμῡκε (pf. 2) the floor echoed all round, Od.

ἀμφι-νεικής, ές, (νεῖκος) contested on all sides, eagerly wooed, Aesch., Soph.

ἀμφι-νείκητος, ον, (νεικέω) = ἀμφινεικής, Soph.

ἀμφι-νέμομαι, Med., of cattle, to feed around : then, of men, to dwell round, c. acc. loci, Il.

ἀμφι-νεύω, f. σω, to nod this way and that way, Anth.

ἀμφι-νοέω, f. ήσω, to think both ways, be in doubt, Soph.

ἀμφι-ξέω, aor. 1 ἀμφέξεσα, to smooth all round with an axe or plane, Od. Hence

ἀμφίξοος, ον, contr. -ξους, polishing all round, Anth.

ἀμφί-παλτος, ον, (πάλλω) tossed about, reëchoing, Anth.

ἀμφι-πᾰτάσσω, f. ξω, to strike on both sides, Anth.

ἀμφί-πεδος, ον, (πέδον) surrounded by a plain, Pind.

ἀμφι-πέλομαι, Dep. to float around, of music, Od.

ἀμφι-πένομαι, Dep. to be busied about, take charge of, c. acc., Hom.; τὸν κύνες ἀμφεπένοντο the dogs made a meal of him, Il.

ἀμφι-πλήγδην, Adv. twined round, Anth.

ἀμφι-περι-στέφομαι, Pass. to be put round as a crown, Od.

ἀμφι-περι-στρωφάω, to keep turning about all ways, Il.

ἀμφι-περι-τρύζω, to chirp or twitter round about, Anth.

ἀμφι-περι-φθῐνύθω [ῠ], to decay all round, h. Hom.

ἀμφι-πιάζω, Dor. for -πιέζω, to squeeze all round, hug closely, Theocr.

ἀμφι-πίπτω, f. -πεσοῦμαι, aor. 2 ἀμφ-έπεσον, to fall around, i. e. to embrace, c. acc., Od.; c. dat., ἀμφιπίπτων στόμασιν embracing so as to kiss, Soph.

ἀμφι-πίτνω (πῐτ), poët. for foreg., Eur.

ἀμφί-πλεκτος, ον, intertwined, Soph.; cf. κλῖμαξ.

ἀμφί-πληκτος, ον, beaten on both sides. II. act. dashing on both sides, Soph.

ἀμφι-πλήξ, ῆγος, ὁ, ἡ, (πλήσσω) striking with both sides, double-edged, Soph.

ἀμφι-πολεύω, f. -σω, (ἀμφίπολος) to be busied about, take care of, c. acc., Od., Hdt.; absol., δοῦναί τινά τινι ἀμφιπολεύειν to give one over to another, to take care of, Od.

ἀμφι-πολέω, (ἀμφίπολος) : I. c. acc. to attend constantly, to attend on, watch, guard, Pind. 2. to tend, treat gently, Lat. fovere, Id. II. c. dat. to minister to, θεαῖς Soph. III. c. gen. rei, to be ministers of, Pind.

ἀμφί-πολις, ὁ, ἡ, poët. ἀμφί-πτολις, ὁ, ἡ, encompassing a city, of a city taken by blockade, Aesch. II. as fem. Subst. a city between two seas or rivers, Thuc.

ἀμφί-πολος, ον, (πολέω) busied about, busy, epith. of Κύπρις, Soph. :—as fem. Subst. a handmaid, Od. :—sometimes joined with another Subst., ἀμφ. ταμίη, ἀμφ. γραῦς the housekeeper, the old woman in waiting, Hom. 2. as masc. an attendant, follower, Pind. :—also a priest, Plut. II. in pass. sense, as Adj. much-frequented, Pind.

ἀμφι-πονέομαι, Dep. (πονέω) to attend to a thing, c. acc., Il.

ἀμφι-ποτάομαι, Dep. to fly round and round, Il.

ἀμφι-πρόσωπος, ον, (πρόσωπον) double-faced, Plut.

ἀμφί-πτολις, poët. for ἀμφίπολις.

ἀμφι-πτυχή, ἡ, a folding round, embrace, Eur.

ἀμφί-πῠλος, ον, (πύλη) with two entrances, Eur.

ἀμφί-πῠρος, ον, (πῦρ) with fire at each end, of the thunder-bolt, Eur.; of Artemis as bearing a torch in either hand, Soph. II. with fire all round, Id.

ἀμφί-ρῠτος, η, ον, (ῥέω) flowed around, sea-girt, of islands, Od., Soph.; so ἀμφίρρυτος, ον, Hes., etc.

ἀμφίς, I. as Adv. (ἀμφί) : 1. on or at both sides, Il.; with both hands at once, Ib. 2. generally, around, round about, Ib. II. apart, asunder, γαῖαν καὶ οὐρανὸν ἀμφὶς ἔχειν to keep heaven and earth asunder, Od.; ἀμφὶς ἀγῆναι to snap in twain, Il.; ἀμφὶς φράζεσθαι or φρονεῖν to think separately, i. e. to be divided, take opposite parts, Ib.

B. as Prep., like ἀμφί, I. c. gen. around, ἅρματος ἀμφὶς all round his chariot, Il. 2. apart from, ἀμφὶς τινος ἧσθαι Ib.; ἀμφὶς ὁδοῦ out of the road, Ib. II. c. acc. about, around, always following its case, Ib.

ἀμφι-σᾰλεύομαι, Pass. to toss about, as on the sea, Anth.

ἀμφί-βαινα, ης, ἡ, (βαίνω) a kind of serpent, that can go either forwards or backwards, Aesch.

ἀμφισβάσίη, ἡ, Ion. for ἀμφισβήτησις, Hdt.

ἀμφισ-βητέω, Ion. -βᾱτέω, f. ήσω : impf. and aor. 1 (with double augm.) ἠμφεσβήτουν, ἠμφεσβήτησα :—

Pass., f. of med. form –ήσομαι : aor. 1 ἠμφισβητήθην or ἠμφεσβ–: (βαίνω) :—literally, *to stand apart*, and so *to disagree with* an argument, c. dat., Hdt. :—c. dat. pers. *to dispute* or *argue with*, τινι Plat.   **2.** absol. *to dispute, wrangle, argue*, Id., etc. :—οἱ ἀμφισβητοῦντες *the opponents*, in a lawsuit, Dem.   **3.** c. gen. rei, *to dispute for* or *about* a thing, Id.; also περί τινος Plat. :—*to lay claim* to the property of a deceased person, τοῦ κλήρου Dem.   **4.** c. acc. rei, *to dispute* a point, Plat.   **5.** c. acc. et inf. *to argue that*, Id.   **II.** Pass. *to be the subject of dispute*, Id.; or impers. ἀμφισβητεῖται περί τι or τινος Id.; ἀμφισβητεῖται μὴ εἶναί τι *it is disputed*, Id.   Hence

ἀμφισβήτημα, ατος, τό, *a point in dispute*, Plat., etc.

ἀμφισβητήσιμος, ον, (ἀμφισβητέω) *disputed, disputable*, Plat., etc.; χώρα ἀμφ. *debatable ground*, Xen.; οὐκέτ᾽ ἐν ἀμφισβητησίμῳ *no longer in doubt*, Dem.

ἀμφισβήτησις, εως, ἡ, (ἀμφισβητέω) *a dispute, controversy, debate*, ἀμφ. γίγνεται (or ἐστι) περί τινος Plat.; ἀμφισβήτησιν ἔχει *it admits of question*, Arist.

ἀμφισβήτητος, ον, (ἀμφισβητέω) *debatable*, γῆ Thuc.

ἀμφι-στέλλομαι, Med. *to fold round oneself*, c. acc., Theocr.

ἀμφι-στεφάνόομαι, Pass. *to stand all round like a crown*, h. Hom.

ἀμφ-ίστημι, f. -στήσω, *to place round*; only used in Pass. ἀμφίσταμαι, with intr. aor. 2 act. ἀμφέστην, Ep. 3 pl. ἀμφέσταν; syncop. 3 pl. pf. ἀμφεστᾶσι (for –εστήκασι) :—*to stand around*, Hom.; c. dat., Soph.

ἀμφί-στομος, ον, (στόμα) *with double mouth*, of a tunnel, Hdt.; λαβαὶ ἀμφίστομοι *handles on both sides of the bowl*, Soph.

ἀμφι-στρᾰτάομαι, Dep. *to beleaguer, besiege*, Ep. 3 pl. impf. ἀμφεστρατόωντο πόλιν Il.

ἀμφι-στρεφής, ές, (στρέφω) *turning all ways*, of a dragon's heads, Il.

ἀμφι-στρόγγυλος, ον, *quite round*, Luc.

ἀμφι-τάμνω, Ion. for ἀμφιτέμνω.

ἀμφι-τανύω, *to stretch all round*, h. Hom.

ἀμφι-τειχής, ές, (τεῖχος) *encompassing the walls*, Aesch.

ἀμφι-τέμνω, Ion. -τάμνω, *to cut off on all sides, intercept*, Il.

ἀμφι-τίθημι [τῐ], imper. ἀμφιτίθει: aor. 1 ἀμφέθηκα, the other moods being supplied by aor. 2 :—*to put round*, Lat. *circumdo*, ἀμφὶ δέ οἱ κυνέην ἔθηκε (in tmesi), Hom.; κόσμον ἀμφ. χροΐ Eur.; also, στέφανον ἀμφὶ κρᾶτα Id. :—Med. *to put round oneself*, Od. :—Pass. *to be put on*, Il.   **2.** *to cover* with a thing, κάρα πέπλοις Eur.

ἀμφι-τῐνάσσω, f. ξω, *to swing round*, Anth.

ἀμφι-τιττῠβίζω, f. σω, *to twitter* or *chirp around*, Ar.

ἀμφι-τόμος, ον, (τέμνω) *cutting with both sides, two-edged*, Aesch., Eur.

ἀμφί-τορνος, ον, *well-rounded*, Eur.

ἀμφι-τρέμω, *to tremble round* one, in tmesi, Il.

ἀμφι-τρέχω, f. -δρᾰμοῦμαι, *to run round, surround*, Pind.

ἀμφι-τρής, ῆτος, ὁ, ἡ, (*τράω) *pierced from end to end*, ἀμφιτρῆς [sc. πέτρα], i. e. a cave *with double entrance*, Eur.; with a neut. noun, ἀμφιτρὴς αὔλιον Soph.

ἀμφί-τρητος, ον, (*τράω) *pierced through*, Anth.

ἀμφι-τρομέω, f. ήσω, *to tremble for*, c. gen., Od.

ἀμφι-φαείνω, *to beam around*, c. acc., h. Hom.

ἀμφί-φᾰλος, ον, *with double crest* (v. φάλος), Il.

ἀμφι-φᾰνής, ές, (φαίνομαι) *visible all round, known to all*, Eur.

ἀμφι-φοβέομαι, Pass. *to tremble all round*, ἀμφεφόβηθεν (Ep. for –ήθησαν, 3 pl. aor. 1) Il.

ἀμφι-φορεύς, gen. έως Ep. ῆος, ὁ: (φέρω) :—*a large jar with two handles*, Lat. *amphora*, Hom.; cf. ἀμφορεύς.

ἀμφι-φράζομαι, f. -σομαι, Med. *to consider on all sides, consider well*, Il.

ἀμφι-χάσκω, aor. 2 ἀμφ-έχᾰνον (no pres. ἀμφι-χαίνω occurs), *to gape round, gape for*, c. acc., Il.; of a child, ἀμφ. μαστόν Aesch.; of an army surrounding a city, Soph.

ἀμφι-χέω, f. -χεῶ, *to pour around, to pour* or *spread over*, Od.   **II.** Pass. *to be poured* or *shed around*, Il.; c. acc., Hom.   **2.** of persons, *to embrace*, c. acc., Od.

ἀμφι-χορεύω, f. σω, *to dance around*, Eur., Anth.

ἀμφι-χρίομαι, Med. *to anoint oneself all over*, Od.

ἀμφί-χρῡσος, ον, *gilded all over*, Eur.

ἀμφίχῠτος, ον, (ἀμφιχέω) *poured around; thrown up around*, of an earthen wall, Il.

ἀμφί-χωλος, ον, *lame in both feet*, Anth.

ἄμφ-οδον, τό, (ὁδός) *a road round houses, a street*, N. T.

ἀμφορεύς, έως, ὁ: acc. ἀμφορέα; pl. ἀμφορῆς:—shortened for ἀμφιφορεύς, *an amphora, jar, urn*, Hdt., etc.   **II.** a liquid measure, = μετρητής = 1½ *amphorae*, or nearly 9 gallons, Id.

ἀμφορίσκος, ὁ, Dim. of ἀμφορεύς, Dem.

ἀμφοτέρῃ, Adv. *in both ways*, Hdt.

ἀμφοτερό-πλοος, ον, contr. -πλους, ουν, *sailing both ways* :—τὸ ἀμφοτερόπλουν (sc. δάνειον), *money lent on bottomry*, when the lender bore the risk *both of the outward and homeward voyage*, Dem.

ἀμφότερος, α, ον, (ἄμφω) *each* or *both of two*, Lat. *uterque*, Hdt., Aesch., etc.   **2.** neut. ἀμφότερον as Adv., ἀμφότερον βασιλεύς τ᾽ ἀγαθὸς κρατερός τ᾽ αἰχμητής *both good king and stout warrior*, Il.; so in neut. pl., ἀμφότερα μένειν πέμπειν τε Aesch.   **3.** κατ᾽ ἀμφότερα *on both sides, utrinque*, Hdt.; ἐπ᾽ ἀμφότερα, *both ways, in utramque partem*, Id.; ἀπ᾽ ἀμφοτέρων *from both sides, ex utraque parte*, Id.; ἀμφοτέραις, Ep. –ῃσι (sc. χερσί), Od.; ἐπ᾽ ἀμφοτέρων βεβακώς (sc. ποδῶν) Theocr.

ἀμφοτέρωθεν, Adv. *from* or *on both sides, utrinque*, Il., Hdt., etc.   **2.** *at both ends*, Od.

ἀμφοτέρωθι, Adv. *on both sides*, Xen.

ἀμφοτέρως, Adv. *in both ways*, Plat.

ἀμφοτέρωσε, Adv. *to both sides*, Il.

ἀμφ-ουδίς, (οὖδας ?) Adv., seems to mean *off* or *from the ground*, Od.

ἀμφράσσαιτο, 3 sing. poët. aor. 1 opt. of ἀναφράζομαι.

ἄμφω, τώ, τά, τώ, dual, οἱ, αἱ, τά, gen. and dat. ἀμφοῖν: (ἀμφί) :—Lat. *ambo, both*, Hom., etc.

ἀμφ-ώβολος, ὁ, (ὀβολός) *a javelin* or *spit with double point*, Eur.

ἀμφ-ώης, ες, (οὖς) = ἄμφ-ωτος, Theocr.

ἄμφ-ωτος, ον, (οὖς) *two-eared, two-handled*, Od.

ἀ-μώμητος, ον, (μωμάομαι) *unblamed, blameless*, Il., etc. :—Adv. -τως, Hdt.

ἄ-μωμος, ον, *without blame, blameless*, Hdt., Aesch.

ἀμῶς or ἀμῶς, Adv. *from* obsol. ἀμός = τις, only in compd. ἀμωσ-γέ-πως, *in some way or other*, Ar., Plat.

῎ΑΝ [ἄ], Ep. and Lyr. κε or κεν, Dor. κα (ᾱ), conditional

Particle. In Att., it is not joined with pres. or pf. indic., nor with imper. of any tense.

Three uses of ἄν must be distinguished in practice: A. in combination with Conjunctions and Relatives. B. in Apodosis. C. in Iterative sentences.

A. in combinations with Conjunctions and Relatives: **I.** such words are regularly foll. by the subj., viz. ἐάν (= εἰ ἄν), ἤν, ἄν, ἐπεάν (= ἐπεὶ ἄν), ἐπήν; ὃς ἄν *quicunque*, πρὶν ἄν, etc.; ἐπειδάν, ὅταν, ὁπόταν: the protasis generally has a fut. in apodosis, εἰ δέ κεν ὡς ἔρξῃς, γνώσῃ if *perchance* thou do thus, thou shalt know, Il. **II.** in Ep. sometimes with Opt., ὥς κε δοίη ᾧ κ᾽ ἐθέλοι that he *might* give her to whomsoever he *might* please, Od.: in such cases κε or ἄν does not affect the Verb. **III.** in Ep., sometimes with εἰ and Indic., οἵ κέ με τιμήσουσι Il. **IV.** in late Greek, ἐάν, etc., take Indic., ἐὰν οἴδαμεν N. T.

B. combined IN APODOSIS with the Verb, denoting that the assertion is dependent on some condition; ἦλθεν he came, ἦλθεν ἄν he *would have come*; ἔλθοι *may he come*, ἔλθοι ἄν he *would come*: **I.** with Indic.: **1.** with impf. and aor., the protasis implies non-fulfilment of a condition, and the apod. expresses what *would be* or *would have been* the case if the condition *were* or *had been* fulfilled. The impf. with ἄν refers to continued action in present or past time, the aor. generally to action in past time; οὐκ ἂν νήσων ἐκράτει, εἰ μὴ ναυτικόν εἶχεν he *would* not *have been* master of islands if he had not had a fleet, Thuc.; εἰ ταύτην ἔσχε τὴν γνώμην, οὐδὲν ἂν ἔπραξεν if he had come to this opinion, he *would have* accomplished nothing, Dem.:—the protasis is often understood, οὐ γὰρ ἦν ὅ τι ἂν ἐποιεῖτε for there was nothing which you *could have* done (i. e. *if you had tried*), Id.:—hence the Indic. with ἄν represents a potential mood; ἦλθε τοῦτο τοὔνειδος τάχ᾽ ἄν this reproach *might perhaps* have come, Soph. **2.** in Ep., with fut. indic., so as to modify the simple fut.; καί κέ τις ὧδ᾽ ἐρέει and some one *will perchance* speak thus, Il. **II.** with Subj., in Ep., much like fut. indic., εἰ δέ κε μὴ δώησιν, ἐγὼ δέ κεν αὐτὸς ἕλωμαι, i. e. *I will* take her myself, Ib. **III.** with Opt.: **1.** after protasis in opt. with εἰ or some relative word, εἴ μοί τι πίθοιο, τό κεν πολὺ κέρδιον εἴη if he should obey me, it *would be* much better, Ib.; sometimes with ind. in protasis, καί νύ κεν ἔνθ᾽ ἀπόλοιτο, εἰ μὴ νόησε he *would have* perished, had she not perceived, Ib.:—sometimes the tense in protasis is pres. or fut., and the opt. with ἄν in apodosi = fut., φρούριον εἰ ποιήσονται, βλάπτοιεν ἄν if they shall build a fort, they *might perhaps* damage, Thuc. **2.** the protasis is often understood: τὸν δ᾽ οὔ κε δύ᾽ ἀνέρε ὀχλίσσειαν two men *could* not heave the stone (i. e. *if they should try*), Il.:—hence the opt. with ἄν becomes a potential mood, βουλοίμην ἄν I *should* like, Lat. *velim* (but ἐβουλόμην ἄν I *should* wish, if it were of any avail, *vellem*). **3.** the opt. with ἄν comes to have the force of a mild command or entreaty, χωροῖς ἂν εἴσω you *may* go in, Soph.; κλύοις ἂν ἤδη hear me now, Id. **IV.** with inf. and part.:—the pres. inf. or part. represents impf. ind., φησὶν αὐτοὺς ἐλευθέρους ἂν εἶναι, εἰ τοῦτο ἔπραξαν he says they *would* (now) be free, if they had done this, Dem.; ἀδυνάτων ἂν ὄντων [ὑμῶν] ἐπιβοηθεῖν when you *would* have been

unable to assist, Thuc.;—or represents pres. opt., φησὶν αὐτοὺς ἐλευθέρους ἂν εἶναι, εἰ τοῦτο πράξειαν he says they *would* (hereafter) be free, *if they should do this*, Xen.;—the aor. inf. or part. represents aor. indic. or opt., οὐκ ἂν ἡγεῖσθ᾽ αὐτὸν κἂν ἐπιδραμεῖν; do you not think he *would* even have run thither? Dem.; οὐδ᾽ ἂν κρατῆσαι αὐτοὺς τῆς γῆς ἡγοῦμαι I think they *would* not even be masters of the land, Thuc.; οὔτε ὄντα οὔτε ἂν γενόμενα, i. e. *things which are not and never could happen*, Id.:—so the pf. (or plqpf.) inf. or partic., πάντα ταῦθ᾽ ὑπὸ τῶν βαρβάρων ἂν ἑαλωκέναι [φήσειεν ἄν] he would say that all these *would* have been destroyed by the barbarians, Dem.

C. with impf. and aor. indic. in the ITERATIVE construction, to express a condition *fulfilled whenever an opportunity offered*; εἶτα πῦρ ἂν οὐ παρῆν then *there would be* no fire at hand, i. e. there never was, Soph.; διηρώτων ἂν αὐτοὺς τί λέγοιεν Plat.

D. GENERAL REMARKS: **I.** Position of ἄν, **1.** ἄν may be separated from its inf. by such verbs as οἴομαι, δοκέω, so that ἄν has the appearance of belonging to the pres. indic., καὶ νῦν ἡδέως ἄν μοι δοκῶ κοινωνῆσαι I think that I *should*, Xen.:—in the peculiar case of οὐκ οἶδ᾽ ἂν εἰ, ἄν belongs not to οἶδα but to the Verb which follows, οὐκ οἶδ᾽ ἂν εἰ πείσαιμι = οὐκ οἶδα εἰ πείσαιμι ἄν, Eur. **2.** ἄν never begins a sentence. **II.** Repetition of ἄν:—in apodosis ἄν may be repeated with the same verb, ὥστ᾽ ἄν, εἰ σθένος λάβοιμι, δηλώσαιμ᾽ ἄν Soph.

ἄν [ᾰ], Att. Conj., = ἐάν, ἤν, often in Plat., etc.; cf. κἄν.

ἄν, crasis for ἃ ἄν, *quaecunque*, Soph.

ἄν, poët. for ἀνά before δ, etc., v. ἀνά A; cf. ἄμ.

ἄν, apocop. for ἄνα, v. ἀνά F. 2.

ἀν- or ἀνα-, the negat. Prefix (of which *a priv.* is a shortened form) before vowels, ἀν-αίτιος, ἀν-ώδυνος (but ἀ-έκων, ἄ-εκτι, ἄ-εργος): the complete form remains in ἀνά-εδνος, ἀνά-ελπτος.

ʹANAʹ [ᾰνᾰ], Prep. governing gen., dat., and acc. Radic. sense *up, upon*, opp. to κατά.

A. WITH GEN., ἀνὰ νηὸς *on board* ship, Od.

B. WITH DAT., *on, upon*, ἀνὰ σκήπτρῳ *upon the sceptre*, Il.; ἀνὰ ὤμῳ *upon the shoulder*, Od.

C. WITH ACC., the comm. usage, implying *motion upwards*: **I.** of Place, *up to, up along*, ἀνὰ τὸν ποταμόν Hdt.; ἀνὰ δῶμα *up and down* the house, *throughout* it, Il.; so, ἀνὰ στρατόν, ἄστυ, ὅμιλον Hom.; ἀνὰ στόμα ἔχειν to have *continually* in the mouth, Id. **II.** of Time, *throughout*, ἀνὰ νύκτα Il.; ἀνὰ τὸν πόλεμον Hdt.; ἀνὰ χρόνον *in course of* time, Id.; ἀνὰ πᾶσαν τὴν ἡμέραν Id.; but, ἀνὰ πᾶσαν ἡμέραν, distributively, day *by* day, Id. **III.** distributively also with Numerals, ἀνὰ πέντε παρασάγγας τῆς ἡμέρας [they marched] *at the rate* of 5 parasangs a day, Xen.; κλισίας ἀνὰ πεντήκοντα companies *at the rate* of 50 in each, N. T.; ἔλαβον ἀνὰ δηνάριον a denarius *apiece*, Ib. **IV.** ἀνὰ κράτος *up to* the full strength, with all might, ἀνὰ κράτος φεύγειν, ἀπομάχεσθαι Xen.; ἀνὰ λόγον *in proportion*, Plat.

D. WITHOUT CASE as Adv. *thereupon*, Hom., etc. **2.** *all over*, μέλανες δ᾽ ἀνὰ βότρυες ἦσαν *all over* there were clusters, Il.

E. IN COMPOS., **1.** *upwards, up*, as ἀναβαίνω, ἀνίστημι. **2.** with a sense of *increase* or *complete-*

ness, as ἀνακρίνω.   3. *again*, as ἀναβλαστάνω, ἀναγινώσκω.   4. *back, backwards*, ἀναχωρέω.

F. ἄνα by anastr. for ἀνάστηθι, *up! arise! ἀλλ' ἄνα* Hom.   2. ἄν apocop. for ἀνέστη, *he stood up*, Il.

ἄνα | ἄνᾰ], voc. of ἄναξ, *king*, Ζεῦ ἄνα Hom.

ἀναβάδην [βᾰ], Adv. (ἀναβαίνω) *going up, mounting*: —in Ar., *aloft, upstairs*.

ἀνα-βαίνω, f. -βήσομαι: (for aor. 1 v. infr. B): aor. 2 ἀνέβην: pf. -βέβηκα:—Med., aor. 1 –εβησάμην, Ep. 3 sing. -εβήσετο, v. infr. B :—*to go up, mount, to go up to,* c. acc. loci, Hom.; φάτις ἀνθρώπους ἀναβαίνει a report *goes up among* men, Od.; with a Prep., ἀν. ἐς δίφρον Il.; ἀν. ἐπὶ οὔρεα Hdt. :—c. dat. *to trample on*, Il. :— c. acc. cogn., ἀν. στόλον *to go up on* an expedition, Pind.   II. Special usages :   1. *to mount* a ship, *go on board, embark*, Hom.; ἐς Τροίην ἀν. *to embark* for Troy, Od., etc.   2. *to mount* on horseback, ἀν. ἐφ' ἵππον, ἐφ' ἵππου Xen.; absol., ἀναβεβηκώς *mounted*, Id.   3. of land-journeys, *to go up* from the coast into Central Asia, Hdt., Xen. ; cf. ἀνάβασις 1. 2.   4. of rivers, *to rise*, Hdt. ; ἀν. ἐς τὰς ἀρούρας *to overflow* the fields, Id.   5. in Att., ἀν. ἐπὶ τὸ βῆμα, or ἀναβαίνειν alone, *to mount* the tribune, Dem. ; ἀν. ἐπὶ or εἰς τὸ πλῆθος, τὸ δικαστήριον *to come* before the people, before the court, Plat.   III. of things and events, *to come to an end, turn out*, like ἀποβαίνω, ἐκβαίνω, Hdt., etc.   2. *to come to, pass over to,* εἴς τινα Id.

B. aor. 1 ἀνέβησα is used as aor. to ἀναβιβάζω in causal sense, *to make to go up*, esp. *to put on shipboard*, Il., Pind. ; so med. ἀνεβήσετο Od.

ἀνα-βακχεύω, f. σω, *to rouse to Bacchic frenzy*, Eur. ; cf. sq.   II. intr. *to break into Bacchic frenzy*, Id.

ἀνα-βακχιόω, =foreg., Eur.

ἀνα-βάλλω, f. -βᾰλῶ : aor. 2 ἀν-έβαλον :—*to throw* or *toss up*, Thuc., Xen.   II. *to put back, put off*, Od.; ἀν. τινα *to put* him *off* with excuses, Dem. :—Pass. *to be adjourned*, Thuc.   III. *to run a risk*, ἐγώ σφε θάψω κἀνὰ κίνδυνον βαλῶ, =καὶ ἀναβαλῶ, Aesch.

B. Med. *to·strike up, begin to play* or *sing* (cf. ἀναβολή II), Od., Ar.   II. *to put off, delay*, Il., Ar., etc.   2. *to throw back* or *refer* a thing to another, Luc.   III. *to throw one's cloak back, throw it over the shoulder*, Ar., Plat.; ἀναβεβλημένος *with one's cloak thrown up* or *back*, Dem. ; cf. ἀναβολή 1. 2.

ἀνα-βαπτίζω, f. σω, *to dip repeatedly*, Plat.

ἀνάβᾱσις, poët. ἄμβᾰσις, εως, ἡ, (ἀναβαίνω) *a going up, mounting* on horseback, Xen. :—πᾶσα ἄμβασις = πάντες ἀναβάται, all *the horsemen*, Soph.   2. *an expedition up* from the coast into Central Asia, as that of the younger Cyrus, Xen.   II. *a way up, ascent* of a tower or mountain, Hdt., Thuc.

ἀνα-βαστάζω, f. σω, *to raise* or *lift up, carry*, Luc.

ἀναβάτης [βᾰ], ου, ὁ, poët. ἀμβάτης, (ἀναβαίνω) *one mounted*, of Pentheus in the tree, Eur. : *a horseman, rider*, Xen.

ἀναβᾰτικός, ή, όν, (ἀναβαίνω) *skilled in mounting*, ἐπὶ τοὺς ἵππους Xen.

ἀναβᾰτός, Ep. ἀμβᾰτός, όν, (ἀναβαίνω) *to be mounted* or *scaled, easy to be scaled*, Hom.

ἀνα-βέβρῡχεν, pf. with no pres. ἀνα-βρύζω in use, ἀναβέβρυχεν ὕδωρ the water *gushed* or *bubbled up*, Il.

ἀνα-βιβάζω, aor. 1 –εβίβασα :—Med., f. Att. -βιβῶμαι :

--Causal of ἀναβαίνω, *to make go up, cause to mount*, ἐπὶ πύργον Hdt., Xen.   II. Special usages :   1. ἀν. τινα ἐφ' ἵππον *to mount* one on horseback, Id. ; ἐπ' ἄρμα Hdt.   2. ἀν. ναῦν *to draw* a ship *up* on land, Xen.   3. Med., ἀναβιβάζεσθαί τινας ἐπὶ τὰς ναῦς *to have* them *put on board* ship, Thuc. ; absol., ἀναβιβασάμενοι Id.   4. at Athens, *to bring up* to the bar as a witness, Plat., etc. : Med., of a culprit, *to bring up* his wife and children to raise compassion, Id.   5. Pass., ἀναβιβάζεσθαι εἰς τιμήν *to ascend* to honour, Plut.   6. ἀν. τοὺς φθόγγους, *to moderate* them, Id. Hence

ἀναβῐβαστέον, verb. Adj. *one must cause to mount*, Plat.

ἀνα-βιόω, = ἀναβιώσκομαι, f. -βιώσομαι : aor. 2 ἀνέβίων or –εβίουν : pf. -βεβίωκα :—*to come to life again, return to life*, Ar., Plat.   Hence

ἀναβίωσις, εως, ἡ, *a reviving*, Plut.

ἀνα-βιώσκομαι, as Pass. = ἀναβιόω, Plat.   II. as Dep., Causal of ἀναβιόω, *to bring back to life*, Id. ; aor. 1 ἀνεβιωσάμην Id.

ἀνα-βλαστάνω [ᾰ], f. -βλαστήσω : aor. 2 –εβλαστον :— *to shoot up, grow up again*, of Plants, Plat. ; of a city, Hdt. ; of misfortunes, *to spring up, be rank*, Id.

ἀνα-βλέπω, f. -βλέψω or -βλέψομαι : aor. 1 –έβλεψα :— *to look up*, Ar., Plat., etc.; ἀν. πρός τινα *to look* him *in the face*, Xen.   2. *to look up at,* c. acc., Eur.; also c. dat., Id.   3. c. acc. cogn., ἀν. φλόγα *to cast up* a glance of fire, Id.   II. *to recover one's sight*, Hdt., Plat.; πάλιν ἀν. Ar.   Hence

ἀνάβλεψις, εως, ἡ, *a looking up*, Arist.   II. *recovery of sight*, N. T.

ἀνάβλησις, εως, ἡ, (ἀναβάλλω) *a putting off, delay*, Il.

ἀνα-βλύζω, poët. ἀμβλ- : aor. 1 ἀνέβλυσα, inf. ἀναβλῦσαι :—*to spout up,* c. acc., Anth.   2. intr. *to gush forth*, Theocr.

ἀναβόᾱμα, poët. ἀμβ-, ατος, τό, *a loud cry*, Aesch. From

ἀνα-βοάω, f. -ήσομαι, Dor. -άσομαι : (ἀναβοάσω is aor. 1 subj.): aor. 1 ἀνεβόησα, Ion. ἀνέβωσα, part. ἀμβώσας : —*to shout aloud, utter a loud cry*, Hdt., Eur. ; of a war-cry, Xen. ; c. inf. *to call out* that . . , Id.   2. c. acc. rei, *to cry out* something, Eur. ; also *to wail aloud over* a misfortune, Aesch., Eur.   3. c. acc. pers. *to call on*, Id.

ἀναβολάς, άδος, ἡ, v. ἀμβολάς.

ἀναβολεύς, έως, ὁ, (ἀναβάλλω) *a groom who helps one to mount*, Plut.

ἀναβολή, poët. ἀμβολή, ἡ, (ἀναβάλλω)   I. of the thing,   1. *that which is thrown up, a mound*, Xen.   2. *that which is thrown back over the* shoulder, *a mantle, cloak*, Plat. :—also *the fashion of wearing it*, Luc. ; cf. ἀναβάλλω B. III.   II. as an action,   1. *a prelude* on the lyre, Pind. ; *a dithyrambic ode*, Ar. ; v. ἀναβάλλω B. I.   2. *a putting off, delaying*, Hdt., Thuc. ; οὐκ ἐς ἀμβολάς *without delay*, Eur. ; v. ἀναβάλλω B. II.   3. intr. *a bursting forth*, Arist.

ἀνα-βράσσω, Att. -βράττω, mostly in pres., *to boil well, seethe,* c. acc., Ar. ; absol., ἀναβράττετ', ἐξοπτᾶτε Id.

ἀνάβραστος, ον, (ἀναβράσσω) *boiled*, Ar.

*ἀναβράχω, v. ἀνέβραχε.

ἀναβρόξειε, ἀναβροχείς, v. βρόχω.

ἀνα-βρῠχάζω, f. ξω, *to neigh aloud*, of horses, Ar.

*ἀναβρύζω, v. ἀναβέβρυχεν.

ἀνα-βρῡχάομαι, Dep. *to roar aloud*, Plat.

ἀν-αγγέλλω, f. ελῶ: aor. 1 -ήγγειλα: pf. -ήγγελκα: —*to carry back tidings of, report*, Aesch., Eur.; τῷ Βρασίδᾳ τὴν ξυνθήκην Thuc. :—Pass., c. part., ἀνηγγέλθη τεθνεώς *was reported* dead, Plut.

ἀν-άγγελος, ον, *from which no messenger returns*, Anth.

ἀνα-γελάω, f. -άσομαι, *to laugh loud*, ἀναγελάσας Xen.

ἀνα-γεννάω, f. ήσω, *to beget anew, regenerate*, N. T.

ἀν-αγέομαι, Dor. for ἀνηγέομαι.

ἀνα-γεύω, f. σω, *to give one a taste*, c. acc. pers., Ar.

ἀνα-γιγνώσκω, Ion. and later -γῑνώσκω: I. Ep. usage, esp. in aor. 2 ἀν-έγνων, *to know well, know certainly*, Hom., Hdt. 2. *to know again, recognise: to acknowledge, own*, Lat. *agnoscere*, Hom., Hdt. II. Att. usage, f. ἀναγνώσομαι: aor. 2 ἀνέγνων: pf. ἀνέγνωκα:— Pass., f. -γνωσθήσομαι: aor. 1 ἀνεγνώσθην: pf. ἀνέγνωσμαι, etc. :—of written characters, *to know* them *again*, and so *to read*, Ar., etc.; ἀναγνώσεται (sc. ὁ γραμματεύς), ἀνάγνωθι, Dem. :—οἱ ἀναγιγνώσκοντες *students*, Plut. III. Ion. usage, aor. 1 ἀνέγνωσα, *to persuade* or *induce* one to do a thing, c. acc. et inf., Hdt. : the inf. is sometimes omitted, ὡς ἀνέγνωσε *when he had persuaded* him, Id.; —the pres. is once so used, ἀναγιγνώσκεις στρατεύεσθαι βασιλέα Id. : —so in aor. 1 pass. ἀνεγνώσθην, *to be persuaded* to do a thing, c. inf., Id.

ἀναγκάζω, f. -άσω: pf. ἠνάγκᾰκα: plqpf. -ειν: (ἀνάγκη):—*to force, compel*, mostly c. acc. pers. et inf., ἀν. τινὰ ποιεῖσθαί τι, λέγειν, etc., Hdt., etc. :—so Pass., ἠναγκάζοντο ἀμύνεσθαι Id.; —without the inf., ἀναγκάζεσθαί τι *to be forced* to do a thing, Plat., etc. :—also, ἀναγκάζειν τινὰ ἔς τι Thuc. 2. c. acc. pers. only, *to constrain* by argument, Plat. : Pass., ἠναγκάσθην *I was constrained, tortured*, Soph. ; ἠναγκασμένος, ἀναγκασθείς *under compulsion*, Thuc. 3. c. acc. rei only, *to carry through by force*, Eur. 4. c. acc. rei et inf. *to prove* that a thing *is necessarily so* and so, Plat.

ἀναγκαίη, ἡ, Ep. and Ion. for ἀνάγκη, Hom., etc.

ἀναγκαῖον, τό, (ἀνάγκη) *a place of constraint, a prison*, Xen. :—others read Ἀνακεῖον.

ἀναγκαῖος, α, ον, and os, ον, (ἀνάγκη) *with* or *by force*: I. act. *constraining, applying force*, Il.; ἦμαρ ἀν. the day *of constraint*, i. e. *slavery*, Ib.; so, ἀναγκαία τύχη the lot *of slavery*, or *a violent death*, Soph.; ῇ τῆς ἀρχῆς ἀναγκαίῳ by the *compulsory nature* of our rule, Thuc.; ἐξ ἀναγκαίου under *compulsion*, Id. 2. of arguments, *forcible, cogent*, Id. II. pass. *constrained, forced*, πολεμιστα ἀν. soldiers *perforce*, whether they will or no, Od. 3. *necessary*, ἀναγκαῖόν [ἐστι], like ἀνάγκη ἐστί, c. inf., *it is necessary* to do a thing, Hdt., etc.; but, ἔνιαι τῶν ἀποκρίσεων ἀναγκαῖαι ποιεῖσθαι *necessarily requiring* to be made, Plat. 3. τὰ ἀναγκαῖα *necessary things, needs*, as food, sleep, Id., Xen.; τὰ ἐκ θεοῦ ἀν. the *appointed order of things, laws of nature*, Id. 4. *absolutely necessary, indispensable, barely sufficient*; ἀν. τροφή = ἡ καθ' ἡμέραν, Thuc.; τὸ ἀναγκαιότατον ὕψος the least height *that was absolutely necessary*, Id.; ἡ ἀναγκαιοτάτη πόλις *the least that could be called* a city, Plat. 5. of persons, *connected by necessary ties*, i. e. *related by blood*, Id., etc. :—οἱ ἀναγκαῖοι, Lat. *necessarii, kinsfolk*, Xen., etc. III. Adv. -ως, *necessarily, of necessity, perforce*, ἀναγκαίως ἔχει it

must be so, Hdt. ; ἀν. φέρειν to bear *as best one can*, opp. to ἀνδρείως, Thuc. 2. ἀν. λέγειν *only so far as is necessary*, Plat.

ἀναγκαστέον, α, ον, verb. Adj. of ἀναγκάζω, *to be compelled*, Plat. II. neut. -έον *one must compel*, Id.

ἀναγκαστός, ή, όν, (ἀναγκάζω) *forced, constrained*, Hdt.; ἀν. στρατεύειν *pressed* into the service, Thuc.

ἀνάγκη, Ion. and Ep. ἀναγκαίη, ἡ, (ἄγχω) *force, constraint, necessity*, Hom., etc.; ἀνάγκῃ *perforce, of necessity*, or in act. sense, *forcibly, by force*, Id.; so, ὑπ' ἀνάγκης, ἐξ ἀνάγκης, δι' ἀνάγκης, πρὸς ἀνάγκην, κατ' ἀνάγκην, Att.; ἀνάγκη ἐστί, c. inf., *it is matter of necessity* to do a thing, Hom., etc.; c. dat. pers., ἀν. μοι σχεθεῖν Aesch. :—in Trag., πολλή γ' ἀνάγκη, πολλή 'στ' ἀνάγκη or πολλή μ' ἀνάγκη, with which an inf. must be supplied. 2. *actual force, violence, torture*, Hdt., etc.; metaph., δολόποιὸς ἀν., i. e. the stratagem of Nessus, Soph. 3. *bodily pain, anguish, distress*, κατ' ἀνάγκην ἔρπειν *painfully*, Id.; ὑπ' ἀνάγκης βοᾶν Id. II. like Lat. *necessitudo, the tie of blood, relationship, kindred*, Lys., etc.

ἀνα-γνάμπτω, f. ψω, *to bend back* : Pass., αἰχμὴ ἀνεγνάμφθη the spear-point *was bent back*, Il. 2. *to undo, loose*, δεσμόν Od.

ἀνα-γνοίην, aor. 2 opt. of ἀναγιγνώσκω.

ἄν-αγνος, ον, *impure, unclean, unholy, defiled*, Aesch. etc.

ἀναγνῶναι, aor. 2 inf. of ἀναγιγνώσκω.

ἀναγνώρισις, εως, ἡ, *recognition*, Plat.; in a tragedy, *recognition*, Arist.

ἀναγνωρισμός, ὁ, = ἀναγνώρισις 1, Arist.

ἀνάγνωσις, εως, ἡ, *recognition*, Hdt. 2. *reading*, Plat.

ἀνάγνωσμα, ατος, τό, (ἀναγιγνώσκω) *a passage read aloud, a lecture*, Luc.

ἀναγνώστης, ου, ὁ, (ἀναγιγνώσκω) *a reader, a slave trained to read*, Plut.

ἀναγνωστικός, ή, όν, (ἀναγιγνώσκω) *suitable for reading*, opp. to ἀγωνιστικός, Arist.

ἀναγόρευσις, εως, ἡ, *a public proclamation*, Decret. ap. Dem. From

ἀν-αγορεύω, impf. -ηγόρευον: f. εύσω: aor. 1 -ηγόρευσα:—Pass., aor. 1 -ηγορεύθην: pf. -ηγόρευμαι: — (but fut. and aor. are mostly supplied by ἀν-ερῶ, ἀν-εῖπον):—*to proclaim publicly*, Aeschin. :—Pass. *to be proclaimed*, ἀναγορευέσθω νικηφόρος Plat.

ἀναγραπτέον, verb. Adj. of ἀναγράφω, *one must register*, εὐεργέτην ἀν. τινά Luc.

ἀνάγραπτος, ον, (ἀναγράφω) *inscribed, registered*, Thuc.

ἀναγραφεύς, έως, ὁ, (ἀναγράφω) *a registrar*, Lysias.

ἀναγραφή, ἡ, (ἀναγράφω) *a registering*, of treaties and the like, Arist. II. *a register*, Plat.

ἀνα-γράφω, f. ψω, *to engrave and set up*, of treaties, laws, etc., *to inscribe, register*, ἀν. τι ἐν στήλῃ or ἐς στήλην, Thuc., Dem. 2. of persons, *to register* his name, Isocr. :—Pass., ἀναγραφῆναι πατρόθεν *to be registered* with his father's name, Hdt.; ἀναγράφεσθαι εὐεργέτης *to be registered* as a benefactor, Id. II. *to describe* mathematically, Plat. (in Med.). III. *to entitle*, Plut.

ἀνα-γρύζω, only in pres., *to keep muttering*, Ar.

ἀνα-γυμνόω, f. ώσω, *to strip naked, unveil*, Plut.

ἀν-άγω, f. -άξω: aor. 2 ἀνήγαγον: I. *to lead up* from a lower place to a higher, Theogn., etc.   2. *to lead up to the high sea, to carry by sea,* Hom., etc.; ἀν. ναῦν *to put* a ship *to sea,* Hdt.; absol. in the same sense, Id.; —this is more common in Med.   3. *to take up* from the coast into the interior, Od., Hdt.; esp. from Asia Minor into Central Asia, Xen.   4. *to bring up* from the dead, Hes., Aesch.   5. ἀν. χορόν *to conduct* the choir, Hes., Eur., etc.; also, ἀν. ὀρτήν *to celebrate* a festival, Hdt.   6. *to lift up, raise,* κάρα, τὸ ὄμμα Soph., etc.   7. ἀν. παιᾶνα *to lift up* the paean, Id.   8. in various senses, ἀν. αἷμα *to bring up* blood, Plut.; ἀν. ποταμόν *to bring* a river *up* [over its banks,] Luc.; ἀν. φάλαγγα, like ἀναπτύσσειν, Plut.; *to bring up* a prisoner for examination, Xen., etc.   II. *to bring back,* Hom., etc.   2. *to refer* a matter to another, Dem.   3. *to rebuild,* Plut.   4. *to reckon* or *calculate,* Id.   5. intr. (sub. ἑαυτόν) *to draw back, withdraw, retreat,* Xen.; ἐπὶ πόδα ἀν. *to retreat* facing the enemy.   6. *to reduce in amount, contract,* Dem.   B. Med. and Pass. *to put out* to sea, set sail, Il., etc.; ἀναχθῆναι Hdt.; ἀναχθείς Aesch.   2. metaph. *to make ready, prepare oneself,* ὡς ἐρωτήσων Plat.

ἀναγωγή, ἡ, (ἀνάγω) *a leading up,* esp. *taking a ship into the high sea, a putting to sea,* Thuc., etc.   II. *a bringing back: restitution* by law, Plat.

ἀν-άγωγος, ον, (ἀγωγή) *ill-trained,* of horses, *ill-broken, unmanageable,* Xen., etc.

ἀν-αγώνιστος, ον, (ἀγωνίζομαι) *without conflict,* Thuc.: *never having contended for a prize,* Xen.

ἀνα-δαίομαι, v. ἀναδατέομαι.

ἀνα-δαίω, f. ἀν-δαίω, only in pres., *to light up,* Aesch.

ἀνα-δάσασθαι, aor. 1 inf. of ἀναδατέομαι.

ἀνα-δασθῆναι, aor. 1 inf. pass. of ἀναδατέομαι.

ἀναδασμός, ὁ, *re-distribution* or *partition* of land, among colonists, Hdt., Plat., etc.; and

ἀνάδαστος, ον, *divided anew, re-distributed,* ἀν. γῆν ποιεῖν (cf. ἀναδασμός) Plat.   II. ἀν. ποιεῖν τι *to rescind,* Luc.   From

ἀνα-δατέομαι: aor. 1 ἀν-εδασάμην :—*to divide anew, re-distribute,* Thuc. :—Pass. ἀναδαίομαι, *to be distributed,* Orac. ap. Hdt.

ἀνα-δέδρακον, aor. 2 of ἀναδέρκομαι.

ἀνα-δέδρομα, pf. of ἀνατρέχω.

ἀνάδειγμα, ατος, τό, *a mouthpiece used by public criers,* Anth. From

ἀνα-δείκνυμι and -ύω, f. -δείξω, Ion. -δέξω :—*to lift up and shew,* πύλας ἀναδεικνύναι *to display by opening* the gates, i.e. *throw wide* the gates, Soph.; (so in Pass., μυστοδόκος δόμος ἀναδείκνυται Ar.); ἀναδέξαι ἀσπίδα *to hold* up a shield *as signal,* Hdt.; ἀνέδεξε σημήϊον τοῖς ἄλλοις ἀνάγεσθαι *made* signal for them to put to sea, Id.   II. *to consecrate,* Anth. Hence

ἀνάδειξις, εως, ἡ, *a proclamation* of an election, *an appointment,* Lat. *designatio,* Plut.   II. (from Pass.) *a manifestation,* N. T.

ἀνα-δέκομαι, Ion. for ἀναδέχομαι.

ἀν-άδελφος, ον, *without brother* or *sister,* Eur.

ἀνάδεμα, poët. ἄνδεμα, ατος, τό, = ἀνάδημα, Anth.

ἀνα-δέξαι, Ion. for -δεῖξαι, aor. 1 inf. of ἀναδείκνυμι.

ἀνα-δέρκομαι, Dep. with aor. 2 act. -δέδρακον, *to look up,* Il.

ἀνα-δέρω, poët. ἀν-δ-, f. -δερῶ: aor. 1 -έδειρα :—*to strip the skin off :* metaph. *to lay bare,* τι Luc. :—so in Med., ἀναδέρεσθον Ar.

ἀνάδεσις, εως, ἡ, (ἀναδέω) *a binding on,* στεφάνων Plut.   2. *a binding up,* τῆς κόμης Luc.

ἀνα-δέσμη, ἡ, *a band for the hair, a head-band,* Il., Eur. :—so, ἀνά-δεσμος, ὁ, (ἀναδέω), Anth.

ἀνάδετος, ον, *binding up the hair,* Eur.

ἀνα-δεύω, f. σω, *to moisten :* metaph. *to imbue,* Plut.

ἀνα-δέχομαι, f. -δέξομαι: aor. 1 ἀνεδεξάμην, Ep. aor. 2 ἀνεδέγμην: pf. ἀναδέδεγμαι: Dep. :—*to take up, catch, receive,* Il.   II. *to take upon oneself, submit to,* ὀϊζύν Od.; ἀν. τι ἐφ' ἑαυτόν Dem.   2. *to undertake, promise to* do, c. fut. inf., Hdt., Xen. :—so, ἀν. τοὺς δανειστὰς *to undertake to satisfy* them, Plut. :—*to be surety to* one, τινι Thuc.

ἀνα-δέω, Att. part. ἀναδῶν : f. -δήσω: aor. 1 ἀνέδησα : —Med. and Pass., Att. contr. ἀναδοῦνται, ἀναδούμενος : pf. pass. -δέδεμαι :—*to bind* or *tie up,* Pind.: Med., ἀναδέεσθαι τὰς κεφαλὰς *to bind their* heads, Hdt.; κρώβυλον ἀναδεῖσθαι τῶν τριχῶν *to bind* one's hair into a knot, Thuc.   2. c. acc. pers. *to crown,* Pind. Thuc.; εὐαγγέλια ἀναδεῖν τινα *to crown* him for good tidings, Ar. :—metaph. in Pass., τροφῇ ἀναδοῦνται *are well furnished* with food, Plat.   II. ἀναδῆσαι τὴν πατρίην ἔς τινα *to attach* one's family to a founder, *trace* it *back,* Hdt.   III. Med., of a ship, ἀναδούμενος ἕλκειν *to take in tow,* Thuc.   IV. metaph. in Pass., ἀναδεδέσθαι ἔκ τινος or εἴς τι *to be dependent* upon, Plut. Hence

ἀνάδημα, poët. ἄνδημα, τό, = ἀναδέσμη, Pind., Eur.

ἀνα-διδάσκω, f. -διδάξω, *to teach otherwise* or *better,* Lat. *dedocere,* Plut. :—Pass. *to be better instructed, change one's mind,* Id.   II. *to shew clearly,* Thuc.: *to expound, interpret,* λόγια ἀν. τινά *to expound* them to one, Ar.

ἀνα-δίδωμι, poët. ἀν-δίδωμι, f. -δώσω, etc., *to hold up and give,* Pind., Xen.   II. *to give forth, send up, yield,* καρπόν Hdt., etc.: of a river, *to yield,* ἀναδιδόναι ἄσφαλτον Id.   2. intr., of springs and fire, *to burst forth,* Id.   III. *to deal round, spread,* Plut.   IV. intr. *to retrograde,* Arist.

ἀνά-δικος, ον, (δίκη) *tried over again,* Andoc., Plat.

ἀνα-διπλόομαι, Pass. *to be made double,* Xen.

ἀνάδοσις, εως, ἡ, (ἀναδίδωμι) *a distribution: digestion,* Polyb.: metaph. *of knowledge,* Plut.

ἀνάδοτος, ον, (ἀναδίδωμι) *to be given up,* Thuc.

ἀναδοχή, ἡ, (ἀναδέχομαι) *a taking up, undertaking,* πόνων Soph.

ἀνα-δραμεῖν, aor. 2 inf. of ἀνατρέχω.

ἀνα-δύω [ῠ], *to come to the top of water,* Batr.

ἀνα-δύομαι, Ep. 3 sing. ἀνδύεται [ῠ]: f. -δύσομαι [ῠ]: aor. 1 ἀνεδυσάμην, Ep. 3 sing. -ετο: Dep. with aor. 2 act. ἀνέδυν, 3 sing. subj. ἀναδύῃ or opt. ἀναδύη [ῠ], inf. ἀναδῦναι: pf. ἀναδέδῠκα :—*to come up, rise* from the sea, c. gen., Hom.; so c. acc., ἀνεδύσατο κῦμα θαλάσσης Il.   II. *to draw back, retire,* Hom.: *to shrink back, hesitate,* Ar. :—of springs, *to fail,* Plut.   2. c. acc. *to draw back from, shun,* πόλεμον Il. Hence

ἀνάδυσις, εως, ἡ, *a drawing back, retreat,* Plat.: *a holding back* from service, Plut.

ἀνά-εδνος, ή, (ἕδνα) without bridal gifts, Il.
ἀν-αείρω, only in pres. and impf. to lift up, of a wrestler, Il.; to carry off, τάλαντα Ib.
ἀνά-ελπτος, ον, (ἔλπομαι) unlooked for, Hes.
ἀν-αερτάω, lengthd. for ἀν-αείρω, Anth.
ἀνα-ζάω, inf. -ζῆν, to return to life, be alive again, N.T.
ἀναξείω, Ep. for ἀναξέω.
ἀνα-ζεύγνυμι and -ύω, f. -ζεύξω, to yoke again, ἀνα-ζευγνύναι τὸν στρατόν to move off the army, Hdt.; ἀν. τὸ στρατόπεδον to break up the camp, Id.; ἀν. τὰς νῆας to move them back, Id. 2. absol. to break up, shift one's quarters, Thuc., Xen. Hence
ἀνάζευξις, εως, ή, a marching off, return home, Plut.
ἀνα-ζέω, f. -ζέσω, to boil up or bubble up, Soph. 2. ἀναζ. εὐλάς to swarm with worms, a kind of disease, Plut.; also, εὐλαὶ ἀναζέουσιν Id.
ἀνα-ζητέω, f. ήσω, to examine into, investigate, τὰ ὑπὸ γῆς Plat.: Pass., Hdt., etc.
ἀνα-ζωγρέω, f. ήσω, to recall to life, Anth.
ἀνα-ζώννυμι or -ύω, f. -ζώσω, to gird up :—Med., ἀν. τὰς ὀσφύας to gird up one's loins, N.T.
ἀνα-ζωπῦρέω, f. ήσω, to rekindle, Eur.:—Pass. to gain fresh life and courage, Plat., Xen.; so, intr. in Act., Plut.
ἀνα-θάλλω, aor. 1 ἀν-έθηλα, to shoot up again : so in f. med., ἀναθαλήσεται Anth.
ἀνα-θαρσέω, Att. -θαρρέω, f. ήσω, to regain courage, Ar., Thuc.; τινι at a thing, Thuc.; πρός τι Plut.
ἀνα-θαρσύνω [ῠ], Att. -θαρρύνω, f. ῠνῶ, to fill with fresh courage, Xen. 2. intr.=foreg., Plut.
ἀνάθεμα, poët. ἄνθεμα, ατος, τό, (ἀνατίθημι)=ἀνάθημα, Theocr., Anth. 2. esp. anything devoted to evil, an accursed thing, N.T. II. a curse, Ib. Hence
ἀναθεμᾰτίζω, f. σω, to devote, ἀναθέματι ἀν. ἑαυτούς to bind themselves by a curse, N.T. II. intr. to swear, Ib.
ἀνα-θερμαίνω, f. ἀνῶ, to warm up, heat again, Anth.
ἀναθετέον, verb. Adj. of ἀνατίθημι, one must attribute, τί τινι Plat.
ἀνα-θηλέω, f. ήσω, (θάλλω) to sprout afresh, Il.
ἀνάθημα, ατος, τό, (ἀνατίθημι) a votive offering set up in a temple, Hdt., Soph., etc. 2. a delight, ornament, Od.
ἀνα-θλίβω [ῑ], f. ψω, to press hard, Anth.
ἄν-αθλος, ον, without contest, not warlike, Luc.
ἀνα-θορεῖν, aor. 2 inf. of ἀναθρώσκω.
ἀνα-θορῠβέω, f. ήσω, to cry out loudly, shout in applause, Plat., Xen. II. c. acc. to applaud, Plat.
ἀνάθρεμμα, ατος, τό, (ἀνατρέφω) a nursling, Theocr.
ἀν-αθρέω, f. ήσω, to look up at, observe closely, Eur., Plat. :—Pass., τὰ ἔργα ἐκ τῶν λόγων ἀναθρούμενα their deeds compared with their words, Thuc.
ἀνα-θρώσκω, poët. and Ion. ἀν-θρώσκω : aor. 2 -έθορον: —to spring up, bound up, rebound, Il., Hdt., etc.; ἀναθρώσκει ἐπὶ τὸν ἵππον springs upon it, Hdt.
ἀνα-θῡμιάω, f. άσω [ᾱ], to make to rise in vapour :— Pass. to rise in vapour, Arist., Luc.
ἀναϊδειά, Ep. and Ion. -είη, Att. also -είᾱ: (ἀναιδής) :— shamelessness, impudence, effrontery, Hom., Plat., etc.
ἀναιδεύομαι, Dep. to behave impudently, Ar. From
ἀν-αιδής, ές, (αἰδώς) shameless, Hom., Soph. 2. c. gen., ἀναιδέα δηϊοτῆτος insatiate of strife, Il. II. of things, λᾶας ἀναιδής the reckless stone, of Sisyphus,

Od.; ἔργ' ἀναιδῆ Soph. : — τὸ ἀναιδές, contr. τἀνειδές, =ἀναίδεια, Eur.; ἐπὶ τὸ ἀναιδέστερον τραπέσθαι Hdt. III. Adv. -δῶς, Soph., etc.
ἀν-αιθύσσω, f. ξω, to stir up, rouse, Soph., Eur.
ἀν-αίθω, only in pres. and impf., to light up, set on fire, Eur.: to inflame to love, Mosch. II. intr. to blaze up, Aesch.
ἀν-αίμακτος, ον, (αἱμάσσω) unstained with blood, Aesch., Eur.
ἀν-αίματος, ον, =ἄναιμος, drained of blood, Aesch.
ἄν-αιμος, ον, (αἷμα) without blood, bloodless, Plat., etc.
ἀν-αίμων, ον, =ἄναιμος, of the gods, Il.
ἀν-αιμωτί, (αἱμόω) Adv., without shedding blood, Il.
ἀν-αίνομαι : impf. ἠναινόμην, Ep. ἀναινόμην : aor. 1 ἠνηνάμην, 3 sing. subj. ἀνήνηται, inf. ἀνήνασθαι : Dep. : ἀν- privat., αἶνος) : 1. c. acc. to reject with contempt, turn one's back on, spurn, Hom. : also simply to refuse, decline, Od., Xen. 2. to renounce, disown, Aesch., Eur. II. c. inf. to refuse, decline to do, Il.; and with pleon. negat., ἀναίνετο μηδὲν ἑλέσθαι he said no, he had received nothing, Ib. III. absol. to refuse, deny, Hom.
ἀν-αίξας, aor. 1 part. of ἀναΐσσω.
ἀναίρεσις, εως, ή, a taking up of dead bodies for burial, Eur., Thuc. :—so, in a sea-fight, ναυαγίων ἀν. Thuc. II. destruction, Xen., Dem. : abrogation of laws, Plut. From
ἀν-αιρέω, f. ήσω : pf. -ῄρηκα : aor. 2 ἀν-εῖλον :—to take up, raise, Lat. tollere. 2. to take up and carry off, bear away, Il., Hdt. 3. to take up bodies for burial, Ar., Xen.; this is more common in Med. II. to make away with, to destroy, kill, Hom., Hdt., etc. 2. of things, to abolish, annul, Xen., etc. 3. to destroy an argument, confute, Plat. III. to appoint, order, of an oracle, c. inf., ἀναιρεῖ παραδοῦναι Thuc.; also c. acc. et inf., ἀνειλέ μιν βασιλέα εἶναι Hdt. 2. absol. to answer, give a response, Id., Att.
B. Med. to take up for oneself, take up ; and then to gain, win, get, achieve, Hom., etc.; ποινήν τινος ἀν. to exact penalty from one, Hdt. 2. to take up and carry off, snatch away, Od. 3. to take up dead bodies for burial, Hdt., Thuc., etc. 4. to take up in one's arms, Il. : hence, to take up new-born children, own them, Lat. tollere, suscipere, Plut. 5. to conceive in the womb, like συλλαμβάνω, Hdt. II. to take upon oneself, undertake, πόνους Id.; πόλεμόν τινι war against one, Id.; ἀν. δημόσιον ἔργον to undertake, contract for the execution of a work, Plat. to accept as one's own, γνώμην Hdt.; ἀν. φιλοψυχίην to entertain a love for life, Id. III. to take back to oneself, cancel, Dem.
ἀν-αίρω, f. -ἀρῶ, to lift up : in Med., Eur.; in Pass., ἀναρθείς carried up, Anth.
ἀναισθησία, ή, want of feeling or perception ; insensibility to pleasure or pain, Arist.; and
ἀναισθητέω, f. ήσω, to want perception, Dem. From
ἀν-αίσθητος, ον, insensate, unfeeling, Xen., etc. :— Adv., ἀναισθήτως ἔχειν to be indifferent, Isocr. 2. senseless, wanting tact, stupid, Thuc., Dem. : — τὸ ἀναίσθητον insensibility, Thuc. II. pass. unfelt, θάνατος Id.
ἀν-αισῑμόω, impf. ἀναισίμουν : 3 pl. aor. 1 subj. ἀναισι-

μώσωσι :--Pass., aor. 1 ἀναισιμώθην, pf. ἀναισίμωμαι : (αἴσιμος ?) :—Ion. Verb = Att. ἀναλίσκω, to use up, use, consume, Hdt. :—Pass., ἀναισιμοῦσθαι ἔς τι to be used for a purpose, or spent upon a thing, Id.; ποῦ ταῦτα ἀναισιμοῦται; where (i. e. how) have these been disposed of? Id.   Hence

ἀναισίμωμα, ατος, τό; consumption, expenditure, Hdt.

ἀν-αΐσσω [ἄνᾱ-], contr. ἀν-ᾴσσω: f. -αΐξω, -ᾴξω : aor. 1 -ῆϊξα, -ῇξα :—to start up, rise quickly, Il.; of thought, Ib.; of a spring, to gush forth, Ib.   2. c. acc. to leap up into, ἅρμα Ib.

ἀναισχυντέω, f. ήσω, to be shameless, behave impudently, Thuc.; πρός τινα Xen.; and

ἀναισχυντία, ἡ, shamelessness, Ar., Plat.   From

ἀν-αίσχυντος, ον, (αἰσχύνω) shameless, impudent, Eur., Ar., etc. :—τὸ ἀναίσχυντον, = ἀναισχυντία, Eur.:—Adv. -τως, Plat.   II. of things, abominable, Eur.

ἀν-αίτιος, ον and α, ον, of persons, not being the cause of a thing, guiltless, Hom., etc.   2. c. gen. rei, guiltless of a thing, Hdt., Aesch., etc. :—οὐκ ἀναίτιόν ἐστι, c. inf. it is blamable to do, Xen.

ἀνα-καγχάζω, f. σω, to burst out laughing, Plat.

ἀνα-κᾰθαίρω, f. -ᾰρῶ, to clear completely :—Pass., of the air, to become quite clear, Plut.   II. Med. to clear or sweep away, Plat.

ἀνα-κάθημαι, Pass. to sit upright, Luc.

ἀνα-κᾰθίζω, f. Att. ιῶ, to set up : Med. to sit up, Plat.   II. intr. to sit up, Plat.

ἀνα-καινίζω, f. σω, = ἀνακαινόω, Plut.

ἀνα-καινουργέω, f. ήσω, = ἀνακαινίζω, Anth.

ἀνα-καινόω, f. ώσω, to renew, restore :—Pass. to be renewed, N. T.   Hence

ἀνακαίνωσις, εως, ἡ, renewal, N. T.

ἀνα-καίω, Att. -κάω : aor. 1 ἀνέκαυσα :—to light up, Od., Hdt., etc. :—Med. to light oneself a fire, Hdt.   2. Pass., metaph. to fire up, with anger, Id.

ἀνα-κᾰλέω, poët. ἀγ-κᾰλέω, f. -έσω : pf. κέκληκα :—to call up the dead, Aesch.; so in Med., Eur.   II. to call again and again : 1. to invoke, appeal to, θεούς Hdt., etc. ;—so in Med., Soph., Eur.   2. to summon, cite, Hdt. :—Med. to call to oneself, send for, summon, Id., Thuc.   3. to call by a name, ἀν. κακούς Eur.; Δαναούς Thuc. :—Pass., Ἀργεῖος ἀνακαλούμενος Soph.   4. to call on, so as to encourage, Thuc.; Med., ἀνακαλεῖσθαι τὰς κύνας to cheer on the hounds, Xen.   III. to call back, recall, mostly in Med., Aesch.; esp. from exile, Plat.; ἀνακαλεῖσθαι τῇ σάλπιγγι to sound a retreat, Xen.

ἀνακᾰλυπτήρια, τά, presents made by the bridegroom, when the bride first took off her veil, Lys.   From

ἀνα-κᾰλύπτω, f. ψω, to uncover, ἀν. λόγους to use open speech, Eur. :—Med. to unveil oneself, unveil, Xen. : —Pass., of a veil, to be uplifted, N. T.

ἀνα-κάμπτω, f. ψω, to bend back : mostly intr. to bend one's steps back, return, Hdt.

ἀν-άκανθος, ον, (ἄκανθα) without spine, of certain fish, Hdt.

ἀνα-κάπτω, f. ψω, to gulp down, Hdt.

ἀνάκᾶται, Ion. for ἀνάκεινται, 3 pl. of sq.

ἀνά-κειμαι, poët. ἀγ-κειμαι, f.-κείσομαι, serving as Pass. to ἀνατίθημι, to be laid up as a votive offering, to be devoted or dedicated, Hdt., etc.   2. to be set up as

a statue, Dem., Theocr.   3. to be ascribed or offered, τινι Plut.   II. to be referred to a person, depend on his will, Hdt.; πάντων ἀνακειμένων τοῖς Ἀθηναίοις ἐς τὰς ναῦς since they had their whole fortunes dependant on their ships, Thuc.; ἐπὶ σοὶ τάδε πάντ' ἀνάκειται Ar.; σοὶ ἀνακείμεσθα Eur.

Ἀνάκειον, τό, (Ἄνακες) the temple of the Dioscuri, Andoc., etc.; cf. ἀναγκαῖον.

ἀνα-κέλᾰδος, ὁ, a loud shout or din, Eur.

ἀνα-κεράννῡμι and -ύω, f. -κεράσω [ᾰ] : to mix up or again, κρητῆρα Od.; οἶνον Ar. :—Pass., aor. 1 -εκεράσθην Plat. ; -εκράθην [ᾱ] Plut.

Ἄνᾱκες, ων, οἱ, old form of ἄνακτες, the Dioscuri, Castor and Pollux, Plut.

ἀνα-κεφᾰλαιόω, f. ώσω, to sum up the argument :— Pass. to be summed up, N. T.

ἀνα-κηκίω, only in pres. and impf., to spout up, gush forth, ἀνακήκϊεν αἷμα Il.

ἀνα-κηρύσσω, Att. -ττω, f. ξω, to proclaim by voice of herald, publish abroad, Soph., Xen.   2. c. acc. pers. to proclaim as conqueror, Ar. :—Pass., aor. 1 inf. ἀνακηρυχθῆναι Hdt.   II. to put up to auction, Hdt.

ἀνα-κινδῡνεύω, f. σω, to run into danger again, to run a fresh risk, Hdt.

ἀνα-κῑνέω, f. ήσω, to sway or swing to and fro, Hdt.   II. to stir up, awaken, νόσον Soph.; πόλεμον Plut.   Hence

ἀνακίνησις [ῐ], εως, ἡ, a swinging to and fro : metaph., excitement, emotion, Soph.

ἀνα-κίρνᾰμαι, Dep. to mix well : metaph., φιλίας ἀνακίρνασθαι to join in closest friendship, Eur.

ἀνα-κλάζω, f. -κλάγξω : aor. 2 ἀνέκλᾰγον :—to cry aloud, scream out, Eur.; of a dog, to bark, bay, Xen.

ἀνα-κλαίω, Att. -κλάω, f. -κλαύσομαι, to weep aloud, burst into tears, Hdt.   2. c. acc. to weep for, Id.; so in Med., Soph.

ἀνα-κλάω, f. -κλάσω [ᾰ], to bend back, δέρην Eur.   2. to break short off, Thuc.

ἀνάκλησις, εως, ἡ, (ἀνακαλέω) a calling on, invocation, θεῶν Thuc.   II. a recalling : retreat, Plut.

ἀνακλητικός, ή, όν, (ἀνακαλέω) fit for exhorting, Plut.   II. fit for recalling, τὸ ἀνακλητικὸν σαλπίζειν to sound a retreat, Anth.

ἀνα-κλίνω [ῑ], poët. ἀγ-κλίνω, f. -κλῑνῶ, to lean one thing upon another, [τόξον] ποτὶ γαίῃ ἀγκλίνας having laid it on the ground, Il. :—Pass. to lean back, to lie on one's back, recline, Lat. resupinari, Od.   II. to push back a trap-door, to open it, Hom., Hdt.   Hence

ἀνάκλῐτος, ον, leaning back : ἀν. θρόνος a seat with a back, Plut.

ἀνα-κλώθω, f. σω, of the Fates, to undo the thread of one's life, to change one's destiny, Luc.

ἀνα-κογχῡλιάζω, f. σω, (κόγχη) to open and counterfeit a seal, Ar.

ἀνα-κοινόω, f. ώσω, to communicate a thing to another, τί τινι Plat.   2. c. dat. pers. to communicate with, take counsel with, ἀν. τοῖς θεοῖς περί τινος Xen.   II. Med., with pf. pass. ἀνακεκοίνωμαι, properly, to communicate what is one's own to another, ἀνακοινοῦται τῷ Ἴστρῳ τὸ ὕδωρ mingles its water with the Ister, Hdt.   2. much like Act., either ἀνακοινοῦσθαί τί τινι

to impart a thing to one; or ἀν. τινι to consult one, Xen.: absol. to hold communication, Ar.

ἀνα-κοιρᾰνέω, f. ήσω, to rule or command in a place, Anth.

ἀνακομῐδή, ή, a carrying away again, recovery, τῶν πλοίων Decret. ap. Dem. From

ἀνα-κομίζω, poët. ἀγ-κομ-, f. Att. -κομιῶ, to carry up, Xen.:—Pass. to be carried up stream, or up the country, Hdt. II. to bring back, recover, Xen.: —Med. (with pf. pass.) to take back with one, Hdt.:— Pass. to be brought back, and of persons, to return, Id., Thuc. 2. Med. also, to bring to pass, Pind.:— to bring back upon oneself, Eur.

ἀν-ᾰκοντίζω, f. σω, intr. to dart or shoot up, Il., Hdt.

ἀνακοπή, ή, a beating back: the recoil of the waves, and the water left after flood-tide, Plut. From

ἀνα-κόπτω, f. ψω, to drive back, Od. 2. to beat back an assailant, Thuc. II. to stop:—Pass. to be stopped, stop short, τινός from a thing, Luc.

ἀνα-κουφίζω, f. Att. -ιῶ, to lift up, Eur.; of a ship, ἀν. κάρα Soph.:—Pass. to be lifted up or lightened, aor. 1 ἀνεκουφίσθην Eur.: to rise in spirits, Xen. Hence

ἀνακούφισις, εως, ή, relief from a thing, c. gen., Soph.

ἀνα-κράζω, aor. 2 ἀνέκρᾱγον, to cry out, lift up the voice, Od., Att.

ἀνάκρᾱσις, εως, ή, (ἀνακεράννυμι) a mixing with others, Plut.

ἀνα-κρέκομαι, Med. to tune up, Anth.

ἀνα-κρεμάννυμι, poët. ἀγ-κρ-: f. -κρεμάσω, Att. -κρεμῶ:—Pass. -κρέμᾰμαι:—to hang up on a thing, c. dat., Od.; ές .. or πρὸς .., Hdt.:—Pass. to be hung up, Id. II. to make dependent, Plat.

ἀνα-κρίνω [ῑ], f. -κρῐνῶ, to examine closely, to question, interrogate, τινά Thuc., Plat. 2. to inquire into a fact, Antipho:—Med., Pind. II. used at Athens in technical sense : 1. to examine magistrates as to their qualification, Dem. 2. of the magistrates, to examine persons concerned in a suit, so as to prepare the matter for trial, Id. III. Med., ἀνακρίνεσθαι πρὸς ἑαυτούς to dispute one with another, Hdt. Hence

ἀνάκρισις, poët. ἄγκρ-, εως, ή, examination of parties concerned in a suit, a preparation of the matter for trial, Xen.; μηδ' εἰς ἄγκρισιν ἐλθεῖν, i. e. not even to begin proceedings, Aesch.

ἀνα-κροτέω, f. ήσω, to lift up and strike together, τὼ χεῖρε Ar.; τὰς χεῖρας Aeschin.: absol. to applaud vehemently, Ar.

ἀνάκρουσις, εως, ή, a pushing back : of a ship, backing water, Thuc.; and

ἀνακρουστέον, verb. Adj. of ἀνακρούω, one must check, Xen. From

ἀνα-κρούω, poët. ἀγ-κρ-, f. σω, to push back, stop short, check, ἵππον χαλινῷ Xen. II. Med., ἀνακρούεσθαι πρύμνην to put one's ship astern, by backing water, Ar.; so ἀνακρούεσθαι alone, Thuc.; also, ἐπὶ πρύμνην ἀν., Hdt.:—metaph. to put back, Plat. 2. in Music, to strike up, Theocr.

ἀνα-κτάομαι, f. -ήσομαι: pf. ἀν-έκτημαι: Dep.:—to regain for oneself, get back again, recover, Hdt., Aesch. II. c. acc. pers. to win a person over, gain his favour or friendship, Hdt., Xen.

ἀνακτορία, ή, (ἀνάκτωρ) management of horses, h. Hom.

ἀνακτόριος, α, ον, (ἀνάκτωρ) belonging to a lord or king, royal, Od.

ἀνάκτορον, τό, a palace ; of gods, a temple, Hdt., Eur. From

ἀνάκτωρ, ορος, ό, = ἄναξ, Aesch., Eur.

ἀνα-κῠκάω, f. ήσω, to stir up and mix, mix up, Ar.

ἀνα-κυκλέω, f. ήσω, to turn round again, Eur.: metaph. to revolve in one's mind, Luc.

ἀνακυκλόομαι, Pass. to revolve, Anth.

ἀνα-κυμβᾰλιάζω, f. σω, (κύμβαλον) to fall rattling over, of chariots, Il.

ἀνα-κύπτω, f. -κύψομαι or -ψω: aor. 1 ἀνέκυψα: pf. ἀνακέκῠφα:—to lift up the head, Hdt.; ἀνακεκυφώς with the head high, of a horse, Xen. II. to come up out of the water, pop up, Ar., Plat. : metaph. to emerge, Plat.

ἀνα-κωκύω [ῡ], f. σω, to wail aloud, Aesch.; ἀνακωκύει φθόγγον utters a loud wail, Soph.

ἀνάκῶς, Adv. (ἄναξ a manager), carefully, ἀνακῶς ἔχειν τινός to look well to a thing, give good heed to it, Hdt., Thuc.

ἀνακωχή, ἀνακωχεύω, v. ἀνοκωχή.

ἀνα-λάζομαι, Dep. only in pres. to take again, Mosch.

ἀν-ᾰλᾰλάζω, f. ξω, to raise a war-cry, cry aloud, Eur., Xen.

ἀνα-λαμβάνω, f. -λήψομαι, to take up, take into one's hands, Hdt. : to take on board ship, Id., Thuc.: generally, to take with one, Thuc. 2. to take up, for the purpose of examining or considering, Plat. 3. to take upon oneself, assume, τὴν προξενίαν Thuc., etc. 4. Med. to take upon oneself, undertake, engage in, κίνδυνον, μάχην Hdt. 5. to learn by rote, Plat. II. to get back, regain, recover, τὴν ἀρχήν Hdt., Xen. 2. to retrieve, make good, τὴν αἰτίην Soph. 3. to restore, repair, Hdt.; ἀν. ἑαυτόν to regain strength, revive, Thuc. 4. to take up again, resume, τὸν λόγον Hdt., Plat.: to recollect, Plut. III. to pull short up, to check a horse, Xen.: ἀν. τὰς κύνας to call them back, Id. IV. to gain quite over, win over, Ar.

ἀνα-λάμπω, f. -ψω, to flame up, take fire, Xen. II. metaph. to break out anew, as war, Plut. 2. to come to oneself again, revive, Id.

ἀν-αλγής, = ἀνάλγητος, painless, Plut.

ἀναλγησία, ή, want of feeling, insensibility, Dem. From

ἀν-άλγητος, ον, (ἀλγέω) without pain, and so : I. of persons, insensible to pain, Arist. 2. unfeeling, hard-hearted, ruthless, Soph.; ἀναλγητότερος εἶναι to feel less grieved, Thuc.: c. gen., ἀν. εἶναί τινος to be insensible to, Plut.:—Adv. -τως, unfeelingly, Soph. II. of things, not painful, Id. 2. cruel, πάθος Eur.

ἀν-αλδής, ές, (ἀλδαίνω) not thriving, feeble, Ar.

ἀνα-λέγω, Ep. impf. ἄλλεγον: f. ἀναλέξω: Ep. aor. 1 inf. ἀλλέξαι:—to pick up, gather up, ὀστέα Il.:—Med. to pick up for oneself, Hdt.; ἀν. πνεῦμα to collect one's breath, Anth. II. to reckon up, τὸν χρόνον Plut.: —Pass., ἀναλεγόμενον being recounted, Xen.

ἀνα-λείχω, f. ξω, to lick up, τὸ αἷμα Hdt.

ἀνάληψις, ή, (ἀναλαμβάνω) a taking up of a child, to acknowledge it, Luc. 2. pass. a being taken up, the Ascension, N. T. II. a taking back, a means

of regaining, Plut. 2. a making good, making amends for a fault, Thuc. : a refreshing, Luc.

ἀν-αλθής, ές, (ἀλθαίνω) powerless to heal, Bion.

ἀν-άλιος, ον, Dor. for ἀν-ήλιος.

ἀν-άλιπος [ἀλ], ον, Dor. for ἀν-ήλιπος.

ἀναλίσκω and ἀναλόω : impf. ἀνήλισκον and ἀνάλουν : f. ἀναλώσω : aor. 1 ἀνήλωσα and ἀνάλωσα [ᾰ] : pf. ἀνήλωκα and ἀνάλωκα [ᾰ] :—Pass., f. ἀναλωθήσομαι : aor. 1 ἀνηλώθην and ἀνάλώθην : pf. ἀνήλωμαι and ἀνάλωμαι. (The quantity of 2nd syll. and the act. form make it doubtful whether this Verb is a compd. of ἀνά, ἀλίσκομαι.) To use up, to spend, lavish or squander money, Thuc. ; εἴς τι upon a thing, Plat., etc. ; πρός τι Dem. ; ὑπέρ τινος Id. :—Pass., τἀνηλωμένα the monies expended, Id. 2. metaph., ἀνάλωσας λόγον hast wasted words, Soph. ; ἀν. σώματα πολέμῳ Thuc. II. of persons, to kill, destroy, Trag. :—Med. to kill oneself, Thuc.

ἀνάλκεια, ἡ, want of strength, feebleness, Ep. dat. pl. ἀναλκείῃσι Il. ; sing. ἀναλκίη [with ῑ] Theogn. From

ἄν-αλκις, ιδος, ὁ, ἡ : acc. -ιδα or -ιν : (ἀλκή) :—without strength, impotent, feeble, of unwarlike persons, Hom., Aesch., etc.

ἀν-άλλομαι, f. -αλοῦμαι, aor. 1 -ηλάμην, Dep. to leap or spring up, Ar., Xen.

ἄν-αλμος, ον, (ἅλμη) not salted, Xen.

ἀναλογία, ἡ, (ἀνάλογος) proportion, Plat., etc.

ἀνα-λογίζομαι, f. Att. -λογιοῦμαι, Dep. to reckon up, sum up, Plat., Xen. 2. to calculate, consider, τι Thuc. 3. foll. by a Conj., ἀναλ. ὡς, ὅτι, to recollect that, Id., Xen. - Hence

ἀναλογισμός, ὁ, reconsideration, Thuc. :—a course or line of reasoning, Xen. 2. κατὰ τὸν ἀναλογισμόν according to proportionate calculation, ap. Dem.

ἀνά-λογος, ον, proportionate, Plat. : neut. as Adv. in proportion, analogously, Arist.

ἀναλόω, old form of ἀναλίσκω.

ἄν-αλτος, ον, (ἀλθαίνω) not to be filled, insatiate, Od.

ἀνάλυσις, εως, ἡ, (ἀναλύω) a loosing, releasing, κακῶν from evils, Soph. II. (from Pass.) retirement, departure, death, N. T.

ἀναλυτήρ, ῆρος, ὁ, a deliverer, Aesch. From

ἀνα-λύω, Ep. ἀλ-λύω : Ep. 3 sing. impf. ἀλλύεσκε : Ep. part. fem. ἀλλύουσα : f. -λύσω :—to unloose, undo, of Penelope's web, Od. 2. to unloose, set free, release, ἐκ δεσμῶν Ib. II. after Hom., ἀν. ὀφθαλμόν, φωνάν, i. e. to restore to a dead man the use of his eyes and voice, Pind. 2. to analyse, Arist. 3. to put an end to a thing, Xen. :—to abolish, cancel, Dem. :—Med. to cancel faults, Xen., Dem. III. intr. to loose a ship from its moorings, weigh anchor, depart, Polyb. : —metaph. of death, N. T. 2. to return, Ib.

ἀνάλωμα, ατος, τό, (ἀναλόω) expenditure, cost, in pl. expenses, Thuc., etc.

ἀνάλωσις, ἡ, (ἀναλόω) outlay, expenditure, Theogn., Thuc.

ἀναλωτής, οῦ, ὁ, (ἀναλόω) a spender, waster, Plat.

ἀναλωτικός, ή, όν, (ἀναλόω) expensive, Plat.

ἀν-άλωτος [ἀλ], ον, (ἁλίσκομαι) not to be taken, invincible, impregnable, Hdt. : also, not taken, still holding out, Thuc. 2. of persons, ἀν. ὑπὸ χρημάτων incorruptible, Xen.

ἀνα-μαιμάω, only in pres. to rage through, c. acc., Il.

ἀνα-μανθάνω, f. -μαθήσομαι, to inquire closely, Hdt.

ἀν-αμάξευτος, ον, (ἁμαξεύω) impassable for wagons, Hdt.

ἀν-αμάρτητος, ον, (ἁμαρτάνω) without missing, unfailing, unerring, Xen. 2. in moral sense, without fault, blameless, Plat., etc. ; ἀν. πρός τινα or τινι having done no wrong to a person, Hdt. ; ἀν. τινός guiltless of a thing, Id. ; τὸ ἀναμάρτητον innocence, Xen. :—Adv. -τως, without fail, unerringly, Id.

ἀνα-μάρυκάομαι, v. ἀναμηρ-.

ἀνα-μᾱσάομαι, v. ἀναμηρ-.

ἀνα-μᾱσάομαι, Dep. to chew over again, ruminate, Ar.

ἀνα-μάσσω, Att. -ττω, f. ξω, to wipe off, ἔργον ὃ σῇ κεφαλῇ ἀναμάξεις a deed which thou wilt wipe off on thine own head (as if it were a stain), Od. ; so, ταῦτα ἐμῇ κεφαλῇ ἀναμάξας Hdt. :—Med., ἀναμάττεσθαι τῷ προσώπῳ τοῦ αἵματος to have [some of] the blood wiped on one's face, Plut.

ἀνα-μάχομαι [ᾰ], f. -μαχέσομαι, Att. -μαχοῦμαι, Dep. to renew the fight, retrieve a defeat, Hdt., Thuc. ; ἀν. τὸν λόγον to fight the argument over again, Plat.

ἀν-αμβᾰτος, ον, of a horse, that one cannot mount, Xen.

ἀνα-μέλπω, f. ψω, to begin to sing, ἀοιδάν Theocr.

ἀνα-μεμίχᾰται, Ion. for ἀναμεμιγμένοι εἰσί, 3 pl. pf. of ἀναμίγνυμι.

ἀνα-μένω, poët. ἀμ-μένω, f. -μενῶ, to wait for, await, c. acc., Od., Hdt., etc. :—c. acc. et inf., ἀν. τινὰ ποιεῖν to await one's doing, Hdt. ; ἀν. τι γίνεσθαι a thing happening, Id. :—absol. to wait, stay, Soph., etc. 2. to await, endure, τί Xen. 3. to put off, delay, Id.

ἀνά-μεσος, ον, in the midland or interior, Lat. mediterraneus, Hdt.

ἀνά-μεστος, ον, filled full, τινός of a thing, Dem.

ἀνα-μεστόω, f. ώσω, to fill up, fill full, Ar., in Pass.

ἀνα-μετρέω, f. ήσω, to re-measure the road one came by, retrace one's steps to a place, ὄφρα ἀναμετρήσαιμι Χάρυβδιν Od. 2. to recapitulate, Eur., in Med. II. to measure over again, to measure carefully, take the measure of, τι Hdt. ; ἀν. ἑαυτόν Ar. :—Med., ἀνεμετρησάμην φρένας τὰς σάς took the measure of thy mind, Eur. 2. ἀναμετρεῖσθαι δάκρυ εἴς τινα to measure out (i. e. pay) to him the tribute of a tear, Id.

ἀναμέτρησις, εως, ἡ, (ἀναμετρέω) a measurement, τινος πρός τι of one thing by another, Plut.

ἀνα-μηρυκάομαι or ἀναμᾱρ-, Dep. to chew the cud, Luc.

ἀνάμιγα, poët. ἀνάμιγα, Adv., = ἀναμίξ, promiscuously, Soph., Anth. ; and

ἀνάμιγδα, = ἀναμίξ, Soph. From

ἀνα-μίγνῡμι and -ύω, poët. ἀμ-μίγνυμι, f. -μίξω : Ep. aor. 1 ἀμμίξας : cf. ἀναμίσγω :—to mix up, mix together, Od., Hdt., etc. :—Pass. to be mixed with others, Hdt., Att. : to have intercourse, Plut.

ἀνα-μιμνήσκω, f. -μνήσω, poët. ἀμμνήσω, to remind one of a thing, c. dupl. acc., ταῦτά μ' ἀνέμνησας Od. ; c. gen. rei, ἀν. τινά τινος Eur. :—c. acc. pers. et inf. to remind one to do, Pind. 2. c. acc. rei, to recall to memory, make mention of, Dem. II. in Pass. to remember, τινός Hdt., etc. ; more rarely τι Ar., Plat. ; περί τι Plat.

ἀνα-μίμνω, poët. for ἀνα-μένω, Il.

ἀναμίξ, (ἀναμίγνυμι) Adv. promiscuously, Hdt., Thuc.

ἀνά-μιξις, εως, ἡ, (ἀναμίγνυμαι) intercourse, Plut.

ἀνα-μίσγω, poët. and Ion. for ἀναμίγνυμι, only in pres.

and impf., *to mix* one thing *with* another, τί τινι Od.:
—Pass. *to have intercourse*, τινι Hdt.

ἀνα-μισθαρνέω, f. ήσω, *to serve again for pay*, Plut.

ἀναμνησθείς, aor. 1 pass. part. of ἀναμιμνήσκω.

ἀνάμνησις, εως, ἡ, (ἀναμιμνήσκω) *a calling to mind*,
recollection, Plat., etc.

ἀναμνηστός, όν, (ἀναμιμνήσκω) *that which one can recollect*, Plat.

ἀνα-μολεῖν, inf. of ἀν-έμολον, aor. 2 of ἀναβλώσκω, *to
go through*, c. acc., Eur.

ἀνα-μορμύρω, *to roar loudly, boil up*, πᾶσ' ἀναμορ-
μύρεσκε (Ion. impf.) of Charybdis, Od.

ἀνα-μοχλεύω, f. σω, *to raise by a lever, to force open*,
πύλας Eur.

ἀν-αμπλάκητος or ἀν-απλάκητος, ον, *unerring, unfailing*, Soph. **2.** of a man, *without error* or *crime*,
Aesch., Soph.

ἀνα-μυχθίζομαι, Dep. only in pres. *to moan loudly*,
Aesch.

ἀν-αμφίβολος, ον, *unambiguous* : Adv. -λως, Luc.

ἀν-αμφίλεκτος, ον, =sq., Luc.

ἀν-αμφίλογος, ον, *undisputed, undoubted*, Xen. Adv.
-γως, *indisputably*, Id.

ἀν-αμφισβήτητος, ον, *undisputed, indisputable*, Thuc.;
ἀν. χώρα *a place about which there is no dispute*, i. e.
well-known, Xen.

ἀνανδρία, ἡ, *want of manhood*, Eur., Plat., etc. **2.**
unmanliness, cowardice, Aesch., etc. From

ἄν-ανδρος, ον, (ἀνήρ) : **I.** =ἄνευ ἀνδρός, *husband-
less*, Trag. **2.** =ἄνευ ἀνδρῶν, *without men*, Ib. **II.**
wanting in manhood, unmanly, Hdt., Plat. ; τὸ ἄναν-
δρον=ἀνανδρία, Thuc.

ἀν-άνδρωτος, ον, (ἀνδρόω) *widowed*, εὐναί Soph.

ἀνα-νεάζω, in pres. *to renew one's youth*, Ar.

ἀνα-νέμω, poët. ἀν-νέμω, f. -νεμῶ, *to divide anew* :
Med. *to count up*, Hdt. (in Ion. fut. -νεμέεται). **2.**
to rehearse, read, Theocr.

ἀνα-νέομαι, Dep. only in pres. *to mount up*, ἀννεῖται
(Ep. for ἀνανεῖται) Od.

ἀνα-νεόομαι, aor. 1 ἀνενεωσάμην, *to renew*, Thuc., etc.

ἀνα-νεύω, f. -νεύσομαι or -νεύσω : aor. 1 ἀνένευσα,
to throw the head back, in token of denial (which we
express by *shaking the head*), Hom., Hdt., etc. **2.**
c. acc. rei, *to deny, refuse*, Il.

ἀνανέωσις, εως, ἡ, (ἀνανεόομαι) *a renewal*, Thuc.

ἀνα-νήφω, only in pres. *to return to sobriety of mind*,
N. T. **2.** trans. *to make sober again*, Luc.

ἀν-ανθής, ές, (ἄνθος) *without bloom, past its bloom*, Plat.

ἄναντα, Adv. of ἀνάντης, *up-hill*, Il.

ἀν-ανταγώνιστος, ον, (ἀγωνίζομαι) *without a rival*,
without a struggle, Thuc. : *uncontested, unalloyed*,
Id.:—Adv. -τως. **II.** *irresistible*, Plut.

ἀν-άντης, ες, (ἀνά, ἀντάω) *up-hill, steep*, Hdt., Plat.,
Xen. ; πρὸς τὸ ἄναντες *to the highest point*, Plat.

ἀν-αντίλεκτος, ον, *incontestable*, Luc.

ἄναξ [ἄ], ἄνακτος, ὁ : voc. ἄνα : (ἀνάσσω) :—*a lord*,
master, being applied to the gods, esp. to Apollo and
Zeus, Hom. ; to the latter in voc., Ζεῦ ἄνα Il. **II.**
among the Homeric heroes Agamemnon is ἄναξ ἀνδρῶν;
but ἄναξ is a title given to all men of rank and note, as to
Teiresias, Od. ; βασιλεὺς ἄναξ *lord king*, Ib. **III.**
the master of the house, esp. as denoting the *relation*

of master to slave, Ib. **IV.** metaph., κώπης, ναῶν
ἄνακτες *lords of the oar, of ships*, Aesch. ; ἄν. ὅπλων
Eur.

ἀνα-ξαίνω, f. -ξανῶ, *to tear open*, a wound, Babr.

ἀνα-ξηραίνω, f. ἀνῶ : aor. 1 ἀνεξήρανα, Ep. 3 sing. subj.
ἀγξηράνῃ :—*to dry up* things, of the wind, Il. ; *to dry
up* a stream, Hdt.

ἀναξία, ἡ, (ἀνάσσω) *a command, behest*, Pind.

ἀν-άξιος, ον and α, ον : **I.** of persons, *unworthy, not
deemed* or *held worthy of*, c. gen., Hdt. ; ἀνάξιον σοῦ
too good for thee, Soph. ; c. inf., ἀνάξιος δυστυχεῖν *undeserving* to suffer, Id. :—Adv., ἀναξίως ἑωυτῶν Hdt. **2.**
absol. *unworthy, worthless*, Id., Soph. :—Adv. -ίως,
Soph. **3.** *undeserving of evil*, Id., Eur. **II.**
of things, *undeserved*, ἀνάξια παθεῖν Eur., etc.

ἀναξι-φόρμιγξ, ιγγος, ὁ, ἡ, *ruled by the lyre*, Pind.

ἀναξυρίδες, ίδων, αἱ, *the trousers* worn by eastern nations,
Hdt., Xen. ; by the Scythians, Hdt. (A Persian word.)

ἀνα-ξύω [ῠ], f. -ξύσω, *to scrape up* or *off* :—Pass., ἀνα-
ξυσθείς (aor. 1 part.) *having the surface scraped off*,
Plut.

ἀνα-οίγω, f. ξω, Ep. for ἀνοίγω, Il.

ἀνα-παιδεύω, f. σω, *to educate afresh*, Ar.

ἀνάπαιστος, ον, *struck back, rebounding* : as Subst. *an
anapaest* (i. e. a dactyl *reversed*), *an anapaestic verse*,
Ar. ; ἀνάπαιστα, τά, *anapaestics, satire*, Plut. From

ἀνα-παίω, f. σω, *to strike back*.

ἀνά-πᾰλιν, Adv. *back again*, Plat., etc. **II.** *over
again*, Id. **III.** *contrariwise, reversely*, Id.

ἀνα-πάλλω, poët. ἀμ-πάλλω : Ep. aor. 2 part. ἀμπεπα-
λών :—*to swing to and fro*, ἀμπεπαλὼν ἔγχος *having
poised and drawn back* the spear before throwing it,
Il. : *to set in motion, urge on*, Eur. ; ἀμπάλλειν τὰ
κῶλα Ar. :—Pass. *to spring up*, ὡς ὅτε ἀναπάλλεται
ἰχθύς, ὡς πληγεὶς ἀνέπαλτο (3 sing. Ep. aor. 2) as
when a fish *springs up*, so he smitten *sprang up*, Il.

ἀνα-πάσσω, f. -πάσω [ᾰ], *to sprinkle upon*, τί τινι Pind.

ἀνάπαυλα, ης, ἡ, (ἀναπαύω) *repose, rest*, Soph. ; κατ'
ἀναπαύλας διῃρῆσθαι *to be divided into reliefs*, of workmen, Thuc. **2.** c. gen. rei, *rest from* a thing, Soph.,
Thuc., etc. **II.** *a resting-place, an inn*, Lat.
deversorium, Eur., Ar.

ἀνάπαυμα, poët. ἄμπ-, ατος, τό, (ἀναπαύω) *a repose,
rest*, Hes. ; μεριμνᾶν *from cares*, Theogn. **2.** *a
resting-place*, Anth.

ἀνάπαυσις, poët. ἄμπ-, εως, ἡ, (ἀναπαύω) *repose, rest*,
Pind., Xen. : *relaxation, recreation*, Xen. **2.** *rest
from* a thing, c. gen., Thuc.

ἀναπαυστήριος —παυτήριος, Ion. ἀμπ-, ον, (ἀναπαύω) *of* or *for resting*, Hdt. **II.** as Subst.
ἀναπαυστήριον, τό, *a time of rest*, Xen. **2.** *a place
of rest*, Luc.

ἀνα-παύω, poët. and Ion. ἀμπ-, f. σω, *to make to cease,
to stop* or *hinder from* a thing, c. gen., Il. ; ἀν. τινά
τινος *to give him rest* or *relief from* a thing, Soph.,
Dem. **2.** c. acc. only, *to stop, put an end to*, βοὴν
Soph. :—more commonly, *to rest, halt*, τὸ στράτευμα,
τοὺς ναύτας Xen. **3.** rarely intr. in sense of Med. *to
take rest*, ἀναπαύοντες Thuc. ; ἀνέπαυεν Xen. **II.**
Med. and Pass. *to desist from* a thing, ἀπὸ ναυμαχίας Thuc. **2.** absol. *to take one's rest, sleep*,
Lat. *pernoctare*, Hdt., Eur., etc. ; of the dead, Theocr. :

—of soldiers, *to halt, rest*, Xen.   3. *to regain strength*, Id.

ἀνα-πείθω, f. -πείσω, *to bring over, convince*, Xen.:—Pass., Thuc.   2. *to persuade, move* to do a thing, c. acc. pers. et inf., Hdt., Att.; ἀν. τινά τι *to persuade one of* a thing, Ar.   3. *to seduce, mislead*, τινά Hdt., etc.

ἀνα-πειράομαι, Dep. *to try* or *attempt again*: as a military and naval term, *to renew* or *continue their exercises*, Hdt., Thuc.

ἀνα-πείρω, poët. ἀμπ-, *to pierce through, fix on a spit*, Il., Ar.   II. *to impale*, ἐπὶ ξύλου τινά Hdt.: Pass., ἀποθανεῖν ἀναπάρεὶς (aor. 2 part.) Id.

ἀναπειστήριος, α, ον, (ἀναπείθω) *persuasive*, Ar.

ἀνα-πεμπάζομαι, Dep. *to count again, count over*, Plat.

ἀνα-πέμπω, poët. ἀμπ-, f. ψω, *to send up* from below, Aesch.: *to send forth*, Pind.:—Med. *to send up from oneself*, Xen.   2. *to send up*, from the coast inland, esp. into Central Asia, Thuc., Xen.   II. *to send back*, Pind.

ἀναπεπταμένος, pf. part. pass. of ἀναπετάννυμι.

ἀναπεσεῖν, aor. 2 inf. of ἀναπίπτω.

ἀνα-πετάννυμι or -ύω, later ἀνα-πετάω: f. -πετάσω [ᾰ], Att. -πετῶ:—poët. ἀμπ-:—*to spread out, unfold, unfurl* sails, Il.; ἀν. βόστρυχον *to let the hair flow loose*, Eur.; φάος ἀμπετάσας *having shed* light *abroad*, Id.; ἀν. τὰς πύλας *to throw wide the gates*, Hdt.:—Pass., ἀναπεπταμένος *thrown open*, Il.; ἀλώπηξ ἀναπιτναμένη *a fox lying on its back*, Pind.:—the part. pf. pass. ἀναπεπταμένος, η, ον, is often a mere Adj. *open*, of the sea, Hdt.; of eyes, Xen.; δίαιτα ἀν. *life in the open air*, Plat.

ἀνα-πέτομαι, f. -πτήσομαι: aor. 2 ἀν-επτόμην or ἀν-επτάμην, also in act. form ἀν-έπτην:—*to fly up, fly away*, Hdt., etc.   2. metaph. *to be on the wing*, ἀνέπταμαν Soph.; ἀνέπταν ὄβῳ Id.

ἀνα-πήγνυμι, f. -πήξω, *to transfix, impale*, Plut.

ἀνα-πηδάω, poët. ἀμπ-, f. -ήσομαι, *to leap up, start up*, Il., Hdt., etc.   II. *to leap back*, from fear, Ar.; ἀνεπήδησεν ἐπὶ τὴν Ἑστίαν, for protection, Xen.

ἀνά-πηρος, ον, *much maimed, crippled*, Plat., etc.

ἀναπῑδύω, of ground, *to send forth water*, Plut.

ἀνα-πίμπλημι, f. -πλήσω, *to fill up*, Lat. *explere*, Epigr. ap. Luc.   2. metaph., πότμον ἀναπλήσαντες *having filled up the full measure* of misery, Il.; so, ἀναπλῆσαι οἶτον, κακά, ἄλγεα, κήδεα Hom., Hdt., etc.   II. c. gen. rei, *to fill full* of a thing, Ar., etc.   2. with a notion of *defiling, infecting*, ὡς πλείστους ἀναπλῆσαι αἰτιῶν Plat.; so Pass. *to be infected with disease*, Thuc., Plat.

ἀνα-πίπτω, poët. ἀμπ-: f. -πεσοῦμαι: aor. 2 -έπεσον:—*to fall back*, Aesch.   2. *to fall back, give ground*, Thuc.: *to flag, lose heart*, Lat. *concidere animo*, Dem.   3. of a plan, *to be given up*, Id.   4. *to recline* at table, like ἀνάκειμαι, N. T.

ἀνα-πίτνημι, poët. for ἀνα-πετάννυμι, Pind.

ἀν-απλάκητος, ον, = ἀναμπλάκητος, q. v.

ἀνα-πλάσσω, Att. -ττω, f. -πλάσω [ᾰ], *to form anew, remodel*, Ar.:—Med. ἀναπλάσασθαι οἰκίην *to rebuild one's house*, Hdt.   2. metaph. *to invent*, in Med., Anth.   II. *to plaster up*: Pass., κηρὸν ἀναπεπλασμένος *having* wax *plastered*, Ar.

ἀνα-πλέκω, f. ξω, *to enwreath*, Pind. :—Med. *to braid one's hair*, Luc.   2. metaph. of writing verses, Anth.   3. Pass., ἀναπεπλεγμένοι *closely engaged*, Plut.

ἀνά-πλεος, α, ον, Att. masc. and neut. -πλεως, ων, also fem. -πλέα: pl., nom. -πλεῳ, neut. -πλεα; acc. masc. -πλεως:—*quite full* of a thing, c. gen., Hdt., Plat.   II. *infected with* or *by* a thing, c. gen., Plat.

ἀνα-πλέω, Ion. -πλώω, Ep. -πλείω: f. -πλεύσομαι :—*to sail up, to go up stream*, c. acc., Od.   2. *to put out to sea*, Il., Dem.   II. *to sail the same way back again, sail back*, Hdt., Xen. :—of fish, *to swim back*, Hdt.

ἀνά-πλεως, v. ἀνάπλεος.

ἀνα-πληρόω, f. ώσω, *to fill up* a void, Plat.   2. *to make up, supply*, Id. :—Med., δώματ᾽ ἀν. *to fill their houses full*, Eur.   3. *to fill up* the numbers of a body, τὴν βουλήν Plut.; ἀν. τὴν συνηγορίαν *to fill the place of advocate*, Id.   4. *to pay in full*, in Med., Dem.   II. Pass. *to be restored to its former size*, of the sun, after an eclipse, Thuc. Hence

ἀναπλήρωσις, εως, ἡ, *a filling up*, Arist., Plut.; and ἀναπληρωτέον, Verb. Adj. *one must fill up*, Plut.

ἀνα-πλῆσαι, aor. 1 inf. of -πίμπλημι : -πλήσω, fut.

ἀνά-πλοος, contr. -πλους, ὁ, (ἀναπλέω) *a sailing upstream*, Hdt.   2. *a putting out* to sea, Polyb.

ἀν-απλόω, f. ώσω, *to unfold, open*, Mosch., Babr.

ἀναπλώω, Ion. for ἀναπλέω.

ἀνάπνευμα, poët. ἄμπν-, ατος, τό, (ἀναπνέω) *a resting-place*, Pind.

ἀνάπνευσις, εως, ἡ, (ἀναπνέω) *recovery of breath, respite from* a thing, c. gen., Il.

ἀνά-πνευστος, ον, *without breath, breathless*, Hes.

ἀνα-πνέω, f. -πνεύσομαι: aor. 1 -έπνευσα: besides the common tenses (v. πνέω), we have three Homeric forms (as if from ἀμ-πνύω), aor. 2 imper. ἄμπνυε, aor. 1 pass. ἀμπνύνθη, and aor. 2 with form of plqpf. ἄμπνυτο :—*to breathe again, take breath*, Il., etc. : *to recover from* a thing, c. gen., Ib., Soph., etc.; so, ἔκ τινος Hdt. :—absol. *to revive*, Xen.; and in this sense Hom. uses ἄμπνυτο, ἀμπνύνθη.   II. *to draw breath, breathe*, Pind., Plat.   III. *to breathe forth, send forth*, καπνόν Pind. Hence

ἀναπνοή, poët. ἄμπν-, ἡ, *recovery of breath, revival*, Pind., Plat.; μόχθων ἀμπνοά *rest* from toils, Pind., Eur.   II. *a drawing breath, respiration*, Ar., Plat.; ἀμπνοὰς ἔχειν = ἀναπνέειν *to breathe*, Soph.; τὴν ἀν. ἀπολαβεῖν τινος *to strangle* him.   III. *a breathing organ*, of the mouth, Luc.; *an air-hole*, Plut.

ἀνα-ποδίζω, f. ίσω, (πούς) *to make to step back, call back, cross-examine*, Hdt., Aeschin.; ἀν. ἑωυτόν *to correct* himself, Hdt.

ἀν-άποινος, ον, (ἄποινα) *without ransom*, only in neut. ἀνάποινον as Adv., Il.

ἀνα-πολέω, poët. ἀμ-πολέω, f. ήσω, properly *to turn up* the ground *again*: hence *to go over again, repeat, reconsider*, Pind., Soph.

ἀναπολίζω = ἀναπολέω, of a field, Pind.

ἀναπομπή, ἡ, (ἀναπέμπω) *a sending up*: ἀν. θησαυρῶν *a digging up* of treasures, Luc.

ἀναπόμπιμος, (ἀναπέμπω) *sent back*, Luc.

ἀναπομπός, ὁ, (ἀναπέμπω) *one that sends up* or *back*, of Hades, *sending up* the shade of Darius, Aesch.

ἀν-απόνιπτος, ον, (ἀπονίζω) *unwashen*, Ar.

ἀνα-πράσσω, Att. -πράττω, f. -πράξω, to exact, levy money or debts, Ar., Thuc.; ἀν. ὑπόσχεσιν to exact the fulfilment of a promise, Thuc.

ἀνα-πρήθω, f. -πρήσω, to blow forth, to let burst forth, δάκρυ ἀναπρήσας with tears bursting forth, Hom.

ἀνα-πτάσθαι or -πτέσθαι, aor. 2 inf. of ἀναπέτομαι.

ἀνα-πτερόω, f. ώσω, properly of a bird, to raise its feathers: hence, ἀν. ἐθείρας Eur. 2. metaph. to set on the wing, excite vehemently, Hdt., Eur., etc.:— Pass. to be in a state of excitement, Aesch., Xen., etc.

ἀνα-πτοέω, poët. -πτοιέω, f. ήσω, to scare exceedingly, Mosch.:—Pass. to be scared, Plut.

ἀνα-πτύσσω, f. -πτύξω, to unfold the rolls on which books were written; and so, to unrol, open for reading, ἀν. βιβλίον Hdt.:—to undo, open, πύλας Eur.; ἀναπτύξας χέρας with arms outspread, Id. 2. to unfold, disclose, reveal, Lat. explicare, Trag. II. as military term, τὴν φάλαγγα ἀναπτ. to fold back the phalanx, i.e. deepen it by wheeling men from both flanks to rear, French replier, Xen.; but conversely, τὸ κέρας ἀναπτ. to open out the wing, i.e. extend the line by wheeling men from rear to front, French déployer, Id. Hence

ἀναπτυχή, poët. ἀμπτυχή, ἡ, αἰθέρος ἀμπτυχαί the expanse of heaven, Eur.; ἡλίου ἀναπτυχαί the sun's expanse, Id.

ἀνα-πτύω, f. ύσω [ῠ], to spit up, sputter, Soph.

ἀν-άπτω, f. -άψω, to make fast on or to a thing, ἐξ ἱστοῦ πεῖρατ' ἀνῆπτον made fast the rope to the mast, Od.:—Med., ἐκ τοῦδ' ἀναψόμεσθα κάλων to him will we make fast our cable, i.e. he shall be our protector, Eur.:—Pass. to fasten oneself on to, cling to a thing, c. gen., Id.; ἀμφί τινι Id.; ἀνῆφθαί τι to have a thing fastened on one, Id. 2. to hang up in a temple, offer up, ἀγάλματα Od. 3. metaph. to attach to, μῶμον ἀνάψαι Ib.; αἷμα ἀν. τινι a charge of bloodshed, Eur. II. to light up, light, λύχνα Hdt.; πῦρ Eur.; also, πυρὶ ἀν. δόμους Id.:—metaph., νέφος οἰμωγῆς ὡς τάχ' ἀνάψει Id.

ἀνα-πυνθάνομαι, f. -πεύσομαι: aor. 2 -επιθόμην:—to inquire closely into, ascertain, Hdt.; τὸν ποιήσαντα Id. 2. to learn by inquiry, Id., Xen. Hence

ἀνάπυστος, ον, ascertained, notorious, Od., Hdt.

ἀν-απαίρηκα, Ion. for ἀν-ήρηκα, pf. of ἀναιρέω.

ἀν-αρθρος, ον, (ἄρθρον) without joints, not articulated, Plat., etc. 2. without strength, nerveless, Soph. II. of sound, inarticulate, Plut.

ἀν-αριθμέομαι, f. ήσομαι, Med. to enumerate, Dem.

ἀν-αρίθμητος, ον, not to be counted, countless, Hdt., Att.: of time, immeasurable, Soph. 2. unregarded, Eur.

ἀν-άριθμος [ᾰ], poët. ἀν-ήρῐθμος, ον, without number, countless, numberless, Sappho, Trag.: c. gen., ἀνάριθμος θρήνων without measure in lamentations, Soph.; μηνῶν ἀνήριθμος without count of months, Id.; πόλις ἀνάριθμος = πολῖται ἀνάριθμοι, Id.

ἄν-αρκτος, ον, (ἄρχω) not governed or subject, Thuc.: not submitting to be governed, Aesch.

ἀν-άρμενος, ον, (ἀραρίσκω) unequipped, Anth.

ἀναρμοστέω, f. ήσω, (ἀνάρμοστος) not to fit or suit, τινί or πρός τι Plat.

ἀναρμοστία, ἡ, discord, of musical sounds, Plat. From

ἀν-άρμοστος, ον, (ἁρμόζω) unsuitable, incongruous, disproportionate, Hdt., Xen.:—of sound, out of tune, Plat.:—Adv. -τως, Id. II. of persons, impertinent, absurd, Ar. 2. unfitted, unprepared, πρός τι Thuc.

ἀναροιβδέω, poët. for ἀναρροιβδέω.

ἀναρπαγή, ἡ, re-capture, Eur. From

ἀν-αρπάζω, f. άσω and άξω, also in med. form -άσομαι: aor. 1 -ήρπασα and αξα:—to snatch up, Il., Xen. II. to snatch away, carry off, Hom., etc.; of slave-dealers, to kidnap, Od.:—Pass., Soph.: in Prose also, to be dragged before a magistrate, carried off to prison, Lat. rapi in jus, Dem. 2. in good sense, to rescue, Plut. III. to take by storm, plunder, Eur.; of persons, ἀναρπασόμενος τοὺς Φωκέας to take them by storm or at once, Hdt. IV. to carry off, steal, Xen., Dem. Hence

ἀναρπαστός, όν, and ή, όν, snatched up, carried off, Eur., Plat. 2. carried up the country, i.e. into Central Asia, Xen.

ἀναρ-ρήγνυμι or -ύω, f. -ρήξω, to break up the ground, Il., Hdt. 2. to break through a wall, Il., Eur.:—Pass., ἡ ναῦς ἀναρρήγνυται τὴν παρεξειρεσίαν the ship has its bow broken through, Thuc. 3. to tear open a carcase, of lions, Il.; of Ajax, δίχα ἀνερρήγνυ was cleaving them asunder, Soph. II. to make to break forth, utter, like Lat. rumpere voces, Ar., Theocr.; ἀν. πόλιν to make it break out, excite greatly, Plut.:—Pass. to burst forth; metaph. of persons, ἀναρρήγνυσθαι πρὸς ὀργήν Id. III. intr. to break forth, Plut.

ἀναρρηθῆναι, aor. 1 pass. inf. of ἀνειπεῖν, q. v.

ἀναρ-ρήξις, εως, ἡ, (ἀναρρήγνυμι) breakage, Plut.

ἀναρ-ρήξω, f. of ἀναρρήγνυμι.

ἀναρ-ρησις, εως, ἡ, a proclamation, Dem.; cf. ἀνεῖπον.

ἀναρ-ρίπτω and -ριπτέω, f. -ρίψω:—to throw up, ἀν. ἅλα πηδῷ to throw up the sea with the oar, i.e. row with might and main, Od.; also without πηδῷ, οἱ δ' ἅλα πάντες ἀνέρριψαν Il. II. ἀν. κίνδυνον, a phrase from the game of dice, to run the hazard of a thing, run a risk, Hdt., Thuc.; περί or ὑπέρ τινος Plut.;— also without κίνδυνον, ἐς ἅπαν τὸ ὑπάρχον ἀναρρίπτειν to throw for one's all, stake one's all, Thuc.; with a second acc. ἀν. μάχην to hazard a battle, Plut.

ἀναρ-ρῑχάομαι, impf. ἀνερριχώμην, to clamber up with the hands and feet, scramble up, Ar. (Deriv. unknown.)

ἀναρ-ροιβδέω and ἀναροιβδέω, f. ήσω, to suck down again, of Charybdis, Od. Hence

ἀνάρ-ρυσις, εως, ἡ, (ῥύομαι) rescue: name of the second day of the festival Ἀπατούρια, Ar.

ἀναρ-ρώννυμι, aor. 1 ἀν-έρρωσα, to strengthen afresh:— Pass. to regain strength, ἀναρρωσθέντες Thuc. 2. intr. in aor. 1 act. to recover, Plut.

ἀν-άρσιος, ον, and α, ον, not fitting, incongruous: hence, I. of persons, hostile, unpropitious, implacable, Hom., Trag. II. of events, untoward, strange, monstrous, Hdt.

ἀν-αρτάω, f. ήσω: Pass., pf. ἀνήρτημαι:—to hang to or upon, to attach to, make dependent upon, ἐς θεοὺς ἀν. τι to leave it depending upon them, Eur.; ἀν. ἑαυτὸν εἰς δῆμον Dem. II. Pass. to be hung up, Plat. 2. metaph. to hang or depend upon, ἔκ τινος Id., Dem.:—ἀνηρτῆσθαι εἰς . . to be referred or referable to . . , Plat.; ἀνηρτημένοι ταῖς ὄψεσιν πρός τινα hanging on one with their eyes, Plut. III. Med. to attach to oneself, make dependent upon one, τινά Xen.

ἀν-αρτέομαι, Ion. Verb, only used in pf. pass. ἀνάρτημαι, *to be ready, prepared* to do, c. inf., Hdt. : cf. ἀρτέομαι.

ἀν-άρτιος, ον, *uneven, odd*, opp. to ἄρτιος (*even*), Plat.

ἀν-αρχαΐζω, f. σω, (ἀρχαῖος) *to make old again*, Anth.

ἀναρχία, ἡ, (ἄναρχος) *lack of a leader*, Hdt. II. *the state of a people without government, anarchy*, Aesch., Thuc., etc. :—at Athens this name was given to the year of the thirty tyrants (B. C. 404), *when there was no archon*, Xen.

ἄν-αρχος, ον, (ἀρχή) *without head* or *chief*, Il., Eur. : τὸ ἄναρχον = ἀναρχία, Aesch.

ἀνα-σἄλεύω, f. σω, *to shake up, stir up*, Luc.

ἀνα-σειράζω, f. σω, (σειρά) *to draw back with a rein, to hold in check*, Anth. II. *to draw aside from the road*, Eur.

ἀνα-σείω, poët. ἀνασ-σείω : 3 sing. Ion. impf. ἀνασσείασκε : f. -σείσω :—*to shake back, swing to and fro, move up and down*, Hes. : esp. as a signal, Thuc. II. *to stir up*, N. T.

ἀνα-σεύομαι, Pass., only in syncop. aor. 2, αἷμα ἀνέσσυτο the blood *sprang forth, spouted up*, Il.

ἀνά-σιλλος or -σῖλος, ὁ, *bristling hair*, Plut.

ἀνα-σκάπτω, f. ψω, *to dig up, to dig up ground*, Plut.

ἀνα-σκεδάννυμι, f.-σκεδάσω [ἄ], *to scatter abroad*, Plut.

ἀνα-σκευάζω, f.-σω : Pass., pf. ἀνεσκεύασμαι :—*to pack up the baggage* (τὰ σκεύη), Lat. *vasa colligere : to carry away*, Xen. :—Med. *to break up one's camp, march away*, Thuc., Xen. 2. *to disfurnish, dismantle* a place, Thuc. : Med. *to dismantle one's house* or *city*, Id. 3. *to waste, ravage, destroy*, Xen. 4. Pass. *to be bankrupt, break*, of bankers, Dem.; metaph., ἀνεσκευάσμεθα *we are ruined*, Eur.

ἀν-άσκητος, ον, (ἀσκέω) *unpractised, unexercised*, Xen.

ἀνα-σκολοπίζω, f. σω : Pass. with fut. med. -σκολοπιοῦμαι : aor. 1 -εσκολοπίσθην : pf. -εσκολόπισμαι :—*to fix on a pole or stake, impale*, Hdt.

ἀνα-σκοπέω, f.-σκέψομαι, aor. 1 ἀνεσκεψάμην :—*to look at narrowly, examine well*, Ar., Thuc.

ἀνα-σοβέω, f. ήσω, *to scare and make to start up, to rouse*, Plat. :—Pass., ἀνασεσοβημένος τὴν κόμην with hair *on end through fright*, Luc.

ἀνα-σπάρασσω, f. ξω, *to tear up*, Eur.

ἀνασπαστός, όν, *drawn up*, Ar. II. *dragged up the country*, of tribes *compelled to emigrate into Central Asia*, Hdt. 2. of a door or gate, *drawn back, opened*, Soph. From

ἀνα-σπάω, poët. ἀν-σπάω, f. -σπάσω [ἄ], *to draw up, pull up*, Solon, Hdt. :—Med., ἐκ χροὸς ἔγχος ἀνεσπάσατο he drew his spear *forth again*, Il. 2. *to draw* a ship *up* on land, Hdt., Thuc. 3. *to draw* or *suck up greedily*, αἷμα Aesch.: but, ὕδωρ ἀν. *to draw water*, Thuc. 4. *to tear up*, Hdt., Att. 5. metaph., ἀνασπᾶν λόγους *to draw forth* words, *to utter violent, offensive* words, Soph. 6. τὰς ὀφρῦς ἀνασπᾶν *to draw up* the eyebrows, and so put on a grave important air, Ar. ; so, τὰ μέτωπα ἀν. Id. II. *to draw back, τὴν χεῖρα* Id. III. *to carry away from home*, Luc.

ἄνασσα, ἡ, fem. of ἄναξ, *a queen, lady, mistress*, addressed to goddesses, Od., Aesch. ; also to a mortal, Od., Trag. II. generally, like ἄναξ IV, ἄνασσα ὀργίων Ar.

ἀν-άσσατος, Dor. for ἀνήσσητος.

ἀνασσείασκον, Ion. impf. of ἀνασείω.

ἀνάσσω, impf. ἤνασσον, Ep. ἄνασσον : f. ἀνάξω : Ep. aor. 1 ἄναξα :—*to be lord, master, owner, to rule, in* a place, c. dat., Ἀργεῖ, νήσοισι ἀν. ; or c. gen. *to be lord of, rule over*, Τενέδοιο, Ἀργείων Hom. : also, μετ' ἀθανάτοισι ἀν. *to be first among* the immortals, Il. :—Med., τρὶς ἀνάξασθαι γένεα ἀνδρῶν *to have been king* for three generations, Od. :—Pass. *to be ruled*, Ib. II. in Trag. metaph. of things, κώπης ἀνάσσειν, etc., Eur., cf. ἄναξ IV :—Pass., παρ' ὅτῳ σκῆπτρον ἀνάσσεται by whom the sceptre *is held as lord*, Soph.

ἀν-ἄσσω, Att. for ἀναΐσσω.

ἀνάστα, for ἀνάστηθι, aor. 2 imp. of ἀνίστημι.

ἀναστἄδόν, Adv. (ἀνίστημι) *standing up, upright*, Il.

ἀνάστἄσις, gen. εως, Ion. ιος, ἡ : I. act. (ἀνίστημι) *a raising up* of the dead, Aesch. 2. *a making men rise and leave their place, removal*, as of suppliants, Thuc. ; ἀν. τῆς Ἰωνίας the *removal* of all the Greeks from Ionia, Hdt. :—*an overthrow, destruction, ruin*, Aesch., Eur. 3. *a setting up, restoration, τειχῶν* Dem. II. (ἀνίσταμαι) *a standing* or *rising up*, in token of respect, Plat. 2. *a rising and moving off, removal*, Thuc. 3. *a rising up, ἐξ ὕπνου* Soph. 4. *a rising again, the Resurrection*, N. T.

ἀναστατήρ and -της, ὁ, (ἀνίστημι) *a destroyer*, Aesch.

ἀνάστἄτος, ον, (ἀνίσταμαι) *made to rise up and depart, driven from one's home*, Hdt. 2. of cities and countries, *ruined, laid waste*, Id., Soph., etc.

ἀναστἄτόω, f. ώσω, (ἀνάστατος) *to unsettle, upset*, N. T.

ἀνα-σταυρόω, f. ώσω, *to impale*, Hdt. : — Pass., Thuc. II. in the Rom. times, *to affix to a cross, crucify*, Plut. 2. *to crucify afresh*, N. T.

ἀνα-στείβω, f. ψω, strengthd. for στείβω, Anth.

ἀνα-στέλλω, f. -στελῶ, *to raise up* :—Med. *to gird up* one's clothes, Eur., Ar. II. *to keep back, repulse* an attack, Eur., Thuc. :—Pass. *to retire*, Thuc.

ἀνα-στενάζω, f. ξω, = ἀναστένω, Hdt. ; τοιάδ' ἀνεστέναζες ἐχθόδοπα such hateful words *didst thou groan forth*, Soph. II. c. acc. pers. *to groan for, lament*, Aesch., Eur.

ἀνα-στενἄχίζω, f. σω, *to groan aloud*, Il.

ἀνα-στενἄχω [ἄ], c. acc. pers. *to groan aloud over, bemoan*, c. acc., Il. ; so in Med., Ib.

ἀνα-στένω, only in pres. *to groan aloud*, Aesch. II. like ἀναστενάχω, c. acc., Eur.

ἀνα-στέφω, f. ψω, *to crown, wreath, κρᾶτα* Eur. :—Pass., ἀνέστεμμαι κάρα *I have* my head *wreathed*, Id.

ἀνα-στηρίζω, f. ξω, *to set up firmly*, Anth.

ἀναστολή, ἡ, (ἀναστέλλω) *a putting back, τῆς κόμης* Plut.

ἀνα-στομόω, f. ώσω, *to furnish with a mouth, ἀν. τάφρον to clear out* a trench, Xen. :—Med., φάρυγος ἀναστόμου τὸ χεῖλος *open the lips of your gullet wide*, Eur.

ἀνα-στρέφω, poët. ἀν-στρέφω, f. ψω, *to turn upside down, upset*, Il., Eur., etc. ; ἀν. καρδίαν *to upset* the stomach, i. e. cause sickness, Eur. :—Pass., ὅρος ἀνεστραμμένον ἐν τῇ ζητήσει *turned up* by digging, Hdt. II. *to turn back, bring back, τινὰ ἐξ Ἅιδου* Soph.; ὄμμ' ἀν. κύκλῳ *to roll* one's eye *about*, Eur. : *to rally* soldiers, Xen. 2. intr. *to turn back, return, retire*, Hdt., Att. III. Pass. *to be* or *dwell in* a place, Lat. *versari, ἄλλην γαῖαν ἀν. to go to* a place *and dwell there*, Od. ; ἀν. ἐν Ἄργει Eur. :—*to conduct*

oneself, ὡς δεσπότης Xen. 2. to revolve,,of the sun, Id. 3. of soldiers, to face about, rally, Id.

ἀν-αστρολόγητος, ον, ignorant of astrology, Strab.

ἀναστροφή, ἡ, (ἀναστρέφω) a turning upside down, upsetting, Eur.; εἰς ἀναστροφὴν διδόναι = ἀναστρέφειν, Id. 2. a turning back, return, Soph.: a wheeling about, of soldiers, whether to flee or rally, Xen.; of a ship, Thuc. II. (from Pass.) a dwelling in a place, Plut.: a mode of life, conversation, N. T. 2. the place where one tarries, an abode, haunt, Aesch.

ἀναστρωφάω, only in pres., Frequentat. of ἀναστρέφω (intr.), to keep turning about, Od.

ἀνα-σύρομαι [ῠ], to pull up one's clothes, Hdt.; pf. part. ἀνασεσυρμένος obscene, Theophr.

ἀνα-σφάλλω, f. -σφᾰλῶ, intr. to rise from a fall or illness, to recover, Babr.

ἀνα-σχεθέειν, contr. -θεῖν, poët. aor. 2 inf. of ἀνέχω.

ἀνα-σχεῖν, -σχέσθαι, aor. 2 inf. act. and med. of ἀνέχω.

ἀνάσχεσις, εως, ἡ, (ἀνέχομαι) a taking on oneself, endurance, τῶν δεινῶν Plut.

ἀνασχετός, Ep. ἀνσχετός, όν, (ἀνέχομαι) to be borne, sufferable, endurable, Theogn., Soph.; mostly with negat., οὐκ ἀνσχετά insufferable, Od.; πτώματ' οὐκ ἀνασχετά Aesch.:—οὐκ ἀνασχετόν [ἐστι], c. inf., Hdt., Soph.

ἀνα-σχίζω, f. σω, to rip up, τὴν γαστέρα Hdt.: to rend, Theocr.

ἀνα-σώζω, f. σω, to recover what is lost, rescue, Soph.: Med., ἀνασώζεσθαί τινα φόβου to recover one from fear, Id.:—Med. in proper sense, ἀν. τὴν ἀρχήν to recover the government for oneself, Hdt.:—Pass. to return safe, of exiles, Xen. 2. in Med. also to preserve in mind, remember, Hdt.

ἀνα-τᾰράσσω, Att. -ττω, f. ξω, to disturb greatly, rouse to frenzy, confound, Soph., Plat.:—Pass., ἀνατεταραγμένος in disorder, Xen.

ἀνατέθραμμαι, pf. pass. of ἀνατρέφω.

ἀνατεί, v. ἀνατί.

ἀνα-τείνω, poët. ἀν-τείνω, f. -τενῶ, to stretch up, hold up, χεῖρα ἀν. to lift up the hand in adjuration or in prayer, Pind.; or as token of ascent in voting, Xen. 2. to stretch forth, τὴν μάχαιραν ἀνατεταμένος with his sword stretched out, Id.; οὐδὲν ἀνατείνασθαι φοβερόν to hold out no alarming threat, Dem. 3. to hold up as a prize, Pind. II. to lift up, exalt, Id. II. to stretch out, extend, e. g. a line of battle, Xen.; ἀετὸς ἀνατεταμένος a spread eagle, Id. III. intr. to reach up, πέδιλα ἐς γόνυ ἀνατείνοντα Hdt.: to extend out, οὖρος ἀν. ἐς Οἴτην Id.

ἀνα-τειχίζω, f. Att. -ιῶ, to rebuild, Xen. Hence

ἀνατειχισμός, ὁ, a rebuilding of the walls, Xen.

ἀνα-τέλλω, poët. ἀν-τέλλω: aor. 1 -έτειλα:—to make to rise up or to grow up, Il.:—Pass., φλὸξ ἀνατελλομένη a flame mounting up, Pind. 2. to give birth to, bring to light, Id.: of events, Soph. II. intr. to rise, of the sun and moon, Hdt., Soph., etc. 2. of a river, to take its rise, Hdt. 3. to grow, of hair, Aesch.

ἀνα-τέμνω, f. -τεμῶ, to cut open, Hdt., Luc.

ἀνατί [ῑ], Adv. of ἄνατος, without harm, with impunity, Trag.: also written ἀνατεί.

ἀνα-τίθημι, f. -θήσω, to lay upon (as a burden), Il., Ar. 2. to refer, attribute, ascribe a thing to a per-

son, Hdt., etc.; οὐ γὰρ ἂν οἱ πυραμίδα ἀνέθεσαν ποιήσασθαι would not have attributed to him the erection of the pyramid, Id.; ἐμοὶ ἀναθήσετε will give me the credit of it, Thuc. :—also, ἀν. τινὶ πράγματα to lay them upon him, entrust them to him, Ar., Thuc. II. to set up as a votive gift, dedicate, τί τινι Hes., Hdt., etc.; hence the votive gift itself was ἀνάθημα :—Pass., aor. 1 inf. ἀνατεθῆναι Ar.; but ἀνάκειμαι is more freq. as the Pass. 2. metaph., ἀν. τι λύρᾳ to commit a song to the lyre, Pind. 3. to set up and leave in a place, Ar. III. to put back, remove, προσθεῖσα κἀναθεῖσα τοῦ γε κατθανεῖν by adding or putting off somewhat of the necessity of death, Soph. B. Med. to put upon for oneself, τὰ σκεύη ἐπὶ τὰ ὑποζύγια Xen. 2. to impart something of one's own, τί τινι N. T. II. to place differently, change about, Orac. ap. Hdt., Plat. 2. metaph. to retract one's opinion, Xen.

ἀνα-τῑμάω, f. ήσω, to raise in price, Hdt.

ἀνα-τῐνάσσω, f. ξω, to shake up and down, brandish, Eur.; of the wind shaking about a sail, Id.

ἀνα-τλῆναι, inf. of ἀν-έτλην, part. ἀνατλάς, aor. 2 with no pres. in use: f. ἀνατλήσομαι :—to bear up against, endure, Od., Att. ; φάρμακ' ἀνέτλη resisted the strength of the magic drink, Od.

ἀνατολή, poët. ἀντολή, (ἀνατέλλω) a rising, rise, of the sun, often in pl., Od.; of the stars, Aesch. 2. the quarter of sunrise, East, Lat. Oriens, Hdt.

ἀνα-τολμάω, f. ήσω, to regain courage, Plut.

ἄν-ατος, ον, (ἄτη) unharmed, Aesch.; c. gen., κακῶν ἄνατος harmed by no ills, Soph.

ἀνατρεπτέον, verb. Adj., one must overthrow, Luc.; and ἀνατρεπτικός, ή, όν, likely to upset a thing, c. gen., Plat. From

ἀνα-τρέπω, poët. ἀν-τρέπω, f. -τρέψω: pf. -τέτροφα :— aor. 2 med. ἀνετράπετο in pass. sense :—to turn up or over, overturn, upset, Archil., etc. :—Pass., ἀνετράπετο = ὕπτιος ἔπεσεν, Il.; of ships, Plat., etc. 2. to overthrow, Lat. evertere, Hdt., Att. 3. to upset in argument, refute, Ar. :—Pass. to be upset, disheartened, ἀνετράπετο φρένα λύπᾳ Theocr. II. to stir up, awaken, Soph.

ἀνα-τρέφω, f. -θρέψω, to feed up, nurse up, educate, Aesch., Ar., Xen.

ἀνα-τρέχω, f. -θρέξομαι and -δρᾰμοῦμαι, to run back, Il. 2. c. acc. to retrace, Lat. repetere, Pind. II. to jump up and run, start up, of men, Hdt., Thuc. 2. of things, ἐγκέφαλος ἀνέδραμε ἐξ ὠτειλῆς the brains spurted up from the wound, Il.; σμώδιγγες ἀνέδραμον weals started up under the blow, Ib. 3. to run up, shoot up, of plants, Ib.; then of cities and peoples, to shoot up, rise quickly, Hdt. 4. ἀναδέδρομε πέτρη the rock ran sheer up, Od.

ἀνάτρησις, εως, ἡ, (ἀνά, τετραίνω) a trepanning, Plut.

ἀνα-τρίβω [ῑ], f. ψω, to rub well, rub clean, κύνας Xen. 2. Pass. to be worn away, Hdt.

ἀνατροπή, ἡ, (ἀνατρέπω) an upsetting, overthrow, Aesch., Plat.

ἀνα-τυλίσσω, Att. -ττω, f. ξω, to unroll, βιβλία Luc.

ἀνα-τῠπόω, f. ώσω, to impress again, Luc.

ἀνα-τυρβάζω, f. σω, to stir up, confound, Ar.

ἀν-αύγητος, ον, (αὐγή) rayless, sunless, Aesch.

ἀν-αύδητος, Dor. -ᾱτος, ον, (αὐδάω) not to be spoken, unutterable, ineffable, Lat. infandus, Aesch., Eur. 2. unspoken, impossible, Soph. II. speechless, Id.

ἄν-αυδος, ον, (αὐδή) speechless, silent, Od., Aesch., etc. 2. preventing speech, silencing, Aesch. II. like ἀναύδητος, unutterable, Soph.

ἄν-αυλος, ον, without the flute, i.e. joyless, melancholy, Eur.: neut. pl. ἄναυλα as Adv., Babr. II. unskilled in flute-playing, Luc.

Ἄναυρος, ὁ, a river in Thessaly, Hes. II. as appellat. ἄναυρος, ὁ, a torrent, Mosch.

ἄ-ναυς, gen. ἄναος, ὁ, ἡ, without ships, νᾶες ἄναες ships that are ships no more, Aesch.

ἀν-αύω, Ep. aor. 1 ἀν-δῦσα, (αὔω) to cry aloud, Theocr.

ἀνα-φαίνω, poët. ἀμ-φαίνω: f. -φᾰνῶ, but -φᾱνῶ in Eur.: aor. 1 ἀνέφηνα or -έφᾱνα:—to make to give light, make to blaze up, ξύλα Od. 2. to bring to light, shew forth, display, Hom., Att.; ἀν. μελέων νόμους Ar. 3. to proclaim, declare, βασιλέα ἀν. τινά Pind.; ἀν. πόλιν to proclaim it victor in the games, Id.:—c. inf., ἀναφανῶ σε τόδε ὀνομάζειν I proclaim that they call thee by this name, i. e. order that thou be so named, Eur. 4. of things, to appoint, νόμους Ar. 5. ἀναφάναντες τὴν Κύπρον having opened, come in sight of, Cyprus, N. T. II. Pass., with f. med. ἀναφᾰνήσομαι or -φανοῦμαι: pf. ἀναπέφαμμαι, or in med. form -πέφηνα:—to be shewn forth, come to light or into sight, appear plainly, Hom., etc. 2. to reappear, Hdt. 3. ἀναφανῆναι μούναρχος to be declared king, Id.; ἀναφαίνεσθαι σεσωσμένος to be plainly in safety, Xen.

ἀναφᾰλαντίας, ου, ὁ, (φάλανθος) bald in front, Luc.

ἀναφανδά, Adv. (ἀναφαίνομαι) visibly, openly, Od.

ἀναφανδόν, Adv. = foreg., Il., Hdt., etc.

ἀνα-φέρω, poët. ἀμ-φέρω: f. ἀν-οίσω: aor. 1 ἀν-ήνεγκα, Ion. ἀνήνεικα, also ἄνῳσα: II. to bring or carry up, Od., etc.; ἀν. τινὰ εἰς Ὄλυμπον Xen.:—to carry up the country, esp. into Central Asia, Hdt.:—Med. to carry up to a place of safety, take with one, Id. 2. to bring up, pour forth, tears, Aesch.:—Med., ἀνενείκασθαι, absol. to fetch up a deep-drawn breath, heave a deep sigh, Il., Hdt.:—c. acc. rei, to utter, ἀνενείκατο φωνάν, μῦθον Theocr. 3. to uphold, take upon one, ἄχθος Aesch.; κινδύνους Thuc. 4. to offer, contribute, εἰς τὸ κοινόν Dem.:—to offer in sacrifice, N. T. 5. intr. to lead up, of a road, Xen. II. to bring or carry back, Eur., etc.; ἀν. τὰς κώπας to recover the oars, at the end of the stroke, Thuc. 2. to bring back tidings, report, Hdt., etc. 3. to bring back from exile, Thuc. 4. to carry back, trace up one's family to an ancestor, Plat. 5. to refer a matter to another, Hdt., etc.: to ascribe, Eur., etc.:—without acc., ἀν. εἴς τινα to appeal to another, make reference to him, Hdt., Plat.:—of things, ἀν. εἴς τι to have reference to a thing, Plat. 6. to bring back, restore, recover, Thuc.:—Pass. to recover oneself, come to oneself, Hdt.:—so also intr. in Act. to come to oneself, recover, Id., etc. 7. to return, yield, as revenue, Xen. 8. to recall a likeness, Plut.

ἀνα-φεύγω, f. -φεύξομαι, to flee up, Xen. 2. to escape, Id. 3. of a report, to disappear gradually, Plut.

ἀν-αφής, ές, (ἁφή) not to be touched, impalpable, Plat.

ἀνα-φθέγγομαι, f. -ξομαι, Dep. to call out aloud, Plut.

ἀνα-φθείρομαι, aor. 2 -εφθάρην [ᾰ], Pass. to be undone, κατὰ τί δεῦρ' ἀνεφθάρης; by what ill luck came you hither? Ar.

ἀνα-φλεγμαίνω, f. -ᾰνῶ, to inflame and swell up, Plut.

ἀνα-φλέγω, f. ξω, to light up, rekindle, Eur.: metaph. ἀν. ἔρωτα Plut.:—Pass. to be inflamed, excited, Anth. Hence ἀνάφλεξις, εως, ἡ, a lighting up, Plut.

ἀνα-φλογίζω, = ἀναφλέγω, Anth.

ἀνα-φλύω, only in impf. to bubble or boil up, Il.

ἀνα-φοβέω, f. ήσω, to frighten away, Ar.

ἀναφορά, ᾶς, ἡ, (ἀναφέρω) a carrying back, reference, Theophr., Plut. 2. recourse to another [in difficulty], Dem. 3. a means of repairing a fault or loss, a means of recovery, Eur., Plut.

ἀνα-φορέω, Frequent. of ἀναφέρω, Hdt., Thuc.

ἀνάφορον, τό, a pole or yoke for carrying things, Ar.

ἀνα-φράζομαι, Ep. aor. 1 -εφρασσάμην, Med. to be ware of a thing, perceive, Od.

ἀν-αφρόδῑτος, ον, (Ἀφροδίτη) without the favour of Venus, Plut., Luc. 2. Lat. invenustus, without charms, Plut.

ἀνα-φρονέω, f. ήσω, to come back to one's senses, Xen.

ἀνα-φροντίζω, f. Att. ιῶ, c. inf., to meditate how to do a thing, Pind.

ἀναφυγή, ἡ, (ἀναφεύγω) escape from a thing, c. gen., Aesch. II. a retreat, Plut.

ἀνα-φύρω [ῡ] -φύρσω, to mix up, confound:—Pass., ἦν πάντα ἀναπεφυρμένα Hdt. 2. to defile, αἵματι ἀναπεφυρμένος Id.

ἀνα-φῡσάω, f. ήσω, to blow up or forth, eject, of volcanoes, Plat. II. metaph. in Pass. to be puffed up, Xen.

ἀνα-φῡσιάω, Ep. part. -φυσιόων, to blow upwards, of a dolphin, Hes.

ἀνα-φύω, f. -φύσω [ῡ], to produce again, to let grow, πώγωνα Theocr. II. Pass., with aor. 2 act. -έφυν, pf. -πέφῡκα, to grow up, Hdt., etc. 2. to grow again, of the hair, Id.

ἀνα-φωνέω, f. ήσω, to call aloud, declaim, Plut. 2. to proclaim, Id. Hence ἀναφώνημα, ατος, τό, a proclamation, Plut.; and ἀναφώνησις, εως, ἡ, an outcry, ejaculation, Plut.

ἀνα-χάζω, to make to recoil, force back, only 3 pl. poët. aor. 1 ἀνέχασσαν, Pind. II. Med. ἀναχάζομαι, Ep. aor. 1 ἀνεχασσάμην:—to draw back, retire, Hom.; ἐπὶ πόδα ἀναχάζεσθαι to retire slowly, of soldiers, Xen. (who also uses Act. in same sense).

ἀνα-χαίνω, v. ἀναχάσκω.

ἀνα-χαιτίζω, f. σω, (χαίτη) of a horse, to throw back the mane, rear up, Eur.: metaph. of men, to become restive, Plut. 2. c. acc. to rear up and throw the rider, Eur.:—metaph. to upset, Id., Dem. 3. c. gen., ἀν. τῶν πραγμάτων to shake off the yoke of business, Plut.

ἀνα-χάσκω, only in pres. and impf., the other tenses being formed from *ἀναχαίνω, -χανοῦμαι: aor. 2 ἀνέχανον: pf. -κέχηνα:—to open the mouth, gape wide, Ar., Luc.

ἀνα-χέω, f. -χεῶ, to pour forth.

ἀνα-χνοαίνομαι, Pass. to get the first down (χνόος), Ar.

ἀνα-χορεύω, f. σω, to begin a choral dance, ἀν. θίασον Eur. 2. to celebrate in the chorus, Βάκχιον Id. 3.

οὐκ ἄν με ἀνεχόρευ' Ἐρινύσι would not scare me away by a band of Furies, Id. **II.** intr. to dance for joy, Id.

ἀνάχυσις, εως, ἡ, (ἀναχέω) effusion : metaph. excess, N. T.

ἀνα-χωνεύω, f. σω, to fuse again, Strab.

ἀνα-χώννυμ, f. -χώσω, to heap up into a mound, Anth.

ἀνα-χωρέω, f. ήσω, to go back, Hom. : esp. to retire or withdraw from battle, Hom., Hdt., Att. **2.** to retire from a place, c. gen., Od. **II.** to come back or revert to the rightful owner, ἐς τὸν παῖδα Hdt. **III.** to withdraw from the world, Ar., Plat. Hence

ἀναχώρησις, εως, Ion. ιος, ἡ, a drawing back, retiring, retreating, Hdt., Thuc. **II.** a means or place of retreat, refuge, Thuc.; and

ἀναχωρητέον, verb. Adj. one must withdraw, retreat, Plat.

ἀνα-χωρίζω, f. σω, to make to go back or retire, Xen.

ἀνα-ψάω, f. ήσω, to wipe up :—Med. to wipe up for oneself, Plut.

ἀνα-ψηφίζω, f. Att. ιῶ, to put to the vote again, Thuc.

ἀναψυχή, ἡ, a cooling, refreshing : relief, recovery, respite, Plat. : from a thing, c. gen., Eur. From

ἀνα-ψύχω [ῡ], f. -ψύξω, to cool, to revive by fresh air, to refresh, Hom., Eur. :—Pass. to be revived, refreshed, Il. **2.** ναῦς ἀν. to let the ships rest and get dry, relieve them, Hdt., Xen.; so, ἀν. τὸν ἱδρῶτα to let it dry off, Plut. **3.** metaph. c. gen., ἀν. πόνων τινα to give him relief from toil, Eur. **II.** intr. in Act. to recover oneself, revive, Anth., Babr.

ἀν-δαίω, poët. for ἀνα-δαίω.

ἀνδάνω [ἄ], impf. ἥνδανον, Ep. ἕήνδανον, Ion. ἑάνδανον: f. ἁδήσω, pf. ἅδηκα or ἕᾱδα: aor. 2 ἕαδον, Ep. εὔαδον and ἅδον [ἄ]. (From Root ΑΔ, whence also ἡδύς, ἡδονή, ἄσμενος.) To please, delight, gratify, c. dat. pers., Hom., etc. :—absol. ἑᾱδότα μῦθον a pleasing speech, Id. **II.** ἀνδάνει, Lat. placet, expressing opinion, οὔ σφι ἥνδανε ταῦτα Hdt.; c. inf., τοῖσι μὲν ἔαδε βοηθέειν it was their pleasure to assist, Id. :—impers., ἐπεί νύ τοι εὔαδεν οὕτως (sc. ποιεῖν) Hom.

ἄν-δεμα, ἀν-δέω, ἄν-δημα, poët. for ἀνά-δεμα, etc.

ἄνδηρον, τό, a raised border, flower-bed, Theocr., Anth. :—any raised bank, a dyke, Mosch. (Perh. akin to ἄνθος.)

ἀν-δίδωμι, poët. for ἀναδίδωμι.

ἄν-δίχα, Adv. (ἀνά, δίχα) asunder, in twain, Il.

ἀνδρ-ἄγαθέω, f. ήσω, = ἀνδραγαθίζομαι :—Pass., ἠνδραγαθημένα brave deeds, Plut.

ἀνδρἄγάθημα, ατος, τό, a brave deed, Plut.; and

ἀνδρἄγἄθία, Ion. -ίη, ἡ, (ἀνήρ, ἀγαθός) bravery, manly virtue, the character of a brave honest man, Hdt., Ar.

ἀνδρ-ἄγἄθίζομαι, (ἀνήρ, ἀγαθός) Dep. to act bravely, honestly, play the honest man, Thuc.

ἀνδρ-ἄγρια, ων, τά, (ἀνήρ, ἄγρα) the spoils of a slain enemy, Il.

ἀνδρἄκάς, Adv. (ἀνήρ) man by man, = κατ' ἄνδρα, Od.

ἀνδρἄπόδεσσι, Ep. dat. pl. of ἀνδράποδον.

ἀνδρᾱποδίζω, f. Att. ιῶ :—aor. 1 ἠνδραπόδισα : Ion. f. med. ἀνδραποδιεῦμαι in pass. sense, Att. ἀνδραποδισθήσομαι : aor. 1 pass. ἠνδραποδίσθην : pf. ἠνδραπόδισμαι : (ἀνδράποδον) :—to reduce to slavery, enslave, esp. to sell the free men of a conquered place into slavery, Hdt.,

Thuc., etc. :—Pass. to be sold into slavery, Hdt., Xen., etc. :—the Med. was also used in act. sense, Hdt. Hence

ἀνδρᾱπόδισις, εως, ἡ, = sq., Xen. ; and

ἀνδρᾱποδισμός, ὁ, a selling free men into slavery, enslaving, Thuc., etc. ; and

ἀνδρᾱποδιστής, οῦ, ὁ, a slave-dealer, kidnapper, Ar., Plat. ; ἀνδρ. ἑαυτοῦ one who sells his own independence, Xen.

ἀνδρᾱποδο-κάπηλος, ὁ, a slave-dealer, Luc.

ἀνδράποδον [δρᾰ], τό, Ep. dat. pl. ἀνδραπόδεσσι, one taken in war and sold as a slave, a captive, Il., Hdt., Att. **II.** generally, a slave, a slavish low fellow, Plat., Xen. (Deriv. uncertain.)

ἀνδρᾱπόδ-ώδης, ες, (εἶδος) slavish, servile, abject, Plat., Xen. Adv. -δῶς, Id.

ἀνδράριον, τό, Dim. of ἀνήρ, a manikin, Ar.

ἀνδρ-αχθής, ές, (ἀνήρ, ἄχθος) loading a man, as much as a man can carry, Od.

ἀνδρεία, Ion. -ηίη, ἡ, (ἀνδρία is a doubtful form), manliness, manhood, manly spirit, Lat. virtus, Trag., etc.

ἀνδρ-είκελον, τό, (ἀνήρ, εἴκελος) an image of a man, Plat. **II.** a flesh-coloured pigment, Id.

ἀνδρ-είκελος, ον, (ἀνήρ, εἴκελος) like a man, Plut.

ἀνδρεῖος, α, ον, Ion. -ήϊος, η, ον, Comp. and Sup. ἀνδρειότερος, -ότατος, even in Hdt. : (ἀνήρ) :—of or for a man, Aesch., etc. ; for αὐλοὶ ἀνδρεῖοι, v. αὐλός. **II.** manly, masculine, Hdt., Att. ; in bad sense, stubborn, Luc. :—neut. τὸ ἀνδρεῖον, by crasis τἀνδρεῖον, = ἀνδρεία, Eur., Thuc. **2.** of things, strong, vigorous, Ar. **III.** ἀνδρεῖα, τά, the public meals of the Cretans, also the older name for the Spartan φειδίτια, Alcman, Plut.

ἀνδρειότης, ητος, ἡ, = ἀνδρεία, Xen.

ἀνδρει-φόντης, ου, ὁ, (ἀνήρ, *φένω) man-slaying, Il.

ἀνδρεῖος, ον, poët. for ἀνδρεῖος, ἀνδρῶν.

ἀνδρεσσι, Ep. dat. pl. of ἀνήρ.

ἀνδρευόμενος, η, ον, Ion. for ἀνδρούμενος, part. pass. of ἀνδρόω.

ἀνδρηϊος, ἀνδρηΐη, ἀνδρήϊος, Ion. for ἀνδρῶν, ἀνδρεία, ἀνδρεῖος.

ἀνδρηλἄτέω, f. ήσω, to banish from house and home, Aesch., Soph. From

ἀνδρ-ηλάτης [ᾰ], ου, ὁ, (ἀνήρ, ἐλαύνω) he that drives one from home, the avenger of blood, Aesch.

ἀνδρία, v. ἀνδρεία.

ἀνδριαντίσκος, ὁ, Dim. of ἀνδριάς, a puppet, Plut.

ἀνδριαντοποιέω, f. ήσω, to make statues, Xen. ; and

ἀνδριαντοποιΐα, ἡ, the sculptor's art, statuary, Plat., Xen. From

ἀνδριαντο-ποιός, οῦ, ὁ, (ἀνδριάς, ποιέω) a statue-maker, statuary, sculptor, Pind., Plat.

ἀνδριάς, ὁ, gen. άντος, (ἀνήρ) the image of a man, a statue, Hdt., Att.

ἀνδρίζω, f. ίσω, (ἀνήρ) to make a man of : Pass. or Med. to come to manhood, behave like a man, play the man, Plat.

ἀνδρικός, ή, όν, (ἀνήρ) of or for a man, masculine, manly, Lat. virilis, Plat. ; ἀνδρ. ἱδρώς the sweat of manly toil, Ar. :—Adv. -κῶς, like a man, Comp. -ώτερον, Sup. -ώτατα, Id. **II.** composed of men, χορός Xen.

ἀνδρίον, τό, Dim. of ἀνήρ, a manikin, Ar., Theocr.

ἀνδριστέον, verb. Adj. of ἀνδρίζομαι, one must play the man, Plat.

ἀνδριστί [ῐ], Adv. (ἀνήρ) like a man, like men, Ar., Theocr.

ἀνδρο-βόρος,ον,(ἀνήρ, βι-βρώσκω) man-devouring,Anth.

ἀνδρό-βουλος, ον, (ἀνήρ, βουλή) of manly counsel, man-minded, Aesch.

ἀνδρο-βρώς, ῶτος, ὁ, ἡ, (ἀνήρ, βι-βρώσκω) man-eating, Eur.

ἀνδρο-γόνος, ον, (ἀνήρ, γί-γνομαι) begetting males, Hes.

ἀνδρό-γῡνος, ὁ, (ἀνήρ, γυνή) a man-woman, hermaphrodite, Plat.   2. a womanish man, effeminate person, Hdt.   II. as Adj. common to men and women, Anth.

ἀνδρο-δάϊκτος, ον, (ἀνήρ, δαΐζω) man-slaying, Aesch.

ἀνδρο-δάμας [ᾰ], αντος, ὁ, ἡ, (ἀνήρ, δαμάζω) man-taming, Pind.

ἀνδρο-θέα, ἡ, the man-goddess, i. e. Athena, Anth.

ἀνδρόθεν, Adv. (ἀνήρ) from a man or men, Anth.

ἀνδρο-θνής, ῆτος, ὁ, ἡ,(ἀνήρ, θνήσκω) murderous,Aesch.

ἀνδρο-κμής, ῆτος, ὁ, ἡ, (ἀνήρ, κάμνω) man-wearying, Aesch. : man-slaying, Id.

ἀνδρό-κμητος, ον, (κάμνω) wrought by men's hands, Il.

ἀνδρο-κτᾰσία, ἡ, (ἀνήρ, κτείνω) slaughter of men in battle, Il., Aesch.

ἀνδροκτονέω, to slay men, Aesch. From

ἀνδρο-κτόνος, ον, (ἀνήρ, κτείνω) man-slaying, murdering, Hdt., Eur.

ἀνδρ-ολέτειρα, ἡ, (ἀνήρ, ὄλλυμι) a murderess, Aesch.

ἀνδροληψία, ἡ, and -λήψιον, τό, (ἀνήρ, λαμβάνω) seizure of men guilty of murdering a citizen abroad, Lex. ap. Dem.

ἀνδρο-μάχος [ᾰ], ον, (ἀνήρ, μάχομαι) fighting with men, Anth.; fem. ἀνδρομάχη Id.

ἀνδρομέος, α, ον, (ἀνήρ) of man or men, human, κρέα Hom.; ψωμοὶ ἀνδρ. goblets of man's flesh, Od.

ἀνδρο-μήκης, ες, (ἀνήρ, μῆκος) of a man's height, Xen.

ἀνδρό-παις, αιδος, ὁ, (ἀνήρ) a man-boy, i. e. a youth near manhood, Aesch.

ἀνδρο-πλήθεια, ἡ, (ἀνήρ, πλῆθος) a multitude of men, Aesch.

ἀνδρό-σῐνις, ιδος, ὁ, ἡ, (ἀνήρ, σίνομαι) hurtful to men, Anth.

ἀνδρο-σφᾰγεῖον, τό, (ἀνήρ, σφάζω) a slaughter-house of men, Aesch.

ἀνδρο-σφιγξ, ιγγος, ὁ, (ἀνήρ) a man-sphinx, sphinx with the bust of a man,not (as usually) of a woman, Hdt.

ἀνδρότης, ητος, ἡ, = ἀνδρεία : cf. ἁδροτής.

ἀνδρο-τῠχής, ές, (ἀνήρ, τυγχάνω) getting a husband, ἀνδρ. βίοτος wedded life, Aesch.

ἀνδροφᾰγέω, f. ήσω, to eat men, Hdt. From

ἀνδρο-φάγος, ον, (φαγεῖν) eating men, Od., Hdt.

ἀνδρο-φθόρος, ον,(φθείρω) man-destroying,murderous, Soph.   II. proparox., ἀνδρόφθορον αἷμα the blood of a slain man, Aesch.

ἀνδροφονία, ἡ, slaughter of men, Arist., Plut. From

ἀνδρο-φόνος, ον, (ἀνήρ, *φένω) man-slaying, Il.   2. of women, murdering husbands, Pind.   II. as law-term, one convicted of manslaughter, a homicide, Plat.,Dem.

ἀνδροφόντης, ου, ὁ, = ἀνδρειφόντης, Aesch.

ἀνδρόω, f. ώσω, (ἀνήρ) to rear up into manhood, Anth. : —Pass. to become a man, reach manhood, Hdt., Eur.   II. in Pass. also of a woman, to be of marriageable age, Eur.

ἀνδρ-ώδης, ες, (ἀνήρ, εἶδος) like a man, manly, Isocr. Adv. -δῶς, Sup. -δέστατα, Xen.

ἀνδρών, ῶνος, ὁ, (ἀνήρ) the men's apartment in a house, the banqueting hall, etc., Hdt., Aesch., etc.; Ion. ἀνδρεών, Hdt.; Ep. -εών, Anth. :—also ἀνδρωνῖτις, ιδος, ἡ, Xen.

ἀν-δύομαι, poët. for ἀνα-δύομαι.

ἀν-δώσειν, poët. for ἀναδώσειν, fut. inf. of ἀνα-δίδωμι.

ἀν-έβην, aor. 2 of ἀναβαίνω.

ἀν-έβρᾰχε, (*βράχω) 3 sing. aor. 2, with no pres. in use, clashed or rung loudly, of armour, Il.; creaked or grated loudly, of a door, Od.

ἀν-έβωσα, Ion. for ἀνεβόησα, aor. 1 of ἀναβοάω.

ἀν-έγγυος, ον, (ἐγγύη) not accredited, Plat.; of a woman, unwedded, Plut.

ἀν-εγείρω, f. ερῶ, to wake up, rouse, ἐξ ὕπνου, ἐκ λεχέων Hom. :—Pass., Eur., Xen.   2. metaph. to wake up, raise, Pind.   3. metaph. also to rouse, encourage, Od.   II. of buildings, to raise, Anth.

ἀν-εγέρμων, ον, (ἀνεγείρω) wakeful, Anth.

ἀν-έγκλητος, ον, (ἐγκαλέω) not accused, without reproach, void of offence, Xen., etc. :—Adv. -τως, Dem.

ἀν-εγνάμφθην, aor. 1 pass. of ἀναγνάμπτω.

ἀν-έγνων, aor. 2 of ἀναγιγνώσκω.

ἀν-εδέγμεθα, Ep. aor. 2 of ἀναδέχομαι.

ἀν-έδειξα, aor. 1 of ἀναδείκνυμι.

ἀνέδην, Adv. (ἀνίημι) let loose, freely, without restraint, Plat., Dem. :—remissly, carelessly, Soph.   II. without more ado, absolutely, Plat.

ἀν-έδρᾰμον, aor. 2 of ἀνατρέχω.

ἀν-έεργω, impf. ἀνέεργον, old Ep. forms of ἀν-είργω.

ἀν-έζησα, aor. 1 of ἀναζάω.

ἀν-έθελητος, ον, (ἐθέλω) unwished for, unwelcome, Hdt.

ἀν-έθηκα, ἀν-έθην, aor. 1 and 2 of ἀνατίθημι.

ἀν-είην, aor. 2 opt. of ἀνίημι.

ἀν-ειλείθυια, ἡ, without the aid of Eileithyia, Eur.

ἀν-ειλέω, f. ήσω, to roll up together :—Pass. to crowd or throng together, Thuc.

ἀν-είληφα, -είλημμαι, pf. act. and pass. of ἀνα-λαμβάνω.

ἀν-ειλίσσω, poët. for ἀνα-λίσσω.

ἀν-εῖλον, aor. 2 of ἀν-αιρέω.

ἀν-είλω, = ἀνειλέω :—Pass. to shrink up or back, Plat.

ἀν-ειμένος, η, ον, part. pf. pass. of ἀν-ίημι, used as Adj. let go free, released from labour, of animals dedicated to the gods, Soph. : metaph., ἀν. ἔς τι devoted to a thing, Hdt.   II. remiss, slack, unconstrained, Thuc.; ἐν τῷ ἀνειμένῳ τῆς γνώμης when their minds are unstrung, Id. :—Adv. ἀνειμένως, at ease, carelessly, without restraint, Thuc., Xen.

ἄν-ειμι, (εἶμι ibo) in Att. serving as f. to ἀνέρχομαι: impf. ἀνῄειν, Ep. and Ion. ἀνήϊον :—to go up, Hom., etc.; ἅμ' ἠελίῳ ἀνιόντι at sun-rise, Il.   2. to sail up, i. e. out to sea, Od.   3. to go up inland, esp. into Central Asia, Plat.   II. to approach, esp. as a suppliant, Il.   III. to go back, go home, return, Od., Hdt., etc.

ἀν-είμων, ον, (εἷμα) without clothing, unclad, Od.

ἀν-ειπεῖν, aor. 2 with no pres. in use, ἀναγορεύω being used instead: aor. 1 pass. ἀναρρήθην (as if from *ἀναρρέω) :—to say aloud, announce, proclaim, Pind., Xen. :—c. acc. et inf. to make proclamation that . . , Ar., Thuc. :—in the Athen. assemblies, ἀνεῖπεν ὁ κῆρυξ Thuc.,

etc. :—Pass. *to be proclaimed*, ἀναρρηθέντος τοῦ στεφάνου *when the crown was proclaimed*, Dem. **II.** *to call upon, invoke*, Plut.

ἀν-είργω, Ep. impf. ἀνέεργον :—*to keep back, restrain*, Hom., Xen.

ἀν-είρομαι, Ep. for ἀν-έρομαι.

ἀν-ειρύω, poët. and Ion. for ἀν-ερύω.

ἀν-είρω, aor. 1 ἄνειρα, *to fasten on* or *to, to string*, Hdt. ; ἀν. στεφάνους *to twine* or *wreathe* them, Ar.

ἀν-είς, aor. 2 part. of ἀν-ίημι.

ἀν-είσοδος, ον, *without entrance* or *access*, Plut.

ἀν-εισφορία, ἡ, *exemption from the* εἰσφορά, Plut. From

ἀν-είσφορος, ον, *exempt from the* εἰσφορά, Plut.

ἀνέκαθεν, (ἀνεκάς) Adv. of Place, *from above*, Hdt., Aesch. **II.** of Time, *from the first, by origin*, Hdt. ; so with Art., τὸ ἀνέκαθεν Id.

ἀν-εκάς, Adv. *upwards*, Lat. *sursum*, Pind., Att.

ἀν-έκβᾰτος, ον, (ἐκβαίνω) *without outlet*, Thuc.

ἀν-εκδιήγητος, ον, (ἐκδιηγέομαι) *ineffable*, N. T.

ἀν-έκδοτος, ον, *not given in marriage*, Dem., etc.

ἀν-έκδρομος, ον, *inevitable*, Anth.

ἀν-εκλάλητος, ον, (ἐκλαλέω) *unspeakable*, N. T.

ἀν-εκλίθην [ῐ], -εκλίνα, aor. 1 pass. and act. of ἀνα-κλίνω.

ἀν-εκπίμπλημι, f. -εκπλήσω, *to fill up* or *again*, Xen.

ἀν-έκπληκτος, ον, (ἐκπλήσσω) *undaunted, intrepid*, Plat. :—τὸ ἀνέκπληκτον *intrepidity*, Xen.

ἀν-έκρᾱγον, aor. 2 of ἀνακράζω.

ἀνεκτέος, ον, verb. Adj. of ἀνέχομαι, *to be borne*, Soph.

ἀνεκτός, όν, verb. Adj. of ἀνέχομαι, *bearable, sufferable, tolerable*, mostly with a negat., Il., Att. **2.** without a negat. *that can be endured*, Od., Thuc. **II.** Adv. -τως, Hom. ; οὐκ ἀνεκτῶς ἔχει it is not *to be borne*, Xen.

ἀν-έλεγκτος, ον, (ἐλέγχω) *not cross-questioned, safe from being questioned*, Thuc. : *unconvicted*, Id. **2.** *not refuted, irrefutable*, Plat. :—Adv. -τως, *without refutation*, Id.

ἀν-ελεῖν, -ελέσθαι, aor. 2 inf. act. and med. of ἀναιρέω.

ἀν-ελέγχω, f. ἔγξω, *to convince* or *convict utterly*, Eur.

ἀν-ελεήμων, ον, ονος, *merciless, without mercy*, N. T.

ἀν-έλεος, ον, *unmerciful*, N. T.

ἀνελευθερία, ἡ, *illiberality*, Plat. From

ἀν-ελεύθερος, ον, *not fit for a free man*, Aesch., Arist. **2.** *illiberal, servile*, Plat., etc. **3.** in money matters, *niggardly, stingy*, Ar. **II.** Adv. -ρως, *meanly*, Xen.

ἀν-ελήφθην, aor. 1 pass. of ἀνα-λαμβάνω.

ἀνέλιγμα, ατος, τό, *anything rolled up, a ringlet*, Anth. ; and

ἀνέλιξις, εως, ἡ, *an unfolding*, Plut. From

ἀν-ελίσσω, Att. -ττω, f. ξω, Ep. and Ion. ἀν-ειλ-:—*to unroll* a book written on a roll, i. e. *to unfold, read, interpret*, Xen. ; ἀν. βίον *to pass* one's whole *life*, Plut. **2.** *to cause to move backward*, πόδα Eur. **II.** *to cause to revolve* :—Pass. *to revolve, move glibly*, Ar.

ἀν-ελκύω, f. Att. -ελκύσω, aor. 1 -είλκυσα :—pf. pass. -είλκυσμαι, Ion. -έλκυσμαι :—*to draw up*, τάλαντα ἀνέλκει *holds* them *up* (in weighing), Il. ; ἀνελκύσαι ναῦς *to haul* them *up high and dry*, Hdt., Thuc. **2.** *to drag up, drag into open court* or *into the witness-box*, Ar. :—Med., ἀνέλκεσθαι τρίχας *to tear* one's own *hair*, Il. **II.** *to draw* a bow, in act *to shoot*, Hom. :—Med., ἔγχος ἀνελκόμενος *drawing back his spear* [out of the corpse], Od.

ἄν-ελπις, ιδος, ὁ, ἡ, *without hope, hopeless*, Eur.

ἀν-έλπιστος, ον, (ἐλπίζω) *unhoped for, unlooked for*, Trag., etc. ; τὸ ἀνέλπιστον τοῦ βεβαίου *the hopelessness of security*, Thuc. **II.** act., **1.** of persons, *having no hope, hopeless*, Theocr. ; c. inf. *having no hope* or *not expecting that* . . , Thuc. **2.** of things or conditions, *leaving no hope, hopeless, desperate*, Soph., Thuc. ; τὸ ἀνέλπιστον *despair*, Thuc. :—Comp. -ότερος *more desperate*, Id.

ἀν-έμβᾰτος, ον, (ἐμβαίνω) *inaccessible*, Babr., Plut. **2.** act. *not going to* or *visiting*, Anth.

ἀ-νέμεσητος, ον, *free from blame, without offence*, Plat.

ἀ-νέμητος, ον, (νέμω) *not distributed*, Dem. **2.** act. *having no share*, Plut.

ἀνεμίζομαι, (ἄνεμος) Pass. *to be driven with the wind*, N. T.

ἀν-εμνήσθην, aor. 1 pass. of ἀνα-μιμνήσκω.

ἀνεμό-δρομος, ον, *running with the wind*, Luc.

ἀνεμόεις, Dor. for ἠνεμόεις.

ἄνεμος [ᾰ], ὁ, (Root AN, cf. ἄημι) *wind*, Hom., etc. ; ἀνέμου κατιόντος *a squall* having come on, Thuc. ; ἀν. κατὰ βορέαν ἑστηκώς *the wind* being settled in the north, Id. ; ἀνέμοις φέρεσθαι παραδοῦναί τι *to cast a thing to the winds*, Lat. *ventis tradere*, Eur. :—Hom. and Hes. mention only four winds, Boreas, Eurus, Notus (or Argestes), Zephyrus ; Arist. gives twelve, which served as points of the compass.

ἀνεμο-σκεπής, ές, (σκέπη) *sheltering from the wind*, Il.

ἀνεμο-σφάρᾰγος, ον, *echoing to the wind*, Pind.

ἀνεμο-τρεφής, ές, (τρέφω) *fed by the wind*, of a wave, Il. ; ἔγχος ἀνεμ. *a spear from a tree reared by the wind*, i. e. *made tough by battling with the wind*, Ib.

ἀνεμόω, f. ώσω, (ἄνεμος) *to expose to the wind* :—Pass., of the sea, *to be raised by the wind*, Hom.

ἀν-έμπληκτος, ον, *intrepid* : in Adv. -τως, Plut.

ἀν-εμπόδιστος, ον, (ἐμποδίζω) *unembarrassed*, Arist.

ἀνεμ-ώκης, ες, (ὠκύς) *swift as the wind*, Eur., Ar.

ἀνεμώλιος, ον, (ἄνεμος) *windy* : metaph., ἀνεμώλια βάζειν *to talk words of wind*, Hom. ; οἱ δ᾽ αὖτ᾽ ἀνεμώλιοι *are like the winds*, i. e. *good for naught*, Il. ; τί νυ τόξον ἔχεις ἀνεμώλιον ; *why bear thy bow in vain ?* Ib. ; ἀνεμώλιος *empty fool !* Anth.

ἀνεμώνη, ἡ, (ἄνεμος) *the wind-flower, anemoné*, Bion.

ἀν-ενδεής, ές, *in want of naught*, Anth.

ἀν-ένδεκτος, ον, (ἐνδέχομαι) *impossible*, N. T.

ἀν-ενδοίαστος, ον, (ἐνδοιάζω) *indubitable*, Luc.

ἀν-ένεικα, -ενεικάμην, -ενείχθην, Ion. aor. 1 act., med. and pass. of ἀνα-φέρω.

ἀν-ενήνοθε, v. ἐνήνοθε.

ἀν-εξάλειπτος, ον, (ἐξαλείφω) *indelible*, Isocr., Plut.

ἀν-εξέλεγκτος, ον, (ἐξελέγχω) *unquestioned, impossible to be questioned* or *refuted*, of statements or arguments, Thuc. ; ἀν. ἔχει τὸ ἀνδρεῖον *leaves their courage without proof*, Id. **2.** of persons, *not to be convicted, irreproachable*, Xen., etc.

ἀν-εξέργαστος, ον, (ἐξεργάζομαι) *unfinished*, Luc.

ἀν-εξέταστος, ον, (ἐξετάζω) *not inquired into* or *examined*, Dem. **II.** *uninquiring*, Plat.

ἀν-εξεύρετος, ον, (ἐξευρίσκω) *not to be found out*, Thuc.

ἀνεξί-κᾰκος, ον, (ἀνέχομαι, κακόν) *enduring evil, forbearing, long-suffering*, N. T., Luc.

ἀν-εξιχνίαστος, ον, (ἐκ, ἴχνιον) not to be traced, unsearchable, inscrutable, N. T.

ἀν-έξοδος, ον, with no outlet, allowing no return, Lat. irremeabilis, Theocr.

ἄνεοι or ἀνεοί, v. ἄνεως.

ἀν-έορτος, ον, (ἑορτή) without festival, c. gen., ἀν. ἱερῶν without share in festal rites, Eur.

ἀν-επαίσθητος, ον, (ἐπαισθάνομαι) unperceived, imperceptible, Plut., Luc.

ἀν-επαίσχυντος, ον, (ἐπαισχύνομαι) having no cause for shame, N. T.

ἀν-έπαλτο, 3 sing. Ep. aor. 2 pass. of ἀναπάλλω.

ἀν-έπαφος, ον, (ἐπαφή) untouched, ἀν. παρέχειν τι rem integram praestare, Dem.

ἀν-επαφρόδῐτος, ον, = ἀναφρόδιτος, Xen.

ἀν-επαχθής, ές, not burdensome, without offence, Plut., Luc. :—Adv. -θῶς, Thuc.

ἀν-επιβούλευτος, ον, (ἐπιβουλεύω) without plots, τὸ ἀνεπιβούλευτον the absence of intrigue, Thuc.

ἀν-επίγρᾰφος, ον, (ἐπιγράφω) without title or inscription : metaph. without noticeable features, Luc.

ἀν-επίδῐκος, ον, (ἐπί, δίκη) not disputed by legal process, undisputed, Dem.

ἀνεπιείκεια, ή, unfairness, unkindness, Dem. From

ἀν-επιεικής, ές, unreasonable, unfair, Thuc.

ἀν-επίκλητος, ον, (ἐπικαλέω) unaccused, unblamed, Xen. II. without preferring any charge :—Adv. -τως, Thuc.

ἀν-επίληπτος, ον, not open to attack, not censured, blameless, Eur., Thuc. : Adv. -τως, Xen.

ἀν-επίμικτος, ον, (ἐπιμίγνυμι) not mixing with others, unsocial, Plut.

ἀν-επίξεστος, ον, (ἐπί, ξέω) not polished or finished, Hes.

ἀν-επίπλεκτος, ον, (ἐπί, πλέκω) without connexion with others, isolated, Strab.

ἀν-επίρρεκτος, ον, (ἐπιρρέζω) not dedicated.

ἀν-επίσκεπτος, ον, (ἐπισκέπτομαι) inattentive, inconsiderate : Adv. -τως, Hdt. II. pass. not examined, unregarded, Xen.

ἀνεπιστημοσύνη, ή, want of knowledge, ignorance, unskilfulness, Thuc. From

ἀν-επιστήμων, ον, gen. ονος, not knowing, ignorant, unskilful, Hdt., Thuc. ; ναῦς ἀνεπιστήμονες ships with unskilful crews, Thuc. ;—c. gen. rei, unskilled in a thing, Plat. ; c. inf. not knowing how to do a thing, Xen. II. without knowledge, unintelligent : Comp. ἀνεπιστημονέστερος less intelligent, Hdt.

ἀν-επίτακτος, ον, subject to no control, Thuc.

ἀν-επιτήδειος, ον, Ion. -επιτήδεος, η, ον, unserviceable, unfit, Xen., Plat., etc. :—mischievous, prejudicial, hurtful, Hdt., Thuc. 2. unkind, unfriendly, Thuc., Xen.

ἀν-επιτήδευτος, ον, (ἐπιτηδεύω) made without care or design, simple, artless, Luc. II. unpractised, untried, Plut.

ἀν-επιτίμητος [τῐ], ον, (ἐπιτιμάω) not to be censured, τινος for a thing, Dem.

ἀν-επίφθονος, ον, without reproach, Soph. ; ἀν. ἐστι πᾶσιν 'tis no reproach to any one, Thuc. ; ἀνεπιφθονώτατον least invidious, Dem. Adv. -νως so as not to create odium, Thuc.

ἀν-έραμαι or ἀν-εράομαι : aor. 1 ἀνηράσθην : (ἐράω) :— to love again, love anew, c. gen., Andoc., Xen.

ἀν-έραστος, ον, not loved, Luc. II. act. not loving, Anth.

ἀν-έργαστος, ον, (ἐργάζομαι) unwrought, untilled, Luc.

ἄν-εργος, ον, (*ἔργω) not done, Eur.

ἀν-έργω, old poët. form of ἀνείργω.

ἀν-ερεθίζω, f. ίσω, to stir up, excite, Plut. :—Pass. to be in a state of excitement, Thuc., Xen.

*ἀν-ερείπομαι, Dep., only used in aor. 1, to snatch up and carry off, ἀνηρείψαντο Hom. ; ἀνερειψαμένη Hes.

ἀν-ερευνάω, f. ήσω, to examine closely, investigate, Plat.

ἀν-ερεύνητος, ον, (ἐρευνάω) not investigated, Plat. 2. that cannot be found out, inscrutable, Eur.

ἀν-έρομαι, Ep. -είρομαι : aor. 2 -ηρόμην, inf. -ερέσθαι : f. -ερήσομαι : 1. c. acc. pers. to enquire of, question, Od., Soph. 2. c. acc. rei, to ask about, Od., Plat. 3. c. dupl. acc. to ask a person about a thing, Il., Soph.

ἀν-έρπω, with aor. 1 ἀνείρπῠσα, to creep up or upwards, Ar., Luc.

ἀν-έρρω, to go quite away : ἄνερρε away with you, Lat. abi in malam rem, Eur.

ἀν-ερυθρῐάω, f. άσω [ᾱ], to begin to blush, blush up, Xen.

ἀν-ερύω, Ion. and Dor. ἀν-ειρύω : f. ύσω [ῠ] :—to draw up, haul up sails, Od. : to haul ships up on land, Hdt. : —Med. to deliver, Anth.

ἀν-έρχομαι (cf. ἄνειμι) : aor. 2 -ήλυθον or -ἦλθον :—to go up, Od., Att. : absol. to mount the tribune, Plut.:— to go up from the coast inland, Od. :—to come up from the nether world, Theogn., Soph. 2. of trees, to grow up, shoot up, Od. : of the sun, to rise, Aesch. :—metaph., ὄλβος ἀν. Eur. II. to go or come back, go or come home again, return, Hom. 2. to come back to a point, recur, Eur., Plat. 3. νόμος εἴς σ' ἀνελθών a law brought home or having relation to you, Eur.

ἀν-ερωτάω, f. ήσω, like ἀνέρομαι : 1. c. acc. pers. to ask or inquire of, question, Od., Plat. 2. c. acc. rei, to ask about, inquire into, Plat. ; so, ἀν. περί τινος Hdt. 3. c. dupl. acc. to question a person about a thing, ask it of him, Eur., Ar.

ἀνέσαιμι, Ep. aor. 1 of ἀνίημι ; ἄνεσαν, 3 pl. ; ἀνέσας, part.

ἄνεσις, gen. εως, Ion. ιος, ή, (ἀνίημι) a loosening, relaxing of strings, Plat., etc. 2. metaph. remission, abatement, κακῶν Hdt. ; ἀν. φόρων, τελῶν remission of tribute, taxes, Plut. 3. relaxation, recreation, Plat., Arist. II. a letting loose, indulgence, license, Plat., Arist.

ἀν-έσσυτο, 3 sing. Ep. aor. 2 pass. of ἀνασεύω.

ἀν-έστιος, ον, (ἑστία) without hearth and home, homeless, Il., Ar.

ἀν-έσχεθον, poët. for ἄνεσχον, aor. 2 of ἀνέχω.

ἀν-ετάζω, f. σω, to examine closely, N. T.

ἀνετέον, verb. Adj. of ἀνίημι, one must dismiss, Plat.

ἄνετος, ον, (ἀνίημι) relaxed, slack, loose, Luc.

ἄνευ, (ἀνα-) Prep. c. gen. without, οὐκ ἄνευ θεῶν, Lat. non sine Diis, not without divine aid, Od. ; ἄνευ ἐμέθεν without my knowledge, Il. ; ἄνευ πολιτῶν without their consent, Aesch. II. away from, far from, ἄνευ δηῶν Il. III. in Prose, except, besides, like χωρίς, Xen.

ἄνευθε, before a vowel -θεν, (ἄνευ) : 1. Prep. c. gen.,

without, Hom. 2. away from, Il. **II.** Adv. far away, distant, Hom.

ἀν-εύθετος, ον, inconvenient, N.T.

ἀν-εύθῦνος, ον, (εὔθυναι) not having to render an account, irresponsible, Hdt., Thuc. 2. guiltless, because such a one is not liable to trial, Luc.; c. gen. guiltless of . . , Id.

ἄν-ευκτος, ον, not wishing, not praying, Anth.

ἀνεύρεσις, εως, ἡ, a discovery, Eur., Plut. From

ἀν-ευρίσκω, f. -ευρήσω, aor. 2 -εῦρον :—Pass., aor. 1 -ευρέθην :—to find out, make out, discover, Hdt., Att. : —Pass. to be found out or discovered, Thuc.; c. part. to be discovered to be . . , Hdt.

ἀν-ευφημέω, f. ήσω, to shout εὐφήμει or εὐφημεῖτε : as this was mainly done on sorrowful occasions, to cry aloud, shriek, Eur., etc.; ἀνευφήμησεν οἰμωγῇ Soph.

ἀ-νέφελος, ον, (νεφέλη) unclouded, cloudless, Od. : metaph. not to be veiled or concealed, Soph.

ἀν-εχέγγυος, ον, not giving surety or confidence, Thuc.

ἀν-έχω, Ep. 3 sing. subj. ἀνέχῃσι :— impf. ἀνεῖχον :—also ἀνίσχω, impf. ἀνῖσχον :—f. ἀνέξω or ἀνασχήσω :—aor. 2 ἀνέσχον, poët. ἀνέσχεθον, Ep. inf. ἀνσχεθέειν :— pf. ἀνέσχηκα :—Med., ἀνέχομαι : impf. ἠνειχόμην (with double augm.): f. ἀνέξομαι or ἀνασχήσομαι: Ep. inf. ἀνσχήσεσθαι : aor. 2 ἀνεσχόμην, with double augm. ἠνεσχόμην, sync. ἠνσχόμην, poët. imper. ἄνσχεο.
A. trans. to hold up one's hands in fight, Od. ; also in token of defeat, Theocr. :—to lift up the hands in prayer, Il., etc. 2. ἀν. φλόγα to hold up a torch at weddings, Eur.; hence ἄνεχε, πάρεχε (sc. τὸ φῶς), i.e. make ready, go on, Id.; also, ἀν. φῶς σωτήριον to hold up a signal fire, Thuc. 3. to lift up, exalt, τινά Pind. 4. metaph. to uphold, maintain, Od., Thuc.; ἀνέχων λέκτρα remaining constant to the bed, Eur.; so, ἀν. κισσόν Soph. 5. to put forth, πτόρθους Eur. **II.** to hold back, Il.; ἀν. Σικελίαν μὴ ὑπό τινα εἶναι to keep it from being subject, Thuc.
B. intr. to rise up, rise, emerge from water, Od., Hdt.:—esp. in form ἀνίσχω, of the sun, Hdt., Xen. 2. of events, to arise, happen, Hdt. 3. to appear, shew oneself, Soph. 4. to project, Il.; of a headland, to jut out, Hdt., Thuc. 5. to hold on, keep doing, c. part., Thuc.; στέρξας ἀνέχει is constant in his love, Soph.; c. acc. et inf. to aver constantly that . . , Id. 6. to hold up, cease, Theogn.:—generally, to wait, delay, Thuc. 7. c. gen. to cease from suffering, get rest from pain, Soph.
C. Med. to hold up what is one's own, ἔγχος, χεῖρας Il.; hence ἀνασχόμενος absol. (sub. ἔγχος etc.), Ib. **II.** to hold oneself up, bear up, hold out, Il.; aor. 2 imper. ἀνάσχεο, Ep. ἄνσχεο, be of good courage, Ib.:—in part., ἀνεχόμενοι with patience, Hdt. 2. c. acc. to bear up against, Il., Hdt., Att. :—so, c. gen., Od., Plat. 3. the dependent clause is added in part., οὔ σε ἀνέξομαι ἄλγε' ἔχοντα I will not suffer thee to have . . , Il., etc.; οὐ σῖγ' ἀνέχει (sc. ὤν) ; Soph. 4. c. inf. to suffer, Aesch.

ἀνεψιά, ᾶς, ἡ, fem. of ἀνεψιός, Xen.

ἀνεψιαδοῦς, οῦ, ὁ, a first-cousin's son, or second cousin, Dem.

ἀνεψιός, ὁ, a first-cousin, cousin, Il., Hdt., Att. 2. a nephew, Hdt. [When the ult. is long, Hom. lengthens

also the penult., ἀνεψιοῦ κταμένοιο.] (From α euphon. or copul., and ΝΕΠ, whence also Lat. nepos, neptis.)

ἀνέψυχθεν, Ep. for -ησαν, 3 pl. aor. 1 pass. of ἀναψύχω.

ἄν-εω, (ἀν- priv., αὔω to cry) without a sound, in silence, in Od. certainly an Adv. ; in other places it may be nom. pl. ἄνεῳ, from ἄν-εως = ἄν-αυος.

ἀν-έῳγα, ἀν-έῳγον, Att. pf. and impf. of ἀν-οίγνυμι.

ἀν-έῳνται, = ἀνεῶνται, 3 pl. pf. pass. of ἀνίημι, as if from *ἀν-έῳω.

ἀν-έῳξα, aor. 1 of ἀν-οίγνυμι.

ἀν-εῴχθην, aor. 1 pass. of ἀν-οίγνυμι.

ἄνη, ἡ, (ἄνω) fulfilment, Aesch.

ἀν-ηβάω, f. ήσω, to grow young again, Theogn., Eur., etc.

ἀν-ηβητήριος, α, ον, (ἀνά, ἡβάω) returning as in youth, Eur.

ἄν-ηβος, ον, (ἥβη) not yet come to man's estate, beardless, Plat., Theocr.

ἀν-ηγεμόνευτος, ον, (ἡγεμονεύω) without leader, Luc.

ἀν-ηγέομαι, f. ήσομαι, Dep. to tell as in a narrative, relate, recount, Pind., Hdt. 2. intr. to advance, Pind.

ἀνήῃ, Ep. 3 sing. aor. 2 subj. of ἀνίημι.

ἀν-ήδυντος, ον, not sweetened or seasoned, Arist. : unpleasant, Plut.

ἀνήθῐνος, η, ον, (ἄνηθον) made of anise or dill, Theocr.

ἄνηθον or ἄννηθον, τό, anise, dill, Ar., Theocr. ; Ion. ἄννησον or ἄνησον, Hdt. ; Aeol. ἄννητον or ἄνητον, Sappho. (Deriv. unknown.)

ἀν-ῆθον, impf. of ἀν-αίθω.

ἀν-ήιξα, aor. 1 of ἀν-αΐσσω.

ἀν-ήιον, Ep. and Ion. impf. of ἄν-ειμι (εἶμι).

ἀν-ήκεστος, ον, (ἀκέομαι) not to be healed, incurable, irreparable, fatal, Il., Hdt., Att.; ἀνήκεστα ποιεῖν τινα to do one irreparable injuries, Xen.; ἀνήκεστα πάσχειν Thuc. 2. of persons, implacable, Xen. **II.** act. damaging beyond remedy, deadly, Soph. :—Adv., ἀνηκέστως διατιθέναι to treat with barbarous cruelty, Hdt.

ἀν-ήκοος, ον, (ἀκοή) without hearing, of the dead, Mosch. 2. c. gen. not hearing a thing, never having heard it, ignorant of it, Xen., etc.:—absol., σκαιὸς καὶ ἀν. ignorant, Dem.

ἀνηκουστέω, f. ήσω, to be unwilling to hear, to disobey, c. gen., Il., Aesch., Thuc.; c. dat., Hdt.; absol., Id. From

ἀν-ήκουστος, ον, (ἀκούω) unheard of, Lat. inauditus, ἤκουσ' ἀνήκουστα Soph. **II.** act. not willing to hear : τὰ ἀνήκουστα disobedience, Xen.

ἀν-ήκω, f. ξω, to have come up to a point, reach up to, of persons, αἱμασιὴν ἀνήκουσαν ἀνδρὶ ἐς τὸν ὀμφαλόν a wall reaching up to a man's middle, Hdt.; ἀν. ἐς τὰ μέγιστα to reach up to the highest point, Id. 2. of things, τοῦτο ἐς οὐδὲν ἀν. amounts to nothing, Id.; αἱ πολλαὶ [ζημίαι] ἐς τὸν θάνατον ἀν. have gone as far as death, Thuc.; ἀν. ἔς σε ἔχειν it has come to you to have, has become yours to have, Hdt. **II.** to appertain, be fit or proper, N.T.; τὸ ἀνῆκον what is fit and proper, Ib.

ἀν-ηλάμην [ᾰ], aor. 1 of ἀνάλλομαι.

ἀν-ηλεής, ές, (ἔλεος) without pity, unmerciful :—Adv. -εῶς, Andoc.

ἀν-ηλέητος, ον, = foreg., Aeschin.

ἀν-ήλιος, Dor. -άλιος, ον, without sun, sunless, Trag.

ἀν-ήλῐπος, Dor. ἀν-άλ-, ον, (ἤλιψ a kind of shoe) unshod, barefoot, Theocr.

ἀνήλωσα, aor. 1 of ἀναλίσκω.

ἀν-ήμελκτος, ον, (ἀμέλγω) unmilked, Od.

ἀν-ήμερος, ον, not tame, wild, savage, of persons and countries, Aesch.

ἀνήνασθαι, aor. 1 inf. of ἀναίνομαι: ἀνήνηται 3 sing. subj.

ἀνηνεμία, ή, =νηνεμία, Anth. From

ἀν-ήνεμος, ον, (ἄνεμος) without wind, ἀνήνεμος χειμώνων without the blast of storms, Soph.

ἀνήνοθε, Ep. pf. with aor. signf., αἷμα ἀνήνοθεν ἐξ ὠτειλῆς blood gushed forth from the wound, Il.; κνίση ἀνήνοθεν the savour mounted up, Od. (Formed as if from *ἀνέθω (ἀνά) to rise up; cf. ἐνήνοθε.)

ἀν-ήνυτος, ον, (ἀνύω) ineffectual, Od.

ἀν-ήνυτος, ον,=ἀνήνυστος, Soph., Plat.   2. endless, Plat.

ἀν-ήνωρ, ορος, ὁ, (ἀνήρ) unmanly, Od., Hes.

ἀν-ῆπται, 3 sing. pf. pass. of ἀν-άπτω.

ἀν-ηπύω, f. σω, to cry aloud, roar, Mosch. [v. ἠπύω.]

ἀνήρ (Root ANEP), ἀνέρος, ὁ, Att. ἀνδρός, ἀνδρί, ἄνδρα, voc. ἄνερ: pl. ἄνδρες, -δρῶν, -δράσι [ᾰ], -δρας: [ᾰ: but in Ep. ἀνέρος, ἀνέρι, ἀνέρες, ᾱ]:—a man, Lat. vir (not homo):   I. a man, opp. to a woman, Hom., etc.   II. a man, opp. to a god, πατὴρ ἀνδρῶν τε θεῶν τε Id.   III. a man, opp. to a youth, a man in the prime of life, Id., etc.; εἰς ἄνδρας ἐγγράφεσθαι to be enrolled among the men, Dem.   IV. a man emphatically, a man indeed, ἀνέρες ἔστε, φίλοι Il.; πολλοὶ μὲν ἄνθρωποι, ὀλίγοι δὲ ἄνδρες many human beings, but few men, Hdt.   V. a man, opp. to his wife, a husband, Hom., etc.; αἰγῶν ἄνερ, Virgil's vir gregis, Theocr.

ἀνήρ [ᾱ], Att. crasis for ὁ ἀνήρ.

ἀν-ήριθμος, poët. for ἀν-άριθμος.

ἀν-ήροτος, ον, (ἀρόω) unploughed, untilled, Od., Aesch.

ἀν-ήρτημαι, pf. pass. of ἀν-αρτάω.

ἄνησον or ἄννησον, v. ἄνηθον.

ἀν-ήσητος, Dor. -ᾱτος, ον,=ἀήσσητος, Theocr.

ἀν-ήφαιστος, ον, without real fire, πῦρ ἀνήφαιστον, i. e. the fire of discord, Eur.

ἀν-ήφθην, aor. 1 pass. of ἀνάπτω.

ἀν-ήφθω, 3 sing. pf. pass. imper. of ἀνάπτω.

ἀνθ-αιρέομαι, f. ήσομαι: aor. 2 -ειλόμην: Dep.:—choose one person or thing instead of another, τινά (or τί) τινος Eur.; to prefer, choose rather, Id.   II. to dispute, lay claim to, τι Id.

ἀνθ-αλοῖεν, 3 pl. aor. 2 opt. of ἀνθ-αλίσκομαι.

ἀνθ-ἁλίσκομαι, f. -αλώσομαι, Pass. to be captured in turn, ἁλόντες αὖθις ἀνθαλοῖεν ἄν Aesch.

ἀνθ-ἁμιλλάομαι, f. -ήσομαι, Dep. to vie one with another, to race one another, Xen.

ἀνθ-άμιλλος [ᾰ], ον,(ἅμιλλα) vying with,rivalling,Eur.

ἀνθ-άπτομαι, Ion. ἀντ-, f. ψομαι, Dep. to lay hold of in turn, c. gen., Hdt., Eur.   II. simply to lay hold of, grapple with, engage in, c. gen., Hdt.,Thuc.: generally, to reach, attain, τερμόνων Eur.   2. to lay hold of, attack, πλευμόνων, φρενῶν, Soph., Eur.

ἄνθειον, τό, (ἄνθος) a flower, blossom, Ar.

ἀνθ-εκτέον, verb. Adj. of ἀντ-έχω, one must cleave to, c. gen., Plat.; so in pl. ἀνθεκτέα, Thuc.

ἀνθ-έλκω, f. -έλξω or ελκύσω [ῡ], to draw or pull against, Thuc.; ἀνθ. ἀλλήλαις to pull against one another, Plat.

ἄνθεμα, ατος, τό, poët. for ἀνάθεμα.

ἀνθέμιον, τό, =ἄνθος, ἀνθέμιον ἐστιγμένος tattooed with flowers, Xen.

ἀνθεμίς, ίδος, ἡ, = ἄνθος, Anth.

ἀνθεμόεις, εσσα, εν and —εις, εν, flowery, of meadows, Il.   II. of works in metal, bright, burnished, or wrought with flowers, Hom.; of tapestry, flowered, Anth. From

ἄνθεμον, τό, (ἀνθέω)=ἄνθος, Sappho, Ar.; ἄνθεμα χρυσοῦ, i. e. the costliest gold, Pind.

ἀνθεμόρ-ρυτος, ον, (ῥέω) flowing from flowers, of honey, Eur.

ἀνθεμ-ουργός, όν, (*ἔργω) working in flowers, of bees, Aesch.

ἀνθεμ-ώδης, ες, (εἶδος) flowery, blooming, Aesch., Eur.

ἄν-θεο, Ep. aor. 2 med. imper. of ἀνα-τίθημι.

ἀνθερεών, ῶνος, ὁ, (ἀνθέω) the chin or part on which the beard grew, Lat. mentum, Il.

ἀνθερίκη [ῐ], ἡ, = ἀνθέριξ, Anth.

ἀνθέριξ, ικος, ὁ, (ἄνθος)=ἀθήρ, the beard of an ear of corn, the ear itself, Lat. spica, Il.   II=the stalk of asphodel, Hdt., Theocr.

ἄν-θεσαν, Ep. for ἀν-έθεσαν, 3 pl. aor. 2 of ἀνατίθημι.

Ἀνθεστήρια, ων, τά, (ἄνθος) the Feast of Flowers, i. e. the three days' festival of Dionysus at Athens, in the month Anthesterion.

Ἀνθεστηριών, ῶνος, ὁ, the month Anthesterion, eighth of the Attic year, answering to the end of February and the beginning of March.

ἀνθ-εστιάω, f. άσω [ᾱ], (ἀντί, ἑστιάω) to entertain in return or mutually, Plut.

ἀνθεσ-φόρος, ον, (ἄνθος, φέρω) bearing flowers, flowering, Eur.

ἄν-θετο, Ep. for ἀν-έθετο, 3 sing. aor. 2 med. of ἀνατίθημι.

ἀνθέω, f. ήσω, (ἄνθος) to blossom, bloom, of the youthful beard, Od.; of flowers and plants, Hes., etc.   II. metaph.,   1. to be bright with colour, ἀνθεῖν φοινίκισι Xen.   2. to be in bloom, Pind.; ἐν ὥρᾳ, ἐφ' ὥρᾳ ἀνθεῖν to be in the bloom of youth, Plat.   3. to flourish in wealth and prosperity, Hes., Hdt., Att.; c. dat., ἀνθ. ἀνδράσι to abound in men, Hdt.   4. to be at the height or pitch, Aesch., Soph.

ἄνθη, ἡ, (ἄνθος) full bloom, Plat.

ἀνθηρός, ά, όν, (ἀνθέω) flowering, blooming, Ar.   II. metaph. blooming, fresh, Eur., Xen.   2. ἀνθηρὸν μένος rage bursting into flower, i. e. at its height, Soph.   3. bright-coloured, bright, Eur.; τὸ ἀνθ. brightness, Luc.

ἀνθ-ησσάομαι, Pass. to give way in turn, τινι Thuc.

ἀνθίζω, f. ίσω, (ἄνθος) to strew or deck with flowers, Eur.   2. to dye with bright colour: Pass., Hdt.; metaph., ἠνθισμένος dyed, disguised, Soph.

ἀνθινός, ή, όν, (ἄνθος) like flowers, blooming, fresh, ἄνθινον εἶδαρ, of the lotus, Od.   II. bright-coloured, Lat. floridus, of women's dress, Plut.

ἀνθ-ιππασία, ἡ, a sham-fight of horse, Xen.

ἀνθ-ιππεύω, f. σω, to ride against, ἀλλήλοις Xen.

ἀνθ-ίστημι, f. ἀντι-στήσω, to set against, Ar., Thuc.: to set up in opposition, Thuc.   2. to match with, compare, Plut.   II. Pass., with intr. aor 2 act. ἀντ-έστην, pf. ἀνθέστηκα, Att. contr. part. ἀνθεστώς: fut. med. ἀντιστήσομαι, aor. 1 ἀντεστησάμην and pass. ἀντ-εστάθην [ᾰ]:—to stand against, esp. in battle, to with-

stand, oppose, τινι Il., Hdt., Att.; also, πρός τινα Thuc., etc.: rarely c. gen., φρενῶν ἀνθίσταται (al. ἀνθάπτεται) Aesch.   2. absol. to make a stand, Il., Hdt.

ἀνθοβολέω, f. ήσω, to bestrew with flowers, Anth.:— Pass. to have flowers showered upon one, Plut. From

ἀνθό-βολος, ον, (βάλλω) garlanded with flowers, Anth.

ἀνθο-δίαιτος, ον, (δίαιτα) living on flowers, Anth.

ἀνθο-δόκος, ον, (δέχομαι) holding flowers, Mosch.

ἀνθοκομέω, f. ήσω, to produce flowers, Anth. From

ἀνθο-κόμος, ον,(κόμη) decked with flowers, flowery, Anth.

ἀνθο-κρατέω, f. ήσω, to govern flowers, Luc.

ἀνθό-κροκος, ον, (κρέκω) worked with flowers or bright-coloured, Eur.

ἀνθολκή, ή, (ἀνθέλκω) a pulling in the contrary direction, resistance, Plut.

ἀνθολογία, ή, a flower-gathering, Luc.: Ἀνθολογίαι were collections of small Greek poems and epigrams by several authors, which the editor made up into a posy or nosegay.

ἀνθο-λόγος, ον, (λέγω) flower-gathering, Anth.; c. gen. culling the flower of . . , Id.

ἀνθ-ομολογέομαι, f. ήσομαι, Med. to make a mutual agreement, πρός τινα Dem.   II. to confess freely and openly, Plut.   III. to return thanks, N. T.

ἀνθ-οπλίζω, f. ίσω, to arm against: Pass. to be arrayed against, τινί Dem.:—Med. to arm oneself, Xen.

ἀν-θορεῖν for ἀνα-θορεῖν, aor. 2 inf. of ἀναθρώσκω.

ἀνθ-ορμέω, f. ήσω, to lie at anchor opposite to, τινί Thuc.; πρός τινα Id.

ΑΝΘΟΣ, εος, τό: gen. pl. ἀνθέων even in Att.:—a blossom, flower, Hom., etc.   2. generally, anything thrown out upon the surface, froth, scum.   II. metaph. the bloom or flower of life, ἥβης ἄνθος Il.; ὥρας ἄνθος Xen.; χροιᾶς ἄνθος the bloom of complexion, Aesch.:—also, the flower of an army and the like, Aesch., Thuc.; τὸ σὸν ἄνθος thy pride or honour, Aesch.   2. the height or highest pitch of anything, bad as well as good, ἔρωτος Id.; μανίας Soph.   III. brightness, brilliancy, Theogn.; in pl. bright colours, Plat.; ἁλὸς ἄνθεα, i. e. purple, Anth.

ἀνθ-οσμίας, ου, ὁ, (ἄνθος, ὀσμή) redolent of flowers, of wine, οἶνος ἀνθ. with a fine 'bouquet,' Ar.; so ἀνθοσμίας alone, Xen., Luc.

ἀνθοσύνη, ή, (ἄνθος) bloom, luxuriant growth, Anth.

ἀνθοφορέω, f. ήσω, to bear flowers, Anth. From

ἀνθο-φόρος, ον, (φέρω) bearing flowers, flowery, Ar., Anth.

ἀνθο-φυής, ές, (φυή) party-coloured, Anth.

ἀνθρᾱκιά, ᾶς, gen. -ιή, ῆς, ή, (ἄνθραξ) a heap of charcoal, hot embers, Il.; ἀνθρακιᾶς ἄπο hot from the embers, Eur.   2. black sooty ashes, Anth.

ἀνθρᾱκίας, ου, ὁ, (ἄνθραξ) a man black as a collier, Luc.

ἀνθρᾱκίζω, f. ίσω, (ἄνθραξ) to make charcoal of, to roast or toast, Ar.

ἀνθρᾱκόομαι, pf. ἠνθράκωμαι, Pass. (ἄνθραξ) to be burnt to cinders, Aesch.

ΑΝΘΡΑΞ, ἄκος, ὁ, charcoal, coal, Ar., Thuc.

ἀνθρήνη, ή, a hornet, wasp, Ar. (Deriv. unknown.)

ἀνθρήνιον, τό, (ἀνθρήνη) a wasp's nest, Ar.

ἀνθρωπ-άρεσκος, ου, ὁ, a man-pleaser, N. T.

ἀνθρωπάριον, τό, Dim. of ἄνθρωπος, a manikin, Ar.

ἀνθρωπέη, contr. -πῆ (sub. δορά), ή, a man's skin, Hdt.

ἀνθρώπειος, α, ον, Ion. -ήϊος, η, ον, of or belonging to man, human, Hdt., etc.; ἀνθρώπεια πήματα such as man is subject to, Aesch.; ἀνθρωπήϊα πρήγματα human affairs, man's estate, Hdt.; τὸ ἀνθρώπειον either mankind or human nature, Thuc.   2. human, of which man is capable, Hdt., Plat.   3. human, as opp. to mythical, Hdt.   II. Adv. -ως, humanly, in all human probability, Thuc.; ἀνθρ. φράζειν to speak as befits a man, Ar.

ἀνθρωπεύομαι, Dep. to be or act as a human being, Arist.

ἀνθρωπίζω, f. ίσω, to be or act like a man, Luc.

ἀνθρωπικός, ή, όν, (ἄνθρωπος) of or for a man, human, Plat. Adv. -κῶς, Luc.

ἀνθρώπινος, η, ον, and ος, ον, (ἄνθρωπος) of, from or belonging to man, human, Hdt., etc.; ἅπαν τὸ ἀνθρώπινον all mankind, Id.; τὸ ἀνθρ. γένος Plat.; τὰ ἀνθρ. πράγματα or τἀνθρώπινα human affairs, man's estate, Id.   2. human, suited to man, Arist.   II. Adv., ἀνθρωπίνως ἁμαρτάνειν to commit human, i. e. venial, errors, Thuc.   2. humanely, gently, Dem.

ἀνθρώπιον, τό, Dim. of ἄνθρωπος, a manikin, Lat. homuncio, Eur., Xen.: a paltry fellow, Xen.

ἀνθρωπίσκος, ὁ, = ἀνθρώπιον, Eur., Plat.

ἀνθρωπο-δαίμων, ονος, ὁ, ή, a man-god, i. e. a deified man, Eur.

ἀνθρωπο-ειδής, ές, (εἶδος) like a man, in human form, Hdt.

ἀνθρωπο-θῠσία, ή, a human sacrifice, Strab.

ἀνθρωπο-κτόνος, ον, (κτείνω) murdering men, a homicide, Eur.   II. proparox. furnished by slaughtered men, Id.

ἀνθρωπο-λόγος, ον, (λέγω) speaking of man, Arist.

ἀνθρωποποιΐα, ή, a making of man or men, Luc. From

ἀνθρωπο-ποιός, όν, (ποιέω) making men, Luc.

ἄνθρ-ωπος, ὁ, (prob. from ἀνήρ, ὤψ, man-faced):—man, Lat. homo (not vir), opp. to gods, ἀθανάτων τε θεῶν, χαμαὶ ἐρχομένων τ' ἀνθρώπων Il.   2. with or without the Art. to denote man generally, Plat., etc.   3. in pl. mankind, ἀνθρώπων, ἀνδρῶν ἠδὲ γυναικῶν Il.; ὁ ἄριστος ἐν ἀνθρώποις ὄρτυξ the best quail in the world, Plat.; μάλιστα, ἥκιστα ἀνθρώπων most, least of all, Hdt., etc.   4. with another Subst., to give it a contemptuous sense, ἄνθρ. ὑπογραμματεύς, συκοφάντης, Oratt.; so homo histrio Cic.:—so, ἄνθρωπος or ὁ ἄνθρωπος was used alone, the man, the fellow, Plat.:—also in vocat. it was addressed contemptuously to slaves, ἄνθρωπε or ὦ ΄νθρωπε, sirrah! you sir! Hdt., Plat.   II. fem. (as homo also is fem.), a woman, Hdt., etc.; with a sense of pity, Dem.

ἄνθρωπος, crasis for ὁ ἄνθρωπος.

ἀνθρωπο-σφᾰγέω, (σφάττω) to slay men, Eur.

ἀνθρωποφᾰγέω, f. ήσω, to eat men or man's flesh, Hdt.

ἀνθρωποφᾰγία, ή, an eating of men, Arist. From

ἀνθρωπο-φάγος, ον, (φαγεῖν) man-eating, Arist.

ἀνθρωπο-φῠής, ές, (φυή) of man's nature, Hdt.

ἀν-θρώσκω, poët. for ἀνα-θρώσκω.

ἀνθ-υβρίζω, f. ίσω, to abuse one another, abuse in turn, Eur., Plut.

ἀνθ-υπάγω [ἄ], f. ξω, to bring to trial in turn, Thuc.

ἀνθυπᾰτεύω, to be proconsul, Plut.; and

ἀνθυπᾰτικός, ή, όν, proconsular. From

ἀνθ-ύπᾰτος, ον, a proconsul, Lat. pro consule, Polyb., etc.

ἀνθ-υπείκω, f. ξω, *to yield in turn*, τινί Plut. From
ἀνθύπειξις, εως, ἡ, *a mutual yielding*, Plut.
ἀνθ-υπηρετέω, f. ήσω, *to serve in turn*, τινί Arist.
ἀνθ-υποκρίνομαι [ῑ], Ion. ἀντυπ-, Med. *to answer in
return*, Hdt. II. *to put on in turn*, ὀργήν Luc.
ἀνθ-υπόμνῡμαι, Med. *to make a counter-affidavit*, Dem.
ἀνθ-υποπτεύω, f. σω, *to suspect mutually* :—Pass., ἀνθ-
υποπτεύεται *he is met by the suspicion that* . . , Thuc.
ἀνθ-υπουργέω, f. ήσω, *to return a kindness*, τινί τι
Hdt., Eur.
ἀνθ-υφίσταμαι, Pass., with aor. 2 act. ἀνθυπέστην :—
ἀνθυποστῆναι (sc. χορηγὸς γενέσθαι) *to undertake to
serve* as choragus *instead of another*, Dem.
ἀνία, Ion. ἀνίη, Aeol. ὀνία, ἡ, *grief, sorrow, distress,
trouble*, Od., Hes., etc. 2. actively, δαιτὸς ἀνίη *the
bane of our feast*, Od. [In Hom. and Soph. ῑ: in
other Poets ῐ.] (Deriv. uncertain.)
ἀνία, Dor. for ἡνία, *a rein*.
ἀνιάζω [ῑ]: aor. 1 ἠνίᾰσα, *to grieve, distress*, c. acc.
pers., Hom. II. intr. *to be grieved* or *distressed,
feel grief*, Id.; c. dat. *at* or *for a thing*, Il.
ἀν-ιάομαι, Dep. *to cure again, repair*, Hdt.
ἀνιᾱρός, ά, όν, Ion. ἀνιηρός, ή, όν, (ἀνιάω) *grievous,
troublesome, annoying*, of persons, Od.; ἐχθροῖς ἀνιαροί
Ar., of animals, Hdt. :—Adv. ἀνιαρῶς Soph. 2. of
things, *painful, grievous, distressing*, Theogn., etc.;
irreg. Comp. ἀνιηρέστερος Od. II. pass. *grieved,
distressed*, Xen. :—Adv. -ρῶς *wretchedly*, Id. [In
Hom. and Soph. always ἀνῑ-, in other Poets ἀνῐ-.]
ἀν-ίᾱτος, Ion. -ίητος, ον, (ἀν- priv., ἰατός) *incurable*,
Plat., etc. 2. of persons, *incorrigible*, Id.; ἀνιάτως
ἔχειν *to be incurable*, Id.
ἀν-ιάχω [ᾰ], *to cry aloud* : c. acc. *to praise loudly*, Anth.
ἀνιάω: 3 sing. impf. ἠνία Il.; ἀνιάσω [ᾱ], Ep. ἀνιήσω:
aor. 1 ἠνίᾱσα, Dor. ἀνίᾱσα :—Pass., ἀνιῶμαι, Ion. 3 pl.
opt. ἀνιῴατο: 3 pl. impf. ἠνιῶντο: f. in med. form
ἀνιάσομαι: 2 sing. ἀνιήσεαι: aor. 1 ἠνιάθην, Ion.
-ήθην: pf. ἠνίημαι: (ἀνία): [ῑ in Hom. and Soph.;
ῐ in other Poets]. Like ἀνιάζω, *to grieve, distress*, c.
acc., Od., etc.; c. dupl. acc., ὁ δρῶν σ᾽ ἀνιᾷ τὰς φρένας
Soph. :—Pass. *to be grieved, distressed*, Od., etc.; with
neut. Adj., τοῦτ᾽ ἀνιῶμαι *I am vexed at* this, Soph.;
aor. 1 part. as Adj., *a sorrowful* man, Hom.
ἀν-ῑδεῖν, aor. 2 inf. of ἀνοράω, *to look up*, Aesch.
ἀν-ίδρῡτος, ον, = ἄϊδρυτος.
ἀν-ῑδρωτί, Adv. (ἱδρόω) *without sweat* : metaph. *without
toil*, Il. : *lazily, slowly*, Xen.
ἀν-ίδρωτος, ον, (ἱδρόω) *without having sweated* or *exercised oneself*, Xen.
ἀν-ιεῖς, -ιεῖ, 2 and 3 sing. of ἀνίημι: ἀν-ίεις, ἀν-ίει,
2 and 3 sing. impf. (as if from ἀνιέω).
ἀν-ίερος, ον, *unholy, unhallowed*, Aesch.; ἀνίερος ἀθύ-
των πελάνων *unhallowed because of* unoffered sacrifices,
Eur. II. *unconsecrated*, Plat.
ἀν-ιερόω, f. ώσω, *to dedicate, devote*, τί τινι Plut.
ἀν-ιεῦνται, Ion. 3 pl. of ἀν-ιάομαι.
ἀν-ίημι, η (also ἀνιεῖς, -εῖ as if from ἀνιέω), ησι:
impf. ἀνίην, 2 and 3 sing. εις, ει, Ion. 3 sing. ἀνίεσκε,
also ἠνίει: f. ἀνήσω: pf. ἀνεῖκα: aor. 1 ἀνῆκα, Ion.
ἀνέηκα :—Hom. also has a 3 sing. fut. ἀνέσει, 3 pl. aor.
ἄνεσαν, opt. ἀνέσαιμι, part. ἀνέσαντες (as if from
ἀν-έζω) :—3 pl. aor. 2 ἀνεῖσαν, imper. ἄνες, Ep. 3 sing.

subj. ἀνήῃ; inf. ἀνεῖναι; part. ἀνείς :—Pass., ἀνί-
εμαι: pf. ἀνεῖμαι, Ion. 3 pl. pf. ἀνέωνται (as if from
ἀν-εόω): aor. 1 part. ἀνεθείς; f. ἀνεθήσομαι. [ἀνῑ-
Ep., ἀνῑ- Att.; but Hom. has ἀνίει, ἀνιέμενος.] *To
send up* or *forth*, Hom., etc.; *of the earth, to make
spring up*, h. Hom.; *of females, to produce*, Soph. :—
Pass. *to be sent up, produced*, Aesch., etc.; *to send up
from the grave* or *nether world*, Id., etc. II.
to send back, put back, open, Hom., Eur. III. *to
let go, leave*, Hom., etc.; c. gen. rei, δεσμῶν ἀνίει
loosed them *from* bonds, Od. : *to let go unpunished*,
Xen. 2. ἀν. τινί *to let loose at* one, ἀν. κύνας, Lat.
canes immittere, Xen.; hence, ἄφρονα τοῦτον ἀνέντες
Il. : c. inf. *to set on* or *urge to do a thing*, Hom. 3.
ἀν. τινὰ πρός τι *to let go for* any purpose, Hdt.; ἀν.
τινὰ μανίας *to set free from* madness, Eur. 4. *to
let, allow* one *to do a thing*, c. acc. et inf., Hdt., etc. :
—so, ἀν. κόμην *to let* it hang, *loosen*, Eur. 5. Med.,
c. acc., κόλπον ἀνιεμένη *baring* her breast, Il.; αἶγας
ἀνιέμενοι *flaying* goats, Od. 6. *to let go free, leave
untilled*, of ground dedicated to a god, Thuc. :—Pass.
to devote oneself, give oneself up, Hdt.; of animals
dedicated to a god, *which are let range at large*, Id.;
esp. in pf. pass. part. ἀνειμένος, Soph., etc. 7. *to
slacken, relax, let down, unstring*, Hdt., Plat. :—then,
to remit, neglect, give up, Soph., Thuc., etc. :—Pass.
to be treated remissly, Thuc. 8. so intr. in Act. *to
slacken, abate*, of the wind, Soph., etc.; οὐδὲν ἀνιέναι
not to give way at all, Xen. :—c. part. *to give up* or
cease doing, ὕων οὐκ ἀνίει [ὁ θεός] Hdt. :—c. gen. *to
cease from a thing*, Eur., Thuc.
ἀνιηρός, ή, όν, Ion. for ἀνιαρός.
ἀνίκα [ῐ], Dor. for ἡνίκα.
ἀν-ίκᾰνος [ῐ], ον, *insufficient, incapable*, Babr.
ἀν-ἱκέτευτος, ον, (ἱκετεύω) *without prayer, not entreating*, Eur.
ἀ-νίκητος [ῑ], Dor. -ᾱτος, ον, (νικάω) *unconquered, unconquerable*, Hes., etc.
ἀν-ίλεως [ῐ], ων, *unmerciful*, N. T.
ἀν-ιμάω, f. ήσω, (ἀνά, ἱμάς) only in pres. and impf., *to
draw up* water, by means of leather straps: generally,
to draw out or *up*, Xen. : also Med. ἀνιμῶμαι, Luc.,
etc. II. intr. (sub. ἑαυτόν), *to mount up*, Xen.
ἄνῑος, ον, (ἀνία) = ἀνιαρός, Aesch.
ἀνίοχος, Dor. for ἡνίοχος.
ἄν-ιππος, ον, *without horse, not serving on horseback*,
Hdt., Soph. : *without a horse to ride on*, Ar. 2. of
countries, *unsuited for horses*, Hdt.
ἀνίπταμαι, Dep. = ἀναπέτομαι.
ἀνιπτό-πους, ὁ, ἡ, gen. πόδος, *with unwashen feet*, Il.
ἄ-νιπτος, ον, (νίζω) *unwashen*, Il. 2. *not to be washed
out*, Aesch.
ἄνις, Megarean for ἄνευ, Ar.
ἄν-ῑσος, ον, (ἴσος) *unequal, uneven*, Plat., etc. :—Adv.,
ἀνίσως, *unfairly*, Dem. Hence
ἀνῑσότης, ητος, ἡ, (ἄνισος) *inequality*, Plat., etc.
ἀνῑσόω, f. ώσω, (ἀνά, ἰσόω) *to make equal, equalise*,
Xen. :—Pass. *to be made equal*, Hdt.
ἀν-ίστημι, A. Causal in pres., impf. ἀνίστην, f. ἀνα-
στήσω, poët. ἀνστήσω, aor. 1 ἀνέστησα, Ep. ἄνστησα; also
in aor. 1 med. ἀνεστησάμην: I. *to make to stand
up, raise up*, χειρός by his hand, Il. :—*to raise from*

sleep, wake up, Il. : metaph., ἀν. *νόσον* Soph. :—*to raise from the dead,* Il., Aesch.; from misery, Soph. 2. of things, *to set up, build,* Hdt., etc.; so, ἀν. *τινὰ χαλκοῦν to set up* a bronze statue of him, Plut.; —aor. 1 med., ἀναστήσασθαι *πόλιν to build oneself* a city, Hdt. 3. *to build up again, restore,* Eur., Dem. 4. *to put up for sale,* Hdt. II. *to rouse to action, stir up,* Il. :—*to rouse to arms, raise* troops, Thuc.; ἀν. *πόλεμον ἐπί τινα* Plut. III. *to make people rise, break up* an assembly, Il., Xen. 2. *to make people rise* from their home, *make them emigrate, transplant,* Od., Hdt., etc. 3. *to make suppliants rise and leave sanctuary,* Hdt., Thuc. 4. of sportsmen, *to put up* game, *spring* it, Xen.
B. Intr. in pres. and impf. ἀνίσταμαι, -μην, in f. ἀναστήσομαι, in aor. 2 ἀνέστην, pf. ἀνέστηκα, Att. plqpf. ἀνεστήκη; also in aor. 1 pass. ἀνεστάθην [ἄ] :—*to stand up, rise,* to speak, Hom., etc.:—*to rise from one's seat* as a mark of respect, Lat. *assurgere,* Il. :—*to rise from bed,* Ib., :—*to rise from the dead,* Ib. :—*to rise from* an illness, *recover,* Hdt. 2. *to rise as a* champion, Il., Soph.: c. dat. *to stand up* to fight against, τινι Il.; *πᾶσιν δὲ ἀνέστη θεοῖς* Aesch. 3. of buildings and statues, *to be set up, to rise up, rear itself,* Eur., Plut., etc. 4. of a river, *to rise,* Plut. II. *to rise to go, set out, go away,* Eur., Thuc., etc. 2. *to be compelled to migrate,* Thuc.; of a country, *to be depopulated,* Hdt., Eur.; *οὐκέτι ἀνισταμένη no longer subject to migration,* Thuc. 3. of a law-court, *to rise,* Dem. 4. of game, *to be put up,* Xen.

ἀν-ιστορέω, f. ήσω, *to make inquiry into, ask about,* Soph.: c. acc. pers. et rei, *to ask a person about a thing,* Aesch., Soph.; so, ἀν. *τινὰ περί τινος* Eur.

ἀν-ιστόρητος, ον, (ἀν- priv., ἱστορέω) *ignorant of history* :—Adv., ἀνιστορήτως ἔχειν τινός *to be uninformed about a thing,* Plut.

ἀν-ίστω, contr. from ἀν-ίστασο, imper. pass. of ἀνίστημι.

ἀν-ίσχω, v. ἀν-έχω.

ἀνίσωσις [ῐ], εως, ἡ, (ἀνισόω) *equalisation,* Thuc.

ἀν-ιχνεύω, f. σω, (ἀνά, ἰχνεύω) *to trace back,* as a hound, Il.: generally, *to trace out,* Plut.

ἀν-ιψάτο, Ion. 3 pl. opt. of ἀνιδομαι.

ἀν-νεῖμαι, poët. for ἀνα-νεῖμαι, aor. 1 inf. of ἀνανέμω.

ἀν-νεῖται, Ep. for ἀνα-νεῖται, 3 sing. of ἀνανέομαι.

Ἀννιβίζω, f. σω, (Ἀννίβας) *to side with Hannibal,* Plut.

ἀν-οδηγέω, f. σω, *to guide back,* Babr.

ἀν-οδος, ον, (ἀν- priv., ὁδός) *having no road, impassable,* Eur., Xen.

ἄν-οδος, ἡ, (ἀνά, ὁδός) *a way up,* as to the Acropolis, Hdt.:—*a journey inland,* esp. into Central Asia, Id., Xen.

ἀν-οδύρομαι [ῠ], f. -ῠροῦμαι, Dep. *to set up a wailing,* Xen.

ἀ-νοήμων, ον, (νοέω) *without understanding,* Od.

ἀ-νόητος, ον, *not thought on, unheard of,* h. Hom. 2. *not within the province of thought, unintelligent,* Plat. II. act. *not understanding, unintelligent,* Lat. *ineptus,* Hdt., Att.; ὦνόητε *oh you fool,* Ar.; ἀνόητα *follies,* Id. :—Adv. -τως, *foolishly,* Plat.

ἄνοιᾰ, old Att. ἄνοιᾱ, Ep. ἄνοίη, ἡ, (ἄνοος) *want of understanding, folly,* Hdt., etc.; ὑπ' ἀνοίας Aesch.; *πολλὴ ἄνοιά [ἐστι] πολεμῆσαι* Thuc.

ἀν-οίγνῡμι and ἀν-οίγω, Ep. ἀνα-οίγω Il. :—impf. ἀν-έῳγον, Ep. also ἀν-ῷγον, rarely ἤνοιγον, Ion. and Ep. ἀνα-οίγεσκον : f. ἀν-οίξω : aor. 1 ἀν-έῳξα or ἤνοιξα, Ion. ἄνοιξα, poët. ἀνῷξα : pf. ἀν-έῳχα or -έῳγα :—Pass. ἀνοίγνυμαι, f. ἀν-εῴξομαι : pf. ἀν-έῳγμαι, -ῷγμαι : 3 sing. plqpf. ἀν-εῴκτο: aor. 1 ἀν-εῴχθην, subj. ἀν-οιχθῶ, opt. ἀν-οιχθείην, ἀν-οιχθείς : aor. 2 ἠνοίγην :—in late Gr., irreg. forms occur, ἠνέῳξα, ἠνέῳγμαι, ἠνεῴχθην :—*to open* doors, etc., ἀναοίγεσκον *κληῖδα they tried to put back the bolt so as to open the door,* Il. ; *πύλας, θύραν* ἀν., Aesch., Ar. 2. *to undo, open,* πῶμ' ἀνέῳγε *took off the cover and opened it,* Il.; metaph., ἀνοίξαντι *κλῇδα φρενῶν* Eur. ; ἀν. *οἶνον to tap* it, Theocr. 3. *to lay open, unfold, disclose,* Soph. 4. as nautical term, absol. *to get into the open sea, get clear of land,* Xen. II. Pass. *to be open, stand open,* of doors, Hdt., Plat. ; *κόλποι δ' ἀλλήλων ἀνοιγόμενοι opening* one into another, Plut.

ἀν-οιδέω, f. ήσω : aor. 1 ἀνῴδησα :—*to swell up,* of a wave, Eur. 2. metaph. of passion, Hdt.

ἀν-οικίζω, f. Att. ἰῶ, *to remove up the country* :—Pass. and Med. *to shift one's dwelling* up the country, *to migrate inland,* Ar. ; and of cities, *to be built up the country, away from the coast,* Thuc. :—generally, *to migrate,* δεῦρ' ἀνοικισθείς Ar., Thuc. II. *to re-settle* :—Pass. *to be re-peopled,* Plut.

ἀν-οικοδομέω, f. ήσω, *to build up,* Hdt. 2. *to wall up,* Ar. II. *to build again, rebuild,* Thuc., Xen.

ἄν-οικος, ον, = ἄ-οικος, *houseless, homeless,* Hdt.

ἀνοικτέον, verb. Adj. of ἀνοίγω, *one must open,* Eur.

ἀν-οικτίρμων, ον, *pitiless, merciless,* Soph., Anth.

ἀν-οίκτιστος, ον, *unpitied, unmourned,* Anth.

ἀνοικτός, ή, όν, (ἀνοίγνυμι) *opened,* Babr., Luc.

ἄν-οικτος, ον, *pitiless, ruthless,* Eur. :—Adv. -τως, *without pity, without being pitied,* Soph., Eur.

ἀν-οιμώζω, fut. ξομαι, *to wail aloud,* Aesch., Thuc.

ἀν-οίμωκτος, ον, (ἀν- priv., οἰμώζω) *unlamented,* Aesch. :—Adv. ἀνοιμωκτί [ῑ], *without need to wail, with impunity,* Soph.

ἄνοιξις, εως, ἡ, (ἀνοίγνυμι) *an opening,* πυλῶν Thuc.

ἀνοιστέον, verb. Adj. of ἀναφέρω, *one must report,* Soph., Eur. :—*one must refer,* τι πρός τι Thuc.

ἄνοιστος, Ion. ἀνώϊστος, ον, (ἀναφέρω, f. ἀνοίσω) *referred,* ἔς τινα *to some one for decision,* Hdt.

ἀν-οιστρέω, f. ήσω, *to goad to madness,* Eur.

ἀνοίσω, f. of ἀναφέρω.

ἄνοιτο, 3 sing. opt. pass. of ἄνω.

ἀνοκωχεύω, f. σω, *to hold back,* ἀν. τὰς νέας *to keep them at anchor,* Hdt. : of a chariot, *to hold it in, keep it back,* Soph. 2. ἀν. τὸν τόνον τῶν ὅπλων *to keep up* the tension of the ropes, *keep them taut,* Ar. II. intr. *to keep back, keep still,* Id. From

ἀν-οκωχή, ἡ, formed by redupl. from ἀν-οχή (cf. ὄκωχα pf. of ἔχω), *a stay, cessation, κακῶν* Thuc. absol. *a cessation of arms, truce,* δι' ἀνοκωχῆς γίγνεσθαί τινι *to be at truce* with one, Id. 2. *a hindrance,* Id. (The forms ἀνακωχή, ἀνακωχεύω are late and corrupt.)

ἀνολβία, ἡ, (ἄνολβος) *misery,* Hes. [ῑ].

ἄνολβος, ον, =sq., Hdt.

ἄν-ολβος, ον, *unblest, wretched, luckless,* Theogn., Trag.

ἀν-όλεθρος, Ep. for ἀνώλεθρος.

ἀνολκή, ἡ, (ἀνέλκω) *a hauling up,* λίθων Thuc.

ἀν-ολολύζω, f. ὔξω, to cry aloud, shout (with joy), Trag.   2. c. acc. to bewail loudly, Soph.   II. in a causal sense, to excite by Bacchic cries, Eur.

ἀν-ολοφύρομαι [ῠ], Dep. to break into loud wailing, Thuc., Xen.

ἄνομαι, v. ἄνω.

ἀν-ομαλίζω, f. σω, to restore to equality, equalise, 1 pf. pass. inf. ἀνωμαλίσθαι Arist.

ἀν-ομαλόω, f. ώσω, = foreg.

ἄν-ομβρος, ον, without rain, of countries, Hdt.; ἄν. ῥοαί streams not fed by showers, Eur.

ἀνομέω, f. ήσω, (ἄνομος) to act lawlessly, περί τι Hdt.

ἀνομία, Ion. -ίη, ἡ, (ἄνομος) lawlessness, Hdt., Eur., etc.

ἀν-ομίλητος [ῑ], ον, having no communion with others, unsociable, Plat.   2. c. gen., ἀνομ. παιδείας unacquainted with education, Luc.

ἀν-όμματος, ον, (ὄμμα) eyeless, sightless, Soph.

ἀν-ομοιο-ειδής, ές, (εἶδος) of unlike kind, heterogeneous, Arist.

ἀν-όμοιος, ον and α, ον, unlike, dissimilar, Pind., Plat.; ἀν. τινι unlike it, Plat. :—Adv. -ως, Thuc.; ἀν. ἔχειν to be unlike, Xen.   Hence

ἀνομοιότης, ητος, ἡ, (ἀνόμοιος) dissimilarity, Plat.; and

ἀνομοιόω, f. ώσω, to make unlike or dissimilar, Plat. : —Pass. to be or become so, Id.

ἀν-ομολογέομαι, f. ήσομαι : pf. ἀνωμολόγημαι : Dep. : — to agree upon a thing, come to an understanding, περί τινος Plat.; πρός τινα with one, Id.   2. to sum up one's conclusions, τὰ εἰρημένα Id.   II. pf. in pass. sense, ἀνωμολόγημαι πράττειν I am allowed to be doing, Dem.   Hence

ἀνομολογητέον, verb. Adj. one must admit, Plat.

ἀνομολογία, ἡ, disagreement, Plut.   From

ἀν-ομόλογος, ον, not agreeing.

ἀν-ομολογούμενος, η, ον, not agreeing, inconsistent, Plat.

ἄ-νομος, ον, without law, lawless, Hdt., Trag., etc. :— Adv. -μως, Eur., etc.; Comp. -ώτερον, Plat.   II. (νόμος II) musical, Aesch.

ἀν-όνητος, Dor. -ᾱτος, ον, (ὀνίνημι) unprofitable, useless, Soph., Eur., etc.; neut. pl. ἀνόνητα as Adv. in vain, Eur.   II. c. gen. making no profit from a thing, Dem.

ἄ-νοος, ον, contr. ἄ-νους, ουν, without understanding, foolish, silly, Il., Soph., etc. :—Comp. ἀνούστερος, Aesch.

ἀνοπαῖα, Adv., either (from ἀν- priv., *ὄπτομαι) she flew away unseen; or = ἄνω, up into the air; or ἀν' ὀπαῖα (= ἀνὰ ὀπήν) up by the smoke-vent, Od. :—others write ἀνόπαια, ἡ, a kind of eagle.

ἄν-οπλος, ον, without the ὅπλον or large shield, Hdt., Plat.

ἀν-όργανος, ον, (ὄργανον) without instruments, Plut.

ἀνορέα, ἡ, Dor. for ἠνορέη.

ἀνορθόω, f. ώσω : aor. 1 ἀνώρθωσα :—to set up again, restore, rebuild, Hdt., Thuc.   2. to restore to health or well-being, πόλιν Soph.   3. to set straight again, set right, correct, τινα Eur.

ἄν-ορμος, ον, without harbour : metaph., ὑμέναιον ἄν. εἰσπλεῖν to sail into a marriage that was no haven for thee, Soph.

ἀν-όρνυμι, f. -όρσω, to rouse, stir up, Pind. :—Pass., Ep. aor. 2 ἀνῶρτο, to start up, Hom.

ἀνορούω, Ep. aor. 1 ἀνόρουσα, to start up, leap up, Hom.; of the sun, ἀνόρουσεν οὐρανὸν ἐς went swiftly up the sky, Od.; ἀνορούσαις (Dor. part. aor. 1) Pind.

ἀν-όροφος, ον, roofless, Eur.

ἀν-ορτᾱλίζω, f. ίσω, (ὀρταλίς) to clap the wings and crow, like a cockrel, Ar.

ἀν-ορύσσω, Att. -ττω : f. ξω : pf. pass. ἀνορώρυγμαι : —to dig up what has been buried, Hdt., Ar.   2. ἀν. τάφον to dig it up, break open, Hdt.

ἀν-ορχέομαι, f. -ήσομαι, Dep. to leap up and dance, Eur.

ἀν-όσιος, ον and α, ον, unholy, profane, Lat. profanus, of persons and things, Hdt., Att.; ἀνόσιος νέκυς a corpse with all the rites unpaid, Soph.:—Adv. -ίως, in unholy wise, Id.: without funeral rites, Eur.   Hence

ἀνοσιότης, ητος, ἡ, (ἀνόσιος) profaneness, Plat.

ἄ-νοσος, Ion. and Ep. ἄ-νουσος, ον, without sickness, healthy, sound, Od., Hdt., Att.   2. c. gen., ἄνοσος κακῶν untouched by ill, Eur.   3. of a season, free from sickness, Thuc.   II. of things, not causing disease, harmless, Eur.

ἀν-όστεος, ον, (ὀστέον) boneless, of the polypus, Hes.

ἀ-νόστητος, ον, (νοστέω) whence none return, Anth.

ἀ-νόστιμος, ον, not returning, κεῖνον ἀν. ἔθηκεν cut off his return, Od.   2. not to be retraced, Eur.

ἄ-νοστος, ον, unreturning, without return, Od.; Sup., ἥβη ἀνοστοτάτη never, never to return, Anth.

ἀν-οτοτύζω, f. ξω, to break out into wailing, Aesch., Eur.

ἀν-ούᾱτος, ον, (οὖς) without ear: without handle, Theocr.

ἄνους, ουν, contr. for ἄνοος.

ἄ-νουσος, ον, Ion. for ἄ-νοσος.

ἀν-ούτᾱτος, ον, (οὐτάω) unwounded by sword, Il.

ἀν-ουτητί [ῑ], Adv. (οὐτάω) without wound, Il.

ἀνοχή, ἡ, (ἀνέχω) a holding back, stopping, esp. of hostilities: pl., like Lat. induciae, an armistice, truce, Xen.   II. (ἀνέχομαι) forbearance, N. T.

ἀν-οχμάζω, f. άσω, to hoist, lift up, Anth.

ἄν-στα, Ep. for ἀνά-στα, -στηθι, aor. 2 imp. of ἀνίστημι :—ἀνα-στάς, part.

ἀν-στήμεναι, Ep. for ἀνα-στῆναι, aor. 2 inf. of ἀνίστημι.

ἀν-στήτην, Ep. for -εστήτην, 3 dual aor. 2 of ἀνίστημι.

ἀν-στρέψειαν, poët. for ἀνα-στρέψειαν.

ἀν-σχεθέειν, Ep. for ἀνα-σχεθεῖν, aor. 2 of ἀνέχω : ἄν-σχεο, for ἀνα-σχοῦ, imperat.

ἀν-σχετός, v. ἀνα-σχετός.

ἀν-σχήσεσθαι, Ep. for ἀνα-σχήσεσθαι.

ἄντα, (ἀντί) Adv. over against, face to face, ἄντα μάχεσθαι to fight man to man; ἄντα ἰδεῖν to look before one; θεοῖς ἄντα ἐῴκει was like the gods to look at, Hom.; ἄντα τιτύσκεσθαι to aim straight at them, Od.   II. as Prep. with gen., over against, Hom.; ἄντα παρειάων before her cheeks; ἀντ' ὀφθαλμοῖιν Od.; ἄντα σέθεν before thee, Ib.   2. in hostile sense, against, Διὸς ἄντα Il.

ἀντ-ᾰγοράζω, f. σω, to buy with money received in payment for something else, Xen. :—Pass., aor. 1 part. ἀντ-αγορασθείς Dem.

ἀντ-ᾰγορεύω, f. σω, to speak against, reply, Pind. :—to gainsay, contradict, τινί Ar.

ἀντ-ᾰγωνίζομαι, f. Att. -ιοῦμαι :—as Dep. to struggle against, prove a match for, τινί Hdt., Thuc. :—generally, to struggle or dispute with, τινί Thuc. :—οἱ ἀνταγωνιζόμενοί τι the parties in a lawsuit, Xen.

ἀνταγωνιστέω, f. ήσω, to oppose, be a rival, Arist.   From

ἀντᾰγωνιστής, οῦ, ὁ, (ἀνταγωνίζομαι) an opponent, competitor, rival, Xen., etc.; ἀντ. ἔρωτος a rival in love, Eur.

ἀντ-αείρω, = ἀντ-αίρω : Med., ἀνταείρεσθαι χεῖράς τινι to raise one's hands against one, Hdt.

ἀντάεις, Dor. for ἀντήεις.

ἄντ-αθλος, ον, contending against, rivalling, τινος Anth.

ἀντ-αιδέομαι, Med. to respect in return, Xen.

ἀνταῖος, α, ον, (ἄντα) set over against, right opposite, ἀνταία πληγή a wound in front, Soph., Eur. 2. opposed to, hostile, hateful, Eur.; τινι to one, Aesch.; τἀνταῖα θεῶν their hostile purposes, Id.

ἀντ-αίρω, f. -ἀρῶ, aor. 1 -ῆρα :—to raise against, χεῖράς τινι Anth.; so in Med., Thuc. II. intr. to rise up against, τινί Plat., Dem.; πρός τι or τινα, Dem., etc. 2. of a cliff, to rise opposite to, πρὸς τὴν Λιβύην Plut.

ἀντ-αιτέω, f. ήσω, to demand in return, Thuc.

ἀντᾰκαῖος, ὁ, a sort of sturgeon, Hdt. (Deriv. unknown.)

ἀντ-ἀκούω, f. -ούσομαι, to hear in turn, τι ἀντί τινος Soph.: absol. to hear in return, Aesch., Xen.

ἀντ-ἀλαλάζω, f. ξω, to return a shout, Aesch.

ἀντάλλαγμα, ατος, τό, (ἀνταλλάσσω) that which is given or taken in exchange, φίλου for a friend, Eur.; τῆς ψυχῆς for one's soul, N. T.

ἀνταλλακτέον, verb. Adj. one must give in exchange, τινός for a thing, Dem. From

ἀντ-αλλάσσω, Att. -ττω, f. ξω, to exchange one thing with another, τί τινι Eur.; τὴν ἀξίωσιν τῶν ὀνομάτων ἀντ. to change the signification of the names, Thuc. II. Med. to take in exchange, τί τινος one thing for another, Eur., Dem.; τι ἀντί τινος Dem.; θάνατον ἀνταλλάξεται shall receive death in exchange, i. e. as a punishment, Eur.:—Pass., ἀντηλλαγμένος τοῦ ἑκατέρου τρόπου having made an interchange of each other's custom, i. e. having each adopted the other's way, Thuc.

ἀντ-ἀμείβομαι, f. -ψομαι, Med. to exchange one thing with another, τί τινι Archil. II. c. acc. pers. to repay, requite, punish, Id., Aesch., etc. III. to answer again, Hdt.; ἀντ. τι πρός τινα Soph.

ἀντ-ἀμύνομαι [ῠ], f. -ῠνοῦμαι, Med. to defend oneself against, resist, Thuc. II. to requite, τινὰ κακοῖς Soph.

ἀντ-ανᾰβῐβάζω, f. -βιβῶ, to make go up in turn, Xen.

ἀντ-ανάγω, f. ξω, to lead up against, ἀντ. νέας to put ships to sea against, Hdt.; but also, ἀντ. ναυσί with ships, Thuc.;—so, ἀντανάγειν or ἀντανάγεσθαι alone, Id., Xen. II. to bring up or out instead, Anth.

ἀντ-αναιρέω, f. ήσω, to take away from the opposite sides of an account, to cancel, Dem.

ἀντ-αναλίσκω, f. -ᾰλώσω, to destroy in return, Eur.

ἀντ-αναμένω, f. -μενῶ, to wait instead of taking active measures, Thuc.

ἀντ-αναπίμπλημι, f. -πλήσω, to fill up in return, Xen.

ἀντ-αναπλέκω, f. ξω, to plait in rivalry with, τινί Anth.

ἀντ-αναπληρόω, f. ώσω, to supply as a substitute or balance, τινὰ πρός τινα Dem.

ἄντ-ανδρος, ον, (ἀνήρ) instead of a man, as a substitute, Luc.

ἀντ-άνειμι, (εἶμι ibo) to rise so as to balance, τινί Thuc.

ἀντ-ανίστημι, f. -στήσω, to set up against, τί τινι Plut. II. Pass., with aor. 2 act., to rise up against, τινί Soph.

ἀντ-άξιος, α, ον, worth just as much as, c. gen., Il.,

Hdt., Att. 2. absol. worth as much, worth no less, Il. Hence

ἀντ-αξιόω, f. ώσω, to demand as equivalent, or in turn, Thuc.

ἀντ-απαιτέω, f. ήσω, to demand in return, Thuc. :— Pass. to be called on for a thing in turn, τι Plut.

ἀντ-απᾰμείβομαι, f. ψομαι, Med. to obey in turn, τινι Tyrtae.

ἀντ-απερύκω [ῠ], f. ξω, to keep off in turn, Anth.

ἀντ-αποδείκνυμι or -ύω, f. -δείξω, to prove in return or answer, Xen.

ἀντ-αποδίδωμι, f. -δώσω, to give back, repay, tender in repayment or requital, Batr., Hdt., Att. :—absol. to make a return, Thuc. II. to make correspondent, Plat. 2. intr. to answer to, correspond with, τοῖς ἑτέροις Id. 3. to give back words, answer, τινί Id. III. to deliver in turn, τὸ σύνθημα Xen. IV. to give back a sound, Plut.

ἀνταπόδομα, ατος, τό, (ἀνταποδίδωμι) repayment, requital, N. T.

ἀνταπόδοσις, εως, ἡ, (ἀνταποδίδωμι) a giving back in turn, Thuc.: a rendering, requiting, repayment, reward, N. T.

ἀντ-αποκρίνομαι [ῑ], Med. to answer again, N. T.: to argue against, τινι Ib.

ἀντ-αποκτείνω, f. -κτενῶ, to kill in return, Hdt., Att.

ἀντ-απολαμβάνω, f. -λήψομαι, to receive or accept in return, Plat., Dem.

ἀντ-απόλλῡμι, f. -απολέσω, to destroy in return, Eur., Plat. II. Pass. and Med., with pf. 2 act. -απόλωλα, to perish in turn, Eur.; ὑπὲρ ἀνδρὸς ἑκάστου δέκα ἀνταπόλυσθαι that ten be put to death in revenge for each man, Hdt.

ἀντ-αποτίω, f. -τίσω [ῑ], to requite, repay, Anth.

ἀντ-αποφαίνω, f. -φᾰνῶ, to shew on the other hand, Thuc.

ἀντ-άπτομαι, Ion. for ἀνθ-άπτομαι.

ἀντ-αρκέω, f. -έσω, to hold out against, τινι Thuc.; πρός τι Plut. II. absol. to hold out, persist, Ar.

ἀντ-ασπάζομαι, f. άσομαι, Dep. to welcome or greet in turn, Xen.; to receive kindly, Id.

ἀνταυγεία, ἡ, reflexion of light, Xen. From

ἀντ-αυγέω, f. ήσω, (αὐγή) to reflect light, φάσγανον ἀνταυγεῖ φόνον flashes back murder, Eur.

ἀντ-αυδάω, f. ήσω, to speak against, answer, τινα Soph.

ἀντ-αύω, f. σω : Dor. aor. 1 -ἄῡσα [ῠ], to sound in turn, answer, τινί Pind.

ἀντ-αφίημι, f. -αφήσω, to let go or let fall in turn, Eur.

ἀντάω, poët. 3 sing. opt. ἀντῴη : Ion. impf. ἤντεον : f. ἀντήσω : Dor. aor. 1 ἄντᾱσα : pf. ἤντηκα : (ἄντα) : I. c. dat. pers. to come opposite to, meet face to face, meet with, Il., Trag. II. c. gen., either 1. gen. pers. to meet in battle, Hom.; or 2. gen. rei, to take part in, partake in or of, Id.; ὅπως ἤντησας ὀπωπῆς how thou hast sped in getting sight of him, Od.; so, ἀντ. ξεινίων Hdt.; κακῶν Soph.; so, ἄντασε Ἐρεχθειδᾶν partook of their blood, Id.

ἀντεβόλησα, aor. 1 of ἀντιβολέω.

ἀντ-εγγράφω, f. ψω, to insert one name instead of another, Dem.

ἀντ-εγκαλέω, f. έσω, to accuse in turn, Dem.

ἀντ-εικάζω, f. άσομαι : aor. 1 -ήκασα :—to compare in return, τινά τινι Ar. : absol., Plat.

ἀν-τείνω, poët. for ἀνα-τείνω.

ἀντ-εῖπον, aor. 2 with no pres. (ἀντ-αγορεύω being used instead, cf. ἀντ-ερῶ) :—to speak against or in answer, gainsay, c. dat., οὐδὲν ἀντ. τινι Aesch. etc.:—absol. to speak in answer, Thuc., etc.; ἀντ. ἔπος to utter a word of contradiction, Eur.   2. ἀντ. τινί τι to set one thing against another, Plat.   3. κακῶς ἀντ. τινά to speak ill of him in turn, Soph.

ἀντ-είρομαι, Ion. for ἀντ-έρομαι.

ἀντ-εισάγω, f. ξω, to introduce instead, substitute, Dem.   II. to bring into office in turn, Plut.

ἀντ-εκκλέπτω, f. ψω, to steal away in return, Ar.

ἀντ-εκκόπτω, f. ψω, to knock out in return, Dem.

ἀντ-εκπέμπω, f. ψω, to send out in return, Xen.

ἀντ-εκπλέω, f. -πλεύσομαι, to sail out against, τινί Thuc.

ἀντ-εκτείνω, -τενῶ, to stretch out in opposition, ἀν. αὑτόν τινι to match oneself with another, Ar.

ἀντ-εκτίθημι, f. -θήσω, to set forth or state instead, Plut.

ἀντεκτρέχω, f. -δρᾰμοῦμαι, to sally out against, Xen.

ἀντ-ελαύνω, f. -ελῶ, intr. to sail against, Plut.

ἀντ-ελπίζω, f. σω, to hope instead or in turn, Thuc.

ἀντ-εμβάλλω, f. -βαλῶ, intr. to make an inroad in turn, Xen.: to attack in turn, Plut.

ἀντ-εμβιβάζω, f. -βιβῶ, to put on board instead, Thuc.

ἀντ-εμπήγνυμαι, aor. -ενεπάγην [ᾰ], Pass. to stick right in, τινί Ar.

ἀντ-εμπίπλημι, f. -πλήσω, to fill in turn, Xen.: to fill in return, by way of compensation, τί τινος Id.

ἀντεμπίπρημι, f. -πρήσω, to set on fire in return, Hdt.

ἀντ-έμφασις, εως, ἡ, (ἐμφαίνω) difference of appearance, Strab.

ἀντ-ενδίδωμι, f. -δώσω, to give way in turn, of sawyers, Ar.

ἀντ-εξάγω, f. ξω, to export in turn or instead, Xen.

ἀντ-εξαιτέω, f. ήσω, to demand in return, Plut.

ἀντ-έξειμι, (εἶμι ibo) to go out against, Xen.

ἀντ-εξελαύνω, f. -ελῶ, to drive, ride, sail out against, Plut.

ἀντ-εξέρχομαι, = ἀντέξειμι, Xen.

ἀντ-εξετάζω, f. άσω, to try one by the standard of another, Aeschin.; τι πρός τι Plut.:—Med. to measure oneself against another, τινί Luc.:—to dispute with him at law, Id.

ἀντ-εξιππεύω, f. σω, to ride out against, Plut.

ἀντ-εξόρμησις, εως, ἡ, (ἐξορμάω) a sailing against, Thuc.: a mode of attack, Plut.

ἀντ-επάγω, f. ξω, to lead against: intr. to advance against, Thuc.

ἀντ-επαινέω, f. έσω, to praise in return, Xen.   II. Pass., ἀντ. τινι to be extolled in comparison with, Luc.

ἀντ-επανάγομαι, Pass. to put to sea against, πρός τινα Thuc.

ἀντ-επαφίημι [ῑ], f. -αφήσω, to let slip against, τινί Luc.

ἀντ-έπειμι, (εἶμι ibo) to rush upon, meet an advancing enemy, c. dat. or absol., Thuc.

ἀντ-επεξάγω, f. ξω, intr., to go out against, Thuc.

ἀντ-επέξειμι, (εἶμι ibo) to march out to meet an enemy, πρός τινα Thuc.; absol., Xen.

ἀντ-επεξελαύνω, f. -ελῶ, = foreg., Thuc.

ἀντ-επεξέρχομαι, = ἀντεπέξειμι, Thuc.

ἀντ-επηχέω, f. ήσω, to clamour against one, Luc.

ἀντ-επιβουλεύω, f. σω, to form counter-designs, Thuc.

ἀντ-επιγράφω, f. ψω, to write something instead, Dem.

ἀντ-επιδείκνυμι, f. -δείξω, to exhibit in turn, Xen.; so Med., Plut.

ἀντ-επιθυμέω, f. ήσω, to desire a thing in rivalry with another, c. gen. rei, Andoc.:—Pass., ἀντεπιθυμεῖσθαι τῆς ξυνουσίας to have one's company desired in turn, Xen.

ἀντ-επικουρέω, f. ήσω, to help in return, τινι Xen.

ἀντ-επιμελέομαι or -μέλομαι, Dep. to attend or give heed in turn, τινός to one, Xen.

ἀντ-επιστέλλω, f. -στελῶ, to write an answer, Luc.

ἀντ-επιστρᾰτεύω, f. σω, to take the field against, Xen.

ἀντ-επιτάσσω, f. ξω, to order in turn, τινι ποιεῖν τι Thuc.

ἀντ-επιτειχίζομαι, f. Att. -ιοῦμαι, Dep. with pf. pass. to build a fort in retaliation, Thuc.

ἀντ-επιτίθημι, f. -θήσω, to entrust a letter in answer, πρός τινα Thuc.

ἀντεπιχειρέω, f. ήσω, to attack in turn, τινι Plut.

ἀντ-ερᾰμαι, aor. 1 -ηράσθην : Dep. to rival another in love for a person, τινί τινος Luc.

ἀντ-ερᾰνίζω, to contribute in turn; Pass. to be repaid, Anth.

ἀντ-εραστής, οῦ, ὁ, a rival in love, τινός for another, Ar.: a rival, Plat.

ἀντ-εράω, to love in return, Aesch.; ἀντερᾶν τινος Luc.: ἀντ. τινί τινος to rival one in love for another, Eur.: absol., τὸ ἀντερᾶν jealous love, Plut.

ἀντ-ερείδω, f. σω, to set firmly against, τί τινι Eur.; ἀντ. ξύλα [τῷ πύργῳ] to set wooden props against it, Xen.; ἀντ. βάσιν to plant it firm, Soph.   II. intr. to stand firm, resist pressure, Xen. From

ἀντέρεισις, εως, ἡ, resistance, Plut.

ἀντ-έρομαι, Ion. -είρομαι, aor. 2 -ηρόμην, Dep. to ask in turn, Hdt., Xen.

ἀντ-ερύομαι, aor. 1 inf. -ερύσασθαι [ῠ], Dep. to make equal in weight with, to value equally with, c. gen., Theogn.

ἀντ-ερῶ, f. with no pres. in use: pf. ἀντείρηκα (cf. ἀντεῖπον):—to speak against, gainsay, Soph.; τι πρός τινα Ar.; c. inf. to refuse, Aesch.:—Pass., οὐδὲν ἀντειρήσεται no denial shall be given, Soph.

ἀντ-έρως, ωτος, ὁ, return-love, Plat.

ἀντ-ερωτάω, f. ήσω, to question in turn, ἐρωτώμενος ἀντερωτᾶν Plat.

ἀντ-ευεργετέω, f. ήσω, to return a kindness, Xen.

ἀντ-ευνοέω, f. ήσω, to wish well in return, τινί Xen.

ἀντ-έχω or ἀντ-ίσχω, f. ἀνθ-έξω: aor. 2 ἀντ-έσχον:—to hold against, c. acc. et gen., χεῖρα ἀντ. κρατός to hold one's hand against one's head, so as to shade the eyes, Soph.; c. dat., ὄμμασι δ' ἀντίσχοις τάνδ' αἴγλαν may'st thou keep this sunlight upon his eyes (al. off his eyes), Id.   II. to hold out against, withstand, c. dat., Hdt., Thuc.; πρός τινα Thuc.; c. acc. to endure, Anth.   2. absol. to hold out, stand one's ground, Hdt., Att.: to hold out, endure, last, Hdt., etc.; of the rivers drunk by the Persian army, to hold out, suffice, Id.   III. Med. to hold before one against something, c. acc. et gen., Od.   2. c. gen. to hold on by, cling to, Hdt., Att.:—metaph., ἀντ. τῶν ὄχθων to cling to the banks, keep close to them, Hdt.; ἀντ. ἀρετῆς, τοῦ πολέμου Id.; τῆς θαλάσσης Thuc.   3. absol. to hold out, Soph.   4. c. dupl. gen. pers. et rei, ἀνθέξεταί σου τῶν χρημάτων will lay claim to the property from you, dispute it with you, Ar.

ἀντήεις, Dor. -άεις, εσσα, εν, (ἄντα) hostile, Pind.
ἀντ-ήλιος (not ἀνθ-ήλιος), ον, opposite the sun, i. e.
facing east, Soph.; δαίμονες ἀντήλιοι statues of gods
which stood in the sun before the door, Aesch.   II.
like the sun, formed like ἀντίθεος, Eur.
ἄντην, (ἀντί) Adv. against, over against, ἄντην στήσομαι I will confront him, Il.; ὁμοιωθήμεναι ἄντην to
match himself against me, Hom.; ἄντην ἔρχεσθαι to go
straight forwards, Il.; ἄντην βάλλεσθαι to be struck in
front, Ib.; ἄντην εἰσιδέειν to look him in the face, Ib.;
ἄντην λόεσθαι to bathe before all, Od.; θεῷ ἐναλίγκιος
ἄντην like a god in presence, Ib.
ἀντ-ήνωρ, ορος, ὁ, ἡ, (ἀνήρ) instead of a man, σποδὸς
ἀντ. dust for men, Aesch.
ἀντ-ηρέτης, ου, ὁ, (ἐρέτης) properly, one who rows
against another: generally an adversary, Aesch.
ἀντ-ήρης, ες, (ἀντί, v. -ήρης) set over against, opposite,
face to face, Eur.:—c. gen. over against, facing, Id.;
ἀντήρεις στέρνων πληγάς aimed straight at the breast,
Soph.:—c. dat., ἀντ. τινί opposite to a thing, Eur.
ἀντ-ηρίς, ίδος, ἡ, (ἀντί, ἐρείδω) a prop, stay, support,
Eur., Xen.; in Thuc., ἀντηρίδες are stay-beams, fixed
so as to strengthen the timbers of the bow.
ἄντησις, εως, ἡ, (ἀντάω) a meeting, Od.
ἀντ-ηχέω, Dor. -αχέω, f. ήσω, to sound or sing in
answer, Eur.   II. of a musical string, to sound re-
sponsively, Plut., Luc.
'ΑΝΤΙ', Prep. c. gen.:—orig. sense over against, opposite.
   A. Usage,   1. of Place, instead, in the place of,
Hom., etc.   2. as good as, equal to, ἀντὶ πολλῶν
λαῶν ἐστίν he is as good as many men, Il.; ἀντὶ κασιγνήτου Od.   3. at the price of, for, ἀντὶ χρημάτων
for money paid, Hdt., etc.   4. for the sake of,
Soph.   5. to mark comparison, ἓν ἀνθ' ἑνός one set
against the other, compared with it, Plat.: so, after
Comparatives, πλέον ἀντὶ σοῦ Soph.; also (esp. after a
negative), ἄλλος ἀντ' ἐμοῦ Aesch.
   B. Position: ἀντί rarely follows its case, and then
does not suffer anastrophé.
   C. IN COMPOS.,   1. over against, opposite, as
ἀντίπορος.   2. against, in opposition to, as ἀντιλέγω.   3. in return, as ἀντιβοηθέω.   4. instead,
as ἀντήνωρ.   5. equal to, like, as ἀντίθεος.   6.
counter, as ἀντίτυπος.
ἀντία, as Adv., v. ἀντίος II.
ἀντιάζω, impf. ἠντίαζον, Ion. ἀντίαζον: f. ἀντιάσω,
Dor. -άξω: aor. 1 ἠντίασα: (ἀντίος):—to meet face to
face,   I. c. acc. pers. to encounter, whether as friend
or foe, Hdt., Aesch.: absol. to meet, answer, Pind.   2.
to approach as suppliants, to entreat, supplicate, Hdt.,
Soph.   II. c. dat. pers. to meet in fight, Pind.
ἀντι-άνειρα, ἡ, (ἀντί, ἀνήρ) fem. Adj., a match for men,
of the Amazons, Il.   II. στάσις ἀντιάνειρα faction
wherein man is set against man, Pind.
ἀντιάω, used by Hom. in Ep. forms ἀντιόω, inf. ἀντιάαν,
3 pl. imp. ἀντιοώντων, part. ἀντιόων, ὅωσα, ὅωντες:—
f. ἀντιάσω [ᾰ]; aor. 1 ἠντίασα:—Med., Ep. 2 pl.
ἀντιάσθε: (ἀντίος).   I. to go for the purpose of
meeting: 1. c. gen. rei, to go in quest of, Hom.; of
an arrow, to hit, Il.; of the gods, to come (as it were) to
meet an offering, to accept it, or to partake of it, Hom.;

then, generally, to partake of, enjoy, obtain, Od.,
Soph.; so in Med., Il.   2. c. gen. pers. to match or
measure oneself with, Ib., Theogn.   II. c. dat. pers.
to meet with, encounter, Hom.   III. c. acc. rei, to
come to, visit, share, ἐμὸν λέχος ἀντιόωσα Il.
ἀντι-βαίνω, f. -βήσομαι, to go against, withstand, resist, c. dat., Hdt., Aesch.; πλευραῖσιν ἀντιβᾶσα having
set her foot against, Hdt., etc.; ἀντι-
βὰς reluctant, Soph.; but, ἀντιβὰς ἐλᾶν to pull stoutly
against the oar, going well back, Ar.
ἀντι-βάλλω, f. -βᾰλῶ, to throw against or in turn,
return the shots, Xen.   II. to put one against the
other, λόγους ἀντ. πρὸς ἀλλήλους to exchange words in
conversation, N. T.
ἀντίβασις, εως, ἡ, (ἀντιβαίνω) resistance, Plut.
ἀντιβᾰτικός, ή, όν, (ἀντιβαίνω) contrary, opposite, Plut.
ἀντι-βιάζομαι, Dep. to use force against, Anth.
ἀντι-βίην, Adv. (βία) against, face to face, Il.
ἀντί-βιος, α, ον and ος, ον, (βία) opposing force to force,
ἀντιβίοις ἐπέεσσι with wrangling words, Hom.:—neut.
as Adv. = ἀντιβίην, Il.
ἀντι-βλέπω, f. -βλέψω or -ομαι, to look straight at,
look in the face, c. dat. pers., Xen.   Hence
ἀντιβλεπτέον, verb. Adj. one must look in the face, Luc.
ἀντίβλεψις, εως, ἡ, a looking in the face, a look, Xen.
ἀντι-βοάω, f. ήσομαι, to return a cry, Bion.
ἀντι-βοηθέω, f. ήσω, to help in turn, τινι Thuc., Xen.
ἀντι-βολέω: impf. ἠντιβόλουν: f. -ήσω: aor. 1 ἀντεβόλησα, with double augm. ἠντεβόλησα: (ἀντι-βάλλω)
—to meet by chance, esp. in battle, c. dat. pers. or
absol., Hom.   2. c. dat. rei, to be present at, φόνῳ
ἀνδρῶν, τάφῳ ἀνδρῶν Od.   3. c. gen. rei, to partake of, have one's share of, μάχης Il.; τάφου Od.   4.
to fall to one's lot, c. gen. pers., γάμος ἀντιβολήσει
ἐμέθεν Ib.   5. c. acc. pers. to meet as a suppliant,
entreat, supplicate, Ar.; c. acc. et inf., Id.:—absol.
to supplicate, entreat, Id.   Hence
ἀντιβόλησις, εως, ἡ, = ἀντιβολία, Plat.
ἀντιβολία, ἡ, (ἀντιβολέω) entreaty, prayer, Thuc.
ἀντιβροντάω, f. ήσω, to rival in thundering, τινί Luc.
ἀντι-γέγωνα, pf. in pres. sense, to return a cry, Anth.
ἀντι-γενεηλογέω, Ion. form, to rival in pedigree, Hdt.
ἀντι-γνωμονέω, f. ήσω, (γνώμων) to be of a different
opinion: ἀντ. τι μὴ οὐκ εἶναι to think that a thing is
otherwise, Xen.
ἀντί-γραμμα, ατος, τό, = ἀντίγραφον, Luc.
ἀντι-γρᾰφεύς, έως, ὁ, a check-clerk, controller, Aeschin.;
ἀντ. τῶν εἰσενεγκόντων one who keeps a check upon
their accounts, Dem.
ἀντι-γρᾰφή, ἡ, a reply in writing, such as Caesar's
Anticato in reply to Cicero's Cato, Plat.   II. as
law-term, a plea, indictment, Plat., Dem.
ἀντί-γρᾰφος, ον, copied, Dem.:—as Subst., ἀντίγραφον,
τό, a transcript, copy, counterpart, Id.   From
ἀντι-γρᾰφω [ᾰ], f. ψω, to write against or in answer,
write back, Thuc., Plut.   II. Med., with pf. pass.,
as law-term, to put in as a plea, to plead against, Dem.
ἀντι-δάκνω, f. -δήξομαι, to bite in turn, Hdt.
ἀντί-δειπνος, ον, (δεῖπνον) taking another's place at
dinner, Luc.
ἀντι-δεξιόομαι, Dep. to salute in return, τινα Xen.
ἀντι-δέομαι, f. δεήσομαι, Dep. to entreat in return, Plat.

ἀντι-δέρκομαι, Dep. =ἀντιβλέπω, c. acc., Eur.
ἀντι-δέχομαι, f. -δέξομαι, Dep. to receive or accept in return, Aesch., Eur.
ἀντι-δημᾰγωγέω, f. ήσω, to rival as a demagogue, Plut.
ἀντι-διαβαίνω, f. -βήσομαι, to cross over in turn, Xen.
ἀντι-διαβάλλω, f. -βᾰλῶ, to attack in return, Arist.
ἀντι-διαπλέκω, f. ξω, to retort, Aeschin.
ἀντι-διατίθεμαι, Med. to offer resistance, τοὺς ἀντιδιατιθεμένους opponents, N. T.
ἀντι-διδάσκω, f. ξω, to teach in turn or on the other side, Anth. :—of poets, to contend for the prize, Ar.
ἀντι-δίδωμι, f. -δώσω, to give in return, repay, τί τινι Hdt., Att.   2. to give for or instead of, τί τινος Eur.; τι ἀντί τινος Ar.   II. at Athens, ἀντ. [τὴν οὐσίαν] to offer to change fortunes with one (cf. ἀντίδοσις), Dem., etc.
ἀντι-διέξειμι, to go through in turn, Aeschin.
ἀντι-δῐκέω, f. ήσω: impf. ἠντιδίκουν, or with double augm. ἠντεδίκουν: aor. 1 ἠντιδίκησα: (ἀντίδικος) :—to dispute, go to law, περί τινος Xen.; οἱ ἀντιδικοῦντες the parties to a suit, Plat.; absol. of the defendant, Ar.; ἀντ. πρός τι or πρός τινα, to urge one's suit against . . , Dem.   From
ἀντί-δῐκος, ον, (δίκη) an opponent in a suit, defendant or plaintiff, Plat., etc.: generally an opponent, Aesch.
ἀντί-δοξος, ον, (δόξα) of a different opinion or sect, Luc.
ἀντί-δορος, ον, (δορά) clothed with something instead of a skin, Anth.
ἀντί-δοσις, εως, ἡ, (ἀντιδίδωμι) a giving in return, exchange, Arist., Luc.   II. at Athens, a form by which a citizen charged with a λειτουργία or public charge might call upon any other citizen, whom he thought richer than himself, either to exchange properties, or to take the charge upon himself, Xen., Dem., etc.
ἀντί-δοτος, ον, (ἀντιδίδωμι) given in lieu of, πυρός Anth.   II. given as a remedy for, κακῶν Id. :—as Subst., ἀντίδοτος, ἡ, an antidote, Id.
ἀντι-δουλεύω, f. σω, to serve in place of, τινός Eur.
ἀντί-δουλος, ον, treated as a slave, Aesch.
ἀντί-δουπος, ον, re-echoing, Aesch.; ἀντίδουπά τινι Id.
ἀντι-δράω, f. -δράσω, to act against, retaliate, Soph., Eur.   II. c. acc. pers. to repay, requite, Soph., Eur.
ἀντι-δωρέομαι, f. ήσομαι, Dep. to present in return, τινά τινι one with a thing, Hdt., Plat., etc.; also, ἀντ. τινί τι to present a thing in turn to one, Eur.
ἀντι-ζητέω, f. ήσω, to seek one who is seeking us, Xen.
ἀντι-ζωγρέω, f. ήσω, to save alive in turn, Babr.
ἀντι-θάπτω, f. ψω, to bury opposite: Pass., aor. 2 ἀντετάφην [ᾰ], Anth.
ἀντί-θεος, η, ον, equal to the gods, godlike, Hom.
ἀντι-θεραπεύω, f. σω, to take care of in return, Xen.
ἀντίθεσις, εως, ἡ, (ἀντιτίθημι) opposition, resistance, Plat., Anth.   2. antithesis, Isocr.
ἀντι-θέω, f. -θεύσομαι, to run against another, compete in a race, Hdt.   II. to run contrary ways, Anth.
ἀντι-θήγω, f. ξω, to whet against another, ὀδόντας ἐπί τινα Luc.
ἀντί-θροος, ον, echoing, Anth.
ἀντί-θῠρος, ον, (θύρα) opposite the door : as neut. Subst., ἀντίθυρον, τό, the part facing the door, the vestibule, Od., Soph.   2. the side of a room facing the door, Luc.

ἀντι-καθεύδω, f. -ευδήσω, to sleep again or instead, Anth.
ἀντι-κάθημαι, Ion. ἀντι-κάτ-, pf. of ἀντικαθίζομαι, used as pres., to be set over against ; of armies or fleets, to lie over against, so as to watch each other, Hdt., Thuc.
ἀντι-καθίζομαι, Ion. ἀντι-κατ-, f. -καθεδοῦμαι, aor. 2 -καθεζόμην :—Med. to sit or lie over against, or armies or fleets watching one another, Hdt., Thuc.
ἀντι-καθίστημι, Ion. ἀντι-κατ-: f. -καταστήσω :—to lay down or establish instead, substitute, replace, Hdt., Thuc.   2. to set against, oppose, τινά πρός τινα Thuc.; τινά τινι Plat.   3. to bring back again, restore, Thuc.   II. Pass., with aor. 2 and pf. act., and aor. 1 pass. κατεστάθην [ᾰ], to be put in another's place, reign in his stead, Hdt., Xen.   2. to stand against, resist, τινί Xen.; absol., Thuc.
ἀντι-κᾰκουργέω, f. ήσω, to damage in turn, τινά Plat.
ἀντι-κᾰλέω, f. έσω, to invite in turn, Xen.
ἀντι-καταθνήσκω, f. -θᾰνοῦμαι: aor. 2 -έθανον :—to die or be slain in turn, Aesch.
ἀντι-καταλείπω, f. ψω, to leave in one's stead, Plat.
ἀντι-καταλλάσσομαι, Att. -ττομαι, f. -αλλάξομαι : Med. :—to exchange one thing for another : 1. to give one thing for another, τί τινος Dem.; τι ἀντί τινος or ὑπέρ τινος Oratt.   2. to receive one thing in exchange for another, τι ἀντί τινος Isocr.
ἀντι-κατατείνω, f. -τενῶ, to stretch out or set directly in contrast, τι παρά τι Plat.
ἀντι-κατηγορέω, f. ήσω, to accuse in turn, recriminate upon, τινός Aeschin.
ἀντι-κάτημαι, -κατίζομαι, -κατίστημι, Ion. for ἀντικάθ-.
ἀντι-κάτων [ᾰ], ωνος, ὁ, Anticato, name of a book written by Caesar in reply to the Cato of Cicero, Plut.
ἀντί-κειμαι, f. -κείσομαι, used as Pass. of ἀντιτίθημι, to be set over against, lie opposite, Plat.: Adv. part. ἀντικειμένως, by way of opposition, Arist.
ἀντι-κελεύω, f. σω, to command in turn, Thuc. :— Pass. to be bidden to do a thing in turn, Id.
ἀντί-κεντρον, τό, something acting as a goad, Aesch.
ἀντι-κηδεύω, f. σω, to tend instead of another, τινός Eur.
ἀντι-κηρύσσω, f. ξω, to proclaim in answer, Eur.
ἀντι-κλάζω, f. -κλάγξω, to sound against, to be echoed by a thing, Eur. :—ἀντ. ἀλλήλαις μέλος to sing against one another, Id.
ἀντι-κλαίω, Att. -κλάω, f. -κλαύσομαι, to weep in return, Id.
ἀντι-κνήμιον, τό, the part of the leg opposite the κνήμη, the shin, Ar.
ἀντι-κολάζομαι, Pass. to be punished in return, Luc
ἀντι-κολᾰκεύω, f. σω, to flatter in turn, Plut.
ἀντι-κομίζω, f. σω, to bring back as an answer, Plut.
ἀντι-κομπάζω, f. άσω, to boast in opposition, τινί Plut.
ἀντι-κόπτω, f. ψω, to beat back, resist, oppose, Xen.   2. impers., ἤν τι ἀντικόψῃ if there be any hindrance, Id.
ἀντι-κορύσσομαι, Med. to take arms against, τινί Anth.
ἀντι-κρᾰτέω, f. ήσω, to hold instead of another, Anth.
ἀντίκρουσις, εως, ἡ, a striking against, hindrance : a repartee, Aeschin.   From
ἀντι-κρούω, f. σω, to strike against, to be a hindrance, counteract, τινί Thuc.; πρός τι Plut.; absol., Dem.
ἀντικρύ, Adv., =ἄντην, over against, right opposite, c.

ῦαῖ., θεοῖς ἀντικρὺ μάχεσθαι Il.; c. gen., Ἕκτορος ἀντικρύ Ib.   **II.** = ἀντίκρυς, *straight on, right on,* Hom.; followed by a Prep., ἀντικρὺ ἀν' ὀδόντας, ἀντικρὺ δι' ὤμου Id.; ἀντικρὺ κατὰ μέσσον *right* in the middle, Il.   **2.** *outright, utterly,* ἀντικρὺ δ' ἀπόφημι Ib.

ἄντικρῦς, Adv. *straight on, right on,* Thuc., etc.   **2.** *outright, openly, without disguise,* Aesch., Thuc., etc.; ἀντ. δουλεία *downright* slavery, Thuc.; οὐκ ἄντικρυς not *at all,* Ar.   **II.** later, = ἀντίκρῦ, *opposite,* Arist., Plut.

ἀντι-κτόνος, ον, (κτείνω) *in requital for murder,* Aesch.

ἀντι-κτυπέω, f. ήσω, *to ring, clash against,* τινί Anth.

ἀντικύρω [ῠ], aor. 1 ἀντέκυρσα, *to hit upon, meet,* τινί Pind., Soph.

ἀντι-κωμῳδέω, f. ήσω, *to ridicule in turn,* Plut.

ἀντιλαβή, ή, (ἀντιλαμβάνω) *a thing to hold by, a handle,* Lat. *ansa,* Thuc. :—metaph., πολλὰς . . ἔχει ἀντιλαβάς gives many *handles against* one, *points of attack,* Plat.

ἀντι-λαγχάνω, f. -λήξομαι : pf. -είληχα :—as law-term, ἀντ. δίαιταν *to have a new* arbitration *granted,* i. e. to get the old one set aside, Dem.; ἀντ. ἔρημον (sc. τὴν δίκην) *to get it set aside* by default, Id.

ἀντι-λάζομαι, -υμαι, Dep. *to take hold of, hold by,* c. gen., Eur.: *to partake in,* πόνων Id.   **2.** c. acc. *to receive in turn,* Id.

ἀντι-λακτίζω, f. σω, *to kick against,* τινί Ar.

ἀντι-λαμβάνω, f. -λήψομαι: aor. 2 -έλαβον: pf.-είληφα: —*to receive instead of,* τί τινος Eur.: *to receive in turn* or *as a return,* τι Id., etc.   **II.** Med., with pf. pass. -είλημμαι, like ἀντέχομαι, c. gen. *to lay hold of,* Theogn., etc.; χώρας ἀντ. *to gain* or *reach* it, Thuc.   **2.** *to help, take part with, assist,* Eur.; c. gen. rei, *to help towards a thing,* Thuc.; c. gen. pers., N. T.   **3.** *to lay claim to,* τοῦ θρόνου Ar.   **4.** *to take part,* or *share in a thing, take in hand,* Lat. *capessere,* τῶν πραγμάτων Xen., etc.   **5.** *to take hold of for the purpose of finding fault, to reprehend,* ἡμῶν Plat.   **6.** *to take fast hold of, to captivate,* ὁ λόγος ἀντιλαμβάνεταί μου Id.   **III.** in Med. also, *to hold against, hold back,* ἵππον Xen.

ἀντι-λάμπω, f. ψω, *to kindle a light in turn,* Aesch.   **II.** intr. *to reflect light, shine,* Xen.   **2.** *to shine opposite to* or *in the face of,* ὁ ἥλιος ἀντ. τινί Plut.

ἀντι-λέγω, f. -λέξω, but the common fut. is ἀντερῶ: aor. 1 -έλεξα (but the aor. commonly used is ἀντεῖπον): so the pf. is ἀντείρηκα, the fut. pass. ἀντειρήσομαι :— *to speak against, gainsay, contradict,* τινί Thuc., etc.; τινὶ περί τινος Xen.; ὑπέρ τινος Id.; πρός τι Ar.; ἀντ. ὡς . . *to declare in opposition* or *answer that . . ,* Hdt., etc.; c. inf. *to reply that . . ,* Thuc.; ἀντ. μὴ ποιεῖν *to speak against* doing, Id.   **2.** c. acc. rei, *to allege in answer,* Soph., Thuc. :—Pass. *to be disputed,* Xen.; of a place, *to be counter-claimed,* Id.   **3.** absol. *to speak one against the other, speak in opposition,* Hdt., etc.; οἱ ἀντιλέγοντες Thuc. Hence

ἀντιλεκτέον, verb. Adj. *one must gainsay,* Eur.

ἀντί-λεκτος, ον, (ἀντιλέγω) *disputably,* Thuc.

ἀντι-λήις, ό, *lion-like,* formed like ἀντίθεος, Ar.

ἀντί-ληξις, εως, ή, (ἀντιλαγχάνω) *a motion for a new* arbitration, Dem.

ἀντιληπτέον, verb. Adj. of ἀντιλαμβάνω, *one must take part in* a matter, Ar.; τῶν πραγμάτων αὐτοῖς ἀντ. Dem.

ἀντίληψις, εως, ή, (ἀντιλαμβάνω) *a receiving in turn* or *exchange,* Thuc.: *a counter-claim,* Xen.   **II.** (from Med.), *a hold, support, defence, succour,* Id.   **2.** *a claim* to a thing, Id.   **3.** *an objection,* Plat.   **III.** (from Pass.) *a being seized, a seizure, attack* of sickness, Thuc.

ἀντιλογέω, f. ήσω, = ἀντιλέγω, *to deny,* Soph.   **2.** = ἀντ.λέγω 3, Ar.

ἀντιλογία, ή, (ἀντιλογέω) *contradiction, controversy, disputation,* Hdt., Thuc.; in pl. *opposing arguments, answering speeches,* Ar., Thuc.

ἀντιλογίζομαι, f. Att. -ιοῦμαι, Dep. *to count up* or *calculate on the other hand,* Xen.

ἀντιλογικός, ή, όν, (ἀντιλέγω) *given to contradiction, contradictory, disputatious,* Ar., etc. :—ή -κή (sc. τέχνη) *the art of contradiction* or *of arguing from contradictories,* Plat.

ἀντίλογος, ον, (ἀντιλέγω) *contradictory, reverse,* Eur.

ἀντι-λοιδορέω, *to rail at* or *abuse in turn,* N. T.; Med., c. acc. rei, Luc.

ἀντι-λῡπέω, f. ήσω, *to vex in return,* Plut.

ἀντί-λῡρος, ον, (λύρα) *responsive to the lyre,* Soph.

ἀντί-λυτρον, ου, τό, *a ransom,* N. T.

ἀντι-μαίνομαι, pf. -μέμηνα, Pass. *to rage* or *bluster against,* τινί Anth.

ἀντι-μανθάνω, f. -μαθήσομαι, *to learn instead,* Ar.

ἀντι-μαρτῠρέω, f. ήσω, *to appear as witness against, to contradict solemnly,* τινί Plut.

ἀντι-μαρτύρομαι [ῠ], f. -ῠροῦμαι, Dep. *to protest on the other hand,* Luc.

ἀντι-μάχομαι, f. -μάχήσομαι, Dep. *to fight against* one, Thuc.

ἀντι-μεθέλκω, f. ξω, *to drag different ways,* Anth.

ἀντι-μεθίστημι, f. -στήσω :—*to move from one side to the other, to revolutionise,* Ar.   **II.** Pass., with aor. 2 and pf. act., *to pass over to the other side,* Luc.

ἀντι-μειρακιεύομαι, Dep. *to behave petulantly in return,* πρός τινα Plut.

ἀντι-μέλλω, f. -μελλήσω, *to wait and watch against* one, aor. 1 inf. ἀντιμελλῆσαι, Thuc.

ἀντι-μέμφομαι, f. ψομαι, Dep. *to blame in turn,* Hdt.

ἀντι-μερίζομαι, Dep. *to impart in turn,* Anth.

ἀντι-μέτειμι, *to compete :* οἱ ἀντιμετιόντες *competitors,* Plut.

ἀντι-μετρέω, f. ήσω, *to measure out in turn, to give in compensation,* Luc.: Pass. *to be measured in turn,* N.T.

ἀντι-μέτωπος, ον, (μέτωπον) *front to front,* Xen.

ἀντι-μηχανάομαι, f. -ήσομαι, Dep. *to contrive against* or *in opposition,* Hdt., Thuc.

ἀντι-μίμησις [μῑ], εως, ή, *close imitation of* a person in a thing, c. dupl. gen., Thuc.

ἀντιμισθία, ή, *a requital, recompense,* N. T.   From

ἀντί-μισθος, ον, *as a reward,* Aesch.

ἀντί-μοιρος, (μοῖρα) Adv. *by way of compensation,* Dem.

ἀντί-μολπος, ον, (μέλπω) *sounding instead of, differing in sound from,* c. gen., Eur.; ὕπνου ἀντίμολπον ἄκος *song,* sleep's *substitute,* Aesch.

ἀντί-μορφος, ον, *corresponding to,* τινί Luc.

ἀντι-ναυπηγέω, f. ήσω, *to build ships against,* Thuc.

ἀντι-νῑκάω, f. ήσω, *to conquer in turn,* Aesch.

ἀντι-νομία, ή, (νόμος) *ambiguity in the law,* ἐν ἀντινομίᾳ γίγνεσθαι to be *in a strait between two laws,* Plut.

ἀντιξοέω, f. ήσω, to set oneself against, Pind. From
ἀντί-ξοος, ον, contr. -ξους, ουν, (ξέω?) opposed, adverse,
Hdt. :—τὸ ἀντίξοον opposition, Id.
ἀντίον, as Adv. = ἄντην, v. ἀντίος.
ἀντιόομαι, f. ώσομαι : aor. 1 ἠντιώθην, Ion. ἀντ-: Dep. :
(ἀντίος) :—to resist, oppose, τινί Hdt., Aesch. :—οἱ ἀν-
τιούμενοι = οἱ ἐναντίοι, Hdt. :—c. acc., once in Hdt.
ἀντίος, ία, ίον, (ἀντί) set against, and so   I. in local
sense, face to face, opposite, esp. in battle, Hom., etc. ;
ἀντίος ἦλθε went to meet him, Il. ; c. gen., Ἀγαμέμνονος ἀντίος Ib. ; usually c. dat., Od., Hdt., Att.   2.
opposite, contrary, Aesch., Eur. : οἱ ἀντίοι = οἱ ἐναντίοι,
Pind., Hdt. : ἐκ τῆς ἀντίης contrariwise, Hdt.   II.
as Adv. in neut. ἀντία and ἀντίον, against, straight at,
right against, ἀντίον ἵζεν Od., etc. ; c. gen., ἀντί᾽ ἐμεῖο
Il. ; so, ἀντία σευ in thy presence, Hdt.; ἀντία τῆς ἵππου
opposite it, Id.   2. against, ἀντίον τινος εἰπεῖν Od. ;
c. dat., ἀντία τοῖς Πέρσῃσι Hdt.   3. τὸν δ᾽ ἀντίον
ηὔδα = ἠμείβετο, answered, Od., Att.
ἀντιο-στᾰτέω, f. ήσω, = ἀνθίσταμαι, to be contrary, of a
wind, Soph.
ἀντι-οχεύομαι, Pass. to drive against, Anth.
ἀντιόω, ἀντιόων, ἀντιώσα, Ep. forms : v. ἀντιάω.
ἀντι-πᾰθής, ές, (πάθος) in return for suffering, Aesch. :
felt mutually, Luc.   II. as Subst., ἀντιπαθές, τό,
a remedy for suffering, Plut.
ἀντι-παίζω, f. -παίξομαι, to play one with another, Xen.
ἀντί-παις, ὁ, ἡ, like a boy or child, Aesch., Eur.
ἀντί-πᾰλος, ον, (πάλη) properly wrestling against :
then, generally, struggling against, antagonistic, rival,
Aesch. ; c. dat. rivalling, a match for another, Eur. ; c.
gen., ὑμεναίων γόος ἀντίπαλος Id.:—as Subst., ἀντίπαλος, ὁ, an antagonist, rival, adversary, mostly in pl.,
Hdt., Att. ; τὸ ἀντίπαλον the rival party, Thuc.   2.
of things, like ἰσόπαλος, nearly balanced, Id. ; ἀντ.
τριήρης equally large, Id. ; ἀντ. δέος fear equal on
both sides, mutual fear, Id. ; ἤθεα ἀντίπαλα [τῇ πόλει]
habits corresponding to the constitution, Id. :—τὸ
ἀντίπαλον τῆς ναυμαχίας the equal balance, undecided
state of the action, Id. :—Adv. -λως, and in neut. pl.
ἀντίπαλα, Id.   II. τὸν ἀμὸν ἀντ. him who fights for
me, my champion, Aesch.
ἀντι-παραβάλλω, f. -βᾰλῶ, to hold side by side, to compare or contrast, τι πρός τι or παρά τι Plat., etc. Hence
ἀντιπαραβολή, ἡ, close comparison or contrast, Arist.
ἀντι-παραγγελία, ἡ, competition for a public office, Plut.
ἀντι-παραγγέλλω, f. -ελῶ, to command in turn or
also, Xen.   II. to compete for a public office, τινί
with one, Plut.
ἀντι-παράγω, f. ξω, intr. (sub. στρατόν) to lead the
army against, advance to meet the enemy, Xen.
ἀντι-παραθέω, f. -θεύσομαι, to outflank, Xen.
ἀντι-παρακᾰλέω, f. έσω, to summon in turn or contrariwise, Thuc., etc.
ἀντι-παρακελεύομαι, f. σομαι, Dep. to exhort in turn
or contrariwise, Thuc., etc.
ἀντι-παρᾰλῠπέω, f. ήσω, to annoy in turn, Thuc.
ἀντι-παραπλέω, f. -πλεύσομαι, to sail along on the
other side, Thuc.
ἀντι-παρασκευάζομαι, Med. to prepare oneself in
turn, arm on both sides, Thuc. ; ἀντ. ἀλλήλοις ὡς ἐς
μάχην Id.

ἀντι-παρασκευή, ἡ, mutual preparation, Thuc.
ἀντι-παρατάσσομαι, Att. -ττομαι, f. άξομαι, Med. and
Pass. to stand in array against, τινι Thuc. ; πρός τι
Aeschin. :—absol. to stand in hostile array, Thuc. ;
ἀπὸ τοῦ ἀντιπαραταχθέντος in hostile array, Id.
ἀντι-παρατείνω, f. -τενῶ, to stretch side by side, so as
to compare, τι πρός τι Plat.
ἀντι-παρατίθημι, f. -θήσω, to contrast and compare,
τινί τι Plat.
ἀντι-πάρειμι (εἶμι ibo), to march so as to meet, of
armies on opposite sides of a river or the like, Xen.
ἀντι-παρεξάγω, f. ξω, to lead on against, Plut.   II.
(sub. στρατόν) to march against, Philipp. ap. Dem.   2.
to march parallel with, τινι Plut.
ἀντι-παρέρχομαι, aor. 2 -παρῆλθον, Dep. to pass by on
the opposite side, N. T.
ἀντι-παρέχω, f. -έξω, to supply in turn, Thuc. :—Med.,
Xen. ; ἀντ. πράγματα to cause trouble in return, Dem.
ἀντι-πάσχω, f. -πείσομαι : aor. 2 -έπαθον :—to suffer
in turn, ἀντιπάσχω χρηστά I receive good for good
done, Soph. ; ἀντ. ἀντί τινος Thuc. : absol. to suffer
for one's acts, Xen.   2. absol., τὸ ἀντιπεπονθός re-
ciprocity, Arist.
ἀντι-πᾰτᾰγέω, f. ήσω, to clatter so as to drown other
sounds, Thuc.
ἀντι-πέμπω, f. ψω, to send back an answer, Hdt.   2.
to send in repayment, Soph.   II. to send against,
στρατιάν τινι Thuc.   III. to send in the place of
another, στρατηγούς Id.
ἀντι-πενθής, ές, (πένθος) causing grief in turn, Aesch.
ἀντι-πέρα, Ep. -πέρη, the opposite coast, Mosch.
ἀντι-πέραιος, α, ον, lying over against : ἀντιπέραια the
lands just opposite, Il.
ἀντι-πέρᾱν, Ion. -ην, Adv., = ἀντιπέρᾱς, Xen.
ἀντι-πέρᾱς, Adv. over against, on the other side, c.
gen., Thuc. ; absol., ἡ ἀντ. Θρᾴκη Id.
ἀντι-πέρηθεν, Adv. from the opposite side, c. gen., Anth.
ἀντι-περιλαμβάνω, f. -λήψομαι, to embrace in turn, Xen.
ἀντι-περιπλέω, f. -πλεύσομαι, to sail round on the
other side, Strab.
ἀντι-περιχωρέω, f. ήσω, to move round in turn or in
opposition, Plut.
ἀντί-πετρος, ον, like stone, rocky, Soph.
ἀντί-πηξ, ηγος, ἡ, (πήγνυμι) a kind of cradle for infants,
on wheels, Eur.
ἀντι-πίπτω, f. -πεσοῦμαι, to fall against, resist, τινί N.T.
ἀντι-πλέω, f. -πλεύσομαι, to sail against an enemy, Thuc.
ἀντι-πλήξ, ῆγος, ὁ, ἡ, beaten by the opposing waves, Soph.
ἀντι-πληρόω, f. ώσω, to man ships against the enemy,
Thuc.   II. to fill up by new members, Xen.
ἀντι-πλήσσω, f. ξω, to strike in turn, Arist.
ἀντι-πνέω, f. -πνεύσομαι, of winds, to be contrary, Plut.,
Luc. Hence
ἀντίπνοος, ον, contr. -πνους, ουν, caused by adverse
winds, Aesch. : adverse, hostile, Id.
ἀντι-ποθέω, f. ήσω, to long for in turn, τι Xen.
ἀντι-ποιέω, f. ήσω, to do in return, τι Plat. : absol. to
retaliate, Xen.   II. Med. to exert oneself about a
thing, seek after, lay claim to, c. gen., Thuc., Plat.,
etc. ; c. inf., ἀντ. ἐπίστασθαί τι to lay claim to knowing, Plat.   2. to contend with one for a thing, ἀντ.
τινὶ τῆς ἀρχῆς Xen. ; τινὶ περί τινος Id.

ἀντί-ποινα, τά, (ποινή) requital, retribution, ἀντίποινα
τίνειν = ἀντι-τίνειν, to atone for, c. acc., Aesch. ; ἀντί-
ποινά τινος πράσσειν to exact retribution for a thing,
Id. ; ἀντίποιν' ἐμοῦ παθεῖν to suffer retribution for the
wrong done me, Soph.

ἀντι-πολεμέω, f. ήσω, to urge war against others,
Thuc., etc. ; c. dat., Xen.

ἀντι-πολέμιος, ον, warring against, οἱ ἀντιπολέμιοι
enemies, Thuc.

ἀντι-πόλεμος, ον, = foreg., Hdt.

ἀντι-πολιορκέω, f. ήσω, to besiege in turn, Thuc.

ἀντί-πολις, εως, ἡ, a rival city, τινι Strab.

ἀντι-πολῑτεύομαι, f. σομαι, Dep. to be a political opponent, Arist. ; ἀντ. τινι to oppose his policy, Plut.

ἀντι-πορεῖν, aor. 2 with no pres. in use, to give instead,
Anth.

ἀντι-πορεύομαι, f. -εύσομαι, aor. 1 -επορεύθην, Pass. to
march to meet another, Xen.

ἀντι-πορθέω, f. ήσω, to ravage in return, Eur.

ἀντί-πορθμος, ον, over the straits, on the opposite side
of the straits, Aesch., Eur.

ἀντί-πορος, ον, on the opposite coast, Aesch. ; Ἄρτεμιν
Χαλκίδος ἀντίπορον, i. e. her temple at Aulis over against
Chalcis, Id.:—simply, over against, opposite to, τινι Xen.

ἀντίπραξις, εως, ἡ, counteraction, resistance, Plut.
From

ἀντι-πράσσω, Att. -ττω, Ion. -πρήσσω : f. ξω :—to act
against, seek to counteract, τινι Xen. :—absol. to act
in opposition, Hdt., etc. ; so in Med., Xen.

ἀντι-πρεσβεύομαι, f. σομαι, Med. to send counter-am-
bassadors, Thuc.

ἀντι-πρόειμι, (εἶμι ibo) to come forward against or to
meet, τινι Thuc.

ἀντί-προικα, Adv. for next to nothing, cheap, Xen.

ἀντι-προκαλέομαι, f. έσομαι, Med. to retort a legal
challenge (πρόκλησις), Dem.

ἀντι-προσαγορεύω, f. σω, to salute in turn, Plut.

ἀντι-πρόσειμι, (εἶμι ibo) to go against, Xen.

ἀντιπροσεῖπον, serving as aor. 2 to ἀντιπροσαγορεύω,
Theophr. : aor. 1 pass. ἀντι-προσερρήθην, Xen.

ἀντι-προσκαλέομαι, f. έσομαι, to summon in turn, Dem.

ἀντι-προσφέρω, to bring near in turn, τί τινι Xen.

ἀντι-πρόσωπος, ον, (πρόσωπον) with the face towards,
facing, τινι Xen. : face to face, Id.

ἀντι-προτείνω, f. -τενῶ, to offer in turn, τὴν δεξιάν Xen.

ἀντί-πρωρος, ον, (πρῷρα) with the prow towards, Hdt.,
Thuc. : prow to prow, Thuc.　2. like ἀντιπρόσωπος,
face to face, Soph.

ἀντί-πῡλος, ον, (πύλη) with gates opposite, ἀλλήλησι
Hdt.

ἀντί-πυργος, ον, like a tower, Eur.

ἀντι-πυργόω, f. ώσω, to build a tower over against, πόλιν τήνδ' ἀντεπύργωσαν reared up this rival city, Aesch.

ἀντιρ-ρέπω, f. ψω, to counterpoise, balance, Aesch. Hence

ἀντίρροπος, ον, counterpoising, compensating for, τινός
Dem. ; λύπης ἀντ. ἄχθος the counterpoising weight of
sorrow, Soph.:—Adv., ἀντιρρόπως πράττειν τινί so as
to balance his power, Xen.

ἀντισεμνύνομαι [ῠ], f. -ῠνοῦμαι, Med. to meet pride
with pride, Arist.

ἀντι-σηκόω, f. ώσω, to counterbalance, compensate for,
c. dat. Aesch. ; c. gen., Eur.　Hence

ἀντισήκωσις, εως, Ion. ιος, ἡ, equipoise, compensation,
Hdt.

ἀντι-σκευάζομαι, f. -άσομαι, Med. to furnish for oneself in turn, Xen.

ἀντι-σκώπτω, f. ψομαι, to mock in return, Plut.

ἀντ-ῑσόομαι (ἰσόω), Pass. to oppose on equal terms, Thuc.

ἀντί-σπαστος, ον, drawn in the contrary direction :
spasmodic, convulsive, Soph.　From

ἀντι-σπάω, f. άσω [ἄ], to draw the contrary way, hold
back, Aesch., Ar. : Pass. to suffer a check, Arist.　2.
to draw to itself, Xen.

ἀντί-σταθμος, ον, (στάθμη) counterpoising : in compensation for, c. gen., Soph.

ἀντι-στασιάζω, f. σω, to form a party against, τινί
Xen. ; οἱ ἀντιστασιάζοντες = οἱ ἀντιστασιῶται, Id.

ἀντί-στασις, εως, ἡ, an opposite party, Plat.　II. a
standing against, resistance, Plut.

ἀντι-στασιώτης, ου, ὁ, one of the opposite faction or
party, Hdt., Xen.

ἀντιστᾰτέω, f. ήσω, to resist, oppose, τινί Plat. ; absol.,
Hdt.　From

ἀντιστάτης [ᾰ], ου, ὁ, (ἀνθίσταμαι) an opponent, adversary, Aesch.

ἀντ-ίστημι, Ion. for ἀνθ-ίστημι.

ἀντιστοιχέω, f. ήσω, to stand opposite in rows or pairs,
ἀλλήλοις Xen. : to stand vis-a-vis in a dance, Id.　From

ἀντί-στοιχος, ον, ranged opposite in rows or pairs,
Arist. : standing over against, Eur.

ἀντι-στρᾰτεύομαι, f. -σομαι, Dep. to make war against,
τινι Xen.

ἀντιστρᾰτηγέω, f. ήσω, to be Propraetor, Plut.　From

ἀντιστράτηγος, ὁ, the enemy's general, Thuc.　II.
the Propraetor or Pro-consul, Polyb.

ἀντιστρᾰτοπεδεία, ἡ, an encamping opposite, Polyb.
From

ἀντι-στρᾰτοπεδεύω, f. σω, to encamp over against, τινί
Isocr., Polyb.: mostly in Med. with pf. pass., Hdt., Att.

ἀντι-στρέφω, f. ψω: pf. -έστροφα :—to turn to the opposite side : intr. to wheel about, face about, Xen.　Hence

ἀντιστροφή, ἡ, a turning about : the antistrophé or returning of the chorus, answering to a previous στροφή,
except that they now moved from left to right instead
of from right to left.

ἀντίστροφος, ον, (ἀντιστρέφω) turned so as to face one
another : correlative, coördinate, counterpart, τινι to
a thing, Plat. : also ἀντίστροφός τινος, as if ἀντ. were
a Subst., the correlative or counterpart of, Id. ; Adv.
-φως, coördinately, τινί Id.

ἀντι-σύγκλητος, ἡ, a counter-senate, Plut.

ἀντι-συλλογίζομαι, f. Att. -ιοῦμαι, Dep. to answer by
syllogism, Arist.

ἀντι-συναντάω, f. ήσω, to meet face to face, Anth.

ἀντι-σφαιρίζω, f. σω, to play at ball against, οἱ ἀντι-
σφαιρίζοντες the parties in a game at ball, Xen.

ἀντι-σχεῖν, -σχέσθαι, aor. 2 act. and med. inf. of ἀντ-
έχω.

ἀντ-ίσχω, collat. form of ἀντέχω, Soph., etc.

ἀντίταγμα, ατος, τό, (ἀντιτάσσω) an opposing force, Plut.

ἀντι-τᾰλαντεύω, f. σω, = ἀντισηκόω, Anth.

ἀντίταξις, εως, ἡ, (ἀντιτάσσω) counter-array, Thuc.

ἀντι-τάσσω, Att. -ττω, f. -τάξω, to set opposite to,
range in battle against, τινά τινι Hdt., Aesch., etc. ; τι

πρός τι Aeschin. :—so in Med., Thuc.   II. Med. also *to set oneself against, meet face to face, meet in battle,* Eur., etc. ; τινι Dem. :—Pass. *to be drawn out against,* τινι Hdt., Xen.; πρός τινα Hdt., Xen.; κατά τινα Xen.

ἀντι-τείνω, f. -τενῶ :—*to stretch out in return, to offer in return, to repay,* τι ἀντί τινος Eur.   II. intr. *to strive against, counteract, resist,* τινί, or absol., Hdt., Att.   2. of places, *to lie over against,* τινί Plut.

ἀντι-τείχισμα, ατος, τό, *a counter-fortification,* Thuc.

ἀντι-τέμνω, f. -τεμῶ : aor. 2 -έτεμον :—*to cut against,* i. e. *to provide a remedy* or *antidote,* Eur.

ἀντι-τεχνάομαι, Dep. *to contrive in opposition, counterplan,* c. acc., Hdt.   Hence

ἀντιτέχνησις, εως, ἡ, *counter-manoeuvring, emulation,* Thuc.

ἀντί-τεχνος, ον, (τέχνη) *rivalling in an art* or *craft,* Ar., Plat. ; c. dat., Plat.

ἀντι-τίθημι, f. -θήσω, *to set against, oppose,* c. dat., Simon. : *to contrast, compare,* τί τινι Hdt., Eur. ; also τί τινος, Thuc. ; τι πρός τι Dem.   2. ἀντ. τινά τινι *to match* one *against* the other in battle, Lat. *committere,* ἴσους ἴσοισι ἀντιθείς Eur. :—Pass. *to be matched* one *against* another, Hdt.   3. *to retort, rejoin,* Eur., Thuc.   II. *to deposit in return,* Eur., Xen. :—*to give in return* or *as a recompense,* τί τινος one thing *for* another, Eur.

ἀντι-τῑμάω, f. ήσω, *to honour in return,* τινά Xen. :— f. med. in pass. sense, Id.   II. Med. as law-term, *to fix a counter-estimate of damages,* c. gen. pretii, Plat.

ἀντι-τῑμωρέομαι, f. ήσομαι, Dep. *to avenge oneself on,* τινα Eur., Thuc. ; absol. *to take vengeance,* Ar.

ἀντι-τίνω [ῑ], f. -τίσω [ῑ], *to pay* or *suffer punishment for* a thing, τι Theogn. ; absol., Soph.   Med. *to exact* or *inflict in turn,* τί τινος one thing *for* another, Aesch., Eur.   2. *to avenge, punish,* σὸν φόνον Eur.

ἀντι-τολμάω, f. ήσω, *to dare to stand against* another, πρός τινα Thuc.

ἀντί-τολμος, ον, (τόλμα) *boldly attacking,* Aesch.

ἀντίτομος, ον, (ἀντιτέμνω) *cut as a remedy for* an evil : —ἀντίτομον, τό, *a remedy, antidote,* Hom.; τινος for a thing, Pind.

ἀντίτονος, ον, (ἀντιτείνω) *strained against, resisting* : as Subst., ἀντίτονα, τά, *cords for a ballista,* Plut.

ἀντι-τοξεύω, f. σω, *to shoot arrows in turn,* Xen.

ἀντι-τορέω, f. ήσω, *to bore right through,* c. gen., Il. ; c. acc. *to break open,* Ib .

ἄν-τιτος, ον, poët. for ἀνά-τιτος, *paid back, requited, avenged* : ἄντιτα ἔργα the work *of revenge* or *retribution,* Od. ; παιδός for her son, Il.

ἀντι-τρέφω, f. -θρέψω, *to maintain in turn,* Xen.

ἀντι-τυγχάνω, aor. 2 -έτυχον, *to meet with in return,* τινός Theogn., Thuc.

ἀντί-τῡπος, ον, rarely η, ον, (τύπτω) *repelled* by a hard body, τύπος ἀντ. *blow and counter-blow,* of hammer and anvil, Orac. ap. Hdt. :—of sound, *echoed, echoing,* στόνος Soph. ; κατὰ τὸ ἀντ. by *repercussion,* of an echo, Luc.   2. *corresponding,* as the stamp to the die, ἀντ. τῶν ἀληθινῶν *figuring* or *representing* the true, N. T.   II. act., of a hard body, *repellent, rigid,* Xen. ; of hard ground, ἀντιτύπα ἐπὶ γᾷ πέσε Soph.   2. metaph. of men, *stubborn, obstinate,* Xen.   3. *opposed to,* τινός Aesch. : *adverse,* of events, Xen.

ἀντι-τῠπόω, f. ώσω, *to express as by a figure,* Anth.

ἀντι-τύπτω, f. ψω, *to beat in turn,* Ar., Plat.

ἀντιφερίζω, f. σω, (ἀντιφέρω) *to set oneself against, measure oneself with,* τινί Il., Ar. ; παρά τινα Pind.

ἀντί-φερνος, ον, (φερνή) *instead of a dower,* Aesch.

ἀντι-φέρω, *to set against,* τι ἐπί τινι Anth. :—Med. or Pass. *to set oneself against, fight against,* Hom.

ἀντι-φεύγω, f. -φεύξομαι, *to go into exile in turn,* Eur.

ἀντί-φημι, f. -φήσω, *to speak against, to contradict,* Plat.

ἀντι-φθέγγομαι, f. -ξομαι, Dep. *to return a sound, echo,* Pind., Eur.   II. *to speak against,* Luc.   Hence

ἀντίφθογγος, ον, *of answering sound, imitative,* Anth.

ἀντι-φῐλέω, f. ήσω, *to love in return,* Plat., Xen. Hence

ἀντιφίλησις, εως, ἡ, *return of affection,* Arist.

ἀντι-φῐλοσοφέω, f. ήσω, *to hold contrary tenets,* Luc.

ἀντι-φῐλοτῑμέομαι, Pass. *to be moved by jealousy against,* πρός τι Plut.

ἀντι-φῐλοφρονέομαι, Dep. *to receive kindly in turn,* Plut.

ἀντί-φονος, ον, *in return for slaughter, in revenge for blood,* Aesch., Soph.   II. θάνατοι ἀντ. deaths *by mutual slaughter,* Aesch.

ἀντι-φορτίζομαι, f. Att. -ιοῦμαι, Med. *to take in a return cargo,* Dem.   II. *to import in exchange for exports,* Xen. : also as Pass., *to be received in exchange for the cargo,* Id.

ἀντι-φράσσω, Att. -φράττω, f. ξω, *to barricade, block up,* Xen.

ἀντι-φῠλᾰκή, ἡ, *a watching* one *against* another, Thuc.

ἀντι-φύλαξ [ῠ], ὁ, *one posted to watch* another, Luc.

ἀντι-φῠλάσσω, Att. -ττω, f. ξω, *to watch in turn,* Plat. :—Med. *to be on one's guard against,* τινά Xen.

ἀντι-φωνέω, f. ήσω, *to sound in answer, reply,* Trag.   2. c. acc. rei, *to utter in reply,* Soph. :—c. acc. pers. *to reply to, answer,* Id.

ἀντί-φωνος, ον, (φωνή) *sounding in answer, responsive to,* c. gen., Eur.

ἀντι-χαίρω, *to rejoice in answer to,* τινί Soph. (in aor. 2 pass. part. ἀντιχαρείς).

ἀντι-χᾰρίζομαι, f. med. -ιοῦμαι, Dep. *to shew kindness in turn,* τινί Hdt., Xen.

ἀντι-χειροτονέω, f. ήσω, *to vote against doing a thing,* ἀντ. μὴ παρέχειν Ar. ; absol., Thuc.

ἀντιχορηγέω, f. ήσω, *to be a rival choragus,* τινί *to* another, Dem.   From

ἀντι-χόρηγος, ὁ, *a rival choragus,* Dem., etc.

ἀντι-χράω, (χράω B) *to be sufficient,* like ἀποχράω, only in aor. 1, ἀντέχρησε Hdt.

ἀντί-χριστος, ὁ, *Antichrist,* N. T.

ἀντι-ψάλλω, *to play a lyre in accompaniment to,* τινί Ar.   Hence

ἀντίψαλμος, ον, *responsive, harmonious,* Eur.

ἀντι-ψηφίζομαι, f. Att. -ιοῦμαι, Dep. *to vote against,* πρός τι Plut.

ἀντλέω, f. ήσω, (ἄντλος) *to bale out bilge-water, bale the ship,* Theogn., Eur.   2. generally, *to draw water,* Hdt.   II. metaph. of toil or suffering, *to exhaust, come to the end of,* like Lat. *exantlare* or *exhaurire labores,* Aesch., Eur.   2. *to squander,* Soph. Hence

ἄντλημα, ατος, τό, *a bucket for drawing water,* N. T.

ἀντλία, ἡ, = ἄντλος, *the hold of a ship,* Soph., Ar.   2. *bilge-water, filth,* Ar.

ἄντλος, ὁ, (perh. for ἀνά-τλος, the Root of -τλος being ΤΛΕ, τλάω) :—the hold of a ship, where the bilge-water settles, Lat. sentina, Od. 2. the bilge-water in the hold, Eur.; ἄντλον οὐκ ἐδέξατο let in no bilge-water, metaph. for 'let no enemy come in,' Aesch.; εἰς ἄντλον ἐμβαίνειν πόδα, metaph. for getting into a difficulty, Eur.

ἀντ-οικτείρω, f. ερῶ, to pity in return, τινά Eur.

ἀντ-οικτίζω, = foreg., Thuc.

ἀν-τολή, ἡ, poët. for ἀνα-τολή.

ἀν-τολίη, ἡ, poët. form of ἀντολή, ἀνατολή, Anth.

ἄντομαι, Dep. only in pres. and impf., (ἀντί) = ἀντάω, to meet, in battle, c. dat., Il. :—absol., διπλόος ἤντετο θώρηξ the breastplate doubled (by the belt) met or stopped (the dart), Ib. II. = ἀντιάζω 1. 2, c. acc. pers. to approach with prayers, entreat, Soph., Eur.

ἀντ-όμνυμι, f. -ομοῦμαι, to swear in turn, c. fut. inf., Xen.

ἀντ-ονομάζω, f. σω, to name instead, call by a new name, Thuc.

ἀντ-οφείλω, f. -ήσω, to owe one a good turn, Thuc.

ἀντ-οφθαλμέω, f. ήσω, (ὀφθαλμός) to meet face to face, to face, τινί Polyb., N. T.

ἀντ-οχέομαι, Pass. to drive or ride against, Mosch.

ἀν-τρέπω, poët. for ἀνα-τρέπω.

ἀντριάς, άδος, ἡ, fem. Adj. of a grotto, Anth.

ἄντρον, τό, Lat. antrum, a cave, grot, cavern, Od., Trag.

ἀντρ-ώδης, ες, (εἶδος) full of caves, Xen.

ἄντυξ, υγος, ἡ, like ἴτυς, the edge or rim of anything round or curved : 1. the rim of the round shield, Il. 2. the rail round the front of the chariot, the chariot-rail, Ib.; sometimes double, and therefore ἄντυγες in pl., Ib., Soph. II. post-Hom. 1. in pl. the chariot itself, Soph., Eur. 2. the frame of the lyre, Eur. 3. the orbit of a planet, h. Hom.; the disk of the moon, Mosch.

ἀντ-υποκρίνομαι, ἀντ-υπουργέω, Ion. for ἀνθ-υπ-.

ἀντ-φδός, όν, (ἄδω) singing in answer, responsive, Ar., Anth.

ἀντωμοσία, ἡ, (ἀντ-όμνυμι) an oath or affidavit made one against the other, i. e. by plaintiff and defendant, Plat., etc.

ἀντ-ωνέομαι, impf. -εωνούμην, Dep. to buy instead, Xen. 2. to bid against, ἀλλήλοις Lys.; ὁ ἀντωνούμενος a rival bidder, Dem.

ἀντ-ωπός, όν, (ὤψ) with the eyes opposite, facing, fronting, Luc., Anth.

ἀντ-ωφελέω, f. ήσω, to assist or benefit in turn, τινά Xen. :—Pass. to derive profit in turn, Id.

ἀν-ύβριστος, ον, (ὑβρίζω) not insulted, Plut. II. act. not insolent, decorous, Id.

ἄν-υδρος, ον, (ὕδωρ) wanting water, waterless, of arid countries, Hdt. :—of a corpse, deprived of funeral lustrations, Eur.

ἀν-ὑμέναιος, ον, without the nuptial song, unwedded, Soph., Eur. : neut. pl. as Adv., Soph., Eur.

ἄνυμες, Dor. for ἀνύομεν, 1 pl. of ἀνύω.

ἀν-υμνέω, f. ήσω, to praise in song, c. acc., Eur.

ἀ-νύμφευτος, ον, (νυμφεύω) unwedded, Soph.; ἀν. γονή birth from an ill-starred marriage, Eur.

ἄ-νυμφος, ον, (νύμφη) not bridal, unwedded, Soph.; νύμφη ἄνυμφος a bride that is no bride, unhappy bride, Eur. II. without bride or mistress, μέλαθρα Id.

ἀν-υπέρβλητος, ον, (ὑπερβάλλω) not to be surpassed or outdone, Xen., etc. :—Adv. -τως, Arist.

ἀν-υπεύθυνος, ον, (εὐθῦναι) not liable to give account, irresponsible, Ar., Plat.

ἀνυποδησία, ἡ, a going barefoot, Plat., Xen.; and

ἀνυποδητέω, f. ήσω, to go barefoot, Luc. From

ἀν-υπόδητος, ον, (ὑποδέω) unshod, barefoot, Plat.

ἀν-υπόδικος, ον, not liable to action, Plut.

ἀν-υπόκρῐτος, ον, (ὑποκρίνομαι) without dissimulation, N. T.

ἀν-υπονόητος, ον, (ὑπονοέω) unsuspected, Dem.

ἀν-ύποπτος, ον, without suspicion, unsuspected, Thuc., Xen. :—Adv. -τως, unsuspectedly, Thuc.

ἀν-υπόστατος, ον, (ὑφίστημι) not to be withstood, irresistible, Xen., etc.

ἀν-υπότακτος, ον, (ὑποτάσσω) not made subject, τινι N. T. II. unruly, refractory, of persons, Ib.

ἀνῦσι-εργός, όν, (ἔργον) finishing work, industrious, Theocr. [ᾰ metri grat.].

ἀνύσιμος [ῠ], ον, (ἀνύω) efficacious, effectual, εἴς τι Xen.: Adv. -μως, Sup. -ώτατα, Plat.

ἄνῠσις, εως, ἡ, (ἀνύω) accomplishment, Hom.

ἀνυστός, όν, (ἀνύω) to be accomplished, practicable, Eur.; ὡς ἀνυστόν, like ὡς δυνατόν, σιγῇ ὡς ἀν. as silently as possible, Xen.

ἀνῠτικός, ή, όν, = ἀνυστικός, Xen.

ἄνῠτο, Dor. for ἤνυτο = ἤνύετο, 3 sing. impf. pass. of ἀνύω.

ἀνύτω or ἀνύτω, Att. form of ἀνύω.

ἀν-ὑφαίνω, f. ἀνῶ, to weave anew, renew, Plat.

ἀν-υψόω, f. ώσω, to raise up, exalt, Anth., in Med.

ἀνύω, Att. ἀνύτω, or ἀνύτω: impf. ἤνυον: f. ἀνύσω [ᾰνῠ-]: aor. 1 ἤνῠσα, Ep. ἄνυσα: pf. ἤνῠκα :—Pass., pf. ἤνῠσμαι: aor. 1 ἠνύσθην. (From the Verb ἄνω): —to effect, achieve, accomplish, complete, Lat. conficere, c. acc. rei, Hom., etc.; absol., οὐδὲν ἤνυε he did no good, Hdt.; c. acc. et inf. to bring to pass that . . , Soph. :—Med. to accomplish for one's own advantage, Od., Plat., etc. 2. to make an end of, destroy, Hom., etc. 3. to finish a journey, ὅσσον νηῦς ἤνυσεν much as a ship can do, Od.; so, ἀν. θαλάσσης ὕδωρ to make its way over the sea water, Ib. 4. in Att. absol. to make one's way, πρὸς πόλιν Soph.; ἐπὶ ἀκτάν Eur.; also, θάλαμον ἀνύτειν to reach the bridal chamber, Soph.; with inf., ἤνυσε περᾶν succeeded in crossing, Aesch.; and with an Adj., εἶναι being omitted, εὐδαίμων ἀνύσει will come to be, happy, Soph. 5. Pass. of Time, to come to an end, Theocr. 6. in Pass. also of persons, to grow up, Aesch. 7. to get, procure, φορβάν Soph., etc. II. with a partic., οὐκ ἀνύω φθονέουσα I gain nothing by grudging, Il. III. to do quickly, make haste, Ar.; then, like φθάνω, ἄνυε πράττων make haste about it, Id.; ἄνυσον ὑποδησάμενος make haste and get your shoes on, Id.; also ἀνύσας with an imper., ἄνοιγ', ἄνοιγ' ἀνύσας make haste and open the door, Id.; ἀνύσας τρέχε, λέγ' ἀνύσας Id., etc.

ΆΝΩ [ᾱ generally], inf. ἄνειν, part. ἄνων, impf. ἦνον :— radic. form of ἀνύω, to accomplish, achieve, finish, ὁδόν Od.; οὐδὲν ἦνον Eur. II. Pass., of the close of a period of time, νὺξ ἄνεται night is drawing to a close, Il.; ἔτος ἀνόμενον the waning year, Hdt. :—generally to be finished, Il.; ἤνετο τὸ ἔργον Hdt.

ἄνω, Adv. : (ἀνά): I. implying Motion, up, upwards,

Hom., etc.; ἄνω ἰόντι going *up the country*,(i.e.*inland*), Hdt.   **II.** implying Rest, *up, aloft, on high*, Soph., Plat., etc.   **2.** *on earth*, as opp. to the world below, Soph.; οἱ ἄνω *the living*, opp. to οἱ κάτω *the dead*, Id.   **3.** *in heaven*, as opp. to earth, οἱ ἄνω θεοί *the gods above*, Lat. *superi*, Id.   **4.** generally of position, ἄνω καθῆσθαι to sit *in the upper quarter* of the city, i. e. the Pnyx, Dem.; ἡ ἄνω βουλή, i. e. the Areopagus, Plut.   **5.** geographically, *on the north, northward*, Hdt.   **6.** *inward from the coast*, Id., Xen.; ὁ ἄνω βασιλεύς the king of Persia, Hdt.   **7.** of Time, *formerly, of old*, Plat., etc.   **8.** *above*, like Lat. *supra*, in referring to a passage, Id.   **9.** of tones in the voice, Plut.   **III.** ἄνω καὶ κάτω, *up and down, to and fro*, Eur., Ar., etc.   **2.** *upside down, topsy-turvy*, Lat. *susque deque*, τὰ μὲν ἄνω κάτω θήσω, τὰ δὲ κάτω ἄνω Hdt.; ἄνω τε καὶ κάτω στρέφων Aesch., etc.
   B. as Prep. with gen. *above*, Hdt.
   C. Comp. ἀνωτέρω, absol. *higher*, Aesch.; *further*, Hdt.   **2.** c. gen. *above, beyond*, Id.   **II.** Sup. ἀνωτάτω *highest*, Id., etc.

ἀν-ῶ [ᾰ], aor. 2 subj. of ἀνίημι.

ἄνωγα, pf. with pres. sense, 1 pl. ἄνωγμεν: imper. ἄνωγε or ἄνωχθι, 3 sing. ἀνωγέτω or ἀνώχθω; 2 pl. ἀνώγετε or ἄνωχθε; 3 sing. subj. ἀνώγῃ; inf. ἀνωγέμεν:—plqpf. with impf. sense, ἠνώγειν and without augm. ἀνώγειν, Ion. ἠνώγεα:—but the form ἀνώγει in most places of Hom. is present, from ἀνώγω, from which also come 2 dual ἀνώγετον, also impf. ἤνωγον or ἄνωγον, fut. ἀνώξω, aor. 1 ἤνωξα, subj. ἀνώξομεν, Ep. for –ωμεν:—lastly the impf. ἠνώγεον implies another pres. ἀνωγέω.   *To command, order*, also *to advise, desire, urge*:—c. acc. pers. et inf., σιωπᾶν λαὸν ἀνώγει *bade the people keep silence*, Il.; also c. dat. pers., Od.; c. acc. pers., without inf., θυμὸς ἄνωγέ με *my spirit bids me*, Hom. (Deriv. uncertain.)

ἀνώ-γαιον or **ἀνώ-γεων**, τό, (ἄνω, γαῖα) *anything raised from the ground; the upper floor of a house*, used as a granary, Xen.; as a dining-room, Lat. *coenaculum*, N. T.

ἀνῶγεν, 3 sing. impf. of ἀνοίγνυμι; but   **II.** ἄνωγεν, of ἄνωγα.

ἄνωγμεν, 1 pl. of ἄνωγα.

ἀνώγω, v. ἄνωγα.

ἀν-ώδυνος, ον, (ὀδύνη) *free from pain*, Soph.   **II.** act. *allaying pain*, Anth.

ἄνωθεν, **-θε**, (ἄνω) Adv. of Place, *from above, from on high*, Hdt., Trag., etc.; ὕδατος ἄνωθεν γενομένου, i. e. *rain*, Thuc.: *from the upper country, from inland*, Id.   **2.** = ἄνω, *above, on high*, Trag.; οἱ ἄν. *the living*, opp. to οἱ κάτω, Aesch.:—c. gen., Hdt.   **II.** of Time, *from the beginning*, Plat., Dem.:—*by descent*, Theocr.; τὰ ἄν. *first principles*, Plat.   **2.** *over again, anew*, N. T.

ἀν-ωθέω, f. ώσω, *to push up, push off from shore*,Od.   **2.** Med. *to push back from oneself, to repel, repulse*, Hdt.

ἀν-ωϊστί [ῐ], Adv. of sq., *unlooked for*, Od.

ἀν-ώϊστος, ον, (οἴομαι) *unlooked for, unexpected*, Il., Mosch.

ἀν-ώϊστος, ον, Ion. for ἀν-οιστός, *referred to* a person, ἔς τινα Hdt.

ἀν-ώλεθρος, ον, (ὄλεθρος) *indestructible*, Plat.; Ep. ἀν-όλεθρος *having escaped ruin*, Il.

ἀνωμᾰλία, ἡ, *unevenness*, Plat., etc.   **2.** of persons, *irregularity*, Aeschin. From

ἀν-ώμᾰλος, ον, (ὁμαλός) *uneven, irregular*, Plat.: τὸ ἀν. *unevenness* of ground, Thuc.   **2.** of fortune, Id.

ἀνωμοτί, Adv. *without oath*, Hdt. From

ἀν-ώμοτος, ον, (ὄμνυμι) *unsworn, not bound by oath*, Eur.; θεῶν ἀνώμοτος *without swearing by* the gods, Id.   **II.** *not sworn to*, εἰρήνη Dem.

ἀν-ωνόμαστος, ον, (ὀνομάζω) *nameless, indescribable, ineffable*, Eur., Ar.

ἀν-ώνῠμος, ον, (ὄνυμα, Aeol. for ὄνομα) *without name, nameless*, Od., Hdt., etc.   **II.** *nameless, inglorious*, Pind., Eur., Plat.

ἀν-ῷξα, aor. 1 of ἀνοίγνυμι.

ἀνῷξαι, aor. 1 inf. of *ἀνώγω: v. ἄνωγα.

ἀνώξω, f. of ἀνώγω: v. ἄνωγα.

ἀνωρία, Ion. **-ίη**, ἡ, *untimeliness*, ἀν. τοῦ ἔτεος *the bad season* of the year, Hdt. From

ἄν-ωρος, ον, = ἄωρος, Hdt.

ἀν-ωρύομαι [ῠ], Dep. *to howl aloud*, Anth.

ἀν-ῶσα, aor. 1 of ἀνωθέω.

ἀνῶσαι, Ion. for ἀνοῖσαι = ἀνενέγκαι, aor. 1 inf. of ἀναφέρω.

ἀνώτατος, η, ον, Sup. Adj. formed from ἄνω, *topmost*, Hdt.:—Adv. ἀνωτάτω, v. ἄνω.

ἀνωτερικός, ή, όν, *upper, inland*, N. T. From

ἀνώτερος, α, ον, Comp. Adj. formed from ἄνω, *higher*, Arist.:—Adv. ἀνωτέρω, v. ἄνω.

ἀν-ωφελής, ές, (ὠφελέω) *unprofitable, useless*, Aesch., Soph., etc.   **2.** *hurtful, prejudicial*, Thuc.; τινι *to one*, Plat.: Adv. –λῶς, Arist.

ἀν-ωφέλητος, ον, (ὠφελέω) *unprofitable, useless*, Soph.; τινι *to one*, Aesch.

ἄνωχθι, **ἀνώχθω**, 2 and 3 sing. imper. of ἄνωγα:—ἄνωχθε, 2 pl.

ἀν-ώχῠρος, ον, (ὀχυρός) *not fortified*, Xen.

ἄξαι, **ἄξασθαι**, aor. 1 inf. act. and med. of ἄγνυμι.

ἄξας, aor. 1 part. of ἀΐσσω.

ἄ-ξεινος, ον, Ion. for ἄ-ξενος.

ἀξέμεν, **ἀξέμεναι**, Ep. fut. inf. of ἄγω.

ἄ-ξενος, Ion. and poët. **ἄ-ξεινος**, ον, *inhospitable*, of persons, Hes., Plat.; of places, Soph., Eur.:—Comp. and Sup. –ώτερος, –ώτατος, Eur.   **II.** Ἄξεινος or Ἄξενος (sc. πόντος), *the Axine*, afterwards called *the Euxine* (*Euxeinus qui nunc Axenus ille fuit* Ov.), Pind., Eur.

ἄ-ξεστος, ον, (ξέω) *unhewn, unwrought*, Soph., Anth.

ἀξία, Ion. **-ίη**, ἡ, (ἄξιος) *the worth* or *value* of a thing, c. gen., Hdt., Eur.; *money-value, price, amount*, Hdt.; τῆς ἀξίας τιμᾶσθαι to estimate the penalty *at the real amount*, Plat.; κατ' ἀξίαν τῆς οὐσίας Xen.   **2.** of persons, *worth, reputation, rank*, Thuc., etc.   **3.** generally, a man's *due*, his *deserts*, τὴν ἀξίαν λαμβάνειν, τῆς ἀξίας τυγχάνειν *to get one's deserts*, Hdt., Ar.; κατ' ἀξίαν according to *desert, duly*, Eur., Plat.; παρὰ τὴν ἀξίαν, οὐ κατ' ἀξίαν Thuc., Dem.

ἀξι-άγαστος, ον, *worth admiring, admirable*, Xen.

ἀξι-άκοῠστος, ον, *worth hearing*, Xen.

ἀξι-ακρόατος, ον, (ἀκροάομαι) *worth listening to*, Xen.

ἀξι-αφήγητος, Ion. **ἀξι-απήγ–**, ον, (ἀφηγέομαι) *worth telling*, Hdt.

ἀξι-έπαινος, ον, *praiseworthy*, Xen.

ἀξι-έραστος, ον, *worthy of love*, Xen.

ἀξίνη [ῐ], ἡ, an axe-head, Il.: battle-axe, Ib.: generally, an axe, Xen., N. T. (Deriv. unknown.)

ἀξιο-βίωτος, ον, worth living for, Xen.

ἀξιο-εργός, όν, (ἔργον) capable of work, Xen.

ἀξιό-ζηλωτος, ον, enviable, Plut.

ἀξιο-θαύμαστος, ον, wonder-worthy, Xen.

ἀξιο-θέᾱτος, Ion. -ητος, ον, well worth seeing, Hdt., Xen.

ἀξιό-θρηνος, ον, worthy of lamentation, Eur.

ἀξιο-κοινώνητος, ον, (κοινωνέω) worthy of one's society, Plat.

ἀξιό-κτητος, ον, (κτάομαι) worth getting, Xen.

ἀξιό-λογος, ον, (λέγω) worthy of mention, noteworthy, Hdt., Plat., etc.; πόλεμος ἀξιολογώτατος Thuc. :—Adv. -γως, Xen.   2. of persons, of note, important, Thuc.

ἀξιο-μᾰκάριστος [κᾰ], ον, worthy to be deemed happy, Xen.

ἀξιό-μᾰχος, ον, (μάχομαι) a match for another in battle or war, τινι Hdt., Thuc.; πρός τινα Plut.: absol., Hdt., etc.   2. c. inf. sufficient in strength or number to do a thing, Id. Adv. -χως, Plut.

ἀξιο-μνημόνευτος, ον, (μνημονεύω) worthy of mention, Plat., Xen.; shapely, beautiful, Manetho.

ἀξιό-νῑκος, ον, (νίκη) worthy of victory, Xen.; c. inf., ἀξιονικότερος ἔχειν τοῦτο τὸ κράτος more worthy to hold this power, Hdt.

ἀξιο-πενθής, ές, (πένθος) lamentable, Eur.

ἀξιό-πιστος, ον, trustworthy, Plat., Dem.; εἴς τι in a thing, Xen.

ἀξιο-πρεπής, ές, (πρέπω) becoming, goodly, Xen.

ἀξι-όρᾱτος, ον, worth seeing, Luc.

ἄξιος, ία, ιον, (ἄγω IV, and so properly) weighing as much, of like value, worth as much as, c. gen., Il., Hdt.; οὐδ' ἑνὸς ἄξιοί εἰμεν Ἕκτορος we are not worth one Hector, Il.; πάντων ἄξιον ἦμαρ, Lat. instar omnium, Ib.; πολλοῦ ἄξιος worth much, Xen.; πλείστου ἄξιον, quantivis pretii, Thuc.; so, παντός, τοῦ παντὸς ἄξιον Plat.; λόγου ἄξιος, = ἀξιόλογος, Hdt., etc. :—opp. to these are οὐδενὸς ἄξ. Theogn.; ὀλίγου, σμικροῦ ἄξ. Plat., etc.   2. c. dat. pers., σοὶ δ' ἄξιόν ἐστιν ἀμοιβῆς 'tis worth a return to thee, i. e. will bring thee a return, Od.; πολλοῦ or πλείστου ἄξιον εἶναί τινι Xen., etc.   3. absol. worthy, goodly, of persons and things, Od., etc.; in Att. it sometimes has an opposite sense, of a proper value, cheap, Ar.   b. of things, deserved, meet, due, δίκη Soph.; χάρις Xen.   4. sufficient for, c. gen., Dem.   II. worthy of, deserving, meet for, c. gen. rei, φυγῆς, γέλωτος Eur.; c. gen. rei et dat. pers., ἡμῖν δ' Ἀχιλεὺς ἄξιος τιμῆς is worthy of honour at our hands, Eur.; πολλῶν ἀγαθῶν ἄξιος ὑμῖν Ar.   2. c. inf., πεφάσθαι ἄξιός worthy to be killed, Il.; ἄξιός εἰμι πληγὰς λαβεῖν I deserve a flogging, Ar.   3. ἄξιόν [ἐστι] 'tis meet, fit, due, Il., Hdt.; c. dat. pers. et inf., τῇ πόλει ἄξιον ξυλλαβεῖν τὸν ἄνδρα 'tis meet for the city, is her duty, to arrest the man, Ar. :—the inf. is sometimes omitted, ἄξιον γὰρ Ἑλλάδι 'tis meet in the eyes of Hellas [so to do], Id.   III. Adv. ἀξίως, c. gen., worthily of, Hdt. :—absol., Soph.

ἀξιό-σκεπτος, ον, (σκέπτομαι) worth considering, Xen.

ἀξιο-σπούδαστος, ον, (σπουδάζομαι) worthy of zealous endeavours, Xen.

ἀξιο-στράτηγος, ον, worthy of being general, Xen.

ἀξιο-τέκμαρτος, ον, (τεκμαίρομαι) worthy of being brought in evidence, credible, Xen.

ἀξιό-φίλητος [ῐ], ον, (φιλέω) worth loving, Xen.

ἀξιό-χρεως, εων, gen. ω: Ion. ἀξιόχρεος, ον, neut. pl. ἀξιόχρεα: (χρέος) :—worthy of a thing, and so,   I. absol., like ἀξιόλογος, note-worthy, considerable, notable, Hdt., Thuc.   2. serviceable, sufficient, αἰτίη Hdt.; ἀξ. ἐγγυηταί trustworthy, substantial, Plat.   II. c. inf. able, sufficient to do, Hdt., Eur., etc.   III. c. gen. rei, worthy, deserving of, Hdt., Dem.

ἀξιόω, f. ώσω: pf. ἠξίωκα :—Pass., f. ἀξιωθήσομαι and in med. form ἀξιώσομαι: aor. 1 ἠξιώθην: pf. ἠξίωμαι: (ἄξιος) :—to think or deem worthy of a thing, whether of reward, Eur., Xen.; or of punishment, Hdt., Plat. :—Pass. to be thought worthy, τινός Hdt., Eur., etc.   2. c. acc. pers. to esteem, honour, Trag.   II. c. acc. pers. et inf. to think one worthy to do or be, Eur., etc.:—Pass., Aesch., etc.   2. to think fit, expect, require, demand that, Lat. postulare, ἀξ. τινα ἐλθεῖν Hdt., etc.   III. c. inf. only, ἀξ. κομίζεσθαι, τυγχάνειν to think one has a right to receive, expect to receive, Thuc. :—Pass. to be required to do, Dem.   2. to think fit, expect, consent, resolve, ἀξιῶ θανεῖν Soph.; εἴ τις ἀξιοῖ μαθεῖν if he deigns to learn, Aesch.:—so in Med., ἀξιοῦσθαι μέλειν to deign to care for, Id., etc.; also as a real Med., οὐκ ἀξιεύμενος not deeming himself worthy, Hdt.   IV. to claim, νικᾶν ἠξίουν claimed the victory, Thuc.: absol. to make a claim, Id.   V. to hold an opinion, Dem.; ἐν τῷ τοιῷδε ἀξιοῦντι in such a state of opinion, Thuc.

ἀξίωμα, ατος, τό, (ἀξιόω) that of which one is thought worthy, an honour, Eur.; γάμων ἀξ. honour of marriage, Id.   2. honour, reputation, Lat. dignitas, Eur., Thuc.   3. rank, position, Thuc.:—of things, worth, quality, Id.   II. that which is thought fit, a decision, purpose, Soph., Dem.   2. in Mathematics, a self-evident theorem, an axiom, Arist.

ἀξίωσις, gen. εως, Ion. ιος, ἡ, (ἀξιόω) a thinking worthy, Hdt.   2. a being thought worthy, reputation, Thuc.   II. a demand or claim, Id.   III. a thinking fit, an opinion, principle, maxim, Id.   IV. ἀξ. τῶν ὀνομάτων the meaning of words, Id.

ἀ-ξόανος, ον, (ξόανον) without carved images, Luc.

ἀξόνιος, ον, (ἄξων) belonging to the axle, Anth.

ἀ-ξυγκρότητος, ον, (συγκροτέω) not welded together by the hammer :—metaph. of rowers, not trained to keep time, Thuc.

ἄ-ξυλος, ον, (ξύλον) with no timber, timberless, ἄξυλος ὕλη a coppice, brushwood, Il. :—others take it to be a wood from which no timber has been cut, a thick wood.   II. without wood, Hdt.

ἀ-ξυμ-, ἀ-ξυν-, v. ἀ-συμ-, ἀ-συν-.

ἀ-ξύστατος, ον, v. ἀ-σύστατος.

ἄξων, ονος, ὁ, (ἄγω) an axle, Lat. axis, Il., etc.   II. οἱ ἄξονες, the wooden tablets of Solon's laws, made to turn upon an axis, Plut.

ἄοζος, ὁ, a servant, attendant, Aesch. (Perh. from ἀ copul., ὄζος; cf. ἀ-κόλουθος.)

ἀοιδή, Att. contr. ᾠδή, ἡ, (ἀείδω) song, a singing, whether the art of song, Hom.; or the act of singing, song, Il.   2. the thing sung, a song, Hom., etc.   3. the subject of song, Od.

ἀοιδιάω, = ἀείδω, to sing, Od.

ἀοίδιμος, ον, (ἀοιδή) sung of, famous in song, Hdt. : in bad sense, notorious, infamous, Il.

ἀοιδο-θέτης, ου, ὁ, (τίθημι) a lyric poet, Anth.

ἀοιδο-μάχος [ᾰ], ον, (μάχομαι) fighting with verses, Anth.

ἀοιδο-πόλος, ὁ, (πολέω) one busied with song, a poet, Anth.

ἀοιδός, ὁ, (ἀείδω) a singer, minstrel, bard, Lat. vates, Hom., Hdt. ; c. gen., χρησμῶν ἀοιδός Eur. ; of the cock, Theocr.   2. as fem. songstress, of the nightingale, Hes.; of the Sphinx, Soph.   3. an enchanter, Lat. incantator, Id.   II. as Adj. tuneful, musical, ὄρνις ἀοιδοτάτη Eur.

ἀοιδο-τόκος, ον, (τίκτω) inspiring song, Anth.

ἀ-οίκητος, ον, (οἰκέω) uninhabited, Hdt.   II. houseless, Dem.

ἄ-οικος, ον, houseless, homeless, Hes., Soph., etc.   II. ἄοικος εἰσοίκησις a homeless, i. e. miserable, home, Soph.

ἄ-οινος, ον, without wine, ἄοινοι χοαί, such as were offered to the Erinyes, Aesch. ; hence Soph. calls the Erinyes ἄοινοι;—ἀοίνοις ἐμμανεῖς θυμώμασιν frantic with sober, deliberate rage, Soph.   2. of men, drinking no wine, sober, Xen. ; of a place, having none, Id.

ἄ-οκνος, ον, without hesitation, untiring, Hes., Soph., Thuc.

ἀ-ολλής, ές, (ᾰ copul., εἴλω, cf. ἀλής) all together, in throngs, shoals or crowds, Hom., Soph., etc.

ἀολλίζω, f. ίσω: Ep. aor. 1 ἀόλλισσα:—Pass., Ep. aor. 1 inf. ἀολλισθήμεναι: (ἀολλής):—to gather together, Il.:—Pass. to come together, assemble, Ib.   II. of things, to gather together, heap up, Anth.

ἄ-οπλος, ον, without shields (ὅπλα), without heavy armour, Thuc., etc.: generally, unarmed, Plat. ; ἅρμα ἄοπλ. a chariot without scythes, Xen.

ἄορ, ἄορος, τό, (ἀείρω) a sword hung in a belt (cf. ἀορτήρ), a hanger, sword, Hom. : he also uses a masc. acc. pl., ἄορας. [ᾰ in ἄορ; but in trisyll. cases also ᾱ.]

ἀ-όρᾱτος, ον, unseen, not to be seen, invisible, Plat., etc.   II. act. without sight, Luc.

ἀοργησία, ἡ, a defect in the passion of anger, 'lack of gall,' Arist. From

ἀ-όργητος, ον, (ὀργή) incapable of anger, Arist.

ἀ-όριστος, ον, (ὁρίζω) without boundaries, Thuc.   II. undefined, indefinite, Dem., etc.

ἄ-ορνος, ον, (ὄρνις) without birds, Soph.   II. Ἄορνος, ὁ, lake Avernus, Strab.

ἀορτέω, lengthd. form of ἀείρω, only in aor. 1 pass. part. ἀορτηθείς, suspended, Anth.

ἀορτή, ῆρος, ὁ, (ἀείρω) a strap to hang anything to, a sword-belt, Hom. : a knapsack-strap, Od.

ἄορτο, Ion. for ἤορτο, 3 sing. plqpf. pass. of ἀείρω.

ἀοσσέω, aor. 1 inf. ἀοσσῆσαι, (ἄοσσος) to help, τινί Mosch. Hence

ἀοσσητήρ, ῆρος, ὁ, an assistant, helper, aider, Hom.

ἄ-ουτος, ον, (οὐτάω) unwounded, unhurt, Il.

ἀ-όχλητος, ον, (ὀχλέω) undisturbed, calm, Luc.

ἀπαγγελία, ἡ, a report, as of an ambassador, Dem.   2. a narrative, recital, Thuc., Plat. From

ἀπ-αγγέλλω, f. -αγγελῶ, Ion. έω: aor. 1 -ήγγειλα:— Pass., pf. -ήγγελμαι: aor. 1 -ηγγέλθην, later -ηγγέ-

λην: 1. of a messenger, to bring tidings, report, announce, τί τινι Il., Hdt., etc. ; τι πρός τινα Aesch., etc.; ἀπ. τι οἴκαδε to carry a report home, Plat. :—absol., πάλιν ἀπ. to bring back tidings, report in answer, Od. :—Pass., ἐξ ὧν ἀπηγγέλλετο as he was reported, Dem. ; c. part., ἀπηγγέλθη ἐκκεκλεμμένος was reported to have been stolen away, Hdt.   2. of a speaker or writer, to relate, narrate, Id., Att.   Hence

ἀπαγγελτήρ, ῆρος, ὁ, a messenger, Anth.

ἄπᾰγε, Adv. (prop. imper. of ἀπάγω, in intr. sense) away! begone! hands off! Lat. apage! Eur., Ar.

ἀ-πᾱγής, ές, (πήγνυμι) not firm or stiff, of Persian caps, Hdt.

ἀπ-ᾱγῑνέω, Ion. for ἀπάγω, only in pres. and impf., esp. of paying tribute, Hdt.

ἀπᾱγόρευσις, εως, ἡ, failure of strength, exhaustion, Plut., Luc. : and

ἀπᾱγορευτέον, verb. Adj. one must give up, Luc. From

ἀπ-ᾱγορεύω, mostly in pres. and impf., (ἀπερῶ is used as fut., ἀπεῖπον as aor., ἀπείρηκα as pf., and ἀπορρηθήσομαι, ἀπερρήθην, ἀπείρημαι as pass. fut., aor. and pf.) : —to forbid, ἀπ. τινὶ μὴ ποιεῖν τι Hdt., Att. ; τινά Xen.   2. to dissuade, Hdt.   II. intr. to bid farewell to, c. dat., ἀπαγ. τῷ πολέμῳ to give up, renounce war, Plat. ; c. part. to give up doing, Xen. :—absol. to give up, fail, sink, Id. ; of things, τὰ ἀπαγορεύοντα worn out and useless, Id.

ἀπ-ᾱγριόομαι, pf. -ηγρίωμαι, Pass. to become wild or savage, Soph.

ἀπ-αγχονίζω, f. σω, (ἀγχόνη) to strangle, Anth.

ἀπ-άγχω, f. -άγξω, to strangle, throttle, Od., Ar. ; to choke with anger, Ar. :—Med. and Pass. to hang oneself, to be hanged, Hdt., Att. : to be ready to choke, Ar.

ἀπ-άγω, f. -άξω, to lead away, carry off, Od., Trag. :— Med. to take away for or with oneself, Hdt., Trag. :— Pass., ἐς ὀξὺ ἀπηγμένος brought to a point, tapering off, Hdt.   2. intr. (sub. ἑαυτόν) to retire, withdraw, march away, Id., Xen. ; cf. ἄπαγε.   II. to bring back, bring home, Hom., Att.   III. to return what one owes, render, ῥαy, τὸν φόρον Ar., Thuc.   IV. to arrest and carry off, παρά τινα Hdt. :—esp. as Att. law-term, to bring before a magistrate and accuse, Dem.:— then, to carry off to prison, Plat., etc.   V. to lead away from the subject, Id., etc.   Hence

ἀπᾱγωγή, ἡ, a leading away, Xen.   II. payment of tribute, Hdt.   III. as Att. law-term, a process by which a person caught in the act (ἐπ' αὐτοφώρῳ) might be arrested and brought before the Magistrates, Oratt. : —the written complaint laid before the Court, Lysias.

ἀπ-ᾱδεῖν, Ion. -έειν, aor. 2 inf. of ἀφ-ανδάνω.

ἀπ-ᾴδω, f. -ᾴσομαι, to sing out of tune, be out of tune, Plat.   II. metaph. to dissent, ἀπ' ἀλλήλων Id.   2. to wander away, ἀπὸ τοῦ ἐρωτήματος Id.

ἀπ-αείρω, aor. 1 -ήειρα, poët. for ἀπαίρω, to depart, Eur. :—Med. to depart from, c. gen., Il.

ἀπ-ᾱθᾰνᾰτίζω, f. σω, to aim at immortality, Plat., Arist.

ἀπάθεια, ἡ, want of sensation, insensibility, Arist. From

ἀ-πᾰθής, ές, (πάθος) not suffering or having suffered, without experience of a thing, c. gen., Theogn., Hdt., Att. :—absol., Ib.   II. without passion or feeling : —Adv., ἀπαθῶς ἔχειν to be without feeling, Plut.

ἀπαί, poët. for ἀπό, Hes.

ἀπ-αιγειρόομαι, Pass. *to be changed into a poplar*, Strab.

ἀ-παιδάγώγητος, ον, *without teacher* or *guide*, Arist. : *uneducated, untaught*, τινος in a thing, Id.

ἀπαιδευσία, ἡ, *want of education*, Thuc., Plat. **2.** *ignorance, boorishness, coarseness*, Plat., etc. **II.** c. gen., ἀπαιδευσίᾳ ὀργῆς *from want of control over passion*, Thuc. From

ἀ-παίδευτος, ον, (παιδεύω) *uneducated*, Eur., Plat. :— c. gen. *uninstructed in* a thing, Xen. **2.** *ignorant, boorish, coarse*, Eur., Plat. **II.** Adv., ἀπαιδεύτως ἔχειν to be *without education*, Eur.

ἀπαιδία, ἡ, (ἄπαις) *childlessness*, Hdt., Soph.

ἀπ-αιθριάζω, f. σω, (αἰθρία) *to clear away* clouds *from the sky*, Ar.

ἀπ-αίνυμαι and ἀπο-αίνυμαι, Dep. *to take away, withdraw*, τί τινος Od. : *to pluck off*, Mosch.

ἀπαιολάω, f. ήσω, *to perplex, confound*, Eur. From

ἀπ-αιόλη, ἡ, (αἰόλος) *cheating, fraud*, personified in Ar.

ἀπαιόλημα, ατος, τό, =foreg., Aesch., Ar.

ἀπ-αιρεθέω, Ion. for ἀφ-αιρεθῶ, aor. 1 pass. subj. of ἀφαιρέω :—ἀπ-αραιρημένος, Ion. pf. part.

ἀπ-αίρω, Ion. impf. ἀπαίρεσκον : f. ἀπᾰρῶ : aor. 1 ἀπῆρα : pf. ἀπῆρκα :—*to lift off, carry off, take away, to remove from*, τί τινος Eur.: absol., Hdt. **II.** *to lead away* a sea or land force, Id.:—intr. (sub. ναῦς, στρατόν, etc.), *to sail* or *march away, depart*, Id., Att. ; c. gen., ἀπαίρειν χθονός *to depart from* the land, Eur. : c. acc. cogn., ἀπ. πρεσβείαν *to set out on* an embassy, Dem.

ἄ-παις, ἄπαιδος, ὁ, ἡ, *childless*, Hdt.; τὰς ἄπαιδας οὐσίας her *childless estate*, Soph. :—c. gen., ἀπ. ἔρσενος γόνου *without* male heirs, Hdt.; τέκνων ἄπαιδα Eur.; etc. **II.** Νυκτὸς παῖδες ἄπαιδες children of Night, *yet children none*, Aesch.

ἀπ-αΐσσω, Att. -ᾴσσω, f. ξω, *to spring from* a height, c. gen., Il. **II.** *to dart away*, Soph. [ἀπᾱ- Hom.]

ἀπ-αισχύνομαι [ῠ], f. -ῠνοῦμαι, Dep. *to refuse through shame*, Plat.

ἀπ-αιτέω, f. ήσω, *to demand back, demand*, Hdt. :—ἀπ. τί τινα *to demand* something *of* one, Id., Att. ; ἀπ. ὅπλα τοῦ πατρός Soph. ; also, χάριν ἀπ. τινα Plat. **II.** Pass., of things, *to be demanded in payment*, Hdt. **2.** of persons, *to have demanded of* one, ἀπαιτεῖσθαι εὐεργεσίαν Xen. Hence

ἀπαίτησις, εως, ἡ, *a demanding back*, Hdt.; ἀπ. ποιεῖσθαι *to make a formal demand*, Dem.

ἀπαιτίζω, only in pres. part., = ἀπαιτέω, *to demand back*, χρήματα Od.

ἀπ-αιωρέομαι, Pass. *to hang down from above, hang suspended, hover about*, Hes.

ἀπ-ακρῑβόομαι, Pass. *to be finished off, highly finished*, Plat., Isocr. **II.** as Med. *to finish off*, Anth., Luc.

ἀ-πάλαιστρος, ον, (πάλαιστρα) *not trained in the palaestra, unskilled in wrestling*, Anth. : *awkward*, Cic.

ἀπ-άλαλκε, 3 sing. aor. 2 opt. ἀπαλάλκοι, (with no pres. in use, v. ἄλαλκε) :—*to ward off* something *from* one, τί τινος Hom. ; Ep. inf. ἀπαλαλκέμεν, Theocr.

ἀ-πάλαμος, ον, poët. for ἀ-πάλαμος, *without hands, helpless, good for naught*, Il. **II.** *impracticable, reckless, lawless*, ἔρδειν ἔργ᾽ ἀπάλαμνα Solon. ; ἀπάλαμνόν τι πάσχειν Eur.

ἀ-πάλᾰμος, ον, (πᾰλάμη) like ἀπάλαμνος, *helpless*, Hes., Pind. [ἀπ- metri grat.]

ἀπ-ᾰλάομαι, Pass. *to go astray, wander*, Hes.

ἀπ-αλγέω, f. ήσω, *to feel no more pain at* a thing, τι Thuc. ; ἀπ. τὸ πένθος *to put away* sorrow, Plut.

ἀπ-αλείφω, f. ψω : pf. -αλήλιφα :—*to wipe off, expunge* from a register, Dem. ; ἀπ. τι *to cancel* it, Aeschin.

ἀπ-αλέξω, f. -αλεξήσω, *to ward* something *off from* a person, τί τινος Il. **2.** *reversely to keep* a person *from suffering* something, τινά τινος Od. **II.** Med. *to defend oneself*, ἀπαλέξασθαί [τι] Soph.

ἀπ-αληθεύω, *to speak the whole truth*, Xen., in Med.

ἀπ-αλθαίνομαι, f. -ήσομαι, Dep. *to heal thoroughly*, Il.

ἀπαλλαγή, ἡ, (ἀπαλλάσσω) *deliverance, release, relief from* a thing, *riddance* of it, πόνων, ξυμφορᾶς Aesch., Soph., etc. **2.** absol. *a divorce*, Eur. **II.** (from Pass.) *a going away, a means of getting away, an escape, departure*, Hdt.; ἡ ἀπ. ἀλλήλων *separation from one another*, of combatants, Thuc. **2.** ἀπ. τοῦ βίου *departure* from life, Xen. ; ψυχῆς ἀπὸ σώματος Plat.

ἀπαλλακτέον, verb. Adj. of ἀπαλλάσσω, *one must release from*, τινά τινος Plut. **II.** (from Pass.) *one must withdraw from, get rid of*, τινός Plut.

ἀπαλλαξείω, Desiderat. of ἀπαλλάσσομαι, *to wish to be delivered from* or *get rid of*, τινός Thuc.

ἀπάλλαξις, εως, ἡ, = ἀπαλλαγή, Hdt. From

ἀπ-αλλάσσω, Att. -ττω : f. ξω : pf. ἀπήλλᾰχα : aor. 1 ἀπήλλαξα :—Pass., pf. ἀπήλλαγμαι, Ion. ἀπάλλαγμαι : aor. 1 ἀπηλλάχθην, Ion. ἀπαλλ— : aor. 2 ἀπηλλάγην [ᾰ] : f. 1 ἀπαλλαχθήσομαι, f. 2 ἀπαλλαγήσομαι :—Med., fut. (in pass. sense) ἀπαλλάξομαι : aor. 1 ἀπηλλαξάμην.

A. Act. *to set free, release, deliver* a person *from* a thing, τινά τινος Hdt., Att. **2.** *to put away* or *remove* a thing *from* a person, τί τινος Eur., etc. **3.** c. acc. only, *to put away, remove, dismiss*, τι or τινα Id., Thuc., etc. : *to destroy*, ἑαυτόν Plut. **II.** intr. *to get off, come off, end* so and so, οὐκ ὡς ἤθελε Hdt. ; κακῶς ἀπ. Plat. ; χαίρων Hdt. :—c. gen. *to depart from*, βίου Eur.

B. Pass. and Med. *to be set free* or *released from* a thing, *get rid of* it, c. gen., Hdt., Att. **2.** *to get off*, καλῶς Eur.; ἀζήμιος Ar. **3.** absol. *to be acquitted*, Dem. **II.** *to remove, depart from*, ἐκ χώρης Hdt., etc. ; γῆς Eur. **2.** ἀπαλλάσσεσθαι τοῦ βίου *to depart* from life, Id. ; and without τοῦ βίου, *to depart, die*, Id., Thuc., etc. **3.** ἀπ. λέχους *to be divorced*, Eur. **4.** ἀπ. τοῦ διδασκάλου *to leave* school, Plat. **5.** ἀπ. ἐκ παίδων *to become a man*, Aeschin. **6.** πολλὸν ἀπηλλαγμένος τινός far *inferior* to him, Hdt. **III.** *to leave off* or *cease from*, τῶν μακρῶν λόγων Soph. ; σκωμμάτων Ar. :—absol. *to have done, give over, cease*, Soph., Plat. :—c. part., εἰπὼν ἀπαλλάγηθι speak *and be done with it*, Plat. ; also in part. with a Verb, οὐκοῦν ἀπαλλαχθεὶς ἄπει ; *have done and begone*, Soph. **2.** *to depart from enmity*, i. e. *to be reconciled*, Plat.

ἀπ-αλλοτριόω, f. ώσω : pf. -ηλλοτρίωκα :—*to estrange, alienate*, Aeschin., Arist. Hence

ἀπαλλοτρίωσις, εως, ἡ, *alienation*, Arist.

ἀπ-ἀλοάω, poët. -οιάω, f. ήσω, *to thresh out*, σῖτος ἀπη-

λοημένος (pf. pass. part.) Dem. :—metaph. *to bruise, crush,* Il.

ἀπᾰλό-θριξ, τρῐχος, ὁ, ἡ, *soft-haired,* Eur.

ἀπᾰλός, ή, όν, Aeol. ἀπ-, *soft to the touch, tender,* of the body, Hom., Soph. ; *of fresh fruit,* Hdt. ; *of tender meat,* Xen. II. metaph. *soft, gentle,* ἀπαλὸν γελάσαι *to laugh gently,* Od. ; ἀπ. δίαιτα *soft, delicate,* Plat. (Deriv. uncertain.) Hence

ἀπᾰλότης, ητος, ἡ, *softness, tenderness,* Xen., etc.

ἀπᾰλο-τρεφής, ές, (τρέφω) *well-fed, plump,* Il.

ἀπᾰλό-φρων, ον, (φρήν) *soft-hearted,* Anth.

ἀπᾰλό-χροος, ον, contr. -χρους, χρουν, with heterocl. gen. ἀπαλόχροος, dat. -χροΐ, acc. -χροα: (χρώς):—*soft-skinned,* h. Hom., Hes., etc.

ἀπᾰλύνω, f. ῠνῶ, (ἀπαλός) *to soften,* Xen. 2. *to make tender,* τοὺς πόδας Id.

ἀπ-ᾰμαλδύνω, *to bring to naught,* Anth.

ἀπ-ᾰμάω, f. ήσω, *to cut off,* Od., Soph. [ᾰπᾱ- Hom., ᾱπᾱ- Soph.]

ἀπ-ᾰμβλίσκω, f. -αμβλώσω: aor. 1 -ήμβλωσα :—*to make abortive,* Plut. II. intr. *to miscarry,* Id.

ἀπ-ᾰμβλύνω, f. ῠνῶ, *to blunt the edge of* a sword: metaph., τεθηγμένον τοί μ' οὐκ ἀπαμβλύνεις λόγῳ Aesch. :—Pass. *to be blunted, lose its edge,* Id., Plat.

ἀπ-αμβροτεῖν, Ep. aor. 2 inf. of ἀφ-αμαρτάνω.

ἀπ-ᾰμείβομαι, f. ψομαι: aor. 1 ἀπημείφθην : 3 sing. plqpf. ἀπάμειπτο: Dep. :—*to reply, answer,* Hom.

ἀπ-ᾰμέρσω, *to deprive one of share in* a thing :—Pass. *to be bereft,* τινός of a thing, Hes.

ἀπ-ᾰμελέομαι, (ἀμελέω) Pass. *to be neglected utterly,* pf. part. ἀπημελημένος Hdt., Soph.

ἀπ-ᾰμμένος, Ion. for ἀφ-ημμένος, part. pf. pass. of ἀφάπτω.

ἀπ-ᾰμπλᾰκεῖν, inf. (with no pres. in use), = ἀφαμαρτεῖν (aor. 2 of ἀμαρτάνω), *to fail utterly,* Soph.

ἀπ-ᾰμύνω, f. ῠνῶ, *to keep off, ward off,* something *for* (i. e. *from)* another, Il. ; τί τινος Luc. : c. acc. *to ward off,* κακά Hdt. ; ἀπ. τὸν βάρβαρον *to repulse* him, Id. II. Med. *to keep off from oneself, to drive back, repel,* τινά Od., Hdt. 2. absol. *to defend or protect oneself,* Hom.

ἀπ-αναίνομαι, aor. 1 -ηνηνάμην, Dor. -ανάμην: Dep. :—*to disown, reject,* Hom., Aesch.

ἀπ-αναισχυντέω, f. ήσω, (ἀναίσχυντος) *to have the effrontery to do or say* a thing, Plat. II. *to deny shamelessly,* Dem.

ἀπ-αναλίσκω, f. -αναλώσω: pf. ἀπανάλωκα:—Pass., aor. 1 -αναλώθην :—*to use quite up, utterly consume,* Thuc.

ἀπ-ανδρόομαι, Pass. *to become manly, come to maturity,* Eur., Luc.

ἀπ-άνευθε and -θεν, Adv. *afar off, far away,* Il. II. Prep. c. gen. *far away from, aloof from,* τῶν ἄλλων θεῶν Ib. ; ἀπ. θεῶν *without* their *knowledge,* Ib. 2. *out from, issuing from,* Ib.

ἀπ-ανθέω, f. ήσω, *to leave off blooming, fade, wither,* Plat., Luc.

ἀπ-ανθίζω, f. ίσω, *to pluck off flowers,* Lat. *decerpere:* metaph., ματαίαν γλῶσσαν ἀπανθίσαι *to cull the flowers of* idle talk, i. e. *talk at random,* Aesch. :—Med. *to gather honey from flowers, to cull the best of,* Luc.

ἀπ-ανθρᾱκίζω, f. σω, *to broil on the coals,* Ar.

ἀπ-ανθρᾰκόω, f. ώσω, *to burn to a cinder,* Luc.

ἀπ-άνθρωπος, ον, *far from* man : I. of places, *desert, desolate,* Aesch. II. of men, *inhuman,* Plut.

ἀπ-ανίστημι, f. -στήσω : aor. 1 -έστησα :—*to make rise up and depart, send away,* τὴν στρατιήν Hdt., Thuc. II. Pass., with aor. 2 and pf. act., and fut. med., *to arise and go away, depart, leave one's country, emigrate,* Hdt., Thuc.

ἀπανταχῇ, Adv. (ἅπας) *everywhere,* Eur. :—ἀπανταχόθεν, *from all sides,* Luc.:—ἀπανταχοῦ, = ἀπανταχοῦ, Id. :—ἀπανταχόσε, *to every place,* Plut. :—ἀπανταχοῦ, *everywhere,* Eur.

ἀπ-αντάω: impf. ἀπήντων, Dor. 3 sing. ἀπάντη: f. ἀπαντήσομαι: aor. 1 ἀπήντησα: pf. ἀπήντηκα: I. *to move from* a place *to meet* a person ; then, generally, *to meet, encounter,* τινί Hdt., Thuc., etc. :—absol., ὁ ἀεὶ ἀπαντῶν *anyone that meets you, any chance person,* Plat. :—often with a Prep., ἀπ. τινι εἰς τόπον *to come or go to* a place *to meet* him, *meet* him at a place, Hdt. : —without a dat. pers., *to present oneself* at a place, Xen. 2. often in hostile sense, *to meet in battle,* Eur. ; ἀπ. Ἀθηναίοις ἐς Τάραντα Thuc. : *to oppose* in any way, Plat. :—absol. *to present oneself* in arms, Eur. 3. as a law term, *to meet in open court,* Plat., Dem. :— absol. *to appear in court,* Dem. 4. ἀπ. εἰς or πρός τι *to enter upon* a thing, *attempt or approach* it, Plat., Aeschin. ; *to have recourse* to . . , Dem. II. of things, *to come upon* one, *happen to* one, Eur., Plat., etc.

ἀπάντη, Adv. (ἅπας) *everywhere,* Hom.

ἀπάντημα, ατος, τό, (ἀπαντάω) *a meeting,* Eur.

ἀπαντικρύ, Adv., strengthd. for ἀντικρύ, *right opposite,* Xen. ; c. gen., Dem.

ἀπ-αντίον, Adv., *right opposite,* ἐς τὴν ἀπ. ἀκτήν Hdt.

ἀπ-αντλέω, f. ήσω, *to draw off water from a ship's hold:* metaph., ἀπ. ὕβρισμα χθονὸς Eur. :—c. acc. only, *to draw off,* Aesch. : *to lighten, lessen,* πόνους Id. ; βάρος ψυχῆς Eur.

ἀπ-άντομαι, = ἀπαντάω, Eur.

ἀπ-ανύω, f. ύσω [ῠ], *to finish entirely,* νῆες ἀπήνυσαν (sc. ὁδόν) the ships *performed the voyage,* Od.

ἅ-πᾰξ, Adv. (ᾰ copul., and Root ΠΑΓ, πήγνυμι, cf. Lat. *sim-plex*) *once, once only, once for all,* like Lat. *semel,* Od., Hdt., Att. 2. c. gen., ἅπ. τοῦ ἐνιαυτοῦ *once* in the year, Hdt. II. *without any notion of number,* after εἴπερ, ἤν, ἐπεί, ὡς, ὅταν, like Lat. *ut semel,* εἴπερ ἐσπείσω γ' ἅπαξ *if once* you have made a treaty, Ar. ; ὡς ἅπαξ ἤρξατο *once* he had begun, Xen.

ἅπαξ-ᾰπᾰς, ᾰσᾰ, ᾰν, *all at once,* mostly in pl., Ar.

ἁπαξ-απλῶς, Adv. *in general,* Luc.

ἀπ-αξιόω, f. ώσω, *to disclaim as unworthy, disown,* τι or τινα Thuc. II. ἀπ. τί τινος *to deem* a thing *unworthy* of one, Luc. :—Med. *to banish from* one's house, Aesch.

ἀπᾰπαῖ, ἀπαππαπαῖ, = ἀπαπαῖ, Soph., Ar.

ἄ-παππος, ον, *with no grandfather :* metaph. *unfathered by* a thing, Aesch.

ἀπ-άπτω, Ion. for ἀφ-άπτω.

ἀ-πᾰράβᾰτος, ον, (παραβαίνω) *not passing over* to another, *not passing away, unchangeable,* N. T.

ἀπ-αραιρημένος, Ion. for ἀφ-ῃρημένος, part. pf. pass. of ἀφαιρέω.

ἀ-πᾰραίτητος, ον, (παραιτέω) : I. of persons, *not to*

be moved by prayer, inexorable, Plat., etc. :—Adv.
-τως, Thuc.　II. of punishments, not to be averted
by prayers, inevitable, unmerciful, Dinarch.

ἀ-παρακάλυπτος, ον, (παρακαλύπτω) uncovered : Adv.
-τως, undisguisedly, Plat.

ἀ-παράκλητος, ον, unsummoned, volunteering, Thuc.

ἀ-παράλλακτος, ον, (παραλλάσσω) unchanged, unchangeable, Plut.

ἀ-παραμύθητος, ον, (παραμυθέομαι) not to be persuaded,
inconsolable, ἀθυμία Plut.

ἀ-πᾰράμῦθος, ον, = foreg., inexorable, Aesch.

ἀ-παρασκεύαστος, ον, (παρασκευάζω) = sq., N. T.

ἀ-παράσκευος, ον, (παρασκευή) without preparation,
unprepared, Thuc., Xen.

ἀπ-ᾰράσσω, Att. -ττω, f. ξω, to strike off, cut off, Il.,
Hdt. : to sweep off from the deck of a ship, ἀπὸ τῆς
νηός Hdt. ; ἀπὸ τοῦ καταστρώματος Thuc.

ἄπαργμα, ατος, τό, = ἀπαρχή, mostly in pl., Ar.

ἀπ-ᾰρέσκω, f. -αρέσω : Ep. aor. 1 inf. med. ἀπαρέσσασ-
θαι :—to be disagreeable to, τινί Thuc.　II. Med.
to shew displeasure, Il.

ἀ-παρηγόρητος, ον, (παρηγορέω) inconsolable, Plut.　II.
not to be advised or controlled, Id.

ἀ-παρθένευτος, ον, (παρθενεύω) unmaidenly, unfitting
a maiden, Eur., in neut. pl. as Adv.

ἀ-πάρθενος, ον, no more a maid, Theocr. ; νύμφην
ἄνυμφον παρθένον τ' ἀπάρθενον 'virgin wife and widow'd
maid,' Eur.

ἀπ-ᾰριθμέω, f. ήσω, to count over, reckon up, Xen.　II.
to reckon or pay back, repay, Id.　Hence

ἀπαρίθμησις, εως, ἡ, a counting over, recounting, Thuc.

ἀπ-αρκέω, f. έσω, to suffice, be sufficient, Trag.　II.
to be contented, acquiesce, Aesch.

ἀπ-αρνέομαι, f. ήσομαι : aor. 1 med. -ηρνησάμην, pass.
-ηρνήθην : Dep. :—to deny utterly, deny, Hdt. ; followed
by μή and inf., Eur., etc. : ἀπαρνηθῆναί τι to refuse,
reject, Thuc.　II. f. ἀπαρνηθήσεται in pass. sense,
shall be denied or refused, Soph., N. T.

ἄπ-αρνος, ον, (ἀρνέομαι) denying utterly, ἄπαρνός ἐστι
μὴ νοέειν he denies that he is ill, Hdt. : c. gen., ἄπαρ-
νος οὐδενός denying nothing, Soph.

ἀ-παρρησίαστος, ον, (παρρησιάζομαι) not speaking
freely, Luc.

ἀπ-αρτάω, f. ήσω, to hang up from, ἀπ. δέρην to strangle,
Eur. :—Pass. to hang loose, Xen.　2. metaph. to
make dependent upon, ἐξ ἑαυτοῦ Luc.　II. to detach,
separate, τί τινος Dem. :—Pass., ἀπηρτημένοι detached,
disunited, Id.　III. intr. in Act. to remove oneself, go away, Thuc.

ἀπ-αρτί [ῐ], Adv. completely, of numbers, exactly, just,
Hdt.　II. of Time, from now, from this time, henceforth, Ar., N. T.　2. just now, even now, N. T.

ἀπ-αρτίζω, f. ίσω, to make even, move regularly,
Aesch.　II. to get ready, complete, Arist.　2.
intr. to be even or exact, Id.

ἀπαρτι-λογία, Ion. -ίη, ἡ, (λόγος) an even number or
sum, Hdt.

ἀπάρτιον, τό, a sale of goods by auction, Plut.

ἀπαρτισμός, ὁ, (ἀπαρτίζω) completion, N. T.

ἀπ-αρύω or -αρύτω [ῠ], f. σω, to draw off, skim off
cream, Hdt. : metaph. to draw off the force of a thing,
in verb. Adj. ἀπαρυστέον, Ar.

ἀπαρχή, ἡ, mostly in pl. ἀπαρχαί, the beginning of a
sacrifice, the primal offering (of hairs cut from the forehead), Eur.　2. the firstlings for sacrifice, first-fruits,
Hdt., Att. :—metaph., ἀπαρχὴ τῆς σοφίας Plat.　From

ἀπ-άρχομαι, f. ξομαι, Dep. to make a beginning, esp. in
sacrifice, τρίχας ἀπάρχεσθαι to begin the sacrifice with
the hair, i. e. by cutting off the hair from the forehead
and throwing it into the fire, Il. : to begin the sacrificial
rites, Od.　II. c. gen. to cut off part of a thing, to
offer it, to offer part of a thing, Hdt., Eur.　III.
to offer the firstlings or first-fruits, Hdt., Ar.　2.
metaph. to take as the first-fruits, as the choice or
best, Theocr.

ἄπαρχος, ὁ, = ἔπαρχος, Aesch.

ἀπ-άρχω, f. ξω, to be the first, be leader, dance, Anth.

ἅ-πᾱς, ἅ-πᾶσα, ἅ-παν, (a copul., πᾶς) quite all, the
whole, and in pl. all together, Hom., etc.　2. with
an Adj., ἀργύρεος ἅπας all silver, i. e. of massive silver,
Od. ; ἅπαν κακόν altogether evil, Ar.　II. in sing.,
like πᾶς, everyone, Lat. unusquisque, πᾶν everything,
unumquodque, Hdt., Att.

ἀπ-ασπαίρω, to gasp away life, Eur.

ἀπαστία, ἡ, an abstaining from food, a fast, Ar. From

ἄ-παστος, ον, (πατέομαι) not having eaten, fasting, Il. :
c. gen., ἄπαστος ἐδητύος ἠδὲ ποτῆτος without having
tasted meat or drink, Od.

ἀπ-αστράπτω, f. ψω, to flash forth, Luc.

ἀπ-ασχολέω, f. ήσω, (ἄσχολος) to leave one no leisure,
Luc. :—Pass. to be wholly occupied, Id.　Hence

ἀπασχολία, ἡ, detention by business, Strab.

ἀπατάω, Ion. -έω : impf. ἠπάτων : f. ήσω : aor. 1 ἠπά-
τησα, Ep. ἀπ— : pf. ἀπάτηκα :—Pass., f. ἀπατηθήσομαι,
and in med. form ἀπατήσομαι : aor. 1 ἠπατήθην : pf.
ἠπάτημαι : (ἀπάτη) :—to cheat, trick, outwit, beguile,
Hom., etc. : Pass. to be deceived, Soph. ; ἀπατᾶσθαι,
ὡς . . , to be deceived into thinking that . . , Plat.

ἀπ-άτερθε and -θεν, Adv. apart, aloof, Il.　II.
Prep. c. gen. far away from, ὁμίλου Ib.

ἀπατεών, ῶνος, ὁ, a cheat, rogue, quack, Plat., Xen.
From

ἀπάτη [ᾰπᾰ-], ἡ, (prob. from ἅπτομαι, cf. ἀπαφίσκω)
a trick, fraud, deceit, Il. : a stratagem, Thuc. : in pl.
wiles, Hom.　2. guile, fraud, deceit, treachery,
Hdt., Att.　Hence

ἀπατήλιος, ον, guileful, wily, ἀπατήλια εἰδώς skilled in
wiles, Od. ; ἀπ. βάζειν Ib.

ἀπατηλός, ή, όν or ος, ον, = foreg., Il., Plat.

ἀπατητικός, ή, όν, (ἀπατάω) fraudulent, Xen.

ἀ-πάτητος, ον, (πᾰτέω) untrodden, Anth.

ἀπ-ᾰτῑμάζω, = sq.: part. pf. pass. ἀπητιμασμένος, Aesch.

ἀπ-ᾰτῑμάω, aor. 1 -ητίμησα, to dishonour greatly, Il.

Ἀπατούρια, ων, τά, the Apaturia, a festival at Athens
in the month Pyanepsion, at which the grown-up youths
(κοῦροι) were enrolled in the φρατρίαι, Oratt. (Prob.
from πατριά, = φρατρία, with a euphon.)

ἀ-πάτωρ, ορος, ὁ, ἡ, (πᾰτήρ) without father, fatherless,
Soph., Eur. : c. gen., ἀπ. ἐμοῦ not having me for a
father, Soph.

ἀπ-αυγάζω, f. σω, to beam forth, Call. (in Med.)　Hence

ἀπαύγασμα, ατος, τό, efflux of light, effulgence, N. T.

ἀπ-αυδάω, f. ήσω, to forbid, Soph. ; ἀπ. μή c. inf. to
prohibit from doing a thing, Id., Eur.　II. to de-

cline, shun, πόνους Eur.: to deny, renounce, νεῖκος Theocr. **III.** to be wanting towards, fail, φίλοισι Eur.; ἀπ. ὑπὸ λιμοῦ Luc.

ἀπ-αυθαδίζομαι, f. ιοῦμαι, Dep. to speak or act boldly, speak out, Plat.

ἀπ-αυθημερίζω, f. σω, (αὐθήμερος) to return the same day, Xen.

ἀπ-αυράω, only used in impf. ἀπηύρων, ας, α, with a part. of aor. form ἀπούρας (as if from ἀπούρημι), and aor. 1 med. part. ἀπουράμενος: (the simple Verb Α'ΥΡΑ'Ω, which is not in use, meant to take):—to take away or wrest from, rob of, c. dupl. acc. pers. et rei, ἄμφω θυμὸν ἀπηύρα Il.; τοὺς μὲν τεύχε' ἀπηύρα Ib. **2.** c. gen. pers., κούρην 'Αχιλῆος ἀπούρας Ib. **3.** c. dat. pers., πολέσσιν θυμὸν ἀπηύρα Ib. **4.** Med., ἀπουράμενοι ψυχάς having lost their lives, Hes. **II.** to receive good or ill, to enjoy or suffer, Id., Eur. Cf. ἐπ-αυρίσκομαι.

ἄ-παυστος, ον, (παύομαι) unceasing, never-ending, Aesch., Soph. **2.** not to be stopped or assuaged, insatiable, δίψα Thuc. **II.** c. gen. never ceasing from, γόων Eur.

ἀπ-αυτομολέω, f. ήσω, to go of one's own accord, desert, Thuc.

ἀπ-αφίσκω, f. -αφήσω: aor. 2 -ήπαφον: (ἅπτομαι, palpare, ἀφή):—like ἀπατάω, to cheat, beguile, Od.

ἀπ-αχθομαι, Dep. to be grievous, τινι Sappho.

ἀπ-έβην, aor. 2 of ἀποβαίνω.

ἀπ-εδήδοκα, pf. of ἀπ-εσθίω.

ἀ-πέδιλος, ον, (πέδιλον) unshod, Aesch.

ἀπ-έδομαι, f. of ἀπ-εσθίω.

ἄ-πεδος, ον, (α copul., πέδον) even, level, flat, Hdt., Thuc., etc.:—ἄπεδον, τό, a plain, flat surface, Hdt.

ἀπ-έῃσιν, Ep. for ἀπ-ῇ, 3 sing. pres. subj. of ἄπειμι (εἰμί sum).

ἀπ-έειπον, Ep. for ἀπ-εῖπον.

ἀπ-έεργον, Ep. for ἀπ-εῖργον, impf. of ἀπείργω.

ἀπ-έθανον, aor. 2 of ἀπο-θνήσκω.

ἀπ-εθίζω, f. ίσω, to disaccustom, ἀπ. τινὰ μὴ ποιεῖν Aeschin.; part. pf. ἀπειθικώς, Plut.

ἀπ-εῖδον, inf. -ιδεῖν, aor. 2 with no pres. in use, ἀφοράω being used instead:—to look away from other things at a thing, and so simply to look at, ἔς or πρός τι Thuc.

ἀπείθεια, ἡ, (ἀπειθής) disobedience, Xen., N. T.

ἀπειθέω, f. ήσω, to be disobedient, refuse compliance, Aesch.; c. dat. to disobey, Eur., Plat.

ἀπ-είθην, Ion. for ἀφ-είθην, aor. 1 pass. of ἀφίημι.

ἀ-πειθής, ές, (πείθομαι) disobedient, τοῖς νόμοις Plat.; of ships, τοῖς κυβερνήταις ἀπειθέστεραι less obedient to them, Thuc. **II.** act. not persuasive, incredible, Theogn.

ἀπ-εικάζω, f. άσομαι:—Pass., aor. 1 ἀπεικάσθην or ἀπηκ-: pf. ἀπείκασμαι or ἀπηκ-:—to form from a model, to express, copy, of painters, Xen., etc.:—Pass. to become like, resemble, ἀπεικασθεὶς θεῷ in a god's likeness, Eur. **2.** to express by a comparison, Plat.:—Pass. to be copied or expressed by likeness, Id. **3.** to liken, compare with, τί τινι Eur., Plat. **II.** ὡς ἀπεικάσαι as one may guess, to conjecture, Soph. Hence

ἀπεικαστέον, verb. Adj. one must represent, Xen.

ἀπ-εικονίζω, f. ίσω, (εἰκών) to represent in a statue, Anth.

ἀπ-εικώς, -εικότως, v. ἀπ-έοικώς.

ἀπ-ειλέω, f. ήσω, to force back; mostly in Pass., ἐς ἀπορίην ἀπειλημένος forced into great difficulties, Hdt.

ἀπειλέω, f. ήσω: (ἀπειλή):—to hold out either in the way of promise or threat: **I.** in good sense, to promise, ἠπείλησεν ἄνακτι ῥέξειν ἑκατόμβην Il.; ἠπείλησας εἶναι ἀρίστους didst profess that they were best, Od. **II.** commonly in bad sense, to threaten, Lat. minari, absol. or c. dat. pers., Hom., etc.; c. acc. cogn., ἠπείλησεν μῦθον spake a threatening speech, Il.—also in Med., N. T. **2.** c. acc. of the thing threatened, θάνατον ἀπ. τινι Hdt. **3.** dependent clauses added in inf. fut., γέρας ἀφαιρήσεσθαι ἀπειλεῖς Il., etc.; Att. also in inf. aor.:—also ἀπ. ὅτι.., ὡς.., Att. **III.** Pass. ἀπειλοῦμαι, of persons, to be terrified by threats, Xen.

ἀπειλή, ἡ, mostly in pl., boastful promises, boasts, Il. **II.** in bad sense, threats, Hom., etc.:—in sing. a threat of punishment, Soph.,Thuc. (Deriv. uncertain.)

ἀπ-ειληθείς, aor. 1 pass. part. of ἀπ-ειλέω:—but ἀπειληθείς, of ἀπειλέω.

ἀπείλημα, ατος, τό,=ἀπειλή, in pl., Soph.

ἀπ-ειλημένος, pf. pass. part. of ἀπειλέω: but ἀπειλημένος of ἀπειλέω.

ἀπ-είλημμαι, pf. pass. of ἀπολαμβάνω.

ἀπειλήτην, Ep. for ἤπ-, 3 dual impf. of ἀπειλέω.

ἀπειλητήρ, ῆρος, ὁ, (ἀπειλέω) a threatener, boaster, Il.

ἀπειλητήριος, α, ον, (ἀπειλέω) of or for threatening, λόγοι Hdt.

ἀπ-είληφα, pf. of ἀπολαμβάνω.

ἀπ-είλλω or -είλω,=ἀπειλέω, to bar the way, Lys.

ἄπ-ειμι (εἰμί sum): impf. ἀπῆν, 2 sing. ἀπῆσθα; Ep. ἀπέην, 3 pl. ἀπέσαν: f. ἀπέσομαι, Ep. ἀπέσσομαι, 3 sing. ἀπεσσεῖται:—to be away or far from, τινος Od., etc.; ἀπό τινος Thuc.: c. dat. to be wanting, φίλοισιν Eur., etc. **2.** absol. to be away or absent, and of things, to be wanting, Soph., etc.; of the dead, Eur.

ἄπ-ειμι (εἶμι ibo), serving as fut. of ἀπέρχομαι, inf. ἀπιέναι, poët. ἀπίναι:—to go away, depart, Od., etc.; οὐκ ἄπει; = ἄπιθι, be gone, Soph.; ἀπ. πάλιν to return, Xen.; ἄπιτε ἐς ὑμέτερα return to your homes, Hdt.; ἄπιμεν οἴκαδε Ar.; ἐπ' οἴκου Thuc.:—of the Nile, to recede, Hdt.; ἐπί τι to go in quest of a thing, Xen.

ἀπ-εῖπον, inf. -ειπεῖν, Ep. ἀπό-ειπεῖν, ἀπό-ειπέμεν, part. ἀπο-ειπών (for εἶπον orig. had a digamma Ϝεῖπον): aor. 1 ἀπεῖπα, med. ἀπειπάμην: fut. in use is ἀπ-ερῶ, pf. ἀπ-είρηκα; and in Pass., pf. ἀπείρημαι, f. ἀπορρηθήσομαι: aor. 1 ἀπερρήθην:—pres. and impf. are supplied by ἀπαυδάω, ἀπόφημι, ἀπαγορεύω:—to speak out, tell out, declare, μῦθον, etc., Hom.; ῥῆσιν Hdt. **II.** to deny, refuse, Il., Plat. **III.** to forbid, ἀπ. τινι μὴ ποιεῖν to forbid one to do, tell him not to do, Hdt., Att.:—Pass., ἀπείρηται τινι ποιεῖν τι it is forbidden him to do, Hdt.; τὸ ἀπειρημένον a forbidden thing, Id. **IV.** to renounce, disown, give up, μῆνιν Il.; τὴν συμμαχίην Hdt.; ἀπ. τὴν στρατηγίαν to resign it, Xen.:—Pass., αἱ σπονδαὶ οὐκ ἀπείρηντο had not been renounced, Thuc.:—so in Med., ἀπείπασθαι ὄψιν to avert a vision (by sacrifice), Hdt. **2.** intr. to give up, to be worn out, fail, sink from exhaustion, Soph., etc.; ἀπεῖπεν φάτις the word failed, was unfulfilled, Aesch.: c. dat. to fail or be wanting to one, οὐκ ἀπειρηκὼς φίλοις Eur.:—c. dat. rei, ἀπειρηκότων χρήμασι, i. e. when they were bankrupt, Dem.; also, ἀπ. κακοῖς, ἄλγει to give way to, sink

under them, Eur.; φέροντες ἀπερούσιν they will be tired of paying, Thuc., Plat.

Ἀπειραῖος, α, ον, Apiraean, and Ἀπείρηθεν, Adv. from Apeiré, Od. (Apeiré = Limitless-land (from ἄ-πειρος B), an imaginary place.)

ἀ-πείραστος, ον, (πειράζω) incapable of being tempted by a thing, c. gen., N. T.

ἀ-πείρᾱτος, ον, Dor. and Att. for ἀπείρητος.

ἀπ-είργάθον, Ep. ἀπο-εργάθον, Ep. aor. 2 of ἀπείργω, to keep away, keep off from, τινά τινος Il.; ῥάκεα ἀπο-έργαθε οὐλῆς pushed back the rags from the scar, Od.; μή σε τῆσδε γῆς ἀπειργαθῆ Soph.

ἀπ-είργω, Ion. ἀπ-έργω, in Hom. also ἀπο-έργω: f. ἀπείρξω: aor. 1 ἀπείρξα Soph.; cf. foreg.:—to keep away from, debar from, τινά τινος Hom., Att.; τινὰ ἀπό τινος Hdt.   2. to keep from doing, prevent, hinder, c. acc. et inf., ἀπ. τινὰ ποιεῖν or μὴ ποιεῖν τι Soph., Eur.   3. c. acc. to keep back, keep off, ward off, Od., Soph., etc.; absol., ἀλλ᾽ ἀπείργοι θεός heaven forfend! Soph.: νόμος οὐδεὶς ἀπ. no law debars, Thuc.: of the Nile, ἀπεργμένος barred or shut off from its old channel, Hdt.   II. to part, divide, separate, κλῇὶς ἀποέργει αὐχένα τε στῆθός τε Il. :—and so to bound, Hdt.   2. of persons travelling, ἐν ἀριστερῇ ἀπέργων Ῥοίτειον keeping Rhoeteium on the left, Id.   III. to shut up, confine, Id.

ἀπειρέσιος, α, ον, lengthd. form of ἄπειρος (B), boundless, immense, countless, Hom., Od.

Ἀπείρηθεν, v. Ἀπειραῖος.

ἀπ-είρηκα, -είρημαι, pf. act. and pass. of ἀπεῖπον.

ἀ-πείρητος, Dor. and Att. -ᾱτος, ον, (πειράομαι) :   I. act. without making trial of a thing, without making an attempt upon, c. gen., Il.   2. without trial or experience of a thing, h. Hom., Pind. :—absol. inexperienced, Od.   II. pass. untried, unattempted, Il., Hdt., Dem.

ἀπειρία, ἡ, (ἄπειρος A) want of skill, inexperience, Plat.; τινός of or in a thing, Eur.

ἀπειρία (ἄπειρος B), ἡ, infinity, Plat.

ἀ-πείρῐτος, ον, = ἀπειρέσιος, Od., Hes.

ἀπειρό-δροσος, ον, unused to dew, unbedewed, Eur.

ἀπειρό-κᾰκος, ον, (κακόν) without experience of evil, unused to evil, Eur.: τὸ ἀπ. ignorance of evil, Thuc.

ἀπειροκᾰλία, ἡ, ignorance of the beautiful, want of taste, Plat.: in pl. vulgarities, Xen. From

ἀπειρό-κᾰλος, ον, (καλόν) ignorant of the beautiful, without taste, tasteless, vulgar, Plat.: τὸ ἀπ., = ἀπειροκαλία, Xen. Adv. -λως, Plat.

ἀπειρό-πλους, ουν, (πλόος) ignorant of navigation, Luc.

ἄπειρος, Dor. for ἤπειρος.

ἄπειρος (A), ον, (πεῖρα) without trial or experience of a thing, unused to, unacquainted with, Lat. expers, c. gen., ἄθλων Theogn.; τυράννων Hdt., etc.   2. absol. inexperienced, ignorant, Pind., Aesch., etc.   II. Adv., ἀπείρως ἔχειν τινός to be ignorant of a thing, Hdt.

ἄπειρος (B), ον, (πεῖρας, πέρας) boundless, infinite, countless, πλῆθος Hdt., Plat.   2. in Trag., of garments, endless, i. e. without end or outlet, inextricable, Aesch., Eur.

ἀπειροσύνη, ἡ, = ἀπειρία, inexperience, Eur.

ἀπειρο-τόκος, ον, (τίκτω) not having brought forth, virgin, Anth.

ἀ-πείρων, ον, (πεῖρα) = ἄπειρος A, without experience, ignorant, Soph.

ἀ-πείρων, ον, (πεῖρας, πέρας) = ἄπειρος B, boundless, endless, countless, Hom.   2. = ἄπειρος B. 2, without end, inextricable, δεσμοί Od.

ἀπ-είς, Ion. for ἀφ-είς, aor. 2 part. of ἀφίημι.

ἀπ-έκ, Prep. with gen., away out of, h. Hom.

ἀπεκ-δέχομαι, f. -δέξομαι, Dep. to expect anxiously, to look for, await, N. T.

ἀπεκ-δύνω, to strip off from, τί τινος Babr.

ἀπεκ-δύομαι, f. -δύσομαι [ῠ]: aor. 1 -εδυσάμην :—to strip off oneself, to put off, as in preparing for single combat, N. T.   II. to strip off for oneself, to despoil, τινα Ib. Hence

ἀπέκδῠσις, εως, ἡ, a putting off (like clothes), N. T.

ἀπ-έκιξα, v. sub *κίκω.

ἀπεκ-λανθάνομαι, Med. to forget entirely, c. gen., only in imperat. of Ep. aor. 2 ἀπεκλελάθεσθε, Od.

ἀ-πέκτητος, ον, (πεκτέω) uncombed, = sq., Anth.

ἀπ-ελαύνω (also ἀπ-ελάω, in imper. ἀπέλα): f. -ελάσω, Att. -ελῶ: pf. -ελήλακα:—Pass., aor. 1 -ηλάθην [ἄ]:— to drive away, expel from a place, τινὰ δόμων, πόλεως, Eur., etc.; ἀπὸ τόπου Xen.: ἀπ. τινά to drive away, banish, expel, Soph., Xen.   2. ἀπ. στρατιήν to lead away an army, Hdt.: then absol. to march or go away, depart, Id.; (sub. ἵππον) to ride away, Xen.   II. Pass. to be driven away, Hdt., Att. :—to be excluded from a thing, Hdt., etc.

ἀπελεγμός, ὁ, refutation: disrepute, N. T.   From

ἀπ-ελέγχω, f. ξω, to refute thoroughly, Antipho.

ἀ-πελέθρος, ον, (πέλεθρον) immeasurable, Hom.: neut. as Adv. immeasurably far, Il.

ἀπ-ελέσθαι, Ion. for ἀφ-, aor. 2 inf. med. of ἀφαιρέω.

ἀπ-ελευθερία, ἡ, the enfranchisement of a slave, Aeschin.

ἀπελευθερικός, ή, όν, in the condition of a freedman, Plut. From

ἀπ-ελεύθερος, ὁ, an emancipated slave, a freedman, Lat. libertus, Plat., Xen. Hence

ἀπελευθερόω, ἡ, f. ώσω, to emancipate a slave, Plat. Hence

ἀπελευθέρωσις, εως, ἡ, emancipation, Dem.

ἀπ-ελθεῖν, aor. 2 inf. of ἀπ-έρχομαι.

ἀπ-έλκω, Ion. for ἀφέλκω.

ἀπ-ελλάζω, Lacon. for ἐκκλησιάζω, Plut.

ἀπ-ελπίζω, f. ίσω, Att. ιῶ: pf. -ήλπικα:—to give up in despair, to despair, N. T.; (others to hope to receive from another); to drive to despair, Lat. Anth.

ἀπ-εμέω, f. έσω, to spit up, vomit forth, Il. evomere, Il.

ἀπ-εμπολάω, f. ήσω: impf. ἀπημπόλων :—to sell, Eur.; ἀπ. τί τινος or ἀντί τινος to sell for a thing, Xen., Eur.; ἀπ. τινὰ χθονός to smuggle one out of the country, Eur. :—Pass., ἀπεμποληθέντες 'bought and sold,' Ar.

ἀπ-έναντι, Adv. (ἔναντι) opposite, against, c. gen., N. T.

ἀπ-εναντίον, Adv. = foreg., ἡ ἀπ. (sc. χώρα) the opposite shore, Hdt.

ἀπ-εναρίζω, f. ξω, (ἔναρα) to strip one of arms, despoil one of a thing, c. dupl. acc., Il.

ἀπ-ενάσσατο, Ep. 3 sing. aor. 1 med. of ἀποναίω.

ἀπ-ένεικα, Ion. for ἀπ-ήνεγκα, aor. 1 of ἀποφέρω: ἀπ-ενείχθην, aor. pass.

ἀπ-ενέπω, v. sub ἀπεννέπω.

ἀ-πενθής, ές, (πένθος) free from grief, Aesch.

ἀ-πένθητος, ον, (πενθέω) = foreg., Aesch.

ἀπ-ενιαυτέω or -ίζω, f. Att. ιῶ, (ἐνιαυτός) to go into banishment for a year, Xen.

ἀπ-εννέπω, rarely ἀπ-ενέπω, to forbid, Aesch. ; ἀπ. τι to forbid it, Soph. ; c. acc. et inf., ἀπ. τινὰ ποιεῖν or μὴ ποιεῖν τι Eur. :—ἀπ. τινὰ θαλάμων to order him from the chamber, Id.　　II. to deprecate, τι Aesch.

ἀπ-έξ, = ἀπέκ, before a vowel.

ἀπεξ-αιρέω, f. ήσω, to take out, remove, τί τινος Eur.

ἀπ-εοικώς, Att. ἀπ-εικώς, υῖα, ός, part. of ἀπέοικα, used as Adj., unreasonable, Antipho :—Adv. ἀπ-εοικότως or -εικότως, unreasonably, Thuc.

ἀ-πέπαντος, ον, (πεπαίνω) not ripened, unripe, Anth.

ἀ-πέπειρος, ον, unripe, untimely.

ἄ-πεπλος, ον, unrobed, clad in the tunic only, Pind. : λευκῶν φαρέων ἄπεπλος not clad in white robes, i. e. in black, Eur.

ἀπ-έπνευσα, aor. 1 of ἀπο-πνέω.

ἀπ-επτάμην [ἄ], aor. 2 of ἀποπέτομαι : also ἀπ-έπτην, in act. form.

ἅ-περ, neut. pl. of ὅσ-περ, used as Adv., = ὥσπερ, as, so as, Att.

ἀπεραντολογία, ἡ, = ἀπειρολογία, Luc.　From

ἀπεραντο-λόγος, ον, (λέγω) talking without end.

ἀ-πέραντος, ον, (περαίνω) boundless, infinite, of space, Pind., Eur., etc. :—of Time, endless, Ar.; —of Number, countless, Plat. ; generally of events, ἀπέραντον ἦν there was no end to it, Thuc.　　II. allowing no escape, Aesch.

ἀπ-εργάζομαι, f. άσομαι : aor. 1 -ειργασάμην : pf. -είργασμαι (which is sometimes act., sometimes pass., aor. 1 -ειργάσθην always pass.) :—to finish off, turn out complete, Ar., Plat.　　2. of a painter, to fill up with colour, express perfectly, Plat.　3. to finish a contract, Xen.　　II. c. dupl. acc. to make so and so, ἀγαθὸν ἀπ. τινα Id. :—so pf. in pass. sense, ἀπειργασμένος τύραννος a finished tyrant, Plat.　Hence

ἀπεργασία, ἡ, a finishing off, completing, of painters, Plat.　　II. a making, producing, Id.　　III. a business, trade, Id.

ἀπεργαστικός, ή, όν, (ἀπεργάζομαι) fit for finishing, causing, c. gen., Plat.

ἀπ-εργμένος, Ion. pf. pass. part. of ἀπ-είργω.

ἀπ-έργω, Ion. for ἀπείργω.

ἀπ-έρδω, f. ξω, to bring to an end, finish, Hdt.

ἀπερ-εί, Adv., (ἅπερ, εἰ) = ὡσπερεί, Soph.

ἀπ-ερείδω, f. σω, to rest, fix, settle, τὴν ὄψιν πρός τι Luc.　2. intr. = Pass. to rest upon, Id.　　II. mostly as Pass., with fut. and aor. 1 med., to support oneself upon, rest upon a thing, c. dat., Xen., etc. ; εἴς τι Plat.

ἀπερείσιος, ον, another Ep. form of ἀπειρέσιος, in Hom. always ἀπερείσι' ἄποινα countless ransom.

ἀ-περιλάλητος, ον, (περιλαλέω) not to be out-talked, Ar.

ἀ-περίληπτος, ον, (περιλαμβάνω) uncircumscribed, Plut.

ἀ-περιμέριμνος, ον, (μέριμνα) free from care :—Adv. -νως, unthinkingly, Luc.

ἀ-περίοπτος, ον, (περιόψομαι, f. of περιοράω) unregarding, reckless of, πάντων Thuc.

ἀ-περίσκεπτος, ον, (περισκέπτομαι) inconsiderate, thoughtless, Thuc.　Adv. -τως ; Comp. -ότερον, Id.

ἀ-περίτμητος, ον, (περιτέμνω) uncircumcised, N. T.

ἀ-περίτροπος, ον, (περιτρέπω) not returning or taking heed, Soph.

ἀπ-έρρω, f. -ερρήσω, to go away, be gone, Eur. : ἄπερρε away, begone, Lat. abi in malam rem, Ar.

ἀπ-ερυθριάω, f. άσω [ᾱσω], to put away blushes, to be past blushing, Ar.

ἀπ-ερύκω [ῠ], f. ξω, to keep off or away, c. acc., Hom. ; c. acc. et gen. to keep away from, Theogn. ; c. acc. et inf. to prevent one from doing, οὔτε σε κωμάζειν ἀπερύκομεν Id. ; also, ἀπ. τινί τι to keep off from, Hdt. ; τι ἀπό τινος Xen. :—Med., ἀπερύκου (sc. φωνῆς) abstain from speech, Soph.

ἀπ-ερύω, f. -ερύσω [ῠ], to tear off from, ῥινὸν ἀπ' ὀστεόφιν ἐρύσαι Od. :—Med., Anth.

ἀπ-έρχομαι, f. -ελεύσομαι (but the Att. fut. is ἄπειμι) : pf. -ελήλυθα : aor. -ῆλθον : Dep. :—to go away, depart from, c. gen., Hom., Att. ; ἀπό or ἐκ τόπου Thuc.　　2. when used with εἰς, departure from one place and arrival at another is implied, ἀπ. ἐς Σάρδις Hdt., etc.　　3. absol. to depart, Id., Thuc., etc. : to depart from life, Anth.

ἀπ-ερῶ, Ion. -ερέω, fut. with no pres. in use : v. ἀπεῖπον.

ἀπερωεύς, έως, ὁ, a thwarter, Il.　From

ἀπ-ερωέω, f. ήσω, to retire or withdraw from, πολέμου Il.

ἀπ-έρωτος, ον, (ἔρως) loveless, unloving, ἔρως ἀπέρωτος, like γάμος ἄγαμος, Aesch.

ἄπ-ες, Ion. for ἄφ-ες, aor. 2 imper. of ἀφίημι.

ἀπ-εσθίω, f. ἀπ-έδομαι : pf. ἀπ-εδήδοκα :—to eat or gnaw off, Ar., Dem.

ἀπ-εσκέδασα, aor. 1 of ἀπο-σκεδάννυμι.

ἀπ-έσκληκα, ἀπ-εσκληκότως, v. ἀπο-σκλῆναι.

ἀπ-έσσεται, Ep. for ἀπ-έσεται, 3 sing. fut. of ἄπ-ειμι (εἰμί sum).

ἀπ-έσσουα, he is gone off, Lacon. for ἀπ-εσσύη or ἀπεσσύθη, 3 sing. aor. 1 pass. of ἀπο-σεύω, Xen.

ἀπ-εσσύμεθα, -σῦτο, 1 pl. and 3 sing. of Ep. aor. 2 pass. of ἀπο-σεύω.

ἀπ-έστην, aor. 2 of ἀφ-ίστημι.

ἀπεστώ, οῦς, ἡ, (ἄπειμι, cf. εὐεστώ) a being away, absence, Hdt.

ἀ-πέτηλος, ον, (πέτηλον) leafless, Anth.

ἀπ-έτραπον, aor. 2 of ἀπο-τρέπω.

ἀ-πευθής, ές, (πυνθάνομαι) not inquired into, unknown, Od.　　II. act. not inquiring, ignorant, Ib.

ἀπ-ευθύνω [ῠ], f. -υνῶ, to make straight again, Plat. ; χέρας δεσμοῖς ἀπ. to bind his arms straight, i. e. behind him, Soph.　2. to guide aright, to direct, govern, Id. ; to correct, chastise, Eur. : c. inf. to direct one to do a thing, Aesch.

ἀπ-ευκτός, ή, όν, to be deprecated, abominable, Aesch.

ἀπ-ευνάζω, f. σω, to lull to sleep, Soph.

ἀπ-εύχετος, ον, = ἀπευκτός, Aesch.

ἀπ-εύχομαι, Dep. to wish a thing away, wish it may not happen, deprecate, c. acc. rei, Eur., Dem. ; c. inf., ἀπ. τι γενέσθαι or μὴ γενέσθαι to pray that it may not happen, Dem.　　II. to reject, despise, τι Aesch.

ἀπ-εφθίθεν, for -ησαν, 1 pl. Ep. aor. 1 of ἀποφθίνω.

ἀπ-εφθῖτο, 3 sing. Ep. aor. 2 pass. of ἀπο-φθίνω.

ἄπ-εφθος, ον, softened form of ἄφ-εφθος, (ἀφ-έψω) boiled down, ἀπ. χρυσός refined gold, Hdt., Thuc.

ἀπ-εχθαίρω, f. -αρῶ : aor. 1 ἀπήχθηρα :—to hate utterly, detest, τινά Il.　　II. to make utterly hateful, τι Od.

ἀπ-εχθάνομαι, impf. ἀπηχθανόμην : f. ἀπεχθήσομαι : pf. ἀπήχθημαι : aor. 2 ἀπηχθόμην, ἀπήχθετο, subj. ἀπέχ-

θῶμαι, inf. ἀπεχθέσθαι: Pass.:—to be hated, incur hatred, be roused to hatred, Od.; c. dat. pers. to be or become hateful to one, Il., Hdt.; ἀπ. πρός τινα to be hateful in his eyes, Eur.:—c. dat. rei, to be hated for a thing, Plat. II. Dep., in causal sense, λόγοι ἀπεχθανόμενοι language that causes hatred, Xen.

ἀπέχθεια, ἡ, (ἀπεχθής) hatred, 1. felt towards another, πρός τινα Eur., etc. 2. felt by others towards one, enmity, odium, opp. to χάρις (popularity), and in pl. enmities, Plat., Dem.; δι᾽ ἀπεχθείας τινὶ ἐλθεῖν to be hated by him, Dem.

ἀπέχθημα, ατος, τό, (ἀπεχθάνομαι) an object of hate, Eur.

ἀπ-εχθής, ές, (ἔχθος) hateful, hostile, Soph., Theocr., etc.: Adv., ἀπεχθῶς ἔχειν τινι to be at enmity with him, Dem.

ἀπ-έχθομαι, later form of ἀπεχθάνομαι, Theocr., etc.: the inf. ἀπέχθεσθαι in Hom., etc. is now written ἀπεχθέσθαι, inf. of ἀπηχθόμην, aor. 2 of ἀπεχθάνομαι.

ἀπ-έχω, f. ἀφέξω and ἀποσχήσω: aor. 2 ἀπέσχον:—to keep off or away from, τινά or τί τινος Il.: absol. to keep off, Eur. 2. to keep apart, part, κληῖδες ἀπ᾽ ὤμων αὐχέν᾽ ἔχουσιν the collar-bones part the neck from the shoulders, Il. II. Med., ἀπὸ χεῖρας ἔχεσθαί τινος (in tmesi) to hold one's hands off or away from, Od.: also, ἀπέχεσθαί τινος to hold oneself off a thing, abstain or desist from it, Hom., Hdt., etc. 2. c. inf., ἀπέχεσθαι ποιεῖν or μὴ ποιεῖν τι to abstain from doing a thing, Thuc., etc. III. intr. in Act. to be away or far from, c. gen. loci, Id.; also, ἀπ. ἀπὸ Βαβυλῶνος, etc., Hdt.: absol. to be distant, Xen. 2. of actions, to be far from, ἀπεῖχον τῆς ἐξευρέσιος were far from the discovery, Hdt.; πλεῖστον ἀπ. τοῦ ποιεῖν to be as far as possible from doing, Xen. IV. to have or receive in full, τὸν μισθόν N.T., Plut. V. impers., ἀπέχει it sufficeth, it is enough, N.T.

ἀπ-έψω, Ion. for ἀφ-έψω.

ἀπ-έωσα, aor. 1 of ἀπωθέω.

ἀπ-ηγέομαι, ἀπ-ήγημα, ἀπ-ήγησις, Ion. for ἀφ-.

ἀπ-ηθέω, f. ήσω, to strain off, filter, Ar.

ἀπ-ηλεγέως, Adv. formed from an Adj. *ἀπ-ηλεγής (ἀπό, ἀλέγω) without caring for anything, reckless of consequences, bluntly, μῦθον ἀπηλεγέως ἀποειπεῖν Hom.

ἀπ-ηλιαστής, οῦ, ὁ, one who keeps away from the Ἡλιαία, i. e. an enemy to law, with a play on ἥλιος, not fond of basking in the sun, Ar.

ἀπ-ήλιξ, Ion. for ἀφ-ῆλιξ.

ἀπ-ηλιώτης, ου, ὁ, (ἥλιος) the wind that comes from the rising sun, the east wind, Lat. subsolanus, Hdt., Thuc.

ἀ-πήμαντος, ον, (πημαίνω) unharmed, unhurt, Od.: ἔστω δ᾽ ἀπήμαντον be misery far away, Aesch.

ἀπ-ήμβροτον, Ep. aor. 2 of ἀφ-αμαρτάνω.

ἀπημοσύνη, ἡ, (ἀπήμων) freedom from harm, Theogn.

ἀπ-ήμπλακε, 3 sing. aor. 2; v. ἀπ-αμπλακεῖν.

ἀ-πήμων, ον, gen. ονος, (πῆμα) unharmed, unhurt, of persons, Hom.; νόστος ἀπ. a safe, prosperous return, Od.: c. gen., ἀπήμων οἰζύος free from distress, Aesch. II. act. doing no harm, harmless, and so kindly, propitious, of a fair wind, of sleep, Hom.; c. gen., νεῶν ἀπ. free from harm to them, Eur.

ἀπήνη, ἡ, a four-wheeled wagon, Hom.: any car or chariot, Aesch., Soph.:—metaph., ναῖα ἀπ. a ship, Eur.; τετραβάμων ἀπήνη, of the Trojan horse, Id. 2. metaph. also, like ζεῦγος, a pair, e. g. of brothers, Id. (Deriv. unknown.)

ἀπ-ηνής, ές, ungentle, harsh, rough, hard, of persons, Hom. (Deriv. of -ηνης, as in προσ-ηνής, uncertain.)

ἀπ-ῆνθον, Dor. for ἀπ-ῆλθον, aor. 2 of ἀπ-έρχομαι.

ἀπ-ήορος, Dor. ἀπ-άορος, ον, (ἀείρω) hanging on high, high in air: also ἀπηόριος, Anth.: cf. ἀπ-ήωρος.

ἄ-πηρος, ον, unmaimed, Hdt.

ἀπ-ηύρων, ας, α, impf. of ἀπ-αυράω.

ἀπ-ηχής, ές, (ἦχος) discordant, ill-sounding, Luc.

ἀπ-ήχθετο, 3 sing. aor. 2 of ἀπ-εχθάνομαι.

ἀπ-ήωρος, ον, = ἀπ-ήορος, high in air, Od.

Ἀπία γῆ, v. ἄπιος.

ἀπ-ιάλλω, Laconic word for ἀποπέμπω, Thuc.

ἀ-πίθανος, ον, of things, not winning belief, incredible, unlikely, improbable, Plat.:—of arguments, not persuasive, unconvincing, Id. 2. of persons, not to be trusted, Aeschin. II. not having confidence to do a thing, c. inf., Plut. Hence

ἀπιθανότης, ητος, ἡ, improbability, Aeschin.

ἀπιθέω, Ep. form of ἀπειθέω, only in aor. 1, c. dat.; οὐκ ἀπίθησε μύθῳ he disobeyed not the words, Il.

ἀ-πιθής, ές, Ep. for ἀπειθής, Anth.

ἀπ-ιθύνω, = ἀπευθύνω, Anth.

ἀ-πινύσσω, (α privat., πινυτός) only in pres. to lack understanding, to be senseless, Hom.

ἄπιξις, εως, ἡ, Ion. for ἄφιξις.

ἄπιον, τό, (ἄπιος) a pear, Lat. pirum, Plat.

ἄπιος [ἄ], ἡ, a pear-tree, Lat. pirus, Arist.

ἄπιος, ον, ον, (ἀπό) far away, far off, distant, ἐξ ἀπίης γαίης Hom. II. Ἄπιος, α, ον, Apian, i. e. Peloponnesian (said to be derived from Ἄπις, a king of Argos), Ἀπία γῆ, Ἀπία χθών, or Ἀπία alone, the Peloponnese, esp. Argolis, Aesch., Soph.: so Ἀπίς, ἰδος, ἡ, Theocr. [The former sense has ἄ, the latter ᾱ.]

ἀπ-ιπόω, f. ώσω, to press the juice from anything, Hdt.

Ἄπις, ιδος, acc. ιν, and Ion. ιος, ὁ, Apis, a bull worshipped in Egypt, Hdt. II. Ἀπίς, = Ἀπία γῆ, cf. ἄπιος II.

ἀπ-ισόω, f. ώσω, to make equal, τινά τινι Plut.:—Pass. to be made equal, τινί to a thing, Hdt.

ἀπιστέω, f. ήσω: pf. ἠπίστηκα:—Pass., f. ἀπιστηθήσομαι, and in med. form ἀπιστήσομαι:—to be ἄπιστος, and so, I. to disbelieve, distrust, mistrust, c. acc., Od., Eur.:—Pass. to be distrusted, Thuc., Xen. 2. c. dat. pers., Hdt., Att.; τινί τι to disbelieve one in a thing, Hdt.; τινι περί τι Id.:—absol. to be distrustful, incredulous, Id. 3. c. inf. to doubt that.., Soph.; ἀπ. μὴ γενέσθαι τι to doubt that it could be, Thuc. II. = ἀπειθέω, to disobey, τινί Hdt., Soph., Eur. III. τὸ σῶμ᾽ οὐκ ἀπιστήσω χθονί, i. e. I will not hesitate to commit it to the earth, Eur.

ἀπιστία, Ion. -ίη, ἡ, (ἄπιστος) disbelief, distrust, mistrust, Hes., Hdt., etc.; ὑπὸ ἀπιστίης μὴ γενέσθαι τι from disbelief that it had happened, Hdt.; ἀπιστίαν ἔχειν περί τινος to be in doubt, Plat. 2. of things, ἐς ἀπιστίην ἀπῖχθαι to have become discredited, Hdt.; πολλὰς ἀπιστίας ἔχει it admits of many doubts, Plat.; εἰς ἀπ. καταπίπτειν Id. II. want of faith, faithlessness, unbelief, Soph.: treachery, Xen.

ἄ-πιστος, ον, I. pass. not to be trusted, and so, 1.

of persons and their acts, *not trusty, distrusted, faithless,* Il., etc.; θράσος ἄπ. *groundless* confidence, Thuc. **2.** of reports and the like, *incredible,* Hdt., Aesch.; τὸ ἐλπίδων ἄπιστον *what one cannot believe even in hope,* Soph. **II.** act. *not believing* or *trusting, mistrustful, incredulous, suspicious,* Od.; ἀπιστότερος *less credulous,* Hdt.; ἄπιστος πρὸς Φίλιππον *distrustful* towards him, Dem.; ἄπιστος σαυτῷ *not believing* what you say yourself, Plat.; τὸ ἀπ. = ἀπιστία, Thuc.:—in N. T., *unbelieving, an unbeliever.* **2.** *not obeying, disobeying,* c. gen., Aesch. **III.** Adv. ἀπίστως, **1.** pass. *beyond belief,* Thuc. **2.** act. *distrustfully, suspiciously,* Id.

ἀπιστοσύνη, ἡ, = ἀπιστία, Eur.

ἀπ-ισχῡρίζομαι, f. Att. -ιοῦμαι, Dep. *to set oneself to oppose firmly, give a flat denial,* πρός τινα Thuc.

ἀπ-ίσχω, = ἀπέχω, *to keep off, hold off,* Od.

ἀπῑτέον, verb. Adj. of ἄπειμι (εἶμι *ibo*), *one must go away,* Xen.

ἀπλακέω, ἀπλακία, v. ἀμπλακέω, ἀμπλακία.

ἀ-πλᾰνής, ές, *not wandering, steady, fixed,* Plat.:—of stars, *fixed,* opp. to πλανῆται, Id., Anth. **II.** of a line, *straight,* Anth.

ἀ-πλάνητος, ον, *that cannot go astray,* Babr.

ἄ-πλαστος, ον, *not moulded,* i. e. *in its natural state, natural, unaffected,* Plut.

ἄ-πλᾶτος, Dor. and Att. for Ep. **ἄ-πλητος,** ον, (πελάζω) for ἀ-πέλατος, *unapproachable, terrible,* Hes., Trag.

ἄ-πλεκτος, ον, (πλέκω) *unplaited,* χαίτη Anth.

ἄ-πλετος, ον, *boundless, immense,* Hdt., Att. (Prob. from ΠΛΕ, πίμπλημι, *not to be filled, beyond measure.*)

ἄ-πλευστος, ον, (πλέω) *not navigated:* τὸ ἄπλ. a part of the sea *not yet navigated,* Xen.

ἄ-πληκτος, ον, (πλήσσω) *unstricken,* of a horse *needing no whip* or spur, Plat.:—*unwounded,* Eur.

ἀ-πλήρωτος, ον, *insatiable,* Luc., Anth.

ἀπληστία, ἡ, *insatiate desire, greediness,* Plat.; τινός of or for a thing, Eur., Plat. From

ἄ-πληστος, ον, (πίμπλημι) *not to be filled, insatiate,* Soph., etc. **2.** c. gen., ἀπλ. χρημάτων *insatiate of money,* Hdt., etc. **II.** Adv., ἀπλήστως ἔχειν *to be insatiate,* Plat.; ἀπλ. διακεῖσθαι or ἔχειν πρός τι Xen.

ἄπλοια, poët. **ἀπλοΐη,** ἡ, (ἄπλους) *impossibility of sailing, detention in port,* esp. from stress of weather, Aesch., Thuc.; ἴσχον αὐτὸν ἄπλοιαι Hdt.

ἀπλοΐζομαι, Dep. (ἀπλοῦς) *to deal openly* or *frankly,* πρὸς τοὺς φίλους Xen.

ἀπλοΐς, ΐδος, ἡ, (ἀπλόος) *simple, single,* of a cloak, Hom.

ἀ-πλόκαμος, ον, *with unbraided hair,* Anth.

Ἁπλο-κύων, ὁ, nickname of *a Cynic who wore his coat single* instead of double, Plut.

ἀπλόος, η, ον, contr. **ἀπλοῦς,** ῆ, οῦν (from ἅμα, as Lat. *simplex* from *simul,* opp. to διπλόος, *duplex, twofold*). **I.** *single,* Soph., Thuc. **II.** *simple, natural, plain, sincere, frank,* Trag., Plat., etc.: in bad sense, *simple,* Isocr. **III.** *simple,* opp. to *compound,* Plat.; ἀπλῆ δημοκρατία *sheer* democracy, Id. **2.** *simple, absolutely true,* Id. **IV.** Adv. ἀπλῶς, v. sub voc. **V.** Comp. and Sup. ἀπλούστερος, ἀπλούστατος, Id.

ἄ-πλοος, ον, contr. **ἄ-πλους,** ουν: (πλέω): **I.** act.

of ships, *not sailing, unfit for sea, not sea-worthy,* Thuc.:—Comp., ἀπλοώτεραι ναῦς *less fit for sea,* Id. **II.** pass., of the sea, *not navigable,* Dem.

ἀπλότης, ητος, ἡ, (ἀπλόος) *singleness: simplicity, frankness,* Xen., etc. **II.** *liberality,* N. T.

ἀπλοῦς, ῆ, οῦν, contr. for ἀπλόος, q. v.

ἄ-πλους, ουν, contr. for ἄ-πλοος, q. v.

ἀπλούστερος, —τατος, v. ἀπλόος signf. v.

ἄ-πλουτος, ον, *without riches,* Soph., Plut.

ἀπλόω, f. ώσω, (ἀπλοῦς) *to make single, to unfold, stretch out,* Batr., Anth.:—Pass., ἡπλώθη [the fish] *lay stretched out,* Babr.

ἀ-πλοώτερος, Comp. of ἄ-πλοος.

ἀπλῡσία, ἡ, *filthiness, filth,* Anth. From

ἄ-πλῠτος, ον, (πλύνω) *unwashen, unwashed,* Ar.

ἀπλῶς, Adv. of ἀπλοῦς, Lat. *simpliciter, singly, in one way,* Plat. **II.** *simply, plainly, openly, frankly,* Aesch., etc. **2.** *simply, absolutely,* ἀπλῶς ἀδύνατον Thuc.; οὐδεμία ἀπλῶς *none at all,* Id.; ὅσ᾽ ἐστὶν ἀπλῶς *simply all there are,* Ar. **3.** *in a word,* Lat. *denique,* Eur., Xen.

ἀπνευστί, Adv. of ἄπνευστος, ἀπ. ἔχειν *to hold one's breath,* Plat.; *without drawing breath,* Dem.

ἄ-πνευστος, ον, (πνέω) *breathless,* Od.

ἄ-πνοος, ον, contr. **ἄ-πνους,** ουν, (πνέω) *without breath, lifeless,* Anth.

᾽ΑΠΟ΄, poët. **ἀπαί,** Prep. c. gen. = Lat. *ab, from.*
I. OF PLACE: **1.** of Motion, *from, away from,* Hom., etc.; of warriors fighting *from* chariots, Hom. **2.** of Position, *away from, far from, apart from,* ἀπὸ ἧς ἀλόχοιο Il.; ἀπ᾽ ὀφθαλμῶν *far from* sight, Ib.; ἀπὸ θαλάσσης Thuc., etc. **3.** of the mind, ἀπὸ θυμοῦ *away from,* i. e. *alien from,* my heart, Il.; οὐκ ἀπὸ τρόπου *not without* reason, Plat.; οὐκ ἀπὸ πράγματος Dem. **4.** in partitive sense, αἶσ᾽ ἀπὸ ληΐδος *a part from* the booty, *a share of* it, Od. **II.** OF TIME, *from, after,* ἀπὸ δείπνου *after supper,* Il.; ἀπὸ δείπνου γενέσθαι *to have done supper,* Hdt., etc.; ἀφ᾽ οὗ (sc. χρόνου), Lat. *ex quo,* Od. **III.** OF ORIGIN, CAUSE, etc.: **1.** of that from which one is born, οὐκ ἀπὸ δρυὸς οὐδ᾽ ἀπὸ πέτρης *not sprung from* oak or rock, Od.; τρίτος ἀπὸ Διός *third in descent from* Zeus, Plat.; οἱ ἀπὸ Σπάρτης *the men from* Sparta, Hdt.:—metaph. of things, κάλλος ἀπὸ Χαρίτων *beauty born of* the Graces, such as they give, Od.; γάλα ἀπὸ βοός Aesch.: —of connexion with the leader of a sect, οἱ ἀπὸ Πλάτωνος, Plato's *disciples;* οἱ ἀπὸ τῆς ᾽Ακαδημίας, ἀπὸ τῆς Στοᾶς, *the* Academics, *the* Stoics, Plut., etc. **2.** of the Material *from* or *of* which a thing is made, ἀπὸ ξύλου Hdt.; ἀπὸ μέλιτος Theocr. **3.** of the Instrument *from* or *by* which a thing is done, ἀπ᾽ ἀργυρέοιο βιοῖο *by* [arrow *shot from*] silver bow, Il. **4.** of the Person *from* whom an act comes, i. e. *by* whom it is done, οὐδὲν μέγα ἔργον ἀπ᾽ αὐτοῦ ἐγένετο Hdt.; ἐπράχθη ἀπ᾽ αὐτοῦ οὐδέν Thuc.;—so that ἀπό came to be used like ὑπό, but implying a *less direct* agency. **5.** of the Source *from* which life or power is sustained, ζῆν ἀπὸ ἰχθύων Hdt.; τρέφειν τὸ ναυτικὸν ἀπὸ τῶν νήσων Xen. **6.** of the Cause, Means, or Occasion *from, by,* or *because of* which a thing is done, ἀπὸ δικαιοσύνης *by reason of* justice, Hdt.; ἀπὸ τῶν αὐτῶν λημμάτων *moved by, for* the same profits, Dem.:—hence in many adverbial usages, ἀπὸ

σπουδῆς in earnest, eagerly, Il. ; ἀπὸ τοῦ ἴσου, ἀπὸ τῆς ἴσης, or ἀπ' ἴσης, equally, Thuc., etc. ; ἀπὸ γλώσσης by word of mouth, Hdt. ; ἀφ' ἑαυτοῦ from or of oneself, Thuc.

B. AS ADVERB, far away, Hom., Hdt.

C. IN COMPOS.: 1. from, asunder, as in ἀποτέμνω : away, off, as in ἀποβαίνω. 2. finishing off, completing, as in ἀπεργάζομαι. 3. ceasing from, leaving off, as in ἀπαλγέω, ἀπολοφύρομαι. 4. back again, as in ἀποδίδωμι, ἀπολαμβάνω : also, in full, or what is one's own, as ἀπέχω. 5. by way of abuse, as in ἀποκαλέω. 6. almost = a priv. ; sometimes with Verbs, as ἀπαυδάω, ἀπαγορεύω ; with Adjectives, as ἀποχρήματος, ἀπόσιτος.

D. ἄπο, by anastrophé for ἀπό, when it follows its Noun, as ὀμμάτων ἄπο Soph.

ἀπο-αίνυμαι, Ep. for ἀπαίνυμαι.

ἀπο-αιρέομαι, Ep. for ἀφαιρέομαι.

ἀπό-βα, = ἀπο-βῆθι, aor. 2 imp. of ἀποβαίνω.

ἀπο-βάθρα, Ion. -βάθρη, ἡ, a ladder for disembarking, a gangway, Hdt., Thuc.

ἀπο-βαίνω, f. -βήσομαι, 3 sing. Ep. aor. 1 -εβήσετο : aor. 2 ἀπ-έβην : pf. ἀπο-βέβηκα :—to step off from a place, to alight or disembark from a ship, Hom., etc. ; absol. to disembark, Hdt., Thuc., etc. :—to dismount from a chariot, ἵππων or ἐξ ἵππων Il. 2. to go away, depart, Ib., Att. ;—c. gen., ἀπ. πεδίων Eur. ; of hopes, to come to naught, Id. II. of events, to issue or result from, τὰ ἔμελλε ἀποβήσεσθαι ἀπὸ τῆς μάχης Hdt. ; τὸ ἀποβαῖνον, contr. τἀποβαῖνον, the issue, event, and τὰ ἀποβαίνοντα, τὰ ἀποβάντα the results, Id., Thuc. ; τὰ ἀποβησόμενα the probable results, Thuc. 2. to turn out so and so, παρὰ δόξαν Hdt. ; τοιόνδε Eur. ; ὡς προσεδέχετο Thuc. :—absol. to turn out well, succeed, Id. 3. of persons, to end by being, ἀπ. κοινοί to prove impartial, Id. ; so, ἐς ἀληθινὸν ἄνδρ' ἀπ. Theocr. ; ἀπέβη ἐς μουναρχίην things ended in a monarchy, Hdt.

B. Causal in aor. 1 ἀπέβησα, to make to dismount, disembark, land, (in which sense ἀποβιβάζω serves as pres.), ἀπ. στρατιήν Hdt.

ἀπο-βάλλω, f. -βαλῶ, to throw off, Il. ; c. gen. to throw off from, ἀπ. ὀμμάτων ὕπνον Eur. ; 2. to throw away, τὴν ἀσπίδα Ar. ; τὸν ἄνδρα ἀπ. to reject him, Eur. :—Med. to cast from one, reject, Theocr. 3. to lose, τὰ πατρῷα, τὸν στρατόν Hdt. ; τὴν οὐσίαν Ar. ; πολλοὺς τῶν στρατιωτῶν Thuc.

ἀπο-βάπτω, f. ψω, to dip quite or entirely, ἑαυτόν Hdt. ; τι εἴς τι Id.

ἀπο-βάς, aor. 2 part. of ἀπο-βαίνω.

ἀπόβασις, εως, ἡ, (ἀποβαίνω) a stepping off, disembarking, ἀπὸ τῶν νεῶν Thuc. ; ἡ ναυτικὴ ἐπ' ἄλλους ἀπόβασις landing from ships in the face of an enemy, Id. ; absol., ποιεῖσθαι ἀπόβασιν to disembark, land, Id. 2. a landing, landing-place, οὐκ ἔχει ἀπόβασιν does not admit of landing, or has no landing-place, Id. ; pl., Id. II. a way off, escape, Plut.

ἀποβάτης [ᾰ], ου, ὁ, (ἀποβαίνω) one who rode several horses leaping from one to the other, Lat. desultor, Plut.

ἀπο-βιάζομαι, f. -άσομαι, Dep. to force away :—Pass. to be forced away or back, Xen. II. absol. to use force, Id.

ἀπο-βιβάζω, Causal of ἀποβαίνω, to make to get off, esp.

from a ship, to disembark, put on shore, Hdt., Thuc., etc. :—Med., ἀποβιβάσασθαί τινας to cause them to be put on shore, Hdt.

ἀπο-βλάπτω, f. ψω, to ruin utterly :—Pass., ἀποβλαφθῆναι φίλου to be robbed of a friend, Soph.

ἀπο-βλαστάνω, aor. 2 -έβλαστον, to shoot forth from, spring from, c. gen., Soph. Hence

ἀπο-βλάστημα, ατος, τό, a shoot, scion, Plat.

ἀπόβλεπτος, ον, gazed on by all, admired, Eur. From

ἀπο-βλέπω, f. -βλέψομαι :—to look away from all other objects at one, to look or gaze steadfastly, ἔς τινα or τι Hdt., Eur. ; πρός τινα or τι Hdt., Plat. 2. to look to, pay attention or regard, ἔς τι Eur., etc. ; πρός τι Plat. 3. to look upon with love or admiration, Lat. observare, suspicere, c. acc., Soph. ; with a Prep., ἔς or πρός τινα Eur., Xen.

ἀποβλητέος, α, ον, verb. Adj. of ἀποβάλλω, to be thrown away, rejected, Plat.

ἀπόβλητος, ον, verb. Adj. of ἀποβάλλω, to be thrown away as worthless, Il.

ἀπο-βλίττω, f. -βλίσω [ῐ], to cut out the comb from the hive : hence to steal, Ar.

ἀπο-βλύζω, f. σω, to spirt out, c. gen. partit., ἀπ. οἴνου to spirt out some wine, Il.

ἀποβολή, ῆς, ἡ, (ἀποβάλλω) a throwing away, Plat. 2. a losing, loss, Lat. jactura, Id.

ἀποβολιμαῖος, ον, (ἀποβάλλω) apt to throw away a thing, c. gen., Ar.

ἀπο-βόσκομαι, Dep. to feed upon, καρπόν Ar.

ἀπο-βουκολέω, f. ήσω, to let cattle stray : to lose (as a bad shepherd does his sheep), εἰ τῇ θυγατρὶ τὸν παῖδα ἀποβουκολήσαιμι if I were to lose my daughter her son, Xen. :—Pass. to lose one's way, Luc.

ἀπο-βρίζω, f. ξω, to go off to sleep, go sound asleep, Od.

ἀπο-βροχίζω, f. ίσω, (βρόχος) to strangle, Anth.

ἀπο-βώμιος, ον, (βωμός) far from an altar, godless, Eur.

ἀπό-γαιος or -γειος, ον, (γῆ) from land : ἀπόγειον or ἀπόγαιον, τό, a morning cable, Luc.

ἀπο-γειόω, f. ώσω, to make to jut out like a cornice (γεῖσον), ὀφρύσι ἀπ. τὸ ὑπὲρ τῶν ὀμμάτων Xen.

ἀπο-γεύω, f. σω, to give one a taste of a thing, c. gen., Anth. :—Med. to take a taste of a thing, c. gen., Plat., Xen.

ἀπο-γεφυρόω, f. ώσω, to bank off, fence with dykes, τὴν Μέμφιν Hdt.

ἀπο-γηράσκω, f. -γηράσομαι [ᾱ], to grow old, Theogn.

ἀπο-γίγνομαι, Ion. and late Att. -γίνομαι : f. -γενήσομαι :—to be away from, have no part in a thing, c. gen., Hdt., Thuc. II. absol. to be taken away, opp. to προσγίγνομαι, Thuc. : generally, to be away, absent, Plat., etc. 2. of death, ἀπ. ἐκ τῶν οἰκιῶν to depart from the house, die out of it, Hdt. ; ἀπογενέσθαι alone, to be dead, οἱ ἀπογενόμενοι the dead, Thuc. ; ὁ ὕστατον αἰεὶ ἀπ. he who died last, Hdt. ; ὁ ἀπογινόμενος one who is dying, Id., Thuc. 3. to be lost, ἀπ. οὐδὲν τοῦ στρατοῦ Thuc.

ἀπο-γιγνώσκω, Ion. and late Att. -γινώσκω, f. -γνώσομαι :—to depart from a judgment, give up a design or intention of doing, ἀπ. τὸ μάχεσθαι Xen. ; ἀπ. μὴ βοηθεῖν to resolve not to help, Dem. II. c. gen. rei, to despair of a thing, c. gen., Lys. :—absol. to despair, Dem. 2. c. acc. to give up as hopeless, Id. :—Pass.

to be so given up, Dem.   **III.** as law-term, *to refuse to receive* an accusation, *reject*, Id.:—ἀπ. τινος (sc. δίκην vel γραφήν) *to reject* the charge *brought against* a man, i. e. *acquit* him, opp. to καταγιγνώσκειν τινός, Id. : also, ἀπ. τινά (sc. τῆς δίκης vel γραφῆς) *to judge* one *free from* the accusation, *to acquit* him, Id.   Hence

ἀπόγνοιά, ἡ, *despair* of a thing, c. gen., Thuc.

ἀπόγονος, ον, (ἀπογίγνομαι) *born* or *descended from*, Lat. *oriundus*, Hdt. : in pl. *descendants*, Id., Thuc. ; ἀπόγονοι τεαί thy *offspring*, Soph.

ἀπογρᾰφή, ἡ, *a writing off*: *a register, list*, of lands or property, Plat., etc. : *a register of persons liable to taxation*, Lat. *census*, N. T.   **II.** as Att. ˙aw-term, *the copy of a* γραφή, *a deposition*, Oratt.   From

ἀπο-γράφω [ᾰ], f. ψω, *to write off, copy* : *to enter in a list, register*, Hdt., Plat.:—Med. *to have* names *registered* by others, or *to register for one's own use*, Hdt., Plat.   **2.** Med. also *to give in one's name, register*, or *enlist oneself*, Xen.   **II.** as Att. law-term,   **1.** ἀπογράφειν τινά *to enter* a person's name *as accused, give in a copy of the charge* against him, *to inform against, denounce*, Id.   **2.** *to give in a list* of property alleged to belong to the state, but held by a private person, Oratt. :—also, ἀπέγραψεν ταῦτα ἔχοντα αὑτόν *gave a written acknowledgment* that he was in possession of this property, Dem.

ἀπο-γυιόω, f. ώσω, *to deprive* one *of the use of his limbs, to enfeeble*, μή μ' ἀπογυιώσῃς Il.

ἀπο-γυμνάζω, f. άσω, *to bring into hard exercise, to ply hard*, Aesch.

ἀπο-γυμνόω, f. ώσω, *to strip quite bare* of arms : Pass. *to be so stripped*, Od. :—Med. *to strip oneself*, Xen.

ἀπο-δάκνω, f. -δήξομαι, *to bite off* a piece of a thing, c. gen. :—Pass., μῆλα ἀποδεδηγμένα with *pieces bitten out*, Luc.   **2.** absol. *to bite hard, gnaw*, Xen.

ἀπο-δακρύω [ῠ], f. -σω, *to weep much for, lament loudly*, τινά Plat.   **2.** ἀπ. γνώμην is *to weep away* one's judgment, Ar.

ἀπο-δαρθάνω, aor. 2 -έδαρθον, *to sleep a little*, Plut.

ἀποδάσμιος, ον, *parted from* the rest, Hdt.   From

ἀποδασμός, ὁ, *a division, part of a whole*, Thuc.   From

ἀπο-δατέομαι, f. -δάσομαι, Ep. -δάσσομαι :—*to portion out* to others, *to apportion*, τί τινι Il.   **II.** *to part off, separate*, Hdt.

ἀποδέδεγμαι, pf. of ἀποδέχομαι.   **II.** Ion. for ἀποδέδειγμαι, pf. pass. of ἀποδείκνυμι.

ἀπο-δεής, ές, (δέω) *wanting much, not fully manned*, Plut.

ἀπο-δειδίσσομαι, Ep. 3 sing. impf. -δειδίσσετο, Dep. *to frighten away*, Il.

ἀπο-δείκνυμι and -ύω : f. -δείξω, Ion. -δέξω : Pass., pf. -δέδειγμαι, Ion. -δέδεγμαι :—*to point away from* other objects at one, and so,   **I.** *to point out, shew forth, exhibit, make known*, by deed or word, τί τινι Hdt. ; τι Aesch.   **2.** *to bring forward, shew, produce*, Lat. *praestare*, μαρτύρια τουτέων Hdt. ; παῖδας Soph. ; ὑγιέα τινὰ ἐόντα ἀπ. *to produce* him safe and sound, Hdt.   **3.** *to produce* or *deliver in* accounts, λόγων Id., Thuc.   **4.** *to publish* a law, Lat. *promulgare*, Xen.   **5.** *to appoint, assign*, τέμενος, βωμὸν ἀπ. τινί Hdt.:—Pass., χῶρος ἀποδεδεγμένος an *appointed* place, Id.   **6.** *to shew by argument, prove, demonstrate*, Ar., Plat., etc.; ἀπ. τινὰ

οὐδὲν λέγοντα *to make it evident* that he says nothing, Hdt.   **II.** *to appoint, name, create*, ἀπ. τινὰ βασιλέα Id., Xen.   **2.** *to make, render*, ἀπ. τινὰ μοχθηρόν *to make* him a rascal, Ar. ; ἀπ. τινὰ κράτιστον Xen.   **3.** *to represent as*, ἀπ. παῖδα Hdt. :—Pass., οὐκ ἐν τοῖσι θεοῖσι ἀποδεδέχαται (Ion. 3 pl. pf.) *have* not *been considered, admitted* among, Id.

    B. Med. *to shew forth, exhibit* something *of one's own*, ἀποδέξασθαι τὴν γνώμην *to deliver one's* opinion, Hdt. ; μνημόσυνα ἀπ. memorials *of oneself*, Id. :—Pass., ἔργα μεγάλα ἀποδεχθέντα Id.   **2.** just like Act., ἀποδ. ὅτι . . , *to declare that* . . , Xen.   Hence

ἀποδεικτέον, verb. Adj. *one must prove*, Plat.   **2.** c. dupl. acc. *one must make* one so and so, Luc.

ἀποδειλίᾱσις, εως, ἡ, *great cowardice*, Plut. ; and

ἀποδειλιᾱτέον, verb. Adj. *one must flinch*, Plat.   From

ἀπο-δειλιάω, f. άσω [ᾱ], *to play the coward, to flinch from danger* or *toil*, Xen., Plat.

ἀπόδειξις, Ion. -δεξις, εως, ἡ, (ἀποδείκνυμι) *a shewing forth, exhibiting*, Eur.   **2.** *a setting forth, exposition, publication*, Hdt., Thuc.   **3.** *a shewing, proving, proof*, Hdt., Att. ; pl. *proofs, arguments in proof* of, τινος Dem.   **II.** (from Med.) ἀπ. ἔργων μεγάλων a *display, performance* of mighty works, Hdt.

ἀπο-δειπνίδιος, ον, (δεῖπνον) *of* or *from supper*, Anth.

ἀπο-δειροτομέω, f. ήσω, *to slaughter by cutting off the head* or *cutting the throat*, Hom.

ἀπο-δείρω, Ion. for ἀπο-δέρω.

ἀποδεκατόω, f. ώσω, *to tithe, pay tithes of*, πάντα N. T. ; ἀπ. τινά *to take tithe* of him, Ib.

ἀπο-δέκομαι, Ion. for ἀπο-δέχομαι.

ἀποδεκτέον, verb. Adj. of ἀποδέχομαι, *one must receive from others*, τι Xen.   **2.** *one must accept, allow, admit*, τι Plat.; c. gen. pers. et part., ἀπ. τινὸς λέγοντος Id.

ἀποδεκτήρ, ῆρος, ὁ, (ἀπο-δέχομαι) *a receiver*, Xen.

ἀποδέκτης, ου, ὁ, *a receiver*, name of a magistrate at Athens who paid the dicasts, Dem.

ἀποδεκτός, όν, (ἀπο-δέχομαι) *acceptable*, N. T.

ἀπο-δενδρόομαι, (δένδρον) Pass. *to be turned into a tree*, Luc.

ἀπο-δέξασθαι, aor. 1 inf. of ἀποδέχομαι.   **II.** Ion. for ἀποδείξασθαι, aor. 1 of ἀποδείκνυμι.

ἀπόδεξις, εως, ἡ, Ion. for ἀπόδειξις.

ἀπόδερμα, ατος, τό, (ἀποδέρω) *a hide stripped off*, Hdt.

ἀπο-δέρω, Ion. -δείρω, f. -δερῶ, *to flay* or *skin completely*, τὸν βοῦν Hdt. ; ἀπ. τὴν κεφαλήν *to take off* the scalp, Id. :—Pass., πρόβατα ἀποδαρέντα Xen.   **II.** ἀπ. τὴν δορήν *to strip off* the skin, Hdt.

ἀπό-δεσμος, ὁ, *a breastband, girdle*, Luc.   **II.** *a bundle, bunch*, Plut.

ἀποδεχθείς, Ion. for ἀποδειχθείς.

ἀπο-δέχομαι, Ion. -δέκομαι : f. -δέξομαι, aor. 1 -εδεξάμην : pf. -δέδεγμαι :—*to accept from* another, *to accept*, Il., Att.   **2.** *to accept* as a teacher, *follow*, Xen.   **3.** *to admit* to one's presence, Plat.   **4.** *to receive favourably, approve, allow, accept, admit*, Thuc., etc. ; οὐκ ἀπ. not *to accept, reject*, Hdt.:—the person *from whom one accepts* in gen., ἀπ. τί τινος Thuc., etc. ; but acc. being omitted, gen. pers. becomes dependent on the Verb, with a partic. added, ἀπ. τινὸς λέγοντος *to accept* [a statement] *from* him, i. e. *to accept* his statements, Plat. :—absol. *to accept a statement, be satisfied*, Dem.   **5.**

to take a thing in a certain way, with an Adv., Xen.; ὕποπτως ἀπ. τι Thuc.; δυσχερῶς Plat. **II.** *to receive back, recover,* Hdt., Thuc.

ἀπο-δέω, f. -δήσω, *to bind fast,* Plat.

ἀπο-δέω, f. -δεήσω, *to be in want of, lack,* τριακοσίων ἀποδέοντα μύρια 10,000 *lacking* 300, Thuc.: *to fall short of, be inferior to,* τινός Luc.

ἀπο-δημέω, Dor. -δᾱμέω, f. ήσω, (ἀπόδημος) *to be away from home, be abroad* or *on one's travels,* Hdt., Att. **2.** *to go abroad,* ἀπ. παρά τινα *to visit him,* Hdt.; ἀπ. ἐς Αἴγιναν κατά τι *to go abroad* to Aegina to fetch a thing, Id. Hence

ἀποδημητής, οῦ, ὁ, *one who goes abroad,* Thuc.; and

ἀποδημητικός, ή, όν, *fond of travelling:* παράστασις ἀπ. banishment *to foreign parts,* i. e. ostracism, Arist.

ἀποδημία, Ion. -ίη, ή, *a being from home, a going* or *being abroad,* Hdt., Att.; περὶ τῆς ἀπ. τῆς ἐκεῖ as to my life in that *foreign land,* i. e. beyond the grave, Plat. From

ἀπό-δημος, Dor. -δᾱμος, ον, *away from one's country, from home, abroad,* Pind., Plut.

ἀπο-διαιτάω, f. ήσω, *to decide for* one *in an arbitration,* opp. to καταδιαιτάω (*to decide against*), Dem.

ἀπο-διατρίβω [ῑ], f. ψω, *to wear quite away, to waste utterly,* Aeschin.

ἀπο-διδράσκω, Ion. -διδρήσκω: f. -δράσομαι, Ion. -δρήσομαι: aor. 2 ἀπ-έδραν, Ion. -έδρην, imperat. ἀπόδρᾱθι, inf. ἀποδρᾶναι, Ion. -δρῆναι, part. ἀποδράς:—*to run away* or *off, escape,* or *flee from, escape. by stealth,* Od., Hdt., Att.; *of runaway slaves,* Xen.; *of soldiers, to desert,* Id. **2.** c. acc. *to flee, shun,* Hdt., Thuc.

ἀπο-δίδωμι [ῐ], f. -δώσω, *to give up* or *back, restore, return,* τί τινι Hom., Att.: esp. *to render what is due, to pay,* as debts, penalties, submission, Il.; ἀπ. τινὶ λώβην *to give* him *back* his insult, i. e. *make atonement for* it, Ib.; ἀπ. ἀμοιβήν τινι Theogn., etc. **2.** *to return, render, yield,* of land, ἐπὶ διηκόσια ἀποδοῦναι (sc. καρπόν) *to yield fruit* two hundred-fold, Hdt. **3.** c. inf. *to suffer* or *allow* a person to do a thing, ἀπ. τισὶ αὐτονομεῖσθαι Thuc., etc.:—so in Pass., ὁ λόγος ἀπεδόθη αὐτοῖς right of speech *was allowed* them, Aeschin. **4.** *to render* so and so, ἀπ. τὴν τέρψιν βεβαιοτέραν Isocr. **5.** *to deliver over, give up,* as a slave, Eur.; ἀπ. ἐπιστολήν *to deliver* a letter, Thuc. **6.** λόγον ἀπ. *to render* or *give in* an account, Lat. *rationes referre,* Dem.: *to give an account of* a thing, Eur. **7.** ἀπ. ὅρκον, v. ὅρκος. **II.** intr. *to increase,* much like ἐπιδίδωμι III, ἢν ἡ χώρα ἐπιδιδῷ ἐς ὕψος καὶ ἀποδιδῷ ἐς αὔξησιν Hdt.;—unless here it means the contrary, if the land *increase* in height and *decrease* in productiveness. **III.** Med. *to give away of one's own will, to sell,* Hdt., Att.; ἀπ. τι Ἑλλάδα *to take* to Greece *and sell it there,* Hdt.; ἀπ. τοῦ εὑρίσκοντος *to sell for* what it will fetch, Aeschin.: at Athens, *to farm out* the public taxes, Dem.

ἀπο-δῐκεῖν, inf. of ἀπ-έδικον, aor. 2 with no pres. in use, *to throw off* or *away,* Aesch., Eur.

ἀπο-δῐκέω, (δίκη) *to defend oneself on trial,* Xen.

ἀπο-δῑνέω, f. ήσω, *to thresh corn* (v. δῖνος II), Hdt.

ἀπο-δίομαι, Dep. = ἀποδιώκω, only in pres., Il.

ἀπο-διοπομπέομαι, f. ήσομαι, Dep. (ἀπό, Διός, πομπή) *to avert threatened evils by offerings to Zeus, to conjure away,* Plat.

ἀπο-διορίζω, f. Att. ιῶ, *to mark off by dividing, to separate,* N. T.

ἀπο-διώκω, f. -διώξομαι, *to chase away,* Thuc.; οὐκ ἀποδιώξει σαυτόν; i. e. *take* yourself *off,* Ar.

ἀπο-δοκεῖ, impers. (δοκέω) *it seems good not* to do a thing, c. inf., ἀπέδοξέ σφι πράττειν or μὴ πράττειν Hdt., Xen.; sometimes with the inf. omitted, ὥς σφι ἀπέδοξε when *they resolved not* (to go on), Hdt.

ἀπο-δοκιμάζω, f. άσω, *to reject on scrutiny, to reject for want of qualification,* Hdt., Att.:—generally, *to reject as unworthy* or *unfit,* Plat., Xen. — Hence

ἀποδοκιμαστέον, verb. Adj. *one must reject,* Xen. **II.** -έος, έα, έον, *to be rejected,* Arist., Luc.

ἀποδοκιμάω, = ἀποδοκιμάζω, *to reject,* Hdt.

ἄπ-οδος, ή, Ion. for ἄφ-οδος.

ἀπόδοσις, εως, ή, (ἀποδίδωμι) *a giving back, restitution, return,* τινος of a thing, Hdt., Att. **2.** *payment,* τοῦ μισθοῦ Thuc.

ἀποδοτέον, verb. Adj. of ἀποδίδωμι, *one must give back, refer, assign,* τί τινι Plat. **2.** *one must describe,* Id.

ἀποδοῦναι, aor. 2 inf. of ἀποδίδωμι.

ἀποδοχή, ή, (ἀποδέχομαι) *a receiving back, having restored to* one, Thuc.

ἀποδραθεῖν, aor. 2 inf. of ἀποδαρθάνω.

ἀποδράς, aor. 2 part. of ἀποδιδράσκω.

ἀπόδρασις, Ion. -δρησις, εως, ή, (ἀποδιδράσκω) *a running away, escape,* Hdt.: c. gen. *escape from,* στρατείας Dem.

ἀπο-δρέπτομαι, f. ψομαι, Dep., = sq., Anth.

ἀπο-δρέπω, f. ψω, *to pluck off,* Pind.; ἀπόδρεπε οἴκαδε βότρυς *pluck and take* them home, Hes.

ἀποδρῆναι, Ion. for -δρᾶναι, aor. 2 inf. of ἀποδιδράσκω.

ἀπόδρησις, Ion. for ἀπόδρασις.

ἀπο-δρύπτω, f. ψω, aor. 1 ἀπέδρυψα: aor. 2 ἀπέδρυφον:—*to tear off the skin, lacerate,* Hom.:—Pass., of the skin, *to be torn off,* Od.

ἀπο-δύομαι [ῠ], = ἀποδύω, *to strip off,* βοείην Od.

ἀπ-οδύρομαι [ῠ], f. -ῠροῦμαι, *to lament bitterly,* Hdt., Att.

ἀποδύς, aor. 2 part. of ἀποδύω.

ἀποδυτέον, verb. Adj. of ἀποδύω, *one must strip,* τινά Luc. **II.** from Pass., ἀπ. ταῖς γυναιξὶν *they must strip off their clothes,* Plat.

ἀποδυτήριον, τό, *an undressing room,* Plat., Xen. From

ἀπο-δύω, f. -δύσω, aor. 1 -έδῠσα:—*to strip off* clothes or armour, Il.:—Pass., f. -δυθήσομαι: aor. 1 -εδύθην [ῠ]: pf. -δέδῠμαι. **2.** *to strip* a person of clothes, ἀπέδυσε τὰς γυναῖκας Hdt., etc.:—Pass. *to be stripped* of one's clothes, Ar. **II.** Med., f. -δύσομαι [ῠ]: aor. 1 -εδυσάμην; also intr. aor. 2 act. ἀπέδυν, pf. ἀποδέδυκα:—*to strip off oneself, take off,* εἵματα Od.:—absol. ἀποδυσάμενος *having stripped,* Ib.; ἀποδύντες *stripped naked,* Thuc.; ἀποδύεσθαι εἴς or πρός τι *to strip for* gymnastic exercises, Plut.: metaph., ἀποδύντες ἐπίωμεν *let us strip and attack,* Ar.

ἀπο-είκω, f. ξω, *to withdraw from* the path, c. gen., Il.

ἀπο-ειπεῖν, Ep. inf. of ἀπ-εῖπον.

ἀπο-εργάθον, ἀπο-έργω, Ep. for ἀπ-είργαθον, ἀπ-είργω.

ἀπό-ερσε, old Ep. aor. 1 only found in 3 pers. ἀπόερσε, *swept away,* subj. ἀποέρσῃ, opt. ἀποέρσειε, all in Il. (Deriv. uncertain.)

ἀπο-ζάω, f. -ζήσω, *to live off,* ὅσον ἀποζῆν *enough to live off,* Thuc. **II.** *to live poorly,* Luc.

ἀπο-ζεύγνῦμαι, aor. 1 -εζεύχθην : aor. 2 -εζύγην [ῠ] : Pass. :—to be parted from, γυναικός Eur. ; εἰ γάμων ἀπεζύγην if I were free from wedlock, Id. ; ἀπεζύγην πόδας I started on foot, Aesch.

ἀπ-όζω, f. -οζήσω, to smell of something, τινος Ibyc. :— impers., ἀπόζει τῆς Ἀραβίης there comes an odour from Arabia, Hdt.

ἀποθάλλω, f. -θάλῶ, to lose the bloom, Anth.

ἀπο-θαρρέω and -θαρσέω, to have full confidence, Xen.

ἀπο-θαυμάζω, Ion. -θωυμάζω or -θωμάζω, f. σω, to marvel much at a thing, c. acc., Od.:—absol. to wonder much, Hdt., Aesch.

ἀπο-θείομαι, Ep. for -θέωμαι, aor. 2 subj. med. of ἀπο-τίθημι.

ἀπο-θειόω, poët. for ἀποθεόω.

ἄποθεν, Adv. (ἀπό) from afar, Thuc., Xen.   II. afar off, Thuc., Xen.

ἀπο-θεόω, f. ώσω, to deify:—Pass., Ep. aor. 1 part. ἀπο-θεωθείς Anth.

ἀπο-θεραπεία, ἡ, regular worship, θεῶν Arist.

ἀπο-θερίζω, poët. aor. 1 ἀπ-έθρῑσα, to cut off, κόμας Eur.

ἀπόθεσις, εως, ἡ, (ἀπο-τίθημι) a laying up in store, Plat.   II. a putting aside, getting rid of a thing, c. gen., N. T.   III. = ἀποδυτήριον, Luc.

ἀπό-θεστος, ον, (θέσσασθαι) despised, Od.

ἀποθέται, ων, αἱ, (ἀποτίθημι) a place in Lacedaemon, into which misshapen children were thrown, Plut.

ἀπόθετος, ον, (ἀποτίθημι) laid by, stored up, Plut., Luc.   2. hidden, secret, mysterious, ἔπη Plat.   3. reserved for occasions, special, Dem.

ἀπο-θέω, f. -θεύσομαι, to run away, Hdt., Xen.

ἀπο-θεώρησις, εως, ἡ, serious contemplation, Plut.

ἀποθέωσις, εως, ἡ, (ἀποθεόω) deification, Strab.

ἀποθήκη, ἡ, (ἀπο-τίθημι) any place wherein to lay up a thing, a barn, magazine, storehouse, Thuc.   II. anything laid by, a store, ἀποθήκην ποιεῖσθαι ἔς τινα to lay up store of favour with him, Hdt.

ἀπο-θηλύνω [ῡ], f. ῠνῶ, to make effeminate, enervate, Plut.

ἀπο-θησαυρίζω, f. σω, to store, hoard up, Luc.

ἀπο-θλίβω [ῑ], f. ψω, to press upon, press, squeeze out, Eur.   II. of a crowd, N. T. Hence

ἀπόθλιψις, εως, ἡ, a squeezing out of one's place, Luc.

ἀπο-θνήσκω, f. -θανοῦμαι, Ion. -θανέομαι or -εῦμαι : aor. 2 -έθανον : pf. -τέθνηκα, Ep. part. -τεθνηώς :—to die off, die, Hom., Att.:—to be ready to die of laughter, Ar.   II. serving as Pass. of ἀποκτείνω, to be put to death, to be slain, ὑπό τινος Hdt., Plat.

ἀπο-θορεῖν, aor. 2 inf. of ἀποθρώσκω.

ἀπο-θρασύνομαι [ῠ], f. -ῠνοῦμαι, Dep. to be very bold, dare all things, Dem.

ἀπο-θραύω, f. σω, to break off, Aesch. :—Pass. to be broken off : metaph., ἀποθραυσθῆναι τῆς εὐκλείας to be broken off from one's fair fame, make shipwreck of it, Ar.

ἀπο-θρηνέω, f. ήσω, to lament much, Babr., Plut.

ἀπο-θριάζω, (θρῖον) properly, to cut off fig-leaves : to cut off, curtail, Ar.

ἀπο-θρύπτω, f. ψω, to crush in pieces :—metaph. in Pass., ἀποτεθρυμμένος broken, enervated, Plat.

ἀπο-θρώσκω, f. -θοροῦμαι : aor. 2 ἀπέθορον :—to leap off from, νηός Il. ; ἀφ' ἵππου, ἀπὸ νεός Hdt.   II. to

leap up from, rise from, καπνὸν ἀποθρώσκοντα γαίης Od. :—absol. to rise sheer up, of rocks, Hes.

ἀπο-θύμιος [ῠ], ον, (θυμός) not according to the mind, unpleasant, hateful, ἀποθύμια ἔρδειν τινί to do one a disfavour, Il. ; ἀποθύμιόν τι ποιῆσαι Hdt.

ἀπο-θύω, f. -θύσω [ῠ], to offer as a votive sacrifice, Xen.

ἀπ-οίδησις, εως, ἡ, abatement of a swelling, Strab.

ἀ-ποίητος, ον, not done, undone, Pind. : not to be done, impossible, Plut.

ἀπ-οικέω, f. ήσω, to go away from home, to settle in a foreign country, emigrate, ἐς Θουρίους Plat.   II. to dwell afar off, to live or be far away, Eur., Thuc. : Pass., ἡ Κόρινθος ἐξ ἐμοῦ μακρὰν ἀπῳκεῖτο Corinth was inhabited far away from me, i. e. I settled far from Corinth, Soph.

ἀποικία, Ion. -ίη, ἡ, (ἄποικος) a settlement far from home, a colony, settlement, Hdt., etc. ; εἰς ἀπ. στέλλειν to send away so as to form a settlement, Id. ; ἀπ. ἐκ-πέμπειν Thuc.

ἀπ-οικίζω, f. Att. ιῶ :—to send away from home, Od., Soph., etc. :—Pass. to be settled in a far land, to emigrate, Plat.   II. to colonise a place, send a colony to it, c. acc., Hdt., Thuc.

ἀποικίς, ίδος, ἡ, fem. of ἄποικος, ἀπ. πόλις a colony, Hdt.

ἀποικισμός, ὁ, the settlement of a colony, Arist.

ἀπ-οικοδομέω, f. ήσω, to cut off by building, wall up, barricade, τὰς θύρας, τὰς ὁδούς Thuc.

ἄπ-οικος, ον, away from home, ἀπ. πέμπειν τινὰ γῆς to send away from one's country, Soph.   II. as Subst., 1. a settler, colonist, Hdt., Thuc., etc.   2. ἄποικος (sub. πόλις), ἡ, a colony, Xen.

ἀπ-οικτίζομαι, f. Att. ιοῦμαι, Dep. to complain loudly of a thing, c. acc., Hdt.

ἀ-ποίμαντος, ον, (ποιμαίνω) unfed, untended, Anth.

ἀπ-οιμώζω, f. ξομαι, to bewail loudly, c. acc., Trag.

ἄ-ποινα, ων, τά, (a copul. or euphon., ποινή) : I. a ransom or price paid, whether to recover freedom or to save one's life or to redeem the corpse of a friend, Il. ; c. gen., ἄποινα κούρης, υἱος ransom for them, Ib.   II. generally, compensation, requital, recompense for a thing, c. gen., Aesch., Eur. Hence

ἀποινάω, f. ήσω, to demand the fine due from the murderer, Lex ap. Dem. :—Med. to hold to ransom, Eur.

ἀποινό-δικος, ον, exacting penalty, Eur.

ἀπ-οϊστεύω, f. σω, to kill with arrows, Anth.

ἀπ-οίσω, fut. of ἀποφέρω.

ἀπ-οίχομαι, impf. -ῳχόμην : f. -οιχήσομαι : Dep. :—to be gone away, to be far from, c. gen., Il., Att.   2. absol. to be gone, to have departed, to be absent, Od. : hence, to be gone, to have perished, ἀποίχεται χάρις Eur. : of persons, to be dead and gone, Pind., Ar.

ἀπο-καθαίρω, f. -καθᾰρῶ, to cleanse or clean quite, ἀπ. τὴν χεῖρα εἰς τὰ χειρόμακτρα upon the towels, Xen.   2. to refine from dross, Strab. : metaph. in Pass., ἀποκεκαθάρθαι τὴν φωνήν to be pure in dialect, Luc.   II. to clear away, τὰς τραπέζας Ar. :—Med., ἀποκαθήρασθαί τινος to rid oneself of a thing, Xen. Hence

ἀποκάθαρσις, εως, ἡ, a clearing off, purging, Thuc.   II. lustration, Plut.

ἀπο-κάθημαι, Pass. to sit apart, ἀτιμώμενοι ἀποκατέαται (Ion. for -κάθηνται) Hdt.

ἀπο-καθίστημι, f. -καταστήσω: aor. 1 -κατέστησα:—
to re-establish, restore, reinstate, Xen.
ἀπο-καίνυμαι, Pass. to surpass or vanquish, c. acc., Od.
ἀπο-καίριος, ον, = ἄκαιρος, unseasonable, Soph.
ἀπο-καίω, Att. -κάω, f. -καύσω: aor. 1 ἀπέκηα and
-έκαυσα:—to burn off, of cautery, Xen.: of intense
cold (like Virgil's frigus adurit), to shrivel up, Id.:—
Pass., ἀπεκαίοντο αἱ ῥῖνες their noses were frozen off, Id.
ἀπο-καλέω, f. έσω, to call back, recall, from exile, Hdt.,
Xen. 2. to call away or aside, Xen. II. to
call by a name, esp. by way of disparagement, to
stigmatise as, τὸν τοῦ μανέντος ξύναιμον ἀποκαλοῦντες
Soph.; σοφιστὴν ἀπ. τινα Xen.
ἀπο-κᾰλύπτω, f. ψω, to uncover, τὴν κεφαλὴν Hdt.,
etc. 2. to disclose, reveal, Plat.:—Med. to reveal
one's whole mind, Plut., N. T.:—Pass. to be disclosed,
made known, N. T.
ἀποκάλυψις, εως, ἡ, an uncovering, a revelation, N.T.:
—the Apocalypse, Ib.
ἀπο-κάμνω, f. -κάμοῦμαι, to grow quite weary, fail or
flag utterly, Soph., Plat.; c. part., ἀπ. ζητῶν to be quite
weary of seeking, Plat. 2. c. inf. to cease to do, Eur.,
Plat. 3. c. acc., ἀπ. πόνον to flinch from toil, Xen.
ἀπο-κάμπτω, f. ψω, intr. to turn off or aside, Xen.
Hence
ἀπόκαμψις, εως, ἡ, a turning off the road, Theophr.
ἀπο-κᾰπύω, to breathe away, ἀπὸ δὲ ψυχὴν ἐκάπυσσεν
(Ep. aor. 1 in tmesi) she gasped forth her life, Il.
ἀπο-κᾰρᾰδοκία, ἡ, (καραδοκέω) earnest expectation, N.T.
ἀπο-καρτερέω, f. ήσω, to kill oneself by abstinence, Plut.
ἀπο-καταλλάσσω, f. ξω, to reconcile again, N. T.
ἀπο-κάτημαι, Ion. for ἀπο-κάθημαι.
ἀπο-καυλίζω, f. Att. ἰῶ, (καυλός) to break off by the
stalk: to break short off, Eur., Thuc. Hence
ἀποκαύλισις, εως, ἡ, a breaking short off, snapping,
Luc.
ἀπο-κάω, Att. for ἀπο-καίω.
ἀπό-κειμαι, f. -κείσομαι, used as Pass. of ἀποτίθημι, to
be laid away, absol. to be laid up in store, Soph., Xen.;
πολύς σοι [γέλως] ἐστὶν ἀποκείμενος you have great
store of laughter in reserve, Xen.
ἀπο-κείρω, f. -κερῶ, Ep. -κέρσω: aor. 1 -έκειρα, Ep.
-έκερσα:—Pass., aor. 2 -εκάρην [ᾰ], pf. -κέκαρμαι:—
to clip or cut off hair, mostly in Med., ἀπεκείρατο χαίτην
cut off his hair, Il.; ἀποκείρασθαι τὰς κεφαλάς to have
their hair shorn close, Hdt.; and absol., ἀποκείρασθαι to
cut off one's hair, Ar.:—Pass., pf. part. ἀποκεκαρμένος
with one's hair cut short, Id. 2. metaph. to cheat,
τοὺς παχεῖς Luc. II. generally, to cut through,
sever, Il. III. to cut off, slay, Aesch.
ἀπο-κερδαίνω, f. -κερδήσω or -κερδᾰνῶ: aor. -εκέρδησα
or -εκέρδᾱνα:—to have benefit, enjoyment from or of
a thing, c. gen., Eur.; absol., Luc.
ἀποκερμᾰτίζω, f. Att. ἰῶ, to change for small coin:
metaph., ἀπ. τὸν βίον to dissipate one's substance, Anth.
ἀπο-κηδέω, f. σω, to cease to mourn for, τινά Hdt.
ἀποκηδέω, f. ήσω, to put away care, be careless, Il.
ἀποκήρυκτος, ον, disinherited, Luc.: and
ἀποκήρυξις, εως, ἡ, public renunciation of a son, dis-
inheriting, Plut., Luc. From
ἀπο-κηρύσσω, Att. -ττω, f. ξω, to sell by auction,
Hdt. II. to renounce publicly, to disinherit,

Plat. III. to forbid by proclamation: impers. in
pf. pass., ἀποκεκήρυκται μὴ στρατεύειν Xen.
ἀποκινδύνευσις, εως, ἡ, a venturous attempt, Thuc. From
ἀποκινδυνεύω, f. σω, to make a bold attempt or venture,
try a forlorn hope, πρός τινα against another, Thuc.;
c. inf., ἀποκινδυνεύετον σοφόν τι λέγειν Ar.:—Pass.,
to be put to the uttermost hazard, Thuc.
ἀπο-κῑνέω, f. ήσω: 3 sing. Ion. aor. 1 ἀποκῑνήσασκεν:
—to remove or put away from, c. gen., Hom.
ἀπό-κῑνος, ὁ, (κινέω) a comic dance:—metaph., ἀπό-
κινον εὑρέ find some way to dance off, Ar.
ἀπο-κλάζω, f. -κλάγξω, to ring or shout forth, Aesch.
ἀπο-κλαίω, Att. -κλάω [ᾰ]: f. -κλαύσομαι:—to weep
aloud, Hdt.; c. acc. cogn., ἀπ. στόνον Soph. 2. ἀπ.
τινα or τι to bewail much, mourn deeply for, Aesch.,
Plat.; so in Med., ἀποκλαίεσθαι κακά Soph.; τὴν πενίαν
Ar. II. Med., also, to cease to wail, Luc.
ἀπο-κλάξω, Dor. for ἀπο-κλείσω, fut. of ἀποκλείω:
ἀπο-κλάξον, for ἀπό-κλεισον, aor. 1 imper.
ἀπόκλᾱρος, ον, Dor. for ἀπόκληρος.
ἀπο-κλάω, f. -κλάσω [ᾰ], to break off:—Med., Anth.:
—Pass., aor. 1 part. ἀποκλασθέντα Theocr.
ἀπο-κλάω, Att. for ἀπο-κλαίω.
ἀπόκλεισις or -κλῃσις, εως, ἡ, (ἀποκλείω) a shutting
up, ἀπόκλ. μου τῶν πυλῶν a shutting the gates against
me, Thuc. II. a shutting out, ἀποκλήσεις γίγνεσθαι (sc. ἔμελλον) there would be a complete stoppage
to their works, Thuc.
ἀπο-κλείω, f. -κλείσω: Ion. ἀπο-κληΐω, fut. -κληΐσω:
Att. ἀποκλῄω, f. -κλήσω:—Dor. f. -κλάξω; aor. 1
imper. -κλᾷξον:—to shut off from or out of, debar,
τινὰ πυλεῶν Hdt.; δωμάτων Aesch.; ἀπ. τινὰ to shut
him out, Ar.:—Med., ἀπ. τινα τῆς διαβάσεως to get
him debarred from passing, Thuc. 2. to shut
out or exclude from a thing, τινός Hdt., etc.; ἀπό
τινος Ar. II. to shut up a gate and the like, to bar,
close, Hdt.:—Pass. to be closed, Id. III. to shut
up one in prison, Soph., Ar., etc. IV. to shut out,
intercept, bar, Hdt., Ar.:—Pass., ἀπ. ὑπὸ τῆς ἵππου Hdt.
ἀποκλῄω, Ion. for ἀποκλείω.
ἀπό-κληρος, Dor. -κλᾱρος, ον, without lot or share of
a thing, c. gen., Pind.
ἀπο-κληρόω, f. ώσω, to choose by lot from a number,
Hdt., Thuc.: to choose or elect by lot, Thuc. 2. to
allot, assign by lot, χώραν τινί Plut. Hence
ἀπο-κλίνω [ῑ], f. ινῶ:—Pass., aor. 1 -εκλίθην [ῑ] or
-εκλίνθην:—to turn off or aside, τι Od.: to turn back,
h. Hom.:—Pass., of the day, to decline, get towards
evening, Hdt. II. Pass. to be upset, Dem. III.
intr. in Act. to turn aside or off the road, Xen.; πρὸς
τὴν ἠῶ ἀποκλίνοντι as one turns to go Eastward,
Hdt. 2. often in bad sense, to fall away, decline,
degenerate, Soph.; ἐπὶ τὸ ῥᾳθυμεῖν Dem.:—and without bad sense, to have a leaning, be favourably disposed, πρός τινα Id. Hence
ἀπόκλῐσις, εως, ἡ, a turning off, declension, sinking,
Plut.
ἀπο-κλύζω, f. ύσω, to wash away: metaph. in Med.
to purge, Plat.:—to avert by purifications, Ar.
ἀπο-κναίω, Att. -κνάω, inf. -κνᾶν:—aor. 1 -έκναισα:—
to wear one out, worry to death, Plat., etc.:—Pass. to
be worn out, Id., Xen.

ἀπ-οκνέω, f. ήσω, to shrink from danger, c. acc., Thuc.:
—c. inf. to shrink from doing, Id., Plat.　2. absol.
to shrink back, hesitate, Thuc., Plat., etc.　Hence
ἀπόκνησις, εως, ή, a shrinking from, c. gen., Thuc.
ἀποκνητέον, verb. Adj. of ἀπ-οκνέω, Plat.
ἀπο-κνίζω, f. ίσω, to nip off.　Hence
ἀπόκνισμα, ατος, τό, that which is nipt off, a little
bit, Ar.
ἀπο-κοιμάομαι, Pass. with f. med. ήσομαι, to sleep away
from home, Plat.　II. to get a little sleep, Hdt., Ar.
ἀποκοιτέω, f. ήσω, to sleep away from one's post, Decret.
ap. Dem.　From
ἀπό-κοιτος, ον, (κοίτη) sleeping away from others, c.
gen., Aeschin.
ἀπο-κολυμβάω, f. ήσω, to dive and swim away, Thuc.
ἀποκομιδή, ή, (ἀποκομίζομαι) a getting away, getting
back, Thuc.
ἀπο-κομίζω, f. Att. ιῶ, to carry away, escort, Xen.: to
carry away captive, Thuc.:—Pass. to take oneself off,
get away, Id.: to return, Hdt.
ἀπόκομμα, ατος, τό, (ἀποκόπτω) a splinter, chip, shred,
Theocr., Luc.
ἀπο-κομπάζω, of lyre strings, to break with a snap, Anth.
ἀποκοπή, ή, (ἀποκόπτω) a cutting off, Aesch.; ἀπ.
χρεῶν, = the Rom. tabulae novae, a cancelling of all
debts, Plat.　II. in Gramm. apocopé, the cutting
off letters from a word.
ἀπο-κόπτω, f. ψω, to cut off, hew off, of men's limbs, Il.,
Hdt.; also, ἀπέκοψε παρήορον he cut loose the trace-
horse, Il. :—Pass., ἀποκοπῆναι τὴν χεῖρα to have it cut
off, Hdt.　II. ἀπ. τινὰ ἀπὸ τόπου to beat off from
a strong place, Xen.　III. Med. to smite the breast
in mourning : c. acc. to mourn for, νεκρόν Eur.
ἀπο-κορυφόω, f. ώσω, to bring to a point :—metaph.,
ἀπεκορύφου σφι τάδε gave them this short answer, Hdt.
ἀπο-κοσμέω, f. ήσω, to restore order by clearing away,
to clear away, Od.
ἀπο-κοτταβίζω, f. Att. ιῶ, to dash out the last drops of
wine, as in playing at the cottabus, Xen.
ἀπο-κουφίζω, f. Att. ιῶ, to lighten, set free from, relieve, τινὰ κακῶν Eur.
ἀπο-κράδιος, ον, (κράδη) plucked from the fig-tree, Anth.
ἀπο-κραιπαλάω, f. ήσω, to sleep off a debauch, Plut.
ἀπο-κρανίζω, (κρανίον) to strike off from the head, Anth.
ἀπο-κρατέω, f. ήσω, to exceed all others, Lat. superare, Hdt.
ἀπο-κρεμάννυμι, f. -κρεμάσω, Att. -κρεμῶ :—Pass. aor. 1
-εκρεμάσθην :—to let hang down, Il.; χορδὰν πλῆκτρον
ἀπεκρέμασε the plectrum broke the string so that it hung
down, Anth.　II. to hang up, suspend, Hdt.
ἀπό-κρημνος, ον, broken sheer off, precipitous, Hdt.,
Thuc., etc. :—metaph. full of difficulties, Dem.
ἀπόκρĭμα, ατος, τό, a judicial sentence, N. T.　From
ἀπο-κρίνω, f. -κρῐνῶ [ῐ], f. to separate, set apart, Plat. :—
Pass., ἀποκρινθέντε parted from the throng, of two heroes
coming forward as champions, Il.; ἀποκρίσθαι εἰς ἕν
ὄνομα to be separated and brought under one name,
Thuc.　2. to mark by a distinctive form, distinguish, Hdt.; pf. pass. part. ἀποκεκριμένος distinct,
Plat.　II. to choose out, choose, Hdt., Plat.　III.
Med. ἀποκρίνομαι, f. -κρῐνοῦμαι : pf. -κέκρῐμαι both in
med. and pass. sense :—to give answer to, reply, Eur.,
etc.; ἀπ. πρός τινα or πρός τι to reply to a questioner

or question, Thuc., etc. :—c. acc., ἀποκρίνεσθαι τὸ ἐρωτηθέν to answer the question, Id. : so in Pass., τοῦτό
μοι ἀποκεκρίσθω let this be my answer, Plat.　2. to
answer charges, defend oneself, Ar.　3. aor. 1 pass.
ἀπεκρίθη, = ἀπεκρίνατο, he answered, first in N. T.
ἀπόκρῐσις, εως, ή, (ἀποκρίνω) a separating.　II.
(from Med.) an answer, Thuc., Xen.
ἀποκρĭτέον, verb. Adj. of ἀποκρίνω, one must reject,
Plat.　II. one must answer, Id.
ἀπό-κροτος, ον, (κροτέω) beaten or trodden hard, of
ground, Thuc.
ἀπο-κρούω, f. σω, to beat off from a place, Xen. :—Med.
to beat off from oneself, beat off an attack, Hdt., Thuc.:
—Pass. to be beaten off, Thuc., Xen., etc.　II. Pass.,
κοτυλίσκιον τὸ χεῖλος ἀποκεκρουμένον a cup with the
lip knocked off, Ar.
ἀπο-κρύπτω, 3 sing. Ep. impf. ἀποκρύπτασκε : f. ψω :—
Pass., aor. 2 -εκρύβην [ῠ] :—to hide from, keep hidden
from, c. acc. et gen., θανάτοιο ἀπ. τινα Il.; c. dupl.
acc., like Lat. celare aliquem aliquid, to keep back from
one, Hdt.; so in Med., ἀποκρύπτεσθαί τινά τι Xen.,
etc.　2. to hide from sight, keep hidden, conceal,
Od., Att.:—Med., ἀποκρύπτεσθαι μὴ ποιεῖν τι to conceal
one's doing, Thuc.　3. to obscure, throw into the
shade, Plat.　II. ἀπ. γῆν to lose from sight, of
ships running out to sea, like Virgil's Phaeacum ab-
scondimus arces, Id., Luc.
ἀπόκρῠφος, ον, (ἀποκρύπτω) hidden, concealed, Eur.;
ἐν ἀποκρύφῳ in secret, Hdt.　2. c. gen. concealed
from, unknown to one, Xen.　II. obscure, hard to
understand, Id.
ἀπο-κτείνω, f. -κτενῶ, Ion. -κτενέω: aor. 1 ἀπέκτεινα
Il.:—pf. ἀπέκτονα: 3 pl. plqpf. -εκτόνεσαν, Ion. 3 sing.
-εκτόνεε: aor. 2 -έκτανον, Ep. 1 pl. ἀπέκταμεν, inf.
ἀποκτάμεναι, -κτάμεν :—Pass. rare (ἀποθνήσκω being
used as Pass.) : med. forms (in pass. sense) 3 sing. Ep.
aor. 2 ἀπέκτατο ; part. ἀποκτάμενος ; cf. ἀποκτίν-
νυμι :—to kill, slay, Hom., Hdt., Att.　2. of judges,
to condemn to death, Plat., Xen., etc.　3. metaph.,
like Lat. enecare, to weary to death, Eur.
ἀπο-κτέννω, late form for ἀποκτείνω, Anth.
ἀπο-κτίννῡμι, = ἀποκτείνω, Plat., Xen.
ἀπο-κυέω, f. ήσω, to bear young, bring forth, c. acc.,
Plut., Luc. :—metaph., ἡ ἁμαρτία ἀπ. θάνατον N. T.
ἀποκῠλίω, f. ίσω [ῐ], to roll away, N. T. :—Pass., Luc.
ἀπο-κωκύω, f. ύσω [ῠ], to mourn loudly over, τινά Aesch.
ἀποκώλῠσις, εως, ή, a hindrance, Xen.　From
ἀπο-κωλύω, f. ύσω [ῠ], to hinder or prevent from a thing,
τινά τινος Xen.; c. inf., ἀπ. τινά ποιεῖν to prevent from
doing, forbid to do, μὴ ποιεῖν τι Eur., Xen.　II.
c. acc. only, to keep off, hinder, Orac. ap. Hdt., Thuc. :
—absol. to stop the way, Thuc. :—impers., οὐδὲν ἀπο-
κωλύει there is no hindrance, Plat.
ἀπο-λαγχάνω, f. -λήξομαι, to obtain a portion of a thing
by lot, τῶν κτημάτων τὸ μέρος ἀπ. Hdt.; generally to
obtain, Eur.　II. to fail in drawing lots, Plut. :
generally to be left destitute, Eur.
ἀπο-λάζῠμαι, poët. for ἀπολαμβάνω, only in pres. and
impf., Eur.
ἀπολακτίζω, f. Att. ιῶ, to kick off or away, shake off,
ὕπνον Aesch.　2. to spurn, Id.
ἀπο-λᾰλέω, f. ήσω, to speak out heedlessly, Luc.

ἀπο-λαμβάνω, f. -λήψομαι, Ion. -λάμψομαι: pf. Att. -είληφα: aor. 2 ἀπ-έλαβον:—Pass., pf. -είλημμαι, Ion. -λέλαμμαι: aor. 1 -ελήφθην, Ion. -ελάμφθην:— to take or receive from another, παρά τινος Thuc.:— to receive what is one's due, μισθόν Hdt., Xen.; ἀπ. ὅρκους to accept oaths tendered, Dem. 2. c. gen. to take of, take part of a thing, Thuc. 3. to hear or learn, Lat. accipio, Plat. II. to take back, get back, regain, recover, τὴν τυραννίδα Hdt. 2. to have an account rendered one, ἀπ. λόγον Aeschin. III. to take apart or aside, ἀπ. τινὰ μοῦνον Hdt.; ἀπολαβὼν σκόπει consider it separately, Plat. IV. to cut off, intercept, arrest, Hdt.; ἀπ. τείχει to intercept by a wall, Thuc.:—Pass. to be arrested or stopped by contrary winds, Hdt.

ἀπο-λαμπρύνω [ῡ], f. ῠνῶ, to make famous:—Pass. to become so, Hdt.

ἀπο-λάμπω, f. ψω, to shine or beam from a thing, of light, Il.; so in Med., χάρις ἀπελάμπετο grace beamed from her, Hom.

ἀπολάπτω, f. ψω, to lap up like a dog, swallow greedily, Ar.

ἀπόλαυσις, εως, ἡ, (ἀπολαύω) enjoyment, fruition, Thuc., Arist. 2. c. gen. advantage got from a thing, Xen.; ἀπόλαυσιν εἰκοῦς (acc. absol.) as a reward for your resemblance, Eur.

ἀπόλαυσμα, ατος, τό, enjoyment, Aeschin.; and

ἀπολαυστικός, ή, όν, devoted to enjoyment, Arist.; producing enjoyment, Id.:—Adv., ἀπολαυστικῶς ζῆν to live a life of pleasure, Id.; and

ἀπολαυστός, όν, enjoyed, enjoyable, Plut. From

ἀπολαύω, f. ἀπολαύσομαι: aor. 1 -έλαυσα: pf. -λέλαυκα. (The simple λαύω is not found, but prob. it was = λάω or λάϝω, to enjoy.) To have enjoyment of a thing, to have the benefit of it, to enjoy, c. gen., Hdt., Att.:—with acc. added, ἀπολαύειν τί τινος to enjoy an advantage from some source, Ar., Thuc. 2. ironically, to have the benefit of, τῶν Οἰδίπου κακῶν Eur.: —absol. to have a benefit, come finely off, Ar.

ἀπο-λάχεῖν, aor. 2 inf. of ἀπολαγχάνω.

ἀπο-λέγω, f. ξω, to pick out from a number, to pick out, choose, Hdt.:—Med. to pick out for oneself, Id., Thuc.; ἀπολελεγμένοι, Att. -ειλεγμένοι, picked men, Hdt., Xen. II. like ἀπαγορεύω, to decline, refuse: —Med. to decline something offered to one, renounce, Plat.:—absol. to give in, Id.

ἀπο-λείβω, f. ψω, to let drop off, to pour a libation, Hes.:—Pass. to drop or run down from, τινός Od.

ἀπο-λείπω, f. ψω: aor. 2 ἀπέλιπον:—to leave over or behind, of meats not wholly eaten, Od.:—Med. to leave behind one, after death, Hdt. 2. to leave hold of, lose, βίον Soph.; also, βίοτος ἀπολείπει τινά Id. 3. to leave behind, as in the race, to distance, and generally to surpass, Xen.; v. infr. II. to leave quite, forsake, abandon, of places one ought to defend, Il., Hdt., etc.: to leave one in the lurch, Hdt., Ar. 2. of things, to leave alone, leave undone or unsaid, Hdt., Att. III. to leave open, leave a space, Hdt., Xen. IV. intr. to fail, to be wanting, Od.; of rivers, to fall, sink, Hdt.; of flowers, to begin to wither, Xen.;—also, like ἀπειπεῖν, to fail, flag, lose heart, Hdt., Xen. 2. to be wanting of or in a thing, c. gen., Thuc.; of measures, ἀπὸ τεσσέ-

ρων πηχέων ἀπ. τρεῖς δακτύλους wanting 3 fingers of 4 cubits, Hdt.: c. inf., ὀλίγον ἀπέλιπον ἀπικέσθαι wanted but little of coming, Id. 3. c. part. to leave off doing, Plat. 4. to depart from, ἐκ τῶν Συρακουσῶν Thuc., Plat.
B. Pass. to be left behind, stay behind, Thuc., Xen. 2. to be distanced by, inferior to, τινος Dem. II. to be parted from, be absent or far from, c. gen., Hdt.: to be deprived of, τάφου Soph.; φρενῶν Eur. 2. to be wanting in, fall short of, παιδείας Dem.; ἀπολειφθεὶς ἡμῶν without our cognisance, Id.; ἀπ. φρενῶν to be bereft of, Eur.

ἀπολείχω, f. ξω, to lick clean, N. T.

ἀπόλειψις, εως, ἡ, (ἀπολείπω) a forsaking, abandonment, of a thing, Thuc.: desertion of a husband by his wife, Dem.; of their post by soldiers, Xen., etc. II. intr. a falling short, deficiency, Thuc.

ἀπόλεκτος, ον, (ἀπολέγω) chosen out, picked, Thuc., Xen.

ἀ-πόλεμος, Ep. ἀ-πτόλεμος, ον, unwarlike, unfit for war, Il., Eur. 2. peaceful, Eur. II. not to be warred on, invincible, Aesch. III. πόλεμος ἀπόλεμος a war that is no war, a hopeless struggle, Id., Eur.

ἀπο-λέπω, f. ψω, to peel off, flay, Eur., Ar.

ἀπ-ολέσθαι, aor. 2 med. inf. of ἀπόλλυμι. II. ἀπολέσκετο, Ep. for ἀπώλετο, 3 sing. ind.

ἀπολήγω, Ep. ἀπολ-λήγω, f. ξω, to leave off, desist from a thing, c. gen., Il., Plat. 2. c. part. to leave off doing, Hom.:—absol. to cease, desist, Id.

ἀπο-ληρέω, f. ήσω, to chatter at random, Dem.

ἀπόληψις, εως, ἡ, (ἀπολαμβάνω IV) an intercepting, cutting off, Thuc.

ἀπο-λῑβάζω, f. ξω, to drop off, vanish, Ar.

ἀπο-λιγαίνω [ῐ], only in pres. to scream aloud, be obstreperous, Ar.

ἀπο-λῑθόομαι, (λίθος) Pass. to become stone, Strab.

ἀπολιμπάνω, late form of ἀπολείπω, Plut., Luc.

ἄ-πολις, neut. ι: gen. ιδος or εως, Ion. ιος: Ion. dat. ἄπολι:—one without city, state or country, an outlaw, Hdt., Soph., etc. II. πόλις ἄπολις a city that is no city, a ruined city, Aesch.

ἀπ-ολισθάνω, f. -ολισθήσω: aor. 2 -ώλισθον:—to slip off or away, Thuc. 2. c. gen. to slip away from, τινός Ar.

ἀπο-λῑταργίζω, f. Att. ιῶ, to pack oneself off, Ar.

ἀ-πολίτευτος, ον, (πολιτεύω) taking no part in public matters, living as a private person, Plut.

ἀπο-λιχμάομαι, Dep. to lick off, αἷμα Il.

ἀπ-όλλῡμι or -ύω, impf. ἀπώλλυν or ἀπώλλυον: f. ἀπολέσω, Ep. ἀπολέσσω, Att. ἀπολῶ, Ion. ἀπολέω: aor. 1 ἀπώλεσα, Ep. ἀπόλεσσα: pf. ἀπολώλεκα:—to destroy utterly, kill, slay, and of things, to destroy, demolish, waste, Hom., Att.; in pregnant sense, γᾶς ἐκ πατρίας ἀπ. to drive me ruined from my fatherland, Eur.; λόγοις ἀπ. τινά Soph.:—to talk or bore one to death, Ar. II. to lose utterly, πατέρα, νόστιμον ἦμαρ Hom.
B. Med. to -ολοῦμαι, Ion. -ολέομαι with part. ἀπολούμενος: aor. 2 -ωλόμην: pf. -όλωλα: plqpf. ἀπολώλειν:—to perish utterly, die, Il.; c. acc. cogn. ἀπ. κακὸν μόρον, αἰπὺν ὄλεθρον Od.; to be undone, Id.; ἀπόλωλας one who is done for, lost, ruined, Ar.; as an imprecation, κάκιστ' ἀπολοίμην Id.; in fut. part., ὦ κάκιστ' ἀπολούμενε oh destined to a miserable end!

i. e. *oh villain, scoundrel!* Ar.   II. *to be lost, slip away, vanish*, of the water eluding Tantalus, Od.; of sleep, Il.

Ἀπόλλων, ὁ, gen. ωνος, acc. Ἀπόλλωνα, apoc. Ἄπολλω, voc. Ἄπολλον [first syll. long in Hom., metri grat.] :— *Apollo*, son of Zeus and Latona, brother of Artemis, Hom., etc. : in Hom. men who die suddenly are said to be slain by his ἀγανὰ βέλεα; cf. Ἄρτεμις.   Hence

Ἀπολλώνιος, α, ον, *of* or *belonging to Apollo,* Pind.   II. Ἀπολλώνιον, τό, *the temple of Apollo,* Thuc.

ἀπολογέομαι, f. ήσομαι: aor. ι med. -ελογησάμην, and pass. -ελογήθην: pf. -λελόγημαι: (ἀπό, λόγος) : Dep. :— *to speak in defence, defend oneself,* περί τινος *about* a thing, πρός τι or τινα *in answer to . .,* Thuc., Plat.; ἀπ.ὑπέρ τινος *to speak* in another's *behalf,* Hom.:—absol. Id.; ὁ ἀπολογούμενος *the defendant,* Ar.   2. c. acc. criminis, *to defend oneself against* a thing, *explain, excuse,* Thuc., Aeschin.   3. ἀπ. τι ἔς τι *to allege in one's defence* against a charge, Thuc., Plat.   4. ἀπ. δίκην θανάτου *to speak against* sentence of death being passed on one, Thuc.   Hence

ἀπολόγημα, ατος, τό, *a plea alleged in defence,* Plut.; and

ἀπολογητέον, verb. Adj. *one must defend,* Plat.; and

ἀπολογία, ἡ, *a speech in defence, defence,* Thuc.

ἀπο-λογίζομαι, f. Att. ιοῦμαι: aor. -ελογισάμην: pf. -λελόγισμαι: Dep.:— *to reckon up, give in an account,* Lat. rationes reddere, Xen.: c. acc. rei, *to give in an account* of the receipts, Aeschin.   II. *to reckon on* a thing, *calculate that* it will be, c. acc. et inf., Dem.   Hence

ἀπολογισμός, ὁ, *a giving account, statement,* Aeschin.   2. *an account kept, record,* Luc.

ἀπό-λογος, ὁ, *a story, tale, fable, apologue,* Plat.

ἀπ-ολεῖσθαι, fut. med. inf. of ἀπ-όλλυμι:—ἀπ-ολοίατο, Ion. for -όλοιντο, 3 pl. aor. 2 med. opt.:—ἀπ-ολόμενος, part.

ἀπο-λούσομαι, Ion. for -ωμαι, pres. med. subj. of sq.

ἀπο-λούω, poët. 3 sing. impf. ἀπέλου: f. -λούσω: aor. ι -έλουσα: I. c. acc. rei, *to wash off* dirt, Il.: Med. ἅλμην ὤμοιιν ἀπολούεσθαι *to wash* the brine *from off my* shoulders, Od.   2. c. acc. pers. *to wash clean,* Ar.:— Med. *to wash* oneself, Il.   3. c. acc. pers. et rei, Πάτροκλον λοῦσαι ἄπο βρότον *to wash* the gore *off* him, Ib.

ἀπ-ολοφύρομαι [ῡ], f. -ῠροῦμαι, Dep. *to bewail loudly,* Xen.   2. in past tenses, *to leave off wailing,* Thuc.

ἀπο-λῡμαίνομαι, Pass. (λῦμα) *to wash dirt off oneself, cleanse oneself by bathing,* Il.

ἀπο-λῡμ ντήρ, ὁ, (λύμη) *a destroyer:* δαιτῶν ἀπολ. *one who destroys* the pleasure of dinner, *a kill-joy,*—or, acc. to others, *a devourer of feasts, lick-plate,* Od.

ἀπόλῠσις, εως, ἡ, (ἀπολύω) *release, deliverance from* a thing, c. gen., Plut.; κατὰ τὴν ἀπόλυσιν τοῦ θανάτου so far as *acquittal from* a capital charge went, Hdt.

ἀπολῠτικός, ή, όν, (ἀπολύω) *disposed to acquit:*—Adv., ἀπολυτικῶς ἔχειν τινός to be *minded to acquit* one, Xen.

ἀπο-λυτρόω, f. ώσω, *to release on payment of ransom,* c. gen. pretii, Philipp. ap. Dem.   Hence

ἀπολύτρωσις, εως, ἡ, *a ransoming,* Plut. : *redemption by payment of ransom,* N. T.

ἀπο-λύω, f. -λύσω [ῠ], etc. : fut. 3 pass. ἀπολελύσομαι: —*to loose from,* τί τινος Od. : *to undo,* Ib.   2. *to set free from, release* or *relieve from,* τινὰ τῆς φρουρῆς, τῆς ἐπιμελείας Hdt., Xen.; τι ἀπό τινος Plat. :—Pass. *to be set free from,* Thuc.   3. in legal sense, ἀπ. τῆς αἰτίης *to acquit* of the charge, Hdt., Xen. :—c. inf., ἀπ. τινὰ μὴ φῶρα εἶναι *to acquit* one *of being* a thief, Hdt. : then absol. *to acquit,* Ar.   II. *to let go free on receipt of ransom, hold to ransom,* Il. :—Med. *to ransom, redeem,* χρυσοῦ by payment of gold, Ib.   III. *to discharge* or *disband* an army, Xen. :—generally, *to dismiss,* Ar.   2. *to divorce* a wife, N. T.

    B. Med. *to redeem,* v. supr. II.   II. *to do away with* charges *against* one, Lat. diluere, Thuc., Plat. :— absol., ἀπολυόμενος *in defence,* Hdt.   III. like Pass. (c. II), *to depart,* Soph.

    C. Pass. *to be released, let off,* τῆς στρατηίης *from* military service, Hdt. ; τῆς ἀρχῆς ἀπολυθῆναι *to be freed from* their rule, Thuc. :—absol. *to be acquitted, discharged,* Id., Plat.   II. of combatants, *to be separated, part,* Thuc.   2. *to depart,* Soph.

ἀπολωβάομαι, Pass. *to be grievously insulted,* Soph.

ἀπ-όλωλα, pf. med. of ἀπόλλυμι.

ἀπο-λωτίζω, f. σω, *to pluck off flowers:* generally, *to pluck off, cut off,* Eur.

ἀπομαγδᾰλία or -ιά, ἡ, (ἀπομάσσω) *the crumb* or *inside of the loaf,* on which the Greeks wiped their hands at dinner, and then threw it to the dogs, *dog's meat,* Ar.

ἀπομαίνομαι, Pass. *to rave, rage to the uttermost,* Luc.

ἀπόμακτρον, τό, (ἀπο-μάσσω) *a strickle,* Ar.

ἀπο-μᾰλᾰκίζομαι, Pass. *to shew weakness,* Plut.

ἀπο-μαλθᾰκόομαι, Pass., = foreg., Plut.

ἀπο-μανθάνω, f. -μᾰθήσομαι, *to unlearn,* Lat. dediscere, Plat., Xen.

ἀπο-μαντεύομαι, Dep. *to announce as a prophet,* τὸ μέλλον ἥξειν Xen.

ἀπόμαξις, εως, ἡ, (ἀπομάσσω) *a wiping off,* Plut.

ἀπο-μᾰραίνομαι, Pass. *to waste* or *wither away, die away,* of a tranquil death, Xen.

ἀπο-μάσσω, Att. -ττω, f. ξω, *to wipe clean,* Dem. :— Med.,Ἀχιλλείων ἀπομάττει *you wipe your hands* on the finest bread, Ar.   II. *to wipe off* or *level corn with a strickle* (ἀπόμακτρον): χοίνικα ἀπ. to give scant measure, as was done in giving slaves their allowance, Luc.; κενεὰν ἀπομάξαι (sc. χοίνικα) *to level* an empty measure, i. e. to labour in vain, Theocr.   III. *to take an impression:* metaph. *to take impression,* Ar.

ἀπο-μαστῑγόω, f. ώσω, *to scourge severely,* Hdt.

ἀπο-ματᾴζω, f. ίσω, *to behave in unseemly fashion,*Hdt.

ἀπο-μάχομαι [ᾰ], f. -μᾰχέσομαι, contr. -μαχοῦμαι, *to fight from the walls,* Thuc. ; τείχεα ἱκανὰ ἀπομάχεσθαι high enough *to fight from,*Xen. :—absol. *to fight desperately,* Id.   II. ἀπ. τι *to fight off* a thing, *decline* it, Hdt. ; absol., Id.   III. ἀπ. τινά *to drive him off in battle,* Xen.

ἀπό-μᾰχος, ον, (μάχη) *past fighting, past service,* Xen.

ἀπο-μείρομαι, Dep. *to distribute,* Hes.   2. Pass. *to be parted from,* Id.

ἀπο-μερίζω, f. Att. ιῶ, *to part* or *distinguish from* a number, Plat.   2. ἀπ. πρός or ἐπί τι *to detach on* some service, Polyb. : *to impart,* Id.

ἀπο-μερμηρίζω, f. ίσω, *to sleep off care,* Ar.

ἀπο-μεστόομαι, Pass. *to be filled to the brim*, Plat.

ἀπο-μετρέω, f. ήσω, *to measure out*, Luc.:—Med., Xen.

ἀπο-μηκύνω [ῡ], f. υνῶ, *to prolong, draw out*, λόγον Plat.: absol. *to be prolix*, Id.:—Pass. *to be extended*, Luc.

ἀπο-μηνίω [ῑ], f. σω, *to be very wroth, to persevere in wrath*, Hom.

ἀπο-μῑμέομαι, f. ήσομαι, Dep. *to express by imitating* or *copying, represent faithfully*, Xen.

ἀπο-μιμνήσκομαι, f. -μνήσομαι, aor. 1 -εμνησάμην: Dep.:—*to remember fully*, χάριν ἀπ. *to recognise, repay* a favour, *feel gratitude*, Il., Thuc.

ἀπό-μισθος, ον, *away from* (i. e. *without*) *pay, unpaid, ill-paid*, Xen., Dem.   II. *paid off*, Dem.

ἀπο-μισθόω, f. ώσω, *to let out for hire*, Thuc.;—c. inf., ἀπ. ποιεῖν τι *to contract for the doing* of a thing, Lex ap. Dem.

ἀπομνημόνευμα, ατος, τό, *a memorial*, Plut.:—in pl. *memoirs*, Lat. *commentarii*, as those of Socrates by Xen. From

ἀπο-μνημονεύω, f. σω, *to relate from memory, relate, recount*, Plat.   2. *to remember, call to mind*, Id.; ὄνομα ἀπεμνημόνευσε τῷ παιδὶ θέσθαι *gave* his son the name *in memory* of a thing, Hdt.   3. ἀπ. τί τινι *to bear* something *in mind against* another, Xen.

ἀπο-μνήσομαι, f. of ἀπομιμνήσκομαι.

ἀπο-μνησικακέω, f. ήσω, *to bear a grudge against*, τινί Hdt.

ἀπ-όμνυμι or -ύω, 3 sing. impf. ἀπώμνυ: f. -ομοῦμαι: —*to take an oath away from* a thing, i. e. *swear that one will not do* it, Od.   2. *to swear one has not done* or *that it is not so, to deny on oath*, Hdt., Att.; with μή added, ἀπ. ἦ μὴν μὴ εἰδέναι Xen.; ἀπ. μηδὲ ὀβολόν (sc. ἔχειν) Id.   3. c. acc. *to disown on oath*: Med., ἀπωμόσατο τὴν ἀρχήν renounced it, Plut.   II. *to take a solemn oath*, ἦ μήν . . Thuc.

ἀπομοίρια, τά, (μοῖρα) *a portion*, Anth.

ἀπο-μονόομαι, (μονόω) Pass. *to be excluded from* a thing, c. gen., Thuc.   2. *to be left alone*, Plut.

ἀπ-ομόργνυμι, f. -ομόρξω:—*to wipe off* or *away from*, τί τινος Il.:—Med. *to wipe off from oneself*, Ib.; ἀπομόρξατο δάκρυ *wiped away* his tears, Od.; absol. in same sense, ἀπομόρξασθαι Ar.; and in Pass., τὴν ὀργὴν ἀπομορχθείς *having* my anger *wiped off*, Id.   2. *to wipe the face clean*, Il.:—Med., ἀπομόρξατο παρειάς *she wiped her* cheeks, Od.

ἀπ-ομόσαι, aor. 1 inf. of ἀπόμνυμι.

ἀπό-μουσος, ον, *away from the Muses, unaccomplished, rude*, Eur.:—Adv., ἀπομούσως *unfavourably*, Aesch.

ἀπο-μῡθέομαι, f. ήσομαι, Dep. *to dissuade*, Il.

ἀπο-μῡκάομαι, f. ήσομαι, Dep. *to bellow loudly*, Anth.

ἀπομυκτέον, verb. Adj. *one must wipe one's nose*, Eur. From

ἀπο-μύσσω, Att. -ττω, f. ξω, *to wipe the nose*, Anth.:— Med. *to blow one's nose*, Ar., Xen.   II. metaph. *to make* him *sharp, sharpen* his *wits*, Plat.; cf. Horace's *vir emunctae naris*.

ἀπ-όναιο, 2 sing. opt. of ἀπονίναμαι:—ἀπ-οναίατο, 3 pl.

ἀπο-ναίω, Ep. aor. 1 ἀπένασσα:—*to remove, to send away*, Il.:—Med. *to wend one's way back*, ἀπενάσσατο Hom.   II. aor. 1 med. in trans. sense, ἀπενάσσατο παῖδα *sent away* her child, Eur.; also, ἀποναςθῆναι, *to be taken away, depart from* a place, c. gen., Id.

ἀπο-ναρκόομαι, (νάρκη) Pass. *to become quite torpid, insensible*, Plat.

ἀπονεμητέον, verb. Adj. *one must assign*, Arist. From

ἀπο-νέμω, f. -νεμῶ, *to portion out, impart, assign*, τί τινι Hdt., Att.:—Med. *to assign* or *take to oneself*, Plat.; ἀπονέμεσθαί τι *to feed on*, Ar.: c. gen. partit. *to help oneself to a share of* a thing, Plat.

ἀπονενοημένως, Adv. part. pf. pass. of ἀπονοέομαι, *desperately*, Xen.

ἀπο-νέομαι, Dep. *to go away, depart*, Hom. [ᾱ metri grat.]

ἀπο-νεύω, f. σω, *to bend away from* other objects towards one, *turn towards*, πρός τι Plat.

ἀπο-νέω, f. -νήσω, *to unload*:—Med. *to throw off* a load from, στέρνων ἀπονησαμένη Eur.

ἀπ-ονήμενος, aor. 2 part. of ἀπονίναμαι.

ἀ-πονητί, (ἀ priv., πονέω) Adv. *without fatigue*, Hdt.

ἀπ-όνητο, Ion. for ἀπώνητο, 3 sing. aor. of ἀπονίναμαι.

ἀ-πόνητος, ον, (πονέω) *without toil*:—Adv. Sup. ἀπονητότατα *with least trouble*, Hdt.   2. *without suffering*, Soph.

ἀπο-νήχομαι, f. ξομαι, Dep. *to escape by swimming, to swim away*, Luc.

ἀπονία, ἡ, (ἄπονος) *non-exertion, laziness*, Xen.: *exemption from toil*, Plut.

ἀπο-νίζω, later -νίπτω: f. -νίψω: aor. 1 -ένιψα:—*to wash off*, ἀπονίψαντες βροτὸν ἐξ ὠτειλῶν Od.:—Med. *to wash off from oneself*, ἱδρῶ ἀπενίζοντο θαλάσσῃ Il.   II. *to wash clean*, properly of the hands and feet, ἀπονίζουσα *as I was washing his feet*, Od.; ἀπονίζῃ καὶ τὼ πόδ' ἀλείφῃ Ar.:—Med. *to wash one's hands and feet*, χεῖράς τε πόδας τε Od.: absol. *to wash one's hands*, Ar.; pf. pass. ἀπονενίμμεθα Id. Hence

ἀπόνιμμα, ατος, τό, *water in which the hands have been washed, dirty water*, Ar. From

ἀπ-ονίναμαι, Med. (ὀνίνημι), f. ἀπο-νήσομαι: Ep. 3 sing. aor. 2 ἀπόνητο; 2 sing. ἀπόναιο, 3 pl. ἀποναίατο; part. ἀπονήμενος:—*to have the use* or *enjoyment of* a thing, c. gen., Hom., Soph.; but the gen. is often omitted, ἦγε μὲν οὐδ' ἀπόνητο *married her but had no joy* [of it], Od.; οὐκ ἀπώνητο (sc. τῆς πόλεως) Hdt.

ἀπόνιπτρον, τό, (ἀπονίζω) *water in which the hands have been washed, dirty water*, Ar. From

ἀπονίπτω, later form of ἀπονίζω.

ἀπο-νίσσομαι, Dep. *to go away*, Theogn.: Ep. aor. 1 part. ἀπονισσάμενος, Anth.

ἀπο-νοέομαι, f. ήσομαι: aor. 1 -ενοήθην: pf. -νενόημαι: —Dep.: (νοέω):—*to have lost all sense*, 1. of fear, *to be desperate*, Xen.; ἄνθρωποι ἀπονενοημένοι *desperate* men, Lat. *perditi*, Thuc.   2. of shame, ἀπονενοημένος *an abandoned fellow*, Theophr. Hence

ἀπόνοια, ἡ, *loss of all sense*, 1. of fear, *desperation*, εἰς ἀπ. καταστῆσαί τινα *to make one desperate*, Thuc.   2. of right perception, *madness*, Lat. *dementia*, Dem.

ἄ-πονος, ον, *without toil* or *trouble, untroubled, quiet*, Aesch., etc.   2. of persons, *not toiling, lazy*, Xen.   II. Adv. -νως, *without trouble*, Hdt., Xen.   III. irreg. Comp. ἀπονέστερος, Pind., but -ώτερος, Thuc.

ἀπο-νοστέω, f. ήσω, *to return, come home*, ἂψ ἀπονοστήσας Il.; ἀπ. ὀπίσω Hdt.

ἀπο-νόσφι, before a vowel -φιν, Adv. *far apart* or *aloof*, Hom.　II. Prep. with gen. *far away from*, Id.

ἀπο-νοσφίζω, f. Att. ιῶ, *to put asunder, keep aloof from*, τινά τινος h. Hom.　2. *to bereave* or *rob of*, ὅπλων τινά Soph. :—Pass. *to be robbed of*, ἐδωδήν h. Hom.　II. c. acc. loci, *to flee from, shun*, Soph.

ἀπο-νυκτερεύω, *to pass a night away from*, τινός Plut.

ἀπ-ονύχίζω, f. Att. ιῶ, *to pare the nails*: Pass. *to have them pared*, Babr.　2. metaph. *to pare down, retrench*, τὰ σιτία Ar.　II. = ὀνυχίζω III, *to try by the nail*, ἀκριβῶς ἀπωνυχισμένος, Horace's *ad unguem factus*, Theophr.

ἀπο-νωτίζω, f. σω, *to make one turn his back and flee*, τινά Eur.

ἀπό-ξενος, ον, *alien to guests, inhospitable*, Soph. :—c. gen. loci, *far from* a country, Aesch. ; πέδου *banished from*, Id.　Hence

ἀποξενόω, f. ώσω, *to drive from house and home, banish*, Plut. :—Pass., γῆς ἀποξενοῦσθαι Eur.　Hence

ἀποξένωσις, εως, ἡ, *a living abroad*, Plut.

ἀπο-ξέω, f. -ξέσω, *to shave off, to cut off*, ἀπὸ δ' ἔξεσε χεῖρα Il.　2. metaph. *to strip off*, Luc.

ἀπο-ξηραίνω, f. ᾰνῶ, *to dry up* a river, Hdt. :—Pass. *to be dried up, run dry*, of rivers, Id.　2. generally *to dry completely*, τὰς ναῦς Thuc.

ἀπ-οξύνω, f. ὐνῶ : aor. 1 inf. -οξῦναι :—*to bring to a point, make taper*, Od.　II. *to make sharp and piercing*, τὴν φωνήν Plut.

ἀπο-ξυράω or -έω, f. ήσω, *to shave clean*, c. dupl. acc., τὸν δοῦλον ἀποξυρήσας τὴν κεφαλήν Hdt.

ἀπό-ξυρος, ον, (ξυρόν) *cut sharp off, abrupt*, Luc.

ἀπο-ξυρόω [ῠ], = ἀποξυράω :—Med. *to have oneself clean shaved*, Plut.

ἀπο-ξύω [ῠ], f. -ξύσω : aor. 1 inf. -ξῦσαι :—*to strip off* as it were a skin, Il.

ἀπο-πάλλω, *to hurl*, Luc. :—Pass. *to rebound*, Plut.

ἀπο-παπταίνω, *to look about one*, as if to flee, Ion. 3 pl. fut. ἀποπαπτανέουσιν Il.

ἀποπατέω, f. ήσομαι : aor. 1 subj. -πατήσω :—*to retire from the way, to go aside to ease oneself*, Ar.　From

ἀπό-πᾰτος, ὁ, also ἡ, *a place out of the way* : *a privy*, Ar.

ἀπο-παύω, f. σω, *to stop* or *hinder from, make to cease from* a thing, τινά, πολέμου Il. ; πένθεος Hdt., etc. : c. inf. *to hinder* from doing, Od. :—Med. and Pass. *to leave off* or *cease from*, c. gen., Hom. ; ἐκ καμάτων Soph. : absol. *to leave off*, Theogn.　2. c. acc. only, *to stop, check*, Il., Eur.

ἀπό-πειρα, ἡ, *a trial, essay*, Hdt., Thuc.

ἀπο-πειράομαι, f. άσομαι [ᾱ] ; aor. 1 pass. ἀπεπειράθην [ᾱ], Ion. -ήθην : Dep. :—*to make trial, essay*, or *proof of* a thing or person, c. gen., Hdt., Att. :—so also in Act., ἀποπειρᾶσαι τοῦ Πειραιῶς *to make an attempt on* the Peiraeus, Thuc.

ἀπο-πελεκάω, f. ήσω, *to hew* or *trim with an axe*, Ar.

ἀπο-πέμπω, f. ψω, *to send off* or *away, to dismiss*, Hom., Hdt., etc. :—Med. *to send away from oneself*, Hdt. ; ἀπ. τὴν γυναῖκα *to put away, divorce* her, Id. : ἀπ. ὕδωρ *to get rid of* it, Id.　II. *to send back*, Od.　2. *to dispatch*, Hdt., Ar.

ἀποπέμψις, εως, ἡ, *a sending off, dispatching*, Hdt.　2. *a divorcing*, Dem.

ἀπο-πενθέω, f. ήσω, *to mourn for*, τινά Plut.

ἀποπεράω, f. άσω, Ion. ήσω, *to carry over*, Plut.

ἀπο-πέρδομαι, f. -παρδήσομαι : Dep., with aor. 2 act. -έπαρδον :—*to break wind*, Lat. *pedo*, Ar.

ἀπο-πέσησι, Ep. 3 sing. aor. 2 subj. of ἀποπίπτω.

ἀπο-πέτομαι, f. -πετήσομαι : aor. 2 -επτάμην, part. -πτάμενος : (cf. πέτομαι) :—*to fly off* or *away*, Hom., Ar.

ἀποπεφασμένως, Adv. pf. pass. part. of ἀποφαίνω, *openly, plainly*, Dem.

ἀπο-πήγνυμι, f. -πήξω, *to make to freeze, to freeze*, Ar. :—Pass., f. -πᾰγήσομαι, *to be frozen*, Xen. : of blood, *to curdle*, Id.

ἀπο-πηδάω, f. -πηδήσομαι, *to leap off from*, ἵππου Plut.　2. *to start off from, turn away from*, τινός Xen.　3. absol. *to leap off, start off*, Plat.

ἀπο-πίμπλημι, poët. -πίπλημι, f. -πλήσω, *to fill up* a number, Hdt.　II. *to satisfy, fulfil*, χρησμόν Id.　2. *to satisfy, appease*, θυμόν, ἐπιθυμίαν Id., Plat.

ἀπο-πίνω [ῐ], f. -πίομαι : aor. 2 -έπιον :—*to drink up, drink off*, Hdt.

ἀπο-πίπτω, f. -πεσοῦμαι : aor. 2 -έπεσον :—*to fall off from*, ἐκ or ἀπό τινος Od., Hdt. ; τινός Hdt. ; absol. *to fall off*, Il.

ἀπο-πιστεύω, f. σω, *to trust fully, rely on*, τινί Polyb.

ἀπο-πλάζω, f. -πλάγξω, *to lead astray from*, τινός Ap. Rh. :—Pass., aor. 1 -επλάγχθην, *to stray away from*, σῆς πατρίδος, Τροίηθεν Od. ; ἀπὸ θώρηκος ἀποπλαγχθείς *having glanced off* from the breastplate, of an arrow, Ib.; absol. τρυφάλεια ἀποπλαγχθεῖσα a helm *struck off* or *falling from the head*, Ib.

ἀπο-πλᾰνάω, f. ήσω, = foreg., *to lead astray*, Aeschin. ; metaph. *to seduce, beguile*, τινά N. T.　Hence

ἀποπλᾰνίας, ου, ὁ, *a wanderer, fugitive*, Anth.

ἀπο-πλέω, Ep. -πλείω, Ion. -πλώω : f. -πλεύσομαι or -πλευσοῦμαι, Ion. -πλώσομαι :—*to sail away, sail off*, Il., Hdt., etc.

ἀπόπληκτος, ον, (ἀποπλήσσω) *disabled by a stroke*, 1. in mind, *struck dumb, astounded, senseless, stupid*, Hdt., Dem.　2. in body, *crippled, palsied*, Lat. *sideratus*, Hdt. ; ἀπ. τὰς γνάθους *struck dumb*, Ar.

ἀπο-πληρόω, f. ώσω, = ἀποπίμπλημι, *to fill up, satisfy*, Lat. *explere*, τὰς ἐπιθυμίας Plat. ; τοῦτό μοι ἀποπλήρωσον *make* this *complete for me, satisfy me in this*, Id.　Hence

ἀποπλήρωσις, εως, ἡ, *a filling up, satisfying*, Plut.

ἀπο-πλήσσω, Att. -ττω, f. ξω, *to strike to earth, disable in body* or *mind* :—Pass. *to lose one's senses, become dizzy* or *astounded*, Soph.

ἀπο-πλίσσομαι, Dep. *to trot off*, Ar. ; v. πλίσσομαι.

ἀπό-πλοος, contr. -πλους, ὁ, (ἀποπλέω) *a sailing away*, Hdt.　2. *a voyage home* or *back*, Xen.

ἀπο-πλύνω [ῠ], f. ῠνῶ : Ion. impf. -πλύνεσκον :—*to wash away*, Od.

ἀπο-πλώω, Ion. for ἀπο-πλέω.

ἀπο-πνέω, Ep. -πνείω : f. -πνεύσομαι : aor. 1 -έπνευσα : —*to breathe forth* fire, etc., Hom. ; θυμὸν ἀπ. *to give up the ghost*, Il. ; ἀπ. τὴν δυσμένειαν *to get rid of it*, Plut.　II. *to blow from* a particular quarter, of winds, Hdt.　III. *to smell of a thing*, c. gen., Plut.

ἀπο-πνίγω [ῐ], f. -πνίξομαι : aor. 1 -έπνιξα :—*to choke, throttle*, Hdt. ; ἀπέπνιγον Ar. ; of plants, N.T. :—Pass.,

f. -πνῑγήσομαι: aor. 2 -επνίγην [ῐ]: pf. part. -πεπνιγ-μένος:—to be choked, suffocated, drowned, Dem.: metaph. to be choked with rage, Id.

ἀπο-πολεμέω, f. ήσω, to fight off from, τοῦ ὄνου from ass-back, Plat.

ἀπό-πολις, poët. ἀπό-πτολις, ι: gen. ιδος and εως:—far from the city, banished, Aesch., Soph.

ἀποπομπή, ή, (ἀποπέμπω) a sending away: getting rid of an illness, Luc.

ἀπο-πορεύομαι, f. σομαι, Pass. to depart, go away, Xen.

ἀπο-πραΰνω [ῡ], f. ῠνῶ, to soften matters down, Plut.

ἀποπρίασθαι, aor. 2 inf. with no pres. in use, to buy off or up, Ar.

ἀπο-πρίζω, aor. ἀπέπρῑσα, late form for -πρίω, Anth.

ἀπο-πρίω, contr. for ἀποπρίασο, v. ἀποπρίασθαι.

ἀπο-πρίω [ῑ], f. ίσω, to saw off, Hdt.

ἀπο-πρό, Adv. far away, afar off, Il. 2. Prep. c. gen. far away from, Ib., Eur.

ἀπο-προαιρέω, f. ήσω, aor. 2 -προεῖλον:—to take away from, σίτου ἀποπροελών having taken some of the bread, Od.

ἀπόπροθε, before vowels -θεν, Adv. (ἀποπρό) from afar, afar off, far away, Hom.

ἀπόπροθι, Adv. (ἀποπρό) far away, Hom.

ἀπο-προΐημι, f. -προήσω: Ep. aor. 1 -προέηκα:—to send away forward, send on, Od.: to send forth, shoot forth, Ib.: to let fall, Ib.

ἀπο-προτέμνω, f. -τεμῶ: aor. 2 -προέταμον:—to cut off from, νώτου ἀποπροταμών after he had cut a slice from the chine, Od.

ἀπο-προφεύγω, f. -φεύξομαι, to flee away from, Anth.

ἀπο-πτάμενος, aor. 2 part. of ἀποπέτομαι.

ἀπόπτολις, poët. for Ἀπόπολις.

ἄποπτος, ον, (ἀπόψομαι, f. of ἀφοράω) out of sight of, far away from, c. gen., Soph.:—absol. out of sight, Id.; ἐξ ἀπόπτου from a distance, Id.

ἀπόπτυστος, ον, spat out: hence loathed, abominated, Trag. From

ἀπο-πτύω [ῡ], f. ύσω: aor. 1 -έπτῡσα:—to spit out, Il.; ἀπ. ἄχνην to vomit forth foam, Ib.; absol. to spit, Xen. 2. to abominate, loathe, spurn, Aesch., Eur.: aor. 1 ἀπέπτυσα, = Lat. omen absit, Eur.

ἀπο-πυνθάνομαι, f. -πεύσομαι, Dep. to inquire or ask of, ἀπ. [αὐτοῦ] εἰ . . asked of him whether . . , Hdt.

ἀπ-οράω, Ion. for ἀφ-οράω.

ἀπο-ρέγχω, f. -ρέγξω, to snore to the end, Anth.

ἀπο-ρέπω, f. ψω, to slink away, Anth.

ἀ-πόρευτος, ον, not to be travelled, Plut.

ἀπ-ορέω, Ion. for ἀφ-οράω.

ἀπορέω, f. ήσω: impf. ἠπόρουν: (ἄπορος):—to be with-out means or resource; and so, 1. to be at a loss, be in doubt, be puzzled, mostly followed by a relative clause, ὅκως διαβήσεται to be at a loss how he shall cross, Hdt.; ἀπ. ὅ τι χρὴ ποιεῖν Xen.; with an acc. added, ἀπ. τὴν ἔλασιν ὅκως διεκπερᾷ to be at a loss about his march, how he shall cross, Hdt.; and with an acc. only, to be at a loss about it, Id.; c. inf. to be at a loss how to do, Ar., Plat.; ἀπ. περὶ τινος Plat.:—also absol., οὐκ ἀπορήσας without hesitation, Hdt., etc.:—Med. in same sense, Id., Plat. 2. in Pass., of things, to be left wanting, left unprovided for, Xen. II. c. gen. rei, to be at a loss for, in want of, Soph., Thuc.,

etc. III. ἀπ. τινι to be at a loss by reason of, by means of something, Xen. IV. absol. to be in want, be poor, Plat. Hence

ἀπορητικός, ή, όν, inclined to doubt, Plat.

ἀ-πόρθητος, ον, rarely ή, ον, (πορθέω) not sacked, un-ravaged, Il., Hdt., Att.

ἀπ-ορθόω, f. ώσω, to make straight, guide aright, Soph.

ἀπορία, Ion. -ίη, ή, (ἄ-πορος) of places, difficulty of passing, Xen. II. of things, difficulty, straits, ἐς ἀπορίην ἀπιγμένος, ἀπειλημένος, ἐν ἀπορίῃ or ἐν ἀπορίῃσι ἔχεσθαι, ἀπορίῃσιν ἐνέχεσθαι Hdt.; ἀπ. τοῦ μὴ ἡσυχά-ζειν impossibility of keeping quiet, Thuc. III. of persons, difficulty of dealing with, τινός Hdt. 2. want of means or resource, embarrassment, difficulty, hesitation, perplexity, Plat., etc. 3. ἀπ. τινός want of a person or thing, Ar., etc. 4. absol. poverty, Thuc.

ἀπ-όρνυμαι, Pass. to start from a place, Λυκίηθεν Il.

ἄ-πορος, ον, without passage, and so: I. of places, impassable, pathless, trackless, Xen., etc. II. of circumstances, hard to see one's way through, imprac-ticable, very difficult, Hdt., Att.; ἄπορα, τά, straits, difficulties, Hdt., Xen.; so, εἰς ἄπορον ἥκειν, πίπτειν Eur., Ar.; ἐν ἀπόρῳ εἶναι at a loss, Thuc. :—Comp., ἀπορώτερος more difficult, Id. 2. hard to get, scarce, Plat. III. of persons, hard to deal with, imprac-ticable, unmanageable, Hdt., Plat.: c. inf., ἀπ. προσ-μίσγειν, προσφέρεσθαι impossible to have any dealings with, Hdt.: so, absol., ἄνεμος ἀπ. Id. 2. without means or resources, at a loss, helpless, Soph., etc.; ἄπορος ἐπὶ φρόνιμα, ἐπ' οὐδέν Id.; of soldiers, οἱ ἀπορώ-τατοι the most helpless, worst equipt, Thuc. 3. poor, needy, Lat. inops, Id., Plat. IV. Adv. ἀπό-ρως, ἀπ. ἔχει μοι I am at a loss, Eur.: Comp. -ώτερον, Thuc.

ἀπ-ορούω, Ep. aor. 1 -όρουσα, to dart away, Hom.

ἀπορρ-, ρ is regularly doubled in all compds. after ἀπό; but in Poets it sometimes remains single.

ἀπορ-ρᾳθῡμέω, f. ήσω, to neglect a thing from faint-heartedness or lasiness, c. gen., Xen.; absol., Plat.

ἀπορ-ραίνω, f. -ρᾰνῶ, to spirt out, shed about, Plat.

ἀπορ-ραίω, f. σω, to bereave one of a thing, c. dupl. acc., Od. Hence

ἀπορραντήριον, τό, (ἀπορραίνω) a vessel for sprinkling with holy water, Eur.

ἀπορ-ράπτω, f. ψω, to sew up again, Hdt., Aeschin.

ἀπορ-ραψῳδέω, f. ήσω, to speak in fragments of Epic poetry, Xen.

ἀπορ-ρέζω, f. -ρέξω, to offer some of a thing, c. gen. partit., Theocr.

ἀπορ-ρέω: fut. and aor. 2 in pass. forms ἀπορρυήσομαι, ἀπερρύην, part. ἀπορρυείς:—to flow or run off, stream forth, Hdt., Aesch.; ἀπό τινος Hdt.; ἔκ τινος Plat. II. to fall off, as fruit, feathers, leaves, etc., Hdt., Att. 2. to die away, fade from remembrance, Soph.

ἀπόρρηγμα, ατος, τό, a fragment, Plut. From

ἀπορ-ρήγνῡμι or -ύω, f. -ρήξω, to break off, snap asunder, Hom., etc.; πνεῦμ' ἀπορρῆξαι βίου to snap the thread of life, Aesch.; ἀπ. βίον Eur. II. Pass., aor. 2 ἀπερράγην [ᾰ], to be broken off, severed, Hdt., Thuc.; ἀπό τινος Hdt. III. intr. in pf. ἀπέρρωγα, to be broken, Archil.

ἀπορ-ρηθῆναι, aor. 1 pass. inf. of ἀπ-ερῶ, cf. ἀπεῖπον.

ἀπόρρησις, εως, ἡ, (ἀπερῶ) a forbidding, prohibition, Plat.   II. a giving up a point, refusal, Id.

ἀπόρρητος, ον, (ἀπερῶ) forbidden, ἀπόρρητον πόλει though it was forbidden to the citizens, Soph. ; τὰ ἀπόρρητα prohibited exports, contraband articles, Ar.   II. not to be spoken, that should not be spoken, Lat. tacendus, ἀπ. ποιεῖσθαι to keep secret, Hdt. ; κύριος καὶ ῥητῶν καὶ ἀπορρήτων, of Philip, like dicenda tacenda, Dem. : ἀπόρρητον, τό, a state-secret, Ar.   2. of sacred things, ineffable, Eur.   3. unfit to be spoken, abominable, Plat.

ἀπορ-ρῑγέω, f. ήσω : pf. 2 ἀπέρρῑγα :—to shrink shivering from a thing, shrink from doing it, c. inf., Od.

ἀπορ-ρῑνάω, f. ήσω, to file off, Strab.

ἀπορ-ρίπτω, poët. ἀπο-ρίπτω, f. -ρίψω : aor. 1 -έρριψα : —Pass., f. ἀπορριφθήσομαι : aor. 1 -ερρίφθην : pf. -έρριμμαι :—to throw away, put away, Il.   II. to cast forth from one's country, Aesch., Soph. ; ἀπερριμμένοι outcasts, Dem.   2. to disown, renounce, Soph.   3. to throw aside, set at naught, Aesch. : Pass., ἀπέρριπται ἐς τὸ μηδέν Hdt.   III. of words, to shoot forth bold, keen words, ἔς τινα at one, Id. :— also, ἀπ. ἔπος to let fall a word, Id.

ἀπορροή and ἀπόρροια, ἡ, (ἀπορ-ρέω) a flowing off, stream, Eur., Xen.   II. an efflux, emanation, Plat.

ἀπορ-ροιβδέω, f. ήσω, to shriek forth, βοᾷς Soph.

ἀπορ-ροφέω or -άω, f. ήσω, to swallow some of a thing, c. gen. partit., Xen.

ἀπορ-ρύπτω, f. ψω, to cleanse thoroughly, Luc. : Med. to cleanse oneself, Plut.

ἀπόρρῠτος, ον, (ἀπορ-ρέω) running, Hes. : ἀπ. σταθμά stables with drains, Aesch.

ἀπορρώξ, ῶγος, ὁ, ἡ, (ἀπορρήγνυμι) broken off, abrupt, sheer, precipitous, Lat. praeruptus, Od., Xen.   II. as fem. Subst. a piece broken off, Στυγὸς ἀπορρώξ a branch or off-stream of the Styx, Il.   2. ἀπ. νέκταρος an efflux, distillation of nectar, Il.

ἀπ-ορφανίζομαι, Pass. to be orphaned or bereaved, Aesch. ; ἀπό τινος ἀπ. to be torn away from one, N.T.

ἀ-πόρφυρος, ον, (πορφύρα) without purple border, Plut.

ἀπ-ορχέομαι, f. ήσομαι, Dep. to dance a thing away, i. e. lose by dancing, τὸν γάμον Hdt.

ἀποσᾰλεύω, f. σω, to lie in the open sea, to ride at anchor, Thuc., Dem.

ἀπο-σᾰφέω, f. ήσω, (σαφής) to make clear, Plat.

ἀπο-σβέννυμι or -ύω, f. -σβέσω, to put out, extinguish, quench, Ar., Plat., etc.   II. Pass., with fut. med. -σβήσομαι, aor. 2 and pf. act. intr., ἀπέσβην, ἀπέσβηκα, and aor. 1 pass. ἀπεσβέσθην :—to be extinguished, go out, cease to exist, Eur., Xen.

ἀπο-σείω, f. σω, to shake off :—Med. to shake off from oneself, Theogn. ; of a horse, to throw his rider, Hdt., Xen. ; metaph., ἀποσείεσθαι λύπην Ar.

ἀπο-σεμνύνω [ῡ], f. ῠνῶ, to make august, glorify, Plat.   II. Pass., with fut. med., to give oneself airs, Ar. ; τι about a thing, Id.

ἀπο-σεύω, to chase away, Anth. :—Pass., with 3 sing. Ep. aor. 2 ἀπέσσῦτο, aor. 1 ἀπεσσύθην [ῠ], to dart away, Il.

ἀπο-σημαίνω, f. ᾰνῶ, to give notice by signs, give notice, περί τινος Hdt. : absol. to give a sign, Plat.   2. c. acc. to indicate by signs, betoken, Plut. :—Med. to show

by signs or proofs, Hdt.   II. ἀπ. εἴς τινα to allude to him, Thuc.   III. Med. to seal up as confiscated, to confiscate, Xen. : of persons, to proscribe, Id.

ἀπο-σήπομαι, Pass., f. -σᾰπήσομαι, aor. 2 -εσάπην [ᾰ], with intr. pf. act. -σέσηπα :—to lose by mortification, or frost-bite, τοὺς δακτύλους Xen.

ἀπο-σῑμόω, f. ώσω, to make flat-nosed : Pass., ἀπου εσιμώμεθα τὴν ῥῖνα we have snub noses, Luc.   II. ἀποσιμοῦν τὰς ναῦς to turn the ships aside, make a sideward movement, so as to avoid the direct shock, Thuc.

ἀπ-οσιόομαι, Ion. for ἀφ-οσιόομαι.

ἀπό-σῑτος, ον, abstaining from food, Luc.

ἀπο-σιωπάω, f. ήσομαι, to cease speaking, maintain silence, Isocr., Plut.   II. trans. to keep secret, Luc. Hence

ἀποσιώπησις, εως, ἡ, a becoming silent, Plut.   2. a rhetorical figure, when the sentence is broken off, as in Il. 1. 342, Virg. Aen. 1. 135.

ἀπο-σκάπτω, f. ψω, to intercept by trenches, Xen.

ἀπο-σκεδάννυμι or -ύω : f. -σκεδάσω, contr. -σκεδῶ :— to scatter abroad, disperse, Hom., Soph. :—Pass. to straggle from the ranks, of soldiers, Xen.

ἀποσκεπτέον, verb. Adj. one must look steadily, Arist.

ἀπο-σκευάζω, f. άσω, to pull off :—Med. to pack up and carry off, to make away with, Luc.

ἀποσκέψομαι, f. of ἀπο-σκοπέω.

ἀποσκηνέω, f. ήσω, to encamp apart from, τινός Xen. From

ἀπό-σκηνος, ον, (σκήνη) encamping apart, messing alone, Xen. Hence

ἀποσκηνόω, f. ώσω, to keep apart from, Plut.   II. = ἀποσκηνέω, Id.

ἀπο-σκήπτω, f. ψω, to hurl from above, ἀπ. βέλεα ἔς τι to hurl thunderbolts upon, Hdt.   II. intr. to fall suddenly, like a thunderbolt, ἔς τινα Eur., Aeschin. ; ἀπ. ἐς φλαῦρον to come to a sorry ending, Hdt.

ἀπο-σκιάζω, f. άσω, to cast a shadow, Plat.   Hence

ἀποσκιασμός, ὁ, the casting a shadow, ἀπ. γνωμόνων measures of time by the shadow on the sun-dial, Plut.

ἀπο-σκίδνᾰμαι, Pass. to be dispersed, Il. ; of soldiers, ἀπ. ἐς τι to disperse for a purpose, Hdt.

ἀπο-σκλῆναι, aor. 2 inf., as if from *ἀπόσκλημι (cf. σκέλλω), to be dried up, to wither, Ar. ; so pf. ἀπέσκληκα Luc. ; f. ἀποσκλήσω Anth.

ἀπο-σκοπέω, f. -σκέψομαι, to look away from other objects at one, to look steadily, πρός τινα or τι Soph., Plat. ; εἴς τι Soph.   2. c. acc. to look to, regard, Eur. ; so in Med., Plut.

ἀπό-σκοπος, ον, (σκοπός) far from the mark, Anth.

ἀπο-σκῠθίζω, f. ίσω, to strip off the scalp in Scythian fashion : metaph. in Pass. to be shaved bare, κρᾶτ' ἀπεσκυθισμένη Eur.

ἀπο-σκῡλεύω, to carry off as spoil from, τί τιν ς Theocr.

ἀπο-σκώπτω, f. -σκώψομαι, to banter, rally, τινά Plat. ; ἀπ. εἴς τινα to jeer at one, Luc.

ἀπο-σμάω, to wipe off dirt, Luc. : Pass. to be wiped clean, Id.

ἀπο-σμήχω, f. ξω, = ἀποσμάω, Luc.

ἀπο-σμῑκρύνω [ῡ], to diminish, Luc.

ἀπο-σμύχομαι [ῠ], aor. 2 -εσμύγην [ῠ], Pass. to be consumed by a slow fire, to pine away, Luc.

ἀπο-σοβέω, f. ήσω, to scare away, as one does birds or

flies, Ar.; metaph., ἀποσοβῆσαι τὸν γέλων Id. II. intr.
to be off in a hurry, οὐκ ἀποσοβήσεις; i. e. be off! Id.
ἀποσπάδιος [ă], η, ον, (ἀποσπάω) torn off or away,
ἀποσπάδιον, τό, = ἀπόσπασμα, Anth.
ἀποσπάραγμα, ατος, τό, = ἀπόσπασμα, Anth. From
ἀπο-σπάράσσω, f. ξω, to tear off, Eur.
ἀποσπάς, άδος, ἡ, a slip torn from a tree, a vine-
branch or bunch of grapes, Anth. : and
ἀπόσπασμα, ατος, τό, that which is torn off, a piece,
rag, shred, Plat. From
ἀπο-σπάω, f. -σπάσω [ă], to tear or drag away from,
τινός Soph., Plat., etc. ; ἀπ. τινα ἀπὸ γυναικός Hdt. ;
τὸ τέκνον ἐκ χερῶν Eur. ; also c. dupl. acc. to tear a
thing from one, Soph. : —ἀπ. τινά to tear him away,
Hdt. : —Med. to drag away for oneself, Plut. : —Pass.
to be dragged away, detached, separated from, τινὸς
Pind., Eur. ; ἐξ ἱροῦ Hdt. ; ἀπὸ τῶν ἱερῶν Thuc. 2.
ἀπ. πύλας to tear off the gates, Hdt. 3. ἀπ. τὸ στρατόπεδον to draw off the army, Xen. ; absol., ἀποσπάσας
having drawn off, Id. : —Pass., of troops, to be separated or broken, Thuc.
ἀπο-σπένδω, f. -σπείσω, to pour out wine as a drink-
offering, Od., Eur.
ἀπο-σπεύδω, f. -σπεύσω, to be zealous in preventing a
thing, Hdt. ; c. acc. et inf., ἀπ. Ξέρξεα στρατεύεσθαι Id.
ἀπο-σποδέω, f. ήσω, to wear quite off, ἀπ. τοὺς ὄνυχας
to walk one's toes off, Ar.
ἀποσ-σεύω, Ep. for ἀπο-σεύω.
ἀπό-στα, for ἀπό-στηθι, aor. 2 imper. of ἀφίστημι.
ἀποστᾰδόν and ἀποσταδά, Adv. (ἀφίστημι) standing
aloof, Hom.
ἀπο-στάζω, f. ξω, to let fall drop by drop, distil,
Theocr. II. intr. to fall in drops, distil, Soph.
ἀποστᾰλάω, = ἀποστάζω I, Anth.
ἀποστᾰσία, ἡ, late form of ἀπόστασις, defection, Plut.
ἀποστᾰσίου δίκη, ἡ, an action against a freedman for
having forsaken or slighted his προστάτης, Dem. ; ἀπο-
στασίου βιβλίον, τό, a writing or bill of divorce, N. T.
ἀπόστᾰσις, εως, ἡ, (ἀφίσταμαι) a standing away from,
and so, 1. a defection, revolt, ἀπό τινος or τινος
Hdt., Thuc. ; πρός τινα Thuc. 2. departure from,
βίου Eur. 3. distance, interval, Plat.
ἀποστᾰτέον, verb. Adj. of ἀφίσταμαι, one must stand
off from or give up a thing. c. gen., Thuc., Dem.
ἀποστᾰτέω, f. ήσω, (ἀφίσταμαι) to stand aloof from,
depart from, be far from, c. gen., Aesch., Soph. ; ἀπ.
φίλων to fall off from one's friends, Ar. II. absol.
to stand aloof or afar off, Aesch.
ἀποστᾰτήρ, ὁ, for (ἀφίστημι) one who has power to dissolve
an assembly, Lycurg. ap. Plut.
ἀποστάτης, ου, ὁ, (ἀφίσταμαι) a runaway slave : a
deserter, rebel, Plut. Hence
ἀποστᾰτικός, ή, όν, of or for rebels, Plut. : —Adv., ἀπο-
στατικῶς ἔχειν to be ready for revolt, Id.
ἀπο-σταυρόω, f. ώσω, to fence off with a palisade, Thuc.
ἀπο-στεγάζω, f. σω, to uncover : to take off a roof, N.T.
ἀπο-στέγω, f. ξω, to keep out water : metaph. to keep
out or off, ὄχλον πύργος ἀποστέγει Aesch. II. to
keep in water, confine it, check its outflow, Plat.
ἀποστεινόω, poët. for ἀποστενόω.
ἀπο-στείχω, aor. 2 -έστιχον, to go away, to go home,
Od., Hdt. ; imper. ἀπόστιχε Il., Hdt.

ἀπο-στέλλω, f. -στελῶ : aor. 1 -έστειλα : pf. -έσταλκα :—
to send off or away from, γῆς, χθονός Soph., Eur. ; ἔξω
χθονός Eur. ; ἐκ τῆς πόλεως Plat. : absol. to send away,
banish, Soph., Eur. :—Pass. to go away, depart, set out,
Soph., Eur. II. to send off, despatch, on some service,
Soph. ; of troops and ships, Hdt., Thuc. III. intr.
to go back, retire, of the sea, Thuc. ; of seamen, Dem.
ἀπο-στενόω, poët. -στεινόω, to straiten, block up :
Pass., 3 sing. plqpf. pass. ἀπεστείνωτο Theocr.
ἀπο-στέργω, f. ξω, to love no more, Theocr. :—hence to
put away from one, reject, Lat. abominari, Aesch.
ἀπο-στερέω, f. ήσω :—Pass., f. -στερηθήσομαι, also in
med. forms -στερήσομαι and -στερουμαι :—to rob, despoil, bereave or defraud one of a thing, c. acc. pers.
et gen. rei, Hdt., Ar.; also, c. acc. pers. et rei, μή μ' ἀπο-
στερήσῃς ἡδονάν Soph., etc. : absol. to defraud, cheat,
Ar. :—Pass. to be robbed or deprived of, c. gen., Ἑλλάδος ἀπεστερημένος Hdt., Att.; also c. acc., ἵππους ἀπε-
στέρηνται Xen. 2. ἀπ. ἑαυτόν τινος to detach, withdraw oneself from . . , Soph., Thuc. 3. c. acc. pers.
to deprive, rob, Hdt., Att. :—τὸ σαφές μ' ἀποστερεῖ
certainty fails me, Eur. 4. c. acc. rei only, to filch
away, withhold, Aesch., etc. Hence
ἀποστέρησις, εως, ἡ, deprivation, τῆς ἀκοῆς Thuc.; and
ἀποστερητής, οῦ, ὁ, a depriver, robber, Plat.; and
ἀποστερητικός, ή, όν, of or for cheating, γνώμη ἀπ.
τόκου a device for cheating one of his interest, Ar.; so
fem. ἀποστερητρίς, ίδος, Id.
ἀποστερίσκω, = ἀποστερέω, Soph.
ἀπόστημα, ατος, τό, (ἀφίσταμαι) distance, interval, τοῖς
ἀπ. πρὸς τοὺς γονεῖς in point of intervals, in relation
to one's parents, Arist.
ἀπο-στηρίζομαι, Med. to fix firmly, Anth.
ἀπο-στιλβόω, to make to shine, Anth.
ἀπο-στίλβω, f. ψω, to be bright from or with oil, c.
gen., ἀπ. ἀλείφατος Od.
ἀπο-στλεγγίζω, f. σω, (στλεγγίς) to scrape with a stri-
gil :—Med. to scrape oneself clean, Xen.; pf. pass.
part. ἀπεστλεγγισμένοι, scraped clean, fresh from the
bath, Ar.
ἀποστολεύς, έως, ὁ, (ἀποστέλλω) at Athens, a magistrate who had to fit out a squadron for service, Dem.,
Aeschin.
ἀποστολή, ἡ, (ἀποστέλλω) a sending off or away,
despatching, Eur., Thuc. II. (from Pass.) a going
away, an expedition, Thuc. 2. the office of an
apostle, apostleship, N. T.
ἀπόστολος, ὁ, (ἀποστέλλω) a messenger, ambassador,
envoy, Hdt. 2. a sacred messenger, an Apostle,
N. T. II. = στόλος, a naval squadron or expedition,
Dem., etc.
ἀπο-στοματίζω, f. σω, (στόμα) to dictate by word of
mouth, teach by dictation, γράμματα Plat. 2. to
question sharply or to provoke one to speak, N. T. 3.
to recite, repeat by heart, Plut.
ἀπο-στράτηγος, ὁ, a retired general, Dem.
ἀπο-στρᾰτοπεδεύομαι, f. -σομαι, Dep. to encamp away
from, τινός Xen.; ἀπ. πρόσω to encamp at a distance, Id.
ἀπο-στρᾰφῶ, aor. 2 pass. subj. of sq.
ἀπο-στρέφω, f. ψω : 3 sing. Ion. aor. 1 ἀποστρέψασκε :
—Pass. and Med., f. -στρέψομαι : aor. 2 -εστράφην [ă] :
pf. -έστραμμαι, Ion. 3 pl. plqpf. -εστράφατο : —to turn

one *back*, i. e. either *to turn to flight, put to flight*, Hom.; or *to turn* him *back from* flight, Xen.; πόδας καὶ χεῖρας *to twist back* the hands and feet so as to bind them, Od.; so τὸν αὐχένα Hdt. : —*to turn back, avert* one's face, Od., Eur. : *to bring back, recall*, Xen. **2.** *to turn away, to divert* the course of a river, Hdt. : *to avert* a danger, Aesch., Thuc. **II.** intr. (sub. ἑαυτόν, ἵππον, ναῦν, etc.), *to turn back*, Hdt., Soph. **B. Pass.**, ἀπεστράφθαι τοὺς ἐμβόλους, of ships, *to have* their beaks *bent back*, Hdt.; ἀποστραφῆναι τὼ πόδε *to have* one's feet *twisted*, Ar. **II.** *to turn away from*, in abhorrence, Lat. *aversari*, c. acc., Soph., Eur.; absol., ἀπεστραμμένοι λόγοι *hostile* words, Hdt. **2.** *to turn oneself about, turn back*, Xen.; *to turn and flee*, Id. **3.** ἀποστραφῆναί τινος *to fall off from* one, *desert* him, Id.

ἀποστροφή, ἡ, (ἀποστρέφομαι) *a turning back*, Xen.; ἀποστροφὴν λαμβάνειν *to have* one's course *turned*, Plut. **II.** *a turning away from, an escape from* a thing, c. gen., Aesch., Eur. **2.** *a resort, resource*, Hdt.:—c. gen. objecti, ὕδατος ἀπ. *a resource* or *means for getting* water, Id.; σωτηρίας ἀπ. Thuc.

ἀπόστροφος, ον, (ἀπο-στρέφομαι) *turned away*, Soph.

ἀπο-στυγέω, f. -στύξω: aor. 1 -εστύγησα: aor. 2 ἀπέστυγον: pf. -εστύγηκα: *to hate violently, abhor, loathe*, Hdt., Soph.; c. inf. *to be disgusted that* . . , Hdt.

ἀπο-στυφελίζω, f. ξω, *to drive away by force from*, τινά τινος Il.

ἀπο-στύφω [ῠ], f. ψω, *to draw up, contract*, of astringents, *to dull* the sense of taste, Anth.

ἀπο-σῡκάζω, f. σω, *to squeeze figs*, to try whether they are ripe, Ar.

ἀπο-σῡλάω, f. ήσω, *to strip off spoils from* a person, *to rob* or *defraud* one of a thing, τινά τινος Soph.; τινά τι Eur., Xen. :—Pass., ἀποσυλᾶσθαί τι *to be robbed of* a thing, Aesch.

ἀπο-συνάγωγος, ον, (συναγωγή) *put out of the synagogue*, N. T.

ἀπο-σῡρίζω, f. ξω, *to whistle aloud* for want of thought, h. Hom. :—Pass. *to sound like whistling*, Luc.

ἀπο-σύρω [ῠ], f. -σῠρῶ :—*to tear away*, Thuc. **II.** *to lay bare*, Theocr.

ἀπο-σφάζω, Att. -σφάττω, f. -σφάξω :—Pass., aor. 2 -εσφάγην [ᾰ]: f. -σφάγήσομαι :—*to cut the throat of* a person, Lat. *jugulo*, ἀποσφ. τινὰ ἐς ἄγγος, so that the blood runs into a pail, Hdt. : generally, *to slay*, Ar., Thuc., etc. :—Med. *to cut one's own throat*, Xen.

ἀπο-σφᾰκελίζω, f. σω, *to have the limbs frost-bitten*, Hdt. **II.** *to fall into convulsions*, Plut.

ἀπο-σφάλλω, f. -σφᾰλῶ: aor. 1 -έσφηλα :—*to lead astray, drive away*, Od.; ἀπ. τινὰ πόνοιο *to baulk* them of the fruits of toil, Il. **II.** Pass., aor. 2 ἀπεσφάλην [ᾰ], *to be baulked* or *disappointed of* a thing, c. gen., Hdt. : *to be deprived of*, Aesch. : *to fail in reaching*, Ἰταλίας Plut. : absol. *to be missing* or *lost*, Dem.

ἀπο-σφάττω, Att. for ἀποσφάζω.

ἀπο-σφήλειε, 3 sing. aor. 1 opt. of ἀποσφάλλω : ἀποσφήλω, subj.

ἀπο-σφίγγω, f. γξω, *to compress*, Luc. : Pass., λόγος ἀπεσφιγμένος *a close-packed* style, Id.

ἀπο-σφρᾱγίζω, Ion. -σφρηγίζω: f. Att. ιῶ :—*to seal up*, Plut. :—so in Med.. Eur.

ἀπο-σχᾰλίδωμα, ατος, τό, (σχαλιδόω) *a forked piece of wood for propping hunting-nets*, Xen.

ἀπο-σχεῖν, -σχέσθαι, aor. 2 inf. act. and med. of ἀπέχω.

ἀπο-σχήσω, f. of ἀπέχω.

ἀπο-σχίζω, f. σω, *to split* or *cleave off*, Od., Eur. **2.** *to sever* or *detach from*, τινὰ ἀπό τινος Hdt. :—Pass., ἀποσχισθῆναί τινος *to be separated from* . . , Id.; of a river, *to be parted from* the main stream, Id. ; of a tribe, *to be detached from* its parent stock, Id. **3.** metaph., ἀπ. τινὰ τοῦ λόγου *to cut* him *off* from his speech, *interrupt* him in it, Ar.

ἀπο-σχοινίζω, f. σω, *to separate by a cord* : generally, *to separate*, Dem.

ἀπο-σώζω, f. σω, *to preserve from, heal from* or *of* a thing, τινός Soph.; ἀπ. οἴκαδε *to bring safe home*, Xen. :—Pass., ἀποσωθῆναι ἐς or ἐπὶ τόπον *to get safe* to a place, Hdt., Xen. : absol. *to get off safe*, Hdt.

ἀπότακτος, ον, or ἀποτακτός, όν, (ἀποτάσσω) *set apart for a special use*, Hdt.

ἀποτάμνω, Ion. for ἀποτέμνω.

ἀπο-τάσσω, Att. -ττω, f. ξω, *to set apart, assign specially*, χώραν τινί Plat. :—Pass., ἀπετέτακτο πρὸς τὸ δεξιόν had *his appointed post* on the right, Xen. **II.** Med. ἀποτάσσεσθαί τινι *to bid farewell to* a person or thing, N. T.

ἀπο-ταυρόομαι, Pass. *to be like a bull* : δέργμα ἀποταυροῦσθαι *to cast savage* glances at . . , Eur.

ἀπο-ταφρεύω, f. σω, *to fence off with a ditch*, Xen.

ἀπο-τέθνᾰσαν, Ep. 3 pl. plqpf. of ἀποθνήσκω.

ἀπο-τεθνειώς, Ep. for τεθνεώς, -τεθνηκώς, pf. part. of ἀποθνήσκω.

ἀπο-τείνω, f. -τενῶ : pf. -τέτᾰκα: 3 pl. pf. pass. ἀποτέτανται :—*to stretch out, extend* :—Pass., Xen. **2.** *to lengthen, extend, prolong*, of the line of an army, Id.; of speeches, ἀπ. τὸν λόγον Plat.

ἀπο-τειχίζω, f. Att. ιῶ, *to wall off*, **1.** so as *to fortify*, τὸν Ἰσθμόν Hdt. **2.** so as *to blockade*, τινάς Ar., Thuc., etc. Hence

ἀποτείχῐσις, εως, ἡ, *the walling off a town, blockading*, Thuc.; and

ἀποτείχισμα, ατος, τό, *a wall built to blockade, lines of blockade*, Thuc., Xen.

ἀποτειχισμός, ὁ, = ἀποτείχισις, Plut.

ἀπο-τελευτάω, f. ήσω, intr. *to end*, εἴς τι in a thing, Plat.

ἀπο-τελέω, f. -τελέσω, Att. -τελῶ, *to bring quite to an end, complete* a work, Hdt., Xen., etc.:—Pass., pf. part. ἀποτετελεσμένος, *perfect*, Xen. **2.** *to pay* or *perform* what one is bound *to pay* or *perform*, as vows to a god, Hdt., Xen. : generally, *to accomplish, perform*, Xen. **3.** *to render* or *make* of a certain kind, τὴν πόλιν ἀπ. εὐδαίμονα *to make* the state *quite* happy, Plat. ; and Med., ἄμεμπτον φίλον ἀποτελέσασθαι *to make* him *without blame towards himself*, Xen.

ἀπο-τέμνω, Ion. -τάμνω: f. -τεμῶ: aor. 2 -έτεμον, -έταμον :—*to cut off, sever*, Il., Hdt., Att. :—Pass., τὴν γλῶτταν ἀποτμηθείς *having* his tongue *cut out*, Aeschin. **2.** *to sever, divide*, in a geographical sense, Hdt. :—Pass., of troops, *to be cut off from* the main body, Xen. **II.** Med. *to cut off for oneself*, Il. ; c. gen. *to cut off a bit* of a thing, Hdt. **2.** *to cut off*, so as *to appropriate*, βοῦς h. Hom., Hdt. ; Φοινίκης ἀπ.

to have a slice or portion of Phoenicia, Theocr.; ἀπ. τῶν Ἀθηναίων to cut off power from the Athenians, Thuc.

ἀπότευξις, εως, ἡ, (ἀπο-τυγχάνω) a failure, Plut.

ἀπο-τηλε, Adv. far from, c. gen., Anth.

ἀπο-τηλοῦ, Adv. far away, Od.

ἀ-ποτίβατος, Dor. for ἀ-πρόσβατος, Soph.

ἀπο-τίθημι, f. -θήσω, to put away, stow away, Il. II. Med. to put away from oneself, lay aside, of arms and clothes, Ib., Hdt.; ἀπ. τὸν νόμον to put aside, i. e. disregard, the law, Thuc. 2. to avoid, escape, of something odious, Il. 3. to put by for oneself, stow away, Ar., Xen. 4. ἀποτίθεσθαι εἰς αὖθις to put off, defer, Eur., Xen., etc.

ἀπο-τίλλω, f. -τῐλῶ: aor. 1 -ἔτῑλα:—to pluck or pull out, τὰς τρίχας Hdt.; οὐδὲν ἀποτίλας without pulling off any of the fur, Id. Hence

ἀπότιλμα, ατος, τό, a piece plucked off, Theocr.

ἀπο-τῑμάω, f. ήσω, to put away from honour, to dishonour, slight, h. Hom. II. Med. to fix a price by valuation, δίμναεις ἀποτιμησάμενοι having fixed their price at two minae a head, Hdt. III. as Att. lawterm, Act. to borrow money on mortgage ; Med. to lend on mortgage ; Pass. of the property, to be mortgaged, Dem. Hence

ἀποτίμημα, ατος, τό, a mortgage, security, Dem.; and

ἀποτίμησις, εως, ἡ, a mortgaging, Dem. II. the Rom. census, Plut.

ἀπό-τῑμος, ον, (τιμή) put away from honour, dishonoured, Hdt., Soph.

ἀπο-τῐνάσσω, f. ξω, to shake off, Eur.

ἀπο-τίνῠμαι, poët. for ἀποτίνομαι; v. ἀποτίνω II.

ἀπο-τίνω [ῑ Ep., ῐ Att.], Ep. inf. -τῑνέμεν: f. -τίσω [ῐ]:—to pay back, repay, return, τί τινι Il. 2. to pay for a thing, τι Hom., Aesch., etc.: absol. to make atonement, Il. 3. to pay in full, Hdt., Att. II. Med. ἀποτίνομαι and ἀποτίνυμαι: f. -τίσομαι:—to get paid one, to exact or require a penalty from a man, ποινήν Il.; δίκην Eur. 2. c. acc. pers., ἀποτίσασθαί τινα to avenge oneself on another, punish him, Od., Xen. 3. c. acc. rei, to take vengeance for a thing, punish it, Od.; so, c. gen. rei, Hdt.:—absol. to take vengeance, Theogn. Hence

ἀποτιστέον, verb. Adj. one must pay, Xen.

ἀπο-τμήγω, f. ξω, Ep. for ἀπο-τέμνω, to cut off from, τινά τινος Il. 2. to cut off, sever, Ib.; κλιτῦς ἀπ. to cut up or plough the hill-sides, Ib.

ἀποτμητέον, verb. Adj. of ἀποτέμνω, one must cut off, τῆς χώρας a portion of it, Plat.

ἄ-ποτμος, ον, unhappy, ill-starred, Hom.,Aesch., Eur.: —Comp. -ότερος ; Sup. -ότατος, Od.

ἀπο-τολμάω, f. ήσω, to make a bold venture, τινί upon one, Thuc.: c. inf., Aeschin.: Pass., τὰ ἀποτετολμημένα what has been hazarded, Plat.

ἀποτομή, ἡ, (ἀποτέμνω) a cutting off, Xen.

ἀπότομος, ον, (ἀποτέμνω) cut off, abrupt, precipitous, Hdt.; ἀπότομον ὤρουσεν εἰς ἀνάγκαν, metaph. from one who comes suddenly to the edge of a cliff, Soph. 2. metaph. severe, relentless, Eur.

ἀπο-τοξεύω, f. σω, to shoot off arrows, Luc. II. to shoot a person, τινά τινι Id.

ἄ-ποτος, ον, not drinkable, Hdt. II. act. never

drinking, Id., Plat. :—not drinking, without drink, Soph., Xen.

ἀπο-τρᾰγεῖν, aor. 2 inf. of ἀποτρώγω.

ἀπο-τρέπω, f. ψω, to turn one away from a thing, c. gen., Il. :—to turn away, deter or dissuade from, Thuc.; also, c. inf., ἀπ. τινὰ ποιεῖν τι Aesch., Dem. 2. c. acc. pers. only, to turn away, turn back, Il. 3. c. acc. rei, to turn aside, avert, prevent, Hdt., Plat.; cf. ἀποτρόπαιος, ἀπότροπος. 4. to turn from others against one, τι ἐπί τινι Soph.:—Med., ἀποτραπόμενος πρός τι turning away from other objects to this one, Plut. II. Med. and Pass. to turn from, to desist from doing a thing, c. part., Il., c. inf., Eur., etc. :—absol. to stop, desist, Thuc. 2. to turn away, turn a deaf ear, Il. 3. c. acc. rei, to turn away from, like Lat. aversari, Aesch., Eur. 4. to turn back, return, Thuc., Xen.

ἀπο-τρέχω, f. -θρέξομαι and -δραμοῦμαι: aor. 2 -ἔδρᾰμον :—to run off or away, Hdt., Att. II. to run hard, of one training for a race, Ar.

ἀπο-τρίβω [ῐ], f. ψω, to wear out, Od. II. to rub clean, to rub down a horse, Xen. III. to rub off, Theocr. :—Med. to get rid of, Dem., Aeschin. : to decline, reject, τὴν πεῖραν Plut.

ἀποτρόπαιος, ον, (ἀποτρέπω) averting evil, of Apollo, Lat. averruncus, Ar., etc. II. pass. that ought to be averted, ill-omened, Luc.

ἀποτροπή, ἡ, (ἀποτρέπω) a turning away, averting, κακῶν Aesch., Eur. 2. a hindering, prevention, Thuc. II. (from Med.) desertion of one's party, Id.

ἀπότροπος, ον, (ἀποτρέπω) turned away, banished, Od. 2. from which one turns away, direful, grim, Aesch., Soph. II. act. turning away, averting, a thing, c. gen., Aesch., Eur.

ἀπό-τροφος, ον, (τρέφω) reared away from home, Hdt.

ἀπο-τρύχω [ῡ], f. ξω, = sq., Plut.

ἀπο-τρύω [ῡ], f. ύσω, to rub away, wear out, Soph. :— Med., γῆν ἀποτρύεσθαι to vex constantly the earth, by working it, Soph.

ἀπο-τρώγω, f. -τρώξομαι: aor. 2 -ἔτραγον :—to bite or nibble off, Ar. 2. c. gen. to nibble at, τᾶς αὔλακος οὐκ ἀποτρώγεις, i. e. you don't get on with your swathe, in reaping, Theocr.

ἀπο-τρωπάω, Frequentat. of ἀποτρέπω, only in pres., Hom.

ἀπο-τυγχάνω, f. -τεύξομαι, to fail in hitting or gaining, to miss, lose, c. gen., Xen., etc. 2. Pass., τὰ ἀποτετευγμένα things not come to pass, Luc. II. absol. to miss one's object, to be unlucky, fail, Xen. : to miss the truth, err, Id. :—c. inf. to fail to do, Id.

ἀπο-τυμπᾰνίζω, f. Att. ιῶ, to cudgel to death, bastinado, Dem.

ἀπο-τῠπόομαι, Med. to stamp an impression as on wax, εἴς τι Plat. II. Act. ἀπ. σφραγῖδα to impress a seal, Luc.

ἀπο-τύπτομαι, Med. to cease to beat oneself, to cease mourning, Hdt.

ἀπ-ούρας, -ουράμενος, aor. 1 part. act. and med. of ἀπ-αυράω.

ἀπ-ουρίζω, Ep. for ἀφ-ορίζω: Ep. fut., ἄλλοι οἱ ἀπουρίσσουσιν ἀρούρας others will mark off, i. e. contract, the boundaries of his fields, Il. : others read ἀπ-ουρήσουσι, = ἀπ-αυρήσουσι (from ἀπ-αυράω) will take away.

ἄπ-ουρος, ον, (ὅρος, Ion. οὖρος) far from the boundaries of one's country, c. gen., Soph.

ἄ-πους, ὁ, ἡ, -πουν, τό, without foot or feet, Plat. 2. without the use of one's feet, halt, lame, Soph.

ἀπουσία, ἡ, (ἄπειμι absum) a being away, absence, Aesch., Eur., etc.

ἀπο-φαγεῖν, aor. 2 inf. of ἀπεσθίω, to eat off, eat up, Ar.

ἀπο-φαιδρύνω [ῡ], f. ὑνῶ, to cleanse off: Med., Anth.

ἀπο-φαίνω, f. -φανῶ:—to shew forth, display, produce, Hdt., Ar.   II. to make known, declare, Hdt.: to give evidence of a thing, Id. 2. to shew by reasoning, shew, represent as doing or being, c. part., Id.; and with part. omitted, ἀπ. ἑωυτὸν αἴτιον (sc. ὄντα) Id.; so, ἀπ. τινα ἐχθρόν Dem. 3. c. acc. et inf. to represent that, Plat.; so, ἀπ. ὡς . . , ὅτι . . , Hdt., Thuc.   III. to give an account of, τὴν οὐσίαν Dem.: to pay in money to the treasury, Id.   IV. to render or make so and so, Ar. 2. to appoint to an office, Plat.
   B. Med. to display something of one's own, Aesch., Plat.: absol. to make a display of oneself, shew off, Xen. 2. to produce evidence, Hdt. 3. ἀποφαίνεσθαι γνώμην to declare one's opinion, Id., Att.:— absol. to give an opinion, Hdt., Att. Hence   II. used like Act., Plat., Xen.

ἀπόφανσις, εως, ἡ, a declaration, statement, Arist.

ἀπόφασις (A), εως, ἡ, (ἀπόφημι) a denial, negation, opp. to κατάφασις, Plat.

ἀπόφασις (B), εως, ἡ, (ἀποφαίνω) a sentence, decision of a court, Dem.   II. a list, inventory, Id.

ἀπο-φάσκω, = ἀπόφημι, only in pres. and impf., to deny, οὔτε δοκοῦντ᾽ οὔτ᾽ ἀποφάσκοντ᾽ neither in assent nor denial, Soph.

ἀπο-φέρβομαι, Dep. to feed on, τι Eur.

ἀπο-φέρω, f. ἀπ-οίσω, Dor. -οισῶ: aor. 1 -ήνεγκα, Ion. -ήνεικα: aor. 2 -ήνεγκον: pf. -ενήνοχα:—to carry off or away, Lat. auferre, Hom., etc.:—Pass. to be carried from one's course, Hdt., Thuc.   II. to carry or bring back, Il., Att.: Pass., of persons, to return, Hdt., Thuc. 2. to pay back, return, Hdt.: hence to pay what is due, Id.   III. as Att. law-term, to give in an accusation, accounts, etc., Dem., etc.   IV. intr. to be off, ἀπόφερ᾽ ἐς κόρακας Ar.
   B. Med. to take away with one, Hdt., etc.: to carry off a prize, Theocr. 2. to take for oneself, gain, obtain, Eur.   II. to bring back for oneself, Hdt.; ἀπ. βίον μητρί, i. e. to return to her alive, Eur.

ἀπο-φεύγω, f. -φεύξομαι and -οῦμαι: pf. -πέφευγα:— to flee from, escape, c. acc., Hdt., etc.:—absol. to get safe away, escape, Id.   II. as law-term, to escape from, τοὺς διώκοντας Id., Att.; also, ἀπ. δίκην Ar., Dem.: —absol. to get clear off, be acquitted, Hdt. Hence

ἀποφευκτικός, ή, όν, useful in escaping: τὰ ἀπ. means of acquittal, Xen.; and

ἀπόφευξις or ἀπόφυξις, εως, ἡ, an escaping, means of getting off, ἀπ. δίκης acquittal, Ar.

ἀπό-φημι, f. -φήσω: aor. 1 -έφησα: aor. 2 -έφην:— to speak out, declare flatly or plainly, Il.; so in Med., Ib.   II. to say No, Soph. 2. c. acc. to refuse, deny, Xen., Plat.

ἀπο-φθέγγομαι, f. -φθέγξομαι, Dep. to speak one's opinion plainly, Luc.:—metaph. to ring, Id.

ἀπό-φθεγκτος, ον, = ἄ-φθεγκτος, Eur.

ἀπόφθεγμα, ατος, τό, (ἀποφθέγγομαι) a terse pointed saying, an apophthegm, Xen. Hence

ἀποφθεγματικός, ή, όν, dealing in apophthegms, sententious, Plut.

ἀπο-φθείρω, f. -φθερῶ, to destroy utterly, ruin, Aesch., Eur.   II. Pass., with fut. med., to be lost, perish, Eur., Thuc.: esp. as interrog. used in an imperat. sense, οὐ γῆς τῆσδ᾽ ἀποφθαρήσεται; i. e. let him begone with a plague to him, Eur.; so, οὐκ εἰς κόρακας ἀποφθερεῖ; Lat. pasce corvos, Ar.

ἀπο-φθινύθω [ῠ], only in pres. to perish, Il.   II. trans. to lose, Ib.

ἀπο-φθίνω [ῑ]:   I. intr. in pres. to perish utterly, die away, Aesch., Soph.   II. Causal in f. -φθίω, aor. 1 -έφθισα [ῑ Ep., ῐ Trag.] to make to perish, waste away, destroy, Hes., Soph.: to lose, βίον Aesch. 2. Pass., = Act. intr., to perish, die, esp. in Ep. aor. 2 -έφθιτο [ῑ], imperat. -φθίσθω, -φθίμην [ῑ], part. -φθίμενος [ῑ], also in 3 pl. Ep. aor. 1 ἀπέφθῐθεν.

ἀποφθορά, ἡ, (ἀπο-φθείρω) utter destruction, Aesch.

ἀποφλαυρίζω, f. ίσω and ίξω, to treat slightingly, make no account of, τι Hdt.

ἀπο-φλοιόομαι, Med. (φλοιός) to strip off oneself, Anth.

ἀπο-φοιτάω, f. ήσω, to cease to go to school, Plat.

ἀπό-φονος, ον, (*φένω) φόνος ἀπ. unnatural murder, Eur.

ἀποφορά, ἡ, (ἀποφέρω) payment of what is due, tax, tribute, Hdt., Att. 2. also, return for money spent, profit, Xen., etc.

ἀπο-φράγνῡμι or -ύω, to fence off, block up, Thuc.: metaph., Soph. Hence

ἀπόφραξις, εως, ἡ, (ἀποφράσσω) a blocking up, Xen.

ἀπο-φράς, άδος, ἡ, (φράζω) not to be mentioned: ἀπο-φράδες ἡμέραι, Lat. dies nefasti, days on which no business was done, Plat.

ἀπο-φράσσω, Att. -ττω, f. ξω, = ἀποφράγνῡμι, Plat., Dem.:—Med., ἀποφράξασθαι αὐτούς to bar their passage, Thuc.

ἀπο-φυγγάνω, = ἀποφεύγω, Dem.

ἀπο-φυγεῖν, aor. 2 inf. of ἀποφεύγω. Hence

ἀποφυγή, ἡ, an escape or place of refuge, ἀποφυγὰς παρέχειν Thuc.; ἀπ. κακῶν escape from ills, Plat.

ἀπόφυξις, v. ἀπόφευξις.

ἀπο-φυσάω, f. ήσω, to blow away, Ar.   II. to breathe out life, Luc.

ἀπο-φώλιος, ον, empty, vain, idle, useless, fruitless, Lat. irritus, Od. (Deriv. unknown.)

ἀπο-χάζομαι, Dep., only in pres., to withdraw from a place, c. gen., Od.

ἀπο-χαλάω, f. άσω [ᾰ], to slack away a rope: metaph., ἀποχάλα τὴν φροντίδα Ar.

ἀπο-χαλινόω, f. ώσω, to unbridle, Xen.

ἀπο-χαλκεύω, f. σω, to forge of copper, Xen.

ἀπο-χαλκίζω, to strip of brass, i. e. money, Anth.

ἀπο-χᾰρᾰκόω, f. ώσω, = ἀποσταυρόω, Plut.

ἀπο-χειρο-βίωτος, ον, (χείρ, βιόω) living by the work of one's hands, Hdt., Xen.

ἀπο-χειροτονέω, f. ήσω, to vote a charge away from one, acquit him, c. gen., Dem.   II. c. acc., ἀπ. τινα τῆς ἀρχῆς to depose him from the command, Plut. 2. of things, to vote against, reject, annul, Ar., Dem.   III. ἀπ. τι μὴ εἶναι to vote that a thing is not, Dem. Hence

ἀποχειροτονία, ἡ, rejection by show of hands, Dem.

ἀπο-χέω, f. -χεῶ : aor. -έχεα, Ep. -έχευα :—to pour out or off, shed, let fall, Od. :—poët. Med. ἀπο-χεύομαι, Eur.

ἀποχή, ἡ, (ἀπέχω) abstinence, Plut.   II. a receipt, quittance, Anth.

ἀπο-χηρόομαι, Pass. to be bereft of, τινος Ar.

ἀπο-χραίνω, to soften away the colour, shade off, Plat.

ἀπο-χράω, Ion. -χρέω, inf. -χρῆν, Ion. -χρᾶν : part. -χρῶν, -χρῶσα : impf. ἀπέχρη, Ion. -έχρα : f. -χρήσω : aor. 1 -έχρησα :—to suffice, be sufficient, be enough : absol., in persons other than 3 sing., δί᾽ ἀποχρήσουσιν μόνω Ar. ; c. inf., ἀποχρέουσι ἑκατὸν νέες χειρώσασθαι are sufficient to subdue, Hdt.   II. mostly in 3 sing. : 1. to suffice, ποταμὸς οὐκ ἀπέχρησε τῇ στρατιῇ πινόμενος was not enough to supply the army with drink, Id. ; ταῦτα ἀποχρᾷ μοι Id., Att. impers., c. inf., ἀποχρᾷ μοι ποιεῖν 'tis sufficient for me to do, Hdt. ; c. part., μέρος ἐχούσῃ ἀπόχρη μοι 'tis sufficient to have a part, Aesch. ;—and without inf., ἀπόχρη τινι it is enough for him, Dem.   III. Pass. to be contented with a thing, c. dat., Hdt.   2. impers., οὐκ ἀπεχρᾶτο Id. ; ἀπεχρέετο, c. inf., Id.   B. Dep. ἀποχράομαι, Ion. -χρέομαι, to use to the full, c. dat. rei or absol., Thuc.   2. to abuse, misuse, Lat. abuti, c. dat., Dem.   II. c. acc. to use up, destroy, Thuc.

ἀποχρήματος, ον, = ἀχρήματος, ζημία ἀποχρ. a penalty but not of money, Aesch.

ἀποχρώντως, Adv. part. pres. of ἀποχράω, enough, sufficiently, Thuc.

ἀπ-οχυρόω, f. ώσω, to secure by fortifications : metaph. in pf. pass. part., ἀπωχυρωμένος πρός τι secure against a thing, Plat.

ἀπο-χωλεύω, f. σω, to make quite lame, Xen.

ἀπο-χωλόομαι, Pass. to be made quite lame, Thuc.

ἀπο-χώννυμι, f. -χώσω, to bank up the mouth of a river, Xen.

ἀπο-χωρέω, f. ήσω and ήσομαι :—to go from or away from a place, c. gen., Ar.   2. absol. to go away, depart, Eur. : to retire, retreat, Thuc., Xen. :—ἀπ. εἴς τι to have recourse to a thing, Dem.   3. ἀπ. ἐκ . . , to withdraw from a thing, i. e. give it up, Xen.   II. to pass off from the bowels, Id. : also, τὰ ἀποχωροῦντα excrements, Id.   Hence

ἀποχώρησις, εως, ἡ, a going off, retreat, Hdt., Thuc. : a place or means of safety, Hdt.

ἀπο-χωρίζω, f. Att. ἰῶ, to part or separate from, τι ἀπό τινος Plat.

ἀπόχωσις, εως, ἡ, (ἀποχώννυμι) the damming up of a river, Hdt.

ἀπο-ψάω, f. ήσω : impf. ἀπέψην : aor. 1 ἀπέψησα.   I. c. acc. rei, to wipe off, Eur. :—Med. to wipe or rub off from oneself, Ar.   II. c. acc. pers. to wipe clean : —Med. to wipe oneself, wipe one's nose, Id. ; also, ἀποψ. τὴν χεῖρα εἴς τι Xen.

ἀπο-ψεύδομαι, Pass. to be quite cheated of a thing, c. gen., Plut.

ἀπο-ψηφίζομαι, f. Att. ἰοῦμαι : Dep. :—to vote away from, θάνατον ἀπ. τινός to vote death away from him, refuse to condemn him to death, opp. to καταψηφίζεσθαι, Lycurg. :—hence ἀπ. τινός to vote a charge away from one, i. e. to acquit him, Dem., etc. :—absol. to vote an acquittal, Plat.   2. to vote the franchise away from one, i. e. to disfranchise by vote, Dem. :— Pass. to be disfranchised, Id.   II. c. acc. rei, of judges, ἀπ. γραφήν to vote against receiving the indictment, Aeschin.   III. ἀπ. μὴ ποιεῖν τι to vote against doing, Xen.

ἀπο-ψιλόω, f. ώσω, to strip bare, Hdt.   II. c. gen. to strip bare of a thing, c. gen., Aesch.

ἀπόψις, εως, ἡ, (ἀπόψομαι, f. of ἀφοράω) an outlook, view, prospect, Hdt.   2. a lofty spot or tower which commands a view, Plut.

ἀπο-ψύχω [ῠ], f. ξω :—Pass., aor. 1 and 2 ἀπεψύχθην and ἀπεψύχην [ῠ] :—to leave off breathing, to faint, swoon, Od., N. T.   2. c. acc., ἀπέψυξεν βίον breathed out life, Soph. : absol., like ἀποπνέω, Lat. exspiro, to expire, die, Thuc.   II. to cool :—Pass., ἱδρῶ ἀπεψύχοντο χιτώνων they got the sweat dried off their tunics, Il. ; ἱδρῶ ἀποψυχθεῖς Ib. ; metaph. ἀπεψυγμένοι cold, indifferent, Arist.   2. impers., ἀποψύχει it grows cool, the air cools, Plat.

ἀππαπαῖ, an exclamation, Ar. : cf. ἀπαπαῖ, ἀτταταῖ.

ἀπ-πέμψῃ], Ep. contr. for ἀπο-πέμψῃ.

ἀ-πρᾱγία, ἡ, (πράσσω) idleness, want of energy, Plut.

ἀπραγμοσύνη, ἡ, freedom from politics and business (πράγματα), love of a quiet life, love of ease, supineness, Lat. otium, Ar., Xen. ; of states that keep clear of foreign politics, Thuc.   From

ἀ-πράγμων, ον, free from business (πράγματα), keeping clear of politics, a good easy quiet man, opp. to πολυπράγμων (a restless meddlesome man), Ar., Thuc., etc. ; πόλις ἀπρ. a country that keeps clear of foreign politics, Thuc. ; τὸ ἄπραγμον = Lat. otium, Id. ; τόπος ἀπρ. a place free from law and strife, Ar.   II. of things, not troublesome or painful, Xen. ; so Adv. -μόνως, without trouble, Thuc.

ἀπρακτέω, f. ήσω, to do nothing, Arist.   II. to gain nothing, παρά τινος Xen.   From

ἄ-πρακτος, Ion. ἄ-πρηκτος, ον :   I. act. doing nothing, ineffectual, unprofitable, Il., Dem.   2. of persons, without success, unsuccessful, ἀπρηκτος νέεσθαι, Lat. re infecta, Il. ; and in Prose, ἄπρ. ἀπιέναι, ἀπελθεῖν, ἀποχωρεῖν Thuc. ; ἀπρ. γίγνεσθαι to gain nothing, Id. ; ἄπρακτον ἀποπέμπειν τινά Id. :—Adv. -τως, unsuccessfully, Id.   II. pass. against which nothing can be done, impracticable, Od.   2. not to be done, impossible, Theogn.   3. not done, left undone, Xen.   4. c. gen., μαντικῆς ἀπρακτος ὑμῖν unassailed by your divining arts, Soph.   Hence

ἀπραξία, ἡ, a not acting, inaction, Eur., Plat.   2. rest from business, in pl. holidays, Plut.   II. want of success, Aeschin.

ἀπρᾱσία, ἡ, want of purchasers, no sale, Dem.   From

ἄ-πρᾱτος, ον, (πιπράσκω) unsold, unsaleable, Dem.

ἀπρέπεια, ἡ, unseemly conduct, indecency, impropriety, Plat.   From

ἀ-πρεπής, ές, (πρέπω) unseemly, unbecoming, indecent, indecorous, Thuc., etc. ; τὸ ἀπρεπές = ἀπρέπεια, Id. :— Adv. -πῶς, -πέως, h. Hom., Plat.   II. of persons, disreputable, Theocr.

ἀπρεπίη, ἡ, poët. for ἀπρέπεια, ugliness, Anth.

ἀ-πρήϋντος, ον, Att. ἀπρά-, (πραΰνω) implacable, Anth.

ἀ-πριάτην [ᾰ], (πρίασθαι) Adv. without purchase-money or ransom, Hom. (In form like μάτην.)

ἄ-πριγδα, = ἀπρίξ, Aesch.

ἀπρικδό-πληκτος, ον, struck unceasingly, Aesch.

ἀ-πρίξ, Adv. (a copulat., πρίω) with closed teeth, Lat. mordicus : hence fast, tight, ἀπρὶξ συλλαβεῖν Soph.

ἀ-προαίρετος, ον, without set purpose, not deliberate, of actions, Arist.

ἀ-προβούλευτος, ον, (προβουλεύω) not planned beforehand, unpremeditated, Arist. 2. not submitted to the βουλή, Dem. II. act. without forethought, Arist. :—Adv. -τως, Plat.

ἀ-πρόβουλος, ον, without premeditation :—Adv. -λως, recklessly, Aesch.

ἀ-πρόθυμος, ον, not eager or ready, unready, backward, Hdt., Thuc.

ἀ-προϊδής, ές, (προϊδεῖν) unforeseen, Anth.

ἄ-προικος, ον, (προίξ) without portion or dowry, ἄπροικον τὴν ἀδελφὴν διδόναι to give her in marriage without dowry, Isae.

ἀ-προμήθεια, ἡ, want of forethought, Plat. From

ἀ-προμήθης, ες, without forethought.

ἀ-προνόητος, ον, (προνοέομαι) unpremeditated, ἀκρασία Arist. II. act. improvident, Xen. :—Adv. -τως, Id.

ἀ-προοιμίαστος, ον, (προοίμιον) without preface, Luc.

ἀ-πρόοπτος, ον, (προόψομαι, f. of προοράω) unforeseen, Aesch.

ἀ-πρόσβατος, Dor. ἀ-ποτίβατος, ον, unapproachable, Soph.

ἀ-προσδεής, ές, without want of more, Luc.

ἀ-προσδιόνυσος, ον, uncongenial to Bacchus : hence, not to the point, out of place, Cic., Luc.

ἀ-προσδόκητος, ον, unexpected, unlooked for, Aesch. etc. ; ἐξ ἀπροσδοκήτου, Lat. necopinato, Hdt. ; so Adv. -τως, Thuc. II. act. not expecting, unaware, Id.

ἀ-προσηγορία, ἡ, want of intercourse by speech, Arist.

ἀ-προσήγορος, ον, not to be accosted, savage, Soph.

ἀ-πρόσικτος, ον, not to be attained, Pind.

ἀ-πρόσιτος, ον, unapproachable, Plut.

ἀ-πρόσκεπτος, ον, (προ-σκοπέω) unforeseen, Xen. II. act. improvident, Dem.

ἀ-πρόσκλητος, ον, (προσκαλέω) of a trial in support of which no summons has been issued, Dem.

ἀ-πρόσκοπος, ον, (προσκόπτω) not stumbling, void of offence, N. T. II. giving no offence, Ib.

ἀ-πρό-σκοπος, ον, = ἀπρόσκεπτος, Aesch.

ἀ-πρόσμαχος, ον, (προσμάχομαι) irresistible, Soph.

ἀ-πρόσμικτος, ον, (προσμίγνυμι) holding no communion with others, c. dat., Hdt.

ἀ-πρόσοιστος, ον, (προσοίσω, f. of προσφέρω) not to be withstood, irresistible, Aesch.

ἀ-προσ-όμιλος, ον, unsociable, Soph.

ἀ-προσπέλαστος, ον, (προσπελάζω) unapproachable, Strab., Plut.

ἀ-προστασίου γραφή, ἡ, (προστάτης) at Athens, an indictment of a μέτοικος for not having chosen a patron from among the citizens, Dem.

ἀ-πρόσφορος, ον, unsuitable, dangerous, Eur.

ἀ-προσωπόληπτος, ον, (προσωπολήπτης) not respecting persons. Adv. -τως, without respect of persons, N. T.

ἀ-πρόσωπος, ον, (πρόσωπον) without a face, i. e. without beauty of face, Plat.

ἀ-προτίμαστος, ον, Dor. for ἀ-πρόσμαστος, (προσμάσσω) untouched, undefiled, Il.

ἀ-προφάσιστος [ᾰ], ον, (προφασίζομαι) offering no excuse, unhesitating, Thuc., Xen. Adv. -τως, without disguise, without evasion, honestly, Thuc.

ἀ-προφύλακτος, ον, (προφυλάσσομαι) not guarded against, unforeseen, Thuc.

ἄ-πταιστος, ον, (πταίω) not stumbling, ἀπταιστότερος less apt to stumble, Xen.

ἄ-πτερος, ον, (πτερόν) without wings, unwinged, in phrase τῇ δ' ἄπτερος ἔπλετο μῦθος, the speech was to her without wings, i.e. did not fly away, sank into her heart, Od. ; ἄπτερα πωτήματα wingless flight, Aesch. II. unfeathered, of the Harpies, Id. ; of arrows, Hdt. 2. of young birds, unfledged, callow, Eur. :—metaph., φάτις ἄπτ. an unfledged, i. e. unconfirmed, report, Aesch.

ἀ-πτήν, ῆνος, ὁ, ἡ, (πτηνός) unfledged, callow, of young birds, Il. II. unwinged, Ar.

ἀ-πτο-επής, ές, (a priv., πτοέω, ἔπος) undaunted in speech, Il.

ἀ-πτόλεμος, ον, poët. for ἀπόλεμος.

ἁπτός, ή, όν, subject to the sense of touch, Plat. From ἅπτω (Root ΑΠ and ΑΦ) : f. ἅψω : aor. 1 ἧψα :—Pass., pf. ἧμμαι, Ion. ἅμμαι (v. ἑάφθη) :—Med., f. ἅψομαι, with pf. pass. ἧμμαι :—to fasten, bind fast, Od., Eur. : Med. to fasten for oneself, Od.,Eur. 2. to join, χορόν Aesch.; πάλην τινὶ ἅπτειν to fasten a contest in wrestling on one, engage with one, Id. II. Med. to fasten oneself to, cling to, hang on by, lay hold of, grasp, touch, c. gen., ἅψασθαι γούνων, as a suppliant, Od. ; so, ἅψ. γενείου Ib. ; ἅπτεσθαι νηῶν Il., etc. :—absol. to reach the mark, Ib. 2. to engage in, take part in, c. gen., βουλευμάτων Soph. ; πολέμου Thuc. ; ἡμμένος φόνου engaged in . . , Plat. ;—but, ἅπτεσθαι τῶν λόγων to lay hold of, dispute the argument of another, Id. ; τούτων ἥψατο touched on these points, Thuc. 3. to set upon, attack, assail, Hdt., Aesch., etc. 4. to touch, affect, ἄγος οὐδὲν ἅπτεται νεκρῶν Aesch., etc. 5. to grasp with the senses, apprehend, perceive, Soph., Plat. 6. to come up to, reach, gain, Plat., Xen.

B. Act., also, to kindle, set on fire, Hdt., Thuc. :— Pass., with fut. med. to be set on fire, catch fire, Od., Hdt. 2. ἅπτειν πῦρ to light a fire, Eur. :—Pass., ἄνθρακες ἡμμένοι red-hot embers, Thuc.

ἀ-πτώς, ῶτος, ὁ, ἡ, (πί-πτω) not liable to fall or fail, Plat.

ἀ-πύλωτος, ον, (πύλόω) not secured by gates, Xen.

ἀ-πύργωτος, ον, (πυργόω) not girt with towers, Od.

ἄ-πυρος, ο ̓, (πῦρ) without fire, of pans and tripods, that have not yet been on the fire, fire-new, brand-new, Il. : —without fire, i. e. cold, cheerless, οἶκος Hes. :—ἄπ. χρυσίον unsmelted, Hdt. :—ἄπυρα ἱερά sacrifices in which no fire was used, Pind. ; but in Aesch. sacrifices without fire, i. e. that will not burn, or unoffered, neglected :—ἄπ. ἄρδις an arrow-point not forged in fire, i. e. the sting of the gad-fly, Aesch.

ἀ-πύρωτος, ον, (πυρόω) not yet exposed to fire, Il.

ἄ-πυστος, ον, (πυνθάνομαι) not heard of, Od. : ἄπυστα φωνῶν speaking what none can hear, Soph. II. act. without hearing or learning a thing, Od. ; c. gen., Ib.

ἀπύω, Dor. for ἠπύω.

ἀπφύς, ύος, ὁ, a term of endearment used by children to their father, papa, Theocr.

ἀπ-ῳδός, όν, (ᾠδή) out of tune, Eur., Luc.

ἄπωθεν, Adv. from afar, Soph., Eur.　2. c. gen. far from, Eur., Thuc.

ἀπ-ωθέω, f. -ώσω: aor. 1 -έωσα:—to thrust away, push back, Il.; to push off, Thuc.: Med. to push away from oneself, Hom.:—c. gen. to drive away from a place; and in Med. to drive away from oneself, to expel, banish, Hom., Hdt., etc.　2. of the wind, to beat from one's course, Od.; so in Med., Ib.　3. in Med., also, to reject, decline, refuse to accept, Hdt., Att.; ἀπ. δουλοσύνην to shake off slavery, Hdt.

ἀπώλεια, ἡ, (ἀπόλλυμι) destruction, N. T.

ἀ-πώμαστος, ον, (πῶμα) without a lid, Babr.

ἀπώμοτος, ον, (ἀπόμνυμι) abjured, declared impossible on oath, βροτοῖσιν οὐδέν ἐστ' ἀπώμοτον Soph.　II. of persons, under oath not to do a thing, Id.

ἀπ-ῶσαι, aor. 1 inf. of ἀπωθέω.

ἄπωσις, εως, ἡ, (ἀπωθέω) a driving away, Thuc.

ἀπωστέον, verb. Adj. of ἀπωθέω, one must reject, Eur.

ἀπωστός, ή, όν, (ἀπωθέω) thrust or driven away from a place, c. gen., Hdt., Soph.　II. that can be driven away, Hdt.

ἀπωτάτω, Sup. Adv. of ἄπωθεν, furthest from, τινός Dem.

ἀπωτέρω, Comp. Adv. of ἄπωθεν, further off, Soph., etc.: proverb., ἀπ. ἢ γόνυ κνήμα Theocr.

ἌΡΑ, Ep. ῥά (enclitic) and before a consonant ἄρ: Inferential Particle:

　A. EPIC USAGE: I. then, straightway, at once, ὣς φάτο, βῆ δ' ἄρ' ὄνειρος Il.: next in order, οἱ δ' ἄρ' Ἀθήνας εἶχον Ib.　2. where attention is called to something startling, τὸν τρεῖς μὲν ἐπιρρήσσεσκον τῶν ἄλλων, Ἀχιλεὺς δ' ἄρ' ἐπιρρήσεσκε καὶ οἶος three men of the common sort were required to do it, but Achilles, mark ye! did it single-handed, Ib.　3. in explanation of a thing going before, εἰ μὴ ὑπερφίαλον ἔπος ἔκβαλε, φῇ ῥ' ἀέκητι θεῶν φυγέειν had he not let fall an impious word,—for he said . . , Ib.:—so, ἄρα makes relat. Pron. more precise, ἐκ δ' ἔθορε κλῆρος, ὃν ἄρ' ἤθελον αὐτοὶ just the one, the very one which . . , Ib.

　B. ATTIC USAGE, much like οὖν, then, therefore: —less strongly, μάτην ἄρ' ἥκομεν so then we have come in vain, Soph.; εἰκότως ἄρα οὐκ ἐγίγνετο Xen.:—in questions, to express the anxiety of the questioner, as τίς ἄρα ῥύσεται; oh! who is there to save? Aesch.

　C. POSITION: ἄρα never begins a sentence, cf. οὖν, Lat. igitur.

ἆρά; interrog. Particle, in accent and sense a stronger form of ἄρα:　1. when it stands alone it usually expects a negative answer, like Lat. num? Att.; so ἆρα μή; num vero? Aesch.:—for an affirmative answer, ἆρ' οὐ; ἆρ' οὐχί; nonne vero? is used, Soph., etc.　2. in prose, ἆρα almost always stands first in the sentence.

ἈΡΑ', Ion. ἀρή, ἡ, a prayer, Il., Hdt.　II. esp. a prayer for evil, a curse, imprecation, mostly in pl., Il., Trag.　2. the effect of the curse, bane, ruin, ἀρὴν καὶ λοιγὸν ἀμῦναι Il.　III. Ἀρά personified as the goddess of destruction and revenge, Lat. Dira, Soph. [ᾰρ- mostly in Ep.: in Att. always ἄρ-.]

ἀραβέω, f. ήσω, (ἄραβος) to rattle, ring, clash, of armour, Il.; of the teeth, to gnash, Theocr.

Ἀραβία, ἡ, Arabia, Hdt., poët. Ἀρραβία Theocr.:— Ἀράβιος, α, ον, Arabian, Hdt.; also -ικός, ή, όν, Plut.

ἄραβος, ὁ, a gnashing or chattering of teeth, Il. (Formed from the sound.)

ἄραγμα, ατος, τό, (ἀράσσω) = sq., τυμπάνων ἄρ. Eur.

ἀραγμός, ὁ, (ἀράσσω) a clashing, clattering, rattling, Aesch.; ἄρ. πετρῶν a crashing shower of stones, Eur.; στέρνων ἄρ. beating of the breast, Lat. planctus, Soph.

ἄραι, aor. 1 inf. of αἴρω.

ἀραίμην, aor. 1 med. opt. of αἴρω.

ἀραῖος, α, ον and ος, ον, (ἀρά): I. pass. prayed to or entreated, Ζεὺς ἀραῖος, = ἱκέσιος, Soph.　2. prayed against, accursed, laden with a curse or curses, Aesch.; μ' ἀραῖον ἔλαβες you adjured me under a curse, Soph.　II. act. cursing, bringing mischief upon a house or person, c. dat., Aesch., Soph.

ἀραιός, ά, όν, thin, narrow, slight, slender, Lat. tenuis, Hom. (Deriv. unknown.)

ἀραίρηκα, redupl. form of ᾕρηκα, pf. of αἱρέω:— ἀραίρημαι, pass.: ἀραίρητο, 3 sing. plqpf. pass.

ἀράμενος, aor. 1 med. part. of αἴρω.

ἀραξί-χειρος, ον, (ἀράσσω) beaten with the hand, τύμπανα Anth.

ἀράομαι, Ion. ἀρέομαι: f. ἀράσομαι [ᾰ], Ion. ἀρήσομαι: aor. 1 ἠρησάμην: Dep.: (ἀρά):—to pray to a god, c. dat., Il.:—c. acc. to invoke, Od.　2. c. acc. et inf. to pray that, Il., Hdt., Soph.:—c. inf. only, to pray to be so and so, Od.　3. to pray something for one, τί τινι; sometimes in good sense, ἀρ. τινι ἀγαθά Hdt.; but usually in bad, to imprecate upon one, ἀρὰς ἀρ. τινι Soph., etc.; without an acc., ἀρᾶσθαί τινι to curse one, Eur.　4. c. inf. fut. to vow that one will or would, ἠρήσατο ῥέξειν Il.

ἄραρε, 3 sing. intr. pf. of ἀραρίσκω.

ἄραρε, 3 sing. poët. aor. 2 of ἀραρίσκω.

ἀραρίσκω, (redupl. form of *ἄρω), impf. ἀράρισκον:— the other tenses are formed from ἄρω, viz.,

　A. TRANS. :—aor. 1 ἦρσα, Ep. ἄρσα: aor. 2 ἤραρον, Ion. ἄραρον, inf. ἀραρεῖν, part. ἀραρών:—Pass., aor. 1 ἤρθην, Ep. 3 pl. ἄρθεν:—to join, join together, fasten, Il.; ἄγγεσιν ἄρσον ἄπαντα pack up everything in the vessels, Od.　II. to fit together, construct, τοῖχον ἀραρεῖν λίθοισιν Il.　2. to prepare, contrive, μνηστήρσιν θάνατον ἀραρόντες Od.　III. to fit, equip, furnish with a thing, νῆα ἄρσας ἐρέτησιν Ib.　2. to please, gratify, favour, Pind., Soph.　IV. to make fitting or pleasing, Il.

　B. INTR. :—pf. ἄραρα in pres. sense, Ion. ἄρηρα, Ep. part. ἀρηρώς, with fem. ἀρηρυῖα and (metri grat.) ἀράρυια: Ep. plqpf. ἀρήρειν, ἠρήρειν, pf. sense: —of the Pass. we only find Ep. aor. 2 part. ἄρμενος, η, ον:—to be joined closely together, to be in close order, close-packed, Hom.　2. to be fixed, of oaths and faith, Trag.:—absol., ἄραρε 'tis fixed, Eur.　II. to fit well or closely, Hom.: to fit or be fitted to a thing, c. dat., Id.　III. to be fitted, furnished with a thing, c. dat.,Il.; κάλλει ἀραρώς endowed with beauty, Eur.　IV. to be fitting, meet or suitable, agreeable or pleasing, like ἀρέσκω, Od., Hes.:—so in Ep. aor. 2 pass. part. ἄρμενος, η, ον, fitting, fitted or suited to, c.dat., Od.; absol. meet, convenient, Lat. habilis, Il.　2. prepared, ready, Hes.　3. agreeable, welcome, ἄρμενα πράξαις = εὖ πράξας, Pind.

ἀραρότως, Adv. of ἀραρώς, pf. part. of ἀραρίσκω, compactly, closely, strongly, Aesch., Eur.

ἀράσσω, Att. -ττω: poët. impf. ἀράσσεσκον: f. ἀράξω, Dor. ἀραξῶ: aor. 1 ἤραξα, Ep. ἄραξα:—Pass., aor. 1 ἠράχθην, Ep. ἀράχθην: (α euphon., ῥάσσω, akin to ῥήσσω):—to strike hard, smite, (Hom. only has it in the compds. ἀπ-, συν-αράσσω); of horses, ὁπλαῖς ἀρ. χθόνα Pind.; θύρας ἀρ. to knock furiously at the door, Eur.; ἀράσσειν στέρνα, κρᾶτα to beat the breasts, the head, in mourning, Lat. plangere, Aesch., Eur.; ἄρασσε μᾶλλον strike harder, Aesch.; ἀρ. ὄψεις, βλέφαρα Soph.   2. c. dat. modi, ἀράσσειν ὀνείδεσι κακοῖς to throw with reproaches or threats, i. e. fling them wildly about, Id.   II. Pass. to be dashed against, πρὸς τὰς πέτρας Hdt.; πέτραις Aesch.

ἀρᾱτός, Ion. ἀρητός, ή, όν, (ἀράομαι) accursed, unblest, Il., Soph.   II. prayed for: hence Ἄρητος, Ἀρήτη, (with changed accent), as prop. n., the Prayed-for, like the Hebrew Samuel, Hom. [ᾱρ- Ep.; ᾰρ- Att.]

ἀραχναῖος, α, ον, of or belonging to a spider, Anth. From

ἀράχνη, ή, fem. of ἀράχνης, Lat. aranea, Aesch., Anth.   II. a spider's web, Id.

ἀράχνης, ὁ, a spider, Lat. araneus, Hes.   (Deriv. uncertain.)   Hence

ἀράχνιον, τό, a spider's web, Lat. aranea, Od., Att.

ἀράω A, = ἀράομαι, only in Ep. inf. ἀρήμεναι, to pray, Od.

ἀράω B, f. ήσω, an old Verb, = βλάπτω, to damage, ἀράσοντι, Dor. for ἀρήσουσι, Inscr.: pf. pass. part. ἀρημένος, βεβλαμμένος, distressed, afflicted, Hom.

ἀρβύλη [ῠ], ή, a strong shoe or half-boot, used by country-people, hunters, travellers, Aesch., Eur. (Deriv. unknown.)

ἀρβυλίς, ίδος, ή, = foreg., Theocr., Anth.

Ἀργάδεῖς, οἱ, (*ἔργω) name of one of the four old Attic tribes, the Workmen, Labourers, Eur.

ἀργάεις, εσσα, εν, Dor. for ἀργήεις.

ἀργάλέος, α, ον, (ἄλγος, as if ἀλγαλέος) painful, troublous, grievous, Lat. gravis, Il., Ar.:—ἀργαλέον ἐστί, c. dat. et inf., 'tis difficult to do a thing, Hom.; rarely c. acc. et inf., Il.   2. of persons, troublesome, Theogn., Ar.

ἀργᾷς, contr. from ἀργάεις.

Ἀργεῖος, α, ον, of or from Argos, Argive: Ἀργεῖοι in Hom., like Ἀχαιοί, for the Greeks in general: ἡ Ἀργεία (sc. γῆ), Argolis, Thuc.

Ἀργει-φόντης, ου, ὁ, (Ἄργος, *φένω) slayer of Argus, i. e. Hermes, Hom.

ἀργέλοφοι, ων, οἱ, the feet of a sheep-skin, and so, generally, offal, Ar. (Deriv. uncertain.)

ἀργεννός, ή, όν, Aeol. for ἀργός, white, of sheep, Il.; of woollen cloths, Ib., Anth.

ἀργεστής, ὁ, (ἀργός) of the South wind, clearing, brightening, like Horace's detergens nubila caelo, Il.   II. ἀργέστης Ζέφυρος (parox.), the North-west wind, Hes.

ἀργέτι, ἀργέτα, Ep. for ἀργῆτι, ἀργῆτα, dat. and acc. of ἀργής.

ἀργέω, f. ήσω, (ἀργός = ἀεργός) to lie idle, be unemployed, do nothing, Eur., Xen.; γῆ ἀργοῦσα land lying fallow, Id.; ἀργεῖ τὸ ἐργαστήριον the shop is out of work, Dem.   II. Pass. to be left undone, to be fruitless, Xen.

ἀργήεις, εσσα, εν, Dor. ἀργάεις, contr. ἀργᾶς, (ἀργός) shining, white, Pind., Aesch.

ἀργής, ῆτος, ὁ, ή; Ep. dat. and acc. ἀργέτι, ἀργέτα: (ἀρ-

γός):—bright, glancing, of vivid lightning, Hom.   2. shining, white, of fat, Il.; of a robe, Ib.

ἀργηστής, οῦ, ὁ, = ἀργής, Aesch.

ἀργία, ή, = ἀεργία, idleness, laziness, Eur., Dem.   2. in good sense, rest, leisure, ἔργων from work, Plat.

ἀργι-κέραυνος, ὁ, wielder of bright lightning, Il.

ἄργιλλα or ἄργῑλα, ή, an underground dwelling, Ephorus ap. Strab.: perh. from

ἄργιλλος or ἄργῑλος, ή, (ἀργός) white clay, potter's earth, Arist.   Hence

ἀργιλλ-ώδης or ἀργῑλ-ώδης, ες, (εἶδος) like clay, clayey, Hdt.

ἀργῑνόεις, εσσα, εν, Ep. form of ἀργός, white, epith. of Rhodian cities, from their chalky hills, Il.

ἀργι-όδους, όδοντος, ὁ, ή, white-toothed, white-tusked Hom.

ἀργι-πόδης, ου, ὁ, = sq., χίμαρος Anth.

ἀργί-πους, ὁ, ή, -πουν, τό, (ἀργός) swift-footed, Il., Soph.

ἄργμα, ατος, τό, (ἄρχω) only in pl. ἄργματα, = ἀπάργματα, ἀπαρχαί, the firstlings at a sacrifice, Od.

Ἀργόθεν, Adv. from Argos, Soph., Eur.

Ἀργολίζω, f. Att. ιῶ, to take part with the Argives, Xen.

Ἀργολίς (sub. γῆ), ίδος, ή, a district in Peloponnesus, Hdt., etc.   2. as Adj., ὁ, ή, of Argolis, Argolic, Aesch.; also Ἀργολικός, ή, όν, Plut.

ἀργο-ποιός, όν, (ποιέω) making idle, Plut.

Ἄργος, εος, τό, name of several Greek cities, of which the Peloponnesian is the best known, called by Hom. Ἀ. Ἀχαικόν, to distinguish it from Ἀ. Πελασγικόν. The former name comprehends all Argolis; the latter, all Thessaly.

ΑΡΓΟΣ, ή, όν, shining, bright, glistening, Lat. nitidus, Il.: white, Arist. (Hence come ἄργυρος, ἄργῑλος.)   II. πόδας ἀργοί, as epith. of hounds, swift-footed, because all swift motion causes a kind of glancing or flickering light, Hom.

ἀργός, όν, (contr. from ἀ-εργός) not working the ground, living without labour, Hdt.; then, generally, inactive, slothful, idle, lazy, Dem., etc.:—c. gen. rei, idle at a thing, free from it, Eur., Plat.;—also, ἀργότεραι ἐς τὸ δρᾶν Thuc.   2. of land, lying fallow or untilled, Xen.; of money, unemployed, yielding no return, Dem.—Adv. ἀργῶς Xen.   II. pass. not done, left undone, Lat. infectus, Soph., Eur.; οὐκ ἐν ἀργοῖς not among things neglected, Soph.

ἀργύρ-αγχη, ή, (ἄργυρος, ἄγχω) silver-quinsy, which Demosthenes was said to have, when he abstained from speaking on the plea of quinsy, but really (it was alleged) because he was bribed, Plut.

ἀργυρ-αμοιβικός, ή, όν, of or for a money-changer, money-changing, Luc.:—Adv. -κῶς, Id. From

ἀργυρ-ἀμοιβός, ὁ, (ἀμείβω) a money-changer, banker, Lat. argentarius, Plat., Theocr., etc.

ἀργύρειος [ῠ], ον, = ἀργύρεος, ἀργύρεια μέταλλα silver-mines, Thuc.; or τὰ ἀργύρεια alone, Xen.

ἀργύρεος, α, ον, contr. ἀργυροῦς, ᾶ, οῦν, (ἄργυρος) silver, of silver, Lat. argenteus, Hom., etc.

ἀργυρεύω, f. σω, to dig for silver, Strab.

ἀργυρ-ήλᾰτος, ον, (ἐλαύνω) of wrought silver, Eur.

ἀργυρίδιον [ρῐ], τό, = ἀργύριον, in contemptuous sense, Ar.

ἀργυρικός, ή, όν, (ἄργυρος) of, for or in silver, Plut.

ἀργύριον [ῠ], τό, *a piece of silver, a silver coin*, Ar., etc. 2. collectively, *money, a sum of money, cash*, as we also say ' silver,' Id., Thuc. II. = ἄργυρος, *silver*, Id., Plat.

ἀργῡρῖτις, ιδος, ἡ, (ἄργυρος) *silver-ore*, Xen.

ἀργυρο-γνώμων, ονος, ὁ, ἡ, *an assayer of silver*, Plat.

ἀργυρο-δίνης [ῐ], ου, ὁ, (δίνη) *silver-eddying*, of rivers, Il.

ἀργυρο-ειδής, ές, (εἶδος) *like silver, silvery*, Eur.

ἀργυρό-ηλος, ον, *silver-studded*, Hom.

ἀργυρο-θήκη, ἡ, *a money-chest*, Theophr.

ἀργυρο-κόπος, ὁ, (κόπτω) *a silver-smith*, N. T.

ἀργυρολογέω, f. ήσω, *to levy money*, Xen. 2. c. acc. pers. *to levy money upon, lay under contribution*, Thuc.; and

ἀργυρολογία, ἡ, *a levying of money*, Xen. From

ἀργυρο-λόγος, ον, (λέγω) *levying money*, Ar., Thuc.

ἀργυρό-πεζα, ἡ, *silver-footed*, Homeric epith. of Thetis.

ἀργυρο-ποιός, ὁ, (ποιέω) *a worker in silver*, Anth.

ἀργυρό-πους, ὁ, ἡ, *with silver feet or legs*, Xen.

ἀργυρορ-ρύτης [ῠ], ου, ὁ, (ῥέω) *silver-flowing*, Eur.

ἄργυρος, ὁ, (ἀργός *white*) *white metal*, i.e. *silver*, Hom., etc. II. *silver-money, money*, like ἀργύριον, Soph.

ἀργυρο-στερής, ές, (στερέω) *robbing of silver*, βίος ἀργ. *a robber's life*, Aesch.

ἀργυρό-τοιχος, ον, *with silver sides*, Aesch.

ἀργυρό-τοξος, ον, (τόξον) *with silver bow*, Hom.

ἀργυρο-φεγγής, ές, (φέγγος) *silver-shining*, Anth.

ἀργυρ-ώδης, ες, (εἶδος) *rich in silver*, Xen.

ἀργυρ-ώνητος, ον, (ὠνέομαι) *bought with silver*, Hdt., Aesch.

ἀργύφεος [ῠ], η, ον, (ἄργυρος) *silver-white*, Hom.

ἄργυφος, ον, = ἀργύφεος, Hom.

Ἀργώ, όος, contr. οῦς, ἡ, (ἀργός *swift*) *the Argo* or *Swift*, the ship in which Jason sailed to Colchis, Od.:— Adj. Ἀργῷος, α, ον, *of the Argo*, Eur.

ἀρδεία, ἡ, (ἄρδω) *a watering* of fields, Strab. From

ἀρδεύω, f. σω, = ἄρδω, *to water*, Lat. *irrigare*, Aesch.

ἄρδην, Adv. contr. for ἀέρδην (as αἴρω for ἀείρω) *lifted up, on high*, Soph., Eur. II. *taken away utterly, wholly*, Lat. *raptim*, Aesch., Eur., etc.

ἄρδις, ἡ, acc. ἄρδιν, Ion. pl. ἄρδις [ῐ], gen. ἀρδέων :— *the point of an arrow*, Hdt., Aesch.

ἀρδμός, ὁ, *a watering-place*, Hom. From

ΆΡΔΩ, impf. ἦρδον, Ion. 3 sing. ἄρδεσκε: aor. 1 ἦρσα :— *to water*, and so, 1. of men, *to water* cattle, h. Hom., Hdt. :—Pass. *to drink*, ἀρδόμενοι h. Hom. 2. of rivers, *to water* land, Lat. *irrigare*, Hdt., Aesch. :— Pass. *to be watered*, of countries or crops, Hdt. II. metaph. *to refresh, cherish*, Lat. *fovere*, Ar., Xen.

Ἀρέθουσα, ἡ, (ἄρδω ?) name of several fountains, the earliest known in Ithaca, Od. :—the most famous in Syracuse, Strab.

ἀρειά [ἀρ], Ion. ἀρειή, ἡ, (ἀρά) *collective noun, menaces, threats*, Il.

Ἀρει-μανής, ές, (μαίνομαι) *full of warlike frenzy*, Anth.

Ἄρειος [ᾰ], ον and α, ον, Ion. Ἀρήιος, η, ον, (Ἄρης) *devoted to Ares, warlike, martial*, Lat. *Mavortius*, Il., Hdt. II. Ἄρειος πάγος, ὁ, *the hill of Ares, Mars-hill*, over against the west side of the Acropolis at Athens, Ἀρήιος π. Hdt.; also Ἄρεος πάγος (where Ἄρεος is gen. of Ἄρης), Soph., Eur. On it was held the highest

judicial court, which took cognisance of murder and other capital crimes, Dem.

ἀρειότερος, α, ον, = ἀρείων, Theogn.

Ἀρεί-τολμος, ον, (τόλμα) *warlike, bold*, Anth.

Ἀρεί-φατος [ἀρ.], Ep. Ἀρηΐ-φατος, ον, (*φένω) *slain by Ares*, i.e. *slain in war*, Il., Eur. II. = Ἄρειος, Aesch.

ἀρείων [ᾰ], ὁ, ἡ, -ον, τό, gen. ονος, as Comp. to ἀγαθός, cf. ἄριστος: (*ἄρω): *better, stouter, stronger, braver, more excellent*, Hom., Aesch.

ἄ-ρεκτος, ον, Ep. for ἄρρεκτος.

ἀρέομαι, Ion. for ἀράομαι.

Ἀρεο-πᾰγίτης, ου, ὁ, (Ἄρειος, πάγος) *a member of the Areopagus*, Aeschin.

ἀρέσαι, ἀρέσασθαι, aor. 1 inf. act. and med. of ἀρέσκω.

ἀρέσκεια, ἡ, *the character of an* ἄρεσκος, *complaisance, obsequiousness*, Arist.

ἀρέσκευμα, ατος, τό, *an act of obsequiousness*, Plut.

ἀρεσκόντως, Adv. part. pres. act. of ἀρέσκω, *agreeably*, Eur., Plat.

ἄρεσκος, η, ον, *pleasing*, but mostly in bad sense, *obsequious, cringing*, Arist., Theophr. From

ἀρέσκω [ᾰ], impf. ἤρεσκον: f. ἀρέσω: aor. 1 ἤρεσα: Med., f. ἀρέσομαι, Ep. ἀρέσσομαι: aor. 1 ἠρεσάμην, Ep. part. ἀρεσσάμενος: aor. 1 pass. in med. sense ἠρέσθην: (*ἄρω): I. *to make good, make up*, ἂψ ἀρέσαι *to make amends*, Il. :—Med., ταῦτα ἀρεσσόμεθα *this will we make up among ourselves*, Hom. 2. Med. *to appease, conciliate*, αὐτὸν ἀρεσσάσθω ἐπέεσσιν Od. 3. after Hom., c. dat. pers. *to please, satisfy, flatter*, Hdt., Att.; ταῦτα ἀρέσκει μοι Hdt.;—so, in Med., Id. II. in Att. also c. acc. pers., οὐ γὰρ μ' ἀρέσκει γλῶσσά σου Soph.; τουτί μ' οὐκ ἀρ. Ar.: hence, in Pass., *to be pleased, satisfied with a thing*, c. dat. rei, Hdt., Thuc. III. ἀρέσκει is used, like Lat. *placet*, to express *the resolution* of a public body, ταῦτα ἤρεσέ σφι ποιέειν Hdt. :—so in Med., Thuc. IV. part. ἀρέσκων, ουσα, ον, *grateful, acceptable*, Soph., Thuc.

ἀρεστός, ή, όν, verb. Adj. of ἀρέσκω, *acceptable, pleasing*, Hdt., Soph. Adv., ἑωυτῷ ἀρεστῶς *quite to his own satisfaction*, Hdt.

ἀρετάω, f. ήσω, *to be fit or proper, to thrive, prosper*, Od.

ἀρετή [ᾰ], ἡ, (Ἄρης) *goodness, excellence*, of any kind, esp. of *manly* qualities, *manhood, valour, prowess*, Hom., Hdt. (like Lat. *vir-tus*, from *vir*). 2. *rank, nobility*, Theogn., Eur. 3. in Prose, generally, *goodness, excellence* in any art, Plat., etc.; of animals or things, Hdt., Att. 4. in moral sense, *goodness, virtue*, Plat., etc.:—also *character for virtue, merit*, Eur., etc. 5. ἀρ. εἴς τινα *service* done him, Thuc.; ἀρ. περί τινα Xen.

ἀρετῇ [ᾱ], crasis for ἡ ἀρετή.

ἄρηαι, Ep. for ἄρῃ, 2 sing. aor. 2 med. subj. of αἴρω.

ἀρηγοσύνη, ἡ, *help, aid*, Anth. From

ἀρήγω [ᾰ], f. ξω, (akin to ἀρκέω) *to help, aid, succour*, esp. in battle, c. dat., Il., Hdt. 2. impers., c. inf., like Lat. *juvat*, *it is good or fit*, σιγᾶν ἀρήγει Aesch. II. c. acc. rei, *to ward off, prevent*, τι Aesch.; also, ἀρ. τί τινι *to ward off from* one, Eur. Hence

ἀρηγών, όνος, ὁ, ἡ, *a helper*, Il.

Ἀρηΐ-θοος [ᾰ], ον, *swift as Ares, swift in battle*, Il.

Ἀρηΐ-κτάμενος [ἀρ-], η, ον, (κτείνω) *slain by Ares or in battle*, Il.

Ἀρήϊος [ᾰ], η, ον, also ος, ον, Ion. for Ἄρειος.

Ἀρηΐφᾰτος [ᾰ], ον, Ion. for Ἀρείφατος.

Ἀρηΐ-φῐλος [ᾰ], η, ον, dear to Ares, favoured of the god of war, Il.

ἀρήμεναι, Ep. inf. of ἀράω A.

ἀρημένος, η, ον, Ep. part. pass. of ἀράω B.

ἄρηξις, εως, ἡ, (ἀρήγω) help, succour, τινος from a person, Aesch., Soph.   II. c. gen. rei, help against a thing, means of averting it, Soph.

ἄρηρα, pf. med. of ἀραρίσκω :—ἀρήρειν, plqpf.

ἀρηρομένος, η, ον, Ion. for ἠρωμένος, pf. pass. part. of ἀρόω.

ΑΡΗΣ, ὁ: gen. Ἄρεως, poët. Ἄρεος: dat. Ἄρεῖ, contr. Ἄρει : acc. Ἄρεα, contr. Ἄρη: voc. Ἄρες, Ep. Ἄρες:— Ion. and Ep. declens. Ἄρης, ηος, ηϊ, ηα :—Ares, called by the Latins Mars, son of Zeus and Hera, god of war and slaughter, also of strife and pestilence, Hom., Trag.   II. in Poets, as appellat., war, battle, discord, slaughter, ξυνάγωμεν Ἄρηα Il.; Ἄρης ἐμφύλιος, Ἄ. τιθασός civil war, Aesch.   2. warlike spirit, Trag. (The Root ΑΡ appears also in ἀρετή, the first notion of goodness (vir-tus) being that of manhood, bravery in war.) [ᾱ in Hom., except in voc. Ἄρες : in Aesch. long or short.]

ἀρητήρ [ᾱ], ῆρος, ἡ, (ἀράομαι) one that prays, a priest, Il.

ἀρητήριον [ᾱ], τό, (ἀράομαι) a place for prayer, Plut.

ἀρητός, ή, όν, Ion. for ἀρατός.

ἄρθεν, Ep. for ἤρθησαν, 3 pl. aor. I of ἀραρίσκω.

ἀρθμέω, f. ήσω, intr. to be united, Il.; and

ἄρθμιος, α, ον, united, ἡμῖν ἄρθμιοι friends with us, in league with us, Od.; ἄρθμια, τά, peaceful relations, friendship, Hdt. From

ἀρθμός, ὁ, (*ἄρω) a bond, league, friendship, Hom., Aesch.

ἄρθρον, τό, (*ἄρω) a joint, Soph.: esp. the socket of the ankle-joint, Hdt., Soph.:—in pl. joined with some other word, ἄρθρα ποδοῖν the ankles, Id.; ἄρθρων ἥλυσις the legs, Eur.; ἄρθρα τῶν κύκλων the eyes, Soph.; ἄρθρα στόματος the mouth, Eur.

ἀρθρο-πέδη, ἡ, a band for the limbs, fetter, Anth.

ἀρθρόω, f. ώσω, (ἄρθρον) to fasten by a joint:—of words, ἡ γλῶσσα ἀρθροῖ τὴν φωνήν the tongue produces articulate sounds, Xen.; but, ἀρθροῦν γλώσσην καὶ νόον to nerve the tongue and mind, Theogn.

ἀρθρ-ώδης, ες, (εἶδος) well-jointed, well-knit, Xen.

ἀρι- [ᾰ], insep. Prefix, like ἐρι-, strengthening the notion conveyed by its compd.: of same Root with Ἄρης, ἀρετή.

ἀρί-γνωτος [ᾰ], ον, or η, ον, easy to be known, Hom.: well-known, far-famed, Id.; and in bad sense, infamous, Lat. nimium notus, Od.

ἀρί-δακρυς, υ, gen. υος, (δάκρυ) much weeping, very tearful, Aesch.

ἀρί-δᾱλος, ον, Dor. for ἀρί-δηλος.

ἀρι-δείκετος, ον, (δείκνυμι) much shewn, hence like Lat. digito monstratus, Od.; as Sup. c. gen., ἀριδείκετος ἀνδρῶν most renowned of men, Il.

ἀρί-δηλος, Dor. -δᾱλος, ον, very distinct, far seen, Simon.   II. quite clear, manifest, Hdt.

ἀρίζηλος, ον and η, ον, Ep. for ἀρίδηλος (v. Ζ ζ. II), conspicuous, very distinct, of a star, Il.; of a voice, Ib.; of persons, conspicuous, remarkable, Ib.:—Adv., ἀριζήλως εἰρημένα a plain tale, Od.

ἀρι-ζήλωτος, ον, much to be envied, Ar.

ἀριθμᾱτός, Dor. for ἀριθμητός.

ἀριθμέω, Ep. impf. ἠρίθμεον as trisyll., f. ήσω, etc. :— Pass., f. med. in pass. sense ἀριθμήσομαι : Ep. aor. I inf. ἀριθμηθήμεναι (for –ῆναι) : (ἀριθμός) :— to number, count or reckon up, Od., etc. :—Med., ἠριθμοῦντο they got them counted, Thuc.   2. to count out, to pay, Xen., Dem.   3. to reckon, count as, ἔν τισι μέρει Id. :—Pass. to be reckoned, ἔν τισι Eur. ; ἀριθμεῖσθαι τῶν φιλτάτων to be counted as one of one's dearest friends, Id.   Hence

ἀρίθμημα, ατος, τό, a reckoning, number, Aesch. ; and

ἀρίθμησις, εως, ἡ, a counting, reckoning up, Hdt.; and

ἀριθμητικός, ή, όν, of or for reckoning, arithmetical, Plat.: ἡ ἀριθμητική (sc. τέχνη) arithmetic, Id.

ἀριθμητός, ή, όν, Dor. -ᾱτός, (ἀριθμέω) easily numbered, few in number, Theocr.: οὐκ ἀριθμητός held in no account, nullo numero habitus, Id.

ἀριθμός [ᾰ], ὁ, (*ἄρω) number, Lat. numerus, Od., etc.; ἀριθμὸν in number, Hdt., Att. ; ἀριθμὸν ἐξ Hdt.; ἐς τὸν ἀρ. τρισχίλια Id.; also, ἐν ἀριθμῷ Id.; so in Att.   2. amount, sum, extent, πολὺς ἀρ. χρόνου Aeschin.; ἀρ. ἀργυρίου a sum of money, Xen.   3. as a mark of station, worth, rank, μετ' ἀνδρῶν ἀριθμῷ among men, Od.; οὐκ ἔχουσιν ἀριθμόν have no account made of them, Eur.; οὐδ' εἰς ἀριθμὸν ἥκεις λόγων you come not into my account, Id.   4. mere number, quantity, opp. to quality, worth, ἀριθμὸς λόγων a mere set of words, Soph.; so of men, οὐκ ἀρ. ἄλλως not a mere lot, Eur.; so ἀριθμός alone, like Horace's nos numerus sumus, Ar.   II. a numbering, counting, ἀριθμὸν ποιεῖσθαι τῆς στρατιῆς to hold a muster of the army, Hdt.; παρεῖναι εἰς τὸν ἀρ. Xen.   III. the science of numbers, numeration, arithmetic, Aesch., Plat.

Ἄριοι, οἱ, the Arians or Aryans, old name of the Medes, Hdt.   II. Ἄριος, α, ον, as Adj. Median, Aesch.

ἀρι-πρεπής, ές, (πρέπω) very distinguished, stately, Hom.   2. (things) very bright, splendid, Id.

ἀρίς, ίδος, ἡ, a carpenter's tool, an auger or drill, Anth.

ἀρί-σημος, Dor. -σᾱμος, ον, (σῆμα) very notable, h. Hom., Tyrtae.   II. very plain, visible, Theocr.

ἀρίστ-αθλος, ον, victorious in the contest, Anth.

ἀρίστ-αρχος, ὁ, (ἄρχω) best-ruling, epith. of Zeus, Simon.

ἀρι-στάφυλος, ον, (στἄφυλή) rich in grapes, Anth.

ἀριστάω [ᾰρ-], f. ήσω: aor. I ἠρίστηκα, pf. ἠρίστηκα, pass. ἠρίσταμαι:—to take breakfast or luncheon, Lat. prandere, Ar., Xen.:—pf. pass. impers., ἠρίστηταί τ' ἐξαρκούντως Ar.

ἀριστεία, ἡ, excellence, prowess, Soph.: Il. 5, in which the prowess of Diomede is described, is called Διομήδους ἀριστεία.

ἀριστεῖα, Ion. -ήϊα, τά, the prize of the best and bravest, the meed of valour, Hdt., Soph., Plat. :—rarely so in sing., Hdt.   2. in sing. a monument of valour, memorial, Dem.

ἀριστερός, ά, όν, left, on the left, Lat. sinister, ἐπ' ἀριστερά towards, i. e. on, the left, Il.; ἐπ' ἀριστερὰ χειρὸς on the left hand, Od.; ἐξ ἀριστερῆς χειρός on the left hand, Hdt.; or simply, ἐξ ἀριστερᾶς Soph.; ἐς ἀριστερήν, ἐν ἀριστερῇ Hdt.   2. metaph. boding ill, ominous, be-

cause to a Greek augur, looking northward, the unlucky signs came from the left, Od. (Deriv. uncertain.)

ἀριστερόφιν, Ep. gen. of ἀριστερός, Il.

ἀριστεύς, έως, ὁ, dual ἀριστέοιν, (ἄριστος) the best man : used by Hom. mostly in Ep. pl. ἀριστῆες, the best or noblest, chiefs, princes ; so Hdt., etc. Hence

ἀριστεύω, f. σω, to be best or bravest, Hom. :—to gain the prize for valour, gain the highest distinction, Hdt. 2. c. gen., ἀριστεύεσκε Τρώων he was the best of the Trojans, Il. ; βουλῆ ἀριστεύεσκεν ἁπάντων Ib. ; c. inf., ἀριστεύεσκε μάχεσθαι was best at fighting, Ib. ; ἀρ. τι to be best in a thing, Theocr.

ἀριστήια, Ion. for ἀριστεῖα.

ἀριστίζω [ᾰρ-], f. ίσω, (ἄριστον) to give one breakfast, c. acc. pers., Ar.

ἀριστό-βουλος, η, ον, (βουλή) best-advising, Plut.

ἀριστο-γένεθλος, ον, (γένεθλον) producing the best, Anth.

ἀριστο-γόνος, ον, (γονή) bearing the best children, Pind.

ἀριστο-κράτέομαι, (κρατέω) Pass. to be governed by the best-born, to live under an aristocratical form of government, Ar., Plat. Hence

ἀριστοκρατία, ἡ, the rule of the best, an aristocracy, Thuc., Plat., etc. ; and

ἀριστοκράτικός, ή, όν, aristocratical, Plat.

ἀριστό-μαντις, εως, ὁ, best of prophets, Soph.

ἀριστό-μάχειος, ον, = sq., Anth.

ἀριστό-μάχος, ον, (μάχομαι) best at fighting, Pind.

ἄριστον [ᾰ Ep., ᾱ Att.], τό, the morning meal, breakfast, taken at sunrise, Hom., Hdt. ; ἄριστα, δεῖπνα, δόρπα θ' αἱρεῖσθαι τρίτον Aesch. :—later, ἄριστον was the mid-day meal, Roman prandium, Thuc. (Perh. akin to ἦρι, early.)

ἀριστό-νοος, ον, of the best disposition, Anth.

ἀριστο-ποιέω, f. ήσω, to prepare breakfast, τὰ ἀριστο-ποιούμενα things prepared for breakfast, Xen. :—mostly in Med. to get one's breakfast, Thuc., Xen.

ἄριστος, η, ον, (Ἄρης) best in its kind, serving as Sup. to ἀγαθός (cf. ἀρείων) : I. best, noblest, bravest, Il. ; βουλῆ, ἔγχεσιν ἄριστος Hom. ; εἶδος ἄριστος Il. :—c. inf., ἄριστοι μάχεσθαι Xen. ; ἀρ. διαβολὰς ἐνδέκεσθαι readiest to give ear to calumnies, Hdt. ; ἀρ. ἀπατᾶσθαι best, i.e. easiest, to cheat, Thuc. 2. best, most virtuous, Eur. II. of animals and things, best, finest, Hom. III. neut. pl. as Adv. ἄριστα, best, most excellently, Il., Hdt.

ἀριστο-τόκος, ον, (τίκτω) bearing the best children :—fem. ἀριστοτόκεια, Theocr. II. pass. ἀριστότοκος (proparox.), ον, born of the best parents, Pind.

ἀριστό-χειρ, ὁ, ἡ, won by the stoutest hand, ἀγών Soph.

ἀριστ-ωδίν, ῖνος, ὁ, ἡ, bearing the best children, Anth.

ἀρι-σφάλής, ές, (σφάλλω) very slippery or treacherous, Od.

ἀρι-φράδής, ές, (φράζομαι) easy to be known, very distinct, manifest, Il. : poët. Adv. -δέως, plainly, Theocr. II. very thoughtful, wise, Soph.

ἀρκεόντως, Att. contr. ἀρκούντως, Adv. part. pres. of ἀρκέω, enough, abundantly, ἀρκούντως ἔχει 'tis enough, Aesch., Thuc.

ἄρκεσις, εως, ἡ, (ἀρκέω) help, aid, service, Soph.

ἀρκετός, ή, όν, sufficient, N. T., Anth.

ἀρκέω, 3 sing. impf. ἦρκε : f. ἀρκέσω : aor. 1 ἤρκεσα : (akin to ἀρήγω) :—to ward off, keep off, a thing from a

person, τί τινι Il. ; ἀρκεῖν τὸ μὴ οὐ θανεῖν to keep off death, Soph. 2. c. dat. only, to defend, assist, succour, Hom., Soph. II. to be strong enough, to be sufficient to suffice, c. inf., Aesch., Soph. ; c. part., ἀρκέσω θνήσκουσα my death will suffice, Id. ; οὐκ ἤρκουν ἰατροὶ θεραπεύοντες Thuc. 2. c. dat. to suffice, be enough for, satisfy, τινι Hdt., Soph. : to be a match for, πρός τινα Thuc. 3. absol. to be enough, be strong enough, avail, hold out, Aesch., etc. :—part., ἀρκῶν, οὖσα, οὖν, sufficient, enough, Hdt., Att. 4. impers., ἀρκεῖ μοι 'tis enough for me, I am content, c. inf., Soph., etc. :—absol., οὐκέτ' ἀρκεῖ there is no help, Id. ; ἀρκεῖν δοκεῖ μοι it seems enough, seems good, Id. III. in Pass. to be satisfied with, c. dat. rei, ἔφη οὐκέτι ἀρκέεσθαι τούτοισι Hdt.

ἄρκιος, α, ον and os, ον, (ἀρκέω) sufficient, sure, certain, νῦν ἄρκιον ἢ ἀπολέσθαι ἠὲ σαωθῆναι one of these is certain, either to perish or be saved, Il. ; μισθὸς ἄρκιος a sure reward, Hom. ; ἄρκιον εὑρεῖν to have enough, Theocr. ; σφίσιν ἄρκιος a match for them, Id.

ἀρκούντως, contr. for ἀρκεόντως.

ἀρκτέον, verb. Adj., I. of ἄρχομαι, one must begin, Soph. II. of ἄρχω, one must govern ; and in pass sense, one must be ruled, i. e. obey, Id.

ΆΡΚΤΟΣ, ἡ, a bear, Od., etc. II. ἄρκτος, ἡ, the constellation Ursa Major, also called ἅμαξα, the Wain, (the star just behind is called Ἀρκτοῦρος the Bearward, or Βοώτης the Wagoner), Hom., etc. 2. the region of the bear, the North, sing., Hdt., Eur.

Ἀρκτ-οῦρος, ὁ, (οὖρος, guard), Arcturus (v. ἄρκτος II), Hes. II. the time of his rising, the middle of September, Soph.

ἀρκτῷος, α, ον, (ἄρκτος II) northern, Luc.

ΆΡΚΥΣ, υος, ἡ : pl., nom. and acc. ἄρκυες, -υας, Att. contr. ἄρκῦς :—a net, hunter's net, Lat. cassis, Aesch. ; oft. in pl., Id., Eur. :—metaph. ἄρκυες ξίφους the toils, i. e. perils, of the sword, Eur.

ἀρκυ-στάσία, ἡ, or -στάσιον, τό, a line of nets, Xen.

ἀρκύ-στατος, η, ον, (ἵστημι) beset with nets, ἀρκυστάτα μηχανά the hunter's toils, Eur. II. ἀρκύστατα, τά, a place beset with nets, a snare, Aesch., Soph.

ἀρκυ-ωρός, ὁ, (οὖρος) a watcher of nets, Xen.

ἅρμα, ατος, τό, (*ἄρω) a chariot, esp. a war-chariot, with two wheels, Hom. ; often in pl. for sing., Il., Trag. 2. chariot and horses, the yoked chariot, Ib. : also the team, the horses, Eur., Ar.

ἀρμαλία, ἡ, (*ἄρω) fitting sustenance, allowance, food, Hes., Theocr.

ἀρμ-άμαξα, ης, ἡ, a covered carriage, borrowed from the Persians, Hdt., Ar. ; used by women, Xen.

ἁρμάτειος, ον, (ἅρμα) of or belonging to a chariot, Xen. ; μέλος ἁρμ. a kind of dirge, Eur.

ἁρμάτεύω, f. σω, (ἅρμα) to drive or go in a chariot, Eur.

ἁρμἄτηλάσία, ἡ, chariot-driving, Xen. ; and

ἁρμἄτηλἄτέω, f. ήσω, to go in a chariot, drive it, Hdt., Xen. From

ἁρμἄτ-ηλάτης, ου, ὁ, (ἐλαύνω) a charioteer, Soph., Xen.

ἁρμἄτ-ήλατος, ον, (ἐλαύνω) driven round by a wheel, of Ixion, Eur.

ἁρμἄτο-δρομία, ἡ, (δρόμος) a chariot race, Strab.

ἁρμἄτό-κτυπος ὄτοβος, the rattling din of chariots, Aesch.

ἀρματο-πηγός, όν, (πήγνυμι) building chariots : ἀρμ. ἀνήρ a wheelwright, chariot-maker, Il.

ἀρματο-τροφέω, f. ήσω, to keep chariot-horses, esp. for racing, Xen. Hence

ἀρματοτροφία, ἡ, a keeping of chariot-horses, Xen.

ἀρματο-τροχιά, ἡ, (τροχός the wheel-track of a chariot, Luc. :—Hom. uses poët. form ἀρματροχιή, Il.

ἀρματωλία, ἡ, = ἀρματηλασία, Ar.

ἅρμενα, τά, the tackling or rigging of a ship, Hes., Theocr. 2. like ὅπλα, any tools, Anth. (Properly neut. of ἅρμενος, v. ἀραρίσκω B. IV.)

ἁρμόδιος, α, ον, (ἁρμόζω) fitting together, Theogn. II. well-fitting, accordant, agreeable, Id. :—Adv. -ως, Plut.

ἁρμόζω, Att. (except in Trag.) ἁρμόττω, Dor. ἁρμόσδω : —impf. ἥρμοζον, Dor. ἅρμ—: f. ἁρμόσω : aor. 1 ἥρμοσα, Dor. ἅρμοξα : pf. ἥρμοκα :—Med., Ep. imper. ἁρμόζεο : aor. 1 ἡρμοσάμην, Dor. ἁρμοξάμην :—Pass., pf. ἥρμοσμαι, Ion. ἅρμοσμαι : aor. 1 ἡρμόσθην, Dor. ἁρμόχθην : f. ἁρμοσθήσομαι : (*ἄρω) :—to fit together, join, esp. of joiner's work, Od. ; so in Med. to join for oneself, put together, Ib. 2. generally, to fit, adapt, prepare, make ready, Soph. :—Med. to suit oneself, πρός τινα Luc. 3. οἱ marriage, ἁρμόζειν τινὶ τὴν θυγατέρα to betroth one's daughter to any one, Hdt. ; also, ἀρμ. γάμους Eur. :—Med. to betroth to oneself, take to wife, τὴν θυγατέρα τινός Hdt. ; (so in Med., N. T.) :— Pass., ἡρμόσθαι θυγατέρα τινὸς γυναῖκα to have her betrothed or married to one, Hdt. 4. to set in order, regulate, govern, Eur. : Pass., Soph. ; κονδύ- λοις ἡρμοττόμην I was ruled or drilled with cuffs, Ar. :—among the Lacedaemonians, to act as harmostes, ἐν ταῖς πόλεσιν Xen. 5. to arrange according to the laws of harmony, to tune instruments, Plat. :— Pass., ἡρμοσμένος in tune, Id. II. intr. to fit, fit well, of clothes or armour, c. dat. pers., Il. 2. to fit, suit, be adapted, fit for, τινί Soph. 3. impers. ἁρ- μόζει, it is fitting, Lat. decet, c. acc. et inf., Id. 4. part., ἁρμόττων, ουσα, ον, fitting, suitable, Plat.; πρός τι Xen.

ἁρμοῖ, Adv. = ἄρτι, ἀρτίως, just, newly, lately, Aesch., Theocr. (In fact, an old dat. of ἁρμός; cf. οἴκοι, πέδοι.)

ἁρμο-λογέω, f. ήσω, (λέγω) to join, pile together, Anth.

ἁρμονία, ἡ, (ἁρμόζω) a fastening to keep ship-planks together, a clamp, Od. 2. a joining, joint, between a ship's planks, τὰς ἁρμ. ἐπάκτωσαν τῇ βύβλῳ caulked the joints with byblus, Hdt. 3. a frame : metaph., δύστροπος γυναικῶν ἁρμ. women's perverse temperament, Eur. II. a covenant, agreement, in pl., Il. :—settled government, order, Aesch. III. harmony, as a con- cord of sounds, first as a mythical personage, Harmonia, Music, companion of Hebé, the Graces and the Hours ; child of the Muses, h. Hom., Eur. 2. metaph., har- mony, concord, Plat.

ἁρμονικός, ή, όν, (ἁρμονία) skilled in music, Plat. :—τὰ ἁρμονικά, music, Id.

ἁρμός, ὁ, (*ἄρω) in pl. the fastenings of a door, Eur. ; ἁρμὸς χώματος λιθοσπαδής a fissure in the tomb made by tearing away the stones at their joinings, Soph.

ἁρμοστήρ, ῆρος, ὁ, = sq., Xen.

ἁρμοστής, οῦ, ὁ, (ἁρμόζω) one who arranges or governs, esp. a harmost or governor of the islands and towns of

Asia Minor, sent out by the Lacedaemonians during their supremacy, Thuc., Xen.

ἁρμόστωρ, ορος, ὁ, (ἁρμόζω) a commander, Aesch.

ἁρμόττω, Att. for ἁρμόζω.

ἄρνα, v. ἀρνός.

ἀρνάκις, ίδος, ἡ, (ἀρνός) a sheep's skin, Ar., Plat.

ἄρνας, ἄρνασι, ἄρνε, v. ἀρνός.

ἄρνειος, α, ον, (ἀρνός) of a lamb or sheep, κρέα Orac. ap. Hdt. ; ἄ. φόνος slaughtered sheep, Soph.

ἀρνειός, ὁ, (ἀρνός) a young ram or wether, just full grown, Il. ; ἀρνειὸς ὄϊς joined, like ὕρηξ κίρκος, Od.

ἀρνεο-θοίνης, ου, ὁ, (θοινάω) feasting on lambs, Anth.

ἀρνέομαι, f. ήσομαι : aor. 1 med. ἠρνησάμην and pass. ἠρνήθην : pf. ἥρνημαι : Dep. :—opp. to φημί, to deny, disown, Hom., etc. 2. opp. to δίδωμι, to decline to give, refuse, Od., etc. 3. absol. to say No, decline, refuse, Il. 4. dependent clauses are put in inf., with or without μή, to deny that, Hdt., Att. (Deriv. unknown.)

ἄρνες, v. ἀρνός.

ἀρνευτήρ, ῆρος, ὁ, (ἀρνεύω) a diver, tumbler, Hom.

ἀρνεύω, (ἀρνός) to butt like a ram, to dive, Lycophr.

ἀρνήσιμος, ον, (ἀρνέομαι) to be denied, Soph.

ἄρνησις, εως, ἡ, (ἀρνέομαι) denial, Aesch., Soph. ; foll. by τὸ μή c. inf., Dem.

ἀρνί, v. ἀρνός.

ἀρνίον, τό, (ἀρνός) a sheep-skin, Luc.

ἀρνός, τοῦ, τῆς, gen. without any nom. in use, ἀμνός being used instead : dat. and acc. ἀρνί, ἄρνα : dual ἄρνε : pl. ἄρνες, gen. ἀρνῶν : dat. ἄρνασι, Ep. ἄρνεσσι ; acc. ἄρνας :—a lamb, Lat. agnus, agna, Il. II. a sheep, whether ram or ewe, Hom. (Prob. akin to ἔρ-ιον, εἶρ-ος, wool.)

ἄρνυμαι, Dep., used only in pres. and impf., lengthd. form of αἴρομαι, to receive for oneself, reap, win, gain, earn, esp. of honour or reward, Hom., Att. :—rarely in bad sense, ἀρνύμενος λώβαν, perh. taking vengeance for my injuries, Eur.

ἀρξεῦμαι, Dor. for ἄρξομαι, f. of ἄρχομαι.

ἆρον, aor. 1 imper. of αἴρω.

ἀρόσιμος, ον, (ἀρόω) arable, fruitful : metaph. fit for engendering children, Soph., in poët. form ἀρώσιμος.

ἄροσις, εως, ἡ, (ἀρόω) arable land, corn-land, Lat. arvum, Hom.

ἀροτήρ, ῆρος, ὁ, (ἀρόω) a plougher, husbandman, Il., Eur. ; Σκύθαι ἀροτῆρες, opp. to νομάδες, Hdt. :—Adj., βοῦς ἀρ ντήρ a steer for ploughing, Hes. II. metaph. a father, Eur.

ἀρότης, ου, ὁ, = foreg., Hdt., Pind.

ἄροτος, ὁ, (ἀρόω) a corn-field, Od. 2. a crop, fruit of the field, Soph. ; metaph., τέκνων ἄροτος Eur. 3. tillage, ploughing, Hes. ; ζῆν ἀπ' ἀρότου to live by husbandry, Hdt. II. the season of tillage, seed- time, Hes. : hence a season, year, Soph.

ἀροτραῖος, η, ον, (ἄροτρον) of corn-land, rustic, Anth.

ἀροτρεύς, έως, ὁ, (ἄροτρον) a ploughman, = sq., Theocr.

ἀροτρεύω, (ἄροτρον) = ἀροτριάω, Anth.

ἀροτρητής, οῦ, ὁ, (ἄροτρον) belonging to the plough, Anth.

ἀροτριάω, f. άσω [ᾱ], = ἀρόω, Babr.

ἀροτρο-δίαυλος, ὁ, a plougher, who goes backwards and forwards like a runner in the δίαυλος, Anth.

ἄροτρον, τό, (ἀρόω) a plough, Lat. arātrum, Hom., etc.

ἀροτρο-πόνος, ον, working with the plough, Anth.

ἀροτρο-φορέω, f. ήσω, (ἄροτρον) to draw the plough, Anth.
ἀροῦμαι [ᾰ], f. med. of ἀείρω: ἀροῦμαι [ᾰ] of αἴρω.
ἀρουρᾰ, ἡ, (ἀρόω) tilled or arable land, seed-land, corn-land, Lat. arvum, and in pl. corn-lands, fields, Il.: then, generally, land, earth, Ib.; πατρὶς ἄρουρα father-land, Od. 2. metaph. of a woman as bearing children, Aesch., Soph. II. a measure of land in Egypt, nearly = the Roman jugerum, Hdt. Hence
ἀρουραῖος, α, ον, of or from the country, rural, rustic, μῦς ἀρ. a field-mouse, Hdt.; ὦ παῖ τῆς ἀρουραίας θεοῦ, of Euripides as the reputed son of a herb-seller, Ar.; ἀρ. Οἰνόμαος, of Aeschines who played the part of Oenomaus in the country, Dem.
ἀρουρείτης (or -ίτης), ὁ, = foreg., Babr.
ἀρούριον, τό, Dim. of ἄρουρα, Anth.
ἀρουρο-πόνος, ον, working in the field, Anth.
ἀρόω, Ep. inf. pres. ἀρόμμεναι: f. ἀρόσω, Ep. -όσσω: aor. 1 ἤροσα:—Pass., aor. 1 ἠρόθην: Ion. part. pf. ἀρηρόμενος:—to plough, Lat. arare, οὔτε φυτεύουσιν, οὔτ᾽ ἀρόωσιν (Ep. for ἀροῦσι) Od.: Pass., πόντος ἠρόθη δορὶ Aesch. II. to sow, ἀροῦν εἰς κήπους Plat. 2. metaph. of the husband, Theogn., Soph.:—Pass., of the child, to be begotten, Id. (The Root is ΑΡΟϝ, cf. ἄρου-ρα, Lat. arv-um.)
ἁρπᾰγή, ἡ, (ἁρπάζω) seizure, rapine, robbery, rape, Solon, Hdt., Att. 2. the thing seized, booty, prey, Aesch., Eur.; ἁρπαγὴν ποιεῖσθαί τι to make booty of a thing, Thuc.; cf. λεία. II. greediness, rapacity, Xen.
ἁρπάγη [ᾰ], ἡ, (ἁρπάζω) a rake, Lat. harpago, Eur.
ἁρπάγιμος, η, ον, (ἁρπάζω) ravished, stolen, Anth.
ἁρπαγμός, ὁ, (ἁρπάζω) a seizing, booty, a prize, N. T.
ἁρπάζω, f. -ξω, Att. -σω and (in med. form) ἁρπάσομαι: —aor. 1 ἥρπαξα, Att. ἥρπασα: pf. ἥρπακα:—Pass., pf. ἥρπασμαι, later ἥρπαγμαι: aor. 1 ἡρπάσθην and -χθην:—to snatch away, carry off, Hom., Hdt., etc.:—absol. to steal, be a thief, Ar. 2. to seize hastily, snatch up, λᾶαν Il.; δόρυ Aesch.; ἁρπ. τινὰ μέσον to seize him by the waist, Hdt.; c. gen. part., ἁρπ. τινὰ ποδὸς by the foot, Eur. 3. to seize, overpower, Aesch.: also to seize a post, Xen. II. to plunder, πόλεις Thuc., etc. (From Root ΑΡΠ come also ἄρπη, Ἅρπυιαι, cf. Lat. rap-io.)
ἁρπάκτειρα, ἡ, fem. of sq., Anth.
ἁρπακτήρ, ὁ, (ἁρπάζω) a robber, Il.
ἁρπακτικός, ή, όν, (ἁρπάζω) rapacious, Luc.
ἁρπακτός, ή, όν, (ἁρπάζω) gotten by rapine, stolen, Hes. 2. to be caught, i. e. to be got by chance, hazardous, Id.
ἁρπαλέος, α, ον, (ἁρπάζω) greedy: Adv. ἁρπαλέως, greedily, eagerly, Od., Theogn. II. attractive, alluring, Od., Pind.
ἁρπαλίζω, f. ίσω, (ἁρπάζω) to catch up, be eager to receive, τινα κωκυτοῖς Aesch. 2. to exact greedily, Id.
ἅρπαξ, αγος, ἡ, (ἁρπάζω) rapacious, Lat. rapax, Ar., Xen. II. as Subst., 1. ἅρπαξ, ἡ, rapine, Hes. 2. ἅρπαξ, ὁ, a robber, plunderer, Ar.
ἁρπαξ-ανδρος, α, ον, (ἀνήρ) snatching away men, Aesch.
ἅρπασμα, ατος, τό, robbery, Plat.
ἁρπαστός, ή, όν, (ἁρπάζω) carried away, Anth.

ἁρπεδόνη, ἡ, a cord, for binding or for snaring game, Xen.: a bowstring, Anth. (Deriv. unknown.)
ἅρπη, ἡ, (v. ἁρπάζω) a bird of prey, a kite, Il. II. a sickle, = δρέπανον, Hes.
Ἅρπυιαι, αἱ, (ἁρπάζω) the Snatchers, a personification of whirlwinds or hurricanes, Od. The Harpies, as described by Virgil, belong to later mythology.
ἀρραβών, ῶνος, ὁ, earnest-money, caution-money, deposited by the purchaser and forfeited if the purchase is not completed, Lat. arrhabo, arrha, Isae., N. T. (A Hebr. word.)
ἄρ-ρατος, ον, (ῥαίω?) firm, hard, solid, Plat.
ἀρ-ραφος, ον, (ῥάπτω) without seam, N. T.
ἄρ-ρεκτος, ον, (ῥέζω) undone, poët. ἄρεκτος, Il.
ἀρρενικός, ή, όν, (ἄρρην) male, Luc.
ἀρρενό-παις, παιδος, ὁ, ἡ, of male children, Anth.
ἀρρενωπία, ἡ, a manly look, manliness, Plat. From
ἀρρεν-ωπός, όν and ή, όν, (ὤψ) masculine-looking, masculine, manly, Plat., Luc.
ἄρ-ρηκτος, ον, (ῥήγνυμι) unbroken, not to be broken, Hom., Hdt., Aesch., etc.: unwearied, Il.
ἄρρην, later Att. for ἄρσην.
ἀρρηής, ές, fierce, savage, Theocr. (Deriv. unknown.)
ἄρ-ρητος, ον and η, ον, unspoken, unsaid, Lat. indictus, Od., etc.: οὐκ ἐπ᾽ ἀρρήτοις λόγοις not without warning spoken, Soph. II. not to be spoken, not to be divulged, of sacred mysteries, Hdt., Eur., etc.; διδακτά τε ἄρρητά τ᾽, i.e. things profane and sacred, Soph. 2. unutterable, inexpressible, horrible, Lat. nefandus, Id., Eur.; ἄρρητ᾽ ἀρρήτων 'deeds without a name,' Soph. 3. shameful to be spoken, Id.; ῥητὰ καὶ ἄρρητα, 'dicenda tacenda,' Dem. III. in Mathem., ἄρρητα, irrational quantities, surds, Plat.
Ἀρρη-φόροι, αἱ, (φέρω) at Athens two maidens of noble birth, chosen in their seventh year, who carried the peplos and other holy things of Athena Polias; hence
ἀρρηφορέω, to serve as Ἀρρηφόρος, Ar.; the procession being called ἀρρηφορία, ἡ, Lysias; the festival Ἀρρηφόρια, τά. (The meaning of Ἀρρη- is uncertain.)
ἀρ-ρίγητος, ον, (ῥιγέω) not shivering, daring, Anth.
ἄρ-ρις, ἰνος, ὁ, ἡ, without power of scenting, Xen.
ἄρριχος, ἡ or ὁ, a wicker basket, Ar., Anth.
ἀρρυθμέω, f. ήσω, not to be in rhythm with, Plat.; and
ἀρρυθμία, ἡ, want of rhythm or proportion, Plat. From
ἄρ-ρυθμος, ον, of sounds, not in rhythm or time, unrhythmical, opp. to εὔρυθμος, Plat.:—metaph. in undue measure, Eur.: ill-proportioned, Xen.
ἀρ-ρυτίδωτος, ον, (ῥυτίς) unwrinkled, Anth.
ἀρρωδέω, ἀρρωδίη, Ion. for ὀρρωδέω, ὀρρωδία.
ἀρ-ρώξ, ῶγος, ὁ, ἡ, (ῥήγνυμι, ἔρρωγα) without cleft or breach, unbroken, γῆ Soph.
ἀρρωστέω, f. ήσω, (ἄρρωστος) to be weak and sickly, Xen., Dem. Hence
ἀρρώστημα, ατος, τό, an illness, a sickness, Dem. 2. a moral infirmity, Plut.
ἀρρωστία, ἡ, weakness, sickness, Thuc., etc.; ἀρρ. τοῦ στρατεύειν inability to serve, Id. From
ἄρ-ρωστος, ον, (ῥώννυμι) weak, sickly:—Adv. ἀρρώστως ἔχειν to be ill, Aeschin. 2. in moral sense, weak, feeble, τὴν ψυχήν Xen.:—remiss, εἴς τι in a thing, Thuc.
ἄρσαι, aor. 1 inf. of ἀραρίσκω. II. also, v. ἄρδω.
ἀρσενο-κοίτης, (κοίτη) lying with men, N. T.

ΑΡΣΗΝ, ὁ, ἡ, ἄρσεν, τό, gen. ἄρσενος; older form of ἄρρην: Ion. ἔρσην:—male, Lat. mas, Il., etc.; ἄρρην, ὁ, or ἄρρεν, τό, the male, Aesch.; οἱ ἄρσενες the male sex, Thuc. **2.** masculine, strong, Eur.: metaph. mighty, κτύπος ἄρσην πόντου Soph. **3.** of the gender of nouns, masculine, ὀνόματα Ar.

ἀρσί-πους, ὁ, ἡ, contr. for ἀερσίπους, raising the foot, active, h. Hom., Anth.

ἄρσις, εως, ἡ, (αἴρω) a raising of the foot in walking, Arist. **II.** in Prosody, arsis, opp. to thesis.

ἄρσω, f. of ἄρδω. **II.** Aeol. for ἀρῶ, f. of αἴρω.

ἀρτάβη [ᾰ], ἡ, a Persian measure, artaba, = 1 medimnus + 3 choenices, Hdt.

ἀρτᾰμέω, f. ήσω, to cut in pieces, rend asunder, Eur. From

ἄρτᾰμος, ὁ, a butcher, cook, Xen. (Deriv. uncertain.)

ἀρτάνη [ᾰ], ἡ, (ἀρτάω) that by which something is hung up, a rope, noose, halter, Aesch., Soph.

ἀρτάω, f. ήσω: aor. 2 ἤρτησα: Pass., pf. ἤρτημαι, Ion. 3 pl. ἀρτέαται: (*ἄρω):—to fasten to or hang one thing upon another, τι ἀπό τινος Thuc.: to fasten in a noose, τὴν δέρην Eur.:—Med., βρόχους ἀρτωμένη fastening halters to one's neck, Id. **II.** Pass. to be hung upon, hang upon, ἠρτῆσθαι ἔκ τινος Id.: hence to depend upon, Lat. pendere ab aliquo, Hdt. Cf. ἀρτέομαι.

ἀρτεμής, ές, (ἄρτιος) safe and sound, Hom. Hence

ἀρτεμία, ἡ, soundness, recovery, Anth.

Ἄρτεμις, ἡ: gen. ιδος: acc. ιν or ιδα:—Artemis, the Roman Diana, goddess of the chase, daughter of Zeus and Latona, sister of Apollo: in Hom., women who die suddenly are said to be slain by her ἀγανὰ βέλεα: cf. Ἀπόλλων. (Deriv. uncertain.) Hence

Ἀρτεμίσιον, τό, a temple of Artemis, Hdt.

ἀρτέμων, ονος, ὁ, (ἀρτάω) prob. a foresail, N. T.

ἀρτέομαι, Ion. Verb, **I.** as Pass. to be prepared, get ready, make ready, c. inf., πολεμεῖν ἀρτέοντο, ἀρτέετο ἐς πόλεμον Hdt.; also, **II.** as Med., c. acc., ναυμαχίην ἀρτέεσθαι to prepare a sea-fight, Id. (Akin to ἀρτύω, not to ἀρτάω.)

ἄρτημα, ατος, τό, (ἀρτάω) a hanging ornament, earring, Hdt.; cf. λίθινος. **II.** any hanging weight, Plut.

ἀρτηρία, ἡ, Ion. -ίη, the wind-pipe or trachea, Plat., etc.; πνεύμονος ἀρτηρίαι the vessels of the lungs, Soph. **II.** an artery, only in late writers. (Deriv. uncertain.)

ἄρτι [ῐ], (*ἄρω) Adv. just, exactly, **1.** of the present, just now, even now, with pres. and pf., Theogn., Aesch., etc. **2.** of the past, just now, just, with impf. and aor., Eur., etc. **3.** in late writers of the future, just now, presently, Luc., etc.

ἀρτιάζω, f. άσω, (ἄρτιος) to play at odd and even, Lat. par impar ludere, Ar. **II.** to count, Anth. Hence

ἀρτιασμός, ὁ, the game of odd and even, Arist.

ἀρτι-βρεχής, ές, (βρέχω) just steeped, Anth.

ἀρτί-γαμος, ον, just married, Anth.

ἀρτι-γένειος, ον, (γένειον) with beard just sprouting, Anth.

ἀρτι-γέννητος, ον, just born, Luc.

ἀρτι-γλῠφής, ές, (γλύπτω) newly carved, Theocr.

ἀρτί-γονος, ον, just born, Anth.

ἀρτι-δᾰής, ές, (δάημι) just taught, Anth.

ἀρτί-δακρυς, υ, (δάκρυ) just weeping, ready to weep, Eur.

ἀρτί-δορος, ον, (δείρω) just stript off or peeled, Anth.

ἀρτί-δροπος, ον, (ἄρτιος, δρέπω) ready for plucking, of tender age, Aesch.: others **ἀρτί-τροπος**, ον, (ἄρτι, τρόπος) just of age, marriageable.

ἀρτιέπεια, ἡ, pecul. fem. of sq., Hes.

ἀρτι-επής, ές, (ἄρτιος, ἔπος) ready of speech, glib or ready of tongue, Il., Pind.

ἀρτιζῠγία, ἡ, (ζυγός) a recent union, ἀνδρῶν ἀρτ., i. e. newly-married husbands, Aesch.

ἀρτίζω, f. ίσω (*ἄρω) to get ready, prepare, Anth.: so in Med., Theocr.

ἀρτι-θᾰλής, ές, (θάλλω) just budding or blooming, Anth.

ἀρτι-θᾰνής, ές, (θνήσκω) just dead, Eur.

ἀρτι-κολλος, ον, (κόλλα) close-glued, clinging close to, ἀρτίκολλος ὥστε τέκτονος χιτών = ἀρτίως κολληθεὶς ὡς ὑπὸ τέκτονος, Soph. **II.** metaph. fitting well together, ἀρτ. συμβαίνει turns out exactly right, Aesch.; ἀρτίκολλόν τι μαθεῖν to hear it in the nick of time, opportunely, Id.

ἀρτι-λόχευτος, ον, (λοχεύω) just born, Anth.

ἀρτι-μᾰθής, ές, (μαθεῖν) having just learnt a thing, c. gen., Eur.

ἀρτι-μελής, ές, (μέλος) sound of limb, Plat.

ἄρτιος, α, ον, (ἄρτι) complete, perfect of its kind, suitable, exactly fitted; ἄρτια βάζειν to speak to the purpose (cf. ἀρτιεπής), Hom.; ἄρτια ἤδη thought things agreeable, was of the same mind, Id.:—meet, right, proper, Solon, Theogn. **2.** c. inf. prepared, ready, to do a thing, Hdt. **II.** of numbers, perfect, i. e. even, opp. to περισσός (odd), Plat., etc. **III.** Adv. ἀρτίως, just, now first, like ἄρτι, used by Soph. both of present time with pres. and pf.; and of past with impf. and aor.

ἀρτιπᾰγής, ές, (πήγνυμι) just put together or made, Theocr., Anth. **II.** freshly coagulated, Id.

ἀρτί-πλουτος, ον, newly gotten, χρήματα Eur.

ἀρτί-πους, ὁ, ἡ, gen. ποδός; Ep. nom. **ἀρτίπος**: (ἄρτιος, πούς) sound of foot, Od., Hdt.:—generally, strong or swift of foot, Il. **II.** (ἄρτι, πούς) coming just in time, Soph.

ἄρτῐσις, εως, ἡ, (ἀρτίζω) equipment, Hdt.

ἀρτί-σκαπτος, ον, (σκάπτω) just dug, Anth.

ἀρτί-στομος, ον, (στόμα) speaking in good idiom, or with precision, Plut.

ἀρτι-τελής, ές, (τέλος) newly initiated, Plat.

ἀρτί-τοκος, ον, (τίκτω) new-born, Anth., Luc. **II.** paroxyt. ἀρτιτόκος, ον, having just given birth, Anth.

ἀρτι-τρεφής, ές, (τρέφω) just nursed, ἀρτιτρεφεῖς βλαχαί the wailings of young children, Aesch.

ἀρτί-φρων, ον, gen. ονος, (ἄρτιος, φρήν) sound of mind, sensible, Od., Eur.: c. gen., γάμων fully conscious of a thing, Aesch.

ἀρτι-φῠής, ές, and **ἀρτί-φῠτος**, ον, (φύομαι) just born, fresh, Anth.

ἀρτι-χᾰνής, ές, (χάσκω) just opening, Anth.

ἀρτί-χνους, ον, gen. ου, with the first bloom on, Anth.

ἀρτί-χριστος, ον, fresh-spread, φάρμακον Soph.

ἀρτίως, Adv., v. ἄρτιος III.

ἀρτο-κόπος, ὁ, ἡ, a baker, Hdt., Xen. (Prob. for ἀρτο-πόπος, from πέπ-τω, cf. Lat. coq-uus.)

ἀρτο-λάγῠνος, ἡ, with bread and bottle in it, πήρα Anth.

ἀρτοποιία, ἡ, a baking, Xen. From

ἀρτο-ποιός, ὁ, (ποιέω) a bread-maker, baker, Xen.

ἀρτοπώλιον, τό, a baker's shop, bakery, Ar. From

ἀρτό-πωλις, ιδος, ἡ, (πωλέομαι) a bread-woman, Ar.

ἄρτος, ὁ, a cake or loaf of wheat-bread (barley-bread is μᾶζα), mostly in pl., Od.; ἄρτος οὖλος soft bread, Ib. (Deriv. uncertain.)

ἀρτο-σῖτέω, f. ήσω, (σιτέομαι) to eat wheaten bread, Xen.

ἀρτοφᾰγέω, f. ήσω, to eat bread, Hdt. From

ἀρτο-φάγος, ον, (φᾰγεῖν) a bread-eater, Batr.

ἄρτῡμα, τό, (ἀρτύω) seasoning, sauce, spice, Batr.

ἀρτύνας [ῠ], ὁ, a magistrate at Argos and Epidaurus, Thuc.; cf. ἁρμοστής. From

ἀρτύνω [ῠ], f. ῠνῶ, Ion. ῠνέω: aor. 1 act. ἤρτῡνα, pass. –ύνθην: (*ἄρω):—Ep. form of ἀρτύω, to arrange, prepare, devise, λόχον ἀρτύνειν, Lat. insidias struere, Od.; μνηστήρσιν θάνατον ἀρτ. Ib.:—Med. to prepare for oneself, Ib.

ἀρτύω, impf. ἤρτῡον: f. ἀρτύσω [ῠ]: aor. 1 ἤρτῡσα:— pf. ἤρτῡκα:—Pass., pf. ἤρτῡμαι: (*ἄρω):—like ἀρτύνω, to arrange, devise, prepare, δόλον, ὄλεθρον, γάμον Hom.; so Hdt., Att.

ἀρύβαλλος [ῠ!], ὁ, a bag or purse, Stesich. II. a bucket shaped like a purse, i. e. narrow at top, Ar. (Deriv. unknown.)

ἀρύσσομαι, (ἀρύω) Med. to draw for oneself, Hdt

ἀρυστήρ, ῆρος, ὁ, (ἀρύω) a cup or ladle, Hdt.

ἀρυστίχος, ὁ, Dim. of ἀρυστήρ, Ar.

ἀρυστρίς, ίδος, ἡ, = ἀρύταινα, Anth.

ἀρύταινα [ῠ], ης, ἡ, (ἀρύω) a small pail, Ar.

ἀρῠτήσιμος, ον, (ἀρύω) fit to drink, Anth.

ἀρύω, Att. ἀρύτω [ῠ], impf. ἤρυον: aor. 1 ἤρῡσα:— Med., f. ἀρύσομαι [ῠ]: aor. 1 ἠρῡσάμην, Ep. part. ἀρυσσάμενος :—Pass., aor. 1 ἠρύθην [ῠ]:—to draw water or any liquor for others, Hes., Xen.:—Med. to draw water for oneself, ἀρυσσάμενος ποταμῶν ἄπο having drawn water from the rivers, Hes.; ἀρύσασθαι ἀπὸ τοῦ ποταμοῦ Xen.; c. acc., ἀρύσασθαι πῶμα Eur.; c. gen. partit., ἀρύτεσθαι Νείλου ὑδάτων to draw of the waters of the Nile, Ar.; ἐς τὸν κόλπον τρὶς ἀρυσάμενος τοῦ ἡλίου having (as it were) drawn the rays of the sun into his bosom, Hdt.

ἀρχ-άγγελος, ον, an archangel, N. T.

ἀρχ-ᾱγέτης, ἀρχ-ᾱγός, Dor. and Att. for ἀρχ-ηγ-.

ἀρχαϊκός, ή, όν, (ἀρχαῖος) old-fashioned, antiquated, primitive, ἀρχαϊκὰ φρονεῖν Ar.

ἀρχαιό-γονος, ον, of ancient race, of old descent, Soph.

ἀρχαιολογέω, f. ήσω, to discuss antiquities or things out of date, Thuc. From

ἀρχαιο-λόγος, ὁ, (λέγω) an antiquary.

ἀρχαιο-μελῑ-σῐδωνο-φρῡνῐχ-ήρᾱτος, ον, μέλη ἀρχ. (μέλι, Σιδών, Φρύνιχος, ἐρατός) dear honey-sweet old songs from Phrynichus' Phoenissae, Ar.

ἀρχαῖον, τό, v. ἀρχαῖος IV.

ἀρχαιό-πλουτος, ον, rich from olden time, of old hereditary wealth, Aesch., Soph.

ἀρχαιο-πρεπής, ές, (πρέπω) distinguished from olden time, time-honoured, Aesch.

ἀρχαῖος, α, ον, (ἀρχή 1) from the beginning: I. of things, ancient, primeval, olden, Hdt., Att. 2. like ἀρχαϊκός, old-fashioned, antiquated, primitive, Aesch., Ar. 3. ancient, former, τὸ ἀρχ. ῥέεθρον Hdt.,

etc. II. of persons, ancient, old, Aesch., Thuc., etc.: οἱ ἀρχαῖοι the Ancients, the old Fathers, Prophets, N. T. III. Adv. ἀρχαίως, anciently, Dem.; so, τὸ ἀρχαῖον, Ion. contr. τώρχαῖον Hdt., Att. τἀρχαῖον Aesch. 2. in olden style, Plat., Aeschin. IV. as Subst., τὸ ἀρχαῖον, the original sum, the principal, Lat. sors, Ar., Oratt.

ἀρχαιοτροπία, ἡ, old fashions or customs, Plut. From

ἀρχαιό-τροπος, ον, old-fashioned, Thuc.

ἀρχ-αιρεσία, ἡ, (αἵρεσις) an election of magistrates, Hdt.; mostly in pl., Xen., etc. Hence

ἀρχαιρεσιάζω, f. σω, to hold the assembly for the election of magistrates, Plut.: to elect, Id. 2. to canvass for election, Id.

ἀρχε–, insep. Prefix (from ἄρχω), implying superiority.

ἀρχεῖον, Ion. ἀρχήϊον, τό, (ἀρχή 11) the senate-house, town-hall, residence of the chief magistrates, Lat. curia, Hdt., Xen. II. the magistracy, Arist.

ἀρχέ-κᾰκος, ον, (κακόν) beginning mischief, Il.

ἀρχέ-λᾱος, ον, leading the people, a chief, Aesch.; contr. ἀρχέλᾱς Ar.

ἀρχέ-πλουτος, ον, = ἀρχαιόπλουτος, Soph.

ἀρχέ-πολις, ον, ruling a city, Pind.

ἀρχέτας, ὁ, Dor. for ἀρχέτης, a leader, prince, Eur.: as Adj., ἀρχ. θρόνος a princely throne, Id.

ἀρχέ-τῡπον, τό, an archetype, pattern, model, Anth.: the figure on a seal, Luc.

ἀρχεύω, only in pres. (ἄρχω) to command, c. dat., Il.

ἀρχέ-χορος, ον, leading the chorus or dance, Eur.

ἀρχή, ἡ, (ἄρχω) a beginning, origin, first cause, Hom., etc.:—with Preps. ἐξ ἀρχῆς - ἀρχῆθεν, from the beginning, from of old, Od., Att.; ἐξ ἀρχῆς πάλιν anew, afresh, Ar.:—so, ἀπ' ἀρχῆς Hdt., Trag.:—κατ' ἀρχάς in the beginning, at first, Hdt.:—absol. in acc. ἀρχήν, to begin with, first, Id.; ἀρχὴν οὐ absolutely not, not at all, Lat. omnino non, Id., Att.; with numerals, ἀρχὴν ἕπτα in all, Hdt. 2. the end, corner, of a bandage, rope, sheet, Id., Eur., N. T. II. the first place or power, sovereignty, dominion, command, Hdt., Att.; c. gen. rei, ἀρχὴ τῶν νεῶν, τῆς θαλάσσης Thuc., etc. 2. a sovereignty, empire, realm, Hdt., Thuc. 3. in Prose, a magistracy, office, Hdt., Att.:—also a term of office, τὴν ἐνιαυσίαν ἀρχήν Thuc.:—these offices were commonly obtained in two ways, χειροτονητῇ by election, κληρωτῇ by lot, Aeschin. 4. in pl., αἱ ἀρχαί (as we say) 'the authorities,' i.e. the magistrates, Thuc., etc.

ἀρχη-γενής, ές, (γίγνομαι) causing the first beginning of a thing, c. gen., Aesch.

ἀρχηγετεύω, f. σω, to be chief leader, τῶν κάτω Hdt.

ἀρχηγετέω, f. ήσω, to make a beginning, Soph.

ἀρχ-ηγέτης, ου, ὁ, fem. ἀρχ-ηγέτις, ιδος: Dor. ἀρχαγέτης: (ἡγέομαι):—a first leader, the founder of a city or family, Hdt., etc. 2. generally, a leader, prince, chief, Aesch., Soph. 3. a first cause, author, τύχης, γένους Eur.

ἀρχ-ηγός, Dor. ἀρχ-ᾱγός, όν, (ἡγέομαι) beginning, originating a thing, c. gen., Eur. II. as Subst., like ἀρχηγέτης, founder, of a tutelary hero, Soph. 2. a prince, chief, Aesch., Simon., Thuc. 3. a first cause, originator, τοῦ πράγματος Xen.

ἀρχῆθεν, Dor. -ᾱθεν, (ἀρχή) Adv. from the beginning,

from of old, from olden time, Hdt. :—with a neg., ἀρχῆθεν μή not *at all,* Id.

ἀρχήιον, Ion. for ἀρχεῖον.

ἀρχήν, Adv., v. ἀρχή I.

ἀρχι-, insep. Prefix, like ἀρχε-.

ἀρχι-γραμμᾰτεύς, έως, ὁ, *a chief clerk,* Plut.

ἀρχίδιον, τό, Dim. of ἀρχή (II. 3), *a petty office, petty officer,* Ar., Dem.

ἀρχιερατικός, ή, όν, *of the high-priest,* N. T. From

ἀρχ-ιερεύς, έως, ὁ : Ion. ἀρχιέρεως, εω, acc. pl. ἀρχιρέας (from ἀρχιρεύς):—*an arch-priest, chief-priest,* Hdt.:— at Rome, the *Pontifex Maximus,* Plut. :—at Jerusalem, the *High-priest,* N. T.

ἀρχ-ιερωσύνη, ή, *the high-priesthood,* Plut.

ἀρχι-θάλασσος, ον, (θάλασσα) *ruling the sea,* Anth.

ἀρχιθεωρέω, f. ήσω, *to be* ἀρχιθέωρος, Dem. From

ἀρχι-θέωρος, ὁ, (θεωρός) *the chief of a* θεωρία *or sacred embassy,* Andoc., Arist.

ἀρχικός, ή, όν, (ἀρχή) *of* or *for rule, royal,* Aesch., Thuc. 2. of persons, *fit for rule, skilled in government* or *command,* Xen., Plat. : c. gen. *having command of,* Arist.

ἀρχι-κῠβερνήτης, ου, ὁ, *a chief pilot,* Plut.

ἀρχί-μῖμος, ὁ, *a chief comedian,* Plut.

ἀρχι-πειρᾱτής, οῦ, ὁ, *a pirate-chief,* Plut.

ἀρχι-πλάνος, ὁ, *a Nomad chieftain,* Luc.

ἀρχι-ποίμην, ὁ, *a chief shepherd,* N. T.

ἀρχ-ιρεύς, ὁ, Ion. for ἀρχιερεύς.

ἀρχι-συνάγωγος, ὁ, (συναγωγή) *the ruler of a synagogue,* N. T.

ἀρχιτεκτονέω, f. ήσω, *to be the architect,* Plut. 2. generally, *to construct, contrive,* Ar. From

ἀρχι-τέκτων, ονος, ὁ, *a chief-artificer, master-builder, director of works, architect, engineer,* Hdt. 2. generally, *a constructor, author,* Eur., Dem. II. at Athens, the *manager of the state theatre* and *of the Dionysia,* Id.

ἀρχι-τελώνης, ου, ὁ, *a chief toll-collector, chief-publican,* N. T.

ἀρχι-τρίκλῑνος, ὁ, *the president of a banquet* (*triclinium*), N. T.

ἀρχι-υπασπιστής, οῦ, ὁ, *chief of the men at arms,* Plut.

ἀρχοντικός, ή, όν, (ἄρχων) *of an archon,* Anth.

ἀρχός, ὁ, *a leader, chief, commander,* Il.

ΆΡΧΩ, Ep. inf. ἀρχέμεναι : impf. ἦρχον, Dor. ἆρχον : f. ἄρξω : aor. 1 ἦρξα : pf. ἦρχα :—Med., f. ἄρξομαι : Dor. ἀρξεῦμαι :—Pass., pf. ἦργμαι (only in med. sense) : aor. 1 ἤρχθην, inf. ἀρχθῆναι : f. ἀρχθήσομαι ; also ἄρξομαι in pass. sense :—*to be first,* I. of Time, *to begin, make a beginning,* both in Act. and Med.: 1. c. gen. *to make a beginning of,* πολέμοιο, μάχης, etc., Hom. ; so Hdt. and Att. :—Med. also in a religious sense, like ἀπάρχεσθαι, ἀρχόμενος μελέων *beginning the sacrifice with* the limbs, Od.; ἄρχειν σπονδῶν Thuc. 2. c. gen. about *to begin from* or *with,* ἐν σοὶ μὲν λήξω σέο δ' ἄρξομαι Il.; so, ἄρχεσθαι ἔκ τινος Od.; ἀρξάμενοι ἀπὸ παιδίων *even from boyhood,* Hdt. 3. c. gen. rei et dat. pers., ἄρχ. θεοῖς δαιτός *to make preparations for a* banquet to the gods, Il.; τοῖσι δὲ μύθων ἦρχε Ib., etc. 4. c. acc., ἄρχειν ὁδόν τινι, like Lat. *praeire viam alicui, to shew* him the way, Od.; absol. (sub. ὁδόν), *to lead the way,* Hom.; then generally ἄρχειν τι

Aesch., Soph. 5. c. inf. *to begin* to do a thing, Hom., etc. ; c. part. of continued action or condition, ἦρχον χαλεπαίνων Il. ; ἄρχ. διδάσκων Xen. 6. absol., ἄρχε *begin!* Hom.; ἄρχει ἡ ἐκεχειρία Thuc.; ἅμα ἦρι ἀρχομένῳ, θέρους ἀρχομένου Id. II. of Authority, *to lead, rule, govern,* only in Act.: 1. c. gen. *to rule, be leader of* . . , τινός Hom., Att. 2. c. dat. *to rule over,* Hom., Aesch. 3. absol. *to rule, govern,* Id.: esp. *to hold a subordinate office,* ὁκοῖον εἴη ἄρχειν μετὰ τὸ βασιλεύειν Hdt. :—at Athens, *to be archon,* Dem.; cf. ἄρχων. 4. Pass. *to be ruled, governed,* Hdt., Att. ; οἱ ἀρχόμενοι *subjects,* Xen.

ἀρχ-ῳδός, ὁ, *a precentor,* Byz.

ἄρχων, οντος, ὁ, (part. of ἄρχω) *a ruler, commander, chief, captain,* Hdt., Aesch., etc. 2. Ἄρχοντες, οἱ, *the chief magistrates at Athens,* nine in number, the first being ὁ Ἄρχων or ᾽Άρχων ἐπώνυμος, the second ὁ Βασιλεύς, the third ὁ Πολέμαρχος, the remaining six οἱ Θεσμοθέται. 3. title of *the chief magistrates* in other places, as the Ephors at Sparta, Hdt.

*ΆΡΩ, radical form of ἀραρίσκω, whence come ἄρθρον, ἁρμόζω, ἄρτι, ἄρτιος, ἀρτύω, etc.

ἀρῶ [ᾰ], f. of ἀείρω : but II. ἀρῶ [ᾰ], of αἴρω.

ἀρωγή, ή, (ἀρήγω) *help, aid, succour, protection,* Ζηνὸς ἀρωγή *aid given* by Zeus, Il.; ἐπ' ἀρωγῇ *in anyone's favour,* Ib.; ἀρ. νόσου, *help against* . . , Plat. II. of persons, *an aid, succour,* Aesch., Soph.

ἀρωγο-ναύτης, ου, ὁ, *helper of sailors,* Anth.

ἀρωγός, όν, (ἀρήγω) *aiding, succouring, propitious, serviceable,* τινι Aesch. ; absol., Id., Soph. 2. c. gen. *serviceable towards* a thing, Aesch., Soph. ; πρός τι Thuc. II. as Subst. *a helper, aid,* esp. in battle, Il. : *a defender* before a tribunal, *advocate,* Ib.

ἄρωμα, ατος, τό, *any spice* or *sweet herb,* Xen.

ἄρωμα, ατος, τό, (ἀρόω) *arable land, corn-land,* Lat. *arvum,* Ar.

ἀρώμεναι, Ep. for ἀροῦν, inf. of ἀρόω.

ἀρωραῖος, Dor. for ἀρουραῖος.

ἀρώσιμος, ον, poët. for ἀρόσιμος.

ἄρωστος, ον, poët. for ἄρρωστος, Anth.

ἃς, also ἅς and ἄς, Aeol. and Dor. for ἕως. II. ἃς, Dor. for ἧς, gen. fem. of ὅς, ἥ, ὅ.

ἄσαι, aor. 1 inf. for ἀδσαι, aor. 1 inf. of ἀδάω, *to hurt.*

ἄσαι, aor. 1 inf. of ἄω, *to satiate* :—ἄσαιμι, opt.

ἄσαι, aor. 1 inf. of ᾄδω.

ἄ-σακτος, ον, (σάττω) *not trodden down,* Xen.

ἀ-σᾰλᾱμίνιος [μῐ], ον, *not having been at Salamis,* Ar.

ἀ-σάλευτος, ον, (σᾰλεύω) *not agitated, tranquil,* of the sea :—metaph. of the mind, Eur.

ἄσαμεν, 1 pl. aor. 1 of ἄω, *to sleep.*

ἀσάμινθος, ή, *a bathing-tub,* Od. (Deriv. unknown.)

ἄ-σᾱμος, Dor. for ἄ-σημος.

ἀ-σάνδᾰλος, ον, (σάνδαλον) *unsandalled, unshod,* Bion.

ἄ-σαντος, ον, (σαίνω) *not to be soothed, ungentle,* Aesch.

ἀσάομαι, Pass. imper. ἀσῶ, part. ἀσώμενος : aor. 1 ἠσήθην, (ἄση) :—*to feel loathing* or *nausea, to be disgusted* or *vexed at* a thing, c. dat., Theogn.; τὴν ψυχὴν ἀσηθῆναι Il.; ἀσώμενοι ἐν φρεσί Theocr.

ἀ-σαρκής, ές, (σάρξ) *not fleshly,* i. e. *spiritual,* Anth.

ἄ-σαρκος, ον, (σάρξ) *without flesh, lean,* Xen.

ἄσασθαι, aor. 1 med. inf. of ἄω, *to satiate.*

ἄσατο, contr. for ἀάσατο, 3 sing. aor. 1 med. of ἀάω, to hurt.

ἀσάφεια, ἡ, indistinctness, obscurity, Plat. From

ἀ-σᾰφής, ές, indistinct to the senses, dim, faint, Thuc.; or to the mind, dim, obscure, Soph., Thuc.; νὺξ ἀσαφεστέρα ἐστίν by night one sees less distinctly, Xen.: —Adv. -φῶς, obscurely, ἀσαφῶς ποτέρων ἀρξάντων without knowing which began, Thuc.

ἀσάω, only in Pass.: v. ἀσάομαι.

ἄ-σβεστος, ον and η, ον, unquenchable, inextinguishable, of fire, Il.; of laughter, etc., Hom.; ἄσβ. πόρος ὠκεανοῦ ocean's ceaseless flow, Aesch. II. as Subst., ἄσβεστος (sc. τίτανος), ἡ, unslaked lime, Plut.

ἄσε, contr. for ἄασε, 3 sing. aor. 1 of ἀάω, to hurt.

ἀσέβεια, ἡ, ungodliness, impiety, profaneness, Eur., Xen., etc.; and

ἀσεβέω, f. ήσω, to be impious, to act profanely, sin against the gods; εἶς τινα or τι Hdt., Eur.; περὶ τινα or τι Hdt., Xen. 2. c. acc. pers. to sin against him, Aesch.; hence in Pass., ἠσέβηται οὐδέν no sin has been committed, Andoc.; and

ἀσέβημα, ατος, τό, an impious or profane act, Thuc., Dem. From

ἀ-σεβής, ές, (σέβω) ungodly, godless, unholy, profane, Soph.: τὸ ἀσεβές = ἀσέβεια, Xen.

ἀ-σείρωτος, ον, (σειρά) not drawn by traces (but by the yoke), Eur.

ἀσελγαίνω, impf. ἠσέλγαινον: f. ἀνῶ:—pf. pass. ἠσέλγημαι:—to behave licentiously, Plat.:—Pass., of acts, τὰ ἠσελγημένα outrageous acts, Dem.; and

ἀσέλγεια, ἡ, licentiousness, Plat., Dem. From

ἀ-σελγής, ές, licentious, wanton, brutal, Dem.:—Adv., ἀσελγῶς πίονες extravagantly fat, Ar.; ἀσ. ζῆν Dem. (The origin of -σελγής is uncertain.)

ἀ-σέληνος, ον, (σελήνη) moonless, νύξ Thuc.

ἀσεπτέω, = ἀσεβέω, Soph. From

ἄ-σεπτος, ον, (σέβω) unholy, Soph., Eur.

ἄσεσθε, 2 pl. f. med. of ἄω, to satiate.

ἀσεῦμαι, Dor. for ἄσομαι, f. of ἅδω.

ἄση [ἄ], ἡ, (ἄω to satiate) nausea, distress, vexation, Hdt., Eur.

ἀσηθῆναι, aor. 1 inf. of ἀσάομαι.

ἀ-σήμαντος, ον, (σημαίνω) without leader or shepherd, Il. II. unsealed, unmarked, Hdt.

ἄ-σημος, Dor. ἄ-σᾱμος, ον, (σῆμα) without mark or sign, ἄσ. χρυσός uncoined gold, Hdt.; ἄσ. ἀργύριον Thuc.; ἄσ. ὅπλα arms without device, Eur. II. of sacrifices or oracles, giving no sign, unintelligible, Hdt., Trag. III. leaving no mark, indistinct, Soph.; of sounds, inarticulate, unintelligible, Hdt.; ἄσημα βοῆς = ἄσημος βοή, Soph.:—generally, unperceived, unnoticed, Aesch., Soph. IV. of persons, cities, etc., of no mark, unknown, obscure, Eur.

ἀ-σήμων, ον, gen. ονος, = ἄσημος III, Soph.

ἀσθένεια, gen. ας, Ion. ης, ἡ, want of strength, weakness, feebleness, sickliness, Hdt., Thuc., etc.; ἀσθένεια βίου poverty, Hdt. 2. sickness, a disease, Thuc.; and

ἀσθενέω, f. ήσω, to be weak, feeble, sickly, Eur., Thuc., etc.; ἠσθένησε he fell sick, Dem. From

ἀ-σθενής, ές, (σθένος) without strength, weak, feeble, weakly, Hdt., etc.; ἀσθενέστερος πόνον ἐνεγκεῖν too weak to bear labour, Dem.:—τὸ ἀσθενές = ἀσθένεια,

Thuc. 2. of property, weak, poor, Hdt., Eur.; οἱ ἀσθενέστεροι the weaker sort, i. e. the poor, Xen. 3. insignificant, οὐκ ἀσθενέστατος σοφιστής Hdt.; of streams, petty, small, Id. II. Adv. ἀσθενῶς, feebly, slightly, Plat.: Comp. -έστερον or -έστερα Id., Thuc. Hence

ἀσθενόω, f. ώσω, to weaken, Xen.

ἄσθμα, ατος, τό, (ἄω, to blow) short breath, panting, from toil, Il., Aesch. II. generally, a breath, breathing, Aesch.: a blast, Anth.

ἀσθμαίνω, (ἄσθμα) to breathe hard, gasp for breath, of one out of breath or dying, mostly in pres. part., Il.

Ἀσία [ἄ], Ion. -ίη, ἡ, Asia, Hdt., Att.:—Adj. Ἀσιᾱνός, ή, όν, Asiatic, Thuc., etc.; fem. Ἀσιάς, άδος, Ἀσίς, ίδος [the latter with ᾱ], Aesch., Eur.; Ἀσιάς (sc. κιθάρα) the lyre as improved in Lesbos:—also Ἀσιάτης, fem. -ᾱτις, Ion. -ήτης, -ῆτις, Aesch., Eur.

Ἀσι-άρχης, ου, ὁ, (ἄρχω) an Asiarch, the highest religious official under the Romans in the province of Asia, N. T.

Ἀσιάς, Ἀσιάτης, v. Ἀσία. Ἀσιᾱτο-γενής, ές, (γίγνομαι) of Asian birth, Aesch.

ἀ-σίδηρος [ῐ], ον, not of iron, Eur.: not made by iron, Anth. II. without sword, unarmed, Eur.

Ἀσιῆτις, Ion. for Ἀσιᾱτις, v. Ἀσία.

ἄ-σικχος, ον, not nice as to food, Plut. (Deriv. uncertain.)

ἀ-σῐνής, ές, (σίνομαι) unhurt, unharmed, of persons, Od., Hdt.: secure, happy of life and fortune, Aesch. 2. of things, undamaged, Hdt. II. act. not harming, Id.: harmless, Xen. 2. protecting from harm, Aesch. III. Adv. ἀσινῶς, innocently, Sup. -έστατα Xen.

Ἄσιος [ᾱ], α, ον, Asian, Il.

ᾹΣΙΣ [ᾰ], εως, ἡ, slime, mud, such as a river brings down, Il.

Ἀσίς [ᾱ], v. Ἀσία.

ἀσῑτέω, f. ήσω, to abstain from food, fast, Eur., Plat.; and

ἀσῑτία, Ion. -ίη, ἡ, want of food, Hdt., Eur. From

ἄ-σῑτος, ον, without food, fasting, Od., Att.

ἀσκᾰλάβώτης, ου, ὁ, the spotted lizard, Lat. stellio, Ar. (Deriv. unknown.)

ἄ-σκᾰλος, ον, (σκάλλω) unhoed, Theocr.

ἀσκάντης, ου, ὁ, a poor bed, pallet, Ar. II. a bier, Anth. (Deriv. unknown.)

ἀσκαρδάμυκτί, Adv., without winking, with unchanged look, Xen. From

ἀ-σκαρδάμυκτος, ον, (σκαρδαμύσσω) not blinking or winking, Ar.

ἀσκεθής, ές, Ep. for ἀσκηθής, Od.

ἀ-σκελής, ές, (ἀ euphon., σκέλλω) dried up, withered, Od. 2. neut. ἀσκελές as Adv. stubbornly, ἀσκελὲς αἰεί Ib.; so, ἀσκελέως αἰεί Il.

ἀ-σκέπαρνος, ον, (σκέπαρνον) without the axe, unhewn, Soph.

ἄ-σκεπτος, ον, (σκοπέω) inconsiderate, unreflecting, Plat.:—Adv. -τως, inconsiderately, Thuc., etc. II. unconsidered, unobserved, Xen.

ἀ-σκευής, ές, (σκευή) without the implements of his art, Hdt.

ἄ-σκευος, ον, (σκευή) unfurnished, unprepared, Soph. : c. gen. unfurnished with a thing, Id.

ἈΣΚΕ'Ω, f. ήσω : aor. 1 ήσκησα : pf. ήσκηκα :—to work curiously, form by art, fashion, Hom. ; ἀσκήσας with skilful art, Id.   2. of adornment, to dress out, trick out, decorate, adorn, deck, Hdt. : Pass., πέπλοισι Περσικοῖς ἠσκημένη Aesch. :—Med., σῶμ' ἠσκήσατο adorned his own person, Eur.   II. in Prose, to practise, exercise, train, Lat. exercere, properly of athletic exercise :   1. of the person trained, Ar. ; ἀσκεῖν τὸ σῶμα εἴς or πρός τι for an object or purpose, Xen., etc.   2. of the thing practised, ἀσκ. τέχνην Hdt. ; metaph., ἀσκ. τὴν ἀλήθειαν Id. ; κακότητα Aesch. ; ἀσέβειαν Eur.   3. c. inf., ἄσκει τοιαύτη μένειν endeavour to remain such, Soph. ; ἀσκ. ἀγαθὰ ποιεῖν to make a practice of doing good, Xen.   4. absol. to practise, go into training, οἱ ἀσκοῦντες those who practise gymnastics, Id.

ἀ-σκηθής, ές, unhurt, unharmed, unscathed, Hom. (Deriv. uncertain.)

ἄσκημα, ατος, τό, (ἀσκέω) an exercise, practice, Xen.

ἄ-σκηνος, ον, (σκηνή) without tents, Plut.

ἄσκησις, εως, ή, (ἀσκέω) exercise, practice, training, Thuc., Xen., etc. ; in pl. exercises, Plat. :—c. gen., ἄσκ. τινος practice of or in a thing, Id.   II. generally, a mode of life, profession, art, Luc.

ἀσκητέος, α, ον, verb. Adj. of ἀσκέω, to be practised, Xen.   II. ἀσκητέον, one must practise, σοφίαν Plat.

ἀσκητής, οῦ, ὁ, (ἀσκέω) one who practises any art or trade, ἀσκ. τῶν πολεμικῶν Xen. : esp. an athlete, one trained for the arena, Ar., Plat.

ἀσκητός, ή, όν, (ἀσκέω) curiously wrought, Od. : adorned, πέπλῳ with a robe, Theocr.   2. to be acquired by practice, Plat., Xen.   II. of persons, practised in a thing, c. dat., Plut.

ἄ-σκιος, ον, (σκιά) unshaded, Pind.

Ἀσκληπιός, ὁ, Asclepius, Lat. Aesculapius, a Thessalian prince, famous as a physician, Il. :—later, son of Apollo, tutelary god of medicine :—Ἀσκληπιάδαι or -ίδαι, οἱ, a name for physicians, Theogn., Soph. :—Ἀσκληπιεῖον, τό, the temple of Asclepius, Luc. :—Ἀσκλήπειος, α, ον, of, belonging to Asclepius, Ἀσκληπίεια (sc. ἱερά) his festival, Plat.

ἄ-σκοπος, ον, (σκοπέω) inconsiderate, heedless, Il. : unregardful of a thing, c. gen., Aesch.   II. pass. unseen, invisible, Soph.   2. not to be seen, unintelligible, obscure, Aesch., Soph. : inconceivable, incalculable, Id.

ἄ-σκοπος, ον, (σκοπός) aimless, random, Luc.

ἈΣΚΟ'Σ, ὁ, a leathern-bag, a wine-skin, Hom. ; ἀσκὸς βοὸς the bag of ox-skin in which Aeolus bottled up the winds, Od. ; ἀσκὸς Μαρσύεω a bag made of the skin of Marsyas, Hdt. :—a bladder, Eur.   2. proverb. usage, ἀσκὸν δείρειν τινά to flay one alive, maltreat wantonly, Ar. ; ἀσκὸς δεδάρθαι Solon.

Ἀσκώλια, τά, (ἀσκός) the 2nd day of the rural Dionysia, when they danced upon greased wine-skins, 'unctos saluere per utres.' Hence

ἀσκωλιάζω, f. σω, to dance as at the Ἀσκώλια, Ar.

ἄσκωμα, ατος, τό, (ἀσκός) the leather padding of the hole which served for the row-lock, put there to make the oar move easily, Ar.

ᾆσμα, ατος, τό, (ᾄδω) a song, a lyric ode or lay, Plat.

ᾀσμᾰτο-κάμπτης, ου, ὁ, (κάμπτω) twister of song, Ar.

ἀσμενίζω, f. σω, to be well-pleased, Polyb. From

ἄσμενος, η, ον : (ἥδομαι, the pf. part. of which would be ἡσμένος) :—well-pleased, glad, always with a Verb, φύγεν ἄσμενος he escaped gladly or he was glad to have escaped, Hom., etc. ; ἐμοὶ δέ κεν ἀσμένῳ εἴη glad would it make me ! Il. ; ἀσμένῳ δέ σοι νὺξ ἀποκρύψει φάος glad wilt thou be when night shuts out the light, Aesch. : —Adv. ἀσμένως, gladly, readily, Id., Eur. : Sup. ἀσμεναίτατα, -έστατα, Plat.

ᾄσομαι, f. of ᾄδω.

ἀσοφία, ή, unwisdom, stupidity, Plut., Luc. From

ἄ-σοφος, ον, unwise, foolish, silly, Theogn.

ἈΣΠΑ'ΖΟΜΑΙ, f. ἀσομαι : Dep. :—to welcome kindly, bid welcome, greet, Lat. salutare, τινα Hom., etc. ; as the common form on meeting, ἀσπάζομαί σε or ἀσπάζομαι alone, Ar. ; πρόσωθεν αὐτὴν ἀσπ. I salute her at a respectful distance, i. e. keep away from her, Eur. :— also to take leave of, Id., Xen.   2. to embrace, kiss, caress, Ar. ; of dogs, Lat. blandiri, Xen.   3. of things, to follow eagerly, cleave to, Lat. amplector, ἀσπ. τὸν οἶνον Plat.   4. ἀσπ. ὅτι to be glad that, Ar.

ἀ-σπαίρω, (α euphon., σπαίρω) to pant, gasp, struggle convulsively, of the dying, Hom., Hdt. ; but, μοῦνος ἤσπαιρε he was the only one who still made a struggle, Hdt.

ἀσπάλᾰθος, ὁ or ή, aspalathus, a prickly shrub, yielding a fragrant oil, Theogn. ; used as an instrument of torture, Plat. (Deriv. unknown.)

ἄ-σπαρτος, ον, (σπείρω) of land, unsown, untilled, Od.   2. of plants, not sown, growing wild, Ib.

ἀσπάσιος, α, ον, and ος, ον, (ἀσπάζομαι) welcome, gladly welcomed, Hom.   II. well-pleased, glad, Id. :— Adv. -ίως, gladly, Id., Hdt.

ἄσπασμα, ατος, τό, (ἀσπάζομαι) a greeting, esp. in pl. embraces, Eur.

ἀσπασμός, ὁ, (ἀσπάζομαι) a greeting, embrace, salutation, Theogn., N. T.

ἀσπαστός, ή, όν, = ἀσπάσιος, welcome, Od., Hdt. Adv. -τῶς, Id.

ἄ-σπειστος, ον, (σπένδω) to be appeased by no libations, implacable, Dem.

ἄ-σπερμος, ον, (σπέρμα) without seed or posterity, Il.

ἀ-σπερχές, (α euphon., σπέρχω) a neut. form used as Adv. hastily, hotly, vehemently, Hom.

ἄ-σπετος, ον, (εἰπεῖν) unspeakable, unutterable, unspeakably great, Hom. :—neut. as Adv. unspeakably, Il.

ἀσπίδ-αποβλής, ή, (ἀποβάλλω) one that throws away his shield, a runaway, Ar.

ἀσπίδη-φόρος, ον, (φέρω) shield-bearing, Aesch., Eur.

ἀσπιδιώτης, ὁ, (ἀσπίς) shield-bearing, a warrior, Il.

ἀσπῐδό-δουπος, ον, clattering with shields, Pind.

ἀσπιδο-πηγεῖον, τό, (πήγνυμι) the workshop of a shield-maker, Dem.

ἀσπιδ-οῦχος, ὁ, (ἔχω) a shield-bearer, Eur.

ἀσπῐδο-φέρμων, ον, (φέρβω) living by the shield, i. e. by war, Eur.

ἄ-σπιλος, ον, (σπίλος) without spot, spotless, Anth., N. T.

ἈΣΠΙ'Σ, ίδος, ή, a round shield, Lat. clipeus, of bull's hide, overlaid with metal plates, with a boss (ὀμφαλός) in the middle, and fringed with tassels (θύσανοι) :

different from the *oblong shield* (ὅπλον, Lat. *scutum*) used by the ὁπλῖται. 2. in Prose, used for *a body of soldiers*, ὀκτακισχιλίη ἀσπίς 8,000 *men-at-arms*, Hdt. 3. military phrases: ἐπ' ἀσπίδας πέντε καὶ εἴκοσι τάξασθαι to be drawn up 25 deep, Thuc.; so, ἐπ' ἀσπίδων ὀλίγων τετάχθαι Id.; ἐπ' ἀσπίδα, παρ' ἀσπίδα (opp. to ἐπὶ δόρυ) *on the left, towards* or *to the left*, because the shield was on the left arm, Xen.; παρ' ἀσπ. στῆναι to stand in battle-array, Eur. II. *an asp*, an Egyptian snake, Hdt. Hence

ἀσπιστής, ῆρος, ὁ, = sq., Soph., Eur.; and

ἀσπιστής, οῦ, ὁ, *one armed with a shield, a warrior*, gen. pl. ἀσπιστάων, Il.:—as Adj., ἀσπισταὶ μόχθοι τευχέων, i. e. the shield of Achilles, Eur.; and

ἀσπίστωρ, ορος, ὁ, = foreg., κλόνοι ἀσπίστορες turmoil of shielded warriors, Aesch.

ἄ-σπλαγχνος, ον, (σπλάγχνον) *without bowels*: metaph. *heartless, spiritless*, Soph.

ἄ-σπονδος, ον, (σπονδή) *without drink-offering*, of a god, *to whom no drink-offering is poured*, ἄσπ. θεός i. e. death, Eur. II. *without a regular truce* (which was ratified by σπονδαί), Thuc.; ἀσπόνδους τοὺς νεκροὺς ἀνελέσθαι to take up their dead *without leave asked*, Id.; τὸ ἄσπονδον *a keeping out of treaty* or *covenant* with others, *neutrality*, Id. 2. *admitting of no truce, implacable, deadly*, Lat. *internecinus*, of war, Aesch., Dem.

ἄ-σπορος, ον, (σπείρω) = ἄσπαρτος, Dem.

ἀ-σπούδαστος, ον, (σπουδάζω) *not to be zealously pursued, not worth pursuing*, Eur.

ἀ-σπουδί [ῑ] or -εί, (σπουδή) Adv. *without zeal, without a struggle, ignobly*, Il.

ἄσσα, Ion. for ἅτινα, neut. pl. of ὅστις, *which, whichsoever, what, whatever*, Il., Hdt. II. ἄσσα, Ion. for τινά, some, ὁπποῖ' ἄσσα *what sort*? Od.; πόσ' ἄττα; Ar.

ἀσσάριον, τό, Dim. of Lat. *as*, a farthing, N. T., Plut.

ἆσσον, Adv. Comp. of ἄγχι, *nearer, very near*, Hom.: c. gen., ἆσσον ἐμεῖο *nearer* to me, Il.; with a double Comp., μᾶλλον ἆσσον Soph.:—hence, as a new Comp., ἀσσοτέρω, with or without gen., Od.; Sup. ἀσσοτάτω, Anth.; whence Adj. ἀσσότατος Id.

Ἀσσύριοι [ῠ], οἱ, the Assyrians, Hdt.:—Ἀσσυρία, Ion. -ίη (sc. γῆ), ἡ, *their country*, Id.

ἄσσω, Att. contr. for ἀΐσσω.

ἀ-σταθής, ές, (ἵσταμαι) *unsteady, unstable*, Anth.

ἀ-στάθμητος, ον, (σταθμάομαι) *unsteady, unstable*, ἀστέρες Xen.; ὁ δῆμος ἀσταθμητότατον πρᾶγμα Dem.: *uncertain of life*, Eur.; τὸ ἀστάθμητον *uncertainty*, Thuc.

ἀστακτί, Adv. *not in drops*, i. e. *in floods*, Soph., Plat. From

ἄ-στακτος, ον, (στάζω) *not in drops, gushing*, Eur.

ἄ-στάλακτος, ον, (σταλάσσω) *not dripping*, Plut.

ἀστάνδης, ὁ, *a courier*, Persian word, Plut.

ἀ-στασίαστος, ον, (στασιάζω) *not disturbed by faction*, Thuc.: of persons, *free from party-spirit, not factious*, Plat.

ἀστατέω, f. ήσω, *to be unstable*, N. T. From

ἄ-στατος, ον, (ἵσταμαι) *unstable*, Plut.

ἀσταφιδίτης [ῐ] ου, ὁ, fem. -ῖτις, ιδος, *of raisins*, Anth.

ἀ-στάφίς, ίδος, ἡ, (ἁ euphon., σταφίς) as collect. noun, *dried grapes, raisins*, Lat. *uva passa*, Hdt.

ἄ-στάχυς, υος, ὁ, (ἁ euphon., στάχυς) *an ear of corn*, Il., Hdt.

ἀ-στέγαστος, ον, (στεγάζω) *uncovered*: διὰ τὸ ἀστέγαστον from their *having no shelter*, Thuc.

ἀστεΐζομαι, Dep. *to talk cleverly*, Plut. From

ἀστεῖος, α, ον, (ἄστυ) *of the town*: hence, like Lat. *urbanus, town-bred, polite, courteous*, opp. to ἄγροικος, Plat.:—*refined, elegant, pretty, witty, clever*, Ar., Plat.:—ironically, ἀστ. κέρδος *a pretty* piece of luck, Ar.

ἀ-στεμφής, ές, (στέμβω) *unmoved, unshaken*, Il.; ἀστεμφὲς ἔχεσκε [τὸ σκῆπτρον] he held it *stiff*, Ib.:—Adv., ἀστεμφέως ἐχέμεν to hold *fast*, Od.: also neut. ἀστεμφές, as Adv. *stiff, stark*, Mosch. 2. of persons, *stiff, unflinching*, Theocr.

ἀ-στένακτος, ον, (στενάζω) *without sigh* or *groan*, Soph., Eur.

ἀστέον, verb. Adj. of ἄδω, *one must sing*, Ar., Plat.

ἄ-στεπτος, ον, (στέφω) *uncrowned*, Eur.

ἀ-στεργ-άνωρ [ἄν], ορος, ὁ, ἡ, (στέργω, ἀνήρ) *without love of man, shunning wedlock*, Aesch.

ἀ-στεργής, ές, (στέργω) *without love, implacable, hateful*, Soph.

ἀστερόεις, εσσα, εν, (ἀστήρ) *starred, starry*, Il. II. *like a star, glittering*, Ib.

ἀ-στεροπή, ἡ, (ἁ euphon., στεροπή) *lightning*, Il. Hence

ἀστεροπητής, οῦ, ὁ, *the lightener*, of Zeus, Il.

ἀστερ-ωπός, όν, (ἀστήρ, ὤψ) *star-faced, bright-shining*, Eur. II. *starry*, Id.

ἀ-στέφανος, ον, *without crown, ungarlanded*, Eur.

ἀ-στεφάνωτος, ον, (στεφανόω) *uncrowned, not to be crowned*, Plat., etc.

ἀστή, ἡ, fem. of ἀστός, Hdt., etc.

ἄ-στηλος, ον, (στήλη) *without tombstone*, Anth.

ἀστήρ, ὁ, gen. έρος, dat. pl. ἀστράσι (not ἀστράσι), *a star*, Il., etc.; cf. ἄστρον. 2. *a flame, light, fire*, Eur. (The Root is ΣΤΕΡ, ἁ being euphon., cf. Lat. *stella*, i. e. *ster-ula*.)

ἀ-στήρικτος, ον, (στηρίζω) *not steady, unstable*, Anth., N. T.

ἀ-στιβής, ές, (στείβω) *untrodden*, Aesch.: *desert, pathless*, Soph. 2. *not to be trodden, holy*, Id.

ἄ-στιβος, ον, = foreg., Anth.

ἀστικός, ή, όν, (ἄστυ) *of a city* or *town*, opp. to country, Aesch.; τὰ ἀστικὰ Διονύσια (also called τὰ κατ' ἄστυ), Thuc. II. *like* ἀστεῖος, *polite, neat, nice*, ἀστικά (as Adv.) Theocr.

ἄ-στικτος, ον, (στίζω) *not marked with* στίγματα, *not tattooed*, Hdt.

ἀ-στλέγγιστος, ον, (στλεγγίς) *not scraped clean*, Anth.

ἄ-στολος, ον, (στέλλω) *unequipped*, of Charon's boat, used in the same way as γάμος ἄγαμος, Aesch.

ἄ-στομος, ον, (στόμα) *without mouth*: of horses, *hard-mouthed, restive*, Soph. II. of dogs, *soft-mouthed, unable to hold with the teeth*, Xen. III. of metal, *soft, incapable of a fine edge*, Plut.

ἀ-στονάχητος, ον, (στοναχέω) *without sighs*, Anth.

ἄ-στοργος, ον, (στοργή) *without natural affection*, Aeschin.; ὤστοργος (i. e. ὁ ἄστ.) *the heartless one*, Theocr.

ἀστός, ὁ, (ἄστυ) *a townsman, citizen*, Hom., Att.

ἆστος, Att. contr. for ἄϊστος.

ἀστοχέω, f. ήσω, to miss the mark, to miss, fail, τινος or περί τινος Polyb.; περί τι N. T. From

ἄ-στοχος, ον, missing the mark, aiming badly at, τινος Plat., Anth.

ἀστράβη, ή, a mule's saddle, an easy padded saddle, Dem. (Deriv. uncertain.)

ἀ-στρᾰβής, ές, = ἀ-στραφής, not twisted, straight, Plat.

ἀστρᾰγᾰλίζω, f. σω, (ἀστράγαλος) to play with ἀστρά-γαλοι, Plat.

ἀστρᾰγάλισις, εως, ή, a playing with ἀστράγαλοι, Arist.

ἀστράγαλος [τρᾰ], ὁ, one of the neck-vertebrae, Hom. II. the ball of the ankle joint, Lat. talus, Hdt., Theocr. III. pl. ἀστράγαλοι, dice or a game played with dice, Il., Hdt. :—they were at first made of knuckle-bones, and never had more than four flat sides, whereas the κύβοι had six. They played with four : the best throw (βόλος), when each die came differently, was called 'Αφροδίτη, Lat. jactus Veneris ; the worst, when all came alike, κύων, Lat. canis. (Deriv. uncertain.)

ἀστραπή [ᾰ], ή, = ἀστεροπή, στεροπή, a flash of light-ning, lightning, Hdt., Att.; in pl. lightnings, Aesch., Soph. 2. any bright light, N. T.

ἀστραπηφορέω, f. ήσω, to carry lightnings, Ar. From

ἀστραπη-φόρος, ον, (φέρω) lightning-bearing, flash-ing, Eur.

ἀστράπτω (a euphon., στράπτω, cf. ἀ-στεροπή), impf. ήστραπτον, Ion. ἀστράπτεσκον : aor. 1 ήστραψα :—to lighten, hurl lightnings, of omens sent by Zeus, Il., Ar. 2. impers., ἀστράπτει it lightens, ήστραψε it lightened, Att. II. to flash like lightning, Soph., Eur., etc. :—c. acc. cogn., ἐξ ὀμμάτων δ' ήστραπτε σέλας (sc. Τυφών) he flashed flame from his eyes, Aesch.

ἄστρασι, (not ἀστράσι) dat. of ἀστήρ.

ἀ-στρᾰτεία, ή, exemption from service, Ar. 2. a shunning of service, which at Athens was a heavy offence, φεύγειν γραφὴν ἀστρατείας to be accused of it, Id.; ἀστρατείας ἁλῶναι, ὀφλεῖν to be convicted of it, Oratt.

ἀ-στράτευτος [ᾰ], ον, (στρατεύω) without service, never having seen service, Ar.

ἀ-στρᾰφής, ές, (στρέφω) = sq., Soph.

ἄ-στρεπτος, ον, = ἄστροφος, Theocr. :—Adv. -τεί, Anth. 2. unbending, inflexible, Id.

ἀστρο-γείτων, ον, gen. ονος, near the stars, Aesch.

ἀστρό-θετος, ον, astronomical, Anth.

ἀστρολογία, ή, astronomy, Xen. From

ἀστρο-λόγος, ον, (λέγω) = ἀστρονόμος, Xen.

ἄστρον, τό, mostly in pl. the stars, Hom., Att.; in sing., mostly of Sirius, Xen., etc.; cf. ἀστήρ.

ἀστρονομέω, f. ήσω, to study astronomy, Ar.; and

ἀστρονομία, ή, astronomy, Ar., Plat., etc.; and

ἀστρονομικός, ή, όν, skilled in astronomy, pertaining to astronomy, Plat. From

ἀστρο-νόμος, ὁ, (νέμω) an astronomer, Plat., etc.

ἄ-στροφος, ον, (στρέφω) without turning away, un-turning, Lat. irretortus, ὄμματα Aesch.; ἀφέρπειν ἄστρ. to go away without turning back, Soph.

ἀστρῷος, α, ον, (ἄστρον) starry, Anth.; ἀστρ. ἀνάγκη the law of the stars, Id.

ἀστρ-ωπός, α, ον, = ἀστερ-ωπός, Eur.

ἄ-στρωτος, ον, without bed or bedding, Plat.: metaph. unsmoothed, rugged, Eur.

ΑΣΤΥ, τό ; Ep. gen. εος, Att. εως : Att. pl. ἄστη :—a city, town, Hom., etc.; Σούσων ἄ. the town of Susa, Aesch.; ἄ. Θήβης Soph. II. the Athenians called Athens "Αστυ, as the Romans called Rome Urbs, mostly without the Art. (as we speak of 'being in town,' 'going to town '), Ar.

ἀστυ-άναξ, ακτος, ὁ, lord of the city, epith. of certain gods, Aesch. : in Hom. only as prop. n.

ἀστῠ-βοώτης, ου, ὁ, (βοάω) crying through the city, of a herald, Il.

ἀστῠ-γείτων, ον, gen. ονος, near or bordering on a city, Hdt., Aesch. 2. as Subst. a neighbour to the city, a borderer, Hdt., Thuc.

ἄστῠ-δε, Adv. into, to, or towards the city, Hom.

ἀστῠ-δρομέομαι, Pass. to have the streets filled with fugitives, Aesch.

ἄ-στῠλος, ον, without pillar or prop, Anth.

ἀστύ-νῖκος πόλις, (νίκη) ή, Athens the victorious city, Aesch.

ἀστυνομέω, f. ήσω, to be ἀστυνόμος, Dem.

ἀστῠνομία, ή, the office of ἀστυνόμος, Arist.

ἀστῠνομικός, ή, όν, of or for an ἀστυνόμος or his office, Plat.

ἀστῠ-νόμος, ὁ, (νέμω) protecting the city, θεοί Aesch.; ὀργαὶ ἀστ. the feelings of social life, Soph. II. as Subst. a magistrate at Athens, who had the care of the police, streets, and public buildings, five for the city and five for Peiraeus, Plat., etc.

ἀστύ-οχος, ον, (ἔχω) protecting the city, Anth.

ἀ-στῠφέλικτος, ον, (στυφελίζω) unshaken, undisturbed, Xen.

ἀ-στῠφελος, η, ον, and ος, ον, not rugged, Theogn., Anth.

ἀ-συγγνώμων, ον, gen. ονος, not pardoning, relentless, Dem.

ἀ-συγκέραννῠμι) unmixed, Anth.

ἀ-συγκόμιστος, ον, (συγκομίζω) not gathered in, Xen.

ἀ-σύγκρῐτος, ον, (συγκρίνω) not to be compared, unlike, Plat.

ἀ-σῠκοφάντητος, ον, (συκοφαντέω) not plagued by in-formers, not calumniated, Aeschin., Luc.

ἀσῡλαῖος, α, ον, (ἄ-συλος) of an asylum, Plut.

ἀ-σύλητος, ον, (συλάω) not inviolate, Eur.

ἀσῡλία, ή, (ἄσυλος) inviolability, of suppliants, Aesch.

ἀ-συλλόγιστος, ον, (συλλογίζομαι) not reasoning justly : —Adv., -τως, ἀσυλλογίστως ἔχειν τινός to be unable to reason about a thing, Plut.

ἄ-σῠλος, ον, (σύλη) safe from violence, inviolate, of persons seeking protection, Eur. :—c. gen., γάμων ἄσυλος safe from marriage, Id. II. of places, γῆν ἄσυλον παρασχεῖν to make the land a refuge, Id.

ἀ-σύμβᾰτος, old Att. ἀ-ξύμβατος, ον, (συμβαίνω) not coming to terms, Thuc. :—Adv., -τως ἔχειν to be irre-concilable, Plut.

ἀ-σύμβλητος, old Att. ἀ-ξύμβλητος, ον, (συμβάλλω) not to be guessed, unintelligible, Soph.

ἀ-σύμβολος, ον, not paying one's scot or share (συμ-βολαί), Lat. immunis, δειπνεῖν ἀσύμβολον Aeschin.

ἀσυμμετρία, ή, want of proportion or harmony, Plat. From

ἀ-σύμμετρος, old Att. ἀ-ξύμμετρος, ον, having no common measure, τινι with a thing, Plat.; πρός τι Plut. II. unsymmetrical, disproportionate, Xen.

ἀ-συμπᾰγής, ές, (συμπήγνυμι) not compact, Luc.
ἀ-συμπᾰθής, ές, without sympathy with, τινι Plut.
ἀ-σύμφορος, old Att. ἀ-ξύμφορος, ον, inconvenient, inexpedient, useless, Hes.: c. dat. inexpedient for, prejudicial to, Eur., Thuc.; also ἔς or πρός τι Id.:— Adv. -ρως, Xen.
ἀ-σύμφωνος, old Att. ἀ-ξύμφωνος, ον, not agreeing in sound, Plat.:—metaph. discordant, at variance, τινι with another, Id.; πρός τινα N. T.
ἀ-σύμψηφος, ον, not agreeing with, τινος Plut.
ἀ-σύνδετος, ον, unconnected, Xen.
ἀ-σύνδηλος, ον, not manifest, Plut.
ἀσυνεσία, old Att. ἀξυνεσία, ή, want of understanding, stupidity, Eur., Thuc. From
ἀ-σύνετος, old Att. ἀ-ξύνετος, ον, void of understanding, stupid, Hdt., Att.; not to be understood, unintelligible, Eur.
ἀσυνήθεια, ή, want of experience in a thing, c. gen., Arist. From
ἀ-συνήθης, ες, gen. εος, unaccustomed, inexperienced, unacquainted with others, Arist.
ἀ-συνήμων, old Att. ἀ-ξυνήμων, ον, = ἀσύνετος, Aesch.
ἀ-σύνθετος, old Att. ἀ-ξύνθετος, ον, (συντίθημι) uncompounded, Plat.   II. (συντίθεμαι) bound by no covenant, faithless, Dem., N. T.
ἀ-σύνοπτος, ον, not easily perceived, Aeschin.
ἀ-σύντακτος, old Att. ἀ-ξύντακτος, ον, not ranged together; of soldiers, not in battle-order, Xen.   2. undisciplined, disorderly, Thuc., Xen.   3. not combined in society, Id.   4. not put on the tax-roll, free from public burdens, Dem.
ἀ-σύντονος, ον, not strained, slack:—Adv. -νως, lazily, Sup. -ώτατα, Xen.
ἀσυσκεύαστος, ον, not arranged, not ready, Xen.
ἀ-σύστᾰτος, old Att. ἀ-ξύστατος, ον, (συνίσταμαι) having no cohesion or consistency, Plat.   2. metaph. incoherent, irregular, Lat. dispar sibi, Ar.; ἀξ. ἄλγος fitful, ever-recurring pain, Aesch.
ἀσύφηλος [ῠ], ον, insolent, degrading, Il. (Deriv. uncertain.)
ἀσυχία, ἄσυχος, Dor. for ἡσυχία, ἥσυχος.
ἀ-σφάδαστος [ᾰδ], ον, (σφαδάζω) without convulsion or struggle, of one dying, Aesch., Soph.
ἄ-σφακτος, ον, (σφάζω) unslaughtered, Eur.
ἀσφάλαξ, ᾰκος, ὁ, (α euphon., σπάλαξ) a mole, Babr.
ἀσφάλεια, gen. ας, Ion. ης, ή, (ἀσφαλής) security against stumbling or falling, ἀσφ. πρὸς τὸν πηλόν Thuc.: stability, Soph.   2. assurance from danger, personal safety, security, Hdt., Thuc., etc.; ἀσφ. διδόναι, παρέχειν Xen.   3. assurance, certainty, ἀσφ. μὴ ἂν ἐλθεῖν αὐτούς certainty that they would not come, Thuc.; ἀσφάλεια λόγου the certainty of an argument, Xen., N. T.
Ἀσφάλειος, ον, of Poseidon, the Securer, Ar. From
ἀ-σφᾰλής, ές, (σφάλλομαι) not liable to fall, immoveable, steadfast, firm, θεῶν ἔδος Od., etc.   2. of friends and the like, unfailing, trusty, Soph., etc.: c. inf., φρονεῖν γὰρ οἱ ταχεῖς οὐκ ἀσφαλεῖς the hasty in council are not safe, Id.: so of things, sure, certain, Thuc., etc.   3. assured from danger, safe, secure, Soph., etc.; ἐν ἀσφαλεῖ in safety, Thuc.; τὸ ἀσφαλές = ἀσφάλεια, Id.; ἀσφαλές [ἐστι], c. inf., it is safe to . . ,

Ar.   4. ἀσφ. ῥήτωρ a convincing speaker, Id.   II. Ep. Adv. ἀσφαλέως ἔχειν or μένειν to be, remain fast, firm, steady, Hom.; so neut. ἀσφαλές as Adv., Id.; ἀσφ. ἀγορεύει without faltering, Od.; ἔμπεδον ἀσφαλέως without fail for ever, Hom.; still further strengthd., ἔμπεδον ἀσφαλὲς ἀεί Il.   III. Att. Adv. ἀσφαλῶς in all senses of the Adj., in safety, with certainty, Soph.:—Comp. -έστερον, Hdt., Plat.; Sup. -έστατα, Id.
ἀσφᾰλίζομαι, Med., f. Att. -ιοῦμαι:—to make safe, secure, N. T.
ἄσφαλτος, ή, asphalt, bitumen, forming in lumps, (θρόμβοι) on the surface of the river Is near Babylon and at Ardericca near Susa, Hdt. (Seems to be a foreign word.)
ἀ-σφᾰρᾰγέω, f. ήσω, (α euphon., σφαραγέω) to resound, clang, of armed men, Theocr.
ἀσφάρᾰγος [φᾰ], ὁ, = φάρυγξ, the throat, gullet, Il.
ἀ-σφάρᾰγος, ὁ, (α euphon., σπαργάω) asparagus, Anth.
ἀσφοδέλῐνος, η, ον, of asphodel, Luc.
ἀσφοδελός, ὁ, asphodel, king's-spear, a plant of the lily kind, Hes., Theocr.   II. oxyt., as Adj., ἀσφοδελὸς λειμών the asphodel mead, which the shades of heroes haunted, Od. (Deriv. unknown.)
ἄ-σφυκτος, ον, (σφύζω) without pulse, lifeless, Anth.
ἀσχᾰλάω, used by Hom. in Ep. forms, 3 sing. ἀσχαλάᾳ, 3 pl. ἀσχαλόωσι, inf. ἀσχαλάαν, part. ἀσχαλόων:—to be distressed, grieved, Hom.: to be vexed at a thing, c. gen., Od. (Deriv. uncertain.)
ἀσχάλλω, f.-ἀλῶ, = ἀσχαλάω, Od., Hdt.; τινι at a thing, Aesch., Eur.; τι Id.
ἄ-σχετος, Ep. also ἀά-σχετος, ον, (σχεῖν) not to be held in or checked, irrepressible, ungovernable, Hom.
ἀ-σχημάτιστος, ον, (σχηματίζω) without form or figure, Plat.
ἀσχημονέω, f. ήσω, to behave unseemly, disgrace oneself, to be put to shame, Eur., Plat.; and
ἀσχημοσύνη, ή, want of form, ungracefulness, Plat.: in moral sense, indecorum, Id. From
ἀ-σχήμων, ον, gen. ονος, (σχῆμα) misshapen, unseemly, shameful, Lat. turpis, Eur.   2. of persons, ἀσχ. γενέσθαι to be indecorous, Hdt.
ἀσχολέω, f. ήσω, to engage, occupy, τινά Luc.
ἀσχολία, ή, an occupation, business, want of leisure, Thuc.; ἀσχ. ἔχειν φιλοσοφίας πέρι to have no leisure for pursuing it, Plat.; ἀσχ. ἄγειν to be engaged or occupied, Id.; ἀσχ. παρέχειν τινι to cause one trouble, Id.
ἄ-σχολος, ον, (σχολή) of persons, without leisure, engaged, occupied, busy, Plat., Dem.; ἀσχ. ἔς τι with no leisure for a thing, Hdt.; ἀσχ. περί τι busy about . . , Plut.:—Adv., ἀσχόλως ἔχειν to be busy, Eur.   II. of actions, allowing no leisure, Id.
ἄσχος, τό, the inspissated juice of a Scythian tree, Hdt.
ἀ-σώμᾰτος, ον, (σῶμα) unembodied, incorporeal, Plat.
ἀσωτεύομαι, Dep. to lead a profligate, wasteful life, Arist.: and
ἀσωτία, ή, prodigality, wastefulness, Plat. From
ἄ-σωτος, ον, (σώζω) having no hope of safety, abandoned, profligate, Lat. perditus, Soph., Arist.   II. act., ἄσωτος γένει bringing ruin on the race, fatal to it, Aesch.

ἀτακτέω, f. ήσω, of a soldier, *to be undisciplined, disorderly*; Xen., Dem.   2. generally, *to lead a disorderly life*, Xen. From

ἄ-τακτος, ον, *not in battle-order*, of troops, Hdt., Thuc., etc.   2. *undisciplined, disorderly, irregular, lawless*, Id., etc.   II. Adv. *-τως, in an irregular, disorderly manner*, of troops, Id. : Comp. ἀτακτότερον, Id.

ἀ-ταλαίπωρος, ον, *without pains or patience, indifferent, careless*, Thuc.

ἀ-τάλαντος, ον, (α copul., τάλαντον) *equal in weight, equivalent or equal to*, τινι Hom.

ἀταλά-φρων, ον, gen. ονος, (φρήν) *tender-minded*, of a child, Il.

ἀτάλλω [ᾰ], only in pres. and impf. *to skip in childish glee, gambol*, Il.   II. Act. *to bring up a child, rear, foster*, like ἀτιτάλλω, Soph. :—Pass. *to grow up, wax*, h. Hom. ; the Act. is so used by Hes. From

ἀταλός [ᾰᾰ], ή, όν, (akin to ἁπαλός) *tender, delicate*, of young creatures, Hom.; ἀταλὰ φρονέοντες *of young, gay* spirit, Il.

ἀταλό-ψῦχος, ον, (ψυχή) *soft-hearted*, Anth.

ἀταξία, Ion. -ίη, ή, (ἄτακτος) *want of discipline, disorderliness*, properly among soldiers, Hdt., Plat., etc.   2. generally *disorder, irregularity*, Plat., etc.

ἀτάομαι [ᾰτ], Pass. (ἄτη) *to suffer greatly, be in dire distress*, ἀτώμενος Soph., Eur.

ἈΤΑ'Ρ, Ep. αὐτάρ, Conjunct. *but, yet*, Lat. *at*, to introduce an objection or correction, Il., Att. ; it always begins a sentence or clause, but is placed after the voc., "Εκτορ, ἀτάρ που ἔφης *still thou didst say*, Il. :—ἀτάρ sometimes answers to μέν, more emphatic than δέ, Hom., Att.   2. in Att. to mark a rapid transition to another thought, Aesch., etc. ; so ἀτὰρ δή Eur.

ἀ-τάρακτος, ον, (ταράσσω) *not disturbed, without confusion, steady*, of soldiers, Xen.

ἀ-τάραχος, ον, = ἀτάρακτος, Arist.

ἀ-ταρβής, ές, (τάρβος) *unfearing, fearless*, Il. ; ἀτ. τῆς θέας *having no fear about the sight*, Soph.   2. *causing no fear*, Aesch. ?

ἀ-τάρβητος, ον, (ταρβέω) *fearless, undaunted*, Soph.

ἀ-τάρμυκτος, ον, *unwincing, unflinching*, Pind. (Deriv. unknown.)

ἀταρπϊτός, ἀταρπός, Ion. for ἀτραπιτός, ἀτραπός.

ἀταρτηρός, όν, Ep. for ἀτηρός, *mischievous, baneful*, Hom.

ἀτασθᾰλία, Ion. -ίη, ή, (ἀτάσθαλος) *presumptuous sin, recklessness, arrogance*, Hom. always in pl. ; in sing., Hes., Hdt.

ἀτασθάλλω, only in pres. part. *acting presumptuously, in arrogance*, Od. From

ἀτάσθαλος [ᾰτ], ον, (ἄτη), though α does not agree in quantity) *presumptuous, reckless, arrogant*, Hom., Hdt.

ἀ-ταύρωτος, ον, (ταυρόομαι) *unwedded, virgin*, Aesch.

ἀτᾰφία, ή, *want of burial*, Luc. From

ἄ-τᾰφος, ον, *unburied*, Hdt., Att.

ἀτάω, v. ἀτάομαι.

ἄτε, properly acc. pl. neut. of ὅστε, used as Adv., *just as, so as*, Il., Hdt., Soph.   II. in causal sense, *inasmuch as, seeing that*, Lat. *quippe*, with part., ἄτε ἔχων Hdt., Thuc., etc. ; with gen. absol., ἄτε τῶν ὁδῶν φυλασσομένων *quippe viae custodirentur*, Hdt. ; with

the part. omitted, δίκτυα δοὺς [αὐτῷ], ἄτε θηρευτῇ [ὄντι] Id.

ἄ-τεγκτος, ον, (τέγγω) *not to be wetted* : metaph. *not to be softened, relentless*, Soph., Eur.

ἀ-τειρής, ές, (τείρω) *not to be worn away, indestructible*, of iron, Hom. : metaph. *stubborn, unyielding*, Il.

ἀ-τείχιστος, ον, (τειχίζω) *unwalled, unfortified*, Thuc.   2. *not walled in, not blockaded*, Id.

ἀ-τέκμαρτος, ον, (τεκμαίρομαι) *not to be guessed, obscure, baffling*, Hdt., Thuc. :—Adv., ἀτεκμάρτως ἔχειν *to be in the dark about a thing*, Xen.   2. of persons, *uncertain, inconsistent*, Ar.

ἀτεκνία, ή, *childlessness*, Arist.   From

ἄ-τεκνος, ον, (τέκνον) *without children, childless*, Hes., Trag.   II. in causal sense, *destroying children*, Aesch.

ἀτεκνόω, f. ώσω, *to make childless* :—Pass. *to be deprived of children*, Anth.

ἀτέλεια, Ion. -ίη, ή, (ἀτελής) *exemption from public burdens* (τέλη), Lat. *immunitas*, granted to those who deserved well of the state, Att. ; c. gen., ἀτ. στρατηίης *exemption* from service, Hdt.

ἀ-τέλεστος, ον, (τελέω) *without end or issue, to no purpose, without effect, unaccomplished*, Hom.   II. *uninitiated* in mysteries, c. gen., Eur. ; absol., Plat.

ἀ-τελεύτητος, ον, (τελευτάω) *not brought to an end or issue, unaccomplished*, Il.   II. of a person, *impracticable*, Soph.

ἀ-τέλευτος, ον, (τελευτή) *endless, eternal*, Aesch.

ἀ-τελής, ές, (τέλος) *without end*, i. e.,   1. *not brought to an end or issue, unaccomplished*, Od., Xen. :—*incomplete*, Soph., Thuc., Plat.   2. act. *not bringing to an end, not accomplishing one's purpose*, Pind., Plat., etc.   II. (τέλος IV) at Athens, *free from tax or tribute, scot-free*, Lat. *immunis*, absol., or c. gen., ἀτ. τῶν ἄλλων *free from* all other taxes, Hdt., Att.   2. of sums, *without deduction, nett, clear*, ὀβολὸς ἀτ. an obol *clear gain*, Xen., Dem.   III. (τέλος V) *uninitiated* in mysteries, c. gen., h. Hom.

ἀτέμβω [ᾰ], only in pres. *to maltreat, to afflict, perplex*, Od. : Pass., c. gen., *to be bereft or cheated of* a thing, Hom. (Deriv. unknown.)

ἀ-τενής, ές, (α copul., τείνω) *strained tight, clinging*, of ivy, Soph. : metaph.   II. of men's minds and speech, *intent, earnest*, Hes., Plat. ; also *stiff, stubborn, inexorable*, Aesch., Ar. :—Adv. ἀτενῶς, *earnestly*, ἀτ. ἔχειν πρός τι Plut.

ἀτενίζω, f. ίσω, (ἀτενής) *to look intently, gaze earnestly*, εἴς τι Arist. ; τινί *upon one*, N. T.

"ΑΤΕΡ [ᾰ], Prep. with gen. *without*, Hom. ; ἄτερ Ζηνός *without his will*, Il.   II. *aloof or apart from*, Ib., Trag.

ἀ-τέραμνος, ον, (τέρην) *unsoftened* : metaph. *stubborn, unfeeling, merciless*, Od., Aesch.

ἀ-τεράμων [ᾰμ], ον, Att. for ἀτέραμνος Ar., Plat.

ἄτερθε, before a vowel -θεν, = ἄτερ, Trag. ; c. gen., Soph.

ἀ-τέρμων, ον, gen. ονος, (τέρμα) *without bounds*; ἀτ. πέπλος *having no end or issue, inextricable*, Aesch. ; ἀτέρμονες αὐγαί the *countless* rays of the mirror, Eur.

ἅτερος [ᾰ], Dor. for ἕτερος, Ar.   2. ἅτερος [ᾱ], Att.

crasis for ὁ ἕτερος, neut. θάτερον [ᾰ], gen. θατέρου, etc.

ἀ-τερπής, ές, (τέρπω) unpleasing, joyless, melancholy, Hom., Aesch.; ἀτερπέστερον εἰς ἀκρόασιν less attractive to the ear, Thuc.

ἄ-τερπος, ον, = ἀ-τερπής, Il. Hence

ἀ-τερψία, ἡ, unpleasantness, Luc.

ἀ-τευκτέω, f. ήσω, to fail in gaining a thing, c. gen., Babr. From

ἄ-τευκτος, ον, (τυγχάνω) not gaining.

ἀ-τευχής, ές, (τεῦχος) unequipped, unarmed, Eur., Anth.: so ἀ-τεύχητος, ον, Id.

ἀ-τεχνής, ές, = ἄτεχνος, Babr.

ἀτεχνία, ἡ, want of art or skill, unskilfulness, Plat. From

ἄ-τεχνος, ον, (τέχνη) without art, ignorant of the rules of art, unskilled, empirical, Plat.

ἀτέχνως, Adv. of ἄτεχνος, without rules of art, empirically, Xen., Plat. II. ἀτεχνῶς (with penult. short), Adv. of ἀτεχνής, simply, i. e. really, absolutely, Lat. plane, omnino, Ar., Plat., etc.; καλὸν ἀτ. simply beautiful, Ar.:—in comparisons, ἀτεχνῶς ὥσπερ just as, Plat.:—with negat., just not, Ar.; ἀτεχνῶς οὐδείς simply no one, Id.

ἀτέω [ᾰ], in part. ἀτέων, fool-hardy, reckless, Il., Hdt.

ἄτη [ᾰ], ἡ, (ἀάω, for ἀάτη) bewilderment, infatuation, reckless impulse, caused by judicial blindness sent by the gods, Hom.:—hence Ἄτη is personified as the goddess of mischief or reckless conduct, Ἄτη, ἡ πάντας ἀᾶται Il.: the Λιταί come slowly after her, undoing the evil she has worked, Ib. II. as a consequence, 1. reckless guilt or sin, as that of Paris, Ib. 2. bane, ruin, Hom., Trag.:—of persons, a bane, pest, Aesch., Soph.

ἄ-τηκτος, ον, not melted or to be melted, Plat.

ἀ-τημελής, ές, neglected, Plut. II. careless :— Adv., ἀτημελῶς ἔχειν Id.

ἀ-τημέλητος, ον, (τημελέω) unheeded, uncared for, Xen. 2. baffled, disappointed, Aesch. II. taking no heed, slovenly, Alciphro:—Adv., ἀτημελήτως ἔχειν to take no heed of a thing, c. gen., Xen.

ἀτηρός [ᾰ], ά, όν, blinded by ἄτη, hurried to ruin, Theogn. II. baneful, ruinous, mischievous, Aesch., Soph.: τὸ ἀτηρόν bane, ruin, Aesch.; ἀτηρότατον κακόν Ar.

Ἀτθίς, ίδος, ἡ, Attic :—as Subst. (sub. γῆ), Attica, Eur.

ἀ-τίετος, ον, (τίω) unhonoured, Aesch. II. act. not honouring or regarding, τινος Eur.

ἀ-τίζω, (τίω, v. a privat.) not to honour, to hold in no honour, θεούς Aesch.: absol. in part., ἀτίζων unheeding, Il.

ἀ-τιθάσευτος, ον, (τιθᾰσεύω) untamable, wild, Plut.

ἀτιμάγελέω, f. ήσω, to forsake the herd, Theocr. From

ἀτιμ-αγέλης, ου, ὁ, (ἀγέλη) despising the herd, i. e. straying, feeding alone, Theocr., Anth.

ἀτιμάζω, f. άσω: aor. 1 ἠτίμᾰσα: pf. ἠτίμᾰκα:—Pass., pf. ἠτίμᾰσμαι: aor. 1 ἠτιμάσθην: f. ἀτιμασθήσομαι: (ἄτιμος):—to hold in no honour, to esteem lightly, dishonour, slight, c. acc., Hom., Att.: so in Med., Soph.:—c. acc. cogn., ἔπη ἀτιμάζεις πόλιν thou speakest words in dishonour of the city, Id.:—Pass. to suffer dishonour, Hdt., Att. 2. c. gen. rei, ἀτ. λόγου to treat

as unworthy of speech, Aesch.; ἀτ. ὦν = ἀτ. τούτων ἅ, Soph.:—also, μή μ' ἀτιμάσῃς τὸ μὴ οὐ θανεῖν deem me not unworthy to die, Id.; οὐκ ἀτιμάσω προσειπεῖν will not disdain to . . , Eur. II. = ἀτιμόω in legal sense, to deprive of civil rights, Xen. Hence

ἀτιμαστέος, α, ον, verb. Adj. to be despised, Plat.; and ἀτιμαστήρ, ῆρος, ὁ, a dishonourer, Aesch.

ἀτιμάω, Ep. impf. ἀτίμων: f. ἀτιμήσω: aor. 1 ἠτίμησα: (ἄτιμος):—to dishonour, treat lightly, Hom.

ἀ-τίμητος, ον, (τιμάω) unhonoured, despised, Il. II. (τιμή II) not valued or estimated, δίκη ἀτ. a cause in which the penalty is not assessed in court, but fixed by law beforehand, Dem.

ἀτιμία, Ion. -ίη [-ῐη Ep.], ἡ, dishonour, disgrace, Od., Soph., etc.; ἐν ἀτιμίῃ τινὰ ἔχειν, ἀτιμίην προστιθέναι τινί Hdt.; ἀτ. τινός dishonour done to one, Eur. 2. at Athens, the loss of civil rights, Lat. deminutio capitis, Aesch., Oratt. II. ἐσθημάτων ἀτ., i. e. ragged garments, Aesch.

ἀτιμο-πενθής, ές, (πένθος) sorrowing for dishonour incurred, Aesch.

ἄ-τιμος, ον, (τιμή I) unhonoured, dishonoured, Il., Trag.; Comp. ἀ-τιμότερος less honourable, Xen.; so gen. without the honour of . . , not deemed worthy of . . , Aesch.; also, χάρις οὐκ ἄτιμος πόνων no unworthy return for . . , Id. 2. at Athens, deprived of privileges, Lat. capite deminutus, opp. to ἐπίτιμος, Ar., etc.; also c. gen., ἀτ. γερῶν deprived of privileges, Thuc.; ἀτ. τοῦ συμβουλεύειν deprived of the right of advising, Dem. II. (τιμή II) without price or value, οἶκον ἄτιμον ἔδεις thou devourest his substance without payment made, Od. 2. unrevenged, Aesch. III. Adv. -μως, dishonourably, ignominiously, Id., Soph.

ἀτιμόω, f. ώσω: aor. 1 ἠτίμωσα: pf. ἠτίμωκα:—Pass., pf. ἠτίμωμαι: aor. 1 ἠτιμώθην:—to dishonour, Aesch.:—Pass. to suffer dishonour or indignity, Hdt., Aesch., Eur. II. at Athens, to punish with ἀτιμία (2), Lat. aerarium facere, Ar., Oratt.

ἀ-τιμώρητος, ον, unavenged, i. e., I. unpunished, ἀτ. γίγνεσθαι to escape punishment, Hdt., Thuc. :— Adv. -τως, with impunity, Plat. II. for which no revenge has been taken, ἀτιμωρητον ἐᾶν θάνατον Aeschin. III. undefended, unprotected, Thuc.

ἀτίμωσις [ῐ], εως, ἡ, a dishonouring, dishonour done to, c. gen., τραπέζης, πατρός Aesch.

ἀτίσῃς [ῐ], 2 sing. aor. 1 subj. of ἀ-τίζω.

ἀτιτάλλω, redupl. form of ἀτάλλω, to rear up a child, foster, cherish, tend, Hom.; of horses, Pass., χην' ἀτιταλλομένην ἐνὶ οἴκῳ Od.

ἀ-τίτης [ῐ], ου, ὁ, (τίομαι) unpunished, Aesch. II. (τίω) unhonoured, Id.

ἄτῐτος, ον, (τίω) unhonoured, unavenged, Il. II. unpaid, Ib. [where ῐ].

ἀ-τίω [ῐ], = ἀ-τίζω, Theogn.

Ἀτλᾱ-γενής, ές, (γίγνομαι) sprung from Atlas, of the Pleiads, Hes.

Ἀτλαντικός, ή, όν, of Atlas, Atlantic, τέρμονες Ἀτλ. the pillars of Hercules, Eur.:—fem. Ἀτλαντίς, ίδος, θάλασσα ἡ Ἀ. καλουμένη Hdt.

Ἄτλας, αντος, ὁ: acc. also Ἄτλαν Aesch.: (a euphon., τλάς, v. *ταλαω):—Atlas, one of the elder gods, who

bore up the pillars of heaven, Od. :—later, one of the Titans, Hes., Aesch.   II. in hist. writers, *Mount Atlas* in Africa, regarded as *the pillar of heaven*, Hdt.

ἀτλητέω, f. *ήσω, to be unable to bear* a thing, *to be impatient*, Soph.   From

ἄ-τλητος, Dor. **ἄ-τλᾱτος**, ον, *not to be borne, insufferable*, Il., Orac. ap. Hdt., Soph.   2. *not to be dared*, ἄτλητα τλᾶσα Aesch.   II. act. *incapable of bearing* a thing, c. gen., Anth.

ἀτμενία, ἡ, (ἀτμήν) *slavery, servitude*, Anth.

ἀτμή, ἡ, = ἀτμός, Hes.

ἀτμήν, ένος, ὁ, *a slave, servant*. (Deriv. uncertain.)

ἄ-τμητος, ον, *not cut up, unravaged*, Thuc., Plut.: of mines, *not yet opened*, Xen.   II. *undivided, indivisible*, Plat.

ἀτμίζω, f. ίσω: pf. ἤτμικα: (ἀτμός):—*to smoke*, Soph.: of water, *to steam*, Xen.

ἀτμίς, ίδος, ἡ, = ἀτμός, Hdt.

ἀτμός, ὁ, (ἄω *to blow*) *steam, vapour*, Aesch.

ἄ-τοιχος, ον, *unwalled*, Eur.

ἄ-τοκος, ον, *having never yet brought forth, never having had a child*, Hdt., Eur.   II. *not bearing interest*, Plat.

ἀ-τόλμητος, Dor. -μᾱτος, ον, = ἄτλητος, *not to be endured, insufferable*, Pind.: of wicked men, Aesch.

ἀτολμία, ἡ, *want of daring, cowardice, backwardness*, Thuc., Dem.   From

ἄ-τολμος, ον, (τόλμα) *daring nothing, wanting courage, spiritless, cowardly*, Ar., Thuc.:—of women, *unenterprising, retiring*, Aesch.:—c. inf. *not having the heart to do* a thing, Id.

ἄ-τομος, ον, (τέμνω) *uncut, unmown*, Soph.   II. *that cannot be cut, indivisible*, Plat.; ἐν ἀτόμῳ *in a moment*, N. T.

ἀτονέω, f. ήσω, *to be relaxed, exhausted*, Plut.   From

ἄ-τονος, ον, (τείνω) *not stretched, relaxed*, Arist.

ἄ-τοξος, ον, (τόξον) *without bow or arrow*, Luc.

ἀτοπία, ἡ, *a being out of the way*, and so :   1. *extraordinary nature* of a thing, Plat.   2. *strangeness, oddness, eccentricity*, Ar., Plat.

ἄ-τοπος, ον, *out of place*, and so,   1. *strange, unwonted, extraordinary*, Eur., etc.   2. *strange, odd, eccentric*, δοῦλοι τῶν ἀεὶ ἀτόπων *slaves to every new paradox*, Thuc.; τῶν ἀτοπωτάτων ἂν εἴη Dem.   3. *unnatural, disgusting, foul*, πνεῦμα Thuc.   II. Adv. -πως, *marvellously* or *absurdly*, Id., Plat.

ἄτος, ον, contr. for ἄατος.

ἀ-τραγῴδητος, ον, (τραγῳδέω) *not treated tragically*, Luc.

ἄτρακτος, ὁ, *a spindle*, Hdt., Ar., etc.   II. *an arrow*, Soph.; cf. ἠλακάτη.   (Deriv. uncertain.)

ἀτρακτῠλίς or **ἀτρακτυλλίς**, ίδος, ἡ, *a thistle-like plant, used for making spindles*, Theocr. (Deriv. unknown.)

ἀτρᾰπῐτός and **ἀταρπιτός**, ἡ, = sq., Od.

ἀ-τραπός, Ep. **ἀ-ταρπός**, ἡ, (τρέπω) *properly a path with no turnings*, generally *a path-way, road*, Hom., Hdt., Thuc., etc.

ἀτράφαξυς, υος, ἡ, *the herb orach*. (Deriv. unknown.)

ἀ-τράχηλος, ον, *without neck*, Anth.

ἀτρέκεια, ἡ, Ion. gen. -είης, *reality, strict truth, certainty*, Hdt.   II. personified Ἀτρέκεια, *severity*, Pind.   From

ἀ-τρεκής, ές, *real, genuine*, Il.   2. *strict, precise*,

exact, ἀριθμός Hdt. :—τὸ ἀτρεκές = ἀτρέκεια, Id.; τὸ ἀτρεκέστερον *greater exactness*, Id.; τὸ ἀτρεκέστατον Id.   3. *sure, certain*, Eur.   II. used by Hom. mostly in Adv. ἀτρεκέως, with ἀγορεύειν, καταλέξαι, *to tell truly, exactly;* so also Hdt.   2. also neut. as Adv., δεκὰς ἀτρεκές *just ten of them*, Od.; so, τὸ ἀτρεκές Theogn. (Deriv. uncertain.)

ἀ-τρέμᾰ, used by Poets for ἀτρέμας *before a conson.*, Il.

ἀτρεμαῖος, α, ον, poët. for ἀτρεμής, Eur.

ἀ-τρέμᾰς, (τρέμω) Adv. *without trembling, without motion*, Hom.; ἀτρέμας εὕδειν Id.; ἀτρέμας ἧσο *sit still*, Il.; ἀτρέμας ἔχειν *to keep quiet*, Hdt.; ἀτρ. ἅπτεσθαί τινος *gently, softly*, Eur.; ἀτρ. πορεύεσθαι *to go softly*, Xen.

ἀτρεμεί or -ί, Adv. of ἀτρεμής, Ar.:

ἀτρεμέω, f. ήσω: aor. 1 ἠτρέμησα:—*not to tremble, to keep still* or *quiet*, Hes.; οὐδαμᾶ κω ἠτρεμήσαμεν, of a *restless* people, Hdt.   From

ἀ-τρεμής, ές, (τρέμω) *not trembling, unmoved*, Plat., Xen.   Adv. ἀτρεμέως Theogn.

ἀτρεμί, v. ἀτρεμεί.

ἀτρεμία, ἡ, (ἀτρεμής) *a keeping still*, ἀτρεμίαν ἔχειν or ἄγειν Xen.

ἀτρεμίζω, f. Att. -ἴῶ, Ion. inf. -ιέειν:—*to keep quiet*, Theogn., Hdt.; οὐκ ἀτρ. *to be restless*, Id.

ἄ-τρεπτος, ον, (τρέπω) *unmoved, immutable*, Plat., Luc.

ἄ-τρεστος, ον, (τρέω) *not trembling, unfearing, fearless*, Lat. *intrepidus*, Trag. : c. gen., ἀτρ. μάχας *fearless of fight*, Aesch.; so, ἀτρ. ἐν μάχαις Soph.; ἀτρ. εὕδειν *securely*, Id.:—also neut. pl. ἄτρεστα as Adv., Eur.

ἀ-τρίακτος, ον, (τριάζω) *unconquered*, Aesch.

ἀ-τρῐβής, ές, (τρίβω) *not rubbed*: of places, *not traversed, pathless*, Thuc.: of roads, *not worn* or *used*, Xen.: generally, *fresh, new*, Lat. *integer*, Id.

ἄτριον, τό, Dor. for ἤτριον.

ἄ-τριπτος, ον, (τρίβω) of hands, *not worn by work*, Od.; of corn, *not threshed*, Xen.; ἀτρ. ἄκανθαι *thorns on which one cannot tread*, or *untraversed* thorns, Theocr.

ἀ-τρόμητος, ον, (τρομέω) = sq., Anth.

ἄ-τρομος, ον, (τρέμω) *intrepid, dauntless*, Il.

ἀτροπία, ἡ, *inflexibility*, Theogn.   From

ἄ-τροπος, ον, (τρέπω) *unchangeable, eternal*, Theocr.   2. *inflexible, unbending*, Anth. :—hence Ἄτροπος, ἡ, *name of one of the* Μοῖραι *or Parcae*, Hes.; v. Κλωθώ.

ἀτροφέω, f. ήσω, *to pine away, suffer from atrophy*, Plut.   From

ἄ-τροφος, ον, (τρέφω) *not fed, ill-fed*, Xen.

ἄ-τρύγετος, η, ον, (τρυγάω) *yielding no harvest, unfruitful*, of the sea, Hom.; of the air, Id.

ἀ-τρύμων [ῠ], ον, = ἄτρυτος, c. gen., ἀτρ. κακῶν *not worn out by ills*, Aesch.

ἄ-τρῠτος, ον, (τρύω) *not worn away, untiring, unwearied*, Aesch. : *indefatigable*, Plut.   2. of things, *unabating*, Soph., Mosch.; of a road, *wearisome*, Theocr.

Ἀ-τρῠτώνη, ἡ, *the Unwearied*, a name of Pallas, Hom. (Lengthd. form of ἀτρύτη, as Ἀϊδωνεύς of Ἄιδης.)

ἄ-τρωτος, ον, *unwounded*, Aesch., Soph.   II *invulnerable*, Eur.

ἄττα, Att. for ἄσσα = τινά, *some*, Plat.

ἄττα, *a salutation used to elders, father*, Hom.

ἀττᾰγᾶς, ᾶ, ὁ, *a bird, prob. a kind of partridge;* **or, as**

others think, the *godwit* or *redshank*, Ar. (Deriv. unknown.)

ἀτταγήν, ῆνος, ὁ, a bird, prob. a kind of *grouse, attagen Ionicus*, Horat.

ἀττἄταῖ, *a cry of pain* or *grief*, Trag., Ar.

ἀττέλαβος, Ion. -εβος, ὁ, a kind of *locust without wings*, Hdt. (Deriv. unknown.)

Ἄττης Ἴτης, a form of exorcism, used by the priests of Cybelé, Dem.

Ἀττικίζω, f. Att. ιῶ, (Ἀττικός) *to side with the Athenians*, Thuc., Xen. Hence

Ἀττικισμός, ὁ, *a siding with Athens, attachment to her*, Thuc.

Ἀττικιστί, Adv., (Ἀττικός) *in the Attic dialect*, Dem.

Ἀττικίων, a comic Dim., *my little Athenian*, Ar. From

Ἀττικός, ή, όν, (ἀκτή) *Attic, Athenian*, Solon, etc.; ἡ Ἀττική (sc. γῆ), *Attica*, Hdt., etc.; cf. Ἀτθίς. II. Adv. -κῶς *in Attic style*, Dem.

Ἀττικωνικός, ή, όν, a comic alteration of Ἀττικός, after the form of Λακωνικός, Ar.

ἄττω, Att. for ᾄσσω, ἀΐσσω.

ἀτύζομαι, in pres., and in aor. 2 part. ἀτυχθείς: Pass.: —*to be distraught from fear, mazed, bewildered*, Hom.; ἀτυζόμενοι πεδίοιο *fleeing bewildered* o'er the plain, Il.: also *to be distraught with grief*, ἀτυζόμενος Soph., Eur.: c. acc., ὄψιν ἀτυχθείς *amazed at the sight*, Il. II. in late Ep. we find the Act. ἀτύζω, with 1 sing. aor. 1 opt. ἀτύξαι, *to strike with terror*, Theocr.

ἀ-τύμβευτος, ον, (τυμβεύω) *without burial*, Anth.

ἄ-τυμβος, ον, *without a tomb*, Luc.

ἀ-τυράννευτος, ον, (τυραννεύω) *not ruled by tyrants*, Thuc.

ἄ-τῡφος, ον, *without pride* or *arrogance, modest*, Plat.

ἀτυχέω, f. ήσω: aor. 1 ἠτύχησα: pf. ἠτύχηκα: (ἀτυχής):—*to be unlucky* or *unfortunate, fail, miscarry*, Hdt., Thuc., etc. 2. c. gen., *to fail of* a thing, *fail in getting* or *gaining* it, τῆς ἀληθείας Xen.; so, c. part., Thuc. 3. ἀτ. πρός τινα *to fail with* another, i. e. to fail in one's request, Xen.:—Pass., τὰ ἀτυχηθέντα *mischances, failures*, Dem. Hence

ἀτύχημα, ατος, τό, *a misfortune, mishap*, Oratt.

ἀ-τυχής, ές, (τυγχάνω) *luckless, unfortunate*, Dem., etc.

ἀτυχία, ἡ, *ill-luck*:—*a misfortune, miscarriage, mishap*, Xen.

ἀτῶμαι, v. ἀτάω.

ΑΥ', Adv., *again, anew, afresh, once more*, Hom., etc.; after numerals, δεύτερον αὖ, τρίτον αὖ, etc., Id. II. generally, *again*, i. e. *further, moreover, besides*, Lat. *porro*, Od., Att. 2. *in turn, on the other hand*, following δέ, Il., Att. III. the pleon. phrases, πάλιν αὖ, αὖ πάλιν, ἔμπαλιν αὖ, αὖθις αὖ, αὖθις αὖ πάλιν, are only Att., mostly Trag.

αὖ, αὖ, *bow wow*, of a dog, Ar.

αὐαίνω, Att. αὖ-: f. αὐανῶ: aor. 1 ηὔηνα or αὖ-:— Pass., aor. 1 ηὐάνθην or αὖ-: f. med. αὐανοῦμαι in pass. sense: (αὔω *to dry*):—*to dry*, Od., Hdt., Xen. 2. *to dry* or *parch up*, αὐανῶ βίον *I shall waste* life *away*, Soph.: Pass., αὐανθείς *withered*, Aesch.; so in f. med., αὐανοῦμαι *I shall wither away*, Soph.

αὐ-αλέος, α, ον, (αὖος) *dry, parched*, Hes.; of eyes, *dry, sleepless*, Anth.

αὐάτα, i. e. ἀϝάτα, Aeol. for ἄτη, Pind.

αὐγάζω, f. άσω, aor. 1 ηὔγασα: (αὐγή):—*to view in the clearest light, see distinctly, discern*, Soph.; so in Med., Il., Hes. II. of the sun, *to beam upon, illumine*, τινά Eur.

ΑΥΓΗ', ἡ, *the light of the sun, sunlight*, and in pl. *his rays* or *beams*, Hom.; ὑπ' αὐγὰς ἠελίοιο, i. e. *still alive*, Od.; so, αὐγὰς ἐσιδεῖν, λεύσσειν, βλέπειν Theogn., Aesch., Eur.; but, ὑπ' αὐγὰς λεύσσειν or ἰδεῖν τι to hold up to *the light* and look at, Id.; κλύζειν πρὸς αὐγάς to rise surging towards *the sun*, Aesch.:—metaph., βίου δύντος αὐγαί 'life's setting sun,' Id.:—αὐγή *the dawn, day-break*, N. T. 2. generally, *any bright light*, as of fire, Hom.; of lightning, Il.; of the eyes, Soph.; hence αὐγαί, like Lat. *lumina*, *the eyes*, Eur. 3. *any gleam* on the surface of bright objects, *sheen*, αὐγὴ χαλκείη Il.; αὐγὰ πέπλου Eur.

αὐδάζομαι, f. -άξομαι, Dep. (αὐδή) *to cry out, speak*, Hdt.: an aor. 1 act. αὔδαξα occurs in Anth.

αὐδάω, impf. ηὔδων: f. αὐδήσω, Dor. άσω [ᾱ], Dor. 3 pl. αὐδασοῦντι: aor. 1 ηὔδησα, Dor. αὔδασα, Ion. 3 sing. αὐδήσασκε:—also as Dep. αὐδάομαι: impf. ηὐδᾶτο: f. ήσομαι: aor. 1 αὐδάθην (pass. only): (αὐδή): I. c. acc. rei, 1. *to utter sounds, speak*, Il., Eur. 2. c. acc. rei, *to speak* or *say something*, Il., Soph.: so as Dep., Id.:—Pass., ηὐδᾶτο γὰρ ταῦτα so 'twas said, Id. 3. of oracles, *to utter, proclaim, tell of*, Id.; *to speak out concerning* a thing, Aesch. II. c. acc. pers., 1. *to speak to, address, accost*, Hom.; *to invoke* a god, Eur. 2. c. acc. et inf. *to tell, bid, order* one to do, Soph.; αὐδ. τινα μὴ ποιεῖν *to forbid* one to do, Aesch.; αὐδῶ σιωπᾶν Soph.: so as Dep., Id. 3. *to call by name, call* so and so, Eur.:—Pass., αὐδῶμαι παῖς Ἀχιλλέως Soph.; κάκιστ' αὐδώμενος most ill reported of, Aesch. 4. like λέγειν, *to mean* such an one, Eur.

ΑΥΔΗ', Dor. αὐδά, ἡ, *the human voice, speech*, opp. to ὀμφή (a divine voice), Il. 2. *the sound* or *twang* of the bowstring, Od.; of a trumpet, Eur.; of the τέττιξ, Hes. = φήμη, *a report, account*, Soph., Eur. 2. *an oracle*, Id. Hence

αὐδήεις, εσσα, εν, *speaking with human voice*, Od.; when θεὸς αὐδήεσσα is applied to Calypso and Circé, it means a goddess *who used the speech of mortals*, Hom.

αὖ-ερύω, Ep. aor. 1 αὐέρυσα, *to draw back* or *backwards*, Il.; *to draw* the bow, Ib.: absol., in a sacrifice, *to draw* the victim's head *back*, so as to cut its throat, Ib. (It can hardly be a compd. of αὖ ἐρύω, for αὖ is never elsewh. used in the local sense of *back*: perh. for ἀν-ερύω, i. e. ἀν-ϝερύω.)

αὐθάδεια, poët. -ία, ἡ, *self-will, wilfulness, stubbornness, contumacy, presumption*, Aesch., etc. From

αὐθ-άδης [ᾰ], ες, (ἥδομαι) *self-willed, wilful, dogged, stubborn, contumacious, presumptuous*, Hdt., etc.:— metaph. of things, *remorseless, unfeeling*, Aesch.:— Adv. -δως, Ar.; Comp. -έστερος, Plat. Hence

αὐθαδίζομαι, Dep. *to be self-willed*, Plat. Hence

αὐθάδισμα [ᾰ], ατος, τό, *an act of self-will, wilfulness*, Aesch.

αὐθαδό-στομος, ον, (στόμα) *self-willed in speech*, Ar.

αὐθ-αίμων, ον, gen. ονος, (αἷμα) *of the same blood, a brother, sister, kinsman*, Soph.; so, **αὔθαιμος**, ον, Id.

αὐθ-αίρετος, ον, *self-chosen, self-elected*, Xen. II. *by free choice, of oneself*, Eur.: *independent*, Thuc. III. *of things taken upon oneself, self-incurred, voluntary*, Soph., Thuc., etc.

αὐθ-έκαστος, ον, *one who calls each thing by its name*, Arist.

αὐθεντέω, f. ήσω, *to have full power over*, τινός N. T.

αὐθ-έντης, ου, ὁ, contr. for **αὐτοέντης**, *one who does anything with his own hand, an actual murderer*, Hdt., Eur., etc.:—more loosely, *one of a murderer's family*, Id. 2. *an absolute master, autocrat*, Id. II. as Adj., **αὐθέντης φόνος**, **αὐθένται θάνατοι** *murder by one of the same family*, Aesch. (The part -έντης is of uncertain deriv.)

αὐθ-ήμερος, ον, (ἡμέρα) *made* or *done on the very day*, Aeschin. II. Adv. **αὐθημερόν** (oxyt.), *on the very day, on the same day, immediately*, Aesch., etc.; Ion. **αὐτημερόν**, Hdt.

αὖθι, Adv. shortened for **αὐτόθι**, of Place, *on the spot, here, there*, Hom.; **αὖθι ἔχειν** *to keep him there, as he is*, Od. 2. of Time, *forthwith, straightway*, Il.

αὐθι-γενής, Ion. **αὐτιγ-**, ές, (γίγνομαι) *born on the spot, born in the country, native*, Lat. *indigena*, Hdt.; **αὐτ. ποταμοί** *rivers that rise in the country*, Id.; **ὕδωρ αὐτ.** *a natural spring*, Id.:—*genuine, sincere*, Eur.

αὖθις, Ion. **αὖτις**, Adv., a lengthd. form of αὖ: I. of Place, *back, back again*, Il.; **ἂψ αὖτις** Ib.; this sense rare in Att. II. of Time, *again, afresh, anew*, Hom., Att.; strengthd., **ὕστερον αὖτις, ἔτ᾽ αὖτις, πάλιν αὖτις** Il., etc.; **βοᾶν αὖθις** *to cry encore!* Xen. 2. of future Time, *again, hereafter*, Il., Aesch. III. of Sequence, *moreover, in turn, on the other hand*, Id., Soph.

αὐθ-όμαιμος, strengthd. for ὅμαιμος, Soph.

ἀ-υΐαχος, ον, (i. e. ἀ-ϝίαχος), epith. of the Trojans in Il., either, 1. (ἀ copul., ἰαχή) *loud-shouting, noisy*, or, 2. (from ἀ privat.) *noiseless, silent*.

αὐλάκ-εργάτης [ᾰ], ου, ὁ, *tracing furrows*, Anth.

αὖλαξ, ἄκος, ἡ, also **ἄλοξ**, οκος with Ep. acc. ὦλκα, **ὦλκας**:—*a furrow* made in ploughing, Lat. *sulcus*, Hom., etc.; **αὔλακ᾽ ἐλαύνειν** *to draw a furrow*, Hes. 2. metaph. of *a wife as the bearer of children*, Soph., Eur. 3. metaph. also, *a furrow in the skin, a gash, wound*, Aesch., Eur. 4. =ὄγμος, *a swathe*, Theocr. (Prob. from same Root as ὁλκός, Lat. *sulcus*, from ἕλκω.)

αὔλειος, α, ον and ος, ον, *of* or *belonging to the αὐλή* or *court*, **ἐπ᾽ αὐλείησι θύρησι** *at the door of the court*, i.e. the *outer door, house-door*, Od.; so in Hdt. and Att.

αὐλέω, f. ήσω, (αὐλός) *to play on the flute*, Hdt., Plat., etc.; **αὐλ. ἔξοδον** *to play a finale*, Ar. II. Pass., of tunes, *to be played on the flute*, Xen.; but, **αὐλεῖται μέλαθρον** *is filled with music*, Eur. 2. in Pass. also of persons, *to be played to, hear music*, Xen.

αὐλή, ἡ, (prob. from ἄημι ᾱ ἄϝημι) *to blow*, for the αὐλή was open to the air):—in Hom. *the court-yard*, surrounded with out-buildings, and having the altar of Ζεὺς Ἑρκεῖος in the middle, so that it was at once the meeting-place of the family, and the cattle-yard, Il.: it had two doors,

viz. the house-door (cf. αὔλειος), and another leading through the αἴθουσα into the πρόδομος, Od. 2. *the wall of the court-yard*, Il. II. after Hom., the **αὐλή** was *the court* or *quadrangle*, round which the house itself was built, having a corridor (περιστύλιον), from which were doors leading into the men's apartments; opposite the house-door (cf. αὔλειος) was the μέσαυλος or μέταυλος (q.v.), leading into the women's part of the house, Hdt., Att. III. generally, *any court* or *hall*, Hom., Trag.

αὔλημα, ατος, τό, (αὐλέω) *a piece of music for the flute*, Ar., Plat.

αὔλησις, εως, ἡ, (αὐλέω) *flute-playing*, Plat.

αὐλητήρ, ῆρος, ὁ, = αὐλητής, Hes., etc.

αὐλητής, οῦ, ὁ, (αὐλέω) *a flute-player*, Lat. *tibicen*, Theogn., Hdt., etc. Hence

αὐλητικός, ή, όν, (αὐλέω) *of* or *for the flute*, Plat.; ἡ -κή (sc. τέχνη) *flute-playing*, Id.

αὐλητρίς, ίδος, ἡ, (αὐλέω) *a flute-girl*, Lat. *tibicina*, Ar., Xen., etc.

Αὐλιάδες Νύμφαι, (αὐλή) Nymphs *protecting cattle-folds*, Anth.

αὐλίδιον, τό, Dim. of αὐλή, Theophr.

αὐλίζομαι: aor. 1 med. ηὐλισάμην, pass. ηὐλίσθην: (αὐλή):—*to lie in the court-yard*, of cattle, Od.; *to pass the night, lodge*, Eur.; of soldiers, *to bivouac*, Hdt.

αὔλιον, τό, (αὐλή) *a country house, cottage*, h. Hom.: *a fold, stable*, Eur., Xen. II. *a chamber, cave, grotto*, Soph.

αὔλιος, α, ον, (αὐλή) *of* or *for farm-yards, rustic*, Eur.

αὖλις, ιδος, ἡ, (αὐλή) *a place for passing the night in, a tent, roosting-place*, Hom., Eur.

αὐλίσκος, ὁ, Dim. of αὐλός, *a small reed, pipe*, Theogn.

αὐλιστρίς, ίδος, ἡ, (αὐλίζομαι) *a house-mate*, Theocr.

αὐλο-δόκη, ἡ, (δέχομαι) *a flute-case*, Anth.

αὐλο-θετέω, (τίθημι) *to make flutes* or *pipes*, Anth.

αὐλοποιϊκή, (sc. τέχνη), ἡ, *flute-making*, Plat. From

αὐλο-ποιός, ὁ, (ποιέω) *a flute-maker*, Plat.

αὐλός, ὁ, (ἄημι *to blow*) *a flute* or rather *clarionet* (for it was played by a mouthpiece, γλωσσίς, Aeschin.), Il., etc.; **αὐλοὶ ἀνδρήϊοι** and **γυναικήϊοι**, Lat. *tibiae dextrae* and *sinistrae, bass* and *treble*, Hdt.; sometimes one person played two αὐλοί at once, Theocr.; **αὐλὸς Ἐνυαλίου**, i. e. *a trumpet*, Anth.:—**ὑπ᾽ αὐλοῦ** *to the sound of the flute*, Hdt.; so, **πρὸς αὐλόν, ὑπὸ τὸν αὐλόν** Xen. 2. *any tube* or *pipe*, as *the socket* of a spear-head, *the groove* into which the tongue of a buckle fitted, Hom.; *the pipe* of bellows, Thuc.:—**αὐλὸς παχύς**, in Od., seems to mean *a jet of blood through the tube* of the nostril.

αὐλών, ῶνος, ὁ, poët. also ἡ, (αὐλός) *a hollow way, defile, glen*, h. Hom., Hdt., Ar. 2. *a canal, aqueduct, trench*, Hdt. 3. *a channel, strait*, Aesch.; **αὐλῶνες πόντιοι** *the sea straits*, i. e. the Archipelago, Soph.

αὐλ-ῶπις, ιδος, ἡ, (ὤψ) *of a helmet, with a tube in front*, to hold the λόφος, Il.

ΑΥΞΑ'ΝΩ and **ΑΥ'ΞΩ**, (poët. ἀέξω, q.v.): f. αὐξήσω: aor. 1 ηὔξησα: pf. ηὔξηκα:—Pass., pf. ηὔξημαι: aor. 1 ηὐξήθην: f. αὐξηθήσομαι and in med. form αὐξήσομαι :—*to make large, increase, augment*, Hdt., etc. (Hom. only uses ἀέξω). 2. *to increase in power, strengthen, exalt*,

aggrandise, Hdt., Att. : also *to promote to honour, glorify, magnify*, Trag., Plat.　II. Pass. *to grow, wax, increase*, Hes., Hdt., etc. ; αὐξ. ἐς πλῆθος, ἐς ὕψος Id. ; of a child, *to grow up*, Id. ; ηὐξανόμην I *grew taller*, Ar.; so with an Adj., αὐξάνεσθαι μέγας *to wax great*, Eur.　Hence

αὔξη, ἡ, = αὔξησις, Plat.

Αὐξησία, ἡ, (αὔξω) *the Goddess of growth*, Hdt.

αὔξησις, εως, ἡ, *growth, increase*, Thuc.; of crops, Hdt.

αὔξιμος, ον, (αὔξω) *promoting growth*, Xen.

αὐξο-σέληνον, τό, (σελήνη) *the waxing moon*, Anth.

αὔξω, *to increase*, v. αὐξάνω.

αὐονή, ἡ, (αὖος) *dryness, withering*, Aesch.

αὖος, η, ον, Att. αὗος, a, ον, (αὔω) *dry*, of timber, Od.: *dried*, of fruit, Hdt.: *withered*, of leaves, Ar.:—neut. as Adv., αὖον αὐεῖν or αὔειν *to ring dry and harsh*, of metal, Il.　2. *dried up, exhausted*, Theocr.

ἀϋπνία, ἡ, *sleeplessness*, Plat.　From

ἄ-ϋπνος, ον, [ῠ], *sleepless, wakeful*, of persons, Od., Att. : metaph. *sleepless, never-resting*, πηδάλια Aesch.; κρῆναι Soph.　2. of *sleepless* nights, Hom.　3. ὕπνος ἄϋπνος a sleep *that is no sleep, from which one easily awakes*, Soph.

αὔρα, Ion. αὔρη, ἡ, (ἄημι) *air in motion, a breeze*, esp. *a cool breeze, the fresh air* of morning, Lat. *aura*, Od., Hdt., Att. Poets ; rare in Prose :—metaph. *steam*, Ar.　2. metaph. also, of *changeful events*, Eur., Ar.; of anything *thrilling*, Eur.

αὔριον, Adv., (akin to ἠώς) *to-morrow*, Lat. *cras*, Hom., etc.; ἐς αὔριον *on the morrow* or *till morning*, Id.　II. as Subst., *the morrow*, Il. ; in Att., ἡ αὔριον (sc. ἡμέρα) *the morrow*, Eur. ; ἡ αὔρ. ἡμέρα Xen. ; ἡ αὔρ. ἡμέρα Soph. ; ὁ αὔριον χρόνος Eur.

ἀῦσαι, aor. 1 inf. of αὔω, *to shout*.

αὔσιος, v. τηΰσιος.

αὐσταλέος, a, ον, Ep. αὐσταλέος, (αὔω *to dry*) *sunburnt, squalid*, Lat. *siccus*, Od., Hes.

αὐστηρός, ά, όν, (αὔω *to dry*) *making the tongue dry and rough, harsh, rough, bitter*, Plat. :—metaph. *austere, harsh*, Id., N. T.　Hence

αὐστηρότης, ητος, ἡ, *harshness, roughness*, οἴνου Xen.: metaph. *austerity, harshness*, Plat.

αὐτ-άγγελος, ὁ, *carrying one's own message, bringing news of what oneself has seen*, Soph., Thuc. ; c. gen. rei, λόγων αὐτ. Soph.

αὐτ-άγρετος, ον, (ἀγρέω) *self-chosen, left to one's choice*, Od., h. Hom.

αὐτ-άδελφος, ὁ, *related as brother* or *sister*, Aesch., Soph.　II. as Subst. *one's own brother* or *sister*, Id.

αὔτ-ανδρος, ον, (ἀνήρ) *together with the men, men and all*, Polyb.

αὐτ-ανέψιος, ὁ, *an own cousin, cousin-german*, Aesch., Eur.

αὐτάρ, Ep. form of ἀτάρ, Hom.

αὐτάρκεια, ἡ, *sufficiency in oneself, independence*, Plat.　From

αὐτ-άρκης, ες, (ἀρκέω) *sufficient in oneself, having enough, independent* of others, Hdt., Plat. ; νηδὺς αὐταρκής *acting of itself*, Aesch. ; χώρα αὐτ. *a country that supplies itself, independent of imports*, Thuc. ; αὐτ. πρός τι *strong enough* for a thing, Id., Xen. ;

c. inf. *able of oneself to do* a thing, Dem. ; αὐτ. βοή a *sufficient, vigorous* shout, Soph.

αὖτε, Adv. (αὖ, τε,—where τε is otiose, as in ὅστε) :　I. of Time, *again*, Il.　II. *to mark Sequence, again, furthermore, next*, Ib., Soph.　2. *on the other hand, on the contrary*, following μέν like δέ, Hom., Att. Poets.

αὐτ-εξούσιος, ον, (ἐξουσία) *in one's own power; τὸ αὐτεξούσιον free power*, Babr.

αὐτ-επάγγελτος, ον, (ἐπαγγέλλω) *offering of oneself, of free will*, Hdt., Eur., Thuc., etc.

αὐτ-επώνυμος, ον, *of the same surname with*, τινος Eur.

αὐτ-ερέτης, ου, ὁ, *one who rows himself*, i.ε. *rower and soldier at once*, Thuc.

ἀῦτέω [ῠ], only in pres. and impf. : (αὔω *to cry*) :—*to cry, shout*, Il., Aesch. :—c. acc. cogn., βοὰν ἀῦτῶ Eur.; ἀῦτεῖ δ' ὀξύ Aesch.　2. c. acc. pers. *to call to*, Il., Eur. :—c. acc. pers. et inf., Eur.　From

ἀϋτή [ῠ], ἡ, (αὔω *to cry*) *a cry, shout*, esp. *battle-shout, war-cry*, Hom. : generally *a sound*, Aesch.

αὐτ-ήκοος, ον, (ἀκούω) *one who has himself heard, an ear-witness*, Thuc., Plat.

αὐτ-ῆμαρ, Adv., = αὐθημερόν, *on the self-same day*, Il.

αὐτ-ημερόν, Ion. for αὐθ-ημερόν.

αὐτι-γενής, ές, Ion. for αὐθι-γενής.

αὐτίκα [ῐ], Adv. (αὐτός) *forthwith, straightway, at once*, Hom., etc.; which notion is strengthened in αὐτίκα νῦν, μάλ' αὐτίκα Od. ; c. partic., αὐτίκ' ἰόντι *immediately* on his going, Ib.; so, αὐτίκα γενόμενος *as soon as born*, Hdt. ; αὐτίκα καὶ μετέπειτα *now* and hereafter, Od. ; so, τὸ αὐτίκα and τὸ μέλλον, Thuc. :—with a Subst., τὴν αὐτίχ' ἡμέραν Soph. ; ὁ αὐτίκα φόβος *momentary fear*, Thuc.　2. also in a slightly *future* sense, *presently*, Lat. *mox*, Soph., etc.　II. *for example, to begin with*, Ar., Plat., etc. ; αὐτίκα δὴ μάλα Dem.

ἀϋτμή, ἡ, (ἄημι) *breath*, Il.; ἀϋτμὴ Ἡφαίστοιο *the fiery breath* of Hephaestus, Ib.; πυρὸς ἀϋτμή Od. ; of bellows, Il. ; of wind, Od.　2. *odour, scent, fragrance*, Hom.

ἀϋτμήν, ένος, ὁ, = ἀϋτμή, Hom.

αὐτο-άνθρωπος, ὁ, *the ideal man, the Form of man*, Arist.

αὐτο-βοεί, (βοή) Adv. *by a mere shout, at the first shout*, Thuc., αὐτ. ἑλεῖν *to take without a blow*, Thuc.

αὐτό-βουλος, ον, *self-willing, self-purposing*, Aesch.

αὐτο-γέννητος, ον, *self-produced*: αὐτογέννητα κοιμήματα μητρός *a mother's intercourse with her own child*, Soph.

αὐτογνωμονέω, f. ήσω, *to act of one's own judgment*, Xen.　From

αὐτο-γνώμων, ον, gen. ονος, *on one's own judgment, at one's own discretion*, Arist. : Adv. -όνως, Plut.

αὐτό-γνωτος, ον, (γνῶναι) *self-determined, self-willed*, Soph.

αὐτό-γυος, ον, (γύης) *of a plough, having the share-beam of one piece with the pole*, Hes.

αὐτο-δαής, ές, (*δάω) *self-taught, unpremeditated*, Soph.

αὐτο-δάϊκτος, ον, (δαΐζω) *self-slain* or *mutually slain*, Aesch.

αὐτ-οδάξ, Adv. *with the very teeth*, ὁ αὐτοδὰξ τρόπος *your ferocious temper*, Ar.

αὐτό-δεκα, *just ten*, Thuc.
αὐτό-δηλος, ον, *self-evident*, Aesch.
αὐτό-δἰδακτος, ον, *self-taught*, Od., Aesch.
αὐτό-δῐκος, ον, (δίκη) *with independent jurisdiction, with one's own law-courts*, Thuc.
αὐτόδιον, Adv. *straightway*, Od. (It seems to be lengthd. from αὐτός, as μαψίδιος from μάψ, μινυνθάδιος from μίνυνθα.)
αὐτο-έκαστος, ον, = αὐθέκαστος : τὸ αὐτ. *the ideal or form of each object*, Arist.
αὐτο-έντης, ου, ὁ, = αὐθέντης, *a murderer*, Soph.
αὐτο-ετεί, Adv. *in the same year*, Theocr. From
αὐτο-ετής, ές, (ἔτος) *in or of the same year* : Adv. αὐτόετες, *in the same year, within the year*, Od.
Αὐτο-θαΐς, ή, *Thaïs herself*, Luc.
αὐτόθε, v. αὐτόθεν.
αὐτοθελεί, Adv. *voluntarily*, Anth. From
αὐτο-θελής, ές, (θέλω) *of one's own will*, Anth.
αὐτόθεν, before a conson. -θε, Adv. : (αὐτοῦ) :—of Place, *from the very spot*, Lat. *illinc*, Hom., Att. ; αὐτ. ἐξ ἕδρης *straight* from his seat, without rising, Il. ; αὐτ. ἐκ Σαλαμῖνος Hdt., etc.; αὐτόθεν *from where thou standest*, Soph. : αὐτ. βιοτεύειν *to find a living from the place*, Thuc. :—οἱ αὐτ. *the natives*, Id.   II. of Time, *on the spot, at once*, Lat. *illico*, Il., Hdt., Att.
αὐτόθῐ, Adv. for αὐτοῦ, *on the spot*, Il., Hdt., Att.
αὐτο-κάβδᾰλος, ον, *wrought or done carelessly, slovenly, random*, Arist. :—Adv. -λως, Id. (Deriv. unknown.)
αὐτο-κᾰσιγνήτη, ή, *an own sister*, Od., Eur.
αὐτο-κᾰσίγνητος, ὁ, *an own brother*, Il., etc.
αὐτο-κατάκρῐτος, ον, (κατακρίνω) *self-condemned*, N. T.
αὐτο-κέλευθος, ον, *going one's own road*, Anth.
αὐτο-κέλευστος, ον, *self-bidden*, i.e. *unbidden, of one's own accord*, Xen., Anth.
αὐτο-κελής, ές, (κέλομαι) = foreg., Hdt.
αὐτό-κλᾰδος, ον, *branches and all*, Luc.
αὐτό-κλητος, ον, *self-called*, i. e. *uncalled, unbidden*, Aesch., Soph.
αὐτό-κομος, ον, (κόμη) *with natural hair, shaggy*, Ar.   II. *hair or leaves and all*, Luc.
αὐτο-κρᾰτής, ές, (κρατέω) *ruling by oneself, absolute, autocratic*, Eur., Plat.
αὐτοκρᾰτορικός, ή, όν, *of or for an autocrat* : Adv. -κῶς, *despotically*, Plut. From
αὐτο-κράτωρ, ορος, ὁ, ή, (κρᾰτέω) *one's own master* : 1. of persons or states, *free and independent*, Lat. *sui juris*, Thuc., Xen.   2. of ambassadors, *possessing full powers, plenipotentiary*, Ar., Thuc., etc.   3. of rulers, *absolute, arbitrary, despotic*, Id., etc.   4. of reasoning, *peremptory*, Id.   II. c. gen. *complete master of*, ἑαυτοῦ Id.; τῆς ἐπιορκίας αὐτ. *at liberty to swear falsely*, Dem.
αὐτό-κτῐτος, ον, (κτίζω) *self-produced*, i. e. *natural*, ἄντρα Aesch.
αὐτοκτονέω, f. ήσω, *to slay one another*, Soph. From
αὐτο-κτόνος, ον, (κτείνω) *self-slaying*; Adv. -νως, *with one's own hand*, Aesch. :—so χεὶρ αὐτ., of Medea, *who slew her own children*, Eur.   2. *slaying one another*, Aesch.; θάνατος αὐτ. *death by each other's hand*, Id.
αὐτο-κῠβερνήτης, ου, ὁ, *one who steers himself*, Anth.

αὐτό-κωπος, ον, (κώπη) *together with the hilt, up to the hilt*, Aesch.
αὐτο-λήκῠθος, ὁ, *one who carries his own oil-flask, a shabby fellow*, Dem.
αὐτο-μᾰθής, ές, (μαθεῖν) *having learnt of oneself, self-taught*, Anth.
αὐτο-μάρτυς, ῠρος, ὁ, ή, *oneself the witness, an eye-witness*, Aesch.
αὐτοματίζω, f. ίσω, *to act of oneself, act unadvisedly*, Xen. From
αὐτόμᾰτος, η, ον, and ος, ον :   1. of persons, *acting of one's own will, of oneself*, Il., etc.   2. of things, *self-moving, self-acting, spontaneous*, of the gates of Olympus, the tripods of Hephaestus, Il. :—of plants, *growing of themselves*, Hdt.   3. *without apparent cause, accidental*, Id. ; αὐτ. θάνατος *a natural death*, Dem.   II. αὐτόματον, τό, *mere chance*, ἀπὸ τοῦ αὐτομάτου or ἀπὸ ταὐτομάτου, Lat. *sponte, by chance, naturally*, Hdt., Thuc.   III. Adv. -τως = ἀπὸ ταὐτομάτου, Hdt.
Αὐτο-μέδων, οντος, ὁ, *Self-ruler*, name of Achilles' charioteer, Il.
Αὐτο-μέλιννα, ή, *Melinna herself*, Anth.
αὐτομολέω, f. ήσω, *to desert*, Hdt., Att.; αὐτ. πρὸς τοὺς Πέρσας Hdt. ; ἐς Ἀθήνας ἐκ Περσέων Id. ; and
αὐτομολία, ή, *desertion*, Thuc. From
αὐτό-μολος, ον, (μολεῖν) *going of oneself, without bidding* : as Subst. *a deserter*, Hdt., Att.
αὐτονομέομαι, f. ήσομαι, Dep. *to live by one's own laws, be independent*, Thuc., Dem.; and
αὐτονομία, ή, *freedom to use one's own laws, independence*, Thuc., etc.
αὐτό-νομος, ον, (νέμομαι) *living under one's own laws, independent*, Hdt., Att.   2. generally, *of one's own free will*, Soph.   3. of animals, *feeding and ranging at will*, Anth.
αὐτό-νοος, ον, contr. -νους, ουν, *self-willed*, Aesch.
αὐτο-νῠχί [ῐ], Adv. (νύξ) *that very night*, Il.
αὐτό-ξῠλος, ον, (ξύλον) *of mere wood*, Soph.
αὐτο-πᾰγής, ές, (πήγνυμι) *self-joined, self-built*, Anth.
αὐτοπάθεια, ή, *one's own feeling or experience*, Polyb. From
αὐτο-πᾰθής, ές, *speaking from one's own feeling or experience* :—Adv. -θως, Polyb.
αὐτό-παις, παιδος, ὁ, ή, *an own child*, Soph.
αὐτο-πήμων, ον, (πῆμα) *for one's own woes*, Aesch.
αὐτό-ποιος, ον, (ποιέω) *self-produced*, as the Athenian olive, Soph.
αὐτό-πολις, ή, *free as a state, independent*, Thuc.
αὐτο-πολίτης, ου, ὁ, *citizen of a free state*, Xen.
αὐτο-πόνητος, ον, (πονέω) *self-wrought*, Anth.
αὐτό-πους, ὁ, ή, -πουν, τό, *on one's own feet*, Luc.
αὐτό-πρεμνος, ον, (πρέμνον) *together with the root, root and branch*, Soph., Ar. ; αὐτ. τι διδόναι *to give in absolute possession*, Aesch.
αὐτο-πρόσωπος, ον, (πρόσωπον) *in one's own person, without a mask*, Luc.
αὐτ-όπτης, ου, ὁ, (ὄψομαι, f. of ὁράω) *seeing oneself, an eyewitness*, Hdt.
αὐτο-πώλης, ου, ὁ, (πωλέω) *selling one's own goods or products*, Plat. Hence

αὐτοπωλικός, ή, όν, = foreg.: ἡ -κη (sc. τέχνη), the trade of an αὐτοπώλης, Plat.

αὐτόρ-ριζος, ον, (ῥίζα) roots and all; poët. αὐτόριζος, Babr. II. self-rooted, self-founded, Eur.

αὐτόρ-ρῦτος, ον, (ῥέω) self-flowing, flowing unbidden, Anth.

ΑΥ'ΤΟ'Σ, αὐτή, αὐτό, reflexive Pron., self, Lat. ipse :— in the oblique cases simply for the personal Pron., him, her, it :—with the Artic. ὁ αὐτός, ἡ αὐτή, τὸ αὐτό (or ταὐτόν), etc., the very one, the same.
I. self, myself, thyself, etc., acc. to the person of the Verb., Hom., etc.: 1. oneself, one's true self, the soul, not the body, Od.; or opp. to others, as king to subjects, parent to children, man to wife, etc., Hom.; hence absol. for the Master, τίς οὗτος;—Αὐτός, i.e. Socrates, Ar.; similarly in neut. αὐτὸ δείξει the result will shew, Eur. 2. of oneself, of one's own accord, Lat. sponte, Hom., Soph. 3. by oneself, alone, αὐτός περ ἐών although alone, Il.; αὐτοί ἐσμεν we are by ourselves, i.e. among friends, Ar. 4. in Plat., τὸ δίκαιον αὐτό right in itself, the idea of right, etc.; cf. αὐτοάνθρωπος. 5. in dat. with Subst., together with, ἀνόρουσεν αὐτῇ σὺν φόρμιγγι he sprang up lyre in hand, Il.; αὐτῇ σὺν πήληκι helmet and all, Ib.; and without σύν, αὐτοῖς ἀνδράσι men and all, Hdt., etc. 6. added to ordinal Numbers, e.g. πέμπτος αὐτός himself the fifth, i.e. himself with four others, Thuc. 7. in connexion with the person. Pron., ἐγὼ αὐτός, ἐμέ σε αὐτῆς, σὲ αὐτόν, etc., Hom.; in Hdt. and Att. it coalesces with oblique cases of Pron., ἐμαυτοῦ, σε-αυτοῦ, ἑ-αυτοῦ :—it is joined with these reflexive Pronouns to add force, αὐτὸς καθ' αὑτοῦ, αὐτοὶ ὑφ' αὑτῶν Aesch., etc. 8. gen. αὐτοῦ is used with the possessive Pron., πατρὸς κλέος ἠδ' ἐμὸν αὐτοῦ Il. 9. αὐτὸς ἑαυτοῦ is also used with Comp. and Sup. Adj. to express something unusual, αὐτὸς ἑωυτοῦ πολλῷ ὑποδεέστερος Hdt.
II. he, she, it, for the simple Pron. of 3 person, only in oblique cases, and never at the beginning of a sentence, Hom., Att.: cf. ἑαυτοῦ.
III. with Article ὁ αὐτός, ἡ αὐτή, τὸ αὐτό, and Att. contr. αὑτός, αὑτή, ταὐτό and ταὐτόν, gen. ταὐτοῦ, dat. ταὐτῷ, pl. neut. ταὐτά: Ion. ὡυτός, τωὐτό :—the very one, the same, Lat. idem, Hom., Hdt., Att.: it freq. takes a dat., like ὅμοιος, to denote sameness, τωὐτὸ ἂν ὑμῖν ἐπρήσσομεν we should fare the same as you, Hdt.; also, ὁ αὐτὸς καί, cf. Lat. simul ac, Id.
IV. αὐτο- in Compos.: 1. of itself, i.e. natural, native, not made, as in αὐτόκτιτος. 2. of mere . ., of nothing but . ., as in αὐτόξυλος. 3. of oneself, self-, as in αὐτοδίδακτος, αὐτόματος: and so independently, as in αὐτόνομος. 4. just, exactly, as in αὐτόδεκα. 5. with reflex. sense of αὑτοῦ and ἀλλήλων, as αὐθέντης, αὐτοκτονέω. 6. together with, as in αὐτόπρεμνος, αὐτόρριζος.
αὐτός, v. sub αὐτός III.

αὐτόσε, Adv. (αὐτοῦ) thither, to the very place, Lat. illuc, Hdt., Thuc.

αὐτο-σίδηρος [ῐ], ον, of sheer iron, with stroke of sword, Eur.

αὐτόσ-σῦτος, ον, (σεύομαι) self-sped, Aesch.

αὐτο-σταδίη, (ἵσταμαι) a stand-up fight, close fight, ἔν γ' αὐτοσταδίῃ Il.

αὐτό-στολος, ον, (στέλλω) self-sent, going or acting of oneself, Soph., Anth.

αὐτό-στονος, ον, (στένω) lamenting by or for oneself, Aesch.

αὐτο-σφαγής, ές, (σφάζω) slain by oneself or by kinsmen, Soph., Eur.

αὐτο-σχεδά, = αὐτοσχεδόν, Il.

αὐτοσχεδιάζω, f. άσω, to act or speak off-hand, Xen. 2. c. acc. to devise off-hand, extemporise, Thuc., Xen. II. in bad sense, to act, speak, or think unadvisedly, try rash experiments, Plat.; and

αὐτοσχεδίασμα, ατος, τό, an impromptu, Arist.; and

αὐτοσχεδιαστής, οῦ, ὁ, one who acts or speaks off-hand: a raw hand, bungler, Lat. tiro, Xen. From

αὐτο-σχέδιος, α, ον and ος, ον, hand to hand, αὐτοσχεδίη (sc. μάχη) in close fight, in the fray, Il.: αὐτοσχεδίην as Adv., = αὐτοσχεδόν, Hom. II. off-hand, of an improvisatore, h. Hom.

αὐτο-σχεδόν, Adv. near at hand, hand to hand, Lat. cominus, of close fight, Hom.

αὐτο-τέλεστος, ον, (τελέω) self-accomplished, spontaneous, Anth.

αὐτο-τελής, ές, (τέλος) ending in itself, complete in itself, supporting oneself, ἱππεῖς Luc. II. (τέλος IV) taxing oneself, self-taxed, Thuc.

αὐτό-τοκος, ον, (τίκτω) young and all, Aesch.

αὐτο-τραγικός, ή, όν, arrant tragic, Dem.

αὐτο-τροπήσας, aor. 1 part. (as if from αὐτο-τροπάω), to turn straightway, h. Hom.

αὐτοῦ, Adv., properly gen. of αὐτός, at the very place, just here, just there, Lat. illico, Hom., Hdt., Att.; with the place added, αὐτοῦ ἐνὶ Τροίῃ Il.; αὐτοῦ τῷδ' ἐνὶ χώρῳ Od.; αὐτοῦ ταύτῃ exactly here, Hdt., etc.

αὐτοῦ, Att. contr. for ἑαυτοῦ.

αὐτουργέω, f. ήσω, (αὐτουργός) to work with one's own hand, Luc. Hence

αὐτούργητος, ον, self-wrought, rudely wrought, Anth.

αὐτουργία, ἡ, a working on oneself, i.e. self-murder or the murder of one's own kin, Aesch. II. personal labour, opp. to slave-labour, Plut. From

αὐτ-ουργός, όν, (*ἔργω) self-working, Soph. 2. as Subst., one who works his land himself (not by slaves), a husbandman, poor farmer, Eur.; of the Peloponnesians, Thuc. :—metaph. αὐτουργὸς τῆς φιλοσοφίας one that has worked at philosophy by himself, without a teacher, Xen. II. pass. self-wrought, simple, native, Anth.

αὐτόφι, -φιν, Ep. gen. and dat. sing. and pl. of αὐτός, Hom.; ἀπ. αὐτόφιν, παρ' αὐτόφιν or -φι, from the very spot, Il.; ἐπ' αὐτόφιν on the spot, Ib.

αὐτό-φλοιος, ον, with the bark on, Theocr.

αὐτο-φόνος, ον, (*φένω) self-murdering, murdering those of one's own family, Aesch.

αὐτο-φόντης, ου, ὁ, = foreg., a murderer, Eur.

αὐτό-φορτος, ον, bearing one's own baggage, Aesch. II. cargo and all, ναῦς Plut.

αὐτο-φυής, ές, (φύομαι) self-grown, Plat. :—of home growth, Xen. 2. natural, opp. to artificial, Hes., Thuc.; κορύνα αὐτοφυής rough as it came from the tree, Theocr. 3. τὸ αὐτοφυές, one's own nature, Plat.

αὐτό-φῠτος, ον, *self-caused*, ἕλκεα Pind.   2. *natural*, αὐτ. ἐργασία, = αὐτουργία, i. e. *agriculture*, Arist.

αὐτό-φωνος, ον, (φωνή) *self-sounding*, χρησμὸς αὐτ. an oracle *delivered by the god himself*, Luc.

αὐτό-φωρος, ον, (φώρ) *self-detected, caught in the act of theft*, Soph.; ἐπ' αὐτοφώρῳ λαμβάνειν to catch *in the act*, Eur., Dem.; ἐπ' αὐτοφώρῳ ἁλῶναι Hdt.: in a more general sense, ἐπ' αὐτοφώρῳ καταλαμβάνειν τινα ἀμαθέστερον ὄντα to detect him *point blank* of ignorance, Plat.; ἐπ' αὐτ. εἴλημμαι πλουσιώτατος ὤν Xen.

αὐτό-χειρ, ρος, ὁ, ἡ, *with one's own hand*, Aesch., Soph., etc.: c. gen. *the very doer* or *author of a thing*, Id., Dem.   II. absol., like αὐθέντης, *one who kills himself* or *one of his kin*, Soph.: then, simply, *a murderer, homicide*, Id., Dem.; in full, τὸν αὐτ. τοῦ φόνου *the perpetrator of* . . , Soph.   III. as Adj. *murderous*, Eur.; πληγέντες αὐτόχειρι μιάσματι *of brothers smitten by mutual slaughter*, Soph. Hence

αὐτοχειρία, ἡ, *murder perpetrated by one's own hand*, Plat.: dat. αὐτοχειρίᾳ, Ion. -ίῃ, *with one's own hand*, αὐτ. κτείνειν Hdt., etc.

αὐτό-χθονος, ον, (χθών) *country and all*, Aesch.

αὐτό-χθων, ον, gen. ονος, *sprung from the land itself*, Lat. *terrigena*: αὐτόχθονες, οἱ, like Lat. *Indigenae, aborigines, natives*, Hdt., Thuc.; of the Athenians, Eur., Ar., etc.   II. as Adj. *indigenous*, Hdt.

αὐτο-χόλωτος, ον, (χολόομαι) *angry at oneself*, Anth.

αὐτο-χόωνος, ον, Ep. for αὐτοχόανος, -χωνος, (χόανος) *rudely cast, massive*, of a lump of iron used as a quoit, Il.

αὐτό-χρημα, Adv. *in very deed, really and truly*, Ar.   II. *just, exactly*, Luc.

αὐτ-οψία, ἡ, (ὄψομαι, f. of ὁράω) *a seeing with one's own eyes*, Luc.

αὐτῶ, Dor. for αὐτοῦ, *there*.

αὔτως, Adv. of αὐτός: I. *in this very manner, even so, just so, as it is*, γυμνὸν ἐόντα, αὔτως—ὥστε γυναῖκα, unarmed *just as I am*—like a woman, Il.   2. in a contemptuous sense, *just so, no better*, τί σὺ κήδεαι αὔτως ἀνδρῶν; why take you *no better* care? Ib.; νήπιος αὔτως *a mere* child, Ib.; αὔτως ἄχθος ἀρούρης Od.   II. in reference to the past, *still so, just as before, as it was*, Hom.; λευκὸν ἔτ' αὔτως *still white as when new*, Il.   III. *in vain, without effect*, οὐκ αὔτως μυθήσομαι Od.

αὐχενίζω, f. Att. ιῶ, (αὐχήν) *to cut the throat of a person, behead*, c. acc., Soph.

αὐχένιος, α, ον, (αὐχήν) *of the neck*, Od.

ΑΥΧΕ'Ω, f. ήσω: aor. 1 ηὔχησα: (αὐχή):—like καυχάομαι, *to boast, plume oneself*, Hdt., Eur.; τινι or ἐπί τινι on a thing, Id., Anth.   II. c. acc. et inf. *to boast* or *declare loudly that, protest that*, Hdt., Thuc., Eur.:—c. inf. only, Aesch.; οὐ γάρ ποτ' ηὔχουν μεθέξειν *I never thought that* . . , Id. Hence

αὐχήεις, εσσα, εν, *braggart, proud*, Anth.; and

αὔχημα, ατος, τό, *a thing boasted of, a pride, boast*, Soph.: *cause for boasting, glory*, Id., Thuc.   II. *boasting, self-confidence*, Id.

αὐχήν, ένος, ὁ, *the neck, throat*, of men and beasts, Hom., etc.   II. metaph. *any narrow passage, a neck of land, isthmus*, Hdt., Xen.   2. *a narrow sea, strait*, Hdt., Aesch.; of the point at which the

Danube spreads into several branches, Hdt.   3. *a narrow mountain-pass, defile*, Id. (Deriv. uncertain.)

αὔχησις, εως, ἡ, (αὐχέω) *boasting, exultation*, Thuc.

αὐχμάω, = αὐχμέω, Luc.

αὐχμέω, f. ήσω, (αὐχμός) *to be squalid* or *unwashed*, Lat. *squaleo*, Od., Ar., Plat.

αὐχμηρός, ά, όν, (αὐχμέω) *dry, dusty, rough, squalid*, Eur., Plat.; esp. of hair, Eur.

αὐχμός, ὁ, (αὔω *to burn*) *drought*, Hdt., Thuc.   2. *the effects of drought, squalor*, Plat.

αὐχμ-ώδης, ες, (εἶδος) *looking dry, squalid*, κόμη Eur.: τὸ αὐχμῶδες *drought*, Hdt.

ΑΥ'Ω, Att. αὔω, *to burn, light a fire, get a light*, Od. (Akin to εὔω: hence αὐαίνω, αὐχμός.)

ΑΥ'Ω, f. αὔσω [ῠ]: aor. 1 ηὖσα:—*to shout out, shout, call aloud*, Hom.; αὖε δ' Ἀθήνη, μακρὸν ἄϋσε, etc., Id.: —also in Trag.; c. acc. cogn. *to utter*, στεναγμόν, αὐδάν Eur.   2. c. acc. pers. *to call upon*, Hom.   3. rarely of things, *to ring*, ἀσπὶς αὖσεν Il.; cf. αὖος. (The Root is Αϝ, akin to ἄημι: hence αὐτή.)

ἀφαγνίζω, Att. f. ιῶ:—Med., aor. 1 -ηγνισάμην:—*to purify*:—Med. *to purify oneself by offerings*, τοῖς θεοῖς to the gods, Eur.

ἀφαίρεσις, εως, ἡ, (ἀφαιρέω) *a taking away, carrying off*, Plat.; and

ἀφαιρέτεον, verb. Adj. *one must take away*, Plat.   II.

ἀφαιρετός, έα, έον, *to be taken away*, Id.; and

ἀφαιρετός, όν, *to be taken away, separable*, Plat. From

ἀφ-αιρέω, Ion. ἀπ-αιρέω: f. ήσω: pf. ἀφήρηκα, Ion. ἀπαραίρηκα: aor. 2 ἀφεῖλον:—*to take from, take away from* a person, τί τινι Od., etc.; also τί τινος, Ar., Xen.; and τί τινα Aesch., Soph.:—c. acc. solo, ἀπελὼν τὰ ἄχθεα having taken them *off*, Hdt.; ὀργήν ἀφ. *to remove* it, Eur.; ἀφ. χωρίς *separate, set aside*, Plat.   II. Med., f. ἀφαιρήσομαι, and later ἀφελοῦμαι: aor. 2 ἀφειλόμην:—*to take away for oneself, take away*, in sense and construction much like Act., Hom., etc.   2. followed by μή c. inf. *to prevent, hinder from doing*, Soph., Eur.   3. ἀφαιρεῖσθαί τινα εἰς ἐλευθερίαν, Lat. *vindicare in libertatem*, *to set a man free*, Plat., Dem.   III. Pass., f. -αιρεθήσομαι: aor. 1 ἀφῃρέθην: pf. ἀφῄρημαι, Ion. ἀπαραίρημαι:—*to be robbed* or *deprived* of a thing, *to have it taken from one*, τι Hdt., Att.   2. c. inf., ἀφῃρέθη εἰσορᾶν *was hindered from* seeing them, Eur.

Ἅφαιστος, Dor. for Ἥφαιστος.

ἀφ-άλλομαι, f. -αλοῦμαι: aor. 1 -ηλάμην: Ep. aor. 2 part. ἀπάλμενος:—*to spring off* or *from*, ἐκ νεώς Aesch.; ἀφήλατο *jumped off*, Ar.   II. *to rebound, glance off*, Anth.

ἄ-φαλος, ον, *without the φάλος* or *boss*, in which the plume was fixed, Il.

ἀφ-αμαρτάνω, f. -αμαρτήσομαι: aor. 2 -ήμαρτον, Ep. -ήμβροτον:—*to miss* one's mark, c. gen., Il., Xen.   II. *to be deprived of* what one has, Il.

ἀφαμαρτο-επής, ές, (ἔπος) *random-talking*, Il.

ἀφ-ανδάνω, f. -αδήσω: Ion. aor. 2 inf. ἀπαδεῖν:—*to displease, not to please*, Od., Hdt., Soph.

ἀφάνεια, ἡ, *obscurity*, ἀξιώματος ἀφ. *want of illustrious birth*, Thuc.   II. *disappearance, utter destruction*, Aesch. From

ἀ-φᾰνής, ές, (φαίνομαι) *unseen, invisible, viewless*, of the nether world, Aesch.: χάσμα ἀφ. *a blind pit*, Hdt.;

ἡ ἀφ. θεός, of Proserpine, Soph. 2. ἀφ. γίγνεσθαι = ἀφανίζεσθαι, to disappear, be missing, Hdt., Eur.:— of soldiers missing after a battle, Thuc.: cf. ἀφανίζω. 3. unseen, unnoticed, secret, Solon, Thuc.: —c. part., ἀφ. εἰμι ποιῶν τι I do it without being noticed, Xen. 4. unknown, uncertain, obscure, Hdt., Att.: of future events, τὸ ἀφανές uncertainty, Hdt.:—Adv. ἀφανῶς, Thuc.; so ἐκ τοῦ ἀφανοῦς as Adv., Id.; and neut. pl. ἀφανῆ, Eur. 5. of persons, unnoticed, obscure, Id., Thuc. 6. ἀφανὴς οὐσία personal property, as money, which can be made away with, opp. to φανερά (real), as land, Oratt.

ἀφᾰνίζω, f. Att. ἰῶ: pf. ἠφάνικα: (ἀφανής):—to make unseen, hide from sight, Xen., Thuc., etc. 2. to do away with, remove, ἄχος Soph.; ἀφ. τινὰ πόλεος to carry off one from the city, Ar.: ἀφ. αὑτὸν εἰς τὸν νεών to disappear into the temple, Ar.:—of state criminals, to remove from sight, make away with, Hdt., Xen.: Pass. to be concealed or suppressed, Thuc. 3. to destroy utterly, rase to the ground, erase writing, Id., Dem.: to obliterate traces, Xen. 4. to obliterate, tarnish one's good name, Thuc., Plat.:—but in good sense, ἀφ. ἀγαθῷ κακόν to wipe out ill deeds by good, Thuc.; δύσκλειαν Id. 5. to disfigure, ἀφ. τὰ πρόσωπα, of hypocritical sadness, N. T. 6. to make away with property, Aeschin., Dem. II. Pass. to become unseen, to disappear, Hdt., Soph.; of persons buried by a sand-storm, Hdt.; or, lost at sea, Thuc., Xen. Hence

ἀφάνισις, εως, ἡ, a getting rid of, τῆς δίκης Ar. II. (from Pass.) disappearance, Hdt.

ἀφᾰνιστέος, έα, έον, verb. Adj. of ἀφανίζω, to be suppressed, Isocr.

ἄ-φαντος, ον, (φαίνομαι) made invisible, blotted out, forgotten, Il.: hidden, Aesch., Soph.; ἀφ. εἶναι, οἴχεσθαι, ἔρρειν, = ἀφανισθῆναι, to disappear, Trag. 2. in secret, Pind. 3. obscure, Id.

ἀφ-άπτω, f. ψω, to fasten from or upon, ἅμματα ἀφ. to tie knots on a string, Hdt.:—Pass. to be hung on, hang on, pf. part. ἀπάμμενος (Ion. for ἀφημμένος), Hdt.; ἀφημμένος ἔκ τινος Theocr.

ἄφαρ [∪ ∪], poët. Adv. straightway, forthwith, at once, quickly, presently, Hom., Trag. 2. thereupon, after that, Hom. II. in Theogn. as Adj. swift, fleet (cf. ἀφάρτερος).

ἄ-φαρκτος, = ἄ-φρακτος, Trag.

ἀφ-αρπάζω, f. Ep. άξω, Att. ἀσομαι:—Pass., pf. –ἥρπασμαι; aor. 1 –ηρπάσθην:—to tear off or from, c. gen., Il.; to snatch away, steal from, τί τινος Ar.: c. acc. only, to snatch eagerly, Soph., Eur.

ἀφάρτερος, α, ον, Comp. Adj. (v. ἄφαρ II), more fleet, Il.

ἀφᾰσία, ἡ, (ἄ-φατος) speechlessness, Eur., Plat.

ἀφάσσω: aor. 1 ἤφᾰσα: (ἀφή, ἅπτομαι):—to handle, feel, c. acc., Hdt.

ἄ-φᾰτος, ον, not uttered, nameless, Hes. 2. untold, unutterable, ineffable, extraordinary, Hdt., Soph.; ἄφατον ὡς there's no saying how, i. e. marvellously, immensely, Ar.

ἀφαυρός, ά, όν, feeble, powerless, παιδὸς ἀφαυροῦ Il.; mostly in Comp. and Sup., Hom., Hes.:—Adv. -ρῶς, Anth. (Deriv. uncertain.)

ἀφ-αύω, (αὔω, Att. αὔω) to dry up, parch, Ar.

ἀφάω, Ep. part. ἀφόων, (ἀφή, ἅπτομαι) to handle, rub, polish, Il.

ἀ-φεγγής, ές, (φέγγος) without light, φῶς ἀφ. a light that is no light (i. e. to the blind), Soph.; νυκτὸς ἀφεγγὲς βλέφαρον, of the moon, as opp. to the sun, Eur. 2. obscure, dim, faint, Aesch. 3. metaph., ill-starred, unlucky, Soph.

ἀφ-εδρών, ῶνος, ὁ, (ἕδρα) a privy, N. T.

ἀφ-έηκα, Ep. for ἀφ-ῆκα, aor. 1 of ἀφ-ίημι.

ἀφειδέω, f. ήσω, to be unsparing or lavish of, ψυχῆς Soph.; ἑαυτοῦ Thuc.:—absol. ἀφειδήσας (sub. ἑαυτοῦ) recklessly, Eur.; but 2. ἀφειδεῖν πόνου to be careless of it, i. e. neglect, avoid, labour, Soph. From

ἀ-φειδής, ές, (φείδομαι) unsparing or lavish of a thing, c. gen., Aesch. 2. of actions, done without regard to cost or risk, Thuc. II. Adv. -δῶς, Ion. -δέως, freely, lavishly Hdt., Dem.:—also sparing no pains, with all zeal, Id. 2. unsparingly, without mercy, Hdt.; Comp. -έστερον, Sup. -έστατα, Xen. Hence

ἀφειδία, ἡ, profuseness, Plat. 2. harsh treatment, neglect, N. T.

ἀφ-είθην, f. ἀσω, aor. 1 pass. of ἀφίημι.

ἀφ-εῖκα, pf. of ἀφίημι.

ἀφ-εῖλον, aor. 2 of ἀφαιρέω.

ἄφ-ειμεν, ἀφ-εῖτε, 1 and 2 pl. aor. 2 of ἀφ-ίημι.

ἀφ-ελεῖν, -ελέσθαι, aor. 2 inf. act. and med. of ἀφαιρέω.

ἀφεκτέον, verb. Adj. of ἀπέχομαι, one must abstain from, τινός Xen.

ἀ-φελής, ές, (φελλεύς?) without a stone, even, smooth, Ar.: metaph. of persons, simple, plain, blunt, Dem., Luc.:—Adv. ἀφελῶς, simply, roughly, Theogn.

ἀφ-έλκω, Ion. ἀπ-έλκω: f. -έλξω: but aor. 1 -είλκυσα: —to drag away suppliants, ἐκ τοῦ ἱροῦ Hdt., etc.; to drag or tow ships away, Thuc.:—to draw aside, ἐπί τι Xen. II. to draw off liquor, drink up, Aesch. 2. Med. to draw off for oneself, Ar.

ἀφελότης, ητος, ἡ, (ἀφελής) simplicity, N. T.

ἀφ-ελών, aor. 2 part. of ἀφ-αιρέω.

᾽ΑΦΕΝΟΣ, τό, riches, wealth, plenty, Il., Theogn. (From same Root as Lat. op-es.)

ἄφερκτος, ον, (ἀπ-είργω) shut out from a place, Aesch.

ἀφ-ερμηνεύω, f. σω, to interpret, expound, Plat.

ἀφ-έρπω, aor. 1 -είρπῦσα:—to creep off, steal away, retire, Soph.

ἄ-φερτος, ον, (φέρω) insufferable, intolerable, Aesch.

ἄφ-ες, aor. 2 imper. of ἀφ-ίημι.

ἄφεσις, εως, ἡ, (ἀφίημι) a letting go, dismissal, Philipp. ap. Dem.:—a quittance or discharge from a bond, Id.: exemption from service, Plut.: a divorce, Id. 2. a letting go (Lat. missio) of horses from the starting-post, and then the starting-post itself, ἰσώσας τἀφέσει τὰ τέρματα having made the winning-post one with the starting-post, i. e. having come back to the starting-post, Soph.

ἀφ-εσταίη, 3 sing. pf. opt. of ἀφ-ίστημι.

ἀφ-εστήξω, old Att. fut. formed from ἀφ-έστηκα (pf. of ἀφίστημι) I shall be absent, away from, τινός Plat., Xen.

ἀφ-ετέον, verb. Adj. of ἀφίημι, one must dismiss, Plat. 2. ἀφετέος, έα, έον, to be let go, Id.

ἀφετήριος, α, ον, (ἀφίημι) for letting go or starting

for a race: ἀφ. Διόσκουροι whose statues stood at the starting place, Anth.

ἄφετος, ον, (ἀφίημι) let loose, at large, ranging at will, of sacred flocks that were free from work, Aesch., Plat.: metaph. of persons, dedicated to a god, Eur.: τὸ ἄφετον, freedom from restraint, Luc.

ἄ-φευκτος, late form of ἄφυκτος.

ἀφ-εύω, aor. 1 ἄφ-ευσα, to singe off, Ar.　2. to fry, toast, Id.

ἀφ-έψω, Ion. ἀπ-έψω, f. -εψήσω, to refine by boiling off the refuse, to boil down, Hdt.:—esp. to boil free of dirt and dross, to refine, χρυσίον Id.: to boil young again, Ar.:—Pass., ὕδωρ ἀπεψημένον Hdt.

ἀφ-έωνται, later form of ἀφ-εῖνται, 3 pl. pf. pass. of ἀφίημι, N. T.; cf. ἀν-έωνται from ἀν-ίημι.

ἀφή, ἡ, (ἅπτω) a lighting, kindling, περὶ λύχνων ἀφάς about lamp-lighting time, Hdt.　II. (ἅπτομαι) a touching, touch, Aesch.: the sense of touch, Plat., etc.

ἀφ-ηγέομαι, Ion. ἀπ-ηγ-, f. ήσομαι, Dep. to lead from a point, and so, generally, to lead the way, go first, οἱ ἀφηγούμενοι the van, Xen.　II. to tell or relate in full, explain, Hdt.: pf. in pass. sense, τὸ ἀπηγημένον what has been told, Id. Hence

ἀφήγημα, Ion. ἀπηγ-, τό, a tale, narrative, Hdt.; and

ἀφήγησις, Ion. ἀπηγ-, εως, Ion. ιος, ἡ, a telling, narrating, ἄξιον ἀπηγήσιος worth telling, Hdt.; and

ἀφηγητήρ, ῆρος, ὁ, a guide, Anth.

ἀφ-ηδύνω, f. ὔνῶ, to sweeten, Plut., Luc.

ἀφ-ῆκα, aor. 1 of ἀφίημι.

ἀφ-ῆκω, to arrive at, Plat.

ἀφ-ῆλιξ, Ion. ἀπ-ῆλιξ, ικος, ὁ, ἡ, beyond youth, elderly, mostly in Comp. ἀπηλικέστερος, Hdt.

ἀφ-ῆμαι, Pass. to sit apart, part. ἀφήμενος Il.

ἀφήτωρ, ορος, ὁ, (ἀφ-ίημι) the archer, of Apollo, Il.

ἀφθαρσία, ἡ, incorruption, N. T. From

ἄ-φθαρτος, ον, (φθείρω) uncorrupted, incorruptible, Arist., etc.

ἄ-φθεγκτος, ον, (φθέγγομαι) voiceless, Aesch., Anth.　II. of places, where none may speak, Soph.　III. pass. unspeakable, Plat.

ἄ-φθῖτος, ον and η, ον, (φθίνω) not liable to perish, imperishable, Hom., Trag.: of persons, immortal, h. Hom.

ἄ-φθογγος, ον, voiceless, speechless, Hdt., Aesch., etc.

ἀ-φθόνητος, ον, (φθονέω) unenvied, Aesch.

ἀφθονία, ἡ, freedom from envy or grudging, readiness, Plat.　II. of things, plenty, abundance, Pind., Plat. From

ἄ-φθονος, ον, without envy: I. act. free from envy, Hdt., Plat.　2. ungrudging, bounteous, Lat. benignus, Trag.　II. pass. not grudged, bounteously given, plentiful, abundant, Hdt., Att.; ἐν ἀφθόνοις βιοτεύειν to live in plenty, Xen.　2. unenvied, provoking no envy, ὄλβος Aesch.　III. irreg. Comp. -έστερος, Sup. -έστατος, Plat.; but -ώτερος, -ώτατος, Xen.　IV. Adv. in abundance, ἀφθ. ἔχειν τινός to have enough of it, Plat.

ἀφθορία, ἡ, incorruption, N. T. From

ἄ-φθορος, ον, uncorrupt, of young persons, Anth.

ἀφ-ῖγμαι, pf. of ἀφικνέομαι.

ἀφ-ιδρύω, f. ύσω [ῡ], to remove to another settlement: Med. to cause to be transported, Eur.

ἀφ-ιερόω, f. ώσω, to purify, hallow: Pass., pf. ταῦτ' ἀφιερώμεθα I have had these expiatory rites performed, Aesch.

ἀφ-ίημι, and (as if from ἀφ-ιέω) 3 sing. ἀφίει, Ion. ἀπίει, imperat. ἀφίει:—impf., ἀφίην, with double augm. ἠφίην, 3 sing. ἀφίει, Ion. ἀπίει, also ἠφίει, ἤφιε, 3 pl. ἀφίεσαν, ἠφίεσαν, ἠφίουν:—f. ἀφήσω, Ion. ἀπ-:—pf. ἀφεῖκα: —aor. 1 ἀφῆκα, Ion. ἀπ-, Ep. ἀφέηκα only in indic.: —aor. 2 ἀφῆν, indic. only in dual and pl., ἀφέτην, ἀφεῖμεν, ἀφεῖτε, ἀφεῖσαν or ἄφετε, ἄφεσαν; imper. ἄφες, subj. ἀφῶ, opt. ἀφείην, inf. ἀφεῖναι, part. ἀφείς:—Med., impf. ἀφιέμην, 3 sing. ἠφίετο: f. ἀφήσομαι: aor. 2 ἀφείμην; imper. ἀφοῦ, ἄφεσθε; inf. -έσθαι, part. -έμενος:— Pass., pf. ἀφεῖμαι:—aor. 1 ἀφείθην, Ion. ἀπείθην: f. ἀφεθήσομαι. [ῐ Ep., except in augm. tenses: ῑ Att.] To send forth, discharge, Lat. emittere, of missiles, Hom., etc.:—hence to let loose, utter, give vent to words, Hdt., Trag.　2. to let fall, Il.　3. to send forth an expedition, dispatch it, Hdt.: Pass., of troops, Id.　4. to give up or hand over to, τινι τί Id., Att.:—Pass., ἡ 'Αττικὴ ἀπεῖτο ἤδη Hdt.　II. to send away, let go, loose, set free, Il., Att.:—c. acc. pers. et gen. rei, to set free from a thing, let off from, Hdt.: in legal sense to release from an engagement, accusation, etc., ἀφ. τινὰ φόνου Dem.　2. to dissolve, disband, break up an army, Hdt.:—to dismiss the council or law-courts, Ar.　3. to put away, divorce, Hdt.　4. to let go as an ἄφετος, consecrate, Xen.　5. of things, to get rid of, δίψαν Il.; to shed its blossoms, of plants, Od.; to slacken its force, of a dart, Il.　6. ἀφ. πλοῖον ἐς . . to loose ship for a place, Hdt.　7. in legal sense, c. dat. pers. et acc. rei, ἀφ. τινὶ αἰτίην to remit him a charge or a fine, Hdt., Dem.　III. to leave alone, give up, let pass, neglect, Hdt., Att.: foll. by a predicate, ἀφύλακτον ἀφ. to leave unguarded.　2. c. acc. et inf., ἀφ. τι δημόσιον εἶναι to give up to be public property, Thuc.; ἀφ. τὸ πλοῖον φέρεσθαι to let the boat be carried away, Hdt.　3. c. acc. pers. et inf. to let, suffer, permit one to do a thing, Id., Plat., etc.　IV. seemingly intr. (sub. στρατόν, ναῦς, etc.), to break up, march, sail, etc., Hdt.

B. Med. to send forth from oneself, send forth, Att.　2. δειρῆς ἀφίετο πήχεε she loosed her arms from off my neck.　3. c. gen. only, τέκνων ἀφοῦ let go hold of the children, Soph., Thuc.

ἀφ-ικάνω [ᾰ], only in pres. and impf. to arrive at, to have come to, c. acc., Hom.

ἀφ-ικνέομαι, Ion. ἀπ-:—f. ἀφίξομαι, Ion. 2 sing. ἀπίξεαι: pf. ἀφῖγμαι, Ion. 3 pl. plqpf. ἀπίκατο: aor. 2 ἀφικόμην Il., Ion. 3 pl. ἀπίκεατο:—to come to one place from another, to arrive at, reach: c. acc. loci, Hom.; or ἀφ. ἐς . . , ἐπί . . , κατά . . , πρός . . , Id., Att. (in Prose the Prep. is seldom omitted); absol. to arrive, Od.:—Hom. also puts the person reached in acc., μνηστῆρας ἀφ. came up to them, Od.; so, to come up to a throw (of the quoit), Ib.:—ἀφ. ἐπὶ or εἰς πάντα to try every means, Soph., Eur.　2. to come into a certain condition, ἀπ. ἐς πᾶν κακόν or κακοῦ, ἐς ἀπορίην, etc., Hdt., Att.　3. ἀπ. τινι ἐς λόγους to hold converse with one, Hdt.; so, ἐς ἔριν, ἐς ἔχθεα ἀφ. τινι Id.; διὰ μάχης, δι' ἔχθρας ἀπ. τινι to come to battle, or into

enmity with one, Id.; διὰ λόγων τινί Eur.　4. ἐς
τόξευμα ἀφ. to come within shot, Xen.

ἀ-φιλ-άγαθος, ον, not loving the good, N. T.

ἀ-φιλ-άργυρος, ον, not loving money, N. T.

ἀ-φίλητος [ῐ], ον, (φιλέω) unloved, Soph.

ἄ-φιλος, ον, of persons, without friends, friendless,
Trag.　II. unfriendly, hateful, Ib.—Adv. ἀφί-
λως in unfriendly manner, Aesch.

ἀ-φιλόσοφος, ον, unphilosophic, Plat.

ἀ-φιλό-σταχυς, ον, without ears of corn, starving,
Anth.

ἀφιλοτιμία, ἡ, want of due ambition, Arist.　From

ἀ-φιλότιμος, ον, without due ambition, Isae., Arist.

ἀ-φιλοχρηματία, ἡ, contempt for riches, Plut.

ἄφιξις, εως, Ion. ἄπιξις, ιος, ἡ, (ἀφικνέομαι) an arrival,
Hdt., Dem.　II. departure, N. T.

ἀφ-ιππάζομαι, Dep. to ride off or away, Plut.

ἀφ-ιππεύω, f. σω, to ride off, away, or back, Xen.

ἀφιππία, ἡ, awkwardness in riding, Xen.　From

ἄφιππος, ον, unsuited for cavalry, χώρα Xen.　II.
of persons, unused to riding, Plat.

ἀφ-ίστημι: 　A. Causal in pres. and impf., in f. ἀπο-
στήσω, aor. 1 ἀπέστησα, as also in aor. 1 med. :—to
put away, remove, c. acc., Aesch., etc. ; ἀφ. τινα
λόγου to hinder from speech, Eur. ; ἀφ. τὴν ἐπιβουλήν
to frustrate it, Thuc. ; ἀφ. τὸν ἄρχοντα to depose him,
Xen.; so in aor. 1 med., δόρυ πυλῶν ἀπεστήσασθε removed war from your own gates, Eur.　2. to make
to revolt, move to revolt, Hdt., Thuc.　II. to weigh
out, Xen. :—aor. 1 med., ἀποστήσασθαι χρεῖος to weigh
out or pay the debt in full, Il.; ἀποστήσασθαι τὸν
χαλκόν to have the money weighed out to one, Dem.
　B. intr., in Pass., as also in aor. 2 act. ἀπέστην,
imperat. ἀπόστηθι, ἀπόστα, pf. ἀφέστηκα in pres. sense,
syncop. pl. ἀφέστάμεν, -στᾶτε, -στᾶσι, inf. ἀφεστάναι,
part. ἀφεστώς, -ῶσα, -ός or -ώς: fut. med. ἀποστή-
σομαι: aor. 1 ἀπεστάθην [ᾰ] :—to stand away or aloof
from, keep far from, c. gen., Hom., Att. ; μακρὰν τόποις καὶ χρόνοις ἀφ. Diod.; ἀφεστάναι φρενῶν to lose
one's wits, Soph. ; ἀφ. πραγμάτων to withdraw from
business, Dem., etc.　2. in Prose, to revolt from, τινος or ἀπό τινος, Hdt., Att.: absol. to revolt, Ib.　3.
ἀφ. τινός τινι to give up a thing to another, Dem.; hence,
ἀφ. τινι to make way for him, give way to him, Eur. ;
c. inf. to shrink from doing, Id.　4. absol. to stand
aloof, Il., Att.

ἀφ-ῖχθαι, pf. inf. of ἀφ-ικνέομαι.

ἄφλαστον, τό, Lat. aplustre, the curved stern of a
ship with its ornaments, Il., Hdt.

ἄ-φλεκτος, ον, (φλέγω) unburnt, unconsumed by fire,
πέλανοι Eur.

ἄ-φλοιος, ον, without bark, Epigr. ap. Plut.

ἀφλοισμός, ὁ, of an angry man, spluttering or perh.
foaming, Il.

ἀφνειός, όν and ἡ, όν, (ἄφενος) rich, wealthy, Il. ; c.
gen., ἀφνειὸς βιότοιο rich in substance, Hom.; c. acc.,
Hes. ; c. dat., Theocr.

ἀφνεός, ά, όν = ἀφνειός, Theogn., Aesch., Soph.

ἌΦΝΩ, Adv. unawares, of a sudden, Eur., Thuc.; cf.
ἐξ-αίφνης.

ἀ-φόβητος, ον, (φοβέομαι) without fear of, δίκης Soph.:
absol. fearless, Anth.

ἀφοβία, ἡ, fearlessness, Plat.　From

ἄ-φοβος, ον, without fear : 　1. fearless, intrepid,
dauntless, Pind., Soph. :—Adv. -βως, Xen.　2.
causing no fear, free from fear, Aesch.　3. ἄφοβοι
θῆρες beasts which no one fears, i. e. cattle, Soph.

ἀφοβό-σπλαγχνος, ον, (σπλάγχνον) fearless of heart, Ar.

ἄφ-οδος, ἡ, a going away, departure, Hdt., Xen.　2.
a going or coming back, return, Ib.

ἀ-φοίβαντος, ον, (φοιβαίνω = φοιβάω) uncleansed, unclean, Aesch.

ἀφ-ομοιόω, f. ώσω, to make like, τί τινι Plat.: to compare, τι Id. :—Pass. to be or become like, τινι Id.　II.
c. acc. rei only, to pourtray, copy, Id., Xen.　Hence

ἀφομοίωμα, ατος, τό, a resemblance, copy, Plat.

ἀφ-οπλίζω, f. ίσω, to strip of arms, τινά τινος Luc. :
to disarm, τινά Anth. :—Med., ἀφοπλίζεσθαι ἔντεα to
put off one's armour, Il.

ἀφ-οράω, Ion. -έω : f. ἀπ-όψομαι : aor. 2 ἀπ-εῖδον : pf.
ἀφ-εόρακα :—to look away from all others at one, to
have in full view, to look at, τι or πρός τι Thuc. ;
also in Med., Ar.　2. to view from a place, ἀπὸ
δενδρέου Hdt.　II. to look away, have the back
turned, Xen.

ἀ-φόρητος, ον, intolerable, insufferable, Hdt., Thuc.

ἀφορία, ἡ, (ἄφορος) a not bearing : 　1. non-pro-
duction, dearth, καρπῶν Xen.　2. barrenness, ste-
rility of land : metaph., ἀφ. φρενῶν Id.

ἀφ-ορίζω, f. Att. ιῶ, to mark off by boundaries, Dem. :
—Med. to mark off for oneself, appropriate, Eur.　2.
to distinguish, determine, define, Plat.　II. c.
acc. pers.,　1. to banish, Eur.　2. to set apart,
separate, N. T.: then,　3. to cast out, excommuni-
cate, Ib.　b. to set apart for some office, to appoint,
ordain, Ib.　Hence

ἀφοριστέον, verb. Adj. one must put aside, Arist.

ἀφ-ορμάω, f. ήσω, to make to start from a place :—
Pass. to go forth, start, depart from a place, c. gen.,
Hom., Att.　II. intr. in same sense as Pass., Eur.,
Thuc.: of lightning, to break forth, Soph. ; c. acc.
cogn., ἀφορμᾶν πεῖραν to begin an enterprise, Id.

ἀφ-ορμή, ἡ, a starting-point, esp. in war, a base of
operations, Thuc. :—also a place of safety, Eur.　2.
generally, a starting-point, the origin, occasion or
pretext of a thing, Id. ; ἀφορμὴν παρέχειν, διδόναι
to give occasion, Dem.　3. the means with which
one begins a thing, resources, Xen., Dem. ; ἀφ. ἔργων
means for undertaking works, Xen.　4. the capital
of a banker, Id., Dem.

ἀ-φόρμικτος, ον, (φορμίζω) without the lyre, Aesch.

ἄφ-ορμος, ον, (ὁρμή) departing from a place, c. gen.,
Soph.

ἄ-φορος, ον, (φέρω) not bearing, barren, Hdt., Xen.　2.
causing barrenness, blighting, Aesch.

ἀ-φόρυκτος, ον, (φορύσσω) unspotted, unstained, Anth.

ἀφ-οσιόω, Ion. ἀποσ-, f. ώσω, to purify from guilt or
pollution, τὴν πόλιν Plat.　II. Med. to purify
oneself from sins of negligence, Id. ; ἀφοσιοῦσθαι
τῇ θεῷ to make expiatory offerings to the goddess,
Hdt.　2. c. acc. rei, to acquit oneself of an obligation, ἀποσιοῦσθαι τὴν ἐξόρκωσιν to quit oneself of one's
oath, Id. ; ἀπ. λογίον quitting oneself of the orders
of an oracle, Id.　Hence

ἀφοσίωσις, εως, ἡ, expiation: ἀφοσιώσεως ἕνεκα for form's sake, Plut.

ἀφόων, Ep. for ἀφῶν, part. of ἀφάω.

ἀφρᾰδέω, only in pres. to be senseless, act thoughtlessly, Hom. From

ἀ-φρᾰδής, ές, (φράζομαι) insensate, reckless, Od.; of the dead, senseless, lifeless, Ib. Adv. ἀφραδέως, senselessly, recklessly, Il. Hence

ἀφρᾰδίᾱ, Ion. -ίη, ἡ, folly, thoughtlessness, mostly in Ep. dat. pl., ἀφραδίῃσι Hom.; δι' ἀφραδίας Od.

ἀ-φράδμων, ον, gen. ονος, = ἀφραδής, without sense, h. Hom.

ἀφραίνω, (ἄφρων) to be silly, senseless, Hom.

ἄ-φρακτος, ον, old Att. ἄφαρκτος, (φράσσω) unfenced, unfortified, unguarded, Thuc.; c. gen., ἄφρ. φίλων by friends, Soph.; c. dat., ἄφρ. ὅρκοις Eur. 2. not to be kept in, irrepressible, Aesch. II. unguarded, off one's guard, Thuc.

ἀφράσμων, ον, Att. for ἀφράδμων, Aesch. Adv. -όνως, Id.

ἄ-φραστος, ον, (φράζω) unutterable, inexpressible, h. Hom., Aesch., Soph. II. (φράζομαι) not perceived or thought of, Aesch.; τὸ ἀφραστότατον χωρίον the place least likely to be thought of, Hdt.:—Adv. -τως, beyond thought, Id.

ἀφρέω, f. ήσω, (ἀφρός) to befoam, cover with foam, ἵπποι ἄφρεον στήθεα Il.

ἀφρη-λόγος, ον, (ἀφρός, λέγω) gathering froth, skimming, τινός Anth.

ἀφρηστής, οῦ, ὁ, (ἀφρός) the foamer, of a dolphin, Anth.

ἀ-φρήτωρ, ὁ, Ion. for ἀ-φράτωρ, without brotherhood (φράτρα), i. e. bound by no social tie, Il.

ἀφρίζω, f. ίσω, (ἀφρός) to foam, Soph.

ἀφριόεις, εσσα, εν, (ἀφρός) foamy, Anth.

ἀφρο-γενής, ές, (γίγνομαι) foam-born, of Aphrodité, Hes.: fem. Ἀφρο-γένεια, Mosch.

Ἀφροδίσια, ων, τά, v. Ἀφροδίσιος.

ἀφροδισιάζω, f. άσω, to indulge lust, Plat., Xen.

Ἀφροδισίας, ἡ, sacred to Aphrodité, name of an island, Hdt.

Ἀφροδίσιος [δῐ], α, ον and ος, ον, belonging to Aphrodité, Plat. II. Ἀφροδίσια, τά, sexual pleasures, Xen. 2. a festival of Aphrodité, Id. III. Ἀφροδίσιον, τό, the temple of Aphrodité. From

Ἀφροδίτη [ῑ], ἡ, (ἀφρός) Aphrodité, Lat. Venus, goddess of love, said to be born from the sea-foam, h. Hom., Hes. II. as appellat. love, pleasure, Od.: —Ἀφρ. κακῶν enjoyment, Eur. 2. attractive beauty, grace, Lat. venustas, Aesch., Luc.; cf. Lat. venus.

ἀφρονέω, f. ήσω, (ἄφρων) to be silly, act foolishly, only in part., Il., Anth.

ἀφροντιστέω, f. ήσω, to have no care of, pay no heed to a thing, c. gen., Xen. From

ἀ-φρόντιστος, ον, (φροντίζω) thoughtless, heedless, taking no care, Lat. securus, Xen., Theocr.:—Adv. -τως, inconsiderately, Soph.; ἀφρ. ἔχειν to be heedless, Xen.; also to be senseless, demented, Soph. II. pass. unthought of, unexpected, Aesch.

ἀφρόνως, Adv., v. ἄφρων.

ΑΦΡΟ'Σ, ὁ, foam, of the sea, Il.: of an angry lion, foam, froth, Ib.; ἀπ' ἀνθρώπων ἀφρόν frothy blood, Aesch.

ἀφροσύνη, ἡ, (ἄφρων) folly, thoughtlessness, senselessness, in sing. and pl., Hom., Soph., Thuc.

ἄ-φρουρος, ον, (φρουρά) unguarded, unwatched, Plat.

ἀφρο-φυής, ές, (φύω) foam-producing, Anth.

ἀφρ-ώδης, ες, (εἶδος) foamy, Eur.

ἄ-φρων, ον, gen. ονος, (φρήν) without sense, of statues, Xen.:—crazed, frantic, or silly, foolish, Hom., Att.: τὸ ἄφρον = ἀφροσύνη, Thuc. Adv. ἀφρόνως, senselessly, Soph.

ἀφ-υβρίζω, f. Att. ιῶ, to give loose to passion, Plut.

ἀφ-υδραίνω, to wash clean from dirt:—Med., aor. 1 -υδρηνάμην, to wash oneself clean, bathe, Eur.

ἀφύη, ἡ, in gen. pl. ἀφύων (not ἀφυῶν), a sort of anchovy or sardine, Ar.

ἀ-φυής, ές, acc. ἀφυῆ, (φυή) without natural talent, witless, dull, Plat.; ἀφυὴς πρός τι naturally unsuited to a thing, Id., Xen. 2. simple, unschooled, Soph.

ἄ-φυκτος, ον, (φεύγω) not to be shunned, from which none escape, Aesch., Soph.; of an arrow, unerring, Id., Eur.; of a question, admitting no escape, inevitable, Plat. II. act. unable to escape, Ar.

ἀφυλακτέω, f. ήσω, to be off one's guard, Xen.: c. gen. to be careless about, Id. From

ἀ-φύλακτος, ον, (φυλάσσω) unguarded, unwatched, Hdt., Thuc. II. (φυλάσσομαι) unguarded, off one's guard, Id.; ἀφύλακτον εὕδειν to sleep securely, Aesch.; ἀφ. τινα λαμβάνειν to catch one off his guard, Xen.; τὸ ἀφ. want of precaution, Thuc.:—Adv. -τως, Xen. III. not to be guarded against, inevitable, Arist.

ἀφ-υλίζω, f. ίσω, to strain off, Anth.

ἄ-φυλλος, ον, (φύλλον) leafless, of dry wood, Il.; ἄφ. στόμα words not seconded by the suppliant's olive-branch, Eur. II. act. stripping off the leaves, blighting, Aesch.

ἀφυξῶ, Dor. f. of ἀφύσσω.

ἀφυπνίζω, f. Att. ιῶ, to wake one from sleep, Eur., Plut.

ἀφυπνόω, f. ώσω, to wake from sleep, Anth. II. to fall asleep, N. T.

ἀφυσγετός, ὁ, the mud and filth which a stream carries with it, rubbish, Il. (Deriv. unknown.)

ἀφύσσω, f. ξω, Dor. -ξω, also ἀφύξω [ῠ]: aor. 1 ἤφυσα, Ep. ἄφυσσα, imper. ἄφυσσον:—Med., aor. 1 ἠφυσάμην, Ep. 3 sing. ἀφύσσατο:—to draw liquids, esp. from a larger vessel with a smaller, οἶνον ἐν ἀμφιφορεῦσιν ἠφύσαμεν Od.:—Pass., πίθων ἠφύσατο οἶνος was drawn from the wine-jars, Ib.:—metaph., πλοῦτον ἀφύξειν to draw full draughts of wealth, i.e. heap it up, τινί for another, Il. II. Med. to draw for oneself, οἶνον Ib.; ῥοὰς Eur.:—metaph., φύλλα ἠφυσάμην I heaped me up a bed of leaves, Od.

ἀ-φώνητος, ον, (φωνέω) voiceless, speechless, Soph.

ἄ-φωνος, ον, (φωνή) voiceless, speechless, dumb, silent, Theogn., Hdt., Dem.: c. gen., ἄφωνος ἀρὰς unable to utter a curse, Soph.:—Adv. -νως, without speaking, Id.; neut. pl. as Adv., Aesch. 2. ἄφωνα (sc. γράμματα), consonants, opp. to φωνοῦντα or φωνήεντα (vowels), Eur., Plat.

ἀχά, Dor. for ἠχή, ἡ.

Ἀχαία, Ion. Ἀχαιίη, ἡ, name of Demeter in Attica, Hdt. (Deriv. unknown.)

Ἀχαιϊκός, ή, όν, (Ἀχαιός) of or for the Achaians, Achaian, Aesch., Eur.

Ἀχαιΐς, ίδος, ἡ, the Achaian land, with or without

γαῖα, Il. 2. (sub. γυνή) an Achaian woman, Ib. ; also Ἀχαιιάς, άδος, Ib.

ἀχαΐνης [ῑ], ὁ, (ἀκίς) with single points to his horns, a young deer, Babr.

Ἀχαιός, ά, όν, Achaian, Lat. Achivus, Hom. :—Ἀχαιοί, οἱ, the Achaians or Greeks generally, Id. :—Ἀχαΐα, ἡ, Achaia in Peloponnese, Thuc.

ἀ-χάλῑνος, ον, unbridled, Eur., Ar., etc.

ἀ-χαλίνωτος [ῑ], ον, without bridle, Xen.

ἀ-χάλκεος, ον, (χαλκοῦς) penniless, Anth.

ἀ-χάλκευτος, ον, (χαλκεύω) not forged of metal, Aesch.

ἀχαλκέω, f. ήσω, to be penniless, Anth. From

ἄ-χαλκος, ον, without brass, ἄχαλκος ἀσπίδων, i. e. ἄνευ ἀσπίδων χαλκείων, Soph.

ἀ-χάλκωτος, ον, (χαλκόω) not brasened; without money, Anth.

ἀχάνη [χᾱ], ἡ, a Persian measure, = 45 μέδιμνοι, Ar.

ἀ-χανής, ές, (χανεῖν, aor. 2 inf. of χάσκω) not opening the mouth, Luc. II. (a euphon.) yawning, wide, Plut., Anth.

ἀ-χᾰράκωτος, ον, (χαρακόω) not palisaded, Plut.

ἄ-χᾰρις, ὁ, ἡ, ἄχαρι, τό, gen. ιτος, without grace or charms, graceless, Theogn. 2. unpleasant, disagreeable, οὐδὲν ἄχαρι παθεῖν Hdt. ; as euphem. for grievous, ἀχ. συμφορή Id. II. ungracious, thankless, Id. ; χάρις ἄχαρις a graceless grace, thankless favour, Aesch., Eur.

ἀχαριστέω, f. ήσω, to be thankless, shew ingratitude, Xen. 2. = οὐ χαρίζομαι, to discourage, τινί Plat. ; and

ἀχαριστία, ἡ, thanklessness, ingratitude, Xen., Dem. 2. ungraciousness, Plat. From

ἀ-χάριστος, ον, (χαρίζομαι) ungracious, unpleasant, unpleasing, Od. ; irreg. Comp., δόρπου ἀχαρίστερον (for -ιστότερον) Ib. : without grace or charms, Xen. II. of persons, ungracious, unfavourable, Theogn. 2. ungrateful, thankless, Hdt., Att. ; τινι Eur. ; πρός τινα Xen. III. Adv. -τως, with an ill-will, Id. ; ἀχαρίστως ἔχει μοι thanks are wanting to me, Id.

ἀ-χάρῑτος, ον, = ἀχάριστος or ἄχαρις, Hdt. 2. ungrateful, thankless, Id. ; χάρις ἀχ., like χάρις ἄχαρις, Eur.

Ἀχαρναί, ῶν, αἱ, Acharnae, a demos of Attica, Thuc. :—Ἀχαρνεύς, έως, ὁ, an inhabitant of Acharnae, pl. Ἀχαρνεῖς, poët. Ἀχαρνῆ͂ιδαι Ar. :—Adj. Ἀχαρνικός, ή, όν, Id.

ἀχεδών [ᾰ], Dor. for ἠχεδών.

ἀ-χείμαντος, ον, (χειμαίνω) not vexed by storms, Alcae.

ἀ-χειροποίητος, ον, not wrought by hands, N. T.

ἄ-χειρος, ον, (χείρ) without hands : τὰ ἄχειρα of the hinder parts of the body, Xen.

ἀ-χείρωτος, ον, (χειρόω) untamed, unconquered, Thuc. II. not planted by man's hand, Soph.

Ἀχελωΐδες (sc. νῆσοι), αἱ, islands at the mouth of the Acheloüs, Aesch.

Ἀχελῷος, poët. Ἀχελώϊος, ὁ, Acheloüs, name of several rivers; the best ran through Aetolia and Acarnania, Il., Hes. II. any stream, or, generally, water, Eur.

ἄχερδος, ἡ, a wild prickly shrub, a wild pear, Od., Soph. ; masc. in Theocr. (Deriv. unknown.)

Ἀχερόντιος, α, ον, of Acheron, Eur.

Ἀχερούσιος, ον, = foreg., Aesch. : fem. Ἀχερουσιάς, άδος, Plat., Xen.

ἀχερωΐς, ΐδος, ἡ, the white poplar, said to have been brought by Hercules from the banks of Acheron, Il.

Ἀχέρων, οντος, ὁ, (ἄχος) Acheron, River of Woe (cf. Κωκυτός), one of the rivers of the world below, Od.

ἀχέτας or ἀχέτᾰ, Dor. and Att. for ἠχέτης.

ἀχεύω and ἀχέω [ᾰ], (ἄχος) only in pres. part. grieving, sorrowing, mourning, Hom. II. from the same Root ΑΧ came also 1. aor. 2 ἤκᾰχον, inf. ἀκαχεῖν, in Causal sense, to grieve, vex, annoy, distress, Hom. : so also, redupl. f. ἀκαχήσω, Ep. aor. 1 ἀκάχησα, Id. ; and a pres. ἀκαχίζω, Od. 2. pass. forms ἄχομαι, ἄχνῠμαι, ἀκαχίζομαι : imper. ἀκαχίζεο, -ίζευ :—pf. ἀκάχημαι, 3 sing. ἀκάχηται, Ep. 3 pl. ἀκηχέδαται, plqpf. ἀκαχείατο ; inf. ἀκάχησθαι ; part. ἀκαχή-μενος (accent. as a pres.), Ep. also ἀκηχέμενος : aor. 2 Ep. 3 pl. ἀκάχοντο :—to be grieved, distressed, Hom. ; c. gen. causae, to grieve for a person, Id. ; rarely c. dat. to grieve at a person's death, Od. ; the cause of grief also in partic., μή τι θανὼν ἀκαχίζεο Ib. 3. later c. acc. to lament, Soph.

ἀχέω [ᾰ], old form for ἰαχέω, h. Hom., Eur.

ἀχέω [ᾱ], Dor. for ἠχέω.

ἀχήν [ᾱ], ὁ, ἡ, poor, needy, Theocr. (Deriv. uncertain.)

ἀχηνία, ἡ, need, want, χρημάτων Aesch. ; ὀμμάτων ἀχηνίαις in the eyes blank gaze, Id.

ἀχθεινός, ή, όν, (ἄχθος) burdensome, oppressive, wearisome, Lat. molestus, of persons, Eur., Xen. :—Adv. -νῶς, unwillingly, Id.

ἀχθείς, aor. 1 pass. part. of ἄγω.

ἀχθηδών, όνος, ἡ, a weight, burden, Aesch. 2. metaph. grievance, distress, vexation, annoyance, Thuc., Plat. ; δι᾽ ἀχθηδόνα for the sake of teasing, Thuc. (ἄχθος, as ἀληδών from ἄλγος.)

ἀχθίζω, f. ίσω, to load, Babr.

ΑΧΘΟΜΑΙ, Pass. : f. ἀχθεσθήσομαι or (in med. form) ἀχθέσομαι : aor. 1 ἠχθέσθην :—to be loaded, νηῦς ἤχθετο Od. II. of mental oppression, to be weighed down, vexed, annoyed, grieved, Hom. ; τινι at a thing, or with a person, Hdt., etc. ; so, ἐπί τινι Xen. ; περί τινος Hdt. ; ὑπέρ τινος Plat. :—also c. acc., ἀχθόμαι ἕλκος Il. ;—also c. part., as of subject, as ἄχθομαι ἰδών Soph. ; or of object, ἤχθετο δαμναμένους at their being conquered, Il. ; but the object is also in gen., οὐδὲν ἤχθετο αὐτῶν πολεμούντων he had no objection to going to war, Xen.

ἄχθος, εος, τό, (ἄχθομαι) a weight, burden, load, Hom.; ἄχθος ἀρούρης a dead weight on earth, cumberers of the ground, Id. II. a load of grief, grief, trouble, distress, sorrow, Trag.

ἀχθοφορέω, f. ήσω, to bear burdens, Plut. 2. to bear as a burden, τι Anth. From

ἀχθο-φόρος, ον, (φέρω) bearing burdens, Hdt.

Ἀχίλλειος, α, ον, Ion. -ήιος, η, ον, of Achilles, Hdt., Eur. II. Ἀχιλλείη κριθή Achilles-barley, a fine kind : hence Ἀχίλλειαι (μᾶζαι) cakes of fine barley, Ar.

Ἀχιλλεύς, gen. Ἀχιλλέως, Ep. ῆος, acc. Ἀχιλλέα, voc. Ἀχιλλεῦ : Ep. nom. also Ἀχιλεύς : (from ἄχος, the grief of the hero being the subject of the Il., cf. Ὀδυσ-

σεύς) :—*Achilles*, son of Peleus and Thetis, prince of the Myrmidons.

ἀ-χίτων [ῐ], ον, gen. ωνος, *without tunic*, i. e. *wearing* the ἱμάτιον only, of Socrates, Xen.

ἀχλαινία, ἡ, *want of a cloak* or *mantle*, Eur. From

ἄ-χλαινος, ον, (χλαῖνα) *without cloak* or *mantle*, Simon.

ἄ-χλοος, ον, contr. ἄχλους, ουν, (χλόα) *without herbage*, Eur.

ἀχλυόεις, εσσα, εν, *gloomy*, Simon. ap. Hdt. From

ἈΧΛΥ῀Σ [ῠ], ύος, ἡ, *a mist*, Lat. *caligo*, Od. ; *a mist over the eyes* of one dying, Il. ; or *of a person deprived of the power of knowing others*, Ib. ʹ—metaph. *gloom, trouble*, Aesch. Hence

ἀχλύω, aor. 1 ἤχλῡσα, *to be* or *grow dark*, Od.

ἈΧΝΗ, Dor. ἄχνα, ἡ, *anything that comes off the surface :*   I. *foam, froth*, of the sea, Od. ; of wine, Eur. ; ἄχνη οὐρανία the *dew of heaven*, Soph. ; δακρύων ἄχνη *dewy tears*, Id.   II. of solids, *the chaff* that flies off in winnowing, in pl., Il. ; *the down* on fruits, Anth.   III. ἄχνην in acc. as Adv., *a morsel, the least bit*, Ar.

ἄ-χνοος, ον, contr. ἄ-χνους, ουν, *without down*, Anth.

ἄχνυμαι, v. ἀχεύω, ἀχέω II. 2.

ἄ-χολος, ον, *allaying bile* or *anger*, Od.

ἄχομαι, v. ἀχεύω, ἀχέω II. 2.

ἀχόρευτος, ον, (χορεύω) *not attended with the dance, joyless, melancholy*, Soph., Eur.

ἄ-χορος, ον, *without the dance*, of death, Soph.: *melancholy*, Eur.

ἈΧΟΣ, εος, τό, *pain, distress*, Hom., Pind., Att. Poets.

ἄχος, Dor. for ἦχος.

ἀ-χρᾱής, ές, gen. έος, = sq., Anth.

ἄ-χραντος, ον, (χραίνω) *undefiled, immaculate*, Plat.

ἀ-χρεῖος, Ion. ἀχρήϊος, ον, *useless, unprofitable, good for nothing*, Hes., Soph., etc.   2. esp. *unserviceable, unfit for war*, Hdt. ; τὸ ἄχρ. τοῦ στρατοῦ *the unserviceable part* of an army, Id., Thuc., etc.   II. in Hom. neut. ἀχρεῖον as Adv., ἀχρεῖον ἰδών giving a *helpless* look, looking *foolish*, of Thersites after being beaten, Il. ; ἀχρεῖον ἐγέλασσε laughing *without cause* or *meaning*, laughed with a *forced* laugh, Od. ; so, ἀχρεῖον κλάζειν to bark *without cause*, Theocr.

ἀχρηματία, ἡ, *want of money*, Thuc. From

ἀ-χρήμᾰτος, ον, (χρήματα) *without money* or *means*, Hdt., Aesch.

ἀχρημοσύνη, ἡ, *want of money*, Od., Theogn. From

ἀ-χρήμων, ον, gen. ονος, (χρήματα) *without money, poor, needy*, Solon, Eur.

ἀχρηστία, ἡ, *uselessness*, Plat.   II. *the non-usance* of a thing, Id. From

ἄ-χρηστος, ον, (χράομαι) *useless, unprofitable, unserviceable*, Hdt., Thuc.: of an oracle, *without effect*, Eur. :—ἄχρ. ἔς or πρός τι *unfit for* a thing, Hdt. ; ἄχρ. τινι *useless* to a person, Id., Eur.   2. like ἀχρεῖος, of *useless, do-nothing* persons, Oratt.   3. act. *making no use of*, c. dat., Eur.   II. (χρηστός) *unkind, cruel*, Hdt.

ἈΧΡΙ, Ep. also ἄχρις :   I. Adv. *to the uttermost, utterly*, Il.   2. after Hom., before Preps., ἄχρι εἰς . . ἄχρι πρός . . , Lat. *usque ad* . . , Xen., Luc.   II. Prep. with gen. *even to, as far as :*   1. of Time, *until*, ἄχρι μάλα κνέφαος *until deep in the night*, Od. ;

ἄχρι τῆς ἡμέρας Dem.   2. of Space, *as far as, even to*, ἄχρι τῆς ἐσόδου Hdt.   3. of Degree, ἄχρι τούτου up to this point, Dem.; ἄχρι τοῦ μὴ πεινᾶν Xen.   III. as Conj., ἄχρι οὗ or ἄχρι alone :   1. of Time, Lat. *donec, until, so long as*, ἄχρι οὗ ὅδε ὁ λόγος ἐγράφετο Id. ; ἄχρι ἄν with Subj., ἄχρι ἄν σχολάσῃ *till he should be at leisure*, Id.   2. of Space, *so far as*, Id., Luc.

ἀ-χρώματος, ον, (χρῶμα) *colourless*, Plat.

ἄ-χρως, ων, gen. ω, *colourless*, Plat.

ἄ-χρωστος, ον, χρώζω) *untouched*, χερῶν ἐμῶν by my hands, Eur.

ἀχῡρῖτις, ιδος, ἡ, fem. Noun, = sq., Anth.

ἀχυρμιά, ἡ, (ἄχυρον) *a heap of chaff*, Il., Anth.

ἀχυρμός, οῦ, ὁ, v. ἀχυρός.

ἄχῡρον [ᾰ], τό, mostly in pl. ἄχυρα, *husks, chaff, bran*, Hdt.; metaph. ἄχυρα τῶν ἀστῶν Ar.

ἀχῡρός or ἄχῠρος, ὁ, *a chaff-heap*, Ar. ; but ἀχυρμός is prob. the true form.

ἀχυρό-τριψ, ῐβος, ὁ, ἡ, (τρίβω) *threshing out the husks*, Anth.

ἀχώ, ἡ, Dor. for ἠχώ.

ἀχώριστος, ον, (χωρίζω) *not parted, not divided*, Plat.   II. (χῶρος) *with no place assigned one*, Xen.

ἄψ, (ἀπό) Adv. of Place, *backwards, back, back again*, Hom.   2. of actions, *again, in return*, Id. ; so, ἂψ αὖτις, ἂψ πάλιν, *yet again*, Il.

ἄ-ψαυστος, ον, (ψαύω) *untouched, not to be touched, sacred*, Thuc.   II. act. *not touching* a thing, c. gen., Soph.

ἀ-ψεγής, ές, (ψέγω) *unblamed, blameless*, Soph.

ἄ-ψεκτος, ον, = ἀψεγής, Theogn.

ἀψεύδεια, ἡ, *truthfulness*, Plat. ; and

ἀψευδέω, f. ήσω, *not to lie, to speak truth*, πρός τινα Soph., Plat. From

ἀ-ψευδής, ές, (ψεῦδος) *without lie and deceit, truthful, sincere, trusty*, Hes., Hdt., etc. :—Adv. -δέως, Att. -δῶς, *really and truly*, Id.

ἄ-ψευστος, ον, = ἀψευδής, Plat., Anth.

ἀ-ψήφιστος, ον, (ψηφίζομαι) *not having voted*, Ar.

ἀψῐδόομαι, pf. ἠψίδωμαι, (ἀψίς) Pass. *to be encircled*, Anth.

ἀψί-κορος, ον, (ἅπτομαι, κόρος) *satisfied with touching*, i. e. *fastidious, dainty*, Plat. :—τὸ ἀψ. *fastidiousness*, Plut., Luc.

ἀψῐμᾰχέω, f. ήσω, *to skirmish with an enemy, lead on to fight*, Plut. ; and

ἀψῐμᾰχία, ἡ, *a skirmishing*, Aeschin. From

ἀψί-μᾰχος, ον, (ἅπτομαι, μάχη) *skirmishing*.

ἀψίνθιον, τό, *wormwood*, Xen. From

ἄψινθος, ἡ, N. T. (Deriv. unknown.)

ἀψίς, Ion. ἀψίς, ῖδος, ἡ, (ἅπτω) *a juncture, loop, mesh*, such as form a net, Il.   2. *the felloe* or *felly* of a wheel, *the wheel* itself, Hes., Hdt., Eur.   3. any *circle* or *disk*, of the sun, Id.   4. *an arch* or *vault*, Plat., Luc.

ἀψ-όρροος, ον, contr. -ρους, ουν, (ἄψ, ῥέω) *back-flowing, refluent*, of Ocean, regarded as a stream *encircling* the earth and *flowing back* into itself, Hom.

ἄψ-ορρος, ον, poët. form of foreg., *going back, backwards*, Il., Soph. :—neut. ἄψορρον as Adv., *backward, back again*, Il., Aesch., Soph.

ἄψος, εος, τό, (ἅπτω) a joint, Od.
ἀ-ψόφητος, ον, (ψοφέω) noiseless ; c. gen., ἀψ. κωκυμάτων without sound of wailings, Soph.
ἄ-ψοφος, ον, = ἀψόφητος, Soph., Eur.
ἄ-ψυκτος, ον, (ψύχω) not capable of being cooled, Plat.
ἀψυχία, ἡ, want of life: want of spirit, faint-heartedness, Aesch., Eur. From
ἄ-ψυχος, ον, (ψυχή) lifeless, inanimate, Simon., Eur., Plat. 2. ἄψ. βορά non-animal food, Eur. II. spiritless, faint-hearted, Aesch.
ΆΩ (A), = ἄημι, to blow. II. = ἰαύω, to sleep, used only in aor. 1 ἄεσα, Ep. ἄεσσα Od. ; also 1 pl. contr. ἄσαμεν, Ib.
ΆΩ (B), to hurt, contr. from ἀάω.
ΆΩ (c), Ep. inf. ἄμεναι (contr. for ἀέμεναι): f. ἄσω: aor. 1 subj. ἄσω, inf. ἄσαι:—Med., Ep. 3 sing. ἄαται: f. ἄσομαι: aor. 1 ἀσάμην: I. trans. to satiate, αἵματος ἄσαι Ἀρῆα to give him his fill of blood, Il. II. intr. to take one's fill of a thing, c. gen., πρὸς ἄμεναι, χροὸς ἄσαι Ib. ; so in Med., ἄσεσθε κλαυθμοῖο, ποτῆτος ἀσασθαι Ib.
ἀῶθεν, Dor. for ἠῶθεν.
ᾠών, ᾠόνος, ἡ, Dor. for ἠϊών.
ἀωρί, Adv. of ἄωρος, at an untimely hour, too early, Luc., Anth. ; ἀωρὶ τῆς νυκτός at dead of night, Antipho, Theocr.
ἀωρία, ἡ, (ἄωρος A) a wrong time: acc. as Adv., ἀωρίαν ἥκειν to have come too late, Ar. ; ἀωρίᾳ at an unseasonable time, so late, Luc.
ἀώριος, α, ον, = ἄωρος, Anth.
ἀωρό-νυκτος, ον, (νύξ) at midnight, Aesch.
ἄ-ωρος (A), ον, (ὥρα) untimely, unseasonable, Lat. intempestivus, Aesch., Eur.:—c. gen., γήρως ἀωρότερα things unbecoming old age, Plut. 2. unripe, ἄωρος πρὸς γάμον Id. II. without youthful freshness, ugly, Xen., Plat.
ἄωρος (B), ον, (ἀείρω, cf. μετ-έωρος) pendulous, waving about, of the πλεκτάναι or polypus-like legs of Scylla, Od.
ἄωρτο, Eq. plqpf. pass. of ἀείρω.
Ἀώς, ἡ, Dor. for Ἠώς, Ἕως.
Ἀωσφόρος, ὁ, Dor. for Ἑωσφόρος.
ἀωτέω, (ἄω to sleep) only in pres., to sleep well, Hom.
ἄωτον, τό, and ἄωτος, ὁ, fine wool, flock, οἶ̓ς ἄωτον, or without οἶός, the sheep's finest wool, Hom. ; λίνοιο λεπτὸν ἄωτον the delicate flock of flax, i. e. the finest linen, Il. II. metaph. the finest, best of its kind, the flower of a thing, ἄωτος ζωᾶς the flower of life, Pind. ; Χαρίτων ἄωτος their choicest gift, Id. (Deriv. uncertain.)

B.

Β, β, βῆτα, indecl., second letter of the Gr. alphabet: hence as numeral, β' = δύο, δεύτερος, ͵β = 2000.
I. β is the medial labial mute, between tenuis π and asp. θ. The dialectic variations of β seem to be mostly due to uncertainties of pronunciation: 1. for γ, as βληχών γληχών, βλέφαρον Dor. γλέφαρον, βουνός γουνός· βεμβράς for μεμβράς, βροτός for μορτός (mort-

alis). 2. β is sometimes inserted between μλ, μρ to give a fuller sound, as in ἄμβροτος, μεσημβρία, γαμβρός, μέμβλεται.
βᾶ, shortd. form of voc. Βασιλεῦ, King! Aesch.
βᾰβαί, Lat. papae! exclamation of surprise, bless me! Eur., Ar.
βᾰβαιάξ, strengthd. for βαβαί, Ar.
βαβύκα, ἡ, Lacon. for γέφυρα, Arist. ap. Plut.
βάγμα, ατος, τό, (βάζω) a speech, Aesch.
βάδην [ᾰ], Adv. (βαίνω) step by step, Lat. pedetentim, Il. ; in marching step, Hdt. ; β. ταχύ at quick step, Xen. 2. gradually, more and more, Ar. II. walking, marching, opp. to riding, driving, sailing, Aesch.
βᾰδίζω, f. Att. βαδιοῦμαι: aor. 1 ἐβάδισα: pf. βεβάδικα: (βάδος, βαίνω):—to go slowly, to walk, Lat. ambulare, h. Hom., Xen.: to go, march, of horsemen, Id.: to go by land, Dem.:—c. acc. cogn., βάδον, ὁδὸν β. Ar., Xen. 2. generally, ἐπ' οἰκίας βαδ. to enter houses, Dem.: to proceed (in argument), Id.:—of things, αἱ τιμαὶ ἐπ' ἔλαττον ἐβάδιζον prices were getting lower, Id. Hence
βάδισις, εως, ἡ, a walking, going, Ar. ; of hares, Xen.; and
βάδισμα, ατος, τό, walk, gait, Xen., Dem. ; and
βαδισμός, ὁ, = βάδισις, Plat.
βαδιστέον, verb. Adj. of βαδίζω, one must walk or go, Soph. :—so pl. βαδιστέα, Ar.
βαδιστής, οῦ, ὁ, (βαδίζω) a goer, ταχὺς βαδ. a quick runner, Eur.
βαδιστικός, ή, όν, (βαδίζω) good at walking, Ar.
βάδος, ὁ, (βαίνω) a walk, βάδον βαδίζειν Ar.
ΒἌΖΩ, chiefly in pres. and impf., 3 sing. pf. pass. βέβακται:—to speak, say, Hom. ; βάζειν τί τινα to say somewhat to a man, Il. ; also, τί τινι Aesch. ; c. dat. modi, χαλεποῖς βάζειν ἐπέεσσι to address with sharp words, Hes. :—Pass., ἔπος βέβακται a word has been spoken, Od.
βαθέως, Adv., v. βαθύς II.
βαθίων, βάθιστος, Comp. and Sup. of βαθύς.
βαθμίς, ἡ, gen. ῖδος and ῖδος, a step, Anth.
βαθμός or βασμός, ὁ, (βαίνω) a step: metaph. a step, degree, N. T.
βάθος, εος, τό, (βαθύς) depth or height, acc. as measured up or down, Lat. altitudo, Ταρτάρου βάθη Aesch. ; αἰθέρος βάθος Eur. : in military sense, the depth of a line of battle, Thuc., Xen. :—β. τριχῶν depth, i.e. thickness or length, of hair, Hdt. :—in N.T., τὸ βάθος the deep water. 2. metaph., κακῶν βάθος Aesch. ; πλούτου βάθος Soph.
βάθρον, τό, shortd. from βατήριον, (βαίνω) that on which anything stands: 1. a base, pedestal, Hdt., Aesch. 2. a stage or scaffold, Hdt. 3. generally solid ground, Σαλαμῖνος β. Soph. ; ἐκ πατρῴων ἑστίας βάθρων i.e. house of my father, Id. :—in pl. foundations, Eur. ; ἐν βάθροις εἶναι to stand firm, Id. 4. a step, Soph. : the round of a ladder, Eur. 5. a bench, seat, Soph., Dem. 6. metaph., κινδύνου βάθρα the verge of danger, Eur.
βαθυ-αγκής, ές, (ἄγκος) with deep dells, Anth.
βαθύ-βουλος, ον, (βουλή) deep-counselling, Aesch.
βαθύ-γαιος, ον, (γαῖα) with deep soil, productive, Hdt.

βαθυ-γήρως, ων, gen. ω, (γῆρας) in great old age, decrepit, Anth.

βᾰθῠ-δίνης [ῑ], ου, ὁ, (δίνη) deep-eddying, Il., Hes. :— so also βᾰθῠ-δῑνήεις, εσσα, εν, Il.

βᾰθΰ-ζωνος, ον, (ζώνη) deep-girded, i.e. girded not close under the breast, but over the hips, so that the gown fell over the girdle in folds (cf. βαθύκολπος), Hom.

βᾰθΰ-θριξ, -τρῐχος, ὁ, ἡ, of sheep, with thick wool, h. Hom.

βᾰθῠ-καμπής, ές, (κάμπτω) strongly curved, Anth.

βᾰθῠ-κήτης, ες, (κῆτος II) deep yawning, of the sea, Theogn.

βᾰθῠ-κλεής, ές, (κλέος) illustrious, Anth.

βᾰθΰ-κολπος, ον, with dress falling in deep folds (cf. βαθύζωνος), of Trojan women, Il.   II. with deep, full breasts, deep-bosomed, Aesch. ; of the earth, Pind. : cf. βαθύστερνος.

βᾰθῠ-κρημνος, ον, with high cliffs, ἅλς Pind. ; β. ἀκταί deep and rugged headlands, Id.

βᾰθῠ-κτέανος, ον, (κτέανον) with great possessions, plenteous, Anth.

βᾰθῠ-λειμος, ον, (λειμών) with deep, rich meadows, Il.:— so, βαθυ-λείμων, ονος, ὁ, ἡ, Pind.

βᾰθῠ-λήϊος, ον, (λήϊον) with deep crop, very fruitful, Il.

βᾰθῠ-νοος, contr. -νους, ουν, of deep mind, Anth.

βᾰθύνω [ῠ], βαθϋνῶ, (βαθύς) to deepen, hollow out, of a torrent, Il.: N. T.   2. as military term, to deepen, τὴν φάλαγγα Xen.

βᾰθῠ-ξῠλος, ον, (ξύλον) with deep wood, Eur.

βᾰθῠ-πελμος, ον, (πέλμα) thick-soled, Anth.

βᾰθῠ-πλουτος, ον, exceeding rich, Aesch.

βᾰθῠ-πόλεμος, ον, plunged deep in war, Pind.

βᾰθυρ-ρείτης, ου, ὁ, (ῥέω) = βαθύρροος, Ep. gen. βαθυρρείταο Il., Hes.

βᾰθύρ-ρηνος, ον, (ῥήν) with thick wool, Anth.

βᾰθύρ-ριζος, ον, (ῥίζα) deep-rooted, Soph.

βᾰθύρ-ροος, ον, contr. -ρους, ουν, (ῥέω) deep-flowing, brimming, Il., Soph.

ΒΑ´ΘΥ´Σ, βαθεῖα Ion. βαθέα, βαθύ : gen. βαθέος, βαθείας Ion. βαθέης : dat. βαθεῖ, βαθείη Ion. βαθέη :—Comp. βαθύτερος, poët. βαθίων [ῑ], Dor. βάσσων : Sup. βαθύτατος, poët. βάθιστος :—deep or high, acc. to one's position, like Lat. altus, Hom., etc. ; βαθέης αὐλῆς from high-fenced court, Il. ; ἠϊόνος προπάροιθε βαθείης the deep, i. e. wide, shore, Ib. ; in Prose, of a line of battle, Xen.   2. deep or thick in substance, of a mist, Hom. ; of ploughed land, opp. to stony ground, Il., Eur. :—deep, thick, of woods, corn, clouds, Il., Hdt., etc. ; of hair, Xen.   3. violent, of a storm, Il.   4. generally, large, copious, abundant, κλέος, κλῆρος Pind. ; βαθεῖα τέρψις Soph. ; βαθὺς ἀνήρ a rich man, Xen. ; β. ὕπνος deep sleep, Theocr.   5. of the mind, deep, Il., Aesch. ; βαθύτερα ἤθεα Hdt.   6. of Time, far-advanced, late, βαθὺς ὄρθρος (v. ὄρθρος) βαθὺ τῆς ἡλικίας Ar. ; β. γῆρας Anth.   II. Adv. βαθέως, Theocr.

βᾰθῠ-σκᾰφής, ές, (σκάπτω) deep-dug, Soph.

βᾰθΰ-σκιος, ον, (σκιά) deep-shaded, h. Hom., Theocr.

βᾰθΰ-σπορος, ον, (σπείρω) deep-sown, fruitful, Eur.

βᾰθΰ-στερνος, ον, (στέρνον) deep-chested, λέων Pind., cf. βαθύκολπος.

βᾰθΰ-στολμος, ον, with deep, full robe, Anth.

βᾰθΰ-στρωτος, ον, deep-strewn, well-covered, Babr.

βᾰθΰ-σχοινος, ον, deep-grown with rushes, Il.

βᾰθΰτης, ητος, ἡ = βάθος, depth, Luc.

βᾰθΰ-φρων, ον, (φρήν) = βαθύβουλος, Solon, Pind.

βᾰθΰ-φυλλος, ον, (φύλλον) thick-leafed, Mosch.

βᾰθΰ-χαίτης, ου, ὁ, (χαίτη) with deep, thick hair, Hes.

βᾰθΰ-χθων, ον, gen. ονος, = βαθύγαιος, Aesch.

βαίνω (Root ΒΑ) : f. βήσομαι, Dor. βάσευμαι, Ep. βέομαι or βείομαι : pf. βέβηκα, Dor. βέβᾱκα, with Ep. syncop. 3 pl. βεβάᾱσι, contr. βεβᾱσι ; inf. βεβάναι [ᾰ], Ep. βεβάμεν [ᾰ] ; part. βεβαώς, -αυῖα, Att. βεβώς: plqpf. ἐβεβήκειν, Ep. βεβήκειν, sync. 3 pl. βέβᾰσαν :—aor. 2 ἔβην, Dor. ἔβᾱν, Ep. 3 sing. βῆ, 3 dual βάτην [ᾰ], 3 pl. ἔβᾰν ; imper. βῆθι, Dor. βᾶθι, 2 pl. βᾶτε ; subj. βῶ, Ep. βείω, 3 sing. βήῃ, Dor. βάμες (for βῶμεν) ; opt. βαίην ; inf. βῆναι, Ep. βήμεναι ; part. βάς βᾶσα βάν :—Med., Ep. 3 sing. aor. 1 ἐβήσετο.

A. in the above tenses,   I. intr. to walk, step, properly of motion on foot, ποσσὶ or ποσὶ βαίνειν Hom., etc. ; c. inf. in Hom., βῆ ἰέναι, βῆ ἰέμεν set out to go, went his way, Il. ; βῆ θέειν started to run, Ib. ; βῆ δ' ἐλάᾱν, Ib., etc. :—c. acc. loci, Soph. ; and with all Preps. implying motion, as, ἐπὶ νηὸς ἔβαινεν was going on board ship, Od. ; ἐφ' ἵππων βάντες having mounted the chariot, Ib. ; βαίνειν δι' αἵματος to wade through blood, Eur., etc.   2. in pf. to stand or be in a place, χῶρος ἐν ᾧ βεβήκαμεν Soph. ; often almost = εἰμί (sum), εὖ βεβηκώς on a good footing, well established, prosperous, Hdt., etc. ; so, οἱ ἐν τέλει βεβῶτες they who are in office, Id., Soph. ; cf. ξυρόν.   3. to go, go away, depart, Il., Soph. ; βέβηκα euphem. for τέθνηκα, Aesch., Soph. :—of things, ἐννέα ἐνιαυτοὶ βεβάᾱσι nine years have come and gone, Il.   4. to come, τίπτε βέβηκας ; Ib. : to arrive, Soph.   5. to go on, advance, ἐς τόδε τόλμης, ἐς τοσοῦτον ἐλπίδων Id.   II. c. acc. to mount, Hom. only in aor. 1 med., βήσασθαι δίφρον :—Pass., ἵπποι βαινόμεναι brood mares, Hdt.   2. χρέος ἔβα με debts came on me, Ar.   3. in Poets, with acc. of the instrument of motion, which is simply pleonastic, βαίνειν πόδα to advance the foot, step on, Eur., etc.

B. Causal, in f. βήσω, aor. 1 ἔβησα :—to make to go, βῆσεν ἀφ' ἵππου, ἐξ ἵππων βῆσε brought them down from the chariot, Il.   The pres. in this sense is βιβάζω.

βάϊον, τό, = βάϊς, N. T.

ΒΑΙΟ´Σ, ά, όν, little, small, scanty, and of number, few, Pind., Aesch., Soph. ; ἐχώρει βαιός he was going with scanty escort, i.e. alone, Id. : of condition, low, mean, humble, Id. : of time, short, Solon, Soph. :— neut. βαιόν, as Adv. a little, Id. ; so pl. βαιά, Ar. Cf. ἠβαιός.

βάϊς, ἡ, a palm-branch, N. T.   (Coptic word.)

βαίτη, ἡ, a shepherd's or peasant's coat of skins, Hdt., Theocr.   (Deriv. unknown.)

βάκηλος, ὁ, an eunuch in the service of Cybelé, Anth., Luc.

βᾰκίζω, to prophesy like Bacis, Ar.   From

Βᾱκίς, ιδος, ὁ, an old Boeotian prophet, Hdt.

βάκλον, τό, Lat. baculum, a stick, Aesop.

βακτηρία, ἡ, = βάκτρον, a staff, cane, Ar., Thuc.: borne as a badge of office by the δικασταί, Dem.

βακτήριον, τό, Dim. of βακτηρία, Ar.

βάκτρευμα, ατος, τό, a staff, βακτρεύματα ποδός support lent to one's foot, Eur. From

βακτρεύω, to lean on a staff.

βάκτρον, τό, (βι-βάζω) Lat. baculus, a staff, stick, cudgel, Aesch., Eur.

βακτρο-προσαίτης, ου, ό, going about begging with a staff, of a Cynic, Anth.

βάκῦλον, τό, = βάκλον : pl. = Lat. fasces, Plut.

Βακχάω, (Βάκχη) to be in Bacchic frenzy, to rave, Aesch.

Βακχέβακχον ᾆσαι, to sing the song Βάκχε Βάκχε! Ar.

Βακχεία, ή, the feast of Bacchus, Bacchic frenzy, revelry, Aesch., Eur. : generally, frenzy, Plat. :—in pl. Bacchic orgies, Eur.

Βακχεῖον, τό, the temple of Bacchus, Ar. II. Bacchic revelry, Eur. :—in pl. Bacchic orgies, Ar. ; also Βάκχια, Eur.

Βάκχειος or Βακχεῖος, in poets also Βάκχιος, α, ον, (Βάκχος) Bacchic, of or belonging to Bacchus and his rites, Eur., Xen. ; frenzied, frenzy-stricken, Hdt., Soph. ; τὸν Β. ἄνακτα, of Aeschylus, Ar. II. as Subst., Βάκχιος, ό, = Βάκχος, Soph., Eur. 2. = οἶνος, Id. 3. Βάκχειος (sc. πούς), ό, a foot of three syllables, – – ◡, opp. to antibacchīus.

Βάκχευμα, ατος, τό, (Βακχεύω) in pl. Bacchic revelries, Eur., Plut.

Βακχεύς, έως, ό, = Βάκχος, Soph., Eur.

Βακχεύσιμος, ον, Bacchanalian, frensied, Eur. ; and

Βάκχευσις, εως, ή, Bacchic revelry, Eur.

Βακχευτής, οῦ, ό, a Bacchanal : as Adj. Bacchanalian, Anth. Hence

Βακχευτικός, ή, όν, disposed to Bacchic revels, Arist.

Βακχεύτωρ, ορος, ό, = Βακχευτής. From

Βακχεύω, f. σω, (Βάκχος) to keep the feast of Bacchus, celebrate his mysteries, Hdt. 2. to speak or act like one frantic, Lat. bacchari, Soph., Eur. II. Causal, to inspire with frenzy, Id. :—Pass., Id.

Βάκχη, ή, a Bacchanté, Aesch., Soph., etc. :—generally, Βάκχη Ἄιδου frantic handmaid of Hades, Eur. ; β. νεκύων Id.

Βακχιάζω, = Βακχεύω, Eur.

Βακχιάς, άδος, ή, poët. fem. of Βάκχειος, Anth.

Βάκχιος, α, ον, = Βάκχειος, q. v.

Βακχίς, ίδος, ή, = Βάκχη, Soph.

Βακχιώτης, ου, ό, = Βακχευτής, Soph.

Βάκχος, ό, Bacchus, a later name of Dionysus, Soph., etc. : called Διόνυσος Βάκχειος and ό Βάκχειος in Hdt. II. as appellat. wine, Eur., etc. III. a Bacchanal, any one inspired, frantic, Id., Plat. (The Root seems to be ϝΑΧ, so that Βάκχος represents ϝάκχος ; and Ἴακχος is for ϝιϝακχος ; prob. from ἰάχω, = ϝιϝάχω, to shout.)

βᾰλᾰν-άγρα, ἡ, a key or hook for pulling out the door-pin (βάλανος II), Hdt., Xen.

βᾰλᾰνεῖον, τό, Lat. balineum, balneum, a bath or bathing-room, Ar. ; in pl., Id. From

βᾰλᾰνεύς, έως, ό, a bath-man, Lat. balneātor, Ar. (Deriv. uncertain.)

βᾰλᾰνεύω, f. σω, (βαλανεύς) to wait upon a person at the bath, β. ἑαυτῷ to be one's own bath-man, Ar.

βᾰλᾰνη-φάγος, ον, (φαγεῖν) acorn-eating, Orac. ap. Hdt.

βᾰλᾰνη-φόρος, ον, (φέρω) bearing dates, Hdt.

βᾰλᾰνίζω δρῦν, to shake acorns from the oak : as a proverb. answer to beggars, ἄλλην δρῦν βαλάνιζε Anth.

βᾰλάνισσα, ἡ, fem. of βαλανεύς, a bathing-woman, Anth.

βᾰλᾰνο-δόκη, ἡ, (δέχομαι) the socket in a door-post to receive the βάλανος (II).

βάλᾰνος [βᾰ], ἡ, an acorn, Lat. glans, the fruit of the φηγός, given to swine, Od. :—any similar fruit, the date, Hdt., Xen. II. from similarity of shape, an iron peg, a bolt-pin, Lat. pessulus, passed through the wooden bar (μόχλος) into the door-post, so that the bar could not be removed till the pin was taken out with a hook (βαλανάγρα), Ar., Thuc. (Deriv. uncertain.)

βᾰλᾰνόω, f. ώσω, to fasten with a bolt-pin (βάλανος II), βεβαλάνωκε τὴν θύραν Ar. :—Pass., βεβαλανωμένος, η, ον, shut close, secured, Id.

βᾰλάντιον, βᾰλαντιοτομέω, βᾰλαντιο-τόμος, ό, v. βαλλ–

βαλβίς, ῖδος, ἡ, properly, the rope drawn across the race-course : mostly in pl., Lat. carceres, the posts marking the line whence the racers started, and to which they returned, Ar. :—then, any starting point, Eur., Ar. ; metaph., πρὸς βαλβῖδα βίον Eur. II. also any point to be gained, as the battlements (by one scaling a wall), Soph. (Deriv. uncertain.)

βαλήν, ό, v. βαλλήν.

βᾰλιός, ά, όν, spotted, dappled, Eur. II. parox. Βαλίος, one of the horses of Achilles, Dapple, Il. (Deriv. uncertain.)

βαλλάντιον, less correctly βαλάντιον, τό, a bag, pouch, purse, Simon., Ar.

βαλλαντιοτομέω, f. ήσω, to cut purses, Plat., Xen. From

βαλλαντιο-τόμος, ό, (τέμνω) a cut-purse, Ar., Plat.

βαλλήν, ό, a king, Aesch. (Prob. from Baal, Bel.)

Βαλλήναδε βλέπειν, a pun between βάλλω and the Attic deme Παλλήνη, Ar.

βάλλεν, Ep. for βάλλου, imper. med. of βάλλω.

βάλλω (Root ΒΑΛ) f. βᾰλῶ, Ion. βᾰλέω, rarely βαλλήσω : aor. 2 ἔβᾰλον, Ion. inf. βαλέειν : pf. βέβληκα : plqpf. ἐβεβλήκειν, Ep. βεβλήκειν :—Med., 3 sing. Ion. impf. βαλλέσκετο : f. βᾰλοῦμαι : aor. 2 ἐβᾰλόμην, Ion. imper. βαλεῦ :—Pass., f. βληθήσομαι and βεβλήσομαι : aor. 1 ἐβλήθην :—Hom. also has an Ep. 3 sing. syncop. aor. 2 pass., ἔβλητο ; subj. βλήεται (for βλῆται), opt. 2 sing. βλῆο or βλεῖο ; inf. βλῆσθαι ; part. βλήμενος : pf. βέβλημαι, Ion. 3 pl. βεβλήαται, plqpf. βεβλήατο.

A. Act. to throw : I. with acc. of person or thing aimed at, to throw so as to hit, to hit one with a missile, opp. to striking (τύπτω, οὐτάω), βλήμενος ἠὲ τυπείς Il. ; c. dupl. acc. pers. et partis, μιν βάλε μηρὸν ὀϊστῷ Ib. : c. acc. cogn. added, ἕλκος, τό μιν βάλε the wound which he gave him, Ib. :—also, βάλε κατ' ἀσπίδα smote upon it, Ib. 2. of things, ἡνίοχον ῥαθάμιγγες ἔβαλλον Ib. :—of the Sun, ἀκτῖσιν ἔβαλλεν [χθόνα] Od. : to strike the senses, of sound, κτύπος οὔατα βάλλει Il. 3. metaph., β. τινὰ κακοῖς to smite with reproaches, Soph., etc. ; φθόνος βάλλει τινά Aesch. II. with acc. of the weapon thrown, to throw, cast, hurl, βαλὼν βέλος Il. ; ἐν νηυσὶν πῦρ βάλλειν Ib. :—with dat. of the weapon, to throw or shoot with a thing,

χερμαδίοισι Ib.; βέλεσι β. τινα Hom.; β. ἐπί τινα to throw at one, Thuc.; ἐπὶ σκοπόν or σκοποῦ Xen. 2. generally of anything thrown, εἰς ἅλα λύματ' ἔβαλλον Il., etc.:—of persons, β. τινὰ ἐν κονίησιν, ἐν δαπέδῳ Hom., etc.; metaph., ἐς κακὸν β. τινά Od.; β. τινὰ ἐς φόβον Eur.; also, ἐν αἰτίᾳ or αἰτίᾳ β. τινά Soph. 3. to let fall, ἑτέρωσε κάρη βάλεν Il.; β. ἀπὸ δάκρυ παρειῶν Od. 4. of the eyes, ἑτέρωσε βάλ' ὄμματα cast them the other way, Ib., etc. 5. in a loose sense, to throw, to put, place, ἐν στήθεσσι μένος βάλε Il.; ὅπως φιλότητα μετ' ἀμφοτέροισι βάλωμεν may put friendship between them, Ib.; β. τί τινι ἐν θυμῷ Od.; ἐς θυμὸν β. to lay to heart, Soph. 6. to put round, ἀμφ' ὀχέεσσι βάλε κύκλα Il.; and of clothes or arms, ἀμφὶ δ' Ἀθήνη ὤμοις βάλ' αἰγίδα Ib. 7. βαλών is sometimes added, like λαβών or ἔχων, at the end of a sentence, almost as an expletive, with, Soph. III. intr., ποταμὸς εἰς ἅλα βάλλων falling, Il.; ἐν πέδῳ βαλῶ (sc. ἐμαυτήν) Aesch. 2. so in familiar language, βάλλ' ἐς κόρακας away with you! be hanged! Lat. pasce corvos! abi in malam rem! Ar.
B. Med. to put for oneself, ἐνὶ θυμῷ βάλλευ lay it to heart, Od.; ἐς θυμὸν βάλλεσθαί τι Hdt.; ἐφ' ἑωυτοῦ βαλόμενος on one's own judgment, of oneself, Id. 2. τόξα or ξίφος ἀμφ' ὤμοις βάλλεσθαι to throw about one's shoulder, Il. 3. ἐς γαστέρα βάλλεσθαι, of a woman, to conceive, Hdt. 4. to lay the foundations of, begin to form, οἰκοδομίαν, στρατόπεδον, Plat., etc.; β. ἄγκυραν to cast anchor, Hdt. II. rarely, χρόα βάλλεσθαι λουτροῖς to dash one's flesh with water, bathe, h. Hom.

βαλός, ὁ, Dor. for βηλός.

βᾰλῶ, f. ind. and aor. 2 subj. of βάλλω.

βᾶμα, τό, Dor. for βῆμα.

βαμβαίνω, only in pres. to chatter with the teeth, Il.: to stammer, Bion. (Formed from the sound.)

βᾶμες, Dor. for βῶμεν, 1 pl. aor. 2 subj. of βαίνω.

βάμμα, ατος, τό, (βάπτω) that in which a thing is dipped, dye, Plat., v. βάπτω I. 3.

βάν [ᾰ], Ep. for ἔβαν, ἔβησαν, 3 pl. aor. 2 of βαίνω.

βᾰναυσία, ἡ, handicraft, the practice of a mere mechanical art, Hdt.; and

βᾰναυσικός, ή, όν, of or for mechanics: τέχνη β. a mere mechanical art, Lat. ars sellularia, Xen. From

βάναυσος, ον, mechanical, and as Subst. a mechanic, Arist. II. τέχνη βάναυσος a mere mechanical art, a base, ignoble art, Soph., Plat. (Deriv. uncertain.)

βαναυσ-ουργία, ἡ, (*ἔργω) handicraft, Plut.

βάξις, εως, ἡ, (βάζω) a saying, esp. an oracular saying, like φήμη, Aesch., Soph. 2. a report, rumour, Theogn., Soph., Eur.; ἁλώσιμος β. tidings of the capture, Aesch.

βαπτίζω, f. Att. ιῶ, to dip in or under water; metaph., βεβαπτισμένοι soaked in wine, Plat.; ὀφλήμασι βεβ. over head and ears in debt, Plut. 2. to baptise, τινά N. T.:—Pass., βαπτίζεσθαι εἰς μετάνοιαν, εἰς ἄφεσιν ἁμαρτιῶν Ib.:—Med. to get oneself baptised, Ib. Hence

βάπτισμα, τό, baptism, N. T.; and

βαπτισμός, ὁ, a dipping in water, ablution, N. T.; and

βαπτιστής, οῦ, ὁ, one that dips: a baptizer, ὁ Β. the baptist, N. T.

βαπτός, ή, όν, dipped, dyed, bright-coloured, Ar. 2. for dyeing, χρώματα Plat. II. of water, drawn by dipping vessels (cf. βάπτω I. 3), Eur. From

βάπτω (Root ΒΑΦ), f. βάψω: aor. 1 ἔβαψα: Pass., f. βαφήσομαι: aor. 1 ἐβάφθην: aor. 2 ἐβάφην [ᾰ]: pf. βέβαμμαι: I. trans. to dip in water, Lat. immergere, Od., Plat.:—of slaughter, ἐν σφαγαῖσι βάψασα ξίφος Aesch.; ἔβαψας ἔγχος Soph.; φάσγανον εἴσω σαρκὸς ἔβαψεν Eur. 2. to dip in poison, ἰούς, χιτῶνα Soph. 3. to dip in dye, to dye, Hdt., Aesch.:—Comic, βάπτειν τινὰ βάμμα Σαρδιανικόν to dye one in the [red] dye of Sardis, i. e. give him a bloody coxcomb, Ar. 4. to draw water by dipping a vessel, Theocr.; βάψασα ἁλός (sc. τὸ τεῦχος) having dipped it so as to draw water from the sea, Eur. II. intr., ναῦς ἔβαψεν the ship dipped, sank, Id.

βάραθρον, Ion. βέρεθρον, τό, a gulf, pit:—at Athens a cleft behind the Acropolis, into which criminals were thrown, Hdt., Ar. 2. metaph. ruin, perdition, Dem. (Deriv. uncertain.)

βαρβᾰρίζω, f. Att. ιῶ, (βάρβαρος) to behave like a barbarian, speak like one, Hdt.: to speak broken Greek, speak gibberish, Plat. II. to hold with the barbarians, i. e. the Persians, Xen.

βαρβᾰρικός, ή, όν, barbaric, foreign, like a foreigner, opp. to Ἑλληνικός, Simon.; τὸ βαρβαρικόν = οἱ βάρβαροι, Thuc.; esp. of the Persians, Xen.:—Adv., βαρβαρικῶς καὶ Ἑλληνικῶς i. e. both in Persian and Greek, Id. Hence

βαρβᾰρισμός, ὁ, (βαρβαρίζω) barbarism, Arist.

βαρβᾰρόομαι, Pass. to become barbarous, Eur.; βεβαρβαρωμένος of barbarous or outlandish sound, Soph.

βάρβᾰρος, ον, barbarous, i. e. not Greek, foreign, known to Hom., as appears from the word βαρβαρόφωνος in Il.:—as Subst. βάρβαροι, οἱ, originally all that were not Greeks, specially the Medes and Persians, Hdt., Att.: so the Hebrews called the rest of mankind Gentiles. From the Augustan age however the name was given by the Romans to all tribes which had no Greek or Roman accomplishments. II. after the Persian war the word took the sense of outlandish, ἀμαθὴς καὶ βάρβαρος Ar.; βαρβαρώτατος Id., Thuc. (Deriv. uncertain.)

βαρβᾰρό-φωνος, ον, (φωνή) speaking a foreign tongue, Κᾶρες Il.

βαρβᾰρόω, v. βαρβαρόομαι.

βάρβῑτος, ἡ or ὁ, a musical instrument of many strings (πολύχορδος Theocr.), like the lyre, and often used for the lyre itself, Anacr., Eur., etc. (Prob. an Oriental word.)

βάρδιστος, η, ον, by Ep. metath. for βράδιστος, Sup. of βραδύς, Il.: βαρδύτερος, for βραδ-, Theocr.

βᾰρέω, f. ήσω: pf. βεβάρηκα: (βαρύς):—to weigh down, depress, Luc. II. intr. in Ep. pf. part. βεβαρηώς, weighed down, heavy, οἴνῳ βεβαρηότες Od.: later in part. pass. βεβαρημένος, Theocr., Anth., etc.

βαρέως, Adv. of βαρύς.

βᾶρις, ιδος Ion. ιος, ἡ: pl. βάρεις, Ion. βάρῑς; poët. dat. pl. βαρίδεσσι:—a flat-bottomed boat, used in Egypt, Hdt., Aesch.

βάρος [ᾰ], εως, τό, (βαρύς) weight, Hdt., etc. II. a weight, burden, load, Aesch., etc. III. metaph. a heavy weight, πημονῆς, συμφορᾶς β. Soph.; then alone for grief, misery, Aesch.; βάρος ἔχειν Arist. IV. abundance, πλούτου, ὄλβου Eur.

βᾰρυ-αλγής, ές, (ἄλγος) = sq., Anth.

βᾰρυ-άλγητος, ον, (ἀλγέω) very grievous, Soph.

βᾰρυ-ᾰχής, ές, (ἄχος) heavy with woe, Soph.

βᾰρυ-αχής, ές, Dor. for βαρυηχής, Ar.

βᾰρυ-βρεμέτης, ου, ὁ, (βρέμω) loud-thundering, Soph.: so, βᾰρυ-βρομήτης (βρομέω), Anth.

βᾰρύ-βρομος, ον, (βρέμω) loud-roaring, loud-sounding, Eur.

βᾰρύ-βρώς, ὁ, ἡ, (βι-βρώσκω) gnawing, corroding, Soph.

βᾰρύ-γουνος, ον, (γόνυ) heavy-kneed, lazy, Call.; and βᾰρύ-γούνατος, Theocr.

βᾰρύ-γυιος, ον, (γυῖον) weighing down the limbs, wearisome, Anth.

βᾰρῠδαιμονέω, f. ήσω, to be grievously unlucky, Ar.

βᾰρυ-δαίμων, gen. ονος, pressed by a heavy fate, luckless, Eur.

βᾰρύ-δακρυς, υ, (δάκρυ) weeping grievously, Anth.

βᾰρύ-δῐκος, ον, (δίκη) taking heavy vengeance, Aesch.

βᾰρύ-δότειρα, ἡ, giver of ill gifts, Aesch.

βᾰρύ-δουπος, ον, loud-sounding, Mosch.

βᾰρύ-ζηλος, ον, exceeding jealous, Anth.

βᾰρύ-θροος, ον, deep or loud-sounding, Mosch.

βᾰρῠθῡμέω, f. ήσω, to be weighed down: to be heavy at heart: in Med., Plut.; and

βᾰρῠθῡμία, ἡ, sullenness, Plut. From

βᾰρύ-θῡμος, ον, heavy in spirit: indignant, sullen, Eur.

βᾰρύθω [ῠ], (βαρύς) only in pres. and impf. to be weighed down, Il., Hes. 2. to be heavy, Anth.

βᾰρύ-κοτος, ον, heavy in wrath, Aesch.

βᾰρύ-κτῠπος, ον, heavy-sounding, loud-thundering, h. Hom., Hes.

βᾰρύ-μήνιος, ον, = sq., Theocr.

βᾰρύ-μηνις, ι, heavy in wrath, exceeding wrathful, Aesch.

βᾰρύ-μισθος, ον, largely paid, Anth.

βᾰρύ-μοχθος, ον, very toilsome, painful, Anth.

βᾰρύνω [ῡ], f. ῠνῶ: aor. 1 ἐβάρῡνα :—Pass., aor. 1 ἐβαρύνθην: (βαρύς) :— to weigh down, oppress by weight, depress, Hom. :—Pass., γυῖα βαρύνεται he is heavy, i. e. weary, in limb, Il.; χεῖρα βαρυνθείς disabled in hand, Ib.; βαρύνεταί τινι τὸ σκέλος Ar.; ὄμμα β., of one dying, Eur. 2. metaph. to oppress, weary, τοὺς δικαστάς Xen. :—Pass. to be oppressed, distressed, Lat. gravari, Aesch., Soph.

βᾰρυ-όργητος, ον, (ὀργάω) exceeding angry, Anth.

βᾰρύ-πάλᾰμος, ον, (παλάμη) heavy-handed, Pind.

βᾰρύ-πενθής, ές, (πένθος) causing grievous woe, Anth.

βᾰρύ-πένθητος, ον, (πενθέω) mourning heavily, Anth.

βᾰρύ-πεσής, ές, (πεσεῖν) heavy-falling, Aesch.

βᾰρύ-ποτμος, ον, = βαρυδαίμων, of persons, Soph.; of sufferings, grievous, Id.: irreg. Sup. βαρυποτμώτατος (metri grat.) Eur.

βᾰρύ-πους, ὁ, ἡ, πουν, τό, heavy at the end, Anth.

ΒΑ'ΡΥ'Σ, εῖα, ύ; poët. gen. pl. fem. βαρεῶν (for -ειῶν) Aesch.: Comp. βαρύτερος, Sup. βαρύτατος :—heavy in weight, opp. to κοῦφος, Hdt., etc.: in Hom. mostly with a notion of strength and force, χεῖρα βαρεῖαν Il., etc.: also, heavy with age or suffering, γήρᾳ, νόσῳ Soph. 2. heavy to bear, grievous, Hom.; βαρὺ or βαρέα στενάχειν to sob heavily, Id. :—in Att., burdensome, grievous, oppressive :—Adv., βαρέως φέρειν τι to take a thing ill, Lat. graviter ferre, Hdt., etc.; βαρέως ἀκούειν to hear with disgust, Xen. 3. violent, Theocr., Plat., etc. 4. weighty, impressive, N. T. II. of persons, severe, stern, Aesch., Soph. :—also, wearisome, oppressive, Eur., Dem.: in good sense, grave, dignified, Arist. 2. of soldiers, heavy-armed, Xen. III. of impressions of the senses, 1. of sound, strong, deep, bass, Od., Aesch., Soph. 2. of smell, strong, offensive, Hdt., Soph.

βᾰρύ-σίδηρος [ῑ], ον, heavy with iron, Plut.

βᾰρύ-σταθμος, ον, weighing heavy, Ar.

βᾰρύ-στονος, ον, (στένω) groaning heavily, bellowing, Dem. :—Adv. -νως, Aesch. II. of things, heavily lamented, grievous, Soph.

βᾰρυ-σφάρᾰγος [ᾰ], ον, loud-thundering, Pind.

βᾰρύτης [ῠ], ητος, ἡ, (βαρύς) weight, heaviness, Thuc. II. of men, importunity, disagreeableness, Dem., Plut. 2. in good sense, gravity, dignity, Arist., Plut. III. of sound, strength, depth, Plat.

βᾰρύ-τῑμος, ον, (τιμή) very costly, N. T.

βᾰρύ-τλητος, ον, bearing a heavy weight, Anth. II. pass. ill to bear, Id.

βᾰρύ-τονος, ον, deep-sounding, Xen.

βᾰρύ-φθογγος, ον, loud-sounding, roaring, h. Hom.

βαρυφροσύνη [ῠ], ἡ, gloominess, indignation, Plut.

βᾰρύ-φρων, ον, gen. ονος, (φρήν) weighty of purpose, grave-minded, Theocr.

βᾰρύ-χειλος, ον, thick-lipped, Anth.

βᾰρύ-χορδος, ον, (χορδή) deep-toned, Anth.

βᾰρύ-ψῡχος, ον, (ψυχή) heavy of soul, dejected, Soph.

βάς, βᾶσα, βάν, aor. 2 part. of βαίνω.

βᾰσᾰνίζω, f. Att. ῐῶ: aor. 1 ἐβασάνισα, ἐβασανίσθην: pf. βεβασάνισμαι:—to rub gold upon the touch-stone (βάσανος), Plat.: hence, to try the genuineness of a thing, to put to the test, make proof of, Id. II. of persons, to examine closely, cross-question, Hdt., Ar. 2. to question by applying torture, to torture, Id. :—Pass. to be put to the torture, for the purpose of extorting confession, Thuc.: to be tormented by disease or storm, N. T. Hence

βᾰσᾰνιστέος, α, ον, verb. Adj. to be put to the proof, Plat. II. βασανιστέον one must put to the torture, τινά Id., Dem.

βᾰσᾰνιστής, οῦ, ὁ, (βασανίζω) questioner, torturer, tormentor, Dem., N. T. :—fem. βᾰσᾰνίστρια, an examiner, Ar.

βάσᾰνος [βᾰ-], ἡ, the touch-stone, Lat. lapis Lydius, a dark-coloured stone on which pure gold, when rubbed, leaves a peculiar mark, Theogn.: hence. II. generally, a test, trial whether a thing be genuine or real, Hdt., Soph. III. inquiry by torture, the 'question,' torture, used to extort evidence from slaves, Oratt. 2. torture of disease, N. T. (Deriv. uncertain.)

βᾰσεῦμαι, Dor. for βήσομαι, f. of βαίνω.

βᾰσίλεᾰ, ή, (βασῐλεύς) a queen, princess, Od., Aesch.
βᾰσῐλείᾱ, Ion. -ηίη, ή, (βασιλεύω) a kingdom, dominion, Hdt.: hereditary monarchy, opp. to τυραννίς, Thuc., etc.
βᾰσῐλείδιον, τό, Dim. of βασιλεύς, a petty king, Plut.
βᾰσίλειον, Ion. -ήϊον, τό, (βασιλεύς) a kingly dwelling, palace, Xen.; mostly in pl., Hdt., etc. 2. the royal treasury, Id.
βᾰσίλειος, ον, or α, ον, Ion. -ήϊος, η, ον, of the king, kingly, royal, Hdt., etc. From
βᾰσῐλεύς, ὁ, gen. έως, Ion. ῆος, acc. βασιλέα, βασιλῆ: nom. pl. βασιλεῖς, Ion. -ῆες, old Att. βασιλῆς; acc. pl. βασιλεῖς, old Att. βασιλῆς:—a king, chief, Hom.: later it was an hereditary king, opp. to τύραννος, Hdt., Att.; ἄναξ β. lord king, Aesch.: c. gen., β. νεῶν Id.; οἰωνῶν β., of the eagle, Id.:—Hom. has a Comp. βασιλεύτερος more of a king, more kingly, Sup. βασιλεύτατος most kingly. 2. of the king's son, prince, or any one sharing in the government, Od. 3. generally, a lord, master, householder, Il., Pind. II. at Athens, the second of the nine Archons was called βασιλεύς; he had charge of the public worship, and the conduct of criminal processes, Plat., etc. III. after the Persian war, the king of Persia was called βασιλεύς (without the Art.), Hdt., Att.; more rarely ὁ βασιλεύς, or ὁ μέγας βασ. Hdt. (Deriv. uncertain.)
βᾰσῐλεύω, f. σω, (βασιλεύς) to be king, to rule, reign, Hom., etc.; of a woman, to be queen, Id.; c. gen. to be king of, Od.; also, ὄφρ' Ἰθάκης κατὰ δῆμον βασιλεύοι Ib.; in aor. to have become king, Hdt.; c. dat. to be king among others, Od.:—Pass. to be governed by a king, Plat.: to submit to the king, Plut. 2. to be master of a thing, c. gen., Theocr.
βᾰσῐλήη, βᾰσῐλήϊος, Ion. for βασιλεία, βασίλειος.
βᾰσῐλῆϊς, ῖδος, ή, poët. fem. of βασίλειος, royal, Il., Eur.
βᾰσῐλίζω, f. σω, (βασιλεύς) to be of the king's party, Plut.
βᾰσῐλικός, ή, όν, like βασίλειος, royal, kingly, Hdt., Att. 2. like a king, kingly, princely, βασιλικώτατος Xen.:—Adv., βασιλικῶς as a king, with kingly authority, Id. II. as Subst., 1. βασιλική (sub. στοά), ή, a colonnade at Athens, Plat.; v. στοά. 2. βασιλικός, ὁ, king's officer, N. T.
βᾰσῐλῑναῦ, barbarism for βασίλιννα, Ar.
βᾰσίλιννα, ή, = βασίλισσα, Dem.
βᾰσῐλίς, ίδος, ή, = βασίλεια, a queen, princess, Soph., Eur., etc. 2. as Adj. royal, Id.
βᾰσίλισσα, ή, later for βασιλεία, a queen, Xen., Theocr.
βάσιμος [ᾰ], ον, (βαίνω) passable, accessible, Dem., Plut.
βάσις [ᾰ], εως, ή, (βαίνω) a stepping, step, and collectively steps, Aesch., Soph., etc.; οὐκ ἔχων βάσιν power to step, Id.; τροχῶν βάσεις the rolling of the wheels, Id. II. that with which one steps, a foot, Eur., N. T. III. that whereon one stands, a base, Plat.
βασκαίνω, f. ᾰνῶ: aor. 1 ἐβάσκηνα, -ᾱνα:—Pass., aor. 1 ἐβασκάνθην:—1. c. acc. to slander, malign, belie, disparage, Dem. 2. c. dat. to envy, grudge, Id. II. to bewitch, by means of spells: Pass., ὡς μὴ βασκανθῶ (aor. 1 subj.) that I be not bewitched, Theocr.

βασκᾰνία, ή, slander, envy, malice, Plat., Dem. From
βάσκᾰνος, ον, slanderous, envious, malignant, Ar., Dem. II. as Subst. a slanderer, Id. 2. a sorcerer, Id. (Deriv. uncertain.)
βασκάς (or -ᾶς), ή, a kind of duck, Ar.
βάσκω (akin to βαίνω, cf. χάσκω, χαίνω), only used in imper., βάσκ' ἴθι, speed thee! away! Il.; also come! Aesch.
βασμός, another form of βαθμός.
βᾶσσα, ή, Dor. for βῆσσα.
βασσάρα [ᾰ], ή, = ἀλώπηξ, a fox. II. a Thracian bacchanal, Anth. (Prob. a foreign word.)
βασσαρικός, ή, όν, = βακχικός, Anth.
βασσάριον, τό, Dim. of βασσάρα I, a little fox, Hdt.
βάσσων, ον, gen. ονος, Dor. Comp. of βαθύς.
βάσταγμα, τό, that which is borne, a burden, Eur. From
βαστάζω: f. άσω: aor. 1 ἐβάστασα, later ἐβάσταξα:—to lift, lift up, raise, Od., Soph., Eur.: to bear, carry, support, Aesch., Soph. 2. to hold in one's hands, Id. 3. βαστάζειν ἐν γνώμῃ to bear in mind, consider, weigh, make proof of, Aesch. II. to carry off, take away, N. T. III. Att. also = ψηλαφάω, to touch, Aesch. (Deriv. uncertain.) Hence
βαστακτός, ή, όν, verb. Adj. to be borne, Anth.
βάτᾰλος, ὁ, (βάττος) a nickname given to Demosthenes, from his stuttering, Aeschin.
βᾶτε, Dor. for βῆτε, aor. 2 imper. of βαίνω.
βᾰτέω, (βαίνω) to tread, cover, of animals, Theocr.
βᾰτην [ᾰ], Ep. for ἐβήτην, 3 dual aor. 2 of βαίνω.
βᾰτηρίς, ίδος, ή, (βατέω) κλῖμαξ β. a mounting ladder, Anth.
βᾰτιδο-σκόπος, ον, looking after skates, Ar.
βᾰτίς, ίδος, ή, a flat fish, perhaps the skate, Ar.
βᾰτο-δρόπος, ον, (δρέπω) pulling berries off, h. Hom.
ΒΑ'ΤΟΣ [ᾰ], ή, a bramble-bush or wild raspberry, Od.
βάτος, ὁ, the Hebrew measure bath, = Att. μετρητής, N. T.
βᾰτός, ή, όν, (βαίνω) passable, Xen.
βατράχειος, ον, (βάτραχος) of or belonging to a frog: βατράχεια (sc. χρώματα), frog-colour, pale-green, Ar.
βατραχίς, ίδος, ή, a frog-green coat, Ar.; and
βατραχο-μυο-μαχία, ή, (μῦς, μάχη) the battle of the frogs and mice. From
βάτραχος [βᾰτρᾰ-], ὁ, a frog, Batr., Hdt., etc. (Deriv. uncertain.)
βαττᾰρίζω, (βάττος) to stutter, Luc.
βαττο-λογέω, f. ήσω (λόγος) to speak stammeringly, say the same thing over and over again, N. T. From
Βάττος, ὁ, Stammerer, name of a king of Cyrené, Hdt. (Formed from the sound.)
βαΰζω, Dor. βαΰσδω, only in pres. to cry βαά βαά, to bark, Theocr.: of angry persons, to snarl, yelp, Aesch.: trans. to shriek aloud for, τινά Id. (Formed from the sound.)
βαύκᾰλις, ή, a wine-cooler, Anth.
βαυκο-πανοῦργος, ὁ, a paltry braggart, Arist.
ΒΑΥΚΟ'Σ, ή, όν, prudish.
βαΰσδω, Dor. for βαΰζω.
βᾰφή, ή, (βάπτω) a dipping of red-hot iron in water, the temper produced thereby, Arist. II. a dipping in dye, dyeing, dye, Aesch., Plat., etc.; κρόκου βαφαί the saffron-dyed robe, Aesch.; βαφαὶ ὕδρας the robe dipped in the hydra's blood, Eur. III. χαλκοῦ βαφαί, in

Aesch., is prob. *the art of tempering* brass, *to express something which no woman could know.* **IV.** in Soph. Aj., βαφῇ σίδηρος ὥς must be construed not with ἐθηλύνθην, but with the preceding words καρτερὸς γενόμενος, for iron becomes harder, not softer, by being dipped. Hence

βᾰφικός, ή, όν, *fit for dyeing,* Luc.

βδάλλω (Root **ΒΔΑΛ**): aor. 1 ἔβδηλα, *to milk* cows, Plat.: *to suck,* Arist. Hence

βδέλλᾰ, ή, *a leech,* Hdt., Theocr.

βδέλυγμα, τό, (βδελύσσομαι) *an abomination,* i. e. *an idol,* N. T.

βδελυγμία, ή, (βδελύσσομαι) *nausea, disgust,* Xen.

βδελυκτός, ή, όν, (βδελύσσομαι) *disgusting, abominable,* N. T.

βδελύκ-τροπος, ον, = foreg., Aesch.

βδελύρεύομαι, Dep. *to behave in a brutal manner,* Dem.; and

βδελυρία, ή, *brutal conduct, want of shame and decency, brutality,* Oratt.

βδελῠρός, ά, όν, (βδέω) *loathsome, disgusting, brutal,* Ar., Oratt.; Sup. -ώτατος, Dem.

βδελύσσομαι, Att. -ττομαι: f. -ύξομαι: aor. 1 ἐβδελύχθην: (βδέω) :—*to feel nausea, to be sick,* Ar. **2.** c. acc. *to feel a loathing at, to loathe,* Id. **II.** *to be loathsome:* οἱ ἐβδελυγμένοι *the abominable* (in ref. to βδέλυγμα), N. T.

ΒΔΕ΄Ω, *to break wind,* Ar. Hence

βδύλλω, Lat. *oppedere, to insult grossly,* τινά Ar. **2.** *to be afraid of,* Id.

βέβαιος, ος, ον and α, ον, (βαίνω) *firm, steady, steadfast, sure, certain,* Aesch., etc.; βεβαιότερος κίνδυνος a *surer* game, Thuc. **2.** of persons, *steadfast, steady, sure, constant,* Aesch., etc.; c. inf., βεβαιότεροι μηδὲν νεωτεριεῖν *more certain* to make no change, Thuc. **3.** τὸ βέβαιον *certainty, firmness, resolution,* Hdt., Thuc. **II.** Adv. -ως, Aesch., etc.; Comp. -ότερον, Thuc.; Sup. -ότατα, Id. Hence

βεβαιότης, ητος, ή, *firmness, steadfastness, stability, assurance, certainty,* Thuc., Plat.; and

βεβαιόω, f. ώσω, *to make firm, confirm, establish, secure, warrant, make good,* Plat., Xen.; ἔργῳ βεβαιούμενα *things warranted by fact,* opp. to ἀκοῇ λεγόμενα, Thuc. **2.** β. τί τινι *to secure* one *the possession of* a thing, Id.:—Med. *to establish for oneself, to confirm, secure,* Id. **II.** Med. also *to secure one's ground* in argument, *to asseverate, maintain, make good,* Plat. **2.** *to guarantee* a title, Isaeus. Hence

βεβαίωσις, εως, ή, *confirmation,* Thuc., Aeschin.

βέβαμεν [ᾰ], sync. for βεβήκαμεν, 1 pl. pf. of βαίνω: so, **βέβᾶσι** for βεβήκασι, **βεβώς** for βεβηκώς.

βέβᾱσαν, sync. for ἐβεβήκεσαν, 3 pl. plqpf. of βαίνω.

βέβηλος, ον, (βηλός, with βε- as a redupl.) *allowable to be trodden, permitted to human use,* Lat. *profanus,* Soph., Eur.; ἐν βεβήλῳ Thuc. **II.** of persons, *unhallowed, impure,* Id., Plat.: c. gen. *uninitiated in* rites, Anth. Hence

βεβηλόω, f. ώσω, *to profane,* N. T.

βεβίηκα, pf. of βιάω.

βέβλαμμαι, pf. pass. of βλάπτω.

βεβλήαται, -ατο, Ep. 3 pl. pf. and plqpf. of βάλλω.

βέβληται, -το, 3 sing. pf. and plqpf. of βάλλω.

βεβολήατο, βεβολημένος, v. *βολέω.

βεβουλευμένως, Adv. part. pf. pass. of βουλεύομαι, *advisedly, designedly,* Dem.

βεβούλημαι, pf. of βούλομαι.

βέβρῖθα, pf. of βρίθω.

βέβρῦχε, v. βρύχω.

βεβρώθοις, v. βιβρώσκω :—**βέβρωκα** pf. of same: **βεβρώσομαι,** f. pass.

βέβυσμαι, pf. pass. of βύω.

βεβώς, Ep. for βεβαώς, βεβηκώς, pf. part. of βαίνω.

βέη, v. βέομαι.

βείομαι, v. βέομαι.

βεκκε-σέληνος, ον, (σελήνη) *superannuated, doting,* Ar. (A word coined from the story about βέκος in Hdt. 2. 2, and the Arcadian claim of being προ-σέληνοι.)

βεκός or **βέκκος,** τό, *bread,* a Phrygian word, Hdt.

βελεη-φόρος, ον, (φέρω) *bearing darts,* Anth.

βέλεμνον, τό, poët. for βέλος, *a dart, javelin,* Il., Aesch.

βελεσσι-χᾰρής, ές, (βέλος, χαίρω) *in darts,* Anth.

βελόνη, ή, (βέλος) *any sharp point, a needle,* Batr., Aeschin.

βελονο-πώλης, ου, ὁ, (πωλέω) *a needle-seller,* Ar.

βέλος, εος, τό, (βάλλω, as Lat. *jaculum* from *jacio*) *a missile, esp. an arrow, dart, bolt,* Hom.; of the rock *hurled* by the Cyclops, Od.; of the ox's leg *thrown* at Ulysses, Ib.; ὑπὲκ βελέων *out of the reach of darts, out of shot,* Il.; so ἔξω βελῶν Xen. **2.** like ἔγχος, used *of any weapon, as a sword,* Ar.: *an axe,* Eur. **3.** the ἀγανὰ βέλεα of Apollo and Artemis in Hom. always denote *the sudden, easy death* of men and women respectively. **4.** after Hom. of *anything swift-darting,* Ζηνὸς βέλη *the bolts* of Zeus, *thunderbolts,* Aesch.; πύρπνουν β. Id.; βέλη πάγων *the piercing frosts,* Soph.:—metaph., ὀμμάτων βέλος *the glance of the eye,* Aesch.; ἱμέρου βέλος *the shaft* of love, Id.; of arguments, πᾶν τετόξευται βέλος Id.

βελο-σφενδόνη, ή, *a dart wrapped with pitch and tow, and thrown while on fire,* Plut.

βέλτερος, α, ον, poët. Comp. of ἀγαθός, *better, more excellent,* βέλτερόν [ἐστι] *it is better,* c. inf., Hom.; in Theogn., Aesch., etc.:—hence Sup. **βέλτατος,** η, ον, Id. (Prob. from same Root as βούλ-ομαι.)

βέλτιστος, η, ον, Dor. βέντ-, Sup. of ἀγαθός, *best,* Ar., Plat., etc.:—ὦ βέλτιστε or βέλτιστε, a common mode of address, *my good friend,* Ar., etc.:—τὸ βέλτιστον *the best, what is best,* Aesch., Plat.:—οἱ βέλτιστοι or τὸ βέλτιστον *the aristocracy,* Lat. *optimates,* Xen. (Cf. βέλτερος.)

βελτίων ῑ', ον, gen. ονος, Att. Comp. of ἀγαθός, *better,* ἐπὶ τὸ βέλτιον χωρεῖν *to improve, advance,* Thuc. (Cf. βέλτερος.)

βεμβῑκιάω, only in pres., (βέμβιξ) *to spin like a top,* Ar.

βεμβῑκίζω, f. Att. ιῶ, (βέμβιξ) *to set a spinning,* Ar.

ΒΕ΄ΜΒΙΞ, ῑκος, ή, Lat. *turbo, a top* spun by whipping, Ar.

βεμβράς, άδος, ή, v. μεμβράς.

βενδῖς, ῖδος, ή, acc. Βενδῖν, *the Thracian Artemis,* Luc.:—hence **Βενδίδειον,** τό, *her temple,* Xen.: **Βενδίδεια,** ων, τά, *her festival,* Plat.

βένθος, εος, τό, poët. for βάθος, as πένθος for πάθος, *the depth* of the sea, Hom.; also in pl., θαλάσσης βένθεα, ἐν βένθεσσιν ἁλός Il., Hom.:—also of a wood, βένθεσιν ὕλης Od.

βέντιστος, α, ον, Dor. for βέλτιστος.

βέομαι and βείομαι, 2 sing. βέῃ, Homeric fut. with no pres. in use, *I shall live* (akin to βιόω):—others regard it Ep. fut. of βαίνω.

βερέσχεθος, ὁ, *a booby*, Ar. (Deriv. unknown.)

βῆ, Ep. for ἔβη, 3 sing. aor. 2 of βαίνω.

βῆ βῆ, *baa*, the cry of sheep, Cratin.

βῆθι, βῆναι, aor. 2 imp. and inf. of βαίνω.

βηλός, Dor. βᾱλός, ὁ, (βαίνω) *that on which one treads, the threshold*, Lat. *limen*, Il., Aesch.

βῆμα, ατος, τό, (βαίνω) *a step, pace, stride*, h. Hom., Aesch., Eur.; Διὸς εὔφρονι βήματι under the kindly *guidance* of Zeus, Soph. II. = βάθρον, *a step, seat*, Id.:—*a raised place* or *tribune* to speak from in a public assembly or law-court, Thuc., Oratt.

βῆμεν, Ep. for ἔβημεν, 1 pl. aor. 2 of βαίνω.

βήμεναι, Ep. for βῆναι, aor. 2 inf. of βαίνω.

βήξ, βηχός, ὁ and ἡ, (βήσσω) *a cough*, Thuc.

βήσετο, Ep. for ἐβήσατο, aor. 1 med. of βαίνω.

βῆσσα, Dor. βᾶσσα, ἡ, *a wooded comb* or *glen*, Hom., Soph. (Deriv. uncertain.) Hence

βησσήεις, εσσα, εν, *of* or *like a glen, wooded*, Hes.

ΒΗ´ΣΣΩ, Att. -ττω: f. βήξω Hipp.: aor. 1 ἔβηξα:—*to cough*, Hdt. (Formed from the sound.)

βητ-άρμων, ονος, ὁ, *a dancer*, Od. (Perh. from βαίνω ἁρμός.)

ΒΙ´Α, Ion. βίη, ἡ: Ep. dat. βίηφι:—*bodily strength, force, power, might*, Hom., etc.; periphr. βίη Ἡρακληείη the strength of Hercules, i. e. the strong Hercules, Il.; βίη Διομήδεος Ib.; Τυδέως βία, Πολυνείκους β. Aesch., etc. 2. of the mind, Il. II. *force, an act of violence*, Od.; in pl., Ib.; in Att., βίᾳ τινός against one's *will, in spite of* him, Aesch., Thuc., etc.; βία φρενῶν Aesch.; also βίᾳ alone as an Adv., *perforce*, Od., etc.; so, πρὸς βίαν τινός and πρὸς βίαν alone, Aesch. Hence

βιάζω, f. σω, = βιάω, *to constrain*, Od.:—Pass., aor. 1 ἐβιάσθην, pf. βεβίασμαι:—*to be hard pressed* or *overpowered*, Il.; βιάζομαι τάδε I *suffer violence* herein, Soph.; βιασθείς Id.; ἐπεὶ ἐβιάσθη Thuc., βεβιασμένοι *forcibly made slaves*, Xen.:—of things, τοὔνειδος βιασθέν *forced from* one, Soph. II. Dep. βιάζομαι, with aor. 1 med. ἐβιασάμην, pf. βεβίασμαι:—*to overpower by force, press hard*, Hom.; βιάζεσθαι νόμους *to do* them *violence*, Thuc.;—β. αὑτόν *to lay violent hands on* oneself, Plat.:—β. τινα, c. inf., *to force* one to do, Xen.; and inf. omitted, β. τὰ σφάγια *to force* the victims [*to be favourable*], Hdt. 2. c. acc. rei, βιάζεσθαι τὸν ἔκπλουν *to force* the entrance, Thuc. 3. absol. *to use force, struggle*, Aesch., Soph., etc.: *to force one's way*, Thuc., Xen.; c. inf., β. πρὸς τὸν λόφον ἐλθεῖν Thuc.: of a famine, *to increase in violence*, Hdt.

βιαιο-μάχας, ὁ, (μάχομαι) *fighting violently*, Anth.

βίαιος, α, ον or and ος, ον, (βία) *forcible, violent, ἔργα βίαια* Od.; β. θάνατος *a violent death*, Hdt., Plat., etc.; ὁ πόλεμος β. διδάσκαλος is a teacher *of violence*, Thuc.:—Adv., βιαίως *by force, perforce*, Od., Aesch., etc.; so, πρὸς τὸ βίαιον Id. II. pass. *constrained, compulsory*, Plat.

βι-αρκής, ές, (βίος, ἀρκέω) *supplying the necessaries of life*, Anth.

βιαστέον, verb. Adj. of βιάζω, *one must do violence to*, Eur.

βιαστής, οῦ, ὁ, (βιάζω) *one who uses force, a violent man*, N. T.

βιάω, f. ἥσω, pf. βεβίηκα, = βιάζω, *to constrain*, Il.:— Pass. *to be forcibly driven*, of fire, Hdt.; θανάτῳ βιηθείς *overpowered*, Id. II. as Dep. in act. sense, *to constrain, press hard, overpower*, Hom.; βιήσατο κῦμ' ἐπὶ χέρσου it *forced* me upon land, Od.; νῶϊ βιήσατο μισθόν he did us *wrong* in respect of our wages, Il.:—*to force* or *urge on*, Aesch.

βιβάζω: f. βιβάσω, Att. βιβῶ: aor. 1 ἐβίβασα:—Med., f. βιβάσομαι, Att. βιβῶμαι: aor. 1 ἐβιβασάμην:— Causal of βαίνω, *to make to mount, to lift up, exalt*, Soph.

βιβάσθω, = βιβάω, βίβημι, μακρὰ βιβάσθων long *striding*, Il.

βιβάω, poët. form of βαίνω, *to stride*, πέλωρα βιβᾷ he *takes* huge *strides*, h. Hom.; ἐβίβασκε, 3 sing. Ion. impf., Id.; elsewhere in part., μακρὰ βιβῶντα, μακρὰ βιβῶσα Hom.

βίβημι, poët. for βαίνω, *to stride*, only in part., μακρὰ βιβάς Il.

βιβλάριον, τό, Dim. of βίβλος, Anth.: βιβλαρίδιον, N. T.

βιβλίδιον [ῐδ], τό, Dim. of βίβλος, Dem., Anth.

βίβλινος οἶνος, ὁ, *Biblian wine*, from Biblis in Thrace, Hes., Theocr.: βύβλινος in Eur.

βιβλιο-κάπηλος [ᾰ], ὁ, *a dealer in books*, Luc.

βιβλίον, τό, Dim. of βίβλος, *a paper, scroll, letter*, Hdt., Ar., etc.; often written βυβλίον.

βίβλος, ἡ, *the inner bark of the papyrus* (βύβλος): generally, *bark*, Plat. II. *a book*, of which the leaves were made of this bark, Dem. (Prob. a foreign word.)

βιβρώσκω, f. βρώσομαι: aor. 1 ἔβρωσα: Ep. aor. 2 ἔβρων: pf. βέβρωκα; syncop. part. βεβρώς, ῶτος: an opt. βεβρώθοις, as if from a pf. βέβρωθα, occurs in Il.:— Pass., f. βεβρώσομαι: aor. 1 ἐβρώθην: pf. βέβρωμαι. (The Root is BOP, v. βορ-ά, Lat. vor-o.) *To eat, eat up*, βεβρωκὼς κακὰ φάρμακ' Il.: c. gen. *to eat of* a thing, βεβρωκὼς βοός Od.:—Pass. *to be eaten*, χρήματα βεβρώσεται *will be devoured*, Ib.

βιη-μάχος, ον, = βιαιο-μάχας, Anth.

βίηφι, Ep. for βίη, Ion. dat. of βία.

βῖκος, ὁ, Oriental word for *a wine-jar*, Hdt., Xen.

ΒΙ-ΝΕ´Ω, *coire*, of illicit intercourse, Ar.

βιο-δότης, ὁ, *giver of life* or *food*, Plat.

βιό-δωρος, ον, *life-giving*, Poëta ap. Plat., Soph.

βιο-δώτης, ου, ὁ, = βιοδότης, Anth.

βιο-θάλμιος, ον, (θάλλω) *lively, strong, hale*, h. Hom.

βιο-θρέμμων, ον, (τρέφω) *supporting life*, Ar.

ΒΙ´ΟΣ, ὁ, *life*, i. e. not animal life (ζωή), but *a course of life, manner of living*, Lat. *vita*, Od., etc.; in pl., τίνες καὶ πόσοι εἰσὶ βίοι; Plat. 2. in Poets = ζωή, βίον ἐκπνεῖν Aesch.; ἀποψύχειν Soph. 3. *life-time*, Hdt., Plat. II. *a living, livelihood, means of living, substance*, Lat. *victus*, Hes., Soph., etc.; τὸν βίον ποιεῖσθαι ἀπό τινος to make one's *living* of a thing, Thuc., etc. III. *a life, biography*, as those of Plut.

ΒΙΟ´Σ, ὁ, *a bow*, Il.

βιο-στερής, ές, (στερέω) *reft of the means of life*, Soph.

βιοτεία, ἡ, (βιοτή) *a way of life*, Xen.

βιοτεύω, f. σω, to live, Eur. 2. to get food, Thuc. : to live by or off a thing, ἀπὸ πολέμου Xen. From
βιοτή, ή, = βίοτος, βίος, Od., Att. Poets. II. a living, sustenance, Soph., Ar.
βιότης, ητος, ή, = foreg., h. Hom.
βιότιον, τό, Dim. of βίοτος, a scant living, Ar.
βίοτος, ό, (βιόω) = βίος I, life, Il., Trag. II. = βίος II, means of living, substance, Lat. victus, Hom. III. the world, mankind, Anth.
βιο-φειδής, ές, (φείδομαι) penurious, Anth.
βιόω, f. βιώσομαι : aor. 1 ἐβίωσα : aor. 2 ἐβίων, 3 sing. imper. βιώτω, subj. βιῶ, opt. βιῴην, inf. βιῶναι, part. βιούς : pf. βεβίωκα : (βίος) :—to live, pass one's life (whereas ζάω properly means to live, exist), Il., etc. ; ἀπ' αὐτῶν ὧν αὐτὸς βεβίωκεν from the very actions of his own life, Dem. ; hence in Pass., τὰ σοὶ κἀμοὶ βεβιωμένα the actions of our life, Id. ; impers., βεβίωταί μοι I have lived, Lat. vixi, Id. :—Med. in act. sense, Hdt.
βιόωνται, Ep. for βιῶνται, 3 pl. med. of βιάω.
βίω, βιώην, βιῶναι, βιώτω, v. βιόω.
βιῴατο, Ep. for βιῷντο, 3 pl. opt. of βιάω.
βιώσιμος, ον, (βιόω) to be lived, worth living, Eur. ; οὐ βιώσιμόν ἐστί τινι 'tis not meet for him to live, Hdt., Soph.
βίωσις, εως, ή, (βιόω) manner of life, N. T.
βιώσκομαι, aor. 1 ἐβιωσάμην, Dep. :—Causal of βιόω, to quicken, make or keep alive, Od.
βιωτέον, verb. Adj. of βιόω, one must live, Plat.
βιωτικός, ή, όν, (βιόω) of or pertaining to life, N. T.
βιωτός, όν, (βιόω) to be lived, worth living, Soph., Ar., etc.
βλάβεν, Ep. for ἐβλάβησαν, 3 pl. aor. 2 of βλάπτω.
βλαβερός, ά, όν, (βλάπτω) hurtful, noxious, disadvantageous, Hes., Xen. From
βλάβη [ᾰ], ή, (βλάπτω) hurt, harm, damage, opp. to wilful wrong (ἀδίκημα), Aesch., etc. :—βλ. τινός damage to a person or thing, φορτίων Ar. ; but, βλάβη θεοῦ mischief from a god, Eur. :—of a person, ή πᾶσα βλάβη who is naught but mischief, Soph. 2. βλάβης δίκη an action for damage done, Dem., etc.
βλάβομαι, = βλάπτομαι, Il.
βλάβος, gen. εος contr. ους, τό, = βλάβη, Hdt., Eur., etc.
βλαισός, ή, όν, having the knees bent inwards, bandy-legged, Lat. valgus, Batr., Xen. :—generally, twisted, crooked, Anth.
βλαίσωσις, εως, ή, (as if from βλαισόω) distortion, retortion, Arist.
βλακεία, ή, laziness, stupidity, Xen., Plat. ; and
βλακεύω, only in pres., to be slack, lazy, Xen. II. c. acc. to lose or waste through laziness, Luc. ; and
βλακικός, ή, όν, lazy, stupid, Plat. : Adv. -κῶς, Ar. ; and
βλακ-ώδης, ες, (εἶδος) lazy-like, lazy, Xen.
βλάξ, βλακός, ό, ή, (μαλακός) slack in body and mind, stupid, a dolt, Plat., Xen. :—Sup. βλακίστατος.
βλάπτω (Root ΒΛΑΒ, v. βλάβη) : f. ψω : aor. 1 ἔβλαψα, Ep. βλάψει : pf. βέβλαφα :—Pass., f. βλαβήσομαι and in med. form βλάψομαι : aor. 1 ἐβλάφθην : aor. 2 ἐβλάβην [ᾰ], Ep. 3 pl. ἔβλαβεν, βλάβεν : pf. βέβλαμμαι :—to disable, hinder, stop, Hom. ; βλ. πόδας to disable the feet, to lame them, Od. :—Pass., ὅτῳ ἔνι βλαφθέντε [the horses] caught in a branch, Il. ; βλάβεν

ἅρματα were stopped, Ib. ; Διόθεν βλαφθέντα βέλεμνα stopped, made frustrate by Zeus, Ib. 2. c. gen. to hinder from, βλάπτουσι κελεύθου Od. :—Pass., βλαβέντα λοισθίων δρόμων arrested in its last course, Aesch. II. of the mind, to distract, delude, deceive, mislead, of the Gods, Hom. ; βλαφθείς, Lat. mente captus, Il. III. after Hom. to damage, hurt, mar, opp. to wilful wrong (ἀδικεῖν), Aesch., etc.
βλαστάνω, f. βλαστήσω : aor. 2 ἔβλαστον : pf. βεβλάστηκα or ἐβλάστηκα : plqpf. ἐβεβλαστήκειν :—to bud, sprout, grow, of plants, Aesch., etc. 2. metaph. to shoot forth, come to light, of men ; ἀνθρώπου φύσιν βλαστών born in man's nature, Soph. ; βλαστάνει ἀπιστία Id. (The Root is ΒΛΑΣΤ, f. βλαστεῖν, βλαστή.)
βλαστέω, late form of βλαστάνω, often introduced by Copyists for the aor. 2 forms βλαστεῖν, βλαστών.
βλάστη, ή, = βλαστός, Plat., etc. ; πετραία βλ. the growing rock, Soph. II. of children, βλάσται πατρός birth from a father, Id. ; παιδὸς βλάσται its growth, Id.
βλάστημα, ατος, τό, = βλάστη I, Eur. II. metaph. offspring, an offshoot, Aesch., Eur. III. an eruption on the skin, Aretae.
βλαστημός, ό, = βλάστη I, Aesch.
βλαστός, ό, (βλαστάνω) a sprout, shoot, sucker, Lat. germen, Hdt.
βλασφημέω : pf. βεβλασφήμηκα : (βλάσφημος) :—to drop evil or profane words, speak lightly or amiss of sacred things, βλ. εἰς θεούς Plat. : to utter ominous words, Aeschin. 2. to speak ill or to the prejudice of one, to speak slander, περί τινος Dem. ; εἴς τινα Id. :—also, βλ. τινα Babr., N. T. :—Pass. to have evil spoken of one, Ib. 3. to speak impiously or irreverently of God, to blaspheme, Ib.
βλασφημία, ή, a profane speech, opp. to εὐφημία, Eur., Plat. 2. defamation, evil-speaking, slander, Dem. 3. impious and irreverent speech against God, blasphemy, N. T. ; τοῦ πνεύματος against the Spirit, Ib. ; πρός τινα Ib. From
βλάσ-φημος, ον, evil-speaking : of words, slanderous, Dem. 2. speaking blasphemy, blasphemous, and as Subst. a blasphemer, N. T. (The origin of βλασ- is uncertain : βλάξ and βλάπτω are both suggested.)
βλαύτη, ή, a kind of slipper worn by fops, Plat. (Deriv. unknown.)
βλαυτίον, τό, Dim. of βλαύτη, Ar.
βλαχά, Dor. for βληχή.
βλάψις, εως, ή, (βλάπτω) a harming, damage, Plat.
βλαψί-φρων, ον, (φρήν) = φρενοβλαβής, mad, Aesch.
βλεῖο, Ep. 2 sing. aor. 2 pass. opt. of βάλλω.
βλεμεαίνω, only in pres. part., to look fiercely, glare around, Il. (Deriv. uncertain.)
βλέμμα, ατος, τό, (βλέπω) a look, glance, Eur., Ar.
βλέπος, τό, = βλέμμα, a look, Ar.
βλεπτέον, verb. Adj. of βλέπω, one must look, Plat.
βλεπτικός, ή, όν, of, of or for sight, Anth.
βλεπτός, ή, όν, to be seen, worth seeing, Soph. From
ΒΛΕ'ΠΩ, f. βλέψομαι : aor. 1 ἔβλεψα :—to see, have the power of sight, Soph. ; μὴ βλέπῃ ὁ μάντις lest he see too clearly, Id. II. to look, εἴς τινα or τι, Aesch., etc. ; πῶς βλέπων ; with what face ? Soph. ;—with an Adv. ἐχθρῶς βλ. πρός τινα Xen. :—foll. by a noun,

φόβον βλ. *to look terror*, i. e. to *look terrible*, Aesch. ; ἔβλεψε νᾶπυ *looked mustard*, Ar. ; πυρρίχην βλέπων *looking like* a war-dancer, Id. ; πεφροντικὸς βλέπειν to look *thoughtful*, Eur.   2. *to look* to some one from whom help is expected, Soph. ; εἴς τινα Id., etc. :— of places, οἰκία πρὸς μεσημβρίαν βλέπουσα *looking towards* the south, Xen.   3. *to look longingly, expect eagerly*, c. inf., Ar.   4. *to look to*, ἑαυτούς N. T. ; also, βλ. ἀπό τινος *to beware of* . . , Ib. ; βλ. ἵνα . . to *see that* . . , Ib.   III. trans. *to see, behold*, c. acc., Trag. : βλ. φάος, φῶς ἠλίου *to see the light of day, to live*, Aesch., Eur. ; and, without φάος, *to be alive, live*, Aesch., etc. ; of things, βλέποντα *actually existing*, Id.

βλεφᾰρίς, ίδος, ἡ, *an eyelash*, in pl. *eyelashes*, Lat. *cilia*, Ar., Xen., etc.

βλέφᾰρον, Dor. γλέφᾰρον, τό, (βλέπω) mostly in pl. *the eyelids*, Hom.   II. *the eyes*, Trag. : ἀμέρας βλέφαρον, νυκτὸς βλέφαρον, i. e. the sun, the moon, Soph., Eur.

βλέψις, εως, ἡ, (βλέπω) *sight*, Plut.

βλήεται, for βλήηται, Ep. 3 sing. aor. 2 pass. of βάλλω.

βληθείς, aor. 1 pass. part. of βάλλω.

βλῆμα, τό, (βάλλω) *a throw, cast*, of dice, Eur.   2. *a shot, wound*, Hdt.   3. *a coverlet*, Anth.

βλήμενος, Ep. aor. 2 pass. part. of βάλλω.

βλῆσθαι, Ep. aor. 2 pass. inf. of βάλλω.

βλητέον, verb. Adj. of βάλλω, *one must put*, N. T.

βλῆτρον, τό, (βάλλω ?) *a fastening, a band* or *rivet*, Il.

βληχάομαι, aor. 1 ἐβληχησάμην, Dep. *to bleat*, of sheep and goats, Ar. ; of infants, Id.   From

ΒΛΗΧΗ´, Dor. βλᾱχά, ἡ, *a bleating*, οἰῶν Od. : *the wailing of children*, Eur. (Formed from the sound.)

βληχρός, ά, όν, (βλάξ) *weak, faint, slight*, Plut. : cf. ἀ-βληχρός.

βληχ-ώδης, ες, (εἶδος) *bleating, sheepish*, Babr.

βλήχων, ἡ, gen. ωνος, or βληχώ, gen. οῦς, Ion. γλήχων, Dor. γλάχων and -ώ, *pennyroyal*, Ar., Theocr. (Deriv. unknown.) Hence

βληχωνίας, ου, δ, *prepared with pennyroyal*, Ar.

βλιστηρίς, ίδος, ἡ, (βλίττω) *honey-taking*, Anth.

βλῑτο-μάμμας, ου, δ, *a booby*, Ar. (Deriv. unknown.)

βλίττω : aor. 1 ἔβλῐσα, *to cut out the comb of bees, take the honey*, Plat. :—metaph., βλ. τὸν δῆμον *to rob the people of their honey*, Ar. :—Pass., μέλι βλίττεται Plat. (The Root is ΒΛΙΤ, of μέλιτ-ος, gen. of μέλι, β being in place of μ, cf: βλώσκω for μλώσκω).

βλοσυρός, ά, όν, and ός, όν, *grim, fierce*, Il. : *terrible*, Aesch. : *bluff, burly, valiant*, Plat. (Deriv. uncertain.)

βλοσύρ-ῶπις, ιδος, ἡ, (ὤψ) *grim-looking*, Γοργώ Il.

ΒΛΥΖΩ, f. βλύσω [ῠ], aor. 1 ἔβλῠσα ; poët. opt. βλύσσειε :—*to bubble* or *gush forth*; c. dat., βλ. Λυαίῳ *with wine*, Anth.   Hence

βλύσις [ῠ], εως, ἡ, *a bubbling up*, Anth.

βλωθρός, ά, όν, *tall, stately*, of trees, Hom. (Deriv. uncertain.)

βλώσκω, f. μολοῦμαι : aor. 2 ἔμολον : pf. μέμβλωκα (for μεμόλωκα) :—*to go* or *come*, Hom., Trag. (The Root is ΜΟΛ, so that βλώσκω is for μολώσκω, μλώσκω ; cf. θρώσκω from ΘΟΡ.)

βοάγριον, τό, *a shield of wild bull's hide*, Il.   From

βό-αγρος, δ, (βοῦς) *a wild bull*.

βόᾱμα, ατος, τό, (βοάω) *a shriek, cry*, Aesch.

βοᾶτις, Dor. fem. of βοητής.

βό-αυλος, δ, (βοῦς, αὐλή) *an ox-stall*, Theocr.

βοάω, Ep. 3 sing. βοάᾳ, 3 pl. βοόωσιν, part. βοόων: Att. f. βοήσομαι, Dor. βοάσομαι; later βοήσω, (βοάσω in Eur. is aor. 1 subj.) : aor. 1 ἐβόησα, Ep. βόησα, Ion. ἔβωσα :—Pass., Ion. aor. 1 ἐβώσθην : pf. βεβόημαι, Ion. part. βεβωμένος : (βοή) :—*to cry aloud, to shout*, Hom., Aesch. ; οἱ βοησόμενοι *men ready to shout* (in the ἐκκλησία), Dem.   2. of things, *to sound, resound, roar, howl*, as the wind and waves, Il., Aesch. ; αὐτὸ βοᾷ *it proclaims* itself, Ar.   II. c. acc. pers. *to call to one, call on*, Eur., Xen.   2. *to call for, shout out for*, Soph.   3. c. acc. cogn., β. βοάν, μέλος, etc., Ar., Soph.   4. *to noise abroad*, βεβωμένα ἀνὰ Ἰωνίην Hdt. ; ἐβώσθησαν ἀνὰ τὴν Ἑλλάδα Id.   5. c. inf. *to cry aloud* or *command in a loud voice* to do a thing, Soph., Eur., Xen.

βοεικός, ή, όν, (βοῦς) = βόειος, of or for oxen, ζεύγη β. *wagons drawn by oxen*, Thuc., Xen.

βόειος, Ion. βόεος, α, ον, (βοῦς) *of an ox* or *oxen*, esp. *of ox-hide*, Hom. ; βόεα κρέα Hdt. ; γάλα βόειον *cows-milk*, Eur. ; metaph., βόεια ῥήματα *great bull-words* (cf. βούπαις, etc.), Ar.   II. βοείη or βοέη (sc. δορή), ἡ, *an ox-hide, ox-hide shield*, Hom. ; gen. pl. βοῶν, contr. for βοέων, Il.

βοεύς, έως, δ, (βοῦς) *a rope of ox-hide*, Od.

ΒΟΗ´, Dor. βοά, ἡ, *a loud cry, shout*, Hom., etc. :—*a battle-cry*, βοὴν ἀγαθός *good at the battle-cry*, Il. ; βοᾶς μηδ' ὄνομ' ἔστω *let there be not even the name of war*, Theocr. ;—also *of the roar* of the sea, Od. ; of the *sound* of musical instruments, Il., Pind. ; the *cry* of birds or beasts, Soph., Eur. ;—ὅσον ἀπὸ βοῆς ἕνεκεν *as far as sound went, only in appearance*, Thuc., Xen.   II. = βοήθεια, *aid called for, succour*, Aesch., Soph.

βοη-γενής, ές, (γίγνομαι) *born of an ox*, of bees, Anth.

βοηδρομέω, f. ήσω, (βοηδρόμος) *to run to a cry for aid, haste to help*, Eur.

Βοηδρόμια, ων, τά, (βοηδρόμος) *games in memory of the succour given* by Theseus against the Amazons, Dem., Plut.

Βοηδρομιών, ῶνος, δ, *the third Attic month*, in which the Βοηδρόμια were celebrated, answering nearly to our September, Dem.

βοη-δρόμος, ον, (βοή, δραμεῖν) *running to a cry for aid, giving succour, a helper*, Eur. : cf. βοη-θόος.

βοήθεια, ἡ, *help, aid, rescue, support*, Thuc., etc.   2. *medical aid, cure*, Plut.   II. *an auxiliary force*, βοήθεια Thuc., Xen.   From

βοηθέω, Ion. βωθέω, f. -ήσω, (βοηθός) :—*to come to aid, to succour, assist, aid*, c. dat. pers., Hdt., Eur., etc. ; πρός τινα Xen.   2. absol. *to give aid, come to the rescue*, Hdt., Thuc., etc.   Hence

βοηθητέον, verb. Adj. *one must help*, Xen., Dem.

βοη-θόος, Dor. βοα-, ον, (βοή, θέω) *hasting to the battle-shout, hasting to battle*, Il.; cf. βοηδρόμος.   II. *aiding, helping*, Pind. ; and as Subst. *an assistant*, Theocr.

βοη-θός, όν, shortened form of βοη-θόος, *assisting, auxiliary*, Thuc. ; and as Subst. *an assistant*, Hdt., Plat.

βοηλᾰσία, ἡ, *a driving of oxen, cattle-lifting*, Il.   II. *a cattle-run*, Anth.   From

βο-ηλάτης, ου, ὁ, fem. -ηλάτις, ιδος, ἡ, (βοῦς, ἐλαύνω) one that drives away oxen, a cattle-lifter, Anth. **II.** ox-driving, Id. Hence

βοηλᾰτικός, ή, όν, of or for cattle-driving:—ἡ -κή (sc. τέχνη) the herdsman's art, Plat.

βοη-νόμος, ὁ, = βου-νόμος, Theocr.

βοητής, οῦ, ὁ, (βοάω) clamorous:—Dor. fem. βοᾶτις Aesch.

βοητύς, ύος, ἡ, (βοάω) a shouting, clamour, Od.

βόθρος, ὁ, any hole or pit dug in the ground, Lat. puteus, Hom.: a natural trough for washing clothes in, Od.:—a hole, such as a fire makes in the snow, Xen. (Prob. from the same Root as βαθύς: cp. also Lat. fod-io.)

βόθυνος, ὁ, = βόθρος, Xen.

βοῖ, like αἰβοῖ, exclam. of disgust, Ar.

βοιδάριον, τό, Dim. of βοῦς, Ar.

βοίδιον, τό, Dim. of βοῦς, Ar.

Βοιωτ-άρχης, ου, ὁ, (ἄρχω) a Boeotarch, one of the chief magistrates at Thebes, Hdt., Thuc., etc.; Βοιώ-ταρχος, Xen.—Hence Βοιωταρχέω, f. ήσω, to be a Boeotarch, Thuc.; and Βοιωταρχία, ἡ, the office of Boeotarch, Plut.

Βοιωτιάζω, f. σω, (Βοιωτός) to play the Boeotian, speak Boeotian, side with the Boeotians, Xen.

Βοιωτίδιον [τῐ], τό, Dim. of Βοιωτός, Ar.

Βοιωτι-ουργής, ές, (*ἔργω) of Boeotian work, Xen.

Βοιωτός, ὁ, a Boeotian, Il., etc.:—Βοιωτία, ἡ, (βοῦς) Boeotia, so called from its cattle-pastures, Hes.:—Adj. Βοιώτιος, α, ον, Boeotian: the Boeotians were proverbially clownish, whence the saying ὗς Βοιωτία:—fem. Βοιωτίς, ίδος, Xen.

βολαῖος, α, ον, (βολή) violent, Trag. ap. Plut.

βόλβα, ἡ, the Lat. vulva, Anth.

βολβίσκος, ὁ, Dim. of βολβός, Anth.

ΒΟΛΒΟ'Σ, ὁ, a bulb: in Theocr. a truffle?

*βολέω, pres. only found in pf. pass. part. βεβολημένος, to be stricken with grief, Hom.; βεβολήατο Ep. 3 pl. plqpf.

βολή, ἡ, (βάλλω) a throw, the stroke or wound of a missile, opp. to πληγή (stroke of sword or pike), Od., Eur., Thuc.: βολαῖς σφόγγος ὤλεσεν γραφήν by its stroke or touch, Aesch. **2.** metaph., like βέλος, a glance from the eyes, Od. **3.** βολαὶ κεραύνιοι thunder-bolts, Aesch.; βολαὶ ἡλίου sun-beams, Soph.; βολὴ χιόνος a snow-shower, Eur.

βολίζω, to heave the lead, take soundings, N. T. From

βολίς, ίδος, ἡ, (βάλλω) a javelin, Plut. **2.** a cast of the dice, a die, Anth.

βολίτινος, η, ον, of cow-dung, Ar. From

βόλιτον, τό, or βόλῐτος, ὁ, (βάλλω?) cow-dung, mostly in pl., Ar.

βολο-κτῠπίη, ἡ, (κτύπος) the rattling of the dice, Anth.

βόλομαι, Ep. form of βούλομαι, Hom.: an impf. ἐβολ-λόμαν in Theocr.

βόλος, ὁ, (βάλλω) a throw with a casting-net, a cast, Orac. ap. Hdt., Theocr.: metaph., εἰς βόλον καθίστασθαι to fall within the cast of the net, Eur. **2.** the thing caught, a draft of fish, Aesch., Id.

βομβ-αύλιος, ὁ, (βομβέω, αὐλός) a bagpiper, with a play on βομβυλιός, Ar.

βομβέω, f. ήσω, (βόμβος) to make a booming, humming noise, to sound deep or hollow, Hom.; βόμβησαν κατὰ ῥόον the oars fell with a loud noise down into the tide, Od.; βόμβησεν λίθος the stone flew humming through the air, Ib.:—of bees, to hum, Theocr.; of mosquitoes, to buzz, Ar.

βομβήεις, εσσα, εν, (βομβέω) humming, buzzing, Anth.

βομβητής, οῦ, ὁ, (βομβέω) a hummer, buzzer, Anth.

ΒΟ'ΜΒΟΣ, ὁ, a booming, humming, Plat. (Formed from the sound.) Hence

βομβῠλιός or -ύλιος, ὁ, an insect that hums or buzzes, a humble-bee, Ar.

βοο-σφᾰγία, ἡ, (σφαγή) slaughter of oxen, Anth.

βορά, ἡ, (v. βι-βρώσκω) eatage, meat, properly of carnivorous beasts, Trag.; of cannibal-like feasts, Hdt., Trag.:—rarely of simple food, Aesch., Soph.

βορβορό-θῡμος, ον, muddy-minded, Ar.

βορβορο-κοίτης, ου, ὁ, (κοίτη) Mudcoucher, name of a frog, Batr.

βόρβορος, ὁ, mud, mire, Lat. coenum, Aesch., Ar., etc.

βορβορο-τάραξις, ὁ, (ταράσσω) a mud-stirrer, mud-lark, Ar.

βορβορ-ώδης, ες, (εἶδος) muddy, miry, Plat.

Βορέας, ου, ὁ; Ion. Βορέης or Βορῆς, έω; Att. Βορρᾶς, ᾶ:—the North wind, Lat. Aquilo, Od.; πρὸς βορῆν ἄνεμον towards the North, Hdt.; πρὸς βορέαν τινός northward of a place, Thuc. (Prob. from ὄρος, ϝόρος, wind from the mountains.) Hence

Βορεάς, Ion. Βορειάς, poët. Βορηϊάς, άδος, ἡ, a Boread, daughter of Boreas, Soph.; and

βόρειος, α, ον and ος, ον, Ion. βορήϊος, η, ον:—from the quarter of the North wind, northern, Hdt.; ἀκτὰ β. exposed to the north, Soph.

Βορηϊάς, βορήϊος, Ion. for Βορεάς, βόρειος.

Βορῆς, έω, ὁ, Ion. contr. for Βορέας.

βορός, ά, όν, (βι-βρώσκω) devouring, gluttonous, Ar.

Βορραῖος, α, ον and ος, ον, = βόρειος, Aesch.

Βορρᾶς, ᾶ, ὁ, Att. contr. for Βορέας.

βόρυες, οἱ, unknown Libyan animals, Hdt.; cf. ὄρυες.

Βορυσθένης, ους, ὁ, the Borysthenes or Dnieper, a river of Scythia, Hdt.:—Βορυσθενείτης, ου, Ion. -είτης, εω, ὁ, an inhabitant of its banks, Id.

βόσις, εως, ἡ, (βόσκω) food, Il.

βοσκή, ἡ, (βόσκω) fodder, food, Aesch., Eur.

βόσκημα, ατος, τό, (βόσκω) that which is fed or fatted: in pl. fatted beasts, cattle, Soph., etc.; of sheep, Eur.; of horses, Id.; of pigs, Ar. **II.** food, Aesch.

βοσκητέον, verb. Adj. of βόσκω, one must feed, Ar.

βοσκός, ὁ, a herdsman, Anth. From

βόσκω, impf. ἔβοσκον, Ep. βόσκον: f. -ήσω:—Pass., Ion. impf. βοσκέσκοντο: f. βοσκήσομαι, Dor. βοσκού-μαι:—**I.** of the herdsman, to feed, tend, Lat. pasco, Od. **2.** generally, to feed, nourish, support, of earth, Ib.; of the Sun, Soph.; of soldiers, to maintain, Hdt., Thuc.: metaph., β. νόσον Soph.; πράγματα β. to feed up troubles, i. e. children, Ar. **II.** Pass., of cattle, to feed, graze, Lat. pascor, Hom., c. acc.:—to feed on, Aesch. **2.** metaph. to be fed or nurtured, Trag.; β. τινί or περί τι to run riot in a thing, Anth. (The Root appears to be BOT, cf. βοτήρ, βοτός, βοτάνη.)

Βόσ-πορος, ὁ, Ox-ford, name of several straits, of which

the Thracian and Cimmerian are best known, Hdt.; also of the Hellespont, Aesch., Soph.

βοστρῠχηδόν, (βόστρυχος) Adv. *like curls,* Luc.

βόστρῠχος, ὁ, pl. βόστρυχα, (βότρυς) *a curl* or *lock of hair,* Aesch., etc. 2. *anything twisted* or *wreathed, πυρὸς β.,* of *a flash of lightning,* Id.

βοτάμια, τά, (βόσκω) *pastures, meadows,* Thuc.

βοτάνη [ᾰ], ἡ, (βόσκω) *grass, fodder,* Il., Plat.; ἐκ βοτάνης from *feeding,* from *pasture,* Theocr.

βοτήρ, ῆρος, ὁ, (βόσκω) *a herdsman, herd,* Od.; οἰωνῶν β. *a soothsayer,* Aesch.; κύων βοτήρ *a herdsman's dog,* Soph. Hence

βοτηρικός, ή, όν, *of* or *for a herdsman,* Plut., Anth.

βοτόν, τό, (βόσκω) *a beast,* Aesch., Soph.: mostly in pl. *grazing beasts,* Il., Trag., etc.; but of birds, Ar.

βοτρῠδόν, Adv. (βότρυς) *like a bunch of grapes, in clusters,* Il.

βοτρύϊος, α, ον, (βότρυς) *of grapes,* Anth.

βοτρυό-δωρος, ον, (δῶρον) *grape-producing,* Ar.

βοτρυόεις, εσσα, εν, (βότρυς) *clustering,* Anth.

βοτρυό-παις, παιδος, ὁ, ἡ, *grape-born, child of the grape,* Anth. 2. act. *bearing grapes,* Theocr.

βοτρυο-χαίτης, ου, ὁ, (χαίτη) *with clustering hair,* Anth.

ΒΟ'ΤΡΥΣ, υος, ὁ, *a cluster* or *bunch of grapes,* Il., Att. 2. = βόστρυχος, Anth. (From same Root as βόστρυχος.)

βότρῠχος, ὁ, = βόστρυχος. Hence

βοτρυχ-ώδης, ες, (εἶδος) *like curls, curly,* Eur.

βοτρυ-ώδης, ες, (εἶδος) *like a bunch of grapes,* Eur.

βου-, often used in compos. to express something *huge* and *monstrous,* e. g. βούπαις, βούγαιος. (From βοῦς, cf. ἵππος IV.)

βούβᾰλις, ιος, ἡ, an African species of *antelope,* prob. the *hartbeeste,* Hdt.

βού-βοτος, ον, *grazed by cattle,* Od.

βού-βρωστις, εως, ἡ, (βι-βρώσκω) *eating enormously*: metaph. *grinding poverty* or *misery,* Il.

ΒΟΥΒΩ'Ν, ῶνος, ὁ, *the groin,* Lat. *inguen,* Il. Hence

βουβωνιάω, *to suffer from swellings in the groin,* Ar.

βου-γάϊος [ᾰ], ὁ, (γαίω) *a great bully* or *braggart,* voc. βουγάϊε Hom.

βου-δόρος, ον, (δέρω) *flaying oxen,* Hes. II. as Subst. *a knife for flaying,* Babr.

βου-θερής, ές, (θέρος) *affording summer-pasture,* Soph.

βου-θοίνης, ου, ὁ, (θοίνη) *beef-eater,* Anth.

βουθυσία, ἡ, *a sacrifice of oxen,* Anth.; and

βουθῠτέω, f. ήσω, *to slay* or *sacrifice oxen,* Soph., Eur.: generally *to sacrifice* any animals, Ar. From

βού-θῠτος, ον, (θύω) *of* or *belonging to sacrifices,* esp. *of oxen,* Aesch., Eur. 2. *on which oxen are offered, sacrificial,* Trag., Ar.

βουκαῖος, ὁ, (βοῦκος) Theocr.

βού-κερως, ων, gen. ω, (κέρας) *horned like an ox* or *cow,* Hdt., Aesch.

βου-κέφᾰλος, ον, (κεφαλή) *bull-headed,* epith. of Thessalian horses, Ar.:—**Βουκεφάλας,** gen. -α, the horse of Alexander the Great, Plut.

βουκολέω, Dor. βωκ-, f. ήσω: Ion. impf. βουκολέεσκον: (βουκόλος):—*to tend cattle,* Il.:—Pass. of cattle, *to range the fields, graze,* Ib. 2. of persons, *to tend, serve, worship,* Ar.: Med., τόνδε βουκολούμενος πόνον *being constantly engaged* in this toil, Aesch. II.

metaph. *to delude, beguile,* Id.; Med., ἐλπίσι βουκολοῦμαι *I feed myself* on hopes, *cheat myself* with them, Eur. Hence

βουκόλημα, ατος, τό, *a beguilement,* τῆς λύπης Babr.; and

βουκολία, ἡ, *a herd of cattle,* h. Hom., Hes. II. *a byre, ox-stall,* Hdt.

βουκολιάζομαι, Dor. βωκ-, Dor. f. βωκολιαξοῦμαι: Dep.: (βουκόλος):—*to sing* or *write pastorals,* Theocr. Hence

βουκολιαστής, Dor. βωκ-, ὁ, *a pastoral poet,* Theocr.

βουκολικός, Dor. βωκ-, ή, όν, *pastoral,* Theocr.; and

βουκόλιον, Dor. βωκ-, τό, *a herd of cattle,* Hdt., Theocr. II. *a means of beguiling,* Anth. From

βου-κόλος, Dor. βωκ-, ὁ, *a cowherd, herdsman,* Hom., Plat. (-κολος is prob. an altered form of -πολος, cf. αἰ-πόλος.)

βοῦκος, Dor. βῶκος, ὁ, = βουκαῖος, Theocr.

βού-κρανος, ον, (κάρα) = βούπρφρος.

βουλαῖος, α, ον, (βουλή) *of the council* : Βουλαία, a name of Vesta, as having a statue in the Senate House, Aeschin.

βουλαρχέω, f. ήσω, *to be a βούλαρχος,* Arist.

βούλ-αρχος, ὁ, *chief of the senate.* II. *adviser of a plan,* Lat. *auctor consilii,* Aesch.

βουλᾱ-φόρος, Dor. for βουληφόρος.

βούλευμα, ατος, τό, (βουλεύω) *a deliberate resolution, purpose, design, plan,* Hdt., Att.

βουλευμάτιον, τό, Dim. of foreg., Ar.

βούλευσις, εως, ἡ, *deliberation,* Arist. II. *the wrongful enrolment* of a person *among the public debtors,* Dem.

βουλευτέον, verb. Adj. of βουλεύω, *one must take counsel,* Aesch., Soph., Thuc.

βουλευτήριον, τό, (βουλεύω) *a council-chamber, senate-house,* Lat. *curia,* Hdt., Att. II. *the council* or *senate itself* : and poët. *a counsellor,* Eur.

βουλευτήριος, ον, (βουλεύω) *advising,* Aesch.

βουλευτής, οῦ, ὁ, (βουλεύω) *a councillor, senator,* Il., Hdt., etc.;—at Athens, *one of the* 500, Oratt.

βουλευτικός, ή, όν, (βουλεύω) *of* or *for the council* or *the councillors,* Xen., Dem. 2. *able to advise* or *deliberate,* Plat., etc. II. as Subst., βουλευτικόν, τό, in the Athen. theatre, *the seats next the orchestra, reserved for the Council,* Ar. 2. *the senatorial order,* Plut.

βουλευτός, ή, όν, *devised, plotted,* Aesch. From

βουλεύω, f. σω: aor. 1 ἐβούλευσα, Ep. βούλευσα: pf. βεβούλευκα: (βουλή):—*to take counsel, deliberate, concert measures,* and in past tenses *to have considered* and *to determine, resolve* : 1. absol., οἷος ἔην βουλευέμεν ἠδὲ μάχεσθαι such as he was *in council* and in battle, Od.; ἔς γε μίαν βουλεύσομεν [sc. βουλήν] *we shall agree* to one plan, Ib. :—in Prose, this sense belongs chiefly to the Med. 2. c. acc. rei, *to deliberate on, plan, devise,* Od., Hdt., Att.:—Pass. with f. med., aor. 1 ἐβουλεύθην: pf. βεβούλευμαι :—*to be determined* or *resolved on,* Aesch., etc.; τὰ βεβουλευμένα = βουλεύματα, Hdt. 3. c. inf. *to resolve* to do, Od., Hdt. II. *to give counsel,* τὰ λῷστα β. Aesch.; c. dat. pers. *to advise,* Il., Aesch. III. in polit. writers, *to be a member of Council,* Hdt.; esp. *of the Council of* 500 at Athens, Plat., Xen., etc.

B. Med., f. -εύσομαι: aor. 1 ἐβουλευσάμην, Ep. βουλ-
or in pass. form ἐβουλεύθην: pf. βεβούλευμαι: 1.
absol. *to take counsel with oneself, deliberate*, Hdt.,
Att. 2. c. acc. rei, *to determine with oneself,
resolve on*, Il., Hdt. 3. c. inf. *to resolve* to do,
Id., Plat.; β. ὅπως .. , Xen.

βουλή, ἡ, Dor. **βωλά** : (βούλομαι): —*will, determination*, Lat. *consilium*, esp. of the gods, Il., etc. 2.
a counsel, piece of advice, plan, design, Ib., Hdt.,
Att. :—in pl. *counsels*, Aesch. II. *a Council of
the elders* or *chiefs, a Senate*, Hom., Aesch. :—at
Athens, *the Council of* 500 created by Cleisthenes,
Hdt., Ar., etc. :—βουλῆς εἶναι to be *of the Council, a
member of it*, Thuc.

βουλήεις, εσσα, εν, (βουλή) *of good counsel*, Solon.

βούλησις, εως, ἡ, (βούλομαι) *a willing* = one's *will,
intention, purpose*, Eur., Thuc., etc. II. *the
purpose* or *meaning* of a poem, Plat.

βουλητός, ή, όν, (βούλομαι) *that is* or *should be willed* :
—τὸ β. *the object of the will*, Plat., Arist.

βουλη-φόρος, ον, (φέρω) *counselling, advising*, Il.; c.
gen. *a counsellor*, Ib.

βου-λιμία, ἡ, (βου-, λιμός) *ravenous hunger*, a disease,
Arist. Hence

βουλιμιάω, *to suffer from* βουλιμία, Ar., Xen.

βούλιος, ον, (βουλή) = βουλευτικός 2, *sage*, Aesch.

βούλομαι, Ion. 2 sing. βούλεαι: impf. ἐβουλόμην, Att.
also ἠβουλόμην, Ion. 3 pl. ἐβουλέατο: f. βουλήσομαι:
aor. 1 ἐβουλήθην, Att. also ἠβ-: pf. βεβούλημαι: Dep.
(The Root is **ΒΟΛ**, which appears in Ep. βόλομαι, Lat.
volo: hence βουλή.) *To will, wish, be willing*,
Hom., etc. :—mostly c. inf. or c. acc. et inf., Id.,
etc. : when βούλομαι is foll. by acc. only, an inf. may
be supplied, Τρώεσσιν ἐβούλετο νίκην he willed victory
to the Trojans, or Τρώεσσιν ἐβούλετο κῦδος ὀρέξαι,—both
in Il. II. Att. usages : 1. βούλει or βούλεσθε
foll. by subj., adds force to the demand, βούλει λά-
βωμαι *would you have* me take hold, Soph. 2. εἰ
βούλει, a courteous phrase, like Lat. *sis* (*si vis*), *if
you please*, Id. 3. ὁ βουλόμενος, Lat. *quivis*, *the
first that offers*, Hdt., Att. 4. βουλομένῳ μοί ἐστι,
nobis volentibus est, c. inf., *it is* according to my
wish that . . , Thuc. 5. *to mean* so and so, τί βούλεται εἶναι; *quid sibi vult haec res?* Plat. :—hence,
βούλεται εἶναι *professes* or *pretends* to be, *would fain*
be, Id. III. followed by ἤ, *to prefer*, for βούλομαι μᾶλλον, βούλομ' ἐγὼ λαὸν σόον ἔμμεναι, ἢ ἀπολέσθαι *I had rather* the people were saved than lost, Il.

βουλό-μᾰχος, ον, (μάχη) *strife-desiring*, Ar.

βου-λῡτός, ὁ, (λύω) *the time for unyoking oxen, evening*, Ar. :—in Hom. as Adv. **βουλῡτόνδε,** *towards
even, at eventide*.

βου-μολγός, ὁ, (ἀμέλγω) *cow-milking*, Anth.

βουνίτης [ῑ], ου, ὁ, (βουνός) *a dweller on the hills*, Anth.

βουνο-βᾰτέω, f. ήσω, (βαίνω) *to walk the hills*, Anth.

βουνο-ειδής, ές, (εἶδος) Plut.

βού-νομος, ον, (νέμομαι) *grazed by cattle*, Soph. 2.
ἀγέλαι βουνόμοι (parox.) herds *of oxen at pasture*, Id.

ΒΟΥΝΟ'Σ, ὁ, *a hill, mound*, Hdt.

βού-παις, αιδος, ὁ, (βου-, παῖς) *a big boy*, Ar. II.
(βοῦς, παῖς) *child of the ox*, of bees, in allusion to their
fabulous origin, Anth.

Βουπάλειος, ον, *like Bupalus*, i. e. *stupid*, Anth.

βού-πᾰλις, εως, ὁ, ἡ, (πάλη) *wrestling like a bull*, i.e.
hard-struggling, Anth.

βου-πάμων [ᾰ], ον, (πάομαι) *rich in cattle*, Anth.

βου-πλάστης, ου, ὁ, (πλάσσω) *cow-modeller*, of the
sculptor Myron, Anth.

βού-πληκτρος, ον, (πλήσσω) *goading oxen*, Anth.

βου-πλήξ, ῆγος, ἡ, (πλήσσω) *an ox-goad*, Lat. *stimulus*, Il. 2. *an axe for felling an ox*, Anth.

βου-ποίητος, ον, = βούπαις II, Anth.

βου-ποίμην, ενος, ὁ, *a herdsman*, Anth.

βου-πόρος, ον, (πείρω) *ox-piercing*, βουπ. ὀβελός a spit
large enough to spit an ox, Hdt., Eur.

βού-πρωρος, ον, (πρῷρα) *with the face of an ox*, Soph.

ΒΟΥ^Σ, ὁ and **ἡ,** gen. βοός, acc. βοῦν, Ep. βῶν, poët.
also βόα :—Dual βόε :—Pl., nom. βόες, rarely βοῦς :
gen. βοῶν, Ep. βῶν: dat. βουσί, Ep. βύεσσι: acc. βόας,
Att. βοῦς :—Lat. *bos* (*bov-is*), *a bullock, bull, ox*, or a
cow, in pl. *oxen* or *kine, cattle*, Hom., etc. II.
= βοείη or βοέη (always fem.), *an ox-hide shield*,
Il. III. proverb., βοῦς ἐπὶ γλώσσῃ βέβηκε, βοῦς
ἐπὶ γλώσσης ἐπιβαίνει, of people who keep silence from
some weighty reason, from the notion of a heavy body
keeping down the tongue, Theogn., Aesch.

βού-σταθμον, τό, and **βού-σταθμος, ὁ,** *an ox-stall*, Eur.

βού-στασις, εως, ἡ, = foreg., Aesch.

βου-στρόφος, ον, (στρέφω) *ox-guiding*, and as Subst.
an ox-goad, Eur.

βου-σφᾰγέω, f. ήσω, (σφαγή) *to slaughter oxen*, Eur.

βούτης, ου, Dor. **βούτας** or **βώτας, α, ὁ,** (βοῦς) *a herdsman*, Aesch., Eur., Theocr. II. as Adj., βούτ.
φόνος the slaughter of *kine*, Eur.

βού-τομον, τό, or **βού-τομος, ὁ,** (τεμεῖν) *butomus, the
flowering rush*, Ar., Theocr.

βου-φάγος [ᾰ], ον, (φαγεῖν) *ox-eating*, Anth.

βουφονέω, f. ήσω, *to slaughter oxen*, Il.; and

βουφόνια (sc. ἱερά), **τά,** *a festival with sacrifices of
oxen*, Ar. From

βου-φόνος, ον, (*φένω) *ox-slaying, ox-offering*, h.
Hom. II. *at* or *for which steers are slain*, Aesch.

βουφορβέω, *to tend cattle*, Eur.; and

βουφόρβια, ων, τά, *a herd of oxen*, Eur. From

βου-φορβός, όν, (φέρβω) *ox-feeding*, and as Subst. *a
herdsman*, Eur., Plat.

βού-φορτος, ον, (βου-, φόρτος) = πολύφορτος, Anth.

βου-χανδής, ές, (χανδάνω) *holding a whole ox*, Anth.

βο-ώνης, ου, ὁ, (ὠνέομαι) at Athens, *an officer who
bought oxen for the sacrifices*, Dem.

βο-ῶπις, ιδος, ἡ, (ὤψ) *ox-eyed*, i. e. *having large, full
eyes*, mostly of Hera, Hom.

βοωτέω, *to plough*, Hes. From

βοώτης, ου, ὁ, (βοῦς) *a ploughman*, Babr. II. *the
name given to the constellation Arcturus*, Od.; v.
ἄρκτος II.

βρᾰβεία, ἡ, (βραβεύς) *arbitration, judgment*, Eur.

βρᾰβεῖον, τό, *a prize in the games*, N. T. From

βρᾰβεύς, έως, ὁ, acc. βραβῆ, Att. pl. βραβῆς, *the judge
who assigned the prizes at the games*, Lat. *arbiter*,
Soph., Plat. 2. generally, *an arbitrator, umpire,
judge*, Eur. : then *a chief, leader*, Aesch. : *an author*,
Eur. (Deriv. unknown.)

βρᾰβευτής, οῦ, ὁ, = foreg., Plat. From

βρᾰβεύω, f. σω, (βραβεύς) to act as a judge or umpire, Isocr.   II. c. acc. to arbitrate, decide on, τὰ δίκαια Dem. :—to direct, arrange, control, Anth.

βράβῠλον, τό, a wild plum, Theocr.

βράβῠλος, ἡ, = βράβυλον, Anth.

βράγχος, ὁ, hoarseness, or sore throat causing hoarseness, Thuc. From

ΒΡΑΓΧΟΣ, ἡ, όν, hoarse, Anth. (Prob. formed from the sound.)

βραδέως, Adv. of βραδύς, q. v.

βράδος, εος, τό, = βράδυτης, Xen.

βρᾰδύνω [ῠ], f. ῠνῶ: aor. 1 ἐβράδῠνα: (βραδύς):— trans. to make slow, delay:—Pass. to be delayed, Soph.   II. intr. to be long, to loiter, delay, Id.: so in Med., Aesch.

βρᾰδῠ-πειθής, ές, (πείθομαι) slow to believe, Anth.

βρᾰδῠ-πλοέω, f. ήσω, πλόος) to sail slowly, N. T.

βρᾰδῠ-πους, ὁ, ἡ, -πουν, τό, slow of foot, slow, Eur.

ΒΡΑΔΥΣ, εῖα, ύ: Comp. βραδύτερος, by metath. βαρδύτερος, Ep. βραδίων and βράσσων: Sup. βραδύτατος, also βράδιστος, by metath. βάρδιστος:—slow, Hom., etc.:—c. inf., ἵπποι βάρδιστοι θείειν slowest at running, Il.; β. λέγειν Eur.:—Adv., βραδέως χωρεῖν Thuc.   2. of the mind, like Lat. tardus, Il.; c. inf., προνοῆσαι βραδεῖς Thuc.; τὸ βραδύ slowness, Id.:—Adv., βραδέως βουλεύεσθαι Id.   II. of Time, tardy, late, Soph., Thuc.

βρᾰδυ-σκελής, ές, (σκέλος) slow of leg, Anth.

βρᾰδυτής, ῆτος, ἡ, (βραδύς) slowness, Il., Att.   2. of the mind, Plat.

βράκος, τό, a rich woman's-garment, Theocr.

ΒΡΑΣΣΩ, Att. ττω: aor. 1 ἔβρᾱσα:—Pass., aor. 1 ἐβράσθην: pf. βέβρασμαι:—to shake violently, throw up, of the sea, Anth.   2. to winnow grain, Plat.

βράσσων, ον, Ep. Comp. of βραδύς.

βράχεα, τά, as if from a nom. βράχος, τό, or βραχέα, neut. pl. of βραχύς, shallows, Lat. brevia, Hdt., Thuc.

βρᾰχείς, aor. 2 part. pass. of βρέχω.

βρᾰχῑονιστήρ, ῆρος, ὁ, an armlet, Plut. From

βρᾰχίων [ῑ, ονος, ὁ, the arm, Lat. brachium, Il.; πρυμνὸς βραχίων the shoulder, Ib. (Deriv. uncertain.)

βρᾰχίων [Ion. ῐ, Att. ῑ], βράχιστος, Comp. and Sup. of βραχύς.

βράχος, εος, τό, v. βράχεα.

βρᾰχύ-βιος, ον, short-lived, Plat.

βρᾰχύ-βωλος, ον, with small or few clods, Anth.

βρᾰχύ-γνώμων, ον, of small understanding, Xen.

βρᾰχύ-δρομος, ον, (δραμεῖν, v. τρέχω) running a short way, Xen.

βρᾰχύ-κωλος, ον, (κῶλον) with short limbs or ends, Strab.   II. consisting of short clauses, περίοδοι Arist.

βρᾰχῠλογία, ἡ, brevity in speech or writing, Plat. From

βρᾰχῠ-λόγος, ον, (λέγω) short in speech, of few words, Plat.

βρᾰχύνω [ῠ], f. ῠνῶ, to shorten, to use as a short syllable, Plut.

βρᾰχύ-πορος, ον, with a short passage, Plat.   2. with narrow passage, Plut.

ΒΡΑΧΥΣ, εῖα, Ion. έα, ύ: Comp. βραχύτερος, βραχίων: Sup. βραχύτατος, βράχιστος:—short, Lat. brevis: 1. of Space and Time, Hdt., Att.; ἐν βραχεῖ (Ion. βρα-

χέι) in a short time, briefly, Hdt., etc.; διὰ βραχέος Thuc. :—Adv. βραχέως, scantily, seldom, Id.   2. of Size, short, small, little, Pind., Soph.; βρ. τεῖχος a low wall, Thuc.; κατὰ βραχύ little by little, Id.   3. of Quantity, few, διὰ βραχέων in few words, Plat.; διὰ βραχυτάτων Dem. :—Adv., βραχέως, briefly, in few words, Xen.   4. of quality, humble, insignificant, Soph.:—of things, small, petty, trifling, Id., etc.:—neut. as Adv., βραχὺ φροντίζειν τινός to think lightly of, Dem.

βρᾰχύ-σύμβολος, ον, (σύμβολον) bringing a small contribution, Anth.

βρᾰχύτης, ητος, ἡ, (βραχύς) shortness, Thuc.   2. narrowness, deficiency, Id.

βρᾰχύ-τονος, ον, (τείνω) reaching but a short way, Plut.

βρᾰχύ-τράχηλος, ον, short-necked, Plat.

βρᾰχύ-φυλλος, ον, (φύλλον) with few leaves, Anth.

ΒΡΑΧΩ, a Root only found in 3 sing. Ep. aor. 2 ἔβραχε or βράχε, to rattle, clash, ring, of arms; of a torrent, to roar; of an axle, to creak; of one wounded, to shriek or roar,—all in Il.

βρέγμα, ατος, τό, the front part of the head, Lat. sinciput, Batr. (Deriv. uncertain.)

βρεκεκεκέξ, formed to imitate the croaking of frogs, Ar.

ΒΡΕΜΩ, only in pres. and impf., Lat. FREMO, to roar, of a wave, Il.; so also in Med., Ib., Soph.   II. in later Poets, of arms, to clash, ring, Eur.; of men, to shout, rage, Aesch., Eur.

βρενθύομαι [ῠ], Dep., only in pres. and impf. to bear oneself haughtily, to hold one's head high, swagger, Ar., Plat.

βρέξις, εως, ἡ, (βρέχω) a wetting, Xen.

βρέτας, τό, gen. βρέτεος: pl., nom. and acc. βρέτεα, contr. βρέτη; gen. βρετέων:—a wooden image of a god, Aesch., Eur., Ar. (Deriv. uncertain.)

ΒΡΕΦΟΣ, εος, τό, the babe in the womb, Lat. foetus: of an unborn foal, Il.   II. the new-born babe, Aesch., Eur. :—of beasts, a foal, whelp, cub, Hdt. :— ἐκ βρέφεος from babyhood, Anth.

βρεφύλλιον, τό, Dim. of βρέφος, Luc.

βρεχμός, ὁ, = βρέγμα, the top of the head, Lat. sinciput, Il.

ΒΡΕΧΩ, f. ξω: aor. 1 ἔβρεξα: Pass., aor. 1 ἐβρέχθην: pf. βέβρεγμαι:—Lat. RIGO, to wet, τὸ γόνυ, of men walking through water, Hdt. :—Pass. to be wetted, get wet, βρεχόμενοι πρὸς τὸν ὀμφαλόν Xen.; βρέχεσθαι ἐν ὕδατι to bathe in water, Hdt.: of hard drinkers, βρεχθεὶς soaked, Eur.   II. to rain, send rain, N. T.; c. acc. cogn., βρ. πῦρ to rain fire, Ib.   2. impers. βρέχει, like ὕει, Lat. pluit, it rains, Ib.

βρῖ, apocop. for βριαρόν, Hes.

Βριάρεως, ὁ, a hundred-handed giant, so called by the gods, but by men Aegaeon, Il. From

βρῐᾰρός, ή, όν, strong, stout, Il. (From same Root as βριθύς, βρίθω, βαρύς.)

βριάω, to make or to be strong and mighty, Hes. (v. βριαρός.)

βρίζω, aor. 1 ἔβριξα: (βριθύς):—to be sleepy, to slumber, nod, Il., Aesch.

βρι-ήπῠος, ον, (ἠπύω) loud-shouting, of Ares, Il.

βρῖθος, εος, τό, (βριθύς) weight, Eur.

βρῑθοσύνη, ἡ, weight, heaviness, Il.

βρῑθύ-νοος, ον, grave-minded, thoughtful, Anth.

βρῑθύς, εῖα, ύ, weighty, heavy, Il.; Comp. βριθύτερος Aesch. (Cf. βριαρός.)

ΒΡΙΘΩ [ῑ], Ep. subj. βρίθῃσι: Ep. impf. βρίθον: f. βρίσω, Ep. inf. -έμεν: aor. 1 ἔβρῑσα: pf. βέβρῑθα: 3 sing. plqpf. βεβρίθει. (From same Root as βριαρός.) To be heavy or weighed down with a thing, c. dat., of fruit-trees, Hom.; metaph., ὄλβῳ βρίθειν Eur.; ξίφεσι βρ. to visit heavily with the sword, Id. 2. c. gen. to groan with weight of a thing, σίτου, οἴνου Od. 3. absol. to be heavy, Il.; rare in Att., βρίθει ὁ ἵππος sinks, Plat. II. of men, to outweigh, prevail, ἐέδνοισι by gifts, Od.: absol. to have the preponderance in fight, to be master, prevail, Il. III. trans. to weigh down, Aesch.:—Pass. to be laden, καρπῷ βριθομένη laden with fruit, Il.:—c. gen., βρίθεσθαι σταχύων Hes.

βρῑμάομαι, Dep. to snort with anger, to be indignant, Ar.

βρίμη, ἡ, strength, bulk, h. Hom. (From same Root as βριαρός.)

βρῑμόομαι, = βριμάομαι, Xen.

βρῑσ-άρματος, ον, (βρίθω) chariot-loading, Hes.

βρόγκος or βρόκχος, ὁ, poët. for βρόχος, Theogn.

βρομέω, = βρέμω, only in pres. and impf., of flies, to buzz, Il.

βρομιάζομαι, Dep., = Βακχεύω, Anth. From

Βρόμιος, α, ον, (βρόμος) sounding, boisterous: whence Βρόμιος, ὁ, as a name of Bacchus, Aesch., Eur.; Βρομίου πῶμα, i. e. wine, Id. 2. as Adj. Βρόμιος, α, ον, Bacchic, Id., Ar.:—so Βρομι-ώδης, ες, (εἶδος) Anth.

βρόμος, ὁ, (βρέμω) Lat. fremitus, any loud noise, as the crackling of fire, Il.; roaring of a storm, Aesch.; neighing of horses, Il. 2. rage, fury, Eur.

βροντάω, f. ήσω: Ep. aor. 1 ἐβρόντησα:—to thunder, Od.; metaph. of Pericles, Ar. 2. impers., βροντᾷ it thunders, Id. From

βροντή, ἡ, thunder, Hom., etc. II. the state of one struck with thunder, astonishment, Hdt. (Akin to βρέμω, βρόμος.)

βρόντημα, ατος, τό, (βροντάω) a thunder-clap, Aesch.

Βρόντης, ὁ, (βροντάω) Thunderer, one of the three Cyclopes, Hes.

βροντησι-κέραυνος, ον, sending thunder and lightning, Ar.

βρόξαι, v. *βρόχω.

βρότειος, ον, or α, ον, (βροτός) mortal, human, of mortal mould, Trag.

βρότεος, η, ον, poët. for βρότειος, Od., Aesch.

βροτήσιος, α, ον, = βρότειος, Hes., Eur.

βροτο-βάμων [ᾱ], ον, (βαίνω) trampling on men, Anth.

βροτό-γηρυς, υ, with human voice, Anth.

βρότος, εσσα, εν, (βρότος) gory, blood-boltered, Il.

βροτοκτονέω, f. ήσω, to murder men, Aesch. From

βροτο-κτόνος, ον, (κτείνω) man-slaying, homicidal, Eur.

βροτο-λοιγός, όν, plague of man, bane of men, of Ares, Hom.

βροτόομαι, Pass. (βρότος) to be stained with gore, Od.

βροτός, ὁ, a mortal man, Hom., Att. Poets. (The orig. form seems to have been μορτός, cf. ἄμβροτος.)

βρότος, ὁ, blood that has run from a wound, gore, Hom. (Deriv. uncertain.)

βροτο-σκόπος, ον, (σκοπέω) taking note of man, Aesch.

βροτο-στυγής, ές, (στυγέω) hated by men or man-hating, Aesch.

βροτο-φεγγής, ές, (φέγγος) giving light to men, Anth.

βροτο-φθόρος, ον, (φθείρω) man-destroying, Aesch.

βροτόω, v. βροτόομαι.

βροχετός, ὁ, (βρέχω) a wetting, rain, Anth.

βροχή, ἡ, (βρέχω) rain, N. T.

βρόχθος, ὁ, the throat, Theocr., Anth. (Deriv. uncertain.)

βροχίς, ἡ, Dim. of sq., Anth. II. (βρέχω) an ink-horn, Id.

ΒΡΟΧΟΣ, ὁ, a noose or slip-knot, for hanging or strangling, Od., Hdt., Soph.:—a snare for birds, Ar.:—the mesh of a net; metaph., ληφθέντες ἐν ταυτῷ βρόχῳ Aesch.

*ΒΡΟΧΩ, to gulp down, a Root only found in aor. 1 ἔβροξα, Anth.:—used by Hom. only in compds., 1. ἀναβρόξαι, to swallow again, suck down again, ὅτ' ἀναβρόξειε ὕδωρ, of Charybdis, Od.; and in aor. 2 part. pass., ὕδωρ ἀναβροχέν Ib. 2. καταβρόξαι, to gulp down, ὃς τὸ καταβρόξειε whoever swallowed the potion, Ib.

ΒΡΥΚΩ or βρύχω [ῠ]: f. βρύξω: aor. 1 ἔβρυξα: (for βέβρυχα, v. βρυχάομαι):—to eat with much noise, to eat greedily, Eur., Ar.:—metaph. to tear in pieces, devour, of a gnawing disease, Soph.; so in Pass., βρύκομαι, Id., Anth.

βρύλλω, to cry for drink, of children, Ar. From

βρῦν, in Ar. βρῦν εἰπεῖν to say bryn, cry for drink. (Formed from the sound.)

βρύον, τό, (βρύω) a kind of mossy sea-weed, Theocr.

βρῡχάομαι, f. -ήσομαι: aor. 1 ἐβρυχησάμην or in pass. form ἐβρυχήθην: Dep. with Ep. pf. act. βέβρυχα (cf. μυκάομαι, μέμυκα):—to roar, bellow, Lat. rugire, of a bull, Soph., Ar.; of elephants, Plut.:—in Il. mostly the death-cry of wounded men, κεῖτο βεβρυχώς; so, βρυχώμενον σπασμοῖσι, of Hercules, Soph.; δεινὰ βρυχηθείς Id.:—in Od. of the roaring of waves. (Formed from the sound.) Hence

βρῡχηδόν, Adv. (βρύχω) with gnashing of teeth, Anth.

βρύχημα, ατος, τό, bellowing, roaring, of men, Plut.: and

βρῡχητής, οῦ, ὁ, a bellower, roarer, Anth.

βρύχιος [ῠ], α, ον and ος, ον, from the depths of the sea, Aesch.; of thunder from the deep, Id. (From *βρύξ, of which an acc. βρύχα occurs in late poets; cf. ὑποβρύχιος.)

βρύχω, v. βρύκω:—for βέβρυχα, v. βρυχάομαι.

ΒΡΥΩ, mostly in pres.:—to be full to bursting: 1. c. dat. to swell or teem with, βρύει ἄνθεϊ teems with bloom, Il.:—metaph., βρύων μελίτταις καὶ προβάτοις Ar.; of men, θράσει βρύων Aesch. 2. c. gen. to be full of, βρύων δάφνης, ἐλαίας, ἀμπέλου Soph.: metaph., νόσου βρ. Aesch. 3. absol. to abound, grow luxuriantly, Soph.: of the earth, to teem with produce, Xen. 4. c. acc. cogn. to send forth water, N. T. (Akin to βλύω, βλύζω, and perh. to φλύω.)

βρῶμα, ατος, τό, (βι-βρώσκω) that which is eaten, food, meat, Thuc., Plat., etc.

βρωμάομαι, Dep. *to bray*, Lat. *rudere*, βρωμησάμενος Ar. (Formed from the sound.)

βρωμᾰτο-μιξ-ᾰπάτη, ἡ, *the false pleasure of eating made dishes*, Anth.

βρώμη, ἡ, (βι-βρώσκω) = βρῶμα, *food*, Od.

βρώσιμος, ον, (βι-βρώσκω) *eatable*, Aesch.

βρῶσις, εως, ἡ, (βι-βρώσκω) *meat*, Od., Thuc., etc.　II. *eating*, Plat.　2. *corrosion, rust*, N. T.

βρωτήρ, ῆρος, ὁ, (βι-βρώσκω) *eating*, Aesch.

βρωτός, ή, όν, verb. Adj. of βι-βρώσκω, *to be eaten*:— βρωτόν, τό, *meat*, Eur., Xen.

βρωτύς [ῠ], ἡ, Ion. for βρῶσις, Hom.

βυβλάριον, τό, Dim. of βύβλος, Anth.

βύβλινος, η, ον, (βύβλος) *made of byblus*, Od., Hdt.

βύβλος, ἡ, *the Egyptian papyrus*, the root and triangular stalk of which were eaten by the poor, Hdt.; cf. βύβλινος.　3. *the outer coat* of the papyrus, used for writing on, hence in pl. *leaves of byblus*, Id.　4. *a paper*, Id.; in this sense more commonly written βίβλος (q. v.):—pl. βύβλα, τά, Anth.

βύζην, (βύω) Adv. *close pressed, closely*, Thuc.

βῠθίζω, f. σω, (βυθός) *to sink* a ship: metaph. *to sink* or *ruin* men, N. T.

βύθιος, α, ον, *in the deep, sunken*, Luc., Anth.　II. *in* or *of the sea*, τὰ βύθια (sc. ζῷα), *water-animals*, Anth.　III. metaph. *of sound, deep*, Plut.; and

βῠθῖτις, ιδος, pecul. fem. of βύθιος, Anth. From

βῠθός, ὁ, *the depth*, esp. of the sea, *the deep*, Aesch., Soph. (Akin to βάθος.)

βύκτης, ου, ὁ, (βύω) *swelling, blustering*, βυκτάων ἀνέμων (Ep. gen.) Od.

βῠνέω, = βύω, *to stuff*, Ar.

βύρσα, ἡ, *the skin stripped off, a hide*, Batr., Hdt.; βύρσης ὄζειν *to smell of leather*, Ar.: *a drum*, Eur.　2. *the skin of a live animal*, Theocr. (Deriv. unknown.)

βυρσ-αίετος, ὁ, *leather-eagle*, nickname of Cleon the tanner, Ar.

βυρσεύς, έως, ὁ, (βύρσα) *a tanner*, N. T.

βυρσίνη [ῐ], ἡ, (βύρσα) *a leathern thong*, Ar.

βυρσοδεψέω, *to dress* or *tan hides*, Ar. From

βυρσο-δέψης, ου, ὁ, (δέψω) *a tanner*, Ar.

βυρσο-πᾰγής, ές, (πήγνυμι) *made of hides*, Plut.

βυρσο-πᾰφλαγών, ὁ, *leather-Paphlagonian*, nickname of Cleon, Ar.

βυρσο-πώλης, ου, ὁ, (πωλέω) *a leather-seller*, Ar.

βυρσο-τενής, ές, and βυρσό-τονος, ον, (τείνω) *with skin stretched over it*, of a drum, Eur.

βύσσινος, η, ον, *made of* βύσσος, σινδών β. *a fine linen bandage*, used for mummy-cloths, Hdt.; *for wounds*, Id.; β. πέπλοι Aesch.

βυσσο-δομεύω, only in pres. part., (δομέω) *to build in the deep*: metaph. *to brood over* a thing *in the depth of one's soul, ponder deeply*, Od.

βυσσόθεν, (βυσσός) Adv. *from the bottom* of the sea, Soph.

βυσσο-μέτρης, ου, ὁ (μετρέω) *measuring the deeps*, epith. of a fisherman, Anth.

βυσσός, ὁ, = βυθός, *the depth of the sea, the bottom*, Il., Hdt.

βύσσος, ἡ, *a fine flax*, and *the linen made from it*, Theocr. (A foreign word; cf. Hebr. *buts*.)

βυσσό-φρων, ον, (φρήν) *deep-thinking*, Aesch.

βύσσωμα, ατος, τό, = βύσμα, of *nets*, which stopped the *passage* of a shoal of tunnies, Anth.

ΒΥ´Ω: f. βύσω [ῠ]: aor. 1 ἔβῡσα:—Pass., aor. 1 ἐβύσθην: pf. βέβυσμαι:—*to stuff*, 1. c. gen. rei, *to stuff full of*, only in Pass., νήματος βεβυσμένος *stuffed full of* spun-work or yarn, Od.; τὸ στόμα ἐβέβυστο [sc. χρυσοῦ] Hdt.　2. c. dat. rei, *to stop* or *bung up with, plug*: Pass., σπογγίῳ βεβυσμένος Ar.　3. absol., βεβ. τὰ ὦτα *deaf*, Luc.

βῶ, aor. 2 subj. of βαίνω.

βωθέω, Ion. contr. for βοηθέω.

βωκολιάσδω, -αστής, Dor. for βουκολιάζω, -αστής.

βωκόλος, βωκολικός, Dor. for βουκ-.

βῶκος, ὁ, Dor. for βοῦκος.

βωλά, Dor. for βουλή.

βῶλαξ, ᾰκος, ἡ, = βῶλος, Theocr.

βωλίον, τό, Dim. of βῶλος, Ar.

ΒΩ̂ΛΟΣ, ἡ, *a lump of earth, a clod*, Lat. *gleba*, Od., Soph., Xen.　2. like Lat. *gleba, land, ground, soil*, Mosch., Anth.　3. generally, *a lump* of anything, *a mass*, of the sun, Eur.

βωλο-τόμος, ον, (τέμνω) *clod-breaking*, Anth.

βώμιος, ον, and α, ον, (βωμός) *of an altar*, Soph., Eur.　2. of a suppliant, βωμία *at the altar*, Id.

βωμίς, ίδος, ἡ, Dim. of βωμός, *a step*, Hdt.

βωμο-ειδής, ές, (εἶδος) *like an altar*, Plut.

βωμολόχευμα, ατος, τό, *a piece of low flattery*, in pl. *base flatteries, ribald jests*, Ar. From

βωμολοχεύομαι, Dep. *to use low flattery, indulge in ribaldry*, Ar., Isocr.; and

βωμολοχία, ἡ, *buffoonery, ribaldry*, Plat.; and

βωμολοχικός, ή, όν, *inclined to ribaldry*, Luc. From

βωμο-λόχος, ὁ, (λοχάω) properly *one that lurked about the altars for the scraps that could be got there, a half-starved beggar*, Luc.　2. metaph. *one who would do any dirty work to get a meal, a lick-spittle, low jester, buffoon*, Ar.:—as Adj., βωμολόχον τι ἐξευρεῖν *to invent some ribald trick*, Id.; *of vulgar* music, Id.

βωμός, ὁ, (βαίνω) *any raised platform, a stand*, Lat. *suggestus*, for chariots, Il.: of a statue, *a base, pedestal*, Od.　2. *a raised place for sacrificing, an altar*, Hom., Trag., etc.　3. *a tomb, cairn*, Anth.

βῶς, Dor. for βοῦς, βόας.

βώσας, βῶσον, Ion. aor. 1 part. and imp. of βοάω.

βῶσι, 3 pl. aor. 2 subj. of βαίνω.

βωστρέω, (βοάω) *to call on*, esp. *to call to aid*, Od., Ar.

βώτας, Dor. for βοότης.

βωτι-άνειρα, ἡ, (βόσκω, ἀνήρ) *man-feeding, nurse of heroes*, Il.

βώτωρ, ορος, ὁ, = βοτήρ, Hom.

Γ.

Γ, γ, γάμμα, indecl., third letter in Gr. alphabet; as Numeral γʹ = *three, third*: but ͵γ = 3000.

I. γ is the medial palatal mute, between tenuis κ and asp. χ. Before the palatals γ, κ, χ and before ξ, pronounced like *n* in *ng*, as in ἄγγος, ἄγκος, ἄγχι, ἄγξω: before the same letters ἐν- in compos. becomes

ἐγ-. II. changes of γ, etc. : 1. γ is sometimes prefixed, αἶα γαῖα, lac γλάγος, γάλακτος, νοέω γνῶναι, νέφος γνόφος. 2. sometimes interchanged with β, v. Β β Ι. 1 ; sometimes with κ, γνάπτω κνάπτω.

γᾰ, Dor. for γε.

γᾶ, Dor. and Aeol. for γῆ, earth.

γάγγᾰμον, τό, a small round net : metaph. a net, δουλείας γ. Aesch. (Deriv. unknown.)

Γάδειρα, Ion. Γήδειρα, ων, τά, Lat. Gades, Cadiz, Hdt. : —Adj. Γαδειραῖος πορθμός the Straits of Gibraltar, Plut. : —Adv. Γαδείρᾱθεν, Anth.

γάζα, ή, Lat. gaza, treasure, Theophr. (A Persian word.) Hence

γαζο-φύλαξ [ῠ], ᾰκος, ὁ, a treasurer, whence γαζοφῠλάκιον, τό, a treasury, N. T.

γᾱθέω, γάθω, Dor. for γηθέω, γήθω.

γαῖα, ή, gen. γαίης Att. γαίας, dat. γαίᾳ, acc. γαῖαν : — poët. for γῆ, a land, country, Hom., Trag. ; φίλην ἐς πατρίδα γαῖαν to one's dear fatherland, Hom. 2. earth, soil, Il. II. Γαῖα, as prop. n., Gaia, Tellus, Earth, spouse of Uranus, mother of the Titans, Hes.

Γαιήϊος, η, ον, (Γαῖα) sprung from Gaia or Earth, Od.

γαιή-οχος, Dor. γαιά-οχος, ον, (ἔχω) poët. for γηοῦχος, earth-upholding, of Poseidon, Hom., Trag. II. protecting the country, Soph.

γάϊος, ον, Dor. for γήϊος, on land, Aesch.

ΓΑΙΩ, to exult, only in part. κύδεϊ γαίων Il. (The Root was ΓΑΥ or ΓΑϜ, cf. γαῦρος, Lat. gaudium.)

γάλα [ῠ ῠ], τό : gen. γάλακτος, rarely γάλατος : —milk, Hom., etc. ; ὀρνίθων γάλα, proverb. of rare and dainty things, Ar. (The Root seems to be ΓΛΑΚ or ΓΛΑΓ, cf. gen. γάλακ-τος, γλάγος, and (with γ drop) Lat. lac, lactis.)

γᾰλᾰ-θηνός, ή, όν, (γάλα, θάω) sucking, young, tender, Od., Theocr. ; γαλαθηνά (sc. πρόβατα), Hdt.

γᾰλάκτινος, η, ον, (γάλα) milky, milk-white, Anth.

γᾰλακτο-πᾰγής, ές, (πήγνυμι) like curdled milk, Anth.

γᾰλακτο-πότης, ου, ὁ, (πίνω) a milk-drinker, Hdt.

γᾰλακτο-φάγος, ον, (φαγεῖν) milk-fed, Strab.

γᾰλάνα, γᾰλᾱνός, Dor. for γαλήνη, γαληνός.

ΓΑΛΕΉ, contr. γαλῆ, ῆς, ή, a weasel, marten-cat or polecat, Lat. mustela, Hdt., Ar.

γᾰλερός, ά, όν, (γαλάω ?) cheerful : Adv. -ρῶς, Anth.

γᾰλεώτης, ου, ὁ, (γαλέη) a spotted lizard, Lat. stellio, Ar.

γᾰλῆ, ή, contr. for γαλέη.

γᾰληναῖος, α, ον, = γαληνός, Anth.

γᾰλήνεια, Dor. γαλάνεια, ή, = γαλήνη, Eur.

γᾰλήνη, ή, stillness of the sea, calm, Od. ; λευκὴ γ. Ib. ; ἐλόωσι γαλήνην will sail the calm sea, i. e. over it, Ib. : —metaph., φρόνημα νηνέμου γαλάνας spirit of serenest calm, Aesch. ; ἐν γαλήνῃ in calm, Soph. (Deriv. uncertain : perh. akin to γελάω.)

γᾰληνιάω, to be calm, Ep. part. γαληνιόωσα Anth.

γᾰληνός, όν, (γαλήνη) calm, γαλήν' ὁρῶ (neut. pl.) I see a calm, Eur. ; of persons, gentle, Id.

γάλοως, ή, gen. γάλοω, dat. and nom. pl. γαλόῳ : Att. γάλως, gen. γάλω : —a husband's sister or brother's wife, a sister-in-law, Lat. glos, Il., etc. (Deriv. uncertain.)

γαμβρός, ὁ, (γαμέω) any one connected by marriage, Lat. affinis, Aesch. : 1. a son-in-law, Lat. gener,

Hom., Hdt., Eur. 2. a brother-in-law, a sister's husband, Il., Hdt. ; or, a wife's brother Soph. 3. = πενθερός, a father-in-law, Eur. 4. Dor. and Aeol. a bridegroom, wooer, suitor, Pind., Theocr.

γᾶμεν, Dor. poët. for ἔγημεν, aor. 1 of γαμέω.

γᾰμετή, ή, fem. of sq., a married woman, wife, γυνὴ γαμ. a wedded wife, Hes.

γᾰμέτης, ου, ὁ, (γαμέω) a husband, spouse, Aesch., Eur. ; Dor. gen. γαμέτα, Id. : —Fem. γᾰμέτις, ιδος, a wife, Anth.

γᾰμέω : f. γαμέω, Att. contr. γαμῶ, aor. 1 ἔγημα : pf. γεγάμηκα : plqpf. ἐγεγαμήκειν : —Med. f. γαμοῦμαι, Ep. 3 sing. γαμέσσεται : aor. 1 ἐγημάμην : —Pass., aor. 1 ἐγαμήθην ; poët. part. γαμεθεῖσα : pf. γεγάμημαι : (γάμος) : —to marry, i. e. to take to wife, Lat. ducere, of the man, Hom., etc. ; ἔγημε θυγατρῶν married one of his daughters, Il. : —c. acc. cogn., γάμον γαμεῖν, Aesch., Eur. : —ἐκ κακοῦ, ἐξ ἀγαθοῦ γῆμαι to marry a wife of mean or noble stock, Theogn. II. Med. to give oneself or one's child in marriage : 1. of the woman, to give herself in marriage, i. e. to get married, to wed, Lat. nubere, c. dat., Od., Hdt. ; γήμασθαι εἰς . . to marry into a family, Eur. : —ironically of a henpecked husband, κεῖνος οὐκ ἔγημεν ἀλλ' ἐγήματο Anacr. ; (cf. Martial, uxori nubere nolo meae) ; so Medea speaks contemptuously of Jason, as if she were the husband, γαμοῦσα σέ Eur. 2. of the parents, to get their children married, or betroth them, to get a wife for the son, Πηλεύς μοι γυναῖκα γαμέσσεται Il.

γᾰμήλευμα, ατος, τό, (γαμέω) = γάμος, Aesch.

γᾰμήλιος, ον, (γαμέω) belonging to a wedding, bridal, Aesch., Eur. 2. γαμηλία (sc. θυσία), a wedding-feast, Dem.

Γᾰμηλιών, ῶνος, ὁ, the seventh month of the Attic year, from γαμέω, because it was the fashionable time for weddings ; —the last half of January and first of February, Arist.

γᾰμίζω, (γάμος) to give in marriage, N. T.

γᾰμικός, ή, όν, (γάμος) of or for marriage, Plat. ; τὰ γαμ. a bridal, wedding, Thuc.

γάμιος, α, ον, = γαμήλιος, Mosch.

γᾰμο-κλόπος, ον, (κλέπτω) adulterous, Anth.

γάμορος, ὁ, for γημόρος.

ΓΑ΄ΜΟΣ, ὁ, a wedding, wedding-feast, Hom., etc. II. marriage, wedlock, Id., etc. ; τὸν Οἰνέως γ. marriage with him, Soph. ; mostly in pl., like Lat. nuptiae, nuptials, Aesch., etc.

γᾰμο-στόλος, ον, (στέλλω) preparing a wedding, Lat. pronuba, epith. of Hera and Aphrodité, Anth.

γαμφηλαί, ῶν, αἱ, the jaws of animals ; of the lion, Il. ; of the horse, Ib. ; of Typhon, Aesch. : the bill or beak of birds, Eur. (Akin to γόμφος.)

γαμψός, ή, όν, (κάμπτω) curved : of birds of prey, = γαμψῶνυξ, Ar.

γαμψ-ῶνυξ, ῠχος, ὁ, ή, (ὄνυξ) with crooked talons, of birds of prey, Hom., Aesch., etc.

γᾶν, Dor. for γῆν.

γᾰνάω, Ep. 3 pl. γανόωσι, part. γανόων, -οωσα, (γάνος) to shine, glitter, gleam, of metals, Hom. : then, like Lat. nitere, to look bright, of garden-beds, Od.

ΓΑ΄ΝΟΣ [ᾰ], εος, τό, brightness, sheen : gladness, joy,

pride, Aesch. ; of water διόσδοτον γάνος, of refreshing rain, Id. ; γ. ἀμπέλον of wine, Id.　Hence

γανόω, f. ώσω, *to make bright* :—Pass. *to be made glad, exult*, Ar. ; part. pf. pass. γεγανωμένος, like Lat. *nitidus, glad-looking, joyous*, Plat. ; and

γανόω, -όωσα, Ep. part. of γανάω : γανόωσι, 3 plur.

γάνῡμαι [ᾰ], Ep. f. γανύσσομαι Il. : Dep. :—*to brighten up*, γάνυται φρένα *he is glad* at heart, Il. ; c. dat., *to be glad at* a thing, Hom. ; c. gen., Aesch.

γάπεδον, τό, Dor. for γήπεδον.

γά-ποτος, ον [ᾰ], *to be drunk up by Earth*, of libations, Aesch.

ΓΑ'Ρ [ᾰ], Conjunct. *for*, Lat. *enim*, and like it, regularly placed after the first word of a sentence : *to introduce the reason* : 　I. ARGUMENTATIVE, *to introduce the reason for* a statement, which usually precedes :—when it precedes the statement, it may be rendered *since, as*, Ἀτρείδη, πολλοὶ γὰρ τεθνᾶσιν Ἀχαιοί, χρὴ πόλεμον παῦσαι Il. 　2. *the statement of which* γάρ *gives the reason may be omitted*, οὐ γάρ τί μοι Ζεὺς ἦν ὁ κηρύξας τάδε [yes], *for* it was not Zeus, etc., Soph. ; ἔστι γὰρ οὕτω [yes], for so it is, i. e. yes certainly, Plat. ; οἶδ' οὐκέτ' εἰσί· τοῦτο γάρ σε δήξεται [I say this], *for* it will sting thee, Eur. : —in Conditional Propositions, where the Condition is omitted, it may be transl. *for otherwise, else*, οὐ γὰρ ἄν με ἔπεμπον πάλιν, (sc. εἰ μὴ ἐπίστευον), Xen. 　II. EPEXEGETIC, where γάρ is used to begin a promised narration, λεκτέα ἃ γιγνώσκω· ἔχει γὰρ ἡ χώρα πεδία κάλλιστα I must relate what I know ; now, the country has most beautiful plains, Xen. ; so, after the introductory forms, σκέψασθε δέ, δῆλον δέ, τεκμήριον δέ, μαρτύριον δέ, τεκμήριον δέ, Plat., etc. ; τούτου δὲ τεκμήριον· τόδε γάρ . . , Hdt. :—in ἀλλὰ γάρ, a clause must be supplied between ἀλλά and γάρ, as, ἀλλὰ γὰρ ἤκουσα *but* [say no more], for I heard, Aesch. 　III. STRENGTHENING. 　1. *a question*, like Lat. *nam*, Engl. *why, what*, τίς γάρ σε ἥκεν ; *why* who hath sent thee ? Il. ; τί γάρ ; *quid enim* ? i. e. it must be so, Soph. 　2. *a wish*, with the opt., κακῶς γὰρ ἐξόλοιο O that you might perish ! Eur. ; in Hom. mostly αἲ γάρ, Att. εἰ or εἴθε γάρ, Lat. *utinam, O that !* so also πῶς γάρ *would that.*

γαργαλίζω, f. σω, *to tickle*, Lat. *titillare*, Plat. :—Pass., generally, *to feel tickling* or *irritation*, Plat.

γάργαρα, τά, *heaps, lots, plenty* ; cf. ψαμμακοσιο-γάργαρα. (Deriv. unknown.)

γαρύω, f. ύσω, Dor. for γηρύω.

γαστήρ, ἡ : gen. έρος, sync. γαστρός : dat. pl. γαστράσι :—*the paunch, belly*, Lat. *venter*, Hom., etc. : hence, γ. ἀσπίδος *the hollow* of a shield, Tyrtae. :—often to express *greed* or *gluttony*, γαστέρες οἶον mere *bellies*, Hes. ; γαστρὸς ἐγκρατής master of *his belly*, γαστρὸς ἥττων a slave to *it*, Xen. 　2. *the paunch stuffed with mince-meat, a black-pudding, sausage*, Od., Ar. 　II. *the womb*, Lat. *uterus*, γαστέρι φέρειν *to be with child*, Il. ; so, ἐκ γαστρός from *the womb, from infancy*, Theogn. ; ἐν γαστρὶ ἔχειν Hdt. (Deriv. uncertain.)

γάστρα, Ion. -τρη, ἡ, *the lower part* of a vessel *bulging out like a paunch* (γαστήρ), Hom.

γαστρίδιον, τό, Dim. of γαστήρ, Ar.

γαστρίζω, f. ίσω, (γαστήρ) *to punch* a man *in the belly*, Ar.

γαστρῑμαργία, ἡ, *gluttony*, Plat.　From

γαστρί-μαργος [ῐ], ον, *gluttonous* (cf. λαίμαργος), Pind.

γάστρις, ιδος, ὁ, *a glutton*, Ar.

γαστρο-βαρής, ές, (βαρύς) *heavy with child*, Anth.

γαστρο-ειδής, ές, (εἶδος) *paunchlike, round*, ναῦς, Plut.

γαστρο-φορέω, f. ήσω, (φέρω) *to bear in the belly*, of a bottle, Anth.

γαστρ-ώδης, ες, = γαστροειδής, *pot-bellied*, Ar.

γάστρων, ωνος, ὁ, = γάστρις, 'fat-guts,' Ar.

γᾱ-τόμος, ον, Dor. for γή-τομος, (τέμνω) *cleaving the ground*, Anth.

γαυλικός, ή, όν, *of* or *for a merchant vessel*, Xen.

γαυλός, ὁ, *a milk-pail*, Od. : *a water-bucket*, Hdt. ; *any round vessel, a bee-hive*, Anth. ; *a drinking-bowl*, Theocr. 　II. **γαῦλος** (properisp.), *a round-built Phoenician merchant vessel*, opp. to the μακρὰ ναῦς used for war, Hdt. (Deriv. uncertain.)

γαυρίᾱμα, ατος, τό, *arrogance, exultation*, Plut.　From

γαυριάω, mostly in pres. act. and med. :—*to bear oneself proudly, prance*, of horses, Plut. ; and in Med., Xen. :—metaph. *to pride oneself* on a thing, c. dat., Dem. ; ἐπὶ σφίσι Theocr.　From

γαυρόομαι, Pass., like γαυριάω, *to exult*, Batr. : *to pride oneself on* a thing, c. dat., Eur. ; and

γαῦρος, ον, (γαίω) *exulting in* a thing, c. dat., Eur. : absol. *haughty, disdainful*, Ar. ; of a calf, *skittish*, Theocr. :—τὸ γ. = γαυρότης, Eur. 　Hence

γαυρότης, ητος, ἡ, (γαῦρος) *exultation, ferocity*, Plut.

γαύρωμα, τό, (γαυρόομαι) *a subject for boasting*, Eur.

γαύσαπος or -άπης, ὁ, *rough cloth*, like *freese*, Strab. (A foreign word.)

γδουπέω, f. ήσω, poët. form for δουπέω, ἐπὶ δ' ἐγδούπησαν Il.

γε, Dor. **γα**, Enclitic Particle, serving to call attention to the word or words which it follows, by limiting the sense (cf. γοῦν), *at least, at any rate*, Lat. *quidem, saltem*, ὧδέ γε so *at least*, i. e. so *and not otherwise*, Il. ; ὁ γ' ἐνθάδε λεώς *at any rate* the people here, Soph. : with negatives, οὐ δύο γε, Lat. *ne duo quidem*, not *even* two, Il. ; οὐ φθόγγος γε not *the least* sound, Eur. 　2. with Pronouns :—with Pron. of 1st Pers. so closely joined, that the accent is changed, ἔγωγε, Lat. *equidem* ; also σύγε, ὄγε, κεῖνός γε, τουτό γε, etc. ; in Att. after relat. Pronouns, ὅς γε, οἵ γε, etc., much like Lat. *quippe qui*, οἵ γέ σου καθύβρισαν Soph. 　3. after Conjunctions of all kinds, πρίν γε, *before at least* ; εἴ γε, ἐάν γε, ἄν γε, Lat. *siquidem*, if *that is to say, if really* ; etc. 　II. exercising an influence over the whole clause : 　1. *namely, that is*, Διός γε διδόντος *that is* if God grant it, Od. ; ἀνήρ, ὅστις πινύτος γε *any man*,—*at least* any wise man, Ib. 　2. in Att. dialogue, where something is added to the statement of the previous speaker, as, ἔπεμψέ τίς σοι ; Answ. καλῶς γε ποιῶν yes *and* quite right too, Ar.; so, πάνυ γε, etc., Plat. 　3. implying concession, εἶμί γε *well then* I will go, Eur.

γέγᾱα, Ep. for γέγονα, pf. of γίγνομαι :—pl. γεγάμεν, γεγάᾱτε, γεγάᾱσι ; part. γεγαώς.

γέγηθα, pf. of γηθέω.

γέγονα, pf. of γίγνομαι.

γέγωνα, Ep. pf. with pres. signf., used by Hom. in 3 sing. γέγωνε and part. γεγωνώς, 3 sing. plqpf. (with impf. signf.) ἐγεγώνειν;—imperat. γέγωνε, subj. γεγώνω, part. γεγωνώς:—absol. *to call out so as to be heard*, ὅσσον τε γέγωνε βοήσας *as far as a man can make himself heard* by shouting, Od. :—c. dat. pers. *to cry out to*, Ib. (Deriv. uncertain.)

γεγωνέω, inf. γεγωνεῖν, Ep. impf. ἐγεγώνευν, γεγώνευν, aor. 1 inf. γεγωνῆσαι, formed from γέγωνα, and used in same sense, Hom. 2. c. acc. rei, *to tell out, proclaim*, Aesch., Soph.

γεγωνίσκω, lengthd. for γεγωνέω, *to cry aloud*, Thuc. 2. c. acc. rei, *to tell out, proclaim*, Aesch., Eur.

γεγωνός, όν, Adj. (from γεγωνώς, part. of γέγωνα) *loud-sounding*, Aesch. : *loud of voice*, Anth. :—Comp. γεγωνότερος, Id.

γεγώνω, = γεγωνέω, in Ep. inf. γεγωνέμεν, Il.

γεγώς, ῶσα, ώς, Att. for γεγαώς, γεγονώς, pf. part. of γίγνομαι.

γέ-εννα, ης, ἡ, = Hebr. gê-hinnôm, i. e. the *valley of Hinnom*, which represented *the place of future punishment*, N. T.

γεη-όχος, ὁ, = γαιηόχος, Hes.

γεη-πόνος, ον, = γεω-πόνος, Babr.

γει-ἀρότης, ου, ὁ, *a plougher of earth*, Anth.

γείνομαι, (from an obsol. act. *γείνω = γεννάω) : I. as Pass., only in pres. and impf., *to be born*, like γίγνομαι, γεινομένῳ at one's *birth*, Hom. ; 1 pl. Ep. impf. γεινόμεθα Il. II. Causal in aor. 1 med. ἐγεινάμην, Ep. 2 sing. γείνεαι (for γείνῃ), of the father, *to beget*, Ib., Trag. ; of the mother, *to bring forth*, Hom. ; ἡ γειναμένη the *mother*, Hdt., Eur. ; and οἱ γεινάμενοι the *parents*, Hdt., Xen. 2. of Zeus, *to bring* men into being, Il.

γειο-φόρος, ον, (γῆ, φέρω) *earth-bearing*, Anth.

γεῖσον or γεῖσσον, τό, *the projecting part of the roof*, the *eaves, cornice, coping*, Eur. (Deriv. unknown.)

γειτνίασις, ἡ, = γειτονία, *neighbourhood : the neighbours*, Plut. From

γειτνιάω, mostly in pres., *to be a neighbour, to border on*, c. dat., Ar., Dem.

γειτονέω, = γειτνιάω, Aesch., Soph. Hence

γειτόνημα, ατος, τό, *neighbourhood : a neighbouring place*, Plat. ; and

γειτόνησις, εως, ἡ, = sq., Luc.

γειτονία, ἡ, *neighbourhood*, Plat. ; and

γειτόσυνος, ον, *neighbouring*, Anth. From

γείτων, ονος, ὁ, ἡ, (γῆ) *one of the same land, a neighbour*, Lat. vicīnus (from vicus), Od. ; γείτων τινός or τινί one's *neighbour*, Eur., Xen. :—ἐκ τῶν γειτόνων or ἐκ γειτόνων *from* or *in the neighbourhood*, Ar., Plat. ; as Adj. *neighbouring*, Aesch., Soph.

γελάσείω, Desiderat. of γελάω, *to be like to laugh, ready to laugh*, Plat.

γελάσκω, = γελάω, Anth.

γέλασμα, ατος, τό, (γελάω) *a laugh*, κυμάτων ἀνήριθμον γέλασμα 'the many-twinkling *smile* of Ocean,' Aesch.

γελαστής, οῦ, ὁ, *a laugher, sneerer*, Soph. ; and

γελαστικός, ή, όν, *inclined to laugh*, Luc. ; and

γελαστός, ή, όν, *laughable*, Od. From

ΓΕΛΑ'Ω, Ep. γελόω, Ep. part. pl. γελόωντες, γελώοντες,

—ώωντες or —οίωντες : Ep. impf. γελοίων or —ώων: Dor. 3 pl. γελᾶντι, part. fem. γελᾶσα:—f. γελάσομαι [ᾰ], later, γελάσω:—aor. 1 ἐγέλᾰσα, Ep. ἐγέλασσα, Dor. ἐγέλαξα:—Pass., aor. 1 ἐγελάσθην : I. absol. *to laugh*, Hom., etc. ; ἐγέλασσεν χείλεσιν, of feigned laughter, Il. :—Pass., ἕνεκα τοῦ γελασθῆναι for the sake of *a laugh being raised*, Dem. II. *to laugh at* a person, Lat. irrideo, ἐπί τινι Il., Aesch. ; also at a thing, Xen. ; so c. dat., Soph., etc. ; rarely, like καταγελάω, c. gen. pers., Id. 2. c. acc. *to deride*, τινά or τι Theocr., Ar. :—Pass. *to be derided*, Aesch., Soph.

ΓΕ'ΛΓΙΣ, ἡ, gen. γέλγιθος, *a clove of garlic*, Anth.

Γελέοντες, οἱ, = Τελέοντες, q. v.

γελοιάω, Ep. for γελάω, h. Hom.

γελοΐιος, Ep. for γέλοιος.

γελοιο-μελέω, f. ήσω, (μέλος) *to write comic songs*, Anth.

γέλοιος or γελοῖος, Ep. γελοΐιος, α, ον, (γελάω) *causing laughter, laughable*, Il., Hdt., etc. ; γελοῖα *jests*, Theogn. II. of persons, *causing laughter, ridiculous*, Plat., etc.

γελοίων, γελοίωντες, γελόω, γελώντες, Ep. forms ; v. sub γελάω.

γελο-ωμῐλία, ἡ, (ὁμιλία) *fellowship in laughing*, Anth.

γέλως, Aeol. γέλος, ὁ: gen. γέλωτος, Att. γέλω : dat. γέλωτι, Ep. γέλῳ or (apocop.) γέλῳ : acc. γέλωτα, poët. γέλων : (γελάω) :—*laughter*, γέλῳ ἔκθανον they were like to die *with laughing*, Od. ; γέλωτα ποιεῖν, κινεῖν, etc., Xen. ;—κατέχειν γέλωτα to restrain one's *laughter*, Id. ; γέλωτα ὀφλεῖν to incur *laughter*, Eur. ; ἐπὶ γέλωτι to provoke *laughter*, Hdt., Ar. ; γέλωτος ἄξια *ridiculous*, Eur. II. *occasion of laughter, matter for laughter*, γ. γίγνομαί τινι Soph.

γελωτο-ποιέω, *to create, make laughter*, esp. by buffoonery, Plat., Xen. ; and

γελωτοποιία, ἡ, *buffoonery*, Xen. From

γελωτο-ποιός, όν, (ποιέω) *exciting laughter* : as Subst. *a jester, buffoon*, Xen.

γελώων, γελώωντες, Ep. forms ; v. sub γελάω.

γεμίζω, f. Att. ιῶ, (γέμω) *to fill full of, to load* or *freight with*, a cargo of a ship, c. gen., Thuc., etc. ; σποδοῦ γ. λέβητας *charging* the urns *with* ashes, Aesch. :—Pass. *to be laden* or *freighted*, Dem. II. later in Pass., c. acc., οἶνον γεμισθείς Anth.

γέμος, τό, *a load, freight*, Aesch. From

ΓΕ'ΜΩ, only in pres. and impf. *to be full*, of a ship, Hdt., Xen. 2. c. gen. rei, *to be full of* a thing, Thuc., etc. ; metaph., Trag.

γενεά, ᾶς, Ion. γενεή, ῆς, ἡ, Ep. dat. γενεῆφι : (γίγνομαι) : I. of the persons in a family, 1. *race, stock, family*, Hom., etc. ; Πριάμου γ. Il. ; ἐκ γενεῆς according to his *family*, Ib. ; γενεῇ by *birth-right*, Od. ; γενεὴν Αἰτωλός by *descent*, Il. :—of horses, *a breed*, Ib. :—generally, *race, kind*, Hdt. :—also a *tribe, nation*, Περσῶν γ. Aesch. 2. *a race, generation*, οἵηπερ φύλλων γενεὴ τοιήδε καὶ ἀνδρῶν Il. ; δύο γενεαὶ ἀνθρώπων Ib. 3. *offspring*, Orac. ap. Hdt. ; and of a single person, Soph. II. of time or place in reference to birth : 1. *a birth-place*, γενεῇ ἐπὶ λίμνῃ Γυγαίῃ Il. ; of an eagle's *eyrie*, Od. 2. *age, time of life*, esp. in phrases γενεῇ νεώτατος, πρεσβύ-

τατος youngest, eldest, *in age*, or *by birth*, Hom. **3.** *time of birth*, ἐκ γενεῆς Hdt. ; ἀπὸ γ. Xen.

γενεᾱλογέω, f. ήσω, *to trace by way of pedigree*, γεν. γένεσιν Hdt. ; γεν. τινα *to draw out* his pedigree, Id. : —Pass., ταῦτα μέν νυν γεγενηλόγηται Id. ; γενεαλογούμενος ἔκ τινος N. T. ; and

γενεᾱλογία, ἡ, *the making a pedigree*, Plat. From

γενεά-λογος, ὁ, (λέγω) *a genealogist*.

γενεῆθεν, (γενεά) Adv. *from birth, by descent*, Anth.

γενέθλη, Dor. -θλα, ἡ, **I.** *of persons, race, stock, family*, Hom. ; *of horses, a breed, stock*, Il. **2.** *race, offspring*, Soph. **II.** *of place or time, birth-place* : metaph., ἀργύρου γ. *a silver-mine*, Il.

γενεθλιᾱκός, ή, όν, (γενέθλιος) *of* or *for a birthday*, Anth.

γενεθλίδιος, ον, = γενέθλιος, Anth.

γενέθλιος, ον, *of* or *belonging to one's birth*, Lat. *natalis*, γ. δόσις *a birthday* gift, Aesch. ; ἡ γενέθλιος (with or without ἡμέρα) *one's birth-day*, Inscrr. ; so τὰ γενέθλια *a birthday feast, birthday offerings*, Eur. **II.** *of one's race* or *family*, esp. *of tutelary gods* (*dii gentiles*), Ζεὺς γ. Pind. ; γ. θεοί Aesch. :— γενέθλιον αἷμα *kindred* blood, Eur. ; γ. ἀραί *a parent's* curse, Aesch. **III.** *giving birth*, γεν. πόρος thy *natal* stream, Id. ; βλασταί γεν. Soph.

γένεθλον, τό, = γενέθλη, *race, descent*, Aesch. **2.** = γέννημα, *offspring*, Id., Soph.

γενειάζω, Dor. -άσδω, = γενειάω, Theocr.

γενειάς, άδος, ἡ, (γένειον) *a beard*, Od., Trag. **2.** in pl. *the sides of the face, cheeks*, Eur. Hence

γενειάσκω, = γενειάζω, *to begin to get a beard*, Plat.

γενειάτης [ᾰ], ου, ὁ, *bearded*, Theocr. From

γενειάω, f. ήσω, (γένειον) *to grow a beard, get a beard*, Od., Xen., etc.

γενειήτης, ου, ὁ, Ion. for γενειάτης.

γένειον, τό, (γένυς) *the part covered by the beard, the chin*, Hom., Trag. :—proverb. of a lean animal, οὐδὲν ἄλλο πλὴν γένειον καὶ κέρατα *nothing but chin* and *horns*, Ar. **2.** = γενειάς, *the beard*, Hdt. **3.** *the cheek*, Anth.

γένεο, Ep. for ἐγένου, 2 sing. aor. 2 of γίγνομαι.

γενέσιος, ον, = γενέθλιος :—but γενέσια, τά, *a day kept in memory of the dead*, Hdt. ; to be distinguished from γενέθλια *a birthday-feast*, though used for it in N. T.

γένεσις, εως, ἡ, (γίγνομαι) *an origin, source, productive cause*, Il. :—*a beginning*, in dual, τοῖν γενεσίοιν, Plat. **II.** *manner of birth*, Hdt. : *race, descent*, Id. ; γένεσιν *by descent*, Soph. **III.** *production, generation*, opp. to φθορά, Plat., etc. **IV.** *creation, created things*, Id. **V.** *a race, kind, family*, Id. **VI.** *a generation, age*, Id.

γενετή, ἡ, = γενεά II. 3, ἐκ γενετῆς *from the hour of birth*, Hom.

γενέτης, ου, ὁ, (γείνομαι) *the begetter, father, ancestor*, Eur., and in pl. *parents*, Id. **2.** (γίγνομαι) *the begotten, the son*, Soph., Eur. **II.** as Adj., = γενέθλιοι θεοί, Aesch., Eur.

Γενετυλλίς, ίδος, ἡ, (γίγνομαι) *goddess of one's birth-hour*, Ar.

γενέτωρ, ορος, ὁ, = γενέτης, Hdt., Eur.

γενηΐς, -ηΐδος, Att. **γενῄς**, ῆδος, ἡ, = γένυς II, *a pickaxe, mattock*, Soph.

γέννᾰ and **γέννᾱ**, ας, ἡ, *descent, birth*, Aesch. **II.**

offspring, Id. : *a generation*, Id. **2.** *a race, family*, Id., Eur. Hence

γεννάδας [ᾰ], ου, ὁ, *noble*, Lat. *generosus*, Ar., Plat.

γενναιο-πρεπής, ές, (πρέπω) *befitting a noble* : Adv. -πῶς, Ar.

γενναῖος, α, ον and ος, ον, (γέννα) *suitable to one's birth* or *descent*, οὔ μοι γενναῖον *it fits not my nobility*, Il. **I.** *of persons, high-born, noble by birth*, Lat. *generosus*, Hdt., Trag. ; so *of animals, well-bred*, Plat., Xen. **2.** *noble in mind, high-minded*, Hdt., Att. : τὸ γ. = γενναιότης, Soph. :—also *of actions, noble*, Hdt., Trag. **II.** *of things, good of their kind, excellent, notable*, Xen. : *genuine, intense*, δύη Soph. **III.** Adv. -ως, *nobly*, Hdt., etc. : Comp. -οτέρως, Plat. : Sup. -ότατα, Eur.

γενναιότης, ητος, ἡ, (γενναῖος) *nobleness of character, nobility*, Eur., Thuc. : *of land, fertility*, Xen.

γεννάω, f. ήσω, (γέννα) Causal of γίγνομαι (cf. γείνομαι II), *of the father, to beget, engender*, Aesch., Soph. ; rarely *of the mother, to bring forth*, Aesch. ; οἱ γεννήσαντες *the parents*, Xen. ; τὸ γεννώμενον *the child*, Hdt. :—like φύω 1. 2, as κἂν σῶμα γεννήσῃ μέγα even if *he grow*, get a large body, i. e. if he be of giant frame, Soph. **2.** metaph. *to produce*, Plat. Hence

γέννημα, ατος, τό, *that which is produced* or *born, a child*, Soph. :—any *product* or *work*, Plat. **2.** *breeding, nature*, Soph. **II.** act. *a begetting*, Aesch. ; and

γέννησις, Dor. -ᾱσις, εως, ἡ, (γεννάω) *an engendering, producing*, Eur., Plat. : *birth*, N. T.

γεννητής, οῦ, ὁ, (γεννάω) *a parent*, Soph., Plat. **II.** γεννῆται, οἱ, (γέννα) at Athens, *heads of families*, Dem. ; οἱ γεννηταὶ γυναικῶν *born of women*, N. T.

γεννητός, ή, όν, (γεννάω) *begotten*, Plat. ; γεννητοὶ γυναικῶν *born of women*, N. T.

γεννήτωρ, Dor. -άτωρ, ορος, ὁ, = γενέτωρ, Eur., Plat.

γεννικός, ή, όν, = γενναῖος, noble, Ar., Plat.

γένος, εος, τό, (γι-γνομαι) *race, stock, family*, Hom., etc. ; absol. in acc., ἐξ Ἰθάκης γένος εἰμί *from Ithaca I am by race*, Od. ; in Att. with the Art., ποδαπὸς τὸ γένος εἶ ; Ar. ; so in dat., γένει πολίτης Dem. ; οἱ ἐν γένει = συγγενεῖς, Soph. ; opp. to οἱ ἔξω γένους, γένους εἶναί τινος *to be of his race*, Id. **II.** *offspring*, even *a single descendant, a child*, Lat. *genus*, σὸν γένος Il. ; θεῖον γένος, Ib. ; so in Trag. **2.** collectively, *offspring, posterity*, Thuc., Dem. **III.** *a race*, in regard to number, γ. ἀνδρῶν *mankind*, Il. ; ἡμιόνων, βοῶν γ. Hom., etc. :—*a clan* or *house*, Lat. *gens*, Hdt. : at Athens as a subdivision of the φρατρία, Plat. : —*a tribe*, as a subdivision of ἔθνος, Hdt. :—*a caste*, Id., Plat. : of animals, *a breed*, Hdt. **2.** *a race* in regard to time, *an age, generation*, Od. ; γ. χρύσειον, Hes. :—hence *age, time of life*, γένει ὕστερος Il. **IV.** *sex*, Plat. : *gender*, in grammar, Arist. **V.** *a class, sort, kind* Xen. **2.** in Logic, *genus*, opp. to εἶδος (*species*), Plat.

γέντο, *he grasped*, = ἔλαβεν, *found only in this form*, Il. :—said to be Aeol. for ἕλετο (ϝέλετο) like ἦνθον for ἦλθον. **II.** syncop. for ἐγένετο, v. γίγνομαι.

ΓΕ΄ΝΥΣ, νος : dat. γένϋΐ :—pl., gen. γενύων, contr. γενῦν, dat. γένυσι, Ep. γέννυσι, acc. γένυας, contr. γένῦς :—*the under jaw*, Od. ; in pl. *the jaws, the mouth*, Il., Trag. ; so in sing., Theogn., Eur. :—gen-

erally, *the side of the face, cheek*, Id. II. *the edge of an axe, a biting axe*, Soph. (Cf. γένειον, γνάθος, Lat. *gena*.)

γεραιός, ά, όν, (γέρων)=γηραιός, *old*, in Hom. and Trag.; of men, with notion of dignity, like *signor*, Id.; ὁ γεραιός *that reverend sire*, Il. :—Comp. γεραίτερος, Hom.; οἱ γεραίτεροι *the elders, senators*, Aesch., Xen.; cf. γέρων:— Sup. γεραίτατος, Ar.; rarely = πρεσβύτατος, *eldest*, Theocr. II. of things, *ancient*, Trag.

γεραιό-φλοιος, ον, *with old, wrinkled skin*, Anth.

γεραίρω: Ep. impf. γέραιρον: f. γεραρῶ: aor. 1 ἐγέρηρα: (γέρας):—*to honour* or *reward with* a gift, τινά τινι Hom., etc. :—Pass. *to be so honoured*, Eur. 2. reversely, γ. τινί τι *to present as an honorary gift*, ap. Dem. II. *to celebrate*, χόροισι *with dances*, Hdt.

γεραίτερος, γεραίτατος, Comp. and Sup. of γεραιός.

ΓΕ'ΡΑ'ΝΟΣ, ή and ὁ, *a crane*, Lat. *grus*, Il.

γεράός, ή, όν, =γεραιός, Soph.

γεραρός, ά, όν, (γεραίρω) *of reverend bearing, majestic*, Il. 2.=γεραιός, Aesch. II. γεραροί, οἱ, *priests*, Id.; γεραραί, *priestesses*, Dem.

ΓΕ'ΡΑ'Σ, αος, ως, τό; nom. pl. γέρᾰ, apoc. for γέραα; Att. γέρᾱ, Ion. γέρεα:—*a gift of honour*, Hom.; τὸ γὰρ γέρας ἐστὶ θανόντων this is *the last honour* of the dead, Il. :—any *privilege* or *prerogative* conferred on kings or nobles, Hom., Hdt., etc. Hence

γεράσμιος, ον, *honouring*, h. Hom. II. =γεραρός, *honoured*, Eur.

γέρεα, Ion. nom. pl. of γέρας.

γεροντ-ἀγωγέω, f. ήσω, (ἀγωγός) *to guide an old man*, Soph.

γεροντία, ή, Lacon. form of γερουσία, Xen.

γερόντιον, τό, Dim. of γέρων, *a little old man*, Ar., Xen.

γεροντο-διδάσκαλος, ὁ, ή, *an old man's master*, Plat.

γερουσία, ή, (γέρων) *a Council of Elders, Senate*, Eur. II. =πρεσβεία, Id.

γερούσιος, α, ον, (γέρων) *for* or *befitting the seniors* or *chiefs*, Il.; γ. ὅρκος *an oath taken by them*, Ib.

γέρρον, τό, (εἴρω) *anything made of wicker-work* : I. *an oblong shield*, covered with ox-hide, such as the Persians used, Hdt., Xen. II. γέρρα, τά, *wattled huts* or *booths*, used in the Athen. market-place, Dem. III. *the wicker body* of a car, Strab.

γερρο-φόροι, οἱ, (φέρω) *a kind of troops that used wicker shields*, Xen.

ΓΕ'ΡΩΝ, οντος, ὁ, *an old man*, Hom., etc. 2. in political sense, γέροντες *the Elders, Seniors*, or *Chiefs*, who formed the King's Council, Hom. :—then, like Lat. *Patres*, the Senators, esp. at Sparta, Hdt. II. as Adj., *old*, mostly with a masc. Noun, Theogn., Aesch., etc. ; but γέρον σάκος occurs in Od.

γεῦμα, ατος, τό, (γεύω) *a taste, smack* of a thing, Eur., Ar.

γεύμεθα, 1 pl. poët. for γευόμεθα, pf. med. of γεύω.

γευστέον, verb. Adj. of γεύω, *one must make to taste*, τινά τινος Plat.

ΓΕΥ'Ω, f. γεύσω: aor. 1 ἔγευσα:—Med., f. γεύσομαι: aor. 1 ἐγευσάμην, subj. γεύσεται, –σόμεθα, Ep. for –ηται, –ώμεθα: pf. γέγευμαι:—*to give a taste of*, τι Hdt.; rarely τινά τι Eur.; or τινά τινος Plat.: cf. γευστέον. II. Med. γεύομαι, with pf. pass., *to taste of*

a thing, c. gen., Od., Thuc. 2. metaph. *to taste, feel*, δουρὸς ἀκωκῆς, ὀϊστοῦ γεύσασθαι Hom.; γευσόμεθ' ἀλλήλων ἐγχείαις *let us try* one another with the spear, Il. : *to taste the sweets of*, ἀρχῆς, ἐλευθερίης Hdt.; *to have experience of*, μόχθων, πένθους Soph., Eur. (The Root was prob. ΓΕΥΣ, cf. Lat. *gus-tare*.)

γέφυρα, ή, *a dyke, dam* or *mound to bar a stream*, in pl., Il.; the phrase πολέμοιο γεφύραι seems to mean *the ground between two lines of battle*, = μεταίχμιον, Ib. II. *a bridge*, to cross a stream, Hdt., Att.; Hom. also seems to recognise this sense in the Verb γεφυρόω. (Deriv. unknown.)

γεφῡρίζω, f. σω, *to abuse from the bridge* : there was a bridge between Athens and Eleusis, and as the people passed it in procession, they had a custom of abusing whom they would : hence *to abuse freely*, Plut. : hence also γεφύριστής, οῦ, ὁ, *a reviler*, Id.

γεφῡρο-ποιός, ὁ, *bridge-maker*, Lat. *Pontifex*, Plut.

γεφῡρόω, f. ώσω, (γέφυρα) *to bridge over, make passable by a bridge*, γεφύρωσε δέ μιν (sc. τὸν ποταμὸν ἡ πτελέη) the fallen tree *made a bridge* over the river, Il.; γ. τὸν ποταμόν *to throw a bridge* over it, Hdt.; ἐγεφυρώθη ὁ πόρος *to make* [a passage] *like a bridge*, γεφύρωσε κέλευθον he made a *bridge*-way, Il.

γεωγρᾰφία, ή, *geography*, Plut. From

γεω-γράφος [ᾰ], ὁ, (γῆ, γράφω) *a geographer*.

γε-ώδης, ες, (γῆ, εἶδος) *earth-like, earthy*, Plat.; *with deep soil*, Xen.

γεωλοφία, ή, *a hill of earth*, Strab., Anth. From

γεώ-λοφος, ον, *crested with earth* : as Subst., *a hill, hillock*, Xen. : so γεώλοφον, τό, Theocr.

γεωμετρέω, f. ήσω, *to measure the earth, to practise* or *profess geometry*, Plat. II. *to measure*, c. acc., Xen. From

γεω-μέτρης, ου, ὁ, (μετρέω) *a land-measurer, geometer*, Plat. Hence

γεωμετρία, ή, *geometry*, Hdt., Plat.; and

γεωμετρικός, ή, όν, *of* or *for geometry, geometrical*, Plat.; γεωμετρική (sc. τέχνη), *geometry*, Id. II. *skilled in geometry, a geometrician*, Id.

γεω-μορία, ή, (γῆ, μείρομαι) *a portion of land*. II. =γεωργία, Anth.

γεώ-πεδον, τό, =γῆ-πεδον, Hdt.

γεω-πείνης, ου, ὁ, (γῆ, πένης) *poor in land*, Hdt.

γεω-πονέω, *to till the ground*; γᾱπονεῖν Eur. From

γεω-πόνος, ὁ, *a husbandman*, Anth.; in Babr. γηπόνος : Dor. form γᾱπόνος = γη-.

γεωργέω, f. ήσω, (γεωργός) *to be a husbandman, farmer*, Plat., Xen., etc. II. c. acc. *to till, plough, cultivate*, Thuc., Dem. 2. metaph. *to work at a thing, practise it*, Lat. *agitare*, Id.; γ. ἔκ τινος *to draw profit* from it, *live* by it, Id. Hence

γεωργία, ή, *tillage, agriculture, farming*, Thuc., Plat. 2. in pl. *farms, tilled land*, Id.; and

γεωργικός, ή, όν, *of* or *for tillage, agricultural*, Ar.; ὁ γ. λεὼς *the country folk*, Id. :—ἡ γ. (sc. τέχνη), *agriculture, farming*, Plat. II. *skilled in farming* : and as Subst. *a good farmer*, Id. From

γε-ωργός, όν, (γῆ, *ἔργω) *tilling the ground*, Ar. :—as Subst. γεωργός, ὁ, *a husbandman*, Hdt., Ar., Plat.

γεωρυχέω, f. ήσω, *to dig in the earth, dig a mine*, Hdt. From

γε-ωρύχος [ῠ], ον, (γῆ, ὀρύσσω) *throwing up the earth*, Strab.

γεω-τόμος, ον, (τέμνω) *cutting the ground, ploughing*, Anth.

ΓΗ͂, ἡ, contr. for γέα : dual gen. and dat. γαῖν : pl. γαῖ, γέαι, Ion. gen. γεῶν, acc. γᾶς :—*earth* opp. to heaven, or *land* opp. to sea, Hom., etc. ; κατὰ γῆν *on land, by land*, Thuc. ; κατὰ γῆς Xen. :—ἐπὶ γῆς *on earth*, Soph. ; κατὰ γῆς *below the earth*, Trag. :—the gen. with local adverbs, ἵνα γῆς, ποῦ γῆς, *ubi terrarum, where in (in what quarter of) the world, where on earth*, Soph., etc.　2. *earth*, as an element, opp. to air, water, fire, Plat.　**II.** *a land, country*, Aesch., etc. ; γῆν πρὸ γῆς *from land to land*, Id.　**III.** *the earth or ground* as tilled, Soph., Plat.　**IV.** *a lump of earth*, in the phrase γῆν καὶ ὕδωρ αἰτεῖν, γῆν καὶ ὕδωρ διδόναι, *in token of submission*, Hdt.

γη-γενής, ές, (γί-γνομαι) like αὐτό-χθων, *earthborn*, of the primeval men, Hdt., Plat.　**II.** *born of Gaia or Tellus*, of the Titans and Giants, Aesch., Soph. ; —so of things, *portentous, furious*, Ar.

γῄδιον, τό, Dim. of γῆ, *a piece of land*, Ar., Xen.

γῆ-θεν, Adv. *out of* or *from the earth*, Aesch., Soph.

γηθέω, Dor. γᾱθέω : f. -ήσω : aor. 1 ἐγήθησα, Ep. γήθησα : pf. γέγηθα, Dor. γέγᾱθα (in pres. sense) : plqpf. ἐγεγήθειν, Ep. γεγήθειν :— (γαίω) :—*to rejoice*, Hom. ; c. acc. rei, τίς ἂν τάδε γηθήσειεν ; Ib. : c. part., γηθήσει προφανεῖσα (dual acc.) *will rejoice* at our appearing, Ib. ; γέγηθας ζῶν *thou rejoicest* in living, Soph. ; γεγηθέναι ἐπί τινι Id. : part. γεγηθώς, like χαίρων, Lat. *impune*, Id.

γῆθος, εος, τό, = sq., (γηθέω) Plut.

γηθοσύνη, ἡ, *joy*, (γηθέω) *delight*, Il.

γηθόσυνος, η, ον and ος, ον, (γηθέω) *joyful, glad* at a thing, c. dat., Il. ; absol., Ib.

γήϊνος, η, ον, (γῆ) *of earth*, Xen., Plat. :—also **γήϊος**, Anth.

γηΐτης, contr. γήτης, ου, ὁ, (γῆ) *a husbandman*, Soph.

γη-λοφος, ὁ, = γεώλοφος, *a hill*, Xen.

γη-μόρος, ὁ, Dor. and Trag. γᾱ-μόρος, Att. γεω-μόρος : (μείρομαι) :—*one who has a share of land*, *a land-owner* : οἱ γ. *the landowners, landlords*, Lat. *optimātes*, Hdt.

γη-οχέω, (ἔχω) *to possess land*, Hdt.

γή-πεδον, Dor. and Trag. γά-πεδον, τό, *a plot of ground*, Aesch. ; cf. γεώ-πεδον.

γη-πετής, ές, (πίπτω) *falling* or *fallen to earth*, Eur.

γη-πόνος, ον, = γεωπ-πόνος.

γή-ποτος, ον, v. γά-ποτος.

γηραιός, ά, όν, (γῆρας) *longer form of* γεραιός, *aged, in old age*, Hes., Hdt., Plat.

γηραλέος, α, ον, = foreg., Aesch.

γηράναι [ᾰ], aor. 2 inf. of γηράσκω, as if from *γήρημι.

γηρᾱός, ον, = γηραιός, Aesch.

γηράς, aor. 2 part. of γηράσκω, as if from *γήρημι.

γῆρας, τό : gen. γήραος, contr. γήρως : dat. γήραϊ, contr. γήρᾳ : (γέρων) :—*old age*, Lat. *senectus*, Hom., etc.

γηράσκω, f. γηράσω and γηράσομαι [ᾰ] : aor. 1 ἐγήρασα : pf. γεγήρακα :—there is also a pres. **γηράω** : there are also some aor. 2 forms, as if from a pres. **γήρημι** or **γήρᾱμι**, 3 sing. ἐγήρα, inf. γηράναι [ᾰ], part. **γηράς**, Ep. dat. pl. γηράντεσσι : (γῆρας) :—*to grow*

old, become old, and in aor. and pf. *to be so*, Hom., etc. ; κηρύσσων γήρασκε *grew old* in his office of herald, Il. ; of things, χρόνος γηράσκων Aesch. ; c. acc. cogn., βίον γηράναι Soph.　**II.** Causal in aor. 1 ἐγήρασα, *to bring to old age*, Aesch., Anth.

γηρο-βοσκέω, f. ήσω, *to feed* or *tend in old age*, Eur. : —Pass. *to be so cherished*, Ar.　From

γηρο-βοσκός, όν, (βόσκω) *feeding* or *tending in old age*, Soph., Eur.

γηρο-κομία, = γηροβοσκία, Plut.　From

γηρο-κόμος, ον, (κομέω) *tending old age*, Hes.

γηρο-τροφέω, f. ήσω, = γηροβοσκέω, Plat. :—f. med. in pass. sense, Dem.　From

γηρο-τρόφος, ον, (τρέφω) = γηροβοσκός, Eur.

γηρυ-γόνη, ἡ, (γενέσθαι) *born of sound*, of echo, Theocr.

γήρῡμα, ατος, τό, (γηρύω) *a voice, sound, tone*, Aesch.

Γηρυόνης, ου, ὁ, (γηρύω) *the three-bodied Giant Geryon*, i. e. *the Shouter*, Pind. ; **Γηρυονεύς**, έως Ep. ῆος, Hes. ; **Γηρυών**, όνος, Aesch.

ΓΗ͂ΡΥΣ, νος, ἡ, *voice, speech*, Il., Soph., Eur.　Hence

γηρύω, Dor. γᾱρύω [ῠ] : f. ύσω [ῡ] : aor. 1 ἐγήρῡσα Ar. :—Med., f. -ύσομαι : aor. 1 ἐγηρυσάμην and in pass. form ἐγηρύθην :—*to sing* or *say, speak, cry*, Trag.; c. acc. cogn. *to utter*, Eur.　**II.** the Med. is used in the same way, *to sing*, h. Hom. : c. acc. cogn., Hes., Eur. ; τοὶ σκῶπες ἀηδόσι γαρύσαιντο let the owls *sing against* the nightingales, Theocr. (Cf. Lat. *garrio, garrulus*.)

γήρως, contr. gen. of γῆρας.

γήτειον, τό, Att. for γήθυον, *a leek*, Ar.

γήτης, ὁ, contr. for γηΐτης.

Γιγάντειος, α, ον, (γίγας) *gigantic*, Luc.

Γιγαντ-ολέτης, ου, (ὄλλυμι) *giantkiller*, Anth. ; -ολέ-τωρ, ορος, ὁ, Luc.

Γιγαντο-φόνος, ον, (*φένω) *giant-killing*, Eur.

γίγαρτον [ῐ], *a grape-stone*, Simon. : in pl. *grapes*, Ar.

ΓΙ͂ΓΑΣ [ῑ], αντος, ὁ : pl., dat. Γίγᾱσιν, Ep. Γιγάντεσσιν : (γῆ, γαῖα ?) :—mostly in pl. Γίγαντες, *the Giants*, a savage race destroyed by the gods, Od. ; *the sons of Gaia*, Hes.　**II.** as Adj. *mighty*, Ζέφυρος γίγας Aesch.

γίγγλῦμος or γιγγλυμός, ὁ, *a hinge joint*: *a joint in a coat of mail*, Xen.

γί-γνομαι, Ion. and in late Gr. γί-νομαι [ῑ], f. γενή-σομαι :—aor. 2 ἐγενόμην, Ion. 2 sing. γένευ, 3 sing. γενέσκετο, syncop. ἔγεντο :—pf. γέγονα : plqpf. ἐγε-γόνειν, Ion. ἐγεγόνεα :—for the Ep. forms γέγαα, γε-γάᾱσι, etc., v. γέγαα :—besides these we have some pass. forms, aor. 1 ἐγενήθην, pf. γεγένημαι : 3 sing. plqpf. ἐγεγένητο or γεγένητο. (γί-γνομαι is syncopated from γι-γένομαι, the Root being ΓΕΝ ; cf. aor. 2 γεν-έσθαι, γένος, etc. ; so Lat. *gi-gno* for *gi-geno*.)

　Radical sense, *to come into being*, Lat. *gigni* :　**1.** of persons, *to be born*, νέον γεγαώς new *born*, Od. ; γεγονέναι ἔκ τινος Hdt. ; more rarely ἀπό τινος Id. ; τινος Eur. :—with Numerals, ἔτεα τρία καὶ δέκα γε-γονώς, Lat. *natus annos tredecim*, Hdt., etc.　**2.** of things, *to be produced*, Plat., Xen., etc. :—of sums, ὁ γεγονὼς ἀριθμός *the result* or *amount*, Plat.　**3.** of events, *to take place, come to pass, come on, happen*, and in past tenses *to be*, Hom., etc. :—ὃ μὴ γένοιτο, Lat. *quod dii prohibeant*, Dem. :—c. dat. et part., γί-γνεταί τί μοι βουλομένῳ, ἀσμένῳ I am glad at *its being*

so, Thuc., etc. :—of sacrifices, omens, etc., to *be favourable, Id., Xen. :—in neut. part., τὸ γενόμενον the event, the fact, Thuc.; τὰ γενόμενα the facts, Xen.; τὰ γεγενημένα former events, the past, Id.; τὸ γενησόμενον the future, Thuc. :—of Time, ὡς τρίτη ἡμέρη ἐγένετο arrived, Hdt. II. followed by a Predicate, to come into a certain state, to become, Lat. fieri, and (in past tenses), to be so and so, Hom., etc.; πάντα γιγνόμενος turning every way, Od.; so, παντοῖος γ. Hdt.; τί γένωμαι; what am I to become? i. e. what is to become of me? Aesch.; οὐκ ἔχοντες ὅ τι γένωνται Thuc. 2. with Adverbs, κακῶς ἐγένετό μοι it went ill with me, Hdt.; εὖ, καλῶς, γίγνεται it goes well, etc., Xen. 3. followed by oblique cases of Nouns, a. c. gen., γ. τῶν δικαστέων to become one of the jurymen, Hdt., etc. :—to fall to the share of, belong to, ἡ νίκη γίγνεταί τινος Xen. :—to be master of, ἑαυτοῦ γ. Soph., etc.; γ. ἐντὸς ἑωυτοῦ Hdt. :—of things, to be at, i. e. to cost, so much, c. gen. pretii, Ar. b. with Preps., ἀπὸ or ἐκ δείπνου to be done supper, Hdt.; γ. εἰς τόπον to be at.., Id. :—γ. ἐξ ὀφθαλμῶν τινι to be out of sight, Id.; γ. ἐν τόπῳ to be in a place, Id.; also, γ. ἐν ποιήσει to be engaged in poetry, Id., etc.; γ. δι' ἔχθρας, δι' ἔριδος γ. τινι to be at enmity with, Ar., etc. :—γ. ἐπί τινι to fall into or be in one's power, Xen. :—γ. μετά τινος to be on his side, Id. :—γ. παρά τινα to come to one, Hdt. :—γ. πρὸς τόπῳ to be at or near.., Plat. :—γ. πρός τινι to be engaged in.., Dem.; πρός τι Plat. :—γ. πρὸ ὁδοῦ to be forward on the way, Il.

γι-γνώσκω, Ion. and in late Gr. γινώσκω, f. γνώσομαι: pf. ἔγνωκα :—aor. 2 ἔγνων (as if from a Verb in -μι), Ep. γνῶν; subj. γνῶ, Ep. γνώω, γνώομεν, γνώωσι; inf. γνῶναι, Ep. γνώμεναι :—Pass., f. γνωσθήσομαι: aor. 1 ἐγνώσθην: pf. ἔγνωσμαι :—to learn to know, to perceive, mark, learn, and in past tenses, to know, c. acc., Hom., etc. :—also to discern, distinguish, ὡς εὖ γιγνώσκῃς ἠμὲν θεὸν ἠδὲ καὶ ἄνδρα that thou mayst discern between gods and men, Il. : c. gen., γνώτην ἀλλήλων were aware of each other, Od.; γνῶ χωομένοιο was aware of his being angry, Il. :—c. part., ἔγνων μιν οἰωνὸν ἐόντα perceived that he was a bird of omen, Od.; ἔγνων ἡττημένος I felt that I was beaten, Ar. :—but c. inf., ἵνα γνῷ τρέφειν that he may learn how to keep, Soph. II. to observe, to form a judgment on a matter, to judge or think so and so, Hdt., Att.: in dialogue, ἔγνων I understand, Soph. :—Pass. to be pronounced, of a sentence or judgment, Thuc., etc. :—also, to judge, determine, decree that.., c. acc. et inf., Hdt., etc. (γι-γνώσκω is redupl. from Root ΓΝΩ, cf. γνῶναι, γνωτός, etc. : so Lat. gnosco.)

γίνομαι, γινώσκω, γίνωσκω, v. γίγνομαι, γιγνώσκω.

γλαγάω, (γλάγος) to be milky, juicy, Anth.

γλᾱγερός, ά, όν, (γλάγος) full of milk, Anth.: so γλᾱγόεις, εσσα, εν, Id.

γλαγο-πήξ, ηγος, ὁ, ἡ, (πήγνυμι) curdling milk, Anth.

γλάγος [ἄ], εος, τό, poët. for γάλα, milk, Il.

γλακτο-φάγος [ἄ], ον, (φαγεῖν) syncop. for γαλακτο-, living on milk, Il.

γλάμων, ον, blear-eyed, Ar.

γλαυκιάω, only in Ep. part. γλαυκιόων, glaring fiercely, of a lion, Il.

γλαυκ-όμματος, ον, (ὄμμα) gray-eyed, Plat.

ΓΛΑΥΚΟΣ, ή, όν, in Hom., prob. without any notion of colour, gleaming, silvery, of the sea, Il., Trag. II. later, certainly, with a notion of colour, bluish green, gray, Lat. glaucus, of the olive, Soph., Eur. :—esp. of the eyes light blue or gray, Lat. caesius, Hdt., Eur..

γλαυκ-ῶπις, ἡ: gen. ιδος: acc. ιδα or ιν: (ὤψ) :—in Hom. as epith. of Athena, with gleaming eyes, bright-eyed; v. γλαυκός.

γλαυκ-ώψ, ῶπος, ὁ, ἡ, = γλαυκῶπις, Pind.

γλαύξ, Att. γλαῦξ, γλαυκός, ἡ, the owl, so called from its glaring eyes (v. γλαυκός, and cf. σκώψ; γλαῦκ' Ἀθήναζε, γλαῦκ' εἰς Ἀθήνας = 'carry coals to Newcastle,' Ar.: Athen. silver coins were called γλαῦκες, because they were stamped with an owl, Id.

γλαφυρία, ἡ, smoothness, polish, Plut. From

γλᾰφῠρός, ά, όν, (γλάφω) hollow, hollowed, of ships, Hom.; of caves, Id.; of the lyre, Od.; γλ. λιμήν a deep harbour or cove, Ib. II. polished, finished: of persons, subtle, critical, nice, exact, Ar. :—Adv. -ρῶς, and neut. as Adv., Luc. Hence

γλαφυρότης, ητος, ἡ, = γλαφυρία, Luc.

ΓΛΑΦΩ [ᾰ], to scrape up the ground, of a lion, Hes.

γλάχων and γλακώ [ᾰ], Dor. for γλήχων, -ώ: v. βλήχων.

γλευκο-πότης, ὁ, drinker of new wine, Anth.

γλεῦκος, εος, τό, (γλυκύς) Lat. mustum, new wine, Arist.

γλέφαρον, τό, Aeol. for βλέφαρον.

γλήνη, ἡ, the pupil of the eye, eyeball, Hom., Soph. II. because figures are reflected small in the pupil, a puppet, doll; as a taunt, ἔρρε, κακὴ γλήνη away, slight girl, Il. (Deriv. uncertain.) Hence

γλήνος, εος, τό, in pl. things to stare at, shows, wonders, Il.

γλήχων, Dor. γλάχων, v. βλήχων.

γλισχρ-αντιλογ-εξ-επίτριπτος, ον, greedy-pettifog-ging-barefaced-knavish, Ar.

γλίσχρος, α, ον, (γλίχομαι) glutinous, sticky, clammy, Plat. :—metaph. 1. sticking close, importunate, Ar.; γλίσχρως ἐπιθυμεῖν Plat. 2. greedy, grasping, niggardly, Arist. :—Adv., Plat., Xen.; hence, with difficulty, hardly, γλισχρῶς καὶ μόλις Dem. 3. of things, mean, shabby, meagre, Id., Plut. Hence

γλίσχρων, ονος, ὁ, a niggard, Ar.

ΓΛΙΧΟΜΑΙ [ῐ], only in pres. and impf. :—to cling to, strive after, long for, a thing, c. gen., Hdt., Plat.; ὡς στρατηγήσεις γλίχεαι art anxious how to become general, Hdt. :—c. inf. to be eager to do, Plat., Dem.

γλοιο-πότις, ιδος, ἡ, sucking up grease, Anth.

ΓΛΟΙΟΣ, ὁ, any glutinous substance, gluten, gum, γλ. ἀπὸ τῆς ὕλης tree-gum, Hdt. II. as Adj., γλοιός, ά, όν, slippery, knavish, Ar.

ΓΛΟΥΤΟΣ, ὁ, the rump, Il. :—pl. the buttocks, Lat. nates, Ib., Hdt.

γλυκαίνω, f. ανῶ, to sweeten :—Pass. to be sweetened, to turn sweet, Mosch.

γλυκερός, ά, όν, = γλυκύς, Od., Eur.

γλυκερό-χρως, ωτος, ὁ, ἡ, with sweet skin, Anth.

γλυκύ-δακρυς, υ, (δάκρυ) causing sweet tears, Anth.

γλυκύ-δωρος, ον, (δῶρον) with sweet gifts, Anth.

γλυκύ-ηχής, ές, (ἦχος) sweet-sounding, Anth.

γλυκυθυμία, ἡ, sweetness of mind: benevolence, Plut.

γλυκύ-θυμος, ον, sweet-minded, sweet of mood, Il. II. act. charming the mind, delightful, Ar.

γλῠκύ-καρπος, ον, *bearing sweet fruit*, Theocr.
γλῠκύ-μᾱλον, Aeol. and Dor. for γλυκύ-μηλον, *sweet-apple*, as a term of endearment, Theocr.
γλῠκύ-μείλιχος, ον, *sweetly winning*, h. Hom.
γλῠκῠμῡθέω, f. ήσω, *to speak sweetly* :—from γλυκύμῡθος, ον, *sweet-speaking*, Anth.
γλῠκύ-παις, ὁ, ή, *having a fair offspring*, Anth.
γλῠκῠ-πάρθενος, ή, *a sweet maid*, Anth.
ΓΛΥ´ΚΥ´Σ, εῖα, ύ, *sweet*, Il., etc. :—metaph. *sweet, delightful*, Hom., etc. :—γλυκύ ἐστι c. inf., Aesch., etc.   2. of water, *sweet, fresh*, opp. to πικρός, Hdt.   3. after Hom., of persons, *sweet, dear*, Soph.; ὦ γλυκύτατε *my dear fellow*, Ar. :—sometimes in bad sense, *simple, silly*, ὡς γλυκὺς εἶ! Plat.   II. Comp. and Sup. γλυκίων [ῐ Att., ῑ Ep.], γλύκιστος; also γλυκύτερος, -τατος, Pind., Att.
γλῠκύτης, ητος, ή, (γλυκύς) *sweetness*, Hdt.
γλυπτήρ, ῆρος, ὁ, (γλύφω) *a graving tool, chisel*, Anth.
γλύπτης, ου, ὁ, (γλύφω) *a carver, sculptor*, Anth.
γλυπτός, ή, όν, (γλύφω) *carved*, Anth.
γλύφανος, ὁ, (γλύφω) *a tool for carving, knife, chisel*, h. Hom., Theocr.; γλ. καλάμου *a pen-knife*, Anth.
γλῠφεῖον, τό, = γλύφανος, Luc.
γλῠφίς, ίδος, ή, mostly in pl. γλυφίδες, *the notched end* of the arrow, Hom., Hdt.; πτερωταὶ γλυφίδες *the arrow itself*, Eur.   From
ΓΛΥ´ΦΩ [ῠ]: f. γλύψω: aor. 1 ἔγλυψα :—Pass., aor. 1 part. γλυφθέν, aor. 2 γλυφέν [ῠ]: pf. γέγλυμμαι: (akin to γλάφω) :—*to carve, cut out with a knife*, Ar.; γλ. σφρηγῖδας *to engrave them*, Hdt.; of sculptors, Id.   II. *to note down* [on tablets], τόκους Anth.
γλώξ, ή, only in pl. γλῶχες, *the beard of corn*, Hes. (Akin to γλωχίν.)
γλῶσσα, Att. γλῶττα, ης, ή, *the tongue*, Hom., etc.   2. *the tongue*, as the organ of speech, γλώσσης χάριν through love *of talking*, Hes., Aesch.; ἀπὸ γλώσσης *by word of mouth*, Hdt., Thuc.; οὐκ ἀπὸ γλώσσης *not by word of mouth*, not from *mere hearsay*, Aesch.; so, οὐ κατὰ γλώσσαν Soph.; ἱέναι γλῶσσαν *to let loose one's tongue*, speak without restraint, Id.; pl., κερτομίοις γλώσσαις, i. e. *with blasphemies*, Id. :—for βοῦς ἐπὶ γλώσσῃ, v. βοῦς.   II. *a tongue, language*, Hom., Hdt., etc.   III. *the tongue* or *mouthpiece* of a pipe, Aeschin. (Deriv. unknown.)
γλωσσαλγία, ή, *endless talking, wordiness*, Eur.
γλώσσ-αλγος, ον, (ἄλγος) *talking till one's tongue aches*.
γλωσσίς, = γλωττίς, Luc.
γλωσσό-κομον, τό, (γλῶσσα III, κομέω) *a case for the mouthpiece of a pipe*: generally, *a case, casket*, N. T.
γλώττα, ης, ή, Att. for γλῶσσα.
γλωττίς, ίδος, ή, = γλῶσσα III, Luc.
γλωχίν or γλωχίς, ή, gen. ῖνος, *any projecting point*, hence,   1. *the end of the yoke-strap*, Il.   2. *the point of* an arrow, Soph., Anth. (Deriv. uncertain.)
γναθμός, ὁ, *the jaw*, poët. form of γνάθος, Hom.; also in pl., Od.: metaph., γναθμοὶ φαρμάκων *the gnawing* of poison, Eur.; for ἀλλοτρίοις γναθμοῖσι, v. ἀλλότριος.
ΓΝΑ´ΘΟΣ [ᾰ], ή, (akin to γένυς) *the jaw*, properly *the lower jaw*, ή κάτω γν. Hdt.; ἔπαγε γνάθον take your *teeth* to it! Ar.; oft. in pl., Plat., etc.   2. metaph. of fire, Aesch.   3. metaph. also, like Lat. *fauces*, of a

narrow *strait*, Id., Xen.   4. *the point* or *edge*, as of a wedge, Aesch.
γναμπτός, ή, όν, (γνάμπτω) *curved, bent*, Hom.   2. *supple, pliant*, of the limbs of living men, Id.   II. metaph. *to be bent*, οὔτε νόημα γναμπτὸν ἐνὶ στήθεσσι (of Achilles), Il.
γνάμπτω, f. ψω: aor. 1 ἔγναμψα Ep. γνάμψα :—poët. form of κάμπτω used by Hom. when a short vowel is to be made long before it, *to bend*; γν. τινα *to bend* his will, Aesch.
γνάπτω, γναφεύς, v. κνάπτω, κναφεύς.
γνήσιος, α, ον, (γένος) *of* or *belonging to the race*, i. e. *lawfully begotten, legitimate*, opp. to νόθος, Hom.; φρονεῖν γνήσια *to have a noble mind*, Eur.; γν. γυναῖκες *lawful wives*, opp. to παλλακίδες, Xen.; γν. τῆς Ἑλλάδος *true sons* of Greece, Dem. :—Adv. -ίως, *lawfully, really, truly*, Eur.
γνοίην, aor. 2 opt. of γιγνώσκω: γνούς, part.
γνόφος, ὁ, = δνόφος, Luc.
γνύξ, Adv. (γόνυ) *with bent knee*: γνὺξ ἐριπεῖν *to fall on the knee*, Il.
γνῶ, Ep. for ἔγνω, 3 sing. aor. 2 of γιγνώσκω :—but γνῷ, 3 sing. subj.
γνῶθι, aor. 2 imper. of γι-γνώσκω.
γνῶμα, ατος, τό, (γι-γνώσκω) *a mark, token*, like γνώρισμα, Hdt., Soph.   II. *an opinion, judgment*, = γνώμη, Aesch., Eur.
γνωμᾰτεύω, f. σω, (γνῶμα) *to form a judgment of, discern*, Plat.
γνώμη, ή, (γι-γνώσκω) *a means of knowing, a mark, token*, Theogn.   II. *the organ by which one knows, the mind*: hence,   1. *thought, judgment, intelligence*, Soph.; acc. absol., γνώμην ἱκανός intelligent, Hdt.; γν. ἀγαθός Soph.; γνώμην ἔχειν to understand, Id.; προσέχειν γνώμην *to give heed, be on one's guard*; ἀπὸ γνώμης *with a good conscience*, Aesch.; but, οὐκ ἀπὸ γν. *not without judgment*, with good *sense*, Soph.   2. *one's mind, will, purpose*, Aesch., etc.; ἐν γνώμῃ γεγονέναι τινί *to stand high in his favour*, Hdt.; τὴν γν. ἔχειν πρός τινα or τι *to have a mind, be inclined towards* .., Thuc.; ἀφ' ἑαυτοῦ γνώμης *of his own accord*, Id.; ἐκ μιᾶς γν. *of one accord*, Dem.; so, μιᾷ γνώμῃ Thuc. :—in pl., φίλιαι γνῶμαι *friendly sentiments*, Hdt.   III. *a judgment, opinion*, πλεῖστός εἰμι τῇ γνώμῃ *I incline mostly to the opinion that* .., Hdt.; so, ταύτῃ πλεῖστος τὴν γν. or ἡ πλείστη γν. ἐστί μοι Id.; γνώμην ἔχειν, like λόγον ἔχ., *to be right*, Ar.; κατὰ γν. τὴν ἐμὴν *mea sententia*, Hdt.; absol., γνώμην ἐμήν Ar.; παρὰ γνώμην *contrary to general opinion*, Thuc. :—of orators, γνώμην ἀποφαίνειν, ἀποδείκνυσθαι *to deliver an opinion*, Hdt.; τίθεσθαι Soph.; δηλοῦν Thuc.   2. like Lat. *sententia*, *a proposition, motion*, γνώμην εἰσφέρειν Hdt.; εἰπεῖν, προθεῖναι Thuc.; γνώμην νικᾶν *to carry a motion*, Ar.   3. γνῶμαι *the opinions* of wise men, *maxims*, Lat. *sententiae*.   4. *a purpose, resolve, intent*, Thuc. :—τινὰ ἔχουσα γνώμην; *with what purpose?* Hdt.; ή ξύμπασα γν. τῶν λεχθέντων *the general purport* .., Thuc.
γνωμίδιον, τό, Dim. of γνώμη III, *a fancy*, Ar.
γνωμολογέω, f. ήσω, (λόγος) *to speak in maxims*, Arist.
γνωμο-λογία, ή, (λέγω) *a speaking in maxims*, Plat.

γνωμονικός, ή, όν, (γνώμων I) fit to give judgment, Xen. : experienced in a thing, c. gen., Plat.   II. (γνώμων II) of or for sun-dials, Anth.

γνωμοσύνη, ή, (γνώμων) prudence, judgment, Solon.

γνωμοτŭπικός, ή, όν, clever at coining maxims, Ar.

γνωμο-τύπος [ŭ], ον, (τύπτω) maxim-coining, sententious, Ar.

γνώμων, ονος, ὁ, (γι-γνώσκω) one that knows or examines, a judge, interpreter, Aesch., Thuc., Xen.   II. the gnomon or index of the sundial, Hdt.   III. οἱ γνώμονες, the teeth that mark a horse's age, Xen.   IV. a carpenter's rule : metaph. a rule of life, Theogn.

γνῶναι, aor. 2 inf. of γι-γνώσκω.

γνώομεν, Ep. for γνῶμεν, pl. aor. 2 subj. of γι-γνώσκω.

γνωρίζω, f. Att. ιῶ : pf. ἐγνώρικα : (γι-γνώσκω) :—to make known, point out, explain, Aesch. :—Pass. to become known, Plat.   2. c. acc. pers. to make known, τινά τινι Plut.   II. to gain knowledge of, discover that a thing is, c. part., Soph., Thuc.   2. to be acquainted with, make acquaintance with, τινά Plat., Dem.

γνώριμος, ον, rarely η, ον, (γι-γνώσκω) well-known, familiar, of persons and things, Plat., etc. :—as Subst. an acquaintance, Od., Xen., etc.   II. known to all, notable, distinguished, οἱ γνώριμοι the notables or wealthy class, opp. to δῆμος, Id. :—Sup., οἱ γνωριμώτατοι Dem.   III. Adv. -μως, intelligibly, Eur.

γνώρισις, εως, ή, (γνωρίζω) acquaintance, τινος with another, Plat. : knowledge, Id.

γνώρισμα, ατος, τό, (γνωρίζω) that by which a thing is made known, a mark, token, Xen. ; γνωρίσματα tokens by which a lost child is recognised, Plut.

γνωριστέον, verb. Adj. of γνωρίζω, one must know, Arist.

γνῶς, γνῷ, 2 and 3 sing. aor. 2 of γι-γνώσκω.

γνωσι-μᾰχέω, (μάχομαι) Ion. Verb, to fight with one's own opinion, i. e. to change one's mind, to recognise one's own fighting power (as compared with the enemy): hence to give way, submit, Hdt., Eur., Ar.; γν. μὴ εἶναι ὁμοῖοι to give way and confess that they are not equal, Hdt.

γνῶσις, εως, ή, (γι-γνώσκω) a judicial inquiry Dem.   II. a knowing, knowledge, Plat., N.T.   2. acquaintance with a person, πρός τινα ap. Aeschin.   3. a knowing, recognising, Thuc.   III. a being known, fame, credit, Luc.

γνωστέον, verb. Adj. of γι-γνώσκω, one must know, Plat.

γνωστήρ, ῆρος, ὁ, (γι-γνώσκω) one that knows : a surety, Lat. cognitor, Xen.

γνώστης, ου, ὁ, (γι-γνώσκω) one that knows, N.T.   II. a surety, Plat.

γνωστικός, ή, όν, (γι-γνώσκω) good at knowing : ἡ –κή (sc. δύναμις) the faculty of knowing, Plat.

γνωστός, ή, όν, later form of γνωτός, known, to be known, Aesch., Soph., Xen.

γνωτός, ή, όν, older form of γνωστός :   I. of things, perceived, understood, known, Hom. ; γνωτὰ κοὺκ ἄγνωτά μοι Soph.   II. of persons, well-known, Od. :—as Subst. a kinsman, brother, γνωτοί τε γνωταί τε brothers and sisters, Il.

γοᾱτάς, Dor. for γοητής.

γοάω, inf. γοᾶν, Ep. γοήμεναι, Ep. part. γοόων, –όωσα : Ep. impf. γόων, Ion. γοάασκεν : Ep. aor. 2 γόον : f. γοήσομαι, later γοήσω : aor. I ἐγόησα : (γόος) :—to wail, groan, weep, Hom. :—c. acc. to bewail, mourn, lament, weep for, Il. ; ὑπέρ τινος Mosch. :—so also in Med., Aesch., Soph. :—Pass., γοᾶται Aesch.

γογγύζω, f. σω, to mutter, murmur, N. T. (Formed from the sound.)

γογγύλος [ŭ], η, ον, = στρογγύλος, round, Ar. (Deriv. uncertain.)

γογγυσμός, ὁ, (γογγύζω) a murmuring, N. T.

γογγυστής, οῦ, ὁ, (γογγύζω) a murmurer, N. T.

γοεδνός, ή, όν, = sq., Aesch.

γοερός, ά, όν, (γόος) of things, mournful, lamentable, Aesch., Eur.   II. of persons, lamenting, Eur.

γοήμεναι, Ep. for γοᾶν, inf. of γοάω.

γοήμων, ον, gen. ονος, = γοερός, Anth.

γόης, ητος, ὁ, (γοάω) one who howls out enchantments, a sorcerer, enchanter, Hdt., Eur. ; γόησι καταείδοντες charming by means of sorcerers, Hdt.   2. a juggler, cheat, Plat., Dem.

γοητεία, ή, (γοητεύω) juggling, cheatery, Plat.

γοητεύω, f. σω, (γόης) to bewitch, beguile, Plat.

γοητής, οῦ, Dor. γοᾱτάς, ᾶ, ὁ, (γοάω) a wailer ; or, in Adv. sense, of lamentation, Aesch.

γοητικός, ή, όν, (γοάω) bewitching : fem. γοῆτις, Anth.

γοῖ, γοῖ, to imitate the sound of pigs grunting, Anth.

γόμος, ὁ, (γέμω) a ship's freight, burden, tonnage, Hdt., Dem.   2. a beast's load, Babr.

γομόω, f. ώσω, (γόμος) to load, Babr.

γομφιό-δουπος, ον, rattling between the teeth, Anth.

γομφίος (sc. ὀδούς), ὁ, (γόμφος) a grinder-tooth, Lat. molaris, Hdt., Ar., etc.

γομφο-πᾱγής, ές, (πήγνυμι) fastened with bolts, well-bolted, Ar.

ΓΟ'ΜΦΟΣ, ὁ, a bolt, for ship-building, Od. ; and for other uses, Hes., Aesch. :—generally, any bond or fastening, of the cross-ribs of canoes, Hdt. (Prob. akin to γαμφηλαί.) Hence

γομφόω, f. ώσω, to fasten with bolts, of ships :—in Pass., γεγόμφωται σκάφος the ship's hull is ready built, Aesch. Hence

γόμφωμα, ατος, τό, that which is fastened by bolts, frame-work, Plut.

γομφωτήρ, ῆρος, ὁ, (γομφόω) a ship-builder, Anth.

γονεύς, έως, ὁ, (γείνομαι II) a begetter, father : in pl. γονεῖς, έων, οἱ, the parents, Hes., Att. : also, a progenitor, ancestor, Hdt.

γονή, ή, (γί-γνομαι) produce, offspring, Hom., etc. ; so in pl., Soph.   2. like γενεά, γένος, a race, stock, family, Trag.   3. a generation, Aesch.   II. that which engenders, the seed, Hes., Hdt., etc.   2. the womb, Eur.   III. of the mother, child-birth, Id., Theocr.   2. of the child, birth, Soph.

γονίας χειμών, perhaps a violent storm, Aesch.

γόνιμος, ον, (γονή) productive, fruitful : γ. μέλεα a parent's limbs, Eur.   2. metaph. of persons, genuine, Ar. ; γ. ὕδωρ Anth.

γόνος, ὁ and ή, (γί-γνομαι) like γονή, that which is begotten, offspring, a child, Il., Hdt. ; ὁ Πηλέως γ. his son, Soph.   2. any product, of the silver mines at Laureion, Aesch. ; of tribute, Ar.   3. ἐς ἔρσενα

γόνον to any of the male *sex*, Hdt. II. like γένος, one's *race, stock, descent*, Od.

ΓΟ'ΝΥ˘, τό : gen. γόνατος, Ion. γούνατος ; Ep. also, γουνός ; dat. γουνί, pl. γοῦνα, γούνων, γούνεσσι :—the Ion. forms γούνατος, -ατι in Trag., but never γουνός, γουνί :—*the knee*, Lat. *genu*, Hom., etc. 2. ἅψα- σθαι γούνων to clasp *the knees* as a suppliant, Il. ; so ἑλεῖν, λαβεῖν, γούνων Ib. ; τῶν γουνάτων λαβέσθαι Hdt. ; περὶ or ἀμφὶ γούνασί τινος χεῖρας βαλεῖν Od. ; ἀμφὶ γόνυ τινὸς πίπτειν Eur. ; γούνων λίσσεσθαι to sup- plicate *by* [*clasping*] *the knees*, Hom. ; ἅντεσθαι or λίσσεσθαι πρὸς τῶν γονάτων Eur. 3. of a sitting posture, γόνυ κάμψειν bend *the knee* so as to sit down, Il. :—ἐπὶ γούνασι on one's *knees*, of a child, Ib. ; πέπ- λον θεῖναι Ἀθηναίης ἐπὶ γούνασιν to lay it on her *lap* (as an offering), Ib. ; metaph., θεῶν ἐν γούνασι κεῖται, i. e. rests on their will and pleasure, Hom. 4. the knees are in Hom. the seat of strength ; hence, γούνατά τινος λύειν to weaken, lame, kill him, Il.: also, metaph., ἐς γόνυ βάλλειν to bring down upon *the knee*, i. e. to humble, conquer, Hdt. 5. proverb., ἀπωτέρω ἢ γόνυ κνήμη 'Charity begins at home,' Theocr. II. the knee or joint of grasses, such as the cane, Lat. *geniculum*, Hdt., Xen.

γονῠπετέω, f. ήσω, *to fall on the knee, to fall down before* one, τινι or τινα N. T. From

γονῠ-πετής, ές, (πί-πτω) *falling on the knee*, ἕδραι γον. a *kneeling posture*, Eur.

γόον, Ep. aor. 2 or impf. of γοάω.

ΓΟ'ΟΣ, ὁ, *weeping, wailing, groaning, howling, mourning, lamentation*, Hom., Trag.

Γόργειος, α, ον, (Γοργώ) *of the Gorgon*, Hom.

Γοργίειος, ον, *of Gorgias, Gorgias-like*, Xen.

Γοργο-λόφας, ον, ὁ, (Γοργώ, λόφος) *he of the Gorgon- crest*, Ar. ; fem. Γοργολόφα, ης, ἡ, Id.

Γοργόνειος, ον, =Γοργεῖος, Aesch.

Γοργό-νωτος, ον, (Γοργώ, νῶτον) *with the Gorgon on it*, of a shield, Ar.

γοργόομαι, Pass. *to be hot* or *spirited*, of a horse, Xen.

ΓΟΡΓΟ'Σ, ή, όν, *grim, fierce, terrible*, Aesch., Eur. ; γοργὸς ἰδεῖν *terrible to behold*, Xen. ; of horses, *hot, spirited*, Id.

Γοργο-φόνος, ον, (*φένω) *Gorgon-killing* : fem. Γοργο- φόνη, as a name of Athena, Eur.

Γοργώ, ἡ, (γοργός) *the Gorgon*, i. e. *the Grim One* (cf. γοργός), Hom. : Hes. speaks of three Gorgons, Euryalé, Stheino, Medusa,—the last being *the Gorgon* ; her snaky head was fixed on the aegis of Athena, and all who looked on it became stone, Eur.—The regular sing. is Γοργώ, gen. Γοργοῦς, dat. Γοργοῖ : later, cases were formed as if from a nom. Γοργών, sc. gen. Γοργόνος ; dat. Γοργόνι :—in pl., Γοργόνες, acc. -ας are the only forms.

γοργ-ωπός, όν, (ὤψ) *fierce-eyed*, Aesch., Eur. :—also γοργώψ, ῶπος, ὁ, ἡ, Eur. ; fem. γοργῶπις, ιδος, of Athena, Soph.

γοῦν, Ion. and Dor. γῶν, (γε οὖν) a stronger form of γε, *at least then, at any rate, any way*, γνώσει ὀψὲ γοῦν τὸ σωφρονεῖν Aesch.; used in quoting an example, Thuc., Xen. ; also in answers, *yes certainly*, τὰς γοῦν Ἀθήνας οἶδα Soph.

γοῦνα, γούνων, poët. pl. of γόνυ.

γουνάζομαι, f. σομαι, Dep. (γόνυ) *to clasp* another's *knees* (v. γόνυ I. 2ˋ), and so *to implore, entreat, sup- plicate*, Il. ; c. inf. *to implore* one *to do* a thing, Ib. ; ὑπέρ τινος *in behalf of* another, Ib. ; πρός τινος *by* another, Od.

γούνατα, γούνασι, Ep. γούνεσσι, Ep. pl. forms of γόνυ.

γουνόομαι, contr. -οῦμαι, Dep. only in pres. and impf., =γουνάζομαι, Hom.

γουνο-παχής, ές, (πάχος) *thick-kneed*, or (better) γουνο- παγής, (πήγνυμι) *cramping the knees*, Hes.

γουνός, a doubtful word, prob.=βουνός (v. Β β. III), a *hill*, γ. Ἀθηνάων *the hill* or *citadel* of Athens, Od. ; ὁ γ. ὁ Σουνιακός *the hill* of Sunium, Hdt. ; ἀνὰ γουνὸν ἀλωῆς up *the slope* of the threshing floor, Od.

γραῖα, Ion. γραίη, ἡ, *an old woman*, fem. of γραῦς, γέρων (v. γεραιά), Od., Soph., Eur. ; γραῖαι δαίμονες, of the Eumenides, Aesch. 2. as Adj. in the obl. cases, *old, withered*, Id., Eur. II. Γραῖαι, αἱ, daughters of Phorcys and Ceto, with fair faces, but *hair gray* from their birth, Hes.

γρᾱΐδιον, τό, Dim. of γραῖα, *an old hag, old woman*, Ar., Xen. : contr. γρᾴδιον, Ar., Dem.

γραιόομαι, (γραῖα) Pass. *to become an old woman*, Anth.

γραῖος, ᾶ, ον, contr. for γεραιός, σταφυλὴ γραίη *raisins*, Anth.

γράμμα, ατος, τό, (γράφω) *that which is drawn*, in pl. *the lines of a drawing* or *picture*, Eur., Theocr. : in sing. *a drawing, picture*, Plat. II. *that which is written, a written character, letter*, Lat. *litera*, Hdt., etc. ; and in pl. *letters*, Aesch. ; hence, *the alphabet*, Hdt., Plat. : γρ. *to have learnt to read*, Id. ; ἐδί- δασκες γράμματα, ἐγὼ δ᾽ ἐφοίτων you *kept school*,—I *went there*, Dem. 2. *a note* in music, Anth. III. in pl. also, *a piece of writing*, and, like Lat. *literae*, a *letter*, Hdt., Eur. : *an inscription, epitaph*, Hdt. 2. *papers* or *documents* of any kind, *records, accounts*, Ar., Oratt. :—in sing. *a bill, account*, N. T. 3. *a man's writings*, i. e. *a book, treatise*, Xen. :—also, *letters, learning*, Plat.

γραμμάτεια, ἡ, *the office of the γραμματεύς*, Plut.

γραμμάτείδιον or -ίδιον, τό, Dim. of γραμματεῖον, *small tablets*, Dem., Plut.

γραμμάτεῖον, τό, (γράμμα) *that on which one writes, tablets*, Plat., etc. 2. *an account-book, register*, Dem.

γραμμάτεύς, έως, ὁ, (γράμμα) *a secretary, clerk*, Lat. *scriba*, Thuc., etc. Hence

γραμμάτεύω, f. σω, *to be secretary*, Thuc., etc. ; c. gen., γρ. τοῦ συνεδρίου Epigr.

γραμμάτη-φόρος, ὁ, (φέρω) *a letter-carrier*, Plut.

γραμμάτίδιον, v. γραμματείδιον.

γραμμάτικεύομαι, Dep. *to be a grammarian*, Anth.

γραμμάτικός, ή, όν, (γράμματα) *knowing one's letters, well grounded in the rudiments, a grammarian*, Xen., etc. :—Adv. -κῶς, Plat. :—ἡ -κή (with or without τέχνη) *grammar*, Id.

γραμμάτιον, τό, Dim. of γράμμα, Luc.

γραμμάτιστής, οῦ, ὁ, =γραμματεύς, Hdt., Plat. II. *one who teaches γράμματα, a schoolmaster*, Xen., Plat.

γραμμά-τόκος, ον, (τίκτω) *mother of letters*, epith. of ink, Anth.

γραμμᾰτο-κύφων [ῠ], ωνος, ὁ, nickname of a γραμματεύς, a porer over records, Dem.

γραμμᾰτο-λικρῐφίς, ίδος, ὁ, a puzzle-headed grammarian, Anth.

γραμμᾰτοφορέω, f. ήσω, to carry or deliver letters, Strab. From

γραμμᾰτο-φόρος, ον, (φέρω) letter-carrying, Polyb.

γραμμᾰτο-φῠλάκιον, τό, (φυλακή) a box for keeping records, Plut.

γραμμή, ή, (γράφω) the stroke of a pen, a line, Plat. II. = βαλβίς, the line across the course, to mark the starting or winning post, Ar.: metaph. of life, Horace's ultima linea rerum, Eur. III. the middle line on a board (like our draught-board), also called ἡ ἱερά, proverb., τὸν ἀπὸ γραμμῆς or ἀφ' ἱερᾶς κινεῖν λίθον to move one's man from this line, i. e. try one's last chance, Theocr. IV. ἡ μακρά (sc. γραμμή), the long line, i. e. the line of condemnation drawn by the dicast, Ar.

γρᾱο-σόβης, ου, ὁ, (γραῦς, σοβέω) scaring old women, Ar.

γραπτέον, verb. Adj. of γράφω, one must describe, Xen. 2. γραπτέος, α, ον, to be described, Luc.

γραπτήρ, ῆρος, ὁ, (γράφω) a writer, Anth.

γραπτός, ή, όν, (γράφω) marked as with letters, ἁ γραπτὰ ὑάκινθος Theocr.

γραπτύς, ύος, ἡ, (γράφω) a scratching, tearing, Od.

γραῦς, gen. γράδς, ἡ: Ion. γρηῦς, γρηός, voc. γρηῦ: poët. also γρηΰς, voc. γρηΰ:—pl., nom. γραῖες, acc. γραῦς: (from same Root as γέρων):—an old woman, Hom., Aesch.; γρ. παλαιή Od.; γραῦς γυνή Eur. II. scum, as of boiled milk, Ar.

γρᾰφεύς, έως, ὁ, (γράφω) a painter, Eur. II. = γραμματεύς, Xen.

γρᾰφή, ή, (γράφω) representation by means of lines: I. drawing or delineation, Hdt.; of painting, Id., Plat. 2. a drawing, painting, picture, ὅσον γραφῇ only in a picture, Hdt.; πρέπουσα ὡς ἐν γραφαῖς Aesch. II. writing, the art of writing, Plat. 2. a writing, a letter, Soph.; so in pl., like γράμματα, Eur.; ψευδεῖς γρ. false statements, Id. III. (γράφομαι) as Att. law-term, an indictment in a public prosecution, a criminal prosecution undertaken by the state, opp. to δίκη (a private action), Plat., etc.

γρᾰφικός, ή, όν, (γράφω) capable of drawing or painting, Plat.:—ἡ -κή (sc. τέχνη), the art of painting, Id. 2. of things, as if painted, as in painting, Plut. II. of or for writing, suited for writing, Arist.: ὑπόθεσις γρ. a subject for description, Plut.: Adv. -κῶς, Id.

γρᾰφίς, ίδος, ή, (γράφω) a stile for writing on waxen tablets, Plat., etc. 2. a needle for embroidering, Anth. II. embroidery, Id.

ΓΡΆΦΩ [ᾰ], f. ψω: aor. 1 ἔγραψα, Ep. γράψα: pf. γέγρᾰφα:—Pass., f. γραφήσομαι and γεγράψομαι: aor. 2 ἐγράφην [ᾰ], later, aor. 1 ἐγράφθην: pf. γέγραμμαι. Orig. sense, to scratch, scrape, graze, αἰχμὴ γράψεν ὀστέον Il.; σήματα γράψας ἐν πίνακι having scratched marks as tokens on a tablet, Ib.:—then, to represent by lines drawn, to delineate, draw, paint, Hdt., Aesch.; εἰκὼν γεγραμμένη Ar.: also in Med., ζῷα γράφεσθαι = ζωγραφεῖν, Hdt. II. to express by written characters, to write, τι Id.; γο. τινά to write a person's name, Xen.; γ. ἐπιστολήν, etc., Id.; γρ. τι εἰς διφθέρας Hdt. 2. to inscribe, like ἐπιγράφω, γρ. εἰς στήλην Eur., Dem. 3. to write down, γρ. τινὰ αἴτιον to set him down as the cause, Hdt. 4. to register, enrol, γρ. τινὰ τῶν ἱππευόντων among the cavalry, Xen.; Κρέοντος προστάτου γεγράψομαι, as a dependent of Creon, Soph. 5. to write down a law to be proposed; hence to propose, move, γνώμην, νόμον Xen.: so, absol., γράφειν (sub. νόμον), Dem.; γρ. πόλεμον, εἰρήνην, etc., Id.; c. inf. to move that . . ; ἔγραψα ἀποπλεῖν τοὺς πρέσβεις Id.

B. Med. to write for oneself or for one's own use, note down, Hdt., Aesch., etc. 2. as Att. law-term, γράφεσθαί τινα to indict one, τινός for some public offence, Plat., etc.; c. acc. et inf., γρ. τινὰ ἀδικεῖν Id.: absol., οἱ γραψάμενοι the prosecutors, Id.:—also, γράφεσθαί τι denounce as criminal, Dem.:—Pass. to be indicted, Id., etc.; τὰ γεγραμμένα the articles of the indictment, Id.; τὸ γεγραμμένον the penalty named in the indictment, Id.:—but γέγραμμαι usually takes the sense of the Med., to indict, Id.

γρᾱ-ώδης, ες, (εἶδος) like an old woman, Strab., N. T.

γρηγορέω, late pres., formed from pf. ἐγρήγορα, to be awake or wakeful, N. T.

γρηῢς, γρηΰς, Ion. for γραῦς.

γρῑπεύς, έως, ὁ, = γρῖπων, Theocr., Mosch.

γρῑπηΐς τέχνη, ἡ, the art of fishing, Anth. From

ΓΡΙ͂ΠΟΣ, ὁ, = γρῖφος, Anth.

γρῖπων, ὁ, (γρῖπος) a fisherman, Anth.

ΓΡΙ͂ΦΟΣ, ὁ, like γρῖπος, a fishing-basket, creel, made of rushes, Plut. 2. metaph. anything intricate, a dark saying, riddle, Ar. (Perh. akin to ῥίψ, ῥιπός.)

γρῦ, a grunt, as of swine: hence οὐδὲ γρῦ ἀποκρίνεσθαι to answer not even with a grunt, Ar.; οὐδὲ γρῦ ἀπαγγέλλειν Dem. (Formed from the sound.)

γρύζω, f. γρύξω and γρύξομαι: aor. 1 ἔγρυξα:—to say γρῦ, to grunt, grumble, mutter, Ar.

γρῡλίζω or γρυλλίζω, Dor. 2 pl. fut. γρυλιξεῖτε, to grunt, of swine, Ar. From

γρῦλος, or γρύλλος, ὁ, a pig, porker, Plut.

γρῡπ-άετος, ὁ, a kind of griffin or dragon, Ar.

ΓΡΥ͂ΠΟ͂Σ, ή, όν, hook-nosed, with aquiline nose, opp. to σιμός, Xen., N. T. 2. generally, curved, γρυπὴ γαστὴρ a round paunch, Xen. Hence

γρῡπότης, ητος, ἡ, hookedness, of the nose, opp. to σιμότης, Xen.

ΓΡΥ͂Ψ, gen. γρῡπός, ὁ, (γρυπός) a griffin or dragon, Hdt., Aesch.

γρώνη, ή, a cavern, a hollow vessel, kneading-trough, Anth. (Deriv. unknown.)

γύα, ή, = γύης II.

γύαια, τά, (γύης II) = πρυμνήσια, Anth.

γύαλον, τό, a hollow, as of the cuirass (θώρηξ), which was composed of a back-piece and breast-piece, called γύαλα, joined at the sides by clasps or buckles (πόρπαι, περόναι), Il. 2. the hollow of a vessel or a hollow vessel, Eur. 3. the hollow of a rock, Soph.: a cavern, grotto, Eur. 4. in pl., vales, dales, dells, Hes., Eur. (Deriv. uncertain.)

ΓΎΗΣ, ου, ὁ, the piece of wood in a plough, to which the share was fitted, the plough-tree, Lat. buris, Hes.

γύης, ὁ, or γύα, ἡ, a piece of land (cf. Lat. juger),

Eur.: mostly in pl. *lands, fields*, Aesch., Soph. :— metaph. of a wife, Id.   (Prob. akin to γέα, γῆ.)

γυιο-βαρής, ές, (βαρύς) *weighing down the limbs*, Aesch.

γυιο-βόρος, ον, (βι-βρώσκω) *gnawing the limbs*, Hes.

ΓΥΪΟΝ, τό, *a limb*, Hom., in pl., γυῖα λέλυντο, τρόμος or κάματος λάβε γυῖα, so Trag.; γυῖα ποδῶν *the feet*, Il.; γυῖα *the hands*, Theocr.; and γυῖον in sing. *the hand*, Id.

γυιο-πᾰγής, ές, (πήγνυμι) *stiffening the limbs*, Anth.

γυιο-πέδη, ἡ, *a fetter*, Aesch.

ΓΥΙΟΣ, ἡ, όν, *lame*, Anth.

γυιο-τᾰκής, ές, (τήκω) *wasting the limbs*, Anth.   II. pass. *with pining limbs*, Id.

γυιό-χαλκος, ον, *of brasen limb*, Anth.

γυιόω, f. ώσω, (γυιός) *to lame*, Il.; γυιωθείς *lame*, Hes.

γῠλι-αύχην, ενος, ὁ, ἡ, *long-necked, scraggy-necked*, Ar. From

γύλιος, ὁ, *a long-shaped wallet*, Ar.

γυμνάζω, f. άσω: aor. 1 ἐγύμνασα: pf. γεγύμνακα :— Pass., aor. 1 ἐγυμνάσθην: pf. γεγύμνασμαι: (γυμνός):— *to train naked, train in gymnastic exercise*: generally, *to train, exercise*, Xen.: c. inf. *to train* or *accustom* persons *to do* a thing, Id.; so also, γ. τινά τινι *to accustom* him *to it*, Id. :—Med. *to exercise for oneself, practise*, γ. τέχνην Plat. :—Pass. *to practise gymnastic exercises*, Hdt., etc.: generally, *to practise, exercise oneself*, Thuc., Xen.; γυμνάζεσθαι πρός τι *to be trained for* a thing, Plat.; περί τι *in* a thing, Xen.   II. metaph. *to wear out, harass, distress*, Aesch. :—Pass., Id.

γυμνάς, άδος, fem. of γυμνός, *naked*, Eur.   II. *trained*, Id.

γυμνασία, ἡ, =γύμνασις, *exercise*, N. T.

γυμνασιαρχέω, f. ήσω, *to be gymnasiarch*, at Athens, Oratt.: Med., Xen. :—Pass. *to be supplied with gymnasiarchs*, Id.

γυμνασι-άρχης or -αρχος, ὁ, *a gymnasiarch*, who superintended the palaestrae, and paid the training-masters, Dem., etc.

γυμνασιαρχία, ἡ, *the office of a gymnasiarch*, Xen.

γυμνασιαρχικός, ή, όν, *of* or *for a gymnasiarch*, Plut.

γυμνάσιον [ᾰ], τό, (γυμνάζω),   I. in pl. *bodily exercises*, Hdt., etc.   II. in sing. *the public place where athletic exercises were practised, the gymnastic school*, Eur., etc.; ἐκ θημετέρου γυμνασίου from our school, Ar.: pl., γ. ἱππόκροτα *the hippodrome*, Eur.

γυμναστέον, verb. Adj. of γυμνάζω, *one must practise*, Xen.

γυμναστής, οῦ, ὁ, (γυμνάζω) *a trainer of professional Athletes*, Xen., Plat.

γυμναστικός, ή, όν, (γυμνάζω) *fond of athletic exercises, skilled in them*, Plat.: ἡ -κή (with or without τέχνη), *gymnastics*, Id. :—Adv. -κῶς, Ar.

γυμνής, ῆτος, ὁ, (γυμνός) *a light-armed foot-soldier, slinger*, Hdt., Eur., Xen. Hence

γυμνητεύω, *to be light-armed*, Plut.

γυμνήτης, ου, ὁ, =γυμνής, Xen. :—as Adj. *naked*, Luc.

γυμνητία, ἡ, (γυμνής) *the light-armed troops*, Thuc.

γυμνητικός, ή, όν, *of* or *for a light-armed soldier* (γύμνης), Xen.

γυμνικός, ή, όν, (γυμνός) *of* or *for gymnastic exercises*, Hdt., Thuc.

γυμνῑτεύω, =γυμνητεύω: *to be naked*, N. T.

Γυμνο-παιδίαι, αἱ, a festival in honour of those who fell at Thyrea, *at which boys went through gymnastic exercises*, Hdt., Thuc., Xen.

ΓΥΜΝΟΣ, ἡ, όν, *naked, unclad*, Od., etc.   2. *unarmed*, Il., etc. :—τὰ γυμνά *the parts not covered by armour, the exposed parts*, Thuc., Xen.: esp. *the right side* (the left being covered by the shields), Thuc.   3. of things, γυμνὸν τόξον an *uncovered bow*, i. e. taken out of the case, Od.   4. c. gen. *stripped of* a thing, Hdt., Aesch.   5. in common language γυμνός meant *lightly clad*, i. e. *in the tunic only* (χιτών), without the mantle (ἱμάτιον), Lat. *nudus*, Hes., Xen.   6. *bare, mere*, N. T.

Γυμνο-σοφισταί, ῶν, οἱ, *the naked philosophers* of India, Plut.

γυμνότης, ητος, ἡ, (γυμνός) *nakedness*, N. T.

γυμνόω, f. ώσω, (γυμνός) *to strip naked*, Soph.; τὰ ὀστέα τῶν κρεῶν γ. *to strip* the bones of their flesh, Hdt. :—in Pass., of warriors, *to be left naked* or *exposed*, Hom.; so, τεῖχος ἐγυμνώθη the wall *was left bare*, i. e. *defenceless*, Il.: but also *to strip oneself naked* or *to be stript naked*, Od.; c. gen., ἐγυμνώθη ῥακέων he stript himself of his rags, Ib.; so later, γυμνωθὲν ξίφος Hdt. Hence

γύμνωσις, εως, ἡ, *a stripping*.   II. *nakedness*: ἐξαλλάσσειν τὴν ἑαυτοῦ γ. his *defenceless side* (cf. γυμνός 2), Thuc.

γυμνωτέος, α, ον, verb. Adj. of γυμνόω, *to be stript of*, τινός Plat.

γυναικεῖος, α, ον or ος, ον: Ion. γυναικήϊος, η, ον: (γυνή) :—*of* or *belonging to women, like women, befitting them, feminine*, Lat. *muliebris*, Od., etc. :— ἡ γ. θεός, the Roman *bona dea*, Plut.: γ. πόλεμος war *with women*, Anth.   2. in bad sense, *womanish, effeminate*, Plat., etc.   II. as Subst., ἡ γυναικηΐη =γυναικών, *the women's apartments, harem*, Hdt.

γυναικίας, ου, ὁ, =γύννις, *a weakling*, Luc.

γυναικό-βουλος, ον, (βουλή) *devised by a woman*, Aesch.

γυναικο-γήρυτος, ον, (γηρύω) *proclaimed by a woman*, Aesch.

γυναικο-κρᾱσία, ἡ, (κρᾶσις) *a woman's nature*, Plut.

γυναικο-κρᾰτία, ἡ, (κρατέω) *the dominion of women*, Arist., Plut.

γυναικό-μῑμος, ον, *aping women*, Aesch., Eur.

γυναικό-μορφος, ον, (μορφή) *in woman's shape*, Eur.

γυναικονομία, ἡ, *the office of γυναικονόμος*, Arist. From

γυναικο-νόμος, ὁ, (νέμω) one of a board of magistrates, appointed *to maintain good manners among the women*, Arist.

γυναικο-πληθής, ές, (πλήθω) *full of women*, Aesch., Eur.

γυναικό-ποινος, ον, (ποινή) *woman-avenging*, Aesch.

γυναικο-φίλης [ῐ], ου, Dor. -ας, α, ὁ, (φιλέω) *woman-loving*, Theocr.

γυναικών, ῶνος, ὁ, =γυναικωνῖτις, Xen.

γυναικωνῖτις, ιδος, ἡ, *the women's apartments* in a house, opp. to ἀνδρών (cf. γυναικών), Lys. :—*the women of the harem*, Luc.

γυναι-μᾰνής, ές, (μαίνομαι) *mad for women*, Il.

γύναιος, α, ον, =γυναικεῖος, γύναια δῶρα presents *made to a woman*, Od.   II. as Subst., γύναιον, τό,

little woman, wifey, as a term of endearment, Ar. :—
in a contemptuous sense, a weak woman, Dem., etc.
γυνή, Dor. γυνά, gen. γυναικός, acc. γυναῖκα, voc.
γύναι : pl. γυναῖκες, etc. (as if from γύναιξ) :—a
woman, Lat. femina, opp. to man, Hom., etc.; with
a second Subst., γυνή ταμίη housekeeper, δέσποινα γ.,
δμωαὶ γυναῖκες, etc., Id. :—in voc. often as a term of
respect, mistress, lady, Theocr. :—πρὸς γυναικός like a
woman, Hom., Xen. II. a wife, spouse, opp. to παρθένος,
Hom., Xen. III. a mortal woman, opp. to a
goddess, Hom. (Prob. from same Root as γί-γνομαι.)
γύννις, ιδος, ὁ, (γυνή) a womanish man, Theocr.
γυπάριον, τό, Dim. of γύπη, a nest, cranny, Ar.
γύπη, ἡ, (γύψ) a vulture's nest : a hole.
γύπινος [ῠ], η, ον, (γύψ) of a vulture, Luc.
γυρεύω, f. σω, (γῦρος) to run round in a circle, Strab.,
Babr.
γυρη-τόμος, ον, (τέμνω) tracing a circle, Anth.
γυρῖνος or γύρῖνος, ὁ, (γυρός) a tadpole, Plat.
γυρο-δρόμος, ον, running round in a circle, Anth.
ΓΥ͂ΡΟΣ, ά, όν, round, γυρὸς ἐν ὤμοισι round-shouldered,
Od.
ΓΥ͂ΡΟΣ, ὁ, a ring, circle, Polyb.
ΓΥ͂Ψ, γυπός, ὁ, a vulture, Il. ; cf. αἰγύπιος.
ΓΥ͂ΨΟΣ, ἡ, chalk, Hdt., Plat. Hence
γυψόω, f. ώσω, to rub with chalk, chalk over, Hdt.
γῶν, Ion. for γοῦν.
γωνία, ἡ, (γόνυ) a corner, angle, Hdt. II. a
joiner's square, Plat. Hence
γωνιασμός, ὁ, a squaring the angles : ἐπῶν γωνιασμοί
the finishing of verses by square and rule, Ar.
γωνίδιον, τό, Dim. of γωνία.
γωνιώδης, ες, (γωνία, εἶδος) angular, Thuc.
γωρῡτός, ὁ, a bow-case, quiver, Od. ; as fem., Anth.
(Deriv. uncertain.)

Δ.

Δ δ, δέλτα, indecl., fourth letter of the Gr. alph.:
as numeral, δ΄ = τέσσαρες and τέταρτος, but ͵δ = 4000.
I. δ is the medial dental mute, between the tenuis
τ and the aspirate θ. II. changes of δ in the
dialects: 1. Aeol. into β, as σάμβαλον for σάνδαλον :—reversely, ὀβελός becomes ὀδελός in Dor. 2.
Aeol. or Dor. into ζ, or ζ into δ and σδ, v. Z ζ.
II. 2. 3. into θ, as ψεῦδος ψύθος. 4. into λ, as
δαήρ, Lat. levir, δάκρυ lacryma, δασύς λάσιος. 5.
into σ, as ὀδμή ὀσμή, ἴδμεν ἴσμεν. 6. sometimes δ
is inserted to give a fuller sound, (ἀνήρ) ἀνέρος ἀνδρός. 7. δ is sometimes lost, cf. διωγμός, δίωξις
with ἰωκή. 8. it sometimes represents j (y), as in
ἤδη or δή, Lat. jam.
δᾰ-, intensive Prefix, = ζα-, as in δά-σκιος, δα-φοινός.
δᾶ, explained by the Scholl. as Dor. for γῆ, in the
phrases δᾶ φεῦ, φεῦ δᾶ Aesch., Eur.; οὐ δᾶν no by
earth, Theocr. But it is prob. that δᾶ or Δᾶ is a Dor.
voc. of Δάν = Ζάν (i. e. Ζήν = Ζεύς), and Δᾶν acc. = Ζῆν
(i. e. Ζῆνα).
δαγύς, ῦδος, ἡ, a wax doll, puppet, Theocr.
δᾳδίον, τό, Dim. of δαΐς, δᾴς, used of firewood, Ar.

δᾳδίς, ίδος, ἡ, a torch-feast, Luc.
δᾳδουχέω, f. ήσω, to hold the office of δᾳδοῦχος, to
carry a torch, esp. in pageants, Eur.
δᾳδ-οῦχος, ὁ, (δᾴς, ἔχω) a torch-bearer, an officer at
the mysteries of Eleusinian Demeter, Arist.
δᾳδο-φορέω, f. ήσω, (δᾴς, φέρω) to carry torches, Luc.
δαείω, Ep. for δαῶ, aor. 2 pass. subj. of *δάω.
δαήμεναι, Ep. for δαῆναι, aor. 2 pass. inf. of *δάω.
δαήμων, ον, gen. ονος, (*δάω, δαῆναι) knowing, experienced in a thing, ἔν τινι Il. ; c. gen., Od. :—δαη-
μονέστατος Xen.
δαῆναι, aor. 2 pass. inf. of *δάω.
ΔΑΗ͂Ρ, έρος, ὁ, voc. δᾶερ, a husband's brother, brother-
in-law, Lat. levir, answering to the fem. γάλως, Il.
δαήσομαι, f. of *δάω.
δαί, colloquial form of δή, used after interrogatives, τί
δαὶ λέγεις σύ; Ar.; τί δαί; what? how? Id., Plat.
δᾱῖ [ῐ], Ep. for δαΐδι, dat. of δαΐς.
δαιδάλεος, α, ον, cunningly or curiously wrought, of
work in metal or wood, Hom. ; of embroidery, Hes.,
Eur. II. cunning, of the artificer's skill, Anth.
δαιδάλλω, mostly in pres. and impf.: (δαίδαλος): to work
cunningly, deck or inlay with curious arts, to embellish, Hom. :—Pass., pf. part. δεδαιδαλμένος, Pind.
δαίδαλμα, ατος, τό, a work of art, Theocr.
δαιδαλόεις, εσσα, εν, = δαιδάλεος, Anth.
δαί-δαλος, ον, (redupl. from Root ΔΑΛ) cunningly or
curiously wrought, Aesch. : in Hom. only in neut.
as Subst., δαίδαλα πάντα all cunning works, Il. ; so in
sing., Od. II. as prop. n., Δαίδαλος, ὁ, Daedalus,
i. e. the Cunning Worker, the Artist, from Cnosus in
Crete, contemporary with Minos, mentioned in Il. as
maker of a χορός for Ariadné.
δαιδαλό-χειρ, ὁ, ἡ, cunning of hand, Anth.
δαΐζω, f. ξω: aor. 1 ἐδάϊξα: (δαίω B) :—to cleave
asunder, cleave, Hom., Aesch. 2. to slay, smite,
Il., Aesch. 3. to rend, tear, χερσὶ κόμην ἤσχυνε
δαΐζων Il. :—Pass., χαλκῷ δεδαϊγμένος Ib. ; δεδαϊγμένος
ἦτορ through the heart, Ib. ; δεδαϊγμένον ἦτορ a heart
torn by misery, Ib. ; δαϊχθεὶς Pind., Eur. 4.
simply, to divide, ἐδαΐζετο θυμὸς ἐνὶ στήθεσσιν his soul
was divided within it, i. e. was in doubt, Il. ; δαϊ-
ζόμενος κατὰ θυμὸν διχθάδια divided or doubting
between two opinions, Ib.
δαϊκτήρ, ῆρος, ὁ, a slayer :—as Adj. heart-rending,
Aesch.
δαιμονάω, to be under the power of a δαίμων, to suffer
by a divine visitation, δαιμονᾶν κακοῖς to be plunged
in heaven-sent woes, Aesch.; so, δ. ἐν ἄτᾳ Id. :—
absol. to be possessed, to be mad, Eur., Xen.
δαιμονίζομαι, Med. to be possessed by a demon or evil
spirit, N. T.
δαιμόνιον, τό, (δαίμων) the Deity, Lat. numen, or
divine operation, Hdt., Eur., etc.: a fatality,
Dem. II. an inferior divine being, a demon,
Xen., Plat. 2. a demon, evil spirit, N. T.
δαιμόνιος, α, ον and ος, ον, of or belonging to a
δαίμων : I. voc. δαιμόνιε, δαιμονίη, mostly in the
way of reproach, thou luckless wight! thou wretch!
sirrah! madam! II. ;—more rarely by way of admiration, noble sir! excellent man! Ib., Hes.; also
by way of pity, poor wretch! so in Hdt., δαιμόνιε

ἀνδρῶν; also in an iron. sense, *my good fellow! good sir! ὦ δαιμόνι' ἀνδρῶν, ὦ δαιμόνι', ὦ δαιμόνι' ἀνθρώπων* Ar., Plat.　　II. *anything proceeding from the Deity, heaven-sent, divine, miraculous,* Hdt., Att.; εἰ μή τι δαιμόνιον εἴη were it not *a divine intervention,* Xen.; τὰ δαιμόνια *visitations of Heaven,* Thuc.　　2. of persons, *divine, excellent,* Plat.　　III. Adv. -ως, by Divine power, marvellously, Ar.:—so neut. pl. δαιμόνια Id., Xen.; δαιμονιώτατα *most clearly by the hand of the gods,* Id.

δαιμονι-ώδης, ες, (εἶδος) *demoniacal, devilish,* N. T.

δαίμων, ονος, ὁ, ἡ, *a god, goddess,* like θεός, θεά, Hom., Trag., etc.:—in Hom. also *Deity* or *Divine power* (θεός denotes *a God in person*), Lat. *numen;* πρὸς δαίμονα *against the Divine power;* σὺν δαίμονι *with it, by its favour,* Il.:—so, κατὰ δαίμονα, nearly =τύχη, by *chance,* Hdt.; ἐν τῷ δ. =θεῶν ἐν γούνασι, Soph.　　2. *one's daemon* or *genius, one's lot* or *fortune,* στυγερὸς δαίμων Od.; δαίμονος αἶσα κακή Ib.: absol. *good* or *ill fortune,* Trag.; esp. of *the evil genius* of a family, Aesch.　　II. δαίμονες, in Hes., are *the souls of men of the golden age,* forming the link between gods and men:—later, of *any departed souls,* Lat. *manes, lemures,* Luc.　　III. in N. T. *an evil spirit, a demon, devil.* (Perh. from δαίω B, *to divide* or *distribute destinies.*)

δαίνυμι, imper. δαίνῦ: Ep. 3 sing. impf. δαίνῦ: f. δαίσω: aor. 1 ἔδαισα: Med., 2 sing. subj. δαινύῃ; Ep. 3 sing. opt. δαινῦτο (for -ύοιτο', 3 pl. δαινύατο: 2 sing. impf. δαίνυ', i. e. -νο: (δαίω B, *to divide*):—*to give a banquet* or *feast,* δαίνυ δαῖτα γέροισιν Il.; δ. γάμον *to give a marriage-feast,* Hom.; δ. τάφον *to give a funeral feast,* Id.　　2. c. acc. pers. *to feast one,* Hdt.; ζὼν μὲ δαίσεις *thou shalt be* my living *feast,* Aesch.　　II. Med. *to have a feast given one, to feast,* Hom., Hdt.　　2. c. acc. *to feast on, consume, eat,* Id.; μίαν δ. τράπεζαν *to eat at a common table,* Theocr.:—also of poison, *to consume,* Soph.

δάϊος [ᾱ], contr. δᾷος, δᾶος, α, ον, Ep. δήϊος, contr. δῇος, η, ον: *hostile, destructive, dreadful,* epith. of πῦρ, *burning, consuming,* Il., Trag.:—δάϊοι, δᾷοι *enemies,* Aesch., Soph.; in sing. *an enemy,* Ar.; hence as Adj. *hostile,* Id.　　2. *unhappy, wretched,* Trag.　　II. *knowing, cunning,* Anth. (In signf. II from *δάω, δαῆναι: in signf. I perh. from δαῖς *battle.*)

δαΐό-φρων, ονος, ὁ, ἡ, (φρήν) *unhappy in mind, miserable,* Aesch.

δαίρω, =δέρω, q. v.

δαΐς, δαΐδος, Att. contr. δᾷς, δᾳδός, ἡ: (δαίω A, *to kindle*):—*a fire-brand, pine-torch,* Lat. *taeda,* Hom.　　2. as collective noun, *pine-wood,* such as torches were made of, Thuc., Xen.

δάϊς (δαίω A), *war, battle,* mostly in apoc. dat. δάϊ, Hom., Aesch.

δαΐς, δαιτός, ἡ, (δαίω B, *to divide*), *a meal, feast, banquet,* often in Hom., who calls the usual meal δαὶς ἐΐση, *equally divided;* Θυέστου δαῖτα παιδείων κρεῶν *the feast* of Thyestes *on* the flesh of his children, Aesch.; in pl., Od.　　2. of the *meat* or *food* itself, Eur.

δαισθείς, aor. 1 pass. part. of δαίω A.

δαιταλεύς, έως, ὁ, (δαίνυμι) *a banqueter, feaster,* Aesch., Ar.

δαίτη, ἡ, poët. for δαίς, *a feast, banquet,* Il.

δαίτηθεν, (δαίς) Adv. *from a feast,* Od., Theocr.

δαιτρεύω, f. σω, (δαιτρός) *to cut up* meat, *cut into joints* or *to carve,* Od.: *to cut up for distribution* among the people, Il.

δαιτρόν, τό, (δαίω B) *one's portion,* δαιτρὸν πίνειν Il.

δαιτρός, ὁ, (δαίω B) *one that carves* meat, *a carver,* Od.

δαιτροσύνη, ἡ, *the art of carving meat, a helping at table,* Od.

δαιτυμών, όνος, ὁ, (δαίς) *one that is entertained, an invited guest,* in pl., Hom., Hdt.:—in sing., Plat.; ὁ ξένων δαιτυμών *who makes his meal* on strangers, Eur.

δαιτύς, ύος, ἡ, Ep. for δαίς, *a meal,* Il.

δαΐ-φρων, ον, gen. ονος, in Il., mostly, of warriors; in Od., of Ulysses. In the first case (from δάϊς *battle,* φρήν) of *warlike mind, warlike;*—in the second (from *δάω, φρήν) *wise of mind, prudent.* Others take *δάω as the Root in all cases, and translate *skilful, proved.*

ΔΑΙΏ (A), Act. only in pres. and impf.:—Pass., 3 sing. aor. 2 subj. δάηται: so also pf. 2 act. δέδηα (used as pres.), plqpf. δεδήειν (as impf.):—aor. 1 part. δαισθείς.　　*To light up, make to burn, kindle,* Lat. *accendo,* Il., Aesch.:—Pass. *to blaze, burn fiercely,* Il.; πυρὶ ὄσσε δεδήει *blazed* with fire, Od.; metaph., πόλεμος, μάχη δέδηε *war blazes forth,* Il.; ὄσσα δεδήει *the report spread like wild-fire,* Lat. *flagrat rumor,* Ib.　　II. *to burn, burn up,* Lat. *uro:*—Pass., δαισθείς Eur. (The Root is ΔΑϜ, which appears in the pf. pass. part. δε-δαυμένος, Simon. Amorg.)

ΔΑΙΏ (B), *to divide;* for the Act., δαίζω is used:—Pass., δαίεται ἦτορ Od.; Ep. 3 pl. pf., διχθὰ δεδαίαται *are divided* in two, Ib.:—Med. *to distribute,* κρέα Ib.—The aor. 1 ἔδαισα, ἐδαισάμην belong to δαίνυμι; f. δάσομαι, aor. 1 ἐδασάμην to δατέομαι.

δακέ-θυμος, ον, *heart-eating, heart-vexing,* Soph.

δάκετόν, τό, =δάκος 1, q. v.

δακνάζομαι, Dep. =δάκνομαι: metaph. *to be afflicted, mournful,* imper. δακνάζου Aesch.

δάκνω (Root ΔΑΚ): f. δήξομαι: pf. δέδηχα: aor. 2 ἔδακον, Ep. δάκε, redupl. δέδακε; Ep. inf. δακέειν:—Pass., f. δηχθήσομαι: aor. 1 ἐδήχθην: pf. δέδηγμαι:—*to bite,* of dogs, Il.; στόμιον δ. *to champ the bit,* Aesch.; χεῖλος ὀδοῦσι δακών, as a mark of determination, Tyrtae.; δ. ἑαυτόν *to bite* one's lips for fear of laughing, Ar.　　II. metaph. of pungent smoke and dust, *to sting* or *prick* the eyes, Ar.　　III. of the mind, *to bite* or *sting,* δάκε φρένας μῦθος Il.; ἔδακε ἡ λύπη Hdt.; so in Trag.:—Pass., of love, δηχθεῖσα Eur.; καρδίαν δέδηγμαι *I was stung, vexed* at heart, Ar.

δάκος, εος, τό, (δάκνω) *an animal of which the bite is dangerous, a noxious beast,* Aesch.; δάκη θηρῶν *ravenous beasts,* Eur.

ΔΑΚΡΥ, τό, poët. for δάκρυον, dat. pl. δάκρυσι, *a tear,* Lat. *lacruma* (v. Δ δ. II. 4), Hom., Trag.　　II. like δάκρυον, *any drop,* δ. πεύκινον Eur.

δάκρυμα, ατος, τό, (δακρύω) *that which is wept for, a subject for tears,* Orac. ap. Hdt.　　II. *that which is wept, a tear,* Aesch., Eur.

δακρυόεις, εσσα, εν, (δάκρυον) 1. of persons, *tearful, much-weeping,* Hom.; δακρυόεν γελάσαι, as Adv., *to smile through tears,* Il.　　2. of things, *tearful, causing tears,* πόλεμος, μάχη Ib.

δάκρυον, τό, Ep. gen. pl. δακρυόφι (-φιν), (δάκρυ) a tear, Hom., Hdt., Att., etc. 2. anything like tears, gum, Hdt. II. = δάκρυμα 1, Anth.

δακρυ-πλώω, (πλέω) to swim with tears, of a drunkard, Od.

δακρυρροέω, f. ήσω, to melt into tears, shed tears, Soph.; ἐπί τινι at a thing, Eur.: of the eyes, to run with tears, Id.

δακρύρ-ροος, ον, (ῥέω) flowing with tears, Eur.

δακρυσί-στακτος, ον, (στάζω) dropping tears, Aesch.

δακρῦτός, όν, (δακρύω) wept over, tearful, Aesch., Anth.

δακρυ-χᾰρής, ές, (χαίρω) delighting in tears, Anth.

δακρυ-χέων, ουσα, a participial form, shedding tears, Hom., Aesch.; τινός for a person, Od.

δακρύω, f. ύσω [ῡ]: aor. 1 ἐδάκρῡσα, Ep. δάκρυσα: pf. δεδάκρῠκα:—Pass., pf. δεδάκρῡμαι: I. intr. to weep, shed tears, Hom., etc.: c. acc. cogn., δ. γόους to lament with tears, Soph.: c. gen. causae, to weep for a thing, Eur.:—also, δ. βλέφαρα to flood them with tears, Id.:—so pf. pass. to be tearful, be all in tears, Il. 2. of trees (cf. δάκρυον), Luc. II. c. acc. to weep for, lament, Aesch., Soph., etc.:—Pass. to be wept for, Aesch., Eur.

δακρυ-ώδης, ες, (εἶδος) tearful, lamentable, Luc.

δακτυλήθρα, ἡ, (δάκτυλος) a finger-sheath, Xen.

δακτυλικός, ή, όν, (δακτύλιος) set in a ring, Anth.

δακτυλιο-γλυφία, ἡ, the art of cutting gems (for rings), Plat. From

δακτυλιο-γλύφος, ὁ, (γλύφω) engraver of gems, Critias.

δακτύλιος [ῠ], ὁ, (δάκτυλος) a ring, seal-ring, Hdt., Ar.

δακτῠλο-δεικτέω, f. ήσω, to point at with the finger, Dem. From

δακτῠλό-δεικτος, ον, (δείκνυμι) pointed at with the finger, Lat. digito monstratus, Aesch.

δακτῠλο-καμψ-όδῠνος, ον, (κάμπτω, ὀδύνη) wearying the fingers by keeping them bent, Anth.

δάκτῠλος, ὁ: poët. pl. δάκτυλα, a finger, Lat. digitus, ἐπὶ δακτύλων συμβάλλεσθαι to reckon on the fingers, Hdt.; ὁ μέγας δ. the thumb, Id. 2. οἱ δ. τῶν ποδῶν the toes, Xen.; also δάκτυλος alone, like Lat. digitus, a toe, Ar. II. the shortest Greek measure of length, a finger's breadth, = about 1/16 of an inch, Hdt. III. a metrical foot, dactyl, - ∪ ∪, Plat. (Deriv. uncertain: perh. from δείκ-νυμι.)

δακτῠλό-τριπτος, ον, (τρίβω) worn by fingers, Anth.

δᾱλέομαι, Dor. for δηλέομαι.

δᾱλίον, τό, Dim. of δαλός, Ar.

Δάλιος, Dor. for Δήλιος : Δᾱλογενής, for Δηλογενής.

δᾱλός, ὁ, (δαίω A) a fire-brand, piece of blazing wood, Hom., Aesch. 2. a thunderbolt, Il. II. a burnt-out torch : metaph. of an old man, Anth.

δαμάζω (Root ΔΑΜ): f. δαμάσω, Ep. 3 sing. δαμάσσει, also δαμῶ, δαμάᾳ, 3 pl. δαμόωσι: aor. 1 ἐδάμασα, Ep. ἐδάμασσα, δάμασσα; imper. δάμασον -ασσον; 3 sing. subj. δαμάσῃ, -άσσῃ; part. δαμάσας, -άσσας:—Med., f. Ep. δαμάσσομαι, 3 sing. aor. 1 ἐδαμάσσατο, part. δαμασσάμενος:—Pass., f. δεδμήσομαι: the aor. has three forms, (1) ἐδαμάσθην, Ep. δαμάσθην; (2) ἐδμήθην, imper. 3 sing. δμηθήτω, part. δμηθείς, Dor. δμᾱθείς; (3) ἐδάμην [ᾰ], Ep. δάμην, 3 pl. δάμεν; Ep. subj. δαμείω, 2 and 3 sing. δαμήῃς -ήῃ, 2 pl. δαμείετε, opt. δαμείην, inf. δαμῆναι, Ep. δαμήμεναι, part. δαμείς:—pf. δέδμημαι :

δάμᾰλη, ἡ, = δάμαλις, Eur., Theocr.

δάμᾰλη-βότος, ον, (βόσκω) browsed by heifers, Anth.

δάμᾰλης, ου, ὁ, (δαμάζω) a young steer, Anth.

δάμᾰλη-φάγος [ᾰ], ον, (φαγεῖν) beef-eating, Anth.

δάμᾰλίζω, poët. form of δαμάζω, to subdue, break in: Med., Eur.

δάμᾰλις, εως, ἡ, (δαμάζω) a heifer, Lat. juvenca, Aesch. II. a girl, Anth.

δάμαρ [ᾰ], αρτος, ἡ, (δαμάζω) a wife, spouse, Il., Trag.

δᾰμᾰσί-μβροτος, ον, taming mortals, man-slaying, Simon.

δᾰμᾰσί-φως, ωτος, ὁ, ἡ, = δαμασίβροτος, Simon.

δᾰμάτειρα, ἡ, (δαμάζω) one who tames, Anth.

Δάμάτηρ, Dor. voc. of Δημήτηρ.

δᾰμάω, a form assumed as the 1st pers. of δαμᾷ, δαμάᾳ, δαμόωσι: but these are Ep. forms of the f. of δαμάζω.

δᾰμείω, Ep. for δαμῶ, aor. 2 pass. subj. of δαμάζω.

δάμεν, Ep. for ἐδάμησαν, 3 pl. aor. 2 pass. of δαμάζω.

δᾰμήμεναι, Ep. for δαμῆναι, aor. 2 pass. inf. of δαμάζω.

δᾰμιοργός, Dor. for δημιουργός; δάμιος, Dor. for δήμιος.

δάμνα, for δάμνασαι, 2 sing. pres. med. of δάμνημι :—also 3 sing. of δαμνάω.

δαμνάω, = δαμάζω, Hom. only in 3 sing. pres. and impf. δάμνᾳ, ἐδάμνα or δάμνα; Ion. δάμνασκε, h. Hom.; 2 sing. pres. δαμνᾷς, Theogn.

δάμνημι, = δαμάζω, Il.:—Med., Hom.:—Pass., ὑφ' Ἕκτορι δάμνατο Il.

δᾱμόσιος, δᾶμος, δᾰμόομαι, Dor. for δημ-.

δᾱμόωσι, δᾰμόωνται, 3 pl. Ep. f. act. and med. of δαμάζω.

δᾰμώματα, τά, = τὰ δημοσίᾳ ᾀδόμενα, songs sung in public, Ar.

δᾶν, v. sub δᾶ.

δάν, δανᾱός, Dor. for δήν, δηναῖος.

Δᾰναοί, οἱ, the Danaäns, subjects of Δάναος, king of Argos; in Il. for the Greeks generally :—Δαναΐδαι, ῶν, οἱ, the sons or descendants of Danaüs, Eur. :—Δαναΐδες, αἱ, his daughters.

δᾰνείζω, f. σω: aor. 1 ἐδάνεισα: pf. δεδάνεικα:—Med., pf. δεδάνεισμαι in med. sense:—Pass., aor. 1 ἐδανείσθην : pf. δεδάνεισμαι: (δάνος):—to put out money at usury, to lend, Plat., etc. 2. Med. to have lent to one, to borrow, Ar.; ἐπὶ μεγάλοις τόκοις at high interest, Dem. 3. Pass., of the money, to be lent out, Ar., Xen.

δάνειον, τό, (δάνος) a loan, Dem.

δάνεισμα, ατος, τό, (δανείζω) a loan, δ. ποιεῖσθαι = δανείζεσθαι (in med. sense), Thuc.

δᾰνεισμός, ὁ, (δανείζω) money-lending, Plat., etc.: metaph., αἵματος δανεισμός Eur.

δᾰνειστής, οῦ, ὁ, (δανείζω) a money-lender, Plut., N.T.

Ep. 3 pl. plqpf. δεδμήατο. To overpower : I. of animals, to tame, break in, to bring under the yoke : Med. to do so for oneself, Hom., Xen. II. of maidens, to make subject to a husband, Il. : Pass. to be forced or seduced, Hom. III. to subdue or conquer, Id. : Pass. to be subject to another, Id. : (hence δμώς, δμωή). 2. to strike dead, kill, Od. 3. of wine and the like, to overcome, overpower, Hom. : Pass. to be overcome, δεδμημένοι ὕπνῳ Il. ; οἱ δμαθέντες the dead, Eur.

δἄνειστικός, ή, όν, (δανείζω) of or for money-lending, Plut.
δἄνός, ή, όν, (δαίω A) burnt, dry, parched, Od.; Sup., δανότατος, Ar.
ΔΑ´ΝΟΣ [ἄ], εος, τό, money lent, a loan, debt, Anth.
δάος [ἄ], εος, τό, (δαίω A) a firebrand, torch, Hom.
δἄπᾰνάω, f. ήσω, etc. :—Pass., aor. 1 ἐδαπανήθην : pf. δεδαπάνημαι :—some pass. tenses are also used in depon. sense, pres., impf., aor. 1: (δαπάνη) :—to spend, Thuc., etc.; δαπ. εἴς τι to spend upon a thing, Id., Xen.; so also as Dep. to spend, Hdt.; ὅσα δεδαπάνησθε εἰς τὸν πόλεμον Dem.   2. to expend, consume, use up, Arist. :—metaph. of persons, ὑπὸ νόσου δαπανᾶσθαι Plut.   II. Causal, τὴν πόλιν δαπανᾶν to put it to expense, Thuc.
δᾰπάνη [ᾰ], ή, (δάπτω) outgoing, cost, expense, expenditure, Hes.; χρημάτων Thuc.; δ. κούφη the cost is little, Eur. :—also in pl., Thuc.   II. money spent, ἵππων on horses, Pind.; δαπάνην παρέχειν money for spending, Hdt.   III. extravagance, Aeschin.
δᾰπάνημα, ατος, τό, (δαπανάω) money spent, Arist.: in pl. costs, expenses, Xen.
δᾰπᾰνηρός, ά, όν, (δαπανάω) of men, lavish, extravagant, Plat., Xen.   II. of things, expensive, Dem., Arist. :—Adv. -ρῶς, Xen.
δάπανος, ον, = δαπανηρός, Thuc.
δάπεδον [ᾰ], τό, (prob. for ζά-πεδον, i. e. διάπεδον, v. ζα-) any level surface : the floor of a chamber, Il., Hdt., Xen.; also, γῆς δάπεδον Ar.; and absol. the ground, Od. : pl. plains, Pind., Eur.
δάπις [ᾰ], ιδος, ή, = τάπης, a carpet, rug, Ar., Xen.
δάπτω (Root ΔΑΠ), Ep. inf. δαπτέμεν : f. δάψω, to devour, as wild beasts, Il.; of fire, Ib.; of a spear, to rend, Ib.: metaph., δάπτει τὸ μὴ 'νδικον injustice gnaws the heart, Soph.; δάπτομαι κέαρ Aesch.
Δάρδανος, ὁ, Dardanus, son of Zeus, founder of Troy, Il. :—as Adj., Δάρδανος ἀνήρ a Trojan, Ib. :—Adj. Δαρδάνιος, α, ον, Trojan, Ib. : fem. Δαρδανίς, ίδος, a Trojan woman, Ib. :—Δαρδανίδης, ου, ὁ, a son or descendant of Dardanus, Δαρδανίωνες, οἱ, Ib.
δαρ-δάπτω, redupl. form of δάπτω, Il. : κτήματα δαρδάπτουσιν they devour one's patrimony, Od.
Δᾱρεικὸς στατήρ or Δᾱρεικός alone, ὁ, a Persian gold coin, a Daric, Hdt., etc.   These are said to have been first coined by Darius Hystaspes.
Δᾱρειο-γενής, ές, (γί-γνομαι) born from Darius, Aesch.
Δᾱρεῖος, ὁ, Darius, name of several kings of Persia; being a Greek form of Persian dará, a king :—also Δαρεαῖος, in Xen.; Δαριάν in Aesch.
δαρθάνω (Root ΔΑΡΘ), aor. 2 ἔδραθον, to sleep, Od.
δᾱρός, ή, όν, Dor. for δηρός, δηρό-βιος.
δᾴς, gen. δᾳδός, ή, Att. contr. for δαΐς (A).
δάσασθαι, aor. 1 inf. of δατέομαι :—Ion. 3 sing. δασάσκετο, 1 pl. opt. δασαίμεθα.
δά-σκιος, ον, (δα-, σκιά) thick-shaded, bushy, Od., Eur.; of a beard, Aesch., Soph.
δάσμευσις, εως, ή, δασμός) a distributing, Xen.
δασμολογέω, f. ήσω, to collect as tribute, τι παρά τινος Dem. :—c. acc. pers. exact tribute from him, Isocr.
δασμολογία, ή, collection of tribute, Plut.   From
δασμο-λόγος, ὁ, (λέγω) a tax-gatherer, Strabo.
δασμός, ὁ, (δατέομαι) a division, distribution, sharing

of spoil, Il., h. Hom.   II. in Att. an impost, tribute, ἀοιδοῦ δ. tribute paid to her, Soph.; δασμὸν τίνειν Id.; δασμὸν φέρειν, ἀποφέρειν, ἀποδιδόναι Xen.
δασμοφορέω, f. ήσω, to be subject to tribute, Aesch. : —Pass., δασμοφορεῖταί τινι tribute is paid one, Xen.
δασμο-φόρος, ον, (φέρω) paying tribute, tributary, Hdt., Xen.
δάσομαι, f. of δατέομαι.
δασ-πλῆτις, ή, horrid, frightful, Ἐρινύς Od.; of Hecaté, Theocr.; so also δασπλής, ῆτος, ὁ, ή, Simon. (Perh. from δα, πλήσσω, σ being inserted.)
δάσσασθαι, Ep. for δάσασθαι.
δᾰσύ-θριξ, ὁ, ή, thick-haired, hairy, Anth.
δᾰσύ-κερκος, ον, bushy-tailed, ἀλώπηξ Theocr.
δᾰσύ-κνημος, ον, (κνήμη) shaggy-legged, of Pan, Anth.
δᾰσύ-κνημος, ον, gen. ονος, = foreg., Anth.
δᾰσύ-μαλλος, ον, thick-fleeced, woolly, Od., Eur.
δᾰσύ-πους, ποδος, ὁ, rough-foot, i. e. a hare, Arist.; λαγωὸς ὁ δ. Babr.
ΔΑ´ΣΥΣ, εῖα, ύ, Ion. fem. δασέα, opp. to ψιλός in all senses :   1. thick with hair, hairy, shaggy, rough, Od.; of young hares, downy, Hdt.   2. thick with leaves, Od.; θρῖδαξ δασέα a lettuce with all the leaves on, Hdt. :—of places, thick with bushes or wood, Id.; διὰ τῶν δασέων through the copses, Ar.; δ. ὕλη thick with copse-wood, Hdt., etc.; rarely c. gen. δασὺς δένδρων Xen. :—τὸ δασύ bushy country, Id.
δασύ-στερνος, ον, (στέρνον) shaggy-breasted, Hes.
δασυ-χαίτης, ον, ὁ, (χαίτη) shaggy-haired, Anth.
δᾰτέομαι, f. δάσομαι : aor. 1 ἐδασάμην (cf. πατέομαι, ἐπασάμην) ; Ion. 3 sing. δασάσκετο, Ep. 3 pl. δάσσαντο, part. δασσάμενος : pf. δέδασμαι, in pass. sense : (δαίω B) :—to divide among themselves, τὰ μὲν εὖ δάσσαντο μετὰ σφισίν Il.; ἄνδιχα πάντα δάσασθαι Hom. ; μένος Ἄρηος δατέονται they share, i. e. are alike filled with, the spirit of Ares, Il.; of persons at a banquet, κρέα δατεῦντο Od. ; διδόναι τινα κυσὶ δάσασθαι to tear in pieces, Il.   2. [ἡμίονοι] χθόνα ποσσὶ δατεῦντο measured the ground with their feet, Lat. carpebant viam pedibus, Ib.   3. to cut in two, Ib.   II. simply, to divide, to divide or give to others, Hdt. :—pf. in pass. sense, to be divided, Il., Hdt., Eur.   Hence
δατήριος, α, ον, dividing, distributing, Aesch.; and
δατητής, οῦ, ὁ, a distributer, Aesch.
Δαυλιάς, ή, a woman of Daulis, epith. of Philomela, who was changed into the nightingale, Thuc.   From
Δαυλίς, ίδος, ή, Daulis, a city of Phocis, Hom., etc. :— Δαύλιος, ὁ, a Daulian, Hdt., Δαυλιεύς, έως, Aesch. : —Δαυλία (sc. χώρα), ή, Phocis, Soph.
δάφνη, ή, the laurel, or rather the bay-tree, Lat. laurus, Od., Hes., etc.; sacred to Apollo, who delivered his oracles ἐκ δάφνης, h. Hom.   (Deriv. uncertain.)
δαφνηφορέω, f. ήσω, to bear a laurel crown, Plut.
δαφνη-φόρος, ον, (φέρω) laurel-bearing, δ. κλῶνες laurel branches borne in worship of Apollo, Eur.
δαφνιακός, ή, όν, (δάφνη) belonging to a laurel, Anth.
δαφνο-γηθής, ές, (γηθέω) delighting in laurel, Anth.
δαφνό-κομος, ον, (κόμη) laurel-crowned, Anth.
δαφν-ώδης, ες, (εἶδος) like laurel : laurelled, Eur.
δαφοινεός, όν, v. δαφοινός.
δᾰ-φοινός, όν, of savage animals, blood-red, tawny, δαφοινὸν δέρμα λέοντος Il.; δράκων ἐπὶ νῶτα δαφοινός Ib.:

the form δαφοινεός bears the same sense, εἷμα δαφοινεὸν αἵματι *red* with blood, Ib. ; δαφοινὸς ἀετός Aesch., etc. **2.** metaph. *savage, cruel*, h. Hom., Aesch.

δαψῐλής, ές, (δάπτω) *abundant, plentiful*, Hdt. :— Adv. -έως, *in abundance*, Theocr. **II.** of persons, *liberal, profuse*, Plut. :—Sup. Adv., δαψιλέστατα ζῆν Xen.

∗ΔΑ'Ω, an old Root, *to learn*, Lat. *disco*, which becomes Causal, *to teach*, Lat. *doceo*, in redupl. aor. 2 δέδαε and in διδάσκω : **I.** intr. in aor. 2 ἐδάην as if from δάημι, subj. δαῶ Ep. δαείω, inf. δαῆναι Ep. δαήμεναι, part. δαείς :—later regul. aor. 2 ἔδαον :—f. (as if from δαέω) δαήσομαι : pf. δεδάηκα, δέδαα and in pass. form δεδάημαι :—*to learn*, and in pf., *to know* ; c. gen. pers. *to learn* from one, Od. ; c. gen. rei, *to hear tidings of* a thing, Il. From δέδαα again is formed a pres. med. inf. δεδάασθαι, *to search out*, c. acc., Od.—The pres. in this sense is διδάσκομαι. **II.** Causal, in redupl. aor. 2 δέδαον, c. dupl. acc. *to teach* a person a thing, Od. ; c. inf. *to teach* one to do a thing, Ib.—The pres. in this sense is διδάσκω.

ΔΕ', *but*: conjunctive Particle, with *adversative* force: it commonly answers to μέν, and may often be rendered by *while, whereas, on the other hand*, v. μέν :—but μέν is often omitted, δέ being used merely to pass on from one thing to another ; ὡς Ἀχιλεὺς θάμβησεν, θάμβησαν δὲ καὶ ἄλλοι Il. ; etc. ; κινεῖ κραδίην κινεῖ δὲ χόλον Eur. **II.** δέ is often redundant, **1.** to introduce the apodosis, where it may be rendered by *then, yet*, εἰ δέ κε μὴ δώωσιν, ἐγὼ δέ κεν αὐτὸς ἕλωμαι if they will not give it, *then* I will take it, Il. ; so *at* in Lat., *si tu oblitus es, at Dii meminerint* Catull. **2.** to resume after interruption caused by a parenthesis, where it may be rendered by *I say, now, so then*, Hdt.

B. POSITION of δέ : properly second, being often put between the Art. and Subst., the Prep. and case.

-δε, enclitic Particle, joined, **I.** to names of Places in the acc., to denote *motion towards* that place, οἴκόνδε (Att. οἴκαδε) *home-wards*, ἅλαδε *sea-wards*, Οὐλυμπόνδε *to* Olympus, θύραζε (for θύρασδε) to the door, Hom. ; sometimes repeated with the possess. Pron., ὅνδε δόμονδε ; and sometimes even after εἰς, as εἰς ἅλαδε Od. ; in 'Αίδόσδε it follows the gen.,= εἰς "Αἰδου (sc. οἶκον). In Att. joined to the names of cities, 'Ελευσῖνάδε, 'Αθήναζε, Θήβαζε (for 'Αθήνασδε, Θήβασδε`. **2.** sometimes it denotes *purpose* only, μή τι φόβονδ' ἀγόρευε speak not aught *tending to* fear, Il. **II.** -δε is also used to strengthen certain Pronouns, ὅ-δε, τοιόσδε, etc.

δέατο, a word of doubtful origin, expl. by ἐδόκει, ἀεικέλιος δέατ' εἶναι *he seemed, methought* he was, a pitiful fellow, Od. : cf. δοάσσατο.

δέγμενος, Ep. aor. 2 part. of δέχομαι.

δεδάασθαι, Ep. pres. med. of ∗δάω :—δέδαα, pf.

δεδαίαται, Ep. 3 pl. pf. pass. of δαίω B, *to divide*.

δέδασμαι, pf. pass. of δατέομαι.

δεδεγμένος, pf. part. of δέχομαι.

δεδειπνάναι, irr. pf. inf. of δειπνέω.

δέδεκα, pf. of δέω A, *to bind*.

δεδέχαται, Ion. 3 pl. pf. of δέχομαι.

δέδηγμαι, pf. pass. of δάκνω.

δέδηε, δεδήει, 3 sing. pf. and plqpf. of δαίω A, *to burn*.

δέδηκα, pf. of δέω A, *to bind*.

δέδια, poët. δείδια, pf. with pres. signf. of δείδω.

δεδίδᾰχα, δεδίδαγμαι, pf. act. and pass. of διδάσκω.

δεδίσκομαι,=δειδίσκομαι, *to greet*, Od.

δεδίττομαι, v. δειδίσσομαι.

δεδίωγμαι, pf. pass. of διώκω.

δεδμήατο, Ion. 3 pl. plqpf. of δαμάζω :—δέδμητο, 3 sing.

δέδμημαι, pf. pass. both of δαμάζω and δέμω.

δέδογμαι, pf. pass. of δοκέω.

δέδοικα, pf. of δείδω.

δέδοικω, Dor. pres.,=δείδω, δέδια, Theocr.

δεδοκημένος, irreg. part. of δέχομαι (Ion. δέκομαι), in act. sense, *waiting, lying in wait*, Il., Hes. ;—not to be confounded with Att. δεδόκημαι from δοκέω.

δεδόνᾱτο, Dor. for -ηντο, 3 sing. plqpf. pass. of δονέω.

δεδραγμένος, pf. pass. part. of δράσσομαι.

δέδρᾱκα, pf. of δράω.

δεδράμηκα, pf. of τρέχω : also **δέδρομα**.

δέδορκα, pf. of δέρκομαι.

δεδουπώς, pf. part. of δουπέω.

δεδύκειν [ῠ], Dor. for δεδυκέναι, pf. inf. of δύω.

δέελος, η, ον, resolved form of δῆλος, Il.

δέημα, ατος, τό, (δέομαι) *an entreaty*, Ar.

δέησις, εως, ἡ, (δέομαι) *an entreating, asking: a prayer, entreaty*, Dem., N. T.

δεητικός, ή, όν, (δέομαι) *suppliant*, Plut.

δεῖ : subj. δέῃ, contr. δῇ ; opt. δέοι ; inf. δεῖν ; part. δέον, contr. δεῖν : impf. ἔδει, Ion. ἔδεε : f. δεήσει : aor. 1 ἐδέησε :—impers. (from δέω A, *to bind*) : **I.** c. acc. pers. et inf., δεῖ τινὰ ποιῆσαι *it is binding* on one to do a thing, *one must, one ought*, Lat. *oportet*, Hom., etc. :—rarely, δεῖ σε ὅπως δείξεις=δεῖ σε δεῖξαι, Soph. :—rarely also c. dat. pers. et inf., *there is need* for one to do, δεῖ τινί ποιῆσαι Eur., Xen. **2.** c. acc. rei et inf., δεῖ τι γενέσθαι Thuc., etc. :—for the phrase οἴομαι δεῖν, v. οἴομαι :—when used absol., an inf. may be supplied, μὴ πεῖθ' ἃ μὴ δεῖ (sc. πείθειν) Soph., etc. **II.** (from δέω B, *to want*), c. gen. rei, *there is need of, there is wanting*, Lat. *opus est re*, οὐδὲν δεῖ τινός Hdt., Att. :—phrases, πολλοῦ δεῖ *there wants much, far from it* ; ὀλίγου δεῖ *there wants little, all but* :—in answers, πολλοῦ γε δεῖ, πολλοῦ γε καὶ δεῖ *far from it*, Ar., Dem ; πλεῦνος δεῖ *it is still further from it*, Hdt :—ὀλίγου δεῖν absol., in same sense, Plat. ; μικροῦ δεῖν Dem. **2.** with a dat. pers. added, δεῖ μοί τινος, Lat. *opus est mihi re*, Aesch., Thuc., etc. **3.** with acc. pers. added, δεῖ σε προμηθέως Aesch. **III.** neut. part. δέον, contr. δεῖν, absol., like ἐξόν, παρόν, *it being needful, quum oporteret*, Plat. ; οὐκ ἀπήντα, δέον, he did not appear in court, *though he ought to have done so*, Dem. ; so, οὐδὲν δέον *there being no need*, Hdt. **2.** for δέον, τό, as Subst., v. sub voce.

δεῖγμα, ατος, τό, (δείκνυμι) *a sample, pattern, proof, specimen*, Lat. *documentum*, Eur., Ar., etc. ; δείγματος ἕνεκα *by way of sample*, Dem. **2.** *a place in the* Peiræus, where merchants set out their wares for sale, *a bazaar*, Xen., Dem.

δειγματίζω, f. σω, (δεῖγμα) *to make a show of*, N. T.

δείδεκτο, 3 sing. plqpf. of δείκνυμι (signf. II) :—**δειδέχαται, δειδέχατο**, Ep. 3 pl. pf. and plqpf.

δειδήμων, ον, gen. ονος, (δείδω) *fearful, cowardly*, Il.

δείδια, Ep. for δέδια, pf. of δείδω : 1 pl. δείδιμεν : Ep. inf. δειδίμεν, (with diff. accent).

δειδίσκομαι, Dep., only in pres. and impf., (δείκνυμι 11) *to meet with outstretched hand, to greet, welcome*, δεξιτερῇ δειδίσκετο χειρί Od. ; *δέπαϊ δειδίσκετο pledged* him in a cup, Ib. ; also, δεδισκόμενος Ib. 2. =δείκνυμι 1, *to shew*, h. Hom.

δειδίσσομαι, Att. δεδίττομαι : f. -ίξομαι : aor. 1 ἐδειδιξάμην : Dep. :—Causal of δείδω, *to frighten, alarm*, μὴ δειδίσσεο λαὸν Ἀχαιῶν Il. ; Ἕκτορα ἀπὸ νεκροῦ δειδίξασθαι *to scare* him *from the corpse*, Ib. ; οὔ σε ἔοικε δειδίσσεσθαι *it beseems not to attempt to frighten* thee, Ib. :—c. inf., φευγέμεν δειδίσσετο Theocr. :—in Att. form, Plat., Dem.

δείδοικα, Ep. pf. of δείδω.

δείδω, pres. only in first pers., δέδοικα or δέδια being always used as pres. in Att. :—f. δείσομαι : aor. 1 ἔδεισα, Ep. ἔδδεισα :—pf. in pres. sense δέδοικα, Ep. δείδοικα ; also δέδια, Ep. δείδια 1, imper. δέδιθι, Ep. δείδιθι, inf. δεδιέναι, Ep. δείδιμεν (to be distinguished from 1 pl. indic. δείδιμεν) ; part. δεδιώς, Ep. pl. δειδιότες :—plqpf. (in impf. sense) ἐδεδοίκειν, also ἐδεδίειν, Ep. pl. ἐδείδιμεν, ἐδείδισαν, δείδισαν. (For the Root, v. δίω.) *To fear*, absol., Hom., etc. ; foll. by a Prep., δ. *περί τινι to be alarmed, anxious about* . . , Il., Att. ; ἀμφί τινι, περί τινος, ὑπέρ τινος Id. :—followed by a relat. clause with μή . . , Lat. *vereor ne* . . , *I fear it is* . . , followed by subj. ; rarely by indic., δείδω μὴ νημερτέα εἶπεν Od. ; δ. μὴ οὐ . . , Lat. *vereor ut* . . , *I fear it is not* . . , foll. by subj., Hdt., etc. 2. c. inf. *to fear to do*, Il., Thuc. 3. c. acc. *to fear, dread*, Hom., etc. 4. τὸ δεδιός, *one's fearing*, = δέος, Thuc.

δειελιάω, f. ήσω, (δείελος) *to wait till evening*, σὺ δ᾽ ἔρχεο δειελιήσας Od.

δειελινός, ή, όν, = δείελος, *at evening*, Theocr.

δείελος, ον, (δείλη) *of or belonging to evening*, δείελον ἦμαρ *eventide*, Od., Theocr. II. as Subst. (sub. χρόνος), *late evening*, εἰσόκεν ἔλθῃ δείελος Il.

δεικανάω, = δείκνυμι, *to point out, shew*, in Ion. impf. δεικανάασκεν Theocr. II. Hom. uses it only in Med. = δειδίσκομαι, *to salute, greet*, δεικανόωντ᾽ ἐπέεσσιν Od. ; δεικανόωντο δέπασσι *pledged* him, Il.

δεικηλίκτης, ὁ, Lacon. for ὑποκριτής, Lat. *mimus, a burlesque actor*, Plut. From

δείκηλον, τό, *a representation, exhibition*, Hdt. : also δείκελον, Anth. From

δείκνῡμι and -ύω (Root ΔΕΙΚ), imper. δείκνυε, δεικνύτω : —impf. ἐδείκνυν and -νον : f. δείξω, Ion. δέξω : aor. 1 ἔδειξα, Ion. ἔδεξα : pf. δέδειχα :—Med., with pf. pass. (v. inf. 11) :—Pass., f. δειχθήσομαι and δεδείξομαι : aor. 1 ἐδείχθην, Ion. ἐδέχθην :—*to bring to light, display, exhibit*, Od., etc. :—Med. *to set before one*, Il. 2. *to shew, point out*, Ib., Soph. :—absol. αὐτὸ δείξει *experiment will shew*, Plat. ; so, δείξει alone, Ar. 3. *to point out by words, to tell, explain, teach*, Lat. *indicare*, ὁδόν Od., etc. :—*to shew, prove*, with part., ἔδειξαν ἕτοιμοι ὄντες *shewed that they were ready*, Thuc. 4. of accusers, *to inform against*, τινά Ar. 5. *to offer, proffer*, τὰ πιστά Aesch. : *to cause*, πήματα Id. II. in Med., like δειδίσκομαι, δεξιόομαι, *to welcome, greet*, τὼ καὶ δεικνύμενος προσέφη Hom. : —so also in pf. and plqpf. pass., δείδεκτ᾽ Ἀχιλῆα he

pledged him, *drank to* him, Il. ; τοὺς μὲν κυπέλλοις δειδέχατο Ib. ; δειδέχαται μύθοισι Od.

δεικτέος, α, ον, verb. Adj. of δείκνυμι, *to be shewn*, Xen. II. δεικτέον μοι *it is* my *duty to shew*, Dem.

δειλαίνω, (δειλός) *to be a coward* or *cowardly*, Arist.

δείλαιος, α, ον, lengthd. form of δειλός, *wretched, sorry, paltry*, mostly of persons, Trag. ; also, δ. χάρις a *sorry kindness*, Aesch. ; δ. σποδός *paltry dust*, Soph., etc. [Penult. is often made short in Att. Poets.]

δειλακρίων, ωνος, ὁ, (δειλός) a *coward :* commonly with a coaxing sense, *poor fellow !* Ar.

δείλ-ακρος, α, ον, very *pitiable*, Ar.

δείλη, ἡ, *afternoon*, ἔσσεται ἢ ἠὼς ἢ δείλη ἢ μέσον ἦμαρ Il. ; divided into *early* and *late* (πρωΐα and ὀψία), περὶ δείλην πρωΐην, or δείλης ὀψίης Hdt. ; τῆς δείλης *in the course of the afternoon*, Xen. 2. *the late afternoon, evening*, Id. (Deriv. uncertain.)

δειλία, Ion. -ίη, ἡ, (δειλός) *cowardice*, Hdt., Soph. ; δειλίην ὀφλεῖν *to be charged with cowardice*, Hdt.

δειλίασις, εως, ἡ, *fright, faintheartedness*, Plut. From

δειλιάω, *to be afraid*.

δειλινός, ή, όν, (δείλη) contr. for δειελινός, Luc.

δείλομαι, Dep. (δείλη) *to verge towards afternoon*, δείλετό τ᾽ ἠέλιος Od.

δειλός, ή, όν, (δέος) : I. of persons, *cowardly, craven*, Il. ; hence, *vile, worthless*, Ib. :—δειλός τινος *afraid of* . . , Anth. 2. *miserable, luckless, wretched*, Hom. ; with a compassionate sense, like Lat. *miser*, δειλοὶ βροτοί *poor mortals !* ἆ δειλέ *poor wretch !* ἆ δειλοὶ *poor wretches !* Id. II. of things, *miserable, wretched*, Hes., Soph.

δεῖμα, ατος, τό, (δείδω) *fear, affright*, Il., Hdt., Att. II. *an object of fear, a terror, horror*, ὦ πῦρ σὺ καὶ πᾶν δ. Soph. : esp. in pl., δειμάτων ἄχη *fearful plagues* or *monsters*, Aesch. ; δείματα θηρῶν Eur.

δειμαίνω, f. ἀνῶ, (δεῖμα) only in pres. and impf., *to be afraid, in a fright*, h. Hom., Hdt., etc. 2. c. acc. *to fear* a thing, Id., Aesch.

δειμαλέος, α, ον, (δεῖμα) *timid*, Mosch. II. *horrible, fearful*, Batr., Theogn.

δειματόεις, εσσα, εν, (δεῖμα) *frightened, scared*, Anth.

δειμάτόω, f. ώσω, (δεῖμα) *to frighten*, Hdt., Ar. :— Pass. *to be frightened*, Aesch., Eur.

δείμομεν, Ep. for δείμωμεν, 1 pl. aor. 1 subj. of δέμω.

δεῖμος, ὁ, (δέος) *fear, terror* :—personified Δεῖμος, Il.

δεῖν, inf. of δέω, v. δεῖ. 2. contr. for δέον neut. part., v. δεῖ III.

δεῖνα, ὁ, ἡ, τό, gen. δεῖνος, dat. δεῖνι, acc. δεῖνα ; pl. οἱ δεῖνες, τῶν δείνων : but sometimes indecl. :—*such an one, a certain one*, whom one cannot or will not name, ὁ δεῖνα Ar., etc. ; ὁ δεῖνα τοῦ δεῖνος τὸν δεῖνα εἰσαγγέλλει Dem. II. δεῖνα in Com. as an interjection, Lat. *malum ! plague on't !* Ar. (Deriv. uncertain.)

δεινο-θέτης, ου, ὁ, (τίθημι) a *knave*, Mosch.

δεινο-λογέομαι, (λέγω) Dep. *to complain loudly*, Hdt.

δεινο-πάθέω, f. ήσω, (παθεῖν) *to complain loudly of sufferings*, Dem.

δεινό-πους, ὁ, ἡ, -πουν, τό, *terrible of foot*, Ἀρὰ δ. (as if she was a hound upon the track), Soph.

δεινός, ή, όν, (from δέος, properly δεινός, cf. ἐλεεινός, ἐλεινός, from ἔλεος) :—*fearful, terrible, dread, dire*, Hom., etc. ; δεινὸν ἀῦτεῖν, βροντᾶν *to shout, thunder*

terribly, Il.; δεινὸν δέρκεσθαι, παπταίνειν, ἰδεῖν to look terrible, Hom.; but, δεινὸς ἰδέσθαι fearful to behold, Od.; δεινὸς μὲν ὁρᾶν, δεινὸς δὲ κλύειν Soph. :—τὸ δεινόν danger, suffering, awe, terror, Hdt., Aesch., etc.; so, τὰ δεινά Soph., etc. :—οὐδὲν δεινοί, μὴ ἀποστέωσιν no fear of their revolting, Hdt. :—δεινὸν ποιεῖσθαι to take ill, complain of, be indignant at a thing, Lat. aegre ferre, Id., etc.; δεινὰ παθεῖν to suffer dreadful, illegal, arbitrary treatment, Att.; so in Adv., δεινῶς φέρειν Hdt.; δ. ἔχειν to be in straits, Xen. II. with a notion of Force or Power, mighty, powerful, δεινὸν σάκος the mighty shield, Il. 2. simply, wondrous, marvellous, strange, τὸ συγγενές τοι δεινόν kin has a strange power, Aesch.; δ. ἵμερος, ἔρως, δέος Hdt.; δεινὸν ἂν εἴη, εἰ . ., it were strange that . ., Eur. :—Adv. -νῶς, marvellously, exceedingly, δ. μέλας, ἄνυδρος Hdt. III. the sense of powerful, wondrous passed into that of able, clever, skilful, Id., Att.; esp. of practical ability, opp. to σοφός, Plat.: c. inf., δεινὸς εὑρεῖν clever at inventing, Aesch.; δεινὸς λέγειν Soph.; δεινὸς πράγμασι χρῆσθαι Dem.: also c. acc., δεινὸς τὴν τέχνην Plat.; δ. περί τι or τινος Id.

δεῖνος, gen. of δεῖνα, q. v.

δεινότης, ητος, ἡ, (δεινός) terribleness, Thuc.: harshness, sternness, severity, νόμων Id. II. natural ability, cleverness, shrewdness, Dem.; esp. in an orator, Thuc., Dem.

δεινόω, f. ώσω, to make terrible: to exaggerate, Thuc.

δειν-ωπός, όν, = δεινώψ, Hes.

δείνωσις, εως, ἡ, (δεινόω) exaggeration, Plat.

δειν-ώψ, ῶπος, ὁ, ἡ, fierce-eyed, of the Erinyes, Soph.

δεῖος, τό, Ep. for δέος, Il.

δειπνέω, f. -ήσω: aor. 1 ἐδείπνησα, Ep. δείπνησα: pf. δεδείπνηκα, syncop. inf. δεδειπνάναι: Ep. plqpf. δεδειπνήκειν :—to make a meal, Hom.: in Att. to take the chief meal, to dine, δ. τὸ ἄριστον to make breakfast serve as dinner, Xen. 2. c. acc., δ. ἄρτον to make a meal on bread, Hes.; also, δ. ἀπό τινος Ar.

δειπνηστός, ὁ, (δειπνέω) meal-time, Od.

δειπνητήριον, τό, (δειπνέω) a dining-room, Plut.

δειπνητικός, ή, όν, (δειπνέω) of or for cookery: Adv. -κῶς, like a cook, artistically, Ar.

δειπνίζω, Att. f. -ιῶ: aor. 1 ἐδείπνισα, Ep. part. δειπνίσσας :—to entertain at dinner, Od., Hdt.

δειπνο-λόχος, η, ον, fishing for invitations to dinner, parasitic, Hes.

δεῖπνον, τό, (δάπτω) in Hom. the principal meal of the day,—sometimes the noonday meal, sometimes = ἄριστον, the morning meal, sometimes = δόρπον, the evening meal. In old Att. the midday or afternoon meal, dinner or supper :—ἀπὸ δείπνου straightway after the meal, Il.; καλεῖν ἐπὶ δεῖπνον; δ. παραθεῖναι, etc. 2. generally, fodder, provender, Il., Aesch.

δειπνο-ποιέω, f. ήσω, to give a dinner :—Med. to dine, Thuc., Xen.

δειπνο-φόρος, ον, (φέρω) carrying meat-offerings, Plut.

δειράς, άδος, ἡ, (δειρή) the ridge of a chain of hills, Hom., Soph. :—in pl., Il., Eur.

δειρ-αχθής, ές, (ἄχθος) heavy on the neck, Anth.

ΔΕΙΡΗ´, ἡ, the neck, throat, Il., Hdt.; Att. -δέρη, (not δέρα) Aesch. (Perh. akin to Lat. dors-um.)

δειρο-τομέω, f. ήσω, (τέμνω) to cut the throat of a person, behead, σὺ δ' ἄμφω δειροτομήσεις Hom.

δείρω, Ion. for δέρω.

δεισ-ήνωρ, ορος, ὁ, ἡ, (δείδω, ἀνήρ) fearing man, Aesch.

δεισιδαιμονία, ἡ, fear of the gods, religious feeling, Polyb.: in bad sense, superstition, Theophr. From

δεισι-δαίμων, ον, (δείδω) fearing the gods: 1. in good sense, like εὐσεβής, pious, religious, Xen. 2. in bad sense, superstitious, bigoted, Theophr.—Comp. -έστερος, somewhat superstitious, N. T.

ΔΕ´ΚΑ, οἱ, αἱ, τά, indecl., ten, Lat. decem, Hom., etc.: —οἱ δέκα the Ten, Oratt.: οἱ δέκα [ἔτη] ἀφ᾽ ἥβης those who are ten years past 20 (the age of military service), Xen. (Some connect it with δάκ-τυλος, from the number of the fingers.)

δεκά-βοιος, ον, (βοῦς) worth ten oxen, τὸ δεκάβοιον a coin attributed to Theseus, Plut.

δεκα-γονία, ἡ, (γένος) the tenth generation, Luc.

δεκαδ-αρχία, ἡ, the government of the ten, Isocr.

δεκάδ-αρχος, ὁ, a commander of ten, Lat. decurio, Xen.

δεκαδεύς, έως, ὁ, (δεκάς) one of a decury, Xen.

δεκά-δυο, οἱ, αἱ, τά, late form for δυώδεκα, N. T.

δεκά-δωρος, ον, (δῶρον II) ten palms long or broad, Hes.

δεκα-έτηρος, ον, (ἔτος) ten-yearly, Plat.

δεκα-ετής, ές, or -έτης, ες, (ἔτος) ten years old, Hdt. II. of or lasting ten years, πόλεμος Thuc.

δεκάζω, f. άσω, (δεκάς I. 2) to bribe or corrupt judges, Isocr., Aeschin. :—Pass. to be bribed, Plut.

δεκάκις, (δέκα) Adv. ten-times, Il.

δεκά-κλινος, ον, (κλίνη) holding ten dinner-couches, Xen.

δεκα-κυμία, ἡ, (κῦμα) the tenth (i. e. an overwhelming) wave, Lat. fluctus decumanus, Luc.: cf. τρικυμία.

δεκά-μηνος, ον, (μήν) ten months old, Xen. 2. in the tenth month, Hdt.

δεκά-μνους, μνουν, (μνᾶ) weighing or worth ten minae, Ar.

δεκ-άμφορος, ον, (ἀμφορεύς) holding ten ἀμφορεῖς (about 90 gallons), Eur.

δεκά-παλαι, Adv. very long ago, like δωδεκάπαλαι, Ar.

δεκά-πηχυς, υ, ten cubits long, Hdt.

δεκα-πλάσιος [ᾰ], ον, tenfold, Lat. decuplus, Plat. :—ἡ δεκαπλασία (sc. τιμή) a fine of ten times the amount, Dem.

δεκά-πλεθρος, ον, enclosing ten πλέθρα, Thuc.

δεκά-πλοος, ον, contr. -πλοῦς, οῦν, = δεκαπλάσιος, Dem.

δεκά-πολις, ἡ, a ten-city land, Decapolis, N. T.

δεκ-άρχης, εως, ὁ, = δεκαδάρχης, Hdt. Hence

δεκαρχία, ἡ, the government of ten, Xen.

δεκάς, άδος, ἡ, (δέκα) a decad : a company of ten, Lat. decuria, Il., Hdt. 2. a bribed company of ten, II. the number ten, Arist.

δεκασμός, ὁ, (δεκάζω) bribery, Plut.

δεκά-σπορος χρόνος, ὁ, a lapse of ten seed-times, i. e. ten years, Eur.

δεκαταῖος, α, ον, (δεκάτη) on the tenth day, Plat. II. ten days old, Luc.

δεκα-τάλαντος, ον, (τάλαντον) worth ten talents : δίκη δεκ. an action in which the damages were laid at ten talents, Aeschin.

δεκατεία, ἡ, = δεκάτευσις, Plut.

δεκατευτήριον, τό, the tenths-office, custom-house, Xen. From

δεκατεύω, f. σω, (δεκάτη) to exact the tenth part from a man, to make him pay tithe, τούτους δεκατεῦσαι τῷ θεῷ to make them pay a tithe to the god, Hdt. :—also of things, δ. τὰ ἐξ ἄγρου ὡραῖα to tithe them (as an offering), Xen. : and so, Pass., δεκατευθῆναι τῷ Διΐ Hdt. : hence proverb., ἐλπὶς ἦν δεκατευθῆναι τὰς Θήβας, i. e. that it would be made to pay tithe, Xen.

δεκάτη, ἡ, v. δέκατος II.

δεκατη-λόγος, ὁ, (λέγω) a tithe-collector, Dem.

δέκατος, η, ον, (δέκα) tenth, Hom., etc.   II. δεκάτη (sc. μέρις), ἡ, the tenth part, tithe, Hdt., etc.   2. δεκάτη (sc. ἡμέρα), ἡ, the tenth day, Hom. ; at Athens, the tenth day after birth, when the child has a name given it, τὴν δ. θύειν to give a naming-day feast, Ar. ; τὴν δ. ἑστιᾶσαι ὑπὲρ τοῦ υἱοῦ Dem.

δεκατό-σπορος, ον, in the tenth generation, Anth.

δεκατόω, f. ώσω, like δεκατεύω, to take tithe of a person, τινα N. T. : Pass. to pay tithe, Ib.

δεκά-φῦλος, ον, (φυλή) consisting of ten tribes, Hdt.

δεκά-χαλκον, τό, the denarius, = ten χαλκοῖ, Plut.

δεκά-χῑλοι, αι, α, (χίλιοι) ten thousand, Il. ; cf. ἐννεά-χιλοι.

Δεκέλεια, Ion. -έη, ἡ, a place in Attica, Hdt., Thuc., etc. :— Δεκελεύς, έως, ὁ, a Decelean, Id. :— Adv., Δεκελεῆθεν, from D., Id.

δεκ-έτηρος, ον, = sq., Anth.

δεκ-έτης, ου, ὁ, (ἔτος) lasting ten years, Soph., Plat.   II. ten years old, Eur. : fem. δεκέτις, ιδος, Plat.

δέκομαι, Ion. for δέχομαι.

δεκτέος, α, ον, verb. Adj. of δέχομαι, to be received, Luc.

δέκτης, ου, ὁ, (δέχομαι) a receiver : a beggar, Od.

δέκτο, 3 sing. Ep. aor. 2 of δέχομαι.

δεκτός, ή, όν, verb. Adj. of δέχομαι, acceptable, N. T.

δέκτωρ, ορος, ὁ, poët. for δέκτης, one who takes upon himself or on his own head, αἵματος δ. νέου Aesch.

δεκ-ώρυγος, ον, (ὀργυία) ten fathoms long, Xen.

δελεάζω, f. άσω, (δέλεαρ) to entice or catch by a bait : —Pass., Xen., Dem.   II. c. acc. cogn., νῶτον ὑὸς περὶ ἄγκιστρον δ. to put it on the hook as a bait, Hdt.

δέλεαρ, ατος, τό, (v. δόλος) a bait, Xen. : metaph., δ. τινος bait for a person, Eur.

δελε-άρπαξ, ὁ, ἡ, snapping at the bait, Anth.

δελέασμα, ατος, τό, = δέλεαρ, Ar.

δέλτα, τό, indecl., delta, v. Δ δ.   II. anything shaped like a Δ, a name for islands formed by the mouths of large rivers, as the Nile, Hdt.

δελτίον, τό, Dim. of δέλτος, Hdt.

δελτο-γράφος [ᾰ], ον, (γράφω) writing on a tablet, re-cording, Aesch.

δέλτος, ἡ, a writing-tablet, from the letter Δ (the old shape of tablets), Hdt., Trag. : metaph., δέλτοις φρε-νῶν on the tablets of the heart, Aesch.

δελφᾰκόομαι, Pass. to grow up to pighood, Ar.   From

δέλφαξ, ᾰκος, ἡ, a young pig, porker, Hdt., etc. (Deriv. uncertain.)

δελφίν, ῖνος, ὁ, later form of δελφίς, Mosch.

Δελφίνιον [ῑ], τό, a temple of Apollo at Athens, τὸ ἐπὶ Δελφινίῳ δικαστήριον the law-court there, Plut.

δέλφιξ, ῑκος, ὁ, a tripod, Plut. (Perh. from Δελφοί.)

δελφίς, ῖνος, ὁ, the dolphin, Hom., etc.   II. a mass of lead, prob. shaped like a dolphin, hung at the yard-arm, and suddenly let down on the decks of the enemy's ships, Ar. :—hence, κεραῖαι δελφινο-φόροι beams with pulleys to let down the δελφίς, Thuc. (Deriv. uncertain.)

Δελφοί, ῶν, οἱ, Delphi, a famous oracle of Apollo in Phocis at the foot of Parnassus (called Pytho by Hom. and Hdt.), h. Hom., Soph.   II. the Del-phians, Hdt. : in sing. Δελφός, king of Delphi, Aesch. :—Adj. Δελφικός, ή, όν, Delphic, Id. ; fem. Δελφίς, Soph.

δελφύς, ύος, ἡ, the womb, Arist. (Deriv. uncertain : hence ἀ-δελφός.)

δέμας, τό, (δέμω) the frame of man, the body, Hom. ; rarely of other animals, Od. ; properly the living body. —Hom. uses it only in acc. sing., absol., μικρὸς δέμας small in stature ; ἄριστος δέμας, δέμας ἀθανάτοισι ἔοικε, etc.   2. in Trag. as a periphrasis, like κάρα, κτανεῖν μητρῷον δ. Aesch. ; Ἡράκλειον δ. Eur. ; Δαμάτρος ἀκτᾶς δ., i. e. bread, Id.   II. as Adv., δέμας πυρὸς αἰθο-μένοιο in form or fashion like burning fire, Lat. instar ignis, Il.

δέμνιον, τό, (δέμω) mostly in pl. δέμνια, the bedstead or matrass, Hom.   2. generally, a bed, bedding, Od., etc.

δεμνιο-τήρης, ες, (τηρέω) keeping one to one's bed, μοῖρα δ. a lingering fate, Aesch.

ΔΕΜΩ, Ep. impf. δέμον : aor. 1 ἔδειμα, Ep. 1 pl. subj. δείμομεν :—Pass., pf. δέδμημαι : 3 sing. plqpf. ἐδέδμητο : —to build, Il., etc. :—Med., ἐδείματο οἴκους he built him houses, Od. :—generally, to construct, δ. ἀλωήν h. Hom. ; δ. ὁδόν, ἁμαξιτόν, Lat. munire viam, Hdt.

δενδίλλω, to turn the eyes or glance quickly, δενδίλλων ἐς ἕκαστον Il. (Deriv. uncertain.)

δένδρεον, τό, Ion. for δένδρον, a tree, mostly in pl., Hom., Hes., Hdt.

δενδρήεις, εσσα, εν, (δένδρον) woody, Od.

δενδρικός, ή, όν, (δένδρον) of a tree, Anth.

δενδρίτης [ῑ], ου, ὁ, of a tree :—fem. δενδρῖτις, Strab.

δενδρο-βᾰτέω, f. ήσω, (βαίνω) to climb trees, Anth.

δενδρο-κόμης, ου, ὁ, (κομέω) of a woodman, Anth.

δενδρο-κόμος, ον, (κόμη) grown with wood, Eur., Ar.

δενδρο-κοπέω, f. ήσω, (κόπτω) to cut down trees, esp. vines and fruit-trees, Xen. ; δ. χώραν to waste a country by cutting down the trees, ap. Dem.

δένδρον, τό, also δένδρος, τό, rare in nom. and acc., but freq. in dat. sing. δένδρει ; nom. and acc. pl. δένδρεα, contr. δένδρη : cf. δένδρεον : gen. δενδρέων ; dat. δένδρεσι :—a tree, Ar. ; δένδρα fruit-trees (opp. to ὕλη timber), Thuc., etc. (Perh. akin to δρῦς.)

δενδρο-πήμων, ον, (πῆμα) blasting trees, Aesch.

δένδρος, εος, τό, v. δένδρον.

δενδροτομέω, f. ήσω = δενδροκοπέω, to lay waste a country, Thuc. : metaph., δ. τὰ νῶτα Ar.

δενδρο-φόρος, ον, (φέρω) bearing trees ; Sup. -ώτατος, Plut.

δενδρό-φῠτος, ον, planted with trees, Plut.

δενδρ-ώδης, ες, (εἶδος) tree-like : δενδρ. Νύμφαι wood-nymphs, Anth.

δενδρῶτις, ιδος, fem. Adj. wooded, Eur.

δεννάζω, f. άσω, to abuse, revile, τινά Theogn., Soph. ;

c. acc. cogn., κακὰ ῥήματα δεννάζειν to utter words of foul reproach, Id. From

ΔΕ'ΝΝΟΣ, ὁ, a reproach, disgrace, Hdt.

δέξαι, aor. 1 imper. of δέχομαι.

δεξαμενή, ἡ, (aor. 1 part. fem. of δέχομαι, with changed accent) a reservoir, tank, cistern, Hdt., Plat.

δεξιά, Ion. -ιή, (fem. of δεξιός), ἡ, the right hand, opp. to ἀριστέρα, Il.; ἐκ δεξιᾶς on the right, Ar.; ἐν δεξιᾷ ἔχειν τὰ οὔρεα to keep them on the right, as you go, Hdt.; ἐν δ. λαβεῖν τὴν Σικελίαν Id.; so, ἐν δ. ἐσπλέοντι on your right as you sail in, Id.; used in welcoming, δεξιὰν διδόναι to salute by offering the right hand, Ar. 2. the right hand given as a pledge or assurance, δεξιαὶ ἧς ἐπέπιθμεν Il.; δεξιὰς δόντες καὶ λαβόντες having exchanged assurances, made a treaty, Xen.; δεξιὰς παρὰ βασιλέως φέρειν μή . . to bring pledges that he would not . . , Id.—Though δεξιά is manifestly fem. of δεξιός, it is always used as a Subst. without χείρ; but δ. χείρ occurs in Soph., Eur., Ar.

δεξί-μηλος, ον, (μῆλον) receiving sheep, i. e. rich in sacrifices, Eur.

δεξιο-λάβος, ὁ, (λαμβάνω) a spearman: in pl. guards, N. T.: others δεξιο-βόλοι, javelin-men.

δεξιόομαι, Ep. 3 pl. δεξιόωνται as if from δεξιάομαι: f. -ώσομαι: aor. 1 ἐδεξιωσάμην: Dep.: (δεξιά):—to greet with the right hand, welcome, greet (cf. δείκνυμι II), c. acc. pers., Ar., Xen.; c. dat. pers., δεξιοῦσθαι θεοῖς to raise one's right hand to the gods, pay honour to them, Aesch.; c. acc. rei, ἄμυστιν δεξιούμενοι pledging one in a bumper, Eur.:—Plat. has aor. 1 δεξιωθῆναι in pass. sense.

δεξιός, ά, όν, (δέχομαι) on the right hand or side, Lat. dexter, opp. to ἀριστερός, Hom., etc.; τὸ δ. (sc. κέρας) the right of an army, Xen.:—adverb. usages, ἐπὶ δεξιά on the right, Il.; ἐπὶ δεξιόφιν (Ep. gen.) towards the right, Ib.; πρὸς δεξιά Hdt. II. fortunate, boding good, of the flight of birds, δεξιὸς ὄρνις, = αἴσιος, Hom. —This sense came from the Greek augurs looking to the North, so that lucky omens, which came from the East, were on the right, while the unlucky ones from the West were on the left. III. metaph. dexterous, ready, opp. to σκαιός (sinister, French gauche); and of the mind, sharp, shrewd, clever, Ar., Thuc., etc.:—Adv. δεξιῶς; Sup. δεξιώτατα, Ar.

δεξιό-σειρος, ὁ, harnessed by a trace on the right side, of a third horse which was outside the regular pair:— hence, generally, spirited, impetuous, Soph.

δεξιότης, ητος, ἡ, (δεξιός) dexterity, cleverness, Hdt., Ar.; opp. to ἀμαθία, Thuc.

δεξιόφιν, Ep. gen. of δεξιός.

δεξιόω, only used as Dep. δεξιόομαι, q. v.

δεξί-πυρος, ον, (πῦρ) receiving fire, Eur.

δεξιτερός, ή, όν, poët. form of δεξιός, right, the right, Hom.: δεξιτερή, like δεξιά (sub. χείρ), the right hand, Il.; Ep. dat. δεξιτερῆφι Ib.

δεξίωμα, ατος, τό, (δεξιόομαι) = δεξίωσις, a pledge of friendship, Soph.

δεξίωσις, εως, ἡ, (δεξιόομαι) a greeting, canvassing, Lat. ambitus, Plut.

δέξο, Ep. aor. 2 imper. of δέχομαι.

δέον, οντος, τό, neut. part. of the impers. δεῖ, made into a Noun, that which is binding, needful, right,

proper, Soph., Xen.; τὰ δέοντα things needful or proper, advantages or duties, Thuc., etc.; ἐν δέοντι (sc. καιρῷ), in good time, Lat. opportune, Eur.; ἐν τῷ δέοντι Hdt.; εἰς τὸ δέον for a needful purpose, Id.; hence (at Athens) the phrase for secret service, εἰς τὸ δέον ἀπώλεσα Ar.

ΔΕ'ΟΣ, gen. δέους, τό; rare in pl. δέη: fear, alarm, affright, Hom., etc.; τεθνάναι τῷ δέει τινά to be dead afraid of a person, Dem. II. awe, reverence, Aesch. III. reason for fear, Il.: a means of inspiring fear, Thuc.

ΔΕ'ΠΑΣ, αος, τό: pl., nom. δέπᾰ; Ep. dat. δεπάεσσι and δέπασσι:—a beaker, goblet, chalice, Hom.

δερ-άγκη, ἡ, (δέρη) a collar, Anth.:—**δερ-αγχής**, ές, (ἄγχω) throttling, Id.

δέραιον, τό, (δέρη) a necklace, Eur.: a collar, Xen.

δέρας, ατος, τό, = δέρος, Eur.

δεράς, άδος, ἡ, = δειράς, Soph.

δέργμα, ατος, τό, (δέρκομαι) a look, glance, Aesch., Eur.

δέρη (not δερά), ἡ, Att. for δειρή, the neck, throat, Trag.

δερκιάομαι, poët. for δέρκομαι, Hes.

ΔΕ'ΡΚΟΜΑΙ, Ion. 3 sing. impf. δερκέσκετο: pf. in pres. sense δέδορκα: aor. 2 ἔδρακον: also aor. 1 in pass. form ἐδέρχθην, poët. δράχθην: Dep.:—to see clearly, see, Hom.; δεδορκώς having sight, opp. to τυφλός, Soph.:—hence to be alive, living, Hom., Trag.:—like βλέπω with a neut. Adj., δεινόν, σμερδαλέον δ. to look terrible, Hom., etc.; c. acc. cogn., πῦρ δεδορκώς flashing fire from the eyes, Od.; Ἄρη δεδορκότων Aesch.; σκότον δεδ. blind, Eur. II. c. acc. to look on or at, Hom., Aesch.:—so, δ. εἴς τινα Eur.; κατά τι Aesch.: generally, to perceive, κτύπον δέδορκα Id.

δέρμα, ατος, τό, (δέρω) the skin, hide, of beasts, Lat. pellis, Hom., etc.; δέρμα κελαινόν, of a shield, Il.:—also of skins prepared for bags or bottles, Od.; of a man's skin stript off, Il., Hdt. 2. later, one's skin, Lat. cutis, περὶ τῷ δέρματι δεδοικέναι Ar.: the shell of a tortoise, Id.

δερμάτινος, η, ον, (δέρμα) of skin, leathern, Od., Hdt.

δέρον, Ep. for ἔδερον, impf. of δέρω.

δέρος and **δέρας**, τό, poët. for δέρμα, but only in nom. and acc., Eur.

δέρρις, εως, ἡ, (δέρος) a leathern covering: in pl. screens of hide, Thuc.: cf. διφθέρα.

δέρτρον, τό, (δέρω) the membrane which contains the bowels, Lat. omentum, δέρτρον ἔσω δύνοντες even to the bowels, Od.

ΔΕ'ΡΩ, Ion. δείρω, Att. also (metri grat.) δαίρω: impf. ἔδερον, Ep. δέρον:—f. δερῶ: aor. 1 ἔδειρα:—Pass., f. δαρήσομαι [ᾰ]: pf. δέδαρμαι:—to skin, flay, of animals, Hom., etc.:—ἀσκὸν δεδάρθαι to have one's skin flayed off, Solon; so, δερῶ σε θύλακον I will make a purse of your skin, Ar. II. also (like the slang words to tan or hide) to cudgel, thrash, Id.

δέσμα, ατος, τό, (δέω) poët. for δεσμός, a bond, fetter, Od. II. a head-band, Il.

δεσμεύω, f. σω, (δεσμός) to fetter, put in chains, h. Hom., Plut.; (δεσμός) to tie together, as corn in the sheaf, Hes.

δεσμέω, f. ήσω, = δεσμεύω, N. T.

δέσμιον, τό, = δεσμός, Anth.

δέσμιος, ον and α, ον, (δεσμός) binding: metaph. binding

as with a spell, enchaining, c. gen., Aesch. II. pass. *bound, in bonds, captive*, Soph., Eur., etc.

δεσμός, ὁ, pl. **δεσμά** as well as **δεσμοί,** (δέω) *anything for binding, a band, bond*, Hom., etc. : *a halter*, Il. : *a mooring-cable*, Od. : *a door-latch*, Ib. ; *a yoke-strap*, Xen. 2. in pl. *bonds, fetters*, Aesch., Thuc. : in sing., collectively, *bonds, imprisonment*, Hdt., etc.

δεσμο-φύλαξ [ῠ], ακος, ὁ, ἡ, *a gaoler*, Luc.

δεσμόω, f. ώσω, = δεσμεύω. Hence

δέσμωμα, ατος, τό, *a bond, fetter*, Aesch.

δεσμωτήριον, τό, (δεσμόω) *a prison*, Hdt., Thuc.

δεσμώτης, ου, ὁ, (δεσμόω) *a prisoner, captive*, Hdt., Att. II. as Adj. *in chains, fettered*, Aesch. : fem. **δεσμῶτις** Soph.

δεσπόζω, f. -όσω : aor. 1 inf. δεσπόσαι : 1. absol. *to be lord* or *master, gain the mastery*, Aesch., Plat. 2. c. gen. *to be lord* or *master of*, h. Hom., Hdt., etc. ; δεσπόζειν φόβης *to own* the lock of hair, Aesch. ; metaph. *to master*, δ. λόγου Id. 3. c. acc. *to lord it over*, Eur.

δέσ-ποινα, ἡ, fem. of δεσπότης, *the mistress, lady of the house*, Lat. *hera*, of Penelopé, Od. 2. in Att. of goddesses, as Artemis, Soph. ; Persephoné, Plat.

δεσποσύνη, ἡ, (δεσπότης) = δεσποτεία, Hdt.

δεσπόσυνος, ον and η, ον, (δεσπότης) *of* or *belonging to the master* or *lord*, h. Hom., Aesch. ; δ. ἀνάγκαι *arbitrary* rule, Id. II. Subst. = δεσπότης, Tyrtae.

δεσποτεία, ἡ, (δεσπότης) *the power of a master* over slaves, or *the relation of master* to slaves, Arist. 2. *absolute sway, despotism*, Isocr.

δεσποτέω, f. ήσω, = δεσπόζω, c. gen., Plat. .—Pass. *to be despotically ruled*, Aesch., Eur.

δεσ-πότης, ου, ὁ, voc. δέσποτα, *a master, lord, the master of the house*, Lat. *herus, dominus*, Aesch., etc. ; properly in respect of slaves, so that the address of a slave to his master was ὦ δέσποτ' ἄναξ or ὦναξ δέσποτα Ar. 2. of Oriental rulers, *a despot, absolute ruler*, whose subjects are slaves, Hdt., Thuc. ; the pl. is used by Poets of single persons, like τύραννοι, Aesch. 3. of the gods, Eur., Xen. II. generally, *an owner, master, lord*, κώμου, Aesch., Soph. (The latter part -πότης is prob. from same Root as πόσις, and Lat. *pot-is, pot-ior* : the syll. δεσ- is uncertain.)

δεσποτικός, ή, όν, (δεσπότης) *of* or *for a master*, δεσποτικαὶ συμφοραί *misfortunes that befall one's master*, Xen. II. of persons, *inclined to tyranny, despotic*, Plat.

δεσπότις, ἡ, = δέσποινα, acc. δεσπότιν, Soph., Eur. ; dat. δεσπότιδι, Anth.

δεσποτίσκος, ὁ, Dim. of δεσπότης, Eur.

δετή, ἡ, (properly fem. of δετός, sub. λαμπάς) *sticks bound up, a fagot, torch*, Il., Ar.

δευήσεσθαι, Ep. f. med. inf. of δεύω, *to want*.

δεῦμα, ατος, τό, (δεύω) *that which is wet*, δεύματα κρεῶν *boiled* flesh, Pind.

δεύομαι, Ep. for δέομαι ; v. δεύω B.

δεῦρο, strengthd. in Att. **δευρί** : Adv. : I. of Place, *hither*, Lat. *huc*, with Verbs of motion, Hom., etc. ; in a pregn. sense with Verbs of Rest, *to* (*have come hither and*) *be here*, πάρεστι δεῦρο Soph. 2. used in calling to one, *here! on! come on!* Lat. *adesdum*, ἄγε δεῦρο,

δεῦρ' ἄγε, δεῦρ' ἴθι, δεῦρ' ἴτω *always with a Verb sing.* (δεῦτε being used with pl.), Hom. ; but with a pl. in Trag. 3. in arguments, μέχρι δ. τοῦ λόγου *up to this point* of the argument, Plat. II. of Time, *until now, up to this time, hitherto*, Trag., Plat. : also, δεῦρ' ἀεί Eur. (Deriv. unknown.)

Δεύς, Aeol. for Ζεύς.

δευσο-ποιός, όν, (δεύω, ποιέω) *deeply dyed, ingrained, fast*, of colours, Plat., Luc.

δεύτατος, η, ον, Sup. of δεύτερος, *the last*, Il.

δεῦτε, Adv., as pl. of δεῦρο, *hither! come on! come here!* just like δεῦρο, with pl. imperat., δεῦτ' ἄγετ' Il. ; δεῦτε φίλοι Ib. ; δεῦτ' ἄγε, Φαιήκων ἡγήτορες Od.

δευτερ-ἀγωνιστής, οῦ, ὁ, *the actor who takes second-class parts* : metaph. *one who seconds a speaker*, Dem.

δευτεραῖος, α, ον, (δεύτερος) *on the second day*, agreeing with the subject of the Verb, δευτεραῖος ἦν ἐν Σπάρτῃ Hdt. ; but also, τῇ δευτεραίῃ [sc. ἡμέρᾳ] Id.

δευτερεῖα (sc. ἆθλα), τά, *the second prize* in a contest ; hence *the second place* or *rank*, δ. νέμειν τινί Hdt.

δευτερεύω, f. σω, (δεύτερος) *to be second* : δευτ. τινί *to play second to . . ,* Plut.

δευτερό-πρωτον σάββατον, τό, *the first* sabbath *after the second day* of the feast of unleavened bread, or *the first sabbath of the second year* (i. e. of the year after the sabbatical year), N. T.

δεύτερος, α, ον, *second*, being Comp. of δύο : I. in point of Order, of one who *comes in second* in a race, Il. : in Att. with Art., ὁ δεύτερος Soph., etc. ; αἱ δεύτεραι φροντίδες *second* thoughts, Eur. ; proverb., τὸν δ. πλοῦν *to try the next best way*, Plat. 2. of Time, δευτέρῃ ἡμέρῃ *on the next day*, Hdt. : c. gen., ἐμεῖο δεύτερος *after my time*, Il. ; δευτέρῳ ἔτεϊ τούτων *in the year after this*, Hdt. : in neut. as Adv., δεύτερον αὖ, δεύτερον αὖτις *secondly, next, afterwards, a second time*, Hom., Att. ; in Prose also δεύτερα :—with Art., τὸ δεύτερον Hdt., Aesch., etc. ; τὰ δεύτερα Thuc. ; ἐκ δευτέρου *for the second time*, N. T. II. in point of Rank, *second,* δ. μετ' ἐκεῖνον Hdt. ; c. gen., δεύτερος οὐδενός *second* to none, Id. ; ἡγεῖσθαι δεύτερον *to think quite secondary*, Soph. 2. *the second of two,* δευτέρη αὐτή *herself with another*, Hdt. III. as Subst., δεύτερα, τά, = δευτερεῖα, *the second prize* or *place*, Il., Hdt.

ΔΕΥ'Ω (Α) : impf. ἔδευον, Ep. δεῦον, Ion. δεύεσκον : f. δεύσω : aor. 1 ἔδευσα :—Pass., aor. 1 ἐδεύθην : pf. δέδευμαι :—*to wet, drench*, Il. :—Med., πτερὰ δεύεται ἄλμῃ *wets his* wings in the brine, Od. 2. *to mix a dry mass with liquid*, so as to make it fit to knead, δ. ἄρτον ὕδατι Xen. II. Causal, *to make to flow, shed*, αἷμα Soph.

δεύω (Β), f. δευήσω, Aeol. and Ep. for δέω, *to miss, want*, ἐδεύησεν ἱκέσθαι *he missed, failed* in reaching, Od. II. as Dep. δεύομαι, f. δευήσομαι, = Att. δέομαι, *to feel the want* or *loss of, be without* a thing, c. gen., Il. : *to stand in need of*, βάκτρου Eur. 2. *to be wanting, deficient in* a thing, c. gen., Il. : absol. δευόμενος, *in need*, Ib. 3. c. gen. pers. *to be inferior to*, Hom.

ΔΕ'ΦΩ, f. ψω, *to soften* by working with the hand, Ar.

δέχαται, Ep. 3 pl. aor. 2 of δέχομαι.

δεχ-ήμερος, ον, (ἡμέρα) *for ten days, lasting ten days,*

ἐκεχειρία δεχ. a truce *terminable on giving ten days' notice*, Thuc.; σπονδαὶ δεχ. Id.

δέχθαι, Ep. aor. 2 inf. of δέχομαι.

δέχνυμαι, poët. for δέχομαι, Anth.

ΔΕΧΟΜΑΙ, Ion. and Aeol. **δέχομαι**: f. δέξομαι, Ep. δεδέξομαι: aor. 1 ἐδεξάμην and ἐδέχθην: pf. δέδεγμαι, Ep. 3 pl. δειδέχαται, plqpf. -ατο: plqpf. ἐδεδέγμην:—there are also several forms of an Ep. aor. 2 ἐδέγμην, viz. 3 sing. ἔδεκτο or δέκτο, 3 pl. δέχαται, imperat. δέξο, inf. δέχθαι, part. δέγμενος: I. of things as the object, *to take, accept, receive* what is offered, Lat. *accipere*, Hom., etc.:—δ. τί τινι *to receive* something *at the hand of* another, Il.; also τί τινος Ib.; τι παρά τινος Hom.; τι ἔκ τινος Soph.:—but also, δ. τί τινος *to receive in exchange for* .., χρυσῷ φίλου ἀνδρὸς ἐδέξατο Od.:—also, μᾶλλον δ., c. inf., *to take rather, to choose* to do or be, Xen.; and instead μᾶλλον, οὐδεὶς ἂν δέξαιτο φεύγειν Thuc. 2. *to accept* graciously, Il.; δ. τὸν οἰωνόν *to accept, hail* the omen, Hdt., etc.:—*to accept* or *approve*, τοὺς λόγους, τὴν ξυμμαχίην Id., Thuc. 3. simply *to give ear to, hear*, Lat. *accipere*, Eur., Thuc. 4. *to take* or *regard* as so and so, μηδὲ συμφορὰν δέχου τὸν ἄνδρα Soph. II. of persons, *to receive hospitably, entertain*, Hom., Att. 2. *to greet, worship*, Il.; δ. τινα ξύμμαχον *to accept* as an ally, Thuc. 3. *to receive an enemy, to await the attack of*, Lat. *excipere*, Il.; of a hunter *waiting for* game or a wild boar *waiting for* the hunters, Ib.; τοὺς πολεμίους δ. Hdt., etc. 4. *to expect*, c. acc. et inf. fut., Od.: or c. acc. *to wait for*, Ib.; μηδὲ συμφορὰν δέχου τὸν ἄνδρα do not *expect* him to be .., Soph. III. absol. *to succeed, come next*, δέχεται κακὸν ἐκ κακοῦ Il.; ἄλλος δ' ἐξ ἄλλου δέχεται ἆθλος Hes.; of places, 'Αρτεμίσιον δέκεται Hdt.

δέψω, aor. 1 ἐδέψησα, as if from δεψέω, (δέψω) *to work* or *knead* a thing *till it is soft*, κηρὸν δεψήσας Od.; δέψει τὸ δέρμα Hdt.

ΔΕΩ (A), imper. 3 pl. δεόντων: f. δήσω: aor. 1 ἔδησα, Ep. δῆσα: pf. δέδεκα or δέδηκα:—Med., aor. 1 ἐδησάμην, Ep. 3 sing. δησάσκετο:—Pass., f. δεθήσομαι, and δεδήσομαι: aor. 1 ἐδέθην: pf. δέδεμαι: plqpf. ἐδεδέμην, Ep. 3 sing. δέδετο, Ion. 3 pl. ἐδεδέατο:—*to bind, tie, fetter, δεσμῷ τινα δῆσαι* Il., etc.:—c. acc. only, *to bind, put in bonds*, Od., Att. 2. metaph. *to bind, enchain*, γλῶσσα δέ οἱ δέδεται Theogn.; ψυχὰ δέδεται λύπῃ Eur. 3. c. gen. *to let* or *stop* one *from* a thing, δῆσε κελεύθου Od. II. Med. *to bind, put on oneself* (cf. ὑποδέω, ποσσὶ δ' ὑπαὶ ἐδήσατο πέδιλα tied them on *his* feet, Il.; and in Pass., περὶ κνήμῃσι κνημῖδας δέδετο he had greaves *bound* round *his* legs, Od.

ΔΕΩ (B), f. δεήσω: aor. 1 ἐδέησα, Ep. δῆσα or δῆσα: pf. δεδέηκα:—Med., f. δεήσομαι and δεηθήσομαι: aor. 1 ἐδεήθην: pf. δεδέημαι:—*to lack, miss, stand in need of* a person or thing, c. gen., Il., Xen.:—πολλοῦ δέω *I want* much, i.e. *am far from*, c. inf., πολλοῦ δέω ἀπολογεῖσθαι *I am* far *from* defending myself, Plat.; μικροῦ ἔδεον εἶναι Xen.; and absol., πολλοῦ γε δέω far from it, Plat.; τοῦ παντὸς δέω Aesch.; v. δεῖ II:—so in partic., δυοῖν δέοντα τεσσαράκοντα forty *lacking* two, thirty-eight, Hdt.; ἑνὸς δέον εἰκοστὸν ἔτος the 20th year *save* one, the 19th, Thuc. II.

as Dep. δέομαι: f. δεήσομαι: aor. 1 ἐδεήθην: 1. *to be in want* or *need, κάρτα δεόμενος* Hdt.:—*to stand in need of* a person or thing, c. gen., Id., Soph.; οὐδὲν δέομαί τινος *I have* no *need* of him, Thuc.: c. inf., τοῦτο ἔτι δέομαι μαθεῖν Plat. 2. *to ask for* a thing *from* a person, c. dupl. gen. rei et pers., Hdt., Thuc.; also, τοῦτο δέομαι ὑμῶν Plat.; and c. acc. cogn., δέημα or δέησιν δεῖσθαί τινος Ar., etc., rarely with gen. pers. only, δεηθεὶς ὑμῶν *having begged a favour* of you, Dem.:—c. gen. pers. et inf. *to beg* a person *to do*, Hdt., Plat. (The Aeol. form δεύω (v. δεύω B) shews that the Root of this word was ΔΕϜ.)

δή, Particle used to give greater *exactness*, to the word or words which it influences (prob. a shortened form of ἤδη, Lat. *jam*) *now, in truth, indeed, surely, really*. I. Usage of δή with single words: 1. after Adjectives, οἷος δή, μόνος δή, *all* alone, Od., etc.: esp. such as imply magnitude, μέγας δή, μικρὸς δή, etc.: often with Superlatives, μέγιστος δή, κράτιστος δή *quite* the greatest, *confessedly* the best, Thuc.; so with Numerals, ὀκτὼ δὴ προέηκα ὀιστούς *I have shot full eight arrows*, Il.; εἷς δή one *only*, Eur., etc. 2. after Adverbs, πολλάκις δή *many times and oft*, often *ere now*, Lat. *jam saepe*, Il.; ὀψὲ δὲ δή *quite late*, Ib.; νῦν δή *even now, now first, now at length*, Xen., etc.:—τότε δή *at that very time*, Thuc.; αὐτίκα δὴ μάλα *on the very spot*, Plat.; also, ναὶ δή *yea verily*, Il.; οὐ δή *surely* not, Soph. 3. with Verbs, δὴ γὰρ ἴδον ὀφθαλμοῖσι *for verily* I saw him, Il. 4. with Substantives, ἐς δὴ τὸ Ἄργος τοῦτο .. *well* to this A. they came, Hdt.; τέλος δή its *complete* end, Aesch.; ironically, Lat. *scilicet*, εἰσήγαγε τὰς ἑταιρίδας δή the *pretended* courtesans, Xen. 5. with Pronouns, to mark strongly, ἐμὲ δή a man *like me*, Hdt.; σὺ δή you *of all persons*, Id.; οὗτος δή this *and no other*, Id.; ὃς δή who *plainly*, Il.:—with indef. Pronouns, ἄλλοι δή others *be they who they may*, Ib.; δή τις some *one or other*, Lat. *nescio quis*, Plat.; δή τι in any way, *whatever it be*, Il., Hdt. II. in reference to whole clauses: 1. *to continue* a narrative, *so then, so*, τότε μὲν δὴ ἡσυχίην εἶχε Hdt.; in summing up, τοιαῦτα μὲν δὴ ταῦτα, Lat. *haec hactenus*, Aesch. 2. in inferences, Hdt., etc.; esp. to express what is unexpected, καὶ σὺ δή *so then* you too! Aesch. 3. with Imper. and Subj., ἐννοεῖτε γὰρ δή for do *but* consider, Xen.; so, ἄγε δή, φέρε δή, ἴθι δή, σκόπει δή, etc. 4. γε δή to express what follows *a fortiori*, μετὰ ὅπλων γε δή *above all* with arms, Thuc.; μή τί γε δή not to mention that, Dem. 5. καὶ δή *and what is more*, Il.: so, ἐς Αἴγυπτον ἀπίκετο, καὶ δὴ καὶ ἐς Σάρδις he came to Egypt, *and what is more* to Sardis also, Hdt.; ἰσχὺς καὶ κάλλος καὶ πλοῦτος δή, and *above all* riches, Plat. b. καὶ δή is also in answers, βλέψον κάτω. Answ. καὶ δὴ βλέπω, *well*, I am looking, Ar. c. in assumptions, καὶ δὴ δέδεγμαι and *now suppose* I have accepted, Aesch.

δηάλωτος, ον, contr. for δηϊάλωτος.

δήγμα, ατος, τό, (δάκνω) *a bite, sting*, Xen.: metaph., δ. λύπης Aesch.

δηγμός, ὁ, (δάκνω) *the act of biting*: in pl. *caustics*, Plut.

δηθά, Ep. Adv., = δήν, *for a long time*, Lat. *diu*, Hom.

δῆθεν, Adv., a strengthd. form of δή, *really, in very truth*, τί δὴ ἀνδρωθέντες δῆθεν ποιήσουσι; *what then will they do when they are really grown up?* Hdt. :—also epexegetic, Lat. *videlicet, that is to say*, Aesch., Eur. :—ironically, Lat. *scilicet*, to imply that a statement is not true, οἵ μιν ἠθέλησαν ἀπολέσαι δῆθεν *as he pretended*, Hdt.; φέροντες ὡς ἄγρην δῆθεν Id.

δηθύνω [ῡ], f. ῠνῶ, (δηθά) *to tarry, be long, delay*, Il.

δηϊ-άλωτος, ον, (δήϊος, ἀλῶναι) *taken by the enemy, captive*, Eur.; contr. δηάλωτος Aesch.

Δηϊ-άνειρα, ἡ, (δήϊος, ἀνήρ) *destroying her spouse*, the wife of Hercules,—her name expressing the legend of his death, Soph.

δήϊος, η, ον, Ep. and Ion. for δάϊος. Hence

δηϊοτής, ῆτος, ἡ, *battle-strife, battle, death*, Hom.

δηϊόω, Ep. 3 pl. opt. δηϊόψεν, part. δηϊόων; Att. pres. **δηῶ**, δηοῦμεν, -οῦτε: impf. ἐδήουν, Ion. ἐδηΐουν or ἐδήευν, Ep. δήουν: f. δηώσω: aor. 1 ἐδήωσα:—Pass., aor. 1 ἐδηϊώθην: pf. δεδήωμαι: (δήϊος):—*to cut down, slay*, Il.: *to cleave asunder*, Ib.: *savage beast, to rend, tear*, Ib.; τὸν πώγωνα δεδηωμένος *having had his beard cut off*, Luc.   II. *to waste* or *ravage* a country, Hdt., Thuc.; ἄστυ δηώσειν πυρί Soph.

δηκτήριος, ον, (δάκνω) *biting, torturing*, c. gen., Eur.

δήκτης, ου, ὁ, (δάκνω) *a biter*, Anth.

δηκτικός, ή, όν, (δάκνω) *able to bite, biting, stinging*, Luc.

δηλαδή or **δῆλα δή**, Adv. *quite clearly, manifestly*, Soph., Eur., etc. :—also iron., προφάσιος τῆσδε δηλαδή *on this pretext forsooth*, Hdt. :—in answers, *yes of course*, Ar.

δηλέομαι, Dor. **δᾱλ-**: f. ήσομαι: aor. 1 ἐδηλησάμην: pf. δεδήλημαι both in act. and pass. sense: Dep.:   I. of persons, *to hurt, do a mischief to*, Hom.; μή με δηλήσεται (Ep. for -ηται) Od.; so in Hdt.; *to hurt* by magic potions, Theocr.   II. Of things, *to damage, spoil, waste*, καρπὸν ἐδηλήσαντ' Il.; γῆν δηλησάμενος Hdt. :—esp. in phrase, ὅρκια δηλήσασθαι *to violate a truce*, Il.   2. absol. *to do mischief, be hurtful*, Hom. (Deriv. uncertain.) Hence

δήλημα, ατος, τό, *a mischief, bane*, Od., Soph.; and

δηλήμων, ον, gen. ονος, *baneful, noxious*, βροτῶν δηλήμονα *baneful* to them, Od.; ἀνθρώπων οὐ δηλήμονες *doing men no hurt*, Hdt.

δηλήσεται, Ep. for -ηται, 3 sing. aor. 1 of δηλέομαι.

δήλησις, εως, ἡ, (δηλέομαι) *mischief, ruin, bane*, Hdt.

δηλητήρ, ῆρος, ὁ, (δηλέομαι) *a destroyer*, Ep. Hom.

Δήλιος, α, ον and os, ον, (Δῆλος) *Delian*, Trag., etc. : —ὁ Δ., name of Apollo, Soph., etc. :—**Δήλιος**, ὁ, *a Delian*, Hdt., etc.: fem. **Δηλιάς**, άδος, ἡ, *a Delian woman*, h. Hom., Eur.   II. **Δηλιάς** (sc. ναῦς), *the Delian ship*, sent from Athens every fourth year in memory of Theseus, Plat.   III. τὰ **Δήλια** (sc. ἱερά) *the quinquennial festival of Apollo at Delos*, Thuc.

Δηλο-γενής, ές, (γί-γνομαι) *Delos-born*, Simon.

δήλομαι, Dor. for βούλομαι, Theocr.

δηλον-ότι, i. e. δῆλον [ἐστιν] ὅτι, used parenthetically, *quite clearly, manifestly, plainly*, Plat., etc.   II. epexegetically, *that is to say, namely*, Lat. *scilicet*, Id., Xen.

δηλο-ποιέω, f. ήσω, *to make clear*, Plut.

Δῆλος, ἡ, *Delos*, one of the Cyclades, birthplace of Apollo and Artemis, Od.; called also Ὀρτυγία. (Prob.

from δῆλος, because of the legend that it became *visible* by rising from the sea.)

δῆλος, η, ον and os, ον: Ep. **δέελος**:   I. properly, *visible, conspicuous*, Il.   II. *clear* to the mind, *manifest, evident*, Od. :—δηλός εἰμι with partic., δηλός ἐστιν ἀλγεινῶς φέρων i.e. *it is clear* that he takes it ill, Soph.; δηλοί εἰσι μὴ ἐπιτρέψοντες *it is clear that they will not permit*, Thuc.; also, acc. to our idiom, δηλόν [ἐστιν] ὅτι . . , v. δηλονότι.   3. δηλον itself is used like δηλαδή, as αὐτὸς πρὸς αὑτοῦ δῆλον, *all by himself, 'tis manifest*, Soph. :—also, δῆλον δέ to introduce a proof, Thuc. (Deriv. uncertain.) Hence

δηλόω, f. ώσω :—Pass., f. δηλωθήσομαι and in med. form δηλώσομαι :—*to make visible* or *manifest, to shew, exhibit*, Soph. :—Pass. *to be* or *become manifest*, Id.   2. *to make known, disclose, reveal*, Aesch., Soph.   3. *to prove*, Id., Thuc.   4. *to declare, explain, set forth, indicate, signify*, Id.; c. part., δηλώσω σε κακόν [ὄντα] Soph.; the partic., if it refers to the nom. of the Verb, is itself in nom., δηλώσει γεγενημένος Thuc.   II. intr. *to be clear* or *plain*, Hdt., Plat.   2. impers., δηλοῖ = δῆλόν ἐστι, Hdt.; f. δηλώσει Plat.; aor. 1 ἐδήλωσε Xen. Hence

δήλωσις, εως, ἡ, *a pointing out, manifestation, explaining, shewing*, Thuc.; δ. ποιεῖσθαι = δηλοῦν, Thuc.

δημᾱγωγέω, f. ήσω, *to lead the people*, in bad sense, Ar.   2. c. acc. pers. *to win by popular arts*, Xen.

δημᾱγωγία, ἡ, *leadership of the people*, Ar.; and

δημᾱγωγικός, ή, όν, *fit for* or *like a demagogue*, Ar. From

δημ-ᾱγωγός, ὁ, *a popular leader*, of Pericles, Isocr.: commonly in bad sense, *a leader of the mob, a demagogue*, such as Cleon, Thuc., Xen.

δημᾱκίδιον [κῐ], τό, Comic Dim. of δῆμος, Ar.

δημ-άρᾱτος, ον, (ἀράομαι) *prayed for by the people*: as prop. n. of a king of Sparta, Hdt.

δημαρχέω, f. ήσω, *to be demarch*, Dem.

δημαρχία, ἡ, *the office* or *rank of δήμαρχος*, Dem.: *the tribunate*, Plut.

δημαρχικός, ή, όν, *tribunician*, Plut.   From

δήμ-αρχος, ὁ, *a governor of the people*:   1. at Athens, *a demarch, the president of a δῆμος*, who managed its affairs, Ar., Dem.   2. at Rome, *a tribune of the plebs*, Plut.

δημ-εραστής, οῦ, ὁ, *a friend of the people*, Plat.

δήμευσις, εως, ἡ, *confiscation of one's property*, Plat.

δημεύω, f. σω, (δῆμος) *to declare public property, to confiscate*, Lat. *publicare*, Thuc., etc.   II. generally, *to make public*, δεδήμευται κράτος *the power is in the hands of the people*, Eur.

δημηγορέω, f. ήσω, (δημηγόρος) *to speak in the assembly*, Lat. *concionari*, Ar., etc. :—Pass., τὰ δεδημηγορημένα *public speeches*, Dem.   II. *to make popular speeches, to speak rhetorically, use clap-trap*, Plat., etc.

δημηγορία, ἡ, *a speech in the public assembly*, Aeschin.   II. *popular oratory, clap-trap*, Plat.

δημηγορικός, ή, όν, *of* or *for public speaking, qualified for it*, Xen.: ἡ -κή (sc. τέχνη), = δημηγορία, Plat. From

δημ-ηγόρος, ὁ, (ἀγορεύω) *a popular orator*, mostly in a bad sense, Plat. :—τιμαὶ δ. *a speaker's honours*, Eur.

Δημήτηρ, gen. τερος and τρος, ἡ, *Demeter*, Lat. *Ceres*,

goddess of agriculture, mother of Persephoné, Hom. (The Deriv. from δῆ=γῆ, quasi Γη-μήτηρ is improbable, v. δᾶ.)

δημίδιον [ῐδ], τό, Comic Dim. of δῆμος, Ar.

δημίζω, f. σω, (δῆμος) to affect popularity, cheat the people, Ar.

δημιο-εργός, όν, poët. for δημιουργός.

δημιο-πληθής, ές, (πλήθω) abounding in public, κτήνη δ. cattle of which the people have large store, Aesch.

δημιό-πρᾱτα, τά, (πρᾱτός) goods sold by public authority : confiscated goods, Ar.

δήμιος, ον, and α, ον, Dor. **δάμιος**: (δῆμος):—belonging to the people, public, Od. ; αἰσυμνῆται δ. judges elected by the people, Ib. ; neut. pl. as Adv., δήμια πίνειν at the public cost, Il.   II. ὁ δήμιος (sc. δοῦλος), the public executioner, Plat., etc.

δημιουργέω, f. ήσω, (δημιουργός) to practise a trade, do work, Plat.   2. c. acc. rei, to work at, fabricate, Id.   II. to be one of the δημιουργοί (II), Id.

δημιουργία, ἡ, a making, creating, Plat.   2. workmanship, handicraft, Id. ; δ. τῶν τεχνῶν practising them, Id.

δημιουργικός, ή, όν, of or for a δημιουργός or handicraftsman, Plat.   From

δημι-ουργός, Ep. **δημιο-εργός**, ὁ: (*ἔργω):—one who works for the people, a skilled workman, handicraftsman, Od., etc. ; of medical practitioners, Plat. ; of sculptors, Id. :—generally, a framer, maker ; λόγων Aeschin. ; πειθοῦς δημιουργὸς ἡ ῥητορική Plat. : metaph., ὄρθρος δημιοεργός morn that calls man to work, h. Hom.   2. the Maker of the world, Xen., Plat.   II. in some Peloponnesian states, the name of a magistrate, Thuc., Dem.

δημο-βόρος, ον, (βι-βρώσκω) devourer of the people, Il.

δημο-γέρων, οντος, ὁ, an elder of the people, chief, Il. : δημογ. θεός, = Lat. deus minorum gentium, Anth.

δημόθεν, (δῆμος) Adv. at the public cost, Od.   II. δημόθεν Εὐπυρίδης an Eupyrian by deme, i. e. by birth, place, Anth.

δημο-θοινία, ἡ, (θοίνη) a public feast, Luc.

δημό-θροος, οον, contr. -θρους, ουν, uttered by the people, Aesch. ; δ. ἀναρχία lawlessness of popular clamour, Id.

δημο-κήδης, ὁ, (κῆδος) friend of the people, Lat. poplicola, Plut.

δημο-κόλαξ, ὁ, a mob-flatterer, Luc.

δημοκοπέω, f. ήσω, to curry mob-favour, Plut. ; and

δημοκοπικός, ή, όν, of or for a demagogue, Plat. From

δημο-κόπος, ὁ, a demagogue.

δημό-κραντος, ον, (κραίνω) ratified by the people, Aesch.

δημο-κρᾰτέομαι, Pass. with f. med. -κρατήσομαι or pass. -κρατηθήσομαι : pf. δεδημοκράτημαι : (δῆμος, κρατέω) :—to have a democratical constitution, live in a democracy, Hdt., Ar., Thuc.   Hence

δημοκρᾰτία, ἡ, democracy, popular government, Hdt., Thuc. ; and

δημοκρᾰτικός, ή, όν, of or for a democracy, Ar., Plat.   II. of persons, favouring democracy, Plat.

δημό-λευστος, ον, (λεύω) publicly stoned, δ. φόνος death by public stoning, Soph.

δημο-λογέω, f. ήσω, (λέγω) = δημόομαι, Anth.

δημόομαι, Dor. δαμ-, (δῆμος) Pass. to talk popularly, Pind., Plat.

δημο-πίθηκος [ῐ], ὁ, a mob-monkey, charlatan, Ar.

δημο-ποίητος, ον, made a citizen, not one by birth, Plut.

δημορ-ρῐφής, ές, (ῥίπτω) hurled by the people, Aesch.

δῆμος, ὁ, a country-district, country, land, Hom.   II. the people of a country, the commons, Lat. plebs, δήμου ἀνήρ, opp. to βασιλεύς, Il., etc. ; of a single person, δῆμος being a commoner, Il. :—in historians, the commons, commonalty, opp. to οἱ εὐδαίμονες, οἱ παχέες, οἱ δυνατοί, Hdt., Thuc. ; of soldiers, opp. to officers, Xen.   2. like πλῆθος, the commons, the democracy, opp. to οἱ ὀλίγοι, Hdt., Ar., etc.   III. in Attica, δῆμοι, οἱ, townships or hundreds, = Dor. κῶμαι, Lat. pagi, ancient divisions of the county, being (in the time of Hdt.) 100 in number, 10 in each φυλή. (Deriv. uncertain.)

δημός, ὁ, fat, Il., Ar., etc. ; δίπλακι δημῷ (of sacrificial meat) with fat above and fat below, Il. (Deriv. unknown.)

Δημοσθενίζω, f. σω, to imitate Demosthenes, Plut.

δημοσίᾳ, Adv., v. δημόσιος.

δημοσιεύω, f. σω, to confiscate, like δημεύω, Xen.: Pass., τὰ δεδημοσιευμένα popular sayings, Arist.   II. intr. to be in the public service, of physicians, Ar., Plat. : generally, to be a public man, opp. to ἰδιωτεύω, Id.   From

δημόσιος, Dor. δαμ-, α, ον, belonging to the people or state, Lat. publicus, opp. to ἴδιος, Hdt., Att. :—δημόσιον εἶναι, γίγνεσθαι to be confiscated, Thuc., Plat.   II. as Subst., ὁ δημόσιος (sc. δοῦλος), a public servant, as the public crier, Hdt. ; a public notary, Dem.   III. as neut., δημόσιον, τό, the state, Lat. respublica, Hdt., Att.   2. any public building, a public hall, Hdt.   3. the treasury, elsewhere τὸ κοινόν, Dem.   4. the public prison, Thuc.   5. τὰ δημόσια (sc. χρήματα) state-property, Ar.   IV. as fem., ἡ δαμοσία (sc. σκηνή) the tent of the Spartan kings, Xen.   V. as Adv. : 1. dat. δημοσίᾳ, Ion. -ίῃ, at the public expense, Hdt. ; by public consent, Dem. ; δ. τεθνάναι to die by the executioner, Id.   2. neut. pl. δημόσια, at the public cost, Ar.

δημοσιόω, f. ώσω, to confiscate, like δημοσιεύω, Thuc.   II. Pass. to be published, Plat.

δημοσι-ώνης, ου, (ὠνέομαι) a farmer of the revenue, Lat. publicanus, Strab.

δημο-τελής, ές, (τέλος) at the public cost, public, national, Hdt., Thuc.

δημότερος, α, ον, = δημόσιος, common, vulgar, Anth.

δημότης, ου, ὁ, (δῆμος) one of the people, a commoner, plebeian, Hdt., Att.   II. one of the same people, a fellow-citizen, Eur.   III. at Athens, one of the same deme, Soph. :—fem. δημότις, ιδος, Theocr.

δημοτικός, ή, όν, (δῆμος) of or for the people, in common use, common, δ. γράμματα in Egypt, opp. to the hieroglyphics, Hdt.   II. of the people, one of them, Lat. plebeius, Xen., Dem.   2. on the popular or democratic side, Lat. popularis, Ar., Thuc., etc. : Adv. -κῶς, affably, kindly, Dem.

δημ-οῦχος, ον, (ἔχω) protecting the people, of guardian deities, Soph. ; δημοῦχοι γᾶς ruling the people or the land, Id.

δημο-φάγος [ᾰ], ον, (φαγεῖν) = δημοβόρος, Theogn.
δημο-χαριστής, οῦ, ὁ, (χαρίζομαι) a mob-courtier, Eur.
δημόω, v. δημόομαι.
δημ-ώδης, ες, (εἶδος) of the people, popular, Plat.
δήμωμα, ατος, τό, (δημόομαι) a popular pastime, χαρίτων δαμώματα odes for public performance, Stesich. ap. Ar.
δημ-ωφελής, ές, (ὔφελος) of public use, Plat.
ΔΗ΄Ν, Dor. δάν, Adv. long, for a long while, Lat. diu, Il. ; οὐ δὴν ἦν he was not long-lived, Ib.   2. long ago, Od.   II. of Place, far, much, δὴν χάζετο Il.
δηναιός, ή, όν, Dor. δᾱναιός, ά, όν : (δήν) :—long-lived, Il., Theocr.   2. old, aged, ancient, Aesch.
δηνάριον, τό, a Roman coin, a denary, nearly = Gr. δράχμη, N. T.
δήνεα, τά, (δήω) only in pl. counsels, plans, arts, whether good or bad, Hom., Hes.
δηξί-θυμος, ον, = δακέ-θυμος, of love, Aesch.
δῆξις, εως, ἡ, (δάκνω) a bite, biting : metaph. of biting jokes, Plut.
δήξομαι, f. of δάκνω.
δήξομᾱρα, Att. crasis for δήξομαι ἄρα.
δηόω, contr. for δηϊόω.
δή-ποθεν or δή ποθεν, indef. Adv., from any quarter, Lat. undecunque, Aesch.
δή-ποτε or δή ποτε, Dor. δή-ποκα, indef. Adv. at some time, once upon a time, Od., Aesch., etc.   2. εἰ δή ποτε, Lat. si quando, Il. ; ὁπόθεν δή ποτε from some quarter or other, Dem.   3. as interrog., τί δή ποτε; what in the world? quid tandem? Id. ; πόσοι δή ποτε; how many do you suppose? Id.
δή-που or δή που, indef. Adv. perhaps, it may be, Il. ; in Att. doubtless, I suppose, I presume, of course, Lat. scilicet, οὐ δήπου τλητόν Aesch., etc. : often in phrases, ἴστε γὰρ δή που, μέμνησθε γὰρ δή που Dem. ; so, as interrog. implying an affirm. answer, τὴν αἰχμάλωτον κάτοισθα δή που; I presume you know, Soph.
δή-πουθεν, indef. Adv. much like δήπου, Ar., Plat.
δηριάομαι, Ep. 3 dual δηριδάσθον, imper. 3 pl. -αάσθων, inf. -άασθαι, 3 pl. impf. δηριόωντο, Dep. (δῆρις) to contend, wrangle, Hom.
δηρίομαι [ῑ], f. δηρίσομαι: Ep. 3 pl. aor. 1 δηρίσαντο, 3 dual pass. δηρινθήτην : Dep., =foreg., Hom. From
δῆρις, ιος, acc. -ιν, ἡ, a fight, battle, contest, Il., Aesch. (Deriv. uncertain.)
δηρί-φατος, ον, (φάω) = ἀρείφατος, Anth.
δηρίω, = δηρίομαι, aor. 1 ἐδήρισα, Theogn., Theocr.
δηρό-βιος, Dor. δαρ-, ον, long-lived, Aesch. From
δηρός, ά, όν, Dor. δᾱρός, (δήν) long, too long, δηρὸν χρόνον Il. ; so, δηρὸν (sub. χρόνον) as Adv. all too long, Ib. ; ἐπὶ δηρόν Ib. ; δαρὸν χρόνον Soph.
δησάσκετο, Ep. for ἐδήσατο, aor. 1 med. of δέω (A).
δῆσε, Ep. aor. 1 of δέω (A).   II. for ἐδήσε, aor. 1 of δέω (B).
δῆτα, Adv., more emphatic form of δή, certainly, to be sure, of course :   1. in answers, added to a word which echoes the question, ἴσασιν ; do they know ? Answ. ἴσασι δῆτα aye they know, Eur. ; often with a negat., οὐ δῆτ᾽ ἔγωγε faith not I, Ar.   2. in questions, mostly to mark an inference or consequence, τί δῆτα ; what then ? πῶς δῆτα ; ἆρα δῆτα, etc. Trag. :— sometimes it expresses indignation, καὶ δῆτ᾽ ἐτόλμας ; and so thou hast dared ? Soph. ; ταῦτα δῆτ᾽ ἀνασχετά ;

Id. ; ironical, τῷ σῷ δικαίῳ δῆτ᾽ ; your principle of justice forsooth, Id.   3. in prayers or wishes, ἀπόλοιο δῆτα now a murrain take thee ! Ar. ; σκόπει δῆτα only look, Plat., etc.
δηχθείς, aor. 1 pass. part. of δάκνω.
δήω, to find, meet with, in pres. with fut. sense, Hom. (Prob. akin to *δάω.)
Δηώ, όος, contr. οῦς, ἡ, = Δημήτηρ, Demeter, h. Hom., Soph., etc. :—Adj. Δηῷος, α, ον, sacred to her, Anth.
δηώσας, δηωθείς, aor. 1 act. and pass. part. of δηϊόω.
Δί, poët. for Διΐ, dat. of Ζεύς :—Δία, acc.
ΔΙΑ΄, poët. διαί, Prep. governing gen. and acc.—Radic. sense, through.
  A. WITH GEN. :   I. of Place or Space :   1. of motion in a line, through, right through, διὰ μὲν ἀσπίδος ἦλθε ἔγχος Il. ; δι᾽ ἠέρος αἰθέρ᾽ ἵκανεν quite through the lower air even to the ether, Ib. ; διὰ πάντων ἐλθεῖν to go through all in succession, Xen.   2. of motion through a space, but not in a line, all through, over, διὰ πεδίοιο Il. ; δι᾽ ἄστεος Od.   3. of Intervals of Space, διὰ δέκα ἐπάλξεων at every 10th battlement, Thuc. ; διὰ πέντε σταδίων at a distance of 5 stades, Hdt.   II. of Time :   1. throughout, during, διὰ παντὸς τοῦ χρόνου Hdt. ; δι᾽ ἡμέρης all day long, Id. ; διὰ παντὸς continually, Aesch. ; δι᾽ ὀλίγου for a short time, Thuc.   2. of the interval between two points of Time, διὰ χρόνου πολλοῦ or διὰ πολλοῦ χρ. after a long time, Hdt. ; διὰ χρόνου after a time, Soph. ; χρόνος διὰ χρόνου time after time, Id.   3. of successive Intervals, διὰ τρίτης ἡμέρης every other day, Hdt. ; δι᾽ ἐνιαυτοῦ every year, Xen.   III. Causal, through, by,   1. of the Agent, δι᾽ ἀγγέλων by the mouth of messengers, Hdt. ; δι᾽ ἑρμηνέως λέγειν Xen.   2. of the Instrument or Means, διὰ χειρῶν Soph. ; διὰ χειρὸς ἔχειν in hand, Id.   3. of the Manner or Way, παίω δι᾽ ὀργῆς through passion, in passion, Soph. ; διὰ σπουδῆς in haste, hastily, Eur.   IV. to express conditions or states, δι᾽ ἡσυχίης εἶναι to be in a state of quiet, to be tranquil, Hdt. ; διὰ πολέμου ἰέναι τινί to be at war with one, Xen. ; δι᾽ ἀπεχθείας ἐλθεῖν τινι to be hated by him, Aesch. ; δι᾽ οἴκτου ἔχειν τινά to feel pity for one, Eur., etc.
  B. WITH ACC. :   I. of Place, in same sense as διά c. gen. :   1. through, ἐξ διὰ πτύχας ἦλθε χαλκός Il.   2. throughout, over, ᾤκεον δι᾽ ἄκριας Od. ; δι᾽ αἰθέρα Soph.   II. of Time, διὰ νύκτα Il. ; διὰ ὕπνον during sleep, Mosch.   III. Causal :   1. of Persons, through, by aid of, by means of, νικῆσαι διὰ Ἀθήνην Od. ; διά σε by thy fault or service, Soph. : through, by reason of, αὐτὸς δι᾽ αὑτόν for his own sake, Plat. ; διὰ τὴν ἐκείνου μέλλησιν Thuc.   2. of things, which express the Cause, Reason, or Purpose, δι᾽ ἐμὴν ἰότητα because of my will, Il. ; δι᾽ ἀχθηδόνα for the sake of vexing, Thuc. ; διὰ τοῦτο, διὰ ταῦτα therefore ; etc.
  C. WITHOUT CASE as Adv. throughout, Hom.
  D. IN COMPOS. :   I. through, right through, as in διαβαίνω.   II. in different directions, as in διαπέμπω :—of separation, asunder, as in Lat. dis-, as in διασκεδάννυμι :—at variance, as in διαφωνέω : or of mutual relation, one with another, as in διαγωνίζομαι, διᾴδω.   III. of preëminence, as in διαπρέπω, δια-

φέρω. **IV.** completion, *to the end, utterly,* as in διαμάχομαι (cf. Lat. *decertare*). **V.** *to add strength, throughly, out and out,* as in διαγαληνίζω. **VI.** of mixture, *between, partly,* as in διάλευκος.

δῖα, ἡ, fem. of δῖος. **II.** **Δία,** acc. of Ζεύς.

δια-βᾰδίζω, f. -ιοῦμαι, *to go across,* Thuc. 2. *to walk to and fro,* Luc.

δια-βάθρα, ἡ, (βαίνω) *a ship's ladder,* Luc.

δια-βαίνω, f. -βήσομαι: aor. 2 -έβην: pf. -βέβηκα: **I.** *to make a stride, walk* or *stand with the legs apart,* εὖ διαβάς of a man *planting himself firmly* for fighting, Il. **II.** c. acc. *to step across, pass over* a ditch or river, Ib. 2. absol. (θάλασσαν or ποταμόν being omitted), *to cross over,* Lat. *trajicere,* ἐς Ἠλίδα Od.; πλοίῳ διαβῆναι Hdt., etc.

δια-βάλλω, f. -βᾰλῶ : pf. -βέβληκα:—*to throw over* or *across, to carry over* or *across,* νέας Hdt. : hence, 2. seemingly intr., like Lat. *trajicere, to pass over, cross, pass,* Id. : also c. acc., δ. γεφύρας Eur.; πέλαγος Thuc. **II.** *to set at variance, make a quarrel between,* ἐμὲ καὶ Ἀγάθωνα Plat. :—Pass. *to be at variance with,* τινί Id. **III.** *to traduce, slander, calumniate,* Hdt., etc.; διέβαλον τοὺς Ἴωνας ὡς .. *traduced* them saying that .., Id. :—Pass., διαβάλλεσθαί τινι to be filled with suspicion against another, Id.; πρός τινα Id.; ἔς τινα Thuc. 2. c. acc. rei, *to misrepresent* a thing, *to state slanderously,* Hdt., Dem. : *to give hostile information, without insinuation of falsehood,* Thuc. **IV.** *to deceive by false accounts, impose upon,* τινά Hdt. :—so in Med., Id. :—Pass., διαβεβλῆσθαι ὡς .. *to be slanderously told that .. ,* Plat.

δια-βαπτίζομαι, f. ίσομαι, Dep. *to dive for a match :* metaph. *to contend in foul language with,* τινι Dem.

δια-βάς, aor. 2 part. of διαβαίνω.

διά-βᾰσις, εως, ἡ, (διαβαίνω) *a crossing over, passage,* δ. ποιεῖσθαι Hdt. 2. *a means* or *place of crossing,* Id. : δ. ποταμοῦ *a ford,* Thuc. : *a bridge,* Xen.

δια-βάσκω, = διαβαίνω, *to strut about,* Ar.

δια-βαστάζω, *to weigh in the hand, estimate,* Plut.

διαβατέος, α, ον, verb. Adj. of διαβαίνω, *that can be crossed* or *passed through,* Xen.

διαβατήρια (sc. ἱερά), τά, *offerings before crossing the border,* τὰ δ. προυχώρει, τὰ δ. ἐγένετο they were favourable, Thuc., Xen.

διαβατός, ή, όν, verb. Adj. of διαβαίνω, *to be crossed* or *passed, fordable,* Hdt., etc.; νῆσον δ. ἐξ ἠπείρου easily got at from the main land, Id.

δια-βεβαιόομαι, Dep. *to maintain strongly,* Dem.

δια-βήμεναι, Ep. for διαβῆναι, aor. 2 of διαβαίνω.

διαβήτης, ου, ὁ, (διαβαίνω) *the compass,* so called from its outstretched legs, Lat. *circinus,* Ar.

διαβιάζομαι, strengthd. for βιάζομαι, Eur.

δια-βῐβάζω, f. Att. -βιβῶ, Causal of διαβαίνω, *to carry over* or *across, to transport,* δ. τὸν στρατὸν κατὰ γεφύρας Hdt. ; ἐς τὴν νῆσον τοὺς ὁπλίτας Thuc.

δια-βιβρώσκω, f. -βρώσομαι: pf. pass. -βέβρωμαι :—*to eat up,* Plat. :—Pass., pf. inf. διαβεβρωσθαι Luc.

δια-βιόω, f. ώσομαι: aor. 2 -εβίων, inf. -βιῶναι :—*to live through, pass,* χρόνον, βίον Plat., etc. :—absol. *to spend one's whole life,* Id., Xen.

δια-βλέπω, f. ψω, *to look straight before one,* Plat.

δια-βοάω, f. ήσομαι, (-βοάσω is aor. 1 subj.) :—*to*

shout out, proclaim, publish, Aesch. :—Pass. *to be the common talk,* Luc. **II.** *to cry out,* Thuc. **III.** Med. *to contend in shouting,* Dem. Hence

διαβόητος, ον, *noised abroad, famous,* Plut.

διαβολή, ἡ, (διαβάλλω) *false accusation, slander, calumny,* ἐπὶ διαβολῇ εἰπεῖν Hdt. ; διαβολὰς ἐνδέχεσθαι *to give ear to false accusations,* Id.; ἐμὴ δ. *the slanders* against me, Plat. **II.** *a quarrel, enmity,* Thuc.

διαβολία, ἡ, poët. διαιβολίη, = διαβολή, Theogn., Pind.

διάβολος, ον, *slanderous, backbiting,* Sup. ; διαβολώτατος Ar. 2. as Subst. *a slanderer,* Arist. : *the Slanderer, the Devil,* N. T. 3. Adv. -λως, *injuriously, invidiously,* Thuc.

διαβόρος, ον, (διαβι-βρώσκω) *eating through, devouring,* Soph. **II.** proparox. διάβορος, ον, pass. *eaten through, consumed,* Id.

δια-βουκολέω, f. ήσω, *to cheat with false hopes,* Luc.

δια-βουλεύομαι, Dep. *to discuss pro and con, discuss thoroughly,* Thuc.

διαβούλιον, τό, *counsel, deliberation,* Polyb.

δια-βρέχω, f. ξω, *to wet through, soak,* Aesch. Hence

διάβροχος, ον, *very wet, moist,* Eur. : ναῦς δ. ships *with their timbers soaked and rotten,* Thuc. :—metaph., ἔρωτι, μέθῃ δ. Luc.

δια-βῠνέω or -βῦνω, only in pres. *to thrust through so as to stop up* :—Med., διαβυνέονται ὀϊστοὺς διὰ τῆς ἀριστερῆς they pass arrows *through their* left hand, Hdt. :—Pass., πηδάλιον διὰ τῆς τρόπιος διαβύνεται is *passed through* the keel, Id.

δια-γαληνίζω, f. ίσω, (γαλήνη) *to make quite calm,* Ar.

δι-ᾰγανακτέω, f. ήσω, *to be full of indignation,* Dem.

διᾰγανάκτησις, εως, ἡ, *great indignation,* Plut.

δι-αγγέλλω, f. ελῶ : aor. 1 διήγγειλα :—*to give notice by a messenger, to send as a message,* Xen. :—generally, *to noise abroad, proclaim,* Eur., Plat. ; c. inf. *to order* to do, Eur. :—Med. *to pass the word of command from man to man, inform one another,* Xen.

δι-άγγελος, ὁ, *a messenger,* Lat. *internuncius,* esp. *a secret informant, go-between, spy,* Thuc.

δια-γελάω, f. άσομαι [ᾰ], *to laugh at,* τινα Eur., Xen.

δια-γίγνομαι, Ion. and in late Gr. -γίνομαι : f. -γενήσομαι : Dep. :—*to go through, pass,* τόσαδε ἔτη Plat. ; τὴν νύκτα Xen. : absol. *to go through life, survive, live,* Ar., etc. ; c. part., διαγίγνεσθαι ἄρχων *to continue in the government,* Xen. ; οὐδὲν ἄλλο ποιῶν διαγεγένηται he never *did anything* else, Id. **II.** *to be between, intervene,* ap. Dem.

δια-γιγνώσκω, Ion. and in late Gr. -γινώσκω : f. -γνώσομαι : aor. 2 -έγνων :—*to distinguish, discern,* Lat. *dignoscere,* διαγνῶναι ἄνδρα ἕκαστον Il. ; δ. εἰ ὁμοῖοί εἰσι whether they are equals or no, Hdt. ; δ. τὸ ὀρθὸν καὶ μή Aeschin. :—δ. τινὰς ὄντας, i. e. δ. οἵτινές εἰσιν, Ar. 2. *to discern exactly,* τι Soph. **II.** *to resolve, vote to do so and so,* c. inf., Hdt. :—Pass., impers. διέγνωστο *it had been resolved,* Thuc. 2. as Athen. law-term, *to decide* a suit, Lat. *dijudicare,* δίκην Aesch. :—*to give judgment,* περί τινος Thuc.

δι-αγκυλίζομαι, Dep. (ἀγκύλη) *to hold a javelin by the thong* :—Pass., pf. part. pass. διηγκυλισμένος, of a man, *ready to shoot,* Xen. :—so (from δι-αγκυλόομαι), διηγκυλωμένος Id.

δια-γλάφω [ᾰ], f. ψω, to scoop out, Od.
διάγλυπτος, ον, carved in intaglio, engraved, Anth.
δια-γλύφω [ῠ], f. ψω, to carve in intaglio, Diod.
διαγνώμη, ἡ, (διαγιγνώσκω) a decree, resolution, Thuc.
δια-γνωρίζω, f. Att. ιῶ, to make known, N. T.
διάγνωσις, εως, ἡ, (διαγιγνώσκω) a distinguishing, discernment, Eur., Dem.   2. power of discernment, Eur.   II. a resolving, deciding, δ. ποιεῖσθαι to decide a matter, Thuc.; δ. περί τινος Dem.
διαγνωστέον, verb. Adj. of διαγιγνώσκω, one must distinguish, Luc.
διαγνωστικός, ή, όν, (διαγιγνώσκω) able to distinguish, Luc.
δια-γογγύζω, to murmur among themselves, N. T.
δι-αγορεύω, f. σω, to speak plainly, declare, Hdt.   II. to speak of, κακῶς δ. τινά Luc.
διάγραμμα, ατος, τό, (διαγράφω) that which is marked out by lines, a figure, plan, Plat.   2. a geometrical figure, diagram, Xen., Plat.   II. a written list, register, Dem.   III. a decree, edict, Plut.
διαγραφή, ἡ, a marking off by lines, Plat. : a geometrical figure, diagram, outline, Plut. From
δια-γράφω, f. ψω, to mark out by lines, delineate, Plat.   II. to draw a line through, cross out, strike off the list, Id.; δ. δίκην to strike a cause out of the list, cancel, quash it, Ar.
δι-αγριαίνω, strengthd. for ἀγριαίνω, Plut.
δι-αγρυπνέω, f. ήσω, to lie awake, Ar.
δι-άγχω, f. -άγξω, strengthd. for ἄγχω, Luc.
δι-άγω, f. -άξω, to carry over or across, Od., Thuc., etc.   II. of Time, to go through, pass, spend, βίοτον, βίον Aesch., etc.   2. intr. (without βίον) to pass life, live, like Lat. degere, Hdt., etc. :—to delay, put off time, Thuc. :—to continue, Xen. : c. part. to continue doing so and so, δ. μανθάνων Id.; also with Adv., ἄριστα Id.   III. to make to continue or keep in a certain state, πόλιν ὀρθοδίκαιον δ. Aesch.; διῆγεν ὑμᾶς Dem.   IV. to entertain a person, Xen.
διᾰγωγή, ἡ, (διάγω II) a passing of life, a way or course of life, Lat. ratio vitae, Plat., etc. ; διαγωγαὶ τοῦ συζῆν public pastimes, Arist. Hence
διαγωγικός, ή, όν, of or for a passage : τέλος δ. a transit duty, Strab.
δι-αγωνίζομαι, f. Att. ιοῦμαι, Dep. to contend, struggle or fight against, τινι and πρός τινα Xen.   II. to fight desperately, contend earnestly, Thuc., Xen.
δια-δάπτω, f. ψω, to tear asunder, rend, Il.
δια-δᾰτέομαι : aor. 1 -δάσασθαι : Dep. :   1. in reciprocal sense, to divide among themselves, διὰ κτῆσιν δατέοντο Il., Hes.   2. in act. sense, to divide, distribute, διὰ παῦρα δασάσκετο (Ion. for ἐδάσατο), Il. ; διεδάσαντο τὴν ληΐην Hdt. ; ἐς φυλὰς διεδάσαντο distributed them among the tribes, Id.
δια-δείκνυμι, f. -δείξω, Ion. -δέξω :—to shew clearly, shew plainly, Hdt.; c. part., διαδεξάτω κηδόμενος let him shew that he cares, Id. :—Pass., διαδεικνύσθω ἐὼν πολέμιος let him be declared the king's enemy, Id.   II. intr. in forms διέδεξε, ὡς διέδεξε, it was clear, manifest, Id.
διαδέκτωρ, ορος, ὁ, (διαδέχομαι) as Adj., πλοῦτος δ. inherited wealth, Eur.
δια-δέξιος, ον, of good omen, Hdt.

δια-δέρκομαι, aor. 2 -έδρακον : Dep. :—to see through, οὐδ᾽ ἂν νῷ διαδράκοι would not see us through (the cloud), Il.
διάδετος, ον, (διαδέω) bound fast, χαλινοὶ διάδετοι γενύων ἱππείων bits firm bound through the horse's mouth, Aesch.
δια-δέχομαι, f. ξομαι, Dep. to receive one from another, Lat. excipere, δ. λόγον to take up the word, i. e. to speak next, Plat. ; so διαδέχεσθαι alone, Hdt.   II. διαδέχεσθαί τινι to succeed one, Xen.   2. absol. to relieve one another, τοῖς ἵπποις with fresh horses, Id. :—part. pf. pass. διαδεδεγμένος, η, ον, in succession, in turns, Soph. ; so, διαδεξάμενος Hdt.
δια-δέω, f. -δήσω, to bind round, τὸ πλοῖον Hdt. :— Pass., διαδεδεμένος fast-bound, Plat.
δια-δηλέομαι, f. ήσομαι, Dep. to do great harm to, tear to pieces, Od., Theocr.
διά-δηλος, ον, distinguishable among others, Thuc.
διά-δηλόω, f. ώσω, to make manifest, Plut.
διάδημα, ατος, τό, (διαδέω) a band or fillet : esp. the band round the τιάρα of the Persian king, Xen.
διαδημᾰτο-φόρος, ον, (φέρω) wearing a diadem, Plut.
δια-διδράσκω, f. -δράσομαι : Ion. διαδιδρήσκω, -δρήσομαι : aor. 2 -έδραν : pf. -δέδρακα :—to run off, get away, escape, Hdt. ; διαδεδρακότες shirkers, Ar.   2. c. acc. to run away from, escape from, Hdt.
δια-δίδωμι, f. -δώσω : aor. 2 διέδων :—to give from hand to hand, to pass on, hand over, Lat. tradere, λαμπάδια διαδώσουσιν ἀλλήλοις Plat. :—Pass., of reports, to be spread abroad, Xen.   2. to distribute, τινί τι Id.   3. δ. κόρας to cast one's eyes around, Eur.
δια-δῐκάζω, f. άσω, to give judgment in a case, Plat. : c. acc. rei, to decide, Xen.   II. Med. to go to law, τινι with another, Plat. ; διαδικάσασθαι τὰ πρὸς ἐμέ to have a matter settled by arbitration, Dem.   2. to submit oneself to trial, Plat., Xen.
δια-δῐκαιόω, f. ώσω, to hold a thing to be right, Thuc.
διαδῐκασία, ἡ, (διαδικάζω) a suit brought to decide who (of several persons) was entitled to any right or privilege, Oratt. :—metaph., δ. τῷ βήματι πρὸς τὸ στρατήγιον a dispute between the orators and the war-office, Aeschin.
διαδίκασμα, ατος, τό, the object of litigation in a διαδικασία, Lys.
δια-διφρεύω, f. σω, to drive horses as in a chariot-race, Eur.
δια-δοκιμάζω, f. άσω, to test closely, Xen.
διά-δος, aor. 2 imper. of διαδίδωμι.
διάδοσις, εως, ἡ, (διαδίδωμι) a distribution, largess, Dem., etc.
δια-δοῦναι, aor. 2 inf. of διαδίδωμι.
διαδοχή, ἡ, (διαδέχομαι) a taking from another, Dem.   2. succession, ἄλλος παρ᾽ ἄλλου διαδοχαῖς by successions or reliefs, Aesch.; ἐκ διαδοχῆς ἀλλήλοις in turns, Lat. vicissim, Dem.; κατὰ διαδοχήν Thuc.   II. in military sense, a relief, relay, Xen.
διάδοχος, ὁ, ἡ, (διαδέχομαι) succeeding a person in a thing :   1. c. dat. pers. et gen. rei, δ. Μεγαβάζῳ τῆς στρατηγίης his successor in the command, Hdt. ; θνητοῖς διάδοχοι μοχθημάτων succeeding them in, i. e. relieving them from, toils, Aesch.   2. c. gen. rei

only, δ. τῆς ναυαρχίας *succeeding to* the command, Thuc. 3. c. gen. pers. only, φέγγος ὕπνου δ. sleep's *successor*, light, Soph. 4. c. dat. pers. only, δ. Κλεάνδρῳ Xen.; so, κακὸν κακῷ δ. Eur.; and in a quasi-act. sense, διάδοχος κακῶν κακοῖς *bringing a* succession of evils *after* evils, Id. 5. absol., διάδοχοι ἐφοίτων they went to work *in relays* or *gangs*, Hdt., Thuc.: neut. pl. as Adv. *in succession*, Eur.

δια-δράκοιμι [ᾰ], aor. 2 opt. of δια-δέρκομαι.

δια-δρᾰμεῖν, aor. 2 inf. of δια-τρέχω.

δια-δρᾶναι, Ion. -δρῆναι, aor. 2 inf. of διαδιδράσκω.

διαδρᾱσι-πολίτης [ῑ], ὁ, *a citizen who shirks all state burdens*, Ar.

δια-δρηπετεύω, *to run off, go over to*, Hdt.:—a correction for δι-επρήστευσε, which has no meaning.

διαδρομή, ἡ, (διαδραμεῖν) *a running about through* a city, Aesch. 2. *a foray*, Plut. II. *a passage through*, Xen.: *an aqueduct*, Plut.

διάδρομος, ον, (διαδραμεῖν) *running through* or *about, wandering*, Aesch.; λέχος δ. *stray, lawless love*, Eur.

δια-δύνω [ῠ] or -δύω: more commonly as Dep. διαδύομαι, f. -δύσομαι: aor. 2 διέδυν:—*to slip through* a hole or gap, Thuc., Xen.: absol. *to slip through, slip away*, Hdt., Ar. 2. c. acc. *to evade, shirk*, Dem.

διάδῡσις, εως, ἡ, *a passage through*: in pl. *evasions*, τινος *from a thing*, Dem.

δια-δωρέομαι, Dep. *to distribute in presents*, Xen.

δια-είδω (i. e. διαϜείδω), f. -είσομαι, *to discern, distinguish*, ἣν ἀρετὴν διαείσεται *will discern, test* his manhood, Il.:—Pass. *to be discerned*, Il.

δι-αείδω, f. -αείσομαι: Att. δι-ᾷδω, -ᾴσομαι:—*to contend in singing*, τινί with one, Theocr.

δια-ειμένος, pf. pass. part. of διίημι.

δια-ειπέμεν, Ep. for δι-ειπεῖν, aor. 2 inf. of διεῖπον.

δι-αέριος, ον, Ion. for διηέριος, *high in air, transcendental*, Luc.

δια-ζάω, Ion. -ζώω, inf. διαζῆν: f. ἥσω:—*to live through, pass*, τὸν βίον Eur.:—then, absol., like Lat. *degere*, Ar., Xen. 2. c. part., like διαβιόω, *to live by doing so and so*, ποιηφαγέοντες διέζων they supported life by eating grass, Hdt.; also, δ. ἀπό τινος *to live off* or *by a thing*, Soph.

δια-ζεύγνῡμαι, aor. 1 -εζεύχθην, Pass. *to be disjoined, separated, parted*, τινος from one, Aeschin.; ἀπό τινος Xen. Hence

διάζευξις, εως, ἡ, *a disjoining, parting*, Plat.

διάζωμα, ατος, τό, *a girdle, drawers*, Lat. *subligaculum*, Thuc. 2. *an isthmus*, Plut. From

δια-ζώννῡμι or -ύω, f. -ζώσω, *to gird round the middle*:—Med. *to gird oneself with*, ἐσθῆτα, Luc.:—Pass., διεζωσμένοι *wearing drawers*, Thuc. II. metaph. *to engirdle, encompass*, Plut.

δια-ζώω, Ion. for δια-ζάω.

δι-άημι, impf. δίαην, *to blow through* trees, etc., c. acc., Od., Hes.

δια-θεάομαι, f. ἄσομαι [ᾱ], Dep. *to look through, examine*, Plat., Xen.:—verb. Adj., διαθεατέον, Plat.

δια-θειόω, f. ώσω, *to fumigate thoroughly*, Od.

δια-θερμαίνω, f. ανῶ, *to warm through*, Plat., etc.:—Pass. *to be heated*, by drinking, Dem.

διά-θερμος, ον, *heated through*: *of a hot temperament*, Arist.

διάθεσις, εως, ἡ, (διατίθημι) *a disposition, arrangement*, Plat. 2. *the composition* in a work of art, as opp. to εὕρεσις, Id. 3. *a disposition* of property, =διαθήκη, Id. 4. *a disposing of, selling, sale*, Plut. II. *a man's disposition*, Plat.

διαθέτης, ου, ὁ, (διατίθημι) *an arranger*, Hdt.

δια-θέω, f. -θεύσομαι, *to run about*, Thuc., etc.; of reports, of panic fear, Xen. II. *to run a race*, τινί with or against another, Plat.:—c. acc. cogn., δ. τὴν λαμπάδα *to run* the torch-race, Plut.

διαθήκη, ἡ, (διατίθημι) *a disposition* of property by will, *a will, testament*, Ar., Oratt. II. *an arrangement between* two parties, *covenant*, Ar., N. T.

δια-θορυβέω, f. ήσω, *to confound utterly*, τινα Thuc.: absol. *to make a great noise*, Plut.

δι-αθρέω, f. ήσω, *to look closely into, examine closely*, Ar.

δια-θροέω, f. ήσω, *to spread a report, give out*, Thuc.

δια-θρῡλέω, f. ήσω, = διαθροέω:—mostly in Pass. *to be commonly reported*, διετεθρύλητο ὡς . . Xen. II. *to be talked deaf*, διαθρυλούμενος ὑπό σου Id.

δια-θρύπτω, f. ψω:—Pass., aor. 2 διετρύφην [ῠ]:—*to break in sunder, break in pieces, shiver*, Luc.:—Pass., τριχθά τε καὶ τετραχθὰ διατρυφὲν [τὸ ξίφος] Il.; ἀσπίδες διατεθρυμμέναι Xen. II. metaph., like Lat. *frangere, to break down* by profligate living and indulgence, *to enervate, pamper, make weak and womanish*, Plat., Xen.:—Pass. *to be enervated, pampered*, Xen. 2. Med. *to give oneself airs*, of a prude, Theocr.; of a singer, διαθρύπτεται ἤδη *is beginning her airs*, Id.

διαί, διαιβολία, poët. for διά, διαβολία.

δια-αιθριάζω, f. ήσω, *to become quite clear and fine*, ἐδόκει διαιθριάζειν it seemed likely *to be fine*, Xen.

δί-αιθρος, ον, (αἴθρα) *quite clear and fine*, Plut.

δί-αιμος, ον, (αἷμα) *blood-stained*, Eur.; δίαιμον ἀναπτύειν *to spit blood*, Plut.

διαίνω, f. διανῶ: aor. 1 ἐδίηνα:—*to wet, moisten*, Il.:—Med., διαίνεσθαι ὄσσε *to wet one's eyes*, Aesch.; absol. *to weep*, Id.

διαίρεσις, εως, ἡ, (διαιρέω) *a dividing, division*, of money, Hdt.; of spoil, Xen.; ἐν διαιρέσει [ψήφων] *in the reckoning* of the votes *on either side*, Aesch.

διαιρετέος, α, ον, verb. Adj. of διαιρέω, *to be divided*, Plat. II. διαιρετέον, *one must divide*, Id.

διαιρετικός, ή, όν, (διαιρέω) *divisible*, Plat.

διαιρετός, ή, όν, (διαιρέω) *divided, separated*, Xen.: *distributed*, Soph. II. *distinguishable*, Thuc. From

δι-αιρέω, f. ήσω: aor. 2 -εῖλον: aor. 1 pass. ἡρέθην:—*to take one from another*, *to cleave in twain*, *to divide into parts*, Il., Hdt.; δ. λαγόν *to cut* it open, Id.; δ. πυλίδα *to break* it open, Thuc.; δ. τὴν ὀροφήν *to tear* it away, Id.; δ. τοῦ τείχους *to take down* part of the wall, *make a breach* in it, Id.; τὸ διῃρημένον *the breach*, Id. II. *to divide*, δύο μοίρας Λυδίαν *into two parts*, Hdt.; so, δ. τριχῇ Plat.; εἰς δύο Dem.:—Med. *to divide for themselves*, ναῦς Thuc.: but also *to divide among themselves*, Hes., Hdt.:—Pass., διῃρημένοι κατ' ἀναπαύλας *divided* into relays, Thuc. 2. *to divide* into component parts, Plat. III. *to distinguish*, Ar. 2. *to determine, decide*, Hdt., Aesch., etc. 3. *to say distinctly, to define, interpret*, Hdt., Att.

δι-αίρω, f. -ᾰρῶ, *to raise up, lift up*, τὸν αὐχένα

Xen.　II. *to separate, remove*, Plut. :—Med., διαρδμένος (sc. τὰ σκέλη) *taking long strides*, Theophr.　2. δ. τὸ στόμα *to open* one's mouth, Dem.

δι-αισθάνομαι, f. ήσομαι, Dep. *to perceive distinctly, distinguish perfectly*, τι Plat.

δι-αΐσσω, f. -άξω : Att. -ᾴσσω or -ᾴττω : f. -άξω : aor. 1 -ῇξα :—*to rush* or *dart through* or *across*, Hdt. : c. acc., ὄρη διᾴσσει Soph. : *of sound*, ἀχὼ διῇξεν μυχόν Aesch. ; and c. gen., σπασμὸς διῇξε πλευρῶν Soph.

δι-αϊστόω, f. ώσω : aor. 1 διηΐστωσα :—*to make an end of*, τινά Soph.

δι-αισχύνομαι, strengthd. for αἰσχύνομαι, Luc.

δίαιτα, ή, (prob. from ζάω, v. Ζ ζ. II. 2) *a way of living, mode of life*, Hdt., Soph., etc. ; δ. ποιεῖσθαι *to pass one's life*, Hdt.　2. *a dwelling, abode, room*, Ar.　II. at Athens, *arbitration*, Soph., Ar., Oratt. Hence

δῖαιτάω, f. ήσω : aor. 1 διῄτησα : pf. δεδιῄτηκα :—Med. and Pass., Ion. impf. διαιτώμην : f. διαιτήσομαι ; and in pass. forms, aor. 1 διῃτήθην, Ion. διαιτήθην : pf. δεδιῄτημαι :—*to feed in a certain way, to diet*, δ. τοὺς νοσοῦντας Plut.　2. Med. and Pass. *to lead a certain course of life, to live*, Hdt., Soph. ; δ. νόμιμα *to live in the observance* of laws, Thuc.　II. *to be arbiter* or *umpire* (διαιτητής), Dem., etc.　2. c. acc. rei, *to determine, decide*, Theocr. Hence

δῐαίτημα, ατος, τό, mostly in pl. *rules of life, a mode* or *course of life*, esp. in regard of *diet*, Xen. : generally, *institutions, customs*, Thuc., Xen.

δῐαιτητήριον, τό, (δίαιτα I. 2) in pl. *the dwelling rooms* of a house, Xen.

δῐαιτητής, οῦ, ὁ, (διαιτάω II.) *an arbitrator, umpire*, Lat. *arbiter*, Hdt., Plat., etc.

διακᾱής, ές, (διακαίω) *burnt through, very hot*, Luc.

δια-κᾰθαίρω, f. ἀρῶ, *to cleanse* or *purge thoroughly*, Plat. Hence

δια-κᾰθᾱρίζω, f. ιῶ, =foreg., N. T. ; and

διακάθαρσις, εως, ἡ, *a thorough cleansing*, Plat.

δια-καθέζομαι and -κάθημαι, Med. *to sit each in his own seat*, Plut.

δια-καθίζω, *to make to sit apart, set apart*, Xen.

δια-καίω, f. -καύσω, *to burn through, heat to excess*, Hdt. :—metaph. *to inflame, excite*, Plut.

δια-καλύπτω, f. ψω, *to reveal to view*, Dem.

δια-κανάσσω, only in aor. 1, μῶν τὸν λάρυγγα διεκάναξέ σου ; has aught *run gurgling through* thy throat ? Eur.

δια-κᾰρᾱδοκέω, f. ήσω, *to expect anxiously*, Plut.

δια-καρτερέω, f. ήσω, *to endure to the end, last out*, Hdt., Xen.

δια-κατελέγχομαι, f. ξομαι, Med. *to confute thoroughly*, τινι N. T.

δια-κεάζω, f. άσω, *to cleave asunder*, Od.

διά-κειμαι, inf. -κεῖσθαι : f. -κείσομαι :—serving as Pass. to διατίθημι, *to be in a certain state, to be disposed* or *affected* so and so, Hdt., etc. : often, like ἔχω, with an Adv., ὁρᾶτε ὡς δ. ὑπὸ τῆς νόσου how *I am affected* by the disease, Thuc. ; κακῶς, μοχθηρῶς, φαύλως δ. *to be in* sorry *plight*, Plat. ; εὖ or κακῶς δ. *to be well* or *ill disposed* towards him, Oratt. ; ἐπιφθόνως δ. τινι *to be envied* by him, ὑπόπτως τινι δ. *to be suspected* by him, Thuc.　II. *of things, to be settled, fixed*, or *ordered*, ὥς οἱ διέκειτο so was it

---

ordered him, Hes. ; τὰ διακείμενα *certain conditions, settled terms*, Hdt. ; *of a gift*, ἄμεινον διακείσεται it *will be* better *disposed of*, Xen.

δια-κείρω, f. -κερῶ and -κέρσω : pf. -κέκαρκα :—*to cut in pieces* : metaph., διακέρσαι ἐμὸν ἔπος *to make it null, frustrate* it, Il. :—Pass., σκευάρια διακεκαρμένος *shorn* of his trappings, Ar.

διακέλευμα or -κέλευσμα, ατος, τό, *an exhortation, command*, Plat. From

δια-κελεύομαι, Dep. *to exhort, give orders, direct*, δ. τινι ποιεῖν τι etc., Hdt., etc. ; also, δ. τινί τι (sc. ποιεῖν), Plat. ; δ. τινι alone, Id.　2. *to encourage one another*, Hdt. ; δ. ἀλλήλοις Xen. ; δ. ἑαυτῷ Id. Hence

διακελευσμός, ὁ, *an exhortation, cheering on*, Thuc.

διακενῆς or διὰ κενῆς, Adv. for διὰ κενῆς πράξεως, *in vain, idly, to no purpose*, Eur., Ar. From

διά-κενος, ον, *quite empty* or *hollow* ; τὸ δ. *the gap, vacuum*, Thuc.　II. *thin, lank*, Plut., Luc.

δια-κερματίζω, f. ιῶ, *to change into small coin*, Ar.

δια-κέρσαι, aor. 1 inf. of διακείρω.

δια-κηρῡκεύομαι, Dep. *to negotiate by herald*, πρός τινα Thuc.

δια-κηρύσσω, f. ξω, *to proclaim by herald*, ἐν διακεκηρυγμένοις *in declared war*, Plut.　2. *to sell by auction*, Id.

δια-κινδῡνεύω, f. σω, *to run all risks, make a desperate attempt, hazard all*, Thuc. ; πρός τινα Id. ; ὑπέρ or πρός τινος Lysias, Xen. ; περί τινος Dem. :—Pass. *of the attempt, to be risked, hazarded*, Id.

δια-κῑνέω, f. ήσω, *to move thoroughly* :—Pass. *to be put in motion*, Hdt.　2. *to throw into disorder, confound*, τὰ πεπραγμένα Thuc.　II. *to sift thoroughly, scrutinise*, Ar.

δια-κίχρημι, *to lend to various persons* :—Pass., διακεχρημένον τάλαντον Dem.

δια-κλᾰπείς, aor. 2 pass. part. of διακλέπτω.

δια-κλάω, f. άσω [ἄ] : Ep. aor. 1 part. διακλάσσας :—*to break in twain*, Il.　II. in Pass., =διαθρύπτομαι : pf. pass. διακεκλασμένος *enervated*, Luc.

δια-κλέπτω, f. ψω, *to steal at different times*, Dem. ; τὸ διακλαπέν *the quantity stolen* [by the soldiers] *and dispersed*, Thuc.　II. *to keep alive by stealth*, τινά Hdt.　III. *to keep back by stealth*, τὴν ἀλήθειαν Dem.

δια-κληρόω, f. ώσω, *to assign by lot, allot*, Aesch.　2. *to choose by lot*, Xen. :—Med. *to cast lots*, Thuc., Xen.

δια-κλίνω [ῑ], f. -κλῑνῶ, *to turn away, retreat*, Polyb.

διάκλῐσις, εως, ἡ, *a retreat*, Plut.

δια-κλύζω, f. ύσω, *to wash, wash out*, Eur.

δια-κναίω, f. σω, *to scrape to nothing*, ὄψιν δ. *to grind out* his eye, Eur. :—Pass. *to be shivered*, Aesch.　2. *to wear out, wear away*, Eur. :—Pass. *to be worn out, destroyed*, Aesch., Eur. ; τὸ χρῶμα διακεκναισμένος *having lost all* one's colour, Id.

δια-κνίζω, f. σω, *to pull to pieces*, Anth.

δῐα-κολλάω, f. ήσω, *to glue together*, Luc.

διακομῐδή, ἡ, *a carrying over*, τινὸς εἰς τόπον Thuc.

δια-κομίζω, f. Att. ιῶ, *to carry over* or *across*, Hdt., Thuc. :—Med. *to carry over what is* one's own, Hdt. :—Pass. *to be carried over, to pass over, cross*, Thuc.

δια-κονέω, Ion. διηκ- : impf. ἐδιακόνουν, later διηκόνουν : f. -ήσω : aor. 1 διηκόνησα : pf. δεδιηκόνηκα :—Pass.,

aor. 1 ἐδιακονήθην: pf. δεδιακόνημαι: (διάκονος):—*to minister, serve, do service,* absol., Eur.; τινι to a person, Dem.; δ. πρός τι *to be serviceable* towards, Plat.:—Med. *to minister to one's own needs,* Soph.; αὐτῷ διακονεῖσθαι Ar. 2. *to be a deacon,* N.T. II. c. acc. rei, *to furnish, supply,* Lat. ministrare, τί τινι Hdt.:—Pass. *to be supplied,* Dem. Hence

διακόνημα, ατος, τό, *servants' business, service,* Plat.

διᾱκονία, ἡ, *the office of a διάκονος, service,* Thuc., Plat. 2. *attendance on a duty, ministration,* Dem.; ἡ δ. ἡ καθημερινή *ministering* to daily wants, N.T.; ἡ δ. τοῦ λόγου *the ministry* of the word, Ib.

διᾱκονικός, ή, όν, *serviceable,* Ar., etc.; Comp. -ώτερος, Plat. From

διάκονος [ᾰ], Ion. διήκονος, ὁ, *a servant, waitingman,* Lat. minister, Hdt., etc.: *a messenger,* Aesch., Soph.:—as fem., Dem. II. *a minister of the church, a deacon,* N.T.: as fem. *a deaconess,* Ib. (Akin to διάκτορος: both perh. from διώκω.)

δι-ᾰκοντίζομαι, Med. *to contend with others at throwing the javelin,* Xen.

διακοπή, ἡ, *a gash, cleft,* Plut.; from

δια-κόπτω, f. ψω, *to cut in two, cut through,* Thuc. 2. *to break through* the enemy's line, τὴν τάξιν Xen.: then, *to break through the line,* Id.

διακορής, ές,=διάκορος, Plat.

δια-κορκορύγέω, *to rumble through,* τὴν γαστέρα Ar.

διά-κορος, ον, *satiated, glutted,* τινός with a thing, Plat.

διᾱκόσιοι, Ion. διηκ-, αι, α, (δίς, ἕκατον) *two hundred,* Lat. ducenti: sing. with n. of multitude, ἵππος διακοσία *two hundred* horse, Thuc.

διᾱ-κοσμέω, f. ήσω, *to divide and marshal, muster in array,* Il., Thuc.:—Pass., εἴπερ ἐς δεκάδας διακοσμηθεῖμεν Ἀχαιοί (Ep. for -είημεν, 1 pl. aor. 1 opt.) Il. 2. generally, *to regulate, set in order,* Hdt., etc.: Med., μέγαρον διεκοσμήσαντο got it set in order, Od. Hence

διακόσμησις, εως, ἡ, *a setting in order, regulating,* Plat.

διάκοσμος, ὁ,=διακόσμησις, *battle-order,* Thuc.

δι-ᾰκούω, f. -ακούσομαι: pf. -ακήκοα:—*to hear through, hear out* or *to the end,* τί Xen.:—*to hear* or *learn* from another, τί τινος Plat. II. c. gen. pers. *to be a hearer of,* Plut.

δια-κράζω, f. ξω, *to scream continually,* Ar. II. δ. τινι *to match* another *at screaming,* Id.

δια-κρᾰτέω, f. ήσω, *to hold fast, hold one's own,* Plut.

δια-κρέκω, f. ξω, *to strike the strings* of the lyre, Anth.

δια-κρηνόω, Dor. -κρᾱνόω, *to make to flow,* Theocr.

δι-ακρῑβόω, f. ώσω, *to examine* or *discuss minutely* or *with precision,* τι Xen.:—Pass. *to be brought to perfection,* Arist. Hence διακρῑβωτέον, verb. Adj. *one must discuss minutely,* Plut.

διακρῑδόν, Adv. (διακρίνω) *eminently, above all,* Lat. eximiè, Il., Hdt.

δια-κρίνεεσθαι, f. med. inf. (in pass. sense) οf διακρίνω.

δια-κρινθήμεναι, Ep. for -ῆναι, aor. 1 pass. inf. of διακρίνω.

δια-κρίνω [ῑ], f. κρῐνῶ, *to separate one from another,* Il.: *to part* combatants, and in Pass. *to be parted,* Hom.; so in f. med. διακρίνεεσθαι, Od.; also, διακριθῆναι ἀπ' ἀλλήλων Thuc.; διακρίνεσθαι πρός . . *to part and join different* parties, Id. 2. Pass. *to be dissolved into elemental parts,* Plat. II. *to distinguish,* Lat. discernere, τὸ σῆμα Od.; οὐ-

δένα διακρίνων *making* no *distinction* of persons, Hdt.: —Pass., διεκέκριτο οὐδέν no *distinction was made,* Thuc. III. *to settle, decide,* of judges, Hdt., Theocr.:—Med., νεῖκος δ. *to get* it *decided,* Hes.: —Pass. *to come to a decision,* Il.; περί τινος Plat.: —*to contend* with one, τινι N.T.; μάχῃ διακρινθῆναι πρός τινα Hdt. IV. Pass. *to doubt, hesitate,* N.T.

Δι-άκριοι, οἱ, (ἄκρα) *the Mountaineers,* one of the three Attic parties after Solon, Ar.

διάκρῐσις, εως, ἡ, (διακρίνω) *separation, dissolution,* Emped. II. *a decision, judgment,* Xen.

διακρῐτέον or -έα, verb. Adj. of διακρίνω, *one must decide,* Thuc.

διάκρῐτος, ον, (διακρίνω) *separated: choice, excellent,* Theocr.

διάκρουσις, εως, ἡ, *a putting off,* Dem. From

δια-κρούω, f. σω, *to prove by knocking* or *ringing,* as one does an earthen vessel, Plat. II. in Med. *to drive from oneself, get rid of, elude,* τινα or τι Hdt., Dem.: *to evade* his creditor *by delays,* of a debtor, Id.: absol. *to practise evasions,* Id.:—Pass., διακρούσθαι τῆς τιμωρίας *to escape from* punishment, Id.

διακτορία, *the office of a διάκτορος, service,* Anth.

διάκτορος, ὁ, epith. of Hermes, *the Messenger* or *Minister of Zeus,* Hom. (Perh. akin to διάκονος.)

διάκτωρ, ορος, ὁ,=foreg., Anth.

δια-κῠβεύω, f. σω, *to play at dice with,* πρός τινα Plut.

δια-κῠκάω, *to mix one with another, jumble,* Dem.

δια-κῡμαίνω, *to raise into waves,* Luc.

δια-κύπτω, f. ψω, *to stoop and creep through* a narrow place, Hdt. 2. *to stoop so as to peep in,* Ar., Xen.

δια-κωδωνίζω, f. σω, strengthd. for κωδωνίζω, Dem.

διακώλῡσις, εως, ἡ, *a hindering,* Plat.; and

διακωλῡτέον, verb. Adj. *one must hinder,* Plat.; and

διακωλῡτής, οῦ, ὁ, *a hinderer,* Hdt., Plat. From

δια-κωλύω [ῡ], f. ύσω, *to hinder, prevent,* τινὰ μὴ ποιεῖν τι; or without μή, Eur., Plat.; δ. τινά Thuc.; δ. φόνον Soph.:—Pass., ἃ διεκωλύθη (sc. ποιεῖν) which *he was prevented* from doing, Dem.

διακωμῳδέω, f. ήσω, *to satirise,* Plat.

διακωχή, v. sub διοκωχή.

δια-λαγχάνω, f. -λήξομαι, *to divide* or *part by lot,* Hdt., Aesch., Xen.; δῶμα σιδήρῳ δ. Eur.:—*to tear in pieces,* Id.

δια-λᾱκέω, f. ήσω, *to crack asunder, burst,* Ar.

δια-λακτίζω, f. σω, *to kick away, spurn,* Theocr.

δια-λᾱλέω, f. ήσω, *to talk over* a thing *with another,* τί τινι Eur.:—Pass. *to be much talked of,* N.T.

δια-λαμβάνω, f. -λήψομαι: aor. 2 διέλαβον: pf. δι-είληφα: pf. pass. -είλημμαι or -λέλημμαι, Ion. -λέλαμμαι:—*to take* or *receive severally,* i.e. *each for himself, each his share,* Xen., etc. II. *to grasp* or *lay hold of separately,* διαλαβόντες τὰς χεῖρας καὶ τοὺς πόδας Hdt.:—generally, *to seize, arrest,* τινά Id. 2. as a gymnastic term, *to seize by the middle,* Ar.: metaph. of the soul, τὴν ψυχὴν ὑπὸ τοῦ σωματοειδοῦς Plat. III. *to divide,* τὸν ποταμὸν ἐς τριηκοσίας διώρυχας δ. Hdt.:—Pass., ποταμὸς διαλελαμμένος πενταχοῦ *divided* into five channels, Id.; θώρακες διειλημμένοι τὸ βάρος breast-plates *having their weight distributed,* Xen. 2. *to mark at intervals,* Decret. ap. Dem. 3. *to cut off, inter-*

cept, Thuc.　　4. *to mark off, distinguish* :—Pass. χρώμασι διειλημμένη, *marked with various colours*, Plat.　　5. *to distinguish* in thought, Id.: *to state distinctly*, ap. Dem.

δια-λάμπω, f. ψω, *to shine through, to dawn*, Ar.

δια-λανθάνω, f. -λήσω : aor. 2 διέλαθον :—*to escape notice*, διαλαθὸν εἰσέρχεται Thuc.: c. acc. pers. *to escape the notice of*, Xen.

δια-λάχεῖν, aor. 2 inf. of διαλαγχάνω.

δι-αλγής, ές, (ἄλγος) *grievous*, Aesch.　　II. *suffering great pain*, Plut.

δια-λέγω, f. ξω, *to pick out one from another, to pick out*, Hdt., Xen.

　　B. Dep. **δια-λέγομαι** : f. -λέξομαι and -λεχθήσομαι : aor. 1 δι-ελεξάμην and διελέχθην : pf. διείλεγμαι : 3 sing. plqpf. διείλεκτο :—*to converse with, hold converse with*, τινί Il., etc. ; πρός τινα Plat. ; δ. τί τινι or πρός τινα *to discuss* a question with another, Xen. ; δ. τινι μὴ ποιεῖν *to argue with one against* doing, Thuc. :—absol. *to discourse, argue*, Plat., Xen.　　II. *to use a dialect or language*, Hdt.

διάλειμμα, ατος, τό, *an interval*, Plat. ; ἐκ διαλειμμάτων *at intervals*, Plut.　From

δια-λείπω, f. ψω : aor. 2 -έλιπον :—*to leave an interval between* :—Pass., διελέλειπτο *a gap had been left*, Hdt.　　2. of Time, διαλιπὼν ἡμέρην *having left an interval* of a day, Hdt. ; ἀκαρῆ διαλιπών *having waited* an instant, Ar. ; διαλιπών absol. *after a time*, Thuc.　II. intr. *to stand at intervals*, δύο πλέθρα ἀπ' ἀλλήλων δ. Thuc.　2. c. part. *to cease* doing a thing, Xen.　3. of Time, διαλιπόντων ἐτῶν τριῶν *after an interval* of three years, Thuc.

δια-λείχω, f. ξω, *to lick clean*, Ar.

διαλεκτέον, verb. Adj. of διαλέγομαι, *one must discourse*, Plat.

διαλεκτικός, ή, όν, (διαλέγομαι) *skilled in logical argument*, Plat. :—ἡ διαλεκτική (sc. τέχνη) *the art of discussion, dialectic*, Id.: Adv. -κῶς, *logically*, Id.

διάλεκτος, ή, (διαλέγομαι) *discourse : discussion, debate, arguing*, Plat.　　II. *language : the language of a country, dialect : a local word* or *phrase*, Plut.　III. *a way of speaking, enunciation*, Dem.

διάλεξις, εως, ή, (διαλέγομαι) *discourse, arguing*, Ar.

δια-λεπτολογέομαι, (λεπτο-λόγος) Dep. *to discourse subtly, chop logic*, τινι with one, Ar.

διαληπτέον, verb. Adj. of διαλαμβάνω, *one must distinguish*, Plat.

διαλλαγή, ή, (διαλλάσσω) *interchange, exchange*, Eur.　　II. *a change* from enmity to friendship, *a reconciliation, truce*, Hdt., Ar. ; in pl., Eur. ; διαλλαγαὶ πρός τινα Dem.

διάλλαγμα, ατος, τό, *a substitute, changeling*, Eur. ; and

διαλλακτήρ, ό, *a mediator*, Hdt., Aesch. ; and

διαλλακτής, οῦ, ό, = διαλλακτήρ, Eur., Thuc.　From

δι-αλλάσσω, Att. -ττω : f. ξω : pf. δι-ήλλαχα :—Pass., f. δι-αλλαχθήσομαι and -αλλάγήσομαι: aor. 1 -ηλλάχθην and -ηλλάγην [ἅ] : pf. -ήλλαγμαι :　I. Med. *to change one with another, interchange*, Hdt. : absol. *to make an exchange*, Xen.　　II. Act. *to exchange*, i. e., 1. *to give in exchange*, τί τινι Eur. ; τι ἀντί τινος Plat.　2. *to take in exchange*, Id.; δ. τὴν χώραν *to change* one land *for* another,

i. e. *to pass through* a land, Xen.　3. simply, *to change*, τοὺς ναυάρχους Id.　III. *to change enmity for friendship, to reconcile* one to another, τινά τινι Thuc. ; τινὰ πρός τινα Ar. ; or c. acc. pl. only, Eur., etc. : absol. *to make friends*, Plat. :—Pass. *to be reconciled, to be made friends*, Aesch., etc.　IV. intr., c. dat. pers. et acc. rei, *to differ from* one *in* a thing, διαλλάσσειν οὐδὲν τοῖσι ἑτέροισι Hdt. : absol., τὸ διαλλάσσον *the difference*, Thuc.　V. Pass. *to be different*, Lat. *distare*, Id.

δι-άλλομαι, aor. 1 -ηλάμην, Dep. *to leap across*, τάφρον Xen.

δια-λογίζομαι, f. Att. ιοῦμαι, Dep. *to balance accounts*, πρός τινα Dem.　　2. *to take full account of, to stop to consider*, Id.: *to distinguish between*, Aeschin.　II. *to converse, debate, argue*, περί τινος Xen.　Hence

διαλογισμός, ό, *a balancing of accounts*, Dem.

διάλογος, ό, (διαλέγομαι) *a conversation, dialogue*, Plat.

δια-λοιδορέομαι, f. ήσομαι, Dep. *to rail furiously at*, τινι Hdt. ; διαλοιδορηθείς Dem.

δια-λυμαίνομαι, Dep. *to maltreat shamefully, undo utterly*, Hdt., Eur.　　2. *to cheat grossly*, Ar.　3. *to falsify, corrupt*, Id.　　II. no Act. occurs, but pf. part. διαλελυμασμένος is used in pass. sense, Hdt.; aor. 1 διελυμάνθην Eur.

διάλυσις [ῠ], εως, ή, (διαλύω) *a loosing one from another, separating, parting*, τῆς ψυχῆς καὶ τοῦ σώματος Plat ; δ. τοῦ σώματος its *dissolution*, Id. ; ἡ δ. τῆς γεφύρας *the breaking* down the bridge, Thuc. : *the disbanding* of troops, Xen. ; ἡ δ. τῆς ἀγορᾶς *the time* of its *breaking up*, Hdt. ; τὴν δ. ἐποιήσαντο *broke off* the action, Thuc. ; δ. γάμου *a divorce*, Plut.　II. *an ending, cessation*, κακῶν Eur. ; πολεμίου Thuc. : absol. *a cessation of hostilities, peace*, Dem.

διαλυτέον, verb. Adj. *one must dissolve*, φιλίαν Arist.

διαλύτης, οῦ, ό, *a dissolver, breaker-up*, Thuc. ; and

διαλυτός, όν, *capable of dissolution*, Plat.　From

δια-λύω, f. -λύσω [ῠ] : pf. -λέλυκα : Pass., aor. 1 -ελύθην [ῠ] : pf. -λέλυμαι :—*to loose one from another, to part asunder, undo*, Hdt. : *to dissolve* an assembly, Id., Thuc., etc. ; τὴν σκηνὴν εἰς κοίτην δ. *to break up* the party and go to bed, Xen. ; δ. τὴν στρατιάν *to disband* it, Thuc. :—Pass., of an assembly, *to break up*, Hdt., etc. : of a man, *to die*, Xen.　2. *to dissolve* into its elements, *to break up*, Plat.　3. *to put an end to* friendship, *break off* a truce, Thuc., etc. :—so in Med., διαλύσασθαι ξεινίην Hdt.　4. *to put an end to* enmity, Thuc. ; and in Med., Dem., etc.　b. c. acc. pers. *to reconcile*, τινὰ πρός τινα Id. ; οὐ γὰρ ἦν ὁ διαλύσων Thuc. :—Pass. and Med., διαλύεσθαι νείκους *to be parted* from quarrel, i. e. *to be reconciled*, Eur., Xen., etc.　5. generally, *to put an end to, do away with*, διαβολήν Thuc. ; so in Med., Id., etc.　6. *to solve* a difficulty, Plat.　7. δ. τιμάς *to pay the full value, discharge* a debt, Hdt., etc. : c. acc. pers. *to pay* him *off*, Dem.　II. absol. *to slacken one's hold, undo*, Theocr.

δι-αλφῑτόω, f. ώσω, (ἄλφιτον) *to fill full of barley meal*, Ar.

διαλωβάομαι, Dep. strengthd. for λωβάομαι, Plut.

δι-ᾰμᾰθύνω, aor. 1 -ημάθῡνα, *to grind to powder, utterly destroy*, Aesch.

δια-μαλάττω, f. ξω, strengthd. for μαλάττω, Luc.

δια-μαντεύομαι, Dep. to determine by an oracle, τι Plat.

δι-αμαρτάνω, f. -αμαρτήσομαι : aor. 2 -ήμαρτον :—to go astray from, τῆς ὁδοῦ Thuc. : to fail of obtaining, τινός Id., Dem. 2. absol. to fail utterly, Plat.

δι-αμαρτία, ἡ, a total mistake, Plut. ; δ. τῶν ἡμερῶν a wrong reckoning of the days, Thuc.

δια-μαρτῠρέω, f. ήσω, as Att. law-term, to use a διαμαρτυρία (q. v.), Dem. 2. c. inf. to affirm by a διαμαρτυρία that a thing is, c. acc. et inf., Id. : Pass., τὰ διαμαρτυρηθέντα things so affirmed, Isocr.

δια-μαρτῠρία, ἡ, as Att. law-term, evidence given to prevent a case from coming to trial, Dem., etc.

δια-μαρτῠρομαι [ῡ], Dep. to protest solemnly, Lat. obtestari, Dem. ; δ. μή . . , c. inf., Id. :—τινι μὴ ποιεῖν to protest against his doing, Aeschin. 2. generally, to protest, asseverate, Plat. 3. absol. to beg earnestly, conjure, Xen.

δια-μάσσω, Att. -ττω, f. -ξω, to knead thoroughly, knead well, Ar.

δια-μαστῑγόω, f. ώσω, to scourge severely, Plat.

δια-μαστροπεύω, f. σω, to pander, δ. τὴν ἡγεμονίαν γάμοις to bargain away the empire by a marriage, Plut.

διαμᾰχητέον or -ετέον, verb. Adj. one must deny absolutely, Plat. From

δια-μάχομαι [μᾰ], f. -μαχέσομαι, Dep. to fight or strive with, struggle against, τινι or πρός τινι Hdt., etc. ; πρός τι Dem. ; δ. μὴ μεταγνῶναι ὑμᾶς I resist to the uttermost your change of opinion, Thuc. ; δ. τὸ μὴ θανεῖν Eur. 2. to fight one with another, Id. 3. to fight it out, contend obstinately, Lat. depugnare, Ar. 4. to exert oneself greatly, ὅπως τι γένηται Plat. 5. in argument, to contend or maintain that . . , δ. τι μὴ εἶναι Thuc. ; or without μή, Plat.

δι-αμάω, f. ήσω, to cut through, Il., Eur. 2. to scrape away, Id. ; Med., διαμᾶσθαι τὸν κάχληκα to get the gravel scraped away, Thuc.

δια-μεθίημι, f. -μεθήσω, to let go, give up, leave off, Eur.

δι-αμείβω, f. ψω, to exchange, τι πρός τι one thing with another, Plat. ; so in Med., διαμείβεσθαί τί τινος or ἀντί τινος, Solon, Plat. :—διαμεῖψαι Ἀσίαν Εὐρώπης to take Asia in exchange for Europe, i. e. to pass into Asia, Eur. 2. δ. ὁδόν to finish a journey, Aesch. ; so in Med., Id. 3. in Med., also, to alter, Hdt.

δια-μειρᾰκιεύομαι, Dep. to strive hotly with, τινί Plut.

διάμειψις, εως, ἡ, (διαμείβω) an exchange, Plut.

δια-μελαίνω, f. ἀνῶ, to make quite black, Plat.

δια-μελεϊστί, Adv. limb by limb, limb-meal, Od.

διαμέλλησις, εως, ἡ, a being on the point to do, πολλὴ δ. φυλακῆς long postponement of precautionary measures, Thuc.

δια-μέλλω, f. -μελλήσω, to be always going to do, i. e. to delay continually, Thuc.

δια-μέμφομαι, f. -ψομαι, Dep. to blame greatly, Thuc.

δια-μένω, f. -μενῶ : pf. -μεμένηκα : to remain by, stand by, τινί Xen. :—to persevere, ἔν τινι Plat. ; ἐπί τινι Xen. :—absol. to stand firm, Dem. :—c. part., δ. λέγων to continue speaking, Id.

δια-μερίζω, f. Att. ιῶ, to distribute, Plat. II. to divide : Med. to divide or part among themselves, N. T. Hence

διαμερισμός, ὁ, division, dissension, N. T.

δια-μετρέω, f. ήσω, to measure through, out or off, χῶρον δ. to measure lists for combat, Il. :—Pass., ἡμέρα διαμεμετρημένη measured by the clepsydra, Dem. 2. to measure out in portions, distribute, Xen., etc. :—Med. to have measured out to one, receive as one's share, Orac. ap. Hdt., Xen. Hence

διαμετρητός, ή, όν, measured out or off, Il.

διά-μετρον, τό, a measured allowance, rations, Plut.

διάμετρος (sc. γραμμή), ἡ, the diameter or diagonal of a parallelogram, Plat. ; κατὰ διάμετρον diametrically, Id. ; so, ἐκ διαμέτρου Luc. II. a rule for drawing the diameter, Ar.

δια-μηχᾰνάομαι, f. ήσομαι, Dep. to bring about, contrive, Ar., Plat.

δια-μῑκρολογέομαι, f. ήσομαι, Dep. to deal meanly, πρός τινα Plut.

δι-ᾰμιλλάομαι, f. ήσομαι : aor. 1 -ημιλλήθην : Dep. :—to contend hotly, strive earnestly, τινι or πρός τινα Plat. ; περί τινος Id.

δια-μιμνήσκομαι, pf. -μέμνημαι, Dep. to keep in memory, Xen.

δια-μῑσέω, f. ήσω, to hate bitterly, Arist., Plut.

διαμιστύλλω, aor. 1 -εμιστῡλα, to cut up piecemeal, Hdt.

διαμνημονεύω, f. σω, to call to mind, remember, Hdt. ; c. gen., Plat. ; c. acc., Xen., etc. 2. to record, mention, Thuc. : Pass., διαμνημονεύεται ἔχειν he is mentioned as having, Xen.

δια-μοιράω, f. ήσω, to divide, rend asunder, Eur. ; so in Med., Id. II. in Med., also, to portion out, distribute, Od.

διαμπάξ, Adv. strengthd. for διά, right through, through and through, c. gen., Aesch., Eur. ; also c. acc., Xen.

δι-αμπερές, (ἀμ-πείρω = ἀνα-πείρω) Adv. 1. of Place, through and through, right through, clean through, c. gen., Il., Soph. :—c. acc., Il., Aesch. II. absol. without break, continuously, Hom. 2. of Time, throughout, for ever, Id. ; διαμπερὲς αἰεί for ever and aye, Il.

δια-μῠδᾰλέος, α, ον, drenching, Aesch.

δια-μῡθολογέω, f. ήσω, to communicate by word, to express in speech, Aesch. : to converse, Plat.

δια-μυλλαίνω, f. ἀνῶ, to make mouths (in scorn), Ar.

δι-αμφίδιος [φῐ], ον, (ἀμφίς) utterly different, Aesch.

δι-αμφισβητέω, f. ήσω, to dispute or disagree, πρός τινα περὶ τινος Dem. :—Pass., τὰ ἀμφισβητούμενα the points at issue, Id. Hence

διαμφισβήτησις, εως, ἡ, a disputing, dispute, Plut.

δι-αναγιγνώσκω, f. -γνώσομαι, to read through, Isocr.

δι-αναπαύομαι, Med. to rest awhile, Plat.

δια-νάσσω, f. ξω, to stop chinks : to caulk ships, Strab.

δια-ναυμᾰχέω, f. ήσω, to maintain a sea-fight, Hdt.

δια-νάω, to flow through, percolate, Plut.

δι-άνδιχα, Adv. two ways, διάνδιχα μερμηρίζειν to halt between two opinions, Il. ; διάνδιχα δῶκε gave one of two things, Ib. ; δ. ἔαξα broke it in twain, Theocr.

διᾱνεκής, ές, Dor. and Att. for διηνεκής.

διανέμησις, εως, ἡ, (διανέμω) a distribution, Plut.

διανεμητέον, verb. Adj. of διανέμω, one must distribute, Thuc.

διανεμητικός, ή, όν, (διανέμω) distributive, Plat.

δι-ανέμομαι, Pass. to flutter in the wind, Luc., Anth.

διανέμω, f. -νεμῶ : pf. -νενέμηκα :—to distribute, af-

portion, τί τινι Ar., Plat. :—Med. *to divide among themselves*, Plat., Arist. :—Pass., aor. 1 inf. διανεμηθῆναι *to be spread abroad*, N. T.

δια-νέομαι, Pass. *to go through*, Anth.

δια-νέω, f. -νεύσομαι, *to swim across*, ἐς Σαλαμῖνα Hdt.   II. c. acc. *to swim through*, Plat.

δια-νήχομαι, f. ξομαι, Dep. = διανέω, Plut.

δι-ανθίζω, f. ίσω, *to adorn with flowers*, Luc. :—Pass. *to be variegated*, Plut.

δι-ανίσταμαι, Pass. with aor. 2 and pf. act. *to stand aloof from, depart from*, τινος Thuc.

δια-νοέομαι, f. -νοήσομαι : aor. 1 διενοήθην : pf. διανενόημαι : Dep. : (νοέω) :—*to be minded, intend, purpose* to do, c. inf., Hdt., etc.   II. *to think over* or *of*, Lat. *meditari*, τι Id. : c. acc. et inf. *to think* or *suppose* that, Plat.   III. with Adv. *to be minded* or *disposed* so and so, καλῶς, κακῶς δ. Id. Hence

διανόημα, ατος, τό, *a thought, notion*, Plat. ; and

διανοητικός, ή, όν, *of* or *for thinking, intellectual*, Plat., Arist. ; and

διάνοιά, ή, *a thought, intention, purpose*, Hdt., Att. ; διάνοιαν ἔχειν = διανοεῖσθαι, c. inf., Thuc.   2. *a thought, notion, opinion*, Lat. *cogitatum*, Hdt., Plat.   II. *intelligence, understanding*, Id.   III. *the thought* or *meaning* of a word or passage, Id. ; τῇ διανοίᾳ as *regards the sense*, Dem.

δι-ανοίγω, f. ξω, *to open*, Plat.   II. *to open and explain*, τὰς γραφάς N. T.

διανομεύς, έως, ὁ, (διανέμω) *a distributer*, Plut.

διανομή, ή, (διανέμω) Aesch., Plat.

δι-ανταῖος, α, ον, *extending throughout, right through*, διανταία πληγή *a home-thrust*, Aesch. ; so, διανταίαν οὐτᾶν Id. ; δ. βέλος Id. ; ὀδύνα Eur. :—metaph., μοῖρα δ. *destiny that strikes home*, Aesch.

δι-αντλέω, f. ήσω, *to drain out, exhaust* : metaph., like Lat. *exhaurire, to drink even to the dregs, endure to the end*, Eur.

δια-νυκτερεύω, f. σω, *to pass the night*, Xen.

δι-ανύω, later -ανύτω [ῠ] : f. -ανύσω [ῠ] :—*to bring quite to an end, accomplish, finish*, κέλευθον, ὁδὸν h. Hom., etc. ;—hence (ὁδόν omitted), διὰ πόντον ἀνύσσας *having finished one's course over* the sea, Hes. :—c. part. *to finish doing* a thing, Od., Hdt.

δια-ξιφίζομαι, (ξίφος) Dep. *to fight to the death*, Ar.

δια-παιδᾰγωγέω, f. ήσω, *to attend children* : generally, *to entertain, amuse*, Plut. ; δ. τὸν καιρόν, Lat. *fallere tempus*, Id.

δια-παιδεύομαι, Pass. *to go through a course of education*, Xen.

δια-πᾰλαίω, f. σω, *to continue wrestling, go on wrestling*, Xen.

δια-πάλη [ᾰ], ή, *a hard struggle*, Plut.

δια-πάλλω, aor. 1 -έπηλα, *to distribute by lot*, Aesch.

δια-πᾰλύνω [ῠ], f. ῠνῶ, *to shiver, shatter*, Eur., Ar.

διαπαντός or διὰ παντός, *throughout*.

δια-παπταίνω, *to look timidly round*, Plut.

δια-παρα-τρίβή, ή, *violent contention*, N. T.

δια-παρθενεύω, f. σω, *to deflower a maiden*, Hdt.

δια-πασσάλεύω, Att. διαπαττ-, f. σω, *to stretch out by nailing the extremities*, as in crucifixion, Hdt. : *to stretch out* a hide *for tanning*, Ar.

δια-πάσσω, Att. -ττω : f. -πάσω [ᾰ] : aor. 1 -έπασα :

—*to sprinkle*, δ. τοῦ ψήγματος ἐς τὰς τρίχας *to sprinkle some dust on the hair*, Hdt.

δια-παύω, f. σω, *to make to cease* :—Med. *to rest between times, pause*, Plat. :—Pass. *to cease to exist*, Xen.

δι-απειλέω, f. ήσω, *to threaten violently*, Hdt. :—so in Med., Aeschin.

δια-πεινάω, inf. -πεινῆν, *to hunger one against the other*, so *to have a starving-match*, διαπεινᾶμες (Dor. 1 pl.), with a play on διαπίνομεν, Ar.

διά-πειρα, ή, *an experiment, trial*, Hdt.

δια-πειράομαι, f. άσομαι : aor. 1 -επειράθην [ᾰ] : pf. -πεπείραμαι : Dep. :—*to make trial* or *proof of, to have experience* of a thing, c. gen., Hdt. ; c. acc., Thuc.

δια-πείρω, f. -περῶ, *to drive through*, τι διά τινος Eur.

δια-πέμπω, f. ψω, *to send off in different directions, send to and fro, send about* or *round*, Hdt., Thuc.   II. *to send over* or *across*, Ar., Thuc. : *to transmit*, ἐπιστολήν Id. ; so in Med., Id.

δια-πενθέω, f. ήσω, *to mourn through*, ἐνιαυτόν Plut.

δια-περαίνω, f. ᾰνῶ, *to bring to a conclusion, discuss thoroughly*, Eur. ; διαπέραινέ μοι *tell me all*, Id. :—Med., διαπεράνασθαι κρίσιν *to get* a question *decided*, Id.

δια-περάω, f. ώσω, *to take across, ferry over*, Plut. :—Pass. *to go across*, Thuc. :—διεπεραιώθη ξίφη *swords were unsheathed*, Soph.

δια-περάω, f. άσω [ᾰ], *to go over* or *across, ῥοάς, οἶδμα* Eur. ; δ. πόλιν *to pass through* it, Ar. ; also, διαπερᾶν Μολοσσίαν *to reign through all* Molossia, Eur.   2. *to pass through, pierce*, Id.   II. trans. *to carry over*, Luc.

δια-πέρθω, aor. 2 -έπρᾰθον, Ep. inf. -πρᾰθέειν : aor. 2 med. -επρᾰθετο in pass. sense :—*to destroy utterly, sack, lay waste*, of cities, Hom.

δι-απέρχομαι, Dep. *to slip away one by one*, Dem.

δια-πέτᾰμαι or -πέτομαι, f. -πτήσομαι : aor. 2 -επτάμην and -επτόμην, and in act. form -έπτην :—*to fly through*, Il., Eur. : c. acc., Id., Ar. ; διὰ τῆς πόλεως Id.   II. *to fly away, vanish*, Eur., Plat.

δια-πεύθομαι, poët. for διαπυνθάνομαι, Aesch.

δια-πήγνυμι, f. -πήξω, *to fix thoroughly* :—Med., δ. σχεδίας *to get* rafts *put together*, Luc.

δια-πηδάω, f. -πηδήσομαι, *to leap across*, τάφρον Ar., Xen. :—absol. *to take a leap*, Id.

δια-πιαίνω, f. ᾰνῶ, *to make very fat*, Theocr.

δια-πίμπλᾰμαι, Pass. *to be quite full of*, τινός Thuc.

δια-πίνω [ῑ], f. -πίομαι : aor. :—*to drink one against another, challenge at drinking*, Hdt., Plat.

δια-πιπράσκω, *to sell off*, Plut.

δια-πίπτω, f. -πεσοῦμαι, *to fall away, slip away, escape*, Xen.   2. of reports and rumours, *to spread abroad*, Id.   II. *to fall asunder, crumble in pieces*, Plat.   2. *to fail utterly, go quite wrong*, Ar., Aeschin.

δια-πιστεύω, f. σω, *to entrust to one in confidence*, τί τινι Aeschin. : Pass. *to have a thing entrusted to* one, Dem.

δι-απιστέω, f. ήσω, *to distrust utterly*, τινι Dem.

δια-πλάσσω, Att. -ττω, f. -πλάσω [ᾰ], *to form completely, mould*, Plut., etc.

δια-πλᾰτύνω [ῠ], f. -ῠνῶ, *to make very wide, dilate*, Xen.

δια-πλέκω, f. ξω, *to interweave, to weave together, plait*, Hdt.   II. metaph., δ. τὸν βίον, Lat. *per-*

texere vitam, to finish the web of one's life, Id.: then, simply, to pass life, live, Ar.

δια-πλέω, f. -πλεύσομαι :—to sail across, Thuc.; εἰς Αἴγιναν Ar. : metaph., δ. βίον to make life's voyage, Plat.

δια-πληκτίζομαι, Dep. to spar with, skirmish with, τινι Plut., Luc.

δια-πλήσσω, Att. -ττω, f. ξω, to break or cleave in pieces, Il.

διά-πλοος, ον, contr. -πλους, ουν : 1. as Adj. sailing continually, διάπλουν καθίστασαν λεών they kept them at the oar, Aesch. II. as Subst., διάπλους, ὁ, a voyage across, passage, πρὸς τόπον Thuc. 2. room for sailing through, passage, δυοῖν νεοῖν for two ships abreast, Id.

δια-πνέω, Ep. -πνείω, f. -πνεύσομαι, to blow through : —Pass., αὔραις διαπνεῖσθαι Xen. II. to breathe between times, get breath, Plut. III. intr. to disperse in vapour, Plat.

δια-ποικίλλω, f. -ιλῶ, to variegate, adorn, Plut.

δια-πολεμέω, f. ήσω, to carry the war through, end the war, Lat. debellare, Hdt.; δ. τινι to fight it out with one, Xen. :—Pass., διαπεπολεμήσεται πόλεμος the war will be at an end, Thuc. II. to carry on the war, continue it, Id. III. to spend some time at war, Plut. Hence

διαπολέμησις, εως, ἡ, a finishing of the war, Thuc.

δια-πολιορκέω, f. ήσω, to besiege continually, to block-ade, Thuc.

δια-πολιτεύομαι, Dep. to be a political rival, Aeschin.

δια-πομπεύω, f. σω, to carry the procession to an end, Luc.

διαπομπή, ἡ, (διαπέμπω) a sending to and fro, interchange of messages, negotiation, Thuc.

δια-πονέω, f. ήσω, to work out with labour, Lat. elaboro, Plat., etc. :—Med. to get worked out, Id., Xen. : —Pass. to be managed, governed, Aesch. 2. Pass. also, to be much grieved, N. T. II. intr. to work hard, toil constantly, Xen., Arist.; οἱ διαπονούμενοι the hardworking, hardy, Xen. Hence

διαπόνημα, ατος, τό, hard labour, exercise, Plat.

διά-πονος, ον, of persons, exercised, Plut.; τι Id. II. of things, toilsome :—Adv. -νως, with toil, Id.

δια-πόντιος, ον, beyond sea, Lat. transmarinus, Aesch., Thuc.

δια-πορεύω, f. σω, to carry over, set across, Xen. II. Pass., with f. med. and aor. 1 pass. διεπορεύθην, to pass across, εἰς Εὔβοιαν Hdt. : c. acc. cogn. to go through, βίον Plat.

δι-απορέω, f. ήσω, to be quite at a loss, Plat. :—so in Med., with aor. and pf. pass., Id. II. to raise an ἀπορία, start a difficulty, Arist. :—so in Med., Plat. : —Pass. to be matter of doubt or question, Id., Arist.

δια-πορθέω, f. ήσω, = διαπέρθω, Il., Thuc. :—Pass. to be utterly ruined, Trag.

δια-πορθμεύω, f. ώσω, to carry over or across a river or strait, Hdt. : to carry a message from one to another, Id. 2. metaph. to translate, interpret, Plat. II. δ. ποταμόν, of ferry-boats, to ply across a river, Hdt.

δι-αποστέλλω, f. -στελῶ, to send off in different directions, dispatch, Dem.

δια-πραγματεύομαι, f. -εύσομαι, Dep. to examine thoroughly, Plat. II. to gain by trading, N. T.

διάπραξις, εως, ἡ, dispatch of business, Plat. From

δια-πράσσω, Att. -ττω, Ion. -πρήσσω : f. -πράξω : —to pass over, c. gen., διέπρησσον πεδίοιο they made their way over the plain, Il.; also, δ. κέλευθον to finish a journey, Od. :—also of Time, c. part., ἤματα διέπρησσον πολεμίζων went through days in fighting, Il.; διαπρήξαιμι λέγων should finish speaking, Od. II. to bring about, accomplish, effect, settle, Hdt.; δ. τί τινι to get a thing done for a man, Id. : —so in Med., Id.; pf. pass. in med. sense, Plat., etc. :—strictly in sense of Med., to effect for oneself, gain one's point, Hdt., Xen. : c. inf. to manage that, Id. III. to make an end of, destroy, slay, Lat. conficere, in part. pf. pass. διαπεπραγμένος, Trag.

δια-πρεπής, ές, (πρέπω) eminent, distinguished, illustrious, Thuc.; τινί or τι in a thing, Eur.; τὸ δ. magnificence, Thuc.

δια-πρέπω, f. ψω, to appear prominent or conspicuous, to strike the eye, h. Hom.; διαπρέπον κακόν Aesch. 2. to be eminent above others, c. gen., Eur.

δια-πρεσβεύομαι, Dep. to send embassies to different places, Xen.

δια-πρηστεύω, v. διαδρηστεύω.

δια-πρίω [ιω], f. -πριοῦμαι, to saw quite through, saw asunder, Ar. :—metaph., διεπρίοντο ταῖς καρδίαις were cut to the heart, N. T. II. δ. τοὺς ὀδόντας to gnash the teeth, Luc.

διαπρό or διὰ πρό, right through, c. gen., Hom.

διαπρύσιος [ῠ], α, ον, (διαπεράω) going through, piercing : neut. as Adv., πρῶν πεδίοιο διαπρύσιον τετυχηκώς a hill running far into the plain, Il. 2. of sound, piercing, thrilling, ἤϋσεν διαπρύσιον he gave a piercing cry, Ib. II. later as Adj., of sound, δ. ὄτοβος Soph.; κέλαδος Eur. 2. metaph., δ. κεραϊστής a manifest thief, h. Hom.

δια-πταίω, f. σω, to stutter much, Luc.

δια-πτάσθαι or -πτέσθαι, aor. 2 inf. of διαπέτομαι.

δια-πτοέω, f. ήσω : Ep. aor. διεπτοίησα :—to scare away, startle and scatter with panic, fear, Od., Eur.

δια-πτύσσω, Att. -ττω, f. ξω, to open and spread out, to unfold, disclose, Soph., Eur. Hence

δια-πτυχή [ῠ], ἡ, a fold, folding leaf, Eur.

δια-πτύω, f. ύσω [ῠ], to spit upon, τινά Dem.

δια-πυκτεύω, f. σω, to spar, fight with, τινί Xen.

δια-πυνθάνομαι, f. -πεύσομαι : pf. -πέπυσμαι : aor. 2 ἐπυθόμην [ῠ] : Dep. :—to search out by questioning, to find out, τι Plat.; τί τινος something from one, Plut.

διά-πυρος, ον, (διά, πῦρ) red-hot, Anaxag. ap. Xen., Eur. 2. metaph. hot, fiery, Plat. Hence

δια-πυρόω, f. ώσω, to set on fire, Eur., in Med.

δια-πυρσεύω, f. σω, to throw a light over, c. acc., Plut.

δια-πωλέω, f. ήσω, to sell publicly, Xen.

δι-αράσσω, f. ξω, to strike through, Hes.

δι-άργεμος, ον, fleckt with white, Babr.

δι-αρθρόω, f. ώσω, to divide by joints, to articulate, Plat. :—Pass., pf. part. διηρθρωμένος well-jointed, well-knit, Id. 2. to endue with articulate speech, Luc.; Med., φωνὴν διηρθρώσατο invented articulate speech, Plat. 3. to complete in detail, Arist.

δι-αριθμέω, f. ήσω, to reckon up one by one, enumerate, Eur. 2. to draw distinctions, distinguish, Plat. : —Pass. to be distinguished, Aeschin.

δι-αρκέω, f. έσω, to have full strength, be quite sufficient, Xen., etc.; δ. πρός τινα to be a match for, Luc. 2. in point of Time, to hold out, endure, last, Aesch.; c. part., δ. πολιορκούμενος Xen. II. to supply nourishment, τινί Plut. Hence

διαρκής, ές, quite sufficient, Thuc. 2. lasting, Dem. :—Adv. -κῶς, Sup. διαρκέστατα in complete competence, Xen.

δι-αρμόζω or -ττω, f. σω, to distribute in various places, dispose, Eur.

δι-αρπάζω, f. άσομαι, to tear in pieces, Il.: to efface, τὰ ἴχνη Xen. II. to spoil, plunder, πόλιν Hdt. 2. to seize as plunder, χρήματα Id.

διαρ-ραίνομαι, Pass. to flow all ways, Soph.

διαρ-ραίω, f. σω, to dash in pieces, destroy, Hom. :—Pass., c. f. med., to be destroyed, perish, Il.; διαρραισθέντας Aesch.

διαρ-ρέω, f. διαρ-ρεύσομαι: aor. 2 δι-ερρύην: pf. δι-ερρύηκα:—to flow through, Hdt. 2. to slip through, τῶν χειρῶν Luc. 3. of a vessel, to leak, Id. 4. of a report, to spread abroad, Plut. 5. χείλη διερρυηκότα gaping lips, Ar. II. to fall away like water, die or waste away, χάρις διαρρεῖ Soph.; of one diseased, Ar.; of money, Dem.

διαρ-ρήγνῡμι, f. -ρήξω :—Pass., f. 2 -ρᾰγήσομαι: aor. 2 δι-ερράγην [ᾰ]:—to break through, cleave asunder, Il. (in Med.), Hdt., Soph.:—Pass. to burst, with eating, Xen.; with passion, Ar.; διαρρᾱγείης, as a curse, ' split you!' Id. :—pf. διέρρωγα, in same sense, Plat.

διαρρήδην, Adv. (v. διεῖπον) expressly, distinctly, explicitly, Lat. nominatim, h. Hom., Att.

διάρριμμα, ατος, τό, a casting about, Xen. From

διαρ-ρίπτω, poët. δια-ρίπτω: Ion. impf. διαρ-ρίπτασκον: f. ψω: in Att. also a pres. διαρριπτέω :—to cast or shoot through, Od. 2. to cast or throw about, a dog, to wag the tail, Xen. 3. to throw about, as nuts or money among a crowd, Ar. II. intr. to plunge, Xen. Hence

διάρριψις, εως, ἡ, a scattering, Xen.

διαρροή, ἡ, (διαρρέω) that through which something flows, a pipe, πνεύματος διαρροαί the wind-pipe, Eur.

διαρ-ροθέω, f. ήσω, to roar through, διαρροθῆσαι κάκην τινί to inspire fear by clamour, Aesch.

διάρροια, ἡ, (διαρρέω) diarrhoea, Thuc.

διαρ-ροιζέω, f. ήσω, to whizz through, c. gen., Soph.

διαρ-ρύδαν, Dor. for -ρύδην, Adv. flowing away, vanishing, Trag.

διαρ-ρυῆναι, aor. 2 pass. inf. of διαρρέω.

διάρρῠτος, ον, intersected by streams, Strab.

διαρρώξ, ῶγος, ὁ, ἡ, (διαρρήγνυμι) rent asunder, Eur.

δι-αρταμέω, f. ήσω, to cut limb from limb, Aesch.

δι-αρτάω, f. ήσω, to suspend, interrupt, Plut. II. to separate, Id.

δια-σαίνω, strengthd. for σαίνω, to fawn upon, Xen.

δια-σαίρω, strengthd. for σαίρω: part. pf. διασεσηρώς, grinning like a dog, sneering, Plut.

δια-σᾰλᾰκωνίζω, f. σω, strengthd. for σαλακωνεύω, Ar.

διᾰ-σᾰλεύω, f. σω, to shake violently: to reduce to anarchy, Luc.; διασεσαλευμένος unsteady, Id.

δια-σᾰφέω, f. ήσω, (σαφής) to make quite clear, shew plainly, Eur., Plat.

δια-σᾰφηνίζω, f. ίσω, to make quite clear, Xen.

διάσειστος, ον, shaken about, Aeschin. From

δια-σείω, f. σω, to shake violently, τι Plat., δ. τῇ οὐρᾷ to wag with the tail, i. e. to keep wagging the tail, Xen. 2. to confound, throw into confusion, Hdt. 3. to extort money from a person, N. T.

δια-σεύομαι, 3 sing. Ep. aor. 2 pass. διέσσυτο: Pass. to dart through, rush across, c. gen., Il.; c. acc., δ. λαὸν Ἀχαιῶν Ib.

δια-σημαίνω, f. ᾰνῶ, to mark out, point out clearly, Hdt., Xen. 2. absol. to beckon, τῇ χειρί Arist.

διά-σημος, ον, (σῆμα) clear, distinct: neut. pl. as Adv., διάσημα θρηνεῖ Soph. II. conspicuous, Plut.

δια-σήπομαι, Pass. with pf. διασέσηπα, to putrefy, decay, Luc.

Διάσια, τά, the festival of Zeus μειλίχιος, Ar.

δια-σίζω, to hiss or whistle violently, Arist.

δια-σιωπάω, f. ήσομαι, to remain silent, Eur., Xen. II. trans. to pass over in silence, Eur.

δια-σκανδῑκίζω, properly, to dose with chervil (σκάνδιξ): in Com. for διευριπιδίζω, to come Euripides over one (his mother was a herb-seller), Ar.

δια-σκάπτω, f. ψω, to dig through, c. gen., Plut.

δια-σκεδάννῡμι, f. Att. -σκεδῶ: aor. 1 -εσκέδᾰσα, 3 sing. opt. -σκεδᾰσείεν:—to scatter abroad, scatter to the winds, disperse, Lat. dissipare, Od., Soph. 2. to disband an army, Hdt.: Pass. to be dispersed, aor. 1 and pf. part. διασκεδασθέντες, διεσκεδασμένοι Id.

δια-σκέπτομαι, late form of διασκοπέω, Luc.

δια-σκευάζω, f. άσω, to get quite ready, equip, Luc. :—Pass., pf. part. διεσκευασμένοι dressed, Plut. : —Med. to prepare for oneself, provide, Thuc. : to equip oneself, Xen. II. Med., διασκευασάμενος τὴν οὐσίαν having disposed of one's property, Dem.

διασκευρέομαι, Med. to set all in order, Plat.

δι-ασκέω, f. ήσω, to deck out, Luc.

δια-σκηνάω or -έω, f. ήσω, to disperse and retire each to his quarters (σκηναί), to take up one's quarters, Xen. II. to leave a comrade's tent, Luc. Hence

διασκηνητέον, verb. Adj. one must take up one's quarters, Xen.

δια-σκηνόω, f. ώσω, = διασκηνάω 1, Xen.

δια-σκηρίπτω, to prop on each side, to prop up, Anth.

δια-σκίδνημι, = διασκεδάννυμι, Il., Hdt. :—Pass., Luc.

δια-σκιρτάω, f. ήσω, to leap about or away, Plut.

δια-σκοπέω, f. -σκέψομαι: pf. δι-έσκεμμαι:—to look at in different ways, to examine or consider well, Hdt., Eur., etc.; also in Med., διασκοπεῖσθαι πρός τι Thuc. II. absol. to keep watching, Xen.

δια-σκοπιάομαι, Dep. to watch as from a σκοπιά, to spy out, Il. :—to discern, distinguish, Ib.

δια-σκορπίζω, f. σω, to scatter abroad, N. T.

δια-σκώπτομαι, f. ψομαι, Med. to jest one with another, pass jokes to and fro, Xen.

δια-σμάω, Ion. -έω, to wipe or rinse out, Hdt.

δια-σμήχω, to rub well: aor. 1 pass. -εσμήχθην, Ar.

δια-σμῑλεύω, f. σω, to polish off with the chisel: metaph., Anth.

δια-σοφίζομαι, f. -ίσομαι, Dep. to quibble like a sophist, Ar.

δια-σπᾰθάω, f. ήσω, to squander away, Plut.

διασπάρακτός, ή, όν, torn to pieces, Eur. From

δια-σπᾰράσσω, Att. -ττω, f. ξω, to rend in sunder or in pieces, Aesch.
διάσπασμα, ατος, τό, a gap, Plut. From
δια-σπάω, f. -σπάσω, Att. -σπάσομαι: aor. 1 -έσπάσα: —Pass., aor. 1 -εσπάσθην, pf. -έσπασμαι:—to tear asunder, part forcibly, Lat. divellere, Hdt., Eur., etc.; δ. τὸ σταύρωμα to tear down the palisade, Xen.: —Pass., pf. part. διεσπασμένος torn asunder, Hdt., Dem. 2. in military sense, to separate part of an army from the rest, Xen.:—Pass., στράτευμα διεσπασμένον scattered and in disorder, Thuc.;—of soldiers, also, to be distributed in quarters, Xen. 3. metaph. to distract, throw into disorder, Id.
δια-σπείρω, f. -σπερῶ:—to scatter abroad, throw about, of money, Hdt.; δ. λόγον Xen.: —Pass., Soph.:—Pass. to be scattered abroad, aor. 2 διεσπάρην [ᾰ], Id.; of soldiers, Thuc. Hence
διασπορά, ἡ, (διασπείρω) dispersion; collectively, = οἱ διεσπαρμένοι, N. T.
δια-σπουδάζω, f. σω, to do zealously: Pass. to be anxiously done or looked to, τί μάλιστα διεσπούδαστο; Dem., who also uses διεσπούδασται in act. sense.
διάσσω, Att. διᾴττω, contr. for διαΐσσω.
διασταθμάομαι, Dep. to order by rule, regulate, Eur.
δια-στασιάζω, to form into separate factions, Arist.
διάστᾰσις, εως, ἡ, (διαστῆναι) a standing aloof, separation, Hdt. 2. difference, Plat.:—in Thuc. it has a causal sense, an attempt to set some against others. 3. divorce, Plut.
διαστᾰτικός, ή, όν, (δι-ίστημι) separative, causing discord, Plut.
δια-σταυρόω, f. ώσω, to fortify with a palisade: Med. διασταυρώσασθαι τὸν ἰσθμόν to have it fortified, Thuc.
δια-στείχω, aor. 2 -έστιχον:—to go through or across, c. acc., Eur. 2. to go one's way, Theocr.
δια-στέλλω, f. -στελῶ, to put asunder, tear open, Plut. 2. to distinguish, define, τὰ λεγόμενα Plat.; so to determine, Id. 3. to give express orders, in Med., N. T.
διάστενος, ον, very narrow, Galen.
δι-άστερος, ον, starred, δ. λίθοις Luc.
διάστημα, ατος, τό, (δια-στῆναι) an interval, Plat. 2. aor. 2 inf. of δι-ίστημι.
δια-στῆναι, aor. 2 inf. of δι-ίστημι.
δια-στηρίζω, f. ξω, to make firm, Anth.
δια-στήτην, Ep. for δι-εστήτην, 3 dual aor. 2 of δι-ίστημι.
δια-στίλβω, f. ψω, to gleam through, Ar., Anth.
δια-στοιβάζω, f. άσω, to stuff in between, Hdt.
δια-στοιχίζομαι, Med. to arrange for oneself regularly, regulate exactly, ἀρχήν Aesch.
διαστολή, ἡ, (διαστέλλω) a notch or nick, Plut.
δια-στρᾰτηγέω, f. ήσω, to serve as a general, assume his duties, Plut. II. trans. to conduct a war to its close, Id.
δια-στρεβλόω, strengthd. for στρεβλόω, Aeschin.
δια-στρέφω, f. ψω, to turn different ways, to twist about, distort, Xen.:—Pass. to be distorted, Plat.: of persons, to have one's eyes distorted, to get a squint, Ar. 2. metaph. to distort, pervert, Dem. Hence
διαστροφή, ἡ, distortion, Arist.; and
δι-άστροφος, ον, twisted, distorted, Hdt., Trag.
δια-σύρω [ῠ], f. -σῠρῶ: pf. -σέσυρκα:—to tear in

pieces: metaph. to pull to pieces, i. e. to disparage, ridicule, Dem.
δια-σφαιρίζω, f. Att. ιῶ, to throw about like a ball, Eur.
διασφακτήρ, ῆρος, ὁ, (σφάζω) murderous, Anth.
δια-σφάλλω, f. -σφᾰλῶ, to overturn utterly, Luc. —Pass. to be disappointed of, τινός Aeschin.
δια-σφάξ, άγος, ἡ, (-σφάζω) any opening made by violence, a cleft, rocky gorge, Hdt.
δια-σφενδονάω, f. ήσω, to scatter as by a sling:— Pass. to fly in pieces, Xen.
διασφηκόομαι: pf. part. δι-εσφηκωμένος: Pass.: (σφηκόω) to be made like a wasp, be pinched in at the waist, Ar.
δια-σχημᾰτίζω, f. σω, to form completely: Pass. to be so formed, Plat.
δια-σχίζω, f. σω, to cleave or rend asunder, Od., Plat., etc.:—Pass. to be cloven asunder, Il.; of soldiers, to be separated, Xen.
δια-σώζω, f. -σώσω, to preserve through a danger, Hdt., Eur.:—Pass. to come safe through, arrive in safety, Thuc., Xen.: to recover from illness, Id. II. of things, to preserve, maintain, Eur., Xen.: to keep in mind, Id.:—Med. to retain, Thuc.
δια-τᾰγεύω, f. σω, to arrange, Xen.
διαταγή, ῆς, ἡ, (διατάσσω) an ordinance, N. T.
δια-τάμνω, f. -τᾰμῶ, Ion. for δια-τέμνω, f. τεμῶ.
διάταξις, εως, ἡ, (διατάσσω) disposition, arrangement, of troops, Hdt., Dem.; of topics, Luc.
δια-τᾰράσσω, Att. -ττω, f. ξω, to throw into great confusion, confound utterly, Xen.
διάτασις, εως, ἡ, (διατείνω) tension, Plat., etc.
δια-τάσσω, Att. -ττω: f. ξω:—Pass., aor. 1 -ετάχθην: pf. -τέταγμαι:—to appoint or ordain severally, dispose, Hes., Hdt.: absol. to make arrangements, Xen.:—Med. to arrange for oneself, get things arranged, Plat.:—Pass. to be appointed, c. inf., Hdt. 2. to draw up an army, set in array, Hdt.: also to draw up separately, Id.:—Med., διαταξάμενοι posted in battle-order, Ar., Xen.; so in pf. pass. διατετάχθαι, Hdt. II. Med. to order by will, Anth.
δια-ταφρεύω, f. σω, to fortify by a ditch, Polyb.
δια-τείνω, f. -τενῶ: pf. -τέτᾰκα:—to stretch to the uttermost, τόξον Hdt.: to stretch out, τὰς χεῖρας Xen. II. intr. to extend, continue, Arist. B. Med. and Pass. to exert oneself, Xen., etc.; διατεινάμενος at full speed, Id.; with all one's force, Theocr.; διατείνεσθαι πρός τι to exert oneself for a purpose, Xen. 2. to maintain earnestly, contend for, τι Dem. II. in strict sense of Med. to stretch out for oneself, δ. τὰ βέλεα to have their lances poised, Hdt.; δ. τὸ τόξον to have one's bow strung, Id.
δια-τειχίζω, f. Att. ιῶ, to cut off and fortify by a wall, Ar. 2. to divide as by a wall, Xen. Hence
διατείχισμα, ατος, τό, a place walled off and fortified, Thuc.
δια-τεκμαίρομαι, Dep. to mark out, Lat. designare, Hes.
δια-τελευτάω, f. ήσω, to bring to fulfilment, Il.
δια-τελέω, f. -τελέσω, Att. -τελῶ, to bring quite to an end, accomplish, Eur., Xen. II. absol., mostly with a part. added, to continue being or doing so and so, Hdt., Plat.:—but the part. is sometimes omitted,

δ. πρόθυμυς to continue zealous, Thuc.: also simply to continue, go on, persevere, Plat.: to live on, Id.

δια-τελής, ές, (τέλος) continuous, incessant, Soph., Plat.

δια-τέμνω, Ion. -τάμνω, f. -τεμῶ, to cut through, cut in twain, dissever, Il., Hdt.; δίχα δ. Plat.:—metaph. to disunite, Aeschin.   2. to cut up, Hdt.:—Pass., διατμηθῆναι λέπαδνα to be cut into strips, Ar.

δια-τετραίνω: f. -τρανέω, Att. -τρανῶ, or -τρήσω:—to bore through, make a hole in, τι Hdt.

δια-τήκω, f. ξω, to melt, soften by heat, Ar.   II. Pass., with pf. -τέτηκα, to melt away, thaw, Xen.

δια-τηρέω, f. ήσω, to watch closely, observe, Plat., etc.   2. to keep faithfully, maintain, Dem., Arist.   3. δ. ἑαυτὸν ἔκ τινος to keep oneself from . . , N. T.

διατί; better written διὰ τί; Lat. quamobrem? wherefore?

δια-τίθημι, f. -θήσω, to place separately, arrange each in their own places, dispose, τὸ μὲν ἐπὶ δεξιά, τὸ δ' ἐπ' ἀριστερά Hdt.; so Xen., etc.   II. to manage well or ill, with an Adv., κράτιστα διατιθέναι τὰ τοῦ πολέμου Thuc.; of persons, δ. τινὰ ἀνηκέστως to treat him barbarously, Hdt, :—Pass., οὐ ῥᾳδίως διετέθη he was not very gently treated or handled, Thuc.   2. οὕτω διατιθέναι τινά to dispose one so or so, Plat., etc.   III. to recite, Id.

B. Med. to arrange as one likes, to dispose of, τὴν θυγατέρα Xen., etc.   2. to dispose of one's property, devise it by will, Plat.: ὁ διαθέμενος the devisor, testator, N. T.   3. to set out for sale, dispose of merchandise, Hdt., Xen.   4. to arrange mutually, δ. διαθήκην τινί to make a covenant with one, Ar., N. T.; πρός τινα Ib.; ἔριν δ. ἀλλήλοις to settle a quarrel with one, Xen.

διά-τιλμα, ατος, τό, (τίλλω) a portion plucked off, Anth.

δι-ατῑμάω, f. ήσω, to continue to dishonour, Aesch.

δια-τῐνάσσω, f. ξω, to shake asunder, shake to pieces, Od., Eur :—f. med. in pass. sense, Id.   II. to shake violently, Id.

δια-τινθαλέος, a, ον, = τινθαλέος, Ar.

δια-τμήγω, aor. 1 -έτμηξα: aor. 2 -έτμάγον, pass. -μάγην:—Ep. for διατέμνω, to cut in twain, διατμήξας having cut [the Trojan host] in twain, Il.; λαῖτμα διέτμαγον I clove the wave, Od.; ὦλκα δ., of ploughing, Mosch. :—Pass., διέτμαγεν (3 pl. aor. 2 for -μάγησαν) they parted, Hom. : they were scattered abroad, Il.

διατομή, ή, (διατέμνω) a severance, Aesch.

δια-τοξεύσιμος, ον, τοξεύω) that can be shot across, δ. χώρα a place within arrow-shot, Plut.

δια-τοξεύω, f. σω, to shoot through.

διά-τορος, ον, (τείρω) piercing, galling, Aesch.; δ. φόβος thrilling fear, Id.; of a trumpet, Id.   II. pass. pierced, bored through, Soph.

διατράγειν, aor. 2 inf. of διατρώγω.

δια-τρέπω, f. ψω, to turn away from a thing :—Pass. with f med., aor 2 med. -ετραπόμην and pass. -ετράπην [ᾰ], to be turned from one's purpose, to be perplexed, Dem.

δια-τρέφω, f. -θρέψω, to sustain continually, Thuc., etc.

δια-τρέχω, f. -θρέξομαι: aor. 2 -έδραμον: pf. -δεδράμηκα:—to run across or over the sea, Od.   2. metaph. to run through, τὸν βίον, τὸν λόγον

Plat.   II. absol. to run about, Lat. discurrere, Ar., Theocr.   2. δ. μέχρι to penetrate to, Plut.

δια-τρέω, f. -τρέσω, to flee all ways, Il.

διατρῐβή, ή, a way of spending time: hence, a pastime (pass-time), amusement, Ar., Dem.   2. serious employment, study, Ar., Plat.,   3. a way of life, living, δ. ἐν ἀγορᾷ Ar.   II. in bad sense, a waste of time, delay, Eur.; in pl., Thuc. From

δια-τρίβω [ῑ], f. ψω :—Pass., aor. 2 -ετρίβην [ῐ]: pf. -τέτριμμαι:—to rub between, rub hard, rub away, consume, waste, Hom. :—Pass., διατρίβῆναι to perish utterly, Hdt.   II. δ. χρόνον, Lat. terere tempus, to spend time, Id., Xen.: Pass., ἐνιαυτὸς διετρίβη Thuc.   2. absol. (without χρόνον), to waste time, pass it away, οὐ μὴ διατρίψεις; i. e. make no more delay, Ar.; δ. ἐν γυμνασίοις to pass all one's time there, Id.; δ. μετ' ἀλλήλων to go on talking, Id.: —hence, to employ oneself on or in a thing, ἔν or ἐπί τινι Plat.; περί τι Id.; c. part., δ. μελετῶν Xen.   b. also absol. to lose time, delay, Il., Ar., etc.: c. gen., δ. ὁδοῖο to lose time on the way, Od.   III. to put off by delay, to thwart, hinder a thing, Hom.; δ. Ἀχαιοὺς ὃν γάμον put them off in the matter of her wedding, Od.   Hence

διατριπτέον, verb. Adj. one must spend time, Arist.

διά-τρῐχα or διὰ τρίχα, Adv., = τρίχα, in three divisions, three ways, Il.

διά-τροπος, ον, various in dispositions, Eur.

διατροφή, ή, (διατρέφω) sustenance, support, Xen.

δια-τροχάζω, f. άσω, of a horse, to trot, Xen.

δια-τρύγιος [ῠ], ον, (τρύγη) bearing grapes in succession, Od.

διατρῠφέν, aor. 2 pass. part. neut. of διαθρύπτω.

δια-τρώγω, f. -τρώξομαι: aor. 2 -έτραγον :—to gnaw through, τὸ δίκτυον Ar.

διάττω or δι-άττω, Att. contr. for δι-αΐσσω.

δια-τῠπόω, f. ώσω, to form perfectly; δ. νόμους to give them a lasting form, Luc.: metaph. to imagine, Id.

διατύπωσις [ῠ], εως, ή, configuration, Plut.

δι-αυγάζω, f. σω, to shine through :—διαυγάζει ἡμέρα day dawns, N. T.

δι-αυγής, ές, (αὐγή) transparent, Anth.

διαυλο-δρόμης, ου, ὁ, (δραμεῖν) a runner in the δίαυλος, Pind.

δί-αυλος, ὁ, (δίς) a double pipe :—in the race, a double course, in which the runner ran to the furthest point of the στάδιον, turned the post (καμπτήρ), and ran back by the other side, Pind., Soph., Eur. :—metaph., κάμψαι διαύλου θάτερον κῶλον to run the backward course, retrace one's steps, Aesch.; also, δίαυλοι κυμάτων ebb and flow, Eur.; δίσσους ἂν ἔβαν διαύλους they would twice return, Id.   II. a strait, Eur.

διαφᾰγεῖν, aor. 2 inf. of διεσθίω, to eat through, Hdt.

δια-φαίνω, f. -φᾰνῶ :—to shew through, let a thing be seen through, Theocr.   II. Pass., aor. 2 -εφάνην [ᾰ], to appear or shew through, νεκύων δ. χῶρος shewed clear of dead bodies, Il.; of things seen through a transparent substance, Hdt.   2. to glow, to be red-hot, Od.   3. metaph. to be proved, shew itself, Thuc.: to be conspicuous among others, Id.   III. absol. in Act. to shew light through, to dawn, ἡμέρα, ἠὼς διέφαινε Hdt.: metaph. to shine through, Xen.

διαφάνεια, ἡ, = διάφασις, transparency, Plat. From
διαφἄνής, ές, (διαφαίνομαι) seen through, transparent,
Ar., Plat. 2. red-hot, Hdt. II. metaph. transparent, manifest, distinct, Soph., Plat. :—Adv. -νῶς,
Thuc., etc. 2. famous, illustrious, Plat.
δια-φαύσκω, Ion. -φώσκω, (φάος, φῶς) only in pres.,
to shew light through, to dawn, Hdt.
διαφερόντως, Adv. part. pres. act. of διαφέρω, differently from, at odds with, διαφερόντως ἤ . . , Plat.; c.
gen., διαφερόντως τῶν ἄλλων above all others, Id. II.
absol. eminently, especially, Thuc., etc.
δια-φέρω, f. -οίσω and -οίσομαι: aor. 1 -ήνεγκα, Ion.
-ήνεικα : aor. 2 -ήνεγκον : pf. -ενήνοχα :—to carry
over or across, δ. ναῦς τὸν Ἰσθμόν Thuc.: to carry
from one to another, κηρύγματα Eur.:—metaph.,
γλῶσσαν διοίσει will put the tongue in motion, will
speak, Soph. 2. of Time, δ. τὸν αἰῶνα, τὸν βίον to
go through life, Hdt., Eur.; absol., ἅπαις διοίσει Id.:
—in Med., διοίσεται will pass his life, Soph.; σκοπούμενος διοίσει Xen. 3. to bear through, bear to the
end, σκῆπτρα Eur., etc. 4. to bear to the end, go
through life, πόλεμον Hdt., Thuc. :—to endure, support, sustain, Lat. perferre, Soph., Eur. II. to
carry different ways, to toss or cast about, Id. 2.
to spread abroad, Dem. 3. to tear asunder, Lat.
differre, Aesch., Eur. 4. δ. τὴν ψῆφον to give one's
vote a different way, i. e. against another, Hdt.: also
simply, to give each man his vote, Eur., Thuc. III.
intr. to differ, make a difference, Pind., Eur.: c. gen.
to be different from, Id., Ar. 2. impers. διαφέρει, it makes a difference, πλεῖστον δ., Lat. multum
interest, βραχὺ δ. it makes little difference, Eur.;
οὐδὲν διαφέρει Plat.;—c. dat. pers., διαφέρει μοι it
makes a difference to me, Id.; αὐτῷ ἰδίᾳ τι δ. he
has some private interest at stake, Thuc. 3. τὸ
δ., τὰ διαφέροντα, the difference, the odds, Id., etc.;
but τὰ δ. also simply points of difference, Id. 4. to
be different from a man, i. e. to surpass, excel him, c.
gen., Id., Plat. :—in a compar. sense, διέφερεν ἀλέξασθαι ἤ . . it was better to defend oneself than . . ,
Xen. 5. to prevail, of a belief, Thuc. IV. Pass.
to differ, be at variance, περί τινος Hdt.; τινι περί
τινος Thuc.: οὐ διαφέρομαι, = οὔ μοι διαφέρει, Dem.
δια-φεύγω, f. -φεύξομαι, to flee through, get away from,
escape, τινά or τι Hdt., Plat. :—absol. to escape, Hdt.,
Thuc.; διαφεύγει οὐδὲ νῦν it is not now too late,
Dem. 2. to escape one, escape one's notice or
memory, Plat., etc. Hence
διάφευξις, εως, ἡ, an escaping, means of escape, Thuc.
δια-φημίζω, f. ίσω, to spread abroad, N. T.
δια-φθείρω, f. -φθερῶ Ερ. -φθέρσω: pf. -έφθαρκα and
διέφθορα :—Pass., f. -φθᾰρήσομαι, Ion. -φθερέομαι: Ion.
3 pl. plqpf. διεφθάρατο :—to destroy utterly, Il., Hdt.,
Att.: to make away with, kill, destroy, ruin, Soph.,
etc.; δ. χέρα to weaken, slacken one's hand, Eur.: to
disable a ship, Hdt. :—absol. to forget, Eur. 2. in
moral sense, to corrupt, ruin, Aesch., Plat., etc. :—
esp. to corrupt by bribes, Hdt., Dem.: to seduce,
Lysias. 3. οὐδὲν διαφθείρας τοῦ χρώματος having
changed nothing of his colour, Plat. II. Pass. to
be destroyed, crippled, disabled, Hdt.; τὴν ἀκοὴν διε-
φθαρμένος deaf, Id.: τὰ σκέλεα δ. with their legs

broken, Id.; τὰ ὄμματα δ. blind, Plat.; τὰς φρένας
Eur.; τὸ φρενῶν διαφθαρέν loss of one's mind,
Id. III. pf. διέφθορα is intr. in Hom., to have
lost one's wits ;—but in Att. trans., Soph., Eur. Hence
διαφθορά, Ion. -ρή, ἡ, destruction, ruin, blight, death,
Hdt., Att. 2. in moral sense, corruption, τῶν νέων
Xen. II. in pass. sense, ἰχθύσιν διαφθ. a prey for
fishes, Soph.; πολεμίοις δ. Eur.; and
διαφθορεύς, έως, ὁ, a corrupter, τῶν νόμων Plat. :—as
fem. in Eur.
δι-αφίημι, f. -αφήσω, to dismiss, disband, Xen.
δια-φῐλονεικέω, f. ήσω, to dispute earnestly, Plut.
δια-φῐλοτῑμέομαι, Dep. to strive emulously, Plut.
δια-φλέγω, f. ξω, to burn through, Plut. :—metaph. to
inflame, Id.
δια-φοιβάζω, to drive mad: Pass., pf. inf. διαπεφοι-
βάσθαι Soph.
δια-φοιτάω, Ion. -έω, f. ήσω, to wander or roam continually, Hdt., Ar.:—of reports, to get abroad, Plut.
διαφορά, ἡ, (διαφέρω) difference, distinction, Thuc. II.
variance, disagreement, Hdt., Eur.
δια-φορέω, f. ήσω, = διαφέρω, to spread abroad, Od. 2.
to carry away, carry off, Thuc.; esp. as plunder,
Hdt. 3. to plunder, οἶκον, πόλιν Hdt. :—Pass.,
διαφορεῖσθαι ὑπό τινος Dem. 4. to tear in pieces,
Eur. :—Pass., Hdt. II. to carry across from one
place to another, Thuc. Hence
διαφόρησις, εως, ἡ, a plundering, Plut.
διάφορος, ον, (διαφέρω) different, unlike, Hdt., Plat.,
etc. 2. differing or disagreeing with another, c.
dat., Eur.; in hostile sense, at variance with, τινι Hdt.,
Plat.; c. gen., δ. τινος one's adversary, Dem. 3.
distinguished, remarkable, Plut. 4. making a difference to one, advantageous, profitable, Thuc. II.
as Subst., διάφορον, τό, 1. a difference, Hdt., Eur.,
Dem. 2. what concerns one, a matter of importance, Thuc., Dem. 3. a difference, disagreement,
Id. 4. in reference to money-matters, one's balance,
expenditure, Id. III. Adv. -ρως, with a difference, variously, Thuc. :—δ. ἔχειν to differ, Plat. 2.
excellently, Id.
διαφορότης, ητος, ἡ, difference, Plat.
διάφραγμα, ατος, τό, a partition-wall, barrier,
Thuc. II. the midriff, diaphragm (Homer's
φρένες), Plat. From
δια-φράγνυμι, f. ξω, (φράσσω) to barricade, Plut.
δια-φράζω, f. σω: Ep. aor. 2 -πέφρᾰδον :—to speak distinctly, tell plainly, Hom.
δια-φρέω, f. ήσω, to let through, let pass, Ar., Thuc.
δια-φυγγάνω, = διαφεύγω, Thuc., Aeschin.
διαφῠγή, ἡ, (διαφεύγω) a refuge, means of escape, τινος
from a thing, Plat.
διαφυή, ἡ, (διαφύομαι) any natural break, a joint,
suture, division, Plat., Xen.
διαφῠλακτέος, α, ον, verb. Adj. to be watched, preserved,
Xen. From
δια-φῠλάσσω, Att. -ττω, f. ξω, to watch closely, guard
carefully, Hdt., etc.; Med. to guard for oneself,
Eur. 2. to observe closely, τὰ μέτρα Hdt. 3. to
observe, maintain, τοὺς νόμους Plat.; δ. τὸ μή, c. inf.,
to guard against being . . , Id.
δια-φύομαι, Pass. with aor. 2 act. διέφῡν, pf. διαπέφῡκα ·

—of time, *to intervene*, Hdt.   **II.** *to be closely connected with*, τινος Plut.

δια-φῡσάω, f. ήσω, *to blow in different directions, disperse*, Plat.   **II.** *to blow through*, Luc.

δι-αφύσσω, f. ξω; aor. 1 -ήφῠσα:—*to draw off* liquids *continually* : Pass., of wine, Od.   **II.** *to draw away, tear away*, πολλὸν διήφυσε σαρκὸς ὀδόντι Ib.

διαφωνέω, f. ήσω, *to be dissonant*, Plat :—generally, *to disagree*, Id. ; τινι *with one*, Id.

διά-φωνος, ον, (φωνή) *discordant*, Luc.

δια-φώσκω, Ion. for δια-φαύσκω.

δια-φωτίζω, f. Att. ιῶ, *to clear completely*, Plut.

δια-χάζομαι, Dep. *to withdraw*, Xen.

δια-χαλάω, f. άσω, *to loosen, unbar*, Eur.   **II.** *to make supple by exercise*, Xen.

δια-χάσκω, aor. 2, -έχανον, *to gape wide, yawn*, Ar.

δια-χέαι, aor. 1 inf. of διαχέω.

δια-χειμάζω, f. άσω, *to pass the winter*, Thuc., Xen.

δια-χειρίζω, f. Att. ιῶ, *to have in hand, conduct, manage, administer*, Oratt. :—Pass., Xen. Hence

διαχείρισις, εως, ή, *management, administration*, Thuc.

δια-χειροτονέω, f. ήσω, *to choose between two* persons or things *by show of hands, to elect*, Dem. ; so in Med., Xen. Hence

διαχειροτονία, ή, *election*, Dem., Aeschin.

δια-χέω, f. -χεῶ: aor. 1 -έχεα, Ep. -έχευα :—*to pour different ways, to disperse*, Hdt. :—*to cut up* a victim, Hom.   **2.** *to dissolve, break up, destroy*, Xen.   **3.** metaph. *to confound*, τὰ βεβουλευμένα Hdt.   **II.** Pass. *to be poured from one vessel into another*, Id.   **2.** *to run through, spread about*, Thuc.   **3.** *to be dissolved, fall away*, of a corpse, Hdt. : *to disperse*, of soldiers, Xen.   **4.** metaph. *to be* or *become diffuse* or *dissipated*, Plat.

δια-χλευάζω, strengthd. for χλευάζω, Dem.

δια-χόω, old form for διαχώννυμι, διαχοῦν τὸ χῶμα *to complete the mound*, Hdt.

δια-χράομαι, Ion. -χρέομαι : f. ήσομαι, Dor. 3 sing. -χρησεῖται :   **I.** Dep., c. dat. rei, *to use constantly* or *habitually*, Hdt. ; τῇ ἀληθείη δ. *to speak the truth*, Id. ; δ. ἀρετῇ *to practise* virtue, Id.   **b.** like Lat. *utor*, of passive states, *to meet with, suffer under*, συμφορᾷ, αὐχμῷ Id.   **2.** c. acc. pers. *to use up, consume, destroy*, Id., Thuc.   **II.** Pass., pf. -κέχρημαι, *to be lent out to different persons*, Dem.

διά-χρῡσος, ον, *interwoven with gold*, Dem.

διάχῠσις, εως, ή, (διαχέω) *diffusion*, Plat. ; δ. λαμβάνειν *to be spread* out, Plut.   **II.** *merriment*, Id.

δια-χώννῡμι, = διαχόω, Strab.

δια-χωρέω, f. ήσω, *to go through, pass through* : impers., κάτω διεχώρει αὐτοῖς they were suffering from *diarrhoea*, Xen.   **2.** of coins, *to be current*, Luc.

δια-χωρίζω, f. Att. ίῶ, *to separate*, Xen. Hence

διαχώρισμα, ατος, τό, *a cleft, division*, Luc.

δια-ψαίρω, mostly in pres., *to brush* or *blow away*, Ar.

δια-ψεύδω, f. -ψεύσομαι, *to deceive utterly*, Dem. :— Pass. also c. mid. : pf. -έψευσμαι: aor. -εψεύσθην :— *to be deceived, mistaken*, Id. ; δ. τινος *to be cheated of, deceived in* a person or thing, Xen., Dem. ; περί τι or τινι Arist.

δια-ψηφίζομαι, f. Att. ιοῦμαι, Dep. *to vote in order*

with ballots (ψῆφοι, *calculi*), Thuc.   **II.** *to decide by vote*, Dem. Hence

διαψήφισις, εως, ή, *a voting by ballot*, Xen.

δια-ψήχω, *to cause to crumble away*, Plut.

δια-ψῐθῠρίζω, f. σω, *to whisper among themselves*, Luc.

δια-ψύχω [ῠ], f. ξω, *to cool, refresh* :—*to dry and clean*, ναῦς Thuc. ; of misers bringing out their hoards, Xen.

διάω, = διάημι.

δί-βᾱμος, ον, (βῆμα) *on two legs*, Eur.

δι-βολία, ή, *a double-edged lance, halbert*, Plut. From

δί-βολος, ον, (δίς, βάλλω) *two-pointed*, Eur., Anth.

δί-γληνος, ον, (γλήνη) *with two eye-balls*, Theocr.

δί-γλωσσος, Att. -ττος, ον, (γλῶσσα) *speaking two languages*, Lat. *bilinguis*, Thuc.   **II.** as Subst. δίγλωσσος, ὁ, *an interpreter*, Plut.

δί-γονος, ον, (γί-γνομαι) *twice-born*, of Bacchus, Anth.   **2.** *twin : double*, Eur.

δίδαγμα, ατος, τό, (διδάσκω) *a lesson*, Ar.

διδακτέον, verb. Adj. of διδάσκω, *one must teach*, Plat.

διδακτικός, ή, όν, (διδάσκω) *apt at teaching*, N. T.

διδακτός, ή, όν, (διδάσκω) :   **I.** of things, *taught, learnt*, Soph.   **2.** *that can* or *ought to be taught* or *learnt*, Pind., Soph., etc.   **II.** of persons, *taught, instructed*, τινός in a thing, N. T.

δίδαξις, εως, ή, (διδάσκω) *teaching, instruction*, Eur.

διδάξω, f. of διδάσκω.

διδασκᾰλεῖον, τό, (διδάσκαλος) *a teaching-place, school*, Thuc., Plat., etc.

διδασκᾰλία, ή, (διδάσκαλος) *teaching, instruction, education*, Lat. *disciplina*, Xen., Plat., etc. ; διδασκαλίαν ποιεῖσθαι or παρέχειν *to serve as a lesson to* one, Thuc.   **II.** *the rehearsing* of a *dramatic* chorus, Plat. : also, *the drama* itself, Plut.

διδασκᾰλικός, ή, όν, (διδάσκω) *fit for teaching, capable of giving instruction, instructive*, Plat., Xen.

διδασκάλιον, τό, (διδάσκαλος) *a thing taught, a science, art, lesson*, Hdt., Xen.   **II.** in pl. *a teacher's fee*, Plut.

διδάσκᾰλος, ὁ and ή, (διδάσκω) *a teacher, master*, h. Hom., Aesch., etc. : εἰς διδασκάλου (sc. οἶκον) φοιτᾶν *to go to* school, Plat. ; διδασκάλων or ἐκ διδασκάλων ἀπαλλαγῆναι *to leave* school, Id. ; ἐν διδασκάλων *at* school, Id.   **II.** *a dramatic poet* was called διδάσκαλος because he *taught the actors*, Ar.

δῐ-δάσκω, Ep. inf. -έμεναι, -έμεν : f. διδάξω: aor. 1 ἐδίδαξα, poët. ἐδίδασκησα : pf. δεδίδαχα :—Med., f. διδάξομαι : aor. 1 ἐδιδαξάμην :—Pass., f. διδαχθήσομαι : aor. 1 ἐδιδάχθην : pf. δεδίδαγμαι : (redupl. form of δάω, in causal sense.) *To teach* (i.e. *instruct*) a person, or *teach* a thing, Hom., etc. : c. dupl. acc., σε . . ἱπποσύνας ἐδίδαξαν *they taught* thee *riding*, Il. ; *to teach* one a thing, Hom., etc. ; also, δ. τινὰ περί τινος Ar. :—c. acc. pers. et inf. *to teach* one *to* be so and so, Od. ; c. inf. only, δίδαξε βάλλειν *taught* him *how to* shoot, Il. :—also with inf. omitted, διδάσκειν τινὰ ἱππέα [sc. εἶναι] *to train* one *as a horseman*, Plat. ; so, δ. τινὰ σοφόν, κακόν Eur. :— Med. *to teach oneself, learn*, Soph. : but the usual sense of the Med. is *to have another taught*, of a father, *to have* his son *taught*, Plat., etc. :—Pass. *to be taught, to learn*, c. gen., διδασκόμενος πολέμοιο *trained in war*, Il. ; also c. acc., Ib., etc. ; c. inf. δεδιδαγμένος εἶναι Hdt. ; διδάσκεται λέγειν ἀκοῦσαί θ'

Eur. II. διδάσκειν is used of dramatic Poets, *who originally taught the actors* their parts, Hdt., Att.

διδαχή, ἡ, = δίδαξις, *teaching*, Hdt., Thuc., etc.

δί-δημι, 3 pl. διδέασι : Ep. 3 sing. impf. δίδη : 3 pl. imper. διδέντων :—Ep. redupl. form of δέω (as τίθημι of *θέω*), *to bind, fetter*, Hom.

διδοῖς, διδοῖ, or διδοῖσθα, Ion. 2 and 3 sing. of δίδωμι.

δι-δράσκω, *to run away* : (redupl. from ΔΡΑ, whence the compds. ἀπο-δρᾶναι, etc.)

δί-δραχμος [ῐ], ον, (δίς, δραχμή) *worth two drachms* : *with pay of two drachms a day*, Thuc. II. as Subst. δί-δραχμον, τό, *a double-drachm* or *half-shekel*, paid to the temple-treasury at Jerusalem, N. T.

διδύμ-άνωρ [ᾰ], ὁ, ἡ, τό, (ἀνήρ) *touching both the men*, Aesch.

διδῡμᾱ-τόκος, ον, Dor. for διδυμητόκος, (τίκτω) *bearing twins*, Theocr., Anth.

διδυμάων [ᾰ], ονος, ὁ, ἡ, (δίδυμος) only in dual nom. and pl. dat. *twin-brothers, twins*, Il.

διδῡμο-γενής, ές, (γί-γνομαι) *twin-born*, Eur.

δίδυμος [ῐ], η, ον and ος, ον, redupl. from δύο, *double, twofold, twain*, Hom., Att., ον, διδύμη ἅλς, i. e. the Pontus and Bosporus, Soph. II. *twin*, Id., Eur. :—as Subst., δίδυμοι *twins*, Il., Hdt. ; also δίδυμα, τά, Id.

δί-δωμι : 3 sing. impf. ἐδίδω, Ep. δίδω, 3 pl. ἐδίδοσαν : (but the more usual forms of the pres. and impf. are from *διδόω, viz. διδοῖς or διδοῖσθα, διδοῖ, διδοῦσι :—imper. δίδου, Ep. δίδωθι ; inf. διδοῦν, Ep. διδοῦναι ; δίδων :—impf. ἐδίδουν, Ep. 3 sing. δίδου, also ἔδιδον, δίδον ; Ep. also δόσκον) :—f. δώσω, Ep. διδώσω : aor. 1 ἔδωκα, Ep. δῶκα : aor. 2 ἔδων, Ep. aor. 2 subj., 3 sing. δώῃ, δώῃσι, δῷσι, 1 pl. δώομεν, 3 pl. δῶωσι, inf. δόμεναι, δόμεν ; pf. δέδωκα : plqpf. ἐδεδώκειν :—Pass., f. δοθήσομαι : aor. 1 ἐδόθην : pf. δέδομαι : 3 sing. plqpf. ἐδέδοτο. (Redupl. from Root ΔΟ, Lat. *do, dare*.)

Orig. sense, *to give*, τί τινι Hom., etc. ; in pres. and impf. *to be ready to give, to offer*, Id. 2. of the gods, *to grant*, κῦδος, νίκην, and of evils, δ. ἄλγεα, ἄτας, κήδεα Id.; later, εὖ διδόναι τινί *to provide* well for . . , Soph., Eur. 3. *to offer to the gods*, Hom., etc. 4. with an inf. added, δῶκε τεύχεα θεράποντι φορῆναι *gave* him the arms *to carry*, Il. ; διδοῖ πιεῖν *gives* to drink, Hdt., etc. 5. Prose phrases, δ. ὅρκον, opp. to λαμβάνειν, *to tender* an oath ; δ. χάριν, = χαρίζεσθαι, as ὀργῇ χάριν δούς *having indulged* his anger, Soph. ;—λόγον τινὶ δ. *to give* one *leave to speak*, Xen. ; but, δ. λόγον ἑαυτῷ *to deliberate*, Hdt. II. c. acc. pers. *to give over, deliver up*, Hom., etc. 2. of parents, *to give* their daughter *to wife*, Id. 3. in Att., διδόναι τινά τινι *to grant* any one to entreaties, *pardon* him, Xen. :—διδόναι τινί τι *to forgive* a thing, *remit* its punishment, Eur., Dem. 4. διδόναι ἑαυτόν τινι *to give* oneself *up*, Hdt., etc. 5. δ. δίκην, v. δίκη IV. 3. III. in vows and prayers, c. acc. pers. et inf. *to grant, allow, bring about that*, Hom., Trag. IV. seemingly intr. *to give oneself up, devote oneself*, τινί Eur.

δῖε, voc. of δῖος. II. δίε, Ep. for ἔδιε, 3 sing. impf. of δίω.

δι-εγγυάω, f. ήσω :—of persons, in Act. *to give bail for* another, and in Med. *to take bail for* him, Isocr. :—Pass. *to be bailed* by any one, Thuc. Hence

διεγγύησις, εως, ἡ, *a giving of bail*, Dem.

δι-έδεξα, Ion. for -έδειξα, aor. 1 of διαδείκνυμι.

δι-έδραμον, aor. 2 of διατρέχω.

δι-έεργω, Ep. for δι-είργω.

δι-έζωσα, aor. 1 of δια-ζώννυμι.

δι-έθετο, 3 sing. aor. 2 med. of δια-τίθημι.

δι-εῖδον, inf. -ιδεῖν, aor. 2 with no pres. in use, διοράω being used instead (cf. διαείδω):—*to see thoroughly, discern*, Ar., Plat. : διιδεῖν περί τινος Id. II. pf. δίοιδα, inf. διειδέναι *to know the difference between, to distinguish*, Eur., etc. : *to decide*, Soph.

διειλημμένως, Adv. (διαλαμβάνω) *distinctly*, Xen.

δι-είληφα, pf. of δια-λαμβάνω.

δί-ειμι, serving as f. to διέρχομαι, impf. διῄειν, *to go to and fro, roam about*, Ar.; of a report, *to spread*, Plut. 2. c. acc. *to go through, go through* a thing, *to narrate, describe, discuss*, Plat.

δι-εῖπον, in Hom. also δια-εῖπον, serving as aor. 2 to διαγορεύω, *to say through, tell fully* or *distinctly*, Hom., Soph. : *to interpret* a riddle, Id. 2. *to speak* one *with another, converse*, διαειπέμεν ἀλλήλοισιν Od. (The f. is δι-ερῶ, aor. 1 pass. δι-ερρήθην.)

δι-είργω, Ep. and Ion. δι-έργω, Ep. also δι-έεργω, *to keep asunder, separate*, Il., Hdt., Thuc. II. seemingly intr. *to lie between*, Xen.

δι-είρηκα, serving as pf. to δι-ερῶ, δι-εῖπον.

δι-είρομαι, aor. 2 inf. δι-ερέσθαι, *to question closely*, Hom., Plat.

δϊ-είρυσα, Ion. for δι-ερύω, *to draw across*, τὰς νέας τὸν ἰσθμόν Hdt.

δι-είρω, pf. διεῖρκα, *to pass* or *draw through*, Xen.

δι-ειρωνό-ξενος, ον, *dissembling with one's guests*, Ar.

δι-είς, aor. 2 part. of δι-ίημι.

δι-έκ, Prep. *through and out of*, c. gen., Hom.

δι-εκδύομαι, aor. 2 διεξέδυν, *to slip out through*, c. acc., Plut. Hence

διέκδυσις, εως, ἡ, *an evasion*, Plut.

δι-εκθέω, f. -θεύσομαι, *to run through*, Plut.

δι-εκπαίω, f. σω, *to break* or *burst through*, Luc.

δι-εκπεραίνω, f. ἄνῶ, *to go through with*, Xen.

δι-εκπεράω, f. ήσω and άσω, *to pass out through, pass quite through*, c. acc., Hdt. :—*to cross over*, Aesch. II. *to pass by, overlook*, Ar.

δι-εκπλέω, f. -πλεύσομαι, aor. 1 -έπλευσα, Ion. -πλώω, aor. 1 -έπλωσα :—*to sail out through*, c. acc., Hdt. : absol. *to sail out*, Id., II. in naval tactics, *to break the enemy's line by sailing through it*, Id., Thuc. Hence

διέκπλοος, contr. διέκπλους, ὁ, *a sailing across* or *through, passing across* or *through*, Hdt. II. *a breaking the enemy's line* in a sea-fight, Id., Thuc.

δι-εκπλώω, Ion. for δι-εκπλέω.

δί-εκροος, ὁ, *a passage for the stream to escape*, Hdt.

δι-εκφεύγω, f. -φεύξομαι, *to escape completely*, Plut.

διεκχέω, strengthd. for ἐκχέω, Aretae. Cur. M. Ac. 2. 5.

δι-ελάσις, εως, ἡ, *a driving through : a charge* or *exercise of cavalry*, Xen. From

δι-ελάθον, aor. 2 of δια-λανθάνω.

δι-ελαύνω, f. διελάσω, Att. διελῶ : aor. 1 διήλασα :—*to drive through* or *across*, c. gen., τάφροιο διήλασεν ἵππους Il. 2. *to thrust through*, λαπάρης διήλασεν ἔγχος Ib. 3. δ. τινὰ λόγχῃ *to thrust* one *through*

with a lance, Plut., Luc.　　**II.** intr. (sub. ἵππον) to ride through, charge through, Xen.

δι-ελέγχω, f. ξω, to refute utterly, Plat.

δι-έλκω, f. -ελκύσω : aor. 1 -είλκῦσα :—to draw asunder, widen, Plat.　　**II.** to pull through a thing, c. gen., Ar.　　**III.** to keep on drinking, Id.

ΔΙ´ΕΜΑΙ, Pass. (as if from an Act. δίημι = δίω), to flee, speed, πεδίοιο over the plain, Il.; δίεσθαι to hasten away, Ib.　　**II.** to fear, c. inf., Aesch.

δι-έμενος, aor. 2 med. part. of δίημι.

δι-εμπολάω, f. ήσω, to sell to different buyers, or sell in lots, Lat. divendere, Eur., Ar. :—metaph. to sell, betray, τινά Soph.

δι-εμφαίνω, f. -φᾰνῶ, to shew through, Luc.

δι-ενέγκαι, Ion. -ενεῖκαι, aor. 1 inf. of διαφέρω.

διενεκτέον, verb. Adj. of διαφέρω, one must excel, Luc.

δι-ενιαυτίζω, f. σω, (ἐνιαυτός) to live out the year, Hdt.

δι-εντέρευμα, ατος, τό, (ἔντερον) a looking through entrails, Comic word for sharp-sightedness, Ar.

δι-εξάίσσω, Att. -άττω, f. ξω, to rush forth, Theocr.

δι-έξειμι, inf. -εξιέναι, Ep. -εξίμεναι : (εἶμι ibo) :—to go out through, pass through, Il., Hdt.　　**II.** to go through in detail, recount in full, relate circumstantially, Id., Plat., etc.; δ. περὶ τινος to go through by way of examining, Eur.

διεξέλᾰσις, εως, ή, = διέλασις, Plut.　From

δι-εξελαύνω, f. -ελάσω, Att. -ελῶ, to drive, ride, march through, absol., Hdt.; c. acc. loci, δ. τὰς πύλας Id.

δι-εξελέγχω, f. ξω, to refute utterly, Luc.

δι-εξελίσσω, Att. -ττω, f. ξω, to unroll, untie, Hdt.

δι-εξερέομαι, to learn by close questioning a person, τινά τι Il.

δι-εξέρχομαι, f. -ελεύσομαι, = διέξειμι, to go through, pass through, τὸ χωρίον Hdt.　　2. to go through, go completely through, πάντας φίλους Eur., etc. : c. part., δ. πωλέων to be done selling, Hdt.　　3. to go through in succession, διὰ πάντων δ. τῶν παίδων, i. e. killing them one after another, Id.; διὰ πασῶν τῶν ζημιῶν, i. e. trying one after another, Thuc.　　4. to go through in detail, recount in full, Hdt., etc.　　**II.** intr. to be past, gone by, of time, Id.　　2. to be gone through, related fully, Dem.

δι-εξηγέομαι, f. ήσομαι, strengthd. for ἐξηγέομαι, Xen.

δι-εξίημι, aor. 1 -εξῆκα, to let pass through, Hdt.　　**II.** intr. (sub. αὑτόν), of a river, to empty itself, Thuc.

διεξοδικός, ή, όν, detailed, Plut.　From

δι-έξοδος, ή, a way out through, an outlet, passage, channel, Hdt.; διέξοδοι ὁδῶν passage-ways, Id.　　2. a pathway, orbit, of the sun, Id., etc.　　3. an issue, event, Id.　　**II.** a detailed narrative, description, Plat.

δι-εξύφαίνω, f. ᾰνῶ, to finish the web, Plut.

δι-εορτάζω, f. σω, to keep the feast throughout, Thuc.

δι-επέφραδον, Ep. redupl. aor. 2 of διαφράζω.

δι-επράθον, -επρᾰθόμην, aor. 2 act. and med. of διαπέρθω.

δι-έπτατο, 3 sing. aor. 2 of διαπέταμαι.

δι-έπω, f. ψω, to manage an affair, order, arrange, Il.; δ. τὰ πρήγματα Hdt.

δι-εργάζομαι, f. άσομαι, Dep. to make an end of, kill, destroy, Lat. conficere, Hdt., Soph. :—plqpf. in pass.

sense, διέργαστο τὰ πράγματα, actum erat de rebus, Hdt.; so in aor. 1 διεργασθεῖτ᾽ ἄν Eur.

διέργω, Ion. for διείργω.

διερείδομαι, f. -είσομαι, Med. to lean upon, τινι Eur.

δι-ερέσσω, f. -ερέσω : aor. 1 -ήρεσα, poët. -ήρεσσα :— to row about, χερσὶ δ. to swim, Od.　　2. c. acc., δ. τὰς χέρας to swing them about, Eur.

δι-ερευνάω, f. ήσω, to search through, examine closely, Plat. : also in Med., Id.　Hence

διερευνητής, οῦ, ὁ, a scout or vidette, Xen.

διερίζω, f. σω, to strive with one another :—Med. to contend with, τινί Plut.

διερμηνευτής, οῦ, ὁ, an interpreter, N. T.　From

δι-ερμηνεύω, f. σω, to interpret, expound, N. T.

ΔΙΕΡΟ´Σ, ά, όν, fresh, active, nimble, of men, Od.; διερῷ ποδί with nimble foot, Ib.　　**II.** after Hom. = liquidus, wet, liquid, Aesch. ; of birds, which float through the air, Ar.; δ. μέλεα of the nightingale's notes, Lat. liquidae voces, Id.; δ. πώγων of one drowned in the sea, Anth.　(The sense of liquid is not in Hom.: his usage seems to connect it with δί-ω, to run, flee.)

δι-έρπω, f. -ερπύσω [ῠ], to creep or pass through, πῦρ δ., of the ordeal of fire, Soph.

δι-έρρωγα, pf. intr. of διαρρήγνυμι.

δι-ερύκω [ῠ], to keep off, to hinder, Plut.

δι-έρχομαι, f. διελεύσομαι (but δίειμι is Att. f., and διήξειν impf.), aor. 2 διῆλθον : Dep. :—to go through, pass through, absol. or c. gen., Il., Soph. :—c. acc., also, Il., Thuc., etc.　　2. to pass through, complete, Hdt., Plat., etc.　　3. of reports, βάξις διῆλθ᾽ Ἀχαιούς Soph.; absol., λόγος διῆλθε went abroad, spread, Thuc., Xen.　　4. of pain, to shoot through one, Soph.; of passion, Id.; ἐμὲ διῆλθέ τι a thought shot through me, Eur.　　5. to go through in detail, tell all through, Aesch., Thuc.　　**II.** intr. of Time, to pass, elapse, Hdt., Dem.; so, σπουδῶν διελθουσῶν Thuc.; but, διελθὼν ἐς βραχὺν χρόνον having waited, Eur.

δι-ερῶ serving as f., διείρηκα as pf., of διαγορεύω, cf. διεῖπον :—to say fully, distinctly, expressly, Plat., Dem. :—Pass., aor. 1 διερρήθην, pf. διείρημαι, Plat.

δι-ερωτάω, f. ήσω, to cross-question, τινα Plat.　　**II.** to ask constantly or continually, Dem.

δίεσθαι, inf. of δίομαι.　　**II.** also of δίεμαι.

δι-εσθίω, f. -έδομαι : aor. 2 διέφᾰγον :—to eat through, δ. τὴν μήτραν, of young vipers, Hdt.

δι-εσκεμμένως, Adv. of διασκοπέω, prudently, Xen.

δι-εσπάρην [ᾰ], aor. 2 pass. of διασπείρω.

διέσσυτο, 3 sing. Ep. aor. 2 of διασεύομαι.

δι-έστειλα, aor. 1 of διαστέλλω.

δι-έστην, aor. 2 of δίίστημι :—δι-εστώς, Ion. δι-εστεώς, pf. part.

δι-έσχον, aor. 2 of διέχω.

δι-ετής, ές, or δι-έτης, ες, (ἔτος) of or lasting two years, Hdt. :—διετές, τό, Lat. biennium, ἐπὶ διετὲς ἡβᾶν to be two years past puberty, Aeschin.

δι-ετήσιος, ον, lasting through the year, Lat. perennis, Thuc.

διετία, ή, (διετής) a space of two years, N. T.

δι-ετμᾶγεν, Ep. for διετμάγησαν, 3 pl. aor. 2 pass. of διατμήγω :— -ετμᾶγον, aor. 2 act.

δι-ευθύνω [ῠ], f. ῠνῶ, to set right, amend, Luc.

δι-ευκρῑνέω, f. ήσω, to separate accurately, arrange carefully, Xen.

δῐ-ευλᾰβέομαι, aor. 1 -ηυλαβήθην, Dep. to take good heed to, beware of, be on one's guard against, c. acc. or gen., Plat. Hence

διευλαβητέον, verb. Adj. one must take heed to, Plat.

δι-ευνάω, f. άσω, to lay asleep, τὸν βίοτον Eur.

δι-ευσχημονέω, f. ήσω, to preserve decorum, Plut.

δι-ευτῠχέω, f. ήσω, to continue prosperous, Dem.

δι-εφθάρᾰτο, Ion. 3 pl. plqpf. pass. of διαφθείρω.

δι-έχω, f. δι-έξω: aor. 2 διέσχον: I. trans. to keep apart or separate, Lat. distinere, Hdt., Plut. 2. to keep off, Id. II. intr. to go through, hold its way, of arrows and lances, Il. :—to extend or reach, Hdt. 2. to stand apart, be separated or distant, Theogn., Thuc. ; διέχοντες ᾖεσαν they marched with spaces between man and man, Id. ; σταδίους ὡς πεντήκοντα διέχει is about 50 stades wide, Xen. 3. of Time, to intervene, Soph. 4. to differ, Arist.

δι-εψευσμένως, Adv. altogether falsely, Strab.

δίζημαι, Ep. 2 sing. δίζηαι, part. διζήμενος: 3 sing. impf. ἐδίζητο : f. διζήσομαι : Dep. :—to seek out, look for, τινά Il. II. to seek for, seek after a thing, Od. ; ἐέδνοισιν διζήμενος seeking to win her by gifts, Ib. ; δ. τὸ μαντήϊον to seek out, seek the meaning of, Hdt. ; ἀγγέλους δ. εἰ . . to inquire of them whether . . , Id. :—c. inf. to seek, desire to do, Id. ; c. acc. et inf. to demand or require that, Id. (Prob. redupl. from the same Root as ζη-τέω.)

δί-ζυξ, ζυγος, ὁ, ἡ, (ζυγόν) double-yoked, ἵπποι Il. : double, Anth.

δίζω, Ep. impf. δίζον, to be in doubt, at a loss, Il., Orac. ap. Hdt. (Prob. from the same Root as δίς ;— but) II. Med. δίζομαι, = δίζημαι, Theocr., Bion.

δί-ζωος, ον, (ζωή) with two lives, Sisyphus, who returned from Hades, Anth.

δι-ηγάγον, aor. 2 of διάγω.

δι-ηγέομαι, f. ήσομαι, Dep. to set out in detail, describe in full, Thuc., etc. Hence

διήγησις, εως, ἡ, narrative, statement, Plat.

δι-ηθέω, f. ήσω, to strain through, filter, Lat. percolare, Plat. 2. to wash out, cleanse, purge, Hdt. II. intr., of the liquid, to percolate, Id.

διηκονέω, διήκονος, Ion. for διᾱκ-.

δι-ηκόσιοι, Ion. for δι-ᾱκ-.

δι-ήκω, f. ξω, to extend or reach from one place to another, Hdt., Thuc. II. c. acc. to go through, pervade, Aesch., Soph. 2. to pass over, Aesch.

δι-ήλᾰσα, aor. 1 of διελαύνω.

δι-ῆλθον, aor. 2 of διέρχομαι.

δι-ημερεύω, f. σω, to stay through the day, pass the day, Plat., Xen.

δι-ήνεγκα, -ήνεικα, aor. 1 of διαφέρω.

δι-ηνεκής, Att. also δι-ᾰνεκής, ές, (δι-ήνεγκα) :—continuous, unbroken, Lat. continuus, Od. ; νώτοισι διηνεκέεσσι with slices cut the whole length of the chine, Il. :—Adv. διηνεκέως, continuously, from beginning to end, Lat. uno tenore, Od. : also distinctly, positively, Ib., Hes.

δι-ήνεμος, ον, (ἄνεμος) blown through, wind-swept, Soph.

δι-ήνοιξα, aor. 1 of διανοίγω.

δι-ῆξα, contr. aor. 1 of διαΐσσω.

δι-ηπειρόω, f. ώσω, to make dry land of, Anth.

δι-ήρεσα, aor. 1 of διερέσσω.

δι-ῄρημαι, pf. pass. of διαιρέω.

δι-ήρης, ες, (*ἄρω) double, μελάθρων διήρες an upper story, upper room, Eur.

δίηται, 3 sing. subj. med. of δίω.

δι-ήφῠσα, aor. 1 of διαφύσσω.

δι-ηχέω, f. ήσω, to transmit the sound of, τι Plut.

δι-θάλασσος, Att. -ττος, ον, (θάλασσα) between two seas, where two seas meet, N. T.

δί-θηκτος, ον, two-edged, ξίφος Aesch.

δί-θρονος, ον, two-throned, Ἀχαιῶν δ. κράτος the two-throned might of the Achaeans, i. e. the brother-kings, Aesch.

Διθύραμβο-γενής, ὁ, (γί-γνομαι) Bacchus-born, Anth.

δῑθῠραμβο-διδάσκαλος, ὁ, the dithyrambic poet who taught his own chorus, Ar.

δῑθύραμβος [ῠ], ὁ, the dithyramb ; a kind of lyric poetry, Hdt., Ar., etc. : its proper subject was the birth of Bacchus, Plat. (Deriv. uncertain.)

δί-θυρος, ον, (θύρα) with two doors, Plut. : with two leaves, of tablets, Luc.

δί-θυρσον, τό, (θύρσος) a double thyrsus, Anth.

Διΐ [υυ], Δί, dat. of Ζεύς.

δι-ιδεῖν, inf. of διεῖδον.

δι-ίημι, f. -ήσω, aor. 1 -ῆκα, to drive or thrust through a thing, c. gen., Od., Eur. ; also c. dupl. acc., λόγχην δ. στέρνα Id. 2. to let people go through a country, give them a passage through, Xen., Dem. :— c. gen. ξυμφορὰς τοῦ σοῦ διῆκας στόματος didst let them pass through thy mouth, gavest utterance to them, Soph. II. to send apart, to dismiss, disband, Xen. 2. to dissolve : in Med., διέμενος ὄξει having diluted it with vinegar, Ar.

δι-ιθύνω [ῠ], to direct by steering, Anth.

δι-ικνέομαι, f. -ίξομαι, aor. 2 -ικόμην : Dep. :—to go through, penetrate, Plut. :—to reach, with missiles, Thuc. 2. in speaking, to go through, recount, Il.

Δῖιος, ον, (Δίς = Ζεύς) of Zeus, Plat.

Διῑ-πετής, ές, (πι-πτω) fallen from Zeus, i. e. from heaven, of streams, fed or swollen by rain, Hom. 2. generally, divine, bright, pure, Eur.

Διῑ-πετής, ές, (πέτομαι) hovering in air, h. Hom.

δι-ιστέον, verb. Adj. of διοῖδα, one must learn, Eur.

δι-ίστημι, f. -στήσω, to set apart, to place separately, separate, Thuc., Dem. 2. to set one at variance with another, τινά τινος Ar., Thuc. ; δ. τὴν Ἑλλάδα to divide it into fractions, Hdt. II. Med. and Pass., with aor. 2, pf., and plqpf. act., to stand apart, to be divided, Il. ; θάλασσα διίστατο the sea made way, opened, Ib. ; τὰ διεστεῶτα chasms, Hdt. 2. of persons, to stand apart, be at variance, Il., Thuc. ; διέστη ἐς ξυμμαχίαν ἑκατέρων sided with one or the other party, Id. :—simply to differ, be different, Xen. 3. to part after fighting, Hdt. 4. to stand at certain distances or intervals, Id. ; of soldiers, δ. κατὰ διακοσίους Thuc. III. aor. 1 med. is trans. to separate, Plat., Theocr.

δι-ισχῡρίζομαι, f. Att. -ιοῦμαι, Dep. to lean upon, rely on, τινι Aeschin. II. to affirm confidently, τι Plat. ; δ. τι εἶναι Id.

δι-ιτέον, verbal of δίειμι, *one must go through*, Plat.

Διϊ-τρεφής, ές, later form of Διοτρεφής, Ar.

δἴκάζω, f. σω, Ion. δικῶ : aor. 1 ἐδίκασα Ep. δίκασα, δίκασσα :—Pass., f. δικασθήσομαι and δεδικάσομαι : aor. 1 ἐδικάσθην : pf. δεδίκασμαι : (δίκη) : **I.** *to judge, to give judgment on* a thing, *decide* or *determine* a point, Il., etc. **2.** c. acc. cogn., δίκας δ., *to adjudge* a penalty, Hdt. ; δ. φυγήν τινι *to decree* it as his punishment, Aesch. ; δ. φόνον ματρός *to ordain* her slaughter, Eur. ; δ. τοῦ ἐγκλήματος [sc. δίκην] Xen. :—Pass. *to be decided*, Thuc. **3.** *to pass judgment on, condemn*, Soph. **4.** φόνον δ. *to plead in* a case of murder, Eur. **5.** c. dat. pers. *to decide between persons, judge* their cause, Τρωσί τε καὶ Δαναοῖσι δικαζέτω Il. ; ἐς μέσον ἀμφοτέροισι δικάσσατε Ib. :—Pass. *to be judged* or *accused*, Xen. **6.** absol. *to be judge, give judgment*, Il. :—*to sit as judges* or *jurymen*, Dem. **II.** Med. of the culprit, *to plead one's own case, defend one's right, have one's case tried, go to law*, Od., etc. :—δίκην δικάζεσθαί τινι *to go to law* with one, Plat. ; πρός τινα Thuc. ; τινος or περί τινος *for* a thing, Dem.

δίκαιεῦν, Ion. for δικαιοῦν, inf. of δικαιόω :—δικαιεῦσι, 3 pl.

δἴκαιο-κρῐσία, ἡ, (κρίσις) *righteous judgment*, N. T.

δἴκαιο-λογέομαι, f. -ήσομαι : aor. 1 ἐδικαιολογησάμην or ἐδικαιολογήθην : (λόγος) : Dep. :—*to plead one's cause before the judge*, Aeschin. **II.** in Act., οἱ δικαιολογοῦντες *advocates*, Luc.

δἴκαιό-πολις, εως, ὁ, ἡ, *strict in public faith*, Pind.

δἴκαιο-πρᾱγέω, f. ήσω, *to act honestly*, Arist. Hence

δἴκαιοπράγημα, ατος, τό, *a just* or *honest act*, Arist. ; and

δἴκαιοπρᾱγία, ἡ, *just* or *honest dealing*, Arist.

δίκαιος [ῐ], α, ον, and ος, ον : (δίκη) : **A.** in Hom. and early writers, **I.** of persons, *observant of custom and social rule, well-ordered, civilised*, Od. ; so, δικαίη ζόη a *regular* way of living, Hdt. :—Adv., δικαίως μνᾶσθαι *to woo in due form, decently*, Od. **2.** *observant of right, righteous*, Hom., etc. :—so of actions, *in accordance with right, righteous*, Id. **B.** later usage : **I.** of things, *even, well-balanced*, ἅρμα δίκαιον Xen.:—*regular, exact, rigid*, ὀργυιαὶ δίκαιαι Hdt. ; τῷ δικαιοτάτῳ τῶν λόγων *to speak quite exactly*, Id. ; πάντα δικαίως τετήρηται Dem. **2.** *right, lawful, just*, τὸ δίκαιον *right*, opp. to τὸ ἄδικον, Hdt., etc. ; also, *a right, a lawful claim*, Thuc., etc.:—Adv. -ως, *rightly, justly*, Hdt., etc. **II.** of persons, *as well as things, like* Lat. *justus, meet, right, fitting*, Aesch. ; ἵππον δ. ποιεῖσθαί τινι to make a horse *fit for* another's *use*, Xen. **2.** *real, genuine, true*, Dem., συγγραφεύς Luc. :—Adv. -ως, *really and truly*, Soph. **3.** *fair, moderate*, like μέτριος, Thuc. :—δικαίως *with reason*, Soph., Thuc.

C. in Prose, δίκαιός εἰμι with inf., δίκαιοί ἐστε ἰέναι you *are bound to come*, Hdt. ; δ. εἰμι κολάζειν I *have a right* to punish, Ar. ; δίκαιοί εἰσι ἀπιστότατοι εἶναι they *have reason* to be most distrustful, Thuc. ; δ. ἐστιν ἀπολωλέναι *dignus est qui pereat*, Dem. :—we should say δίκαιόν ἐστι, which also occurs.

δἴκαιοσύνη, ἡ, *righteousness, justice*, Theogn., Hdt., etc. ; and

δικαιότης, ητος, ἡ, = δικαιοσύνη, Xen., Plat., etc.

δἴκαιόω, Ion. impf. δικαιεῦν : f. ώσω and ὥσομαι : aor. 1 ἐδικαίωσα:—Pass., aor. 1 ἐδικαιώθην : (δίκαιος): **I.** *to set right* : Pass., δικαιωθείς *proved, tested*, Aesch. **II.** *to hold* or *deem right, think fit, demand*, c. inf., Hdt., etc. ; inf. omitted, as οὕτω δικαιοῦν (sc. γενέσθαι) Id. :—*to consent*, δουλεύειν Id. ; οὐ δ. *to refuse*, Thuc. :—c. acc. pers. et inf. *to desire* one to do, Hdt. **III.** *to do a man right* or *justice, to judge*, i. e., **1.** *to condemn*, Thuc. : *to chastise, punish*, Hdt. **2.** *to deem righteous, justify*, N. T. Hence

δικαίωμα, ατος, τό, *an act by which wrong is set right* : —*a judgment, punishment, penalty*, Plat. **2.** *a plea of right*, Thuc. : *justification*, N. T. : and **3.** *an ordinance, decree*, Ib.

δικαίωσις, εως, ἡ, *a setting right, doing justice to* : *punishment*, Thuc. **2.** *a deeming righteous, justification*, N. T. **II.** *a demand of right* or *as of right, a just claim*, Thuc. **III.** *judgment of what is right*, Id.

δικαιωτήριον, τό, (δικαιόω) *a house of correction*, Plat.

δἴκᾱνικός, ή, όν, **I.** of persons, *skilled in law, versed in pleading, lawyer-like*, Plat., Xen., etc. **II.** of things, *belonging to trials, judicial*, Ar., Plat., etc. : *like a lawyer's speech, tedious*, Id.

δἴ-κάρηνος, ον, *two-headed*, (δίς, κάρηνον) Batr., Anth.

δίκασ-πόλος, ὁ, (πολέω) *one who administers law, a judge*, Hom.

δικαστήρ, ῆρος, ὁ, = δικαστής, Babr.

δικαστηρίδιον [ρῐ], τό, Dim. of δικαστήριον, Ar.

δικαστήριον, τό, (δικάζω) *a court of justice*, Hdt., Ar., etc. :—ὑπὸ δ. ἄγειν, ὑπάγειν τινά Hdt. ; εἰς δ. ἄγειν Plat. **2.** *the court*, i. e. *the judges*, Ar., Dem.

δἴκαστής, οῦ, ὁ, (δικάζω) *a judge*, Hdt., Aesch., etc. **2.** at Athens, the δικασταί, like the Roman *judices*, were more like our *jurymen* (the *presiding judge* being ὁ κριτής), Soph., etc. **II.** δ. αἵματος *an avenger*, Eur. Hence

δἴκαστικός, ή, όν, *of* or *for law* or *trials, practised in them*, Xen. **II.** as Subst., τὸ δ. *the juror's fee*, at first *one obol*, then *three obols*, Ar.

δἴκάστρια, ἡ, (δικαστής) *a she-judge*, Luc.

ΔΙ'ΚΕΙΝ, inf. of ἔδικον, aor. 2, with no pres. in use, *to throw, cast*, Aesch., Eur. **2.** *to strike*, Pind., Eur.

δί-κελλα [ῐ], ης, ἡ, (δίς, κέλλω) *a mattock, a two-pronged hoe*, Soph., Eur. Hence

δῐκελλίτης [λῑ], ου, ὁ, *a digger*, Luc.

δῐ-κέραιος, ον, (κέρας) *two-horned, two-pointed*, Anth.

δί-κερως, ωτος, ὁ, ἡ, (κέρας) *two-horned*, h. Hom.

ΔΙ'ΚΗ [ῐ], ἡ, *custom, usage*, αὕτη δίκη ἐστὶ βροτῶν this is the custom of mortals, Od. ; ἡ γὰρ δίκη ἐστὶ γερόντων Ib. :—acc. δίκην as Adv., *after the manner of*, c. gen., δίκην ὕδατος Aesch., Plat. **II.** *right as dependent on custom, law, right*, Hom., etc. **2.** δίκη ἐστί, like δίκαιόν ἐστι, Aesch. :—δίκῃ *duly, rightly*, Il., Trag. ; κατὰ δίκην Hdt. ; μετὰ δίκης Plat. ; πρὸς δίκης Soph. **III.** *a judgment*, δίκην εἰπεῖν *to give judgment*, Il.: pl. *righteous judgments*, Hom. **IV.** after Hom., *a lawsuit*, properly, *a private suit* of *action*, opp. to γραφή (*a public suit* or *indictment*), Plat., etc. **2.** *the trial* of the case, πρὸ δίκης

Thuc. 3. *the penalty awarded by the judge*, δίκην τίνειν, ἐκτίνειν Hdt., Soph. ; δίκην or δίκας διδόναι to *make amends*, suffer *punishment*, Lat. *poenas dare*, Hdt., Att. ; δίκας δοῦναι, also, to submit to *trial*, Thuc. :—δίκας λαμβάνειν is sometimes = δ. διδόναι, Lat. *dare poenas*, Hdt., Dem.; but also like Lat. *sumere poenas*, to inflict *punishment*, take *vengeance*, λαβεῖν δίκην παρά τινος Id. :—also, δίκας or δίκην ὑπέχειν to stand *trial*, Hdt., Soph.; δίκην παρέχειν Eur. :—δίκην ὀφλεῖν ὑπό τινος to incur *penalty*, Plat. ; δίκην φεύγειν to be the defendant in *the trial* (opp. to διώκειν to prosecute), Dem. :—δίκας αἰτέειν to demand *satisfaction*, τινός for a thing, Hdt. ; δίκην τίσασθαι, v. τίνω II :—δίκας διδόναι καὶ λαμβάνειν παρ' ἀλλήλων to have their causes tried, of subject-states whose causes were tried in the courts of the ruling state, Id.; δ. δοῦναι καὶ δέξασθαι to submit differences to a peaceful settlement, Thuc.

δίκη-φόρος, ον, (φέρω) *bringing justice, avenging*, Ζεύς Aesch.; ἡμέρα δ. the day of *vengeance*, Id. :—as Subst. *an avenger*, Id.

δικίδιον [ῐδ], τό, Dim. of δίκη, *a little trial*, Ar.

δικλίς, ίδος, ἡ, (κλίνω) *double-folding*, of doors or gates, in pl., Od. ; rarely in sing., Theocr., Anth.

δικο-γραφία, ἡ, (γράφω) *the composition of law-speeches*, Isocr.

δικο-λέκτης, ου, ὁ, = δικολόγος, Anth.

δικο-λόγος, ὁ, (λέγω) *a pleader, advocate*, Plut.

δικορράφέω, f. ήσω, *to get up a lawsuit*, Ar. From

δικορ-ράφος [ᾰ], ὁ, (ῥάπτω) *a pettifogger*.

δι-κόρυμβος, ον, *two-pointed, two-peaked*, Luc.

δι-κόρυφος, ον, (κορυφή) *two-peaked*, of Parnassus, Eur.

δί-κρανον, τό, (δίς, κάρα) *a pitch-fork*, Luc.

δι-κράτής, ές, (κράτος) *co-mate in power*, Soph. ; δικρατεῖς λόγχαι *double-slaying* spears, Id.

δί-κροος, contr. **δίκρους**, α, ουν; or **δικρόος**, contr. **δικροῦς**, ᾶ, οῦν, *forked, cloven, bifurcate*, Xen.

δί-κροτος, ον, *double-beating*, κῶπαι Eur. 2. of ships, *double-oared* or *with two banks of oars*, Xen. II. δ. ἁμαξιτός a road *for two cars*, Eur.

δικτάτωρ [ᾱ], οπος or ωρος, ὁ, the Roman *dictator*, Polyb. Hence

δικτᾱτωρεία or -ία, ἡ, *the dictatorship*, Plut.

δικτῠβολέω, f. ήσω, *to cast the net*, Anth. From

δικτῠ-βόλος, ον, (βάλλω) *a fisherman*, Anth.

Δίκτυννα, ἡ, (δίκτυον) Artemis as *goddess of the chase*, Hdt., Eur.

δικτῠό-κλωστος, ον, (κλώθω) *woven in meshes*, σπεῖραι δ. the net's meshy coils, Soph.

δίκτυον, τό, (δικεῖν) *a casting-net, a net*, Od., Aesch. : *a hunting-net*, Hdt., Ar. :—metaph. δ. ἄτης, Ἅιδου Aesch.

δικτυόομαι, Pass. *to be caught in a net*, Babr.

δίκτυς, υος, ὁ, an unknown Libyan animal, Hdt.

*δίκω, v. δικεῖν.

δικωπία, ἡ, *a pair of sculls*, Luc. From

δί-κωπος, ον, (δίς, κώπη) *two-oared*, σκάφος Eur.

δῑλογέω, f. ήσω, *to say again, repeat*, Xen. ; and

δῑλογία, ἡ, *repetition*, Xen. From

δί-λογος, ον, (δίς) *double-tongued, doubtful*, N. T.

δί-λογχος, ον, (δίς, λόγχη) *double-pointed, two-fold*, Aesch.

δί-λοφος, ον, *double-crested*, of Parnassus, Soph.

δι-μναῖος, α, ον, or **δι-μνέως**, ων, (δίς, μνᾶ) *worth* or *costing two minae*, διμναίους ἀποτιμήσασθαι to value *at two minae*, Hdt.

δῐμοιρία, ἡ, *a double share*, Xen. : *double pay*, Id. From

δί-μοιρος, ον, (δίς, μοῖρα) *divided in two, double*, Aesch.

δί-μορος, ον, = foreg., Aesch.

δίνευμα [ῐ], τό, *a whirling round*, in dancing, Xen.

δινεύω, Ion. impf. δινεύεσκον : f. εύσω :—also **δῑνέω**, impf. ἐδίνεον, Ep. δίνεον : f. ήσω : aor. 1 ἐδίνησα :—Pass., aor. 1 ἐδινήθην : pf. δεδίνημαι : (δίνη):—*to whirl* or *twirl round*, or *spin round*, Hom. : *to drive round a circle*, Il. :—Pass. *to whirl* or *roll about*, Hom. : of a river, *to eddy*, Eur. : *to whirl round* in the dance, Xen. 2. Pass., also, *to roam about*, Lat. *versari*, Od. II. intr. in Act., just like Pass. *to whirl about*, of dancers or tumblers, Il. ; of a pigeon *circling in its flight*, Ib. ; generally, *to roam about*, Hom. ; δινεύειν βλεφάροις to look wildly about, Eur.

ΔΙ΄ΝΗ [ῑ], ἡ, *a whirlpool, eddy*, Lat. *vortex*, Il., etc. 2. *a whirlwind*, Ar. 3. generally, *a whirling, rotation*, Id., Plat. : metaph., ἀνάγκης δίναι Aesch. Hence

δινήεις, Dor. -άεις, εσσα, εν, *whirling, eddying*, Hom. II. *rounded*, Mosch.

δινητός, ή, όν, (δινέω) *whirled round*, Anth.

ΔΙ΄ΝΟΣ, ὁ, *a whirling, rotation*, Ar. II. *a round area*, where oxen trod out the corn, *a threshing-floor*, Xen. III. *a large round goblet*, Ar.

δίνω, only in pres. *to thresh out on the δῖνος* (II), Hes.

δῑν-ώδης, ες, (εἶδος) *eddying* ; τὰ δινώδη eddies, Plut.

δῑνωτός, ή, όν, (as if from δινόω) *turned, rounded*, Hom. : νώροπι χαλκῷ δινωτήν [sc. ἀσπίδα] *covered all round* with brazen plates, Il.

διό, Conjunct., for δι' ὅ, *wherefore, on which account*, Lat. *quapropter, quocirca, quare*, Thuc., Plat., etc.

Διό-βολος, ον, (βάλλω) *hurled by Zeus*, Soph., Eur.

Διο-γενέτωρ, ορος, ὁ, *giving birth to Zeus*, Eur.

Διο-γενής [ῑ in Hom.], ές, (γί-γνομαι) *sprung from Zeus*, of kings and princes, *ordained and upheld by Zeus*, Hom. ; of gods, Trag.

Διό-γνητος, ον, contr. for Διογένητος, = Διογενής, Hes.

Διό-γονος, ον, = Διογενής, Eur. [with ῐ].

δι-οδεύω, f. σω, *to travel through*, c. acc., Plut.

δι-οδοιπορέω, f. ήσω, = διοδεύω, Hdt.

δί-οδος, ἡ, *a way through, thoroughfare, passage*, Hdt., etc.; ἄστρων δίοδοι their *pathways*, Aesch.; δ. αἰτεῖσθαι, to demand *a passport* or *safe-conduct*, Ar.

Διό-δοτος, ον, = διόσδοτος, Aesch.

Διόθεν, (Διός, gen. of Ζεύς) Adv. *sent from Zeus, by his will* or *favour*, Il., Trag.

δι-οίγνυμι, f. ξω, *to open*, Ar. :—also **διοίγω**, Soph., Eur.

δίοιδα, pf. : v. διείδω.

δι-οιδέω, f. ήσω, strengthd. for οἰδέω, Luc.

δι-οικέω, impf. διῴκουν : f. -ήσω : aor. 1 διῴκησα : pf. διῴκηκα :—Pass., aor. 1 διῳκήθην : pf. διῴκημαι :—properly *to manage a house* : then generally, *to manage, control, govern, administer*, τὴν πόλιν Thuc., etc.; esp. of financial matters, Dem. :—Med. *to manage after one's own will and pleasure*, τὰ πράγματα Id.; pf. pass. (in same sense), Id. 2. *to provide, furnish*, Id. II. *to inhabit distinct places*, Plat. :—Med. *to live apart*, Xen. Hence

διοίκησις, εως, ἡ, government, administration, τῆς πόλεως Plat., etc.; esp. the treasury-department, Dem.; ὁ ἐπὶ τῆς διοικήσεως the controller, treasurer, ap. Dem.   II. one of the lesser Roman provinces, Cic.   2. as an Eccles. division, a diocese.

δι-οικίζω, f. Att. ιῶ, to cause to live apart, Dem.: —Pass., Xen. Hence

διοικισμός, ὁ, a dispersion, Plut.

δι-οικοδομέω, f. ήσω, to build across, wall off, Thuc.

δι-οιστέον, verb. Adj. of διαφέρω (διοίσω, f. of διαφέρω) one must move round, Eur.

δι-οϊστεύω, f. σω, to shoot an arrow through, c. gen., Od.   καί κεν διοϊστεύσειας thou mightest reach it with an arrow, i. e. but a bow-shot off, Ib.

δι-οίσω, δι-οίσομαι, f. act. and med. of διαφέρω.

δίοιτο, 3 sing. opt. med. of δίω.

δι-οιχνέω, f. ήσω, to go through, c. acc., Aesch.   II. absol. to wander about, h. Hom.

δι-οίχομαι, f. -οιχήσομαι: pf. -οίχημαι: Dep. :—to be quite gone by, of time, Hdt.: of persons, to be clean gone, to have perished, Lat. periisse, Soph., Eur.   II. to be gone through, ended, Soph., Eur.

διοκωχή, ἡ, (διέχω) a cessation, Thuc.

δι-ολισθάνω, f. -ολισθήσω, to slip through, to give one the slip, c. acc., Ar. : absol. to slip away, Luc.

δι-όλλυμι or -ύω: f. -ολέσω, Att. -ολῶ :—to destroy utterly, bring to naught, Soph., Plat., etc. :—Pass., with fut. -ολοῦμαι, pf. -όλωλα, to perish utterly, come to naught, Trag., Thuc.   II. to blot out of one's mind, forget, Soph.

δι-ομᾰλίζω, f. σω, to be always evenminded, Plut.

Διομει-αλαζών, ὁ, a braggart of the deme Diomeia, Ar.

Διομήδειος, α, ον, of or like Diomedes, ἡ Διομήδεια λεγομένη ἀνάγκη, i. e. absolute, fatal necessity, Plat.

Διο-μήδης (μήδος), εος, ὁ, Jove-counselled ; in Hom. as prop. n. Diomedes.

δι-όμνυμι, f. -ομόσω : aor. 1 -ώμοσα : pf. -ομώμοκα : —to swear solemnly, to declare on oath that . . , c. inf. fut., Soph. :—Med. διόμνυμαι, f. -ομοῦμαι, Id., Plat., etc. ; διομνύμενος on oath, Dem.

δι-ομολογέω, f. ήσω, to make an agreement, undertake, Xen. :—Pass. to be agreed on, Plat. :—Med. to agree mutually, to agree upon certain points, take as granted, concede, δ. τι εἶναι Id. ; περί τινος Id.

διομολόγησις, εως, ἡ, a convention, Polyb.

διομολογητέον, verb. Adj. one must concede, Plat.

διομολογία, ἡ, = διομολόγησις, Isaeus.

δίον, acc. of δῖος ; but   II. δίον, Ep. impf. of δίω.

δι-ονομάζω, f. σω, to distinguish by a name, Plat.   II. Pass. to be widely known, Isocr.

Διονύσια [ῠ], (sc. ἱερά), τά, the feast of Dionysus or Bacchus at Athens, of which there were four: viz. 1. τὰ κατ' ἀγρούς or τὰ μικρά, in Poseideon (December). 2. τὰ ἐν Λίμναις or τὰ Λήναια (in the suburb Λίμναι, where the Λήναιον stood), in Gamelion (January). 3. τὰ 'Ανθεστήρια in Anthesterion (February). 4. τὰ ἀστικά or τὰ κατ' ἄστυ, also called τὰ μέγαλα or simply τὰ Διονύσια, in Elaphebolion (March), when Athens was full of strangers, and new Dramas were performed. Hence

Διονῡσιάζω, f. σω, to keep the Dionysia : hence to live extravagantly, Luc.

Διονυσιακός, ή, όν, belonging to Dionysus, Thuc., Arist.

Διονῡσιάς, άδος, ἡ, fem. of Διονυσιακός, Eur.

Διόνῡσος, Ep. also Διώνῡσος, ὁ, Dionysus, Od., etc. : v. Βάκχος. (Deriv. uncertain.)

Διό-παις, παιδος, ὁ, son of Zeus, Anth.

διόπερ or δι' ὅπερ, = διό, Thuc.

Διο-πετής, ές, (πί-πτω) that fell from Zeus, Eur. From

διοπεύω, to be in charge of a ship, ap. Dem. From

δίοπος, ὁ, (διέπω) a ruler, commander, Aesch., Eur.

διοπτεύω, f. σω, to watch accurately, spy about, Il. : to look into, στέγος Soph. From

δι-οπτήρ, ῆρος, ὁ, (ὄψομαι, f. of ὁράω) a spy, scout, Il.

δι-όπτης, ου, ὁ, (ὄψομαι, f. of ὁράω) a looker through, ὦ Ζεῦ διόπτα! says Dicaeopolis, holding up a ragged garment to the light, Ar.   II. = foreg., Eur.

δι-όπτρα, ἡ, (ὄψομαι, f. of ὁράω) an instrument for measuring heights, a Jacob's staff, Polyb. Hence

διοπτρικός, ή, όν, of, belonging to the use of the διόπτρα, Strab.

δι-οράω, f. -όψομαι, to see through, see clearly, Xen.

δι-όργυιος, ον, (ὄργυια) two fathoms long, high, Hdt.

δι-ορθεύω, f. σω, to judge rightly, Eur.

δι-ορθόω, f. ώσω, to make quite straight, set right, amend, δ. ἔριν to make up a quarrel, Eur. :—Med. to amend for oneself, διορθοῦσθαι περί τινος to take full security for . . , Dem. Hence

διόρθωμα, τό, a making straight, amendment, Plut.; and

διόρθωσις, εως, ἡ, a making straight, restoration, reform, Arist. ; and

διορθωτής, οῦ, ὁ, a corrector, reformer, Plut.

δι-ορίζω, Ion. δι-ουρίζω, f. Att. -οριῶ, to draw a boundary through, divide by limits, separate, Hdt., Plat. 2. to distinguish, determine, define, Hdt., Aesch., etc. 3. to determine, declare, Soph. ; c. inf. to determine one to be so and so, Dem. ; with inf. omitted, μικρὸν καὶ μέγαν διώρισαν με Soph. :—Med., with pf. pass. in med. sense, Dem. 4. absol. to draw distinction, lay down definitions, Id. :—so in Med., Ar., etc.   II. to remove across the frontier, to banish, Eur., Plat. : generally, to carry abroad, Eur. ; δ. πόδα to depart, Id. Hence

διόρισις, εως, ἡ, and διορισμός, ὁ, distinction, Plat.

διόρυγμα, ατος, τό, a through-cut, canal, Thuc. From

δι-ορύσσω, Att. -ττω, f. ξω, to dig through or across, τάφρον Od. ; τοῖχον δ. = τοιχωρυχέω, Hdt., Ar.

δι-ορχέομαι, f. ήσομαι, Dep. to dance a match with one, τινί Ar.

δῖος, δῖα, δῖον (fem. δῖος and δία in Eur.), contr. for δῖιος: (Διός, gen. of Δίς) :—god-like, divine, Il. ; δῖα γυναικῶν noblest of women, Od. :—also worthy, trusty, the swineherd, Ib. ; of whole nations or cities, Hom. ; of a noble horse, Il. 2. of things, like θεῖος, θεσπέσιος, ἱερός, divine, wondrous, Hom.   II. in literal sense, of or from Zeus, Aesch.

Διός [ῑ], gen. of Ζεύς, from *Δίς.

Διόσ-δοτος, ον, (δί-δωμι) given by Zeus, Aesch.

Διο-σημία, ἡ, (σῆμα) a sign from Zeus, an omen from the sky, of a sudden storm, Ar.

Διοσκόρειον, τό, the temple of the Dioscuri, Thuc. From

Διόσ-κοροι, Ion. -κουροι, οἱ, the sons of Zeus and Leda, Castor and Pollux, h. Hom.   II. the con-

stellation named from them, *the Twins*, Lat. *Gemini*, Luc.

δι-ότι, Conjunct. for διὰ τοῦτο ὅτι, *for the reason that, since*, Hdt., etc. 2. indirect, *wherefore, for what reason*, μανθάνειν διότι Id. II. = ὅτι, *that*, Id., Dem.

Διο-τρεφής, ές, (τρέφω) *cherished by Zeus*, of kings and nobles, Hom.

διουρίζω, Ion. for διορίζω.

δι-οχετεύομαι, Pass. *to be watered by canals* (ὀχετοί), Strab.

δι-οχλέω, f. ήσω, *to trouble* or *annoy exceedingly*, Dem.

δι-όψομαι, f. of διοράω.

δί-παις, παιδος, ὁ, ἡ, *with two children*, Aesch. 2. δ. θρῆνος a dirge *chanted by one's two children*, Id.

δι-πάλαιστος, ον, (παλαιστή) *two palms broad*, Xen.

δί-παλτος, ον, (πάλλω) *brandished with both hands, two-handed*, Eur. :—δίπαλτος ἄν με φονεύοι would kill me *each with two spears*, Soph.

δί-πηχυς, υ, *two cubits long, broad*, etc., Hdt., etc.

διπλάδιος [ᾰ], ον, *double*, poët. for διπλάσιος, Anth.

διπλάζω, = διπλασιάζω, *to double*, Eur. II. intr., τὸ δίπλαζον κακόν the *twofold evil*, Soph.

δί-πλαξ, ᾰκος, ὁ, ἡ, *twofold, double, in double folds*, Il. II. as Subst., δίπλαξ, ἡ, a *double-folded mantle*, Hom. 2. in pl. *ship-planks* (doubled one over the one below), Aesch.

διπλᾰσιάζω, f. άσω, *to double*, Xen.; and

διπλᾰσιόομαι, Pass. *to become twofold*, Thuc. From

δι-πλάσιος [ᾰ], α, ον, Ion. **δι-πλήσιος**, η, ον, (δίς) *twofold, double, twice as much as, twice as many as, as long as*, etc., Hdt., etc.; as Comp. foll. by ἤ . . , Id.; or c. gen. *twice the size of*, Id. 2. as Subst., διπλάσιον, τό, *as much again*, Lat. *duplum*, Id. 3. διπλασίαν (sc. ζημίαν), ap. Dem. 4. Adv. -ως, *doubly*, Thuc., Aeschin. (The deriv. of -πλάσιος is uncertain.)

δί-πλεθρος, ον, *two πλέθρα long* or *broad*, Luc.

διπλῆ, Adv. *twice, twice over*, Soph., Eur.

διπλήσιος, Ion. for διπλάσιος.

διπλοΐζω, = διπλασιάζω, Aesch.; and

διπλοΐς, ίδος, ἡ, a *double cloak*, like δίπλαξ, Anth. From

δι-πλόος, η, ον, contr. **δι-πλοῦς**, ῆ, οῦν: (δίς, cf. ἁπλόος) :—*twofold, double*, Lat. *duplex*, of a cloak, Hom.; ὅθι δίπλοος ἤντετο θώρηξ where the cuirass met [the buckle] *so as to be double*, Il. :—παῖσον διπλῆν (sc. πληγήν), Soph.; διπλῆ ἄκανθα spine *bent double* by age, Eur.; διπλῇ χερί by *mutual* slaughter, Soph. II. in pl., = δύο, Aesch., Soph. III. *double-minded, treacherous*, Plat., Xen.

διπλός, ή, όν, poët. for διπλόος, Anth., N. T.

διπλόω, f. ώσω, (διπλόος) *to double*, Xen. :—Pass., of a sword, *to be bent double*, Plut. II. *to repay twofold*, N. T. Hence

δίπλωμα, ατος, τό, a *doubled* or *folded paper*, a *letter of recommendation, diploma*, Cic., Plut.; and

δίπλωσις, εως, ἡ, a *compounding of words*, Arist.

δι-πόδης, ες, (πούς) *two feet long, broad*, etc., Xen.

Δϊ-πόλεια or **Δι-πόλια**, τά, contr. from Διϊ-π-, (*Δίς) an ancient *festival of Zeus* at Athens, Ar. Hence

Δϊπολι-ώδης, ες, (εἶδος) *like the Διπόλια*, i. e. *obsolete, out of date*, Ar.

δί-πορος, ον, *with two roads* or *openings*, Eur.

δί-ποτάμος, ον, *between two rivers*, Eur.

δί-πους, ποδος, ὁ, ἡ, *two-footed*, Lat. *bipes*, Aesch., Plat., etc. 2. δίπους, ὁ, *the jerboa*, which springs from its two hind feet, like the kangaroo, Hdt. II. *two feet long*, Lat. *bipedalis*, Plat.

δί-πτῠχος, ον, (πτυχή) *double-folded, doubled*, Od.; δ. δελτίον a pair of tablets, Hdt. :—neut. pl. as Adv., δίπτυχα ποιήσαντες [τὴν κνῖσαν], *having doubled* the fat, i. e. putting one layer of fat under the thighs (μηροί) and another over them, Il. II. *twofold*, Lat. *geminus*, Eur. : and in pl. = δισσοί, *two*, Id.

δί-πῠλος, ον, (πύλη) *double-gated, with two entrances*, Soph. II. δίπυλον, τό, a gate at Athens, Plut.

δί-πῠρος, ον, (πῦρ) *with double flame*, Ar.

δίρ-ρῠμος, ον, *with two poles*, i. e. *three horses*, Aesch.

δίς (for δϝίς, from δύο), Adv. *twice, doubly*, Lat. *bis*, Od., Hdt., Att.

-δις, inseparable Suffix, signifying *motion to a place*, like -δε, as in ἄλλυδις, οἴκαδις, χαμάδις, etc.

***Δίς**, an old nom. for Ζεύς, which appears in the oblique cases Διός, Διΐ, Δία, and Lat. *Dis, Dies-piter, Djovis*.

δισ-ᾱβος [ῐ], ον, Dor. for δίσηβος, *twice young*, Anth.

δίσ-ευνος, ον, (εὐνή) *with two wives*, Anth.

δισ-θᾰνής, ές, (θανεῖν, θνήσκω) *twice dead*, Od.

δισκεύω, f. σω, = δισκέω : Pass. *to be pitched*, Eur.

δισκέω, f. ήσω, *to pitch the quoit* (δίσκος), *play at quoits*, Od. :—Pass. *to be pitched*, Anth. Hence

δίσκημα, ατος, τό, a *thing thrown*, Eur.

δί-σκηπτρος, ον, (σκῆπτρον) *two-sceptred*, Aesch.

δισκο-βόλος, ὁ, (βάλλω) *the quoit-thrower*, a famous statue by Myron, Luc.

δίσκος, ὁ, (δικεῖν) *a sort of quoit*, made of stone, Od. II. *anything quoit-shaped, a trencher*, Anth. :—*a mirror*, Id.

δίσκ-ουρα, τά, (οὖρος) *a quoit's cast*, as a measure of distance, Il.

δισκο-φόρος, ον, (φέρω) *bringing the discus*, Luc.

δισ-μύριοι [ῠ], αι, α, *twenty thousand*, Hdt., etc.

δισσ-άρχης, ου, ὁ, (ἄρχω) *joint-ruling*, Soph.

δισσός, Att. **διττός**, Ion. **διξός**, ή, όν, (δίς) *two-fold, double*, Hdt. II. in pl. *two*, Id., Trag., etc. III. metaph. *double, divided, doubtful*, Aesch., Soph.

διστάζω, f. άσω, (δίς) *to be in doubt, hesitate*, Plat.

δί-στιχος, ον, *of two verses*, Anth. II. as Subst., δίστιχον, τό, a *distich*, Id.

δί-στολος, ον, (στέλλω) *in pairs, two together*, Soph.

δί-στομος, ον, (στόμα) *double-mouthed, with two entrances*, Soph.; δίστομοι ὁδοί *branching* roads, Id. II. of a weapon, *two-edged*, Eur.

δι-σύλλαβος, ον, (συλλαβή) *of two syllables*, Luc.

δισ-χίλιοι [ῑ], αι, α, *two thousand*, Hdt. :—sing. with collective nouns, δισχιλίη ἵππος 2000 horse, Id.

δί-τάλαντος, ον, (τάλαντον) *worth* or *weighing two talents*, Hdt. : *costing two talents*, Dem.

διττός, Att. for δισσός.

δι-υλίζω, f. σω, *to strain off*, τι N. T.

δι-υπνίζω, f. σω, (ὕπνος) *to awake from sleep*, Luc.

δι-υφαίνω, f. ᾰνῶ, *to fill up by weaving*, Luc.

δι-φάσιος [ᾰ], α, ον, = διπλάσιος, *two-fold, double*, Lat. *bifarius*, Hdt. II. in pl. = δύο, Id.

διφάω, only in pres., *to search after*, Il., Hes. :—Ion.

διφέω, Anth. Hence

διφήτωρ, opos, ὁ, a searcher, χρυσοῦ after gold, Anth.

διφθέρα, ἡ, (δέφω) a prepared hide, tanned skin, piece of leather, Hdt.; opp. to δέρρις (an undressed hide), Thuc. :—διφθέραι were used for writing-material in ancient times, before papyrus came in, Hdt. II. a leathern garment such as peasants wore, Ar., Plat. 2. a wallet, bag, Xen. 3. in pl. skins used as tents, Id. Hence

διφθερίας, ου, ὁ, one clad in leather, Luc.; and

διφθέρινος, η, ον, of tanned leather, Xen.

διφθερίς, ίδος, ἡ, = διφθέρα, Anth.

δίφραξ, ακος, ἡ, poët. for δίφρος, a seat, chair, Theocr.

διφρεία, ἡ, (διφρεύω) chariot-driving, Xen.

διφρ-ελάτειρα, ἡ, poët. fem. of διφρηλάτης, Anth.

διφρευτής, οῦ, ὁ, a charioteer, Soph. From

διφρεύω, f. σω, (δίφρος) to drive a chariot, Eur.; αἴγλαν ἐδίφρευε drove his beaming car, Id.

διφρηλάτέω, f. ήσω, to drive a chariot through, τὸν οὐρανόν, of the Sun, Soph. From

διφρ-ηλάτης [ᾰ], ου, ὁ, (ἐλαύνω) a charioteer, Trag.

δίφριος, α, ον, of a chariot : neut. pl. as Adv., δίφρια συρόμενος dragged at the chariot wheels, Anth.

διφρίσκος, ὁ, Dim. of δίφρος, Ar.

δί-φροντις, ιδος, ὁ, ἡ, divided in mind, distraught, Aesch.

δίφρος, ὁ, (syncop. for διφόρος) the chariot-board, on which two could stand, the driver (ἡνίοχος) and the combatant (παραιβάτης), Hom. 2. the war-chariot itself, Il. :—in Od. a travelling-chariot. II. a seat, chair, stool, Hom., Att.

διφρ-ουλκέω, f. ήσω, (ἕλκω) to draw a chariot, Anth.

διφρο-φορέω, f. ήσω, to carry in a chair or litter :— Pass. to travel in one, Hdt. II. to carry a camp-stool, Ar. From

διφρο-φόρος, ον, (φέρω) carrying a camp-stool ; of the female μέτοικοι, who carried seats for the κανηφόροι, Ar. II. carrying another upon a δίφρος, Plut.

δι-φυής, ές, (φυή) of double form, Hdt., Soph.

δί-φυιος [ῐ], ον, = διφυής : also = δύο, Aesch.

δίχᾰ [ῐ], (δίς), I. Adv. in two, asunder, Od., etc. :—generally, apart, aloof, Hdt., etc. 2. metaph. in two ways, at variance or in doubt, Hom., etc. II. Prep. with gen. apart from, Aesch., Soph. :—differently from, unlike, Id.; τοῦ ἑτέρου from the other, Thuc. 2. πόλεως δ. against the will of, Soph. 3. besides, except, like χωρίς, Aesch.

δίχα, Dor. for διχῇ.

διχάδε, Adv., = δίχα, Plat.

διχάζω, f. άσω, (δίχα) to divide in two, Plat. : δ. τινὰ κατά τινος to divide one against another, N. T.

δί-χαλκον, τό, a double chalcos, = ¼ of an obol, Anth.

δίχαλος, Dor. for δίχηλος.

διχαστής, οῦ, ὁ, (διχάζω) a divider, Arist.

διχῇ, Adv. = δίχα, in two, asunder, Aesch., Plat., etc. 2. in two ways, Id., Dem.

δί-χηλος, ον, Dor. δίχαλος, (χηλή) cloven-hoofed, Hdt., Eur. II. δίχηλον, τό, a forceps, pincers, Anth.

δῐχ-ήρης, ες, (*ἄρω) dividing the month in twain, c. gen., of the moon, Eur.

διχθά, Adv., Ep. for δίχα, δ. δεδαίαται they are parted in twain, Od.; δ. κραδίη μέμονε my heart is divided, Il.

διχθάδιος, α, ον, twofold, double, divided, Il.

διχογνωμονέω, f. ήσω, to differ in opinion, Xen. From

δῐχο-γνώμων, ὁ, ἡ, (γνώμη) divided between two opinions, Plut.

δῐχόθεν, (δίχα) Adv. from both sides, both ways, Aesch., Thuc., etc.

δί-χοίνῑκος, ον, holding 2 χοίνικες, near 3 pints, Ar.

δῐχομηνία, ἡ, the fullness of the moon, Plut.; and

δῐχό-μηνις, ιδος, ὁ, ἡ, = sq., Eur. From

δῐχό-μηνος, ον, (μήν) dividing the month, i. e. at or of the full moon, h. Hom., Plut.

δῐχό-μῡθος, ον, double-speaking, λέγειν διχόμυθα to speak ambiguously, Eur.

δῐχόνοια, ἡ, discord, disagreement, Plat. From

δῐχό-νοος, ον, contr. -νους, ουν, double-minded.

δῐχο-ρραγής, ές, (ῥήγνυμι) broken in twain, Eur.

δῐχόρ-ροπος, ον, (ῥέπω) oscillating : Adv. -πως, waveringly, doubtfully, Aesch.

δῐχοστᾰσία, ἡ, a standing apart, dissension, Hdt. : sedition, Solon, Theogn. From

δῐχο-στᾰτέω, f. ήσω, (στῆναι) to stand apart, disagree, Aesch. ; πρός τινα Eur.

δῐχοτομέω, f. ήσω, to cut in two, cut in twain, Plat., N. T. From

δῐχό-τομος, ον, (τέμνω) cut in half, divided equally, Arist.

δῐχοῦ, Adv., = δίχα, Hdt.

δῐχό-φρων, ον, gen. ονος, (φρήν) at variance, discordant, Aesch.

δί-χρωμος, ον, (χρῶμα) two-coloured, Luc.

δῐχῶς, (δίχα) Adv. doubly, in two ways, Aesch.

ΔΙ'ΨΑ [ᾰ], ης, ἡ, thirst, Il., etc. ; ποτοῦ for drink, Plat.

διψᾰλέος, α, ον, = δίψιος, thirsty, Batr.

διψάς, άδος, fem. of δίψιος, Anth.

διψάω (forms in αε contr. into η not α, as in πεινάω), 3 sing. διψῇ, inf. διψῆν: 3 sing. impf. ἐδίψη : f. -ήσω : aor. 1 ἐδίψησα : pf. δεδίψηκα : (δίψα) :—to thirst, διψῶν [ᾱ] Od. ; of the ground, to be thirsty, parched, Hdt. 2. metaph. to thirst after a thing, c. gen., Plat. : later c. acc., Anth., N. T. ; c. inf. to long to do, Xen.

δίψιος, α, ον, and ος, ον, (δίψα) thirsty, athirst, and of things, thirsty, dry, parched, Trag.

δίψος, εος, τό, = δίψα, Thuc., etc.

δί-ψῡχος, ον, (ψυχή) = δίθυμος, double-minded, N. T.

ΔΙ'Ω [ῐ], only in pres. and Ep. impf. δίον, (for δέδια, etc., v. δείδω) : 1. to run away, take to flight, flee, like δίεμαι Il. 2. to be afraid, δίε ποιμένι λαῶν μήτι πάθῃ Il. II. Causal in Med., subj. δίωμαι, δίηται, δίωνται, opt. δίοιτο, inf. δίεσθαι, to drive away, chase, put to flight, Hom., Aesch. :—simply to drive horses, Il. 2. to pursue, give chase, ἐπί τινα Aesch. : δ. λάχος to pursue, discharge an office, Id.

δι-ωβελία, ἡ, (δίς, ὀβολός) at Athens, the allowance of two obols to each citizen during the festivals, to pay for their seats in the theatre, Xen.

δίωγμα, ατος, τό, (διώκω) a pursuit, chase, Aesch., Eur. II. that which is chased, ' the chase,' Xen.

διωγμός, ὁ, (διώκω) the chase, Xen. II. pursuit, persecution, harassing, Aesch., Eur.

δι-ώδῑνος, ον, (ὀδύνη) with thrilling anguish, Soph.

δι-ωθέω, f. -ωθήσω and -ώσω, to push asunder, tear away, Il., Eur. 2. to thrust through, Plut. II.

Med. *to push asunder for oneself, force one's way through, break through*, c. acc., Hdt., Xen. **2.** *to push from oneself, push one another away*, of seamen keeping ships from collision, Thuc. :—*to drive back, repel, repulse*, Hdt., Eur. :—absol. *to get rid of danger*, Hdt. **3.** *to reject*, Lat. *respuere*, Id., Thuc. :—absol. *to refuse*, Hdt.

δι-ωθισμός, ὁ, *a pushing about, a scuffle*, Plat.

διωκαθεῖν [ᾰ], aor. 2 inf. of διώκω, cf. ἀμυναθεῖν.

διωκτέος, α, ον, verb. Adj. of διώκω, *to be pursued*, Hdt., Ar. **II. διωκτέον,** *one must pursue*, Plat.

διωκτήρ, ῆρος, ὁ, (διώκω) *a pursuer*, Babr. :—**διώκτης, ου, ὁ,** N. T.

διώκω, Ep. inf. διωκέμεναι, -έμεν : f. ξω and -ξομαι : aor. 1 ἐδίωξα : aor. 2 ἐδιώκάθον, inf. διωκαθεῖν :—Pass., f. διωχθήσομαι and in med. form διώξομαι : aor. 1 ἐδιώχθην : pf. δεδίωγμαι : (δίω II) :—*to pursue* a person, *to chase, hunt*, Il., etc. :—so in Med., διώκεσθαί τινα πεδίοιο *to chase* one over or across the plain, Hom.: —*to be a follower of* a person, *attach oneself* to him, Xen. **2.** *to pursue* an object, *seek after*, Od., etc. ; δ. τὰ συμβάντα *to follow* or *wait for* the event, Dem. **II.** *to drive* or *chase away, banish*, Od., Hdt. **III.** of the wind, *to drive* a ship, of rowers, *to impel, speed on her way*, Od. ; of a chariot, *to drive*, Orac. ap. Hdt. ; δ. πόδα *to urge on*, Aesch. :—then, intr. *to drive, drive on*, Il. : *to gallop, speed, run*, Aesch. **IV.** as law-term, *to prosecute, bring an action against* a man, ὁ διώκων *the prosecutor* (opp. to ὁ φεύγων the defendant), Hdt., etc. ; ὁ διώκων τοῦ ψηφίσματος *he who impeaches the words* of the decree, Dem. ; c. gen. poenae, θανάτου or περὶ θανάτου δ. τινά, Lat. *capitis accusare*, Xen. : but c. gen. criminis, *to accuse of, to prosecute for*, δ. τινὰ τυραννίδος Hdt. ; δειλίας Ar. ; φόνου Plat. ; but, φόνον τινὸς δ. *to avenge* another's murder, Eur.

δι-ωλένιος, ον, (ὠλένη) *with out-stretched arms*, Anth.

διωλύγιος, α, ον, *far-sounding, enormous, immense*, Plat. (Deriv. unknown.)

δι-ώμοσα, aor. 1 of διόμνυμι.

διωμοσία, ἡ, *an oath taken by both parties before the trial came on*, Oratt.

διώμοτος, ον, (διόμνυμι) *bound by oath*, Lat. *juratus*, c. inf., Soph.

δι-ώνῠμος, ον, (δίς, ὄνυμα = ὄνομα) *with two names*, or, of two persons, *named together*, Eur. **II.** (διά) *far-famed*, Plut.

Διώνυσος, etc., Ep. for Διόνυσος.

δῐωξι-κέλευθος, ον, *urging on the way*, Anth.

διώξ-ιππος, ον, *horse-driving*, Anth.

δίωξις, εως, ἡ, (διώκω) *chase, pursuit*, of persons, Thuc. **2.** *pursuit* of an object, Plat. **II.** as law-term, *prosecution*, Dem., etc.

διώρυγος, ον, = διόργυιος, Xen.

διῶρυξ, ὕχος, ἡ, (διορύσσω) *a trench, conduit, canal*, Hdt., Thuc. ; κρυπτὴ δ. *an underground passage*, Hdt.

διωρυχή, ἡ, (διορύσσω) *a digging through*, Dem.

δι-ῶσα, aor. 1 of διωθέω.

δίωσις, εως, ἡ, *a pushing off, delaying*, Arist.

δί-ωτος, ον, (δίς, οὖς) *two-eared* : *two-handled*, Plat.

δμηθῆναι, aor. 1 pass. inf. of δαμάζω.

δμῆσις, εως, ἡ, (δαμάζω) *a taming, breaking*, ἵππων Il.

δμητήρ, ῆρος, ὁ, (δαμάζω) *a tamer*, ἵππων h. Hom. :— fem., νὺξ δμητείρα θεῶν Il.

δμωή, ἡ, (δαμάζω) *a female slave taken in war*, Il. :— then, generally, *a female slave, serving-woman*, Lat. *ancilla*, Hom., Trag.

δμώϊος, ον, *in servile condition*, βρέφος Anth. ; and **δμωῖς, ίδος, ἡ,** = δμωή, Aesch., Eur. From

δμώς, ωός, ὁ, (δαμάζω) *a slave taken in war*, Od. :— then, generally, *a slave*, Ib., Soph., Eur. ; Ep. dat. pl. δμώεσσι Od.

δνοπᾰλίζω, f. ξω, *to shake violently, fling down*, Il. ; τὰ σὰ ῥάκεα δνοπαλίξεις ' *wrap* thy old cloak *about thee*,' Od. (Deriv. unknown.)

δνοφερός, ά, όν, *dark, dusk, murky*, Hom., Trag. From

δνόφος, ὁ, *darkness, dusk, gloom*, Simon., Aesch. (Akin to κνέφας.)

δνοφ-ώδης, ες, = δνοφερός, Eur.

δοάσσατο, 3 sing. Ep. aor. 1 med., = Att. ἔδοξε, *it seemed*, Hom. ; ὥς ἄν σοι πλήμνη δοάσσεται ἱκέσθαι (Ep. subj. for -ηται) *till the nave appear* to graze, Il. : cf. δέατο.

δόγμα, ατος, τό, (δοκέω) *that which seems to one, an opinion, dogma*, Plat. **2.** *a public decree, ordinance*, Xen., Dem. Hence

δογματίζω, f. σω, *to decree*, δ. τινὰ καλήν *to declare* her beautiful, Anth. **2.** in Pass., of persons, *to submit to ordinances*, N. T.

δοθήσομαι, f. pass. of δίδωμι.

δόθι, δός, 2 sing. aor. 2 imper. of δίδωμι.

δοθιήν, ῆνος, ὁ, *a small abscess, boil*, Ar. (Deriv. unknown.)

δοιδῠκο-ποιός, ὁ, (ποιέω) *a pestle-maker*, Plut. From

δοΐδυξ, ῠκος, ὁ, *a pestle*, Ar., etc. (Deriv. unknown.)

δοιή, ἡ, (δύο) *doubt, perplexity*, ἐν δοιῇ Il.

δοιοί, αί, ά, Ep. for δύο, *two, both*, Il., Hes., etc. : neut. δοιά as Adv. *in two ways, in two points*, Od. **II.** *two-fold, double*, Anth. Hence

δοιο-τόκος, ον, (τίκτω) *bearing twins*, Anth.

δοιώ, = δοιοί (of which it is properly the dual), = δύο, indecl., Hom.

***δοκάω,** assumed as pres. of δεδοκημένος : v. δέχομαι.

δοκεύω, f. σω, (δέχομαι) *to keep an eye upon, watch narrowly*, Il., Pind., Eur.

ΔΟΚΕΏ, impf. ἐδόκουν : f. and other tenses are two-fold, **1.** from *δόκω, f. δόξω, aor. 1 ἔδοξα, pass. ἐδόχθην : pf. pass. δέδογμαι. **2.** from δοκέω, f. δοκήσω, Dor. δοκησῶ or -ᾱσῶ : aor. 1 ἐδόκησα, Ep. δόκησα, pass. ἐδοκήθην ; pf. δεδόκηκα, pass. δεδόκημαι.

I. = *videor mihi, to think, suppose, imagine, expect*, c. acc. et inf., δοκέω νικησέμεν Il. ; οὔ σε δοκέω πείθεσθαι Hdt. ; τεκεῖν δράκοντ' ἔδοξεν *she thought* a serpent bare young ones, Aesch. ; ἔδοξα ἰδεῖν, Lat. *visus sum videre, methought* I saw, Eur. ; ἀείδειν δοκῶ *I think* to sing, Aesch. **2.** absol. *to have* or *form an opinion*, περί τινος Hdt. ; in parenthetic phrases, ὡς δοκῶ Trag. ; πῶς δοκεῖς ; *how think you?* Eur. **3.** δοκῶ μοι in Att., just like δοκεῖ μοι, as Lat. *videor mihi* for *videtur mihi*, *I seem to myself, methinks*, c. inf., Hdt., etc. ; also, *I am determined, resolved*, c. inf., Ar. **4.** c. inf., also, *to seem* or *pretend* to be doing, Lat. *simulo* ; or with a negat. *to seem* or *pretend* not to be doing, Lat. *dissimulo ;* ἤκουσά του λέγοντος, οὐ δοκῶν κλύειν Eur. **II.** = *videor, to*

seem to one, δοκέεις δέ μοι οὐκ ἀπινύσσειν Od.,
etc.　2. absol. *to seem*, as opp. to reality, οὐ δοκεῖν,
ἀλλ' εἶναι θέλει Aesch.　3. *to seem good*, Lat.
placere, εἰ δοκεῖ σοι ταῦτα Id.　4. impers., δοκεῖ μοι
much in the same sense as δοκῶ μοι (supr. I. 3), *it
seems to me*, *meseems*, *methinks*, ὥς μοι δοκεῖ εἶναι
ἄριστα Il., etc.:—in decrees and the like, ἔδοξε τῇ
βουλῇ, *placuit senatui*, Ar., Thuc., etc.; τὸ δόξαν
the decree, Hdt.; τὰ δόξαντα Soph.; παρὰ τὸ δοκοῦν
ἡμῖν Thuc.:—so in Pass., δέδοκται, Lat. *visum est*,
Hdt., Trag., etc.　b. acc. absol. δόξαν, *when it
was decreed* or *resolved*, δόξαν αὐτοῖς ὥστε διαναυ-
μαχεῖν* (i. e. ὅτε ἔδοξεν αὐτοῖς) Thuc.; so, δεδογμένον
αὐτοῖς Id.　5. *to be thought* or *reputed* so and
so, ἄξιοι δοκοῦντες Id.; οἱ δοκοῦντες εἶναί τι *men
who are held to be something*, *men of repute*, Plat.;
so οἱ δοκοῦντες alone, Eur.; τὰ δοκοῦντα, opp. to τὰ
μηδὲν ὄντα, Id.; also in Pass., οἱ δεδογμένοι ἀνδρόφονοι
those who have been found guilty of homicide, Dem.
δοκή, ἡ, (δοκέω) = δόκησις, *a vision*, *fancy*, Aesch.
δόκημα, ατος, τό, (δοκέω) *a vision, fancy*, Eur.; οἱ
δοκήμασιν σοφοί *the wise in appearance*, Id.　2.
opinion, expectation, Id.
δόκησις, εως, ἡ, (δοκέω) *an opinion, belief, conceit,
fancy*, Hdt., Soph.; δ. ἀγνὼς λόγων ἦλθε a vague
suspicion was thrown out, Id.　2. *an apparition,
phantom*, Eur.　II. *good report, credit*, Id., Thuc.
δοκησί-σοφος, ον, *wise in one's own conceit*, Id.
δοκιμάζω, f. άσω, (δόκιμος) *to assay* or *test* metals, to
see if they be pure, Isocr., etc.　II. of persons, *to put
to the test, make trial of, scrutinise*, Hdt., Thuc.:
—then, *to approve*, Id., Plat., etc.; c. inf.; ἐκπονεῖν
ἐδοκίμαζε he approved of *their working*, Xen.　III.
at Athens, *to approve as fit* for an office, and in Pass.
to be approved as fit, Plat., etc.; c. inf.; ἱππεύειν δε-
δοκιμασμένος Xen.　2. *to examine and admit* boys
to the class of ἔφηβοι or ἔφηβοι *to the rights of manhood*; and in Pass. *to be so admittd*, Ar., etc.; ἕως
ἀνὴρ εἶναι δοκιμαθείην Dem.　IV. c. inf. *to think
fit* to do, or with negat. *to refuse* to do, N.T.　Hence
δοκιμασία, ἡ, *an assay, examination, scrutiny*:　1.
of magistrates, to see if they fulfil the legal requirements, Plat., etc.　2. δ. τῶν ἐφήβων, before admission to the rights of manhood, Dem.　3. δ. τῶν
ῥητόρων, a process *to determine the right to speak* in
the ἐκκλησία or law-courts, Aeschin.
δοκιμαστής, οῦ, ὁ, (δοκιμάζω) *an assayer, scrutineer*,
Plat., Dem.　II. *an approver, panegyrist*, Id.
δοκιμεῖον or δοκίμιον, τό, (δόκιμος) *a test, means of
testing*, Plat., N.T.　From
δοκιμή, ἡ, *a proof, test: tried character*, N.T.　From
δόκιμος, ον, (δέχομαι) *assayed, examined, tested*, properly of metals, Dem.　II. generally, 1. of
persons, *approved, esteemed, notable*, Lat. *probus*,
Hdt.; δοκιμώτατος Ἑλλάδι *most approved* by Hellas,
Eur.　2. of things, *excellent, notable, considerable*,
Hdt.　3. Adv. -μως, *really, truly*, Aesch., Xen.
δοκίς, ίδος, ἡ, Dim. of δοκός, Xen.
δοκός, ἡ, later ὁ, (δέχομαι) *a bearing-beam*, in the roof
or floor of a house, Od.: generally, *a balk* or *beam*,
Il., Thuc.: *the bar* of a gate or door, Ar.
δοκώ, οος, contr. οῦς, ἡ, = δόκησις, Eur.

δολερός, ά, όν, (δόλος) *deceitful, deceptive, treacherous*,
Hdt., Soph., etc.
δολιό-πους, ὁ, ἡ, πουν, τό, *stealthy of foot*, Soph.
δόλιος, α, ον, and ος, ον, *crafty, deceitful, treacherous*,
Od., Trag.
δολιό-φρων, ὁ, ἡ, (φρήν) *crafty of mind*, Aesch., Eur.
δολιόω, f. ώσω, *to deal treacherously with* one, N.T.
δολίχ-αυλος, ον, *with a long tube* or *socket*, Od.
δολίχ-εγχής, ές, (ἔγχος) *with tall spear*, Il.
δολιχεύω, f. σω, = δολιχοδρομέω, Anth.
δολίχ-ήρετμος, ον, (ἐρετμός) *long-oared*, of a ship, Od.;
of men, *using long oars*, Il.
δολιχο-γραφία, ἡ, (γράφω) *prolix writing*, Anth.
δολιχό-δειρος, Ep. δουλ-, ον, (δειρή) *long-necked*, Il.
δολιχοδρομέω, f. ήσω, *to run the* δόλιχος, Aeschin. From
δολιχό-δρομος, ον, (δόλιχος, ὁ, δραμεῖν) *running the
long course*, Plat., Xen.
δολίχόεις, εσσα, εν, Ion. δουλ-, = δολιχός, Anth.
ΔΟΛΙΧΟΣ, ή, όν, *long*, Hom.: neut. δολιχόν as Adv.,
Il., Plat.　Hence
δόλιχος, ὁ, *the long course*, opp. to στάδιον, Plat., Xen.
δολιχό-σκιος, ον, (δολιχός, σκία) epith. of ἔγχος,
casting a long shadow; or for δολιχ-όσχιος (ὅσχος)
long-shafted, Il.
δολόεις, εσσα, εν, (δόλος) *subtle, wily*, Od.　II. of
things, *craftily contrived*, Eur.
δολο-μήτης, ου, ὁ, and δολό-μητις, ὁ, *crafty of counsel,
wily*, Hom.
δολό-μῦθος, ον, *subtle-speaking*, or *conveyed in crafty
speech*, Soph.
δολοπλοκία, ἡ, *subtlety, craft*, Theogn.　From
δολο-πλόκος, ον, (πλέκω) *weaving wiles*, Sappho,
Arist.
δολο-ποιός, όν, (ποιέω) *treacherous, ensnaring*, Soph.
δολορ-ράφος [ᾰ], ον, (ῥάπτω) *contriving wiles*.
δόλος, ὁ, (from Root ΔΕΛ, v. δέλ-εαρ) properly, *a bait
for fish*, Od.: then, *any cunning contrivance for deceiving* or *catching*, as the Trojan horse, the robe of
Penelopé, Ib.:—generally, *any trick* or *stratagem*,
Il.; in pl., *wiles*, Ib.　2. *guile, craft, cunning,
treachery*, Lat. *dolus*, Hom., Trag.
δολοφονέω, f. ήσω, *to murder by treachery*, Dem. From
δολο-φόνος, ον, (*φένω) *slaying by treachery*, Aesch.
δολο-φραδής, ές, (φράζω) *wily-minded*, h. Hom.
δολοφρονέων, ουσα, ον, only as a partic., *planning
craft, wily-minded*, Hom.
δολοφροσύνη, ἡ, *craft, subtlety, wiliness*, Il.　From
δολό-φρων, ον, (φρήν) = δολοφραδής, Aesch., Anth.
δολόω, f. ώσω, (δόλος) *to beguile, ensnare, take by
craft*, Hes., Hdt., Att.　II. *to disguise*, Soph. Hence
δόλωμα, ατος, τό, *a trick, deceit*, Aesch.
δόλων, ωνος, ὁ, (δόλος) *a secret weapon, poniard,
stiletto*, Plut.
δολ-ῶπις, ιδος, ἡ, (ὤψ) *artful-looking, treacherous*, Soph.
δόλωσις, εως, ἡ, (δολόω) *a tricking*, Xen.
δομαῖος, α, ον, (δομή) *for building*, Anth.
δόμεναι, δόμεν, Ep. aor. 2 inf. of δίδωμι.
δομή, ἡ, (δέμω) *a building*.
δόμονδε, Adv. *home, homeward*, Hom.; ὅνδε δόμονδε
to his own house, Od.
δόμος, ὁ, (δέμω) Lat. *domus:*　1. *a house*, Hom.,
etc.: also *part of a house, a room, chamber*, Od.:—

hence in pl. for *a house*, Hom., Trag.   **2.** *the house of a god, a temple*, Hom., Trag.   **3.** of animals, *a sheep-fold*, Il. : *a wasps'* or *bees' nest*, Ib.   **4.** κέδρινοι δόμοι *a closet* or *chest* of cedar, Eur.   **II.** *the house*, i. e. *the household, family*, Trag. :—also *one's father's house*, Aesch.   **III.** *a layer* or *course* of stone or bricks in a building, διὰ τριήκοντα δόμων πλίνθου at every thirtieth *layer* of brick, Hdt.

δομο-σφᾰλής, ές, (σφάλλω) *shaking the house*, Aesch.

δονακεύομαι, Dep. *to fowl with reed and birdlime*, Anth.   From

δονᾰκεύς, έως, ὁ, (δόναξ) *a thicket of reeds*, Il.   **II.** =δόναξ, Anth.

δονακῖτις, ιδος, ἡ, (δόναξ) *of reed*, Anth.

δονᾰκο-γλύφος [ῠ], **ον,** (γλύφω) *reed-cutting, pen-making*, Anth.

δονᾰκόεις, εσσα, εν, (δόναξ) *reedy*, Eur. ; δόλος δ., of a reed covered with birdlime, Anth.

δονᾰκο-τρόφος, ον, (τρέφω) *producing reeds*, Theogn.

δονᾰκό-χλοος, ον, contr. **-χλους, ουν,** (χλόη) *green with reeds*, Eur.

δόναξ, ᾰκος, ὁ, Ion. **δοῦναξ,** Dor. **δῶναξ** : (from δονέω, 'a reed *shaken* by the wind,' cf. ῥίψ from ῥίπτω) :—*a reed*, Hom. ; δόνακες καλάμοιο reed-stalks, h. Hom.   **II.** *anything made of reed*, **1.** *the shaft of an arrow*, Il.   **2.** *a shepherd's pipe*, Aesch., Theocr.   **3.** *a fishing-rod* or *limed twig* (cf. δονακόεις), Anth.   **4.** *the bridge of the lyre*, Ar.

δονέω, f. ήσω :—Pass., Dor. 3 sing. plqpf. δεδόνατο :— *to shake*, of wind, Il. ; δ. γάλα *to shake* it, as to make butter, Hdt.   **2.** *to drive about*, Lat. *agitare*, Od., Pind. :—Pass., ἡ Ἀσίη ἐδονέετο Asia *was in commotion*, Hdt. ; αἰθὴρ δονεῖται Ar.   Hence

δόνημα, ατος, τό, *an agitation, waving*, δένδρου Luc.

δόξᾱ, ἡ, (δοκέω) *a notion*, true or false : and so,   **1.** *expectation*, ή δόξης otherwise than *one expects*, Hom. ; παρὰ δόξαν ἤ . . Hdt. ; opp. to κατὰ δόξαν, Plat., etc. ; ἀπὸ δόξης πεσέειν, Lat. *spe excidere*, Hdt. ; δόξαν παρέχειν τινί *to make one expect* that, c. inf., Xen.   **2.** *an opinion, judgment*, Pind., Att.   **3.** like δόκησις, *a mere opinion, conjecture*, Aesch., etc. ; δόξῃ ἐπίστασθαι *to imagine, suppose* (but wrongly), Hdt. :—also, *a fancy, vision, dream*, Aesch., Eur.   **II.** *the opinion which others have of one, estimation, reputation, credit, honour, glory*, Lat. *existimatio*, Solon, Aesch., etc. ; δόξαν φέρεσθαι, ἔχειν Thuc., etc. ; τινός for a thing, Eur. :—rarely of *ill repute*, Dem.   **2.** *the estimate popularly formed of a thing*, Id.   **III.** of external appearance, *glory, splendour, effulgence*, N. T.   Hence

δοξάζω, f. άσω, *to think, imagine, suppose, fancy, conjecture*, c. acc. et inf., Aesch., etc. ; inf. omitted, πῶς ταῦτ' ἀληθῆ δοξάσω; how can I suppose this to be true? Id. :—Pass., δοξάζεται (sc. εἶναι) is supposed to be, Plat.   **2.** c. acc. cogn., δόξαν δοξάζειν *to entertain* an opinion, Id.   **3.** absol. *to hold an opinion*, Soph., Thuc.   **II.** *to magnify, extol*, Id.   Hence

δόξασμα, ατος, τό, *an opinion, notion, conjecture*, Thuc., etc. :—*a fancy*, Eur. : and

δοξαστός, ή, όν, *matter of opinion, conjectural*, Plat.

δοξοκοπέω, f. ήσω, *to court popularity*, Plut. ; and

δοξοκοπία, ἡ, *thirst for popularity*, Plut.   From

δοξο-κόπος, ον, (κόπτω) *thirsting for popularity*.

δοξο-μᾰνής, ές, (μαίνομαι) *mad after fame*.   Hence

δοξομᾰνία, ἡ, *mad desire for fame*, Plut.

δοξο-μᾰταιό-σοφος, ον, *a would-be philosopher*, Anth.

δοξόομαι, pf. δεδόξωμαι : Pass. :—*to have the character* or *credit* of being, c. inf., Hdt.

δοξοσοφία, ἡ, *conceit of wisdom*, Plat.   From

δοξό-σοφος, ον, *wise in one's own conceit*, Plat.

δορά, ἡ, (δέρω) *a skin, hide*, Theogn., Hdt.

δοράτιον, τό, Dim. of δόρυ, Hdt., Thuc.

δορᾱτισμός, ὁ, *a fighting with spears*, Plut.

δορᾰτο-πᾰχής, ές, (πάχος) *of a spear's thickness*, Xen.

δόρᾱτος, gen. of δόρυ.

δορήϊος, α, ον, (δόρυ) *wooden*, Anth.

δορι-άλωτος, ον, (ἁλῶναι) *captive of the spear, taken in war*, Hdt., Eur. ; Ion. **δουριάλωτον** λέχος, of Tecmessa, Soph.

δορι-γαμβρος [ῐ], **ον,** *bride of battles*, i. e. *causing war by marriage*, or *wooed by battle*, of Helen, Aesch.

δορι-θήρᾱτος, ον, (θηράω) *taken by the spear*, Eur.

δορί-κᾰνής, ές, (κανεῖν) *slain by the spear*, Aesch. :— so **δορι-κμής, ῆτος, ὁ, ἡ,** Ion. δουρ-, Id.

δορί-κρᾱνος, ον, (κάρα) *spear-headed*, Aesch.

δορί-κτητος, ον, *won by the spear*, Eur. : Hom. has Ion. fem. δουρικτητή.

δορί-ληπτος, ον, (λαμβάνω) *won by the spear*, Soph., Eur. ; Ion. **δουρίλ-,** Soph.

δορί-μᾰνής, ές, (μαίνομαι) *raging with the spear*, Eur.

δορί-μαργος, ον, *raging with the spear*, Aesch.

δορί-μήστωρ, ορος, ὁ, *master of the spear*, Eur.

δορί-παλτος, ον, (πάλλω) *wielding the spear*, ἐκ χερὸς δοριπάλτου, i. e. on the right hand, Aesch.

δορῐ-πετής, ές, (πί-πτω) *fallen by the spear*, Eur.

δορί-πονος, ον, *toiling with the spear*, Aesch., Eur.

δορι-πτοίητος, ον, (πτοιέω) *scattered by the spear*, Anth.

δορισθενής, ές, (σθένος) *mighty with the spear*, Aesch.

δορι-στέφανος, ον, *crowned for bravery*, Anth.

δορῐ-τίνακτος [τῐ], **ον,** (τινάσσω) *shaken by battle*, Aesch.

δορί-τμητος, ον, (τέμνω) *pierced by the spear*, Aesch.

δορί-τολμος, ον, (τόλμα) *bold in war*, Anth.

δορκάδειος [ᾰ], **α, ον,** (δορκάς) *of an antelope*, Theophr.

δορκᾰλίς, ίδος, ἡ, =δορκάς, Anth. : παίγνια δορκαλίδων dice *made of the vertebrae of an antelope*, Id.

δορκάς, άδος [ᾰ], **ἡ,** (δέ-δορκα) *a kind of deer* (so called from its large bright eyes), in Greece, *the roe-deer*, Eur., Xen. ; in Syria and Africa, *the gazelle*, Hdt. :— so **δόρξ, δορκός, ἡ,** ζορκάς, Hdt.

δορός, ὁ, (δέρω) *a leathern bag* or *wallet*, Od.

δορπέω, f. ήσω, (δόρπον) *to take supper*, Hom.

δορπηστός, ὁ, *supper-time, evening*, Ar., Xen.

δορπία, ἡ, *the eve* of a festival, Hdt.

δόρπον, τό, in Hom. *the evening meal*, whether called *dinner* or *supper*, Lat. *coena* :—later, generally, *a meal*, h. Hom. (Deriv. uncertain.)

δόρπος, =foreg., Anth.

δόρυ, τό, gen. δόρατος :—Ep. decl., gen. δούρᾱτος, dat. δούρᾱτι, pl. δούρᾱτα, δούρᾱσι ; also δουρός, δουρί, dual δοῦρε, pl. δοῦρα, δούρων, δούρεσσι :—in Att. Poets, gen. δορός, dat. δορί or δόρει, pl. nom. δόρη : (from same Root as δρῦς) :   **I.** *a stem, tree*, Od. :—commonly *a plank* or *beam*, Hom. ; δόρυ νήϊον a ship's *plank*, Id. :—

hence, 2. *a ship* is called δόρυ, like Lat. *trabs*, Aesch., Eur.　II. *the shaft of a spear*, Il. : then, generally, *a spear, pike*, Hom., etc. ; εἰς δόρυ ἀφικνεῖσθαι to come within *a spear's* throw, Xen. ; ἐπὶ δόρυ *to the spear-side*, i. e. *the right hand*, opp. to ἐπ' ἀσπίδα, Id. :—also, *the pole* of a standard, Id.　2. metaph., δουρὶ κτεατίζειν *to win wealth by the spear*, Il. ; δορὶ ἑλεῖν Thuc. ; in Trag. to express *an armed force.*

δορυ-δρέπανον, τό, a kind of *halbert*, Plat.

δορῠ-θαρσής, ές, (θάρσος) = δορίτολμος, Anth.

δορῠ-κρανος, δορῠ-κτητος, δορῠ-παλτος, δορυ-σθενής, less correct forms for δορι-.

δορῠ-ξενος, ὁ, ἡ, *a spear-friend*, i. e., properly, *one who having been captive to one's spear becomes one's friend*; then generally, *a firm friend*, Aesch., Soph.: as Adj., δόμοι δορύξενοι Aesch. ; ἑστία Soph.

δορυ-ξόος, contr. -ξοῦς, ὁ, (ξέω) *a maker of spears*, Plut. : also, δορυξός, ὁ, Ar.

δορύ-σοος, ον, = δορύσσοος, Aesch.

δορυσσ-σόης, ητος, ὁ, = δορύσσοος, μόχθων δορυσσοήτων of the toils *of battle*, Soph.

δορυσσ-σόος, ον, (σεύομαι) *charging with the lance*, Hes., Theogn. ; δορυσσούς, Soph.

δορῠφορέω, f. ήσω, (δορυφόρος) *to attend as a body-guard*, τινα Hdt., Thuc. : generally, *to keep guard over*, Dem. :—Pass. *to be guarded*, Id.　II. δ. τινι *to serve as guard*, Xen.　Hence

δορῠφόρημα, ατος, τό, *a body of guards*, Luc.

δορῠφορία, ἡ, *guard kept over*, τινός Xen.　From

δορῠ-φόρος, ον, (φέρω) *spear-bearing*, Aesch.　II. as Subst. *a spearman, pikeman*, Xen.　2. δορυφόροι, οἱ, *the body-guard*, of kings and tyrants, Lat. *satellites*, Hdt., etc. :—metaph., ἡδοναὶ δ. *satellite pleasures*, Plat.

δόσις, εως, ἡ, (δί-δωμι) *a giving*, Hdt., etc.　II. *a gift*, Hom., etc.

δόσκον, Ion. aor. 2 of δίδωμι.

δότειρα, ἡ, fem. of δοτήρ, Hes.

δοτέος, α, ον, verb. Adj. of δίδωμι, *to be given*, Hdt.　II. δοτέον, *one must give*, Id.

δοτήρ, ῆρος, ὁ, (δί-δωμι) *a giver, dispenser*, Il., Aesch.

δότης, ου, ὁ, late form of δοτήρ, N. T.

δουλ-ἀγωγέω, f. ήσω, (ἀγωγός) *to make a slave, treat as such*: metaph. *to bring into subjection*, N. T.

δουλεία, ἡ, Ion. δουληΐη, (δουλεύω) *servitude, slavery, bondage*, Hdt., etc.　II. in collect. sense, *the slaves, slave-class*, Ib.

δούλειος, α, ον and ος, ον, (δοῦλος) *slavish, servile*, Od., Theogn., Att.

δούλευμα, ατος, τό, *a service*, Eur.　II. *a slave*, Soph. ; and

δουλευτέον, verb. Adj. *one must be a slave*, Eur.　From

δουλεύω, f. σω, (δοῦλος) *to be a slave*, τινί to one, Plat., etc. ; παρά τινι Dem. ; c. acc. cogn., δουλείαν δ. Xen.　2. *to serve* or *be subject to*, opp. to ἄρχω, Hdt., etc. ; τῇ γῇ δ. *to be a slave* to one's land, i. e. submit to indignities that one may keep it, Thuc.

δούλη, ἡ, v. δοῦλος.

δουλικός, ή, όν, (δοῦλος) *of* or *for a slave, servile*, Xen., Plat. : Adv. -κῶς, Xen.

δούλιος, α, ον, (δοῦλος) *slavish, servile*, δούλιον ἦμαρ the day *of slavery*, Il. : δ. φρήν a slave's *mind*, Aesch.

δουλίς, ίδος, ἡ, = δούλη, Anth.

δουλῐχό-δειρος, ον, Ion. for δολῐχό-δειρος.

δουλῐχόεις, Ion. for δολιχόεις.

δουλο-πρέπεια, ἡ, *a slavish spirit*, Plat.　From

δουλο-πρεπής, ές, (πρέπω) *befitting a slave, servile*, Hdt., Xen., etc.

δοῦλος, ὁ, properly, *a born bondman* or *slave*, opp. to *one made a slave* (ἀνδράποδον), Thuc. ; then, generally, *a bondman, slave*, Hdt. : Hom. has only the fem.

δούλη, ἡ, *a bondwoman* :—χρημάτων δ. *slave to* money, Eur.　II. as Adj., δοῦλος, η, ον, *slavish, servile, subject*, Soph., etc.　III. τὸ δοῦλον = οἱ δοῦλοι, Eur. : also = δουλεία, Id. (Deriv. uncertain.)

δουλοσύνη, ἡ, *slavery, slavish work*, Od., Aesch., Eur.

δουλόσυνος, ον, δοῦλος II, *enslaved*, τινι Eur.

δουλόω, f. ώσω, (δοῦλος) *to make a slave of, enslave*, Hdt., Att. :—Pass. *to be enslaved*, Hdt., Thuc. :—Med., with pf. pass. *to make one's slave, make subject to oneself, enslave*, Thuc., etc.　Hence

δούλωσις, ἡ, *enslaving, subjugation*, Thuc.

δοῦναι, aor. 2 inf. of δίδωμι.

δοῦναξ, δουνακόεις, Ion. for δον-.

δουπέω, f. ήσω : Ep. aor. 1 δούπησα, also ἐγδούπησα (as if from γδουπέω) : pf. δέδουπα : (δοῦπος) :—*to sound heavy* or *dead*, δούπησεν πεσών *with a thud he fell*, Il. ; δουπεῖ χεὶρ γυναικῶν *falls with heavy sound* upon their breasts, Eur.　Hence

δουπήτωρ, ορος, ὁ, *a clatterer*, Anth.

ΔΟΥ~ΠΟΣ, ὁ, *any dead, heavy sound, a thud*, Il. ; of *the distant din of battle*, the sound of footsteps, of *the measured tread* of infantry, *the hum* of a multitude, *the roar* of the sea, Hom. : rare in Trag. (The form γδουπ-έω, connects the word with κτύπ-ος.)

δοῦρας, τό, formed from Homeric pl. δούρατα, Anth.

δουράτεος, α, ον, (δόρυ) *of planks* or *beams of wood*, ἵππος δ. *the wooden horse*, Od.

δούρειος, α, ον, = δουράτεος, Eur., Plat.

δουρ-ηνεκής, ές, (ἐνεγκεῖν) *a spear's throw off* or *distant*, only in neut. as Adv., Il.

δουρι-άλωτος, ον, Ion. for δοριάλ-.

δουρι-κλειτός and δουρι-κλῠτός, όν, *famed for the spear*, Hom.

δουρι-κμής, -κτητός, -ληπτος, -μανής, Ion. for δορι-.

δούριος, α, ον, = δούρειος, Ar.

δουρι-πηκτος, ον, *fixed on spears*, Aesch.

δουρι-τῠπής, ές, (τύπτω) *wood-cutting*, Anth.

δουρο-δόκη, ἡ, (δέχομαι) *a case* or *stand for spears*, Od.

δουρο-μανής, ές, Ion. for δοριμανής, Anth.

δουρο-τόμος, Ion. for δοριτόμος, *cutting wood*, Anth.

δοχή, ἡ, (δέχομαι) *a receptacle*, Eur.　II. *a reception, entertainment*, N. T.

δοχεῖον, τό, Ion. for δοχεῖον, *a holder* : μέλανος δ. an ink-horn, Anth.

δοχμή or δόχμη, ἡ, (δέχομαι) *the space contained in a hand's breadth*, the same as παλαστή, Ar.

δόχμιος, α, ον, (δοχμός) *across, athwart, aslant*, like πλάγιος, Lat. *obliquus*, Il., Eur.

δοχμό-λοφος, ον, *with slanting, nodding plume*, Aesch.

δοχμόομαι, Pass. *to turn sideways*, δοχμωθείς, of a boar *turning* to rip up his enemy, Hes. ; so of Hermes *turning* to dart through the key-hole, h. Hom.

ΔΟΧΜΟΣ, όν, Lat. *obliquus*, δοχμὼ ἀΐσσοντε rushing on *slantwise*, Il. (Deriv. uncertain.)

δράγμα, ατος, τό, (δράσσομαι) as much as one can grasp, a handful, truss of corn, Lat. manipulus, Il. :—also a sheaf, = ἄμαλλα, Xen. II. uncut corn, Anth., Luc.

δραγμάτη-φόρος, ον, (φέρω) carrying sheaves, Babr.

δραγμεύω, f. σω, (δράγμα) to collect the corn into sheaves, Il.

δραγμός, ὁ, (δράσσομαι) a grasping, Eur.

δραθεῖν, aor. 2 inf. of δαρθάνω.

δράθι, aor. 2 imper. of διδράσκω :—δραίην opt.

δραίνω, much like δρασείω, to be ready to do, Il.

δράκαινα, ης, ἡ, fem. of δράκων (cf. Λάκαινα), a she-dragon, h. Hom., Aesch., Eur.

δρᾰκεῖν, δρᾰκῆναι, aor. 2 inf. act. and pass. of δέρκομαι :—δράκον, Ep. aor. 2 of act. form.

δρᾰκόντειος, ον, (δράκων) of a dragon, Eur., Anth.

δρᾰκοντ-ολέτης, ου, ὁ, (ὄλλυμι) serpent-slayer, Anth.

δρᾰκοντό-μαλλος, ον, with snaky locks, Aesch.

δρᾰκοντ-ώδης, ες, (εἶδος) snake-like, Eur.

δρᾰκών, aor. 2 part. of δέρκομαι.

δράκων [ᾰ], οντος, ὁ, (δρᾰκεῖν) a dragon, or serpent of huge size, a python, Hom., etc.

δρᾶμα, ατος, τό, (δράω) a deed, act, Aesch., Plat. II. an action represented on the stage, a drama, Ar. ; δρ. διδάσκειν to bring out a play, v. διδάσκω II :—metaph. stage-effect, Plat.

δρᾱμάτιον, τό, Dim. of δρᾶμα, Plut.

δρᾱμᾰτουργία, ἡ, dramatic work, a drama, Luc. From

δρᾱμᾰτ-ουργός, όν, (*ἔργω) a dramatist.

δρᾰμεῖν, inf. aor. 2 of τρέχω.

δράμημα or δρόμημα, ατος, τό, (δραμεῖν) a running, course, a race, Hdt., Trag.

δρᾰμοῦμαι, f. of τρέχω : δραμών, aor. 2 part.

δρᾶναι, aor. 2 inf. of δι-δράσκω.

δράξ, ἄκός, ἡ, = δράγμα, Batr.

δρᾱπετεύω, σω, to run away, Xen. ; τινά from one, Plat. ; δραπετεύσουσι ὑπὸ ταῖς ἀσπίσιν will skulk behind their shields, Xen. From

δρᾱπέτης, ου, Ion. δρηπέτης, εω, ὁ, (δι-δράσκω) a run-away, Lat. fugitivus, βασιλέος from the king, Hdt. :—a runaway slave, Id. 2. as Adj., runaway, fugitive, δραπέτης κλῆρος a lot of fugitive kind, i.e. crumbling clod of earth, which could not be drawn out of the urn, Soph. Hence

δρᾱπετίδης, ου, ὁ, = foreg., Mosch.

δρᾱπετικός, ή, όν, of or for a δραπέτης, δρ. θρίαμβος a triumph over a runaway slave, Plut.

δρᾱπέτις, ιδος, ἡ, fem. of δραπέτης, Anth.

δρᾱπετίσκος, ὁ, Dim. of δραπέτης, Luc.

δρασείω, Desiderat. of δράω, to have a mind to do, to be going to do, Soph., Eur.

δράσιμος [ᾰ], ον, = δραστήριος : τὸ δρ. activity, Aesch.

δρασμός, Ion. δρησμός, ὁ, (διδράσκω) a running away, flight, Hdt., Aesch. ; in pl., Eur.

ΔΡΑ'ΣΣΟΜΑΙ, Att. δράττομαι : f. δράξομαι : aor. 1 ἐδραξάμην : pf. δέδραγμαι or δέδαργμαι, 2 pers. δέδαρξαι : Dep. :—to grasp, c. gen. rei, κόνιος δεδραγμένος clutching a handsful of dust, Il. ; so, ἐλπίδος δεδραγμένος Soph. 2. to lay hold of, τί μου δέδραξαι ; Eur. ; δραξάμενος φάρυγος having seized [them] by the throat, Theocr. II. c. acc. rei, to take by handsful, Hdt.

δράστεος, α, ον, verb. Adj. of δράω, to be done, Soph. II. δραστέον, one must do, Id., Eur.

δραστήριος, ον, (δράω) vigorous, active, efficacious, Aesch., Eur. : τὸ δρ. activity, energy, Thuc. 2. in bad sense, audacious, Eur.

δραστικός, ή, όν, = δραστήριος, Plat.

δρᾱτός, ή, όν, metath. for δαρτός, verb. Adj. of δέρω, skinned, flayed, Il.

δραχμή, ἡ, (δράσσομαι) properly, a handful, like δράγμα :—an Attic weight, a drachm, weighing about 66½ grains, the Aeginetan being = ⅔ Attic. 2. an Att. silver coin, a drachma, worth 6 obols, i.e. 9¾d., nearly = Roman denarius and Fr. franc, Hdt., etc. Hence

δραχμιαῖος, α, ον, worth a drachma, to the amount of a drachma, Arist.

ΔΡΑ'Ω, subj. δρῶ, δρᾷς, δρᾷ : opt. δρῴμι, Ep. δρώοιμι : impf. ἔδρων : f. δράσω : aor. 1 ἔδρασα, Ion. ἔδρησα : pf. δέδρᾱκα :—Pass., aor. 1 ἐδράσθην : pf. δέδρᾱμαι :—to do, esp. to do some great thing, good or bad, cf. Lat. facinus, Att. ; often opp. to πάσχω, ἄξια δράσας ἄξια πάσχων Aesch. ; κακῶς δράσαντες οὐκ ἐλάσσονα πάσχουσι Id. ; proverb., 'δράσαντι παθεῖν' doers must suffer, Id. ; πεπονθότα μᾶλλον ἢ δεδρακότα things of suffering rather than of doing, Soph. ; so, τὸ δρῶν the doing of a thing, Id. :—εὖ or κακῶς δρᾶν τινα to do one a good or ill turn, Theogn., Soph.

δρεπάνη [ᾰ], ἡ, (δρέπω) = δρέπανον, a sickle, reaping-hook, Il. : a pruning-hook, Hes.

δρεπανη-φόρος, ον, (φέρω) bearing a scythe, ἅρμα δ. a scythed car, Xen.

δρεπᾰνο-ειδής, ές, (εἶδος) sickle-shaped, Thuc.

δρέπᾰνον, τό, (δρέπω) = δρεπάνη, Od., Hdt., Att. : a scythe, Xen. 2. a curved sword, scimitar, Hdt.

δρεπᾰν-ουργός, ὁ, (*ἔργω) a sword-maker, armourer, Ar.

δρέπτω, poët. for δρέπω, to pluck, Ep. impf. δρέπτον, Mosch. : so in Med., Anth.

ΔΡΕ'ΠΩ, Ep. impf. δρέπον : aor. 1 ἔδρεψα : aor. 2 ἔδρᾰπον :—Med., Dor. f. δρεψεῦμαι :—to pluck, cull, Lat. carpo, Hdt., Eur., etc. :—metaph. to cull flowers from a field, δρ. λειμῶνα Μουσῶν, of a poet, Ar. II. Med. to pluck for oneself, cull, Od. : metaph., δρεπόμενοι τὰ μέλη Plat. ; even, αἷμα δρέψασθαι to shed it, Aesch.

δρηπέτης, δρησμός, Ion. for δραπέτης, δρασμός.

δρησμοσύνη, ἡ, = δρηστοσύνη, Lat. cultus, h. Hom.

δρηστήρ, ῆρος, ὁ, (δράω) a labourer, working man, Od. : fem. δρήστειρα, a workwoman, Ib. II. (διδράσκω) a runaway, Babr. : fem. δρῆστις, Anth.

δρηστοσύνη, ἡ, Ion. for δραστ-, (δράω) service, Od.

δρῐμύλος [ῠ], ον, = δριμύς, piercing, Mosch.

ΔΡΙΜΥ'Σ, εῖα, ύ, piercing, sharp, keen, Lat. acer, of a dart, Il. : metaph., δριμεῖα μάχη, δριμὺς χόλος Ib. ; δριμὺ μένος Od. II. of things which affect the eyes or taste, pungent, acrid, as smoke, Ar. ; herbs, Xen. ; smell, Ar. III. metaph. of persons, keen, bitter, Aesch., Ar. ; also keen, shrewd, Eur. :—δριμὺ βλέπειν to look bitter, Ar. Hence

δρῐμύτης, ητος, ἡ, pungency : metaph. keenness, vehemence, Plat.

δρίος, τό, a copse, wood, thicket, δρίος ὕλης copse-wood,

Od.; δρίος ὕλην Anth. :—in pl. δρία, τά, (as if from δρίον), Hes., Soph., Eur. (From same Root as δρῦς.)

δροίτη, ἡ, *a bath*, Aesch. (Deriv. unknown.)

δρομαῖος, α, ον and ος, ον, (δρόμος) *running at full speed, swift, fleet*, Soph., Eur.; δρ. κάμηλος *a dromedary*, Plut.

δρομάς, άδος, ὁ, ἡ, (δραμεῖν) *running*, Eur.; ἄμπυξ δρ. *the whirling wheel*, Soph.; also with a neut. Noun, Eur.   2. like φοιτάς, *wildly roaming, frantic*, Id.

δρομάω, Frequent. of δράμεῖν, *to run*, only in pf. δεδρόμηκα, Aeol. -ἄκα, Sapph., Babr.

δρομεύς, έως, ὁ, (δραμεῖν) *a runner*, Eur., Ar.

δρόμημα, τό, v. δράμημα.

δρομικός, ή, όν, (δραμεῖν) *good at running, swift, fleet*, Plat.; τὰ δρομικὰ τοῦ πεντάθλου *the race*, Xen.

δρομο-κῆρυξ, ῡκος, ὁ, *a runner, postman*, Aeschin.

δρόμος, ὁ, (δραμεῖν) *a course, running, race*, Hom. (v. τείνω); οὐρίῳ δρόμῳ in straight *course*, Soph. :—of *any quick movement*, e. g. *flight*, Aesch. :—of time, ἡμέρης δρ. *a day's running*, i. e. the distance one can go in a day, Hdt. :—δρόμῳ *at a run*, Id., Att.   2. *the foot-race* :—proverb., περὶ τοῦ παντὸς δρόμον θεῖν *to run for one's all*, Hdt.; τὸν περὶ ψυχῆς δρόμον δραμεῖν Ar.   3. *the length of the stadium, a course* or *heat* in a race, Soph.   II. *a place for running, a run* for cattle, Od.   2. *a race-course*, Hdt.: *a public walk*, Lat. *ambulatio*, Eur., Plat. :—proverb., ἔξω δρόμου or ἐκτὸς δρόμου φέρεσθαι, Lat. *extra oleas vagari*, to get off the course, i. e. wander from the point, Aesch., Plat.; ἐκ δρόμου πεσεῖν Aesch.

δροσερός, ά, όν, (δρόσος) *dewy, watery*, Eur., Ar.

δροσίζω, f. σω, (δρόσος) *to bedew, besprinkle*, Ar.

δροσινός, ή, όν, = δροσερός, Anth.

δροσόεις, εσσα, εν, = δροσερός, Eur.

ΔΡΟ'ΣΟΣ, ἡ, *dew*, Lat. *ros*, Hdt.; in pl., Aesch., etc.   2. *pure water*, Aesch., Eur.   3. of other liquids, δρ. φονία, of blood, Aesch.   II. *any thing tender*, like ἔρση II, *the young of animals*, Id.

δροσ-ώδης, ες, (εἶδος) *like dew, moist*, Eur.

Δρυάς, άδος, ἡ, (δρῦς) *a Dryad*, nymph whose life was bound up with that of her tree, Plut.; cf. Ἁμαδρυάς.

δρύϊνος, η, ον, (δρῦς) *oaken*, Od., Eur.; δρ. πῦρ *a wood* fire of oak-wood, Theocr.; μέλι δρ. *honey from the hollow of an oak*, Anth.

δρυ-κολάπτης, ὁ, = δρυοκολάπτης, Ar.

δρυμός, ὁ, heterog. pl. δρυμά, (δρῦς) *an oak-coppice*; and, generally, *a coppice, wood*, only in pl. δρυμά, Hom.; δρυμός in Soph., Eur. Hence

δρῦμών, ῶνος, ὁ, = δρυμός, Babr.

δρυο-κοίτης, ου, ὁ, (κοίτη) *dweller on the oak*, τέττιξ Anth.

δρυο-κολάπτης, ου, ὁ, (κολάπτω) *the woodpecker*, Arist.; δρυκολάπτης in Ar.

δρυόχοι, οἱ, (δρῦς, ἔχω) *the props* or *trestles* upon which was laid the keel (τρόπις) of a new ship, Od.: metaph., δρυόχους τιθέναι δράματος *to lay the keel* of a new play, Ar.; ἐκ δρυόχων *from the beginning*, Plat.   II. = δρυμά, *woods*, Anth.; so heterog. pl. δρύοχα Eur.

δρυόψ, οπος, ὁ, a kind of *woodpecker*, Ar.

δρύππα, ἡ, Lat. *druppa*, an *over-ripe olive*, Anth.

δρύπτω (Root ΔΡΥΦ) : f. δρύψω : aor. 1 ἔδρυψα, Ep. δρύψα :—Pass., aor. 1 ἐδρύφθην Babr. :—*to tear, strip*,

---

II. :—Med., δρυψαμένω παρειάς *tearing each other's* cheeks, Od.; in sign of mourning, δρύπτεσθαι παρειάν *to tear one's cheek*, Eur.

ΔΡΥ'Σ, ἡ, gen. δρυός, acc. δρῦν : pl., nom. and acc. δρῦς or δρύες, δρύας; gen. δρυῶν :—originally *a tree* (which indeed comes from the same Root), commonly *the oak*, Lat. *quercus*, Hom., etc.; sacred to Zeus, who gave his oracles from the oaks of Dodona, Od.;—hence, αἱ προσήγοροι δρύες Aesch. :—proverb., οὐ γὰρ ἀπὸ δρυός ἐσσι οὐδ᾽ ἀπὸ πέτρης thou art no foundling from *tree* or rock, i. e. thou hast parents and a country, Od.; οὐ νῦν ἐστιν ἀπὸ δρυὸς οὐδ᾽ ἀπὸ πέτρης 'tis no time now to talk at ease from *tree* or rock, Il.   II. of other trees, πίειρα δρῦς the resinous *wood* (of the pine), Soph.; of the olive, Eur.   III. metaph. *a worn-out old man*, Anth.

δρῠ-τόμος, ὁ, (τέμνω) *a wood-cutter*, Il.

δρύ-φακτος, ὁ, for δρύ-φρακτος, (δρῦς, φράσσω) *a fence* or *railing*, serving as *the bar* of the law-courts or council-chamber, Ar.; in pl., like Lat. *cancelli*, Id.

δρύψα, Ep. for ἔδρυψα, aor. 1 of δρύπτω.

δρύψια, τά, (δρύπτω) *parings*, Anth.

δρώοιμι, Ep. for δρῷμι, opt. of δράω.

δρωπακίζω, f. σω, *to get rid of hair by pitch-plasters*, Luc. From

δρῶπαξ, ἄκος, ὁ, (δρέπω) *a pitch-plaster*.

δῦ, Ep. for ἔδυ, 3 sing. aor. 2 of δύω.

δύα, Dor. for δύη.

δυάς, άδος, ἡ, (δύο) *the number two*, Plat.

δυάω, (δύη) *to plunge in misery*, Ep. 3 pl. δυόωσιν Od.

ΔΥ'Η, Dor. δύα, ἡ, *woe, misery, anguish, pain*, Od., Trag.; δυηπαθίη, ἡ, *misery*, Anth.

δύην, Ep. aor. 2 opt. of δύω.

δυη-πάθος, ον, (παθεῖν) *much-suffering*, h. Hom.

δῦθι, aor. 2 imper. of δύω.

δύμεναι [ῠ], Ep. for δῦναι, aor. 2 inf. of δύω.

ΔΥ'ΝᾸΜΑΙ, Dep., decl. in pres. and impf. like ἵσταμαι ; 2 sing. δύνασαι, Att. δύνᾳ, Ion. δύνῃ, Ion. 3 pl. δυνέαται ; subj. δύνωμαι, Ep. 2 sing. δύνηαι, Att. δύνῃ :—impf. 2 sing. ἐδύνω, Ion. 3 pl. ἐδυνέατο :—f. δυνήσομαι :—aor. 1 ἐδυνησάμην, Ep. δυνησάμην ; also ἐδυνάσθην, Ep. δυνάσθην, in Att. ἐδυνήθην :—pf. δεδύνημαι. The aor. 1 also has double augm., ἠδυνάμην, ἠδυνήθην.

I. *to be able, capable, strong enough to* do, c. inf., Hom., etc.; but the inf. is often omitted, Ζεὺς δύναται ἅπαντα [sc. ποιεῖν] Od.; so also, μέγα δυνάμενος *very powerful, mighty*, Ib.; οἱ δυνάμενοι *men of power*, Eur., Thuc.; δυνάμενος παρά τινι *having influence* with him, Hdt., etc.   2. *to be able*, i. e. *to dare* or *bear* to do a thing, οὐδὲ ποιήσειν δύναται Od.; οὐκέτι ἐδύνατο βιοτεύειν Thuc.   3. with ὡς and a Sup., ὡς ἐδύναντο ἀδηλότατα as secretly as *they could*, Id.; ὡς δύναμαι μάλιστα as much as *I possibly can*, Plat.; or simply ὡς ἐδύνατο in the best way *he could*, Xen.   II. *to pass for*, i. e.   1. of money, *to be worth* so much, c. acc., ὁ σίγλος δύναται ἑπτὰ ὀβολούς the shekel *is worth* 20 obols, Id.   2. of number, *to be equivalent to*, τριηκόσιαι γενεαὶ δυνέαται μύρια ἔτεα Hdt.   3. of words, *to signify, mean*, Lat. *valere*, Id., etc.; ἴσον δύναται, Lat. *idem valet*, Id.; τὴν αὐτὴν δύνασθαι δουλείαν *to mean the same slavery*, Thuc. :—also *to avail*, οὐδένα καιρὸν δύναται *avails* to

no good purpose, Eur.   III. impers., οὐ δύναται,
c. inf., *it cannot be, is not to be*, Hdt.   Hence
δύνᾰμις [ῠ], ἡ, gen. εως, Ion. ιος, Ion. dat. δυνάμι, Ion. dat. δυνάμι, *power,
might, strength*, Hom. : then, generally, *strength,
power, ability* to do a thing, Id. ; παρὰ δύναμιν beyond
one's *strength*, Thuc. ; ὑπὲρ δ. Dem. ; κατὰ δ. as
far as lies in one, Lat. *pro virili*, Hdt.   2. *power,
might, authority*, Aesch., etc.   3. *a force for war,
forces*, Xen.   4. *a quantity*, Lat. *vis*, χρημάτων δ.
Hdt., etc.   II. *a power, faculty, capacity*, αἱ τοῦ
σώματος δυνάμεις Plat., etc. ; also of plants, etc.,
Xen.   III. *the force* or *meaning* of a word, Plat.,
etc.   2. *the worth* or *value* of money, Thuc.   Hence
δῠνᾰμόω, f. ώσω, *to strengthen* : Pass., N. T.
δύνᾰσις [ῠ], εως, ἡ, poët. for δύναμις, Soph., Eur.
δυναστεία, ἡ, *power, lordship, sovereignty*, Soph.,
Thuc., etc.   II. *an oligarchy*, Id., Xen.   From
δυναστεύω, f. σω, *to hold power* or *lordship, be powerful*, Hdt., Thuc., etc.   From
δυνάστης, ου, ὁ, (δύναμαι) *a lord, master, ruler*, of
Zeus, Soph. ; οἱ δ., Lat. *optimates*, Hdt. : in Aesch.,
the stars are λαμπροὶ δύνασται.   Hence
δυναστικός, ή, όν, *arbitrary*, Arist.
δῠνᾰτέω, f. ήσω, (δυνατός) *to be powerful, mighty*, N.T.
δῠνάτης [ᾰ], ου, ὁ, poët. for δυνάστης, Aesch.
δῠνᾰτός, ή, όν, and ος, ον, (δύναμαι) *strong, mighty, able*,
esp. in body, τὸ δυνατώτατον *the ablest-bodied men*,
Hdt. : —of ships, *fit for service*, Thuc.   2. c. inf.
able to do, Hdt., etc.   3. *powerful*, Id. ; οἱ δυνατοί
the chief men of rank and influence, Thuc.   II.
pass., of things, *possible*, Lat. *quod fieri possit*, Hdt.,
etc. : —δυνατόν [ἐστι], c. inf., Id., Aesch., etc. ; ὁδὸς
δυνατὴ καὶ τοῖς ὑποζυγίοις πορεύεσθαι *practicable*, Xen. :
—κατὰ τὸ δυνατόν, *quantum fieri possit*, Plat., etc. ;
so, ἐς τὸ δ. Hdt. ; ὅσον δυνατόν Eur., etc.   III.
Adv. —τῶς, *strongly, powerfully*, Aeschin. ; δ. ἔχει it
is possible, Hdt.
δῦνε, Ep. for ἔδυνε, 3 sing. impf. of δύνω.
δυνέαται, Ion. for δύνανται, 3 pl. of δύναμαι.
δύνηαι, Ion. for δύνῃ, 2 sing. subj. of δύναμαι.
δύνω, v. sub δύω.
ΔΥ'Ο, Ep. δύω : gen. and dat. δυοῖν :—Ion. also gen. pl.
δυῶν, dat. δυοῖσι, and in later Att. δυσί :—and indecl.,
like ἄμφω, by Hom., τῶν δύο μοιράων, δύω κανόνεσσι Il. ;
so in Hdt. and Att. Prose ; but declined in Trag. :—*two*,
Il., etc. ;—in Poets δύο or δύω may be joined with pl.
Nouns, δύο δ' ἄνδρες Ib. :—εἰς δύο *two and two*, Xen. ;
σὺν δύο *two together*, Il., Hdt.
δυο-καί-δεκα, οἱ, αἱ, τά, *twelve*, Il.
δυοκαιδεκά-μηνος, ον, (μήν) = δωδεκάμηνος, Soph.
δύρομαι [ῠ], poët. for ὀδύρομαι.
δυόωσιν, Ep. for δυῶσι, 3 pl. of δυάω.
δύς, δῦσα, δύν, aor. 2 part. of δύω.
δῠσ-, insepar. Prefix, like *un-* or *mis-* (in *un-lucky,
mis-chance*), *destroying the good sense* of a word, or
increasing its bad sense.
δυσ-αγκόμιστος, poët. for δυσ-ανακόμιστος.
δύσ-αγνος, ον, *unchaste*, Luc.
δυσαγρέω, f. ήσω, *to have bad sport in fishing*, Plut.
δυσ-αγρής, ές, (ἄγρα) *unlucky in fishing*.
δυσ-άγων, ωνος, ὁ, ἡ, *having seen hard service*, Plut.
δυσ-άδελφος, ον, *unhappy in one's brothers*, Aesch.

δυσ-αής, ές, (ἄημι) *ill-blowing, stormy*, of winds,
Hom. ; Ep. gen. pl. δυσ-αήων for –αέων, Od.
δυσ-άθλιος, ον, *most miserable*, Soph.
δυσ-αιανής, ές, *most melancholy*, Aesch.
δυσ-αίθριος, ον, *not clear, murky*, Eur.
δυσ-αίων, ωνος, ὁ, ἡ, *living a hard life, most miserable*, Aesch., Soph. ; αἰὼν δυσαίων a life *that is no
life*, Eur.
δυσ-αλγής, ές, (ἄλγος) *very painful*, Aesch.
δυσ-άλγητος, ον, (ἀλγέω) *hard-hearted*, Soph.
δυσ-άλιος, ον, Dor. for δυσ-ήλιος.
δυσ-άλωτος, ον, (ἁλῶναι) *hard to catch* or *take*, ἄγρα
Plat.   2. *hard to conquer*, Aesch. ; c. gen., δ.
κακῶν *beyond reach* of ills, Soph.
δυσαμερία, Dor. for δυσημερία.
δῠσ-άμμορος, ον, *most miserable*, Il.
δυσ-ανάκλητος, ον, (ἀνακαλέω) *hard to call back*, Plut.
δυσανακόμιστος, ον, (ἀνακομίζω) *hard to bring back*
or *recal*, Plut. ; poët. δυσαγκόμιστος, Aesch.
δυσ-ανάπλους, ουν, (ἀναπλέω) *hard to sail up*, Strab.
δυσ-ανάπλωτος, ον, = foreg., Strab.
δυσανασχετέω, f. ήσω, *to bear ill*, Lat. *aegre ferre*,
Thuc. : *to be greatly vexed*, ἐπί τινι Plut.   From
δυσ-ανάσχετος, ον, *hard to bear*.
δυσ-ανάτρεπτος, ον, (ἀνατρέπω) *hard to overthrow*, Plut.
δυσ-άνεκτος, ον, = δυσανάσχετος, Xen.
δυσ-άνεμος [ᾰ], ον, Dor. for δυσ-ήνεμος, Soph.
δυσ-άντητος, ον, (ἀντάω) *disagreeable to meet, boding
of ill*, Luc.
δυσ-αντίβλεπτος, ον, (ἀντιβλέπω) *hard to look in the
face*, Plut.
δύσαντο, Ep. for ἐδύσαντο, 3 pl. aor. 1 med. of δύω.
δυσ-απάλλακτος, ον, (ἀπαλλάσσω) *hard to get rid of*,
Soph.
δυσ-άπιστος, ον, *very disobedient*, Anth.
δυσ-απόδεικτος, ον, (ἀποδείκνυμι) *hard to demonstrate*, Plat.
δυσ-απόκρῐτος, ον, (ἀποκρίνωμαι) *hard to answer*, Luc.
δυσ-απότρεπτος, ον, (ἀποτρέπω) *hard to dissuade*, Xen.
δυσ-άρεστος, ον, *hard to appease, implacable*, Aesch. :
—*ill to please, peevish, morose*, Eur., Xen.   2. *ill-
pleased*, τινι *with one*, Eur. : τὸ δυσάρεστον *displeasure*, Plut.
δυσ-άριστο-τόκεια, ἡ, (τίκτω) *unhappy mother of the
noblest son*, Il.
δύσ-αρκτος, ον, (ἄρχω) *hard to govern*, Aesch., Plut.
δυσαρμοστία, ἡ, *disagreement*, Plut.   From
δυσ-άρμοστος, ον, (ἁρμόζω) *ill-united*, Plut.
δυσαυλία, ἡ, *ill* or *hard lodging*, Aesch.   From
δύσ-αυλος, ον, (αὐλή) *inhospitable*, Soph.
δύσ-αυλος ἔρις, *an unhappy* contest *with the flute*
(αὐλός), Anth.
δυσ-αφαίρετος, ον, (ἀφαιρέω) *hard to take away*, Arist.
δυσ-αχής, ές, (ἄχος) *most painful*, Aesch.
δυσ-βάστακτος, ον, (βαστάζω) *grievous to bear*, N. T.
δυσβατο-ποιέομαι, Med. *to make impassable*, Xen.
δύσ-βᾰτος, ον, *inaccessible, impassable*, Xen.   II.
trodden in sorrow, Aesch.
δυσ-βάϋκτος, ον, (βαΰζω) *sadly wailing*, Aesch.
δυσ-βίοτος, ον, *making life wretched*, πενίη Anth.
δυσβουλία, ἡ, *ill counsel*, Aesch., Soph.   From
δύσ-βουλος, ον, (βουλή) *ill-advised*.

δύσ-βωλος, ον, of ill soil, unfruitful, Anth.

δύσ-γᾰμος, ον, ill-wedded, Eur.

δυσ-γάργαλις, ι, (γαργαλίζω) very ticklish, skittish, Xen.

δυσγένεια, ἡ, low birth, Soph., etc. II. meanness, Eur. From

δυσ-γενής, ές, (γένος) low-born, Eur., etc. II. low-minded, low, mean, Id.

δυσ-γεφύρωτος, ον, hard to bridge over, Strab.

δύσ-γνοια, ἡ, (γι-γνώσκω) ignorance, doubt, Eur.

δυσ-γνωσία, ἡ, (γι-γνώσκω) difficulty of knowing, Eur.

δυσ-γοήτευτος, ον, (γοητεύω) hard to seduce by enchantments, Plat.

δυσδαιμονία, ἡ, misery, Eur. From

δυσ-δαίμων, ον, of ill fortune, ill-fated, Trag., etc.

δυσ-δάκρῦτος, ον, sorely wept, Aesch. II. act. sorely weeping, Anth.

δύσ-δᾱμαρ, αρτος, ὁ, ἡ, ill-wived, ill-wedded, Aesch.

δυσ-διάθετος, ον, (διατίθεμαι) hard to settle, Plut.

δυσ-διαίτητος, ον, (διαιτάω) hard to decide, Plut.

δυσ-διάλῦτος, ον, hard to reconcile, Arist.

δυσ-διερεύνητος, ον, (διερευνάω) hard to search through, Plat.

δυσ-δίοδος, ον, hard to pass through, Polyb.

δύσ-εδρος, ον, (ἕδρα) bringing evil by one's abode, Aesch.

δυσ-ειδής, ές, (εἶδος) unshapely, ugly, Hdt., Plat.

δυσ-είμᾰτος, ον, (εἷμα) meanly clad, Eur.

δυσ-είσβολος, ον, (εἰσ-βάλλω) hard to enter: Sup. -ώτατος, ον, least accessible, Thuc.

δυσ-είσπλους, ουν, hard to sail into, Strab.

δυσ-έκθῦτος, ον, (ἐκ-θύομαι) hard to avert by sacrifice, Plut.

δυσ-έκλῦτος, ον, (ἐκλύω) hard to undo: Adv. -τως, indissolubly, Aesch.

δυσ-έκνιπτος, ον, (ἐκνίζω) hard to wash out, Plat.

δυσ-εκπέρᾱτος, ον, hard to pass out from, Eur.

δυσ-έκφευκτος, ον, (ἐκφεύγω) hard to escape from: Adv. -τως, Anth.

δυσ-έλεγκτος, ον, (ἐλέγχω) hard to refute, Luc.

Δυσ-ελένα, ἡ, ill-starred Helen, Eur.

δύσ-ελπις, ιδος, ὁ, ἡ, hardly hoping, desponding, Aesch., Xen.

δυσ-ελπιστος, ον, = δύσελπις, Plut. II. unhoped for, ἐκ δυσελπίστων, unexpectedly, Xen.

δυσ-έμβᾰτος, ον, hard to walk on, Thuc.

δυσ-έμβολος, ον, hard to enter, inaccessible, Xen.

δυσ-εντερία, ἡ, (ἔντερον) dysentery, Hdt., Plat.

δυσ-έντευκτος, ον, hard to speak with, Theophr.

δυσ-εξᾰπάτητος, ον, hard to deceive, Plat., Xen.

δυσ-έξαπτος, ον, hard to loose from bonds, Plut.

δυσ-εξαρίθμητος, ον, hard to enumerate, Polyb.

δυσ-εξέλεγκτος, ον, (ἐξελέγχω) hard to refute, Plat.

δυσ-εξέλικτος, ον, (ἐξελίσσω) hard to unfold, Plut.

δυσ-εξερεύνητος, ον, hard to investigate, Arist.

δυσ-εξημέρωτος, ον, (ἐξημερόω) hard to tame, Plut.

δυσ-εξήνυστος, ον, (ἐξανύω) indissoluble, Eur.

δυσ-έξοδος, ον, hard to get out of, Arist.

δύσεο, Ep. aor. 1 med. imper. of δύω.

δυσ-επιβούλευτος, ον, hard to attack secretly, Xen.

δυσ-έραστος, ον, (ἔραμαι) unfavourable to love, Anth.

δυσεργία, ἡ, difficulty in acting, Plut. From

δύσ-εργος, ον, (*ἔργω) unfit for work, Plut.

δυσ-έρημος, ον, very lonely, desolate, Anth.

δύσ-ερις, ι, gen. ιδος, very quarrelsome, contentious, Plat. II. act. producing unhappy strife, Plut.

δυσ-έριστος, ον, shed in unholy strife, Soph.

δυσ-ερμήνευτος, ον, (ἑρμηνεύω) hard to interpret, N.T.

δύσ-ερως, ωτος, ὁ, ἡ, sick in love with, τινος Eur., Thuc. II. hardly loving, stony-hearted, Theocr.

δυσ-εννήτωρ, Dor. -άτωρ, ορος, ὁ, (εὐνάω) an ill bedfellow, Aesch.

δυσ-εύρετος, ον, hard to find out, Aesch. 2. hard to find or get, Xen. 3. hard to find one's way through, impenetrable, Eur.

δύσ-ζηλος, ον, exceeding jealous, Od., Plut. :—Adv., δυσζήλως ἔχειν πρός τινα Plut.

δύσ-ζήτητος, ον, hard to seek or track, Xen.

δύσ-ζωος, ον, (ζωή) wretched, Anth.

δυσ-ήκεστος, ον, hard to heal or cure, Anth.

δυσ-ήκοος, ον, (ἀκούω) hard of hearing, Anth.

δυσ-ηλεγής, ές: (λέγω to lay asleep, cf. ταν-ηλεγής): —laying one on a hard bed, of death, Hom., Hes.

δυσ-ήλιος, Dor. -άλιος, ον, sunless, Aesch., Eur.

δυσ-ηνιόχητος, ον, (ἡνιοχέω) ungovernable, Luc.

δύσ-ηρις, ιδος, ὁ, ἡ, poët. for δύσερις 1, Pind.

δυσ-ηχής, Dor. δυσ-ᾱχής, ές, (ἠχέω) ill-sounding, hateful, Il.

δυσ-θαλπής, ές, (θάλπω) hard to warm: chilly, Il.

δυσ-θᾰνᾰτέω, f. ήσω, to die hard, die a lingering death, Hdt.: to struggle against death, Plat. From

δυσ-θάνατος, ον, bringing a hard death, Eur.

δυσ-θᾰνής, ές, (θανεῖν) having died a hard death, Anth.

δυσ-θέᾱτος, ον, ill to look on, Aesch., Soph.

δύσ-θεος, ον, godless, ungodly, Aesch.; hateful to the gods, Soph.

δυσ-θεράπευτος, ον, (θεραπεύω) hard to cure, Soph.

δυσθετέομαι, Dep. to be much vexed, Xen. From

δύσ-θετος, ον, (τίθημι) in bad case.

δυσ-θήρᾱτος, ον, (θηράω) hard to catch, Plut.

δυσ-θνήσκω, = δυσθανατέω, only in part., Eur.

δυσ-θρήνητος, ον, (θρηνέω) loud-wailing, most mournful, Soph., Eur.

δύσ-θροος, ον, ill-sounding, Aesch.

δυσ-θῡμαίνω, to be dispirited, to despond, h. Hom.

δυσθῡμέω, f. ήσω, = foreg., Hdt., Plut. :—Med. to be melancholy, angry, Eur.; and

δυσθῡμία, ἡ, despondency, despair, Eur., Plat., etc. From

δύσ-θῡμος, ον, desponding, melancholy, repentant, Soph., etc.: τὸ δύσθυμον = δυσθυμία, Plut. Adv. -μως, Comp. -ότερον, Plat.

δυσ-ίᾱτος [ῐ], ον, hard to heal, incurable, Aesch., Eur.

δυσ-ιερέω, f. ήσω, (ἱερά, τά) to have bad omens in a sacrifice, Plut.

δῦσι-θάλασσος, Att. -ττος, ον, (δύω, θάλασσα) dipped in the sea, Anth.

δύσ-ιππος, ον, hard to ride in; τὰ δ. parts unfit for cavalry-service, Xen., Plut.

δύσις [ῠ], εως, ἡ, (δύω) a setting of the sun or stars, Aesch., etc. 2. the quarter in which the sun sets, the west, Thuc., etc.

δυσ-κάθαρτος, ον, (καθαίρω) hard to satisfy by purification or atonement, Soph., Ar.

δυσ-κάθεκτος, ον, (κατέχω) hard to hold in, ἵπποι Xen.

δύσ-καπνος, ον, noisome from smoke, smoky, Aesch. ∗

δυσ-καρτέρητος, ον, (καρτερέω) hard to endure, Plut.

δυσ-καταμάθητος, ον, (καταμανθάνω) hard to learn or understand, Isocr. Adv., –τως ἔχειν Id.

δυσ-κατάπαυστος, ον, (καταπαύω) hard to check, restless, Aesch., Eur.

δυσ-κατάπρακτος, ον, (καταπράσσω) hard to effect, Xen.

δυσ-κατάστατος, ον, (καθ-ίστημι) hard to restore or rally, Xen.

δυσ-καταφρόνητος, ον, not to be despised, Xen.

δυσ-κατέργαστος, ον, = δυσκατάπρακτος, Xen.

δύσκε, Ion. for ἔδυ, 3 sing. aor. 2 of δύω.

δυσ-κέλᾰδος, ον, ill-sounding, shrieking, discordant, Il., Aesch., Eur.

δυσ-κηδής, ές, (κῆδος) full of misery, Od.

δύσ-κηλος, ον, (κηλέω) past remedy, Aesch.

δυσ-κίνητος, ον, (κῑνέω) hard to move, Plat. :—immovable, resolute, Plut. : inexorable, Anth.

δυσ-κλεής, ές, (κλέος) poët. acc. δυσκλεέα for δυσκλεέα : —infamous, shameful, Il., Aesch., Xen. Adv. –εῶς, Soph., Eur. Hence

δύσκλεια, ἡ, ill-fame, an ill name, infamy, Eur., Thuc. : ἐπὶ δυσκλείᾳ tending to disgrace him, Soph.

δυσ-κλής, poët. for δυσ-κλεής.

δυσ-κοινώνητος, ον, (κοινωνέω) unsocial, Plat.

δυσκολαίνω, f. ᾰνῶ, (δύσκολος) to be peevish or discontented, Ar. : to shew displeasure, Xen.

δυσκολία, ἡ, (δύσκολος) discontent, peevishness, Ar., Plat. II. of things, difficulty, Dem.

δυσ-κόλλητος, ον, (κολλάω) ill-glued or fastened, loose, Luc.

δυσκολό-καμπτος, ον, (κάμπτω) hard to bend : δ. καμπή an intricate flourish in singing, Ar.

δυσκολό-κοιτος, ον, (κοίτη) making bed uneasy, Ar.

δύσ-κολος, ον, opp. to εὔκολος, I. of persons, properly, hard to satisfy with food ; then, generally, hard to please, discontented, fretful, peevish, Eur., Ar., etc. :—Adv., δυσκόλως ἔχειν, διακεῖσθαι to be peevish, Plat. II. of things, troublesome, harassing, Id.; generally, unpleasant, Dem. :—δυσκολόν ἐστι it is difficult, N. T. :—Adv. –λως, hardly, with difficulty, Ib. (Deriv. of –κολος uncertain.)

δύσ-κολπος, ον, with ill-formed womb, Anth.

δυσ-κόμιστος, ον, (κομίζω) hard to bear, intolerable, Soph., Eur.

δυσκρασία, ἡ, bad temperament, Lat. intemperies, of the air, Plut. From

δύσκρᾱτος, ον, (κεράννυμι) of bad temperament, Strab.

δύσ-κρῐτος, ον, hard to discern or interpret, Aesch., Soph. : δύσκριτόν ἐστι, c. inf., Plat. Adv. –τως, doubtfully, darkly, Aesch.; δ. ἔχειν to be in doubt, Ar.

δυσ-κύμαντος, ον, arising from the stormy sea, Aesch.

δυσκωφέω, f. ήσω, to be stone-deaf, Anth. From

δύσ-κωφος, ον, stone-deaf.

δύσ-λεκτος, ον, hard to tell, Lat. infandus, Aesch.

δύσ-ληπτος, ον, (λαμβάνω) hard to catch, Luc.

δυσ-λόγιστος, ον, (λογίζομαι) ill-calculating, Soph.

δύσ-λοφος, ον, hard for the neck, hard to bear, Theogn., Aesch. II. impatient of the yoke : Adv., impatiently, Eur.

δύσ-λῠτος, ον, (λύω) indissoluble, Aesch., Eur.

δυσμᾰθέω, to be slow at recognising, Aesch. From

δυσ-μᾰθής, ές, (μανθάνω) hard to learn, Aesch. ; δ. ἰδεῖν hard to know at sight, Eur. : τὸ δυσμαθές difficulty of knowing Id. II. act. slow at learning, Plat. :—Adv., δυσμαθῶς ἔχειν to be so, Id. Hence

δυσμᾰθία, ἡ, slowness at learning, Plat.

δυσμᾰχέω, f. ήσω, to fight in vain against, or, to fight an unholy fight with, τινί Soph. : so verb. Adj. δυσμᾰχητέον, one must fight desperately with, Id.

δύσ-μᾰχος, ον, (μάχομαι) hard to fight with, unconquerable, Aesch., Eur., etc. : generally, difficult, Aesch.

δυσμεναίνω, to bear ill-will, τινί against another, Eur., Dem.; and

δυσμένεια, ἡ, ill-will, enmity, Soph., Eur., etc. ; and

δυσμενέων, a participial form only in masc., bearing illwill, hostile, Od.

δυσ-μενής, ές, (μένος) full of ill-will, hostile, Il., Hdt., Trag. ; rarely c. gen., ἄνδρα δ. χθονός an enemy of the land, Soph. II. rarely of things, Id., Xen.

δυσ-μεταχείριστος, ον, (μεταχειρίζω) hard to manage : hard to attack, Xen.

δυσμή, ἡ, (δύω) = δύσις, mostly in pl., Soph., etc. ; ἐπὶ δυσμῇσιν at the point of setting, Hdt. II. the quarter of sunset, the west, Id., Aesch.

δύσ-μηνις, ι, wrathful, Anth.

δυσ-μήνῑτος, ον, (μηνίω) visited by heavy wrath, Anth.

δυσ-μήτηρ, ερος, ἡ, not a mother, Od.

δυσμηχανέω, f. ήσω, to be at loss how to do, c. inf. Aesch. From

δυσ-μήχανος, ον, (μηχανή) hard to effect, Anth.

δυσ-μίμητος, ον, (μῑμέομαι) hard to imitate, Luc.

δύσ-μοιρος, ον, (μοῖρα) = δύσμορος, Soph.

δυσμορία, ἡ, a hard fate, Anth. From

δύσ-μορος, ον, = δύσ-μοιρος, ill-fated, ill-starred, Il., Soph. :—Adv. –ρως, with ill fortune, Aesch.

δυσμορφία, ἡ, badness of form, ugliness, Hdt. From

δύσ-μορφος, ον, (μορφή) misshapen, ill-favoured, ἐσθής Eur.

δύσ-μουσος, ον, (μοῦσα) = ἄμουσος, unmusical, Anth.

δυσ-νίκητος, ον, (νῑκάω) hard to conquer, Plut.

δύσ-νιπτος, ον, (νίζω) hard to wash out, Soph.

δυσνοέω, f. ήσω, (δύσνοος) to be ill-affected, τινί Plut.

δύσνοια, ἡ, (δύσνοος) disaffection, ill-will, malevolence, Soph., Eur.

δυσνομία, ἡ, lawlessness, a bad constitution, Solon.

δύσ-νομος, ον, lawless, unrighteous, Anth.

δύσ-νοος, ον, contr. –νους, ουν, ill-affected, disaffected, τινί Soph., Eur., etc.

δύσ-νοστος νόστος, a return that is no return, Eur.

δυσ-νύμφευτος, ον, (νυμφεύω) unpleasing to marry, Anth.

δύσ-νυμφος, ον, (νύμφη) ill-wedded or ill-betrothed, Eur.

δυσ-ξύμβολος, ον, (συμβάλλω) hard to deal with, driving a hard bargain, Plat., Xen.

δυσξύνετος, ον, (συνίημι II) hard to understand, unintelligible, Eur., Xen.

δύσ-ογκος, ον, over heavy, burdensome, Plut.

δυσ-οδέω, f. ήσω, to make bad way, get on slowly, Plut.

δύσοδμος, Ion. for δύσοσμος.

δυσ-οδο-παίπᾰλος, ον, (ὁδός, παιπαλόεις) difficult and rugged, Anth.

δύσ-οδος, ον, hard to pass, scarce passable, Thuc.

δυσ-οίζω, to be distressed, to fear, Eur. :—δυσοίζω φόβῳ

to tremble with fear at a thing, c. acc., Aesch. (οἴζω is formed from οῖ oh! as οἰμώζω from οἴμοι.)

δυσ-οίκητος, ον, bad to dwell in, Xen.

δύσ-οιμος, ον, = δύσοδος, Aesch.

δύσ-οιστος, ον, hard to bear, insufferable, Aesch., Soph.

δύσομαι, f. med. of δύω.

δύσ-ομβρος, ον, stormy, wintry, Soph.

δυσ-όμῑλος, ον, hard to live with, bringing evil in one's company, Aesch.

δυσ-όμματος, ον, (ὄμμα) scarce-seeing, purblind, Aesch.

δυσ-όρᾱτος, ον, hard to see, Xen.

δυσ-όργητος, ον, = δύσοργος, Babr.

δύσ-οργος, ον, (ὀργή) quick to anger, Soph.

δύσ-ορμος, ον, with bad anchorage, Aesch.: — τὰ δύσορμα rough ground, where one can scarce get footing, Xen. II. act., πνοαὶ δ. that detained the fleet in harbour, Aesch.

δύσ-ορνις, ῑθος, ὁ, ἡ, ill-omened, boding ill, Aesch., Eur.: — with ill auspices, Plut.

δυσ-όρφναιος, α, ον, (ὄρφνη) dusky, Eur.

δυσοσμία, ἡ, an ill smell, ill savour, Soph. From

δύσ-οσμος, Ion. –οδμος, ον, (ὀσμή) ill-smelling, stinking, Hdt. II. bad for scent, in hunting, Xen.

δυσ-ούριστος, ον, (οὐρίζω) driven by a too favourable wind, fatally favourable, Soph.

δυσπάθεια, ἡ, firmness in resisting, Plut. From

δυσπᾰθέω, f. ήσω, to suffer a hard fate, Mosch. II. to be impatient, ἐπί τινι, πρός τι Plut. From

δυσ-πᾰθής, ές, (παθεῖν) impatient of suffering, Plut.: hardly feeling, impassive, Luc.

δυσ-πάλαιστος, ον, (πᾰλαίω) hard to wrestle with, Aesch., Eur., Xen.

δυσ-πάλᾰμος, ον, (πᾰλάμη) hard to conquer, Aesch.

δυσ-πᾰλής, ές, (πάλη) hard to wrestle with, Aesch.

δυσ-παράβλητος, ον, (παραβάλλω) incomparable, Plut.

δυσ-παραίτητος, ον, (παραιτέομαι) hard to move by prayer, inexorable, Aesch., Plut.

δυσ-παρακόμιστος, ον, (παρακομίζω) hard to carry along, difficult, Polyb.

δυσ-παραμύθητος, ον, hard to appease, Plut.

δυσ-πάρευνος, ον, ill-mated, Soph.

δυσ-παρήγορος, ον, hard to appease, Aesch.

δυσ-πάρθενος, ον, unhappy maiden, Anth.

Δύσ-παρις, ιδος, ὁ, unhappy Paris, ill-starred Paris, Il.; cf. Δυσελένα.

δυσ-πάρῐτος, ον, (παριέναι) hard to pass, Xen.

δυσ-πειθής, ές, (πείθομαι) hardly obeying, self-willed, intractable, Xen.: — Adv., δυσπειθῶς ἔχειν Plut.

δύσ-πειστος, ον, = foreg., Xen.

δύσ-πεμπτος, ον, (πέμπω) hard to send away, Aesch.

δυσ-πέμφελος, ον, (perh. from same Root as πέμφ-ιξ): —of the sea, rough and stormy, Il., Hes.: — metaph. rude, uncourteous, Hes.

δυσ-πενθής, ές, bringing sore affliction, direful, Pind.

δυσ-πέρατος, ον, hard to get through, Eur.

δυσ-περίληπτος, ον, hard to encompass, Arist.

δυσ-πετής, ές, (πί-πτω) falling out ill, most difficult, Soph. Adv. δυσπετῶς, Ion. –έως, Aesch.

δυσ-πήμαντος, ον, (πημαίνομαι) full of grievous evil, disastrous, Aesch.

δυσ-πῐνής, ές, (πίνος) squalid, Soph.

δύσ-πλᾰνος, ον, (πλάνη) wandering in misery, Aesch.

δυσπλοΐα, Ion. –πλοίη, ἡ, difficulty of sailing, Anth.

δύσ-πλοος, ον, contr. –πλους, ουν, bad for sailing, Anth.

δύσ-πλωτος, ον, = δύσπλοος, Anth.

δυσπνοια, ἡ, difficulty of breathing, Xen. From

δύσ-πνοος, ον, contr. –πνους, ουν, scant of breath, Soph. II. δ. πνοαί contrary winds, Id.

δυσ-πολέμητος, ον, (πολεμέω) hard to war with, Dem.

δυσ-πόλεμος, ον, unlucky in war, Aesch.

δυσπολιόρκητος, ον, hard to take by siege, Xen.

δυσ-πονής, ές, (πονέω) toilsome, Od.

δυσ-πόνητος, ον, (πονέω) bringing toil and trouble, Aesch. 2. laborious, Soph.

δύσ-πονος, ον, toilsome, Soph.

δυσ-πόρευτος, ον, (πορεύομαι) hard to pass, Xen.

δυσπορία, ἡ, (δύσπορος) difficulty of passing, Xen.

δυσ-πόριστος, ον, (πορίζω) gotten with much labour: τὸ δ. difficulty of getting, Plut.

δύσ-πορος, ον, hard to pass, scarce passable, Xen.

δύσ-ποτμος, ον, unlucky, ill-starred, unhappy, wretched, Trag.; δ. εὐχαί i. e. curses, Aesch.; Comp. δυσποτμώτερος Eur. Adv. –μως, Aesch.

δύσ-ποτος, ον, unpalatable, Aesch.

δυσ-πρᾱγέω, f. ήσω, (πρᾶγος) to be unlucky, Aesch., Plut.

δυσ-πραξία, ἡ, (πράσσω) ill success, ill luck, Aesch., Soph.

δυσ-πρεπής, ές, (πρέπω) base, undignified, Eur.

δυσ-πρόσβατος, ον, hard to approach, Thuc.

δυσ-πρόσῐτος, ον, difficult of access, Eur.

δυσ-πρόσμαχος, ον, (προσμάχομαι) hard to attack, Plut.

δυσ-πρόσοδος, ον, hard to get at, difficult of access, Thuc.: of men, unsocial, Id., Xen.

δυσ-πρόσοιστος, ον, (προσοίσομαι, f. med. of προσφέρω) hard to approach, Soph.

δυσ-πρόσοπτος, ον, (προσόψομαι, f. of προσ-οράω) hard to look on, horrid to behold, Soph.

δυσ-προσπέλαστος, ον, hard to get at, Plut.

δυσ-πρόσωπος, ον, (πρόσωπον) of ill aspect, Plut.

δυσ-ρᾱγής, ές, (ῥήγνυμι) hard to break, Luc.

δύσ-ρῑγος, ον, impatient of cold, Hdt.

δυσσέβεια, ἡ, impiety, ungodliness, Trag. 2. a charge of impiety, Soph.; and

δυσσεβέω, f. ήσω, to think or act ungodly, Trag. From

δυσ-σεβής, ές, (σέβω) ungodly, impious, profane, Trag.

δυσσεβία, ἡ, poët. for δυσσέβεια, Aesch.

δύσ-σοος, ον, hard to save, ruined, Theocr.

δυσ-σύμβολος, Att. for δυσ-ξύμβολος.

δυσ-σύνοπτος, ον, hard to get a view of, Polyb.

δυσ-τάλᾱς, αινα, ᾰν, most miserable, Soph., Eur.

δυσ-τέκμαρτος, ον, (τεκμαίρομαι) hard to make out from the given signs, hard to trace, inexplicable, Trag.

δύσ-τεκνος, ον, (τέκνον) unfortunate in children, Soph.

δυσ-τερπής, ές, (τέρπω) ill-pleasing, Aesch.

δύστηνος, Dor. δύστᾱνος, ον, wretched, unhappy, unfortunate, disastrous, mostly of persons, Hom., Trag.; δυστήνων δέ τε παῖδες ἐμῷ μένει ἀντιόωσιν unhappy are they whose sons encounter me, Il. 2. of things, Trag., Ar.: Sup. Adv., δυστᾱνοτάτως Eur. II. after Hom., in moral sense, wretched, like Lat. miser (a wretch), Soph. (Prob. for δύσ-στηνος; but the origin of –στηνος is uncertain.)

δυσ-τήρητος, ον, (τηρέω) hard to keep, Plut.

δυσ-τλήμων, ον, suffering hard things, h. Hom.

δύσ-τλητος, ον, *hard to bear*, Aesch.

δυσ-τοκεύς, έως, ό, *an unhappy parent*, Anth.

δυστοκέω, f. ήσω, *to be in sore travail*, of women :— metaph., δυστοκεῖ πόλις Ar. From

δύσ-τοκος, ον, (τίκτω) *bringing forth with pain.*

δυστομέω, *to speak evil of*, τινά τι Soph. From

δύ-στομος, ον, (δυσ-, στόμα) *bad of mouth : hard-mouthed*, Anth.

δύ-στονος, ον, for δύσ-στονος, *lamentable*, Aesch.

δυσ-τόπαστος, ον, (τοπάζω) *hard to guess*, Eur.

δυ-στόχαστος, ον, (δυσ-, στοχάζομαι) *hard to hit*, Plut.

δυσ-τράπεζος, ον, *fed on horrid food*, Eur.

δυσ-τράπελος, ον, (τρέπω) *hard to deal with, intractable, stubborn*, Soph. :—Adv. -λως, *awkwardly*, Xen.

δύσ-τροπος, ον, (τρέπω) *hard to turn, intractable*, Eur., Dem.

δυστῠχέω, Ion. impf. ἐδυστύχεον: f. ήσω: aor. 1 ἐδυστύχησα: pf. δεδυστύχηκα: (δυστυχής) :—*to be unlucky, unhappy, unfortunate*, Hdt., Att.; τινι in a thing, Eur.; περί τινος Id.; ἔν τινι Ar.; also, πάντα δυστυχεῖν Eur. Hence

δυστύχημα [ῠ], τό, *a piece of ill luck, a failure*, Plat.

δυσ-τῠχής, ές, (τύχη) *unlucky, unfortunate*, Trag., etc.; τὰ δυστυχῆ = δυστυχίαι, Aesch. :—Adv. -χῶς, Id. 2. *ill-starred, harbinger of ill*, Id. Hence

δυστῠχία, ή, *ill luck, ill fortune*, Eur., Thuc., etc.

δυσ-υπόστᾰτος, ον, *hard to withstand*, Plut.

δυσ-φαής or -φᾰνής, ές, (φάος or φαίνομαι) *scarce visible*, Plut.

δύσ-φᾰτος, ον, *hard to speak, unutterable*, Lat. nefandus, Aesch.

δυσφημέω, f. ήσω, (δύσφημος) *to use ill words*, esp. *words of ill omen*, Trag. II. trans. *to speak ill of*, Soph., Eur. Hence

δυσφημία, ή, *ill language, words of ill omen*, Soph.

δύσ-φημος, Dor. -φᾱμος, ον, (φήμη) *of ill omen, boding*, Hes., Eur. II. *slanderous*, Theogn.

δυσ-φῐλής, ές, (φιλέω) *hateful*, Aesch., Soph.

δυσφορέω, f. ήσω, impf. ἐδυσφόρουν : (δύσφορος) :—*to bear with pain, bear ill*, Lat. aegre ferre : intr. *to be impatient, angry, vexed*, Hdt., Soph.; τινι at a thing, Aesch., Eur.; ἐπί τινι Aesch. Hence

δυσφόρητος, ον, *hard to bear*, Eur.

δυσ-φόρμιγξ, ιγγος, ὁ, ή, *unsuited to the lyre*, Eur.

δύσ-φορος, ον, (φέρω) *hard to bear, heavy*, Xen. 2. mostly of sufferings, *hard to bear, grievous*, Trag.; δύσφοροι γνῶμαι *false, blinding* fancies, Soph.; τὰ δύσφορα *our troubles, sorrows*, Id. :—δύσφορόν [ἐστι] Xen. :—Adv. 3. of food, *oppressive*, Xen. II. (from Pass.) *moving with difficulty, slow of motion*, Id.

δυσφρόνη, ή, = δυσφροσύνη : in pl. *troubles*, Hes.

δυσφρόνως, Adv. of δύσφρων, *rashly*, Id.

δυσφροσύνη, ή, *anxiety, care*, Hes., in Ep. gen. pl. δυσφροσυνάων. From

δύσ-φρων, ον, gen. ονος, (φρήν) *sad at heart, sorrowful, melancholy*, Trag. II. *ill-disposed, malignant*, Aesch., Eur. III. = ἄφρων, *insensate*, Aesch., Soph.

δυσ-φύλακτος, ον, *hard to keep off* or *prevent*, Eur.

δυσ-χείμερος, ον, (χεῖμα) *suffering from hard winters, very wintry, freezing*, Il., Hdt., Aesch.

δυσ-χείρωμα, ατος, τό, *a thing hard to be subdued, a hard conquest*, Soph.

δυσ-χείρωτος, ον, (χειρόω) *hard to subdue*, Hdt., Dem.

δυσχεραίνω, f. -ᾰνῶ: aor. 1 ἐδυσχέρᾱνα: (δυσχερής) :—*to be unable to endure* a thing, *bear with an ill grace*, Lat. aegre ferre, c. acc., Plat.; c. acc. et part. *to be annoyed* at his doing, Aeschin. 2. intr. *to feel annoyance, to be discontented, displeased, vexed*, τινός *for* or *because of* a thing, Plat., etc.; τινί at a thing, Dem. :—Pass. *to be hated*, Plut. 3. c. inf. *to scorn* to do a thing, Plat. II. Causal, *to cause vexation*, ῥήματα τέρψαντα ἢ δυσχεράναντ' Soph. III. δ. ἐν τοῖς λόγοις *to make difficulties* in argument, *to be captious*, Plat.

δυσχέρεια, ή, of things, *annoyance* or *disgust* caused by a thing, Soph. 2. *difficulty* in doing a thing, Plat. II. of persons, *peevishness, ill temper : loathing, nausea*, Id., Theophr. From

δυσ-χερής, ές, (χείρ) *hard to take in hand* or *manage*, of things, *annoying, vexatious, discomfortable*, Trag.: τὸ δυσχερές, = δυσχέρεια, Eur.; δυσχερὲς ποιεῖσθαί τι, Lat. aegre ferre, Thuc.; τὰ δυσχερῆ *difficulties*, Dem. 2. of arguments, *contradictory, captious*, Plat., etc. II. of persons, *ill tempered, unfriendly, hateful*, τινι to one, Soph., Eur., etc.; δ. περί τι *fastidious*, Plat. III. Adv., δυσχερῶς ἔχειν *to be annoyed*, Id.

δύσ-χιμος, ον, (χεῖμα, cf. μελάγχιμος) *wintry, troublesome, dangerous, fearful*, Lat. horridus, Trag.

δυσ-χλαινία, ή, (χλαῖνα) *mean clothing*, Trag.

δύσ-χορτος, ον, *with little grass, ill off for food*, Eur.

δυσχρηστέω, f. ήσω, *to be in difficulty* or *distress*, Polyb. From

δύσ-χρηστος, ον, (χράομαι) *hard to use, nearly useless*, Xen.; *intractable*, Id. :—Adv. -τως ἔχειν *to be in distress*, Plut.

δυσ-χωρία, ή, (χώρα) *difficult, rough ground*, Xen.

δυσ-ώδης, ες, (ὔζω) *ill-smelling*, Hdt., Soph., Thuc.

δυσ-ώδῑνος, ον, (ὠδίν) *causing grievous pangs*, Anth.

δυσωνέω, *to beat down the price, cheapen*, Anth.

δυσ-ώνης, ου, ὁ, (ὠνέομαι) *one who beats down the price.*

δυσ-ώνῠμος, ον, (ὄνυμα, Aeol. for ὄνομα) *bearing an ill name, ill-omened*, Hom., Soph., etc.; esp. *bearing a name of ill omen*, such as Αἴας, Id.

δυσ-ωπέω, f. ή̆σω, (ὤψ) *to put out of countenance, put to shame*, τινά Luc. : absol. *to be importunate*, Plut. II. in good authors only Pass. *to be put out of countenance, to be troubled*, Plat.; of animals, *to be shy, timid*, Xen. 2. *to be ashamed of*, τι Plut.

δυσ-ωρέομαι, f. ήσομαι : (ὦρος = οὖρος *a watcher*) :—*to keep painful watch*, Il.

δύτης [ῠ], ου, ὁ, (δύω) *a diver*, Hdt.

δύω, Ep. for δύο.

δύω, δύνω [ῠ]: A. Causal in f. and aor. 1, *to strip off* clothes, etc., Od. (in compd. ἐξ-έδῡσα).

B. Non-causal, pres. δύω, or δύνω [ῠ] : Ep. impf. δῦνον : — Med. δύομαι, impf. ἐδυόμην, Ep. 3 pl. δύοντο : —f. δύσομαι [ῠ] :—aor. 1 ἐδυσάμην : Ep. 2 and 3 sing. ἐδύσεο, ἐδύσετο, imperat. δύσεο : aor. 2 ἔδῡν (as if from *δῦμι) : 3 dual ἐδύτην [ῠ], pl. ἔδῡμεν, ἔδῦτε, ἔδῡσαν Ep. ἔδῠν ; Ion. 3 sing. δύσκεν ; imperat. δῦθι, δῦτε ;

subj. δύω [ῠ], Ep. opt. δύην [ῠ] (for δυίην), inf. δῦναι, Ep. δύμεναι [ῠ], part. δύς, δῦσα : pf. δέδῡκα, Ep. inf. δεδῡκεῖν : 　　I. of Places or Countries, to enter, make one's way into, τείχεα δύω (aor. 2 subj.) Il. ; ἔδυ νέφεα plunged into the clouds, of a star, Ib. ; δῦτε θαλάσσης κόλπον plunge into the lap of Ocean, Ib. ; δύσεο μνηστῆρας go in to them, Od. : also with a Prep., δύσομαι εἰς Ἀΐδαο Ib. ; δύσετ' ἁλὸς κατὰ κῦμα Il. ; ὑπὸ κῦμα ἔδυσαν Ib. ; δύσκεν εἰς Αἴαντα he got himself unto Ajax, i. e. got behind his shield, Ib.　　2. of the sun and stars, to sink into [the sea, v. supr.], to set, ἠέλιος μὲν ἔδυ Ib. ; Βοώτης ὀψὲ δύων late-setting Boötes, Od. ; πρὸ δύντος ἠλίου Hdt. :—metaph., βίου δύντος αὐγαί Aesch. ; ἔδυ δόμος the house sank, Id.　　II. of clothes and armour, to get into, put on, Il. ; metaph., εἰ μὴ σύγε δύσεαι ἀλκήν if thou wilt not put on strength (cf. ἐπιειμένος ἀλκήν) :—ἀμφ' ὤμοισιν ἐδύσετο τεύχεα Ib. ; ὤμοιϊν τεύχεα δῦθι Ib.　　III. of sufferings, passions, and the like, to enter, come over or upon, κάματος γυῖα δέδυκε Il. ; ἄχος ἔδυνεν ἦτορ, etc., Ib. ; δῦ μιν Ἄρης the spirit of war filled him, Ib.

δυώ-δεκα, poët. for δώ-δεκα (δύο καὶ δέκα), twelve, in all genders, Lat. duo-decim, Hom., etc.

δυωδεκά-βοιος, ον, (βοῦς) worth twelve beeves, Il.

δυωδεκά-μηνος, ον, (μήν) twelve months old, Hes.

δυωδεκά-μοιρος, ον, divided into twelve parts, Anth.

δυω-δεκάς, -δεκαταῖος, -δέκατος, Ep. for δωδεκ-.

δυω-και-εικοσί-μετρος, ον, (μέτρον) holding 22 measures, Il.

δυω-και-εικοσί-πηχυς, υ, 22 cubits long, Il.

δῶ, τό, shortd. Ep. nom. and acc. for δῶμα, a house, dwelling, Hom.

δῶ, 1 sing. aor. 2 subj. of δίδωμι :—δῷ 3 sing.

δώ-δεκα, οἱ, αἱ, τά, (δύο, δέκα) twelve, Hom., etc.: v. δυώδεκα.

δωδεκα-γναμπτος, ον, (γνάμπτω) bent twelve times, δωδεκ. τέρμα the post (in the race-course) that has been doubled twelve times, Pind.

δωδεκάδ-αρχος, ὁ, a leader of twelve, Xen.

δωδεκα-δραχμος, ον, (δράχμη) sold at 12 drachmae, Dem.

δωδεκά-δωρος, ον, (δῶρον II) twelve palms long, Anth.

δωδεκ-άεθλος, ον, (ἄεθλον) conqueror in 12 contests, Anth.

δωδεκα-ετής, ές, or -έτης, ες, (ἔτος) 12 years old, Plut.

δωδεκάκις, (δώδεκα) Adv. twelve times, Ar.

δωδεκά-λινος, ον, (λίνον) of twelve threads, Xen.

δωδεκα-μήχανος, ον, (μηχανή) knowing twelve arts or tricks, Ar.

δωδεκά-παις, ὁ, ἡ, with twelve children, Anth.

δωδεκά-πἄλαι, Adv. twelve times long ago, ever so long ago, Ar.

δωδεκά-πηχυς, υ, twelve cubits long, Hdt.

δωδεκά-πολις, ιος, formed of twelve united states, Hdt.

δωδεκ-άρχης, ου, ὁ, (δωδεκάδαρχος, Xen.

δωδεκάς, άδος, ἡ, the number twelve, Anth.

δωδεκά-σκαλμος, ον, twelve-oared, Plut.

δωδεκά-σκῡτος, ον, of twelve pieces of leather, Plut.

δωδεκᾰταῖος, α, ον, on the twelfth day, Plat.　　II. twelve days old, Hes. (in Ep. form δυωδ-).

δωδέκατος, η, ον, the twelfth, Hom., etc.: Ep. δυωδ-, Id.

δωδεκά-φορος, ον, bearing twelve times a year, Luc.

δωδεκά-φῡλος, ον, (φυλή) of twelve tribes, τὸ δ. the twelve tribes of Israel, N. T.

δωδεκ-έτης or -ετής, ὁ, twelve years old, Plut. :—fem. -έτις, ιδος, Anth.

Δωδώνη, ἡ, Dodona, in Epirus, the seat of the most ancient oracle of Zeus, Hom., etc. :—Soph. uses the heterocl. forms Δωδῶνος, -ῶνι, -ῶνα (as if from Δωδών). —Adj. Δωδωναῖος, α, ον, Il., Aesch.

δώῃ, δώῃσι, Ep. for δῷ, 3 sing. aor. 2 subj. of δώην = δοίην, aor. 2 opt. of δίδωμι.

δῶκα, Ep. for ἔδωκα, aor. 1 of δίδωμι.

δώλα, δῶλος, Dor. for δούλη, δοῦλος.

δῶμα, ατος, τό, (δέμω) a house, Hom., Trag. : part of a house, the chief room, hall, Hom. :—hence in pl. for a single house, Od., Trag.　　II. a house, household, family, Aesch., Soph.

δωμάτιον, τό, Dim. of δῶμα, Ar.　　II. a chamber, bed-chamber, Plat.

δωματῖτις, ιδος, fem. Adj. of the house, Aesch.

δωματο-φθορέω, f. ήσω, (φθορά) to ruin the house, Aesch.

δωμάω, f. ήσω, to build : Med. to cause to be built, Anth.

δῶναξ, ὁ, Dor. for δόναξ.

δώομεν, Ep. for δῶμεν, pl. aor. 2 subj. of δίδωμι.

δωρεά, Ion. -εή, ἡ, a gift, present, esp. a free gift, bounty, Lat. beneficium, Hdt., Aesch., etc.　　II. acc. δωρεάν as Adv. as a free gift, freely, Lat. gratis, Hdt.　　2. to no purpose, in vain, N. T.

δωρέω, f. ήσω (δῶρον) to give, present, Hes., Pind. :— Pass., aor. 1 ἐδωρήθην, to be given or presented, Hdt. ; of persons, to be presented with a thing, Soph.　　II. also as Dep., Il. ; δωρέεσθαί τί τινι to present a thing to one, Lat. donare aliquid alicui, Hdt., Aesch., etc. ; also, δ. τινά τινι to present one with a thing, Lat. donare aliquem aliquo, Id. ; δ. τινά to make him presents, Hdt.　Hence

δώρημα, ατος, τό, that which is given, a gift, present, Hdt., Trag. ; and

δωρητήρ, ῆρος, ὁ, a giver, Anth. ; and

δωρητός, όν, of persons, open to gifts or presents, Il.　　II. of things, freely given, Soph., Plut.

Δωριάζω, = Δωρίζω, Anacreon.

Δωριεύς, έως, ὁ, a Dorian, descendant of Dorus : pl. Δωριεῖς, Att. -ῆς, οἱ, the Dorians, Od., Hdt., etc.

Δωρίζω, Dor. -ίσδω, f. ίσω, to imitate the Dorians in life, dialect, or music, to speak Doric Greek, Theocr.

Δωρικός, ή, όν, Doric, Hdt., Trag., etc.

Δώριος, α, ον, and os, ον, Dorian, Pind., Arist.

Δωρίς, ίδος, ἡ, fem. Adj. Dorian, Hdt., Thuc. : hence,　1. Δωρὶς νᾶσος the Dorian island, i. e. Peloponnesus, Pind., Soph.　2. (with or without γῆ) Doris, in Northern Greece, Hdt., Thuc., etc.　3. Δ. κόρα a Dorian damsel, Eur.

Δωρίσδω, Dor. for Δωρίζω.

Δωριστί [ῐ], Adv. in Dorian fashion : ἡ Δ. ἁρμονία the Dorian mode or measure in music, Plat., etc.

δωροδοκέω, f. ήσω, (δωροδόκος) to accept as a present, esp. to take as a bribe, ἀργύριον, χρυσόν Hdt., Plat.　2. absol. to take bribes, Hdt., Ar.　　II. Pass., 1. of persons, to have a bribe given one, δεδωροδόκηνται Dem.　2. of the bribe, τὰ δωροδοκηθέντα the bribes received, Aeschin.　Hence

δωροδόκημα, ατος, τό, *acceptance of a bribe, corruption*, Dem.; and
δωροδοκία, ἡ, *a taking of bribes, openness to bribery*, Oratt.
δωροδοκιστί, Adv. *in bribe-fashion*, Ar., with a play on Δωριστί. From
δωρο-δόκος, ον, (δέχομαι) *taking presents* or *bribes*, Plat., Dem.
δωρο-δότης, ου, ὁ, *a giver of presents, a giver*, Anth.
δῶρον, τό, (δί-δωμι) *a gift, present*, Hom.: *a votive gift*, Il.:—δωρά τινος *the gifts of*, i.e. *given by*, him, δῶρα θεῶν Hom.; δῶρ' Ἀφροδίτης, i.e. *personal charms*, Il.; c. gen. rei, ὕπνου δ. *the blessing of sleep*, Ib. 2. δῶρα, *presents* given by way of bribe, Dem., etc.; δώρων ἑλεῖν τινα to convict him of *receiving presents*, Ar. II. *the breadth of the hand, the palm*, as a measure of length; v. ἐκκαιδεκάδωρος.
δωρο-φάγος [ᾰ], ον, (φαγεῖν) *greedy of presents*, Hes.
δωροφορέω, f. ήσω, *to bring presents*, τινι Plat.: *to give as presents* or *bribes*, τί τινι Ar. From
δωρο-φόρος, ον, (φέρω) *bringing presents*, Pind., Anth.
δωρύττομαι, Dor. for δωρέομαι, Theocr.
δώς, ἡ, Lat. *dos*, = δόσις, only in nom., Hes.
δωσί-δικος, ον, (δίκη) *giving oneself up to justice, abiding by the law*, Hdt.
δώσων, οντος, ὁ, f. part. of δίδωμι, *always going to give*: Δώσων as a name of Antigonus II, *Promiser*, Plut.
δωτήρ, ῆρος, ὁ, (δί-δωμι) *a giver*, Od., Hes.:—so δώτης, ου, ὁ, Hes.
δωτινάζω, *to receive* or *collect presents*, Hdt. From
δωτίνη [ῑ], ἡ, (δί-δωμι) *a gift, present*, Hom., Hdt.
Δωτώ, οῦς, ἡ, (δί-δωμι) *Giver*, a Nereid, Il., Hes.
δώτωρ, ορος, ὁ, = δωτήρ, Od., h. Hom.

E.

Ε ε, fifth letter of the Gr. alphabet: as numeral ε' = πέντε and πέμπτος, but ͵ε = 5000. The ancients called this vowel εἶ (as they called ο, οὖ). When in the archonship of Euclides (B.C. 403) the Athenians adopted *long e* (Η η) from the Samian alphabet, the Gramm. gave to *short e* the name of ἒ ψιλόν, i.e. ε *without the aspirate*, because Ε had been used for the aspirate.
  In Ion., ε sometimes stood for ἄ, βέρεθρον ἔρσην τέσσερες for βάραθρον ἄρσην τέσσαρες, and in contr. Verbs in -δάω, as δρέω φοιτέω.
ἒ ἕ, or ἒ ἒ ἒ ἕ, an exclamation, *woe! woe!* Aesch., etc.
ἕ, Lat. *se*, v. sub οὗ, *sui*.
ἔα, exclam. of surprise or displeasure, *ha! oho!* Lat. *vah!* esp. before a question, ἔα, τί χρῆμα; Aesch.; ἔα, τίς οὗτος . . ; Eur.
ἔα, Ion. for ἦν, impf. of εἰμί (*sum*).
ἔα, Ion. for εἴα, 3 sing. impf. of ἐάω. II. ἐᾷ, Ep. ἐάᾳ, 3 sing. pres.
ἔαγα [ᾰ], pf. (with pres. signf.) of ἄγνυμι:—ἐάγην [ᾰ], aor. 2 pass.
ἔαδώς, part. ἐαδώς, pf. of ἀνδάνω:—ἔαδον, aor. 2.
ἐάλην or ἐάλην [ᾰ], aor. 2 pass. of εἴλω.
ἑάλωκα [ᾰ], pf. of ἁλίσκομαι:—ἑάλων, aor. 2.
ἐάν [ᾰ], Conjunct. compounded of εἰ ἄν, also contracted into ἤν and ἄν, *if haply, if*, followed by subj. (whereas εἰ is foll. by indic. or opt.), Ep. εἴ κε, αἴ κε. II. in N.T. ἐάν is used just like the adverb ἄν after relative Pronouns and Conjunctions, as ὃς ἐάν *whosoever*, ὅσος ἐάν, ὅστις ἐάν, ὅπου ἐάν, etc.
ἔανδανε, Ion. for ἥνδανε, 3 sing. impf. of ἀνδάνω.
ἐανός, ή, όν, (ἔννυμι) *fit for wearing*, ἐανῷ λιτί with linen *good for wear*, i.e. *fine and white*, Il.; πέπλος ἐανός *a fine, light veil*, Ib.; ἐανοῦ κασσιτέροιο tin *beat out* and so made *fit for wear*, Ib. II. as Subst., ἐανός, ὁ, *a fine robe, fit* for the *wear of* goddesses and great ladies, Hom.
ἔαξα, Ep. for ἦξα, aor. 1 of ἄγνυμι.
ἘΑΡ, ἔαρος, τό, later Ep. εἶαρ, εἴαρος; contr. ἦρ, ἦρος:—Lat. *ver, spring*, ἔαρος νέον ἱσταμένοιο in time of *early spring*, Od.; ἅμα τῷ ἔαρι at the beginning of *spring*, Hdt.; ἐξ ἦρος εἰς Ἀρκτοῦρον Soph.:—metaph. of the *prime* or *flower* of anything, Hdt., etc.; ἔαρ ὁρᾶν to look *fresh and bright*, Theocr.; γενύων ἔαρ, i.e. *the first down* on a youth's face, Anth. Hence
ἐαρίζω, f. Att. ιῶ, *to pass the spring*, Xen.
ἐαρινός, ή, όν, Ep. εἰαρινός; in other Poets, ἠρινός:—Lat. *vernus, of spring*, εἰαρινὴ ὥρη *spring*-time, Il., etc.:—neut. ἠρινόν, -νά, as Adv., *in spring-time*, Eur.; ἠρινὰ κελαδεῖν, of the swallow, Ar.
ἐαρο-τρεφής, ές, (τρέφω) *flourishing in spring*, Mosch.
ἔας, Ion. 2 sing. impf. of εἰμί (*sum*). II. ἐᾷς, 2 sing. of ἐάω.
ἔασι, Ep. for εἰσί, 3 pl. of εἰμί (*sum*).
ἔασκον, Ion. and Ep. impf. of ἐάω.
ἔασσα, Dor. part. fem. of εἰμί (*sum*).
ἔαται, ἔατο, Ion. for ἧνται, ἧντο, 3 pl. pres. and impf. of ἧμαι.
ἔατε, Ion. 2 pl. impf. of εἰμί (*sum*).
ἐατέος, α, ον, verb. Adj. of ἐάω, *to be suffered*, Hdt., Eur. 2. ἐατέον, *one must suffer*, Id., Plat.
ἑ-αυτοῦ, ῆς, οῦ, dat. ἑαυτῷ, ῇ, ῷ, acc. ἑαυτόν, ήν, ό: pl. ἑαυτῶν, ἑαυτοῖς, ἑαυτούς -άς : Ion. ἑωυτοῦ, etc.: Att. contr. αὑτοῦ, etc.:—reflex. Pron. of 3rd pers., Lat. *sui, sibi, se, of himself, herself, itself*, etc.; first in Hdt. and Att.; Hom. has ἕο αὑτοῦ, οἷ αὑτῷ, ἓ αὑτόν:—αὐτὸ ἐφ' ἑαυτό itself by *itself, absolutely*, Plat.; so τὸ καθ' ἑαυτόν Thuc.; αὐτὸ καθ' αὑτό Plat.; ἀπ' ἑαυτοῦ of *himself*, Thuc., etc.; ἐν ἑαυτοῦ, ἐντὸς ἑαυτοῦ, Lat. *sui compos*:—παρ' ἑαυτῷ at *his own house*, Xen.; often with Comp. and Sup., ἐγένοντο ἀμείνονες αὐτοὶ ἑωυτῶν they surpassed themselves, Hdt.; πλουσιώτεροι ἑαυτῶν, i.e. *continually richer*, Thuc. II. in Att. αὐτοῦ, sometimes for 1st or 2nd pers., Aesch., Soph.
ἐάφθη, prob. Ep. for ἥφθη, aor. 1 pass. of ἅπτω, ἐπ' αὐτῷ ἀσπὶς ἐάφθη upon him his shield *was fastened upon* or *clung* to him, i.e. *they fell together*, Il.
ἘΑΏ, Ep. εἰῶ, Ep. 2 and 3 sing. ἐᾷς, ἐᾷ, inf. ἐᾶν:—impf. εἴων, ας, α, Ion. and Ep. ἔων, ἔασκον or εἴασκον:—f. ἐάσω [ᾰ]:—aor. 1 εἴασα, Ep. ἔασα:—pf. εἴᾱκα:—Pass., f. ἐάσομαι in pass. sense, aor. 1 εἰάθην:—pf. εἴᾱμαι:—*to let, suffer, allow, permit*, Lat. *sinere*, c. acc. pers. et inf., Hom., Att.:—Pass. *to be given up*, Soph. 2. οὐκ ἐᾶν *not to suffer*, and then *to forbid, hinder, prevent*, c. acc. et inf., Hom., etc.: often an inf. may be supplied, οὐκ ἐάσει σε τοῦτο will not *allow* thee [to do] this, Soph. II. *to let*

alone, let be, c. acc., Hom., etc.;—absol., ἔασον *let be*, Aesch.:—Pass., ἢ δ᾽ οὖν ἐάσθω Soph.   2. in same sense, c. inf., κλέψαι μὲν ἐάσομεν *we will have done with stealing*, Il.; θεὸς τὸ μὲν δώσει, τὸ δ᾽ ἐάσει [sc. δοῦναι] he will give one thing, the other he will *let alone*, Od.; v. χαίρω fin.

ἐάων [ᾱ], Ep. for ἐήων, gen. pl. of ἐΰς.

ἔβᾰλον, aor. 2 of βάλλω.

ἔβᾰν, Ep. for ἔβησαν, 3 pl. aor. 2 of βαίνω.

ἐβδομ-ᾱγέτης, ου, ὁ, (ἄγω) name of Apollo, to whom the Spartans *sacrificed on the 7th of every month*, Aesch.

ἑβδομαῖος, α, ον, *on the seventh day*, Thuc., Xen.

ἑβδομάς, άδος, ἡ, *the number seven* or *a number of seven*, Anth.   II. *a period of seven days, a week*, Arist.: also *of seven years, a septenary*, Id.

ἑβδόμᾰτος, ον, = ἕβδομος, *the seventh*, Il.

ἑβδομήκοντα, οἱ, αἱ, τά, (ἕβδομος) indecl. *seventy*, Hdt., etc.

ἑβδομηκοντ-ούτης, ου, ὁ, (ἔτος) *seventy years old*: fem. -οῦτις, Luc.

ἕβδομος, η, ον, (ἑπτά) *seventh*, Lat. *septimus*, Hom., etc.; ἡ ἑβδόμη *the seventh day*, Hdt.

ΕΒΕΝΟΣ, ἡ, *the ebony-tree, ebony*, Hdt., Theocr.

ἔβην, aor. 2 of βαίνω.

ἔβησα, aor. 1 (in causal sense) of βαίνω.

ἐβήσετο, Ep. for -ατο, 3 sing. aor. 1 med. of βαίνω.

ἐβίων, aor. 2 of βιόω.

ἐβιώσαο, Ep. for ἐβιώσω, 2 sing. aor. 1 of βιώσκομαι.

ἔβλᾰβεν, Ep. for -ησαν, 3 pl. aor. 2 pass. of βλάπτω.

ἐβλάστησα, ἔβλαστον, aor. 1 and 2 of βλαστάνω.

ἔβλητο, 3 sing. Ep. aor. 2 pass. of βάλλω.

ἐβουλήθην, aor. 1 pass. of βούλομαι.

Ἑβραῖος, ὁ, *a Hebrew*, N.T.:—Adj. Ἑβραϊκός, ή, όν, with fem. Ἑβραΐς, ίδος, *Hebrew*, Ib.:—Adv. Ἑβραϊστί, *in the Hebrew tongue*, Ib.

ἔβρᾰκε, 3 sing. aor. 2 of *βράχω.

ἐγ, for ἐν in compos. before γ κ ξ χ.

ἔγ-γαιος, α, ον, and ἔγ-γειος, ον, (γαῖα, γῆ) *in or of the land, native*, Lat. *indigena*, Aesch.   II. of *property, in land, consisting of land*, Dem., etc.   III. *in or of the earth*, Plat.

ἐγ-γέγᾱα, Ep. pf. of ἐγ-γίγνομαι.

ἐγ-γείνωνται, 3 pl. aor. 1 subj. in causal sense (no pres. ἐγ-γείνομαι being found), μὴ μυῖαι εὐλὰς ἐγγείνωνται *lest the flies breed maggots in* [the wounds], Il.

ἔγ-γειος, ον, (γέα, γῆ) v. ἔγγαιος.

ἐγγελαστής, οῦ, ὁ, *a mocker, scorner*, Eur. From

ἐγ-γελάω, f. άσομαι [ᾰ], *to laugh at, mock*, Lat. *irridere*, τινί Soph., Eur.; κατά τινος Soph.

ἐγ-γενής, ές, (γί-γνομαι) *inborn, native*, Lat. *indigena*, Hdt., Att.; θεοὶ ἐγγενεῖς *gods of the race* or *country*, Aesch.   2. *born of the same race, kindred*, Soph.:—Adv. -νῶς, *like kinsmen*, Id.   II. of qualities, *inborn, innate*, Trag.

ἐγγήρᾱμα, τό, *a comfort for old age*, Plut. From

ἐγ-γηράσκω, f. άσομαι [ᾱ], *to grow old in one, decay*, Thuc.

ἐγ-γίγνομαι, Ion. and later -γίνομαι [ῑ]: f. -γενήσομαι: 3 pl. Ep. pf. ἐγγεγάᾱσι: Dep.:—*to be born* or *bred in* a place, c. dat., Hom., Hdt.   2. of qualities, *to be inborn, innate*, Id., Eur.   3. of events

and the like, to happen in or *among*, τισι Hdt.   II. *to come in, intervene, pass*, of Time, Id., Thuc.   III. ἐγγίγνεται, impers., *it is allowed* or *possible*, c. inf., Hdt., Att.

ἐγγίων [ῑ], ον, ἔγγιστος, η, ον, Comp. and Sup. Adj., from Adv. ἐγγύς, *nearer, nearest*: neut. ἔγγῑον, ἔγγιστα, as Adv., Dem., etc.

ἐγ-γλύσσω, only in pres. (γλυκύς) *to have a sweet taste*, Hdt.

ἐγ-γλύφω [ῠ], f. ψω, *to cut in, carve*, Hdt.

ἐγ-γλωττο-γάστωρ, ορος, ὁ, ἡ, *one who lives by his tongue*, Ar.

ἐγ-γλωττο-τῠπέω, *to talk loudly of*, Ar.

ἔγ-γονος, ὁ, ἡ, *a grandson, granddaughter*, Plut.

ἐγγρᾰφή, ἡ, *a registering, registration*, Dem. From

ἐγ-γράφω [ᾰ], f. ψω, *to mark in* or *on*, Hdt.   II. *to inscribe, write in* or *on*, Id.:—Pass., ἐγγεγραμμένος τι *having something written on it*, Soph.; so Virg. *flores inscripti nomina*.   2. *to enter in the public register*, ἐγγρ. τὸν υἱὸν εἰς ἄνδρας Dem.:—Pass., εἰς τοὺς δημότας ἐγγραφῆναι Id.   3. *to enter on the judge's list, to indict*, Ar., Dem.

ἐγ-γυᾰλίζω, f. ξω, (γύαλον) properly, *to put into the palm of the hand, put into one's hand*, Hom.

ἐγγυάω, f. ήσω: aor. 1 ἠγγύησα:—Med., f. -ήσομαι: —the forms ἐν-εγγύων, ἐν-εγύησα, ἐγ-γεγύηκα (as if the Verb were a compd. with Prep. ἐν or ἐγ) are erroneous: (ἐγγύη):—*to give* or *hand over as a pledge*, Lat. *spondere*, and in Med. *to have a thing pledged* to one, *accept as a surety*, Od., Plat.   2. of a father *to give his daughter in marriage, to plight, betroth*, Hdt., Eur.:—Med. *to have a woman betrothed to one*, Dem.   II. Med. also *to pledge oneself, give security*, Plat., etc.: c. acc. et inf. f. *to promise* or *engage that* .., Ar., Xen.   2. c. acc. rei, *to answer for*, Dem.

ἐγ-γύη, not ἐγγύᾰ, ἡ, (ἐν, γύ-αλον) *a pledge put into the hand: surety, security*, Lat. *vadimonium*, Od., Att.

ἐγγύησις, εως, ἡ, (ἐγγυάω) *betrothed*, Isaeus.

ἐγγυητής, οῦ, ὁ, (ἐγγυάω) *one who gives security, a surety*, Hdt., Att.

ἐγγυητός, ή, όν, (ἐγγυάω) of a wife, *wedded*, Dem.

ἐγγύθεν [ῠ], Adv. (ἐγγύς) *from nigh at hand*, Il., Att.   2. with Verbs of rest, *hard by, nigh at hand*, Hom.   3. c. dat., ἐγγύθεν τινί *hard by him*, Il.; also c. gen., Ib.

ἐγγύθι [ῠ], Adv. *hard by, near*, c. gen., Il.; also c. dat., Ib.   II. of Time, *nigh at hand*, Ib.

ἐγ-γυμνάζω, f. άσω, *to exercise* a person in a thing, c. dat., Luc.:—Med. *to practise oneself in*, Plut.

ἔγγυος, ον, (ἐγγύη) *giving security*, Theogn., Xen.

ἐγγύς [ῠ], Adv.: Comp. ἐγγυτέρω, Sup. ἐγγυτάτω or -ύτατα; also ἔγγῑον, ἔγγιστα: I. of Place, *near, nigh, at hand*, Hom.; c. gen. *hard by, near to*, Id., Soph.; also c. dat., Eur.   II. of Time, *nigh at hand*, Hom., Xen.   III. of Numbers, etc., *nearly*, Thuc., Xen.; οὐδ᾽ ἐγγύς i.e. *not by a great deal, nothing like it*, Plat., Dem.; ἐγγὺς τοῦ τεθνάναι *very nearly dead*, Plat.   IV. of Relationship, *akin to*, Aesch., Plat. (From the same Root as ἄγχι, cf. ἄγχιστος, ἔγγιστος.)

ἐγγύτατος, η, ον, Sup. Adj., δι᾽ ἐγγυτάτου = ἐγγυτάτω, Thuc.

ἐγ-γώνιος, ον, (γωνία) forming an angle, esp. a right angle, λίθοι ἐν τομῇ ἐγγώνιοι cut square, Thuc.

ἐγδούπησα, Ep. for ἐδούπησα, aor. 1 of δουπέω.

ἐγείρω (Root ΕΓΕΡ): Ep. impf. ἔγειρον:—f. ἐγερῶ: aor. 1 ἤγειρα, Ep. ἔγειρα: pf. ἐγήγερκα:—Pass., f. ἐγερθήσομαι: aor. 1 ἠγέρθην, Ep. 3 pl. ἔγερθεν:—pf. ἐγήγερμαι:—Ep. aor. 2 ἠγρόμην, 3 sing. ἔγρετο, imper. ἔγρεο, inf. ἐγρέσθαι:—intr. pf. ἐγρήγορα (as pres.): plqpf. ἐγρηγόρη or -ειν (as impf.), Ep. 3 pl. ἐγρηγόρθασι, 2 pl. imper. ἐγρήγορθε, inf. ἐγρήγορθαι: I. Act. to awaken, wake up, rouse, Il., Trag. 2. to rouse, stir up, ἐγείρειν Ἄρηα to stir the fight, Il., etc. 3. to raise from the dead, N.T.; or from a sick bed, Ib. 4. to raise or erect a building, Ib. II. Pass., with pf. act. ἐγρήγορα, to awake, Od., Hdt., etc.: in aor. 2 also to keep watch or vigil, Il.:—in pf. to be awake, Hom., Att. 2. to rouse or stir oneself, be excited by passion, Hes., Thuc.

ἔγεντο, Ep. for ἐγένετο, 3 sing. aor. 2 of γίγνομαι.

ἐγερσί-γελως, ωτος, ὁ, ἡ, laughter-stirring, Anth.

ἐγερσῐ-θέατρος, ον, exciting the theatre, Anth.

ἐγερσῐ-μάχας, ου, ὁ, fem. -μάχη, battle-stirring, Anth.

ἐγέρσῐμος, ον, from which one wakes, ὕπνος ἐγ., opp. to the sleep of death, Theocr. From

ἔγερσις, εως, ἡ, a waking from sleep, Plat.:—awaking from death, N.T.

ἐγερσῐ-φαής, ές, (φάος) light-stirring, ἐγ. λίθος the flint, Anth.

ἐγερτέον, verb. Adj. of ἐγείρω, one must raise, Eur.

ἐγερτί [ῐ], (ἐγείρω) Adv. eagerly, busily, Soph.: wakefully, Eur.

ἐγερτικός, ή, όν, (ἐγείρω) waking, stirring, τινος Plat.

ἐγήγερμαι, pf. pass. of ἐγείρω.

ἔγηρα, 3 sing. aor. 2 of γηράσκω.

ἐγ-καθέζομαι, —ἐδούμαι, Dep. to sit or settle oneself in a place, εἰς θᾶκον Ar.:—to encamp in a place, Thuc.

ἐγ-καθηβάω, f. ήσω, to pass one's youth in, Eur.

ἐγ-κάθημαι, Dep. to sit in or on, Xen.: to lie in ambush, Eur.

ἐγ-καθιδρύω, f. ύσω [ῡ], to erect or set up in, Eur.

ἐγ-καθίζω, Ion. -κατίζω, f. Att. ἰῶ, to seat in or upon, Plat.:—so in aor. 1 med., ναὸν ἐγκαθείσατο founded a temple there, Eur. II. Med. to take one's seat on, Hdt.

ἐγ-καθίημι, f. -καθήσω, to let down: to send in as a garrison, Plut.

ἐγ-καθίστημι, f. -καταστήσω, to place or establish in a place, as king or chief, Eur., Thuc.: to place as a garrison in a place, Dem. II. Pass., with aor. 2, pf. and plqpf. act., to be established in a place, Thuc.

ἐγ-καθοράω, to look closely into, Plut. II. to remark something in a person or thing, Id.

ἐγ-καθορμίζομαι, f. Att. ιοῦμαι, Med. to run into harbour, come to anchor, Thuc.

ἐγ-κᾰθυβρίζω, f. σω, to riot or revel in a thing, Eur.

ἐγκαίνια, τά, (καινός) a feast of renovation, esp. that established by Judas Macc. at the re-consecration of the Temple, N.T.

ἐγ-καινίζω, ον, to renovate, consecrate:—Pass., N.T.

ἐγ-καίω, f. -καύσω, to burn or heat in fire, Eur. II. to make a fire in a place, Plut.

ἐγ-κᾰκέω, f. ήσω, (κακός) to lose heart, grow weary, N.T.

ἐγ-κᾰλέω, f. -έσω: pf. -κέκληκα:—to call in a debt, Xen., etc. II. to bring a charge against a person, φόνον ἐγκαλεῖν τινι to bring a charge of murder against one, Soph., Plat.:—to accuse, τινί Thuc., etc.:—ἐγκ. τι to bring as a charge, Soph., Thuc.

ἐγ-καλλωπίζομαι, Pass. to take pride or pleasure in a thing, c. dat., Plut.

ἐγκαλλώπισμα, τό, an ornament, decoration, Thuc.

ἐγκαλυμμός, ὁ, a covering, wrapping up, Ar. From

ἐγ-καλύπτω, f. ψω, to veil in a thing, to wrap up, Ar.: —Pass. to be veiled or enwrapt, Id., Xen. II. Med. to hide oneself, hide one's face, Ar., etc.; of persons at the point of death, Xen., Plat.; as a mark of shame, Id.

ἐγκάμπτω, f. ψω, to bend in, bend, Xen.

ἐγ-κᾰνάσσω, f. ξω, to pour in wine, Eur., Ar.

ἐγ-κᾰνᾰχάομαι, Dep. to make a sound in a thing, ἐγκ. κόχλῳ to blow on a conch, Theocr.

ἐγ-κάπτω, f. ψω: pf. -κέκαφα:—to gulp in greedily, snap up, Ar.

ἔγ-κᾰρος, ὁ, (κάρ, κάρα) the brain, Anth.

ἔγ-καρπος, ον, containing fruit, Soph.

ἐγ-κάρσιος, α, ον, (v. ἐπι-κάρσιος) athwart, oblique, Thuc.

ἐγ-καρτερέω, f. ήσω, to persevere or persist in a thing, c. dat., Thuc., Xen. 2. c. acc. to await stedfastly, Eur. 3. absol. to hold out, remain firm, Plut.

ἔγκᾰτα, τά, (ἐγκάσι, ἐν) the inwards, entrails, bowels, Lat. intestina, Hom.

ἐγ-καταγηράσκω, f. άσομαι, to grow old in, ἐν πενίᾳ Plut.

ἐγ-καταδέω, f. -δήσω, to bind fast in, Plat.

ἐγ-καταδύνω, aor. 2 -κατέδυν, sink beneath, ὕδασιν Anth.

ἐγ-καταζεύγνυμι, f. -ζεύξω, to adapt to, τί τινι Soph.

ἐγ-κατάθοιτο, 3 sing. aor. 2 opt. of ἐγκατατίθεμαι.

ἐγ-κατακαίω, f. -καύσω, to burn in, Luc.

ἐγ-κατάκειμαι, Pass. to lie in, c. dat., Theogn. 2. to lie in bed, sleep, Ar.

ἐγ-κατακλίνω [ῑ], f. -κλῑνῶ, to put to bed in a place, Ar.:—Pass. to lie down in, Id.

ἐγ-κατακοιμάομαι, Pass. to lie down to sleep in a place, Hdt.

ἐγ-κατακρούω, f. σω, to hammer in: ἐγκ. χορείαν τοῖς μύσταις to tread a measure among the mystae, Ar.

ἐγ-καταλαμβάνω, f. -λήψομαι, to catch in a place, to hem in, Thuc.; ἐγκ. τινὰ ὅρκοις to trammel by oaths, Aeschin.

ἐγ-καταλέγω, f. ξω, to build in: Pass., 3 pl. aor. 2 ἐγκατελέγησαν were built into the wall, Thuc. II. to count among, Luc.: to enlist soldiers, Anth.

ἐγ-καταλείπω, f. ψω, to leave behind, Hes., Thuc., etc. 2. to leave in the lurch, Id., etc. 3. to leave out, omit, Hdt. II. Pass. to be left behind in a race, Id.

ἐγ-κατάληψις, εως, ἡ, a being caught in a place, a being hemmed in, interception, Thuc.

ἐγ-καταλογίζομαι, Dep. to reckon in or among, Isae.

ἐγ-καταμίγνυμαι, Pass. to be mixed in or with, c. dat., Isocr.

ἐγ-καταπήγνυμι, f. -πήξω, to thrust firmly in or into, c. dat., Od.

ἐγ-καταπίπτω, poët. aor. 2 ἐνικάππεσον, to fall in or upon, c. dat., Anth.

ἐγ-καταπλέκω, f. -πλέξω, to interweave, entwine, Xen.

ἐγ-καταρράπτω, f. ψω, to sew in, Xen.

ἐγ-κατασκήπτω, f. ψω, to fall upon, like lightning: of epidemics, to break out among, Thuc. II. trans. to hurl down among or upon, properly of a thunder-bolt, Aesch., Soph.

ἐγ-κατασπείρω, f. -σπερῶ, to disperse in or among,Plut.

ἐγ-καταστοιχειόω, f. ώσω, to implant as a principle in, τί τινι Plut.

ἐγ-κατασφάττω, f. ξω, to slaughter in a place, Plut.

ἐγ-κατατέμνω, f.-τεμῶ, to cut up among a number, Plat.

ἐγ-κατατίθεμαι, Med., ἱμάντα τέῳ ἐγκάτθεο κόλπῳ (Ep. aor. 2 imper.) put the band upon or round thy waist, Il.; ἄτην ἑῷ ἐγκάτθετο θυμῷ stored up, devised mischief in his heart, Od.; τελαμῶνα ἐῇ ἐγκάτθετο τέχνῃ designed the belt by his art, Ib.

ἐγ-καταχέω, f. -χεῶ, to pour in besides, Anth.

ἐγ-κάτθεο, Ep. for ἐγ-κατάθου, aor. 2 imper. of ἐγκατατίθεμαι :—ἐγκάτθετο, 3 sing. indic.

ἐγ-κατιλλώπτω, f. ψω, to scoff at, τινί Aesch.

ἐγ-κατοικέω, f. ήσω, to dwell in a place, Hdt.

ἐγ-κατοικοδομέω, f. ήσω, to build in a place, Thuc. II. to immure, Aeschin.

ἔγκάτον, v. ἐγκατα.

ἔγ-καυμα, ατος, τό, (ἐγκαίω) a sore from burning, Luc.

ἔγ-κειμαι, f. -κείσομαι: used as Pass. of ἐντίθημι: I. to lie in, be wrapped in clothes, Il., Hdt. 2. ἐγκεῖσθαί τινι to be involved in a thing, Eur. II. to press upon, of troops pressing the enemy, Thuc. :—with an Adj. or Adv., πολλὸς ἐνέκειτο was very urgent, Hdt.; πολὺς ἔγκειται he insists much upon a thing, c. dat., Dem. 2. to be devoted to one, Theocr.

ἐγ-κείρω, only in pf. pass. part., ἐγκεκαρμένῳ κάρᾳ with shorn head, Eur.

ἐγ-κέκλιμαι, pf. pass. of ἐγκλίνω.

ἐγ-κεκόλαμμαι, pf. pass. of ἐγκολάπτω.

ἐγκέλευμα or -ευσμα, τό, an encouragement, Xen.; and

ἐγκέλευστος, ον, urged on, bidden, commanded, Xen. From

ἐγ-κελεύω, f. σω, to urge on, cheer on, Aesch.; c. dat., Xen.; to sound a charge, Plut.

ἐγ-κεντρίς, ίδος, ἡ, (κέντρον) a sting, Ar.: a goad, Xen.

ἐγ-κεράννῦμι or -ύω, f. -κεράσω [ᾰ], to mix in, mix, esp. wine, Il.:—Med. to mix for oneself: metaph. to concoct, Hdt.

ἐγ-κερτομέω, f. ήσω, to abuse, mock at, τινί Eur.

ἐγ-κέφαλος, ὁ, (κεφαλή) that which is within the head, the brain, Hom., etc. II. the edible pith of young palm-shoots, Xen.

ἐγ-κεχρημένος, pf. part. pass. of ἐγχράω.

ἐγ-κῐθᾰρίζω, f. ίσω, to play the harp among, h. Hom.

ἐγ-κλείω, Ion. -κληΐω, Att. -κλῄω: f. -κλείσω, Ion. -κληΐσω :—to shut in, close gates, Hdt., Plat. II. to shut or confine within: Pass., ἑρκέων ἐγκεκλημένος (for ἐντὸς ἑρκέων κεκλημένος), Soph.; δόμοις ἐγκεκλημένος Id. 2. generally to confine, γλῶσσαν ἐγκλῄσας Id. III. Med. to shut oneself up in, Xen.

ἔγκλημα, ατος, τό, (ἐγκαλέω) an accusation, charge, complaint, Soph., etc.; ἐγκλήματα ἔχειν τινός = ἐγκαλεῖν τινι, Thuc.; ἔγκλημα διαλύεσθαι Id. Hence

ἐγκληματικός, ή, όν, litigious, Arist.

ἔγ-κληρος, ον, having a lot or share in a thing, c. gen., Soph.; λαχεῖν ἔγκληρά τινι to have an equal share with another, Id. 2. having a share of an inheritance, an heir, heiress, Eur. 3. ἔγκληρος εὐνή a marriage which brings wealth, Id.; ἔγκ. πεδία land possessed as an inheritance, Id.

ἐγκλῄω, Att. for ἐγκλείω.

ἐγκλῐδόν, Adv. leaning, bent down, h. Hom. From

ἐγ-κλίνω [ῑ]: f. -κλῐνῶ: pf. pass. -κέκλῐμαι :—to bend in or inwards, Xen. 2. Pass. to lean on, rest or weigh upon one, Id.; metaph., πόνος ὔμμι ἐγκέκλιται labour lies upon you, Il. 3. ἐγκλίνειν νῶτόν τινι to turn one's back towards another, Eur. II. intr. to give way, flee, Lat. inclinari, Xen., etc. 2. to decline, become worse, Plut.

ἐγ-κοιλαίνω, f. ἀνῶ, to hollow or scoop out, Hdt.

ἔγ-κοιλος, ον, sinking in hollows, hollow, Plat.

ἐγ-κοιμίζω, f. ίσω, to lull to sleep in a place, Anth.

ἐγ-κοισῦρόομαι, Pass. to be luxurious as Coesyra (a woman of the Alcmaeonid family), ἐγκεκοισυρωμένη Ar.

ἐγ-κοιτάς, άδος, ἡ, (κοίτη) serving for a bed, Anth.

ἐγ-κολάπτω, f. ψω, to cut or carve upon stone, Hdt.

ἐγ-κοληβάζω, to fall heavily upon, or to gulp down, swallow up, Ar. (Deriv. unknown.)

ἐγ-κολπίζω, f. ίσω, to form a bay, Strab.

ἐγ-κομβόομαι, Med. to bind a thing on oneself, gird oneself, N. T.

ἐγ-κονέω, f. ήσω, to be quick and active, make haste, hasten, Hom., Soph., etc.

ἐγ-κονίομαι, Med. (κονίω) to sprinkle sand over oneself before wrestling, Xen.

ἐγκοπεύς, έως, ὁ, a tool for cutting stone, chisel, Luc.; and

ἐγκοπή, ἡ, a hindrance, N. T.; and

ἔγκοπος, ον, wearied, Anth. From

ἐγ-κόπτω, f. ψω, to hinder, thwart, N. T.

ἐγ-κορδυλέω, f. ήσω, (κορδύλη) to wrap up in coverlets: Pass., ἐγκεκορδυλημένη Ar.

ἐγ-κοσμέω, f. ήσω, to arrange in a place, c. dat., Od.

ἐγ-κοτέω, f. ήσω, to be indignant at, τινί Aesch.

ἔγ-κοτος, ον, bearing a grudge, spiteful, malignant, Aesch. II. as Subst., a grudge, ἔγκοτον ἔχειν τινί to bear a grudge against one, Hdt.

ἐγ-κράζω, f. -κράξομαι: aor. 2 -έκραγον :—to cry aloud at one, τινί Ar.; ἐπί τινα Thuc.

ἐγκράτεια, ἡ, mastery over a person or thing, ἐγκρ. ἑαυτοῦ self-control, Plat. II. absol. self-control, Lat. continentia, Xen. From

ἐγ-κρᾰτής, ές, (κράτος) in possession of power, Soph. II. holding fast, stout, strong, Aesch., Soph. III. c. gen. rei, having possession of a thing, master of it, Lat. compos rei, Hdt., Soph.; ἐγκρατῆ πόδα the sheet that controls the ship, Id.; ἐγκρατὴς ἑαυτοῦ master of oneself, Plat. IV. Adv. -τῶς, with a strong hand, by force, Thuc.

ἐγ-κρίνω [ῑ], f. -κρῐνῶ, to reckon in or among, Eur. II. to admit as elected, εἰς τὴν γερουσίαν Dem.: generally, to admit, accept, Plat. Hence

ἔγκρῐσις, εως, ἡ, admission to the contest, Luc.; and

ἐγκρῐτέος, verb. Adj. one must admit, Plat.

ἐγ-κροτέω, f. ήσω, to strike on the ground, to beat time, Theocr. :—Med. to dash one against the other, Eur.

ἐγ-κρούω, f. σω, to knock or hammer in, Ar. : to strike, Anth.　II. to dance, Ar.

ἐγ-κρύπτω, f. ψω : aor. 1 -έκρυψα :—to hide or conceal in a place, c. dat., Od.　2. to keep concealed, Ar.

ἐγ-κρῠφιάζω, (κρύφιος) intr. to keep oneself hidden, act underhand, Ar.

ἐγ-κρῠφίας ἄρτος, ὁ, (κρύφιος) a loaf baked in the ashes, Luc.

ἐγ-κτάομαι, f. ήσομαι, Dep. to acquire possessions in a foreign country, Hdt., Dem.　Hence

ἔγκτημα, ατος, τό, land held in a district by a person not belonging to it, Dem.; and

ἔγκτησις, εως, ἡ, Dor. ἔγκτᾱσις, εως, ἡ, tenure of land in a place by a stranger, Xen. :—the right of holding such land, granted to foreigners, Decret. ap. Dem.

ἐγ-κῠκάω, f. ήσω, to mix up in, Ar.

ἐγ-κυκλέομαι, Pass. to rotate in the sockets : metaph. to turn in, Ar.

ἐγ-κύκλιος, ον, (κύκλος) circular, rounded, round, Eur., Aeschin.　II. revolving in a cycle, periodical, Dem. :—ordinary, Lat. quotidianus, Isocr., etc.

ἐγ-κυκλόω, f. ώσω, to move round in a circle, τι Eur.　II. Pass. to encircle, φωνή μέ τις ἐγκεκύκλωται a voice has echoed around me, Ar.　III. Med. to roam about a place, c. acc., Plut.　Hence

ἐγκύκλωσις, εως, ἡ, a surrounding, Strab.

ἐγ-κῠλίνδω, f. -κυλίσω [ῑ], to roll up in : metaph. in Pass. to be involved in, εἴς τι Xen.

ἐγ-κύμων, ον, gen. ονος, (κῦμα II) pregnant, Xen.; ἐγκύμων τευχέων big with arms, of the Trojan horse, Eur.

ἔγ-κυος, ον, (κύω) = foreg., Hdt.

ἐγ-κύπτω, f. ψω, to stoop down and peep in, Plat.; ἐγκ. εἴς τι to look closely into, Hdt. :—absol., ἐγκεκῠφότες stooping to the ground, Ar., Thuc.

ἐγ-κυρέω, f. ήσω, = ἐγκύρω, Aesch.

ἐγ-κύρω [ῡ], f. -κύρσω: aor. 1 -έκυρσα :—to fall in with, light upon, meet with, c. dat., Il., Hes., Hdt.

ἐγκωμιάζω, impf. ἐν-εκωμίαζον: f. -άσω and -άσομαι : pf. ἐγκεκωμίακα : (the augmented tenses are formed as if the Verb were a compound of ἐν and κῶμος, not a deriv. from ἐγκώμιον):—to praise, laud, extol one, ἐπί τινι for a thing, Plat. :—Pass. to be praised, Hdt.

ἐγ-κώμιος, ον, (κώμη) in or of the same village, native, Hes.　II. (κῶμος) of or belonging to a Bacchic revel, in which the victor was led home in procession with music and dancing :—hence　2. ἐγκώμιον, τό, a song in honour of a conqueror, an eulogy, Ar., Plat.

ἔγνωκα, ἔγνωσμαι, pf. act. and pass. of γι-γνώσκω.

ἔγνων, aor. 2 of γι-γνώσκω.

ἐγράφην [ᾰ], aor. 2 pass. of γράφω.

ἔγραψα, aor. 1 act. of γράφω.

ἐγρε-κύδοιμος, ον, rousing the din of war, Hes.

ἐγρε-μάχης, ου, ὁ, (μάχη) rousing the fight, Soph.

ἔγρεο, ἔγρετο, 2 and 3 sing. Ep. aor. 2 pass. of ἐγείρω.

ἐγρεσί-κωμος, ον, stirring up to revelry, Anth.

ἐγρήγορα, ἐγρήγορθε, -θαι, -θασι, pf. forms of ἐγείρω.

ἐγρηγορόων, Ep. part., as if from a pres. ἐγρηγοράω, (= ἐγείρομαι), watching, waking, Od.

ἐγρηγορτί [ῑ], (ἐγρήγορα) Adv. awake, watching, Il.

ἐγρήσσω, (ἐγείρω) to be awake or watchful, Hom.

ἔγρω, later form of ἐγείρω; imper. ἔγρετε.

ἔγροιτο, 3 sing. Ep. aor. 2 pass. opt. of ἐγείρω :—ἐγρόμενος part.

*ἐγχαίνω, v. sub ἐγχάσκω.

ἐγ-χᾰλῑνόω, f. ώσω, to put a bit in the mouth of a horse, c. acc., Babr. :—Pass. of horses, to have the bit in their mouths, Hdt., Xen.

ἔγ-χαλκος, ον, in or with brass : moneyed, rich, Anth.

ἐγ-χάνῃ, 3 sing. aor. 2 subj. of ἐγ-χάσκω :—ἐγ-χᾰνοῦμαι, fut.

ἐγ-χᾰράσσω, f. -ξω, to engrave upon a thing, Plut.

ἐγ-χάσκω, f. -χανοῦμαι: aor. 2 inf. ἐγχανεῖν (as if from *ἐγχαίνω):—to gape, Luc.　II. to grin or scoff at one, c. dat., Ar.

ἐγ-χέζω, f. -χέσω or -χεσοῦμαι: pf. ἐγκέχοδα:—Lat. incacare, Ar.: c. acc. to be in a horrid fright at one, Id.

ἐγχείη, ἡ, Ep. form of ἔγχος, a spear, lance, Hom.; gen. pl. ἐγχειάων, dat. ἐγχείῃσι.

ἐγ-χείῃ, Ep. for ἐγ-χέῃ, 3 sing. pres. subj. of ἐγ-χέω.

ἐγ-χειρέω, f. ήσω, (χείρ) to put one's hand in or to a thing, to attempt it, c. dat. rei, Eur., Thuc.; c. inf., Xen., etc.: absol. to make an attempt or beginning, Soph., Thuc.　2. to lay hands on, attack, assail, τινι Id., Xen.　Hence

ἐγχείρημα, ατος, τό, an undertaking, attempt, Soph., Plat., etc.; and

ἐγχείρησις, εως, ἡ, a taking in hand, undertaking, Thuc., Plut.; and

ἐγχειρητέον, verb. Adj. one must undertake, Xen.; and

ἐγχειρητής, οῦ, ὁ, an undertaker, an adventurer, Ar.; and

ἐγχειρητικός, ή, όν, enterprising, adventurous, Xen.

ἐγ-χειρίδιος, ον, (ἐν, χείρ) in the hand, Aesch.　II. as Subst., ἐγχειρίδιον, τό, a hand-knife, dagger, Hdt.

ἐγ-χειρίζω, f. Att. -ιῶ: pf. -κεχείρικα:—to put into one's hands, entrust, τί or τινά τινι Hdt., Thuc., etc.: —Pass., ἐγχειρισθαί τι to be entrusted with a thing, Luc.　II. Med. to take in hand, encounter, κινδύνους Thuc.

ἐγ-χειρί-θετος, ον, put into one's hands, Hdt.

ἐγχέλειος, α, ον, of an eel, τἀγχέλεια (sub. κρέα) eel's flesh, Ar.

ἔγχελυς or ἐγχέλυς, ἡ, rarely ὁ, gen. εως or υος: pl. ἐγχέλεις, -νες or -υς, gen. -έων or -ύων, dat. -εσι or -υσι: (v. ἔχις) :—an eel, Lat. anguilla, Il., Ar., etc.

ἐγχελυ-ωπός, όν, (ὤψ) eel-faced, Luc.

ἐγχεσί-μωρος, ον, eager with the spear, Hom. (The deriv. of -μωρος is uncertain, cf. ἰό-μωρος, ὑλακό-μωρος.)

ἐγχέσ-πᾰλος, ον, (πάλλω) wielding the spear, Il.

ἐγ-χέω: f. -χεῶ: aor. 1 ἐν-έχεα, Ep. ἐν-έχευα, Ep. 3 sing. subj. ἐγχήῃ, Ep. ἐγχείη: pf. pass. -κέχυμαι:—to pour in, μέθυ ἐγχ. δεπάεσσι Od.; οἶνον ἐς κύλικα Ar.: ἐγ-χεῖν alone, to pour in wine, to fill the cup, Xen., etc.: —Med. to fill one's cup, Ar.　2. of dry things, to pour in, shoot in, Od.　II. with acc. of the cup, to fill by pouring in, Xen.　III. ἐγχεῖν ὕδωρ τινί, i. e. to fill the κλεψύδρα (q. v.), Dem.

ἐγ-χθόνιος, ον, in or of the country, Anth.

ἔγχος, τό, a spear, lance, often in Hom., consisting of two parts, αἰχμή and δόρυ, head and shaft, Il.　II. any weapon, a sword, Soph., Eur.:—metaph. φροντίδος ἔγχος Soph. (Prob. akin to Root ΑΚ, in ἀκή, ἀκών.)

ἔγχουσα, ἡ, the plant *alkanet*, the root of which yields a red dye, Xen. (Deriv. unknown.)

ἐγ-χράω and **-χραύω**, like ἐγχρίμπτω, *to dash against*, Lat. *impingere*, Hdt. :—pf. part. pass., ἔσαν ἐγκεχρημένοι (sc. πόλεμοι) *there were wars urged on*, Id.

ἐγ-χρέμπτομαι, Dep. *to expectorate*, Luc.

ἐγ-χρῄζω, *to have need*: ἐγχρῄζοντα *necessaries*, Luc.

ἐγ-χρίμπτω or **-χρίπτω**: aor. 1 -έχριμψα :—Pass., aor. 1 ἐνεχρίμφθην:—*to bring near to*, τῷ [τέρματι] ἐγχρίμψας *so as almost to touch the post*, Il.; ἐγχρ. τὴν βᾶριν τῇ γῇ *to bring* the boat *close to* land, Hdt. II. intr. *to come near, approach*, τινί Soph. :—so in Pass., ἐγχριμφθεὶς πύλῃσιν Il.; αἰχμὴ ὀστέῳ ἐγχριμφθεῖσα the point *driven to* the very bone, Ib.; ἀσπίδ᾽ (i.e. ἀσπίδι) ἐνιχριμφθείς *dashed against* his shield, Ib.

ἔγχριστος, ον, *rubbed in as an ointment*, Theocr. From

ἐγ-χρίω [ῑ], f. σω, *to rub, anoint*, τινί *with* a thing, Anth. II. *to sting, prick*, τινί Plat.

ἐγ-χρονίζω, f. Att. ιῶ, *to be long about* a thing, *to delay*, Thuc. :—Pass. *to become chronic*, Plat.

ἐγ-χρώζομαι, pf. ἐγκέχρωσμαι, Pass. *to be engrained*: —metaph. *to be amalgamated with*, c. dat., Arist.

ἐγ-χύνω, late form of ἐγχέω, Luc.

ἐγ-χυτρίζω, f. σω, *to expose children in an earthenware vessel*: hence, *to make an end of*, Ar.

ἐγ-χωρέω, f. ήσω, *to give room* for doing a thing, *to allow, permit*, Hdt., Xen. :—ἐγχωρεῖ, impers. *it is possible* or *allowable*, c. dat. pers. et inf., Plat., Xen., etc.: absol., ἔτι ἐγχωρεῖ *there is yet time*, Plat.

ἐγ-χώριος, ον, and **α, ον**, (χώρα) *in* or *of the country*, Hdt., Att. 2. as Subst. *a dweller in* the land, *inhabitant*, Soph., Eur. 3. τὸ ἐγχώριον as Adv. *according to the custom of the country*, Thuc.

ἔγ-χωρος, ον, (χώρα) = foreg., Soph.

ἘΓΩ´, Ep. ἐγών before vowels, pron. of the first person; Lat. *ego*, *I* :—strengthd. ἔγωγε, Lat. *equidem*, *I at least, for my part, for myself*, Hom., Att.; Dor. ἐγώγα, Dor. ἐγώνγα Ar.: Boeot. ἰώνγα, ἰώγα Id. II. a Root ΜΕ appears in the oblique cases, viz. Gen. ἐμοῦ, enclit. μου, Ion. and Ep. ἐμέο, ἐμεῦ, μευ, Ep. also ἐμέθεν:—Dat. ἐμοί, enclit. μοί, Dor. ἐμίν, Acc. ἐμέ, enclit. με. III. Dual, nom. and acc. ΝΩ´, Ion. and Ep. νῶι (cf. Lat. *nos*), gen. and dat. νῶν, Ep. νῶιν. IV. Pl., nom. ἩΜΕΙΣ; Aeol. ἄμμες; Dor. ἅμες :—Gen., ἡμῶν, Ion. ἡμέων, Ep. ἡμείων, Dor. ἁμῶν :—Dat., ἡμῖν, in Att. Poets also ἡμίν (ῐ) or ἥμιν; Aeol. and Dor. ἄμμιν, ἄμμι, Dor. also ἁμίν :—Acc. ἡμᾶς, Ion. ἡμέας; Aeol. ἄμμε, Dor. ἁμέ.

ἐγᾦδα, ἐγᾦμαι, crasis for ἐγὼ οἶδα, ἐγὼ οἶμαι.

ἐγών, ἔγωγα, ἐγώνγα, dialectic forms of ἐγώ, ἔγωγε.

ἐδάην, aor. 2 of *δάω.

ἔδαισα, aor. 1 of δαίνυμι.

ἔδακον, aor. 2 of δάκνω.

ἐδάμην [ᾰ], Ep. aor. 2 pass. of δαμάζω.

ἐδανός, ή, όν, (ἔδω) *eatable*: ἐδανόν, τό, *food*, Aesch.

ἐδάρός, ή, όν, (prob. from ἀδεῖν, ἡδύς) *sweet, delicious*, Il.

ἐδάρην [ᾰ], aor. 2 pass. of δείρω.

ἔδαρθον, metath. form of ἐδράθον, aor. 2 of δέρκομαι.

ἐδασάμην, aor. 1 med. of δατέομαι.

ἐδαφίζω, f. Att. ιῶ, *to dash to the ground*, N.T. From

ἔδαφος, εος, τό, (prob. from same Root as ὁδός, οὖδας) *the bottom, foundation, base* of anything, Thuc.;

ἔδαφος νηός *the bottom, hold* of a ship, Od.; ἔδ. ποταμοῦ Xen. 2. *the ground-floor, pavement*, οἴκου Hdt.; καθαιρεῖν εἰς τὸ ἔδαφος *to rase to the ground*, Thuc. 3. *ground, soil, land*, Aeschin., Dem.

ἔδεισα, Ep. for ἔδεισα, aor. 1 of δείδω.

ἐδέδμην, Ep. sync. aor. 2 of δέχομαι.

ἐδεδέατο, Ion. for -εντο, 3 pl. plqpf. pass. of δέω *to bind*.

ἐδεδμήατο, Ion. for ἐδέδμηντο, 3 pl. plqpf. pass. of δέμω.

ἐδεήθην, aor. 1 of δέομαι *to want*.

ἐδέθην, aor. 1 pass. of δέω *to bind*.

ἔδεθλον, τό, (ἕδος) *a seat, abode*, Aesch.

ἔδειρα, aor. 1 of δέρω.

ἐδείδιμεν, -δῑσαν, Ep. 1 and 3 pl. plqpf. of δείδω.

ἔδεκτο, 3 sing. Ep. sync. aor. 2 of δέχομαι.

ἔδεσμα, ατος, τό, (ἔδω) *meat*: pl. *meats*, Batr., Plat.

ἐδεστέον, verb. Adj. of ἔδω, *one must eat*, Plat.

ἐδεστής, οῦ, ὁ, (ἔδω) *an eater*, Hdt.

ἐδεστός, ή, όν, (ἔδω) *eatable*: *eaten, consumed*, Soph.

ἐδήδεσμαι, pf. pass. of ἐσθίω: ἐδήδοκα, pf. act.

ἐδήδοται, 3 sing. pf. pass. of ἔδω.

ἐδηδώς, pf. part. of ἔδω.

ἐδητύς, ύος, ἡ, *meat, food*, (ἔδω) Hom.

ἐδήχθην, aor. 1 pass. of δάκνω.

ἐδίδαξα, pf. of διδάσκω.

ἔδμεναι, Ep. for ἔδειν, inf. of ἔδω.

ἐδμήθην, aor. 1 pass. of δαμάω.

ἐδνάομαι, = ἑδνόομαι, Eur.

ἔδνον, τό, (prob. from ἀδεῖν, ἡδύς) mostly in pl. ἕδνα, Ep. ἔεδνα, *a wedding-gift*, presented by the suitor to the bride or her parents (φερνή being the bride's *portion*), Hom., Aesch. II. of *wedding-gifts* made to the bride *by those of her own household*, Od., Eur.

ἑδνόω, f. ώσω, (ἕδνον) *to promise for wedding-presents, to betroth* one's daughter, Theocr. :—so in Med., Od. II. in Med. also, *to marry*, Anth. Hence

ἑδνωτής, Ep. ἐεδν-, οῦ, ὁ, *a betrother*, Il.

ἐδοκεύμες, Dor. for ἐδοκοῦμεν, 1 pl. impf. of δοκέω.

ἔδομαι, f. of ἔδω and ἐσθίω.

ἔδοντι, Dor. for ἔδουσι, 3 pl. of ἔδω.

ἔδοξα, aor. 1 of δοκέω.

ἕδος, εος, τό, (ἕζομαι) *a sitting-place*: 1. *a seat, chair, stool, bench*, Il. 2. *a seat, abode, dwelling-place*, Hom., etc. :—*a temple*, Plat., Xen., etc. 3. *a foundation, base*, Hes., Anth. II. *the act of sitting*, οὐχ ἕδος ἐστί 'tis no *time to sit still*, Il.

ἑδοῦμαι, f. of ἕζομαι.

ἕδρα, Ep. and Ion. ἕδρη, ἡ : (ἕδος) : I. *a sitting-place*: 1. *a seat, chair, stool, bench*, Hom. : *a seat of honour*, Il., Xen. 2. *a seat*, of the gods, *a sanctuary, temple*, Pind., Trag. 3. *the seat* or *place* of anything, Hdt.; ἐξ ἕδρας out of its *right place*, Eur. :—*a foundation, base*, Plut. 4. ἡ ἕδρα τοῦ ἵππου *the back* of the horse, *on which the rider sits*, Xen. 5. ἕδραι are the quarters of the sky in which omens appear, Aesch., Eur. II. *a sitting*, Aesch., Soph. : of a position, γονυπετεῖς ἕδραι *kneeling*, Eur. 2. *a sitting still, inactivity, delay*, Hdt., Thuc.; οὐχ ἕδρας ἀκμή 'tis not the season *for sitting still*, Soph. 3. *the sitting* of a council, Id. III. *the seat, breech, fundament*, Hdt. Hence

ἐδράζω, f. άσω, *to make to sit, place,* Anth.

ἔδρᾰθον, poët. for ἔδαρθον, aor. 2 of δαρθάνω.

ἑδραῖος, α, ον, and ος, ον, (ἕδρα) *sitting, sedentary,* Xen., Plat.   **2.** ἑδραία ῥάχις the horse's back *on which the rider sits,* Eur.   **II.** *sitting fast, steady, steadfast,* Id., Plat.   Hence

ἑδραίωμα, ατος, τό, *a foundation, base,* N. T.

ἔδρᾰκον, aor. 2 of δέρκομαι.

ἔδρᾰμον, aor. 2 of τρέχω.

ἔδρᾱν, aor. 2 of διδράσκω :—ἔδρᾱν, 3 pl.

ἔδρᾰνον, τό, poët. form of ἕδρα, *a seat, abode,* Aesch., Soph.   **II.** *a stay, support,* of an anchor, Anth.

ἔδρη, ἡ, Ep. and Ion. for ἕδρα.

ἔδρησα, Ion. for ἔδρᾱσα, aor. 1 of δράω.

ἑδριάω, *to seat* or *set* :—Pass. *to sit,* in Ep. forms 3 pl. pres. and impf. ἑδριόωνται, ἑδριόωντο, Hom., Hes.; inf. ἑδριάασθαι, Id.   **II.** intr. in Act. *to sit,* Theocr.

ἑδρο-στρόφος, ὁ, (ἕδρα, στρέφω) *a wrestler who throws his adversary by a cross-buttock,* Theocr.

ἔδῠν, aor. 2 of δύω :—also Ep. 3 pl. for ἔδυσαν.

ἐδύνατο, Ion. for ἐδύναντο, 3 pl. impf. of δύναμαι.

ΈΔΩ, old Ep. pres. for Att. ἐσθίω (q. v.), Ep. inf. ἔδμεναι : impf. ἔδω, Ion. sing. 3 ἔδεσκε : f. ἔδομαι, pf. part. ἐδηδώς :—Pass., pf. ἐδήδοται :—*to eat,* Hom. : of beasts, *to eat, devour,* Id.; of worms, *to gnaw,* Id.   **II.** *to eat up, devour, consume,* βίοτον, κτήματα Od. : also, ἄλγεσι θυμὸν ἔδοντες Ib.   Hence

ἐδωδή, ἡ, *food, meat, victuals,* Hom., Plat.   **2.** *fodder* for cattle, Il.   **3.** *a bait* for fish, Theocr.

ἐδώδιμος, ον, in Hdt. η, ον, *eatable,* Hdt., Thuc., etc. : ἐδώδιμα, τά, *eatables, provisions,* Thuc.

ἔδωκα, aor. 1 of δίδωμι.

ἐδώλιον, τό, (ἕδος) *a seat,* mostly in pl., *abodes,* Aesch., Soph.   **II.** in a ship, ἐδώλια are *the rowing-benches,* or rather *a half-deck,* Hdt., Soph., Eur.

ἑέ, poët. for ἕ, *him,* acc. of οὗ.

ἕεδνα, Ep. for ἕδνα : ἑεδνόω, -ωτής, Ep. for ἑδν-.

ἐεικοσάβοιος, ἐείκοσι, ἐεικόσορος, ἐεικοστός, Ep. for εἰκοσ-.

ἐείλεον, Ep. for εἴλεον, impf. of εἴλω.

ἔειπα, ἔειπον, Ep. for εἶπα, εἶπον, qq. v.

ἔεις, Ep. for εἷς.

ἐεισάμην, -αο, Ep. aor. of εἴδομαι (v. *εἴδω A) :—part. ἐεισάμενος.

ἐείσατο, 3 sing. Ep. aor. of εἶμι (ibo) : ἐεισάσθην, 2 dual.

ἐέλδομαι, ἔελδωρ, Ep. for ἔλδομαι, ἔλδωρ.

ἐέλμεθα, Ep. 1 pl. pf. pass. of εἴλω : part. ἐελμένος.

ἐέλπομαι, Ep. for ἔλπομαι.

ἔελσαι, Ep. aor. 1 inf. of εἴλω.

ἐεργάθω, ἔεργε, ἐεργμένος, ἐέργνυμι, ἐέργω, Ep. for εἰργ-.

ἐερμένος, Ep. pf. pass. part. of εἴρω.

ἐέρση, ἐερσήεις, Ep. for ἕρση, ἑρσήεις.

ἐέρτο, Ep. 3. sing. plqpf. pass. of εἴρω.

ἐέρχατο, Ep. 3 pl. plqpf. pass. of εἴργω.

ἐέσσατο, Ep. 3 sing. aor. 1 med. of ἵζω.

ἐέσσατο, Ep. 3 sing. aor. med. of ἕννυμι.

ἔεστο, Ep. 3 sing. plqpf. pass. of ἕννυμι.

ἔζευγμαι, pf. pass. of ζεύγνυμι.

ἐζεύχθην, aor. 1 pass. of ζεύγνυμι.

ἕζομαι (Root ΕΔ) : impf. and aor. 2 ἑζόμην : aor. 1

---

pass. ἕσθην :—*to seat oneself, sit,* ἐν λέκτρῳ, ἐπὶ δίφρῳ, κατὰ κλισμούς Hom.; ἐπὶ χθονὶ ἑζέσθην they sank to the earth, of a pair of scales, Il. :—cf καθέζομαι.   **II.** there is no act. pres., ἕζω, *to set, place ;* though, as if from it, we have trans. tenses εἷσα, med. εἱσάμην, f. med. εἵσομαι, pf. pass. εἷμαι; v. εἷσα.

ἔζωσμαι, pf. pass. of ζώννυμι.

ἐή, fem. of ἑός, *his.*

ἐή, exclam., like ἔ or ἒ ἔ.

ἔη, Ion. for ᾖ, 3 sing. subj. of εἰμί (*sum*).

ἔην, Ep. for ἦν, 3 sing. impf. for εἰμί (*sum*).

ἐήνδανον, Ep. for ἥνδανον, impf. of ἁνδάνω.

ἐῆος, gen. masc. of ἐΰς.

ἐῆς, Ep. for ἧς, gen. fem. of ὅς, *who ;*—but ἑῆς, gen. of ὅς, *his.*

ἔησθα, 2 sing. Ep. for ἦς, 2 sing. impf. of εἰμί (*sum*).

ἔῃσι, Ep. for ᾖ, 3 sing. pres. subj. of εἰμί (*sum*).

ἔθανον, aor. 2 of θνήσκω.

ἐθάς, άδος, ὁ, ἡ, (ἔθος) *customary, accustomed to* a thing, c. gen., Thuc., Plut.

ἔθειρα, ἡ, *hair,* used by Hom. in pl., either of *a horse's mane,* or of the *horsehair crest* on helmets :—later in sing. and pl. of the *hair of the head,* Aesch., Eur., etc.; of a lion's *mane,* Theocr.   Hence

ἐθειράζω, f. άσω, *to have long hair,* Theocr.

ἐθείρω, once in Hom., *to tend, take care of* a field. (Deriv. unknown.)

ἐθελημός, όν, (ἐθέλω) *willing, voluntary,* Hes.

ἐθέλησθα, Ep. for ἐθέλῃς, 2 sing. subj. of ἐθέλω.

ἐθελοδουλεία, ἡ, *willing slavery,* Plat.   From

ἐθελό-δουλος, ον, *a willing slave,* Plat.

ἐθελο-θρησκεία, ἡ, *will-worship,* N. T.

ἐθελοκᾰκέω, f. ήσω, *to be slack in duty, play the coward purposely,* Hdt.   From

ἐθελό-κᾰκος, ον, *wilfully bad* or *cowardly.*

ἐθελοντηδόν, (ἐθέλω) Adv. *voluntarily,* Thuc.

ἐθελοντήν, (ἐθέλω) Adv. *voluntarily,* Hdt.

ἐθελοντήρ, ῆρος, ὁ, (ἐθέλω) *a volunteer,* Od.

ἐθελοντής, οῦ, ὁ, later form of foreg., Hdt., Thuc., etc.

ἐθελοντί, Adv., = ἐθελοντηδόν, Thuc.

ἐθελό-πονος, ον, *willing to work,* Xen.

ἐθελο-πρόξενος, ον, one who voluntarily charges himself with the office of πρόξενος (q. v.), Thuc.

ἐθελ-ουργός, όν, (*ἔργω) *willing to work,* Xen.

ἐθελούσιος, α, ον, (ἐθέλω) *voluntary,* Xen.   **II.** of things, *optional, matter of free choice,* Id.

ΈΘΕΛΩ or **ΘΕΛΩ,** Ep. subj. ἐθέλωμι :—impf. ἤθελον, Ep. also ἔθελον, Ion. ἐθέλεσκον :—f. ἐθελήσω and θελήσω : aor. 1 ἠθέλησα, Ep. ἐθέλησα :—pf. ἠθέληκα :—*to will, wish, purpose,* c. acc. et inf. *to wish that . . ,* c. inf. *to wish to do,* Hom., Att.; c. acc., inf. being omitted, τί θέλων (sc. πρᾶξαι) Aesch.   **2.** with a negat., almost = δύναμαι, μίμνειν οὐκ ἐθέλεσκον they cared not to make a stand, i. e. *they were unable,* Il.   **II.** of things,   **1.** much like μέλλω, merely to express a *future* event, εἰ θελήσει ἀναβῆναι ἡ τυραννίς if the monarchy *will revert,* Hdt.   **2.** *to be wont* or *accustomed,* c. inf., Id., Thuc.   **3.** *to mean, purport,* τί ἐθέλει τὸ ἔπος; Lat. *quid sibi vult?* French *que veut-il dire?* Hdt., etc.

ἐθέλχθην, aor. 1 pass. of θέλγω.

ἔθεν, poët. gen. for ἕο, οὗ, *his, her, of him, of her.*

ἔθεντο, 3 pl. aor. 2 med. of τίθημι.

ἐθηεῖτο, ἐθηεύμεθα, ἐθηεῦντο, Ion. for ἐθεᾶτο, ἐθεώμεθα, ἐθεῶντο, 3 sing., 1 and 3 pl. of θεάομαι.

ἐθηήσαντο, Ion. for ἐθεάσαντο, 3 pl. aor. 1 of θεάομαι.

ἔθηκα, aor. 1 of τίθημι.

ἐθημο-λογέω, (ἔθος, λέγω) to gather customarily, Anth.

ἔθην, aor. 1 pass. of ἵημι:—but　　II. ἔθην, aor. 2 act. of τίθημι.

ἔθιγον, aor. 2 of θιγγάνω.

ἐθίζω, f. Att. ἐθιῶ: aor. 1 εἴθισα: pf. εἴθικα: Pass., aor. 1 εἰθίσθην: pf. εἴθισμαι: (ἔθος):—to accustom, use, ἐθ. τινὰ ποιεῖν τι Plat., Xen.:—Pass. to be or become accustomed or used to do, c. inf., Thuc. Hence

ἐθιστέον, verb. Adj. one must accustom, Xen.; and

ἐθιστός, ή, όν, to be acquired by habit, Arist.

ἐθν-άρχης, ου, ὁ, (ἄρχω) an ethnarch, N. T., Luc.

ἐθνικός, ή, όν, (ἔθνος) foreign, heathen, gentile, N. T.: Adv. -νικῶς, Ib.

ἔθνος, εος, τό, (ἔθω) a number of people accustomed to live together, a company, body of men, Il., etc.; ἔθνος λαῶν a host of men, Ib.; also of animals, swarms, flocks, Ib., Soph.　　2. after Hom., a nation, people, Hdt., etc.:—in N. T. τὰ ἔθνη the nations, Gentiles, i. e. all but Jews and Christians.　　3. a special class of men, a caste, tribe, Plat., Xen.　　4. sex, Id.

ἔθορον, aor. 2 of θρώσκω.

ἔθος, εος, τό, (ἔθω) custom, habit, Aesch., etc.; ἐν ἔθει εἶναι to be in the habit, Thuc.; ἔθει habitually, Arist.

ἐθρέφθην, aor. 1 pass. of τρέφω:—ἔθρεψα, aor. 1 act.

ἐθρίσα, poët. for ἐθέρισα, aor. 1 of θερίζω.

ἘΘΩ, to be accustomed: the pres. only in partic., κακὰ πόλλ' ἔρδεσκεν ἔθων much ill he wrought by custom, i. e. was accustomed to work, Il.; otherwise, pf. εἴωθα, Ion. ἔωθα is used as a pres., and plqpf. εἰώθειν, Ion. ἐώθεα, as impf.:—to be wont or accustomed, be in the habit, c. inf., Il., Hdt., etc.:—in part. absol. accustomed, customary, usual, Il., Soph., etc.; in neut., κατὰ τὸ εἰωθός according to custom, παρὰ τὸ εἰωθός contrary to custom, Thuc.:—Adv. εἰωθότως, more solito, Soph.

ΕΙ', Ep. and Dor. also αἰ, a Conditional Conjunction, Lat. si, if; and in indirect questions, whether.

A. with a verb in protasis, answered by a similar tense in apodosis:　　1. with pres. and fut. indic., to express mere Possibility, εἰ τοῦτο ποιεῖ (or ποιήσει), ἁμαρτάνει (or ἁμαρτήσεται) if he is doing (or shall do) this, he is (or will be) wrong.　　2. with impf. and aor. indic., to express Impossibility, εἰ τοῦτο ἐποίει, ἡμάρτανεν ἄν if he was doing this, he would be wrong; εἰ τοῦτο ἐποίησεν, ἥμαρτεν ἄν if he did (or had done) this, he would be wrong.　　3. with optat. to express a mere Assumption, εἰ τοῦτο ποιοῖ, ἁμαρτάνοι ἄν if he were to do this, he would be wrong.　　II. with Subjunctive, to express Possibility with some degree of Probability: in this case ἄν is always added, and εἰ ἄν becomes εἰ ἐάν, ἤν, ἄν, (Ep. εἴ κεν), ἐὰν τοῦτο ποιῇ, ἁμαρτήσεται if he do this, he will be wrong.　　II. sometimes the apodosis is omitted, so that εἰ expresses a wish, εἴ μοι γένοιτο φθόγγος if I had a voice, [I would . .], i. e. Oh that I had a voice! so εἰ γάρ, εἴθε, Ep. αἰ γάρ, αἴθε.　　2. sometimes the protasis is

omitted, εἰ δ' ἄγε come on, = εἰ δὲ [βούλει], ἄγε, Od.; εἰ δέ, σὺ μὲν ἄκουσον Il.　　3. εἰ δὲ μή = Lat. sin minus, otherwise, for εἰ δὲ μή [τοῦτό ἐστι], Hdt., etc.

B. In Indirect Questions, whether, Lat. an, followed by the indic., subj., or opt., according to the principles of oratio obliqua:　　1. with INDIC. or SUBJ. after primary tenses, οὐκ οἶδ', εἰ θεός ἐστιν whether he is a god, Il.; οὐκ οἶδ' εἰ δῶ whether I shall give, Xen.　　2. with OPTAT. after past tenses, ἤρετο εἴ τις ἐμοῦ εἴη σοφώτερος he asked whether any one was wiser than I, Plat.　　II. after Verbs expressive of wonder, indignation, etc., θαυμάζω εἰ μηδεὶς ὀργίζεται, where εἰ nearly = ὅτι, Dem.; ἀγανακτεῖ εἰ μὴ στεφανωθήσεται Aeschin.

εἶα, poët. trisyll. ἔϊα, Lat. eia, Interj. on! up! away! with imper., Trag.; εἶα δή come then! Aesch.; εἶα νῦν well now! Ar., etc.

εἰαμενή, ἡ, a river-side pasture, meadow, ἐν ἐλαμενῇ ἔλεος in a marshy meadow, Il. (Deriv. uncertain.)

εἰανός, ή, όν, Ep. for ἑανός, Il.

εἶαρ, εἴαρινός, Ep. for ἔαρ, ἐαρινός.

εἰαρό-μασθος, ον, with youthful breasts, Anth.

εἴας, 2 sing. impf. of ἐάω.

εἴασκον, Ion. impf. of ἐάω.

εἴαται, εἴατο, Ep. for ἧνται, ἧντο, 3 pl. pres. and impf. of ἧμαι.

εἴατο, Ep. for εἶντο, 3 pl. plqpf. pass. of ἕννυμι.

ΕΙ'ΒΩ, Ep. form of λείβω, to drop, let fall in drops, Hom.:—Pass. to trickle down, Hes.

εἰ γάρ, in wishes, v. εἰ A. II. 1.

εἰ δ' ἄγε, v. εἰ A. II. 2.

εἰδάλιμος, η, ον, (εἶδος) shapely, comely, Od.　　II. like, looking like, Anth.

εἶδαρ, ατος, τό, (εἴδω) food, and of horses, fodder, Hom.

εἰδείην, opt. of οἶδα, εἰδέναι, inf.: v. *εἴδω B.

εἰ δὲ μή, v. εἰ A. II. 3.

εἴδετε, Ep. for εἴδητε, 2 pl. subj. of οἶδα: v. *εἴδω B.

εἰδήμων, ον, gen. ονος, (*εἴδω B) knowing or expert in a thing, τινός Anth.

εἰδησέμεν, Ep. f. inf., v. *εἴδω B

εἰδοί, ῶν, αἱ, the Roman Idus, Plut.

εἴδομαι, εἶδον, v. sub *εἴδω A.

εἴδομεν, Ep. for εἴδωμεν, 1 pl. subj. of οἶδα: v. *εἴδω B.

εἰδο-ποιέω, f. ήσω, to make an image of a thing, to mould, Plut.; and

εἰδοποιΐα, ἡ, the specific nature of a thing, Strab. From

εἰδο-ποιός, όν, (ποιέω) forming a species, specific, Arist.

εἶδος, εος, τό, (*εἴδω A) that which is seen, form, shape, figure, Lat. species, forma, Hom.; absol. in acc., εἶδος ἄριστος, etc.　　II. a form, sort, particular kind or nature, Hdt., etc.　　2. a particular state of things or course of action, Thuc.　　III. a class, kind, sort, whether genus or species, Plat., etc.

εἰδότως, Adv. of εἰδώς, knowingly, Aeschin.

εἰδύλλιον, τό, Dim. of εἶδος: a short descriptive poem, mostly on pastoral subjects, an idyll, Theocr., etc.

*εἴδω (Root ϜΙΔ, Lat. vid-eo) to see: not used in act. pres., ὁράω being used instead; but pres. is used in Med., v. infr.:—aor. 2 εἶδον retains the proper sense of to see: but pf. οἶδα (I have seen) means I know, and is used as a pres.

A. aor. 2 εἶδον, Ep. without augm. ἴδον, Ion. 3 sing. ἴδεσκε; imper. ἴδε (as Adv. ἰδέ, ecce); subj. ἴδω, Ep. ἴδωμι; opt. ἴδοιμι; inf. ἰδεῖν, Ep. ἰδέειν; part. ἰδών:— hence is formed a fut. ἰδησῶ:—aor. 2 med. is used in same sense, εἰδόμην, Ep. ἰδόμην; imper. ἰδοῦ (as Adv. ἰδού, ecce); subj. ἴδωμαι; opt. ἰδοίμην; inf. ἰδέσθαι; part. ἰδόμενος:—ὄψομαι is used as fut., ἑόρακα or ἑώρακα as pf.: **1.** to see, perceive, behold, Hom., etc.; after a Noun, θαῦμα ἰδέσθαι a marvel to behold, Il.; οἰκτρὸς ἰδεῖν Aesch. **2.** to look at, εἰς ὦπα ἰδέσθαι to look him in the face, Il., etc. **3.** to look so and so, ἀχρεῖον ἰδών looking helpless, Ib. **4.** to see mentally, ἰδέσθαι ἐν φρεσίν 'to see in his mind's eye,' Hom. **II.** Med., pres. εἴδομαι, Ep. 3 sing. ἐείδεται; aor. 1 εἰσάμην, Ep. 2 and 3 pers. ἐείσαο, ατο, Lat. videor, to be seen, appear, εἴδεται ἄστρα they are visible, appear, Il. **2.** c. inf. to appear or seem to be, τοῦτό μοι κάλλιστον εἴδεται εἶναι Od.; also with inf. omitted, τόγε κέρδιον εἴσατο Ib.; also, εἴσατ' ἴμεν he made a show of going, Ib. **3.** in strictly middle sense, c. dat., ἐείσατο φθογγὴν Πολίτῃ she made herself like Polites in voice, Il.:—also to be like, Ib.

B. pf. οἶδα I have seen, i.e. I know, as pres.; plqpf. ᾔδειν, ᾔδεα, Att. ᾔδη, I knew, as impf.; 2 sing. οἶσθα, rarely οἶδας; pl. ἴσμεν (Ep. and Dor. ἴδμεν), ἴστε, ἴσασι, rarely οἴδαμεν, -ατε, -ᾱσι:—imperat. ἴσθι, ἴστω (Boeot. ἴττω):—subj. εἰδῶ, Ep. ἰδέω; pl. εἴδομεν Ep. for εἰδῶμεν, εἴδετε for εἰδῆτε:—optat. εἰδείην; inf. εἰδέναι, Ep. ἴδμεναι, ἴδμεν:—part. εἰδώς, εἰδυῖα, Ep. ἰδυῖα:—Plqpf. ᾔδη, ᾔδησθα (rarely ᾔδης), ᾔδη; Att. also ᾔδειν, Ion. ᾔδεα, ᾔδεε, ᾔδεε; ᾔειδον Att. 1 pl. ᾔδειμεν, ᾔδεμεν, 2 pl. ᾔδειτε, 3 pl. ᾔδεσαν; also shortened ᾖσμεν, ᾖστε, ᾖσαν, Ep. 3 pl. ἴσαν.—The fut., in this sense, is εἴσομαι or εἰδήσω, Ep. inf. εἰδησέμεν. To know, εὖ οἶδα I know well; εὖ ἴσθι be assured: often c. acc. rei, νοήματα οἶδε, μήδεα οἶδε he is versed in counsels, Hom.; with neut. Adjs., πεπνυμένα, φίλα, ἀθέμιστα εἰδώς Id.; also c. gen., τόξων εὖ εἰδώς cunning in the use of the bow; οἰωνῶν σάφα εἰδώς Od.:—χάριν εἰδέναι τινί to acknowledge a debt to another, thank him, Il., etc.:—the Imperat. in protestations, ἴστω Ζεὺς αὐτός be Zeus my witness, Ib.; Dor. ἴττω Ζεύς, ἴττω Ar.:—εἰδώς absol. one who knows, εἰδυίῃ πάντ' ἀγορεύω Il.; ἰδυίῃσι πραπίδεσσι with knowing mind, Ib. **2.** c. inf. to know how to do, Ib., Att. **3.** with the part. to know that so and so is the case, ἴσθι μοι δώσων know that thou wilt give, Aesch.; τὸν Μῆδον ἴσμεν ἐλθόντα Thuc. **4.** οὐκ οἶδ' εἰ, I know not whether, expresses disbelief, like Lat. nescio an non, οὐκ οἶδ' εἰ πείσαιμι Eur. **5.** οἶδα or ἴσθι are often parenthetic, οἶδ' ἐγώ Id.; οἶδ' ὅτι, οἶσθ' ὅτι, ἴσθ' ὅτι, πάρειμι Soph.; so, εὖ οἶδ' ὅτι Dem.:—in Trag. also, οἶσθ' ὃ δρᾶσον; equivalent to δρᾶσον —οἶσθ' ὅ; do—know'st thou what? i.e. make haste and do; οἶσθ' ὡς ποίησον, Id.

εἰδωλεῖον, τό, (εἴδωλον) an idol's temple, N.T.

εἰδωλό-θυτος, ον, (θύω) sacrificed to idols: εἰδωλόθυτα, τά, meats offered to idols, N.T.

εἰδωλολατρεία, ἡ, idolatry, N.T. From

εἰδωλο-λάτρης, ου, ὁ, ἡ, (λάτρις) an idol-worshipper, idolater, N.T.

εἴδωλον, τό, (εἶδος) an image, a phantom, Hom., Hdt.;

βροτῶν εἴδωλα καμόντων phantoms of dead men, Od.; of any unsubstantial form, σκιᾶς εἴδωλον Aesch.; οὐδὲν ἄλλο πλὴν εἴδωλα Soph. **II.** an image in the mind, idea, Xen.:—also a fancy, Plat. **III.** an image, likeness, Hdt. **IV.** an image, idol, N.T.

εἰδωλοποιέω, f. ήσω, to form an image in the mind, Plat.; and

εἰδωλοποιΐα, ἡ, formation of images, as in a mirror, Plat. From

εἰδωλο-ποιός, ὁ, (ποιέω) an image-maker, Plat.

εἰδώς, part. of οἶδα: v. *εἴδω B.

εἶεν, Particle, only used in Att. dialogue, well! Lat. esto! be it so! εἶεν· τί δῆτα; Soph.; εἶεν· καὶ δὴ τεθνᾶσι Eur.

εἴην, opt. of εἰμί (sum):—εἶεν 3 pl., for εἴησαν.

εἵην, aor. 2 opt. of ἵημι.

εἶθαρ, Adv. (εὐθύς) at once, forthwith, Il., Theocr.

εἴθε, Ep. and Dor. αἴθε, interj. would that? Lat. utinam: v. εἰ A. II. 1.

εἰθίζω, f. ίσω, poët. for ἐθίζω.

εἶκα, Att. for ἔοικα, but, **II.** εἶκα, pf. of ἥμι.

εἰκάζω, impf. ᾔκαζον, Ion. εἴκαζον:—f. -άσω:—aor. 1 ᾔκασα, Ion. εἴκασα:—Pass., f. εἰκασθήσομαι: aor. 1 ᾐκάσθην: pf. ᾔκασμαι, Ion. εἴκασμαι:—to make like to, represent by a likeness, portray, Xen.; εἰκὼν γραφῇ εἰκασμένη a figure painted to the life, Hdt.; αἰετὸς εἰκασμένος a figure like an eagle, Id. **II.** to liken, compare, τί τινι Aesch., Ar.; εἰκ. τι καί τι Hdt.: to describe by a comparison, Id.:—Pass. to resemble, τινι Eur. **III.** to infer from comparison, form a conjecture, Hdt., Soph.; ὡς εἰκάσαι, so far as one can guess, Hdt.:—c. acc. et inf. to guess that it is so, guess it to be, Id., Thuc.:—εἰκ. τι ἔκ τινος Aesch., Thuc.; ἀπό τινος Id.; εἰκ. τι to make a guess about it, Aesch.

εἰκαθεῖν, inf. of εἴκαθον, poët.aor. 2 of εἴκω to yield, Soph.

εἰκαῖος, α, ον, (εἰκῇ) random, purposeless, Luc.

εἰκάς, άδος, ἡ, (εἴκοσι) the twentieth day of the month (sub. ἡμέρα), Hes.: the days from 21 to 30 were called αἱ εἰκάδες Ar. **II.** the sixth day of the Eleusinian mysteries, Eur.

εἰκάσδω, Aeol. and Dor. for εἰκάζω.

εἰκασία, ἡ, (εἰκάζω) a likeness, image, Xen. **II.** a comparison, a conjecture, Plat.

εἴκασμα, ατος, τό, (εἰκάζω) a likeness, image, Aesch.

εἰκασμός, ὁ, (εἰκάζω) a conjecturing, Plut., Luc.

εἰκαστής, οῦ, ὁ, (εἰκάζω) one who conjectures, a diviner, τῶν μελλόντων Thuc.

εἰκαστικός, ή, όν, able to represent or conjecture: τὸ εἰκαστικόν the faculty of conjecturing, Luc.

εἰκαστός, ή, όν, (εἰκάζω) comparable, similar, Soph.

εἴκατι, Dor. for εἴκοσι.

εἴ κε, εἴ κεν, v. εἰ A. I. 4.

εἰκελ-όνειρος, ον, dream-like, Ar.

εἴκελος, η, ον, (εἰκός) like, Lat. similis, τινι Hom., Hdt.

εἰκελό-φωνος, ον, (φωνή) of like voice, Anth.

εἰκέναι, Att. for ἐοικέναι, inf. of ἔοικα.

ΕΙΚΗ͂, Adv. without plan or purpose, heedlessly, rashly, at random, at a venture, Lat. temere, Aesch., etc.

εἰκονικός, ή, όν, (εἰκών) counterfeited, pretended, Anth.

εἰκός, Ion. οἰκός, ότος, τό, neut. partic. of εἶκα or ἔοικα, like truth, i.e. likely, probable, reasonable, Lat. veri-

simile, Trag.　2. as Subst. εἰκός, τό, a likelihood or probability, τὰ οἰκότα likelihoods, Hdt.; κατὰ τὸ εἰκός in all likelihood, Thuc.; ἐκ τοῦ εἰκότος Id.; ἤν γ' ἐρωτᾷς εἰκότ', εἰκότα κλύεις Eur.　II. reasonable, fair, equitable, Thuc.

εἰκοσά-βοιος, Ep. ἐεικ-, ον, (βοῦς) worth twenty oxen, Od.

εἰκοσα-ετής, ές, or -έτης, ες, (ἔτος) of twenty years, Hdt.

εἰκοσάκις, (εἴκοσι) twenty times, Il.

εἰκοσά-μηνος, ον, (μήν) twenty months old, Anth.

εἰκοσά-πηχυς, υ, = εἰκοσιπ-, Luc.

εἰκοσάς, άδος, ἡ, = εἰκάς, Luc.

εἰκοσ-έτης, ὁ, = εἰκοσαετής, Anth.; fem. -ετίς, ίδος, Ib.

ΕΙΚΟΣΙ, indecl., twenty, Lat. viginti, Il., etc.; also in Ep. form ἐείκοσι, before a vowel ἐείκοσιν, Ib.

εἰκοσι-ετής, ές, εἰκοσα-ετής, Plat.

εἰκοσι-νήριτος, ον, twenty-fold without dispute, Il.

εἰκοσί-πηχυς, υ, of twenty cubits, Hdt.

εἰκοσί-ορος, poët. ἐεικ-, ον, (εἴκοσι, ἐρ-έσσω) with twenty oars, Od.

εἰκοστή, ἡ, v. εἰκοστός II.

εἰκοστο-λόγος, ὁ, ἡ, (λέγω) one who collects the twentieth, a tax or toll collector, Ar.

εἰκοστός, ή, όν, (εἴκοσι) the twentieth, Od.; Ep. also ἐεικοστός, Il.　II. εἰκοστή, ἡ, a tax of a twentieth, Lat. vicesima, levied by the Athenians on imports and exports from the allies in lieu of tribute, Thuc.

εἰκοσ-ώρυγος, ον, (ὀργυιά) of 20 fathoms, Xen.

εἰκότως, Adv. of εἰκώς, Att. pf. part. of ἔοικα, in all likelihood, suitably, fairly, reasonably, naturally, Aesch., etc.; εἰκότως ἔχει 'tis reasonable, Eur.; οὐκ εἰκότως unreasonably, Thuc.

εἴκτον, ἐίκτην, 3 dual pf. and impf. of ἔοικα:—ἔικτο, 3 sing. plqpf.

*ΕΙΚΩ, to be like, seem likely, v. ἔοικα.

εἴκω (Root ϜΙΚ, cf. Lat. vi-to for vic-to): f. εἴξω: aor. 1 εἶξα, Ion. 3 sing. εἴξασκε; cf. εἰκαθεῖν:—to yield, give way, draw back, retire, Il.　2. c. dat. pers. et gen. loci, μηδ' εἴκετε χάρμης Ἀργείοις shrink not from the fight for them, Ib.; εἴκειν τινὶ τῆς ὁδοῦ, Lat. concedere alicui de via, Hdt.　3. with dat. pers. only, to yield to, give way to, either in battle or a mark of honour, Hom.:—then, to give way to any passion or impulse, ᾧ θυμῷ εἴξας Il.; αἰδοῖ Od.:—also of circumstances, πενίῃ εἴκων Ib.; κακοῖς, ἀνάγκῃ Aesch.　4. εἴκειν τινί τι, where the acc. is adverbial, μένος οὐδένι εἴκων yielding to none in force, Hom.; c. acc. cogn., εἴξαντας ἃ δεῖ yielding in . . , Soph.　II. trans. to yield up, give up, εἶξαί τέ οἱ ἡνία give the horse the rein, Il.:—to grant, allow, Lat. concedere, ὁπηνίκ' ἂν θεὸς πλοῦν ἡμῖν εἴκῃ Soph.　III. impers., like παρείκει, it is allowable or possible, Il.

εἰκών, ἡ, gen. όνος, acc. όνα, etc.: poët. and Ion. forms (as if from εἰκώ) gen. εἰκοῦς, acc. εἰκώ, pl. εἰκούς: (*ἔικω, ἔοικα):—a likeness, image, portrait, Hdt., Aesch.　2. an image in a mirror, Eur., Plat.　II. a semblance, phantom, Eur., Plat., etc.: an image in the mind, Id.　III. a similitude, simile, Ar., Plat.

εἰκώς, part. of ἔοικα: cf. εἰκός, εἰκότως.

εἰλαδόν, Adv. εἴλη) = ἰληδόν, Hdt.

εἰλαπινάζω, only in pres., to revel in a large company, Od.; and

εἰλαπιναστής, οῦ, ὁ, a feaster, guest, boon-companion, Il. From

εἰλαπίνη [ῐ], ἡ, a feast or banquet, given by a single host, opp. to ἔρανος (q. v.), Hom., Eur. (Deriv. uncertain.)

εἶλαρ, τό, only in nom. and acc. sing., (εἴλω) a close covering, shelter, defence, εἶλαρ νηῶν τε καὶ αὐτῶν shelter for ship and crew, Il.; εἶλαρ κύματος a fence against the waves, Od.

εἰλ-άρχης, ου, ὁ, (εἴλη, ἄρχω) a commander of a troop of horse, esp. at Thebes, Plut.

εἰλάτινος, Ep. for ἐλάτινος.

εἴλεγμαι, for λέλεγμαι, pf. pass. of λέγω.

Εἰλείθυια, ἡ, Ilithyia, the goddess who comes to aid women in child-birth, Lat. Lucina, Il.: Εἰλήθυια Theocr. (A quasi-participial form, as if ἐληλυθυῖα, the Ready-comer.)

εἰλεός, ὁ, (εἴλέω) a lurking-place, den, hole, Theocr.

εἰλεῦντο, Ion. for εἰλοῦντο, 3 pl. impf. pass. of εἰλέω.

εἴλεω, Att. εἰλέω, lengthd. form of εἴλω.

εἴλη, ἡ, = ἴλη, Hdt.; κατ' εἴλας in troops, Id.

ΕΙΛΗ, ἡ, the sun's heat or warmth, Ar.

εἴληγμαι, pf. pass. of λαγχάνω.

εἰληδόν, -δά, Adv. (εἰλέω) by twisting round, Anth.

εἰληθερέομαι, Med. to bask in the sun, Luc.

εἰλη-θερής, ές, (θέρω) warmed by the sun.

εἰλήλουθα, εἰληλούθειν, Ep. for ἐλήλυθα, -ύθειν, pf. and plqpf. of ἔρχομαι:—εἰλήλουθμεν, Ep. 1 pl. pf.

εἴλησις, εως, ἡ, (εἴλη) sun-heat, heat, Plat.

εἴληφα, εἴλημμαι, pf. act. and pass. of λαμβάνω.

εἴληχα, pf. of λαγχάνω.

εἰλι-κρῑνής, ές, unmixed, without alloy, pure, Lat. sincerus, Xen., Plat.; εἰλικρινεῖ τῇ διανοίᾳ χρώμενος using pure intellect, Id.; εἰλ. ἀδικίαsheerinjustice, Xen.　II. Adv. -νῶς, without mixture, of itself, simply, absolutely, Plat. (The origin of εἰλι- is uncertain.)

εἰλιξ, ικος, ἡ, Ion. and poët. for ἕλιξ.

εἰλί-πους [ῐ], ὁ, ἡ, πουν, τό: gen. ποδος: (εἴλω, πούς) —rolling in their gait, with rolling walk, Hom.

εἰλίσσω, poët. and Ion. for ἑλίσσω.

εἰλι-τενής, ές, epith. of the plant ἄγρωστις, Theocr., prob. (from ἕλος, τείνω) spreading through marshes.

εἰλίχατο, Ion. 3 pl. plqpf. pass. of ἑλίσσω.

εἴλιξα, aor. 1 of ἕλκω.

εἴλλω, v. εἴλω.

εἶλον, εἰλόμην, aor. 2 act. and med. of αἱρέω:—εἶλευ, Ion. 2 sing. aor. 2 med.

εἰλύαται, Ion. 3 pl. pf. pass. of εἰλύω.

εἴλῦμα, ατος, τό, a wrapper, Od.

εἰλυός, ὁ, (εἰλύω) a lurking place, den, Xen.

εἰλυσπάομαι, = ἰλυσπάομαι.

εἴλῦτο, 3 sing. plqpf. pass. of εἰλύω.

εἰλυφάζω = εἰλύω, only in pres. and impf., to roll along (trans.), Il.　II. intr. to roll or whirl about, of a torch, Hes.

εἰλυφάω, = foreg., Ep. part. εἰλυφόων, Il., Hes.

εἰλύω, f. εἰλύσω [ῦ]:—Pass., pf. εἴλῦμαι Ep. 3 pl. εἰλύαται [ῠ]; plqpf. εἴλῦτο: (εἴλω) —to enfold, enwrap, Il.:—Pass. to be wrapt or covered, νεφέλῃ εἰλυμένος ὤμους, etc., Hom.　II. Pass., also, = ἰλυσπάομαι, to crawl or wriggle along, of a lame man, Soph.　2. in Theocr. εἰλυσθείς means rolled up, crouching.

ΕΙΛΩ, also εἰλέω, ἴλλω or εἴλλω: Ep. aor. 1 ἔλσα,

inf. ἕλσαι, ἐέλσαι :—Pass., aor. 2 ἐάλην [ἄ], inf.
ἀλῆναι, Ep. ἀλήμεναι, part. ἀλείς : Ep. pf. ἔελμαι : 3
sing. Ep. plqpf. ἐόλητο.— From εἰλέω, come f. εἰλήσω,
aor. 1 εἴλησα ;—Med., Ep. 3 pl. impf. εἰλεῦντο ; part.
εἰλεύμενος ;—Pass., pf. εἴλημαι.   To roll up, pack
close, Lat. conglobare, κατὰ τείχεα λαὸν ἐέλσαι to roll
up the host and force it back to the walls, Il. ; Ἀχαιοὺς
ἐπὶ πρύμνησιν ἐείλεον Ib. ; εἰλεῖν ἐν μέσσοισι to coop
up or hem in on all sides, Ib. ; θῆρας ὁμοῦ εἰλεῖν to
drive game together, Od. :—Pass. to be cooped or
huddled up, εἰς ἄστυ ἄλεν (for ἀλησαν) Ib. ;
ἐπὶ γλαφυρῇσιν ἐελμένοι Ib. :—metaph., Διὸς βουλῇσιν
ἐελμένος straitened, held in check by the counsels of
Zeus, Ib.   2. to smite, νῆα κεραυνῷ Ζεὺς ἔλσας
having smitten the ship with lightning, Ib.   II.
to collect : Pass., ἀλὲν ὕδωρ water collected, ponded,
Il.   III. Pass., also, to draw oneself up, shrink
up, ἀλῆναι ὑπ’ ἀσπίδι Ib ; Ἀχιλῆα ἀλεὶς μένεν collecting
himself he waited the attack of Achilles, Ib.   IV.
Pass. also, to go to and fro, like Lat. versari,
Hdt.   V. to wind, turn round :—Pass. to turn
round, revolve, ἰλλομένων ἀρότρων moving to and
fro, Soph. ; ἕλιξ εἰλεῖται is twined round, Theocr.

Εἵλως, ωτος, and Εἱλώτης, ου, ὁ, a Helot, name of the
Spartan serfs, Hdt., Thuc., etc. (Deriv. uncertain.)
Εἱλωτεία, ἡ, the condition of a Helot, Plat. ; and
Εἱλωτεύω, f. σω, to be a Helot or serf, Isocr. ; and
Εἱλωτικός, ή, όν, of Helots, Plut.
εἶμα, ατος, τό, (ἕννυμι) a garment, in pl. clothes, clothing,
Hom., etc.   II. a cover, rug, carpet, Aesch., Soph.
εἶμαι, pf. pass. of ἕννυμι.   II. pf. pass. of
ἵημι.   III. pf. pass. of ἕζω, rarer form of ἧμαι.
εἵμαρται, εἵμαρτο, 3 sing. pf. and plqpf. of μείρομαι :
—εἱμαρμένος, part.
εἰμέν, Ep. and Ion. for ἐσμέν, 1 pl. of εἰμί (sum).   II.
εἶμεν, εἴμεναι, Dor. inf. of same.
εἱμένος, pf. pass. part. of ἕννυμι.
εἰμές, Dor. for ἐσμέν, 1 pl. of εἰμί (sum).
εἰμί (sum), Aeol. ἐμμί (the orig. form being ΕΣ-ΜΙ) ;
2nd pers. εἶ, Ion. εἶς, Dor. ἐσσί ; 3rd ἐστί, Dor. ἐντί ;
3 dual ἐστόν ; pl. 1 ἐσμέν, Ion. εἰμέν, Dor. εἰμές ; 3rd
εἰσί (-ἰν), Ep. ἐασί (-ἰν), Dor. ἐντί :—Imper. ἴσθι, Ep.
also in med. form ἔσσο ; 3 sing. ἔστω (ἤτω in N. T.) ;
3 pl. ἔστωσαν or ἔστων, Att. ὄντων :—Subj. ὦ, ᾖς, ᾖ,
Ep. ἔω, ἔῃς, ἔῃ or ἔῃσι, Ep. also εἴω, ἔῃς, etc. :—Opt.
εἴην, -ης or -ησθα, Ep. ἔοις, ἔοι ; 2 dual εἴητην for
εἴητην ; pl. εἴημεν, εἶτε, εἴησαν or εἶεν :—Inf. εἶναι, Ep.
ἔμμεναι, ἔμμεν, ἔμεναι, ἔμεν, Dor. εἶμεν, εἴμεναι :—
Part. ὤν, Ep. ἐών, ἐοῦσα, ἐόν ; Dor. neut. pl. ἐῦντα :—
Impf. ἦν or ἔον, in old Att. also ἦ, contr. from the Ion.
ἔα, Ep. also ἦα, ἤην ; 2 sing. ἦσθα, Ep. ἔησθα ; 3
sing. ἦν, Ep. ἔην, ἤην, ἦεν, Dor. ἦς ; 3 dual ἤτην or
ἤστην ; 3 pl. ἦσαν, Ion. and poët. ἔσαν : a med. form
ἤμην occurs in N. T. ; Ep. 3 pl. εἴατο for ἦντο ; Ion.
and Ep. also ἔσκον :—Fut. ἔσομαι, ἔσται, Ep. also
ἔσσομαι, ἔσσεται, ἔσσεται ; Dor. 2 and 3 sing. ἐσσῇ,
ἐσσεῖται (as if from ἐσσοῦμαι).—The whole of the pres.
indic. (except 2 sing. εἶ) may be enclitic when εἰμί is
the Copula ; but the 3 sing. is written ἔστι in certain
cases of emphasis. e. g. ἔστι μοι, I have : when used as
Verb Subst., it retains the accent in all persons.   To
be :   A. as Substantive Verb, to be, to exist, οὐκ

ἔσθ’ οὗτος ἀνήρ, οὐδ’ ἔσσεται Od. ; τεθνηῶτος, μηδ’ ἔτ’
ἐόντος Ib. ; οὐκέτ’ ἔστι he is no more, Eur. ; θεοὶ αἰὲν
ἐόντες Il. ; ἐσσόμενοι posterity, Ib. ; ζώντων καὶ ὄντων
Ἀθηναίων Dem. :—so of cities, etc., ὄλωλεν, οὐδ’ ἔτ’
ἔστι Τροία (cf. Troja fuit), Eur.   II. of things, to
be, exist, εἰ ἔστιν ἀληθέως [ἡ τράπεζα] Hdt. ; ἕως ἂν ὁ
πόλεμος ᾖ so long as it last, Thuc.   III. to be, opp.
to appearing to be, as esse to videri, τὸν ἐόντα λόγον
the true story, Hdt. ; τὰ ὄντα ἀπαγγέλλειν Thuc. ; τῷ
ὄντι, Lat. revera, in reality, in fact, Plat.   IV. foll.
by the Relative, οὐκ ἔστιν ὅς, no one, Il., etc. ; ἐστὶν οἵ,
Lat. sunt qui, Thuc., etc. ; ἐστὶν ἅ some things, Id. ;
also ἔστιν οἵ, for εἰσὶν οἵ, Hdt., etc. : — so with relat.
Particles, ἔστιν ἔνθα, Lat. est ubi, Xen., etc. ; ἔστιν
ὅπη, ἔσθ’ ὅπου, somewhere, or somehow, Plat., etc. ;
ἔστιν ὅπως in some manner, Hdt., etc. ; ἔστιν ὅτε,
ἔσθ’ ὅτε, sometimes, Soph., etc.   V. ἔστι impers.,
c. inf., like πάρεστι, it is possible, Hom., Att.
     B. to be, Copula connecting predicate with subject,
both being in the same case, Hom., etc.   2. sometimes εἶναι with Part. represents finite Verb, ἦν τε-
θνηκώς, for ἐτεθνήκει, Aesch. ; πεφυκός ἐστι = πέφυκε,
Ar.   II. the Inf. is redundant in some phrases, ἑκὼν
εἶναι (v. ἑκών II) ; τὸ ἐπ’ ἐκείνοις εἶναι quantum in illis
esset, Thuc. ; τὸ σύμπαν εἶναι Hdt. ; τὸ νῦν εἶναι Plat., etc.

εἶμι, (ibo, Root Ι), 2 sing. εἶ, Ep. and Ion. εἶς, εἶσθα, 3
sing. εἶσι ; pl. ἴμεν, ἴτε, ἴασι, ἴσι or εἶσι :—imper. ἴθι, 3
pl. ἴτωσαν, ἴτων, ἰόντων :—subj. ἴω, Ep. 2 and 3 sing.
ἴῃσθα, ἴῃσι ; Ep. pl. ἴομεν (for -ωμεν) :—opt. ἴοιμι, ἰοίην ;
Ep. ἰείην :—inf. ἰέναι, Ep. ἴμεναι, ἴμεν, ἴμμεναι :—part.
ἰών, ἰοῦσα, ἰόν.—Impf. ᾔειν, ᾔεις or ᾔεισθα, ᾔει or -ειν ;
Ep. and Ion. ἤϊα, 3 sing. ἤϊε, contr. ᾔε ; dual ᾔτην ;
pl. 1 and 2 ᾖμεν, ᾖτε, 3 pl. Ep. and Ion. ἤϊσαν, ἴσαν,
Att. ᾖσαν :—also 3 sing. ἴεν, ἴε Hom. ; Ep. 1 pl. ᾔομεν,
3 dual ἴτην :—There is also an Ep. fut. med.
εἴσομαι, aor. 1, 3 sing. εἴσατο, ἐείσατο, 3 dual ἐεισάσθην.—In Prose εἶμι serves as fut. to ἔρχομαι, I shall
go, shall come.   To come or go, Hom., etc. ; c.
acc. cogn., ὁδὸν ἰέναι to go a road, Od. :—in Hom., c.
gen., ἰὼν πεδίοιο going across the plain ; χροὸς εἴσατο
went through the skin.   2. to go in a ship, Od. ; of
birds, to fly, Ib. : of things, πέλεκυς εἶσι διὰ δουρὸς the
axe goes through the beam, Il. ; φάτις εἶσι the report
goes, Od. ; metaph. usages, ἰέναι ἐς λόγους τινί to
enter on a conference with one, Thuc., etc. ; ἰέναι ἐς
χεῖρας to come to blows, Id. ; ἰέναι διὰ δίκης πατρί to
contest the point with him, Soph. ; ἰέναι διὰ μάχης, διὰ
φιλίας to live in conflict, in friendship with others,
etc.   II. the Imper. ἴθι is used like ἄγε, Lat.
age, come, come now, mostly followed by 2 sing. imper. ;
ἴθι λέξον Ar., etc. ; with 1 pl. ἴθι ἐπεσκεψώμεθα Xen.   2.
ἴτω let it pass, well then, Soph., Eur.   III. the
part. is added by Trag. to Verbs, φρονείτω ἰών let him
go and think, Soph.

εἰν, Ep. and Lyric for ἐν, in, Hom.
εἰνά-ετής, ές, or -έτης, ες, (ἔτος) of nine years : neut.
εἰνάετες, as Adv. nine years long, Od.
εἶναι, inf. of εἰμί (sum).   II. in Hes., for ἰέναι, inf.
of εἶμι (ibo).
εἶναι, aor. 2 inf. of ἵημι to send.
εἰνάκις, εἰνάκισ-χίλιοι, εἰνακόσιοι, v. sub ἐνάκις.
εἰνάλιος, η, ον, poët. for ἐνάλιος.

εἰναλί-φοιτος, ον, *roaming the sea*, of nets, Anth.
εἰνά-νυχες [ᾰ], as Adv. *nine nights long*, Il.
εἰνάς, άδος, ἡ, (ἐννέα) *the ninth day of the month*, Hes.
εἰνάτερες [ᾰ], αἱ, *sisters-in-law*, Il.
εἴνατος, η, ον, Ion. for ἔνατος, *ninth*, Il., Hdt.
εἵνεκα, εἵνεκεν, Ion. and poët. for ἕνεκα.
εἰνί, Ep. and Lyr. for ἐν, *in*.
εἰνόδιος, Ep. and Lyr. for ἐνόδιος.
εἰνοσί-φυλλος, ον, (ἔνοσις) *with quivering foliage*, Il.
εἴξασι, Att. for ἐοίκασι, 3 pl. of ἔοικα.
εἴξασκε, Ion. 3 sing. aor. 1 of εἴκω.
εἷο, Ep. for οὗ, *of him*.
εἰοικώς, Ep. for ἐοικώς, part of ἔοικα.
εἷος, old Ep. form of ἕως, *until*, Hom.
εἶπα, aor. 1 = εἶπον: imper. εἶπον, part. εἴπας.
εἰπέμεν, -έμεναι, Ep. for εἰπεῖν, inf. of εἶπον.
εἴπερ, strengthd. for εἰ, *if really, if indeed*, Hom., etc. ; also, *even if, even though*, Ib.   **II.** in Att. *if that is to say*, implying doubt of the fact, εἴπερ ἦν πέλας *if I had been* (but I was not), Soph.
εἶπον, aor. 2 of *ἔπω (pres. in use being φημί, ἀγορεύω, f. ἐρέω, ἐρῶ, pf. εἴρηκα); Ep. ἔειπον; imper. 2 pl. Ep. ἔσπετε, subj. εἴπω, Ep. εἴπωμι, ἦσθα, -ησι: opt. εἴποιμι : inf. εἰπεῖν, Ep. -έμεναι, -έμεν :—*to speak, say*, Hom., etc. ; in parenthesis, ὡς ἔπος εἰπεῖν *so to say*, Lat. *ut ita dicam*, Thuc., etc. ; so, ὡς εἰπεῖν, ὡς ἔπος εἰπεῖν Id.   **II.** c. acc. pers. *to speak to, address, accost* one, Il.   **2.** *to name, mention*, Ib.   **3.** *to call* one so and so, πολλοὶ δέ μιν ἐσθλὸν ἔειπον Od.   **4.** c. dupl. acc. pers. et rei, *to say* or *tell of* one, ἀπάσθαλόν τι εἰπεῖν τινα Ib. ; κακὰ εἰπεῖν τινα Ar.   **III.** at Athens, *to propose* or *move* a measure in the ἐκκλησία, Thuc., etc.
εἰπόμην, impf. med. of ἔπω.
εἴ-ποτε, *if ever*, Lat. *si-quando*, Hom.   **II.** indirect, *if* or *whether ever*, Ib.
εἴ-που, *if anywhere, if at all*, Lat. *si-cubi*, Hom., etc. ; εἴ τί που ἐστίν, *if it is any way* possible, Od.
εἰργαθεῖν, poët. aor. 2 inf. of εἴργω.
εἴργασμαι, pf. of ἐργάζομαι.
εἰργμός or εἰργμός, ὁ, (εἴργω) *a cage, prison*, Plat.
εἰργμο-φύλαξ [ῠ], ᾰκος, ὁ, ἡ, *a gaoler*, Xen.
εἴργνῡμι, = εἴργω, ἔργω, *to shut in* or *up*, Ep. impf. ἐέργνυν, Od.
εἴργω or εἵργω, Att. for the earlier form ἔργω, q. v.
εἰρέαται, Ion. for εἴρηνται, 3 pl. pf. pass. of ἐρῶ.
εἵρερος, ὁ, (εἴρω) *bondage, slavery*, Od.
εἰρεσία, Ion. -ίη, ἡ, (ἐρέσσω) *rowing*, Od., Hdt., etc. : —metaph., εἰρ. πτερῶν Luc.   **II.** in collective sense, *the rowers, oarsmen*, Lat. *remigium*, Eur., Thuc.   **2.** *a boat-song*, Plut., Luc.
εἰρεσιώνη, ἡ, (εἶρος) *a harvest-wreath* of olive or laurel *wound round with wool*, borne about by singing boys at the Πυανέψια and Θαργήλια and then hung up at the house door, Ar.
εἰρέω, Ion. for ἐρέω, *to say*, Ep. part. fem. εἰρεῦσαι Hes.
εἴρη, ἡ, (εἴρω B) Ion. for ἀγορά, *a place of assembly*, Ep. gen. pl. εἰράων Il.
εἴρην, ενος or ἰρήν, ενος, ὁ, *a Lacedaemonian youth who had completed his* 20th *year*, when he was entrusted with authority over his juniors, Plut. (Deriv. uncertain.)

εἰρηναῖος, α, ον, *peaceful, peaceable*, Hdt. : τὰ εἰρηναῖα *the fruits of peace*, Id. : Adv. -ως, Id. ; and
εἰρηνεύω, f. σω, *to bring to peace, reconcile*, Babr.   **II.** intr. *to keep peace, live peaceably*, Plat., N. T. From
εἰρήνη, ἡ, *peace, time of peace*, Hom., etc. ; ἐπ᾽ εἰρήνης *in peace*, Il. ; εἰρ. γίγνεται *peace is made*, Hdt. ; εἰρήνην ποιεῖν or ποιεῖσθαι *to make a peace* ; εἰρ. ἄγειν *to keep peace*, Ar. ; λύειν *to break it*, Dem.   (Deriv. uncertain.)
εἰρηνικός, ή, όν, *of* or *for peace, peaceful*, Plat., etc. : Adv. -κῶς, *peaceably*, Xen.
εἰρηνο-ποιός, ὁ, (ποιέω) *a peace-maker*, Xen.
εἰρηνο-φύλαξ [ῠ], ᾰκος, ὁ, ἡ, *a guardian of peace*, Xen.
εἰρίνεος, εἴριον, Ion. for ἐρίνεος, ἔριον.
εἰρκτέον, verb. Adj. of εἴργω, *one must prevent*, Soph.
εἱρκτή, Ion. ἑρκτή, ἡ, (εἴργω) *an inclosure, prison*, Hdt. :—also *the inner part of the house, the women's apartments*, Xen.
εἱρο-κόμος, ον, (κομέω) *dressing wool*, Il.
εἴρομαι, Ion. for ἔρομαι, *to ask* ; v. εἴρω (B).
εἰρο-πόκος, ον, *wool-fleeced, woolly*, Hom.
εἶρος, τό, *wool*, Od.   (From Root ΕΡ, cf. ἔριον.)
εἰρο-χαρής, ές, (χαίρομαι) *delighting in wool*, Anth.
εἱρύαται, Ion. for εἴρυνται, 3 pl. pf. of ἐρύω.
εἰρύω, εἰρύομαι, Ep. for ἐρύω, ἐρύομαι.
εἴρω (A): aor. 1 εἶρα or ἔρσα :—Pass., pf. part. ἐρμένος, Ep. ἐερμένος :—*to fasten together in rows, to string*, ἠλέκτροισιν ἐερμένος *a necklace strung* with pieces of electron, Od.   (The Root is prob. ΣΕΡ, cf. Lat. *ser-o, serui, σειρά*.)
εἴρω (B): *to say, speak, tell*, Od. : so in Med., Hom. : but in Ion. Prose, the Med. means *to cause to be told one*, i. e. *to ask*, like Att. ἐροῦμαι.   (The Root is ϜΕΡ, cf. Lat. *verbum*, our *word*.)
εἴρων, ωνος, ὁ, *a dissembler, one who says less than he thinks*, Lat. *dissimulator*, Arist., etc.   Hence
εἰρωνεία, ἡ, *dissimulation*, i. e. *assumed ignorance, irony*, Plat, etc. ; and
εἰρωνεύομαι, Dep. *to dissemble*, i. e. *feign ignorance*, Plat., etc. : generally, *to dissemble, shuffle*, Ar.
εἰρωνικός, ή, όν, (εἴρων) *dissembling, putting on a feigned ignorance*, Plat. : Adv. -κῶς, Ar.
εἰρωτάω Ep., and εἰρωτέω Ion., for ἐρωτάω.
ΕΙΣ or **ΕΣ**, Prep. with acc. only. Radical sense, *into*, and then *to* :   **I.** of Place, the commonest usage, εἰς ἅλα *into* or *to the sea*, Hom., etc. :—properly opposed to ἐκ, ἐς σφυρὸν ἐκ πτέρνης from head to foot, Il. ; εἰς ἔτος ἐξ ἔτεος from year *to* year, Theocr. :—then, with all Verbs implying motion or direction, ἰδεῖν εἰς οὐρανόν Il. ; εἰς ὦπα ἰδέσθαι to look in the face, Ib. :—in Hom. and Hdt. also c. acc. pers., where the Att. use ὡς, πρός, παρά.   **2.** with Verbs which express *rest* in a place, when a previous motion *into* or *to* it is implied, ἐς μέγαρον κατέθηκε, i. e. he brought it *into* the house, and put it *there*, Od. ; παρεῖναι ἐς τόπον to go to a place and be there, Hdt.   **3.** with Verbs of saying or speaking, λόγους ποιεῖσθαι εἰς τὸ πλῆθος *to come before the people and speak*, Id., etc.   **4.** elliptical usage εἰς Ἀΐδαο, Att. εἰς Ἅιδου [δόμους], ἐς Ἀθηναίης [ἱερόν] to the temple of Athena, etc. ; as in Lat. *ad Apollinis, ad Castoris* (sc. *aedem*); so with appellatives, ἀνδρὸς ἐς ἀφνειοῦ to a rich man's, Il.   **II.** of

TIME, 1. to denote a certain point or limit of time, *to*, *up to*, *until*, ἐς ἠῶ (Att. εἰς τὴν ἕω) Od. ; ἐς ἥλιον καταδύντα *till* sun-set, Ib. ; ἐς ἐμέ *up to* my time, Hdt. :—so with Advs., εἰς ὅτε (cf. ἔς τε) *against* the time when, Od. ; so, εἰς πότε ; *until* when? how long? Soph. ; ἐς ὅ *until*, Hdt. 2. to determine a period, εἰς ἐνιαυτόν *for a year*, i.e. a whole year, Hom. ; ἐς θέρος ἢ ἐς ὀπώρην *for* the summer, Od. ; εἰς ἑσπέραν ἥκειν to come *at* even, Ar. ; εἰς τρίτην ἡμέραν or εἰς τρίτην alone, *on the third day*, in three days, Plat. ; ἐς τέλος *at* last, Hdt. ; οὐκ ἐς ἀναβολάς *with* no delay, Id. ;—so with Advs., ἐς αὔριον Il. ; ἐς αὖθις or ἐσαῦθις Thuc. ; εἰς ἔπειτα Soph., etc. ; cf. εἰσάπαξ, εἰσότε. III. to express MEASURE OR LIMIT, ἐς δίσκουρα λέλειπτο *was left behind as far as* a quoit's throw, Il. ; ἐς δράχμην ἐδίδωκε *paid them as much as* a drachma, Thuc. 2. with Numerals, ναῦς ἐς τὰς τετρακοσίους *to the number of* 400, Id. ; εἰς ἕνα, εἰς δύο, *one, two deep*, etc., Xen. IV. to express RELATION, *to* or *towards*, ἁμαρτάνειν εἴς τινα Aesch. ; ἔχθρα ἔς τινα Hdt. 2. *in regard to*, like Lat. *quod attinet ad*, εὐτυχεῖν ἐς τέκνα Eur. ; τὰ ἄλλα Thuc. ; τό γ' ἐς ἑαυτόν, τὸ εἰς ἐμέ Soph., Eur. 3. periphr. for Advs., ἐς κοινόν = κοινῶς, Aesch. ; ἐς τὸ πᾶν = πάντως, Id. ; εἰς τάχος = ταχέως, Ar. V. of an END, ἔρχεσθαι, τελευτᾶν ἔς . ., to end in . ., Hdt., etc. ; καταξαίνειν ἐς φοινικίδα to cut *into* red rags, Ar. :—also, of a Purpose, εἰς ἀγαθόν *for good*, *for* his good, Il. ; εἰς κάλλος ζῆν to live *for* show, Xen.

ΕΙ῝Σ, μία, ἕν ; gen. ἑνός, μιᾶς, ἑνός :—Ep. lengthd. ἕεις :—Ep. fem. ἴα, gen. ἰῆς ; dat. ἰῇ ; a neut. dat. (ἰῷ κίον ἤματι) also occurs in Il. (The orig. form was prob. ΕΝ-Σ, cf. Lat. *un-us*. The fem. μία points to a second Root, cf. οἷος with μόνος.) 1. *one*, Hom., etc. ; εἷς οἷος, μία οἴη *a single one*, one alone, Id. ; εἷς μόνος Hdt. 2. with a Sup., like Lat. *unus omnium maxime*, εἷς ἀνὴρ πλεῖστον πόνον παρασχών Aesch. ; κάλλιστ' ἀνὴρ εἷς Soph. ; πάντων εἷς ἀνὴρ τῶν μεγίστων αἴτιος κακῶν Dem. 3. in oppos., made emphatic by the Art., ὁ εἷς, ἡ μία Hom., Att. 4. with a negat., εἷς οὐδείς *nullus unus*, no *single* man, Hdt., Thuc. ; οὐχ εἷς, is more than one, Aesch. ; and more emphatic, οὐδὲ εἷς, μηδὲ εἷς, v. οὐδείς, μηδείς. 5. εἷς ἕκαστος *each one*, each *by himself*, Lat. *unusquisque*, Hdt., Plat. 6. often with κατά, καθ' ἕκαστον, each *singly*, piece by piece, etc. ; so, καθ' ἕνα, καθ' ἕν *one by one*, Plat. 7. with other Preps., ἐν ἀνθ' ἑνός *above all*, Id. :—ἓν πρὸς ἕν, *in comparisons*, Hdt., Plat. ; εἷς πρὸς ἕνα Dem. ; παρ' ἕνα *alternately*, Luc. II. *one*, i.e. *the same*, εἷς καὶ ὅμοιος Plat. : c. dat. *one with* . ., Eur. III. *one*, as opp. to *another* ; so, ὁ μὲν . ., εἷς δὲ . ., εἷς δ' αὖ . ., Od. ; εἷς μέν . ., ἕτερος δέ . ., Xen. IV. indefinitely, εἷς τις, *some one*, Lat. *unus aliquis*, Soph., Plat. ;—then alone, like our indef. Art. *a*, *an*, (as *faber unus* Horat.), Eur. V. οὐδὲ εἷς οὐδὲ δύο *not one* or two only, Dem.

εἷς, 2 sing. of εἰμί (*sum*). II. of εἶμι (*ibo*).
εἶσα, aor. 1 of ἵζω, *to place*.
εἰσαγγελεύς, έως, ὁ, *one who announces, a gentleman-usher* at the Persian court, Hdt. ; and
εἰσαγγελία, ἡ, at Athens, *an impeachment*, brought

---

before the Senate of 500, or (sometimes) the ἐκκλησία, Xen. From

εἰσ-αγγέλλω, f. ελῶ, *to go in and announce* a person (cf. εἰσαγγελεύς), Hdt., Eur., etc. 2. *to announce, report* a thing, Thuc. :—Pass., ἐσαγγελθέντων ὅτι . . *information having been given that* . ., Id. II. *to impeach*, Dem., etc. ; cf. εἰσαγγελία. Hence
εἰσαγγελτικός, ή, όν, *of* or *for impeachment*, ap. Dem.
εἰσ-αγείρω, f. ερῶ, *to collect into* a place, Hom. :—Med., νέον δ' ἐσαγείρατο θυμόν *he gathered* fresh *courage*, Il. : but also in pass. sense, θοῶς δ' ἐσαγείρατο λαὸς [εἰς τὰς ναῦς] Od.
εἰσ-άγω [ᾰ], f. ξω : pf. -αγήοχα :—*to lead in* or *into, to introduce*, c. dupl. acc., αὐτοὺς εἰσῆγον δόμον Od. ; also, εἰσάγειν τινὰ ἐς . . , Hdt. ; or c. dat., τινὰ δόμοις Eur. :—Med. *to admit* forces into a city, Thuc. : also *to introduce into* a league, Hdt. 2. ἐσάγειν or ἐσάγεσθαι γυναῖκα *to lead* a wife *into one's house*, *ducere uxorem*, Id. 3. *to import* foreign wares, Id., Att. ; so in Med., Hdt., etc. 4. ἰατρὸν εἰσάγειν τινί *to call in* a physician, Xen. 5. *to introduce new customs*, Hdt., Eur. II. *to bring in*, *bring forward*, esp. on the stage, Ar., Plat. 2. εἰσάγειν τι ἐς τὴν βουλήν *to bring before* the Council, Xen. 3. as law-term, εἰσάγειν δίκην or γραφήν *to bring* a cause *into court*, Lat. *litem intendere*, Aesch., Dem. : εἰσ. τινὰ *to bring into court, prosecute*, Plat. Hence
εἰσᾰγωγεύς, έως, ὁ, *one who brings cases into court*, Dem. ; and
εἰσᾰγωγή, ἡ, *importation* of goods, Plat. II. as law-term, *a bringing causes into court*, Id. ; and
εἰσᾰγώγιμος, ον, *that can* or *may be imported*, Plat. II. as law-term, *within the jurisdiction of the court*, δίκη Dem.
εἰσ-αεί, for εἰς ἀεί, *for ever*, Aesch., Soph.
εἰσ-αείρομαι, Med. *to take to oneself*, Theogn.
εἰσ-αθρέω, f. ήσω, *to discern, descry*, Il.
εἰσ-αίρω, -αρῶ, *to bring* or *carry in*, Ar.
εἰσᾴσσω, contr. -ᾴσσω, Att. -ᾴττω, f. -ᾴξω, *to dart in* or *into*, Ar.
εἴσαιτο, aor. 1 opt. med. of *εἴδω.
εἰσ-αΐω, *to listen* or *hearken to*, c. gen., Theocr.
εἰσ-ακοντίζω, f. Att. ιῶ, *to throw* or *hurl javelins at*, τινά Hdt. ; εἰς τὰ γυμνά Thuc. 2. absol. *to dart* or *spout*, of blood, Eur.
εἰσ-ακούω, f. σομαι, *to hearken* or *give ear to one*, Il. ; c. acc. rei, h. Hom. ; c. gen. pers., Soph., Eur., etc. 2. in Poets, simply, *to hear*, Soph., Eur. II. c. dat. pers. *to hearken to*, *give heed to*, Hdt.
εἰσακτέον, verb. Adj. *one must bring into court* (v. εἰσάγω II. 3), Ar., Xen.
εἰσ-άλλομαι, f. -αλοῦμαι : Ep. 3 sing. aor. 2 ἐσᾶλτο : aor. 1 med. -ηλάμην : Dep. :—*to spring* or *rush into*, c. acc., Il. ; ἐσάλλ. ἐς τὸ πῦρ *to leap into* it, Hdt.
εἰσ-αμείβω, f. ψω, *to go into*, *enter*, Aesch.
εἰσάμην, Ep. aor. 1 of εἶμι (*ibo*). II. of *εἴδω II.
εἰσάμην, aor. 1 med. of ἵζω.
εἰσ-αναβαίνω, *to go up to* or *into*, c. acc., Hom.
εἰσ-αναγκάζω, f. άσω, *to force into* a thing, *to constrain*, τινά Aesch.
εἰσ-ανάγω, f. ξω, *to lead up into*, c. acc., Od.
εἰσ-ανεῖδον, aor. 2 (v. *εἴδω) *to look up to*, c. acc., Il.

εἰσ-άνειμι, to go up into, c. acc., Il.

εἰσανῑδών, part. of εἰσανεῖδον.

εἰσανιών, part. of εἰσάνειμι.

ἴσ-αντα, Ep. ἔσ-αντα, Adv. right opposite, ἔσ. ἰδεῖν to look in the face, Hom.

εἰσ-άπαξ, for εἰς ἅπαξ, at once, once for all, Hdt., Att.

εἰσ-αράσσω, Att. -ττω, f. ξω, to drive or force in upon, Hdt.

εἰσάττω, Att. for εἰσαΐσσω.

εἰσ-αυγάζω, f. σω, to look at, view, Anth.

εἰσ-αῦθις, for εἰς αὖθις, hereafter, afterwards, Eur., Plat.

εἰσ-αύριον, for εἰς αὔριον, on the morrow, Ar.

εἰσ-αῦτις, Dor. and Ion. for εἰσ-αῦθις.

εἰσ-αφίημι, f. -αφήσω, to let in, admit, Xen.

εἰσ-αφικάνω [ᾰ], to come to, τινά Od.

εἰσ-αφικνέομαι, Ion. ἐσ-απικνέομαι, f. -αφίξομαι: aor. 2 -αφικόμην: Dep.:—to come into or to, reach or arrive at a place, c. acc., Od., Eur.; ἐσαπ. ἐς τόπον Hdt.; also c. dat., Id.

εἰσ-βαίνω, f. -βήσομαι, to go into a ship, to go on board ship, embark, Od.; ἐσβ. ἐς ναῦν Hdt.   2. generally, to go into, enter, δόμους Eur.; ἐσβ. κακά to come into miseries, Soph.   II. Causal in aor. 1 ἀνέβησα, to make to go into, put on board, Il.

εἰσ-βάλλω, f. -βαλῶ, to throw into, put into, foll. by εἰς, Hdt., Att.:—Med. to put on board one's ship, Hdt.   II. intr. to throw oneself into, make an inroad into, εἰς χώραν Id., Att.; πρὸς πόλιν ἐσβ. to fall upon it, Thuc. :—poët. c. acc., to come upon, fall in with, Eur.   2. of rivers, to empty themselves into, fall into, Hdt.

εἴσβᾱσις, εως, ἡ, (εἰσβαίνω) an entrance, means of entrance, Eur.: embarkation, Thuc.

εἰσβᾱτός, ή, όν, (εἰσβαίνω) accessible, Thuc.

εἰσ-βιάζομαι, Dep. to force one's way into, εἰς οἶκον Plut.   2. to force oneself into the citizenship, Ar.

εἰσ-βῑβάζω, Att. f. -βιβῶ, Causal of εἰσβαίνω, to put on board ship, τὸν στρατὸν ἐς τὰς νέας Hdt.   2. generally, to make to go into, ἐς τόπον Id.

εἰσβλέπω, f. ψω, to look at, look upon, mostly with εἰς, Hdt.; but c. acc., Eur.

εἰσβολή, ἡ, (εἰσβάλλω II) an inroad, invasion, attack, Hdt., Eur.   2. an entrance, pass, ἡ ἐσβ. ἡ Ὀλυμπική the pass of Mount Olympus, Hdt.: a strait, Eur. :—so in pl., of Thermopylae, Hdt. :—in pl. also, the mouth of a river, Id.   3. an entering into a thing, a beginning, Eur., Ar.

εἰσ-γράφω [ᾰ], f. ψω, to write in, inscribe :—Med., ἐς τὰς σπονδὰς ἐσγράψασθαι to have oneself written or received into the league, Thuc.

εἰσ-δέρκομαι, Dep., with aor. 2 act. -έδρακον, pf. εἰσδέδροκα :—to look at or upon, Hom., Eur.

εἰσ-δέχομαι, Ion. ἐσ-δέκομαι: f. -δέξομαι: Dep. :—to take into, admit, ἐς τὸ ἱρόν Hdt.; c. acc., Eur.; c. dat., ἄντροις εἰσδέξασθαί τινα to receive him in the cave, Id.; εἰσδ. τινα ὑπόστεγον Soph.

εἰσ-δίδωμι, used intr. like εἰσβάλλω II. 2, of rivers, to flow into, Hdt.

εἰσδοχή, ἡ, (εἰσδέχομαι) reception, εἰσδοχαὶ δόμων a hospitable house, Eur.

εἰσδραμεῖν, aor. 2 inf. of εἰστρέχω. Hence

εἰσδρομή, ἡ, an inroad, onslaught, Eur., Thuc.

εἰσ-δύνω [ῡ], and as Dep. εἰσ-δύομαι (v. δύω): f. -δύσομαι, with aor. 2 act. -έδυν, pf. -δέδυκα :—to get or go into, with εἰς, Od., Hdt., etc.   2. c. acc. to enter, Lat. subire, Il., Hdt. :—of feelings, εἰσέδυ με μνήμη κακῶν Soph.; also c. dat., δεινόν τι ἐσέδυνε σφίσι great fear came upon them, Hdt.

εἴσεαι, Ep. 2 sing. fut. of *εἴδω II.

εἰσέδραμον, aor. 2 of εἰστρέχω.

εἰσέδῡν, aor. 2 of εἰσδύνω.

εἰσ-εῖδον, Ep. -ίδον, serving as aor. 2 to εἰσοράω.

εἴσ-ειμι, inf. -ιέναι, serving as fut. to εἰσέρχομαι: impf. εἰσῄειν :—to go into, οὐκ Ἀχιλῆος ὀφθαλμοὺς εἴσειμι I will not come before Achilles' eyes, Il. :—more commonly with a Prep., εἰσ. μετ᾽ ἀνέρας Od.; παρὰ βασιλέα Hdt.; εἰς .. or πρός .., Id., Att.; εἰσ. εἰς σπονδὰς to enter into a treaty, Thuc.   II. of the Chorus or of actors, to come upon the stage, to enter, Plat.   2. as Att. law-term, to come into court, Dem.   3. to enter on an office, ὁ ἐσιών the new king, Hdt.   III. metaph. to come into one's mind, c. acc., Id., Att., Eur.; also c. dat., Id. :—impers., εἰσῄει αὐτοὺς ὅπως .. , it came into their minds that .. , Xen.   IV. of things, τὰ εἰσιόντα what enters into one, food, Id.

εἰσ-ελαύνω, Ep. -ελάω: f. -ελάσω [ᾰ], Att. -ελῶ :—to drive in, of a shepherd driving in his flock, Od.   II. intr. to row or sail in, Ib.: to ride in, Xen. :—to enter in triumphal procession, Plut.

εἰσελθεῖν, aor. 2 inf. of εἰσέρχομαι.

εἰσ-έλκω, to draw, haul, drag in or into: aor. 1 -είλκῠσα, Hdt., Ar.

εἰσ-εμβαίνω, to go on board, Anth.

εἰσενεγκεῖν, aor. 2 inf. of εἰσφέρω.

εἰσ-ένθωμες, Dor. for εἰσέλθωμεν, 1 pl. aor. 2 of εἰσέρχομαι.

εἰσ-έπειτα, Adv. for hereafter, Soph.

εἰσέπτατο, 3 sing. aor. 2 of εἰσπέτομαι :—εἰσ-έπτη, act. form of same.

εἰσ-έργνῡμι, to shut up in (a mummy-case), Hdt.

εἰσ-έρπω, aor. 1 εἰσείρπῠσα, to go into, Plut.

εἰσ-έρρω, to go into, get in; aor. 1 εἰσήρρησα, Ar.

εἰσ-ερύω, f. σω, to draw into, Od.

εἰσ-έρχομαι, f. -ελεύσομαι: aor. 2 -ήλῠθον, -ήλθον: but Att. fut. is supplied by εἴσειμι, and impf. by εἰσῄειν: Dep. :—to go in or into, enter, c. acc., Il., etc.; in Prose, εἰσ. εἰς .. , Xen., etc.; εἰσ. εἰς τὰς σπονδὰς to come into the treaty, Thuc.; εἰσ. εἰς τοὺς ἐφήβους to enter the Ephebi, Xen.: of money, to come in, Id.   II. of the Chorus or of actors, to come upon the stage, to enter, Plat., Xen. :—to enter the lists, Soph.   2. as Att. law-term, of the accuser, to come into court, Plat., Dem.   III. metaph., [μένος] ἄνδρας ἐσέρχεται courage enters into the men, Il.; Κροῖσον γέλως ἐσῆλθε :—also c. dat., δέος εἰσ. τινι Plat. :—also to come into one's mind, Hdt.; so, impers., εἰσῆλθε αὐτόν, c. inf., it comes into one's head that .. , Id.

εἰσ-έσθαι, aor. 2 med. inf. of εἴσημι.

εἰσ-έτι, Adv., still yet, Theocr.

εἰσ-έχω, f. ξω, intr. to stretch into, reach, extend, ἐπὶ Αἰθιοπίης towards Ethiopia, Hdt.; θάλαμος ἐσέχων ἐς τὸν ἀνδρεῶνα a chamber opening into the men's apartment, Id.

εἰσ-ηγέομαι, Dor. εἰσᾱγ-: f. ήσομαι: Dep. :—to bring

in, introduce a practice, Hdt. 2. to propose, Thúc., etc.; εἰσηγουμένου τινός on his motion, Id. 3. εἰσηγεῖσθαί τινι to represent a matter to a person, Id. 4. to relate, narrate, explain, τινί τι Plat. Hence

εἰσήγημα, ατος, τό, a proposition, motion, Aeschin.; and
εἰσήγησις, εως, ἡ, a proposing, moving, Thuc.; and
εἰσηγητέον, verb. Adj. one must move, Thuc.; and
εἰσηγητής, οῦ, ὁ, one who brings in, a mover, author, κακῶν Thuc.

εἰσ-ηθέω, f. ήσω, to inject by a syringe, Hdt.
εἰσ-ήκω, f. ξω, to have come in, Ar.:—in fut. to be about to come in, Aesch.
εἰσ-ήλῦθον, -ήλθον, aor. 2 of εἰσ-έρχομαι. Hence
εἰσηλῦσία, ἡ, a coming in, entrance, Anth.
εἴσθα, Aeol. and Ep. for εἶς, 2 sing. of εἶμι (ibo).
εἴσθαι, pf. pass. inf. of ἵημι.
εἰσ-θέω, f. -θεύσομαι, to run into, run up to him, Ar.
εἰσ-θρώσκω, aor. 2 -έθορον, to leap into or in, Il.; c. acc., ἐσθορεῖν δόμον Aesch.
εἰσί, εἰσίν, 3 pl. of εἰμί (sum).
εἶσι, εἶσιν, 3 sing. of εἶμι (ibo).
εἰσ-ῐδεῖν, Ep. -ιδέειν, aor. 2 inf. of εἰσεῖδον: v. εἰσοράω.
εἰσιδρύω, pf. pass. εἰσίδρῦμαι, to build in, Hdt.
εἰσ-ίζομαι, Med. to sit down in, c. acc., Il.
εἰσ-ίημι, f. ήσω, to send into, ἐς τὴν [λίμνην] εἰσ. τὸ ὕδωρ, of rivers, Hdt.; εἰσ. τοὺς Πέρσας ἐς τὸ τεῖχος to let them in, Id.:—Med. to let in, Xen. II. in Med. also, to betake oneself into, enter, c. acc., Od.
εἰσίθμη, ἡ, (εἴσειμι) an entrance, Od.
εἰσ-ικνέομαι, f. -ίξομαι, Dep. to go into, penetrate, Hdt.
εἰσῐτήριος, ον, (εἴσειμι) belonging to entrance:—εἰσιτήρια (sc. ἱερά), τά, a sacrifice at entrance on an office, Dem.
εἰσῐτητέον, verb. Adj. of εἴσειμι, one must go in, Luc.
εἰσ-κᾰλᾰμάομαι (κάλαμος II. 2) Dep. to haul in as an angler the fish which he has hooked, Ar.
εἰσ-κᾰλέω, f. έσω, to call in, Ar., Xen.
εἰσ-καταβαίνω, to go down into, c. acc., Od.
εἴσ-κειμαι, as Pass. of εἰστίθημι, to be put on board ship, Thuc.
εἰσ-κηρύσσω, Att. -ττω, f. ξω, to summon by public crier, Soph., Ar.
εἰσκομιδή, ἡ, importation of supplies, Thuc. From
εἰσ-κομίζω, f. Att. ιῶ, to carry into the house, carry in, Hes., Aesch. etc.:—Med. to bring in for oneself, import, Thuc.:—Pass., εἰσκομίζεσθαι εἰς τόπον to get into a place for shelter, Id.
εἰσ-κυκλέω, f. ήσω, in a theatre, to turn a thing inwards by machinery, of changing scenes in a theatre:—metaph., δαίμων πράγματα εἰσκεκύκληκεν εἰς τὴν οἰκίαν some spirit has brought scenes of trouble into the house, Ar.
ἔίσκω, Ep. Verb, only in pres. and impf., to make like (cf. ἴσκω), Od. II. to deem like, liken, compare, τινά or τί τινι Hom. 2. c. acc. et inf. to deem, suppose, Id. 3. absol., ὡς σὺ ἔίσκεις as thou deemest, Od. (Deriv. uncertain.)
εἰσ-λεύσσω, to look into, Soph.
εἰσ-μαίομαι, 3 sing. Ep. aor. 1, ἐσεμάσσατο:—to touch to the quick, affect greatly, Il. II. to put in the hand to feel, ἐσεμάξατο χεῖρας (Dor. form) Theocr.
εἰσ-νέομαι, Pass. to go into, Anth.

εἰσ-νέω, f. -νεύσομαι, to swim into, Thuc.
εἰσ-νοέω, f. ήσω, to perceive, remark, Hom.
εἴσ-οδος or ἔσοδος, ἡ, a way in, entrance, i. e., place of entrance, entry, Od., Hdt., etc. II. entrance, a right or privilege of entrance, Id., Xen.
εἰσ-οικειόω, f. ώσω, to bring in as a friend, Plut.:—Pass. to become intimate with another, Xen.
εἰσ-οικέω, f. ήσω, to settle in, Anth. Hence
εἰσοίκησις, εως, ἡ, a place for dwelling in, a home, Soph.
εἰσ-οικίζω, f. Att. ιῶ, to bring in as a settler:—Med. and Pass. to establish oneself in, settle in, εἰς τόπον Hdt.; c. acc., Plut.
εἰσ-οικοδομέω, f. ήσω, to build into, εἰς τεῖχος Thuc.
εἰσοιστέος, α, ον, verb. Adj. of εἰσφέρω, to be brought in, Dem.
εἰσ-οιχνέω, Aeol. 3 pl. -οιχνεῦσι, to go into, enter, c. acc., Od.
εἰσ-όκε, before a vowel, -κεν, Dor. εἰσ-όκα, (εἰς ὃ κε) until, with subj., Il., (in 3. 409, ποιήσεται is Ep. for ποιήσηται). II. so long as, Il.
εἴσομαι, f. of οἶδα (v. *εἴδω B). II. Ep. f. of εἶμι (ibo).
εἶσον, imperat. of εἷσα (v. ἵζω).
εἰσ-οπίσω [ῐ], Adv. in time to come, hereafter, h. Hom., Soph.
εἴσοπτος, ον, (εἰσόψομαι, f. of εἰσοράω) visible, Hdt.
εἰσοπτρίς, ίδος, ἡ, = εἴσοπτρον, Anth.
εἴσ-οπτρον, always in the form ἔσ-οπτρον, τό, (ὄψομαι, f. of εἰσοράω) a mirror, Pind.
εἰσ-οράω, Ep. part. εἰσορόων, inf. med. εἰσοράασθαι: f. -όψομαι: aor. 2 -εἶδον, Ep. inf. -ιδεῖν:—to look into, look upon, view, behold, c. acc., Hom., etc.:—so in Med., Il. 2. to look upon with admiration, Lat. suspicere, θεοὺς ὣς εἰσορόωσιν Ib.:—hence to pay regard to, respect, τι Soph., Eur.; so, ἐσ. ἔς τι Hdt.; εἰσορ. πρός τι to look at, eye eagerly, Soph. 3. to look on with the mind's eye, perceive, Id. 4. of angry gods, to visit, punish, Id. 5. followed by μή, to take care lest . . , Id.
εἰσ-ορμάω, f. ήσω, to bring forcibly into, Anth.:—Pass. to force one's way into, c. acc., Soph.
εἰσ-ορμίζω, f. Att. ιῶ, to bring into port:—Pass. and Med. to run into port, Xen., Plut.
ἔίσος, η, ον [ῐ], Ep. form of ἴσος, alike, equal: 1. of a feast, equal, i. e. equally shared, of which each partakes alike, Il. 2. of ships, even or well-balanced, Hom. 3. of a shield, equal all ways, i. e. perfectly round, Il. 4. of the mind, even, well-balanced, Lat. aequus, Od.
εἰσ-ότε or εἰς ὅτε, against the time when, Od.
εἰσοχή, ἡ, (εἰσέχω) a hollow, recess, Strab.
εἴσοψις, εως, ἡ, a spectacle, Eur. From
εἰσ-όψομαι, f. of εἰσοράω: v. ὁράω.
εἰσ-παίω, aor. 1 -έπαισα, to burst or rush in, Soph.; c. acc. loci, Eur.
εἰσ-πέμπω, f. ψω, to send in, bring in, let in, Eur., Thuc.: to prompt or suborn agents, Soph.
εἰσ-περάω, f. άσω [ᾰ], Ion. ήσω, to pass over into, c. acc., Hes.
εἰσ-πέτομαι, f. -πτήσομαι: aor. 2 εἰσ-επτάμην (as if from εἰσ-ίπταμαι), also in act. form -έπτην:—to fly into, c. acc., Il.; metaph. of reports, Hdt.

εἰσ-πηδάω, f. -πηδήσομαι, to leap into, c. acc., Hdt. ; εἰς τόπον Xen.   2. to burst in upon, πρός τινα Dem.

εἰσ-πίπτω, f. -πεσοῦμαι : aor. 2 -έπεσον :—to fall into, but generally with a notion of violence, to rush or burst in, ἐς πόλιν Hdt. ; ἐς οἴκημα Thuc. :—poët. c. dat., ἐσπίπτει δόμοις Eur.   2. simply to fall into, ἐς χαράδρας Thuc. ; εἰσπ. εἰς εἱρκτήν to be thrown into prison, Id. ; in Poets, c. acc., Eur.   3. to fall into a certain condition, ξυμφοράν Id.   II. to fall upon, attack, τινά Hdt., Soph.

εἰσ-πίτνω, poët. form of εἰσ-πίπτω (v. πίτνω), Eur.

εἰσ-πλέω, f. -πλεύσομαι, to sail into, enter εἰς τόπον Thuc. : poët. c. acc., Soph., Eur. :—absol., ἐπ' ἀριστερὰ ἐσπλέοντι on the left as one sails in, Hdt. ; οὐδὲν εἰσπλεῖ nothing comes into port, Thuc. : of corn, to be imported, Dem.   Hence

εἴσπλοος, contr. -πλους, ὁ, a sailing in of ships, Thuc., Xen.   II. the entrance of a harbour, Thuc.

εἰσ-πνέω, f. -πνεύσομαι, to breathe upon, τινά Ar. Hence

εἰσπνήλας, ὁ, one who inspires love, a lover, Theocr.

εἰσ-ποιέω, f. ήσω, to give in adoption, εἰσποιεῖν υἱόν τινι Plat. ; εἰσπ. ἑαυτὸν Ἀμμῶνι to make himself son to Ammon, Plut. :— Med. to adopt as one's son, Dem.   2. generally, εἰσπ. τινας εἰς λειτουργίαν to introduce new persons into the public service, Dem.

εἰσποιητός, ή, όν, adopted, Dem.

εἰσ-πορεύω, f. σω, to lead into, Eur. :—Pass. with f. med. to go into, enter, Xen.

εἴσπραξις, εως, ἡ, a getting in or collection of dues, Thuc., Dem.   From

εἰσ-πράσσω, Att. -ττω, f. ξω, to get in or exact debts, taxes, dues, Dem. ; τινά from a person, Id. :—Med. to exact for oneself, have paid one, Eur. :—Pass., of the money, to be exacted, Dem.

εἰσ-ρέω, f. -ρεύσομαι : aor. 2 pass. (in same sense) -ερρύην :—to stream in or into, Eur., Plat.

εἰσ-τίθημι, f. -θήσω, to put into, place in, τινα or τι εἰς χεῖράς τινι Hdt., Thuc. ; τινὰ ἐς ἄμαξαν Hdt.   2. ἐστ. ἐς ναῦν to put on board ship, Lat. navi imponere, Id. ; τέκνα ἐσθέσθαι (aor. 2 inf.) to put their children on board, Id.

εἰσ-τοξεύω, f. σω, to shoot arrows at, Hdt.

εἰσ-τρέχω, f. -δραμοῦμαι : aor. 2 -έδραμον :—to run in, Thuc. ; c. acc. to run into, Theocr.

εἰσ-φέρω, f. -οίσω ; aor. 1 -ήνεγκα ; pf. -ενήνοχα : plqpf. -ενηνόχειν :—to carry into or to, Od., Hdt.   2. to bring in, contribute, Plat., Xen., etc. :—at Athens, to pay the property-tax (v. εἰσφορά II), Thuc.   3. to bring (suffering) in or upon, πένθος εἰσφ. δόμοις Eur., etc.   4. to introduce, bring forward, propose, Hdt. ; γνώμην ἐσφ. ἐς τὸν δῆμον Thuc. ; εἰσφ. νόμον, Lat. legem rogare, Dem. :—absol., like Lat. referre ad senatum, Thuc.   II. Med. with pf. pass. εἰσενήνεγμαι, to carry with one, sweep along, Il.   2. to bring in for oneself, to import, Hdt., Thuc.   3. to bring in with one, introduce, Hdt., Eur.   III. Pass. to be brought in, introduced, Hdt.   2. to rush in, Thuc.

εἰσ-φοιτάω, f. ήσω, to go often to or into, Eur., Ar.

εἰσφορά, ἡ, (εἰσφέρω) a gathering in, Xen.   II.

at Athens, a property-tax levied to supply a deficit in the revenue, to meet the exigencies of war, Thuc., etc.

εἰσ-φορέω, = εἰσφέρω, Od., Thuc.

εἰσ-φρέω, impf. -έφρουν : f. -φρήσω and -φρήσομαι : impf. med. εἰσ-εφρούμην :—to let in, admit, Lat. admittere, Ar., Dem. :—Med. to bring in with one, Eur. (The Root φρέω, prob. akin to φέρω, is only found in compos. with δια-, εἰσ-, ἐπεισ-, ἐκ-.)

εἰσ-χειρίζω, f. Att. ιῶ, = ἐγχειρίζω, to put into one's hands, entrust, τί τινι Soph.

εἰσ-χέω, f. -χεῶ, to pour in or into, Hdt., Eur. :— Pass. with Ep. syncop. aor. 2 ἐσεχύμην [ῠ], to stream in, ἐσέχυντο ἐς πόλιν Il.

εἴσω, ἔσω, Adv. of εἰς, ἐς to within, into, absol., μή πού τις ἐπαγγείλησι καὶ εἴσω lest some one may carry the news into the house, Od. ; εἴσω ἀσπίδ' ἔαξε he brake it even to the inside, Il.   2. c. acc., δῦναι δόμον Ἄϊδος εἴσω Il., etc. ; Ἄϊδος εἴσω (sc. δόμον) Ib.   II. = ἔνδον, inside, within, Od., etc.   2. c. gen., μένειν εἴσω δόμων Aesch. ; εἴσω τῶν ὅπλων within the heavy-armed troops, i. e. encircled by them, Xen.

εἰσ-ωθέω, f. -ωθήσω and -ώσω, to thrust into :—Med. to press in, Xen.

εἰσ-ωπός, όν, (ὤψ) in sight of, εἰσωποὶ δ' ἐγένοντο νεῶν [the Greeks] stood facing the ships, Il.

ΕἸ'ΤΑ, Adv.   I. to denote Sequence of Time, then, next, Lat. deinde, πρῶτα μὲν . . , εἶτα . . , Soph., Plat., etc. : soon, presently, Soph.   II. to denote Consequence, and so, then, therefore, accordingly, esp. in questions or exclamations to express surprise or sarcasm, and then . . ? and so . . ? κᾆτ' οὐ δέχονται λίτας ; Soph. ; εἶτ' οὐκ αἰσχύνεσθε ; Dem.

εἶται, 3 sing. pf. pass. of ἕννυμι.

εἴ-τε, Dor. αἴ-τε, (εἰ, τε) generally doubled, εἴτε . . , εἴτε . . , Lat. sive . . , sive, either . . , or . . , whether . . , or . . :—the first εἴτε is sometimes omitted in Poets :—the first εἴτε is sometimes replaced by εἰ, as εἰ . . , εἴτε . . , Hdt., Trag.   II. also used, like εἰ, in indirect questions, Od., etc.

εἶτε, for εἴητε, 2 pl. pres. opt. of εἰμί (sum).

εἴω, Ep. for ἔω, ὦ, pres. subj. of εἰμί (sum).

εἴωθα, pf. 2 (in pres. signf.) of ἔθω.

εἰωθότως, Adv. of εἴωθα, in customary wise, as usual, Soph., Plat.

εἴωσι, Ep. for ἐῶσι, 3 pl. of ἐάω.

εἴως, Ep. for ἕως.

'ΕΚ, before a vowel 'ΕΞ, and 'ΕΓ before β γ δ λ μ :— Prep. governing GEN. only, Lat. e, ex :—Radical sense, from out of, opp. to εἰς :   I. OF PLACE :   1. of Motion, out of, forth from, Hom., etc. : ἐκ θυμοῦ φίλεον I loved her from my heart, with all my heart, Il.   2. to denote change from one place or condition to another, κακὸν ἐκ κακοῦ one evil from (or after) another, Ib. ; λόγον ἐκ λόγου λέγειν Dem.   3. to express distinction from a number, ἐκ πόλεων πίσυρες four out of many, Il.   4. of Position, like ἔξω, outside of, beyond, ἐκ βελέων out of shot, Ib. ; ἐκ καπνοῦ out of the smoke, Od.   5. with Verbs of Rest, ἐκ ποταμοῦ χρόα νίζετο washed his body with water from the river, Ib. :—with Verbs signifying to hang or fasten, ἐκ πασσαλόφι κρέμασεν φόρμιγγα he hung his lyre from (i. e. on) the peg, Ib. ; ἐκ τοῦ

βραχίονος ἐπέλκουσα leading it [by a rein] *upon* her arm, Hdt. :— also, *sitting* or *standing*, στᾶσ' ἐξ Οὐλύμποιο from Olympus where she stood, Il. ; καθῆσθαι ἐκ πάγων to sit *on* the heights and look *from* them, Soph.   II. OF TIME, ἐξ οὗ or ἐξ οὗτε [χρόνου], Lat. *ex quo, since,* Hom., Att. ; ἐκ τοῦ or ἐκ τοῖο *from* that time, Il. ; ἐκ πολλοῦ (sc. χρόνου) *for* a long time, Thuc.   2. of particular points of time, ἐκ νέου or ἐκ παιδός *from* boyhood ; ἐξ ἀρχῆς, etc. ; so, ἐκ θυσίας γενέσθαι to have *just finished* sacrifice, Hdt. ; ἐκ τοῦ ἀρίστου *after* breakfast, Xen.   3. when we say *in* or *by*, ἐκ νυκτῶν Od. ; ἐκ νυκτός Xen., etc.   III. OF ORIGIN,   1. of the Material, *out of* or *of* which things are made, ποιεῖσθαι ἐκ ξύλων τὰ πλοῖα Hdt.   2. of the Father, ἔκ τινος εἶναι, γενέσθαι, φῦναι, etc., Il. ; ἀγαθοὶ καὶ ἐξ ἀγαθῶν Plat.   3. of the Author or Occasion of a thing, ὄναρ ἐκ Διός ἐστιν Il. ; θάνατος ἐκ μνηστήρων death *by the hand of* the suitors, Od. ; τὰ ἐξ Ἑλλήνων τείχεα walls *built by* them, Hdt.   4. with the agent after Pass. Verbs, where ὑπό is more common, ἐφιλήθεν ἐκ Διός they were beloved *of* (i. e. *by*) Zeus, Il.   5. of the Cause, Instrument or Means *by* which a thing is done, ἐκ πατέρων φιλότητος *in consequence of* our father's friendship, Od. ; so, ἐκ τίνος ; ἐκ τοῦ ; *wherefore?* Eur. ; ποιεῖτε ὑμῖν φίλους ἐκ τοῦ Μαμωνᾶ τῆς ἀδικίας make yourselves friends *of* (i. e. *by means of*), N. T.   6. *from*, i. e. *according to*, ἐκ τῶν λογίων *according to* the oracles, Hdt. ; ἐκ νόμων Aesch.   7. periphr. for an Adv., (as in Lat. *ex consulto, ex composito*), ἐκ βίας *by force*, = βιαίως, Soph. ; ἐκ τοῦ φανεροῦ = φανερῶς, Thuc., etc.   8. with numerals, ἐκ τρίτου in the third place, Eur.

Ἑκά-εργος, ὁ, (ἑκάς, *ἔργω) *the far-working :* of Apollo, *the far-shooting, far-darting*, like ἐκηβόλος, Hom.

ἑκάην, aor. 2 pass. of καίω.

ἔκαθεν, Adv. (ἑκάς) *from afar*, Il. ; c. gen., ἔκαθεν πόλιος Ib.   II. = ἑκάς, *far off, far away*, Od.

ἐκάθηρα, aor. 1 of καθαίρω.

ἐκάμμυσα, poët. for κατ-έμυσα, aor. 1 of κατα-μύω.

ἔκαμον, aor. 2 of κάμνω.

ἙΚΑΣ [ἄ], Att. ἕκας, Adv. *far, afar, far off*, Lat. *procul*, Hom., Trag. ; οὐχ ἑκάς Thuc. :—c. gen. *far from, far away from*, Il. ; also, ἑκὰς ἀπὸ τοῦ τείχεος Ib.   2. Comp. ἑκαστέρω, *farther*, Od., etc. :—c. gen., Hdt. ; also ἑκαστοτέρω Theocr. :—Sup. ἑκαστάτω, *farthest*, Il., Hdt. ; ἑκαστάτω τινος *farthest from* . . , Id.   II. of Time, οὐχ ἑκὰς χρόνου in no *long* time, Id.

ἑκαστάτω, Sup. of ἑκάς, q. v.

ἑκασταχόθεν, (ἕκαστος) Adv. *from each side*, Thuc., Xen.

ἑκασταχόθι, (ἕκαστος) Adv. *on each side*, Plut.

ἑκασταχοῖ, (ἕκαστος) Adv. *to each side, every way*, Plut.

ἑκασταχοῦ, (ἕκαστος) Adv. *everywhere*, Thuc., etc.

ἑκαστέρω, Comp. of ἑκάς, q. v.

ἑκάστοθι, Adv. *for each* or *every one*, Od.   From

ἙΚΑΣΤΟΣ, η, ον, *every, every one, each, each one*, Lat. *quisque*, Hom., etc. ; the sing. is often joined with a pl. Verb, ἔβαν οἴκονδε ἕκαστος they went home *every one of them*, Il. ; ἕκαστος ἐπίστασθε Xen. :—the sing. is also put in apposition with a pl. Noun, Τρῶας ἕκαστον ὑπήλυθε τρόμος (for Τρώων ἕκαστον) fear seized

them *every one*, Il.   II. in pl. *all and each one*, Hom.   III. more definitely, εἷς ἕκαστος, Lat. *unusquisque, every single* one, Hdt., etc. :—καθ' ἕκαστον *singly, by itself*, Lat. *singulatim*, Plat., etc.   2. ὡς ἕκαστοι *each by himself*, Hdt., etc.

ἑκάστοτε, (ἕκαστος) Adv. *each time, on each occasion*, Hdt., etc. ; ἑκάστοτ' ἀεί Ar.

ἑκαστοτέρω, Adv., like ἑκαστέρω, v. sub ἑκάς.

Ἑκαταῖος, α, ον, *of Hecaté* : Ἑκάταιον or Ἑκάτειον, τό, *a statue* or *chapel of Hecaté*, Ar.

ἑκατεράκις [ἄ], Adv. (ἑκάτερος) *at each time*, Xen.

ἑκάτερθε [ἄ], before a vowel -θεν, Adv. for ἑκατέρωθεν, *on each side, on either hand*, Lat. *utrinque*, Hom. : —c. gen. *on each side of*, Id.

ἙΚΑΤΕΡΟΣ [ἄ], α, ον, *each of two, either, each singly*, Hdt., etc. :—in sing., with a pl. noun, like Lat. *uterque*, ταῦτα εἰπόντες ἀπῆλθον ἑκάτεροι Xen. ; except when each party is a plur., Plat.   Hence

ἑκατέρωθεν, Adv. *on each side, on either hand*, like the poët. ἑκάτερθεν, Hdt., Thuc. ; c. gen., ἐκ. τῆς πόλεως Id.

ἑκατέρωθι, Adv. *on each side*, Hdt. ; and

ἑκατέρωσε, Adv. *to each side, each way, both ways*, Plat., Xen.

Ἑκάτη, ἡ, (ἕκατος) *Hecaté, the Far-darter*, Hes. ; later, identified with Artemis.   II. Ἑκάτης δεῖπνον *Hecaté's dinner*, a meal set out by rich persons at the foot of her statue on the 30th of each month for beggars and paupers, Ar.

ἑκατη-βελέτης, ου, ὁ, = sq., Il.

ἑκατη-βόλος, ον, (ἑκάς, βάλλω) *far-shooting*, epith. of Apollo, Hom., Hes. ; as Subst. *the Far-darter*, Il.

ἕκατι, Dor. and Att. for ἕκητι.

ἑκατογ-κάρηνος, ον, (κάρηνον) = sq., Aesch.

ἑκατογ-κεφάλας, gen. α, ὁ, (κεφαλή) *hundred-headed*, Pind. : so ἑκατογ-κέφαλος, ον, Eur., Ar.

ἑκατόγ-χειρος, ον, (χείρ) *hundred-handed*, of Briareus, Il. :—ἑκατόγ-χειρ, ὁ, ἡ, Plut.

ἑκατό-ζυγος, ον, (ζυγόν) *with 100 benches for rowers*, Il.

ἑκατομβαιών, ῶνος, ὁ, *the month Hecatombaeon*, the first of the Att. year, answering to the last half of July and the first half of August, Att.   From

ἑκατόμ-βη, ἡ, (ἑκατόν, βοῦς) properly *an offering of a hundred oxen*,—but generally, *a great public sacrifice* :—thus, in Il. we find a hecatomb of *twelve* oxen, in Od. of *eighty-one*.

ἑκατόμ-βοιος, ον, (βοῦς) *worth a hundred beeves*, Il.

ἑκατόμ-πεδος, ον, (πούς) *measuring a hundred feet*, Il.

ἑκατόμ-πολις, ον, *with a hundred cities*, Il.

ἑκατόμ-πους, ὁ, ἡ, *hundred-footed*, Soph.

ἑκατόμ-πυλος, ον, (πύλη) *hundred-gated*, Il.

ἙΚΑΤΟΝ, οἱ, αἱ, τά, indecl. *a hundred*, Lat. *centum*, Il., etc.

ἑκατοντα-ετηρίς, ίδος, ἡ, (ἔτος) *a term of 100 years*, Plat.

ἑκατόν-τάλαντος, ον, *rated at 100 talents*, Ar.

ἑκατοντα-πλάσίων, ον, gen. ονος, *a hundred times as much* or *many*, Xen.

ἑκατοντά-πυλος, ον, (πύλη) = ἑκατόμπυλος, Anth.

ἑκατοντ-άρχης, ου, ὁ, (ἄρχω) *leader of a hundred*, Hdt.

ἑκατόντ-αρχος, ὁ, = ἑκατοντάρχης, Xen.

ἑκατοντάς, άδος, ἡ, *the number a hundred*, Hdt.

ἑκατοντ-όργυιος, ον, *of 100 fathoms*, Ar.

ἑκατοντ-ούτης, ου, ὁ, contr. for ἑκατονταετής, Luc.

ἕκᾰτος, ὁ, (ἑκάς) far-shooting, epith. of Apollo, Il.

ἑκᾰτό-στομος, ον, (στόμα) hundred-mouthed, Eur.

ἑκᾰτοστός, ή, όν, the hundredth, Lat. centesimus, Hdt., etc.; ἐπ' ἑκατοστά a hundred-fold, Id.   II.
ἑκατοστή, ή, the hundredth part, a tax or duty at Athens, Ar., Xen.

ἑκᾰτοστύς, ύος, ή, = ἑκατοντάς, Xen.

ἐκ-βάζω, f. ξω, to speak out, declare, Aesch.

ἐκ-βαίνω, f. -βήσομαι : aor. 2 ἐξέβην :—to step out of or off from a place, c. gen., Il., etc.; ἐκβ. ἐκ . . , Thuc. :—absol. to disembark, dismount, Il., etc.   2. to go out of a place, c. gen. or ἐκβ. ἐκ . . , Eur., etc.   3. c. acc. to outstep, overstep, Id., Plat.   4. in Poets, the instrument of motion is added in acc., ἐκβὰς πόδα Eur.; cf. βαίνω A. II. 3.   II. metaph., 1. to come out so and so, come to pass, turn out, Hdt., Thuc. :—to be fulfilled, of prophecies, Dem.; κάκιστος ἐκβ. to prove a villain, Eur. :—τὰ ἐκβησόμενα things likely to happen, Hdt., etc.   2. to go out of due bounds, to go far, ἐς τοῦτ' ἐκβέβηκ' Eur.
B. Causal, in aor. 1 -έβησα, to make to go out, to put out of a ship, Hom., Eur.

ἐκ-βακχεύω, f. σω, to excite to Bacchic frenzy, to make frantic, Eur., Plat. :—Pass. to be frenzied, Id.; so in Med., Eur.

ἐκ-βάλλω, f. -βᾰλῶ, pf. -βέβληκα : aor. 2 ἐξέβαλον :—to throw or cast out of a place, c. gen., Il., etc.; or absol. to throw out, throw overboard, Od. : also, like Lat. ejicere, to throw ashore, Ib., Hdt.; but, ἐκβ. ἐς τὸ πέλαγος carry out to sea, Id. :—Med. to put ashore, Id.   2. to cast out of a place, banish, Id., etc.   3. to expose on a desert island, Soph.; to expose a dead body, Id.   4. to divorce a wife, Dem.,   5. to cast out of his seat, depose a king, Aesch., etc.   II. to strike out of, Lat. excutere, χειρῶν ἔκβαλλε κύπελλα Od. ;—absol., δοῦρα ἐκβ. to fell trees (properly, to cut them out of the forest), Ib.   2. to strike open, break in, πύλας Eur.   III. to let fall, χειρὸς ἐκβαλεν ἔγχος Il. :—metaph., ἔπος ἐκβ. to let fall a word, Hom., etc. : so, δάκρυα ἐκβ. Od.; ἐκβ. ὀδόντας to cast one's teeth, Eur.   IV. to throw away, reject, Soph., etc. :—to reject a candidate for office, Dem.; to drive an actor from the stage, Lat. explodere, Id.   V. to lose, properly by one's own fault, Soph., etc.   VI. to produce, of women, Plut.; so, of wheat, ἐκβ. σταχύν Eur.   VII. intr. (sub. ἑαυτόν) to go out, depart, Id.; of a river, to empty, discharge itself, Plat.

ἐκβαλεῖν, aor. 2 inf. of ἐκβάλλω.

ἐκβάς, aor. 2 part. of ἐκβαίνω.

ἔκβασις, εως, ἡ, (ἐκβαίνω) a way out, egress, Od., Xen.   2. a going out of, escape from, c. gen., Eur.

ἐκ-βάω, Dor. for ἐκβαίνω, ἐκβῶντας Foed. in Thuc.

ἐκ-βεβαιόω, f. ώσω, to establish, Plut.; in Med., Id.

ἐκ-βιάζω, to force out :—Pass., τόξον χειρῶν ἐκβεβιασμένον the bow forced from mine hands, Soph.

ἐκ-βῐβάζω, f. Att. -βιβῶ, Causal of ἐκβαίνω, to make to step out, Ar.; ἐκβ. ποταμόν to turn a river out of its channel, Hdt. :—metaph., ἐκβ. τινὰ δικαίων λόγων to stop one from discussing the question of justice, Thuc.   2. to land one from a ship, disembark, Id.

ἐκ-βιβρώσκω, pf. -βέβρωκα, to devour, Soph.

ἐκ-βλαστάνω, aor. 2 ἐξ-έβλαστον, to sprout out, Plat.

ἐκβλητέον, Verbal of ἐκβάλλω, one must cast out, Plat.

ἔκβλητος, ον, (ἐκβάλλω) thrown out or away, Eur.

ἐκ-βλύζω, to gush out, Plut.

ἐκ-βοάω, to call out, cry aloud, Xen., Plat.

ἐκβοήθεια, ἡ, a going out to aid, a sally of the besieged, Thuc. From

ἐκ-βοηθέω, f. ήσω, to march out to aid, Hdt. : to make a sally, Thuc.

ἐκ-βολβίζω, f. Att. ιῶ, (βολβός) to peel, as one does an onion of its outer coats, Ar.

ἐκβολή, ή, (ἐκβάλλω) a throwing out, ψήφων ἐκβ. turning the votes out of the urn, Aesch.   2. a throwing the cargo overboard, Id.   II. ejectment, banishment, Id., Plat.   III. a letting fall, δακρύων Eur.   IV. a bringing forth :—ἐκβ. σίτου the time when the corn comes into ear, Thuc.   V. (from intr. signf. of ἐκβάλλω) a going out, outlet, Lat. exitus, ἐκβ. ποταμοῦ the discharge of a river from between mountains, Hdt. : a mountain-pass, Id. : the mouth of a river, Thuc.   2. ἐκβ. λόγου a digression, Id.   VI. (from Pass.), that which is cast out, ἐκβ. δικέλλης earth cast or scraped up by a hoe or mattock, Soph.; οὐρεία ἐκβολή children exposed on the mountains, Eur.   2. a cargo cast overboard, ἐκβολαὶ νεώς wrecked seamen, Id.

ἔκβολος, ον, (ἐκβάλλω) cast out of a place, c. gen., Eur. :—as Subst., ἔκβολον, τό, an outcast, Id. :—but, ναὸς ἔκβολα rags cast out from the ship, Id.

ἐκ-βράζω or -βράσσω, f. -βράσω, to throw out foam, of the sea :—Pass., of ships, to be cast ashore, Hdt.

ἐκ-βροντάω, f. ήσω, to strike out by lightning, ἐξεβροντήθη σθένος he had strength struck out of him by lightning, Aesch.

ἐκ-βρυχάομαι, Dep. to bellow forth or aloud, Eur.

ἔκβρωμα, ατος, τό, (ἐκβιβρώσκω) anything eaten out, πρίονος ἐκβ. saw-dust, Soph.

ἐκ-γαμίζω, f. σω, to give in marriage, and Pass. to be given in marriage, N. T. :—so, ἐκγαμίσκομαι, Ib.

ἐκ-γαυρόομαι, Pass. to exult greatly in, c. acc., Eur.

ἐκγέγάα, poët. pf. of ἐκγίγνομαι.

ἐκ-γελάω, f. άσομαι, to laugh out, laugh loud, Od., Xen.: metaph. of a liquid, to rush gurgling out, Eur.

ἐκγενέσθαι, aor. 2 inf. of ἐκγίγνομαι.

ἐκγενέτης, ου, ὁ, = ἔκγονος, Eur.

ἐκ-γίγνομαι, later and Ion. ἐκ-γίν- [ῑ] : f. -γενήσομαι : Ep. pf. ἐκγέγάα, 3 dual ἐκγεγάτην [ᾰ], part. ἐκγεγαώς : Dep. :—to be born of a father, c. gen., Ἑλένη Διὸς ἐκγεγαυῖα Il.   2. c. dat. to be born to, Πορθεῖ τρεῖς παῖδες ἐξεγένοντο Il.   II. in aor. 2 to have gone by, χρόνου ἐκγεγονότος time having gone by, Hdt. : c. gen., ἐκγενέσθαι τοῦ ζῆν to have departed this life, Xen.   III. impers., ἐκγίγνεται, like ἔξεστι, it is allowed, it is granted, c. dat. pers. et inf.; mostly with a negat., οὐκ ἐξεγένετό τινι ποιεῖν it was not granted him to do, Hdt. : absol., οὐκ ἐξεγένετο it was not in his power, Id.

ἐκ-γλύφω [ῠ], f. ψω, to scoop out : irr. pf. pass. ἐξέγλυμμαι Plat.   II. to hatch, Plut.

ἔκγονος, ον, (ἐκ-γίγνομαι) born of, sprung from, τινός Hom.   II. as Subst. a child, whether son or

daughter, Id.; and in pl. ἔκγονοι, descendants, Hdt., etc.; neut., ἔκγονά τινος one's offspring, Aesch.

ἐκ-γράφω [ᾰ], f. ψω, to write out :—Med. to write out or copy for oneself, Ar., Dem. Pass. to be stript utterly, Babr.

ἐκ-γυμνόομαι, Pass. to be stript utterly, Babr.

ἐκ-δακρύω, f. σω, to burst into tears, weep aloud, Soph., Eur.

ἐκδεδαρμένος, pf. pass. part. of ἐκδέρω.

ἐκδεδωριεῦνται, 3 pl. pf. of ἐκδωριεύομαι.

ἐκ-δεής, ές, (δέομαι) defective. Hence

ἔκδεια, ἡ, a falling short, being in arrear, Thuc.

ἐκ-δείκνῡμι, f. -δείξω, to shew forth, exhibit, display, Soph., Eur.

ἐκ-δειματόω, f. ώσω, strengthd. for δειματόω, Plat.

ἐκδέκομαι, Ion. for ἐκδέχομαι.

ἔκδεξις, εως, ἡ, (ἐκδέχομαι) a receiving from another : succession, Hdt.

ἐκδέρω, Ion. -δείρω: f. -δερῶ:—to strip off the skin from a person, c. acc., Hdt.: also c. acc. rei, to strip off, βύρσαν ἐκδ. Eur. II. to cudgel soundly, to ' hide,' Ar.

ἔκδετος, ον, (ἐκδέω) fastened to, Anth.

ἐκ-δέχομαι, Ion. ἐκδέκ-: f. -δέξομαι : Dep. : I. mostly of persons, 1. to take or receive from another, τί τινι Il., Aesch. 2. to take up, of a successor, τὴν ἀρχὴν παρά τινος Hdt., etc.; often also with the acc. omitted, ἐξεδέξατο Σαδυάττης (sc. τὴν βασιληΐην) he succeeded, Id. 3. to take up the argument, ὥσπερ σφαῖραν ἐκδ. τὸν λόγον Plat. 4. to wait for, expect, Soph. II. of events, to await, Lat. excipere, Hdt. III. of contiguous countries, to come next, Id.

ἐκ-δέω, f. -δήσω, to bind so as to hang from, to fasten to or on, c. gen., Il.: absol. σανίδας ἐκδῆσαι to bind planks (to his back), Od. :—Med. to bind a thing to oneself, hang it round one, Hdt.

ἔκ-δηλος, ον, conspicuous, Il. :—quite plain, Dem.

ἐκ-δημέω, f. ήσω, to be abroad, to be on one's travels, Hdt., Soph.; and

ἐκδημία, ἡ, a being abroad, exile, Plat. From

ἔκ-δημος, ον, from home, gone on a journey, Xen.; ἐκδ. στρατεῖαι service in foreign lands, Thuc.; ἐκδ. φυγή Eur. II. c. gen. departed from, Id.

ἐκ-διαβαίνω, aor. 2 -διεξέβην, to pass quite over, c. acc., Il.

ἐκ-διαιτάομαι, f. ήσομαι, Pass. to depart from one's accustomed mode of life, change one's habits, Thuc.

ἐκδιαίτησις, εως, ἡ, change of habits, Plut.

ἐκδίδαγμα, ατος, τό, prentice-work, a sampler, Eur.

ἐκ-διδάσκω : f. ξω :—to teach thoroughly, Lat. edocere, Aesch., etc.; ἐκδ. τινά τι Soph. :—Med. to have another taught, of the parents, Hdt., Eur.:—Pass., αἰσχρὰ ἐκδιδάσκεται is taught disgraceful things, Soph.; ἐκδιδαχθεὶς τῶν κατ' οἶκον having learnt of things at home, Id. 2. c. acc. pers. et inf. to teach one to be so and so, Id.; inf. omitted, γενναῖόν τινα ἐκδ. Soph.

ἐκ-διδράσκω, Ion. -διδρήσκω : f. -δράσομαι [ᾱ]: aor. 2 ἐξ-έδραν, part. ἐκδράς:—to run out from, run away, escape, ἐκ τόπου Hdt.; absol., Ar.

ἐκ-δίδωμι, 3 sing. ἐκδιδοῖ (as if from -διδόω) : f. -δώσω :—to give up, surrender, esp. something seized unlawfully, Lat. reddere, Il., Hdt. :—ἐκδ. δοῦλον to give up a slave to be examined by torture, Dem. 2. ἐκδ.

θυγατέρα to give one's daughter in marriage, Lat. nuptum dare, Hdt., Att.; so in Med., ἐκδίδοσθαι θυγατέρα Hdt., Eur. 3. to give out for money, let out for hire, Hdt.:—c. inf., like Lat. locare aliquid faciendum, Dem. 4. to lend out money on security, such as the cargo of a ship, ap. Dem. II. intr. (sub. ἑαυτόν or -ούς) of rivers, to empty themselves, Hdt.

ἐκ-δικάζω, f. άσω, to decide finally, settle, of a judge, Ar. II. to avenge, Eur. Hence

ἐκδικαστής, οῦ, ὁ, an avenger, Eur.

ἐκ-δικέω, f. ήσω, (ἔκδικος) to avenge, punish a crime, N. T.: also to exact vengeance for a crime, Ib. II. to avenge a person, Ib.; ἐκδ. τινὰ ἀπό τινος to avenge one on another, Ib. Hence

ἐκδίκησις, εως, ἡ, an avenging, ἐκδίκησιν ποιεῖν τινι to avenge him, N. T.

ἔκ-δικος, ον, (δίκη) without law, lawless, unjust, Lat. exlex, Aesch., etc. :—Adv. -κως, Id. II. maintaining the right, avenging, Anth.

ἐκ-διφρεύω, f. σω, to throw from a chariot, Luc.

ἐκ-διώκω, f. -διώξομαι, to chase away, banish, Thuc.

ἐκ-δονέω, f. ήσω, to shake utterly, confound, Anth.

ἔκδοσις, εως, ἡ, (ἐκδίδωμι) a giving out or up, surrendering, Hdt., Plat. 2. a giving in marriage, portioning out, Id. 3. a lending money on ships or exported goods, bottomry, Dem.

ἐκδοτέον, verb. Adj. of ἐκδίδωμι, one must give up, Plut. 2. one must give in marriage, Ar.

ἔκδοτος, ον, (ἐκδίδωμι) given up, delivered over, surrendered, Hdt., Att.

ἐκδοχή, ἡ, (ἐκδέχομαι) a receiving from another, succession, Aesch., Eur. II. = προσδοκία, N. T.

ἐκδόχιον, τό, (ἐκδέχομαι) a reservoir, Anth.

ἐκ-δρακοντόομαι, (δράκων) Pass. to become a very serpent, Aesch.

ἐκδράμεῖν, aor. 2 inf. of ἐκτρέχω. Hence

ἐκδρομή, ἡ, a running out, sally, charge, Xen. 2. a party of skirmishers, Thuc.; and

ἔκδρομος, ὁ, that sallies out from the ranks, a skirmisher, Thuc., Xen.

ἔκδῠμα, ατος, τό, that which is stript off, a skin, garment, Anth.; and

ἐκδῦμεν, Ep. for ἐκδῦναι, aor. 2 inf. of ἐκδύω.

ἐκδύνω [ῡ], v. ἐκδύω II.

ἔκδῠσις, εως, ἡ, a getting out, way out, Hdt. From

ἐκ-δύω and -δύνω [ῡ]: I. Causal in pres. ἐκδύω, impf. ἐξέδυον, f. ἐκδύσω, aor. 1 ἐξέδῡσα:—to take off, strip off, Lat. exuere, c. dupl. acc. pers. et rei, ἐκ μέν με χλαῖναν ἔδυσαν they stripped me of my cloke, Od.: c. acc. pers. only, to strip him, Xen., etc. 2. Med. ἐκδύομαι, aor. 1 ἐξεδυσάμην :—to strip oneself of a thing, put off, Il., etc.: absol. to put off one's clothes, strip, Ar., Xen. II. in pres. ἐκδύνω, impf. ἐξέδυνον, aor. 2 ἐξέδυν, pf. ἐκδέδῡκα, in same sense as Med. ἐκδύομαι, to put off, Od., Hdt. 2. in aor. 2 ἐξέδυν, pf. ἐκδέδῡκα, to go or get out of, c. gen., ἐκδὺς μεγάροιο Od.; ἐκδ. τῆς θαλάσσης to emerge from the sea, Plat. b. c. acc. to escape, ἐκδῦμεν ὄλεθρον Il.

ἐκ-δωριεύομαι, (Δώριος) Pass. to become a thorough Dorian, Hdt.

ἐκέασσα, Ep. aor. 1 of κεάζω.

ἐκέατο, Ion. for ἔκειντο, 3 pl. impf. of κεῖμαι.

ἐκεῖ, Dor. τηνεί, Adv. *there, in that place*, Lat. *illic*, Att. 2. euphem. for ἐν Ἅιδου, *in another world*, Aesch., etc.; οἱ ἐκεῖ, i. e. *the dead*, Id. II. with Verbs of motion, for ἐκεῖσε, as we say *there* for *thither*, ἐκεῖ πλέειν Hdt., etc. Hence

ἐκεῖθεν, poët. κεῖθεν, Dor. τηνῶθεν :—Adv. *from that place, thence*, Lat. *illinc*, opp. to ἐκεῖσε, Soph., etc. 2. = ἐκεῖ, Aesch., Thuc. :—c. gen., τοὐκεῖθεν ἄλσους on *yon* side of the grove, Soph. II. *thence, from that fact*, Isocr., Dem. III. of Time, *thereafter, next*, Il.

ἐκεῖθι, poët. κεῖθι : Dor. τηνόθι = ἐκεῖ, Hom.

ἐκείνῃ, v. sub ἐκεῖνος III.

ἐκεῖνος, poët. κεῖνος, η, ο, Aeol. κῆνος, Dor. τῆνος :— in Att. strengthd. ἐκεινοσί : Demonstr. Pron. : (ἐκεῖ) : —*the person there, that person* or *thing*, Hom., etc. : when οὗτος and ἐκεῖνος refer to two things before mentioned, ἐκεῖνος, *ille*, belongs to *the more remote*, i. e. *the former*, οὗτος, *hic*, to *the nearer*, i. e. *the latter*. 2. like *ille*, to denote well-known persons, ἐκεῖνος Θουκυδίδης Ar. 3. with demonstr. force, Ἶρος ἐκεῖνος ἧσται Irus sits *there*, Od. 4. in Att. the Subst. with ἐκεῖνος properly has the Article, and ἐκεῖνος may precede or follow the Subst., ἐκείνῃ τῇ ἡμέρᾳ, τῇ ἡμέρᾳ ἐκείνῃ : when the Art. is omitted in Prose, ἐκείνῃ follows the Subst., νῆες ἐκεῖναι Thuc. II. Adv. ἐκείνως, *in that way, in that case*, Id. III. dat. fem. ἐκείνῃ as Adv., 1. of Place (sub. ὁδῷ), *there, at that place; on that road*, Hdt., Thuc. 2. of Manner, *in that manner*, Plat., etc. IV. with Preps., ἐξ ἐκείνου from *that time*, Xen. ; so, ἀπ' ἐκείνου Luc. ; κατ' ἐκεῖνα in *that place, there*, Xen. : μετ' ἐκεῖνα *afterwards*, Thuc.

ἐκεῖσε, poët. κεῖσε, Adv. *thither, to that place*, Lat. *illuc*, opp. to ἐκεῖθεν, Hom., etc. 2. *to the other world*, Eur., Plat. ; cf. ἐκεῖ I. 2. 3. c. gen., ἐκ. τοῦ λόγου from *that part* of the story, Hdt.

ἐκέκαστο, 3 sing. plqpf. of καίνυμαι.

ἐκεκεύθει, 3 sing. plqpf. of κεύθω.

ἐκέκλετο, 3 sing. Ep. aor. 2 of κέλομαι.

ἐκέκλῑτο, 3 sing. plqpf. of κλίνω.

ἐκεκοσμέᾱτο, Ion. for ἐκεκόσμηντο, 3 pl. plqpf. of κοσμέω.

ἐκέλευ, Dor. for ἐκέλου, 2 sing. impf. of κέλομαι.

ἐκέλσαμεν, 1 pl. aor. 1 of κέλλω.

ἐκε-χειρία, ἡ, (ἔχω, χείρ) *a holding of hands, a cessation of hostilities, armistice, truce*, Thuc., Xen. 2. generally, *rest from work, vacation, holiday*, Luc.

ἐκ-ζέω, f. -ζέσω, *to boil out* or *over, break out*, of curses, Aesch. 2. c. gen., εὐλέων ἐξέζεσε *boiled over* with worms, i. e. *bred worms*, Hdt.

ἐκ-ζητέω, f. ήσω, *to seek out, enquire*, N. T. II. *to demand an account of* a thing, c. acc., Ib.

ἐκ-ζωπυρέω, f. ήσω, *to rekindle*, Ar., Plut.

ἔκηα, Ep. aor. 1 of καίω.

ἐκηβολία, ἡ, *skill in archery*, Il. From

ἐκη-βόλος, Dor. ἑκᾱ-βόλος, ον, (ἑκάς, βάλλω) *fardarting, far-shooting*, epith. of Apollo, Il.

ἔκηλος, Dor. ἔκᾱλος, ον, = εὔκηλος, *at rest, at one's ease*, Lat. *securus*, of persons enjoying themselves, Hom. ; ἕκηλοι συλήσετε ye will plunder them *at your ease*, i. e. *without let* or *hindrance*, Il. ; ἔκ. εὕδειν Soph. ; neut. as Adv., Id.

ΕΚΗΤΙ, Dor. and Att. ἕκᾱτι, *by means of, by virtue of, by the aid of*, Διὸς ἕκητι Od., etc. II. = ἕνεκα, *on account of, for the sake of*, Trag. : also, *as to*, Lat. *quod attinet ad*, Aesch., Eur.

ἐκθαμβέομαι, Pass. *to be amazed*, N. T. From

ἔκ-θαμβος, ον, *amazed, astounded*, N. T.

ἐκ-θαμνίζω, (θάμνος) *to root out, extirpate*, Aesch.

ἐκθανεῖν, aor. 2 inf. of ἐκθνήσκω.

ἐκ-θαρρέω, f. ήσω, strengthd. for θαρρέω, *to have full confidence* in a person, c. dat., Plut.

ἐκ-θεάομαι, Dep. *to see out, see to the end*, Soph.

ἐκ-θεατρίζω, f. σω, *to make a public show of, to expose to public shame*, N. T.

ἐκ-θειάζω, f. σω, *to make a god of, deify*, Luc. : *to worship as a god*, Plut. II. of things, *to make matter of religion*, Plut.

ἐκθείς, aor. 2 part. of ἐκτίθημι.

ἐκ-θέμεναι or -θέμεν, Ep. for ἐκθεῖναι, aor. 2 inf. of ἐκτίθημι.

ἐκ-θεραπεύω, f. σω, strengthd. for θεραπεύω, *to gain over entirely*, Aeschin., Plut.

ἐκ-θερίζω, f. Att. ιῶ, *to reap* or *mow completely*, Dem.

ἐκθέσθαι, aor. 2 inf. med. of ἐκτίθημι.

ἔκθεσις, εως, ἡ, (ἐκτίθημι) *a putting out, exposing*, of a child, Hdt., Eur.

ἐκ-θεσμος, ον, *out of law, lawless : horrible*, Plut.

ἔκθετος, ον, (ἐκτίθημι) *exposed*, Eur.

ἐκ-θέω, f. -θεύσομαι, *to run out, make a sally*, Xen.

ἐκ-θηράομαι, Dep. *to hunt out, catch*, Xen., Plut.

ἐκ-θηρεύω, f. σω, = foreg., Hdt.

ἐκ-θηριόομαι, Pass. *to become quite savage*, Lat. *efferari*, Eur.

ἐκ-θλίβω [ῑ], f. ψω, *to squeeze much : to distress greatly*, Xen.

ἐκ-θνήσκω : f. -θανοῦμαι : aor. 2 ἐξέθανον :—*to die away*, γέλῳ (for γέλωτι) ἔκθανον were like to die with laughing, Od. 2. *to be in a death-like swoon, be at the point of death*, Soph.

ἐκ-θοινάομαι, f. ήσομαι, Dep. *to feast on*, c. acc., Aesch.

ἔκ-θορον, Ep. for ἐξ-έθορον, aor. 2 of ἐκθρώσκω.

ἐκ-θρηνέω, f. ήσω, *to lament aloud*, Luc.

ἐκ-θρώσκω, f. -θοροῦμαι : aor. 2 ἐξέθορον :—*to leap out of*, c. gen., ἔκθορε δίφρου Il. ; κραδίη δέ μοι ἔξω στηθέων ἐκθρώσκει *of the violent beating of the heart*, Ib. :— rarely c. acc., Anth.

ἐκ-θυμιάω, f. άσω, *to burn as incense*, Eur.

ἔκ-θυμος, ον, *out of one's mind, senseless*, Lat. *demens*, Aesch. II. *very spirited, ardent*, Plut.

ἔκθῡσις, εως, ἡ, *atonement*, Lat. *expiatio*, Plut. From

ἐκ-θύω, f. ύσω [ῠ], *to offer up, sacrifice, slay*, Soph., Eur. 2. Med. *to atone for, expiate by offerings*, Lat. *lustrare, expiare*, c. acc. rei, Hdt. ; but c. acc. pers. *to propitiate, appease*, Eur.

ἔκιχον, aor. 2 of κιχάνω.

ἐκ-καγχάζω, f. σω, *to burst into loud laughter*, Xen.

ἐκ-κᾰθαίρω, f. -κᾰθᾰρῶ, *to cleanse out :* 1. with acc. of the thing cleansed, *to clear out* ditches, etc., Il. ; χθόνα ἐκκαθαίρει κνωδάλων he clears this land of monsters, Aesch. :—Pass. *to be purified*, Xen. 2. with acc. of the dirt removed, *to clear away*, Plat.

ἐκ-καθεύδω, f. -ευδήσω, *to sleep out of one's quarters*, Xen.

ἐκ-καί-δεκα, indecl. *sixteen*, Lat. *sedecim*, Hdt., etc.

ἐκκαιδεκά-δωρος, ον, (δῶρον) *sixteen palms long*, Il.

ἐκκαιδεκά-λῖνος, ον, (λίνον) *consisting of sixteen threads*, Xen.

ἐκκαιδεκά-πηχυς, Dor. -πᾶχυς, υ, gen. εος, contr. ους, *sixteen cubits long* or *high*, Decret. ap. Dem.

ἐκ-και-δέκατος, η, ον, *sixteenth*, Hdt., etc.

ἐκκαιδεκ-έτης, ου, ὁ, fem. -έτις, ιδος, 16 *years old*, Anth.

ἐκ-καιρος, ον, *out of date, antiquated*, Anth.

ἐκ-καίω, Att. ἐκ-κάω: f.-καύσω: aor. 1 part. ἐκκέας:—*to burn out*, Hdt., Eur. II. *to light up, kindle*, Hdt., Ar.

ἐκκακέω, f. ἥσω, *to be faint-hearted*, N. T.

ἐκ-καλάμάομαι, (κάλαμος II. 2) Dep. *to pull out with a fishing-rod*, Ar.

ἐκ-κᾰλέω, f. έσω, *to call out* or *forth, summon forth*, Hom., Hdt., Eur. II. Med. *to call out to oneself*, Od., Hdt. 2. *to call forth, elicit*, Aesch., etc. 3. c. inf. *to call on* one *to do*, Soph.

ἐκ-κᾰλύπτω, f. ψω, *to uncover*, Hdt.: *to disclose*, Aesch., Soph.:—Med. *to uncover one's head, unveil oneself*, Od., Plat.

ἐκ-κάμνω, f. -κᾰμοῦμαι, *to grow quite weary of* a thing, c. acc., Thuc.; c. part., ἐξέκαμον πολεμοῦντες Plut.; ἐκκ. πληγαῖς *to yield to* blows, Id.

ἐκ-καρπίζομαι, Med. *to yield as produce*, Aesch.

ἐκ-καρπόομαι, f. ώσομαι, Med. *to enjoy the fruit of*, ἄλλης γυναικὸς παῖδας ἐκκ. *to have children by another wife*, Eur. II. *to derive advantage from being*, c. part., Thuc.

ἐκ-κατεῖδον, aor. 2 with no pres. ἐκκαθοράω in use, *to look down from* a place, c. gen., Il.

ἐκ-κατα-πάλλομαι, Ep. 3 sing. aor. -κατέπαλτο, Pass. *to leap down from* a place, c. gen., Il.

ἐκ-καυλίζω, f. σω, *to pull out the stalk*: metaph. *to pull up root and branch*, Ar.

ἐκ-καυχάομαι, f. ήσομαι, *to boast loudly*, c. inf., Eur.

ἐκκάω, Att. for ἐκκαίω.

ἔκ-κειμαι, serving as Pass. of ἐκτίθημι, *to be cast out* or *exposed*, Hdt. 2. *of public notices, to be set up in public, posted up*, Dem. II. c. gen. *to fall from out, be left bare of*, Soph.

ἐκ-κενόω, poët. ἐκ-κεινόω, f. ώσω, *to empty out, leave desolate*, Aesch.; ἐκκενοῦν θυμὸν ἐς σχεδίαν γέροντος *to pour out* one's spirit *into Charon's boat*, i. e. give up the ghost, Theocr.; ἐκκ. ἰούς *to shoot all* one's arrows, Anth. :—Pass. *to be left desolate*, Aesch.

ἐκ-κερατίζω, f. σω, *to cut off root and branch*, Anth.

ἐκ-κέχυμαι, pf. pass. of ἐκχέω. Hence

ἐκκεχῠμένως, Adv. part. pf. pass. *profusely*, Plat.

ἐκ-κηραίνω, *to enfeeble, exhaust*, Aesch.

ἐκ-κηρύσσω, Att. -ττω, f. ξω, *to proclaim by voice of herald*, Soph. II. *to banish by proclamation*, Hdt. :—Pass., ἐξεκηρύχθην φυγάς Soph.

ἐκ-κῑνέω, f. ήσω, *to move out of* his lair, *to put up*, ἔλαφον Soph. : metaph. *to stir up, rouse, excite*, Plut.

ἐκ-κίω, *to go out*, Od.

ἐκ-κλάζω, f. -κλάγξω, *to cry aloud*, Eur.

ἐκ-κλείω, Ion. -κληίω, Att. -κλήω: f. Att. -κλήσω: —*to shut out from* a place, c. gen., Eur. 2. metaph. *to exclude from* a thing, Hdt., Aeschin. :— Pass., ἐκκληϊόμενοι τῇ ὥρῃ *being hindered* by [want of] time, Hdt.

ἐκ-κλέπτω, f. ψω, *to steal and bring off secretly, to purloin*, Il., Hdt., etc.; ἐκκλ. πόδα *to steal away*, Eur.: —ἐκκλ. μὴ θανεῖν Id. II. ἐκκλ. τινὰ λόγοις *to deceive* him, Soph.; μὴ ἐκκλέψῃς λόγον *disguise* not the matter, speak not falsely, Id.

ἐκκληΐω, Ion. for ἐκκλείω.

ἐκκλησία, ἡ, (ἔκκλητος) *an assembly of the citizens regularly summoned, the legislative assembly*, Thuc., etc. :—at Athens, the ordinary Assemblies were called κύριαι, the extraordinary being σύγκλητοι, ap. Dem. ; ἐκκλ. συναγείρειν, συνάγειν, συλλέγειν, ἀθροίζειν *to call an assembly*, Hdt., etc.; ἐκκλ. ποιεῖν 'to make a house,' Ar.; ἐκκλ. γίγνεται, καθίσταται *an assembly is held*, Thuc.; ἐκκλ. διαλύειν, ἀναστῆσαι *to dissolve it*, Id., etc. ; ἀναβάλλειν *to adjourn it*, Id. II. in N. T. *the Church*, either *the body*, or *the place*.

ἐκκλησιάζω: f. -άσω, impf. ἐκκλησίαζον, aor. 1 ἐκκλήσιασα, but also in irr. form, ἐξεκλησίαζον, ἐξεκλησίασα : (cf. ἐγκωμιάζω) :—*to hold an assembly, debate therein*, Ar., Thuc., etc. 2. *to be a member of the Assembly*, ἐκκλ. ἀπὸ τιμήματος οὐθένος Arist. Hence

ἐκκλησιαστής, οῦ, ὁ, *a member of the* ἐκκλησία, Plat.

ἐκκλησιαστικός, ή, όν, *of* or *for the* ἐκκλησία, Dem. :— τὸ ἐκκλησιαστικὸν [ἀργύριον] *the public pay received by each citizen who sat in the* ἐκκλησία, Luc.

ἐκ-κλητεύω, f. σω, *to summon into court*, Aeschin.

ἔκκλητος, ον, (ἐκκαλέω) *selected to judge* or *arbitrate on a point*, ἐκκλ. πόλις *an umpire city*, Aeschin. :—οἱ ἔκκλητοι, *in Sparta, a committee of citizens chosen for special business*, Xen.

ἐκκλήω, f. ήσω, old Att. for ἐκκλείω.

ἐκ-κλίνω, f. ῐνῶ, *to bend out of the regular line* : intr. (sub. ἑαυτόν) *to turn away, give ground, retire*, Thuc., Xen. :—also c. acc. *to avoid, shun*, τι Plat. 2. *to turn aside towards*, κατά τι Xen.

ἐκ-κλύζω, f. ύσω, *to wash out* stains, Plat.

ἐκ-κλαίω, *to wear out* : metaph. *to wear out* in loquacity, like Lat. *enecare*, Theocr., in Dor. fut. 3 pl. ἐκκναισεῦντι.

ἐκ-κνάω, f. ήσω, *to scrape off from*, c. gen., Hdt.

ἐκ-κοβᾰλικεύομαι, Dep. *to cheat by juggling tricks, cajole*, Ar.

ἐκ-κοκκίζω, f. Att. ιῶ, *to take out the kernel*: metaph., ἐκκ. σφυρόν *to put out* one's ankle, Ar.; ἐκκ. τὰς πόλεις *to sack, gut the cities*, Id.

ἐκ-κολάπτω, f. ψω, *to scrape out, obliterate*, Thuc.

ἐκ-κολυμβάω, f. ήσω, *to swim out of*, c. gen., Eur.

ἐκκομῐδή, ἡ, *a carrying out*, Hdt. : *of a corpse, burial*, Anth. From

ἐκ-κομίζω, f. Att. ιῶ, *to carry out*, esp. *to a place of safety*, Hdt.; ἐκκ. τινὰ ἐκ πρήγματος *to keep* him *out* of trouble, Id. : so in Med., Id., Thuc. 2. *to carry out a corpse, bury*, Lat. *efferre*, Plut. II. *to endure to the end*, τι Eur.

ἐκκομπάζω, f. σω, *to boast loudly*, Soph.

ἐκ-κομψεύομαι, Med. *to set forth in fair terms*, Eur.

ἐκκοπή, ἡ, *a cutting out* of an arrow-point from the body, Plut. From

ἐκ-κόπτω, f. ψω: pf. -κέκοφα: aor. 2 pass. ἐξ-εκόπην :—*to cut out, knock out* :—Pass., ἐξεκόπη τὠφθαλμώ he had both his eyes knocked out, Ar. 2. *to cut* [trees] *out of* a wood, *to fell* (cf. ἐκβάλλω), Hdt., Xen. ; ἐκκ.

τὸν παράδεισον cut down all the trees in the park, Xen. 3. metaph. to cut off, make an end of, Hdt., etc. 4. as military term, to beat off, repulse, Xen. 5. to cut off, N. T.

ἐκ-κορέω, f. ήσω, to sweep out, to sweep clean, Ar.

ἐκ-κορίζω, f. σω, (κόρις) to clear of bugs, Anth.

ἐκ-κορύφόω, to tell summarily, sum up, Hes.

ἐκ-κουφίζω, f. Att. ιῶ, to raise up, exalt, Plut. II. to relieve, Id.

ἐκκράζω, to cry out, Plut.

ἐκ-κρέμαμαι, Pass. to hang from, depend upon, c. gen., Plut.

ἐκ-κρεμάννῦμι, f. -κρεμάσω, to hang from or upon a thing; τι ἔκ τινος Ar. II. Pass. to hang on by, cling to, c. gen., Thuc. :—metaph. to be devoted to, Eur. Hence

ἐκκρεμής, ές, hanging from or upon, τινος Anth.

ἐκ-κρήμναμαι, = ἐκκρέμαμαι, c. gen., Eur.; ῥόπτρων χέρας ἐκκρημνάμεσθα we hang on to the door-handle by the hands, Id.

ἐκ-κρίνω [ῑ], f. ἰνῶ, to choose or pick out, to single out, Thuc. :—Pass., aor. 1 part. ἐκκριθείς Soph. 2. to single out for disgrace, expel, like Lat. tribu movere, Xen. 3. to secrete, separate, ὅταν ὁ νοῦς ἐκκριθῇ Id. Hence

ἔκκρῐτος, ον, picked out, select, Aesch., Soph. :—neut. ἔκκριτον, as Adv. above all, eminently, Eur.

ἔκκρουσις, εως, ἡ, a beating out, driving away, Xen.

ἔκκρουστος, ον, beaten out, embossed, Aesch.

ἐκ-κρούω, f. σω, to knock out, τι ἐκ τῶν χειρῶν Xen. 2. to drive back, repulse, Thuc., Xen. : metaph. to frustrate one of a thing, c. gen., Plut. 3. to hiss an actor off the stage, explodere, Dem. 4. to put off, adjourn by evasions, Id.; ἐκκρ. τοὺς λόγους to baffle by putting off, elude, Plat.

ἐκ-κυβεύομαι, Pass. to lose at play, c. acc., Plut.

ἐκ-κυβιστάω, f. ήσω, to tumble headlong out of a chariot, c. gen., Eur.; ἐκκ. ὑπέρ τινος to throw a somersault over a thing, Xen.

ἐκ-κυέω, f. ήσω, to put forth as leaves, Anth.

ἐκ-κυκλέω, f. ήσω, to wheel out, esp. by means of the ἐκκύκλημα (q. v.): ἀλλ᾽ ἐκκυκλήθητι come, wheel yourself out! i. e. shew yourself, Ar. Hence

ἐκκύκλημα, ατος, τό, a theatrical machine, which served the purpose of drawing back the scenes, and disclosing the interior to the spectators.

ἐκ-κῠλίνδω, f. -κυλίσω [ῑ]: aor. 1 pass. ἐξεκυλίσθην: —to roll out, Ar. :—to overthrow, Anth. :—Pass., ἐκ δίφροιο ἐξεκυλίσθη rolled headlong from the chariot, Il. 2. to extricate :—Pass. to be extricated from, τῆσδ᾽ ἐκκυλισθήσει τύχης Aesch.; ἐκκυλισθῆναι εἰς ἔρωτας to plunge headlong into intrigues, Xen.

ἐκ-κῠμαίνω, f. ἀνῶ, to wave from the straight line, of a line of soldiers, Xen.

ἐκ-κῠνέω, f. ήσω, (ἔκκυνος) to keep questing about, of hounds, Xen.

ἐκ-κῠνηγετέω, f. ήσω, to pursue in the chase, hunt down, τινα Eur.

ἔκ-κυνος, ον, (κύων) of a hound, questing about, not keeping on one scent, Xen.

ἐκ-κύπτω, f. ψω, to peep out of a place, c. gen., Babr.

ἐκ-κωμάζω, f. σω, to rush wildly out, Eur.

ἐκ-κωφέω, f. ήσω, to make quite deaf, Ar. :—Pass., metaph., ἐκκεκώφηται ξίφη swords are blunted, Eur.

ἐκ-κωφόω, f. ώσω, to make quite deaf, Plat. :—Pass. to become so, Luc.

ἐκ-λαγχάνω, f. -λήξομαι, to obtain by lot or destiny, Soph.

ἐκ-λακτίζω, f. σω, to kick out, fling out behind, Ar.

ἐκ-λᾰλέω, f. ήσω, to speak out, blab, divulge, Dem.

ἐκ-λαμβάνω, f. -λήψομαι, to receive from others, receive in full, Soph., etc. II. ἔργα ἐκλ. = ἐργολαβέω, to contract to do work, opp. to ἐκδίδωμι (to let it out), Hdt. III. to take in a certain sense, to understand, Lat. accipere, Plat. ; ἐκλ. τι ἐπὶ τὸ χεῖρον Arist.

ἐκ-λάμπω, f. ψω, to shine or beam forth, Hdt., Aesch., etc.

ἐκ-λανθάνω, aor. 2 ἐξ-έλᾰθον: —to escape notice utterly: —Med., with pf. pass. ἐκλέλησμαι, to forget utterly, c. gen. rei, Soph. II. Causal in pres. ἐκληθάνω, with aor. 1 ἐξέλησα, Dor. ἐξέλᾱσα; Ep. redupl. aor. 2 ἐκλέλᾰθον: —to make one quite forgetful of a thing, c. gen. rei, Od. : c. acc. rei, ἐκλέλαθον κιθαριστύν made him quite forget his harping, Il.

ἐκ-λᾰπάζω, to cast out from a place, c. gen., Aesch.

ἐκ-λάπτω, f. -λάψομαι, to drink off, Ar.

ἐκ-λέγω, f. ξω : pf. pass. ἐξείλεγμαι and ἐκλέλεγμαι: —to pick or single out, Thuc., Xen. :—Med. to pick out for oneself, choose out, Hdt., Plat., etc. 2. Med. also, ἐκλέγεσθαι τὰς πολιὰς τρίχας to pull out one's gray hairs, Ar. II. to levy taxes or tribute, Thuc.; c. acc. pers., ἐκλ. τέλη τινάς to levy tolls on them, Aeschin.; so c. gen. pers., Xen.

ἐκ-λείπω, f. ψω, to leave out, omit, pass over, Hdt., Aesch., etc. :—Pass., ὄνειδος οὐκ ἐκλείπεται fails not to appear, Aesch. 2. to forsake, desert, abandon, Hdt., Aesch., etc. 3. in elliptic phrases, ἐκλείπειν τὴν πόλιν εἰς τὰ ἄκρα to abandon the city and go to the heights, Hdt.; εἴ τις ἐξέλιπε τὸν ἀριθμόν (of the Persian immortals) if any one left the number incomplete, Id. II. intr. of the sun or moon, to suffer an eclipse, Thuc.; —in full, ὁ ἥλιος ἐκλιπὼν τὴν ἐκ τοῦ οὐρανοῦ ἕδρην Hdt.; cf. ἔκλειψις. 2. to die, οἱ ἐκλελοιπότες the deceased, Plat.; in full, ἐκλ. βίον Soph. 3. generally, to leave off, cease, stop, Hdt., etc. 4. to fail, be wanting, Eur.

ἔκλειψις, εως, ἡ, abandonment, τῶν νεῶν Hdt. II. (from intr.) of sun or moon, an eclipse, Thuc.

ἐκλεκτός, ή, όν, (ἐκλέγω) picked out, select, Thuc., Plat., etc. II. οἱ ἐκλεκτοί, the elect, N. T.

ἐκλελᾰθεῖν, Ep. redupl. aor. 2 of ἐκλανθάνω.

ἐκλέλῠμαι, pf. pass. of ἐκλύω. Hence

ἐκλελῠμένως, Adv. loosely, carelessly, Plut.

ἔκλεο, Ep. for ἐκλέεο, 2 sing. impf. of κλέω.

ἐκ-λέπω, f. ψω, to bring the young brood out of the shell, to hatch, Hdt., Ar.

ἐκ-λευκαίνω, to make quite white, Eur.

ἐκ-λήγω, f. ξω, to cease utterly, Soph.

ἐκ-ληθάνω, v. ἐκλανθάνω II.

ἐκλήθην, aor. 1 pass. of καλέω.

ἔκλησις, εως, ἡ, (ἐκλαθέσθαι) a forgetting and forgiving, Od.

ἐκ-λιμπάνω, = ἐκλείπω, to abandon, Eur. 2. intr. to cease, Id.

ἐκλινθῆμες, Dor. for -ημεν, 1 pl. aor. 1 pass. of κλίνω.

ἐκ-λῑπαίνω, to fatten :—Pass. to grow fat, Plut.

ἐκ-λῐπεῖν, aor. 2 inf. of ἐκλείπω. Hence

ἐκλῐπής, ές, failing, deficient, ἡλίου ἐκλιπές τι ἐγένετο =ἔκλειψις, Thuc. II. omitted, overlooked, Id.

ἐκλογή, ἡ, (ἐκλέγω) a picking out, choice, election, Plat. II. that which is chosen out, an extract, choice collection of passages, Horat.

ἐκ-λογίζομαι, f. Att. -ιοῦμαι, Dep. to compute, calculate, Plut. 2. to consider, reflect on, τι Hdt., Eur.; περί τινος Thuc. 3. to reckon on, οὐδεὶς αὑτοῦ θάνατον ἐκλογίζεται Eur. Hence

ἐκλογισμός, ὁ, a computation, calculation, Plut.

ἐκλόμην, sync. for ἐκελόμην, aor. 2 of κέλομαι.

ἐκ-λοχεύω, f. σω, to bring forth, Eur., in Med. :—Pass. to be born, Id.

ἔκλυσις, εως, ἡ, (ἐκλύω) release or deliverance from a thing, c. gen., Aesch., etc. II. feebleness, faintness, Dem.

ἐκλῠτήριος, ον, (ἐκλύω) of or for release :—ἐκλυτήριον, τό, a release, Soph.: an expiatory offering, Eur.

ἔκλῠτος, ον, (ἐκλύω) easy to let go, light, buoyant, of missiles, Eur. II. Adv. ἐκλύτως, remissly, Plut.

ἐκ-λύω, f. ύσω [ῠ]: pf. pass. ἐκλέλῠμαι: aor. 1 ἐξελύθην [ῠ]:—to loose, release, set free, from a thing, c. gen., Aesch., Soph.:—Pass. to be set free, Plat.:—Med. to get one set free, to release from, c. gen., Od., etc. II. to unloose, unstring a bow, Hdt.; ἐκλύσων στόμα likely to let loose the tongue, Soph. 2. to put an end to, Id., Eur. 3. to relax, enfeeble :—Pass. to be faint, fail, give way, Dem. 4. to pay in full, Plut.

ἐκ-λωβάομαι, aor. 1 ἐξελωβήθην, Pass.to sustain grievous injuries, Soph.

ἐκ-λωπίζω, f. σω, (λῶπος) to lay bare, Soph.

ἐκμᾱγεῖον, τό, (ἐκμάσσω) that on or in which an impression is made : also the impression made, an impress, mould, Plat. :—metaph., ἐκμαγεῖον πέτρης counterfeit of rock, of a fisherman who is always on them, Anth.

ἐκ-μαίνω, f. ᾰνῶ, to drive mad with passion, Eur., Theocr.; ἐκμῆναί τινα δωμάτων to drive one raving from the house, Eur. :—Pass., with pf. 2 act. ἐκμέμηνα, to go mad with passion, be furious, Hdt. 2. c. acc. rei, ἐκμῆναι πόθον to kindle mad desire, Soph.

ἔκμακτρον, τό, (ἐκμάσσω) an impress, Eur.

ἐκ-μανθάνω, f. -μᾰθήσομαι, to learn thoroughly, and, in past tenses, to have learnt thoroughly, to know full well, Hdt., Aesch., etc. II. to examine closely, search out, Hdt., Eur., etc.

ἐκμάξαι, aor. 1 inf. of ἐκμάσσω.

ἐκ-μᾰραίνω, f. ᾰνῶ, to make to wither away, Anth. :—Pass. to wither away, Theocr.

ἐκμαργόομαι, Pass. to go raving mad, Eur.

ἐκμαρτῠρέω, f. ήσω, to bear witness to a thing, c. acc., Aesch. Hence

ἐκμαρτῠρία, ἡ, the deposition of a witness, Dem.

ἐκ-μάσσατο, 3 sing. aor. 1, he devised or invented, τι h. Hom.; v. μαίομαι.

ἐκ-μάσσω, Att. -ττω, f. ξω, to wipe off, wipe away, Soph., Eur. :—Med. to wipe away one's tears, Anth. II. of an artist, to mould or model in wax or plaster, Lat. exprimere, Plat.:—Med.,τοκέων ἐκμάσσεται

ἴχνη he impresses anew the footsteps of his fathers, i. e. walks in their steps, Theocr.

ἐκ-μεθύσκω, f. ύσω [ῠ], to make quite drunk, to saturate with a thing, c. gen., Anth.

ἐκ-μείρομαι, in pf. 2 ἐξέμμορε τιμῆς obtained a chief share of honour, Od.

ἐκ-μελετάω, f. ήσω, to train carefully, τινα Plat. 2. to learn perfectly, con over, practise, τι Id.

ἐκ-μελής, ές, (μέλος) out of tune, dissonant, Plut.

ἐκ-μετρέω, f. ήσω, to measure out, measure, χρόνον Eur. :—Med. to measure for oneself, take measure of, τι Xen.; ἄστροις ἐκμετρούμενος χθόνα calculating its position by the stars, Soph.

ἐκ-μηνος, ον, (ἕξ, μήν) of six months, half-yearly, Soph.

ἐκ-μηνύω, f. ύσω [ῠ], to inform of, betray, Plut.

ἐκ-μηρύομαι, Dep. to wind out like a ball of thread : of an army, to make it defile out of a place, c. gen., Polyb., Plut. II. intr., of the army, to defile, Xen.

ἐκ-μῑμέομαι, f. ήσομαι, Dep. to imitate faithfully, represent exactly, Eur., Xen.

ἐκ-μῑσέω, f. ήσω, to hate much, Plut.

ἐκ-μισθόω, f. ώσω, to let out for hire, τί τινι Xen.

ἐκ-μολεῖν, inf. of aor. 2 ἐξέμολον, Ep. 3 sing. ἔκμολε : —to go out, go forth, Il. :—For the pres., v. βλώσκω.

ἐκ-μουσόω, f. ώσω, to teach fully, τινά τι Eur.

ἐκ-μοχθέω, f. ήσω, to work out with toil, Lat. elaborare, Eur. 2. to struggle through, πόνους Id. 3. to win by labour, achieve, Id. 4. to struggle out of danger, c. acc., Id.

ἐκ-μῠζάω, f. ήσω, to squeeze out, Il.

ἐκ-μυκτηρίζω, f. σω, to turn up one's nose at, mock at, N. T.

ἐκ-ναρκάω, f. ήσω, to become quite torpid, Plut.

ἐκ-νέμομαι, Med. with aor. 1 pass. ἐξενεμήθην, to go forth to feed : metaph., ἐκνέμεσθαι πόδα to turn away one's foot, Soph.

ἐκνεοττεύω, to hatch, Arist.

ἐκ-νευρίζω, f. σω, (νεῦρον) to cut the sinews :—Pass., ἐκνενευρισμένοι unnerved, Dem.

ἐκ-νεύω, f. σω, aor. 1 ἐξένευσα (cf. ἐκνέω):—to turn the head aside, Xen. 2. c. acc. to shun, avoid, Orph. II. to fall headlong, Eur. III. to give one a sign to move away, c. inf., Id.

ἐκ-νέω, f. -νεύσομαι, aor. 1 ἐξένευσα:—to swim out, swim to land, escape by swimming, Eur., Thuc.: generally, to escape, Eur.

ἐκ-νήφω, f. ψω, to sleep off a drunken fit, become sober again, Anth.

ἐκ-νήχομαι, f. ξομαι: Dep. = ἐκνέω, to swim out or away, Luc.

ἐκ-νίζω, f. -νίψω (formed from -νίπτω), to wash out, purge away, Eur. :—Med. to wash off from oneself, Lat. diluere, οὐδέποτε ἐκνίψῃ τὰ πεπραγμένα Dem. II. to wash clean, purify, Anth.

ἐκ-νῑκάω, f. ήσω, to achieve by force, Eur.: to carry one's point, Plut. II. intr. to win a complete victory : metaph. to gain the upper hand, prevail, Thuc.

ἐκνίψω, fut. of ἐκνίζω.

ἐκ-νόμιος, ον, (νόμος) unusual, marvellous : Adv. -ίως, Ar.; Sup. ἐκνομιώτατα Id.

ἔκ-νομος, ον, outlawed, Lat. exlex, Aesch. :—Adv. -μως, out of tune, discordantly, Id.

ἔκ-νοος, ον, contr. -νους, ουν, senseless, Lat. amens, Plut.
ἐκ-νοσφίζομαι, Dep. to take for one's own, Anth.
ἑκοντί, Adv. willingly, Plut.
ἑκούσιος, α, ον and ος, ον, (ἑκών) of actions, voluntary, Soph., Eur., etc.; τὰ ἑκούσια voluntary acts, opp. to τὰ ἀκούσια, Xen. 2. rarely, like ἑκών, of persons, willing, acting of free will, Soph.,Thuc. II. Adv. -ίως, Eur., etc.; so, ἐξ ἑκουσίας (sc. γνώμης) Soph.; καθ' ἑκουσίαν Thuc.
ἐκπαγλέομαι, Pass. to be struck with amazement, to wonder greatly, only in part., Hdt. II. to wonder at, admire exceedingly, c. acc., Aesch., Eur.
ἔκπαγλος, ον, metath. for ἔκπλαγος (from ἐκπλήσσω) terrible, fearful, of persons; Superl. ἐκπαγλότατος Il.: —of things, Od. 2. as Adv. terribly, vehemently, exceedingly, Hom.: — also neut. as Adv., ἔκπαγλον and ἔκπαγλα, Il. II. in later Poets, marvellous, wondrous, Aesch., Soph.; Adv. ἔκπαγλα marvellously, Id.
ἐκπαίδευμα, ατος, τό, a nursling, a child, Eur. From
ἐκ-παιδεύω, f. σω, to bring up from childhood, educate completely, Eur., Plat.
ἐκ-παιφάσσω, to rush madly to the fray, Il.
ἐκ-παίω, f. -παιήσω: aor. 1 ἐξ-έπαισα: —like ἐκβάλλω, to throw out of a thing, dash one from it, c. gen., Eur. II. Med. to dash out, escape, Plut.
ἐκ-πάλλω, to shake out: —Pass. to spurt out from, c. gen., ἔκπαλτο (syncop. Ep. aor. 2 med. as pass.) Il.
ἐκ-πατάσσω, f. ξω, to strike, afflict, Eur.: —Pass., φρένας ἐκπεπαταγμένος stricken in mind, Od.
ἐκ-πάτιος [ᾰ], α, ον, (πάτος) out of the common path: excessive, vehement, Aesch.
ἐκ-παύω, f. σω, to set quite at rest, put an end to, Eur.: —Med. to take one's rest, Thuc.
ἐκ-πείθω, f. σω, to over-persuade, Soph., Eur.
ἐκ-πειράζω, f. άσω, to tempt, c. acc., N. T.
ἐκ-πειράομαι, f. άσομαι [ᾱ], aor. 1 ἐξεπειράθην [ᾱ] : to make trial of, prove, tempt, c. gen. pers., Hdt.; c. inf., ἐκπειρᾷ λέγειν; art thou tempting me to speak? Soph. 2. to inquire of another, τί τινος Ar.
ἐκ-πέλει, impers., = ἔξεστι, 'tis permitted, Soph.
ἐκ-πέμπω, f. ψω: I. of persons, to send out or forth from a place, c. gen., Hom., Aesch., etc.: —Med., Od., Soph., etc. 2. to bring out by calling, call or fetch out, Id.; so in Med., Id.: —Pass. to go forth, depart, Id. 3. to send forth, dispatch, Thuc. 4. to send away, cast out, Hdt., Aesch.; to divorce a wife, Hom.: —so in Med., Soph. II. of things, to send out, send abroad, Il., Hdt. 2. to send forth, give out, σέλας Aesch. Hence
ἔκπεμψις, εως, ἡ, a sending out or forth, Thuc.
ἐκ-πεπαίνω, to make quite ripe or mellow, Theophr.
ἐκπεπέτασμαι, pf. pass. of ἐκπετάννυμι.
ἐκπεπληγμένως, Adv. pf. pass. of ἐκπλήσσω, in panic fear, Dem.
ἐκπέποται, 3 sing. pf. pass. of ἐκπίνω, Od.
ἐκπεπταμένως, Adv. pf. pass. of ἐκπετάννυμι, extravagantly, Xen.
ἐκ-πέπτω, later form of ἐκ-πέσσω.
ἐκπέπτωκα, pf. of ἐκπίπτω.
ἐκ-περαίνω, f. ἀνῶ, to finish off, Eur.: —Pass. to be accomplished, Id., Xen.

ἐκπέρᾱμα, τό, a coming out of, δωμάτων Aesch. From
ἐκ-περάω, f. άσω [ᾰ], Ion. ήσω, to go out over, pass beyond, Od., Aesch.; ἐκπ. βίον to go through life, Eur. 2. absol. of an arrow, to pass through, pierce, Il. 3. to go or come out of a place, c. gen., Eur.
ἐκ-περδικίζω, f. σω, (πέρδιξ) to escape like a partridge, Ar.
ἐκ-πέρθω, f. -πέρσω, to destroy utterly, Il., Aesch.
ἐκ-περίειμι, to go out and round, go all round, Xen.
ἐκ-περιπλέω, f. -πλεύσομαι, to sail out round, so as to attack in flank, Plut.
ἐκ-περισσῶς, Adv. more exceedingly, N. T.
ἐκ-πέρυσι, Adv. more than a year ago, Luc.
ἐκ-πετάννυμι, f. -πετάσω: aor. 1 pass. ἐξεπετάσθην: pf. ἐκπεπέτασμαι: —to spread out, of a sail, Eur.; of wings, Anth.; of a net, Orac. ap. Hdt. 2. metaph., ἐπὶ κῶμον ἐκπετασθείς wholly given up to revel, Eur.
ἐκπετήσιμος, ον, ready to fly out, just fledged, Ar.
ἐκ-πέτομαι or -πέταμαι: f. -πτήσομαι: aor. 2 ἐξεπτόμην or -άμην, and in act. form ἐξέπτην: —to fly out or away, Hes., Eur.
ἐκπεύθομαι, = ἐκπυνθάνομαι, Aesch.
ἐκπεφυῖαι, pf. part. pl. fem. of ἐκφύω.
ἐκ-πηδάω, f. -πηδήσομαι: —to leap out, Hdt. 2. to make a sally, Xen. 3. to leap up, start up, Soph.
ἐκπήδημα, ατος, τό, a leap out, ὕψος κρεῖσσον ἐκπηδήματος a height too great for out-leap, Aesch.
ἐκ-πηνίζομαι, f. Att. -ιοῦμαι, to spin out: —metaph. of an advocate, αὐτοῦ ἐκπηνιεῖται ταῦτα will wind these things out of him, Ar.
ἐκ-πῑδύομαι [ῠ], Dep. to gush forth, Aesch.
ἐκ-πίμπλημι, f. -πλήσω, to fill up a bowl, Eur.; ἐκπ. κρατῆρας δρόσου to fill them full of liquid, Id. 2. to satiate, Id., Thuc. II. to fulfil, Hdt.; ἁμαρτάδα ἐξέπλησε paid the full penalty of sin, Id. III. to accomplish, complete, Trag.
ἐκ-πίνω [ῑ]: f. -πίομαι: aor. 2 ἐξέπιον, Ep. ἔκπιον: —to drink out or off, quaff liquor, Od.: so, in pf. pass., ἐκπέποται Ib., Hdt.; αἵματ' ἐκποθένθ' ὑπὸ χθονός Aesch. 2. to drain a cup dry, πλῆρες ἐκπ. κέρας Soph.: metaph. ἐκπ. ὄλβον Eur.
ἐκ-πιπράσκω, to sell out, sell off, Dem.
ἐκ-πίπτω, f. -πεσοῦμαι: aor. 2 ἐξέπεσον: pf. -πέπτωκα: —to fall out of a chariot, c. gen., Hom., etc.; c. dat. pers., τόξον δέ οἱ ἔκπεσε χειρός Il. 2. of seafaring men, to be thrown ashore, Lat. ejici, Od., Hdt., etc.: of things, to suffer shipwreck, Xen. 3. to fall from a thing, i. e. be deprived of it, Lat. excidere, τινός or ἔκ τινος Aesch., etc. 4. to be driven out, of persons banished, Hdt., etc. 5. to go out or forth, sally out, Id., Xen. 6. to come out, of votes, Id. 7. to escape, Thuc. 8. of oracles, to issue from the sanctuary, be imparted, Luc. 9. to depart from, digress, Xen., Aeschin. 10. to fall off, come to naught, N. T. 11. of actors, to be hissed off the stage, Lat. explodi, Dem.
ἐκπίτνω, = ἐκπίπτω, Aesch.
ἐκπλᾱγείς, aor. 2 pass. part. of ἐκπλήσσω.
ἔκ-πλεθρος, ον, (ἓξ, πλέθρον) six plethra long, Eur.
ἔκ-πλεος, ον, ποët. -πλειος, α, ον, Att. -πλεως, ων: — quite full of a thing, c. gen., Eur. 2. complete, of a body of soldiers, Xen.: abundant, Id.

ἐκ-πλέω, f. -πλεύσομαι : Ion. -πλώω, aor. 1 -έπλωσα : —to sail out, sail away, weigh anchor, Hdt., etc. : c. gen. to sail away from, Soph. 2. metaph., ἐκπλεῖν τοῦ νοῦ, τῶν φρενῶν to go out of one's mind, lose one's senses, Hdt. II. ἐκπλ. τὰς ναῦς to outsail the ships, Thuc.

ἔκπλεως, ων, Att. for ἔκπλεος : nom. pl. ἔκπλεῳ.

ἔκπληγεν, Ep. for -εσαν, 3 pl. aor. 2 pass. of ἐκπλήσσω.

ἐκ-πλήγνῡμι, = ἐκπλήσσω, Thuc.

ἐκπληκτικός, ή, όν, (ἐκπλήσσω) striking with consternation, astounding, Thuc.

ἔκπληκτος, ον, terror-stricken, amazed, Luc.

ἔκπληξις, εως, ἡ, (ἐκπλήσσω) consternation, Thuc., etc. ; ἔκπλ. κακῶν terror caused by misfortunes, Aesch.

ἐκ-πληρόω, f. ώσω, = ἐκπίμπλημι, to fill quite up, Eur. 2. to make up to a certain number, Hdt., Soph. 3. to man completely, ναῦς Hdt. 4. to fulfil, Id. II. ἐκπλ. λιμένα to make one's way over the harbour, Lat. emetiri, Eur.

ἐκ-πλήσσω, Att. -ττω : f. ξω : —to strike out of, drive away from, Aesch. : —absol. to drive away, Thuc. II. to drive out of one's senses, to amaze, astound, Od., Eur. : —often in aor. 2 pass., Ep. ἐξεπλήγην, Att. ἐξεπλάγην [ᾰ] ; aor. 1 ἐξεπλήχθην ; pf. ἐκπέπληγμαι : —to be panic-struck, amazed, astonied, Il., Soph., etc. ; ἐκπλαγῆναί τινι to be astonished at a thing, Hdt., so διά τι, ἐπί τινι, etc. ; ἐκπλαγῆναί τινα to be struck with panic fear of . . , Soph., Thuc. 2. generally, of sudden passion, to be stricken, Aesch., etc.

ἔκπλοος, contr. -πλους, ὁ, (ἐκπλέω) a sailing out, leaving port, Aesch., Thuc., etc. II. a passage out, entrance of a harbour, Aesch., Xen.

ἐκ-πλύνω [ῡ], aor. 1 ἐξέπλυνα : —to wash out, esp. to wash out colours from cloths, Plat. : —Pass. to be washed out, Hdt. II. to wash clean, Ar. Hence

ἔκπλῠτος, ον, to be washed out, of colours, Plat. : —metaph. washed out, Aesch.

ἐκπλώω, Ion. for ἐκπλέω.

ἐκ-πνέω, Ep. -πνείω : f. -πνεύσομαι or -οῦμαι : —to breathe out or forth, Plat. ; κεραυνὸς ἐκπνέων φλόγα Aesch. 2. βίον ἐκπν. to breathe one's last, expire, Id., Eur. ; also, ἐκπν. θυμόν, ψυχήν Id. II. absol. to cease blowing, to become calm, Id. 2. to blow outwards, of wind, Hdt., Thuc. : to burst out, Soph.

ἐκπνοή, ἡ, a breathing out, expiring, Plat.

ἐκ-ποδών, Adv. (ἐκ ποδῶν) opp. to ἐμποδών, away from the feet, i. e. out of the way, Hdt., Aesch., etc. : —c. dat., ἐκπ. χωρεῖν τινι to get out of his way, Eur. : —ἐκποδὼν ποιεῖσθαι to put out of the way, Xen. : c. gen., ἐκπ. χθονός far from it, Eur.

ἐκ-ποιέω, f. ήσω, to put out : I. to put out a child, i. e. give him in adoption, Isae. II. Med. to produce, bring forth, Ar. III. to make complete, finish, finish off, Hdt. : —c. gen. materiae, Παρίου λίθου τὸ ἔμπροσθε ἐξηποίησαν they made all the front of Parian marble, Id. Hence

ἐκποίησις, εως, ἡ, a putting forth, emission, Hdt.

ἐκποίητος, ον, given in adoption, Aeschin.

ἐκ-πολεμέω, f. ήσω, to excite to war, make hostile, Xen.

ἐκ-πολεμόω, f. ώσω, to make hostile, to involve in war, Hdt., Thuc. : —Pass. to become an enemy to, be at feud with, τινι Hdt. Hence

ἐκπολέμωσις, εως, ἡ, a making hostile, Plut.

ἐκ-πολιορκέω, f. ήσω, to force a besieged town to surrender, Thuc., Xen. : —Pass. to be forced to surrender, Thuc.

ἐκ-πομπεύω, f. σω, to walk in state, to strut, Luc.

ἐκπομπή, ἡ, (ἐκπέμπω) a sending out or forth, Thuc.

ἐκ-πονέω, f. ήσω, to work out, finish off, Lat. elaborare, Ar. ; κῆμέ μαλθακὸν ἐξεπόνασε σιδαρέῳ wrought me soft-hearted from iron-hearted, Theocr. ; ἐκπ. τινά to deck him out, Eur. : —Pass. to be brought to perfection, Thuc.; ἐκπεπονημένος σῖτος corn fully prepared for use, Xen. ; ἐκπεπονῆσθαι τὰ σώματα to be in good training or practice, Id. 2. to execute, Eur. ; so in Med., Id. 3. to provide by labour, earn, Id. : —c. acc. et inf., τοὺς θεοὺς ἐκπ. φράζειν to prevail on the gods to tell, Id. 4. absol. to work hard, Id., Xen. 5. to work out by searching, to search out, Eur. 6. of food, to digest it by labour, Xen. 7. to work at, work well, Theocr. 8. in Pass. to be worn out, Lat. confici, Plut.

ἐκ-πορεύω, f. σω, to make to go out, fetch out, Eur. : —Med., with fut. med. and aor. 1 pass., to go out or forth, march out, Xen.

ἐκ-πορθέω, f. ήσω, to pillage, Eur., etc. : —Pass., of a person, to be undone, Soph., Eur. II. to carry off as plunder, Thuc. Hence

ἐκπορθήτωρ, ορος, ὁ, a waster, destroyer, Eur.

ἐκ-πορθμεύω, f. σω, to carry away by sea : —Eur. has pf. pass. ἐκπεπόρθμευται in both pass. and med. sense.

ἐκ-πορίζω, f. Att. ιῶ, to invent, contrive, Eur. II. to provide, furnish, Soph., Ar., etc. : —Med. to provide for oneself, procure, Thuc.

ἐκ-πορνεύω, f. σω, to commit fornication, N. T.

ἐκ-ποτάομαι, Ion. -έομαι, Dep. to fly out or forth, of snow-flakes, Il. : metaph., πᾶ τὰς φρένας ἐκπεπότασαι (2 sing. Dor. pf.) = quae te dementia cepit? Theocr.

ἐκ-πράσσω, Att. -ττω, f. ξω, to do completely, to bring about, achieve, Lat. efficere, Aesch., etc. ; τὸν καλλίνικον ἐξεπράξατε ἐς γόον γε have made the hymn of triumph end in wailing, Eur. II. to make an end of, kill, destroy, Lat. conficere, Trag. III. to exact, levy, Eur. ; c. dupl. acc., χρήματα ἐκπρ. τινά to exact money from a person, Thuc. 2. to exact punishment for a thing, to avenge, Soph., Eur. : —so in Med., Hdt.

ἐκπρεπής, ές, (ἐκπρέπω) distinguished out of all, pre-eminent, remarkable, Il. ; μεγέθει ἐκπρεπεστάτη Aesch. ; εἶδος ἐκπρεπεστάτη Eur. II. = ἔξω τοῦ πρέποντος, unseemly, monstrous, Thuc. : so Adv. -πῶς, without reasonable grounds, Id.

ἐκ-πρέπω, to be excellent in a thing, τινί Eur.

ἔκπρησις, εως, ἡ, (ἐκ, πίμπρημι) a setting on fire, inflaming, Plut.

ἐκπρήσσω, Ion. for ἐκπράσσω.

ἐκ-πρίασθαι, aor. 2 (v. *πρίαμαι), to buy off, Oratt.

ἐκ-πρίω, f. -πρίουμαι, to saw out, Thuc.

ἐκ-πρόθεσμος, ον, beyond the appointed day, too late for a thing, c. gen., Luc.

ἐκ-προθυμέομαι, to be very zealous, Eur.

ἐκ-προΐημι, f. -προήσω, to send forth, Eur.

ἐκ-προκαλέομαι, Med. to call to oneself or summon out of, ἐκπροκαλεσσαμένη μεγάροιο Od.

ἐκ-προκρίνω [ῐ], f. -κρῐνῶ, to choose out, πόλεος ἐκπροκριθεῖσα Eur.

ἐκ-προλείπω, f. ψω, to forsake, abandon, Od.

ἐκ-προρέω, f. -ρεύσομαι, to flow forth from, Anth.

ἐκ-προτῑμάω, f. ήσω, to honour above all, Soph.

ἐκ-προφεύγω, f. -φεύξομαι, to flee away from, Anth.

ἐκ-προχέω, f. -χεῶ, to pour forth, Anth.

ἐκ-πτερύσσομαι, Dep. to spread the wings, Luc.

ἐκ-πτήσσω, f. ξω, to scare out of, οἴκων με ἐξέπταξας (Dor.) Eur.

ἐκ-πτοέω, f. ήσω, = foreg., Tzetz. :—Pass. to be struck with admiration, Eur.

ἐκ-πτύω, f. ύσω, also -ύσομαι [ῠ], to spit out of, c. gen., Od.　II. to spit in token of disgust, Ar. :— to spit at, abominate, N. T.

ἐκ-πῠθέσθαι, aor. 2 inf. of sq.

ἐκ-πῠνθάνομαι, f. -πεύσομαι : aor. 2 ἐξεπῠθόμην : Dep. : —to search out, make enquiry, Il., Eur.　2. c. acc. to enquire about, hear of, learn, Soph. ; ἐκπ. τινος to make inquiry of him, Ar.

ἐκ-πῠρόω, f. ώσω, to burn to ashes, consume utterly, Eur. : Pass. to catch fire, be burnt up, Id.　Hence

ἐκπύρωσις [ῠ], εως, ή, a conflagration, Luc.

ἔκπυστος, ον, (ἐκπυνθάνομαι) discovered, Thuc.

ἔκπωμα, ατος, τό, (ἐκπίνω) a drinking-cup, beaker, Hdt., Soph., etc.

ἐκπωτάομαι, poët. for ἐκποτάομαι, Babr.

ἐκράανθεν, Ep. for -ησαν, 3 pl. aor. 1 pass. of κραίνω.

ἐκρᾰγῆναι, aor. 2 pass. inf. of ἐκρήγνυμι.

ἐκρᾰγήσομαι, fut. 2 pass. of ἐκρήγνυμι.

ἔκρᾱνα, for ἐκρήηνα, Ep. aor. 1 of κραίνω.

ἐκράθην [ᾱ], aor. 1 pass. of κεράννυμι.

ἐκ-ραίνω, f. ᾰνῶ, to scatter out of, make to fall in drops from, Soph.

ἐκρέμω, for ἐκρέμασο, 2 sing. of κρέμαμαι.

ἐκ-ρέω, f. -ρεύσομαι : pf. ἐξερρύηκα : aor. 2 pass. ἐξερρύην in act. sense :—to flow out or forth, Il., Hdt., Plat.　2. of feathers, to fall off, Ar.　3. metaph. to fall away, disappear, Lat. effluere, Plat.　II. c. acc. cogn. ἐκρεῖ, let fall, χάριν Anth.

ἐκ-ρήγνῡμι, f. -ρήξω, to break off, snap asunder, Il. ; c. gen., ὕδωρ ἐξέρρηξεν ὁδοῖο the water broke off a piece of the road, Ib. :—Pass. to break or snap asunder, Hdt.　II. c. acc. cogn. to let break forth, break out with, Plut., Luc. :—Pass. to break out, of an ulcer, Hdt., Aesch. ; of a quarrel, ἐς μέσον ἐξερράγη it broke out in public, Hdt. ; of persons, to break out into passionate words, Id.　III. sometimes also intr. in Act., οὔ ποτ' ἐκρήξει μάχη Soph.

ἐκ-ριζόω, f. ώσω, to root out, N. T.

ἐκ-ριπίζω, f. ίσω, to fan the flame, stir up, Plut.

ἐκ-ρίπτω, f. ψω, to cast forth, Aesch., Soph.

ἐκροή, ή, (ἐκρέω) = ἔκροος, Plat.　II. an issue, Id.

ἔκροος, contr. -ρους, ὁ, (ἐκρέω) a flowing out, outflow, outfall, Hdt.

ἐκ-ροφέω, f. ήσω, to drink out, gulp down, Ar.

ἐκρύβην [ῠ], aor. 2 pass. of κρύπτω.

ἐκ-ρύομαι, f. -ρύσομαι [ῠ], to deliver, Eur.

ἐκρύφθην, aor. 1 pass. of κρύπτω.

ἐκ-σᾰλάσσω, to shake violently, Anth.

ἐκσᾰόω, aor. 1 ἐξεσάωσα, Ep. for ἐκσώζω, Hom.

ἐκ-σείω, f. σω, to shake out of, τί τινος Hdt. :—Pass., Ar.

ἐκ-σεύομαι : pf. ἐξέσσῠμαι : 3 pl. plqpf. ἐξέσσῠτο : aor. 1 ἐξεσύθην [ῠ] :—to rush out or burst forth from a place, c. gen., Hom. : absol. to rush out, Id.

ἐκ-σημαίνω, f. -ᾰνῶ, to disclose, indicate, Soph.

ἐκ-σῑγάομαι, Pass. to be put to utter silence, Anth.

ἐκ-σκεδάννῡμι, f. -σκεδάσω, to scatter to the wind, Ar.

ἐκ-σκευάζω, f. σω, to disfurnish of tools and implements, Dem.

ἐκ-σμάω, to wipe out, wipe clean, Hdt.

ἐκ-σοβέω, f. ήσω, to scare away, Anth.

ἐκ-σπάω, f. άσω, to draw out, Il. ; so in Med., ἐκσπασσάμενος ἔγχεα having drawn out their spears, Ib.

ἐκ-σπένδω, f. -σπείσω, to pour out as a libation, Eur.

ἔκ-σπονδος, ον, (σπονδή) = ἔξω τῶν σπονδῶν, out of the treaty, excluded from it, Thuc., Xen.

ἐκ-στάδιος, ον, (ἑξ, στάδιον) six stades long, Luc.

ἔκστᾰσις, εως, ή, (ἐξίστημι) any displacement : entrancement, astonishment, N. T. ; a trance, Ib.

ἐκστᾰτικός, ή, όν, inclined to depart from, c. gen., Arist.

ἐκστέλλω, f. -στελῶ, to fit out, equip, Soph.

ἐκ-στέφω, f. ψω, to deck with garlands, Eur. ; of suppliants, κρᾶτας ἐξεστεμμένοι Id. ; but, ἱκτηρίοις κλάδοισιν ἐξεστεμμένοι with garlands on the suppliant olive-branches, Soph.

ἐκστρᾰτεία, ή, a going out on service, Luc.　From

ἐκ-στρᾰτεύω, f. σω, to march out, Thuc., Xen.　II. in Med., absol. to take the field, Hdt., Thuc.　2. to have ended the campaign, Id.

ἐκ-στρᾰτοπεδεύομαι, f. -εύσομαι, Dep. with pf. pass. to encamp outside, Thuc., Xen.

ἐκ-στρέφω, f. ψω, to turn out of, root up from a place, c. gen., Il.　II. to turn inside out, Ar. : metaph. to alter entirely, Id.

ἐκ-σῡρίσσω, Att. -ττω, f. -ξω, to hiss off the stage, Lat. explodere, Dem.

ἐκ-σύρω [ῠ], to drag out, Anth., in aor. 2 pass. ἐξεσύρην [ῠ].

ἐκσφρᾱγίζομαι, f. Att. -ιοῦμαι, Pass. to be shut out from, Eur.

ἐκ-σώζω, f. -σώσω, to preserve from danger, keep safe, Hdt., Soph., etc. ; ἐκσ. τινά τινος to save one from another, Eur. ; ἐκσ. τινὰ ἐς φάος to bring one safe to light, Id. :—Med. to save oneself, Hdt. ; or to save for oneself, Aesch. :—Pass. to flee for safety, Id.

ἐκ-σωρεύω, f. σω, to heap or pile up, Eur.

ἔκτᾰ, Ep. 3 sing. aor. 2 of κτείνω :—ἔκτᾰμεν, ἔκτᾰν, 1 and 3 pl.

ἐκτάδην [ᾰ], Adv. (ἐκτείνω) outstretched, Eur.

ἐκτάδιος [ᾰ], η, ον, (ἐκτείνω) outstretched, outspread, Il.

ἔκτᾰθεν, Ep. for ἐκτάθησαν, 3 pl. aor. 1 pass. of κτείνω.

ἐκτᾰθήσομαι, fut. pass. of ἐκτείνω.

ἐκταῖος, α, ον, (ἑξ) on the sixth day, Xen.　II. = ἕκτος, sixth, Anth.

ἐκτάμην, Ep. aor. 2 med. of κτείνω.

ἐκτάμνω, Ion. for ἐκτέμνω.

ἔκτᾰμον, Ep. for ἐξέταμον, aor. 2 of ἐκτέμνω.

ἔκτᾰν, Ep. 3 pl. aor. 2 of κτείνω.

ἔκτᾰνον, aor. 2 of κτείνω.

ἐκ-τᾰνύω, f. ύσω : Ep. aor. 1 ἐξετάνυσσα, = ἐκτείνω, to stretch out (on the ground), lay low, Il. :—Pass. to lie outstretched, ἐξετανύσθη Ib.　2. to stretch tight, Od.

ἐκ-τᾰράσσω, Att. -ττω, f. ξω, to throw into great trouble, to agitate, Plut.

ἔκτᾰσις, εως, ἡ, (ἐκτείνω) extension, Plat.

ἐκ-τάσσω, Att. -ττω, f. ξω, to draw out in battle-order, of the officers :—Med. to draw themselves out, of the soldiers, Xen.

ἐκτέατο, Ion. for ἔκτηντο, 3 pl. plqpf. of κτάομαι.

ἐκ-τείνω, f. -τενῶ: pf. -τέτᾰκα, pass. -τέτᾰμαι :—to stretch out, Hdt., Att.: τὰ γόνατα ἐκτ. to straighten the knees, Ar. : ἐκτ. νέκυν to lay one dead, Eur. :—Pass. to be outstretched, lie at length, Soph.   2. to stretch or spread out a net, Aesch. : to extend the line of an army, Eur.   II. to stretch out, prolong, λόγον Hdt., Att.   III. to put to the full stretch, of a horse put to full speed, Xen. ; πᾶσαν προθυμίην ἐκτ. to put forth all one's zeal, Hdt. :—metaph. in Pass. to be on the rack, Soph.

ἐκ-τειχίζω, f. Att. ἰῶ, to fortify completely, Thuc., Xen.; τεῖχος ἐκτ. to build it from the ground, Ar.

ἐκ-τεκνόω, f. ώσω, to generate, Eur., in Med.

ἐκ-τελευτάω, f. ήσω, to bring quite to an end, accomplish, Aesch. :—Pass. to be quite the end of, τινός Soph.

ἐκ-τελέω, Ep. impf. ἐξετέλειον : f. -τελέσω :—to bring quite to an end, to accomplish, achieve, Hom., Hdt. : —Pass., f. inf. ἐκτελέεσθαι, to be accomplished, Il., etc.

ἐκ-τελής, ές, (τέλος) brought to an end, perfect, Aesch. ; of corn, ripe, Hes. ; of persons, Eur.

ἐκ-τέμνω, Ep. and Ion. τάμνω : f. -τεμῶ :—to cut out, Il., Hdt. ; ὀϊστὸν ἐκτάμνειν μηροῦ to cut an arrow from the thigh, Il.   2. to cut trees out of a wood, cut down, Il. ; of planks, to hew out, hew into shape, ὃς νήϊον ἐκτάμνῃσιν (Ep. for -τέμνῃ) Ib.   3. to cut away, sever, Pind., Plat.   II. to castrate, Hdt.

ἐκτένεια, ἡ, intensity, zeal, earnestness, N. T. From

ἐκτενής, ές, (ἐκτείνω) intense, zealous, instant, N. T.

ἐκτέος, α, ον, verb. Adj. of ἔχω, to be held, Ar.   II. ἐκτέον, one must have, Xen.

ἐκτεφρόω, f. ώσω, to burn to ashes, calcine, Strab.

ἐκ-τήκω, f. ξω : aor. 2 ἐξέτᾰκον :—to melt out, destroy by melting, Eur., Ar.   2. metaph. to let melt away, let pine or waste away, Eur.   II. Pass., with pf. ἐκτέτηκα, aor. 2 ἐξετάκην [ᾰ], to melt, pine or waste away, Id. ; τόδ' μήποτ' ἐκτακείη may it never melt from my remembrance, Aesch.

ἔκτημαι, for κέκτημαι, pf. of κτάομαι.

ἐκτη-μόριοι, οἱ, those who paid ⅙th of the produce, Plut.

ἐκτησάμην, aor. 1 of κτάομαι.

ἐκ-τίθημι, f. -θήσω, to set out, place outside, Od. : to expose on a desert island or to expose a new-born child, Hdt., Att. :—Med. to export, Plut.   II. to set up in public, exhibit publicly, νόμους Dem.

ἐκ-τίλλω, f. -τῐλῶ, to pluck out hair :—Pass., κόμην ἐκτετιλμένος having one's hair plucked out, Anacr.

ἐκ-τῑμάω, to honour highly, Soph.

ἔκ-τῑμος, ον, (τιμή) not shewing honour, Soph.

ἐκ-τῐνάσσω, f. ξω, to shake out :—Pass., ἐκ δ' ἐτινάχθεν (Ep. for -ησαν) ὀδόντες Il.   2. to shake off dust from one's feet, N. T. : so in Med., Ib.

ἐκ-τίνω [ῐ], f. -τίσω [ῑ] : aor. 1 ἐξέτισα :—to pay off, pay in full, Hdt., Att. ; δίκην ἐκτ. to pay full penalty, Eur. ; τινός for a thing, Hdt.   II. Med.

to exact full payment for a thing, avenge, c. acc. rei, Soph., Eur. ; to take vengeance on, τινά Id.

ἐκ-τιτρώσκω, f. -τρώσω, to bring forth untimely : to miscarry, Hdt.

ἔκτοθεν, poët. Adv. (ἐκτός) = ἔκτοσθεν, from without, outside, c. gen., ἔκτοθεν ἄλλων μνηστήρων outside their circle, apart from them, Od. ; πύργων δ' ἔκτ. βαλών having struck them from the wall, Aesch.   2. absol. outside, Trag. ; ἔκτ. γαμεῖν to marry from an alien house, Eur.

ἐκ-τόθι, for ἐκ τόθεν, v. τόθεν.

ἔκτοθι, Ep. Adv. (ἐκτός) out of, outside, c. gen., Il.

ἐκ-τολῠπεύω, f. σω, to wind a ball of wool quite off : metaph. to bring quite to an end, Hes., Aesch.

ἐκτομή, ἡ, (ἐκτεμεῖν) a cutting out, Plut.   2. castration, Hdt., etc.   II. a segment, piece, Plut.

ἐκτομίας, ου, ὁ, (ἐκτέμνω) a eunuch, Hdt.

ἐκτομίς, ίδος, (ἐκτέμνω) fem. Adj. cutting down, Anth.

ἐκ-τοξεύω, f. σω, to shoot out, shoot away, Hdt. :— metaph. ἐξετόξευσεν has shot away all its arrows, i. e. has no resource left, Eur.   II. absol. to shoot from a place, shoot arrows, Xen.

ἐκ-τοπίζω, f. σω, to take oneself from a place, go abroad, like ἀποδημέω, Arist. :—metaph. of a speaker, to wander from the point, Id.

ἐκτόπιος, α, ον, = ἔκτοπος, Soph. ; ἠνύσατ' ἐκτοπίαν φλόγα ye have put away the fire, Id.

ἔκ-τοπος, ον, away from a place, away from, c. gen., Soph.   2. absol. distant, Id. ; ἔκτοπος ἔστω let him leave the place, Eur.   II. foreign, strange, οὐδενὸς πρὸς ἐκτόπου by no strange hand, Soph.   2. out of the way, strange, extraordinary, Ar.

ἐκ-τορέω, f. ήσω, to kill by piercing, h. Hom.

ἕκτος, η, ον, (ἕξ) sixth, Lat. sextus, Hom., etc.

ἐκτός, Adv., (ἐκ) outside, opp. to ἐντός :   1. as Prep. with gen. outside, out of, far from, c. gen., Hom. : outside of, free from, Hdt., Att. ; ἐκτὸς ἐλπίδος beyond hope, Lat. praeter spem, Soph.   2. of Time, beyond, Hdt.   3. except, ἐκτὸς ὀλίγων Xen.   II. absol., τὰ ἐκτός external things, Eur.   III. with Verbs of motion, ῥίπτειν ἐκτός to throw out, Soph., etc. Hence

ἔκτοσε, Adv. outwards, c. gen. out of, Od.

ἔκτοσθε and before vowels -θεν, Adv., = ἔκτοθεν, outside, c. gen., Hom. :—absol., Od.

ἐκ-τρᾳγῳδέω, f. ήσω, to deck out in tragic phrase, exaggerate, Luc.

ἐκ-τράπεζος, ον, (τράπεζα) banished from the table, Luc.

ἐκτράπελος [ᾰ], ον, (ἐκτρέπομαι) turning from the common course, devious, strange, Theogn.

ἐκτράπω, Ion. for ἐκτρέπω.

ἐκ-τρᾰχηλίζω, f. Att. ἰῶ, of a horse, to throw the rider over its head, Xen. :—Pass. to break one's neck, Ar. : metaph. to plunge headlong into destruction, Dem.

ἐκτρᾱχύνω [ῠ], f. ῠνῶ, to make rough, Luc. :—metaph. to exasperate, Plut.

ἐκ-τρέπω, Ion. -τράπω, f. ψω, to turn out of the course, to turn aside, c. acc., Hdt., Att. :—Pass. and Med., c. gen. to turn aside from, Soph. : absol. to turn aside, Hdt., Xen.   2. to turn a person off the road, order him out of the way, Soph. :—Pass. and Med. ἐκτοέπεσθαί τινα to get out of one's way,

avoid him, Dem.　3. τὴν δρῶσαν ἐκτρέπειν *to prevent* her from acting, Soph.　4. ἀσπίδας θύρσοις ἔκτρ. *to turn* shields *and flee before* the thyrsus, Eur.

ἐκ-τρέφω, f. -θρέψω, *to bring up from childhood, rear up*, Hdt., Att. :—Med. *for oneself*, h. Hom., Soph.

ἐκ-τρέχω, f. -θρέξομαι and -δρᾰμοῦμαι :—*to run out or forth, make a sally*, Il., Thuc.　2. *to run off or away*, Ar.　3. *to run beyond bounds, exceed bounds*, Soph.

ἐκ-τρίβω [ῑ], f. ψω: f. 2 pass. -τρῐβήσομαι : pf. -τέτρῐμμαι :—*to rub out*, πῦρ ἐκτρ. *to produce* fire *by rubbing*, Xen.:—*to rub hard*, Soph.　II. *to rub out*, i. e. *to destroy root and branch*, Hdt., Eur. ; βίον ἐκτρ. *to bring* life *to a wretched end*, Soph. :—Pass., πρόρριζος ἐκτέτριπται Hdt.　III. *to rub constantly, wear out*, Eur.

ἐκτροπή, ή, (ἐκτρέπω) *a turning off or aside*, Thuc.　II. (from Med.) *a turning aside, escape*, μόχθων *from* labours, Aesch.　2. ἐκτρ. ὁδοῦ *a place to which one turns from* the road, *a resting-place*, Lat. *deverticulum*, Ar.

ἐκ-τρύχόω, f. ώσω, *to wear out, exhaust*, Thuc.

ἐκ-τρώγω, f. -τρώξομαι, *to eat up, devour*, Ar.

ἔκτρωμα, τό, *a child untimely born, an abortion*, N. T.

ἔκτῠπον, Ep. aor. 2 of κτυπέω.

ἐκ-τῠπος, ον, *worked in high relief*: ἔκτυπος, ὁ, *a figure worked in relief, a cameo*, Inscr. Hence

ἐκ-τῠπόω, f. ώσω, *to model or work in relief*, Xen.

ἐκ-τυφλόω, f. ώσω, *to make quite blind*, Hdt., Xen., etc. Hence

ἐκτύφλωσις, εως, ή, *a making blind*, Hdt.

ἐκῠρά, ή, *a mother-in-law, step-mother*, = πενθερά, Il.

ἐκῠρός, ὁ, *a father-in-law, step-father*, = πενθερός, Il.

ἔκῠσα, aor. 1 of κυνέω :—but ἔκῠσα, aor. 1 of κύω.

ἐκφᾰγεῖν, used as aor. 2 of ἐξεσθίω.

ἐκ-φαιδρύνω [ῠ], *to make quite bright, clear away*, Eur.

ἐκ-φαίνω, f. -φᾰνῶ, Ion. -φανέω : aor. 1 ἐξέφηνα :—*to shew forth, bring to light, disclose, reveal, make manifest*, Il., Hdt., etc. :—Pass. *to shew oneself, shine forth, come forth to view*, Il.　2. *to exhibit*, κακότητα Hdt.　3. ἐκφ. πόλεμον *to declare* war, Xen. Hence

ἐκφᾰνής, ές, *shewing itself, manifest*, Aesch., Plat.

ἐκφάσθαι, inf. med. of ἔκφημι.

ἔκφᾰσις, εως, Ion. ιος, ή, (ἔκφημι) *a declaration*, Hdt.

ἔκ-φᾰτος, ον, *beyond power of speech* : Adv. -τως, *ineffably, impiously*, Aesch.

ἐκ-φαυλίζω, f. Att. ιῶ, *to depreciate*, Luc.

ἐκ-φέρω, f. ἐξοίσω : fut. med. ἐξοίσομαι in pass. sense :—*to carry out of* a place, c. gen., or ἐκ τόπου, Il., Hdt.　2. *to carry out* a corpse for burial, Lat. *efferre*, Il., etc.　3. *to carry off* as prize or reward, Ib. : so in Med., Hdt., Att.　4. *to carry out of* the sea, *to throw ashore*, Hdt., Eur. :—Pass., with fut. med., *to come to land, be cast ashore*, Hdt.　II. *to bring forth*,　1. of women, of the earth, *to bring forth, produce*, Id.　2. *to bring about, accomplish*, Il.　3. *to bring out, publish*, Ar. : ἐκφ. χρηστήριον *to deliver* an oracle, Hdt. :—of public measures, *to bring forward*, ἐκφ. ἐς τὸν δῆμον Id., Dem.　4. generally *to disclose, tell, betray*, Hdt. :—Med., ἐκφέρεσθαι γνώμην *to declare one's* opinion, Id.　5. *to put forth, exert*, δύναμιν Eur. ;

and in Med., Soph.　6. ἐκφέρειν πόλεμον, Lat. *inferre bellum, to begin* war, Hdt., Xen.　7. *to bear the marks of* a thing, Eur.　III. Pass. *to be carried beyond bounds, be carried away*, Soph., Thuc., etc.　IV. *to carry to a certain point*, Soph., Plat.　V. intr. (sub. ἑαυτόν) *to shoot forth* (before the rest), Il. : *to run away*, Xen.　2. *to come to fulfilment, come to an end*, Soph.

ἐκ-φεύγω, f. ξομαι and ξοῦμαι, *to flee out or away, escape*, Od., Aesch., etc. :—*to be acquitted*, Ar.　2. c. gen. *to escape out of, flee from*, Hom.　3. c. acc. *to escape*, Il., Hdt., etc.　b. of things, ἐκφεύγει μέ τι something *escapes* me, Soph., Eur.

ἔκ-φημι, *to speak out or forth, speak loudly* : Med., ἔπος ἐκφάσθαι (aor. 2 inf.) Od.

ἐκ-φθείρω, f. -φθερῶ : aor. 2 pass. ἐξέφθαρην [ᾰ] :—*to destroy utterly* :—Pass. ἐκφθείρομαι, *to be undone, ruined*, Eur. : *to vanish, pack off*, Ar.

ἐκ-φθίνω [ῐ], in 3 plqpf. pass., ἐξέφθῐτο οἶνος νηῶν the wine had all been *consumed out of* the ships, *had vanished from* the ships, Od. ; 3 pl. pf. pass. ἐξέφθινται they *have utterly perished*, Aesch.

ἐκ-φῐλέω, f. ήσω, *to kiss heartily*, Anth.

ἐκ-φλαυρίζω, Att. for ἐκφαυλίζω, Plut.

ἐκ-φλέγω, f. ξω, *to set on fire*, Ar.

ἐκ-φοβέω, f. ήσω, *to frighten away, affright*, Aesch., Plat., etc. ; τὸ ἐκφοβῆσαι so *as to cause alarm*, Thuc. ; ἐκφ. τινὰ ἐκ δεμνίων Eur. :—Pass. *to be much afraid, to fear greatly*, c. acc., Soph.

ἔκ-φοβος, ον, *affrighted*, N. T.

ἐκ-φοινίσσω, f. ξω, *to make all red or bloody*, Eur.

ἐκ-φοιτάω, Ion. -έω, f. ήσω, *to go out constantly, be in the habit of going out*, Hdt., Eur.　2. of things, *to be spread abroad*, Plut.

ἐκφορά, ή, (ἐκφέρω) *a carrying out* of a corpse to burial, Aesch., Ar.　II. (from Pass.) of horses, *a running away*, Xen.

ἐκ-φορέω, f. ήσω, = ἐκφέρω, *to carry out* a corpse for burial, Od. :—generally *to carry out*, Hdt. :—Med. *to take out with one*, Eur., etc. :—Pass. *to move forth*, Il.　2. *to carry quite out, leave none behind*, of earth dug from a trench, Hdt.　3. Pass. *to be cast on shore*, Id.

ἐκφόριον, τό, (ἐκφέρω) *payment on produce, rent, tithe*, Hdt.

ἔκφορος, ον, (ἐκφέρω) *to be carried out, exportable*, Ar.　2. *to be made known or divulged*, Eur.　II. act. *prepared to weed out*, as a gardener does noxious plants, Aesch.

ἐκ-φορτίζομαι, Pass. *to be sold for exportation, to be kidnapped, betrayed*, Soph.

ἐκ-φράζω, f. σω, *to tell over, recount*, Aesch., Eur.

ἔκφρασις, εως, ή, *a description*, Luc.

ἐκ-φρέω (v. εἰσφρέω) : poët. 1 pl. impf. ἐξεφρείομεν : f. -φρήσω: aor. 1 -έφρησα :—*to let out, bring out*, Eur., Ar.

ἐκ-φροντίζω, f. Att. ιῶ, *to think out, discover*, Lat. *excogitare*, Eur., Ar., etc.

ἔκ-φρων, ον, gen. ονος, (φρήν) *out of one's mind, senseless*, Dem. : also, *frensied, enthusiastic*, of poets, Plat.

ἐκφυγγάνω, = ἐκφεύγω, Aesch.

ἔκφυγον, Ep. for ἐξέφυγον, aor. 2 of ἐκφεύγω.

ἐκ-φῠλάσσω, f. ξω, *to watch carefully*, Soph., Eur.

ἐκ-φυλλο-φορέω, f. ήσω, to condemn by leaves, used of the Athen. βουλή, which gave their votes written on olive-leaves, Aeschin.

ἔκ-φῦλος, ον, (φυλή) out of the tribe, alien :—metaph. strange, unnatural, Plut.

ἐκφῦναι, aor. 2 inf. of ἐκφύω.

ἐκ-φυσάω, f. ήσω, to blow out, ποταμὸς ἐκφυσᾶ μένος pours forth its strength, Aesch. : metaph., ἐκφ. πόλεμον to blow up a war from a spark, Ar. II. to breathe out, ὕπνον ἐκφ. i. e. to snore, Theocr.

ἐκ-φυσιάω, poët. for ἐκφυσάω, Aesch.

ἐκ-φύω, f. ύσω [ῡ], to generate from another, to beget, of the male, Soph., etc. 2. of the female, to bear, Id. : also, to produce a plant, Dem. II. Pass., with pf. and aor. 2 act., to be born from another, c. gen., Il., Soph., etc. ; λάδημα ἐκπεφυκός a tattler by nature, Id.

ἐκ-φωνέω, f. ήσω, to cry out, Plut.

ἐκ-χαλάω, f. άσω [ἄ], to let go from, τί τινος Anth.

ἐκ-χαλινόω, f. ώσω, to unbridle, Plut.

ἐκ-χαυνόω, f. ώσω, to stuff out, to make vain and arrogant, Eur.

ἐκ-χέω, f. -χεῶ: aor. 1 ἐξέχεα, Ep. ἔκχενα, med. ἐκ-χευάμην :—to pour out, properly of liquids, Il., Aesch., etc. : metaph., (in Med.) ἐκχέυατ᾽ ὀϊστούς he poured forth his arrows, Od. 2. of words, Aesch., etc. 3. to pour out like water, squander, waste, one's substance, Id., etc. II. Pass., 3 pl. plqpf. ἐξεκέχυντο, Ep. syncop. aor. 2 ἐξέχυτο or ἔκχῦτο, part. ἐκχύμενος [ῠ] :—to pour out, stream out or forth, properly of liquids, Hom. :—metaph. of persons, Id. : —generally, to be spread out, Od. 2. to be poured out like water, forgotten, Theogn., Plat. 3. to give oneself up to joy, to be overjoyed, Ar. ; ἐκχ. γελῶν to burst out laughing, Anth. 4. to lie languidly, Id.

ἐκ-χορεύω, f. σω, to break out of the chorus : Med. to drive out of the chorus, Eur.

ἐκ-χράω, f. -χρήσω : aor. 2 ἐξέχρην :—to declare as an oracle, tell out, Soph. II. to suffice, Hdt. :—impers., like ἀποχρᾷ, c. inf., κῶς βασιλέϊ ἐκχρήσει ; how will it suffice him ? how will he be content to . . ? Id.

ἐκ-χρηματίζομαι, Dep. to squeeze money from, levy contributions on, τινα Thuc.

ἐκχύτης [ῠ], ου, ὁ, (ἐκχέω) a spendthrift, Luc.

ἔκχυτο, 3 sing. Ep. aor. 2 pass. of ἐκχέω.

ἔκχῦτος, ον, (ἐκχέω) poured forth, unconfined, outstretched, Anth.

ἐκ-χώννυμαι, pf. -κέχωσμαι : aor. 1 ἐξεχώσθην :—Pass. to be raised on a bank or mound, Hdt.

ἐκ-χωρέω, f. ήσω, to go out and away, depart, emigrate, Hdt. 2. to slip out of, ἐξεχώρησεν ἐξ ἄρθρων was dislocated, Id. 3. to give way, Soph., Eur.

ἐκ-ψύχω [ῡ], f. ξω, to give up the ghost, expire, N. T.

ἘΚΩ´Ν, ἑκοῦσα, ἑκόν, willing, of free will, readily, Hom., etc. 2. wittingly, purposely, ἑκὼν ἡμάρτανε φωτός Il., Att. 3. in Prose, ἑκὼν εἶναι or ἑκών, as far as depends on my will, as far as concerns me, mostly with a negat., Hdt., Plat.

ἐλάα, Att. for ἐλαία.

ἐλάαν, Ep. for ἐλᾶν, inf. pres. of ἐλάω ; also Ep. fut. inf. of ἐλαύνω.

ἘΛΑΙ´Α, Att. ἐλάα [ᾱᾱ], ἡ, the olive-tree, Lat. olea,

oliva, Hom., etc. ; said to have been produced by Athena in her contest with Poseidon, Hdt., Soph. ; φέρεσθαι ἐκτὸς τῶν ἐλαῶν to run beyond the olives, which stood at the end of the Athenian race-course, i. e. to go too far, Ar. II. the fruit of the olive-tree, an olive, Id. Hence

ἐλαιήεις, εσσα, εν, planted with olives, Anth.

ἐλαιηρός, ή, όν, oily, of oil, Anth.

ἐλάϊνεος, α, ον, = sq., Od.

ἐλάϊνος, η, ον, (ἐλαία) of olive-wood, Hom.

ἐλαιο-λόγος, Att. ἐλαο-, ον, (λέγω) an olive-gatherer, Ar.

ἔλαιον, τό, (ἐλαία) olive-oil, Lat. oleum, olivum, Hom.

ἐλαιο-πώλης, ου, ὁ, (πωλέομαι) an oil-merchant, Dem.

ἔλαιος, ὁ, (ἐλαία) the wild olive, Lat. oleaster, Soph.

ἐλαιο-φόρος, Att. ἐλαο-φόρος, ον, olive-bearing, Eur.

ἐλαιο-φυής, ές, (φύω) olive-planted, Eur.

ἐλαιό-φυτος, ον, olive-planted, Aesch.

ἐλαΐς, ίδος, ἡ, (ἐλαία) an olive-tree : Att. pl. ἐλᾷδες Ar.

ἐλαιών, ῶνος, ὁ, (ἐλαία) an olive-yard, Lat. olivetum : the Mount of Olives, Olivet, N. T.

ἔλ-ανδρος, ον, (ἑλεῖν) man-destroying, of Helen, Aesch.

ἐλαολόγος, ἐλαοφόρος, v. sub ἐλαιο-.

ἔλασα, Ep. for ἤλασα, aor. 1 of ἐλαύνω : Ion. 3 sing.

ἐλάσασκε :—Ion. 3 pl. opt. ἐλασαίατο.

ἐλασᾶς, ὁ, an unknown bird, Ar.

ἐλᾰσείω, (ἐλαύνω) Desiderat. to wish to march, Luc.

ἐλᾰσίη, ἡ, = ἔλασις : riding, Xen.

ἐλᾰσί-βροντος, ον, (ἐλαύνω, βροντή) hurled like thunder, Ar.

ἔλᾰσις, εως, ἡ, (ἐλαύνω) a driving away, banishing, Thuc. 2. (sub. στρατοῦ), a march, expedition, Hdt. : a procession, Xen. :—(sub. ἵππου) a riding, Id.

ἔλασσα, Ep. for ἤλασα, aor. 1 of ἐλαύνω.

ἐλασσόω, Att. -ττόω : aor. 1 ἠλάττωσα :—Pass., f. ἐλασσωθήσομαι, in med. form ἐλασσώσομαι : aor. 1 ἠλασσώθην, -ττώθην :—to make less or smaller, to lessen, diminish, lower, Oratt.: c. gen. to detract from, Thuc. II. Pass. 1. absol. to become smaller, be lessened, suffer loss, be depreciated, Id. : —also to take less than one's due, waive one's rights or privileges, Id. 2. c. dat. rei, to have the worst of it, to be inferior, τινι in a thing, Id., Xen. 3. c. gen. pers. to be at disadvantage with a person, Dem.

ἐλάσσων, Att. -ττων, ον, gen. ονος :—smaller, less, formed from ἐλαχύς (with Sup. ἐλάχιστος, q. v.), but serving as Comp. to μικρός, Il. : ἔλασσον ἔχειν to have the worse, be worse off, τινί in a thing, Hdt., Dem.: so, ἐλάττω γίγνεσθαι Ar. 2. c. gen. pers. worse than, inferior to, Thuc., etc.; but c. gen. rei, like ἥσσων, subservient to, Id. 3. in neut. with Preps., ἐλάσσονα ποιεῖσθαι to consider of less account, Hdt.; παρ᾽ ἔλαττον ἡγεῖσθαι Plat.; δι᾽ ἐλάττονος at less distance, Thuc. II. of Number, fewer, οἱ ἐλάσσονες the smaller number, Hdt., Thuc. III. neut. ἔλασσον, as Adv. less, Aesch., etc.

ἐλαστρέω, Ep. and Ion. for ἐλαύνω, to drive, Il.; ἐλ. τινα to drive about, of the Furies, Eur. :—Pass., of ships, to be rowed, Hdt.

ἐλάσω [ἄ], f. of ἐλαύνω.

ἐλᾰτέον, verb. Adj. of ἐλάω, ἐλαύνω, one must ride, Xen.

ἘΛΑ´ΤΗ [ἄ], ἡ, the silver fir, pinus picea, Il. II. an oar, Hom. : also a ship or boat, like Lat. abies, Eur.

ἐλᾰτήρ, ῆρος, ὁ, (ἐλάω, ἐλαύνω) *a driver* of horses, *a charioteer*, Il., Aesch. **II.** *a sort of broad, flat cake*, Ar.

ἐλᾰτήριος, ον, (ἐλαύνω) *driving away*, c. gen., Aesch.

ἐλάτινος [ᾰ], Ep. ἐλάτινος, η, ον, (ἐλάτη) *of the fir*, Lat. *abiegnus*, Il., Eur. :—*of fir* or *pine-wood*, Od., Eur.

ἐλάττωμα, ατος, τό, (ἐλαττόω) *a disadvantage*, Dem.

ἐλάττων, ἔλαττόω, Att. for ἐλάσσων, ἐλασσόω.

ἘΛΑΥΝΩ (ἐλάω q. v.), f. ἐλάσω [ᾰ], Ep. ἐλάσσω and ἐλόω, Att. ἐλῶ :—aor. 1 ἤλᾰσα, Ep. ἔλᾰσα and ἔλασσα, Ion. 3 sing. ἐλάσασκεν :—pf. ἐλήλᾰκα : plqpf. ἐληλάκειν :—Pass., aor. 1 ἠλάθην [ᾰ], later ἠλάσθην :—pf. ἐλήλαμαι : 3 sing. plqpf. ἠλήλᾰτο, Ep. ἐλήλατο ; 3 pl. ἠλήλαντο, Ep. ἐληλέδατ'. Radic. sense : *To drive, drive on, set in motion*, of driving flocks, Hom. ; so aor. med. ἠλασάμην Il. : often of chariots, *to drive*, Ib., Hdt. ; also, ἐλ. ἵππον *to ride* it, Id. ; ἐλ. νῆα *to row* it, Od. :—in this sense the acc. was omitted, and the Verb became intr., *to go in a chariot, to drive*, μάστιξεν δ' ἐλάαν (sc. ἵππους) he whipped them *on*, Il. ; βῆ δ' ἐλάαν ἐπὶ κύματα he *drove on* over the waves, Ib. ; διὰ νύκτα ἐλάαν *to travel* the night through, Od. ; —*to ride*, Hdt., etc. ; *to march*, Id. ; *to row*, Od. **b.** in this intr. sense, it sometimes took an acc. loci, γαλήνην ἐλαύνειν *to sail* the calm sea, i. e. over it, Ib. ; ἐλαύνειν δρόμον *to run* a course, Ar. **2.** *to drive away*, like ἀπελαύνω, of stolen cattle, Hom., Xen. :—so in Med., Hom. **3.** *to drive away, expel*, Il., Trag. **4.** *to drive* to extremities, ἄδην ἐλόωσι πολέμοιο will *harass* him till he has had enough of war, Il. ; ἄδην ἐλάαν κακότητος shall *persecute* him till he has had enough, Od. :—then in Att. *to persecute, attack, harass*, Soph., etc. **5.** intr. in expressions like ἐς τοσοῦτον ἤλασαν, they *drove* it so far (where πρᾶγμα must be supplied), Hdt. :—hence, *to push on, go on*, Eur., Plat. **II.** *to strike*, ἐλάτῃσιν πόντον ἐλαύνοντες, cf. Lat. *remis impellere*, Il. **2.** *to strike* with a weapon, but never with a missile, Ib. :— c. dupl. acc., τὸν μὲν ἔλασ' ὦμον him *he struck* on the shoulder, Ib. ; χθόνα ἤλασε μετώπῳ struck earth with his forehead, Od. **3.** *to drive* or *thrust* through, δόρυ διὰ στήθεσφιν ἔλασσε Il. ; and in Pass. *to go through*, Ib. **III.** in metaph. senses : **1.** *to beat* with a hammer, Lat. *ducere*, *to beat out* metal, Il. ; περὶ δ' ἕρκος ἔλασσε κασσιτέροιο around *he made* a fence of beaten tin, Ib. **2.** *to draw a line* of wall or a trench, Lat. *ducere murum*, Hom., etc. ; τεῖχος ἐς τὸν ποταμὸν τοὺς ἀγκῶνας ἐλήλαται the wall *has* its angles *carried down* to the river, Hdt. ; ὄγμον ἐλαύνειν *to work* one's way down a ridge or swathe in reaping or mowing, Il. ; ὄρχον ἀμπελίδος ἐλ. *to draw* a line of vines, i. e. *plant* them *in line*, Ar. **3.** κολφὸν ἐλαύνειν *to prolong* the brawl, Il.

ἐλαφᾰ-βόλος, ον, Dor. for ἐλαφη-βόλος.

ἐλάφειος, ον, (ἔλαφος) *of a stag*, ἐλ. κρέα *venison*, Xen.

ἐλάφη-βολία, ἡ, *a shooting of deer*, Soph. ; and

ἐλᾰφηβολιών, ῶνος, ὁ, the ninth month of the Attic year, in which the *Elaphebolia* were held, answering to the last half of March and first of April, Thuc. From

ἐλᾰφη-βόλος, ον, (ἔλαφος, βάλλω) *shooting deer*, Il., Soph.

ἐλᾰφο-κτόνος, ον, (κτείνω) *deer-killing*, Eur.

ἘΛΑ'ΦΟΣ, ὁ and ἡ, *a deer*, whether male, *a hart* or *stag*, or female, *a hind*, Il. :—κραδίην ἐλάφοιο [ἔχων] with heart *of deer*, i. e. a coward, Ib.

ἐλᾰφοσ-σόα, ἡ, (σεύω) *deer-hunting*, Anth.

ἐλαφρία, ἡ, *lightness : levity*, N. T. From

ἘΛΑΦΡΟ'Σ, ά, όν, (ἐ-λαφ-ρός = Lat. *lev-is*) *light in weight*, Il., Hdt., Att. : — Adv. *lightly, buoyantly*, Od. **2.** *light to bear, not burdensome, easy*, Il. ; ἐλαφρόν [ἐστι] 'tis *light, easy*, Aesch., etc. ; ἐν ἐλαφρῷ ποιεῖσθαί τι to make *light* of a thing, Hdt. **II.** *light in moving, nimble*, Lat. *agilis*, Hom., Aesch. ; ἐλαφρὰ ἡλικία the age of *active* youth, Xen. ; οἱ ἐλαφροί *light troops*, Lat. *levis armatura*, Id. **III.** *light-minded, thoughtless*, Eur. Hence

ἐλαφρύνω [ῡ], *to make light, lighten*, Babr.

ἐλάχιστος [ᾰ], η, ον, Sup. of ἐλαχύς, Comp. ἐλάσσων, *the smallest, least*, οὐκ ἐλ. h. Hom., Hdt., etc. ; ἐλαχίστου λόγου of *least* account, Id. ; περὶ ἐλαχίστου ποιεῖσθαι Plat. **2.** of Time, *shortest*, δι' ἐλαχίστου [sc. χρόνου] Thuc. ; ἐξ ἐλαχίστης βουλῆς with *shortest* deliberation, Id. **3.** of Number, *fewest*, Plat. **II.** τὸ ἐλάχιστον, τοὐλάχιστον, *at the least*, Hdt., Xen., etc. ; also ἐλάχιστα, Thuc., Plat. **III.** there is also a new Comp. ἐλαχιστότερος, *less than the least*, N. T.

ἘΛΑΧΥ'Σ, ἐλάχεια (not -εῖα), ύ, *small, short, little*, old Ep. Positive, whence ἐλάσσων, ἐλάχιστος are formed, h. Hom. : cf. λάχεια.

ἘΛΑΩ, old form of ἐλαύνω, Ep. inf. ἐλάαν (which is also fut.) Hom. ; 3 pl. impf. ἔλων Od.

ἜΛΔΟΜΑΙ, Ep. ἐέλδομαι, only in pres. and impf. *to wish, long* to do a thing, c. inf., Hom. :—c. gen. *to long for*, Id. : c. acc. *to desire*, Id :—as Pass., νῦν τοι ἐελδέσθω πόλεμος be war now *welcome*, Il. Hence

ἔλδωρ, only found in Ep. form ἐέλδωρ, τό, *a wish, longing, desire*, Il., Hes.

ἐλεαίρω, = ἐλεέω, *to take pity on*, τινά Hom., Ar.

ἐλεᾶς, ὁ, *a kind of owl*, Ib.

ἐλεγεία, ἡ, *an elegy*, Plut.

ἐλεγεῖον, τό, (ἔλεγος) *a distich consisting of hexameter and pentameter, the metre of the elegy*, Thuc. **II.** in pl., ἐλεγεῖα, τά, *an elegiac poem*, Plat., etc. :—so in sing., Plut.

ἐλέγευ, Dor. for ἐλέγου, 2 sing. impf. pass. of λέγω.

ἐλεγκτήρ, ῆρος, ὁ, ἐλεγκτής, οῦ, ὁ, *one who convicts* or *detects*, τῶν ἀποκτεινάντων Antipho.

ἐλεγκτικός, ή, όν, (ἐλέγχω) of persons, *fond of cross-questioning* or *examining* :—Adv. -κῶς, Xen.

ἐλεγμός, ὁ, = ἔλεγξις, N. T.

ἐλεγξί-γᾰμος, ον, *proving a wife's fidelity*, Anth.

ἔλεγξις, εως, ἡ, = ἔλεγχος, ὁ, *a conviction*, N. T.

ἘΛΕΓΟΣ, ὁ, *a song of mourning, a lament* : at first without reference to metrical form, later always in alternate *hexameters and pentameters*, Eur., etc.

ἐλεγχείη, ἡ, *reproach, disgrace*, Il. ; and

ἐλεγχής, ές, *worthy of reproof ;* of men, *cowardly*, Il. :—Irreg. Sup. ἐλέγχιστος, Ib. From

ἔλεγχος, τό, (ἐλέγχω) *a reproach, disgrace, dishonour*, Hom. : of men, κάκ' ἐλέγχεα base *reproaches* to your name, Il.

ἔλεγχος, ὁ, (ἐλέγχω) *a cross-examining, testing*, for purposes of *disproof* or *refutation*, ἔχειν ἔλεγχον to admit of *disproof*, Hdt., Thuc. ; ἐλ. διδόναι τοῦ βίου to give *an account* of one's life, Plat. ; εἰς ἔλ. πίπτειν to

be convicted, Eur.; οἱ περὶ Παυσανίαν ἔλ. *the evidence on which* he *was convicted*, Thuc.

ΈΛΕ'ΓΧΩ, f. ἐλέγξω: aor. 1 ἤλεγξα:—Pass., f. ἐλεγχθήσομαι: aor. 1 ἠλέγχθην: pf. ἐλήλεγμαι:—*to disgrace, put to shame*, μῦθον ἔλ. *to treat* a speech *with contempt*, Il.; ἔλ. τινά *to put* one *to shame*, Od. II. *to cross-examine, question*, for the purpose of *disproving* or *reproving, to censure, accuse*, Hdt., Att.; c. acc. et inf. *to accuse* one of doing, Eur.:—Pass. *to be convicted*, Hdt., Xen., etc. 2. of arguments, *to bring to the proof, to disprove, confute*, Aesch., Dem.:—absol. *to bring convincing proof*, Hdt.: then generally *to prove*, Lat. *arguere*, Thuc.

ἐλέειν, Ep. for ἐλεῖν, aor. 2 inf. of αἱρέω.

ἐλεεινός, ή, όν, in Att. Poets ἐλεινός: (ἔλεος):—*finding pity, pitied* or *moving pity, pitiable, piteous*, Hom., etc.; ἐλεινὸς εἰσορᾶν *piteous* to behold, Aesch.; ἐλεινὸν ὁρᾷς thou lookest *piteous*, Soph.; ἐσθῆτ' ἐλεινήν Ar.; ποιῶν ἑαυτὸν ὡς ἐλεεινότατον Dem. 2. *shewing pity, pitying*, ἐλ. δάκρυον a tear *of pity*, Od.; οὐδὲν ἐλεεινὸν *no feeling of pity*, Plat. II. Adv. ἐλεεινῶς, in Att. Poets ἐλεινῶς, *pitiably*, Soph.; neut. pl. ἐλεεινά as Adv., Il.

ἐλεέω, impf. ἠλέουν: f. ήσω: aor. 1 ἠλέησα: (ἔλεος):—like ἐλεαίρω, *to have pity on, shew mercy upon*, c. acc., Od., Att.:—Pass. *to be pitied, have pity* or *mercy shewn one*, Plat. 2. absol. *to feel pity*, Ar.

ἐλεημοσύνη, ἡ, *pity, mercy: a charity, alms* (which is a corruption of the word), N. T., etc. From

ἐλεήμων, ον, gen. ονος, (ἐλεέω) *pitiful, merciful, compassionate*, Od., Dem.

ἐλεητύς, ύος, ἡ, Ion. for ἔλεος, *pity, mercy*, Od.

Ἐλείθυια, ἡ, poët. for Εἰλείθυια.

ἐλεῖν, aor. 2 inf. of αἱρέω.

ἐλεινός, ή, όν, in Att. Poets for ἐλεεινός.

ἐλειο-βάτης [ᾰ], ου, ὁ, (βαίνω) *walking the marsh, marsh-dwelling*, Aesch.

ἔλειος, ον or α, ον, (ἕλος) *of the marsh* or *meadow*, ἔλ. δάπεδον the surface *of the meads*, Ar. 2. *growing* or *dwelling in the marsh*, Aesch., Thuc.

ἔλεκτο, Ep. syncop. aor. 2 pass. of λέγω, *he lay down*.

ἐλελεῦ, or doubled ἐλελεῦ ἐλελεῦ, a war-cry, Ar.: generally *any cry*, Aesch.

ἐλελήθεε, Ion. for ἐλελήθει, Ep. 3 sing. plqpf. of λανθάνω.

ἐλελίζω (A), Ep. lengthd. form of ἑλίσσω: aor. 1 ἐλέλιξα:—sync. aor. 2 pass. ἐλέλικτο:—*to whirl round*, Od. 2. *to rally* soldiers, Il.: Pass., οἱ δ' ἐλελίχθησαν Ib. 3. generally, *to make to tremble* or *quake*, Ib.:—Pass. *to tremble, quiver*, Ib. II. Med. and Pass. *to move in coils* or *spires*, of a serpent, Ib.

ἐλελίζω (B): aor. 1 ἠλέλιξα: (ἐλελεῦ):—*to raise the battle-cry*, Xen.: generally, *to raise a loud cry*, Eur.: —in Med., of the nightingale, *to trill her sad lay*, Id.; c. acc., Ἴτυν ἐλελιζομένη *trilling her lament for* Itys, Ar.

ἐλέλικτο, 3 sing. Ep. aor. 2 pass. of ἐλελίζω (A).

ἐλελίχθην, aor. 1 pass. of ἐλελίζω (A).

ἐλελί-χθων, ον, (ἐλελίζω A) *shaking the earth*, Soph.

ἐλελόγχειν, plqpf. of λαγχάνω.

ἐλέ-ναυς, ἡ, (ἑλεῖν) *ship-destroying*, of Helen, Aesch.

ἐλεό-θρεπτος, ον, (ἕλος, τρέφω) *marsh-bred*, Il.

ἐλεόν, Adv., like ἐλεεινόν, *piteously*, Hes.

ΈΛΕΟ'Σ, ὁ, *a kitchen-table, a board on which meat was cut up, a dresser*, Hom.:—also ἐλεόν, τό, Ar.

ΈΛΕΟΣ, ὁ, *pity, mercy, compassion*, Il., Att.; ἔλ. τινος *pity for* . . , Eur.:—in N. T. also ἔλεος, τό. II. *an object of compassion, a piteous thing*, Eur.

ἐλέ-πολις, poët. ἑλέ-πτολις, ι, εως, (ἑλεῖν) *city-destroying*, of Helen, Aesch., Eur.

ἑλέσθαι, aor. 2 med. inf. of αἱρέω.

ἑλετός, ή, όν, (ἑλεῖν) *that can be taken* or *caught*, Il.

ἐλευθερία, Ion. -ίη, ἡ, (ἐλεύθερος) *freedom, liberty*, Hdt., Aesch., etc.; δι' ἐλευθερίας μόλις ἐξῆλθες, i. e. μόλις ἠλευθερώθης, Plat. 2. *licence*, Plat.

ἐλευθέριος, ον, α, ον, *speaking* or *acting like a freeman, free-spirited, frank*, related to ἐλεύθερος, as Lat. *liberalis* to *liber*, Plat., Xen. b. *freely giving, bountiful, liberal*, Id. 2. of pursuits, *fit for a freeman, liberal*; τὸ ἐλευθέριον = ἐλευθεριότης, Id. 3. of appearance, *free, noble*, Id. II. Ζεὺς Ἐλευθέριος Jove *the Deliverer*, Hdt.

ἐλευθεριότης, ητος, ἡ, *the character of an* ἐλευθέριος, *liberality*, Plat.

ἐλευθερό-παις, ὁ, ἡ, *having free children*, i. e. *a free man*, Anth.

ἐλευθερο-πρεπής, ές, (πρέπω) *worthy of a freeman*, Plat.

ΈΛΕΥ'ΘΕΡΟΣ, α, ον, or ος, ον: (ἐ-λεύθερ-ος = Lat. *liber*):—*free*, opp. to δοῦλος: ἐλεύθερον ἦμαρ the day *of freedom*, i. e. *freedom*, Il.; κρητὴρ ἐλεύθερος the cup drunk *to freedom*, Ib.: of persons, Hdt., Att.: —τὸ ἐλ. *freedom*, Hdt.:—c. gen. *free* or *freed from a thing*, Trag. 2. of things, *free, open to all*, Xen. II. like ἐλευθέριος, *fit for a freeman, free, frank*, Hdt., Att.:—Adv., ἐλευθέρως εἰπεῖν Hdt., Soph.

ἐλευθερο-στομέω, f. ήσω, (στόμα) *to be free of speech*, Aesch., Eur.

ἐλευθερ-ουργός, όν, (*ἔργω) *bearing himself freely* or *nobly*, of the mind, Plat.

ἐλευθερόω, f. ώσω, (ἐλεύθερος) *to free, set free*, Hdt., Aesch., etc.; ἐλ. τὸν ἔσπλουν *to set the entrance free, clear it*, Thuc.; ἐλευθεροῖ στόμα *he keeps his tongue free*, i. e. *does not commit himself by speech*, Soph.: *to free from blame, acquit*, τινά Xen.:—Pass. *to be set free*, Hdt. 2. c. gen. *to set free, loose* or *release from*, Eur.; so, ἐλευθεροῦντες ἐκ δρασμῶν πόδα, i. e. *ceasing to flee*, Id. Thence

ἐλευθέρωσις, εως, ἡ, *a setting free*, Hdt., Thuc.; and

ἐλευθερωτής, οῦ, ὁ, *a liberator*, Luc.

Ἐλευσίνιος, α, ον, *of Eleusis*, h. Hom., Hdt., etc. From

Ἐλευσίς, ῖνος, ἡ, *Eleusis*, an old city of Attica, sacred to Demeter and Proserpine, h. Hom., etc.:—Advs., Ἐλευσῖνι *at Eleusis*, Andoc., Xen., etc.: Ἐλευσίνάδε, Adv. *to Eleusis*, Id.: Ἐλευσινόθεν, *from Eleusis*, Lys., etc.

ἔλευσις, εως, ἡ, *a coming* :—the *Advent* of our LORD, N. T.

ἐλεύσομαι, fut. of ἔρχομαι.

ἐλεφαίρομαι, aor. 1 part. ἐλεφηράμενος:—Ep. Dep. *to cheat with empty hopes*, said of the *false dreams* that come through the *ivory gate* (ἐλέφας), Od.: generally, *to cheat, overreach*, Il. II. *to destroy*, Hes.

ἐλεφαντ-άρχης, ου, ὁ, *the commander of a squadron of elephants*, Plut.

ἐλεφαντίνεος, α, ον, = sq., Anth.

ἐλεφάντῖνος, η, ον, (ἐλέφας) of ivory, ivory, Lat. eburneus, Ar.

ἐλεφαντό-δετος, ον, inlaid with ivory, Ar.

ἐλεφαντό-κωπος, ον, (κώπη) ivory-hilted, Luc.

ἐλεφαντο-μᾰχία, ἡ, (μάχη) a battle of elephants, Plut.

ἐλεφαντό-πους, ὁ, ἡ, ivory-footed, Luc.

ΕΛΕΦΑΣ, αντος, ὁ, the elephant, Hdt.   II. the elephant's tusk, ivory, Il., Hes.

ἔλῃ, 3 sing. aor. 2 subj. of αἱρέω :—but also, with Ep. form ἔληαι, 2 sing. aor. 2 med. subj.

ἐλήλᾰκα, ἐλήλαμαι, pf. act. and pass. of ἐλαύνω.

ἐλήλεγμαι, pf. pass. of ἐλέγχω.

ἐληλέδατο, Ep. 3 pl. plqpf. pass. of ἐλαύνω.

ἐλήλιγμαι, pf. pass. of ἑλίσσω.

ἐλήλῠθα Ep. εἰλήλουθα, pf. of ἔρχομαι.

ἐλήφθην, aor. 1 pass. of λαμβάνω.

ἐλθεῖν, Ep. ἐλθέμεναι, ἐλθέμεν, aor. 2 inf. of ἔρχομαι.

ἐλίγδην, Adv. (ἑλίσσω) whirling, rolling, Aesch.

ἔλιγμα, ατος, τό, (ἑλίσσω) a curl, lock of hair, Anth.

ἐλιγμός, ὁ, (ἑλίσσω) a winding, convolution, as of the Labyrinth, Hdt., Xen.

ἑλῐκο-βλέφᾰρος, ον, (βλέφαρον) with ever-moving eyelids, quick-glancing, h. Hom.

ἑλῐκο-δρόμος, ον, running in curves, circular, Eur.

ἑλῐκο-ειδής, poët. εἱλικ-, ές, (εἶδος) of winding or spiral form, Plut.

ἑλικτός, ή, όν, (ἑλίσσω) curved, twisted, wreathed, h. Hom., Soph. ; ἑλ. κύτος a wheeled ark, Eur. ; σῦριγξ περὶ χεῖλος ἑλικτά·moving quickly, Theocr.   II. metaph. tortuous, Eur.

Ἑλικών, ῶνος, ὁ, Helicon, a hill in Boeotia, Hes. Hence Ἑλῐκωνιάδες (sc. παρθένοι), αἱ, the dwellers on Helicon, the Muses, Hes. : so, Νύμφαι Ἑλικωνίδες Soph.

ἑλίκ-ωψ, ωπος, ὁ, ἡ, fem. ἑλικῶπις, ιδος, with rolling eyes, quick-glancing, Il.

ΕΛΙ˘ΝΥ˘Ω : f. –ύσω [ῠ] : aor. 1 ἐλίνυσα :—to keep holiday, to take rest, be at rest, keep quiet, stand idle, Hdt., Aesch.   2. c. part. to rest or cease from doing, Id.

ἕλιξ, ῑκος, ὁ, ἡ, (ἑλίσσω) Adj. twisted, curved, of oxen, either with twisted, crumpled horns, or rolling as they walk, Hom., etc. :—later, ἕλικα ἀνὰ χλόαν on the tangled grass, Eur.

ἕλιξ, poët. εἷλιξ, ῑκος, ἡ, (ἑλίσσω) anything which assumes a spiral shape :   1. an armlet or earring, Il.   2. a twist, whirl, convolution, ἕλικες στεροπῆς flashes of forked lightning, Aesch.   3. the tendril of the vine, Eur. : of ivy, Id.   4. a curl or lock of hair, Anth.   5. the coil or spire of a serpent, Eur.

ἑλιξό-κερως, ω, ὁ, ἡ, with crumpled horns, Anth.

ἔλῐπον, aor. 2 of λείπω.

ἑλίσσω, Ep. inf. –έμεν ; Ion. εἱλίσσω : f. ἑλίξω : aor. 1 εἵλιξα :—Pass., aor. 1 εἱλίχθην : pf. ἑλίγμαι, Ion. 3 pl. εἱλίχατο : 3 sing. plqpf. εἵλικτο : (ἕλω) :—to turn round, to turn a chariot round the doubling-post, Il. ; so of the chariot of Day, Aesch., Eur. ; ἑλ. κόνιν to roll the eddying dust, Aesch. ; ἑλ. δίνας of the Euripus, Eur. ; ἑλ. βλέφαρα Id.   2. of any rapid motion, esp. of a circular kind, ἑλ. πλάταν to ply the oar swiftly, Soph. ; ἑλ. πόδα to move the swift foot, Eur. : absol. to dance, Id.   3. to roll or wind round, as the wool round the distaff, Hdt., Eur.   4. metaph. to turn in one's mind, revolve, Soph. ; ἑλ.

λόγους to speak wily words, Eur.   II. Pass. and Med. to turn oneself round, turn quick round, turn to bay, Il. ; of a serpent, to coil himself, Ib. ; of a missile, to spin through the air, Ib.   2. to turn hither and thither, go about, Ib. :—also, like Lat. versari, to be busy about a thing, Ib.   3. to whirl in the dance, Eur.   4. Med. in Act. sense, with a whirl, like a sling, Il.   5. τὰς κεφαλὰς εἱλίχατο μίτρῃσι have their heads rolled round with turbans, Hdt.

ἑλί-τροχος, ον, (ἑλίσσω) whirling the wheel, Aesch.

ἔλιφθεν, Aeol. for ἐλείφθησαν, 3 pl. aor. 1 pass. of λείπω.

ἑλί-χρῡσος, ὁ, a creeping plant with yellow flower or fruit, Theocr.

ἑλκαίνω, (ἕλκος) to fester, Aesch.

ἑλκεσί-πεπλος, ον, trailing the robe, with long train, Il.

ἑλκεσί-χειρος, ον, drawing the hand after it, Anth.

ἑλκε-χίτων [ῐ], ωνος, ὁ, trailing the tunic, with long tunic, Il.

ἑλκέω, f. ήσω, strengthd. for ἕλκω, to drag about, tear asunder, Il. : to attempt violence to one, Od.

ἑλκηδόν, Adv. by dragging or pulling, Hes.

ἑλκηθμός, ὁ, (ἑλκέω) a being carried off, violence suffered, Il.

ἕλκημα, ατος, τό, (ἑλκέω) that which is torn in pieces, a prey, Eur.

ἑλκητήρ, ῆρος, ὁ, one that drags, Anth.

ἑλκήτον, 3 dual subj. of ἕλκω.

ἑλκο-ποιέω, f. ήσω, to make wounds or sores : metaph. to rip up old sores, Aeschin.

ἑλκο-ποιός, όν, (ποιέω) having power to wound, Aesch.

ἕλκος, εος, τό, (ἕλκω) a wound, Il., Att.   2. a festering wound, ἕλκος ὕδρου the festering bite of a serpent, Il. : of plague-ulcers, Thuc.   II. metaph. a wound, loss, Aesch., Soph.

ἑλκόω, f. ώσω, (ἕλκος) to wound sorely, lacerate, Eur. :—metaph., ἑλκ. φρένας οἴκους Id.

ἑλκτέον, verb. Adj. of ἕλκω, one must drag, Plat.

ἑλκτικός, ή, όν, (ἕλκω) fit for drawing, attractive, Plat.

ἑλκύδριον, τό, Dim. of ἕλκος, a slight sore, Ar.

ἑλκυστάζω, Frequentat. of ἕλκω, to drag about, Il.

ἑλκυστέος, α, ον, verb. Adj. of ἕλκω, to be dragged, Xen.

ἝΛΚΩ : impf. εἷλκον, Ep. ἕλκον :—f. ἕλξω :—aor. 2 εἵλκῠσα (as if from ἑλκύω) ; later εἷλξα, poët. ἕλξα :— pf. εἵλκῠκα, f. ἑλκύσω :—Pass., f. ἑλκυσθήσομαι : aor. 1 εἱλκύσθην : pf. εἵλκυσμαι, Ion. ἕλκυσμαι. To draw, drag, Lat. traho, with a notion of force, ποδὸς ἕλκε began to drag [the dead body] by the foot, Il. ; to draw ships down to the sea, Od. ; of mules, to draw a chariot, Ib. ; to draw the plough through the field, Ib.   2. to draw after one, Il. ; πέδας ἕλκ. to trail fetters after one, Hdt.   3. to tear in pieces, Id., Eur. :—Med., ἕλκεσθαι χαίτας to tear one's hair, Il.   4. to draw a bow, Hom., etc.   5. to draw a sword, Soph. ; and in Med., to draw one's sword, Il.   6. ἕλκ. ἱστία to hoist or haul up the sails, Od.   7. to hold up scales, so as to poise or balance them, Il.   II. after Hom., in many ways :   1. to pull an oar, Hdt.   2. to drag into court, Ar. : to drag about, esp. with lewd violence, Dem., etc.   3. to draw or suck up, Hdt. : of persons drinking, to drink 'n long draughts, quaff, Eur., etc. ; ἕλκ.

μαστόν to suck the breast, Id. 4. ἕλκ. βίοτον, ζόην to drag out a weary life, Id. : to drag on, prolong tediously, Hdt. : κόρδακα ἑλκύσαι to dance in long, measured steps, Ar. 5. to draw to oneself, attract, Hdt., etc. 6. ἕλκ. σταθμόν to draw down the balance, i. e. to weigh so much, Id. ; absol., τὸ δ᾽ ἂν ἑλκύσῃ whatever it weigh, Id. 7. ἑλκύσαι πλίνθους, like Lat. ducere, to make bricks, Id. 8. Med. to draw to oneself, amass riches, Theogn.

ἑλκώδης, ες, (εἶδος) like a sore, ulcerated, Eur.

ἕλκωσις, εως, ἡ, (ἑλκόω) ulceration, Thuc.

ἔλλαβον, Ep. for ἔλαβον, aor. 2 of λαμβάνω.

ἐλ-λαμπρύνομαι, (ἐν, λαμπρύνω) Pass. to gain distinction, Thuc.

ἐλ-λάμπω, f. ψω, (ἐν) to shine upon, to illuminate :— metaph. in Med. to distinguish oneself, gain glory in or with a thing, Hdt.

Ἑλλάνιος, Dor. for Ἑλλήνιος.

Ἑλλᾱνο-δίκαι, ων, οἱ, the chief judges at the Olympic games, Pind. II. at Sparta, a court-martial to try disputes among the allied troops, Xen.

ΕΛΛΑ'Σ, άδος, ἡ, Hellas, a city of Thessaly, founded by Hellen, Il. 2. that part of Thessaly in which the Myrmidons dwelt, also called Phthiotis, Hom. 3. Northern Greece, as opp. to Peloponnesus, Od. 4. later, the name for Greece, from the South to Epirus and Thessaly inclusively, Hes., Hdt., etc. II. as Adj. with a fem. Subst. Hellenic, Greek, Id., etc.

ἔλλαχον, Ep. for ἔλαχον, aor. 2 of λαγχάνω.

ἐλλέβορος, ὁ, hellebore, Lat. veratrum, a plant used as a specific for madness, πῖθ᾽ ἐλλέβορον drink hellebore, i. e. you are mad, Ar. (Deriv. unknown.)

ἐλλεδανός, ὁ, (εἴλω) the band for binding corn-sheaves, Il.

ἐλ-λείπω, f. ψω, (ἐν) to leave in, leave behind, Eur. 2. to leave out, leave undone, Lat. omitto, Soph., etc. II. intr. to fall short, fail, h. Hom., Soph.; τὸ ἐλλεῖπον τῆς ἐπιστήμης deficiency of knowledge, Thuc. 2. c. gen. rei, like δέω, to be in want of, fall short of, lack, Aesch., Thuc.: πολλοῦ ἐλλείπω I am far from it, Aesch. 3. c. gen. pers. to be inferior to, Plat. 4. foll. by μή c. inf., τί γὰρ ἐλλ. μὴ παραπαίειν; in what does he fall short of madness? Aesch. 5. with a part., οὐκ ἐλλείπει εὐχαριστῶν he fails not to give thanks, ap. Dem. 6. of things, to be wanting or lacking to . . , c. dat., Xen. III. Pass. to be left behind in a race, Soph.: to be surpassed, Xen. 2. to be left wanting, to fail, Id.

ἐλ-λεσχος, ον, (ἐν, λέσχη) commonly talked of, Hdt.

Ἕλλην, ηνος, ὁ, Hellen, son of Deucalion, Hes. 2. the Ἕλληνες of Hom. are the Thessalian tribe of which Hellen was the reputed chief (cf. Ἑλλάς 1), Il. 3. later, Ἕλληνες was the regul. name for Greeks, opp. to βάρβαροι, Hdt., etc. 4. later still, of Gentiles, opp. to Jews, N. T. II. as Adj. = Ἑλληνικός, Thuc., etc. :—even with a fem. Subst., Aesch., Eur. Hence

Ἑλληνίζω, f. σω: Pass. aor. 1 without augm. :—to speak Greek, Plat. :—Pass., Ἑλληνισθῆναι τὴν γλῶσσαν to be made Greeks in language by another, Thuc.

Ἑλληνικός, ή, όν, (Ἕλλην) Hellenic, Greek, Hdt., Att. 2. τὸ Ἑλληνικόν the Greeks collectively, Hdt.; the Greek soldiery, Xen. 3. τὰ Ἑλληνικά the

history of Grecian affairs, Thuc. II. like the Greeks, Eur., Ar. :—Adv. -κῶς, in Greek fashion, Hdt.

Ἑλλήνιος, α, ον, =foreg., Hdt., etc. II. Ἑλλήνιον, τό, the temple of the Hellenes in Egypt, Id. III. Ἑλλανία, ἡ, = Ἑλλάς, Eur.

Ἑλληνίς, Dor. Ἑλλᾱνίς, ίδος, ἡ, fem. of Ἕλλην, Att. II. Ἑλληνίς (sub. γυνή) a Grecian woman, Eur.

Ἑλληνιστής, οῦ, ὁ, (Ἑλληνίζω) one who uses the Greek language ; i. e., in N. T., a Hellenist, a Greek-Jew.

Ἑλληνιστί, Adv. in Greek fashion, Luc. ; Ἑλλ. ξυνιέναι to understand Greek, Xen.

Ἑλληνο-τᾰμίαι, ων, οἱ, the stewards of Greece, i. e. officers appointed by Athens B. C. 477 to levy the contributions paid by the Greek states towards the Persian war, Thuc.

Ἑλλησποντιακός, ή, όν, of the Hellespont, Xen. :—so Ἑλλησπόντιος, α, ον, Hdt., Xen. ; and

Ἑλλησποντίᾱς, Ion. -ίης (sc. ἄνεμος), a wind blowing from the Hellespont, i. e. from the N. E., Hdt. From

Ἑλλήσ-ποντος, ὁ, the Hellespont or sea of Hellé (daughter of Athamas, who was drowned therein), now the Dardanelles, Hom., Hdt., etc.

ἐλ-λιμενίζω, (ἐν, λιμήν) to collect harbour-dues. Hence

ἐλλιμενιστής, οῦ, ὁ, a collector of harbour-dues, Dem.

ἐλλιπεῖν, aor. 2 inf. of ἐλλείπω.

ἐλλιπής, ές, (ἐλλείπω) pass. wanting, lacking, defective, Thuc., etc. ; also c. dat. ; τὸ μὴ ἐπιχειρούμενον ἀεὶ ἐλλιπὲς ἦν τῆς δοκήσεως whatever was not attempted was so much lost of their reckoning, Thuc. ; τὸ ἐλλιπές defect, failure, Id.

ἐλλισάμην, Ep. for ἐλισάμην, aor. 1 of λίσσομαι.

ἐλλιτάνευον, Ep. for ἐλιτ-, impf. of λιτανεύω.

ἐλλόβιον, τό, (ἐν, λοβός) that which is in the lobe of the ear, an earring, Lat. inauris, Luc.

ἐλλογάω, (ἐν, λόγος) to reckon in, to impute, N. T.

ἐλ-λόγιμος, ον, held in account (ἐν λόγῳ), notable, famous, Hdt., Plat.

ἐλλοπιεύω, (ἔλλοψ) to fish, Theocr.

ΕΛΛΟ'Σ or ἐλλός, ὁ, a young deer, fawn, Od.

ἐλλός, ή, όν, = ἔλλοψ, Soph.

ἐλ-λοχίζω, (ἐν) to lie in ambush, Eur. : c. acc. to lie in wait for, Plut.

ΕΛΛΟ'Ψ, οπος, mute, of fish, Hes.

ἐλ-λύχνιον, τό, (ἐν, λύχνος) a lamp-wick, Hdt.

ἕλξις, εως, ἡ, (ἕλκω) a drawing, dragging, trailing, Plat.

ἑλοίμην, aor. 2 med. opt. of αἱρέω.

ἕλοιμι, aor. 2 opt. of αἱρέω.

ἕλον, ἑλόμην, Ep. for εἷλ-, aor. 2 act. and med. of αἱρέω.

ΕΛΟΣ, εος, τό, low ground by rivers, a marsh-meadow, Hom., Hdt., etc.

ἑλοῦσα, aor. 2 part. fem. of αἱρέω :—but II. ἔλουσα, aor. 1 of λούω.

ἔλοωσι, Ep. for ἐλῶσι, 3 pl. fut. of ἐλαύνω.

ἐλπίδο-δώτης, ου, ὁ, giver of hope, Anth.

ἐλπίζω, f. Att. ἰῶ : aor. 1 ἤλπισα : pf. ἤλπικα :—Pass., aor. 1 ἠλπίσθην : (ἔλπω) :—to hope for, look for, expect, τι Aesch., etc. : c. inf. fut. or aor. to hope or expect that, Hdt., Att. 2. of evils, to look for, fear, Soph., etc. 3. with inf. pres. it means little more than to think, deem, suppose, believe that, Hdt.,

Att. 4. c. dat. *to hope in* . . , τῇ τύχῃ Thuc. ; εἴs τινα, ἐπί τινα N. T.

ἐλπίς, ίδος, ἡ, (ἔλπω) *hope, expectation,* Od. ; in pl., πολλῶν ῥαγεισῶν ἐλπίδων *after the wreck of many hopes,* Aesch. ;—with gen. both of subject and object, Πελοποννησίων τὴν ἐλπίδα τοῦ ναυτικοῦ *the hope* of the P. *in their navy,* Thuc. 2. *the object of hope, a hope,* Ὀρέστης, ἐλπὶς δόμων Aesch. II. *apprehension, fear,* Id.

ἜΛΠΩ, only in pres. *to make to hope,* πάντας ἔλπει *feeds* all *with hope,* Od. II. Med. ἔλπομαι, Ep. ἐέλπομαι : 3 sing. impf. ἤλπετο, Ep. also ἔλπετο and ἐέλπ– : pf. ἔολπα ; 3 sing. plqpf. ἐώλπει :—*to hope or expect, indulge hope,* Hom., Hdt. ; like Att. ἐλπίζω. 2. *to expect anxiously, to fear,* Hom., Hdt. 3. *generally, to think, deem, suppose,* Il.

ἐλπωρή, ἡ, Ep. form of ἐλπίς, Od.

ἔλσαι, aor. 1 inf. of εἴλω :—**ἔλσας,** part.

ἔλῦμα, ατος, τό, (ἐλύω) *the tree* or *stock of the plough,* on which the share was fixed, Lat. *dentāle,* Hes.

ἔλῦτρον, τό, (ἐλύω II) *the case* of *a spear,* Ar. 2. *the body* as *the case of the soul,* Plat. ap. Luc. II. *a place for holding water, a reservoir,* Hdt.

ἐλύω, Att. ἐλύω, *to roll round* (cf. εἰλύω) :—only in aor. 1 pass. ἐπὶ γαῖαν ἐλύσθη *rolled* to the ground, Il. ; προπάροιθε ποδῶν Ἀχιλῆος ἐλυσθείς *rolled up, crouching* before Achilles' feet, Ib. ; ὑπὸ γαστέρ' ἐλυσθείς *huddled* under [the ram's] belly, Od. II. = εἰλύω, *to wrap up, cover,* Ap. Rh.

ἔλωρ, τό, only in nom. and acc. sing. and pl. : (ἑλεῖν) :—*booty, spoil, prey,* of unburied corpses, Hom. II. in pl., Πατρόκλοιο ἕλωρα *penalty for the slaughter* of Patroclus, Il.

ἐλώριον, τό, = foreg., Il.

ἔμαθον, aor. 2 of μανθάνω.

ἐμάνην [ᾰ], aor. 2 of μαίνομαι.

ἐμάρνατο, 3 sing. impf. of μάρναμαι.

ἐμᾰσάμην, aor. 1 of μαίομαι.

ἐμαυτοῦ, ἐμαυτῆς, Ion. ἐμεωυτοῦ (or ἐμωυτοῦ), ῆς :—Reflexive Pronoun of first person, *of me, of myself :* only used in gen., dat., and acc. sing., Hom., etc.

ἔμβᾱ, Att. for ἔμβηθι, aor. 2 imperat. of ἐμβαίνω.

ἐμβάδιον [ᾰ], τό, Dim. of ἐμβάς, Ar.

ἐμβαδόν, Adv. (ἐμβαίνω) *on foot, by land,* Il.

ἐμ-βαίνω, f. –βήσομαι : pf. –βέβηκα, Homeric part. –βεβαώς : aor. 2 ἐνέβην, Ep. 3 sing. ἔμβη, dual ἔμβητον: (ἐν) :—*to step in,* μή τις ἐμβήῃ *let none step in* (to interfere), Il. 2. *to go on, go quickly,* ἔμβητον, says Antilochus to his horses, Ib. ; ἔμβα *advance,* Eur. 3. *to step into a ship, embark, go on board,* Hom., etc. : — pf. *to be mounted on,* ἐμβεβαὼς ἵπποισι Il. ; also c. acc., Ἴλιον ἐμβεβαώς Eur. 4. *to step upon,* c. dat., Od., Aesch. 5. *to enter upon,* εἰς κίνδυνον Xen. ; c. acc., ἐμβ. κέλευθον Eur., Plat. 6. rarely c. gen. *to step upon,* γῆς ὅρων Soph. 7. in Poets, with acc. of the instrument of motion (cf. βαίνω II. 3`), ἐμβήσει (2 sing.) πόδα Eur. II. Causal in aor. 1 ἐνέβησα, *to make to step in, put in,* Od., Eur. ; ἐμβῆσαί τινα εἰς φροντίδα to make him anxious, Hdt.

ἐμ-βάλλω, f. –βᾰλῶ : pf. –βέβληκα : aor. 2 ἐνέβαλον : (ἐν) :—*to throw in, put in,* Il., etc. ; ἐμβ. τινὰ εἰς τὸ

δεσμωτήριον *to throw* one into prison, Dem. ; ἔμβαλλε χεῖρα δεξιάν, as a pledge of good faith, Soph. 2. ἐμβ. τινί τι θυμῷ *to put* it *into* his mind, Hom. ; so, ἐμβ. ἵμερον, μένος τινί Id. ; βουλὴν ἐμβ. περί τινος *to give* one counsel about a thing, Xen. 3. *to throw at, upon* or *against,* νηΐ κεραυνόν Od. ; ἐμβ. πληγάς *to inflict* stripes, Xen. ; ἐμβ. πῦρ *to apply* it, Thuc. :—metaph., ἐμβ. φόβον τινί *to strike* fear into him, Lat. *incutere timorem,* Hdt. II. intr. (sub. στρατόν) *to make an inroad* or *invasion,* Id. b. generally *to break, burst, rush in,* Aeschin. ; ἐμβάλωμεν εἰς ἄλλον λόγον Eur. 2. *to strike* a ship *with the ram, to charge* or *ram* it, c. dat., Hdt., Thuc. 3. κώπῃ ἐμβάλλειν (sub. χεῖρας) *to lay oneself* to the oar, Lat. *incumbere remis,* Od. ; and ἐμβάλλειν alone, *to lay to, pull hard,* Ar. 4. of a river, *to empty itself,* Plat. III. Med. *to throw in what is one's own,* Dem. 2. metaph., ἐμβάλλεσθαί τι θυμῷ *to lay* it to heart, *consider* it, Il. 3. c. gen., ἐμβάλεσθε τῶν λαγῴων *fall upon* the hare's flesh, Ar. IV. Pass. of ships, *to charge,* Thuc.

ἔμβαμμα, ατος, τό, (ἐμβάπτω) *sauce, soup,* Xen.

ἐμβαπτίζω, = sq., Plut.

ἐμ-βάπτω, f. ψω, (ἐν) *to dip in,* Ar.

ἐμβάς, άδος, ἡ, (ἐμβαίνω) *a felt-shoe,* Hdt., Ar.

ἐμβάς, aor. 2 part. of ἐμβαίνω.

ἐμ-βᾰσἴλεύω, f. σω, (ἐν) *to be king in* or *among* others, c. dat., Hom.

ἔμβᾰσις, εως, ἡ, (ἐμβαίνω) *that on which one goes* or *steps,* ἔμβασις ποδός, i. e. *a shoe,* Aesch. 2. *the foot, hoof,* Eur. 3. *a bath,* Anth.

ἐμβᾰσί-χῠτρος, ὁ, (ἐμβαίνω) *name* of a mouse in Batr.

ἐμ-βᾰτεύω, f. σω, (ἐμβάτης) *to step in* or *on, to frequent, haunt* a place, c. acc., of tutelary gods, Aesch., etc. :—c. gen., simply, *to set foot upon,* Soph. II. ἐμβατ. κλήρους *to enter on, come into possession of,* Eur. ; so, ἐμβ. φς τι Dem.

ἐμβᾰτήριος, ον, (ἐμβαίνω) *of* or *for marching in,* ἐμβ. παιάν *a march,* Plut.

ἐμβάτης [ᾰ], ου, ὁ, (ἐμβαίνω) *a half-boot of felt,* Xen.

ἐμβάφιον, τό, (ἐμβάπτω) *a flat vessel for sauces,* Hdt.

ἐμβέβᾰα, Ep. pf. of ἐμβαίνω :—ἐμβέβᾰσαν, 3 pl. plqpf.

ἔμβη, Ep. for ἐνέβη, 3 sing. aor. 2 of ἐμβαίνω :—**ἔμβητον,** 3 dual :—**ἐμβήῃ,** 3 sing. subj.

ἐμβῑβάζω, Att. f. –βιβῶ, Causal of ἐμβαίνω, *to set in* or *on,* Plat. :—*to put on board ship, cause to embark,* Thuc., Xen. 2. *to lead* to a thing, Eur., Dem.

ἔμβλεμμα, ατος, τό, (ἐμβλέπω) *a looking straight at,* Xen. From

ἐμ-βλέπω, f. ψω, (ἐν) *to look in the face, look at,* τινι or εἴς τινα Plat. ; absol., Xen.

ἔμβλημα, ατος, τό, (ἐμβάλλω) *an insertion,* τὸ εἰς τὸν σίδηρον ἔμβλ. *the shaft fitted into* the spear-head, Plut.

ἐμ-βοάω, f. ήσομαι, (ἐν) *to call upon, shout to,* τινί Xen. ; absol., Thuc.

ἐμβολεύς, έως, ὁ, (ἐμβάλλω) *anything put in : a dibble for setting plants,* Anth.

ἐμβολή, ἡ, (ἐμβάλλω) *a putting into* its place, *insertion* of a letter, Plat. II. intr. *a breaking in, inroad into an enemy's country, foray,* Xen. 2. *an assault, attack, charge,* Eur. :—esp. *the charge made by one ship upon another,* Aesch., Thuc. ; ἐμβολαῖς χαλκοστόμοις *with shocks of brasen beaks,*

Aesch. 3. *the stroke* of a missile, Eur. 4. *a way into, entrance, pass*, Hdt., Xen. III. *the head of a battering-ram*, Thuc.

ἐμβόλιμος, ον, (ἐμβάλλω) *inserted, intercalated*, Hdt.

ἔμβολος, ὁ, or **ἔμβολον, τό,** (ἐμβάλλω) *anything pointed so as to be easily thrust in:* τῆς χώρης ἔμβολον *a tongue* of land, Hdt. 2. *in ships of war, the beak* or *ram* of a ship of war, masc. in Hdt.; neut. in Thuc. b. οἱ ἔμβολοι *the rostra* in the Roman forum, Plut. 3. *the wedge-shaped order of battle*, Lat. *cuneus*, neut. in Xen. 4. *a bolt, bar*, neut., Eur.

ἐμ-βραδύνω [ῡ], f. ῠνῶ, (ἐν) *to dwell on*, τινί Luc.

ἔμ-βραχυ, (ἐν) Adv. *in brief, shortly*, Ar., Plat.

ἔμ-βρεφος, ον, (ἐν) *boy-like*, Anth.

ἐμβρῑθής, ές, (ἐν, βρίθω) *weighty*, Hdt., Plat. 2. metaph., like Lat. *gravis, weighty, grave, dignified*, Plut. 3. *in bad sense, heavy, grievous*, Aesch.

ἐμ-βρῑμάομαι, (ἐν) Dep. c. aor. med. et pass., *to snort in*, of horses, Aesch. 2. of persons, *to be deeply moved*, N. T. II. c. dat. pers. *to admonish urgently, rebuke*, Ib.

ἐμ-βροντάομαι, (ἐν, βροντάω) Pass. *to be stricken by lightning*, Xen. Hence

ἐμβρόντητος, ον, *thunderstruck, stupefied, stupid*, Lat. *attonitus*, Xen., Dem.

ἐμ-βρύ-οικος [ῠ], **ον,** (ἐν, βρύον, οἰκέω) *dwelling in sea-weed*, Anth.

ἔμβρυον, τό, (ἐν, βρύω) *a young one*, Od. II. *an embryo*, Lat. *foetus*, Aesch.

ἐμβύθιος, α, ον, or **ος, ον,** (ἐν, βυθός) *at the bottom* of the sea, Anth.

ἐμ-βύω [ῠ], f. ύσω, (ἐν) *to stuff in, stop with* a thing, Ar.

ἐμέγηρα, aor. 1 of μεγαίρω.

ἔμεινα, aor. 1 of μένω.

ἐμέθεν, ἐμεῖο, Ep. genitive of ἐγώ.

ἐμέλλησα, aor. 1 of μέλλω.

ἐμέμηκον, Ep. redupl. aor. 2 of μηκάομαι.

ἐμέμικτο, 3 sing. plqpf. pass. of μίγνυμι.

ἐμέν, poët. for ἐσμέν, 1 pl. of εἰμί (*sum*).

ἔμεν, ἔμεναι, Ep. for εἶναι, inf. of εἰμί (*sum*).

ἔμεν, ἔμεναι, Ep. for εἶναι, aor. 2 inf. of ἵημι:—**ἔμενος,** part. med.

ἐμέο, Ep. gen. of ἐγώ.

ἐμέσαι, aor. 1 of ἐμέω.

ἐμετικός, ή, όν, *one who uses emetics*, like the Roman gourmands, Plut. From

ἔμετος, ὁ, (ἐμέω) *vomiting*, Lat. *vomitus*, Hdt.

ἐμεῦ, Ep. gen. of ἐγώ: **ἐμεῦς,** Dor.

ἘΜΕ'Ω, impf. ἤμουν, Ion. ἤμεον: f. ἐμέσω, Att. ἐμῶ, med. ἐμοῦμαι: aor. 1 ἤμεσα, Ep. ἔμεσσα: pf. ἐμήμεκα:—*to vomit, throw up*, Il., Hdt., etc.: absol. *to vomit, to be sick*, Hdt., Att.; ἐμ. πτίλῳ *to make oneself sick* with a feather, Ar.

ἐμεωυτοῦ, Ion. for ἐμαυτοῦ.

ἔμηνα, aor. 1 in causal sense, of μαίνομαι.

ἔμικτο, 3 sing. Ep. aor. 2 pass. of μίγνυμι.

ἐμίν, ἐμίγα, Dor. for ἐμοί, ἐμοίγε, dat. of ἐγώ.

ἐμ-μαίνομαι, (ἐν) Dep. *to be mad at* a thing, c. dat., N.T.

ἐμ-μαλλος, ον, (ἐν) *woolly, fleecy*, Luc.

ἐμ-μανής, ές, (ἐν μανίᾳ ὤν) *in madness, frantic, raving*, Hdt., Aesch., etc.

ἐμ-μαπέως, Adv. *quickly, readily, hastily*, Hom. (Perh. from μαπέειν, μάρπτω, *to seize eagerly*.)

ἐμ-μάττομαι, Dep. *to knead bread in*, Ar.

ἐμ-μάχομαι [ᾰ], (ἐν) Dep. *to fight a battle in*, Hdt.

ἐμ-μειδιάω, f. άσω [ᾱ!], (ἐν) *to smile* or *be glad at*, Xen.

ἐμμέλεια, ἡ, (ἐμμελής) *harmony: a stately Tragic dance*, Plat.: *the tune of this dance*, Hdt.

ἐμ-μελετάω, f. ήσω, (ἐν) *to exercise* or *train in* a thing, Plat. Hence

ἐμμελέτημα, ατος, τό, *an exercise, a practice*, Anth.

ἐμ-μελής, ές, (ἐν, μέλος) *sounding in unison, in tune* or *time, harmonious*, Plat. II. metaph., of persons, *in tune* or *harmony, orderly, suitable, proper*, Plat.:—*graceful, elegant*, Id. III. Adv. -λῶς, Ion. -έως, *harmoniously, suitably, decorously*, Simon., Plat.

ἐμ-μεμαώς, υῖα, ός, (ἐν, *μάω) *in eager haste, eager*, of persons, Il.

ἐμ-μέμονα, (ἐν) *to be lost in passion*, Soph.

ἔμμεν, ἔμμεναι, Ep. for εἶναι, inf. of εἰμί (*sum*).

ἐμμενής, ές, *abiding in:* neut. ἐμμενές as Adv., ἐμμενὲς αἰεί *unceasing ever*, Hom.:—so ἐμμενέως, Hes. From

ἐμ-μένω, f. -μενῶ, (ἐν) *to abide in* a place, Thuc. 2. *to abide by, stand by, cleave to, be true to* one's word, oath, etc., c. dat., Hdt., Att.: also, ἐμμ. ἐν σπονδαῖς Thuc.:—absol. *to stand fast, be faithful*, Eur. 3. of things, *to stand fast, hold good, be fixed*, Aesch., etc.

ἐμμετρία, ἡ, *fit measure, proportion*, Plat. From

ἔμ-μετρος, ον, (ἐν, μέτρον) *in measure, proportioned, suitable, moderate*, Plat. II. *in metre, metrical*, Id.

ἐμμετρότης, ητος, ἡ, *proportion, fitness*, Aristaen.

ἐμ-μηνος, ον, (ἐν, μήν) *in a month, done* or *paid every month, monthly*, Soph., Theocr.

ἔμ-μητρος, ον, (ἐν, μήτρα) *with pith in it*, Theocr.

ἐμμί, Aeol. for εἰμί (*sum*).

ἐμ-μίγνυμαι, (ἐν) Pass. *to be mixed* or *mingled in*, Aesch. II. intr. in Act. *to encounter*, c. dat., Soph.

ἔμ-μισθος, ον, (ἐν) *in pay, in receipt of pay, hired*, Thuc.

ἐμμονή, ἡ, (ἐμμένω) *an abiding by, cleaving to*, τινος Plat.

ἔμμονος, ον, (ἐμμένω) *abiding by, steadfast*, Xen.; ἔμμ. τινι *abiding by* a thing, Id.

ἔμμορα, pf. 2 of μείρομαι.

ἔμ-μορος, ον, (ἐν, μείρομαι) *partaking in, endued with* a thing, c. gen., Od. II. (μόρος) *fortunate*, Anth.

ἔμ-μορφος, ον, (ἐν, μορφή) *in bodily form*, Plut.

ἔμ-μοτος, ον, (ἐν, μοτός) *needing to be stopped with lint:* metaph. ἔμμοτον τῶνδ᾽ ἄκος *a cure to heal these wounds*, Aesch.

ἔμ-μοχθος, ον, (ἐν) *toilsome*, βίοτος Eur.

ἐμ-μυέομαι, f. ήσω, (ἐν) *to initiate in:* Pass., μῶν ἐνεμυήθης δῆτ᾽ ἐν αὐτῷ τὰ μεγάλα; *what, were you initiated at the great mysteries in that shabby coat?* Ar.

ἔμνησα, aor. 1 of μιμνήσκω: ἐμνήσθην aor. 1 pass.

ἐμνώοντο, Ep. for ἐμνῶντο, 3 pl. impf. of μνάομαι.

ἐμοί, dat. of ἐγώ.

ἔμολον, aor. 2 of βλώσκω.

ἐμός, ή, όν, possess. Pron. of first pers., (ἐγώ, ἐμοῦ) *mine*, Lat. *meus*, Hom., etc.; by crasis with the Art., οὑμός, τοὐμόν, τοὐμοῦ, τᾠμῷ, τἀμά:—to strengthen the possessive notion, ἐμὸν αὐτοῦ *mine own*, Il.; τὸν ἐμὸν αὐτοῦ βίον Ar. 2. objectively, *to me, relating to me, against*

me, ἐμὴ ἀγγελίη Hom.; τὴν ἐμὴν αἰδῶ respect for me, Aesch.; αἱ ἐμαὶ διαβολαί slanders against me, Thuc.; τοὐμὸν αἷμα πατρός his blood shed by me, Soph.   3. τὸ ἐμόν, τὰ ἐμά my property, Ar., etc. :—but also, τὰ ἐμά or τὸ ἐμόν, my part, my affairs, my interest, οὕτω τὸ ἐμὸν ἔχει things stand thus with me, Hdt.; ἔρρει τἀμά Xen.;—hence periphr. for ἐγώ or ἐμέ, Soph.; or absol., τό γε ἐμόν, τὸ μὲν ἐμόν, for my part, as far as concerns me, Hdt., etc.   4. ἡ ἐμή (sub. γῆ) my country, Thuc.

ἐμοῦμαι, f. med. of ἐμέω.

ἔμπᾰ, Adv., v. ἔμπᾱς.

ἐμπᾰγείς, aor. 2 pass. part. of ἐμπήγνυμι.

ἐμπάζομαι, (perh. from ἔμπαιος) Dep. only in pres. to busy oneself about, take heed of, care for a thing, c. gen., Hom.; once c. acc. pers., Il.

ἐμ-πᾰθής, ές, (πάθος) in a state of emotion, much affected by or at a thing, Plut.

ἔμπαιγμα, τό, and ἐμπαιγμονή, ἡ, mockery, N. T. From

ἐμ-παίζω, f. ξοῦμαι, (ἐν) to mock at, mock, Lat. illudere, τινί Hdt.: absol., Soph.   II. to sport in or on a place, c. dat., Eur.   Hence

ἐμπαίκτης, ου, ὁ, a mocker, deceiver, N. T.

ἐμπαῖξαι, aor. 1 inf. of ἐμπαίζω.

ἔμπαιος, ον (A), possessed of or practised in a thing, c. gen., Od. (Perh. from ἐν, πάομαι.)

ἔμ-παιος, ον (B), (παίω) bursting in, sudden, Aesch.

ἐμπαίω, f. -παίσω or -παιήσω, to strike in, stamp, emboss, Ath.   II. intr. to burst in upon, c. dat., Soph.

ἐμ-πακτόω, f. ώσω, (ἐν) to close by stuffing in or caulking, Hdt.

ἐμ-πᾰλάσσομαι, Pass. to be entangled in, Hdt.: absol., ἐμπαλασσόμενοι entangled one with another, Thuc.

ἔμπᾰλιν, (ἐν) Adv., in Att. and Prose often with the Art., τὸ ἔμπαλιν or τοὔμπαλιν, τὰ ἔμπαλιν or τἄμπαλιν:—backwards, back, h. Hom., Hes., etc.   II. contrariwise, the opposite way, ἐκ τοὔμπαλιν from the opposite side, Thuc.   2. c. gen. contrary to, Hdt.; τοὔμπ. οὗ βούλονται Xen.

ἐμ-πᾰνηγῠρίζω, f. σω, (ἐν) to hold assemblies in, Plut.

ἐμ-παρέχω, f. ξω, (ἐν) to give into another's hands, put into his power to do, c. inf., Thuc.

ἐμ-παροινέω, (ἐν) to behave like one drunken, Luc.

ΈΜΠΑΣ, Ep. ἔμπης, poët. also ἔμπᾰ, Adv. notwithstanding, nevertheless, Hom.; with a negat., not at all, Id.; after a part. with περ, like ὅμως, πίνοντά περ ἔμπης, busy though he was with drinking, Il. :—so in Trag., at any rate, yet.

ἐμ-πάσσω, Att. -ττω: f. -πάσω [ᾰ], (ἐν) to sprinkle in or on, Plat.: metaph. to weave as patterns in a web of cloth, Il.

ἐμ-πᾰτέω, f. ήσω, (ἐν) to walk in or into a place, enter, c. acc., Aesch.

ἔμπεδα, Adv., v. ἔμπεδος.

ἐμπεδ-ορκέω, f. ήσω, to abide by one's oath, Hdt., Xen.

ἔμ-πεδος, ον, (ἐν, πέδον) in the ground, firm-set, steadfast, Hom.; of events, sure and certain, Od.   2. of Time, lasting, continual, Hom.   II. neut. ἔμπεδον as Adv., μένειν ἔμπεδον to stand fast, Il.; θέειν ἔμπεδον to run on and on, run without resting, Ib.;

strengthd., ἔμπεδον αἰέν Ib. :—so in pl., τίκτει δ' ἔμπεδα μῆλα the flocks bring forth without fail, Od. :—also in Att. Poets, of a surety, Soph.; but more often ἐμπέδως, Aesch., Soph.   Hence

ἐμπεδόω, impf. ἠμπέδουν, f. ώσω, to fix in the earth: generally, to make firm and fast, establish, Eur., Xen.

ἐμπείρᾱμος, ον, poët. for ἐμπέραμος.

ἐμπειρία, ἡ, experience, Eur., Thuc., etc.   2. c. gen. rei, experience in, acquaintance with, Thuc., etc.; also, ἐμπ. περί τι Xen.   From

ἔμ-πειρος, ον, (ἐν, πεῖρα) experienced or practised in a thing, acquainted with it, c. gen., Hdt., Att. :—absol., οἱ ἔμπειροι the experienced, Soph., Plat., etc.; ναυσὶν ἐμπείροις with ships proved by use, Thuc. :—τὸ ἐμπειρότερον αὐτῶν their greater experience, Id.   II. Adv., ἐμπείρως τινὸς ἔχειν to know a thing by experience, by its issue, Xen.

ἐμπελᾰδόν, Adv., near, hard by, c. dat., Hes.   From

ἐμ-πελάζω, f. σω, (ἐν) to bring near, Hes. :—Pass. to come near, approach, c. gen., Soph.   II. intr. in Act., like Pass. to approach, c. dat., h. Hom., Soph.

ἐμπεπλησμένος, pf. pass. part. of ἐμπίπλημι.

ἐμπέρᾱμος, ον, = ἔμπειρος, skilled in the use of a thing, c. gen., Anth.; also ἐμπείρᾱμος, Id.

ἐμ-περιπᾰτέω, f. ήσω, (ἐν) to walk about in, Luc. :—absol. to walk about, Id.

ἐμ-περόνημα, Dor. -ᾱμα, ατος, τό, (ἐν) a garment fastened with a brooch on the shoulder, Theocr.

ἔμπεσον, Ep. for ἐνέπεσον, aor. 2 of ἐμπίπτω.

ἐμ-πεσοῦμαι, f. of ἐμπίπτω.

ἐμ-πετάννῡμι or -ύω, f. -πετάσω, (ἐν) :—to unfold and spread in or on, Il.

ἔμπετες, Dor. for ἐνέπεσες, 2 sing. aor. 2 of ἐμπίπτω.

ἐμ-πήγνῡμι and -ύω: f. -πήξω, (ἐν) to fix or plant in, c. dat., Il. :—Pass., with pf. and plqpf. act. to be fixed or stuck in, to stick in, τινί or ἐν τινι Ar.

ἐμ-πηδάω, f. ήσομαι, (ἐν) to jump upon a person, c. dat., Hdt.   2. to leap in or into, absol. in aor. 1 part. ἐμπηδήσας, eagerly, greedily, Luc.

ἔμ-πηρος, ον, (ἐν) crippled, maimed, Hdt.

ἔμπης, Ep. for ἔμπας.

ἐμ-πικραίνομαι, (ἐν, πικρός) Med. or Pass. to be bitter against a person, c. dat., Hdt.

ἐμ-πίμπλημι, -πίμπρημι, v. ἐμ-πίπλημι, -πίπρημι.

ἐμ-πίνω [ῑ], f. -πίομαι: aor. 2 ἐνέπιον: pf. ἐμπέπωκα: (ἐν): — to drink in, drink greedily, Eur., etc.; ἐμπ. τοῦ αἵματος to drink greedily of the blood, Hdt.   2. absol. to drink one's fill, Theogn., Xen.

ἐμ-πίπλημι, not ἐμ-πίμπλημι but impf. med. ἐνεπιμπλάμην; imper. ἐμπίπληθι, Att. ἐμπίπλη: f. ἐμπλήσω: pf. ἐμπέπληκα :—Pass., aor. 1 ἐνεπλήσθην: Ep. aor. 2 ἐμπλήμην: (ἐν) :—to fill quite full, Od., Xen.   2. c. gen. to fill full of a thing, Hom., etc.   II. Med. to fill for oneself or what is one's own, ἐμπλήσατο νηδὺν Od.; μένεος ἐμπλήσατο θυμόν he filled his heart with rage, Il.   III. Pass. to be filled full of a thing, c. gen., Hom. :—metaph., υἷος ἐνιπλησθῆναι to take my fill of my son, i.e. to sate myself with looking on him, Od.; so c. part. to be satiated with doing, Eur., Xen.   2. c. dat., καρπῷ ἐμπ. to be filled with . . , Hdt.   3. absol. to eat one's fill, Id., etc.

ἐμ-πίπρημι, not ἐμπίμπρημι: also (as if from ἐμπι-

πράω)inf. ἐμπιπρᾶν: impf. ἐνεπίμπρων, 3 pl. –πίμπρασαν: f. ἐμπρήσω: aor. 1 ἐνέπρησα:—Pass., f. ἐμπεπρήσομαι or (in med. form) ἐμπρήσομαι: aor. 1 ἐνεπρήσθην. pf. ἐμπέπρησμαι: (ἐν):—to kindle, burn, set on fire, Il., Hdt., Soph.; also c. gen., πυρὸς νῆας ἐνιπρῆσαι to burn them by force of fire, Il.:—Pass. to be on fire, Hdt.

ἐμ-πίπτω, f. –πεσοῦμαι: aor. 2 ἐνέπεσον, Ep. ἔμπεσον: —to fall in or upon or into, c. dat., Hom., etc. **2.** to fall upon, attack, Id.; also ἐμπ. εἰς . . , Hdt., etc.; rarely c. acc., Soph., Eur. **3.** to light or chance upon a thing, to fall in with, τινί Hdt., etc.; more commonly ἐμπ. εἰς . . , Lat. incidere in . . , Soph., etc. **4.** to break in, burst in or into, c. dat., Id., etc.; aor. 2 part. ἐμπεσών violently, Hdt.

ΕΜΠΙ͂Σ, ίδος, ὁ, a mosquito, gnat, Lat. culex, Ar.

ἐμ-πιστεύω, f. σω, (ἐν) to entrust, τινί τι Plut.:—Pass. to be entrusted with, τι Luc.

ἐμπίτνω, poët. for ἐμπίπτω, to fall upon, τινί Aesch., Soph.

ἐμ-πλάσσω, f. –πλάσω [ă], to plaster up, Hdt.

ἔμ-πλειος, η, ον, Ep. for ἔμπλεος.

ἐμ-πλέκω, Ep. ἐνι-πλέκω, f. ξω:—Pass., aor. 2 ἐνεπλάκην, part. ἐμπλακείς: (ἐν):—to plait or weave in, Lat. implicare, χεῖρα ἐμπ. to entwine one's hand in another's clothes, so as to hold him, Eur.:—Pass. to be entangled in a thing, c. dat., Soph., Eur.

ἔμπλεος, α, ον: Att. –πλεως, ων: Ep. ἔμπλειος, ἐνίπλειος, η, ον:—quite full of a thing, Od., Hdt., etc.

ἐμ-πλέω, f. –πλεύσομαι, (ἐν) to sail in, πλοίῳ Hdt.: absol., οἱ ἐμπλέοντες the crews, Thuc.

ἐμπλήγδην, Adv. (ἐμπλήσσω) madly, rashly, Od.

ἐμπληκτικός, ή, όν, (ἐμπλήσσω) easily scared, Plut.

ἔμπληκτος, ον, (ἐμπλήσσω) stunned, amazed, stupefied, Lat. attonitus, Xen., Plut. **2.** unstable, capricious, Soph., Eur. **II.** Adv. –τως, rashly ; τὸ ἐμπλήκτως ὀξὺ startling rapidity of action, Thuc.

ἐμπλήμενος, Ep. aor. 2 part. 2 pass. of ἐμπίπλημι.

ἔμπλην, Adv. near, next, close by, c. gen., Il. (Prob. from ἐμπελάζω.)

ἔμπλην, Adv. strengthd. for πλήν, besides, except, c. gen., Archil.

ἔμπληντο, Ep. 3 pl. aor. 2 pass. of ἐμπίπλημι.

ἐμπληξία, ἡ, amazement, stupidity, Aeschin.

ἐμπλήσας, –σάμενος, aor. 1 part. act. and med. of ἐμπίπλημι:—ἐμπλήσατο, Ep. for ἐνεπλήσατο.

ἐμ-πλήσσω, Att. –ττω, ἐνιπλ–, f. ξω, to strike against, fall upon or into, c. dat., Hom.

ἐμπληστέος, α, ον, verb. Adj. of ἐμπίπλημι, to be filled with, τινός Plat.

ἔμπλητο, 3 sing. Ep. aor. 2 pass. of ἐμπίπλημι.

ἐμ-πνέω, poët. –πνείω: f. –πνεύσομαι: aor. 1 ἐνέπνευσα: —to blow or breathe upon, c. dat., Il., Eur. **2.** absol. to breathe, live, be alive, Aesch., Soph., Plat., etc.; βραχὺν βίοτον ἐμπνέων ἔτι Eur. **3.** c. gen. to breathe of, φόνου, Lat. caedem spirare, N.T. **II.** trans. to blow into, ἱστίον ἐμ. to swell the sail, h. Hom. **2.** to breathe into, inspire, μένος or θάρσος τινί Hom. Hence

ἔμπνοια, ἡ, inbreathing, inspiration, Luc.; and

ἔμπνοος, ον, contr. –πνους, ουν, with the breath in one, breathing, alive, Hdt., Att.

ἐμ-ποδίζω, f. Att. ιῶ: Pass., pf. –πεπόδισμαι: (ἐν, πούς):—to put the feet in bonds, to fetter, Hdt.: —Pass., ἐμπεποδισμένος τοὺς πόδας Id. **II.** generally, to hinder, thwart, impede, Lat. impedire, τινά Ar., Xen.; πρός τι in a thing, Isocr.:—Pass., Soph. **III.** ὥσπερ ἐμποδίζων ἰσχάδας like one stringing figs or treading figs flat for packing, Ar.

ἐμπόδιος, ον, at one's feet, coming in the way, meeting, ap. Plut. **2.** in the way, impeding, c. dat. pers., Eur.:—c. gen. rei, ἐμπ. εἶναι εἰρήνης Thuc.

ἐμ-ποδών, Adv. = ἐν ποσὶν ὤν, but formed by anal. to ἐκποδών:—at the feet, in the way, in one's path, Hdt., etc. **2.** in one's way, presenting an hindrance, ἐμπ. εἶναι to be in the way, Aesch.; ἐμπ. στῆναί τινι Id.; κεῖσθαι Eur.:—c. inf., ἐμπ. εἶναι τῷ ποιεῖν Xen.; ἐμπ. εἶναι or γίγνεσθαί τινι μὴ πράττειν to prevent a person's doing, Thuc., etc.:—τὸ ἐμπ. the hindrance, obstacle, Hdt.

ἐμ-ποιέω, f. ήσω, (ἐν) to make in, Il.:—Pass., χελιδὼν ἐμπεποιημένη introduced by the poet's art, Ar. **2.** to foist in, interpolate, Hdt. **II.** to produce or create in, of states of mind, ἐπιθυμίαν τοῖς Ἀθηναίοις ἐμπ. Thuc.; κακόν τι ἐμπ. ταῖς ψυχαῖς Plat. **2.** of conditions, to introduce, produce, cause, φθόρον, στάσιν Thuc.

ἐμπολαῖος, α, ον, concerned in traffic, Ar. From

ἐμπολάω: impf. ἠμπόλων: f. ήσω: aor. 1 ἠμπόλησα: pf. ἠμπόληκα:—Pass., aor. 1 ἠμπολήθην: pf. ἠμπόλημαι, Ion. ἐμπ–: (ἐμπολή):—to get by barter or traffic, earn, Soph., Xen.:—Med., βίοτον πολὺν ἐμπολόωντο they were getting much substance by traffic, Od. **2.** to deal or traffic in a thing, to purchase, buy, Soph.:—metaph., ἐμπ. τὴν ἐμὴν φρένα to make profit of my mind, by dealing with me, Id. **II.** absol. to deal as a merchant, traffic, Ar.:—metaph., ἠμποληκὼς τὰ πλεῖστ' ἀμείνονα having dealt in most things with success, Aesch.

ἐμ-πολέμιος, ον, (ἐν) pertaining to war, Hdt.

ἐμπολεύς, έως, ὁ, a merchant, trafficker, Anth. From

ἐμ-πολή, ἡ, (ἐν, πωλέω) merchandise, Ar., Xen. **II.** traffic, purchase, Eur., Xen.

ἐμπόλημα, ατος, τό, (ἐμπολάω) matter of traffic, the freight of a ship, merchandise, Soph. (metaph.), Eur. **II.** gain made by traffic, Theophr.

ἐμπολητός, ή, όν, (ἐμπολάω) bought, οὑμπολητὸς Σισύφου Λαερτίῳ the son of Sisyphus bought by or palmed off upon Laërtes, Soph.

ἔμ-πολις, εως, ὁ, ἡ, (ἐν) in the city or state: ὁ ἐμπ. τινι one's fellow-citizen, Soph.

ἐμ-πολῖτεύω, f. σω, (ἐν) to be one of a state, to be a citizen, hold civil rights, Thuc.

ἐμπολόωντο, Ep. for –ῶντο, 3 pl. pres. med. of ἐμπολάω.

ἐμ-πομπεύω, f. σω, (ἐν) to swagger in procession, Luc.

ἐμπόρευμα, ατος, τό, merchandise, Xen. From

ἐμ-πορεύομαι, f. –πορεύσομαι: aor. 1 ἐνεπορεύθην: (ἐν): Dep.:—to travel, Soph. **II.** to travel for traffic, to be a merchant, to trade, traffic, Thuc. **2.** c. acc. rei, to import, Luc. **3.** c. acc. pers. to make gain of, to overreach, N.T. Hence

ἐμπορευτέα, verb. Adj. one must go or tramp, Ar.

ἐμπορία, Ion. –ίη, ἡ, (ἔμπορος) commerce, trade, traffic, Hes., etc. **2.** a trade or business, N.T., Anth. **II.** merchandise, Xen., Dem.

ἐμπορικός, ή, όν, commercial, mercantile, Stesich.;

ἐμπ. τέχνη = ἐμπορία, Plat.; ἐμπ. δίκαι *mercantile* actions, Dem.; τὰ ἐμπ. χρήματα money *to be used in trade*, Id. 2. *imported, foreign*, Ar.; and

ἐμπόριον, τό, Lat. *emporium, a trading-place, mart, factory*, such as were formed by the Phoenicians and Carthaginians, Hdt., etc. 2. τὸ ἐμπ., at Athens, *the Exchange*, where the merchants resorted, Dem. II. ἐμπόρια, τά, *merchandise*, Xen. From

ἔμ-πορος, ον, (ἐν, πόρος, cf. περάω) *one who goes on shipboard as a passenger*, Lat. *vector*, Od. II. = ὁ ἐν πόρῳ ὤν, *any one on a journey, a traveller, wanderer*, Trag. III. *a merchant, trader*, Lat. *mercator*, Hdt., etc.:—metaph., ἔμπορος βίου *a trafficker* in life, Eur.

ἐμ-πορπάω, Ion. -έω, f. ήσω, (ἐν) *to fasten with a brooch*:—Pass., εἵματα ἐνεπορπέατο (Ion. for -ηντο) they wore garments *fastened with a brooch*, Hdt.

Ἔμπουσα, ἡ, *Empusa, a hobgoblin* assuming various shapes, Ar. (Deriv. unknown.)

ἔμ-πρακτος, ον, (ἐν) *practicable*:—Adv. -τως, Plut.

ἐμ-πρέπω, (ἐν) *to be conspicuous in*, c. dat., Aesch.; Βάκχαις among them, Ar. 2. *to be conspicuous* or *famous for* a thing, Trag. 3. *to suit*, τινί Plut.

ἐμ-πρήθω, f. σω, (ἐν) *to blow up, inflate*, Il.:—Pass., ἐμπεπρημένη ὗς *a bloated* sow, Ar. II. = ἐμπίπρημι, *to burn*, Il. Hence

ἔμπρησις, εως, Ion. ιος, ἡ, *a conflagration*, Hdt.

ἐμ-πρίω [ῑ], f. ίσω (ἐν) *to saw into, to gnash* the teeth *together*, Luc.

ἐμπροθεν, poët. for ἔμπροσθεν, Theocr.

ἐμ-πρόθεσμος, ον, (ἐν) *within the stated time*, Luc.

ἔμ-προσθεν, poët. -θε: I. Adv.: 1. of Place, *before, in front*, Hdt., Xen.: τὸ and τὰ ἔμπροσθεν *the front, fore-side*, Hdt., etc.; εἰς τὸ ἔμπρ. *forwards*, Id.; ἐκ τοῦ ἔμπρ. *opposite*, Xen. 2. of Time, *before, earlier, of old*, Plat. II. as Prep. with gen. *before, in front of*: 1. of Place, ἔμπρ. αὐτῆς (sc. τῆς νηός) Hdt. 2. of Time, ἔμπρ. ταύτης (sc. τῆς γνώμης) Id. Hence

ἐμπρόσθιος, ον, *fore, front*, of an animal's feet, Hdt., Xen.

ἐμ-πτύω, f. σω, (ἐν) *to spit into*, ἐς ποταμόν Hdt. II. *to spit upon*, N.T.

ἐμ-πυκάζω, (ἐν) *to wrap up in*:—Pass., νόος οἱ ἐμπεπύκασται his mind *is veiled, dark*, Mosch.

ἔμ-πυος, ον, (ἐν, πύον) *suppurating*, Soph.

ἐμ-πυρεύω, (ἐν) *to roast in* or *on the fire*, Ar.

ἐμ-πυρῐ-βήτης, ου, ὁ, (ἐν, πῦρ, βαίνω) *made for standing on the fire*, of a tripod, Il.

ἔμ-πυρος, ον, (ἐν, πῦρ) *in the fire*, ἡ ἔμπ. τέχνη the work of *the fire, the forge*, Plat.; also *the art of divining by fire*, Eur. II. *exposed to fire* or *sun, scorched, burnt*, Id. 2. *burning, fiery*, of the sun, Anth. 3. *lighted*, of a lamp, Id. III. *of* or *for a burnt-offering*, Eur. 2. as Subst., ἔμπυρα (sc. ἱερά), τά, *burnt sacrifices*, Soph., Eur.

ἐμ-φαγεῖν, inf. of aor. 2 ἐν-έφαγον, no pres. ἐν-εσθίω being in use:—*to eat hastily*, Xen. II. *to eat in* or *upon*, Luc.

ἐμ-φαίνω, f. -φᾰνῶ, (ἐν) *to let* a thing *be seen in* a mirror, Plat.:—*to exhibit, display*, Plut., etc. II. Pass., with fut. med. *to be seen in* a mirror, *to be reflected*, Plat., Xen. 2. *to become visible*, Id.

ἐμφᾰνής, ές, *shewing in* itself, *reflecting*, of mirrors, Plat. II. *visible to the eye, manifest*, esp. of the gods *appearing bodily* among men, Soph., etc.; so, ἐμφανῆ τινα ἰδεῖν *to see him bodily*, Id.:—of things, τἀμφανῆ κρύπτειν Id.; ἐμφ. τεκμήρια *visible* proofs, Id.; τὰ ἐμφ. κτήματα the *actual* property, Xen. 2. ποιεῖν τι ἐμφανές *to do it in public*, Lat. *in propatulo*, Hdt.; τὸ ἐμφ. opp. to τὸ μέλλον, Thuc.; εἰς τοὐμφανὲς ἰέναι *to come into light*, Xen. 3. *open, actual, palpable*, Ar., Thuc., etc. 4. *manifest, well-known*, τὰ ἐμφανῆ Hdt. III. Adv. -νῶς, Ion. -νέως, *visibly, openly*, Lat. *palam*, Id., Aesch., etc.; *openly*, i. e. *not secretly* or *treacherously*, Soph.; οὐ λόγοις ἀλλ' ἐμφανῶς but *really*, Ar. 2. so in neut. Adj., ἐξ ἐμφανέος or ἐκ τοῦ ἐμφ., Hdt.; ἐν τῷ ἐμφανεῖ Thuc.

ἐμφᾰνίζω, f. Att. ιῶ, *to make manifest, exhibit*, ἐμφ. τινὰ ἐπίορκον, φίλον *to represent* him as . . , Xen.:—Pass. *to become visible*, N. T. 2. *to make clear* or *plain*, τινί τι Xen.

ἐμφέρβομαι, poët. ἐνιφ-, Pass. *to feed in* a place, c. dat., Mosch.

ἐμφέρεια, ἡ, *likeness*, Plut. From

ἐμφερής, ές, (ἐμφέρω) *answering to, resembling*, τινί, Hdt., Att.: cf. προσφερής.

ἐμ-φέρω, f. ἐν-οίσω, *to bear* or *bring in*, cf. ἐμφορέω. II. ἐνεφέρετο an account was given, Not. ad Polyb.

ἐμ-φεύγω, f. -ξομαι, (ἐν) *to fly in* or *into*, Luc.

ἐμ-φῐλοχωρέω, f. ήσω, (ἐν) *to be fond of dwelling in, to dwell in*, τῇ μνήμῃ Luc.

ἐμ-φλέγω, f. ξω, (ἐν) *to kindle in*, τινί Anth.

ἔμ-φλοξ, ογος, ὁ, ἡ, (ἐν) *with fire in it*, πέτρος Anth.

ἔμ-φοβος, ον, (ἐν) *terrible*, Lat. *formidolosus*, Soph.

ἐμ-φορβιόομαι, (ἐν, φορβειά) Pass. *to have the mouth-band on*, Ar.

ἐμ-φορέω, = ἐμφέρω:—Pass. *to be borne about in* or *on*, c. dat., Od. II. *to pour in*, ἄκρατον Diod.:— Med. and Pass. *to take one's fill* or *make much use of* a thing, c. gen., Hdt., Plut. III. metaph. *to put upon, inflict on*, ἐμφορεῖν πληγάς τινι Id. 2. *to object to, throw in one's teeth*, Soph.

ἐμ-φράσσω, Att. -ττω, f. ξω, (ἐν) *to block up*, Thuc.

ἐμ-φρουρέω, f. ήσω, (ἐν) *to keep guard* in a place, Thuc.

ἔμ-φρουρος, ον, (ἐν) *on guard* in a place; οἱ ἔμφρουροι *the garrison*, Xen. II. pass. *garrisoned*, Dem.

ἔμ-φρων, ον, gen. ονος, (ἐν, φρήν) *in one's mind* or *senses*, Aesch., Soph. 2. *alive*, Id. II. *rational, intelligent*, Xen., Plat. 2. *sensible, shrewd, prudent*, Theogn., Soph., etc.

ἐμφύλιος, ον, = sq., ἐμφύλιοι *kinsfolk*, Soph.; αἷμ' ἐμφύλιον Id.; γῆ ἐμφύλιος *one's native* land, Id. II. *in one's tribe*, Ἄρης ἐμφύλιος Aesch.; μάχη Theocr.

ἔμ-φῦλος, ον, (ἐν, φῦλον) *of the same tribe* or *race*, Od. II. *in one's tribe*, ἐμφ. στάσις *civil* strife, Hdt.

ἐμ-φῡσάω, f. ήσω, (ἐν) *to blow in*: *to play the flute*, Ar.

ἐμ-φῡσιόω, (ἐν, φύσις) *to implant, instil into*, Xen.

ἔμ-φῠτος, ον, *implanted, innate, natural*, Hdt., Att.

ἐμ-φύω, f. -φύσω, (ἐν) *to implant*, τί τινι Od., Xen. II. Pass., with pf. ἐμπέφῡκα and aor. 2 ἐνέφῦν: 1. *to grow in* or *on*, c. dat., ὅθι τρίχες κρανίῳ ἐμπεφύασι (Ep. for ἐμπεφύκασι) Il.:—of qualities, φθόνος ἐμφύεται ἀνθρώπῳ is *implanted* in him, Hdt.; οὐδεὶς χαρακτὴρ ἐμπέφυκε σώματι no mark *is set by nature*

on the body, Eur. 2. *to be rooted in, cling closely,* ὡς ἔχετ' ἐμπεφυῖα (Ep. for ἐμπεφύκυῖα) she hung on *clinging,* Il.; ἔφυν ἐν χερσί *clung* to his hand, Od.; ἐμφὺς ὡς βδέλλα *clinging* like a leech, Theocr.

ἔμ-φωνος, ον, (ἐν, φωνή) *loud of voice,* Xen.

ἔμ-ψοφος, ον, (ἐν) *sounding,* Anth.

ἔμ-ψῡχος, ον, (ἐν, ψυχή) *having life in one, alive, living,* Hdt., Att. 2. of a speech, *animated,* Luc.

ἐμψῡχόω, *to animate,* Anth.

ἐν, Aeol. and Dor. for εἰς *into,* v. εἰς sub init.

'ΕΝ, poët. Ep. and poët. ἐνί, εἰν, εἰνί, Lat. *in.*
PREP. WITH DAT.: I. OF PLACE, 1. *in,* ἐν νήσῳ, ἐν Τροίῃ, etc., Hom., etc.:—elliptic, ἐν 'Αλκινόοιο (sc. οἴκῳ) Od.; εἰν 'Αἴδαο Il.; ἐν παιδο- τρίβου *at the school of* the training master, Ar. 2. *in, upon,* ἐν οὔρεσι Hom., etc. 3. *in the num- ber of, amongst,* ἐν Δαναοῖς, etc., Hom.; and with Verbs of ruling, ἄρχειν, ἀνάσσειν ἐν πολλοῖς to be first or lord *among* many, i. e. *over* them, Id.; cf. ὁ, ἡ, τό B. III. 3. 4. *in one's hands, within* one's reach or power, Lat. *penes,* Hom., etc.; ἐν σοὶ γάρ ἐσμεν Soph.; ἐν τῷ θεῷ τὸ τέλος ἦν Dem. 5. *in respect of,* ἐν γήρᾳ *in point of* age, Soph. 6. when ἐν is used with Verbs of motion, where we use the Prep. *into,* the construction is called *pregnant,* πίπτειν ἐν κονίῃσι *to fall* [to the dust and lie] *in* it; οἶνον εἶναι ἐν δέπαϊ Od., etc. II. OF THE STATE, CONDITION, POSITION, in which one is: 1. *of outward circumstances,* ἐν πολέμῳ, etc., Hom.; ἐν λόγοις εἶναι to be engaged *in* oratory, Plat.; οἱ ἐν τοῖς πράγμασι ministers of state, Thuc.; οἱ ἐν τέλει the magistrates, Id. 2. *of inward states,* of feeling, etc., ἐν φιλότητι Il.; ἐν φόβῳ εἶναι to be *in* fear, ἐν αἰσχύνῃ, etc.; also, ἐν ὀργῇ ἔχειν τινά to have him the object of one's anger, Thuc.; ἐν αἰτίᾳ ἔχειν τινά to blame him, Hdt. 3. often with a neut. Adj., ἐν βραχεῖ = βραχέως, Soph.; ἐν τάχει = ταχέως, Id.; ἐν ἐλαφρῷ ποιεῖσθαι Hdt.; ἐν ἴσῳ = ἴσως, Thuc. III. OF THE INSTRUMENT, MEANS or MANNER, *in* or *with,* ἐν πυρὶ πρῆσαι Il.; ἐν ὀφθαλμοῖς or ἐν ὄμμασιν ὁρᾶν have the object *in* one's eye, Lat. *in oculis,* Hom.; ἐν λιταῖς by prayers, ἐν δόλῳ by deceit, Aesch., etc. IV. OF TIME, *in, in the course of,* ὥρῃ ἐν εἰαρινῇ Il.; ἐν ἡμέρᾳ, ἐν νυκτί Hdt., Att.; ἐν ᾧ (sc. χρόνῳ), *while,* Hdt.:—ἐν ταῖς σπονδαῖς *in the time of* the truce, Xen. 2. *in, within,* ἐν ἔτεσι πεντήκοντα Thuc.; ἐν τρισὶ μησί Xen.

B. WITHOUT CASE, AS ADVERB, in the phrase ἐν δέ .. : 1. *and therein,* Hom. 2. *and among* them, Il. 3. *and besides, moreover,* Hom., Soph.

C. IN COMPOS.: 1. with Verbs, the Prep. retains its sense of being *in* or *at* a place, etc., c. dat., or foll. by εἰς or ἐν. 2. with Adjs., it qualifies, as in ἔμπικρος, *rather* better; or expresses the possession of a quality, as in ἔναιμος, *with blood in it,* ἔμφωνος *with* a voice. II. ἐν becomes ἐμ- before the labials β μ π φ ψ; ἐγ- before the gutturals γ κ ξ χ; ἐλ- before λ; and in a few words ἐρ- before ρ.

ἔν, neut. of εἶς.

ἐναβρύνομαι, Pass. *to be conceited in* or *of* a thing, τινι Luc.

ἐν-άγής, ές, = ἐν ἄγεϊ ὤν, (ἄγος) *under a curse, excom- municate, accurst,* Lat. *piacularis,* Hdt., etc.

ἐν-αγίζω, f. σω, *to offer sacrifice to the dead* or *manes,* Lat. *parentare,* τινί Hdt., etc. Hence

ἐνάγισμα, ατος, τό, *an offering to the manes,* Luc.; and

ἐναγισμός, ὁ, *an offering to the manes,* Plut.

ἐν-αγκαλίζομαι, Med. *to take in one's arms,* Anth.

ἐν-αγκυλάω, f. ἥσω, *to fit thongs* (ἀγκύλαι) *to* javelins, for throwing them by, Xen.

ἐναγρόμενος, η, ον, Ep. aor. 2 part. pass. of ἐναγείρω.

ἔν-αγχος, Adv. (ἄγχι) *just now, lately,* Ar., Plat.

ἐν-άγω, f. ξω, *to lead in* or *on,* Lat. *inducere,* Hdt., Thuc., etc.; mostly c. inf., μαίνεσθαι ἐνάγει ἀνθρώπους (sc. Bacchus) Hdt. 2. c. acc. rei, *to urge on, pro- mote,* τὸν πόλεμον Thuc.

ἐν-αγωνίζομαι, Ion. f. -ιεῦμαι, Dep. *to contend* or *fight among* others, c. dat., Hdt. II. γῆ εὐμενὴς ἐναγωνίζεσθαι favourable *to fight in,* Thuc.

ἐν-αγώνιος, ον, *of* or *for a contest,* Plut., Luc.:—of gods *who presided over games,* Simon., etc.

ἐν-αέριος, ον, *in the air,* Luc.

ἐν-αθλέω, = ἀθλέω ἐν: absol. in Med., Anth.

ἐν-αιμήεις, εσσα, εν, = sq., Anth.

ἔν-αιμος, ον, (αἷμα) *with blood in one,* Hdt.

ἐναίρω, Ep. ἐνναίρω, Ep. inf. ἐναιρέμεν: aor. 2 ἤναρον, inf. ἐναρεῖν:—Med., aor. 1 3 sing. ἐνήρατο (ἔναρα):— poët. *to slay in battle,* generally, *to kill, slay,* Il., Soph.; of things, *to destroy,* Od.

ἐν-αίσιμος, ον, *ominous, boding, fateful,* Lat. *fatalis,* Od.; neut. ἐναίσιμον and -μα as Adv. *ominously,* Hom.: — in good sense, *seasonable,* Lat. *opportunus,* of omens, Il. II. of persons, *righteous,* Hom. 2. of things, *fit, proper,* Il.:—Adv. -ως, *fitly, becomingly,* Aesch., Eur.

ἐναίσιος, ον, = foreg. II, Soph.

ἐν-αιχμάζω, f. σω, *to fight in,* Anth.

ἐν-αιωρέομαι, Pass. *to float* or *drift about in* the sea, c. dat., Eur.

ἐνάκις [ᾰ], Ep. εἰνάκις, (ἐννέα) Adv. *nine times,* Od., Plat. Hence

ἐνακισ-χίλιοι, αι, α, *nine thousand,* Ion. εἰνακισχίλιοι, Hdt.

ἐνακόσιοι, Ion. εἰν-, αι, α, (ἐννέα, ἕκατον) *nine hun- dred,* Hdt., Thuc.

ἐν-ακούω, f. σομαι, *to listen to* a thing, c. gen., Soph.

ἐν-αλείφω, f. ψω: pf. pass. -αλήλιμμαι:—*to anoint with* ointment, c. dat., Plat.:—Med. *to anoint oneself,* Anth.

ἐν-αλήθης, ες, *in accordance with truth:* Adv. -θως, *probably,* Luc.

ἐν-αλίγκιος, ον, *like, resembling,* c. dat., Hom.; θεοῖς ἐναλίγκιος αὐδήν *like* the gods in voice, Od.

ἐν-άλιος [ᾰ], α, ον or ος, ον, poët. εἰνάλιος: (ἅλς):— *in, on, of the sea,* Lat. *marinus,* Od., Aesch., etc.; ἐν. λεώς seamen, Soph.; πόντου εἰναλία φύσις, i. e. fish, Id.

ἐναλλάγῆναι, aor. 2 pass. inf. of ἐναλλάσσω.

ἐναλλάξ, Adv. *crosswise,* Ar. 2. *alternately,* Lat. *vicissim,* πρήσσειν ἐν. to have alternations of fortune, Hdt. From

ἐν-αλλάσσω, Att. -ττω: f. ξω: pf. -ήλλαχα, pass. -ήλ- λαγμαι: aor. 2 -ηλλάγην [ᾰ]:—*to exchange,* φόνον θανάτῳ ἐν., i. e. *to pay* for murder by death, Eur.; ἐνήλλαξεν τὴν ὕβριν *diverted* his assault, Soph. II.

Pass. *to be changed*, τί δ' ἐνήλλακται τῆς ἡμερίας νὺξ ἥδε βάρος; what heavy *change* from the day *hath* this night *suffered?* Soph.　　2. *to have dealings with*, τινι Thuc.

ἐν-άλλομαι, f. -ᾰλοῦμαι : aor. 1 -ηλάμην, aor. 2 -ηλόμην : Dep. :—*to leap in* or *upon*, c. dat., Aesch., Soph.　2. *to rush against*, Id.　　3. absol. *to dance*, Ar.

ἔν-αλλος, ον, *changed, contrary*, Theocr., Anth.

ἔν-ᾰλος, ον, = ἐνάλιος, h. Hom., Eur.

ἐν-αμβλύνω [ῡ], *to deaden* or *discourage besides*, Plut.

ἐν-ᾰμέλγω, f. ξω, *to milk into*, γαυλοῖς Od.

ἐν-άμιλλος [ᾰ], ον, (ἅμιλλα) *engaged in equal contest with, a match for*, τινι Plat.

ἔν-αντα, Adv. *opposite, over against, face to face*, c. gen., Il. ; ἔν. προσβλέπειν νεκρόν Soph. ; ἔν. ἐλθεῖν Eur.

ἔν-αντι, Adv., *in the presence of*, c. gen., N. T.

ἐν-αντίβιος, ον, *set against, hostile*, Anth. :—as Adv. *face to face, against*, μαχέσασθαι, πολεμίζειν Il.

ἐναντίον, Adv., v. ἐναντίος.

ἐναντιόομαι, f. -ώσομαι : aor. 1 ἠναντιώθην : pf. ἠναντίωμαι : Dep. :—*to set oneself against, oppose, withstand*, τινι Hdt., Thuc., etc. ; οὐκ ἐναντιώσομαι τὸ μὴ οὐ γεγωνεῖν I will not *refuse* to speak, Aesch. ; τοῦτό μοι ἐναντιοῦται πράττειν this *prevents* me from doing, Plat.　　2. *to contradict, gainsay*, Eur., Thuc., etc.　　3. of the wind, *to be adverse*, Soph., Thuc.

ἐν-αντίος, α, ον, *opposite*, Lat. *adversus* :　　1. of Place, *over against, opposite*, c. dat., Hom. : *fronting, face to face*, Od., Eur. :—with Verbs of motion, *in opposite directions, meeting*, Il.　　2. in hostile sense, *opposing, facing* in fight, Ib., etc. ; c. gen., ἐναντίοι Ἀχαιῶν Ib., etc. : also c. dat., Ib. :—οἱ ἐν. one's *adversaries*, Aesch., etc. :—generally, *opposed to*, τινί Soph., Xen.　　3. of qualities, acts, etc., *the opposite, contrary, reverse*, Aesch., Soph. ; mostly c. gen., τὰ ἐν. τούτων the very *reverse* of these things, Hdt., etc. ; also c. dat., Aesch.　　II. in Adv. usages : ἐναντίον, *opposite, face to face*, Od., Att. :—as Prep. c. gen. *in the presence of, before*, Lat. *coram*, c. gen., Soph., Thuc., etc.　　b. in hostile sense, *against*, c. gen., Il. ; also c. dat., Ib., Eur.　　c. *contrariwise*, in Att. τοὐναντίον, *on the other hand* : so also neut. pl. ἐναντία Hdt., Thuc., etc.　　2. ἐκ τοῦ ἐναντίου, *over against, opposite*, Lat. *ex adverso, e regione*, Xen., etc. : so, ἐξ ἐναντίας, Ion. -ίης, Hdt., Thuc.　　3. regul. Adv. ἐναντίως, *contrariwise*, c. dat., Aesch. : —also c. gen., Plat. :—ἐν. ἔχειν to be *exactly opposed*, Dem. Hence

ἐναντιότης, ητος, ἡ, *contrariety, opposition*, Plat.

ἐναντιόω, not used in Act. ; v. ἐναντιόομαι.

ἐναντίωμα, ατος, τό, (ἐναντιόομαι) *an obstacle, hindrance*, Thuc., Dem.　　2. *a contradiction, discrepancy*, Plat.

ἐναντίωσις, εως, ἡ, (ἐναντιόομαι) *a contradiction*, Thuc.

ἔναξα, aor. 1 of νάσσω.

ἐναπῆκε, Ion. for ἐναφῆκε, 3 sing. aor. 1 of ἐναφίημι.

ἐναπῆπτε, Ion. for ἐναφῆπτε, 3 sing. impf. of ἐναφάπτω.

ἐν-αποδείκνῠμαι, Med. or Pass. *to gain distinction among* others, ἐναπεδείκνυατο (Ion. 3 pl. impf.) Hdt.

ἐν-αποθνήσκω, *to die in* a place, Hdt., Thuc.

ἐνα-ποθραύω, f. σω, *to break off in* a wound, c. dat., Plut.

ἐν-απόκειμαι, Pass. *to be stored up in*, c. dat., Plut.

ἐν-αποκλάω, f. σω, *to break off short in* a shield, Thuc.

ἐν-απόλλῠμαι, f. -απολοῦμαι, Pass. *to perish in* a place, c. dat., Xen.

ἐν-απολογέομαι, Dep. *to defend oneself in*, Aeschin.

ἐν-απονίζω, f. -νίψω, *to wash clean in* a thing :—Med., ἐναπονίζεσθαι τοὺς πόδας ἐν τῷ ποδανιπτῆρι to wash one's feet in the foot-pan, Hdt.

ἐν-αποπνέω, f. -πνεύσομαι, *to expire in the act of* doing a thing, c. dat., Plut.

ἐν-αποπνίγομαι, Pass. *to be suffocated in*, Luc.

ἐν-αποσημαίνω, f. ᾰνῶ, *to indicate* or *point out in*, Plut.

ἐν-αποτίνω, f. -τίσω [ῐ], *to spend on law in* a place, Ar.

ἐν-αποψύχω [ῠ], f. ξω, *to give up the ghost in* a place, Hes., Anth.

ἐν-άπτω, f. ψω, *to bind on* or *to a person*, Eur. :— Pass., pf. ἐνημμαι, of persons, *to be fitted with, clad in*, c. acc., λεοντέας ἐναμμένοι (Ion. for ἐνημμ-) Hdt., Ar.　　II. *to kindle, set on fire*, Id.

ἔΝΑΡΑ, ων, τά, only in pl., *the arms and trappings of a slain foe, spoils, booty*, Lat. *spolia*, Il.

ἐν-ᾰράρίσκω : aor. 1 ἐνῆρσα, *to fit* or *fasten in*, Od.　　II. ἐνάρηρα, intr., *to be fitted in*, Ib.

ἐνάργει, Dor. for ἐνήργει, impf. of ἐνεργέω.

ἐν-αργής, ές, (ἀργός) *visible, palpable, in bodily shape*, properly of gods appearing in their own forms, Hom. ; so of a dream or vision, Od., Hdt., etc. ; ἐναργὴς ταῦρος in visible form a bull, a *very* bull, Soph.　　2. *manifest to the mind's eye, distinct*, Id., Dem. :— Adv. -γῶς, *manifestly*, Aesch., etc.　　3. of words, etc., *distinct, manifest*, Id., Plat., etc. :—Adv., ἐναργέως λέγειν Hdt.

Ἐνᾰρέες or -ίες, οἱ, prob. a Scythian word, answering to the Greek ἀνδρόγυνοι, a band who plundered the temple of Aphrodité at Ascalon, Hdt.

ἐνᾰρεῖν, aor. 2 inf. of ἐναίρω.

ἐνᾰρηρώς, pf. 2 part. of ἐναραρίσκω.

ἐνᾰρη-φόρος, ον, (φέρω) *wearing the spoils*, Anth.

ἐνᾰρίζω, f. -ίξω : aor. 1 ἠνάριξα, Ep. ἐνάριξα :—Pass., aor. 1 ἠναρίσθην, pf. ἠνάρισμαι :—*to strip a slain foe of his arms* (ἔναρα), Lat. *spoliare*, ἔντεα ἐν. τινά Il. :— hence, *to slay in fight*, and, generally, *to slay*, Ib., Aesch. :—Pass., νὺξ ἐναριζομένα night *when dying*, i. e. when yielding to day, Soph.

ἐν-ᾰριθμέω, f. ήσω, *to reckon in* or *among* : *to reckon, account*, οὐδέν *as nothing*, Soph. :—Med., = ἐν ἀριθμῷ ποιεῖσθαι, *to make account of*, Eur.

ἐν-ᾰρίθμιος, ον, (ἀριθμός) *in the number, to make up the number*, Od. : *counted among*, i. e. *among*, c. dat., Theocr.　　II. *taken into account*, Lat. *in numero habitus*, Il.

ἐν-αρμόζω and -ττω, f. σω, *to fit* or *fix in* a thing, c. dat., Eur.　　2. metaph. *to fit, adapt*, τι εἴς τι Plat. ; ἐν. αὑτόν *to make* himself *popular*, Plut. :—Med., τὰν Δωριστὶ (sc. ἁρμονίαν) ἐναρμόττεσθαι τὴν λύραν to have it *tuned* to the Dorian mode, Ar.　　II. intr. *to fit, suit, be convenient*, Id. :—c. dat. pers. *to please*, Plut.

ἐν-αρμόνιος, ον, (ἁρμονία) *in accord* or *harmony*, Luc.

ἐναρμόττω, v. ἐναρμόζω.

ἔναρον, τό, sing. of ἔναρα, but not in use.

ἐν-αρφόρος, ον, syncop. for ἐναρηφόρος, Hes.

ἐν-άρχομαι, f. ξομαι, Dep. in sacrifices, *to begin the*

offering, by taking the barley (οὐλοχύται) from the basket (κανοῦν), Eur. :—pf. in pass. sense, Id.

ἐν-ασκέω, f. ήσω, to train or practise in a thing, Plut. : Pass. with fut. med., to be so practised, Luc.

ἐν-ασπῐδόομαι, (ἀσπίς) Pass. to fit oneself with a shield, Ar.

ἔνασσα, aor. 1 of ναίω ΙΙ.

ἐν-ασχημονέω, to behave oneself unseemly in, Plut.

ἐνἄταῖος, a, ον, (ἔνατος) on the ninth day, Thuc.

ἔνᾰτος, Ion. and Ep. εἴνατος, η, ον, (ἐννέα) ninth, Lat. nonus, Il., Hes.   II. in pl. = ἐννέα, Anth.

ἐν-αυλᾰκο-φοῖτις, ἡ, (αὔλαξ, φοιτάω) wandering in the fields, Anth.

ἐναύλειον, τό, = ἔναυλος (A). ΙΙ.

ἐν-αυλίζω, f. σω, intr. to dwell or abide in a place, Soph.   II. Dep. ἐναυλίζομαι, to take up one's quarters in a place during night, to take up night-quarters, bivouac, Hdt., Thuc., Xen., etc.   Hence

ἐναυλιστήριος, ον, habitable, Anth.

ἔν-αυλον, τό, (αὐλή) an abode, Anth.

ἔναυλος, ὁ, (A) Subst. :   I. (αὐλός) the bed of a stream, a torrent, mountain-stream, Il.   II. (αὐλή) in pl. the haunts of the country-gods, Hes., Eur.

ἔναυλος, ον, (B) Adj. :   I. (αὐλός) on or to the flute : metaph., λόγοι ἔν. words ringing in one's ears, Plat. : hence fresh in memory, Aeschin.   II. (αὐλή), dwelling in dens, Eur. : in one's den, Soph.

ἐν-αυξάνω, f. -αυξήσω, to increase, enlarge, Xen.

ἔναυρος, ον, (αὔρα) exposed to the air, Theophr.

ἔναυσις, ἡ, a kindling, Plut.

ἔναυσμα, ατος, τό, (ἐναύω) a spark, remnant, Plut.

ἐν-αυχένιος, ον, or η, ον, (αὐχήν) on the neck, Anth.

ἐν-αύω, impf. ἔναυον : aor. 1 ἔναυσα :—to kindle, ἐν. πῦρ τινι to light one a fire, give him a light, Xen. :—Med., πῦρ ἐναύεσθαι to get a light, Plut., Luc.

ἐν-αφάπτω, Ion. ἐναπ-, to fasten up in a thing, Hdt.

ἐν-αφίημι, f. -αφήσω, to let drop into, v. l., Hdt.

ἔν-δαις, αιδος, or ἔν-δας, ᾳδος, ὁ, ἡ, with lighted torch, Aesch.

ἐν-δαίω, to kindle in : Med. to burn or glow in, Od.

ἐν-δάκνω, f. δήξομαι : aor. 2 ἔδακον [ᾰ] :—to bite into, ἐνδ. στόμια γνάθοις to take the bit between the teeth, of runaway horses, Eur.

ἐν-δακρύω, f. σω, to weep in : ἐνδ. ὄμμασι to suffuse them with tears, Aesch.

ἐνδᾱμέω, ἐνδᾱμία, Dor. for ἐνδημ-.

ἐν-δάπιος, a, ον, (ἔνδον) native of the country, Mosch.

ἐν-δᾰτέομαι, Dep. to divide, δὶς τοὐνόμ' ἐνδατούμενος dividing the name of Polynices (into πολὺ νεῖκος), Aesch. : ἐνδ. λόγους ὀνειδιστῆρας to distribute or fling about reproaches, Eur.   2. c. acc. objecti, to speak of in detail, i. e., in bad sense, to reproach, revile, or, in good sense, to tell of, celebrate, Soph.

ἐνδέδημαι, pf. pass. of ἐνδέω.

ἐνδεής, ές: neut. pl. ἐνδεᾶ : (ἐνδέω) :—in need of a thing, c. gen., Hdt., Att.   2. absol. in need, indigent, Xen., Plat., etc.   b. lacking, deficient, mostly in Comp., Hdt., Thuc. ; τινι in a thing, Id. :—τὸ ἐνδεές lack, want, defect, deficiency, Id.   3. inferior to, c. gen., Xen. ; τῆς δυνάμεως ἐνδεᾶ πρᾶξαι to act short of your real power, Thuc. ; τούτου ἐνδεᾶ ἐφαίνετο (sc. τὰ πράγματα) their power was unequal to the

purpose, Id.   4. insufficient, Id. :—Adv., ἐνδεῶς, defectively, insufficiently, Plat. ; μὴ ἐνδεῶς γνῶναι to judge not insufficiently, Thuc.

ἔνδεια, ἡ, (ἐνδεής) want, need, lack, Thuc., etc.   2. defect, deficiency, Plat.   3. want of means, need, poverty, Lat. egestas, Id., Dem.

ἔνδειγμα, ατος, τό, a proof, token, Dem.   From

ἐνδείκνῡμι or -ύω, -δείξω, to mark, point out, Lat. indicare, Soph., etc.   2. as Att. law-term, to inform against one, Plat. ; so in Med., Plut. :—in Pass., ἐνδεδειγμένοι Plat. ; ἐνδειχθέντα δεκάζειν being informed against for bribing, Dem., Aeschin.   II. Med. to shew forth oneself or what is one's own, Πηλείδη ἐνδείξομαι I will declare myself to Achilles, Il. ; ἐνδείκνυσθαί τὴν γνώμην Hdt.   2. with a part. to shew, give proof of doing, Eur., etc.   3. c. acc. rei, to display, exhibit, Lat. prae se ferre, Aesch., Thuc.   4. ἐνδείκνυσθαί τινι to display oneself to one, make a set at him, court him, Dem., Aeschin.

ἔνδειξις, εως, ἡ, a pointing out :—as Attic law-term, a laying information against one who discharged public functions for which he was legally disqualified, Dem., etc.   II. a display of good will, Aeschin.

ἔν-δεκα, οἱ, αἱ, τά, indecl. eleven, Lat. undecim, Hom., etc.   II. at Athens, οἱ ἔνδεκα, the Eleven, the Police-Commissioners, who had charge of the prisons, and the punishment of criminals, Ar., etc.   Hence

ἐνδεκά-πηχυς, υ, gen. εος, eleven cubits long, Il.

ἐνδεκάς, άδος, ἡ, the number Eleven, Plat.

ἐνδεκαταῖος, α, ον, on the eleventh day, Thuc. ; and

ἐνδέκᾰτος, η, ον, the eleventh, Hom., etc.

ἐνδέκομαι, Ion. for ἐνδέχομαι.

ἐνδελεχής, ές, continuous, perpetual, Plat., etc.   Adv. -χῶς, Id.   (Deriv. uncertain.)

ἐν-δέμω, f. δεμῶ, to wall up, Hdt.   II. to build in a place, Theocr.

ἐν-δεξιόομαι, Dep. to grasp with the right hand, Eur.

ἐνδέξιος, α, ον, towards the right hand, from left to right : neut. pl. as Adv., θεοῖς ἐνδέξια φνοχόει he filled for the gods from left to right, Il. :—contrary procedure was avoided as unlucky, hence, ἐνδέξια σήματα propitious omens, Ib.   2. = δεξιός, on the right, Eur.   II. clever, expert, h. Hom.

ἔν-δετος, ον, bound to, entangled in, τινι Anth.

ἐν-δέχομαι, Ion. -δέκομαι: f. -ξομαι : pf. -δέδεγμαι: Dep. :—to take upon oneself, Lat. suscipere, Hdt.   II. to accept, admit, approve of, Lat. accipere, Id., Thuc.   2. to give ear to, believe, Hdt. : absol. to give ear, attend, Eur.   III. of things, to admit, allow of, Thuc., Plat. :—c. inf., οὐκ ἐνδέχεται μελετᾶσθαι does not admit of being practised, Thuc.   2. absol. to be possible, ἐνδέχεται Id. : esp. in part. ἐνδεχόμενος, η, ον, possible, ἐκ τῶν ἐνδεχομένων by all possible means, Xen. :—ἐνδέχεται impers., it admits of being, it is possible that, c. acc. et inf., Thuc., etc.

ἐνδεχομένως, Adv. of foreg., as far as possible, ap. Dem.

ἐν-δέω (A), f. -δήσω, to bind in, ὄν or to, τι ἔν τινι Od. ; τί τινι Ar., etc. ; so in Med., ἐνεδήσατο δεσμῷ bound them fast, Theocr. ; ἐνδησάμενος having packed it up, Ar. :—Pass., ἱρὰ ἐνδεδεμένα ἐν καλάμῃ Hdt. ; ἐνδεθῆναι εἰς σῶμα or ἐν τῷ σώματι Plat.   II. metaph., Ζεύς

με ἄτη ἐνέδησε *entangled* me in it, Il. :—Pass., ἐνδεδέσθαι ὁρκίοις, etc., Hdt. ; ἐνδεδέσθαι τὴν ἀρχήν *to have the government secured*, Id. :—Med. *to bind to oneself*, Eur.

ἐν-δέω (Β\, f. -δεήσω, *to be in want of* a thing, c. gen., Eur., Plat. ; ΄c. inf., τίνος ἐνδέομεν μὴ οὐ χωρεῖν; *what do we lack* of going? Eur. :—so in Med., Xen. ; and in Pass., στρωμάτων ἐνδεηθέντες Id. 2. of things, *to be wanting* or *lacking*, Hdt. :—impers. ἐνδεῖ, *there is need* or *want*, c. gen. rei, Plat., Xen.

ἐνδεῶς, Adv. of ἐνδεής, q. v.

ἔν-δηλος, ον, = δῆλος, *visible, manifest, clear*, Soph., Thuc. 2. of persons, *manifest, discovered, known*, Ar., Thuc. II. Adv. -λως, Sup. -ότατα, Id.

ἐνδημέω, Dor. -δᾱμέω, *to live in* a place, Lys. From

ἔν-δημος, ον, *dwelling in* a place, *a native*, Hes., etc. ; ἐνδημότατος *the greatest 'stay-at-home,'* Thuc. II. *of* or *belonging to a people, national*, Id.

ἐνδιάασκον, Ep. impf. of ἐνδιάω.

ἐν-διαβάλλω, *to calumniate* in a matter, Luc.

ἐνδιάζω, (ἔνδιος I) *to pass the noon*, Plut.

ἐν-διαθρύπτομαι, Pass. *to play the prude towards, trifle with*, τινι Theocr.

ἐν-δίαιτάομαι, Ion. -έομαι, Dep. *to live* or *dwell in* a place, Hdt., Thuc., etc.

ἐν-διατάσσω, f. ξω, *to draw an army up in*, Hdt.

ἐν-διατρίβω [ῑ], f. ψω, *to spend* or *consume in* doing, χρόνον Ar., Thuc. II. absol. (sub. χρόνον), *to spend time in* a place, Dem. 2. *to waste time by staying in* a place, *linger there*, Thuc., Plat. 3. *to continue in the practice of* a thing ἔν τινι Xen. :— absol. *to dwell upon a point* (in speaking), Aeschin.

ἐνδιατριπτέον, Verbal, *one must dwell upon*, τινί Luc.

ἐνδιάω, Ep. impf. ἐνδιάασκον, (ἔνδιος) *to stay in the open air ; generally, to linger in* or *haunt* a place, c. dat., Anth. :—in Med., h. Hom. II. trans., ποιμένες μῆλα ἐνδιάασκον *shepherds were driving* their *sheep afield*, Theocr.

ἐν-διδύσκω, *to put on* another, τινά τι N. T. :—Med. *to put on oneself*, Ib.

ἐν-δίδωμι, f. -δώσω, *to give in* : I. *to give into* one's hands, *give up to*, τινά or τί τινι Eur., etc. ; a city, esp. by treachery, Thuc., Xen. II. like Lat. *praebere, to give, lend, afford*, ἐνδιδόναι τινὶ χέρα *to lend* him a hand, Eur. ; ἐνδ. λαβήν τινι *to give* one a handle, Ar. :—*to cause, excite*, Thuc. III. *to shew, exhibit*, Hdt., Eur., etc. IV. *to allow, grant, concede*, Eur., Thuc. V. intr. *to give in, allow, permit*, Hdt. : *to give in, give way*, Thuc. :— ἐνδ. τινι *to yield to*, Id.

ἐν-διημερεύω, *to pass the day in*, Theophr.

ἐνδίημι, *to chase, pursue*, 3 pl. impf. ἐνδίεσαν, Ep. for ἐνεδίεσαν, Il.

ἔν-δικος, ον, (δίκη) : I. of things, *according to right, right, just, legitimate*, Trag. :—τὸ μὴ 'νδικον = τὸ ἄδικον, Soph. ; μὴ λέγων γε τοὔνδικον *not speaking truth*, Id. II. of persons, *righteous, just, upright*, Aesch., etc. ; τίς ἐνδικώτερος ; *who has better right* or *more reason ?* Id. III. Adv. -κως, *right, with justice, fairly*, Id. 2. *truly, indeed*, Eur. 3. *justly, naturally, as one has a right to expect*, Trag.

ἔνδῑνα, τά, (ἔνδον) *the entrails*, or rather *the body enclosed in armour*, Il.

ἐν-δῑνέω, f. ήσω, *to revolve, go about*, ἐνδινεῦντι, Dor. for ἐνδινοῦσι, Theocr.

ἔν-διος, ον, (ἐν, Διός, cf. Lat. *sub divo*) :—*at midday*, *at noon*, Hom., Theocr. II. ἔνδιος, *in the open air*, Anth. : neut. ἔνδῑον, *an abode*, Id.

ἐν-δίφριος, ον, (δίφρος) *sitting on the same seat with* another, c. dat., Xen.

ἔνδοθεν, (ἔνδον) Adv. *from within*, Lat. *intrinsecus*, Od., Trag., etc. :—c. gen., ἔνδοθεν στέγης *from inside the tent*, Soph. 2. like οἴκοθεν, *of oneself, by one's own doing*, Aesch. II. *within*, c.gen., Il., Hes. 2. absol., Hdt. ; οἱ ἔνδοθεν *the domestics*, Ar. ; or *the people inside the city*, Thuc.

ἔνδοθι, (ἔνδον) Adv. *within, at home*, Lat. *intus*, Hom. 2. c. gen., Il.

ἔνδοι, Aeol. and Dor. for ἔνδοθι, Theocr.

ἐνδοιάζω, = ἐν δοίῃ εἰμί, *to be in doubt, at a loss* how to do a thing, c. inf., Thuc. : absol., οἱ ἐνδοιάζοντες *the waverers*, Id. :—Pass. *to be matter of doubt*, ἐνδοιασθῆναι Id. Hence

ἐνδοιάσιμος, ον, *doubtful*, Luc. ; and

ἐνδοιαστός, ή, όν, *doubtful, ambiguous* : Adv. -τῶς, *doubtfully*, προθύμως Hdt., Thuc.

ἐνδόμησις, εως, ἡ, (ἐν, δόμος) *structure*, N. T.

ἐνδό-μυχος, ον, *in the inmost part of a dwelling, lurking within*, Soph.

ἔνδον, Adv. (ἐν) *in, within, in the house, at home*, Lat. *intus*, Hom., etc. ; τἄνδον as Adv. *in one's heart*, Eur. :—οἱ ἔνδον *those of the house, the family*, Soph. : τὰ ἔνδον *family matters*, Id. 2. c. gen., Διὸς ἔνδον *in the house of* Zeus, Il. ; σκηνῆς ἔνδον Soph. ; φρενῶν ἔνδον *in one's senses*, Eur.

ἔν-δοξος, ον, (δόξα) *held in esteem* or *honour, of high repute*, Xen., Plat. 2. of things, *notable*, Aeschin. : —Adv. -ξως, hence Sup., ἐνδοξότατα Dem.

ἐνδοτέρω, Adv. Comp. of ἔνδον, *quite within*, Plut.

ἐν-δουπέω, f. ήσω, *to fall in with a heavy sound*, Od.

ἐν-δρομίς, ίδος, ἡ, (δρόμος) *a high shoe*, worn by Artemis, Anth. II. *a thick wrapper worn by runners*, after exercise, Juven.

ἔν-δροσος, ον, *bedewed*, Hes.

ἔν-δρυον, τό, (δρῦς) *the oaken peg* or *pin by which the yoke is fixed to the pole* (ἱστοβοεύς), Hes.

ἐν-δῠκέως, (ἐν, δοκέω) Adv. *thoughtfully, carefully, sedulously*, Hom.

ἔνδῠμα, ατος, τό, (ἐνδύω) *a garment*, N. T., Plut.

ἐνδῠνάμόω, f. ώσω, (δύναμις) *to strengthen*, N. T.

ἐν-δῠναστεύω, f. σω, *to exercise dominion in* or *among* people, c. dat., Aesch. II. *to procure by one's authority*, Xen.

ἐνδύνω [ῠ], v. ἐνδύω.

ἔνδῠσις, εως, ἡ, (ἐνδύομαι) *a putting on*, N. T.

ἐν-δυστῠχέω, f. ήσω, *to be unlucky in* or *with*, c. dat., Eur.

ἐνδῠτήρ, ῆρος, ὁ, *for putting on*, Soph. ; and

ἐνδῠτός, όν, *put on*, Aesch., Eur. 2. ἔνδυτον (sc. ἔσθημα), τό, *a garment, dress*, Id. :—metaph., ἐνδ. σαρκός, i. e. *one's skin*, Id. II. *clad in, covered with*, στέμμασιν Id. From

ἐν-δύω and -δύνω [ῠ], with Med. ἐνδύομαι, f. -δύσομαι,

aor. 1 -εδυσάμην and aor. 2 act. -ἔδυν: I. c. acc., to go into,   1. of clothes, to put on, Lat. induere sibi, ἔνδυνε χιτῶνα Il.; πέπλον Soph. :—so in Med., Il.,etc.:—pf. ἐνδεδύκα, to wear κιθῶναs Hdt.:—metaph. to put on, assume the person of . . , N. T.   2. to enter, to press into, c. acc., Il., etc. :—also, ἐνδ. εἰs . . , Thuc., etc. :—also c. dat., Xen. :—absol. to enter, Hdt.   II. Causal in pres. ἐνδύω, f. -δύσω, aor. 1 -ἔδυσα :—Lat. induere alicui, to put on another, τὸ clothe in, c. dupl. acc., Xen.   2. to clothe, τινά Hdt.

ἐνέβαλον, aor. 2 of ἐμβάλλω.

ἔνεγκαι, ἐνεγκεῖν, aor. 1 and 2 inf. of φέρω.

ἐνεγύησα, irreg. aor. of ἐγγυάω.

ἐνέδρα, ἡ, a sitting in: a lying in wait, ambush, Thuc., Xen.   2. the men laid in ambush, Id.

ἐνεδρεύω, impf. ἐνήδρευον: f. ἐνεδρεύσω: aor. 1 ἐνήδρευσα :—to lie in wait for, Lat. insidiari, τινά Dem.: —Pass. to be caught in an ambush, to be ensnared, Xen.   2. absol. to lay or set an ambush, Thuc., Xen.; so in Med., Id. :—Pass. to lie in ambush, Id.

ἔν-εδρος, ον, (ἕδρα) an inmate, inhabitant, Soph.

ἔνεδυν, aor. 2 of ἐνδύω.

ἐν-έζομαι, f. -εδοῦμαι, Dep. to have one's abode in a place, c. acc., Aesch.

ἐνέηκα, Ep. for ἐνῆκα, aor. 1 of ἐνίημι.

ἐνέην, Ep. for ἐνῆν, impf. of ἔνειμι (εἰμί sum).

ἐνεῖδον, aor. 2 with no pres. in use, ἐνοράω being used instead, to observe something in a person, τι ἔν τινι Thuc.; τί τινι Xen. : absol. to observe, Soph.

ἐν-ειδο-φορέω, of a sculptor, to work into shape, Anth.

ἔνεικα, Ep. for ἤνεγκα, Ep. imper. ἔνεικε, inf. -έμεν, aor. 1 of φέρω.

ἐνείκεον, Ion. impf. of νεικέω.

ἐν-ειλέω, f. ἤσω, = ἐνείλλω, to wrap in: metaph. in Pass. to be engaged in or with, τοῖς πολεμίοις Plut.

ἐνειλίσσω, Ion. for ἐνελίσσω.

ἔνειμεν, Ep. for ἐνέσμεν, 1 pl. of ἔνειμι (εἰμί, sum): but II. ἔνειμεν, 3 sing. aor. of νέμω.

ἔν-ειμι (εἰμί sum), f. -έσομαι, to be in a place, c. dat., Hom., etc.: c. dat. pl. to be among, Hdt.   2. absol. to be there, be in abundance, Od., etc.; σίτου οὐκ ἐνόντος as there was no corn there, Thuc.; ἱερῶν τῶν ἐνόντων of the temples that were in the place, Id.   II. to be possible, Trag., etc.   2. impers. c. dat. pers. et inf. it is in one's power, one may or can, Soph., etc.   3. part. neut. ἐνόν absol. since it was in them, was possible, Luc.   4. τὰ ἐνόντα all things possible, Dem.

ἐν-είρω, to string on a thing, Pass., Hdt.

ἐν-εῖς, aor. 2 part. of ἐνίημι.

ἔνεκα or -κεν, Ion. and poët. εἵνεκα or -κεν :—Prep. with gen., mostly after its case, Il., etc. : on account of, for the sake of, because of, for, Lat. gratia, Ib., etc.   2. as far as regards, as for, ἐμοῦ γε ἕνεκα as far as depends on me, Ar.; εἵνεκέν γε χρημάτων Hdt., etc.   3. pleon. ἀμφὶ σοὕνεκα Soph.; ὅσον ἀπὸ βοῆς ἕνεκα as far as shouting went, Thuc.   II. as Conjunct., for οὕνεκα, because, h. Hom.

ἐνέκυρσα, aor. 1 of ἐγκύρω.

ἐν-ελαύνω, f. -ελάσω, Att. -ελῶ, to drive in or into, c. dat., Il.

ἐν-ελίσσω, Ion. εἰλ-, f. ξω, to roll up in :—Med. to wrap oneself in, Hdt.

ἐν-εμέω, f. έσω, to vomit in or into, εἴs τι Hdt.

ἐνενήκοντα, οἱ, αἱ, τά, (ἐννέα) indecl. ninety, Il., etc.

ἐνενηκοντα-ετής, ές, ninety years old, Luc.

ἐνένιπε, 3 sing. Ep. redupl. aor. 2 of ἐνίπτω.

ἐνεώκα, Ion. for ἐνενόηκα, pf. of ἐννοέω.

ἐνένωτο, Ion. for ἐνενόητο, 3 sing. plqpf. of ἐννοέω.

ἐν-εορτάζω, f. σω, to keep holiday in, Plut.

ἘΝΕΟΣ or ἐννεός, ά, όν, dumb, deaf and dumb, Xen.

ἐν-επ-άγομαι, Med. to make an irruption among, Aesop.

ἐν-επαίχθην, aor. 1 pass. of ἐμπαίζω.

ἐν-επιορκέω, to forswear oneself by a god, Aeschin.

ἐνεπλάκην [ἄ], aor. 2 pass. of ἐμπλέκω.

ἐνέπλησα, aor. 1 of ἐμπίπλημι.

ἐνέπνευσα, aor. 1 of ἐμπνέω.

ἐνέπρησα, aor. 1 of ἐμπίπρημι.

ἐνέπτυσα, aor. 1 of ἐμπτύω.

ἐνέπω, lengthd. ἐννέπω : aor. 2 ἔνισπον, imperat. ἔνισπες and ἔνισπε: fut. ἐνισπήσω and ἐνίψω :—a lengthd. form of *ἔπω, εἰπεῖν, to tell, tell of, relate, describe, Hom., Trag. :—absol. to tell news or tales, Od.   2. simply to speak, Hes., Trag.   3. c. acc. et inf. to bid one do so and so, Soph.   4. to call so and so, ἐνν. τινὰ δοῦλον Eur.   5. = προσεννέπω, to address, τινά Soph.

ἐν-εργάζομαι, f. σομαι, Dep. to make or produce in, c. dat., Xen., etc. :—aor. 1 ἐνειργάσθην in pass. sense, to be placed in, Id.   2. to work for hire in a place, Hdt.; ἐνεργ. τῇ οὐσίᾳ to trade with the property, Dem.

ἐνέργεια, ἡ, action, operation, energy, Arist.; and

ἐνεργέω, f. ήσω, to be in action, to operate, Arist.; so in Med., N. T.   From

ἐνεργής, ές, = ἐνεργός: of land, productive, Plut.

ἐνεργο-λαβέω, f. ήσω, to make profit of a thing, Aeschin.

ἐν-εργός, όν, (ἔργον) at work, working, active, busy, Hdt., etc. : of soldiers, ships, effective, fit for service, Thuc., Xen.   II. of land, in work, productive, opp. to ἀργός, Id.; ἐν. χρήματα capital which brings in a return, Dem.   III. Adv. ἐνεργῶς with activity, Xen.

ἐν-ερείδω, f. σω, to thrust in, fix in, τί τινι Od. :— Med. ἐνερεισάμενος πέτρᾳ γόνυ having planted his own knee on the rock, Theocr.

ἐν-ερεύγομαι, Dep. with aor. 2 act. -ήρῦγον, to belch on one, c. dat., Ar.

ἐν-ερευθής, ές, somewhat ruddy, Luc.

ἔνερθε, before a vowel -θεν, poët. also νέρθε, -θεν: (from ἐν, ἔνερ-οι, cf. ὑπέρ, ὕπερθε):   I. Adv., from beneath, up from below, Il., Aesch., Eur.   2. without sense of motion, beneath, below, Hom.; οἱ ἔνερθε θεοί the gods below, Lat. dii inferi, Il.   II. as Prep. with gen. beneath, below, Hom., Trag.   2. subject to, in the power of, Soph.

ἔνεροι, ων, οἱ, (ἐν) Lat. inferi, those below, those beneath the earth, Il., Hes., Aesch.

ἔνερσις, εως, ἡ, (ἐνείρω) a fitting in, fastening, Thuc.

ἐνέρτερος, α, ον, Comp. of ἔνεροι, lower, of the world below, Il., Aesch. : c. gen. below, Il. Cf. νέρτερος.

ἔνεσαν, Ep. for ἐνῆσαν, 3 pl. impf. of ἔνειμι (εἰμί, sum).

ἐνεσία, Ep. ἐννεσία, ἡ, (ἐνίημι) a suggestion, κείνης ἐννεσίῃσι (Ep. dat. pl.) at her suggestion, Il.

ἐνέσκληκα, pf. of ἐνσκέλλω.

ἐνέστακται, 3 sing. pf. pass. of ἐνστάζω.

ἐνεστεώς, Ion. for ἐνεστηκώς, pf. part. of ἐνίστημι.

ἐνεστήρικτο, 3 sing. plqpf. pass. of ἐνστηρίζω.

ἐνέτειλα, aor. 1 of ἐντέλλω.

ἐνετή, ἡ, (ἐνετός) a pin, brooch, Il.

ἐνετύλιξα, aor. 1 of ἐντυλίσσω.

ἐνέτυχον, aor. 2 of ἐντυγχάνω.

ἐν-ευδαιμονέω, f. ήσω, to be happy in one's life, Thuc.

ἐν-ευδοκιμέω, f. ήσω, to gain glory in another's ill fortune, Dem.

ἐν-εύδω, f. -ευδήσω, to sleep in or on a thing, c. dat., Od.

ἐν-ευλογέομαι, Pass. to be blessed in one, c. dat., N. T.

ἐν-εύναιος, ον, (εὐνή) on which one sleeps, for sleeping on, Od. ; ἐνεύναια, bed-furniture, Ib.

ἐνέχεα, aor. 1 of ἐγχέω : ἐν-εχευάμην, Ep. aor. 1 med.

ἐνεχθῆναι, aor. 1 pass. inf. of φέρω : ἐνέχθητι imper. ; ἐνεχθείην opt. ; ἐνεχθῶ, subj.

ἐνεχθήσομαι, f. pass. of φέρω.

ἐν-εχυράζω, f. άσω, (ἐνέχυρον) to take a pledge from one, τινός Lex ap. Dem. 2. c. acc. rei, to take in pledge, Dem., Aeschin. :—Pass. to have one's goods seized for debt, Ar. :—Med. to have security given one, take it for oneself, Id.

ἐνεχῠρασία, ἡ, a taking in pledge, a security, pledge, Plat.

ἐνεχῠρασμός, ὁ, = ἐνεχυρασία, Plut. From

ἐν-έχυρον, τό, (ἐχυρός) a pledge, surety, security, Hdt., Xen. ; ἐν. τιθέναι τι to make a thing a pledge, put it in pawn, Ar.

ἐν-έχω, f. -έξω or -σχήσω, to hold within, χόλον ἐνέχειν τινί to lay up, cherish inward wrath at one, Hdt. II. Pass., with f. and aor. med., to be held, caught, entangled in a thing, c. dat., Id., Xen. : metaph., ἐνέχεσθαι ἀπορίησιν Hdt. ; ἐν κακῷ Id. ; ἐν θωύματι ἐνέσχετο was seized with wonder, Id. 2. to be obnoxious, liable or subject to, ζημίᾳ, αἰτίᾳ Plat., etc. III. intr. to enter in, pierce, εἴς τι Xen. 2. to press upon, be urgent against, τινί N. T.

ἐν-ζεύγνῡμι, f. -ζεύξω, to yoke in, bind, involve in misfortune, Aesch. II. to bind fast, Soph.

ἔνη, ἔνη καὶ νέα, v. ἔνος, η, ον.

ἐν-ηβητήριον, τό, (ἡβάω) a place of amusement, Hdt.

ἐνηείη, ἡ, (ἐνηής) kindness, gentleness, Il.

ἔνηεν, Ep. for ἐνῆν, 3 sing. impf. of ἔνειμι (εἰμί, sum).

ἐνηής, ές, gen. ἐνῆεος, kind, gentle, Hom. (Perh. akin to ἀπ-ηνής, προσ-ηνής.)

ἐνήλᾰτον, τό, (ἐνελαύνω) anything driven in : as Subst., ἐνήλατα (sc. ξύλα), τά, the rounds of a ladder, which are fixed in the sides, Eur. II. ἀξόνων ἐνήλατα the pins driven into the axle, linchpins, Id.

ἐνήλικος, ον, of age, in the prime of manhood, Plut.

ἐνήλλαγμαι, pf. pass. of ἐναλλάσσω.

ἐνήλλου, 2 sing. pres. imper. of ἐνάλλομαι.

ἔνημαι, properly pf. of ἐνέζομαι, to be seated in, Od.

ἐνῆμμαι, pf. pass. of ἐνάπτω.

ἐνήνεγμαι, pf. pass. of φέρω.

ἐνήνοθε, 3 sing. pf. without any pres. ἐνέθω in use : only found in compds. : I. ἐπενήνοθε, of Thersites' head, ψεδνὴ ἐπ. λάχνη a thin coat of downy hair grew

thereon, Il. ; of a cloak, οὐλὴ ἐπενήνοθε λάχνη a thick pile was on it, Ib. ; c. acc., of ambrosial unguent, οἷα θεοὺς ἐπενήνοθε such as is on the gods, Od. II.

κατ-ενήνοθε, to be over, lie upon, Hes., Hom.

ἐνήνοχα, pf. of φέρω.

ἐνήραμην, aor. 1 med. of ἐναίρω.

ἐν-ήρης, ες, (*ἄρω) with oars, Plut.

ἔνθα, (ἐν) Adv. : I. Demonstr., 1. of Place, there, Lat. ibi, Hom., etc. :—also with Verbs of motion, thither, Lat. illuc, Id. ; ἔνθα καὶ ἔνθα here and there, hither and thither, Lat. hic illic, huc illuc, Id. 2. of Time, thereupon, then, just then, Id., etc. II. Relat., 1. of Place, where, Lat. ubi, Il., etc. ; c. gen., γαίας ἔνθα in that spot of earth in which, Soph. ; ἔνθα πημάτων κυρῶ at what point of misery I am, Eur. : —with Verbs of motion, whither, Lat. quo, Soph. 2. of Time, when, Xen. ; ἔστιν ἔνθα, Lat. est ubi, sometimes, Soph.

ἐνθάδε, Adv. : I. of Place, thither, hither, Lat. illuc, huc, Od., etc. 2. in Att. like ἔνθα, here or there, Lat. hic, Ar., etc. ; οἱ ἐνθάδε those here, opp. to οἱ κάτω, Soph. ; also the people of this country, Id. II. of circumstances, in this case or state, Xen. ; so, ἐνθάδ' ἥκων having come to this point, Soph. ; c. gen., ἐνθάδε τοῦ πάθους at this stage of my suffering, Id. 2. of Time, here, now, Id., Xen.

ἐνθαδί, Att. strengthd. for foreg., Ar.

ἐν-θᾱκέω, f. ήσω, to sit in or on a thing, c. dat., Soph.

ἐνθάκησις [ᾰ], εως, ἡ, a sitting in, ἡλίου ἐνθ. a seat in the sun, Soph.

ἔνθα-περ, Adv. there where, where, stronger form of ἔνθα, Il., etc. : whither, Soph.

ἐν-θάπτω, f. ψω, to bury in a place : aor. 2 pass. ἐνετάφην Aeschin.

ἐνθαῦτα, ἐνθεῦτεν, Ion. for ἐνταῦθα, ἐντεῦθεν.

ἐνθεάζω, f. σω, to be inspired, Hdt.

ἐνθέμεν, -θέμεναι, Ep. for ἐνθεῖναι, aor. 2 inf. of ἐντίθημι.

ἔνθεν, (ἐν) Adv. : I. Demonstr., 1. of Place, Lat. inde, thence, Hom. ; ἔνθεν μὲν .., ἑτέρωθι δέ .., on the one side and the other, Od. ; ἔνθεν καὶ ἔνθεν on this side and on that, Lat. hinc illinc, Hdt., etc. :— c. gen., ἔνθεν καὶ ἔνθεν τῶν τροχῶν on both sides of the wheels, Xen. 2. of Time, thereupon, thereafter, Il., Aesch. 3. of occasion, thence, from that point, Od. II. Relat., for ὅθεν, 1. of Place, Lat. unde, whence, from which, Ib., Soph. 2. of occasion, whence, like Lat. unde, Aesch., Eur. Hence

ἐνθένδε, Adv. hence, from this quarter, Lat. hinc, Hom., Att. ; ἐνθένδ' αὐτόθεν from this very city, Ar. 2. of Time or Consequence, from that time, Thuc. ; ἐνθένδε or τοὐνθένδε, thereafter, Soph., Eur. ; τἀνθένδε what followed, the event, Id.

ἔν-θεος, ον, full of the god, inspired, possessed, Trag., Xen. :—c. gen. rei, ἔνθεος τέχνης gifted of heaven with prophetic art, Aesch. II. of divine frenzy, inspired by the god, Id.

ἐν-θερμαίνω, to heat :—Pass., ἐντεθέρμανται πόθῳ is heated by passion, Soph.

ἔνθεσις, εως, ἡ, (ἐντίθημι) a putting in : also a piece put in, a mouthful, Ar.

ἔν-θεσμος, ον, lawful, like ἔννομος, Plut.

ἔνθετος, ον, (ἐντίθημι) put in, implanted, Theogn·

ἐνθεῦτεν, Ion. for ἐντεῦθεν.
ἔν-θηρος, ον, (θήρ) full of wild beasts, infested by them, Eur. II. metaph. savage, wild, rough, Aesch.: untended, undressed, Soph.
ἐν-θνήσκω, f. -θανοῦμαι, to die in a place, Soph., Eur. 2. of the hand, to grow torpid in, τινί Id.
ἐνθουσιάζω and ἐνθουσιάω, (ἔνθεος) to be inspired or possessed by the god, be rapt, be in ecstasy, Xen., Plat. :—c. dat., ἐνθουσιᾶν κακοῖς Eur. Hence
ἐνθουσιαστικός, ή, όν, inspired, Plat., etc.
ἐνθουσιάω, v. ἐνθουσιάζω.
ἐνθουσιώδης, ες, (ἐνθουσιάω, εἶδος) possessed, Plut.
ἐνθρέψασθαι, aor. 1 med. inf. of ἐντρέφω.
ἔνθρυπτος, ον, (θρύπτω) crumbled and put into liquid : τὰ ἔνθρυπτα sops, Dem. From
ἐν-θρώσκω, f. -θοροῦμαι : aor. 2 ἐνέθορον, Ep. ἔνθορον : —to leap in, on, or among, c. dat., Il., Eur.:—λὰξ ἔνθορεν ἰσχίῳ leapt with his feet against his, Od.
ἐν-θῡμέομαι, f. -ήσομαι : aor. 1 ἐνεθυμήθην : pf. ἐντεθύμημαι : (θυμός) :—to lay to heart, consider well, reflect on, ponder, Aesch., Thuc., etc. b. c. gen., ἐνθυμεῖσθαί τινος to think much or deeply of a thing, Id., Xen. c. foll. by a relative, as by ὅτι, to consider that, Ar., etc. d. with part., οὐκ ἐντεθύμηται ἐπαιρόμενος was not conscious that he was becoming excited, Thuc. 2. to take to heart, be hurt or angry at, τι Aesch., Dem. 3. to think out a thing, form a plan, Thuc. 4. to infer, conclude, Dem. Hence
ἐνθύμημα, τό, a thought, piece of reasoning, argument, Soph., Aeschin. II. an invention, device, Xen.
ἐνθύμησις [ῡ], εως, ἡ, consideration, esteem, Thuc.; and
ἐνθύμητος, verb. Adj. one must consider, Dem.; and
ἐνθῡμία, ἡ, a scruple, misgiving, Thuc.
ἐν-θύμιος [ῡ], ον, (θυμός) taken to heart, μή σοι ἐνθύμιος ἔστω take not much thought for him, Od.; ἐνθύμιόν οἱ ἐγένετο he had trouble of heart, Hdt.; τί δ᾽ ἐστί σοι τοῦτ᾽ ἐνθύμιον; what is᾽t that weighs upon thy heart? Soph.; ἐνθύμιον ποιεῖσθαί τι to have a scruple about it, Thuc.
ἐν-θύμιστός, ή, όν, = ἐνθύμιος, taken to heart, Hdt.
ἔνθω, Dor. for ἔλθω, aor. 2 subj. of ἔρχομαι.
ἐν-θωρακίζω, f. Att. ιῶ, to arm, equip with armour : part. pf. pass. ἐντεθωρακισμένος mailed, Xen.
ἐνί, poët. for ἐν. II. ἐνί, dat. of εἷς.
ἔνι, for ἔνεστι or ἔνεισι, 3 sing. and pl. of ἔνειμι (εἰμί sum).
ἐνιαύσιος, α, ον, or ος, ον, of a year, one year old, σῦς Od., Dem., etc. II. yearly, annual, year by year, Hdt. :—neut. pl. as Adv., Hes. III. for a year, lasting a year, Eur., Thuc.; κἀνιαύσιος βεβώς gone, absent for a year, Soph. From
ἐνιαυτός, ὁ, (ἔνος = annus) any long period of time, a cycle, period, περιπλομένων ἐνιαυτῶν as times rolled on, Od.; ἐτῶν ἐνιαυτούς Ar. II. = ἔτος, a year, Hom., etc.; ἐνιαυτόν during a year, Od.; τοῦ ἐνιαυτοῦ every year, Xen.; εἰς ἐνιαυτόν for a year, Il.;—κατ᾽ ἐνιαυτόν for a year, Thuc.; or every year, Att.
ἐν-ιαύω, f. -ιαύσω, to sleep among others, c. dat., Od.
ἐνιαχῇ, Adv. (ἔνιοι) in some places, Hdt.; c. gen. loci, Id.
ἐνιαχοῦ, Adv. (ἔνιοι) in some places, here and there, now and then, Plat.
ἐνιβάλλω, ἐνιβλάπτω, poët. for ἐμβάλλω, ἐμβλάπτω.

ἐνῐδεῖν, inf. of ἐνεῖδον.
ἐν-ιδρόω, f. ώσω, to sweat in, labour hard in, Xen.
ἐν-ιδρύω, f. ύσω [ῡ], to set in a place :—Med. to found or build for oneself, Hdt. :—Pass. to be placed or settled in a place, Id.
ἐνι-ζεύγνυμι, poët. for ἐν-ζεύγνυμι.
ἐν-ίζω, to sit in or on a seat, c. acc., Eur. ; c. dat., Plat.
ἐν-ίημι [ῑ], f. -ήσω : aor. 1 -ἦκα, Ep. -έηκα :—to send in or into, Hom. 2. to put in, implant, inspire, c. acc. rei et dat. pers., καί οἱ θάρσος ἐνὶ στήθεσσιν ἐνῆκε Il. ; ἐνεὶς λύσσαν Eur. 3. reversely, c. acc. pers. et dat. rei, to plunge into, τὸν Ζεὺς ἐνέηκε πόνοισι Il. 4. generally, to throw in or upon, c. dat., Hom. :—of ships, to launch them into the sea, Od. :—metaph. to incite one to do a thing, c. inf., Mosch. 5. to send into the assembly, employ, Thuc. 6. to inject poison, Xen. II. intr. to press on, fall in.
ἐνι-θνήσκω, ἐνι-θρύπτω, Ep. for ἐν-θνήσκω, ἐν-θρύπτω.
ἐνικάββαλον, Ep. for ἐγκατέβαλον, aor. 2 of ἐγκαταβάλλω.
ἐνικάππεσον, Ep. for ἐγκατέπεσον, aor. 2 of ἐγκαταπίπτω.
ἐνικάτθανον, Ep. for ἐγκατέθανον, aor. 2 of ἐγκαταθνήσκω.
ἐνικάτθεο, ἐνικάτθετο, Ep. for ἐγκαταθοῦ, ἐγκατέθετο 2 sing. aor. 2 med. of ἐγκατατίθημι.
ἐνι-κλάω, poët. for ἐγκ-, to break in, break off : metaph., ἐνικλᾶν ὅττι νοήσω to frustrate what I devise, Il.
ἐνι-κλείω, Ep. for ἐγ-κλείω.
ἐνι-κνώσσω, poët. for ἐγ-κνώσσω.
ἐνι-ναιετάεσκον, Ep. impf. of ἐν-ναιετάω.
ἔνιοι, αι, α, some, Lat. aliqui, = ἔστιν οἵ, Hdt., Xen., etc.
ἐνίοτε, Adv. for ἔνι ὅτε = ἔστιν ὅτε, sometimes, Eur., etc.
ἐνῑπή, ἡ, (ἐνίπτω) a rebuke, reproof ; also abuse, contumely, Hom.
ἐνί-πλειος, ον, Ep. for ἔμ-πλεος.
ἐνιπλήσασθαι, -σθῆναι, aor. 1 med. and pass. inf. of ἐμπίπλημι.
ἐνι-πλήσσω, Ep. for ἐμ-πλήσσω.
ἐν-ιππάζομαι, Dep. = sq., Plut.
ἐν-ιππεύω, f. σω, to ride in, Hdt.
ἐνιπρῆσαι, Ep. aor. 1 inf. of ἐμπίπρημι.
ΕΝΊΠΤΩ, f. ἐνίψω : Ep. aor. 2 ἠνίπαπον [ῑ], and also ἐνένιπον :—to reprove, upbraid, Lat. objurgo, Hom.
ἐνι-σκέλλω, ἐνι-σκήπτω, ἐνι-σκίμπτω, Ep. for ἐν-σκέλλω, etc.
ἐνισπεῖν, aor. 2 inf. of ἐνέπω.
ἐνισπήσω, fut. of ἐνέπω :—aor. 2 ἔνισπον.
ἐνίσσω, collat. form of ἐνίπτω, to attack, reproach, Hom. :—Ep. inf. ἐνισσέμεν Il. :—Pass., ἐνισσόμενος misused, Ib.
ἐν-ίστημι, Causal in pres., fut. and aor. 1 act., and in aor. 1 med. :—to put, set, place in, ἐν λίθοις Xen.; ἐς τὰς χώρας Hdt. 2. aor. 1 med. to begin, Dem.
B. Pass., with aor. 2 pf. and plqpf. act. :—to be set in, to stand in a place, c. dat., Eur. ; ἐν τῷ νηῷ Hdt. II. to be appointed, βασιλεὺς ἐνίστασθαι Id. III. to be upon, to threaten, Lat. imminere, c. dat. pers., Id. :—absol. to be at hand, begin, arise, Ar., Dem. :—of time, ὁ ἐνεστὼς πόλεμος the present war, Aeschin. ; τὰ ἐνεστηκότα πράγματα present circumstances, Xen. IV. to stand in the way, resist, τινι Thuc. :—absol. to stand in the way, Att.

ἐν-ίσχω, = ἐνέχω : Med., ἐνίσχεσθαι τὴν φωνήν to keep in one's voice, Plut. :—Pass. to be held fast, Hdt., Xen.

ἐνι-τρέφω, ἐνι-τρίβω, Ep. for ἐν-τρέφω, ἐν-τρίβω.

ἐνι-φέρβομαι, Ep. for ἐμ-φέρβομαι.

ἐνι-χραύω, ἐνι-χρίμπτω, Ep. for ἐγ-χραύω, ἐγ-χρίμπτω.

ἐνίψω, fut. both of ἐνέπω and ἐνίπτω.

ἐνναετήρ, ῆρος, ὁ, also ἐνναέτειρα, (ἐνναίω) an inmate, inhabitant, Anth.

ἐννα-ετηρίς, ίδος, ἡ, (ἔτος) a period of nine years, Plat.

ἐννα-έτηρος, ον, (ἔτος) = sq., nine years old, Hes.

ἐννα-ετής, ές, (ἔτος) nine years old, Theocr. :—neut. ἐννάετες, as Adv. for nine years, Hes. :—fem. ἐννάετις, ιδος, Anth.

ἐνναέτης, ου, ὁ, (ἐνναίω) an inhabitant, Anth.

ἐνναίρειν, Ep. for ἐναίρειν, Batr.

ἐν-ναίω, to dwell in a place, c. dat., Eur. ; ἐνν. ἐκεῖ Soph. :—c. acc. loci, to inhabit, Mosch.

ἐννάκις [ἄ], Adv. = ἐνάκις nine times, Anth.

ἐν-ναυπηγέομαι, Pass. to have ships built in it, of a place, Thuc.

ΈΝΝΕΆ·, indecl. nine, Lat. novem, Hom., etc.

ἐννεά-βοιος, ον, (βοῦς) worth nine beeves, Il.

ἐννεα-καί-δεκα, indecl. nineteen, Il., etc.

ἐννεακαιδεκά-μηνος, ον, (μήν) nineteen months old, Anth.

ἐννεα-και-δεκ-ετής, ές, (ἔτος) eleven years old, Anth.

ἐννεά-κρουνος, ον, with nine springs, name of a well at Athens, also called Καλλιρρόη, Hdt., Thuc.

ἐννεά-λῖνος, ον, (λίνον) of nine threads, Xen.

ἐννεά-μηνος, ον,˘ (μήν) of or in nine months, Hdt.

ἐννεά-πηχυς, υ, nine cubits broad or long, Il.

ἐννεάς, άδος, ἡ, (ἐννέα) a body of nine, Theocr.

ἐννεά-φωνος, ον, (φωνή) = ἐννεάφθογγος, Theocr.

ἐννεά-χῖλοι, αι, α, Ep. for ἐνάκις χίλιοι, nine thousand, Il.

ἐν-νενόηκασι, Ion. for ἐν-νενοήκασι, 3 pl. pf. of ἐννοέω.

ἔννεον, Ep. for ἔνεον, impf. of νέω to swim.

ἐννε-όργυιος, ον, (ὄργυια) nine fathoms long, Od.

ἐν-νεοσσεύω, Att. ἐν-νεοττεύω, f. εύσω, to hatch young in a place, Ar. II. c. acc. to hatch as in a nest, Plat.

ἐννέπω, lengthd. for ἐνέπω.

ἐννεσία, ἡ, Ep. for ἐνεσία.

ἐν-νεύω, f. σω, to make signs to, to ask by signs, N. T.

ἐννέ-ωρος, ον, (ὥρα) of or for nine years, Hom. 2. nine years old, Od.

ἐννήκοντα, Ep. for ἐνενήκοντα.

ἐννῆμαρ, Ep. Adv. for nine days, Il.

ἔννηιν, v. sub ἔνος.

ἐν-νοέω, f. ήσω· Ion. aor. 1 part. ἐννώσας, pf. ἐννένωκα:—in Att. also as Dep. ἐννοοῦμαι, with aor. pass. ἐνενοή-θην· Ion. 3 sing. plqpf. ἐννένωτο—to have in one's thoughts, to think, consider, reflect, Hdt., Plat. ; ἐνν. μή . . , to be anxious lest . . , Xen. 2. c. acc. to think or reflect upon, consider, Hdt., Soph. ; ἐννοεῖν περί τινος Eur. 3. c. gen. to have thought of a thing, Id., Xen. II. to understand, Trag. III. to intend to do, c. inf., Hdt., Soph. IV. to think of, invent, Lat. excogitare, Id., Xen. V. to have in one's mind, to conceive, form a notion of, τι Plat., Xen. Hence

ἔννοια, ἡ, a thought in the mind, notion, conception, Plat. 2. a thought, intent, design, Eur., Xen.

ἔν-νομος, ον, within the law, lawful, legal, Trag., etc. ; ἔννομα πάσχειν to suffer lawful punishment, Thuc. 2.

of persons, keeping within the law, upright, Aesch, etc. :—subject to law, N. T.

ἔν-νοος, ον, contr. ἔν-νους, ουν, thoughtful, intelligent, sensible, Aesch., etc.; ἔννους γίγνομαι I come to my senses, Eur.

ἔννος, v. sub ἔνος.

Ἐννοσί-γαιος, ὁ, Ep. for Ἐνοσί-γαιος, (ἔνοσις, γαῖα) the Earth-shaker, name of Poseidon, Hom.

ἐν-νοχλέω, poët. for ἐνοχλέω.

ἔννῡμι, ον, Ion. εἵνυμι, εἵνύω : f. ἔσω, Ep. ἕσσω : Ep. aor. 2 ἕσσα:—Med., Ep. fut. 3 sing. ἕσατο, Ep. ἕσσατο, ἑέσσατο :—Pass., pf. εἷμαι, εἷται, Ep. 2 sing. ἕσσαι: 2 and 3 sing. plqpf. ἕσσο, ἕστο, Ep. ἕεστο, 3 dual ἕσθην, 3 pl. εἵατο. (The Root was ϜΕΣ, cf. Lat. vestio). To put clothes on another, c. dupl. acc., κεῖνός σε χλαῖνάν τε χιτῶνά τε ἕσσει he will clothe thee in cloak and frock, Od. II. Med. and Pass., c. acc. rei, to clothe oneself in, to be clad in, put on, to wear, Hom. ; ἀσπίδας ἑσσάμενοι, of tall shields which covered the whole person, Il. ; [ξυστὰ] εἱμένα χαλκῷ shafts clad with brass, Ib. ; and by a strong metaph., λάϊνον ἕσσο χιτῶνα thou hadst been clad in coat of stone, i. e. stoned by the people, Ib. :—metaph. also, φρεσὶ εἱμένοι ἀλκήν Ib.

ἐν-νὔχεύω, f. σω, to sleep in or on a place, Soph.

ἐννὔχιος [ῠ], α, ον, or ος, ον, (νύξ) in the night, by night, nightly, Lat. nocturnus, Hom., Soph. :—ἐννύχιοι dwellers in the realms of Night, the dead, Id.

ἔν-νῠχος, ον, = foreg., Il., Aesch. :—Adv. ἔννυχον or -χα, N. T. II. epith. of Hades, Soph.

ἐννῶσαι, -νώσας, Ion. for ἐννοῆσαι, -νοήσας, aor. 1 inf. and part. of ἐννοέω.

ἐν-όδιος, α, ον, Ep. εἰν-όδιος, η, ον, (ὁδός) in or on the way, by the way-side, Il., Aesch. :—epith. of gods, who had their statues by the way-side, Lat. triviales, as of Hecaté, Soph., Eur. ; Ἐνοδία, = Lat. Trivia, Id.

ἐν-οικέω, f. ήσω, to dwell in a place, c. dat., Eur.; ἐν τόπῳ Xen. ; [Θυρέαν] ἔδοσαν ἐνοικεῖν gave it them to dwell in, Thuc. II. c. acc. loci, to inhabit, Hdt., Soph., etc. ; οἱ ἐνοικοῦντες the inhabitants, Hdt., Thuc., etc.

ἐνοίκησις, εως, ἡ, a dwelling in a place, Thuc.

ἐν-οικίζω, f. Att. ιῶ, to settle in a place :—Pass. to be settled in a place, to take up one's abode there, Hdt. ; so in Med., Thuc.

ἐν-οίκιος, ον, (οἶκος) in the house, keeping at home, ἐν. ὄρνις a dunghill cock, Aesch. II. as Subst., ἐνοίκιον, τό, house-rent, Dem., Anth.

ἐν-οικοδομέω, f. ήσω, to build in a place, Thuc. :—Med., ἐν. τεῖχος to build themselves a fort there, Id. II. to build up, block up, Id.

ἔν-οικος, ον, in-dwelling : an inhabitant, Trag., Thuc., etc. 2. pass. dwelt in, Eur.

ἐν-οικουρέω, f. ήσω, to keep house, dwell in a place, Luc.

ἐν-οινοχοέω, f. ήσω, to pour in wine, Hom.

ἐνο-λισθάνω or -αίνω, f. -ολισθήσω, aor. 2 -ώλισθον, to fall in, of the ground, Plut. : to slip and fall, Id.

ἐνομῑλέω, = ὁμιλέω ἐν, to be well acquainted with a thing, c. dat., Plut.

ἐν-ομόργνῠμαι, Med. to impress, Plut.

ἐνοπή, ἡ, (ἐνέπω) a crying, screaming, as of birds, Il. : a war-cry, Ib. 2. generally, a voice, Od., Eur. 3. of things, a sound, Il., Eur.

ἐνόπλιος, ον, = sq. :—ἐνόπλιος (sc. ῥυθμός), ὁ, a war-tune, march, Ar., Xen.

ἔν-οπλος, ον, (ὅπλον) in arms, armed, Soph., Eur. II. with armed men within, of the Trojan horse, Id.

ἔν-οπτρον, τό, (ὄψομαι, f. of ὁράω) a mirror, Eur.

ἐν-οράω, Ion. -έω : f. -όψομαι : aor. 2 -εἶδον :—to see, remark, observe something in a person or thing, τί τινι Thuc., etc. ; τι ἔν τινι Hdt., etc. ; c. acc. et part. fut., ἐνεώρα τιμωρίην ἐσομένην he saw that vengeance would come, Id. II. to look at or upon, Xen.

ἔν-ορκος, ον, bound by oath, Lat. juratus, Soph., Thuc. : c. dat. pers., Lat. addictus, Soph. II. that whereto one is sworn, Id., etc.

ἐν-ορμίζω, f. Att. ιῶ, to bring a ship to harbour :—Pass. to come to anchor, Theogn. Hence

ἐνορμίτης [ῑ], ου, ὁ, in harbour, Anth.

ἐν-όρνυμι, aor. 1 -ῶρσα : Ep. aor. 2 pass. ἐνῶρτο :—to arouse, stir up in a person, Il. :—Pass. to arise in or among, ἐνῶρτο γέλως θεοῖσιν Ib.

ἐν-ορούω, f. ούσω, to leap in or upon another, c. dat., Il.

ἐνόρχης, ου, ὁ, = ἔνορχος, Ar. :—a he-goat, Theocr.

ἔνορχις, ιος, ὁ, ἡ, Ion. for ἐνόρχης, Hdt.

ἔν-ορχος, ον, (ὄρχις) uncastrated, entire, ἔνορχα μῆλα rams, Il.

*ἜΝΟΣ, ὁ, = the Lat. annus, a year, hence ἐνιαυτός, cf. ἄφ-ενος, Lat. bi-ennis, etc.

ἜΝΟΣ, η, ον, the day after to-morrow, Lat. perendie, only in oblique cases of fem., gen. ἔνης Ep. ἔννηφι (sub. ἡμέρας) Hes. ; Dor. ἔνας Theocr. ; εἰς ἔνην Ar.

ἜΝΟΣ, η, ον, belonging to the former of two periods, last year's, ἔναι ἀρχαί last year's magistrates, Dem. :—dat. ἔνῃ as Adv., long ago, Ar. 2. ἔνη καὶ νέα (sc. ἡμέρα), the old and new day, i. e. the last day of the month, which consisted of two halves, one belonging to the old, the other to the new moon, Id.

ἑνός, gen. of εἷς and ἕν, one.

ἔνοσις, εως, ἡ, a shaking, quake, Hes., Eur. (From an obsol. Root *ἐνόθω to shake.)

Ἐνοσί-χθων, ονος, ὁ, Earth-shaker, of Poseidon, Hom.

ἐν-ουράνιος, ον, in heaven, heavenly, Anth.

ἐνοχλέω, poët. 2 sing. ἐνοχλεῖς : impf. with double augm. ἠνώχλουν : f. ἐνοχλήσω : aor. 1 ἠνώχλησα : pf. ἠνώχληκα :—to trouble, disquiet, annoy, τινά Plat., Xen., etc. :—Pass. to be troubled or annoyed, Id. 2. c. dat. to give trouble or annoyance to, Id., Dem., etc. 3. absol. to be a nuisance, Ar.

ἔνοχος, ον, (ἐνέχω) held in, i. e. liable to, subject to, c. dat., Plat. ; ἔν. θανάτου (sc. ζημίᾳ) liable to the penalty of death, N. T.

ἐν-ράπτω, f. ψω, to sew up in, τι εἴς τι ; so Med., Hdt. : —Pass. to be sewed up in, c. dat., Eur.

ἐν-ρῑγόω, f. ώσω, to shiver or freeze in a garment, Ar.

ἐν-σείω, f. σω, to shake in or at, Soph. ; κέλαδον ἐνσ. πώλοις to drive a sound into their ears, Id. 2. c. acc. pers. to drive into, ἐνσ. τινὰ ἀγρίαις ὁδοῖς Id.

ἐν-σημαίνομαι, f. -ανοῦμαι, Med. to intimate, Xen.

ἐν-σκέλλω, pf. ἐνέσκληκα, to be dry, withered, Anth.

ἐν-σκευάζω, f. άσω, to get ready, prepare, Ar. 2. to dress in a garment, Plut. ; Ἡρακλέα 'νεσκεύασα dressed you up as Hercules, Ar. :—Med. to dress one-self up in other clothes, Id. : to arm oneself, Xen. : —Pass. to be equipped, Hdt.

ἐν-σκήπτω, f. ψω, to hurl, dart in or upon, τί τινι Hdt. II. intr. to fall in or on, Id., Soph.

ἐν-σκίμπτω, poët. ἐνι-σκ-, Ep. form of foreg., to let fall upon, οὖδει ἐνισκίμψαντε κάρηατα, of horses hanging their heads in grief for their master's loss, Il. :—Pass. to stick in the ground, Ib.

ἐν-σκιρρόω, f. ώσω, to harden :—Pass. to become in-veterate, of diseases, Xen.

ἔν-σοφος, ον, wise in a thing, Anth.

ἔν-σπονδος, ον, (σπονδή) included in a truce or treaty, Thuc. ; ἔνσπ. τινί in alliance with one, Eur., Thuc. ; and as Subst. an ally, Id. II. under truce or safe-conduct, Eur.

ἐν-στάζω, f. ξω, to drop in or into a thing, c. dat., Ar. : —Pass. to be instilled into, Od., Hdt.

ἐν-σταλάζω, f. ξω, = ἐνστάζω, εἴς τι Ar.

ἔνστασις, εως, ἡ, (ἐνίσταμαι) a beginning, plan, management, Aeschin.

ἐνστάτης [ᾰ], ου, ὁ, (ἐνίσταμαι) an adversary, Soph.

ἐν-στέλλω, f. -στελῶ, to dress in :—Pass., στολὴν ἐνε-σταλμένος clad in a dress, Hdt.

ἐν-στηρίζω, f. ξω, to fix in :—Pass., γαίῃ ἐνεστήρικτο it stuck fast in earth, Il.

ἐν-στρατοπεδεύομαι, Dep. to encamp in, Hdt. ;—so in Act., Thuc.

ἐν-στρέφω, f. ψω, to turn in :—Pass. to turn or move in a place, c. dat., Il. 2. c. acc. loci, σηκοὺς ἐνστρέ-φειν to visit them, Eur.

ἐν-σφρᾱγίζω, Ion. -σφρηγίζω, to impress on a thing, c. dat., Anth.

ἔνταλμα, ατος, τό, = ἐντολή, N. T.

ἐν-τάμνω, Ion. for ἐν-τέμνω.

ἐν-τᾰνύω, f. σω, poët. and Ion. for ἐντείνω, to stretch or strain tight with cords or straps, Hom. ; ἐντανύσας [τὸν θρόνον ἱμᾶσιν] to cover it with stretched straps, Hdt. 2. to stretch a cord tight, of the bow-string, Od. : also to stretch a bow tight, i. e. to string it, Ib. :—Med., δυνήσεαι ἐντανύσασθαι to string one's bow, Ib.

ἔντασις, εως, ἡ, (ἔντασις) tension : limitation, Plat.

ἐν-τάσσω, Att. -ττω, f. ξω, to place or post in :—Pass., σφενδονᾶν ἐντεταγμένος posted to use the sling, Xen.

ἐνταῦθα, Ion. ἐνθαῦτα, Adv., (ἔνθα) : I. of Place, here, there, Lat. hic, illic, Hdt., etc. ; ἐνταῦθά που here-abouts, Ar. 2. like ἐνταυθοῖ, with sense of motion towards, hither, thither, Lat. huc, illuc, Il., Att. 3. c. gen., ἐντ. τῆς ἠπείρου Thuc. ; ἔντ. τῆς πολιτείας in department of government, Dem. II. of Time, at the very time, then, Aesch. etc. 2. c. gen., ἐντ. ἡλικίας, Lat. ad hoc aetatis, Plat. III. of Sequence, = Lat. deinde, thereupon, then, Hdt. IV. generally, herein, Soph., Plat., etc. : in this state of things, in this position, Dem.

ἐνταυθῖ [ῑ], Att. strengthd. form of foreg., Ar.

ἐνταυθοῖ, Adv. (ἔνθα) hither, here, Hom.

ἐντᾰφιάζω, to prepare for burial, N. T. ; and

ἐνταφιασμός, ὁ, burial, N. T. From

ἐν-τάφιος [ᾰ], ον, (τάφος) of or used in burial : hence as Subst., ἐντάφιον, τό, a shroud, winding-sheet, Simon., Anth. 2. ἐντάφια, τά, offerings to the dead, obsequies, Soph.

ἜΝΤΕΑ, ων, τά, fighting gear, arms, armour, Hom. II. furniture, appliances, ἔντεα δαιτός Od. ;

ἔντεα νηός rigging, tackle, h. Hom.; ἔντη δίφρου the harness, Aesch.

ἐν-τείνω, f. -τενῶ: pf. -τέτἄκα, pass. -τέτᾰμαι:—to stretch or strain tight:—Pass., δίφρος ἱμᾶσιν ἐντέταται is hung on tight-stretched straps, Il.; γέφυραι ἐντεταμέναι a bridge with the mooring-cables made taught, Hdt.; ἐντεταμένου τοῦ σώματος being braced up, Plat. 2. to stretch a bow tight, i.e. string it for shooting (cf. ἐντανύω), Eur.; so in Med. to string one's bow, Id.:—Pass., τόξα ἐντεταμένα bows ready strung, Hdt. 3. ἐντείνειν ναῦν ποδί to keep a ship's sail taught by the sheet, Eur. 4. to tie tight, Id. II. metaph. to strain, exert:—so in Med., φωνὴν ἐντεινάμενος Aeschin.; ἐντεινάμενοι τὴν ἁρμονίαν pitching the tune high, Ar.;—and in Pass., ἐντεινόμενος, on the stretch, eager, Xen. 2. to carry on vigorously, Plut. 3. so intr. in Act. to exert oneself, be vehement, Eur. III. to stretch out at or against, πληγὴν ἐντείνειν τινί, Lat. plagam intendere, to lay a blow on him, Xen. IV. to put into verse, Plat.

ἐν-τειχίζω, f. Att. ιῶ, to build or fortify in a place, Xen. II. in Med. to wall in, i. e. blockade, Thuc.

ἐντεκνόομαι, Dep. to beget children in, Plut. From

ἔν-τεκνος, ον, (τέκνον) having children, Luc.

ἐν-τελευτάω, f. ήσω, to end one's life in a place, Thuc.

ἐν-τελής, ές, (τέλος) complete, full, Ar., Thuc. 2. of victims, perfect, unblemished, Soph. 3. of soldiers and their equipments, in good condition, effective, Thuc. 4. of men, full-grown, Aesch.

ἐν-τέλλω, mostly in Med., f. -τελοῦμαι, to enjoin, command, τί τινι Hdt., etc.; ἐντέλλεσθαι ἀπὸ γλώσσης to command by word of mouth, Id.:—Pass., τὰ ἐντεταλμένα commands, Id., Xen.

ἐν-τέμνω, Ion. -τάμνω, f. -τεμῶ, to cut in, engrave upon, ἐν τοῖσι λίθοισι γράμματα Hdt. II. to cut up, 1. to cut up the victim, sacrifice, Thuc. 2. to cut in, shred in, as herbs in a medical mixture, ἄκος ἐντ. Aesch. 3. to cut in two, Luc.

ἔντερον, τό, (ἐντός) an intestine, piece of gut, ἔντερον οἰός a string of sheep's gut, Od.:—mostly in pl. ἔντερα, the guts, bowels, Il., Att. Hence

ἐντερόνεια, ἡ, the timber of a ship, belly-timber, Ar.

ἐντεσι-εργός, όν, (ἔργον) working in harness, ἡμίονοι ἐντ. draught-mules, Il.

ἐντέτᾰμαι, pf. pass. of ἐντείνω. Hence

ἐντεταμένως, Adv. vehemently, vigorously, Hdt.

ἐντεῦθεν, Ion. ἐνθεῦτεν, Adv. (ἔνθεν): I. of Place, hence or thence, Lat. hinc or illinc, Od., etc. II. of Time, henceforth, thenceforth, thereupon, Hdt., etc.; τοὐντεῦθεν Eur.; τἀντεῦθεν what remains, Aesch. III. Causal, from that source, Thuc.

ἐντευθενί [ῑ], strengthd. form of foreg., Ar.

ἐντευκτικός, ή, όν, affable, Plut. From

ἔντευξις, εως, ἡ, (ἐντυγχάνω) a lighting upon, meeting with, converse, intercourse, τινος with a person, Aeschin. 2. a petition, Plut.: intercession for a person, N. T.

ἐν-τευτλᾰνόομαι, Pass. to be stewed in beet (τεῦτλον), Ar.

ἔν-τεχνος, ον, (τέχνη) within the province of art, artificial, artistic, Plat.

ἐν-τήκω, f. ξω, to pour in while molten, μόλιβδον Plut. II. Pass., with pf. act. ἐντέτηκα, 1. of

feelings, to sink deep in, Soph. 2. of persons, to be absorbed by a thing, Id.

ἐντί, Dor. for ἐστί or εἰσί, 3 sing. and pl. of εἰμί (sum).

ἐν-τίθημι, f. -θήσω: poët. aor. 1 inf. ἐνθέμεν:—to put in or into a ship, Od., Att.; so in Med., Od.:—then, generally, to put in or into, Hes., Hdt., etc. 2. metaph. to put into a person, inspire, Theogn., Xen.;—Med., χόλον ἔνθεο θυμῷ thou didst store up wrath in thy heart, Il.; πατέρας ἔνθεο τιμῇ hold our fathers in honour, Ib. 3. to put in the mouth, τί τινι Ar.; and in Med., ἔνθου, put in, i. e. eat, Id.

ἐν-τίκτω, f. -τέξομαι, to bear or produce in a place, c. dat., Eur.; ᾠὰ ἐντ. ἐς τὴν ἰλύν to drop eggs into the mud, Hdt. 2. to create or cause in a person, τί τινι Eur. II. pf. part. ἐντετοκώς intr., inborn, innate, Ar.

ἐντῑλάω, f. ήσω, Lat. incacare, to squirt upon, τί τινι Ar.

ἐν-τῑμάω, f. ήσω, to value in or among, Dem.

ἔν-τῑμος, ον, (τιμή) 1. of persons, in honour, honoured, prised, Soph., etc.:—c. dat. rei, honoured with or in a thing, Eur.:—οἱ ἔντιμοι men in office, men of rank, Xen. 2. of things, honoured, held in honour, Soph. 3. Adv., ἐντίμως ἔχειν to be in honour, Xen.

ἔντμημα, ατος, τό, (ἐντέμνω) an incision, notch, Xen.

ἔντο, 3 pl. aor. 2 med. of ἵημι.

ἐντολή, ἡ, (ἐντέλλω) an injunction, order, command, behest, Hdt., etc.

ἔντομος, ον, (ἐντέμνω) cut in pieces, cut up: neut. pl., ἔντομα victims, Hdt.

ἔντονος, ον, (ἐντείνω) of persons, well-strung, sinewy: metaph. intense, earnest, eager, vehement, Hdt., Att.: —Adv. ἐντόνως, eagerly, violently, Thuc., Xen.

ἔν-τοπος, ον, in or of a place, Soph.

ἐντορεύω, f. σω, to carve in relief on a thing, Plut.

ἔντος, τό, v. ἔντεα, τά.

ἐντός, Adv. (ἐν) within, inside, Lat. intus, opp. to ἐκτός: I. as Prep. with gen., τείχεος ἐντός Il.; ἐντὸς Ὀλύμπου Hes., etc.; ἐντὸς ἐμαυτοῦ in my senses, Hdt.; so absol. ἐντὸς ὤν Dem.:—also with Verbs of motion, τείχεος ἐντὸς ἰέναι Il. 2. within, i. e. on this side, Lat. citra, ἐντὸς τοῦ Ἅλυος ποταμοῦ Hdt., etc. 3. of Time, within, ἐντὸς εἴκοσιν ἡμερῶν Thuc.; ἐντὸς ἑσπέρας short of, i.e. before, evening, Xen. II. absol. within, ἐντὸς ἐέργειν Hom.; ἐντὸς ἔχειν Thuc.; τὰ ἐντός the inner parts, inwards, Id.

ἔντοσθε, before a vowel -θεν, Adv. from within, Od.: —also = ἐντός, within, absol. or c. gen., Il.

ἐντράγειν, aor. 2 inf. of ἐντράγω.

ἐν-τρᾰγῳδέω, f. ήσω, to strut among, τισί Luc.

ἐν-τρέπω, f. -τρέψω, to turn about, τὰ νῶτα Hdt.: to alter, Luc. II. Med. or Pass., aor. 2 ἐνετράπην [ἄ], to turn about, linger, hesitate, Soph. 2. c. gen. pers. to turn towards, give heed to, pay regard to, to respect or reverence, Hom., Trag. 3. c. inf. to take care that, Theogn. 4. absol. to feel shame or fear, N. T.

ἐν-τρέφω, f. -θρέψω, to bring up in the house, Eur.:— so in Med., Hes.:—Pass. to be reared in a place, c. dat., Eur.

ἐν-τρέχω, f. -δρᾰμοῦμαι, to run in, εἰ ἐντρέχοι ἀγλαὰ γυῖα if his limbs moved freely in [the armour], Il. II. to slip in, enter, Anth.

ἐντρῐβής, ές, metaph. from the touchstone, proved by rubbing, versed in a thing, c. dat., Soph. From
ἐν-τρίβω [ῐ], f. ψω, to rub in or into a thing, c. dat., Luc. 2. metaph., ἐντρ. κόνδυλόν τινι to give him a drubbing, Plut.; so in Med., Luc. II. c. acc. pers. to rub one with cosmetics, Xen. :—Pass. to have cosmetics rubbed in, to be anointed, painted, Id. III. to wear away by rubbing, Ar. Hence
ἔντρῐμμα, ατος, τό, a cosmetic, Plut.
ἐντρῐτωνίζω, (ἐν, τρίτος) to third with water, i. e. to mix three parts of water with two of wine,—with a pun on ἡ Τριτογενής, Ar.
ἔν-τρῐχος, ον, (θρίξ) hairy, Anth.
ἔντριψις, εως, ἡ, (ἐντρίβω) a rubbing in, Xen.
ἔν-τρομος, ον, (τρέμω) trembling, Plut., N. T.
ἐν-τροπᾰλίζομαι, Pass., Frequent. of ἐντρέπω, to keep turning round, of men retreating, Il.
ἐντροπή, ἡ, (ἐντρέπω) a turning towards, ἐντροπήν τινος ἔχειν respect or reverence for one, Soph.: shame, reproach, N. T. Hence
ἐντροπία, ἡ, a trick, dodge, h. Hom.
ἔντροφος, ον, (ἐντρέφω) living in or acquainted with a thing, c. dat., Soph. 2. as Subst., nursling, Anth.
ἐν-τρυφάω, f. ήσω, to revel in a thing, c. dat., Menand. :—absol. to be luxurious, Xen. II. to mock at, τινί Eur.
ἐν-τρώγω, f. ξομαι: aor. 2 ἐνέτρᾰγον :—to eat greedily, to gobble up, Ar. :—c. gen. to eat greedily of, Luc.
ἐν-τυγχάνω, f. -τεύξομαι: aor. 2 ἐνέτῠχον: pf. ἐντετύχηκα: aor. 1 pass. part. ἐντευχθείς in act. sense :— to light upon, fall in with, meet with a person or thing, c. dat., Hdt., etc. :—absol. ὁ ἐντυχών the first who meets us, any chance person, Thuc.; of thunder, to fall upon, c. dat., Xen.; so of misfortunes, Aesch. 2. rarely, like τυγχάνω, c. gen., λελυμένης τῆς γεφύρης ἐντυχόντες having found the bridge broken up, Hdt.; ἐντυχὼν Ἀσκληπιδῶν having fallen in with them, Soph. II. to converse with, talk to, τινί Plat. 2. to intercede with, intreat, τινί N. T., Plut. :—c. inf. to intreat one to do, Id. III. of books, to meet with, Plat.: hence, to read, Luc.
ἐν-τῠλίσσω, f. ξω, to wrap up, Ar.
ἐν-τύνω [ῠ], impf. ἐντύνω: f. ἐντῠνῶ: aor. 1 ἔντῡνα: —also ἐντύω [ῠ], impf. ἔντῠον :—to equip, deck out, get ready, Hom.; δέπας δ' ἔντυνον (aor. 1 imperat.) prepare the cup, i. e. mix the wine, Il.; εὖ ἐντύνασαν ἑ αὐτήν having decked herself well out, Ib. :—Med., ὄφρα τάχιστα ἐντύνεαι (Ep. for ἐντύνῃ) may'st get thee ready, Od. :—Med., c. acc., to prepare for oneself, ἐντύνεσθαι δαῖτα, δεῖπνον Hom.
ἐν-τῠπάς, (τύπος) Adv., ἐντυπὰς ἐν χλαίνῃ κεκαλυμμένος (of Priam in his grief), wrapt up in his mantle so closely as to shew his limbs, Il.
ἐν-τῠπόω, f. ώσω, to cut in intaglio, Plut.
ἐν-τύφω [ῠ], f. -θύψω, to smoke as one does wasps, Ar.
ἐντύω, v. ἐντύνω.
Ἐνῡάλιος [ᾰ], ὁ, the Warlike, name of Ares (Mars), Il., Soph., etc. 2. as appellat. war, battle, Eur. II. as Adj. warlike, furious, Theocr.
ἐν-ὑβρίζω, f. Att. ιῶ, to insult or mock one in a thing, c. dat., Soph.; τινὰ ἐν κακοῖς Eur.
ἔν-υδρις, ἡ, gen. ιος, (ὕδωρ) an otter, Hdt.

ἐνυδρό-βῐος, ον, living in the water, Anth.
ἔν-υδρος, ον, (ὕδωρ) with water in it, holding water, ἔν. τεῦχος, i. e. a bath, Aesch.; of countries, well-watered, Hdt.; ἔν. φρούριον provided with water, Xen. 2. of water, watery, Eur. 3. living in or by water, of Nymphs, Soph.; of plants, Ar.
ἔνυξα, aor. 1 of νύσσω.
ἐν-ύπνιον, τό, (ὕπνος) a thing seen in sleep, ἐνύπνιον ἦλθεν ὄνειρος a dream or vision in sleep came to me, Od. :—hence as Adv., ἐνύπνιον ἐστιᾶσθαι 'to feast with the Barmecide,' Ar. 2. simply a dream, Hdt., Att.
ἐν-ύπνιος, ον, (ὕπνος) in dreams appearing, Aesch.
ἐνύσταξα, aor. 1 of νυστάζω.
ἐν-ὑφαίνω, f. ᾰνῶ, to weave in as a pattern :—Pass. to be inwoven, Hdt. Hence
ἐνῠφαντός, όν, inwoven, Theocr.
Ἐνῡώ, gen. όος contr. οῦς, ἡ, Enyo, goddess of war, answering to the Roman Bellona, Il., Aesch.
ἐν-ωθέω, aor. 1 -έωσα, to thrust in or upon, Plut., Luc.
ἐνωμοτ-άρχης or -αρχος, ον, ὁ, leader of an ἐνωμοτία, Thuc., Xen.
ἐνωμοτία, ἡ, a band of sworn soldiers, a company in the Spartan army, the λόχος contained 4 πεντηκοστύες, each πεντηκοστύς 4 ἐνωμοτίαι, and each ἐνωμοτία 32 men, Thuc., Xen. From
ἐν-ώμοτος, ον, (ὄμνυμι) bound by oath, Soph. :—Adv. -τως, on oath, Plut. II. a conspirator, Id.
ἐνωπᾰδίως, Adv. in one's face, to one's face, Od. From
ἐν-ωπή, ἡ, (ὤψ) the face, countenance, dat. ἐνωπῇ as Adv., before the face, openly, Il.
ἐνώπια, τά, the inner wall fronting those who enter a building or the side-walls of the entrance, Hom. From
ἐν-ώπιος, ον, (ὤψ) face to face, Theocr. II. neut. ἐνώπιον, Prep. with gen., like Lat. coram, N. T.
ἔνωρσα, aor. 1 of ἐνόρνυμι :—ἐν-ῶρτο, 3 sing. Ep. aor. 2 pass.
ἔνωσα, Ion. contr. for ἐνόησα, aor. 1 of νοέω.
ἐν-ωτίζομαι, Dep. (οὖς) to hearken to a thing, τι N. T.
ἐξ, Lat. ex, out of the form of the Prep. ἐκ, before a vowel and before some consonants, as ρ σ.
Ἕ Ξ, οἱ, αἱ, τά, indecl. six, Hom., etc.—In composition, before δ κ π, it becomes ἐκ, as ἕδραχμος, ἐκκαίδεκα, ἕκπλεθρος; or has σ inserted, as ἑξάκλινος, etc.
ἐξαγγελία, ἡ, information sent out to the enemy, Xen.
ἐξ-αγγέλλω, f. ελῶ, to send out tidings, report, of traitors and the like, Il., Att. :—Med. to cause to be proclaimed, Hdt., Soph.; c. inf. to promise to do, Eur. :— Pass. to be reported, Hdt.; impers., ἐξαγγέλλεται it is reported, Id.
ἐξ-άγγελος, ὁ, ἡ, a messenger who brings out news from within, an informer, Thuc., etc. II. on the Greek stage, ἄγγελοι told news from a distance, ἐξάγγελοι what was a-doing behind the scenes, as in Soph. Hence
ἐξάγγελτος, ον, told of, denounced, Thuc.
ἐξ-ἄγίζω, to drive out as accursed :—Pass., aor. 1 part. ἐξαγισθείς, Aesch.
ἐξἄγινέω, Ion. for ἐξάγω, to lead forth, Hdt.
ἐξ-άγιστος, ον, (ἐξαγίζω) devoted to evil, accursed, abominable, Dem., Aeschin. II. ἐξάγιστα holy things, matters of religion, Soph.
ἐξ-άγνυμι, f. -άξω, to break and tear away, to rend, Il.

ἐξ-ἀγοράζω, f. σω, *to buy up*, Plut.　II. *to redeem*, N. T.; so in Med., Ib.

ἐξἀγορευτικός, ή, όν, *fit to explain*, τινος Luc. From

ἐξ-ἀγορεύω (the aor. is supplied by ἐξεῖπον, the fut. and pf. by ἐξερῶ, ἐξείρηκα), *to tell out, make known, declare*, Od. : *to betray* a secret or mystery, Hdt.

ἐξ-αγριαίνω, f. ἄνῶ, *to make savage*, Plat. :—Pass. *to be or become savage*, Id.

ἐξ-αγριόω, f. ώσω, *to make wild* or *waste* :—Pass. *to be or be made so*, Aeschin.　II. like foreg. *to make savage, exasperate*, Hdt., Eur.

ἐξ-άγω, f. ξω : aor. 2 -ήγᾰγον :—*to lead out* :　I. of persons, *to lead* or *carry out from* a place, Hom., etc.: *to bring forth into the world*, Il. : *to lead out to execution*, Hdt.　b. *to march out* (sub. στρατόν), Xen.: generally, *to go out*, Id.　2. *to eject* a claimant from property, Dem., etc.　II. of merchandise, *to carry out, export*, Ar., etc. :—Pass., τὰ ἐξαγόμενα exports, Xen.　2. *to draw off* water, Id.　3. of building, *to carry further out*, Thuc.　III. *to call forth, excite*, δάκρυ Eur. :—Med., γέλωτα ἐξάγεσθαι Xen.　IV. *to lead on, carry away, excite*, τινά Eur., Thuc.; and in bad sense, *to lead on, tempt*, Id. :—Pass. *to be led on*, c. inf., Xen.　Hence

ἐξ-αγωγή, ή, *a leading out* of soldiers, Xen.　2. *a drawing out* of a ship to sea, Hdt.　3. *a carrying out, exportation*, Id., Att.

ἐξ-ἀγωνίζομαι, f. Att. ιοῦμαι, Dep. *to struggle hard*, Eur.

ἐξ-ἀγώνιος, ον, *beside the mark, irrelevant*, Luc.

ἐξάδ-αρχος, ον, (ἑξάς) *leader of a body of six*, Xen.

ἐξ-ἀδω, f. -άσομαι, *to sing out, sing one's last song*, of the swan, Plat.　II. trans. *to sing of, laud*, Eur.

ἐξαείρω, Ion. for ἐξαίρω.

ἐξ-ἀερόω, f. ώσω, (ἀήρ) *to make into air, volatilise*, Luc.

ἐξα-ετής, ές, or -έτης, ες, (ἔτος) *six years old* : fem. ἐξαέτις, ιδος, Theocr.　II. *of six years*, χρόνος Plut. :—Adv., ἐξέτες, *for six years*, Od.

ἐξ-ἀθροίζομαι, Med. *to seek out and collect*, Eur.

ἐξ-ἀθῦμέω, f. ήσω, *to be quite disheartened*, Plut.

ἐξ-αιάζω, *to wail loudly*, Eur.

ἐξ-αιμάσσω, Att. -ττω, f. ξω, *to make quite bloody*, Xen.

ἐξ-αίνῦμαι, Ep. Dep. *to carry off*, Od. ; c. dupl. acc., ἐξαίνυτο θυμὸν ἀμφοτέρω took away life *from* both, Il.

ἐξαίρεσις, εως, ή, *a taking out*, Hdt. :—*a way of taking out*, Id.; and

ἐξαιρετέος, α, ον, verb. Adj. *to be taken out* or *removed*, Xen.　II. ἐξαιρετέον, *one must take out* : *one must pick out, select*, Id.; and

ἐξαιρετός, ή, όν, *that can be taken out, removable*, Hdt.　II. ἐξαίρετος, ον, *taken out, picked out, chosen*, Lat. *eximius*, Hom., etc.　2. *excepted*, Eur., Thuc., etc.: *special, remarkable*, Dem.　From

ἐξ-αιρέω, f. ήσω: aor. 2 ἐξεῖλον, Ep. ἔξελον, inf. ἐξελεῖν :—Pass., pf. ἐξῄρημαι, Ion. -αραίρημαι Hdt. :—*to take out of* a thing, τί τινος Hom., etc.; ἔκ τινος Hdt., etc. :—simply *to take out*, νηδύν Id. :—Med. *to take out for oneself*, Il. ; ἐξ. τὰ φορτία *to discharge their cargoes*, Hdt.　II. *to take from among others, to pick out, choose*, Hom., etc. :—Med. *to choose for oneself, carry off as booty*, Id. :—Pass. *to be given as a special honour*, τινι to one, Thuc.; ἐξαραιρημένος Ποσειδέωνι *dedicated* to him, Hdt.　2. *to take out*

of a number, *to except*, Id., Att.　III. *to expel people from their seats*, Hdt., Thuc.　2. *to take out, remove*, Hdt., Att.　3. in Med. *to bereave a person* of life, c. dupl. acc., μιν ἐξείλετο θυμόν Il., Att. ; or c. gen. pers., μευ φρένας ἐξέλετο Il. ; rarely c. dat. pers., Ib. :—Med. *to take away from one*, Soph. :—Pass., ἐξαιρεθέντες τὸν Δημοκήδεα having had him *taken out of their hands*, Hdt.　IV. in Med. *to set free, deliver*, Aesch., Dem.　V. *to make away with, annul*, Soph. : *to demolish* a city, Hdt., etc.　2. *to bring to an end, accomplish*, Eur.

ἐξ-αίρω, f. -ἀρῶ, contr. from Ion. ἐξαείρω, *to lift up, lift off the earth*, Hom., Hdt. ; ἐξάραντες having bade me *rise* (from suppliant posture), Soph.　2. *to raise in dignity, exalt*, Hdt., Aeschin.　3. *to raise, arouse, stir up*, Theogn., Soph. ; ἐξ. σε θανεῖν excites thy wish to die, Eur.　II. Med., 3 sing. aor. 1 ἐξήρατο, *to carry off for oneself, earn, win, gain*, Od.　2. *to take on oneself*, Soph.　III. Pass. *to be raised*, Hdt. : *to rise up, rise*, Eur. :—*to be excited, agitated*, Soph.

ἐξ-αίσιος, ον, or α, ον, *beyond what is ordained* or *fated* : hence,　1. *lawless*, Od.　2. *extraordinary, violent*, Hdt., Xen. ; ἐξ. φυγή *headlong* flight, Id.

ἐξ-αΐσσω, Att. -άσσω and -άττω, f. ξω, *to rush forth, start out from*, c. gen., Il. ; ἐκ τοῦ νεώ Ar. :—so in Pass., Il.

ἐξ-αϊστόω, f. ώσω, *to utterly destroy*, Aesch.

ἐξ-αιτέω, f. ήσω, *to demand* or *ask for from* another, c. dupl. acc., τήνδε μ' ἐξαιτεῖ χάριν Soph. ; ἐξ. τινα πατρός *to ask her in marriage* from . . , Id. :—ἐξ. τινα *to demand the surrender* of a person, Hdt., Dem. ;—σμικρὸν ἐξ. *to beg for little*, Soph.　II. Med. *to ask for oneself, demand*, Hdt., Soph., etc.　2. in Med. also, = παραιτοῦμαι, *to beg off, gain* his *pardon* or *release*, Lat. *exorare*, Aesch., Xen. ; c. inf. *to beg that one may obtain*, Eur. :—c. acc. rei, *to avert by begging*, Lat. *deprecari*, Id.　Hence

ἐξαίτησις, εως, ή, *a demanding* one *for punishment*, Dem.　II. *intercession*, Id.

ἐξ-αιτος, ον, (αἰτέω) *much asked for, much desired, choice, excellent*, Hom.

ἐξ-αίφνης, (ἄφνω) Adv. *on a sudden*, Il., Att. ; ἐξ. ἀποθανόντος *the moment* he is *dead*, Plat.

ἐξ-ἀκέομαι, f. έσομαι, Dep. *to heal completely, heal the wound, make amends*, Il.　II. c. acc. *to appease*, Hom. ; *to make up for*, Xen.　2. *to mend clothes*, Plat.　Hence

ἐξάκεσις [ᾰ], εως, ή, *a thorough cure*, Ar.

ἐξάκῐς [ᾰ], Adv. (ἕξ) *six times*, Lat. *sexies*, Plat., etc. : poët. ἐξάκι, Anth.

ἐξάκισ-μύριοι [ῠ], *sixty thousand*, Hdt., Xen.

ἐξάκισ-χίλιοι [ῑ], αι, α, *six thousand*, Hdt., Thuc., etc.

ἐξ-ἀκοντίζω, f. Att. ιῶ, *to dart* or *hurl forth*, Xen. ; φάσγανον πρὸς ἧπαρ ἐξ. *to strike* it home, Eur.　2. metaph., ἐξ. κῶλον τῆς γῆς i. e. *to flee precipitately*, Id. ; τοὺς πόνους ἐξ. *to proclaim loudly*, Id.

ἐξακόσιοι, αι, α, (ἕξ) *six hundred*, Hdt.

ἐξ-ἀκούω, f. -ακούσομαι, *to hear a sound*, esp. *from a distance*, Aesch., Soph. ; c. gen. pers., Xen. ; rei, Plut.

ἐξ-ακρῑβόω, f. ώσω, *to make exact*, ἐξ. λόγον *to make a distinct* or *precise* statement, Soph.

ἐξ-ακρίζω, f. σω, to reach the top of, ἐξ. αἰθέρα to skim the upper air, Eur.

ἐξακτέον, Verbal, (ἐξάγω I. 1. b) one must march out, Xen.

ἐξ-αλαόω, f. ώσω, to blind utterly, Od.　II. to put an eye quite out, Ib.

ἐξ-αλαπάζω, f. ξω, to sack a city, Il., etc. :—also, to empty a city of its inhabitants, clear it out, so as to plant new settlers in it, μίαν πόλιν ἐξαλαπάξας Od. : generally, to destroy utterly, Il.

ἐξάλειπτρον, τό, an unguent-box, Ar.　From

ἐξ-αλείφω, f. ψω : Pass. pf. ἐξ-ήλιμμαι, Att. -αλήλιμμαι : —to plaster or wash over, Hdt., Thuc.　II. to wipe out, obliterate, Eur. :—ἐξ. τινά to strike his name off the roll, Ar., etc.　2. metaph., like Lat. delere, to wipe out, destroy utterly, Aesch., Eur. :—Med. ἐξαλείψασθαι φρενός to blot it out of one's mind, Id.

ἐξ-αλέομαι, Dep. to beware of, avoid, escape, Il. ; Ep. aor. 1 inf. ἐξαλέασθαι, Hes., Ar.

ἐξαλεύομαι, = foreg., Soph.

ἐξ-αλίνδω, only in aor. 1 part. ἐξαλίσας [ῑ], pf. ἐξήλικα : —to roll out or thoroughly, ἄπαγε τὸν ἵππον ἐξαλίσας take him away when you have given him a good roll on the ἀλινδήθρα, Ar. ; ἐξήλικας ἐμέ γ' ἐκ τῶν ἐμῶν you have rolled me out of house and home, Id.

ἐξαλλᾰγή, ἡ, a complete change, alteration, Plat. From

ἐξ-αλλάσσω, Att. -ττω, f. ξω, to change utterly or completely, Eur. :—Med. μηδὲν ἐξαλλάσσεται he sees no change take place, Soph.　2. to withdraw from a place, c. acc., Eur.　II. ἐξαλλάσσειν τί τινος to remove from, c. gen., Thuc.　2. intr. to change, turn another way, move back and forward, Eur. ; ποίαν ἐξαλλάξω ; which other way shall I take ? Id. ; ἐξαλλάσσουσα χάρις unusual grace, Id.

ἐξ-άλλομαι, f. -ᾰλοῦμαι : Ep. aor. 2 part. ἐξάλμενος : Dep. :—to leap out of or forth from a place, c. gen., Il. ; προμάχων ἐξάλμενος springing out from the front rank, Ib. ; ἐξάλατο ναός (Dor. for ἐξήλατο νηός) Theocr. :—absol. to jump off, hop off, Ar. ; ἵν' ἐξήλου ; to what point didst thou leap forth ; i. e. to what misery hast thou come ? Soph. ; of wheels, to start from the axle, Xen.　II. to leap up, Id. : of horses, to rear, Id.

ἐξ-αλύσκω, f. ύξω : aor. 1 ἐξήλυξα :—like ἐξαλέομαι, to flee from, c. acc., Eur. ; absol. to escape, Aesch., Eur.

ἐξαλύω, = ἐξανύσκω, h. Hom.

ἐξ-ᾰμαρτάνω, f. ήσομαι : aor. 2 -ήμαρτον :—to err from the mark, fail, Xen. : to miss one's aim, Soph.　2. to err, do wrong, sin, Hdt., Att. ; c. acc. cogn., ἐξ. τι to commit a fault, Hdt., Soph., etc.　II. in Pass. to be mismanaged, Plat.　Hence

ἐξαμαρτία, ἡ, an error, transgression, Soph.

ἐξ-ᾰμάω, f. ήσω, to mow or reap out, to finish mowing or reaping, Trag. :—metaph. to cut out, in Med., Eur. :—Pass., γένους ῥίζαν ἐξημημένος (part. pf.) having the race cut off root and branch, Soph.

ἐξ-αμβλόω, f. ώσω, to make to miscarry, Eur.　2. to make abortive, Ar.

ἐξ-αμβλύνω [ῡ], to blunt, weaken, Plut.

ἐξ-ᾰμείβω, f. ψω, to exchange, alter, ἐξαμείψασαι τρόμον having put away fear from one, Eur. :—Med. to take the place of, c. gen., Id. ; so intr. in Act., c. dat., φόνῳ φόνος ἐξαμείβων murder following after murder,

Id.　II. of Place, to change one for another, pass over, c. acc., Aesch., Eur. : absol. to withdraw, depart, Id.　III. in Med. also to requite, repay, Aesch.

ἐξ-ᾰμέλγω, f. ξω, to milk out, suck out, Aesch.　II. to press out, Eur.

ἐξ-ᾰμελέω, to be utterly careless of a thing, c. gen., Hdt.

ἑξά-μετρος [ᾰ], ον, of six metres, hexameter, Hdt., etc.

ἑξά-μηνος [ᾰ], ον, of six, lasting six months : ἑξάμ. (sc. χρόνος), ὁ, a half-year, Xen. ; ἡ ἑξάμ. (sc. ὥρη), Hdt.

ἐξ-ᾰμηχᾰνέω, f. ήσω, to get out of a difficulty, c. gen., Eur.

ἐξ-ᾰμιλλάομαι, f. ήσομαι : aor. 1 part. ἐξαμιλλησάμενος and -ηθείς : Dep. :—to struggle vehemently, c. acc. cogn., τὰς τεθρίππους ἁμίλλας ἐξαμιλληθείς having contested the chariot-race, Eur.　II. to drive out of a place, c. gen., Id. : to drive out of his wits, Id.　III. aor. 1 in pass. sense, to be forced out, of the Cyclops' eye, Id.

ἐξ-ᾰμύνομαι [ῡ], f. -ᾰμῠνοῦμαι, Med. to ward off from oneself, drive away, Aesch., Eur.

ἐξ-αναβρύω, to gush or cause to gush forth, Aesch.

ἐξ-αναγιγνώσκω, f. -γνώσομαι, to read through, Plut.

ἐξ-αναγκάζω, f. άσω, to force or compel utterly, τινὰ ποιεῖν τι Soph., Eur., etc. ; c. acc. only, Soph.　II. to drive away, Xen.

ἐξ-ανάγω, f. άξω, to bring out of or up from, c. gen., Eur. :—Pass. to put out to sea, set sail, Hdt., etc.

ἐξ-αναδύομαι, Dep. with aor. 2 act. ἐξανέδυν, to rise out of, emerge from water, c. gen., Od.　2. to escape from, c. gen., Theogn., Plut.

ἐξ-αναζέω, f. -ζέσω, to boil up with, c. acc. cogn., ἐξαναζέει χόλον will let fury boil forth, Aesch.

ἐξαναιρέω, to take out of, c. gen., h. Hom. ; Med., Eur.

ἐξ-ανακρούομαι, f. σομαι, Med. to retreat out of a place by backing water, Hdt.

ἐξ-αναλίσκω, f. -αναλώσω : pf. pass. -ανήλωμαι :—to spend entirely, Dem. :—to exhaust, Plut.　2. to destroy utterly, Aesch. :—Pass., Dem.

ἐξ-αναλύω, f. ύσω [ῡ], to set quite free from, c. gen., Il.

ἐξανάλωσις, εως, ἡ, (ἐξαναλίσκω) entire consumption, Plut.

ἐξ-ανάπτω, f. ψω, to hang from or by a thing, c. gen., Eur. :—Med. to attach to oneself, τι Id.　II. to rekindle, Anth.

ἐξ-αναρπάζω, f. σω or ξω, to snatch away, Eur.

ἐξ-ανασπάω, f. άσω [ᾰ], to tear away from, Hdt., Eur. : to tear up from, χθονός Id.

ἐξανάστᾰσις, εως, ἡ, (ἐξανίσταμαι) a rising up from, resurrection from the dead, N. T.

ἐξ-αναστέφω, f. ψω, to crown with wreaths, Eur.

ἐξ-αναστρέφω, f. ψω, to hurl headlong from a place, c. gen., Aesch.

ἐξ-ανατέλλω, f. -τελῶ, intr. to spring up from a place, c. gen., Mosch.

ἐξ-αναφανδόν, Adv. all openly, Od.

ἐξ-αναφέρω, f. -ανοίσω, to bear up out of the water, Plut.　II. intr. to recover from an illness, Id.

ἐξ-αναχωρέω, f. ήσω, to go out of the way, withdraw, retreat, Hdt.　2. c. acc. to evade, Thuc.

ἐξ-ανδρᾰποδίζω, and in Med. ἐξανδραποδίζομαι, f. Att. -ιοῦμαι, to reduce to utter slavery, Hdt., Xen., etc.　II. also as Pass., Hdt., Dem.　Hence

ἐξανδρᾱπόδισις, εως, ἡ, a selling for slaves, Hdt.

ἐξ-ανδρόομαι, pf. -ήνδρωμαι, Pass. *to come to man's years*, Hdt., Eur.   II. ὀδόντων ὄφεος ἐξηνδρωμένος *having grown to men* from serpent's teeth, Id.

ἐξ-ανεγείρω, f. -εγερῶ, *to excite*, Eur.

ἐξ-άνειμι, *to rise from the* horizon, of stars, Theocr.   II. *to come back from,* ἄγρης h. Hom.

ἐξ-ανεμόω, f. ώσω, *to blow out with wind, inflate*, Eur. : —metaph., ἐξηνεμώθην *I was puffed up*, Id.

ἐξ-ανέρχομαι, *to come forth from*, c. gen., Eur.

ἐξ-ανευρίσκω, *to find out, invent*, Soph.

ἐξ-ανέχω, f. -έξω : *to hold up from* : but mostly intr. *to jut out from*, c. gen., Theocr.   II. Med., impf. and aor. 2 with double augm. ἐξηνειχόμην, ἐξηνεσχόμην, *to bear up against, endure*, with part., ἐξανασχοίμην κλύων Soph. ; ταῦτα παῖδας ἐξανέξεται πάσχοντας Eur. ; ταῦτα δόξαντ' ἐξηνέσχετο *endured* that these things should be decreed, Id.

ἐξ-ανθέω, f. ήσω, *to put out flowers*, Xen.   2. metaph. *to burst forth*, like an efflorescence, *bloom forth*, Aesch., Eur. :—of ulcers, *to break out*, Thuc., Luc.

ἐξ-ανίημι, f. -ανήσω or -ήσομαι, *to send forth, let loose*, Il., Soph. :—c. gen. *to send forth from*, Eur.   2. *to let go*, Id.   3. *to slacken, undo*, Id. :—and intr. *to slacken, relax*, Soph. ; c. gen., ὀργῆς ἐξανείς Eur.

ἐξ-ανίστημι,   I. Causal in pres., impf., fut. and aor 1 :   1. *to raise up* : *to make one rise* from his seat, *bid* one *rise* from suppliant posture, Eur. ; ἐξ. τὴν ἐνέδραν *to order* the men in ambush *to rise*, Xen.   2. *to make* a tribe *emigrate, to remove* or *expel*, Hdt., Soph.   3. *to depopulate, destroy, πόλιν* Hdt., Eur., etc.   4. ἐξ. θηρία *to rouse* them *from their lair*, Xen.   II. intr. in Pass., with aor. 2, pf. and plqpf. act. :   1. *to stand up from one's seat*, Hdt., etc. ; *to rise* to speak, Soph. ; from ambush, Eur., Thuc. ; from bed, Eur.   2. c. gen. *to arise and depart from, emigrate from*, Hdt. :—absol. *to break up, depart*, Thuc., etc.   3. *to be driven out* from one's home, *to be forced to emigrate*, Hdt., Aesch.   4. of places, *to be depopulated*, Hdt., Eur.

ἐξ-ανοίγω, f. ξω, *to lay open*, Ar.

ἐξ-αντλέω, f. ήσω, *to draw out* water :—metaph. *to endure to the end, see out*, Lat. *exantlare, exhaurire*, Eur.   2. metaph. also *to rob, plunder*, Luc.

ἐξ-ανύω, Att. -ανύτω [ῠ] : f. ύσω [ῠ] :—*to accomplish, fulfil, make effectual*, Il., Soph. :—Med. *to accomplish* or *finish for oneself*, Eur.   2. *to finish* or *dispatch*, i. e. *kill*, Lat. *conficere*, Il.   3. of Time and Distance, *to bring to an end, finish, accomplish*, βίοτον Soph. ; δρόμον Eur. :—absol. *to finish one's way to* a place, *arrive at* it, ἐς or ἐπὶ τόπον Hdt. ; also c. acc. loci, Soph., Eur.   4. c. inf. *to manage* to do, Id.   5. Med. *to obtain*, τι παρά τινος Id.

ἐξᾱ-πάλαιστος, ον, (παλαιστή) *of six hands-breadth*, Hdt.

ἐξ-απαλλάσσω, Att. -ττω, f. ξω, *to set free from, remove from, κακῶν* Eur. :—Pass. *to ged rid of, escape from*, Hdt., Thuc.

ἐξ-απαρτάομαι, Pass. *to hang from* or *on*, c. gen., Luc.

ἐξ-ᾰπᾰτάω, Ion. impf. ἐξαπάτασκον : f. ήσω :—Pass., fut. -απατηθήσομαι or in med. form -απατήσομαι :—*to deceive* or *beguile thoroughly*, Hom., Hdt., etc. :— also, ἐξ. τινά τι *in* a thing, Xen.

ἐξ-ᾰπάτη, ή, *gross deceit*, Hes., Xen.

ἐξᾰπᾱτητέον, Verbal of ἐξαπατάω, *one must deceive*, Plat.

ἐξᾰπᾱτητικός, ή, όν, *calculated to deceive*, Xen.

ἐξᾰπᾰτύλλω, Comic Dim. of ἐξαπατάω, *to cheat a little, humbug*, Ar.

ἐξᾰπᾰφίσκω, Ep. form of ἐξαπατάω, Hes. : aor. 2 ἐξήπᾰφον : subj. ἐξαπάφω, part. ἐξαπαφών, Od., etc. : 3 sing. aor. 2 med. opt. ἐξαπάφοιτο in act. sense, Il.

ἐξά-πεδος, ον, (πούς) *six feet long*, Hdt.

ἐξ-απεῖδον, inf. -απιδεῖν, aor. 2 without any pres. ἐξαφοράω in use, *to observe from afar*, Soph.

ἐξά-πηχυς, υ, *six cubits long*, Hdt., Xen.

ἐξάπῖνα, later form of ἐξαπίνης, N. T.

ἐξαπίναιος, α, ον, or ος, ον, = ἐξαιφνίδιος, Xen.   Adv. -ως, Thuc.   From

ἐξᾰπίνης [ῐ], Adv., = ἐξαίφνης, Il., Hdt., Thuc.

ἐξᾰ-πλάσιος, α, ον, Ion. -πλήσιος, η, ον, *six times as large as*, τινος Hdt.

ἐξά-πλεθρος, ον, (πλέθρον) *six πλέθρα long*, i. e. about 1200 feet, Hdt.

ἐξᾰπλήσιος, η, ον, Ion. for ἐξαπλάσιος.

ἐξ-αποβαίνω, f. -βήσομαι, *to step out of*, νηός Od.

ἐξ-αποδύνω [ῠ], *to put off*, εἵματα Od.

Ἑξά-πολις, εως, ή, *a League of six cities*, of the Asiatic Dorians, Hdt.

ἐξ-απόλλῡμι, f. -ολέσω, Att. -ολῶ, *to destroy utterly*, Trag., etc.   II. Med., with pf. 2 ἐξαπόλωλα, aor. 2 ἐξαπωλόμην :—*to perish utterly out of* a place, c. gen., Hom., Aesch. :—absol. *to perish utterly*, Hdt.

ἐξ-απονέομαι, Pass. *to return out of*, Il.

ἐξ-απονίζω, f. -νίψω, *to wash thoroughly*, Od.

ἐξ-αποξύνω [ῠ], *to sharpen well*, Eur.

ἐξ-απορέω, f. ήσω, *to be in great doubt* or *difficulty* : so in Med. and Pass., N. T., Plut.

ἐξ-αποστέλλω, f. -στελῶ, *to send quite away* :—Pass. *to be dispatched*, Philipp. ap. Dem.

ἐξ-αποτίνω [ῑ], *to satisfy in full*, Il.

ἐξά-πους, ὁ, ἡ, πουν, τό, = ἐξάπεδος, Plut.

ἐξ-αποφαίνω, strengthd. for ἀποφαίνω, Luc.

ἐξ-αποφθείρω, f. -φθερῶ, *to destroy utterly*, Aesch., Soph.

ἐξ-άπτω, f. ψω, *to fasten from*, i. e. *to*, a thing, c. gen. ; Hom., Eur. ; τι ἔκ τινος Hdt.   2. metaph., ἐξ. στόματος λιτάς *to let* prayers *fall from* one's mouth, Eur.   3. ἐξ. τί τινι *to place upon*, Id.   II. Med. *to hang on*, Il.   2. *to hang* a thing *to oneself, carry it about* one, *wear*, Eur.

ἐξ-απωθέω, f. -ώσω and -ωθήσω, *to thrust away*, Eur.

ἐξᾰραίρημαι, pf. pass. of ἐξαιρέω.

ἐξ-αράομαι, Dep. *to utter curses*, Soph.

ἐξ-ἄράσσω, Att. -ττω, f. ξω, *to dash out, shatter*, Od., Ar.   II. c. acc. pers. *to assail furiously*, Id.

ἐξ-αργέω, f. ήσω, *to be quite torpid* :—Pass. *to be quite neglected*, Soph.

ἐξ-αργῠρίζω, f. σω, *to turn into money*, Thuc., Dem.

ἐξ-αργῠρόω, f. ώσω, = foreg., Hdt.

ἐξ-αρέσκομαι, Dep. = ἔσομαι, *to make oneself acceptable*, Xen.   2. c. acc. pers. *to win over*, Dem.

ἐξ-ᾰριθμέω, f. ήσω, *to count throughout, number*, Lat. *enumerare*, Hdt., Att.   II. *to count out, pay in ready money*, Lat. *numeratim solvere*, Dem.

ἐξ-αρκέω, f. έσω :   I. of objects, *to be quite enough for, suffice for*, τινί Soph., Plat., etc. ; πρός τι Xen. : absol. *to suffice, be sufficient*, Eur., Dem.   2. impers.,

ἐξαρκεῖ it is enough for, suffices for, c. dat. pers., Hdt., Att. II. of persons, to be satisfied with, to be a match for, c. dat., Eur. :—c. part. to be content with having, Id. Hence

ἐξαρκής, ές, enough, sufficient, Aesch., Soph.

ἐξαρκούντως, Adv. part. pres. of ἐξαρκέω, enough, sufficiently, Ar.

ἐξ-αρνέομαι, f. ήσομαι, aor. 1 ἐξηρνησάμην and ἐξηρνήθην : Dep. :—to deny utterly, Hdt., Eur. Hence

ἐξάρνησις, εως, ἡ, a denying, denial, Plat.; and

ἐξαρνητικός, ή, όν, apt at denying, negative, Ar.

ἔξ-αρνος, ον, (ἀρνέομαι) denying ; ἔξαρνός εἰμι or γίγνομαι = ἐξαρνέομαι, Ar., etc. ; foll. by μή c. inf., ἐξ. ἦν μὴ ἀποκτεῖναι he denied that he had killed, Hdt., etc.

ἐξ-αρπάζω, f. ξω and σω, also -άσομαι : aor. 1 ἐξήρπαξα, or -ασα :—to snatch away from a place, c. gen., Od. ; τι παρά τινος Hdt. ; τι ἐκ χερῶν τινος Eur. :—to rescue, Il. :—Pass., οἱ ἐξηρπασμένοι the captured ones, Soph. II. to tear out, Ar.

ἐξ-αρτάω, f. ήσω, to hang upon, to make dependent upon, c. gen., Plut. : also in Med., Eur. II. Pass., f. in med. form -αρτήσομαι, pf. -ήρτημαι :—to be hung upon, hang upon, χειρός Id. 2. to depend upon, be dependent upon, be attached to, σοῦ γὰρ ἐξηρτήμεθα Id. 3. of countries, to border upon, τινος Plut. 4. to be hung up or exposed to view, Thuc. 5. pf. pass. part., c. acc. rei, having a thing hung on one, be furnished with, Ar., Aeschin.

ἐξ-αρτίζω, f. Att. ιῶ, to complete, finish, τὰς ἡμέρας N. T. :—Pass. to be thoroughly prepared or furnished, Ib. :—Med. to provide oneself with, τι Luc.

ἐξαρτύω [ῠ], f. ύσω, to get ready, equip thoroughly, fit out, Eur., Thuc. :—Med. to get ready for oneself, fit out, Id. : c. inf., ἐξαρτύεται γαμεῖν Aesch. :—Pass. to be got ready, πάντα σφι ἐξήρτυτο Hdt. :—in pf. pass. part., equipt, harnessed, Eur. ; c. dat. rei, furnished or provided with, Hdt., Aesch., etc.

ἔξ-αρχος, ὁ, ἡ, a leader, beginner, Lat. auctor, Il. 2. the leader of a chorus, Lat. coryphaeus, Dem.

ἐξ-άρχω, f. ξω, to begin with, make a beginning of, Lat. auctor esse, c. gen., ἐξῆρχε γόοιο Il., etc. :—so in Med., ἐξήρχετο βουλῆς Od. 2. c. acc., βουλὰς ἐξάρχων Il. ;—also ἐξάρχειν or ἐξάρχεσθαι παιᾶνά τινι to begin a hymn, address it to him, Xen.

ἑξάς, άδος, ἡ, (ἕξ) the number six, Plut., etc.

ἐξ-ασκέω, f. ήσω, to adorn, deck out, equip, Soph.; c. dupl. acc., ἀγώ νιν ἐξήσκησα with which I equipped him, Eur. II. to train or teach thoroughly, τινά Plat. 2. to practise, τι Plut.

ἐξ-αστράπτω, f. ψω, to flash as with lightning, N. T.

ἐξ-ατῑμάζω, f. σω, to dishonour utterly, Soph.

ἐξ-άττω, Att. contr. for ἐξαΐσσω.

ἐξ-αυαίνω, f. ἀνῶ, to dry quite up, Hdt.

ἐξ-αυγής, ές, (αὐγή) dazzling white, Eur.

ἐξ-αυδάω, f. ήσω, to speak out, Il., Soph. :—so in Med., Aesch.

ἐξ-αυλίζομαι, f. ίσομαι, Dep. to leave one's quarters, to go out of camp into villages, Xen.

ἐξ-αυτῆς, Adv., for ἐξ αὐτῆς [τῆς ὥρας], at the very point of time, at once, Theogn.

ἐξ-αῦτις, Adv. over again, once more, anew, Il. II. of place, back again, backwards, Ib.

ἐξ-αυτομολέω, f. ήσω, to desert from a place, Ar.

ἐξ-αυχέω, f. ήσω, aor. 1 -ηύχησα, to boast loudly, profess, Trag.

ἐξ-αύω, f. σω, to cry out, Soph.

ἐξ-αφαιρέω, f. ήσω, to take right away : in Med., aor. 2 -αφειλόμην Od.

ἐξ-αφίημι, f.-αφήσω, to send forth, discharge, Xen. II. to set free from labour, c. gen., Soph.

ἐξ-αφίσταμαι, Pass., with aor. 2, pf., and plqpf. act., to depart or withdraw from, τινος Soph., Eur.

ἐξ-ᾰφρίζομαι, Med. to throw off by foaming :—metaph. from a horse, ἐξαφρίζεσθαι μένος Aesch.

ἐξ-ᾰφύω, (ἀφύσσω) to draw forth liquor, Od.

ἐξά-χειρ, ειρος, ὁ, ἡ, six-handed, Luc.

ἐξά-χοος, οον, contr. -χους, ουν, holding six χόες, Plut.

ἐξέβαλον, aor. 2 of ἐκβάλλω.

ἔξ-εβαν, Aeol. of -έβησαν, 3 pl. aor. 2 of ἐκβαίνω.

ἐξ-εγγυάω, f. ήσω, to free a person by giving bail, Dem. :—Pass. to be bailed, Id. Hence

ἐξεγγύησις, εως, ἡ, a giving of bail, Dem.

ἐξ-εγείρω, f. ερῶ, to awaken, Soph. :—Pass. to be awaked, wake up, Hdt., etc. ; syncop. aor. 2 ἐξηγρόμην Ar. ; Ep. 3 pl. ἐξέγροντο Theocr. ; pf. 2 ἐξεγρήγορα Ar. 2. to raise from the dead, Aesch. 3. metaph. to awake, arouse, bring on, Eur.

ἐξέγλυμμαι, pf. pass. of ἐκ-γλύφω.

ἔξέδομαι, fut. of ἐξεσθίω.

ἐξέδρα, ἡ, Lat. exhedra, a hall or arcade in the gymnasia, a sort of cloister, Eur.

ἔξ-εδρος, ον, (ἕδρα) away from home, Soph. 2. c. gen. out of, away from, Eur. : metaph., ἔξεδροι φρενῶν λόγοι insensate words, Id. II. of birds of omen, ἐξ. χώραν ἔχειν to be in an unlucky quarter, Ar.

ἐξεθέμην, aor. 2 med. of ἐκτίθημι.

ἐξέθορον, aor. 2 of ἐκθρώσκω.

ἔξει, for ἔξιθι, imperat. of ἔξειμι (εἶμι ibo).

ἔξ-εῖδον, inf. -ιδεῖν, aor. 2 in use of the pres. ἐξοράω, to look out, see far, Il. : also imperat. med., ἔξιδοῦ see well to it, Soph.

ἐξείης, Adv., poët. for ἑξῆς.

ἐξ-εικάζω, f. άσω, to make like, to adapt, Xen. :—Pass., ἐξείκαστό τινι was like it, Id. ; part. pf., οὐδὲν ἐξηκασμένα not mere semblances, but the things themselves, Aesch. ; στέρνα ἐξηκασμένα portrayed, Eur. ; οὐκ ἐξηκασμένος not represented by a portrait-mask, Ar.

ἐξ-ειλέω, f. ήσω, = ἐξείλλω, to unfold, Luc.

ἐξ-είλλω, to disentangle, Xen. II. to keep forcibly from, debar from, τινά τινος Dem.

ἐξεῖλον, aor. 2 of ἐξαιρέω.

ἐξ-ειλύω, to unwrap :—Pass. to glide along, aor. 1 ἐξειλύσθην, Theocr.

ἔξ-ειμι (εἶμι ibo) Ep. 2 sing. ἔξεισθα : Att. imper. ἔξει, for ἔξιθι : serving as Att. fut. of ἐξέρχομαι, but with impf. ἔξηειν, Ion. ἐξήϊα :—to go out, come out of the house, Hom. ; c. gen. loci, Od., Soph. ; ἐξ. ἐκ τῶν ἱππέων to leave the knights, Hdt. ; εἰς ἔλεγχον ἐξιέναι to come forth to the trial, Soph. 2. to march out with an army, Thuc., Xen. :—c. acc. cogn. to go out on an expedition or enterprise, Soph., Eur.,etc. 3. to come forward on the stage, Ar. II. of Time or incidents, to come to an end, expire, Hdt., Soph.

ἔξ-ειμι (εἰμί sum), only used in impers. forms, v. ἔξεστι.

ἐξ-εῖπον, inf. -ειπεῖν, aor. 2 in use of ἐξαγορεύω, ἐξερέω (q. v.) being the fut.: also 2 sing. aor. 1 ἐξεῖπας Soph.:—to speak out, tell out, declare, Lat. effari, Hom., Thuc.   2. c. dupl. acc. to tell something of a person, Soph., Eur.

ἐξειργασμένως, Adv. part. pf. pass. of ἐξεργάζομαι, carefully, accurately,.fully, Plut.

ἐξείργω, Att. for ἐξέργω.

ἐξείρομαι, Ion. for ἐξέρομαι.

ἐξείρύω, Ion. for ἐξερύω.

ἐξ-είρω, aor. 1 -εῖρα, to put forth, Lat. exsero, τὴν χεῖρα Hdt.; τὸ κέντρον Ar.   II. to pull out, τὴν γλῶσσαν Id.

ἔξεισθα, Ep. for ἔξει, 2 sing. of ἔξειμι (εἶμι ibo).

ἐξεκέχυντο, 3 pl. Ep. aor. 2 pass. of ἐκχέω.

ἐξελάαν, Ep. pres. inf. of ἐξελαύνω:—ἐξελᾶν, Att. fut. inf. of same.

ἐξέλᾰσις, εως, ἡ, a driving out, expulsion, Hdt.   II. intr. a marching out, expedition, Id., Xen. From

ἐξ-ελαύνω, f. -ελάσω, contr. -ελῶ: pf. -ελήλᾰκα:—an Ep. part. ἐξελάων, inf. ἐξελάαν, occurs in Hom.:—to drive out from, ἄντρου ἐξήλασε μῆλα Od.; absol. to drive afield, of a shepherd, Ib.:—esp. to drive out or expel from a place, Ib., Aesch., etc.   2. to drive out horses or chariots, Il.: Med. to drive out one's horses, Theocr.; so, ἐξελαύνειν στρατόν to lead out an army, Hdt.: hence   3. intr. to march out, Hdt.: to drive or ride out, Thuc.   II. to knock out, Od.   III. to beat out metals, Hdt.

ἐξελεγκτέος, α, ον, verb. Adj. to be refuted, Plat. From

ἐξ-ελέγχω, f. ξω, to convict, confute, refute, Soph., Ar., etc.   2. c. dupl. acc. pers. et rei, to convict one of a thing, Plat.: Pass. to be so convicted of, Dem.   3. with predicate added in part. to convict one of being . . , Plat.:—Pass., κἀξελέγχεται κάκιστος ὤν Eur.   II. to search out, put to the proof, Aesch:—Pass., ᾖσαν ἐξεληλεγμένοι all had had their sentiments well ascertained, Dem.; ἐξηλέγχθη ἐς τὸ ἀληθές was fully proved to be true, Thuc.

ἐξελεῖν, aor. 2 inf. of ἐξαιρέω.

ἐξελευθερικός, ὁ, of the class of freedmen or their offspring, Lat. libertinus, Plut. From

ἐξ-ελεύθερος, ὁ, ἡ, set at liberty, a freedman, Lat. libertinus, libertinus, Cic.

ἐξελευθερο-στόμεω, f.ήσω,to be very free of speech,Soph.

ἐξελεύσομαι, fut. of ἐξέρχομαι.

ἐξελθεῖν, aor. 2 inf. of ἐξέρχομαι.

ἐξ-ελίσσω, Att. -ττω, f. ξω, to unroll, Eur.: metaph. to unfold, Lat. explicare, Id.   2. of any rapid motion, ἴχνος ἐξ. ποδός to evolve the mazy dance, Id.:—hence intr. to wheel about, Plut.   II. as military term, = ἀναπτύσσειν, Lat. explicare, to extend the front by bringing up the rear men, to deploy, Xen.   2. to draw off, Plut.

ἐξελκτέον, verb. Adj. one must drag along, Eur. From

ἐξ-έλκω, aor. 1 -είλκυσα, and 3 sing. pass. subj. -ελκυσθῇ (formed from ἑλκύω):—to draw or drag out, Il.   2. to drag out from a place, c. gen., Od., Eur.   II. to drag along, Soph., Eur.

ἐξ-ελληνίζω, f. σω, to turn into Greek, to trace to a Greek origin, Plut.

ἔξελον, Ep. for ἐξεῖλον, aor. 2 of ἐξαιρέω.

ἐξέμεν, Ep. for ἐξεῖναι, aor. 2 inf. of ἐξίημι.

ἐξέμεν, Ep. for ἔξειν, fut. inf. of ἔχω.

ἐξ-εμέω, f. έσω, to vomit forth, disgorge, Od.:—metaph. to disgorge ill-gotten gear, Ar.   2. absol. to vomit, be sick, Id.

ἐξέμμορε, 3 sing. pf. of ἐκμείρομαι.

ἐξ-εμπεδόω, to keep quite firm, strictly observe, Xen.

ἐξ-εμπολάω, Ion. -έω, f. ήσω, to traffic, κέρδος ἐξ. to drive a gainful trade, Soph.; ἐξημπόλημαι I am bought and sold, betrayed, Id.   II. to sell off, Hdt.

ἐξ-εναίρω, to kill outright, aor. 2 inf. ἐξενάρεῖν Hes.

ἐξ-εναρίζω, f. ίξω, to strip or spoil a foe slain in fight, Il.; τεύχεα ἐξ. to strip off his arms, Ib.   2. to kill, slay, Hom.

ἐξενεῖκαι, Ion. for -ενέγκαι, aor. 1 inf. of ἐκφέρω.

ἐξένευσα, aor. 1 of ἐκνέω.

ἐξένθοις, ἐξ-ενθών, Dor. for ἐξ-ελθ-, aor. 2 opt. and part. of ἐξέρχομαι.

ἐξ-επᾴδω, f. -ᾴσομαι, to charm away, Plat.:—Pass., ἐξεπᾴδεσθαι φύσιν to be charmed out of their nature, Soph.

ἐξ-επεύχομαι, Dep. to boast loudly that, c. inf., Soph.

ἐξ-επι-και-δέκατος, η, ον, = ἐκκαιδέκατος, Anth.

ἐξεπίσταμαι, Dep. to know thoroughly, know well, Hdt., Att.; c. inf. to know well how to do, Soph.

ἐξεπίτηδες, Adv. of set purpose, Ar., Plat.: with malice prepense, Dem.

ἐξεπλάγην [ᾰ], aor. 2 pass. of ἐκπλήσσω.

ἐξέπνευσα, aor. 1 of ἐκπνέω.

ἐξεπόνᾱσα, Dor. for -ησα, aor. 1 of ἐκπονέω.

ἐξέπρᾱθον, aor. 2 of ἐκπέρθω.

ἐξέπταξα, Dor. for -ηξα, aor. 1 of ἐκπτήσσω.

ἐξέπτην, aor. 2 act. of ἐκπέτομαι.

ἐξέρᾱμα, ατος, τό, a vomit, thing vomited, N. T. From

ἐξ-εράω, aor. 1 ἐξήρᾱσα:—to disgorge, Ar.; φέρ' ἐξεράσω τὰς ψήφους let me disgorge the ballots from the urn (in order to count them), Id.; ἐξέρα τὸ ὕδωρ pour it out, Dem.

ἐξ-εργάζομαι, f. -άσομαι: pf. -είργασμαι, Ion. -έργασμαι (both in act. and pass. sense):—to work out, make completely, finish off, bring to perfection, Hdt., Att.   2. to accomplish, perform, achieve a work, Soph.; κακὸν ἐξ. τινα to work him mischief, Hdt.:—as Pass., ἔργον ἐστὶν ἐξειργασμένον Aesch.; ἐπ' ἐξειργασμένοισι after the deed had been done, Hdt.   3. to work at: as Pass., ἀγροὶ εὖ ἐξειργασμένοι well cultivated lands, Id.; [ἡ γῆ] ἐξείργασται Thuc.   II. to undo, destroy, overwhelm, ruin, Hdt., Eur.:—as Pass., ἐξειργάσμεθα we are undone, Id.   Hence

ἐξεργαστικός, ή, όν, able to accomplish, τινος Xen.

ἐξ-έργω, Att. ἐξ-είργω, to shut out from a place, debar, Hdt., etc.; ἐξείργειν τινα χθονός Eur.; ἐκ τοῦ θεάτρου Dem.:—Pass., ἐξείργεσθαι πάντων Thuc.   2. to debar, hinder, prevent, preclude, Soph., Eur.   3. to force:—Pass. to be constrained, Hdt., Thuc.

ἐξ-ερείνω, Ep. Verb,   1. c. acc. rei, to inquire into, Od.   2. c. acc. pers. to inquire after, Ib.: absol. to make inquiry, Il.; so in Med., Ib.   II. to search thoroughly, Od.

ἐξ-ερέθω, to irritate greatly, Anth.

ἐξ-ερείπω, to strike off: intr. in aor. 2 ἐξήριπον, inf. ἐξερίπεῖν, to fall to earth, Il.; χαίτη ζεύγλης ἐξεριποῦσα the mane streaming downwards from the yoke, Ib.

ἐξ-ερεύγομαι, Pass., of rivers, to empty themselves, Hdt.

ἐξ-ερευνάω, f. ήσω, to search out, examine, Soph., Eur.

ἐξ-ερέω (A), Att. contr. -ερῶ, fut. of ἐξεῖπον, I will speak out, tell out, utter aloud, Hom., Soph.: so in pf. act. ἐξείρηκα Id.; 3 sing. plqpf. pass. ἐξείρητο Id.; fut. pass. ἐξειρήσεται Id.

ἐξ-ερέω (B), = ἐξέρομαι (of which it is the Ep. form): 1. to inquire into a thing, Od.; so in Med., Ib. 2. to inquire of a person, Ib.; and in Med., Ib. II. to search through, Ib.

ἐξ-ερημόω, f. ώσω, to make quite desolate, leave destitute, abandon, Soph., Eur.; ἐξ. γένυν δράκοντος making it destitute of teeth, Id. :—Pass. to be left destitute, Ar.

ἐξ-ερίζω, f. σω, to be contumacious, Plut. Hence

ἐξεριστής, οῦ, ὁ, a stubborn disputant, Eur.

ἐξ-ερμηνεύω, f. σω, to interpret accurately, Luc.

ἐξ-έρομαι, Ion. εἴρομαι, f. -ερήσομαι: aor. 2 -ηρόμην, inf. -ερέσθαι: Dep.: 1. to inquire into a thing, Od., Soph. 2. to inquire of a person, Il., Soph.

ἐξ-έρπω: aor. 1 -είρπυσα:—to creep out of, ἔκ τινος Ar. 2. absol. to creep out or forth, Soph., Ar.; of an army, οὐ ταχὺ ἐξέρπει Xen.

ἐξέρρω, only in imperat., ἔξερρε γαίας away out of the land! Eur.

ἐξ-ερύκω [ῠ], f. ξω, to ward off, repel, Soph.

ἐξ-ερύω, Ion. -ειρύω: aor. 1 -είρυσα, Ep. -έρυσα and -είρυσσα, Ion. 3 sing. aor. 1 -ερύσασκε:—to draw out of, c. gen., Il.; ἰχθύας ἔκτοσθε θαλάσσης ἐξέρυσαν Od. :—also, to snatch out of, ἐξείρυσσε χειρὸς τόξον Il. : to tear out, Od.

ἐξ-έρχομαι, f. -ελεύσομαι (but in Att. ἔξειμι supplies the fut., as also the impf. ἐξῄειν): aor. 2 ἐξῆλθον: Dep.: to go or come out of, c. gen. loci, Hom., Hdt., etc.; of an actor, to come out on the stage, Ar. :—also c. acc., ἐξ. τὴν χώρην Hdt. :—absol. to go away, march off, Il. : also, to march out, go forth, ἐπί τινα Hdt. :—c. acc. cogn. to go out on an expedition, Xen. : to go through a work, Soph. 2. ἐξ. εἰς ἔλεγχον to stand forth and come to the trial, Eur. : to turn out so and so, Soph. 3. c. acc. rei, to execute, Thuc. II. of Time, to come to an end, expire, Hdt., Soph. III. of prophecies, dreams, events, to be accomplished, come true, Hdt.; ὀρθὸν ἐξ. to come out right, Soph.; μὴ ἐξέλθῃ σαφής lest he turn out a true prophet, Id.

ἐξερῶ, v. ἐξερέω A.

ἐξ-ερωέω, f. ήσω, to swerve from the course, Il.

ἐξεσάωσα, aor. 1 of ἐκσαόω.

ἐξ-εσθίω, f. -έδομαι: pf. -εδήδοκα: aor. 2 -έφαγον:— to eat away, eat up, Ar.

ἐξ-έσθω, = foreg., Aesch.

ἐξεσία, Ion. -ίη, ἡ, (ἐξίημι) a sending out, mission, embassy, Hom.

ἔξεσις, εως, ἡ, (ἐξίημι) a dismissal, divorce, Hdt.

ἐξέσσυτο, 3 sing. Ep. aor. 2 pass. of ἐκσεύω.

ἐξεστάναι [ᾰ], for ἐξεστηκέναι, pf. inf. of ἐξίστημι.

ἔξ-εστι, imper. ἐξέστω, subj. ἐξῇ, opt. ἐξείη, inf. ἐξεῖναι, part. ἐξόν: impf. ἐξῆν: f. ἐξέσται, opt. ἐξέσοιτο: impers. (the only forms in use of ἔξ-ειμι) :—it is allowed, it is in one's power, is possible, c. inf., Hdt. : c. dat. pers. et inf., Id., Att.; ἐξ. σοι ἀνδρὶ γενέσθαι Xen. :— c. acc. pers. et inf., Ar. :—part. neut. absol., ἐξόν since it was possible, Hdt., Aesch., etc.

ἐξ-ετάζω: f. -ετάσω: aor. 1 -ήτασα, Dor. -ήταξα: pf. -ήτακα:—Pass., f. -ετασθήσομαι: aor. 1 -ητάσθην: pf. -ήτασμαι:—to examine well or closely, inquire into, scrutinise, review, Theogn., Att. 2. of troops, to inspect, review, Thuc., etc. :—generally, to pass in review, enumerate, Dem. II. to examine or question a person closely, Hdt., Soph., etc. III. to estimate, compare, τι πρός τι one thing by or with another, Id. IV. to prove by testing, of gold, Id. : —in Pass. with part., ἐξετάζεται παρών he is proved to have been present, Plat.; ἐξετάζεσθαι φίλος (sc. ὤν) Eur. ; c. gen., τῶν ἐχθρῶν ἐξετάζεσθαι to be found in the number of the enemies, Dem. 2. to present oneself, appear, Id. Hence

ἐξετάκην [ᾰ], aor. 2 pass. of ἐκτήκω.

ἐξέταμον, aor. 2 of ἐκτέμνω.

ἐξέτᾰσις, εως, ἡ, (ἐξετάζω) a close examination, scrutiny, review, Thuc., Plat., etc. 2. a military inspection or review, Thuc., Xen.

ἐξετασμός, ὁ, = foreg., Dem.

ἐξεταστέον, Verbal, one must scrutinise, Plat.

ἐξεταστής, οῦ, ὁ, (ἐξετάζω) an examiner, inquirer, Plut. : at Athens, a paymaster, Aeschin.

ἐξεταστικός, ή, όν, (ἐξετάζω) capable of examining into, τινός Xen. :—absol. inquiring, Id. :—Adv. -κῶς, Dem. II. ἐξ. (sc. ἀργύριον), τό, the salary of an ἐξεταστής, Id.

ἐξετέλειον, Ep. for -ετέλεον, impf. of ἐκτελέω.

ἐξετελεῦντο, Ep. for -οῦντο, 3 pl. impf. pass. of ἐκτελέω.

ἐξετετόξευτο, 3 sing. plqpf. pass. of ἐκτοξεύω.

ἐξ-έτης, ες, (ἔτος) six years old, Il., Ar.

ἐξ-έτι, Prep. with gen., even from, ἐξέτι πατρῶν even from the fathers' time, Od.

ἐξ-ευλᾰβέομαι, f. ήσομαι, to guard carefully against, τι Eur., Plat.

ἐξ-ευμᾰρίζω, f. σω, to make light or easy, Eur. II. Med. to prepare, Lat. expedire, Id.

ἐξ-ευμενίζω, (εὐμενής) to propitiate :—Med., Plut.

ἐξεύρεσις, εως, ἡ, a searching out, search, Hdt. 2. a finding out, invention, Id.

ἐξευρετέος, α, ον, verb. Adj. to be discovered, Ar. II. ἐξευρετέον, one must find out, Plat.; and

ἐξεύρημα, ατος, τό, a thing found out, an invention, Hdt., Aesch. From

ἐξ-ευρίσκω, f. -ευρήσω: aor. 2 -εῦρον :—to find out, discover, Il., Thuc., etc. 2. to invent, Hdt., Aesch. 3. simply to find, Soph. 4. to seek out, search after, Hdt. 5. to find out, win, get, procure, Soph.

ἐξ-ευτελίζω, f. σω, (εὐτελής) to disparage greatly, Plut.

ἐξευτρεπίζω, to make quite ready, Eur.

ἐξ-εύχομαι, f. -ξομαι, Dep. to boast aloud, proclaim, Aesch. II. to pray earnestly, Id., Eur.

ἐξεφαάνθην, Ep. for -εφάνθην, aor. 2 pass. of ἐκφαίνω: Ep. 3 pl. -φάανθεν.

ἐξεφάνην [ᾰ], aor. 2 pass. of ἐκφαίνω.

ἐξέφθαρμαι, pf. pass. of ἐκφθείρω.

ἐξέφθινται, Ep. 3 pl. pf. pass. of ἐκφθίνω.

ἐξέφθῖτο, 3 sing. plqpf. pass. of ἐκφθίνω.

ἐξ-εφίημι, strengthd. for ἐφίημι :—Med. ἐξεφίεμαι, to enjoin, command, Soph., Eur.

ἐξεφρείομεν, poët. for -εφρέομεν, 1 pl. impf. of ἐκφρέω.

ἐξέφρησα, aor. 1 of ἐκφρέω.

ἐξέχεα, aor. 1 of ἐκχέω :—ἐξεχύθην [ῠ], aor. 1 pass.

ἐξέχρην, ἐξέχρησα, aor. 1 and 2 of ἐκχράω.

ἐξ-έχω, f. -έξω, to stand out or project from, τινός Ar. 2. absol. to stand out, appear, Id.

ἐξ-έψω, f. -εψήσω, to boil thoroughly, Hdt.

ἐξ-ήβος, ον, (ἥβη) past one's youth, Aesch.

ἐξήγᾰγον, aor. 2 of ἐξάγω.

ἐξ-ηγέομαι, f. ήσομαι, Dep. to be leader of others, c. gen., Il. :—also c. acc. pers. to lead, direct, govern, Thuc. II. to go first, lead the way, h. Hom., Hdt. 2. c. dat. pers. to shew one the way, go before, lead, Id., Soph., etc. 3. c. gen. rei, to conduct a business, Xen. 4. ἐξ. εἰς τὴν Ἑλλάδα to lead an army into Greece, Id. III. like Lat. praeïre verbis, to prescribe or dictate a form of words, Eur., Dem.:—generally to prescribe, order, Hdt., Aesch., etc.:—to prescribe or expound the form to be observed in religious ceremonies, Hdt., Att. IV. to tell at length, relate in full, Hdt., Att. Hence

ἐξήγησις, εως, ἡ, a statement, narrative, Thuc. II. explanation, interpretation, Plat. ; and

ἐξηγητής, οῦ, ὁ, one who leads on, an adviser, Lat. auctor, Hdt., Dem. II. an expounder, interpreter, of oracles, dreams, omens, and sacred customs, Hdt., Plat., etc. ; and

ἐξηγητικός, ή, όν, of or for interpretation, Plut.

ἐξηγρόμην, aor. 2 med. of ἐξεγείρω.

ἐξήκοντα, οἱ, αἱ, τά, (ἕξ) indecl. sixty, Hom., etc.

ἐξηκοντα-έτης, ες, (ἔτος) sixty years old, Mimnerm.

ἐκηκοντα-ετία, ἡ, a time of sixty years, Plut.

ἐξηκοντα-τάλαντα, ἡ, (τάλαντον) a company contributing a sum of 60 talents to the state, Dem.

ἐξηκοστός, ή, όν, (ἑξήκοντα) sixtieth, Hdt., etc.

ἐξ-ήκω, f. ξω, to have reached a certain point, Soph., Plat. II. of Time, to have run out or expired, to be over, Hdt., Soph., etc. 2. of prophecies, dreams, etc. to turn out true, Id., Hdt.

ἐξήλασσα, Ep. for ἐξήλᾰσα, aor. 1 of ἐξελαύνω.

ἐξήλᾰτος, ον, (ἐξελαύνω) beaten out, of metal, Il.

ἐξῆλθον, aor. 2 of ἐξέρχομαι.

ἐξήλῠσις, εως, ἡ, (ἐξήλῠθον aor. 2 of ἐξέρχομαι) a way out, outlet, Hdt.

ἐξ-ῆμαρ, Adv. for six days, six days long, Od.

ἐξ-ημερόω, f. ώσω, to tame or reclaim quite, Hdt., Eur. :—metaph. to soften, humanise, Plut. Hence

ἐξημέρωσις, εως, ἡ, a reclaiming, humanising, Plut.

ἐξημημένος, pf. pass. part. of ἐξαμάω.

ἐξημοιβός, όν, (ἐξαμείβω) serving for change, εἵματα δ' ἐξημοιβά changes of raiment, Od.

ἐξήνεγκα and ἐξήνεγκον, aor. 1 and 2 of ἐκφέρω.

ἐξήπαφον, aor. 2 of ἐξαπαφίσκω.

ἐξήραμμαι, ἐξηράνθην, pf. and aor. 1 pass. of ξηραίνω.

ἐξήρᾱτο, 3 sing. aor. 1 med. of ἐξαίρω.

ἐξ-ήρετμος, ον, (ἐρετμός) of six banks of oars, Anth.

ἐξ-ήρης, ες, (*ἄρω) with six banks of oars, ναῦς, Plut.

ἐξηρώησα, aor. 1 of ἐξερωέω.

ἑξῆς, Ep. also ἑξείης, Adv. : (ἕξω, fut. of ἔχω):—one after another, in order, in a row, Hom. : in order, in a regular manner, Plat. 2. of Time, thereafter, next, Aesch., etc. ; ἡ ἑξῆς ἡμέρα the next day,

---

N. T. II. c. gen. next to, Ar. ; τούτων ἑξῆς next after this, Dem. ; c. dat. next to, Plat.

ἐξήταξα, aor. 1 of ἐξετάζω.

ἐξηττάομαι, strengthd. for ἡττάομαι, Plut.

ἐξήῡνα, aor. 1 of ἐξαυαίνω.

ἐξήφυσσα, Ep. for -ήφῠσα, aor. 1 of ἐξαφύσσω.

ἐξ-ηχέω, f. ήσω, to sound forth :—Pass. to be made known, N. T.

ἐξ-ιάομαι, f. -άσομαι, Ion. -ήσομαι, Dep. to cure thoroughly, Hdt., Plat.

ἐξιδεῖν, inf. of ἐξεῖδον.

ἐξ-ῑδιόομαι, to appropriate, Xen.

ἐξ-ῑδίω, f. ίσω [ῑ], to exsude, Ar.

ἐξ-ῑδρύω, f. ύσω [ῠ], to make to sit down, Soph.

ἐξιέναι, inf. of ἔξειμι (εἶμι ibo).

ἐξ-ίημι, f. -ήσω, Ep. aor. 2 inf. ἐξ-έμεναι, -έμεν :—to send out, let one go out, Od. ; γόου ἐξ ἔρον εἵην had dismissed, satisfied the desire of lamentation, Il. ; ἐξιέναι πάντα κάλων (v. sub κάλως):—to take out, Hdt. 2. intr. of rivers, to discharge themselves, Id., Thuc. II. Med. to put off from oneself, get rid of, πόσιος καὶ ἐδητύος ἐξ ἔρον ἕντο Hom. 2. to send from oneself, divorce, γυναῖκα Hdt.

ἐξ-ῑθύνω [ῑ], f. ῠνῶ, to make straight, Il.

ἐξ-ῑκετεύω, f. σω, to intreat earnestly, Soph.

ἐξ-ῑκνέομαι, f. -ίξομαι : aor. 2 -ῑκόμην [ῑ]: Dep. :—to reach, arrive at a place, c. acc., Hom., Trag. II. c. acc. pers. to come to as a suppliant, Od. 2. c. acc. rei, to arrive at or reach an object, to complete, accomplish, Thuc. ; so c. gen., Eur. 3. absol. to reach, Hdt., Xen. :—of mental operations, ὅσον δυνατός εἰμι ἐξικέσθαι so far as I can get by inquiry, Hdt. b. of things, to be sufficient, Plat.

ἐξ-ῑλάσκομαι, f. άσομαι [ᾰ], Ep. άσσομαι, Dep. to propitiate, Orac. ap. Hdt., Xen.

ἐξίμεναι, Ep. for ἐξιέναι, inf. of ἔξειμι (εἶμι ibo).

ἐξ-ιππάζομαι, f. άσομαι, Dep. to ride out or away, Plut.

ἕξις, εως, ἡ, (ἕξω, fut. of ἔχω) : I. (trans.) a having, possession, Plat. II. (intr.) a habit of body, esp. a good habit, Xen., Plat. 2. a habit of mind, Id.

ἐξ-ῑσόω, f. ώσω, to make equal or even, bring to a level with, Lat. exaequare, τινά or τί τινι Soph., Thuc. :—Med. to make oneself equal, Babr. :—Pass. to be or become equal, τινι Plat., etc. ; to be a match for, to rival, τινι Thuc. 2. to put on a level, τοὺς πολίτας Ar. II. intr. to be equal or like, μητρὶ δ' οὐδὲν ἐξισοῖ acts in no way like a mother, Soph. ; ἐξ. τοῖς ἄλλοις Thuc. : so in Pass., Soph.

ἐξιστάνω, later form of ἐξίστημι, N. T.

ἐξ-ίστημι, A. Causal in pres., impf., fut., aor. 1 : —to put out of its place, to change or alter utterly, Arist., Plut. 2. metaph., ἐξιστάναι τινὰ φρενῶν to drive one out of his senses, Eur. ; τοῦ φρονεῖν Xen. ; absol. to derange, Dem.

 B. intr. in Pass. and Med., with aor. 2, pf., and plqpf. act. : 1. of Place, to stand aside from, ἐκστάντες τῆς ὁδοῦ out of the way, Hdt. ; so, ἐκστῆναί τινι Soph., etc. :—metaph., ἐξ ἕδρας ἐξέστηκε is displaced, disordered, Eur. 2. c. acc. to shrink from, shun, Soph., Dem. II. c. gen. to retire from, give up possession of, τῆς ἀρχῆς Thuc. : —to cease from, abandon, τῶν μαθημάτων Xen. 2.

ἐκστῆναι πατρός to lose one's father, give him up, Ar. 3. φρενῶν ἐξεστάναι to lose one's senses, Eur.: —then, absol. to be out of one's wits, to be astonished, amazed, N. T. 4. to degenerate, οἶνος ἐξεστηκώς changed, sour wine, Dem.; πρόσωπα ἐξεστηκότα disfigured faces, Xen. 5. absol. to change one's position, one's opinion, Thuc.

ἐξ-ιστορέω, f. ήσω, to search out, inquire into, Aesch. 2. to inquire of, τινά τι Hdt., Eur.

ἐξ-ισχύω [ῡ], f. ύσω, to have strength enough, to be quite able to do, c. inf., N. T.

ἐξ-ίσχω, = ἐξέχω, to put forth, Od.

ἐξίσωσις, εως, ἡ, (ἐξισόω) equalisation, Plut. Hence

ἐξῑσωτέον, verb. Adj. one must make equal, Soph.

ἐξίτηλος [ῐ], ον, (ἐξιέναι) going out, losing colour, fading, evanescent, Xen. :—metaph., ἐξ. γενέσθαι, of a family, to become extinct, Hdt.; of things, lost to memory, forgotten, Id.

ἐξιτητέον, verb. Adj. of ἔξειμι (εἶμι ibo) one must go forth, Xen.

ἐξιτός, ή, όν, verb. Adj. of ἔξειμι (εἶμι ibo), to be come out of, τοῖς οὐκ ἐξιτόν ἐστι for whom there is no coming out, Hes.

ἐξιχνευτέον, verb. Adj. one must trace out, Luc. From

ἐξ-ιχνεύω, f. σω, to trace out, Aesch., Eur.

ἐξ-ιχνοσκοπέω, f. ήσω, to seek by tracking, Soph.; so in Med., Id.

ἐξ-μέδιμνος, ον, of, holding six medimni, Ar.

ἐξ-ογκόω, f. ώσω, to make to swell: metaph., μητέρα τάφῳ ἐξογκοῦν to honour her by raising a tomb, Eur.: Pass. to be swelled out, πάντα ἐξώγκωτο he had all his garments stuffed out, Hdt. :—metaph. to be puffed up, elated, Id., Eur.; τὰ ἐξωγκωμένα full-sailed prosperity, Id.; so in fut. med., Id. Hence

ἐξόγκωμα, ατος, τό, anything swollen, ἐξ. λάινον a mound of stones, Eur.

ἐξοδάω, f. ήσω, to sell, Eur.

ἐξοδία, Ion. -ίη, ἡ, = ἔξοδος I. 2, Hdt.

ἐξόδιος, ον, (ἔξοδος) of or belonging to an exit :—as Subst., ἐξόδιον (sc. μέλος), τό, the finalé of a tragedy, Plut. : metaph. a catastrophe, Id.

ἐξ-οδοιπορέω, f. ήσω, to get out of, c. gen., Soph.

ἔξ-οδος, ἡ, a going out, Hdt., Att. 2. a marching out, military expedition, Hdt., Att. 3. a solemn procession, Hdt., Dem. II. a way out, outlet, Lat. exitus, Hdt., Aesch., etc. III. like Lat. exitus, an end, close, Thuc., Xen.: the end or issue of an argument, Plat.: absol. departure, death, N. T. 2. the end of a tragedy, or music played at its close, Ar.

ἐξ-οδῠνάω, f. ήσω, to pain greatly, Eur.

ἐξ-όζω, intr. to smell, κακὸν ἐξόσδειν (Dor.) to smell foully, Theocr.

ἐξ-οιδα, -οισθα, pf. in pres. sense, plqpf. ἐξῄδη as impf., 2 sing. -ῄδησθα: (v. *εἴδω):—to know thoroughly, know well, Il., Soph., etc.

ἐξ-οιδέω, f. ήσω, to swell or be swollen up, Eur., Luc.

ἐξ-οικέω, f. ήσω, to emigrate, Dem. II. Pass. to be completely inhabited, Thuc. Hence

ἐξοικήσιμος, ον, habitable, inhabited, Soph.

ἐξ-οικίζω, f. Att. ιῶ, to remove one from his home, eject, banish, Eur., Thuc. :—Pass. and Med. to go

from home, remove, emigrate, Ar., Aeschin. II. to dispeople, empty, Eur.

ἐξ-οικοδομέω, f. ήσω, to build completely, finish a building, Hdt., Ar.

ἐξ-οιμώζω, f. -οιμώξομαι, to wail aloud, Soph.

ἐξ-οινόομαι, Pass. to be drunk, pf. part. ἐξῳνωμένος drunken, Eur.

ἐξοιστέος, α, ον, verb. Adj. of ἐξοίσω (fut. of ἐκφέρω), to be brought out: ἐξοιστέον, one must bring out, Eur.

ἐξ-οιστράω or -έω, f. ήσω, to make wild, madden, Luc.

ἐξ-οίσω, fut. of ἐκφέρω.

ἐξ-οιχνέω, to go out or forth, ἐξοιχνεῦσι (Ion. for -οῦσι), Il.

ἐξ-οίχομαι, to have gone out, to be quite gone, Il., Soph.

ἐξ-οιωνίζομαι, Dep. to avoid as ill-omened, Plut.

ἐξ-οκέλλω, aor. 1 -ώκειλα, intr., of a ship, to run aground or ashore, Hdt., Aesch. II. trans. to run (a ship) aground :—metaph. to drive headlong, Eur.

ἐξ-ολισθάνω, f. -ολισθήσω: aor. 2 -ώλισθον :—to glide off, slip away, Il.: to glance off, as a spear from a hard substance, Eur. : to slip out, escape, Ar. :—c. acc. to elude, Id.

ἐξ-όλλυμι and -ύω: f. -ολέσω, Att. -ολῶ: aor. 1 -ώλεσα: pf. -ολώλεκα :—to destroy utterly, Od., Eur., etc. II. Med., with pf. 2 ἐξόλωλα, to perish utterly, Soph., etc.

ἐξ-ολοθρεύω, f. σω, to destroy utterly, N. T.

ἐξ-ολολύζω, f. σω, to howl aloud, Batr.

ἐξ-ομᾰλίζω, f. σω, to smooth away, Babr.

ἐξομήρευσις, ἡ, a demand of hostages, Plut. From

ἐξ-ομηρεύομαι, Med. to take as hostages, Plut.

ἐξ-ομῑλέω, f. ήσω, to have intercourse, live with, τινι Xen. : to bear one company, Eur. II. Med. to be away from one's friends, be alone in the crowd, Id.

ἐξ-όμῑλος, ον, out of one's own society, alien, Soph.

ἐξ-ομμᾰτόω, f. ώσω, to open the eyes of: Pass. to be restored to sight, Soph. ap. Ar. II. metaph. to make clear or plain, Aesch.

ἐξ-όμνῡμι and -ύω: f. ἐξομοῦμαι: aor. 1 ἐξώμοσα :— to swear in excuse, Eur. : to swear in the negative, ἐξ. τὸ μὴ εἰδέναι Soph. :—mostly in Med., to deny or disown upon oath, swear formally that one does not know a thing, Dem., etc. 2. to decline an office by oath that one cannot perform it, Aeschin., etc.

ἐξ-ομοιόω, f. ώσω, to make quite like, to assimilate, Hdt., Plat. :—Pass. to become or be like, Soph., Eur.

ἐξομοίωσις, εως, ἡ, a becoming like, Plut.

ἐξομολογέομαι, f. ήσομαι, Dep. to confess in full, Plut., N. T. 2. to make full acknowledgments, give thanks, Ib. II. in Act. to agree, promise, Ib.

ἐξ-ομόργνῡμι, f. -ομόρξω :—to wipe off from, Eur. :— Med. to wipe off from oneself, purge away a pollution, Id. II. metaph. ἐξομόρξασθαί τινι μωρίαν to wipe off one's folly on another, i. e. give him part of it, Id. 2. to stamp or imprint upon, Plat.

ἐξ-ονειδίζω, f. Att. ιῶ, 1. c. acc. rei, to cast in one's teeth, Soph., Eur. ; ἐξονειδισθεὶς κακά having foul reproaches cast upon one, Soph. :—simply, to bring forward, Lat. objicere, Eur. 2. c. acc. pers. to reproach, Soph.

ἐξ-ονομάζω, f. σω, to utter aloud, announce, Hom. II. to call by name, Plut.

ἐξ-ονομαίνω, f. ἀνῶ, to name, speak of by name, Hom.

ἐξ-ονομα-κλήδην, Adv. (καλέω) by name, calling by name, Hom.

ἐξόπῐθεν and -θε, Adv., Ep. for ἐξόπισθεν, behind, in rear, Il. 2. as Prep. with gen. behind, ἐξ. κεράων Ib.

ἐξόπιν, Adv., = foreg. 1, Aesch.

ἐξόπισθεν, poët. -θε, Adv., Att. for ἐξόπιθεν, Ar. 2. as Prep. with gen., Id.

ἐξοπίσω [ῐ], Adv., I. of Place, backwards, back again, Il. 2. as Prep. with gen. behind, Ib. II. of Time, hereafter, Od.

ἐξ-οπλίζω, f. σω, to arm completely, accoutre, Hdt., Xen.: —Med. and Pass. to arm or accoutre oneself, Eur.: to get under arms, stand in armed array, Id., Xen.:— generally, ἐξωπλισμένος fully prepared, all ready, Ar.

ἐξοπλῐσία, ἡ, a being under arms, Xen.; and

ἐξόπλῐσις, εως, ἡ, a getting under arms, Xen.

ἐξ-οπτάω, f. ήσω, to bake thoroughly, Hdt., Eur. 2. to heat violently, Hdt.

ἐξ-οράω, to see from afar: Pass., Eur.:—cf. ἐξεῖδον.

ἐξ-οργίζω, f. Att. ιῶ, to enrage, Xen., Aeschin.:—Pass. to be furious, Batr.

ἐξ-ορθιάζω, to lift up the voice, to cry aloud, Aesch.

ἐξ-ορθόω, f. ώσω, to set upright: metaph. to set right, secure, restore, Soph.: Pass., Eur.

ἐξ-ορίζω, f. Att. ιῶ, to send beyond the frontier, banish, Lat. exterminare, Eur., etc. 2. to expose a child, Id. 3. to get rid of a thing, Plat. II. c. acc. loci only, ἄλλην ἀπ' ἄλλης ἐξ. πόλιν to pass from one to another, Eur. III. in Pass. to come forth from, τινος Id.

ἐξ-ορίνω [ῑ], to exasperate, Aesch.

ἐξόριστος, ον, (ἐξορίζω) expelled, banished, Dem.

ἐξ-ορκίζω, f. Att. ιῶ, = ἐξορκόω, to adjure, N.T. Hence

ἐξορκιστής, οῦ, ὁ, an exorcist, N.T.

ἐξ-ορκόω, f. ώσω, to swear a person, administer an oath to one, c. acc. pers., or absol., ἐξορκούντων οἱ πρυτάνεις Foed. ap. Thuc., Dem.; followed by ἢ μήν (Ion. ἢ μέν) c. inf. fut., Hdt., etc.: c. acc. rei, to make one swear by a thing, Id. Hence

ἐξόρκωσις, εως, ἡ, a binding by oath, Hdt.

ἐξ-ορμάω, f. ήσω, to send forth, send to war, Aesch., Eur.; ἐξ. τὴν ναῦν to start the ship, set it agoing, Thuc.:—Pass. to set out, start, Hdt., Eur., etc.; of arrows, to spring from the bow, Id. 2. to excite to action, urge on, Id., Thuc. II. intr., like Pass., to set out, start, of a ship, Od., Xen.: c. gen. to set out from, Eur.:—metaph. to break out, of a disease, Soph.; σφοδρὸς ἐφ' ὅ τι ἐφορμήσειε eager in all that he attempted, Plat.

ἐξ-ορμέω, f. ήσω, to be out of harbour, run out, Aeschin.

ἐξ-ορμίζω, f. Att. ιῶ, to bring out of harbour, Dem. 2. to let down, Eur.: pf. pass. in med. sense, ἐξώρμισαι σὺν πόδα thou hast come forth, Id.

ἐξ-ορμος, ον, sailing from a harbour, c. gen., Eur.

ἐξ-ορούω, f. ήσω, to leap forth, Hom.

ἐξ-ορύσσω, Att. -ττω, f. ξω, to dig out the earth from a trench, Hdt. II. to dig out of the ground, dig up, Id., Ar.: metaph., ἐξ. αὑτῶν τοὺς ὀφθαλμούς Hdt.

ἐξ-ορχέομαι, f. ήσομαι, Dep. to dance away, hop off, Dem. II. c. acc. rei, to dance out, i.e. to let out, betray secrets, Luc.

ἐξόσδω, Dor. for ἐξόζω.

ἐξ-οσιόω, f. ώσω, to dedicate, devote, Plut.

ἐξ-οστρᾰκίζω, f. σω, to banish by ostracism, Hdt., Plat. Hence

ἐξοστρᾰκισμός, ὁ, banishment by ostracism, Plut.

ἐξ-ότε, Adv., (ἐξ ὅτε) = ἐξ οὗ, from the time when, Ar.

ἐξ-οτρύνω [ῡ], f. ῠνῶ, to stir up, urge on, excite, τινὰ ποιεῖν τι Aesch., Eur.; τινὰ ἐπί τι Thuc.

ἐξ-ουδενόω, f. ώσω, (οὐδείς) to set at naught, N.T.

ἐξ-ουθενέω, f. ήσω, (οὐθείς) = ἐξουδενόω, N.T.

ἐξούλης δίκη, ἡ, (ἐξείλλω) an action against exclusion, brought by one who was excluded from property by the defendant in a suit, Dem.

ἐξουσία, ἡ, (ἔξεστι) power or authority to do a thing, c. inf., Thuc., Xen.; c. gen. power over, licence in a thing, Thuc., Plat. II. absol. power, authority, might, as opp. to right, Thuc.: also licence, Dem. 2. an office, magistracy, Lat. potestas, Plat. 3. as concrete, also like Lat. potestas, the body of the magistrates, in pl., the authorities, N.T. III. abundance of means, resources, Thuc. IV. pomp, Plut.

ἐξουσιάζω, f. σω, to exercise over, c. gen., N.T.

ἐξ-οφέλλω, to increase exceedingly, ἐξώφελλεν ἔεδνα offered still higher dowry, Od.

ἐξ-όφθαλμος, ον, with prominent eyes, Xen.

ἔξοχα, Adv., v. sub ἔξοχος.

ἐξοχή, ἡ, (ἐξέχω) prominence: οἱ κατ' ἐξοχήν the chief men, N.T.

ἔξοχος, ον, (ἐξέχω) standing out: metaph. eminent, excellent, Hom. 2. c. gen. standing out from, most eminent, greatest, mightiest, used like a Superl., ἔξοχος ἡρώων, ἐξ. ἄλλων Il.; as a real Sup. ἐξοχώτατος Aesch., Eur.:—also c. dat., μέγ' ἔξοχοι αἰπολίοισιν eminent among the herds, Od.; so, ἐν πολλοῖσι ἔξοχος ἡρώεσσιν Il. II. neut. pl. ἔξοχα as Adv., especially, above others, Hom.; μοι δόσαν ἔξοχα gave me as a high honour, Od.; ἔξοχ' ἄριστοι beyond compare the best, Hom. 2. c. gen., ἔξοχα πάντων far above all, Id.

ἐξ-οχῠρόω, f. ώσω, to fortify strongly, Plut.

ἐξ-υβρίζω, f. Att. ιῶ, to break out into insolence, to run riot, wax wanton, Hdt., Thuc., etc.; ἐξ. ἐς τόδε to come to this pitch of insolence, Id.: with an Adj. neut., παντοῖα ἐξ. to commit all kinds of violence, Hdt.

ἐξυνῆκα, ἐξυνῆκα, for ξυνῆκα, poët. aor. 1 with double augm. of συνίημι.

ἐξ-υπᾰνίστημι, only in intr. aor. 2, σμῶδιξ μεταφρένου ἐξυπανέστη a weal started up from under the skin of the back, Il.

ἐξ-υπειπεῖν, = ὑπειπεῖν, to advise, Eur.

ἐξ-ύπερθε [ῠ], Adv., = ὕπερθε, from above, Soph.

ἐξ-υπηρετέω, f. ήσω, to assist to the utmost, Soph.

ἐξ-υπνίζω, f. σω, (ὕπνος) to awaken from sleep, N.T.: —Pass. to wake up, Plut.

ἐξ-υπνος, ον, awakened out of sleep, N.T.

ἐξ-υπτιάζω, f. σω, to turn upside down, Lat. resupinare, Aesch.; ἐξ. ἑαυτόν throwing back his head haughtily, Luc.

ἐξῠράμην, aor. 1 med. of ξυρέω:—ἐξύρημαι, pf. pass.

ἔξυσμαι, pf. pass. of ξύω.

ἐξ-υφαίνω, f. ἀνῶ, to finish weaving, Hdt. Hence

ἐξύφασμα [ῠ], ατος, τό, a finished web, Eur.

ἐξ-υφηγέομαι, f. ήσομαι, to lead the way, Soph.

ἔξω, Adv. of ἐξ, as εἴσω of εἰς: **I.** of Place, **1.** with Verbs of motion, out, ἔξω ἰών Od.; χωρεῖν ἔξω Hdt., etc.:—c. gen. out of, Hom., etc.:—c. acc., ἔξω τὸν Ἑλλήσποντον outside the H., Hdt. **2.** without any sense of motion, like ἐκτός, outside, without, Od.: τὸ ἔξω the outside, Thuc.; τὰ ἔξω things outside the walls, Id.; τὰ ἔξω πράγματα foreign affairs, Id.;—οἱ ἔξω those outside, Id. (in N. T. the heathen); —ἡ ἔξω θάλασσα, the Ocean, opp. to ἡ ἐντός (the Mediterranean sea), Hdt.:—c. gen., οἱ ἔξω γένους Soph.; ἔξω τοξεύματος, ἔξω βελῶν out of shot, Thuc., Xen.; ἔξω τινὸς εἶναι to have nothing to do with it, Thuc.; ἔξω τοῦ φρονεῖν out of one's senses, Eur.:—proverb., ἔξω τοῦ πηλοῦ αἴρειν πόδα to keep clear of difficulties, Aesch.; πημάτων ἔξω πόδα ἔχειν Id. **II.** of Time, beyond, over, ἔξω μέσου ἡμέρας Xen. **III.** without, but, except, c. gen., Hdt., Thuc.

ἕξω, fut. of ἔχω.

ἔξωθεν, Adv. (ἔξω) from without, Trag., Plat., etc.:— c. gen., ἐξ. δόμων from without the house, Eur. **II.** = ἔξω, Hdt., Plat., etc.; οἱ ἔξωθεν foreigners, Hdt.; τὰ ἔξωθεν matters outside the house, Aesch., etc.:—c. gen. without, free from, Soph., Eur.

ἐξ-ωθέω, f. -ωθήσω and -ώσω: aor. 1 ἐξέωσα:—to thrust out, force out, wrench out, Il.: to expel, eject, banish, Soph.:—to thrust back, Id., Thuc.:—Pass., ἐξωθέεσθαι ἐκ τῆς χώρης Hdt.; πατρίδος ἐξωθούμενος Soph. **2.** ἐξ. γλώσσας ὀδύναν to put forth painful words, to break forth into cruel words, Id. **II.** to drive out of the sea, drive on shore, Lat. ejicere, Thuc.: metaph., ἐξωσθῆναι ἐς χειμῶνα Id.

ἐξώλεια, ἡ, utter destruction, κατ' ἐξωλείας ὀμόσαι to swear with deadly imprecations against oneself, Dem.; ἐπαρᾶσθαι ἐξώλειαν αὑτῷ Id. From

ἐξώλης, ες, (ἐξόλλυμι) utterly destroyed, Hdt., Dem.: in imprecations, ἐξ. ἀπόλοιο Ar.; cf. προώλης.

ἐξ-ωμίας, ου, ὁ, (ὦμος) one with arms bare to the shoulder, Luc.

ἐξωμιδο-ποιία, ἡ, (ποιέω) the making of an ἐξωμίς, Xen.

ἐξ-ωμίς, ίδος, ἡ, (ὦμος) a man's vest without sleeves, leaving both shoulders bare, or with one sleeve, leaving one shoulder bare, Ar., Xen.

ἐξωμοσία, ἡ, (ἐξόμνυμι) denial on oath that one knows anything of a matter, Ar., Dem. **II.** a declining an office on oath, in case of ill health, Id.

ἐξ-ωνέομαι, f. ήσομαι, Dep. to buy off, redeem:— generally, to buy, Hdt., Aeschin.

ἐξ-ωνωμένος, pf. pass. part. of ἐξοινόω.

ἐξ-ώπιος, ον, (ὤψ) out of sight of, c. gen., Eur.

ἐξ-ωριάζω, (ὥρα) to leave out of thought, Aesch.

ἐξ-ώριος, ον, (ὥρα) untimely, out of season, unfitting, Soph.:—superannuated, Aeschin.

ἐξῶσαι, aor. 1 inf. of ἐξωθέω.

ἐξώστης, ου, ὁ, (ἐξωθέω) one who drives out, Eur.:— ἐξ. ἄνεμοι violent winds which drive ships ashore, Hdt.

ἐξωτάτω, Adv., Sup. of ἔξω, outermost, Plat.

ἐξωτέρω, Adv., Comp. of ἔξω, more outside, c. gen., Aesch.:—hence Adj. ἐξώτερος, outer, utter, N. T.

ἔο, Ep. for οὗ, Lat. sui:—ἐοῖ, Ep. for οἷ, Lat. sibi.

ἔοι, Ep. for εἴη, 3 sing. pres. opt. of εἰμί (sum).

ἜΟΙΚΑ, ας, ε, pf. with pres. sense, to be like, (from

εἴκω, of which we have 3 sing. impf. εἶκε, it seemed good, Il.; fut. εἴξω, will be like, Ar.):—besides the common forms ἔοικα, ας, ε, we have Ep. 3 dual εἴκτον for ἐοίκατον, 1 pl. ἔοιγμεν, 3 pl. εἴξασι; inf. εἰκέναι; part. εἰκώς:—Ion., οἶκα, part. οἰκώς:—plqpf. ἐῴκειν, εις, ει; 3 pl. ἐῴκεσαν, Ep. ἐοίκεσαν; Ep. 3 dual εἴκτην, for ἐῳκείτην; plqpf. ἤϊκτο, εἴκτο: **I.** to be like, look like, τινι Hom., etc.:—with the part., where we use the inf., αἰεὶ γὰρ δίφρου ἐπιβησομένοισι εἴκτην always just about to set foot upon the chariot, Il.; ἔοικε σπεύδοντι seems anxious, Plat. **II.** to seem likely, c. inf., in phrases which we render by making the Verb impersonal, as in the Lat. videor videre, methinks I see, χλιδᾶν ἔοικας methinks thou art delicate, Aesch.; ἔοικα οὐκ εἰδέναι Soph. **2.** impers., ἔοικε it seems; ὡς ἔοικε as it seems, Id., etc.; ὡς ἔοικε used to modify a statement, probably, I believe, Plat.:—so also personal, ὡς ἔοικας Soph. **III.** to beseem, befit, c. dat. pers., Xen. **2.** impers., ἔοικε it is fitting, right, seemly, reasonable, mostly with a negat. and foll. by inf., οὐκ ἔστ', οὐδὲ ἔοικε, ἀρνήσασθαι it is not possible, nor is it seemly, to deny, Hom. **IV.** part. ἐοικώς, εἰκώς, Ion. οἰκώς, υἶα, ός, **1.** seeming like, like, Id., etc. **2.** fitting, seemly, meet, Id. **3.** likely, probable, εἰκός ἐστι, for ἔοικε, Soph.; also ὡς εἰκός, Ion. ὡς οἰκός, for ὡς ἔοικε, Hdt., etc.

ἐοικότως, Att. εἰκότως, Ion. οἰκότως, Adv. of part. ἐοικώς, similarly, like, Aesch. **2.** reasonably, fairly, naturally, Hdt.; οὐκ εἰκότως unfairly, Thuc.

ἐοῖο, Ep. for ἐοῦ, gen. of ἐός:—ἐοῖς, dat. pl.

ἔοις, Ep. for εἴης, 2 sing. opt. of εἰμί (sum).

ἐοῖσα, Dor. for ἐοῦσα, οὖσα, part. fem. of εἰμί (sum).

ἐόλητο, Ep. 3 sing. plqpf. pass. of εἴλω.

ἔολπα, Ep. pf., with pres. sense, of ἔλπω.

ἔον, Ep. for ἦν, 1 sing. impf. of εἰμί (sum). **II.** ἐόν, Ion. for ὄν, part. neut.

ἔοργα, Ep. pf. of ἔρδω: Ion. 3 sing. plqpf. ἐόργεε.

ἑορτάζω, Ion. ὁρτάζω: impf. ἑώρταζον (with irreg. augm. in second syll.): f. άσω: aor. 1 ἑώρτασα (with irreg. augm.), inf. ἑορτάσαι: (ἑορτή):—to keep festival or holiday, Hdt., Eur. **II.** to celebrate as or by a festival, Plut.

ἑορτάσιμος, ον, of or for a festival, Luc.

ἑορτή, Ion. ὁρτή, ἡ, a feast or festival, holiday, Od., Hdt., etc.; ὁρτὴν or ἑορτὴν ἄγειν to keep a feast, Thuc.; ἑορτὴν ἑορτάζειν Xen. **2.** generally, holiday-making, amusement, pastime, Aesch., Thuc.

ἑός, ἑή, ἑόν, Ep. for ὅς, ἥ, ὅν: (ἕ, ἕο, = οὗ):—possessive Adj. of 3 pers. sing. his, her own, Lat. suus, Hom., etc.; never in Att. Prose.

ἐοῦσα, Ion. and Ep. for οὖσα, part. fem. of εἰμί (sum).

ἐπ-αγάλλομαι, Pass. to glory in, exult in a thing, c. dat., Il.; ἐπί τινι Xen.

ἐπ-αγανακτέω, f. ήσω, to be indignant at, Plut.

ἐπαγγελία, ἡ, a public denunciation of one who, being subject to ἀτιμία, yet takes part in public affairs, Aeschin., Dem. **2.** an offer, promise; profession, Id. From

ἐπ-αγγέλλω, f. -ελῶ; aor. 1 -ήγγειλα: pf. -ήγγελκα: —to tell, proclaim, announce, Od., Hdt., etc.:— Med. to let proclamation be made, Id. **2.** to give orders, command, Id., Thuc.; c. acc., στρατιὰν

ἐπ., like Lat. *milites imperare, to order* an army to be furnished, Thuc. :—also in Med., Hdt.   **3.** *as* Att. law-term, *to denounce* one who, having incurred ἀτιμία, yet takes part in public affairs, Aeschin., etc.   **4.** *to promise,* τί τινι Aesch. :—so in Med., Hdt., Att. :—absol. *to make offers,* Hdt.   **5.** *to profess, make profession of,* τι Dem. :—so in Med., like Lat. *profiteri,* Xen., Plat.   **6.** *to demand, require,* Foed. ap. Thuc. ; so in Med., Dem. Hence

ἐπάγγελμα, ατος, τό, *a promise, profession,* Dem. :— *one's profession,* Plat.

ἐπ-αγείρω, f. -αγερῶ, *to gather together, collect,* of things, Il. :—Pass., of men, *to assemble,* Od. Hence

ἐπάγερσις, εως, ἡ, *a mustering* of forces, Hdt.

ἐπάγην [ᾰ], aor. 2 pass. of πήγνυμι.

ἐπ-αγῑνέω, Ion. for ἐπάγω, *to bring to,* Hdt.

ἐπ-αγλαΐζω, f. Att. ιῶ, *to honour still more :*—Pass. *to pride oneself on* a thing, *glory* or *exult in* it, Il.

ἐπ-άγνυμι, *to break :* pf. ἐπέαγα intr., Hes.

ἐπ-αγρυπνέω, f. ήσω, *to keep awake and brood over,* τινί Plut., Luc.

ἐπ-άγω [ᾰ], f. ξω: aor. 2 ἐπήγαγον :—*to bring on,* Od., Aesch. : *to bring upon,* τί τινι Hes., Att.   **2.** *to set on, urge on,* as hunters do dogs, Od., Xen.   **b.** *to lead on* an army *against* the enemy, Hdt., Thuc., etc.   **3.** *to lead on by persuasion, influence,* Od., Eur. ; c. inf. *to induce* him to do, Id.   **4.** *to bring in, invite* as aiders or allies, Hdt., Dem.   **5.** *to bring to* a place, *bring in,* Hdt., etc. :—*to bring in, supply,* Thuc.   **6.** *to lay on* or *apply* to one, ἐπ. κέντρον ἵπποις, of a charioteer, Eur. ; ἔπαγε γνάθον *lay* your jaws *to* it, Ar.   **7.** *to bring forward, propose* a measure, Thuc., Xen. ; so, ἐπ. δίκην, γραφήν τινι, Lat. *intendere litem alicui,* Plat., etc.   **8.** *to bring in over and above, to add,* τι Aesch., Ar. :—*to intercalate* days in the year, Hdt.   **II.** Med. *to procure* or *provide for oneself,* Thuc. :—metaph. Ἄϊδα φεῦξιν ἐπ. *to devise, invent* a means of shunning death, Soph.   **2.** of persons, *to bring into* one's country, *bring in* or *introduce* as allies, Hdt., Thuc.   **3.** *to call in* as witnesses, *adduce,* Plat., etc.   **4.** *to bring upon oneself,* φθόνον Xen. ; δουλείαν Dem.   **5.** *to bring with one,* Xen.   **6.** *to bring over to oneself, win over,* Thuc. Hence

ἐπαγωγή, ἡ, *a bringing in, supplying,* Thuc.   **2.** *a bringing in to* one's aid, *introduction,* Id.   **3.** *a drawing on, alluring,* Dem.

ἐπαγώγιμος, ον, (ἐπάγω) *imported,* Plut.

ἐπαγωγός, όν, (ἐπάγω) *attractive, tempting, alluring, seductive,* Hdt., Thuc. :—ἐπαγωγόν ἐστι, c. inf., it is *a temptation,* Xen.

ἐπαγωνίζομαι, Dep. *to contend with,* τινι Plut.   **2.** c. dat. rei, *to contend for* a thing, N. T.

ἐπ-αγώνιος, ον, (ἀγών) *helping in the contest,* Aesch.

ἐπ-αείδω, contr. Att. -ᾴδω: f. -ᾴσομαι :—*to sing to* or *in accompaniment,* Hdt., Eur.   **2.** *to sing as an incantation,* Xen., Plat. ;—absol., ἐπαείδων *by means of charms,* Aesch.

ἐπ-αείρω, poët. for ἐπαίρω.

ἐπ-αέξω, *to make to grow* or *prosper,* Od.

ἔπ-αθλον, τό, *the prize* of a contest, Plat.

ἔπᾰθον, aor. 2 of πάσχω.

ἐπ-αθροίζομαι, Pass. *to assemble besides,* N.T., Plut.

ἐπ-αιάζω, f. ξω, *to cry* αἰαῖ *over, mourn over,* τινί Luc.   **II.** *to join in wailing,* Bion.

ἐπ-αιγιαλῖτις, ιδος, ἡ, (αἰγιαλός) *on the beach,* Anth.

ἐπ-αιγίζω, f. σω, (αἰγίς II) *to rush furiously upon,* of a stormy wind, Hom.

ἐπ-αιδέομαι, f. -αιδεσθήσομαι: aor. 1 -ῃδέσθην : Dep. : —*to be ashamed,* c. inf., Eur. ; σὺ δ' οὐκ ἐπαιδεῖ, εἰ . ., *te non pudet, si* . . , Soph.

ἐπ-αίθω, *to kindle, set on fire,* Anth.

ἐπαίνεσις, εως, ἡ, *praise,* Eur. ; and

ἐπαινετέον, verb. Adj. *one must praise,* Plat. ; and

ἐπαινέτης, ου, ὁ, *a commender, admirer,* Thuc. ; and

ἐπαινετός, ή, όν, *to be praised, laudable,* Plat. From

ἐπ-αινέω, Ep.impf. ἐπῄνεον : f. -έσω or -έσομαι, poët. (but not Att.) ᾔσω: aor. 1 ἐπῄνεσα, poët. (but not Att.) ἐπῄνησα: pf. ἐπῄνεκα :—Pass., fut. -αινεθήσομαι: aor. 1 ἐπῃνέθην :—*to approve, applaud, commend,* Lat. *laudare,* Hom., etc. ; ἐπ. τινά τι *to commend* one *for* a thing, Aesch.   **2.** *to compliment publicly, panegyrise,* Thuc.   **3.** *to undertake to do,* c. inf., Eur.   **4.** the aor. ἐπῄνεσα is in Att. used in a pres. sense, ἐπῄνεσ' ἔργον I commend it, Soph. : and absol., *well done!* Ar.   **II.** *to recommend, exhort, advise,* c. inf., Soph.   **III.** as a civil form of declining an offer, *I thank you, I am much obliged,* κάλλιστ', ἐπαινῶ Ar. ; so, ἐπ. τὴν κλῆσιν *to decline* it, Xen.   **IV.** of Rhapsodists, *to declaim,* Plat.

ἔπ-αινος, ὁ, *approval, praise, commendation,* Hdt., Att.

ἐπ-αινός, only found in fem. ἐπαινή, *dread,* Hom.

ἐπ-αίρω, Ion. and poët. ἐπαείρω: f. -αρῶ: aor. 1 -ῆρα :—Pass., aor. 1 ἐπήρθην :—*to lift up and set on* a car or stand, c. gen., Il.   **2.** *to lift, raise,* Ib., Soph., etc. : Med., ὅπλα ἐπαίρεσθαι Eur.   **3.** *to exalt, magnify,* Xen.   **4.** intr. *to lift up one's leg* or *rise up,* Hdt.   **II.** *to stir up, excite,* Id., Soph., etc. : —*to induce* or *persuade* one to do, c. inf., Hdt., Ar. : —Pass. *to be led on, excited,* Hdt., etc.   **2.** Pass., also, *to be elated at* a thing, Id., Thuc., etc. :—absol. *to be conceited* or *proud,* Ar.

ἔπαισδον, Dor. for ἔπαιζον, impf. of παίζω.

ἐπ-αισθάνομαι, f. -αισθήσομαι: aor. 2 -ῃσθόμην : Dep. : —*to have a perception* or *feeling of,* c. gen., Soph.   **2.** c. acc. *to perceive, hear,* Aesch., Soph.

ἐπ-αΐσσω, f. ξω: contr. Att. -ᾴσσω or -ᾴττω, f. -ᾴξω : —*to rush at* or *upon,* c. gen., Il.   **2.** c. dat. pers. *to rush upon* her, Od.   **3.** c. acc. *to assail, assault,* Ἕκτορα Il. :—Med., ἐπαΐξασθαι ἄεθλον *to rush at* (i. e. *seize upon*) the prize, Ib.   **4.** absol., of a hawk, ταρφέ ἐπαΐσσει makes frequent *swoops,* Ib. ; of the wind, Ib., Att.   **II.** c. acc. πόδα *to move with hasty step,* Eur. :—Pass., χεῖρες ἐπαΐσσονται they *move lightly,* Il.

ἐπάϊστος, ον, (ἐπαΐω) *heard of, detected,* Hdt.

ἐπ-αισχύνομαι, f. -αισχυνθήσομαι, Dep. : — *to be ashamed at* or, c. inf., Hdt. ; τινα or τι Xen. :—c. inf. *to be ashamed to do,* Aesch. ; c. part. *to be ashamed of* doing or having done a thing, Hdt., Soph., etc.

ἐπ-αιτέω, f. ήσω, *to ask besides,* Il., Soph. :—so in Med., Hdt.

ἐπ-αιτιάομαι, f. -άσομαι [ᾱ], Ion. -ήσομαι : Dep. :—*to bring a charge against, accuse,* τινα Hdt., Att. ; ἐπ. τινά τινος *to accuse* one *of* a thing, Thuc., Dem. ; c.

inf. *to accuse* one *of doing* a thing, Soph., etc. :—c. acc. rei, *to lay the blame upon*, Thuc., Plat.

ἐπ-αίτιος, ον, (αἰτία) *blamed for* a thing, *blameable, blameworthy*, Il., Aesch., etc.

ἐπ-αΐω, contr. ἐπᾴω, *to give ear to*, c. gen., Aesch., Eur.   2. *to perceive, feel*, c. gen., Hdt.   3. *to understand*, c. acc., Soph., Ar.   4. *to profess knowledge, to be a professor* in any subject, Plat.

ἐπ-αιωρέω, f. ήσω, *to keep hovering over, keep in suspense*, Anth.   II. Pass. *to hover over, to buoy up*, Luc.   2. *to overhang, threaten*, τινί Plut.

ἐπ-ακμάζω, f. άσω, *to come to its bloom*, Luc.

ἐπ-ἀκολουθέω, f. ήσω, *to follow close upon, follow after*, τινί Ar., Plat.;—absol., Thuc., etc.   2. *to pursue* as an enemy, Id., etc.   3. *to follow mentally*, τῷ λόγῳ Plat.   4. *to follow*, i.e. *comply with*, τοῖς πάθεσι Dem.   Hence

ἐπἀκολούθημα, ατος, τό, *a consequence*, Plut.

ἐπἀκουός, όν, *attentive to*, c. gen., Hes.   From

ἐπ-ἀκούω, f. -ακούσομαι, *to listen* or *hearken to, to hear*, c. acc., Hom., Att. : also c. gen., Hdt., Eur. :—c. acc. rei et gen. pers. *to hear* a thing *from* a person, Od.   2. absol. *to give ear, hearken*, Aesch., etc.   II. *to obey*, τινός Il., Soph.

ἐπ-ἀκρίζω, f. σω, *to reach the top of* a thing, αἱμάτων ἐπήκρισε he *reached the highest point* in deeds of blood, Aesch.

ἐπακτέον, verb. Adj. of ἐπάγω, *one must apply*, Luc.

ἐπακτήρ, ῆρος, ὁ, = ὁ κύνας ἐπάγων, *a hunter*, Hom.

ἐπάκτιος, ον, and α, ον, (ἀκτή) *on the shore*, Soph., Hdt.

ἐπακτός, όν, (ἐπάγω) *brought in, imported*, Thuc., etc.   2. of persons, *alien*, Eur.;—of foreign allies or mercenaries, Aesch., Soph.;—also, ἐπακτὸς ἀνήρ, i.e. *an adulterer*, Id. ; ἐπ. πατήρ *a false father*, Eur.   II. *brought upon oneself*, Soph., Eur.

ἐπακτρίς, ίδος, ἡ, (ἐπάγω) *a light vessel, skiff*, Xen. :—so, ἐπακτρο-κέλης, ὁ, *a light piratical skiff*, Aeschin.

ἐπ-ἀλαλάζω, f. ξω, *to raise the war-cry*, Aesch., Xen.

ἐπἀλαλκέμεν, Ep. for -αλαλκεῖν, aor. 2 inf. of ἐπαλέξω.

ἐπ-ἀλάομαι, Dep. with aor. 1 pass. *to wander about* or *over*, πόλλ᾽ ἐπαληθείς Od.

ἐπ-ἀλαστέω, f. ήσω, (ἄλαστος) *to be full of wrath at* a thing, Od.

ἐπ-ἀλγέω, f. ήσω, *to grieve over*, c. gen., Eur.

ἐπ-ἀλείφω, f. ψω, *to smear over, plaster up*, Od.

ἐπ-ἀλέξω, f. -αλεξήσω, *to defend, aid, help*, τινί Il.   II. *to ward off, keep off*, c. acc., Ib.

ἐπἀληθείς, aor. 1 part. of ἐπαλάομαι: -αληθῇ, 3 sing. subj.

ἐπ-ἀληθεύω, f. σω, *to prove true, verify*, Thuc.

ἐπ-ἀλής, ές, (ἀλέα) *open to the sun, sunny*, Hes.

ἐπ-ἀλκής, ές, (ἀλκή) *strong*, Aesch.

ἐπαλλαγή, ἡ, (ἐπαλλάσσω) *an interchange*, Hdt.

ἐπ-αλλάξ, Adv. , = ἐναλλάξ, Xen.

ἐπ-αλλάσσω, Att. -ττω, f. άξω : pf. -ήλλᾰχα, pass. -ήλλαχμαι : aor. 1 and 2 pass. -ηλλάχθην, -ηλλάγην [ᾰ] :—*to interchange*, πολέμιο πεῖραρ ἐπαλλάξαντες *making* the rope-end of war *go now this way, now that*, i.e. *fighting* with doubtful victory, (metaph. from a game like 'soldiers and sailors'), Il. :—Pass. *to cross one another*, Xen. ; ποὺς ἐπαλλαχθεὶς ποδί *closely joined*, Eur. : *to be entangled, perplexed*, Xen.

ἐπάλληλος, ον, (ἀλλήλων) *one after another*, ἐπαλλήλοιν χεροῖν *by one another's* hands, Soph.

ἐπάλμενος, Ep. aor. 2 part. of ἐφάλλομαι.

ἐπάλξις, εως, ἡ, (ἐπαλέξω) *a means of defence* : in pl. *battlements*, Il., Hdt., etc. :—in sing. *the battlements, parapet*, Il., Thuc.   2. generally, *a defence, protection*, Aesch., Eur.

ἐπ-ᾶλτο, Ep. 3 sing. aor. 2 of ἐφ-άλλομαι : but ἔπαλτο, aor. 2 pass. of πάλλω.

ἐπἀμαξεύω, f. σω, Ion. for ἐφαμ-, *to traverse with cars*, γῆ ἐπημαξευμένη τροχοῖσι *marked with the tracks* of wheels, Soph.

ἐπ-ἀμάομαι, f. ήσομαι, Med. *to scrape together for oneself*, εὐνὴν ἐπαμήσατο *heaped him up* a bed (of leaves), Od. ; γῆν ἐπαμησάμενος *having heaped up* a grave, Hdt.

ἐπ-αμβάτήρ, ῆρος, ὁ, poët. for ἐπ-αναβάτης, *one who mounts upon, an assailant*, Aesch.

ἐπ-ἀμείβω, f. ψω, *to exchange, barter*, Il. :—Med. *to come one after another, come in turn to*, Ib.

ἐπαμμένος, Ion. for ἐφημμένος, pf. pass. part. of ἐφάπτω.

ἐπαμμένω, poët. for ἐπαναμένω, Aesch.

ἐπἀμοιβᾰδίς, Adv. (ἐπαμείβω) *interchangeably*, Od.

ἐπἀμοίβιος, ον, (ἐπαμείβω) *in exchange*, h. Hom.

ἐπ-αμπέχω, f. -αμφέξω : aor. 2 -ήμπισχον, inf. -αμπισχεῖν :—*to put on over*, Eur.

ἐπἀμύντωρ, ορος, ὁ, *a helper, defender*, Od.   From

ἐπ-ἀμύνω, f. -ὕνῶ, *to come to aid, defend, assist*, τινί Il., Thuc., etc. :—absol., Il., Hdt., etc.

ἐπ-ἀμφέρω, poët. for ἐπαναφέρω.

ἐπ-ἀμφοτερίζω, f. Att. ιῶ, (ἀμφότερος) of words, *to admit a double sense*, Plat. ; of persons, *to play a double game*, Thuc.

ἐπάν, Conjunct., later form of ἐπήν.

ἐπ-αναβαίνω, f. -βήσομαι, *to get up on, mount*, Ar. ; ἐπαναβεβηκότες *mounted* on horseback, Hdt.   II. *to go up* inland, Thuc. :—*to go up, ascend*, Xen.

ἐπ-αναβάλλω, -βᾰλῶ, *to throw back over* : in Med. *to throw back, defer*, Hdt.

ἐπ-αναβἴβάζω, Causal of ἐπαναβαίνω, *to make to mount upon*, Thuc.

ἐπαναβληδόν, Adv. *thrown over*, Hdt.

ἐπ-αναβοάω, f. -βοήσομαι, *to cry out*, Ar.

ἐπ-ανἀγκάζω, f. άσω, *to compel by force, constrain* to do a thing, c. inf., Aesch., Ar.

ἐπ-ανάγκης, (ἀνάγκη) only in neut. : ἐπάναγκες [ἐστί] *it is necessary*, c. inf., etc. : as Adv. *by compulsion*, Hdt.

ἐπ-αναγορεύω, *to proclaim publicly* :—impers. in Pass., ἐπαναγορεύεται *proclamation is made*, Ar.

ἐπ-ανάγω, f. -άξω, *to bring up* : *to stir up, excite*, Hdt.   II. *to draw back* an army, Thuc.   2. *to bring back to the point*, Xen., Dem.   3. intr. *to withdraw, retreat*, Xen.   III. *to put out to sea*, ναῦς Id. ; and without ναῦς, N. T. : so in Pass. *to put to sea against*, τινι Hdt. ; absol., Id., Thuc.

ἐπ-αναθεάομαι, Dep. *to contemplate again*, Xen.

ἐπ-αναιρέομαι, Med. *to take upon one, enter into*, Lat. *suscipere*, Plat.   2. *to withdraw*, Plut.

ἐπαναίρω, *to lift up*, Xen. :—Med. *to raise one against another*, Soph., Thuc. :—Pass. *to rise up*, Ar.

ἐπ-ανακᾰλέω, f. έσω, *to invoke besides*, Aesch.

ἐπ-ανάκειμαι, Pass. *to be imposed upon* as punishment, τινι Xen.

ἐπ-ανακλαγγάνω, *to give tongue again and again*, Xen.

ἐπ-ανακύπτω, f. ψω, *to have an upward tendency*, Xen.

ἐπ-αναλαμβάνω, f. -λήψομαι, *to take up again, resume, repeat*, Plat. ·   II. *to revise, correct*, Id.   ·

ἐπ-ανᾱλίσκω, *to consume still more*, χρόνον Dem.

ἐπ-αναμένω, poët. -αμμένω, *to wait longer*, Hdt.   II. *to wait for* one, τινά Ar. :—impers., τί μ' ἐπαμμένει παθεῖν; what *is there in store* for me *to suffer?* Aesch.

ἐπ-αναμιμνήσκω, f. -αναμνήσω, *to remind* one *of*, τινά τι Plat.

ἐπ-ανανεόομαι, Med. *to renew, revive*, Plat.

ἐπ-αναπαύομαι, Med. *to rest upon, depend upon*, τινι and ἐπί τινα N. T.

ἐπ-αναπηδάω, f. ήσομαι, *to leap upon*, Ar.

ἐπ-αναπλέω, Ion. -πλώω : f. -πλεύσομαι :—*to put to sea against*, ἐπί τινα Hdt. ; ἐπί τι *for* a purpose, Xen.   2. *to sail back again*, Id.   II. metaph., ἐπαναπλώει ὑμῖν ἔπεα κακά ill language *floats upwards, rises, to* your *tongue*, Hdt.

ἐπ-αναρρήγνῡμι, f. -ρήξω, *to tear open again*, Plut.

ἐπ-αναρρίπτω, f. ψω, *to throw up in the air* : intr. (sub. ἑαυτόν) *to spring high in the air*, Xen.

ἐπανάσεισις, εως, ἡ, *a brandishing against*, Thuc. From

ἐπ-ανασείω, *to lift up and shake*.

ἐπ-ανασκοπέω, f. -ανασκέψομαι, *to consider yet again*, Plat.

ἐπ-ανάστασις, εως, ἡ, *a rising up against, an insurrection*, Hdt., Thuc.; ἐπαναστάσεις θρόνων *rebellions* (i. e. *rebels*) *against the throne*, Sóph.

ἐπαναστήσομαι, fut. med. of ἐπ-ανίστημι.

ἐπ-αναστρέφω, f. ψω, intr. *to turn back upon* one, *wheel round* and *return to the charge*, Ar., Thuc. :—so in Pass., Ar.

ἐπ-ανατείνω, f. -ανατενῶ, *to stretch out and hold up*, Xen.; ἐπ. ἐλπίδας *to hold out* hopes, Id.   II. Med. *to hold over* as a threat, Luc.

ἐπ-ανατέλλω, poët. -αντέλλω, aor. 1 -ανέτειλα, *to lift up, raise*, Eur.   II. intr. *to rise*, of the sun, Hdt. ; *to rise* from bed, Aesch. :—*to appear*, Id., Eur.

ἐπ-ανατίθημι, f. -αναθήσω, *to lay upon*, τί τινι Ar.

ἐπ-ανατρέχω, = ἀνατρέχω, *to recur*, πρός τι Luc.

ἐπ-αναφέρω, poët. -αμφέρω, f. -ανοίσω, *to throw back upon, ascribe, refer*, τι τίνι or εἴς τινα Solon, Ar., etc.   2. *to put into the account*, Dem.   3. *to bring back a message*, in Med., Xen.   II. intr. *to come back, return*, ἐπί τι Plat.   III. Pass. *to rise*, as an exhalation, Plat.

ἐπ-αναχωρέω, f. ήσω, *to go back again, to retreat, return*, Hdt., Att.   Hence

ἐπαναχώρησις, εως, ἡ, *a return*, Thuc.

ἐπ-ανδιπλάζω, poët. for ἐπ-αναδιπλάζω, *to reiterate questions*, Aesch.

ἐπ-άνειμι, (εἶμι, *ibo*) used as fut. of ἐπ-ανέρχομαι, *to go back, return*, Thuc. :—in writing or speaking, *to return* to a point, Hdt., etc.   2. c. acc. rei, *to recapitulate*, Plat.

ἐπ-ανεῖπον, aor. 2 with no pres. in use, *to offer by public proclamation*, Thuc.

ἐπ-ανέρομαι, Ion. -ανείρομαι, Med., *to question again and again*, Hdt. :—Att. aor. 2 ἐπανηρόμην Aesch.,

Ar.; τὸν θεὸν ἐπανήροντο εἰ . . Thuc.   2. *to ask again*, ἐπ. τινά τι Plat.

ἐπ-ανέρχομαι, f. -ανελεύσομαι (but v. ἐπάνειμι) : Dep. with aor. 2 and pf. act. :—*to go back, return*, ἐκ τόπου Thuc. :—in writing or speaking, *to return to* a point, Eur., Xen., Dem.   2. c. acc. rei, *to recapitulate*, Xen.   II. *to go up, ascend*, Id. : *to go up* or *pass* from one place to another, Hdt.

ἐπ-ανερωτάω, f. ήσω, of persons, *to question again*, Xen.   2. of things, *to ask over again*, Plat.

ἐπ-ανέχω, f. -ανέξω, *to hold up, support*, Plut.

ἐπανήκω, *to have come back, to return*, Dem.

ἐπ-ανηλογέω, aor. 1 ἐπανηλόγησα, *to recount, recapitulate*, Hdt. : but perh. ἐπαλιλλόγησα is the true form : v. παλιλ-λογέω.

ἐπ-ανθέω, f. ήσω, *to bloom, be in flower*, Theocr.   II. metaph. of *any thing that forms on the surface*, as a salt crust, Hdt. ; *the down on fruit*, Ar., etc. : generally, *to be upon the surface, shew itself, appear plainly*, Id.   III. *to be bright*, Babr.

ἐπ-ανθίζω, f. σω, *to deck as with flowers, to make bright-coloured*, Luc. :—metaph. *to decorate*, Aesch.

ἐπ-ανθοπλοκέω, *to plait of* or *with* flowers, Anth.

ἐπ-ανθρᾱκίδες, ων, αἱ, (ἀνθρακίς) *small fish for frying, small fry*, Ar.

ἐπ-ανίημι, f. -ανήσω : aor. 1 -ανῆκα :—*to let loose at*, τινά τινι Il.   II. *to let go back, relax*, Dem.   2. intr. *to relax, leave off* doing, c. part., Plat. : absol., ἐπανῆκεν ὁ σῖτος corn *fell in price*, Dem.

ἐπ-ανισόω, f. ώσω, *to make quite equal, to balance evenly, equalise*, τινα πρός τινα Thuc. : absol. *to provide compensation*, Plat.

ἐπ-ανίστημι, f. -αναστήσω : aor. 1 -ανέστησα :—*to set up again*, Plat.   2. *to make to rise against*, Plut.   II. Pass., with fut. med., aor. 2 and pf. act. *to stand up after* another or *at* his *word*, Il. : *to rise from bed*, Ar. : *to rise* to speak, Dem. :—of buildings, *to be raised*, Ar.   2. *to rise up against, rise in insurrection against*, τινι Hdt., Thuc. : absol. *to rise in insurrection*, Id.

ἐπανῑτέον, verb. Adj. of ἐπάνειμι one must return *to* a point, Plat.

ἐπ-άνοδος, ἡ, *a rising up*, Plat.   II. in speaking, *recapitulation*, Id.

ἐπ-ανορθόω, f. ώσω, impf. and aor. 1 with double augm., ἐπηνώρθουν, ἐπηνώρθωσα :—Med., f. -ανορθώσομαι : impf. ἐπηνωρθούμην : aor. 1 ἐπηνωρθωσάμην :—Pass., f. -ανορθωθήσομαι : aor. 1 ἐπηνωρθώθην : pf. ἐπηνώρθωμαι :—*to set up again, restore*, Thuc., etc.   2. *to correct, amend, revise*, Plat. ; so in Med., Id.   Hence

ἐπανόρθωμα, ατος, τό, *a correction*, Plat., Dem. ; and

ἐπανόρθωσις, εως, ἡ, *a correcting, revisal*, Dem.

ἐπ-αντέλλω, poët. and Ion. for ἐπ-ανατέλλω.

ἐπ-άντης, ες, (ἄντα) = ἀνάντης, *steep*, Thuc.

ἐπαντιάζω, f. σω, *to fall in with* others, h. Hom.

ἐπαντλέω, f. ήσω, *to pump over* or *upon, pour over*, Plat. :—Pass. *to be filled*, Id.

ἐπ-ανύω, f. -ύσω [ῠ], *to complete, accomplish*, Hes. :—Med. *to procure*, Soph.

ἐπ-άνω [ᾰ], Adv. (ἄνω) *above, atop, on the upper side* or *part*, Plat. ; ὁ ἐπάνω πύργος *the upper tower*, Hdt.   2. c. gen. *above*, Id., Plat.   II. *above,*

in a book, Lat. *supra*, Xen.
ἐπ-άνωθεν, before a vowel -θε, Adv. *from above, above,* Eur., Thuc. 2. οἱ ἐπ. *men of former time,* Theocr.
ἐπ-άξιος, α, ον, *worthy, deserving of,* τινος Aesch., Eur.:—c. inf., Soph. II. *of things, deserved, meet,* Aesch., Soph., etc.; κυρεῖν τῶν ἐπαξίων *to meet with one's deserts,* Aesch.:—so, Adv. -ίως, Soph. 2. *worth mentioning,* Hdt. Hence
ἐπ-αξιόω, f. ώσω, *to think right, deem right* to do a thing, c. inf., Soph. 2. *to expect, believe,* c. acc. et inf., Id.; ἐπ. τινά *to deem* one *worthy of honour,* Id.
ἐπ-αξόνιος, ον, (ἄξων) *upon an axle,* δίφρος Theocr.
ἐπάξω, Dor. for ἐπήξω, 2 sing. aor. 1 med. of πήγνυμι.
ἐπαοιδή, ἡ, Ion. and poët. for ἐπῳδή.
ἐπ-απειλέω, f. ήσω, *to hold out as a threat* to one, τί τινι Hom., Hdt., Soph.:—c. dat. only, *to threaten,* Il.:—c. inf. *to threaten* to do, Hdt., Soph.; inf. omitted, ὡς ἐπαπείλησεν *as he threatened,* Il.:—Pass. *to be threatened,* Soph.
ἐπαποδύομαι, Med. *to strip and set upon,* τινι Plut.
ἐπ-αποθνήσκω, f. -θανοῦμαι, *to die after,* τινι Plat.
ἐπ-αποπνίγω [ῑ], *to choke besides:*—Pass. aor. 2 opt., ἐπαποπνῑγείης, *may you be choked besides,* Ar.
ἐπάπτω, Ion. for ἐφάπτω.
ἐπᾱπύω, Dor. for ἐπηπύω.
ἐπ-αρά, Ion. -αρή [ᾰ], ἡ, *an imprecation,* Il.
ἐπ-αράομαι: f. -άσομαι, Ion. -ήσομαι: pf. -ήραμαι: Dep.:—*to imprecate curses upon,* τινι Hdt.; ἐπ. λόγον *to utter an imprecation,* Soph.
ἐπ-αραρίσκω, f. -άρσω: aor. -ήραρον:—*to fit to* or *upon, fasten,* τί τινι Il. II. intr. in Ion. pf. ἐπάρηρα, plqpf., *to fit tight* or *exactly, be fitted therein,* Ib.: ἐπάρμενος, η, ον, Ep. aor. 2 pass. part. *prepared,* Hes.
ἐπ-αράσσω, Att. -ττω, f. ξω, *to dash to,* θύραν Plat.
ἐπάρᾱτος, ον, (ἐπαράομαι) *accursed, laid under a curse,* Thuc.; ἐπάρατον ἦν μὴ οἰκεῖν *there was an imprecation against inhabiting it,* Id.
ἐπ-άργεμος, ον, *having a film over the eye:* metaph. *dim, obscure,* Aesch.
ἐπ-άργυρος, ον, *overlaid with silver,* Hdt.
ἐπ-άρδω, f. σω, *to irrigate, refresh,* Luc.
ἐπ-αρήγω, f. ξω, *to come to aid, help,* τινί Hom., Eur.: absol., aor. 1 imper. ἐπάρηξον Aesch.
ἐπάρην [ᾰ], aor. 2 pass. of πείρω.
ἐπᾰρήρα, Ion. pf. of ἐπαραρίσκω:—ἐπαρήρειν plqpf.
ἐπ-ᾰριστερά, ων, *towards the left, on the left hand,* τὰ ἐπαρίστερα as Adv., Hdt. II. metaph. *left-handed, awkward,* French *gauche,* Plut.
ἐπάρκεσις, εως, ἡ, *aid, succour,* Soph., Eur. From
ἐπ-αρκέω, f. έσω, *to ward off* a thing from a person, τί τινι Il. 2. c. acc. rei only, *to ward off, prevent,* Od.; ἐπ. μὴ πεσεῖν, *prohibere quominus,* Aesch. 3. c. dat. pers. only, *to help, assist,* Hdt., Ar.:—rarely c. acc. pers., like ὠφελεῖν, Eur.:—absol., τίς ἄρ' ἐπαρκέσει; *who will aid?* Aesch. II. *to supply, furnish,* τι Id.; ἐπ. τινί τινος *to impart* to him *a share of,* Xen.; c. dat. rei, *to supply with* a thing, Eur. III. absol. *to be sufficient, to prevail,* Soph.
ἐπ-άρκιος, ον, *sufficient,* Anth.

ἐπαρκούντως, Adv. part. of ἐπαρκέω, *sufficiently,* Soph.
ἐπ-άρουρος, ον, (ἄρουρα) *attached to the soil* as a serf, *ascriptus glebae,* Od.
ἐπ-αρτάω, *to hang on* or *over,* ἐπ. φόβον τινί Aesch.: —Pass. *to hang over, impend,* Lat. *imminere,* Dem.
ἐπ-αρτής, ές, (ἀρτάω) *ready for work, equipt,* Od.
ἐπ-αρτύω and -ύνω [ῡ], *to fit on,* Od. II. *to prepare,* Ib.:—Med. *to prepare for oneself,* h. Hom.
ἐπαρχία, ἡ, *the government of a province,* Plut.; and
ἐπαρχικός, ή, όν, *provincial,* Plut. From
ἔπ-αρχος, ον, (ἀρχή) *a commander,* Aesch. 2. *the* Roman *praefectus,* Plut.
ἐπ-άρχω, f. ξω, *to be governor of,* τῆς χώρας Xen.; *of* consular authority, Plut. 2. *to rule in addition to* one's own dominions, Xen. II. Med. in the phrase δεπάεσσιν ἐπάρχεσθαι, *to begin with the cups,* i. e. by offering libations to the gods before the wine was served, Hom. 2. generally, *to offer,* h. Hom.
ἐπᾰρωγή, ἡ, *help, aid,* against a thing, Luc.
ἐπ-ᾰρωγός, ὁ, *a helper, aider,* Od., Eur.
ἐπ-ασκέω, f. ήσω, *to labour* or *toil at, finish carefully,* Od., etc. II. *to practise,* τέχνην Hdt., Ar.
ἐπ-ασσύτερος [ῠ], α, ον, (ἆσσον, ἀσσύτερος) *one upon another, one after another,* mostly in pl., Hom.; in sing., κῦμα ὄρνυτ' ἐπασσύτερον *wave upon wave,* Il.
ἐπασσῠτερο-τρῐβής, ές, (τρίβω) *following close one upon another,* Aesch.
ἐπαστέος, verb. Adj. of ἐπᾴδω, *one must enchant,* Plat.
ἐπ-αστράπτω, f. ψω, *to lighten upon,* Anth.; ἐπ. πῦρ *to flash* fire, Id.
ἐπ-άττω, Att. for ἐπαΐσσω.
ἐπ-αυγάζομαι, Med. *to look at by the light,* Anth.
ἐπ-αυδάομαι, Med. *to call upon, invoke,* Soph.
ἐπαύθην or ἐπαύσθην, aor. 1 pass. of παύω.
ἐπ-αυλέω, f. ήσω, *to accompany on the flute,* c. dat., Luc. 2. Pass. *to be played on the flute,* Eur.
ἐπ-αυλίζομαι, Dep. with aor. med., *to encamp on the field,* Thuc. 2. *to encamp near,* τινι Plut.
ἔπ-αυλις, εως, ἡ, = sq., Hdt.; *a fold,* Il.
ἔπ-αυλος, ὁ, (αὐλή) *a fold* for cattle at night, ἔπαυλοι Od.; heterog. pl. ἔπαυλα Soph. 2. generally, *a dwelling, home,* Aesch., Soph.
ἐπαυξάνω or -αύξω: f. -αυξήσω:—*to increase, enlarge, augment,* Thuc., Dem.:—Pass. *to grow, increase,* Xen.
ἐπ-αύξησις, εως, ἡ, *increase, increment,* Plat.
ἐπαύρεσις, εως, ἡ, *fruition,* Hdt., Thuc. From
ἐπ-αυρέω and -αυρίσκω, aor. 2 -ηῦρον, poët. -αῦρον, Ep. inf. -αυρέμεν:—Med., -αυρίσκομαι: f. -αυρήσομαι: aor. 1 -ηυράμην: aor. 2 -ηυρόμην, Ep. 2 sing. subj. -αύρηαι. (For the Root, v. ἀπ-αυράω.) I. Act. *to partake of, share,* c. gen. rei, Il. 2. *of* physical contact, *to touch, graze,* c. acc., esp. *of* slight wounds, Ib.; also c. gen. *to touch,* Ib. II. Med. *to reap the fruits of* a thing, whether good or bad: 1. c. gen., *in good sense,* Ib., Eur. 2. *in bad sense,* Il.; ἵνα πάντες ἐπαύρωνται βασιλῆος *that all may enjoy their* king, i. e. feel what it is to have such a king, Il.; c. acc. et gen., τοιαῦτ' ἐπηύρω τοῦ φιλανθρώπου τρόπου *such profit didst thou gain from . . ,* Aesch.; and absol. ἐπαυρήσεσθαι ὀΐω *I doubt not he will feel* the consequences, Il.
ἐπαύσας [ῠ], aor. 1 part. of ἐπαύω.

ἐπ-αϋτέω [ῠ], to creak besides, Hes.　　**II.** to shout in applause, Theocr.

ἐπ-αυχένιος, ον, (αὐχήν) on or for the neck, Anth.

ἐπ-αυχέω, aor. 1 -ηύχησα, to exult in or at a thing, c. dat., Soph.　　**2.** c. inf. to be confident that, Id.

ἐπ-αύω, to shout over a thing, c. dat., Aesch.

ἐπ-αφαναίνομαι, Pass. to be withered, ἐπαφανάνθην γελῶν I was quite spent with laughing, Ar.

ἐπ-ἀφάω (v. ἀφάω), to touch on the surface, stroke, Aesch. :—Med., c. gen., Mosch. Hence

ἐπᾰφή, ἡ, touch, touching, handling, Aesch.

ἐπ-ἀφίημι, f. -ἀφήσω, to discharge at, c. dat., Xen.

ἐπ-ἀφρίζω, f. σω, to foam up or on the surface, Mosch.

ἐπ-ἀφρόδῑτος, ον, (Ἀφροδίτη) lovely, charming, Lat. venustus, of persons, Hdt., etc.　　**II.** used to translate Sulla's epithet Felix, favoured by Venus, i. e. fortune's favourite, Plut.

ἐπ-ἀφύσσω, aor. 1 -ήφῠσα, to pour over, Od.

ἐπ-ἀχθής, ές, (ἄχθος) heavy, ponderous, Ar.　　**II.** metaph. burdensome, annoying, grievous, Aesch., Plat.　　**2.** of persons, Thuc., Dem.

ἐπ-ἄχθομαι, Pass. to be annoyed at a thing, c. dat., Eur.

ἐπ-αχνίδιος, α, ον, (ἄχνη) lying like dust upon, Anth.

ἐπεάν, i. e. ἐπεὶ ἄν, Ion. for ἐπήν.

ἐπέβᾰλον, aor. 2 of ἐπιβάλλω.

ἐπέβην, aor. 2 of ἐπιβαίνω: ἐπεβήσετο Ep. 3 sing. aor. 1 med.

ἐπέβρᾰχε, v. sub ἐπιβραχεῖν.

ἐπ-εγγελάω, f. ἀσομαι, to laugh at, exult over a person, c. dat., Soph., Xen.; κατά τινος Soph.

ἐπ-εγείρω, f. -εγερῶ, to awaken, rouse up, τινά Od., Hdt., etc. :—Pass. to be roused, wake up, Hom., in forms ἐπέγρετο, ἐπεγρόμενος (which are from an Ep. aor. ἐπ-ηγρόμην).　　**II.** metaph. to awaken, excite, Solon, Soph.;—Pass., ἐπηγέρθη μῆνις Hdt.

ἐπ-εγήθει, 3 sing. impf. of ἐπι-γηθέω.

ἐπ-εγκάπτω, f. ψω, to snap up besides, Ar.

ἐπ-εγκελεύω, f. σω, to give an order to others, Eur.

ἐπέγνων, aor. 2 of ἐπιγιγνώσκω.

ἐπέγρετο, Ep. 3 sing. aor. 2 pass. of ἐπεγείρω.

ἐπεγρόμενος, Ep. aor. 2 pass. part. of ἐπεγείρω.

ἐπ-εγχέω, f. -χέω, to pour in besides, Aesch., Eur.

ἐπέδρᾰμον, aor. 2 of ἐπιτρέχω.

ἐπέδρη, ἡ, Ion. for ἐφέδρα.

ἐπέδῡν, aor. 2 of ἐπιδύω.

ἐπέδωκα, aor. 1 of ἐπιδίδωμι.

ἐπέην, Ep. 3 sing. impf. of ἔπειμι (εἰμί sum).

ἐπέθηκα, aor. 1 of ἐπιτίθημι.

ἐπεί, Ion. ἐπείτε, also ἐπειδή, conjunct., temporal and causal, like Lat. quum :

A. OF TIME, after that, after (postquam), since, when (quum), with aor. to express a complete action, or impf. to express one not yet complete, ἐπεὶ ὑπηντίαζεν ἡ φάλαγξ καὶ ἡ σάλπιγξ ἐφθέγγατο after the phalanx began to advance and the trumpet had sounded, Xen.　　**2.**= ἐξ οὗ, from the time when, ever since, ἐπείτε παρέλαβον τὸν θρόνον since I came to the throne, Hdt.　　**II.** with Subjunct., ἄν or κε being added, so that ἐπεί becomes ἐπάν, ἐπήν, Ion. ἐπεάν, or ἐπεί κε :—referring to future time, ἐπήν κε ἕλωμεν when we shall have taken the city, Il. :—also whenever, ἐπεί κε λίπῃ ὄστεα θυμός Od.　　**III.** with Opt. without ἄν, re-

ferring to future time, ἐπειδὴ πρὸς τὸ φῶς ἔλθοι after he had come into the light, Plat. :—also whenever, ἐπεὶ πύθοιτο Xen.　　**2.** in oratione obl. after past tenses, representing a subj. in orat. rect., ἐπεὶ διαβαίης, the direct form being ἐπὴν διαβῶ, Id.　　**IV.** with other words, ἐπεὶ τάχιστα, as soon as, Lat. quum primum, Id.; ἐπεὶ εὐθέως Id.; ἐπειδὴ τάχιστα Plat.; ἐπειδὴ θᾶττον Dem.

B. CAUSAL, since, seeing that, with Indic. or Opt. with ἄν, Hom., etc.; with Imp., ἐπεὶ δίδαξόν for teach me, Soph.; ἐπεὶ πῶς ἂν καλέσειας; for how would you call him? Ar. :—sometimes it may be rendered by although, or by else, otherwise.　　**2.** with other Particles, ἐπεὶ ἄρα, ἐπεὶ ἂρ δή since then, Od.; ἐπεί γε, Lat. quandoquidem, since indeed, Hdt.; ἐπείπερ seeing that, Aesch., etc.; ἐπεί τοι since surely, Soph.

ἘΠΕΙΓΩ, impf. ἤπειγον, Ep. ἔπειγον: aor. 1 ἤπειξα :— Med. and Pass., f. ἐπείξομαι: aor. 1 ἠπείχθην: pf. ἤπειγμαι :—to press down, weigh down, Il.　　**2.** to press in pursuit, to press hard, press upon, absol. and c. acc., Hom.　　**II.** to drive on, urge forward, ἐρετμὰ χερσὶν ἔπειγον Od.; of a fair wind, Ib., Soph.　　**2.** to urge on, hurry on a thing, Od., Soph. :—Pass., of a ship, Il. :—Med. to urge on for oneself, τὸν ἐμὸν γάμον Od.; τὴν παρασκευήν Thuc.; ἐπειγομένων ἀνέμων by the force of winds, Il.; ὀπὸς γάλα ἐπειγόμενος συνέπηξεν the fig-juice by its force curdled the milk, Ib.　　**3.** Pass. to hurry oneself, haste to do, c. inf., Ib. :—absol. to hasten, hurry, speed, make haste, Ib., etc. : part., ἐπειγόμενος in eager haste, eagerly, Ib.; c. inf., δῦναι ἐπειγόμενος eager for its setting, Od.; c. gen., ἐπειγόμενος περ ὁδοῖο longing for the journey, Ib.　　**III.** intr. in Act., to hasten to a place, Soph., Eur. :—τὰ ἐπείγοντα necessary matters, Plut.

ἐπειδ-άν, i. e. ἐπειδὴ ἄν, = ἐπεάν, ἐπήν, whenever.

ἐπει-δή or ἐπεὶ δή, a stronger form of ἐπεί.

ἐπ-εῖδον, inf. ἐπ-ιδεῖν, aor. 2 with no pres. in use, ἐφοράω being used instead :—to look upon, behold, Il.; also in Med., Eur., Ar. :—of the gods, to look upon human affairs, Aesch.　　**2.** to continue to see, i. e. to live to see, Hdt. : to experience, χαλεπά Xen.

ἐπεὶ ἦ, not ἐπειή, (εἶ in Hom.) since in truth, Hom.

ἐπείη, 3 sing. opt. of ἔπειμι (εἰμί sum).

ἐπ-εικάζω, f. σω, to make like or liken, δάμαρτα τήνδ' ἐπεικάζων κυρῶ; am I right in identifying her with his wife, i.e. in conjecturing that she is so? Soph.　　**II.** to conjecture, ὡς ἐπεικάσαι as far as one may guess, Hdt., Soph.

ἐπεί-κεν, ἐπεί-κε, or rather ἐπεί κεν, ἐπεί κε, Ep. for ἐπεάν, ἐπήν.

ἐπεικώς, Att. part. of ἐπέοικα.

ἐπ-είληφα or -είλημμαι, pf. act. and pass. of ἐπιλαμβάνω.

ἔπ-ειμι (εἰμί sum), inf. -εῖναι: f. -έσομαι, Ep. -εσσομαι :—to be upon, c. dat., Il., Aesch.; but in Prose with Prep. ἐπὶ τοῦ καταστρώματος Hdt.; ἐπὶ ταῖς οἰκίαις Xen.　　**2.** to be set upon, Hdt. :—of rewards and penalties, to be affixed or attached, Aesch., etc.　　**II.** of Time, to be hereafter, remain, Od.; ἐπεσσόμενοι ἄνθρωποι generations to come, Orac. ap. Hdt. :—also to be at hand, Soph., Xen.　　**III.**

to be set over, Lat. *praeesse*, τισι Hdt.   **IV.**
to be added, be over and above, of numbers, Id.
ἔπειμι (εἶμι *ibo*), inf. -ιέναι, serving iu Att. as fut. of
ἐπέρχομαι :—Ep. 3 sing. impf. **ἐπήϊεν**, pl. **ἐπήϊσαν** and
ἐπῆσαν, Att. **ἐπῄειν**, 3 pl. **ἐπῄεσαν** : f. **ἐπείσομαι**, part.
fem. aor. 1 med. **ἐπιεισαμένη** :—*to come upon* :   **1.**
come near, approach, Od.   **b.** mostly in hostile sense,
to come or *go against, attack, assault*, c. acc., Il. ;
c. dat., Ib., Hdt., Att. ; absol., Hom. ; οἱ ἐπιόντες *the
invaders, assailants*, Hdt. ; but ὁ ἐπιών = ὁ τυχών,
the first comer, Soph.   **c.** *to get on the βῆμα to
speak*, Thuc. : *to come on the stage*, Xen.   **2.** of
events, etc., *to come upon* one, *overtake*, c. acc., Il.,
Aesch. : c. dat. *to come near, threaten*, Il., etc.   **b.**
c. dat. pers. *to come into* one's head, *occur to* one,
Plat., Xen. ;—absol., τοὐπιόν *what occurs to* one,
Plat.   **II.** of Time, *to come on* or *after* : mostly in
part. ἐπιών, οὖσα, όν, *following, succeeding, instant*,
ἡ ἐπιοῦσα ἡμέρα *the coming* day, Hdt. ; ὁ ἐπιών βίοτος
Eur. ; τὰ ἐπιόντα *the consequences*, Dem. ; ὁ ἐπιών *the
successor*, Soph.   **III.** *to go over* a space, *to
traverse, visit*, c. acc., Od., Hdt., etc.   **2.** *to go
over*, i. e. *count over*, Od.
ἐπείνυσθαι, Ion. for ἐφηνύσθαι, inf. med. of ἐφέννυμι.
ἔπειξις, εως, ἡ, (ἐπείγω) *haste, hurry*, Plut.
ἐπεί-περ or **ἐπεί περ**, Conj. *seeing that*, Aesch., etc.
ἐπ-εῖπον, aor. 2 with no pres. in use, *to say besides*,
Hdt., Thuc.
ἐπ-είρομαι, Ion. for ἐπ-έρομαι.
ἐπειρύω, Ion. for ἐπερύω.
ἐπ-ειρωτάω, -είρώτημα, Ion. for ἐπερ-.
ἐπ-εισάγω, f. ξω, *to bring in besides, to bring in
something new*, Aeschin. :—Med. *to introduce besides*,
Plat.   Hence
ἐπεισαγωγή, ἡ, *a bringing in besides, a means of
bringing* or *letting in*, Thuc.   Hence
ἐπ-εισάγώγιμος, ον, *brought in besides* the products of
the country ; τὰ ἐπ. *imported wares*, Plat.
ἐπ-είσακτος, ον, *brought in besides*: *brought in from
abroad, imported, alien, foreign*, Eur., Dem.
ἐπ-εισβαίνω, f. -βήσομαι, *to go into upon*, ἵππῳ εἰς
θάλασσαν Xen. ; ἐπ. ἐς τὴν θάλασσαν *to go into the
sea so as to board ships*, Thuc.
ἐπ-εισβάλλω, f. -βάλῶ, *to throw into besides*, τί τινι
Eur.   **II.** intr. *to invade again*, Thuc.
ἐπεισβάτης [ᾰ], ου, ὁ, (ἐπεισβαίνω) *an additional
passenger, supernumerary on board* ship, Eur.
ἐπ-είσειμι (εἶμι *ibo*), *to come in* or *besides*, in battle,
Hdt. : *to come next upon the stage*, Aeschin.
ἐπ-εισέρχομαι, Dep. with aor. and pf. act. :—*to come
in besides*, Thuc. ; as stepmother, Hdt.   **2.** *to come
in after*, Id.   **3.** *to come into besides*, c. acc., or dat.,
Eur. : of things, *to be imported*, Thuc.   **II.** *to
come into* one's head, *occur to* one, Luc.
ἐπ-εισκυκλέω, f. ήσω, *to roll* or *bring in one upon
another*, Luc. :—Pass. *to come in one upon another*, Id.
ἐπ-εισκωμάζω, f. σω, *to rush in like revellers*, Plat.
ἐπ-εισόδιος, ον, *coming in besides, adventitious*,
Plut.   **II.** as Subst., **ἐπεισόδιον**, τό, *an addition,
episode*, Anth.   From
ἐπ-είσοδος, ἡ, *a coming in besides, entrance*, Soph.
ἐπ-εισπαίω, f. σω, *to burst in*, εἰς τὴν οἰκίαν Ar.

ἐπεισπηδάω, f. -ήσομαι, *to leap in upon*, εἴς τι Xen. ;
absol., Ar.
ἐπ-εισπίπτω, f. -πεσοῦμαι, *to fall in upon*, c. dat.,
Eur., Xen. ; c. acc., Eur. :—absol. *to burst in*,
Soph.   **2.** *to fall upon*, of lightning, Hdt.
ἐπ-εισπλέω, f. -πλεύσομαι, *to sail in after*, Thuc.,
Xen.   **II.** *to sail against, attack*, Thuc.
ἐπ-εισρέω, f. -ρεύσομαι, *to flow in upon* or *besides*,
Plut., Luc.
ἐπ-εισφέρω, f. -οίσω, *to bring in besides* or *next*,
Aesch., Ar. :—Med. *to bring in for oneself*, Thuc. :—
Pass., τὸ ἐπεισφερόμενον πρῆγμα whatever *comes upon
us, occurs*, Hdt.
ἐπ-εισφρέω, aor. 1 -έφρησα, *to introduce besides*, Eur.
ἔπ-ειτα, Ion. -ειτεν, Adv. : (ἐπί, εἶτα) :—marks
sequence, *thereupon*, Lat. *deinde*, when strongly
opposed to the former act or state, with past tenses,
thereafter, afterwards, with future, *hereafter*, Hom.,
etc. ; in narrative, πρῶτον μέν . . , followed by ἔπειτα
δέ . . , Lat. *primum* . . , *deinde* . . , Thuc., etc. ; πρὶν
μὲν . . , ἔπ. δὲ . . Soph. :—with the Article, τὸ ἔπ.
what follows, Id. ; οἱ ἔπ. *future generations*,
Aesch. ; ὁ ἔπ. βίος Plat. ; ἐν τῷ ἔπ. (sc. χρόνῳ)
Id.   **2.** like εἶτα, with a Verb after a part., μειδήσασα
δ᾽ ἔπ. ἐῷ ἐγκάτθετο κόλπῳ she smiled and *then* placed
it in her bosom, Il. ; often to mark surprise or the like,
and then, and yet, ἣ μητρὸς αἷμα ἐκχέας ἔπειτα
οἰκήσεις πατρός ; after shedding thy mother's blood,
wilt thou *yet* dwell in thy father's house ? Aesch.   **3.**
after a Temporal Conjunct. *then, thereafter*, ἐπειδὴ
σφαίρῃ πειρήσαντο, ὠρχείσθην δὴ ἔπ. when *they had
done playing* at ball, *then* they danced, Od.   **4.**
after εἰ or ἤν, *then surely*, εἰ δ᾽ ἐτεὸν ἀγορεύεις, ἐξ ἄρα
δή τοι ἔπ. θεοὶ φρένας ὤλεσαν if thou speakest sooth,
then of a surety have the gods infatuated thee, Il. ; so
when the apodosis is a question, εἰ κελεύετε, πῶς ἂν
ἔπειτ᾽ Ὀδυσῆος λαθοίμην ; how can I *in such a case?*
Ib.   **II.** of Consequence or Inference, *why then,
therefore*, οὐ σύ γ᾽ ἔπειτα Τυδέος ἔκγονός ἐσσι Ib.   **2.**
to begin a story, *well then*, Od.   **3.** in Att. to introduce emphatic questions, *why then* . . ? ἔπ. τοῦ δέει ; Ar.;
to express surprise, *and so forsooth? and so really?*
ἔπειτ᾽ οὐκ οἴει φροντίζειν [τοὺς θεοὺς τῶν ἀνθρώπων] ;
Xen. ; ἔπειτα δῆτα δοῦλος ὢν κόμην ἔχεις ; Ar.
ἐπεί-τε or **ἐπεί τε**, Ion. for ἐπεί.
ἔπειτεν, Ion. for ἔπειτα.
ἐπ-εκβαίνω, f. -εκβήσομαι, aor. 2 -εξέβην, *to go out
upon, disembark*, Thuc.
ἐπ-εκβοηθέω, f. ήσω, *to rush out to aid*, Thuc.
ἐπεκδιδάσκω, f. -ξω, *to teach* or *explain besides*, Plat.
ἐπ-εκδιηγέομαι, f. ήσομαι, Dep. *to explain besides*,
Plat.
ἐπ-εκδρομή, ἡ, *an excursion, expedition*, Thuc.
ἐπ-έκεινα, Adv., for ἐπ᾽ ἐκεῖνα, *on yonder side, beyond*,
Lat. *ultra*, c. gen., Plat., Xen. :—with Article, τὸ
ἐπέκεινα, Att. τοὐπ., or τὰ ἐπ., Att. τἀπ., *the part
beyond, the far side*, τὰ ἐπ. τῆς Εὐρώπης Hdt. ; τοὐπ.
τῆσδε γῆς *beyond* it, Eur. : absol., ἐν τῷ ἐπ. *on the
far side*, Thuc. ; εἰς τὸ ἐπ. Plat.
ἐπεκέκλετο, 3 sing. Ep. aor. 2 of ἐπικέλομαι.
ἐπ-εκθέω, f. -εκθεύσομαι, = ἐπεκτρέχω, Thuc., Xen.
ἐπ-εκπίνω [ῑ], f. -εκπίομαι, *to drink off after*, Eur.

ἐπ-έκπλοος, contr. -πλους, ὁ, a sailing out against, an attack by sea, Thuc.

ἐπ-εκτείνω [ῑ], f. -εκτενῶ, to extend :—Pass. to be extended, reach out towards, τινί N. T.

ἐπ-εκτρέχω, f. -εκδραμοῦμαι: aor. 2 -εξέδραμον :—to sally out upon or against, τινί Xen.

ἐπ-εκφέρω, f. -εξοίσω,·to carry out far, Plut.

ἐπ-εκχωρέω, f. -ήσω, to advance next or after, Aesch.

ἐπελάβον, aor. 2 of ἐπιλαμβάνω.

ἐπελάθον, aor. 2 of ἐπιλανθάνω.

ἐπέλᾰσις, εως, ἡ, a charge, of cavalry, Plut. From

ἐπ-ελαύνω, f. -ελάσω [ᾰ], Att. -ελῶ : pf. -εξελήλακα : —to drive upon, τὰς ἁμάξας ἐπελαύνουσι, i. e. upon the ice, Hdt. 2. to lay metal beaten out into plates over a surface (cf. ἐλαύνω III. 1), ἐπὶ δ' ὄγδοον ἤλασε χαλκόν ll. 3. metaph., ὅρκον ἐπελαύνειν τινί to force an oath upon one, Hdt. II. to ride or lead against, ἵππον στρατίην τινί Xen., Hdt. 2. intr. to march against, Id.; to charge, Id.: of ships, to drive upon a rock, Id. Hence

ἐπελήκεον, impf. of ἐπιληκέω.

ἐπελήλᾰτο, 3 sing. plqpf. pass. of ἐπελαύνω.

ἐπελήλῠθα, pf. of ἐπέρχομαι.

ἐπέλησα, aor. 1 of ἐπιλήθω.

ἐπελθεῖν, aor. 2 inf. of ἐπέρχομαι.

ἐπ-ελίσσω, ἐπ-έλκω, Ion. for ἐφελ-.

ἐπέλλᾰβε, Ep. for ἐπέλαβε, 3 sing. aor. 2 of ἐπιλαμβάνω.

ἐπελπίζω, f. σω, to buoy up with hope, to cheat with false hopes, Thuc. II. intr. = ἐλπίζω, Eur.

ἐπ-έλπομαι, Ep. ἐπι-έλπομαι, (ἔλπω) to have hopes of, to hope that . ., c. inf. fut., Hom., Aesch.

ἐπεμασσάμην, aor. 1 of ἐπιμαίομαι.

ἐπ-εμβάδόν, Adv. step upon step, ascending, Anth.

ἐπ-εμβαίνω, f. -εμβήσομαι, aor. 2 -ενέβην, to step or tread upon, and in pf. to stand upon, c. gen., Il., Soph. : also c. dat., Aesch., etc. ; sometimes c. acc., Eur. 2. to embark on ship-board, Dem. II. c. dat. pers. to trample upon, Lat. insultare, Soph., Eur. 2. τῷ καιρῷ ἐπ. to take advantage of the opportunity, Dem.

ἐπ-εμβάλλω, f. -εμβαλῶ, to put on, τί τινι Eur. : to throw down upon, δόμους Id. 2. to throw against, c. acc., Id. 3. to put in besides, insert, Hdt. :— metaph., σωτῆρα σαυτὸν ἐπεμβάλλεις thou intrudest thyself as saviour, Soph. II. intr. to flow in besides, of rivers, Xen.

ἐπ-εμβάτης [ᾰ], ου, ὁ, one mounted, c. gen., Eur.

ἐπεμβαώς, pf. part. of ἐπεμβαίνω.

ἐπεμηνάμην, aor. 1 of ἐπιμαίνομαι.

ἐπ-εμπηδάω, f. -εμπηδήσομαι, to trample upon, τινί Ar.

ἐπ-εμπίπτω, f. -εμπεσοῦμαι, to fall upon besides, attack furiously, τινί Soph. 2. to fall to, set to work, Lat. incumbere, Ar.

ἐπεναρίζω, f. ξω, to kill one over another, Soph.

ἐπ-ενδίδωμι, f. -δώσω, to give over and above, Aesch.

ἐπένδῠμα, ατος, τό, an upper garment, Plut. From

ἐπ-ενδύνω [ῠ] or -ενδύω, to put on one garment over another, Hdt. :—Pass. to have on over, Plut.

ἐπενεῖκαι, Ion. for ἐπενέγκαι, aor. 1 inf. of ἐπιφέρω.

ἐπενήνεον, impf. of ἐπινηνέω.

ἐπ-ενήνοθε, pf. with no pres. in use, v. ἐνήνοθε.

ἐπ-ενθρώσκω, f. -ενθοροῦμαι : aor. 2 -ενέθορον :— to

leap upon a thing, c. dat., Aesch. ; ἐπ. ἐπί τινα to leap upon one, as an enemy, Soph.

ἐπενθών, Dor. for ἐπελθών, aor. 2 part. of ἐπέρχομαι.

ἐπ-εντᾰνύω : f. ύσω [ῠ], Ep. -ύσσω, to make fast, Od.

ἐπ-εντείνω, f.-εντενῶ, to stretch tight upon: Pass., ἐπεντᾰθείς stretched upon his sword, Soph. II. intr. to press on amain, Ar.

ἐπ-εντέλλω, f. -τελῶ, to command besides, Soph.

ἐπ-εντύνω [ῠ] and -εντύω, to set right, get ready, Il.; χεῖρα ἐπεντύνειν ἐπί τινι to arm it for the fight, Soph. : —Med. to prepare or train oneself for, ἄεθλα Od.

ἐπ-εξάγω [ᾰ], f. ξω, to lead out an army against the enemy, Thuc. 2. intr. (sub. τάξιν) to extend the line of battle (by taking ground to right or left), Id. ; so of ships, to extend their line, Id. Hence

ἐπεξᾰγωγή, ἡ, extension of a line of battle, Thuc.

ἐπ-εξᾰμαρτάνω, f. ήσομαι, to err yet more, one must err yet more, Dem.

ἐπ-έξειμι (εἶμι ibo), serving as Att. fut. to ἐπεξέρχομαι: impf. -ήειν, Ion. 3 pl. -ήϊσαν :—to go out against an enemy, c. dat., Hdt., Thuc. II. to proceed against, take vengeance on, Hdt.: in legal sense, to prosecute, τινι Dem. :—also c. acc. pers., Eur., Dem. III. to go over, traverse, go through in detail, c. acc., Hdt., Ar. 2. to go through with, execute, παρασκευάς, τιμωρίας Thuc.

ἐπ-εξελαύνω, f. Att. -εξελῶ, to send on to the attack, ἱππεῖς Xen.

ἐπ-εξεργάζομαι, f. -εξεργάσομαι, Dep. to effect besides, Dem. 2. to slay over again, Soph.

ἐπ-εξέρχομαι, (v. ἐπέξειμι), to go out against, make a sally against, τινι Hdt., Thuc., etc. ; of a message, ἐπ. τινι to reach him, Hdt. 2. to proceed against, prosecute, τινι Thuc., etc. :—c. acc. pers. to punish, Eur. 3. to proceed to an extremity, Soph., Eur. II. c. acc. loci, to go through or over, traverse, Hdt. 2. to carry out, accomplish, execute, Thuc. ; πᾶν ἐπεξ. to try every course. 3. to discuss, relate or examine accurately or fully, Aesch., Thuc. ; ἀκριβείᾳ περὶ ἑκάστου ἐπ. Id.

ἐπ-εξέτᾰσις, εως, ἡ, a fresh review or muster, Thuc.

ἐπ-εξευρίσκω, f. -εξευρήσω, to invent besides, Hdt.

ἐπ-εξηγέομαι, Dep. to recount in detail, Plut.

ἐπεξῆς, Ion. for ἐφεξῆς.

ἐπ-εξιακχάζω, to shout in triumph over another, Aesch.

ἐπεξόδιος, ον, of a march : ἐπεξόδια (sc. ἱερά), τά, sacrifices before the march of an army, Xen. From

ἐπ-έξοδος, ἡ, a march out against an enemy, Thuc.

ἐπ-έοικε, pf. with no pres. in use, to be like, to suit, c. dat. pers., ὅστις οἷ τ᾽ ἐπέοικε Il. II. mostly impers. it is fit, proper, c. dat. pers. et inf., Ib. ; νέῳ ἐπέοικε κεῖσθαι 'tis a seemly thing for a young man to lie dead, Ib. :—c. acc. pers. et inf., λαοὺς δ᾽ οὐκ ἐπέοικε ἐπαγείρειν Ib. :—c. inf. alone, ἀποδώσομαι ὅσσ᾽ ἐπέοικε [ἀποδόσθαι] Ib. :—part. pl. ἐπεικότα, seemly, fit, Aesch.

ἐπέπεσον, aor. 2 of ἐπιπίπτω.

ἐπεπήγειν, plqpf. of πήγνυμι.

ἐπέπιθμεν, Ep. for ἐπεποίθαμεν, pl. pf. of πείθω.

ἐπέπλως, 2 sing. Ep. aor. 2 of ἐπιπλέω.

ἐπεποίθειν, plqpf. of πείθω.

ἐπεπόνθειν, plqpf. of πάσχω.

ἐπέπταρον, aor. 2 of ἐπιπταίρω.

ἐπεπτάμην, aor. 2 of ἐπιπέτομαι.
ἐπέπυστο, 3 sing. plqpf. of πυνθάνομαι.
ἐπ-έπω, Ion. for ἐφ-έπω.
ἐπ-έραστος, ον, (ἐράω) lovely, amiable, Luc.
ἐπ-εργάζομαι, f. -άσομαι, Dep. to cultivate besides, encroach upon ground consecrated to a god, Aeschin.
ἐπεργᾰσία, ἡ, cultivation of another's land, encroachment upon sacred ground, Thuc. II. the right of mutual tillage on each other's ground, Xen.
ἐπ-ερεθίζω, f. σω, to stimulate, urge on, Plut.
ἐπ-ερείδω, f. -ερείσω, to drive against, drive home, ἔγχος Il.; ἐπέρεισε δὲ ἶν' ἀπέλεθρον put vast strength to it, Hom.:—ἐπ. τὴν φάλαγγά τινι to bring the whole force of the phalanx against, Plut.:—Med., λαίφη προτόνοις ἐπερειδόμεναι staying their sails on ropes, Eur.:—Pass. to lean or bear upon, τινί Ar.: absol. to resist with all one's force, Id.
ἐπ-ερέφω, f. ψω, to put a cover upon, deck, Il.
ἐπ-έρομαι, Ion. -είρομαι, f. -ερήσομαι:—aor. 2 -ηρόμην, inf. -ερέσθαι:—to ask besides or again, Xen. II. to question a person besides about a thing, consult him about, τινά τι Hdt.; to enquire of a god, θεόν Id., Thuc.
ἐπερρώσαντο, 3 pl. aor. 1 of ἐπιρρώομαι.
ἐπερρώσθην, aor. 1 pass. of ἐπιρώννυμι.
ἐπ-ερύω, Ion. -ειρύω: f. ὕσω [ῠ]: aor. 1 -είρυσα, Ep. -έρυσσα:—to pull to a door, Od.: to drag to a place, Ib.:—Med. to draw on one's clothes, Hdt.
ἐπ-έρχομαι, impf. ἐπηρχόμην, but the Att. impf. is ἐπῄειν, and the fut. ἔπειμι: (εἶμι ibo): Dep., with act. aor. 2 ἐπῆλθον, Ep. -ήλυθον, pf. -ελήλυθα: I. to come upon, come near, come suddenly upon, τινί Hom., Hdt.:—to come to for advice, Lat. adire aliquem, Eur. b. in hostile sense, to go or come against, to attack, assault, absol. or c. dat., Il., Eur., etc.; c. acc., τὴν τῶν πέλας ἐπ. to invade it, Thuc.; hence, to visit, reprove, τινα Eur. c. to come forward to speak, Id., Thuc.; also, ἐπ. ἐπὶ τὸν δῆμον Hdt. 2. of conditions, events, etc., to come suddenly upon, ὕπνος ἐπήλυθέ τινα or τινι Od. b. c. dat. pers. to come into one's head, occur to one, ἵμερος ἐπῆλθέ μοι ἐπείρεσθαι Hdt.; or impers. c. inf., καί οἱ ἐπῆλθε πταρεῖν it happened to him to sneeze, Id. II. of Time, to come on, return, of the seasons, Od.; so, νὺξ ἐπῆλθε Ib. 2. to come in after or over another, of a second wife, Hdt. III. to go over or on a space, to traverse, Lat. obire, c. acc., Od.:—of water, to overflow, Hdt.:—so in Att. to go the round of, visit, Soph., Eur. 2. to go through, treat of, recount, Id., Ar. 3. to go through, execute, Thuc.
ἐπερωτάω, Ion. ἐπειρ-, f. ήσω, to inquire of, question, consult, τὸν θεόν Hdt., Thuc., etc.; τινὰ περί τινος Hdt.:—Pass. to be questioned, asked a question, Thuc. 2. c. acc. rei, to ask a thing or about a thing, Hdt.:—c. acc. pers. et rei, ἐπ. τοὺς προφήτας τὸ αἴτιον Id.:—absol. to put the question, Dem. Hence
ἐπερώτημα, Ion. ἐπειρ-, τό, a question, Hdt., Thuc.; and
ἐπερώτησις, Ion. ἐπειρ-, εως, ἡ, a questioning, consulting, Hdt., Thuc.
ἔπεσαν, Ep. for ἐπῆσαν, 3 pl. impf. of ἔπειμι (εἰμί sum).
ἐπεσβαίνω, = ἐπεισβαίνω.
ἐπεσβολία, ἡ, hasty speech, scurrility, Od. From

ἐπεσ-βόλος, ον, (ἔπος, βάλλω) throwing words about, rash-talking, abusive, scurrilous, Il.
ἐπ-εσθίω, f. -έδομαι: aor. 2 ἐπ-έφαγον:—to eat after or with other food, Xen. II. to eat up, Ar.
ἐπεσκεψάμην, aor. 1 med. of ἐπισκοπέω.
ἔπεσον, aor. 2 of πίπτω.
ἐπέσσομαι, aor. 2 of ἐφέπω.
ἐπέσσεται, Ep. for ἐπέσεται, 3 sing. fut. of ἔπειμι (εἰμί sum).
ἐπέσσευον, impf. of ἐπισεύω: 3 pl. med. ἐπεσσεύοντο.
ἐπέσσῦται, ἐπέσσῠτο, 3 sing. pf. and plqpf. of ἐπισεύω.
ἐπεστεώς, Ion. part. pf. of ἐφίστημι.
ἐπέστην, aor. 2 of ἐφίστημι.
ἐπεσφέρω, = ἐπεισφέρω.
ἐπ-εσχάριος, ον, (ἐσχάρα) on the hearth, Anth.
ἐπέσχον, -εσχόμην, aor. 2 act. and med. of ἐπέχω: ἐπέσχεθον, poët.
ἐπ-έτειος, ον, or α, ον, Ion. ἐπ-έτεος:—annual, yearly, Hdt.: ἐπέτειοι τὴν φύσιν changeful as the seasons, Ar. 2. annual, lasting for a year, Hdt., Dem.
ἐπετήσιος, ον, = ἐπέτειος, from year to year, yearly, Od.
ἐπέτρᾰπον, aor. 2 of ἐπιτρέπω: ἐπιτρᾰπόμην, aor. 2 med.: ἐπετράπην, aor. 2 pass.
ἔπευ, Ion. for ἔπου, imperat. of ἕπομαι.
ἐπ-ευθύνω [ῡ], to guide to a point: to administer, Aesch.
ἐπ-ευκλεΐζω, f. σω, to make illustrious, Simon.
ἐπ-ευρίσκω, Ion. for ἐφ-ευρίσκω.
ἐπ-ευφημέω, f. ήσω, to shout assent, Il. 2. c. acc. rei, to sing over or with a thing, c. dat., Aesch., Eur. 3. c. dupl. acc., ἐπ. παιᾶνα Ἄρτεμιν to sing a paean in praise of her, Id.
ἐπ-εύχομαι, f. ξομαι, Dep. to pray or make a vow to a deity, c. dat., Hom., Hdt., etc.:—c. inf. to pray to one that . . , Od., etc.:—c. acc. rei, to pray for, Aesch.: also, c. acc. cogn., ἐπ. λιτάς Soph. II. to imprecate a curse upon, τί τινι Aesch.; c. inf., ἐπεύχομαι [αὐτῷ] παθεῖν Soph.: absol. to utter imprecations, Id. III. to glory over, τινι Il. IV. to boast that, c. inf., h. Hom., Aesch., etc.
ἐπ-εωνίζω, f. σω, to lower the price of a thing, Dem.
ἐπέφαντο, 3 sing. plqpf. pass. of φαίνω.
ἔπεφνον, Ep. redupl. aor. 2 of *φένω.
ἐπεφόρβειν, plqpf. of φέρβω.
ἐπέφρᾰδον, Ep. redupl. aor. 2 of φράζω.
ἐπεφύκον, Ep. for ἐπεφύκεσαν, 3 pl. plqpf. of φύω.
ἐπεχεύατο, 3 pl. Ep. aor. of ἐπιχέω.
ἐπέχυντο, 3 pl. Ep. aor. 2 pass. of ἐπιχέω.
ἐπέχθην, aor. 1 pass. of πέκω.
ἐπ-έχω, f. ἐφ-έξω, aor. ἐπ-έσχον, imperat. ἐπίσχες, inf. ἐπισχεῖν: poët. ἐπ-εσχέθον:—to have or hold upon, πόδας θρόνῳ Il. II. to hold out to, present, offer, οἶνον Ib., Eur.; so c. inf., πιεῖν ἔπεσχον Ar.:—Med., ἐπισχόμενος (sc. τὴν κύλικα) having put it to his lips, Plat. III. to direct towards, τόξα ἐπ. τινί Eur.:—intr. to aim at, attack, τινί Od.; ἐπί τινα Hdt.:—ἐπί τινι Thuc.:—aor. 2 med. part. ἐπισχόμενος having aimed at him, Od. 2. ἐπέχειν (sc. τὸν νοῦν), to intend, purpose, c. inf., Hdt. 3. to stand facing, to face in a line of battle, τινάς Id. IV. to keep in, hold back, check, Lat. inhibere, Il., Soph., etc. 2. ἐπέχειν τινά τινος to stop him, hinder him from it, Id., Eur.: so c. inf., ἐπ. τινὰ μὴ πράσσειν τι

Soph. :—absol. *to stay* proceedings, Thuc.   2. absol. also *to stay, stop, wait, pause*, Od., Hdt.; ἐπίσχες ἔστ᾽ ἂν προσμαθῇς Aesch.; ἐπ. ἕως .. Dem.   b. c. gen. rei, *to stop* or *cease from*, ἐπίσχες τοῦ δρόμου Ar. ; τῆς πορείας Xen. :—so c. inf. *to leave off* doing, Id.   V. *to reach* or *extend over* a space, ἐπτὰ δ᾽ ἐπέσχε πέλεθρα Il. ; ὁπόσσον ἐπέσχε πῦρ so far as the fire *reached*, Ib. ; aor. 2 med., ἐπέσχετο he lay outstretched, Il.   VI. *to occupy* a country, τὴν Ἀσίην Hdt., etc. :—of things, ἡ ὀπώρη ἔπεσχεν αὐτούς *occupied* or *engaged* them, Id.   2. absol. *to prevail, predominate*, of a wind, Id. ; of an earthquake, Thuc.

ἐπ-ηβάω, Ion. for ἐφ-ηβάω.

ἐπή-βολος, ον, poët. for ἐπί-βολος, (ἐπιβάλλω) *having achieved* or *gained* a thing, c. gen., Od., Hdt., Aesch. ; ἐπ. φρενῶν compos mentis, Id.   2. of things, *pertaining to, befitting*, c. dat., Theocr.

ἐπηγκενίδες [ῐ], αἱ, *the long side-planks bolted to the ribs* (σταμῖνες) of the ship, Od. (Prob. from ἐνεγκεῖν.)

ἐπ-ηγορεύω, *to state objections against*, τί τινι Hdt.

ἐπήειν, impf. of ἔπειμι (εἶμι ibo).

ἐπῆεν, Ep. 3 sing. impf. of ἔπειμι (εἰμί sum).

ἐπηετανός, όν, also ἡ, όν, *abundant, ample, sufficient*, Od. ; πλυνοὶ ἐπ. troughs *always full*, Ib. ; ἐπηετανὸν γὰρ ἔχεσκον for they had *great store*, Ib. ; ἐπηεταναὶ τρίχες *thick, full* fleeces, Hes. ; ἐπηεταναὶ πλατάνιστοι Theocr.: —neut. as Adv. *abundantly*, Od. (Deriv. uncertain : that from ἔτος, *sufficient the whole year through*, will not suit all passages and is not necessary in any.)

ἐπήῐεν, -ἤῐσαν, Ep. 3 sing. and pl. impf. of ἔπειμι (εἶμι ibo).

ἐπῆκα, Ion. for ἐφῆκα, aor. 1 of ἐφίημι.

ἐπήκοος, Dor. ἐπάκοος, ον, (ἐπακούω) *listening* or *giving ear to* a thing, c. gen., Aesch., Plat. ; also c. dat., Id.   II. *within hearing, within ear-shot*, εἰς ἐπήκοον Xen.

ἔπηλα, aor. 1 of πάλλω.

ἐπήλθον, aor. 2 of ἐπέρχομαι.

ἐπ-ηλυγάζω, (ἠλύγη) *to overshadow* :—Med., τῷ κοινῷ φόβῳ τὸν σφέτερον ἐπηλυγάζεσθαι *to throw a shade over* (i. e. *conceal*) one's own fear by that of others, Thuc.; ἐπηλυγάζεσθαί τινα *to put him as a screen before one*, Plat.

ἐπήλυθον, Ep. aor. 2 of ἐπέρχομαι.

ἐπήλυξ, υγος, ὁ, ἡ, *overshadowing, sheltering*, Eur.

ἔπηλυς, υδος, ὁ, ἡ, ἔπηλυ, τό, (ἐπήλυθον) *one who comes to a place*, ἐπήλυδες αὖθις *coming back to me*, Soph.   II. *an incomer, stranger, foreigner*, Lat. advena, opp. to αὐτόχθων, Hdt., Aesch.

ἐπηλυσίη, ἡ, (ἐπήλυθον) *a coming over one by spells, a bewitching*, h. Hom.

ἐπήλυσις, εως, ἡ, (ἔπηλυς) *an approach, assault*, Anth.

ἐπηλύτης [ῠ], ου, ὁ, = ἔπηλυς II, Thuc.

ἐπ-ημοιβός, όν, (ἀμείβω) *alternating, crossing*, of door-bolts, Il.   2. *serving for change*, χιτῶνες Od.

ἐπ-ημύω [ῠ], *to bend* or *bow down*, of a corn-field, Il.

ἐπήν, Conj. = ἐπεὶ ἄν, v. ἐπεί A. II.

ἐπήνεον, impf. of ἐπαινέω :—ἐπήνεσα and -νησα, aor. 1.

ἔπηξα, aor. 1 of πήγνυμι.

ἐπ-ηόνιος, ον, (ἠών) *on the beach* or *shore*, Anth.

ἐπ-ηπύω, *to shout in applause*, Il.

ἐπ-ήρᾰτος, ον, (ἐράω) *lovely, charming*, Hom.

ἐπηπείλησα, aor. 1 of ἐπαπειλέω.

ἐπηρεάζω, *to threaten abusively*, Hdt.   II. *to deal despitefully with, act despitefully towards*, τινί Xen., Dem. :—absol. *to be insolent*, Xen. From

ἐπήρεια, ἡ, *despiteful treatment, spiteful abuse*, Lat. contumelia, Dem., etc. ; κατ᾽ ἐπήρειαν *by way of insult*, Thuc.; ἐν ἐπηρείας τάξει Dem. (Deriv. uncertain.)

ἐπ-ήρετμος, ον, (ἐρετμός) *at the oar*, Od.   2. *equipt with oars*, νῆες Ib.

ἐπ-ηρεφής, ές, (ἐρέφω) *overhanging, beetling*, of cliffs, Hom.   II. pass. *covered, sheltered*, Hes.

ἐπῆρα, aor. 1 of ἐπαίρω : ἐπήρθην, pass.

ἐπῆρσα, Ep. aor. 1 of ἐπαραρίσκω.

ἐπῆσαν, Ep. 3 pl. impf. of ἔπειμι (εἶμι ibo).

ἐπησθεῖεν, Ion. 3 pl. opt. aor. 1 of ἐφήδομαι.

ἐπησθόμην, aor. 2 of ἐπαισθάνομαι.

ἐπήσκημαι, pf. pass. of ἐπασκέω.

ἐπητής, οῦ, ὁ, (ἔπος) *affable, gentle*, Od.

ἐπητιασάμην, aor. 1 of ἐπαιτιάομαι.

ἐπ-ήτρῐμος, ον, (ἤτριον) properly, *woven upon, closely woven* : then, *close-thronged, one upon another*, Il.

ἐπητύς [ῠ], ύος, ἡ, (ἐπητής) *courtesy, kindness*, Od.

ἐπήυρον, -όμην, aor. 2 act. and med. of ἐπαυρίσκομαι.

ἐπηχέω, f. ήσω, *to resound, re-echo*, Eur.

ἐπήφῠσα, aor. 1 of ἐπαφύσσω.

ἘΠΙ΄, Prep. with gen., dat., and acc. : Radic. signf. *upon*.

A. WITH GEN. : I. of Place, 1. with Verbs of Rest, *upon* or *on*, κεῖσθαι ἐπὶ χθονός Il. ; ἐφ᾽ ἵππου *on horse-back*, etc. ; ἐπὶ γῆς *upon earth*, Soph. ; ἐπ᾽ ἀγροῦ *in the country*, Od. ; also *at* or *near*, ἐπὶ Λήμνου *off Lemnos*, Hdt., etc. ; with Verbs of motion, the sense is pregnant, ἐπ᾽ ἠπείροιο ἔρυσσαν drew the ship *upon the land and left it there*, Il., etc. ; ἀναβῆναι ἐπὶ τῶν πύργων Xen.   2. not strictly of Place, μένειν ἐπὶ τῆς ἀρχῆς *to remain in* the command, Id. ; ἐπὶ τῶν πραγμάτων *engaged in* business, Dem. : —of ships, ὁρμεῖν ἐπ᾽ ἀγκύρας *to ride at* (i. e. *in dependence on an*) anchor, Hdt.   3. with the person. and reflex. Pron., ἐφ᾽ ὑμέων *by yourselves*, Il. ; ἐφ᾽ αὑτοῦ *by himself*, Thuc. ; αὐτὸς ἐφ᾽ ἑαυτοῦ Xen.   4. with numerals, to denote the *depth* of a body of soldiers, ἐπὶ τεττάρων *four deep*, Id. ; ἐπ᾽ ὀλίγων i. e. *in a long thin file*, Id. ; ἐφ᾽ ἑνός *in single file*, Id.   5. c. gen. pers. *before, in presence of*, Lat. coram, ἐπὶ πάντων Dem.   6. with Verbs of observing, *in*, ὁρᾶν τι ἐπί τινος Xen.   7. of motion *towards*, προτρέποντο ἐπὶ νηῶν Il. ; πλεῖν ἐπὶ Χίου *to sail for* Chios, Hdt. ; ἡ ἐπὶ Βαβυλῶνος ὁδός *the road leading to* B., Xen.   II. of Time, *in the time of*, ἐπὶ προτέρων ἀνθρώπων Il. ; ἐπὶ Κύρου Hdt. ; ἐπ᾽ ἐμοῦ *in my time*, Id.   III. in various Causal senses : 1. *over*, of persons in authority, ὁ ἐπὶ τῶν ὁπλιτῶν, ὁ ἐπὶ τῶν ἱππέων Dem. ; ὁ ἐπὶ τῆς διοικήσεως *the paymaster*, Id.   2. κεκλῆσθαι ἐπί τινος *to be called after* him, Hdt. ; ἡ ἐπ᾽ Ἀνταλκίδου εἰρήνη καλουμένη Xen.   3. of occasions, and the like, ἐπὶ πάντων *on* all occasions, Dem. ; so in phrases which became adverbial, ἐπ᾽ ἴσης (sc. μοίρας) *equally*, Soph.

B. WITH DAT. : I. of Place, *upon*, ἕζεσθαι ἐπὶ δίφρῳ Il. :—with Verbs of Motion, Ib. ; in pregnant construction, πέτονται ἐπ᾽ ἄνθεσιν *fly on to* the flowers *and settle there*, Ib. :—*at* or *near*, ἐπὶ θύρῃσι

Ib. :—on or over, ἐπ' Ἰφιδάμαντι over the body of Iphidamas, Ib.   2. in hostile sense, against, Hdt.   3. towards, in reference to, ἐπὶ πᾶσι Il. ; νόμον τίθεσθαι ἐπί τινι to make a law for his case, whether for or against, Plat.   4. of accumulation, upon, after, ὄγχνη ἐπ' ὄγχνη one pear after another, Od.   5. in addition to, ἐπὶ τοῖσι besides, ἐπὶ τούτοις Att.   6. of position, after, behind, of soldiers, Xen.   7. in dependence upon, in the power of, Lat. penes, ἐπί τινί ἐστι 'tis in his power to do, c. inf., Hdt. ; τὸ ἐπ' ἐμοί as far as is in my power, Xen.   8. of condition or circumstances, Il., etc.; ἐπὶ τῷ παρόντι Thuc.   II. of Time, ἐπὶ νυκτί by night, Il. ; αἰεὶ ἐπ' ἤματι every day, Od.   2. after, ἕκτῃ ἐπὶ δεκάτῃ or τῇ ἕκτῃ ἐπὶ δέκα, on the 16th of the month, ap. Dem.; τὰ ἐπὶ τούτοις, Lat. quod superest, Thuc. ; τοὐπὶ τῷδε Eur.   III. in various Causal senses :   1. of the occasion or cause, ἐπὶ σοί for thee, Il. ; μέγα φρονεῖν ἐπί τινι to be proud at or of a thing, Plat. ; ἀγανακτεῖν ἐπί τινι Xen.   2. of an end or purpose, ἐπὶ δόρπῳ for supper, Od. ; ἐπὶ κακῷ for mischief, Hdt. ; δῆσαι ἐπὶ θανάτῳ Id., Xen. ; ἐπ' ἐξαγωγῇ for exportation, Hdt.   3. of the condition upon which a thing is done, ἐπὶ τούτοις on these terms, Id. ; ἐφ' ᾧ or ἐφ' ᾧτε on condition that, Id. ; ἐπὶ οὐδενί on no account, Id. ; ἐπ' ἴσῃ καὶ ὁμοίᾳ on fair and equal terms, Thuc.   4. of price, ἔργον τελέσαι μεγάλῳ ἐπὶ δώρῳ Il. ; ἐπὶ πόσῳ ; Plat. ; ἐπ' ἀργυρίῳ Dem. ; of the interest payable on money, δανείζεσθαι ἐπὶ τοῖς μεγάλοις τόκοις Id.   5. κεκλῆσθαι ἐπί τινι to be called after, Plat.   6. of persons in authority, ἐπὶ βουσὶν over the kine, Od. ; ἐπὶ ταῖς ναυσίν Xen. ; οἱ ἐπὶ τοῖς πράγμασιν Dem.
C. WITH ACC. :   I. of Place, upon or on to a height, ἐπὶ πύργον ἔβη Il. ; προελθεῖν ἐπὶ τὸ βῆμα Thuc. ; ἀναβαίνειν ἐπὶ τὸν ἵππον Xen. : simply to, ἦλθε θοὰς ἐπὶ νῆας Il., etc. :—metaph. ἐπὶ ἔργα τρέπεσθαι Ib. ; ἐπὶ τὴν τράπεζαν ὀφείλειν to owe to the bank, Dem.   2. up to, as far as, ἐπὶ θάλασσαν Thuc. :—in measurements, πλέον ἢ ἐπὶ δύο στάδια Xen. ; with a neut. Adj., ὅσον τ' ἔπι as far as, Il. ; ἐπὶ πᾶν ἐλθεῖν Xen. ; ἐπὶ σμικρόν, a little way, a little, Soph. ; ἐπ' ἔλαττον, ἐπ' ἐλάχιστον Plat., etc.   3. ἐπὶ πλέον still more, Hdt. ; before, Lat. coram, ἦγον αὐτὸν ἐπὶ τὰ κοινά Id.   4. in Military phrases, ἐπ' ἀσπίδας πέντε καὶ εἴκοσιν, i.e. 25 in file, Thuc.   5. towards, to, ἐπὶ δεξιά, ἐπ' ἀριστερά Hom., etc. :—also in Military phrases, ἐπὶ δόρυ ἀναστρέψαι, ἐπὶ ἀσπίδα μεταβαλέσθαι, to the spear or shield side, i.e. to right or left, Xen. ; ἐπὶ πόδα ἀναχωρεῖν to retire on the foot, i.e. facing the enemy, Xen. ; ἐπὶ μεῖζον, with exaggeration, Thuc. ; ἐπὶ τὰ γελοιότερα so as to provoke laughter, Plat.   6. in hostile sense, against, Il., etc.   7. of extension over a space, ἐπ' ἐννέα κεῖτο πέλεθρα nine acres he lay stretched, Ib. ; ἐπὶ πολύ over a large space, Thuc. :—so in many cases, where we say on, rather than over, δράκων ἐπὶ νῶτα δαφοινός Il.; ἵππους ἐπὶ νῶτον ἐΐσας Ib.   II. of Time, for or during a certain time, πολλὸν ἐπὶ χρόνον Ib. ; ἐπὶ δέκα ἔτη Thuc.   2. up to or till a certain time, ἐπ' ἠῶ καὶ μέσον ἦμαρ Od   III. in various Causal senses :   1. of the object or purpose for which one goes, ἐπὶ Τυδῆ for

(i.e. to bring) tidings of Tydeus, Il. ; ἐλθεῖν ἐπ' ἀργύριον Xen. :—with neut. Pron., ἐπὶ τοῦτο ἐλθεῖν for this purpose, Id. ; ἐπὶ τί ; to what end ? Lat. quorsum ? Ar. ; ἐπὶ τόκον for (i.e. to gain) interest, Dem.   2. as regards, τοὐπ' ἐμέ, τοὐπί σε Eur.   3. of persons set over others, ἐπὶ τοὺς πεζοὺς καθιστάναι ἄρχοντα Xen.   4. according to, by, ἐπὶ στάθμην by the rule, Od.
D. POSITION :—ἐπί may follow its case, when it becomes ἔπι by anastrophé.
E. ABSOL., ἐπί without anastrophé, esp. ἐπὶ δέ, and besides, Hdt.   II. ἔπι, for ἔπεστι, 'tis here, Hom.
F. IN COMPOS. :   I. of Place, denoting Rest upon, as in ἐπίκειμαι, or Motion, upon or over, as in ἐπιβαίνω ; to or to vards, as in ἐπαρίστερος, ἐπιδέξιος ; against, as in ἐπαΐσσω, ἐπιστρατεύω ; up to a point, as in ἐπιτελέω ; over or beyond boundaries, as in ἐπινέμομαι, ἐπεργασία.   2. Extension over a surface, as in ἐπαλείφω, ἐπάργυρος, ἐπίχρυσος.   3. Accumulation or addition, as in ἐπιβάλλω, ἐπίκτητος.   4. Accompaniment, to, with, as in ἐπᾴδω, ἐπαυλέω.   5. Interest, ἐπίτριτος one and ⅓ more, 1 + ⅓, Lat. sesquitertius ; so ἐπιτέταρτος, etc.   II. of Time and Sequence, after, as in ἐπιγίγνομαι.   III. in Causal senses, of Superiority felt over or at, as in ἐπιχαίρω, ἐπιγελάω ; of Authority, over, as in ἐπικρατέω, ἐπιβούκολος ; of Motive, for, as in ἐπιθυμέω, ἐπιθάνατος ; to give force or intensity to the Verb, as in ἐπαινέω, ἐπιμέμφομαι.
ἐπι-άλλομαι, Ep. for ἐφ-άλλομαι, of which Hom. has Ep. aor. 2 part. ἐπιάλμενος.
ἐπι-άλλω, f. -ιαλῶ : aor. 1 -ίηλα [with ῐ] :—to send upon, lay upon, ἑτάροις ἐπὶ χεῖρας ἴαλλεν laid hands upon them, Od. ; ἐπίηλεν τάδε ἔργα brought these deeds to pass, Ib. ; ἐπιαλῶ (sc. τὸ κέντρον) I will lay it on, Ar.
ἐπιανδάνω, Ep. for ἐφανδάνω.
ἐπ-ιαύω, to sleep among, c. dat., Od.   2. to sleep upon, Anth.
ἐπ-ιάχω [ᾰ], to shout out, to shout applause after a speech, Il. : also simply to shout aloud, Ib.
ἐπιβᾱ, for ἐπίβηθι, aor. 2 imper. of ἐπιβαίνω.
ἐπιβάθρα, ἡ, (ἐπιβαίνω) a ladder or steps : metaph. a means of approach, τινός towards .., Plut.
ἐπίβαθρον, τό, (ἐπιβαίνω) a passenger's fare, Lat. naulum, Od.   II. a roosting-place, perch, Anth.
ἐπι-βαίνω, f. -βήσομαι : pf. -βέβηκα : aor. 2 -έβην, imper. ἐπίβηθι or ἐπίβᾱ : aor. 1 med., ἐπεβησάμην (of which Hom. always uses the Ion. form ἐπεβήσετο, imper. ἐπιβήσεο) :   A. In these tenses, intr., to go upon :   I. c. gen. to set foot on, tread or walk upon, Hom., Att. :—also, ἐπ. ἐπί τινος Hdt.   2. to get upon, mount on, νεῶν, ἵππων Hom., Hdt. ;—also, ἐπ. ἐπὶ νηός Hdt.   3. of Time, to arrive at, Plat.   4. metaph., ἐπ' ἀναιδείης ἐπ. to indulge in impudence, Od. ; εὐσεβίας ἐπ. to observe piety, Soph.   II. c. dat. to mount upon, get upon, ναυσί Thuc. :—also, ἐπ. ἐπὶ πύργῳ Hdt.   2. c. dat. pers. to set upon, attack, assault, τινί Xen.   III. c. acc. loci, to light upon, Hom. : simply, to go on to a place, to enter it, Hom.   2. c. acc. to attack, like ἐπέρχομαι, Soph.   3. to mount, νῶ' ἵππων Hes. ; ἵππον Hdt.   IV. absol. to get a footing, Od.   2. to step onwards, advance, Hes., Soph.   3. to mount

on a chariot or on horseback, be mounted, Il., Hdt.:
to go or be on board ship, Il., Soph., etc.
　　B. Causal in aor. 1 act. (ἐπιβιβάζω serves as pres.),
to make one mount, set him upon, ἵππων ἐπέβησε Il.;
πυρῆς ἐπέβησε Ib.　2. metaph., εὐκλέης ἐπίβησον
bring to great glory, Ib.; σαοφροσύνης ἐπέβησαν they
bring him to sobriety, Od.

ἐπι-βάλλω, f. -βᾰλῶ; aor. 2 ἐπέβᾰλον:　I. trans. to
throw or cast upon, Lat. injicere, τρίχας ἐπ. (sc. πυρί)
Il.; ἐπ. ἑωυτὸν ἐς τὸ πῦρ Hdt.　2. to lay on, Lat.
applicare, [ἵπποις] ἐπέβαλλεν ἱμάσθλην Od.; ἐπιβ.
πληγάς τινι Xen.:—to lay on as a tax, tribute, fine or
penalty, τί τινι Hdt., Att.　3. ἐπιβ. σφραγῖδα to
affix a seal, Hdt.　4. to add, ἐπ. (sc. χοῦν) to throw
on more and more earth, Thuc.:—metaph. to mention,
Lat. mentionem injicere rei, τι Soph.　II. intr.
(sub. ἑαυτόν), to throw oneself upon, go straight towards, c. acc., Od.　2. to fall upon or against,
τινί Plat.　3. (sub. τὸν νοῦν) to apply oneself to
a thing, devote oneself to it, c. dat., Plut.: to give
one's attention to, think on, N. T.　4. to follow,
come next, Plut.　5. to belong to, fall to, τινί
Hdt., Dem.:—also impers. c. acc. et inf. it falls to
one's very lot, it concerns one to do a thing, Hdt.:—
τὸ ἐπιβάλλον (sc. μέρος) the portion that falls to one,
Id., N. T.　III. Med., c. gen., to throw oneself
upon, desire eagerly, Il.　2. c. acc. to put upon
oneself, Eur.: metaph. to take possession of, take
upon oneself, Thuc.　IV. in Pass. to be put upon,
ἐπιβεβλημένοι τοξόται archers with their arrows on
the string, Xen.

ἐπιβάς, aor. 2 part. of ἐπιβαίνω.

ἐπίβασις, εως, ἡ, (ἐπιβαίνω) a stepping upon, approaching: a means of approach, access, Plat.; εἰς
τινα ποιεῖσθαι ἐπ. to find a means of attacking one, Hdt.

ἐπι-βάσκω, Causal of ἐπιβαίνω, c. gen., κακῶν ἐπι-
βασκέμεν υἷας Ἀχαιῶν to lead them into misery, Il.

ἐπι-βαστάζω, f. σω, to weigh in the hand, Eur.

ἐπι-βᾰτεύω, f. σω, (ἐπιβάτης) to set one foot upon a
place, c. gen., Plut.:—metaph. to take one's stand
upon, οὐνόματος ἐπ. to usurp a name, Hdt.; ῥήματος
ἐπ. to rely upon a word, Id.　II. to be a soldier
on board ship, Id.

ἐπιβάτης [ᾰ], ου, ὁ, (ἐπιβαίνω) one who mounts or
embarks; 1. ἐπιβάται, οἱ, the soldiers on board
ship, the fighting men, as opp. to the rowers and seamen, Hdt.　b. a merchant on board ship, supercargo, Dem.　2. the fighting man in a chariot, Plat.

ἐπιβᾰτός, ή, όν, (ἐπιβαίνω) that can be climbed, accessible, Hdt.; χρυσίῳ ἐπ. accessible to a bribe, Plut.

ἐπιβείομεν, Ep. for -βῶμεν, aor. 2 subj. of ἐπιβαίνω:
ἐπιβήμεναι, Ep. for -βῆναι, inf.

ἐπιβήσσω, to cough after or besides, Hipp.

ἐπιβήτωρ, ορος, ὁ, (ἐπιβαίνω) one who mounts, ἐπ.
ἵππων a mounted horseman, Od.　2. of male animals,
e. g. a boar, Ib.; a bull, Theocr.

ἐπι-βιβάζω, Causal of ἐπιβαίνω, to put one upon, τοὺς
ὁπλίτας ἐπὶ τὰς ναῦς Thuc.

ἐπι-βιόω, f. -βιώσομαι: aor. 2 -εβίων:—to live over or
after, survive, Thuc.

ἐπι-βλέπω, f. ψομαι, to look upon, look attentively,
εἴς τινα Plat.; τινί Luc.　2. c. acc. to look well at,

observe, Plat.　II. to eye with envy, Lat. inviaere,
c. dat., Soph.　Hence
ἐπίβλεψις, εως, ἡ, a looking at, gazing, Plut.
ἐπίβλημα, ατος, τό, (ἐπιβάλλω) that which is thrown
over, tapestry, hangings, Plut.　II. that which is
put on, a patch, N. T.
ἐπιβλής, ῆτος, ὁ,(ἐπιβάλλω) a bar fitting into a socket,Il.
ἐπι-βλύζω, to well or gush forth, Anth.
ἐπι-βοάω: f. -βοήσομαι, Ion. -βώσομαι:—to call upon
or to, cry out to, ἐπ. τινί ὅτι . . , or c. inf., Thuc.　2.
to utter or sing aloud over, τί τινι Ar.:— so in
Med., Id.　3. to cry out against, τινά: Pass.
ἐπιβοώμενος cried out against, Id.　II. to invoke, call upon, θεούς Od.; so in Med., ἐπιβοᾶσθαι Θέμιν
Eur.:—to call to aid, τὴν στρατιὴν ἐπεβώσαντο Hdt.
ἐπιβοήθεια, ἡ, a coming to aid, succour, Thuc., Xen.
ἐπι-βοηθέω, Ion. -βωθέω, f. σω, to come to aid, to
succour, τινί Hdt., Thuc.
ἐπιβόημα, ατος, τό, (ἐπιβοάω) a call or cry to one, Thuc.
ἐπιβόητος, Ion. -βωτος, ον, (ἐπιβοάω) cried out
against, ill spoken of, Thuc.
ἐπιβολή, ἡ, (ἐπιβάλλω) a throwing or laying on,
ἱματίων Thuc.; χειρῶν σιδηρῶν of grappling-irons,
Id.　2. a hostile attempt, Plut.　II. that which
is laid on, ἐπιβολαὶ πλίνθων layers or courses of
bricks, Thuc.　2. a penalty, fine, Ar., Xen.:—an
impost, public burden, Plut.
ἐπι-βομβέω,f.ήσω,to roar in answer to or after,τινί Luc.
ἐπι-βόσκομαι, Med., c. dat., of cattle, to graze or feed upon,τινί
Batr.　II. to feed among the herd, c. dat., Mosch.
ἐπι-βουκόλος, ὁ, an over-herdsman, Od.
ἐπιβούλευμα, ατος, τό, a plot, attempt, scheme, Thuc.;
and
ἐπιβουλευτής, οῦ, ὁ, one who plots against, c. gen.,
Soph.　From
ἐπι-βουλεύω, f. σω, to plan or contrive against, κακὸν
πόλει Tyrtae.; θάνατόν τινι Hdt.:—c. dat. pers. only,
to plot against, lay snares for, τῇ πόλει Aesch.; τῷ
πλήθει Ar.;—absol. οὑπιβουλεύων the conspirer, Soph.:
—c. acc. rei only, to plan secretly, scheme, plot, τὸν
ἔκπλουν Thuc.　2. c. dat. rei only, to form designs
upon, aim at, πρήγμασι μεγάλοισι Hdt.; τυραννίδι
Plat.　3. c. inf. to purpose or design to do, Hdt.,
Thuc.　II. Pass., with f. med. -εύσομαι: aor. 1
-εβουλεύθην:—to have plots formed against one, to
be the object of plots, Id.　2. of things, to be
designed against, πρᾶγμα, ὃ τοῖς θεοῖς ἐπιβουλεύεται
Ar.; τὰ ἐπιβουλευόμενα plots, Xen.
ἐπι-βουλή, ἡ, a plan against another,a plot, Hdt.,Thuc.
ἐπί-βουλος, ον, (ἐπί, βουλή) plotting against, τινι
Plat.: treacherous, Xen.
ἐπι-βρέμω, to make to roar, Il.:—Med.to roar,Ar.　II.
c. acc. cogn. to roar out, Eur.
ἐπιβρῑθής, ές, falling heavy upon, Aesch.　From
ἐπι-βρίθω [ῑ], f. ίσω, to fall heavy upon, fall heavily,
of rain, Il.; in good sense, ὁπότε δὴ Διὸς ὧραι ἐπι-
βρίσειαν when the seasons produce heavy crops, Od.:
—metaph., of war, Il.; of persons, ἐπέβρισαν ἀμφὶ
ἄνακτα pressed closely round him, Ib.
ἐπι-βροντάω,f.ήσω, to thunder in response,Plut.　Hence
ἐπιβρόντητος, ον, = ἐμβρόντητος, frantic, Soph.
ἐπι-βρύκω [ῠ], f. ξω, to gnash, Anth.

ἐπι-βρύω, f. υσω [ῠ], to burst forth, of flowers, Theocr.

ἐπι-βύω, f. ύσω [ῡ], to stop up, τὸ στόμα τινός Ar. :—Med., ἐπιβύσασθαι τὰ ὦτα to stop one's ears, Luc.

ἐπιβωθέω, Ion. for ἐπιβοηθέω.

ἐπι-βώμιος, ον, (βωμός) on or at the altar, Eur.; ἐπιβώμια ῥέζειν Theocr.

ἐπιβωμιοστᾰτέω, (as if from a Subst. ἐπιβωμιο-στάτης) to stand suppliant at the altar, Eur.

ἐπιβώσομαι, Ion. for ἐπιβοήσομαι, fut. of ἐπιβοάω.

ἐπι-βωστρέω, Ion. and Dor. for ἐπιβοάω, to shout to, call upon, τινά Theocr.

ἐπίβωτος, ον, Ion. for ἐπιβόητος.

ἐπι-βώτωρ, ορος, ὁ, (βώτης) an over-shepherd, Od.

ἐπί-γαιος, ον, (γῆ, γαῖα) upon the earth, τὰ ἐπίγαια the parts on or near the ground, Hdt.

ἐπι-γαμβρεύω, f. σω, (γαμβρός) to marry as the next of kin, γυναῖκα N. T.

ἐπι-γᾰμέω, f. -γαμέσω, Att. -γᾰμῶ :—to marry besides, ἐπ. πόσει πόσιν to wed one husband after another, Eur.; ἐπ. τέκνοις μητρυιὰν to marry and set a step-mother over one's children, Id.

ἐπι-γᾰμία, ἡ, = Lat. connubium, the right of inter-marriage between states, Xen. :—generally, inter-marriage, Hdt., Xen.

ἐπί-γᾰμος, ον, (γαμέω) marriageable, Hdt., Dem.

ἐπιγαυρόομαι, Pass. to exult in, τινι Xen.

ἐπι-γδουπέω, Ep. for ἐπι-δουπέω, to shout in applause, Il.

ἐπί-γειος, ον, (γέα, = γῆ) terrestrial, Plat.

ἐπι-γελάω, f. άσομαι [ᾰ], to laugh approvingly, Lat. arrideo, Il., Att.   II. = ἐπεγγελάω, Luc.

ἐπι-γεραίρω, to give honour to, τινά Xen.

ἐπι-γηθέω, f. ήσω, to rejoice or triumph over, τινι Aesch.

ἐπι-γίγνομαι, Ion. and later -γίνομαι [ῑ]: f. -γενήσομαι: aor. -εγενόμην: pf. -γέγονα: I. of Time, to be born after, come into being after, ἔαρος δ' ἐπιγίγνεται ὥρη other [leaves] come on in spring time, Il.; οἱ ἐπιγιγνόμενοι ἄνθρωποι posterity, Hdt.; οἱ ἐπιγενόμενοι τούτῳ σοφισταὶ who came after him, Id.; τῇ ἐπιγενομένῃ ἡμέρᾳ the following day, Thuc.; χρόνου ἐπιγιγνομένου as time went on, Hdt., Thuc.   II. of events, to come upon, be incident to, Lat. supervenire, χειμών, νὺξ ἐπεγένετο Hdt.; ἄνεμος ἐπιγένετο τῇ φλογί seconded the flame, Thuc.; τὰ ἐπιγιγνόμενα each in succession, Id.   2. to come in after, ἐπὶ τῇ ναυμαχίῃ Hdt.: to come upon, assault, attack, τινι Thuc.   3. to befall, come to pass, Id.

ἐπι-γιγνώσκω, Ion. and later -γίνώσκω: f. -γνώσομαι: aor. 2 ἐπ-έγνων, Ep. 3 pl. subj. ἐπιγνώωσι: pf. ἐπ-έγνωκα:—to look upon, witness, observe, Od., Xen.   II. to recognise, know again, Od., Soph. : to acknowledge or approve a thing, N. T.   2: of things, also to find out, discover, detect, Aesch., Thuc.   III. to come to a decision, to resolve, decide, τι περί τινος Id.

ἐπι-γλωσσάομαι, Att. -ττάομαι, Dep., (γλῶσσα) to throw forth ill language, utter abuse, Aesch. : c. gen. io vent reproaches against a person, Id.

ἐπιγναμπτός, ή, όν, curved, twisted, h. Hom.   From

ἐπι-γνάμπτω, f. ψω, to bend towards one, Il. :—metaph. to bow or bend to one's purpose, Ib.

ἐπι-γνάπτω, f. ψω, to clean clothes : to vamp up, Luc.

ἐπι-γνώμων, ονος, ὁ, ἡ, an arbiter, umpire, judge, c.

gen. rei, Plat. ; ἐπ. τῆς τιμῆς an appraiser, Dem.   II. = συγγνώμων, pardoning, τινι Mosch.

ἐπι-γνωρίζω, f. Att. ιῶ, to make known, announce, Xen.

ἐπίγνωσις, εως, ἡ, (ἐπιγιγνώσκω) full knowledge, N. T.

ἐπιγνώωσι, Ep. 3 pl. subj. aor. 2 of ἐπιγιγνώσκω.

ἐπι-γονή, ἡ, increase, growth, produce, Plut., Luc.

ἐπί-γονος, ον, (ἐπιγίγνομαι) born besides :—as Subst., ἐπίγονοι, οἱ, offspring, posterity, Aesch. : a breed [of bees], Xen.   II. οἱ Ἐπίγονοι the Afterborn, sons of the chiefs who fell in the first war against Thebes, Hdt.   2. the Successors to Alexander's dominions.

ἐπι-γουνίς, ίδος, ἡ, (γόνυ) the part above the knee, the great muscle of the thigh, μεγάλην ἐπιγουνίδα θεῖτο he would grow a stout thigh-muscle, Od.

ἐπιγράβδην, Adv. (ἐπιγράφω) scraping the surface, grasing, Lat. strictim, Il.

ἐπίγραμμα, ατος, τό, (ἐπιγράφω) an inscription, Hdt., Thuc. :—esp. in verse, an epigram, commonly in Elegiacs.   II. a written estimate of damages, Dem.

ἐπιγραμμάτιον, τό, Dim. of ἐπίγραμμα, Plut.

ἐπιγραφή, ἡ, an inscription, στηλῶν on stones, Thuc.

ἐπι-γράφω [ᾰ], f. ψω, to mark the surface, just pierce, graze, ὀϊστὸς ἐπέγραψε χρόα Il.   2. to mark, put a mark on the lot, Ib.—In Hom. the word has not any notion of writing.   II. to write upon, inscribe, Hdt. :—Pass., of the inscription, to be inscribed upon, Id.; also, ἐπεγράφου τὴν Γοργόνα hadst the Gorgon painted on thy shield, Ar.   III. in Att. law phrases :   1. to set down the penalty or damages in the title of an indictment, Id. ; τὰ ἐπιγεγραμμένα the damages claimed, Dem. :—so in Med., Aeschin.   2. to register, Oratt. :—Med. to have one's name registered, Thuc.; also, ἐπεγράψαντο πολίτας had them registered as citizens, Id.   3. προστάτην ἐπιγράψασθαι to choose a patron, and have his name entered in the public register, as all μέτοικοι at Athens were obliged to do, Ar. ;—so, ἐπιγράψασθαί τινα κύριον Dem.   IV. ἐπιγράψαι ἑαυτὸν ἐπί τι to lend one's name to a thing, to endorse it, Aeschin. ;—so in Pass. and Med., to inscribe one's name on, Id.   V. Med. to assume a name, Plut.

ἐπί-γρυπος, ον, somewhat hooked, of the beak of the ibis, Hdt. ; of men, Plat.

ἐπι-δαίομαι, Dep. (δαίω B) to distribute, h. Hom. :—Pass., pf. δέδασμαι, Hes.

ἐπι-δακρύω, f. ύσω [ῡ], to weep over, absol., Ar.

ἐπι-δάμναμαι, Med. to subdue, Anth.

ἐπίδαμος, ον, Dor. for ἐπίδημος.

ἐπι-δᾰνείζω, f. σω, to lend money on property already mortgaged, Dem. :—Med. to borrow on such property, Id.

ἐπι-δαψιλεύομαι, Dep. to lavish upon a person, bestow freely, τί τινι Hdt. ; ἐπιδ. τινί τινος to give him freely of it, Xen. :—metaph. to illustrate more richly, Luc.

ἐπιδέδρομα, pf. 2 of ἐπιτρέχω.

ἐπιδεής, ές, (ἐπιδέομαι) in want of, τινος Plat., Xen. :—Comp., ἐπιδεέστερος ἐκείνων inferior to them, Plat. : Sup. -έστατος Id.

ἐπιδεῖ, impers., v. ἐπιδέω B.

ἐπίδειγμα, ατος, τό, (ἐπιδείκνυμι) a specimen, pattern, Xen., Plat.

ἐπιδείελος, ον, at even, about evening; neut. ἐπιδείελα as Adv., Hes.

ἐπι-δείκνῡμι and -ύω : f. -δείξω : aor. 1 -έδειξα, Ion. -έδεξα :—to exhibit as a specimen, Ar. : generally, to shew forth, display, exhibit, Plat., Xen., etc.   2. Med. to shew off or display for oneself or what is one's own, Hdt., Plat., etc.; ἐπιδείξασθαι λόγον to exhibit one's eloquence, Id. :—absol. to shew off, make a display of one's powers, Ar., Plat., etc.   II. to shew, point out, τί τινι Id. :—c. part. to shew that a thing is, Hdt., etc.; also in Med., Xen.; ἐπ. τινὰ δωροδοκήσαντα to prove that one took bribes, Ar.   2. absol. to lay informations, Id. Hence

ἐπιδεικτέον, verb. Adj. one must display, Xen., etc.

ἐπιδεικτικός, ή, όν, fit for displaying, c. gen., Luc.; ἡ ἐπιδεικτική display, Lat. ostentatio, Plat.   2. ἐπιδ. λόγοι speeches for display, declamations, Dem., etc. : —Adv. -κῶς, Plut.

ἐπ-ιδεῖν, inf. of ἐπ-εῖδον.

ἐπίδειξις, Ion. ἐπίδεξις, εως, ἡ, (ἐπι-δείκνῡμι) a shewing forth, making known, ἐς ἐπίδειξιν ἀνθρώπων ἀπίκετο became notorious, Hdt.   2. an exhibition, display, Thuc.; ἐπ. ποιεῖσθαι to make a demonstration, in military sense, Id.; ἐλθεῖν εἰς ἐπίδειξίν τινι to come to display oneself to one, Ar.   3. a show-off speech, declamation, Thuc., Plat., etc.   II. an example, Lat. specimen, Eur., Aeschin.

ἐπι-δειπνέω, f. ήσω, to eat at second course, eat as a dainty, Ar.

ἐπι-δέκατος, η, ον, one in ten : τὸ ἐπιδέκατον the tenth, tithe, Xen., Dem., etc.

ἐπι-δέμνιος, ον, (δέμνιον) on the bed or bed-clothes, Eur.

ἐπι-δέξιος, ον, towards the right, i.e. from left to right :   I. neut. pl. as Adv., ὄρνυσθ' ἑξείης ἐπιδέξια rise in order beginning with the left hand man, Od. : —hence auspicious, lucky, ἀστράπτων ἐπιδέξια Il.   2. after Hom., on the right hand, Xen.; τἀπιδέξια the right side, Ar.   II. as Adj., of persons, dexterous, capable, clever, Aeschin., etc. Hence

ἐπιδεξιότης, ητος, ἡ, dexterity, cleverness, Aeschin.

ἐπίδεξις, ἡ, Ion. for ἐπίδειξις.

ἐπι-δέρκομαι, Dep. to look upon, behold, τινα Hes.

ἐπι-δεσμεύω, f. σω, to bind up, Anth.

ἐπί-δεσμος, ὁ, an upper or outer bandage, Ar.

ἐπι-δεσπόζω, f. σω, to be lord over, στρατοῦ Aesch.

ἐπιδευής, ές, poët. and Ion. for ἐπιδεής, in need or want of, c. gen., Hom., Hdt. : absol. in want, Il.   II. lacking, failing in a thing, c. gen., Od.; βίης ἐπιδευέες Ὀδυσῆος inferior to U. in strength, Ib.; absol., ἐπιδευέες ἦμεν too weak were we, Ib.

ἐπι-δεύομαι, f. -δευήσομαι, Ep. for ἐπιδέομαι, to be in want of, to lack a thing, c. gen., Hom., Hdt. : to need the help of, c. gen. pers., Il.   II. to be lacking in, fall short of a thing, c. gen., Ib. : also c. gen. pers., κείνων ἐπιδεύεαι ἀνδρῶν fallest short of them, Ib.; or both together, μάχης ἐπιδεύετ' Ἀχαιῶν Ib.

ἐπι-δεύω, to moisten, Anth.

ἐπι-δέχομαι, Ion. -δέκομαι, f. ξομαι, Dep. to admit besides or in addition, Hdt. : to allow of, admit of, Lat. recipere, Dem.

ἐπι-δέω (A), f. -δήσω, to bind or fasten on, τὸν λόφον Ar.; and in Med., λόφους ἐπιδέεσθαι to have crests

fastened on, Hdt.   II. to bind up, bandage : —Pass., ἐπιδεδεμένος τὰ τραύματα with one's wounds bound up, Xen.; ἐπιδεδεμένοι τὴν χεῖρα Id.

ἐπιδέω (B), f. -δεήσω, to want or lack of a number, τετρακοσίας μυριάδας, ἐπιδεούσας ἑπτὰ χιλιαδέων 4,000,000 lacking 7000, Hdt.   II. Med., like Ep. ἐπιδεύομαι, to be in want of, τινος Id., Xen.

ἐπί-δηλος, ον, (εἶδον) seen clearly, manifest, Hdt.   2. distinguished, remarkable, Xen.   II. like, resembling, τινι Ar.

ἐπιδημέω, f. σω, (ἐπίδημος) to live among the people, live in the throng, opp. to living in the country, Od.

ἐπιδημέω, f. ήσω, (ἐπίδημος) to be at home, live at home, opp. to ἀποδημέω, Thuc., Xen.   II. to come home from foreign parts, Id., Aeschin.   III. of foreigners, to stay in a place, ἐν τόπῳ Xen.; ἐπ. τοῖς μυστηρίοις to attend them, Dem. :—absol. to be in town, Plat. Hence

ἐπιδημία, ἡ, a stay in a place, Plat., Xen.

ἐπι-δήμιος, ον, (δῆμος) among the people, ἐπιδήμιοι ἁρπακτῆρες plunderers of one's own countrymen, Il.; πόλεμος ἐπ. civil war, Ib.; ἐπιδήμιον εἶναι to be at home, Od.; ἐπ. ἔμποροι resident merchants, Hdt.

ἐπι-δημιουργοί, οἱ, magistrates sent annually by Doric states to their colonies, Thuc.

ἐπί-δημος, ον, = ἐπιδήμιος, Ar.; ἐπίδαμος φάτις (Dor.) popular, current report, Soph.

ἐπι-διαβαίνω, f. -βήσομαι, to cross over after another, Hdt.; ἐπ. τάφρον Thuc.; ποταμόν Xen.

ἐπι-διαγιγνώσκω, Ion. -γινώσκω, to consider anew, Hdt.

ἐπι-διαιρέω, f. ήσω, to divide anew :—Med. to distribute among themselves, Hdt.

ἐπι-διακρίνω, f. -κρινῶ, to decide as umpire, Plat.

ἐπι-διαρρήγνῡμαι, aor. 2 -διερράγην [ᾰ], Pass. to burst at or because of a thing, Dem.

ἐπι-διατάσσομαι, Med. to add an order, N. T.

ἐπι-διατίθεμαι, Med. to deposit as security, Dem.

ἐπι-διαφέρομαι, Pass. to go across after, Thuc.

ἐπι-διδάσκω, f. ξω, to teach besides, Xen.

ἐπι-δίδωμι, f. -δώσω, to give besides, τί τινι Il., Hdt., Att.   2. to give in dowry, Il., Xen.   3. to give freely, Thuc., Ar. :—esp. to contribute as a 'benevolence,' for state necessities, opp. to εἰσφέρειν (which was compulsory), Xen., Dem.; cf. ἐπίδοσις.   II. Med. to take as witness, θεοὺς ἐπιδώμεθα Il.; (others take it to be ἐπ-ιδώμεθα let us look to the gods).   III. intr. to increase, advance, ἐς ὕψος Hdt.; ἐπὶ τὸ μεῖζον Thuc., etc.; absol. to grow, wax, advance, improve, Id.

ἐπι-δίζημαι, Dep. to inquire besides, to go on to inquire, Hdt.   2. to seek for or demand besides, Id.; so, ἐπιδίζομαι Mosch.

ἐπι-δικάζω, f. ἄσω, to adjudge property to one, of the judge, Dem. :—Pass., ἐπιδεδικασμένου τὸν κλῆρον having had it adjudged to one, Id.   II. Med., of the claimant, to go to law to establish one's claim, Plat.   2. c. gen. to sue for, claim at law, Dem., etc.

ἐπί-δικος, ον, (δίκη) disputed at law :—ἐπίδικος, ἡ, an heiress, whose hand is claimed by her next of kin, Oratt.   2. generally, disputed, Plut.

ἐπι-δῑνέω, f. ήσω, to whirl or swing round before throwing, Hom. :—Med. to turn over in one's mind,

revolve, Od. :—Pass., aor. 1 ἐπεδινήθην, *to wheel about*, as birds in the air, Ib.

ἐπι-διορθόομαι, Med. *to set in order also*, N. T.

ἐπι-διπλοΐζω, *to redouble*, Aesch.

ἐπι-διφριάς, άδος, ἡ, (δίφρος) *the rail upon the car*, Il.

ἐπι-δίφριος, ον, (δίφρος) *on the car*, Od.

ἐπι-διώκω, f. ξω, *to pursue after*, τινά Hdt.

ἐπι-δόντες, pl. nom. aor. 2 part. of ἐπι-δίδωμι : but 2. ἐπ-ιδόντες, of ἐπ-εῖδον.

ἐπί-δοξος, ον, (δόξα) of persons, *likely* or *expected to do* or *be* so and so, c. inf., ἐπίδοξοι πείσεσθαι *likely to suffer*, Hdt. 2. of things, *likely, probable*, c. inf., ἐπ. γενέσθαι Id. : absol., κακὰ ἐπίδοξα *such as might be expected*, Id.

ἐπι-δορπίδιος, ον, = ἐπιδόρπιος, Anth.

ἐπι-δόρπιος, ον, (δόρπον) *for use after dinner*, Theocr.

ἐπίδοσις, εως, ἡ, (ἐπιδίδωμι) *a giving over and above, a voluntary contribution* to the state, *a 'benevolence,'* Dem. II. (ἐπιδίδωμι intr.) *increase, growth, advance, progress*, Plat., etc.

ἐπι-δουπέω, f. ήσω, *to make a noise* or *clashing*, τινι with a thing, Plut.

ἐπιδοχή, ἡ, (ἐπιδέχομαι) *the reception of something new*, Thuc.

ἐπι-δραμεῖν, aor. 2 inf. of ἐπιτρέχω : -δραμέτην, 3 dual.

ἐπι-δράσσομαι, Att. -ττομαι : Dep. *to lay hold of*, τινος Plut.

ἐπιδρομή, ἡ, (ἐπιδραμεῖν) *a sudden inroad, a raid, attack*, Thuc. ; ἐξ ἐπιδρομῆς ἁρπαγή *plundering by means of an inroad*, i. e. *a plundering inroad*, Hdt. ; hence, ἐξ ἐπιδρομῆς *on the sudden, off-hand*, Dem. II. *a place to which ships run in, a landing-place*, Eur.

ἐπίδρομος, ον, (ἐπιδραμεῖν) *that may be overrun*, τεῖχος ἐπ. *a wall that may be scaled*, Il. ; ἐπίδρ. Ζεφύροισι *overrun by the W. winds*, Anth. II. ἐπίδρομος, ὁ, *a cord which runs along the upper edge of a net*, Xen.

ἐπι-δύω, aor. 2 ἐπέδυν, *to set upon* an action, so as to *interrupt* it, Il., N. T.

ἐπιδώμεθα, v. ἐπιδίδωμι II.

ἐπιείκεια, ἡ, (ἐπιεικής) *reasonableness, fairness, equity*, Thuc., Plat., etc. : *clemency, goodness*, Dem.

ἐπι-είκελος, ον, = εἴκελος, *like, resembling*, τινι Hom.

ἐπι-εικής, ές, (εἰκός) *fitting, meet, suitable*, τύμβον ἐπιεικέα *meet in size*, Il. ; ἐπιεικέ' ἀμοιβήν *a fair recompence*, Od. ; ὡς ἐπιεικές *as is meet*, Hom. ; c. inf., ὅν κ' ἐπιεικὲς ἀκούειν *which word it is meet to hear*, Il. II. after Hom., 1. of statements, rights, etc., a. *reasonable, specious, plausible*, Hdt., Thuc. b. *fair, equitable*, τῶν δικαίων τὰ ἐπιεικέστερα προτιθέασι Hdt. ; πρὸς τὸ ἐπ. = ἐπιεικῶς 3, Thuc. 2. of persons, *able, capable*, Hdt., Xen. b. in moral sense, *reasonable, fair, kind, gentle, good*, Thuc., Plat., etc. : τοὐπιεικὲς *goodness*, Soph. III. Adv. -κῶς, Ion. -κέως, *fairly, tolerably, moderately*, Lat. *satis*, Hdt., Ar. ; τέως μὲν ἐπ. *for some little time*, Plat. 2. *probably, reasonably*, Id. 3. *with moderation, kindly*, Plut.

ἐπι-εικτός, ή, όν, (εἴκω) *yielding* : with negat. *unyielding, unflinching*, Hom. ; ἔργα οὐκ ἐπιεικτά *not yielding, harsh*, Od.

ἐπι-ειμένος, Ion. for ἐφ-ειμένος, pf. pass. part. of ἐπιέννυμι.

ἐπιείσομαι, fut. of ἔπειμι (εἶμι *ibo*) :—ἐπιεισάμενος, aor. 1 part.

ἐπι-έλπομαι, Ep. for ἐπ-έλπομαι.

ἐπι-έννυμι, Ep. for ἐφ-έννυμι : aor. 1 ἐπί-εσσα :—Med., Ion. pres. inf. ἐπ-είνυσθαι : aor. 1 ἐπι-εσσάμην :— Pass., 3 sing. pf. ἐπί-εσται ; aor. 1 ἐπι-ειμένος :—*to put on besides* or *over*, Od. : Pass., pf. part. metaph., ἐπιειμένος ἀλκήν *clad in* strength, Il., etc. ; χαλκὸν ἐπιέσται *has* brass *upon* or *over it*, Orac. ap. Hdt. :—Med. *to put on oneself besides, put on* as an *upper* garment or *covering*, Il., Hdt.

ἐπιζάνω, Ion. for ἐφιζάνω.

ἐπι-ζαρέω, = ἐπι-βαρέω, Eur. : v. Ζ ζ.

ἐπι-ζάφελος [ἄ], ον, *vehement, violent*, Il. :—Adv. ἐπιζαφελῶς (as if from ἐπιζαφελής), *vehemently, furiously*, Hom. (The simple ζάφελος never occurs : it is connected with the Prefix ζα-.)

ἐπι-ζάω, Ion. -ζώω, f. -ζήσω, Ion. -ζώσω :—*to overlive, survive*, Hdt., Plat.

ἐπι-ζεύγνυμι and -ύω, f. -ζεύξω, *to join at top*, Hdt., Plut.; simply *to bind fast*, Theocr. 2. *to join to*, Lat. *adjungere*, Aesch. :—metaph. in Pass., μηδ' ἐπιζευχθῇς στόμα φήμαις πονηραῖς nor *let thy mouth be given* to evil sayings, Id.

ἐπι-ζέφυρος, ον, *towards the west* :—the Italian Locrians were called Ἐπιζεφύριοι, Hdt.

ἐπι-ζέω, f. -ζέσω, *to boil over* :—metaph., ἡ νεότης ἐπέζεσε *my youthful spirit boiled over*, Hdt. ; κέντρ' ἐπιζέσαντα, of the poison *working out of the skin*, Soph. ; πῆμα Πριαμίδαις ἐπέζεσε Eur. II. Causal, *to make to boil, heat*, c. acc., ἐπιζεῖν λέβητα Id.

ἐπί-ζηλος, Dor. -ζᾱλος, ον, *enviable, happy*, Aesch.

ἐπι-ζήμιος, Dor. -ζάμιος, ον, (ζημία) *bringing loss upon, hurtful, prejudicial*, Thuc., Xen. 2. *penal* :—ἐπιζήμια, τά, *penalties*, Dem. II. *liable to punishment*, Aeschin.

ἐπι-ζημιόω, f. ώσω, *to mulct*, στατῆρι κατὰ τὸν ἄνδρα *every man a stater*, Xen.

ἐπι-ζητέω, f. ήσω, *to seek after, wish for, miss*, Lat. *desiderare*, τινά Hdt. ; ἐπ. τινά *to make further search* for him, Dem. :—absol., οἱ ἐπιζητοῦντες *the beaters* for game, Xen.

ἐπι-ζώννυμι, f. -ζώσω, *to gird on* :—Pass., ἐπεζωσμέναι *with their clothes girt on* so as to leave the breast bare, Hdt. ; ἐπιζωσμένος ἐγχειρίδιον *girt with a dagger*, Xen.

ἐπιζώω, Ion. for ἐπιζάω.

ἐπίηλα [ῐ], aor. 1 of ἐπιάλλω.

ἐπ-ίημι, Ion. for ἐφ-ίημι.

ἐπι-ήνδανον, Ep. for ἐφήνδανον, impf. of ἐφανδάνω.

ἐπί-ηρα, τά, (ἦρα) *acceptable gifts*, Soph., Anth.

ἐπι-ήρανος, ον, (ἦρα) *pleasing, acceptable*, Od. II. *assisting against*, c. gen., Anth. : *defending, governing*, also c. gen., Id.

ἐπίηρος, ον, v. sub ἐπίηρα.

ἐπι-θάλαμιος, ον, (θάλαμος) *nuptial*, Luc. : as Subst., ἐπιθαλάμιος, ὁ or ἡ (sub. ὕμνος or ᾠδή), *the bridal song*, Theocr., Luc.

ἐπι-θαλασσίδιος, Att. -ττίδιος, ον, = sq., Thuc., Xen.

ἐπι-θαλάσσιος, Att. -ττιος, α, ον, or ος, ον, *lying* or *dwelling on the coast*, Lat. *maritimus*, Hdt., Thuc.

ἐπι-θάνᾰτος, ον, sick to death, at death's door, Dem.

ἐπι-θαρσέω, Att. -ρρέω, to put trust in, τινί Plat.

ἐπι-θαρσύνω [ῡ], Att. -ρρύνω, to cheer on, encourage, τινά Il., Plut.

ἐπι-θαυμάζω, f. σω, to pay honour to, τινά Ar.

ἐπι-θεάζω, = sq., ἐπιθεάζων with imprecations, Plat.

ἐπι-θειάζω, f. σω, to call upon in the name of the gods, to adjure, conjure, Lat. obtestari per deos, Thuc. II. to lend inspiration, τινί Plut. Hence

ἐπιθειασμός, ὁ, an appeal to the gods, Thuc.

ἐπιθείην, aor. 2 opt. of ἐπιτίθημι :—ἐπιθεῖναι, inf.

ἐπιθεῖτε, Ep. for ἐπιθείητε, 2 pl. aor. 2 opt. of ἐπιτίθημι.

ἐπι-θερᾰπεύω, f. σω, to serve diligently, work zealously for, τι Thuc.

ἐπιθές, aor. 2 imper. of ἐπιτίθημι.

ἐπίθεσις, εως, ἡ, (ἐπιτίθημι) a laying on, τῶν χειρῶν N. T. II. (from Med.) a setting upon, attack, Xen.

ἐπι-θεσπίζω, f. σω, of the Pythian Priestess, to prophesy or divine upon, τῷ τρίποδι Hdt.

ἐπιθετέον, verb. Adj. of ἐπιτίθημι, one must impose, δίκην Plat. II. one must set to work at, τινί Id.

ἐπιθετικός, ή, όν, (ἐπιτίθεμαι) ready to attack, θηρίοις Xen.: enterprising, Id.

ἐπίθετος, ον, (ἐπιτίθημι) added, assumed, Plut.

ἐπι-θέω, f. -θεύσομαι, to run at or after, Hdt., Xen.

ἐπιθήκη, ή, (ἐπιτίθημι) an addition, increase, Hes.: acc. as Adv., κἀπιθήκην τέτταρας and 4 drachmas into the bargain, Ar.

ἐπίθημα, ατος, τό, something put on, a lid, cover, Il., Hdt. 2. a sepulchral figure, Plut.

ἐπι-θιγγάνω, aor. 2 ἐπέθῐγον, to touch on the surface, touch lightly, c. gen., Plut.

ἐπι-θοάζω, only in pres., to sit as a suppliant at an altar, Aesch., Eur.

ἐπι-θορῠβέω, f. ήσω, to shout to, Lat. acclamare, in token either of approval or of displeasure, Xen.

ἐπι-θραύω, f. σω, to break besides, Anth.

ἐπιθρέξας, aor. 1 part. of ἐπιτρέχω.

ἐπι-θρηνέω, f. ήσω, to lament over, c. acc., Babr.

ἐπι-θρώσκω· f. -θορούμαι: aor. 2 -έθορον :—to leap upon a ship, c. gen., Il.: also c. dat. to leap (contemptuously) upon, Lat. insultare, τύμβῳ ἐπιθρώσκων Μενελάου Ib. II. to leap over, τόσσον ἐπιθρώσκουσι so far do [the horses] spring at a bound, Ib.

ἐπι-θῡμέω, f. ήσω, (θυμός) to set one's heart upon a thing, lust after, long for, covet, desire, c. gen., Hdt., Aesch., etc.; also c. gen. rerum, Xen.:—c. inf. to desire to do, Hdt., Soph.:—absol. to desire, covet, Thuc., etc.; τὸ ἐπιθυμοῦν τοῦ πλοῦ = ἐπιθυμία, eagerness for it, Id. Hence

ἐπιθύμημα [ῡ], ατος, τό, an object of desire, Xen.; and

ἐπιθῡμητής, οῦ, ὁ, one who longs for or desires a thing, c. gen., Hdt., etc. 2. absol. a lover, Xen.; and

ἐπιθῡμητικός, ή, όν, desiring, coveting, lusting after a thing, c. gen., Plat., etc.:—Adv., ἐπιθυμητικῶς ἔχειν τινός = ἐπιθυμεῖν, Id.

ἐπιθυμία, Ion. -ίη, ή, (ἐπιθυμέω) desire, yearning, longing, Hdt., Plat., etc.; ἐπιθυμίᾳ by passion, opp. to προνοίᾳ, Thuc. 2. c. gen. a longing after a thing, desire of or for it, Id., etc.; so, ἐπ. πρός τι Id.

ἐπιθυλάμᾰτα, ατος, τό, an incense-offering, Soph. From

ἐπι-θυμιάω, f. άσω, to offer incense, Plut.

ἐπ-ῑθύνω [ῡ], to guide straight, direct, Soph.

ἐπῐ-θύω, (θύω A. I. 3) f. ύσω [ῡ] to sacrifice besides or after, Aesch., Eur.:—so in Med., Plut. II. to offer incense on the altar; generally to offer, Ar.

ἐπι-θύω, (θύω B) only in pres., to rush eagerly at, Od. 2. c. inf. to strive vehemently to do a thing, Il., h. Hom. [ἐπῑ-θύω in Hom.]

ἐπι-θωρᾱκίδιον, τό, a tunic worn over the θώραξ.

ἐπι-θωρᾱκίζομαι, Med. to put on one's armour, Xen.

ἐπι-θωΰσσω, f. ξω, to shout aloud, give loud commands, Aesch.; ἐπεθώϋξας τοῦτο didst urge this upon us, Id.

ἐπι-ίδμεν, ον, gen. ονος, = ἐπιΐστωρ, τινός Anth.

ἐπι-ίζομαι, Ion. for ἐφ-έζομαι, Anth.

ἐπι-ίστωρ, ορος, ὁ, ἡ, privy to a thing, c. gen., Od. 2. acquainted with, practised in a thing, c. gen., Anth.

ἐπι-καθαιρέω, f. ήσω, to pull down or destroy besides, Thuc.

ἐπι-καθέζηται, 3 sing. aor. 2 subj. of ἐπικαθίζομαι.

ἐπι-καθεύδω, f. -καθευδήσω, to sleep upon, τινί Luc.

ἐπι-κάθημαι, Ion. -κάτημαι, to sit upon, τινι Hdt., Ar.: to press upon, be heavy upon, ἐπί τινι Id. 2. ἐπ. ἐπὶ τῆς τραπέζης to sit at his counter, of a money-changer, Dem. II. to sit down against a place, besiege, Thuc.

ἐπι-καθίζω, to set upon, τινά ἐπί τι Hipp. :—Med., aor. 2 -καθέζομην, φυλακὴν ἐπεκαθίσαντο had a guard set, Thuc. II. intr. to sit upon, light upon, Plut.

ἐπι-καινόω, f. ώσω, to innovate upon, Aesch.

ἐπι-καίνυμαι, pf. -κέκασμαι, Dep. to surpass, excel, c. acc., Il. II. as Pass. to be adorned or furnished with a thing, c. dat., Ib.

ἐπι-καίριος, ον, = ἐπίκαιρος, Xen. 2. important, οἱ ἐπικαιριώτατοι the most important officers, Id.; c. inf., οἱ θεραπεύεσθαι ἐπικαίριοι those whose cure is all-important, Id.

ἐπί-καιρος, ον, in fit time or place, in season, seasonable, opportune, convenient, Soph., Thuc.; of places, ἐπικαιρότατον χωρίον ἀποχρῆσθαι most convenient to use, Id.; τοὺς ἐπικαίρους τῶν τόπων Dem. :—also c. gen., λουτρῶν ἐπίκαιρος convenient for . . , Soph. 2. of parts of the body, vital, Xen.

ἐπι-καίω, Att. -κάω, f. -καύσω, to light up a place, πῦρ h. Hom.: to burn on an altar, μηρία Hom.

ἐπι-κᾰλᾰμάομαι, (καλάμη) Dep. to glean after the reapers, Luc.

ἐπι-κᾰλέω, f. έσω, to call upon a god, invoke, appeal to, Hdt., Dem.; θεόν τινι to invoke a god, to watch over him, Hdt. :—so in Med., Id., Xen. 2. to invite, Od.; in Med., Hdt. 3. Med. to call in as a helper or ally, Id., Thuc. 4. Med. to call before one, summon, of the Ephors, Hdt. 5. Med. to challenge, Id. II. Pass. to be called by surname, Id.: to be nicknamed, Xen. III. to bring as an accusation against, τί τινι Thuc.; ταῦτ' ἐπικαλεῖς; is this your charge? Ar. :—Pass., τὰ ἐπικαλεύμενα χρήματα the money he was charged with having, Hdt.

ἐπι-κᾰλύπτω, f. ψω, to cover over, cover up, shroud, Hes., Plat. II. to put as a covering over, βλεφάρων ἐπ. φᾶρος Eur.

ἐπικαμπή, ή, (ἐπικάμπτω) the bend, return or angle of a building, Hdt.; ἐπ. ποιεῖσθαι to draw up their army angular-wise, i. e. with the wings advanced at angles

with the centre, so as to take the enemy in flank, Xen.

ἐπικαμπής, ές, curved, curling, Plut., Luc. From

ἐπι-κάμπτω, f. ψω, to bend into an angle:—Pass. to move the wings of an army forward, so as to form angles with the centre and take the enemy in flank, Xen.

ἐπι-καμπύλος [ῠ], ον, crooked, curved, h. Hom.

ἐπί-κάρ, Adv. head-foremost, v. κάρ II.

ἐπι-καρπία, (καρπός) the usufruct of a property, revenue, profit, opp. to the principal (τὰ ἀρχαῖα), Dem.

ἐπι-καρπίδιος, ον, (καρπός) on fruit, Anth.

ἐπι-κάρσιος, α, ον, = ἐγ-κάρσιος, athwart, cross-wise, at an angle, Od., Hdt.; τὰ ἐπικάρσια the country measured along the coast, opp. to τὰ ὄρθια (at right angles to the coast), Id.:—c. gen., τριήρεας τοῦ Πόντου ἐπικαρσίας forming an angle with the current of the Pontus, Id. (Deriv. of -κάρσιος uncertain.)

ἐπι-καταβαίνω, f. -βήσομαι, to go down to a place, Hdt., Thuc. 2. to go down against an enemy, Id.

ἐπι-καταβάλλω, f. -καταβαλῶ, to let fall down at a thing, τὰ ὦτα Xen.

ἐπι-κατάγομαι, Pass. to come to land along with or afterwards, Thuc.

ἐπι-καταδαρθάνω, aor. 2 -έδαρθον, to fall asleep afterwards, Thuc., Plat.

ἐπι-καταίρω, intr. to sink down upon, τινί Plut.

ἐπι-κατακλύζω, to overflow besides, τὴν Ἀσίην Hdt.

ἐπι-κατακοιμάομαι, Dep. to sleep upon, Hdt.

ἐπι-καταλαμβάνω, f. -λήψομαι, to catch up, overtake, τινά Thuc., Plat.

ἐπι-καταλλαγή, ἡ, money paid for exchange, discount, Theophr.

ἐπι-καταμένω, f. -μενῶ, to tarry longer, Xen.

ἐπι-καταπίπτω, f. -πεσοῦμαι, to throw oneself upon, Luc.

ἐπι-κατάρατος, ον, yet more accursed, N. T.

ἐπι-καταρρέω, f. -ρεύσομαι, to fall down upon, τινί Plut.

ἐπι-καταρρήγνυμαι, Pass. to fall violently down, Plut.

ἐπι-καταρριπτέω, to throw down after, Xen.

ἐπι-κατασφάζω, Att. -ττω, f. ξω, to slay upon or over, τινὰ τῷ νεκρῷ, ἑαυτὸν τῷ τύμβῳ Hdt.

ἐπι-κατατέμνω, f. -τεμῶ, to carry the workings of a mine beyond one's boundaries, Dem.

ἐπι-καταψεύδομαι, Dep. to tell lies besides, Hdt., Thuc.

ἐπι-κάτειμι, (εἶμι ibo) to go down into, Thuc.

ἐπι-κατέχω, to detain still, Luc.

ἐπίκαυτος, ον, (ἐπικαίω) burnt at the end, Lat. praeustus, Hdt.

ἐπικάω [ᾱ], Att. for ἐπικαίω.

ἐπί-κειμαι, inf. -κεῖσθαι, Ion. -κέεσθαι, serving as Pass. to ἐπιτίθημι, to be laid upon: I. of doors, to be put to or closed, Od., Theogn. 2. to be placed in or on, c. dat., Hes., Theocr. 3. of islands, νῆσοι ἐπὶ Λήμνου ἐπικείμεναι lying off Lemnos, Hdt.; so, ἐπ. τῇ Θρηίκῃ Id.; αἱ νῆσοι αἱ ἐπικείμεναι the islands off the coast, Thuc. II. to press upon, be urgent in intreaty, Hdt.: to press upon a retreating enemy, c. dat., Id., Ar., etc. 2. to hang over, Lat. imminere, c. dat., Xen.; of penalties, θάνατος ἢ ζημίη ἐπικέεται the penalty imposed is death, Hdt.; ζημία ἐπέκειτο στατήρ Thuc. III. c. acc. rei, ἐπικείμεναι κάρα κυνέας having their heads covered with helmets, Eur.;

πρόσωπον ἐπικείμενος under an assumed character, Plut.

ἐπι-κείρω, Ep. aor. 1 ἐπέκερσα, to cut off, cut down, Il. II. metaph. to cut short, Lat. praecidere, Ib.

ἐπικέκλετο, 3 sing. Ep. aor. 2 of ἐπικέλομαι.

ἐπικέκλιμαι, pf. pass. of ἐπικλίνω.

ἐπι-κελάδέω, f. ήσω, to shout to, shout in applause, Il.

ἐπικέλευσις, εως, ἡ, a cheering on, exhortation, Thuc.

ἐπι-κελεύω, f. σω, to encourage besides, to cheer on again, absol. or c. dat., Eur.; also c. acc. pers., Thuc.

ἐπι-κέλλω, f. -κέλσω, aor. 1 -έκελσα, to bring to shore, Lat. appellere, Od. 2. absol. to run ashore, Ib.

ἐπι-κέλομαι, Ep. 3 sing. aor. 2 ἐπικέκλετο: Dep. to call upon, τινα Il.

ἐπι-κεντρίζω, f. σω, to apply the spur, Anth.

ἐπι-κεράννῦμι, aor. 1 inf. -κρῆσαι (Ep. for -κεράσαι):—to mix in addition, Od.

ἐπι-κερδαίνω, to gain in addition, Plut.

ἐπι-κέρδια, τά, (κέρδος) profit on traffic or business, Hdt.

ἐπι-κερτομέω, f. ήσω, to mock, ἐπικερτομέων in mockery, Hom.; in milder sense, laughingly, Il. II. c. acc. to reproach one, Hdt.:—to tease, plague, Theocr.

ἐπι-κεύθω, f. σω, to conceal, hide, Hom.

ἐπι-κήδειος, ον, (κῆδος) of or at a burial, funeral, Eur.; ἐπικήδειον, τό, a dirge, elegy, Plut.

ἐπικήριος, ον, = sq., Heraclit. ap. Luc.

ἐπίκηρος, ον, (κήρ) subject to death, perishable, Arist.

ἐπικηρῦκεία, ἡ, the sending an embassy to treat for peace, entering into negotiation, Dem.; and

ἐπι-κηρῦκευμα, ατος, τό, a demand by herald, Eur. From

ἐπι-κηρῦκεύομαι, (κηρυκεύω) Dep. to send a message by a herald, τινι or πρός τινα Hdt.; ὥς τινα Thuc.:—c. dat. et inf. to send a message calling on them to do a thing, Id.; ἐπικηρυκευομένων messages being sent, Id. 2. to send ambassadors to treat for peace, to make proposals for a treaty of peace, Hdt., Thuc. 3. of private affairs, to negociate, τινι with one, Dem.

ἐπι-κηρύσσω, Att. -ττω, f. ξω, to announce by proclamation, Aesch., in Pass. 2. of penalties, ἐπ. θάνατον τὴν ζημίαν to proclaim death as the penalty, Xen.; ἐπ. ἀργύριον ἐπί τινι to set a price on his head, Hdt. 3. to offer as a reward, Plut. II. to put up to public sale, Id.

ἐπι-κίδνημι, to spread over, Orac. ap. Hdt.:—Pass., ὕδωρ ἐπικίδναται αἶαν is spread over the earth, Il.; ὅσον τ' ἐπικίδναται ἠώς far as the morning light is spread, Ib.

ἐπι-κινδῦνεύομαι, Pass. to be risked, Dem.

ἐπι-κίνδῦνος, ον, in danger, dangerous, insecure, precarious, Hdt., Thuc., etc.; of a person, ἐπικίνδυνος ἦν μὴ λαμφθείη was in danger of being taken, Hdt.:—Adv. -νως, in a precarious or critical state, Soph.: at one's risk, Thuc.

ἐπι-κίρνημι, Ion. for ἐπικεράννυμι:—Pass., ἐπι-κίρνάμαι Hdt.

ἐπι-κίχρημι, aor. 1 ἐπ-έχρησα, to lend, τί τινι Plut.

ἐπίκλᾱρος, Dor. for ἐπίκληρος.

ἐπίκλαυτος, ον, tearful, Ar.

ἐπι-κλάω [ᾱ], f. άσω [ᾱ], to bend to or besides:—Pass. to be bent double, Luc. II. metaph. to bow down, τινα Plut.:—Pass., ἐπικλασθῆναι τῇ γνώμῃ to be broken in spirit, Thuc.; but also, to be bent or turned to pity, Id.

ἐπι-κλείω, Att. -κλήω, f. -κλείσω, -κλήσω :—to shut to, close, as a door, Ar. :—Med., Luc.

ἐπι-κλείω, to extol or praise the more, Od.

ἐπίκλημα, ατος, τό, (ἐπικαλέω) an accusation, charge, Soph., Eur.

ἐπίκλην, Adv. (ἐπικαλέω) by surname, by name, Plat.

ἐπί-κληρος, Dor. -κλᾶρος, ἡ, an heiress, Ar., etc.

ἐπι-κληρόω, Dor. -κλαρόω, f. ώσω, to assign by lot, τί τινι Dem., etc.

ἐπίκλησις, εως, ἡ, (ἐπικαλέω) a surname or additional name ; the acc. being used absol. as Adv., by surname, 'Αστυάναξ, ὃν Τρῶες ἐπίκλησιν καλέουσι Astyanax, as they call him by surname (his name being Scamandrius), Il., etc. 2. generally, a name, Thuc. 3. an imputation, Id. II. a calling upon, invocation, appeal, Plut., Luc.

ἐπίκλητος, ον, (ἐπικαλέω) called upon, called in as allies, Hdt., Thuc. 2. specially summoned, Hdt. ; ἐπίκλητοι privy-councillors, among the Persians, Id. 3. a supernumerary guest, Lat. umbra, Ar.

ἐπικλῑνής, ές, (ἐπι-κλίνω) sloping, Thuc., Plut.

ἐπι-κλίνω, f. -κλῑνῶ, to put a door to : Pass., pf. part. ἐπικεκλῑμέναι σανίδες closed doors, Il. II. to bend towards, τὰ ὦτα ἐπ. to prick the ears, Xen. :— Pass., κεραῖαι ἐπικεκλιμέναι spars inclined at an angle to the wall, Thuc. 2. intr. to incline towards, πρός τι Dem. III. Pass. to lie over against a place, c. dat., Eur. IV. in Pass., also, to lie down at table, both.

ἐπί-κλοπος, ον, (κλέπτω) thievish, wily, Od., Aesch. 2. c. gen., ἐπίκλοπος μύθων cunning in speech, Hom.

ἐπι-κλύζω, f. ύσω, to overflow, Il., Thuc. 2. metaph. to deluge, swamp, Eur. ; ἐπ. τινὰ κακοῖς Luc. 3. metaph., also, to sweep away, liquidate the expenses, Aeschin. Hence

ἐπίκλυσις, εως, ἡ, an overflow, flood, Thuc.

ἐπι-κλύω, = ἐπακούω, c. acc., Il. ; c. gen., Od.

ἐπι-κλώθω, f. -κλώσω, to spin to one, of the Fates who spun the thread of destiny : then, generally, to assign as one's lot or destiny, Od., Aesch. :—so in Med., Hom. :—Pass., aor. 1 part., τὰ ἐπικλωσθέντα one's destinies, Plat.

ἐπι-κνάω, Ep. 3 sing. impf. ἐπικνῆ (for ἐπέκναε), to scrape or grate over, Il., Ar.

ἐπι-κνέομαι, Ion. for ἐφ-ικνέομαι.

ἐπι-κνίζω, f. σω, to cut on the surface, Anth.

ἐπι-κοιμάομαι, f. ήσομαι, Pass. to fall asleep over a thing, c. dat., Plat., Luc.

ἐπι-κοινόομαι, Med. to consult with, τινι περί τινος Plat.

ἐπί-κοινος, ον, common to many, promiscuous, Hdt. : —sharing equally in a thing, c. gen., Eur. :—neut. pl. ἐπίκοινα as Adv. in common, Id.

ἐπι-κοινωνέω, f. ήσω, to communicate with a person, c. dat., Plat., etc. 2. to have a share of a thing in common with another, τινός τινι Id.

ἐπι-κομπάζω, f. σω, to add boastingly, Eur., Plut.

ἐπι-κομπέω, f. ήσω, = foreg. 1, Thuc. 2. to boast of, τι Id.

ἐπίκοπος, ον, fit for cutting : as Subst., ἐπίκοπον, τό, a chopping-block, Luc. From

ἐπι-κόπτω, f. ψω, to strike upon (i. e. from above), to fell, Od. 2. metaph. to cut short, reprove,

Plut. 3. in Med. to smite one's breast, mourn for another, c. acc., Eur.

ἐπι-κορύσσομαι, Med. to arm oneself against, τινι Luc.

ἐπι-κοσμέω, f. ήσω, to add ornaments to, to decorate after or besides, Hdt. ; θεὰν ἐπ. to honour, celebrate, Ar., Xen.

ἐπί-κοτος, ον, wrathful, vengeful, Aesch. ; ἐπίκοτος τροφᾶς in wrath at the sons he had bred, Id.—Adv. -τως, wrathfully, Id.

'Επικούρειος, ον, Epicurean, Anth. ; οἱ 'Επ. the Epicureans, Luc.

ἐπικουρέω, f. ήσω, (ἐπίκουρος) to act as an ally, Il., Hdt., etc. ; τινι to one, Thuc., etc. II. generally, to aid or help at need, τινί Eur., Ar. : c. dat. rei, νόσοις ἐπικουρεῖν to aid one against them, Xen. ; ἐσθὴς ἐπικουρεῖ τινι does him good service, Id. ; ἐπ. τροφῇ to make provision for it, Aeschin. 2. c. acc. rei, ἐπικουρεῖν τινι χειμῶνα to keep it off from one, Lat. defendere, Xen. Hence

ἐπικούρημα, ατος, τό, protection, χιόνος against snow, Xen. ; and

ἐπικούρησις, εως, ἡ, protection, κακῶν against evils, Eur.

ἐπικουρία, Ion. -ίη, ἡ, (ἐπικουρέω) aid, succour, Hdt., Aesch., etc. II. an auxiliary or mercenary force, Hdt., Thuc.

ἐπικουρικός, ή, όν, (ἐπικουρέω) serving for help, assistant, Plat. 2. of troops, auxiliary, allied, Thuc. : τὸ ἐπικουρικόν, = ἐπικουρία II, Id.

ἐπί-κουρος, ὁ, an assister, ally, Il., Hdt. : of the allies of Troy, Τρῶες ἠδ' ἐπίκουροι Il. 2. in Att., ἐπίκουροι were mercenary troops, opp. to the citizen-soldiers (πολῖται), Thuc., Xen. 3. = δορυφόροι, the body-guards of kings, Hdt. II. as Adj. assisting, aiding, c. dat. pers., Il., Ar., etc. c. gen. rei, defending or protecting against, Soph., Eur., Xen.

ἐπι-κουφίζω, f. Att. ιῶ, to lighten a ship by throwing out part of its cargo, Hdt. : metaph., ἐπ. τοὺς πόνους to lighten one's labours, Xen. :—c. gen. rei, to relieve of a burden, Eur. II. to lift up, support, Soph. : metaph. to lift up, encourage, Xen.

ἐπι-κράζω, pf. -κέκραγα, to shout to or at, τινί Luc.

ἐπι-κραίνω, Ep. -κραιαίνω: f. -κρᾰνῶ: aor. 1 -έκρᾱνα, Ep. -έκρηνα and -εκρήηνα :—to bring to pass, accomplish, fulfil, Il. ; νῦν μοι τόδ' ἐπικρήηνον ἐέλδωρ grant me now this prayer, fulfil it, Ib. :—Pass., χρυσῷ δ' ἐπὶ χείλεα κεκράαντο were finished off with gold, Od.

ἐπί-κρανον, τό, (κράς) that which is put on the head, a head-dress, cap, Eur. II. the capital of a column, Id.

ἐπικράτεια, ἡ, (ἐπικρατής) mastery, dominion, possession, Xen. II. of a country, a realm, dominion, Id.

ἐπι-κρᾰτέω, f. ήσω, to rule over, c. dat., Hom. : absol. to have or hold power, Od. II. to prevail in battle, be victorious, conquer, Il., Hdt. 2. c. gen. to prevail over, get the mastery of an enemy, Id., Att. :—also to become master of, Lat. potiri, τῆς θαλάσσης, τῶν 'Ελλήνων Hdt., etc. 3. generally, to be superior, τῷ ναυτικῷ Thuc. ; κατὰ θάλασσαν Xen.

ἐπι-κρᾰτής, ές, (κράτος) master of a thing: only in Comp., ἐπικρατέστερος superior, Thuc. :—Adv., ἐπικρατέως, with overwhelming might, impetuously, Il., Hes.

ἐπικράτησις, εως, ἡ, victory over, τινος Thuc.

ἐπι-κρεμάννῦμι and -ύω : f. -κρεμάσω [ᾰ], Att. -κρεμῶ : aor. 1 -εκέρᾰσα, Ep. inf. -κρῆσαι :—to hang over, τί τινι Theogn. II. Pass. ἐπικρέμαμαι, aor. 1 -εκρεμάσθην :—to overhang, of a rock, h. Hom., Plut. : —metaph. to hang over, Lat. imminere, Thuc.

ἐπικρήηνον, Eṗ. aor. 1 imper. of ἐπικραίνω :—ἐπικρήνειε 3 sing. opt.

ἐπι-κρῆσαι, Ep. for -κεράσαι, aor. 1 inf. of ἐπικεράννυμι.

ἐπι-κρίνω [ῑ], f. -κρῐνῶ, to decide, determine, Plat., etc.

ἐπ-ίκριον, τό, the yard-arm of a ship, Od.

ἐπι-κροτέω, f. ήσω, to rattle over the ground, Hes.

ἐπί-κροτος, ον, trodden hard, of ground, Xen.

ἐπι-κρούω, f. -σω, to strike upon, ἐπ. χθονὰ βάκτροις to strike the earth with staffs, Aesch.

ἐπι-κρύπτω, f. ψω: aor. 2 ἐπέκρῠφον :—to throw a cloak over, conceal, Aesch., Plat.:—Med. to disguise, Id., Dem.:—to disguise oneself, conceal one's purpose, Thuc., Plut.; ἐπικρυπτόμενος with concealment or secrecy, Xen. Hence

ἐπίκρῠφος, ον, unknown, inglorious, Plut.; and

ἐπίκρυψις, εως, ἡ, concealment, Plut.

ἐπι-κρώζω, to caw or croak at, Ar.

ἐπι-κτάομαι, f.-κτήσομαι, Dep. to gain or win besides, Hdt., Aesch., etc.

ἐπι-κτείνω, f. -κτενῶ, to kill besides or again, Soph.

ἐπι-κτέονται, Ion. for -κτῶνται.

ἐπίκτησις, εως, ἡ, further acquisition, fresh gain, Soph.

ἐπί-κτητος, ον, gained besides or in addition, newly acquired, Hdt., Att.; ἡ γῆ, of the Delta of Egypt, Hdt.

ἐπι-κτῠπέω, f. ήσω, to make a noise after, re-echo, Ar.

ἐπι-κῠδής, ές, (κῦδος) glorious, brilliant, successful, Xen.

ἐπι-κυΐσκομαι, Pass. to become doubly pregnant, Hdt.

ἐπι-κυκλέω, intr. to come round in turn upon, Soph.

ἐπι-κῦμαίνω, f. ᾰνῶ, to flow in waves over, Plut.

ἐπι-κύπτω, f. ψω, to bend oneself or stoop over, ἐπ. ἐπί τι to stoop down to get something, Xen.:—to lean upon, τινί Luc.

ἐπι-κῡρόω, f. ώσω, to confirm, sanction, ratify, Thuc., Xen., etc.; c. inf., Eur.

ἐπι-κυρτόω, f. ώσω, to bend forward, Hes.

ἐπι-κύρω [ῠ], Ep. impf. ἐπίκῦρον, Ep. aor. 1 ἐπίκυρσα or ἐπικύρησα :—to light upon, fall in with, c. dat., Il., Hes. II. c. gen. to have a share of, Aesch.

ἐπι-κυψέλιος, ὁ, (κυψέλη) a guard of beehives, Anth.

ἐπι-κωκύω, f. ύσω [ῠ], to lament over a person or thing, c. acc., Soph.

ἐπι-κωλύω, f. ύσω [ῠ], to hinder, check, Soph., Thuc.

ἐπι-κωμάζω, f. σω, to rush in like revellers, to make a riotous assault, Ar.; εἰς τὰς πόλεις Plat. :—Pass. to be grossly maltreated, Plut.

ἐπι-κωμῳδέω, f. ήσω, to satirise in comedy, Plat.

ἐπί-κωπος, ον, (κώπη) up to the hilt, through and through, Ar.

ἐπιλᾰβεῖν, aor. 2 inf. of ἐπιλαμβάνω.

ἐπι-λαγχάνω, f. -λήξομαι, to obtain the lot, to succeed another, Aeschin. II. pf. ἐπι-λέλογχα, to fall to one's lot next, Soph.

ἐπι-λάζῠμαι, Dep. to hold tight, close, Eur.

ἐπιλᾰθεῖν, -λᾰθέσθαι, aor. 2 inf. act. and med. of ἐπι-λανθάνω.

ἐπιλάθεται [ᾱ], Dor. for -λήθεται.

ἐπι-λαμβάνω, f. -λήψομαι: aor. 2 -έλᾰβον: pf. -είληφα, pass. -είλημμαι :—to lay hold of, seize, attack, as a disease, Hdt., Thuc. :—Pass., τὴν αἴσθησιν ἐπιληφθείς Lat. sensibus captus, Plut. b. of events, to overtake, surprise, interrupt, Thuc. 2. to attain to, reach, Xen.; ἔτη ὀκτὼ ἐπ. to live over eight years, Thuc. 3. to seize, stop, esp. by pressure, Ar., etc.; ἐπ. τινὰ τῆς ὀπίσω ὁδοῦ to stop him from getting back, Hdt. 4. metaph., πολὺν χῶρον ἐπ. to get over much ground, traverse it rapidly, as in Virgil corripere campum, Theocr. II. Med., with pf. pass., to hold oneself on by, lay hold of, catch, c. gen., Hdt., Thuc. 2. to attack, τινος Xen. 3. to make a seisure of, τινος Dem. 4. to lay hold of, get, obtain, προστάτεω a chief, προφάσιος a pretext, Hdt. 5. of place, to gain, reach, τῶν ὀρῶν Plut. 6. to attempt a thing, c. gen., Id. 7. to take up, interrupt in speaking (cf. ὑπολαμβάνω), Plat. : to object to, Xen.

ἐπι-λαμπρύνω, f. ῠνῶ, to make splendid, adorn, Plut.

ἐπίλαμπτος, ον, Ion. for ἐπίληπτος.

ἐπι-λάμπω, f. ψω, to shine after or thereupon, Il., etc.; ἐπιλαμψάσης ἡμέρης when day had fully come, Hdt. 2. to shine upon, c. dat., Plut., Anth.

ἐπιλανθάνομαι, to forget, v. sub ἐπιλήθω.

ἐπι-λεαίνω, aor. 1 -ελέηνα, to smoothe over, ἐπιλεήνας τὴν Ξέρξεω γνώμην, i. e. making it plausible, Hdt.

ἐπι-λέγω, f. ξω, to choose, pick out, select, Hdt. :— Med., τῶν Βαβυλωνίων ἐπελέξατο he chose him certain of the Babylonians, Id. in Att. :—Pass., ἐπιλελεγμένοι or ἐπειλεγμένοι chosen men, Xen. II. to say in addition, add further, Hdt. 2. to call by name, Id. III. in Ion. Gr. also, in Med. 1. to think upon, think over, τι Hdt.; οὐκ ἐπ., nihil curare, Id.; c. inf. to deem or expect that, Id.; so also in Aesch. 2. to con over, read, Hdt.

ἐπι-λείβω, to pour wine over a thing, Il. ; to pour a libation, Od.

ἐπι-λείπω, f. ψω, to leave behind, Od., Xen. 2. to leave untouched, Plat. II. of things, to fail one, Lat. deficere, c. acc. pers.; ὕδωρ μιν ἐπέλιπε the water failed him, Hdt.; ἐπιλείψει με λέγοντα ἡ ἡμέρα Dem. 2. in Hdt., often of rivers, ἐπ. τὸ ῥέεθρον to leave their stream empty, run dry, Hdt.; and so without ῥέεθρον, to fail, run dry, Id. 3. generally, to fail, be wanting, Id., Xen., etc. Hence

ἐπίλειψις, εως, ἡ, a deficiency, lack, Thuc.

ἐπίλεκτος, ον, (ἐπιλέγω) chosen, picked, of soldiers, Xen.

ἐπι-λέπω, f. ψω, to strip of bark, h. Hom.

ἐπι-λεύσσω, to look towards or at, τόσσον τίς τ' ἐπιλεύσσει one can only see so far before one, Il.

ἐπίληθος, ον, causing to forget, τινος Od. From

ἐπι-λήθω, f. σω, to cause to forget a thing, τινος, Od.: —Pass. to be forgotten, pf. part. ἐπιλελησμένος N. T. II. Med. ἐπι-λήθομαι and -λανθάνομαι, f. -λήσομαι: aor. 2 -ελᾰθόμην : with pf. act. -λέληθα and pass. -λέλησμαι: plqpf. -ελελήσμην :—to let a thing escape one, to forget, lose thought of, c. gen., ὅπως Ἰθάκης ἐπιλήσεται (Ep. for -ηται) Od.; so Hdt., Att. :—also c. acc., Hdt., Eur., etc. :—c. inf., Ar., Plat. 2. to forget wilfully, ἑκὼν ἐπιλήθομαι Hdt.

ἐπι-ληΐς, ΐδος, ἡ, (λεία) obtained as booty, Xen.

ἐπι-ληκέω, to beat time to dancers, Od.

ἐπι-ληκὔθίστρια, ἡ, (λήκυθος) nickname of the Tragic muse, *the bombastical*, Anth.

ἐπίληπτος, Ion. ἐπίλαμπτος, ον, (ἐπιλαμβάνω) *caught* or *detected* in anything, Soph.; c. part., ἐπίλαμπτος ἀφάσσουσα *caught* in the act of feeling, Hdt.   II. *suffering*, Dem.

ἐπιλήπτωρ, ορος, ὁ, *a censurer*, Timo ap. Plut.

ἐπιλησμονή, ἡ, *forgetfulness*, N. T.   From

ἐπιλήσμων, ον, gen. ονος, (ἐπιλήθομαι) *apt to forget*, *forgetful*, Ar., Plat., etc.; c. gen. rei, Xen., in Comp. ἐπιλησμονέστερος, whereas Ar. has ἐπιλησμότατος (as if from ἐπίλησμος).

ἐπιλήσομαι, f. med. of ἐπιλήθομαι.

ἐπίληψις, εως, ἡ, *a seizing*, *seizure*, Plat.   II. *epilepsy*, Lat. *morbus comitialis*.

ἐπι-λίγδην, Adv. *grazing*, Il.

ἐπι-λιμνάζομαι, (λίμνη) Pass. *to be overflowed*, Plut.

ἐπι-λῑπαίνω, *to make fat* or *sleek*, Plut.

ἐπιλῑπής, ές, (ἐπιλείπω II) = ἐλλιπής, Plut.

ἐπι-λιχμάω, (λιχμάομαι) = ἐπιλείχω, Babr.

ἐπ-ιλλίζω, only in pres., *to make signs to* one *by winking*, Od.: *to wink roguishly*, h. Hom.

ἐπι-λογίζομαι, f. Att. -λογιοῦμαι: aor. 1 -ελογισάμην and -ελογίσθην: Dep.:—*to reckon over*, *conclude*, ὅτι . . Hdt.; ἐπ. τι *to take account* of a thing, Xen.

ἐπίλογος, ὁ, (ἐπιλέγω) *a conclusion*, *inference*, Hdt.

ἐπί-λογχος, ον, (λόγχη) *barbed*, Eur.

ἐπί-λοιπος, ον, *still left*, *remaining*, Hdt., Att.   2. of Time, *to come*, *future*, χρόνος Hdt., Plat., etc.

ἐπι-λῡπέω, f. ήσω, *to annoy* or *offend besides*, τινα Hdt.

ἐπίλῡσις, εως, ἡ, *release from* a thing, c. gen., Aesch.

ἐπι-λύω, f. -λύσω [ῡ], *to loose*, *untie*, Theocr.: *to set free*, *release*, Luc.: so in Med., Plat.; ἐπιλύεσθαι ἐπιστολάς *to open* letters, Hdt.

ἐπι-λωβεύω, *to mock at* a thing, Od.

ἐπι-μάζιος, ον, (μαζός) = ἐπιμαστίδιος, Anth.

ἐπι-μαίνομαι, Pass., with aor. 2 -εμάνην [ᾰ], but also med. -εμηνάμην: pf. -μέμηνα:—*to be mad after*, *dote upon*, c. dat., Il., Ar.:—absol. *to be mad*, *to rage*, Aesch.   II. *to attack furiously*, τινι Anth.

ἐπι-μαίομαι: Ep. f. -μάσσομαι, aor. 1 -εμασσάμην: Dep.:—*to strive after*, *seek to obtain*, *aim at*, c. gen., σκοπέλου ἐπιμαίεο *make for* (i. e. *steer for*) the rock, Od.; metaph. ἐπιμαίεο νόστου *strive after* a return, Ib.   II. c. acc. *to lay hold of*, *grasp*, ἐπεμαίετο κώπην he clutched his sword-hilt, Ib.; χείρ' (i. e. χειρί) ἐπιμασσάμενος *having clutched* [the sword] with my hand, Ib.   2. *to handle*, *feel*, Ib.; ἕλκος ἰητὴρ ἐπιμάσσεται *will probe* the wound, Ib.

ἐπι-μανθάνω, f. -μαθήσομαι, *to learn besides* or *after*, Hdt., Thuc.

ἐπι-μαρτῠρέω, f. ήσω, *to bear witness to* a thing, *to depose*, Plat., etc.   II. in Med. *to adjure*, τινὶ μὴ ποιεῖν τι Hdt.   Hence

ἐπιμαρτῠρία, ἡ, *a witness*, *testimony*, Thuc.

ἐπι-μαρτύρομαι [ῡ], f. -μενῶ, Dep. *to call to witness*, *appeal to*, τοὺς θεούς Xen.:—also, *to call a person as one's witness*, Lat. *antestari*, Ar.   2. *to call on earnestly*, *to conjure*, Lat. *obtestari*, Hdt.; ἐπιμ. τινα μὴ ποιεῖν τι *to call on* one not *to do*, Id.   3. *to affirm* or *declare before witnesses that* . . , Dem.

ἐπι-μάρτῠρος, ὁ, *a witness to* one's word, Hom.

ἐπιμάρτυς, ὔρος, ὁ, = foreg., Ar.; acc. -μάρτυρα, Anth.

ἐπιμάσσομαι, Ep. fut. of ἐπιμαίομαι.

ἐπι-μάσσομαι, Med. *to knead again*, *stroke*, Anth.

ἐπι-μαστίδιος, ον, (μαστός) *at the breast*, *not yet weaned*, Trag.

ἐπίμαστος, ον, (ἐπιμαίομαι) *seeking for help*, *begging*, Od.

ἐπιμᾰχέω, f. ήσω, *to help one in war*, τῇ ἀλλήλων ἐπιμαχεῖν *to make a league for* the mutual *defence* of their countries, Thuc.; and

ἐπιμᾰχία, ἡ, *a defensive alliance*, Thuc., Dem.   From

ἐπί-μᾰχος, ον, (μάχομαι) *easily attacked*, *assailable*, Hdt., Thuc., etc.: of a country, *open to attack*, Id.

ἐπι-μειδάω, f. ήσω, *to smile at*, ἐπιμειδήσας προσέφη *addressed him with a smile*, Il.

ἐπι-μειδιάω, f. άσω [ᾰ], *to smile upon*, Xen.

ἐπι-μείζων, ον, gen. ονος, strengthd. for μείζων, *still larger* or *greater*, Democr.

ἐπι-μείλια, τά, = μείλια, Il.

ἐπιμέλεια, ἡ, (ἐπιμελής) *care*, *attention*, Att. Prose; also in Hdt.; pl. *cares*, *pains*, Xen., etc.:—c. gen. *care for* a thing, *attention paid to* it, Hdt., Thuc., etc.; also, περί τινος Id.; πρός τινα or τι Dem.   II. *a public charge* or *commission*, Lat. *procuratio*, Aeschin.: *any pursuit*, Lat. *studium*, Xen., etc.

ἐπι-μελέομαι and -μέλομαι:—f. -μελήσομαι: aor. 1 -εμελήθην: pf. -μεμέλημαι: Dep.:—*to take care of*, *have charge of*, *have the management of* a thing, c. gen., Hdt., Att.; περί τινος, ὑπέρ τινος Xen.:—c. acc. et inf. *to take care that* . . , Thuc., etc.; so, ἐπ. ὅπως Plat.:—absol. *to give heed*, *attend*, Hdt.   II. in public offices, *to be curator of*, Xen., Plat.   Hence

ἐπιμέλημα, ατος, τό, *a care*, *anxiety*, Xen.

ἐπι-μελής, ές, (μέλομαι) *careful* or *anxious about*, *put in charge of* a thing, c. gen., Plat., Xen.:—τὸ ἐπιμελές τινος = ἐπιμέλεια, Thuc.   2. absol. *careful*, *attentive*, Ar., Xen.   II. Pass. *cared for*, *an object of care*, Hdt.; ἐπιμελές μοι ἦν it was my business, Id., Att.

ἐπιμελητέον, verb. Adj. of ἐπιμελέομαι, one must take care, *pay attention*, Plat., Xen.

ἐπιμελητής, οῦ, ὁ, (ἐπιμελέομαι) one who has charge of a thing, *a governor*, *manager*, *curator*, *superintendent*, Ar., Xen., etc.   Hence

ἐπιμελητικός, ή, όν, *able to take charge*, *managing*, Xen.

ἐπιμέλομαι, v. ἐπιμελέομαι.

ἐπι-μέλπω, f. ψω, *to sing to*, Aesch.

ἐπι-μέμονα, poët. pf. 2 with pres. sense, *to desire* to do a thing, Soph.

ἐπι-μέμφομαι, f. ψομαι, Dep. *to cast blame upon* a person, c. dat., Od., Hdt., etc.; rarely c. acc. pers., Soph.:—c. gen. rei, *to find fault for* or *because of* a thing, *complain of* it, εὐχωλῆς ἐπιμέμφεται *complains* of the vow [neglected], Il.:—absol. *to find fault*, *complain*, Hdt., etc.   2. *to impute as matter of blame*, τί τινι Id.

ἐπι-μένω, f. -μενῶ: aor. 1 -έμεινα:—*to stay on*, *tarry* or *abide still*, Hom., Att.; ἐπίμεινον *wait*, Il.   2. absol. *to remain in place*, *continue as they are*, of things, Thuc., Plat.:—*to keep his seat*, of a horseman, Xen.   3. *to continue* in a pursuit, ἐπί τινι Plat., etc.   4. *to abide by*, ταῖς σπονδαῖς Xen.   II. c. acc. *to await*, Eur., Plat.: so c. inf., Thuc.

ἐπι-μεταπέμπομαι, Med. *to send for a reinforcement*, Thuc.

ἐπι-μετρέω, f. ήσω, *to measure out besides*, Hes. :— Pass., ὁ ἐπιμετρούμενος σῖτος the corn *paid by measure* to the Persians, Hdt.   II. *to add to the measure*, *give over and above*, Plut., Luc.

ἐπί-μετρον, τό, *over-measure, excess*, Theocr.

ἐπι-μήδομαι, Dep. *to contrive against* one, τί τινι Od.

Ἐπι-μηθεύς, έως, ὁ, (μῆδος) *Epi-metheus, After-thought*, brother of *Pro-metheus, Fore-thought*, Hes.

ἐπι-μηθής, ές, (μῆδος) *thoughtful*, Theocr.

ἐπιμηθικῶς, Adv. *like Epimetheus*, Eust.

ἐπι-μήκης, ες, (μῆκος) *longish, oblong*, Luc.

Ἐπι-μηλίδες, αἱ, (μῆλα) *Flock-protectors, Nymphs*, Theocr.

ἐπι-μήνιος, ον, (μήν) *monthly*: as Subst., ἐπιμήνια, τά, (sub. ἱερά), *monthly offerings*, Hdt.

ἐπι-μηνίω, *to be angry with*, Πριάμῳ ἐπεμήνϊε Il.

ἐπι-μηχανάομαι, Dep. *to devise plans against, take precautions*, Hdt., Luc.   II. *to devise besides*, Xen.

ἐπι-μήχανος, ον, (μηχανή) *craftily devising*, κακῶν ἐπιμήχανος ἔργων *contriver* of ill deeds, Orac. ap. Hdt.

ἐπιμίγνυμι and –ύω: f. –μίξω :—*to add to by mixing*, *mix with*, τί τινι Plat.   II. intr. *to mingle with* others, *to have intercourse* or *dealings* with them, τισί Thuc.; πρός τινας Xen. :—so also in Pass., ἐπιμίγνυσθαι ἀλλήλοις Id.; παρ' ἀλλήλους Thuc.

ἐπι-μιμνήσκομαι, Ion. also –μνάομαι, –μνῶμαι: f. –μνήσομαι or –μνησθήσομαι: aor. 1 ἐπεμνήσθην or ἐπεμνησάμην: pf. ἐπιμέμνημαι: Pass. :—*to bethink oneself of*, *to remember, think of* a person or thing, c. gen., Hom.   2. *to make mention of*, τινος Od., Hdt., etc.; περί τινος Id., Xen.

ἐπι-μίμνω, poët. for –μένω, *to continue in* a work, c. dat., Od.

ἐπιμίξ, Ep. Adv. (ἐπιμίγνυμι) *confusedly, promiscuously, pêle-mêle*, Hom.

ἐπιμιξία, Ion. –ίη, ἡ, (ἐπιμίγνυμι) *a mixing with* others, *intercourse, dealings*, Lat. *commercium*, πρός τινας Hdt., Xen.; παρ' ἀλλήλους Thuc.

ἐπίμιξις, εως, ἡ, = foreg., Theogn., Babr.

ἐπι-μίσγω, older form of ἐπιμίγνυμι, intr. *to have intercourse*, παρ' ἀλλήλους Thuc. :—so Pass. in same sense, c. dat. pers., Od., Hdt., etc.; αἰεὶ Τρώεσσ' ἐπιμίσγομαι I have always *to be dealing with* the Trojans, am always *clashing with* them, Il.: absol. *to associate together*, Hdt., Thuc.

ἐπι-μοίριος, ον, (μοῖρα) *fated*, Anth.

ἐπιμολεῖν, inf. aor. 2 of ἐπιβλώσκω, *to come upon*, *befall*, Soph.

ἐπί-μολος, ὁ, (μολεῖν) *an invader*, Aesch.

ἐπί-μομφος, ον, (μέμφομαι) *inclined to blame*, Eur.   II. *blameable, unlucky*, Aesch.

ἐπιμονή, ἡ, (ἐπιμένω) *a staying on, tarrying, delay*, Thuc.

ἐπι-μύζω, f. ξω, *to murmur at* one's words, Il.

ἐπι-μῦθέομαι, Dep. *to say besides*, Il.

ἐπι-μύθιος, ον, (μῦθος) *coming after the fable*: τὸ ἐπ. *the moral*, Luc.

ἐπίμυκτος, ον, (ἐπιμύζω) *scoffed at*, Theogn.

ἐπι-μύω, f. ύσω [ῠ], *to wink* in token of assent, Ar.

ἐπι-μωμητός, ή, όν, *blameworthy*, Hes., Theocr.

ἐπιμώομαι, Dor. for ἐπιμαίομαι II.

ἐπινάχομαι, Dor. for ἐπινήχομαι.

ἐπί-νειον, τό, (ναῦς) *the sea-port* where the navy lies, *the state harbour*, Hdt., Thuc.

ἐπινέμησις, εως, ἡ, (ἐπινέμομαι) *a spreading*, Plut.

ἐπινέμω, f. –νεμῶ and –νεμήσω: aor. ἐπένειμα :—*to allot, distribute*, Hom.   II. *to turn* one's cattle *to graze over the boundaries*, Plat. :— in Med., of cattle, *to feed over the boundaries, trespass on* one's neighbour's lands: metaph., of fire, *to spread* over a place, Hdt. :—so of an infectious disease, Thuc.; in Pass., ὅρος ἐπινέμεται the boundary *is exposed to encroachment*, Aesch. : cf. ἐπινομία.

ἐπι-νεύω, f. –νεύσω, *to nod*, in token of approval, *to nod assent*, Il.; ἐπ. τι *to approve, sanction, promise*, Eur.; ἐπένευσεν ἀληθὲς εἶναι he nodded in sign that it was true, Aeschin.   2. *to make a sign* to another to do a thing, *to order* him to do, Hom.   3. *to nod forwards*, κόρυθι ἐπένευε he nodded with his helmet, i. e. it nodded, Il.   4. *to incline towards*, Ar.

ἐπι-νέφελος, ον, (νεφέλη) *clouded, overcast*, ἐπινεφέλων ὄντων (gen. absol.) the weather being *cloudy*, Hdt.

ἐπι-νεφρίδιος, ον, (νεφρός) *upon the kidneys*, Il.

ἐπι-νέω (Α), f. –νήσω, *to allot by spinning*, of the Fates, Il.

ἐπι-νέω (Β), *to heap up* or *load with* a thing, c. gen., Hdt.

ἐπι-νήϊος, ον, (ναῦς, νηῦς) *on board ship*, Anth.

ἐπι-νήω, only in impf., *to heap* or *pile upon* a thing, c. gen., Il.

ἐπι-νήχομαι, f. ξομαι, Dep. *to swim upon*, Batr.; ἐπενήχετο φωνά the voice *came up* to earth, Theocr.

ἐπινίκειος, ον, = sq., Soph.

ἐπινίκιος [ῐ], ον, (νίκη) *of victory, triumphal*, Pind., etc.   II. as Subst., ἐπινίκιον (sc. μέλος), τό, *a song of victory, triumphal ode*, Aesch.; ἐπινίκια (sc. ἱερά), τά, *a sacrifice for a victory* or *feast in honour of it*, Plat., etc.   b. (sc. ἆθλα) *the prize of victory*, Soph.

ἐπι-νίσσομαι, Dep. *to go over*, c. gen., Soph.   2. *to visit*, Theocr.

ἐπι-νίφω [ῐ], *to snow upon*: impers., ἐπινίφει fresh snow falls, or it keeps snowing, Xen.

ἐπι-νοέω, f. ήσω, *to think on* or *of, contrive*, Hdt., Att. : —c. inf., Ar. :—absol. *to form plans, to plan, invent*, Thuc.   2. *to have in one's mind, intend, purpose*, Id., etc. : c. inf., Hdt., Xen.   II. aor. 1 pass. ἐπινοήθην is used like Act., Hdt. Hence

ἐπίνοια, ἡ, *a thinking on* or of a thing, *a thought, notion*, Thuc.   2. *power of thought, inventiveness, invention*, Ar.   3. *a purpose, design*, Eur.   II. *after-thought, second thoughts*, Soph.

ἐπινομή, ἡ, (ἐπινέμομαι) *a grazing over the boundaries*: —metaph., ἐπ. πυρός *the spreading* of fire, Plut.

ἐπινομία, ἡ, (ἐπινέμομαι) *a grazing over the boundaries*: *a mutual right of pasture*, vested in the citizens of two neighbouring states, Xen.

ἐπι-νύκτιος, ον, (νύξ) *by night, nightly*, Anth.

ἐπι-νύμφειος, ον, = sq., Soph.

ἐπι-νυμφίδιος, ον, *of* or *for a bride, bridal*, Anth.

ἐπι-νυστάζω, f. σω and ξω, *to drop asleep over*, c. dat., Plut., Luc.

ἐπι-νωμάω, f. ήσω, *to bring* or *apply to*, Soph., Eur.   II. *to distribute, apportion*, Aesch., Soph.

ἐπι-νωτίδιος, ον, (νῶτον) on the back, Anth.
ἐπι-νωτίζω, f. σω, to set on the back, Eur
ἐπι-νώτιος, ον, (νῶτον) on the back, Batr.
ἐπί-ξανθος, ον, inclining to yellow, tawny, of hares, Xen.
ἐπι-ξενόομαι, pf. ἐπεξένωμαι, Pass. to have hospitable relations with, be intimate with, Dem.   II. as Med. to claim friendly services, Aesch.
ἐπί-ξηνον, τό, (ξηνός) a chopping-block: the executioner's block, Aesch., Ar.
ἐπί-ξυνος, ον, poët. for ἐπίκοινος, a common, Il.
ἐπί-οίνιος, ον, (οἶνος) at or over wine, Theogn.
ἐπι-οινοχοεύω, to pour out wine for others, h. Hom.
ἐπι-ορκέω, f. ήσω: aor. 1 -ώρκησα: pf. -ώρκηκα: (ἐπίορκος):—to swear falsely, forswear oneself, πρὸς δαίμονος by a deity, Il.; c. acc., τοὺς θεοὺς by the gods, Ar., Xen.; and
ἐπιορκία, ἡ, a false oath, Lat. perjuria, Xen., Plat.
ἐπί-ορκος, ον, sworn falsely, of oaths, Il.: as Subst., ἐπίορκον ὀμνύναι to take a false oath, swear falsely, Il., Hes.: but also, ἐπ. ἐπώμοσε he swore a bootless oath, Il.   II. of persons, forsworn, perjured, Hes., Eur., etc.
ἐπιορκοσύνη, ἡ, = ἐπιορκία, Anth.
ἐπι-όσσομαι, Dep. to have before one's eyes, Il.
ἐπί-ουρα, v. οὖρον.
ἐπί-ουρος, ὁ, an over-keeper, a guardian, watcher, ward, c. gen.; υἶῶν ἐπίουρος Od. etc.; c. dat., Κρήτῃ ἐπ. guardian over Crete, of Minos, Il.
ἐπιούσιος, ον, for the coming day, sufficient for the day, N. T. (From ἡ ἐπιοῦσα [ἡμέρα] the coming day.)
ἐπι-όψομαι, poët. for ἐπ-όψομαι, fut. of ἐφοράω.
ἐπί-παγχυ, Adv. altogether, Theocr.
ἐπι-παιανίζω, f. σω, to sing a paean over, Plut.
ἐπι-πάλλω, to brandish at or against, Aesch.
ἐπίπαν or ἐπὶ πᾶν, Adv. upon the whole, in general, on the average, Hdt., Thuc.; ὡς ἐπίπαν, also τὸ ἐπ. and ὡς τὸ ἐπ. Hdt.   2. altogether, Aesch.
ἐπι-παρανέω, to heap up still more, to heap up, Thuc.
ἐπι-παρασκευάζομαι, Med. to provide oneself with besides, Xen.
ἐπι-πάρειμι, (εἰμί sum) to be present besides or in addition, Thuc.
ἐπι-πάρειμι, (εἶμι ibo) to march on high ground parallel with one below, Xen., etc.:—to assail in flank, c. dat., Thuc.   2. to come to one's assistance, Id., Xen.   3. to come to the front of an army, so as to address it, Thuc.
ἐπι-πάσσω, Att. -ττω, f. -πάσω [ă], to sprinkle upon or over, Hom. Hence
ἐπίπαστος, ον, sprinkled over:—as Subst. ἐπίπαστον, τό, a kind of cake with comfits (or the like) upon it, Ar.   2. a plaster, Theocr.
ἐπίπεδος, ον, (πέδον) to the level of the ground, level, Xen., etc.:—irreg. Comp. -πεδέστερος, Id.
ἐπι-πείθομαι, f. σω: Pass., f. med. -πείσομαι, to be persuaded to a certain end, Hom.   2. to trust to, put faith in, c. dat., Aesch.   3. to comply with, obey, Hes., Soph.
ἐπι-πελάζω, f. σω, to bring near to, Eur.
ἐπι-πέλομαι, Dep., (πέλω) to come to or upon a person, c. dat., Od.; Ep. syncop. part. aor. 2 ἐπιπλόμενος, coming

on, approaching, ἐπιπλόμενον ἔτος the coming year, Ib.; of a storm, like Lat. ingruens, Soph.
ἐπίπεμπω, f. ψω, to send besides or again, of messages, Hdt.   2. of the gods, to send upon or to, Id.; esp. by way of punishment, to send upon or against, let loose upon, Eur., Plat. Hence
ἐπίπεμψις, εως, ἡ, a sending to a place, Thuc.
ἐπιπέπτωκα, pf. of ἐπιπίπτω.
ἐπιπέπωκα, pf. of ἐπιπίνω.
ἐπι-περκάζω, to turn dark, of grapes ripening; ἐπιπερκάζειν τριχί to begin to get a dark beard, Anth.
ἐπί-περκνος, ον, somewhat dark, of the colour of certain hares, Xen.
ἐπιπεσοῦμαι, fut. of ἐπιπίπτω:—ἐπιπεσών, aor. 2 part.
ἐπι-πετάννυμι, f. -πετάσω [ă], to spread over, Xen.
ἐπι-πέτομαι, f. -πτήσομαι: aor. 2 ἐπεπτάμην or -όμην, also in act. form ἐπέπτην, part. ἐπιπτάς: Dep.:—to fly to or towards, Hom., etc.   2. c. acc. to fly over, πεδία Eur., etc.
ἐπι-πήγνυμι, f. -πήξω, to freeze at top, Xen.
ἐπι-πηδάω, f. ήσομαι, to leap upon, assault, Ar., Plat.
ἐπι-πιέζω, to press upon, press down, Od.
ἐπι-πίλναμαι, Dep. only in pres. and impf., to come near, Od.
ἐπιπίμπλημι, to fill full of, τί τινος Ar.
ἐπι-πίνω [ĭ], f. -πίομαι: aor. 2 ἐπέπιον: pf. -πέπωκα:—to drink afterwards or besides, esp. to drink after eating, Od., Att.
ἐπι-πίπτω, f. -πεσοῦμαι, to fall upon or over another, c. dat., Thuc.   II. to fall upon, attack, assail, τινί Hdt., Thuc., etc.; of storms, Hdt., Plat.: of disease and accidents, Thuc., Eur.
ἔπιπλα, τά, (from ἐπί, as δίπλα from δίς) implements, utensils, furniture, moveable property, Hdt., Att.
ἐπι-πλάζομαι: aor. 1 ἐπεπλάγχθην:—Pass.:—to wander about over, πόντον ἐπιπλαγχθείς Od.
ἐπι-πλάσσω, Att. -ττω, f. άσω [ă], to spread as a plaster over, Hdt. Hence
ἐπίπλαστος, ον, plastered over:—metaph. feigned, false, Luc.
ἐπι-πλᾰτᾰγέω, f. ήσω, to applaud loudly, τινί Theocr.
ἐπι-πλέκω, f. ξω, to wreathe into a chaplet, Anth.   II. Pass. to be interwoven with, Luc.
ἐπί-πλεος, έα Ion. έη, εον, quite full of a thing, c. gen., Hdt.
ἐπί-πλευσις, εως, ἡ, a sailing against, ἐπ. ἔχειν to have the power of attacking, Thuc. From
ἐπι-πλέω, Ion. -πλώω: f. -πλεύσομαι: Ep. 2 sing. aor. 2 ἐπέπλως, part. ἐπιπλώς: aor. 1 part. ἐπιπλώσας:—to sail upon or over, πόντον Hom.   II. to sail against, to attack by sea, c. dat., Hdt., Thuc.   III. to sail on board, Id.   IV. to float on the surface, Hdt.
ἐπίπλεως, ων, Att. for ἐπίπλεος, Plut.
ἐπιπλήκτειρα, ἡ, (ἐπιπλήσσω) Anth.
ἐπίπληξις, εως, ἡ, (ἐπιπλήσσω) rebuke, reproof, Aeschin.
ἐπι-πληρόω, f. ώσω, to fill up again:—Med., ἐπιπληρωσόμεθα τὰς ναῦς we shall man our ships afresh, Thuc.
ἐπι-πλήσσω, Att. -ττω, f. ξω, to strike at, strike smartly, Il.   II. to chastise with words, to rebuke, reprove, c. acc., Ib., Plat.: also c. dat., Il.   2. ἐπ. τί τινι to cast a thing in one's teeth, Hdt., Aesch.:—c. acc. rei only, Soph.
ἐπίπλοα, τά, longer form of ἔπιπλα, Hdt.

ἐπιπλόμενος, Ep. sync. part. aor. 2 of ἐπιπέλομαι.
ἔπιπλον, ἐπίπλοον, τό, v. ἔπιπλα, ἐπίπλοα.
ἐπίπλοος, ὁ, (ἐπί) the membrane enclosing the entrails, the caul, Lat. omentum, Hdt.
ἐπίπλοος, contr. ἐπίπλους, ὁ, (ἐπιπλέω) a sailing against, bearing down upon, Thuc., Xen.　II. of friends, a sailing towards, approach, Thuc.
ἐπιπλώς, Ep. aor. 2 part. of ἐπιπλέω.
ἐπιπλώσας, Ep. for -πλεύσας, aor. 1 part. of ἐπιπλέω.
ἐπι-πλώω, Ion. for ἐπιπλέω.
ἐπι-πνέω, Ep. -πνείω: f. -πνεύσομαι: aor. 1 ἐπέπνευσα:—to breathe upon, to blow freshly upon, Il.; τινί on one, Ar.:—to blow fairly for one, τινί Od.　2. to blow furiously upon, τινί Hdt., Aesch.　3. c. acc. to blow over, Hes.　II. metaph. to excite, inflame, τινά τινι one against another, Eur.; τινὰ αἵματι one to slaughter, Id.　2. to inspire into, Anth.　Hence
ἐπίπνοια, ἡ, a breathing upon, inspiration, Lat. afflatus, Aesch., Plat.; and
ἐπίπνοος, ον, contr. -πνους, ουν, breathed upon, inspired, Plat.
ἐπι-πόδιος, α, ον, (πούς) upon the feet, Soph.
ἐπι-ποθέω, f. ήσω, to yearn after, Hdt., Plat.　Hence
ἐπιπόθησις, εως, ἡ, a longing after, N. T.; and
ἐπιπόθητος, ον, longed for, desired, N. T.
ἐπιποθία, ἡ, = ἐπιπόθησις, N. T.
ἐπι-ποιμήν, ένος, ὁ, ἡ, a chief shepherd, Od.
ἐπιπολάζω, f. σω, (ἐπιπολή) to come to the surface, float, Xen.　2. to be uppermost, to be prevalent, Id.　3. to be forward; c. dat. pers. to behave insolently to, Luc.　II. to be engaged upon a thing, c. dat., Id.
ἐπιπόλαιος, ον, on the surface, superficial, Luc.:—metaph. superficial, common-place, Dem.　2. prominent, Xen.　From
ἐπιπολή, ἡ, (ἐπιπέλομαι) a surface: mostly in gen. ἐπιπολῆς as Adv. on the surface, a-top, Hdt., Xen.　2. ἐπιπολῆς also as Prep. c. gen. on the top of, above, Hdt., Ar.　II. Ἐπιπολαί, αἱ, an eminence near Syracuse, with a flat surface, Thuc.
ἐπίπολος, ον, (πολέω) = πρόσπολος, a companion, Soph.
ἐπιπολύ, Adv. for ἐπὶ πολύ, to a great extent, generally, Hdt., etc.
ἐπι-πομπεύω, f. σω, to triumph over, τινί Plut.
ἐπι-πονέω, f. ήσω, to toil on, persevere, Xen.
ἐπί-πονος, ον, painful, toilsome, laborious, Soph., Thuc., etc.: — rarely in good sense, Xen.:—ἐπίπονόν [ἐστι] 'tis a hard task, Thuc.　2. of persons, laborious, patient of toil, Ar.　3. of omens, portending distress, Xen.　II. Adv. -νως, Lat. aegre, Thuc., Xen.:—Sup. -ώτατα, Id.
ἐπι-πορεύομαι, f. εύσομαι: aor. 1 ἐπεπορεύθην: Dep.: (πορεύω):—to travel, march to, march over, Plut.
ἐπι-πόρπημα, Dor. -άμα, ατος, τό, any garment buckled over the shoulders, a mantle, Plut.
ἐπι-ποτάομαι, pf. -πεπότημαι, Dep., lengthd. for ἐπιπέτομαι, to fly or hover over, Aesch.
ἐπιπρεπής, ές, becoming: — τὸ ἐπιπρεπές, propriety, Luc.　From
ἐπι-πρέπω, to be manifest on the surface, to be conspicuous, Od., Theocr.　II. to beseem, fit, suit, τινί Xen.

ἐπι-πρεσβεύομαι, Dep. to send an embassy, Plut.
ἐπι-πρίω, to grind the teeth with rage at a thing, Anth.
ἐπι-προβάλλω, to throw forward, ap. Plut.
ἐπιπροέηκα, Ep. for -προῆκα, aor. 1 of ἐπιπροΐημι.
ἐπιπροέμεν, Ep. for -προεῖναι, aor. 2 inf. of ἐπιπροΐημι.
ἐπι-προΐαλλω, to set out or place before one, τί τινι II.　II. to send on one after another, Hom.
ἐπι-προΐημι, to send forth, Il.; Μενελάῳ ἐπιπροέμεν ταχὺν ἰόν to shoot an arrow at him, Ib.　II. νήσοισιν ἐπιπροέηκε (sc. τὴν ναῦν) he steered straight for them, Od.
ἐπί-προσθεν, poët. -προσθε: Adv.:　I. of Place, before, Eur., Xen.; γεωλόφους ἐπ. ποιεῖσθαι to make the hills cover one, Id.　II. of Degree, ἐπ. εἶναί τινος to be better than another, Eur.　Hence
ἐπιπροσθέω, to be before, ἐπ. τοῖς πύργοις to be in a line with them, so as to cover one with the other, Polyb.
ἐπι-προχέω, f. -χεῶ, to pour forth, h. Hom.
ἐπι-πταίρω, aor. 2 -έπταρον, to sneeze at, ἐπέπταρε ἔπεσσιν he sneezed as I spoke the words, a good omen, Od.:—metaph. of the gods, to be gracious to, τινί Theocr.
ἐπιπτέσθαι, aor. 2 inf. of ἐπιπέτομαι.
ἐπι-πτυχή, ἡ, an over-fold, a flap, Plut., Luc.
ἐπι-πωλέομαι, Dep. to go about, go through, Lat. obire, c. acc., ἐπεπωλεῖτο στίχας ἀνδρῶν, of the general inspecting his troops, Il.;—but also to reconnoitre an enemy, Ib.　Hence
ἐπιπώλησις, εως, ἡ, a going round, inspection, name given to the latter half of Il. 4.
ἐπι-πωτάομαι, lengthd. form of ἐπιποτάομαι, Anth.
ἐπιρ-ραβδοφορέω, f. ήσω, to urge a horse by the whip, Xen.
ἐπιρ-ραθυμέω, f. ήσω, to be careless about a thing, Luc.
ἐπιρ-ραίνω, to sprinkle upon or over, τί τινι Theocr.
ἐπιρ-ράπτω, f. ψω, to sew or stitch on, N. T.
ἐπιρ-ράσσω, f. ξω, = ἐπιρρήσσω, to dash to, slam to, πύλας Soph.　II. intr. to break or burst upon one, Id.
ἐπιρ-ραψῳδέω, f. ήσω, to recite in accompaniment, Luc.
ἐπιρ-ρέζω, Ep. impf. -ρέζεσκον: — to offer sacrifices at a place, Od.　2. to sacrifice besides, Theocr.
ἐπιρρεπής, ές, leaning towards, Lat. proclivis, Luc.
ἐπιρ-ρέπω, f. ψω, to lean towards, fall to one's lot, Il.; c. inf., ἐπιρρέπει τινὶ ποιεῖν τι Aesch.　II. trans. ἐπ. τάλαντον to force down one scale, Theogn.: metaph. to weigh out to one, allot, Aesch.
ἐπιρ-ρέω, f. -ρεύσομαι and in pass. form -ρυήσομαι: aor. 2 pass. also in act. sense ἐπερρύην:—to flow upon the surface, float a-top, like oil on water, Il.　2. to flow in besides, flow fresh and fresh, Ar.:—metaph. of large bodies of men, to stream on and on, Il., Hdt.; also, οὑπιρρέων χρόνος onward-streaming time, i. e. the future, Aesch.; ὄλβου ἐπιρρυέντος if wealth flows on and on, increases continually, Eur.
ἐπιρ-ρήγνυμι, f. -ρήξω: aor. 1 ἐπέρρηξα:—to rend, Aesch.
ἐπιρ-ρήσσω, f. ξω. Ep. impf. -ρήσσεσκον:—Ion. for ἐπιρράσσω, to dash to, shut violently, θύρην Il.
ἐπιρ-ρητορεύω, f. σω, to declaim over, τί τινι Luc.
ἐπίρ-ρητος, ον, exclaimed against, infamous, Xen.
ἐπίρ-ρικνος, ον, shrunk up, Luc.
ἐπιρ-ριπτέω, = sq., only in pres. and impf., Xen.　2. intr. to throw oneself upon the track, Id.
ἐπιρ-ρίπτω, f. ψω, to cast at another, c. dat., Od.; χεῖρα

ἐπ. to lay hand upon, Anth. :—metaph. to throw upon one, τί τινι Aesch.

ἐπιρροή, ή, (ἐπιρρέω) afflux, influx, Aesch. :—metaph., ἐπ. κακῶν Eur.

ἐπιρ-ροθέω, f. ήσω, to shout in answer or in approval (cf. ἐπευφημέω), Trag.; ἐπ. κτύπῳ to answer to, ring with the sound, Aesch.   2. c. acc., λόγοις ἐπιρροθεῖν to inveigh against him, Soph.

ἐπίρ-ροθος, ον, hasting to the rescue, a helper, Il., Hes.: —c. gen. giving aid against, Aesch.   II. ἐπ. κακά reproaches bandied backwards and forwards, abusive language, Soph. Cf. ἐπιτάρροθος.

ἐπιρ-ροίβδην, (ῥοῖβδος) Adv. with noisy fury, Eur.

ἐπιρ-ροιζέω, f. ήσω, to shriek at one, c. acc. cogn., ἐπ. φυγάς τινι to shriek or forebode flight at him, Aesch.

ἐπιρ-ροφέω, f. ήσω, to swallow besides, Plut.

ἐπιρ-ρύζω, to set a dog on one, Ar.

ἐπιρρυείς, aor. 2 pass. part. of ἐπιρρέω.

ἐπιρ-ρυθμίζω, f. σω, to bring into form, arrange, Luc.

ἐπιρ-ρύομαι, Dep. to save, preserve, Soph.

ἐπίρρυτος, ον, (ἐπιρρέω) flowing in or to : metaph. over-flowing, Aesch.   II. pass. overflowed, Xen.

ἐπιρ-ρώννυμι and -ύω : aor. 1 ἐπέρρωσα :—to add strength to, strengthen or encourage for an enterprise, Hdt., Thuc.   II. Pass., pf. ἐπέρρωμαι, plqpf. ἐπερ-ρώμην used as pres. and impf. : fut. ἐπιρρωσθήσομαι : aor. 1 ἐπερρώσθην :—to recover strength, pluck up courage, Thuc., Xen.; κείνοις ἐπερρώσθη λέγειν (impers.) they took courage to speak, Soph.

ἐπιρ-ρώομαι : aor. 1 -ερρωσάμην :—Med. to flow or stream upon, χαῖται ἐπερρώσαντο ἀπὸ κρατός his locks flowed waving from his head, Il.   2. to move nimbly, Hes. : c. acc. cogn., ἐπίρρωσαι χορείην urge the rapid dance, Anth.   II. to apply one's strength to a thing, work lustily at it, c. dat., Od.

ἐπίσαγμα, ατος, τό, a load on a beast's back :—metaph., τοὐπίσαγμα τοῦ νοσήματος the burden of the disease, Soph. From

ἐπίσα, aor. 1 of πιπίσκω.

ἐπι-σάττω, f. ξω : pf. pass. -σέσαγμαι :—to pile a load upon a beast's back, Hdt.; ἵππον ἐπ. to saddle it, Xen.

ἐπίσειστος, ον, waving over the forehead, Luc. From

ἐπι-σείω, Ep. ἐπισσ-, f. σω, to shake at or against, with the view of scaring, τί τινι Il., Eur.; Πέρσας ἐπ. to hold them out as a threat, Plut.; but, ἐπ. τὴν χεῖρα, in token of assent, Luc.   2. to set upon one, c. dat., Eur.

ἐπι-σεύω, Ep. ἐπισσ-, to put in motion against, set upon one, c. dat., Od.   II. Pass. to hurry or hasten to or towards, Hom. ; in hostile sense, to rush upon or at, c. dat., Il.   2. part. pf. pass. ἐπεσσύμενος, with 3 sing. pf. and plqpf. ἐπέσσυται, -το :—mostly in hostile sense, to rush on, Ib.; c. dat., αὐτῷ μοι ἐπέσσυτο Ib.; c. acc. to assault, Ib.; c. gen., ἐπεσσύμενος πεδίοιο rushing, hurrying over the plain, Ib. :—also, without hostile sense, to express rapid motion, ἐπέσσυτο δέμνια swept over the clothes, Od. ; c. inf., ἐπέσσυτο διώκειν he hasted on to follow, Il. :—metaph. to be excited, eager, θυμὸς ἐπέσσυται Ib.

ἐπί-σημον, τό, = ἐπίσημον, Aesch., Eur.

ἐπι-σημαίνω, f. ἄνῶ, to set a mark upon a person, of a disease, Thuc., Xen. : Pass. to have a mark set on one, Eur.   II. to indicate, Plut.   III. Med.

to mark for oneself, signify, indicate, Plat.   2. to set one's seal to a thing, approve it, Dem., Aeschin.

ἐπίσημον, τό, = ἐπίσημα, any distinguishing mark, a device or badge, the bearing on a shield, the ensign of a ship, Hdt. From

ἐπί-σημος, ον, (σῆμα) having a mark on it, of money, stamped, coined, Hdt., Thuc., etc. ; ἀναθήματα οὐκ ἐπ. offerings with no inscription on them, Hdt.   2. notable, remarkable, Lat. insignis, Id., Att. : in bad sense, notorious, Eur.

ἐπ-ίσης, for ἐπ' ἴσης (sc. μοίρας), v. sub ἴσος.

ἐπι-σίζω, to set on a dog, Ar.

ἐπι-σιμόω, f. ώσω, to bend inwards : intr. to turn aside one's course, Xen.

ἐπι-σιτίζομαι, f. Att. -ιοῦμαι, Ion. -ιεῦμαι : Med. :—to furnish oneself with food or provender, Hdt., Thuc., etc.   2. c. acc. rei, ἐπ. ἄριστον to provide oneself with breakfast, Id. ; ἐπισ. ἀργύριον Xen.   3. c. acc. pers. to supply with provisions, Id. Hence

ἐπισιτισμός, ὁ, a furnishing oneself with provisions, foraging, Xen.   2. a stock or store of provisions, Id.

ἐπι-σκάπτω, f. ψω, to dig superficially, Anth.

ἐπι-σκεδάννυμι, f. -σκεδάσω [ἄ], to scatter or sprinkle over :—Pass. to be sprinkled over, τινι Plut.

ἐπι-σκέλίσις, εως, ή, (σκέλος) the first bound, in a horse's gallop, Xen.

ἐπισκεπτέος, α, ον, verb. Adj. to be considered or ex-amined, Thuc., Plat.   II. neut. ἐπισκεπτέον, one must consider, Id. From

ἐπισκέπτομαι, a pres., which furnishes its tenses to ἐπισκοπέω ; v. σκέπτομαι.

ἐπι-σκέπω, to cover over, Anth.

ἐπι-σκευάζω, f. σω, to get ready, to equip, fit out, Thuc., Xen. :—Med., ἐπισκευάζεσθαι ναῦν to have a ship equipped, Thuc.   2. τὰ χρήματα ἐφ' ἁμαξῶν ἐπισκευάσαι to pack them upon wagons, Xen.   II. to make afresh, to repair, Lat. reficere, Thuc., Xen.

ἐπισκευαστής, οῦ, ὁ, one who equips or repairs, Dem.

ἐπισκευαστός, ή, όν, repaired, restored, Plat.

ἐπισκευή, ή, repair, restoration, Hdt., Dem.   II. materials for repair or equipment, stores, Thuc., Dem.

ἐπίσκεψις, εως, ή, (ἐπισκέπτομαι) inspection, visita-tion, Xen., Plut.   2. investigation, inquiry, Xen.

ἐπί-σκηνος, ον, (σκηνή) at or before the tent, i. e. public, Soph.

ἐπι-σκηνόω, f. ώσω, to be quartered in a place : metaph. to dwell upon, N. T.

ἐπι-σκήπτω, f. ψω, to make to lean upon, make to fall upon, Aesch. : impose on, τί τινι Soph.   2. intr. to fall upon, like lightning : metaph., δεῦρ' ἐπέσκηψεν it came to this point, Aesch.   II. to lay it upon one to do a thing, to enjoin, lay a strict charge upon, c. dat. pers. et inf., Id., Soph. ; c. acc. et inf., Hdt., Eur.   III. as Att. law-term, generally in Med. to denounce a person, so as to begin a prosecu-tion, Plut., etc. :—Pass. to be denounced as guilty of a crime, c. gen., Soph.

ἐπίσκηψις, εως, ή, an injunction, Plut.   II. as law-term, a denunciation, Dem.

ἐπι-σκιάζω, f. άσω, to throw a shade upon, overshadow, Hdt., N. T. :—Pass. λαθραῖον ὄμμ' ἐπεσκιασμένη keep-ing a hidden watch, Soph.

ἐπί-σκιος, ον, (σκιά) shaded, dark, obscure, Plat. **II.** act. shading, c. gen., χεὶρ ὀμμάτων ἐπίσκιος Soph.

ἐπι-σκοπέω: f. -σκέψομαι, later -σκοπήσω: aor. 1 -εσκεψάμην: pf. ἐπέσκεμμαι:—to look upon or at, inspect, observe, examine, regard, Hdt., Eur.: to watch over, of tutelary gods, Soph., Eur. **2.** to visit, Soph., Xen., etc.:—Pass., εὐνὴν ὀνείροις οὐκ ἐπισκοπουμένην visited not by dreams, i. e. sleepless, Aesch. **3.** of a general, to inspect, review, Xen. **4.** to consider, reflect, Soph., Xen.:—Med. to examine with oneself, meditate, Plat.

ἐπισκοπή, ἡ, a watching over, visitation, N. T. **II.** the office of ἐπίσκοπος, Ib.: generally, an office, Ib.

ἐπισκοπία, ἡ, (ἐπισκοπέω) a looking at, Anth.

ἐπί-σκοπος, ὁ, one who watches over, an overseer, guardian, Hom., Soph.:— of tutelary gods, Solon, etc. **2.** ἐπ. Τρώεσσι one set to watch them, Il. **3.** a public officer, intendant, sent to the subject states, Ar. **4.** a bishop, N. T.

ἐπί-σκοπος, ον, hitting the mark: metaph. reaching, touching a point, c. gen., Aesch., Soph.:—neut. pl. ἐπίσκοπα, as Adv. successfully, with good aim, Hdt.

ἐπι-σκοτέω, f. ήσω, (σκότος) to throw a shadow over, c. dat., Dem.; ἐπ. τινὶ τῆς θέας to be in the way of one's seeing, Plat. Hence

ἐπισκότησις, εως, ἡ, a darkening, obscurity, of the sun or moon in eclipse, Plut.

ἐπί-σκοτος, ον, in the dark, darkened, Plut.

ἐπι-σκύζομαι, Dep. to be indignant at a thing, Il.; ἐπισκύσσαιτο (Ep. aor. 1 opt.) Od.

ἐπι-σκυθίζω, f. ιῶ, to ply with drink in Scythian fashion, i. e. with unmixed wine, Hdt.

ἐπι-σκυθρωπάζω, f. σω, to look gloomy or stern, Xen.

ἐπι-σκύνιον [ῠ], τό, the skin of the brows which is knitted in frowning, Il., Ar. **2.** superciliousness, Anth. (Deriv. uncertain.)

ἐπι-σκώπτω, f. ψω, to laugh at, quiz, make game of, τινά Plat., Xen.:—absol. to joke, make fun, Ar.; ἐπισκώπτων jestingly, Xen.

ἐπίσκωψις, εως, ἡ, mocking, raillery, Plut.

ἐπι-σμυγερός, ά, όν, gloomy, Hes.:—Adv., ἐπισμυγερῶς ἀπέτισεν sadly did he pay for it, Od.; ἐπισμυγερῶς ναυτίλλεται to his cost doth he sail, Ib.

ἐπισπαστήρ, ῆρος, ὁ, (ἐπισπάω) the latch or handle by which a door is pulled to, Hdt. **II.** the angler's rod or line, Anth.; and

ἐπισπαστός, ή, όν, drawn upon oneself, Od. **II.** tight-drawn, of a noose, Eur. From

ἐπι-σπάω, f. -σπάσω [ᾰ], to draw or drag after one, Hdt.; and in Med., Xen.; ἐπισπάσας κόμης by the hair, having dragged her by the hair, Eur.:—metaph. to bring on, cause, πλῆθος πημάτων Aesch. **2.** to pull to, τὴν θύραν Xen.; ἐπισπασθέντος τοῦ βρόχου the noose being drawn tight, Dem. **3.** to attract, gain, win, Soph.:—so in Med., ἐπισπᾶσθαι κέρδος Hdt. **4.** in Med. to draw on, allure, persuade, Thuc.:—c. inf., ἐπισπάσασθαι [ἂν] αὐτοὺς ἡγεῖτο προθυμήσεσθαι he thought it would induce them to make the venture, Id.:—Pass., φοβοῦμαι μὴ πάντες ἐπισπασθῶσιν πολεμῆσαι Dem. **5.** Pass., of the sea, ἐπισπωμένη returning with a rush, Thuc. **II.** in Med. to become uncircumcised, N. T.

ἐπισπεῖν, ἐπισπών, aor. 2 inf. and part. of ἐφέπω.

ἐπι-σπείρω, f. -σπερῶ, to sow with seed, Hdt.

ἐπίσπεισις, εως, ἡ, a libation over a sacrifice, Hdt.

ἐπισπένδω, f. -σπείσω, to pour upon or over the head of a victim, at a sacrifice, Aesch.:—absol. to make a libation, Hdt.:—metaph., ἐπ. δάκρυ Theocr. **II.** in Med. to make a fresh treaty, Thuc.

ἐπισπερχής, ές, hasty, hurried: Adv. -χῶς, Xen. From

ἐπι-σπέρχω, f. σω, to urge on horses, Il.; generally, to urge on, press forward, Aesch., Thuc. **II.** intr. to rage furiously, of storms, Od.

ἐπισπέσθαι, aor. 2 med. inf. of ἐφέπω.

ἐπι-σπεύδω, f. σω, to urge on, further or promote an object, Hdt., Soph.: of persons, to urge on, Xen. **II.** intr. to hasten onward, Eur.; ἐπισπ. εἴς τι to be zealous for, aim at an object, Xen.

ἐπισπόμενος, aor. 2 med. part. of ἐφέπω.

ἐπισπονδή, ἡ, (ἐπισπένδω) a renewed or renewable truce, Thuc.

ἐπισπορία, ἡ, = foreg., Hes.

ἐπίσπορος, ον, (ἐπισπείρω) sown afterwards, οἱ ἐπ. posterity, Aesch.

ἐπι-σπουδάζω, f. σω, intr. to make haste in a thing, Luc.

ἐπίσπω, -σποιμι, aor. 2 subj. and opt. of ἐφέπω:— ἐπισπών part.

ἐπισ-σείω, ἐπισ-σεύω, Ep. for ἐπισείω, ἐπισεύω.

ἐπίσσυτος, ον, (ἐπέσσυμαι, pf. of ἐπισεύω) rushing, gushing, of tears, Aesch.: violent, sudden, of misfortunes, Id.: c. acc. rushing upon, τὰς φρένας Eur.

ἐπίσσωτρον, τό, Ep. for ἐπίσωτρον.

ἐπίστα, for ἐπίστασαι, 2 sing. of ἐπίσταμαι.

ἐπισταδόν, Adv. (ἐπιστῆναι) standing over each in turn, i. e. one after another, successively, Od.

ἐπι-σταθμάομαι, Dep. to weigh well, ponder, Aesch.

ἐπι-σταθμεύω, f. σω, (σταθμός) to be quartered upon others, Plut. **II.** Pass. to be assigned as quarters, Id.

ἐπισταθμία, ἡ, a liability to have persons quartered on one, Plut.

ἐπί-σταθμος, ον, at the door, Anth.

ἐπι-σταλάζω, f. ξω, to drop over, τί τινι Luc.

ἐπι-σταλάω, to fall in drops over, c. acc., Anth.

ἐπίσταλμα, ατος, τό, (ἐπιστέλλω) a commission, Theophr.

ἐπ-ίσταμαι, 2 pers. -ασαι, also ἐπίστᾳ, ἐπίστῃ, Ion. ἐπίστεαι: imperat. ἐπίστασο, Ion. ἐπίστᾱ, contr. ἐπίστω: subj. ἐπίστωμαι, Ion. -έωμαι:—impf. ἠπιστάμην, ασο, ατο, Ion. ἐπίστατο, Ion. 3 pl. ἠπιστέατο or ἐπιστέατο:—fut. ἐπιστήσομαι, aor. 1 ἠπιστήθην: (prob. = ἐφ-ίσταμαι): Dep.: **I.** c. inf. to know how to do, to be able to do, capable of doing, Hom., Att. **2.** to be assured or believe that a thing is, Hdt. **II.** c. acc. to understand a matter, know, be versed in or acquainted with, Hom., etc.:—after Hom. to know as a fact, know for certain, know well, Hdt., Att. **2.** rarely, to know a person, Eur. **III.** c. part., to know that one is, has, etc., Hdt., Att. **IV.** part. pres. ἐπιστάμενος, η, ον, is often also used as an Adj. knowing, understanding, skilful, Hom.:—c. gen. skilled or versed in a thing, Id.:—Adv. ἐπισταμένως, skilfully, expertly, Id., Hes.

ἐπι-στάς, aor. 2 pass. of ἐφίστημι.

ἐπιστασία, Ion. -ίη, ἡ, (ἐπιστῆναι) authority, dominion, Plut.

ἐπιστάσιος Ζεύς, ὁ, *Jupiter Stator*, Plut. (From ἐφίστημι, *he that makes to stand firm*.)

ἐπίστᾰσις, εως, ἡ, (ἐπιστῆναι) *a stopping, halting, a halt*, Xen.; φροντίδων ἐπιστάσεις *haltings* of thought, Soph.   2. *attention, care, anxiety*, N. T.   3. *superintendence* of works, Xen.

ἐπιστᾰτέω, f. ήσω, (ἐπιστάτης) *to be set over*, c. dat., Soph., Plat.: also *to stand by, to support, second*, Aesch.   2. c. gen. *to be in charge of, have the care of*, Hdt., Xen.   II. at Athens, *to be* Ἐπιστάτης or *President* of the βουλή and ἐκκλησία, Thuc., etc.

ἐπιστάτης, ου, ὁ, (ἐφίσταμαι) *one who stands near* or *by, a suppliant*, Od.   2. in battle-order, *one's rear-rank man* (as παραστάτης is *the right-* or *left-hand man*, προστάτης *the front-rank man*), Xen.   II. *one who stands* or *is mounted upon* a chariot, c. gen., Soph., Eur.   2. *one who is set over, a commander*, Trag.; ἐπιστ. Κολωνοῦ, of a tutelary god, Soph.; ἐπ. ἄθλων *president, steward* of the games, *a training-master*, Xen.   III. at Athens *the President* of the βουλή and ἐκκλησία, Aeschin., Dem.   2. *an overseer, superintendent*, in charge of any public works, Id.   IV. *the caldron for the hot bath which stood over* the fire, Ar.

ἐπιστᾰτητέον, verb. Adj. of ἐπιστατέω, *one must superintend*, c. dat., Plat.; c. gen., Xen.

ἐπιστέαται, Ion. for ἐπίστανται, 3 pl. of ἐπίσταμαι.

ἐπι-στείβω, f. ψω, *to tread upon, stand upon* a place, c. acc., Soph.

ἐπι-στείχω, f. ξω, *to approach*, c. acc., Aesch.

ἐπι-στέλλω, f. -στελῶ, *to send to, send as a message* or *letter*, Hdt., Att.:—absol. *to send a message, write word*, Eur., Thuc.   2. *to enjoin, command*, τινί τι Id.; τινά τι Xen.; also, ἐπ. τινὶ or τινὰ ποιεῖν τι Soph., Xen.: — so, in Pass., ἐπέσταλτό οἱ .. c. inf., he *had received orders* to do, Hdt.; ἐπέσταλται τί τινι a matter *has been committed* to one, Aesch.; τὰ ἐπεσταλμένα *orders given*, Id.   3. *to order by will*, Xen.

ἐπι-στενάζω, f. άξω, *to groan over*, τινί Aesch.

ἐπι-στενάχω, =foreg., τινί Aesch.:—absol., Soph.   2. Med. *to groan in answer*, Il.

ἐπι-στένω, *to groan* or *sigh in answer*, Il.   2. *to lament over*, τινί Eur.   3. c. acc. *to lament*, Soph.

ἐπιστεφής, ές, of bowls, ἐπιστεφέες οἴνοιο *crowned* (i. e. *brimming high*) *with* wine, Hom. From

ἐπι-στέφω, f. ψω, *to surround with* or *as with a chaplet*: metaph. in Med., κρητῆρας ἐπιστέψαντο ποτοῖο *crowned* them *to the brim, filled* them *brimming high*, with wine, Hom.   II. χοὰς ἐπιστέφειν *to offer* libations *as an honour* to the dead, Soph.

ἐπιστέωνται, Ion. for ἐπίστωνται, 3 pl. of ἐπίσταμαι.

ἐπίστῃ, for ἐπίστασαι, 2 sing. of ἐπίσταμαι.

ἐπι-στηλόομαι, (στήλη) Pass. *to be set up as a column upon*, Anth.

ἐπιστήμη, ἡ, (ἐπίσταμαι) *acquaintance with* a matter, *skill, experience*, as in archery, Soph.; in war, Thuc., etc.   II. generally, *knowledge*, Soph.: esp. *scientific knowledge, science*, Plat., etc.

ἐπιστήμων, ον, gen. ονος, (ἐπίσταμαι) *knowing, wise, prudent*, ἐπ. βουλῇ τε νόῳ τε Od.   2. *acquainted with* a thing, *skilled* or *versed in*, c. gen., Thuc., etc.   3. c. inf. *knowing how to do*, Plat., etc.—

Adv., ἐπιστημόνως *with knowledge*: Comp. -έστερον, Xen.; Sup. -έστατα, Plat.   II. *possessed of perfect knowledge*, Id.

ἐπι-στηρίζω, f. ξω, *to make to lean on*:—Pass. *to lean upon*, τινι Luc.

ἐπι-στίλβω, *to glisten on the surface*, Plut.

ἐπίστιον, τό, in Od. means *a shed* in which a ship is laid up. (Deriv. uncertain.)

ἐπ-ίστιος, ον, Ion. for ἐφέστιος.

ἐπιστολάδην [ᾰ], Adv. (ἐπιστέλλω II), *girt up, neatly*, of dress, Hes.

ἐπιστολεύς, έως, ὁ, *secretary*: also *a courier*, Xen.   II. among the Spartans, *a vice-admiral*, Id. From

ἐπιστολή, ἡ, (ἐπιστέλλω) *a message, command, commission*, whether verbal or in writing, Hdt., Att.; ἐξ ἐπιστολῆς *by command*, Hdt.   2. *a letter*, Lat. *epistola*, Thuc., etc. Hence

ἐπιστολιμαῖος, ον, *commanded*:—δυνάμεις ἐπ. forces decreed, but never sent, *paper*-armies, Dem.

ἐπιστόλιον, τό, Dim. of ἐπιστολή, Plut.

ἐπι-στομίζω, f. Att. ιῶ, (στόμα) *to curb in* a horse: metaph. *to curb, bridle*, τινά Ar., Dem.   II. *to put on the mouth-piece* of a flute; and of a flute, *to stop the voice*, Plut.   III. *to throw on his face*, τινά Luc.

ἐπιστονάχέω, = ἐπιστένω, of waves, Il.:—so ἐπιστονᾰχίζω, Hes.

ἐπι-στορέννῡμι: f. -στρώσω: aor. 1 -εστόρεσα or -έστρωσα:—*to strew* or *spread upon*, Od.   2. *to saddle*, Luc.

ἐπι-στρᾰτεία, Ion. -ηίη, ἡ, *a march* or *expedition against*, Hdt.; c. gen., Thuc.

ἐπιστράτευσις, εως, ἡ, = foreg., Hdt.

ἐπι-στρᾰτεύω, f. σω, *to march against, make war upon*, τινί Eur., etc.:—*to make an expedition*, εἰς Θετταλίαν Aesch.; c. acc., Soph.:—absol., Aesch.:—so in Med., with pf. pass., ἐπιστρατεύεσθαι ἐπ' Αἴγυπτον Hdt.; c. dat., Eur., etc.

ἐπίστρεπτος, ον, (ἐπιστρέφω) *to be turned towards, to be looked at, conspicuous*, Aesch.

ἐπιστρεφής, ές, *turning one's eyes* or *mind* to a thing, *attentive*, Xen.   2. *earnest, vehement*: Adv. -φῶς, Ion. -φέως, *earnestly, sharply*, Hdt., Aeschin. From

ἐπι-στρέφω, f. ψω, *to turn about, turn round*, Eur.; ἐπ. τὰς ναῦς *to make a sudden tack*, Thuc.; but also *to put* an enemy *to flight*, Xen.   b. intr. *to turn about, turn round*, Il., Hdt., Att.:—*to return*, N. T.   2. *to turn towards*, τὸ νόημα Theogn.; πρός τι, εἴς τινα Plut.:—ἐπ. πίστιν *to press* a pledge upon one, Soph.   b. intr. *to turn towards*, Xen.   3. *to turn* from an error, *to correct, make to repent*, Luc.   b. intr. *to repent*, N. T.   4. *to curve, twist, torment*, Ar.   II. Med. and Pass., esp. in aor. 2 pass. ἐπεστράφην [ᾰ]:—*to turn oneself round, turn about*, ἐπιστρεφόμενος *constantly turning*, *to look behind one*, Hdt.; with acc., θάλαμον ἐπεστράφη *turned to gaze on* it, Eur.; δόξα ἐπεστράφη *turned about, changed*, Soph.   2. *to go back- and for-wards, wander over* the earth, Hes.:—c. acc. loci, *to turn* to a place, Eur.   3. *to turn the mind towards, to pay attention to*, c. gen., Theogn., Soph.: —absol. *to recover oneself, pay attention*, Hdt., Dem.   4. c. acc. *to visit*, Eur.   5. part. pf.

pass. ἐπεστραμμένος, = ἐπιστρεφής, earnest, vehement, Hdt. Hence

ἐπιστροφάδην [ᾰ], Adv. turning this way and that way, right and left, Hom.: also, ἐπ. βαδίζειν back-and for-wards, h. Hom.

ἐπιστροφή, ἡ, (ἐπιστρέφω) a turning about, twisting, Plat. II. intr. a turning or wheeling about, of men turning to bay, Soph.; ἐπιστροφαὶ κακῶν renewed assaults of ills, Id.:—of ships, a putting about, tacking, Thuc. 2. a turn of affairs, reaction, Id. 3. attention paid to a person or thing, regard, Soph., Xen. 4. a moving up and down in a place, δωμάτων ἐπιστροφαί occupation of them, Aesch.; ξενοτίμους ἐπ. δωμάτων, of the duties of hospitality, Id.

ἐπίστροφος, ον, (ἐπιστρέφω) having dealings with, conversant with, c. gen., Od., Aesch.

ἐπιστρώννυμι or –ύω, v. ἐπιστορέννυμι.

ἐπι-στρωφάω, Frequentat. of ἐπιστρέφω, to visit or frequent a place, c. acc. loci, Od.:—Med. to go in and out of, frequent, visit, occupy, Aesch., Eur.

ἐπιστύλιον, τό, (στῦλος) the lintel on the top of pillars, the epistyle, architrave, Plut.

ἐπίστω, for ἐπίστασο, 2 sing. imper. of ἐπίσταμαι.

ἐπι-συκοφαντέω, f. ήσω, to harass yet more with frivolous accusations.

ἐπι-συνάγω, f. ξω, to collect and bring to a place, to gather together, N. T. Hence

ἐπισυνᾰγωγή, ἡ, a gathering or being gathered together, N. T.

ἐπι-συνάπτω, f. ψω, to renew a war, Plut.

ἐπι-συνδίδωμι, to push forward together, Plut.

ἐπι-συντρέχω, to run together to a place, N. T.

ἐπίσυρμα, ατος, τό, the trail or track made by dragging a thing, Xen. From

ἐπι-σύρω [ῡ], to drag or trail after one, in Med., Luc.: —Pass. to crawl along, Xen. II. to do anything in a slovenly way, to slur over, Lys.; ἐπισύροντες confusedly, Dem.; often in part. pf. pass. slovenly, careless, Luc.

ἐπι-σύστασις, εως, ἡ, a gathering together against, a riotous meeting, N. T.

ἐπι-σφάζω, later –σφάττω, f. ξω, to slaughter over or upon, of sacrifices offered at a tomb, Eur., Xen. II. to kill after or besides, Id.

ἐπι-σφᾰλής, ές, (σφάλλω) prone to fall, unstable, precarious, Plat., Dem.:—Adv., ἐπισφαλῶς διακεῖσθαι to be in danger, Plut.

ἐπι-σφάττω, later form of ἐπι-σφάζω.

ἐπι-σφίγγω, f. ξω, to bind, clasp tight, Anth.

ἐπι-σφραγίζω, f. Att. ιῶ, to put a seal on, to confirm, ratify, Anth. II. as Dep. ἐπισφραγίζομαι, to put as a seal upon, impress upon, Plat.; also as Pass. to be impressed, marked, Anth. Hence

ἐπισφρᾱγιστής, οῦ, ὁ, one who seals or signs, Luc.

ἐπισφύρια [ῠ], τά, (σφυρόν) bands, clasps or hooks, which fastened the greaves (κνημῖδες) over the ankle, Il. II. the ankle, Anth.

ἐπι-σφύριος, ον, and -σφύρος, ον, on the ankle, Anth.

ἐπι-σχεδόν, Adv. near at hand, hard by, h. Hom.

ἐπισχεθεῖν, poët. for ἐπισχεῖν, aor. 2 of ἐπέχω, to hold in, check, Aesch.

ἐπι-σχερώ, Adv. (σχερός) in a row, one after another, Il. II. of Time, by degrees, Theocr.

ἐπισχεσία, Ion. -ίη, ἡ, (ἐπέχω) a thing held out, a pretext, Od.

ἐπίσχεσις, εως, ἡ, (ἐπέχω) a checking, hindrance, delay, reluctance, lingering, Od., Thuc.

ἐπ-ισχύω, f. ύσω [ῡ], to make strong or powerful, Xen. II. intr. to prevail, be urgent, N. T.

ἐπ-ίσχω, strengthd. for ἐπ-έχω, to hold or direct towards, Il.; τινί against one, Hes. II. to restrain, withhold, check, Id., Att.:—c. gen. to restrain from a thing, Od. 2. intr. to leave off, stop, wait, Thuc.; imper. ἔπισχε, hold, Eur.

ἐπισχών, aor. 2 part. of ἐπέχω.

ἐπί-σωτρον, Ep. ἐπίσ-σωτρον, τό, the metal hoop round the felloe (σῶτρον), the tire of a wheel, Il.

ἐπίταγμα, ατος, τό, (ἐπιτάσσω) an injunction, command, Plat., Aeschin. II. a reserve force, Plut.

ἐπιτακτήρ, ῆρος, ὁ, (ἐπιτάσσω) a commander, Xen.

ἐπίτακτος, ον, (ἐπιτάσσω) drawn up behind, οἱ ἐπίτακτοι the reserve of an army, Thuc.

ἐπι-τᾰλαιπωρέω, f. ήσω, to labour yet more, Thuc.

ἐπιτάμνω, Ion. for ἐπιτέμνω.

ἐπι-τᾰνύω, = ἐπιτείνω, to push home a bolt, Od.

ἐπίταξις, εως, ἡ, (ἐπιτάσσω) an injunction, ἡ ἐπ. τοῦ φόρου the assessment of the tribute, Hdt.

ἐπιτάραξις, εως, ἡ, disturbance, confusion, Plat. From

ἐπι-τᾰράσσω, Att. -ττω, f. ξω, to trouble or disquiet yet more, Hdt., Luc.

ἐπιτάρροθος, ὁ, ἡ, Ep. for ἐπίρροθος, a helper, defender, ally, Hom.; μάχης ἐπ. in fight, Il. 2. a master, lord, Orac. ap. Hdt.

ἐπίτᾰσις, εως, ἡ, (ἐπιτείνω) a stretching of strings, Plat.

ἐπι-τάσσω, Att. -ττω, f. ξω, to put upon one as a duty, to enjoin, τί τινι Hdt., etc. :—c. dat. pers. et inf. to order one to do, Id., Att.:—absol. to impose commands, Thuc.; τινί on one, Soph.:—Pass. with f. med. -τάξομαι, aor. 1 -ετάχθην, pf. -τέταγμαι:—to accept orders, submit to commands, Eur., Ar.; c. acc. rei, Thuc.:—of things, to be ordered, ὁ στρατὸς ὁ ἐπιταχθεὶς ἑκάστοισι Hdt.; τὰ ἐπιτασσόμενα orders given, Id. II. to place next or beside, Id., Xen.:— Med. τοὺς ἱππέας ἐπετάξαντο they had the cavalry placed next, Thuc. 2. to place behind, c. gen., Hdt.: absol. to place in reserve, Plut. :—Med., Xen. 3. to set in command over, οἱ ἐπιτεταγμένοι set as guards over the waggons, Xen.

ἐπι-τάφιος [ᾰ], ον, (τάφος) over a tomb, λόγος ἐπ. a funeral oration, spoken over citizens who had fallen in battle, such as that of Pericles in Thuc.

ἐπι-τᾰχύνω [ῠ], f. υνῶ, to hasten on, urge forward, Thuc.

ἐπιτεῖλαι, aor. 1 inf. of ἐπιτέλλω.

ἐπιτείνω, f. -τενῶ: Ion.impf. ἐπιτείνεσκον :—to stretch upon or over a place, Hdt. :—Pass., in tmesi, ἐπὶ νὺξ τέταται βροτοῖσι Od. 2. to stretch as on a frame, tighten, of musical strings, Plat.: metaph. to increase in intensity, to increase, augment, Id. 3. to urge on, incite, τινὰ ποιεῖν τι Xen.; ἐπ. ἑαυτόν to exert himself, Plut. II. Pass. to be stretched as on the rack, Plat. 2. to be on the stretch, to be strained or con-

tracted, Id.; ἐπ. βιβλίοις to devote oneself to books, Luc. 3. to hold out, endure, Xen.

ἐπι-τειχίζω, f. Att. ιῶ, to build a fort on the frontier as a basis of operations against the enemy, Thuc., Xen.:—metaph., ἐπ. τυράννους to plant them like such forts, Dem. · Hence

ἐπιτείχισις, εως, ἡ, the building a fort on the enemy's frontier, the occupation of it, Thuc.; and

ἐπιτείχισμα, ατος, τό, a fort placed on the enemy's frontier, Thuc., Xen., etc.; c. gen., ἐπιτειχίσματα τῆς αὑτοῦ χώρας fortresses which command his country, Dem. 2. metaph., ἐπ. πρός τι a barrier or obstacle to a thing, Id.; and

ἐπιτειχισμός, ὁ, = ἐπιτείχισις, Thuc., Xen.

ἐπι-τελειόω, f. ώσω, to complete a sacrifice, Plut. Hence

ἐπιτελείωσις, εως, ἡ, accomplishment, completion, Plut.

ἐπι-τελέω, f. έσω, to complete, finish, accomplish, Hdt., Thuc.: esp. of the fulfilment of oracles, visions, vows or promises, Id. II. to discharge a religious service, Hdt. III. to pay in full, Id.:—metaph. in Med., ἐπιτελεῖσθαι τὰ τοῦ γήρως to have to pay, be subject to, the burdens of old age, Xen.; ἐπ. θάνατον to have to pay the debt of death, Id.

ἐπι-τελής, ές, (τέλος) brought to an end, completed, accomplished, Hdt., etc.

ἐπι-τέλλω: aor. 1 ἐπ-έτειλα: pf. -τέταλκα, pass. -τέταλμαι:—to lay upon, enjoin, prescribe, ordain, command, τι or τί τινι Hom.:—c. dat. pers. only, to give orders to, Il.:—c. dat. pers. et inf. to order him to do, Ib.:—also in Med., just like the Act., Ib. II. Pass. to rise, of stars, Hes.:—metaph., of love, Theogn.

ἐπι-τέμνω, Ion. -τάμνω: f. -τεμῶ: aor. 2 ἐπέταμον:—to cut on the surface, make an incision into, gash, Lat. incidere, Hdt., Aeschin.:—Med., ἐπιτάμνεσθαι τοὺς βραχίονας to gash their arms, Hdt. II. to cut short, to abridge, Plut.

ἐπι-τέξ, εκος, ἡ, (τίκτω) at the birth, about to bring forth, Hdt., Luc.

ἐπι-τερπής, ές, (τέρπω) pleasing, delightful, h. Hom., Plut.:—Adv. -πῶς, Id. II. devoted to pleasure, Id.

ἐπι-τέρπομαι, Pass. to rejoice or delight in a thing, c. dat., Od., Hes.

ἐπιτέταμαι, pf. pass. of ἐπιτείνω.

ἐπιτέτραμμαι, pf. pass. of ἐπιτρέπω: ἐπιτετράφαται, Ion. 3 pl.

ἐπι-τεχνάομαι, f. -ήσομαι, Dep. to contrive for a purpose or to meet an emergency, to invent, Hdt. 2. to contrive against, τί τινι Luc. Hence

ἐπιτέχνησις, εως, ἡ, contrivance for a purpose, invention, Thuc.; and

ἐπιτέχνητός, όν, artificially made, Luc.

ἐπιτήδειος, α, ον, Ion. -εος, έη, εον: regul. Comp. and Sup. -ειότερος, Ion. -εώτερος, -εώτατος: (ἐπιτηδές):—made for an end or purpose, fit or adapted for it, suitable, convenient, ἔς τι, πρός τι Hdt., Plat.; c. inf., χωρίον ἐπ. ἐνιππεῦσαι fit to ride in, Hdt.; ἐπ. ὑπεξαιρεθῆναι convenient to be put out of the way, Thuc.; ἐπ. ξυνεῖναι a pleasant person to live with, Eur.; ἐπ. παθεῖν deserving to suffer, Dem., also, ἐπιτήδεόν [ἐστί] μοι, c. inf., Hdt. II. useful, serviceable, necessary, 1. of things, fit or serviceable for, c. dat., Thuc.; ἐς τὸ

ἐπ. to their advantage, Id.; of treaties, omens, favourable, Hdt. :—esp. as Subst., τὰ ἐπιτήδεια necessaries, provisions, Lat. commeatus, Id., Thuc., etc. 2. of persons, serviceable, friendly, Hdt., Thuc.; τῷ πατρί conformable to his will, Hdt.: as Subst., c. gen., a close friend, Lat. necessarius, Thuc. III. Adv. -έως, Ion. -έως, studiously, carefully, Hdt. · 2. suitably, conveniently, fitly, Id.;—Comp. -ειότερον, Id. Hence

ἐπιτηδειότης, ητος, ἡ, fitness, suitableness, Plat.

ἐπιτηδές, Adv. such as may serve the purpose, enough, or of set purpose, advisedly, studiously, Lat. consulto, de industria, Hom.;—in Hdt. and Att. written proparox., ἐπίτηδες Hdt.; Dor. ἐπίτᾱδες Theocr.:—also designedly, deceitfully, Eur. (Deriv. uncertain.)

ἐπιτήδευμα, ατος, τό, a pursuit, business, practice, Lat. studium, Thuc., Plat.; and

ἐπιτήδευσις, εως, ἡ, devotion or attention to a pursuit, Thuc., Plat., etc.; βίοτου ἐπιτηδεύσεις refinements of life, Eur. From

ἐπιτηδεύω, impf. ἐπετήδευον: aor. 1 ἐπ-ετήδευσα: pf. -τετήδευκα, pass. -τετήδευμαι, (as if it were a compd. of ἐπί, τηδεύω, but there is no such Verb; and ἐπιτηδεύω must be formed directly from ἐπιτηδές):—to pursue or practise a thing, make a practice of, make it one's business, Lat. studere rei, c. acc., Hdt., Att. :—also, ἐπ. τι πρός τι to invent for a purpose, Hdt. :—Pass. to be done with pains and practice, to be made so and so by art, Id.; of dogs, to be trained, Xen. 2. c. inf. to take care to do, use to do, Hdt., Plat.

ἐπιτηδέως, Adv. of ἐπιτήδεος, Ion. for ἐπιτήδειος.

ἐπιτήκτος, ον, overlaid with gold: metaph. counterfeit, Anth. From

ἐπι-τήκω, f. ξω, to melt upon, pour when melted over a thing, Plut.

ἐπι-τηρέω, f. ήσω, to look out for, Ar., Thuc., etc.

ἐπι-τίθημι, f. -θήσω: pf. -τέθεικα: the Pass. is mostly furnished by ἐπίκειμαι: A. Act. to lay, put or place upon, of offerings laid on the altar, meats on the table, etc., c. dat., Od., Att.; also c. gen., Il., Hdt.:—c. acc. only, ἐπ. φάρμακα to apply salves, Il.; ἐπ. στήλην to set it up, Hdt. II. to put on a covering or lid, Od.; λίθον ἐπέθηκε θύρῃσιν, i. e. put a stone as a door to the cave, put it before the door, Ib.: to put a door to, shut it, Il., Hom. III. to put to, grant or give besides, Il. 2. of Time, to add, bring on, Od. IV. μύθῳ or μύθοις τέλος ἐπιθεῖναι to put an end to them, Il. 2. to put on as a finish, ἐπέθηκε κορώνην Ib.; ἐπ. κεφαλαῖον (v. sub κεφαλαῖον) Dem. V. to impose or inflict a penalty, θωὴν σοι ἐπιθήσομεν Od.; δίκην, ζημίαν ἐπ. τινί Hdt. VI. like ἐπιστέλλω, to dispatch a letter, Id., Dem. VII. to give a name, Hdt., Plat.

B. Med. to put on oneself or for oneself, Il., Eur. II. to set oneself to, apply oneself to, employ oneself on or in, c. dat., Hdt., Thuc., etc. 2. to make an attempt upon, attack, τῇ Εὐβοίῃ Hdt., Thuc., etc. 3. absol., δικαιοσύνην ἐπιθέμενος ἤσκεε he practised justice with assiduity, Hdt. IV. to bring on oneself, ἀράς Aesch.: also to cause a penalty to be imposed, Thuc. V. to lay commands on, τί τινι Hdt. VI. to give a name, Od.

ἐπι-τῑμάω, f. ήσω, to lay a value upon, Lat. aestimare : hence, 1. to shew honour to, τινά Hdt. 2. to raise in price :—Pass. to rise in price, Dem. II. of judges, to lay a penalty on a person, Hdt. 2. c. acc. to censure, Dem. ; also c. dat., Id. : absol., Thuc. Hence

ἐπιτίμησις, εως, ή, censure, criticism, Thuc. ; and

ἐπιτῑμητής, οῦ, ὁ, a chastiser, censurer, Aesch., Eur.

ἐπιτῑμήτωρ, ορος, ὁ, an avenger, Od.

ἐπιτῑμία, ή, the condition of an ἐπίτιμος, the enjoyment of civil rights, opp. to ἀτιμία, Aeschin., Dem.

ἐπιτίμιον, τό, mostly in pl. ἐπιτίμια, τά, the value, price, or estimate of a thing, i. e., 1. the honours paid to a person, Soph. 2. assessment of damages or penalties, Hdt., Eur. ; τῶνδε for these things, Aesch. ; ἐπ. δυσσεβείας the wages of ungodliness, Soph. ; in sing., τοὐπιτίμιον λαβεῖν to exact the penalty, Aesch.

ἐπί-τῑμος, ον, (τιμή) of a citizen, in possession of his rights and franchises (τιμαί⟩, opp. to ἄτιμος, Ar., Thuc.

ἐπι-τίτθιος, ον, at the breast, a suckling, Theocr.

ἐπι-τιτρώσκω, f. -τρώσω, to wound on the surface, Anth.

*ἐπι-τλάω, only in aor. 2 ἐπ-έτλην, inf. -τλῆναι :—to bear patiently, be patient, Il.

ἐπιτολή, ή, (ἐπιτέλλω II) the rising of a star, Eur., Thuc.

ἐπι-τολμάω, f. ήσω, to submit or endure to do, c. inf., Od. : absol., ἐπετόλμησε he stood firm, Ib.

ἐπιτομή, ή, (ἐπιτέμνω) a cutting on the surface, incision, Aesch. II. an epitomé, abridgment, Cic.

ἐπίτονος, ον, (ἐπιτείνω) on the stretch, strained :—ἐπίτονος (sc. ἱμάς), ὁ, a rope for stretching or tightening, the back-stay of a mast (opp. to πρότονος), Od. 2. ἐπίτονοι, οἱ, the sinews of the shoulder and arm, Plat.

ἐπι-τοξάζομαι, Dep. to shoot at, c. dat., Il., Luc.

ἐπιτόσσαις, Dor. part. of ἐπέτοσσε, q. v.

ἐπι-τραγῳδέω, f. ήσω, to make into a tragic story, exaggerate, Luc. : to add in exaggeration, Plut.

ἐπι-τραπέζιος, ον, (τράπεζα) on or at table, Luc.

ἐπιτράπέουσι, Ep. for ἐπιτρέπουσι.

ἐπιτρεπτέον, verb. Adj. one must permit, Xen. ; so in pl. ἐπιτρεπτέα Hdt. From

ἐπι-τρέπω, Ion. -τράπω : f. -τρέψω : aor. 1 -έτρεψα, Ion. -έτραψα : aor. 2 -έτραπον :—Pass. and Med., Ion. aor. 1 -ετράφθην : aor. 2 pass. -ετράπην, med. -ετράπόμην :—properly to turn towards, in aor. 2 med., θυμὸς ἐπετράπετο εἴρεσθαι thy mind inclined itself to ask, Od. 2. to turn over to, to commit or entrust to another as trustee, guardian, or vicegerent, Hom., Hdt., Att. ; c. inf. σοὶ ἐπέτρεψεν πονέεσθαι he left it to you to work, Il. 3. c. dat. only, to trust to, rely upon, Hom., Hdt. : to refer the matter to a person, leave it to his judgment, Ar., Thuc. :—so in Med. to entrust oneself, leave one's case to, τινι Hdt. 4. Pass. to be entrusted, ᾧ λαοὶ τ' ἐπιτετράφαται (3 pl. pf. for ἐπιτετραμμένοι εἰσί) Il. ; τῆς (sc. Ὥραις) ἐπιτέτραπται οὐρανός heaven's gate is committed to them (to open and to shut), Ib. ;—also c. acc. rei, ἐπιτρέπομαί τι I am entrusted with a thing, Hdt., Thuc. II. to give up, yield, Ποσειδάωνι νίκην ἐπέτρεψας Il. ; so τινί c. inf. to permit, suffer, Hdt., Att. III. intr. to yield, give way, Il., Hdt. III. to command, τινὶ ποιεῖν τι Xen.

ἐπι-τρέφω, f. -θρέψω : pf. -τέτροφα : aor. 2 pass. ἐπετράφην [ᾰ] :—to rear upon :—generally, to support, maintain, Hdt. II. Pass. to grow up after, as posterity, Lat. succrescere, Id. ; to grow up as a successor, Id.

ἐπι-τρέχω : f. -δράμοῦμαι : aor. 2 -έδραμον : rarely aor. 1 -έθρεξα : pf. -δεδράμηκα Xen. ; poët. -δέδρομα :— to run upon or at, for the purpose of attack, Il.; of dogs, Od. ; so in Att. to make an assault upon, τινί Thuc., Xen. 2. to run after, ἐπιδραμών in haste, eagerly, Hdt., Plat. II. to run over a space, Il. : to run over or graze the surface, Ib. 2. to be spread over, of a mist, Od. :—c. acc., οἶδμα ὅταν ἔρεβος ἐπιδράμῃ when the billow runs over the deep, Soph. 3. to overrun, as an army does a country, Hdt., Thuc. 4. to run over, to treat lightly of, Lat. percurrere, Xen. III. to run close after, Il.

ἐπι-τρίβω [ῑ], f. ψω : aor. 2 pass. ἐπετρίβην [ῑ] :—to rub on the surface, to crush, Ar. :—Pass. to be galled, Id. 2. metaph. to afflict, distress, destroy, ruin, Hdt., Ar. ; of an actor, to murder a character, Dem. : —Pass. to be utterly destroyed or undone, Solon, Ar. ; ἐπιτριβείης be hung ! Ar.

ἐπι-τριηραρχέω, f. ήσω, to be trierarch beyond the legal time, Dem. Hence

ἐπιτριηράρχημα, ατος, τό, the burden of a trierarchy continued beyond the legal term, Dem.

ἐπίτριπτος, ον, (ἐπιτρίβω) rubbed down, well worn : metaph. of persons, practised, cunning, Soph. ; οὑπίτριπτος the rogue, Ar.

ἐπί-τρῐτος, ον, one and a third, i. e. 1 + ⅓ or ⁴⁄₃, Plat. II. ἐπίτριτον (sc. δάνεισμα), τό, a loan of which ⅓ is paid as interest, i. e. 33⅓ p. cent., Xen.

ἐπιτροπαῖος, α, ον, (ἐπιτροπή) delegated, Hdt.

ἐπιτροπεύω, (ἐπίτροπος) to be a trustee, administrator, guardian, governor, Hdt., Xen. 2. c. acc. to govern, administer, πατρίδα Hdt., Ar., etc. ; ἐπ. τινά to be his guardian, Thuc. :—Pass., κακῶς ἐπιτροπευθῆναι to be ill treated by one's guardians, Dem.

ἐπιτροπή, ή, (ἐπιτρέπω) a reference to an arbiter, Thuc., Dem. II. an action against a guardian, Id.

ἐπίτροπος, ον, (ἐπιτρέπω) one to whom a charge is entrusted, a trustee, administrator, Hdt. : a governor, viceroy, Id., Dem. 2. a guardian, Hdt., Thuc.

ἐπιτροχάδην [ᾰ], (ἐπιτρέχω) Adv. trippingly, fluently, glibly, Hom.

ἐπίτροχος, ον, (ἐπιτρέχω) voluble, glib, Luc.

ἐπι-τρύζω, to murmur beside or over, τινί Babr.

ἐπι-τρώγω, f. -τρώξομαι : aor. 2 -έτραγον :—to eat with or after, Luc.

ἐπι-τυγχάνω : aor. 2 ἐπέτυχον :—properly to hit the mark : hence to light or fall upon, meet with, 1. c. dat., Hdt., Thuc., etc. 2. c. gen., Ar., Thuc. 3. absol., ὁ ἐπιτυχών, like ὁ τυχών, the first person one meets, any one, Hdt., Plat. II. to attain to, reach, gain one's end, c. gen. rei, Xen., Dem. 2. c. part. to succeed in doing, Hdt. 3. c. dat. modi, to be successful in a thing, μάχῃ Aeschin. : absol. to succeed, be successful, Plat., Xen. III. ἐπ. βιβλίῳ to read it, Luc.

ἐπι-τυμβίδιος, α, ον, (τύμβος) at or over a tomb, Aesch. II. crested, a name given to larks, Theocr.

ἐπιτύμβιος, ον, = foreg., Aesch., Soph.
ἐπιτύφομαι [ῡ], Pass. to be inflamed; ἐπιτεθυμμένος furious, rabid, Plat.
ἐπιτυχεῖν, aor. 2 inf. of ἐπιτυγχάνω.
ἐπιφαγεῖν, aor. 2 inf. of ἐπεσθίω.
ἐπι-φαίνω, f. -φᾰνῶ: aor. 1 -έφηνα, later -έφᾱνα:— to shew forth, display, shew off, Theogn. :—Pass. to come into light, come suddenly into view, Il., Hdt. : —to present oneself, shew oneself, appear, Id. II. intr. to shew light, shine upon, c. dat., N. T.
ἐπιφάνεια [ᾰ], ἡ, manifestation, Plut. II. visible surface: outward show, distinction, Plat.
ἐπιφᾰνῆναι, aor. 2 pass. inf. of ἐπιφαίνω.
ἐπιφᾰνής, ές, coming to light, appearing, of gods, Hdt., etc. 2. in full view, πόλις ἐπ. ἔξωθεν, of a place commanded by another, Thuc. 3. manifest, evident, of proofs, Id. II. of men, conspicuous, famous, distinguished by rank, Hdt.; notable, for well or ill, Thuc., Xen. 2. of things, remarkable, Hdt. III. Adv. -νῶς, openly, Thuc. : Sup. -έστατα, Id.
ἐπίφαντος, ον, (ἐπιφαίνομαι) in the light, alive, Soph.
ἐπι-φατνίδιος, ον, (φάτνη) at the manger, Xen.
ἐπι-φαύω, (φάος) to shine upon, τινι N. T.
ἐπι-φέρω, f. ἐποίσω: aor. 1 ἐπήνεγκα : aor. 2 ἐπήνεγκον :—to bring, put or lay upon, τί τινι Il., etc. ; ἐπιφέρειν τινὶ πόλεμον, Lat. bellum inferre, to make war upon him, Hdt., Att. ; so, ἐπ. δόρυ Aesch., etc. :— absol. to attack, assail, Ar. 2. to bring offerings to the grave, Thuc. 3. to bring as a charge against, Hdt., Att.; so, ἐπ. μωρίην, μανίην τινί to impute it to him, Hdt., etc. 4. to confer or impose upon, in good or bad sense, Thuc. 5. to add to, increase, Id. II. Med. to bring with or upon oneself, bring as dowry, Dem. III. Pass. to rush upon or after, attack, assault, Il., Hdt., Att. 2. to be borne onwards, Hdt. 3. to come after or next, ensue, τὰ ἐπιφερόμενα coming events, Id.
ἐπι-φημίζω, f. σω, to utter words ominous of the event, in Med., Hdt. 2. to promise according to an omen, c. inf., Eur. II. to assign as authority to a thing, τοὺς θεούς Dem. 2. c. acc. et inf. to allege that, Plut. III. to dedicate or devote to a god, Luc. Hence
ἐπιφήμισμα, ατος, τό, a word of ominous import, Thuc.
ἐπι-φθάνω [ᾰ], to reach first, part. aor. 2 ἐπιφθάς, Batr.
ἐπι-φθέγγομαι, f. γξομαι, Dep. to utter after or in accordance, Lat. accinere, Aesch., Plat. 2. to utter, pronounce, Id. II. to call to, Luc.
ἐπι-φθονέω, f. ήσω, to bear grudge against, τινι Od., Hdt.
ἐπί-φθονος, ον, liable to envy or jealousy, regarded with jealousy, odious, Hdt., Att. :—ἐπίφθονόν ἐστι, c. inf. 'tis invidious, hateful to, Hdt., Ar. :—τὸ ἐπίφθονον jealousy, odium, Thuc. 2. act. bearing a grudge against, τινι Aesch.: absol. injurious, Id. II. Adv., ἐπιφθόνως διακεῖσθαί τινι to be liable to his hatred, Thuc.; ἐπ. ἔχειν πρός τινα Xen.; ἐπ. διαπράξασθαί τι in an odious manner, Thuc.
ἐπι-φθύζω, = ἐπιπτύω, to spit at, so as to avert a spell, ἐπιφθύζοισα (Dor. part.) Theocr. :—also to mutter, Id.
ἐπι-φῐλοπονέομαι, Dep. to labour earnestly at, τινι Xen.

ἐπι-φλέγω, f. ξω, to burn up, consume, Il., Hdt.; ἐπ. τὴν πόλιν to set fire to it, Thuc. 2. metaph. to inflame, excite, Aesch., Plut. II. intr. to be scorching hot, Luc.
ἐπί-φοβος, ον, frightful, terrible, Aesch.
ἐπι-φοιτάω, f. ήσω, to come habitually to, visit again and again, τὸ ἐπιφοιτέον or οἱ ἐπιφοιτέοντες the visitors, Hdt. ; ὁ ἐπιφοιτέων κέραμος the wine-jars which are regularly imported, Id. ; ἐπ. ἐς . . to go about to different places, Thuc. 2. c. dat., σπάνιος ἐπ. σφι visits them rarely, of the Phoenix, Hdt. 3. c. acc. pers., of visions, to haunt, Id.
ἐπιφορά, ἡ, (ἐπιφέρω) a bringing to or besides : a donative, addition made to one's pay, Thuc.
ἐπι-φορέω, f. ήσω, = ἐπιφέρω, to put upon, lay over, Hdt., Ar., etc. Hence
ἐπιφόρημα, ατος, τό, in pl. dishes served up besides or after, dessert, Hdt., etc.
ἐπίφορος, ον, (ἐπιφέρω) carrying towards, Thuc. : favourable, Aesch. II. of ground, sloping, Plut. III. near the time of bringing forth, Xen.
ἐπι-φράζω, f. σω, to say besides, Hdt. II. Med. with aor. 1 med. ἐπεφρασάμην and pass. ἐπεφράσθην : 1. c. inf. to think of doing, take into one's head to do, Hom. 2. absol. to think on, devise, contrive, Od., Hdt. :—absol., ὧδε ἐπιφρασθεὶς having come to this conclusion, Id. ; ἐπιφρασθεῖσα αὐτὴ by her own mother wit, Id. 3. to notice, observe, Hom. :—to recognise, Od. :—to acquaint oneself with, take cognisance of, Il.
ἐπι-φράσσω, Att. -ττω, f. ξω, to block up, Theophr. : —Med., ἐπ. τὰ ὦτα to stop one's ears, Luc.
ἐπιφρασσαίατο, Ep. for -φράσαιντο, 3 pl. aor. 1 med. opt. of foreg.
ἐπι-φρονέω, to be shrewd, prudent; in part. fem. ἐπιφρονέουσα, carefully, Od.
ἐπιφροσύνη, ἡ, (ἐπίφρων) thoughtfulness, Od.
ἐπί-φρουρος, ον, keeping watch over, τινι Eur.
ἐπί-φρων, ον, (φρήν) thoughtful, sage, Od.
ἐπι-φύλιος, ον, (φυλή) distributed to the tribes, Eur.
ἐπι-φυλλίς, ίδος, ἡ, (φύλλον) the small grapes left for gleaners, Anth. : hence, Ar. calls poetasters ἐπιφυλλίδες, mere gleanings.
ἐπι-φῠτεύω, f. σω, to plant over or upon a thing, Ar.
ἐπι-φύω, f. ύσω [ῡ], to produce on or besides, Theophr. II. Pass., with aor. 2 and pf. act. ἐπέφυν, ἐπιπέφυκα, to grow upon, c. dat., Hdt. : — of dogs, to stick close to, Plut. 2. to be born after, Id.
ἐπι-φωνέω, f. ήσω, to mention by name, tell of, Soph. 2. to say upon or with respect to, τινί or εἴς τι Plut. 3. to call out or address to, Id. Hence
ἐπιφώνημα, ατος, τό, a witty saying, Plut. ; and
ἐπιφώνησις, εως, ἡ, acclamation, a cry, Plut.
ἐπι-φώσκω, (φάος, φῶς) to draw towards dawn, N. T.
ἐπι-χαίνω, later form of ἐπιχάσκω, Luc.
ἐπι-χαίρω, to rejoice over, exult over, mostly of malignant joy, c. dat., Soph., Dem. ; absol., Ar., etc. 2. rarely in good sense, to rejoice in another's joy, c. acc., σὲ μὲν εὖ πράσσοντ' ἐπιχαίρω Soph.
ἐπι-χαλαζάω, to shower hail upon, τινά Luc.
ἐπι-χαλάω, f. άσω [ᾰ], to loosen, slacken, Luc. II. intr. to give way, relax, Aesch.

ἐπι-χαλκεύω, f. σω, to forge upon an anvil : metaph., ἐπ. τινά to forge or mould to one's purpose, Ar.

ἐπί-χαλκος, ον, covered with copper or brass, Hdt., Ar.

ἐπι-χαράσσω, Att. -ττω, to engrave upon, Plut.

ἐπι-χαρής, ές, (χαρά) gratifying, agreeable, Aesch.

ἐπι-χαριεντίζομαι, Dep. to quote as a good joke, Luc.

ἐπι-χαρίζομαι, f. Att. ιοῦμαι, Dep. to make a present of a thing, c. acc., Xen. 2. intr., ἐπιχάριττα (Boeot. for ἐπιχάρισαι, aor. 1 imper.) τῷ ξένῳ be civil to him, Ar.

ἐπί-χαρις, ό, ή, neut. -χαρι, pleasing, agreeable, charming, Aesch., Xen.:—τὸ ἐπίχαρι pleasantness of manner, Id.—The Comp. and Sup. are ἐπιχαριτώτερος, -τατος (as if from ἐπιχάριτος), Id. : Adv. is also ἐπιχαρίτως, Id.

ἐπιχαρίττως, Boeot. Adv. of ἐπίχαρις.

ἐπίχαρμα, ατος, τό, (ἐπιχαίρω) an object of malignant joy, Eur., Theocr. II. malignant joy, Eur.

ἐπίχαρτος, ον, (ἐπιχαίρω) wherein one feels joy, delightsome, Soph. 2. wherein one feels malignant joy, ἐχθροῖς ἐπίχαρτα sufferings that afford triumph to my enemies, Aesch. ; οἱ δικαίως τι πάσχοντες ἐπίχαρτοι to see people justly punished is a satisfaction, Thuc.

ἐπι-χειλής, ές, (χεῖλος) full to the brim, brim-full, Ar.

ἐπι-χειμάζω, f. σω, to pass the winter at a place, Thuc.

ἐπι-χειρέω, f. ήσω, (χείρ) to put one's hand on a thing, c. dat., Ar. 2. to put one's hand to a work, set to work at, attempt, c. dat., Hdt., Att. :—rarely c. acc., Theogn., Plat.:—Pass. to be attempted, Thuc. 3. c. inf. to endeavour or attempt to do, Hdt., Att. II. to make an attempt on, to set upon, attack, τινί Hdt., Att.; πρός τινα Thuc. ;—absol., Hdt., etc. Hence

ἐπιχείρημα, ατος, τό, an attempt, enterprise, Thuc., Xen.

ἐπιχείρησις, εως, ή, an attempt, attack, Hdt., Thuc. ; ἐπ. ποιεῖσθαί τινος to attempt a thing, Id.

ἐπιχειρητέον or -έα, verb. Adj. of ἐπιχειρέω, one must attempt or attack, τινί Thuc., Plat.

ἐπιχειρητής, οῦ, ό, an enterprising person, Thuc.

ἐπί-χειρον, τό, (χείρ) only in pl. ἐπίχειρα, τά, wages of manual labour : generally wages, pay, guerdon, reward, Ar., Plat. :—also in bad sense, τῆς ὑψηγόρου γλώσσης ἐπ. rewards for proud speech, Aesch. ; ξιφέων ἐπ. the wages of the sword, i. e. slaughter by it, Soph.

ἐπι-χειροτονέω, f. ήσω, to vote in favour of a proposed decree, to sanction by vote, Dem. 2. of magistrates, to admit one elected to office, ap. Dem. Hence

ἐπιχειροτονία, ή, a voting by show of hands, Dem.

ἐπι-χέω: f. -χεῶ (v. χέω), 2 pers. ἐπιχεῖς : aor. 1 ἐπέχεα :—Ep. pres. ἐπιχεύω, aor. 1 ἐπέχευα, inf. ἐπιχεῦαι : —to pour water over the hands, Hom., Att. :—metaph. to pour or shed over, ὕπνον τινί, etc., Hom. 2. of solids, like χώννυμι, Id. B. Med. to pour or throw over oneself or for himself, Od. II. to have poured out for one to drink, ἐπ. ἀκρατόν τινος to drink it to any one's health, Theocr. C. Pass. to be poured over, Xen. : aor. 1 ἐπεχύθην [ῠ], pf. -κέχυμαι :—metaph., of a crowd of persons, to stream to a place, ἐπέχυντο (Ep. aor. 2 pass.), Il. :— to come like a stream over, Hdt.

ἐπι-χθόνιος, ον, and later α, ον, upon the earth, earthly,

as epith. of mortals, Hom. ; absol., ἐπιχθόνιοι earthly ones, men on earth, Il.

ἐπι-χλευάζω, f. σω, to make a mock of, τι Plut. : to say scornfully, Babr.

ἐπι-χλιαίνω, f. ἄνῶ, to warm slightly, Luc.

ἐπί-χολος, ον, (χολή) act. producing bile, ποίη ἐπιχολωτάτη Hdt.

ἐπι-χορεύω, f. σω, to dance to or in honour of a thing, Ar. II. to come dancing on, Xen.

ἐπι-χορηγέω, f. ήσω, to supply besides, τί τινι N. T. : —Pass., Ib. Hence

ἐπιχορηγία, ή, additional help, N. T.

ἐπι-χράω (χράω B), only in impf. or aor. 2 ἐπέχραον, to attack, assault, c. dat., Il. ; μητέρι μοι μνηστῆρες ἐπέχραον beset her, Od.

*ἐπι-χράω, to lend besides, cf. ἐπικίχρημι. II.

ἐπιχράομαι, Dep. to make use of besides, c. dat., Eur. 2. c. dat. pers., Lat. uti, to have dealings with, be friends with, Hdt., Thuc.

ἐπι-χρέμπτομαι, Dep. to spit upon, τινι Luc.

ἐπί-χριστος, ον, smeared over :—metaph. spurious, Lat. fucatus, Luc.

ἐπι-χρίω, f. ίσω [ι], to anoint, besmear, Od. :—Med. to anoint oneself, Ib. 2. to plaster over, τι ἐπί τι N. T. ; τινί with a thing, Luc.

ἐπί-χρῡσος, ον, overlaid with gold, Hdt., Xen.

ἐπι-χρωματίζω, f. σω, to lay in like colour, Plat.

ἐπι-χρώννῡμι and -ύω, f. -χρώσω, to smear over, colour on the surface, tinge, τινί with a thing, Luc.

ἐπι-χωρέω, f. ήσω, to give way, yield, τινί to one, Soph. 2. to forgive, Plut. II. to come towards, join as an ally, Lat. accedere alicui, Thuc., Xen. III. to go against the enemy, Id.

ἐπιχωριάζω, to be in the habit of visiting, Plat. ; ἐπ. τοῖς ἄνω πράγμασι to be occupied with, Luc. From

ἐπι-χώριος, εως, α, ον, or ος, ον, (χώρα) in or of the country : 1. of persons, οἱ ἐπ. the people of the country, natives, Hdt., al. ; οἱ ἐπιχώριοι χθονός Soph., Eur. 2. of things, of or used in the country, Hdt., Ar. ;—often, τὸ ἐπιχώριον, τοὐπιχώριον the custom of the country, custom, fashion, Id., Thuc., etc. ; ἐπιχώριον ὂν ἡμῖν, c. inf., as is the custom of our country, Thuc. II. Adv. -ίως, Ar.

ἐπι-ψᾱκάζω, old Att. for ἐπι-ψεκάζω.

ἐπι-ψαύω, f. σω, to touch on the surface, touch lightly, handle, c. gen., Hes., Hdt., Att. ; κᾶν ὀλίγον νυκτός τις ἐπιψαύσῃσι, i. e. if one gets ever so little of the night, i. e. sleeps ever so little, Theocr. :—metaph. to touch lightly upon, Lat. strictim attingere, Hdt. II. intr., ὅσσ' ὀλίγον περ ἐπιψαύῃ πραπίδεσσιν who can reach ever so little way by his wits, Od.

ἐπι-ψεκάζω, old Att. -ψακάζω, to keep dropping, ὁ θεὸς ἐπιψακάζει, of small rain, 'tis drizzling, Ar.

ἐπι-ψέλιον, τό, a curb-chain, Anth.

ἐπι-ψεύδομαι, Dep. to lie still more, Xen. II. to attribute falsehood to, τί τινι Luc. III. to falsify a number, Plut.

ἐπι-ψηλᾰφάω, to feel by passing the hand over the surface, Plat. ; ἐπ. τινός to feel for it, Id.

ἐπι-ψηφίζω, f. Att. ιῶ, to put a question to the vote (the office of the President) in the Athenian Senate or Assembly, ἐπ. τὰς γνώμας Aeschin., Dem.; c. inf. to

put it to the vote that .., Thuc.　2. absol. to put the question, Id., Xen.　3. ἐπ. τινί to put the question for or at the instance of any one, Hdt.　4. ἐπ. τοὺς παρόντας to put the question to them, take their votes, Plat.　II. Pass. to be put to the vote, Aeschin.　III. Med., of the voters, to vote, Luc.

ἐπί-ψογος, ον, exposed to blame, blameworthy, Xen. : —Adv. -γως, Plut.　II. act. censorious, Aesch.

ἐπι-ψύχω [ῠ], to cool, Plut.

ἐπ-ιωγαί, ῶν, αἱ, places of shelter for ships, roadsteads, Od.

ἐπ-ιών, part. of ἔπ-ειμι (εἶμι ibo).

ἐπλάγχθην, aor. 1 pass. of πλάζομαι.

ἐπλάθην [ᾰ], aor. 1 pass. of πελάζω.

ἔπλᾰσα, aor. 1 of πλάσσω.

ἔπλε, syncop. for ἔπελε, aor. 2 act. of πέλω :—ἔπλεο or ἔπλευ, ἔπλετο, sync. for ἐπέλεο, ἐπέλου, ἐπέλετο, 2 and 3 sing. aor. 2 med.

ἔπλεξα, aor. 1 of πλέκω.

ἐπλήγην, aor. 2 pass. of πλήσσω.

ἔπληντο, 3 pl. Ep. aor. pass. of πελάζω.

ἔπλωον, Ion. impf. of πλέω.

ἔπνευσα, ἐπνεύσθην, aor. 1 act. and pass. of πνέω.

ἐπ-όγμιος, ον, (ὄγμος) presiding over the furrows, Anth.

ἐπόδια, ἀποδιάζω, Ion. for ἐφοδ-.

ἐπ-οδύρομαι [ῠ], Dep. to lament over a thing, Anth.

ἐποδώκει, v. ποδοχέω.

ἐπόθην, v. for πίνω.

ἐποικέω, f. ήσω, (ἔποικος) to go as settler or colonist to a place, to settle in a place, c. acc., Eur.; ἐν τόπῳ Xen.　II. to be settled with hostile views against, ὑμῖν Thuc. : Pass., ἡ Δεκέλεια τῇ χώρᾳ ἐποικεῖται De-celeia is occupied as a base of operations against the country, Id.

ἐπ-οικοδομέω, f. ήσω, to build up, Thuc.　2. to build upon, Xen.　II. to rebuild, Id., Dem.

ἐπ-οικος, ὁ, one who has settled among strangers, a settler, alien, Soph., Plat.　2. a colonist, Ar., Thuc.　II. as Adj. neighbouring, Aesch. : hence again as Subst. a neighbour, one near, Soph.

ἐπ-οικτείρω, to have compassion on, τινά Soph.; absol., Aesch.

ἐπ-οικτίζω, f. σω, to compassionate, c. acc., Soph.

ἐποίκτιστος, ον, pitiable, piteous, Aesch.

ἐπ-οικτος, ον, piteous, Aesch.

ἐπ-οιμώζω, f. -οιμώξομαι, to lament over, πάθει Aesch.

ἐποίσω, fut. of ἐπιφέρω.

ἐπ-οιχνέω, =sq., Anth.

ἐπ-οίχομαι, Dep. to go towards, approach, c. acc., Od., Theogn.　2. to approach with hostile purpose, set on, attack, c. acc., Il.　3. to go over, traverse, Ib.　2. to go round, visit in succession (cf. ἔπειμι (εἶμι ibo) III), of one who hands round wine, ἐπῴχετο οἰνοχοεύων Od.; of a general, to go round, inspect, στίχας Hom.; and absol. to go the rounds, Il.　3. of Apollo and Artemis to visit with death, Hom.　4. to go over or ply one's work, Id.; ἱστὸν ἐπ. to ply the loom, Lat. percurrere telam, Id. :—absol. in partic., busily, Il.

ἐπ-οκέλλω, = ἐπικέλλω, to run a ship ashore, Hdt., Thuc.　2. of the ship, to run aground, Id.

ἐπ-οκριόεις, εσσα, εν, uneven, projecting, Anth.

ἐπ-ολισθάνω, f. -ολισθήσω, to slip or glide upon, Anth.

ἐπ-ολολύζω, f. ξω, to shout for joy, τινί at or to one, Aesch.; τι over or at a thing, Id.;—also in Med., Id.

ἔπομαι, to follow : v. ἕπω.

ἐπ-ομβρέω, f. ήσω, to pour rain upon, Anth.

ἐπομβρία, ἡ, heavy rain, abundance of wet, wet weather, Ar.　From

ἐπ-ομβρος, ον, very rainy, Arist.

ἐπ-όμνυμι and -ύω : f. -ομοῦμαι : aor. 1 -ώμοσα :—to swear after, swear accordingly, Od. : to take an oath besides, Thuc.　2. c. acc. pers., to swear by, Hdt., Eur., etc. : so in Med., ap. Dem.　3. c. acc. rei, to swear to a thing, Xen.　4. c. inf. to swear that, Hdt., Eur. : so in Med., Dem.　5. absol. in aor. 1 part., ἐπομόσας upon oath, Hdt., Xen.

ἐπ-ομφάλιος, α, ον, (ὀμφαλός) on the navel or central point, on the boss of the shield (Lat. umbo), Il.

ἐπόνᾱσα, Dor. for -ησα, aor. 1 of πονέω.

ἐπ-ονείδιστος, ον, (ὀνειδίζω) to be reproached, shameful, ignominious, Eur., Plat. ; ἐπονείδιστόν ἐστι is matter of reproach, Dem.

ἐπ-ονομάζω, f. σω, to give a surname : to name or call so and so, Thuc., Plat. :—Pass. to be named, ἀπό τινος or τινος after one, Thuc., Eur. :—to be surnamed, Thuc.　II. to pronounce a name, Hdt.

ἐπ-οπίζομαι, Dep., only in pres. and impf. to regard with awe, to reverence, Od., Theogn.

ἐποποῖ, a cry to mimic that of the hoopoe (ἔποψ), Ar.

ἐποποιΐα, ἡ, epic poetry or an epic poem, Hdt.　From

ἐπο-ποιός, ὁ, (ποιέω) an epic poet, Hdt.

ἐπ-οπτάω, f. ήσω, to roast besides or after, Od.

ἐποπτεύω, f. σω, (ἐπόπτης) to look over, overlook, watch, of an overseer, Od., Aesch., etc. :—also, to visit, punish, Id., Plat.　II. to become an ἐπόπτης, be ad-mitted to the highest mysteries, Ep. Plat. ; proverb. to attain to the highest earthly happiness, Ar.

ἐποπτήρ, ῆρος, ὁ, = sq., of tutelary gods, λιτῶν Aesch.

ἐπόπτης, ου, ὁ, (ἐπόψομαι, f. of ἐφοράω) an overseer, watcher, ἐπ. πόνων a spectator, Aesch. ; ἐπ. τῶν στρα-τηγουμένων Dem.　II. one admitted to the highest mysteries, Plut. Hence

ἐποπτικός, ή, όν, of or for an ἐπόπτης, τὰ τέλεα καὶ ἐπ. the highest mysteries, Plat.

ἐποράω, Ion. for ἐφοράω.

ἐπ-ορέγω, f. ξω, to hold out to, give yet more, Il. ; so in Med., Solon.　II. Med. to stretch oneself to-wards, ἐπορεξάμενος reaching forward to strike, Il.　2. metaph. to rise in one's demands, Hdt.

ἐπορέω, Ion. for ἐφοράω.

ἐπ-ορθιάζω, to set upright, of the voice, to lift up, Aesch. ; absol., ἐπορθ. γόοις to lift up the voice in wailing, Id.

ἐπ-ορθο-βοάω, to utter aloud, Eur.

ἐπ-ορμάω, ἐπ-ορμέω, Ion. for ἐφ-.

ἐπ-όρνυμι and -ύω : f. -όρσω : aor. 1 -ῶρσα :—to stir up, arouse, excite, Il.　2. to rouse and send against, c. dat., ὕπνον ἐπῶρσε sent sleep upon her, Od.　II. Pass. ἐπόρνυμαι, with pf. 2 act. ἐπόρωρα, 3 sing. Ep. aor. 2 pass. ἐπῶρτο :—to rise against, assault, fly upon one, c. dat., Il. ; absol., Ib. :—of things, c. inf., Od.

ἐπ-ορούω, f. σω, to rush violently at or upon, c. dat., Il. ; absol., Ib. : to rush after, i. e. to seek him, Ib. ; of sleep, to overtake, Od.

ἔπορσον, aor. 1 imper. of ἐπόρνυμι.

ἐπ-ορχέομαι, Dep. to dance to the tune of, c. gen., Dem.

ἔπος, εος, τό, (ἔπω A): **I.** a word, Od., etc.:—a tale, story, lay, Ib. **2.** a pledged word, promise, Il., etc. **3.** a word of advice, counsel, Ib. **4.** the word of a deity, a prophecy, oracle, Od., Hdt., Trag.:—later also, a saying, saw, proverb, Hdt. **5.** the meaning, substance, subject of a speech, a thing or matter, Il. **II.** Phrases:—ἅμα ἔπος τε καὶ ἔργον ἐποίεε 'no sooner said than done,' Hdt. **2.** κατ' ἔπος word by word, exactly, Ar. **3.** οὐδὲν πρὸς ἔπος nothing to the purpose, Plat. **4.** ὡς ἔπος εἰπεῖν or ὡς εἰπεῖν ἔπος, so to say, as the saying is, Eur., etc. **5.** ἑνὶ ἔπει in one word, briefly, Hdt. **III.** in pl. poetry in heroic verse, epic poetry, opp. to μέλη (lyric poetry), etc., Id., Att.: also, generally, poetry, Pind. **2.** in sing. a verse or line of poetry, Hdt., Ar.

ἐπ-οτοτύζω, f. ξω, to yell out, utter lamentably, Eur.

ἐπ-οτρύνω [ῠ], f. ῠνῶ, to stir up, excite, urge on, Hom., Hdt., etc.; c. inf., Il., etc.; c. dat. et inf., ἑτάροισιν ἐποτρῦναι κατακῆαι to urge them to burn, Od. **2.** c. acc. rei, to stir up against, Ib.; ἀγγελίας ἐπ. sends urgent messages, Ib.; ξύνοδον ἐπώτρυνον τοῖς ὁπλίταις gave the signal for engagement to the men-at-arms, Thuc.:—Med., ἐποτρυνώμεθα πομπήν let us urge on our escort, Od.:—Pass. to press on, hasten, Aesch.

ἐπ-ουραῖος, α, ον, (οὐρά) on the tail, Anth.

ἐπ-ουράνιος, ον, in heaven, heavenly, Hom. **2.** οἱ ἐπουράνιοι the gods above, Theocr.:—τὰ ἐπ. the phenomena of the heavens, Plat.

ἐπ-ουριάζω, = sq., to waft onwards, Luc.

ἐπ-ουρίζω, f. σω, to blow favourably upon, of a fair wind (οὖρος), ἐπ. τὴν ὀθόνην to fill the sail, Luc.:—metaph., φρόνημα ἐπ. to turn one's mind successfully to a thing, Eur.: c. acc. cogn., πνεῦμα αἱματηρὸν ἐπ. τινί (of the Erinyes) to send after him a gale of murderous breath, Aesch.

ἔπ-ουρος, ον, blowing favourably, Soph.

ἐπ-οφείλω, to owe besides or still, Thuc.

ἐπ-οφθαλμιάω, to cast longing glances at, c. dat., or πρός τι Plut.

ἐπ-οχέομαι, Pass. with fut. med., to be carried upon, ride upon, c. dat., Il.; absol., κάμηλον ὥστε ἐποχεῖσθαι a camel to ride on, Xen.

ἐπ-οχετεύω, f. σω, to carry water by sluices or courses, Lat. derivare, Plat.

ἐποχή, ἡ, (ἐπέχω) a check, cessation: the epoch of a star, i. e. the point at which it seems to halt after reaching the zenith, Plut.

ἐπ-οχθίδιος, α, ον, (ὄχθη) on or of the mountains, Anth.

ἔποχος, τό, the saddle-cloth, housing, Xen. From

ἔποχος, ον, (ἐπέχω) mounted upon a horse, chariot, ship, c. gen. vel dat., ναῶν ἔποχοι, ἅρμασιν ἔποχοι Aesch.: metaph., λόγος μανίας ἐπ. words borne on madness, i. e. frantic words, Eur. **2.** absol. having a good seat on horseback, Xen. **II.** pass., ποταμὸς ναυσὶ ἐπ. navigable by ships, Plut.

ἜΠΟΨ, οπος, ὁ, the hoopoe, Lat. upupa, Ar.

ἐπ-οψίδιος, ον, (ἐπόψομαι) for eating with bread, Anth.

ἐπόψιμος, ον, (ἐπόψομαι) that can be looked on, Soph.

ἐπόψιος, ον, (ὄψις) full in view, conspicuous, Soph. **II.** act. overlooking all things, of gods, Id.

ἐπ-οψις, εως, ἡ, a view over, ἐπ' ὅσον ἐπ. τοῦ ἱροῦ εἶχε so far as the view from the temple reached, Hdt.; τὴν ἔποψιν τῆς ναυμαχίας ἔχειν to view the sea-fight, Thuc.

ἐπόψομαι, fut. of ἐφοράω, with no pres. in use.

ἐπράθην [ᾰ], aor. 1 pass. of πιπράσκω.

ἔπρᾱθον, aor. 2 of πέρθω.

ἔπρεσα, Ep. for ἔπρησα, aor. 1 of πρήθω, Hes.

ἐπρήθην, Ion. for ἐπράθην, aor. 1 pass. of πιπράσκω.

ἔπρηξα, Ion. for ἔπραξα, aor. 1 of πράσσω.

ἔπρησα, aor. 1 of πρήθω.

ἐπριάμην [ᾰ], aor. 2 of ὠνέομαι.

ἙΠΤΆ, οἱ, αἱ, τά, indecl. seven, Lat. septem, Hom., etc.

ἑπτα-βόειος, ον, of seven bulls'-hides, Il.

ἑπτά-βοιος, ον, = foreg., Soph.

ἑπτά-δραχμος, ον, worth seven δραχμαί, Theocr.

ἑπτα-ετής, ές, = ἑπτέτης, seven years old, Plat.:—fem. -έτις, ιδος, Anth. **II.** parox. ἑπταέτης, ες, of seven years: neut. ἑπτάετες as Adv. for seven years, Od.

ἑπτά-και-δεκα, οἱ, αἱ, τά, indecl. seventeen, Hdt., etc.

ἑπτακαιδεκά-πους, ὁ, ἡ, neut. -πουν, 17 feet long, Plat.

ἑπτακαιδέκατος, η, ον, seventeenth, Thuc.

ἑπτά-και-είκοσι, οἱ, αἱ, τά, seven and twenty. Hence

ἑπτακαιεικοσ-έτης, ες, 27 years old, Anth.

ἑπτάκις, poët. -κι [ᾰ], Adv. seven times, Lat. septies, Ar., etc.

ἑπτάκις-μύριοι [ῠ], αι, α, seventy-thousand, Hdt., etc.

ἑπτάκις-χίλιοι [χῑ], αι, α, seven-thousand, Hdt., etc.

ἑπτά-κλῑνος, ον, with seven couches or beds, Xen.

ἑπτακόσιοι, αι, α, seven hundred, Hdt., etc.

ἑπτά-λογχος, ον, (λόγχη) of seven lances, i. e. seven bodies of spearmen, Anth.

ἑπτά-λοφος, ον, on seven hills, of Rome, Anth.

ἑπτά-μηνος, ον, (μήν) born in the seventh month, Hdt.

ἑπτά-μιτος, ον, seven-stringed, Luc., Anth.

ἑπτά-μοιρον, τό, the seven districts, Plut.

ἔπταξαν, Dor. for ἔπτηξαν, 3 pl. aor. 1 of πτήσσω.

ἑπτά-πηχυς, υ, gen. εος, seven cubits long, Hdt., etc.

ἑπτά-πόδης, ου, ὁ, (πούς) seven feet long, Hes.

ἑπτά-πορος, ον, with seven paths, of the Pleiads, Eur.

ἑπτά-πῠλος, ον, (πύλη) with seven gates, epith. of Boeotian Thebes, Hom., etc.;—Egyptian Thebes being ἑκατόμπυλοι.

ἑπτά-πυργος, ον, seven-towered, of Thebes, Eur., etc.

ἔπταρον, aor. 2 of πταίρω, Od.

ἑπτά-στομος, ον, (στόμα) seven-mouthed, with seven portals, of Thebes, Eur.

ἑπτα-τείχης, ές, with seven walls, of Thebes, Aesch.

ἔπτατο, 3 sing. aor. 2 of πέτομαι or πέταμαι.

ἑπτά-τονος, ον, seven-toned, Eur.

ἑπτά-φθογγος, ον, seven-toned, Eur.

ἑπτά-φωνος, ον, (φωνή) seven-voiced, Luc.

ἑπτᾰχᾶ, (ἑπτά) Adv. in seven parts, Od.

ἑπτ-έτης, = ἑπταετής, seven years old, Ar.; nom. pl. ἑπτέτεις Plat.

ἔπτηξα, aor. 1 of πτήσσω.

ἔπτῑσα, aor. 1 of πτίσσω.

ἐπτοιήθην, aor. 1 pass. of πτοιέω (πτοέω).

ἐπτόμην, aor. 2 of πέτομαι.

ἔπυδρος, ον, Ion. for ἔφυδρος.

ἐπύλλιον, τό, Dim. of ἔπος, a versicle, scrap of poetry, Ar.

ἐπῠθόμην, aor. 2 of πυνθάνομαι.

ἜΠΩ (A), to say; v. εἶπον.

ἜΠΩ (B), to be about, be busy with, τεύχε' ἔποντα busy with his armour, Il.: cf. ἀμφι-έπω, δι-έπω, ἐφ-έπω, μεθ-έπω, περι-έπω.
B. Med. ἕπομαι:—impf. εἱπόμην, Ep. ἑπόμην:—fut. ἕψομαι:—aor. 2 with aspirate ἑσπόμην, 2 sing. ἕσπεο, inf. ἑσπέσθαι, part. ἑσπόμενος, imper. ἕπεο, σπεῖο:—to follow, whether after or in company with, Hom.; c. dat. pers., Id.:—also ἕπεσθαι ἅμα τινί Il., etc.; μετά τινι or τινα Ib., etc. 2. to follow, as attendants, Od.:—also to escort, attend, by way of honour, Lat. prosequi, Il. 3. in hostile sense, to pursue, τινι Ib. 4. to keep pace with, ἕπεθ' ἵπποις Hom.: metaph. of a man's limbs, they do his bidding, Id. 5. to follow the motions of another, τρυφάλεια ἕσπετο χειρί the helm went with his hand, i. e. came off in his hand, Il. 6. to follow, obey, submit to, τῷ νόμῳ Hdt., Att. 7. simply, to come near, approach, only in imper., ἕπεο προτέρω come on nearer, Hom. 8. to follow up, esp. in mind, to understand, Plat. II. of Things, as of honour, glory, etc., τούτῳ κῦδος ἅμ' ἕψεται Il., etc. 2. to follow upon, τῇ ἀχαριστίᾳ ἡ ἀναισχυντία ἕπ. Xen.
ἐπ-ωβελία, ἡ, (ὀβελός) an assessment of an obol in the drachma, to be paid by the plaintiff, in case he failed to gain ⅕ of the votes, Dem.
ἐπ-ῳδή, Ion. and poët. ἐπαοιδή, ἡ, a song sung to or over: an enchantment, charm, spell, Od., Hdt., Att.: c. gen. objecti, a charm for or against a thing, Aesch.
ἐπ-ῳδός, όν, (ἐπᾴδω) singing to or over: as Subst. an enchanter, Eur.: c. gen. acting as a charm for or against, Aesch., Plat. 2. pass. sung or said after, μορφῆς ἐπῳδόν called after this form, Eur. II. in metre, ἐπῳδός, ὁ, a verse or passage returning at intervals, a chorus, burden, refrain, as in Theocr. 1.
ἐπ-ῴζω, to cluck, like a sitting bird, Ar.
ἐπ-ωθέω, f. ήσω, to push on, thrust in, Plut.
ἐπώκειλα, aor. 1 of ἐπ-οκέλλω.
ἐπ-ωλένιος, ον, (ὠλένη) upon the arm, h. Hom.
ἐπ-ωμάδιος, ον, (ὦμος) on the shoulders, Theocr. 1.
ἐπ-ωμαδόν, Adv. on the shoulder, Anth.
ἐπ-ωμίς, ίδος, ἡ, (ὦμος) the point of the shoulder, where it joins the collar-bone, the acromion, Xen.: the shoulder, Anth. 2. the front or the uppermost part of a ship, Id. II. the shoulder-strap of a tunic, Eur.
ἐπώμοσα, aor. 1 of ἐπόμνυμι.
ἐπώμοτος, ον, (ἐπόμνυμι) on oath, sworn, Soph. II. pass. witness of oaths, Id.
ἐπωνυμία, Ion. -ίη, ἡ, (ἐπώνυμος) a surname, name given after some person or thing, Lat. cognomen, as Polynices, (from πολύς, νεῖκος), Aesch.; ἐπ. ποιεῖσθαι, θέσθαι to take a surname, Hdt.; καλεῖσθαι ἐπωνυμίην ἐπί τινος after some one, Id.; ἔχειν ἐπ. ἀπό τινος Id., Thuc.; ἐπ. σχεῖν χώρας to have the naming of it, i. e. have it named after one, Id.; with inf. added, ἐπ. ἔχει εἶναί τι he has a name for being, may be said to be, Plat. 2. generally, a name, Hdt.; and
ἐπωνύμιον, τό, = foreg., Plut.; and
ἐπ-ώνυμος, α, ον, poët. for sq., called by the name of, τινός Hdt. From
ἐπ-ώνῠμος, ον, (ὄνυμα, Aeol. for ὄνομα) given as a name,

τῷ Ὀδυσεὺς ὄνομ' ἐστὶν ἐπώνυμος Odysseus is the name given him, Od.; Ἀλκυόνην καλέεσκον ἐπώνυμον Alcyoné they called her by name, Il.; Ἀρήτη δ' ὄνομ' ἐστὶν ἐπώνυμον Arētē (the Desired) is the name given her, Od. 2. named besides, surnamed, Hdt. 3. named after a person or thing, c. gen., Id., Trag.; also, ἐπ. ἐπί τινος Hdt. II. act. giving one's name to a thing or person, ἐπώνυμον (sc. τὸ σάκος), which gives thee thy name (of Eurysaces), Soph. 2. at Athens, οἱ ἐπώνυμοι (sc. ἥρωες), the heroes after whom the Attic φυλαί had their names, Dem. b. ἄρχων ἐπ. the first Archon, who gave his name to the current year.
ἐπ-ωπάω, (ὠπάομαι) to observe, watch, Aesch.
ἐπώπτων, impf. of ἐποπτάω.
ἐπῶρσα, aor. 1 of ἐπόρνυμι; ἐπῶρτο, 3 sing. Ep. aor. 2 pass.
ἐπ-ωρύω [ῠ], to howl at, Anth.
ἐπωτίδες, αἱ, (οὖς) beams projecting like ears on each side of a ship's bows, whence the anchors were let down, cat-heads, Eur., Thuc.
ἐπ-ωφελέω, f. ήσω, to aid or succour one in a thing, τινά τι Soph., etc.; ἐπ. τινα to aid or succour, Id.; also τινι Id., Eur. II. δῶρον, ὃ μήποτ' ἐπωφέλησα ἐξελέσθαι a gift, which would that I never had received, Id. Hence
ἐπωφέλημα, ατος, τό, a help, store, βορᾶς Soph.; and
ἐπωφελία, ἡ, help, succour, Anth.
ἐπ-ώχατο, Ep. 3 pl. plqpf. pass. of ἐπ-έχω, πᾶσαι γὰρ [πύλαι] ἐπώχατο all the gates were kept shut, Il.
ἐπ-ῳχόμην, impf. of ἐπ-οίχομαι.
*ἜΡΑ, ἡ, the Lat. terra, earth:—hence Adv. ἔραζε, to earth, to the ground, Hom.; Dor. ἔρασδε Theocr.
ἔρᾰμαι, 2 sing. ἔρασαι, Ep. ἔρασσαι: 2 pl. ἔρασθε (like ἀγάασθε); 3 sing. subj. ἔρηται, Dor. ἔρᾱται; opt. ἐραίμην: impf. ἠράμην [ᾰ]: fut. ἐρασθήσομαι: aor. 1 ἠράσθην; also in med. form ἠρασάμην, Ep. 3 sing. ἠράσσατο, ἐράσσατο:—to love, to be in love with, c. gen. pers., Hom., Eur. II. of things, to love passionately, long for, lust after, Il., Hdt., Att. 2. c. inf. to desire eagerly, Theogn., Soph., etc.
ἐρᾰνίζω, f. σω, (ἔρανος) lay under contribution, τινά Dem. 2. c. acc. rei, to collect by contributions, to beg, borrow, Aeschin.: metaph. to combine, Anth.:—Med. to collect for oneself, borrow, Luc. II. to assist by contribution, τινί Dem.
ἐρᾰννός, ή, όν, (ἐράω) lovely, of places, Hom., Theocr.
ἔρᾰνος, ὁ, a meal to which each contributed his share, Lat. coena collaticia, a pic-nic, Od., Eur. 2. any contribution, Lat. symbola, such as Athenians paid to pay for the support of the poor or state-necessities, Ar.; ἐράνους λέλοιπε he has left his sub-scriptions unpaid, Dem.; ἔρανον φέρειν, simply, to contribute freely, Id. 3. a kindness, service, favour, Eur., Thuc., etc. II. a society of subscribers to a common fund, a club, Dem. (Perh. from ἐράω.)
ἔρασδε, Dor. for ἔραζε.
ἐράσι-χρήματος, ον, (χρήματα) loving money, Xen.
ἐράσμιος, ον, lovely, Xen.:—beloved, desired, Aesch., Xen.: neut. as Adv., Anth.
ἐραστεύω, = ἐράω, to long for, c. gen., Aesch. From
ἐραστής, οῦ, ὁ, (ἔραμαι) a lover, properly of persons, Ar., etc.:—metaph. of things, τυραννίδος Hdt.; πολέ-

μων Eur. ; ἐρ. πραγμάτων = πολυπράγμων, Ar. ; ἐρ. τοῦ πονεῖν fond of work, Id. ; ἐρ. ἐπαίνου Xen.

ἐραστός, ή, όν, = ἐρατός, beloved, lovely, Plat.

ἐρᾶται, 3 sing. of ἔραμαι; but ἐρᾶται, pass. indic. of ἐράω.

ἐρᾰτεινός, ή, όν, lovely, charming, Hom. ; of a man, ἑτάροις ἐρατεινός welcome to his comrades, Od.

ἐρᾰτίζω, Ep. form of ἐράω, κρειῶν ἐρατίζων greedy after meat, Hom.

ἐρᾰτός, ή, όν, (ἐράω) lovely, charming, Il., Hes., etc. : —neut. as Adv., ἐρατὸν κιθαρίζειν h. Hom.   2. beloved, Tyrtae.

ἐρᾰτό-χροος, ον, (χρόα) fair of face, Anth.

ἐρᾰτύω, Dor. for ἐρητύω.

Ἐρᾰτώ, οῦς, ἡ, Erato, the Lovely, one of the Muses, Hes.   2. one of the Oceanides, Id.

ΈΡΑ'Ω (Α), used in Act. only in pres. and impf. (which in Poetry are ἔραμαι, ἠράμην): impf. ἤρων :—Pass., 2 sing. opt. ἐρῷο, inf. ἐρᾶσθαι, part. ἐρώμενος :—but ἐράομαι also as Dep., 3 sing. ἐρᾶται :—to love, to be in love with, c. gen. pers., Xen., etc. : c. acc. cogn., ἐρᾶν ἔρωτα Eur. :—absol., ἐρῶν a lover, opp. to ἡ ἐρωμένη the beloved one, Hdt.   II. of things, to love or desire passionately, τυραννίδος Archil. ; μάχης Aesch. ; and c. inf. to desire to do, Soph., Eur.

ΈΡΑ'Ω (Β), to pour out, vomit forth, Aesch.

ἐργάζομαι, f. άσομαι, Dor. ἐργαξοῦμαι : aor. 1 εἰργασάμην : pf. εἴργασμαι, Ion. ἔργ—:—these tenses are all depon. ; but some tenses take a pass. sense, v. infr. III : (ἔργον) :—to work, labour, properly of husbandry, Hes., Thuc., etc. ; but also of all manual labour, Od., Hdt. :—also of things, as Vulcan's bellows, Il.   II. trans. to work at, make, build, Od., Att.   2. to do, perform, accomplish, Hom., Att. :—c. dupl. acc. to dᵒ something to another, Hdt., etc. ; κακὰ ἐργάζεσθαί τινα Soph., Thuc.   3. to work a material, χρυσῷ εἰργάζετο Od. ; ἐργ. γῆν to work the land, Hdt.   4. to earn by working, χρήματα Id., Att.   5. to work at, practise, Lat. exercere, τέχνην Plat.   6. absol. to work at a trade or business, to traffic, trade, Dem.   III. the pf. pass. εἴργασμαι is used in act. sense, as Hdt., Soph. ; but also in pass. sense,   1. to be made or built, ἔργαστο τὸ τεῖχος Hdt. ; ἐκ πέτρας εἰργασμένος Aesch., etc.   2. to be done, Id. —The fut. ἐργασθήσομαι always in pass.sense, Soph.,etc.

ἐργᾰθεῖν, Ep. ἐεργαθεῖν, Att. εἰργαθεῖν, poët. aor. 2 inf. of εἴργω, to sever, cut off, Il.   II. to hold back, check, Soph., Eur.

ἐργᾰλεῖον, Ion. -ήϊον, τό, (ἔργον) a tool, instrument, Hdt., Thuc., etc.

ἐργᾰσείω, Desiderat. of ἐργάζομαι, to be about to do, Soph.

ἐργᾰσία, Ion. -ίη, ἡ, (ἐργάζομαι) work, daily labour, business, Lat. labor, h. Hom., Att. ; δὸς ἐργασίαν, c. inf., Lat. da operam ut . . , N. T.   II. a working at, making, building, τειχῶν Thuc. ; ἱματίων, ὑποδημάτων Plat., etc.   2. a working of a material, τοῦ σιδήρου Hdt. ; τῶν χρυσείων μετάλλων Thuc., Ar., etc.   3. generally, trade, commerce, Xen., Dem.   4. a practising, exercising, τῶν τεχνῶν Plat.   5. a work of art, production, τετράγωνος ἐργ., of the Hermae, Thuc.

ἐργάσιμος [ᾰ], ον, (ἐργάζομαι) of land, arable, Xen., etc.

ἐργαστέον, verb. Adj. of ἐργάζομαι, one must work the

land, Xen.   II. τοὖργον ἔστ' ἐργ. it must be done or one must do it, Aesch., Eur.

ἐργαστήρ, ῆρος, ὁ, (ἐργάζομαι) a workman, husbandman, Xen.

ἐργαστήριον, τό, any place in which work is done : a workshop, manufactory, Hdt., Att. : a mine, quarry, Dem. :—a butcher's shop, Ar.

ἐργαστικός, ή, όν, (ἐργάζομαι) able to work, working, industrious, Plat., Xen.

ἐργάτης [ᾰ], ου, ὁ, a workman : esp. one who works the soil, a husbandman, Hdt., Att. ; οὑργάτης λεώς the country-folk, Ar.   2. as Adj. hard-working, strenuous, Xen.   II. one who practises an art, c. gen., Id.   III. a doer, worker, Soph., Xen.

ἐργᾰτήσιος, α, ον, producing an income, Plut. ; and

ἐργᾰτικός, ή, όν, given to labour, diligent, active, Plat. ; of the Nile, from its activity in depositing silt, Hdt. : Adv. -κῶς τι advantageously, Plut.

ἐργᾰτίνης [ῐ], ου, ὁ, = ἐργάτης, a husbandman, Theocr.   2. as Adj., active, laborious, Anth.   II. c. gen. making a thing or practising an art, Id.

ἐργᾰτῐς [ᾰ], ιδος, fem. of ἐργάτης, a workwoman : as Adj. laborious, industrious, active, Hdt., Soph.   II. c. gen. working at or producing a thing, Aesch. ; νέκταρος ἐργ., of bees, Anth.

ἔργμα, ατος, τό, (*ἔργω) a work, deed, business, Theogn., Aesch., etc.

ἔργνῡμι, = εἴργω, to confine, Ep. impf. ἐέργνυν, Od.

ἐργο-δότης, ου, ὁ, one who lets out work, opp. to ἐργολάβος, Xen.

ἐργολᾰβέω, f. ήσω, to contract for the execution of work, ἐργ. ἀνδριάντας, Lat. statuas conducere faciendas, Xen. :—absol. to work for hire, ply a trade, Dem.

ἐργο-λάβος, ὁ, (λαβεῖν) one who contracts for the execution of work, a contractor, Lat. conductor, redemptor, opp. to ἐργοδότης, Plat.

ἔργον, τό, (*ἔργω) :—work, Hom., etc. ; τὰ σαυτῆς ἔργα κόμιζε mind your own business, Hom. :   1. in Il. mostly of deeds of war, πολεμήϊα ἔργα Il., etc. ; so, ἐν τῷ ἔργῳ during the action, Thuc. ; ἔργου ἔχεσθαι to engage in battle, Id.   2. of works of industry, tilled lands, fields, farms, Hom. ; οὔτε βοῶν οὔτ' ἀνδρῶν ἔργα (cf. Virgil's hominumque boumque labores), Il. ; ἔργα Ἰθάκης the tilled lands of Ithaca, Od. ; so in Att. τὰ κατ' ἀγροὺς ἔργα, etc. :—then, generally, property, wealth, possessions, ἔργον ἀέξειν Od.   b. of women's work, weaving, Hom.   c. of other occupations, θαλάσσια ἔργα fishing, as a way of life, Od. ; periphr. ἔργα δαιτός works of feasting, Il. ; so, ἔργα θήρας, etc., Xen., etc. :—in Att. also of all kinds of works, such as mines, iron-works, Id., Dem.   3. a hard piece of work, a hard task, Il. : also, a shocking deed or act, Lat. facinus, Od. :—also, χερμάδιον λάβε Τυδείδης, μέγα ἔργον a huge mass, Il.   4. a deed, action, often, as opp. to ἔπος, deed, not word, Hom.   II. a thing, matter, πᾶν ἔργον in every point, Il. ; ἄκουε τοὖργον Soph., etc.   III. pass. that which is wrought, a work, of the arms of Achilles, Il. ; metal-work is called ἔργον Ἡφαίστοιο Od., etc.   2. the result of work, ἔργον χρημάτων profit on money, Dem.   IV. the following pecul. Att. phrases arise from signf. I :   1.

ἔργον ἐστί, **a.** c. gen. pers. *his business, his proper work*, ἔργον ἀγαθοῦ πολίτου Plat.; so, σὸν ἔργον ἐστί *it is your business*, Aesch. **b.** c. gen. rei, *there is need of, use of* a thing, Eur. **c.** c. inf. *it is hard work, difficult* to do, πολὺ ἔργον ἂν εἴη διεξελθεῖν Xen., etc.; οὐκ ἔργον θρηνεῖσθαι 'tis no *use* to lament, Soph. **2.** ἔργα παρέχειν τινί to give one *trouble*, Ar.; ἔργον ἔχειν to take *trouble*, Xen.

ἐργο-πόνος, ὁ, *a husbandman*, Anth.

ΈΡΓΩ, ἔεργω, Ep. form for the Att. εἴργω or εἴργω:
—fut. ἔρξω, Att. εἴρξω or εἴρξω, aor. 1 ἔρξα, Att.
εἶρξα:—aor. 2 εἰργάθον (v. sub ἐργαθεῖν):—cf. Med. and Pass., f. ἔρξομαι, Att. εἴρξομαι:—aor. 1 ἔρχθην, Att. εἴρχθην:—pf. ἔργμαι, Ep. 3 pl. ἔρχαται, Att. εἴργμαι, Ep. part. ἐεργμένος:—plqpf., Ep. 3 pl. ἔρχατο, ἐέρχατο:—*to bar one's way* either *by shutting in* or *shutting out*: **I.** *to shut in, shut up*, Lat. *includere*, Hom.; ἐντὸς ἐέργειν *to enclose, bound*, Il.; ἂψ ἐπὶ νῆας ἔεργε drove them to the ships *and shut them up* there, Ib.:—of things, δόμον ἐέργειν *to shut it up*, Od.:—Pass., ἔρχατο *were fenced in*, Il.; γέφυραι ἐεργμέναι *well-secured, strong-built*, Ib. **II.** *to shut out*, Lat. *excludere*, Hom.; ἐκτὸς ἐέργειν Od. **2.** c. gen. *to shut out* or *keep away from*, Il., Hdt., Att.; and with Preps., ἔργ. τι ἀπό τινος Il.; c. dat. pers., εἴργειν μητρὶ δόρυ *to keep it off* from her, Aesch.:—Pass., εἰργόμενον θανάτου *short of* death, Aeschin.:—Med. *to keep oneself* or *abstain from*, Hdt., Soph. **3.** *to hinder, prevent from* doing, Theogn.:—Pass., οὐδὲν εἴργεται *nothing is barred*, i. e. all things are permitted, Soph.: c. inf., mostly with μή added: εἴργει με θανεῖν νόμος Eur.; c. inf. only, οὐδὲν εἴργει τελειοῦσθαι τάδε Soph.

*ἔργω, *to do work*, obsol. Root, for which ἔρδω, ῥέζω, ἐργάζομαι are used in the pres.: for the fut., aor. 1 and pf., v. ἔρδω.

ἐργ-ώδης, ες, (εἶδος) *irksome, troublesome*, Xen., etc.

ΈΡΔΩ, impf. ἔρδον, Ion. ἔρδεσκον:—fut. ἔρξω:—aor. 1 ἔρξα:—pf. ἔοργα, Ion. 3 sing.: ἔόργεε: (v. *ἔργω):—*to do*, Hom., etc.; often c. dupl. acc., *to do* something *to a* person, κακὰ πολλὰ ἔοργεν Τρῶας Il.; also, εὖ or κακῶς ἔρδειν τινά Theogn., etc.; simply, ἔρδ. τινά *to do* one *harm*, Soph.: 2. πήματα *to work* mischief, Aesch.; ἔρδοι τις ἣν ἕκαστος εἰδείη τέχνην *let* each man *practise* the art he knows, Ar. **2.** *to make* or *offer* a sacrifice (v. ῥέζω), Hom., Hdt.:—absol., like Lat. *facere, operari*, Hes.

ἐρεβεννός, ή, όν, (Ἔρεβος) *dark, gloomy*, Il., Hes.

Ἐρέβεσφιν, Ep. gen. of Ἔρεβος.

ἐρέβινθος, ὁ, *a kind of pulse, chick-pea*, Lat. *cicer*, Il., Ar. Cf. ὄροβος.

ἐρεβο-διφάω, *to grope about in darkness*, Ar.

ἐρεβόθεν, *from nether gloom*, Eur. From

ΈΡΕΒΟΣ, τό: Att. gen. Ἐρέβους, Ion. Ἐρέβευς, Ep. Ἐρέβεσφιν:—*Erebus*, a place of nether darkness, above Hades, Hom., etc.:—metaph., ἔρεβος ὕφαλον *the darkness* of the deep, Soph.

Ἐρεβόσδε, Adv. *to* or *into Erebus*, Od.

ἐρεείνω, (ἔρομαι) like ἔρομαι, *to ask*, c. acc. pers. *to ask of* one, Od.; c. acc. rei, *to ask* a thing, Hom.; c. dupl. acc., ἐρ. τινά τι *to ask* one a thing, Od.:—so in Med., Ib.

ἐρεθίζω, Dor. -ίσδω, Ep. inf. -ιζέμεν: impf. ἠρέθιζον, Ep. ἐρ-: aor. 1 ἠρέθισα, poët. ἐρ-:—pf. ἠρέθικα:—Pass., aor. 1 ἠρεθίσθην; pf. ἠρέθισμαι: (ἐρέθω):—*to rouse to anger, rouse to fight, irritate*, Hom., Hdt., etc.: *to provoke to curiosity*, Od.; metaph., ἐρ. χορούς *to stir* them, Eur.:—Pass. *to be provoked, excited*, Hdt., Ar.; of fire, φέψαλος ἐρεθιζόμενος ῥιπῖδι a spark kindled by the bellows, Il.; αἰθὴρ ἐρεθιζέσθω βροντῇ Aesch.; of one who is out of breath, Eur. Hence

ἐρέθισμα, ατος, τό, *a stirring up, exciting*, Ar.

ΈΡΕ'ΘΩ, impf. ἤρεθον, Ion. ἐρέθεσκον, *to stir to anger, provoke, irritate*, Hom.: c. acc. rei, ἤρεθον ᾠδάν they *raised* a song, Theocr.

ΈΡΕΊΔΩ: Ep. impf. ἔρειδον: f. ἐρείσω: aor. 1 ἤρεισα, Ep. ἔρεισα, Ep. aor. 1 ἐρείσθην:—pf. ἐρήρεισμαι, Ep. 3 pl. ἐρηρέδαται: 3 sing. plqpf. ἠρήρειστο, Ep. 3 pl. ἐρηρέδατο:—*to make one thing lean against* another, τι πρός τι or τι ἐπί τινι Hom.; of Atlas supporting heaven, Aesch., Eur., etc.:—generally, *to fix firmly*, ἐρ. ὄμμα, Lat. *figere oculos*, εἴς τι Id. **2.** *to prop, stay, support*, ἀσπὶς ἄρ' ἀσπίδ' ἔρειδε, κόρυς κόρυν, ἀνέρα δ' ἀνήρ, of close ranks of men-at-arms, Il. **3.** *to hurl forth*, Ar.; and in Med., Id. **4.** *to infix, plant in*, τί τινι Soph.; ἐρ. πληγήν *to inflict* a blow, Eur. **5.** of wagers or matches, *to set* one pledge *against* another, Theocr. **II.** intr. *to lean against, jostle*, c. dat., Od. **2.** *to set upon, press hard*, c. dat., Il.; εἴς τινα Ar.; absol., of an illness, Aesch. **3.** generally, *to go to work, fall to*, of eating, Ar. **III.** Med. and Pass. *to lean upon*, c. dat., Il.; ἐπί τινος and τινος, Ib.: absol. *to plant oneself firmly, take a firm stand*, Ib.; οὔδει χαῖται ἐρηρέδαται their hair *rests* on the ground, Ib. **2.** *to be fixed firm, planted*, ἔγχος διὰ θώρηκος ἠρήρειστο had been *fixed*, Il., etc.; λᾶε ἐρηρέδαται the stones *are firmly set*, Ib. **IV.** Med., **1.** in recipr. sense, *to strive* one with another, *contend*, Ib. **2.** c. acc. *to support for oneself*, βάκτρῳ ἐρείδου στίβον Eur.; ἐρ. ἐπὶ τοῖχῳ λίθον Theocr.

ΈΡΕΊΚΗ, ἡ, *heath, heather*, Lat. *erīca*, Aesch., Theocr.

ΈΡΕΊΚΩ, aor. 1 ἤρειξα:—*to rend*, Hes., Aesch.: Pass., ἐρεικόμενος περὶ δουρί Il. **2.** *to bruise, pound, shatter*, Aesch. **II.** intr. only in aor. 2 ἤρῐκον, *to be rent, to shiver*, Il.

ἔρειο, Ep. for ἔροιο, imperat. of ἔρομαι.

ἐρειοί, οἱ, a term of insult to Egyptians, Theocr.

ἐρείομεν, Ep. for ἐρέωμεν, 1 pl. subj. of ἐρέω.

ἐρείπιον, τό, (ἐρείπω) *a fallen ruin, wreck*, mostly in pl., ναυτικὰ ἐρ. pieces of wreck, Aesch., Eur.; also, οἰκημάτων ἐρ. ruins of houses, Hdt.; ἐρ. πέπλων *fragments*, Eur.; cf. ἐρείπω.

ΈΡΕΊΠΩ: Ep. impf. ἔρειπον: f.ἐρείψω:—aor. 1 ἤρειψα:
—intr. in aor. 2 ἤρῐπον, and pf. ἐρήρῐπα :—Pass., aor. 1 ἠρείφθην: aor. 2 ἠρίπην [ῐ]: pf. pass. ἐρήριμμαι, Ep. 3 sing. plqpf. ἐρέριπτο:—*to throw* or *dash down, tear down*, Il., Hdt.: metaph., ἐρείπει γένος θεῶν τις some god*brings* the family *to ruin*, Soph.:—Pass. *to be thrown down, fall in ruins*, Il.; ἐν ἐρειπίοις νεκρῶν ἐρειφθεὶς *a ruin* amid the ruins of the dead, Soph.; ἐρείπεται κτύπος the thunder *comes crashing down*, Id. **II.** intr., in aor. 2 ἤρῐπον, Ep. ἔρῐπον, *to fall down, tumble, fall headlong*, Hom.

ἔρεισα, Ep. for ἤρεισα, aor. 1 of ἐρείδω.

ἔρεισμα, ατος, τό, (ἐρείδω) a prop, stay, support, Lat. columen, Soph., Eur.:—in pl. the props to keep a boat on shore upright, Theocr.

ἐρείψιμος, ον, (ἐρείπω) thrown down, in ruins, Eur.

ἐρείψί-τοιχος, ον, overthrowing walls, c. gen., Aesch.

ἐρεμνός, ή, όν, syncop. from ἐρεβεννός (cf. Ἔρεβος), black, swart, dark, Hom., Aesch., etc.:—metaph., ἐρεμνὴ φάτις a dark, obscure rumour, Soph.

ἔρεξα, aor. 1 of ῥέζω.

ἐρέομαι, Ep. for εἴρομαι, ἔρομαι, to ask.

ἐρέπτομαι, Dep. to feed on, c. acc., λωτόν, κρῖ λευκόν, πυρὸν ἐρεπτόμενοι Hom. (Deriv. uncertain.)

ἐρέριπτο, Ep. for ἐρήριπτο, 3 sing. plqpf. of ἐρείπω.

ἐρέσθαι, inf. aor. 2 of the Ion. pres. εἴρομαι, to ask, which Att. writers use only in aor. 2 ἠρόμην, inf. ἐρέσθαι, with ἐρωτάω for its pres. (Distinguished by the accent from the pres. inf. ἔρεσθαι, to say.)

ΕΡΕΣΣΩ: Ep. inf. ἐρεσσέμεναι, impf. ἔρεσσον: aor. 1 ἤρεσα:—to row, Hom., Soph.; of birds flying, πτεροῖς ἐρ. Eur. II. trans. to speed by rowing; metaph., γόων ἐρέσσετ᾿ πίτυλον ply the measured stroke of lamentation, Aesch.:—Pass. to be rowed, Id.; of birds, πτερύγων ἐρετμοῖσιν ἐρεσσόμενοι with the oarage of wings (cf. Virgil's remigio alarum), Id. 2. generally, to put in quick motion, ply, τὸν πόδα Eur.:—metaph., ἐρ. ἀπειλάς to set threats in motion, Soph.; ἐρ. μῆτιν Id.:—Pass., of a bow, to be plied, handled, Id. III. to row through the sea, Anth.

ἐρεσχηλέω, only in pres. to talk lightly, to be jocular, Plat. II. trans. to jest upon, quiz, banter, τινά Id.

ἐρέτης, ου, ὁ, (ἐρέσσω) a rower, Od., Hdt., Att. II. in pl. also, oars, Anth. Hence

ἐρετικός, ή, όν, of or for rowers, ἐρ. πληρώματα crews of rowers, Plut.

ἐρετμόν, τό, (ἐρέσσω) Lat. remus, an oar, Od., Eur.:—of wings, v. ἐρέσσω II. 1.

ἐρετμόω, f. ώσω, to furnish with oars, set to row, Eur.

Ἐρετριεύς, ὁ, an Eretrian, Hdt., etc.

ἐρέττω, late Att. for ἐρέσσω, Luc.

ΕΡΕΥΓΟΜΑΙ, to spit or spew out, to disgorge, Lat. eructare, c. acc., Il.:—absol. to belch, Lat. ructare, Od. 2. metaph. of the sea, to surge, break in foam against the land, Hom. II. in aor. 2 act. ἤρυγον, inf. ἐρυγεῖν, part. ἐρυγών, to bellow, roar, properly of oxen (cf. ἐρύγμηλος), ἤρυγεν ὡς ὅτε ταῦρος ἤρυγεν Il.

ἐρευθέδανον, τό, madder, Hdt. From

ἐρεύθω, aor. 1 inf. ἐρεῦσαι, to make red, stain red, Il.:—Pass. to be or become red, Theocr.

ἔρευνα, ης, ἡ, (ἔρομαι) inquiry, search, ἐρ. ἔχειν τινός to make search for one, Soph.; ἄσσειν εἰς ἔρευναν Eur.

ἐρευνάω, f. ήσω, to seek or search for, search after, track, Hom., Att.; ὧν χρείαν ἐρευνᾷ the things whereof he seeks after the use, i. e. whatever things he finds serviceable, Soph. 2. to search a place, Hdt., Theocr. 3. to enquire after, examine, Eur., Plat. 4. c. inf. to seek to do, Theocr. Hence

ἐρευνητέον, verb. Adj. one must seek out, Xen.

ἐρεῦσαι, aor. 1 inf. of ἐρεύθω.

ἐρέφω· f. ἐρέψω: aor. 1 ἤρεψα, Ep. ἔρεψα:—to cover with a roof, ἔρεψαν ὄροφον made a roof, Il.: θάλαμον ἐρ. Od. 2. to cover with a crown, to crown, Soph.:—Med. to crown oneself, Eur.

Ἐρεχθεύς, έως, Ep. ῆος, ὁ, an ancient hero of Attica, the Render (from ἐρέχθω): hence Ἐρεχθεῖδαι, οἱ, as a name of the Athenians, Trag.

ΕΡΕΧΘΩ, to rend, break, Od.:—Pass., of a ship, to be shattered by the winds, Il.

ἔρεψις, εως, ἡ, (ἐρέφω) a roofing, roof, Plut.

ἐρέω (A), Ep. Verb, = ἐρεείνω, ἔρομαι, ἐρωτάω (not to be confounded with ἐρέω (B)):—to ask, enquire, τι about a thing, Hom. 2. c. acc. pers. to question, μάντιν ἐρείομεν (Ep. for ἐρώωμεν) Il.; ἀλλήλους ἐρέοιμεν Od.

ἐρέω (B), Ion. for ἐρῶ, I will say: v. Att. ἐρῶ.

ἐρημάζω, (ἔρημος) to be left lonely, go alone, ἐρημά-ζεσκον (Ion. impf.) Theocr.

ἐρημαῖος, α, ον, poët. for ἔρημος, desolate, solitary, Mosch.: c. gen. bereft of, Anth.

ἐρήμη (sc. δίκη), ἡ, v. ἐρῆμος II.

ἐρημία, ἡ, I. of places, a solitude, desert, wilderness, Hdt., Aesch., etc. II. as a state or condition, solitude, loneliness, ἐρημίαν ἄγειν, ἔχειν to keep alone, Eur.; of persons, isolation, desolation, Soph.; δι᾽ ἐρημίαν from being left alone, Thuc. 2. c. gen. want of, absence, Eur., Thuc., etc.; τὴν ἐρ. ὁρῶν τῶν κωλυσόντων seeing that there would be none to hinder him, Dem.; ἐρ. κακῶν freedom from evil, Eur.

ἐρημιάς, άδος, ἡ, (ἔρημος) a solitary devotee, Theocr.

ἐρημο-κόμης, εс, gen. ου, (κόμη) void of hair, Anth.

ἐρημο-λάλος [ᾰ], ον, chattering in the desert, Anth.

ἐρημό-νομος or -νόμος, ον, haunting the wilds, Anth.

ἐρημό-πολις, ι, gen. ιδος, reft of one's city, Eur.

ΕΡΗΜΟΣ, ον, or η, ον, desolate, lone, lonely, lonesome, solitary: 1. of places, Hdt., Att.; τὰ ἐρ. desert parts, Hdt., etc.; ἡ ἔρημος (sc. χώρα), Id. 2. of persons or animals, Il., Aesch., etc.: desolate, helpless, Soph., Dem.:—neut. pl. as Adv., ἔρημα κλαίω I weep in solitude, Eur. 3. of conditions, Soph. II. c. gen. reft of, void or destitute of, Hdt., Att. 2. of persons, with no bad sense, wanting, without, ἔρημος ὅπλων οἰκεῖ Eur. III. ἐρήμη δίκη, ἡ, an undefended action, in which one party does not appear, and judgment goes against him by default, Thuc., etc.: so ἐρήμη or ἔρημος (without δίκη), ἐρήμην εἷλον I got judgment by default, Dem.; ἐρήμην ὦφλε he let it go by default, Id.; ἐρήμην κατηγορεῖν to accuse in a case where there was no defence, Plat.

ἐρημοσύνη, ἡ, solitude, Anth.

ἐρημο-φίλης [ῐ], ου, ὁ, (φιλέω) loving solitude, Anth.

ἐρημόω, f. ώσω, (ἔρημος) to strip bare, to desolate, lay waste, ἱερά Thuc.:—Pass., Hdt., etc. II. to bereave one of a thing, c. gen., ἐρ. ναυβατῶν ἐρετμά to leave the oars without men, Eur.:—Pass. to be bereft of, c. gen., Hdt., Aesch. 2. to set free or deliver from, c. gen., Eur. III. to abandon, desert, c. acc., Aesch., Eur.; ἐρ. Συρακοσίας to evacuate it, Thuc. IV. to keep in solitude, isolate, Eur.:—Pass. to be isolated from, c. gen., Hdt.

ἐρημωτής, οῦ, ὁ, (ἐρημόω) a desolator, Anth.

ἐρηρέδαται, -ατο, Ep. 3 pl. pf. and plqpf. pass. of ἐρείδω.

ἐρήρεισμαι, pf. pass. of ἐρείδω.

ἐρήριμμαι, pf. pass. of ἐρείπω.

ἐρήριπτο, 3 sing. plqpf. pass. of ἐρείπω.

ἐρητύω, Dor. ἐρᾱτύω : impf. ἐρήτυον : f. ύσω [ῡ] : aor. 1 ἐρήτῡσα, Ion. ἐρητύσασκον :—Pass., aor. 1 ἐρητύθην, Ep. 3 pl. -ύθεν :—to keep back, restrain, check, Hom. ; πολλὰ κέλευθος ἐρατύοι let a long distance bar thy approach, Soph. 2. c. gen. to keep away from, Eur.

ἐρῐ-, insepar. prefix, like ἀρι-, to strengthen the sense of a word, very, much.

ἐρι-αύχην, ενος, ὁ, ἡ, with high-arching neck, of horses, Il.

ἐρι-βόας, ου, ὁ, (βοάω) loud-shouting, Anth.

ἐρι-βρεμέτης, ου, ὁ, of Zeus, loud-thundering, Il. : loud-sounding, αὐλός Anth.

ἐρι-βρεμής, ές, = ἐρίβρομος, Anth.

ἐρί-βρομος, ον, (βρέμω) loud-shouting, h. Hom.

ἐρι-βρύχης, gen. ου, Ep. -εω, ὁ, = sq., Hes.

ἐρί-βρῡχος, ον, (βρύχω) loud-bellowing, h. Hom. : loud-braying, of the trumpet, Anth.

ἐρι-βῶλαξ, ακος, ὁ, ἡ, with large clods, very fertile, Od. :—so, ἐρί-βωλος, ον, Hom.

ἐρί-γδουπος, ον, = ἐρίδουπος, loud-thundering, Hom.

ἐρῐδαίνω, Ep. aor. 1 ἐρίδηνα :—Med., Ep. aor. 1 inf. ἐριδήσασθαι : (ἐρίζω) :—to wrangle, quarrel, dispute, Hom. ; c. dat. :—and in Med., ποσσὶν ἐριδήσασθαι Ἀχαιοῖς to contend with them in the foot-race, Ib.

ἐριδμαίνω, = ἐρεθίζω, to provoke to strife, irritate, Il. II. intr. = ἐριδαίνω, to contend, Theocr., Mosch.

ἐρί-δμᾱτος, ον, (δέμω) strongly-built, i. e. unconquerable, or (from δαμάω) all-subduing.

ἐρί-δουπος, ον, = ἐρίγδουπος, Hom.

ἐρίζω, Ep. inf. ἐριζέμεναι -έμεν, Dor. ἐρίσδεν : impf. ἤριζον, Ep. ἔριζον, Ion. ἐρίζεσκον : fut. ἐρίσω :—Ep. aor. 1 ἤρισα, Ep. opt. ἐρίσσειε :—pf. ἤρικα Polyb. :—Med., Ep. aor. 1 subj. ἐρίσσεται (for ἐρίσηται) : pf. ἐρήρισμαι : (ἔρις) :—to strive, wrangle, quarrel, τινί with one, Hom., Att. ; πρός τινα Hdt., Plat. 2. to rival, vie with, be a match for, τινί Hom. :—c. acc. rei, to contend with one in a thing, Id. ; —also, c. dat. rei, Od., Att. 3. absol. to engage in a contest, keep the contest up, Il. II. Hom. sometimes uses the Med., like the Act.

ἐρί-ηρος, ον, (*ἄρω, cf. ἦρα) fitting exactly : as epith. of ἑταῖρος, faithful, trusty, Il. ; pl. in heterocl. form, ἐρίηρες ἑταῖροι, ἐρίηρας ἑταίρους Hom.

ἐρῐθᾰκίς, ίδος, ἡ, fem. of ἔριθος, Theocr.

ἐρῐ-θηλής, ές, (θάλλω) very flourishing, luxuriant, of plants, Il., Hes.

ἔρῐθος, ὁ, a day-labourer, hired servant of any sort ; in Il., ἔριθοι are mowers or reapers : later, ἔριθοι, αἱ, spinsters, workers in wool, Dem., Theocr. (Deriv. uncertain.)

ἐρῐκεῖν, aor. 2 inf. of ἐρείκω.

ἐρί-κλαυστος and -κλαυτος, ον, much-weeping, Anth.

ἐρί-κτῠπος, ον, loud-sounding, Hes.

ἐρι-κῠδής, ές, (κῦδος) very famous, glorious, splendid, Hom.

ἐρι-κύμων [ῡ], ον, (κύω) big with young, Aesch.

ἐρί-μῡκος, ον, (μυκάομαι) loud-bellowing, Hom., Hes.

ἘΡἼΝΕὌΣ, ὁ, the wild fig-tree, Il., Theocr.

ἐρίνεος [ῐ], α, ον, Ion. εἰρίνεος, η, ον, (ἔριον) of wool, woollen, Hdt.

Ἐρῑνῡ̄́ς (not Ἐρινύς), gen. ύος, ἡ : pl. Ἐρῑνύες, Att. Ἐρῑνῡ̄́ς : Att. gen. Ἐρῑνῡ̄́ν :—the Erinys or Fury, an avenging deity, in sing. and pl., Hom., Trag. :—the number Three first in Eur. ; the names Tisiphoné, Megaera, Alecto only in late writers. At Athens they were called Εὐμενίδες, Σεμναί. II. as appellat., μητρὸς Ἐρινύες curses from one's mother, Hom. ; but Ἐρινῦς πατρός the blood-guiltiness of his sire, Hes. ; φρενῶν Ἐρινύς distraction, Soph. :—in Trag. persons sent to be curses to men are called Ἐρινύες.

ἔριον, τό, Ion. εἴριον, (ἔρος, εἶρος) wool, in sing. and pl., Hom., Att. :—εἴρια ἀπὸ ξύλου cotton (Germ. Baumwolle, tree-wool), Hdt.

ἐριο-πωλικῶς, (πωλέω) Adv. like a wool-dealer, roguishly, Ar.

ἐρι-ούνης and ἐρι-ούνιος, ὁ, Homeric epith. of Hermes (prob. from ἐρι-, ὀνίνημι), the ready helper, luck-bringer, Il.

ἐριουργέω, f. ήσω, to work in wool, Xen. From ἐρι-ουργός, όν, (ἔριον, *ἔργω) working in wool.

ἐρίπνη or ἐρίπνα, ἡ, (ἐρείπω) a broken cliff, crag, scaur, Eur. : a steep side, sheer ascent, Id.

ἔρῐπον, Ep. for ἤρῐπον, aor. 2 of ἐρείπω : inf. ἐριπεῖν.

ἐρῐπών, aor. 2 part. of ἐρείπω.

ἘΡΙΣ, ιδος, ἡ : acc. ἔριν and ἔριδα : pl. ἔριδες, later ἔρεις :—strife, quarrel, debate, contention : I. in Il. mostly of battle-strife, ἔριδι or ἐξ ἔριδος μάχεσθαι ; ἔριδι ξυνιέναι to meet in battle ; θεοὺς ἔριδι ξυνελάσσαι to set them a-fighting, etc. II. in Od. mostly of contention, rivalry, ἔργοιο in work ; ἀέθλων for prizes, etc. :—later much like ἀγών, a contest, ἔριν ἔχειν ἀμφὶ μουσικῇ Hdt. ; ἔρις ἀγαθῶν zeal for good, Aesch. III. after Hom. of political or domestic strife, discord, quarrel, wrangling, disputation, Hdt., Att. IV. as pr. nom. Eris, a goddess who excites to war, sister and companion of Ares, Il.

ἐρίσδεν, Dor. for ἐρίζειν :—ἐρίσδομες for ἐρίζομεν.

ἐρι-σθενής, ές, very mighty, of Zeus, Hom., Hes. : of the Furies, Orph.

ἔρισμα, ατος, τό, (ἐρίζω) a cause of quarrel, Il.

ἐρι-σμάραγος, ον, loud-thundering, of Zeus, Hes.

ἐρι-στάφυλος, ον, (σταφυλή) of wine, made of fine grapes, Od. II. rich in grapes, of Bacchus, Anth.

ἐριστός, ή, όν, (ἐρίζω) matter for contest, Soph.

ἐρί-τῑμος, ον, (τιμή) highly-prized, precious, Il., Ar.

ἐρίφειος, ον, (ἔριφος) of a kid, Xen.

ἐρίφιον, τό, Dim. of ἔριφος, a kid, N. T.

ἘΡἼΦΟΣ, ὁ, a young goat, kid, Hom. II. ἔριφοι, οἱ, Lat. hoedi, a constellation (rising in Oct.) which brought storms, Theocr.

ἐρί-χρῡσος, ον, rich in gold, Anth.

ἐριώλη, ἡ, a hurricane, applied to Cleon by Ar. :— deriv. uncertain ; for the deriv. in Ar. from ἔριον ὀλλύναι, wool-consumption, is a mere pun.

ἑρκεῖος, ον, or α, ον, of or in the ἕρκος or front court, Ζεὺς Ἑρκεῖος, the household god, because his statue stood in the ἕρκος, Od., Hdt., etc. 2. πύλαι, θύρα ἕρκ. the gates, door of the court, Aesch. ; ἑρκεῖος στέγη the court itself, Soph.

ἑρκίον, τό, (ἕρκος) a fence, inclosure, Hom.

ἕρκος, εος, τό, (ἔργω, εἴργω) a fence, hedge, wall,

Hom.; esp. round the court-yards of houses, Od. :—also *the place enclosed, the court-yard*, Hom.; Κίσσινον ἔρκος, i. e. Susa, Aesch.; γαίας ἔρκος a fenced city, Eur.; ἔρκος ἱρόν, i. e. the altar, Soph.; ἔρκος ὀδόντων *the ring* or *wall* which the teeth make round the gums, i. e. *the teeth*, Hom.; σφραγῖδος ἔρκος, i. e. a seal, Soph. 2. metaph. *any fence*, ἔρκος ἀκόντων *a defence against* javelins, Il.; ἔρκος βελέων Ib. :—of persons, ἔρκος Ἀχαιῶν, of Ajax, ἔρκος Ἀχαιοῖσιν πολέμοιο, of Achilles, Ib. 3. *a net, toils, snare* for birds, Od.; mostly in pl., Ar. :—metaph., τῆς Δίκης ἐν ἕρκεσιν Aesch.

ἑρκ-οῦρος, ον, *watching an enclosure*, Anth.

ἑρκτή, ή, Ion. for εἱρκτή.

ἕρμα, ατος, τό, *a prop, support*, used to keep ships upright when ashore, Il.: metaph. of men, ἕρμα πόληος *prop* or *stay* of the city, Lat. *columen*, Hom.; μελαινέων ἔρμ᾽ ὀδυνάων, of a sharp arrow, *the foundation*, i. e. *the cause*, of pangs, Il. II. *a sunken rock, reef*, on which a vessel may strike, Hdt., Aesch., etc. III. *a mound, cairn, barrow*, Soph. IV. *that which keeps a ship steady, ballast*, Plut. (Deriv. uncertain.)

ἕρμα, ατος, τό, (εἴρω Α) in pl. ἕρματα, *earrings*, Hom.

ἑρμ-ἀγέλη, ή, *a herd of Hermae*, Anth.

ἕρμαιον, τό, *a god-send, wind-fall*, reputed to be *a gift of the god* Hermes, as in Latin of Hercules, Soph., Plat.; Ἕρμαια, (sc. ἱερά), τά, *a feast of Hermes*, Aeschin.

Ἑρμαῖος, α, ον, *called after Hermes*, Od., Aesch. 2. *of* or *from Hermes, gainful*, Id.

Ἑρμ-αφρόδιτος, ὁ, *an Hermaphrodite, a person partaking of the attributes of both sexes*, so called from Hermaphroditus, son of Hermes and Aphrodité, Luc.

Ἑρμέας, Ep. for Ἑρμῆς :—also Ἑρμείας, αο.

Ἑρμήδιον, = Ἑρμίδιον, Luc.

ἑρμηνεία, ή, (ἑρμηνεύω) *interpretation, explanation*, Plat., Xen.

ἑρμήνευμα, ατος, τό, (ἑρμηνεύω) *an interpretation, explanation*, Eur. II. *a symbol, monument*, Id.

ἑρμηνεύς, έως, ὁ, (Ἑρμῆς, *the messenger* of the gods), *an interpreter*, esp. of foreign tongues, *a dragoman*, Hdt., Xen. II. *an interpreter, expounder*, Aesch.

ἑρμηνευτικός, ή, όν, *of* or *for interpreting*, Luc. From

ἑρμηνεύω, f. σω, (ἑρμηνεύς) *to interpret* foreign tongues, Xen. II. *to interpret, put into words, give utterance to*, Thuc., etc. 2. *to explain*, Soph., Plat.

Ἑρμῆς, οῦ, ὁ, acc. Ἑρμῆν, dat. Ἑρμῇ, voc. Ἑρμῆ : Ep. gen. Ἑρμέω, Ἑρμείω :—*Hermes*, the Lat. *Mercurius*, son of Maia and Zeus; messenger of the gods (διάκτορος); giver of good luck (ἐριούνιος, ἀκάκητα); god of all secret dealings, cunning, and stratagem (δόλιος); bearing a golden rod (χρυσόρραπις); conductor of defunct spirits (ψυχοπομπός, πομπαῖος); tutelary god of all arts, of traffic, markets, roads (ἀγοραῖος, ἐμπολαῖος, ὅδιος, ἐνόδιος), and of heralds. His bust, mounted on a four-cornered pillar, was used to mark boundaries. —Proverb., κοινὸς Ἑρμῆς *shares in your luck!* Theophr.: cf. ἕρμαιον.

Ἑρμίδιον [ῐδ], τό, Dim. of Ἑρμῆς, *a little Hermes*, Ar.

ἑρμίς or -ίν, ῖνος, ὁ, dat. pl. ἑρμῖσι, *a bed-post*, Od.

ἑρμογλῦφεῖον, τό, *a statuary's shop*, Plat. From

ἑρμο-γλῦφεύς, έως, ὁ, *a carver of Hermae* : generally, *a statuary*, Luc. Hence

ἑρμογλῦφικός, ή, όν, *of* or *for a statuary* : ἡ -κη (sc. τέχνη), *the art of statuary*, Luc.

ἑρμο-γλῦφος, ὁ, = ἑρμογλυφεύς, Luc.

ἑρμο-κοπίδης, ου, ὁ, (κόπτω) *a Hermes-mutilator*, Plut.

ΈΡΝΟΣ, εος, τό, *a young sprout, shoot, scion*, Hom.; ἀνέδραμεν ἔρνεϊ ἶσος shot up like *a young plant*, Il. II. metaph. of *a child, a scion*, Trag.

ἕρξα, Ep. for εἷρξα, aor. 1 of ἔργω, εἴργω :—also of ἔρδω.

Ἐρξείης or Ἐρξίης, ὁ, in Hdt., as a translation of the Persian name Darius : (either from *ἔργω, ἔρδω *the worker, doer;* or from ἔργω, εἴργω, Lat. *coercitor*).

ἔρξω, εἴρξω, fut. of ἔργω, εἴργω :—also ἔρξω, fut. of ἔρδω.

ἐρόεις, εσσα, εν, (ἔρος) poët., *lovely, charming*, Hes., etc.

ἔρομαι, 2 sing. ἔρεαι; Ion. and Ep. εἴρομαι, = ἐρωτάω : impf. εἰρόμην : f. ἐρήσομαι, Ion. εἰρήσομαι : aor. 2 ἠρόμην, imper. ἐροῦ, inf. ἐρέσθαι (not ἔρεσθαι) :—also Ep. pres. ἐρέομαι, subj. ἐρέωμαι, inf. ἐρέεσθαι, impf. ἐρέοντο : —*to ask, enquire*, Od., Thuc. 2. c. acc. objecti, *to learn by enquiry*, Od. : *to ask after* or *for*, Il. 3. c. acc. pers. *to enquire of, question*, Ib., Hdt. 4. c. dupl. acc. *to ask one about* a thing, Od.

ἔρος, ὁ, acc. ἔρον, dat. ἔρῳ, poët. form of ἔρως (cf. γέλως), *love, desire*, Hom., etc. II. as nom. pr. *Eros*, the god of love, Hes.

ἔρος, τό, *wool*, only occurs in the Ion. for εἶρος.

ἔροτις, ή, Aeol. for ἑορτή, Eur.

ἑρπετόν, τό, (ἕρπω) *a walking animal, quadruped*, Od.; ἑρπετά, opp. to πετεινά, Hdt. II. *a creeping thing, reptile*, Eur., etc.

ἑρπηστής, οῦ, ὁ, = ἑρπετόν, of a mouse, Anth. 2. Adj. *creeping*, Id.

ἕρπω, used by Hom. in pres. (cf. ἔρπω) :—*to creep, crawl*, of persons weighed down by age or distress.

ἕρπυλλος, ὁ, and ή, *creeping thyme*, Lat. *serpyllum*, Ar., Theocr.

ἑρπυστής, οῦ, ὁ, (ἑρπύζω) *a crawling child*, Anth.

ΈΡΠΩ, impf. εἷρπον : Dor. f. ἑρψῶ : Att. f. aor. 1 εἵρπυσα, inf. ἑρπύσαι (supplied by ἑρπύζω) :—*to creep, crawl*, Lat. *serpo, repo*, and generally *to move slowly, walk*, Hom., Trag. :—also simply, *to go* or *come*, Id. II. variously, of a tear, *to steal* from the eye, Soph.; of reports, *to creep on, spread*, like Lat. *serpit rumor*, Id.; ὁ πόλεμος ἑρπέτω let it take its course, Ar.; of calamities, Soph.

ἐρράγην [ᾰ], aor. 2 pass. of ῥήγνυμι.

ἐρράδᾰται, -ατο, Ep. 3 pl. pf. and plqpf. pass. of ῥαίνω.

ἔρραμμαι, pf. pass. of ῥάπτω.

ἐρράπισα, aor. 1 of ῥαπίζω.

ἐρρήθην, aor. 1 pass. of ἐρῶ.

ἔρρηξα, aor. 1 of ῥήγνυμι.

ἔρρῑγα, pf. with pres. signf. of ῥιγέω :—ἐρρίγησα, aor. 1.

ἔρριμμαι, pf. pass. of ῥίπτω :—ἔρριψα, aor. 1.

ἐρρύηκα, pf. of ῥέω :—ἐρρύην, aor. 2 pass.

ΈΡΡΩ, f. ἐρρήσω : aor. 1 ἤρρησα : pf. ἤρρηκα :—*to go slowly, wander about*, Od.; of slow, halting gait, whence Hephaestus is called ἔρρων, *limping*, Il. II. *to go* or *come to one's own loss* or *harm*, Ib.; ἔρρων ἐκ ναός *gone, fallen* from a ship, Aesch. 2. imperat. ἔρρε, Lat. *abi in malam rem, away! begone!* Il.,

etc.; so, ἔρροις Eur.; in pl. ἔρρετε Il.; and in 3 sing. ἐρρέτω, *away with him*, Hom.; ἐρρέτω Ἴλιον *perish Troy!* Soph.; ἔρρ' ἐς κόρακας, Lat. *pasce corvos, be thou hung*, Ar.; so, οὐκ ἐρρήσετε; οὐκ ἐς κόρακας ἐρρήσετε; Id. 3. in Att. of persons and things, *to be clean gone, to be lost, perish, disappear,* Trag.; ἐξ οἵων καλῶν ἔρρεις from what fortunes *hast thou fallen,* Eur.; ἔρρει τὰ ἐμὰ πράγματα, Lat. *actum est de me!* Xen.

ἔρρωγα, pf. intr. of ῥήγνυμι.

ἐρρωμένος, η, ον, part. pf. pass. of ῥώννυμι, used as Adj. *in good health, stout, vigorous,* opp. to ἄρρωστος, Plat., Dem.; irreg. Comp., ἐρρωμενέστερος, Hdt., Xen.: —Sup. -έστατος, Plat. :—Adv. ἐρρωμένως, *stoutly, manfully, vigorously,* Aesch., Ar., etc.

ἐρρώμην, v. sub ῥώννυμι.

ἐρρώοντο, 3 pl. impf. of ῥώομαι :—ἐρρώσαντο, aor. 1; ἐρρώσθην, aor. 1 of pass. form.

ἐρρῶσθαι, pf. pass. inf. of ῥώννυμι :—ἔρρωσο, ἔρρωσθε, 2 sing. and pl. imperat.

ἜΡΣΗ, Ep. ἐέρση, Dor. ἔρσα, ἡ, *dew,* Lat. *ros,* Hom., etc. :—in pl. *rain-drops,* Il. **II.** metaph. of *young and tender animals,* Od.; cf. δρόσος. Hence

ἐρσήεις, Ep. ἐερσ-, εσσα, εν, *dewy, dew-besprent,* Il.: metaph. of a corpse, *fresh,* Ib.

ἔρσην, ενος, ὁ, Ion. for ἄρσην, ἄρρην.

ἐρυγγάνω, = ἐρεύγομαι, *eructare,* οἶνον ἐρυγγ. Eur.

ἐρύγειν, aor. 2 inf. of ἐρεύγομαι.

ἐρύγμηλος, η, ον, (ἐρυγεῖν) *loud-bellowing,* Il.

ἐρυθαίνομαι, Pass. *to become red* with blood, Il. Hence

ἐρύθημα, ατος, τό, *a redness on the skin,* Thuc.; ἐρ. προσώπου *a blush,* Eur. :—absol. *redness,* Il.

ἐρυθραίνομαι, Pass. *to become red, to blush,* Xen.

ἐρυθριάω, impf. ἠρυθρίων : aor. 1 ἠρυθρίασα : pf. ἠρυθρίακα :—*to be apt to blush, to colour up,* Ar., etc.

ἐρυθρό-πους, ὁ, ἡ, neut. -πουν, *red-footed* :—name of a bird, *the redshank,* Ar.

ἘΡΥΘΡΟΣ, ά, όν : [ῠ by nature, so that the correct forms of the Comp. and Sup. are -ώτερος, -ώτατος] :— *red,* Lat. *ruber,* of the colour of nectar and wine, Hom.; of copper, Il.; of gold, Theogn.; of minium, Hdt.; of blood, Aesch. **II.** Ἐρυθρὴ θάλασσα in Hdt. *the Erythraean sea,* including not only the *Red Sea* or *Arabian Gulf,* but also the *Indian Ocean* :—later also of *the Persian Gulf,* Xen.

ἐρυκάνάω, *to restrain, withhold,* Ep. part. fem. ἐρυκανόωσ' : impf. ἐρύκανε (from ἐρυκάνω), Ib.

ἐρύκω [ῠ, Ep. inf. ἐρυκέμεν :—f. ἐρύξω : aor. 1 ἤρυξα, Ep. ἔρυξα : Ep. aor. 2 ἠρύκάκον or ἐρύκάκον, inf. ἐρυκάκέειν : (akin to ἐρύω) :—τ· *keep in, hold back, keep in check, curb, restrain,* Hom. :—c. gen., μή με ἔρυκε μάχης *keep me not from* fight, Il. :—c. inf. *to hinder from* doing, Eur. :—absol. *to hinder,* Il. **2.** *to detain* a guest, Hom. :—but also, *to detain by force, to withhold, confine,* Id. **3.** *to ward off,* Lat. *arcere,* ἄκοντα, Λιμόν Id. **4.** *to keep apart, separate,* Il. **II.** Pass. *to be held back, detained,* Od. :— *to hold back, keep back,* Ib. **2.** *to be kept away,* Hdt. **3.** ἀνέδην χῶρος ἐρύκεται *the place is remissly guarded,* i. e. *is open to all,* Soph.

ἔρυμα, ατος, τό, (ἐρύομαι) *a fence, guard,* ἔρυμα χροός, of defensive armour, Il., Xen.; τὸ ἔρ. τοῦ τείχεος *the*

defence given by it, Hdt. : absol. *a bulwark, breast-work,* Thuc. **2.** *a safeguard,* of the Areopagus, Aesch.; παῖδας ἔρ. δώμασι Eur.

ἐρυμνό-νωτος, ον, *with fenced back,* of a crab, Anth.

ἐρυμνός, ή, όν, (ἐρύομαι) *fenced, fortified,* by art or nature, Eur., Thuc.; τὰ ἐρυμνά *strong positions,* Xen.

ἐρυμνότης, ητος, ἡ, *strength* or *security* of a place, Xen.

ἐρυσαίατο, Ion. for -αιντο, 3 pl. aor. 1 med. opt. of ἐρύω.

ἐρῡσ-άρμάτες, acc. -άτας, (ἐρύω, ἅρμα) no sing. in use, *chariot-drawing,* of horses, Il.

ἐρυσίβη [ῑ], ἡ, (ἐρυθρός) *red blight,* Lat. *robīgo,* Plat.

ἐρῡσί-θριξ ψήκτρα, *a comb for drawing through the hair, a small-tooth comb,* Anth.

ἐρῡσί-νηΐς, ΐδος, ἡ, (νηῦς, ναῦς) *preserving ships,* Anth.

ἐρῡσί-πτολις, ὁ, ἡ, (ἐρύομαι) *protecting the city,* Il.

ἐρυσμός, ὁ, *a safeguard* against witchcraft, h. Hom.

ἐρυστός, ή, όν, *drawn,* Soph. From

ἐρύω, Ion. εἰρύω ; Ep. inf. εἰρύμεναι [ῠ] : impf. εἴρυον, Ep. ἔρυον : f. ἐρύω : aor. 1 εἴρυσα, Ep. ἔρυσα and εἴρυσσα :—*to drag along the ground, drag, draw,* a ship in to the sea or on to land, Hom.; νεκρὸν ἐρ., *to drag* a body *away, rescue,* Il.; or to *drag off for plunder,* Ib.; of dogs and birds of prey, *to drag and tear,* Ib. :—also, *to tear away* battlements, Il. **2.** without any sense of violence, φᾶρος κὰκ κεφαλῆς εἴρυσσε *drew* it *over* his head, Od.; χλαίνης ἐρύων *plucking* him by the cloak, Il.; τόξον Hdt.; πλίνθους εἰρύειν, Lat. *ducere lateres,* Id.

B. Med. ἐρύομαι, Ion. εἰρύομαι : Ep. f. ἐρύομαι and ἐρύσσομαι or εἰρύσσομαι :—aor. 1 εἰρυσάμην, Ep. 3 sing. εἰρύσσατο : Ep. pf. 3 pl. εἰρύαται, inf. εἰρύσθαι : plqpf. 2 and 3 sing. εἴρυσο, ἔρυτο or εἴρῡτο, pl. εἴρυντο, -ύατο :—*to draw for oneself,* Hom.; ἐρύσασθαι νῆας *to launch us* ships, Il.; ξίφος ἐρύεσθαι *to draw one's* sword, Ib.; ἐρύσσεσθαι τόξον *to prepare to draw one's* bow, i. e. *to string* it, Od. **2.** *to draw towards oneself,* Ib. **II.** *to draw out of* the press, ἐρύσασθαί τινα μάχης Il.; hence, *to rescue, deliver,* of captives, *to redeem, ransom,* Ib. **2.** simply *to protect, guard,* of armour, Ib. **III.** c. acc. rei, *to keep off, ward off,* Ib. **2.** *to thwart, check, curb,* Ib. **3.** *to keep guard upon, watch over,* νῆας, δῶμα Od.; εἰρύαται οἴκαδ' ἰόντα *lie in wait for* me, Ib.; φρεσὶν ἐρύσασθαι *to keep in one's* heart, *to conceal,* Ib. **4.** *to support, hold in honour,* with notion of obedience, Ib.

C. Pass. *to be drawn ashore, drawn up in line,* of ships, Il.; νῆες δ' ὁδὸν εἰρύαται *are drawn up along* the road, Od.

ἔρχάται, ἔρχάτο, Ion. 3 pl. pf. and plqpf. pass. of ἔργω.

ἐρχάτάομαι, (ἔργω, εἴργω) Pass. *to be kept* or *shut up,* Ep. 3 pl. ἐρχατόωντο Od.

ἜΡΧΟΜΑΙ, impf. ἠρχόμην : fut. (as if from ἐλεύθομαι) ἐλεύσομαι :—act. forms, aor. 2 ἦλθον, ἦλθον ; Ep. inf. ἐλθέμεναι, -έμεν ; Dor. ἤνθον :—pf. ἐλήλῦθα, Ep. εἰλήλουθα, 1 pl. ἐλήλυθμεν, Ep. εἰλήλουθμεν, Ion. 3 sing. ἐλήλύθεε, Ep. εἰλήλουθεῖ :—*to come* or *go,* Hom., etc. **2.** *to come* or *go back, return,* Od.; in full, αὖτις, ἄψ, πάλιν ἐλθεῖν Ib. **3.** c. acc. cogn., ὁδόν or κέλευθον ἐλθεῖν *to go* a journey, Hom., Aesch.; ἀγγελίην ἐλθεῖν *to go* a message, Il. **4.** c. gen. loci, πεδίοιο ἐλθεῖν *over* or *across* the plain, Ib. **5.** c. part. fut., *to denote the object,* ἔρχομαι οἰσόμενος *I go to fetch,* Ib.;

μαρτυρήσων ἦλθον Aesch., etc. :—like an auxiliary Verb, ἔρχομαι λέξων *I am going to* tell, *I intend* to say (as in French *je vais dire*), Hdt. 6. the aor. part. ἐλθών is often added to another Verb, κάθηρον ἐλθών *come and* cleanse, Il., etc. II. Post-Homeric phrases: 1. εἰς λόγους ἔρχεσθαί τινι *to come to* speech with, Hdt., Soph. 2. εἰς χεῖρας, so, ἐς μάχην ἐλθεῖν τινι *to come* to blows with one, Aesch., Hdt. 3. ἐπὶ μεῖζον ἔρχ. *to increase*, Soph. ; εἰς πᾶν ἐλθεῖν *to try everything*, Xen. 4. ἐς τὸ δεινόν, ἐς τὰ ἀλγεινὰ ἐλθεῖν *to come* into danger, etc., Thuc., etc. 5. παρὰ μικρὸν ἐλθεῖν, c. inf. *to come within a little of, be near* a thing, Eur. ; παρὰ τοσοῦτον ἦλθε κινδύνου so narrow was her escape, Thuc. 6. with διά and gen., periphr. for a Verb, διὰ μάχης τινι ἔρχεσθαι, for μάχεσθαί τινι, Eur., etc.
ἐρψῶ, Dor. fut. of ἕρπω.
ἘΡΩ͂, Ion. and Ep. ἐρέω, fut. of εἴρω (B) ; pf. εἴρηκα, pass. εἴρημαι, Ion. 3 pl. εἰρέαται : 3 pl. plqpf. εἴρητο : —Pass., aor. 1 ἐρρήθην, Ion. εἰρέθην : fut. εἰρήσομαι, rarely ῥηθήσομαι :—the place of the pres. εἴρω (rare even in Ep. and never in Att.) is supplied by φημί, λέγω or ἀγορεύω ; and εἶπον serves as the aor.: I. *I will say* or *speak*, Att. : c. acc. pers. *to speak of*, κακῶς ἐρεῖν τινα Theogn., Eur. ; c. dupl. acc., ἐρεῖν τινά τι Id., etc. II. *I will tell, proclaim*, Il., etc. ; φόως ἐρέουσα *to announce* the dawn, Ib. ; ἐπὶ ῥηθέντι δικαίῳ upon *clear right*, Od. 2. εἰρημένος *promised*, μισθός Hes., Hdt. ; εἰρημένον, absol., *when it had been agreed*, Thuc. 3. *to tell, order* one to do, c. dat. et inf., Xen. ; c. acc. et inf., Id. :—so in Pass., εἴρητό οἱ, c. inf., *orders had been given* him to do, Hdt. III. in Pass. *to be mentioned*, Id.
ἐρωδιός, ὁ, *the heron* or *hern*, Lat. *ardea*, Il., Ar.
ἐρωέω, f. ήσω : aor. 1 ἠρώησα :—*to rush, rush forth*, Hom. ; ἠρώησαν ὀπίσσω, of horses, *they started* back, Il. 2. c. gen. rei, *to draw back* or *rest from*, πολέμοιο, χάρμης Ib. ; νέφος οὔποτ᾽ ἐρωεῖ the cloud never *fails from* (the rock), Od. :—c. acc. *to leave, quit*, Theocr. II. trans. *to drive* or *force back*, Il. From
ἐρωή, ἡ, *any quick motion, rush, force*, Il. ; mostly of things, δουρός, βελέων ἐρ. Ib. ; λείπετο δουρὸς ἐρωήν war left a spear's *throw* behind, Ib. ; λικμητῆρος ἐρωή *the force* or *swing* of the winnower's (shovel), Ib. II. c. gen. rei, *a drawing back from, rest from*, πολέμου Ib.
ἐρωμένιον, τό, *a little love, darling*, Anth. From
ἐρώμενος, ὁ, ἐρωμένη, ἡ, *one's love*: v. ἐράω.
ἔρως, ωτος, ὁ : for dat. ἔρω = ἔρωτι, v. ἔρος: (ἔραμαι): —*love*, Trag. :—*love of* a thing, *desire for* it, τινός Hdt., Aesch., etc. :—in pl. *loves, amours*, Eur. ; in Soph. of *passionate joy*, cf. φρίσσω II. 3. II. as prop. n. *the god of love*, Eros, Amor, Id., Eur.
ἐρωτάριον, τό, Dim. of ἔρως, *a little Cupid*, Anth.
ἐρωτάω, Ep. εἰρωτάω, Ion. -έω : impf. ἠρώτων, εἰρώτων, Ion. εἰρώτεον or -ευν : f.. ήσω : (ἔρομαι):—*to ask*, τινά τι *something of* one, Od., Soph., etc. :—Pass. *to be asked*, τι Xen. 2. ἐρ. τι *to ask about* a thing, Aesch. :— Pass., τὸ ἐρωτηθέν *the question*, Thuc., Xen. II. *to enquire* of a person, *question* him, Od., Eur., etc. :—Pass. *to be questioned*, Id. III. = αἰτέω, *to ask*, i. e. *to beg, solicit*, N. T.

ἐρώτη, Dor. for ἐρώτα, 3 sing. impf. of ἐρωτάω, Ar.
ἐρώτημα, ατος, τό, (ἐρωτάω) *that which is asked, a question*, Thuc. ; τὰ ἐρ. τοῦ ξυνθήματος asking *for* the watchword, Id.
ἐρώτησις, εως, ἡ, (ἐρωτάω) *a questioning*, Plat., Xen.
ἐρωτιάς, άδος, ἡ, special fem. of ἐρωτικός, Anth.
ἐρωτικός, ή, όν, (ἔρως) *amatory*, Thuc., etc. II. of persons, *amorous*, Plat., Xen. :—Adv. -κῶς, Thuc. ; ἐρ. ἔχειν τινός *to be eager for*, Xen.
ἐρωτίς, ίδος, ἡ, (ἔρως) *a loved one, darling*, Theocr. II. as Adj., *of love*, Anth.
ἐρωτο-γράφος, ον, (γράφω) *for writing of love*, Anth.
ἐρωτο-πλάνος [ᾰ], ον, *beguiling love*, Anth.
ἐρωτύλος [ῠ], ὁ, Dor. word, *a darling, sweetheart*, Theocr. II. as Adj., ἐρωτύλα ἀείδειν *to sing love-songs*, Bion.
ἐς, Ion. and old Att. form of εἰς : compounds must be sought under εἰσ-.
ἐσ-αγείρω, ἐσ-άγω, v. εἰσ-.
ἐσ-αεί, *for ever*, v. ἀεί.
ἐσ-αθρέω, ἐσ-ακούω, etc., v. εἰσ-.
ἐσ-ᾶλτο, v. εἰσάλλομαι.
ἔσαν, Ep. and Ion. for ἦσαν, 3 pl. impf. of εἰμί (*sum*).
ἐσ-άντα, ἐσ-άπαξ, v. εἰσ-.
ἐσ-απικνέομαι, Ion. for εἰσ-αφικνέομαι.
ἔσας, aor. part. of ἵζω (signf. 1).
ἐσ-αῦθις, v. εἰσ-αῦθις.
ἐσάωθην, aor. 1 pass. of σαόω :—ἐσάωσα, aor. 1 act.
ἐσβαίην, aor. 2 opt. of εἰσβαίνω.
ἐσ-βαίνω, ἐσ-βάλλω, etc., v. εἰσ-.
ἐσβάς, aor. 2 part. of εἰσβαίνω.
ἔσβην, aor. 2 of σβέννυμι.
ἐσ-βιβάζω, ἐσ-βολή, ἐσ-δέχομαι, ἐσ-δίδωμι, v. εἰσ-.
ἔσδομαι, Dor. for ἕζομαι.
ἐσ-δύω, v. εἰσ-.
ἔσεαι, Ep. 2 pers. fut. of εἰμί (*sum*) :—ἔσεται, for ἔσται.
ἐσέδρακον, aor. 2 of εἰσδέρκομαι.
ἔσ-ειμι, v. εἰσ-.
ἐσελεύσομαι, fut. of εἰσέρχομαι.
ἐσ-έρχομαι, v. εἰσ-.
ἐσεμασσάμην, v. εἰσμαίομαι.
ἐσέπτατο, v. εἰσπέτομαι.
ἐσεργνύναι, Ion.for εἰσ-εἴργειν,*to shut in, enclose*, Hdt.
ἐσεσάχατο, Ion. 3 pl. plqpf. pass. of σάττω.
ἐσέχυντο, 3 pl. Ep. aor. 2 pass. of εἰσχέω.
ἐσ-έχω, ἐσ-ηγέομαι, ἐσ-ηθέω, ἐσ-ήκω, v. εἰσ-.
ἐσήλατο, v. εἰσάλλομαι.
ἐσηλϋσίη, ἡ, = εἰσέλευσις, Anth.
ἐσήμηνα, aor. 1 of σημαίνω.
ἔσηνα, aor. 1 of σαίνω.
ἐσθέω, (ἐσθής) *to clothe* :—only used in pf. and plqpf. pass., ἤσθημαι, Ion. ἔσθημαι, *clothed* or *clad*, τι *in* a thing, ἐσθῆτα ἐσθημένος Hdt. ; ῥάκεσι ἐσθημένος Id. ; ἠσθημένοι πέπλοισι Eur.
ἔσθημα, ατος, τό, *a garment*, in pl., *clothes, raiment*, Trag., Thuc., etc.
ἔσθην, 3 dual plqpf. pass. of ἕννυμι.
ἐσθής, ῆτος, Dor. ἐσθάς, ᾶτος, ἡ, (ἕννυμι) *dress, clothing, raiment*, Hom., Hdt., Att. ; in pl., of *the clothes of several* persons, Aesch. II. collectively, *clothes*, Od., Hdt.

ἔσθησις, εως, ἡ, (ἐσθέω) clothing, raiment, N. T.
ἐσθίω : impf. ἤσθιον :—fut. ἔδομαι from ἔδω :—pf. ἐδήδοκα, Ep. part. ἐδηδώς :—plqpf. ἐδηδόκειν Luc.:—Pass., pf. ἐδήδεσμαι, Ep. 3 sing. ἐδήδοται :—the aor. 2 is supplied by φαγεῖν, q. v. :—to eat, Lat. edo (cf. ἔδω), Hom., etc. ; ἐσθ. τινός to eat of a thing (partitive gen.), Xen. :—Pass., οἶκος ἐσθίεται the house is eaten up, we are eaten out of house and home, Od. 2. metaph., πάντας πῦρ ἐσθίει the fire devours all, Il. ; ἐσθ. ἑαυτόν to vex oneself (like Homer's ὃν θυμὸν κατέδων), Ar. ; ἐσθ. τὴν χελύνην to bite the lip, Id.
ἘΣΘΛΟΣ, ή, όν, Dor. ἐσλός, ά, όν, much like ἀγαθός, good of his kind, good, brave, esp. in Il. ; —also, rich, wealthy, Hes. : noble, opp. to κακός (v. ἀγαθός I), εἶτ' εὐγενὴς πέφυκας εἶτ' ἐσθλῶν κακή Soph. 2. of things, Hom., etc. 3. good, fortunate, lucky, Od., Trag. 4. as Subst., ἐσθλά, τά, goods, Od. :—but ἐσθλόν, τό, good luck, Hom. 5. ἐσθλόν [ἐστι], c. inf. it is good, expedient to do, Il.
ἔσθορον, Ep. for εἰσέθορον, aor. 2 of εἰσθρώσκω.
ἔσθος, εος, τό, = ἔσθημα, Il., Ar.
ἔσθ' ὅτε, for ἐστὶν ὅτε, Lat. est quum, there is a time when, i. e. now and then, sometimes, Soph., Xen.
ἐσ-θρώσκω, v. εἰσ-.
ἔσθω, Ep. inf. ἐσθέμεναι : impf. ἦσθον :—poët. form of ἐσθίω, to eat, Hom. : to eat up, consume one's substance, Id.
ἐσῑγάθην [ᾰ], Dor. for –ήθην, aor. 1 pass. of σιγάω.
ἐσῐδεῖν, aor. 2 inf. of εἰσεῖδον :—ἐσιδέσθην, 2 dual aor. 2 med.
ἐσῑέμενος, pres. med. part. of εἰσίημι.
ἐσίζηται, 3 sing. of εἰσίζομαι.
ἐσικνέομαι, v. εἰσίκταμαι, v. εἰσ-.
ἔσις, εως, ἡ, (ἵημι) a sending forth. 2. (ἵεμαι) an impulse, tendency, only in Plat. : but the compd. ἔφεσις is found. II. (ἕζω) a sitting.
ἐσ-καταβαίνω, v. εἰσ-.
ἐσκάτθετο, 3 sing. aor. 2 med. of εἰσκατατίθημι.
ἐσκεμμένος, Adv. pf. pass. part. deliberately, Dem.
ἐσκίδναντο, 3 pl. impf. pass. of σκίδνημι.
ἔσκληκα, intr. pf. of σκέλλω.
ἐσ-κομιδή, ἐσ-κομίζω, v. εἰσ-.
ἔσκον, Ep. and Ion. impf. of εἰμί (sum).
ἐσλός, Dor. for ἐσθλός.
ἔσμηχον, impf. of σμήχω.
ἑσμός, ὁ, (ἵημι) anything let out, Lat. scaturigo : esp. a swarm of bees or wasps, Hdt., Ar. :—of things, ἑσμοὶ γάλακτος streams of milk, Eur.
ἑσμο-τόκος, ον, (τεκεῖν) producing swarms of bees, Anth.
ἔσο, Ep. for ἴσθι, imper. of εἰμί (sum).
ἐσ-όδος, ἐσ-οικέω, v. εἰσ-.
ἔσ-οπτρον, ἐσοράω, v. εἰσ-.
ἐσοῦμαι, Dor. for ἔσομαι, fut. of εἰμί (sum).
ἐσόψομαι, fut. of εἰσοράω.
ἐσπάρην [ᾰ], aor. 2 pass. of σπείρω :—ἔσπαρμαι, pf. 1 of σπείρω.
ἔσπεισα, aor. 1 of σπένδω.
ἑσπέρα, Ion. -έρη, ἡ, Lat. vespera, properly fem. of ἕσπερος : I. (sub. ὥρα), evening, eventide, eve, Hdt. ; ἑσπέρας at eve, Plat., etc. ; ἀπὸ ἑσπέρας εὐθύς just at nightfall, Thuc. ; πρὸς ἑσπέρα Ar. ; ἐπεὶ πρὸς ἑσπέραν ἦν Xen. ; ἑσπέρας γιγνομένης Plat. II. (sub. χώρα), the west, Lat. occidens, Eur. ; ἡ πρὸς

ἑσπέρην χώρη the country to the west, Hdt. ; τὸ πρὸς ἑσπέρης Id. ; τὰ πρὸς ἑσπέραν Thuc.
ἑσπερῑνός, ή, όν, = sq., Xen.
ἑσπέριος, α, ον, and ος, ον : (ἕσπερος): I. of Time, at even, at eventide, Hom. ; ἑσπέριος ἦλθεν Od., etc. II. of Place, western, Lat. occidentalis, Ib., Eur. ; τὰ ἑσπ. the western parts, Thuc.
Ἑσπερίς, ίδος, in nom. pr., Ἑσπερίδες, αἱ, the Hesperides, daughters of Night, who dwelt in an island in the west, and guarded a garden with golden apples, Hes.
ἙΣΠΕΡΟΣ, ον, of or at evening, ἕ. ἀστήρ the evening-star, Il. ; as Subst., without ἀστήρ, Hesperus, esp. of the planet Venus, Eur., Bion ; but, ἕσπ. θεός the god of darkness, i. e. Hades, death, Soph. 2. as Subst. evening (v. ἑσπέρα), ἐπὶ ἕσπερος ἦλθε Od. ; ποτὶ ἕσπερον at eventide, Hes. ; also heterog. pl., ποτὶ ἕσπερα Od. II. western, Aesch., Soph.
ἔσσομαι, Ep. form of ἔπομαι, Od.
ἑσπόμην, inf. ἑσπέσθαι, part. ἑσπόμενος, aor. 2 of ἕπομαι.
ἔσπον, an aor. 2 used by Hom. only in 2 pl., ἔσπετε νῦν μοι, Μοῦσαι tell me now, ye Muses, Il.
ἔσσα, aor. 1 of ἕννυμι : inf. ἔσσαι : ἐσσάμενος, part. aor. 1 med.
ἐσσεῖται, 3 sing. of ἐσσοῦμαι, Dor. fut. of εἰμί (sum).
ἔσσεσθαι, Ep. for ἔσεσθαι, fut. inf. of εἰμί (sum).
ἔσσευα, Ep. aor. 1 of σεύω.
ἐσσί, Dor. 2 sing. of ἐμί, Dor. for εἰμί (sum).
ἔσσο, ἔσσο, 2 and sing. plqpf. pass. of ἕννυμι.
ἔσσομαι, Ep. for ἔσομαι, fut. of εἰμί (sum).
ἐσσόομαι, Ion. for ἡσσάομαι.
ἔσσυμαι, syncop. pf. pass. of σεύω.
ἐσσύμενος, η, ον, part. pf. pass. of σεύω, hurrying, vehement, eager, impetuous, Il. :—eager, yearning for a thing, c. gen., Hom. ; also c. inf., Id. II. Adv. ἐσσυμένως, hurriedly, furiously, Id.
ἔσσυο, -το, 2, 3 sing. plqpf., or Ep. aor. 2 pass. of σεύω.
ἔσσων, ον, Ion. for ἥσσων.
ἐστάλᾱτο, Ion. 3 pl. plqpf. pass. of στέλλω.
ἐστάλην [ᾰ], aor. 2 pass. of στέλλω.
ἐστάμεν, -άμεναι [ᾰ], Ep. for ἑστάναι, syncop. pf. inf. of ἵστημι : but, II. ἕσταμεν, 1 pl. indic.
ἔσταν, Ep. for ἔστησαν, 3 pl. aor. 2 of ἵστημι.
ἑστάναι, for ἑστηκέναι, pf. inf. of ἵστημι.
ἑσταότως, Adv. on one's feet, Il.
ἕστᾰσαν, 3 pl. syncop. plqpf. of ἵστημι, they stood. II.
ἔστᾰσαν, for ἔστησαν, 3 pl. aor. 1, they set or placed.
ἑστάτον, for ἑστήκατον, dual of ἵστημι :—ἕστᾰμεν, ἕστατε, ἑστᾶσι, of same.
ἐσταύρωμαι, pf. pass. of σταυρόω.
ἑσταώς, pl. -αότες, poët. for ἑστηκώς, -ηκότες, pf. part. of ἵστημι.
ἔσ-τε (ἔσ-οτε): I. CONJUNCTION, = ἕως : 1. up to the time that, until, with indic. or optat., etc. ; ἔστ' ἄν, with subj., Aesch., etc. 2. so long as, while, with same tenses, etc. II. ADVERB, even to, up to, ἔστε ἐπί, Lat. usque ad, Xen. :—also of Time, ἔστε ἐπὶ κνέφας Id.
ἔστειλα, aor. 1 of στέλλω.
ἔστεμμαι, pf. pass. of στέφω.
ἐστέρημαι, pf. pass. of στερέω.
ἐστεφάνωτο, 3 sing. plqpf. pass. of στεφανόω.

ἔστηκα, -ειν, intr. pf. and plqpf. of ἵστημι :—ἔστην aor. 2 :—ἔστηξω, -ομαι, fut.

ἐστήρικται, -το, 3 sing. pf. and plqpf. pass. of στηρίζω.

ἔστησα, -άμην, aor. 1 act. and med. of ἵστημι.

ἑστηώς, Ep. for -ηκώς, pf. part. of ἵστημι.

ἑστία, Ion. ἱστίη, ἡ, the hearth of a house, fireside, Hom., Aesch., etc.; the shrine of the household gods, and a sanctuary for suppliants (ἐφέστιοι), ἐπὶ τὴν ἑστίαν καθίζεσθαι Thuc. 2. the house itself, a dwelling, home (as we say fireside), Hdt., Trag.: metaph. of the last home, the grave, Soph. 3. a household, family, Hdt. 4. an altar, shrine, Trag.; γᾶς μεσόμφαλος ἑστ., of the Delphic shrine, Eur. II. as nom. pr. Ἑστία, Ion. Ἱστίη, Vesta, daughter of Kronos and Rhea, guardian of the hearth, h. Hom., Hdt., etc. (Deriv. uncertain.)

ἑστίαμα, ατος, τό, (ἑστιάω) an entertainment, banquet, Eur.

Ἑστιάς, άδος, ἡ, (Ἑστία) a Vestal virgin, Plut.

ἑστίασις, εως, ἡ, a feasting, banqueting, entertainment, Thuc., Plat.; and

ἑστιάτωρ [ᾱ], ορος, ὁ, one who gives a banquet, a host, Plat. :—at Athens, the citizen whose turn it was to give a dinner to his tribe, Dem. From

ἑστιάω, Ion. ἱστιάω : impf. εἱστίων, Ion. 3 sing. ἱστία : —f. ἑστιάσω [ᾱ] : aor. 1 εἱστίᾱσα :—pf. εἱστίᾱκα : (ἑστία) :—to receive at one's hearth or in one's house : to entertain, feast, regale, Hdt., Att. :—absol. to give a feast, Plat. 2. c. acc. cogn., γάμους ἑστιᾶν to give a marriage feast, Eur., Ar.; ἑστ. νικητήρια Xen. II. Pass., with fut. med. ἑστιάσομαι, aor. 1 εἱστιάθην : pf. εἱστίαμαι, Ion. inf. ἱστιῆσθαι :—to be a guest, be feasted, feast, Hdt., Plat.; ἑστ. ἐνύπνιον to have a visionary feast, 'feast with the Barmecide,' Ar.

ἑστιόομαι, Pass. (ἑστία) to be founded or established (by children), Eur.

ἑστι-οῦχος, ον, (ἔχω) guarding the house, a guardian, Eur. 2. having an altar or hearth, Trag.

ἐστιχόωντο, 3 pl. Ep. impf. med. of στιχάω.

ἔστο, 3 sing. plqpf. of ἕννυμι.

ἔστοργα, pf. of στέργω.

ἐστόρεσα, aor. 1 of στορέννυμι.

ἔστραμμαι, pf. pass. of στρέφω.

ἐστρατόωντο, Ep. 3 pl. impf. of στρατάομαι.

ἐστράφην [ᾰ], aor. 2 pass. of στρέφω.

ἔστρωμαι, pf. pass. of στορέννυμι : ἔστρωσα, aor. 1 act.

ἔστρωτο, 3 sing. plqpf. pass. of στρώννυμι.

ἔστυγον, aor. 2 of στυγέω.

ἔστωρ, ορος, ὁ, a peg at the end of the pole, passing through the yoke and having a ring (κρίκος) affixed, Il. (Deriv. uncertain.)

ἐσύνηκα, aor. 1 with double augm. of συνίημι.

ἐσ-ύστερον, Adv. for εἰς ὕστερον, hereafter, Od., Hdt.

ἔσφαγμαι, pf. pass. of σφάζω.

ἐσφαίρωσα, 3 sing. plqpf. pass. of σφαιρόω.

ἔσφᾱλα, Dor. for ἔσφηλα, aor. 1 of σφάλλω, Pind.

ἐσφαλμένως, Adv. part. pf. pass. erringly, amiss, Anth.

ἐσφέρω, ἐσφορά, v. εἰσ-.

ἐσφήκωντο, 3 pl. plqpf. pass. of σφηκόω.

ἐσ-φορέω, v. εἰσ-.

ἐσφράγισμαι, pf. pass. of σφραγίζω.

ἐσχάρα, Ion. -άρη [ᾰ], ἡ : Ep. gen. and dat. ἐσχαρό-φιν :—the hearth, fire-place, Hom.; the sanctuary of suppliants, καθέζετο ἐπ᾽ ἐσχάρῃ ἐν κονίῃσιν Od. :—a pan of coals, a brasier, Ar. 2. πυρὸς ἐσχάραι the watch-fires of the camp, Il. II. an altar for burnt-offerings, Od., Soph.

ἐσχαρεών, ῶνος, ὁ, = ἐσχάρα I, Theocr.

ἐσχάριος, ον, (ἐσχάρα) of or on the hearth, Anth.

ἐσχαρίς, ίδος, ἡ, (ἐσχάρα) a pan of coals, Plut.

ἐσχαρόφιν, Ep. gen. and dat. sing. of ἐσχάρα.

ἐσχατάω, (ἔσχατος) to be at the edge, on the border, Il.; Ep. part. ἐσχατόων straying about the edge of the camp, Ib.

ἐσχατιά, Ion. -ιή, ἡ, (ἔσχατος) the furthest part, edge, border, verge, Hom., Hdt., Att.: in pl. the borders, Hdt.; the extremities of the world, Id.

ἐσχάτιος, ον, poët. for ἔσχατος, Anth.

ἐσχατόεις, εσσα, εν, = ἔσχατος, Theocr.

ἔσχατος, η, ον, (prob. from ἐκ, ἐξ, as if ἔξατος, outermost) : I. of Space, as always in Hom. the furthest, uttermost, extreme, Id., Hdt., Att.; ἔσχατοι ἄλλων, of the Thracians who were the last in the Trojan lines, Il.; ἔσχατοι ἀνδρῶν, of the Aethiopians, Od.: ἔσχατα, τά, extremities, ἐσχ. γαίης Hes.; τὰ ἔσχ. τοῦ στρατοπέδου Thuc. II. the furthest in each direction. 2. the uppermost, Soph. 3. lowest, deepest, Lat. imus, Ἀΐδας Theocr. 4. innermost, Lat. intimus, Soph. 5. the last, hindmost, Id. III. of Degree, the uttermost, utmost, last, worst, πόνος, κίνδυνος Plat. :—as Subst., τὸ ἔσχατον, τὰ ἔσχατα, the utmost, Hdt.; of suffering, pain, etc., Id., Att.; ἐπ᾽ ἔσχατα βαίνεις Soph.; ἐσχατ᾽ ἐσχάτων κακὰ worst of possible evils, Id.; so in Sup., τὰ πάντων ἐσχατώτατα the extremest of all, Xen. IV. of Time, last, ἐς τὸ ἔσχ. to the end, Hdt., Thuc.; ἐσχάτας ὑπὲρ ῥίζας the last scion of the race, Soph. : —neut. ἔσχατον as Adv., for the last time, Id. V. Adv. -τως, to the uttermost, exceedingly, Xen. :—so, ἐς τὸ ἔσχ. Hdt., Xen.

ἐσχατόων, όωσα, Ep. part. of ἐσχατάω.

ἔσχεθον, poët. for ἔσχον, aor. 2 of ἔχω.

ἐσ-χέω, v. εἰσ-.

ἔσχηκα, -ημαι, pf. act. and pass. of ἔχω.

ἐσχίσθην, aor. 1 pass. of σχίζω :—ἔσχισμαι, pf.

ἔσχον, ἐσχόμην, aor. 2 act. and med. of ἔχω.

ἔσχων, impf. of *σχάω, = σχάζω.

ἔσω, older form of εἴσω, cf. ἔς, εἰς :—Comp., ἐσωτέρω τῆς Ἑλλάδος to the interior of Greece, Hdt.

ἔσωθεν, poët. -θε, Adv. from within, Hdt., Att. 2. within, Hdt., Aesch. :—c. gen., ἔσωθεν ἄντρων Eur.

ἐσώτατος, η, ον, Sup. of ἔσω, innermost, Lat. intimus : —ἐσώτερος, α, ον, interior, N. T.

ἐσωτέρω, Comp. of ἔσω.

ἐτάγην [ᾰ], aor. 2 pass. of τάσσω.

ἐτάζω, to examine, test, Anth.

ἐτάθην [ᾰ], aor. 1 pass. of τείνω.

ἑταίρα, Ion. -ρη, ἡ, v. ἑταῖρος II.

ἑταιρεία or ἑταιρία, Ion. -ηΐη, ἡ, (ἑταῖρος) companionship, association, brotherhood, Hdt., Att. 2. at Athens, a political club or union for party purposes, Thuc., etc. II. generally, friendly connexion, friendship, Dem.

ἑταιρεῖος, α, ον, Ion. -ήϊος, η, ον, of or belonging to

companions, Ζεὺς ἑτ. presiding over fellowship, Hdt.; φόνος ἑτ. the murder of a comrade, Anth.

ἑταιρέω, f. ήσω, (ἑταίρα) to keep company, of courtesans, Aeschin., etc.

ἑταιρήΐη, ἑταιρήΐος, Ion. for ἑταιρεία, ἑταιρεῖος.

ἑταίρησις, εως, ἡ, (ἑταιρέω) unchastity, Aeschin.

ἑταιρία, ἡ, v. ἑταιρεία.

ἑταιρίζω, f. ἴσω, (ἑταῖρος) to be a comrade to any one, c. dat., Il.   2. trans. in Med. to associate with oneself, choose for one's comrade, ἤ τινά που Τρώων ἑταρίσσαιτο (Ep. for ἑταιρίσαιτο) Ib.

ἑταιρικός, ή, όν, of or befitting a companion : τὸ ἑταιρικόν, = ἑταιρεία 2, Thuc.: hence the ties of party, Id.   II. of or like an ἑταίρα, meretricious Plut.:— Adv. -κῶς, Id., Luc.

ἑταιρίς, ίδος, ἡ, = ἑταίρα, Xen.

ἑταῖρος, Ep. and Ion. ἕταρος, ὁ, (ἔτης) a comrade, companion, mate, Hom.; a common way of addressing people, ὦ 'ταῖρε my good friend, Ar.; φίλ' ἑταῖρε Theogn.; pupils or disciples were the ἑταῖροι of their masters, as those of Socrates, Xen.:—c. gen., δαιτὸς ἑταῖρε partner of my feast, h. Hom.; πόσιος καὶ βρώσιος ἑταῖροι messmates, Theogn.   2. metaph. of things, ἐσθλὸς ἑταῖρος, of a fair wind, Od.; c. dat., βίος ὁ σοφοῖς ἕταρος Anth.: as Adj. associate in a thing, c. gen., Plat.: Sup., ἑταιρότατος Id.   II.

ἑταίρα, Ion. ἑταίρη, Ep. ἑτάρη [ἄ], ἡ, a companion, Il.; φόρμιγξ, ἣν δαιτὶ θεοὶ ποίησαν ἑταίρην Od.; πενία σφιν ἑταίρα Theocr.   2. opp. to a lawful wife, a concubine, a courtesan, Hdt., Att.   Hence

ἑταιρόσυνος, η, ον, friendly, a friend, Anth.

ἑτάκεο, Dor. for ἑτήκου, 2 sing. impf. of τήκω.

ἑτάλασσα, Ep. aor. 1 of *τλάω.

ἕταμον, Ion. and Dor. aor. 2 of τέμνω.

ἑταρίσσας, ἑτᾱρίσσαιτο, Ep. aor. 1 part. and opt. med. of ἑταιρίζω II.

ἕταρος, ἑτάρη, Ep., and Ion. for ἑταῖρος, ἑταίρη.

ἕτας, acc. pl. of ἔτης.

ἐτάτυμος, Dor. for ἐτήτυμος.

ἑτάφην [ἄ], aor. 2 pass. of θάπτω.

ἐτέθαπτο, 3 sing. plqpf. pass. of θάπτω.

ἐτέθην, aor. 1 pass. of τίθημι.

ἐτεθήπεα, Ep. for ἐτεθήπειν, plqpf. of τέθηπα.

ἔτειος, α, ον, (ἔτος) yearly, from year to year, Lat. annuus, Aesch., Eur.   II. of one year, yearling, Xen.

ἔτεκον, aor. 2 of τίκτω.

ἐτελείετο, Ep. 3 sing. impf. pass. of τελέω.

ἐτελέσθην, aor. 1 pass. of τελέω.

ἔτεμον, aor. 2 of τέμνω.

Ἐτεο-βουτάδης, ου, ὁ, a genuine son of Butes (one of the hereditary priests of Athena Polias), Dem.

Ἐτεό-κρητες, οἱ, true Cretans, of the old stock, Od.

ΕΤΕΟ'Σ, ά, όν, true, real, genuine, Hom.; ἐτεὸν μαντεύεται prophesies truth, Il.; ὡς ἐτεόν περ as the truth is, Hom.   II. ἐτεόν as Adv., in truth, really, verily, Lat. revera, Id.; rightly, Theocr.:—Att. as an interrog., often in iron. sense, really? indeed? so? Lat. itane? Ar.

ἑτερ-αλκής, ές, (ἀλκή) giving strength to one of two, Δαναοῖσι μάχης ἑτεραλκέα νίκην δοῦναι to give victory in battle inclining to the side of the Danai, Il.; ἑτ. σῆμα a sign that victory was changing sides, Ib.; so without

μάχης, δίδου ἑτεραλκέα νίκην Hom.   2. act., δῆμος ἑτ. a body of men which decides the victory, Il.   II. inclining first to one side then to the other, doubtful, Lat. anceps, Hdt.; so in Adv., ἑτεραλκέως ἀγωνίζεσθαι, ancipiti Marte pugnare, Il.

ἑτερ-ήμερος, ον, (ἡμέρα) on alternate days, day and day about, of the Dioscuri, Od.

ἑτέρηφι, Ep. dat. fem. of ἕτερος.

ἑτερό-γλωσσος, Att. -ττος, ον, (γλῶσσα) of other tongue, ἐν ἑτερογλώσσοις by men of foreign tongue, N.T.

ἑτερό-γνᾰθος, ὁ, with one side of the mouth harder than the other, ἵππος Xen.

ἑτεροδιδασκᾰλέω, to teach differently, to teach errors, N.T.   From

ἑτερο-διδάσκαλος, ὁ, one who teaches error.

ἑτερό-ζηλος, ον, zealous for one side, leaning to one side, of the balance:—Adv. -λως, unfairly, Hes.   II. zealous in another pursuit, Anth.

ἑτεροζῠγέω, to be yoked in unequal partnership with another, N.T.   From

ἑτερό-ζῠγος, ον, (ζυγόν) coupled with an animal of diverse kind, Lxx.

ἑτερό-ζυξ, ῠγος, ὁ, ἡ, (ζυγῆναι) yoked singly, without its yokefellow, metaph., Ion ap. Plut.

ἑτεροῖος, α, ον, of a different kind, Hdt.   Hence

ἑτεροιόω, f. ώσω, to make of different kind:—Pass. to be changed or altered, to alter, Hdt.

ἑτερο-κλῐνής, ές, (κλίνω) leaning to one side, sloping, Xen.

ἑτερο-μήκης, ες, (μῆκος) with sides of uneven length, i. e. oblong, rectangular, Xen.

ἑτερό-πλοος, ον, contr. -πλους, ουν, of money lent on a ship and cargo with the risk of the outward, but not of the homeward, voyage, Dem.

ἕτερος, α, ον: Dor. ἅτερος [ἄ]: but ἄτερος [ἄ], Att. crasis for ὁ ἕτερος, Ion. οὕτερος, Dor. ὥτερος; neut. θάτερον Att., Ion. τοὔτερον: pl. ἄτεροι, θάτερα, for οἱ ἕτεροι, τὰ ἕτερα; gen. θατέρου: dat. θατέρῳ: fem. nom. ἀτέρα, dat. θατέρα: I. Lat. alter, the other, one of two, χειρὶ ἑτέρῃ Hom., v. infr. IV; χωλὸς ἕτερον πόδα, etc.:—then of all persons or things of which there are two, Lat. alteruter, Il.; τὴν ἑτ. πύλην one of the two gates, Hdt.; δυοῖν ἀγαθοῖν τὸ ἕτ. Thuc., etc.:—in pl. one of two parties, each of which is plur., Lat. alterutri, Hom.   2. in double clauses, ἕτερος (in Prose ὁ ἕτερος) is repeated, ἕτερον μὲν ἔδωκε, ἕτερον δ' ἀνένευσε Il., etc.   3. often repeated in the same clause, ἐξ ἑτέρων ἕτερ' ἐστίν one depends upon the other, Od.; ἕτεροι ἑτέρων ἄρχουσι the one rule the other, Thuc.   4. like Lat. alter, = δεύτερος, second, ἣ μὲν . . , ἣ δ' ἑτέρη . . , ἣ δὲ τρίτη . . , Od., etc.; ἡ ἑτέρα (sc. ἡμέρα), the second day, i. e. day after to-morrow, Xen.:—so with Pronouns of quantity, ἕτερον τοσοῦτο another of the same size, Hdt.   II. put loosely for ἄλλος, Lat. alius, another, Hom., Att.   III. other than usual, different, Od., etc.; ἑτ. καὶ οὐχ ὁ αὐτός Dem.:—c. gen. other than, different from, ἑτέρους τῶν νῦν ὄντων Thuc.; so, ἕτερον ἤ . . , Eur.   2. other than should be, other than good, euphem. for κακός, as Lat. sequior for malus, ἀγαθῇ ἢ θατέρα Dem.; and alone, ἑτ. θυσία Aesch., etc.   IV. Special Phrases: 1. elliptical, τῇ ἑτέρᾳ (sc. χειρί), Ep. τῇ

ἑτέρῃ or ἑτέρηφι with one hand, Il.; esp. with the left hand, Hom. **b.** (sub. ἡμέρᾳ) on the next day, Soph., Xen. **c.** (sub. ὁδῷ) in another or a different way, Soph., Ar. **2.** Adverbial with Preps., ἐπὶ θάτερα to or on the other side, Thuc., etc. **b.** κατὰ θάτερα on the one or other side, Dem. **V.** Adv. ἑτέρως, in one or the other way, Plat. **2.** differently, Ar., Dem.

ἑτερό-τροπος, ον, of different sort or fashion, Ar. **II.** turning the other way, uncertain, Anth.

ἑτερ-όφθαλμος, ον, one-eyed, Lat. unoculus, luscus, Dem.

ἑτερό-φρων, ον, (φρήν) of other mind, raving, Anth.

ἑτερό-φωνος, ον, (φωνή) of different voice: foreign, Aesch.

ἕτερσετο, 3 sing. aor. 2 med. of τερσαίνω.

ἑτέρωθεν, (ἕτερος) Adv. from the other side, Il. **2.** in pregnant sense with Verbs of rest, as if for ἑτέρωθι, on the other side, opposite, Ib.

ἑτέρωθι, (ἕτερος) Adv. on the other side, Od., Hdt. **II.** = ἄλλοθι, elsewhere, Hom., etc.:—c. gen., ἑτ. τοῦ λόγου in another part of my story, Hdt. **III.** at another time, Id.

ἑτέρως, v. ἕτερος V.

ἑτέρωσε, (ἕτερος) Adv. to the other side, Hom.:—on one side, Id. **2.** in pregnant sense with Verbs of Rest, as if for ἑτέρωθι, on the other side, Il., Dem. **II.** = ἄλλοσε, elsewhither, Il., Hom.

ἑτέρωτα, Aeol. for ἑτέρωθι.

ἐτέταλτο, 3 sing. plqpf. pass. of τέλλω.

ἐτετεύχατο, Ep. 3 pl. plqpf. pass. of τεύχω.

ἔτετμε, 3 sing. aor. 2; v. τέτμον.

ἐτέτυξο, -υκτο, 2 and 3 sing. plqpf. pass. of τεύχω.

ἐτέχθην, aor. 1 pass. of τίκτω.

ἛΤΗΣ, ου, ὁ, mostly in pl. ἔται, οἱ:—the ἔται were clansmen, i. e. the kinsmen of a great house, cousins, παῖδές τε κασίγνητοί τε ἔται τε Hom.; ἔται καὶ ἀνεψιοί Il. **II.** later, = δημότης, a townsman, neighbour, Thuc.:—in sing. a private citizen, Aesch. **III.** for ὦ τάν or ὦ 'τάν, v. sub τάν.

ἐτησίαι, οἱ, (ἔτος) with or without ἄνεμοι, periodic winds: of the Egyptian monsoons, which blow from the North-west during the summer, Hdt.; of northerly winds, which blow in the Aegean for 40 days from the rising of the dog-star, Id., Dem.

ἐτήσιος, ον, (ἔτος) lasting a year, a year long, πένθος Eur., Thuc. **2.** every year, annual, Id.

ἐτητυμία, ἡ, truth, Anth. From

ἐτήτυμος, ον, lengthd. poët. for ἔτυμος, true, Hom.; τοῦτ' ἀγόρευσον ἐτήτυμον tell me this true, Od.; εἰ λέγεις ἐτήτυμα Soph. **2.** of persons, truthful, Eur. **3.** true, genuine, real, Lat. sincerus, κείνῳ δ' οὐκέτι νόστος ἐτ. for him there remains no true, real return, Od.; ἐτ. Διὸς κόρα Aesch.; παῖς χρυσός Theocr. **II.** as Adv., in neut. ἐτήτυμον, truly, really, in truth and in deed, Hom.:—regul. Adv. -μως, Aesch., Soph.

ἛΤΙ, Adv.: **I.** of Time, **1.** of the Present, yet, as yet, still, Lat. adhuc, Il., Att.; cf. οὐκέτι. **2.** of the Past, mostly with impf., ἀήθεσσον γὰρ ἔτι they were yet unaccustomed, Il.; προορωμένοις ἔτι Thuc. **3.** of the Future, yet, further, ἄλγε' ἔδωκεν, ἠδ' ἔτι δώσει Il.:—also hereafter, Aesch., Soph. **II.** of

Degree, yet, still, besides, further, moreover, Lat. praeterea, insuper, Hom., etc.; ἔτι δέ and besides, nay more, Thuc. **2.** often to strengthen a Comp., ἔτι μᾶλλον yet more, Il.; μᾶλλον ἔτι Od.; ἔτι πλέον Hdt., etc. **3.** with the posit., ἔτι ἄνω yet higher up, Xen.

ἔτλην, ης, η, aor. 2 of *τλάω.

ἔτμαγεν, Aeol. for -γησαν, 3 pl. aor. 2 pass. of τέμνω.

ἐτνήρυσις, εως, ἡ, (ἀρύω) a soup-ladle, Ar.

ἐτνο-δόνος, ον, (δονέω) soup-stirring, τορύνη Anth.

ἛΤΝΟΣ, εος, τό, a thick soup of pulse, pea-soup, Ar., Plat.

ἑτοιμάζω, f. άσω, etc.:—Med., Ep. aor. 1 ἑτοιμασσάμην:—Pass., pf. ἡτοίμασμαι: (ἕτοιμος):—to make or get ready, prepare, provide, Il., Hdt., Att.; c. inf., κάπρον ἑτοιμασάτω ταμέειν Il. **II.** Med. to cause to be prepared, Ib. **2.** with pf. pass. ἡτοίμασμαι, to prepare for oneself, τἆλλα ἡτοιμάζετο made his other arrangements, Thuc.; ἡτοιμασμένοι Xen. **3.** to prepare oneself, c. inf., Id.

ἛΤΟΙ͂ΜΟΣ, ον, or η, ον, in Att. also ἕτοιμος:—at hand, ready, prepared, of food, Od., Hdt.; ἑτ. χρήματα ready money, money in hand, Id.; ἑτ. ποιεῖσθαι to make ready, Id.; ἐξ ἑτοίμου off-hand, forthwith, Xen.:—τὰ ἑτοῖμα what comes to hand, Thuc. **2.** of the future, sure to come, certain, Il.:—also easy to be done, feasible, Ib. **3.** of the past, carried into effect, made good, Hom. **II.** of persons or the will, ready, active, zealous, Lat. paratus, promptus, Att., Aesch.; εἴς or πρός τι Hdt., Xen.:—c. inf. ready to do, Hdt., Att.: τὸ ἑτοῖμον readiness, Eur. **III.** Adv. -μως, readily, Thuc., etc. Hence

ἑτοιμότης, ητος, ἡ, a state of preparation, readiness, Plut.

ἑτοιμο-τόμος, ον, (τέμνω) ready for cutting, Anth.

ἛΤΟΣ, εος, τό, a year, Hom., etc.; τῶν προτέρων ἐτέων in bygone years, Il.; ἑκάστου ἔτους every year, Plat.; ἀνὰ πᾶν ἔτος Anth.; ἀνὰ πέντε ἔτεα every five years, Hdt.; δι' ἔτους πέμπτου every fifth year, Ar.; κατὰ ἔτος every year, Thuc.; ἔτος εἰς ἔτος year after year, Soph.; in acc., ἔτος τόδ' ἤδη δέκατον now for these ten years, Id.

ἐτός, Adv., = ἐτωσίως, without reason, for nothing, only with negat. οὐκ ἐτός, Lat. non temere, Ar., Plat.; οὐκ ἐτὸς ἄρ' ἦλθεν it was not for nothing then that he came? Ar. (Deriv. uncertain.)

ἔτραγον, aor. 2 of τρώγω.

ἔτραπον, ἐτράπην, aor. 2 act. and pass. of τρέπω.

ἐτράφην [ᾰ], aor. 2 pass. of τρέφω:—act. ἔτραφον in same sense.

ἔτρωσα, aor. 1 of τιτρώσκω.

ἐτύθην [ῠ], aor. 1 pass. of θύω.

ἔτυμος, ον, like ἐτός, ἐτήτυμος, true, real, actual, ψεύσομαι ἦ ἔτυμον ἐρέω; shall I lie or speak truth? Hom.; οἳ ῥ' ἔτυμα κραίνουσι those [dreams] have true issues, Od.; ἐτ. ἄγγελος, φήμη Aesch., Eur. **2.** neut. ἔτυμον as Adv., like ἐτεόν, truly, really, Hom.; also pl. ἔτυμα Anth.; the regular Adv. -μως, Aesch., etc.

ἐτύπην [ῠ], ἐτύφθην, aor. 2 and 1 pass. of τύπτω.

ἐτύχησα, ἔτυχον, aor. 1 and 2 of τυγχάνω.

ἐτωσιο-εργός, όν, (*ἔργω) working fruitlessly, Hes.

ἐτώσιος, ον, (ἐτός Adv.), fruitless, useless, unprofitable, Lat. irritus, ἐτώσιον ἄχθος ἀρούρης Il., etc.

εὖ, Ep. ἐΰ, Adv. (neut. of ἐΰς), well, Lat. bene, opp. to κακῶς, Hom., etc.; with another Adv., εὖ καὶ ἐπιστα-

μένως *well* and workmanlike, Hom. ; so, εὖ κατὰ κόσμον *well* and in order, Il. :—also, *luckily, happily, well off,* Od. :—in Prose, εὖ ἔχειν to be *well off,* Att.; c. gen., εὖ ἥκειν τοῦ βίου to be *well off* for livelihood, Hdt. 2. εὖ γε, oft. in answers, v. εὖγε. 3. with Adjectives or Adverbs, to add to their force, εὖ πάντες, like μάλα πάντες, Od. ; εὖ μάλα Ib.; εὖ πάνυ Ar. ; εὖ σαφῶς Aesch. II. as Subst., τὸ εὖ the *right,* the *good cause,* τὸ δ᾽ εὖ νικάτω Id. III. as the Predicate of a propos., τί τῶνδ᾽ εὖ; which of these things is *well?* Id.; εὖ εἴη may it be *well,* Id. IV. in Compos., it has all the senses of the Adv., but commonly implies *greatness, abundance, prosperity, easiness,* opp. to δυσ-. (Like α- privat., Lat. *in-,* δυσ-, it is properly compounded with Nouns only, Verbs beginning with εὖ being derived from a compd. Noun, as, εὐπαθέω from εὐπαθής. εὐ-δοκέω is an exception.)

εὖ, Ion. for οὗ, Lat. *sui,* gen. of reflexive Pron. of 3d pers.

εὐαγγελίζομαι, (εὐάγγελος), Dep. *to bring good news, announce them,* Ar., Dem., etc. II. *to proclaim as glad tidings,* τὴν βασιλείαν τοῦ Θεοῦ N. T. 2. absol. *to preach the gospel,* Ib. :—c. acc. pers. *to preach the gospel to* persons, Ib. ;—so also in Act., Ib. :—Pass. *to have the gospel preached to* one, Ib. ; of the gospel, *to be preached,* Ib.

εὐαγγέλιον, τό, *the reward of good tidings,* given to the messenger, Od.; in pl., εὐαγγέλια θύειν to make a thankoffering for *good tidings,* Xen., etc. ; εὐαγγελίων θυσίαι Aeschin.; εὐαγγέλια στεφανοῦν τινα to crown one for *good news,* Ar. II. in Christian sense, *the Glad Tidings,* i. e. the Gospel (Saxon *gode-spell*), N.T.; and

εὐαγγελιστής, οῦ, ὁ, *the bringer of good tidings, an evangelist, preacher of the gospel,* N.T. From

εὐ-άγγελος, ον, *bringing good news,* Aesch.

εὐαγέω, *to be pure, holy,* Theocr. From

εὐ-αγής (A), ές, (ἄγος) *free from pollution, guiltless, pure, undefiled,* ὅσιος καὶ εὐαγής Lex Solonis ; of snow, Eur. 2. of actions, *holy, righteous,* Soph., Dem. ; —so Ep. Adv. εὐαγέως, h. Hom. 3. in act. sense, *purificatory,* Soph.

εὐ-αγής (B), ές, (ἄγω) *moving well, nimble,* Anth.

εὐ-αγής (C), ές, (αὐγή) *bright, far-seen, conspicuous,* ἕδραν εὐαγῆ στρατοῦ a seat *in full view* of the army, Aesch. ; πύργον εὐαγῆ a *lofty* town, Eur.

εὐ-άγητος, ον, = εὐαγής (C), *bright,* of clouds, Ar.

εὐ-άγκαλος, ον, (ἀγκάλη) *easy to bear in the arms,* Aesch.

εὐαγορέω, εὐαγορία, Dor. for εὐηγ-.

εὐαγρεσία, ἡ, = εὐαγρία, Theocr.

εὐαγρέω, f. ήσω, *to have good sport,* Anth.; and

εὐαγρία, ἡ, *good sport,* Anth. From

εὔ-αγρος, ον, (ἄγρα) *lucky in the chase, blessed with success,* Soph., Anth.

εὐαγωγία, ἡ, *good education,* Aeschin. From

εὐ-άγωγος, ον, (ἀγωγή) *easy to lead, easily led, ductile,* ἐπί τι, εἴς τι, πρός τι Plat., Xen.

εὔάδον, Aeol. for ἔαδον, aor. 2 of ἀνδάνω.

εὐάζω, (εὐοῖ) *to cry evoe to Bacchus,* Soph., Eur.

εὐ-αής, ές, (ἄημι) *well ventilated, fresh, airy,* Hes. II. act., of a wind, *favourably blowing, fair,* Hdt., Eur. : —metaph. *favourable,* Soph.

εὔ-αθλος, ον, *happily won,* Anth.

εὐ-αίρετος, ον, (αἱρέω) *easy to be taken,* Hdt.

εὐ-αίων, ωνος, ὁ, ἡ, *happy in life,* Eur. ; of life itself, *happy, fortunate, blessed,* Aesch., Soph.; ὕπνος εὐ. *blessed* sleep, Soph.

εὐᾱκής, ές, Dor. for εὐηκής.

εὐᾱκοέω, εὐάκοος, ον, Dor. for εὐηκ-.

εὐᾱλάκατος, ον, Dor. for εὐηλ-.

εὐ-αλδής, ές, (ἀλδαίνω) *well-grown, luxuriant,* Anth.

εὐάλιος, ον, Dor. for εὐήλιος.

εὐ-άλφῖτος, ον, (ἄλφιτον) *of good meal,* Anth.

εὐ-άλωτος, ον, *easy to be taken* or *caught,* Xen., etc.

εὐαμερία, εὐάμερος, Dor. for εὐημ-.

εὐ-άμπελος, ον, *with fine vines,* Anth.

εὐάν [ᾰ], *evan,* a cry of the Bacchanals, like εὐοῖ, Eur.

εὐ-ανάκλητος, ον, *easy to call out,* of the names of dogs, Xen. II. *easy to recall,* Plut. :—Adv., εὐανακλήτως ἔχειν πρός τινα Id.

εὐανδρέω, f. ήσω, *to abound in men,* Plut. II. *to be in full vigour,* Id. ; and

εὐανδρία, ἡ, *abundance of men, store of goodly men,* Xen. ; in pl., πληρωμάτων εὐανδρίαις by the crews *being able-bodied men,* Plut. II. *manhood, manliness, manly spirit,* Eur. From

εὔ-ανδρος, ον, (ἀνήρ) *abounding in good men,* Tyrtae., Eur., etc. II. *prosperous to men,* Aesch.

εὐάνεμος, Dor. for εὐήνεμος.

εὐ-άνθεμος, ον, (ἄνθεμον) *flowery, blooming,* Anth.

εὐανθέω, *to be flowery* or *blooming,* Luc. From

εὐ-ανθής, ές, (ἄνθος) *blooming, budding,* Od. II. *rich in flowers, flowery,* Theogn., Ar. 2. *flowered, gay-coloured, gay, bright,* Plat., Anth. III. metaph. *blooming, fresh, goodly,* Ar.

εὐᾱνορία, ἡ, Dor. for εὐηνορία.

εὐ-άντητος, ον, (ἀντάω) *accessible, gracious,* Anth.

εὐ-άντυξ, ῠγος, ὁ, ἡ, *finely vaulted,* Anth.

εὐάνωρ [ᾱ], ορος, ὁ, ἡ, Dor. for εὐήνωρ.

εὐ-απάλλακτος, ον, *easy to part with,* Xen.

εὐ-ἀπάτητος, ον, (ἀπατάω) *easy to cheat,* Plat.

εὐαπήγητος, ον, Ion. for εὐαφήγητος.

εὐ-απόβατος, ον, (ἀποβαίνω) *easy to disembark on, convenient for landing,* Thuc.

εὐ-απολόγητος, ον, (ἀπολογέομαι) *easy to excuse,* Plut.

εὐ-αποτείχιστος, ον, (ἀποτειχίζω) *easy to wall off, easy to blockade by circumvallation,* Thuc., Xen.

εὐ-άρεσκος, ον, = εὐάρεστος, Xen.

εὐ-άρεστος, ον, (ἀρέσκω) *well-pleasing, acceptable,* N.T. :—Adv., εὐαρεστοτέρως διακεῖσθαί τινι to be *more popular* with one, Xen.

εὐ-ἀρίθμητος, ον, *easy to count,* i. e. *few in number,* Plat.

εὔ-αρκτος, ον, (ἄρχω) *easy to govern, manageable,* of a horse's mouth, Aesch.

εὐ-άρμᾰτος, ον, (ἅρμα) *with beauteous car,* Soph.

εὐαρμοστία, ἡ, *easiness of temper,* Plat., Dem.

εὐ-άρμοστος, ον, (ἁρμόζω) *well-joined, harmonious,* Eur., Plat. II. of men, *accommodating,* Plat.

εὔ-αρνος, ον, *rich in sheep* or *lambs,* Anth.

εὐ-άροτος, ον, (ἀρόω) *well-ploughed* or *easy to be ploughed,* Anth.

εὔ-αρχος, ον, (ἄρχω) *beginning well, making a good beginning,* Anth.

εὖος, ὁ, the Roman *ovatio,* Plut.

εὔασμα, ατος, τό, (εὐάζω) *a Bacchanalian shout,* Eur.

εὐασμός, ὁ, (εὐάζω) *a shout of revelry,* Plut.

εὐαστήρ, ῆρος, ὁ, = sq., Anth.
εὐαστής, οῦ, or parox. εὐάστης, ου, ὁ, (εὐάζω) a Bacchanal, Anth.
εὐάτριος [ᾱ], ον, Dor. for εὐήτριος.
εὐ-αφήγητος, Ion. εὐαπ-, ον, easy to describe, Hdt.
εὐ-ᾰφής, ές, (ἀφή) touching gently: metaph., εὐ. μετάβασις an easy, unforced transition, Luc.:—τὸ εὐαφές delicate touch, Id.:—φῶς, Id.
εὐᾱχής, εὐάχητος, Dor. for εὐηχ-.
εὐ-βάστακτος, ον, easy to carry or move, Hdt.
εὔ-βᾰτος, ον, (βαίνω) accessible, passable, Aesch.; Comp. -ώτερος, Xen.
εὐ-βλέφᾰρος, ον, (βλέφαρον) with beautiful eyes, Anth.
Εὔβοια, gen. as Ion. ης, ἡ, Euboea, now Negropont (i. e. Egripo or Evripo, from Euripus), an island lying along the coast of Boeotia and Attica, Hom., etc.:—Εὐβοεύς, έως, ὁ, acc. Εὐβοᾶ, pl. -οᾶς, an Euboean, Hdt., etc.:—Adj., Εὐβοϊκός, Εὐβοεικός, ή, όν, Id., etc.; fem. Εὐβοΐς, Id.; lengthd. Εὐβοιΐς, Soph.
εὔ-βολος, ον, throwing luckily (with the dice): Adv., ἦν γὰρ εὐβόλως ἔχων he was in luck, Aesch.
εὔ-βοτος, ον, (βόσκω) with good pasture, Od. II. well-fed, thriving, Theocr.
εὔ-βοτρυς, υ, gen. υος, rich in grapes, Soph.
εὐβουλία, ἡ, good counsel, prudence, Aesch., Soph., etc.
εὔ-βουλος, ον, (βουλή) well-advised, prudent, Theogn., Hdt., Aesch.
εὔ-βους, ὁ, ἡ, rich in cattle, h. Hom.
εὔ-βροχος, ον, well-noosed, well-knit, Anth.
εὐγᾱθής, εὐγάθητος, Dor. for εὐγηθ-.
εὖγε or εὖ γε, Adv. well, rightly, to confirm or approve what has been said, Ar., Plat.:—ironically, Eur., Ar. 2. without a Verb, good! well said! well done! bravo! Lat. euge! Id.
εὐγένεια, ἡ, (εὐγενής) nobility of birth, high descent, Aesch., Eur.; εὐγένεια παίδων = εὐγενεῖς παῖδες, Id.
εὔ-γένειος, Ep. ἠΰγεν-, ον, (γένειον) of a lion, well-maned, Hom.; of men, well-bearded, Plat.
εὐγενέτης, ου, ὁ, = sq., Eur.: fem. εὐγενέτειρα, Anth.
εὐ-γενής, ές, (γένος) well-born, of noble race, of high descent, Lat. generosus, Trag.; εὐγενές [ἐστι] is a mark of nobility, Hdt. 2. noble-minded, generous, Soph., Plat. 3. of animals, high-bred, noble, generous, Theogn., Aesch., etc.; of a country, fertile, Plut. 4. of outward form, noble, Eur. II. Adv. -νῶς, nobly, bravely, Id.
εὐγενία, ἡ, = εὐγένεια, Eur., Anth.
εὐ-γηθής, ές, (γηθέω) joyous, cheerful, Eur.
εὐ-γήθητος, Dor. εὐ-γάθ-, ον, = foreg., Eur.
εὔ-γηρυς, υ, sweet-sounding, Ar.
εὐ-γλᾱγής, ές, (γάλα) abounding in milk:—a metapl. dat. εὐγλάγι, as if from εὔγλαξ, Anth.
εὔ-γλυπτος, ον, and εὐ-γλυφής, ές, (γλύπτω) well-carved, well-engraved, Anth.
εὐγλωσσία, Att. -ττία, ἡ, glibness of tongue, Ar.
εὔγλωσσος, Att. -ττος, ον, good of tongue, eloquent, Aesch.: glib of tongue, voluble, Ar. 2. sweet-sounding, Anth. II. act. loosing the tongue, making eloquent, Id.
εὔγμα, ατος, τό, (εὔχομαι) like εὖχος, a boast, vaunt, Od. II. like εὐχή, but always in pl. prayers, wishes, Aesch., Soph.

εὔγναμπτος, Ep. ἔϋγν-, ον, well-bent, Od.
εὐγνωμονέω, to be fair and honest, shew good feeling, Plut.; and
εὐγνωμοσύνη, ἡ, kindness of heart, considerateness, indulgence, Aeschin. 2. prudence, Plut. From
εὐ-γνώμων, ον, gen. ονος, (γνώμη) of good feeling, kind-hearted, considerate, reasonable, indulgent, Xen., etc. 2. wise, prudent, thoughtful, Anth. II. Adv. -μόνως, indulgently, fairly, candidly, Luc. 2. prudently, Xen.
εὔ-γνωστος, ον, well-known, familiar, Soph., Eur. 2. easy to discern, Dem.
εὔ-γομφος, ον, well-nailed, well-fastened, Eur.
εὐγονία, ἡ, fruitfulness, Xen. From
εὔ-γονος, ον, productive.
εὔ-γραμμος, ον, (γραμμή) well-drawn, Luc.; τῶν ὀφρύων τὸ εὔγραμμον their fine lines, Id.
εὐ-γρᾰφής, ές, (γράφω) well-painted, Anth. II. act. writing well, Id.
εὔ-γυρος, ον, well-circling, Anth.
εὐγωνία, ἡ, regularity of angles, Eur. From
εὐ-γώνιος, ον, (γωνία) with regular angles, Xen.
εὐ-δαίδᾰλος, ον, beautifully wrought, Anth.
εὐδαιμονέω, f. ήσω, (εὐδαίμων) to be prosperous, well off, happy, Hdt., Att.:—εὐδαιμονοίης, as a form of blessing, Eur. Hence
εὐδαιμονία, Ion. -ίη, ἡ, prosperity, good fortune, wealth, weal, happiness, h. Hom., Hdt., Att.
εὐδαιμονίζω, f. Att. ιῶ, (εὐδαίμων) to call or account happy, Eur., Xen., etc.; c. gen., μοίρας for his fortune, Soph.; ὑπέρ τινος Dem.; ἐπί τινι Dem.
εὐδαιμονικός, ή, όν, conducive to happiness, Plat.; τὰ εὐδ. the constituents thereof, Xen. From
εὐ-δαίμων, ον, blessed with a good genius; hence fortunate, happy, blest, Lat. felix, Hes., Theogn., Trag., etc.:—τὸ εὔδαιμον = εὐδαιμονία, Thuc.:—Adv. -μόνως, Eur., etc. 2. of outward prosperity, well off, wealthy, Hdt., Thuc., etc.
εὐ-δάκρῡτος, ον, (δακρύω) tearful, lamentable, Aesch.
εὐ-δάπᾰνος, ον, (δαπάνη) of much expense, liberal, Plut.
εὐ-δείελος, ον, (δείελος = δέελος, δῆλος) very clear, distinct, far-seen, epith. of Ithaca and other islands, Od.
εὔ-δειπνος, ον, (δεῖπνον) with goodly feasts, Eur.
εὔ-δενδρος, ον, (δένδρον) well-wooded, abounding in fair trees, Pind., Eur.
εὔ-δηλος, ον, quite clear, manifest, Aesch., etc.: εὔδηλός [ἐστι] ποιῶν may see him doing, Ar.
εὔδησθα, Ep. for εὔδης, 2 sing. subj. of εὔδω.
εὐδία, ἡ, (εὔδιος) fair weather, Xen. 2. metaph. tranquillity, calm, Aesch., Xen.
εὐ-διάβᾰτος, ον, easy to cross, ποταμός Xen.
εὐ-διάβολος, ον, easy to misrepresent, Plat.
εὐδιαίτερος, α, ον, irreg. Comp. of εὔδιος.
εὐ-δίαιτος, ον, (δίαιτα) living temperately, Xen.
εὐδιάλλακτος, ον, easy to reconcile, placable: Adv. -τως, Plut.
εὐδι-άναξ, ακτος, ὁ, ruler of the calm, Luc.
εὐδιεινός, ή, όν, = εὔδιος, Plat.; ἐν εὐδιεινοῖς in sheltered spots, Xen.
εὐ-δικία, Ion. -ίη, ἡ, (δίκη) righteous dealing, Od.
εὐ-δίνητος [ῐ], ον, easily-turning, Anth.
εὔ-διος, ον, (δῖος) calm, fine, clear, of weather, sea,

etc., Xen., Theocr. :—neut. εὔδιον, εὔδια, as Adv.,
Anth. :—irreg. Comp. εὐδιαίτερος, Xen.

εὔ-δμητος, Ep. ἐΰ-δμητος, ον, (δέμω) well-built, Hom.

εὐ-δοκέω, impf. εὐδόκουν or ηὐδόκουν : f. ήσω :—to be
well pleased, ἔν τινι with a person or thing, N. T.　2.
c. inf. to consent to do, be glad to do, Ib.　Hence

εὐδοκία, ἡ, satisfaction, approval, N. T.

εὐδοκιμέω : impf. ηὐδοκίμουν : aor. 1 ηὐδοκίμησα : pf.
ηὐδοκίμηκα : the augm. is omitted in Ion. : (εὐδόκι-
μος) :—to be of good repute, to be held in esteem,
honoured, famous, popular, Theogn., Eur., Ar., etc. :
—εὐδ. ἔν τινι to be distinguished in a thing, Hdt.,
Thuc. ; ἐπί τινι Plat. :—εὐδ. παρὰ τῷ βασιλεῖ to have
influence with him, Hdt.　Hence

εὐδοκίμησις, εως, ἡ, good repute, credit, Plat.

εὐ-δόκιμος, ον, in good repute, honoured, famous,
glorious, Aesch., Eur. ; πρός τι in a thing, Plat.

εὐδοξέω, f. ήσω, to be in good repute, to be honoured,
famous, Eur., Xen. ; and

εὐδοξία, ἡ, good repute, credit, honour, glory, Simon.,
Dem.　2. approval, τοῦ πλήθους Plat.　II.
good judgment, Id.　From

εὔ-δοξος, ον, (δόξα) of good repute, honoured, famous,
glorious, Theogn., Thuc., etc. ; νέες εὐδοξόταται ships
of best repute, Hdt.

εὐ-δρᾰκής, ές, (δέρκομαι) sharp-sighted, Soph.

εὔ-δρομος, ον, (δραμεῖν) running well, swift of foot,
Anth.　2. εὔδρ. πόλις a city with fair race-courses, Id.

εὔ-δροσος, ον, with plenteous dew, abounding in water,
Eur., Ar.

ΕΥ´ΔΩ : impf. ηὗδον, Ep. εὗδον, Ion. 3 sing. εὔδεσκε :—
f. εὐδήσω Aesch. :—to sleep, lie down to sleep, Hom.,
etc. ; c. acc. cogn., εὕδειν ὕπνον Od., Eur., Theocr. ;
also, ὕπνῳ εὕδειν Soph. ; βραδὺς εὕδει, i. e. sleep detains
him, Id.　2. of the sleep of death, Il., Soph.　II.
metaph. to be still, be hushed, of wind, sea, etc., Il.,
Aesch. ; of the mind, to be at ease, content, Plat., Theocr.

εὔ-έανος, ον, richly-robed, Mosch.

εὔ-εδρος, ον, (ἕδρα) with beautiful seat, on stately
throne, of gods, Aesch.　2. of a ship, = εὔσσελμος,
Theocr.　II. pass. easy to sit, ἵππος Xen.

εὐ-ειδής, ές, (εἶδος) well-shaped, goodly, beautiful,
beauteous, Il., Hdt., Att.

εὔ-ειλος, ον, (εἵλη) sunny, warm, Lat. apricus, Eur.

εὔ-είμων, ον, (εἷμα) well-robed, Aesch.

εὔ-ειρος, ον, (εἶρος, ἔριον) with or of good wool, fleecy,
Anth. :—Att. εὔερος, Soph.

εὐ-έλεγκτος, ον, easy to refute : easy to test, Plat.

εὔ-ελπις, ὁ, ἡ, neut. εὔελπι, of good hope, hopeful,
cheerful, sanguine, Thuc., Xen., etc. :—c. inf. fut.,
εὔελπις ἰσχύσειν Aesch. ; εὔελπις σωθήσεσθαι in good
hope to be saved, Thuc.

εὐ-εξάλειπτος, ον, (ἐξαλείφω) easy to wipe out, Xen.

εὐ-εξαπάτητος, ον, (ἐξαπατάω) easily deceived, Plat.,
Xen.

εὐ-εξία, ἡ, (ἕξις) a good habit of body, good state of
health, high health, Plat. :—generally, vigour, Id.

εὐ-έξοδος, ον, easy to get out of or escape from,
Aesch.

εὐέπεια, ἡ, beauty of language, eloquence, Plat.　II.
kind words, Soph.　From

εὐ-επής, ές, (ἔπος) well-speaking, eloquent, melodious,

Xen.　2. making eloquent, of Helicon, Anth.　II.
pass. well-spoken, acceptable, λόγος Hdt.

εὐ-επίβᾰτος, ον, easy of attack, Luc.

εὐ-επιβούλευτος, ον, (ἐπιβουλεύω) exposed to treachery
or stratagem, Xen.

εὐεπίη, ἡ, Ion. for εὐέπεια, Anth.

εὐ-επίθετος, ον, easy to set upon or attack, Thuc. ;
εὐεπίθετον τοῖς πολεμίοις easy for them to make an
attack, Xen.

εὐ-επίτακτος, ον, easily put in order, docile, Anth.

εὐέργεια, Ion. -είη, ἡ, = εὐεργεσία I, Anth.

εὐεργεσία, Ion. -ίη, ἡ, well-doing, Od., Theogn.,
etc.　II. good service, a good deed, kindness,
bounty, benefit, Od., Hdt. ; εὐ. καταθέσθαι ἔς τινα
Thuc. ; εὐ. ὀφείλεταί μοι Id., etc.

εὐεργετέω : impf. εὐεργέτουν : f. -ήσω : aor. 1 εὐεργέ-
τησα : pf. εὐεργέτηκα :—Pass., aor. 1 part. εὐεργετηθείς : pf. εὐεργέτημαι : (εὐεργέτης) :—to do well, do
good, Soph.　II. c. acc. pers. to do good services
or shew kindness to one, Aesch., Eur. ; εὐεργεσίαν
εὐεργ. τινά to do one a kindness, Plat. :—Pass. to have
a kindness done one, εὐεργεσίαν εὐεργετηθείς Id.

εὐεργέτημα, ατος, τό, a service done, kindness, Xen.

εὐεργέτης, ου, ὁ, (*ἔργω) a well-doer, benefactor,
Soph. ; τινί to one, Hdt., Eur. ; more commonly, τινός
Id., etc.　2. a title of honour of such persons as
had 'done the state some service,' εὐ. βασιλέος ἀνε-
γράφη was registered as the King's benefactor, Id. ;
so Xen., etc.

εὐεργετητέον, verb. Adj. of εὐεργετέω, one must shew
kindness to, τοὺς φίλους Xen.

εὐεργέτις, ιδος, fem. of εὐεργέτης, Eur.

εὐ-εργής, ές, (*ἔργω) well-wrought, well-made, of
chariots, ships, etc., Hom. ; of gold, wrought, Od.　2.
well-done : pl. εὐεργέα = εὐεργεσίαι, benefits, services,
Ib.

εὐ-εργός, όν, (*ἔργω) doing good or well, upright,
Od.　II. pass. well-wrought, well-tilled, Theocr.　2. easy to work, Hdt.

εὐ-ερκής, ές, (ἕρκος) well-fenced, well-walled, Hom.,
Aesch.　II. act. fencing well, well-closed, of
doors, Od.

εὐ-ερκτής, ου, ὁ, poët. for εὐεργέτης, Anth.

εὐ-ερνής, ές, (ἔρνος) sprouting well, flourishing, Eur.

εὔερος, ον, Att. for εὔειρος.

εὐ-εστώ, οῦς, ἡ, (ἐστώ being, from εἰμί sum) well-being,
tranquillity, prosperity, Hdt., Aesch.

εὐ-ετηρία, ἡ, (ἔτος) goodness of season, a good season
(for the fruits of the earth), Xen., etc.

εὐ-ετία, ἡ, = foreg., Anth.

εὐ-εύρετος, ον, (εὑρίσκω) easy to find, χώρα εὐεύρετος a
place in which it will be easy to find things, Xen.

εὐ-έφοδος, ον, easy to come at, assailable, accessible,
of places, Xen.

εὔ-ζηλος, ον, emulous in good : Adv. -λως, Anth.

εὔ-ζῠγος, Ep. ἐΰζ-, ον, (ζυγόν III) of ships, well-
benched, Od.

εὔ-ζωνος, Ep. ἐΰζ-, ον, (ζώνη) well-girdled, of women,
Il.　2. of men, girt up for exercise, dressed for walking, active, Horace's alte praecinctus, Hdt., Thuc. ; of
light troops, unincumbered, Lat. expeditus, Xen.　3.
metaph. unincumbered, πενία Plut.

εὔ-ζωρος, ον, quite pure, unmixed, of wine, Eur.; Comp. -ότερος and -έστερος.

εὐ-ηγενής, ές, Ep. for εὐγενής, Il., Theocr.

εὐ-ηγεσία, ἡ, (ἡγέομαι) good government, Od.

εὐήθεια and εὐηθία, Ion. -ίη, ἡ, goodness of heart, good nature, guilelessness, simplicity, honesty, Hdt., Att. 2. in bad sense, simplicity, silliness, Hdt., Att.

εὐ-ήθης, ες, (ἦθος) good-hearted, open-hearted, simple-minded, guileless, Plat.; τὸ εὐηθες = εὐήθεια, Thuc. 2. in bad sense, simple, silly, Hdt., Att.: —as Subst. a simpleton, Xen. II. Adv. -θως, Plat. :—Comp. -έστερα, Id.; Sup. -έστατα, Eur.

εὐηθία, Ion. -ίη, = εὐήθεια.

εὐηθίζομαι, Pass. (εὐήθης) to play the fool, Plat.

εὐηθικός, ή, όν, (εὐήθης) good-natured, Plat.:—Adv. -κῶς, Ar.

εὐ-ήκης, ες, (ἀκή) well-pointed, Il.

εὐ-ήκοος, ον, (ἀκοή) inclined to give ear, of gods, Anth.

εὐ-ηλάκατος, Dor. εὐάλακ-, ον, spinning well, Theocr.

εὐ-ήλατος, ον, (ἐλαύνω) easy to drive or ride over, πεδίον εὐ. a plain fit for cavalry, Xen.

εὐ-ήλιος, Dor. εὐ-άλ- [ᾱ], ον, well-sunned, sunny, genial, Lat. apricus, Eur., Ar.; εὐήλιον πῦρ the sun's heat, Eur. —Adv. -ίως, with bright sunshine, Xen.

εὐημερέω, f. ήσω, (εὐήμερος) to spend the day cheerfully, live happily from day to day, Soph.; ταῖσι Θήβαις εὐημερεῖ τὰ πρὸς σέ 'tis fair weather for Thebes in relation to thee, Id. 2. to be successful in a thing, gain one's point, Aeschin.

εὐημερία, Dor. εὐαμ- [ᾱ], ἡ, fineness of the day, good weather, εὐημερίας οὔσης Xen. II. good times, health and happiness, health and wealth, Eur. From

εὐ-ήμερος, Dor. εὐ-άμ- [ᾱ], ον, (ἡμέρα) of a fine day, εὐ. φάος a happy day, Soph. 2. enjoying a lucky day, cheerful, happy, Ar., Plat.

εὐ-ήνεμος, Dor. εὐ-άνεμος, ον, well as to the winds, i.e., I. sheltered from the wind, calm, Eur. II. open to the wind, Soph.

εὐ-ήνιος, ον, (ἡνία) obedient to the rein, tractable, Plat.

εὐηνορία, ἡ, manliness, manly virtue, Eur. From

εὐ-ήνωρ, Dor. -άνωρ [ᾱ], ορος, ὁ, ἡ, man-exalting, glorious, Od.

εὐ-ήρετμος, ον, (ἐρετμός) well fitted to the oar, Aesch. 2. well-rowed, Soph., Eur.

εὐ-ήρης, ες, (*ἄρω) well-fitted, of the oar, well-poised, easy to handle, Od., Eur.

εὐ-ήρυτος, ον, (ἀρύω) easy to draw out, h. Hom.

εὐ-ήτριος, Dor. εὐ-άτρ-[ᾱ], ον, (ἤτριον) with good thread, well-woven, Plat. II. act. well-weaving, Anth.

εὐ-ήχητος, Dor. εὐ-άχ- [ᾱ], ον, (ἠχέω) well-sounding, tuneful, Eur.: loud-sounding, Id.

εὐ-θάλασσος, ον, (θάλασσα) prosperous by sea, δῶρον εὐθ. the gift of seamanship, Soph.

εὐ-θαλής, ές, (θάλλω) blooming, flourishing, Mosch.

εὐθαλής, ές, Dor. for εὐθηλής.

εὐ-θαρσής, ές, (θάρσος) of good courage, h. Hom.,Aesch., etc. 2. giving courage, secure, Xen.

εὐθεῖα, ἡ, v. εὐθύς.

εὐ-θεράπευτος, ον, (θεραπεύω) easily won by kindness or attention, Xen.

εὐθετέω, f. ήσω, = sq., Luc.

εὐθετίζω, f. σω, to set in order, arrange well, Hes., Luc.

εὔ-θετος, ον, well-arranged or easily stowed, Aesch.; εὔθ. σάκος well-fitting, ready for use, Lat. habilis, Id.

εὐθέως, Adv. of εὐθύς, q. v.

εὐ-θηγής, ές, (θήγω) sharpening well, Anth.

εὐ-θηλήμων, ον, rare form for sq., Anth.

εὐ-θηλής, Dor. -θᾱλής, ές, (θηλή) well-nurtured, thriving, goodly, Eur., Ar.

εὔ-θηλος, ον, (θηλή) with distended udder, Eur.

εὐθημοσύνη, ἡ, good management, Hes. 2. a habit of good order, tidiness, Xen. From

εὐ-θήμων, ον, gen. ονος, (τίθημι) setting in order, c. gen., δωμάτων εὔθ. Aesch.

εὐθηνέω, Att. εὐθενέω, only in pres., to thrive, flourish, prosper, Lat. florere, vigere, Hdt., Aesch., Dem. :—c. dat. to abound in a thing, h. Hom. II. Pass. in same sense, οἱ Λακεδαιμόνιοι εὐθηνήθησαν Hdt.; τὴν πόλιν εὐθενεῖσθαι Dem. (Deriv. uncertain.)

εὐ-θήρᾱτος, ον, easy to catch or win, Anth.

εὔ-θηρος, ον, (θήρα) lucky or successful in the chase, Eur.; εὔθ. ἄγρη successful sport, Anth.; εὔθ. κάλαμοι unerring arrows, Id. II. (θήρ) abounding in game, good for hunting, Id.

εὐ-θήσαυρος, ον, well-stored, precious, Anth.

εὐ-θικτος, ον, (θιγεῖν) touching the point, clever, Anth.

εὐ-θνήσιμος, ον, (θανεῖν) in or with easy death, Aesch.

εὔ-θοινος, ον, with rich banquet: sumptuous, Aesch.

εὔ-θριγκος, ον, well-coped, of high walls, Eur.

εὔ-θριξ, Ep. ἐΰ-θρ-, -τρίχος, ὁ, ἡ, with beautiful hair : in Il. always of horses, with flowing mane ; of dogs, Xen.; of birds, well-plumed, Theocr. II. made of good hair, of a fishing line, Aesch.

εὔ-θρονος, Ep. ἐΰ-θρ-, ον, with beautiful throne, Hom.

εὔ-θροος, Ep. ἐΰ-θρ-, ον, loud-sounding, Anth.

εὔ-θρυπτος, ον, (θρύπτω) easily broken, crumbling, Plut.

εὐθύ, neut. of εὐθύς, used as Adv.: v. εὐθύς B.

εὐθυβολία, ἡ, a direct throw, Plut. From

εὐθυ-βόλος, ον, (βάλλω) throwing straight.

εὐθυ-δίκαιος, ον, = εὐθύδικος, Aesch.

εὐθυδικία, ἡ, an open, direct trial, on the merits of the case, Dem.

εὐθύ-δικος, ον, (δίκη) righteous-judging, Aesch., Anth.

εὐθυ-εργής, ές, (*ἔργω) accurately wrought, Luc.

εὐθυ-θάνατος, ον, quick-killing, mortal, Plut.

εὐθυ-μάχης, ον, ὁ, fighting openly, Pind.

εὐθυμάχια, ἡ, a fair fight, Plut. From

εὐθυ-μάχος [ᾰ], ον, = εὐθυμάχης, Anth.

εὐθυμέω, f. ήσω, (εὔθυμος) to be of good cheer, Eur., Anth. :—to be gracious, Theocr. II. trans. to make cheerful, cheer, delight, τινά Aesch. :—Pass. to be cheerful, Xen.

εὐθυμητέον, verb. Adj. one must be cheerful, Xen.

εὐθυμία, ἡ, cheerfulness, tranquillity, Xen. From

εὔ-θυμος, ον, bountiful, generous, Od. II. of good cheer, cheerful, in good spirits, Xen. :—of horses, spirited, Id.;—Adv. -μως, cheerfully, Aesch., Xen.

εὔθῡνα, ἡ,—εΐται-ης, acc. -αν· (εὐθύνω) :—a setting straight, correction, chastisement, Plat. II. at Athens, an examination of accounts, audit, Ar., etc.; in pl. Id., etc.; εὔθυναι τῆς πρεσβείας an account of one's embassy, Dem.; εὐθύνας ἀπαιτεῖν to call for one's accounts, Id.; εὐθύνας διδόναι to give them in, Ar.; εὐθύνας ὀφλεῖν Lys., etc.

εὔθυνος, ὁ, (εὐθύνω) a corrector, chastiser, judge, Aesch.   II. at Athens, an examiner, auditor, Plat.

εὐθυντήρ, ῆρος, ὁ, (εὐθύνω) a corrector, chastiser, Theogn.

εὐθυντήριος, α, ον, (εὐθύνω) directing, ruling, Aesch.   II. εὐθυντηρία, ἡ, the part of a ship wherein the rudder was fixed, Eur.

εὐθυντής, οῦ, ὁ, (εὐθύνω) a ruler, Eur.

εὐθύνω [ῡ], impf. ηὔθυνον: f. ῠνῶ: (εὐθύς):—like Homeric ἰθύνω, to guide straight, direct, Aesch., Ar.; εὐθ. δόρυ to steer the bark straight, Eur.; εὐθ. πλάταν Id.; εὐθ. χερσί to manage or guide him, Soph.   2. metaph. to direct, govern, Trag.   II. to make or put straight, Plat.; εὐθ. δίκας σκολιάς to make crooked judgments straight, Solon.   III. at Athens, to audit the accounts (cf. εὔθυνα) of a magistrate, call him to account, Plat.   2. c. gen. to call to account for an offence, εὐθ. τινὰ κλοπῆς Plut.:—Pass., τῶν ἀδικημάτων εὐθύνθη Thuc.

εὐθυπορέω, to go straight forward, πότμος εὐθυπορῶν (metaph. from a ship), unswerving destiny, Aesch. From

εὐθύ-πορος, ον, going straight: metaph. straight-forward, Plat.

εὐθυρρημονέω, to speak in a straightforward manner, Cic.: to speak off-hand, From

εὐθυρ-ρήμων, ον, (ῥῆμα) plain-spoken, Cic.

εὔ-θυρσος, ον, with beautiful shaft, Eur.

ΕΥ'ΘΥ'Σ, εῖα, ύ, Ion. and Ep. ἰθύς (q.v.), straight, direct, Thuc., etc.:—εὐθεῖα (sc. ὁδῷ) by the straight road, Plat.; so, τὴν εὐθεῖαν Eur.   2. in moral sense, straightforward, open, frank, Tyrtae., Aesch., etc.; ἀπὸ τοῦ εὐθέος, ἐκ τοῦ εὐθέος openly, without reserve, Thuc.

  B. as Adv., εὐθύς and εὐθύ, the former properly of Time, the latter of Place: I. εὐθύ, of Place, straight, εὐθὺ Πύλονδε straight to P., h. Hom.; εὐθὺ πρὸς τὰ λέχη Soph.; εὐθὺ ἐπὶ Βαβυλῶνος straight towards B., Xen.; so c. gen., εὐθὺ Πελλήνης Ar., etc.   II. εὐθύς, 1. of Time, straightway, forthwith, at once, Aesch., etc.; εὐθὺς ἐκ παιδίου Xen.; with a part., εὐθὺς νέοι ὄντες Thuc.; τοῦ θέρους εὐθὺς ἀρχομένου just at the beginning of summer, Id.   2. rarely, like εὐθύ, of Place, ὑπὲρ τῆς πόλεως εὐθύς just above the city, Id.; τὴν εὐθὺς Ἄργους ὁδόν the road leading straight to Argos, Eur.   3. of Manner, directly, simply, Plat.

  C. εὐθέως, Adv., is used just as the Adv. εὐθύς, Soph., etc.; ἐπεὶ εὐθέως as soon as, Xen.

εὐ-θύσανος [ῠ], ον, well-fringed, Anth.

εὐθύ-φρων, ον, (φρήν) right-minded, Aesch.

εὐθύ-ωρος, ον, in a straight direction: in neut. εὐθύωρον as Adv. = εὐθύς, Xen. (Deriv. uncertain.)

εὐ-θώρηξ, ὁ, ἡ, well-mailed, Anth.

εὐιάζω, = εὐάζω, Eur.

εὐιακός, ή, όν, Bacchic, Anth.: fem. εὐιάς, άδος, Id.

εὐ-ίᾱτος, ον, (ἰάομαι) easy to heal, Soph.

εὐ-ίερος, ον, very holy, Lat. sacrosanctus, Anth.

Εὔιος, ὁ, Euios, Evius, name of Bacchus, from the cry, εὐοῖ, Soph., Eur.: Εὔιος = Βάκχος, Id.   II. εὔιος, ον, as Adj. Bacchic, Soph., Eur.

εὔ-ιππος, ον, of persons, well-horsed, delighting in horses, h. Hom.: Sup., Xen.   2. of places, famed for horses, Soph.

εὔ-ιστος, ὁ, (ἴσημι) for good knowledge, Anth.

εὐ-καθαίρετος, ον, easy to conquer, Thuc.

εὐ-κάθεκτος, ον, (κατέχω) easy to keep under, Xen.

εὐκαιρέω, f. ήσω, to devote one's leisure, εἴς τι N.T.

εὐκαιρία, Ion. -ίη, ἡ, good season, opportunity, Plat.

εὔ-καιρος, ον, well-timed, in season, seasonable, Soph.: neut. εὔκαιρον in season, Anth.:—Adv. -ρως, seasonably, opportunely, -ότερον, Plat.

εὐκᾱλος, εὐκᾱλία, Dor. for εὔκηλ-.

εὐ-κάματος, ον, of easy labour, easy, Eur.; εὐκ. ἔργα well-wrought works, Anth.; εὐκ. στέφανος a crown won by noble toils, Id.

εὐ-καμπής, ές, (κάμπτω) well-curved, curved, Od., Mosch., etc.   II. easy to bend, flexible, Plut.

εὐ-κάρδιος, ον, (καρδία) good of heart, stout-hearted, Lat. egregie cordatus, Soph., etc.; of a horse, spirited, Xen.:—Adv. -ίως, with stout heart, Eur.

εὔ-καρπος, ον, rich in fruit, fruitful, h. Hom., Soph.; of Demeter, Anth.

εὐ-κατάλυτος, ον, (καταλύω) easy to overthrow, Xen.

εὐ-καταφρόνητος, ον, (καταφρονέω) easy to be despised, contemptible, despicable, Xen., Dem.

εὐ-κατέργαστος, ον, (κατεργάζομαι) easy to work: of food, easy of digestion, Xen.   2. easy of accomplishment, Id.   3. easy to subdue, Plut.

εὐ-κατηγόρητος, ον, (κατηγορέω) easy to blame, open to accusation, Thuc.

εὐ-κέᾱτος, ον, (κεάζω) easy to cleave or split, Od.

εὐ-κέλᾰδος, ον, well-sounding, melodious, Eur., Ar.

εὔ-κεντρος, ον, (κέντρον) pointed, Anth.

εὐ-κέραος, ον, (κέρας) with beautiful horns, Mosch.: —contr. εὔκερως, ων, Soph.

εὐ-κηλήτειρα, ἡ, (κηλέω) she that lulls or soothes, Hes.

εὔκηλος, Dor. εὔκᾱλος, ον, (lengthd. from ἕκηλος) free from care, at one's ease, Lat. securus, Hom., Soph.; εὔκηλοι πολέμιζον were fighting undisturbed, Il.   2. of night, still, silent, Theocr.

εὐ-κίνητος, ον, (κινέω) easily moved, εἴς τι Anth.

εὔ-κισσος, ον, ivied, Anth.

εὐ-κίων [ῑ], ον, with beautiful pillars, Eur., Anth.

εὐκλεής, Ep. ἐϋ-κλ-, ές: poët. acc. sing. εὐκλέα, for εὐκλεέα or -εᾶ, pl. εὐκλέας, for εὐκλεέας or -εεῖς, Ep. also ἐϋκλεῖας: (κλέος):—of good report, famous, glorious, Hom., etc.; εὐκλεέστατος βίος Eur. Adv. -εῶς, Ep. -ειῶς, Il.; κατθανεῖν Aesch.; Sup. εὐκλεέστατα, Xen.

εὔκλειᾰ, ἡ, Ep. ἐϋκλείη, good repute, glory, Hom., Trag.

εὐκλεΐζω, Ion. -ηΐζω, contr. -ῄζω, f. σω, to praise, laud, Tyrtae.

εὐκλειής, Adv. ἐϋκλειῶς, Ep. for εὐκλεής, εὐκλεῶς.

εὔ-κλεινος, ον, much-famed, Anth.

εὐκληρέω, f. ήσω, to have a good lot, Anth. From

εὔ-κληρος, ον, fortunate, happy, Anth.

εὔ-κλωστος, ον, well-spun, h. Hom., Anth.

ἐϋ-κνήμις, ῖδος, ἡ, well-equipped with greaves, well-greaved, Ep. nom. and acc. pl. ἐϋκνήμῑδες, -ῖδας, Hom.

εὔ-κνημος, ον, (κνήμη) with beautiful legs, Anth.

εὐ-κοινώνητος, ον, (κοινωνέω) easy to deal with, Arist.

εὐκολία, ἡ, (εὔκολος) contentedness, good temper, Plat., etc.   2. of the body, agility, facility, Plut.

εὔ-κολλος, ον, (κόλλα) gluing well, sticky, Anth.

εὔ-κολος, ον, (κόλον):   I. of persons, easily satisfied, contented with one's food, Anth., Plut.   2.

easily satisfied, contented, good-natured, peaceable, Lat. *facilis, comis*, Ar.; c. dat., **εὔκολος πολίταις** *friendly* to them, *at peace with* them, Id.:—Adv. -λως, *tranquilly, calmly*, Xen. **3.** *willing, agile*, Anth. **4.** in bad sense, *easily led, prone*, πρὸς ἀδικίαν Luc. **II.** of things, *easy*, Plat.

εὔ-κολπος, ον, *with fair bosom*, Anth. **2.** *in goodly folds*, of a net, Id.

εὔ-κομῐδής, ές, (κομῐδή) *well cared for*, Hdt.

εὔ-κομος, Ep. ἠΰ-κ-, ον, (κόμη) *fair-haired*, Hom., Hes.: of sheep, *well-fleeced*, Anth.

εὔ-κομπος, ον, *loud-sounding*, Eur.

εὔ-κοπος, ον, *with easy labour, easy*, εὐκοπώτερόν [ἐστι], c. inf., N. T.

εὔ-κόσμητος, ον, (κοσμέω) *well-adorned*, h. Hom.

εὐκοσμία, ἡ, *orderly behaviour, good conduct, decency*, Eur., Xen., etc. From

εὔ-κοσμος, ον, *behaving well, orderly, decorous*, Solon, Att., Thuc.; τὸ εὔκοσμον = εὐκοσμία, Thuc. **2.** *well-adorned, graceful*, Eur. **II.** Adv. -μως, *in good order*, Od.; Sup. -ότατα, Xen. **2.** *gracefully*, Plut.

εὔ-κραιρος, Ep. ἐΰκρ-, η, ον, (κραῖρα) *with fine horns*, esp. of oxen, h. Hom.

εὐ-κράς, ᾶτος, ὁ, ἡ, = εὔκρατος, Plat. **2.** of persons, *mixing readily with others*, Anth. Hence

εὐκρᾱσία, ἡ, *a good temperature, mildness*, Plat.

εὔ-κρᾱτος, Ion. εὔ-κρητος, ον, (κεράννυμι) *well-mixed, temperate*, Plat.

εὔ-κρεκτος, ον, (κρέκω) *well-struck, well-woven*, of the threads of the warp, Anth.

εὔ-κρηνος, ον, (κρήνη) *well-watered*, Anth.

εὔκρητος, ον, Ion. for εὔκρατος.

εὔ-κρῑθος, ον, (κριθή) *rich in barley*, Theocr., Anth.

εὐκρῑνέω, f. ήσω, *to keep distinct, keep in order*, Xen.

εὐ-κρῑνής, ές, (κρίνω) *well-separated*, Xen. **II.** *well-arranged, in good order*, Hdt., Xen.:—*regular, steady*, of winds, Hes.

εὐ-κρότᾰλος, Ep. ἐΰ-κρ-, ον, *accompanied by castanets*, Anth.: *rattling*, πλατάγη Id.

εὐ-κρότητος, ον, *well-hammered, well-wrought*, of metal, Soph., Eur.

εὔ-κρυπτος, ον, *easy to hide*, Aesch.

εὐκταῖος, α, ον, (εὔχομαι) *of or for prayer, votive*, Aesch., Ar.: *devoted*, Eur.:—εὐκταῖα, τά, *votive offerings, vows, prayers*, Aesch., Soph. **2.** of gods, *invoked by prayer*, Aesch., Eur. **3.** *prayed for*, Anth.

εὐ-κτέανος, ον, (κτέανον) *wealthy*, Aesch., Anth.

εὐ-κτέᾱνος, ον, (κτείς) *with straight fibres, slender, tall*, Plut.

ἐΰ-κτήμων, ον, (κτῆμα) *wealthy*, Pind.

εὔ-κτητος, ον, *easily gotten*, Anth.

εὐκτικός, ή, όν, (εὐκτός) *expressing a wish, votive*, Anth.

ἐΰ-κτῐμενος, η, ον, (κτίζω) *well-built*, Il.; νῆσος ἐΰκτιμένη *furnished with goodly buildings*, Od.; ἐΰκτ. ἐν ἀλῳῆ on *well-made* threshing-floor, Il.; of a garden, *well-wrought*, Od.

ἐΰ-κτῐτος, ον, = ἐΰκτίμενος, Il., h. Hom.

εὐκτός, ή, όν, (εὔχομαι) *wished for*, ὄφρ᾿ εὐκτὰ γένηται *that what they wish for* may happen, Il. **2.** *to be wished for*, εὐκτὸν ἀνθρώποις Eur.:—εὐκτόν ἐστι, c. inf., Id., Xen. **II.** *vowed, dedicated*, Anth.

εὔ-κυκλος, ον, *well-rounded, round*, of a shield, Il., Aesch.; of a chariot, *well-wheeled*, Id., Od.

εὐ-κύλῐκος, η, ον, (κύλιξ) *suited to the wine-cup*, Anth.

εὐλάβεια, Ion. -ίη, ἡ, (εὐλαβής) *discretion, caution, circumspection*, Theogn., Soph., etc.; εὐλάβειαν ἔχειν μή . . = εὐλαβεῖσθαι μή . ., Plat.; εὐλαβείας δεῖται *it requires caution*, Dem.; ἐπ᾿ εὐλαβείᾳ *by way of caution*, Plat. **2.** c. gen. *caution or discretion in a thing*, Soph. **3.** *reverence, piety*, περὶ τὸ θεῖον Plut.: absol. *godly fear*, N. T. **4.** in bad sense, *over-caution, timidity*, Plut.

εὐλᾰβέομαι: impf. ηὐλαβούμην: f. -ήσομαι: aor. 1 ηὐλαβήθην or εὐλ-:—*to behave like the* εὐλαβής, *have a care, to be discreet, cautious, circumspect, to beware*, Lat. *cavere*, foll. by μή or ὅπως μή with subj., Soph., Eur., etc.; c. inf., with or without μή, Soph., Eur.:—absol., εὐλαβήθητι Soph.; μηδὲν εὐλαβηθέντα *without reserve*, Dem. **II.** c. acc. *to have a care of, beware of*, Aesch., Plat., etc. **2.** *to reverence, pay honour to*, Id. **3.** *to watch for, await quietly*, Eur.

εὐ-λᾰβής, ές, (λαβεῖν) *taking hold well, holding fast*:—then metaph. *undertaking prudently, discreet, cautious, circumspect*, Plat. **2.** in bad sense, *over-cautious, timid*, Plut.:—Adv. εὐλαβῶς, Comp. -εστέρως, Eur. **3.** *reverent, pious, religious, devout*, N. T. **II.** pass. *easy to get hold of*, Luc.

εὐλαβητέον, verb. Adj. of εὐλαβέομαι, *one must beware*, c. inf., Plat. **II.** *one must beware of*, c. acc., Id.

εὐλᾰβίη, Ion. for εὐλάβεια.

εὐ-λάϊγξ, ὁ, ἡ, poët. for εὔ-λιθος, Anth.

εὐλάζω, f. ξω, *to plough*, Orac. ap. Thuc.; and

εὐλάκα, ἡ, *a ploughshare*, Orac. ap. Thuc.—(Old Lacon. forms, prob. akin to αὖλαξ.)

εὔ-λᾰλος, ον, *sweetly-speaking*, Anth. **II.** = εὔγλωσσος II, Id.

εὐ-λάχᾰνος, ον, (λάχανον) *fruitful in herbs*, Anth.

εὔ-λειμος, ον, = sq., Eur.

εὐ-λείμων, ον, *with goodly meadows*, Od., h. Hom.

εὔ-λεκτρος, ον, (λέκτρον) *bringing wedded happiness, blessing marriage*, Soph.

εὐ-λεχής, ές, = εὔλεκτρος, Anth.

ΕΥΛΗ΄, ἡ, *a worm or maggot*, Il., Hdt.

εὔ-ληπτος, ον, *easily taken hold of*: Adv. -τως *so that one can easily take hold*, Sup. εὐληπτότατα Xen. **2.** *easy to be taken or reduced*, Thuc.:—*easy to gain or obtain*, Luc.

εὔληρα, ων, τά, old word for ἡνία, *reins*, Il. (Deriv. unknown.)

εὐ-λίμενος, ον, (λιμήν) *with good harbours*, Eur., Plat.

εὐλογέω: impf. εὐλόγουν or ηὐλ-: f. -ήσω: aor. 1 εὐλόγησα or ηὐλ-:—*to speak well of, praise, honour*, Trag.; δίκαια εὐλ. τινα *to praise* him *justly*, Ar.:—Pass. *to be honoured*, Soph. **II.** *to bless*, N. T.

εὐλογητός, ή, όν, *blessed*, N. T.

εὐλογία, ἡ, *good or fine language*, Plat.: *a fair speech, specious talk*, N. T. **II.** *eulogy, panegyric*, Pind.; *blessing* (as an act) or *a blessing* (as an effect) Id.:—*of the alms collected* for poor brethren, N. T.

εὐ-λόγιστος, ον, *rightly reckoning, thoughtful*, Arist.

εὔ-λογος, ον, *having good reason, reasonable, sensible*, Aesch.; εὐλόγον [ἐστι], c. inf., *it is reasonable that*, Ar. **2.** *reasonable, fair*, Thuc., etc.: τὸ εὐλ. a

fair reason, Id.　　**II.** Adv. -γως, with good reason, reasonably, Aesch., Thuc.; εὐλ. ἔχειν to be reasonable, Plat.

εὔ-λογχος, ον, (λαγχάνω) propitious, Plut.

εὐ-λοέτειρα, ἡ, (λοετρον) with fine baths, Anth.

εὔ-λοφος, ον, well-plumed, Soph.

εὔ-λοχος, ον, (λοχεύω) helping in childbirth, Eur.

εὔ-λύρας [ῠ], ὁ, =sq., name of Apollo, Eur.

εὔ-λύρος, ον, (λύρα) playing well on the lyre, skilled in the lyre, Ar., Anth.

εὔ-λῠτος, ον, (λύω) easy to untie or loose, Xen.; εὐλ. πρὸς λοιδορίαν easily breaking into abuse, Theophr.　**2.** metaph. easily dissolved or broken, Eur., Xen.

εὐμάθεια and **-ία,** Ion. -ίη, ἡ, readiness in learning, docility, Plat., Anth. From

εὐ-μαθής, ές, (μανθάνω) ready or quick at learning, Lat. docilis, Plat., Dem. :—Adv. -θῶς, Aeschin.　**II.** pass. easy to learn or discern, intelligible, Aesch.: well-known, Soph.

εὐμᾰθία, Ion. -ίη, = εὐμάθεια, Plat.

εὐμᾰκής, ές, Dor. for εὐμηκής.

εὔ-μαλλος, ον, of fine wool, Pind.

εὔμᾱλος, Dor. for εὔμηλος.

εὐ-μάρᾰθος, ον, abounding in fennel, Anth.

εὐμάρεια, ἡ, Ion. -ίη, easiness, ease, opportunity, τινος for doing a thing, Soph.　**2.** ease of movement, dexterity, Eur.　**3.** of condition, ease, comfort, εὐμαρείᾳ χρῆσθαι to be at ease, in comfort, Soph. ; but also, εὐμαρίη χρᾶσθαι euphem. for alvum exonerare, to ease oneself, Hdt. ; εὐμ. πρός τι provision for, protection against, Plat. From

εὐ-μᾰρής, ές, (μάρη obsol. word for χείρ) easy, convenient, without trouble, Theogn. ; εὐμ. χείρωμα an easy prey, Aesch. :—εὐμαρές [ἐστι], c. inf., 'tis easy, Pind., Eur. ; so, ἐν εὐμαρεῖ [ἐστι] Id.　**II.** Adv. -ρῶς, Ep. -ρέως, mildly, Theogn.　**2.** easily, Plat.

εὐμᾰρίη, Ion. for εὐμάρεια.

εὐμᾰρις, ιδος, ἡ, acc. ιν, an Asiatic shoe or slipper, Aesch., Eur.　(A foreign word.)

εὐμάχᾰνος [ᾱ], ον, Dor. for εὐμήχανος.

εὐ-μεγέθης, ες, (μέγεθος) of good size, very large, Ar.

εὐ-μέλᾱνος, ον, (μέλας) well-blackened, inky, Anth.

εὐ-μελής, ές, (μέλος) musical, rhythmical, Arist.

εὐμένεια, ἡ, poët. -ία, (εὐμενής) the character of the εὐμενής, goodwill, favour, grace, Hdt., Soph., etc.

εὐμενέτης, ου, ὁ, Ep. for εὐμενής, a well-wisher, εὐμενέτῃσι (Ep. dat. pl.) Od.

εὐμενέω, to be gracious, Theocr.　**II.** c. acc. to deal kindly with, Pind. From

εὐ-μενής, ές, (μένος) well-disposed, favourable, gracious, kindly, h. Hom., Att.　**2.** of places, γῆ εὐμ. ἐναγωνίσασθαι favourable to fight in, Thuc. ; of a river, kindly, bounteous, Aesch.; of a road, easy, Xen.　**II.** Adv. -νῶς, Ion. -έως, Aesch., Plat., etc. :—Comp. -έστερον, Eur.

εὐμενία, ἡ, poët. form of εὐμένεια, Pind.

Εὐμενίδες (sc. θεαί), ίδων, αἱ, (εὐμενής) the gracious goddesses, euphem. name of the Ἐρινύες or Furies, Aesch., etc.

εὐμενίζομαι, (εὐμενής) Med. to propitiate, ἥρωας Xen.

εὐ-μετάβλητος, ον, (μεταβάλλω) easily changed, Arist.

εὐ-μετάβολος, ον, = foreg., changeable, Plat., Xen., etc.

εὐ-μετάδοτος, ον, (μεταδίδωμι) readily imparting, generous, N. T.

εὐ-μετάπειστος, ον, (μεταπείθω) easy to persuade, Arist.

εὐ-μεταχείριστος, ον, (μεταχειρίζω) easy to handle or manage, manageable, Plat., Xen.　**2.** easy to deal with or master, Thuc., Xen.

εὔ-μετρος, ον, (μέτρον) well-measured, well-calculated, Aesch. : well-proportioned, Theocr.

εὐ-μήκης, ες, Dor. -μάκης [ᾱ], ες, (μῆκος) of a good length, tall, Plat., Theocr.

εὔ-μηλος, Dor. -μᾱλος, ον, rich in sheep, Od., Pind.

εὐ-μήρῠτος, ον, (μηρύω) easy to spin out, Luc.

εὔ-μητις, ιδος, ὁ, ἡ, of good counsel, prudent, Anth.

εὐμηχᾰνία, Dor. εὐμᾱχ-, ἡ, inventive skill, Pind., Plut. From

εὐ-μήχᾰνος, Dor. εὐ-μάχ- [ᾱ], ον,　**I.** of persons, skilful in contriving, ingenious, inventive, Aesch., Plat.　**II.** pass., of things, skilfully contrived, ingenious, Ar., Plat.

εὐ-μίμητος [ῑ], ον, easily imitated, Plat.

εὐ-μίσητος [ῑ], ον, exposed to hatred, Xen.

εὐμῑτος, ον, with fine threads, εὐμίτοις πλοκαῖς = τὸν μίτον εὖ πλέκουσα, Eur.

εὔ-μιτρος [ῑ], ον, with beautiful μίτρα, Mosch.

εὔμ-μελίης, ὁ, (εὖ, μελία) Ep. for εὐ-μελίης, armed with good ashen spear, Hom.; εὐμμελίω Ep. gen., Il.

εὔ-μναστος, Dor. for εὔ-μνηστος.

εὐμνημόνευτος, ον, easy to remember, Dem.; Comp. -ότερος, Arist.

εὐ-μνήμων, ον, easy to remember :—Comp. Adv. εὐμνημονέστερως ἔχειν to be easier to remember, Xen.

εὔ-μνηστος, Dor. -μναστος, ον, well-remembering, mindful of a thing, c. gen., Soph.

εὐμοιρία, ἡ, happy possession of a thing, wealth or weal, Luc. From

εὔμοιρος, ον, (μοῖρα) blest with possessions, Plat.

εὐμολπέω, to sing well, h. Hom. From

εὔ-μολπος, ον, (μολπή) sweetly singing, Anth.

εὐμορφία, ἡ, beauty of form, symmetry, Eur., Plat., etc.; symmetry in the σπλάγχνα, which was required for good omens, Aesch. From

εὔ-μορφος, ον, (μορφή) fair of form, comely, goodly, Hdt., Aesch.

εὔ-μουσος, ον, (μοῦσα) skilled in the arts, esp. in poetry and music : hence musical, melodious, Eur., Anth.

εὔ-μοχθος, ον, laborious, Anth.

εὔ-μῡθος, ον, eloquent, Anth.

εὔ-μῡκος, ον, (μυκάομαι) loud-bellowing, Anth.

εὐνάζω, f. άσω [ᾰ] : aor. 1 ηὔνᾰσα or εὔνᾰσα :—Pass., aor. 1 ηὐνάσθην or εὐν-, Ep. 3 pl. εὔνασθεν : (εὐνή) :　**1.** to lay or place in ambush, Od.　**2.** to put to bed : of animals, to lay their young in a form, Xen. : metaph. of death, to lay asleep, Soph. : —Pass. to go to bed, sleep, Od., Att. ; of fowls, Od. : —of pain, εὐναθέντος κακοῦ Soph.　**II.** intr., like Pass., to sleep, Id.

εὐ-ναιετάων, ουσα, ον, (ναιετάω) well-situated, of cities and houses, Hom. :—so also **εὐ-ναιόμενος, η, ον,** Il.

εὐναῖος, α, ον, (εὐνή) in one's bed, εὐν. λαγώς a hare in its form, Xen.　**2.** wedded, Aesch., Eur.　**3.** λύπη εὐν. making one keep one's bed (cf. δεμνιοτήρης), Id. ; εὐν. πτέρυγες brooding, of a bird on the nest,

Anth.   II. (εὐνή II) *of* or *for anchorage*: generally, *steadying, guiding a ship*, of the rudder, Eur.
εὐνάσιμος, ον, (εὐνάζω) *good for sleeping in*: εὐνάσιμα, τά, *convenient sleeping places*, Xen.
εὐνατήρ, εὐνάτειρα, εὐνάτωρ, v. sub εὐνητ–.
εὐνατήριον, τό, *a sleeping-place, bed-chamber*, Trag.
εὐνάω, f. ήσω: aor. 1 εὔνησα:—Pass., aor. 1 εὐνήθην: pf. εὔνημαι: (εὐνή):—poët. for εὐνάζω: 1. *to lay* or *place in ambush*, Od.   2. *to lay asleep, lull to sleep*, metaph., εὔνησε γόον Ib.:—Pass. *to lie asleep*, of a dog, *to lie kennelled*, Soph.: of the winds, Od.
εὐνέτης, ου, ὁ, (εὐνή) = εὐναστήρ, Eur., Anth.
εὔνεως, ων, (ναῦς) *well furnished with ships*, Max.
ΕΥΝΗ', ἡ: Ep. gen. sing. and pl. εὐνῆφι, -φιν:—*a bed*, Hom.; εὐνῆς ἐπιβήμεναι Il.; ἐξ εὐνῆς ἀναστᾶσα Ib., etc.   2. *the bedding*, as opp. to λέχος (the bedstead), Od.   3. εὐναὶ Νυμφάων *their abode*, Il.:—of animals, *the lair* of a deer, Hom.; *the seat* of a hare, Xen.; *the nest* of a bird, Soph.   4. *the marriage-bed*, Hom., etc.   5. *one's last bed, the grave*, Aesch., Soph.   II. pl. εὐναί, *stones used as anchors* in the times of Hom. and Hes., and thrown out from the prow, while the stern was made fast to land, ἐκ δ' εὐνὰς ἔβαλον κατὰ δὲ πρυμνήσι' ἔδησαν Hom.   Hence
εὐνῆθεν, Adv. *from* or *out of bed*, Od.
εὐνηθῆναι, aor. 1 pass. inf. of εὐνάω.
εὔνημα, ατος, τό, (εὐνάω) *marriage*, Eur.
εὐνητήρ, Dor. -ᾱτήρ, ῆρος, ὁ, (εὐνάω) *a bedfellow, husband*, Aesch.:—Dor. fem. εὐνάτειρα, θεοῦ μὲν εὐν. *partner* of his *bed*, Id.; εὐν. Διὸς λεχέων Id.
εὐνήτης, ου, ὁ, = foreg., Eur.:—fem. εὐνήτρια, Soph.
εὐνήτωρ, Dor. -άτωρ, ορος, ὁ, = εὐνητήρ, Aesch., Eur.
εὐνῆφι, εὐν. Ep. gen. sing. and pl. of εὐνή.
εὖνις, ὁ, ἡ, acc. εὖνιν: pl. εὔνιδες:—*reft of, bereaved of*, c. gen., Hom., Aesch.:—absol. *bereaved of children*, Id.   (Deriv. uncertain.)
εὖνις, ιδος, ἡ, = εὐνέτις, *a bedfellow, wife*, Soph., Eur.
ἐΰ-νητος, ον, Ep. for εὔ-νητος, (νέω) *well-spun*, Hom.
εὐνοέω, f. ήσω, (εὔνοος) *to be well-inclined*, Hdt., Att.
εὐνοιά, ἡ, poët. sometimes εὐνοιά, Ion. εὐνοίη, poët. εὐνοίη: (εὔνους):—*good-will, favour, kindness*, κατ' εὔνοιαν *out of kindness* or *good-will*, Hdt.; δι' εὐνοίας Thuc.; δι' εὔνοιαν Plat.; εὐνοίας ἕνεκα Dem.; μετ' or ὑπ' εὐνοίας Id.; ἐπ' εὐνοίᾳ χθονός *for love of fatherland*, Aesch.; εὔνοιαν ἔχειν εἴς τινα ap. Dem.:—in pl. *feelings of kindness, favours*, Aesch.   II. *a gift in token of good-will*, esp. of presents to the Athenian commanders from the subject states, Dem.
εὐνοϊκός, ή, όν, *well-disposed, kindly, favourable*, Dem.:—Adv., εὐνοϊκῶς ἔχειν τινί or πρός τινα *to be kindly disposed to* . . , Xen.
εὐνομέομαι, -ήσομαι: aor. 1 εὐνομήθεν: Dep.:—*to have good laws, to be orderly*, Hdt., Thuc., etc.
εὐνομία, Ion. -ίη, ἡ, *good order, order*, Od., Hdt., Att.   2. personified by Hes. as daughter of Themis.
εὔ-νομος, ον, *under good laws, well-ordered*, Pind., Plat.
εὔ-νοος, ον, Att. εὔνους, ουν: gen. pl. εὐνόων (poët.):—*well-minded, well-disposed, kindly, friendly*, Hdt., Att.; τινι *to one*, Hdt., etc.; οἱ ἐμοὶ εὖνοι *my well-wishers*, Xen.; τὸ εὔνουν = εὔνοια, Soph., etc.—Comp. εὐνούστερος Id., Ion. εὐνοέστερος Hdt.; Sup. εὐνούστατος Ar.

εὐν-οῦχος, ὁ, *a eunuch*, employed to take charge of the women and act as *chamberlains* (whence the name, οἱ τὴν εὐνὴν ἔχοντες), Hdt., Ar., etc.
εὖντα, Dor. for ἐόντα, neut. pl. of part. ὤν.
εὐ-νώμας, ου, ὁ, (νωμάω) *moving well* or *regularly*, εὐνώμᾳ χρόνῳ by the *steady* march of time, Soph.
εὔ-ξαντος, ον, (ξαίνω) *well-carded*, of wool, Anth.
εὔξεαι, Ep. 2 sing. aor. 1 subj. of εὔχομαι.
εὔ-ξενος, Ion. εὔ-ξεινος, ον, *kind to strangers, hospitable*, ἀνδρῶνας εὐξένους δόμων the *guest*-chambers, Aesch.; λιμὴν εὐξεινότατος ναύταις Eur.   II. πόντος εὔξεινος the Euxine, now *the Black sea*, Hdt., etc.:—anciently called ἄξενος, *the inhospitable* (*dictus ab antiquis Axenus ille fuit*, Ovid.).
εὔ-ξεστος, Ep. ἐΰ-ξεστος, η, ον, or ος, ον: (ξέω):—*well-planed, well-polished*, of carpenters' work, Hom.
εὔ-ξοος, Ep. ἐΰ-ξοος, ον: contr. gen., εὔξου Il.: (ξέω):—*just like* εὔξεστος, often in Hom.; σκέπαρνον εὔξοον an axe *with polished haft*, Od.
εὐ-ξύμβλητος, εὐ-ξύμβολος, εὐ-ξύνετος, Att. for εὐ-σύμβλητος, etc.
εὐοδέω, f. ήσω, (εὔοδος) *to have a free course* or *passage*, of running water, Dem.
εὐοδία, ἡ, (εὔοδος) *a good journey, wishes for a good journey*, Aesch. ap. Ar.
εὔοδμος, v. εὔοσμος.
εὔ-οδος, ον, *easy to pass*, of mountains, Xen.; of a road, *easy to travel*, Id.
εὐ-οδόω, f. ώσω, *to help on the way*, c. dat. pers., Soph.   2. Pass. *to have a prosperous journey*, N. T.:—metaph. *to prosper, be successful*, Hdt., N. T.
εὐοῖ, Bacchanalian exclamation, Lat. *evoe*, Soph., etc.
εὔ-οινος, ον, *producing good wine*, Anth.
εὔ-ολβος, ον, *wealthy, prosperous*, Eur.
εὐ-ομολόγητος, ον, *easy to concede, indisputable*, Plat.
εὐοπλέω, *to be well-equipt*, Anth.; and
εὐοπλία, ἡ, *a good state of arms and equipments*, Xen.
εὔ-οπλος, ον, (ὅπλον) *well-armed, well-equipt*, Ar., Xen.
εὐοργησία, ἡ, *gentleness of temper*, Eur.   From
εὐ-όργητος, ον, (ὀργή) *good-tempered*:—Adv. -ως, *with good temper*, Thuc.
εὐορκέω, f. ήσω, *to be faithful to one's oath*, Eur., Thuc.
εὐορκία, ἡ, *fidelity to one's oath*, Pind.   From
εὔ-ορκος, ον, *keeping one's oath, faithful to one's oath*, Hes., Att.   II. of oaths, εὔορκα ὀμνύναι *to swear faithfully*, Att.; εὔορκόν [ἐστι] it is *in accordance with one's oath, no breach of oath*, Thuc.; εὔορκα ταῦθ' ὑμῖν ἐστι Dem.; so in Adv., τάδ' εὐόρκως ἔχει Aesch.
εὔ-όρκωμα, ατος, τό, *a faithful oath*, Aesch.
εὔ-ορμος, ον, *with good mooring-places*, Hom., Soph.   2. *well-moored*, of ships, Anth.
εὔ-ορνις, ιθος, ὁ, ἡ, *abounding in birds*, Anth.
εὔ-οροφος, ον, *well-roofed*, Anth.
εὔ-οσμος or -οδμος, ον, (ὀσμή, ὀδμή) *sweet-smelling, fragrant*, Theocr.
εὐ-όφθαλμος, ον, *with beautiful eyes*, Xen.: *keen-eyed*, Id.
εὐ-οφρυς, v, *with fine eyebrows*, Anth.
εὐοχθέω, f. ήσω, *to be in good case*, Hes.   From
εὔ-οχθος, ον, *with goodly banks, fertile*, Ep. Hom.:—generally *abundant, rich*, Eur.

εὐ-πᾰγής, ές, (πήγνυμι) of the body, compact, firm, strong, Xen., Theocr.

εὐπάθεια, Ion. -ίη, ἡ, the enjoyment of good things, comfort, ease, Xen. :—esp. in pl. enjoyments, luxuries, ἐν εὐπαθίησι εἶναι to enjoy oneself, Hdt. ; also delicacies, dainties, Xen. ; and

εὐπᾰθέω, f. ήσω, to be well off, enjoy oneself, make merry, Hdt., Plat. From

εὐ-πᾰθής, ές, (πάσχω) enjoying good things, easy.   II. easily affected, Plut.

εὐπᾰθίη, Ion. for εὐπάθεια.

εὐπαιδία, ἡ, a goodly race of children, Eur. ; εὐπαιδίαν ἔχων blest in his children, Id. From

εὐ-παις, παιδος, ὁ, ἡ, blest in one's children, i. e. with many or good children, h. Hom., Hdt., Att. ; γόνος εὔπαις noble offspring, Eur.

εὔπακτος, Dor. for εὔπηκτος.

εὐ-πάλᾰμος, ον, (παλάμη) handy, skilful, ingenious, inventive, Aesch., Anth.

εὐ-πάξ, πᾱγος, ὁ, ἡ, Dor. for εὐ-πήξ, = εὐπᾱγής, Eur.

εὐ-παράγωγος, ον, (παράγω) easy to lead astray, Ar.

εὐ-παραίτητος, ον, (παραιτέομαι) placable, Plut.

εὐ-παρᾰκολούθητος, ον, (παρακολουθέω) easy to follow, of an argument, Arist.

εὐ-παρᾰκόμιστος, ον, (παρακομίζω) easy to convey, Plut.

εὐ-πάραος, ον, Dor. for εὐπάρειος (παρειά), with beauteous cheeks, Pind.

εὐ-παράπειστος, α, ον, easily led away, Xen.

εὐ-πάρεδρος, ον, constantly attending, τὸ εὐπ. τῷ Κυρίῳ constant waiting on the Lord, N. T.

εὐ-πάρθενος, ον, = καλὴ πάρθενος, Eur.

εὐ-παρόξυντος, ον, (παροξύνω) rendered irritable, Plut.

εὐ-παρόρμητος, ον, (παρορμάω) easily excited, Arist.

εὐ-πάρυφος, ον, (παρυφή) with fine purple border, Plut.   2. of persons, wearing such a garment, Lat. praetextatus, a grandee, Luc.

εὐ-πᾰτέρεια, ἡ, (πατήρ) daughter of a noble sire, Hom.   2. of places, of a noble father, Eur.

εὐ-πᾰτρίδης, ου, Dor. -δας, α, ὁ, (πατήρ) of good or noble sire, of noble family, of persons, Soph., Eur., etc. ; εὐπατρίδαι οἶκοι Eur.   II. at Athens in the old time, the εὐπατρίδαι formed the first class (the Nobles), the γεωμόροι the second, the δημιουργοί the third, Xen.   2. at Rome, the Patricians, Id.

εὐπᾰτρις, ιδος, ἡ, (πατήρ) born of a noble sire, Eur. ; τίς ἂν εὔπατρις ὧδε βλάστοι ; who could be born so worthy of a noble sire ? Soph. ; ἐλπίδων εὐπατρίδων of hopes derived from those of noble birth, Id.

εὐ-πάτωρ [ᾰ], ορος, ὁ, ἡ, (πατήρ) born of a noble sire, Aesch.

εὐ-πειθής, ές, (πείθω) ready to obey, obedient, τινι Aesch., Plat. ; also τινος, Id.   II. act. persuasive, Aesch.

εὔπειστος, ον, (πείθομαι) easily persuaded, Arist.

εὐ-πέμπελος, ον, a word of uncertain meaning in Aesch., either tranquil, placable, as if it were εὐπέμφελος (cf. δυσπέμφελος), or easy to be sent away (cf. δύσπεμπτος).

εὐ-πένθερος, ον, with a good father-in-law, Theocr.

εὔ-πεπλος, ον, beautifully robed, Hom.

εὔ-πεπτος, ον, (πέσσω) easy of digestion, Arist.

εὐ-περιάγωγος, ον, (περιάγω) easily turned round, Luc.

εὐ-περίγραφος, ον, (περιγράφω) easy to sketch out, with a good outline, Luc.

εὐ-περίσπαστος, ον, (περισπάω) easy to pull away, Xen.

εὐ-περίστατος, ον, (περιστῆναι) easily besetting, N. T.

εὐ-πέτᾱλος, ον, (πέταλον) with beautiful leaves, Anth.

εὐπέτεια, ἡ, ease, δι' εὐπετείας easily, Eur. :—pl., εὐπετείας διδόναι to give facilities, Plat.   2. easiness of getting or having a thing, c. gen., Hdt., Xen. From

εὐ-πετής, ές, (πίπτω) of the dice, falling well ; metaph. favourable, Aesch. ; so in Adv., εὐπετῶς ἔχειν Id.   2. easy, without trouble, Lat. facilis, Hdt., Att. :—Adv. εὐπετῶς, Ion. -έως, easily, Hdt., Att. ; with numerals, ἑξακοσίους ἀμφορέας εὐπ. χωρέει it easily holds 600 amphorae, i. e. full 600, Hdt. :—Comp. -εστέρως Id.   II. of persons, easy-tempered, accommodating, Eur.

εὔ-πετρος, ον, of good hard stone, Anth.

εὐ-πηγής, ές, = εὐπᾱγής, well-built, stout, Od.

εὔ-πηκτος, ον, (πήγνυμι) well-built, Hom.

εὔ-πηλης, ὁ, ἡ, with beautiful helmet, Anth.

εὔ-πηνος, ον, (πήνη) of fine texture, Eur.

εὔ-πηχυς, υ, with beautiful arms, Eur.

εὔ-πῖδαξ, ᾰκος, ὁ, ἡ, abounding in fountains, Anth.

εὔ-πῐθής, ές, = εὐπειθής I, Aesch.

εὔ-πιστος, ον, trustworthy, trusty, Xen. ; εὔπιστα things easy to believe, Soph.   II. act. easily believing, credulous, Arist.

εὐ-πίων [ῐ], ον, gen. ονος, very fat : very rich, Anth.

εὐ-πλᾰτής, ές, (πλάτος) of a good breadth, Xen.

εὔ-πλειος, α, ον, well filled, Od.

εὔ-πλεκής, ές, (πλέκω) = sq., Il.

εὔ-πλεκτος, Ep. εὔ-πλ—, ον, (πλέκω) well-plaited, well-twisted, of wicker-work and ropes, Il. ; of nets, Eur.

εὔπλοια, poët. -οίη, ἡ, (εὔπλοος) a fair voyage, Il., Soph.

εὐ-πλοκᾰμίς, ῖδος, Ep. fem. of sq., Od.

εὐ-πλόκᾰμος, Ep. εὔ-πλ—, ον, with goodly locks, fair-haired, Hom. ; εὐπλ. κόμαι goodly tresses, Eur.

εὔ-πλοκος, ον, (πλέκω) = εὔπλεκτος, Anth.

εὔ-πλοος, ον, (πλέω) good for sailing, εὔπλοον ὅρμον ἵκοιτο may he reach a friendly port, Theocr.

εὐ-πλῠνής, ές, (πλύνω) well-washed, well-cleansed, Od.

εὔ-πλοῠτος, ον, favourable to sailing, Anth.

εὔπνοια, poet. -ίη, ἡ, easiness of breathing.   2. fragrance, Anth. From

εὔ-πνοος, ον, contr. εὔ-πνους, ουν ; Ep. εὔ-πνοος : (πνέω) :—breathing well, breathing a sweet smell, sweet-smelling, Mosch., Anth.   II. affording a free passage to the air, Lat. perflabilis, Xen.

εὐποδία, ἡ, (εὔπους) goodness of foot, Xen.

εὐ-ποιητικός, ή, όν, beneficent, Arist.

εὐ-ποίητος, ον, well-made, well-wrought, Od., Hes.

εὐ-ποιΐα, ἡ, (ποιέω) beneficence, Luc.

εὐ-ποίκῐλος, ον, much varied, variegated, Anth.

εὔ-ποκος, ον, rich in wool, fleecy, Aesch.

εὐ-πόλεμος, ον, good at war, successful in war, h. Hom., Xen.

εὔ-πομπος, ον, conducting to a happy issue, Aesch., Soph.

εὐπορέω, f. ήσω : aor. 1 εὐπόρησα : pf. εὐπόρηκα : (εὔπορος) :—to prosper, thrive, be well off, Xen. ; ὅθεν ὁ πόλεμος εὐπορεῖ from which sources war is successfully maintained, Thuc.   b. c. gen. rei, to have plenty of, to have store of, to abound in a thing, c. gen., Xen., etc.   2. to find a way, find means, Thuc. :

c. inf. *to be able* to do, Plat. **II.** c. acc. rei, *to supply, furnish*, Thuc., Dem., etc.

εὐπορία, ἡ, (εὔπορος) *an easy way* of doing a thing, *facility* or *faculty* for doing, c. inf., Thuc.; absol., Xen.:—c. gen. rei, *easy means* of providing, Thuc., etc. **2.** *plenty, store, abundance, wealth*, Xen.:— in pl. *advantages*, Isocr., Dem. **II.** *the solution* of *doubts* or *difficulties*, Xen., etc.

εὐ-πόριστος, ον, (πορίζω) *easy to procure;*—εὐπόριστα (sc. φάρμακα), τά, *common medicines*, Plut.

εὔ-πορος, ον, *easy to pass* or *travel through*, Aesch.; τὰ εὔπορα *open ground*, Xen. **2.** *easily gotten, easily done, easy*, Hdt., Thuc., etc.:—τὸ εὔπορον = εὐπορία, Id.; εὐπορόν ἐστι it is *easy*, c. inf., Id. **II.** *going easily, ready, glib, γλῶττα* Ar. **2.** of persons, *full of resources* or *devices, ingenious, inventive, ready*, opp. to ἄπορος, Ar., Plat. **III.** εὔπ. τινι *well-provided with, rich in* a thing, Thuc.:—absol. *well off, wealthy*, Dem. **IV.** Adv. -πως, *easily*, Xen.; Comp. -ώτερον, Plat. **2.** *in abundance*, εὐπ. ἔχειν πάντα Thuc.

εὐποτμέω, f. ήσω, *to be lucky, fortunate*, Plut.; and εὐποτμία, ἡ, *good fortune*, Plut., Luc. From εὔ-ποτμος, ον, *happy, prosperous*, Aesch.

εὔ-ποτος, ον, *easy to drink, pleasant to the taste*, Aesch.

εὔ-πους, ὁ, ἡ, πουν, τό, *with good feet*, Xen. **II.** of verses, *with good feet, flowing*, Anth.

εὐπραγέω, f. = εὖ πράσσω, *to do well, be well off, flourish*, Thuc., Xen., etc. Hence

εὐπρᾱγία, ἡ, = εὐπραξία, *well-doing, well-being, welfare, success*, Thuc., etc.

εὔ-πρακτος, ον, *easy to be done*, Xen.

εὐπραξία, Ion. εὐπρηξίη, ἡ, = εὐπραγία, Hdt., Trag. **II.** *good conduct*, Xen.

εὔπραξις, ἡ, poët. for εὐπραξία.

εὔ-πρεμνος, ον, (πρέμνον) *with good stem*, Anth.

εὐπρέπεια, ἡ, *goodly appearance, dignity, comeliness*, Thuc. **II.** *colourable appearance, speciousness, plausibility*, Id., Plat. From

εὐ-πρεπής, ές, (πρέπω) *well-looking, goodly, comely*, of outward appearance, Hdt., Att.; εὐπρ. ἰδεῖν *fair* to look on, Xen.; εἶδος εὐπρεπής Eur. **2.** *decent, seemly, fitting, becoming*, Hdt., Aesch., Eur.; τελευτή εὐπρεπεστάτη *a most glorious* end, Thuc. **3.** *specious, plausible*, Hdt., Thuc.; ἐκ τοῦ εὐπρεποῦς in *pretence*, Id. **II.** Adv. -πῶς, Ion. -πέως, Hdt., Aesch., etc.; Comp. -πέστερον, Eur.; Sup. -πέστατα, Thuc.

εὐπρηξίη, Ion. for εὐπραξία.

εὔ-πρηστος, ον, (πρήθω) *well-blowing, strong-blowing*, Il.

εὐ-πρόσδεκτος, ον, (προσδέχομαι) *acceptable*, N. T.

εὐπρόσεδρος, ον, = εὐπάρεδρος, N. T.

εὐ-προσήγορος, ον, *easy of address*, i. e. *affable, courteous*, Eur.; οὐκ εὐπρ. ἆται *miseries that forbid my being spoken to*, Id.

εὐ-πρόσιτος, ον, *easy of access*, of places, Luc.

εὐ-πρόσοδος, ον, of persons, *accessible, affable*, Lat. *qui faciles aditus habet*, Thuc., Xen. **2.** of places, *easily accessible*, Id.

εὐ-πρόσοιστος, ον, *easy of approach: generally, easy*, Eur.

εὐπροσωπέω, f. ήσω, *to make a fair show*, N. T.

εὐπροσωπο-κοίτης, ὁ, (κοίτη) *lying so as to present a fair face*, Aesch.

εὐ-πρόσωπος, ον, (πρόσωπον) *fair of face*, Ar., Xen.: *with glad countenance*, Soph. **2.** metaph. *fair in outward show, specious*, Hdt., Eur., etc.

εὐ-προφάσιστος, ον, *with good pretext, plausible*, Thuc.

εὔ-πρυμνος, ον, (πρύμνα) *with goodly stern*, Il., Eur.

εὔ-πρῳρος, ον, (πρῷρα) *with goodly prow*, Eur.

εὔ-πτερος, ον, (πτερόν) *well-winged, well-plumed*, Soph., Eur.; metaph., of *high-plumed* dames, Ar.

εὐ-πτέρυγος, ον, (πτέρυξ) = foreg., of ships, Anth.

εὔ-πτορθος, ον, *finely branching*, of horns, Anth.

εὔ-πυργος, ον, *well-towered*, of fortified towns, Il.

εὔ-πώγων, ὁ, *well-bearded*, Anth.

εὔ-πωλος, ον, *abounding in foals* or *horses*, Il.: *breeding noble horses*, Soph.

εὐρ-ακύλων, v. εὐροκλύδων.

εὐράμην, aor. 1 med. of εὑρίσκω.

εὐράξ, Adv. (εὖρος) *on one side, sideways*, Il. **II.** εὐρὰξ πατάξ, an exclamation to frighten away birds, Ar.

εὑρέθην, aor. 1 pass. of εὑρίσκω:—εὑρεῖν, Ep. εὑρέμεναι, aor. 2 inf.

εὕρεσις, εως, ἡ, (εὑρεῖν) *a finding, discovery*, Plat.

εὑρετέος, α, ον, verb. Adj. of εὑρίσκω, *to be discovered, found out*, Thuc.

εὑρετής, οῦ, ὁ, (εὑρεῖν) *an inventor, discoverer*, Plat.

εὑρετικός, ή, όν, (εὑρεῖν) *inventive, ingenious*, Plat.

εὕρετο, 3 sing. aor. 2 med. of εὑρίσκω.

εὑρετός, ή, όν, verb. Adj. of εὑρίσκω, *discoverable*, Xen.

εὕρηκα, -ημαι, pf. act. and pass. of εὑρίσκω.

εὕρημα, ατος, τό, (εὑρεῖν) *an invention, discovery*, Eur., Ar., etc. **2.** c. gen. *an invention for* or *against* a thing, *a remedy*, Eur., Dem. **II.** *that which is found unexpectedly*, i. e., much like Ἕρμαιον, *a piece of good luck, godsend, windfall, prize*, Hdt., Eur., etc. **III.** of a child, *a foundling*, Soph., Eur.

εὕρην, Dor. for εὑρεῖν.

εὑρησι-επής, ές, (ἔπος) *inventive of words, fluent*, Pind.: *wordy, sophistical*, Ar.

εὑρήσω, fut. of εὑρίσκω.

εὑρήτωρ, ορος, ὁ, = εὑρετής, Anth.

εὔ-ρινος, Ep. ἐΰρ-ρ-, ον, (ῥίς) = εὔρις, Babr., etc.

εὔ-ρινος, Ep. ἐΰρ-ρ-, ον, (ῥινός) *of good leather*, Anth.

Εὐριπίδειος, α, ον, *of* or *like Euripides*, Plat.

Εὐριπίδιον, τό, *little Euripides*, term of endearment, Ar.

εὔ-ριπος, ὁ, (ῥιπίζω) *a place where the flux and reflux is strong*, esp. *the strait which separates Euboea from Boeotia*, where the current was said to change seven times a day, Xen.:—proverb of *an unstable man*, Aeschin. **II.** generally, *a canal, ditch*, Anth.

εὔ-ρις, ἰνος, ὁ, ἡ, (ῥίς) *with a good nose*, i. e. *keen-scented*, Aesch., Soph.

ΕΥΡΙ'ΣΚΩ: impf. ηὔρισκον or εὕρ-: f. εὑρήσω: aor. 2 εὗρον or ηὗρον, Ep. inf. εὑρέμεναι:—pf. εὕρηκα:—Med., f. εὑρήσομαι: aor. 2 εὑρόμην or Att. ηὑρ-: aor. 1 εὑράμην:—Pass., f. εὑρεθήσομαι: also med. (in pass. sense) εὑρήσομαι: aor. 1 εὑρέθην: pf. ηὕρημαι or εὕρ-. *To find*, Hom., etc.:—c. part. *to find that*, Hdt.; and in Pass., ἢν εὑρεθῇς δίκαιος ὤν Soph. **2.** c. inf., εὕρισκε πρῆγμά οἱ εἶναι *found* that the thing for him was, Hdt. **II.** *to find out, discover*, Hom., etc.; cf. εὕρημα II.:—so in Med. *to find out for oneself*, Od. **III.** *to devise, invent*, Aesch., etc.:—Med., τὰ δ' ἔργα τοὺς λόγους. εὑρίσκεται deeds *make them-*

selves words, i. e. speak for themselves, Soph.　　IV.
to find, get, gain, procure, Pind., Soph., etc. :—Med.
to get for oneself, bring on oneself, κακὸν εὕρετο Od.;
αὑτὸς εὑρόμην πόνους Aesch.　　V. of merchandise,
to find a purchaser, *to fetch, earn,* πολλὸν χρυσίον
εὑροῦσα having fetched a large sum, Hdt.; ἀποδίδοται
τοῦ εὑρόντος sells *for what it will fetch,* Xen.

εὑροέω, f. ήσω, (εὖρος) *to flow well* or *abundantly ;*
metaph. *to go on well, be favourable,* Eur.　　II. *to
be fluent, speak successfully,* Plut.　　Hence

εὕροια, ἡ, *a good flow, free passage,* Plat.　　II.
fluency, Id.　　III. *successful progress,* Id.

εὑ-ροίζητος, ον, (ῥοιζέω) *loud-whizzing,* Anth.

εὕροιμι, ·οίμην, aor. 2 act. and med. opt. of εὑρίσκω.

εὑρο-κλύδων, ωνος, ὁ, in Act. Ap., probably *a storm
from the East ;* but the prob. reading is εὐρ-ακύλων,
Euro-aquilo, a N. E. wind.

εὗρον, aor. 2 of εὑρίσκω :—εὕρομες, Dor. 1 pl.

εὕ-ροος, Ep. ἐΰρ-poos, ον, contr. εὕ-ρους, ουν, *flowing
well* or *plentifully, fair-flowing,* Il., Soph., Eur.　　II.
of words, *flowing, fluent, glib,* Id.

εὕ-ροπος, ον, (ῥέπω) *easily inclining, easy-sliding,* Anth.

Εὗρος, ὁ, *the East wind,* or more exactly E. S. E., Lat.
Eurus, Il. (Probably akin to ἠώς, ἕως, *the morning-
wind,* as Ζέφυρος is to ζόφος, *the evening-wind.*)

ΕΥ̓ΡΟΣ, τό, *breadth, width,* absol., εὗρος *in breadth,*
Od., Hdt., etc.; so, τὸ εὖρος Xen.; εἰς εὖρος Eur.

ἐϋρ-ραφής, ές, (ῥάπτω) *well-stitched,* Il.

ἐΰρ-ρεής, ές, (ῥέω) *fair-flowing,* Ep. gen. ἐϋρρεῖος ποταμοῖο, contr. for εὐρρέος, Il.

ἐΰρ-ρείτης, ου, ὁ, (ῥέω) = ἐΰρρεής, Hom., Eur.

ἐΰρ-ρηνος, ον, (ῥήν) *of a good sheep,* Anth.

ἐΰρ-ρῖν, ἐΰρ-poos, Ep. for εὔ-ριν, εὔ-poos.

εὐρύ-άγυιᾰ, fem. Adj. used only in nom. and acc., *with
wide streets,* in epith. of great cities, Hom.

εὐρύ-άλος, ον, (ἅλως) *with wide threshing-floor,* generally, *broad,* Anth.

εὐρυ-βίας, Ion. -βίης, ου, ὁ, = εὐρυσθενής, Hes., Pind.

εὐρυθμία, ἡ, *rhythmical order* or *movement,* Plat., etc.

εὕ-ρυθμος, ον, *rhythmical,* of musical time or cadence,
Ar., etc.　　2. *well-proportioned,* Xen., of armour,
fitting well, Id.

εὐρύ-κολπος, ον, = εὐρύστερνος, Pind.

εὐρύ-κρειων, οντος, ὁ, *wide-ruling,* of Agamemnon, Hom.

εὐρυ-λείμων, ον, *with broad meadows,* Pind.

εὐρυ-μέδων, οντος, ὁ, = εὐρυκρείων, Pind.

εὐρυ-μέτωπος, ον, *broad-fronted,* of oxen, Hom.

εὐρύνω [ῦ], f. ῠνῶ (εὐρύς) *to broaden,* εὐρῦναι ἀγῶνα *to
clear* the arena (for dancing), Od.; τὸ μέσον εὐρύνειν
to leave a wide space in the middle, Hdt.　　2. metaph.
to extend, Anth. :—Pass. *to be spread abroad,* Luc.

εὐρύ-νωτος, ον, (νῶτον) *broad-backed,* Soph.

εὐρυ-όδεια, ἡ, (ὁδός) fem. Adj. *with broad, open ways,*
only used in gen. fem., χθονὸς εὐρυοδείης Hom.

εὐρυ-οπα, Ep. for -όπης, ὁ, (ὄψομαι) *the far-seeing,* of
Zeus, εὐρύοπα Ζεύς Hom.; also in voc., εὐρύοπα Ζεῦ
Il. ;—in Il. there is also an acc. (as if from a nom.
εὐρύοψ) εὐρύοπα Ζῆνα.

εὐρύ-πεδος, ον, (πέδον) *with broad surface,* Anth.

εὐρύ-πορος, ον, *with broad ways,* of the sea, *where all
may roam at will,* Hom., etc.

εὐρυπρωκτία, ἡ, *lewdness,* Ar.

εὐρύ-πρωκτος, ον, *lewd, filthy,* Ar.

εὐρυ-πῠλής, ές, (πύλη) *with broad gates,* Hom.

εὐρυ-ρέεθρος, ον, (ῥέεθρον) *with broad channel, broad-
flowing,* Il.

εὐρυ-ρέων, ουσα, ον, (ῥέω) *broad-flowing,* Il.—There is
no such *Verb* as εὐρυρέω, v. εὖ fin.

ΕΥ̓ΡΥ̓Σ, εὐρεῖα, εὐρύ : Ion. fem. εὐρέα : gen. εὐρέος,
είας, έος : acc. sing. εὐρύν and εὐρέᾰ :—*wide, broad,*
Hom., etc.　　2. *far-reaching, far-spread,* κλέος εὐρύ
Od.; ἐλπίδες Anth.　　II. as Adv. the neut. εὐρύ is
mostly used, Il., etc.

εὐρυ-σάκης [ᾰ], ες, (σάκος) *with broad shield,* name of
Ajax' son, Soph.

εὐρυ-σθενής, ές, (σθένος) *of far-extended might, mighty,*
Hom., Pind.

εὐρύ-σορος, ον, *with wide bier* or *tomb,* Anth.

εὐρύ-στερνος, ον, (στέρνον) *broad-breasted,* Hes.

εὐρύ-στομος, ον, (στόμα) *wide-mouthed,* Xen., etc.

εὐρύ-τιμος, ον, (τιμή) *wide, far-honoured,* Pind.

εὐρυ-φάρέτρης, ου, ὁ, (φαρέτρα) *with wide quiver,* Pind.

εὐρυ-φυής, ές, (φύομαι) *broad-growing,* of the manner
in which the grains of barley are set on the stalk, Od.

εὐρυχάδής, ές, (χαδεῖν) *wide-mouthed,* of cups, Anth.

εὐρυ-χαίτης, ου, ὁ, *with wide-streaming hair,* Pind.

εὐρύ-χορος, ον, Ep. for εὐρύ-χωρος, *with broad places,
spacious,* of cities, Hom., etc. : cf. καλλίχορος.

εὐρυχωρία, Ion. -ίη, ἡ, *open space, free room,* Hdt.,
Dem.　　2. *of an open field* for battle, Xen.; ἐν εὐρυ-
χωρίῃ ναυμαχέειν *to fight with plenty of sea-room,* Hdt.

εὐρύ-χωρος, ον, (χώρα) *roomy, wide,* Arist.

εὐρύ-οψ, οπος, ὁ, ἡ, v. εὐρύοπα.

εὐ-ρώγης, (ῥώξ) *abounding in grapes,* Anth.

εὐρ-ώδης, ες, (εἶδος) poët. for εὐρύς, Soph.

εὐρώεις, εσσα, εν, (εὐρώς) *mouldy, dank,* οἰκία εὐρώεντα
(Virgil's *loca senta situ*), of the world below, Hom.;
τάφον εὐρώεντα Soph.

εὐρών, οῦσα, όν, aor. 2 act. part. of εὑρίσκω.

Εὐρώπη, ἡ, *Europa, Europe,* as a geograph. name, first
in the Homeric Hymn to Apollo.

εὐρ-ωπός, ή, όν, (εὐρύς, ὤψ) poët. for εὐρύς, Eur.

ΕΥ̓ΡὨΣ, ῶτος, ὁ, *mould, dank decay,* Lat. *situs,
squalor,* Theogn., Eur., etc.

εὐρωστία, ἡ, *stoutness, strength,* Plut.　　From

εὔ-ρωστος, ον, (ῥώννυμι) *stout, strong,* Xen.　　Adv.
·τως, Id.

εὐρωτιάω, (εὐρώς) *to be* or *become mouldy,* βίος εὐρωτιῶν
the life of the unwashed, Ar.

ΕΥ̓Σ, ὁ, acc. ἐΰν : Ep. neut. ἠΰ (εὖ being used only as
Adv. : Ep. gen. ἑῆος, pl. ἐάων : (v. εὖ) :—*good, brave,
noble,* Hom. :—Ep. gen. pl. ἐάων, *of good things, good
fortune,* Id.

εὖσα, Dor. fem. part. of εἰμί (*sum*).

εὖσα, aor. 1 of εὕω.

εὔσαρκος, ον, (σάρξ) *fleshy, in good case, plump,* Xen.

εὐσέβεια, poët. εὐσεβίη, ἡ, *reverence towards the gods,
piety, religion,* Trag.; εὐσ. Ζηνός *towards* him, Soph.;
πρὸς εὐσέβειαν = εὐσεβῶς, Id. :—also, like Lat. *pietas,
reverence towards parents, filial respect,* Plat.　　2.
credit or *character for piety,* Soph.; and

εὐσεβέω, f. ήσω, *to live* or *act piously and religiously,*
Theogn., Soph., etc.; εἴς τινα *towards* one, Id.;
εὐσ. τὰ πρὸς θεούς *in matters that respect the gods,*

Id.:—also, εὐσ. θεούς to reverence them, Aesch. From

εὐ-σεβής, ές, (σέβω) Lat. pius, pious, religious, Theogn., Hdt., Att.; εὐσεβὴς χεῖρα righteous in act, Aesch. II. of acts, things, etc., holy, hallowed, held sacred, Id., Eur.:—εὐσεβές [ἐστι], c. inf., Anth.; so, ἐν εὐσεβεῖ [ἐστι] Eur.:—τὸ εὐσ. = εὐσέβεια, Soph., etc. III. Adv. εὐσεβέως, Att. -βῶς, Pind., etc.; εὐσεβῶς ἔχει, for εὐσεβές ἐστι, Soph.:—Comp. -έστερον, Xen.: Sup. -έστατα, Isocr.

εὐσεβία, ἡ, poët. for εὐσέβεια, Theogn., Soph., etc.

εὔ-σελμος, Ep. ἐΰσ-σελμος, ον, (σέλμα) well-benched, with good banks of oars, Hom., Eur.

εὔ-σεπτος, ον, (σέβω) much reverenced, holy, Soph.

εὔ-σημος, ον, (σῆμα) of good signs or omens, Eur. II. easily known by signs, clear to be seen, Aesch. 2. clear to understand, distinct, Soph.

εὐσθενέω, to be strong, healthy, Eur. From

εὐ-σθενής, Ep. ἐΰ-σθ-, ές, (σθένος) stout, lively, Eur.

εὐ-σίπνος, ον, (σίπνα) with full bread-basket, Anth.

εὔ-σκάνδιξ, ῑκος, ὁ, ἡ, abounding in chervil, Anth.

εὔ-σκαρθμος, ον, (σκαίρω) swift-springing, bounding, Il.

εὔ-σκέπαστος, ον, (σκεπάζω) well-protected, Thuc.

εὐσκευέω, (as if from εὔ-σκευος) to' be well equipt, Soph.

εὔ-σκίαστος, ον, (σκιάζω) well-shaded, shadowy, Soph.

εὔ-σκιος, ον, (σκιά) = foreg., Pind., Xen.

εὔ-σκοπος, Ep. ἐΰ-σκ-, ον, (σκοπέω) sharp-seeing, keen-sighted, watchful, Hom. II. far-seen or command-ing a wide view, Xen. II. (σκοπός) shooting well, of unerring aim, Orac. ap. Hdt., Aesch.

εὔσοια, ἡ, happiness, prosperity, Soph. From

εὔ-σοος, ον, safe and well, happy, Theocr.

εὐ-σπειρής, ές, and εὔ-σπειρος, ον, (σπεῖρα) well-turned, wreathing, winding, Anth.

εὐσπλαγχνία, ἡ, good heart, firmness, Eur. From

εὔ-σπλαγχνος, ον, with healthy bowels, Medic. II. metaph. compassionate, N. T.

εὔ-σπορος, Ep. ἐΰ-σπ-, ον, well-sown, Ar., Anth.

ἐΰσ-σελμος, ἐΰσ-σωτρος, Ep. for εὔ-σελμος, εὔ-σωτρος.

εὐστάθεια, Ion. -ίη, ἡ, stability: good health, vigour, Anth.; and

εὐσταθέω, to be steady, favourable, Eur.:—to be calm, tranquil, of the sea, Luc. From

εὐ-σταθής, ές, Ep. ἐΰ-στ-, (ἵσταμαι) well-based, well-built, Hom.

εὐστάθίη, ἡ, Ion. for εὐστάθεια.

εὐστάλεια, ἡ, light equipment, Plut. From

εὐ-σταλής, ές, (στέλλω) well-equipt, Aesch.; of troops, light-armed, Lat. expeditus, Thuc., Xen. 2. well-conducted, favourable, Soph. 3. well-packed, compact, Plut. 4. well-behaved, mannerly, Plat.: —in dress, neat, trim, Luc.

εὔ-στάχυς, υ, rich in corn, Anth.: metaph. blooming, fruitful, Anth.

εὐ-στέφανος, Ep. ἐΰ-στ-, ον, well-crowned or well-girdled, Hom., Hes. II. crowned with walls and towers, Od., Pind.

εὐ-στῐβής, ές, (στίβος) well-trodden, Anth.

εὔστολος, ον, (στολή) = εὐσταλής, Soph.

εὐστόμᾰχος, ον, with good stomach: Adv. -χως, Anth.

εὐστομέω, to sing sweetly, Soph. 2. generally, = εὐφημέω, to refrain from speech, Aesch., Ar. From

εὔ-στομος, ον, (στόμα) with mouth of good size, of dogs, Xen. II. speaking well, eloquent, Anth.; of the cup, making eloquent, Id. 2. like εὔφημος, avoiding words of ill omen, περὶ τούτων εὔστομα κείσθω on these things let me keep a religious silence, Hdt.; εὔστομ' ἔχε peace, be still! Soph.

εὔ-στοος, ον, (στοά) with goodly colonnades, Anth.

εὐ-στόρθυγξ, Ep. ἐΰ-στ-, ὁ, ἡ, from a good trunk, Anth.

εὐστοχία, ἡ, skill in shooting at a mark, good aim, Eur.; χερὸς εὐστ., periphr. for a bow, Id. II. metaph. quickness in guessing, sagacity, Arist.

εὔ-στοχος, ον, well-aimed, Eur., Xen. II. aiming well, Id.:—Adv. εὐστόχως βάλλειν Id. 2. metaph. guessing well, sagacious, Arist.

εὔστρα or εὔστρα, (εὔω) the place for singeing slaugh-tered swine, Ar.

εὔ-στρεπτος, Ep. ἐΰ-στρ-, ον, (στρέφω) well-twisted, of ropes, Od. II. well-plied, nimble, πόδες Anth.

ἐΰ-στρεφής, ές, (στρέφω) well-twisted, of cords, Hom.

εὐ-στροφάλιγξ [ᾰ], ὁ, ἡ, curly, of hair, Anth.

εὔ-στροφος, Ep. ἐΰ-στρ-, ον, (στρέφω) well-twisted, Il. II. easily turning, active, nimble, Eur.

εὐ-στρωτος, ον, well spread with clothes, h. Hom.

εὔ-στῡλος, ον, with goodly pillars, Eur.

εὐ-σύμβλητος, old Att. εὐ-ξύμβ-, ον, = sq., Hdt., Aesch.

εὐ-σύμβολος, old Att. εὐ-ξύμβ-, ον, easy to divine or understand (cf. συμβάλλω III), Aesch. II. easy to deal with, honest, upright, Xen. III. (σύμβολον) affording a good omen, auspicious, Plut.

εὐσυνεσία, ἡ, shrewdness, Arist. From

εὐ-σύνετος, old Att. εὐ-ξύν-, ον, quick of apprehen-sion, Arist.:—Adv. -τως, with intelligence, Comp. -τώτερον, Thuc. II. easily understood, Eur.

εὐ-σύνθετος, ον, well-compounded, Arist.

εὐ-σύνοπτος, ον, (συνόψομαι) easily taken in at a glance, seen at once, Aeschin., etc.

εὔ-σφῡρος, Ep. ἐΰ-σφ-, ον, (σφυρόν) with beautiful ankles, Hes., Eur.

εὔ-σχημος, ον, = εὐσχήμων: Adv. -μως, with decency, Eur.

εὐσχημοσύνη, ἡ, gracefulness, decorum, Xen., Plat.

εὐ-σχήμων, ον, gen. ονος, (σχῆμα) elegant in figure, mien and bearing, graceful, Plat.; Comp. -έστερος, Sup. -έστατος, Id., Xen. 2. in bad sense, with an outside show of goodness, specious, Eur. II. of things, decent, becoming, Id., etc.; τὸ εὔσχημον, Lat. decorum, Plat.:—Adv. -μόνως, with grace and dignity, like a gentleman, Ar., Xen. III. noble, honourable, in rank, N. T.

εὐ-σχῐδής, ές, = sq., Anth.

εὔ-σχιστος, ον, easily split, Anth.

εὐσωμάτέω, (as if from εὐ-σώματος) to be well-grown, to be strong and lusty, Eur., Ar.

εὔ-σωτρος, Ep. ἐΰ-σ-, ον, with good felloes (σῶτρα), i. e. with good wheels, Hes.

εὐ-τᾰκής, ές, (τήκω) easy to soften by heat, Luc.

εὐτακτέω, f. ήσω, to be orderly, behave well, Thuc., Xen., etc.: of soldiers, to obey discipline, Id. From

εὔ-τακτος, ον, well-ordered, orderly, Ar. 2. of soldiers, orderly, well-disciplined, Id., Thuc., etc. II. Adv. -τως, in order, Aesch., Ar.: Comp. -ότερον Dem., -τέρως Xen. Hence

εὐταξία, ἡ, *good arrangement, good condition*, Xen.   2. *good order, discipline*, Thuc.

εὔ-ταρσος, ον, *delicate-footed*, Anth.

εὖτε, relat. Adv. :   **I.** *of Time*, poët. for ὅτε, *when, at the time when :*   2. with Opt., *whenever*, referring to instances in past time, Hes., Aesch.   3. with Subj., εὖτ' ἄν, like ὅταν, *whenever, so often as*, Od.   **II.** *Causal, since, seeing that*, Soph.   **III.** as Adv. of Comparison, for ἠΰτε, *as, even as*, twice in Hom.

εὐ-τείχεος, ον, (τεῖχος) *well-walled*, Il.

εὐτειχής, ές, = foreg., Pind., Eur. ; but in Il. the acc. is εὐτείχεα, not εὐτειχέα.

εὐ-τείχητος, ον, = εὐτείχεος, h. Hom.

εὐτεκνία, ἡ, *the blessing of children, a breed of goodly children*, Eur.

εὔ-τεκνος, ον, (τέκνον) *blest with children*, Eur., etc. ; εὔτ. χρησμός an oracle *that gives promise of fair children*, Id. ; εὔτ. ξυνωρίς a pair *of fair children*, Id. : —Sup. -ώτατος Id.

εὐτέλεια, Ion. -ίη, ἡ, *cheapness*, Hdt. ; εἰς εὐτέλειαν *cheaply*, i. e. *vilely*, Ar.   **II.** *thrift, economy*, ἐπ' εὐτελείᾳ *economically*, Id. ; μετ' εὐτελείας Thuc. ; εἰς εὐτ. συντέμνειν to cut down *to an economical standard*, Id. From

εὐ-τελής, ές, (τέλος) *easily paid for, cheap*, Hdt., Plat., etc. ; εὐτελέστερα δὲ τὰ δεινά the danger would be *more cheaply* met, Thuc. :—Adv. -λῶς, *at a cheap rate*, Xen.   2. *mean, paltry, worthless*, Aesch. ; εὐτελεστέρα ἄσκησις *paltry, requiring no exertion*, Xen.   **II.** *thrifty, frugal*, Id.

εὐ-τερπής, ές, (τέρπω) *delightful*, Pind., Anth.

εὐ-τέχνητος, ον, (τεχνάομαι) *artificially wrought*, Anth.

εὐτεχνία, ἡ, *skill in art*, Luc., Anth. From

εὔ-τεχνος, ον, (τέχνη) *ingenious*, Anth.

εὐ-τλήμων, Dor. -τλάμων [ᾱ], ον, gen. ονος, (τλῆναι) *much-enduring, steadfast*, Aesch., Eur.

ἐΰ-τμητος, ον, (τέμνω) *well-cut*, of leatherwork, Il.

εὐτοκία, ἡ, *happy child-birth*, Anth. From

εὔ-τοκος, ον, (τίκτω) *bringing forth easily*, Arist.

εὐτολμία, ἡ, *courage, boldness*, Eur. From

εὔ-τολμος, ον, (τόλμα) *brave-spirited, courageous*, Aesch., Xen. Adv. -μως, Tyrtae., Aesch.

εὔ-τονος, ον, (τείνω) *well-strung, vigorous*, Plat. :—Adv. -νως, *vigorously*, Ar.

εὐ-τόρνευτος, ον, = sq., Anth.

εὔ-τορνος, ον, *well-turned, rounded, circular*, Eur.

εὐ-τράπεζος, ον, (τράπεζα) *hospitable*, Aesch.

εὐτραπελία, ἡ, *wit, liveliness*, Lat. *urbanitas*, Arist., Plut.   2. in bad sense, *jesting, ribaldry*, N. T.

εὐ-τράπελος, ον, (τρέπω) *easily turning* or *changing*, λόγος εὐτρ. a *dexterous, ready* plea, Ar. :—Adv. -λως, *dexterously, without awkwardness*, Thuc.   2. *ready with an answer, witty*, Lat. *lepidus*, Arist.   **b.** in bad sense, *jesting, ribald*, Isocr.   3. *tricky, dishonest*, Pind.

εὐ-τράφής, ές, (τρέφω) *well-fed, well-grown, thriving, fat*, Eur., etc.   **II.** act. *nourishing*, Aesch.

εὐ-τρεπής, ές, (τρέπω) *readily turning* : generally, *ready*, Eur. ; εὐτρεπὲς ποιεῖσθαί τι Id. :—Adv., εὐτρεπῶς ἔχειν to be *in a state of preparation*, Dem.

εὐτρεπίζω, f. Att. ιῶ, to *make ready, get ready*, ξίφος

Aesch., Eur., etc. ; εὐτρ. τὰ τείχη to *restore* them, Xen. :—Pass. *to be made ready*, Eur. :—Med. *to get ready for oneself*, or something *of one's own*, Thuc.   **II.** to *win over, conciliate*, τινά τινι Xen. ; so in Med., Id. ; in pf. pass., ἅπαντας ηὐτρέπισται Dem.

εὔ-τρεπτος, ον, (τρέπω) *easily changing*, Plut.

εὐ-τρεφής, Ep. ἐΰ-τρ-, ές, (τρέφω) *well-fed*, Od., Eur.

εὔ-τρητος, Ep. ἐΰ-τρ-, ον, (τιτράω) *well-pierced*, of ears for earrings, Il. : *porous*, Anth.

εὐ-τρίαινα, ὁ, Aeol. for -νης, *with goodly trident*, Pind.

εὔ-τρῐχος, ον, = εὔθριξ, Eur. From

εὔ-τροπος, ον, (τρέπω) *versatile*, Arist.

εὐτροφία, ἡ, *good nurture, thriving condition*, Plat.

εὔ-τροφος, ον, (τρέφω) *well-nourished*.

εὐ-τρόχᾰλος, Ep. ἐΰ-τρ-, ον, (τρέχω) *running well, quick-moving*, Anth.   **II.** *well-rounded*, Hes.

εὔ-τροχος, Ep. ἐΰ-τρ-, ον, *well-wheeled*, Hom., Eur.   2. *quick-running, running easily*, of a running cord, Xen. ; εὔτροχος γλῶσσα a *ready, glib tongue*, Eur.   **II.** *well-rounded, round*, Anth.

εὐτῠκάζομαι, Dep. *to make ready*, Aesch. From

εὔτῠκος, ον, rare form for sq., *ready*, Aesch., Theocr.

εὔ-τυκτος, ον, (τεύχω) *well-made, well-wrought*, Hom.   2. *ready*, Hdt.

εὐτῠχέω : impf. ηὐτύχουν or εὐτ- : f. ήσω : aor. 1 ηὐτύχησα or εὐτ- : pf. ηὐτύχηκα or εὐτ- : 3 pl. plqpf. ηὐτυχήκεσαν : (εὐτυχής) :—to *be well off, successful, prosperous*, Hdt., etc. ; c. part. *to succeed in doing*, Eur., etc. :—εὐτύχει, like Lat. *vale*, at the close of letters, etc. ; so, ἀλλ' εὐτυχοίης Trag. :—Pass., ἱκανὰ τοῖς πολεμίοις εὐτύχηται (impers.) they *have had success* enough, Thuc.   2. of things, *to turn out well, prosper*, Aesch., Soph., etc. Hence

εὐτύχημα, ατος, τό, *a piece of good luck, a happy issue, a success*, Eur., Xen., etc.

εὐ-τῠχής, ές, (τυγχάνω) *well off, successful, lucky, fortunate, prosperous*, Hdt., Att. ; εὐτ. ἱκέσθαι τινί to *come with blessings to him*, Soph. :—τὸ εὐτυχές, = εὐτυχία, Thuc.   **II.** Adv. -χῶς, Pind., Trag., etc. ; Ion. -χέως, Hdt. : Comp. -έστερον, Eur., etc. ; Sup. -έστατα, Hdt. Hence

εὐτῠχία, ἡ, *good luck, success, prosperity*, Hdt., Trag., etc. ; εὐτυχίᾳ χρῆσθαι Plat. :—in pl. *successes*, Thuc.

εὔ-υδρος, ον, (ὕδωρ) *well-watered, abounding in water*, Pind., Hdt.   2. of a river, *with beautiful water*, Eur.

εὔ-υμνος, ον, *celebrated in hymns*, h. Hom.

εὐ-ὑπέρβλητος, ον, (ὑπερβάλλω) *easily overcome*, Arist.

εὐ-ὕφής, ές, (ὑφή) *well-woven*, Arist.

εὐφάμέω, εὔφᾱμος, Dor. for εὐφημ-.

εὐ-φᾰρέτρης, ου, ὁ, Dor. -ας, α, (φαρέτρα) *with beautiful quiver*, Soph.

εὐ-φεγγής, ές, (φέγγος) *bright, brilliant*, Aesch.

εὐφημέω, Dor. εὐφᾱμέω, f. ήσω, (εὔφημος) to *use words of good omen*, opp. to δυσφημέω :   **I.** *to avoid all unlucky words*, Horace's *male ominatis parcere verbis* : hence, *to keep a religious silence*, Il., Hdt., etc. ; Imper., εὐφήμει, εὐφημεῖτε *hush! be still!* Lat. *favete linguis*, Ar., Plat.   **II.** *to shout in praise* or *honour* of any one, or *in triumph*, Aesch., Ar.   2. c. acc. *to honour by praise, speak well of*, Xen.   **III.** *to sound triumphantly*, Aesch.

εὐφημία, ἡ, *the use of words of good omen*, opp. to

δυσφημία: **I.** *abstinence from inauspicious language, religious silence,* Trag.; εὐφημίαν ἴσχε =εὐφήμει, Soph.; εὐφημία 'στω, a proclamation of *silence* before a prayer, Ar. **II.** *in positive sense, auspiciousness, fairness,* Aeschin. :—esp. *a fair name* for a bad thing, *euphemism,* Id. **III.** *prayer and praise, worship, honour,* Eur.; in pl. *songs of praise, lauds,* Pind.

εὔ-φημος, Dor. **εὔ-φᾶμος, ον,** (φήμη) *uttering sounds of good omen,* or *abstaining from inauspicious words,* i. e. *religiously silent,* opp. to δύσφημος, Aesch., etc.; εὐφήμου στόμα φροντίδος ἱέντες *uttering words of religious* thought, i. e. *keeping a holy silence,* Soph.; so, ὑπ᾽ εὐφήμου βοῆς, i. e. *in silence,* Id.; εὔφημα φώνει, *like* εὐφήμει, Id. **II.** in positive sense, *auspicious,* Aesch., Eur., etc. :—so Adv. *-μως, with* or *in words of good omen,* h. Hom., Aesch.

εὔ-φθογγος, ον, *well-sounding, cheerful,* Theogn., Aesch.

εὐ-φιλής, ές, (φιλέω) *well-loved,* Aesch. **II.** act. *loving well,* c. gen., Id.

εὐ-φίλητος, η, ον, (φιλέω) *well-beloved,* Aesch.

εὐ-φιλό-παις, ὁ, ἡ, *the children's darling,* of a lion's whelp, Aesch.

εὐ-φιλοτίμητος, ον, *ambitious,* Arist.

εὔ-φλεκτος, ον, (φλέγω) *easily set on fire,* Xen.

εὐ-φόρητος, ον, *easily borne, endurable,* τινι Aesch.

εὐ-φόρμιγξ, ιγγος, ὁ, ἡ, *with beautiful lyre* or *playing beautifully on it,* Anth.

εὔ-φορος, ον, (φέρω) *well* or *patiently borne,* Pind. **2.** *easy to bear* or *wear, manageable, light,* ὅπλα Xen. **3.** *spreading rapidly,* of diseases, Luc. **2.** act. *bearing well ;* of a breeze, *favourable,* Xen. **2.** of the body, *active, vigorous,* Id. **3.** *able to endure, patient ;* Adv., εὐφόρως Soph.

εὔ-φορτος, ον, *well-freighted, well-ballasted,* Anth.

εὐ-φραδής, ές, (φράζω) *well-expressed :* Adv., εὐφραδέως ἀγορεύειν *to speak in set terms, eloquently,* Od.

εὐφράδίη, ἡ, Ion. and poët. for εὐφράδεια, Anth.

εὐ-φραίνω, Ep. **ἐΰ-φρ-:** f. Att. εὐφρανῶ, Ion. and Ep. εὐφρανέω, ἐϋφρανέω: aor. 1 εὔφρᾱνα or ηὔφρ-, Ep. εὔφρηνα :—Pass., with fut. med. εὐφρανοῦμαι, Ion. 2 sing. εὐφράνεαι, pass. εὐφρανθήσομαι: aor. 1 εὐφράνθην or ηὔφρ-: (εὔφρων) :—*to cheer, delight, gladden,* Hom., Trag., etc. **II.** Pass. *to make merry, enjoy oneself, be happy,* Od., Hdt.; ἐπί τινι Ar.; ἔν τινι, διά τινος, ἀπό τινος Xen.; c. part., εὐφράνθη ἰδών *was rejoiced at seeing,* Pind.

εὔ-φραστος, ον, (φράζω) *easy to speak* or *utter,* Arist.

εὐ-φρονέων, Ep. **ἐΰ-φρ-,** *well-meaning, well-judging,* Hom. No Verb εὐφρονέω occurs.

εὐφρόνη, ἡ, (εὔφρων) *the kindly time,* euphem. for νύξ, *night,* Hes., Hdt., etc.

εὐφρόνως, Adv. of εὔφρων.

εὐφροσύνη, Ep. **ἐΰφρ-, ἡ,** (εὔφρων) *mirth, merriment,* Od. :—of a banquet, *good cheer, festivity,* Ib. :—in pl. *glad thoughts,* Ib.; *festivities,* Aesch., etc.

εὐφρόσυνος, η, ον, also ος, ον, poët. for εὔφρων :—Adv. *-νως, in good cheer,* Theogn.

εὔ-φρων, Ep. **ἐΰ-φρ-,** (φρήν) *cheerful, gladsome, merry,* of persons making merry, Hom., etc. : Adv. εὐφρόνως, *with good cheer,* Pind., etc. **2.** act. *cheer-*

ing, making glad or *merry,* Il., Aesch., etc. **II.** *later, well-minded, favourable, gracious,* Pind., Aesch., etc. :—Adv., *in this sense,* Id. **III.** =εὔφημος, Id.

εὐ-φυής, ές, (φυή) *well-grown, shapely, goodly,* Il., Eur. **II.** *of good natural disposition,* Xen.; of horses and dogs, Id. **2.** *naturally suited* or *adapted,* εἴς or πρός τι Plat.; c. inf., εὐφυὴς λέγειν Aeschin. :—Adv. εὐφυῶς Dem. **III.** *of good natural parts, clever,* Arist. :—Adv. εὐφυῶς, Plat. Hence

εὐφυΐα, ἡ, *natural goodness of shape, shapeliness,* Plut. **II.** *good natural parts, cleverness, genius,* and morally, *goodness of disposition,* Arist.

εὐ-φύλακτος, ον, (φυλάσσω) *easy to keep* or *guard,* Aesch. :—ἐν εὐφυλάκτῳ εἶναι *to be on one's guard,* Eur.; εὐφυλακτότερα αὐτοῖς ἐγίγνετο *it was easier for them to keep a look-out,* Thuc.

εὔ-φυλλος, ον, (φύλλον) *well-leafed,* Pind., Eur.

εὐφυῶς, Adv. of εὐφυής.

εὐφωνία, ἡ, *goodness of voice,* Xen. From

εὔ-φωνος, ον, (φωνή) *sweet-voiced, musical,* Pind., Aesch. **2.** *loud-voiced,* of a herald, Xen., Dem.

εὐ-χαίτης, ου, ὁ, (χαίτη) *with beautiful hair :* of trees, *with beautiful leaves,* Anth.

εὔ-χαλκος, ον, *wrought of fine brass* or *well-wrought in brass,* Hom., Aesch.

εὐ-χάλκωτος, ον, (χαλκόω)=foreg., Anth.

εὔ-χαρις, neut. εὔχαρι, gen. ιτος, *pleasing, engaging, winning, gracious, popular,* Eur., Plat. :—τὸ εὔχαρι *popularity, urbanity,* Xen.

εὐχάριστέω, f. ήσω, *to be thankful, return thanks,* ap. Dem.; and

εὐχαριστία, ἡ, *thankfulness, gratitude,* Decret. ap. Dem. **2.** *a giving of thanks.* From

εὐ-χάριστος, ον, (χαρίζομαι)=εὔχαρις, *winning,* Xen.: of things, *agreeable, pleasant,* Id. :—Adv., τελευτᾶν τὸν βίον εὐχαρίστως *to die happily,* Hdt. **II.** *grateful, thankful,* Lat. *gratus,* Id., Xen.

εὔ-χειρ, ειρος, ὁ, ἡ, *quick* or *ready of hand, expert, dexterous,* Pind., Soph.

εὐ-χείρωτος, ον, (χειρόω) *easy to master* or *overcome,* Aesch., Xen.

εὐχέρεια, ἡ, *dexterity,* Plat., etc. **II.** *readiness, proneness,* εὐχ. πονηρίας *proclivity to evil,* Id. **2.** *licentiousness, recklessness,* Aesch.

εὐ-χερής, ές, (χείρ) *easily handled, easy to deal with, easy,* εὐχερές ἐστι, c. inf., Batr.; πάντα ταῦτ᾽ ἐν εὐχερεῖ ἔθου *didst make light of them,* Soph. :—Adv. *-ρῶς,* Id. **2.** of persons, *manageable, accommodating, kind, yielding,* Soph. :—Adv., εὐχερῶς φέρειν Plat., etc.; Comp. *-έστερον,* Xen. **3.** *in bad sense, unscrupulous, reckless,* Dem. :—Adv. *-ρῶς,* Id.

εὐχετάομαι, Dep., only in Ep. pres. and impf. εὐχετόωνται, -όωντο, inf. *-άασθαι:* (εὔχομαι) :—*to pray,* Il.; *to make vows,* Hom. **II.** *to boast oneself, profess, brag, boast,* c. inf., τίνες ἔμμεναι εὐχετόωνται; Od., etc.; ἐπ᾽ ἀνδράσιν εὐχ. *to glory over them,* Ib.

εὐχή, ἡ, (εὔχομαι) *a prayer, vow,* Od., etc. : (but the common Homeric words are εὖχος and εὐχωλή); εὐχὴν ἐπιτελέσαι, Lat. *vota persolvere,* Hdt.; ἀποδιδόναι Xen.; κατὰ χιλίων εὐχὴν ποιήσασθαι χιμάρων *to make a vow of a thousand goats,* Ar. **2.** *a mere wish, an aspiration,* as opp. to reality, εὐχαῖς ὅμοια λέγειν *to*

build castles in the air, Plat.　3. *a prayer for evil,*
i.e. *an imprecation,* Aesch., Eur.

εὔ-χῑλος, ον, of a horse, *feeding well,* Xen.

εὔ-χίμᾰρος [ῐ], **ον,** *rich in goats,* Anth.

εὔ-χλοος, ον, contr. **-χλους, ουν, (χλόα)** *verdant,* Soph.

ΕΥΧΟΜΑΙ, Ep. 2 sing. **εὔξεαι:** impf. **ηὐχόμην** or **εὐ-:**
f. **εὔξομαι:** aor. 1 **ηὐξάμην** or **εὐ-:** pf. **εὔγμαι,** plqpf.
ηὔγμην (v. sub fin.) : Dep. : — *to pray, offer prayers,
pay one's vows, make a vow,* Lat. *precari, vota facere,*
θεῷ or **θεοῖς** Hom., etc. ; **πρὸς τοὺς θεούς** Xen., etc. : — c.
dat. commodi, *to pray for one,* Il.　2. c. inf. *to pray
that,* Hom., etc. ; also, **εὔχ. τοὺς θεοὺς δοῦναι** *to pray*
them *to give,* Xen.　3. c. acc. objecti, *to pray for* a
thing, *long* or *wish for,* Pind., Att. ; **εὔχ. τινί τι** *to
pray for* something *for* a person, as Soph.　II. *to
vow* or *promise to do,* c. inf., Hom., Att.　2. c. acc.
rei, like Lat. *vovere, to vow* a thing, Aesch., Ar.　III.
to profess loudly, to boast, vaunt, Il. ; mostly of something of which one has a right to be proud, **πατρὸς ἐξ
ἀγαθοῦ γένος εὔχομαι εἶναι** Ib.　2. simply *to profess*
or *declare,* Od.　IV. as a Pass., **ἐμοὶ μετρίως
εὖκται** I have prayed sufficiently, Plat. : — but Soph.
uses plqpf. **ηὔγμην** in act. sense.

εὔ-χορδος, ον, (χορδή) *well-strung,* Pind.

εὖχος, εος, τό, (εὔχομαι) *the thing prayed for, object of
prayer,* **εὖχος δοῦναι, πορεῖν** to grant one's *prayer,*
Hom. ; **εὖχος ἀρέσθαι** to obtain *it,* Il.　II. *a boast,
vaunt,* Ib., Pind.　III. *a vow, votive offering,* Anth.

εὔ-χρηστος, ον, (χράομαι) *easy to make use of, useful,
serviceable,* Xen., etc.

εὔ-χροής, ές, Ep. for **εὔχροος, δέρμα βόειον εὔχροές** Od.

εὔ-χροος, ον, contr. **-χρους, ουν,** Ion. **-χροιος, ον** :
(χρόα) : — *well-coloured, of good complexion, fresh-
looking, healthy,* Xen., etc. : — Comp. **-οώτερος,** Id.

εὔ-χρῡσος, ον, *rich in gold,* of the Pactolus, Soph.

εὔ-χρως, ων, = **εὔχροος,** Ar.

εὐχωλή, ἡ, (εὔχομαι) Ep. form of **εὐχή,** *a prayer, vow,*
Hom.　II. *a boast, vaunt,* Il. : *a shout of triumph,*
Ib.　2. *an object of boasting, a boast, glory,* **καδ δέ
κεν εὐχωλὴν Πριάμῳ λίποιεν Ἑλένην** Ib.　Hence

εὐχωλιμαῖος, α, ον, *bound by a vow,* Hdt.

εὔ-ψάμᾰθος, ον, *sandy,* Anth.

εὐψῡχέω, f. ήσω, *to be of good courage,* N. T.　II.
imper. **εὐψύχει** farewell, Inscr. on tombs, Anth.

εὐψῡχία, ἡ, *good courage, high spirit,* Aesch., etc. From

εὔ-ψῡχος, ον, (ψυχή) *of good courage, stout of heart,
courageous,* Lat. *animosus,* Aesch., etc. ; **τὸ ἐς τὰ ἔργα
εὔψυχον** Thuc. ; **εὐψυχότατοι πρὸς τὸ ἐπιέναι** Id. : —
Adv. **-χως,** Xen.

ΕΥΩ, f. εὔσω: aor. 1 **εὖσα:** — *to singe,* of singeing off
swine's bristles, Hom.

εὐ-ώδης, ες, (ὄδωδα) *sweet-smelling, fragrant,* Hom.,
etc. ; **εὐωδέστατος** Hdt.　Hence

εὐωδία, Ion. **-ίη, ἡ,** *a sweet smell,* Hdt., Xen.

εὐ-ώδῑν, ῑνος, ὁ, ἡ, *happy as a parent, fruitful,* Anth.

εὐ-ώλενος, ον, (ὠλένη) *fair-armed,* Pind., Eur.

εὔ-ωνος, ον, *of fair price, cheap* (Fr. *à bon marché*),
Xen., Dem., etc.

εὐ-ώνῠμος, ον, (ὄνυμα, Aeol. for **ὄνομα)** *of good name,
honoured,* Hes., Pind., etc.　2. *of good omen,
prosperous, fortunate,* Id., Plat.　II. euphemistic
for **ἀριστερός** (which was a word of ill omen), *left,* on

the left hand, Hdt., Soph., etc. ; **ἐξ εὐωνύμου χειρός** or
ἐξ εὐωνύμου, *on the left,* Hdt.

εὐ-ῶπις, ιδος, ἡ, (ὤψ) *fair to look on,* Od., Pind.

εὐ-ωπός, όν, = **εὐώψ,** Eur. ; **εὐ. πύλαι** *friendly gates,* Id.

εὐωρῐάζω, *to be negligent,* Aesch.　From

εὔ-ωρος, ον, (ὤρα) *careless, τινος* about a thing.

εὐ-ωχέω, f. ήσω : — Med., f. **-ήσομαι :** aor. 1 **εὐωχησάμην,**
also in pass. form **εὐωχήθην :** (**εὖ, ἔχω**) : — *to treat*
or *feed well, entertain sumptuously,* Hdt., Att. : —
Med. *to fare sumptuously, feast,* Hdt. ; **κρέα εὐωχ.**
to feast upon, enjoy, Xen. ; of animals, *to eat their
fill,* Ar., Xen.　II. metaph., **εὐωχεῖν τινα καινῶν λόγων** *to entertain* him *with* novelties, Theophr. : —
Med. *to relish, enjoy,* c. gen., **τοῦ λόγου** Plat.
Hence

εὐωχία, ἡ, *good cheer, feasting,* Ar., etc. : — metaph.
λόγων εὐωχίαι feasts of reason, Anth.

εὐ-ώψ, ῶπος, ὁ, ἡ, (ὤψ) *fair to look on,* Soph.

ἐφᾱ, Dor. for **ἔφη,** 3 sing. aor. 2 of **φημί.**

ἐφαάνθη, Ep. for **ἐφάνθη,** 3 sing. aor. 1 of **φαίνω.**

ἔφαβος, ἐφαβικός, Dor. for **ἐφηβ-.**

ἐφ-αγιστεύω, f. σω, *to perform obsequies over* the grave,
Soph.

ἐφ-αγνίζω, f. σω, = foreg., **τὰ πάντ' ἐφαγνίσαι** to perform
all *the obsequies,* Soph.

ἔφαγον, aor. 2 of **ἐσθίω.**

ἐφαιρέομαι, Pass. *to be chosen to succeed* another, Thuc.

ἐφ-άλλομαι: 3 sing. Ep. aor. 2 **ἐπ-ᾶλτο** (cf. **ἀναπάλλω**),
with part. **ἐπ-άλμενος, ἐπι-άλμενος :** Dep. : — *to spring
upon, assail,* c. dat., **Τρώεσσιν ἐπάλμενος** Il. : — also,
without hostile sense, c. gen., **ἐπιάλμενος ἵππων** *having
leaped upon* the chariot, Ib.

ἔφ-αλος, ον, (ἅλς) *on the sea,* of seaports, Il., Soph.

ἐφ-ᾱλόω, Dor. for **ἐφ-ηλόω.**

ἐφ-άμαν [φᾰ], Dor. for **ἐφάμην,** aor. 2 med. of **φημί.**

ἐφ-άμερος, ἐφ-ᾱμέριος, Dor. for **ἐφ-ημ-.**

ἐφ-άμιλλος [ᾰ], **ον, (ἅμιλλα)** *a match for, equal to,
rivalling,* **ἐφ. γίγνεσθαί τινι** Xen.　II. pass. *regarded
as an object of rivalry* or *contention,* Dem.

ἔφᾰν, Aeol. and Ep. for **ἔφασαν,** 3 pl. aor. 2 of **φημί.**

ἐφ-ανδάνω, f. -αδήσω : Ep. **ἐπι-ανδάνω :** — *to please, be
grateful to,* c. dat., **ἐμοὶ δ' ἐπιανδάνει οὕτως** Il. ; **τοῖσιν
δ' ἐπιήνδανε μῦθος** Od.

ἐφ-άπαξ, Adv. *once for all,* N. T., etc.　II. *at
once, at the same time,* Ib.

ἐφ-απλόω, f. ώσω, *to spread* or *fold over,* Babr.

ἐφ-άπτω, Ion. **ἐπ-άπτω:** f. **ψω:** — *to bind on* or *to,
λύουσα ἢ 'φάπτουσα* undoing or *making fast,* Soph. ;
τοῦργον ὡς ἐφάψειεν τόδε that she *had made fast* (i. e.
perpetrated) the deed, Id. : — Pass., 3 sing. pf. and
plqpf. **ἐφῆπται, -το,** *is* or *was hung over* one, *impends
over, is fixed as* one's *doom,* c. dat., **Τρώεσσι κήδε' ἐφῆπται** Il.　II. Med. *to lay hold of, grasp, reach,* c.
gen., Od., Theogn., Soph.　2. *to lay hold of* with
the mind, *attain to,* Lat. *assequi,* c. gen., Plat.　3.
in Pind. also c. dat. (like **θιγγάνω, ψαύω**), *to apply oneself to.*　4. Hdt. uses part. pf. pass. with gen.,
εἴδεος ἐπαμμένος *possessed of* a certain degree of
beauty.　5. *to follow, come next,* Theocr.

ἐφ-αρμόζω, Att. **-όττω,** Dor. **-όσδω:** f. **-αρμόσω :**　I.
intr. *to fit on* or *to, to fit* one, c. dat., Il.　2. *to be
adapted to,* **τινί** Arist.　II. trans. *to fit* one thing

to another, *fit on, put on*, τί τινι Hes., Theocr. :— Med. *to put on oneself*, Anth. 2. *to suit, accommodate*, Xen.; πίστιν ἐφαρμόσαι *to add fitting* assurance, Soph. Hence

ἐφαρμοστέον, verb. Adj. *one must adapt*, τί τινι Luc.

ἐφ-έδρα, Ion. ἐπ-έδρη, ἡ, *a sitting by* or *before* a place : *a siege, blockade*, Lat. *obsessio*, Hdt.

ἐφεδρεία, ἡ, *a sitting upon*. II. *a sitting by, waiting for one's turn*, of pugilists, Plat. : *a lying in wait*, Plut. From

ἐφεδρεύω, f. σω, (ἔφεδρος) *to sit upon, rest upon*, Eur. II. *to lie by* or *near, lie in wait*, of an enemy waiting to attack, Thuc.; ἐφ. τινί *to keep watch over*, Eur.: generally, *to watch for*, Dem. III. *to halt*, Plut.

ἐφεδρήσσω, poët. for foreg., *to sit by*, τινί Anth.

ἔφ-εδρος, ον, (ἕδρα) *sitting* or *seated upon*, c. gen., λεόντων ἔφεδρε, of Cybelé, Soph.; ἔφ. ἵππου Eur. II. *sitting by, at*, or *near*, τῶν πηδαλίων, of a pilot, Plat.; also c. dat., Eur. : absol. *close at hand*, Soph. 2. *posted in support* or *reserve*, Eur. 3. *lying by*, of a third combatant (pugilist or wrestler), *who sits by to fight the conqueror*, Pind., Ar., Xen. :—μόνος ὢν ἔφεδρος δισσοῖς, i. e. one *against* two, with no one to take his place if beaten, Aesch. 4. *a successor*, Hdt.

ἐφ-έζομαι, Dep., chiefly used in part. and 3 sing. impf.; inf. ἐφέζεσθαι :—*to sit upon*, c. dat., Hom., Ar. ;—also c. gen., Pind. ; and c. acc., Aesch., Eur. 2. *to sit by* or *near*, Od., Aesch.

ἐφῆκα, Ep. for ἐφῆκα, aor. 1 of ἐφίημι.

ἐφείην, aor. 2 opt. of ἐφίημι :—ἐφείω, Ep. subj.

ἐφεῖναι, aor. 2 inf. of ἐφίημι.

ἐφείς, aor. 2 part. of ἐφίημι.

ἐφείω, Ep. for ἐφέω, aor. 2 subj. of ἐφίημι.

ἔφ-εκτος, ον, *containing* 1 + ⅙ : τόκος ἔφ. when ⅙ of the principal was paid as interest, = 16⅔ p. cent., Dem.

ἐφ-έλκω, Ion. ἐπ-: f. ἐφέλξω: but the aor. 1 in use is ἐφείλκυσα (cf. ἕλκω) :—*to draw on, drag* or *trail after* one, *ἐπ. τὰς οὐράς*, of long-tailed sheep, Hdt.; ἵππον ἐκ τοῦ βραχίονος ἐπ. *to lead* a horse by a rein upon the arm, Id.; ναῦς ὡς ἐφέλξω *will take in tow*, Eur. 2. *to bring on, bring in its train*, Id. 3. *to drink off*, Id. II. Pass., ἐφελκομένοιο πόδεσσι *with feet trailing after* him, of one who is dragged lifeless away, Il.; ἐφέλκετο ἔγχος, i. e. sticking in his hand, Ib.; ἐπελκόμενος *trailing behind*, of a boat, Hdt.; οἱ ἐπελκόμενοι *the stragglers* of an army, Id. 2. *to be attracted*, h. Hom., Thuc. III. Med. *to draw to oneself, attract*, αὐτὸς γὰρ ἐφέλκεται ἄνδρα σίδηρος *the very sight of arms attracts* men, i. e. *tempts* them *to use it*, Od. 2. *to draw* or *pull over*, Plut.; ἐφ. ὀφρῦς *to frown*, Anth. 3. *to bring on consequences*, Eur., Xen. 4. *to assume*, Plat., Theocr.

ἐφέμεν, Ep. for ἐφεῖναι, aor. 2 inf. of ἐφίημι.

ἐφ-έννυμι, v. ἐπιέννυμι.

ἐφ-εξῆς, Ion. ἐπ-εξῆς : Adv. *in order, in a row, one after another*, Hdt., Eur., Xen. 2. c. dat. *next to*, Plat. II. *in succession, without exception*, πᾶσαν τὴν γῆν ἐφ. Xen.; τὴν Ἑλλάδα πᾶσαν ἐφ. Dem. 2. of Time, τρεῖς ἡμέρας ἐπεξῆς Hdt.; τέσσαρες ἐφ. Ar. 3. *thereupon, after*, εὐθὺς ἐφ. Dem.

ἐφεξις, εως, ἡ, (ἐπέχω) *an excuse, pretext*, τοῦ ἔφεξιν ; =τίνος χάριν ; Ar.

ἐφ-έπω : impf. Ep. ἔφεπον, Ion. ἐφέπεσκον : f. ἐφέψω : aor. 2 ἐπέσπον, inf. ἐπισπεῖν, part. ἐπισπών :—*to go after, follow, pursue*, c. acc., Il. II. *to drive on, urge on*, [ἵππους] ἐφέπων μάστιγι Ib.; and c. dat. pers., Πατρόκλῳ ἔφεπε ἵππους *drove* them *against* him, Ib. III. *to follow* a pursuit, *busy oneself about* it, c. acc., Hom.; ἐφ. Θήβας *to administer, govern* it, Aesch. 2. c. acc. loci, *to search, explore, traverse*, Lat. *obire*, Hom., Hes. IV. *to come suddenly upon, encounter, incur*, πότμον ἐπισπεῖν Hom.; ὀλέθριον ἦμαρ ἐπ. Il.

B. Med. ἐφέπομαι : impf. -ειπόμην : f. -έψομαι : aor. 2 -εσπόμην, imper. ἐπί-σπου, inf. ἐπι-σπέσθαι :—*to follow, pursue*, c. dat., Od., Hdt., etc. II. *to follow, accompany, attend*, Il., Hdt.; ἐπισπέσθαι ποσίν *to follow* on foot, i. e. keep up with, Hdt. ; εἴ οἱ τύχη ἐπίσποιτο if fortune *attend* him, Id. :—absol., Thuc. 2. *to obey, attend to*, θεοῦ ὀμφῇ Od.; ἐπισπόμενοι μενεῖ σφῷ *giving the reins to* their passion, Ib.; βουλῇ ἐπισπέσθαι πατρός Aesch., etc. :—absol., ὁ ἐπισπόμενος, opp. to ὁ πείσας, Thuc. :—also *to agree, approve*, in tmesi, ἢν δ' ἔσπωνται θεοὶ ἄλλοι Od. 3. *to follow* an argument, Plat.

ἐφ-ερπύζω, later pres. for sq., Anth.

ἐφ-έρπω : f. ψω, but the aor. 1 in use is ἐφείρπυσα :—*to creep upon*, Ar. II. poët. *to come on* or *over, come gradually* or *stealthily upon*, τινά Aesch.; ἐπ' ὅσσοισι νὺξ ἐφέρπει Eur. 2. absol. *to go forth, proceed*, Aesch.; in part. *advancing, future*, Pind.

ἔφες, aor. 2 imper. of ἐφίημι.

Ἐφέσια, ίων, τά, *the feast of Ephesian Artemis*, Thuc.

ἐφέσιμος δίκη, ἡ, *a suit in which there was the right of appeal*, Dem. From

ἔφεσις, εως, ἡ, (ἐφίημι) *a throwing* or *hurling at, a shooting*, Plat. 2. as Att. law-term, *an appeal to another court*, Dem. II. (ἐφίεμαι) *appetite, desire*, Arist.

ἐφ-έσπερος, ον, (ἑσπέρα) *western*, Soph.

ἐφέσσαι, -ασθαι, Ep. aor. 1 act. and med. inf. of ἐφίζω :—ἔφεσσαι, imper. med. :—ἐφέσσεσθαι, fut. inf. med.

ἐφ-εστᾰότες, Ep. for -ηκότες, pf. part. pl. of ἐφίστημι : —ἐφ-έστασαν, for -εστήκεσαν, 3 pl. plqpf. :—ἐφ-εστᾶσιν, for -εστήκᾰσι, 3 pl. pf.

ἐφ-έστιος, Ion. ἐπ-ίστιος, ον, (ἑστία) *at one's own fireside, at home*, Od.; ἐφέστιοι ὅσσοι ἔασιν *as many as have a home of their own*, Il.; ἐφέστιον πῆξαι σκῆπτρον (i. e. ἐπὶ τῇ ἑστίᾳ) Soph. :—of suppliants who claim protection by *sitting by the fireside*, Hdt.; δόμων ἐφ. *an inmate* of the temple, Aesch.; also merely of *guests*, Soph. II. generally, *of* or *in the house* or *family*, Lat. *domesticus*, πόνοι δόμων ἐφέστιοι Aesch. ; ἐφ. δόμοι *the chambers of the house*, Id. :—Ion. ἐπίστιον, τό, *a household, family*, Hdt. : —θεοὶ ἐφ. *the household gods*, Lat. *Lares* or *Penates*, Ζεὺς ἐπίστιος, ἐφέστιος, *as presiding over hospitality*, Id., Soph.

ἐφεστρίδιον, τό, Dim. of sq., Luc.

ἐφεστρίς, ίδος, ἡ, (ἐφέννυμι) *an upper garment, wrapper*, Xen., Plut.

ἐφέτης, ου, ὁ, (ἐφίημι) a commander, Aesch.   II.
ἐφέται, οἱ, at Athens, the Ephetae, a court of Eupa-
tridae, created by Draco to try cases of homicide, Plut.
ἐφετμή, ἡ, (ἐφίημι) a command, behest, Hom., etc.
ἐφευρετής, οῦ, ὁ, an inventor, contriver, N. T.   From
ἐφ-ευρίσκω, Ion. ἐπ-: f. ἐφευρήσω: aor. 2 ἐφηῦρον or
ἐφεῦ-:—to light upon, discover, Od.; with a partic.
to find one doing so and so, Hom., Soph.:—so in
Pass., μὴ ἐπευρεθῇ πρήσσων Hdt.   II. to invent
or bring in besides, generally to invent, Pind., Eur.
ἐφ-εψιάομαι, Dep. to mock or scoff at, τινι, Lat. illudere, Ep. 3 pl. ἐφεψιόωνται Od.
ἐφεώρων, impf. of ἐφοράω.
ἐφ-ηβάω, Ion. ἐπ-, f. ήσω, to come to man's estate,
grow up io manhood, Hdt., Aesch., Xen.
ἐφηβεία, ἡ, (ἐφηβεύω) puberty, man's estate, Anth.
ἐφήβειος, α, ον, (ἔφηβος) youthful, Anth.
ἐφηβεύω, (ἔφηβος) to arrive at man's estate.
ἐφηβικός, ή, όν, Dor. ἐφαβ-, ά, όν, of or for an ἔφηβος,
Theocr. From
ἔφ-ηβος, Dor. ἔφ-ᾱβος, ὁ, one arrived at puberty
(ἥβη) a youth of 18 years when the Athen. youth
underwent his δοκιμασία and was registered as a citizen, Xen., etc.   II. a throw on the dice, Anth.
ἐφηβοσύνη, ἡ, the age of an ἔφηβος, puberty, Anth.
ἐφ-ηγέομαι, f. -ήσομαι, Dep. to lead to a place: esp. to
lead the magistrate to a house where a criminal lay
concealed, Dem.
ἐφ-ήδομαι, Pass. to exult over a person, τινι Xen.
ἐφῆκα, aor. 1 of ἐφίημι.
ἐφ-ήκω, f. ξω, to have arrived, Soph., Thuc.   2. ὅσον ἂν
ἡ μόρα ἐφήκῃ so far as the division reaches, so much
space as it occupies, Xen.
ἐφ-ῆλιξ, ἴκος, ὁ, ἡ, = ἔφηβος, Anth.
ἔφ-ημαι, pf. pass. used as a pres., (cf. ἧμαι) to be set
or seated on, to sit on, θρόνῳ Od.; also c. gen., θινὸς
ἐφήμενος Soph.:—to be seated at or in, δόμοις Aesch.:
—also c. acc., βρέτας ἐφήμενος Id.   II. to act as
assessor (cf. ἔφεδρος), Παλλὰς οἵ τ᾽ ἐφήμενοι Id.
ἐφημερία, ἡ, (ἐφ᾽ ἡμέραν) a division (of the priests)
for the daily service of the temple, N. T.
ἐφ-ημέριος, Dor. ἐφ-ᾱμ-, ον and α, ον, (ἡμέρα) on,
for or during the day, the day through, Od.; by
day, Pind.   2. for a day only, for the day, ἐφημέρια φρονέοντες taking thought for the day only,
Od.:—often of men, ἐφημέριοι creatures of a day,
Aesch., etc.   3. hired for the day, Theogn.
ἐφ-ημερίς, ίδος, ἡ, (ἡμέρα) a diary, journal, such as
Caesar's Commentarii, Plut.
ἐφ-ήμερος, ον, Dor. ἐφ-ᾱμ-, Aeol. ἐπ-άμ-, (ἡμέρα)
living but a day, short-lived, Pind., Eur., etc.   2.
of men, ἐφήμεροι creatures of a day, Pind., Aesch.   II.
for the day, daily, Plut., etc.   III. φάρμακον ἐφ.
killing on the same day, Id.
ἐφημοσύνη, ἡ, (ἐφίημι) = ἐφετμή, Pind., Soph.
ἔφηνα, aor. 1 of φαίνω.
ἐφῆπται, -ῆπτο, 3 sing. pf. and plqpf. of ἐφάπτω.
ἔφησθα, Ep. and Aeol. for ἔφης.
ἐφήσω, fut. of ἐφίημι.
ἐφθάρην [ᾰ], aor. 2 pass. of φθείρω: ἔφθαρμαι, pf.
pass., Ion. 3 pl. ἐφθάραται.
ἔφθασα, Dor. ἔφθαξα, aor. 1 of φθάνω.

ἐφθεγξάμην, aor. 1 of φθέγγομαι.
ἐφθ-ημίμερής, containing seven halves, i. e. 3½, of the
first 3½ feet of a Hexameter or Iambic Trimeter.
ἔφθην, aor. 2 of φθάνω.
ἔφθῐθεν, Ep. for -ησαν, 3 pl. aor. 1 pass. of φθίω, φθίνω:
—ἔφθῐται, 3 sing. pf. pass.:—ἔφθῖσο, -ιτο, 2 and
3 sing. plqpf. pass.:—ἐφθίατο, Ion. for ἔφθιντο, 3 pl.
plqpf.
ἑφθός, ή, όν, verb. Adj. of ἕψω, boiled, dressed, Hdt.,
Eur., etc.   2. ἑφθὸς χρυσός refined gold, Simon.
ἐφίδρωσις, εως, ἡ, (ἱδρόω) superficial perspiration, Plut.
ἐφ-ιζάνω, only in pres. and impf., to sit at or in a
place, c. dat., Il.; ὕπνος ἐπὶ βλεφάροισιν ἐφίζανεν
sleep sate upon, Ib.
ἐφ-ίζω, Dor. -ίσδω: I. Causal, in Ep. aor. 1,
to set upon, ἐφέσσαι to set me ashore, Od.:—Med.,
γούνασιν οἷσιν ἐφεσσάμενος having set [me] on his
knees, Ib.; imperat., ἔφεσσαί με νηὸς set me on board
the ship, Ib.   II. intr. in pres. and impf. ἐφῖζον, Ion.
ἐφίζεσκον, to sit at or by, Ib., Pind., etc.
ἐφ-ίημι, Ion. ἐπ-, f. ἐφήσω, aor. 1 ind. ἐφῆκα, Ep.
ἐφέηκα, aor. 2 imperat. ἔφες, subj. ἐφείω, ῃς, Att.,
ἐφῇς, part. ἐφείς:—Med., part. ἐφιέμενος, f. ἐφή-
σομαι:—3 sing. impf. ἐφίει, as if from ἐφιέω:—to
send to one, Il.   2. c. inf. to set on or incite to do,
ἐφῆκε ἀείσαι Od.; ἐφ. τινὰ χαλεπῆναι, etc., Il.   3.
of things, to throw or launch at one, ὅς τοι ἐφῆκε
βέλος Ib., etc.; ἐφ. οἰστὸν ἐπί τινι Eur.; ἐφ. χεῖράς
τινι to lay hands on him, Od.   4. of events,
destinies, etc., to send upon one, τοῖσιν πότμον ἐφῆκεν
Il., etc.   5. to send against, in hostile sense,
Hdt., etc.:—ἐφ. τὸν ποταμὸν ἐπὶ τὴν χώρην Id.; ἐφῆ-
κας γλῶσσαν did'st let loose, Eur.   6. to throw
into, ἐς λέβητ᾽ ἐφῆκεν μέλη Id.   II. to let go,
loosen, esp. the rein, Plat.:—hence to give up, yield,
Lat. concedere, τινὶ τὴν ἡγεμονίαν Thuc.:—c. inf. to
permit, allow, τινὶ ποιεῖν τι Hdt., Soph., etc.   2.
to give up, leave as a prey, Soph.:—then, seemingly
intr. (sub. ἑαυτόν), to give oneself up to, οὐρίᾳ a fair
wind, Plat.   III. to put the male to the female,
Hdt.   IV. as law-term, to leave to another
to decide, δίκας ἐφ. εἴς τινα Dem.:—and absol. to
appeal, εἰς τοὺς δικαστάς Id.
  B. Med. to lay one's command or behest upon,
Hom., Aesch., etc.:—c. inf., ἐφ. τινὶ ποιεῖν τι Soph.,
Ar.; ἐς Λακεδαίμονα to send orders to L., Thuc.   2.
to allow or permit one to do, Soph., etc.   II. c.
gen. to aim at, Arist.:—to long after, desire, Soph.,
Eur., etc.; c. inf. to desire to do, Eur.
ἐφίητι, Dor. for ἐφίησι.
ἐφ-ικάνω, = sq., Od.
ἐφ-ικνέομαι, Ion. ἐπ-: f. ἐφίξομαι: aor. 2 ἐφικόμην,
Ion. ἐπ-: Dep.:—to reach at, aim at, c. gen., Il.,
Plat., etc.   2. to reach or extend, ἐφ᾽ ὅσον
μνήμη ἐφ. Xen., etc.   3. metaph. to hit or touch
the right points, Lat. rem acu tangere, τῷ λόγῳ ἐφ.
τῶν ἐκεῖ κακῶν Dem.; —so, ἐς τὰ ἄλλα ἐπίκεο Hdt.   4.
to reach, gain, attain to, ἀνδραγαθίας Aeschin.,
etc.   II. c. acc. to come upon, εἴ σε μοῖρ᾽ ἐφίκοιτο
Pind.; dupl. acc., ἐπικέσθαι πληγὰς τὸν Ἑλλησπόντον
to visit it with blows, Hdt. Hence
ἐφικτός, ή, όν, easy to reach, accessible, Plut.

ἐφίλᾱθεν, Dor. and poët. for ἐφιλήθησαν, 3 pl. aor. 1 pass. of φιλέω.

ἐφίλᾱσα, Dor. for ἐφίλησα, aor. 1 of φιλέω.

ἐφίλᾱτο [ῐ], irreg. 3 sing. aor. 1 med. of φιλέω.

ἐφ-ῑμείρω, strengthd. for ἱμείρω, c. gen., Anth.

ἐφ-ίμερος [ῐ], ον, longed for, desired, charming, Hes., Aesch.; c. inf., ἐφ. προσλεύσσειν Soph.

ἐφῑμώθην, aor. 1 pass. of φιμόω.

ἐφ-ιππάζομαι, Dep. to ride upon, Luc.

ἐφ-ιππεύω, to ride upon, Babr.

ἐφ-ίππιος, ον, (ἵππος) for putting on a horse, Xen.:— ἐφίππιον (sc. στρῶμα) τό, a saddle-cloth, Id.

ἐφ-ιππος, ον, on horseback, riding: ἀνδριὰς ἔφ. an equestrian statue, Plut.   II. κλύδων ἔφιππος a rushing wave of horses, Soph.

ἐφ-ίπταμαι, late form of ἐπιπέτομαι, Mosch.

ἐφίσδω, Dor. for ἐφίζω.

ἐφ-ίστημι, Ion. ἐπ–:   A. Causal in pres., impf., fut., and aor. 1:   I. to set or place upon, τί τινι Thuc.; τι ἐπί τινι Xen.: metaph., ἐφ. μοῖραν βίῳ Plat.   II. to set over, Lat. praeficere, ἐφ. τινὰ ὑπαρχόν τισι Hdt., etc.   III. to set up, establish, institute games, Id.   IV. to set by or near to, ἱππέας ἐπιστήσαντες κύκλῳ τὸ σῆμα (= περὶ τὸ σ.) Id.   V. to stop, make halt, Lat. inhibere, Xen.: —absol., ἐπιστήσας (sc. ἑαυτόν, τὸν ἵππον) having halted, Id.   VI. ἐφίστημι τὴν γνώμην κατά τι to fix one's mind upon it, attend to it, and then absol. to give attention, Arist. 2. c. acc. pers. to arrest the attention of, Plut.

B. intr. in Med. and Pass., ἐφίσταμαι, aor. 1 ἐπεστάθην, with pf., plqpf. and aor. 2 act.:—to stand upon, πύργῳ, δίφρῳ, ἐπὶ βηλῷ Il. 2. to be imposed upon, τινι Soph. 3. to stand on the top or surface, τὸ ἐπιστάμενον τοῦ γάλακτος, i.e. cream, Hdt.   II. to be set over, Lat. praeesse, c. dat., Aesch., etc.; also c. gen., Hdt., Eur.:—absol. to be in authority, Hdt., etc.   III. to stand by or near, ἀλλήλοισι Il., etc.: of dreams or visions, to appear to, εὕδοντι ἐπέστη ὄνειρος Hdt. 2. in hostile sense, to stand against, oppose, Hom.: to come upon by surprise, Thuc. 3. of events, to impend, be at hand, Lat. instare, Κῆρες ἐφεστᾶσιν θανάτοιο Il.; πρίν μοι τύχη ἐπέστη Soph.   IV. to halt, stop, in a march, Xen.:— c. gen., ἐπ. τοῦ πλοῦ Thuc.   V. to fix one's mind on, give one's attention to, τινι Eur., Dem.

C. the aor. 1 med. is used in causal sense, to set up, τὰς θύρας Xen.: to set, post, φρουρούς Id.

ἐφλάδον, aor. 2 of φλάζω.

ἐφόβηθεν, Ep. 3 pl. aor. 1 pass. of φοβέω.

ἐφοδεύω, f. σω, (ἔφοδος) to visit, go the rounds, patrol, Xen.:—Pass., ἐφοδεύεται the rounds are made, Ar.   II. c. dat. to watch over, ἀγῶσιν Aesch.

ἐφοδιάζω, Ion. ἐποδ–, f. άσω, (ἐφόδιον) to furnish with supplies for a journey, Lat. viaticum dare, Hdt.   II. Med., πενταδραχμίαν ἑκάστῳ ἐφοδιασάμενος having seen that five drachms were paid to each, Xen.:—metaph. to maintain, ἀργίαν Plut.

ἐφ-όδιον, τό, mostly in pl. ἐφόδια, Ion. ἐπόδια, τά, (ἐφ' ὁδοῦ) like Lat. viaticum, supplies for travelling, money and provisions, Hdt., Dem.:—of an ambassador's travelling-allowance, Ar.; sometimes in sing.,

Thuc., Xen. 2. generally, ways and means, maintenance, support, ἐφόδια τῷ γήρᾳ Dem.; of public money, μιᾶς ἡμέρας ἐφόδια ἐν τῷ κοινῷ Id.

ἔφ-οδος, ον, accessible, Thuc.

ἔφ-οδος, ὁ, one who goes the rounds, Xen.

ἔφ-οδος, ἡ, a way towards, approach, Thuc., Xen.:— access for traffic and intercourse, communication, παρ' ἀλλήλους Thuc. 2. importation, Xen.   II. an onset, attack, assault, Aesch., Thuc., etc.

ἐφοίτη, Dor. for ἐφοίτα, 3 sing. impf. of φοιτάω.

ἐφόλκαιον, τό, (ἐφέλκω) a rudder, Od.

ἐφόλκιον, τό, (ἐφέλκω) a tow-boat: metaph. an appendage, Anth., Plut.

ἐφολκίς, ἡ, = foreg., a burdensome appendage, Eur.

ἐφολκός, όν, (ἐφέλκω) drawing on or towards, enticing, alluring, Thuc.   II. requiring to be drawn on, a laggard, Ar.

ἐφ-ομαρτέω, f. ήσω, to follow close after, Il.

ἐφ-οπλίζω, f. σω: Ep. aor. 1 inf. ἐφοπλίσσαι:—to equip, get ready, prepare, Hom.; so in Med., δόρπα τ' ἐφοπλισόμεθα we will get ready our suppers, Il. 2. to arm against, τινά τινι, so in Med., Anth.

ἐφορᾱτικός, ή, όν, fit for overlooking, ἔργων Xen. From

ἐφ-οράω, Ion. 3 sing. ἐπορᾷ; 3 pl. ἐπορῶσι: —impf. ἐφεώρων, Ion. 3 sing. ἐπώρα:—f. ἐπόψομαι, Ep. also ἐπιόψομαι; the aor. is ἐπεῖδον (q.v.): —to oversee, observe, survey, of the sun, Hom.:—then of the gods, to watch over, observe, take notice of, Od., Hdt., etc.: of a general going his rounds, Thuc.; to visit the sick, Xen. 2. simply, to look upon, view, behold, Od., etc.:—Pass., ὅσον ἐφεωρᾶτο τῆς νήσου as much of it as was in view, Thuc.   II. to look out, choose, ἐπιψόμαι ἥτις ἀρίστη Od., etc.

ἐφορεία, ἡ, (ἐφορεύω) the ephoralty, Xen.

ἐφορεῖον, τό, (ἔφορος) the court of the ephors, Xen.

ἐφορεύω, = ἐφοράω, c. acc., Aesch.; c. gen., Id.   II. (ἔφορος) to be ephor, Thuc., Xen.

ἐφορικός, ή, όν, (ἔφορος) of or for the ephori, Xen.

ἐφ-όριος, α, ον, (ὅρος) on the border or frontier, ap. Dem.

ἐφ-ορμαίνω, to rush on, Aesch.

ἐφ-ορμάω, Ion. ἐπ–, f. ήσω, to stir up, rouse against one, Hom.; ἐπορμῆσαι τοὺς λύκους to set them on, Hdt.; ναύτας ἐφορμήσαντα τὸ πλεῖν having urged them on to sail, Soph.   II. intr. to rush upon, attack, τινι Eur.   III. Pass. and Med. to be stirred up; c. inf. to be eager or desire to do, Hom.:—absol. to rush furiously on, ἔγχει ἐφορμᾶσθαι Il.; ἐφορμηθείς Ib.; and, without hostile sense, to spring forward, Od.:— c. acc. to rush upon, make a dash at, Il.

ἐφ-ορμέω, Ion. ἐπ–, f. ήσω, to lie moored at or over against a place, to blockade it, λαθὼν τοὺς ἐφορμέοντας having escaped the blockading fleet, Hdt.; ἐφ. τῷ λιμένι Thuc. 2. generally, to lie by and watch, Soph., Dem.

ἐφ-ορμή, ἡ, a way of attack, μία δ' οἴη γίγνετ' ἐφορμή only room for one to attack, Od. 2. an assault, attack, Thuc.

ἐφόρμησις, εως, ἡ, (ἐφορμέω) a lying at anchor so as to watch an enemy, blockading, Thuc.: a means of so doing, Id.

ἐφ-ορμίζω, Att. ιῶ, to bring a ship to its moorings (ὅρμος):—Med. and Pass. to come to anchor,

Thuc.　　　II. intr. in Act. *to seek refuge in* a place, c. dat., Anth.

ἔφ-ορμος, ον, *at anchor,* Thuc.

ἔφ-ορμος, ὁ, = ἐφόρμησις, Thuc.

ἔφορος, ὁ, (ἐφοράω) *an overseer, guardian, ruler,* Aesch., Soph.　　II. at Sparta, **ἔφοροι, οἱ,** *the Ephors,* a body of five magistrates, who controlled even the kings, Hdt., etc.

ἐφρασάμην, aor. 1 med. of φράζω.

ἔφριξα, aor. 1 of φρίσσω.

ἐφρύαξα, aor. 1 of φρυάσσω.

ἐφ-υβρίζω, f. σω, *to insult over* one, Il.; c. dat., Soph.; c. acc., in Med., μὴ 'φυβρίζεσθαι νεκρούς Eur.; ἐφύβριζον ἄλλα τε καὶ εἰ *they used insulting language, asking especially whether,* Thuc.　　II. *to exult maliciously over,* Soph.

ἔφυγον, aor. 2 of φεύγω.

ἐφυδριάς, άδος, ἡ, *of the water,* Νύμφη Anth.　From

ἔφ-υδρος, Ion. ἔπ-, ον, (ὕδωρ) *wet, moist, rainy,* of the west wind, Od.　　2. *well-watered,* Hdt.

ἐφ-υμνέω, f. ήσω, *to sing* or *chant after* or *over,* τί τινι Aesch., Soph.　　II. *to sing a dirge besides,* Soph.　　III. *to sing of, descant on,* c. acc., Id.

ἐφ-ύπερθε [ῠ], before a vowel -θεν, Adv. *above, atop, above,* Hom.:—*from above,* Od.:—c. gen., Theocr.

ἐφ-υπνόω, *to sleep meantime,* Aesop.

Ἐφύρα [ῠ], Ion. -ρη, ἡ, *Ephyra,* old name of Corinth, Il.

ἐφύση [ῠ], Dor. for ἐφύσα, 3 sing. impf. of φυσάω.

ἐφ-υστερίζω, f. σω, *to come later,* τὰ ἐφυστερίζοντα = αἱ ὑστεροῦσαι πόλεις, Thuc.

ἐφ-ύω, *to rain upon:*—pf. pass. part. ἐφυσμένος *rained upon, exposed to the rain,* Eur.

ἐφ-ώριος, ον, (ὥρα) *mature,* Anth.

ἔχαδον, aor. 2 of χανδάνω.

ἐχάρην [ᾰ], aor. 2 pass. of χαίρω.

ἔχεα, aor. 1 of χέω.

ἐχ-έγγυος, ον, (ἐγγύη) *having given* or *able to give security, trust-worthy, secure,* Eur.; ζημία ἐχ. a penalty *to be relied on* (for the prevention of crime), Thuc.: τὸ ἐχέγγυον *security,* Hdt.: c. inf. *sufficiently strong* to do, Plut.　　II. pass. *having received a pledge, secured against danger,* Soph.

χέ-θῡμος, ον, *master of one's passion,* Od.

ἔχεισθα, poët. 2 sing. of ἔχω.

ἐχεμῡθέω, f. ήσω, *to hold one's peace,* Luc.; and

ἐχεμῡθία, ἡ, *silence, reserve,* Plut.　From

ἐχέ-μῡθος, ον, *restraining speech, taciturn.*

ἐχε-νηΐς, ΐδος, contr. -νῇς, ῇδος, ἡ, (ναῦς) *ship-detaining,* Aesch., Anth.

ἐχε-πευκής, ές, (πεύκη) Homeric epith. of a dart, *bitter,* or rather *sharp-pointed, piercing,* Il.

ἔχεσκον, Ion. impf. of ἔχω.

ἐχέ-στονος, ον, *bringing sorrows,* Theocr.

ἐχέτης, ου, ὁ, = ὁ ἔχων, *a man of substance,* Pind.

ἐχέτλη, ἡ, (ἔχω) *a plough-handle,* Lat. *stiva,* Hes.

ἐχετλήεις, εσσα, εν, *of* or *belonging to a plough-handle,* Anth.

ἔχευα, Ep. for ἔχεα, aor. 1 of χέω: med. **ἐχευάμην.**

ἐχεφρονέω, *to be prudent,* Anth.; and

ἐχεφροσύνη, ἡ, *prudence, good sense,* Anth.　From

ἐχέ-φρων, ον, gen. ονος, (φρήν) *sensible, prudent, discreet,* Hom.

ἔχησθα, Ep. 2 sing. subj. of ἔχω.

ἐχθαίρω, Dor. 3 pl. -οντι: impf. ἤχθαιρον: aor. 1 ἤχθηρα, Dor. ἤχθᾱρα: (ἔχθος) :—*to hate, detest,* Hom., Trag.; c. acc. cogn., ἔχθος ἐχθήρας μέγα *hating with great hatred,* Soph.:—Pass. *to be hated, hateful,* Trag.; so in fut. med., ἐχθαρεῖ μὲν ἐξ ἐμοῦ Soph. Hence

ἐχθαρτέος, α, ον, verb. Adj. *to be hated,* Soph.

ἐχθές, Adv. (v. χθές), *yesterday,* Ar.; ἀπ' ἐχθές Anth.; νῦν τε καὶ χθές *to-day* or *yesterday,* Soph.; cf. πρώην.

ἐχθεσινός, ή, όν, = χθεσινός, *yesterday's,* Anth.

ἐχθέω, = ἐχθῶ: imper. ἔχθει Theogn.

ἔχθιστος, η, ον, irreg. Sup. of ἐχθρός, *most hated, most hateful,* Il., Trag.　　2. *most hostile,* Thuc.; c. gen., as if a Subst., οἱ ἐκείνου ἔχθ. his *bitterest enemies,* Xen.

ἐχθίων, ον, gen. ονος, irreg. Comp. of ἐχθρός, *more hated, more hateful,* Trag.　Adv. ἐχθιόνως ἔχειν *to be more hostile,* Xen.

ἐχθοδοπέω, f. ήσω, *in hostility with* another, c. dat., Il.

ἐχθοδοπός, όν, lengthd. form of ἐχθρός, *hateful, detestable,* Soph., Ar., Plat.

ἘΧΘΟΣ, εος, τό, *hate, hatred,* Hom., etc.; ἔχθος τινός *hatred for* one, Hdt., Thuc.; ἐς ἔχθος ἀπικέσθαι τινί *to incur his hatred* or *enmity,* Hdt.; εἰς ἔχθος ἐλθεῖν τινί Eur.　　II. of persons, ὦ πλεῖστον ἔχθος *object of* direst *hate,* Aesch.

ἔχθρα, Ion. ἔχθρη, ἡ, (ἐχθρός) *hatred, enmity,* Hdt., Att.; ἔχθρα τινός *hatred for, enmity to* one, Thuc.; κατ' ἔχθραν τινός Ar.; ἔχθρα ἔς τινα Hdt.; ἔχθρα πρός τινα Aesch.; δι' ἔχθρας ἀφικέσθαι, ἐλθεῖν τινί *to be at feud with* one, Eur., etc.; ἔχθραν συμβάλλειν, συνάπτειν τινί *to engage in hostility with* . ., Id.; ἔχθραν λύειν, διαλύεσθαι Id., Thuc.

ἐχθραίνω, impf. ἤχθραινον, (ἐχθρός) later form of ἐχθαίρω, *to hate,* Xen., Plut.

ἐχθρο-δαίμων, ον, *hated of the gods,* Soph.

ἐχθρό-ξενος, ον, *hostile to guests, inhospitable,* Aesch., Eur.

ἐχθρός, ά, όν, (ἔχθος) *hated, hateful,* Hom., etc.; ἐχθρόν μοί ἐστιν, c. inf., 'tis *hateful* to me to . ., Il.　　II. act. *hostile, at enmity with,* τινι Thuc., etc.　　III. as Subst., ἐχθρός, ὁ, *one's enemy,* Hes., etc.; ὁ Διὸς ἐχθρός Aesch.; οἱ ἐμοὶ ἐχθροί Thuc.　　IV. the regul. Comp. and Sup. ἐχθρότερος, -τατος are rare: the irreg. ἐχθίων, ἔχθιστος being more used.　　V. Adv. ἐχθρῶς, Plat., etc.; Comp. ἐχθροτέρως, Dem.

ἔχθω, (ἔχθος) *to hate,* Soph., Eur. :—Pass. *to be hated, detested,* Hom., Aesch.

ἔχιδνα, ἡ, (ἔχις) *an adder, viper,* Hdt., Trag., etc.; metaph. of a treacherous wife or friend, Aesch., Soph.

ἐχιδναῖος, α, ον, *of* or *like a viper,* Eur.

Ἐχῖναι, ῶν, αἱ, *the islands in the Ionian sea,* Il., Eur., etc.; commonly called **Ἐχῖνάδες, αἱ,** Hdt., etc.

ἐχῖνέες or **ἐχῖνες, οἱ,** *a kind of mouse with bristly hair,* in Libya, Hdt.

ἘΧῖΝΟΣ, ὁ, *the urchin, hedgehog,* Ar., etc.　　2. *the sea-urchin,* Plat.　　II. *the shell of the sea-urchin,* often used as *a cup:* then like Lat. *testa, a pot, jug, pitcher,* Lat. *echinus,* Ar., etc.:—*the vase* in which the notes of evidence were deposited, Dem.　　III. in pl. *sharp points* at each end of a bit, Xen.

ΈΧΙΣ, εως, ὁ, gen. pl. ἐχέων, an adder, viper, Plat. ; metaph., συκοφάντης καὶ ἔχις τὴν φύσιν Dem.

ἔχμα, ατος, τό, (ἔχω) that which holds ; and so, **I.** a hindrance, obstacle, Il. 2. c. gen. a bulwark, defence against a thing, c. gen., h. Hom. **II.** a hold-fast, stay, ἔχματα πέτρης bands of rock, Il ; ἔχματα πύργων stays of the towers, Ib. ; ἔχματα νηῶν props for the ships, to keep them upright, Ib.

ἐχῡρός, ά, όν, (ἔχω) strong, secure, of Places, Thuc., etc. ; ἐν ἐχυρῷ εἶναι to be in safety, Id. ; ἐν ἐχυρωτάτῳ ποιεῖσθαί τι Xen. 2. of reasons, etc., trustworthy, Thuc. **II.** Adv. -ρῶς, Id. ; Comp. -ώτερον, Id.

ΈΧΩ, impf. εἶχον, Ep. ἔχον, Ion. ἔχεσκον :—fut. ἕξω or σχήσω : aor. 2 ἔσχον ; imperat. σχές ; inf. σχεῖν :—(for the poët. form ἔσχεθον v. *σχέθω) : pf. ἔσχηκα ; Ep. ὄχωκα :—Med., fut. ἕξομαι or σχήσομαι : aor. 2 ἐσχόμην, Ep. 3 sing. σχέτο ; imper. σχοῦ, σχέσθον σχέσθε ; inf. σχέσθαι :—Pass., aor. 1 ἐσχέθην :—the aor. 2 med. is also used in pass. sense.

A. Trans., in two senses, to have or to hold : **I.** to have, possess, Hom., etc. ; ὁ ἔχων a wealthy man, Soph. ; οἱ οὐκ ἔχοντες the poor, Eur. :—c. gen. partit., μαντικῆς ἐχ. τέχνης Soph. :—Pass. to be possessed by, belong to, τινι Il. 2. to have charge of, keep, πύλας Ib. ; φυλακὰς ἔχον kept watch, Ib., etc. 3. c. acc. loci, to dwell in, inhabit, haunt, Hom., etc. 4. to have to wife, Id., etc. 5. to have in one's house, to entertain, Od. 6. the pres. part. is joined with a Verb, ἔχων ἀτίταλλε kept and made much of, i. e. kept with special care, Il. ; ὃς ἂν ἥκῃ ἔχων στρατόν whoever may have come with an army, Hdt. 7. of Habits or Conditions, γῆρας ἔχ., periphr. for γηράσκειν, Od. 8. like Lat. teneo, to know, understand, Il., Aesch. ; ἔχεις τι ; tenes? d' ye understand ? Ar. 9. to involve, imply, give cause for, ἀγανάκτησιν Thuc. 10. ἔχειν σταθμόν to weigh so much, Hdt. **II.** to hold, Hom., etc. ; ἐχ. ἐν χερσίν Hdt. ; μετὰ χερσίν Il. ; διὰ χειρός Soph., etc. 2. to hold fast, ἔχειν τινὰ χειρός, ποδός to hold him by the hand, by the foot, Il. ; ἔχειν τινὰ μέσον to grip one by the middle, of wrestlers, Ar. 3. of a woman, to be pregnant, Lat. utero gestare, Hdt. ; ἐν γαστρὶ ἔχειν Id. 4. to hold out, bear up against, support, sustain an attack, Lat. sustinere ; in which sense Hom. uses fut. σχήσω, σχήσομαι. 5. to hold fast, keep close, as bars do a gate, Il. : to enclose, Hom. 6. to hold or keep in a certain direction, like ἐπέχω, ὀϊστὸν ἔχε he aimed it, Il. ; of horses or ships, to guide, drive, steer, Ib. ; then absol., τῇ ῥ' ἔχε that way he held his course, Ib. :—also to put in, land, εἰς or πρὸς τόπον Hdt. ; δεῦρο νοῦν ἔχε attend to this, Eur. ; πρός τι τὸν νοῦν ἔχ. Thuc. 7. to hold in, stay, keep back, ἵππους Il., etc. ; οὐ σχήσει χεῖρας will not withhold his hands, Od. ; ὀδύνας ἔχ. to allay, assuage them, Il., etc. 8. to keep away from, c. gen. rei, τινὰ ἀγοράων, νεῶν Ib. :—in Att. to stop or hinder from doing, τοῦ μὴ καταδῦναι Xen. ; ἔσχον μὴ κτανεῖν Eur. 9. to keep back, withhold a thing, χρήματα Od., etc. 10. to hold in guard, keep safe, protect, Il. **III.** c. inf. to have means or power to do, to be able, c. inf., Hom., etc. :—with inf. omitted, οὔπως εἶχε he could not, Il. 2. after Hom., οὐκ

ἔχω ὅπως I know not how, etc., Soph., etc. ; οὐκ ἔχω ὅ τι χρὴ λέγειν Xen.

B. intrans. to hold oneself, to keep so and so, ἔξω, ὡς ὅτε τις λίθος . . I will hold fast, as a stone . . , Od. ; σχὲς οὗπερ εἶ keep where thou art, Soph. ; ἔχειν κατὰ χώραν to keep in one's place, Ar., etc. ; διὰ φυλακῆς ἔχειν to keep on one's guard, Thuc. 2. c. gen. to keep from, πολέμου Id. 3. c. gen., also, to take part in, have to do with, τέχνης Soph. : to be engaged or busy, ἀμφί τι Aesch. ; περί τι Xen. **II.** simply to be, often with Advs. of manner, εὖ ἔχει Od. ; καλῶς ἔχει, κακῶς ἔχει, Lat. bene habet, male habet, it is going on well, Att. ; οὕτως ἔχει so the case stands, Ar., etc. :—a gen. modi is often added, εὖ ἔχειν τινός to be well off for a thing, abound in it, Hdt. ; ὡς ποδῶν εἶχον as fast as they could go, Id. ; ὥς τις εὐνοίας ἢ μνήμης ἔχοι as each man felt disposed or remembered, Thuc. **III.** to lead towards, ἐπὶ τὸν ποταμόν Hdt. ; ἔχ. εἴς τι, to point towards, tend towards, Id. ; τὸ ἐς Ἀργείους ἔχον what concerns them, Id. ; also, ἐπ' ὅσον ἔποψις εἶχε so far as the view extended, Id. 2. ἐπί τινι ἔχειν to have hostile feelings towards . . , Id., Soph. **IV.** after Hom., ἔχω is joined with aor. part. of another Verb, κρύψαντες ἔχουσι for κεκρύφασι, Hes. ; ἀποκλήσας ἔχεις for ἀποκέκλεικας, Hdt. ;—sometimes it gives a pres. sense to the aor., θαυμάσας ἔχω I am in a state of wonderment, Soph. ; ὅς σφε νῦν ἀτιμάσας ἔχει who now treats her with dishonour, Eur. 2. the part. ἔχων, with the pres., adds a notion of duration, as, τί κυπτάζεις ἔχων ; why do you keep poking about there ? Ar. ; φλυαρεῖς, ληρεῖς ἔχων you keep chattering, trifling, Plat. 3. pleonast., ἐστὶν ἔχον = ἔχει, Hdt. ; ἐστὶν ἀναγκαίως ἔχον = ἔχει ἀναγκαίως, Aesch.

C. Med. to hold on by, cling to, c. gen., Hom., etc. 2. metaph. to cleave or cling to, ἔργου Hdt. ; ἐλπίδος Eur. ; τῆς αὐτῆς γνώμης Thuc. : to lay claim to a thing, Hdt. ; to be zealous for, μάχης Soph. 3. to come next to, follow closely, Xen. ; τῆς πληγῆς ἔχεται follows up the blow, Dem. :—of peoples or places, to be close, touch, border on, τινος Hdt., etc. ; οἱ ἐχόμενοι the neighbouring people, Id. : of Time, τὸ ἐχόμενον ἔτος the next year, Thuc. 4. to depend on, τινος or ἔκ τινος Hom. 5. to pertain to, τινος Hdt. **II.** to bear or hold for oneself, Hom. **III.** to maintain oneself, hold one's ground, Il. 2. c. acc. to keep off from oneself, repel, Ib. **IV.** to stop oneself, stop, Ib. :—to keep oneself back, abstain or refrain from, Hom., etc.

ἔχωντι, Dor. for ἔχωσι, 3 pl. subj. of ἔχω.

ἐψάλαται, Ion. 3 pl. pf. pass. of ψάλλω.

ἐψ-άνδρα, ἡ, (ἀνήρ) cooking men, of Medea, Anth.

ἐψεύσμαι, pf. of ψεύδομαι :—ἐψεύσω, 2 sing. aor. 1.

ἐψέω, v. sub ἕψω.

ἔψημα, ατος, τό, anything boiled : pl. vegetables for kitchen use, Plat.

ἔψησις, εως, ἡ, (ἕψω) a boiling, Hdt.

ἐψητήρ, ῆρος, ὁ, (ἕψω) a pan for boiling, Anth.

ἐψητός, ή, όν, (ἕψω) boiled, Xen. ; ἐψητοί, ῶν, οἱ, boiled fish, Ar.

ΈΨΙΑ, Ion. -ίη, ἡ, a game played with pebbles. Hence ἐψιάομαι, Dep. to play with pebbles, generally, to amuse

oneself, ἐψιάσθων (Ep. 3 dual imper.), Od. ; ἐψιάασθαι μολπῇ καὶ φόρμιγγι (Ep. inf.) Ib.

ΈΨΩ, 3 sing. impf. ἦψε :—the other tenses are formed from ἑψέω, f. ψήσω : aor. 1 ἥψησα :—Med., f. ἑψήσομαι :—Pass., aor. 1 ἡψήθην :—*to boil, seethe*, Hdt., Att. : proverb. of useless labour, λίθον ἕψεις Ar. ; c. gen. partit., ἥψομεν τοῦ κορκόρου *we boiled some pimpernel*, Id. :—Pass. *to be boiled*, Hdt. 2. of metals, *to smelt, refine*, Pind. 3. metaph., γῆρας ἀνώνυμον ἕψειν *to cherish an inglorious age*, Id.

ἕῳ, Ion. for ᾦ, pres. subj. of εἰμί (*sum*).

ἑῶ, contr. for ἐάω.

ἕῳ, Ion. for ᾦ, aor. 2 subj. of ἵημι. II. gen. and acc. of ἕως, *the dawn*.

ἐῷ, contr. 3 sing. opt. of ἐάω. II. ἑῷ, dat of ἑός.

ἔῳγα, pf. 2 of οἴγνυμι :—ἔῳγμαι, pf. pass.

ἔῳθα, Ion. pf. of ἔθομαι, in pres. sense :—ἐῶθεα, plqpf.

ἔῳθεν, Ep. ἠῶθεν (q. v.), Adv. (ἔως) *from morn*, i. e. *at earliest dawn, early in the morning*, Plat. ; ἔ. εὐθύς Ar. 2. αὔριον ἔ. *to-morrow early*, Xen. ; so ἔῳθεν *alone*, Ar.

ἑῳθῑνός, ή, όν, (ἔως) *in the morning, early*, Hdt., Ar. : —τὸ ἑῳθινόν, as Adv., *early in the morning*, Hdt. ; so, ἐξ ἑῳθινοῦ=ἕῳθεν, Xen.

ἐῶθουν, impf. of ὠθέω.

ἐῴκει, 3 sing. plqpf. of ἔοικα.

ἑῳλο-κρᾱσία, ἡ, (κρᾶσις) *a mixture of the dregs and heel-taps*, with which the drunken were dosed at the end of a revel ; metaph., ἑωλοκρασίαν μου τῆς πονηρίας κατασκεδάσας having discharged *the stale dregs* of his rascality over me, Dem.

ἕῳλος, ον, (prob. from ἕως, ἠώς) *a day old, kept till the morrow, stale*, Comici ; ἕῳλος θρυαλλίς a *stinking wick* (after the lamp has been blown out), Luc. 2. of actions or events, *stale, out of date*, Dem. 3. of men, *coming a day too late*, Plut.

ἑῶλπει, 3 sing. plqpf. of ἔλπομαι.

ἑῶμεν, a 1 pl. subj. found in Il., ἐπεί χ' ἑῶμεν πολέμοιο when we *have enough of* war :—but prob. it should be written ἕωμεν, Ion. for ᾦμεν, 1 pl. subj. of ἄω (c. II.), *to take one's fill* of a thing.

ἑῶμεν, contr. 1 pl. of ἐάω :—ἑῶμι, 1 sing. opt.

ἑών, Ion. for ὤν, part. of εἰμί (*sum*).

ἐώνημαι, ἐωνήμην, pf. and plqpf. of ὠνέομαι.

ἐῳνοχόει, 3 sing. impf., with double augm. of οἰνοχοέω.

ἔῳξα, aor. 1 of οἴγνυμι.

ἐῷος, α, ον or ος, ον, poët. ἑῶϊος, Ion. ἠοῖος (ἔως) :— *in or of the morning, at morn, early*, πάχνη ἐῴα the *morning* rime, Aesch. ; ἑῷος ἐξαναστῆναι to get up *early*, Eur. 2. *eastern*, Xen.

ἑώρα, ἡ, collat. form of αἰώρα, *a halter*, Soph.

ἑώρᾱ, 3 sing. impf. of ὁράω :—ἑώρᾱκα, pf.

ἑώργει, 3 sing. plqpf. of *ἔργω=ἔρδω.

ἑώρταζον, impf. of ἑορτάζω.

ἔωρτο, for ἤωρτο, 3 sing. plqpf. pass. of ἀείρω.

ἑώρων, impf. of ὁράω.

ἕως, ἡ, Att. form of Ion. ἠώς, q. v.

ΈΩΣ, Ep. εἴως and εἶος, Conjunction, *until, till*, Lat. *donec, dum*, Hom. :—in Hom. sometimes use =τέως, *for a time* :—to express a fact, ἔως is foll. by Indic., εἶος φίλον ὤλεσε θυμόν Il. ; when the event is uncertain, by the opt., ἕως ὅ γε μιγείη *till he should reach*,

Od. b. ἔως ἄν or κε with Subj., relating to an uncertain event in *future* time, μαχήσομαι, εἴως κε κιχείω *till* I find, Il. 2. *while, so long as*, εἴως πολεμίζομεν Od. ; ἔως ἔτι ἐλπίς [ἦν] Thuc. II. as Adv., Lat. *usque*, mostly with Advs. of Time, ἔως ὅτε, Lat. *usque dum, till the time when*, Xen. ; so, ἔως οὖ Hdt. ; ἔως ὀψέ *till late*, Thuc. :—c. gen., ἔως τοῦ ἀποτῖσαι *till* he made payment, ap. Aeschin.

ἕωσα, ἑώσθην, aor. 1 act. and pass. of ὠθέω.

ἔωσι, Ion. for ὦσι, 3 pl. pres. subj. of εἰμί (*sum*).

ἕωσ-περ, strengthd. for ἕως, *even until*, Thuc.

Ἑωσ-φόρος, Dor. Ἀωσφόρος, ὁ, *Bringer of morn*, Lat. *Lucifer, the Morning-star*.

ἑωυτοῦ, ἑωυτέων, Ion. for ἑαυτοῦ, ἑαυτῶν.

Z.

Z, ζ, ζῆτα, τό, indecl., sixth letter of Gk. Alphabet : as numeral ζ'=ἑπτά and ἕβδομος (the obsol. ϛ', i. e. ϝ, *vau*, the digamma, being retained to represent ἕξ, ἕκτος), but ͵ζ = 7000.

Ζ ζ is composed of σ and δ, so that in Aeol. it becomes σδ, as Σδεύς κωμάσδω ψιθυρίσδω for Ζεύς κωμάζω ψιθυρίζω :—reversely, in Att., σδ becomes ζ, Ἀθήναζε θύραζε for Ἀθήνασδε θύρασδε. But σ often disappears in Aeol., where ζά=δια, see ζά, ζα-:—so in Aeol. and Dor., as we have Δεύς Δάν for Ζεύς Ζάν, δορκάς=ζορκάς :—so also ἀρίζηλος for ἀρίδηλος ; ἀλαπαδνός from ἀλαπάζω, παιδνός from παίζω :—Dor., in the middle of words, it becomes δδ, as θερίδδω for -ίζω, μάδδα for μᾶζα.

Zeta, being a double conson., made a short vowel at the end of the foregoing syllable long by position. But Homer used the vowel short before two prop. names, which could not otherwise come into the Hexam., viz. ἄστυ Ζελείης, ὑλήεσσα Ζάκυνθος.

ζά [ᾰ], Aeol. for διά, ζὰ τὰν σὰν ἰδέαν Theocr. II.

ζα- insep. Prefix, =δα-, ἀρι-, ἐρι-, *very*, as in ζά-θεος, ζά-κοτος, ζα-μενής, etc.

ζάγκλον, τό, *a reaping-hook* or *sickle*, Lat. *falx*, Sicilian word for δρέπανον, Thuc. Hence Ζάγκλη, the ancient name for Messana.

ζα-ής, ές, acc. ζαῆν, (ἄημι) *strong-blowing, stormy*, Hom.

ζά-θεος [ᾰ], α, ον and ος, ον, *very divine, sacred*, Il., etc.

ζα-θερής, ές, (θέρος) *very hot, scorching*, Anth.

ζά-κορος, ὁ and ἡ, *a temple-servant*, being perh. a form of διάκονος, Plut. For -κορος cf. νεω-κόρος.

ζά-κοτος [ᾰ], ον, *exceeding wroth*, Il., Theocr.

ζάλη [ᾰ], ἡ, (perh. from ζέω) *the surging* of the sea, *surge, spray*, Aesch., Soph., etc. ; πύρπνοος ζάλη, of the fiery rain from Aetna, Aesch. :—metaph. ζάλαι *storms, distresses*, Pind.

ζᾶλος, ζᾶλόω, ζᾶλωτός, Dor. for ζῆλος, etc.

ζᾰμενέω, *to put forth all one's might*, Hes. From

ζᾰ-μενής, ές, (μένος) poët. Adj. *very strong, mighty, raging*, h. Hom., Pind.

ζᾱμία, ζᾱμιόω, etc., Aeol. and Dor. for ζημία, etc.

Ζάν, Ζανός, ὁ, Dor. for Ζήν, Ζηνός.

ζᾰ-πληθής, ές, (πλήθω) *very full*, ζ. γενειάς a *thick beard*, Aesch. ; ζ. Μούσης στόμα *full-sounding*, Anth.

ζά-πλουτος, ον, very rich, Hdt., Eur.
ζά-πρέπω, Aeol. for διαπρέπω.
ζά-πυρος [ἄ], ον, (πῦρ) very fiery, Aesch.
ζᾱτεύω, Dor. for ζητεύω.
ζά-τρεφής, ές, (τρέφω) well-fed, fat, goodly, Hom.
ζά-φλεγής, ές, (φλέγω) full of fire, of men at their prime, Il.
ζά-χολος [ἄ], ον, (χολή) = ζάκοτος, Anth.
ζα-χρεῖος, ον, (χρεία) wanting much : c. gen., ζαχρ. ὁδοῦ one who wants to know the way, Theocr.
ζα-χρηής, ές, (χράω B) only in pl. attacking violently, furious, raging, Hom.
ζά-χρυσος, ον, rich in gold, Eur.
ΖΑ'Ω, ζῇς, ζῇ, ζῆτε, imper. ζῆ, inf. ζῆν (αει and αε being contr. into η) ; opt. ζῴην :—impf. ἔζων : f. ζήσω or ζήσομαι : aor. 1 ἔζησα :—Ep. and Ion. ζώω, Ep. inf. ζωέμεναι, -έμεν : impf. ἔζωον, Ion. ζώεσκον : aor. 1 ἔζωσα :—later we find a pres. ζόω. To live, Hom., etc. ; ἐλέγχιστε ζωόντων vilest of living men, Od. ; ζώειν καὶ ὁρᾶν φάος ἠελίοιο Il. ; ῥεῖα ζώοντες living at ease, of the gods, Ib. ; ζῶν κατακαυθῆναι to be burnt alive, Hdt. :—also, ζῆν ἀπό τινος to live off or on a thing, Theogn., Hdt., etc. :—τὸ ζῆν = ζωή, Aesch., etc. :—in a quasi-trans. sense, ἐκ τῶν ἄλλων ὧν ἔζης (= ἃ ἐν τῷ βίῳ ἔπραττες) from the other acts of your life, Dem.　II. metaph. to be in full life and strength, to be fresh, be strong, ἄτης θύελλαι ζῶσι Aesch. ; ἀεὶ ζῇ ταῦτα [νόμιμα] Soph. ; ζώσα φλόξ living fire, Eur.
-ζε, inseparable Suffix, denoting motion towards :—properly it represents -σδε, as in Ἀθήναζε, θύραζε for Ἀθήνασδε, θύρασδε :—but sometimes found with sing. Nouns, as Ὀλυμπίαζε, Μουνυχίαζε.
ζεγέριες, without mark of gender, a Libyan word = βουνοί, a kind of mouse, Hdt.
ΖΕΙΑ', ἡ, mostly in pl. ζειαί, a kind of grain, spelt, a coarse wheat, used as fodder for horses, Od. ; like ὀλύραι in Il. ; and Hdt. expressly asserts their identity.
ζεί-δωρος, ον, (δῶρον) sea-giving, as epith. of the earth, ζείδωρος ἄρουρα fruitful corn-land, Hom.
ζειρά, ἡ, a wide upper garment, girded about the loins and falling over the feet, Hdt., Xen. (A foreign word.)
ζέσσα, Ep. for ἔζεσα, aor. 1 of ζέω.
ζευγάριον [ἄ], τό, Dim. of ζεῦγος, a puny team, Ar.
ζευγηλατέω, f. ήσω, to drive a yoke of oxen, Xen. From
ζευγ-ηλάτης [ᾰ], ου, ὁ, (ἐλαύνω) the driver of a yoke of oxen, teamster, Xen.
ζευγίτης [ῑ], ου, ὁ, fem. ζευγῖτις, ιδος, (ζεῦγος) yoked in pairs, of soldiers, in the same rank, Plut.　II. ζευγῖται, οἱ, the third of Solon's four classes of Athenian citizens, so called from their being able to keep a team of oxen, ap. Dem. : cf. πεντακοσιομέδιμνοι.
ζευγλά, ἡ, poët. for sq., Anth.
ζεύγλη, ἡ, the strap or loop of the yoke (ζυγόν) through which the beasts' heads were put, so that the ζυγόν had two ζεύγλαι, Il., Hdt., etc.　II. the cross-bar of the double rudder, Eur.
ζεῦγμα, ατος, τό, (ζεύγνυμι) that which is used for joining, a band, bond, τὸ ζ. τοῦ λιμένος the barrier of ships moored across the harbour, Thuc. :—a bridge of boats, Anth. :—a platform formed by lashing several vessels together, Plut.　2. metaph., ζεύγματ' ἀνάγκης the bonds of necessity, Eur.

ζεύγνῡμι or -ύω, inf. -ύναι [ῠ], Ep. ζευγνύμεν, part. ζευγνύς ; impf. 3 pl. ἐζεύγνῠσαν, Ep. ζεύγν- : f. ζεύξω : aor. 1 ἔζευξα :—Pass., aor. 1 ἐζεύχθην : aor. 2 ἐζύγην [ῠ] : (from Root ΖΥΓ, as in ζυγῆναι) :—to yoke, put to, ἵππους Hom., etc. ; ζ. ἵππους ὑφ' ἅρματα, ὑφ' ἅρμασιν, ὑπ' ὄχεσφιν, ὑπ' ἀμάξησιν Il. ;—(so in Med., ἵππους ζεύγνυσθαι to put to one's horses, Hom.) ;—also of riding horses, to harness, saddle and bridle, ζεῦξαι Πάγασον Pind. :—of chariots, to put to, get ready, Id., Eur.　2. to bind, bind fast, Xen. :—Pass., φάρη ἐζευγμέναι having them fastened, Eur.　3. metaph., πότμῳ ζυγείς in the yoke of fate, Pind. ; ἀνάγκῃ, ὁρκίοις ζευγείς Soph., Eur.　II. to join together, σανίδες ἐζευγμέναι well-joined, Il.　2. to join in wedlock, Eur. :—in Med., of the husband, to wed, Id. :—Pass. to be married, Soph., Eur.　3. to join opposite banks by bridges, τὸν Ἑλλήσποντον ζεῦξαι Hdt., etc. : — also, γέφυραν ζεῦξαι to form a bridge, Id.　4. to undergird ships with ropes, Thuc.
ζεῦγος, εος, τό, (ζεύγνυμι) a yoke of beasts, a pair of mules, oxen or horses, Il., etc.　2. the carriage drawn by a pair, a chariot, car, Hdt., etc.　II. a pair or couple of any things, Id., Aesch.
ζευγο-τρόφος, ον, keeping a yoke of beasts, Plut.
ζευκτήριος, α, ον, (ζεύγνυμι) fit for joining or yoking, γέφυραν γαῖν δυοῖν ζ. Aesch.　II. as Subst., ζευκτήριον, τό, = ζυγόν, a yoke, Id.
ζεῦξαι, aor. 1 inf. of ζεύγνυμι.
ζεῦξις, εως, ἡ, (ζεύγνυμι) a yoking or manner of yoking oxen, Hdt.　II. a joining, as by a bridge, Id.
Ζεύς, ὁ, voc. Ζεῦ : the obl. cases (formed from Δίς), gen. Διός ; dat. Διΐ, Διΐ [ῑ], acc. Δία :—in Poets also, Ζηνός, Ζηνί, Ζῆνα, in later Dor. Ζάν, Ζανός, etc. :—Zeus, Lat. Ju-piter, father of gods and men, son of Kronos and Rhea, hence called Κρονίδης, Κρονίων, husband of Hera : —Hom. makes him rule in the lower air (ἀήρ) ; hence rain and storms come from him, Ζεὺς ὕει, etc. :—in oaths, οὐ μὰ Ζῆνα Hom., Att. ; so μὰ Δία, νὴ Δία, Att.　II. Ζεὺς καταχθόνιος, Pluto, Il.
Ζεφύρη (sc. πνοή), ἡ, = Ζέφυρος, the west wind, Od.
Ζέφυρος, ὁ, Zephyrus, the west wind, Lat. Favonius, Hom., etc. ; westerly wind, often represented as stormy, Od. ; but also as clearing, ὁπότε νέφεα Ζ. στυφελίξῃ Il. (From ζόφος night, the region of darkness, as Εὖρος from ἔως, the morn.)
ΖΕ'Ω, 3 sing. Ep. : impf. ἔζεε : f. ζέσω : aor. 1 ἔζεσα, Ep. ζέσσα :—to boil, seethe, of water, Hom. ; λέβης ζεῖ the kettle boils, Il.　2. metaph. to boil or bubble up, of the sea, Hdt. ; of passion, like Lat. fervere, Aesch., Soph.　3. c. gen. to boil up or over with a thing, ζεῖν ὕδατος καὶ πηλοῦ Plat. ; also c. dat., ζ. φθειρσί Luc.　II. Causal, to make to boil, θυμόν Anth.
ζῆ, ζῆθι, imperat. of ζάω.
ζηλαῖος, α, ον, (ζῆλος) jealous, Anth.
ζηλήμων, ον, gen. ονος, (ζηλέω) jealous, Od.
ζηλο-δοτήρ, ῆρος, ὁ, giver of bliss, Anth.
ζηλο-μανής, ές, (μαίνομαι) mad with jealousy, Anth.
ζῆλος, ου, ὁ, later εος, τό, (prob. from ζέω) eager rivalry, zealous imitation, emulation, a noble passion, opp. to φθόνος (envy), Plat., etc. :—but also jealousy, Hes.　2. c. gen. pers. zeal for one, Soph., Plut.　3. c. gen. rei, rivalry for a thing, Eur. ; ζ.

πλούτου Plut., etc.　　　II. pass. *the object of emulation* or *desire, happiness, bliss, honour, glory*, Soph., Dem.　　　III. *of style, extravagance*, Plut. :—also, *fierceness*, N. T.

ζηλοσύνη, ή, poët. for ζῆλος, h. Hom.

ζηλοτὕπέω, f. ήσω, *to be jealous of, to emulate, rival*, c. acc. pers., Plat.　　II. c. acc. rei, *to regard with jealous anger*, Aeschin.　　2. *to pretend to*, ἀρετήν Id.

ζηλοτὕπία, ή, *jealousy, rivalry*, Aeschin., Plut.　From

ζηλό-τῠπος, ον, (τύπτω) *jealous*, Ar., Anth.

ζηλόω, f. ώσω, (ζῆλος) :　　I. c. acc. pers. *to rival, vie with, emulate*, Lat. *aemulari*, Soph., Thuc., etc.:— in bad sense, *to be jealous of, envy*, Hes., Theocr.:— absol. *to be jealous*, N. T.　　2. *to esteem* or *pronounce happy, admire, praise*, τινά τινος one *for a thing*, Soph., Ar.: ironical, ζηλῶ σε happy in your ignorance! Eur.　　II. c. acc. rei, *to desire emulously, strive after*, Dem. :—Pass., Plat., etc.　　2. Pass. also of persons, *to be impelled by zeal*, N. T.

ζήλωμα, ατος, τό, *that which is emulated*: in pl. *high fortunes*, Eur.　　II. in pl. also *emulous efforts, rivalries*, Aeschin., Dem.; and

ζήλωσις, εως, ή, *emulation, imitation*, Thuc.; and

ζηλωτής, οῦ, ὁ, *an emulator, zealous admirer* or *follower*, Plat., etc.　　II. *a zealot*, used to translate Καναvίτης or Καναναῖος (from the Hebr. *gânâ, to glow, be zealous*), N. T.

ζηλωτικός, ή, όν, *emulous*, Arist.　From

ζηλωτός, ή, όν and ος, ον : Dor. ζᾱλ-, (ζηλόω) *to be emulated, worthy of imitation*, Plat., Dem.　　2. *to be deemed happy, to be envied*, Theogn., Aesch., etc.　　3. of conditions, *enviable, blessed*, Eur., Ar.

ζημία, Dor. ζᾱμία, ή, *loss, damage*, Lat. *damnum*, opp. to κέρδος, Plat., etc.; ζημίαν λαβεῖν to sustain *loss*, Dem.　　II. *a penalty in money, a fine, mulct*, ζημίην ἀποτίνειν Hdt.; ὀφείλειν Id.; καταβάλλειν Dem.; ζημία ἐπίκειται στατήρ *a fine* of a stater is imposed, Thuc.　　2. generally *a penalty*, ζ. ἐπιτιθέναι τινί Hdt.; ζ. πρόσκειται τινι Xen.; θάνατον ζημίαν ἐπιτίθεσθαι, προτιθέναι, τάττειν to make death *the penalty*, Thuc., etc.　　III. φανερὰ ζᾱμία a mere *good-for-nothing*, a dead *loss*, Ar. (Deriv. uncertain.) Hence

ζημιόω, f. ώσω : aor. 1 ἐζημίωσα : pf. ἐζημίωκα :—Pass., f. ζημιωθήσομαι, but more often in med. form ζημιώσομαι : aor. 1 ἐζημιώθην : pf. ἐζημίωμαι :—*to cause loss* or *do damage to* any one, τινά Plat., etc. :—Pass., μεγάλα ζημιώσεται will suffer great losses, Thuc.　　II. *to fine, amerce, mulct in* a sum of money, c. dat. rei, ζ. τινὰ χιλίῃσι δραχμῇσι Hdt.; χρήμασιν Thuc. :— Pass. *to be fined* or *amerced in* a thing, c. dat., Plat.; c. acc., τὴν ψυχὴν ζημιώσεαι wilt lose thy life, Hdt.　　2. generally *to punish*, Id., Thuc.

ζημι-ώδης, ες, (εἶδος) *causing loss, ruinous*, Xen.

ζημίωμα, ατος, τό, (ζημιόω) *a penalty, fine*, Luc.; τῆς ἀταξίας *for* their disorder, Plat.

Ζήν, ὁ, gen. Ζηνός, poët. for Ζεύς.

Ζηνό-φρων, ον, gen. ονος, (Ζήν, φρήν) *knowing the mind of Zeus*, of Apollo, Anth.

ζήσομαι, fut. of ζάω.

ζητεύω, poët. for sq., Hes.: Dor. ζᾱτεύω, Theocr.

ζητέω, Dor. part. fem. ζᾱτεῦσα : impf. ἐζήτουν, Ep. 3

sing. ζήτει : aor. 1 ἐζήτησα : pf. ἐζήτηκα :—*to seek, seek for*, Il., Aesch., etc.; μὴ ζητῶν without *seeking*, Xen.; τὸ ζητούμενον ἀλωτόν what is sought for may be found, Soph.　　2. *to enquire for*, Xen. : *to ask about* a thing, Id.　　3. *to search after, search out*, Soph., Thuc.　　4. *to search* or *inquire into, investigate*, Plat., etc.; ζ. τὰ θεῖα Xen., etc.　　5. *to require, demand*, παρὰ τοῦ στρατηγοῦ λόγον ζητοῦντες Dem.　　II. *to seek after, desire*, ἀμήχανα Eur.　　2. c. inf. *to seek to do*, Hdt., Aesch., etc.　　III. *to have to seek, feel the want of*, Lat. *desidero*, Hdt. Hence

ζήτημα, ατος, τό, *that which is sought, οὐ ῥᾴδιον ζ. a thing* not easy *to find*, Eur.　　II. *an inquiry, question*, Soph., Plat., etc.　　2. *a search, μητρός after* her, Eur.

ζητήσιμος, ον, (ζητέω) *to be searched, τὰ ζ. places to be beaten for game*, Xen.

ζήτησις, εως, ή, (ζητέω) *a seeking, seeking for, search for* a thing, c. gen., Hdt., Soph., etc.　　2. *a searching, search*, ποιέεσθαι ζήτησιν τῶν νεῶν *to search* the ships, Hdt.　　3. *inquiry, investigation*, Plat.

ζητητέος, α, ον, verb. Adj. of ζητέω, *to be sought*, Soph.　　II. ζητητέον one must seek, Ar.

ζητητής, οῦ, ὁ, (ζητέω) *a seeker, inquirer*, Plat.　　II. in pl. *commissioners to inquire into state-offences*, Dem.

ζητητικός, ή, όν, (ζητέω) *disposed to search* or *inquire, searching, inquiring*, Plat.

ζητητός, ή, όν, verb. Adj. of ζητέω, *sought for*, Soph.

ζιζάνιον, τό, *a weed that grows in wheat*, prob. Lat. *lolium, darnel*, in pl., N. T.

ζόη, ζόα, ζοία, v. sub ζωή.

ζόος, ά, όν, poët. for ζωός, Theocr.

ζορκάς, άδος, ή, v. δορκάς.

ζοφερός, ά, όν, (ζόφος) *dusky, gloomy*, Hes., Luc.:— metaph., ζ. φροντίδες Anth.

ΖΟΦΟΣ, ὁ, *the gloom of the world below, nether darkness*, Hom., Aesch. :—generally, *gloom, darkness*, Hes., Pind.　　II. *the dark quarter*, i. e. *the West*, opposed to ἠώς, Hom. : cf. Ζέφυρος.

ζοφόω, *to darken* :—Pass. *to be* or *become dark*, Anth.

ζόω, Ion. for ζάω.

ζύγαστρον [ῠ], τό, (ζεύγνυμι) *a chest* or *box* (of board strongly fastened together), Soph., Xen.

ζυγείς, aor. 2 pass. part. of ζεύγνυμι.

ζυγῆναι, aor. 2 pass. part. of ζεύγνυμι.

ζῠγη-φόρος, ον, poët. for ζυγοφόρος, Eur.

ζύγιος, α, ον and ος, ον, (ζυγόν) of or *for the yoke*, ζ. ἵππος a *draught-horse, wheeler*, Ar. :—c. gen., θηρῶν ζυγίους ζεύξασα σατίνας having yoked cars *to teams of* beasts, Eur.

ζῠγό-δεσμον, τό, *a yoke-band*, i. e. a band for fastening the yoke to the pole, Il., Plut.

ζῠγο-μᾰχέω, f. ήσω, (μάχομαι) *to struggle with one's yoke-fellow*, generally, *to struggle*, Dem.

ΖΥΓΟΝ, τό, and ΖΥΓΟΣ, ὁ, (cf. ζεύγνυμι) *anything which joins two bodies*; and so,　　I. *the yoke* of cross-bar tied by the ζυγόδεσμον to the end of the pole, and having ζεῦγλαι (collars or loops) at each end, by which two horses, mules or oxen drew the plough or carriage, Hom., etc. :—metaph., τὸ δούλιον ζ. *the yoke* of slavery, Hdt.; δουλείας, ἀνάγκης ζ. Soph., Eur. ;

ἐπιτιθέναι τινὶ ζυγὰ τοῦ μὴ . . , so as to prevent . . , Xen.   2. *a pair*, Eur.; κατὰ ζυγά in *pairs*, Theocr.   II. *the cross-bar joining* the horns of the φόρμιγξ, along which the strings were fastened, Il.   III. in pl. *the thwarts joining* the opposite sides of a ship or boat, *the benches*, Lat. *transtra*, Od., Hdt.; in sing., Soph.:—metaph., τὸ πόλεος ζ. Eur.   2. *the middle of the three banks* in a trireme; metaph., οἱ ἐπὶ ζυγῷ δορός those on the upper bench, Aesch.   IV. *the beam of the balance*, Dem.: —*the balance* itself, Plat.   V. καρχασίου ζ. *the yard-arm* at the masthead, Pind.   VI. *a rank* or *line* of soldiers, opp. to a *file*, Thuc.

ζῠγοστᾰτέω, f. ήσω, *to weigh by the balance*, Luc.

ζῠγο-στάτης [ᾰ], ου, ὁ, (ἵστημι) *a public officer, who looked to the weights.*

ζῠγόφιν, Ep. gen. of ζυγόν.

ζῠγο-φόρος, ον, (φέρω) *bearing the yoke*, Eur.

ζῠγόω, f. ώσω, (ζυγόν) *to yoke together*, ζ. κιθάραν *to put the cross-bar to the lyre*, Luc.

ζῠγωθρίζω, (ζυγόν IV) *to weigh, examine*, Ar.

ζῠγωτός, ή, όν, (ζυγόω) *yoked*, Soph.

ζύμη [ῠ], ή, (ζέω) *leaven*:—metaph. of *corruption, falsehood*, N.T.   Hence

ζῠμίτης [ῑ], masc. Adj. *leavened*, Xen.

ζῠμόω, f. ώσω, (ζύμη) *to leaven*, N.T.

ζω-άγρια, ων, τά, (ζωός, ἀγρεύω) *reward for life saved*, Od., Hdt.; also, like θρεπτήρια, *a reward for nursing and rearing one*, Il.: c. gen. rei, ζωάγρια μόχθων, νούσων Anth.

ζω-άγριος, α, ον, *for saving life*, Babr.: v. foreg.

ζωγρᾰφέω, f. ήσω, *to paint from life, to paint*, Plat.

ζωγρᾰφία, ή, *the art of painting*, Plat., Xen.; and

ζωγρᾰφικός, ή, όν, *skilled in painting*, Plat., Xen.   From

ζω-γράφος, ὁ, (ζωός, γράφω) *one who paints from life* or *from nature, a painter*, Hdt., Plat., etc.

ζωγρέω, f. ήσω, (ζωός, ἀγρεύω) *to take alive, take captive* instead of killing, Il., Hdt., etc.:—Pass., Id.   II. (ζωή, ἀγείρω) *to restore to life, revive*, Il.   Hence

ζωγρία, Ion. -ίη, ή, *a taking alive*, ζωγρίη λαμβάνειν or αἱρεῖν = ζωγρεῖν, Hdt.

ζῴδιον, τό, Dim. of ζῷον II, *a small figure*, Hdt.   II. in pl. *the signs of the Zodiac*, Arist.

ζωέμεν, -έμεναι, Ep. for ζώειν, inf. of ζώω = ζάω.

ζωή, Dor. ζωά; Ion. ζόη, Dor. ζόα; Aeol. ζοΐα; ή: (ζάω):—*a living*, i. e. one's *means of life, substance*, Od.; τὴν ζόην ποιεῖσθαι ἀπό or ἐκ τινος *to get one's living* by . . , Hdt., etc.   2. *life, existence*, Tyrtae., Trag., etc.   3. *a way of life*, Hdt.

ζω-θάλμιος, ον, (ζωή, θάλλω) *giving the bloom and freshness of life*, Pind.

ζῶμα, ατος, τό, (ζώννυμι) *that which is girded, a girded frock* or *doublet*, Od.   2. in Il. *the lower* part of the θώρηξ, round which the ζωστήρ passed, Il.   3. *the drawers* worn . by athletes, in Prose διάζωμα, Ib.   II. = ζώνη, *a woman's girdle*, Soph., Anth.

ζώμευμα, ατος, τό, *soup*, ζωμεύματα put by way of joke for ὑποζώματα νεώς, Ar.   From

ζωμεύω, (ζωμός) *to boil into soup*, Ar.

ζωμ-ήρῠσις, εως, ή, (ζωμός, ἀρύω) *a soup-ladle*, Anth.

ζωμίδιον, τό, Dim. of ζωμός, *a little sauce*, Ar.

ΖΩΜΟ'Σ, ὁ, Lat. *jus, sauce* to eat with meat, fish, etc., Ar.; ὁ μέλας ζ. *the black broth* of Spartans, Plut.

ζώνη, ή, (ζώννυμι) *a belt, girdle*:   I. properly *the lower girdle* worn by women above the hips, (the *upper-girdle*, the στρόφιον, being worn *under the breasts*), Hom.   2. Phrases, λῦσε δὲ παρθενίην ζώνην *unloosed her maiden girdle*, of the bridegroom, Od.; Med. of the *bride*, Anth.:—of men on a march, ζ. λύεσθαι *to slacken one's belt*, i. e. *rest oneself*, Hdt.:— of pregnant women, φέρειν ὑπὸ ζώνης, τρέφειν ἐντὸς ζώνης Aesch., Eur.:—εἰς ζώνην δεδόσθαι *to be given for girdle-money* (as we should say, *pin-money*), of Oriental queens who had cities given them, Xen.   II. *the man's belt* (in Hom. commonly ζωστήρ), Il., Xen., etc.   2. *the part round which the girdle past, the waist, loin*, Il.

ΖΩ'ΝΝῡ-ΜΙ, f. ζώσω: aor. 1 ἔζωσα:—Pass., aor. 1 ἐζώσθην: pf. ἔζωσμαι:—*to gird*, esp. *to gird round the loins* for a pugilistic conflict, Od., Hes.; ζ. γαῖαν, of Ocean, Anth.   II. Med. ζώννῠμαι, *to gird oneself, gird up one's loins*, of wrestlers and pugilists, who in early times wore a linen cloth (ζῶμα, διάζωμα) round their loins.   2. generally, *to gird up one's loins, prepare for battle*, Il.; also c. acc., ζωννύσκετο μίτρην *girded on his belt*, Ib.; χαλκὸν ζ. *to gird on one's* sword, Ib.

ζωο-γλύφος [ῠ], ὁ, (γλύφω) *a sculptor*, Anth.

ζωογονέω, f. ήσω, (ζωός) *to produce alive*, Luc.   II. *to preserve alive*, N.T.   From

ζωο-γόνος, ον, (ζῷον, *γείνω) *producing animals, generative*, name of Apollo, Anth.   II. ζωο-γόνος, (ζωή) *life-bringing*, Id.

ζωο-γράφος, ον, poët. for ζω-γράφος.

ζωο-θετέω, f. ήσω, (τίθημι) *to make alive*, Anth.

ζωό-μορφος, ον, (μόρφη) *in the shape of an animal*, Plut.

ζῷον, (as if contr. from ζώϊον), τό, (ζάω) *a living being, animal*, Hdt., Ar., etc.   II. in painting and sculpture, *a figure, image*, not necessarily of animals, Hdt.; mostly in pl. ζῷα ἐς τὴν ἐσθῆτα ἐγγράφειν Id., Plat., etc.; ζῷα γράφεσθαι, = ζωγραφεῖν, with a second acc. of the thing painted, ζῷα γράψασθαι τὴν ζεῦξιν τοῦ Βοσπόρου *to have the passage of the Bosporus painted*, Hdt.

ζωο-ποιέω, f. ήσω, (ζῷον) *to produce animals*, Arist., Luc.   II. ζωο-ποιέω, (ζωός) *to make alive*, N.T.

ζωός, ή, όν, (ζάω) *alive, living*, Hom., Hdt., etc.; ζωὸν ἑλεῖν τινά *to take prisoner*, Il.; ζωὸν λαβεῖν Xen.

ζωό-σοφος, ον, *wise unto life*, Anth.

ζωο-τόκος, ον, (τίκτω) *producing its young alive, viviparous*, Theocr.

ζωο-τύπος [ῠ], ον, *describing to the life*, Anth.

ζωο-φόρος, ον, (ζωή, φέρω) *life-giving*, Anth.   II. ζωοφόρος, ον, (ζῷον) *bearing animals*: ὁ ζ. (sc. κύκλος), *the zodiac*, Anth.

ζω-πονέω, f. ήσω, (ζώς) *to represent alive*, Anth.

ζωπῠρέω, *to kindle into flame, light up*: metaph., ζ. τάρβος Aesch.; νείκη Eur.

ζώ-πῠρον, τό, (πῦρ) *a spark, ember*, Plat., etc.

ζωροποτέω, *to drink sheer wine*, Anth.   From

ζωρο-πότης, ου, ὁ, *drinking sheer wine, drunken*, Anth.

ζωρός, όν, (ζάω?) *pure, sheer*, properly of wine without water, Anth.; absol., ζωρός (sc. οἶνος) Id.:—Compar.

in Hom., ζωρότερον δὲ κέραιε mix the wine *more pure*, i. e. add less water, Il. As the Greeks mixed their wine with water, the phrase ζωρότερον πίνειν came to mean not only, as in Hdt., *to drink purer wine than common*, but, generally, *to drink hard, be a drunkard*, like ἀκρατοποτεῖν, Theophr., Luc.

ζώς, neut. ζών, gen. ζώ, = ζωός, Il., Hdt.

ζῶσαι, aor. 1 inf. of ζώννυμι.

ζωστήρ, ῆρος, ὁ, (ζώννυμι) *a girdle*, in Il. always a *warrior's belt* or *baldric*, which passed round the loins and secured the bottom of the θώραξ :—in Od., *the belt* with which the swineherd girds up his frock. 2. later, = ζώνη, *a woman's girdle*. 3. metaph. of the encircling sea, Anth.

ζωστός, ή, όν, (ζώννυμι) *girded*, Plut.

ζῶστρον, τό, (ζώννυμι) *a belt, girdle*, Od.

ζωτικός, ή, όν, (ζάω) *full of life, lively*, Lat. *vivax*, Plat.:—Adv., ζωτικῶς ἔχειν to be *fond of life*, Plut. 2. of works of Art, *true to life*, τὸ ζωτικὸν φαίνεσθαι πῶς ἐνεργάζῃ τοῖς ἀνδριᾶσιν; how do you produce *that look of life* in your statues? Xen.

ζώ-φυτος, ον, (φύω) *giving life to plants, fertilising, generative*, Aesch., Plut.

ζώω, Ep. and Ion. for ζάω.

H.

H, η, ἦτα, τό, indecl., seventh letter of the Gr. alphabet; as numeral η' = ὀκτώ and ὄγδοος, but ͵η = 8000. The uncial form of Eta (H) was a double ε (Ε Ǝ) and prob. it was pronounced as a long ε, cf. δῆλος (from δέελος). The old Alphabet had only one sign (Ε) for the ε sound, till the long vowels η and ω were introduced from the Samian Alphabet in the archonship of Euclides, B. C. 403. The sign H, before it was taken to represent the double ε, was used for the spiritus asper, as ΗΟΣ for ὅς, (which remains in the Latin H). When H was taken to represent ē, it was at the same time cut in two, so that ⊢ represented the spir. asper, ⊣ the spir. lenis; whence came the present signs for the breathings.

As to dialectic changes, 1. the vowel η was much used by the Ion., being in Aeol. and Dor. replaced by ᾱ, as also in Att., but mostly after ρ or a vowel, πρήσσω θώρηξ ἰητρός, Att. πράσσω θώραξ ἰατρός. 2. in Att., ει and ηι were not seldom changed into η, as κλεῖθρα κλῇθρα, Νηρηΐδες Νηρῇδες. 3. Dor. and Aeol. for ει, as τῆνος, κῆνος for κεῖνος.

ἤ, Ep. also ἠέ, Conjunction with two chief senses, Disjunctive and Comparative.
  A. DISJUNCTIVE, *or*, Lat. *vel*, to subjoin one or more clauses differing from the first, ἤκουσας ἢ οὐκ ἤκουσας ἢ κωφῇ λέγω; Aesch.:—ἤ . . , ἤ . . , *either* . . , *or* . . , Lat. *aut* . . , *aut* . . , Hom., etc.   II. in indirect Questions, εἰ . . , ἤ . . , *whether* . . , *or* . . , Lat. *utrum* . . , *an* . . , εἰδῶμεν εἰ νικῶμεν ἢ νικώμεθα Aesch.:—but in Hom. ἤ . . , ἤ (or ἦ) . . is used for εἰ, Lat. *an*, εἰπὲ ἤ . . , say *whether* . . , Od.
  B. COMPARATIVE, *than, as*, Lat. *quam*, Hom., etc.: after Adjs. which imply comparison, as ἄλλος,

ἕτερος, ἀλλοῖος, διπλάσιος, ἐναντίος, ἴδιος, πολλαπλάσιος, and after the Advs. πρίν, πρόσθεν; so, after Verbs implying comparison, βούλεσθαι ἤ . . to wish *rather than* . . ; φθάνειν ἤ . . to come *sooner than* . . , etc. 2. ἤ sometimes joins two Comparatives, when they both refer to the same subject, ἐλαφρότεροι ἢ ἀφνειότεροι to be swifter *rather* than richer, Od.; ταχύτερα ἢ σοφώτερα Hdt. 3. rarely after a Sup., πλεῖστα θωυμάσια ἔχει Αἴγυπτος ἢ ἄλλη πᾶσα χώρη Id. 4. ἤ is often omitted with numerals after πλέων, ἐλάττων, μείων, as, ἔτη πλέω ἑβδομήκοντα Plat. [When ἢ οὐ, ἢ οὐκ come together in a verse, the two coalesce into one syll.]

ἤ, an exclamation, to call one's attention to a thing, ἤ, ἤ, σιώπα Ar.

ἦ, Adv., with two chief senses, Confirmative and Interrogative:
  I. TO CONFIRM an assertion, *in truth, truly, verily, of a surety*, Hom., etc.; often strengthd. by other Particles, as ἦ ἄρα, ἦ δή, ἦ δή που, ἦ μάλα, etc. ;—and to express doubt, ἦ που ;—ἦ μήν, Ion. and Ep. ἦ μέν, ἦ μάν, used in protestations and oaths, σὺ μοι ὀμόσσον, ἦ μέν μοι ἀρήξειν Hom., etc.
  II. in INTERROG. sentences, Lat. *num? pray?* or *can it be?*—also ἦ οὐκ . . ; Lat. *nonne?* Particles are often added to this ἦ, ἦ ῥα, ἦ ἄρα δή, etc.

ἦ, for ἔφη, 3 sing. impf. or aor. 2 of ἠμί.

ἦ, Att. contr. from Ion. ἔα, impf. of εἰμί (*sum*).

ᾖ, 3 sing. pres. act. subj. of εἰμί (*sum*).

ἥ, fem. of Artic. ὁ :—in Hom. also for αὕτη.

ἥ, fem. of relat. Pron. ὅς.

ᾗ, dat. sing. fem. of possess. Pron. ὅς, ἥ, ὅν, *his*.

ᾗ, dat. sing. fem. of relat. Pron. ὅς, ἥ, ὁ, Hom.: freq. in adverb. sense, 1. of Place, *which way, where, whither, in* or *at what place*, relat. to τῇ, Il., Soph. II. of Manner, as, ᾗ καὶ Λοξίας ἐφήμισεν Aesch., Thuc., etc. 2. *wherefore*, Lat. *quare*, Id. 3. *in so far as*, Lat. *qua, quatenus*, Xen. III. joined with a Sup., ᾗ ἐδύνατο τάχιστα as quick as he was able, Id.; ᾗ ῥᾷστά τε καὶ ἥδιστα Id.

ἦα, ἦεν, Ep. for ἦν, 1 and 3 sing. impf. of εἰμί (*sum*).

ἦα, contr. for ἤϊα, Ep. impf. of εἶμι (*ibo*).

ἦα, τά, contr. from ἤϊα, τά, q. v.

ἠβαιός, ά, όν, Ion. for βαιός, *little, small, poor, slight*, with negat. οὐδέ, οὔ οἱ ἔνι φρένες, οὐδ᾽ ἠβαιαί no sense is in him, no not *the least*, Hom.; οὔ οἱ ἔνι τρίχες, οὐδ᾽ ἠβαιαί no not even *a few*, Od.:—neut. as Adv., οὐδ᾽ ἠβαιόν not *in the least*, not *at all*, Lat. *ne tantillum quidem*, Hom.; rarely without a negat., ἠβαιὸν ἀπὸ σπείους *a little* from the cave, Od.

ἠβάσκω, Incept. of ἠβάω, *to come to man's estate, come to one's strength*, Lat. *pubescere*, Xen. :—metaph. *to be new*, ἠβάσκει πενίη Anth.

ἠβάω: Ep. opt. ἡβώοιμι, part. ἡβώων: f. -ήσω, Dor. -άσω [ᾱ]: aor. 1 ἤβησα: pf. ἥβηκα: (ἥβη):—*to be at man's estate, to be in the prime of youth*, ἀνὴρ οὐδὲ μάλ᾽ ἡβῶν not even *in the prime and pride of life*, Hom.; γυνὴ τέτορ᾽ ἡβώωσα (sc. ἔτη) i. e. *being four years past puberty*, Hes.; ἡβῶν when *I was young*, Ar.; οἱ ἡβῶντες *the young*, Id. :—of plants, ἡμερὶς ἡβώωσα *a young luxuriant* vine, Od. 2. metaph. *to be young*, ἀεὶ γὰρ ἡβᾷ τοῖς γέρουσιν εὖ μαθεῖν learning

is young even for the old, i.e. 'tis never too late to learn, Aesch.; ἥβᾳ δῆμος the people is like a young man, Eur.

῾ΗΒΗ, Dor. ἥβα, rarely ἄβα, ἡ, manhood, youthful prime, youth, Lat. pubertas, νεηνίη ἀνδρὶ ἐοικώς, τοῦπερ χαριεστάτη ἥβη Od.; ἥβης μέτρον ἱκέσθαι or ἱκάνειν = ἡβάσκειν, Ib. b. youthful strength, vigour, πειρώμενος ἥβης Il.; ἥβη πεποίθεα Od. c. legally, ἥβη was the time before manhood, at Athens 16 years of age; at Sparta, 18, so that τὰ δέκα ἀφ' ἥβης were men of 28, τὰ τετταράκοντα ἀφ' ἥβης men of 58, and so on, Xen.: cf. ἔφηβος. 2. metaph. youthful cheer, merriment, δαιτὸς ἥβη Eur.: also youthful passion, fire, spirit, Pind. 3. a body of youth, the youth, Lat. juventus, Aesch. II. as femin. prop. n., ῝Ηβη, Hebé, daughter of Zeus and Hera, wife of Hercules, Hom. Hence

ἡβηδόν, Adv. from the youth upwards, Hdt.

ἡβητήρ, ῆρος, ὁ, = ἡβητής, Anth.

ἡβητήριον, τό, a place where young people meet, to eat and drink, exercise and amuse themselves, Plut. From

ἡβητής, οῦ, (ἡβάω) masc. Adj. youthful, at one's prime, h. Hom., Eur.

ἡβητικός, ή, όν, youthful, Lat. juvenilis, Xen.

ἡβός, ή, όν, Dor. ἀβός, = ἡβῶν, Theocr.

ἡβυλλιάω, Comic Dim. of ἡβάω, to be youngish, Ar.

ἡβῷμι, opt. of ἡβάω, Ep. ἡβώοιμι, Att. ἡβῴην.

ἡβώων, -ώωσα, Ep. for ἡβῶν, -ῶσα, part. of ἡβάω.

ἡγάσθε, Ep. for ἥγασθε, 2 pl. of ἄγαμαι.

ἡγαγόμην, ἥγαγον, aor. 2 med. and act. of ἄγω.

ἡγά-θεος, η, ον, Dor. ἀγάθ-, (ἄγαν, θεῖος) very divine, most holy, Hom.

ἡγαλλῖασα, aor. 1 of ἀγαλλιάω.

ἡγάπευν, Dor. for ἡγάπων, impf. of ἀγαπάω.

ἡγάσσατο, Ep. for ἡγάσατο, 3 sing. aor. 1 of ἄγαμαι.

ἤγγειλα, aor. 1 of ἀγγέλλω.

ἤγγικα, ἤγγισα, pf. and aor. 1 of ἐγγίζω.

ἤγειρα, aor. 1 of ἀγείρω.

ἡγεμόνευμα, ατος, τό, a leading: in Eur. ἀγεμόνευμα νεκροῖσι = ἡγεμὼν νεκρῶν.

ἡγεμονεύς, έως, Ep. for ἡγεμών, Ep. acc. ἡγεμονῆα, -ῆας, Anth., etc.

ἡγεμονεύω, Dor. ἀγεμ-, f. σω, to be or act as ἡγεμών, to go before, lead the way, Hom.; ὁδὸν ἡγ. Od.; c. dat. pers. to lead the way for him, ῥόον ὕδατι ἡγεμόνευεν made a course for the water, Il. II. to lead in war, to rule, command, c. dat., Ib.; elsewhere, like most Verbs of ruling, c. gen., Ib., Hdt., etc.:—absol. to have or take the command, Hdt., Plat.:—Pass. to be ruled, Thuc.; to be governor, τῆς Συρίας N. T.

ἡγεμονία, ἡ, (ἡγεμών) a leading the way, going first, Hdt. II. chief command, Id., Thuc., etc.; ἡγ. δικαστηρίων authority over them, Aeschin. 2. the hegemony or sovereignty of one state over a number of subordinates, as. of Athens in Attica, Thebes in Boeotia:—the hegemony of Greece was wrested from Sparta by Athens; and the Peloponn. war was a struggle for this hegemony. b. = Roman imperium, Plut.: the reign of the Emperor, N. T. III. a division of the army, a command, Plut.

ἡγεμονικός, ή, όν, ready to lead or guide, Xen. II.

fit to command, authoritative, leading, Id., etc. 2. = Rom. Consularis, Plut.

ἡγεμόσυνα (sc. ἱερά), τά, thank-offerings for safe-conduct, Xen. From

ἡγεμών, Dor. ἀγεμ-, όνος, ὁ, also ἡ:—one who leads, Lat. dux: and so, I. in Od., a guide to shew the way, so Hdt., etc.; ἡγ. γενέσθαι τινὶ τῆς ὁδοῦ Id. 2. one who is an authority to others, Lat. dux, auctor, τοῖς νεωτέροις ἡγ. ἠθῶν γίγνεσθαι Plat.; ἡγεμόνα εἶναί τινος to be the cause of a thing, Xen., etc. II. in Il., a leader, commander, chief, ἡγεμόνες Δαναῶν, φυλάκων, Il., etc.; ἔχοντες ἡγεμόνας τῶν πάνυ στρατηγῶν having some of the best generals as commanders, Thuc.: a chief, sovereign, Pind., Soph., etc. b. = Rom. Emperor, Plut.: also a provincial governor, N. T.

ἡγέομαι, Dor. ἀγ-: impf. ἡγούμην, Ion. -εόμην or -εύμην: f. ἡγήσομαι: aor. 1 ἡγησάμην: pf. ἥγημαι: Dep.: (ἄγω):—to go before, lead the way, Hom., etc.:—c. dat. pers. to lead the way for him, guide, conduct, Id.:—also, ὁδὸν ἡγήσασθαι to go before on the way, Lat. praeire viam, Od. 2. c. dat. pers. et gen. rei, to be one's leader in a thing, ἀοιδὸς ἡμῖν ἡγείσθω ὀρχηθμοῖο Ib.; ἡγ. τινι σοφίας, ᾠδῆς Pind., etc.:—and c. gen. rei only, ἡγ. νόμων to lead the song, Id., etc. 3. c. acc. rei, to lead, conduct, τὰς πομπάς Dem., etc. II. to lead an army or fleet, c. dat., Hom., etc.:—c. gen. to be the leader or commander of, Id. 2. absol., οἱ ἡγούμενοι the rulers, Soph.; ἡγούμενοι ἐν τοῖς ἀδελφοῖς leading men, N. T. III. to suppose, believe, hold, Lat. ducere, Hdt., etc.; ἡγ. τι εἶναι Id. 2. with an attributive word added, ἡγ. τινα βασιλέα to hold or regard as king, Thuc. 3. ἡγ. τι περὶ πολλοῦ Id.; περὶ πλείστου Thuc. 3. ἡγ. θεούς to believe in gods, Eur., etc.; cf. νομίζω II. 4. ἡγοῦμαι δεῖν, to think it fit, deem it necessary to do, c. inf., Dem.; without δεῖν, παθεῖν μᾶλλον ἡγησάμενοι ἤ.. Thuc. IV. the pf. is used in pass. sense, τὰ ἡγημένα = τὰ νομιζόμενα, ap. Dem.

ἡγερέθομαι, Ep. form of ἀγείρομαι (Pass.), to gather together, assemble, Hom., only in 3 pl. pres. and impf. ἡγερέθονται, ἡγερέθοντο, and inf. ἡγερέθεσθαι.

ἡγέρθην, aor. 1 pass. of ἀγείρω and of ἐγείρω:—Ep. 3 pl. ἤγερθεν.

ἡγέτης, ου, ὁ, Dor. ἀγέτα, (ἡγέομαι) a leader, Anth.

ἤγηλα, aor. 1 of ἀγάλλω.

ἡγηλάζω, Ep. collat. form of ἡγέομαι, to guide, lead, Od.; κακὸν μόρον ἡγ. to lead a wretched life, Ib.

ἥγημαι, pf. of ἡγέομαι.

ἡγήτειρα, ἡ, fem. of ἡγητήρ, Anth.

ἡγητέον, verb. Adj. of ἡγέομαι, one must lead, Xen. II. one must suppose, Plat.

ἡγητήρ, Dor. ἀγ-, ῆρος, ὁ, a guide, Soph. 2. a commander, Pind.

ἡγήτωρ, ορος, ὁ, a leader, commander, chief, Il.

ἡγιασμένος, pf. pass. part. of ἁγιάζω.

ἥγνισα, 2 sing. aor. of ἁγνίζω.

ἠγνόουν, impf. of ἀγνοέω.

ἦγξα, aor. 1 of ἄγχω.

ἦγον, impf. of ἄγω.

ἡγορόωντο, Ep. for ἠγορῶντο, 3 pl. impf. of ἀγοράομαι.

ἤγουν, Conjunct., (ἤ γε οὖν) that is to say, or rather, to define a word more correctly, Xen.

ἠγώ, crasis for ἢ ἐγώ.

ἠγωνισάμην, aor. 1 of ἀγωνίζομαι.

ἠ-δέ, and, properly correlative to ἠ-μέν v. sub ἠμέν :—but, often without ἠμέν, just like καί, and, Il. :—ἠδὲ καί conjoined and also, Hom.

ἦδε, fem. of ὅδε.

ἤδεα, Ion. plqpf. of οἶδα: v. *εἴδω.

ἠδέσθην, aor. 1 of αἰδέομαι.

ἡδέως, Adv. of ἡδύς, v. ἡδύς III.

ἬΔΗ, Adv. (related to νῦν, as Lat. jam to nunc), by this time, before this, already, or of the future, now, presently, forthwith, Hom.; νὺξ ἤδη τελέθει 'tis already night, Il.; ἔτος τόδ' ἤδη δέκατον Soph. :—so in a local relation, ἀπὸ ταύτης ἤδη Αἴγυπτος directly after this is Egypt, Hdt. 2. of the future, λέξον ὄφρα κεν ἤδη ταρπώμεθα Il.; στείχοις ἂν ἤδη Soph. II. often joined with other words of time, ἤδη νῦν now already, Hom.; νῦν ἤδη Soph., etc.; ἤδη πάλαι Id.; ἐπεὶ ἤδη, Lat. quum jam, Od., etc.

ἤδη, ἤδησθα or ἤδεισθα, ἤδη, plqpf. of οἶδα: v. *εἴδω.

ἥδιστος, ἡδίων, Sup. and Comp. of ἡδύς.

ἬΔΟΜΑΙ, Dor. ἅδομαι: f. ἡσθήσομαι: aor. 1 ἥσθην, med. ἡσάμην: Dep. :—to enjoy oneself, take delight, take one's pleasure, Od., etc.—Construction : 1. with participle, ἥσατο πίνων Od.; ἥσθη ἀκούσας he was glad to have heard, Hdt., etc. 2. c. dat., ἥδεσθαί τινι to delight in or at a thing, Id., etc.; ἐπί τινι Xen., etc.; rarely c. gen.; ἥσθη ἥσθη ποτάματος he enjoyed the draught, Soph. 3. c. acc. and part., ἥσθην πατέρα τὸν ἀμὸν εὐλογοῦντά σε I was pleased to hear you praising him, Id. 4. part. as an Adj. glad, delighted, Ar.: also, like βουλομένῳ, ἀσμένῳ, in the phrase ἡδομένῳ ἐστί μοί τι I am well pleased at the thing happening, Hdt., Plat.

ἡδομένως, Adv. of foreg., with joy, gladly, Xen.

ἡδονή, Dor. ἁδονά or ἁδονά, ἡ, (ἥδομαι) delight, enjoyment, pleasure, Lat. voluptas, Hdt., etc.; ἡδονῇ ἡσσᾶσθαι, χαρίζεσθαι to give way to pleasure, Thuc., Plat., etc. :—often with Prepositions in Adv. sense, πρὸς or καθ' ἡδονὴν λέγειν to speak so as to please another, Hdt., Att.; καθ' ἡδονὴν κλύειν, ἀκούειν Soph., Dem.; καθ' ἡδονήν or πρὸς ἡδ. ἐστί μοι Aesch.; ὃ μὲν ἐστι πρὸς ἡδ. that which is agreeable, Dem.; ἐν ἡδονῇ ἐστί τινι it is a pleasure or delight to another, Hdt., etc. 2. a pleasure, a delight, Soph., Ar. 3. in pl. pleasures, pleasant lusts, Xen., N. T.

ἧδος, εος, τό, (ἀνδάνω) delight, enjoyment, pleasure, δαιτὸς ἧδος pleasure from or in the feast, Hom.; ἀλλὰ τί μοι τῶν ἧδος; what delight have I therefrom? Il.

ἣ δ' ὅς, for ἔφη ἐκεῖνος, v. ἠμί.

ἡδύ-βόης, Dor. -βόας, ου, ὁ, sweet-sounding, Eur., Anth.

ἡδύ-γαμος, ον, sweetening marriage, Anth.

ἡδύ-γελως, ων, gen. ω, sweetly laughing, h. Hom., Anth.

ἡδύ-γλωσσος, ον, (γλῶσσα) sweet-tongued, Pind.

ἡδύ-γνώμων, ον, (γνώμη) of pleasant mind, Xen.

ἡδύ-επής, Dor. ἁδυ-, ές, (ἔπος) sweet-speaking, Il., etc.: sweet-sounding, Pind. :—poët. fem. ἡδύνεπεια, Hes.

ἡδύ-θροος, ον, contr. -θρους, ουν, sweet-strained, Eur.

ἡδύ-λογος, Dor. ἁδυλ-, ον, sweet-speaking, sweet-voiced, Pind., Anth. 2. of persons, flattering, fawning, Eur.

ἡδύ-λύρης [ῠ] ου, ὁ, singing sweetly to the lyre, Anth.

ἡδυ-μελής, Dor. ἁδυ-μ-, ές, (μέλος) sweet-strained, sweet-singing, Pind.

ἡδυ-μελί-φθογγος, ον, of honey-sweet voice, Anth.

ἡδύ-μιγής, ές, (μίγνυμι) sweetly-mixed, Anth.

ἤδυμος, ον, poët. for ἡδύς, sweet, pleasant, h. Hom.

ἡδύνω [ῡ] : aor. 1 ἥδῡνα :—Pass., aor. 1 ἡδύνθην : pf. ἥδυσμαι : (ἡδύς) :—to sweeten, season, give a flavour or relish to a thing, c. acc., Xen., etc.

ἡδύ-οινος, ον, producing sweet wine, Xen. :—ἡδύοινοι, οἱ, dealers in sweet wine, Id.

ἡδυπάθεια, ἡ, (ἡδυπαθής) pleasant living, luxury, Xen.

ἡδυπαθέω, f. ήσω, (ἡδυπαθής) to live pleasantly, enjoy oneself, be luxurious, Xen. Hence

ἡδυπάθημα, ατος, τό, enjoyment, Anth.

ἡδυ-παθής, ές, (παθεῖν) living pleasantly, luxurious.

ἡδύ-πνευστος, ον, = sq., Anth.

ἡδύ-πνοος, Dor. ἁδύπν-, ον, contr. -πνους, ουν, (πνέω) sweet-breathing, Eur.; of musical sound, Pind.; of dreams, Soph. 2. sweet-smelling, fragrant, Anth.

ἡδύ-πολις, Dor. ἁδ-, ὁ, ἡ, dear to the people, Soph.

ἡδύ-πότης, ου, fond of drinking, Anth.

ἡδύ-ποτος, ον, sweet to drink, Od.

ἡδύς, ἡδεῖα, ἡδύ, also ἡδύς as fem. : Dor. ἁδύς, irreg. acc. ἀδέα for ἡδύν and for ἡδεῖαν : Ion. fem. ἡδέα, Dor. ἁδέα :—Comp. ἡδίων [ῑ], Sup. ἥδιστος, later ἡδύτερος, ἡδύτατος: (ἀνδάνω): I. sweet to the taste or smell, Hom.; to the hearing, Id.; then of any pleasant feeling or state, as sleep, Id. :—c. inf., ἡδὺς δρακεῖν Aesch.; ἡδὺς ἀκοῦσαι λόγος Plat. :—ἡδύ ἐστι or γίγνεται it is pleasant, Hom., etc. :—so, οὔ μοι ἡδιόν ἐστι λέγειν I had rather not say, Hdt. :—neut. as Subst., τὰ ἡδέα pleasures, Thuc. :—neut. as Adv., sweetly, Il., etc. II. after Hom., of persons, pleasant, welcome, Soph. 2. well-pleased, glad, Id., Dem.; in addressing a person, ὦ ἥδιστε, Horace's dulcissime rerum, Plat. 3. like εὐήθης, innocent, simple, ὡς ἡδὺς εἶ Id. III. Adv. ἡδέως, sweetly, pleasantly, with pleasure, Soph., Eur., etc.; ἡδέως ἂν ἐροίμην I would gladly ask, should like to ask, Dem.; ἡδέως τι to be pleased or content with, Eur.; ἡδ. ἔχειν πρός τινα or τινί to be kind, well-disposed to one, Dem. :—Comp. ἥδιον Plat., etc. :—Sup. ἥδιστα Id.

ἥδυσμα, ατος, τό, (ἡδύνω) that which gives a relish or flavour, seasoning, sauce, Ar., Xen., etc.

ἡδύ-φαής, ές, (φάος) sweet-shining, Anth.

ἡδύ-φρων, ονος, ὁ, ἡ, (φρήν) sweet-minded, Anth.

ἡδυφωνία, ἡ, sweetness of voice or sound, Babr. From

ἡδύ-φωνος, ον, (φωνή) sweet-voiced, Sappho.

ἡδύ-χαρής, ές, (χαίρω) sweetly joyous, Anth.

ἡδύ-χροος, ον, contr. -χρους, ουν, (χρόα) of sweet complexion, Anth.

ἠέ, poët. for ἤ, or, whether.

ἠέ, exclam., ah! Aesch.

ἦε, Ep. for ἤει, 3 sing. impf. of εἶμι (ibo).

ἤειδειν, Ep. for ᾔδειν, plqpf. of οἶδα, v. *εἴδω.

ἤειδον, impf. of ἀείδω.

ἤειρα, aor. 1 of ἀείρω.

ἠέλιος, ὁ, Ep. and Ion. for ἥλιος.

ἠελιῶτις, Ep. fem. of ἡλιώτης.

ἦεν, Ep. for ἦν, impf. of εἰμί (sum).

ἠέ-περ, Ep. for ἤ-περ, Hom.

ἠέρα, Ion. and Ep. acc. of ἀήρ.

ἠερέθομαι, Ep. for ἀείρομαι, Pass., only found in 3 pl. pres. and impf. ἠερέθονται, -οντο:—*to hang floating or waving in the air*, Il.:—metaph., ὁπλοτέρων ἀνδρῶν φρένες ἠερέθονται *young men's minds turn with every wind*, Ib.

ἠέρι, Ion. and Ep. dat. of ἀήρ.

ἠέριος, α, ον, (ἀήρ) *early, with early morn*, Il. **II.** *in the air, high in air*, Anth.

ἠερο-δίνης [ῑ], ες, *wheeling in mid air*, Anth.

ἠερο-ειδής, ές, Ep. for ἀερο-, (ἀήρ, εἶδος) *of dark and cloudy look, cloud-streaked*, of the sea, Od.: generally, *dark, murky*, Ib.:—neut. as Adv., *in the far distance, dimly*, ὅσσον τ' ἠεροειδὲς ἀνὴρ ἴδεν Il.

ἠερόεις, εσσα, εν, Ep. for ἀερ-, (ἀήρ) *hazy, murky*, Il.; ἠερόεντα κέλευθα *the murky* road (i. e. death), Od.

ἠερόθεν, Ep. for ἀερ-, (ἀήρ) *from air*, Anth.

ἠέρος, Ep. gen. of ἀήρ.

ἠερο-φοῖτις, ιδος, (φοιτάω), fem. Adj. *walking in darkness*, Il.

ἠερό-φωνος, ον, *sounding through air, loud-voiced*, Il.

ἠέρτησα, aor. 1 of ἀερτάζω:—ἠέρτημαι, pf. pass.

ἤεσαν, 3 pl. impf. of εἶμι (*ibo*).

ἤήδει, poët. 3 sing. plqpf. of οἶδα; v. *εἴδω.

ἤην, Ep. for ἦν, impf. of εἰμί (*sum*).

ἤήρ, v. sub ἀήρ.

ἠθαῖος, α, ον, Dor. for ἠθεῖος, Pind.

ἠθάς, άδος, ὁ, ἡ, (ἦθος II) *accustomed to* a thing, *acquainted with* it, c. gen., Soph. **2.** absol. *accustomed, usual*, Eur.: of animals, *tame, domestic*, Lat. mansuetus, Ar.:—as neut., = ἦθος, τὰ καινά γ' ἐκ τῶν ἠθάδων ἡδίον' ἐστί Eur.

ἠθεῖος, Dor. ἠθαῖος, α, ον, (ἦθος) *trusty, honoured*, ἠθεῖε sir, Il.; ἠθείη κεφαλή Ib.; ἀλλά μιν ἠθεῖον καλέω *I will call him my honoured lord*, Od.

ἤθελον, impf. of ἐθέλω.

ἤθεος, ὁ, ἡ, Att. for ἠΐθεος.

ἠθέω, f. ήσω, (ἦθω):—*to sift, strain*:—Pass. *to be strained*, Plat.

ἠθικός, ή, όν, (ἦθος II) *of or for morals, ethical, moral*, Arist.; τὰ ἠθικά *a treatise on morals*, Id. **II.** *shewing moral character, expressive thereof*, Id.:—Adv., ἠθικῶς λέγειν Id.

ἠθμός, ὁ, (ἦθω) *a strainer*, Eur.; of the eyelashes, Xen.

ἠθοποιέω, *to form manners or character*, Plut. From ἠθο-ποιός, όν, (ποιέω) *forming character*, Plut.

ἦθος, εος, τό, lengthd. form of ἔθος, *an accustomed place*: in pl. *the haunts or abodes* of animals, Hom., Hdt. **II.** *custom, usage*, Hes., Pind. **2.** of man, *his disposition, character*, Lat. ingenium, mores, Hes., Att.; ὦ μιαρὸν ἦθος, addressed to a person, Soph. **3.** in pl., generally, of *manners*, like Lat. mores, Hes., Hdt., Thuc.

ἦθω, rare collat. form of ἠθέω.

ἤϊα, contr. ᾖα, τά, *provisions for a journey*, Ep. word for ἐφόδια, Lat. viaticum, Hom.:—generally, λύκων ἤϊα *food for wolves*, Il. **II.** *husks or chaff*, Od.

ἤϊα, Ion. for ᾖειν, impf. of εἶμι (*ibo*).

ἠΐθεος [ῑ], Att. contr. ᾖθεος, ὁ, *a youth just come to manhood, but not yet married*, παρθένος ἠΐθεός τε Hom.; χόρους παρθένων τε καὶ ἠϊθέων Hdt. **II.** rare as fem., ἠΐθεη = παρθένος. (Deriv. uncertain.)

ἤϊκτο, 3 sing. plqpf. pass. of ἔοικα.

ἤϊξα, aor. 1 of ἀΐσσω.

ἠϊόεις, εσσα, εν, (ἠϊών) *with banks, high-banked*, Il.

ἤϊον, Ep. for ᾖεσαν, 3 pl. impf. of εἶμι (*ibo*).

ἤϊος, ὁ, epith. of Phoebus, ἤϊε Φοῖβε Il. (Prob. from the cry ἤ, ἤ, cf. λήϊος, εὔϊος.)

ἤϊσαν, Ep. for ᾖεσαν, 3 pl. impf. of εἶμι (*ibo*).

ἤϊσαν, Ep. for ᾖδεσαν, 3 pl. impf. of οἶδα, v. *εἴδω.

ἠΐχθην, aor. 1 pass. of ἀΐσσω.

ἠϊών, Att. ᾐών, ή: Ep. dat. pl. ἠϊόνεσσι:—*a sea-bank, shore, beach*, Hdt., etc.; *a river-bank*, Aesch.

ἦκα (*ἀκή 2), Adv., **I.** of Place or Motion, *slightly, a little, softly, gently*, Hom. **II.** of Sound, *stilly, softly, low*, Il. **III.** of Sight, *softly, smoothly*, ἦκα στίλβοντες ἐλαίῳ *with oil soft shining*, Ib. **IV.** of Time, *by little and little*, Anth.

ἦκα, aor. 1 of ἵημι.

ἠκαζον, impf. of εἰκάζω:—ἤκασα, aor. 1.

ἠκάχον, Ep. aor. 2 of ἀχέω II.

ἠκέσατο, 3 sing. aor. 1 of ἀκέομαι.

ἤ-κεστος, η, ον, (Ep. for ἄ-κεστος) *untouched by the goad*, of young heifers reserved for sacrifices, Il.

ἠκηκόειν, old Att. -όη, plqpf. of ἀκούω.

ἤκιστος, η, ον, sup. Adj. from Adv. ἦκα, ἤκιστος ἐλαυνέμεν *the gentlest or slowest* in driving, Il.

ἤκιστος, η, ον, Sup. of the Comp. ἥσσων, the Posit. in use being μικρός, *least*:—as Adv. ἤκιστα, *least*, Soph., etc.; οὐχ ἤκιστα, ἀλλὰ μάλιστα Hdt.; ὡς ἥκιστα *as little as possible*, Thuc. **2.** often in reply to a question, *nay not so, not at all*, Lat. minime, Soph., etc.; ἥκιστά γε minime vero, Id.

ἤ-κου, Ion. and Dor. for ἤ-που.

ἤκουσα, aor. 1 of ἀκούω:—ἤκουσμαι, pf. pass.

ἭΚΩ, impf. ἧκον: f. ἥξω, Dor. ἥξω:—*to have come, be present, be here*, Lat. adesse, properly in a pf. sense, with the impf. ἧκον as plqpf., *I had come*, and fut. ἥξω as fut. pf. *I shall have come*, directly opp. to οἴχομαι *to be gone*, while ἔρχομαι *to come or go* serves as pres. to both, Hom., etc.:—*to return*, Xen. **2.** *to have reached a point*, ἐς τοσήνδ' ὕβριν Soph.; ἐς τοσοῦτον ἀμαθίας Plat. **3.** δι' ὀργῆς ἥκειν *to be angry*, Soph.; cf. διά A. IV. **4.** like ἔχω B. II, εὖ ἥκειν τινός *to be well off for a thing, have plenty of* it, as, εὖ ἥκ. τοῦ βίου Hdt.; καλῶς αὐτοῖς ἧκον βίου *as they had come to a good age*, Eur.; ὧδε γένους ἥκ. τινί *to be* this degree of kin to him, Id.:—also, εὖ ἥκειν, absol., *to be well off, flourishing*, Hdt.:—c. gen. only, σὺ δὲ δυνάμιος ἥκεις μεγάλης *thou art in great power*, Id. **II.** of things, *to be brought*, Id., etc.; ἵν' ἥκει τὰ μαντεύματα *what they have come to*, Soph. **2.** *to concern, relate*, or *belong to*, εἴς ἐμ' ἥκει τὰ πράγματα Ar. **3.** *to depend upon*, ἐπί τι Dem.

ἠλάθην [ᾰ], aor. 1 pass. of ἐλαύνω.

ἠλαίνω, Ep. for ἀλαίνω, *to wander, stray*, Theocr.

ἠλάκατα, τά, only in pl. *the wool on the distaff*, Od.

ἠλᾰκάτη [κᾰ], ἡ, Dor. ἠλακάτα or ἀλακάτα:—*a distaff*, Lat. colus, on which the wool is put, Hom., etc.; ἡ ἠλ. τοῦ ἀτράκτου *the stalk* of the spindle, Plat. (Deriv. uncertain.)

ἠλάμην, aor. 1 of ἅλλομαι.

ἤλᾰσα, -άμην, aor. 1 act. and med. of ἐλαύνω:—ἠλάσθην, pass.

ἠλασκάζω, lengthd. form of ἠλάσκω, Il.　**II**. c. acc. *to flee from, shun*, Od.

ἠλάσκω, (ἀλάομαι) *to wander, stray, roam about*, Il.

ἠλᾶτο, 3 sing. impf. of ἀλάομαι.

ἤλδανε, 3 sing. aor. 2 of ἀλδαίνω.

ἤλειψα, aor. 1 of ἀλείφω.

ἠλέκτρινος, *ον, made of* ἤλεκτρον, Luc.

ἤλεκτρον, *τό*, and **ἤλεκτρος**, *ὁ* or *ἡ*, *electron*, a word sometimes used to denote *amber*, as prob. in Hom., Hes. and Hdt.;—sometimes *pale gold*, a compound of 1 part of silver to 4 of gold, Soph., etc.—In Ar. ἐκπιπτουσῶν τῶν ἠλέκτρων, the ἤλεκτροι are prob. the pegs of the lyre *made of* or *inlaid with electron*. (Deriv. uncertain.)

ἠλέκτρο-φαής, *ές*, (φάος) *amber-gleaming*, Eur.

ἠλέκτωρ, *opos, ὁ, the beaming sun*, Il.; as Adj., ἠλέκτωρ Ὑπερίων *beaming* Hyperion, Ib. (Deriv. uncertain.)

ἠλέματος, Dor. **ἀλέματος**, *ον*, (ἠλεός) *idle, vain, trifling*, Theocr., Anth.

ἠλεός, *ή, όν*, (ἀλάομαι) *astray, distraught, crazed*, Od.; also in apocop. form ἠλέ, Il.: ἠλεά as Adv. *foolishly*, Anth.　**2**. act. *distracting, crazing*, οἶνος Od.

ἠλεύατο, Ep. 3 sing. aor. 1 of ἀλέομαι.

ἠλήλαντο, Ep. 3 pl. plqpf. pass. of ἐλαύνω.

ἦλθα, late aor. 1 of ἔρχομαι, N. T.

ἡλιάζομαι, f. άσομαι: aor. 1 -ασάμην: Dep.:—*to sit in the court* Ἡλιαία, *be a Heliast*, Ar.

ἡλιαία, *ἡ*, at Athens, *a public place* or *hall*, in which the chief law-court was held, Ar.　**2**. *the supreme court*, ap. Dem.

ἡλιάς, *άδος*, fem. Adj. *of the sun*, ap. Luc.

ἡλιαστής, *οῦ, ὁ, a juryman of the court* ἡλιαία, *a Heliast*, Ar. Hence

ἡλιαστικός, *ή, όν, of, for*, or *like a Heliast*, Ar.

ἠλίβᾰτος, Dor. **ἀλίβ**-, *ον, high, steep, precipitous*, epith. of rocky crags, Hom., Hes., etc.; of the throne of Zeus, Ar.　**2**. in Od. 9. 243 ἠλίβατος πέτρη, it seems to mean *enormous, huge*.　**II**. = Lat. *altus, deep, profound*, Hes., Eur. (Deriv. uncertain.)

ἤλιθα, Adv. (ἅλις) *enough, sufficiently*, Lat. *satis*, ληὶς ἤλιθα πολλή Il.; δύη ἤλιθα πολλή Od., etc.

ἠλιθιάζω, *to speak* or *act idly, foolishly*, Ar. From

ἠλίθιος, Dor. **ἀλίθ**-, *α, ον*, (ἤλιθα) *idle, vain, random*, Pind., Aesch.　**II**. of persons, *stupid, foolish, silly*, like μάταιος, Hdt., Ar., etc. Adv. -ίως, Plat.; neut. ἠλίθιον as Adv., Ar. Hence

ἠλιθιότης, *ητος, ἡ, folly, silliness*, Plat.; and

ἠλιθιόω, f. ώσω, *to make foolish, distract, craze*, Aesch.

ἡλικία, Ion. -ίη, Dor. **ἁλικία**, *ἡ*, (ἧλιξ) *time of life, age*, Lat. *aetas*, Il.;—acc. used absol. *in age*, οὐκ ἡλικίην Hdt.; so in dat., ἡλικίᾳ ὢν νέος Thuc.; πόρρω τῆς ἡλ. advanced in *years*, Plat.　**2**. mostly, *the flower* or *prime of life* from about 17 to 45, *man's estate, manhood*, ἐν ἁλικίᾳ πρώτᾳ Pind.; ἐν ἡλικίᾳ εἶναι to be of age, Plat., etc.; so, ἡλικίαν ἔχειν, εἰς ἡλ. ἐλθεῖν Id.; ἡλικίαν ἔχειν, c. inf., to be *of fit age* for doing, Hdt.; οἱ ἐν ἡλικίᾳ men *of serviceable age*, Thuc.　**3**. *youthful heat and passion*, ἡλικίη ἐπιτρέπειν Hdt.　**II**. as collective Noun, = οἱ ἥλικες, *those of the same age, fellows, comrades*, Il., Thuc.　**III**. *time*, ταῦτα ἡλικίην ἂν εἴη κατὰ Λάϊον about the *time* of Laius, Hdt.　**2**. *an age, genera-*

tion, Lat. *saeculum*, Dem., etc.　**IV**. *of the body, stature, growth*, as a sign of age, Hdt., Plat.

ἡλικιώτης, *ου, ὁ, an equal in age, fellow, comrade*, Lat. *aequalis*, Hdt., Ar., etc.:—fem. **ἡλικιῶτις**, *ιδος*, Luc.; ἡλ. ἱστορία *contemporary* history, Plut.

ἡλίκος [ῐ], *η, ον, as big as*, Lat. *quantus*, Ar., Dem.　**2**. *of age, as old as*, Ar., etc.　**3**. in expressions of wonder, θαυμάσια ἡλίκα *extraordinarily great*, as in Lat. *mirum quantum*, Dem. From

ἨΛΙΞ, Dor. **ἆλιξ**, *ῖκος, ὁ, ἡ, of the same age*, Od., Pind.: c. gen. *of the same age with*, Aesch.　**2**. as Subst. *a fellow, comrade*, Hdt., Aesch., etc.

ἡλιό-βλητος, *ον, sun-stricken, sun-burnt*, Eur.

ἡλιο-ειδής, *ές*, (εἶδος) *like the sun, beaming*, Plat.

ἡλιό-καυστος, *ον*, (καίω) *sun-burnt*, Theocr.

ἡλιο-μᾰνής, *ές*, (μαίνομαι) *sun-mad, mad for love of the sun*, Ar.

ἡλιόομαι, Pass. *to live in the sun*, Plat.; τὸ ἡλιούμενον *a sunny spot*, Xen.

ἨΛΙΟΣ, *ὁ*, Dor. **ἅλιος**, Ep. **ἠέλιος**: Dor. **ἀέλιος**:—*the sun*, Lat. *sol*, Hom., etc.; ὁρᾶν φάος ἠελίοιο, i. e. to be alive, Il.—The Sun furnished the earliest mode of determining the points of the heaven, πρὸς ἠῶ τ᾽ ἠέλιόν τε, i. e. towards the *East*, opp. to πρὸς ζόφον, Hom.; πρὸς ἠῶ τε καὶ ἡλίου ἀνατολάς, opp. to πρὸς ἑσπέρην, Hdt.　**2**. *day, a day*, like Lat. *soles*, Pind., Eur.: so in pl. *hot sunny days*, Thuc.　**II**. as prop. n., *Helios, the sun-god*, Hom.; in later Poets = *Apollo*, Aesch., etc.

ἡλιο-στερής, *ές*, (στερέω) *depriving of sun*, i. e. *shading from the sun*, Soph.

ἡλιο-στῐβής, *ές*, (στείβω) *sun-trodden*, Aesch.

ἡλιόω, only used in Pass. ἡλιόομαι, q. v.

ἤλῐτον, aor. 2 of ἀλιταίνω.

ἠλῐτο-εργός, *όν*, (ἤλιτον, ἔργον) *missing the work, failing in one's aim*, Anth.

ἠλῐτό-μηνος, *ον*, (ἤλιτον, μήν) *missing the right month*, i. e. *untimely born*, Il.

ἡλιώτης, *ου, ὁ*, fem. **-ῶτις**, *ιδος*, (ἥλιος) *of the sun*, Ep. ἠελιῶτις Anth.:—οἱ ἠλιῶται *the inhabitants of the sun*, Luc.

ἥλκησα, aor. 1 of ἑλκέω.

ἥλκωσα, aor. 1 of ἑλκόω.

ἠλλάγην [ᾰ], -άχθην, aor. 2 and 1 pass. of ἀλλάσσω.

ἤλλαγμαι, pf. pass. of ἀλλάσσω:—ἤλλακτο, 3 sing. plqpf.

ἠλλοίωμαι, pf. pass. of ἀλλοιόω.

ἨΛΟΣ, Dor. **ἆλος**, *ὁ, a nail*: in Hom. only for ornament, *a nail-head* or *stud*.　**2**. after Hom. *a nail* to fasten with, Pind., Xen., etc.

ἠλός, supposed nom. of the vocat. ἠλέ, v. ἠλεός.

ἤλπετο, 3 sing. impf. of ἔλπομαι.

ἤλπῑσα, aor. 1 of ἐλπίζω.

ἠλύγη [ῠ], *ἡ, a shadow, shade*: metaph., δίκης ἠλύγη *the obscurity* of a lawsuit, Ar. (Deriv. uncertain.)

ἤλῠθον, Ep. aor. 2 of ἔρχομαι.

ἤλυξα, aor. 1 of ἀλύσκω.

Ἠλύσιον πεδίον, *τό, the Elysian fields*, Lat. *Elysium*, Od.; in pl., Anth. Hom. places it on the west border of the earth, near to Ocean; Hesiod's Elysium is in the μακάρων νῆσοι. Hence

Ἠλύσιος, *α, ον, Elysian*, Anth.

ἤλῠσις, εως, ἡ, = ἔλευσις, a step, Eur.
ἤλφον, aor. 2 of ἀλφαίνω.
ἠλώμην, impf. of ἀλάομαι.
ἤλων, Ion. for ἑαλών, aor. 2 of ἀλίσκομαι.
ἦμα, τό, (ἵημι) that which is thrown, a dart, javelin, Il.
ἠμᾰθόεις, εσσα, εν, Ep. for ἀμ-, (ἄμαθος) sandy, Hom.
'ΗΜΑΙ, ἧσαι, ἧσται, ἥμεθα, ἧστε, ἧνται, Ep. εἵαται and ἕαται; imperat. ἧσο, ἥσθω; inf. ἧσθαι; part. ἥμενος:—impf. ἥμην, ἧσο, ἧστο, dual ἥσθην, pl. ἥμεθα poët. ἥμεσθα, ἧσθε, ἧντο, Ep. εἵατο and ἕατο:—to be seated, sit, Hom. etc.:—to sit still, sit idle, Il., etc.: of an army, to lie encamped, Ib.:—of a spy, to lurk, Ib.:—later, of places, to lie, be situated, Hdt.; ἡμένῳ ἐν χώρῳ = εἱαμενῇ, in a low, sunken place, Theocr.:—rarely c. acc., σέλμα ἧσθαι to be seated on a bench, Aesch.; ἧσθαι Σιμόεντος κοίτας Eur.
'ΗΜΑΡ, ατος, Dor. ἆμαρ, τό, poët. for ἡμέρα, day, Hom.; νύκτας τε καὶ ἦμαρ by night and day, Il.; ἦμαρ by day, Hes.; μέσον ἦμ. mid-day, Il.; δείελον ἦμ. evening, Od. 2. in Hom. with Adjs. to describe a state or condition, αἴσιμον, ὀλέθριον, μόρσιμον, νηλεὲς ἦμαρ the day of destiny, of death; ἐλεύθερον, δούλιον, ἀναγκαῖον ἦμαρ the day of freedom, of slavery; νόστιμον ἦμαρ, etc. 3. of the seasons, ἦμαρ' ὀπωρινῷ, ἤματι χειμερίῳ Il. II. with Preps., ἐπ' ἤματι day by day, daily, Od.; also, in a day, for a day, Hom.:—so, ἐπ' ἦμαρ by day, Soph.; for a day, Eur.:—κατ' ἦμαρ day by day, Lat. quotidie, Soph.; κατ' ἦμαρ ἀεί Id.; but κατ' ἦμαρ, also, this day, to-day, Lat. hodie, Id.:—παρ' ἦμαρ every other day, Pind., Soph.
ἡμάτιος [ᾰ], α, ον, (ἦμαρ) by day, Od. II. day by day, daily, Il.
ἤμβλωκα, pf. of ἀμβλίσκω.
ἤμβροτον, Ep. for ἥμαρτον, aor. 2 of ἁμαρτάνω.
ἡμεδᾰπός, ή, όν, (ἡμεῖς) of our land or country, native, Lat. nostras, Ar.
ἡμεῖς, ἡμᾶς, nom. and acc. pl. of ἐγώ.
ἠμελημένως, Adv. part. pf. pass. of ἀμελέω, carelessly; ἡμ. ἔχειν Xen.
ἤμελλον, impf. of μέλλω.
ἠ-μέν, Ep. Conjunction, correlative to ἠ-δέ, as well . . , as also . . , Lat. et . . , et . . , but sometimes disjunctive, like Lat. vel . . , vel . . , Hom.
ἤμεν, 1 pl. impf. of εἰμί (sum).
ἤμεν, 1 pl. impf. of εἶμι (ibo).
'ΗΜΕ'ΡΑ, Ion. ἡμέρη, Dor. ἀμέρα, ἡ:—day, Hom., etc.:—phrases for day-break, ἅμα ἡμέρᾳ or ἅμα τῇ ἡμέρᾳ Xen.; ἡμ. διαλάμπει or ἐκλάμπει Ar.; ἡμ. ὑποφαίνεται Xen.; γίγνεται or ἐστὶ πρὸς ἡμέραν Id. 2. with Adjs. to describe a state or time of life, ἐπίπονος ἡμ. a life of misery, Soph.; λυπρὰν ἄγειν ἡμ. Eur.; αἱ μακραὶ ἡμέραι length of days, Soph.; νέα ἡμ. youth, Eur. 3. poët. for time, ἡμ. κλίνει τε κἀνάγει πάλιν ἅπαντα τἀνθρώπεια Soph. II. absol. usages, 1. in gen., τριῶν ἡμερέων within three days, Hdt.; ἡμερῶν ὀλίγων within a few days, Thuc.:—also, ἡμέρας by day, Plat.; δὶς τῆς ἡμέρης ἑκάστης twice every day, Hdt. 2. in dat., τῇδε τῇ ἡμέρᾳ on this day, Soph.; so, τῇδ' ἐν ἡμέρᾳ Id. 3. in acc.,

πᾶσαν ἡμ. all day, Hdt.; τρίτην ἡμ. ἥκων three days after one's arrival, Thuc.; τὰς ἡμέρας in daytime Xen. III. with Preps.; ἀνὰ πᾶσαν ἡμ. every day, Hdt.:—δι' ἡμέρης, Att. -ρας, the whole day long, Id.; διὰ τρίτης ἡμ. every third day, Lat. tertio quoque die, Id.; δι' ἡμ. πολλῶν at a distance of many days, Thuc.:—ἐξ ἡμέρας by day, Soph.:—ἐφ' ἡμέραν sufficient for the day, Hdt., etc.; but, τοὐφ' ἡμέραν day by day, Eur.:—καθ' ἡμέραν by day, Aesch.; but commonly day by day, daily, Soph., etc.; τὸ καθ' ἡμ., absol., every day, Ar., etc.;—μεθ' ἡμέραν at mid-day, Hdt., etc.
ἡμερεύω, f. σω, (ἡμέρα) to spend the day, Xen., etc.:—absol. to travel the whole day, Aesch. 2. to pass one's days, live, Soph.
ἡμερήσιος, Dor. ἀμερ-, α, ον, (ἡμέρα) for the day, by day, ἡμ. φάος light as of the day, Aesch. II. a day long, ἡμ. ὁδός a day's journey, Hdt., Plat., etc.
ἡμερία (sc. ὥρα), ἡ, = ἡμέρα, Soph.
ἡμερινός, ή, όν, (ἡμέρα) of day, Plat.; ἄγγελος ἡμ. a day-messenger, Xen.
ἡμέριος, Dor. ἀμ-, ον, (ἡμέρα) for a day, lasting but a day, Soph., Eur.
ἡμερίς, ίδος, fem. of ἥμερος:—as Subst., ἡμερίς (sc. ἄμπελος), ἡ, the cultivated vine, opp. to ἀγριάς, Od.: but distinguished from ἄμπελίς by Ar.
ἡμεροδρομέω, to be an ἡμεροδρόμος, Luc.
ἡμερο-δρόμος, ὁ, (δραμεῖν) as Subst. a courier, Hdt.
ἡμερό-κοιτος, Dor. ἀμερ-, ον, sleeping by day, Hes., Eur.
ἡμερο-λεγδόν, Adv. (λέγω) by count of days, Aesch.
ἡμερο-λογέω, (λέγω) to count by days, Hdt.
ἡμερο-λόγιον, τό, (λέγω) a calendar, Plut.
'ΗΜΕΡΟΣ, Dor. ἄμ-, ον, and α, ον, tame, tamed, reclaimed, Lat. mansuetus, of animals, Od., Plat.; so, τὰ ἥμερα alone, Xen. 2. of plants and trees, cultivated, Lat. sativus, Hdt., etc. 3. of men, civilised, gentle, Id., Dem.; so of a lion, Aesch.
ἡμερο-σκόπος, ὁ, watching by day, Aesch., Ar.:—as Subst., a day-watcher, Hdt., Soph., etc.
ἡμερότης, ητος, ἡ, (ἥμερος) tameness:—of men, gentleness, kindness, Xen.
ἡμερό-φαντος, ον, (φαίνομαι) appearing by day, Aesch.
ἡμερο-φύλαξ [ῠ], ᾰκος, ὁ, = ἡμεροσκόπος, Xen.
ἡμερόω, f. ώσω, (ἥμερος) to tame, make tame, of wild beasts, Plat. 2. of countries, to clear them of robbers and wild beasts, as Hercules and Theseus did, Pind., Aesch.:—also, to tame by conquest, subdue, Hdt. 3. of men also, to soften, civilise, Plat.
ἡμέρωσις, εως, ἡ, a taming: civilising, Plut.
ἥμες, Dor. for εἶναι, inf. of εἰμί (sum).
ἡμέτερος, Dor. ἀμετ-, α, ον, (ἡμεῖς) our, Lat. noster, Hom., etc.; εἰς ἡμέτερον (sc. δῶμα) Od.; so, ἡμέτερόνδε Ib.; ἡ ἡμετέρα (sc. χώρα) Thuc.; τὰ ἡμέτερα φρονεῖν to take our part, Xen. II. sometimes for ἐμός, Od.
ἡμέων, Ion. for ἡμῶν, gen. pl. of ἐγώ.
ἥμην, impf. of ἧμαι.
ἤμησα, aor. 1 of ἀμάω.
'ΗΜΙ', I say, Lat. inquam, used to repeat something with emphasis, παῖ ἠμί, παῖ boy I say, boy! Ar.:—impf. ἦν, 3 sing. ἦ, καὶ σχέθε χεῖρα he spake and held

his hand, Il.; in Att., ἦν δ' ἐγώ said I, Plat.; ἦ δ' ὅς said he, Ar., Plat.

ἡμῐ-, Insep. Prefix, half-, Lat. semi-.

ἡμι-άνθρωπος, ὁ, a half-man, Luc.

ἡμι-βρᾰχής or -βρεχής, ές, (βρέχω) sodden, Anth.

ἡμι-βρώς, ῶτος, ὁ, ἡ, = sq., Anth.

ἡμί-βρωτος, half-eaten, Xen.

ἡμι-γένειος, ον, (γένειον) but half-bearded, Theocr.

ἡμί-γυμνος, ον, half-naked, Luc.: so ἡμι-γύναιος, ον, Suid.; ἡμίγυνος, ον, Synes.

ἡμι-δαής, ές, (δαίω) half-burnt, Il.   II. (δατέομαι) half-divided, half-mangled, Anth.

ἡμι-δᾰρεικόν, τό, a half-daric, Xen.

ἡμι-δεής, ές, (δέω) wanting half, half-full, Xen., Anth.

ἡμί-δουλος, ον, a half-slave, Eur.

ἡμι-εκτέον, τό, = sq., Ar.

ἡμι-εκτον, τό, a half-ἑκτεύς, i.e. ₁⁄₁₂ of a medimnus, Dem.

ἡμι-έλλην, ηνος, ὁ, ἡ, a half-Greek, Luc.

ἡμι-εργής, ές, (*ἔργω) half-made, half-finished, Luc.

ἡμί-εργος, ον, = foreg., Hdt.

ἡμι-εφθος, ον, (ἕψω) half-boiled, half-cooked, Luc.

ἡμι-θᾰλής, ές, (θάλλω) half-green, Anth.

ἡμι-θᾰνής, ές, (θνήσκω) half-dead, Anth.

ἡμίθεος, Dor. ἁμίθεος, ὁ, a half-god, demigod, Il., Hes.

ἡμι-θνής, ῆτος, ὁ, ἡ, = ἡμιθανής, Ar., Thuc., etc.

ἡμί-θραυστος, ον, (θραύω) half-broken, Eur., Anth.

ἡμι-κλήριον, τό, (κλῆρος) half the inheritance, Dem.

ἡμίκυκλον, τό, (κύκλος) a semicircle, the front seats in the theatre, Plut.

ἡμί-λευκος, ον, half-white, Luc.

ἡμι-μᾰνής, ές, (μαίνομαι) half-mad, Aeschin., Luc.

ἡμι-μάραντος, ον, (μαραίνω) half-withered, Luc.

ἡμι-μέδιμνον, τό, a half-μέδιμνος, Dem.

ἡμι-μεθής, ές, (μέθη) half-drunk, Anth.

ἡμι-μναῖον, τό, a half-mina, Xen., etc.

ἡμι-μόχθηρος, ον, half-evil, half a villain, Plat.

ἡμί-ξηρος, ον, half-dry, Anth.

ἡμι-όλιος, α, ον, Dor. ἁμι-όλιος, ον: (ὅλος):—containing one and a half, half as much again, Lat. sesquialter, Plat.:—c. gen. half as large again as, half as much again as, Hdt., Xen.   II. ἡμιολία ναῦς a ship with one and a half banks of oars, Theophr.

ἡμιόνειος, α, ον, (ἡμίονος) belonging to a mule, ἄμαξα ἡμ. a car drawn by mules, Hom.

ἡμιονικός, ή, όν, = ἡμιόνειος, Xen.

ἡμί-ονος, ὁ, ἡ, a half-ass, i.e. a mule, Hom., etc.:— proverb., ἐπεὰν ἡμίονοι τέκωσι, i.e. never, Hdt.   2. the ἡμ. ἀγροτέρα of Il. 2. 851 is prob. the wild ass.   II. as Adj., βρέφος ἡμίονον a mule-foal, Il.; ἡμ. βασιλεύς a mule-king, half-Mede half-Persian, Orac. ap. Hdt.

ἡμί-οπτος, ον, half-roasted, Luc.

ἡμι-πέλεκκον (κ doubled metri grat.), τό, (πέλεκυς) a half-axe, i.e. a one-edged axe, Il.

ἡμι-πέφθος, ον, (πέσσω) half-cooked, Plut.

ἡμί-πλεθρον, τό, a half-πλέθρον, Hdt., Xen.

ἡμι-πλίνθιον, τό, (πλίνθος) a half-plinth, a brick (two of which formed a plinth), Hdt.

ἡμί-πνοος, ον, (πνέω) half-breathing, half-alive, Batr.

ἡμι-πόνηρος, ον, half-evil, Arist.

ἡμι-πύρωτος, ον, (πυρόω) half-burnt, Anth.

ἡμίσεια, ἡ, ἡμίσεον, τό, v. sub ἡμισυς.

ἡμί-σπαστος, ον, (σπάω) half-pulled down, Anth.

ἡμι-στάδιαῖος, α, ον, (στάδιον) of half a stadium, Luc.

ἡμι-στρᾰτιώτης, ου, ὁ, a half-soldier, Luc.

ἡμι-στρόγγῡλος, ον, half-round, Luc.

ἡμῐσυς, εια, υ : gen. ἡμίσεος : nom. and acc. pl. masc., Ion. ἡμίσεες, -εας, Att. -εις; neut. ἡμίσεα, contr. -η:— Ion. fem. ἡμίσέα, gen. -έας, dat. -έᾳ, etc. : (ἡμι-):— half, Lat. semis, used both as Adj. and Subst. :   I. as Adj., ἡμίσεες λαοί half the people, Hom.; ἥμισυς λόγος half the tale, Aesch., etc.;—c. gen., like a Comp., ἥμισυ οὗ διενοεῖτο half of what he intended, Thuc. :— also with its Subst. in gen., τῶν νήσων τὰς ἡμίσεας half of the islands, Hdt.; αἱ ἡμίσειαι τῶν νεῶν Thuc.; ὁ ἥμισυς τοῦ ἀριθμοῦ Plat.   II. as Subst.,   1. neut., ἥμισυ τιμῆς, ἐνάρων, ἀρετῆς Hom.; πλέον ἥμισυ παντός Hes.; ἡμίσεα, τὸ ἡμ. τοῦ στρατοῦ Thuc., etc. ;—also in pl., ἄρτων ἡμίσεα Xen.   2. fem., ἡ ἡμ. τοῦ τιμήματος Plat.; ἐφ' ἡμισείᾳ up to one half, Dem.

ἡμι-τάλαντον, τό, a half-talent, as a weight, Il.; τρία ἡμιτάλαντα three half-talents, Hdt., but τρίτον ἡμιτάλαντον two talents and a half, Id.

ἡμι-τέλεια, ἡ, a remission of half the tribute, Luc.

ἡμι-τέλεστος, ον, (τελέω) half-finished, Thuc.

ἡμι-τελής, ές, (τέλος) half-finished, δόμος ἡμ. a house but half complete, i.e. wanting its lord and master, Il.; ἡμ. ἀνήρ, opp. to τελείως ἀγαθός, Xen.

ἡμίτομος, ον, (τέμνω) half cut through, cut in two, Mosch.   II. as Subst., ἡμίτομον, τό, a half, Hdt.

ἡμιτύβιον [ῠ], τό, a stout linen cloth, towel, napkin, Ar. (An Egypt. word.)

ἡμι-φαής, ές, (φάος) half-shining, Anth.

ἡμι-φάλακρος, ον, half-bald, Anth.

ἡμί-φαυλος, ον, half-knavish, Luc.

ἡμί-φλεκτος, ον, (φλέγω) half-burnt, Theocr., Luc.

ἡμι-ωβολιαῖος, α, ον, worth half an obol, Ar.: as large as a half-obol, Xen. From

ἡμι-ωβόλιον or -ωβέλιον, τό, (ὄβολος) a half-obol, Xen.

ἧμμαι, pf. pass. of ἅπτω.

ἦμος, Dor. ἆμος, poët. Adv. relative to τῆμος, at which time, when, Hom.   2. while, so long as, Soph.

ἡμός, ή, όν, Aeol. ἁμός, = ἡμέτερος.

ἠμπεσχόμην, aor. 2 med. with double augm. of ἀμπέχω.

ἤμπλᾰκον, aor. 2 of ἀμπλακίσκω.

ἠμύω, aor. 1 ἤμῡσα, to bow down, sink, drop, ἑτέρωσ' ἤμυσε κάρη his head dropped to one side, Il.; ἤμυσε καρήατι bowed with his head, of a horse, Ib.; of a corn-field, ἐπὶ δ' ἠμύει ἀσταχύεσσι it bows or waves with its ears, Ib.: metaph. of cities, to nod to their fall, totter, Ib. (Deriv. uncertain.)

ἠμφεγνόουν, impf. with double augm. of ἀμφιγνοέω.

ἠμφεσβήτουν, ἠμφεσβήτησα, impf. and aor. 1, with double augm. of ἀμφισβητέω.

ἠμφίεσμαι, pf. pass. of ἀμφιέννυμι.

ἤμων, impf. of ἀμάω.

ἥμων, ονος, ὁ, (ἵημι) a thrower, darter, slinger, Il.

ἤν, contr. for ἐάν, Hom., Hdt., etc.

ἤν, Interject. see! see there! lo! Lat. en! Ar. :—also ἠνίδε (i. e. ἦν ἴδε) Theocr.

ἦν, 1 and 3 sing. impf. of εἰμί (sum) :—3 pl. in Hes.

ἦν, impf. of ἠμί.

ἥν, acc. sing. fem. of relat. Pron. ὅς, and of possess. Pron. ὅς, ἑός.

ἠναίνετο, 3 sing. impf. of ἀναίνομαι.

ἤνδᾰνον, impf. of ἀνδάνω.

ἤνεγκα, ἤνεγκον, aor. 1 and 2 of φέρω :—Ion. ἤνεικα.

ἠνειχόμην, impf. med., with double augm., of ἀνέχω.

ἤνεκα, pf. of αἰνέω.

ἠνεμόεις, Dor. ἀνεμόεις, εσσα, εν, (ἄνεμος) windy, airy, Hom., etc. II. of motion, rapid, rushing, Aesch.

ἤνεον, ἤνεσα, impf. and aor. 1 of αἰνέω.

ἠνεσχόμην, aor. 2 med., with double augm., of ἀνέχω.

ἤνετο, 3 sing. impf. pass. of ἄνω = ἀνύω.

ἠνέχθην, aor. 1 pass. of φέρω.

ἠνηνάμην, aor. 1 of ἀναίνομαι.

ἠνθισμένος, pf. pass. part. of ἀνθίζω.

ἤνθον, ες, ε, Dor. for ἦλθον : 1 pl. ἤνθομες.

ἠνθρᾰκωμένος, pf. part. of ἀνθρακόομαι.

'ΗΝΙ'Α, ίων, τά, reins, Hom., Hes., Pind.

'ΗΝΙ'Α, Dor. ἀνία, ἡ, the bridle (in riding), the reins (in driving), like the Homeric ἡνία (τά) mostly in pl., Pind., etc. ; πρὸς ἡνίας μάχεσθαι Aesch. ; in sing., ἐπισχὼν ἡνίαν Soph. 2. metaph., χαλάσαι τὰς ἡνίας τοῖς λόγοις to give one's words free reins, Plat. ; τῆς Πυκνὸς τὰς ἡνίας παραδοῦναί τινι Id. 3. as a military term, ἐφ' ἡνίαν to the left, Plut.

ἠν-ίδε, v. sub ἤν (Interject.), see there !

ἡνίκᾰ [ῐ], Dor. ἀνίκα, Adv. of Time, relat. to τηνίκα, at which time, when, Od., Trag. : also causal, since, Pind., Att. 2. with Opt. in orat. obl., or to denote an uncertain or repeated occurrence in past time, whenever, Soph., etc. 3. ἡνίκ' ἄν, like ὅταν, with Subj., of the future, whenever, Id., etc.

ἠνίον, τό, v. ἡνία, τά.

ἡνιο-ποιεῖον, τό, (ποιέω) a saddler's shop, Xen.

ἡνιοστροφέω, to guide by reins, Aesch., Eur. From

ἡνιο-στρόφος, ὁ, (στρέφω) one who guides by reins, a charioteer, Soph.

ἡνιοχεία, ἡ, (ἡνιοχέω) chariot-driving, Plat.

ἡνιοχεύς, έως, Ερ. ῆος, ὁ, poët. for ἡνίοχος, Il.

ἡνιοχεύω, Dor. ἀν-, f. σω, poët. form of ἡνιοχέω, to act as charioteer, Hom. :—metaph. to guide, Anth.

ἡνιοχέω, f. ήσω, prose form of ἡνιοχεύω, to hold the reins, Xen. 2. c. acc. to drive, guide, Hdt. : metaph. to direct, Ar. :—Pass. to be guided, Xen.

ἡνιοχικός, ή, όν, of or for driving, Plat. : ἡ -κή (sc. τέχνη) the art of driving, Id.

ἡνί-οχος, Dor. ἀνί-οχος, ὁ, (ἔχω) one who holds the reins, a driver, charioteer, opp. to παραιβάτης (the warrior by his side), Il. 2. generally a charioteer, as in the games, Pind., Att. :—in Theogn., a rider. 3. metaph. a guide, governor, Pind., Ar.

ἠνίπᾰπε, 3 sing. aor. 2 of ἐνίπτω.

ἠνῖς, ἡ, pl. ἤνῑς (ἔνος) a year old, yearling, Hom.

ἤνοιξα, aor. 1 of ἀνοίγνυμι.

ἤνον, impf. of ἄνω = ἀνύω.

ἠνορέη, Dor. ἀνορέα, ἡ, (ἀνήρ), Ep. for ἀνδρεία, manhood, Hom. : manly beauty, Il. :—in pl. praises of manhood, Pind.

ἤνουν, impf. of αἰνέω.

ἤνοψ, οπος, ὁ, ἡ, in Hom., always in phrase ἤνοπι χαλκῷ, with gleaming, glittering brass. (Deriv. uncertain.)

ἤν-περ, related to εἴπερ, as ἤν (ἐάν) to εἰ, Xen.

ἠνσχόμην, syncop. for ἠνεσχόμην.

ἠντεβόλησα, ἠντεβόλουν, aor. 1 and impf., with double augm., of ἀντιβόλεω.

ἤντεον, ἤντησα, impf. and aor. 1 of ἀντάω.

ἤντληκα, pf. of ἀντλέω.

ἧντο, 3 pl. impf. of ἧμαι.

ἤνῠκα, ἤνῠσα, pf. and aor. 1 of ἀνύω.

ἤνυστρον, τό, (ἀνύω) the fourth stomach of ruminating animals, a favourite dish at Athens, tripe, Ar.

ἤνῠτο, Ep. for ἠνύετο, 3 sing. impf. pass. of ἀνύω :—ἠνυτόμην, impf. med.

ἠνώγεα, Ep. plqpf. of ἄνωγα ; 3 sing. ἠνώγει : aor. 1 ἤνωξα.

ἠνώχλουν, ἠνώχλησα, -ηκα, impf., aor. 1, and pf., with double augm., of ἐνοχλέω.

ἧξα, aor. 1 of ἀΐσσω, ἄσσω. II. ἧξα, aor. 1 of ἄγνυμι and of ἄγω.

ἠξίωσα, -ώθην, aor. 1 act. and pass. of ἀξιόω.

ἥξω, Dor. for ἥξω, f. of ἥκω.

ἠοῖ, dat. of ἠώς.

ἠοῖος, α, ον, Ion. ἠόϊος, η, ον, = ἑῷος, morning, Ar. :—ἡ ἠοίη (sc. ὥρα), the morning, Od. II. toward morning, eastern, Ib., Hdt. II. αἱ 'Ηοῖαι was a poem of Hesiod, in which each sentence began with ἢ οἵη.

ἤομεν, 1 pl. impf. of εἶμι (ibo).

ἠόνιος, α, ον, (ἠών) on the shore, Anth.

ἠπανία, ἡ, want, Anth. (Deriv. uncertain.)

ἠπάομαι, v. ἠπήσασθαι.

'ΗΠΑΡ, ατος, τό, the liver, Hom., etc. :—ὑφ' ἥπατος φέρειν, of pregnant women, Eur. :—in Trag. as the seat of the passions, anger, fear, etc., answering therefore to our 'heart.'

ἤπαφον, aor. 2 of ἀπαφίσκω.

ἠπεδᾰνός, ή, όν, weakly, infirm, halting, Hom. 2. c. gen. void of a thing, Anth. (Deriv. uncertain.)

ἠπείλεον, ἠπείλησα, impf. and aor. 1 of ἀπειλέω.

ἠπειρο-γενής, ές, (γίγνομαι) born or living in the mainland, Aesch.

ἤπειρόνδε, to the mainland, Od.

ἤπειρος, Dor. ἄπ- [ᾱ], ἡ, terra-firma, the land, as opp. to the sea, Hom., Hes., etc. ; κατ' ἤπειρον by land, Hdt. ; μήτ' ἐν θαλάττῃ μήτ' ἐν ἠπείρῳ Ar. :— hence in Od., even an island is called ἤπειρος. II. the mainland of Western Greece, opp. to the neighbouring islands (afterwards called Ἤπειρος as n. pr.), Od. :—then, generally, the mainland, Hdt., Att. III. later, a Continent : Asia was esp. called the Continent, Hdt., etc. ; also Europe, Aesch. ; whence Soph. speaks of δισσαὶ ἤπειροι, i.e. Europe and Asia. (Deriv. uncertain.) Hence

ἠπειρόω, to make into mainland, Anth. :—Pass. to become so, Thuc. ; and

ἠπειρώτης, ου, ὁ, fem. -ῶτις, ιδος, of the mainland, living there, opp. to νησιώτης, Hdt. : αἱ ἠπειρώτιδες πόλιες, opp. to those in islands, Id., etc. ; ἠπ. ξυμμαχία alliance with a military power, opp. to ναυτική, Thuc. II. of or on the mainland of Asia, Asiatic, Eur. III. an Epirote, Luc. Hence

ἠπειρωτικός, ή, όν, continental, Xen. II. of Epirus, Thuc.

ἤ-περ, poët. ἠέ-περ, (ῆ) than at all, than even, Hom.

ἤ-περ, (ῇ) in the same way as, v. ὥσπερ.

ἠπεροπεύς, έως, Ep. ῆος, ὁ, a cheat, deceiver, cozener, Od., Anth. (Deriv. uncertain.)

ἠπεροπευτής, οῦ, ὁ, = foreg., ἠπεροπευτά (Ep. voc.) Il.

ἠπεροπεύω, (ἠπεροπεύς) only in pres. and impf. *to cheat, cajole, deceive, cozen*, Hom.

ἠπήσασθαι, (aor. 1, with no pres. ἠπάομαι in use), *to mend, repair*, Ar. (Deriv. uncertain.) Hence

ἠπητής, οῦ, ὁ, *a mender, cobbler*, Batr., Xen.

ἠπιαλέω, f. ήσω, *to have a fever* or *ague*, Ar. From

ἠπίαλος, ὁ, *a fever with shivering, ague*, Ar.   II. = ἐφιάλτης, *night-mare*, Id. (Deriv. unknown.)

ἠπϊο-δίνητος [ῑ], ον, (δινέω) *softly-rolling*, Anth.

ἠπιό-δωρος, ον, (δῶρον) *soothing by gifts, bountiful*, Il.

ἠπιό-θῡμος, ον, *gentle of mood*, Anth.

ἤπϊος, α, ον, and ος, ον :   1. of persons, *gentle, mild, kind*, πατήρ δ᾽ ὡς ἤπιος ἦεν Hom. :—c. dat. pers., Id., Trag.   2. of sentiments, ἤπια εἰδέναι *to have kindly feelings*, Hom.; πρὸς τὸ ἠπιώτερον καταστῆσαί τινα *to bring him to a milder mood*, Thuc.   II. act. *soothing, assuaging*, of medicines, Il., etc.   2. ἤπιον ἦμαρ, c. inf., a day *favourable* for beginning a thing, Hes.   III. Adv. ἠπίως, Hdt., Soph.

ἠπιό-χειρ, ειρος, ὁ, ἡ, *with soothing hand*, Anth.

ἦπου or ἦ που, = ἦ, modified by που, or *perhaps, as perhaps*, Hom.

ἦπου or ἦ που, *I suppose, I ween*, Il., Soph., etc.: after a negat., *much less*, Thuc.   II. to ask a question, *is it possible that . . ? can it be that . . ?* Od., Aesch.

ἠπύτᾰ [ῠ], ὁ, Ep. for ἠπύτης, (ἠπύω) *calling, crying*, ἠπύτα κῆρυξ *the loud-voiced herald*, Il. From

ἠπύω, Dor. ἀπύω [ᾱ], f. ύσω [ῡ] : aor. 1 ἤπῡσα: (εἰπεῖν?) :—*to call to, call on, call*, Od., Aesch., etc.:—c. dupl. acc., τί με τόδε χρέος ἀπύεις; *why callest thou on me for this?* Eur.   2. absol. *to call out, shout*, Od.; of the wind, *to roar*, Il.; of the lyre, *to sound*, Od.   3. *to utter, speak*, πατρὸς ὄνομ᾽ ἀπύεις Aesch.; τί ποτ᾽ ἀπύσω; Eur.

ἦρ, contr. for ἔαρ.

ἦρᾱ, 3 sing. impf. of ἐράω.

ἦρᾰ, aor. 1 of αἴρω :—but   II. ἦρα᾽, i. e. ἦραο, Ep. for ἤρω, 2 sing. aor. 1 med. of αἴρω; so ἦρᾱ, Boeot.

ἦρα, a neut. Adj. pl., *acceptable gifts, kindnesses*, ἦρα φέρειν Hom.   II. = χάριν, c. gen., *on account of*, Anth.

Ἥρα, Ion. Ἥρη, ἡ, *Hera*, the Lat. *Juno*, queen of the gods, daughter of Kronos and Rhea, sister and wife of Zeus, Hom., etc.; νὴ τὴν Ἥραν, an oath of Athen. women, Xen. Hence

Ἡραῖος, α, ον, *of Hera*: Ἡραῖον (sc. ἱερόν), τό, *the temple of Hera, Heraeum*, Il.

Ἡρα-κλῆς, contr. Ἡρᾰ-κλῆς, ὁ : Att. gen. Ἡρακλέους, dat. Ἡρακλέει, acc. Ἡρακλέᾱ, voc. Ἡρακλέες, -εῖς : Ion. and Ep., Ἡρακλῆος, -κλῆι, -κλῆα :—the Att. forms are further shortd., Ἡρακλέος, Ἡρακλέῑ, Ἡρακλέᾱ and Ἡράκλῆ :—irreg. acc. Ἡρακλέην :—*Heracles*, Lat. *Hercules*, son of Zeus and Alcmena, the most famous of the Greek heroes, Hom., etc. (The name signifies *Hera's glory*, Ἥρας κλέος, from the power she obtained over him at birth.) Hence

Ἡράκλειδαι, οἱ, *the Heraclidae* or *descendants of Hercules*, Hdt.; and

Ἡράκλειος, α, ον, and ος, ον : Ep. -ήειος, Ion. -ήιος, η, ον : —*of Hercules*, Lat. *Herculeus*, βίη Ἡρακληείη, i. e. *Hercules himself*, Hom. :—Ἡρ. στῆλαι the opposite headlands of Gibraltar and Apes' Hill near Tangier,

Hdt.   II. as Subst., Ἡράκλειον, Ion. -ήιον (sc. ἱερόν), τό, *the temple of Hercules, Heracleum*, Id., etc.   2. Ἡράκλεια (sc. ἱερά), τά, *his festival*, Ar.

Ἡρακλείτειος, α, ον, *of Heraclitus*, Plat.

Ἡρᾰκλῆς, ὁ, contr. from Ἡρακλέης.

Ἡρακλίσκος, ὁ, Dim. of Ἡρακλῆς, Theocr.

ἤραρον, aor. 2 of ἀραρίσκω.

ἠράσάμην, aor. 1 of ἔραμαι, Ep. 3 sing. ἠράσσατο :— pass. in med. sense ἠράσθην.

ἦρᾰτο, 3 sing. aor. 1 med. of αἴρω.

ἠρᾱτο, 3 sing. impf. of ἀράομαι.

ἠρέθην, aor. 1 pass. of αἱρέω :—ἤρει, 3 sing. impf. act.

ἠρέμᾱ, Adv., like ἀτρέμας, *stilly, quietly, gently, softly*, Ar., Plat.   2. *a little, slightly*, Id.   3. *slowly*, opp. to τάχιστα, Id. (Deriv. uncertain.)

ἠρεμαῖος, α, ον, Adj. of ἠρέμα, *still, quiet, gentle*, Plat. :—irreg. Comp. ἠρεμέστερος, Xen. Adv. -αίως, = ἠρέμα, Id.; Comp. -εστέρως Id.

ἠρεμέω, f. ήσω, *to keep quiet, be at rest*, Xen., Plat.

ἠρέμησις, εως, ἡ, *quietude*, Arist.

ἠρεμί [ῑ], Adv. = ἠρέμα, Ar.

ἠρεμία, ἡ, *rest, quietude*, ἐπὶ ἠρεμίας ὑμῶν leaving you at rest, Dem.

ἠρεμίζω, *to make still* or *quiet*, Xen.   II. intr. = ἠρεμέω, Id.

ἤρεμος, ον, = ἠρεμαῖος, N. T.

ἤρεσα, aor. 1 of ἀρέσκω.

ἠρέτισα, aor. 1 of αἱρετίζω.

ἤρευν, Ion. for ᾕρουν, impf. of αἱρέω.

Ἥρη, Ion. for Ἥρα.

ἤρηκα, -ημαι, pf. act. and pass. of αἱρέω :—ᾕρηντο, 3 pl. plqpf.

ἠρήρει, 3 sing. plqpf. of ἀραρίσκω B.

ἠρήρειστο, 3 sing. plqpf. pass. of ἐρείδω.

-ήρης, an Adj. termin.,   1. from ἀραρ-εῖν, ἀραρ-ίσκω, as in ἐρι-ήρης, θυμ-άρης.   2. from ἐρ-έσσω, as in ἀμφ-ήρης, ἁλι-ήρης, τρι-ήρης, etc.

ἠρησάμην, aor. 1 of ἀράομαι.

ἦρι, Ep. Adv. *early*, Hom.; ἦρι μάλ᾽, μάλ᾽ ἦρι Id.

ἠρι-γένεια, ἡ, (γίγνομαι) *early-born, child of morn*, epith. of Ἠώς, Hom.; also absol., = Ἠώς, *Morn*, Od.; ἠριγενείας at morn, Theocr.

Ἠρῐδᾰνός, ὁ, *Eridanus*, a river famous in legends, Hes., Hdt.; later authors mostly took it for *the Po*, as Eur.; others for *the Rhone* or *Rhine*, as perh. in Hdt.

ἤριζον, ἤρισα, impf. and aor. 1 of ἐρίζω.

ἠρίθμεον, -ουν, impf. of ἀριθμέω.

ἤρϊκε, 3 sing. aor. 2 of ἐρείκω.

ἠρῐνός, ή, όν, (ἦρ) = ἐαρινός, *of* or *in spring*, Solon, Eur.: —neut. pl. as Adv., *in spring*, Ar.

ἠρίον, τό, *a mound, barrow, tomb*, Il., Theocr. (Deriv. uncertain.)

ἤρϊπε, 3 sing. aor. 2 of ἐρείπω.

ἠρι-πόλη, ἡ, (πολέω) *early-walking*: as Subst. *the morn*, Anth.

ἠρίστηται, 3 sing. pf. pass. of ἀριστάω.

ἠρνήθην, ἤρνημαι, aor. 1 and pf. of ἀρνέομαι :—ἠρνησάμην, aor. 1 med.

ἤρόθην, aor. 1 pass. of ἀρόω.

ἤρπαξα and ἥρπᾰσα, aor. 1 of ἁρπάζω.

ἤρρησα, aor. 1 of ἔρρω.

ἦρσα, aor. 1 of ἀραρίσκω.   II. of ἄρδω.

ἤρτησα, aor. 1 of ἀρτάω:—ἤρτημαι, pf. pass.
ἤρτῡνα, ἠρτῡνάμην, aor. 1 act. and med. of ἀρτύνω.
ἤρτῦσα, aor. 1 of ἀρτύω.
ἠρῡγον, aor. 2 (in act. form) of ἐρεύγομαι II.
ἠρύκακον, Ep. aor. 2 of ἐρύκω.
ἥρῳ, poët. dat. sing. of ἥρως : ἥρῳ, gen. and acc. of same.
ἤρω, 2 sing. impf. of ἀράομαι.
ἠρωῆσα, aor. 1 of ἐρωέω.
ἡρωικός, ή, όν, (ἥρως) of or for a hero, heroïc, Plat., etc. II. metrically, ἡρ. στίχος the heroïc verse, the hexameter, Id.
ἡρωίνη [ῐ], ἡ, fem. of ἥρως, a heroïne, Theocr.; contr. ἡρώνη, Ar.
ἡρώιος, α, ον, = ἡρωικός, Pind.
ἡρωΐς, ίδος, ἡ, = ἡρωίνη, Pind. II. as fem. of ἡρωϊκός, Anth.
ἡρώμην, impf. of ἀράομαι.
ἡρῷον, Ion. -ώιον, τό, (ἥρως) 1. (sub. ἱερόν) the temple or chapel of a hero, Hdt., etc. ; θἠρῷον, i. e. τὸ ἡρῷον, Ar. 2. (sub. μέτρον), an hexameter, Plut.
ἡρῷος, α, ον, contr. for ἡρώιος ; ὁ ἡρ. (sc. ῥυθμός), the heroïc measure, hexameter, Plat., etc. ; πους ἡρ. the dactyl, Anth.
ἭΡΩΣ, ὁ, gen. ἥρωος, Att. also ἥρω : dat. ἥρωϊ, ἥρῳ : acc. ἥρωα, ἥρω, rarely ἥρων:—Plur., nom. ἥρωες, rarely ἥρως, dat. ἡρώων: acc. ἥρωας, rarely ἥρως :—(akin to Lat. vir), a hero, in Hom. used of the Greeks before Troy, then of warriors generally ; and then of all free men of the heroïc age, as the minstrel Demodocus, the herald Mulius, even the unwarlike Phaeacians. 2. in Hes. the Blessed Heroes are the Fourth Age of men, who fell before Thebes and Troy, and then passed to the Islands of the Blest. 3. heroes, as objects of worship, demigods or men born from a god and a mortal, as Hercules, Aeneas, Memnon, Hdt., Pind. ; then of such as had done great services to mankind, as Daedalus, Triptolemus, Theseus, Anth. 4. later, the heroes are inferior local deities, patrons of tribes, cities, guilds, founders of cities, etc. ; as at Athens the ἥρωες ἐπώνυμοι were the heroes after whom the φυλαί were named, Hdt.
ἡρώσσα, ἡ, = ἡρωίνη, Anth.
ἧς, Dor. for ἦν, 3 sing. impf. of εἰμί (sum).
ἧς, Dor. for εἷς, one, Theocr.
ἧσα, aor. 1 of ᾄδω : but, II. ἧσα, aor. 1 of ἥδω.
ἧσαι, 2 sing. of ἧμαι.
ἦσαν, 3 pl. impf. of εἰμί (sum).
ἦσαν, Att. for ᾔδεσαν, 3 pl. plqpf. of οἶδα. II. for ἤισαν, 3 pl. impf. of εἶμι (ibo).
ἥσατο, 3 sing. aor. of ἥδομαι.
ἥσειν, fut. inf. of ἵημι.
ἦσθα, Aeol. and Att. for ἦς, 2 sing. impf. of εἰμί (sum).
ἦσθαι, inf. of ἧμαι.
ἠσθένησα, -ένουσα, aor. 1 and impf. of ἀσθενέω.
ἥσθην, aor. 1 of ἥδομαι: but II. ἤσθην, aor. 1 pass. of ᾄδω.
ἠσθόμην, aor. 2 of αἰσθάνομαι.
ἧσι, Ep. for ᾗς, 3 sing. aor. 2 subj. of ἵημι.
ἤσκειν, for ἤσκεεν, 3 sing. impf. of ἀσκέω.
ᾔσμεν, Att. for ᾔδειμεν, 1 pl. plqpf. of οἶδα, v. *εἴδω.
ἧσο, 2 sing. imper. of ἧμαι.

ἧσσα, Att. ἧττα, ης, ἡ, (ἥσσων) a defeat, discomfiture, opp. to νίκη, Thuc., etc. :—c. gen. rei, a giving way to a thing, ἡδονῶν, ἐπιθυμιῶν Plat.
ἡσσάομαι, Att. ἡττ-: f. ἡσσηθήσομαι or med. ἡττήσομαι in pass. sense : aor. 1 ἡσσήθην : pf. ἥσσημαι :—Ion. ἑσσόομαι, part. ἑσσούμενος : 3 sing. impf. ἑσσοῦτο (without augm.) : aor. 1 ἑσσώθην : pf. ἕσσωμαι :—Pass. to be less than another, inferior to him, c. gen. pers., Eur., Xen., etc. ; c. gen. rei, ἡσσ. ῥήματος to yield to the power of a word, Thuc. ; ὁ ἡττᾶτο wherein he had proved inferior, Xen. 2. as a real Pass. to be defeated, discomfited, worsted, beaten, ὑπό τινος Hdt. Att. ; also c. gen. pers., Eur., etc. ;—ἡσσᾶσθαι μάχῃ or μάχην Hdt., Dem. 3. to give way, yield, to be a slave to passion and the like, c. gen., ἡσσημένος ἔρωτος Eur. ; τῶν ἡδονῶν Xen. :—also c. dat. to be overcome by, ἡδονῇ ἡσσώμενοι Thuc.
ἡσσητέος, α, ον, neut. pl. ἡσσητέα, verb. Adj. one must be beaten, γυναικός by a woman, Soph.
ἥσσων, ἧσσον, gen. ονος : Att. ἥττων : Ion. ἕσσων : Comp. of κακός or μικρός (but formed from ἧκα, softly, so that the orig. form was ἡκίων, with Sup. ἥκιστος) : I. c. gen. pers. less, weaker, less brave, Hom., etc. ; c. inf., ἕσσων θεῖν not so good at running, Hdt. ; οὐδενὸς ἥσσων γνῶναι 'second to none' in judging, Thuc. 2. absol. of the weaker party, ἥσσους γενέσθαι to have the worst of it, Id. ; τὰ τῶν ἡττόνων the fortunes of the vanquished, Xen. ; of things, τὸν ἥττω λόγον κρείττω ποιεῖν 'to make the worse appear the better reason,' Plat. II. c. gen. rei, yielding to a thing, a slave to, ἔρωτος Soph. ; κέρδους Ar., etc. :—generally, yielding to, unable to resist, τοῦ πεπρωμένου Eur. III. neut. ἧσσον, Att. ἧττον, as Adv., less, Od., Thuc., etc. :—with a negat., οὐχ ἧσσον, οὐδ' ἧσσον not the less, just as much, Aesch., etc.
ἧσται, 3 sing. of ἧμαι.
ἦστε, Att. for ᾔδειτε, 2 pl. plqpf. of οἶδα, v. *εἴδω.
ἤστην, for ἤτην, 3 dual impf. of εἰμί (sum).
ᾔστην, Att. for ᾐδείτην, 3 dual plqpf. of οἶδα.
ἧστο, 3 sing. impf. of ἧμαι.
ἤστον, for ἤτον, 2 dual impf. of εἰμί (sum).
ᾔστωσα, aor. 1 of ἀιστόω.
ἥσυχα, neut. pl. of ἥσυχος, as Adv.
ἡσυχάζω, f. -άσω, -άσομαι: aor. 1 ἡσύχασα : (ἥσυχος):—to be still, keep quiet, be at rest, Aesch.; ἡ ἀπορία τοῦ μὴ ἡσυχάζειν the difficulty of finding rest, Thuc. :—often in part., ἡσυχάζων προσμένω Soph. ; ἡσυχάσασα by resting from war, Thuc. ; τὸ ἡσυχάζον τῆς νυκτός the dead of night, Id. II. Causal in aor. 1, to make still, lay to rest, Plat.
ἡσυχαῖος, Dor. ἁσυχ-, α, ον, poët. for ἥσυχος, Soph.
ἡσυχαίτερος, -τατος, irreg. Comp. and Sup. of ἥσυχος.
ἡσυχῇ, Dor. ἁσυχᾷ, Adv. stilly, quietly, softly, gently, Pind. ; ἔχ' ἡσυχῇ keep quiet, Plat. ; ἡ. γελάσαι Id.
ἡσυχία, Ion. -ίη, Dor. ἁσυχία, ἡ, stillness, rest, quiet, Od., Hdt., Att. :—c. gen. rest from a thing, Hdt., Plat. 2. with Preps., δι' ἡσυχίης εἶναι to keep quiet, Hdt. :—ἐν ἡσ. ἔχειν τι to keep it quiet, not speak of it, Id. :—ἐφ' ἡσυχίας Ar. :—κατ' ἡσυχίην πολλὴν quite at one's ease, Hdt. ; καθ' ἡσυχίαν at leisure, Thuc. :—μεθ' ἡσυχίας quietly, Eur. 3. with Verbs, ἡσυχίαν ἄγειν to keep quiet, be at rest, keep silent,

Hdt., Att.:—so ἡσυχίαν ἔχειν Hdt., Att.   II. solitude, a sequestered place, h. Hom., Xen.
ἡσύχιμος, Dor. ἀσύχ-, ον, = ἥσυχος, Pind.
ἡσύχιος [ῠ], Dor. ἀσύχ-, ον, = ἥσυχος, still, quiet, at
rest, at ease, Il.; also in Prose, τρόπου ἡσυχίου of a
quiet disposition, Hdt.; τὸ ἡσύχιον τῆς εἰρήνης Thuc.
Adv. -ίως, h. Hom.
ἡσυχιότης, ητος, ἡ, = ἡσυχία, Plat.
ἩΣΥ´ΧΟΣ, Dor. ἄσυχος, ον, still, quiet, at rest, at
ease, at leisure, Hes., Hdt., Att.; ἡσύχῳ βάσει φρενῶν, i. e. in thought, Aesch.; ἐν ἡσύχῳ quietly,
Soph.   2. quiet, gentle, of character, Aesch., Eur.,
etc.; τοὺς ἀφ' ἡσύχου ποδός those of quiet life, Id.;
ὀργῇ ὑπόθες ἥσυχον πόδα, i. e. moderate thy anger,
Id.; τὸ ξύνηθες ἥσυχον their accustomed quietness,
Thuc.   II. the common Att. Comp. and Sup.
were ἡσυχαίτερος, -αίτατος, but the regular form -ώτε-
ρος is also found.   III. Adv. -χως, Eur., etc.:
gently, cautiously, Id.:—Sup. ἡσυχαίτατα Plat.—The
neut. ἥσυχον, Dor. ἄσυχον, is also used as Adv.,
Theocr.; and pl. ἄσυχα, Id.
ἡσχυμμένος, pf. pass. part. of αἰσχύνω.
ἥσω, fut. of ἵημι.
ἤ-τε (ἤ τε), or also, Il.
ἦτε or ἦ τε, surely, doubtless, Hom.
ἤτε, ἤτην, Att. for ἤειτε, ἠείτην, 2 pl. and 3 impf. dual
of εἶμι (ibo).
ἤτην, 3 dual impf. of εἰμί (sum).
ἠτιάασθε, Ep. for ἠτιᾶσθε, 2 pl. impf. of αἰτιάομαι:—
ἠτιασάμην and -άθην, aor. 1 : ᾐτίαμαι, pf.
ἤ-τοι: I. = ἦ τοι, now surely, truly, verily, Il.;
after ἀλλ' εἰ . ., nevertheless, Ib.   II. = ἤ τοι,
either in truth, followed by ἤ, or, Hdt., etc.
ἮΤΟΡ, τό, in Hom. always in nom. or acc.:—the heart
as a part of the body, Il.:—then, as the seat of life,
life, ἦτορ ὀλέσσαι Ib.:—as the seat of feeling, the
heart, Ib., etc.
ἬΤΡΙΟΝ, Dor. ἄτριον, τό, the warp in a web of cloth,
Plat., Theocr.:—in pl. a thin, fine cloth, such that one
could see between the threads, Eur.; ἤτρια βύβλων
leaves made of strips of papyrus, Anth.
ἮΤΡΟΝ, τό, the part below the navel, the abdomen,
Plat., Xen., etc.
ἧττα, ἡττάομαι, ἡττάω, ἥττων, Att. for ἧσσ-.
ἥττημα, ατος, τό, = ἧσσα, N. T.
ἤτω, for ἔστω, 3 sing. imperat. of εἰμί (sum).
ἠυ-γένειος, -γενής, -κάρηνος, -κομος, -πυργος, etc.,
Ep. and Lyr. for εὐ-γένειος, etc.
ηὐλάβεια, crasis for ἡ εὐλάβεια.
ηὔλησα, aor. 1 of αὐλέω; ηὐλεῖτο, 3 sing. impf. pass.
ηὐλισάμην, -ίσθην, aor. 1 med. and pass. of αὐλίζομαι.
ηὐξάμην [ᾰ], aor. 1 of εὔχομαι.
ηὔξανον, impf. of αὐξάνω; ηὔξησα, -ήθην, aor. 1 act.
and pass.
ἠΰς, neut. ἠΰ, Ep. for εὔς, good, brave, Hom., Il.
ηὗσα [ῠ], aor. 1 of αὔω.
ἠΰτε, Ep. Particle, as, like as, Il., etc.; often in Hom.
in similes for ὡς ὅτε.   II. in Il. 4. 277 after a Comp.,
μελάντερον ἠΰτε πίσσα very black, like as pitch, or = ἤ,
blacker than pitch.
ηὐτρέπισται, 3 sing. pf. pass. (in med. sense) of εὐτρεπίζω.

ἠύ-χορος, ον, Ep. for εὔχορος, with fair dances, Anth.
Ἡφαίστειος, α, ον, of Hephaestus: Ἡφαιστεῖον or
Ἡφαίστειον (sc. ἱερόν), τό, temple of Hephaestus, Hdt.,
Dem., etc.:—Ἡφαίστεια (sc. ἱερά), τά, his festival,
the Lat. Vulcanalia, Xen.
Ἡφαιστό-πονος, ον, wrought by Hephaestus, Eur.
Ἥφαιστος, ου, ὁ, Hephaestus, Lat. Vulcanus, son of
Zeus and Hera, lame from birth, master of metal working, Hom., etc.   II. meton. for πῦρ, fire, Il., Soph.
(Perh. from ἅπ-τω, to kindle fire.)
Ἡφαιστό-τευκτος, ον, wrought by Hephaestus, Soph.
ἤφθᾱ, Dor. for ἥφθη, 3 sing. aor. 1 pass. of ἅπτω.
ἦφι, Ep. for ᾗ, dat. fem. of ὅς (suus).
ἠφίουν, impf. (with double augm.) of ἀφίημι; 3 sing.
ἠφίει, later ἤφιε; 3 pl. ἠφίεσαν.
ἤφυσα, aor. 1 of ἀφύσσω.
ἠχεῖον, τό, (ἦχος) a kind of kettle-drum or gong, Plut.
ἠχέτης, ου, ὁ, Ep. ἠχέτᾰ, Dor. ἀχέτας, ἀχέτᾱ: (ἠχέω):
—clear-sounding, musical, Aesch., Eur.:—of the grasshopper, chirping, Hes., Anth.; and ἀχέτας, ὁ, alone,
the chirper, the grasshopper, Ar.
ἠχέω, Dor. ἀχέω [ᾱ], f. ήσω,   I. intr. to sound,
ring, peal, Hes.; often of metal, ἤχεσκε (Ion. impf.)
Hdt.; τὰ χαλκεῖα πληγέντα μακρὸν ἠχεῖ Plat.; of the
grasshopper, to chirp, Theocr.   II. c. acc. cogn.,
ἀχεῖν ὕμνον to let it sound, Aesch.; κωκυτὸν Soph.;
χαλκίον ἄχει sound the cymbal, Theocr.:—Pass., ἠχεῖ-
ται κτύπος a sound is made, Soph.
ἨΧΗ´, Dor. ἀχά, ἡ, a sound or noise of any sort, Hom.,
Att.; of the confused noise of a crowd, the roar of the
sea, the groaning of trees in a wind, Il., etc.:—in
Trag., like ἰαχή, a cry of sorrow, wail; but, σάλπιγγος
ἠχή Eur.:—rarely of articulate sounds, Id.   Hence
ἠχήεις, εσσα, εν, sounding, ringing, roaring, Hom.
ἤχημα, Dor. ἄχ-, τό, (ἠχέω) a sound, sounding, Eur.
ἤχθετο, 3 sing. impf. of ἄχθομαι.   2. of ἔχθω.
ἤχθηρα, aor. 1 of ἐχθαίρω.
ἧχι (not ἦχι), Ep. for ᾗ, Adv. where, Hom.
ἠχμᾱσα, aor. 1 of αἰχμάζω.
ἦχος, ὁ, later form of ἠχή, Theocr., Mosch.
ἠχώ, Dor. ἀχώ: ἡ: gen. (ἠχόος) ἠχοῦς, Dor. ἀχῶς: acc.
ἠχώ, Dor. ἀχώ: Dor. voc. ἀχοῖ: like ἠχή, a sound, but
properly of a returned sound, echo, h. Hom., Hes.,
etc.   2. generally, a ringing sound, Soph., Trag.;
τὴν Βοιωτίην κατεῖχε ἠχὼ ὡς . . Boeotia rang with the
news that . . , Hdt.
ἤψα, aor. 1 of ἅπτω.
ἦψε, 3 sing. impf. of ἕψω: 1 pl. ἥψομεν:—ἥψησα,
aor. 1.
ἠῶθεν, Dor. ἀῶθεν, Adv. (ἠώς) like ἕωθεν, from morn,
i. e. at dawn, at break of day, Hom., etc.; this morning, Od.
ἠῶθι, Ep. gen. of ἠώς.
ἠών, όνος, ὁ, contr. from ἠϊών.
ἠῷος, ῴα, ῷον, = ἠοῖος, at morn, at break of day, h.
Hom., Hes.   2. from the east, eastern, Hdt. From
ἩΏΣ, ἡ: gen. (ἠόος) ἠοῦς, Ep. ἠῶθι: dat. ἠοῖ: acc.
ἠῶ:—Att. ἕως, gen. ἕω, acc. ἕω, like λεώς:—Dor. ἀώς:
—Aeol. ἄυως (i. e. ἄϝως), not αὔως:—the morning-
red, daybreak, dawn, Hom., Hdt., etc.:—morning
as a time of day, opp. to μέσον ἦμαρ and δείλη, Il.;
gen. ἠοῦς at morn, early, Ib.; ἠῶ the morning long,

Od. :—ἐξ ἠοῦς μέχρι δείλης ὀψίης Hdt. :—ἅμα ἠοῖ at daybreak, Id.; ἅμ᾽ ἔῳ or ἅμα τῇ ἔῳ Thuc.; Ep. ἠῶθι πρό Hom.; ἐς ἀῶ to-morrow, Theocr. 2. since the Greeks counted their days by mornings, ἠώς often denoted a day, Hom. II. the East, Id.; ἀπὸ ἠοῦς πρὸς ἑσπέρην Hdt., etc. III. as prop. n. Ἠώς, Aurora, the goddess of morn, who rises out of her ocean-bed, Il., Eur.

Θ.

Θ, θ, θῆτα, τό, indecl., eighth letter of the Gr. alphabet: as numeral θ´ = ἐννέα, ἔνατος, but ͵θ = 9000.—θ is the aspirated dental mute, related to the tenuis τ and the medial δ. θ is sometimes represented by φ, as θλάω φλάω; so in Lat. θήρ (Aeol. φήρ) fera; θύρα fores; by b, as ἐ-ρυθρός ruber, οὖθαρ uber. II. changes of θ in the Gr. dialects: 1. Lacon., into σ, as σάλασσα σεῖος Ἀσάνα παρσένος for θάλασσα θεῖος Ἀθάνα παρθένος. 2. Aeol. and Dor. into τ, as αὖτις ἐντεῦθεν for αὖθις ἐντεῦθεν. 3. when θ was repeated in two foll. syllables, the former became τ, as Ἀτθίς.
θαάσσω, Ep. form of θάσσω, only in pres. and impf., to sit, Hom.; Ep. inf. θαασσέμεν Od.
θᾰδώλια, crasis for τὰ ἐδώλια.
θάεο [ᾱ], imperat. of θάομαι.
θαέομαι, Dor. for θηέομαι (Ion. form of θεάομαι), Pind., Theocr.; aor. 1 imper. θάησαι Anth.
θάημα, ατος, τό, Dor. for θέαμα, a sight, wonder, Theocr.
θαητός, ή, όν, Dor. for θηητός.
θαἱμάτια, θαἱματίδια, crasis for τὰ ἱμάτια, etc.
ΘΑΙΡΟΣ, ὁ, the hinge of a door or gate, Il.
θᾱκεύω, = sq., Plut.
θᾱκέω, Ion. and Dor. θωκέω, (θᾶκος) to sit, Hdt., Trag.; c. acc. cogn., θακοῦντι παγκρατεῖς ἕδρας sitting on imperial throne, Aesch.: suppliants, Soph., Eur. Hence
θάκημα, ατος, τό, a sitting, esp. as a suppliant, Soph. 2. a seat, Id., Eur.: and
θάκησις, εως, ἡ, a sitting, sitting-place, Soph.
θᾶκος, Ion. and Ep. θῶκος, Ep. also θόωκος, ὁ, (θάσσω) a seat, chair, Hom.; θῶκοι ἀμπαυστήριοι seats for resting, Hdt.; θᾶκος κραιπνόσυτος, of a winged car, Aesch., etc. 2. a chair of office, Ar. 3. a privy, Theophr. II. in Hom. a sitting in council, a council, Od.; θῶκόνδε to the council, Ib.; ἐν θώκῳ κατήμενος sitting in council, Hdt.
θάλαμαξ, ἄκος, ὁ, = θαλαμίτης, Ar.
θαλάμευμα, ατος, τό, = θαλάμη, Eur.
θᾰλάμη [ᾰ], ἡ, a lurking-place, den, hole, cave, Od., Eur.; of the grave, Id. II. = θάλαμος III., Luc.
θαλάμήϊος, η, ον, of or for a θάλαμος, Hes.
θαλάμη-πόλος, ἡ, (πολέομαι) a chamber-maid, waiting-maid, Od., Aesch. 2. ὁ, a eunuch of the bed-chamber, Plut. II. rarely, a bridegroom, Soph. 2. as Adj. bridal, Anth.
θᾰλᾱμιός, ά, όν, of or belonging to the θάλαμος:—as Subst., I. θαλαμιός, ὁ, = θαλαμίτης, Thuc. II. θαλαμία, Ion. -ιή (sub. κώπη), ἡ, the oar of the θαλαμίτης, Ar. 2. (sub. ὀπή) the hole in the ship's side, through which this oar worked, διὰ θαλαμιῆς

διελεῖν τινα to place a man so that his upper half projected through this hole, Hdt.
θᾰλᾰμίτης [ῑ], ου, ὁ, (θάλαμος III) one of the rowers on the lowest bench of a trireme, who had the shortest oars and the least pay; cf. ζυγίτης, θρανίτης.
θαλαμόνδε, Adv. to the bed-chamber, Od. From
ΘΑΛΑΜΟΣ, ὁ, an inner room or chamber: 1. generally, the women's apartment, inner part of the house, Hom., Hdt. 2. a chamber in this part of the house: a. a bed-room, Il.:—the bride-chamber, Ib., Soph., etc. b. a store-room, Hom., Xen. c. generally, a chamber, room, Od. II. metaph., ὁ παγκοίτας θ. of the grave, Soph.; τυμβήρης θ. of the ark of Danaë, Id.; θάλαμοι ὑπὸ γῆς the realms below, Aesch.; θ. Ἀμφιτρίτης of the sea, Soph.; ἀρνῶν θ. their folds or pens, Eur., etc. III. the lowest part of the ship, in which the θαλαμῖται sat, the hold. IV. a shrine, temple, Anth.
ΘΑΛΑΣΣΑ [θᾰ], later Att. -ττα, ἡ, the sea, Hom., etc.; when he uses it of a particular sea, he means the Mediterranean, opp. to Ὠκεανός;—Hdt. calls the Mediterranean ἥδε ἡ θάλασσα; so, ἡ παρ᾽ ἡμῖν θάλ. Plat.; κατὰ θάλασσαν by sea, opp. to πεζῇ by land, Hdt.; τὸ κατὰ γῆς, Thuc. :—metaph., κακῶν θ. a sea of troubles, Aesch. 2. a well of salt water, said to be produced by a stroke of Poseidon's trident, in the Acropolis at Athens, Hdt.
θαλασσαῖος, α, ον, = θαλάσσιος, Pind.
θαλασσεύω, to be at sea, keep the sea, Thuc.; τὰ θαλαττεύοντα τῆς νεὼς μέρη the parts under water, Plut.
θαλάσσιος, later Att. -ττιος, α, ον and ος, ον: (θάλασσα):—of, in, on or from the sea, belonging to it, Lat. marinus, οὕ σφι θαλάσσια ἔργα μεμήλει, οἳ the Arcadians, Il.; κορώναι τῇσίν τε θαλ. ἔργα μέμηλεν, i.e. which live by fishing, Od. :—θαλάσσια sea-animals, opp. to χερσαῖα, Hdt.; πεζοί τε καὶ θαλ. landsmen and seamen, Aesch.; θαλ. ἐκρίπτειν τινά to throw one into the sea, Soph. II. skilled in the sea, nautical, Hdt., Thuc.
θαλασσο-κοπέω, f. ήσω, (κόπτω) to strike the sea with the oar: metaph. to make a splash, Ar.
θαλασσο-κρατέω, to be master of the sea, Hdt., Thuc.
θαλασσο-κράτωρ, ορος, ὁ, ἡ, (κρατέω) master of the sea, Hdt., Thuc., Xen.
θαλασσό-πλαγκτος, ον, (πλάζω) made to wander o'er the sea, sea-tost, Aesch., Eur.
θαλασσο-πληκτος, ον, (πλήσσω) sea-beaten, Aesch.
θαλασσο-πόρος, ον, sea-faring, Anth.
θαλασσ-ουργός, ὁ, (*ἔργω) one who works on the sea, a fisherman, seaman, Xen.
θαλασσόω, to make or change into sea: Med. to be a sea-faring man, Luc.
θάλαττα, -ττεύω, -ττιος, etc., Att. for θάλασσα, etc.
θάλεα [ᾰ], τά, (θάλλω) good cheer, happy thoughts, θαλέων ἐμπλησάμενος κῆρ Il.
θᾰλέθω, poët. lengthd. for θάλλω, to bloom, flourish, Hom. only in part.; of trees, Od.; of men, Ib.; of swine, μαλέθοντες ἀλοιφῇ swelling, wantoning in fat, Il.
θάλεια, fem. Adj. blooming, luxuriant, goodly, bounteous, of banquets, θεῶν ἐν δαιτὶ θαλείῃ Od., etc. No masc. θάλυς occurs, θαλερός being used instead. II.

as prop. n. Θάλεια, ἡ, one of the Muses, the *blooming one*, Hes.; also Θαλίη, Anth. From
θᾰλεῖν, aor. 2 inf. of θάλλω.
θᾰλερός, ά, όν, (θάλλω) *blooming, fresh*, of young persons, Hom.; θ. γάμος the marriage *of a youthful pair*, Od. II. of the body, *fresh, vigorous*, Il.; θ. χαίτη *luxuriant* hair, Ib.; θ. ἀλοιφή *rich, abundant* fat, Od.;—then of other things, θαλερὸν κατὰ δάκρυ χέουσα *shedding big* tears, Il.; θ. γόος *the thick and frequent* sob, Od.; θαλερὴ φωνή *a full, rich* voice, Hom.
θᾰλερ-ῶπις, ιδος, ἡ, (ὤψ) = θαλερόμματος, Anth.
θᾰλέω, Dor. for θηλέω.
Θᾰλῆς, ὁ, gen. Θάλεω, dat. Θαλῇ, acc. Θαλῆν:—*Thales* of Miletus, Hdt.
Θᾰλία, Ion. -ίη, ἡ, (θάλλω) *abundance, plenty, good cheer*, Il.; in pl. *festivities*, Od., Hdt.
θαλλός, ὁ, (θάλλω) *a young shoot, young branch*, Od., Soph., etc.:—of *the young olive-shoot* carried by suppliants, Hdt., Trag.; ἱκτὴρ θ. Eur.; also, θαλλοῦ στέφανος the *olive*-wreath worn at festivals, Aeschin.
θαλλο-φόρος, ον,(φέρω) *carrying young olive-shoots*,Ar.
ΘΑΛΛΩ, f. θαλλήσω: aor. 1 ἔθηλα: aor. 2 ἔθαλον: pf. τέθηλα: 3 sing. plqpf. τεθήλει:—*to bloom, abound, to be luxuriant*, of fruit-trees, Od., Soph., etc.; often in part. pf. τεθηλώς, Ep. fem. τεθαλυῖα, as Adj. *luxuriant, exuberant*, Hom.; c. acc. cogn., οὐ δένδρε᾽ ἔθαλλεν χῶρος the place *grew* no trees, θαλλούσης βίον ἐλαίας Aesch. b. of other natural objects, τεθαλυῖα ἔρση the *fresh* or *copious* dew, Od.; τεθαλυῖα ἀλοιφῇ *rich* with fat, Il.; εἰλαπίνη τεθαλυίη at a *sumptuous* feast, Ib. 2. of men, *to bloom, flourish*, Hes., Soph., etc. 3. in bad sense, *to be active*, νόσος ἀεὶ τέθηλε Soph.; ῥήματα ἀεὶ θάλλοντα Id. Hence
θᾶλος [ᾰ], εος, τό, like θαλλός, only in nom. and acc., in metaph. sense of *young persons*, like ἔρνος (q. v.), φίλον θάλος dear *child* of mine, Il.; τοίονδε θάλος so fair *a scion* of their house, Od.:—v. Θάλεα.
θαλπιάω, (θάλπω) *to be* or *become warm*, εὖ θαλπιόων (Ep. part.) right *warm and comfortable*, Od.
θαλπνός, ή, όν, (θάλπω) *warming, fostering*, Pind.
θάλπος, εος, τό, (θάλπω) *warmth, heat*, esp. *summer-heat*, Aesch.; θ. θεοῦ the sun's *heat*, Soph.; μεσημβρινοῖσι θάλπεσιν with the meridian *rays* (cf. Lat. *soles*), Aesch. 2. metaph. *a sting, smart*, caused by an arrow, Soph., Anth.
θαλπτήριος, ον, *warming*, Anth. From
ΘΑΛΠΩ, f. ψω, *to heat, soften by heat*, Od.:—Pass., ἐτήκετο, κασσίτερος ὣς θαλφθείς Hes.: metaph. *to be softened*, λόγοις Ar. II. *to heat, warm*, without any notion of *softening*, καῦμ᾽ ἔθαλπε (sc. ἡμᾶς) Soph.: —Pass., θάλπεσθαι τοῦ θέρους *to be warm* in summer, Xen.:—metaph. *to be alive*, Pind. 2. *to warm* at the fire, *dry*, Soph., Eur. III. metaph. of passion, *to heat, inflame*, Aesch., Soph. 2. *to cherish, comfort, foster*, Theocr. Hence
θαλπωρή, ἡ, *warming*: metaph. *comfort, consolation, source of hope*, Hom.
θᾰλύσια [ῠ], τά, (θάλος) *the firstlings of the harvest, offerings of firstfruits*, Il., Theocr. Hence
θᾰλῠσιάς, άδος, fem. Adj. *of* or *for the θαλύσια*, Theocr.
θᾰμά, Adv. (ἅμα) *often, oft-times*, Hom., etc.
θᾰμάκις [ᾰ], Adv., = θαμά, Pind.

θαμβαίνω, = θαμβέω, *to be astonished at*, h. Hom.
θαμβέω, f. ήσω: aor. 1 ἐθάμβησα, Ep. θάμβησα: (θάμβος):—*to be astounded, amazed*, Hom., Soph., Eur. 2. c. acc. *to be astonished at, marvel at*, Od., Pind. II. Causal, *to surprise*:—Pass., τεθαμβημένος astounded, Plut.
θάμβος, εος, τό, (from Root ΤΑΦ, v. τέθηπα), = τάφος (τό), *astonishment, amazement*, Hom., Att.
θᾰμέες, οἱ, dat. θαμέσι, acc. -έας (from θαμύς): fem. nom. and acc. θαμειαί, -άς (from θαμειός):—poët. Adj. only in pl., *crowded, close-set, thick*, Hom.
θᾰμίζω, (θαμά) *to come often*, Lat. *frequentare*, Hom., Xen. 2. *to be often* or *constantly engaged* with or in a thing, Od.; οὔτι κομιζόμενός γε θάμιζεν he *was* not *wont* to be so cared for, Ib.; μινύρεται θαμίζουσα ἀηδών *mourns often* or *constantly*, Soph.
θᾰμινός, ή, όν, *frequent*, in neut. pl. θαμινά as Adv. = θαμά, Pind., Att.: v. θαμέες.
θάμνος, ὁ, (θαμινός) *a bush, shrub*, Lat. *arbustum*, Hom.; in pl. *a copse, thicket*, Id., Att.
θᾰμύς, v. θαμέες.
***θᾰνάσιμος** [νᾰ], ον, (θνήσκω) *deadly*, Trag., etc. 2. *of* or *belonging to death*, θαν. αἷμα (as we say) *the life*-blood, Aesch.; μέλψασα θ. γόον having sung my *death*-song, Id. II. of persons, *near death*, Soph., Plat.: *subject to death, mortal*, Plat.: also *dead*, Soph.
θᾰνᾰτάω, Desiderat. of θανεῖν, *to desire to die*, Plat.
θᾰνᾰτη-φόρος, ον, (φέρω) *death-bringing, mortal*, Aesch., Soph., etc.
θᾰνᾰτιάω, = θανατάω, Luc.
θᾰνᾰτικός, ή, όν, *deadly*, θ. δίκη sentence *of death*, Plut.
θᾰνᾰτόεις, εσσα, εν, *deadly*, Soph., Eur. From
θάνᾰτος, ὁ, (θνήσκω) *death*, Hom., etc.; θ. τινος the death threatened by him, Od.; θάνατόνδε *to death*, Il., etc. 2. in Att., θάνατον καταγιγνώσκειν τινός *to pass sentence of death* on one,Thuc.; θανάτου κρίνεσθαι *to be tried for one's life*, Id.:—ellipt., τὴν ἐπὶ θανάτῳ κεκοσμημένος (sc. στολήν) Hdt.; δῆσαί τινα τὴν ἐπὶ θανάτου (sc. δέσιν) Id.; τοῖς Ἀθηναίοις ἐπιτρέψαι περὶ σφῶν αὐτῶν πλὴν θανάτου for any penalty short of death, Thuc. 3. pl. θάνατοι, *kinds of death*, Od.; or *the deaths* of several persons or even of one person, Trag. II. as prop. n., Θάνατος *Death*, twin-brother of Sleep, Il. III. = νεκρός, Anth.
θᾰνᾰτούσια (sc. ἱερά), τά, *a feast of the dead*, Luc.
θᾰνᾰτο-φόρος, ον, = θανατηφόρος, Aesch.
θᾰνᾰτόω, f. ώσω:—Pass., aor. 1 ἐθανατώθην: f. med. in pass. sense θανατώσομαι Xen.:—*to put to death*, τινά Hdt., Att. 2. metaph. *to mortify* the flesh, N. T. II. *to put to death by sentence* of law, Plat.:—Pass., Xen. Hence
θᾰνάτωσις, εως, ἡ, *a putting to death*, Thuc.
θᾰνεῖν, aor. 2 inf. of θνήσκω.
θᾰνεῖσθαι, Ep. -έεσθαι, fut. inf. of θνήσκω.
θᾰνοῦσα, Dor. for -οῦσα, aor. 2 part. fem. of θνήσκω.
θάνον, Ep. for ἔθανον, aor. 2 of θνήσκω.
ΘΑΟΜΑΙ: aor. 1 ἐθησάμην: Dep.:—*to wonder at, admire*, Od. 2. later, *to gaze on, see*, 2 pl. θᾶσθε, Ar.; imperat. θάεο Anth.: Dor. fut. part. θασόμενος Theocr.; aor. 1 imper. θάσαι Ar.; inf. θάασθαι Theocr.
θαπτέον, verb. Adj. *one must bury*, Soph. From
θάπτω (from Root ΤΑΦ, cf. τάφηναι, τάφος): f. θάψω:

aor. 1 ἔθαψα:—Pass., f. τᾰφήσομαι and τεθάψομαι: aor. 1 ἐθάφθην: aor. 2 ἐτάφην [ἄ]:—pf. τέθαμμαι, Ion. 3 pl. τεθάφαται: 3 sing. plqpf. pass. ἐτέθαπτο:—to pay the last dues to a corpse, to honour with funeral rites, i. e. in early times by burning the body, Hom.: then, simply, to bury, inter, Hdt., Att.

Θαργήλια (ἱερά), ων, τά, a festival of Apollo and Artemis held in the month Thargelion, Lex ap. Dem.:—Θαργηλιών, ῶνος, ὁ, the 11th month of the Attic year, from mid-May to mid-June, Att.

Θαρρᾰλέος, θαρρέω, θάρρος, etc., Att. for θαρσ-, etc.

θαρσᾰλέος, Att. θαρραλέος, α, ον, (θάρσος) bold, of good courage, ready, daring, undaunted, Il., Att.: —τὸ θαρσαλέον confidence, Thuc.:—so in Adv., θαρραλέως ἔχειν to be of good courage, Plat., Xen. 2. in bad sense, overbold, audacious, Od. II. that which may be ventured on, Plat.

θαρσᾰλεότης, Att. θαρραλ-, ητος, ἡ, boldness, Plut.

θαρσέω, Att. θαρρέω, f. ήσω, (θάρσος) to be of good courage, take courage, Il., etc.:—in bad sense, to be over-bold, audacious, Thuc., Plat.; θάρσει, θαρσεῖτε, take courage! cheer up, Hom., etc.; θαρσήσας with good courage, Il.; so, θαρσῶν Hdt., Att.:—also, τὸ τεθαρρηκός confidence, Plut. 2. c. acc. θάρσει τόνδε γ᾽ ἄεθλον take heart for this struggle, Od.; θ. θάνατον Plat.; θ. μάχην to venture a fight, Xen.:—c. acc. pers. to have confidence in, Id.:—so also, θαρσεῖν τινι Hdt. 3. c. inf. to believe confidently that, Soph.; also, to make bold or venture to, Xen. Hence

θάρσησις, εως, ἡ, confidence in a thing, Thuc.

θάρσος, Att. θάρρος, τό, (θρασύς) courage, boldness, Hom., Att.; θ. τινός courage to do a thing, Aesch., Soph. 2. that which gives courage, θάρση grounds of confidence, Eur., Plat. II. in bad sense, audacity, Il.: cf. θράσος.

θαρσούντως, Att. θαρρ-, Adv. pres. part. of θαρσέω, boldly, courageously, Xen.

θάρσῡνος, ον, =θαρσαλέος, Il.; c. dat. relying on a thing, Ib.

θαρσῡ́νω [ῡ], Att. θαρρῡ́νω, Causal of θαρσέω, to encourage, cheer, θάρσυνον (aor. 1 imper.) Il.; θαρσύνεσκε (Ion. impf.) Ib.; so Hdt., Thuc., etc. II. intr. θάρσυνε be of good courage, Soph.

θᾶσαι, Dor. for θήσαι, aor. 1 imp. of θάομαι.

Θάσιος [ᾰ], α, ον, of or from Thasos, Thasian, οἶνος Ar.:—ἡ Θασία ἅλμη Thasian pickled fish, Id.

θάσομαι, Dor. for θήσομαι, fut. of θάομαι.

θᾶσσον, Att. θᾶττον, neut. of θάσσων, as Adv.

ΘΆΣΣΩ, Ep. θαάσσω, to sit, sit idle; — c. acc. sedis, θάσσειν θρόνον Soph., etc.; c. acc. cogn., θ. δυστήνους ἕδρας to sit in wretched posture, Eur.

θάσσων, Att. θάττων, Comp. of ταχύς, quicker, swifter: neut. θᾶσσον as Adv., more quickly.

θάτερον, crasis for τὸ ἕτερον.

θᾶττον, Att. for θᾶσσον.

θαῦμα, ατος, τό, Ion. θώϋμα or θῶμα, (θάομαι): I. of objects, whatever one regards with wonder, a wonder, marvel, Hom., Hes.; θαῦμα, of Polypheme, Od.; θαῦμα βροτοῖσι, of a beautiful woman, Ib.; c. inf., θαῦμα ἰδέσθαι or ἰδεῖν a wonder to behold, Ib., Eur.; καὶ θαῦμά γ᾽ οὐδέν and no wonder, Ar.:—θῶμα ποιεῖσθαί τι Hdt.:—in pl., θαύματ᾽ ἐμοὶ κλύειν Aesch.; θαυμάτων

κρείσσονα or πέρα things more than wondrous, Eur. 2. in pl. also jugglers' tricks, mountebank-gambols, Xen., etc. II. of the feeling, wonder, astonishment, Od., etc.; ἐν θώματι εἶναι or γίγνεσθαι to be astonished, Hdt., Thuc.; τινός at a thing, Hdt. Hence

θαυμάζω, Ion. θωϋμ- or θωμ-: Att. f. θαυμάσομαι, Ep. θαυμάσσομαι: aor. 1 ἐθαύμασα: pf. τεθαύμακα:—Pass., f. -ασθήσομαι: aor. 1 ἐθαυμάσθην: 1. absol. to wonder, marvel, be astonied, Il., etc. 2. c. acc. to look on with wonder and amazement, to wonder at, marvel at, Hom., Hdt., Att. b. to honour, admire, worship, Lat. admirari, observare, Od., Hdt., Att.: —θ. τινά τινος for a thing, Thuc.; ἐπί τινι Xen. 3. c. gen. to wonder at, marvel at, Thuc., etc.; θ. σοῦ λέγοντος Plat. 4. c. dat. rei, to wonder at, Thuc. 5. c. acc. et inf., θ. σε πενθεῖν Eur. II. Pass. to be looked at with wonder, Hdt.; θαυμάζεται μὴ παρών, i. e. I keep wondering that he is not present, Soph. 2. to be admired, Hdt.; τὰ εἰκότα θ. to receive proper marks of respect, Thuc.

θαυμαίνω, Ep. f. -ανέω, = θαυμάζω 2, to admire, gaze upon, Od., Pind.

θαυμάσιος, α, ον, Ion. θωϋμ- or θωμ-, (θαῦμα) wondrous, wonderful, marvellous, Hes., Hdt.; θαυμάσια wonders, marvels, Hdt., Plat.: θαυμάσιόν [ἐστι], c. inf., Ar.; θαυμάσιος τὸ κάλλος marvellous for beauty, Xen.; θαυμάσιον ὅσον wonderfully much, Plat.; θαυμάσια ἡλίκα Dem. 2. Adv. -ίως, wonderfully, i. e. exceedingly, Ar.; often with ὡς added, θ. ὡς ἄθλιος marvellously wretched, Plat. II. admirable, excellent, with slight irony, Id., Dem.; ὦ θαυμασιώτατε ἄνθρωπε, in scorn, Xen.

θαυμασι-ουργέω, (*ἔργω) to work wonders, Xen.

θαυμασμός, ὁ, (θαυμάζω) a marvelling, Plut., etc.

θαυμαστέος, α, ον, verb. Adj. of θαυμάζω, to be admired, Plat. II. neut. θαυμαστέον, one must admire, Eur.

θαυμαστής, οῦ, ὁ, (θαυμάζω) an admirer, Arist.

θαυμαστικός, ή, όν, (θαυμάζω) inclined to wonder or admire, Arist.

θαυμαστός, Ion. θωϋμ- or θωμ-, ή, όν, (θαυμάζω) wondrous, wonderful, marvellous, h. Hom., Hdt., Att.:—c. acc., θαυμαστὸς τὸ κάλλος Plat.; c. gen., θ. τῆς ἐπιεικείας Plut.; c. dat., πλήθει Id.:—foll. by a Relat., θαυμαστὸν ὅσον Lat. mirum quantum, Plat., etc.; θαυμαστὸν ἡλίκον Dem.:—Adv. -τῶς, θαυμαστῶς ὡς σφόδρα Plat. II. admirable, excellent, Pind., Soph.

θαυμᾰτοποιέω, to work wonders, Luc.; and

θαυμᾰτοποιία, ἡ, conjuring, juggling, Plat. From

θαυμᾰτο-ποιός, όν, (ποιέω) wonder-working:—as Subst. a conjuror, juggler, Plat., Dem.

θαύψῐνος, η, ον, yellow-coloured, yellow, sallow, Ar.

θάψος, ἡ, a plant or wood used for dyeing yellow, brought from Thapsos, Theocr.

*ΘΆΩ, Ep. for the prose θηλάζω: only in Med., παρέχουσι γάλα θῆσθαι they give milk to suck, Od.; aor 1, θήσατο μαζόν he sucked the breast, Il.; part., θησάμενος sucking, h. Hom. II. Causal, to suckle a child, Il.

-θε, inseparable suffix, v. -θεν.

ΘΕΆ, ἡ, fem. of θεός, a goddess, Hom.; often with

another Subst., θεὰ μήτηρ Il. :—τὰ θεά in dual are Demeter and Persephoné (Ceres and Proserpine) Soph. ; αἱ σεμναὶ θεαί the Furies, Id.

θέᾱ, Ion. θέη, ἡ, (θάομαι, θεάομαι) a seeing, looking at, view, θέης ἄξιος = ἀξιοθέητος, Hdt. ; θέαν λαβεῖν to take or get a view, Soph.   2. aspect, διαπρεπὴς τὴν θέαν Eur.   II. that which is seen, a sight, spectacle, Trag.,   III. the place for seeing from, a seat in the theatre, Aeschin., Dem.

θέαινᾰ, ἡ, Ep. for θεά, a goddess, Hom.

θέᾱμα, Ion. θέημα, ατος, τό, (θεάομαι) that which is seen, a sight, show, spectacle, Trag., Thuc., etc.

θεάμων [ᾱ], Ion. θεήμων, ὁ, ἡ, a spectator, Anth. From θεάομαι, Ion. θηέομαι: imper. θεῶ; Ep. 2 sing. opt. θηοῖο (for θεῷο); Ion. part. θηεύμενος; Ion. impf. 3 sing. and pl. ἐθηεῖτο, ἐθηεῦντο, Ep. θηεῖτο, θηεῦντο :— fut. θεάσομαι [ᾱ], Ion. -ήσομαι: aor. 1 ἐθεασάμην, Ion. ἐθηησάμην : pf. τεθέαμαι: Dep. :—to look on, gaze at, view, behold, Hom., Hdt., Att. ; ἐθεᾶτο τὴν θέσιν τῆς πόλεως reconnoitred it, Thuc.   2. to view as spectators, οἱ θεώμενοι the spectators in a theatre, Ar. :—metaph., θ. τὸν πόλεμον to be spectators of the war, Hdt.   3. θ. τὸ στράτευμα to review it, Xen.

θέαριον [ᾱ], τό, Dor. for θεώριον, the place where the θεωροί met, Pind. From θεᾱρός, ὁ, Dor. for θεωρός.

θεᾱτέος, α, ον, verb. Adj. of θεάομαι, to be seen, Plat.   II. θεατέον, one must see, Id.

θεᾱτής, Ion. θεητής, ὁ, (θεάομαι) one who sees, a spectator, Hdt., Eur., etc.

θεᾱτός, ή, όν, to be seen, Soph., Plat.

θεᾱτρίζω, f. σω, (θέατρον) to bring on the stage :— Pass. to be made a show of, a gazing-stock, N. T.

θεᾱτρικός, Ion. θεητρικός, ή, όν, (θέατρον) of or for the theatre, theatrical, Arist., Plut.

θέᾱτρον, Ion. θέητρον, τό, (θεάομαι) a place for seeing, esp. a theatre, Hdt., Thuc., etc.   2. collective for οἱ θεαταί, the people in the theatre, the spectators, 'the house,' Hdt., Ar.   3. = θέαμα, a show, spectacle, θ. γενηθῆναι = θεατρίζεσθαι, N. T.

θέειον, Ep. for θεῖον (sulphur).

θεεῖος, η, ον, Ep. for θεῖος, α, ον.

θεειόω, f. ώσω, Ep. for θειόω.

θέη, ἡ, Ion. for θέα.

θεήϊος, η, ον, Ion. for θέειος, θεῖος, divine, Bion.

θε-ήλᾰτος, ον, (ἐλαύνω) driven or hunted by a god, Aesch.   II. sent or caused by a god, Hdt., Soph. ; ἔκ τινος θεηλάτου from some destiny, Eur.   III. built for the gods, like θεόδμητος, Id.

θεη-μάχος, ον, poët. for θεο-μ-, Anth.

θεημοσύνη, ἡ, contemplation : a problem, Anth.

θεήμων, ονος, ὁ, Ion. for θεάμων, Anth.

θεητής, θέητρον, Ion. for θεατής, θέατρον.

θειάζω, f. σω, (θεῖος) to practise divinations, Thuc.

θειασμός, οῦ, ὁ, practice of divination, Thuc.

Θείβᾰθεν, Adv., Boeot. for Θήβηθεν, from Thebes, Ar. : so, Θείβᾶθι, at Thebes, Id.

θείην, aor. 2 opt. of τίθημι :—θεῖεν, 3 pl.

θειλό-πεδον, τό, (εἵλη) a sunny spot in the vineyard, on which the grapes were suffered to dry, so as to make raisins, Od.

θεῖμεν, for θείημεν, 1 pl. opt. aor. 2 act. of τίθημι.

θεῖναι, aor. 2 inf. of τίθημι.   II. aor. 1 inf. of θείνω.

ΘΕΙ'ΝΩ, Ep. inf. θεινέμεναι: impf. ἔθεινον : f. θενῶ: aor. 1 ἔθεινα; the other moods are taken from an aor. 2 ἔθενον (which does not occur in indic.), imper. θένε, subj. θένω, inf. θενεῖν, part. θενών :—to strike, wound, Hom., Eur. :—Pass., θεινομένου πρὸς οὔδεϊ stricken to earth, Od.   2. metaph., θείνειν ὀνείδει Aesch.   3. intr. of ships, θ. ἐπ' ἀκτᾶς to strike on the shore, Id.

θειό-δομος, ον, (δέμω) built by gods, Anth.

θεῖομεν, Ep. for θέωμεν, 1 pl. aor. 2 subj. of τίθημι.

θεῖον, Ep. θέειον, θήϊον, τό, brimstone, Lat. sulfur, used to fumigate and purify, Hom. ; δεινὴ δὲ θεείου γίγνεται ὀδμή, from a thunderbolt, Il.

θεῖον, τό, the divinity, v. θεῖος II.

θεῖος, α, ον : Ep. θέειος, θήϊος : Lacon. σεῖος : Comp. and Sup. θειότερος, -ότατος, θεώτερος being Comp. of θεός : (θεός) :   1. of or from the gods, sent by the gods, issuing from them, divine, Hom., Hdt., Att. ; θ. νόσος of a whirlwind, Soph. ; θείᾳ τινὶ μοίρᾳ by divine intervention, Xen. ; so, θείῃ τύχῃ Hdt. :— appointed of God, βασιλῆες Od.   2. belonging or sacred to a god, in honour of a god, holy, Hom. : under divine protection, δόμος Id. ; of heralds and minstrels, Id.   3. like θεσπέσιος, ἱερός, Lat. divinus, of anything more than human, wondrous : of heroes, divinely strong, great, beautiful, etc., Hom. ; and as a mere mark of respect, excellent, θεῖος ὑφορβός Od. ; so, θ. πρήγματα marvellous things, Hdt. ; ἐν τοῖσι θειότατον one of the most marvellous things, Id. ; so, at Sparta, θεῖος (or rather σεῖος) ἀνήρ was a title of distinction, Plat., Arist.   II. as Subst., θεῖον, τό, the Divine Being, the Divinity, Deity, Hdt., Aesch.   2. θεῖα, τά, divine things, the acts and attributes of the gods, the course of providence, Soph., Ar., etc. : religious observances, Xen. ; ἔρρει τὰ θεῖα religion is out of date, Soph.   III. Adv. θείως, by divine providence, Xen. ; θεῖοι ἔρως by special providence, Hdt.

ΘΕΙ'ΟΣ, ὁ, one's father's or mother's brother, uncle, Lat. patruus and avunculus, Eur., etc.

θειότης, ητος, ἡ, divine nature, divinity, Plut.

θεῖτο, 3 sing. aor. 2 med. opt. of τίθημι.

θειόω, Ep. θεειόω, f. ώσω) to smoke with brimstone, fumigate and purify thereby, Od. :—Med., δῶμα θειοῦται he fumigates his house, Ib. : generally, to purify, hallow, Eur.

θεῖς, θεῖσα, aor. 2 part. of τίθημι.

θείω, Ep. for θέω, to run.

θείω, Ep. for θέω, θῶ, aor. 2 subj. of τίθημι.

θείως, v. θεῖος III.

θελγεσί-μῦθος, ον, soft-speaking, Anth.

θέλγητρον, τό, (θέλγω) a charm or spell, Eur., Luc.

ΘΕ'ΛΓΩ, Ion. impf. θέλγεσκε Od. : f. θέλξω, Dor. -ξῶ: aor. 1 ἔθελξα :—Pass., aor. 1 ἐθέλχθην, Ep. 3 pl. -χθεν : —properly, to stroke or touch with magic power, Lat. mulcere, and so to charm, enchant, spell-bind, of Hermes, who with his magic wand ἀνδρῶν ὄμματα θέλγει, lays men in a charmed sleep, Hom. ; of the sorceress Circé, Od., etc.   2. in bad sense, to cheat, cozen, Hom., Soph.   II. to produce by spells, ἀοιδαὶ θέλξαν νιν (sc. εὐφροσύναν) Pind. ; [γαλήνη] θ. ἀνηνεμίην Anth.

θέλημα, ατος, τό, (θέλω) will, N. T.

θέλησις, εως, ἡ, (θέλω) a willing, will, N. T.

θελκτήρ, ῆρος, ὁ, (θέλγω) a soother, charmer, h. Hom.

θελκτήριον, τό, (θέλγω) a charm, spell, enchantment, of the girdle of Aphroditè, Il. ; θεῶν θελκτήριον a means of soothing the gods, Od. ; νεκροῖς θελκτήρια, of offerings to the Manes, Eur.

θελκτήριος, ον, (θέλγω) charming, enchanting, soothing, Aesch., Eur.

θέλκτρον, τό, = θελκτήριον, Soph.

θέλξαι, aor. 1 inf. of θέλγω.

θελξί-νοος, ον, charming the heart, Anth.

θελξί-πικρος, ον, sweetly painful, Anth.

θελξί-φρων, ον, (φρήν) = θελξίνοος, Eur., Anth.

θέλοισα, Dor. for θέλουσα, part. fem. of θέλω.

θέλω, f. θελήσω, shortened form of ἐθέλω, q. v.

θέμεθλα, τά, (ΘΕ, Root of τίθημι) the foundations, lowest part, bottom, ὀφθαλμοῖο θέμεθλα the very bottom, roots of the eye, Il. ; Ἄμμωνος θέμ. the place where Ammon stands, i. e. his temple, Pind. ; Παγγαίου θέμ. the roots of Mt. Pangaeus, Id.

θεμείλια, τά, = θέμεθλα, Il. : also θέμειλα, Anth.

θεμέλιος, ον, (ΘΕ, Root of τίθημι) of or for the foundation, Ar. : —as Subst., θεμέλιος (sub. λίθος) a foundation, οἱ θεμέλιοι the foundations, Thuc. ; ἐκ τῶν θεμελίων from the foundations, Id. Hence

θεμελιόω, f. ώσω, to lay the foundation of, found firmly, Xen. : —Pass. to have the foundations laid, N. T. : metaph., βασιλεία καλῶς θεμελιωθεῖσα Diod.; ἡγεμονία κάλλιστα τεθεμελιωμένη Id. ; ἐν ἀγαπῇ τεθ. N. T.

θέμεν, θέμεναι, Ep. for θεῖναι, aor. 2 inf. of τίθημι : — θέμενος, part. med.

θεμερός, όν, = σεμνός, Anth. (Deriv. uncertain.)

θεμερ-ῶπις, ιδος, ἡ, (ὤψ) of grave and serious aspect, Aesch.

θεμίζω, (θέμις) to judge : —Med., θεμισσάμενοι ὀργάς controlling our wills, Pind.

θεμί-πλεκτος, ον, (πλέκω) rightly plaited, θ. στέφανος a well-earned crown, Pind.

ΘΕ'ΜΙΣ, ἡ, old Ep. gen. θέμιστος, acc. θέμιστα, Att. θέμιν : (ΘΕ, Root of τί-θημι) : I. that which is laid down or established by custom, Lat. jus or fas, as opp. to lex, θέμις ἐστί 'tis meet and right, Lat. fas est, Hom. ; ἡ θέμις ἐστί as 'tis right, as the custom is, Id. ; ἡ θέμις ἐστὶ γυναικός as is a woman's custom, Od. ; so in Att., ὅ τι θέμις αἰνεῖν what it is right to praise, Aesch., etc. : —also indeclin., θέμις being used as acc., φασὶ θέμις εἶναι Plat., etc. 2. = δίκη, right, law, Aesch., Soph. II. pl. θέμιστες, the decrees of the Gods, oracles, Διὸς θέμιστες Od. ; θέμισσιν by oracles, Pind. 2. rights of the chief, prerogatives, σκῆπτρόν τ' ἠδὲ θέμιστες Il. 3. laws or ordinances, οἵτε θέμιστας εἰρύαται who maintain the laws, Ib. 4. claims to be decided by the kings or judges, οἱ σκολιὰς κρίνωσι θέμιστας Ib. III. as prop. n., gen. Θέμιστος, Θέμιδος; Θέμιτος, voc. Θέμι, Themis, goddess of law and order, Il.

θεμι-σκόπος, ον, seeing to law and order, Pind.

θεμισ-κρέων, οντος, ὁ, reigning by right, Pind.

θέμιστα, θέμιστας, Ep. acc. sing. and pl. of θέμις.

θεμιστεῖος, α, ον, (θέμις) of law and right, θ. σκᾶπτον the sceptre of righteous judgment, Pind.

θεμιστεύω, f. σω, (θέμις) to declare law and right, Lat. jus dicere, Od. : c. gen. to claim right over, to govern, Ib. II. to give by way of answer or oracle, h. Hom. : —absol. to deliver oracles, Eur.

θεμιστέων, Ep. gen. pl. of θέμις.

θεμιστο-πόλος, ον, (πολέω) ministering law, h. Hom.

θεμιστός, ή, όν, = θεμιτός, Aesch. : —Adv. -τῶς, Id.

θεμῐτεύω, = θεμιστεύω, Eur. From

θεμῐτός, ή, όν, (θέμις) like θεμιστός, allowed by the laws of God and men, righteous, h. Hom.; οὐ θεμιτόν [ἐστι], like οὐ θέμις, Pind., Hdt., Att.

ΘΕΜΟ'Ω, Ep. aor. 1 θέμωσα, to drive or bring, νῆα θέμωσε χέρσον ἱκέσθαι forced, urged the ship to come to land, or simply, brought it to land, Od.

-θεν, old termin. of the genit., as in ἐμέθεν, σέθεν, Διόθεν, θεόθεν; sometimes after Preps., ἀπὸ Τροίηθεν Od. ; ἐξ οὐρανόθεν Il. II. as insep. Particle, denoting motion from a place, opp. to -δε, as in ἄλλοθεν, οἴκοθεν, from another place, from home.

ΘΕ'ΝΑΡ, ἄρος, τό, the palm of the hand, Il. 2. metaph., θ. βωμοῦ the flat top of the altar, Pind. ; ἁλὸς θ. the surface of the sea, Id.

θένω, late form of θείνω, Theocr.

θέο, Ep. for θοῦ, aor. 2 med. imp. of τίθημι.

θεοβλάβεια, ἡ, madness, blindness, Aeschin.; and

θεοβλᾰβέω, to offend the Gods, Aesch. From

θεο-βλᾰβής, ές, (βλάπτω) stricken of God, infatuated, Hdt.

θεο-γεννής, ές, (γεννάω) begotten of a god, Soph.

θεό-γλωσσος, ον, (γλῶσσα) with the tongue of a god, Anth.

θεογονία, Ion. -ίη, ἡ, (γενέσθαι) the generation or genealogy of the gods, Hes., Hdt.

θεό-γονος, ον, (γίγνομαι) born of God, divine, Eur.

θεο-δήλητος, ον, (δηλέομαι) by which the gods are injured, Anth.

θεο-δίδακτος, ον, taught of God, N. T.

θεό-δμητος, ον, Dor. -δμᾱτος, ον, and α, ον, (δέμω) god-built, made or founded by the gods, Il., Pind., etc.

θεό-δοτος, ον, (δίδωμι) = θεόσδοτος, Pind.

θεο-ειδής, ές, (εἶδος) divine of form, Hom., Plat.

θεο-είκελος, ον, godlike, Hom.

θεο-εχθρία, ἡ, = θεοσεχθρία.

θεόθεν, old gen. of θεός, used as Adv. (v. -θεν), from the gods, at the hands of the gods, Lat. divinitus, Od. 2. by the help or favour of the gods, Pind., Aesch., etc. : by the gods, Soph.

θε-οίνια, τά, (οἶνος) the feast of the wine-god, ap. Dem.

θεοισία, Dor. for θεοῦσα, part. fem. of θέω.

θεοισ-εχθρία, ἡ, = θεοσεχθρία, Ar.

θεοκλῠτέω, f. ήσω, to call on the gods, Aesch. ; c. acc., Eur. 2. c. acc. rei, to call aloud, declare, Plut.

θεό-κλῠτος, ον, (κλύω) calling on the gods, Aesch.

θεό-κραντος, ον, (κραίνω) wrought by the gods, Aesch.

θεό-κρῐτος, ον, (θεοκρίτης) judging between gods, Anth.

θεό-κτῐτος, ον, (κτίζω) created by God, Solon.

θεο-μᾰνής, ές, (μαίνομαι) maddened by the gods, Aesch., Eur.; λύσσα θ. madness caused by the gods, Eur.

θεό-μαντις, εως, ἡ, one who has a spirit of prophecy, an inspired person, Plat.

θεομᾰχέω, f. ήσω, to fight against the gods, Eur.; and θεομᾰχία, ή, a battle of the gods, as certain books of the Il. were called, Plat. From

θεο-μάχος, ον, (μάχομαι) fighting against God, N. T., Luc.

θεο-μήστωρ, ορος, ό, like the gods in counsel, Aesch.

θεο-μῑσής, ές, (μῖσος) abominated by the gods, Ar., Plat.

θεομορία, Ion. θευμορίη, ή, destiny, Anth. From

θεό-μορος, ον, Dor. θεύ-μ-, destined by the gods, imparted by them, Pind.   II. blessed by the gods, Id.

θεό-μορφος, ον, (μορφή) of form divine, Anth.

θεο-μῦσής, ές, (μύσος) abominated by the gods, Aesch.

θεό-παις, παιδος, ό, ή, child of the gods, Anth.

θεό-πεμπτος, ον, (πέμπω) sent by the gods, Arist.

θεό-πνευστος, ον, (πνέω) inspired of God, N. T.

θεοποιέω, f. ήσω, to make into gods, deify, Luc. From

θεο-ποιός, όν, (ποιέω) making gods, Anth.

θεό-πομπος, ον, = θεόπεμπτος, Pind.

θεο-πόνητος, ον, (πονέω) prepared by the gods, Eur.

θεο-πρεπής, ές, (πρέπω) meet for a god, Pind. Adv. -πῶς, Luc.

θεοπροπέω, to prophesy, only in part. masc., θεοπροπέων ἀγορεύεις Hom., Pind., etc.; and

θεοπροπία, ή, a prophecy, oracle; and

θεοπρόπιον, τό, a prophecy, oracle, Il.; ἐκ θεοπροπίου according to an oracle, Hdt. From

θεο-πρόπος, ον, (πρέπω) foretelling things by a spirit of prophecy, prophetic, Il., Soph.   2. as Subst. a seer, prophet, diviner, Hom.   II. a public messenger sent to enquire of the oracle, Il., Hdt., Aesch.

θεό-πτυστος, ον, (πτύω) detested by the gods, Aesch.

θεό-πῠρος, ον, (πῦρ) kindled by the gods, Eur.

θέ-ορτος, ον, (ὄρνυμαι) sprung from the gods, celestial, Pind., Aesch.

ΘΕΟ'Σ, ό, Lacon. and Boeot. σιός, God, Hom., both in general sense, Θεὸς δώσει God will grant, and in particular sense, θεός τις a god; πατήρ ἀνδρῶν τε θεῶν τε Hom.:—things are said to happen σὺν θεῷ, σύν γε θεοῖσιν by the will of God, Id., etc.; οὐκ ἄνευ θεοῦ, Lat. non sine diis, Od.; οὐκ ἄνευθε θεοῦ Il.; οὐ θεῶν ἄτερ Pind.;—ἐκ θεόφι Il.;—ὑπὲρ θεόν against his will, Ib.;—κατὰ θεόν τινα, Lat. divinitus, Eur.:—as an oath, πρὸς θεῶν by the gods, in God's name, Trag.; θεὸς ἴστω Soph., etc.   II. θεός as fem. for θεά, θέαινα, a goddess, Hom.; θήλεια θεός Il.; ἡ νερτέρα θ. Proserpine, Soph.; often in oaths, νὴ τὼ θεώ Id.; ναὶ τὼ σιώ, with the Spartans, of Castor and Pollux, Xen.; with the Boeotians, of Amphion and Zethus, Id.   III. as Adj. in Comp. θεώτερος, more divine, θύραι θ. doors more used by the gods, Od.

θεόσ-δοτος, ον, (δίδωμι) poët. for θεόδοτος, given by the gods, Hes., Pind.

θεοσέβεια, ή, the service or fear of God, religiousness, Xen. From

θεο-σεβής, ές, (σέβω) fearing God, religious, Hdt., Soph., etc. Adv. -βῶς, Xen.

θεόσ-σεπτος, ον, feared as divine, Ar.

θεοσέπτωρ, ορος, ό, = θεοσεβής, Eur.

θεοσ-εχθρία, ή, (ἐχθρός) hatred of the gods, Dem.

θεόσ-σῠτος, poët. for θεόσυτος.

θεο-στήρικτος, ον, (στηρίζω) supported by God, Anth.

θεο-στῠγής, ές, (στύγος) hated of the gods, Eur.: hated of God, N. T.

θεο-στύγητος [ῠ], ον, (στυγέω) = foreg. 1, Aesch.

θεό-σῠτος, ον, (σεύω) sent by the gods, Aesch.

θεό-ταυρος, ό, the god-bull, a name for Zeus, Mosch.

θεο-τείχης, ές, (τεῖχος) walled by gods, of Troy, Anth.

θεο-τερπής, ές, (τέρπω) fit for the gods, Anth.

θεό-τευκτος, ον, made by God, Anth.

θεότης, ή, (θεός) divinity, divine nature, Luc.

θεο-τίμητος [ῑ], ον, honoured by the gods, Tyrtae.

θεότῑμος, ον, = foreg., Pind.

θεό-τρεπτος, ον, turned or directed by the gods, Aesch.

θεο-τρεφής, ές, (τρέφω) feeding the gods, Anth.

θεου-δής, ές, prob. = θεοδεής (θεός, δέος), fearing God, Od.

θεο-φάνια (sc. ἱερά), τά, (θεός, φαίνω) a festival at Delphi, at which the statues of Apollo and other gods were shewn to the people, Hdt.

θεο-φῐλής, ές, (φίλος) dear to the gods, highly favoured, Hdt., Pind., Att. Adv. θεοφιλῶς πράττειν to act as the gods will, Plat.

θεόφιν, Ep. gen. and dat. sing. and pl. of θεός.

θεοφορέω, f. ήσω, (θεόφορος) to bear God within one: Pass. to be possessed by a god, Luc.

θεο-φόρητος, ον, possessed by a god, inspired, Aesch.

θεοφορία, Ep. θευφορίη, ή, inspiration, Anth.

θεό-φορος, ον, (φέρω) possessed by a god, inspired, θ. δίναι the pains of inspiration, Aesch.

θεό-φρων, ον, gen. ονος, (φρήν) godly-minded, Pind.

θεράπαινα, ή, fem. of θεράπων, a waiting maid, handmaid, Hdt., Xen., etc.

θεραπαινίδιον, τό, Dim. of sq., Plut., Luc.

θεράπαινίς, ίδος, ή, = θεράπαινα, Plat.

θεραπεία, Ion. -ηίη, ή, (θεραπεύω) a waiting on, service, θ. θεῶν service done to the gods, divine worship, Plat.   2. service done to gain favour, a courting, paying court, θ. τῶν ἀεὶ προεστώτων Thuc.; ἐν πολλῇ θεραπείᾳ ἔχειν to court one's favour, Id.   II. of things, a fostering, tending, nurture, care, τοῦ σώματος Plat.   2. medical treatment, service done to the sick, tending, Thuc., Plat.   III. of animals or plants, a rearing or bringing up, tendance, Id.   IV. in collective sense, a body of attendants, suite, retinue, Hdt., Xen.

θεράπευμα, ατος, τό, medical treatment, Arist.

θεραπευτέον, verb. Adj. of θεραπεύω, one must do service to, τοὺς θεούς Xen.   II. one must cultivate, τὴν γῆν Plat.   2. one must cure, Id.

θεραπευτήρ, ῆρος, ό, = sq., ὁ περὶ τὸ σῶμα θ. Xen.

θεραπευτής, οῦ, ό, one who serves the gods, a worshipper, Plat.   2. one who serves a great man, a courtier, Xen.   II. one who attends to anything, c. gen., Plat.

θεραπευτικός, ή, όν, inclined to serve a person, c. gen., Xen.: inclined to court, Plut.   2. absol. courteous, courtier-like, obedient, obsequious, Xen., Plut.; and

θεράπευτός, όν, that may be fostered, Plat. From

θεράπεύω, f. -εύσω, (θεράπων) to be an attendant, do service, Od.   2. to do service to the gods, Lat. colere deos, Hes., Hdt., Att.:—to do service or honour to one's parents or masters, Eur., Plat.   3. to serve, court, pay court to, τινά Hdt., Ar., etc.; and in bad sense, to flatter, wheedle, Thuc.: to conciliate, Id.;

τὸ θεραπεῦον = οἱ θεραπεύοντες, Id.　4. of things, *to consult, attend to,* Lat. *inservire,* Id. ; ἡδονὴν θερ. *to indulge* one's love of pleasure, Xen. ; τὰς θύρας τινὸς θερ. *to wait at* a great man's door, Id.　II. *to take care of, provide for* men, of the gods, Id.　2. of things, *to attend to, provide for,* Soph., Thuc., etc.　3. θερ. τὸ σῶμα *to take care* of one's person, Lat. *cutem curare,* Plat.　4. *to treat medically, to heal, cure,* Thuc., Xen.　5. θ. ἡμέρην *to observe* a day, *keep* it *as* a *feast,* Hdt. ; θ. τὰ ἱερά = Lat. *sacra procurare,* Hdt.　6. of land, *to cultivate,* Xen. ; δένδρον θερ. *to train* a tree, Hdt.

θεραπηΐη, ἡ, Ion. for θεραπεία.

θερᾰπήϊος, α, ον, Ion. for θεραπευτικός, Anth.

θερᾰπίδιον, τό, (θεραπεύω) *a means of cure,* Luc.

θεράπνη, ἡ, poët. contr. from θεράπαινα, *a handmaid,* h. Hom., Eur.　II. *a dwelling, abode,* Id.

θεραπνίς, ίδος, ἡ, poët. contr. from θεραπαινίς, Anth.

ΘΕΡΑ'ΠΩΝ [ᾰ], οντος, ὁ: poët. dat. pl. θεράποντεσσι: — *a waiting-man, attendant,* Od., etc. ; differing from δοῦλος, as implying *free service ;* and in Hom. *a companion in arms,* though inferior in rank ; as Patroclus is *the companion* or *esquire* of Achilles ; Meriones of Idomeneus, Il. ; so *the charioteer* is ἡνίοχος θεράπων ; kings were Διὸς θεράποντες ; warriors θεράποντες Ἄρηος, etc. :—c. dat., οἶκος ξένοισι θεράπων *devoted to the service of* its guests, Pind.　II. later, simply, *a servant,* Hdt. :—in Chios, θεράποντες was the name for their slaves, Thuc.

θέραψ, ᾰπος, ὁ, rare poët. form for θεράπων : nom. pl. θέραπες Eur., Anth.

θερεία, ἡ, v. θέρειος.

θέρειος, α, ον, (θέρος) *of summer, in summer :*—θερεία, Ion. -είη, (sc. ὥρα), ἡ, = θέρος, *summer-time, summer,* Hdt. ; ταῖς θερείαις Pind.

θερέω, Ep. for θερῶ, aor. 2 pass. subj. of θέρω.

θερίζω, Boeot. inf. θερίδδεν :—fut. Att. θεριῶ :—aor. 1 ἐθέρισα, syncop. ἔθρισα :—Med., aor. 1 ἐθερισάμην :— Pass., aor. 1 ἐθερίσθην : pf. τεθέρισμαι : (θέρος) :—*to do summer-work,* i. e. mow, reap, σῖτον, κριθάς, καρπόν Hdt., Ar., etc. :—Med., καρπὸν Δηοῦς θερίσασθαι Id.　2. metaph. *to cut off,* Soph., Eur.　3. metaph. *to reap a good harvest,* Ar.　4. ὁ θερίζων (with or without λόγος) a kind of syllogism, Luc.　II. intr. *to pass the summer,* Xen. ; cf. ἐαρίζω, χειμάζω.

θερίνεος, α, ον, = sq. : θ. τροπαί *the summer* solstice, i. e. June 21st, Hdt.

θερῐνός, ή, όν, = θέρειος, Pind., Xen., etc.

θερισμός, ὁ, (θερίζω) *reaping-time, harvest,* N. T.　2. *the harvest, crop,* Ib.

θεριστής, οῦ, ὁ, (θερίζω) *a reaper, harvester,* Eur., Xen.

θεριστόν, τό, (θερίζω) *a light summer garment,* opp. to χειμάστριον, Theocr. :—so θέριστρον, τό, Anth.

θερμαίνω, f. ᾰνῶ : aor. 1 ἐθέρμηνα, later ἐθέρμᾱνα : pf. pass. τεθέρμασμαι : (θερμός) :—*to warm, heat,* Il., Aesch., etc. :—Pass. *to be heated, grow hot,* Od.　2. metaph. *to heat,* ἕως ἐθέρμην' αὐτὸν φλὸξ οἴνου Eur. ; σπλάγχνα θ. Ar. ; πολλὰ θ. φρενί *to cherish hot feelings,* Aesch. :—Pass., θερμαίνεσθαι ἐλπίσι *to glow* with hope, Soph. ; χαρᾷ θ. καρδίαν *to have* one's heart *warm* with joy, Eur.

θερμᾰσία, ἡ, = θερμότης, Xen.

θέρμη, ἡ, (θερμός) *heat, feverish heat,* Thuc., etc.

θέρμῑνος, η, ον, *of lupines* (θέρμος), Luc.

θερμο-βᾰφής, ές, *dyed hot,* opp. to ψυχροβαφής, Theophr.

θερμό-βλυστος, ον, *hot-bubbling,* Paul. S. Therm.

θερμό-βουλος, ον, (βουλή) *hot-tempered,* Eur. ap. Ar.

θερμο-δότης, ου, ὁ, *one who brought the hot water at baths,* Lat. *caldarius ;* fem. θερμοδότις, ιδος, Anth.

θερμό-νους, ουν, *heated in mind,* Aesch.

θερμο-πύλαι [ῠ], ῶν, αἱ, literally *Hot-Gates,* i. e. *a narrow gate-like pass, in which were hot springs,* name of the famous pass from Thessaly to Locris, the key of Greece, also called simply Πύλαι, Hdt.

θερμός, ή, όν, and ος, ον, (θέρω) *hot, warm,* θερμὰ λοετρά Hom. ; of tears, Id., etc.　II. metaph. *hot, hasty, rash, headlong,* like Lat. *calidus,* Aesch., Ar., etc.　2. *still warm, fresh,* ἴχνη Anth.　III. τὸ θερμόν, = θερμότης, *heat,* Lat. *calor,* Hdt., Plat., etc.　2. θερμόν (sc. ὕδωρ), τό, *hot water,* θερμῷ λοῦσθαι Ar.　3. τὰ θερμά (sub. χωρία), Hdt. : but (sub. λουτρά), *hot baths,* Xen.　IV. Adv. -μῶς, Plat.

ΘΕ'ΡΜΟΣ, ὁ, *a lupine,* Anth.

θερμότης, ητος, ἡ, (θερμός) *heat,* Lat. *calor,* Plat.

θερμ-ουργός, όν, (*ἔργω) *doing hot and hasty acts, reckless,* Xen., Luc.

θέρμω, (θέρω) *to heat, make hot,* Od., Ar. :—Pass. *to be heated, grow hot,* Hom.

θέρος, τό, Ion. gen. θέρευς, (θέρω) *summer, summertime,* χείματος οὐδὲ θέρευς in winter nor *in summer,*Od.; οὔτ' ἐν θέρει οὔτ' ἐν ὀπώρῃ Ib. ; τὸ θέρος *during the summer,* Hdt. ; θέρους μεσοῦντος *about* mid*summer,* Luc.　2. *summer-fruits, harvest, a crop,* Aesch., Ar., etc. ; metaph., δράκοντος θ. Eur.

Θερσίτης, ου, ὁ, *Thersites,* i. e. *the Audacious* (from θέρσος, Aeol. for θάρσος), Hom.

ΘΕ'ΡΩ, *to heat, make hot* :—Pass. θέρομαι, with fut. med. θέρσομαι, aor. 2 ἐθέρην, Ep. subj. θερέω (for θερῶ) :—*to become hot* or *warm, warm oneself,* Od. ; πυρός at the fire, Ib. ; θέρου *warm yourself,* Ar.　2. of things, μὴ ἄστυ πυρὸς θέρηται lest the city *be burnt* by fire, Il.

θές, aor. 2 imper. of τίθημι.

θέσαν, Ep. for ἔθεσαν, 3 pl. aor. 2 of τίθημι.

θέσθαι, aor. 2 med. inf. of τίθημι.

θέσθε, 2 pl. aor. 2 med. imper. of τίθημι :—θέσθω, 3 sing.

θέσις, εως, ἡ, (τίθημι) *a setting, placing, arranging,* Pind., Plat. ; θ. νόμων *lawgiving,* Dem.　II. *a deposit of money, preparatory to a law-suit,* Ar. ; *money paid in advance, earnest-money,* Dem.　III. *position, situation,* Lat. *situs,* of a city, Thuc., etc.

θέσκελος, ον, = θεοείκελος, *marvellous, wondrous,* θέσκελα ἔργα *works of wonder,* Hom. :—as Adv., ἔϊκτο δὲ θέσκελον αὐτῷ 'twas *wondrous* like him, Il.

θέσμιος, Dor. τέθμιος, ον, (θεσμός) *according to law, lawful,* Pind., Aesch.　II. θέσμια, τά, as Subst. *laws, customs, rites,* Hdt., etc. ; also in sing., Eur.

θεσμοθετέω, *to be* a θεσμοθέτης, Dem.　From

θεσμο-θέτης, ου, ὁ, (τίθημι) *a lawgiver :*—at Athens, the θεσμοθέται were *the six junior archons,* who judged causes assigned to no special court, Aeschin., etc.

θεσμο-ποιέω, f. ήσω, *to make laws,* Eur.

θεσμός, Dor. τεθμός, ὁ : pl. θεσμοί, poët. θεσμά Soph. : (τίθημι) :—like θέμις, *that which is laid down and*

established, a law, ordinance, Lat. *institutum,* λέκτροιο θεσμὸν ἵκοντο, i. e. they fulfilled *the established law* of wedlock, Od.; so in Hdt. and Att.   2. at Athens, Draco's laws were called θεσμοί, because each began with the word θεσμός (cf. θεσμοθέτης), while Solon's laws were named νόμοι.   II. *an institution, ordinance,* as the court of Areopagus, Aesch.; of the great games, Pind.   Hence

θεσμοσύνη, ἡ, *justice,* like δικαιοσύνη, Anth.

θεσμοφόρια, ων, τά, *the Thesmophoria,* an ancient festival held by the Athenian women in honour of Demeter Θεσμοφόρος, Hdt., Ar.   Hence

θεσμοφοριάζω, *to keep the Thesmophoria,* Ar., Xen.; and

θεσμοφόριον, τό, *the temple of Demeter* Θεσμοφόρος, Ar.

θεσμο-φόρος, ον, (φέρω) *law-giving,* an ancient name of Demeter (Ceres), Hdt.; τὼ θεσμοφόρω Ceres and Proserpine, Ar.

θεσμο-φύλακες, οἱ, *guardians of the law,* Thuc.

θεσ-πέσιος, α, ον, or ος, ον: (θεός, ἔσπον = εἶπον, v. θέσπις):—properly of the voice, *divinely sounding, divinely sweet,* Hom., Pind.   II. *that can be spoken by none but God,* i. e. *unspeakable, ineffable;* hence,   1. like θεῖος, *divine,* Hom.; dat. fem. θεσπεσίῃ (sc. βουλῇ) *by the will of God,* Id.; θ. ὁδός the way *of divination,* of Cassandra, Aesch.   2. *wondrous, marvellous, portentous, awful,* of things, Hom.; θ. χαλκός *marvellous fine* brass, Od., Il.; θ. ὀδμή a smell *divinely sweet,* Od.; so in Hdt., θεσπέσιον ὡς ἡδύ:—of human affairs, θ. φόβος Il., etc.   III. Adv. -ίως, θ. ἐφόβηθεν they trembled *unspeakably,* Ib.: so neut. as Adv., Theocr.

θεσπῐ-δαής, ές, (δαίω) *kindled by a god,* θ. πῦρ *furious, portentous* fire, such as seems *more than natural,* Hom.

θεσπι-έπεια, fem. Adj. (ἔπος) *oracular, prophetic,* Soph.

θεσπίζω, f. Att. ιῶ, Ion. inf. θεσπιέειν: Dor. aor. 1 ἐθέσπιξα: (θέσπις):—*to declare by oracle, prophesy, divine,* Hdt., Trag.; Pass., τί δὲ τεθέσπισται; Soph.

θέσπιος, ον, = θεσπέσιος, Orac. ap. Ar.

θέσ-πις, ιδος, ὁ, ἡ, (θεός, ἔσπον = εἶπον, cf. θεσπέσιος) *having words from God, inspired,* Od., Eur.   2. generally, *divine, wondrous, awful,* θέσπις ἄελλα h. Hom.

θέσπισμα, ατος, τό, (θεσπίζω) in pl., *oracular sayings,* Hdt., Soph.

θεσπιῳδέω, (θεσπιῳδός) *to prophesy, sing in prophetic strain,* Aesch., Eur., Ar.   From

θεσπι-ῳδός, όν, *singing in prophetic strain, prophetic,* Eur.   II. *caused by prophecy,* φόβος Aesch.

Θεσσᾰλός, Att. Θεττ-, ὁ, *a Thessalian,* Hdt., etc.; proverb., Θεσσαλὸν σόφισμα a *Thessalian trick,* from the faithless character of the people, Eur.   II. fem., Θεσσαλὶς κυνῆ a Thessalian cap, Soph.

θέσσασθαι, defect. aor. 1, *to pray,* Pind.   (Deriv. uncertain.)

θεσφᾰτη-λόγος, ον, *prophetic,* Aesch.

θέσ-φᾰτος, ον, (θεός, φημί) *spoken by God, decreed, ordained, appointed,* Lat. *fatalis,* Aesch., Soph.: θέσφατόν ἐστι it is *ordained,* Il.; σοὶ δ' οὐ θ. ἐστι θανέειν 'tis not *appointed* thee to die, Il.   2. as Subst., θέσφατα, τά, *divine decrees, oracles,* Ib., Trag., etc.   II. generally, like θεῖος, *divine,* Od.

θετέος, α, ον, verb. Adj. *to be laid down,* Arist.   II. θετέον, one must *lay down,* Xen.

Θετίδειον [ῐ], τό, *the temple of Thetis,* Eur.

θετικός, ή, όν, (τίθημι) *of* or *for adoption,* Arist.

Θέτις, ιδος, Dor. ιος, ἡ, *Thetis,* one of the Nereïds, wife of Peleus, mother of Achilles: Hom. uses Θετῐ for dat. and vocat.; Θέτιν for acc.

θετός, ή, όν, verb. Adj. of τίθημι, *taken as one's child, adopted,* Pind., Hdt., etc.

Θεττᾰλός, Θετταλικός, etc., later Att. for Θεσσ-.

θεῦ, Dor. and Ion. for θέο, θοῦ, aor. 2 med. imp. of τίθημι.

θευμορία, θεύμορος, Dor. for θεομορία, θεόμορος.

θευφορία, ή, Dor. for θεοφορία, Anth.

ΘΕ´Ω, Ep. also θείω; Ep. 3 sing. subj. θέῃσι: 3 sing. impf. ἔθει, Ion. impf. θέεσκον: f. θεύσομαι:—the other tenses are supplied by τρέχω and *δρέμω:—the syllables εο, εου remain uncontracted even in Att. :—*to run,* Hom., etc.; θέειν πεδίοιο *to run over* the plain, Il.: in part. with another Verb, ἦλθε θέων, ἦλθε θέουσα came *running,* Ib.; θέων Αἴαντα κάλεσσον *run and* call him, Ib.   2. περὶ τρίποδος θεύσεσθαι *to run for* a tripod, Ib.; περὶ ψυχῆς θέον Ἕκτορος they were *running for* Hector's life, Ib.   II. of other kinds of motion, as,   1. of birds, θεύσονται δρόμῳ Ar.   2. of ships, ἔθεε κατὰ κῦμα Il.; of a potter's wheel, Ib.; of a quoit, ῥίμφα θέων ἀπὸ χειρός *flying* lightly, Od.   III. of things which (as we say) *run* in a continuous line, though not actually in motion, φλὲψ ἀνὰ νῶτα θέουσα Il.; esp. of anything circular, which *runs round into* itself, ἄντυξ, ἡ πυμάτη θέεν ἀσπίδος Ib.   IV. c. acc. loci, *to run over,* τὰ ὄρη Xen.

θέω, for θέαου, imperat. of θεάομαι, *behold!*

θεωρέω, f. ήσω, (θεωρός) *to look at, view, behold,* Hdt., Aesch., etc.: *to inspect* or *review* soldiers, Xen.   2. of the mind, *to contemplate, consider, observe,* Plat., etc.   II. *to view* the public games, of spectators, θ. τὰ Ὀλύμπια Hdt.; θ. τινά *to see* him *act,* Dem.: —absol. *to go as a spectator,* ἐς τὰ Ἐφέσια Thuc.   III. *to be a* θεωρός or *state-ambassador to the oracle* or *at the games,* Ar., Thuc.   IV. in θεωρήσασα τοὐμὸν ὄμμα Soph., the acc. ὄμμα may be taken as in βαίνειν πόδα, *having beheld with* mine eye.   Hence

θεώρημα, ατος, τό, *that which is looked at, viewed, a sight, spectacle,* Dem., etc.   2. *a principle thereby arrived at, a rule,* Lat. *praeceptum :* in Mathematics, *a theorem,* Eucl.

θεωρητήριον, τό, (θεωρέω) *a seat in a theatre,* Plut.

θεωρητικός, ή, όν, *fond of contemplating* a thing, c. gen., Arist.: absol. *speculative,* Id., Plut., etc.

θεωρία, Ion. -ίη, ἡ, (θεωρέω) *a looking at, viewing, beholding,* θεωρίης εἵνεκεν ἐκδημεῖν *to go abroad to see the world,* Hdt.; so Thuc., etc.: of the mind, *contemplation, speculation,* Plat., etc.   2. pass. = θεώρημα, *a sight, show, spectacle,* Aesch., Eur., etc.; esp. at a theatre, Ar., Xen.   II. *the being a spectator* at *the theatre* or *the public games,* Soph., Plat.   III. *the* θεωροί or *state-ambassadors* sent to the oracles or games, *a mission,* Id., Xen.   2. *the office of* θεωρός, *discharge of that office,* Thuc., etc.

θεωρικός, ή, όν, *of* or *for* θεωρία (signfs. II and III), πεπλώματ' οὐ θεωρικά *no festal* robes, Eur.   II. θεωρικά (sc. χρήματα), τά, *the money,* which, from the time of Pericles, was given to the poor citizens *to pay for seats in the theatre* (at 2 obols the seat), but

aiso for other purposes, Dem.: in sing., τὸ θεωρικόν *the theatric fund,* Id.

θεωρίς, ίδος, ἡ,   1. (with and without ναῦς), *a sacred ship, which carried the* θεωροί (cf. θεωρός 11) *to their destination,* but was also used for other state-purposes, Hdt., Plat. : metaph. *of Charon's bark,* Aesch.   2. (sub. ὁδός) *the road by which the* θεωροί *went.*

θεωρός, Dor. **θεᾱρός,** ὁ, *a spectator,* Theogn., Aesch., etc. ; θ. εἰκάδων *viewing the festivals* or *present at them,* Eur.   II. *an ambassador sent to consult an oracle* or *to present an offering,* Soph., ap. Dem. The Athenians sent θεωροί to Delphi, to Delos, and to the four great games, the Olympian, Pythian, Nemean and Isthmian. (Derived in first sense from θεάομαι; in second perh. from θεός, ὥρα, cura.)

θεώτερος, α, ον, Comp. of θεός, *more divine*: v. θεός.

Θηβᾱ-γενής, ές, *sprung from Thebes, Theban,* Hes.

Θῆβαι, ῶν, αἱ, *Thebes,* the name of several cities, the most famous being the Egyptian (ἑκατόμπυλοι), and the Boeotian (ἑπτάπυλοι), Hom.

Θηβαι-γενής, ές, = Θηβα-γενής, Eur.

Θηβαιεύς, έως, Ion. έος, ὁ, epith. of Zeus, *the Theban,* Hdt.

Θηβαῖος, α, ον, *Theban,* Hom., etc. ; **Θηβαϊκός,** ή, όν, Hdt.

Θηβαΐς, ΐδος, ἡ, *the Thebaïs,* i.e. territory of Thebes (in Egypt), Hdt.; (in Boeotia), Thuc.

Θήβασδε, Adv. *to Thebes,* Il.

Θήβη, ἡ, poët. form of Θῆβαι, Hom.:—hence **Θήβηθεν** or -θε, Adv. *from Thebes,* Anth. ; Aeol. **Θείβᾱθεν,** Ar. :—**Θήβησιν** or -σι, *at Thebes,* Hom.; Aeol. **Θείβᾱθι,** Ar.

θηγάλέος, α, ον, (θήγω) *pointed, sharp,* Anth.   II. act. *sharpening,* c. gen., Id.

θηγάνη [ἄ], ἡ, *a whetstone,* Aesch., Soph. : metaph., αἱματηραῖς θηγάναι *incentives* to bloodshed, Aesch.

θηγάνω, = θήγω, Aesch.

ΘΗΓΩ, f. θήξω: aor. 1 ἔθηξα: Pass., pf. τέθηγμαι:—*to sharpen, whet,* Il. ; θήγων λευκὸν ὀδόντα Ib. ; θ. φάσγανον, ξίφος Aesch., Eur.:—in Med., δόρυ θηξάσθω *let him whet his spear,* Il.   2. metaph. *to sharpen, excite, provoke,* like Lat. *acuere,* τὰς ψυχὰς εἰς τὰ πολεμικά Xen. :—Pass., λόγοι τεθηγμένοι *sharp, biting* words, Aesch. ; γλῶσσα τεθηγμένη Soph.

θηέομαι, Ion. form of θεάομαι :—θηεῖτο, 3 sing.

θήῃς, Ep. for θῇς, 2 sing. aor. 2 subj. of τίθημι.

θηητήρ, ῆρος, ὁ, Ion. for θεατής, *one who gazes at, an admirer,* Od.

θηητός, ή, όν, Ion. for θεατός, Dor. θᾱητός, *gazed at, wondrous, admirable,* Lat. *spectandus,* Hes., Pind.

θήϊον, τό, Ep. for θεῖον, *brimstone,* Od.

θήϊος, Ep. for θεῖος, *divine.*

θηκαῖος, α, ον, *like a chest* or *coffin,* οἴκημα θ. *a burial vault,* Hdt. From

θήκη, ἡ, (τίθημι) *a case to put anything in, a box, chest,* Hdt., Eur.   II. *a place for corpses, a grave, tomb,* Hdt., Aesch.   2. *a mode of burial,* Thuc.

θηκτός, ή, όν, verb. Adj. of θήγω, *sharpened,* Aesch., Eur.

θηλάζω, f. άσω, Dor. άξω, (θηλή) :   I. *of the mother, to suckle,* Lat. *lactare,* Lysias, N.T.   II. *of the young animal, to suck,* Lat. *lactere ;* θηλάζων χοῖρος *a sucking* pig, Theocr. : c. acc., μασδὸν ἐθήλαζεν Id.

θηλασμός, ὁ, *a giving suck, suckling,* Plut.

θήλεα, Ion. for θήλεια, fem. of θῆλυς.

θηλέω, Dor. **θᾱλέω :** Ep. impf. θήλεον : f. θηλήσω : Dor. poët. aor. θάλησα : (θάλλω) :—*to be full of,* c. gen., λειμῶνες ἴου ἠδὲ σελίνου θήλεον *the meadows were full* of violets and parsley, Od. ; so c. dat., θάλησε σελίνοις Pind.   2. absol. *to flourish,* Anth.

θηλή, ἡ, (*θάω) *the part of the breast which gives suck, the teat, nipple,* Eur., Plat.

θηλυ-γενής, ές, (γίγνομαι) *of female sex, womanish,* Eur.

θηλύ-γλωσσος, ον, *with woman's tongue,* Anth.

θηλυδρίας, ου, Ion. -ίης, εω, ὁ, (θῆλυς) *a womanish, effeminate person,* Hdt., Luc.

θηλυ-κράτής, ές, (κρατέω) *swaying women,* Aesch.

θηλυ-κτόνος, ον, (ἔκτονα, pf. of κτείνω) *slaying by woman's hand,* Aesch.

θηλυ-μελής, ές, (μέλος) *singing in soft strain,* Anth.

θηλυ-μίτρης, ου, ὁ, (μίτρα) *with a woman's head-band,* Luc.: fem. -μίτρις, ιδος, ὁ, ἡ, Id.

θηλύ-μορφος, ον, (μορφή) *woman-shaped,* Eur.

θηλύ-νοος, contr. -νους, ουν, *of womanish mind,* Aesch.

θηλύνω [ῦ] : aor. 1 ἐθήλυνα :—Pass., aor. 1 ἐθηλύνθην : pf. τεθήλυμμαι : (θῆλυς) :—*to make womanish, to enervate,* Eur., Xen. : metaph. *to soften,* Ζέφυρος κῦμα θηλύνει Anth. :—Pass. *to become weak and womanish,* Soph. : *to play the coquet,* Bion.

θηλυ-πρεπής, ές, (πρέπω) *befitting a woman,* Anth.

θῆλυς, θήλεια, θῆλυ Hom.; θῆλυς also as fem. :—in Ion. the fem. forms are θήλεα, θήλειαν, θηλέης, θηλέῃ, pl. θήλεαι, θήλεας, θηλέων : (*θάω *to suckle*) :—*of female sex, female,* θήλεια θεός a goddess, Il.; θήλειαι ἵπποι mares, Od.; σύες θήλειαι sows, Ib.; ὄϊς θῆλυς a ewe, Il.; ἄπαις θήλεος γόνου without *female* issue, Hdt.:—ἡ θήλεα, Att. -εια, *the female,* Id., Aesch. ; χρῆμα θηλειῶν *woman-kind,* Eur. ; τὸ θῆλυ γένος or τὸ θῆλυ *the female sex, woman-kind,* Id.   2. *of* or *belonging to women,* Hdt., Aesch. ; θ. φόνος *murder by women,* Eur.   3. in Gramm. *feminine.*   II. applied to persons and things,   1. *fresh, refreshing,* of dew, Hes.   2. *tender, delicate, gentle,* θηλύτεραι γυναῖκες, θηλύτεραι θεαί (where the Comp. is used much like a Positive), Hom. ; θῆλυς ἀπὸ χροιᾶς *delicate* of skin, Theocr. ; of character, *soft, yielding, weak,* γυνὴ θῆλυς οὖσα Soph.

θηλύ-σπορος, ον, (σπείρω) *of female kind,* Aesch.

θηλύτης, ητος, ἡ, (θῆλυς) *womanishness, delicacy, effeminacy,* Plut.

θηλυ-τόκος, ον, (τίκτω) *giving birth to girls,* Theocr.

θηλυ-φᾱνής, ές, (φαίνομαι) *like a woman,* Plut., Anth.

θηλῠ-χίτων [ῐ], ὁ, ἡ, *with woman's frock,* Anth., Luc.

θἠμέρᾳ, crasis for τῇ ἡμέρᾳ.

θἠμετέρου, crasis for τοῦ ἡμετέρου.

θἤμισυ, crasis for τὸ ἥμισυ.

θημο-λογέω, f. ήσω, (θημών, λέγω) *to collect in a heap,* shortened from θημωνολογέω, Anth.

θημών, ῶνος, ὁ, (τίθημι) *a heap,* Od.

θήν, enclitic Particle, chiefly Ep., = δή, expressing strong conviction, *surely now,* Hom., Theocr. ; ironically, λείψετέ θην νέας *so then you will* leave the ships, Il. ; strengthd., ἦ θην *in very truth,* Ib. ; οὔ θην *surely not,* Hom.

θηξάσθω, 3 sing. aor. 1 med. imper. of θήγω.

θηοῖο, Ep. for θεῷο, 2 sing. pres. opt. of θηέομαι.

ΘΗΡ, θηρός, Ep. dat. pl. θήρεσσι, ὁ :—*a wild beast,*

beast of prey, Il., etc.; joined with λέων, Eur.; with λέαινα, Anth.; also of Cerberus, Soph.:—in pl. beasts, as opp. to birds and fishes, Od., etc.　　2. of any animal, as of birds, Ar., etc.　　3. any fabulous monster, as the sphinx, Aesch.; esp. a centaur, Soph. (cf. Φήρ); a satyr, Eur.

θήρα, Ion. **θήρη, ἡ,** a hunting of wild beasts, the chase, Hom., Hdt., etc.　　2. metaph. eager pursuit of anything, Soph.　　II. the beasts taken, spoil, booty, prey, game, Od., Aesch., etc.; in pl., ὦ πτανὰ θῆραι, of birds, Soph.

θηρ-αγρέτης, ου, ὁ, (ἀγρέω) a hunter, Eur., Anth.

θήραμα, ατος, τό, (θηράω) that which is caught, prey, spoil, booty, Eur., Anth.

θηράσιμος [ᾰ], **ον,** (θηράω) to be hunted down or caught, Aesch.

θηρατέος, α, ον, verb. Adj. to be hunted after, sought eagerly, Soph., Xen.　　II. θηρατέον one must hunt after, Xen.

θηρατήρ, Ion. **-ητήρ, ῆρος, ὁ,** (θηράω) a hunter, Il.

θηρατής, οῦ, ὁ, = foreg.; metaph., θ. λόγων one who hunts for words, Ar.

θηρατικός, ή, όν, = θηρευτικός: metaph., τὰ θ. τῶν φίλων the arts for winning friends, Xen.

θήρατρον, τό, an instrument of the chase, a net, trap, Xen.; and

θηράτωρ, Ion. **-ήτωρ, ορος, ὁ,** = θηρατήρ, Il.　　From

θηράω: f. **ἀσω** [ᾱ]: aor. 1 ἐθήρασα: pf. τεθήρᾱκα:—Med., f. θηράσομαι, aor. 1 ἐθηρᾱσάμην:—Pass., aor. 1 ἐθηράθην [ᾱ]: (θήρα):—to hunt or chase wild beasts, Soph., Xen.:—of men, to catch, capture, Xen.: metaph. to captivate, Id.:—θ. πόλιν to seek to destroy it, Aesch.　　2. metaph., like Lat. venari, to hunt after a thing, pursue it eagerly, Trag.:—c. inf. to seek or endeavour to do, Eur.; and in Med., Soph., Eur.　　II. Med. much like Act. to hunt for, fish for, ἐγχέλεις Ar.; absol., οἱ θηρώμενοι hunters, Xen.　　2. metaph. to cast about for, seek after, Hdt., Eur., etc.　　III. Pass. to be hunted, pursued, Aesch., etc.

θῆρε, dual of θήρ.

θήρειος, ον and **α, ον,** (θήρ) of wild beasts, Lat. ferīnus, θήρειον γραφήν the figures of animals worked upon the cloak, Aesch.; θ. δάκος = θήρ, Eur.; θ. βία, periphr. for ὁ θήρ, the centaur, Soph.; θ. κρέα game, Xen.

θήρευμα, ατος, τό, (θηρεύω) = θήραμα, spoil, prey, Eur.

θήρευσις, εως, ἡ, (θηρεύω) hunting, the chase, Plat.

θηρευτής, οῦ, ὁ, (θηρεύω) = θηρατής, a hunter, huntsman, Il.; κυσὶ θηρευτῇσι Ib.; also of a fisher, Hdt.

θηρευτικός, ή, όν, of or for hunting, κύνες θ. hounds, Ar., Xen.; βίος θ. the life of hunters, Arist.; and

θηρευτός, ή, όν, = θηρατός, Arist.　　From

θηρεύω, f. **σω:**—Pass., aor. 1 ἐθηρεύθην:—like θηράω, to hunt, go hunting, Od., Hdt.　　II. c. acc. to hunt after, chase, catch, Id., Xen., etc.:—of men, to hunt down, Hdt.; to lay wait for, Xen.:—Pass. to be hunted, Hdt.: to be caught, Aesch.　　2. metaph. to hunt after, Id., Eur., etc.

θηρητήρ, -ήτωρ, Ion. for θήρᾱτηρ, -άτωρ.

θηρέω, Ion. for θηράω.

θηρίον, τό, in form a Dim. of θήρ, but in usage equiv. to it, a wild animal, beast, of a stag, Od.;—of savage beasts, Hdt., Xen., etc.; but, of a pig, Plat.; of a dog,

Theocr.:—in pl. beasts, opp. to men, birds, and fishes, wild animals, game, Hdt., Plat.:—proverb. ἢ θηρίον ἢ θεός, i. e. either below or above the nature of man, Arist.　　2. an animal, Hdt., Plat.　　3. a poisonous animal, reptile, serpent, N. T.　　II. also as real Dim. a little animal, insect, of bees, Theocr.　　III. as a term of reproach, beast! like Lat. bellua, French bête, Ar., Plat.　　Hence

θηριότης, ητος, ἡ, the nature of a beast, brutality, Arist.

θηριόω, f. ώσω, (θηρίον) to make into a wild beast.

θηρι-ώδης, ες, (εἶδος) full of wild beasts, infested by them, Lat. belluosus, of countries, Hdt.　　II. of men, beast-like, wild, savage, brutal, Lat. belluīnus, Eur., Plat., etc.:—τὸ θ. the animal nature, Eur.

θηριωδία, ἡ, = θηριότης, Arist.

θηρίωσις, εως, ἡ, (θηριόω) a turning into a beast, Luc.

θηρο-βολέω, f. ήσω, (βάλλω) to slay wild beasts, Soph.

θηρό-βοτος, ον, (βόσκω) where wild beasts feed, Anth.

θηρό-θυμος, ον, with brutal mind, brutal, Anth.

θηρο-κτόνος, ον, (κτείνω) killing wild beasts, ἐν φοναῖς θηροκτόνοις, i. e. in the chase, Eur.

θηρ-ολέτης, ου, ὁ, (ὄλλυμι) slayer of beasts, Anth.

θηρ-όλετος, ον, (ὄλλυμι) slain by beasts, Anth.

θηρο-μῖγής, ές, (μίγνυμι) half-beast, θηρ. τις ὠρυγή a cry of beasts, Plut.

θηρο-νόμος, ον, (νέμω) tending wild beasts, Anth.

θηρο-σκόπος, ον, looking out for wild beasts, h. Hom.

θηροσύνη, ἡ, (θήρ) the chase, Anth.

θηρο-τόκος, ον, (τίκτω) producing beasts, ἄλση Anth.

θηρο-τρόφος, ον, (τρέφω) feeding wild beasts, Eur.　　II. proparox. θηρότροφος, feeding on beasts, Id.

θηρο-φόνος, ον, and **η, ον,** killing wild beasts, Eur.

θηρσί, dat. pl. of θήρ.

θηρῶν, crasis for τὸ ἡρῶον.

θής, θητός, ὁ, a serf or villain, bound to till his lord's land, Lat. ascriptus glebae, opp. to a mere slave, θῆτές τε δμῶές τε Od.: also a hired farm-servant or bailiff, Lat. villicus, Hes., Plat.　　2. at Athens, by the constitution of Solon, the θῆτες were the fourth class, (the other three being πεντακοσιομέδιμνοι, ἱππεῖς, ζευγίται), including all whose property in land was under 150 medimni, Plut.: they were employed as light-armed and seamen.　　II. fem. **θῆσσα,** new Att. **θῆττα, ἡ,** a poor girl, one obliged to go out for hire, Plut.　　2. as Adj. θῆσσα τράπεζα menial fare, Eur. (From ΘΕ, Root of τίθημι, a settler.)

θῆσαι, aor. 1 inf. of *θάω, to suckle:—**θήσατο,** 3 sing. aor. 1 med.

θησαυρίζω, f. σω, (θησαυρός) to store or treasure up, Hdt., Xen., etc.　　Hence

θησαύρισμα, ατος, τό, a store, treasure, Soph., Eur.; and

θησαυρισμός, ὁ, a laying up in store, Arist.

θησαυρο-ποιός, όν, (ποιέω) laying up in store, Plat.

θησαυρός, ὁ, (from ΘΕ, Root of τίθημι) a store laid up, treasure, Aesch., Ar.:—metaph., θ. ὕμνων Pind.; Διὸς θ., of fire, Eur.; οἰωνοῖς γλυκὺς θ., of a dead body, Soph.　　II. a store-house, treasure-house, magazine, Hdt.: the treasury of a temple, Id., Xen.　　2. any receptacle for valuables, a chest, casket, Hdt.; θ. βελέεσσιν, of a quiver, Aesch.

Θησεῖδαι, οἱ, sons of Theseus, i. e. the Athenians, Soph.

Θησεῖον, τό, the temple of Theseus, a sanctuary for

criminals and runaway slaves, Ar. II. τὰ Θησεῖα (sc. ἱερά, the festival of Theseus, Id.

θησεῖς, Dor. 2 sing. fut. of τίθημι.

θησέμεναι, Dor. for θήσειν, fut. inf. of τίθημι.

θησεύμεθα, Dor. for θησόμεθα, 1 pl. fut. med. of τίθημι.

Θησεύς, ὁ, gen. έως, Theseus, the famous ancestral hero of Athens, Il., etc. (From ΘΕ, Root of τίθημι, the Settler; cf. θής.)

Θησηΐς, ΐδος, contr. Θησῆς, ῆδος, fem. of Θήσειος, of Theseus, Aesch. II. as Subst. the Theseïd, a poem on Theseus, Arist. 2. name of a mode of hair-cutting, first used by Theseus, Plut.

θῆσθαι, pres. pass. inf. of *θάω to suckle.

θῆσσα, fem. of θής, q. v. II. Greek form of Lat. thensa, a sacred car, Plut.

θήσω, f. of τίθημι: Dor. θησῶ.

θητεία, ἡ, (θητεύω) hired service, service, Soph.

θητεύω, Ep. inf. θητευέμεν: f. σω: (θής) to be a serf or menial, serve for hire, Hom., Hdt., Att.

θητικός, ή, όν, (θής) of or for a hireling, menial, Arist. 2. τὸ θητικόν, the class of θῆτες, Id.

θῆττα, ἡ, Att. for θῆσσα.

-θι, originally a termin. of the gen., as in Ἰλιόθι πρό, ἠῶθι πρό Il. II. insepar. Affix of several Substs., Adjs., and Pronouns, to which it gives an adv. sense, denoting the place at which, οἴκοθι, ἄλλοθι, etc.

θίασ-άρχης, ου, ὁ, the leader of a θίασος, Luc.

θιασεύω, to bring into the Bacchic company, Eur.:— Pass. to be of the Bacchic company, to be hallowed by Bacchic rites, Id. From

ΘΙ'ΑΣΟΣ, ὁ, a band or company marching through the streets with dance and song, esp. in honour of Bacchus, a band of revellers, Hdt., Eur., etc. 2. generally, any party, company, troop, Eur., Xen.

θιάσως, Dor. for θιάσους, acc. pl. of θίασος.

θιασώτης, ου, ὁ, the member of a θίασος, Ar., etc.:— c. gen., θιασῶται τοῦ Ἔρωτος followers of Love, Xen.; ὁ ἐμὸς θ. Eur. 2. of Bacchus, leader of θίασοι, Anth.

θιγγάνω [ἄ], f. θίξομαι: aor. 2 ἔθῐγον: (lengthd. from Root ΘΙΓ, cf. θιγεῖν, Lat. te-tig-i):—to touch, handle, c. gen., Trag. 2. to take hold of, τινός Soph., etc.; ὠλέναις θ. τινός to embrace, Eur. 3. to touch, attempt, τινός Soph.:—in hostile sense, to attack, θηρός Eur. II. metaph. of the feelings, to touch, Id.; ψυχῆς, φρενῶν θ. Id.; πολλὰ θιγγάνει πρὸς ἧπαρ reach to the heart, Aesch. 2. to reach, gain, win, τινός Pind., etc.:—Pind. uses it in this sense, as he does ψαύω, c. dat.

θιγεῖν, aor. 2 inf. of θιγγάνω.

θίξομαι, fut. of θιγγάνω.

ΘΙ'Σ [ῑ], θῑνός, ὁ, and ἡ, a heap, Od., Aesch.:—in pl. sand-heaps, sand-banks, Hdt., etc. 2. the beach, shore, παρὰ θῖνα θαλάσσης Il.; παρὰ θῖν' ἁλός Ib.; so, ἐπὶ θινί Od. 3. sand or mud at the bottom of the sea, οἶδμα κυλίνδει βυσσόθεν θῖνα Soph.; metaph., τὸν θῖνά μου ταράττεις you trouble the very bottom of my heart, Ar.

θλάσσε, Ep. for ἔθλασε, 3 sing. aor. 1 of θλάω.

ΘΛΑ'Ω, θλῶ, inf. θλάσω: aor. 1 ἔθλᾰσα, Ep. θλάσσα: —Pass., pf. τέθλαγμαι:—to crush, bruise, Hom.

ΘΛΙ'ΒΩ [ῑ]: f. θλίψω: aor. 1 ἔθλιψα:—Pass., pf. τέθλιμμαι:—to press, squeeze, pinch, Ar., Dem.:—Pass. of a

person heavy-laden, ὡς θλίβομαι! Ar.:—Med., πολλῇσι φλιῇσι θλίψεται ὤμους he will rub his shoulders against many doorposts, of a beggar, Od. II. to pinch, compress, straiten, Plat.:—Pass. to be compressed, θλιβομένα καλύβα a small, close hut, Theocr.; ὁδὸς τεθλιμμένη a narrow way, N. T. 2. metaph. to oppress, afflict, distress, Arist.

θνάσκω, Dor. for θνήσκω:—θνατός for θνητός.

θνήσκω, Dor. θνάσκω: f. θανοῦμαι, Ep. inf. -έεσθαι:— aor. 2 ἔθἄνον, Ep. and Ion. θανέειν inf. also θανέμεν:— pf. τέθνηκα, with syncop. forms, 1 dual τέθνᾰτον, 1 pl. τέθνᾰμεν, 3 pl. τεθνᾶσι; 3 pl. plqpf. ἐτέθνᾰσαν; imper. τέθνᾰθι, τεθνάτω; opt. τεθναίην; inf. τεθνάναι [ἄ], Ep. τεθνάμεναι, -άμεν; part. τεθνεώς, τεθνεῶσα, τεθνεός; Ep. τεθνηώς or -ειώς, -υῖα; gen. τεθνηῶτος and τεθνηότος:—from τέθνηκα arose the Att. fut. forms τεθνήξω, τεθνήξομαι. (The Root is ΘΑΝ, found in aor. 2 θανεῖν, etc.):—in pres. and impf. to die, be dying, in aor. 2 and pf. to be dead, Hom., etc.; the pres. sometimes takes a pf. sense, θνήσκουσι γάρ, for τεθνήκασι, Soph., Eur. 2. often used like a pass. Verb, χερσὶν ὑπ' Αἴαντος θανέειν to fall by his hand, be slain by him, Il., etc.:—note the phrase of Dem., τεθνᾶσι τῷ δέει τοὺς τοιούτους, where τεθνᾶσι τῷ δέει must be taken as a single Verb, are in mortal fear of. II. metaph. of things, to die, perish, Aesch., Soph., etc.

θνητο-γενής, Dor. θνᾱτ-, ές, (γίγνομαι) of mortal race, Soph., Eur.

θνητο-ειδής, ές, (εἶδος) of mortal nature, Plat.

θνητός, ή, όν, and ός, όν: Dor. θνατός: (θνήσκω):— liable to death, mortal, Hom., etc.:—as Subst., θνητοί mortals, Od., Trag. 2. of things, befitting mortals, human, Pind., Eur., etc.

θοάζω, only in pres., (θοός) trans. to move quickly, ply rapidly, πτέρυγας Eur.; τίς ὅδ' ἀγὼν θοάζων σε; what task is thus hurrying thee on? Id.; θ. θοάζω πόνον I urge it on, Id.; θ. σῖτα to dispatch food quickly, Id. 2. intr. to move quickly, hurry along, rush, dart, Id. II. = θάσσω, to sit, τίνας ποθ' ἕδρας θοάζετε; why sit ye in this suppliant posture? Soph.

θοιμάτιον, θοιματίδιον, crasis for τὸ ἱμάτ-.

θοίνα, ἡ, Dor. for θοίνη. Hence

θοινάζω, = θοινάω, Xen.

θοίναμα, ατος, τό, (θοινάω) a meal, feast, Eur.

θοινᾱτήρ, ῆρος, ὁ, (θοινάω) lord of the feast, Aesch.

θοινᾱτήριον, τό, = θοίνη, Eur.; and

θοινᾱτικός, ή, όν, of or for a feast, Xen.; and

θοινάτωρ [ἄ], ορος, ὁ, = θοινατήρ, Eur. From

θοινάω, f. ήσω, (θοίνη) to feast on, eat, ἰχθῦς Hes. II. to feast, entertain, φίλους Eur.; τὸ δεῖπνον, τό μιν ἐκεῖνος ἐθοίνησε the feast, which he gave him, Hdt. 2. Med. and Pass., f. ήσομαι and ἄσομαι [ᾱ]: aor. 1 ἐθοινήθην and -ησάμην: pf. τεθοίνᾱμαι:— absol. to be feasted, to feast, banquet, Hom., Od., Eur.:—c. acc. to feast on, Eur.; so c. gen., Anth.

θοίνη, Dor. θοίνα, ἡ, a meal, feast, banquet, dinner, Hes., Hdt., Att. (Deriv. uncertain.)

θοινήτωρ, ὁ, = θοινάτωρ, θοινατήρ, Anth.

θοῖτο, for θεῖτο, 3 sing. aor. 2 med. opt. of τίθημι.

θολερός, ά, όν, (θολός) muddy, foul, thick, troubled, Lat. turbidus, properly of water, Hdt., Thuc., etc. II. metaph. troubled by passion or mad-

ness, θολεροὶ λόγοι Aesch. ; θολερῷ χειμῶνι with *turbid* storm of madness, Soph.

θολία, ἡ, (θόλος) *a conical hat with a broad brim* to keep the sun off, Theocr. From

ΘΟ'ΛΟΣ, ἡ, *a round building with a conical roof, a vaulted chamber*, Od.   2. at Athens, *the Rotunda*, in which the Prytanes dined, Plat., etc.

ΘΟΛΟ'Σ, ὁ, *mud, dirt*, esp. *the thick, dark juice of the cuttle-fish* (*sepia*), which it emits to trouble the water and hide himself, Lat. *loligo*, Arist.   Hence

θολόω, f. ώσω, *to make turbid*, properly of water : metaph., θ. καρδίαν Eur.

θοός, ή, όν, (θέω *to run*) *quick, nimble, active*, Il. ; θοὴ νύξ *swift* Night, because she drove a car, or came on suddenly, Hom. ; θοὴν ἀλεγύνετε δαῖτα prepare a *hasty* meal, Od., etc. :—Adv. θοῶς, *quickly, in haste*, Hom. ; *soon*, Od.   II. of the Echinades, islands with *sharp-peaks*, Ib.

θοόω, f. ώσω, (θοός 11) *to make sharp* or *pointed*, Od.

θορεῖν, inf. aor. 2 of θρώσκω :—**θόρε,** Ep. for ἔθορε, 3 sing.

θορή, ἡ, = θορός, Hdt.

Θορῐκόνδε, Adv. *to Thoricus*, h. Hom.

θόρνυμαι or **-ύομαι,** Dep., = θρώσκω II, 3 pl. subj. θορνύωνται Hdt.

θορός, ὁ, *semen genitale*, Hdt.

θορούμαι, f. of θρώσκω.

θορυβάζομαι, Pass. *to be troubled*, N. T.   From

θορῠβέω, f. ήσω, (θόρυβος) *to make a noise* or *uproar*, of a crowd, Ar.   2. like Lat. *acclamare*, *to shout in token either of approbation* or *the contrary* :   a. *to cheer, applaud*, Plat.   b. *to raise clamours against*, c. dat., Thuc., Plat., etc. :—Pass. *to have clamours raised against one*, Soph.   II. trans. *to confuse by noise* or *tumult, to trouble, throw into confusion*, Thuc. :—Pass. *to be thrown into confusion*, Hdt., etc.   Hence

θορῠβητικός, ή, όν, *uproarious, turbulent*, Ar.

θορῠβο-ποιός, όν, (ποιέω) *making an uproar*, Plut.

θόρῠβος, ὁ, (θρόος) *a noise, uproar, clamour*, Pind., Eur., Thuc., etc. ; θόρυβος βοῆς a confused *clamour*, Soph.   2. *in token of approbation* or *the contrary :*   a. *applause, cheers*, Ar., Plat., etc.   b. *groans, murmurs*, Soph.   II. *tumult, confusion*, Hdt., Thuc.

θορῠβ-ώδης, ες, (εἶδος) *noisy, uproarious, turbulent*, Plat.   II. *causing alarm*, Xen.

θορών, οῦσα, aor. 2 part. of θρώσκω.

θοῦ, aor. 2 imper. of τίθημι.

θοὔδωρ, θοὔδατος, crasis for τὸ ὕδωρ, τοῦ ὕδατος.

Θουριό-μαντις, εως, ὁ, *a Thurian prophet*, of Lampon who led the colony to Thurium, Ar.

θούριος, α, ον, in Att. Poets for θοῦρος, Aesch., etc.

θοῦρις, ιδος, ἡ, fem. of sq., Hom. ; θοῦρις ἀσπίς, the shield *with which one rushes to the fight*, Il.

θοῦρος, ὁ, (cf. θρώσκω) *rushing, raging, impetuous, furious*, Il., Aesch.

θόωκος, ὁ, Ep. lengthd. form of θῶκος ; v. θᾶκος.

Θόωσα, ἡ, (θοός) *Speed*, as prop. n., Od.

Θράκη, ἡ, *Thrace*, Ar., Thuc., etc. : Ion. **Θρηίκη,** Hdt. ; Ep. contr. **Θρήκη,** Il., Trag. ; **Θράκη** in Ar. :—**Θρήκηθεν,** *from Thrace*, Il. :—**Θρήκηνδε,** *to Thrace*, Od.

Θράκιος, α, ον, *Thracian*, Thuc., etc. : Ion. **Θρηίκιος** [ῑ], η, ον, Il., Hdt. ; contr. **Θρήκιος, α, ον,** Trag. :— Σάμος Θρηίκίη = Σαμοθράκη, Il.

Θρακιστί, (Θράκη) Adv. *in Thracian fashion*, Theocr.

θρανεύομαι, Pass. with fut. med. -εύσομαι : (θρᾶνος) :— *to be stretched on the tanner's board, to be tanned*, Ar.

θρανίον, τό, Dim. of θρᾶνος, Ar.

θρανίτης [ῑ], ου, ὁ, (θρᾶνος) *one of the rowers on the topmost of the three benches* in a trireme, who had the longest oars and most work, *a top-rower*, Ar., Thuc.: —cf. ζυγίτης, θαλαμίτης.

θρᾶνος, ὁ, or τό, (*θράω) *a bench, form*, Ar.

Θρᾷξ, Θρᾳκός, ὁ, *a Thracian* ; Ion. **Θρῆΐξ,** ικος, pl. **Θρῆΐκες** [ῑ], Il., Hdt., etc. ; Ep. contr. **Θρῇξ, Θρῃκός,** Il., Trag., etc.

θρᾶξαι, aor. 1 inf. of θράσσω :—**θρᾶξον,** imper.

ΘΡΑ'ΣΟΣ [ᾰ], εος, τό, (Θράκη) θρασύς = θάρσος, *courage, boldness*, Il., Soph. ; θρ. ἰσχύος *confidence* in strength, Soph.   II. in bad sense, *over-boldness, daring, rashness, audacity, impudence*, Att., Hdt.

Θρᾷσσα, ἡ, Att. **Θρᾷττα,** Trag. **Θρᾴσσα,** Dor. **Θρεῖσσα,** (Θρᾷξ) *a Thracian woman*, Soph., etc.

θράσσω, Att. **θράττω:** f. ξω : aor. 1 inf. θράξαι :— contr. from ταράσσω, *to trouble, disquiet*, Aesch., Eur., Plat., etc.   2. *to destroy*, rare, Anth.

θρασύ-βουλος, ον, (βουλή) *bold in counsel*, Arist.

θρᾰσύ-γυιος, ον, (γυῖον) *strong of limb*, Pind.

θρᾰσύ-δειλος, ὁ, ἡ, *an impudent coward*, Arist.

θρᾰσύ-κάρδιος, ον, (καρδία) *bold of heart*, Il.

θρασύ-μᾰχος, ον, (μάχομαι) *bold in battle*, Arist.

θρᾰσύ-μέμνων, ον, *bravely steadfast* (cf. **Μέμνων**), Hom.

θρᾰσύ-μηδης, ες, (μῆδος) *bold of thought* or *plan, daring, resolute*, Pind.

θρᾰσύ-μητις, ιδος, ὁ, ἡ, = foreg., Anth.

θρᾰσύ-μήχᾰνος, Dor. -μάχανος, ον, (μηχανή) *bold in contriving, daring in design*, Pind.

θρᾰσύ-μῡθος, ον, *bold of speech, saucy*, Pind.

θρᾰσύνω [ῡ', f. ῠνῶ, (θρασύς) = θαρσύνω, *to make bold, embolden, encourage*, Aesch., Thuc. :—Pass. and Med., *to be bold* or *ready, take courage*, Aesch., Eur., etc.   II. Pass., in bad sense, *to be over-bold, audacious, to speak boldly* or *insolently*, Soph., Ar.

θρᾰσύ-πονος, ον, *bold* or *ready at work*, Pind.

θρασυ-πτόλεμος, ον, *bold in war*, Anth.

ΘΡΑ'ΣΥ'Σ, εῖα, ύ, *bold, spirited, courageous, confident*, Hom., Hdt., Att. ; θρασεῖα τοῦ μέλλοντος *full of confidence* for the future, Thuc.   2. in bad sense, *over-bold, rash, venturous*, Lat. *audax*, Od., Att.   II. of things, *to be ventured*, c. inf., θρασύ μοι τόδ' εἰπεῖν this I am *bold* to say, Pind. ; οὐκ ἄρ' ἐκείνῃ προσμῖξαι θρασύ ; Soph.   III. Adv. -έως : Comp. θρασύτερον, *too boldly*, Thuc.

θρᾰσύ-σπλαγχνος, ον, (σπλάγχνον) *bold-hearted*, Eur. Adv. -ως, Aesch.

θρᾰσυστομέω, *to be over-bold of tongue*, Trag. ; and

θρᾰσυστομία, ἡ, *insolence*, Anth.   From

θρᾰσύ-στομος, ον, (στόμα) *bold of tongue, insolent*, Aesch.

θρᾰσύτης, ητος, ἡ, *over-boldness, audacity*, Thuc.

θρᾰσύ-χειρ, χειρος, ἡ, ὁ, *bold of hand*, Anth.

Θρᾴττα, ης, ἡ, Att. for Θρᾷσσα.

θράττω, Att. for θράσσω.

θραῦμα, ατος, τό, (θραύω) = θραῦσμα.

θραυσ-άντυξ, ὕγος, ὁ, ἡ, (θραύω) breaking wheels, Ar.

θραῦσμα or θραῦμα, ατος, τό, that which is broken, a fragment, wreck, piece, Aesch. From

ΘΡΑΥΏ, f. σω: aor. 1 ἔθραυσα:—Pass., aor. 1 ἐθραύσθην: pf. τέθραυσμαι:—to break in pieces, shatter, shiver, Hdt., Aesch., Eur. :—Pass. to fly into pieces, Hdt.   II. metaph., like Lat. frangere, = θρύπτω, to break down, enfeeble, Pind., Eur., etc.

*ΘΡΑΏ, to set.

Θρεῖσσα, ἡ, Dor. for Θρῆσσα, Θρᾶσσα.

θρέμμα, ατος, τό, (τρέφω) a nursling, creature, of sheep and goats, Xen., Plat.   2. of men, Soph., etc.   3. of wild beasts, Id.   4. as a term of reproach, a creature, θρέμματ' οὐκ ἀνασχετά Aesch.; ὦ θρέμμ' ἀναιδές Soph.   5. ὕδρας θρ., periphr. for ὕδρα, Id.

θρέξασκον, Ion. aor. of τρέχω:—θρέξομαι, fut.

ΘΡΕΌΜΑΙ, Dep. only in pres. to cry aloud, shriek forth, Aesch., Eur.

θρέπτειρα, ἡ, fem. of θρεπτήρ, Eur., Anth.

θρεπτέος, α, ον, verb. Adj. of τρέφω, to be fed, Plat.   II. θρεπτέον, one must feed, Xen.   2. from Pass., one must be fed, one must live, Id.

θρεπτήρ, ῆρος, ὁ, (τρέφω) a feeder, rearer, Anth.

θρεπτήριος, ον, (τρέφω) able to feed or rear, feeding, nourishing, Aesch.   II. πλόκαμος θρ. hair let grow as an offering, Id.   III. θρεπτήρια, τά, rewards for rearing, h. Hom.; but also, the returns made by children for their rearing, Hes.   2. = τροφή, nourishment, Soph.

θρεπτικός, ή, όν, (τρέφω) promoting growth, Arist.; τὸ θρεπτικόν the principle of growth, Id.

θρέπτρα, τά, (τρέφω) the returns made by children to their parents for their rearing, Il.

θρεττανελό, a sound imitative of the cithara (as tra lira of the horn), Ar.

θρέττε, τό, in Ar., οὐκ ἔνι μοι τὸ θρέττε, the spirit's not in me; a barbarism for τὸ θράσος.

θρέψα, Ep. for ἔθρεψα, aor. 1 of τρέφω:—θρέψω, fut.

ΘΡΕΏ, v. θρέομαι.

Θρηϊκίη, Θρηΐκιος, η, ον, Ion. for Θρακία, Θράκιος.

Θρηῖξ, ῖκος, ὁ, Ep. and Ion. for Θρᾷξ.

Θρηῖσσα, ἡ, Ep. and Ion. for Θρᾶσσα.

Θρήκη, ἡ, Θρήκηθεν, Θρήκηνδε, v. Θράκη.

Θρήκιος, Ion. and old Att. for Θράκιος.

θρηνέω, f. -ήσω, (θρῆνος) to sing a dirge, to wail, Od., Aesch. :—c. acc. cogn., ἀοιδὴν ἐθρήνεον were singing a dirge, Il. ; ᾠδάς, ἐπῳδὰς θρ. Soph. :—Pass., ἅλις μοι τεθρήνηται, impers., Id.   2. c. acc. objecti, to wail for, lament, Aesch., etc.; so also Med., Id. :—Pass. to be lamented, Soph.   Hence

θρήνημα, νος, ατος, τό, a lament, dirge, Eur.; and

θρηνητήρ, ῆρος, ὁ, a mourner, wailer, Aesch.

θρηνητής, οῦ, ὁ, = θρηνητήρ, Aesch.

θρηνητικός, ή, όν, (θρηνέω) querulous, Arist.

θρῆνος, ὁ, (θρέομαι) a funeral-song, dirge, lament, Lat. naenia, Il., Hdt., Trag.; θρῆνος οὑμός for me, Aesch.   2. a complaint, sad strain, Pind., etc.

θρῆνυς, νος, ὁ, (*θράω) a footstool, Hom.   II. θρ. ἑπταπόδης the seven-foot bench, the seat of the helmsman or the rowers, Il.

θρηνῳδέω, f. ήσω, to sing a dirge over, τινά Eur.

θρην-ώδης, ες, (εἶδος) like a dirge, μι for a dirge, Plat.

θρηνῳδία, ἡ, lamentation, Plat.   From

θρην-ῳδός, ὁ, ἡ, (ἀοιδός) one who sings a dirge, Arist.

Θρῇξ, ηκός, ὁ, Ion. for Θρᾷξ; fem. Θρῇσσα.

θρησκεία, Ion. -ηΐη or -ίη, ἡ, religious worship or usage, Hdt.: religion, N.T.; θρ. τῶν ἀγγέλων worshipping of angels, Ib.   From

θρησκεύω, f. σω, (θρῆσκος) to hold religious observances, observe religiously, Hdt.   II. to be a devotee, Plut.

θρῆσκος, ον, religious, N.T.   (Deriv. uncertain.)

Θρῇσσα, ἡ, Ion. for Θρᾶσσα.

θριαμβευτικός, ή, όν, of triumphal families, Plut.

θριαμβεύω, f. σω, pf. τεθριάμβευκα: (θρίαμβος) :—to triumph, Plut., etc.; θρ. ἀπό τινος or κατά τινος, Lat. triumphare de aliquo, Id.; also, θρ. τινά N.T.   II. to lead in triumph, τινά Plut.

θριαμβικός, ή, όν, triumphal, ἀνὴρ θρ. = Lat. vir triumphalis, Plut.

θρίαμβος, ὁ, a hymn to Bacchus, Cratin.: also a name for Bacchus, Plut., etc.   II. used to express the Roman triumphus, Id.   (Deriv. unknown.)

θριγκίον, τό, Dim. of sq., Luc.

ΘΡΙΓΚΟΌΣ, ὁ, the topmost course of stones in a wall, which projected over the rest, the eaves, cornice, coping, Od., Eur.; θριγκὸς κυάνοιο a cornice of blue metal, Od.   2. metaph. the coping-stone, culmination, θριγκὸς κακῶν Eur.   II. a wall, fence of any sort, Id.   Hence

θριγκόω, f. ώσω, to surround with a coping, [αὐλὴν] ἐθρίγκωσεν ἀχέρδῳ he fenced it at top with thornbushes, Od.   II. to build even to the coping-stone: metaph. to put the finishing stroke to a thing, Aesch. ; δῶμα κακοῖς θριγκοῦν to bring the house to the height of misery, Eur.   Hence

θρίγκωμα, ατος, τό, a coping, cornice, Eur.

θρῑδάκῐνος, η, ον, of lettuce, Luc.   From

ΘΡΙΔΑΞ [ῐ], ᾰκος, ἡ, lettuce, Hdt., etc.

θρίζω, syncop. for θερίζω, Aesch.

Θρῑνᾰκίη, ἡ, (θρῖναξ) an old name of Sicily, from its three promontories, Od., etc. :—in later times, the old form Θρινακίη was altered into Τρινακρία, Lat. Trinacria, as if it were compounded of τρεῖς ἄκραι.   From

θρῖναξ, ᾰκος, ὁ, (τρεῖς, ἀκή) a trident, Ar.

ΘΡΙΞ, ἡ, gen. τρῐχός, dat. pl. θριξί, the hair of the head, used by Hom. only in pl.; Att. also in sing.: Hom. etc. :—also sheep's wool, Il.; pig's bristles, Hom.; οὐραῖαι τρίχες the hair of a horse's tail, Il.   2. a single hair, proverb., θρὶξ ἀνὰ μέσσον only a hair's breadth between, Theocr.; ἄξιον τριχός, i.e. good for nothing, Ar.

ΘΡΙΟΝ, τό, a fig-leaf, Ar.   II. a mixture of eggs, milk, lard, flour, honey, and cheese, a kind of omelette, so called because it was wrapped in fig-leaves, Id.   (Prob. from τρίς, from the three lobes of the fig-leaf.)

θρίψ, gen. θρῑπός, ὁ, (τρίβω) a wood-worm, Anth.

θροέω, f. ήσω: aor. 1 ἐθρόησα: (θρόος) :—to cry aloud, Soph. :—to speak, say, utter, Trag. ;—and in Med., Aesch.   2. to tell out, declare, Id., Soph.   II. Pass. to be troubled, N.T.

θρόμβος, ὁ, (τρέφω) a lump, piece, Lat. grumus, as of asphalt, Hdt. : a clot or gout of blood, Aesch.

θρομβ-ώδης, ες, (εἶδος) like clots, clotted, Soph.

θρόνα, τά, only in pl., flowers embroidered on cloth, patterns, Il.　　II. flowers or herbs used as drugs and charms, Theocr. (Deriv. uncertain.)

θρόνος, ὁ, (*θράω) a seat, chair, Hom. : a throne, chair of state, Hdt., 'Att. :—in pl. also, the throne, i. e. the king's estate or dignity, Soph.　　2. the oracular seat of Apollo or the Pythia, Aesch., etc.　　3. the chair of a teacher, Lat. cathedra, Plat. Hence

θρόνωσις, εως, ἡ, the enthronement of the newly initiated at the mysteries, Plat.

θρόος, Att. θροῦς, ὁ, (θρέομαι) a noise as of many voices, Il.; of musical sounds, Pind.　　2. the murmuring of a crowd, Thuc.　　II. a report, Lat. rumor, Xen.

θρυαλλίδιον, τό, Dim. of θρυαλλίς, Luc.

θρυαλλίς, ίδος, ἡ, a plant which, like our rush, was used for making wicks, a wick, Ar. (Deriv. unknown.)

θρυλέω (vulg. θρυλλέω), f. ήσω, to make a confused noise, chatter, babble, Ar., Theocr.　　II. c. acc. rei, to be always talking about a thing, repeat over and over again, Lat. decantare, Eur., Plat., etc. :—Pass., τὸ θρυλούμενον the common talk, what is in every one's mouth, Dem.

θρυλίζω (vulg. θρυλλ-), to make a false note, h. Hom.

θρυλίσσω (vulg. θρυλλ-), to crush, shiver, smash :—Pass., θρυλίχθη δὲ μέτωπον (Ep. for ἐθρυλίχθη) Il.

θρῦλος (vulg. θρύλλος), ὁ, (θρέομαι) a noise as of many voices, a shouting, murmuring, Batr.

θρύμμα, ατος, τό, (θρύπτω) that which is broken off, a piece, bit, Ar., Anth.

ΘΡΥ'ΟΝ, τό, a rush, Lat. juncus, Il.

θρυπτικός, ή, όν, easily broken : metaph. delicate, effeminate, Xen. From

ΘΡΥ'ΠΤΩ, f. θρύψω: aor. 1 ἔθρυψα :—Pass. and Med., f. θρύψομαι: aor. 2 ἐτρύφην [ῠ] : (akin to θραύω) :—to break in pieces, break small, Plat., Theocr.　　II. metaph., like Lat. frangere, to break, crush, enfeeble : Pass., with fut. med., to be enfeebled, enervated, unmanned, Xen.; τεθρυμμένος Luc.　　2. in Pass. also, to play the coquet, be coy and prudish, give oneself airs, bridle up, Ar., Xen.; θρύπτεσθαι πρός τινα to give oneself airs toward him, Plut.

θρύψις, εως, ἡ, a breaking in small pieces :—metaph. softness, weakness, debauchery, Xen., Plut., etc.

θρώσκω : Ep. impf. θρῶσκον : f. θοροῦμαι : aor. 2 ἔθορον, Ep. θόρον, Ion. inf. θορέειν. (From Root ΘΟΡ, which appears in fut. and aor. 2.)　　To leap, spring, ἐκ δίφροιο, ἀπὸ λέκτροιο Hom.; of arrows, ἀπὸ νευρῆφι θρῶσκον Il.; of the oar, Soph.　　2. foll. by Prep. to leap upon, i. e. attack, assault, ἐπὶ Τρώεσσι θόρον Il. : —of a recurring illness, to attack, Soph.　　3. generally, to rush, dart, Pind., Soph. :—metaph., πεδάρσιοι θρώσκουσι leap up into air, i. e. vanish away, Aesch.　　II. trans. to mount, ὁ θρώσκων the sire, Id. Hence

θρωσμός, ὁ, ground rising from the plain, an eminence, Il.

ΘΥ'ΓΑΤΗΡ, ἡ : gen. θυγάτερος, contr. θυγατρός ; dat. θυγάτερι, θυγατρί ; acc. θυγάτερα but Ep. θύγατρα : voc. θύγατερ :—a daughter, Hom., etc. Hence

θυγατρίδη, ἡ, a daughter's daughter, granddaughter, Att.; and

θυγατρίδοῦς, οῦ, ὁ, a daughter's son, grandson, Att.; Ion. -ιδέος, Hdt.

θυεία, Ion. -είη, ἡ, (θύω) a mortar, Ar.

θυείδιον, τό, Dim. of θυεία, Ar.

θύελλα, ἡ, (θύω, as ἄελλα from ἄημι) a furious storm, hurricane, Hom.; πυρὸς θύελλαι thunderstorms, Od.; ποντία θ. Soph.; metaph., ἄτης θύελλαι Aesch.

Θυέστειος, α, ον, of Thyestes, Ar.

θυη-δόχος, ον, (θύος, δέχομαι) receiving incense, Anth.

θυήεις, εσσα, εν, (θύος) smoking or smelling with incense, fragrant, Hom., Hes.

θυηλή, ἡ, (θύω) the part of the victim that was burnt, the primal offering, mostly in pl., Il., Ar. :—metaph., θυηλὴ Ἄρεος, an offering to Ares, i. e. the blood of the slain, Soph.

θυηπολέω, f. ήσω, to busy oneself with sacrifices, Aesch., Eur.　　2. trans. to sacrifice :—Pass., θυηπολεῖται δ' ἄστυ is filled with sacrifices, Id. From

θυη-πόλος, ον, (θύος, πολέω) busy about sacrifices, sacrificial, Aesch. :—as Subst. a diviner, soothsayer, Eur., Ar.

θυη-φάγος [ἄ], ον, (θύος, φαγεῖν) devouring offerings, Aesch.

θυία or better θύα, ἡ, an African tree with scented wood, a kind of juniper or cedar, Theophr.

θυιάς, άδος, ἡ, (θύω) a mad or inspired woman, a Bacchante, Aesch.

θύϊνος, η, ον, of the tree θυία, of cedar, N. T.

θύϊω or θυίω, = θύω, to be inspired, h. Hom.

θυλάκιον, τό, Dim. of θύλακος, a little bag, Hdt., Ar.

ΘΥ'ΛΑ'ΚΟΣ [ῠ], ὁ, a bag, pouch, wallet, Hdt., Ar.; δερῶ σε θύλακον I'll make a bag of your skin, Id.　　II. in pl. the trousers of the Persians, Eur., Ar.

θύλαξ, άκος, ὁ, = θύλακος, Aesop. :—θῡλάς, άδος, ἡ, Anth.

θυλέομαι, (θύος) to offer. Hence

θύλημα, ατος, τό, that which is offered ; mostly in pl. θυλήματα, cakes, incense, etc., Ar.

θῦμα, ατος, τό, (θύω A) that which is slain or offered, a victim, sacrifice, offering, Trag., Thuc., etc. ; πάγκαρπα θ. offerings of all fruits, Soph.　　II. sacrifice, as an act, Id. : metaph., θ. λεύσιμον a sacrifice to be avenged by stoning [the murderers], Aesch.

θυμαίνω, f. ἀνῶ, (θυμός) to be wroth, angry, Hes., Ar.

θυμ-αλγής, ές, (ἀλγέω) heart-grieving, Hom., Hdt.　　II. pass. inly grieving, καρδία Aesch.

θυμάλωψ [ᾰ], ωπος, ὁ, (τύφω) a piece of burning wood or charcoal, a hot coal, Ar.

θυμᾰρέω, to be well-pleased, Theocr. From

θύμ-ᾱρής, ές, (v. -ήρης) suiting the heart, i. e. well-pleasing, dear, delightful, Hom. :—neut. as Adv. in the form θυμήρες, Od.

ΘΥ'ΜΒΡΑ, ἡ, a bitter herb, savory, Eupol. Hence

θυμβρ-επίδειπνος, ον, supping on bitter herbs, i. e. living poorly, Ar.

Θύμβρις, ιδος, ἡ, the Tiber, Anth.

θυμβρο-φάγος, ον, (φαγεῖν) eating savory, θυμβροφάγον βλέπειν to look as if one had eaten savory, make a savory or (as we might say) a verjuice face, Ar.

θυμέλη, ἡ, (θύω) a place for sacrifice, an altar, Aesch., Eur.　　2. θυμέλαι Κυκλώπων, supposed to be the

Cyclopian *walls* at Mycenae, Eur.   II. in the Athenian theatre, *a platform* in the orchestra, on the steps of which stood the leader of the Chorus, Plut. :—generally, *a raised seat* or *stage*, Id.   Hence

θῡμελικός, ή, όν, of or *for the thymelé, scenic, theatric*, Plut. :—οἱ θυμελικοί, i. e. *the chorus* or *musicians*, Id.

θῡμ-ηγερέων, (ἀγείρω) a part. with no pres. in use, *gathering breath, collecting oneself*, Od.

θῡμ-ηδής, ές, (ἧδος) *well-pleasing*, Od., Aesch.

θῡμ-ήρης, v. θυμάρης.

θῡμίαμα, Ion. -ημα, ατος, τό, *that which is burnt as incense*: in pl. *fragrant stuffs* for burning, Hdt., Soph., etc.   2. *stuff for embalming*, Hdt.

θῡμιατήριον, Ion. θυμιητ-, τό, *a vessel for burning incense, a censer*, Hdt., Thuc., etc.

θῡμιάω, f. σω: Ion. aor. 1 ἐθυμίησα: (θῦμα :—*to burn so as to produce smoke, burn*, Hdt. :—Pass. *to be burnt*, 3 sing. θυμιῆται (Ion. for -ᾶται) Id.

θῡμίδιον, τό, Dim. of θυμός, Ar.

θῡμίημα, Ion. for θυμίαμα.

θῡμιητήριον, Ion. for θυμιατήριον.

θῡμιῆται, Ion. for -ᾶται, 3 sing. pres. pass. of θυμιάω.

θῡμικός, ή, όν, (θυμός) *high-spirited, passionate*, Arist.

θῡμίτης [ῑ], ου, ὁ, (θύμον) *flavoured with thyme*, Ar.

θῡμο-βαρής, ές, (βαρύς) *heavy at heart*, Anth.

θῡμοβορέω, *to gnaw* or *vex the heart*, Hes.   From

θῡμο-βόρος, ον, (βι-βρώσκω) *eating the heart*, Il.

θῡμο-δακής, ές, (δάκνω) *biting the heart*, Od., Anth.

θῡμο-ειδής, ές, (εἶδος) *high-spirited, courageous*, Lat. *animosus*, Plat., Xen.   2. *hot-tempered, restive*, Ib.

θῡμο-λέων, οντος, ὁ, *lion-hearted, Coeur-de-lion*, Il.

θῡμό-μαντις, εως, ὁ, ἡ, *prophesying from one's own soul* (without inspiration, like the θεόμαντις), Aesch.

θῡμο-μάχέω, *to fight desperately*, N. T., Plut.

θύμον [ῠ] or θύμος, εος, τό, *thyme*, Ar., etc.   2. *a mixture of thyme with honey and vinegar*, Id. (Deriv. uncertain.)

θῡμο-πληθής, ές, (πλῆθος) *wrathful*, Aesch.

θῡμο-ραϊστής, οῦ, ὁ, (ῥαίω) *life-destroying*, Il.

θύμος, τό, v. θύμον.

θῡμός, ὁ, (θύω B) *the soul*:   I. like Lat. *anima, the soul, breath, life*, θυμὸν ἀπαυρᾶν, ἀφελέσθαι, ἐξελέσθαι, ἐξαίνυσθαι, ὀλέσαι *to take away life*, Hom.; θυμὸν ἀποπνείειν *to expire*, Il.; θυμὸν ἀγείρειν *to collect oneself*, Ib., etc.; θυμὸς τείρετο καμάτῳ *his spirit* was *wearied by toil*, Ib.   II. like Lat. *animus, the soul, heart;* and so,   1. of desire for meat and drink, ἔπιον θ' ὅσον ἤθελε θυμός Ib. :—c. inf., βαλέειν δέ ἑ θυμὸς ἀνώγει *his heart* bade him *shoot*, Ib.; ἤθελε θυμῷ he wished *in his heart* or *with all his heart*, Ib.; θυμῷ βουλόμενος wishing *with all one's heart*, Hdt.; so, ἐκ θυμοῦ φιλέειν Il. :—θυμός ἐστί μοι, θ. γίγνεταί μοι, c. inf., I have *a mind* to do .., Id., Xen., etc. :—also as the seat of *sorrow* or *joy*, χαῖρε δὲ θυμῷ Il.; ἄχνυτο θυμός Ib., etc.   2. *mind, temper, will*, θ. πρόφρων, νηλεής, σιδήρεος Hom.; ἕνα θυμὸν ἔχειν *to be of one mind*, Il.; δόκησε δ' ἄρα σφίσι θυμὸς ὣς ἔμεν it pleased them *to be of this mind*, Od.; ἐδαΐζετο θωμός their *mind* was divided, Il.   3. *spirit, courage*, μένος καὶ θυμός Ib.; θυμὸν λαμβάνειν *to take heart*, Od.; παραὶ ποσὶ κάππεσε θυμός Il., etc.   4. *as the seat of anger*, νεμεσίζεσθαι ἐνὶ θυμῷ Ib. :—hence, *anger, wrath*, δάμα-

σον θυμόν Ib.; θυμὸς μέγας ἐστὶ βασιλῆος Ib.   5. *the soul as the agent of thought*, ᾔδεε γὰρ κατὰ θυμόν Ib.; φράζετο θυμῷ Ib.

θῡμοσοφικός, ή, όν, *like a clever fellow*, Ar.   From

θῡμό-σοφος, ον, *wise from one's own soul*, i.e. *naturally clever, a man of genius*, Ar., Plut.

θῡμοφθορέω, f. ήσω, *to torment the soul, break the heart*, Soph.   From

θῡμο-φθόρος, ον, (φθείρω) *destroying the soul, life-destroying*, Od. :—*heart-breaking*, Ib.; of persons, *troublesome, annoying*, Ib. :—θυμοφθόρα πολλά (sc. σήματα) tokens *poisoning* the king's *mind* (against Bellerophon), Il.

θῡμόω, f. ώσω, (θυμός) *to make angry* :—Med. and Pass., f. -ώσομαι: aor. 1 ἐθυμωσάμην and ἐθυμώθην: pf. inf. τεθυμῶσθαι :—*to be wroth* or *angry*, absol., Hdt., Trag.; of animals, *to be wild, restive*, Soph.; θυμοῦσθαι εἰς κέρας *to vent fury* with the horns, Virgil's *irasci in cornua*, Eur.; τὸ θυμούμενον *passion*, Thuc. :—θυμοῦσθαί τινι *to be angry with* one, Aesch., etc.; εἴς τινα Hdt.; c. dat. rei, *to be angry at* a thing, Ar.

θῡμ-ώδης, ες, = θυμο-ειδής, Arist.

θύμωμα [ῠ], ατος, τό, (θυμόω) *wrath, passion*, Aesch.

θῡνέω, = θύνω, only in impf., *to dart along*, Hes.

θυννάζω, f. σω, (θύννος) *to spear a tunny-fish*, Ar.

θύννειος, α, ον, (θύννος) *of the tunny-fish*: τὰ θύννεια (sc. κρέα) its *flesh*, Ar.

θυννευτικός, ή, όν, (θύννος) *for tunny-fishing*, Luc.

θυννο-κέφαλος, ὁ, (κεφαλή) *tunny-headed*, Luc.

θύννος, ὁ, *the tunny-fish*, a large fish, used for food in the Mediterranean, Orac. ap. Hdt., Aesch., etc. (From θύνω, because of its quick, darting motion.)

θυννοσκοπέω, f. ήσω, *to watch for tunnies*, Ar.   From

θυννο-σκόπος, ὁ, *a tunny-watcher*, i.e. one who was posted on a high place, from which he could see the shoals coming, and make a sign to the fisherman to let down their nets, Theocr.

θύννως, Dor. for θύννους, acc. pl. of θύννος.

θύνω [ῠ], only in pres. and impf., = θύω B, *to rush* or *dart along*, mostly of warriors in battle, Hom., Pind.

θυο-δόκος, ον, (θύος, δέχομαι) *receiving incense, full thereof, odorous*, Eur.

θυόεις, εσσα, εν, (θύος) *laden with incense, odorous, fragrant*, Il., Eur.

θύον, τό, (θύω A) *a tree*, the wood of which was burnt as a perfume, Od.

θύον, Ep. for ἔθυον, impf. of θύω A.   2. of θύω B.

θύος, εος, τό, (θύω A) dat. pl. θύεσσι, Ep. θνέεσσι, Hes.; Ep. gen. θυέων; acc. θύη :—*a sacrifice, offering*, Hom., etc.

θυοσκέω, *to make burnt-offerings*, Aesch.   From

θυοσ-κόος, ον, ὁ, (κέω = καίω) *the sacrificing priest*, Hom., Eur.

θυόω, f. ώσω, (θύος) *to fill with sweet smells*: pf. pass. part., ἔλαιον τεθυωμένον *fragrant* oil, Il.

ΘΎΡΑ [ῠ], Ion. θύρη, ἡ, Ion. gen. pl. θυρέων :—*a door*, Hom., mostly in pl. *double* or *folding doors*, in full δικλίδες θύραι Od.: θύρην ἐπιτιθέναι, *to put to* the door, opp. to ἀνακλίνειν: so, τὴν θ. προστιθέναι Hdt.; ἐπισπάσαι Xen.; θύραν κόπτειν, πατάσσειν, κρούειν, Lat. *januam pulsare*, *to knock, rap at the door*, Ar., Plat.; metaph., ἐπὶ ταῖς θύραις *at the*

door, i. e. close at hand, Xen.   2. from the Eastern custom of receiving petitions *at the gate* αἱ τοῦ βασιλέως θύραι became a phrase, βασιλέως θύραις παιδεύονται are educated at *court*, Id.; αἱ ἐπὶ τὰς θύρας φοιτήσεις dangling after *the court*, Id.   3. proverb., γλώσσῃ θύραι οὐκ ἐπίκεινται (cf. ἀθυρότομος) Theogn.; ἐπὶ θύραις τὴν ὑδρίαν to break the pitcher *at the* very door, = 'there's many a slip 'twixt cup and lip,' Arist.   4. *the door* of a carriage, Xen.   5. θύρη καταπακτή *a trap-door*, Hdt.   6. *a frame of planks, a raft*, φραξάμενοι τὴν ἀκρόπολιν θύρῃσί τε καὶ ξύλοις *with planks and logs*, Id.   II. generally, *an entrance*, as to a grotto, Od.

θύραζε, Adv. properly θύρασ-δε, *out to the door, out of the door*, Lat. *foras*, Hom.   2. generally, *out*, Id.; θ. ἐξιέναι to go *out of* the ship, Il.:—so in Att., ἐκφέρειν θ., ἐξέλκειν τινὰ θ. Ar.; οἱ θ. those *outside*, Id.   3. c. gen., ἁλὸς θ. *out of* the sea, Od.; θ. τῶν νόμων, like ἔξω, Eur.

θύραθεν, Ep. θύρηθε, (θύρα) Adv. *from outside the door, from without*, Eur.   2. *outside the door, outside*, θύρηθ' ἔα was *out of* the sea, Od.:—οἱ θ. aliens, the enemy, Aesch.

θυραῖος, α, ον, and ος, ον, (θύρα) *at the door* or *just outside the door*, Aesch., Soph.; θ. οἰχνεῖν to go *to the door, go out*, Id.; θ. πόλεμος, opp. to civil war, Aesch.   2. *absent, abroad*, Id.; *from abroad*, Eur.; ἄνδρες θ. *strangers, other men*, Id.; θυραῖα φρονήματ' the thoughts *of strangers*, Id. = ἀλλότριος, Lat. *alienus*, ὄλβος θ. *the luck of other men*, Aesch.; πῆμα Eur.

θύρασι, -σιν, Adv. (θύρα) *at the door, outside, without*, Lat. *foris*, Ar.   2. *out of doors, abroad*, Eur.

θυραυλέω, f. ήσω, *to live in the open air, to camp out*, Xen., etc.: in war, *to keep the field*, Arist.

θυραυλία, ἡ, *a living out of doors, camping out*, Luc.

θύρ-αυλος, ον, (αὐλή) *living out of doors*, Hesych.

θυρέ-ασπις, ιδος, ἡ, *a large shield*, Anth.; cf. θυρεός II.

θυρεός, ὁ, (θύρα) *a stone put against a door* to keep it shut, *a door-stone*, Od.   II. *a large oblong shield* (*like a door*), opp. to ἀσπίς (the round shield), as Lat. *scutum* to *clipeus*, ap. Plut.   Hence

θυρεο-φόρος, ον, (φέρω) *bearing a shield*, Plut.

θύρετρα, τά, = θύρα, *a door*, Hom., etc.

θύρη, **θύρηθε**, Ion. and Ep. for θύρα, θύραθεν.

θύρηφι, Ep. dat. of θύρα, used as Adv. *outside*, Od., Hes.

θύριον, τό, Dim. of θύρα, *a little door, wicket*, Ar.

θυρίς, ίδος, ἡ, Dim. of θύρα, Plat.; *a window*, Ar.

θυροκοπέω, f. ήσω, *to knock at the door, break it open*, Ar.   From

θυρο-κόπος, ον, (κόπτω) *knocking at the door, begging*, Aesch.

θυρόω, f. ώσω, (θύρα) *to furnish with doors, shut close*, Ar.: metaph. *to close as with a door*, βλεφάροις θυρῶσαι τὴν ὄψιν Xen.

θυρσο-μανής, ές, (μαίνομαι) *he who raves with the thyrsus*, Eur.

ΘΥΡΣΟΣ, ὁ, with heterog. pl. θύρσα, *the thyrsus* or *Bacchic wand*, being a wand wreathed in ivy and vine-leaves with a pine-cone at the top, Eur., Anth.

θυρσοφορέω, f. ήσω, *to assemble* or *regulate with the thyrsus*, Eur.   From

θυρσο-φόρος, ον, (φέρω) *thyrsus-bearing*, Eur., Anth.

θυρσο-χαρής, ές, (χαίρω) *delighting in the thyrsus*, Anth.

θυρώματα, τά, (θυρόω) *a room with doors to it, a chamber*, Hdt.   II. *a door with posts and frame*, Thuc., Dem.

θυρών, ῶνος, ὁ, (θύρα) *the part outside the door, a hall, antechamber*, Lat. *vestibulum*, Soph.

θυρωρέω, *to be a door-keeper*, Luc.   From

θυρ-ωρός, ὁ, ἡ, (ὤρα or οὖρος) *a door-keeper, porter*, Lat. *janitor*, Hdt., Att.

θυρωτός, όν, (θυρόω) *with a door* or *aperture*, Babr.

θῦσαι [ῠ], aor. 1 inf. of θύω A.

θυσανόεις, Ep. θυσσανόεις, εσσα, εν, *tasseled, fringed*, of the aegis, Il.   From

θύσανος [ῠ], ὁ, (θύω B) *a tassel*, in pl. *tassels, fringe*, Hdt.; of the tufts of the golden fleece, Pind.

θυσανωτός, ή, όν, (as if from θυσανόω), = θυσανόεις, Hdt.

θύσθλα, ων, τά, (θύω A) *the implements of Bacchus, the thyrsi and torches* of the Bacchantes, Il.

θυσία, Ion. -ίη, ἡ, (θύω A) *an offering* or *mode of offering*, Hdt.   2. in pl. *offerings, sacrifices, sacred rites*, Batr., Hdt., Att.; θυσίῃσι (Ion. dat. pl.) ἱλάσκεσθαι τὸν θεόν Hdt.; θυσίας ἔρδειν, ἐπιτελέειν, ἀνάγειν Id.; of the gods, θυσίαν δέχεσθαι Aesch.   3. *a festival*, at which *sacrifices* were offered, Plat.   II. *the victim* or *offering* itself, Luc.

θυσιάζω, f. σω, *to sacrifice*, Lysias.   Hence

θυσιαστήριον, τό, *an altar*, N. T.

θυσίμος, ον, (θύω A) *fit for sacrifice*, Hdt., Ar.

θυσσανόεις, Ep. for θυσανόεις.

θυστάς, άδος, ἡ, (θύω A) *sacrificial*, Aesch., Soph.

θυτεῖον, τό, (θύω A) *a place for sacrificing*, Aeschin.

θυτέον, verb. Adj. of θύω A, *one must sacrifice*, Ar.

θυτήρ, ῆρος, ὁ, (θύω A) *a sacrificer, slayer*, Aesch., Soph.

θυτήριον, τό, = θῦμα, Eur.

θυτικός, ή, όν, (θύω A) of or *for sacrifice*, Luc.

θύψαι, aor. 1 inf. of τύφω:—θύψω, fut.

ΘΥΩ (A), Ep. impf. θῦον· f. θύσω [ῠ], Dor. θυσῶ· aor. 1 ἔθῦσα, Ep. θῦσα· pf. τέθῠκα:—Med., f. θύσομαι, also in pass. sense: aor. 1 ἐθυσάμην:—Pass., aor. 2 ἐτύθην [ῠ]: pf. τέθῠμαι, also used in med. sense: I. Act. *to offer* part of a meal to the gods, Hom. (who used the word only in the sense of *offering* or *burning*, never = σφάξαι, *to slaughter for sacrifice*); θ. πέλανον, δεῖπνα Aesch.; κριθάς, πυρούς Ar.   2. *to sacrifice*, i. e. by slaying a victim, τῷ ἡλίῳ θ. ἵππους Hdt.; θ. αὐτοῦ παῖδα Aesch.; ἱερεῖα Thuc.: — also simply, *to slaughter, slay*, Hdt.: — Pass., τὰ τεθυμένα *the flesh of the victim*, Xen.   3. absol. *to sacrifice, offer sacrifices*, Hdt., Aesch., etc.   4. *to celebrate* with offerings or sacrifices, c. acc., Hdt., Xen.   5. c. dupl. acc., εὐαγγέλια θ. ἑκατὸν βοῦς *to sacrifice* a hundred oxen *for* the good news, Ar.   II. Med. *to cause to be offered, to have a victim slain*, and so *to take the auspices*, Hdt., Aesch., etc.:—rarely c. inf., θύομαι ἰέναι *I consult the auspices* about going, *to know whether I may go or not*, Xen.; so, θύεσθαι ἐπ' ἐξόδῳ Id.:—metaph. *to tear in pieces*, Aesch.

ΘΥΩ (B) [ῠ], f. σω, like θύνω, *to rush on* or *along*, of a rushing wind, Od.; of a swollen river, Il.; of the sea, Od.; δάπεδον αἵματι θῦεν the ground *boiled* with blood, Ib.:—generally, *to storm, rage*, Il., Aesch.

θυ-ώδης, ες, (θύος, ὄζω, cf. εὐ-ώδης, δυσ-ώδης):—smelling of incense, sweet-smelling, Od., Eur.,

θύωμα, ατος, τό, (θυόω) that which is burnt as incense; in pl. spices, Hdt.

θώ, ὁ, apocop. for θώραξ, Anth.

θωή or θωή (v. ἄθως), ἡ, a penalty, Hom. (Perh. from τί-θημι to impose.)

θωκέω, θῶκος, Ion. and Dor. for θᾱκέω, θᾶκος.

θῶμα, θωμάζω, θωμάσιος, Ion. for θαῦμα, etc.

θῶμιγξ, ιγγος, ὁ, a cord, string, Hdt.: a bow-string, Aesch. (Deriv. uncertain.)

θώμισυν, crasis for τὸ ἥμισυ.

θωμός, ὁ, = σωρός, a heap, Aesch. (Like θημών, from τί-θημι.)

θωπεία, ἡ, flattery, adulation, Eur., Ar.; and

θώπευμα, ατος, τό, a piece of flattery, Ar.; pl. caresses, Eur.:—Dim. θωπευμάτια, τά, bits of flattery, Ar.

θωπεύω, f. σω, (θώψ) to flatter, fawn on, cajole, wheedle, Lat. adulari, Soph., Eur., etc.; σὺ ταῦτα θώπευ᾽ be it thine to flatter thus, Soph.:—to caress or pat a horse, Xen.

θῶπλα, crasis for τὰ ὅπλα.

θώπτω, = θωπεύω, Aesch.

θωρᾱκεῖον, τό, = θώραξ III, a breast-work, Aesch.

θωρᾱκίζω, f. ίσω, (θώραξ) to arm with a breastplate or corslet, Xen.:—Med. to put on one's breastplate, Id.:—Pass., θωρακισθείς with one's breastplate on, Id.; οἱ τεθωρακισμένοι cuirassiers, Thuc., Xen. II. generally, to cover with defensive armour, ἐθωράκισε πλὴν τῶν ὀφθαλμῶν Xen.

θωρᾱκο-ποιός, όν, (ποιέω) making breastplates, Xen.

θωρᾱκο-πώλης, ου, ὁ, (πωλέω) a dealer in breastplates, Ar.

θωρᾱκο-φόρος, Ion. θωρηκ-, ον, (φέρω) wearing a breastplate, a cuirassier, Hdt., Xen.

θώραξ, ᾱκος, Ion. and Ep. θώρηξ, ηκος, ὁ: (θωρήσσω): —a breastplate, cuirass, corslet, Lat. lorica, Il.:— the breast and back pieces which composed it were called γύαλα, which were fastened by clasps (ὀχεῖς) on both sides. II. the part covered by the breastplate, the trunk, Eur., Plat. III. the breastwork of a wall, the outer wall, Hdt.

θωρηκοφόρος, ον, Ion. for θωρακοφόρος.

θωρηκτής, οῦ, ὁ, (θωρήσσω) armed with breastplate, Il.

θώρηξ, ηκος, ὁ, Ion. for θώραξ.

θωρήσσω, Ep. aor. 1 θώρηξα, subj. θωρήξομεν (for -ωμεν): = θωρακίζω, to arm with breastplate: and, generally, to arm, get men under arms, Il. 2. Med. and Pass., θωρήσσομαι, f. ξομαι: aor. 1 ἐθωρήχθην :—to arm oneself, put one's harness on, Hom.; τεύχε᾽ ἐνείκω θωρηχθῆναι I will bring you arms to arm yourselves withal, Od.; πρὸς τοὺς πολεμίους θωρήξομαι Ar. II. to make drunk, to intoxicate, Theogn.:— Med. to drink unmixed wine, to get drunk, Id.

ΘΩΣ, θωός, ὁ, also ἡ, the jackal, Il., Hdt.

θωυκτήρ, ῆρος, ὁ, a barker, roarer, crier, Anth.

θωῦμα, θωυμάζω, incorrect forms for θῶμα, θωμάζω.

θωΰσσω, f. ξω, make a noise, of a gnat, to buzz, Aesch.; of men, to cry aloud, shout out, Trag. 2. c. acc. pers. to call on, call, Soph.; also c. dat., θ. κυσί to shout to dogs, Eur. (Deriv. uncertain.)

ΘΩ΄Ψ, gen. θωπός, ὁ, a flatterer, fawner, false friend, Hdt.:—as Adj., θῶπες λόγοι fawning speeches, Plat.

I.

Ι, ι, ἰῶτα, τό, indecl., ninth letter of the Gr. alphabet: as numeral ι΄ = 10, but ͺι = 10,000.

The ι subscriptum was called ι προσγεγραμμένον, adscriptum, and was so written till the 13th century, τῶι (not τῷ), as is still done in capital letters ΤΩΙ. Changes of ι: 1. Dor., ι for υ in the 3 pl. and part. pres., as φιλέοισι ἐοῖσα for φιλέουσι, etc.; so also Μοῖσα Ἀρέθοισα for Μοῦσα, etc.:—it was added to α in some Adjs., and in the aor. 1 part., as μέλαις τάλαις ῥίψαις for μέλας, etc.; and in the acc. pl. fem. of 1st decl., as ταὶς νύμφαις for τὰς νύμφας. 2. Boeot. and Lacon. as σιός, σεῖος, for θεός, θεῖος. 3. ῑ easily passes into ει, whence forms like εἵλω ἵλλω, εἵλη ἵλη, εἵρην ἰρήν; ῑ was sometimes exchanged with ε, as in ἑστία, Ion. ἱστίη:—often inserted to lengthen the syll., e.g. εἰν εἰς ξεῖνος κεινός πνείω ὑπείρ διαί μεταί παραί, for εν, ες, etc. The Quantity of ι varies.

-ῑ [ῑ], iota demonstrativum, in familiar Att. (not in Trag.), is attached to demonstr. Pronouns, to strengthen their force, as οὑτοσί αὑτηῒ τουτί, Lat. hicce; ἐκεινοσί ὁδί ταδί τοσουτονί τοσονδί τυννουτοσί, etc.; also to demonstr. Advs., as οὑτωσί ὡδί ἐνθαδί δευρί νυνί.

Ἵ, nom. of the reflex. Pron. οὗ, sui, Plat.:—dat. ἵν αὑτῷ, sibi ipsi, Hes.; ἵν (enclit.) Pind.

ἸΑ΄, Ion. ἰή, ἡ, a voice, cry, Orac. ap. Hdt., Aesch., Eur.

ἴα, ἴης, ἴῃ, ἴαν, old Ion. fem. of εἷς, for μία, μιῆς, etc.

ἰά [ῑ], τά, heterocl. pl. of ἰός, an arrow, Il.

ἰάθην [ᾱ], aor. pass. of ἰάομαι.

ἰαιβοῖ [ῑ], Comic exclamation for αἰβοῖ, Ar.

ἸΑΙ΄ΝΩ, aor. 1 ἵηνα, Dor. ἵᾱνα:—Pass., aor. 1 ἰάνθην:— to heat, Od. 2. to melt:—Pass. to be melted, Ib. 3. to warm, cheer, Lat. fovere, θυμὸν ἰαίνειν Ib., etc.:—Pass., ἐν φρεσὶ θυμὸς ἰάνθη Ib.; μέτωπον ἰάνθη her brow unfolded, Il.; c. dat. rei, to take delight in, Od.

ἰαχάζω, to shout Ἴακχος; c. acc. cogn., ἰακχάζειν φωνήν to utter the cry Ἴακχος, Hdt.

ἰακχεῖον, τό, (Ἴακχος) a temple of Bacchus, Plut.

ἰακχέω, ἰακχή, v. ἰαχέω, ἰαχή.

ἰάκχιος, ία, ιον, Bacchanalian, Soph. From

Ἴακχος, ὁ, (ἰαχέω) Iacchus, mystic name of Bacchus, Ar., etc. 2. a festal song in his honour, Hdt., etc.

ἰαλεμίστρια, Ion. ἰηλ-, ἡ, a wailing woman, Aesch.

ἰάλεμος [ᾱ], Ion. ἰήλ-, ὁ, a wail, lament, dirge, Aesch., Eur. II. as Adj., hapless, melancholy, Theocr. (Prob. from the cry ἰή.)

ἸΑ΄ΛΛΩ, f. ἰᾱλῶ: aor. 1 ἵηλα:—to send forth, ὀϊστὸν ἀπὸ νευρῆφιν ἴαλλεν Il.; ἐπ᾽ ὀνείατα χεῖρας ἴαλλον they put forth their hands to the dishes, Hom.; περὶ χερσὶ δεσμὸν ἵηλα threw chains around thy arms, Il. 2. to attack, assail, ἀτιμίῃσιν ἰάλλειν τινά to assail him with reproaches, Od. 3. to send, Theogn., Aesch. II. intr. (sub. ἑαυτόν, to send oneself on, i.e. to flee, run, fly, Hes. Hence

ἰαλτός, ή, όν, verb. Adj. *sent forth*, Aesch.

ἴαμα, Ion. ἴημα, ατος, τό, (ἰάομαι) *a means of healing, remedy, medicine*, Hdt., Thuc. II. = ἴασις, N.T.

ἰαμβεῖος, ον, (ἴαμβος) *iambic, μέτρον* Arist. II. as Subst., ἰαμβεῖον, τό, *an iambic verse*, Ar., Plat. 2. *iambic metre*, Arist. Hence

ἰαμβειο-φάγος, ὁ, (φαγεῖν) *a glutton at iambics*, or perhaps *a murderer of them*, Dem.

ἰαμβιάζω, =sq., Anth.

ἰαμβίζω, *to assail in iambics, to lampoon*, Arist.

ἰαμβικός, ή, όν, *iambic*, Arist.

ἰαμβοποιέω. *to write iambics*, Arist. From

ἰαμβο-ποιός, ὁ, (ποιέω) *a writer of iambics*, Arist.

ἴαμβος, ὁ, *an iambus*, a metrical foot consisting of a short and long syll., as ἐγώ, Plat., etc. II. *an iambic verse*, the trimeter or *senarius*, Hdt., Ar. 2. *an iambic poem, lampoon*, Plat. (From ἰάπτω 2, because iambics were first used by the satiric poets Archilochus and Hipponax; *criminosi iambi*, Horat.)

Ἰάν, ὁ, contr. for Ἰάων, *an Ionian*, Aesch. [who has gen. pl. Ἰάνων with ᾰ].

ἰάνθην, aor. 1 pass. of ἰαίνω.

ΙΑ'ΟΜΑΙ, imper. ἰῶ: f. ἰάσομαι [ᾱ], Ion. ἰήσομαι: aor. 1 ἰᾱσάμην, Ion. ἰησάμην:—Pass., v. infr.—[ῑᾱ– Hom., etc.; later also ῐ]:—*to heal, cure*, Hom., etc.:—metaph., ἀδικίαν ἰᾶσθαι Eur.: proverb., μὴ τῷ κακῷ τὸ κακὸν ἰῶ, i. e. do not make bad worse, Hdt. II. the aor. 1 ἰάθην [ᾱ] is always pass., *to be healed, to recover*, Andoc., N. T.; so pf. ἴαμαι N. T.

Ἰάοναῦ, barbarism for Ἰάον (voc.), *O Ionian*, Ar.

Ἰάονες [ᾰ], οἱ, lengthd. for Ἴωνες, *the Ionians*, including, Il.:—in Persian it was=Ἕλληνες, Aesch.:—sing. Ἰάων rare, Theocr.:—Ἰαόνιος, α, ον, *Ionian, Greek*, Aesch.; *Athenian*, Orac. ap. Plut.

ΙΑ'ΠΤΩ, f. ψω, *to send on, put forth*, Hom.; κατὰ χρόα ἰάπτειν (sc. τὰς χεῖρας) *to put forth* (her hands) *against her body*, i. e. smite her breasts for grief, Od.:—of missiles, *to send forth, shoot*, Aesch.; ἰάπτειν ὀρχήματα *to begin the dance*, Soph. 2. *to assail, attack*, Id.: *to wound*, ἰ. τινὰ ἐς ὀστέον ἄχρις Theocr.: Pass., ἰάπτομαι ἄλγεσιν ἦτορ Mosch.

Ἰᾶπυξ, Ion. Ἰῆπυξ, ῡγος, ὁ, *the NW* or *WNW wind*, Arist. II. Ἰάπυγες, Ion. Ἰῆπ–, οἱ, *a people of Southern Italy*, Hdt.:—ἡ Ἰᾱπυγία, Ion. Ἰηπ–, *their country*, Id.:—Adj. Ἰᾱπύγιος, α, ον, *Iapygian*, Thuc.

Ἰάς, άδος, ἡ, Adj. fem. of Ἰάων, Ἴων, *Ionian, Ionic*, Hdt., Thuc. II. as Subst. (sub. γυνή), *an Ionian woman*, Hdt. 2. (sub. γλῶσσα) *the Ionic dialect*, Luc.

ἴᾱσι [ῐ], 3 pl. pres. of εἶμι (*ibo*).

ἰᾶσι [ῐ], for ἰέασι, 3 pl. pres. of ἵημι.

ἰάσιμος [ᾱ], ον, (ἰάομαι) *to be cured, curable*, opp. to ἀνίατος, Aesch., Plat., etc.: metaph. *appeasable*, Eur.

ἴᾱσις [ῐ], εως, ἡ, (ἰάομαι) *healing, a mode of healing, cure, remedy*, Lat. *medela*, Soph., Plat., etc.

ἴασπις, ιδος, ἡ, *jasper*, Anth. (A foreign word.)

Ἰαστί [τῐ], Adv. (Ἰάς) *in Ionic fashion*, Plat. 2. *in the Ionic mode* (of music), Id. 3. *in the Ionic dialect*, Luc.

Ἰασώ, όος, contr. οῦς, ἡ, voc. Ἰασοῖ, (ἰάομαι) *Iāso, the goddess of healing*, Ar.

ἰᾱτήρ [ῐ], Ep. ἰητήρ, ῆρος, ὁ, poët. for ἰατρός, Il., etc.: metaph., ἰ. κακῶν Od., Soph.

ἰᾶτο, 3 sing. impf. of ἰάομαι.

ἰᾱτορία, ἡ, *the art of healing, surgery*, Soph.

ἰᾱτός, ή, όν, (ἰάομαι) *curable*, Pind., Plat.

ἰᾱτρεία, ἡ, (ἰατρεύω) *medical treatment*: metaph. *a curing, correcting*, Arist.

ἰᾱτρεῖον, τό, (ἰατρός) *a surgery*, Plat., etc.

ἰᾱτρευμα, ατος, τό, = ἴαμα: in Rhet. *a means of healing disaffection in the hearers*, Arist.

ἰᾱτρευσις, εως, ἡ, = ἰατρεία, Plat.

ἰᾱτρεύω, f. σω, (ἰατρός) *to treat medically, to cure*, Plat.:—Pass. *to be under medical care*, Id. 2. absol. *to practise medicine*, Arist.

ἰᾱτρικός, Ion. ἰητρ–, ή, όν, (ἰατρός) *of* or *for a surgeon*: —ἡ -κή (sc. τέχνη), *surgery, medicine*, Hdt., Plat., etc. II. *skilled in the medical art*, Plat.: metaph., ἰ. περὶ τὴν ψυχήν Id.

ἰᾱτρό-μαντις, εως, ὁ, *physician and seer*, of Apollo and Aesculapius, Aesch., Ar.: metaph., Ar.

ἰᾱτρός [ῐ], Ion. ἰητρός, ὁ, (ἰάομαι) like ἰατήρ, *one who heals, a mediciner, physician* or *surgeon* (for there seems to have been no professional distinction), Il., etc.: —ἰ. ὀφθαλμῶν, ὀδόντων *an oculist, dentist*, Hdt. II. metaph., ἰατρ. πόνων Pind.; ὀργῆς Aesch.

ἰᾱτρο-τέχνης, ου, ὁ, (τέχνη) *a practiser of medicine*, Ar.

ἰαττᾱταί, Interj. *alas! ah! woe's me!* Ar.; so, ἰατταταιάξ Id.

ἰαῦ, *a shout in answer to one calling, ho! holla!* Ar.

ἰαυοῖ, *exclamation of joy, ho ho!* Ar.

ἰαύω, Ion. impf. ἰαύεσκον: f. σω: aor. 1 ἴαυσα: (ἄω, ἄημι):—*to sleep, to pass the night*, Hom.:—c. acc. cogn., ἐννυχίαν τέρψιν ἰαύειν *to enjoy* the night's sleep, Soph.

ἰ-ἀφέτης [ῐ], ου, ὁ, (ἰός, ἀφίημι) *an archer*, Anth.

ἰᾱχέω, f. ήσω: aor. 1 ἰάχησα:—*to cry, shout, shriek*, like ἰάχω, Eur., etc.:—c. acc. cogn., ἰαχεῖν μέλος Id.; ἀοιδάν Ar. 2. *to bewail, lament*, Eur. II. of things, *to sound*, h. Hom., Eur. From

ἰᾱχή, ἡ, (ἰάχω) *a cry, shout, wail, shriek*, Hom.: also *a joyous sound*, ἰαχὰ ὑμεναίων Pind., Trag. Hence

ἰάχημα, ατος, τό, (ἰαχέω) *a cry*: *the hissing* of a serpent, Eur.: *the sound* of an instrument, Anth.

ΙΑ'ΧΩ [ᾰ]: Ion. impf. ἰάχεσκον: pf. ἴαχα, Ep. part. fem. ἰαχυῖα:—*to cry, shout, shriek*, in sign either of joy or grief, like ἰαχέω, Hom. 2. of articulate speech, Eur., Anth. 2. of things, *to ring, resound*, Hom.; of waves and of fire, *to roar*, Id.; of a bowstring, *to twang*, Il.; of hot iron in water, *to hiss*, Od. 3. c. acc. cogn., ἰ. ἀοιδήν, μέλος *to sound forth* a strain, h. Hom.; ἰ. λογίων ὁδόν *to proclaim* the sense of oracles, Ar.; ἴαχον Ἀπόλλω *were sounding* his praises, Id.

Ἰάων, ονος, ὁ, v. Ἰάονες.

ἶβις, ἡ: gen. ἴβιος, acc. ἴβιν: pl. ἴβιες, Ion. ἴβῑς:—*the ibis*, an Egyptian bird, Hdt., Ar.

ΙΓΔΙΣ, ἡ, *a mortar*, Solon, Anth.

ἴγμαι, pf. of ἱκνέομαι:—ἱγμένος, part.

ἰγνύα, Ion. ἰγνύη, ἡ, =sq., *the part behind the thigh and knee, the ham*, Lat. *poples*, Il., Theocr.

ἰγνύς, ύος, ἡ, =foreg., from a nom. dat. pl. ἰγνύσι h. Hom.; acc. ἰγνύα Theocr. (Deriv. unknown.)

Ἰδαῖος, α, ον, (Ἴδη) *of Ida*, Il.

ἰδάλιμος, ον, (ίδος) *causing sweat*, Hes.

ἰδέ [ῐ], Ep. Conjunction=ἠδέ, *and*, Hom., Soph.

ἰδέ, imperat. aor. of εἶδον, lo, behold, Hom. : later ἴδε.
ἴδε, Ep. 3 sing. of aor. 2 εἶδον, he saw.
ἰδέα [ῐ], Ion. ἰδέη, ἡ, (ἰδεῖν) = εἶδος, form, Pind., Ar., etc. 2. the look of a thing, as opp. to its reality, Lat. species, γνώμην ἐξαπατῶσ' ἰδέαι outward appearances cheat the mind, Theogn. 3. a kind, sort, nature, Hdt.; ἐφρόνεον διφασίας ἰδέας they conceived two modes of acting, Id.; τὰ ὀργι' ἐστὶ τίν' ἰδέαν ἔχοντα; what is their nature or fashion? Eur.; καινὰς ἰδέας εἰσφέρειν to bring in new fashions, Ar.; πᾶσα ἰδέα θανάτου every form of death, Thuc. II. in Logic, = εἶδος, a class, kind, sort, species, Plat.
ἰδεῖν, aor. 2 inf. of εἶδον; Ep. ἰδέειν; Dor. ἰδέμεν.
ἰδέσθαι, inf. med. of εἶδον.
ἴδεσκον, Ion. for εἶδον.
ἰδέω, Ion. for ἴδω, aor. 2 subj. of εἶδον. II. Ep. for εἰδῶ, pf. subj. of οἶδα, to know.
ἼΔΗ, Dor. ἴδα, ἡ, Ion. dat. pl. ἴδῃσι :—a timber-tree, in pl., Hdt. :—in sing., a wood, ἐν τῇ ἴδῃ τῇ πλείστῃ in the thick of the wood, Id. II. as prop. n., Ἴδη, Ida, i. e. the wooded hill, Mt. Ida, Il.; Ep. gen., Ἴδηθεν μεδέων ruler of Ida, Ib.; as Adv. from Ida, Ib.
ἴδηαι, Ep. for ἴδῃ, 2 sing. subj. aor. 2 med. εἰδόμην.
ἰδησῶ, Dor. f. of εἶδον, I shall see, Theocr.
ἰδίᾳ, v. ἴδιος IV. 2.
ἰδιαίτερος, -ατος, irreg. Comp. and Sup. of ἴδιος.
ἰδιο-βουλέω or -εύω, (βουλή) to follow one's own counsel, take one's own way, Hdt.
ἰδιο-γνώμων, ον, holding one's own opinion, Arist.
ἰδιό-μορφος, ον, (μορφή) of peculiar form, Plut.
ἴδιον, τό, v. ἴδιος I. 2.
ἰδιόομαι, (ἴδιος) Med. to appropriate to oneself, Plat.
ἼΔΙΟΣ [ῐδ], α, ον, and ος, ον : I. one's own, pertaining to oneself : and so, 1. private, personal, πρῆξις ἥδ' ἰδίη οὐ δήμιος this business is private, not public, Od.; ἴδιος ἐν κοινῷ σταλείς embarking a private man in a public cause, Pind.; πλοῦτος ἴδιος καὶ δημόσιος private and public wealth, Thuc.; τὰ ἱρὰ καὶ τὰ ἴδια temples and private buildings, Id. 2. τὰ ἴδια, either private affairs, private interests, Thuc.; or one's own property, Id.; ἴδια πράττειν to mind one's own affairs, Eur.; τὰ ἐμὰ ἴδια Dem. :—in sing., τὸ ἡμέτερον ἴδιον Id.; εἰς τὸ ἴδιον for oneself, Xen.; τοὐμὸν ἴδιον for my own part, Luc. II. peculiar, separate, distinct, ἔθνος ἴδιον Hdt.; ἴδιοί τινες θεοί Ar.; ἴδιον ἢ ἄλλοι peculiar and different from others, Plat.; strange, unaccustomed, ἰδίοισιν ὑμεναίοισι Eur. III. regul. Comp. is ἰδιώτερος; Sup. ἰδιώτατος, Dem.; later ἰδιαίτερος, -αίτατος, Arist. IV. Adv. ἰδίως, especially, peculiarly, Plat., etc. 2. also ἰδίᾳ, Ion. -ίῃ, as Adv. by oneself, privately, separately, on one's own account, Hdt., etc.; οὔτε ἰδίᾳ οὔτε ἐν κοινῷ Thuc.; καὶ ἰδίᾳ καὶ δημοσίᾳ Id. :—c. gen. apart from, Ar.
ἰδιό-στολος, ον, (στέλλω) equipt at one's own expense, Plut.; ἰδ. ἔπλευσα sailed in his own ship, Id.
ἰδιότης, ητος, ἡ, (ἴδιος) peculiar nature, property, Xen.
ἰδίω [ῐδ-], only used in Med. ἰδίομαι, q. v.
ἰδίω [ῐδ-], (ἴδος) to sweat, Od., Ar.
ἰδίως, Adv. of ἴδιος IV.
ἰδίωσις, εως, ἡ, (ἰδιόομαι) distinction between, Plat.

ἰδιωτεία, ἡ, private life or business, Xen., Plat. II. uncouthness, want of education, Luc.; and
ἰδιωτεύω, f. σω, to be a private person, i. e. to live in retirement, Plat., Xen. :—of a country, to be of no consideration, Xen. II. to practise privately, of a physician, Plat. III. c. gen. rei, to be unpractised in a thing, Id. From
ἰδιώτης, ου, ὁ, (ἴδιος) a private person, an individual, ξυμφέροντα καὶ πόλεσι καὶ ἰδιώταις Thuc., etc. II. one in a private station, opp. to one taking part in public affairs, Hdt., Att.; opp. to στρατηγός, a private soldier, Xen. 2. a common man, plebeian, Plut. 3. as Adj., ἰδ. βίος a private station, homely way of life, Plat. III. one who has no professional knowledge, as we say 'a layman,' ἰατρὸς καὶ ἰδιώτης Thuc.; opp. to ποιητής, a prose-writer, Plat.; to a trained soldier, Thuc.; to a skilled workman, Plat. 2. c. gen. rei, unpractised, unskilled in a thing, Lat. expers, rudis, ἰατρικῆς Id.; also, ἰδ. κατά τι Xen. 3. generally, a raw hand, an ignorant, ill-informed man, Id., Dem. IV. ἰδιῶται one's own countrymen, opp. to ξένοι, Ar. Hence
ἰδιωτικός, ή, όν, of or for a private person, private, Hdt., Att. II. not done by rules of art, unprofessional, unskilful, rude, Plat. :—Adv., ἰδιωτικῶς τὸ σῶμα ἔχειν, i. e. to neglect gymnastic exercises, Xen.
ἴδμεν, Ion. and Dor. for ἴσμεν, 1 pl. of οἶδα. II.
ἴδμεν, ἴδμεναι, Ep. for εἰδέναι, inf. of οἶδα.
ἰδμοσύνη, ἡ, knowledge, skill, Hes. From
ἴδμων, ον, gen. ονος, (ἴδμεν II) skilled, skilful, τινός in a thing, Anth.
ἸΑΝΟΌΜΑΙ, aor. 1 ἰανώθην, Pass. to bend oneself, double oneself up, shrink up, esp. for pain, Il.; ἰανωθεὶς ὀπίσω bent back, of one throwing up a ball, Hom.
ἰδοίατο, Ion. for ἴδοιντο, 3 pl. opt. med. of εἶδον.
ἰδοῖσα, Dor. for ἰδοῦσα, part. fem. of εἶδον.
Ἰδο-μενεύς, έως Ep. ῆος, ὁ, the chief of the Cretans, properly Strength of Ida (in Crete), Il.
ἴδον, Ep. for εἶδον.
ἼΔΟΣ, εος, τό, 2. violent heat, as of the dog-days, Hes. II. sweat.
ἰδού, imper. of aor. 2 med. εἰδόμην :—as Adv. lo! behold! see there! Soph.; ἰδού, δέχου there! take it! Lat. en tibi! Id., etc. :—well, as you please! Ar. 2. in repeating another's words quizzingly, ἰδού γ' ἄκρατον oh yes, wine, Id.
ἰδρεία, Ion. -είη, ἡ, skill, ἰδρείῃ πολέμοιο Il. From
ἴδρις, gen. ἴδριος Att. ἴδρεως, ὁ, ἡ, neut. ἴδρι : voc. ἴδρι : pl. ἴδριες : (ἴδμεν II) :—experienced, knowing, skilful, Od.; c. gen. rei, Hes., Trag., etc.; c. inf. knowing how to do, Od. 2. ἴδρις alone, the provident one, i. e. the ant, Hes.
ἰδρόω [ῐ], Ep. part. ἰδρώων : f. ώσω : aor. 1 ἵδρωσα : pf. ἵδρωκα : (ἴδος) :—to sweat, perspire, Hom. (esp. in Il.); ἵππους ὑπὸ ζυγοῦ ἰδρώοντας Od.; ἰδρώσει τελαμὼν it shall reek with sweat, Il.; c. acc. cogn., ἱδρῷ θ' ὃν ἵδρωσα Ib. :—This Verb, like its oppos. ῥιγόω, is contracted Ep. into ω and φ instead of ου and οι, part. fem. ἱδρώσα Il., lengthd. ἱδρώωσα, masc. acc. ἱδρώοντα, -οντας; but in Xen. we find ἱδροῦντι, not ἱδρῶντι.
ἰδρύθην [ῡ], aor. 1 pass. of ἱδρύω.
ἵδρυμα, ατος, τό, (ἱδρύω) a thing founded or built, a

foundation, Plut.   **2.** like ἕδος, *a temple, shrine,* Hdt., Aesch., Eur.   **3.** τὸ σὸν ἵδρυμα πόλεως the *stay, support* of thy city, Lat. *columen rei,* Eur.

ἵδρῦμαι, pf. pass. of ἱδρύω.

ἵδρῦσις, εως, ἡ, (ἱδρύω) *a founding, building,* of temples, Plat.   **2.** Ἑρμέω ἱδρύσιες his *statues,* Anth.

ἱδρῦτέον, verb. Adj. of ἱδρύω, *one must inaugurate a* statue, Ar.   **II.** pass., ἱδρυτέον *one must sit idle,* Soph.

ἱδρύω, f. ύσω : aor. 1 ἵδρῦσα : pf. ἵδρῦκα :—Pass., aor. 1 ἱδρύθην (not ἱδρύνθην) : pf. ἵδρῦμαι, inf. ἱδρῦσθαι : (ἵζω) : —*to make to sit down, to seat,* Hom., etc.; αὐτός τε κάθησο καὶ ἄλλους ἵδρυε λαούς Il.; ἵδρυσε τὴν στρατιήν *encamped* the army, Hdt.:—Pass. *to be seated, sit still,* Il., Eur.; of an army, *to lie encamped,* Hdt.; ἀσφαλῶς ἱδρυμένος *seated, steady, secure,* Id.   **2.** like Lat. *figere, to fix* or *settle* persons in a place, εἰς δόμον Eur.—Pass. *to be settled,* Hdt., Soph., etc.   **3.** in Med. *to establish,* ἱδρ. τινὰ ἄνακτα Eur.; τινὰ ἐς οἰκόν Id.   **4.** pf. pass. ἵδρῦμαι, of places, *to be situated, to lie,* Hdt.   **II.** *to set up, found,* esp. *to dedicate* temples, statues, Eur., Ar.:—Pass., ἱρόν, βωμὸς ἵδρυται Hdt.:—Med. *to set up for oneself, to found,* Id., Eur.; pf. pass. in med. sense, Hdt., Plat.

ἱδρώην, Att. opt. of ἱδρόω.

ἱδρώς [ῑ], ῶτος, ὁ, dat. ἱδρῶτι, acc. ἱδρῶτα, Ep. shortd. ἱδρῷ, ἱδρῶ : (ῖδος) :—*sweat,* Lat. *sudor,* Hom., Att.   **2.** the *exudation* of trees, *gum,* σμύρνης Eur.

ἱδρῶσαι, part. pl. fem. of ἱδρόω.

ἰδυῖα [ῐ], ἡ, Ep. for εἰδυῖα, part. fem. of οἶδα :—as Adj., ἰδυίῃσι πραπίδεσσιν with *knowing, skilful mind,* Il.

ἴδω, Ep. ἴδωμι, subj. of εἶδον.

ἰδών, οῦσα, όν, part. of εἶδον.

ἱέ, ἱέν, Ep. 3 sing. impf. of εἶμι (*ibo*).

ἵει, Ion. and Att. 3 sing. impf. of ἵημι (from ἱέω).

ἱείη, Ep. for ἵοι, 3 sing. pres. opt. of εἶμι (*ibo*).

ἱείς, εἶσα, ἔν, part. of ἵημι.

ἱεῖσι, for ἵᾶσι, 3 pl. of ἵημι.

ἵεμαι, pass. of ἵημι.

ἱέμεν, ἱέμεναι, Ep. inf. pres. of ἵημι :—ἱέμενος, part. pres. pass.

ἵεν, Aeol. for ἵεσαν, 3 pl. impf. of ἵημι.

ἱέναι, inf. of εἶμι (*ibo*).

ἱέναι, inf. of ἵημι.

ἱεράκίσκος, ὁ, Dim. of ἱέραξ, Ar.

ἹΕ'ΡΑΞ, ᾱκος, Ion. and Ep. ἵρηξ, ηκος, ὁ, *a hawk, falcon,* Il., Ar.

ἱεράομαι, Ion. ἱρ-, f. άσομαι [ᾱ], (ἱερεύς, ἱέρεια) Pass. *to be a priest* or *priestess,* Hdt., Thuc.

ἱερᾱτεία, ἡ, the *priest's office, priesthood,* Arist., N. T.

ἱεράτευμα, ατος, τό, *a priesthood,* N. T.; and **ἱερᾱτευματικός, ἡ, όν,** *priestly,* Plut. From **ἱερᾱτεύω,** f. σω, (ἱερεύς) *to be a priest,* N. T.

ἱερᾱτικός, ἡ, όν, (ἱερεύς) *of* or *for the priest's office, priestly,* Arist., Plut.   **II.** *devoted to sacred purposes,* Luc.

ἱέρεια, ἡ, Ion. ἵρεια, ἱερείη or ἱρήτη, in Trag. also ἱερία :—fem. of ἱερεύς, *a priestess,* Il., Att.

ἱερεῖον, Ion. ἱερήιον or ἱρήιον, τό, *a victim, an animal for sacrifice* or *slaughter,* Hom., Hdt., Att.   **2.** *an*

offering for the dead, Od.   **II.** of *cattle slaughtered for food,* mostly in pl., Hdt., Xen.

ἱερεύς, έως Ion. ῆος, ὁ, Att. pl. ἱερῆς : Ion. nom. ἱρεύς : (ἱερός) :—*a priest, sacrificer,* Il., etc.   **2.** metaph., ἱερεύς τις ἄτης *a minister* of woe, Aesch.; and, comically, λεπτοτάτων λήρων ἱερεῦ Ar.

ἱερεύω, Ion. ἱρεύω : Ion. impf. ἱρεύεσκον : f. εύσω, Ep. inf. -ευσέμεν : 3 sing. plqpf. pass. ἱέρευτο : (ἱερός) :— *to slaughter* for sacrifice, *to sacrifice,* Hom.   **2.** *to slaughter* for a feast, Od. : Med. *to slaughter for oneself,* Ib.

ἱερή, ἡ, = ἱέρεια, Anth.

ἱερήιον, τό, Ion. for ἱερεῖον.

ἱερία, poët. for ἱέρεια.

ἱερογλῠφικός, ή, όν, *hieroglyphic ;* ἱερογλυφικά (sc. γράμματα), τά, *a way of writing on monuments* used by the Egyptian priests, Luc.

ἱερό-γλωσσος, ον, (γλῶσσα) *of prophetic tongue,* Anth.

ἱερο-γραμματεύς, έως, ὁ, *a sacred scribe,* a lower order of the Egyptian priesthood, Luc.

ἱερό-θῠτος, ον, (θύω Α) *offered to a god,* ἱερ. καπνός smoke *from the sacrifices,* Ar.

ἱερο-κῆρυξ, ῠκος, ὁ, the *herald at a sacrifice,* Dem.

ἱερολογία, Ion. ἱρολογίη, ἡ, (λόγος) *sacred* or *mystical language,* Luc.

ἱερο-μηνία, ἡ, (μήν, μήνη) the *holy time of the month,* during which the great festivals were held and hostilities suspended, ἱερ. Νεμέας, of the Nemean games, Pind., Thuc. :—ἱερομήνια, τά, of the Carneian festival at Sparta, Thuc.

ἱερομνημονέω, *to be* ἱερομνήμων, Ar.

ἱερο-μνήμων, ονος, ὁ, Dor. -μνάμων, ονος, ὁ, the *sacred Secretary* or *Recorder* sent by each Amphictyonic state to their Council, Dem. :—generally, *a recorder, notary,* Arist.

ἱερόν, τό, v. ἱερός III. 2.

ἱερο-νίκης [νῑ], ου, ὁ, *conqueror in the games,* Luc.

ἱεροποιέω, f. ήσω, *to offer sacrifices, to sacrifice,* Dem.

ἱερο-ποιός, όν, (ποιέω) *managing sacred rites :* at Athens, the ἱεροποιοί were *ten magistrates,* one from each tribe, *who saw that the victims were perfect,* Plat., Dem.

ἱερο-πρεπής, ές, (πρέπω) *beseeming a sacred place, person* or *matter, holy, reverend,* Plat., Luc. ; ἱεροπρεπέστατος Xen.

ἱερ-οργίη, *a false form for* ἱρ-ουργίη in Hdt.

ἹΕΡΟ'Σ, ά, όν and ός, όν : Ion. and poët. ἱρός, ή, όν : —*super-human, mighty, divine, wonderful,* Hom. ; often like θεσπέσιος, to express wonder or admiration, ἱερὸν τέλος, ἱερὸς στρατός *a glorious* band, Id. ; ἱερὸς δίφρος *a splendid* chariot, Il. ; οὐχ ἱερόν no *mighty matter !* Theocr.   **II.** *holy, hallowed,* Lat. *sacer,* Hom., etc. ; ἱερὸς πόλεμος *a holy war,* Ar., etc. : ἱρὰ γράμματα, = ἱερογλυφικά, Hdt. ; ἱερὸν τὸ σῶμα διδόναι, of one *dedicated* to a god, Eur. ; ἱερὸς νόμος the law *of sacrifice,* Dem. ; of the Roman Tribunes, to express *sacrosanctus,* Plut. ; for ἱερὰ καὶ ὅσια, v. ὅσιος.   **2.** of kings, heroes, etc., from a notion of ' the divinity that doth hedge a king,' Pind., Soph.   **III.** as Subst.   **1.** ἱερά, Ion. ἱρά, τά, *offerings, sacrifices, victims,* ἱερὰ ῥέξειν, Lat. *sacra facere, operari,* Il. ; ἔρδειν Hes. ; θῦσαι Hdt. :—after Hom. the *inwards*

of the victim, the auspices, τὰ ἱερὰ καλὰ ἦν Xen. ; or, simply, τὰ ἱερὰ γίγνεται Id. :—generally, sacred things or rites, Lat. sacra, Hdt. 2. ἱερόν, Ion. ἱρόν, τό, a temple, holy place, Id., Att. 3. ἱρὸν τῆς δίκης a sacred principle of right, Eur. IV. special phrases: 1. ἱερὸς λόχος, v. λόχος I. 4. 2. ἱερὰ νόσος the awful disease, epilepsy, Hdt. 3. ἡ ἱ. ὁδός the sacred road to Delphi, Id. 4. ἡ ἱερά (sc. τριήρης), of the Delian ship, or one of the state-ships (Salaminia or Paralos), Dem. 5. Ἱερὰ νῆσος, one of the Liparean group, Thuc. V. Adv. -ρῶς, holily, Plut.

ἱεροσῡλέω, f. ήσω, to rob a temple, commit sacrilege, Ar., Plat.:—c. acc., ἱερ. τὰ ὅπλα to steal the sacred arms, Dem.

ἱεροσῡλία, ἡ, temple-robbery, sacrilege, Xen., Plat.

ἱερό-σῡλος, ὁ, (συλάω) a temple-robber, sacrilegious person, Lat. sacrilegus, Ar., Plat.

ἱερουργέω, f. ήσω, to perform sacred rites : c. acc., ἱερ. τὸ εὐαγγέλιον to minister the gospel, N. T. ; so in Med., ἱερουργίας ἱερουργεῖσθαι Plut. ; and

ἱερουργία, Ion. ἱροεργίη, ἡ, religious service, worship, sacrifice, Hdt. From

ἱερ-ουργός, ὁ, (*ἔργω) a sacrificing priest.

ἱεροφαντέω, to be a hierophant, Luc. From

ἱερο-φάντης, Ion. ἱρ-, ου, ὁ, (φαίνω) a hierophant, one who teaches the rites of sacrifice and worship, Hdt., Plut. :—at Rome, the Pontifex Maximus, Plut. Hence

ἱεροφαντία, ἡ, the office of hierophant, Plut. ; and

ἱεροφαντικός, ή, όν, of a hierophant, Luc. ; βίβλοι ἱερ. the Libri pontificales, Plut. Adv. -κῶς, Luc.; and

ἱερόφαντις, ιδος, fem. of -φάντης, Plut.

ἱερο-φύλαξ [ŭ], poët. ἱρ-, ἄκος, ὁ, a keeper of a temple, temple-warden, Lat. aedituus, Eur.

ἱερό-χθων, poët. ἱρ-, ὁ, ἡ, of hallowed soil, Anth.

ἱερόω, f. ώσω, (ἱερός) to hallow, consecrate, dedicate, Plat. :—pf. pass. inf. ἱερῶσθαι Thuc.

ἱερωσύνη, Ion. ἱρ-, ἡ, (ἱερεύς) the office of priest, priesthood, Hdt., Att.

ἵεσθαι, inf. med. of ἵημι.

ἱεῦ, an ironical exclamation, whew ! Lat. hui ! Ar.

ἱζάνω, (ἵζω) : I. Causal, to make to sit, Il. II. intr. to sit, Lat. sedere, Od. ; ἐπ' ὅμμασιν ὕπνος ἱζάνει Il. 2. of soil, to settle down, sink in, Thuc.

ἼΖΩ, Dor. ἴσδω, imperat. ἵζε : impf. ἵζον, Ion. ἵζεσκον : aor. 1 εἷσα : (cf. ἕζομαι.) I. Causal, to make to sit, seat, place, μή μ' ἐς θρόνον ἵζε Il. ; ἵζει μάντιν ἐν θρόνοις Aesch. :—the Ion. and poët. aor. 1 εἷσα is always causal (as in the compds. ἐφ-, καθ-εῖσα), εἷσεν ἐν κλισμοῖς, κατὰ κλισμούς, ἐπὶ θρόνου, ἐς δίφρον Hom. ; εἷσέ μ' ἐπὶ βουσί set me over the oxen, Il. ; λόχον εἷσαν laid an ambush, Ib. ; εἷσεν ἐν Σχερίῃ settled [them] in Scheria, Od. ; imperat. εἷσον Ib. ; part. ἕσας Ib. ; so in Hdt., τοῦτον εἷσε ἐς τὸν θρόνον Id. ; ἐπὶ δεῖπνον ἵζειν τοὺς βασιλέας Id. ; inf. ἕσσαι in Pind. ; rare in Att. σὺ γάρ νιν εἷσας ἐς τόδε for thou didst bring it to this, Soph. ; cf. καθίζω. 2. the aor. 1 med. εἱσάμην is used in the sense of ἱδρύω, to dedicate temples statues, etc., to gods, Theogn., Hdt. ; part. εἱσάμενος Thuc. II. intr. to sit, sit down, Lat. sedere, Il. ; ἵζειν ἐς θρόνον Od. ; ἐς θᾶκον Soph. ; also, ἐπὶ θρόνου Hom. ; ἐπὶ τὸ δεῖπνον Hdt. ; ἐπὶ κώπην, of rowers,

Ar. :—c. acc. loci, ἵζειν θρόνον Aesch. ; βωμόν Eur. 2. to sit still, be quiet, h. Hom. III. Pass. also in signf. II, to sit, πάροιθ' ἵζευ ἐμεῖο sit down before me, Il. : to lie in ambush, Ib. : of an army, to sit down, take up a position, ἵζεσθαι ἀντίοι τινί Hdt. ; ἵζεσθαι ἐν τῷ Τηϋγέτῳ or ἐς τὸ Τηΰγετον Id.

ἰή, Lat. io ! exclam. of joy, ἰή, ἰή, ἰή, Ar. ; ἰὴ παιών Id. 2. of grief, Aesch.

ἰή, ἡ, Ion. for ἰά.

ἰήιος, α, ον, and ος, ον, invoked with the cry ἰή, of Apollo, Aesch., etc. II. mournful, grievous, Soph. ; ἰήιος βοά a cry of mourning, Eur.

ἴηλα, aor. 1 of ἰάλλω.

ἰήλεμος, Ion. for ἰάλ-.

ἼΗΜΙ, ἵης, ἵησι, 3 pl. ἱᾶσι, Ion. ἱεῖσι ; imper. ἵει ; subj. ἱῶ ; opt. ἱείην ; inf. ἱέναι, Ep. ἱέμεναι, ἱέμεν ; part. ἱείς : impf. 3 sing. ἵη (also 2 sing. ἵει, as if from ἱέω), 3 pl. ἵεσαν :—aor. 1 ἧκα, Ep. ἕηκα, only in Indic. : aor. 2 ἧν never in Indic., Ep. 3 sing. subj. ᾗσι ; inf. εἷναι : pf. εἷκα : —Med., pres. ἵεμαι, impf. ἱέμην : f. ἥσομαι : aor. 2 εἵμην, Ep. and Ion. ἕμην, 3 pl. ἕντο ; imper. ἕο ; subj. ὧμαι ; opt. εἵμην or ἥμην ; inf. ἕσθαι ; part. ἕμενος :—Pass., f. ἑθήσομαι : aor. 1 εἵθην : pf. εἷμαι. Radical sense : to set a going, put in motion, being the Causal of εἶμι (ibo), ἧκα πόδας καὶ χεῖρε φέρεσθαι Od. ; ἱ. πόδα Eur. : hence 1. to send, Hom., etc. 2. of sounds, to send forth, utter, Id., etc.; Ἑλλάδα γλῶσσαν ἱ. to speak Greek, Hdt. ; φωνὴν Παρνησίδα Aesch. ; τὸ τᾶς εὐφήμου στόμα φροντίδος ἱέντες, i. e. speaking not in words, but in silent thought, Soph. 3. to send forth, throw, hurl, of stones or javelins, Hom. ; c. gen. pers. to throw or shoot at one, Il. b. like βάλλω, c. dat. instrumenti, ἵησι τῇ ἀξίνῃ he throws [at him] with his axe, Xen. c. the acc. is often omitted, so that ἵημι sometimes seems intr., to throw, shoot, Hom. ; c. gen. objecti, τῶν μεγάλων ψυχῶν ἱείς shooting at great souls, Soph. 4. of water, to let flow, let burst or spout forth, Il., Aesch., etc. ; ὕδωρ omitted, ποταμὸς ἐπὶ γαῖαν ἵησιν the river pours over the land, Od. ; so, of fire, Eur. 5. to let fall, κὰδ δὲ κάρητος ἧκε κόμας made his locks flow down from his head, Od. ; ἐκ δὲ ποδοῖιν ἄκμονας ἧκα δύω I let two anvils hang from his two legs, Ib. ; ἧκαν ἑαυτούς let themselves go, Xen. II. Med. to send oneself, hasten, οἴκαδε ἱέμενος hastening homewards, Hom. ; ἱέμενος Τροίηνδε Od. ; so, δρόμῳ ἵεσθαι ἐπί τινα Hdt. ; etc. 2. metaph. to be set upon doing a thing, to desire to do it, c. inf., ἵετο γὰρ βαλέειν Il. :—c. gen. to long for, ἱέμενοι νίκης Ib. :—absol. in part., ἱέμενός περ eager though he was, Od. 3. the 3 pl. aor. 2 med. ἕντο is used by Hom. in the phrase ἐπεὶ πόσιος καὶ ἐδητύος ἐξ ἔρον ἕντο, when they had put away the desire of meat and drink, i. e. eaten and drunk enough, Virgil's postquam exempta fames epulis.

ἵηνα, aor. 1 of ἰαίνω.

Ἰη-παιήων, ὁ, epith. of Apollo, from the cry ἰὴ παιάν, h. Hom. II. a hymn sung to him, Id. Hence

ἰηπαιωνίζω, f. ίσω, to cry ἰὴ παιών ! Ar.

ἰήσασθαι, Ion. aor. 1 inf. of ἰάομαι.

ἵησι, 3 sing. of ἵημι.

ἵησι, Ep. for ἵῃ, 3 sing. subj. of εἶμι (ibo).

ἰήσιμος, ἴησις, Ion. for ἰασ-.

Ἰησοῦς, οῦ, dat. οῖ, Jesus, Greek form of Hebrew Joshua or Jehoshua, Saviour, N. T.

ἰητήρ, ἰητρικός, ἰητρός, Ion. for ἰατ-.

ἰθᾱ-γενής, ές, Ep. ἰθαι-γ-, (ἰθύς, γένος) born in lawful wedlock, legitimate, ἀλλά με ἶσον ἰθαιγενέεσσιν ἐτίμα honoured me like his true-born sons, Od. :—so, of a nation, from the ancient stock, genuine, ἰθ. Αἰγύπτιοι Hdt. ; of some mouths of the Nile, natural, original, opp. to ὀρυκτά, Id.

Ἰθάκη [ῐ], ἡ, Ithăca, the home of Ulysses, an island on the West coast of Greece, Hom. :—hence he is called Ἰθᾰκήσιος, Ithacan, Id. :—Ἰθάκηνδε, to Ithaca, Od.

ἰθέα, Ion. for ἰθεῖα, fem. of ἰθύς.

ἰθέως, Adv. of ἰθύς, v. ἰθύς II. 3.

ἴθῑ, imperat. of εἶμι (ibo), come, go, Hom., Att.   II. like ἄγε, as Adv. come! well then! Il. ; ἴθι νυν Ar.

ἴθμα, ατος, τό, (εἶμι ibo) a step, motion, Il.

ἰθύ, as Adv. of ἰθύς, v. ἰθύς II.

ἰθῠ-δίκης [ῐθ], ου, ὁ, (δίκη) giving right judgment, Hes.

ἰθύ-δῐκος, ον, = foreg., Anth.

ἰθυ-δρόμος [ῐ], ον, (δραμεῖν) straight-running, Anth.

ἰθύ-θριξ [ῐ], τρίχος, ὁ, ἡ, straight-haired, opp. to οὐλόθριξ (woolly-haired), Hdt.

ἰθῠμᾰχία, Ion. -ίη, ἡ, a fair, stand-up fight, Hdt.   From

ἰθύ-μᾰχος [ῐ], ον, (μάχομαι) fighting fairly, Simon.

ἰθυνθήτην, 3 dual aor. 1 pass. of ἰθύνω.

ἰθύντατα, Adv., Sup. of ἰθύ: v. ἰθύς I. 2.

ἰθυντήρ [ῐ], ῆρος, ὁ, a guide, pilot, Anth.   From

ἰθύνω [ῑ, ῡ]: aor. 1 ἴθυνα :—Pass., aor. 1 ἰθύνθην :— Ion. for εὐθύνω, to make straight, straighten, ἐπὶ στάθμην ἴθυνεν by the rule, Od. :—Pass. to run evenly, of horses yoked abreast, Il.   2. to guide in a straight line, ἵππους ἰθύνομεν (Ep. for -ωμεν) let us drive them straight, Ib. ; νῆα ἰθύνει [the pilot] keeps it straight, Ib. ; βέλος ἴθυνεν she sped it straight, Ib. :—Med. to guide or steer for oneself, ἰθύνετο ὀϊστὸν aimed his arrow straight, Od. ; πηδαλίῳ ἰθύνετο (sc. νῆα) Ib. ; c. gen., ἀλλήλων ἰθυνομένων δοῦρα as they drove their spears straight at each other, Il. :—Pass., of a boat, to be guided, steered, Hdt.   3. to guide, direct, rule, Il., Aesch. : of a judge, μύθους ἰθύνειν to rectify unjust judgments, Hes. ; ἰθ. τὸ πλέον τινί to adjudge the greater part to him, Theocr. :—Pass., ἰθύνεσθαι θανάτῳ to be punished with death, Hdt.

ἰθῠ-πόρος, ον, going straight on, Anth.

ἰθυ-πτίων [πτῐ], ωνος, ὁ, ἡ, (πέτομαι) straight-flying, of a javelin, Il.

ΙΘΥΣ, ἰθεῖα, ἰθύ, Ion. fem. ἰθέα, Ion. for εὐθύς :   1. of motion, straight, direct, Lat. rectus, used by Hom. in this sense only in Adv. ἰθύς (infr. II) ; ἰθείῃ τέχνῃ straightway, forthwith, Hdt.; ἰθεῖαν (sc. ὁδόν) straight on, Lat. recta (sc. via), Id. ; ἐκ τῆς ἰθείης (sc. ὁδοῦ) outright, openly, Id. ; κατ' ἰθύ εἶναι to be right over against, opposite, Id.   2. in moral sense, straight, straight-forward, just, ἰθεῖα γὰρ ἔσται [ἡ δίκη] Il. ; ἰθείῃσι δίκαις Hes. : so in Sup. Adv., δίκην ἰθύντατα εἰπεῖν to give judgment most fairly, Il. ; so, πρήξιες ἰθύτεραι [ῠ] Theogn. ; ἰθύς τε καὶ δίκαιος Hdt.   II. ἰθύς, or less commonly ἰθύ, as Adv., straight at, right at, c. gen. objecti, ἰθὺς Δαναῶν Il. ; ἰθὺς κίεν οἴκου

went straight towards the home, Ib. ; ἰθὺ τοῦ Ἴστρου Hdt. ;—also, ἰθὺς πρὸς τεῖχος Il. ; ἰθὺς ἐπὶ Θεσσαλίης Hdt.   2. absol., ἰθὺς φρονέων resolving to go straight on, Il. ; ἰθὺς μαχέσασθαι to fight hand to hand, Ib. ; τέτραπτο πρὸς ἰθύ οἱ, i. e. προσετέτραπτό οἱ ἰθύ, he fronted him face to face, Ib. :—of Time, straightway, Hdt.   3. ἰθέως, regul. Adv., Hdt.

ἰθύς [- -], ἡ, only in acc. ἰθύν, a straight course, ἀν' ἰθύν straight upwards, on high, Hom.   2. a direct attempt, purpose, πᾶσαν ἐπ' ἰθύν Id. ; γυναικῶν γνώομεν ἰθύν Od.

ἰθῠ-τενής, ές, (τείνω) stretched out, straight, Anth.: upright, perpendicular, Id.

ἰθύ-τονος [ῐ], ον, = ἰθυτενής, Anth.

ἰθύτρῐχες, pl. of ἰθύθριξ.

ἰθύ-φαλλος, ὁ, the phallos carried in the festivals of Bacchus: metaph. a lewd fellow, Dem.

ἰθύω, aor. 1 ἴθυσα, (ἰθύς) to go straight, press right on, Il. ; ἴθυσε μάχη πεδίοιο the tide of war set straight over the plain, Ib. :—c. gen. objecti, ἴθυσε νεός made straight for the ship, Ib. ; ἴθυσαν δ' ἐπὶ τεῖχος Ib. ; ἴθυσαν πρός . . Hdt.   II. c. inf. to strive or struggle to do, Od. ; ὅκη ἰθύσειε στρατεύεσθαι whichever way he purposed to march, Hdt.

ἱκᾰνός [ῐ], ή, όν, (ἵκω, ἱκάνω) becoming, befitting, sufficing: I. of persons, sufficient, competent, c. inf., Hdt. ; ἱκ. τεκμηριῶσαι sufficient to prove a point, Thuc. ; ἱκ. ζημιοῦν with sufficient power to punish, Xen. ; c. acc. rei, ἀνὴρ γνώμην ἱκανός a man of sufficient prudence, Hdt. ; ἱκ. τὴν ἰατρικήν sufficiently versed in medicine, Xen. :—c. dat. pers. a match for, equivalent to, εἷς πολλοῖς ἱκανός Plat. :—absol., ἱκανὸς Ἀπόλλων Soph. ; ἱκ. ἂν γένοιο σύ Eur. ; ἱκανοὶ ὡς πρὸς ἰδιώτας very tolerable in comparison with common men, Plat.   II. of things, sufficient, adequate, enough, Eur. ; ἱκανὰ τοῖς πολεμίοις εὐτύχηται they have had successes enough, Thuc. :—of size, large enough, οὐχ ἱκανῆς οὔσης τῆς Ἀττικῆς Id. ; ἱκανά σοι μέλαθρα ἐγκαθυβρίζειν large enough to riot in, Eur. :—of Time, considerable, long, Ar.   2. sufficient, satisfactory, ἱκανὴ μαρτυρία Plat. :—τὸ ἱκανὸν λαμβάνειν to take security, N. T.   III. Adv. -νῶς, sufficiently, adequately, enough, Thuc., etc.   2. ἱκ. ἔχειν to be sufficient, to be far enough advanced, Id., Xen., etc. : —Sup. ἱκανώτατα Plat.   Hence

ἱκᾰνότης, ητος, ἡ, sufficiency, fitness, Plat.   II. a sufficiency, sufficient supply, Id. ; and

ἱκᾰνόω, f. ώσω, to make sufficient, qualify, N. T.

ἱκάνω [ῑκᾰ-], impf. ἵκανον [ῑ by the augm.] : other tenses are supplied by ἱκνέομαι :—lengthd. form of ἵκω, to come, arrive, Hom., Aesch. : c. acc. to come to, reach, ἱκάνω νῆας Ἀχαιῶν Il., etc. ; of a tall tree, δι' ἠέρος αἰθέρ' ἵκανεν Ib. ; ἥβης μέτρον ἱκ. reached, attained to the age of youth, Od.   II. with a person for the object, often of grief, hardship, and the like, ἄχος κραδίην καὶ θυμὸν ἱκάνει Il. ; so, ἄλγος, γῆρας, κάματος, χόλος ἱκάνει τινά Hom. ; παλαίφατα θέσφατ' ἱκάνει με they are fulfilled upon me, Od.   2. of a suppliant, σὰ γούνατ' ἱκάνω Il. ; cf. ἱκνέομαι III.   III. also in Med., χρειὼ γὰρ ἱκάνεται Ib. ; τὰ σὰ γούναθ' ἱκάνομαι Hom.

Ἰκάριος [ῑκᾰ], α, ον, Icarian, πόντος Ἰκ. the Aegean

between the Cyclades and Caria, where Icarus son of Daedalus was drowned, Il. ; 'Ικ. πέλαγος Hdt.

ἴκελος [ῐ], η, ον, poët. and Ion. form of εἴκελος, *like, resembling*, τινι Il., Hdt., Pind.   Hence

ἰκελόω [ῐ], f. ώσω, *to make like*, Anth.

ἰκέσθαι, aor. 2 inf. of ἱκνέομαι :— ἱκέσθω, 3 sing. imper.

ἱκεσία, ἡ, (ἱκέτης) *the prayer of a suppliant*, Eur. ; ἱκεσίαισι σαῖς at thy entreaties, Id.

ἱκέσιος [ῐ], α, ον or ος, ον, (ἱκέτης) -- ἱκετήσιος, Trag.   2. *of* or *consisting of suppliants*, Aesch.   3. *suppliant*, of prayers, Soph., Eur. ; of persons, Soph., Eur.

ἱκετεία [ῐ], ἡ, = ἱκεσία, *supplication*, Thuc. ; ἱκετείαν ποιεῖσθαί τινος *to supplicate him*, Id.

ἱκέτευμα [ῐ], ατος, τό, *a mode of supplication*, Thuc.

ἱκετευτέος, α, ον, *to be besought* or *entreated*, Luc.

ἱκετεύω [ῐ], f. σω : aor. 1 ἱκέτευσα: (ἱκέτης) :— *to approach as a suppliant*, ἐπεί σε ἱκέτευσα Od. ; ἐς Πηλῆ' ἱκέτευσε Il. ; ἱκ. τινὰ γονάτων or πρὸς γονάτων Eur.   2. *to supplicate, beseech* one to do a thing, c. acc. et inf., Od., Hdt., Att. :--also c. gen. pers. et inf. *to beg of* one that . . , Eur.   3. c. acc. rei, *to ask* a thing *as a suppliant*, Id., Thuc.

ἱκετήριος, sync. ἱκτήριος, α, ον, (ἱκέτης) :— *of* or *fit for suppliants*, ἱκτ. θησαυρός, of hair offered to a god, Soph. ; ἱκτήριοι = ἱκέται, Id.   II. ἱκετηρία, Ion. -ίη, (sub. ῥάβδος), ἡ, *an olive-branch which the suppliant held* as a symbol of his condition, Hdt., Ar., etc. ; so, κλάδοι ἱκτήριοι Soph. :—metaph., ἱκετηρίαν ὑπὸ γόνασιν ἐξάπτω σέθεν *τὸ σῶμα τοὐμὸν* I attach my body to thy knees *as a suppliant olive-branch*, Eur. ; so, νομίζετε τὸν παῖδα ἱκτηρίαν προκεῖσθαι Dem.

ἱκέτης [ῐ], ου, ὁ, (ἵκω) *one who comes to seek protection, a suppliant* or *fugitive*, who lays his ἱκετηρία on the altar or hearth, after which his person was inviolable ; esp. *one who seeks purification after homicide*, Hom., etc.

ἱκετήσιος [ῐ], α, ον, epith. of Zeus, as *tutelary god of suppliants*, Od.

ἱκέτις [ῐ], ιδος, ἡ, fem. of ἱκέτης, Hdt., Soph., etc.

ἵκμαι, Ερ. for ἵκη, 2 sing. aor. 2 of ἱκνέομαι.

ΙΚΜΑ'Σ, άδος, ἡ, *moisture, juice*, Il., Hdt. :—comic metaph., τὴν ἰκμάδα τῆς φροντίδος Ar. ; ἰ. Βάκχου, i.e. *wine*, Anth. ; ἰ. δρυός, i.e. *gum*, Id.

ἵκμενος, only in the phrase ἵκμενος οὖρος (from ἵκω, ἱκνέομαι) *a following, favourable wind*, Hom.

ἱκνέομαι, Dep. lengthd. form of ἵκω, ἱκάνω : f. ἵξομαι, Dor. ἱξοῦμαι: aor. 2 ἱκόμην [with ῐ, except when lengthd. by augm.]: pf. ἷγμαι, part. ἱγμένος : 3 sing. plqpf. ἷκτο :—*to come* to a place, c. acc. loci, or foll. by a prep., ἵκετο νῆας or ἐπὶ νῆας Hom., etc.   2. *to come to*, ἵκετο χρόα, of a spear, Il. ; τέλος ἵκεο μύθων Ib. ; ἠῶ ἱκέσθαι, *to live* till morning, Od. ; λέκτροιο θεσμὸν ἱκ., i.e. *to wed*, Ib. ; ὅ τι χεῖρας ἵκοιτο, *whatever came to hand*, Ib. ; ἱκ. ἐς λόγους τινός *to speak with* one, Soph., etc.   II. of suffering, sorrow, etc., *to come upon*, πένθος ἱκ. τινά Il. ; ἄχος, χόλος τινὰ ἱκ. θυμόν or κραδίην Hom.   III. *to approach as suppliant*, Id. ; τὰ σὰ γοῦνα ἱκόμεθ' Od. :—hence, like ἱκετεύω, *to supplicate, beseech*, τὰς θεὰς ἱκνοῦμαι Soph. ; καί σε πρὸς θεῶν ἱκνοῦμαι Id. :—c. inf., πάντες σ' ἱκνοῦνται θάψαι νεκρούς Eur.   IV. impers. like προσήκει, *it becomes, befits*, φαμὲν ἡμέας ἱκνέεσθαι ἡγεμονεύειν we say *that it befits* us to take the lead,

Hdt. ; τοὺς μάλιστα ἱκνέεται (sc. κεκάρθαι) *whom it most concerns*, Id. ; so, ἐς τὸν ἱκνέεται he *to whom it belongs*, Id.   2. in part., τὸ ἱκνεύμενον *that which is fitting, proper*, Id. ; ὁ ἱκν. χρόνος the *fit, proper time*, Id. ; τὸ ἱκν. ἀνάλωμα the *proportionate* expense, Thuc. :—hence Adv. ἱκνευμένως, *fittingly, aright*, Hdt.

ἱκνεύμεσθα, Ion. for ἱκνούμεθα, 1 pl. of ἱκνέομαι :—Ion. part. ἱκνεύμενος.

'ΙΚΡΙΑ, τά, *the half-decks* fore and aft of Homeric ships, Hom. : *the planks of the deck*, Od.   II. generally, *a platform, stage*, Hdt.

ἴκταρ, Adv., (ἵκω) *following closely*, Hes.   II. of Place, *close to, hard by*, Aesch., Plat. ; c. gen., Aesch.

ἱκτήρ, ῆρος, ὁ, = ἱκέτης, *a suppliant*, Soph., Eur.   II. as Adj. = ἱκετήριος, Aesch.

ἱκτήριος, α, ον, v. ἱκετήριος.

ἱκτίδεος, α, ον, (ἱκτίς), v. κτίδεος.

ἰκτῖνος, ὁ, *a kite*, Hdt., Ar., Plat.

'ΙΚΤΙ'Σ, ῖδος, ἡ, *the yellow-breasted marten, the marten-cat*, (cf. γαλέη), Lat. *mustela*, Ar.

ἵκτο, 3 sing. plqpf. of ἱκνέομαι.

ἵκτωρ, ορος, ὁ, poët. for ἱκέτης : as Adj. *suppliant*, Eur.

'ΙΚΩ [ῐ] : impf. ἷκον : Dor. f. ἱξῶ : aor. 2 ἷξον : for ἵξομαι, ἷγμαι, v. sub ἱκνέομαι :—*to come to, reach*, c. acc. or with a Prep., ἵκειν ἐς πατρίδα, ἵκειν κατὰ νῆας or ἵκειν δόμον, Τροίην, κλισίην Hom.   2. of sufferings, feelings, etc., ὅτε κέν τινα χόλος ἵκοι *whenever anger come upon* him, Il. ; χρειὼ ἵκει με *necessity is upon* me, Od.

ἱλᾶ [ῐ], ἡ, Dor. for ἵλη.

ἱλαδόν [ῐ], Adv. (ἵλη) *in troops*, Lat. *turmatim*, Il., Hdt. : generally, *in abundance, in a mass*, Hes.

ἵλαθι, v. sub ἵλημι.

ἵλαμαι, = ἱλάσκομαι, h. Hom.

ἱλάομαι [ῐλᾱ], = ἱλάσκομαι, Il.

'ΙΛΑΟΣ [ῑ], ον, Att. ἵλεως, ων, dual ἵλεω : nom. pl. ἵλεῳ, neut. ἵλεα :—of gods, *propitious, gracious*, Il., Hes., etc.   II. of men, *gracious, kindly, gentle*, θυμὸς ἐνὶ φρεσὶν ἵλαος ἔστω Il. ; so in Soph.

ἱλαρός [ῐ], ά, όν, (ἵλαος) *cheerful, gay, merry, joyous*, Lat. *hilaris*, Ar., Xen. :—τὸ ἱλαρόν = ἱλαρότης, Plut.   Adv. -ρῶς, Xen.   Hence

ἱλαρότης, ητος, ἡ, *cheerfulness*, Lat. *hilaritas*, Plut.

ἱλάσκομαι [ῐ]; f. ἱλάσομαι [ᾰ], Ep. ἱλάσσομαι : aor. 1 ἱλασάμην, Ep. 2 sing. subj. ἱλάσσεαι : Dep. : (ἵλαος) :—*to appease*, θεὸν ἱλάσκεσθαι *to make him propitious to one, conciliate* him, win his favour, Hom. ; μολπῇ θεὸν ἱλάσκοντο Il. ; ὄφρ' ἧμιν 'Εκάεργον ἱλάσσεαι Ib. ; so of men, Hdt., Plat.   II. in N. T. *to expiate*, τὰς ἁμαρτίας.   III. in N. T. also, an aor. 1 imperat. pass. ἱλάσθητι, *be gracious*.   Hence

ἱλασμός [ῐ], ὁ, *a means of appeasing*, Plut. :—a *propitiation*, N. T. ; and

ἱλαστήριος, α, ον, *propitiatory*.   II. as Subst., **ἱλαστήριον** (sub. ἐπίθεμα), τό, *the mercy-seat*, covering of the ark in the Holy of Holies, N. T.   2. (sub. ἀνάθημα), *a propitiation*, Ib.

ἵλεως, ων, Att. for ἵλαος.

ἵλη [ῐ], Dor. ἵλα, Ion. εἵλη, ἡ, (ἵλλω, εἵλω) :—*a crowd, band, troop* of men, Hdt., Soph. : εὔφρονες ἷλαι *merry companies*, Pind. ; also, ἵλη λεόντων Eur.   2. *a troop of horse*, Lat. *turma, ala*, κατ' ἵλας = ἱλαδόν, Xen.

ἰλήκω [ῐ], (ἴλαος) to be gracious, εἴ κεν Ἀπόλλων ἡμῖν ἰλήκῃσι (Ep. 3 sing. subj.) Od.

ἴλημι [ῐ], = foreg., imperat. ἴληθι, in prayers, be gracious! Od.; Dor. ἴλᾶθι Theocr.

Ἰλιάδαι [ῐ], οἱ, descendants of Ilos, i. e. Trojans, Eur.

Ἰλιακός [ῐ], ή, όν, (Ἴλιον) Ilian, Trojan, Anth.

Ἰλιάς [ῐ], άδος, ἡ, fem. of Ἰλιακός, Hdt., Trag. II. as Subst.: 1. (sub. γῆ), Troy, the Troad, Hdt. 2. (sub. γυνή), a Trojan woman, Eur. 3. (sub. ποίησις), the Iliad, Arist.; proverb., Ἰλιὰς κακῶν, i. e. an endless string of woes, Dem.

ἰλιγγιάω [ῐ], to be or become dizzy, lose one's head, caused by looking down from a height or by drunkenness, Plat.; by fear, Ar., etc.

ἴλιγγος, ὁ, (ἴλλω, εἴλω) a spinning round: esp. a swimming in the head, Lat. vertigo, Plat.

Ἰλιο-ραΐστης, ὁ, (ῥαίω) destroyer of Troy, Anth.

Ἴλιος [ῐ], ον, ἡ, Ilios or Ilium, the city of Ilus, Troy, Hom., Eur. :—Ἴλιον, τό, Il., Trag. :—hence the Ep. genitives, Ἰλιόθεν from Troy, Hom.; Ἰλιόθι πρό before Troy, Od., etc.; Ἰλιόφι τείχεα the walls of Troy, Il. II. as Adj., Ἴλιος, α, ον or ος, ον, Ilian, Trojan, Eur.

ἰλλάς, άδος, ἡ, (ἴλλω, εἴλω) a rope, band, Il.

ἴλλω, to roll, v. sub εἴλω.

ἰλυόεις [ῐ], εσσα, εν, (ἰλύς) muddy, impure, Anth.

ΙΛΥΣ [ῐ], ύος, ἡ, mud, slime, dirt, Il., Hdt. [Gen. ἰλύος Hom., ἰλύος Anth.]

ἱμάντινος, η, ον, (ἱμάς) of leathern thongs, Hdt.

ἱμαντο-πέδη, ἡ, a leathern noose, of a polypus' leg, Anth.

ἱμάς [ῐ], ὁ, gen. ἱμάντος: dat. pl. ἱμᾶσι, Ep. ἱμάντεσσι: —a leathern strap or thong, Il.: in pl. the traces by which horses were attached to the chariot, Ib.: also, the reins, Ib., Soph., Eur. 2. the straps on which the body of the chariot was hung, Il. 3. the lash of a whip, Ib. 4. the caestus of boxers, consisting of straps put round the hand, Ib. II. in sing. the magic girdle of Aphroditè, Lat. cestus, Ib. 2. the chin-strap of the helmet, Ib. 3. in Od. a latchet or thong, by which the bolt was shot home into the socket, and which was then fastened to the κορώνη, Od. 4. after Hom. the thong or latchet of a sandal, Xen. 5. a dog-leash, Id.: proverb., ἱμὰς κύνειός ἐστι he's as tough as a dog-leash, Ar.

ἱμάσθλη [ῐ], ἡ, the thong of a whip, a whip, Hom.

ἱμάσσω [ῐ], f. ἱμάσω [ᾰ]: aor. 1 ἵμασα: (ἱμάς) :—to flog horses, Hom.; generally, to scourge, smite, Il.

ἱμάτιδιον [τῐ], τό, Dim. of ἱμάτιον, Ar.

ἱματίζω (ἱμάτιον) to clothe : part. pf. pass. ἱματισμένος.

ἱματιο-κάπηλος, ὁ, a clothes-seller, Luc. From

ἱμάτιον [ῐμᾰ-], τό, in form a Dim. of ἷμα (i. e. εἷμα), an outer garment, a cloak or mantle worn above the χιτών, the same as Homer's χλαῖνα, Hdt., Ar. :—used of the Roman toga, ἐν ἱματίοις, Lat. togati, Plut. 2. ἱμάτια, τά, generally, clothes, Hdt., Dem. II. generally, a cloth, Hdt.

ἱματιο-φῠλακέω, (φύλαξ) to take care of clothes, Luc.

ἱματισμός, ὁ, (ἱματίζω) clothing, apparel, Theophr.

ἱμείρω [ῐ], (ἵμερος) to long for, yearn after, desire a thing, c. gen., Od., Aesch., etc. :—c. inf. to long or wish to do, Solon, Aesch., etc. II. as Dep. ἱμείρομαι, aor. 1 med. ἱμειράμην, pass. ἱμέρθην :—to desire, c. gen., ὁππότ' ἂν ἧς ἱμείρεται αἴης (Ep. for -ηται) Od.; χρημάτων ἱμ. μεγάλως Hdt.

ἴμεν, 1 pl. of εἶμι (ibo). II. ἴμεν, ἴμεναι [ῐ], Ep. inf.

ἱμερόεις [ῐ], εσσα, εν, (ἵμερος) exciting love or desire, lovely, delightsome, charming, Hom., Theocr. :—Sup. ἱμεροέστατος Theogn.

ἱμερο-θᾰλής, ές, (θάλλω) Dor. for -θηλής, sweetly blooming, Anth.

ἵμερος [ῐ], ὁ, a longing or yearning after a thing, Lat. desiderium, c. gen., Il.; γόου ἵμερον ὦρσεν raised [in them] a yearning after tears, i. e. a desire to weep, Ib.; and with a second gen., πατρὸς ὑφ' ἵμερον ὦρσε γόοιο for his father, Od.; ἵμερον ἔχειν = ἱμείρεσθαι, Hdt. :—in pl., πολλοὶ ἵμεροι various emotions, Aesch. 2. absol. desire, love, Il., etc. II. as Adj., but only in neut. as Adv., ἵμερον αὐλεῖν Anth.; ἵμερα μελίζεσθαι, δακρύειν Id.

ἱμερό-φωνος, ον, (φωνή) of lovely voice or song, Theocr.

ἱμέρρω [ῐ], Aeol. for ἱμείρω.

ἱμερτός [ῐ], ή, όν, (ἱμείρω) longed for, lovely, Il., Hes.

ἴμμεναι, poët. for ἴμεναι, ἰέναι, inf. of εἶμι (ibo).

ἱμονιά [ῐ], ἡ, (ἱμάς) the rope of a draw-well, Ar. Hence

ἱμονιο-στρόφος, ὁ, (στρέφω) a water-drawer, Ar.

ἴν, dat. and acc. of the old pers. Pron. ἵ.

ἽΝΑ: A. Adverb, I. of Place, 1. demonstr. in that place, there, only in Il. 10. 127. 2. relat., = ὅπου, in which place, where, Hdt., etc. ;—so, ἵνα τε Il.; ἵνα περ Hom. :—c. gen., ἵνα γῆς in whatever part of the land, Hdt.; ἔμαθε ἵνα ἦν κακοῦ in what a calamity, Id.; οὐχ ὁρᾷς ἵν' εἶ κακοῦ Soph. :—so, = ὅποι, with Verbs of motion, whither, Od.; ὁρᾷς ἵν' ἥκεις Soph. II. of circumstance, when, at which, Od.

B. Final Conjunction, = ὅπως, that, in order that, Lat. ut, Hom.: 1. with subj., a. after principal tenses of indic., Id., etc. b. after historical tenses, in similes, where the aor. refers to any possible time, Od. c. after optat. and ἄν, ἔδωκε μένος, ἵνα γένοιτο she gave him vigour, that he might become, Il. 2. with optat., a. after historical tenses, Hom., etc. 3. with past tenses of ind., to express a consequence which has not followed or cannot follow, ἵν' ἦν τυφλός in which case he must be blind, Soph., etc. 4. ἵνα μή as the negat. of ἵνα, that not, Lat. ut ne or ne, Il., Att. II. elliptical usages, 1. where the purpose only is stated, Ζεὺς ἔσθ', ἵν' εἰδῇς 'tis Zeus, [I tell thee this] that thou may'st know it, Soph.; so, ἵνα συντέμω Dem. 2. ὅρα or βλέπε being understood, ἵνα ἐλθὼν ἐπιθῇς τὰς χεῖρας αὐτῇ see that thou come and lay hands on her, N. T. 3. ἵνα τί (sc. γένηται); to what end? Ar., Plat.

ἰνδάλλομαι, Dep., hardly used, save in pres. and impf.: (from εἴδομαι, videor) :—to appear like, look like, ἀθάνατοι ἰνδάλλεται εἰσοράασθαι he is like the immortals to look upon, Od.; ἰνδάλλετο δέ σφισι μεγαθύμῳ Πηλείωνι he seemed to them like the son of P., Il. 2. to appear, seem, Ib.; ὥς μοι ἰνδάλλεται ἦτορ as my heart seems to me [to say], i. e. as the matter

seems to me, Od. ; ἰνδάλλεται ὁμοιότατος κλητῆρος he seems most like a summoner, Ar.   Hence

ἴνδαλμα, ατος, τό, an appearance, Lat. species, Anth., Luc.

Ἰνδικός, ή, όν, (Ἰνδός) Indian, Hdt., etc.

Ἰνδ-ολέτης, ου, ὁ, (ὀλέσαι) Indian-killer, Anth.

Ἰνδός, ὁ, an Indian, Hdt., etc.   2. the river Indus, Id.   II. as Adj. = Ἰνδικός, Anth.

ἰνίον [ῑν-], τό, (ῑς) the muscle at the back of the neck, the nape of the neck, Il.

ἼΝΙΣ, ὁ, a son, Aesch., Eur. :— ῑνις, ή, a daughter, Eur.

Ἰνώ [ῑ], όος contr. οῦς, ή, Ino, daughter of Cadmus, worshipped as a sea-goddess by the name of Leucothea, Od., Hes.

ἰν-ώδης [ῑ], ες, (εἶδος) fibrous, of parts of animals, Xen.

ἴξαλος, ον, of the ibex (v. αἴξ), bounding, springing, Il.   (Deriv. uncertain.)

ἰξευτής, οῦ, ὁ, (ἰξεύω) a fowler, bird-catcher, Bion, Anth.   II. as Adj. catching with birdlime, Id.

ἰξεύω, (ἰξός) to catch by birdlime.

Ἰξίων [ῑ], ονος, ὁ, Ixion, a king of Thessaly: his name prob. was = ἱκέτης, for he was the first homicide, and therefore the first suppliant, Pind., Aesch.

ἰξοβολέω, to catch with limed twigs : to catch, Anth.

ἰξο-βόλος, ον, (βάλλω) setting limed twigs.

ἰξο-εργός, ὁ, (*ἔργω) one who uses birdlime, Anth.

ἴξομαι, fut. of ἱκνέομαι.

ἴξον, ξος, ε, aor. 2 of ἵκω.

ἸΞΟΣ, ὁ, mistletoe, Lat. viscum, Arist.   II. birdlime prepared from the mistletoe berry, Eur.   2. metaph., ἐκφυγὼν τὸν ἰξὸν τὸν ἐν πράγματι Luc.

ἰξο-φορεύς, έως, Ep. ῆος, ὁ, (φέρω) limed, Anth.

ἸΞΥΣ, ύος, dat. ἰξυῖ, ή, the waist, Od.

Ἰόβακχος, ὁ, Bacchus invoked with the cry of Ἰώ, Anth.

ἰο-βλέφαρος, ον, (ἴον, βλέφαρον) violet-eyed, Luc.

ἰοβολέω [ῑ], to shoot arrows, dart, Anth.   From

ἰο-βόλος [ῑ], ον, (ἰός, βάλλω) shooting arrows, Anth.   II. shedding venom, poisonous, Id.

ἰο-βόστρυχος, ον, (ἴον) dark-haired, Pind.

ἰο-δνεφής, ές, (δνόφος) violet-dark, purple, Od.

ἰο-δόκος [ῑ], ον, (ἰός, δέχομαι) holding arrows, Hom. : —as Subst. a quiver, Anth.

ἰο-ειδής, ές, (ἴον, εἶδος) like the violet, purple, of the sea, Hom.

ἰόεις, εσσα, εν, (ἴον) violet-coloured, dark, Il.

ἰο-μῐγής [ῑ], ές, (ἰός, μιγῆναι) mixed with poison, Anth.

ἰό-μωροι, οί, (ἰός arrow?) warlike or ill-fated, miserable, Hom.   (Sense and deriv. both uncertain.)

ΙΟΝ [ῑ], τό, the violet, Theocr.:—once in Hom., λειμῶνες ἴου ἠδὲ σελίνου θήλεον the meadows were blooming with ἴον and parsley;—but whether it is here violet or some other dark blue flower is doubtful.

ἰονθάς, άδος, ή, shaggy, epith. of the wild goat, Od. From

ἴονθος, ὁ, the root of hair.

Ἰόνιος [ῑ], α, ον, (Ἰώ) of or called after Io, Ἰόνιος κόλπος or πόρος, the sea between Epirus and Italy, across which Io swam, Hdt., Aesch., etc.

ἰο-πλόκος, ον, (πλέκω) weaving violets, Anth.

ἸΟΣ [ῑ], ὁ: pl. ἰοί, also ἰά :—an arrow, Il., Trag.

ἸΟΣ [ῑ], ὁ, rust, Theogn., Plat.   II. poison, as of serpents, Trag.

ἰος, ἴα, Ep. for εἷς, μία : v. εἷς.

ἰο-στέφανος, ον, violet-crowned, h. Hom., Solon, etc.

ἰότης, ητος, ή, will, desire, θεῶν ἰότητι by the will or hest of the gods, Hom.   II. = ἕκατι II, for the sake of, ἰότᾱτι γάμων Aesch.   (Deriv. uncertain.)

ἰού or ἰοῦ, Interj. a cry of woe, Lat. heu ! Trag.   II. like ἰώ, a cry of surprise, ho ! Aesch., Ar., etc.

Ἰουδαῖος, ὁ, a Jew : Ἰουδαία, a Jewess ; ἡ Ἰουδαία (sub. γῆ), Judaea :— Ἰουδαϊκός, ή, όν Jewish : Ἰουδαΐζω, to side with or imitate the Jews, N. T.

ἴουλος, ὁ, = οὖλος, the young hair at the side of the face, the whiskers, Od., Aesch.

ἰο-χέαιρα [ῑ], ή, arrow-pourer, shooter of arrows, of Artemis, Hom.   (Prob. from χέω, not from χαίρω.)

ἱπνίτης [ῑ], ου, ὁ, (ἱπνός) baked in the oven, Anth.

ἱπνο-ποιός, όν, (ποιέω) one who works at an oven, Luc.

ἹΠΝΟΣ, ὁ, an oven or furnace, Hdt., Ar.   II. the place of the oven, i. e. the kitchen, Ar.   III. a lantern, Id.

ἱπόομαι, Pass. to be weighed down, Aesch., Ar.   From

ἶπος, ὁ or ή, (ἵπτομαι) in a mouse-trap, the piece of wood that falls and catches the mouse : generally any weight, Pind.   Hence

ἱππ-αγρέται, ῶν, οἱ, (ἀγείρω) three officers at Lacedaemon, who chose 300 ἔφηβοι, to serve as a body-guard for the kings, Xen.

ἱππ-άγωγός, όν, carrying horses, of ships used as cavalry transports, Hdt., Thuc., etc.

ἱππάζομαι, f. άσομαι: Dep.: (ἵππος) :—to drive horses, drive a chariot, Il.: later, to ride, Hdt., Ar.   2. Pass., of the horse, to be ridden or driven, Plat.: to be broken in for riding, Xen.   II. ἱππάζεσθαι χώραν to ride over a country, Plut.

ἱππ-αλεκτρυών, όνος, ὁ, a horse-cock, gryphon, a fabulous animal, Aesch.

ἱππᾰλίδας, ου, ὁ, poët. lengthd. form for ἱππεύς, Theocr.

ἱππᾰπαί, a cry of the Ἱππεῖς, a parody of the boatmen's cry (ῥυππαπαί), Ar.

ἱππάριον, τό, Dim. of ἵππος, a pony, Xen.

ἱππ-αρμοστής, οῦ, ὁ, Laced. for ἵππαρχος, a commander of cavalry, Xen.

ἱππαρχέω, f. ήσω, (ἵππαρχος) to command the cavalry, c. gen., Hdt., Dem.; and

ἱππαρχία, ή, the office of ἵππαρχος, Xen.; and

ἱππαρχικός, ή, όν, of or for a ἵππαρχος : ἱππαρχικόν ἐστι it is part of his duty, Xen.   From

ἵππ-αρχος, ὁ, a general of cavalry, Hdt.: at Athens there were two, with 10 φύλαρχοι under them, Ar.

ἱππάς, άδος, ή, fem. of ἱππικός, ἱππὰς στολή a riding-dress, Hdt.

ἱππᾰσία, ή, (ἱππάζομαι) riding, horse-exercise, Ar., Xen.   2. chariot-driving, Luc.

ἱππάσιμος [ᾰ], η, ον, (ἱππάζομαι) fit for horses, fit for riding, Hdt., Xen.: — metaph., κόλαξιν ἱππάσιμος ridden by flatterers, Plut.

ἱππαστής, οῦ, ὁ, = ἱππευτής, Luc.   II. as Adj. fit for riding, of a horse, Xen.

ἱππαστικός, ή, όν, (ἱππάζομαι) fond of riding, Plut.

ἱππάστρια, ή, fem. of ἱππαστής II, Plut.

ἱππ-άφεσις, εως, ή, the starting-post in a race, Anth.

ἱππεία, ή, (ἱππεύω) a riding or driving of horses, horsemanship, Soph., Eur.   II. cavalry, Xen.

ἵππειος, α, ον, (ἵππος) of a horse or horses, Hom., Soph.; ἱππ. λόφος a horse-hair crest, Il.

ἵππ-ερος, ὁ, horse-love, horse-fever, Ar.
ἵππευμα, ατος, τό, (ἱππεύω) a ride on horseback or journey in a chariot, Eur.
ἱππεύς, gen. έως Ep. ῆος, ὁ, (ἵππος) a horseman, either of the charioteer or of the hero who fights from a chariot, Il.　2. a horseman, i. e. rider, first in Hdt.　II. in Solon's constitution, the ἱππεῖς, Att. ἱππῆς, Horsemen or Knights, were the 2d class, required to possess land producing 300 medimni, and a horse, Ar., Thuc.　2. at Sparta 300 chosen men, the King's Body Guard, Hdt.
ἱππευτήρ, ῆρος, ὁ, = sq., Anth.
ἱππευτής, οῦ, ὁ, a rider, horseman, Eur.　From
ἱππεύω, f. σω: aor. 1 ἵππευσα: (ἱππεύς):—to be a horseman or rider, to ride, Hdt., Att.:—so in Med., Hdt.　2. metaph. of the wind, Eur.　II. to be a trooper, serve in the cavalry, Xen.　III. of a horse, as we say 'the horse rides (i. e. carries his rider) well,' Id.
ἱππηδόν, (ἵππος) Adv. like a horse, Aesch.　II. as on horseback, like a horseman, Ar.
ἱππ-ηλάσιος, α, ον, (ἐλαύνω) = ἱππήλατος, ἱππ. ὁδός a chariot-road, Il.
ἱππηλάτᾰ, ὁ, Ep. for ἱππηλάτης.
ἱππηλᾰτέω, f. ήσω, to ride or drive, Ar.　From
ἱππ-ηλάτης [ᾰ], ου, ὁ, (ἐλαύνω) a driver of horses, one who fights from a chariot, a Knight, Hom.
ἱππ-ήλᾰτος, ον, (ἐλαύνω) fit for horsemanship or driving, of countries, Od.
ἱππ-ημολγοί, οἱ, (ἀμέλγω) the Mare-milkers, a Scythian or Tartar tribe, Il.
ἱππι-άναξ [ᾰ], ακτος, ὁ, king of horsemen, Aesch.
ἱππικός, ή, όν, (ἵππος) of a horse or horses, Hdt., Att.　2. of horsemen or chariots, ἱππικὸς ἀγών, δρόμος Hdt., Soph.　II. skilled in riding, equestrian, Plat.; ἡ ἱππική Ar.　III. τὸ ἱππικόν, the horse, cavalry, Hdt., Xen.　2. a course of four stadia, Plut.　IV. Adv. -κῶς, like a horseman: Sup. -κώτατα, with best horsemanship, Xen.
ἵππιος, α, ον, (ἵππος) of a horse or horses, Eur.; epith. of the Queen of the Amazons, Id.; of Poseidon as creator of the horse, Aesch., etc.
ἱππιο-χαίτης, ου, ὁ, (χαίτη) shaggy with horse-hair, Il.
ἱππιο-χάρμης, ου, ὁ, (χάρμη) one who fights from a chariot, Hom.: later, a horseman, rider, Aesch.　II. as Adj., ἱππ. κλόνοι the tumult of the horse-fight, Id.
ἱππο-βάμων [ᾰ], ον, gen. ονος, (βαίνω) going on horseback, equestrian, Aesch., Soph.　2. metaph., ῥήματα ἱππ. great high-paced words, bombast, Ar.
ἱππο-βάτης [ᾰ], ου, ὁ, (βαίνω) a horseman, Aesch.
ἱππο-βότης, ου, ὁ, (βόσκω) feeder of horses, Eur.　II. the ἱπποβόται at Chalcis in Euboea were a class, like the ἱππεῖς at Athens, Lat. Equites, the Knights, Hdt.
ἱππό-βοτος, ον, (βόσκω) grazed by horses, Hom., Eur.
ἱππο-βουκόλος, ὁ, a horse-herd, horse-keeper, Eur.
ἱππο-γέρανοι, οἱ, crane-cavalry, Luc.
ἱππό-γυποι, οἱ, (γύψ) vulture-cavalry, Luc.
ἱππό-δαμος, ον, (δαμάω) tamer of horses, Hom.
ἱππο-δάσεια [ᾰ], as fem. without any masc. in use, bushy with horse-hair, of helmets, Hom.
ἱππό-δεσμα, ων, τά, (δεσμός) horse-bands, reins, Eur.
ἱππο-δέτης, ου, ὁ, (δέω to bind) binding horses, Soph.

ἱππο-διώκτης, ου, ὁ, Dor. -τας, a driver or rider of steeds, Theocr.
ἱπποδρομία, ή, a horse-race or chariot-race, Ar., Thuc.
ἱππό-δρομος, ὁ, a chariot-road, Il.　2. a race-course for chariots, Lat. curriculum, Plat., etc.
ἱππο-δρόμος, ὁ, a light horseman, Hdt.
ἱππόθεν, Adv. (ἵππος) forth from the horse, Od.
ἱπποϊΐν, Ep. gen. and dat. dual of ἵππος.
ἱππο-κάνθᾰρος, ὁ, a horse-beetle, Ar.
ἱππο-κέλευθος, ον, travelling by means of horses, a driver of horses, Il.
ἱππο-κένταυρος, ὁ, a horse-centaur, half-horse half-man, Xen.
ἱπποκομέω, f. ήσω, to groom horses, ἱπποκομεῖν κάνθαρον to groom one's beetle, Ar.
ἱππο-κόμος, ὁ, (κομέω) a groom or esquire, who attended the ἱππεύς in war, Lat. equiso, Hdt., Thuc., etc.
ἱππό-κομος, ον, (κόμη) decked with horse-hair, of a helmet, Il., Soph.
ἱππο-κορυστής, οῦ, ὁ, (κορύσσω) equipt or furnished with horses, Il.
ἱππο-κρᾰτέω, f. ήσω, to be superior in horse, Dem.:—Pass. to be inferior in horse, Thuc.　Hence
ἱπποκρᾰτία, ή, victory in a cavalry action, Xen.
ἱππό-κρημνος, ον, tremendously steep, ἱππόκρημνον ῥῆμα a neck-breaking word, Ar.
ἱππό-κροτος, ον, sounding with horses, Eur.
ἱππό-λοφος, ον, with horse-hair crest, Ar., Anth.
ἱππο-μᾰνής, ές, (μαίνομαι) of a meadow, in which horses take mad delight, or, swarming with horses, Soph.　II. as Subst., ἱππομανές, έος, τό, an Arcadian plant, which makes horses mad, Theocr.　Hence
ἱππο-μᾰνία, ή, mad love for horses, Luc.
ἱππομᾰχέω, f. ήσω, to fight on horseback, Thuc., Xen.
ἱππομᾰχία, ή, a horse-fight, an action of cavalry, Thuc., etc.　From
ἱππο-μάχος, ον, (μάχομαι) fighting on horseback, a trooper, Simon., Luc.
ἱππο-μύρμηξ, ὁ, a horse-ant: pl. ant-cavalry, Luc.
ἱππο-νώμας, ὁ, (νωμάω) guiding or keeping horses, Soph., Eur.
ἱππο-πόλος, ον, (πολέω) busied with horses, Il.
ἵΠΠΟΣ, ὁ, ή, a horse, mare, Lat. equus, equa, Hom., etc.:—the pl. ἵπποι in Hom. are the chariot-horses, Il.:—hence ἵπποι is used for the chariot itself, καθ' ἵππων ἅλλεσθαι, ἐξ ἵππων βῆσαι, ἵππων ἐπεβήσετο Ib.:—the art of riding, though known to Hom., was an uncommon practice, cf. κέλης, κελητίζω.　II. as Collective Noun, ἵππος, ή, horse, cavalry, Lat. equitatus, Hdt., Att.; always in sing., as ἵππος χιλίη a thousand horse, Hdt.　III. ὁ ἵππος ὁ ποτάμιος the hippopotamus, Id.　IV. in Compos., ἵππος expressed anything large or coarse, as in our horse-chestnut, horselaugh, v. ἱππόκρημνος, etc.
ἱππό-στᾰσις, εως, ή, a stable:—metaph., Ἀελίου κνεφαία ἱππόστασις the dark stable of the Sun, i. e. the West, Eur.
ἱπποσύνη, ή, (ἵππος) the art of chariot-driving, horse-manship, Hom.　II. = ἵππος II, horse, cavalry, Orac. ap. Hdt.
ἱππόσυνος, η, ον, = ἱππικός, Eur.
ἱππότης, ου, ὁ, Ep. ἱπποτᾰ, ὁ, (ἵππος) ὁ, a driver or

rider of horses, a horseman, knight, Lat. eques, Hom., Hdt., etc. II. as Adj., ἱππότης λεώς the horse, the horsemen, Aesch., Soph.

ἱππο-τοξότης, ου, ὁ, a mounted bowman, horse-archer, Hdt., Thuc.

ἱπποτροφία, ἡ, a breeding or keeping of horses, esp. for racing, Simon., Thuc. From

ἱππο-τρόφος, ον, (τρέφω) horse-feeding, abounding in horses, Hes. II. of persons, breeding and keeping race-horses, Dem., Plut.

ἱππο-τῡφία, ἡ, (τῦφος) horse-pride, i.e. excessive pride, Luc.

ἵππ-ουρις, ιδος, (οὐρά) fem. Adj. horse-tailed, decked with a horse-tail, of helmets, Hom.

ἱπποφόρβιον, τό, a lot of horses out at grass, a troop of horses, Hdt., Xen. II. a stable, Eur. From

ἱππο-φορβός, όν, (φέρβω) a horse-keeper, Plat.

ἱππ-ώδης, ες, (εἶδος) horse-like, Xen.

ἱππών, ῶνος, ὁ, a place for horses: 1. a stable, Xen. 2. a posting-house, station, Id.

ἱππωνεία, ἡ, a buying of horses, Xen. From

ἱππ-ωνέω, (ὠνέομαι) to buy horses, Xen.

ἵπταμαι, Dep., late form of the pres. πέτομαι, Mosch.

ΊΠΤΟΜΑΙ, f. ἵψομαι: Ep. 2 sing. aor. 1 ἵψαο: Dep. :— to press hard, oppress, Il., Theocr.

ἱρά, τά, Ion. for ἱερά.

ἱράομαι, Ion. for ἱεράομαι.

ἱρεία or ἱρηίη, Ion. for ἱέρεια.

ἱρεύς, ἱρηύς, ἱρήιον, Ion. for ἱερεύς, ἱερεύω, ἱερεῖον.

ἱρήν, ένος, ὁ, Ion. for εἰρήν.

ἵρηξ, ηκος, ὁ, Ion. for ἱέραξ.

Ἶρις, ιδος, ἡ, acc. Ἶριν, voc. Ἶρι:—Iris, the messenger of the gods, Il. II. as Appellat. ἶρις, ἡ:—the rainbow, iris, in Hom., as in the Bible, a sign to men, τέρας μερόπων ἀνθρώπων Il. 2. any bright-coloured circle as that round the eyes of a peacock's tail, Luc. 3. the plant Iris, Theophr.

ἱρόν, τό, Ion. for ἱερόν:—ἱρογίη, for ἱερουργία.

ἱρός, Ion. and poët. for ἱερός.

ἱρο-φάντης, ὁ, Ion. for ἱεροφάντης.

ἱρωσύνη, ἡ, Ion. for ἱερωσύνη.

ΊΣ [ῑ], ἡ, gen. ἰνός, acc. ἶνα, nom. pl. ἶνες, dat. ἴνεσι or ἰσί:—a muscle, esp. the muscle at the back of the neck, Il.:—in pl. the muscles, Hom. II. strength, force, Lat. vis, Hom.:—in periphr. like βίη, ἱερὴ ἲς Τηλεμάχοιο the strong Telemachus, Od., etc.

ἰσ-άγγελος, ον, like an angel, N. T.

ἰσ-άδελφος [ἰσᾰ], ον, like a brother, Eur.

ἰσάζω, f. άσω:—Pass., aor. 1 ἰσάσθην: pf. ἴσασμαι: (ἴσος):—to make equal, to balance, of a person holding scales, Il.; ἰσ. τὰς κτήσεις to equalise them, Arist.: —Med. to make oneself equal to another, Il.

ἰσαίτερος, ἰσαίτατος, Comp. and Sup. of ἴσος.

ἴσᾱμι, Dor. for ἴσημι.

ἰσ-άμιλλος, ον, equal in the race: neut. pl. as Adv., Anth.

ἴσαν, they went, Ep. 3 pl. impf. of εἶμι (ibo). II. they knew, Ep. 3 pl. plqpf. of οἶδα.

ἴσαντι, Dor. 3 pl. of ἴσημι.

ἰσ-άργυρος, ον, worth its weight in silver, Aesch.

ἰσ-άριθμος [ἰσᾰ], ον, equal in number.

ἴσας [ᾱ], Dor. 2 sing. of ἴσημι.

ἰσάσκετο [ῐ], Ep. 3 sing. impf. med. of ἰσάζω.

ἴσᾱτι, Dor. 3 sing. of ἴσημι.

ἰσ-ηγορία, Ion. -ίη, ἡ, (ἀγορεύω) equal freedom of speech, equality, Hdt., Xen.

ἰσ-ῆλιξ, ικος, ὁ, ἡ, of the same age with, τινι Xen.

ἴσημι, I know, only in Dor. forms, ἴσᾱμι, ἴσας, ἴσᾱτι, ἴσαντι, Theocr.

ἰσ-ήρης, ες, (*ἄρω) = ἴσος, Eur.

ἰσήριθμος, ον, poët. for ἰσάριθμος, Anth.

ἴσθι, know, imperat. of οἶδα. II. ἴσθι, be, imperat. of εἰμί (sum).

Ἴσθμια, ων, τά, v. Ἴσθμιον II.

Ἰσθμιάς, άδος, ἡ, (ἴσθμιον II) Isthmian, Thuc.

ἴσθμιον, τό, (ἰσθμός) anything on the neck, a necklace, Od. II. Ἴσθμια (sc. ἱερά), τά, the Isthmian games, holden on the Isthmus of Corinth, Ar., etc.

ἴσθμιος, α, ον, or ος, ον, Isthmian, Soph.

Ἰσθμόθεν, Adv. from the Isthmus, Anth.; and

Ἰσθμόθι, Adv. on the Isthmus, Anth.; and

Ἰσθμοῖ, Adv. on the Isthmus, ap. Plut. From

ἰσθμός, οῦ, ὁ, (εἶμι ibo) : any narrow passage: esp. a neck of land between two seas, an isthmus, Hdt., Aesch., etc. 2. ὁ Ἰσθμός was the Isthmus of Corinth, Hdt.

ἰσθμ-ώδης, ες, (εἶδος) like an isthmus, Thuc.

Ἰσιακός [ῐ], ή, όν, of or for Isis:—fem. Ἰσιάς, άδος, ἡ, Anth. From

Ἶσις, ἡ, gen. Ἴσιδος, Ion. Ἴσιος, dat. Ἴσι, acc. Ἶσιν:— Isis, an Egypt. goddess, answering to the Greek Demeter, Hdt.

ἴσκε, ἴσκεν, Ep. for ἔνισπεν, he said, he spake, Od.; 1 pers. ἴσκον in Theocr.

ἴσκω, = ἐΐσκω, to make like, τί τινι Od.; ἴσκε ψεύδεα πολλὰ λέγων ἐτύμοισιν ὁμοῖα speaking many lies he made them like truths, i.e. seemed to speak truth, Ib. II. to think like, τινά τινι Il.: absol., ἴσκεν ἕκαστος ἀνήρ every one fancied, i.e. took false for real, Od. 2. to deem, suppose, Anth.

ἰσο-βᾰσιλεύς, έως, ὁ, ἡ, equal to a king, Plut.

ἰσό-γαιος, ον, (γαῖα) like land, Luc.

ἰσο-γονία, ἡ, (γονή) equality of kind, Plat.

ἰσο-δαίμων, ον, gen. ονος, godlike, Aesch.

ἰσο-δίαιτος, ον, (δίαιτα) living on an equality, Thuc.

ἰσό-δρομος, ον, running equally, of equal length, Anth.

ἰσο-ζῠγής, ές, (ζυγόν) evenly balanced : equal, Anth.

ἰσό-θεος, ον, equal to the gods, godlike, Hom., Att.

ἰσοθεόω, to make equal to the gods, Aesop.

ἰσο-κίνδῡνος, ον, equal to the danger or risk, a match for, Thuc.

ἰσό-κληρος, ον, equal in property, Plut.

ἰσο-κρᾰτής, ές, (κράτος) of equal power, possessing equal rights with others, Il.

ἰσο-μάτωρ [ᾱ], Dor. for -μήτωρ, ὁ, ἡ, like one's mother, Theocr.

ἰσό-μᾰχος, ον, (μάχομαι) equal in battle, Xen.

ἰσο-μεγέθης, ες, (μέγεθος) equal in size, Xen.

ἰσο-μέτωπος, ον, (μέτωπον) with equal front, Xen.

ἰσο-μήκης, ες, (μῆκος) equal in length, Plat.

ἰσομοιρέω, f. ήσω, to have an equal share, Thuc., Xen.; and

ἰσομοιρία, Ion. -ίη, ἡ, an equal share, partnership, τινός in a thing, Thuc. From

ἰσό-μοιρος, ον, (μοῖρα) *sharing equally* or *alike*, c. gen., Xen.   **2.** *coextensive*, Aesch.; γῆς ἰσόμοιρ' ἀήρ earth's *equal partner* air, Soph.

ἰσό-μορος, ον, = ἰσόμοιρος, used by Poseidon of himself as ἰσόμορος with Zeus, Il.

ἰσ-όνειρος, ον, *dream-like, empty,* Aesch.

ἰσό-νεκυς, υος, ὁ, ἡ, *dying equally* or *alike,* Eur.

ἰσο-νομέομαι, (νόμος) Pass. *to have equal rights,* Thuc.

ἰσονομία, Ion. -ίη, ἡ; *equality of rights, the equality* of a Greek democracy, Hdt., Thuc.

ἰσό-νομος, ον, of states, *having equal rights,* Scol. Gr.

ἰσό-παις, ὁ, ἡ, *like a child, as of a child,* Aesch.

ἰσο-πάλαιστος, ον, (παλαιστή) *a span long,* Anth.

ἰσο-πᾰλής, ές, (πάλος) *equal in the struggle, well-matched,* Hdt.   **2.** generally, *equivalent,* Thuc.

ἰσό-πᾰλος, ον, = foreg., Luc.

ἰσό-πεδον, τό, *level ground, a flat,* Il., Xen.

ἰσό-πεδος, ον, (πέδον) *of even surface, level* or *even with,* c. dat., Hdt.

ἰσο-πλᾱτής, ές, (πλάτος) *equal in breadth,* τινι to a thing, Thuc.

ἰσο-πλάτων, ωνος, ὁ, *another Plato,* Anth.

ἰσο-πληθής, ές, *equal in number* or *quantity,* τινι to a person or thing, Thuc.

ἰσό-πρεσβυς, υ, *like an old man,* Aesch.

ἰσορροπία, ἡ, *equipoise, equilibrium,* Plat.   From

ἰσόρ-ροπος, ον, (ῥοπή) *equally balanced, in equipoise,* of the balance, Plat.; metaph. of fortune, Aesch.; *of a* conflict, Eur.:—c. dat. *equally matched with,* Hdt.; so, c. gen., *in equipoise with,* Thuc.

ΊΣΟΣ, η, ον, Ep. **ἶσος** and **ἔϊσος:**—*equal to, the same as,* c. dat., or absol. *equal, like,* Hom., etc.:—ἴσα πρὸς ἴσα '*measure* for *measure,*' Hdt.; of the mixture of wine with water, ἴσος οἶνος ἴσῳ ὕδατι κεκραμένος Comici; metaph., μηδὲν ἴσον ἴσῳ φέρων not mixing *half and half,* i. e. not giving *tit for tat,* Ar.   **II.** *equally divided, equal,* Hom., Soph.:—τὰ ἴσα *an equal share, fair measure,* Hdt., Soph.:—ἴσαι (sc. ψῆφοι) *votes equally divided,* Ar.   **2.** at Athens, of *the equal division of all civic rights,* Thuc., etc.:—τὰ ἴσα *equal rights, equality,* Dem.:—also, ἡ ἴση καὶ ὁμοία (sc. δίκη) Thuc., etc.; ἐπ' ἴσῃ τε καὶ ὁμοίῃ *on fair and equal* terms, Hdt.   **III.** of persons, *fair, impartial,* Soph., Plat., etc.   **IV.** of ground, *even, level, flat,* Lat. *aequus,* εἰς τὸ ἴσον καταβαίνειν, of an army, Xen.   **V.** Adv., ἴσως, v. sub voc.:—but there are other adverbial forms, **1.** neut. sing., ἴσον Κηρὶ *even as Death,* Il.; ἴσον ἐμοί *like me,* Ib.; ἴσον τῷ πρίν *equally as before,* Eur.; followed by καί, ἴσα καί . . *like as, as if,* Lat. *aeque ac,* Soph., etc.:—absol. *alike,* Id.   **2.** with Preps.:—ἀπὸ τῆς ἴσης *equally,* Lat. *ex aequo,* Thuc.; ἀπ' ἴσης Dem.:—ἐν ἴσῳ *equally,* Thuc., etc.;—ἐξ ἴσου Hdt., Att.:—ἐπὶ ἴσης, later ἐπίσης, Hdt., Att.   **VI.** Att. Comp. ἰσαίτερος Eur., etc.

ἰσο-σκελής, ές, (σκέλος) *with equal legs, isosceles,* Plat.   **2.** of numbers, *that can be divided into two equal parts, even* (as 6 = 3 + 3), Id.

ἰσο-στάσιος, ον, (ἵστημι) *in equipoise with, equivalent to,* τινι Plut., Luc.

ἰσοτέλεια, ἡ, *the condition of an* ἰσοτελής, *equality in tax and tribute,* Xen.

ἰσοτέλεστος, ον, (τελέω) *fulfilled alike,* ὁ ἐπίκουρος ἰσ., the ally *that comes to all alike,* of Death, Soph.

ἰσο-τελής, ές, (τέλος) *paying alike, bearing equal burdens:* at Athens, the ἰσοτελεῖς were a class of μέτοικοι, who needed no patron (προστάτης), and paid no alien-tax (μετοίκιον), Lys., etc.

ἰσότης, ητος, ἡ, (ἴσος) *equality,* Eur., etc.

ἰσοτιμία, ἡ, *equality of privilege,* Luc.   From

ἰσό-τιμος, ον, (τιμή) *held in equal honour, having the same privileges,* Plut., etc.

ἰσο-φᾰρίζω, (φέρω) *to match oneself with, be a match for, cope with,* c. dat., Il.

ἰσο-φόρος, ον, (φέρω) *bearing* or *drawing equal weights, equal in strength,* Od.

ἰσο-χειλής, ές, (χεῖλος) *level with the brim,* Xen.

ἰσό-χνοος, ον, *equally woolly with,* τινι Anth.

ἰσοψηφία, ἡ, *equal right to vote,* Plut.   From

ἰσό-ψηφος, ον, *with* or *by an equal number of votes,* Aesch.   **II.** *having an equal vote with others, equal in authority,* Eur., Thuc.

ἰσό-ψῡχος, ον, (ψυχή) *of equal spirit,* κράτος ἰσ. Aesch.   **2.** *of like soul* or *mind,* N. T.

ἰσόω [ῐ], f. -ώσω, (ἴσος) *to make equal,* Soph., Ar., etc.:—Med., ὄνυχας χεῖράς τε ἰσώσαντο, i. e. used them in like manner, Hes.:—Pass. *to be made like* or *equal to,* c. dat., Od., Soph.

ἰστάμεν, ἰστάμεναι, Ep. for ἱστάναι, inf. of ἵστημι.

ἰστάνω, late form of ἵστημι, N. T., etc.

ἵστᾰσο, pres. imper. pass. of ἵστημι.

ἰστάω, collat. form of ἵστημι, Hdt.

ἴστε, 2 pl. of οἶδα.

ἵ-στημι (for σί-στημι, redupl. from ΣΤΑ):   **I.** Causal Tenses, *to make to stand,* Lat. *sisto,* pres. ἵστην, imper. ἵστη or ἵστα: impf. ἵστην, Ep. 3 sing. ἵστασκε:—f. στήσω, Dor. στάσῶ:—aor. 1 ἔστησα, Ep. 3 pl. ἔστᾰσαν for ἔστησαν; so aor. 1 med. ἐστησάμην.   **II.** intr. *to stand,* Lat. *sto,* **1.** of the Act., aor. 2 ἔστην Ep. στάσκον, 3 pl. ἔστησαν Ep. also ἔσταν, στάν [ᾰ]; imper. στῆθι, Dor. στᾶθι; subj. στῶ, Ep. 2 and 3 sing. στήῃς, στήῃ (for στῇς, στῇ), στέωμεν and στείομεν for στῶμεν; opt. σταίην, inf. στῆναι, Ep. στήμεναι; part. στάς:—pf. ἕστηκα, plqpf. ἑστήκειν, Att. also εἱστήκειν; Ion. 3 sing. ἑστήκεε: the usual dual and pl. forms of pf. are ἕστᾰτον, ἕστᾰμεν, ἕστᾰτε, ἕστᾰσι Ion. ἑστέᾱσι; imperat. ἕστᾰθι; subj. ἑστῶ; opt. ἑσταίην; inf. ἑστάναι, Ep. ἑστάμεν, ἑστάμεναι, part. ἑστώς, ἑστῶσα, ἑστός, Ion. ἑστεώς, ῶτος, Ep. ἑστηώς, gen. ἑστᾰότος, acc. ἑστᾰότα, nom. pl. ἑστᾰότες, plqpf., ἑστήκη [ᾰ], ἕστᾰμεν, ἕστᾰτε, ἕστᾰσαν.   **2.** Pass., ἵστᾰμαι: imper. ἵστω, Ep. ἵστασο: impf. ἱστάμην: f. στᾰθήσομαι and in med. form στήσομαι; also (from pf. ἕστηκα) a 3 fut. ἑστήξω, ἑστήξομαι:—aor. 1 ἐστάθην [ᾰ]: pf. ἕσταμαι.

    A. Causal, *to make to stand, set,* Hom., etc.:—*to set men in array, post them,* Il., Xen.   **II.** *to make to stand, stop, stay, check,* Hom., etc.; στῆσαι τὴν φάλαγγα *to halt it,* Xen.; στ. τὰ ὄμματα *to fix them,* of a dying man, Plat.; ἱ. τὸ πρόσωπον, Lat. *componere vultum,* Xen.   **III.** *to set up,* ἱστ. ἱστόν *to set up* the loom, or *to raise* the mast, Hom.; *to raise* buildings, statues, trophies, etc., Hdt., Att.; ἱστάναι τινὰ χαλκοῦν *to set* him *up* in brass, raise a brasen

statue to him, Dem. **2.** *to raise, rouse, stir up,* Hom., etc.; φυλόπιδα στήσειν *to stir up* strife, Od.; in aor. 1 med., στήσασθαι μάχην Ib. **3.** *to set up, appoint,* τινὰ βασιλέα Hdt.; Pass., ὁ σταθεὶς ὕπαρχος Id. **4.** *to establish, institute* a festival, Id., Att. **IV.** *to place in the balance, weigh,* Il., etc.; ἱστάναι τι πρός τι *to weigh* one thing *against* another, Hdt. **B.** Pass. and intr. tenses of Act. *to be set* or *placed, to stand,* Hom.:—often merely for εἶναι, *to be there,* Od., etc.; with an Adv. *to be in a* certain *state* or *condition,* ἵνα χρείας ἕσταμεν *in* what a state of need we are, Soph., etc. **2.** *to lie, be situated,* Thuc. **II.** *to stand still, stop, halt,* Hom.: *to stand idle,* Il.: *to stop, cease, be at rest,* Ib. **2.** metaph. *to stand firm,* Xen. **III.** *to stand up, rise up,* Il.; of a horse, ἵστασθαι ὀρθός *to rear up,* Hdt. **2.** *to arise, begin,* Il. **3.** in marking Time, ἔαρος ἱσταμένοιο as spring *was beginning,* Od.; ἕβδομος ἑστήκει μείς *the seventh month began,* Il.; τοῦ μὲν φθίνοντος μηνός, τοῦ δ' ἱσταμένοιο as one month ends and the next *begins,* Od.; the month in Hom. being divided into *two* parts, ἱστάμενος and φθίνων; but in the Att. Calendar, it fell into *three* decads, ἱστάμενος, μεσῶν, φθίνων, Thuc. **4.** *to be appointed,* στῆναι ἐς ἀρχήν Hdt.

ἱστίη, Ion. for ἑστία:—and as prop. n. Ἱστίη for Ἑστία.

ἱστίον, τό, (ἱστός) any *web,* a *sail,* ἱστία στέλλεσθαι, μηρύεσθαι, καθελεῖν *to lower* or *furl sail,* Od.; ἄκροισι χρῆσθαι ἱστίοις *to keep* the *sails* close-reefed, Il.

ἱστο-βοεύς, Ion. gen. ῆος, ὁ, (βοῦς) the *plough-tree* or *pole,* Hes.

ἱστο-δόκη, ἡ, (δέχομαι) the *mast-crutch,* on which the mast rested when let down, Il.

ἵστον, 2 and 3 dual of οἶδα.

ἱστο-πέδη, Dor. -πέδα, ἡ, a *hole* in the keel *for stepping* the *mast,* Od.

ἱστό-ποδες, οἱ, (πούς) the *long beams of the loom,* Anth.

ἱστό-πόνος, ον, *working at the loom,* Anth.

ἱστορέω, f. ήσω, (ἵστωρ) *to inquire into* a thing, *to learn by inquiry,* Hdt., Aesch., etc.; *to examine,* and in pf. sense, *to know,* Aesch. **2.** c. acc. pers. *to inquire of, ask,* Hdt., Eur.:—Pass. *to be questioned,* Eur. **b.** c. acc. pers. also *to inquire about* one, Soph., Eur. **3.** c. dupl. acc. *to inquire of* one *about* a thing, Eur. **4.** absol. *to inquire,* Hdt. **II.** *to narrate what one has learnt,* Arist., Luc. Hence

ἱστορία, Ion. -ίη, ἡ, a *learning by inquiry, inquiry,* Hdt., Plat. **2.** the *knowledge so obtained, information,* Hdt. **II.** an *account of one's inquiries, a narrative, history,* Arist.

ἱστορικός, ή, όν, *of* or *for inquiry : historical,* Plut.

ἱστός, ὁ, (ἵστημι) anything *set upright :* **I.** a ship's *mast,* ἱστὸν στῆσαι or στήσασθαι *to step* the *mast,* Hom.:—a *rod, pole,* Hdt. **II.** the *beam* of the loom, which *stood upright,* instead of lying horizontal as in our looms, Hom.; ἱστὸν στήσασθαι *to set up* the *beam* and so begin a web, Hes.; ἱστὸν ἐποίχεσθαι *to traverse the loom,* because the weaver was obliged to walk to and fro, Hom. **2.** the *warp that was fixed to the beam,* the *web,* Id.

ἱστό-τονος, ον, (τείνω) *stretched in the loom,* Ar.

ἱστουργέω, f. ήσω, *to work at the loom,* Soph.; and

ἱστουργία, ἡ, *weaving,* Plat. From

ἱστ-ουργός, ὁ or ἡ, (*ἔργω) a *worker at the loom.*

ἴστω, 3 sing. imperat. of οἶδα.

ἱστῶ, Dor. for ἱστοῦ, gen. of ἱστός.

ἵστωρ or ἴστωρ, ορος, ὁ, ἡ, (οἶδα) a *wise man, one who knows right, a judge,* Il. **II.** as Adj. *knowing,* Hes.; ἵστωρ τινός *knowing* a thing, Soph.

ἰσχάδιον [ἄ], τό, Dim. of ἰσχάς, Hdt.

ἰσχ-αιμος, ον, (ἴσχω, αἷμα) *staunching blood,* Luc.

ἰσχαλέος, α, ον, poët. for ἰσχνός, *thin,* Od.

ἰσχανάω, Ep. for ἰσχάνω, Ep. 3 sing. -άᾳ, impf. -άασκον:—Pass., Ep. 3 pl. pres. and impf. - όωνται, -όωντο:—*to hold back, check,* Hom. **II.** c. gen. *to cling to, long after, desire eagerly,* Id.

ἰσχάνω [ἄ], Ep. lengthd. form of ἴσχω, *to check, hinder,* Il.:—c. gen. *to keep back from,* Hes.

ἰσχάς, άδος, ἡ, (ἰσχνός) a *dried fig,* Ar.

ἰσχίον, τό, the *hip-joint,* Hom. **2.** in pl. the *fleshy parts round the hip-joint,* the *haunches, hams,* Il., etc. (Deriv. uncertain.)

ἰσχναίνω, f. -ᾰνῶ : aor. 1 ἴσχνᾱνα, Ion. -ηνα: (ἰσχνός):—*to make dry* or *withered, to dry up,* Hdt., Att.:—metaph., θυμὸν ἰσχναίνειν *to bring down* a proud stomach, Aesch.; τὴν τέχνην ἴσχνανα *I refined* the art (Tragedy), Aesch.

ἰσχνο-πάρειος, ον, (παρειά) *with withered cheeks,* Anth.

ἰσχνός, ή, όν, (ἴσχω) *dry, withered, lean, meagre,* Ar.

ἰσχνό-φωνος, ον, (φωνή) *checked in one's voice, stuttering, stammering,* Hdt.

ἰσχῡρίζομαι, f. Att. ιοῦμαι: aor. 1 ἰσχῡρισάμην: Dep.: (ἰσχυρός):—*to make oneself strong, to be strong, gain force,* Xen. **II.** *to contend stoutly, to persist obstinately in* doing, c. part., Thuc.: esp. *to maintain stiffly, obstinately,* Id., Plat. **2.** *to put firm trust in* a thing, c. dat., Dem. Hence

ἰσχῡριστέον, verb. adj. *one must maintain,* Plat.

ἰσχῡρός, ά, όν, (ἰσχύς) *strong, mighty,* Hdt., Soph.; τὸ ἰσχυρόν *strength, vigour,* Thuc.; τὰ ἰσχυρότατα *your strongest points,* Id.:—*hard,* χθών Aesch. **2.** *obstinate, stiff, stubborn, inveterate, excessive, severe,* Hdt., Thuc. **II.** Adv. -ρῶς, *strongly, with all force,* Thuc.:—*exceedingly,* Hdt., Xen.

ἰσχύς [ῡ], ύος [ῠ], ἡ, (perh. akin to ἔχω, ἴσχω) *strength* of body, Att., Hes.; a fortified *place,* Thuc. **2.** *might, power, force,* Aesch., etc.; κατ' ἰσχύν *perforce,* Id.; πρὸς ἰσχύος χάριν Eur. **II.** a *force of soldiers,* Xen. Hence

ἰσχύω [ῡ], f. ύσω [ῡ]: aor. 1 ἴσχῡσα: pf. ἴσχῡκα: (ἰσχύς):—*to be strong* in body, Soph., Xen., etc. **2.** *to be strong, mighty, powerful, prevail,* Aesch., etc.; πλέον, μεῖζον ἰσχ. Eur.; ἰσχ. παρά τινι *to have power* or *influence* with one, Thuc.

ἴσχω, a form of ἔχω only in pres. and impf. ἴσχον, Ep. inf. ἰσχέμεναι, ἰσχέμεν:—*to hold, check, curb, keep back, restrain,* Hom.:—c. gen. *to keep from,* Il., Eur., etc.; also, ἴσχ. τινὰ μὴ πράσσειν Id. **2.** intr., ἴσχε *hold, stay, stop,* Aesch.; of ships, *to lie at anchor,* Thuc.:—so in Pass., ἴσχεσθ' Ἀργεῖοι, μὴ φεύγετε Od.; ἴσχεο Hom.:—c. gen. *to desist from,* Od.; ἴσχετο impers., *here it stopped,* Xen. **II.** *to hold fast, hold, maintain,* Il., Soph. **III.** like ἔχω, *to hold* or *have in possession,*

to have, Hdt., Att.: *to have* a wife, Hdt.: *to have* a child, Id. 2. intr., with an Adv., *to be so and so*, Thuc.

ἰσ-ωνία, ἡ, (ὠνή) *sameness of price, fair price,* Ar.

ἴσως, Adv. of ἴσος, *equally, in like manner,* Soph.: Sup. ἰσαίτατα Plat. **II.** *equally, fairly, equitably,* Dem. **III.** *probably, perhaps,* Hdt., Att. ;—in Att. often joined with ἄν or τάχ' ἄν, Soph., etc. **IV.** with numerals, *about,* Ar.

ἴσωσα, aor. 1 of ἰσόω.

Ἰταλία, Ion. -ίη, ἡ, *Italy,* Hdt., etc. Hence

Ἰταλιώτης, ου, ὁ, *an Italiote,* i. e. *a Greek inhabitant of Italy,* Thuc. :—fem. -ῶτις, ιδος, Adj. *Italian,* Id.

Ἰταλός, ὁ, *Italian :—*as Adj., Anth.

ἰταλός, ὁ, = ταῦρος, whence Italy is said to be derived, cf. Lat. *vitulus.*

ἰταμός [ῐ], η, όν, (εἶμι *ibo*) *headlong, hasty, eager, ready for anything, reckless,* Lat. *audax,* Aesch., Dem.

ἸΤΕ'Α, Ion. ἰτέη, ἡ, *a willow,* Lat. *salix,* Il., Hdt., etc. **II.** *a wicker shield, target,* Eur. Hence

ἰτεΐνος [ῐτ], η, ον, *of willow,* Lat. *salignus,* Hdt. ; *made of wicker,* Theocr.

ἰτέον, verb. Adj. of εἶμι (*ibo*), *one must go,* Plat.

ἴτην, 3 dual of εἶμι (*ibo*).

ἴτης, ου, ὁ, = ἰταμός, Ar., Plat.

ἰτητέον, = ἰτέον, Ar.

ἰτός, ή, όν, (εἶμι *ibo*) *passable,* Anth.

ἰτρίνεος, α, ον, *like a cake,* Anth. From

ἼΤΡΙΟΝ, τό, *a cake* of sesamé and honey, Ar.

ἴττω, Boeot. for ἴστω, 3 sing. imperat. of οἶδα, ἴττω Ζεύς Zeus *be witness!* Ar., Plat.

ἰτῦς [ῐ], υος, ἡ, *a circle made of willow* (cf. ἰτέα) : of the felloe of a wheel, Il. :—*the edge* or *rim* of a shield, Hes., Hdt. ; *the round shield* itself, Eur., Xen.

ἴτω [ῐ], 3 sing. imperat. of εἶμι (*ibo*), *let him* or *it go,* Hom., Att.

ἴτων, 3 dual and also pl. of εἶμι (*ibo*).

ἰυγή [ῠ], ἡ, (ἰύζω) *a howling, shrieking, yelling,* as of men in pain, Orac. ap. Hdt., Soph.

ἰυγμός, ὁ, (ἰύζω) *a shouting, shout of joy,* Il. **II.** *a cry of pain, shriek,* Aesch., Eur.

ἴυγξ, ἴυγγος, ἡ, (ἰύζω) *the wryneck,* so called from its cry. The ancient witches used to bind it to a wheel, believing that, as it turned, it drew men's hearts along with it, Xen., Theocr. 2. metaph. *a spell, charm, passionate yearning for,* c. gen., Aesch.

ἰύζω, aor. 1 ἴυξα, (ἰού) *to shout, yell,* Hom. :—later *to yell* or *cry* from grief or pain, Aesch., Soph. [ῐ, Ep. and Pind. ; ῑ in Soph.]

ἰυκτής [ῑ], οῦ, ὁ, (ἰύζω) *one who shouts* or *yells :* also, *a singer, whistler, piper,* Theocr.

ἴφθιμος, η, ον, or ος, ον, (ἶφι, ἴφιος) *stout, strong, stalwart,* Il. :—of women, *comely, goodly,* Hom.

ἶφι, Ep. Adv., an old dat. of ἴς, *strongly, stoutly, mightily,* Hom.

ἰφι-γένεια, ἡ, (γίγνομαι) *strong-born :—*as prop. n. Iphigeneia, Agamemnon's daughter, Trag. ; called Ἰφιάνασσα by Hom.

ἴφιος, α, ον, (ἶφι) *stout, fat, goodly,* of sheep, Hom.

ἰχθυάζομαι, Dep. = sq., Anth.

ἰχθυάω, (ἰχθύς) *to fish, angle,* Ep. impf. ἰχθυάασκον Od. ; c. acc. *to fish for,* Ep. 3 sing. ἰχθυάᾳ Ib. **II.** *to sport,* of fish, Hes.

ἰχθυβολεύς, έως, ὁ, = ἰχθυβόλος, Anth.

ἰχθυβολέω, f. ήσω, *to strike fish,* Anth. From

ἰχθυ-βόλος, ον, (βάλλω) *striking fish,* ἰχθ. μηχανή, of the trident, Aesch. 2. as Subst. *a fisher, angler,* Anth. **II.** pass., ἰχθ. θήρα *a spoil of speared fish,* Id.

ἰχθυ-βόρος, ον, (βιβρώσκω) *fish-eating,* Anth.

ἰχθύδιον, τό, Dim. of ἰχθύς, *a little fish,* Anth.

ἰχθυ-δόκος, ον, (δέχομαι) *holding fish,* Anth.

ἰχθυηρός, ά, όν, (ἰχθύς) *fishy, scaly,* i.e. *foul, dirty,* Ar.

ἰχθυο-ειδής, ές, (εἶδος) *fish-like, of fishes,* Hdt.

ἰχθυόεις, εσσα, εν, (ἰχθύς) *full of fish, fishy,* Hom. **II.** *consisting of fish,* Anth.

ἰχθυο-θηρητήρ, ῆρος, ὁ, (θηράω) *a fisherman,* Anth.

ἰχθυο-λύμης [λῠ], ου, ὁ, (λύμη) *plague of fish,* of a fish-eater, Ar.

ἰχθυο-τρόφος, ον, *feeding fish : full of fish,* Plut.

ἰχθυο-φάγος, ον, (φαγεῖν) *fish-eating :—*οἱ Ἰχθ. ἄνδρες *the Fish-eaters,* a tribe on the Arabian Gulf, Hdt.

ἰχθυ-πάγης, ές, (πήγνυμι) *piercing fish,* Anth.

ἸΧΘΥ'Σ [ῠ], ύος [ῠ], ὁ: acc. ἰχθύν, later ἰχθύα : voc. ἰχθύ: —pl. ἰχθύες, acc. ἰχθύας, contr. ἰχθῦς :—*a fish,* Hom., etc. **II.** in pl., οἱ ἰχθῦς *the fish-market,* Ar.

ἰχθῦσι-ληϊστήρ, ῆρος, ὁ, *a stealer of fish,* Anth.

ἰχθῡ-φάγος [ᾰ], ον, = ἰχθυοφάγος, Anth.

ἰχθυώδης, ες, = ἰχθυοειδής, *full of fish,* Hdt.

ἰχναῖος, α, ον, (ἴχνος) *following on the track,* h. Hom.

ἰχνεία, ἡ, (ἴχνος) *a casting about for the scent,* of hounds, Xen.

ἰχν-ελάτης, ου, ὁ, *one who pursues* the track, Anth.

ἰχνεύμων, ονος, ὁ, (ἰχνεύω) *the tracker :* an Egyptian animal of the weasel-kind, *which hunts out* crocodile's eggs, *the ichneumon, Pharaoh's rat,* Arist.

ἴχνευσις, εως, ἡ, *a tracking,* Xen. ; and

ἰχνευτής, οῦ, ὁ, *a tracker,* ἰχν. κύων a hound *that hunts by nose,* Anth. **II.** = ἰχνεύμων, Hdt.

ἰχνεύω, f. σω, (ἴχνος) *to track out, hunt after, seek out,* Soph., Eur. : metaph. τὴν ψῆφον ἰχν. *seeking for* the vote of condemnation, Ar. 2. ἰχν. ὄρη *to hunt* the mountains, Xen.

ἴχνιον, τό, (ἴχνος) *a track, trace, footstep,* Hom.

ἰχνο-πέδη, ἡ, *a kind of fetter* or *trap,* Anth.

ἼΧΝΟΣ, εος, τό, *a track, footstep,* Od., Hdt., etc. : metaph. *a track, trace, clue,* Trag. 2. poët. *a foot* or *leg,* Eur.

ἰχνο-σκοπέω, f. ήσω, *to examine the track,* Aesch.

ἸΧΩ'Ρ [ῑ], ῶρος, ὁ, *ichor, the etherial juice,* that flows in the veins of gods, Il. ;—Ep. acc. ἰχῶ for ἰχῶρα, Ib. : later *blood,* Aesch.

ἴψ, ὁ, gen. ἰπός [ῑ], nom. pl. ἶπες : (ἴπτομαι) :—*a worm that eats horn and wood,* Od.

ἴψαο, Ep. 2 sing. aor. 1 of ἴπτομαι.

ἴω, subj. of εἶμι (*ibo*).

ἰῶ, contr. for ἰδοῦ, imper. of ἰάομαι.

ἰώ, an exclamation of joy, as in Lat. *io triumphe!* Trag. 2. of grief or suffering, *oh !* Ib.

Ἰώ [ῑ], 'Ιοῦς, ἡ, acc. Ἰοῦν, voc. Ἰοῖ Aesch. :—*Io,* daughter of Inachus, Hdt., etc.

ἰωά, = ἰώ, Aesch.

ἰώγα, Boeot. for ἔγωγε.

ἰωγή, ἡ, *shelter,* Βορέω ὑπ' ἰωγῇ *under shelter* from the north-wind, Od. (Deriv. uncertain.)

ἰωή, ἡ, (ἀύω) *any loud sound: the shout* or *cry* of

men, Il. ; *the sound* of the lyre, Od. ; of the wind, of a fire, Il.

ἰωκή, ἡ, (διώκω) *rout, pursuit*, Il. :—Ἰωκή is personified Ib. :—metaplast. acc. ἰῶκα (as if from ἰώξ), Ib.

Ἴων, ωνος, ὁ, *Ion*, the son of Xuthus (or Apollo) and Creüsa, from whom sprung the Ionian race, Hdt. :—οἱ Ἴωνες *the Ionians*, etc. Hence

ἰώγα, Boeot. for ἔγωγε.

ἰωνιά, ᾶς, ἡ, (ἴον) *a violet-bed*, Lat. *violarium*, Ar.

Ἰωνικός, ή, όν, *Ionic, Ionian*, i. e. *effeminate*, Ar.

ἰῶτα, the letter iota, proverb. of anything very small, *the smallest letter, a jot* (the Hebr. *yôd*), N. T.

ἰωχμός [ῐ], ὁ, = ἰωκή, Il., Hes.

K.

Κ, κ, κάππα, τό, indecl., tenth letter in Gr. alphabet : as numeral κ΄ = 20, but ͵κ = 20,000 :—κ is the tenuis guttural mute, related to the medial γ and the aspir. χ. Changes of κ in the Gr. dialects : 1. Ion. κ replaces χ, as κιθών δέκομαι κύθρη for χιτών δέχομαι χύτρα :—it represents π, as κου κοτε κως, etc., for που ποτε πως, etc. ; so, ἴσκε = ἔσκεν, ἵππος Lat. *equus*. 2. Dor. κ is interchanged with τ, as ὅκα ἄλλοκα τῆνος for ὅτε ἄλλοτε κεῖνος.

κᾱ, Dor. for Ion. κε, = Att. ἄν, Ar., etc.

κάββαλε, Ep. for κατέβαλε, 3 sing. aor. 2 of καταβάλλω.

καββάς, Ep. for καταβάς, aor. 2 part. of καταβαίνω.

Κάβειροι, οἱ, *the Cabeiri*, divinities worshipped in Lemnos and Samothrace, reputed to be sons of Hephaestus or Vulcan, from their skill in working metals, Hdt.

κάγ, Ep. for κατά before γ, κὰγ γόνυ for κατὰ γόνυ, Il.

κάγκανος, ον, (καίω) *fit for burning, dry*, Hom., Theocr.

καγχάζω, later form for καχάζω, Babr.

καγχαλάω, *to laugh aloud*, Lat. *cachinnari*, in Ep. forms, 3 pl. καγχαλόωσι Il. ; part. καγχαλόων, -όωσα Hom. (Like καχάζω, formed from the sound.)

κάγχρυς, late form of κάχρυς.

κἀγώ [ᾰ], crasis for καὶ ἐγώ.

κάδ, Ep. for κατά before δ, κὰδ δώματα Od. ; κὰδ δύναμιν Hes. ; κὰδ δ᾽ ἔβαλε by tmesis for κατέβαλε δέ, Od.

κἀδάπανα, crasis for καὶ ἀδάπανα.

καδδραθέτην, Ep. for κατεδραθέτην, 3 dual aor. 2 of καταδαρθάνω.

καδδῦσαι, Ep. for καταδῦσαι, aor. 2 part. fem. of καταδύω.

κἀδίσκος, ὁ, Dim. of κάδος, *an urn* or *box* : there were two, in which the dicasts placed their votes of *guilty* or *not guilty*, Ar.

Καδμεῖος, α, ον, *Cadmean*, Hes., Trag. ; poët. Καδμεῖος, Pind., Soph., Ion. for Καδμήιος, η, ον :—Καδμεῖοι, οἱ, *the Cadmeans* or *ancient inhabitants of Thebes*, Hom., etc. ; also Καδμείωνες, Il. :—ἡ Καδμεία *the citadel of Thebes*, Xen. :—proverb., Καδμεία νίκη a dear-bought victory (from the story of the Σπαρτοί, or that of Polynices and Eteocles), Hdt.

Καδμηΐς, ίδος, fem. of Καδμεῖος, h. Hom., Hes. ; also in Att., Thuc.

Καδμο-γενής, ές, (γίγνομαι) *Cadmus-born*, Trag.

Κάδμος, ὁ, *Cadmus*, Od., Hes. : son of the Phoenician king Agenor, brother to Europa, founder of Boeotian Thebes. Cadmus brought from Phoenicia the old Greek alphabet of sixteen letters, hence called Καδμήια or Φοινικήια γράμματα (Hdt.) ; which was afterwards increased by the eight (so called) Ionic, η ω θ φ χ ζ ξ ψ.

κάδος [ᾰ], ὁ, (χαδεῖν ?) *a jar* or *vessel for water* or *wine*, Lat. *cadus*, Hdt., etc. 2. *a liquid measure*, = ἀμφορεύς, Anth. II. *an urn* or *box for collecting the votes*, like καδίσκος, Ar.

κάδος, Dor. for κῆδος.

Κάειρα, ἡ, fem. from Κάρ, *a Carian woman*, Il. II. Adj. fem. = Καρική, *Carian*, Hdt.

κάεις, aor. 2 pass. part. of καίω :—καήμεναι, Ep. for καῆναι, inf.

κάθά [ᾰ], Adv., for καθ᾽ ἅ, *according as, just as*, Xen. :—so καθάπερ, Ion. κατάπερ, Hdt., Ar., etc. :—strengthd., καθάπερ εἰ, Ion. κατάπερ εἰ, *like as if, exactly as*, Hdt., Plat. ; καθάπερ ἄν Dem. ; καθάπερ ἂν εἰ Plat., etc.

καθ-αγίζω, f. ίσω, Att. κατ- : *to devote, dedicate, offer to a god*, τί τινι Hdt., Ar., etc. :—*of a burnt offering*, Hdt. :—*to make offerings* to the manes, Lat. *parentare*, Luc. II. generally, *to burn*, καταγιζομένου τοῦ καρποῦ Hdt. :—*to burn* a dead body, and even *to bury*, Plut. :—so, ὅσων σπαράγματ᾽ ἢ κύνες καθήγισαν whose mangled bodies dogs *have buried*, i. e. *devoured*, Soph. Hence

καθάγισμός, ὁ, *funeral rites*, Lat. *parentalia*, Luc.

καθ-αγνίζω, f. Att. ιῶ, *to purify, hallow*, Luc. :—Pass., μήτηρ πυρὶ καθήγνισται δέμας, i. e. has been burnt on the funeral-pyre, Eur. II. *to offer as an expiatory sacrifice*, Eur.

καθαιμακτός, όν, *bloodstained, bloody*, Eur. From

καθ-αιμάσσω, f. ξω, *to make bloody, sprinkle* or *stain with blood*, Aesch., Eur.

καθ-αιμάτόω, = foreg., Eur., Ar.

κάθ-αιμος, ον, (αἷμα) *bloodstained, bloody*, Eur.

καθαίρεσις, εως, ἡ, (καθαιρέω) *a pulling down, rasing to the ground*, Thuc., Xen. : *destruction*, N. T.

καθαιρετέος, α, ον, verb. Adj. of καθαιρέω, *to be put down*, Thuc.

καθαιρέτης, ου, ὁ, *a putter down, overthrower*, Thuc. ; and

καθαιρετός, ή, όν, *to be taken* or *achieved*, Thuc. From

καθ-αιρέω, Ion. κατ- : f. ήσω : f. 2 καθελῶ : aor. 2 καθεῖλον, inf. καθελεῖν :—Pass., aor. 1 καθῃρέθην : pf. -ῄρημαι :—*to take down*, καθείλομεν ἱστία we lowered sail, Od. ; κ. ἄχθος *to take* a load down, Dem., etc. : *to take* off one's shoulders, Ar. :—Med., καταιρεῖσθαι τὰ τόξα *to take down* one's bow, Hdt. 2. *to put down* or *close* the eyes of the dead, Hom. 3. of sorcerers, *to bring down*, Lat. *caelo deducere*, σελήνην Id., Plat. 4. κατά με πέδον γᾶς ἕλοι (in tmesi) may earth *swallow* me! Eur. II. *to put down by force, destroy*, Od., Trag. : simply *to kill, slay*, Eur. 2. in a milder sense, *to put down, reduce*, Hdt., Dem., etc. : *to depose, dethrone*, Hdt. ; κ. τὸ ληστικόν *to remove* it utterly, Thuc. 3. *to rase to the ground, pull down*, τὰς πόλεις Id. ; τῶν τειχῶν a part of the walls, Xen. 4. *to cancel, rescind*, τὸ ψήφισμα Thuc. 5. as Att. law-term, *to condemn*, Soph. 6. *to reduce in flesh*, Plut. III. *to overpower, seize*, κὰδ δέ μιν ὕπνος ᾕρει (in tmesi) Od. ; καθ. τινὰ ἐν ἀφροσύνῃ *to*

*ratch in the act of folly, Soph. : c. gen. partis, κ. τῶν ὤτων to seize by the ears, Theocr. IV. to fetch down as a reward or prize, καθαιρεῖν ἀγῶνα or ἀγώνισμα Plut. : metaph. to achieve, Pind. ; so in Med., φόνῳ καθαιρεῖσθ᾽, οὐ λόγῳ, τὰ πράγματα Eur. ; in Pass., Hdt. V. more rarely like the simple αἱρέω, to take and carry off, seize, Id.

κᾰθαίρω: f. κᾰθᾰρῶ : aor. 1 ἐκάθηρα : Med., f. καθαροῦμαι : aor. 1 ἐκαθηράμην : —Pass., aor. 1 ἐκαθάρθην : pf. κεκάθαρμαι : (καθαρός) : I. of the person or thing purified, to make pure or clean, cleanse, clean, purge, καθήραντες χρόα ὕδατι Od. :—to purge, clear a land of monsters and robbers, Soph. 2. in religious sense, to cleanse, purify, [δέπας] ἐκάθηρε θεείῳ purified it by fumigating with sulphur, Il. ; καθ. τινὰ φόνου to purify him from blood, Hdt. ; Δῆλον κ. Id. :—Med. to purify oneself, get purified, Id. ; οἱ φιλοσοφίᾳ καθηράμενοι Plat. :—so Pass., κεκαθαρμένος Id. 3. to prune a tree, i. e. clear it of superfluous wood, N. T. 4. metaph., = μαστιγόω, like our vulgar phrase 'to rub down,' Theocr. II. of the thing removed by purification, to purge away, wash off or away, λύματα Il. ; ῥύπα Od. ; φόνον Aesch. III. c. dupl. acc., αἷμα κάθηρον Σαρπηδόνα cleanse Sarpedon of blood, wash the blood off him, Il. :—Pass., φόνον καθαρθείς Hdt.

καθ-άλλομαι, f. -άλοῦμαι : aor. 1 -ηλάμην : Dep. :—to leap down, Xen. : metaph. of a storm, to rush down, Il.

καθ-άπαν, Adv. on the whole ; divisim καθ᾽ ἅπαν.

καθ-άπαξ, Adv. once for all, Od., Dem. :—then, like ἁπλῶς, once for all, absolutely, Dem.

καθάπερ, καθαπερεί, καθαπερανεί, v. sub καθά.

καθαπτός, ή, όν, bound with, equipt with a thing, c. dat., Ar. From

καθ-άπτω, Ion. κατ-, f. ψω :—to fasten, fix or put upon, τί τινι Soph. ; so, κ. τι ἀμφί τινι Eur. ; ἐπί τι Xen. :—Pass., βρόχῳ καθημμένος (pf. part.) fastened with a halter, i. e. hung, Soph. 2. to dress, clothe, in Med., σκευῇ σῶμ᾽ ἐμὸν καθάψομαι Eur. 3. intr. in sense of Med. (II), to lay hold of, τινός N. T. II. Med., καθάπτεσθαί τινα ἐπέεσσι, in good or bad sense, as, σὺ τόν γ᾽ ἐπέεσσι καθάπτεσθαι μαλακοῖσι or μειλιχίοις do thou accost or address him with gentle words, Hom. ; or, ἀντιβίοις ἐπέεσσι καθαπτόμενος assailing or attacking . . , Od. : also without qualifying words, to accost or assail, γέροντα καθαπτόμενος προσέειπεν Id. 2. c. gen. to assail, attack, upbraid, Hdt., Att. :—also, like Lat. antestari, θεῶν καταπτόμενος appealing to them, Hdt. 3. to lay hold of, τυραννίδος Solon ; βρέφεος Theocr.

κᾰθάρειος, and **καθάριος**, ον, (καθαρός) of persons, cleanly, neat, nice, tidy, Lat. mundus, Arist. :—Adv. -είως or -ίως, Xen., etc.

κᾰθάρευτέον, one must keep oneself clean, Luc.

κᾰθάρεύω, f. σω, (καθαρός) to be clean or pure, Plat. : —c. gen. to be clean or free from guilt, Plat. ; also, κ. ἀπ᾽ αὐτοῦ (sc. τοῦ σώματος) Plat. ; also, καθ. γνώμῃ to be pure or clear in mind, Ar.

κᾰθᾰρίζω, f. Att. ιῶ, (καθαρός) to make clean, to cleanse, N. T. :—Pass. to be or become clean from disease, Ib. ; and of the disease, to be purged away, Ib.

κᾰθάριος, = καθάρειος.

κᾰθᾰριότης, ητος, ή, cleanliness, purity, Hdt., Xen.

κᾰθᾰρισμός, ό, later form for καθαρμός, N. T.

κάθαρμα, ατος, τό, (καθαίρω) that which is thrown away in cleansing ; in pl. the offscourings, refuse of a sacrifice, Aesch. 2. metaph. a castaway, outcast, Ar., Dem., etc. II. in pl. = κάθαρσις, purification, Eur. III. purified ground, ἐντὸς καθάρματος within the hallowed space, Ar.

καθ-αρμόζω, f. σω, to join or fit to, τί τινι Eur.

κᾰθᾰρμός, ό, (καθαίρω) a cleansing, purification from guilt, Soph. :—hence, a means of purification, purifying sacrifice, atonement, expiation, καθαρμὸν τῆς χώρης ποιεῖσθαί τινα to make him an atonement for his country, Hdt. ; μύσος ἐλαύνειν καθαρμοῖς by purifying rites, Aesch. ; θοῦ νῦν καθαρμὸν δαιμόνων avert their wrath by purification, Soph. ; καθαρμὸν θύειν to offer a purifying sacrifice, Eur. 2. applied to rites of initiation, Plat., Dem.

ΚΑΘΑΡΟ΄Σ, ά, όν : 1. clear of dirt, clean, spotless, unsoiled, Od., Hdt., Eur. 2. clear, open, free, ἐν καθαρῷ (sc. τόπῳ) in a clear, open space, Il. ; ἐν καθαρῷ βῆναι to leave the way clear, Soph. ; διὰ καθαροῦ ῥέειν, of a river whose course is clear and open, Hdt. ; τὸ ἐμποδὼν ἐγεγόνεε καθαρόν the hindrance was cleared away, Id. :—c. gen., γλῶσσα καθαρὴ τῶν σημηΐων clear of the marks, Id. 3. in moral sense, clear from shame or pollution, pure, καθαρῷ θανάτῳ Od. : esp. clear of guilt or defilement, clean, pure, Theogn., Aesch. ; καθαρὸς χεῖρας Hdt. :—so, of persons purified after pollution, ἱκέτης προσῆλθες κ. Aesch. ; of things, βωμοί, θύματα, δόμοι, μέλαθρα Id., Eur. :—c. gen. clear of or from a charge, κ. ἐγκλημάτων, ἀδικίας, κακῶν, etc., Horace's sceleris purus, Plat., Xen. 4. opp. to θολερός, clear of admixture, clear, pure, of water, Hdt., Eur. ; so, κ. φάος, φέγγος Pind. ; κ. ἄρτος χρυσός Hdt. ; ἀργύριον Theocr. 5. of birth, opp. to ξένος, pure, genuine, Pind., Eur. ; τῶν Ἀθηναίων ὅπερ ἐστράτευε καθαρὸν ἐξῆλθε, i. e. who were citizens of pure blood, Thuc. :—καθαρόν a real, genuine saying, Id. 6. without blemish, τὸ καθαρὸν τοῦ στρατοῦ the sound portion of the army, Hdt. 7. clear, exact, ἂν καθαραὶ ὦσιν αἱ ψῆφοι if the accounts are clear, exactly balanced, Dem. II. Adv. καθαρῶς, Hes. ; καθαρῶς γεγονέναι to be of pure blood, Hdt. 2. with clean hands, honestly, Theogn., Plat. 3. clearly, plainly, λέγειν Ar. ; γνῶναι, εἰδέναι Id., Plat. Hence

κᾰθᾰρότης, ητος, ή, cleanness, purity, in moral sense, Plat.

καθ-αρπάζω, f. άξω or άσω, to snatch down, Eur.

κᾰθάρσιος, ον, (καθαίρω) cleansing from guilt or defilement, purifying, Hdt., Soph. :—of sacrifice, αἷμα Aesch. ; πῦρ, φλόξ Eur. 2. c. gen., κ. φόνου cleansing or purifying from blood, Aesch. ; but, κ. οἴκων purifying them, Eur. II. as Subst., καθάρσιον (sc. ἱερόν), τό, a purifying sacrifice, Aeschin. :—hence, purification, Hdt.

κάθαρσις, εως, ή, (καθαίρω) a cleansing from guilt or defilement, purification, Lat. lustratio, Hdt., Plat.

κᾰθαρτής, οῦ, ὁ, (καθαίρω) a cleanser from guilt or defilement, purifier, Soph., Ar., etc. Hence

κᾰθαρτικός, ή, όν, for cleansing or purifying, Plat.

καθεδοῦμαι, fut. of καθέζομαι.

καθ-έδρα, ἡ, a seat, κ. τοῦ λαγῶ a hare's seat or form, Xen. II. the posture of sitting, ἐν τῇ καθέδρᾳ while they were sitting idle, Thuc.

καθ-έζομαι: impf. ἐκαθεζόμην (as if the Verb were not a compd.), Xen.: f. καθεδοῦμαι: aor. 1 part. καθεσθείς: Dep.:—to sit down, take one's seat, Hom., Trag. 2. to sit as suppliants, Eur., Thuc. 3. to sit down in a country, encamp, Thuc.

καθέηκα, Ep. for καθῆκα, aor. 1 of καθίημι.

καθείατο, Ep. for ἐκάθηντο, 3 pl. impf. of κάθημαι.

καθεῖλον, aor. 2 of καθαιρέω.

καθεῖμαι, pf. pass. of καθίημι.

καθείμαρται, pf. pass., used impers. it is ordained to one's ruin, Plut., Luc.

καθ-είργνῡμι, Ion. κατ-: aor. 1 καθεῖρξα:—to shut in, enclose, confine, imprison, Od., Hdt., Att.

καθεῖς, for καθ' εἷς, one by one, εἷς καθεῖς, for εἷς καθ' ἕνα, N. T.

καθεῖσα, aor. 1 of καθίζω. II. καθεῖσαν, 3 pl. aor. 2 of καθίημι.

καθέκαστα, v. ἕκαστος.

καθεκτέον, verb. Adj. of κατέχω, one must keep back, Plut.

καθ-εκτός, ή, όν, (κατ-έχω) to be held back or checked, Dem.: to be retained, Plut.

καθελεῖν, aor. 2 of καθαιρέω.

καθ-ελίσσω, Ion. κατ-ειλίσσω, f. ξω, to wrap with bandages, enfold, swathe, Hdt.:—Pass., τὰς κνήμας ῥάκεσι κατειλίχατο (Ion. 3 pl. plqpf.), they have their legs swathed in rags, Id.

καθ-έλκω, f. -έλξω Ar. and -ελκύσω: aor. 1 καθείλκῠσα: pf. -είλκῠκα:—Pass., aor. 1 -ειλκύσθην: pf. -είλκυσμαι: 1. of ships, to draw them to the sea, launch them, Lat. deducere, Hdt., Att. 2. to draw down or depress the scale, Ar.

καθελοῦσα, Dor. for -οῦσα, aor. 2 part. fem. of καθαιρέω.

καθελῶ, fut. 2 of καθαιρέω:—καθελών, aor. 2 part.

κάθεμεν, Ep. 1 pl. aor. 2 of καθίημι.

καθέν, for καθ' ἕν, one by one.

καθέννῡμι, to clothe, v. καταέννυμι.

κάθεξις, εως, ἡ, (κατέχω) a holding, retention, Thuc.

καθέξω, fut. of κατέχω.

καθ-έρπω, aor. 1 καθείρπυσα, to creep down, Ar., Xen.

κάθες, imperat. aor. 2 of καθίημι.

κάθεσσα, poët. for καθεῖσα, aor. 1 of καθίζω.

καθεστάμεν, sync. for καθεστήκαμεν, 1 pl. pf. of καθίστημι.

καθεστηκότως, Adv. part. pf. act. of καθίστημι, steadily, calmly, Arist.

καθεστήξω, fut. 3 of καθίστημι, with intr. sense.

καθεστῶτα, ων, τά, syncop. for καθεστηκότα, pf. part. pl. neut. of καθίστημι.

κάθετος, ον, (καθίημι) let down, of a fishing-line, Anth.

καθευδητέον, verb. Adj. one must sleep, Plat. From

καθ-εύδω, Ion. κατ-εύδω: impf. καθεῦδον, Att. also καθηῦδον and ἐκάθευδον: f. καθευδήσω:—to lie down to sleep, sleep, Hom., etc.:—ἐκ τοῦ καθεύδοντος (part. neut.) from a sleeping state, Plat. II. metaph. to lie asleep, lie idle, Aesch., etc.:—also of things, to sleep, lie still, be at rest, ἐλπίδες καθεύδουσιν Eur.

καθ-ευρίσκω, f. -ευρήσω, to discover, Luc.:—Pass.,

καθευρέθη κοσμοῦσα she was found in the act of adorning, Soph.

καθ-εψιάομαι, Dep., to mock at, Lat. illudere, c. gen., Od.

καθ-έψω, f. -εψήσω, to boil down, Ar. II. metaph. to soften, temper, Xen.

κάθη, Att. for κάθησαι, 2 sing. of κάθημαι.

καθ-ηγεμών, όνος, ὁ, ἡ, a leader, a guide, Hdt.

καθ-ηγέομαι, Ion. κατ-ηγ-: f. ήσομαι: Dep.:—to go before, act as guide, lead the way, absol., Hdt., Thuc.; οἱ κατηγεόμενοι the guides, Hdt.:—c. dat. to guide a person, Id. 2. c. acc. rei, to go before and teach a thing, to explain, expound, Id. 3. c. gen., καθ. τοῦ λόγου to begin the discourse, Plat. 4. to be the first to do, to establish, institute, Hdt.; οὐ κατηγήσομαι τὸν νόμον τόνδε τιθείς I will not begin establishing this law, Id.

καθ-ηδυπάθέω, f. ήσω, to squander in luxury, Xen., Plut.

καθῆκα, aor. 1 of καθίημι.

καθ-ήκω, Ion. κατ-ήκω, f. -ήξω, to have come or gone down, esp. to fight, Aesch. 2. to come down to, come or reach to, Hdt. 3. to have come to any one, καθῆκεν ἐς ἡμᾶς ὁ λόγος the turn of speaking came to us, Aeschin. 4. of Time, ὁ χρόνος καθήκει the time is come, Xen.; ὅταν ἐκ τῶν νόμων καθήκῃ when [the time] appointed by the law comes, Dem. II. to be meet, fit, proper, τοῦ καθήκοντος χρόνου Soph.; αἱ καθ. ἡμέραι the regular, proper days, Dem. 2. impers., καθήκει μοι it belongs to me, beseems me, c. inf., οἷς καθήκει ἀθροίζεσθαι whose duty it is to assemble, Xen.:—in part. τὸ καθῆκον, τὰ καθήκοντα, Ion. τὰ κατήκοντα, that which is meet, fit or proper, one's due or duty, Hdt., Xen.; also the present state of things, circumstances, Hdt.

καθ-ηλιάζω, f. σω, to bring the sun down upon, to illuminate, Anth.

καθ-ηλόω, f. ώσω, to nail on or to, Plut.

κάθ-ημαι, Ion. κατ-; 2 sing. κάθησαι or κάθη, Ion. 3 pl. κατέαται: imper. κάθησο or καθοῦ, 3 sing. καθήσθω; opt. καθοίμην; inf. καθῆσθαι; part. καθήμενος: —impf. ἐκαθήμην, Ion. 3 pl. ἐκατέατο; Ion. κατῆστο, Ep. 3 pl. καθείατο, Ion. κατέατο:—to be seated, Hom., etc. 2. to be seated in court, Ar.; οἱ καθήμενοι the judges, the court, Thuc., etc. 3. to sit still, sit quiet, Lat. desidere, Hom., Hdt.: in bad sense, to sit or lie idle, Il., etc. 4. of a besieging army, to sit down or lie before a place, Eur., Thuc. 5. to lead a sedentary life, Hdt., Aesch., etc. 6. of people, to be settled, Hdt.

καθ-ημέριος, Dor. καθ-αμ-, α, ον, day by day, daily (καθ' ἡμέραν) Eur.:—later also καθημερινός, ή, όν, Plut. II. on this day, Soph.

κάθηραι, κάθηρας, aor. 1 inf. and part. of καθαίρω.

καθῆσθαι, inf. of κάθημαι.

κάθησο, imper. of κάθημαι:—κάθηστο, 3 sing. impf.

καθηῦδον, impf. of καθεύδως.

καθ-ιδρύω, f. ύσω [ῡ], Causal of καθέζομαι, to make to sit down, Od., Eur.:—Pass. to sit down, settle, Ar.; κ. ἐς Ἀργώ to take one's seat in Argos, Theocr. 2. to consecrate, dedicate: so in aor. 1 med. -ιδρυσάμην and pf. pass. -ίδρυμαι, Eur.

καθ-ιερεύω, f. σω, to sacrifice, offer, Plat., Arist.

καθ-ιερόω, Ion. **κατ-ῑρόω**, f. ώσω :—*to dedicate, devote, hallow*, Hdt., Att. Hence

καθιέρωσις, εως, ἡ, *a dedication*, Aeschin., Plut.

καθ-ιζάνω [ἄ], *to sit down*, θῶκόνδε καθῖζανον they *went* to the council *and took their seats*, Od. ; μάντις ἐς θρόνους κ. Aesch.

καθ-ίζω, Ion. **κατ-**: impf. καθῖζον or κάθιζον, Att. ἐκάθιζον (as if the Verb were not a compd.) :—f. Att. καθιῶ Xen., Dor. καθιξῶ :—aor. ι ἐκάθισα, Ep. κάθῖσα Il., Att. also καθῖσα, Ion. κατῖσα, Ep. part. καθίσσας, Dor. καθῖξας : —another aor. ι is καθεῖσα or -θεσσα :—Med., impf. ἐκαθιζόμην : f. καθιζήσομαι, later καθίσομαι :—aor. ι ἐκαθισάμην : **I.** Causal, *to make to sit down*, seat, Il., Hdt. ; καθίσαι τινὰ εἰς θρόνον Xen. **2.** *to set* or *place*, Hom. ; καθίσαι στρατόν *to encamp* it, Eur., Thuc. **b.** *to set* or *place* for *any purpose*, post, Od. ; καθίσαι φύλακους, φύλακας *to set* guards, Hdt., Aesch. **3.** *to set up*, ἀνδριάντα κάθεσσαν Pind. **4.** *to make* an assembly *take their seats*, Od. ; κ. τὸ δικαστήριον *to hold* the court, Ar. **5.** *to put into a certain condition*, κλαίοντά τινα κ. *to set* him a-weeping, Plat. ; also, κλαίειν τινὰ κ. *to make* him weep, Xen. **II.** intr., like καθέζομαι, *to sit down, be seated, take one's seat, sit*, Hom., etc. :—c. acc., καθ. τρίποδα, βωμόν, (as we say 'to sit at a horse'), Eur. **2.** *to sit at* meals, Lat. *discumbere*, Xen. **3.** *to sit as judge*, Hdt., Dem. **4.** *to sit down in a country, encamp*, Thuc. **5.** *to settle, sink in*, Plat. **III.** the Med. is also used in intr. sense, Il., Theocr., etc. ; καθίζεσθαι *to take their seats* (in the theatre), Dem.

καθ-ίημι, Ion. **κατ-**: f. καθήσω: aor. ι καθῆκα, Ep. καθέηκα: pf. καθεῖκα, etc. ; [ἱστία] ἐς νῆας κάθεμεν (ι pl. aor. 2) *we let down*, lowered the sails, Od. ; κ. ἄγκυραν Hdt. ; κ. καταπειρητηρίην *to let down* a sounding-line, Id. ; καθιέναι *to sound*, Plat. ; καθῆκε τὰ σκέλη *to let down* his legs, of one who had been lying down, Id. ; κ. δόρυ *to let down* one's pike, *bring* it *to the rest*, Xen. ; κ. τὰς κώπας *to let down* the oars, so as to stop the ship's way, Thuc. :—rarely of striking, δι' ὀμφαλοῦ καθῆκεν ἔγχος Eur. ; γόνυ καθεῖσαν sank on their knee, Id. :— Pass. *to come down*, of a cow's udder, Hdt. ; καθεῖτο τὰ τείχη the walls *were carried down* to the water, Thuc. **2.** *to send down* into the arena, enter for racing, ἅρματα, ζεύγη Id. ; τοῦτον τὸν λόγον καθεῖκε *has entered* this plea, Dem. **3.** *to set at*, Lat. *immittere*, Luc. :—Pass. *to be put in motion*, ἡ στρατηλασίη κατίετο ἐς τὴν Ἑλλάδα Hdt. **II.** seemingly intr. (sub. ἑαυτόν), *to swoop down* like a wind, Ar. ; of rivers, *to run down*, Plat. ; κ. εἰς γόνυ *to sink* on the knee, Plut.

καθίκεο [ῐ], 2 sing. aor. 2 of καθικνέομαι.

καθ-ικετεύω, Ion. **κατ-**, f. σω, *to beg earnestly*, Eur. **2.** *to offer earnest prayers*, Hdt.

καθ-ικνέομαι, f. -ίξομαι, aor. 2 -ἱκόμην : Dep. :—*to come down* to : metaph. *to reach, touch*, με καθίκετο πένθος Od. ; καθίκεο θυμόν *hast touched* my heart, Il. ; κάρα μου καθίκετο *came down* upon my head, Soph.

καθ-ιμάω [ῑ], f. ήσω, *to let down by a rope*, Ar.

καθίξω, Dor. aor. ι subj. of καθίζω :—**καθίξας**, part.

καθ-ιππάζομαι, f. άσομαι, Dep. *to ride down*, over-

run with horse, Hdt. **2.** *to ride down, trample under foot*, Aesch.

καθ-ιππεύω, f. σω, = καθιππάζομαι 2, Eur.

καθιστάνω, = καθίστημι Lys. :—also **καθιστάω**, N: T.

καθίστημι, **A.** in Causal sense ; of Act., pres. impf., fut. ; of Med., the aor. ι, and sometimes pres. : —*to set down, place*, Il. ; νῆα κατάστησον *stop* it, *bring* it *to land*, Od. ; κ. δίφρον *to station* it, before starting for the race, Soph. :—Med., [λαῖφος] κατεστήσαντο *steadied* the sails, h. Hom. **2.** *to bring down* to a place, Od., etc. :—*to restore*, ἐς φῶς σὸν κατ. βίον Eur. :—Pass., οὐκ ἂν χάρις καθίσταιτο *would* not *be returned*, Thuc. **3.** *to bring before* a magistrate or king, Hdt. **II.** of soldiers, *to set in order, to set* as guards, Xen. **2.** *to ordain, appoint*, Hdt., etc. :—in aor. ι med. *to appoint for oneself, establish, institute*, Hdt., Aesch. **b.** esp. of political constitutions, *to settle, establish*, νόμους Eur., etc. ; κατ. πολιτείαν, Lat. *constituere rempublicam*, Plat., etc. :— so in Med., φρούρημα γῆς καθίσταμαι Aesch. ; καθίστατο τὰ περὶ τὴν Μιτυλήνην Thuc. **3.** *to bring into* a certain state, κατ. δῆμον ἐς μοναρχίαν Eur. ; κ. τινὰ ἐς ἀπόνοιαν, ἐς φόβον, ἐς ἀπορίαν Thuc. ; so, κ. τοὺς φίλους ἐν ἀκινδύνῳ Xen. :—also, κ. ἑαυτὸν ἐς κρίσιν *to present* himself for trial, Thuc. **4.** *to make* or *render* so and so, κ. τινα ψευδῆ Soph. ; ἄπιστον Thuc. :—rarely c. inf., καθ. τινὰ φεύγειν *to make* him fly, Id. :—Med., τὴν ναυμαχίαν πεζομαχίαν καθίστασθαι Id. **5.** τὴν ζόην καταστήσασθαι ἀπ' ἔργων ἀνοσιωτάτων *to get one's* living by most unhallowed deeds, Hdt. **6.** *to make, continue*, Aesch. ; so in Med., Id.

B. intr. in aor. 2, pf., and plqpf. of Act. (also in fut. καθεστήξω), and in all tenses of Med. (except aor. ι), and all of Pass. :—*to be set, set oneself down, settle, arrive*, ἐς τόπον Hdt., Soph. **b.** *to come before* another, *stand* in his presence, Hdt. ; καταστὰς ἐπὶ τὸ πλῆθος ἔλεγε Thuc. **2.** *to be set* as guard, Hdt., etc.: *to be appointed*, Eur., etc. **3.** *to stand quiet, be calm*, of water, Ar. ; so, πνεῦμα καθεστηκός Id. ; ὁ θόρυβος κατέστη abated, Hdt. ; so, of persons, καταστάς composedly, Aesch. ; ἡ καθεστηκυῖα ἡλικία *middle* age, Thuc. **4.** in pf. *to come into a certain state, to become*, and in aor. 2 and plqpf. *to be*, Hdt., etc. ; καταστάντων εὖ τῶν πρηγμάτων *being* in a good state, Id. ; τίνι τρόπῳ καθέστατε ; in what case *are ye?* Soph. ; ἀρξάμενος εὐθὺς καθισταμένου (sc. τοῦ πολέμου) from its first commencement, Thuc. **5.** *to be established* or *instituted, to prevail, exist*, Hdt., etc. : in pf. part. *existing, established, prevailing*, τὸν νῦν κατεστεῶτα κόσμον Id. ; οἱ καθεστῶτες νόμοι Soph. ; τὰ καθεστῶτα *the present state of life*, Id. ; so, τὰ κατεστεῶτα, *existing laws, customs*, Hdt. **6.** Pass. *to stand against, oppose*, Τιτήνεσσι κατέσταθεν Hes.

καθό, Adv. for καθ' ὅ, = καθά, *in so far as, according as*, Lys., etc. **II.** *so that*, Plat.

καθ-οδηγέω, f. ήσω, *to guide*, Plut.

κάθ-οδος, Ion. **κάτ-οδος**, ἡ, *a going down, descent*, Luc.: *a way down*, Id. **II.** *a coming back, return*, Eur., Thuc. ; of an exile, Hdt., Thuc.

καθ-όλου, (ὅλος) as Adv. *on the whole, in general*, for καθ' ὅλου, Arist., etc. ; οὐ καθόλου, *not at all*, Dem.

καθ-ομῑλέω, f. ήσω, to conciliate by daily intercourse, to win the favour of, Arist.

καθ-ομολογέω, f. ήσω, to confess or allow, esp. to one's detriment, Plat. II. to promise, vow, Luc. 2. to betroth, Plut.

καθ-οπλίζω, f. Att. ιῶ, to equip or arm fully, τῇ πανοπλίᾳ Aeschin. :—Pass. to be so armed, Xen. II. τὸ μὴ καλὸν καθοπλίσασα having taken arms against dishonour, Soph. Hence

καθόπλῐσις, εως, ἡ, a mode of arming, armour, Xen.

καθ-οράω, Ion. κατ- : impf. καθεώρων, Ion. 3 sing. κατώρα : pf. καθεόρακα :—also from the Root ΟΠ, f. κατόψομαι : pf. κατῶμμαι : aor. ι κατώφθην :—for the aor. 2, v. κατεῖδον :—to look down, Il., Hdt. ; so in Med., Il. II. c. acc. to look down upon, ὁπόσους ἥλιος καθορᾷ Theogn., etc. 2. to have within view, to perceive, Hdt., Ar., etc. 3. to look to, observe, Pind., Ar. 4. to explore, τὰ ἄλλα Hdt.

καθ-ορμάω, = ὁρμάω, Anth.

καθ-ορμίζω, f. Att. ιῶ, to bring a ship into harbour, bring to anchor, Plut. :—Pass., with aor. ι med., to come into harbour, put in, Thuc. 2. metaph., ἐς τάσδε σαυτὸν πημονὰς καθώρμισας hast brought thyself to such miseries, Aesch.

καθ-οσιόομαι, Med. to dedicate, θεῷ Eur. :—Pass., καθωσιώθη Ar. 2. κ. πόλιν καθαρμοῖς to purify, Plut.

καθόσσον, for καθ' ὅσον, in so far as, inasmuch as, Thuc.

καθότι, Ion. κατότι, for καθ' ὅ τι, in what manner, Hdt., Thuc.

καθοῦ, aor. 2 med. imper. of καθίημι. II. imper. of κάθημαι.

καθ-υβρίζω, Ion. κατ-, f. Att. ιῶ, to treat despitefully, to insult or affront wantonly, τινά Soph., etc. ; also τινός Id. :—Pass., absol., to wax wanton, Id.

κάθ-υδρος [ῠ], ον, (ὕδωρ) full of water, κάθυδρος κράτηρ, poët. for water itself, Soph.

καθ-υπερακοντίζω, f. σω, to overshoot completely, Ar.

καθ-ύπερθε, poët. before a vowel -θεν : Ion. κατύπερθε : Adv. :—from above, down from above, Hom., etc. :—c. gen., κ. μελαθρόφιν Od. 2. on the top or upper side, above, Ib. ; καθ. ἐπιρρέει floats atop, Il. :—to denote geographical position, Φρυγίη καθύπερθε Ib.; c. gen., καθύπερθε Χίου above, i. e. north of, Chios, Od. ; τὰ κ. the upper country, i. e. further inland, τὰ κ. τῆς λίμνης Hdt. ; καθύπερθε γενέσθαι τινός, properly, of a wrestler who falls atop of his opponent ; hence, to have the upper hand of, Id. II. of Time, before, o. gen.

καθ-υπέρτερος, α, ον, Ion. κατ-υπ-, η, ον, Comp. Adj. : (καθύπερθε) :—above : metaph. having the upper hand, superior, κ. γίγνεσθαι Hdt., Thuc., etc. : c. gen., πόλις κ. τῶν ἀντιπάλων Xen. :—neut. καθυπέρτερον as Adv., = καθύπερθε, Theocr. :—Sup. καθυπέρτατος, η, ον, highest, ἐν τῇ κατυπερτάτῃ τῆς γῆς Hdt.

καθ-υπισχνέομαι, strengthd. for ὑπισχ-, Luc.

καθ-υπνόω, Ion. κατ-, f. ωσω, to be fast asleep, fall asleep, Hdt., Xen. :—Pass., pf. part. κατυπνωμένος asleep, Hdt.

καθ-υποκρίνομαι [ῐ], f. -κρῐνοῦμαι, Dep. to subdue by histrionic arts, Dem. II. c. inf. to pretend to be some one else, Luc.

καθ-υστερέω, f. ήσω, to come far behind, Plut. : absol. to be behind-hand, Menand.

καθ-υφίημι, f. -υφήσω, to give up treacherously, Dem.; καθ. τὸν ἀγῶνα to conduct it treacherously, compromise it, Dem. ; so also in Med., with pf. pass., Id. II. Med., καθυφίεσθαί τινι to give way to any one, Xen.

καθ-ώς, Adv., = καθά, Hdt., N.T. II. how, N.T.

καί, crasis for καὶ αἱ.

ΚΑΙ', Conjunction, used in two principal senses, either copulative, to join words and sentences, and, Lat. et ; or making a single word or clause emphatic, also, even, Lat. etiam.

A. copulative, and, merely joining words or sentences, Lat. et, while τε answers to que, Hom., etc. : to combine more closely, τε . . , καὶ . . are used, ἄρκτοι τε καὶ λέοντες both bears and lions, etc. ; often to add epithets after πολύς, πολλὰ καὶ ἐσθλά Il. ; πολλὰ καὶ μεγάλα Dem., etc. :—θεοὶ καὶ Ζεύς all the gods, and above all Zeus, Aesch. ; ἄλλοι τε καί . . , ἄλλως τε καί . . , v. ἄλλος, ἄλλως :—ὀλίγου τινὸς ἄξια καὶ οὐδενός worth little or nothing, Plat. II. in questions, to introduce an objection, καὶ πῶς . . ; but how . . ? nay how can it be ? Eur., etc. :—also = καίτοι, and yet, Ar. III. after words implying sameness or likeness, καί must be rendered by as, like Lat. atque or ac after aeque, perinde, simul, γνώμῃσι ὁμοίῃσι καὶ σύ the same opinion as you, Hdt. ; ἴσον or ἴσα καί . . , Soph., etc. : in Att., καί . . , καί . . answer to the Lat. cum, tum, not only, but also, Plat., etc.

B. influencing single words or clauses, also, even, Lat. etiam, ἔπειτά με καὶ λίποι αἰών then let life also forsake me, i. e. life as well as all other goods, Il. ; καὶ αὐτοί they also, they likewise, Xen. ; εἴπερ τις καὶ ἄλλος Plat., etc.

καιάδας, gen. ου Dor. α, ὁ, a pit at Sparta, into which criminals were thrown, like the Athen. βάραθρον, Thuc., Plut. (Lacon. word.)

καὶ γάρ, for truly, to confirm a proposition, Lat. etenim, Hom., etc. :—also καὶ γὰρ δή for of a surety, Il. ; καὶ γάρ ῥα Ib. ; καὶ γὰρ οὖν, καὶ γάρ τοι, Lat. etenim profecto, Plat., etc.

καὶ δέ, but also, Hom.

καὶ δή, nay further, Hdt.

καὶ εἰ, by crasis κεἰ, even if, although, Hom.

καϊκᾶ, crasis for καὶ αἶκα.

καικίας, ου, ὁ, the north-east wind, Ar.

καὶ μήν, v. sub μήν II. 2.

καινίζω, f. Att. ιῶ, (καινός) to make new : hence, καί τι καινίζει στέγη and the house has something strange about it, Soph.; καίνισον ζυγόν try on thy new yoke, handsel it, Aesch.; κ. εὐχὰς to offer new, strange prayers, Eur.

Καινόν, τό, the New Court, at Athens, Ar.

καινο-παθής, ές, (παθεῖν) newly suffered : unheard of, Soph.

καινο-πηγής, ές, (πήγνυμι) newly put together, new-made, Aesch.

καινο-πήμων, ον, (πῆμα) new to misery, Aesch.

καινο-ποιέω, f. ήσω, to make new, to bring about new things, to make changes, innovate, Luc. :—Pass., τί καινοποιηθὲν λέγεις ; what new-fangled, strange words art thou using ? Soph. Hence

καινοποιητής, οῦ, ὁ, *an inventor of new pleasures*, Xen.

ΚΑΙΝΟΣ, ή, όν, *new, fresh*, Lat. *recens, novus*, καινὰ καὶ παλαιὰ ἔργα Hdt.; καινοὺς λόγους φέρειν *to bring news*, Aesch.; λέγεταί τι καινόν; Dem.; ἐκ καινῆς (sc. ἀρχῆς) *anew, afresh*, Lat. *de novo*, Thuc. :—esp. of dramas *produced for the first time*, Aeschin., Dem. **II.** *newly-invented, new-fangled, novel*, Eur., etc.; κ. θεοί *strange gods*, Plat.; καινὰ innovations, Xen.; οὐδὲν καινότερον εἰσέφερε τῶν ἄλλων *he introduced as little of anything new as others*, Id.; τὸ καινὸν τοῦ πολέμου *the unforeseen turn which war often takes*, Thuc. **III.** κ. ἄνθρωπος = *novus homo*, Plut.

καινό-τᾰφος, ον, *of a new tomb*, Anth.

καινότης, ητος, ἡ, (καινός) *newness, freshness*, Plut. **2.** *novelty*, Thuc., etc.

καινοτομέω, f. ήσω, (τέμνω) *to cut fresh into*, in mining, *to open a new vein*, Xen. **II.** metaph. *to begin something new, institute anew*, Ar.: absol. *to make innovations in the state*, Lat. *res novare*, Arist.; also, κ. περὶ τὰ θεῖα Plat.; and

καινοτομία, ἡ, *innovation*, Plut. **2.** *novelty*, Id.

καινο-τόμος, ον, (τέμνω) *innovating*, Arist.

καινουργέω, *to begin something new*, τί καινουργεῖς; *what new plan art thou meditating?* Eur.; κ. λόγον *to speak new, strange words*, Id.: *to make innovations*, Xen.; and

καινουργία, ἡ, *innovation*, Isocr. From

καιν-ουργός, όν, (*ἔργω) *producing changes* : τὸ κ. a *novelty*, Luc.

καινόω, f. ώσω, (καινός) *to make new, innovate* :—Pass., of political changes, Thuc.; καινοῦσθαι τὰς διανοίας *to have their minds revolutionised*, Id. **II.** =καινίζω, *to use for the first time, to handsel*, Hdt.

καί νύ κε, *and now perhaps*, Il.

ΚΑΙΝΥΜΑΙ, 3 sing. impf. ἐκαίνῦτο : pf. κέκασμαι, Dor. κέκαδμαι (as pres.) : 3 sing. plqpf. ἐκέκαστο (as impf.) : Dep. :—*to surpass, excel*, ἐκαίνυτο φῦλ' ἀνθρώπων νῆα κυβερνῆσαι *he surpassed mankind in steering*, Od.; ἐγχείῃ δ' ἐκέκαστο Πανέλληνας *he excelled all the Hellenes in throwing the spear*, Ib.; ὁμηλικίην ἐκέκαστο γνῶναι *surpassed them all in knowledge*, Ib.: esp. in part., δόλοισι κεκασμένε *excellent in wiles*, Ib.; τέχνῃσι κεκασμένος Hes.; φρουραῖς κέκασται *is well furnished with*, Eur.

καὶ νῦν, *and now, even now*, Hom.

ΚΑΙΝΩ, f. κᾰνῶ : aor. 2 ἔκᾰνον, inf. κᾰνεῖν Dor. κανῆν: pf. κέκονα :—collat. form of κτείνω, *to kill, slay*, Trag., Xen.

καίπερ, *although, albeit*, mostly with a part., καίπερ πολλὰ παθών Od.; often divided, καὶ οὐκ ἀγαθόν περ ἐόντα Il.; καὶ κρατερός περ ἐών Ib.; in Trag., with ὅμως added, καίπερ οὐ στέργων ὅμως Id., etc.

καί ῥα, Ep., *to make a transition*, *and so*, Il.

καίριος, α, ον, and ος, ον: (καιρός Β): **I.** of Place, *in* or *at the right place*, hence of parts of the body, ἐν καιρίῳ, κατὰ καίριον *in a vital part*, Il.; also, of wounds, πέπληγμαι καιρίαν πληγήν, καιρίας πληγῆς τυχεῖν Aesch.; πληγή is sometimes omitted, Hdt. :—Adv. -ίως, *mortally*, Aesch. **II.** of Time, *in season, seasonable, timely, opportune*, Hdt., Trag., etc.; τὰ καίρια *timely circumstances, opportunities*,

Thuc. **2.** *lasting but for a season*, Anth. **3.** Adv. -ρίως, *in season, seasonably*, Aesch.: Comp. -ωτέρως Xen. :—so also, πρὸς τὸ καίριον Soph.

ΚΑΙΡΟΣ (Α), ὁ, *the row of thrums* in the loom, to which the threads of the warp are attached, Lat. *licia*.

ΚΑΙΡΟΣ (Β), ὁ, *due measure, proportion, fitness*, Hes., etc.; καιροῦ πέρα *beyond measure, unduly*, Aesch., etc.; μείζων τοῦ καιροῦ, Lat. *justo major*, Xen. **II.** of Place, *a vital part* of the body, like τὸ καίριον, Eur. **III.** of Time, *the right point of time, the proper time* or *season* of action, *the exact* or *critical time*, Lat. *opportunitas*, καιρὸς βραχὺ μέτρον ἔχει 'time and tide wait for no man,' Pind.; καιρὸν παριέναι *to let the time go by*, Thuc.; καιροῦ τυχεῖν Eur.; καιρὸν λαμβάνειν Thuc.; ἔχειν καιρόν *to be in season*, Id.: καιρός ἐστι, c. inf., *it is time to do*, Hdt., etc. **2.** adverbial usages, εἰς or ἐς καιρόν *in season, at the right time, opportune*, Hdt., etc.; so, ἐπὶ καιροῦ Dem.;—κατὰ καιρόν Hdt.; πρὸς καιρόν Soph., etc.; and, without Preps., καιρῷ or καιρόν *in season*, Att.;—all these being opp. to ἀπὸ καιροῦ, Plat.; παρὰ καιρόν Eur.; πρὸ καιροῦ *prematurely*, Aesch. **3.** pl., ἐν τοῖς μεγίστοις κ. *at the most critical times*, Xen., etc. **IV.** *advantage, profit, fruit*, τινος *of* or *from a thing*, Pind.; τί καιρὸς καταλείβειν; *what avails it to ..?* Eur.; οὗ κ. εἴη *where it was convenient* or *advantageous*, Thuc.; μετὰ μεγίστων καιρῶν *with the greatest odds, the most critical results*, Id.

καιροσέων, a fem. gen. pl. in Od. 7. 107, καιροσέων ὀθονέων ἀπολείβεται ἔλαιον *from the close-woven linen trickles off the oil* ;—i. e. the linen is so well-woven, that oil does not ooze through. It seems to be for καιροεσσέων, Ep. gen. pl. of an Adj. καιρόεις, from καῖρος Α.

καιρο-φυλᾰκέω, f. ήσω, (φύλαξ) *to watch for the right time*, Dem. :—also, *to attend on*, Luc.

καί τοι or **καίτοι**, *and indeed, and further*, Hom., Eur. **II.** *and yet*, to mark an objection, καίτοι τί φημι; Aesch.; καίτοι τί φωνῶ; Soph. :—also, strengthd. καίτοι γε Ar.

ΚΑΙΩ, old Att. **κάω** [ᾱ]: impf. ἔκαιον, old Att. ἔκαον Ep. καῖον :—f. καύσω and καύσομαι: aor. 1 ἔκαυσα, Ep. ἔκηα or ἔκεια and without augm. κῆα, imper. κῆον, 1 pl. subj. κήομεν; opt. κήαι, κήαιεν; inf. κῆαι, Att. part. κέας, κέαντες: pf. κέκαυκα :—Med., aor. 1 ἐκαυσάμην, Ep. 3 pl. κήαντο :—Pass., fut. 2 κᾰήσομαι :—aor. 1 ἐκαύθην, aor. 2 ἐκάην [ᾰ], Ep. inf. καήμεναι :—pf. κέκαυμαι : **I.** *to light, kindle*, πυρὰ πολλὰ Il.; πῦρ κῆαι Od.; Med., πῦρ κήαντο *they lighted them* a fire, Hom. :—Pass. *to be lighted, to burn*, Il., Hdt., etc. **II.** *to set on fire, burn up, burn*, Hom. **2.** *to burn, scorch*, of the sun, Hdt. :—also of extreme cold (as Virg. *penetrabile frigus adurit*), Xen. **3.** Pass., of fever-heat, *to be burnt* or *parched up*, Thuc.: metaph. of passion, Pind., etc. **III.** *to burn and destroy* (in war), τέμνειν καὶ κ., καὶ κ. καὶ πορθεῖν *to waste with fire and sword*, Xen. **IV.** of surgeons, *to cauterise*, τέμνειν καὶ κάειν *to use knife and cautery*, Plat., Xen.

κάκ, for κατά before κ, as κὰκ κεφαλῆς Hom.

κἀκ, crasis for καὶ ἐκ.

κᾰκ-άγγελος, ον, *bringing ill tidings*, Aesch.

κἄκ-άγγελτος, ον, (ἀγγέλλω) caused by ill tidings, Soph.

κακαγόρος, Dor. for κακηγόρους, acc. pl. of κακήγορος.

κἄκ-ανδρία, ἡ, unmanliness, Soph.. Eur.

κἄκεῖ, κἄκεῖθεν, κἄκεῖνος, Att. crases for καὶ ἐκεῖ, etc.

κἄκ-έσχᾰτος, ον, extremely bad, Menand.

κάκη, ἡ, (κἄκός) wickedness, vice, Eur., Ar., etc. 2. baseness of spirit, cowardice, sloth, Aesch., Eur.

κἄκηγορέω, to speak ill of, abuse, slander, Plat. ; and

κἄκηγορία, ἡ, evil-speaking, abuse, slander, Pind., Plat. :—κακηγορίας δίκη an action for defamation, Dem. ; also κἄκηγορίου δίκη, ap. Dem. From

κἄκ-ήγορος, ον, (ἀγορεύω) evil-speaking, abusive, slanderous, Pind., Plat.

κἄκη-λόγος, ον, (λέγω) evil-speaking, Menand.

κἄκία, ἡ, (κακός) badness in quality, opp. to ἀρετή (excellence), Theogn., Soph. :—pl. κακίαι defects, Luc. 2. cowardice, sloth, Thuc., Plat. 3. moral badness, wickedness, vice, Plat., Xen. II. ill-repute, Thuc. III. evil suffered, N. T.

κἄκίζω, f. Att. ιῶ, (κακός) to abuse, reproach, accuse, Hdt., Thuc., etc. II. to make cowardly, Eur. :— Pass. to play the coward, Il., Eur. ; κακίζεσθαι τύχῃ to be worsted by fortune alone, Thuc.

κἄκιστέον, verb. Adj. one must bring reproach on, τινά Eur.

κἄκίων, κάκιστος, irreg. Comp. and Sup. of κακός.

κακκάω, (κάκκη) cacare, Ar.

κακκεῖαι or κακκῆαι, Ep. for κατακαῦσαι, aor. 1 inf. of κατακαίω.

κακκείοντες, Ep. for κατακείοντες, part. of κατακείω.

κακκεφᾰλῆς, for κὰκ κεφαλῆς, i. e. κατὰ κεφαλῆς.

ΚΑ΄ΚΚΗ, ἡ, ordure, dung, Ar.

κακκῆαι, v. κακκεῖαι.

κακκόρυθα, κακκορύφήν, for κὰκ (i. e. κατὰ) κόρυθα, etc.

κακκρύπτω, Ep. for κατακρ-.

κἄκκυνηγετῶ, crasis for καὶ ἐκκυνηγετῶ.

κἄκό-βιος, ον, living ill or poorly, Hdt., Xen.

κἄκόβουλεύομαι, aor. 1 ἐκακοβουλεύθην, Pass. to be ill-advised, Eur. From

κἄκό-βουλος, ον, (βουλή) ill-advised, Eur., Ar.

κἄκό-γαμβρος γόος, distress for her wretched brother-in-law, Eur.

κἄκο-γᾰμίου δίκη, ἡ, (γάμος) an action for forming an unlawful marriage, Plut. (No nom. -γάμιον.)

κἄκογείτων, ον, gen. ονος, a bad neighbour or a neighbour to his misery, Soph.

κἄκό-γλωσσος, ον, (γλῶσσα) ill-tongued, βοὴ κ. a cry of misery, Eur.

κἄκοδαιμονάω, to be tormented by an evil genius, be like one possessed, Ar., Xen., etc. ; and

κἄκοδαιμονέω, to be unfortunate, Xen. ; and

κἄκοδαιμονία, Ion. -ίη, ἡ, unhappiness, misfortune, Hdt., Xen., etc. II. possession by a demon, raving madness, Ar., Xen. From

κἄκο-δαίμων, ον, gen. ονος, possessed by an evil genius, ill-fated, ill-starred, miserable, Eur., Ar. :—Adv. -μόνως, Luc. II. as Subst. an evil genius, Ar.

κἄκοδοξέω, to be in bad repute, Xen. ; and

κἄκοδοξία, ἡ, bad repute, infamy, Xen., Plat. From

κἄκό-δοξος, ον, (δόξα) in ill repute : i. e., 1. with-

out fame, unknown, Theogn. 2. infamous, discreditable, Eur., Xen.

κἄκο-δρομία, ἡ, (δρόμος) a bad passage (by sea), Anth.

κἄκο-είμων, ον, gen. ονος, (εἷμα) ill-clad, Od.

κἄκο-εργία, κἄκο-εργός, Ep. for κακ-ουργία, -γος.

κἄκοζηλία, ἡ, unhappy imitation, affectation, Luc.

κἄκό-ζηλος, ον, imitating unhappily.

κἄκοήθεια, Ion. -ίη, ἡ, badness of disposition, malignity, Plat., etc. II. bad manners or habits, Xen. ; and

κἄκοήθευμα, ατος, τό, a malicious deed, Plut. From

κἄκο-ήθης, ες, (ἦθος) ill-disposed, malicious, Ar., Dem. 2. as Subst., τὸ κακόηθες wickedness, an ill habit or itch for doing a thing, Plat. II. of diseases, malignant :—Adv. -θως, ap. Dem.

κἄκο-θημοσύνη, ἡ, (τί-θημι) disorderliness, Hes.

κἄκό-θροος, ον, contr. -θρους, ουν, evil-speaking, slanderous, Soph.

κἄκο-θῡμία, ἡ, (θυμός) malevolence, Plut.

Κἄκ-οίλιος, ἡ, (Ἴλιος) evil or unhappy Ilium, Od.

κἄκοκέρδεια, ἡ, base love of gain, Theogn. From

κἄκο-κερδής, ές, (κέρδος) making base gain.

κἄκό-κνημος, Dor. -κνᾱμος, ον, (κνήμη) weak-legged, thin-legged, Theocr.

κἄκο-κρῑσία, ἡ, (κρίσις) a bad judgment, Anth.

κἄκολογέω, to speak ill of, to revile, abuse, Lysias, N. T. ; and

κἄκολογία, ἡ, evil-speaking, reviling, Hdt., Xen., etc.

κἄκο-λόγος, ον, (λέγω) evil-speaking, Pind., Plat.

κἄκό-μαντις, εως, ὁ, ἡ, prophet of ill or evil, Aesch.

κἄκο-μᾰχέω, f. ήσω, to behave ill in fight, Luc.

κἄκο-μέλετος, ον, (μέλομαι) busied with evil, Aesch.

κἄκο-μηδής, ές, (μῆδος) contriving ill, deceitful, h. Hom.

κἄκο-μήτης, ου, ὁ, = foreg., Eur.

κἄκομηχᾰνία, ἡ, a practising of base arts, Luc. From

κἄκο-μήχᾰνος, Dor. κακομᾱχ-, ον, (μηχανή) mischief-plotting, mischievous, baneful, Hom.

κἄκο-μίμητος [ῑ], ον, (μιμέομαι) imitating ill ; Adv. -τως, Arist.

κἄκο-μοιρος, ον, (μοῖρα) ill-fated, Anth.

κἄκόνοια, ἡ, ill-will, malignity, malice, Xen., Dem.

κἄκονομία, ἡ, a bad system of laws and government, a bad constitution, Xen. From

κἄκό-νομος, ον, with bad laws, ill-governed, Hdt.

κἄκό-νοος, ον, contr. -νους, ουν : Att. pl. κακόνοι :—ill-disposed, disaffected, Ar., Thuc., etc.:—bearing malice against, τινι Xen. :—Sup. κακονούστατος Dem.

κἄκό-νυμφος, ον, (νύμφη) ill-married, of unhappy wedlock, Eur. II. as Subst. an ill or unhappy bridegroom, Id.

κἄκό-ξενος, Ion. -ξεινος, ον, unfortunate in guests, in irreg. Ep. κακοξεινώτερος, Od. II. unfriendly to strangers, inhospitable, Eur., Anth.

κἄκο-ξύνετος, ον, wise for evil, Thuc.

κἄκοπάθεια, ἡ, ill plight, distress, Thuc. ; and

κἄκοπαθέω, f. ήσω, to suffer ill, to be in ill plight, be in distress, Thuc., Xen., etc. From

κἄκο-πᾰθής, ές, (πάσχω) suffering ill, in ill plight ; Adv. -θῶς, miserably, Arist.

κἄκο-πάρθενος, ον, unbecoming a maid, Anth.

κἄκό-πατρις, ιδος, ὁ, ἡ, (πατήρ) having a mean father, low-born, Theogn.

κᾰκο-πῑνής, ές, (πίνος) exceeding filthy, loathsome, Sup. κακοπινέστατος Soph.

κᾰκοποιέω, f. ήσω, to do ill, play the knave, Ar.: to manage one's affairs ill, Xen.   II. trans. to do mischief to, maltreat, Id.; and

κᾰκοποιΐα, ή, evil-doing, injury, Isocr. From

κᾰκο-ποιός, όν, (ποιέω) ill-doing, mischievous, Pind.

κᾰκο-πονητικός, ή, όν, (πονέω) unfit for toil, Arist.

κᾰκό-ποτμος, ον, ill-fated, ill-starred, Aesch., Eur.

κᾰκό-πους, ὁ, ἡ, πουν, τό, with bad feet, Xen.

κᾰκο-πρᾱγέω, f. ήσω, (πρᾶγος) to fare ill, fail in an enterprise, to be in ill plight, Thuc. Hence

κᾰκοπρᾱγία, ή, misadventure, failure, Thuc.

κᾰκο-πράγμων, ον, (πράσσω) = κακοποιός, Xen.

κᾰκορ-ρᾰφία, Ion. -ίη, ή, (ῥάπτω) contrivance of ill, mischievousness, Hom.

κᾰκορ-ρήμων, ον, (ῥῆμα) telling of ill, ill omened, Aesch.

κᾰκορ-ροθέω, f. ήσω, (ῥόθος) to speak evil of, abuse, revile, Eur., Ar.

κᾰκό-ρυπος, very filthy, Babr.

ΚΑ'ΚΟΣ, ή, όν, bad, Lat. malus: I. of persons, 1. opp. to καλός, mean, ugly, Il.   2. opp. to ἀγαθός, ἐσθλός, ill-born, mean, ignoble, Hom., Soph.   3. craven, cowardly, base, Hom., Hdt., Att.   4. bad of his kind, i.e. worthless, sorry, poor, κ. ἀλήτης a sorry beggar, Od.; κ. ἰατρός Aesch.; κ. ναύτης Eur.; πάντα κακός bad in all things, Od.; κακὸς γνώμην Soph.; — c. inf., κακὸς μανθάνειν bad at learning, Id.   5. in moral sense, bad, evil, wicked, Od., Att.   II. of death, disease, etc., bad, evil, baneful, Hom., Att.; of omens, bad, unlucky, Att.; of words, evil, abusive, Soph.; κ. ποιμήν, i.e. the storm, Aesch.

B. κακόν, τό, and κακά, τά, as Subst. evil, ill, Od., Hdt., etc.; δυοῖν ἀποκρίνας κακοῖν having chosen the least of two evils, Soph.:—κακόν τι ἔρδειν or ῥέζειν τινά to do evil or ill to any one, Il.; κακὸν (or κακὰ) ποιεῖν τινά Att.; κακὰ κακῶν = τὰ κάκιστα, Soph.   2. κακά, τά, also evil words, reproaches, Hdt., Trag.

C. degrees of Comparison: 1. regul. Comp. κακώτερος Od., Theocr.; but never in Att.:—irreg. κακίων, ον, [with ῑ], Hom., [with ῑ], Att.   2. Sup. κάκιστος, Hom., etc.:—but χείρων, χείριστος, and ἥσσων, ἥκιστος, are also used as Comp. and Sup.

D. Adv. κακῶς, Lat. male, ill, Il., etc.:—κακῶς ποιεῖν τινα to treat one ill; κακῶς ποιεῖν τινά τι to do one any evil, Att.; κακῶς πράσσειν to fare ill, Aesch.; κακῶς πάσχειν Id.; κακῶς γίγνεταί τινι Hdt.; κακῶς ἐκπέφευγα, Lat. vix demum effugi, Dem.:—Comp. κάκιον, Hdt., Att.: Sup. κάκιστα, Ar., etc.

E. in Compos., when added to words already signifying something bad, it increases this property, as in κακο-πινής: but added to words signifying something good, it implies too little of this property, as in κακό-δοξος. Once or twice it stands merely as an Adj. agreeing with the Subst. with which it is compounded, as Κακοΐλιος for κακὴ Ἴλιος, κακόνυμφος for κακὸς νύμφιος.

κᾰκό-σῑτος, ον, eating badly, i.e. having no appetite, fastidious, Plat.

κᾰκο-σκελής, ές, (σκέλος) with bad legs, Xen.

κᾰκο-σκηνής, ές, (σκῆνος) of a bad, mean body, Anth.

κάκ-οσμος, ον, (ὀσμή) ill-smelling, Ar.

κᾰκό-σπλαγχνος, ον, (σπλάγχνον) faint-hearted, Aesch.

κᾰκό-σπορία, ή, (σπόρος) a bad sowing or crop, Anth.

κᾰκό-στόμᾰχος, ον, with bad stomach, fastidious, Anth.

κᾰκοστομέω, to speak evil of, abuse, τινά Soph. From

κᾰκό-στομος, ον, (στόμα) evil-speaking, Eur.

κᾰκό-στρωτος, ον, ill-spread, i.e. rugged, Aesch.

κᾰκο-σύνθετος, ον, ill put together, Luc.

κᾰκό-σχολος, ον, (σχολή) using one's leisure ill, indolent, lazy, Anth.   II. act., κ. πνοαί winds that wear men out in idleness, Aesch.

κᾰκοτεχνέω, f. ήσω, (κακότεχνος) to use base arts, act basely or meanly, deal fraudulently, Hdt., Dem.

κᾰκοτεχνής, ές, v. κακότεχνος fin.

κᾰκοτεχνία, ή, bad art: I. often in pl., forgeries, falsifications, Plat., Dem.   II. bad, base art, Luc. From

κᾰκό-τεχνος, ον, (τέχνη) using bad arts or evil practices, artful, wily, δόλος Il.:—irreg. Comp. -τεχνέστερος, as from κακοτεχνής, Luc.

κᾰκότης, ητος, ή, (κακός) :—badness: I. of character, baseness, weakness, cowardice, Hom., Thuc.   2. badness, wickedness, Il., Hdt., Att.; κακότητι λειφθῆναι to have been absent by malice prepense, Hdt.   II. of condition, evil condition, distress, misery, Od., Hdt.

κᾰκοτροπία, ή, badness of habits, mischievousness, maliciousness, wickedness, Thuc. From

κᾰκό-τροπος, ον, mischievous, malignant.

κᾰκοτῠχέω, f. ήσω, to be unfortunate, Thuc. From

κᾰκο-τῠχής, ές, (τύχη) unfortunate, Eur.

κᾰκουργέω, f. ήσω, (κακοῦργος) to do evil, work wickedness, deal basely, Eur., etc.; of a horse, to be vicious, Xen.   II. c. acc. pers. to do evil or mischief to one, to maltreat, Eur., Plat.:—to ravage a country, Thuc.: —to corrupt, falsify, τοὺς νόμους Dem. Hence

κᾰκούργημα, ατος, τό, an ill deed, fraud, Plat.

κᾰκουργία, Ep. κακοεργίη [ῐ], ή, the character and conduct of a κακοῦργος, ill-doing, wickedness, villany, malice, Od., Thuc., etc.; of a horse, viciousness, Xen.   II. in pl. malpractices, Id.

κᾰκουργικός, ή, όν, malicious, Arist. From

κᾰκ-οῦργος, Ep. κακο-εργός, ον, (*ἔργω) doing ill, mischievous, knavish, villanous, γαστὴρ κακοεργός importunate, Od.; κακούργοι κλῶπες Hdt.; ἀνήρ Soph.; κακουργότατος λόγος Dem.   2. as Subst. a malefactor, criminal, Thuc., etc.: esp. a thief, robber, Dem.   II. doing harm, hurtful, c. gen., κ. εἶναί τινος to hurt any one, Xen.

κᾰκ-ουχία, ή, (ἔχω) ill-treatment, ill-conduct, Plat.; χθονὸς κ. devastation of it, Aesch.

κᾰκό-φᾰτις, ιδος, ή, ill-sounding, ill-omened, Aesch.

κᾰκο-φρᾰδής, ές, (φράζομαι) bad in counsel, Il.

κᾰκοφρᾰδία, Ion. -ίη, ή, badness of counsel, folly, h. Hom.

κᾰκοφρονέω, f. ήσω, to bear ill-will, Aesch. From

κᾰκό-φρων, ον, (φρήν) ill-minded, malicious, malignant, Aesch., Eur.   II. imprudent, thoughtless, heedless, Soph., Eur.

κᾰκο-φυής, ές, (φυή) of bad natural qualities, Plat.

κᾰκό-χαρτος, ον, (χαίρω) rejoicing in men's ills, Hes.

κᾰκό-χρησμων, Dor. -χράσμων, ον, (χράομαι) difficult to live with, Theocr.

κᾰκό-ψογος, ον, malignantly blaming, Theogn.

κᾰκόω, f. ώσω, (κακός) of persons, *to treat ill, maltreat, afflict, distress*, Hom., Aesch., etc.:—Pass. *to suffer ill, be in ill plight, be distressed*, Hom., etc.; κεκακωμένος ἁλμῇ *befouled* with brine, Od. 2. of things, *to spoil, ruin*, Hdt., Thuc.

κακτάμεναι, Ep. for κατα-κτανεῖν, aor. 2 inf. of κατακτείνω:—κάκτανε, Ep. for κατάκτανε, aor. 2 imperat., and for κατέκτανε 3 indic.:—κάκτεινε, Ep. for κατέκτεινε, 3 sing. impf.

κᾰκύνω [ῠ], *to damage*:—Pass., in moral sense, *to become bad, behave badly, act basely*, Eur.: of soldiers, *to be mutinous*, Xen. II. Pass. also, *to be reproached*, Eur.

κακχεῦαι, Ep. for καταχεῦαι, aor. 1 inf. of καταχέω.

κακχύδην [ῠ], poët. for καταχύδην.

κακῶς, Adv. of κακός (D).

κάκωσις, εως, ἡ, (κᾰκόω) *ill-treatment*, τοῦ ἡγεμόνος Xen.: *a distressing, harassing*, τῶν πληρωμάτων of the crews, Thuc. 2. in Att. law, κακώσεως δίκη an action *for ill-usage* or *neglect of parents*, Dem., etc. II. *damage, misfortune*, Thuc.

κᾰλᾰθίσκος, ὁ, Dim. of κάλαθος, Ar. From

ΚΑ'ΛΑ'ΘΟΣ [κᾰ], ὁ, *a vase-shaped basket*, Lat. *calathus*, Ar. II. *a cooling-vessel, cooler*, Virg.

κᾰλάϊνος or καλλάϊνος, η, ον, *like the κάλαϊς, of changeful hue*, of the cock, Anth. From

κάλαϊς, ἡ, *a precious stone of a greenish blue* (v. foreg.), *the turquoise* or *chrysolite*, Plin.

κᾰλᾰμαία, ἡ, (κᾰλάμη) *a kind of grasshopper*, Theocr.

κᾰλᾰμευτής, οῦ, ὁ, (as if from *καλαμεύω) *a reaper, mower*, Theocr. II. *an angler*, Anth.

κᾰλάμη [ᾰ], ἡ, (v. κάλαμος) *the stalk* or *straw of corn*: metaph., αἶψα φυλόπιδος πέλεται κόρος, ἧς τε πλείστην μὲν καλάμην χθονὶ χαλκὸς ἔχευεν, ἄμητος δ' ὀλίγιστος *men are soon satiated with battle, where the sword throws much straw on the ground, and there is little harvest*, i. e. *much slaughter and little profit*, Il.; κ. πυρῶν *wheatstraw*, Hdt. 2. *the stalk without the ear, stubble*; metaph. of an old man, καλάμην γέ σ' ὀΐομαι εἰσορόωντα γιγνώσκειν *thou mayst still, I ween, perceive the stubble* (i. e. *the residue*) of former strength, Od.; ἀπὸ τῆς καλάμης τεκμαίρεσθαι *to judge from the remains*, Luc.

κᾰλᾰμη-τομία, ἡ, (τέμνω) *a reaping*, Anth.

κᾰλᾰμη-φάγος [ᾰ], ον, (φαγεῖν) *devouring stalks*, i. e. *cutting them*, Anth.

κᾰλᾰμη-φόρος, ον, (φέρω) *carrying reeds*, Xen.

κᾰλάμῐνος, η, ον, (κάλαμος) *made of reed*, Hdt. II. *made of cane*, Id.

κᾰλᾰμίς, ῖδος, ἡ, (κάλαμος) *a reed fishing-rod*, Anth.

κᾰλᾰμίσκος, ὁ, Dim. of κάλαμος, *a bit of reed*, used as a phial, Ar.

κᾰλᾰμῖτις, ιδος, ἡ, = καλαμαία, Anth.

κᾰλᾰμόεις, εσσα, εν, *of reed*, Eur. From

ΚΑ'ΛΑ'ΜΟΣ [κᾰ], ὁ, *a reed*, larger than the δόναξ, Lat. *arundo*, being used for thatching houses or even for making the walls, Id., Thuc. II. *anything made of reed* or *cane*: 1. *a reed-pipe, flute*, Pind., Eur. 2. *a fishing-rod*, Theocr. 3. *an arrow*, Horat. III. collectively, of plants, which are neither bush (ὕλη), nor tree (δένδρον), Xen. 2. *a mat of reeds*, Plat. IV. = κᾰλάμη, *the stalk* of wheat, Xen.

κᾰλάμο-στεφής, ές, (στέφω) *covered with reed*, Batr.

κᾰλᾰμό-φθογγος, ον, *played on a reed*, of tunes, Ar.

κᾰλᾰμ-ώδης, ες, (εἶδος) *like reed, full of reeds*, Anth.

κᾰλάπους, ποδος, ὁ, (κᾱλον) *a shoemaker's last*, Plat.

κᾰλάσῖρις, ιος, ἡ, *a long garment, with fringe at bottom*, Hdt. II. the Καλασίριες were a branch of the military caste in Egypt, Id. (Egypt. word.)

κᾰλαῦροψ, οπος, ἡ, *a shepherd's staff*, which was thrown so as to drive back the cattle to the herd, Il., Anth. (Deriv. unknown.)

κᾰλέοντι, Dor. for καλέουσι, καλοῦσι.

κᾰλεῦνται, Dor. for καλοῦνται.

κᾰλεῦντο, Dor. for ἐκαλέοντο, 3 pl. impf. pass. of sq.

ΚΑ'ΛΕ'Ω, Ep. inf. καλήμεναι: Ion. impf. καλέεσκον; fut. Ion. καλέω, Att. καλῶ (καλέσω is aor. 1 subj.): aor. 1 ἐκάλεσα, Ep. ἐκάλεσσα, κάλεσσα: pf. κέκληκα: —Med., f. Att. καλοῦμαι (also in pass. sense), later καλέσομαι: aor. 1 ἐκαλεσάμην, Ep. καλεσσάμην:—Pass., f. κεκλήσομαι: aor. 1 ἐκλήθην: pf. κέκλημαι, Ion. 3 pl. κεκλέαται; Ep. 3 pl. plqpf. κεκλήατο; opt. κεκλήμην, κεκλῇο: I. *to call, summon*, Hom., etc.: Med. *to call to oneself*, Id. 2. *to call to a repast, to invite*, Od.; κ. ἐπὶ δεῖπνον Hdt., Xen.; κληθέντες πρός τινα *invited* to his house, Dem. 3. *to call on, invoke*, τοὺς θεούς Hdt., Att.; so in Med., Aesch., etc.:—but ἀράς, ἅς σοι καλοῦμαι *curses, which I call down* on thee, Soph.:—in Pass., of the god, *to be invoked*, Aesch. 4. as law-term, of the judge, *to cite* or *summon* before the court, Ar., Dem.; πρὶν τὴν ἐμὴν δίκην καλεῖσθαι before it *is called on*, Ar. b. of the plaintiff, in Med., καλεῖσθαί τινα *to sue* at law, Lat. *vocare in jus*, Id., etc. II. *to call by name, to call, name*, Il., Trag:—ὄνομα καλεῖν τινά *to call* him a *name* (i. e. by name), Od.; so, without ὄνομα, τί νιν καλοῦσα τύχοιμ' ἄν; Aesch.:—Pass., τύμβῳ δ' ὄνομα σῷ κεκλήσεται *a name shall be given* to thy tomb, Eur. 2. in pf. pass. κέκλημαι, *to have received a name, to bear it*, often = εἰμί, *to be*, οὕνεκα σὴ παράκοιτις κέκλημαι *because I am thy wife*, Il.; πόσις κεκλημένος εἴη *were to be* my spouse, Od.;—rarely in pres., γαμβρὸς καλέεσθαι Ib.; poët. Ἀλεισίου ἔνθα κολώνη κέκληται *where is the hill called* the hill of Aleisios, Il. b. foll. by a dependent clause, καλεῖ με, πλαστὸς ὡς εἴην πατρί *he calls me a suppositious son*, Soph.

κᾰλήμεναι, Ep. for καλεῖν, inf. pres. act. of καλέω.

κᾰλ-ήμερος, ον, (ἡμέρα) *with fortunate days*, Anth.

κάλημι, Aeol. for καλέω.

κᾰλήτωρ, ορος, ὁ, (καλέω) *a crier*, Lat. *calator*, Il.

κᾰλιά, Ion. -ιή, ἡ, *a wooden dwelling, hut, barn*, Hes.: *a bird's nest*, Theocr. [ῐ Hes.; ῑ Theocr.]

κᾰλιάς, άδος, ἡ, = foreg., *a hut*, Anth.: *a chapel*, Plut.

κᾰλινδέομαι, Dep. only in pres. and impf., *to lie rolling about* or *wallowing*, Lat. *volutari*, Hdt., Thuc.:—hence, *to be constantly engaged in* a thing, Lat. *versari in aliqua re*, Xen., etc.

κάλλαιον, τό, *a cock's comb*: pl. κάλλαια, τά, *the wattles*, Lat. *palea*, Ar.

κᾰλλείπω, Ep. for καταλείπω.

καλλι-, the first part in compds., where the notion of *beautiful* is added to the simple notion: καλο- is later

and less common.   2. sometimes like a mere Adj. with its Subst., as καλλίπαις = καλὴ παῖς.

καλλι-βλέφᾰρος, ον, (βλέφαρον) with beautiful eyelids, beautiful-eyed, Eur.

καλλι-βόας, ου, ὁ, (βοάω) beautiful-sounding, Soph., Ar.

καλλί-βοτρυς, υ, beautiful-clustering, Soph.

καλλί-βωλος, ον, (βῶλον) with fine, rich soil, Eur.

καλλι-γάληνος [ᾰ], **ον,** (γαλήνη) beautiful in calm, Eur.

καλλί-γᾰμος, ον, happy in marriage, Anth.

καλλι-γένεια, ἡ, (γένος) bearer of a fair offspring, name of Demeter at the Thesmophoria, Ar.

καλλι-γέφῡρος, ον, (γέφυρα) with beautiful bridges, Eur.

*****καλλι-γύναιξ** [ῠ], **ὁ, ἡ,** (γυνή) with beautiful women, only in the obl. cases, Ἑλλάδα καλλιγύναικα Ἀχαιΐδα κ., Σπάρτην κ. Hom.

καλλι-δίνης [ῑ], **ου, ὁ,** (δίνη) beautifully flowing, Eur.

καλλί-διφρος, ον, with beautiful chariot, Eur.

καλλι-δόναξ, ὁ, ἡ, with beautiful reeds, Eur.

καλλι-επέομαι, (ἔπος) Med. to say in fine phrases, Thuc.: to use fine language, Arist.:—Pass., λόγοι κεκαλλιεπημένοι ῥήμασί τε καὶ ὀνόμασι decked out with verbs and nouns, Plat.

καλλ-ιερέω, Ion. **καλλ-ιρέω :** pf. κεκαλλιέρηκα : (ἱερόν) :—to have favourable signs in a sacrifice, to obtain good omens for an undertaking, Lat. litare, perlitare, Xen.; so in Med., Hdt., etc.   2. c. acc. to sacrifice with good omens, Theocr. :—so in Med., Ar.   **II.** of the offering, to give good omens, be favourable, καλλιρῆσαι οὐκ ἐδύνατο [τὰ ἱρά] the sacrifices would not give good omens, Hdt.; ὥς σφι ἐκαλλιέετο [τὰ ἱρά] Id.; also c. inf., οὐκ ἐκαλλίρεε διαβαίνειν μιν the sacrifices were not favourable for his crossing, Id. :—in Med., ὡς οὐδὲ ταῦτα ἐκαλλιερεῖτο Xen.

καλλι-ζῠγής, ές, (ζυγόν) beautifully yoked, Eur.

καλλι-ζωνος, ὁ, ἡ, (ζώνη) with beautiful girdles, Hom.

καλλι-θριξ, τρίχος, ὁ, ἡ, with beautiful manes, of horses, Hom.; of sheep, with fine wool, Od.

καλλι-θῠτέω, f. ήσω, (θύω A) to offer in auspicious sacrifice, κάπρον Anth.

καλλί-καρπος, ον, with beautiful fruit, Aesch., Eur.

καλλί-κερως, ὁ, ἡ, (κέρας) with beautiful horns, Anth.

Καλλι-κολώνη, ἡ, Fair-hill, a place near Troy, Il.

καλλι-κόμας, ὁ, = sq., Eur.

καλλί-κομος, ὁ, ἡ, (κόμη) beautiful-haired, of women, Hom., Hes., Ar.

καλλι-κρήδεμνος, ὁ, ἡ, (κρήδεμνον) with beautiful head-band, Od.

καλλι-λογέομαι, Med. to use specious phrases, Luc.

καλλί-μορφος, ον, (μορφή) beautifully shaped or formed, Eur.

κάλλῑμος, ον, Ep. = for καλός, beautiful, Od.

καλλί-νᾰος, ον, beautiful-flowing, Eur.

καλλί-νῑκος, ον, (νίκη) with glorious victory, κῦδος κ. the glory of noble victory, Pind.: c. gen., τῶν ἐχθρῶν κ. triumphant over one's enemies, Eur.   **II.** adorning or ennobling victory, ὕμνος, ᾠδή, μοῦσα Pind., Eur. :—τὸ καλλίνικον the glory of victory, Pind.; so, καλλίνικος (sub. ὕμνος) Id.

κάλλῑον, neut. of καλλίων, used as Adv., v. καλός C.

Καλλι-όπη, ἡ, (ὄψ) Calliopé, the beautiful-voiced, chief of the nine Muses, the Epic Muse, Hes., h. Hom.: also **Καλλιόπεια,** Anth.

καλλί-παις, παιδος, ὁ, ἡ, with beautiful children, blessed with fair children, Aesch., Eur.   **II.** a beautiful child, Eur.; v. καλλι- 2.

καλλι-πάρῃος, ον, (παρειά) beautiful-cheeked, Hom.

καλλι-πάρθενος, ον, with beautiful nymphs, Eur.; δέρη κ. necks of beauteous maidens, Id.

κάλλιπε, Ep. for κατέλιπε, 3 sing. aor. 2 of καταλείπω : —**καλλιπέειν,** Ep. inf.

καλλι-πέδῑλος, ὁ, ἡ, (πέδιλον) with beautiful sandals, h. Hom.

καλλί-πεπλος, ὁ, ἡ, with beautiful robe, Pind., Eur.

καλλί-πετηλος, ον, (πέτηλον) with beautiful leaves, Anth.

καλλι-πηχυς, υ, gen. εως, with beautiful elbow, Eur.

καλλι-πλόκᾰμος, ὁ, ἡ, with beautiful locks, Hom., Eur.

καλλί-πλουτος, ον, adorned with riches, Pind.

καλλί-πολις, εως, ἡ, fair-city, Plat.

κάλλῐπον, Ep. for κατέλιπον, aor. 2 of καταλείπω.

καλλι-πότᾰμος, ον, of beautiful rivers, Eur.

καλλι-πρῳρος, ον, (πρῴρα) with beautiful prow, Eur. :—metaph. with beautiful face, beautiful, Aesch.

καλλί-πῠλος, ον, (πύλη) with beautiful gates, Anth.

καλλί-πυργος, ον, with beautiful towers, Eur.; κ. σοφία high-towering, Ar.

καλλί-πύργωτος, ον, = foreg., Eur.

καλλί-πωλος, ον, with beautiful steeds, Pind.

καλλι-ρέεθρος, ον, (ῥέεθρον) beautiful-flowing, Od., Eur.

καλλιρέω, Ion. for καλλιερέω.

καλλίροος, ον, poët. for καλλίρροος.

καλλιρρημοσύνη, ἡ, elegance of language, Luc.   **II.** braggart language, Id.   From

καλλι-ρήμων, ον, (ῥῆμα) in elegant language.

καλλί-ρροος, ον, poët. also **καλλί-ροος,** beautiful-flowing, Hom., Aesch. :—metaph. of the flute, Pind.— Fem. Καλλιρόη, one of the Oceanids, h. Hom., Hes. :— but Καλλιρρόη, also, a spring at Athens, later Ἐννεάκρουνος (but now again Καλλιρρόη), Thuc.

καλλι-στάδιος, ον, (στάδιον) with a fine race-course, Eur.

κάλλιστα, Adv. Sup., v. καλός C.

καλλιστεῖον, (καλλιστεύω) the prize of beauty, Eur.   **II.** in pl. = ἀριστεῖα, the meed of valour, Soph.

καλλίστευμα, ατος, τό, exceeding beauty, Eur.   **II.** the first-fruits of beauty or the most beautiful, Id.   From

καλλιστεύω, f. σω, (κάλλιστος) to be the most beautiful, Hdt., Eur.; c. gen., καλλιστεύσει πασέων τῶν γυναικῶν Hdt. :—also in Med., δῶρ' ἃ καλλιστεύεται Eur.

καλλι-στέφανος, ον, beautiful-crowned, h. Hom., Eur.

Καλλιστώ, οῦς, ἡ, Most-beautiful, daughter of Lycaon, Eur., in voc. Καλλιστοῖ.

καλλίσφῠρος, ὁ, ἡ, (σφυρόν) beautiful-ankled, Hom.

καλλί-τεκνος, ον, (τέκνον) with fair children, Plut., Luc.

καλλι-τεχνία, ἡ, (τέχνη) beauty of workmanship, Plut.

καλλί-τοξος, ὁ, ἡ, (τόξον) with beautiful bow, Eur.

κάλλιφ', i. e. κάλλιπε, Ep. for κατέλιπε, 3 sing. aor. 2 of καταλείπω.

καλλι-φεγγής, ές, (φέγγος) beautiful-shining, Eur.

καλλι-φθογγος, ον, (φθογγός) beautiful-sounding, Eur.

καλλί-φλοξ, ον, (φλόξ) auspiciously burning, Eur.

καλλιφωνία, ἡ, beauty of sound, Luc.   From

καλλί-φωνος, ὁ, ἡ, (φωνή) with a fine voice, Plat.

καλλί-χορος, ον, Ep. for καλλί-χωρος, with beautiful

places, as εὐρύχορος for εὐρύχωρος, epith. of large cities, Od., Pind. II. (χόρος) of or for beautiful dances, Eur., Ar. :—ὁ κ. a spring near Eleusis, the fount of goodly dances, h. Hom., Eur. 2. beautiful in the dance, of Apollo, Eur.

καλλίων [ῑ], ον, gen. ονος, Comp. of καλός : v. καλός B.

καλλονή, ἡ, (κάλλος) beauty, Hdt., Eur.

κάλλος, εος, Att. ους, τό, (καλός) beauty, Hom., etc. :— ἐς κάλλος with an eye to beauty, so as to set off her beauty, Eur. ; but, εἰς κ. ζῆν for pleasure, Xen. 2. of persons, a beauty, Id., Luc. 3. in pl. also rich garments and stuffs, Aesch., Plat. ; κάλλεα κηροῦ beautiful works of wax, i. e. honeycombs, Anth.

καλλοσύνη, ἡ, poët. for κάλλος, Eur.

κάλλυντρον, τό, an implement for cleaning, broom, Plut.

καλλύνω [ῡ], f. ῠνῶ, (καλός) to beautify: metaph. to gloss over, Soph. 2. Med. to pride oneself in a thing, Plat.

καλλ-ωπίζω, f. ίσω, (ὤψ) properly, to make the face beautiful ; hence, to beautify, embellish, Plat. :—Pass., κεκαλλωπισμέναι τὸ χρῶμα, i. e. painted, Xen. II. Med. to adorn oneself, make oneself fine or smart, Plat. : metaph. to pride oneself in or on a thing, τινι or ἐπί τινι Id. :—absol. to make a display, shew off, of a horse, Xen. 2. to be coy, play the prude, τινι or πρός τινα towards another, Plat. ; c. inf., κ. παραιτεῖσθαι to affect to deprecate, Plut. Hence

καλλώπισμα, τό, ornament, embellishment, Plat. ; and

καλλωπισμός, ὁ, an adorning oneself, making a display, Plat., Xen. II. ornamentation, εἰς κ. for ornament, Xen. ; καλλωπισμοὶ περὶ τὸ σῶμα Plat.

κᾰλο-διδάσκαλος, ὁ, a teacher of virtue, N. T.

κᾰλοκᾰγᾰθία, ἡ, the character and conduct of a καλὸς κἀγαθός, nobleness, goodness, Xen., Dem. ; and

κᾰλοκᾰγᾰθικός, ή, όν, beseeming a καλὸς κἀγαθός, honourable :—Adv. -κῶς, Plut. 2. inclined to κα-λοκἀγαθία, Id. From

κᾰλοκἀγᾰθός, όν, in good writers written divisim καλὸς κἀγαθός, beautiful and good, noble and good, used in earlier times of the nobles or gentlemen, Hdt., Att. optimates, Hdt., Att. ; later, καλὸς κἀγαθός was a perfect man, a man as he should be, also applied to qualities and actions, Plat., Xen. ; to an army, Xen., etc.

κᾰλον, τό, wood, but only used in pl. κᾶλα, logs for burning (prob. from καίω), h. Hom. : seasoned wood, for joiner's work, κάμπυλα κ. Hes.

κᾰλο-πέδῑλα, τά, (κᾶλον) wooden shoes, used to keep a cow still while milking, Theocr.

κᾰλο-ποιέω, f. ήσω, to do good, N. T.

κάλος, ὁ, Ep. and Ion. for κάλως, a rope.

ΚΑΛΟ´Σ, ή, όν, beautiful, beauteous, fair, Lat. pulcher, of outward form, Hom., etc. ; καλὸς δέμας beautiful of form, Od. ; so, εἶδος κάλλιστος Xen. ; καλὸς τὸ σῶμα Id. ; c. inf., κ. εἰσοράασθαι Hom. 2. τὸ καλόν, like κάλλος, beauty, Eur., etc. : τὰ καλά the decencies, proprieties, elegancies of life, Hdt., etc. 3. in reference to use, beautiful, fair, good, κ. λιμήν Od. ; καλὸς εἴς τι Xen. ; πρός τι Plat. ; c. inf., κάλλιστος τρέχειν Xen. ;—esp. in the foll. phrases, ἐν καλῷ [τόπῳ] in a good place, Thuc. ; ἐν καλῷ τοῦ κόλπου, τῆς πόλεως Xen. ; ἐν κ. (sub. χρόνῳ), in good time, in season, Eur. :—so, καλόν ἐστι, c. inf., Soph. 2.

of sacrifices, good, auspicious, Aesch., etc. III. in moral sense, beautiful, noble, καλόν [ἐστι] c. inf., Hom., etc. ; καλὰ ἔργματα noble deeds, Pind., etc. 2. τὸ καλόν moral beauty, virtue, opp. to τὸ αἰσχρόν (Cicero's honestum and turpe), Xen., Plat. IV. in Att. not seldom ironically, like Lat. praeclarus, admirable, specious, fair, κ. γὰρ οὑμὸς βίοτος, ὥστε θαυμάσαι Soph. ; μετ' ὀνομάτων καλῶν Thuc.

B. Degrees of Compar. : Comp. καλλίων [ῑ], ον, Sup. κάλλιστος, η, ον, Hom., etc.

C. Adv. :—καλόν as Adv., καλὸν ἀείδειν, etc., Hom. ; so καλά Il. ; τὸ καλόν Theocr. II. regul. Adv. καλῶς, mostly in moral sense, well, rightly, Od. ; καλῶς ζῆν, τεθνηκέναι, etc., Soph., etc. ; οὐ καλῶς ταρβεῖς Id. ; often in phrase καλῶς καὶ εὖ, καλῶς τε καὶ εὖ Plat. 2. of good fortune, well, happily, κ. πράσσειν = εὖ πρ. to fare well, Aesch., etc. ; κ. ἔχειν to be well, Id. ; κ. ἔχει, c. inf., 'tis well to . . , Xen. 3. καλῶς = πάνυ, right well, κ. ἔξοιδα Soph. ; so in Comp., κάλλιον εἰδέναι Plat. ; and in Sup. κάλλιστα, Soph., etc. 4. κ. ποιῶν, as Adv., rightly, deservedly, Lat. merito, κ. ποιῶν ἀπόλλυται Ar. 5. in answers, to approve the words of the former speaker, well said! Lat. euge, Eur., Dem. :—but, also, to decline an offer courteously or ironically, thank you ! Lat. benigne, Ar. ; and in Sup., κάλλιστ', ἐπαινῶ Id. 6. ironically, finely, Lat. belle, Soph., Eur.

D. Quantity : ᾰ in Ep. Poets : ᾰ in Att. : in later Poets ᾰ or ᾱ, as the verse requires.

ΚΑ´ΛΠΙΣ, ιδος, ἡ : acc. κάλπιν and κάλπιδα : - a vessel for drawing water, a pitcher or ewer, Od., Att. :—an urn for drawing lots or collecting votes, Anth., Luc. :—a cinerary urn, Anth.

κάλτιος, ὁ, Sicil. form of Lat. calceus, a shoe, Plut.

κᾰλύβη [ῠ], ἡ, (καλύπτω) a hut, cabin, cell, Lat. tugurium, Hdt., Thuc., etc. II. a cover, screen, Anth.

κᾰλύβιον, τό, Dim. of foreg., Plut.

κᾰλῠκο-στέφᾰνος, ον, crowned with flower-buds, Anth.

κᾰλῠκῶπις, ιδος, ἡ, (ὤψ) like a budding flower in face, i. e. blushing, roseate, h. Hom.

κάλυμμα, ατος, τό, (καλύπτω) a head-covering used by women, a hood or veil, Il. ; worn by brides, Aesch. ; a covering put over the face of the dead, Soph. 2. a grave, Anth.

κάλυξ [ᾰ], ῠκος, ἡ, (καλύπτω) a covering, used only of flowers and fruit : 1. the shell or pod of plants, Hdt. ; κάλυκος ἐν λοχεύμασι, i. e. when the fruit is setting, Aesch. 2. the calyx of a flower, a bud, a rose-bud, h. Hom., Theocr. II. in Il. 18. 401, κάλυκες seem to be earrings like flower-cups.

κᾰλύπτειρα, ἡ, = καλύπτρα, a veil, Anth.

κᾰλυπτός, ή, όν, verb. Adj. of καλύπτω II, put round so as to cover, enfolding, enveloping, Soph.

κᾰλύπτρα, Ion. -πτρη, ἡ, a woman's veil, Hom., Aesch. :—metaph. δνοφερὰ κ. the dark veil of night, Aesch. 2. of land given to queens as veil-money (cf. ζώνη I. 2), Plat. II. the cover or lid of a quiver, Hdt.

κᾰλύπτω (lengthd. from Root ΚΑΛΥΒ, v. καλύβη) : Ep. impf. κάλυπτον : f. ψω : aor. 2 ἐκάλυψα, Ep. κάλ- : Med., aor. 1 ἐκαλυψάμην :—Pass., fut. καλυ-φθήσομαι : aor. 1 ἐκαλύφθην : pf. κεκάλυμμαι : 3 sing.

plqpf. κεκάλυπτο: I. *to cover with* a thing, παρδαλέῃ μετάφρενον κάλυψεν Il.; νυκτὶ καλύψας Ib.: simply, *to cover*, μέλαν δέ ἑ κῦμα κάλυψεν Ib.; πέτρον χεὶρ ἐκάλυψεν his hand *covered, grasped* a stone, Ib.; of death, τέλος θανάτοιο κάλυψεν ὀφθαλμούς Ib., etc.; of grief, τὸν δ᾿ ἄχεος νεφέλη ἐκάλυψε Ib.; κ. χθονὶ γυῖα, i.e. *to be buried*, Pind.; also, χθονί, τάφῳ κ. *to bury* another, Aesch.:—Med. *to cover* or *veil one-self*, Hom.:—Pass., ἀσπίδι κεκαλυμμένος ὤμους Il.; ἐν χλαίνῃ κεκαλ. Ib., etc. 2. like κρύπτω, *to cover* or *conceal*; κ. καρδίᾳ τι Soph.; Pass., κεκαλυμμένοι ἵππῳ *concealed in* the horse, Od. 3. *to cover with* dishonour, *throw a cloud over*, σὺ μὴ κάλυπτε ᾿Αθήνας Soph. II. *to put over as a covering*, Lat. *cir-cumdare*, οἱ πέπλοιο πτύγμ᾿ ἐκάλυψεν Il.; οἳ ἄσιν καθύ-περθε καλύψω *I will put* mud *over* him, Ib.; ἀμφὶ Με-νοιτιάδῃ σάκος εὐρὺ καλύψας Ib.

Κᾰλυψώ, όος, contr. οῦς, ἡ, *Calypso*, a nymph, daughter of Atlas, who lived in the island Ogygia; so called be-cause *she hid* (ἐκάλυψε) Ulysses there, Od.

καλχαίνω, (κάλχη) properly, *to make purple*: metaph. *to make dark and troublous* like a stormy sea, *to ponder deeply*, Soph., Eur. Hence

Κάλχας, αντος, ὁ, *Calchas* the Greek Seer at Troy, properly *the Searcher*.

ΚΑ῎ΛΧΗ, ἡ, *the murex* or *purple limpet*.

κᾰλώδιον, τό, Dim. of κάλως, *a small cord*, Ar., Thuc.

καλῶς, Adv. from καλός; v. καλός c.

κάλως [ᾰ], ὁ, gen. κάλω, acc. κάλων: Ep. and Ion. κάλος, ου, ὁ, *a reefing rope, reef*, Od., where the κάλοι are distinguished from πόδες (sheets) and ὑπέραι (braces); κάλως ἐξιέναι *to let out the reefs*, i.e. *to set all sail*, Eur.; metaph., ἐχθροὶ γὰρ ἐξίασι πάντα δὴ κάλων are letting out every *reef*, i.e. using every effort, Id.; φόνιον ἐξίει κάλων give a loose to slaughter, Id.; so, πάντα ἐξίεναι κάλων Ar. II. generally, *a rope, line*, κάλων κατιέναι to let down a *sounding-line*, Hdt. 2. *a cable*, Id.; πρυμνήτης κ. a stern *cable*, Eur.; ἀπὸ κάλω παραπλεῖν to be towed along shore, Thuc.

κᾰλω-στρόφος, ὁ, (στρέφω) *a rope-maker*, Plut.

κάμ, Ep. for κατά before μ, as κὰμ μέν for κατὰ μέν, κὰμ μέσον for κατὰ μέσον, Hom.

κᾰμάκῐνος, ον, (κάμαξ) *made of reed* or *cane*, Xen.

ΚΑ῎ΜΑΞ [κᾰ], ᾰκος, ἡ and ὁ, *a vine-pole, vine-prop*, Il., Hes. 2. *the shaft of a spear*, Aesch., Eur. 3. *the tiller* of the rudder, Luc.

ΚΑ῝ΜΑ῎ΡΑ, Ion. -ρη [μᾰ], ἡ, Lat. *camera, anything with an arched cover, a covered carriage*, Hdt.

κᾰμᾰσῆνες, ων, οἱ, *a kind of fish*, Anth. (Foreign word.)

κᾰμᾰτηρός, ά, όν, *toilsome, troublesome, wearisome*, h. Hom.:—*tiring, exhausting*, Luc. II. pass. *bowed down with toil, broken down, worn out*, Hdt. From

κάμᾰτος, ὁ, (κάμνω) *toil, trouble, labour*, Od., Soph., Eur. 2. *the effects of toil, distress, weariness*, Hom.; ὕπνῳ καὶ καμάτῳ ἀρημένος (so Hor., *ludo fati-gatumque somno*), Od. II. *that which is earned by toil*, ἡμέτερος κάματος our *hard-won earnings*, Ib.; ἀλλότριος κάματος *the earnings* of other men's *toil*, Hes. 2. *the result of labour, a work, a thing wrought* by the lathe, Anth.

κᾰμᾰτ-ώδης, ες, (εἶδος) *toilsome, wearisome*, Hes., Pind.

κάμε, Ep. for ἔκαμε, aor. 2 of κάμνω. II. **κᾰμέ**, crasis for καὶ ἐμέ.

κᾰμεῖν, aor. 2 inf. of κάμνω.

κᾰμεῖται, 3 sing. f. med. of κάμνω.

κάμηλος [ᾰ], ὁ and ἡ, *a camel*, Hdt., etc.; κ. ἀμνός α camel-lamb, i.e. *young camel*, Ar. 2. ἡ κ. (like ἡ ἵππος) *the camels in an army*, as one might say *the camelry, camel-brigade*, Hdt. (Cf. Hebr. *gâmal*.)

κᾰμῑνευτήρ, ῆρος, ὁ, = foreg.; αὐλὸς κ. the pipe *of a smith's bellows*, Anth.; and

κᾰμῑνευτής, οῦ, ὁ, = καμινεύς, Luc. From

κᾰμῑνεύω, f. σω, *to heat in a furnace*, Arist. From

κάμῑνος, ἡ, (καίω) *an oven, furnace, kiln*, for baking, smelting metals, for burning bricks, Hdt. Hence

κᾰμῑνώ, οῦς, ἡ, *a furnace-woman*, Od.

κᾰμμέν, v. κάμ.

κάμμες, crasis for καὶ ἄμμες, Aeol. for καὶ ἡμεῖς.

κάμμεσον, v. κάμ.

κᾰμμίξας, Ep. for καταμίξας, aor. 1 part. of καταμίγνυμι.

κᾰμμονίη, ἡ, Ep. for καταμονή, *the reward of endur-ance*, Il.

κάμμορος, ον, Ep. for κατάμορος, *subject to destiny*, i.e. *ill-fated*, Od.

κᾰμμύω, Ep. and poët. for καταμύω.

κάμνω, (lengthd. from the Root ΚΑΜ): κᾰμοῦμαι:—aor. 2 ἔκᾰμον, inf. κᾰμεῖν, Ep. subj. redupl. κεκάμω, 3 sing. κεκάμῃσι, 3 pl. κεκάμωσι:—pf. κέκμηκα; 3 pl. plqpf. ἐκεκμήκεσαν; Ep. part. κεκμηώς, κεκμηῶτι, κεκ-μηῶτα, acc. κεκμηῶτας:—Med., Ep. aor. 2 κᾰμό-μην: I. trans. *to work*, of smith's work, σκῆπτρον, τὸ μὲν ῞Ηφαιστος κάμε which he *wrought*, Il.; κ. νῆας Od. II. Med. *to win by toil*, τὰς (sc. γυναῖκας) αὐτοὶ καμόμεσθα Il. 2. *to work* or *till by labour*, Od. III. intr. *to work, labour*, Thuc.:—then, *to be weary*, ἀνδρὶ δὲ κεκμηῶτι μένος οἶνος ἀέξει Il.; οὐδέ τι γυῖα κάμνω nor is he *weary* in limb, Ib.; περὶ δ᾿ ἔγχεῖ χεῖρα καμεῖται he will have his hand *weary* in grasping the spear, Ib.:—c. part., κάμνει πολεμίζων, ἐλαύνων is *weary* of fighting, rowing, Ib.; οὐκ ἔκαμον τανύων *I found no trouble* in stringing the bow, i.e. did it without trouble, Od.; οὔτοι καμοῦμαι λέγουσα *I shall never be tired* of saying, Aesch., etc. 2. *to be sick* or *ill, suffer under illness*, οἱ κάμνοντες *the sick*, Hdt., etc.; so, κάμνειν νόσον Eur.; κ. τοὺς ὀφθαλμούς Hdt. 3. generally, *to suffer, be distressed* or *afflicted*, στρατοῦ καμόντος Aesch.; οὐ καμεῖ will not *have to complain*, Soph.; οὐκ ἴσον καμὼν ἐμοὶ λύπης not *having borne an equal share of grief* with me, Id. 4. οἱ καμόντες (aor. part.) *those who have done their work*, Lat. *defuncti*, i.e. *the dead*, Hom.; so, κεκμηκότες Eur., Thuc.

καμπή, ἡ, (κάμπτω) *a bending, winding*, of a river, Hdt. II. *the turning in a race-course, turning-post*, Ar.: metaph., μῦθον ἐς καμπὴν ἄγειν to bring a speech to *its middle* or *turning point*, Eur.; καμπὰς ποιεῖσθαι Plat. Hence

κάμπιμος, η, ον, *bent, turning*, Eur.

καμπτήρ, ῆρος, ὁ, (κάμπτω) *a bend, an angle*, Xen. II. *the turning-point in the* δίαυλος, *the goal*, Arist.: metaph., κ. πύματος *life's last turn* or *course*, Anth.

κάμπτω, (lengthd. from Root ΚΑΜΠ, v. κάμψω): f. κάμψω, Ep. inf. -έμεν: aor. 1 ἔκαμψα: Pass., aor. 1 ἐκάμφθην:—*to bend, curve*, ὄφρα ἴτυν κάμψῃ that he may bend

it into a chariot-rail, Il.; γόνυ κ. to bend the knee so as to sit down and rest, Ib.; οὐ κάμπτων γόνυ, i. e. never resting, Aesch.; so, κ. κῶλα Soph.; then, κάμπτειν alone, to sit down, rest, Id.;—also, γόνυ κ. to bend the knee in worship, N. T. II. to turn or guide a horse or chariot round the turning-post (καμπή 11); hence, of the horse or chariot, κάμψαι διαύλου θάτερον κῶλον πάλιν to double the post (καμπτήρ) and return along the second half of the δίαυλος, Aesch.; κάμπτοντος ἵππου as the horse was turning, Soph.:—metaph., κ. βίον to make the last turn in the course of life, Id.; κ. βίου τέλος Eur. 2. so also of seamen, to double a headland, ἄκρην κ. Hdt.; also, κ. περὶ ἄκραν Ar.; κ. κόλπον to wind round the bay, Hdt. 3. absol., πάλιν κ. to turn back, Eur.; ἐγγὺς τῶν ἐμῶν κάμπτεις φρενῶν thou comest near my meaning, Id. III. metaph., like Lat. flectere, κάμπτειν τινά to bend or bow one down, Pind.:—Pass. to be bowed down, Aesch., Thuc.; κάμπτομαι I submit, Plat.

καμπῠλόεις, εσσα, εν, poët. for καμπύλος, Anth.

καμπὔλος [ῠ], η, ον, (κάμπτω) bent, crooked, curved, of a bow, Il.; of wheels, Ib.; of chariots, Ib.

καμψί-πους, ὁ, ἡ, πουν, τό, bending the foot, i. e. swift-running, Aesch.

κᾰμών, aor. 2 part. of κάμνω.

κάν, poët. for κατά before ν, as κὰν νόμον Pind.

κᾶν, crasis for καὶ ἐν.

κᾶν, crasis, I. for καὶ ἄν, Hes., Att.; κακὸν δὲ κᾶν ἐν ἡμέρᾳ γνοίης μιᾷ Soph.:—later, κᾶν came to be used, even when the Verb in apodosi was of a tense that could not be joined with ἄν, as, κᾶν εἰ πολλαὶ [αἱ ἀρεταί] εἰσιν, for ὦσι, Plat. II. for καὶ ἄν or καὶ ἐάν, and if, even if, although, Soph., Ar., etc.

κᾰνάβῐνος, η, ον, of or for a block-figure, σῶμα κ. a body so lean as to be a mere skeleton, Anth. From

κάνᾰβος, ὁ, a wooden block round which artists moulded wax or clay, a block-figure.

κάνᾰθρον or rather **κάνναθρον**, τό, (κάννα) a cane or wicker carriage, Xen.

κᾰνᾰκωκύσας, crasis for καὶ ἀνακωκύσας.

κάνᾰστρον, τό, = κάνεον, a dish, Ep. Hom.

κᾰνᾰχέω, f. ήσω: Ep. aor. 1 κανάχησα:—to ring, clash, clang, of metal, Od. From

ΚΑ˘ΝΑ˘ΧΗ', ἡ, a sharp sound: the ring or clang of metal, Il., Soph.; καναχὴ δ᾽ ἦν ἡμιόνοιϊν loud rang their tramp, Od.; ὀδόντων καναχή a gnashing of teeth, Il.; καναχὰ αὐλῶν the sound of flutes, Pind. (For Verb κανάσσω v. ἐγ-κάνασσω.)

κᾰνᾰχηδά, Adv. with a sharp loud noise, of water, Hes.

κᾰνᾰχής, ές, of water, plashing, Aesch.

κᾰνᾰχίζω, only in impf., = καναχέω, to ring, Hom.

κάνδυς, υος, ὁ, a Median cloak with sleeves, Xen.

κᾰνεῖν, fut. inf. of καίνω.

κάνεον [ᾰ], τό, Ep. also **κάνειον**, Att. κανοῦν : (κάννα): —a basket of reed or cane, a bread-basket, Lat. canistrum, Hom., Hdt., Att.; also made of metal, Hom.: —it was used for the sacred barley at sacrifices, ἔχεν οὐλὰς ἐν κανέῳ Od.

κᾰνέπτυε, crasis for καὶ ἀνέπτυε.

ΐανῆν, Dor. for κανεῖν, aor. 2 inf. of καίνω.

κάνης, ητος, ὁ, (κάννα) a mat of reeds such as the

Athen. women took with them when they went out, Lex Solonis ap. Plut.

κᾰνηφορέω, f. ήσω, to carry the sacred basket in procession, Ar.; and

κᾰνηφορία, ἡ, the office of κανηφόρος, Plat. From

κᾰνη-φόρος, ον, (φέρω) carrying a basket :— Κανηφόροι, αἱ, Basket-bearers, at Athens, maidens who carried on their heads baskets containing the sacred things used at the feasts of Demeter, Bacchus and Athena, Ar.

ΚΑ'ΝΘΑ˘ΡΟΣ, ὁ, Lat. cantharus, a beetle worshipped in Egypt, Aesch., etc. II. a Naxian boat, Ar. III. a mark or knot like a beetle, on the tongue of the Egyptian god Apis, Hdt.

κάνθεν, crasis for καὶ ἔνθεν.

κανθήλια, ων, τά, Lat. clitellae, a pack-saddle, or the panniers at the sides of a pack-saddle, Ar.

κανθήλιος, ὁ, = κάνθων, a large sort of ass for carrying burdens, a pack-ass, Xen., Plat., etc.

κάνθων, ωνος, ὁ, = κανθήλιος, a pack-ass, Ar., Anth.

κἀνιαύσιος, crasis for καὶ ἐνιαύσιος.

κἄνις, crasis for καὶ ἄνις = καὶ ἄνευ.

ΚΑ'ΝΝΑ or **κάννη**, ης, ἡ, a reed, Lat. canna : in pl. a reed-fence, railing, Ar.

κανναβῐνος, η, ον, hempen, of hemp, like it, Anth. From

ΚΑ'ΝΝΑ˘ΒΙΣ, ἡ, gen. ιος, acc. κάνναβιν or κανναβίδα :— hemp, Hdt., etc.;—it was burnt, so as to medicate vapour-baths, Id.

κάνναβος, ὁ, = κάναβος.

καννεύσας, Ep. for κατανεύσας, aor. 1 part. of κατανεύω.

κάννεώσασθαι, crasis for καὶ ἀνανεώσασθαι.

καννόμον, for κὰν (i. e. κατά) νόμον.

κἀνόνητα, crasis for καὶ ἀνόνητα.

κᾰνονίζω, f. ίσω, (κανών) to measure by rule, Longin. : to regulate, square, Arist., Anth.

κᾰνονίς, ίδος, ἡ, a ruler, Anth.

κᾰνόνισμα, ατος, τό, = κανών 1. 3, Anth.

κἀνταῦθα, crasis for καὶ ἐνταῦθα.

κἀντῐβάς, crasis for καὶ ἀντιβάς.

κἄνω, fut. of καίνω.

Κάνωβος or **Κάνωπος**, ὁ, Canopus, a town in lower Egypt, Hdt., etc.; famed for its temple of Serapis, who was called Κανωβίτης, Anth.:—the Westernmost mouth of the Nile was called the Κανωβικὸν στόμα, Hdt.

κᾰνών, aor. 2 part. of καίνω.

κᾰνών, όνος, ὁ, (κάννα) any straight rod or bar : 1. in Hom. the κανόνες of a shield seem to have been two rods running across the hollow of the shield, through which the arm was passed. 2. a rod used in weaving, the shuttle or quill, by which the threads of the woof (πηνίον) were passed between those of the warp (μίτος), Il. 3. a rule used by masons or carpenters, Eur., Xen., etc. b. a ruler, Anth. c. metaph., ἀκτὶς ἡλίου, κανὼν σαφής, Milton's ʻlong-levelled rule of light,ʼ Eur. 4. the beam or tongue of the balance, Anth. 5. in pl. the keys or stops of the flute, Id. II. metaph., like Lat. regula, norma, a rule, standard of excellence, Eur. ;—in Chronology, κανόνες χρονικοί were chief epochs or eras, Plut.

κἀξ, crasis for καὶ ἐξ.

κάπ, Ep. for κατά before π, φ, as κὰπ πεδίον, κὰπ φάλαρα Il.

κἄπαγε, crasis for καὶ ἄπαγε.

κἀπαγώνιος, crasis for καὶ ἐπαγώνιος.
κἄπειτα, crasis for καὶ ἔπειτα.
κάπετον, Dor. for κατέπεσον, Pind.
κάπετος, ἡ, (for σκάπετος, from σκάπτω), a ditch, trench, Il. :—a hole, grave, Ib., Soph.
ΚΑΠΗ [ă], ἡ, Ep. dat. pl. κάπῃσι : (v. κάπτω) :—a crib for the food of cattle, manger, Hom.
κἄπηλεία, ἡ, retail trade, tavern-keeping, Plat.; and
κἄπηλεῖον, τό, the shop of a κάπηλος, esp. a tavern, Lat. caupona, Ar. From
κἄπηλεύω, f. εύσω, (κάπηλος) to be a retail-dealer, Hdt.; δι' ἀψύχου βορᾶς σίτοις καπήλευ' drive a trade, chaffer with your vegetable food, Eur. II. c. acc. to sell by retail, Hdt. :—metaph., καπηλεύειν μάχην to make a trade of war, Lat. cauponari bellum, Aesch.; καπηλεύουσα τὸν βίον playing tricks with life, corrupting it, Anth.; κ. τὸν λόγον τοῦ θεοῦ N. T.
κἄπηλικός, ή, όν, (κάπηλος) of or for a retail dealer : —ἡ καπηλική (sc. τέχνη) = καπηλεία, Plat. 2. like a petty trader, knavish, Anth. :—Adv., καπηλικῶς ἔχειν to be vamped up for sale, Ar.
κἄπηλίς, ίδος, ἡ, fem. of κάπηλος, Lat. copa, Ar.
ΚΑΠΗΛΟΣ, ὁ, a retail-dealer, huckster, hawker, peddlar, higgler, Lat. institor, Hdt., Att.; opp. to the merchant (ἔμπορος), Xen., etc.; applied to Darius because of his finance-regulations, Hdt. :—κ. ἀσπίδων, ὅπλων a dealer in . . , Ar. 2. a tavern-keeper, publican, Lat. caupo, Id., etc. 3. metaph., κ. πονηρίας a dealer in petty rogucry, Dem.
κἄπιβῶ, crasis for καὶ ἐπιβῶ (contr. from ἐπιβόα).
καπίθη, ἡ, a measure containing two χοίνικες, Xen. (Prob. a Persian word.)
κἄπικείμεναι, crasis for καὶ ἐπικείμεναι.
κἄπιπείσομαι, crasis for καὶ ἐπιπείσομαι.
κἄπισημανθήσομαι, crasis for καὶ ἐπισημανθήσομαι.
κάπνη, ἡ, = καπνοδόχη, Ar.
καπνίζω, f. Att. ιῶ : aor. 1 ἐκάπνισα, Ep. 3 pl. κάπνισσαν : (καπνός) :—to make smoke, i. e. to make a fire, Il. II. to smoke, blacken with smoke, Dem. 2. intr. to be black with smoke, Ar. Hence
κάπνισμα, ατος, τό, incense, Anth.
καπνο-δόκη, later -δόχη, ἡ, (δέχομαι) properly, a smoke-receiver, i. e. a hole in the roof for the smoke to pass through, Hdt.
καπνόομαι, Pass. to be turned into smoke, burnt to ashes, Pind., Eur. From
ΚΑΠΝΟΣ, ὁ, smoke, Hom., etc.; proverb., καπνοῦ σκιά shadow of smoke, of things worth nothing, Soph.; περὶ καπνοῦ στενολεσχεῖν to quibble about smoke, Ar.; γραμμάτων καπνοί learned trifles, Eur.
κᾶπος, Dor. for κῆπος.
κάππα, τό, v. sub Κ κ.
Καππαδόκαι, οἱ, the Cappadocians, notorious as knaves and cowards, Hdt. Hence
Καππᾰδοκίζω, f. σω, to favour the Cappadocians, Hdt. :—Pass. to play the Cappadocian, Hdt.
κάππᾰρις, εως, ἡ, the caper-plant, or its fruit, the caper, Lat. capparis, Arist. (Deriv. unknown.)
καππεδίον, for κὰπ (i. e. κατὰ) πεδίον.
κάππεσον, Ep. for κατέπεσον, aor. 2 of καταπίπτω.
καππο-φόρος, ον, (φέρω) marked with a κάππα, Luc.

καππῠρίζω, for καταπυρίζω, to catch, take fire, aor. 1 part. καππυρίσασα Theocr.
καπράω, (κάπρος) metaph. to be lewd or lecherous, Ar.
κάπριος, ὁ, poët. for κάπρος, a wild boar, Il.; also, σῦς κάπριος Ib. II. as Adj. κάπριος, ον, like a wild boar, Hdt.
ΚΑΠΡΟΣ [ă by nature], ὁ, the boar, wild boar, Lat. aper, Il., etc.; also, σῦς κάπρος Ib.
καπρο-φόνος, ον, (*φένω) killing wild boars, Anth.
κάπτω (lengthd. from Root ΚΑΠ, v. κάπη) : f. κάψω : —to gulp down, Ar., etc. : cf. κεκαφηώς.
ΚΑΠΥΡΟΣ, ά, όν, dried by the air, dry, Theocr. 2. act. drying, parching, Id. II. metaph. of sound, καπυρὸν γελᾶν to laugh loud, Anth.; κ. στόμα a loud, clear-sounding voice, Theocr., Mosch.; κ. συρίζειν to play clearly on the syrinx, Luc.
καπφάλαρα, for κἀπ (i. e. κατὰ) φάλαρα.
κάρ, for κατά before ρ, as κὰρ ῥόον, κάρ ῥα Il.
ΚΑΡ, hair cut off, a lock of hair, (cf. κείρω, ἀ-καρής), τίω δέ μιν ἐν καρὸς αἴσῃ I value him but at a hair's worth, flocci eum facio, Il. II. also = κάρα, κάρη, head, ἐπὶ κάρ head-long, Il.
Κάρ, ὁ, gen. Καρός, pl. Κᾶρες, a Carian, Il., etc.; fem. Κάειρα, Ib. :—the Carians hired themselves out as mercenaries, and were used to spare the lives of the citizen-soldiers; hence, ἐν τῷ Καρὶ κινδυνεύειν to make the risk, not with one's own person, but with a Carian, Lat. experimentum facere in corpore vili, Eur.
κάρᾱ, Ion. κάρη [ă], τό, (on the forms and Root, v. infr.) :—poët. for κεφαλή, the head, Il., etc. 2. the head or top of anything, as of a mountain, Hes.; the edge or brim of a cup, Soph. 3. in Att. Poets, it is used like κεφαλή, periphr. for a person, Οἰδίπου κάρα, i. e. Οἰδίπους, Soph.; ὦ κασίγνητον κ., for ὦ κασίγνητε, Id., etc.—Hom. used κάρη only in nom. and acc. sing. and pl., and supplied the obl. cases from decl. 5, gen. and dat. κάρητος, κάρητι, also κάρηατος, κάρητι; pl. κάρηατα (formed as if from a nom. κάρηαρ or κάρηας) : later Poets inflected κάρη as of decl. 1, viz. κάρης, κάρῃ, κάρην; Trag. dat. κάρᾳ.
κᾰράβο-πρόσωπος, ον, with the face of a κάραβος, Luc.
ΚΑΡΑΒΟΣ [κᾱ-], ὁ, the stag-beetle, Arist.
κᾰρᾱ-δοκέω, f. ήσω, to watch with outstretched head, i. e. to watch eagerly or anxiously, Hdt., Eur., Xen. : —also, κ. εἴς τινα to look eagerly at one, Ar.
καράκαλλον, τό, a hood, Lat. caracalla, Anth.
κᾰρᾱνιστήρ, ῆρος, ὁ, beheading, capital, Aesch.
κᾰρᾱνιστής, οῦ, ὁ, = foreg., Eur.
κάρᾱνον, τό, v. κάρηνον.
κάρᾱνος, ὁ, (κάρα) a chief, Xen.
κᾰρᾱνόω, f. ώσω, (κάρανον) to achieve, Aesch.
κᾰρᾱτόμος, f. ήσω, to cut off the head, behead, Eur.
κᾰρᾱ-τομος [ρᾱ], ον, (τέμνω) beheaded, Eur.; κ. ἐρημία νεανίδων, i. e. their slaughter, Id. 2. cut off from the head, κ. χλιδαί one's shorn locks, Soph.
κάρβᾰνος, ον, = βάρβαρος, outlandish, foreign, Aesch. (Foreign word.)
καρβάτιναι, αἱ, shoes of undressed leather, brogues, Xen. (Deriv. unknown.)
ΚΑΡΔΑΜΟΝ, τό, a kind of cress, Lat. nasturtium, or its seed, which was eaten like mustard by the Persians,

Xen.; in pl. cresses, Ar.;—metaph., βλέπειν κάρδαμα, i. e. look sharp and stinging, Id.

ΚΑΡΔΙΑ, ή, Ion. καρδίη, Ep. also κρἄδίη :—the heart, ἐν στέρνοισι κραδίη πατάσσει Il.; κραδίη ἔξω στήθεος ἐκθρώσκει, of one panic-stricken, Ib.; οἰδάνεται κραδίη χόλῳ Ib., etc.; ἐκ τῆς καρδίας φιλεῖν Ar.; τἀπὸ καρδίας λέγειν, Lat. ex animo, to speak freely, Eur.   II. the stomach, Thuc.

καρδιο-γνώστης, ου, ὁ, knower of hearts, N. T.

καρδιό-δηκτος, ον, (δάκνω) gnawing the heart, Aesch.

καρδι-ουλκέω, (ἕλκω) to draw the heart out of the victim, Luc.

ΚΑΡΔΟΠΟΣ, ἡ, a kneading-trough, Ar.

κάρη, τό, Ion. for κάρα, the head.

*κάρηαρ, assumed nom. of the Ep. forms καρήατος, -ήατι, -ήατα, v. κάρα.

κἄρη-κομόωντες, οἱ, (κομάω) with hair on the head, long-haired, of the Achaians, who let all their hair grow (whereas the Abantes, who wore theirs long only at the back of the head, were called ὄπιθεν κομόωντες), Il.

κάρηναι, aor. 2 pass. inf. of κείρω.

κάρηνον, τό, Dor. κάρᾱνον, (κάρη) the head, mostly in pl., ἀνδρῶν κάρηνα periphr. for ἄνδρες, Il.; νεκύων κ., for νέκυες, Od.; βοῶν κ., as we say, so many head of cattle, Il.   2. metaph. of mountain-peaks, Οὐλύμποιο κ. Ib.; and of towns, a citadel, Ib.

κάρητος, κάρητι, gen. and dat. of κάρη, v. κάρα.

Κᾱρικός, ή, όν, Carian, Soph.; Κ. αὐλήματα dirges, Ar.

Κᾱρίνη [ῑ], ἡ, a Carian woman, Phan. ap. Plut.

Κάριος [ᾰ], α, ον, = Καρικός, Hdt.

ΚΑΡΙΣ, gen. καρίδος [ῐ], ἡ, a shrimp or prawn, Ar.

καρκαίρω, to quake under the feet of men and horses, Lat. tremere, Il. (Formed from the sound.)

καρκίνος [ῐ], ὁ, with heterog. pl. καρκίνα, a crab, Lat. cancer, Batr., Ar., Plat.:—proverb., οὔποτε ποιήσεις τὸν καρκίνον ὀρθὰ βαδίζειν Ar.   II. a pair of tongs, Anth.; καρκίνα compasses, Id.

καρκῑνό-χειρες, ων, with crab's claws for hands, Luc.

Κάρνεια, poët. Κάρνεα, τά, a festival held in honour of Apollo Κάρνειος by the Spartans, during nine days of the Att. month Metageitnion, called by them Καρνεῖος μήν, Eur., Thuc.

Κάρπᾰθος, Ep. Κρἄπαθος, ἡ, an island between Crete and Rhodes, Hom.

καρπαία, ἡ, a mimic dance of the Thessalians, Xen. (Perh. from ἁρπ-άζω.)

καρπάλιμος, ον, (v. κραιπνός) swift, Lat. rapidus, Il.:—Adv. -μως, swiftly, rapidly, Ib.   2. in Pind., γένυες κ. eager jaws.

καρπίζω, f. σω, (καρπός) to make fruitful, fertilise, Eur.

κάρπιμος, ον, fruit-bearing, fruitful, Aesch., Eur., etc.:—κάρπιμα, τά, fruit-trees or corn-fields, Ar.; κάρπιμα ἀγαθά property that yields a produce, opp. to ἄκαρπα, Arist.:—metaph., τῶν ξένων τοὺς κ. rich foreigners from whom money can be wrung, Ar.

καρπο-γένεθλος, ον, fruit-producing, Anth.

ΚΑΡΠΟΣ (A), ὁ, fruit, καρπὸς ἀρούρης, i. e. corn, Il.; so, κ. Δήμητρος Hdt., etc.; of trees, Od., etc.   II. generally, produce, returns, profits, Hdt., etc.; οἱ καρποὶ ἐκ τῶν ἀγελῶν the produce of the herds, Xen.   III. of actions, fruit, result, profit, εἰ καρπὸς ἔσται θεσφάτοισι if his oracles shall bear fruit,

i. e. be fulfilled, Aesch.; γλώσσης ματαίας κ., i. e. curses, Id.; κ. ἐπέων οὐ κατέφθινε, i. e. poesy, Pind.; κ. φρενῶν wisdom, Id.

ΚΑΡΠΟΣ (B), ὁ, the wrist, Hom., etc.

καρπο-τόκος, ον, (τίκτω) bearing fruit, Anth.

καρπο-φάγος, ον, (φαγεῖν) living on fruit, Arist.

καρπο-φθόρος, ον, (φθείρω) spoiling fruit, Anth.

καρποφορέω, to bear fruit, Xen.   From

καρπο-φόρος, ον, (φέρω) fruit-bearing, fruitful, of trees, Hdt., Xen.; of lands, Pind., Eur.; of Demeter, Ar.

καρπο-φύλαξ [ῠ], ᾰκος, ὁ, watcher of fruit, Anth.

καρπόω, f. ώσω, (καρπός A) to bear fruit or bear as fruit, Aesch.   II. Med. to get fruit for oneself, i. e., 1. to reap crops from land, Hdt., Aesch.: metaph. to exhaust or drain, τὴν Ἑλλάδα Ar.   2. to enjoy the interest of money, Dem.; so in pf. pass., τὸ ἐργαστήριον κεκαρπωμένος enjoying the profits of the shop, Id.:—absol. to make profit, Ar.   3. to reap the fruits of, enjoy the free use of, Thuc., etc.: —then,   4. simply, to enjoy, Soph., Eur., etc.: — sometimes in bad sense, καρποῦσθαι τὴν ἁμαρτίαν Aesch.; πένθη Eur.   Hence

κάρπωσις, εως, ἡ, use or profit, Xen.

καρρέζουσα, Ep. for καταρρ-, part. fem. of καταρρέζω.

κάρτᾰ, (κάρτος = κράτος), Adv. very, very much, extremely, Lat. valde, admodum.   2. beyond measure, in good earnest, κ. ἐγχώριος a thorough native, Aesch.; κ. ὢν ἐπώνυμος true to thy name, Id.; κ. δ' εἰμὶ τοῦ πατρός all on my father's side, Id.   3. καὶ κάρτα, used to increase the force of a previous statement, really and truly, most certainly, Hdt., Soph.; so, τὸ κάρτα, with iron. sense, in good sooth, with a vengeance, Hdt.

καρτερέω, f. ήσω, (καρτερός) to be steadfast, patient, staunch, Soph., etc.; with a Prep., κ. πρός τι to hold up against a thing, Xen., etc.:—with a part. to persevere in doing, Eur.: absol., τὰ δεῖν' ἐκαρτέρουν was strangely obdurate or obstinate, Soph.   II. c. acc. rei, to bear patiently, Eur., Xen.:—Pass., κεκαρτέρηται τἀμά my time for patience is over, Eur.   Hence

καρτέρημα, ατος, τό, an act of patience, Plat.; and

καρτέρησις, εως, ἡ, a bearing patiently, patience, Plat.   2. c. gen. patient endurance of a thing, Id.

καρτερία, ἡ, (καρτερός) patient endurance, patience, opp. to μαλακία, Xen., Plat.

καρτερικός, ή, όν, (καρτερός) capable of endurance, patient, Xen., Arist.

καρτερό-θῡμος, ον, stout-hearted, Hom., Hes.: generally, strong, mighty, ἄνεμοι Hes.

καρτερός, ά, όν, (κάρτος) = κρατερός, strong, staunch, stout, sturdy; c. inf., καρτερὸς ἐναίρειν strong to kill, Il.; τὰ καρτερώτατα the strongest, Soph.   2. c. gen. possessed of a thing, lord or master of it, Theogn., Theocr.   3. like καρτερικός, steadfast, patient, πρὸς πάντα Xen.: obstinate, Plat.   4. of things, strong, mighty, potent, ὅρκος Il.; κ. ἔργα deeds of might, Ib.; κ. μάχη strongly contested, desperate, Hdt., Thuc. —τὸ καρτερόν, τόλμης τὸ κ. the extremity of daring, Eur.:—κατὰ τὸ καρτερόν by force, Hdt., Ar., etc.; so, πρὸς τὸ καρτερόν Aesch., absol., Theocr.   5. of place, like ὀχυρός, strong, Thuc.; τὸ καρτερώτερον τοῦ χωρίου Id.   II. Adv. -ρῶς, strongly, etc., κ. ὑπνοῦσθαι to sleep soundly, Hdt.   III.

the common Comp. and Sup. are κρείσσων and κράτιστος (qq. v.): but the regular forms καρτερώτερος, -ώτατος, occur now and then, Pind., Att.

καρτερούντως, Adv. of καρτερέω, strongly, stoutly, Plat.

καρτερό-χειρ, χειρος, ὁ, ἡ, strong-handed, h. Hom.

κάρτιστος, Ep. for κράτιστος.

κάρτος, εος, τό, Ep. for κράτος, dat. κάρτεϊ, strength, vigour, courage, Hom., Hes.

καρτύνω [ῡ], Ep. for κρατύνω.

Καρύαι, ῶν, αἱ, a place in Laconia with a famous temple of Artemis, Thuc. :—hence, II. Καρυᾶτις, ἡ, a name of Artemis: whence Καρυᾶτίζω, to dance the Caryatic dance, Luc.

κᾰρύκη [ῠ], ἡ, a Persian dish, composed of blood and rich spices, Luc. Hence

κᾰρύκινος, η, ον, dark-red, Xen.

κᾰρῡκο-ποιέω, f. ήσω, to make a καρύκη or rich sauce, Ar.

κάρυξ, Dor. for κῆρυξ.

ΚΑ'ΡΥΟΝ [ᾰ], τό, any kind of nut, Ar., Xen.; distinguished into various kinds, as κ. βασιλικά or Περσικά, walnuts, also called simply κάρυα, Batr.; κ. κασταναϊκά or κασταναῖα chestnuts, etc.

κᾰρύο-ναύτης, ου, ὁ, one who sails in a nut-shell, Luc.

καρύσσω, Dor. for κηρύσσω.

καρφᾰλέος, α, ον, (κάρφω) dry, parched, Od. :—of sound, καρφαλέον ἀσπὶς αὖσε the shield rang dry, i. e. hollow, Il.

κάρφη, ἡ, (κάρφω) dry grass, hay, Xen.

καρφηρός, ά, όν, of dry straw, Eur.; and

καρφίτης, ου, ὁ, built of dry straws, Anth. From

κάρφος, εος, τό, a dry stalk, Lat. palea, stipula, a chip of wood, Ar.: in pl. the dry sticks of cinnamon, Hdt.; dry twigs, chips, straws, bits of wool, such as birds make nests of, Ar. From

ΚΑ'ΡΦΩ, f. κάρψω, to dry up, wither, κάρψω χρόα καλόν I will wither the fair skin, wrinkle it, Od.; ἠέλιος χρόα κάρφει Hes.

καρχᾰλέος, α, ον, rough, δίψῃ καρχαλέοι rough in the throat with thirst, Virgil's siti asper, Il. (Deriv. uncertain.)

καρχᾰρ-όδους, ὁ, ἡ, -ουν, τό, with sharp, jagged teeth, of dogs, Il.; applied to Cleon by Ar.; and

καρχᾰρ-όδων, οντος, ὁ, ἡ, =foreg., Theocr. From

ΚΑ'ΡΧΑ'ΡΟΣ, α, ον, sharp-pointed, jagged, with sharp or jagged teeth, κάρχαρον μειδήσας, of the wolf, Babr.: —metaph. sharp, biting, of language, Luc.

Καρχηδονίζω, f. ίσω, to side with the Carthaginians, Plut. From

Καρχηδών, όνος, ἡ, Carthage, Hdt. :—Adj. Καρχηδόνιος, α, ον, Carthaginian, Id.

καρχήσιον, Dor. -άσιον [ᾱ], τό, a drinking-cup narrower in the middle than the top and bottom, Sappho, etc. II. the mast-head of a ship, Pind., etc.; in pl., Eur.

κᾱς, crasis for καὶ εἰς or καὶ ἐς.

κᾰσαλβάζω, f. σω, to abuse in harlot fashion, Ar. From

κᾰσαλβάς, άδος, ἡ, like κάσσα, a courtesan, harlot, Ar.

κάσας, ου, or κασᾶς, οῦ, ὁ, a carpet or skin to sit upon, a saddle, Xen. (Prob. a Persian word.)

κᾰσία, Ion. -ίη, ἡ, cassia, an Arabian spice like cinnamon, but of inferior quality, Hdt. (A foreign word.)

κᾰσιγνήτη, ἡ, fem. of κασίγνητος, a sister, Hom., etc.

κᾰσί-γνητος, ὁ, (κάσις, γίγνομαι), a brother, Hom.,

etc. :—in more general sense, a cousin, Il. II. as Adj., κασίγνητος, η, ον, brotherly, sisterly, Soph., Eur.

ΚΑ'ΣΙΣ [ᾰ], κάσιος, voc. κάσι, ὁ, a brother, Aesch., Soph. :—ἡ, a sister, Eur.

Κασσῐτερίδες, ων, αἱ, the Cassiterides or Tin-islands, prob. the Scilly islands and Cornwall, Hdt. From

κασσίτερος [ῐ], Att. καττ-, ὁ, tin, Lat. stannum, Il. It was melted, and then cast upon χαλκός, hence χεῦμα κασσιτέροιο a plating of tin, Ib. (A foreign word.)

κάσσῡμα, Att. κάττ-, ατος, τό, anything stitched, esp. the sole stitched under a shoe or sandal, a shoe-sole, Ar.; metaph., ὑποδύσασθαι ἐχθρῶν παρ' ἀνδρῶν καττύματα to put on shoes made by an enemy, Id. From

κασσύω [ῠ], Att. καττ-, prob. for κατα-σύω (though σύω only occurs in Lat. suo), to stitch or sew together like a shoemaker, Plat. II. metaph. to stitch up a plot, like Lat. dolos suere, Ar.

Κασταλία, Ion. -ίη, ἡ, the famous spring of the Muses on Mt. Parnassus, Hdt., Soph., etc. (Prob. akin to καθαρός, Lat. castus.)

κᾰστίν, crasis for καὶ ἐστίν.

κᾰστόν, crasis for καὶ ἐστόν.

Καστόρειος, ον, of or for Castor;—τὸ Κ. μέλος, a martial song, set to the flute, used in celebrating victories in the chariot-race (Castor being the inventor of the ξυνωρίς), Pind., Plut.; ὁ Κ. ὕμνος Pind.

καστορίδες, αἱ, a Laconian breed of hounds, first reared by Castor, Anth.: also καστόριαι κύνες Xen.

Κάστωρ, ορος, ὁ, Castor, son of Zeus (or Tyndareus) and Leda, brother of Pollux, Hom.

ΚΑ'ΣΤΩΡ, ορος, ὁ, the beaver, Hdt.

κάσχεθον, Ep. for κατέσχεθον, poët. aor. 2 of κατέχω.

κάτ, for κατά before τ, v. sub καττά.

κατά [κᾰτᾰ], Prep. with gen. or acc. Radical sense down, downwards.

A. WITH GENIT., I. denoting motion from above, down from, βῆ δὲ κατ' Οὐλύμποιο καρήνων Il., etc. II. denoting downward motion, 1. down upon or over, κατὰ χθονὸς ὄμματα πήξας Il.; of the dying, κατ' ὀφθαλμῶν κέχυτ' ἀχλύς a cloud settled upon the eyes, Ib.; so, ὕδωρ κατὰ χειρός, v. χείρ II. 6. 2. down into, νέκταρ στάξε κατὰ ῥινῶν Od.; so, κατὰ χθονὸς (or γῆς) δῦναι Trag.; κατὰ χθονὸς κρύπτειν to bury, Soph., etc. 3. ἔχεσθαι or ὀμόσαι κατά τινος to vow or swear by a thing (because one calls down the vengeance of the gods upon it), Thuc., Dem. :—also to make a vow towards something, i. e. make a vow of offering it, Ar. 4. in hostile sense, against, Aesch., etc.; esp. of judges giving sentence against a person, Id.; λόγος κατά τινος a speech against one accused, Lat. in aliquem; λόγος πρός τινα an answer to an opponent, Lat. adversus aliquem. 5. Lat. de, upon, in respect of, concerning, σκοπεῖν κατά τινος Plat.; ἔπαινος κατά τινος praise bestowed upon one, Aeschin., etc.

B. WITH ACCUS., I. of motion downwards, κατὰ ῥόον down stream, Hdt.; κατ' οὖρον ἰέναι, ῥεῖν to sail down (i. e. with) the wind, Aesch. 2. of motion, on, over, throughout a space, Hom., etc.; καθ' Ἑλλάδα Aesch.; κατὰ γῆν καὶ θάλασσαν by land and sea, Il. :—also to hit upon the shield, Il. 3. opposite, over against, κατὰ Σινώπην πόλιν Hdt.; ἀνὴρ κατ' ἄνδρα

Aesch. 4. κατὰ τὸ προάστειον *somewhere in* the suburb, Hdt. II. *distributively*, of a whole divided into parts, κατὰ φῦλα, κατὰ φρήτρας *by* tribes, *by* clans, Il.; κατὰ κώμας κατῳκῆσθαι to live *in separate* villages, Hdt.; κατ' ἄνδρα man *by* man, Id. 2. so of parts of Time, καθ' ἡμέραν, κατ' ἦμαρ day *by* day, daily, v. ἡμέρα III, ἦμαρ. 3. of numbers, *by* so many *at a time*, καθ' ἕνα one *at a time*, Hdt.; κατὰ τὰς πέντε καὶ εἴκοσι μνᾶς πεντακοσίας δραχμὰς εἰσφέρειν to pay 500 drachmae *on every* 25 minae, Dem., etc. III. of direction towards an object, πλεῖν κατὰ πρῆξιν *on* a business, *for* or *after*, Od.; κατὰ ληίην *in quest of* booty, Hdt.; κατὰ θέαν ἥκειν to have come *for the purpose* of seeing, Thuc. 2. of pursuit, κατ' ἴχνος *on* the track, Soph. IV. *according to*, κατὰ θυμόν Hom.; καθ' ἡμέτερον νόον *after* our liking, Il.; κατὰ μοῖραν *as is* meet and right, Hom.; so, κατ' αἶσαν, κατὰ κόσμον Id.; καθ' ἡδονήν *so as to* please, Aesch.; κατὰ δύναμιν to the best of one's power, etc. 2. *in relation to, concerning*, τὰ κατ' ἀνθρώπους = τὰ ἀνθρωπινά, Aesch.; so, τὸ καθ' ὑμᾶς *as far as concerns* you, Hdt.; κατὰ τοῦτο *according to* this way, in this view; κατὰ ταὐτά *in* the same *way*, καθ' ὅτι so far as, etc. 3. implying comparison, κατὰ λοπὸν κρομύοιο *like* the coat of a leek, Od.; κατὰ Μιθραδάτην *answering to the description of* him, Hdt.; κατὰ πνιγέα *very like* an oven, Ar.; κηδεῦσαι καθ' ἑαυτόν to marry in one's own rank of life, Aesch.; κατ' ἄνθρωπον *like* a man, *as befits* a man, Id.; κατ' ἄνδρα, μὴ θεόν Id.:—after a Compar., μείζων ἢ κατ' ἀνθρώπου greater than *befits* a man, Hdt.; μείζω ἢ κατὰ δάκρυα too great to weep for, Thuc. V. *by the favour* of a god, κατὰ δαίμονα, Lat. *non sine numine*, Pind.; κατὰ θεόν Hdt. VI. of loosely stated numbers, *nearly, about*, κατὰ ἑξακόσια ἔτεα 600 years *more or less*, Id. VII. of Time, *during*, *sometime* in a period, κατὰ τὸν πόλεμον *in the course of* the war, Id.; καθ' ἡμέραν *by* day, Aesch. 2. *about*, κατὰ τὸν αὐτὸν χρόνον Hdt.; κατὰ ᾽Άμασιν βασιλεύοντα *about the time* of Amasis, Id. VIII. used periphr. for Adverbs, as, καθ' ἡσυχίην, κατὰ τάχος, etc., for ἡσύχως, ταχέως, Id.; κατὰ μέρος *partially*; κατὰ φύσιν *naturally*; etc. C. Position: when κατά follows its case it is written with anastr. κάτα. D. absol. as Adv. like κάτω, *downwards*, Hom. E. κατά in Compos., I. *downwards, down*, as in καταβαίνω. II. *in answer to, in accordance with*, as in κατᾴδω, καταθύμιος. III. *against*, in hostile sense, as καταγιγνώσκω, κατακρίνω. IV. often only to strengthen the notion of the simple word, as κατακόπτω, καταφαγεῖν. F. κατά as a Prep. was sometimes shortened, esp. in Ep. into κάγ, κάκ, κάμ, κάν, κάπ, κάρ, κάτ, before γ, κ, μ, ν, π (or φ), ρ, τ (or θ), respectively; see these forms in their own places. Mss. and the older Edd. join the Prep. with the following word, as καγγόνυ, καδδέ, κακκεφαλῆς, καππεδίον, καππέδιλα, καρρόον, καττάδε, καττόν, etc. In compd. Verbs, κατά sometimes changes into καβ, καλ, καρ, κατ, before β, λ, ρ, θ, respectively, as κάββαλε, κάθανε, κάλλιπε, καρρέζουσα; and before στ, σχ, the second syll. sometimes

disappears, as in καστορνῦσα, κάσχεθε, κασσύω, as also in Doric forms καβαίνων, κάπετον.

κατά, Ion. for καθ' ἅ.

κᾷτα, crasis for καὶ εἶτα.

κατάβα, for κατάβηθι, aor. 2 imp. of καταβαίνω.

καταβάδην [βᾰ], Adv. *going down* or *downstairs*: cf. ἀναβάδην.

καταβαθμός, Att. -βασμός, ὁ, *a descent*, name *of the steep descent from Nubia to* Egypt, Aesch.

κατα-βαίνω: f. -βήσομαι: pf. -βέβηκα: aor. 2 κατέβην, poët. 3 pl. κατέβαν; imper. κατάβηθι or κατάβᾱ; Ep. 1 pl. subj. καταβείομεν (for -βῶμεν):—Med., Ep. 3 sing. aor. 1 κατεβήσετο; imperat. καταβήσεο:—*to step down, go* or *come down*, Lat. *descendere*, ἐξ ὄρεος *from* the mountain, Il.; κ. πόλιος *to go down from* the city, Ib.; κ. δίφρου *to dismount* from the chariot, Ib.; c. acc. loci, θάλαμον κατεβήσετο she *came down* to her chamber, Od.:—but also c. acc., κατέβαιν' ὑπερώϊα she *came down from* the upper floor, Ib.; κλίμακα κατεβήσετο *came down* the ladder, Ib.; absol. *to come down stairs*, Ar.; hence in Pass., ἵππος καταβαίνεται the horse *is dismounted from*, Xen. 2. *to go down from the inland parts to the sea*, esp. from central Asia (cf. ἀναβαίνω II. 3), Hdt.; κ. ἐς Πειραιᾶ, Plat. 3. *to come to land, get safe ashore*, Pind. 4. *to go down into the arena*, κ. ἐπ' ἄεθλα Hdt.; and absol., like Lat. *in certamen descendere*, Soph., Xen. 5. of an orator, *to come down from the tribune*, κατάβα᾽ —answer, καταβήσομαι Ar. 6. πόσσω κατέβα τοι ἀφ' ἱστῶ; at what price did [the robe] *come down from* the loom? Theocr. II. metaph., καταβαίνειν εἴς τι *to come to* a thing *in the course of speaking*, κατέβαινε ἐς λιτάς he *ended* with prayer, Hdt.; c. part., κατέβαινεν παραιτεόμενος *ended* in begging, Id.; κ. ἐπὶ τελευτήν Plat. B. trans. *to bring down*, Pind.

κατα-βακχιόομαι, (Βάκχος) Pass. *to be full of Bacchic frenzy*, καταβακχιοῦσθε δρυὸς κλάδοις in oak-wreaths ye rave with Bacchic fury, Eur.

κατα-βάλλω, f. -βαλῶ: aor. 2 κατέβαλον, Ep. 3 sing. κάββαλε:—*to throw down, overthrow*, Hom., etc.; κ. εἰς τὸ μηδέν *to bring down* to nothing, Hdt.; *to strike down* with a weapon, *to slay*, Il., Hdt., etc. 2. *to throw* or *bring into* a certain state, Eur., Plat. 3. *to cast down* or *away, cast off, reject*, Xen. II. in milder sense, *to let fall, drop down*, Hom.; κ. ἱστία *to lower* sail, Theogn.; τὰς ὀφρῦς κ. Eur. 2. *to lay down, set down*, Lat. *deponere*, Il., Ar. 3. *to bring* or *carry down*, esp. *to the sea-coast*, Hdt. 4. *to pay down, yield* or *bring in*, Id.:—Med. *to pay down, pay*, Thuc., etc.:—Med. *to cause to be deposited*, Dem. 5. *to put in, render*, μαρτυρίαν Id. 6. *to throw down seed, sow*, Id.; κ. φάτιν, Lat. *spargere voces*, Hdt. 7. *to lay down as a foundation*, mostly in Med., Eur.:—Pass., καταβεβλημένος *laid down, ordinary*, Arist.

κατα-βάπτω, f. ψω, *to dip down into*, Luc.

κατα-βαρέω, f. ήσω, *to weigh down, overload*, Luc.

καταβάς, aor. 2 part. of καταβαίνω.

κατάβασις, εως, ἡ, (καταβαίνω) *a going down, way down, descent*, Hdt., Att.; cf. καταίβασις. 2. *the descent from* Central Asia, Xen.

κατάβασμός, ὁ, Att. for καταβαθμός.
καταβάτέον, verb. Adj. of καταβαίνω, one must descend, Ar., Plat.　II. one must attack, Ar.
κατά-βαύζω, f. ξω, to bark at, τινός Anth.
κατα-βεβαιόομαι, Dep. to affirm strongly, Plut.
καταβείομεν, Ep. for καταβῶμεν, 1 pl. aor. 2 subj. of καταβαίνω:—καταβήμεναι, for καταβῆναι, aor. 2 inf. :—καταβήσεο, for κατάβηναι, aor. 1 med. imper.
καταβήσομαι, f. of καταβαίνω.
κατα-βιάζομαι, f. άσομαι, Dep. to constrain, Thuc.　II. Pass. to be forced, Plut.
κατα-βῑβάζω, f. Att. -βιβῶ, Causal of καταβαίνω, to make to go down, bring down, Hdt., Plut.　2. to bring down by force, Xen. Hence
κάταβῑβαστέος, a, ον, verbal, to be brought down, Plat.
κατα-βιβρώσκω, f. -βρώσομαι: aor. 2 -έβρων: pf. pass. -βέβρωμαι: aor. 1 -εβρώθην:—to eat up, devour, Hdt., Plat.
κατα-βιόω, f. ώσομαι: aor. 2 κατεβίων, later aor. 1 -εβίωσα:—to bring life to an end, Plat.
κατα-βλάπτω, f. ψω, to hurt greatly, damage, h. Hom., Plat.
κατα-βλέπω, f. ψω, to look down at, Plut.
καταβλητέον, verb. Adj. of καταβάλλω, Plat.
καταβλητικός, ή, όν, (καταβάλλω) fit for throwing off horseback, Xen.
κατα-βληχάομαι, Dep. to bleat loudly, Theocr.
κατα-βλώσκω, to go down through a place, c. acc., Od.
κατα-βοάω, f. -βοήσομαι, Ion. -βώσομαι, to cry down, cry out against, c. gen., Hdt.; κ. τινῶν ὅτι τὰς σπονδὰς λελυκότες εἶεν Thuc.; c. acc. to bawl down, outcry, Ar.
κατα-βοή, ῆς, ἡ, an outcry against, c. gen., Thuc.
καταβόησις, εως, ἡ, a crying out against, Plut.
καταβολή, ἡ, (καταβάλλω) a throwing or laying down, N. T.　II. metaph., 1. a foundation, beginning, Pind., N. T.　2. a paying down, by instalments, Dem.　III. a periodical attack of illness, a fit, access, Plat.
κατα-βόσκω, f. -βοσκήσω, to feed flocks upon or in a place, Lat. depascere, χὠ τὰν Σαμίαν καταβόσκων the shepherd of Samos, Theocr.
κατα-βόστρυχος, ον, with flowing locks, Eur.
κατα-βρᾱβεύω, f. σω, to give judgment against, c. acc., N. T. :—Pass. to have judgment given against one, Dem.
κατα-βρέχω, f. ξω : Pass., aor. 1 κατεβρέχθην :—to wet through, drench :—metaph., μέλιτι καταβρέχειν Pind.
κατα-βρίθω [ῑ], f. -βρίσω : pf. -βέβρῑθα :—intr. to be heavily laden or weighed down by a thing, c. dat., Hes., Theocr.　II. trans. to weigh down, to outweigh, ὄλβῳ κ. βασιλῆας Theocr.
κατα-βρόξειε, v. *βρόχω 2.
κατα-βροχθίζω, f. ίσω, to gulp down, Ar.
κατα-βρύκω [ῠ], to bite in pieces, eat up, Anth.
κατα-βρώθω, late form for καταβιβρώσκω, Babr.
καταβρώσομαι, fut. of καταβιβρώσκω.
κατα-βυρσόω, f. ώσω, to cover quite with hides, Thuc.
καταβώσομαι, Ion. for -βοήσομαι, fut. of καταβοάω.
κατάγαιος, ον, Ion. for κατάγειος.
καταγγελεύς, έως, ὁ, = κατάγγελος, N. T.
καταγγελία, ἡ, proclamation, Luc. From

κατ-αγγέλλω, f. ελῶ, to denounce, betray, Xen.　2. to declare, πόλεμον Lys. Hence
κατάγγελτος, ον, denounced, betrayed, Thuc.
κατά-γειος, Ion. κατά-γαιος, ον, (γῆ) in or under the earth, underground, subterranean, Hdt., Xen., etc.
Κατα-γέλα, ἡ, Comic name of a supposed town, with a play on the Sicil. Gela, Γέλα καὶ Καταγέλα Ar.
καταγέλαστος, ον, ridiculous, absurd, Hdt., Ar. : Adv. -τως, Sup. -τότατα, Plat. From
κατα-γελάω, f. άσομαι : Pass., pf. -γεγέλασμαι :—to laugh at, jeer or mock at, c. gen., Hdt., Ar., etc.; also c. dat., Hdt. :—absol. to laugh scornfully, Eur., Ar., etc.　2. c. acc. to laugh down, deride, Eur. :—Pass. to be derided, Aesch., Ar., etc.
κατά-γελως, ωτος, ὁ, mockery, derision, ridicule, Lat. ludibrium, ἐμαυτοῦ καταγέλωτα τάδε ; these ornaments which bring ridicule upon me ? Aesch. ; κ. πλατύς sheer mockery, Ar. ; ὁ κ. τῆς πράξεως the crowning absurdity of the matter, Plat.
κατα-γηράσκω and -γηράω : f. -γηράσομαι [ᾱ], and άσω : aor. 1 -εγήρασα :—to grow old, Lat. senescere, Od., Hdt.
κατα-γίγνομαι, Ion. and later -γίνομαι [ῑ] :—to abide, dwell, ap. Dem.
κατα-γιγνώσκω, Ion. and later -γινώσκω : f. -γνώσομαι :—to remark, discover, esp. something to one's prejudice, οὐκ ἐπιτήδεα κατά τινος κ. having formed unfavourable prejudices against one, Hdt. ; καταγνοὺς τοῦ γέροντος τοὺς τρόπους having observed his foibles, Ar.　II. c. acc. criminis, to lay as a charge against a person, κακίαν, ἀδικίαν κ. τινός Plat. :—Pass., pf. part. κατεγνωσμένος condemned, N. T.　2. c. gen. criminis, παρανόμων κ. τινός Dem.　3. c. inf., κ. ἑαυτοῦ ἀδικεῖν to charge oneself with wrong-doing, Aeschin. ; so, κ. ἑαυτοῦ μὴ περιέσεσθαι he passed sentence of non-survival against himself, Thuc. : Pass., καταγνωσθεὶς νεώτερα πρήσσειν being suspected of doing, Hdt.　III. c. acc. poenae, to give as judgment or sentence against a person, κ. τινὸς θάνατον to pass sentence of death on one, Lat. damnare aliquem mortis, Thuc. :—Pass., θάνατός τινος κατέγνωστο ap. Dem.　2. of a suit, to decide it against one, δίκην Ar. :—Pass. to be decided, Aesch.
κατ-αγίζω, Ion. for καθ-αγίζω.
κατ-αγῑνέω, Ion. for κατάγω, to bring down, Od.　II. to bring back, recall, Hdt.
κατ-αγλαΐζω, to glorify, Anth.
κατα-γλωττίζομαι, pf. κατεγλώττισμαι, Pass. to be talked down, Ar.
κάταγμα, ατος, τό, (κατάγω) wool drawn or spun out, worsted, Plat. : a flock of wool, Soph.
κατα-γνάμπτω, f. ψω, to bend down, Anth.
κατα-γνάφω, to comb away, lacerate, Hdt.
κατ-άγνυμι, inf. -ύναι [ῠ], or καταγνύω : f. κατάξω : aor. 1 κατέαξα, part. κατάξας :—Pass., aor. 2 κατεάγην [ᾱ], opt. καταγείην :—pf. κατέαγα, Ion. κατέηγα (in pass. sense) :—to break in pieces, shatter, shiver, crack, Hom., Att.　2. to break up, weaken, enervate, Eur., Plat.　II. Pass. with pf. act. to be broken, δόρατα κατεηγότα Hdt. ; κατεαγέναι or καταγῆναι τὴν κεφαλήν to have the head broken, Ar., etc. ; c. gen., τῆς κεφαλῆς κατέαγε he has got a bit of his head broken, Id.

κατάγνωσις, εως, ἡ, (καταγιγνώσκω) *a thinking ill of, a low* or *contemptuous opinion of,* c. gen., Thuc.   **II.** *judgment given against* one, *condemnation,* Id., Dem.; τοῦ θανάτου *to death,* Xen.

καταγνωστέον, verb. Adj. of καταγιγνώσκω, *one must condemn,* τινός Luc.

κατα-γοητεύω, f. σω, *to enchant, bewitch* : *to cheat* or *blind by trickery,* τινά Xen.

κατ-ἀγοράζω, f. ἀσω, *to buy up,* φορτία Dem.

κατ-ἀγορεύω, f. σω, *to denounce,* τί τινι Ar., Thuc.; τι πρός τινα Xen.

καταγράφος, ον, *embroidered,* Luc. From

κατα-γράφω [ᾰ], f. ψω, *to scratch away, lacerate,* Hdt.   **2.** *to engrave, inscribe,* νόμους Plut.   **3.** *to paint over,* Luc.   **II.** *to fill* tablets *with writing,* Eur.   **2.** *to write down, register, record,* Plat.

κατα-γυμνάζω, *to exercise much, discipline,* Luc.

κατ-άγω : f. ξω, Ep. inf. -αξέμεν (in aor. sense) : aor. 1 κατήγαγον : pf. καταγήοχα :—*to lead down,* Lat. *deducere,* Od., etc. ; esp. *into the nether world,* Ib. ; εἰς Ἀΐδαο Ib.   **2.** *to bring down to the sea-coast,* Il., Xen.   **3.** *to bring down from the high seas to land,* Od. ; κατ. ναῦν *to bring a ship into port,* Hdt., Att. :—Pass. *to come to land, land,* opp. to ἀνάγεσθαι, Od., Hdt., Att.   **b.** καταγεσθαι παρά τινι *to turn in and lodge in* a person's house, Lat. *deversari apud aliquem,* Dem.   **4.** *to draw down* or *out, spin,* Lat. *deducere filum,* Plat.   **5.** *to reduce* to a certain state, ἐς κίνδυνον κ. τὴν πόλιν Thuc.   **6.** κ. θρίαμβον, Lat. *deducere triumphum,* Plut. : *to escort,* like πομπεύω, Id.   **7.** κ. γένος *to derive* a pedigree, Id.   **8.** κατ. βοὴν *to lower* the voice, Eur.   **II.** *to bring back,* Lat. *reducere,* Od. : *to bring home, recall,* Hdt., Att. : generally, *to restore,* Hdt. :—Pass. *to return,* Plat., Xen. Hence

καταγωγή, ἡ, *a bringing down from* the high sea: *a landing, landing-place,* Thuc. :—generally, *a halting-place, inn,* Lat. *statio,* Hdt., Plat. ; and

καταγώγιον, τό, *a place to lodge in, an inn, hotel,* Thuc., Xen., etc.

κατ-αγωνίζομαι, f. Att. ιοῦμαι, Dep. *to struggle against, prevail against, conquer,* Luc. : as Pass., καταγωνισθεὶς ὑπό τινα Id.

κατα-δαίνυμαι, f. -δαίσομαι, Dep. *to devour,* Theocr.

κατα-δάκνω, f. -δήξομαι, *to bite in pieces,* Batr., Theocr.

κατα-δακρύω, f. σω, *to bewail,* τὴν τύχην Xen. : absol. *to weep bitterly,* Eur.

κατα-δᾰμάζομαι, aor. 1 inf. -δαμάσασθαι, Med. *to subdue utterly,* Thuc.

κατα-δάμναμαι : foreg., h. Hom.

κατα-δᾰπᾰνάω, f. ήσω, *to squander, lavish,* Xen. :—Pass., [τὰ χρήματα] καταδεδαπάνητό σφι Hdt.   **II.** *to consume entirely,* of an army, Xen.

κατα-δάπτω, f. -ψω, *to rend in pieces, devour,* Hom. : metaph. in Med., καταδάπτεται ἦτορ Od.

κατα-δαρθάνω, aor. 2 -έδαρθον metaph. -έδραθον, 2 pl. καδραθέτην : pf. -δεδάρθηκα :—*to fall asleep,* in aor. *to be asleep, sleep,* Od. :—pf. καταδεδαρθηκώς *having fallen asleep,* Id.   **2.** simply *to pass the night,* κατέδαρθον ἐν ὅπλοις Thuc.

κατα-δᾰτέομαι, f. -δάσομαι [ᾰ], Med. *to divide among themselves, tear and devour,* Il.

καταδεής, ές, (καταδέω B) *wanting* or *failing in, lacking* a thing, c. gen., Hdt. : absol., *needy,* Dem.   **2.** Comp. καταδεέστερος, *weaker, inferior,* Id., etc.   **II.** Adv. -δεῶς, mostly in Comp., καταδεεστέρως ἔχειν περί τι *to be very ill off* in a thing, Id.

κατα-δεῖ, impers. *there is wanting,* v. καταδέω B.

κατα-δείδω, f. -δείσω : aor. 1 inf. -δεῖσαι :—*to fear greatly,* τι Ar., Thuc.

κατα-δείκνῡμι and -ύω, f. δείξω : Ion. aor. 1 κατέδεξα :—Pass., κατέδέδεκτο :—*to discover and make known,* Hdt., Plat., etc. ; c. inf. *to give notice that* . . , Aeschin. :—Pass., c. part., κατεδέδεκτο ἐοῦσα χρηστή *had been proved* to be good, Hdt.   **2.** *to invent and teach, introduce, exhibit,* Ar., Plat. ; c. inf. *to shew how to do,* Hdt., Ar.

κατα-δειλιάω, f. άσω [ᾰ], *to shew signs of fear,* Xen.

κατα-δέομαι, Dep. *to intreat earnestly,* Lat. *deprecari,* c. gen. pers., Plat.

κατα-δέρκομαι : aor. 1 κατεδέρχθην : Dep. :—*to look down upon,* Od., Soph.

κατά-δεσμος, ὁ, *a tie, band* : *a magic knot,* Plat.

κατα-δεύω, f. σω, *to wet through,* Il., Hes. :—of a river, *to water,* πεδία Eur.

κατα-δέχομαι, -δέξομαι, Dep. *to receive, admit,* Plat., etc.   **2.** *to receive back, take home again,* Oratt. :—aor. 1 pass. καταδεχθῆναι in pass. sense, Luc.

κατα-δέω (Α), f. -δήσω, *to bind on* or *to, bind fast,* Hom., Hdt. :—Pass., καταδεδεμένος τοὺς ὀφθαλμούς, *having* his eyes *bound,* Hdt. ; ὁ φόβῳ καταδεθεῖσα Eur. ; καταδεῖται ψυχὴ ὑπὸ τοῦ σώματος Plat. :—Med. *to bind to oneself,* Eur.   **2.** *to put in bonds, imprison,* Hdt., Thuc., etc. ; κ. τὴν ἐπὶ θανάτῳ (sc. δέσιν) *to bind* him *for execution,* Hdt.   **3.** *to convict and condemn of* a crime, κ. τινα φῶρα εἶναι Id.   **II.** *to tie down, stop, check,* ἀνέμων κατέδησε κελεύθους Od.; κατέδησε κέλευθα *stopped* my course, Ib.

κατα-δέω (Β), f. -δεήσω, *to want, lack, need,* c. gen., esp. of numbers, καταδέει πεντεκαίδεκα σταδίων ὡς μὴ εἶναι πεντακοσίων *it wants* 15 stadia of being 500, Hdt.

κατά-δηλος, ον, *quite manifest, plain, visible,* Hdt., Thuc. ; κατάδηλον ποιεῖν *to make known, discover,* Hdt., Soph. ; κ. εἶναι *to be discovered,* Hdt., Plat.

κατα-δημαγωγέω, f. ήσω, *to conquer by the arts of a demagogue* :—Pass. *to be so conquered,* Plut.

κατα-δημοβορέω, f. ήσω, (δημοβόρος) *to consume publicly,* Il.

κατα-διαιτάω, f. ήσω : pf. -δεδιῄτηκα, (v. διαιτάω) *to decide as arbitrator against, give judgment against* c. gen., Dem. : Pass. *to be decided against* one, Id.

κατα-διαλλάσσω, f. ξω, *to reconcile again,* Ar.

κατα-δίδωμι, f. -δώσω, *to give away,* intr. *to open into,* ἡ Προποντὶς καταδιδοῖ ἐς τὸν Ἑλλήσποντον Hdt.

κατα-δῐκάζω, f. σω : aor. 1 κατεδίκασθην : pf. καταδεδίκασμαι :—*to give judgment against* a person, *pass sentence upon* him, *condemn* him, opp. to ἀποδικάζω, c. gen. pers. et acc. rei, κ. τινὸς θάνατον *to pass sentence* of death upon him, Hdt. ; c. inf., κ. τινὸς τὰ ἔσχατα παθεῖν *to condemn* him *to suffer extreme penalties,* Xen. :—Med. *to get sentence given against* one, δίκην καταδικάζεσθαί τινος Thuc. :—Pass., καταδικασθεὶς con-

demned, Plat. ; c. inf., καταδικάζεται ἀποθανεῖν Luc. ; of the sentence, ἀντέλεγον μὴ δικαίως σφῶν καταδεδικάσθαι they contended that judgment had been given against them unjustly, Thuc.　　　II. to declare by express judgment, Xen.

κατα-δίκη [ῐ], ἡ, judgment given against one : the damages awarded, Thuc.

κατα-διώκω, f. ξω or ξομαι, to pursue closely, Thuc.

κατα-δοκέω, f. -δόξω, to suppose a thing to any one's prejudice, c. inf., κ. τινα ποιεῖν τι to suspect one of doing so and so, Hdt. ; κ. σφέας εἶναι κλῶπας to suspect them of being thieves, Id. ; also, οὐκ ἄν κοτε κατέδοξα ἔνθεν ἦν should never have guessed whose son he was, Id.

κατα-δοξάζω, f. άσω, = καταδοκέω, Xen.

κατα-δουλόω, f. ώσω, to reduce to slavery, enslave, Hdt., Thuc. :—Pass., καταδεδούλωντο, κατεδουλώθησαν Hdt.　　2. Med. to make a slave to oneself, to enslave, Id., Xen. : so in pf. pass., Eur., Plat.　　II. to enslave in mind :—Pass., Xen., Plat. Hence

καταδούλωσις, εως, ἡ, enslavement, subjugation, Thuc.

κατα-δουπέω, f. ήσω, to fall with a heavy sound, Anth.

Κατάδουποι, ων, αἱ, the Cataracts of the Nile, Hdt. (Commonly derived from καταδουπέω, as if Downroars.)

καταδράθω [ᾰ], aor. 2 subj. of καταδαρθάνω.

κατα-δραμεῖν, aor. 2 inf. of κατα-τρέχω.

κατα-δρέπω, f. ψω, to strip off from, τί τινος Hdt.

κατάδρομή, ἡ, (καταδραμεῖν) an inroad, raid, Thuc., etc. :—metaph. a vehement attack, invective, Aeschin.

κατάδρομος, ον, (καταδραμεῖν) overrun, wasted, Eur.

κατάδρυμμα, ατος, τό, a tearing or rending, Eur. From

κατα-δρύπτω, f. -ψω, to tear in pieces, rend, Anth. :— Med., Hes.

κατα-δυναστεύω, f. σω, to exercise power over, Xen.

καταδύνω, v. καταδύω.

κατάδυσις, εως, ἡ, (καταδύω) a going down into, descent, Luc.

κατα-δυσωπέω, f. ήσω, to put to the blush by earnest intreaty, Luc.

καταδύω or -δύνω [ῡ] :　　I. intr., in act. pres. καταδύνω and med. καταδύομαι : f. -δύσομαι : aor. i med. -ἐδῡσάμην, Ep. 2 and 3 sing. -δύσεο, -δύσετο : aor. 2 act. κατέδυν : pf. καταδέδῡκα :—to go down, sink, set, of the sun, ἥλιος κατέδυ Il. ; ἐς ἠέλιον καταδύντα till sunset, Od. ; of ships, to be sunk or rather to be disabled (v. infr. 11), Hdt., Thuc. :—of persons, καταδεδυκώς having popped down, Ar.　　2. to go down into, plunge into, c. acc., καταδῦναι ὅμιλον, μάχην, δόμον, πόλιν Hom. ; foll. by a Prep., καταδυσόμεθ' εἰς 'Αΐδαο δόμους we will go down into . . , Od., etc. :—with a notion of secrecy, to insinuate oneself, steal into, Plat.　　3. to slink away and lie hid, καταδύομαι ὑπὸ τῆς αἰσχύνης Xen.　　4. to get into, put on, τεύχεα Hom.　　II. Causal, to make to sink, Lat. submergere, ἐμὲ καταδύουσι τῷ ἄχει Xen. ; mostly in aor. 1, τοὺς γαυλοὺς καταδύσας Hdt. ; καταδῦσαι ναῦν to cut it down to the water's edge, disable it, Id., Thuc.

κατ-ᾴδω, Ion. -αείδω, f. -ᾴσομαι, to sing to, Lat. occinere, and so,　　I. trans. to charm or appease by singing, Luc. ; c. dat. to sing a spell or incantation (ἐπῳδή) to another, Hdt.　　2. to deafen by singing, Luc. : Pass. to have another sing before one, Id.　　II. to sing by way of incantation, βάρβαρα μέλη Eur.

κατα-δωροδοκέω, f. ήσω, to take presents or bribes, Ar. ; so in Med., Id.

κατ-αείδω, Ion. for κατᾴδω.

καταειμένος, η, ον, part. pf. pass. of κατα-έννυμι.

καταείνυον, Ep. impf. of κατα-έννυμι.

καταείσατο, Ep. 3 sing. aor. i of κάτειμι.

κατα-έννυμι or -εινύω, only in impf., aor. i and pf. pass. :—to clothe, cover, θριξὶ νέκυν καταείνυσαν Il. :— Pass., ὅρος καταειμένον ὕλῃ Od.

κατ-αξαίνω, to make quite dry, parch quite up, καταζήνασκε δὲ δαίμων (Ion. aor. 1), Od.

κατα-ζάω, f. -ζήσω, to live on, Eur., Plat.

κατα-ζεύγνῡμι and -ύω, f. -ζεύξω, to yoke together, yoke, Pind. :—Pass. to be united, Plat.　　2. Pass., also, to be straitened, confined, imprisoned, Hdt., Soph. Hence

κατάζευξις, εως, ἡ, a yoking together :—opp. to ἀνάζευξις, encamping, Plut.

κατ-αζήνασκε, 3 sing. Ion. impf. of κατ-αζαίνω.

κατα-ζώννῡμι and -ύω, f. -ζώσω, to gird fast ; Med. to gird for oneself.

κατα-θαμβέομαι, Pass. to be astonished at, c. acc., Plut.

κατα-θάπτω, f. ψω, to bury, Il., Aesch.

κατα-θαρσύνω [ῠ], f. ῠνῶ, to embolden or encourage against, τινὰ πρὸς τὸ μέλλον Plut. :—Pass., in form καταθρασύνομαι, Luc.

κατα-θεάομαι, f. άσομαι [ᾱ], Dep. to look down upon, watch from above, Xen. :—generally, to contemplate, Id.

καταθεῖναι, aor. 2 inf. of κατα-τίθημι.

καταθεῖο, 2 sing. aor. 2 med. opt. of κατα-τίθημι.

καταθείομαι, Ep. for κατα-θέωμαι, -θῶμαι, aor. 2 med. subj. of κατα-τίθημι :—καταθείομεν, for κατα-θέωμεν, -θῶμεν, 1 pl. aor. 2 subj.

κατα-θέλγω, f. ξω, to subdue by spells or enchantments, Od. Hence

κατάθελξις, εως, ἡ, enchantment, Luc.

καταθεματίζω, = ἀναθεματίζω, to curse, N. T.

κατα-θέω, f. -θεύσομαι, to run down, Thuc., Xen. : of ships, to run into port, Xen.　　II. to make inroads, Id. :—c. acc. to overrun a country, Thuc., Xen.

κατα-θεωρέω, f. ήσω, to contemplate from above, Plat.

κατα-θήγω, f. ξω, to sharpen, whet, Anth.

κατα-θηλύνω [ῠ], f. ῠνῶ, to make womanish, Luc.

*καταθήπω, obsol. pres. of κατατέθηπα.

κατ-αθλέω, f. ήσω, to exercise oneself much, ἠθληκότες well-trained, of soldiers, Plut.

κατα-θλίβω [ῐ], f. ψω, to press down, press out : aor. 2 pass. part. καταθλῐβείς, Plut.

κατα-θνήσκω, f. κατα-θανοῦμαι, sync. κατθανοῦμαι : aor. 2 κατέθανον, Ep. κάτθανον : pf. -τέθνηκα :—to die away, be dying, and in aor. 2 and pf. to be dead, Il., Trag.　　2. to die away, disappear, Mosch., Bion.

κατα-θνητός, ή, όν, mortal, Il.

καταθορεῖν, aor. 2 inf. of καταθρώσκω.

κατα-θορυβέω, f. ήσω, to cry down, Plat.

κατα-θρασύνω, v. καταθαρσύνω.

κατα-θραύω, f. σω, to break in pieces, shatter, Plat.

κατα-θρηνέω, f. ήσω, to bewail, lament, mourn, Eur.

κατα-θρώσκω, f. -θορούμαι :—aor. 2 κατέθορον :—to leap down, Il. ; c. acc., κ. τὴν αἱμασιήν to leap down the wall, Hdt.

κατ-αθῡμέω, f. ήσω, to be quite cast down, lose all heart, Xen.

κατα-θύμιος [ῡ], α, ον, (θυμός) in the mind or thoughts, Od. ; μηδέ τί τοι θάνατος κατ. ἔστω let not death sit heavy on thy heart, Il. II. according to one's mind, satisfactory, Theogn., Hdt.

κατα-θύω, f. σω, to sacrifice, Hdt., Xen. 2. to offer, dedicate, τὴν δεκάτην Xen. II. Med., φίλτροις καταθύσομαι I will compel by magic sacrifices, Theocr.

κατα-θωρᾱκίζομαι, Pass. to be armed at all points, Xen.

καταί-βᾰσις, εως, ἡ, poët. for κατάβασις, Anth.

καταιβάτης [ᾰ], poët. for καταβάτης, ου, ὁ, (καταβαίνω) a name of Zeus as descending in thunder and lightning, Ar. :—also of his thunder, descending, hurled down, Aesch. 2. of Ἀχέρων, that to which one descends, downward, Eur.

καταιβᾰτός, ή, όν, poët. for καταβατός, θύραι κ. gates by which men descend, downward-leading, Od.

κατ-αιγίζω, f. Att. ιῶ, to rush down like a storm, Aesch. :—generally, to be tempestuous, Anth.

κατ-αιδέομαι, Dep. with fut. med. -αιδέσομαι, aor. 1 pass. -δέσθην :—to feel shame or reverence before another, stand in awe of him, Hdt., Soph., etc.: c. inf. to be ashamed to do a thing, Eur.

κατ-αιθᾰλόω, f. ώσω, to burn to ashes, Eur., Ar. :— Pass., [Τροίας] πυρὶ κατηθαλωμένης Eur.

κατ-αιθύσσω, f. ξω, to wave or float adown, πλόκαμοι νῶτον καταιθύσσον Pind. ; Κάστωρ καταιθύσσει ἐστίαν Castor sheds his lustre down upon the hearth, Id.

κατ-αίθω, to burn down, burn to ashes, Aesch., Eur. : —metaph. of love, Theocr.

κατ-αικίζω, f. Att. ιῶ: Pass., pf. κατῄκισμαι :—to wound severely, to spoil utterly, Od. ; so Med., Eur.

καταίνεσις, εως, ἡ, an agreement : a betrothal, Plut.

κατ-αινέω, f. έσω, poët. ήσω, to agree to a thing, approve of it, c. acc. rei, Hdt. ; also σω, Thuc. 2. to agree or promise to do, c. inf., Pind., Soph. ; also, κ. τοῦτον βασιλέα σφίσι εἶναι to agree that he should be king, Hdt. 3. to grant, promise, Soph. : to promise in marriage, betroth, Eur.

κατ-αιρέω, Ion. for καθ-αιρέω.

κατ-αίρω, f. -ᾰρῶ, intr. to come down, make a swoop, of birds, Ar. ; of persons, Eur., etc. II. of ships, to put into port, put in, Thuc.

κατ-αισθάνομαι, f. -αισθήσομαι, Dep. to come to full perception of, Soph.

κατ-αίσιος, ον, all righteous, Aesch.

κατ-αισχύνω [ῡ], f. ῠνῶ, to disgrace, dishonour, put to shame, Od., Hdt., Att. ; τὴν σὴν οὐ κατ. φύσιν I put not thy nature to shame, i. e. show myself un-worthy of thee, Soph. ; ἐμὸν κατῄσχυνε χρέος covered me with dishonour in that my debt remained unpaid, Pind. II. Med. to feel shame before, θεούς Soph. ; so in aor. 1 pass., καταισχυνθῆναι, ὅπως μὴ δόξει . . to be ashamed of being thought, Thuc.

κατα-ἴσχω, Ep. for κατ-ίσχω, Od.

κατ-αιτιάομαι, f. άσομαι [ᾱ], Dep. to accuse, arraign, reproach, Hdt., Dem. :—Med. to accuse one another, Hdt. 2. c. acc. rei, to lay something to one's charge, impute, ἀμαθίαν Thuc. II. part. aor. 1

pass. καταιτιαθείς is used in pass. sense, an accused person, defendant, Id., Xen.

καταῖτυξ, ῠγος, ἡ, a low helmet or skull-cap of neat's leather, Il. (Deriv. uncertain.)

κατ-αιωρέομαι, Pass. to hang down, κατηωρεῦντο (Ion. impf.) Hes.

κατα-καγχάζω, f. σω, to laugh aloud at, τινός Anth.

κατα-καιέμεν, Ep. for -καίειν, inf. of κατακαίω.

κατα-καίνω, = κατακτείνω, only in aor. 2 κατέκανον, Xen.

κατα-καίριος, ον, = καίριος, Anth.

κατα-καίω, Att. -κάω [ᾰ], Ep. inf. κατακαιέμεν : f. -καύσω : aor. 1 κατέκαυσα, Ep. κατέκηα, 1 pl. subj. κατακήομεν or -κείομεν (for -κήωμεν), inf. κατακῆαι, syncop. κακκῆαι : pf. -κέκαυκα :—Pass., f. -κανθήσομαι : aor. 1 κατεκαύθην, aor. 2 κατεκάην : pf. -κέκαυμαι : (cf. καίω) :—to burn down, burn completely, Hom., Il., Hdt. ; κ. τοὺς μάντιας to burn them alive, Hdt. ; ζῶντα κατακαυθῆναι Id. II. Pass., of fire, in tmesi, κατὰ πῦρ ἐκάη had burnt down, burnt out, Il.

κατα-κᾰλέω, f. έσω, to call down, summon, invite, Thuc. :—Med., Plut.

κατα-κᾰλύπτω, f. ψω, to cover up, Il., Hdt., Att. :— Med., in tmesi, κατὰ κρᾶτα καλυψάμενος having covered his head, Od. ; so -καλυψάμενος alone, having veiled oneself, Hdt. ; and -κεκαλυμμένος Id., Plat.

κατα-κάμπτω, f. ψω, to bend down, so as to be con-cave, Plat. :—metaph. μ. ἐλπίδας to bend down, over-throw hopes, Eur. :—Pass. to be bent (by intreaty), Aeschin.

κατα-κάρφομαι, Pass. to wither away, Aesch.

κατα-καύσας, aor. 1 part. of κατακαίω.

κατα-καυχάομαι, f. ήσομαι, Dep. to boast against one, exult over him, τινος or κατά τινος N. T. : to have no fear of, τινος Ib.

κατακεῖαι, Ep. aor. 1 inf. of κατακαίω.

κατά-κειμαι, Ep. 3 pl. κατακείαται, Ion. -κέαται ; subj. -κέωμαι : Pass., only in pres. and impf. with fut. med. -κείσομαι :—to lie down, lie outstretched, Hom., Ar. 2. to lie hid, lurk, Hom. 3. to lie stored up, Lat. reponi, Il., Hes. 4. to lie sick, Hdt. :— also to lie idle, Xen. 5. to recline at meals, Lat. accumbere, πῖνε, κατάκεισο Ar. 6. of land, to lie sloping to the sea (so Horat. Usticae cubantis), Pind.

κατα-κείομεν, Ep. for -κέωμεν, aor. 1 subj. of κατα-καίω. II. also Ep. for -κείωμεν, aor. 1 subj. of κατακείω.

κατα-κείρω, f. -κερῶ, to shear off :—Med., κ. τὰς κεφα-λάς to crop their heads close, Hdt. II. metaph. to cut away, destroy, squander, Plat.

κατα-κείω, used as fut. of κατάκειμαι, κατακείετε οἴκαδ' ἰόντες Od. ; σπείσαντες κατακείομεν (Ep. for -κείωμεν) Ib. ; κακκείοντες ἔβαν (Ep. part.) they went to lie down, Hom.

κατακεκράκτης, ου, voc. -κέκρακτα, ὁ, one who cries down, a bawler, Ar.

κατακέκλῑσο, 2 sing. plqpf. pass. of κατακλίνω.

κατα-κελεύω, f. σω, to command silence, Ar. : gener-ally, to command, c. inf., Plut. II. of the κελευστής, to give the time in rowing, Ar.

κατα-κερδαίνω, f. ἀνῶ, to make gain of a thing wrong-fully, Xen.

κατα-κερματίζω, f. Att. ιῶ, to change into small coin : generally, to divide into small parts, to cut up, Plat.

κατα-κερτομέω, f. ήσω, to rail violently, Hdt.
κατα-κηλέω, f. ήσω, to charm away, Lat. delinire, Soph.
κατακήομεν, Ep. for -κήωμεν, 1 pl. aor. 1 subj. of κατακαίω.
κατα-κηρόω, f. ώσω, to cover with wax, Hdt.
κατα-κηρύσσω, Att. -ττω, f. ξω, to proclaim or command by public crier, Xen.　　II. in an auction, κ. τι εἴς τινα to order it to be knocked down to one, Plut.
κατα-κλαίω, Att. -κλάω [ᾰ]: f. κλαύσομαι :—to bewail loudly, lament, Ar.; so in Med., Eur.　　2. absol. to wail aloud, Id.
κατα-κλάξασθαι, Dor. for -κλήσασθαι, aor. 1 med. inf. of κατακλείω.
κατα-κλάω [ᾰ], Att. for κατακλαίω.
κατα-κλάω [ᾰ], impf. κατέκλων: aor. 1 -έκλᾰσα :—Pass., aor. 1 -εκλάσθην: pf. -κέκλασμαι :—to break down, break short, snap off, Il., Hdt.　　II. metaph. to break down, οὐδένα ὅντινα οὐ κατέκλασε he broke us all down, broke all our hearts, Plat.: Pass., κατεκλάσθη φίλον ἦτορ Od.; φρένας κατεκλάσθη Eur.
κατα-κλείς, εῖδος, ἡ, an instrument for fastening doors, a key, Ar.
κατα-κλείω, Ion. -κληΐω, old Att. -κλήω: fut. Ion. -κληΐσω, Dor. κατακλάξω :—Med., aor. 1 κατεκλεισάμην, Dor. κατεκλαξάμην :—Pass., aor. 1 κατεκλείσθην, Ion. κατεκληΐσθην: pf. κατα-κέκλειμαι or -κέκλεισμαι:　　I. c. acc. pers. to shut in, inclose a mummy in its case, Hdt.; τοὺς Ἕλληνας ἐς τὴν νῆσον κ. to drive them into the island and shut them up there, Thuc. :—Med. to shut oneself up, Xen.; κατακλάξασθαι to shut up the bride with oneself, Theocr.　　2. metaph., νόμῳ κ. to shut up, i. e. to compel, oblige, Dem.; also, εἰς κίνδυνον μέγιστον κατακεκλεῖσθαι to be reduced, Id.　　II. c. acc. rei, to shut up, close, τὰς πυλίδας Hdt.; τὰ ἱρά Id., etc.
κατα-κληρο-δοτέω, (κλῆρος, δίδωμι), f. ήσω, to distribute by lot, N. T.
κατα-κληρονομέω, f. ήσω, to obtain by inheritance, Plut.
κατα-κληρόω, f. ώσω, to portion out :—Med. to receive as one's portion, Plut.
κατακλιθείς, aor. 1 pass. part. of κατακλίνω :—κατακλινείς, aor. 2.
κατακλϊνής, ές, sloping, Anth. From
κατα-κλίνω [ῑ], f. -κλῐνῶ :—Pass., aor. 1 κατ-εκλίθην [ῐ]: aor. 2 κατ-εκλίνην [ῐ], part. -κλινείς: f. -κλῐνή-σομαι :—to lay down, [δόρυ] κατακλίνας ἐπὶ γαίῃ Od.; κατ. τοὺς Πέρσας εἰς λειμῶνα having made them recline (for dinner) in a meadow, Hdt.; κ. τινα εἰς Ἀσκληπιοῦ to lay a sick person in the temple of Aesculapius, that he might sleep there and so be cured, Ar. : —Pass. to lie at table, sit at meat, Lat. accumbere, Hdt., Ar., etc.　　II. metaph. to lay prostrate, overthrow, Theogn. Hence
κατάκλῐσις, εως, ἡ, a making one to lie down, seating him at table, Plat.; ἡ κ. τοῦ γάμου the celebration of the marriage feast, Hdt.　　II. (from Pass.) a lying at table, sitting at meat, Plat.
κατα-κλύζω: f. -κλύσω [ῠ], poët. -κλύσσω, to dash over, flood, deluge, inundate, Hdt., etc. :—metaph. to deluge, overwhelm, Eur., Plat. :—Pass., κύματι κατακλυσθῆν (aor. 1 inf., poët. for -κλυσθῆναι),

Aesch.　　II. to wash down or away, Pind.　　2. to wash out, wash away, Xen.
κατακλυσμός, ὁ, a deluge, inundation : metaph., Dem.
κατα-κνάω, f. -κνήσω, to scrape away, make away with, Ar.
κατα-κνήθω, = foreg. :—Pass., Ar.
κατα-κνίζω, f. Att. ιῶ, to pull to pieces, shred small, Luc.　　II. to tickle : Pass. to itch, Ar.
κατα-κοιμάω, f. ήσω :　　I. intr. to sleep through, κ. τὴν φυλακήν to sleep out the watch, i. e. sleep all the time of one's watch, Hdt.; so, κατακοιμῆσαι τὴν ἡμέραν Xen.: absol. to go to sleep, Hdt.　　II. in Causal sense, to put to sleep, Soph. :—Pass., aor. 1 κατα-κοιμηθῆναι, to go to sleep, sleep, Il., Hdt.
κατα-κοιμίζω, f. σω, = κατακοιμάω II, Plat., Luc.
κατα-κοινωνέω, f. ήσω, to make one a partaker, Dem.; κ. τὰ τῆς πόλεως to share the public property among themselves, Aeschin.
κατ-ἀκολουθέω, f. ήσω, to follow after, obey, Plut.
κατα-κολπίζω, f. Att. ιῶ, (κόλπος) to run into a bay, Thuc.
κατα-κολυμβάω, f. ήσω, to dive down, Thuc.
κατακομϊδή, ἡ, a bringing down to the sea-shore for exportation, Thuc. From
κατα-κομίζω, f. Att. ιῶ, to bring down, esp. from the inland to the coast, Thuc.　　2. κ. ναῦν to bring it into harbour, Dem.　　3. metaph. to bring into a place of refuge, Id.
κατά-κομος, ον, (κόμη) with long falling hair, Eur.
κατἄκονά, ἡ, (κατακαίνω) = διαφθορά, destruction, Eur.
κατα-κονδϋλίζω, (κόνδυλος) to buffet sharply, Aeschin.
κατ-ἀκοντίζω, f. Att. -ιῶ, to shoot down, Hdt., Dem.
κατα-κόπτω, f. ψω, to cut down, cut in pieces, cut up, Hdt., Ar., etc.: Pass., aor. 2 part. κατακοπείς cut in pieces, Hdt.　　2. to kill, slay, Id., Att.　　3. in a military sense, to cut in pieces, 'cut up,' Dem.; Pass., aor. 2 inf. κατακοπῆναι Xen.　　4. generally, to break in pieces, destroy, Dem.　　II. to coin into money, Hdt., Xen.
κατα-κορής, ές, (κορέννυμι) satiated, glutted : metaph. insatiable, excessive, wearisome, Plat.
κατάκορος, ον, = κατακορής :—Adv. -ρως, to excess, intemperately, ap. Dem.
κατα-κοσμέω, f. ήσω, to set in order, arrange, Od. (in Med.); ἐπὶ νευρῇ κατακόσμει ὀϊστόν was fitting it on the string, Il.　　2. to fit out completely, adorn, Ar., Plat.　　II. to reduce to order, Plut.
κατ-ἀκούω, f. σομαι, to hear and obey, be subject to another, c. dat., Hdt.; c. gen.; c. acc., τινός Dem.　　2. to hearken or give ear to one, Id.　　3. to hear plainly, τι or τινά, Eur., Thuc., etc.; τινός Ar.
κατα-κράζω, f. -κεκράξομαι, to cry down, outdo in crying, Ar.
κατα-κρᾰτέω, f. ήσω, to prevail over, τινός: absol. to prevail, gain the mastery, Hdt., Aesch.; of a name, to prevail, become current, Hdt.
κατα-κρέμαμαι, Pass. to hang down, be suspended, Hdt.
κατα-κρέμαννυμι, f. -κρέμασω, to hang up, Od., Hdt.
κατακρῆθεν, Adv. better κατὰ κρῆθεν, v. κράς II.
κατα-κρήμναμαι, Pass., = κατακρέμαμαι, Ar.
κατα-κρημνίζω, f. σω, to throw down a precipice, Dem., Plut.　　2. generally, to throw headlong down, ἐκ τριηρέων Xen. :—Pass. to be so thrown down, Id.

κατά-κρημνος, ον, *steep and rugged*, Batr.

κατάκρης, Adv., better κατ' ἄκρης, v. ἄκρα.

κατάκρῖμα, τό, *condemnation, judgment*, N. T. From

κατα-κρίνω [ῑ], f. -κρῐνῶ :— *to give as sentence against*, τινός :—Pass., τοῖσι κατακέκρῖται θάνατος *sentence of* death *has been passed upon* them, Hdt.; κατακεκριμένων οἱ τούτων *when this sentence has been given against* him, Id.; impers., ἢν κατακριθῇ μοι *if sentence be given against* me, Xen. 2. c. acc. pers. *to condemn*, κατέκρινάν μιν ἔκδοτον ἄγεσθαι Hdt.; κ. τινὰ θανάτῳ N. T.:—Pass. *to be condemned*, Eur., Xen.

κατα-κρύπτω, poët. part. κακκρύπτων, f. ψω, *to cover over, hide away, conceal*, Hom., etc. II. absol. *to use concealment, to conceal oneself*, of the gods, Od. Hence

κατακρυφή, ή, *concealment : a subterfuge*, Soph.

κατα-κρώζω, *to croak at : croak down*, like jackdaws, Ar.

κατα-κτάμεν, -κτάμεναι, Ep. for -κτανεῖν, aor. 2 inf. of κατακτείνω.

κατα-κτάομαι, f. -κτήσομαι, Dep. *to get for oneself entirely, gain possession of*, and in past tenses, *to have in full possession*, Soph., etc.

κατα-κτάς, Ep. aor. 2 part. of sq. : -κτάμενος, med.

κατα-κτείνω : f. -κτενῶ, Ion. -κτᾰνῶ, Ep. -κτᾰνέω : aor. 1 κατέκτεινα : aor. 2 κατέκτᾰνον, Ep. imperat. κάκτανε, poët. κατέκτᾰν, ας, α, Ep. inf. κακτάμεναι, κατακτάμεν, part. κατακτάς : pf. κατέκτονα :—Pass., fut. med. in pass. sense κατακτανέεσθε :—aor. 1 κατεκτάθην [ᾰ], 3 pl. -θεν ; part. med. κατακτάμενος (in pass. sense) :—*to kill, slay, murder*, Hom., Hdt.

ⲕατακτός, ή, όν, (κατάγω) *to be sunk* or *let down*, Ar.

κατα-κῠβεύω, f. σω, *to lose in dicing* :—Pass. *to be gambled away*, Aeschin.

κατα-κυκλόω, f. ώσω, *to encircle;* in Med., Plut.

κατα-κῠλίνδω or -κυλίω, f. -κυλίσω [ῐ] : aor. 2 pass. -εκυλίσθην :—*to roll down* :—Pass. *to be rolled down* or *thrown off*, Hdt., Xen.

κατα-κύπτω, f. ψω, *to bend down, stoop*, Il. :—*bend down and peep into* a thing, Luc.

κατα-κῠριεύω, *to gain dominion over*, c. gen., N. T.

κατα-κῡρόω, f. ώσω, *to confirm, ratify*, Soph. :—Pass., ψήφῳ θανάτου κατακυρωθείς, = κατακριθείς, *condemned* to death, Eur.

κατα-κωλύω, f. ύσω [ῠ], *to hinder from doing*, Ar.: *to detain, keep back*, Xen. :—Pass., c. gen. rei, κατεκωλύθη τοῦ πλοῦ Dem.

κατα-κωμάζω, f. σω, *to burst riotously in upon*, τὸ δαιμόνιον κατεκώμασε δώμασιν Eur.

κατακωχή, κατακώχιμος, incorrect forms for κατοκωχή, κατοκώχιμος.

καταλᾰβεῖν, aor. 2 inf. of καταλαμβάνω.

κατ-αλαζονεύομαι, Dep. *to boast* or *brag largely*, Dem.

κατα-λᾰλέω, f. ήσω, *to talk loudly, to blab*, Ar.

καταλᾰλιά, ή, *evil report, slander*, N. T. From

κατά-λᾰλος, ό, *a slanderer*, N. T.

κατα-λαμβάνω, -λήψομαι, Ion. -λάμψομαι : pf. -είληφα : Ion. plqpf. -λελαβήκεε :—Pass., Ion. aor. 1 -ελάμφθην :—*to seize upon, lay hold of*, Lat. *occupare*, Od., Hdt., Att. :—Med. *to seize for oneself*, Lat. *capesso*, Hdt. 2. *to seize, overpower*, of death and fatigue, Hom. 3. *to seize with the mind, apprehend, comprehend*, Plat. II. *to catch, overtake, come*

up with, τοὺς φεύγοντας Hdt. : of mischances, *to overtake, befall*, Id. 2. *to surprise, catch, find*, Lat. *deprehendo*, with a partic., κ. τινὰ ζῶντα Id. ; καταλαμβάνει τοὺς ἄρχοντας ἐξιόντας Dem., etc. 3. impers., καταλαμβάνει τινά, c. inf., like the Att. συμβαίνει, *it happens to one, it is* one's *fortune to do so and so*, τοῦτον κατέλαβε κεῖσθαι Hdt. 4. absol., τὰ καταλαβόντα = τὰ συμβάντα, *what happened, the circumstances*, Id. ; ἢν πόλεμος καταλαβῇ Thuc. III. *to repress, arrest, check*, τὴν δύναμιν Κύρου Hdt. ; κ. τὸ πῦρ *to get* it *under*, Id. ; κ. ἑαυτόν Id. ; κ. τὰς διαφοράς *to put an end to* them, Id. :—Pass., ὁ θάνατος καταλαμφθεὶς ἐσιγήθη *inquiries about the death being checked*, Id. 2. *to bind*, κ. πίστι, ὁρκίοις, Lat. *jurejurando adstringere, to bind* by oath, Id., Thuc. 3. *to force* or *compel* one *to do*, c. inf. ἀναγκαίη μιν κ. φαίνειν *forces* him *to bring out the truth*, Hdt. :—Pass., καταλαμβανόμενος *being constrained*, Id. Hence

καταλαμπτέος, α, ον, Ion. for καταληπτέος, *to be arrested*, Hdt.

κατα-λάμπω, f. -λάμψω, *to shine upon* or *over*, c. gen., Plat. : c. acc., κ. τοὺς στενωπούς *to light them*, Plut. II. absol. *to shine*, Eur. ; so in Med., Id.

κατ-αλγέω, f. ήσω, *to suffer much, feel sore pain*, Soph.

κατα-λέγω, f. ξω, *to lay down* : Med. and Pass. *to lie down, go to bed*, aor. 1 κατελέξατο Hom. ; Ep. syncop. aor. 2 pass. κατέλεκτο Il., etc. ; part. καταλέγμενος and inf. καταλέχθαι Od. ; f. καταλέξομαι Hes. II. *to pick out, choose out of many*, Hdt. :— *to choose* as soldiers, *to enrol, enlist*, Ar., Thuc. ; Med. *to choose for himself*, Hdt., Thuc., etc. :—Pass. *to be enlisted* or *enrolled*, Lat. *conscribi*, Hdt., etc. III. *to recount, tell at length* or *in order*, in fut. or aor. 1, ταῦτα καταλέξω Il. ; πᾶσαν ἀληθείην κατάλεξον Ib. :—Pass., τούτων δὴ τῶν καταλεχθέντων *of those which have been recounted*, Hdt. 2. *to reckon up*, Od., Hdt., etc.

κατα-λείβω, f. ψω, *to pour down ;* absol. *to shed tears*, Eur. : —Pass. *to drop down*, Il., Eur. Hence

κατ-άλειπτος, ον, *anointed*, Ar.

κατα-λείπω, Ep. also καλλείπω, f. καλλείψω, aor. 2 κάλλιπον ; Ion. impf. καταλείπεσκον :—Med. and Pass., fut. med. (in pass. sense), also fut. καταλειφθήσομαι : —*to leave behind*, Il. ; esp. of persons dying or going into a far country, οἷόν μιν Τροίηνδε κιὼν κατέλειπεν Ὀδυσσεύς Od. ; κ. τινὰ μόνον Soph., etc. ; so in Med., καταλείπεσθαι παῖδας *to leave behind one*, Hdt., etc. : —Pass., καταλελειμμένος τοῦ ἄλλου στρατοῦ *being part of the army left behind*, Id. 2. *to leave as an heritage*, Od., Att. ; καταλείψει οὐδὲ ταφῆναι *will leave not enough to be buried with*, Ar. 3. in Med., *simply, to leave* in a certain state, Hdt. II. *to forsake, abandon, leave in the lurch*, Hom., Att. III. *to leave remaining*, ὀκτὼ μόνον Xen. : Med. *to reserve for oneself*, Id. :—Pass., καταλείπεται μάχη *yet remains to be fought* Id. 2. *to leave alone*, Id.

κατα-λειτουργέω, f. ήσω, *to spend all* one's *substance in bearing the public burdens* (λειτουργίαι), Dem.

κατάλειψις, εως, ή, (καταλείπω) *a leaving behind*, Plat.

κατα-λεπτολογέω, f. ήσω, *to waste in subtle talk*, Ar.

κατα-λεύω, f. σω, *to stone to death*, Hdt., Ar., etc.

κατ-ᾰλέω, f. έσω, *to grind down*, Od., Hdt.

κατα-λήγω, f. ξω, *to leave off, end, stop*, Aesch.; ποῖ καταλήξει; at what point *will it cease?* Id.:—τὰ καταλήγοντα the limits of a district, Plut.

κατα-λήθομαι, Dep. *to forget utterly*, τινός Il.

καταληπτέος, α, ον, verb. Adj. of καταλαμβάνω, *to be seized* or *occupied*, Plut.

καταληπτικός, ή, όν, (καταλαβεῖν) *able to keep down* or *check*, c. gen., Ar.

καταληπτός, ή, όν, verb. Adj. of καταλαμβάνω, *to be achieved*, Thuc. **II.** act. *seizing suddenly;* πένθος θεόθεν καταληπτόν grief *that falls on us* from the gods, Eur.

κατάληψις, εως, ἡ, (καταλαμβάνω) *a seizing*, ἐν καταλήψει within one's grasp, Thuc.:—*an assaulting*, Ar. **2.** *a taking possession, occupation*, Plat., Dem., etc.

κατα-λῐθάζω, =καταλιθόω, N.T.

κατα-λῐθόω, f. ώσω, *to stone to death*, Dem.

καταλιμνάζω, *to make into a lake* or *swamp*, Byz.

καταλιμπάνω, =καταλείπω, Thuc.

κατα-λῑπᾰρέω, f. ήσω, *to entreat earnestly*, Luc.

καταλλᾰγή, ἡ, *exchange*, esp. of money: *the profits of the money-changer*, Dem. **II.** *a change from enmity to friendship, reconciliation*, Aesch., etc. **2.** *reconciliation* of sinners *with God*, N.T.

καταλλακτικός, ή, όν, *easy to reconcile, placable*, Arist.

κατ-αλλάσσω, Att. -ττω, f. άξω, *to change* money, Plut., etc.; and so in Med., Dem.:—Med. *to exchange* one thing *for* another, Plat. **II.** *to change* a person *from enmity to friendship, reconcile*, Hdt., N.T.:— Med., καταλλάσσεσθαι τὴν ἔχθρην τινί *to make up* one's enmity with any one, Hdt.:—Pass., esp. in aor. 1 κατηλλάχθην or aor. 2 κατηλλάγην [ᾰ], *to become reconciled*, Soph., Eur., etc.

κατ-ᾰλοάω, f. ήσω, *to crush in pieces, make an end of*, Xen., Aeschin.

καταλογάδην [ᾰ], Adv. (καταλέγω) *by way of conversation, in prose*, Plat.

κατ-ᾰλογέω, v. sub κατηλογέω.

κατα-λογίζομαι, f. Att. ιοῦμαι, Dep. *to count up, number, reckon*, Xen.; κ. τὸ εὐεργέτημα πρός τινα *to put it down* to his *account*, Dem.; καταλογιζέσθω μηδεὶς τοῦθ' ὑμῖν ἐν ἀρετῇ *let* no one *impute* it to you as a virtue, Aeschin. **II.** *to count* or *reckon among*, Lat. *annumerare*, τοὺς ἀχαρίστους ἐν τοῖς ἀδίκοις Xen.

κατάλογος, ὁ, (καταλέγω) *an enrolment, register, list, catalogue*, Plat.; κ. νεῶν *the catalogue* of ships in Il. 2. **2.** at Athens, *the register of citizens*, Ar., etc.: [ὁπλῖται] ἐκ καταλόγου soldiers *on the list for service*, Thuc., etc.; οἱ ἐν τῷ καταλόγῳ Xen.; οἱ ἔξω τοῦ κ., or, οἱ ὑπὲρ τὸν κ., *the superannuated*, Lat. *emeriti*, Id.; καταλόγοις χρηστοῖς ἐκκριθέν, of picked troops, Thuc.

κατ-ᾰλοκίζω, f. σω, *to cut into furrows*, Eur.

κατα-λόσμαι, v. -λούομαι.

κατα-λούομαι, Med. *to spend in bathing*, καταλόει [metri grat. pro -λούει] Ar.

κατα-λοφάδεια, Adv. =κατὰ τὸν λόφον, *on the neck*, βῆν δὲ καταλοφάδεια φέρων (sc. τὸν ἔλαφον) Od.

κατα-λοχίζω, f. σω, *to distribute into* λόχοι, and generally *to distribute*, Plut. Hence

καταλοχισμός, ὁ, *distribution into bodies*, Plut., Luc.

κατάλῠμα, ατος, τό, (καταλύω II) *an inn, lodging*, N.T.

κατα-λῡμαίνομαι, Dep. *to ruin utterly, destroy*, Xen.

καταλύσιμος, ον, *to be dissolved* or *done away*, Soph.

κατάλῠσις, εως, ἡ, (καταλύω) *a dissolving, dissolution* of governments, Thuc., etc. **2.** *the dismissal* or *disbanding* of a body of men, στρατιᾶς Xen.; εἰς κατάλυσιν till *dismissal*, of soldiers at a review, Id. **3.** κ. τοῦ πολέμου *an ending* of the war, *pacification*, Thuc., Xen. **4.** generally, *an end, termination*, Xen. **II.** *a resting, lodging, rest*, Eur. **2.** = κατάλυμα, *a resting-place, guest-chamber, quarters, lodging*, καταλύσιες (Ion. for -λύσεις), Hdt., Plat.

κατα-λύω, f. -λύσω [ῠ]: Pass., f. -λῠθήσομαι: pf. -λέλῠμαι:—*to put down, destroy*, Il., Eur. **2.** of governments, *to dissolve, break up, put down*, Hdt., Ar., etc.; κ. τύραννον *to put down*, *to depose*, Thuc.; κ. τινὰ τῆς ἀρχῆς Xen.:—Pass., τῶν ἄλλων καταλελυμένων στρατηγῶν having been dismissed, Hdt. **b.** *to dissolve, dismiss, disband* a body, καταλύειν τὴν βουλὴν Id.; τὸ ναυτικόν Dem. **c.** τὴν φυλακὴν κ. *to neglect* the watch, Ar. **3.** *to end, bring to an end*, βίοτον Eur.; τὸν βίον Xen. **b.** κ. τὴν εἰρήνην *to break* the peace, Aeschin. **c.** κ. τὸν πόλεμον *to end* the war, make peace, Thuc., Xen., etc.; and absol. (sub. τὸν πόλεμον) καταλύειν τινί or πρός τινα *to make peace with* him, Thuc.:—so in Med., Id., etc.; καταλύεσθαι τὰς ἔχθρας Hdt. **II.** *to unloose, unyoke*, ἵππους Od.; τὸ σῶμα τοῦ ἀδελφέου κ. *to take* it *down* from the wall, Hdt. **2.** intr. *to take up one's quarters, to lodge*, παρ' ἐμοὶ καταλύει he *is my guest*, Plat.; κ. παρά τινα *to go and lodge* with him, Thuc.: absol. *to take one's rest*, Ar.; Med., θανάτῳ καταλυσαίμαν *may I take my rest* in the grave, Eur.

κατα-λοφάω, Ion. -έω, f. ήσω, *to rest from* a thing, c. gen., Od.

κατα-μᾰγεύω, f. σω, *to bewitch*, Luc.

κατα-μᾰθεῖν, aor. 2 inf. of κατα-μανθάνω.

κατα-μᾰλᾰκίζω, f. Att. ιῶ, *to make soft* or *effeminate*, Jo. Chrys.:—Pass. *to be* or *become so*, Xen.

κατα-μᾰλάσσω, Att. -ττω, f. ξω, *to soften much*, Luc.; metaph. *to appease*, Id.

κατα-μανθάνω, f. -μᾰθήσομαι: aor. 2 κατ-εμᾰθον:—*to observe well, examine closely*, Hdt., Xen. **2.** *to learn thoroughly*, τι Plat., etc. **3.** *to perceive, understand*, Id., etc. **4.** *to discover, find*, c. part., καταμαθόντες μιν ἀγοράζοντα Hdt.; κ. τινὰ θύοντα Xen. **5.** *to learn thoroughly*, and in pf. *to have learnt, to be aware*, Id. **6.** *to consider*, τι Id.

κατα-μαντεύομαι, Dep. *to divine, surmise*, Arist.

κατα-μαργάω, Ion. -έω, f. ήσω, *to be stark mad*, Hdt.

κατα-μάρπτω, f. ψω, *to catch*, Lat. *deprehendo*, Il.; esp. *to catch* one running away, Hom., Pind.

κατα-μαρτῠρέω, f. ήσω, *to bear witness against*, τινός or κατά τινος Oratt.; c. acc. pers. et inf., καταμαρτυροῦσιν αὐτὸν λαβεῖν Dem. :—Pass. *to have evidence given against* one, Id. **2.** Pass. also of the evidence, *to be given against* one, Id.

κατα-μάχομαι, f. -μᾰχοῦμαι, Dep. *to subdue, conquer*, Plut.

κατ-αμάω, used by Hom. only once in Ep. aor. 1 med. κατ-ἄμήσατο, *to scrape over, pile up, heap up*, Il. **II.** in Act., *to cut down, reap like corn* (cf. ἀμάω), Soph.

κατ-αμβλύνω [ῠ], to blunt or dull, Soph. : aor. 1 pass. κατημβλύνθην Anth.

κατα-μεθύσκω, aor. 1 -εμέθῠσα, Causal, to make quite drunk, Hdt., Plat.

καταμεῖναι, aor. 1 inf. of καταμένω.

κατ-ἀμελέω, f. ήσω, to take no care of, c. gen., Xen. : absol. to pay no heed, be heedless, Soph., Xen.

κατα-μελῐτόω, f. ώσω, to spread over with honey, metaph. of the nightingale's voice, Ar.

κατάμεμπτος, ον, blamed by all, abhorred, Soph. : neut. pl. as Adv. so as to have cause to find fault, Il.

κατα-μέμφομαι, f. ψομαι : aor. 1 -εμεμψάμην or -εμέμφθην : —to find great fault with, blame greatly, accuse, Thuc., Plat. Hence

κατάμεμψις, εως, ή, a blaming, finding fault, Thuc.; οὐκ ἔχει τινὶ κατάμεμψιν it leaves him no ground for censure, Id.

κατα-μένω, f. -μενῶ : aor. 1 κατ-έμεινα :—to stay behind, stay, Hdt., Att. 2. to remain fixed, continue in a certain state, Xen.

κατα-μερίζω, f. Att. ιῶ, to cut in pieces, Luc. 2. to distribute, Xen.

κατα-μετρέω, f. ήσω, to measure out to, Hdt., Xen.

κατα-μηλόω, f. ώσω, to put in a probe : metaph., κημὸν κ. to use the ballot-box as a probe, i.e. make a peculator disgorge what he has stolen, Ar.

κατα-μηνύω [ῠ], f. ύσω, to point out, make known, indicate, Hdt. 2. to inform against, τινός Xen.

κατα-μιαίνω, f. -ᾰνῶ, to taint, defile, Pind., Plat. :— Pass. to wear squalid garments as a sign of grief, wear mourning (cf. Lat. sordidatus), Hdt.

κατα-μίγνῡμι or -ύω, f. -μίξω : Ep. aor. 1 part. καμμίξας :—to mix up, mingle the ingredients, Il., Ar.

καταμίσγω=foreg. : Med. in pass. sense, h. Hom.

κατα-μισθοφορέω, f. ήσω, to spend in paying public servants or soldiers, Ar., Aeschin.

κατάμομφος, ον, (καταμέμφομαι) liable to blame, inauspicious, Aesch.

καταμόνᾱς, Adv. better divisim κατὰ μόνας, v. μόνος.

κατα-μονομάχέω, to conquer in single combat, Plut.

κατ-αμπέχω and -ίσχω, to encompass, κ. ἐν τύμβῳ, i. e. to bury him, Eur.

κατάμῠσις, ή, (καταμύω) a closing of the eyes, Plut.

κατ-ἀμύσσω, f. ξω, to tear, scratch, Theocr. :—Med., καταμύξατο χεῖρα she scratched her hand, Il.

κατα-μυττωτεύω, f. σω, to make mincemeat of, Ar.

κατα-μύω, f. ύσω : aor. 1 ἐκάμμῠσα, Ep. inf. καμμῦσαι : —to shut or close the eyes, Xen., N. T. :—hence to drop asleep, doze, Batr., Ar.

κατ-αμφικαλύπτω, f. ψω, to put all round, Od.

κατα-μωκάομαι, Dep. to mock at, τινος Plut.

κατ-ἀναγκάζω, f. σω, to overpower by force, confine, Eur. 2. to coerce, τινὰ ἐς ξυμμαχίαν Thuc.

κατ-ανάθεμα, a curse, N. T. Hence

καταναθεμᾱτίζω, f. σω, to curse, N. T.

καταναίω, to make to dwell, settle, only used in aor. 1 κατένασσα Hes. :—Med., aor. 1 κατανασσαμένη Aesch. : —Pass. to take up one's abode, dwell, only in aor. 1 κατενάσθην, Eur.; poët. 3 pl. κατένασθεν Ar.

κατ-αναλίσκω, f. -ἀναλώσω : aor. 1 -ηνάλωσα :—Pass., aor. 1 -αναλωθῆναι :—to use up, spend, lavish, Xen., Plat. :—Pass., with pf. act., to be lavished, Plat.

κατα-ναρκάω, f. ήσω, to be slothful towards, press heavily upon, c. gen., N. T.

κατα-νάσσω, f. ξω, to stamp or beat down firmly, Hdt.

κατα-ναυμᾰχέω, f. ήσω, to conquer in a sea-fight, Xen., etc. :—Pass. to be so conquered, Luc.

κατα-νέμω, f. -νεμῶ, to distribute, allot, assign, esp. as pasture-land, Hdt., Dem. 2. to distribute, divide into separate bodies, Xen. :—of a single person, κ. τινὰ εἰς τὴν τάξιν to assign him to his post, Aeschin. II. Med. or Pass. to divide among themselves, Thuc., Plat. 2. to occupy with cattle, to graze land, Lat. depasci, Isocr. :—metaph. to plunder, Babr.

κατα-νεύω : f. νεύσομαι : aor. 1 κατένευσα, Ep. part. καννεύσας :—to nod assent, Il. : c. acc. to grant, promise, Ib. ; so c. inf., generally, to make a sign by nodding the head, Od.

κατα-νέω, Ion. -νήω, aor. 1 -ένησα, to heap up, Hdt.

κατ-ανθρᾰκίζω, f. ίσω, to burn to cinders, Anth.

κατ-ανθρᾰκόομαι, Pass. to be burnt to cinders, pf. part. κατηνθρακωμένος Soph. ; aor. 1 κατηνθρακώθην Eur.

κατα-νίφω [ῐ], f. -νίψω, to cover with snow, Ar. : metaph. to sprinkle as with snow, Luc. II. absol. κατανίφει it snows, κεἰ κριμνώδη κατανίφοι even were it to snow thick as meal, Ar.

κατα-νοέω, f. ήσω, to observe well, to understand, Hdt., Plat. 2. to perceive, Thuc. 3. to learn, Id. 4. to consider, περί τινος Xen. Hence

κατανόησις, εως, ή, observation : means of observing, Plut.

κατ-άνομαι, Pass. (ἄνω) to be used up or wasted, Od.

κατα-νοτίζω, f. σω, to bedew, Eur.

κάτ-αντα, Adv. down-hill, Il.

κατ-άντης, ες, (ἄντα) down-hill, downward, steep, Ar. ; εἰς τὸ κάταντες downwards, Xen. II. metaph. prone, inclined, πρός τι Eur.

κατάντηστιν, Adv., better κατ' ἄντηστιν, so as to face, right opposite, Od.

κατ-αντικρύ [ῐ Att.], Prep. with gen. straight down from, Od. 2.=ἀντικρύ, right opposite, ἐς τὰ κ. Κυθήρων to the parts opposite Cythera, Thuc. ; κατ. ᾗ εἰσρεῖ exactly opposite to the point at which it flows in, Plat. II. as Adv. of Place, right opposite, ἡ ἤπειρος ἡ κ. Thuc. ; ἐκ τοῦ κ. from the opposite side, Plat. 2. straightforward, downright, Thuc.

κατ-αντίον, Adv. over against, right opposite, facing, c. gen., Hdt. ; c. dat., Id. ; absol., Soph.

κατ-αντιπέρας, = καταντικρύ II, c. gen., Xen.

κατ-αντλέω, f. ήσω, to pour water over :—metaph. to pour a flood of words over, τινός Ar.

κατάνυξις, εως, ή, stupefaction, slumber, N. T.

κατα-νύσσομαι, aor. 2 -ενύγην [ῠ], Pass. to be sorely pricked, κατενύγησαν τῇ καρδίᾳ N. T. II. to be stupefied, to slumber, Lxx. Hence

κατ-ανύω, Att. -ύτω [ῠ] : f. -ανύσω [ῠ] :—to bring to quite an end : esp., 1. to accomplish a certain distance, δρόμον, ὁδόν Hdt., Xen. 2. (the acc. being omitted) intr. to arrive at a place, Hdt., Soph., etc. II. to accomplish, perpetrate, Eur. ; κ. αἷμα to murder, Id.

κατα-ξαίνω, f. -ξᾰνῶ, to card or comb well : to tear in pieces, rend in shreds, Eur. ; καταξαίνειν τινὰ εἰς φοι-

νικίδα to pound him to red rags, Ar. :—Pass., κατα-ξανθείς crushed to atoms, Soph. ; πρὶν κατεξάνθαι Eur.   2. to wear or waste away, Lat. atterere, Aesch. : Pass., κατεξάνθην πόνοις, δακρύοις Eur.

κατάξειε, 3 sing. aor. 1 opt. of κατάγνυμι.

κατα-ξενόομαι, (ξενόω) Pass. to be received as a guest, pf. part. κατεξενωμένος Aesch.

κατ-άξιος, ον, quite or very worthy of, c. gen., Soph. ; absol., Eur. Adv. -ίως, Id.

κατ-αξιόω, f. ώσω, to deem worthy, Plat. :—Med. to hold in high esteem, Aesch.   II. πολλὰ χαίρειν ξυμφοραῖς καταξιῶ I bid a long farewell to calamities, Id. ; σύ τοι κατηξίωσας thou would'st have it so, Soph.

κατάορος, ον, Dor. for κατήορος.

κατα-παίζω, f. -παίξομαι, to mock at, τινός Anth.

καταπακτός, ή, όν, (καταπήγνυμι) shutting down-wards, καταπακτή θύρα a trap-door, Hdt.

κατα-παλαίω, f. σω, to throw in wrestling, Ar. : metaph. to overthrow, Eur., Plat.

κατα-πάλλομαι, Pass. to vault or leap down, οὐρανοῦ ἐκ κατέπαλτο (Ep. syncop. aor. 2 for κατεπάλετο), Il.

κατα-πάσσω, Att. -ττω, f. -πάσω, to besprinkle or bespatter, Ar. :—Pass., καταπάττομενος Id.   II. c. acc. rei, to sprinkle or strew over, Id. Hence

κατάπαστος, ον, besprinkled, Ar.   2. embroidered, Id.

κατα-πατέω, f. ήσω, to trample down, trample under foot, Thuc., etc. ; κ. ὑσὶ τὸ σπέρμα to trample down the seed (i. e. have it trampled down) by swine, Hdt.: —Pass., Id., Thuc., etc.   2. metaph. in tmesi, κατὰ δ' ὅρκια πιστὰ πάτησαν Il.

καταπαυέμεν, Ep. for -παύειν, -inf. of καταπαύω.

κατάπαυμα, ατος, τό, a means of stopping, Il. ; and

κατάπαυσις, εως, ἡ, a putting to rest : a putting down, deposing, Hdt.   II. a cessation, calm, N. T.

κατα-παύω, poët. καπ-παύω, f. σω, Ep. inf. -παυσέ-μεν, to lay to rest, put an end to, Hom., Hdt. :— Med., Eur.   II. c. acc. pers. to lay to rest, i. e. kill, Il.   2. to make one stop from a thing, hinder or check from, c. gen., Hom. :—and c. acc. only, to stop, keep in check, Id., Hdt.   3. like καταλύω, to put down or depose from power, κ. τινὰ τῆς ἀρχῆς, τῆς βασιληίης Hdt. ; κ. τοὺς τυράννους Id. :—Pass., τῆς βασιληίης κατεπαύθη Id.   b. to put down, τὴν Κύρου δύναμιν Id. ; τὸν δῆμον Thuc.   III. Pass. and Med. to leave off from, cease from, τινος Hdt., etc.   2. absol. to leave off, cease, Ar., etc.   3. the Act. is also used intr. like Med., Eur.

κατα-πεδάω, f. ήσω, to fetter, hamper, Hom.

κατα-πείθω, f. -πείσω, to persuade, Luc.

κατ-απειλέω, f. ήσω, to threaten loudly, κατ. ἔπη to use threatening words, Soph. ; τὰ κατηπειλημένα the threats uttered, Id.

κατα-πειρατηρία, Ion. -πειρητηρίη, ἡ, (πειράω) a sounding-line, Hdt.

καταπελτάζω, f. άσομαι, to overrun with light-armed troops (πελτασταί), Ar.

καταπεμπτέος, α, ον, verb. Adj. to be sent down, Luc.

κατα-πέμπω, f. ψω, to send down, Hes. ; esp. from the inland to the sea-coast, Xen.   II. to send from head-quarters, to dispatch, Dem.

κατα-πενθέω, f. ήσω, to mourn for, bewail, Anth.

καταπεπτηυῖα, Ep. for -πεπτηκυῖα, pf. part. fem. of κατα-πτήσσω.

κατάπερ, Ion. for καθάπερ.

κατα-πέρδω, mostly in Med. -πέρδομαι ; aor. 2 κατέ-παρδον : pf. καταπέπορδα :—to break wind at, τινός Ar.

κατα-πέσσω, f. -πέψω, to boil down, to digest food, Arist. :—metaph. to digest, keep from rising, Lat. concoquere, κ. χόλον Il. ; κ. μέγαν ὕλβον, i. e. to bear great fortune meekly, Pind.

κατα-πετάννυμι and -ύω, f. -πετάσω [ᾰ], to spread out over, Il., Eur.   II. to spread or cover with, τί τινι Ar., Xen. Hence

καταπέτασμα, ατος, τό, a curtain, veil, N. T.

κατα-πέτομαι, f. -πτήσομαι : 3 sing. aor. 2 κατέπτατο, part. καταπτάμενος, subj. καταπτώμαι : also aor. 2 act. κατέπτην :—to fly down, Hdt., Ar., etc.

κατα-πετρόω, f. ώσω, to stone to death, Xen.

καταπεφθῇ, aor. 1 pass. subj. of καταπέσσω.

καταπέφνων, part. of κατέπεφνον.

καταπεφρονηκότως, Adv. part. pf. act. of καταφρονέω, contemptuously, Dem.

καταπέψῃ, 3 sing. aor. 1 subj. of καταπέσσω.

κατα-πήγνυμι and -ύω : f. -πήξω, to stick fast in the ground, plant firmly, Il., Hdt., etc.   II. Pass., with pf. and plqpf. act., to stand fast or firm in, Il. ; absol., στήλη καταπεπηγυῖα Hdt.

κατα-πηδάω, f. ήσομαι, to leap down, Xen.

κατα-πίμπλημι, f. -πλήσω, to fill full of a thing, c. gen., Plat.

κατα-πίμπρημι, f. -πρήσω, to burn to ashes, Anth.

κατα-πίνω [ῐ], f. -πίομαι, later -πιοῦμαι : aor. 2 κατ-έπιον, Ep. κάππιον :—to gulp or swallow down, Hes., Hdt., Att.   II. metaph., κ. Εὐριπίδην to drink in Euripides, i. e. imbibe his spirit, Ar.   2. to swallow up, consume, Id.   3. to spend in tippling, Aeschin.

κατα-πιπράσκω, to sell outright, καταπραθείς Luc.

κατα-πίπτω, f. -πεσοῦμαι : aor. 2 κατ-έπεσον, poët. κάπ-πεσον, 3 dual καπ-πεσέτην : pf. πέπτωκα :—to fall or drop down, Hom., Hdt., Att. :—used as Pass., κάππεσε = κατεβλήθη, Aesch.   2. metaph., κάππεσε θυμός their spirit fell, Il. ; κ. εἰς ἀπιστίαν Plat.   II. to have the falling sickness, Luc.

κατα-πισσόω, Att. -ττόω, f. ώσω, to cover with pitch, to pitch over and burn (as a punishment), Plat.

κατα-πιστεύω, f. σω, to trust, Plut.

κατα-πλάσσω, Att. -ττω, f. -πλάσω [ᾰ], to plaster over with clay, etc., Hdt., Ar. :—Med., καταπλάσσεσθαι τὴν κεφαλήν to plaster one's own head, Hdt. ; τοῦτο καταπλάσσονται ὅλον τὸ σῶμα this they plaster over their whole body, Id. Hence

καταπλαστός, όν, plastered over, καταπλαστὸν φάρμακον a plaster, Ar.

καταπλαστύς, ύος, ἡ, Ion. for κατάπλασμα, Hdt.

κατα-πλέκω, f. ξω, to entwine, plait, Hdt.   2. metaph. to implicate, κ. τινὰ προδοσίᾳ Hdt.   II. to finish twining : metaph. to bring to an end, τὴν ζόην, τὴν ῥῆσιν Id.

κατά-πλεος, ον, Att. -πλεως, ων, gen. ω, quite full, τινος of a thing :—fouled or stained with a thing, γῆς κατάπλεως καὶ αἵματος Xen.

κατα-πλέω, f. -πλεύσομαι : Ion. -πλώω :—to sail down : i. e.,   1. to sail from the high sea to shore,

sail to land, put in, Od., Hdt., Att.; νεωστὶ καταπεπλευκώς having lately come ashore, Plat. 2. to sail down stream, κατ. τὸν Εὐφρήτην Hdt. II. to sail back, Id.

κατάπλεως, ων, gen. ω, Att. for κατάπλεος.

καταπλήξ, ῆγος, ὁ, ἡ, stricken with amazement, astounded, Lysias. 2. shy, bashful, Arist.; and

κατάπληξις, εως, ἡ, amazement, consternation, Thuc.

κατα-πλήσσω, Att. -ττω, f. ξω, to strike down : metaph. to strike with amazement, astound, terrify, Thuc., Xen., etc. :—Pass. to be panic-stricken, amazed, astounded, κατεπλήγη (aor. 2) Il.; Att. aor. 2 inf., καταπλαγῆναι Thuc.; 2 pl. pf. καταπέπληχθε Id.; c. acc., καταπλαγέντες τὸν Φίλιππον Dem.

κατά-πλοος, contr. -πλους, ὁ, (καταπλέω) a sailing down to land, a putting ashore, putting in, Thuc. II. a sailing back, return, Xen.

κατα-πλουτίζω, f. ιῶ, to enrich greatly, Hdt., Xen.

κατα-πλύνω [ῡ], to wash by pouring over, to drench, Xen. II. to wash out :—Pass., metaph., τὸ πρᾶγμα καταπέπλυται the affair is washed out, i. e. forgotten, Aeschin. Hence

κατάπλυσις, ἡ, a bathing in water, Xen.

καταπλώω, Ion. for καταπλέω.

κατα-πνέω, Ep. -πνείω : f. -πνεύσομαι :—to breathe upon or over, c. gen., Eur. 2. to inspire, Aesch.; θεὸς καταπνεῖ σε Eur.

καταπνοή, ἡ, (καταπνέω) a blowing, Pind.

καταπόδα, -πόδας, less correct forms for κατὰ πόδα, κατὰ πόδας.

καταποθῇ, 3 sing. aor. 1 subj. pass. of καταπίνω.

κατα-πολεμέω, f. ήσω, to war down, i. e. to exhaust by war, subdue completely, reduce, Lat. debellare, Thuc., Xen. : in pres. to attempt to subdue, Thuc. :—Pass., ἐλπίζοντες [τὴν πόλιν] καταπεπολεμῆσθαι Id.

κατα-πολιτεύομαι, Dep. to subdue by policy, Dem.

καταπολύ, less correct form for κατὰ πολύ.

κατα-πονέω, f. ήσω, to subdue after a hard struggle : —Pass. to be so subdued, Aeschin.

κατά-πονος, ον, tired, wearied, Plut.

κατα-ποντίζω, f. σω, to throw into the sea, drown therein, Dem. Hence

καταποντιστής, οῦ, ὁ, one who throws into the sea, Dem.

κατα-ποντόω, f. ώσω, = καταποντίζω, Hdt., Plat.

κατα-πορνεύω, f. σω, to prostitute, Plut.

κατα-πράσσω, Att. -ττω, f. ξω, to accomplish, execute, Xen. 2. to achieve, gain, Id. :—Med. to achieve for oneself, Id. :—Pass., τὰ καταπεπραγμένα Id.

κατα-πραΰνω [ῡ], f. ῠνῶ, to soften down, appease, Plat.

κατα-πρηνής, ές, down-turned, of the hand as used in striking or grasping, χειρὶ καταπρηνεῖ with the flat of his hand, Il.; χείρεσσι καταπρηνέσσι Od.

κατα-πρηνόω, f. ώσω, to throw headlong down, Anth.

κατα-πρίω [ῑ], f. -πριοῦμαι, to saw up, Hdt. 2. to cut or bite into pieces, Theocr.

κατα-προδίδωμι, f. -προδώσω, to betray utterly, leave in the lurch, Hdt., Att.

κατα-προΐξομαι. Att. -προίξομαι, (προῖξ) a fut. without any pres. in use, to do a thing without return, i. e. with impunity, used with a negat., οὐκ ἐμὲ λωβησάμενος καταπροΐξεται he shall not escape for having insulted me, Hdt.; οὐ καταπροΐξονται ἀποστάν-

τες, Id.; οὔ τοι καταπροΐξει πολλὰ κλέψας Ar. :— absol., ἐκείνους οὐ καταπροΐξεσθαι ἔφη he said that they should not get off scot-free, Hdt. 2. c. gen. pers., οὔ τοι ἐμοῦ καταπροΐξει you will not escape for this despite done to me, Ar.

καταπτάκών, poët. aor. 2 part. of καταπτήσσω.

κατά-πτερος, ον, (πτερόν) winged, Aesch., Eur.

καταπτήσομαι, fut. of καταπέτομαι.

κατα-πτήσσω, f. -πτήξω : 3 dual Ep. aor. 2 καταπτήτην, poët. part. καταπτάκών : pf. κατέπτηχα, Ep. part. καταπεπτηώς :—to crouch down, to lie crouching or cowering, Hom., Hes. 2. c. acc. to cower beneath, Plut.

κατάπτομαι, Ion. for καθάπτομαι.

κατάπτυστος, ον, (καταπτύω) to be spat upon, abominable, despicable, Aesch., Eur., Dem.

κατα-πτυχής, ές, (πτύχη) with ample folds, Theocr.

κατα-πτύω, f. ύσω [ῠ], to spit upon or at, esp. as a mark of abhorrence, c. gen., Dem., Aeschin.

κατα-πτώσσω, = καταπτήσσω, Il.

κατα-πτωχεύω, f. σω, to reduce to beggary, Plut.

καταπτυγοσύνη, ἡ, brutal lust, Ar. From

κατα-πύγων, ὁ, (πυγή) a lewd fellow, Ar.

κατα-πύθω [ῡ], f. ύσω, to make rotten, h. Hom. :— Pass. to become rotten, Il.

κατά-πυκνος, ον, very thick, Theocr. Hence

καταπυκνόω, f. ώσω, to stud thickly with a thing, Plut.

καταπῠρίζω, v. καππυρίζω.

κᾰτ-άρα [ᾰρ], Ion. -άρη, ἡ, a curse, κατάρην ποιεῖσθαί τινι to lay a curse upon one, Hdt.; διδόναι τινὰ κατάρᾳ Eur.

κατ-άραιρημένος, Ion. for καθ-, pf. pass. part. of καθαιρέω.

κατ-αράομαι [ᾰρ Hom., ᾱρ Att.], Ion. -αρεόμαι : f. ἀσομαι, Ion. ήσομαι : Dep. :—to call down curses upon, imprecate upon, τί τινι Hom., Hdt. :—c. inf., καταρῶνται ἀπολέσθαι they pray that he may perish, Theogn. :—c. dat. pers. only, to curse, execrate, Hdt., Ar., etc.; later, c. acc. pers., Plut., N. T. 2. absol. to utter imprecations, Ar. 3. pf. pass. part. κατ-ηράμένος in pass. sense, accursed, Id.

κατ-αράσσω, Att. -ττω, f. ξω, to dash down, break in pieces, τοὺς λοίπους κατήραξεν ἐς τὸν Κιθαιρῶνα drove them shattered to Cithaerae, Hdt.; τὸ στράτευμα κατηράχθη εἰς τὰ τειχίσματα Thuc. II. intr. to fall down, fall headlong, Plut.

κατάρᾱτος, ον, (καταράομαι) accursed, abominable, Eur., Ar.; Comp. -ότερος Dem.; Sup. -ότατος Soph.

κατ-αργέω, f. ήσω, to leave unemployed or idle, Eur.; κ. τὴν γῆν to occupy the ground uselessly, cumber it, N. T. II. to make of none effect, Ib. :—Pass., καταργηθῆναι to be abolished, cease, Ib.; κ. ἀπὸ τοῦ νόμου to be set free from the law, Ib.

κατ-αργίζω, to make to tarry, v. sub ἀπαρτίζω.

κάταργμα, τό, (κατάρχω ΙΙ) only in pl. κατάργματα, the first offerings, Eur. 2. the purifications made by such offerings, Plut.

κατ-αργῠρόω, f. ώσω, to cover with silver :—Pass., καταργυρωμένος (Ion. for κατηργυρ-) silvered, Hdt. II. to buy or bribe with silver, κατηργυρωμένος Soph.

κατ-άρδω, f. -άρσω, to water :—metaph. to besprinkle with praise, Ar.

καταρέζω, Ep. for καταρρέζω.

καταρέομαι, Ion. for καταράομαι, Hdt.

κατα-ρῖγηλός, ή, όν, making one shudder, horrible, Od.

κατ-άριθμέω, f. ήσω, to count or reckon among, Eur., Plat.   2. to recount in detail, Plat. :—in Med. to recount, enumerate; Id.

κατ-αρκέω, f. έσω, to be fully sufficient, Hdt., Eur.

καταρμόζω, Ion. for καθαρμόζω.

κατ-αρνέομαι, f. -ήσομαι, to deny strongly, persist in denying, Soph.

κατ-αρόω, f. -όσω, to plough up, τὴν γῆν Ar.

καταρ-ραθυμέω, f. ήσω, to lose from carelessness, Xen., Dem. :—Pass., τὰ κατερραθυμημένα things lost through negligence, Dem.   II. intr. to be very careless, καταρραθυμήσαντες through carelessness, Xen.

καταρ-ράκόω, to tear into shreds : pf. pass. part. κατερρακωμένος in rags or tatters, Soph.

καταρ-ράκτης, ου, (καταρ-ρήγνυμι), or κατ-αράκτης (κατ-αράσσω) :   I. as Adj. down-rushing, τὸν καταρράκτην ὁδόν (Att. for οὐδόν) to the downward entrance [of Hades], Soph.   II. as Subst. broken water, a waterfall, Lat. cataracta, Strab.   2. a kind of portcullis, Plut.   3. a sea-bird, so called from rushing down upon its prey, a gull, Ar.

καταρρακτός, ή, όν, = foreg., κ. θύρα a trap-door, Plut.

καταρ-ράπτω, f. ψω, to stitch on or over, θύρη κατερ-ραμμένη ῥιπεῖ καλάμων a frame lashed to a crate of reeds, Hdt.   II. to stitch tight, Plut.   2. metaph. to devise, compass, Aesch. From

κατάρράφος, ον, sewn together, patched, Luc.

καταρ-ρέζω, f. ξω, to pat with the hand, to stroke, caress, like Lat. mulcere, Lat. mulcere, χειρὶ δέ μιν κατέρεξε (Ep. for κατερρ-) Hom.; also καρρέζουσα (Ep. for καταρρ-) Il.

καταρ-ρέπω, f. ψω, to make to incline downwards, make to fall, Soph.

καταρ-ρέω, f. -ρεύσομαι and -ρυήσομαι : pf. -ερρύηκα : aor. 2 in pass. form -ερρύην :—to flow down, Il., Hdt., Att.   2. of men, to stream or rush down, Ar., Thuc.   3. of fruit, leaves, etc., to fall off, Xen.   4. to fall in ruins, Dem.   5. κ. εἴς τινα to come to, fall to the lot of, Theocr., Bion.   II. κ. φόνῳ to run down with blood, Eur. ; so in Med., Plut.

καταρ-ρήγνυμι and -ύω, f. -ρήξω, to break down, τὴν γέφυραν Hdt. ; μέλαθρα Eur.   2. to tear in pieces, rend, Dem. :—Med., κατερρήξαντο τοὺς κιθῶνας they rent their coats, Hdt.   3. in Soph. Ant. 675 τροπὰς καταρρήγνυσι [ἡ ἀναρχία] breaks up armies and turns them to flight.   II. Pass., aor. 2 κατερράγην [ἄ], with pf. act. κατέρρωγα :—to be broken down, to be thrown down and broken, Hdt.   2. to fall or rush down, to break or burst out, of storms, Eur. : of tears, Eur. :—metaph., ὁ πόλεμος κατερράγη Ar.   3. to be broken in pieces, Αἴγυπτος μελάγγαιός τε καὶ κατερρηγμένη with black and crumbling soil, Hdt.

καταρ-ρίνάω or -έω, f. ήσω, (ῥίνη) to file down :—metaph., κατερρινημένον τι polished, elegant, Ar.

καταρ-ρίπτω, f. ψω, to throw down, overthrow, Aesch.

κατάρροος, contr. -ρους, ὁ, (καταρρέω) a running from the head, a catarrh, Plat.

καταρ-ροφέω, f. ήσω, to gulp or swallow down, Xen.

καταρρυῆναι, inf. aor. 2 pass. of καταρρέω.

καταρρυής, ές, (καταρρέω) falling away, Soph.

κατάρ-ρὔτος, ον, irrigated, watered, Eur.   II. carried down by water, alluvial, of the Delta, Hdt.

κατ-αρρωδέω, Ion. for κατορρωδέω, to fear, dread, Hdt.

καταρρώξ, ῶγος, ὁ, ἡ, (καταρρήγνυμι) jagged, broken, Soph.

κάταρσις, εως, ἡ, (καταίρω) a landing-place, Thuc.

κατ-αρτάω, f. ήσω, to hang down from, hang on or append, Plut.   II. to adjust, χρῆμα κατηρτη-μένον a well-adjusted or convenient thing, Hdt.

κατ-αρτίζω, f. ίσω, to adjust or put in order again, restore, Hdt. ; κ. δίκτυα to put nets to rights, mend them, N. T. :—metaph. to restore to a right mind, Ib.   II. to furnish completely : pf. pass. part. κατηρτισμένος, absol., well-furnished, complete, Hdt., N. T. Hence

κατάρτἴσις, εως, ἡ, restoration, N. T.   II. a train-ing, education, discipline, Plut. ; and

καταρτιστήρ, ῆρος, ὁ, one who restores order, a medi-ator, Hdt.

κατ-αρτύω, f. ύσω [ὔ], to prepare, dress, of food, Luc.   2. generally, to train, educate, discipline : —Pass. to be trained, disciplined, Solon, Soph.   3. c. inf., κ. μολεῖν to procure his coming, Soph.   II. intr. in part. pf., κατηρτυκὼς ἱκέτης, metaph., a com-plete suppliant, one who has done all that is required, Aesch.

κατάρὔτος, ον, poët. for κατάρρυτος, Eur.

κατ-αρχαιρεσιάζω, f. σω, to defeat in an election, esp. by unfair means, Plut.

καταρχάς, less correct form for κατ' ἀρχάς.

κατ-άρχω, f. ξω, to make beginning of a thing, c. gen., Aesch. ; ὁδοῦ κατάρχειν to lead the way, Soph. :— rarely c. acc. to begin a thing, Plat. :—c. part. to begin doing, Xen.   2. to honour, Eur.   II. Med. to make a beginning, to begin, like Act., c. gen., Id., Plat. ; also c. acc., Eur. : absol., κατάρχεται μέλος is beginning, Id.   2. in religious sense, to begin the sacrificial ceremonies, Νέστωρ χέρνιβά τ' οὐλοχύτας τε κατήρχετο Nestor began [the sacrifice] with the washing of hands and sprinkling the barley on the victim's head, Od. ; κατάρχομαι I begin the function, Eur. :—c. gen., κατάρχεσθαι τοῦ τράγου to make a beginning of the victim, i. e. consecrate him for sacri-fice by cutting off the hair of his forehead, Ar. ; πῶς δ' αὖ κατάρξει θυμάτων ; Eur.   b. to sacrifice, slay, Id. :—Pass., σὸν κατήρκται σῶμα hath been devoted, Id.   c. simply, to strike, Plut.

κατα-σβέννῡμι or -ύω, f. -σβέσω, to put out, quench, Lat. extinguere, Il., Eur., etc. :—metaph., ἔστιν θάλ-ασσα, τίς δέ νιν κατασβέσει ; who shall dry it up ? Aesch. ; κ. βοήν, ἔριν to quell noise, strife, Soph.   II. Pass., aor. 1 κατ-εσβέσθην, with intr. aor. 2 act. κατ-έσβην, inf. κατα-σβῆναι, pf. act. κατ-έσβηκα :—to go out, be quenched, Hdt. :—metaph., κλαυμάτων πηγαὶ κατε-σβήκασι Aesch.

κατα-σείω, f. -σείσω, to shake down, throw down, Thuc.   II. κατασεῖσαι τὴν χεῖρα to shake or make a motion of the hand ; so, κ. τὰ ἱμάτια, by way of signal, Plut. ; but also κ. τῇ χειρί to beckon with the

hand, N. T.: absol., κατασείειν τινί to beckon to another, as a sign for him to be silent, Xen.

κατασεύομαι, Pass., to rush back into, c. acc., κῦμα κατέσσυτο (Ep. aor. 2) ῥέεθρα Il.

κατα-σημαίνω, f. ᾰνῶ, to seal up : Med. to have a thing sealed up, Plat.

κατα-σήπω, to make rotten, let rot, Xen. : —Pass., aor. 2 κατ-εσάπην [ᾰ], Ep. 3 sing. subj. -σαπῇ, with pf. 2 act. κατα-σέσηπα, to grow rotten, rot away.

κατ-ασθενέω, f. ήσω, to weaken, Anth.

κατ-ασθμαίνω, to pant and struggle against a thing, c. gen., Aesch.

κατα-σῑγάω, f. ήσομαι, to become silent, Plat.

κατα-σῑκελίζω τυρόν, to Sicilise (i. e. to consume) the cheese (in allusion to the peculations of Laches in Sicily), Ar.

κατα-σῑτέομαι, f. ήσομαι, Dep. to eat up, feed on, Hdt.

κατα-σῐωπάω, f. ήσομαι, to be silent about a thing, Dem. II. Causal, to make silent, silence, Xen.: Med. to cause silence, Id.

κατα-σκάπτω, f. ψω, to dig down, destroy utterly, rase to the ground, overthrow, Hdt., Soph., etc. :— Pass., οἰκία οἱ κατεσκάφη (aor. 2) Hdt. Hence

κατασκᾰφή, ἡ, a rasing to the ground, destruction, Trag. II. γῆς κατασκαφαία grave deep dug in earth, Aesch.; θανόντων ἐς κατασκαφάς, i. e. to the grave, Soph.; and

κατασκᾰφής, ές, dug down, κ. οἴκησις the deep-dug dwelling, i. e. the grave, Soph.

κατα-σκεδάννῡμι and -ύω, f. -σκεδάσω [ᾰ], to scatter, or pour upon or over, τι κατά τινος Ar.; also τί τινος, Dem., etc. 2. κ. φήμην to spread a report against one, Plat. 3. Med. to pour or sprinkle about, Xen.

κατα-σκέλλομαι, Pass. to become a skeleton, wither or pine away, Aesch.: —so in pf. act. κατέσκληκα and plqpf. κατεσκλήκει, Babr.

κατα-σκέπτομαι, a late form, = κατασκοπέω, q. v.

κατα-σκευάζω, f. -σκευάσω: —to equip or furnish fully, Dem.; so in Med., Xen. : —Pass., σκηνὴ χρυσῷ κατεσκευασμένη Hdt., etc. 2. to get ready, make, build, Id., Plat., etc. : — hence, to prepare, arrange, δημοκρατίαν Xen.; συμπόσιον Plat., etc.: —Med. to prepare for oneself, esp. to build a house and furnish it, Thuc.: to pack up, also opp. to ἀνα-σκευάζεσθαι, Xen. 3. of fraudulent transactions, to get up, trump up, Id., etc.; of persons, to suborn, Arist. 4. to make so and so, with a second acc., εἰ μὴ Γοργίαν Νέστορά τινα κατασκευάζεις unless you make Gorgias a kind of Nestor, Plat.: also, to represent as so and so, κ. τινὰ πάροινον, Dem. 5. in Logic, to construct an argument, Arist. 6. absol. in Med. to make ready for doing, ὡς πολεμήσοντες Thuc.; ὡς οἰκήσων Xen. Hence

κατασκεύασμα, ατος, τό, that which is prepared or made, a building, structure, edifice, Dem. II. an arrangement, contrivance, device, Id.; and

κατασκευασμός, ὁ, contrivance, Dem.; and

κατασκευαστέον, one must prepare or make, Xen.

κατα-σκευή, ἡ, preparation, ἐν κατασκευῇ τοῦ πολέμου in preparing for it, Thuc.; the equipment of ships, engines, etc., Id. II. any kind of furniture that is fixed, opp. to what is movable (παρασκευή),

buildings, fixtures, Id.; but also, like παρασκευή, any furniture, Hdt., Thuc. III. the state, condition, constitution of a thing, Eur., Plat. IV. a device, trick, Aeschin.

κατ-ασκέω, f. ήσω, to practise much : part. pf. pass. κατησκημένος, regular, ascetic, Plut.

κατα-σκηνάω, f. ήσω, = κατασκηνόω, Xen.

κατα-σκηνόω, f. ώσω, to pitch one's camp or tent, take up one's quarters, encamp, Xen.; generally, to rest, lodge, settle. Hence

κατασκήνωμα, ατος, τό, a covering, veil, Aesch.; and

κατασκήνωσις, εως, ἡ, an encamping : —of birds, a resting-place, nest, N. T.

κατα-σκήπτω, f. ψω, to rush down or fall upon, c. dat., of lightning and storms, Hdt.; of divine wrath, Id.; of the plague, Thuc. : —rarely, κατασκήψαί τινα to fall on one, Eur. II. κ. λιταῖς to storm or importune with prayers, Soph.

κατα-σκιάζω, f. -σκιάσω, contr. -σκιῶ, to overshadow, cover over, Hes.; κ. κόνει to bury one, Soph.

κατα-σκιάω, poët. for κατασκιάζω, impf. κατ-εσκίαον, Od.

κατά-σκιος, ον, (σκιά) shaded or covered with something, Hes., Hdt., Aesch. II. trans. overshadowing, Aesch., Eur., Ar.

κατα-σκοπέω, f. -σκέψομαι: aor. 1 -εσκεψάμην : — to view closely, spy out, Eur.: to reconnoitre, Xen. :— also in Med., Id. Hence

κατασκοπή, ἡ, a viewing closely, spying, Soph., Eur.; ἐπὶ κατασκοπῇ, κατασκοπῆς ἕνεκα Xen.

κατά-σκοπος, ὁ, one who keeps a look out, a scout, spy, Hdt., Eur.: —in Thuc., a person sent to examine and report, an inspector.

κατα-σκώπτω, f. -σκώψομαι, to make jokes upon, to jeer or mock, Hdt.

κατα-σμῑκρίζω, f. σω, to disparage, depreciate, Arist.

κατα-σμύχω [ῡ], f. ξω, to burn with a slow fire, burn up, Il.; metaph. of love, Theocr.; in Pass., of a lover, to smoulder away, Id.

κατα-σοφίζομαι, f. -ίσομαι, Dep. to conquer by sophisms or fallacies, to outwit, Luc. : —also as Pass. to be outwitted, Id.

κατ-ασπάζομαι, f. άσομαι, Dep. to embrace, Plut.

κατα-σπαράσσω, Att. -ττω, f. ξω, to tear down, pull to pieces, Ar.

κατα-σπᾰτᾰλάω, to live wantonly, to wanton, Anth.

κατα-σπάω, f. άσω [ᾰ], to draw or pull down, κ. τὰς νῆας to haul ships down to the sea, Hdt.; κ. σημεῖα to pull the flags down (in token of defeat), Thuc.; κ. τινὰ ἀπὸ τοῦ ἵππου Xen. II. to quaff or swallow down, Lat. deglutire, Ar.

κατα-σπείρω, f. -σπερῶ, to sow thickly : metaph., ἀνίας κ. to sow a crop of sorrows, Soph. 2. to beget, τέκνα Eur. II. to scatter over, as in sowing, c. gen., Plut. III. to besprinkle, Anth.

κατάσπεισις, εως, ἡ, self-devotion, Plut. From

κατα-σπένδω, f. -σπείσω, to pour as a drink-offering, Lat. libare, Eur., Ar. : —absol. to pour drink-offerings, Hdt. II. c. acc., κ. τινὰ δακρύοις to honour with offerings of tears, Eur.; κ. τινὰ to lament with tears, Anth. III. to consecrate, Plut., Anth.

κατα-σπέρχω, f. ξω, to urge on, Ar.; —absol., κατασπέρχον urgent, pressing, causing anxiety, Thuc.

κατα-σπεύδω, f. σω, to press, urge, or hasten on, Aeschin.

κατα-σποδέω, f. ήσω, to throw down in the dust: Pass., pf. part. κατεσποδημένοι Aesch.

κατα-σπουδάζομαι, Dep., with aor. 1 and pf. pass., to be very earnest or serious, Hdt.; οὐδαμῶς κατεσπουδασμένος ἀνήρ Id.

κατα-στάζω, f. ξω: I. of persons, 1. to let fall in drops upon, pour upon, shed over, τί τινος Eur. 2. c. dat. rei, to run down with a thing, νόσῳ κ. πόδα to have one's foot running with a sore, Soph.; κ. ἀφρῷ to run down with foam, Eur. II. of the liquid, 1. intr. to drop down, drip or trickle down, Eur., Xen. 2. trans. to drop down over, wet, ἱδρὼς καταστάζει δέμας Soph.

κατα-σταθείς, aor. 1 pass. part. of καθίστημι.

κατα-στασιάζω, f. άσω, to form a counter-party in the state, Plut. II. Pass. to be factiously opposed or overpowered, Xen., Dem.

κατά-στᾰσις, εως, ή, I. trans. a settling, appointing, appointment, institution, Aesch., Dem.; δαιμόνων κατ. their ordinance, Eur. 2. appointment of magistrates, Plat. 3. a bringing of ambassadors before the senate or assembly, an introduction, presentation, Hdt. 4. κ. ἐγγυητῶν a bringing one's bail forward, Dem. 5. a putting down, calming, Arist. II. intr. a standing firm, a settled condition, fixedness, Soph. 2. a state, condition, Hdt., Eur., etc. 3. a constitution, system, Hdt., Plat.

κατασ-τατέον, verb. Adj. of καθίστημι, one must appoint, Plat., Xen.

καταστάτης [ᾰ], ου, ὁ, (καθίστημι) an establisher, restorer, Soph.

καταστᾰτικός, ή, όν, (καθίστημι) fitted for calming: τὸ κ. a power to calm, of music, Plut.

κατα-στεγάζω, f. σω, to cover over, Hdt., Plat. Hence

κατα-στέγασμα, ατος, τό, a covering, Hdt.

κατά-στεγος, ον, (στέγη) covered in, roofed, Hdt., Plat.

κατα-στείβω, f. ψω, to tread down, κ. πέδον to tread the ground, Soph.

κατα-στείχω, f. ξω, = κατέρχομαι, Anth.

κατα-στέλλω, f. -στελῶ, to put in order, arrange, Eur. II. to keep down, repress, check, Eur., N. T.

κατα-στένω, to sigh over or lament, τινά Soph., Eur.; ὑπέρ τινος Eur.

κατα-στεφᾰνόω, f. ώσω, to crown, Anth.

καταστεφής, ές, crowned, Soph.; of suppliant branches, wreathed with wool, Eur. From

κατα-στέφω, f. ψω, to deck with garlands, crown, wreath, Eur.; κ. νεκρόν (with libations), Id.; κ. τινά to supplicate him, Id.:—Pass., pf. inf., κατεστέφθαι Aeschin.

κατάστημα, ατος, τό, (καθίσταμαι) a condition or state of health, Plut. Hence

καταστηματικός, ή, όν, established: sedate, Plut.

κατα-στίζω, f. ξω, to cover with punctures. Hence

κατάστικτος, ον, spotted, speckled, brindled, Eur.

κατα-στιλβόομαι, Pass. to be brilliant, Greg.

κατα-στίλβω, f. ψω, to send beaming forth, σέλας h. Hom. II. intr. to beam brightly, Anth.

κατα-στονάχέω, f. ήσω, to bewail, Anth.

καταστορέννῦμι; part. fem. καστορνῦσα (as if from καταστόρνυμι): f. -στορέσω:—to over-spread or cover

with a thing, τί τινι Il. II. to spread upon, Od. III. to throw down, lay low, Hdt.; καταστ. κύματα, Lat. sternere aequor, Anth.

κατ-αστράπτω, f. ψω, to hurl down lightning, κατὰ τόπον upon a place, Soph.; absol., καταστράπτει it lightens, Plut. II. trans. to strike with lightning, dazzle, τὰς ὄψεις Id.

κατα-στρᾰτοπεδεύω, f. σω, to put into cantonments, encamp, Xen.: to station a fleet, Id. II. Med. to take up quarters, encamp, Id.

κατα-στρέφω, f. ψω, to turn down, trample on, h. Hom.: to turn the soil, Xen. II. to upset, overturn, Ar. 2. Med. to subject to oneself, to subdue, Hdt., Thuc., etc.; κατεστρέψατο ἐς φόρου ἀπαγωγὴν subdued and made them tributary, Hdt.; so, Ἰωνίην κατεστρέψατο δασμοφόρον εἶναι Id. 3. Pass., in aor. 1 and pf., to be subdued, Id.; ἀκούειν σοῦ κατέστραμμαι am constrained to hear, Aesch.:—but the pf. pass. is also used in sense of Med., Hdt., Dem. III. to turn back, bring back, κατέστρεψε λόγους εἰς φιλανθρωπίαν Aeschin. IV. to turn round, bring to an end, Aesch.:—absol. to come to an end, die, Plut. V. to twist up: metaph., λέξις κατεστραμμένη a close periodic style, opp. to a loose running style (εἰρομένη) Arist.

κατα-στρηνιάω, to behave wantonly towards, τινός N. T.

καταστροφή, ή, (καταστρέφω) an overturning, Aesch. 2. a subduing, subjugation, reduction, Hdt., Thuc. II. a sudden turn or end, a close, conclusion, Aesch.; of death, Soph., Thuc.: in drama, the catastrophé, Luc.

κατάστρωμα, ατος, τό, that which is spread over: in a ship, the deck, Hdt., Thuc.; οἱ ἀπὸ τῶν καταστρωμάτων the marines, opp. to the rowers, Thuc. From

κατα-στρώννῦμι and -ύω: f. -στρώσω: aor. 1 pass. -εστρώθην:—to lay low, Eur., Xen.:—Pass., κατέστρωντο οἱ βάρβαροι Hdt.

κατα-στὔγέω, f. ήσω, aor. 2 κατέστυγον:—to shudder at, abhor, abominate, Hom.

κατα-στὔφελος [ῠ], ον, very hard or rugged, Hes.

καταστύφω [ῠ], to make sour: Pass., pf. part., τὸ κατεστυμμένον sourness, harshness, Plut.

κατα-στωμύλλομαι, Dep. to chatter: pf. part. κατεστωμυλμένος a chattering fellow, Ar.

κατα-σύρω [ῠ], f. -σύρω, aor. 1 -έσυρα:—to pull down, lay waste, ravage, Hdt. 2. to drag away, N. T.

κατα-σφάζω, later -σφάττω: f. ξω:—to slaughter, murder, Hdt.: Pass., aor. 2 κατεσφάγην [ᾰ], Trag.

κατα-σχεθεῖν, inf. of κατέσχεθον, poët. aor. 2 of κατέχω:—to hold back, Od., Soph.; κάσχεθε (Ep. for κατέσχεθε), Il. II. intr., Θορικόνδε κατέσχεθον they held on their way to Thoricum, h. Hom.

κατάσχετος, ον, poët. for κάτοχος, held back, Soph.

κατα-σχηματίζω, f. Att. ιῶ, to dress up or invest with a certain form or appearance, Isocr., Plut.:—Med. or Pass. to conform oneself, Plut.

κατα-σχίζω, f. -σχίσω, to cleave asunder, split up, Ar.; Med., κατεσχίσω τὸ ῥάκος Id.; κατασχ. τὰς πύλας to burst them open, Xen.

κατα-σχολάζω, f. σω, to pass the time in idleness, χρόνῳ τι κ. to tarry somewhat too long, Soph.

κατασχόμενος, part. aor. 2 med., in pass. sense, v. κατέχω C. II.

κατασχῶμεν, pl. aor. 2 subj. of κατέχω.

κατα-σώχω, to rub in pieces, grind down, Hdt.

κατατάκω [ᾱ], Dor. for κατατήκω.

κατατάμνω, Ion. and Dor. for κατατέμνω.

κατατάνύω [ῠ], =κατατείνω, h. Hom.

κατα-τάσσω, Att. -ττω, f. ξω, to draw up in order, arrange, τὴν στρατιάν Xen. **2.** to appoint, ἐπί τι to do a thing, Dem. **II.** κατατάξασθαί τινι to make arrangements with one, Id.

κατα-τεθνεώς, Ep. -ηώς, pf. part. of καταθνήσκω.

κατατέθνηκα, pf. of καταθνήσκω.

κατα-τείνω: f. -τενῶ: aor. 1 -έτεινα: pf. -τέτᾰκα:— to stretch or draw tight, Il., Hdt.; κ. τὰ ὅπλα to draw the cables taut, Dem., etc. **2.** to stretch so as to torture, Dem., etc. **3.** to stretch or draw in a straight line, Hdt. **4.** to hold tight down, Plut. **II.** intr. to stretch oneself: hence, **1.** to extend or run straight towards, Lat. tendere, Hdt., Xen. : absol. to extend, Hdt. **2.** to strive against, strive earnestly, be vehement, Eur., Xen.: aor. 1 part., with all one's might, λέγω κατατείνας Plat.

κατα-τέμνω: f. -τεμῶ: aor. 2 κατέτᾰμον:—to cut in pieces, cut up, Hdt., Ar., etc.: so in Med., Eur.:— Pass., τελαμῶσι κατατετμημένοις with regularly cut bandages, Hdt.; σπλάγχνα κατατετμημένα Ar. **2.** κ. χώρην ἐς διώρυχας to cut it up into ditches or canals, Hdt.; κατετέτμηντο τάφροι ἐπὶ τὴν χώραν Xen. **3.** c. dupl. acc., κ. τινὰ καττύματα to cut him into strips, Ar. :—Pass., κατατμηθείην λέπαδνα may I be cut up into straps, Id. **4.** κ. τὸν Πειραιᾶ to lay it out for building, Arist.:—Pass., ἡ πόλις κατατέτμηται τὰς ὁδοὺς ἰθείας has its streets cut straight, Hdt. **5.** to cut into the ground, κατετέτμηντο τάφροι there were trenches cut, Xen.

κατα-τήκω, Dor. -τάκω [ᾱ], f. -τήξω, trans. to melt away, to make to fall away, Hdt. **II.** Pass., with pf. act. κατατέτηκα, to melt or be melting away, Od., Hdt., Att.

κατα-τίθημι, f. -θήσω: aor. 2 κατ-έθην: Ep. forms, pl. κάτ-θεμεν, κάτ-θετε, κάτ-θεσαν, inf. κατ-θέμεν, 1 pl. subj. κατα-θείομεν (for κατα-θῶμεν):—Med. κατ-θέμεθα, κατ-θέσθην, part. καταθείομαι, subj. for καταθῶμαι, part. κατ-θέμενος:—to place, put, or lay down, Hom. **2.** to propose as a prize, Id.; κ. ἄεθλον to propose a contest, Od.; κ. τι ἐς μέσον to put it down in the midst, i. e. for common use, Eur.; but, ἐς μέσον Πέρσῃσι κ. τὰ πρήγματα to communicate power to them, give them a common share of it, Hdt. **3.** to put down as payment, pay down, Id., Ar., etc.:— to redeem a promise, ἃ δ᾽ ὑπέσχεο ποῖ καταθήσεις; Soph. **4.** to lay up, lay by, Theogn., Hdt.; so in Med., v. infr. II. 4. **II.** Med. to lay down from oneself, put off, lay aside, Lat. deponere, of arms or clothes, Hom., etc. **2.** metaph. to put an end to, arrange, settle, τὸν πόλεμον Thuc. **b.** to put aside, treat negligently, Xen. **3.** to lay down in a place, Hes., etc.: of the dead, to bury, Od. **4.** to deposit for oneself, lay up in store (v. supr. I. 4), Ib., etc.: —metaph., κατατίθεσθαι κλέος to lay up store of glory, Hdt.; χάριτα or χάριν κατατίθεσθαί τινι or πρός τινα

to lay up a store of gratitude or favour, Lat. collocare gratiam apud aliquem, Id., etc.; so, εὐεργεσίαν κ. Thuc., etc. **5.** to deposit in a place of safety, Id., Xen. **6.** to lay up in memory or as a memorial, Theogn., Plat.

κατα-τῑλάω, f. ήσω, to make dirt over, c. gen., Ar.

κατα-τιτρώσκω, f. -τρώσω, to wound severely, Xen.

κατα-τοκίζω, to beggar by usurious interest:—Pass. to be thus beggared, Arist.

κατατομή, ἡ, (κατατέμνω) abscission, concision, as opp. to true circumcision, N. T.

κατα-τοξεύω, f. σω, to strike down with arrows, shoot dead, Hdt., Thuc., etc.

κατατρᾰγεῖν, aor. 2 inf. of κατατρώγω.

κατα-τραυματίζω, Ion. -τρωματίζω, f. Att. ιῶ, to cover with wounds, Hdt., Thuc.:—of ships, to disable utterly, cripple, Thuc.

κατα-τρέχω: f. -δρᾰμοῦμαι: aor. 2 κατ-έδρᾰμον:—to run down, Hdt., Xen. **2.** of seamen, to run to land, to disembark in haste, Xen.:—metaph., κ. ἄστυ to come to a haven in.., Pind. **II.** trans. to overrun, ravage, χώραν Thuc.

κατα-τρίβω [ῑ], f. ψω: pf. -τέτρῑφα:—to rub down or away; hence, **1.** of clothes, to wear out, Theogn., Plat. **2.** of persons, to wear out, exhaust, Thuc.: —Pass. to be quite worn out, Ar., Xen. **3.** of Time, to wear it away, get rid of it, Lat. diem terere, Dem., Aeschin.: κ. τὸν βίον to employ it fully, Xen.; so in pf. pass. to pass one's whole time, κατατέτριμμαι στρατευόμενος Id. **4.** of property, to squander, Id.

κατα-τρίζω, to squeak or scream loudly, Batr.

κατα-τρύζω, to chatter against, τινὸς Anth.

κατα-τρύχω [ῠ], f. ξω, to wear out, exhaust, Hom., Theocr.:—Pass., κατατρυχόμενοι Eur.

κατατρύω, =foreg.: Pass., pf. inf. κατατετρῦσθαι, Xen.

κατα-τρώγω, f. -τρώξομαι, aor. 2 κατ-έτρᾰγον, to gnaw in pieces, eat up, Ar.; c. gen., Plut.

κατατρωματίζω, Ion. for κατατραυμ-.

κατα-τυγχάνω, f. -τεύξομαι, to hit one's mark, to be successful, Dem.

κατ-αυγάζω, f. σω, to shine upon: Med. to gaze at, see, Anth. Hence

καταυγασμός, ὁ, a shining brightly, Plut.

κατ-αυδάω, f. ήσω, to speak out, speak plainly, Soph.

κατ-αυλέω, f. ήσω, to play upon the flute to, τινός Plat.:—Pass., of persons, to have it played to one, Id.:—Pass. to resound with flute-playing, Plut. **II.** c. acc. pers. to overpower by flute-playing:—generally, to overpower, strike dumb, Eur.

κατ-αυλίζομαι: aor. 1 κατηυλίσθην, later κατηυλισάμην: Dep.:—to be under shelter of a hall, house, tent, Soph., Eur.

κατ-αυχέω, f. ήσω, to exult in a thing, c. dat., Aesch.

κατα-φᾰγεῖν, serving as aor. 2 to κατ-εσθίω, to devour, eat up, Il., Hdt. **2.** to spend in eating, waste, devour, Od., Aeschin.

κατα-φαίνω, f. -φᾰνῶ, to declare, make known, Pind. **II.** Pass., f. -φᾰνήσομαι, aor. 2 κατ-εφάνην [ᾰ], to become visible, appear, h. Hom., Hdt. **2.** to be quite clear or plain, Hdt., Plat.; κατεφάνη τῷ Δαρείῳ τεχνάζειν it was apparent to Darius that he was playing tricks, Hdt. Hence

καταφᾰνής, ές, clearly seen, in sight, Xen. ; ἐν καταφανεῖ in an open place, Id. 2. manifest, evident, καταφανὲς ποιεῖν or ποιεῖσθαί τι Hdt., Xen. ; καταφανέστερος εἶναι κακουργῶν Thuc :—Adv. -νῶς, evidently, plainly, Ar. ; καταφανέστερον ἢ ὥστε λανθάνειν too manifestly to escape detection, Thuc.

κατάφαρκτος, ον, = κατάφρακτος.

κατα-φαρμᾰκεύω, f. σω, to anoint with drugs or charms, to enchant, bewitch, Plat.

κατα-φαρμάσσω, f. ξω, to bewitch with drugs, Hdt.

κατα-φᾰτίζω, f. σω, to protest, promise, Plut.

κατα-φαυλίζω, f. σω, to depreciate, Plut.

κατα-φερής, ές, (φέρομαι) going down, εὖτε ἂν κ. γίνηται ὁ ἥλιος when the sun is near setting, Hdt. ; of ground, sloping downwards, Lat. declivis, Xen. II. inclined, Lat. proclivis, pronus, πρὸς οἶνον Plut.

κατα-φέρω, f. κατ-οίσω, Ep. -οίσομαι :—to bring down, ἄχος με κατοίσεται Ἄϊδος εἴσω grief will bring me down to the grave, Il. ; καταφέρω ποδὸς ἀκμάν I bring down my foot, Aesch. :—Pass. to be brought down by a river, of gold dust, Hdt. 2. of a storm, to drive ships to land, Thuc. 3. to pay down, Plut. 4. Pass. to be weighed down by sleep, N.T. II. to carry home, Ar. :—Pass. to return, Id.

κατα-φεύγω, f. -φεύξομαι, to flee for refuge, Hdt. ; c. acc., κ. βωμόν to flee for refuge to the altar, Eur. ; κ. ἐν τόπῳ to flee and take refuge in a place, Xen. ; to flee for protection, ὃς ἂν καταφυγῇ ἐς τούτους Hdt. ; so, κ. ἐπί τινα, πρός τινα Dem. 2. ἐκ τῆς μάχης κ. to escape from . . , Hdt. 3. to have recourse to, εἰς τοὺς λόγους Plat. ; ἐπὶ τὸν δικαστήν Arist. 4. εἰς τὴν τοῦ βίου μετριότητα to fall back upon, appeal to, Dem. Hence

καταφευκτέον, verb. Adj. one must have recourse to, Luc. ; and

κατάφευξις, εως, ἡ, flight for refuge, Thuc. II. a place of refuge, Id.

κατά-φημι, to say yes, assent, Soph.

κατα-φημίζω, f. σω: aor. 1 -εφήμισα, Dor. -εφάμιξα : —to spread a report abroad, announce, Pind.

κατα-φθᾰτέομαι, (φθάνω ?) to take first possession of, γῆν καταφθατουμένη Aesch.

κατα-φθείρω, f. -φθερῶ, to destroy or spoil utterly, bring to naught, Aesch., Soph., etc.

κατα-φθῐνύθω [ῠ], = καταφθίω, h. Hom.

κατα-φθίνω [ῐ], to waste away, decay, perish, Hdt., Trag. ; κ. νόσῳ, γήρᾳ Soph., Eur.

κατα-φθίω, I. Causal in fut. κατα-φθίσω [ῑ], aor. 1 κατ-έφθῑσα, to ruin, destroy, Od., Aesch. II. Pass., Ep. aor. 2 κατ-εφθίμην [ῐ], inf. καταφθίσθαι ; poët. κατ-έφθῐμενος :—to be ruined, to waste away, perish, ἥϊα πάντα κατέφθιτο the provisions were all consumed, Od. ; ὡς καὶ σὺ καταφθίσθαι ὤφελες oh that thou hadst perished, Ib. ; σεῖο καταφθιμένοιο if thou wert dead, Il. ; ἐκεῖ κατέφθιτο there he died, Aesch. ; φέγγος ἡλίου κατέφθιτο the sun's light was gone, Id.

καταφθορά, ἡ, (καταφθείρω) destruction, death, Eur. 2. metaph. confusion, φρενῶν Aesch.

κατ-αφίημι, to let slip down, κατηφίει (impf.) Plat.

κατα-φῐλέω, f ήσω, to kiss tenderly, to caress, Xen.

κατα-φλέγω, f. ξω, to burn down, burn up, consume, πυρί Il., Hes., etc. :—Pass. to be burnt down, Thuc.

κατα-φοβέω, f. ήσω, to strike with fear, Thuc. :— Pass., c. fut. med. to be greatly afraid of, τι Ar. ; absol., καταφοβηθείς Thuc.

κατα-φοιτάω, Ion. -έω, f. ήσω, to come down constantly or regularly, as wild beasts from the mountains to prey, Hdt.

κατα-φονεύω, f. σω, to slaughter, Hdt., Eur., etc.

κατα-φορέω, f. ήσω, Frequent. of καταφέρω, of a river, to carry down gold dust, Hdt. 2. to pour like a stream over, τί τινος Plat.

κατα-φράζω, f. σω, to declare, Pind. :—Med., with aor. 1 pass. and med., to consider, think upon, ponder, Hes. ; καταφρασθείς observed, Hdt.

κατάφρακτος, old Att. -φαρκτος, ον, shut up, confined, Soph. ; πλοῖα κ. decked vessels, Thuc. From

κατα-φράσσω, Att. -ττω, f. ξω, to cover with mail ; ἵπποι καταπεφραγμένοι Plut.

κατα-φρονέω, f. ήσω, to think down upon, i. e. to look down upon, think slightly of, τινός Hdt., Eur., etc. 2. c. acc. to regard slightly, despise, Hdt., Att. :—Pass. to be thought little of, despised, Xen., etc. 3. absol. to be disdainful, deal contemptuously, Thuc. 4. c. inf. to think contemptuously that, to presume, καταφρονήσαντες κρέσσονες εἶναι Hdt. ; καταφρονοῦντες κἂν προαισθέσθαι Thuc. II. c. acc. rei, only in Ion. writers (cf. κατανοέω), to fix one's thoughts upon, aim at, Lat. affectare, τὴν τυραννίδα Hdt. : also to observe with contempt, τι Id. Hence

καταφρόνημα, ατος, τό, contempt of others, μὴ φρόνημα μόνον, ἀλλὰ καταφρ. not only spirit, but a spirit of disdain ; and

καταφρόνησις, εως, ἡ, contempt, disdain, Thuc., Plat. 2. without any bad sense, opp. to αὔχημα, Thuc. ; and

καταφρονητής, οῦ, ὁ, a despiser, Plut. ; and

καταφρονητικός, ή, όν, contemptuous, Arist. Adv. -κῶς, Xen.

κατα-φροντίζω, Att. f. ιῶ, τὸ ἱμάτιον οὐκ ἀπολώλεκ', ἀλλὰ καταπεφρόντικα I have not lost it, but I've thought it away, lost it in the schools, Ar.

κατα-φρύγω [ῠ], f. ξω, to burn to ashes, Ar.

καταφυγγάνω, = καταφεύγω, Hdt., Aeschin.

καταφυγεῖν, aor. 2 inf. of καταφεύγω. Hence

καταφῠγή, ἡ, a refuge, place of refuge, Hdt., Eur. : c. gen., κ. κακῶν refuge from evils, Eur., Thuc. II. a way of escape, excuse, Dem.

κατα-φῦλᾰδόν, (φῦλον) Adv. in tribes, by clans, Il.

κατα-φυλλοροέω, f. ήσω, to shed the leaves : metaph. to lose its splendour, Pind.

κατα-φῠτεύω, f. σω, to plant, Plut., Luc.

κατα-φύομαι, Pass., with aor. 2 act. κατ-έφυν, pf. -πέφυκα, to be produced, Plut.

κατάφῠτος, ον, all planted with a thing, c. dat., Luc.

κατα-φωράω, f. άσω [ᾱ], to catch in a theft : to catch in the act, detect, discover, Thuc., Xen.

κατάφωρος, ον, detected : manifest, Plut.

κατα-φωτίζω, f. σω, to illuminate, light up, Anth.

κατα-χαίρω, to exult over, c. dat., Hdt. ; absol., καταχαίρων with malignant joy, Id.

κατα-χᾰλαζάω, f. ήσω, to shower down like hail upon, τί τινος Luc.

κατά-χαλκος, ον, overlaid with brass or copper, Eur. :

κατ. πεδίον ἀστράπτει the plain flashes *with gleaming arms*, Id. ; δράκων κ. a serpent *lapt in mail*, i. e. scales, Id.

κατα-χαλκόω, f. ώσω, *to cover with brass*, Hdt.

κατα-χαρίζομαι, f. Att. ιοῦμαι, Dep. *to do* or *give up* a thing *out of courtesy*, Aeschin. ; κ. τὰ δίκαια *to give* judgment *by private interest*, Plat. 2. *to shew favour* to a person, c. dat., Dem.

κατάχαρμα, ατος, τό, (καταχαίρω) *a mockery*, Theogn.

κατα-χέζω, aor. 1 κατ-έχεσα :—*to befoul*, τινός Ar.

κατα-χειροτονέω, f. ήσω, *to vote against, to vote in condemnation of*, τινός Dem. ; c. inf., ἀδικεῖν Εὐάνδρου κατεχειροτόνησεν ὁ δῆμος Id. :—Pass., καταχειροτονηθὲν αὐτοῦ καὶ ταῦτα ἀσεβεῖν *a vote of condemnation having been passed against* him, and that for sacrilege, Id.

καταχειροτονία, ἡ, *a vote of condemnation*, Dem.

καταχεῦαι, Ep. for -χέαι, aor. 1 inf. of καταχέω.

κατα-χεύω, Ep. for sq. : Ep. impf. med., τέττιξ καταχεύετ᾽ ἀοιδήν Hes.

κατα-χέω, f. -χεῶ : aor. 1 κατέχεα, Ep. κατέχευα : Pass., 3 sing. and pl. Ep. aor. 2 κατέχῦτο, κατέχυντο : —*to pour down upon, pour over*, τί τινι Hom. ; also, κατ. τί τινος Hdt., Att. :—κατὰ ταῖν κόραιν ὕπνου τι καταχεῖται a bit of sleep *is poured over* the eyes, Ar. 2. *to pour* or *shower down*, Hom. : *to throw* or *cast down*, Id. ; πέπλον κατέχευεν ἐπ᾽ οὔδει *let the* robe *fall upon* the pavement, Il. 3. Pass. *to be poured over* the ground, *lie in heaps*, ὁ χῶρος, ἐν ᾧ αἱ ἄκανθαι [τῶν ὀφίων] κατακεχύαται (Ion. 3 pl. pf. pass.), Hdt. II. *to melt down*, χρυσὸν ἐς πίθους Id. ; and in Med., χρυσὸν καταχέασθαι *to have it melted down*, Id.

κατα-χήνη, ἡ, (χανεῖν) *derision, mockery*, Ar.

κατα-χηρεύω, f. σω, *to pass in widowhood*, Dem.

κατ-αχής, ές, Dor. for κατ-ηχής, *sounding*, Theocr.

κατα-χθόνιος, ον, *subterranean*, Ζεὺς καταχθόνιος, i. e. Pluto, Il. ; δαίμονες κ. *Dii Manes*, Anth.

κατα-χορδεύω, f. σω, *to mince up as for a sausage*, Hdt.

κατα-χορηγέω, f. ήσω, *to lavish as* χορηγός : generally, *to spend lavishly, squander*, Plut.

κατα-χραίνομαι, Dep. *to besprinkle*, Anth.

κατα-χράομαι, f. -χρήσομαι : pf. -κέχρημαι both in act. and pass. senses : aor. 1 -εχρήσθην : Dep. :—*to make full use of, apply*, c. dat., Plat., Dem. 2. *to use to the uttermost, use up*, c. acc., Dem. 3. *to misuse, abuse*, c. dat., Plat. 4. of persons, *to make away with, destroy, kill*, c. acc., Hdt. ;—so aor. 1 καταχρησθῆναι, in pass. sense, Id. II. *to pretend, allege*, Dem.

B. Act. **καταχράω** only in Ion. writers in 3 sing., ἀντὶ λόφου ἡ λοφιὴ κατέχρα the mane *sufficed* them for a crest, Hdt. :—impers., οὐδέ οἱ καταχρήσει ὑμέων ἀπέχεσθαι nor *will it suffice* him to keep his hands off you, Id.

κατα-χρειόομαι, (χρέος) Pass. *to be ill-treated*, pf. part. κατηχρειωμένη Anth.

κατα-χρέμπτομαι, Dep. *to spit upon*, τινος Ar.

κατά-χρῡσος, ον, *overlaid with gold-leaf, gilded*, Luc.

κατα-χρῡσόω, f. ώσω, *to cover with gold-leaf, gild*, Hdt. II. *to make golden* (i. e. *splendid*), Plut.

κατα-χρώζω or **-χρώννῡμι**, f. -χρώσω, *to colour* :— Pass. *to be stained*, Eur.

κατάχυσμα, ατος, τό, *that which is poured over, sauce*, Ar. 2. in pl. *handfuls* of nuts, figs, etc.; Lat. *bellaria*, which used to be *showered over* a bride or a new slave on entering the house (cf. Virg. *sparge, marite, nuces*), Ar., Dem.

κατα-χωνεύω, f. σω, *to melt down*, Dem.

κατα-χώννῡμι, f. -χώσω, *to cover with a heap*, ὁ νότος κατέχωσέ σφεας the South wind *buried* them in sand, Hdt. ; κ. τινὰ λίθοις Id.

κατα-χωρίζω, f. Att. ιῶ, *to set in a place, place in position*, Xen. :—Pass. *to take up a position*, Id.

καταχῶσαι, aor. 1 inf. of καταχώννυμι.

κατα-ψακάζω, Att. for κατα-ψεκάζω.

κατα-ψάλλομαι, Pass. *to resound with music*, Plut.

κατα-ψάω, f. ήσω, *to stroke with the hand, to stroke, caress*, καταψῶσα αὐτοῦ τὴν κεφαλήν Hdt. ; καταψῶν αὐτὸν [τὸν κάνθαρον], ὥσπερ πωλίον Ar.

κατα-ψεκάζω, Att. ψακάζω, f. σω, *to wet by continual dropping*, Aesch., Plut.

κατα-ψεύδομαι, Dep., with f. med. -ψεύσομαι, pf. pass. -έψευσμαι, aor. 1 -εψεύσθην :—*to tell lies against, speak falsely of*, τινος Ar., Plat., etc. 2. *to allege falsely against*, τί τινος Plat., Dem. 3. *to say falsely, pretend*, Eur.: *to feign, invent*, τι Dem. II. also as Pass. *to be falsely reported* : of writings, *to be spurious*, Plut.

κατα-ψευδομαρτυρέω, f. ήσω, *to bear false witness against*, τινός Xen. ; so in Med., Dem. :—Pass. *to be borne down by false evidence*, Plat.

κατα-ψηφίζομαι, f. Att. ιοῦμαι, Med. *to vote against* or *in condemnation of*, τινος Plat., Xen. ; κ. τινος κλοπὴν *to find* him *guilty* of theft, Plat. ; so in pf. pass., κατεψηφισμένοι αὐτοῦ θάνατον Xen. 2. Pass., in pf. and aor. 1 pass., *to be condemned*, Plat., Dem. :—of the sentence, *to be pronounced against*, δίκη κατεψηφισμένη τινός Thuc. ; κατεψηφισμένος ἦν μου ὁ θάνατος Xen. II. *to vote in affirmation*, Arist. Hence

καταψηφιστέον, verb. Adj. *one must condemn*, Xen.

κατα-ψήχω, f. ξω, *to rub down, pound in a mortar* :—Pass. *to crumble away*, pf. κατέψηκται Soph. II. *to stroke down, caress*, Lat. *mulceo*, ἵππους Eur.

κατα-ψύχω [ῠ], f. ξω, *to cool, chill*, Arist. :—Pass., pf. κατέψυγμαι, aor. 1 κατεψύχθην and 2 κατεψύγην [ῠ]: —*to be chilled, become cold*, of persons, Id., Plut. II. Pass., of a country, *to be dried* or *parched up*, Plut.

κατέᾱγα, intr. pf. of κατάγνυμι :—**κατεάγην** [ᾰ], aor. 2 pass., 3 pl. subj. κατεαγῶσιν :—**κατέαξα**, aor. 1 act.

κατέβᾱ, Dor. for -έβη, 3 sing. aor. 2 of καταβαίνω : —**κατέβᾱν**, Dor. 3 pl. for -έβησαν.

κατ-εβλάκευμένως, Adv. pf. pass. part. of κατα-βλακεύω, (βλάξ) *slothfully, tardily*, Ar., Anth.

κατ-εγγυάω, f. ήσω : aor. 1 κατηγγύησα :—*to pledge, betroth*, παῖδά τινι Eur. II. as Att. law-term, *to make responsible, to compel to give security*, Dem. : —Med. or Pass. *to give* or *find security*, Id. 2. *to seize as a security*, Id.

κατ-εγγύη, ἡ, *bail* or *security given*, Dem.

κατ-έδω, Ep. pres., = κατεσθίω, *to eat up, devour*, Il. ; metaph., οἶκον, κτῆσιν κατέδειν *to eat up* house,

goods, Od. ; ὃν θυμὸν κατέδων *eating* one's heart for grief, Il.

κατεηγώς, Ion. for κατεαγώς, intr. pf. part. of κατάγνυμι.

κατ-είβω, poët. for κατα-λείβω, *to let flow down, shed,* Od. :—Med. *to flow apace,* Hom. ; metaph., κατείβετο αἰών life *ebbed, passed away,* Od.

κατειδέναι, inf. of κάτοιδα.

κατ-εῖδον, inf. κατ-ιδεῖν, part. κατιδών, aor. 2 with no pres. in use, καθοράω being used instead :—*to look down,* Il., Hdt., etc. II. c. acc. *to look down upon,* Ar. : simply *to behold, regard, perceive,* Theogn., Aesch. ; κατιδεῖν βίον *to live,* Aesch.—Also in aor. 2 med. κατειδόμην, inf. κατιδέσθαι, Hdt., Soph.

κατ-είδωλος, ον, (εἴδωλον) *full of idols, given to idolatry,* N. T.

κατ-εικάζω, f. σω, *to liken* :—Pass., aor. 1 κατ-εικάσθην, *to be* or *become like,* Soph. II. *to guess, surmise,* Hdt. : *to suspect* evil, Id.

κατ-ειλέω, f. ήσω, *to force into a narrow space, to coop up,* ἐς τὸ τεῖχος, ἐς τὸ ἄστυ Hdt. :—Pass., κατειλήθη-σαν ἐς Διὸς ἱρόν Id. ; ἐν ὀλίγῳ χώρῳ πολλαὶ μυριάδες κατειλημέναι Id.

κατείλημμαι, -είληφα, pf. pass. and act. of καταλαμβάνω.

κατ-ειλίσσω, Ion. for καθ-ελίσσω.

κατειλίχατο, Ion. for καθειλιγμένοι ἦσαν, 3 pl. plqpf. of καθελίσσω.

κατ-ειλύω, f. ὕσω [ῡ], *to cover up,* Il. : Pass., ὅρος ψάμμῳ κατειλυμένον (pf. part.) Hdt.

κάτ-ειμι, Ep. aor. 1 καταείσατο: (εἶμι *ibo*) :—*to go* or *come down,* Hom., etc. :—esp. *to go down* to the grave, Il. ; of a ship, *to sail down* to land, Od. ; of a wind, *to come sweeping down,* Thuc. II. *to come back, return,* Od. ; of exiles, *to return home,* Hdt., Att.

κατεῖναι, Ion. for καθεῖναι, aor. 2 inf. of καθίημι.

κατ-είνυμι, Ion. for καθ-έννυμι.

κατ-εῖπον, inf. κατειπεῖν, used as aor. 2 to καταγορεύω, (κατερῶ being the fut.) : also in form κατεῖπα :—*to speak against* or *to the prejudice of, accuse, denounce,* τινος Hdt., Eur., etc. II. c. acc. *to speak out, tell plainly, declare, report,* Eur., Ar. 2. absol. *to tell,* Hdt., etc. ; κάτειπέ μοι tell me, Ar.

κατειργάθόμην, poët. aor. 2 med. of κατείργω.

κατ-είργνυμι, Ion. 3 pl. -ειρνῦσι, = sq., Hdt.

κατ-είργω, Ion. -έργω : f. -είρξω, Ion. -έρξω :—*to drive into, shut in,* Hdt. :—generally, *to press hard, reduce to straits,* Id. :—Pass. *to be hemmed in, kept down,* Thuc. ; τὸ κατειργόμενον what is done under necessity, Id. II. *to hinder, prevent,* Eur.

κατ-ειρύω, Ion. for κατερύω.

κατ-ειρωνεύομαι, Dep. *to use irony towards, to dissemble,* Plut.

κατ-εισάγω, f. ξω, *to betray to one's own loss,* Anth.

κατέκειρα, aor. 1 of κατακείρω.

κατέκηα, aor. 1 of κατακαίω.

κατεκλᾶσα, aor. 1 of κατακλάω :—**κατεκλάσθην,** aor. 1 pass.

κατέκλων, impf. of κατα-κλάω.

κατεκρίθην [ῐ], aor. 1 pass. of κατα-κρίνω.

κατέκτα, 3 sing. aor. 2 of κατα-κτείνω :—**κατ-έκταν,** 3 pl. :—**κατ-έκτάθεν,** Aeol. and Ep. 3 pl. aor. 1 pass.

κατέκτἄνον, aor. 2 of κατακτείνω.

κατέλἄβον, aor. 2 of καταλαμβάνω.

κατ-ελαύνω, *to draw down,* Plut.

κατ-ελέγχω, f. γξω, *to convict of falsehood, to belie,* Hes. II. *to disgrace,* Pind.

κατ-ελέω, f. ήσω, *to have compassion upon,* τινά Plat.

κατελεύσομαι, fut. of κατέρχομαι.

κατελήφθην, aor. 1 pass. of καταλαμβάνω.

κατελθεῖν, aor. 2 inf. of κατέρχομαι.

κατ-έλκω, Ion. for καθέλκω.

κατ-ελπίζω, f. σω, *to hope* or *expect confidently,* Hdt.

κατέμεν, Ion. 1 pl. aor. 2 of καθίημι.

κατ-εμπίπρημι, f. -εμπρήσω, *to burn up,* Eur.

κατ-εναίρομαι, aor. 1 -ενηράμην, Dep. *to kill, slay, murder,* Od. :—an aor. 2 act. κατήνἄρον occurs in Soph., Anth.

κατ-έναντι, Adv., = sq., c. gen., N. T.

κατ-εναντίον, Adv. *over against, opposite, before,* τινί Il., Hes. ; τινός Hdt., etc.

κατ-εναρίζω, f. σω, *to kill outright* : aor. 1 pass. κατηναρίσθην Aesch. ; pf. part. κατηναρισμένος Soph.

κατέναασσα, aor. 1 of καταναίω.

κατενεχθείς, aor. 1 pass. part. of καταφέρω.

κατ-ενήνοθε, v. ἐνήνοθε II.

κατενήρατο, 3 sing. aor. 1 of κατεναίρομαι.

κατενθῆν, Dor. for κατελθεῖν, aor. 2 inf. of κατέρχομαι.

κατενύγησαν [ῠ], 3 pl. aor. 2 pass. of κατανύσσω.

κατ-ένωπα or **-ενῶπα,** Adv. (ἐνωπή) *right over against, right opposite,* c. gen., Il.

κατ-ενώπιον, = foreg., N. T.

κατ-εξανίσταμαι, Pass. with aor. 2 act. κατ-εξανέστην :—*to rise up against, struggle against,* τινός Plut.

κατ-εξενωμένος, pf. pass. part. of κατα-ξενόω.

κατ-εξουσιάζω, f. σω, *to exercise lordship over,* τινός N. T.

κατ-επαγγέλλομαι, Med. with pf. pass. -επήγγελμαι, *to make promises* or *engagements,* τινι with one, Dem. ; πρός τινα Aeschin.

κατ-επάγω [ᾰ], f. ξω, *to bring* one thing *quickly upon* or *after* another, *to repeat quickly,* Ar.

κατ-επᾴδω, f. -άσομαι, *to subdue by charms,* τινά Plat.

κατ-επάλμενος, v. sub κατ-εφάλλομαι :—but for κατέπαλτο, v. sub καταπάλλω.

κατ-επείγω, f. ξω, *to press down, depress,* Il. 2. *to press much, press hard, drive on, urge on, impel,* Hdt., Thuc., etc. II. intr. *to hasten, make haste,* Xen.

κατέπεσον, aor. 2 of καταπίπτω.

κατεπέστην, aor. 2 of καθεφίστημι.

κατ-έπεφνον, aor. 2 with no pres. in use (v. *φένω), *to kill, slay,* Hom., Soph.

κατέπηκτο, 3 sing. plqpf. pass. of καταπήγνυμι.

κατ-έπηξα, aor. 1 of κατα-πήγνυμι.

κατ-επιορκέομαι, Med. *to effect by perjury,* Dem.

κατεπλάγην [ᾰ], Ep. -επλήγην, aor. 2 pass. of καταπλήσσω.

κατέπλευσα, aor. 1 of καταπλέω.

κατ-εργάζομαι, f. άσομαι, aor. 1 -ειργασάμην, and (in pass. sense) -εργάσθην : pf. -είργασμαι both in act. and pass. sense: Dep. :—*to effect by labour, to achieve, accomplish,* Hdt., Soph., etc.—so pf. κατείργασμαι, Xen. ; but in pass. sense, *to be effected* or *achieved,* Hdt., Eur. b. *to earn* or *gain by labour, to achieve, acquire,* τὴν ἡγεμονίην Hdt. ; σωτηρίαν Eur. ; in

pass. sense, ἀρετὴ ἀπὸ σοφίης κατεργασμένη Hdt. c. absol. *to be successful*, Id. 2. c. acc. pers., like Lat. *conficere, to make an end of, finish, kill*, Id., Soph., Eur. b. *to overpower, subdue, conquer*, Hdt., Ar., Thuc. :—pf. pass. *to be overcome*, Thuc.; κατείργασται πέδον *is subdued, brought under cultivation*, Aesch. c. *to prevail upon*, Hdt., Xen. : —aor. 1 pass., οὐκ ἐδύνατο κατεργασθῆναι *could not be prevailed upon*, Hdt. II. *to work up for use*, Lat. *concoquere*, κ. μέλι *to make* honey, Id.

κατέργνυμι, κατέργω, Ion. for κατείρ-.

κατ-ερεικτός, v. κατερικτός.

κατ-ερείκω, f. ξω, *to grind down* :—metaph., κ. θυμόν *to fritter* it *away, smooth* it *down*, Ar. :—Med. *to rend one's* garments, in token of sorrow, Hdt., Aesch.

κατ-ερείπω, f. ψω, *to throw* or *cast down*, Orac. ap. Hdt. :—Pass. *to fall in ruins*, of Troy, Eur. II. intr. in aor. 2 κατ-ήριπον, *to fall down, fall prostrate*, Il., Theocr. ; so in pf., τεῖχος κατ-ερήριπεν Il.

κατέρεξα, aor. 1 of καταρρέζω.

κατ-ερεύγω, aor. 2 -ήρῠγον, *to belch over*, τινός Ar.

κατ-ερέφω, f. ψω, *to cover over, roof*, Plut. :—Med. *to roof over for oneself* or *what is one's own*, Ar.

κατ-ερέω, Att. κατ-ερῶ, serving as fut. of the aor. 2 κατεῖπον : pf. κατείρηκα:—*to speak against, accuse*, τινός Xen., Plat. 2. c.acc. *to denounce*, Hdt. II. *to say* or *tell plainly, speak out*, Il., Eur., etc. :— Pass., κατειρήσεται *it shall be declared*, Hdt.

κατερήρῐπε, 3 sing. pf. intr. of κατερείπω.

κατ-ερητύω, f. ύσω [ῠ], *to hold back*, Hom., Soph.

κατ-ερικτός or -ερεικτός, όν, (κατ-ερείκω) *bruised, ground*, of pulse, Ar.

κατ-ερῠκάνω [ᾰ], = sq., Il.

κατ-ερύκω [ῠ], f. ξω, *to hold back, detain*, Hom., Theogn., Ar. :—Pass., κατερύκεται εὐρέϊ πόντῳ Od.

κατ-ερύω, Ion. -ειρύω, f. ύσω [ῠ], *to draw* or *haul down*, of ships, Lat. *deducere naves*, Od., Hdt. :—Pass., νῆῦς τε κατείρυσται Od. 2. κ. τόξα *to draw* a bow, Anth.

κατ-έρχομαι, κατελεύσομαι (but in good Att. κάτειμι): aor. 2 κατήλῠθον, κατῆλθον, inf. κατελθεῖν : Dep. :—*to go down from* a place, c. gen., Il. ; *to go down to the grave*, κ. Ἄϊδος εἴσω, Ἀϊδόσδε Ib. ;—also from high land to the coast, Od. 2. of things, κατερχομένης ὑπὸ πέτρης *by the descending* rock, Ib. ; of a river, κατέρχεται ὁ Νεῖλος πληθύων *comes down* in flood, Hdt. II. *to come back, return*, πόλινδε Od. : esp. *to come back from exile*, Hdt., Att. ; in pass. sense, ὑπό τινος κατελθεῖν *to be brought back* by him, Thuc.

κατ-ερῶ, v. κατ-ερέω.

κἀτέρωτα, Aeol. for καὶ ἑτέρωθε, Sappho.

κατέσβεσα, aor. 1 of κατασβέννυμι:—κατέσβηκα, intr.pf.

κατ-εσθίω, f. κατέδομαι : aor. 2 κατέφαγον (v. καταφαγεῖν) : pf. κατεδήδοκα, Ep. κατέδηδα : pf. pass. κατεδήδεσμαι:—*to eat up, devour*, of animals of prey, Hom. ; of men, *to eat up*, Od., Hdt. 2. *to eat up* or *devour* one's substance, Ar., Dem. 3. λίθοι κατεδηδεσμένοι ὑπὸ σηπεδόνος *corroded*, Plat.

κατ-εσθω, poët. for foreg., Anth.

κατεσκαμμένος, pf. pass. part. of κατασκάπτω.

κατεσκεύασμαι, pf. pass. of κατασκευάζω.

κατεσκεψάμην, aor. 1 med. of κατασκοπέω.

κατέσκληκα, pf. of κατασκέλλομαι.

κατέσσῠτο, 3 sing. Ep. aor. 2 of κατασεύομαι.

κατέστᾰθεν, Aeol. for -εστάθησαν 3 pl. aor. 1 pass. of καθίστημι.

κατέσταλμαι, pf. pass. of καταστέλλω.

κατεστεώς, Ion. for -εστηκώς, pf. part. of καθίστημι.

κατέστην, aor. 2 of -καθίστημι :—κατέστησα, aor. 1.

κατεστόρεσα, aor. 1 of καταστορέννυμι.

κατεστράφατο, Ion. 3 pl. plqpf. pass. of καταστρέφω.

κατέστῠγον, aor. 2 of καταστυγέω.

κατέσχεθον, poët. aor. 2 of κατέχω.

κατετάκετο, Dor. for -ετήκετο, 3 sing. impf. pass. of κατατήκω.

κάτευγμα, τό, always in pl. *vows*, Aesch. :—*votive offerings*, Soph. II. *imprecations, curses*, Aesch., Eur.

κατ-ευημερέω, f. ήσω, *to be quite successful, carry one's point*, Aeschin.

κατ-ευθύ, Adv. *straight forward*, Xen.

κατ-ευθύνω [ῠ], f. υνῶ, *to make* or *keep straight, to set right, guide aright*, Plat. II. intr. *to make straight towards* a point, Plat.

κατ-ευνάζω, f. άσω, *to put to bed, lull to sleep*, Soph. ; of death, Id. ; ἐκτὸς αὐτὸν τάξεων κατηύνασεν *assigned* him *quarters* outside the army, Eur. ; κ. τινὰ μόχθων *to give* one rest from . . , Anth. :—Pass. *to lie down to sleep*, Il. Hence

κατευναστής, οῦ, ὁ, *one who conducts to bed, a chamberlain*, Plut.

κατ-ευνάω, f. ήσω, *to put to sleep*, Il. : metaph. *to lull* pain *to sleep*, Soph. :—Pass. *to be asleep*, Od.

κατ-ευορκέω, f. ήσω, *to swear solemnly*, Gorg. ap. Arist.

κατ-ευστοχέω, f. ήσω, *to be quite successful*, Plut.

κατ-ευτρεπίζω, f. ίσω, *to put in order again*, Xen.

κατ-ευτυχέω, f. ήσω, *to be quite successful, prosper*, Plut.

κατ-ευφημέω, f. ήσω, *to applaud, extol*, Plut.

κατ-ευχή, ἡ, *a prayer, vow*, Aesch.

κατ-εύχομαι, f. -εύξομαι, Dep. *to pray earnestly*, Hdt., Trag. ; κ. τινι *to pray to* one, Aesch., Eur. 2. absol. *to make a prayer or vow*, Hdt., Aesch., etc. II. in bad sense. 1. c. gen. pers. *to pray against* one, *imprecate* curses on one, Lat. *imprecari*, Plat. ; also, κατ. τί τινι Aesch.; c. acc. et inf., Soph. 2. absol., Eur. III. *to boast that* . . , Theocr.

κατ-ευωχέομαι, Dep. *to feast and make merry*, Hdt.

κατ-εφάγον, v. καταφαγεῖν.

κατ-εφάλλομαι, Dep. *to spring down upon, rush upon*, κατεπάλμενος (aor. 2 part. syncop.) Il., Anth. II. for κατ-έπαλτο, v. καταπάλλω.

κατ-έφθῐτο, 3 sing. Ep. aor. 2 pass. of καταφθίω.

κατ-εφίσταμαι, Pass., with aor. 2 act. *to rise up against*, N. T.

κατ-έχω, f. καθέξω and κατασχήσω : aor. 2 κατέσχον, poët. κατέσχεθον, Ep. 3 sing. κάσχεθε : I. trans. *to hold fast*, Hes. 2. *to hold back, withhold*, Hom. :—*to check, restrain, control, bridle*, Hdt., Att. :—Pass. *to be held down, to be bound, kept under*, Hdt. 3. *to detain*, Id., Xen. :—Pass. *to be detained, to stay, stop, tarry*, Hdt., Soph. II. *to have in possession, possess, occupy*, Trag. 2. of sound, *to fill*, ἀλαλητῷ πεδίον κατέχουσι Il. ; κ. στρατόπεδον δυσφημίαις *to fill* it with his grievous cries, Soph. 3. βιοτὰν κ. *to continue* a life, Id. 4

to occupy, be spread over, cover, νὺξ κατέχ' οὐρανόν Od.; ἡμέρα κάτεσχε γαῖαν Aesch.:—in Med., κατέσχετο πρόσωπα *covered her* face, Od. **5.** of the grave, *to confine, cover,* Hom. **6.** of conditions and the like, *to hold down, overpower, oppress, afflict,* Od., Soph.:—of circumstances, *to occupy* or *engage* one, Hdt. **7.** *to occupy,* in right of *conquest,* Id., Soph., etc. **8.** *to master, understand,* Plat. **9.** in Pass., of persons, *to be possessed, inspired,* Xen., Plat. **III.** *to follow close upon, press hard,* Lat. *urgere,* Xen. **IV.** *to bring a ship to land, bring it in* or *to,* Hdt.
B. intr. : **1.** (sub. ἑαυτόν) *to control oneself,* Soph., Plat.:—*to hold, stop, cease,* of the wind, Ar. **2.** *to come from the high sea to shore, put in,* h. Hom., Hdt., Att. **3.** *to prevail,* ὁ λόγος κατέχει the report *prevails, is rife,* Thuc.; σεισμοὶ κατ. earthquakes *prevail, are frequent,* Id. **4.** *to have the upper hand,* Theogn., Arist.
C. Med. *to keep back for oneself, embezzle,* Hdt. **2.** *to cover oneself,* v. supr. A. II. 4. **3.** *to hold, contain,* Polyb. **II.** the aor. med. is also used like a Pass., *to be stopped, to stop,* Od. :—κατασχόμενος *subdued,* Pind.
κατήγαγον, aor. 2 of κατάγω.
κατ-ηγεμών, κατ-ηγέομαι, Ion. for καθ-.
κατήγετο, 3 sing. impf. pass. of κατάγω.
κατ-ηγορέω, f. ήσω, (ἀγορεύω) *to speak against, to accuse,* τινός Hdt.; κατά τινος Xen. **2.** κ. τί τινος, *to state* or *bring as a charge against* a person, *accuse* him *of* it, Hdt., Soph., etc. **3.** c. acc. rei only, *to allege in accusation, allege,* Lat. *objicere,* Eur., Xen., etc. :—Pass. *to be brought as an accusation against,* Soph., Thuc., etc. :—impers., c. inf., σφέων κατήγορητο μηδίζειν a charge had been brought against them that they *favoured* the Medes, Hdt.; so, κατηγορεῖταί τινος ὡς βαρβαρίζει Xen. **4.** absol. *to be an accuser, appear as prosecutor,* Ar., Plat. **II.** *to signify, indicate, prove,* Lat. *arguo,* c. acc. rei, τι Xen. : c. gen. *to tell of,* Aesch. Hence
κατηγόρημα, ατος, τό, *an accusation, charge,* Plat., Dem.
κατηγορία, Ion. -ίη, ἡ, *an accusation, charge,* Hdt., Thuc., etc.
κατήγορος, ον, *an accuser,* Hdt., Soph. :—*a betrayer,* Aesch.
κατήδη, plqpf. of κάτοιδα.
κατήκοος, ον, (κατακούω) *listening :* as Subst. *a listener, eaves-dropper,* Hdt. **II.** *hearkening to, obeying, obedient, subject,* Id., Soph.; τινος *to* another, Hdt.; also c. dat., Κύρῳ κ. Id. **III.** *giving ear to,* εὐχωλῇσι Anth.
κατήκω, Ion. for καθήκω.
κατήλθον, aor. 2 of κατέρχομαι.
κατ-ηλιψ, ιφος, ἡ, *the upper story* of a house, or *a stair-case* or *ladder,* Ar. (Deriv. uncertain.)
κατηλλάγην [ᾰ], -ηλλάχθην, aor. 2 and 1 pass. of κατ-αλλάσσω.
κατ-ηλογέω, f. ήσω, (ἀλογέω) *to make of small account, take no account of, neglect,* Hdt.
κατήλυθον, impf. of κατέρχομαι. Hence
κατήλῠσις, εως, ἡ, *a going down, descent,* Anth.
κάτημαι, Ion. for κάθημαι.

κατήνεγκα, pf. of καταφέρω.
κατήορος or **κατήορος,** Dor. -άορος or -άορος, ον, (ἀείρω) *hanging down, hanging on their mother's neck,* of children, Eur.
κατ-ηπιάω, *to assuage, allay* Ep. 3 pl. impf. pass., κατηπιόωντο Il.
κατηράμενος, pf. part. of καταράομαι.
κατηράσω [ᾱ], 2 sing. aor. 1 of καταράομαι.
κατηρᾶτο, 3 sing. impf. of καταράομαι.
κατ-ηρεμίζω, f. ίσω, *to calm, appease,* Xen.
κατ-ηρεφής, ές, (ἐρέφω) *covered over, vaulted, overhanging,* Hom., Hes. ; κ. πέτρος, of a cave, Soph. :—of trees, *thick-leaved,* Theocr. :—κ. πόδα τιθέναι *to keep the foot covered,* of Pallas when seated, and the robe falls over her feet, opp. to ὀρθὸν πόδα τ., when she steps forward, Aesch. **2.** *covered* by a thing, c. dat., σπέος δάφνῃσι κατηρεφές *shaded* by laurels, *embowered* in them, Od. ; τύμβῳ κ., i.e. *buried,* Soph. : —also c. gen., *covered with* or *by* a thing, Eur.
κατήρης, ες, (*ἄρω) *fitted out* or *furnished* with a thing, c. dat., Eur. :—of ships, *furnished with oars,* πλοῖον κατήρες a *rowing* boat, Hdt. ; but, τάρσος κ. a *well-fitted* oar, Eur.
κατηρίθμημαι, pf. pass. of καταριθμέω.
κατήρῐπον, aor. 2 intr. of κατερείπω.
κατήρτισμαι, pf. pass. of καταρτίζω.
κατηρτίσω, 2 sing. aor. 1 med. of καταρτίζω.
κατήφεια, Ion. and Ep. -είη or -ίη [ῐ], ἡ, (κατηφής) : —*dejection, sorrow, shame,* Il., Thuc.
κατηφέω, f. ήσω, *to be downcast, to be mute* with horror or grief, Hom., Eur. From
κατ-ηφής, ές, *with downcast eyes, downcast, mute,* Od., Eur. **2.** metaph. *dim, obscure, dusk,* Anth. (Deriv. uncertain.)
κατηφιάω, = κατηφέω, Anth.
κατηφίη [ῐ], ἡ, Ep. for κατήφεια.
κατηφών, όνος, ὁ, (κατηφέω) *one who causes grief* or *shame,* as Priam calls his sons κατηφόνες, *dedecora,* Il.
κατ-ηχέω, f. ήσω, *to sound* a thing *in one's ears, to teach by word of mouth,* Luc. :—Pass. *to be informed,* N. T. **2.** in Christian writers, *to instruct in the elements of religion,* Ib.
κατήχθην, aor. 1 pass. of κατάγω.
κάτ-θανον, Ep. for κατ-έθανον, aor. 2 of καταθνήσκω.
κατ-θάψαι, Ep. for κατα-θάψαι, aor. 1 inf. of καταθάπτω.
κατ-θείην, poët. for κατα-θείην, aor. 2 opt. of κατατίθημι.
κατ-θέμεθα, -θέσθην, Ep. 2 and 3 pl. aor. 2 med. of κατα-τίθημι.
κάτ-θεμεν, Ep. for κατα-θέμεν, 1 pl. aor. 2 of κατατίθημι : but **II. κατ-θέμεν,** for κατα-θεῖναι, inf.
κατ-θέμενος, aor. 2 med. of κατα-τίθημι.
κάτ-θετε, -θεσαν, Ep. 2 and 3 pl. aor. 2 of κατα-τίθημι.
κάτ-θεο, Ep. aor. 2 med. imper. of κατα-τίθημι.
κατ-ιάπτω, ψω, *to harm, hurt,* Od., Mosch.
κατίᾰσι, 3 pl. of κάτειμι (εἶμι *ibo*).
κατίᾰσι, Ion. for καθίᾰσι, 3 pl. of καθίημι.
κατιδεῖν, aor. 2 inf. of κατεῖδον : **κατιδέσθαι,** aor. 2 inf. med.
κατ-ιδρύω, κατ-ίδρῠσις, Ion. for καθ-.
κατ-ιερόω, κατι-έρωσις, Ion. for καθ-.
κατ-ῑθύνω [ῠ], Ion. for κατ-ευθύνω, Hdt.

κατ-ῑκετεύω, Ion. for καθ-ικετεύω.

κατ-ῑλύω, f. ύσω [ῡ], to fill with mud or dirt, Xen.

κατ-ίμεν [ῐ], Ep. inf. of κάτ-ειμι (εἶμι ibo).

κατ-ιππάζομαι, κατ-ῑρόω, κατ-ίστημι, Ion. for καθ-.

κάτ-ισθι, imperat. of κάτοιδα.

κατ-ισχάνω, Ep. for κατίσχω, Od.

κατ-ισχναίνω; f. ᾰνῶ, to make to pine or waste away, Aesch. :—fut. med. κατισχνᾰνεῖσθαι in pass. sense, Id.

κατ-ισχύω, f. ύσω [ῡ], to have power over, overpower, prevail against one, c. gen., N.T. II. to come to one's full strength, Soph.

κατ-ίσχω, collat. form of κατέχω, to hold back, Lat. detinere, Il., Hdt. :—Med. to keep by one, Il. II. to occupy : Pass. to be occupied, Od. III. to direct or steer to a place, Ib., Hdt., etc. IV. intr., to come down, Hdt.

κάτ-οιδα, -οισθα, inf. -ειδέναι, part. -ειδώς, pf. (in pres. sense), plqpf. κατῄδη (in impf. sense) :—to know well, understand, Aesch., Soph. 2. c. acc. pers. to know by sight, recognise, Soph., Eur. 3. absol. οὐ κατειδώς unwittingly, Eur. 4. c. part. to know well that, Soph. ; c. inf. to know how to do, Id.

κατ-οικέω, f. ήσω, to dwell in as a κάτοικος, to settle in, colonise, Hdt., Eur. : generally, to inhabit, Soph., Eur., etc. 2. absol. to settle, dwell, Soph., Eur., etc. :—so in pf. and plqpf. pass. to have been settled, to dwell, Hdt. II. in Pass., of a state, to be administered, governed, Soph., Plat. III. intr. of cities, to lie, be situate, Plat. Hence

κατοίκησις, εως, ἡ, a settling in a place, Thuc. ; and

κατοικητήριον, τό, a dwelling-place, abode, N.T. ; and

κατοικία, ἡ, a settlement, colony : the foundation of a colony, Plut.

κατ-οικίδιος, ον, living in or about a house, domestic, οἱ κατοικίδιοι home birds, Luc.

κατ-οικίζω, f. Att. ιῶ :—to remove to a place, plant, settle or establish there as colonists, κ. τινὰ εἰς τόπον Hdt., Ar.; γυναῖκας ἐς φῶς ἡλίου κατ. Eur. :—also, κ. τινὰ ἐν τόπῳ to settle or plant one in, Soph. ; ἐλπίδας ἔν τινι κ. to plant them in his mind, Aesch. 2. c. acc. loci, to colonise, people a place, Hdt., Aesch., etc. II. Pass., 1. of persons, to be placed or settled, ἐν τόπῳ Hdt. ; ἐς τόπον Thuc. 2. of places, to have colonies planted there, to be colonised, Id. III. to bring home and re-establish there, to restore to one's country, Aesch. Hence

κατοίκισις, εως, ἡ, a planting with inhabitants, foundation of a state, colonisation, Thuc., Plat.

κατ-οικοδομέω, f. ήσω, to build upon or in a place, Xen. II. to build away, i.e. to squander in building, Plut.

κατ-οικονομέω, f. ήσω, to manage well, Plut.

κάτ-οικος, ὁ, a settler, Aesch.

κατ-οικοφθορέω, f. ήσω, to ruin utterly, Plut.

κατ-οικτείρω, f. ερῶ, to have mercy or compassion on, τινά Hdt., Soph., Eur., etc. II. intr. to feel or shew compassion, Hdt.

κατ-οικτίζω, f. σω, =κατοικτείρω, Soph. :—Med. to bewail oneself, utter lamentations, Hdt., Aesch. ; so in aor. 1 pass. κατῳκτίσθην, Eur. :—c. acc. rei, as in Act., Aesch. II. Causal, to excite pity, Soph. Hence

κατ-οίκτισις, εως, ἡ, compassion, Xen.

κατ-οιμώζω, f. ώξομαι, to bewail, lament, Eur.

κατοίσεται, 3 sing. fut. med. of καταφέρω.

κατ-οίχομαι, Dep. to have gone down, οἱ κατοιχόμενοι the departed, dead, Dem.

κατ-οκνέω, to shrink from doing or undertaking, c. inf., Soph., Thuc. ;—absol. to shrink back, Aesch., Thuc.

κατοκωχή, ἡ, Att. for κατοχή, a being possessed, possession (i.e. inspiration), Plat. Hence

κατοκώχιμος, η, ον, capable of being possessed, Arist.

κατ-ολισθάνω, f. -ολισθήσω, to slip or sink down, Luc.

κατ-όλλυμι, to destroy utterly :—Pass., with pf. acc. to perish utterly, Aesch.

κατ-ολολύζω, f. ξω, to shriek over a thing, c. gen., Aesch.

κατ-ολοφύρομαι, Dep. to bewail, c. acc., Eur., Xen.

κατ-ομβρέομαι, Pass. to be rained on, drenched, Anth.

κατ-όμνῡμι, f. -ομοῦμαι : aor. 1 -ώμοσα :—to confirm by oath, τί τινι Ar. ; c. inf. to swear that .., Dem. 2. c. acc. to call to witness, swear by, τὴν ἐμὴν ψυχὴν Eur. :—so in Med., Dem. II. in Med. also, c. gen. to take an oath against, accuse on oath, Hdt.

κατ-όνομαι, aor. 1 κατ-ωνόσθην, Dep. to censure bitterly, depreciate, abuse, Hdt.

κάτ-οξυς, εια, υ, very sharp, piercing, of sound, Ar.

κατ-οπάζω, to follow hard upon, Hes.

κατ-όπιν, Adv. (ὄπις), by consequence, behind, after, Theogn., Att. :—c. gen., Ar., Plat. II. of Time, after, Plat.

κατ-όπισθεν, in Poets also -θε, Adv. behind, after, in the rear, Hom.; c. gen., Od. II. of Time, hereafter, afterwards, henceforth, Ib.

κατ-οπτεύω, f. σω, (κατόπτης) to spy out, reconnoitre, Xen. :—Pass. to be observed, Soph.

κατ-οπτήρ, ῆρος, ὁ, =sq., Aesch.

κατ-όπτης, ου, ὁ, (ὄψομαι, fut. of ὁράω) a spy, scout, h. Hom., Hdt., Aesch., etc. II. an overseer, τῶν πραγμάτων Aesch.

κάτοπτος, ον, (ὄψομαι, f. of ὁράω) to be seen, visible, Thuc. II. c. gen. in view of or looking down over, Aesch.

κατοπτρίζω, f. σω, to shew as in a mirror :—Med. κατοπτριζόμενοι τὴν δόξαν beholding as in a mirror, or rather reflecting as a mirror, N.T. From

κάτ-οπτρον, τό, (ὄψομαι, f. of ὁράω) a mirror, Lat. speculum, Eur. II. metaph. a mere reflexion (not a reality), Aesch.

κατ-οργᾰνίζω, to sound with music through, Anth.

κατ-οργάς, άδος, ἡ, (ὄργια) celebrating orgies, Anth. Hence

κατ-οργιάζω, to initiate in orgies, Plut.

κατ-ορθόω, f. ώσω, to set upright, erect, Eur. :—metaph. to keep straight, set right, Soph. 2. to accomplish successfully, bring to a successful issue, Plat., Dem. : —Pass. to succeed, prosper, Hdt., Eur. ; δρᾶν κατώρθωσαι thou hast rightly purposed to do, Aesch. II. intr. as in Pass. to go on prosperously, succeed, Thuc., Xen. ; τὸ κατορθοῦν success, Dem. Hence

κατόρθωσις, εως, ἡ, a setting straight : successful accomplishment of a thing, success, Arist. ; and

κατορθωτικός, ή, όν, likely or able to succeed, Arist.

κατ-οροúω, f. σω, to rush downwards, h. Hom.

κατ-ορρωδέω, Ion. κατ-αρρ-, f. ήσω, to be dismayed

at, dread greatly, c. acc., Hdt. II. absol. to be afraid, be in fear, Id.

κατ-ορύσσω, Att. -ττω : f. ξω : fut. pass. -ορύχήσομαι : —to bury in the earth, Hdt. ; ἐπὶ κεφαλὴν κατώρυξε buried head downwards, Id. ; ἐν τῇ κεφαλῇ Ar.

κατ-ορχέομαι, f. ήσομαι, Dep. to dance in triumph over, treat despitefully, Lat. insultare, Hdt.

κατ-όσσομαι, Dep. to contemplate, behold, Anth.

κατ-ότι, Adv., Ion. for καθ-ότι or καθ᾽ ὅ τι.

κατ-ουδαῖος, ον, (οὖδας) under the earth, h. Hom.

κατ-ουλόομαι, Pass. to cicatrise, heal over, Anth.

κατ-ουρίζω, f. ίσω, to bring into port with a fair wind : metaph., τάδ᾽ ὀρθῶς ἔμπεδα κατουρίζει the oracle brings these things safe to port or to fulfilment, or intr. these things come to fulfilment, Soph.

κατοχή, ἡ, (κατέχω) a holding fast, detention, Hdt. II. possession by a spirit, inspiration, Plut.

κάτοχος, ον, (κατέχω) holding down, holding fast, tenacious, Plut. II. pass. kept down, held fast, overpowered, overcome, Aesch., Soph. ; κάτοχος subject to him, Eur.

κατ-όψιος, ον, (ὄψις) in sight of, opposite, τινος Eur.

κατ-οψοφᾶγέω, f. ήσω, to spend in eating, Aeschin.

καττά, Dor. for κατὰ τά, and **καττάδε** for κατὰ τάδε, ap. Thuc.

κατ-τάνῦσαν, Ep. for κατ-ετάνυσαν, 3 pl. aor. 1 of καταταννύω.

καττίτερος, καττιτέρινος, Att. for κασσ-.

κάττῦμα, καττύω, Att. for κάσσυμα, κασσύω.

κατ-υβρίζω, κατ-ύπερθε, κατ-υπέρτερος, κατ-υπνόω, Ion. for καθ-.

κάτω, Adv. (κατά) : I. with verbs of Motion, down, downwards, Hom., Hdt., Att. II. with Verbs of Rest, beneath, below, underneath, opp. to ἄνω, Hes. : —esp. in the world below, Soph., Plat. b. geographically below, southward, Hdt. ; but also, on the coast, Thuc. III. as a Prep. c. gen. under, below, Trag. IV. Comp. κατωτέρω, lower, further, downwards, Ar. ; c. gen. lower than, below, Hdt. 2. Sup. κατωτάτω, at the lowest part, Id.

κάτωθεν, (κάτω) Adv. from below, up from below, Aesch., Plat. :—also, from the low country, from the coast, Hdt. II. below, beneath, where κάτω would be required by our idiom, Soph., Plat., etc.

κατ-ωθέω, aor. 1 -έωσα, to push down, Il.

κάτω-κάρα [κᾰ], Adv. head downwards, Ar.

κατ-ωμάδιος [ᾰ], α, ον, (ὦμος) from the shoulder, δίσκος κ. a quoit thrown from the shoulder, i. e. from the upturned hand held above the shoulder, Il. ; cf. sq. II. worn or borne on the shoulder, Anth.

κατ-ωμᾰδόν, Adv. (ὦμος) from the shoulders, with the arm drawn back to the shoulder, Il.

κατ-ωμοσία, Ion. -ίη, ἡ, (ὄμνυμι) an accusation on oath, Hdt.

κατ-ωράϊζομαι, Ion. for καθ-ωραΐζομαι.

κατῶρυξ, ὑχος, ὁ, ἡ, (κατορύσσω) sunk or imbedded in the earth, ἀγορὴ λάεσσι κατωρυχέεσσ᾽ ἀραρυῖα (as if from κατωρυχής), Od. II. underground, in caves, Aesch. ; ἐκ κατώρυχος στέγης, i. e. from the grave, Soph. III. as Subst., κατῶρυξ, ἡ, a pit, cavern, Id. 2. a buried treasure, Eur.

κατώτατος, η, ον, Sup. Adj. from κάτω, lowest, Xen.: neut. pl. as Adv., Hdt.

κατω-φᾱγᾶς, οῦ or ᾶ, ὁ, (φαγεῖν) eating with the head down to the ground, gluttonous, Ar.

κατω-φερής, ές, = κάτω φερόμενος, sunken, Xen.

κα-νάξαις, Ep. for κατ-ϝάξας, 2 sing. aor. 1 opt. of κατάγνυμι.

Καύκασος, ὁ, Mt. Caucasus between the Euxine and Caspian, Hdt. ; a gen. **Καυκάσιος** (as if from Καύκασις) Id. ; τὸ Καυκάσιον ὄρος Hdt.

καύλινος, η, ον, (καυλός) made of a stalk or stick, Luc.

καυλο-μύκητες, οἱ, stalk-fungi, Luc.

ΚΑΥΛΟΣ, ὁ, the shaft of a spear, Il. : the hilt of a sword, Ib. II. the stalk of a plant, Ar., etc.

καῦμα, ατος, τό, (καίω) burning heat, esp. of the sun, καύματος in the sun-heat, Il. ; καῦμ᾽ ἔθαλπε Soph. 2. fever-heat, Thuc. :—metaph. of love, Anth. Hence

καυμᾰτίζω, f. ίσω, to burn or scorch up, N. T. :—Pass. to be burnt up, Ib.

καννάκης [ᾰ], ου, ὁ, a thick cloak, Ar. (Prob. a Persian word.)

καύσῐμος, ον, (καίω) fit for burning, combustible, Xen.

καῦσις, εως, ἡ, (καίω) a burning, Hdt. :—in surgery, cautery, Plat.

καυσόομαι, Pass. to burn with intense heat, N. T.

καῦσος, ὁ, = καῦμα, burning heat.

καύστειρα, (καίω) fem. Adj. burning hot, raging, in gen. καυστείρης κάχης Il.

καυστηριάζω, καυστήριον, v. καυτ-.

καυστός or **καυτός, ή, όν,** (καίω) burnt, red-hot, Eur.

Καύστριος, α, ον, of or from the river Caÿster (in Lydia), Ar.

καύσω, fut. of καίω.

καύσων, ωνος, ὁ, (καίω) burning heat, N. T.

καυτήρ, ῆρος, ὁ, (καίω) a burner, Pind.

καυτηριάζω, f. άσω, to cauterise, brand : metaph. in Pass., N. T.

καυτήριον, τό, (καίω) a branding iron, Luc., N. T.

καύτης, ου, ὁ, = καυτήρ, Anth.

καυτός, ή, όν, another form of καυστός.

καὐτός, crasis for καὶ αὐτός.

καυχάομαι, 2 sing. καυχᾶσαι in late Gr. : f. ήσομαι aor. 1 ἐκαυχησάμην : pf. κεκαύχημαι : (akin to αὐχέω, εὔχομαι) :—to speak loud, be loud-tongued, Pind. : to boast or vaunt oneself, c. inf., to boast that, Hdt. :— c. acc. to boast of a thing, c. acc., N. T. From

καύχη, ἡ, = sq., Pind.

καύχημα, ατος, τό, (καυχάομαι) a boast, vaunt, Pind. 2. a subject of boasting, N. T.

καυχήμων, ον, (καυχάομαι) boastful, Babr.

καύχησις, εως, ἡ, (καυχάομαι) reason to boast, N. T.

κάφαγιστρευσας, crasis for καὶ ἐφαγιστρεύσας.

κᾰχάζω, Dor. fut. καχαξῶ, to laugh aloud, Soph., Theocr. (Formed from the sound, cf. Lat. cachinnari.)

κᾰχασμός, ὁ, = καγχασμός (q. v.), Ar.

κᾱχ-εξία, ἡ, (ἕξις) a bad habit of body, opp. to εὐεξία, Plat., etc.

κᾰχ-ήμερος, ον, (ἡμέρα) living bad days, wretched, Anth.

καχλάζω, redupl. form of χλάζω, only used in pres. and impf., to plash, of wine poured into a cup, Pind. ; of

the sea, Aesch., Theocr. :—c. acc. cogn., κῦμα ἀφρὸν
καχλάζον a wave *frothing with* foam, Eur.

κάχληξ, ηκος, ὁ, *a pebble* in the beds of rivers :—collectively, *gravel, shingle*, Thuc. (Prob. akin to χάλιξ, Lat. *calx, calculus*.)

κάχ-ορμισία, ἡ, (ὅρμισις) *unlucky harbourage*, Anth.

ΚΑΧΡΥΣ, υος, ἡ, *parched barley*, from which pearlbarley (ἄλφιτα) was made, Ar.

κάχ-υποπτος, ον, *suspecting evil, suspicious*, Plat.

κάχ-υπότοπος, ον, =foreg., Plat.

κάω [ᾰ], Att. for καίω, *to burn*.

κε, and before a vowel **κεν**, Ep. and Ion. for ἄν, Aeol. and old Dor. **κᾱ** ; always enclitic.

ΚΕΑΖΩ, Ep. aor. 1 κέασα, κέασσα, ἐκέασσα :—Pass., Ep. aor. 1 κεάσθην : pf. part. κεκεασμένος :—*to split, cleave* wood, Od. ; of lightning, *to shiver, shatter*, Ib. ; of a spear, κέασσε δὲ ὀστέα λευκά Il. ; [κεφαλὴ] ἄνδιχα κεάσθη was *cloven* in twain, Ib.

κέαρ, contr. κῆρ, q. v.

κέαται, κέατο, Ep. for κεῖνται, ἔκειντο, 3 pl. pres. and impf. of κεῖμαι.

κεβλή-πυρις, (πῦρ) *the redcap, redpoll*, Ar.

κεγχριαῖος, α, ον, (κέγχρος) *of the size of a grain of millet*, Luc.

κεγχρο-βόλοι, οἱ, (βάλλω) *millet-throwers*, Luc.

ΚΕΓΧΡΟΣ, ὁ, *millet*, Hes., Hdt., etc.; of a single grain, Hdt. II. *anything in small grains*, as *the spawn of fish*, Id. Hence

κεγχρώματα, ων, τά, *things of the size of millet-grains* :—in Eur., *eyelet-holes* in the rim of the shield, through which a soldier could view his enemy without exposing his person.

κεδάννυμι, poët. for σκεδάννυμι, Ep. aor. 1 ἐκέδασσα, pass. ἐκεδάσθην : —*to break asunder, break up, scatter*, Hom. :—Pass., κεδασθείσης ὑσμίνης when the battle *was broken up*, i. e. when the combatants were no longer in masses, Il.

ΚΕΔΝΟΣ, ή, όν, *careful, diligent, sage, trusty*, Hom., Aesch., Eur. 2. pass. *cared for, cherished, dear*, Hom. II. of things, κέδν' εἰδυῖα knowing *her duties*, Od. ; κ. φροντίς, βουλεύματα *sage, wise*, Aesch. ; of news, *good, joyful*, Id.

κεδρία, Ion. -ίη, ἡ, *cedar resin* or *oil*, Hdt. ; and

κέδρινος, η, ον, of *cedar*, Il., Eur. From

ΚΕΔΡΟΣ, ἡ, *the cedar-tree*, Lat. *cedrus*, Od., Hdt. II. *anything made of cedar-wood; a cedar-coffin*, Eur. ; *a cedar-box*, for a bee-hive, Theocr. III. *cedar-oil*, Luc. Hence

κεδρωτός, ή, όν, *made of* or *inlaid with cedar-wood*, Eur.

κέεσθαι, κέεται, Ion. for κεῖσθαι, κεῖται, inf. and 3 sing. of κεῖμαι.

κειάμενος, Ep. aor. 1 Med. part. of καίω :—κείαντες, aor. 1 act. part. pl.

κεῖθεν, κεῖθι, Ion. and Ep. for ἐκεῖθεν *thence*, ἐκεῖθι *there*.

ΚΕΙΜΑΙ, κεῖσαι, κεῖται, Ion. κέεται ; pl., κεῖνται, Ion. κέαται : imperat. κεῖσο, κείσθω :—subj., 3 sing. κέηται, Ep. κῆται :—opt. κεοίμην :—inf., κεῖσθαι, Ion. κέεσθαι :—part. κείμενος :—impf., ἐκείμην, Ep. κείμην, Ep. 3 sing. κεῖτο :—fut. κείσομαι, Dor. κεισεῦμαι. Radical sense, *to be laid* (used as a Pass. to τίθημι), and so *to lie, lie outstretched*, Hom., etc. ; ὁ δ' ἐπ' ἐννέα κεῖτο

πέλεθρα *lay stretched* over nine plethra, Od. ; κειμένῳ ἐπιπηδᾶν *to kick him when he's down*, Ar. 2. *to lie asleep, repose*, Hom., etc. :—also, *to lie idle, lie still*, Id. ; ὑπὸ γαστέρ' ἐλυσθεὶς κείμην of Ulysses under the ram's belly, Od. ; κακὸν κείμενον *a sleeping evil*, Soph. 3. *to lie sick* or *wounded, lie in misery*, Hom., Soph., etc. ; *to lie at the mercy of* the conqueror, Aesch. 4. *to lie dead*, like Lat. *jacere*, Hom., Hdt., Trag. 5. *to lie neglected* or *uncared for*, of an unburied corpse, Il. ;—so also of places, *to lie in ruins*, Aesch. 6. of wrestlers, *to have a fall*, Id., Ar. II. of places, *to lie, be situated*, Od., Hdt., Att. III. *to be laid up, be in store*, of goods, property, Hom. ;—also of things dedicated to a god, Hdt. ; of money, κείμενα *deposits*, Id. IV. *to be set up*, proposed, κεῖται ἄεθλον Il. ; ὅπλων ἔκειτ' ἀγὼν πέρι Soph. 2. of laws, κεῖται νόμος the law *is laid down*, Eur., Thuc. ; οἱ νόμοι οἱ κείμενοι the *established* laws, Ar. ; κεῖται ζημία the penalty is *fixed by law*, Thuc. 3. of names, κεῖται ὄνομα the name *is given*, Hdt., Xen. V. metaph., πένθος ἐνὶ φρεσὶ κεῖται grief *lies heavy* on my heart, Od. ; ταῦτα θεῶν ἐν γούνασι κεῖται, i. e. these things are yet in the power of the gods, to give or not, Il. 2. κεῖσθαι ἔν τινι *to rest entirely* or *be dependent on him*, Pind. ; θεῷ κείμεθα Soph. 3. *to be so and so*, Hdt., Aesch. :—simply, *to be*, νεῖκος κ. τισι there is strife between them. Hence

κειμήλιον, τό, (κεῖμαι) *anything stored up* as valuable, *a treasure, heirloom*, Hom., Hdt., Soph., Eur.

κείμᾱν, Dor. and poët. for ἐκείμην, impf. of κεῖμαι.

κεῖνος, η, ο, Ion. and poët. for ἐκεῖνος :—κείνη *by that way*, Od. : κείνως *in that manner*, Hdt.

κεινός, ή, όν, Ion. and poët. for κενός.

Κεῖος, v. Κέος.

κειρία, ἡ, *the cord* or *girth of a bedstead*, Lat. *instita*, Ar. II. in pl. *swathings, grave-clothes*, N. T.

κείρυλος, ὁ, v. κηρύλος.

ΚΕΙΡΩ, f. κερῶ, Ion. κερέω : aor. 1 ἔκειρα, Ep. ἔκερσα : pf. κέκαρκα :—Med., fut. κεροῦμαι : aor. 1 ἐκειράμην, Ep. ἐκερσάμην :—Pass., aor. 1 part. κερθείς ; aor. 2 subj. κάρῇ, inf. κάρῆναι, part. καρείς : pf. κέκαρμαι :—*to cut the hair short, shear, clip*, Il., Hdt., Eur. :—Med. *to cut off one's hair* or *have it cut off*, as in deep mourning, Hom., Eur., etc. :—Pass., βοστρύχους κεκαρμένος *having one's locks cut off*, Eur. ; κεκάρθαι τὰς κεφαλὰς *to have their heads shorn*, in sign of mourning, Hdt. ; of the hair, *to be cut off*, Pind. II. *to cut* or *hew out*, Il. ; ὕλην Soph. III. *to ravage* a country, *by cutting down* the crops and fruit-trees, Hdt., Thuc. :—Pass., of a country, *to be ravaged*, Thuc. :—Med., Ἄρης πλάκα κερσάμενος *having had* the plain *swept clean* (by destroying the men), Aesch. IV. generally, *to destroy*, and so, 1. *to tear, eat greedily*, Lat. *depasci*, of beasts, Hom. ; ἔκειρε πολυκέρων φόνον, i. e. he slaughtered many a horned beast, Soph. 2. of the suitors, *to consume, waste* one's substance, Od.

κεῖς, crasis for καὶ εἰς.

κεῖσε, Adv., Ion. and Ep. for ἐκεῖσε, *thither*.

κεισεῦμαι, Dor. for κείσομαι, fut. of κεῖμαι.

κεῖσο, κείσθω, 2 and 3 sing. imper. of κεῖμαι.

ΚΕΙ´Ω, Desiderat. of κεῖμαι, βῆ δ' ἰμέναι κείων he went to lie down, went to bed, Od.; ἴομεν κείοντες Il.

ΚΕΙ´Ω, to cleave, radic. form of κεάζω, Od.

κεκαδήσομαι, Ep. fut. pass. of κήδω.

κεκαδήσω, Ep. fut. of χάζω.

κεκαδμένος, Dor. pf. part. of καίνυμαι.

κέκαδον, Ep. aor. 2 part. of χάζω.

κεκάδοντο [ᾰ], 3 pl. Ep. aor. 2 of χάζομαι.

κεκάλυμμαι, pf. pass. of καλύπτω:—**κεκάλυπτο**, 3 sing. Ep. plqpf.

κέκαμον, Ep. aor. 2 of κάμνω:—**κεκάμω**, subj.; 3 pl. **κεκάμωσι**.

κεκάρθαι, pf. pass. inf. of κείρω:—**κεκαρμένος**, part.

κέκασμαι, pf. of καίνυμαι: 3 sing. Ep. plqpf. **κέκαστο**: part. κεκασμένος.

κέκαυμαι, pf. pass. of καίω.

κεκαφηώς, an Ep. pf. part. with no pres. in use, only found in phrase κεκαφηὼς θυμόν breathing forth one's life, Lat. animam agens, Hom.—Commonly referred to κάπτω.

κεκεύθει, 3 sing. Ep. plqpf. of κεύθω.

κέκλαυμαι, pf. pass. of κλαίω.

κεκλέᾱται, Ion. 3 pl. pf. pass. of καλέω.

κέκλειμαι and **κέκλεισμαι**, pf. pass. of κλείω (to shut).

κέκλετο, 3 sing. Ep. aor. 2 of κέλομαι.

κεκλήᾱτο, Ion. 3 pl. plqpf. of καλέω.

κέκληγα, pf. of κλάζω: part. κεκληγώς, with Ep. pl. κεκλήγοντες.

κέκληκα, pf. act. of καλέω:—**κέκλημαι**, pf. pass.; opt. **κεκλήμην**.

κεκλίᾱται, Ion. for κέκλινται, 3 pl. pf. pass. of κλίνω.

κέκλῐκα, pf. of κλίνω: **κέκλῐμαι**, pass.: **κέκλῐτο**, Ep. 3 sing. plqpf. pass.

κεκλόμενος, Ep. aor. 2 part. of κέλομαι.

κέκλοφα, pf. of κλέπτω.

κέκλῠθι, κέκλῠτε, poët. 2 sing. and pl. aor. 2 of κλύω.

κέκλυσμαι, pf. pass. of κλύζω.

κέκμηκα, pf. of κάμνω:— Ep. part. κεκμηώς, ῶτος.

κέκομμαι, pf. pass. of κόπτω.

κεκονίᾱμαι, pf. pass. of κονιάω.

κεκονῑμένος, pf. pass. part. of κονίω:—**κεκόνῑτο**, Ep. 3 sing. plqpf.

κεκοπώς, pf. part. of κόπτω.

κεκόρημαι, Ion. for κεκόρεσμαι, pf. pass. of κορέννυμι.

κεκορηώς, dual -ηότε, Ep. pf. act. intr. part. of κορέννυμι.

κεκόρυθμαι, Ep. pf. pass. of κορύσσω.

κεκοτηώς, Ep. pf. part. of κοτέω.

κεκράαντα, -αντο, Ep. 3 pl. pf. and plqpf. of κραίνω.

κέκρᾱγα, pf. of κράζω. Hence

κέκραγμα, ατος, τό, a scream, cry, Ar.; and

κεκραγμός, ὁ, = foreg., Eur.

κεκράκτης, ου, ὁ, a bawler, Ar.

κέκρᾱμαι, pf. pass. of κεράννυμι.

κεκραξι-δάμᾱς, αντος, ὁ, (κέκραγα, δαμάω) he who conquers all in bawling, the blusterer, Ar.

κεκράξομαι, Att. fut. of κράζω.

κεκρασπεδωθαι, pf. pass. inf. of κρασπεδόομαι.

κέκραχθι, imper. of κέκραγα, pf. of κράζω.

κέκρῑγα, pf. of κρίζω.

κέκρῐκα, κέκρῐμαι, pf. act. and pass. of κρίνω.

κεκρόταμαι, Dor. pf. pass. of κροτέω.

Κέκροψ, οπος, ὁ, a mythical king of Athens, Hdt.:

hence **II**. Adj. **Κεκρόπιος**, α, ον, Cecropian, Athenian, πέτρα Κ. the Acropolis, Eur.; (also simply Κεκροπία, ἡ, used for Athens itself, Id.); Κ. χθών Attica, Id.; Κεκρόπιοι, οἱ, the Athenians, Anth. **2**. fem. **Κεκροπίς**, name of a tribe, Ar. **3**. **Κεκροπίδαι**, οἱ, the Athenians, Hdt., Eur.

κέκρυμμαι, pf. pass. of κρύπτω.

κεκρύφαλος [ῠ], ὁ, (κρύπτω) a woman's head-dress of net, to confine the hair, Lat. reticulum, Il., Anth. **2**. part of the headstall of a bridle, Xen. **II**. the pouch or belly of a hunting-net, Id., Plut.

κεκρύφαται [ῠ], Ion. 3 pl. pf. pass. of κρύπτω.

κέκτημαι, pf. of κτάομαι.

κεκύθωσι [ῠ], 3 pl. Ep. redupl. aor. 2 subj. of κεύθω.

κεκύλισμαι, pf. pass. of κυλίνδω.

κελάδεινός, ή, όν, sounding, noisy, Il.; epith. of Artemis, from the noise of the chase, Hom.:—Dor. **κελαδεννός**, Pind.

κελάδέω, f. -ήσω: poët. aor. 1 κελάδησα: (κέλαδος):— to sound as rushing water, Orac. ap. Aeschin.:—to shout aloud, in applause, Il.; κ. παιᾶνα to sound the loud paean, Eur. **2**. of various sounds, to utter a cry, cry aloud, Aesch., Ar., etc.; of bells, to ring, tinkle, Eur.; of the flute, κ. φθόγγον κάλλιστον Id. **II**. trans. to sing of, celebrate loudly, τινά Pind., Eur., etc. Hence

κελάδημα, ατος, τό, a rushing sound, Eur., Ar.

κελάδητις, ιδος, ἡ, loud-sounding, Pind.

ΚΕ´ΛΑΔΟΣ, ὁ, a noise as of rushing waters: a loud noise, din, clamour, Il. **II**. a loud clear voice, a shout, cry, Aesch., Soph., etc. **III**. the sound of music, Eur.

κελάδω, Ep. form of κελαδέω, used in part. only, sounding, roaring, Hom., Theocr.

κελαιν-εγχής, ές, with black (i. e. bloody) spear, Pind.

κελαι-νεφής, ές, sync. for κελαινο-νεφής, (νέφος) black with clouds, of Zeus, shrouded in dark clouds, cloud-wrapt, Hom.:—generally, dark-coloured, αἷμα Id.; πεδίον κ. black, rich soil, Pind.

κελαινό-βρωτος, ον, black and bloody with gnawing, Aesch.

κελαινόομαι, Pass. to grow black or dark, Aesch.

ΚΕΛΑΙΝΟ´Σ, ή, όν, black, swart, dark, murky, Hom., etc.

κελαινο-φαής, ές, (φάος) black-gleaming, ὄρφνα κ. murky twilight, Ar.

κελαινό-φρων, ον, (φρήν) black-hearted, Aesch.

κελαινό-χρως, ωτος, ὁ, ἡ, black-coloured, Anth.

κελαιν-ώπας, α, ὁ, (ὤψ) black-faced, swarthy, gloomy, Soph.: fem., κελαινῶπις Pind.

κελαιν-ώψ, ῶπος, ὁ, ἡ, = foreg., Pind.

κελᾰρύζω: Dor. aor. 1 κελάρυξα:—to murmur, of running water, Hom.; Dor. 3 sing. impf. κελάρυσδε Theocr.

κελέβη, ἡ, a cup, jar, pan, Theocr.

κελέοντες, ων, οἱ, the beams in the upright loom of the ancients, between which the web was stretched, Theocr. (Deriv. unknown.)

κελευθήτης, ου, ὁ, a wayfarer, Anth.

κελευθο-ποιός, όν, (ποιέω) road-making, Aesch.

κελευθο-πόρος, ὁ, a wayfarer, Anth.

ΚΕ´ΛΕΥΘΟΣ, ἡ, heterog. pl. κέλευθα, a road, way, path, track, Hom., etc.; ὑγρὰ κέλευθα, ἰχθυόεντα κέλευθα, of the sea, Od.; ἀνέμων κέλευθα or κέλευθοι Hom.;

ἐγγὺς γὰρ νυκτός τε καὶ ἤματός εἰσι κέλευθοι i. e. night and day follow closely, Od. ; ἄρκτου στροφάδες κ. their paths or orbits, Soph.   II. *a journey, voyage,* Hom. ; πολλὴ κ., i. e. a great distance, Soph.   2. *an expedition,* Aesch.   III. *a way of going, walk, gait,* Eur. :—metaph. *a way of life,* Aesch., Eur.

κέλευσμα or κέλευμα, ατος, τό, (κελεύω) *an order, command, behest,* Aesch., Soph., etc. ; *a call, summons,* Aesch. :—*the word of command* in battle, Hdt. ; also *the call* of the κελευστής (q. v.), which gave the time to the rowers, ἀπὸ ἑνὸς κελεύσματος *all at once,* Thuc. ; ἐκ κελεύσματος *at the word of command,* Aesch.

κελευσμός, ὁ, (κελεύω) *an order, command,* Eur.

κελευσμοσύνη, ἡ, Ion. for κέλευσμα, Hdt.

κελευστής, οῦ, ὁ, (κελεύω) *the signalman* on board ship, *who gave the time to the rowers,* Eur., Thuc.

κελευστός, ή, όν, (κελεύω) *ordered, commanded,* Luc.

κελευτιάω, Frequentat. of κελεύω, as πνευστιάω from πνέω, only used in Ep. part., κελευτιόωντε (dual) *continually urging on* [the men], Il.

κελεύω, Ep. impf. κέλευον : f. -σω, Ep. inf. -σέμεναι : aor. 1 ἐκέλευσα, Ep. κέλ- : pf. κεκέλευκα :—Pass., aor. 1 ἐκελεύσθην : pf. κεκέλευσμαι : (κέλομαι) :—*to urge* or *drive on, urge, exhort, bid, command, order,* Hom., etc. : c. acc. pers. et inf. *to order* one to do, Il. ; (also c. dat. pers., Hom.) :—c. acc. pers. et rei, τί με ταῦτα κελεύεις (sc. ποιεῖν) ; also c. acc. pers. only, θυμός με κελεύει (sc. φείδεσθαι) Od. ; ἐκέλευσε τοὺς ἕνδεκα ἐπὶ τὸν Θηραμένην *ordered* them [to go] against him, *ordered* them to seize him, Xen. ; c. acc. rei only, *to command* a thing, Aesch. :—Pass., τὸ κελευόμενον, τὰ -να, *commands, orders,* Xen.

κελέων, ὁ, obsol. sing. of κελέοντες, q. v.

κέλης, ητος, ὁ, (κέλλω) *a courser, riding-horse,* Od., Hdt., etc.   II. *a fast-sailing yacht* with one bank of oars, *a light vessel,* Lat. *celox,* Hdt., Thuc.

κελήσομαι, fut. of κέλομαι.

κελητίζω, f. ίσω, (κέλης) *to ride,* of one who rides one or more horses, leaping from one to the other, Il.

ΚΕ´ΛΛΩ, f. κέλσω, aor. 1 ἔκελσα :—*to drive on,* νῆα κέλσαι *to run* a ship to land, *put* her *to shore,* Lat. *appellere,* Od. :—metaph., Ἄργει κ. πόδα Eur.   II. intr., of ships or seamen, *to put to shore* or *into harbour,* Od., Aesch., etc. :—metaph., πᾶ ποτε κέλσαντ' *having reached* what port ? Aesch. ; πᾶ κέλσω ; *where shall I find a haven ?* Eur.

ΚΕ´ΛΟΜΑΙ, Ep. 2 sing. κέλεαι ; imperat. κελέσθω, -εσθε, opt. -οίμην, inf. -εσθαι : Ep. impf. κελόμην, Dor. 2 sing. ἐκέλευ, Ep. 3 κέλετο :—f. κελήσομαι : aor. 1 ἐκελησάμην, κελήσατο, Pind. :—Ep. 3 sing. aor. 2 ἐκέκλετο, κέκλετο ; opt. κεκλοίμην ; part. κεκλόμενος :—*to urge on, exhort, command,* in Hom. ; constructed like κελεύω.   II. much like καλέω, *to call, call to,* Il. : also, *to call on for aid,* Soph.   2. *to call by name, call,* Pind.

Κελτιστί, Adv. *in the language of the Celts,* Luc.

Κελτοί, οἱ, *the Kelts* or *Celts,* Hdt., Xen. :—hence Κελτικός, ή, όν, *Celtic, Gallic,* fem. Κελτίς, ίδος, Anth.

κελύφανον [ῠ], τό, = κέλυφος, Luc.

κέλῡφος, εος, τό, *a sheath, case, pod, shell,* Arist. : *the hollow* of the eye, Anth.   2. metaph. of old dicasts,

ἀντωμοσιῶν κελύφη *mere affidavit-husks,* Ar. ;—of an old man's *boat,* which served as his *coffin,* Anth. (Deriv. uncertain.)

κέλωρ, ωρος, ὁ, *son,* Eur. (Deriv. unknown.)

κεμάς, άδος, ἡ, *a young deer, a pricket,* Il. :—also κεμμάς, Anth. (Deriv. unknown.)

κεν, before a vowel for κε.

κεν-αγγής, ές, (κενός, ἄγγος) *emptying vessels : breeding famine,* Aesch.

κενανδρία, ἡ, *lack of men, dispeopled state,* Aesch. From κέν-ανδρος, ον, (ἀνήρ) *empty of men, dispeopled,* Aesch., Soph.

κεν-αυχής, ές, v. = κενε-αυχής, Anth.

κενε-αυχής, ές, (αὐχή) *vain-glorious,* Il.

κενέβρειος, ον, — νεκριμαῖος, dead : κενέβρεια, τά, *carrion, dog's-meat,* Ar. (Deriv. unknown.)

κεν-εμβατέω, f. ήσω, *to step on emptiness, step into a hole,* Plut., Luc.

κενεό-φρων, ον, (φρήν) *empty-minded,* Theogn., Pind.

κενεών, ῶνος, ὁ, (κενός) *the hollow below the ribs, the flank,* Hom., Xen.   II. *any hollow, a glen,* Anth.

κεν-οδοντίς, ίδος, ἡ, (ὀδούς) *toothless,* Anth.

κενολογέω, f. ήσω, *to talk emptily,* Arist. From κενο-λόγος, ον, (λέγω) *talking emptily, prating.*

ΚΕΝΟ´Σ, Ion. and poët. κεινός, ή, όν ; Ep. also κενεός, ά, όν :   I. of things, *empty,* opp. to πλέως or πλήρης, Hom., Hdt., Att.   2. metaph. *empty, vain,* κενὰ εὔγματα Od. ; κ. ἐλπίς Aesch., etc. :—in adverbial usages, neut. pl., κενεὰ πνευσαις Pind. ; διὰ κενῆς *to no purpose, in vain,* Ar., Thuc.   II. of persons,   1. c. gen. *void, destitute, bereft,* τοῦ νοῦ, φρενῶν Soph. ; συμμάχων Eur.   2. *empty-handed,* Hom., Hdt., Att. :—*bereft of* her mate, λέαινα Soph. :—*empty of wit, empty-headed,* Id., Ar.   III. Comp. and Sup. κενώτερος, -ώτατος, Plat., etc.

κενο-τᾰφέω, f. ήσω, (τάφος) *to honour with an empty tomb,* Eur.

κενο-τάφιον, τό, (τάφος) *an empty tomb, cenotaph,* Xen.

κενότης, ητος, ἡ, (κενός) *emptiness, vanity,* Plat.

κενοφροσύνη, ἡ, *emptiness of mind,* Plut. From κενό-φρων, ον, (φρήν) *empty-minded,* Aesch.

κενο-φωνία, ἡ, (φωνέω) *vain talking, babbling,* N. T.

κενόω, Ion. and poët. κειν- : f. ώσω : aor. 1 ἐκένωσα : —Pass., aor. 1 ἐκενώθην : pf. κεκένωμαι, Ion. κεκείνωμαι : (κενός) :—*to empty out, drain,* opp. to πληρόω, Aesch., Eur., etc. ; c. gen. *to empty of* a thing :— Pass. *to be emptied, made* or *left empty,* Soph. ; ἐς τὸ κενούμενον *into the space continually left empty,* Thuc. ; c. gen., κεκεινωμένος πάντων *stripped of all things,* Hdt.   2. *to make* a place *empty by leaving* it, *desert* it, Eur.   II. metaph. *to make empty, to make of no account* or *of no effect,* N. T. :—Pass. *to be* or *become so,* Ib.

κένσαι, Ep. aor. 1 inf. of κεντέω.

κέντᾰσε, Dor. and poët. 3 sing. aor. 1 of κεντέω.

Κενταύρειος, α, ον, *Centaurian, of Centaurs,* Eur.

Κενταυρίδης, ου, ὁ, *of* or *from Centaurs,* ἵππος Κ. *a Thessalian* horse, Luc.

Κενταυρικός, ή, όν, *like a Centaur,* i. e. *savage, brutal :* Adv. -κῶς, Ar.

Κενταυρο-μᾰχία, ἡ, (μάχη) *a battle of Centaurs,* Plut.

Κενταυρο-πληθής, ές, *full of Centaurs,* Eur.

Κένταυρος, ὁ, (κεντέω) *a Centaur :* the Centaurs were a savage Thessalian race, between Pelion and Ossa, extirpated in a war with their neighbours the Lapithae, Hom. **II.** in later Poets they are monsters of double shape, *half-man and half-horse,* Pind., etc.

κεντεύω, = κεντέω 3, Hdt.

ΚΕΝΤΕ΄Ω, f. ήσω : aor. 1 ἐκέντησα, Ep. inf. κένσαι (as if from κέντω) :—*to prick, goad, spur on,* Il., Ar. **2.** of bees and wasps, *to sting,* Ar., Theocr. **3.** generally, *to prick, stab,* Pind., Soph., etc. : *to torture,* Xen. : metaph., σὺν δόλῳ κ. *to stab in the dark,* Soph.

κεντρ-ηνεκής, ές, (*ἐνέγκω) *spurred* or *goaded on,* Il.

κεντρίζω, f. ίσω, = κεντέω, *to prick, goad* or *spur on,* Xen. ; metaph., ἔρως κ. Id.

κεντρο-μανής, ές, (μαίνομαι) *madly spurring,* or *spurring to madness,* Anth.

κέντρον, τό, (κεντέω) *any sharp point :* **1.** *a horse-goad,* Lat. *stimulus,* Il., etc. : also *an ox-goad,* Plat. ; —proverb., πρὸς κέντρα λακτίζειν, v. λακτίζω 2. **b.** metaph. *a goad, spur, incentive,* Aesch., Eur. **2.** *an instrument of torture,* Hdt. :—metaph. in pl. *tortures, pangs,* Soph. **3.** *the sting* of bees and wasps, Ar. ; of a scorpion, Dem. ; metaph. of the impression produced by Socrates, ὥσπερ μέλιττα τὸ κ. ἐγκαταλιπών Plat. **4.** *the stationary point of a pair of compasses, the centre* of a circle, Id.

κεντρο-τυπής, ές, (τύπτω) *struck by the goad,* Anth.

κεντρόω, f. ώσω, (κέντρον) *to furnish with a sting :*—Pass. *to be so furnished, to sting,* Plat. **2.** *to strike with a goad,* Hdt.

κέντρων, ωνος, ὁ, *one that bears the marks of the κέντρον, a rogue that has been put to the torture,* Ar.

κεντυρίων, ωνος, ὁ, the Lat. *Centurio,* N. T.

κέντωρ, ορος, ὁ, (κεντέω) *a goader, driver,* Il.

κένωσις, εως, ἡ, (κενόω) *an emptying,* Plat.

κεοίμην, opt. of κεῖμαι.

κέοντο, Ion. 3 pl. of κεῖμαι.

ΚΕ΄ΠΦΟΣ, ὁ, *a sea-bird :*—metaph. *a booby,* Ar.

κεραία, ἡ, (κέρας) *any thing projecting like a horn ; a yard-arm,* (as Lat. *cornua antennarum*), Aesch., Thuc., etc. **2.** *the projecting beam of a crane,* Thuc. **3.** *a branching stake of wood,* Plut. :—*of the forked ends of the ancilia,* Id. **4.** *the apex* of a letter, *a dot, tittle,* N. T. **5.** *the projecting spur* of a mountain, Anth. **II.** *a bow of horn,* Id.

κεραΐζω, Ep. impf. κεράϊζον : aor. 1 ἐκεράϊσα : (κείρω) :—*to ravage, despoil, plunder,* Hom., Hdt. **2.** of ships, *to sink* or *disable* them, Hdt. **3.** of living beings, *to assail fiercely, to slaughter,* Il., Hdt. **II.** *to carry off as plunder,* Hdt. Hence

κεραϊστής, οῦ, ὁ, *a ravager, robber,* h. Hom.

κεραίω, Ep. for κεράω, ζωρότερον κέραιε *mix* the wine stronger, Il.

κεραμεία, ἡ, (κεραμεύς) *the potter's art* or *craft,* Plat.

Κεράμεικός, ὁ, the *Potter's Quarter :* in Athens two places were called Cerameicus, one within and the other without the Dipylon or Thriasian Gate, Thuc., etc.

κεραμεῖον, τό, *a potter's work-shop,* Aeschin.

κεραμεούς, ᾶ, οῦν, (κέραμος) *of clay, earthen,* Plat.

κεραμεύς, έως, ὁ, (κέραμος) *a potter,* Lat. *figulus,* Il. :—proverb., κεραμεὺς κεραμεῖ κοτέει ' *two of a trade*

never agree,' Hes. **II. Κεραμεῖς**, Att. **Κεραμῆς**, οἱ, name of an Attic deme, Ar., etc.

κεραμεύω, f. σω, (κεραμεύς) *to be a potter, work in earthenware,* Plat., etc. **2.** c. acc., κ. τὸν κεραμέα *to make a pot* of the potter, Id.

κεραμικός, ή, όν, (κέραμος) *of* or *for pottery,* Xen., etc.

κεράμινος, η, ον, —κεραμεοῦς, Hdt., Xen.

κεράμιον, τό, (κέραμος) *an earthenware vessel, a jar,* Lat. *testa,* Hdt., Xen.

κεραμίς, ἡ, ἰδος [ῐ] and —ῖδος (κέραμος), *a roof-tile* or *coping tile,* Ar., Thuc.

ΚΕ΄ΡΑ˙ΜΟΣ, ὁ, *potter's earth, potter's clay,* Plat. **II.** *anything made of this earth,* as, **1.** *an earthen vessel, wine-jar,* Il., Hdt. : also in collective sense, *pottery,* Ar. ; κ. ἐσάγεται πλήρης οἴνου *jars* full of wine, Hdt. **2.** *a tile,* and in collective sense, *the tiles, tiling,* Ar., Thuc. **III.** *a jar,* used to confine a person in, Il.

κεράννυμι, and —ύω : impf. ἐκεράννυν : f. κεράσω : aor. 1 ἐκέρασα, poët. κέρασα, Ep. κέρασσα :—Med., aor. 1 ἐκερασάμην, Ep. 3 sing. κεράσσατο :—Pass., f. κράθήσομαι aor. 1 ἐκράθην [ᾱ], also ἐκεράσθην : pf. κέκρᾱμαι, also κεκέρασμαι : (κεράω) :—*to mix, mingle,* (cf. κρᾶσις) : **1.** mostly of *diluting* wine with water, Od., Att. ;—so in Med., ὅτε περ οἶνον κέρωνται when they *mix their* wine, Il. ; κρητῆρα κεράσσατο he mixed him a bowl, Od. :—Pass., κύλιξ ἴσον ἴσῳ κεκρᾱμένη a cup *mixed* half and half, Ar. **2.** *to temper* or *cool by mixing,* θυμῆρες κεράσασα having mixed (the water) *to an* agreeable *temperature,* Od. **3.** generally, *to mix, blend, temper, regulate,* Lat. *tempero,* of climates, ὥραι μάλιστα κεκραμέναι most *temperate* seasons, Hdt. ; οὐ γήρας κέκραται γενεᾷ no old age *is mingled with* the race, i. e. it knows no old age, Pind. :—of tempers of mind, Plat. **11.** generally, *to mix, compound,* Lat. *attempero,* ἔκ τινος of a thing, Id. ; φωνὴ μεταξὺ τῆς τε Χαλκιδέων καὶ Δωρίδος ἐκράθη Thuc.

κεραο-ξόος, ον, (ξέω) *polishing* or *working horn,* esp. for bows, Il.

κεραός, ά, όν, (κέρας) *horned,* Hom., Theocr. **II.** *of horn, made of horn,* Anth.

κερα-οῦχος, ον, (ἔχω) = κερούχος, Anth.

ΚΕ΄ΡΑΣ, τό : gen. κέρᾱτος, Ερ. κέραος, Att. also κέρως : dat. κέρᾱτι, κέραϊ, κέρᾳ :—dual κέραε, κέρᾱ, κεράοιν : pl. nom. κέραα, κέρᾱ, gen. κεράων, κερῶν, dat. κέρᾱσι (κέρᾱσι in Hom.), Ep. κεράεσσι :—the Ion. decl. is κέρας, κέρεος, κέρεῖ, pl. κέρεα, κερέων : **I.** *the horn* of an animal, as of oxen, Il. ; ὀφθαλμοὶ δ' ὡσεὶ κέρα ἕστασαν his eyes stood fixed and stiff like *horns,* Od. **II.** *horn,* as a material, αἱ μὲν γὰρ [αἱ πύλαι] κεράεσσι τετεύχαται, through which the *true* dreams came, Ib. **III.** *anything made* of *horn,* **1.** *a bow,* Il., Hom., Theocr. **2.** of musical instruments, *a horn for blowing,* Xen. : *a flute,* Luc. **3.** *a drinking-horn,* Xen. **IV.** βοὸς κ. *a horn guard* or *pipe* to which the lead-weight (μολύβδαινα) of *a fishing-line* was attached, Hom. **V.** κέρατα *the horn points* with which the *writing-reed* was tipped, Anth. **VI.** *an arm* or *branch of a river,* Hes., Thuc. **VII.** *the wing of an army* or *fleet,* Hdt., Att. ; κατὰ κέρας

προσβάλλειν, ἐπιπίπτειν to attack *in flank*, Thuc., Xen. ; ἐπὶ κέρας ἄγειν to lead *towards the wing*, i. e. *in column*, not with a broad front, Lat. *agmine longo*, Hdt., Att.   VIII. *any projection*, e. g. *a mountain-peak*, Xen.

κέρασσε, Ep. for ἐκέρασε, 3 sing. aor. 1 of κεράννυμι.

κεράστης, ου, voc. κεράστα, ὁ, *horned*, ἔλαφος Soph., Eur. :—fem. **κεραστίς, ίδος**, of Io, Aesch.

κεραστός, ή, όν, (κεράννυμι) *mixed, mingled*, Anth.

κερασ-φόρος, ον, (φέρω) *horn-bearing, horned*, Eur.

κερατέα or **-ία, ἡ**, *the carob* or *locust-tree* (Arab. (kharoob) :—its fruit κεράτια, τά, is called *St. John's bread*, from a notion that it was the fruit he ate in the wilderness, N. T.

κεράτινος [ᾰ], η, ον, (κέρας) *of horn*, Xen.

κεράτιον [ᾰ], τό, Dim. of κέραα, v. sub κερατέα.

κερατών, ῶνος, ὁ, (κέρας) *made of horns*, Plut.

κεραύνειος, ον, (κεραυνός) *wielding the thunder*, Anth.

κεραύνιος, α, ον, and **ος, ον**, *of a thunderbolt*, Aesch., Eur.   **2.** *thunder-smitten*, Soph., Eur.

κεραυνοβολέω, to hurl the thunderbolt, Anth.   **II.** trans. *to strike therewith*, Il.   From

κεραυνο-βόλος, ον, (βάλλω) *hurling the thunder*, Anth.   **II.** proparox. κεραυνό-βολος, ον, pass. *thunder-stricken*, Eur.

κεραυνο-βρόντης, ου, ὁ, (βροντάω) *the lightener and thunderer*, Ar.

κεραυνο-μάχης, ὁ, *fighting with thunder*, Anth.

ΚΕΡΑΥΝΟ'Σ, ὁ, *a thunderbolt*, Lat. *fulmen*, Hom., etc. : generally, *thunder* :—but *thunder* properly was βροντή, Lat. *tonitru ; lightning* was στεροπή, Lat. *fulgur*.   **II.** metaph., κεραυνὸν ἐν γλώσσῃ φέρειν, of Pericles, Plut.

κεραυνο-φαής, ές, (φάος) *flashing like thunder*, Eur.

κεραυνο-φόρος, ον, *wielding the thunderbolt*, Plut.

κεραυνόω, f. ώσω, *to strike with thunderbolts*, Hdt. :—Pass., κεραυνωθείς Hes., Plat., etc.

ΚΕΡΑ'Ω, Ep. radic. form of κεράννυμι, part. κερῶν Od. ; Med., in imper. κεράασθε (lengthd. from -ᾶσθε) Ib. ; 3 pl. impf. κερόωντο Il.

ΚΕ'ΡΒΕΡΟΣ, ὁ, *Cerberus*, the fifty-headed dog of Hades, which guarded the gate of the nether world, Hes. ; later, with three heads or bodies, Eur.

κερδαίνω, f. -ᾰνῶ, Ion. -ανέω, also κερδήσω, and κερδήσομαι :—aor. 1 ἐκέρδᾱνα, Ion. -ηνα, also ἐκέρδησα : —pf. κεκέρδηκα : (κέρδος) :—*to gain, derive profit* or *advantage*, κακὰ κ. *to make unfair gains*, Hes. ; ἔκ or ἀπό τινος Hdt., Att. ; πρός τινος Soph. ; τί κερδανῶ ; what *shall I gain by* it ? Ar. :—c. part. *to gain by* doing, οὐδὲν ἐκμαθοῦσα κερδανεῖς Aesch., etc.   **2.** absol. *to make profit, gain advantage*, Hdt., Att. :— *to traffic, make merchandise*, Soph. ; κ. ἔπη *to receive fair words*, Id.   **II.** like ἀπολαύω, *to gain a loss, reap* disadvantage from a thing, as, δάκρυα κ., Eur. ; κ. ζημίαν N. T.

κερδᾰλέος, α, ον, (κέρδος) *having an eye to gain, wily, crafty, cunning*, Hom. :—of the fox, Archil. ap. Plat.   **II.** of things, *gainful, profitable*, κερδαλεώτερον Hdt. :—τὸ κ. = κέρδος, Aesch., Thuc. : Adv. -λέως, *to one's advantage*, Thuc.

κερδᾰλεό-φρων, ον, (φρήν) *crafty-minded*, Il.

κερδίων, ον [ῐ Ep., ῑ Att.], gen. ονος, Comp. (with no

Posit. in use, formed from κέρδος), *more profitable*, Hom., etc.   **II.** κέρδιστος, η, ον, Sup. *most cunning* or *crafty*, Il.   **2.** of things, *most profitable*, Aesch., Soph.

ΚΕ'ΡΔΟΣ, εος, τό, *gain, profit, advantage*, Lat. *lucrum*, Od. ; ποιεῖσθαί τι ἐν κέρδει, Horace's *lucro apponere*, Hdt. ; so, κέρδος ἡγεῖσθαι or νομίζειν τι Eur., Thuc.   **2.** *desire of gain, greed of gain*, Pind., Trag.   **II.** in pl. *cunning arts, wiles, tricks*, Hom.

κερδοσύνη, ἡ, like κερδαλεότης, *cunning, craft* : dat. κερδοσύνῃ as Adv., *by craft, cunningly*, Hom.

κερδώ, όος, contr. οῦς, ἡ, (κέρδος) *the wily one*, i. e. *the fox*, Pind., Ar.

κερδῷος, α, ον, (κέρδος) *bringing gain*, of Hermes, Luc., etc.   **II.** (κερδώ) *foxlike, wily*, Babr.

κέρεα, τά, Ion. for κέραα, pl. of κέρας.

κερέω, Ep. for κερῶ, fut. inf. of κείρω.

κερκίδο-ποιϊκή (sc. τέχνη), ἡ, *the art of the shuttle-maker* (κερκιδοποιός), Arist.

κερκίζω, *to make the web close with the* κερκίς, Plat.

κερκίς, ίδος, ἡ, (κρέκω ?) *in the loom, the rod* or *comb* by which the threads of the woof were driven home, so as to make the web even and close, Hom., Soph., etc.   **II.** *any rod, a measuring-rod*, Anth.   **2.** *the great bone of the leg, the tibia*, Plut.

ΚΕ'ΡΚΟΣ, ἡ, *the tail* of a beast, Ar., Plat., etc.

κέρκουρος or **κερκοῦρος, ὁ**, *a light vessel, boat*, esp. of the Cyprians, Hdt.

Κέρκῡρα, ἡ, the island *Corcyra*, now *Corfu*, Hdt., etc. : —Adj. Κερκυραῖος, α, ον, *Corcyraean*, Id., etc. :— τὰ Κερκυραϊκά, *the affairs of Corcyra*, Thuc.

Κέρκ-ωψ, ωπος, ὁ, (κέρκος) :—*the Cercopes* were a kind of *men-monkeys*, Hdt.   **2.** metaph. *a mischievous fellow, knave*, Aeschin.

κέρμα, ατος, τό, (κείρω) *a slice* : hence, *a small coin, mite*, in pl. *small coin, small change*, Ar.   **2.** generally, *small wares*, Anth.   Hence

κερμᾰτίζω, f. Att. ιῶ, *to cut small, mince, chop up*, Plat.   **II.** *to coin into small money*, Anth.

κερμάτιον, τό, Dim. of κέρμα, Anth.

κερμᾰτιστής, οῦ, ὁ, (κερματίζω) *a money-changer*, N. T.

κέρνος, εος, τό, *a large earthen dish*, in which fruits were offered to the Corybantes, borne by a priest or priestess called κερνᾶς, Anth.

κερο-βάτης [ᾰ], ου, ὁ, (κέρας, βαίνω) *horn-footed, hoofed*, Ar.

κερο-βόας, ου, ὁ, (βοάω) *horn-sounding*, of a horn flute, Anth.

κερό-δετος, ον, *bound with* or *made of horn*, Eur.

κερόεις, -όεσσα (contr. -οῦσσα), -οεν, (κέρας) *horned*, Eur.   **II.** *of horn*, of a flute, Anth.

κερ-οίαξ, ᾰκος, ὁ, *a rope belonging to the sailyards*, Luc.

κερο-τῠπέω, (τύπτω) *to butt with the horns* :—Pass., of ships in a storm, *buffeted*, Aesch.

κερ-ουλκός, ή, όν, (ἕλκω) *drawn by the horns*, pass. of a bow, because *tipped with horn*, Eur.

κερουτιάω, (κέρας) *to toss the horns*, Lat. *cornua tollere*: metaph. of persons, *to toss the head, give oneself airs*, Ar.

κερουχίς, ίδος, fem. of sq., Theocr.

κερ-οῦχος, ον, (ἔχω) *having horns, horned*, Babr.

κερο-φόρος, ον, (φέρω) = κερασφόρος, *horned,* Eur.

κέρσα, Ep. aor. 1 of κείρω.

κερτομέω, f. ήσω, (κέρτομος) *to taunt* or *sneer at,* c. acc. pers., Od., Aesch., Eur.: absol. *to sneer,* Od. :— Pass. *to be scoffed at,* Eur.   Hence

κερτόμησις, εως, ή, *jeering, mockery,* Soph. ; and

κερτομία, ή, = foreg. ; in pl., κερτομίας ήδ᾽ αἴσυλα μυθήσασθαι Il. ; κερτομίας καὶ χεῖρας ἀφέξω Od.

κερτόμιος and **κέρτομος, ον,** (κέαρ, τέμνω) *heart-cutting, stinging, reproachful,* Od. ; Δία κερτομίοις ἐπέεσσι Hom. ; also, κερτομίοισι (without ἐπέεσσι) Id. ; κέρτομα βάζειν Hes. ; χόροι κέρτομοι *abusive,* Hdt.   II. *mocking, delusive,* κέρτομος χαρά Eur.

κέρχνη, ή, a kind of *hawk, the kestrel;* also **κερχνηΐς,** contr. **κερχνής, ῆδος, ή,** Ar.

κέσκετο, Ion. 3 sing. impf. of κεῖμαι.

κεστός, ή, όν, (κεντέω) *stitched, embroidered,* κεστὸς ἱμάς of Aphrodite's *charmed girdle,* Il.   2. later, κεστός, ὁ, as Subst., Lat. *cestus,* Anth., Luc.

κέστρα, ή, (κεντέω) *a fish* held in esteem among the Greeks, Ar.

κευθάνω, poët. for κεύθω, Il.

κευθμός, ὁ, = sq., Il.

κευθμών, ῶνος, ὁ, (κεύθω) *a hiding place, hole, corner,* Od.; κευθμῶνες ὀρέων the *hollows* of the mountains, Pind., Eur.   2. of the nether world, *the abyss,* Hes., Aesch.   3. in Aesch. Eum. 805 = ἄδυτον, *a sanctuary.*

κεύθοισα, Dor. for -ουσα, part. fem. of κεύθω.

κεῦθος, εος, τό, = κευθμών, ὑπὸ κεύθεσι γαίης in the *depths* of the earth, Hom. ; in sing., κ. νεκύων Soph. ; κ. οἴκων the innermost chambers, like μυχός, Eur.

ΚΕΥ´ΘΩ, f. κεύσω: aor. 1 ἔκευσα: Ep. redupl. aor. 2 subj. κεκύθω: pf. κέκευθα: plqpf. ἐκεκεύθειν, Ep. κεκεύθειν:— *to cover quite up, to cover, hide,* of the grave, ὅπου κύθε γαῖα where earth *covered* him, Od. ; so, ὃν οὐδὲ κατθανόντα γαῖα κ. Aesch. ; also, ὁπότ᾽ ἄν σε δόμοι κεκύθωσι, i. e. when thou hast entered the house, Od. : Soph. :—pf. *to contain,* Hom., Soph.   2. *to conceal,* and in pf. *to keep concealed,* Hom. ; οὐκέτι κεύθετε βρωτὺν οὐδὲ ποτῆτα no more can ye *disguise* your eating and drinking, Od. ; κ. τι ἔνδον καρδίας Aesch. ; κ. μῆνιν *to cherish* anger, Eur.   3. c. dupl. acc., οὐδέ σε κεύσω [ταῦτα] nor will *I keep* them *secret from* thee, Od.   II. in Trag. sometimes intr. *to be concealed, lie hidden,* esp. in pf., Aesch., Soph.

κεφαλάδιον, τό, Dim. of κεφάλαιον.

κεφάλαιος, α, ον, (κεφαλή) *of the head :* metaph., like Lat. *capitalis, principal,* Ar.   II. as Subst., κεφάλαιον, τό, *the head,* Id.   2. *the chief* or *main point, the sum of the matter,* Pind., Thuc., etc. ; ἐν κεφαλαίῳ, or ὡς ἐν κ., εἰπεῖν *to speak summarily,* Xen., etc. ; ἐν κεφαλαίοις ὑπομνῆσαι, ἀποδεῖξαι, περιλαβεῖν τι Thuc.   3. of persons, *the head* or *chief,* Luc.   4. of money, *the capital,* Lat. *caput,* opp. to interest, Plat., etc. : *the sum total,* Dem.   5. *the crown, completion* of a thing, *a crowning act* of wrong, Id. ; κ. ἐπιτιθέναι ἐπί τινι, Lat. *corollam imponere rei,* Plat.   Hence

κεφάλαιόω, f. ώσω, *to bring under heads, sum up, state summarily,* Thuc.   II. *to smite on the head,* N. T.

κεφάλαι-ώδης, ες, (εἶδος) *capital, principal, chief,* Luc. :—Adv. -δῶς, *summarily,* Arist.

κεφαλαίωμα, ατος, τό, (κεφαλαιόω) *the sum total,* Hdt.

κεφάλ-αλγής, ές, (ἀλγέω) *causing headache,* Xen. Hence

κεφαλαλγία, ή, *head-ache :* later **-αργία, ή,** Luc.

ΚΕΦΑ´ΛΗ´, ή, *the head* of man or beast, Hom., etc. ; κατὰ κεφαλῆς, Ep. κὰκ κεφαλῆς, over the head, Id.; κὰκ κεφαλήν *on the head,* Il. :—ἐς πόδας ἐκ κεφαλῆς from *head* to foot, Ib. :—ἐπὶ κεφαλήν *head foremost, head downwards, headlong,* Hdt., Plat., etc.   2. *the head,* put for the whole person, Hom. ; ἴσον ἐμῇ κεφαλῇ *like myself,* Il. ; φίλη κ., Lat. *carum caput,* Ib. : in bad sense, ὦ κακαὶ κεφαλαί Hdt. ; ὦ μιαρὰ κ. Ar.   3. *the head,* i. e. *the life,* παρθέμενοι κεφαλάς setting *their heads* on the cast, Od. :—in imprecations, ἐς κεφαλὴν τρέποιτ᾽ ἐμοί *on my head be it!* Ar., etc.   II. generally, κ. σκορόδου *a head* of garlic, Id. : *the top* or *brim* of a vessel, Theocr. : *the coping* of a wall, Xen. :—in pl. *the head* or *source* of a river, Hdt.   III. metaph., like κεφάλαιον, *the crown, completion* of a thing, Plat.

κεφᾰλῆφι, -ῆφι, Ep. gen. and dat. of κεφαλή.

κεφάλῖνος, ὁ, *a sea-fish,* = βλεψίας, Dorio ap. Ath.

κεφάλιον, ά, τό, Dim. of κεφαλή, Plut.

κεφᾰλίς, ίδος, ή, Dim. of κεφαλή.   II. *part of a shoe,* Arist.   III. *a head, chapter,* N. T.

κέχανδα, pf. of χανδάνω.

κεχάρηκα, κεχάρημαι [ἄ], pf. act. and pass. of χαίρω.

κεχάρήσεμεν, Ep. fut. inf. of χαίρω.

κεχάρήσεται, 3 sing. Ep. fut. med. of χαίρω.

κεχάρητο [ἄ], **-ηντο,** Ep. 3 sing. and pl. plqpf. pass. of χαίρω.

κεχαρηώς, Ep. pf. part. of χαίρω.

κεχαρισμένος, pf. pass. part. of χαρίζομαι.

κεχάριστο, 3 sing. plqpf. pass. of χαρίζομαι.

κεχᾰρῑτωμένος, pf. pass. part. of χαριτόω.

κεχαροίατο, Ep. for -οιντο, 3 pl. plqpf. pass. of χαίρω.

κεχάροντο [ἄ], 3 pl. Ep. redupl. aor. 2 med. of χαίρω.

κέχηνα, pf. of χάσκω.   Hence

Κεχηναῖοι, ων, οἱ, Comic word for Ἀθηναῖοι, *Gapenians* for *Athenians,* Ar.

κέχλᾰδον, poët. redupl. aor. 2 of χλάδω.

κεχλᾰδώς, pf. part. of χλάζω.

κεχλίαγκα, pf. of χλιαίνω.

κεχλῖδώς, pf. part. of χλίω.

κεχρημένος, *needy,* pf. pass. part. of χράω c.

κεχολῶσθαι, pf. pass. inf. of χολόω.

κεχολώσομαι, fut. 3 pass. of χολόω.

κεχρηματισμένος, pf. pass. part. of χρηματίζω.

κέχῦμαι, pf. pass. of χέω.

κέχῦτο, -υντο, 3 sing. and pl. Ep. plqpf. of χέω.

κεχωρίδαται, Ion. 3 pl. pf. pass. of χωρίζω.

κεχωρισμένως, Adv. (χωρίζω) *separately,* Arist.

κεχωσμένος, pf. pass. part. of χώννυμι.

κέωμαι, subj. of κεῖμαι.

κέων, part. of κέω = κεῖμαι, q. v.

Κέως, Ion. **Κέος, ή,** *Ceos,* one of the Cyclades, Hdt., etc.: —hence **Κεῖος,** Ion. **Κήϊος, ὁ,** *a Ceian,* Id., etc. ; οὐ Χῖος, ἀλλὰ Κεῖος not a (roguish) *Chian,* but an (honest) *Ceian,* proverb in Ar.

κῆ, Ion. for πῇ or ποῖ : but κη enclit. for πῃ or που, Hdt.

κῆαι, (Ep. aor. 1 inf. of καίω) 3 sing. opt.   II. **κήαι,** 3 sing. opt.

κῆγώ or κῆγών, Dor. crasis of καὶ ἐγώ.

κηδεία, ἡ, (κῆδος) connexion by marriage, alliance, Lat. affinitas, Eur., Xen.

κήδειος, ον, (κῆδος) cared for, dear, beloved, Il.   2. careful of, or caring for, c. gen., Eur.   II. of a funeral or tomb, mourning, sepulchral, Aesch., Eur.

κηδεμονεύς, έως, ὁ, = κηδεμών, Anth.

κηδεμονία, ἡ, (κηδεμών) care, solicitude, Plat.; and

κηδεμονικός, ή, όν, provident, careful: Adv. -κῶς, Luc. From

κηδεμών, όνος, ὁ, (κηδέω) one who is in charge, esp. for burial, Il.   2. generally, a protector, guardian, Theogn., Soph., etc.:—also of a female, Soph.   II. = κηδεστής, Eur., Ar.

κήδεος, ον, = κήδειος, given in charge for burial, Il.

κήδεσκον, aor. 1 med. imper. of κήδω.

κήδεσκον, Ion. impf. of κήδω:—κηδέσκετο, 3 sing. impf. med.

κηδεστής, οῦ, ὁ, (κῆδος) a connexion by marriage, Lat. affinis, Xen., etc.: esp. a son-in-law, father-in-law, a step-father, Dem.:—a brother-in-law, Eur. Hence

κηδεστία, ἡ, connexion by marriage, Xen.

κήδευμα, ατος, τό, connexion or alliance by marriage, Lat. affinitas, Eur.   2. poët. for κηδεστής, one who is so connected, Soph., Eur.

κηδευτής, ὁ, = κηδεμών, Anth.

κηδεύω, f. σω, (κῆδος) to take charge of, attend to, tend, Soph., Eur.   2. esp. to attend to a corpse, close the eyes, bury, mourn, Eur., etc.   II. to contract a marriage, ally oneself in marriage, Aesch., Eur.; κ. λέχος to marry, Soph.:—Pass. to be so allied, Eur.   2. c. acc. to make one's kinsman by marriage, Id.   3. absol., οἱ κηδεύσαντες those who formed the marriage, Id.

κηδήσω, fut. of κήδω.

κήδιστος, η, ον, Sup. formed from κῆδος, most worthy of our care, most cared for, Hom.   II. nearest allied by marriage, Od.

κῆδος, Dor. κᾶδος, εος, τό, (κήδω) care for others, c. gen., Od.   2. trouble, sorrow; mostly in pl. troubles, Hom.   3. esp. cares for the dead, mourning, Id., Aesch., etc.; also in sing., κᾶδος φθιμένου Pind.; ἄμα κήδεϊ when there is a death in the family, Hdt.; ἐς τὸ κ. ἰέναι to attend the funeral, Id.   4. an object of care, a care, Aesch.   II. connexion by marriage, Lat. affinitas, Hdt., Att.

κηδόσυνος, ον, anxious, Eur.

κήδω: impf. ἔκηδον, Ion. κήδεσκον: f. κηδήσω (from a form κηδέω):—Med. and Pass., Ep. impf. κηδέσκετο: f. κεκαδήσομαι (for κεκαδήσω, κέκαδον, v. χάζω B): aor. 1 imper. κήδεσαι: pf. κέκηδα (in pres. sense):   I. Act. to trouble, distress, vex, Hom.   II. Med. and Pass. to be troubled or distressed for others, c. gen. pers., Il., etc.: also c. gen. rei, τῶν ἀλφίτων Ar.:—absol. in part. κηδόμενος, η, ον, caring for a person, anxious, Il.

κήδωκε, Dor. crasis for καὶ ἔδωκε.

κῆεν, 3 sing. Ep. aor. 1 of καίω.

κηθάριον, τό, a vessel into which the ψῆφοι were cast in voting, Ar. (Deriv. uncertain.)

κῆκ, Dor. crasis for κὰκ, i. e. καὶ ἐκ.

κηκίς [ῑ], ῖδος, ἡ, anything oozing forth, ooze, Aesch.;

κ. φόνου oozing blood, Id.; μυδῶσα κ., of the juices drawn by fire from a sacrificial victim, Soph.   II. the dye made from sap oozing from the gall-nut, Dem.; κ. πορφύρας the dye of the purple-fish, Aesch.

κηκίω, only in pres. and Ep. impf. κήκιον, (κηκίς) to gush or ooze, Od., Soph.:—Pass., αἷμάς κηκιομένα ἑλκέων Soph. [ῑ Ep.; ῐ Att.]

κήλεος, ον, (καίω) burning, Il.:—so κήλειος, Ib.

ΚΗΛΕ´Ω, f. ήσω, to charm, bewitch, enchant, beguile, fascinate, esp. by music, Lat. mulcere, Eur., Plat.

κήλη, Att. κάλη [ᾱ], ἡ, a tumor, esp. a rupture, Lat. hernia, Anth.

κηληθμός, ὁ, (κηλέω) enchantment, fascination, Od.

κήλημα, ατος, τό, a magic charm, spell, Eur.

κήλησις, εως, ἡ, an enchanting, fascination, Plat.

κηλητήριος, α, ον, better ος, ον, charming, appeasing, Eur.; τὸ κ. = κήλημα, Soph.

κηλήτης, ου, ὁ, (κήλη) one who is ruptured, Anth.

κηλιδόω, f. ώσω, to stain, sully, soil, Eur. From

ΚΗΛΙ´Σ [ῑ], ῖδος, ἡ, a stain, spot, defilement, esp. of blood, Trag.   2. metaph. a stain, blemish, dishonour, Soph., Xen.

ΚΗ´ΛΟΝ, τό, a shaft, an arrow, Il., Hes.

ΚΗ´ΛΩΝ, ωνος, ὁ, a swipe or swing-beam, for drawing water, Lat. tolleno:—so, κηλώνειον, Ion. -ήιον, τό, Hdt.

κημαυτόν, κημέ, κημοί, Dor. crasis for καὶ ἐμαυτόν, καὶ ἐμέ, καὶ ἐμοί.

ΚΗΜΟ´Σ, ὁ, a muzzle, put on a led horse, Xen., Anth.   II. the funnel-shaped top to the voting-urn (κάδος, καδίσκος) in the Athen. law-courts, through which the ballots (ψῆφοι) were dropt, Ar.

κημόω, (κημός) to muzzle a horse, Xen.

κήν, Dor. crasis for καὶ ἐν:—but κήν for καὶ ἄν.

κηνιαυτός, Dor. crasis for καὶ ἐνιαυτός.

κῆνος, Aeol. for κεῖνος, ἐκεῖνος.

κῆνσος, ὁ, Lat. census, registration of taxation, N. T.: —the tax itself, Ib.

ΚΗ´Ξ, κηκός, ἡ, a sea-bird that dashes into the sea to seize its prey, perh. the tern or gannet, Od.

κήξ, Dor. crasis for καὶ ἐξ.

κηξαπίνας, Dor. crasis for καὶ ἐξαπίνης.

κήομεν, Ep. for κήωμεν, 1 pl. aor. 1 subj. of καίω.

κῆπε, Dor. crasis for καὶ εἶπε.

κηπεί, κήπειτα, Dor. crasis for καὶ ἐπεί, καὶ ἔπειτα.

κήπευμα, ατος, τό, (κηπεύω) a garden-flower, Ar.

κηπεύς, έως, ὁ, (κῆπος) a gardener, Anth.

κηπεύω, f. σω, (κῆπος) to rear in a garden, Luc.: metaph. to tend, cherish, freshen, Eur.

κηπί, Dor. crasis for καὶ ἐπί.

κηπίον, τό, Dem. of κῆπος: a parterre: metaph. a decoration, appendage, Thuc.

κήπιχάριτται, Boeot. crasis for καὶ ἐπιχάρισαι.

κηπο-λόγος, ον, (λέγω) teaching in a garden, Anth.

ΚΗ´ΠΟΣ, Dor. κᾶπος, ὁ, a garden, orchard, plantation, Od.:—of any fertile region, Ἀφροδίτης κᾶπος, i. e. Cyrene, Pind.; also, i. e. Libya, Id., etc.:—οἱ Ἀδώνιδος κῆποι, v. Ἄδωνις 2.

κηπουρικός, ή, όν, of or for gardening, Plat. From

κηπ-ουρός, ὁ, keeper of a garden, a gardener.

ΚΗ´Ρ, ἡ, Κηρός, acc. Κῆρα, the goddess of death, hence doom, fate, Hom.; in full, Κὴρ Θανάτοιο Od.; Κῆρες Θανάτοιο Il.: generally, bane, ruin, βαρεῖα μὲν κὴρ

τὸ μὴ πιθέσθαι grievous *ruin* it were not to obey, Aesch. ; **κὴρ οὐ καλή** an unseemly *calamity*, Soph.

ΚΗ῀Ρ, τό, contr. from **κέαρ** (as **ἦρ** from **ἔαρ**), *the heart*, Lat. *cor*, Hom. ; dat. **κῆρι** as Adv., *with all the heart, heartily*, Id. :—in Trag. always **κέαρ**.

κηραίνω, f. **ᾰνῶ**, (**κήρ**) *to be sick at heart, to be disquieted, anxious*, Eur.

Κηρεσσι-φόρητος, ον, (**κήρ**, **φορέω**) *urged on by the Κῆρες*, Il.

κήρῐνος, η, ον, (**κηρός**) *of wax, waxen*, Plat. : metaph. *pliable as wax* (Horat., *cereus in vitium flecti*), Id.

κηριο-κλέπτης, ου, ὁ, *stealer of honeycombs*, Theocr.

κηρίον, τό, (**κηρός**) *a honeycomb*, Lat. *favus*, Hes., Hdt., etc. ; also, **κηρίον σφηκῶν** Hdt.   2. *a wax tablet*, Anth.

κηρι-τρεφής, ές, (**τρέφω**) *born to misery*, Hes.

κηρο-δέτης, ου, ὁ, Dor. **κηροδέτας**, = sq., Eur.

κηρό-δετος, Dor. **καρ-**, ον, (**δέω**) *wax-bound*, **μέλι** Anth.

κηρόθῐ, Adv. (**κήρ**) *in the heart, with all the heart, heartily*, Hom., Hes.

κηρόομαι, Pass. (**κηρός**) Med. *to form for oneself of wax*, Anth.

κηρο-παγής, ές, (**πήγνυμι**) *fastened with wax*, Anth.

κηρό-πλαστος, ον, *moulded of wax, waxen*, Anth.   2. = **κηρόδετος**, Aesch.

ΚΗΡΟ῀Σ, ὁ, *bees-wax*, Lat. *cera*, Od., Plat.

κηρο-τέχνης, ου, ὁ, *a modeller in wax*, Anacreon.

κηρο-τρόφος, ον, (**τρέφω**) *producing wax, waxen*, Anth.

κηρο-χίτων [ῐ], ωνος, ὁ, ἡ, *clad in wax*, Anth.

κηρο-χῠτέω, *to make waxen cells*, Anth. From

κηρό-χῠτος, ον, *moulded of wax*.

κηρόω, v. **κηρόομαι**.

κήρυγμα, ατος, τό, (**κηρύσσω**) *that which is cried by a herald, a proclamation, public notice*, Hdt., Att.   2. *a reward offered by proclamation*, Xen., Aeschin.

κηρῡκεία, Ion. -**ηΐη**, ἡ, (**κήρυξ**) *the office of herald* or *crier*, Hdt., Plat.

κηρῡκειον [ῠ], Ion. -**ήϊον**, Dor. **κᾱρύκειον**, τό, (**κήρυξ**) *a herald's wand*, Lat. *caduceus*, Hdt., Thuc.

κηρῡκευμα [ῠ], ατος, τό, *a proclamation, message*, Aesch.

κηρῡκεύω, f. **σω**, (**κήρυξ**) *to be a herald* or *crier, fulfil the office of one*, Plat.   II. trans. *to proclaim, notify*, τί τινι Aesch., Eur.

κηρῡκίη, -**ηΐον**, Ion. for **κηρῡκεία**, -**ειον**.

κηρῡκικός, ή, όν, (**κήρυξ**) *of heralds*, Plat.

κηρύλος [ῠ], ὁ, *the halcyon*. The form **κείρυλος** is a joke in Ar., the barber Sporgilos being called (from **κείρω**), *rasor-bird*.

κῆρυξ, Dor. **κᾱρυξ**, ῡκος, ὁ, *a herald, pursuivant, marshal, public messenger*, Hom., etc. In Hom. they summon the assembly, separate combatants, have charge of sacrifices, act as envoys, and their persons were sacred. After Hom., Hermes is called the **κῆρυξ** of the gods, Hes., etc.   2. at Athens, *a crier*, who made proclamation in the public assemblies, Ar., etc. From

κηρύσσω, Il., Att. -**ττω**, Dor. **κᾱρύσσω** : f. -**ξω** : aor. 1 **ἐκήρυξα** :—Pass., f. **κηρυχθήσομαι** ; fut. med. in pass. sense **κηρύξομαι** : aor. 1 **ἐκηρύχθην** : pf. **κεκήρυγμαι** :—*to be a herald, officiate as herald*, Il.; **λαὸν κηρύσσοντες ἀγειρόντων** let them convene the people *by voice of herald*, Ib.; **κήρυσσε, κήρυξ** Aesch., etc. :—impers., **κηρύσσει**

(sc. ὁ **κῆρυξ**) *he gives notice, proclamation is made*, Xen.   II. c. acc. pers. *to summon by voice of herald*, Hom., Ar.   2. *to proclaim* as conqueror, Xen., etc. : *to extol*, Eur.   3. *to call upon, invoke*, Aesch., Eur.   III. c. acc. rei, *to proclaim, announce*, τί τινι Trag. :—*to proclaim* or *advertise* for sale, Hdt. ; **κ. ἀποικίαν** *to proclaim* a colony, i. e. *to invite* people to join as colonists, Thuc.   2. *to proclaim* or *command publicly*, Lat. *indicere*, Aesch., Soph., etc. ; **τὰ κηρυχθέντα** *the public orders*, Soph.

κηρωτός, ή, όν, (**κηρόω**) *covered with wax* : **κηρωτή**, ἡ, *a cerate* or *salve*, Ar.

κής, Dor. crasis for **καὶ εἰς**.

κῆται, contr. from **κέηται**, 3 sing. subj. of **κεῖμαι**.

κήτειος, α, ον, (**κῆτος**) *of sea monsters*, Mosch.

ΚΗ῀ΤΟΣ, εος, τό, *any sea-monster* or *huge fish*, Hom., Hdt.   II. *an abyss, hollow*, cf. **κήτωεις**.

κητο-φόνος, ον, (***φένω**) *killing sea-monsters*, Anth.

κητώεις, εσσα, εν, (**κῆτος** II), as epith. of Lacedaemon, *full of hollows* or *ravines*, Hom. ; cf. **μεγακήτης**.

κηῠ, Dor. crasis for **καὶ εὖ**.

κηφᾶ, Dor. crasis for **καὶ ἔφη**.

ΚΗΦΗ῀Ν, ῆνος, ὁ, *a drone*, Lat. *fucus* : metaph. *a drone, a lazy fellow*, Hes., Ar.

κηφην-ώδης, ες, (**εἶδος**) *like a drone*, Plat.

κηφθᾶ, Dor. crasis for **καὶ ἤφθη** from **ἅπτομαι**.

Κηφῑσός, Dor. **Κᾱφ-**, ὁ, *the Cephisus*, a river of Phocis, Il. :—fem. **λίμνη Κηφῑσίς** Ib.   2. the more famous river of Athens, Soph., etc.

κηώδης, ες, (**κῆαι**, aor. 1 inf. of **καίω**) *smelling as of incense, fragrant*, Il.

κηώεις, εσσα, εν, = **κηώδης**, Il.

κιβδηλεύω, (**κίβδηλος**) *to adulterate* coin, Ar., etc.   II. metaph. *to palm off*, Eur.

κιβδηλία, ἡ, *adulteration, trickery, dishonesty*, Ar. From

κίβδηλος, ον, *adulterated, spurious, base*, of coin, Theogn., Eur.   II. metaph. *base, false, spurious, fraudulent*, of men, Theogn., Eur. ; of oracles, *deceitful*, Hdt. ; **ἐν κιββήλῳ** Eur. From

ΚΙ῀ΒΔΟΣ, ὁ, *dross, alloy*.

κίβῑσις [κῐ], ἡ, *a pouch, wallet*, Hes. (A Cyprian word.)

κιβώτιον, τό, Dim. of **κιβωτός**, Ar.

κιβωτός, ἡ, *a wooden box, chest, coffer*, Ar. (Deriv. uncertain.)

κιγκλίζω, (**κίγκλος**) *to wag the tail* :—metaph. *to change constantly*, Theogn.

ΚΙΓΚΛΙ῀Σ, ῖδος, ἡ, mostly in pl. **κιγκλίδες**, *the latticed gates* in the law-courts or council-chamber, through which the members passed, Ar. ; metaph., means *waitings at the bar, the law's delays*, Plut. ; in sing., **ἐντὸς τῆς κιγκλίδος διατρίβειν** *to live in court*, Luc.

ΚΙ῀ΓΚΛΟΣ, ὁ, prob. *a kind of wagtail*, Theogn.

κιγχάνω [ᾰ], v. sub **κιχάνω** [ᾰ].

κίδναμαι, Pass. = **σκεδάννυμαι**, only in pres. and impf., *to be spread abroad* or *over*, of the dawning day, Il. ; **ὕπνος ἐπ' ὄσσοις κ.** Eur.

ΚΙΘΑ῀ΡΑ, Ion. -**ρη** [θᾰ], ἡ, the Lat. *cithara* (whence *guitar*), a kind of *lyre* or *lute*, h. Hom., Hdt., Att. : —it was of triangular shape, with seven strings, Eur. Cf. sq.

κῐθαρίζω, f. **ίσω**, (**κίθαρις**) *to play the cithara*, **φόρμιγγι**

κιθάριζε Il., Hes. ; λύρη ἐρατὸν κιθαρίζων h. Hom. ; (so that there can have been no great difference between the κιθάρα, λύρα, and φόρμιγξ) ; κιθαρίζειν οὐκ ἐπίσταται, of an uneducated person, Ar.

κίθαρις, ιος, ἡ, acc. κίθαριν, = κιθάρα, Hom., etc. II. =κιθαριστύς, Id.

κιθάρισις [ᾰ], εως, ἡ, (κιθαρίζω) a playing on the cithara, Plat.; and

κιθάρισμα [ᾰ], ατος, τό, (κιθαρίζω) that which is played on the cithara, a piece of music for it, Plat.

κιθαριστής, οῦ, ὁ, (κιθαρίζω) a player on the cithara, Hes., Att. Hence

κιθαριστικός, ή, όν, skilled in harp-playing, Plat. : ἡ -κή (sc. τέχνη) — sq., Id.

κιθαριστύς, ύος, ἡ, (κιθαρίζω) the art of playing the cithara, Il.

κιθαρῳδέω, f. ήσω, to sing to the cithara, Plat. ; and

κιθαρῳδία, ἡ, a singing to the cithara, Plat. ; and

κιθαρῳδικός, ή, όν, of or for harp-playing, Ar. 2. ἡ -κή (sc. τέχνη) = κιθαρῳδία, Plat. From

κιθαρ-ῳδός, ὁ, (κιθάρα, ἀοιδός) one who plays and sings to the cithara, a harper, Hdt., Plat., etc.

κιθών, Ion. for χιτών.

ΚΙ'ΚΙ, τό, the castor berry, Hdt.

κίκιννος [κῐ], ὁ, a ringlet, Lat. cincinnus, Ar., Theocr.

κικκάβαῦ, onomatop., a cry in imitation of the screech-owl's note, toowhit, toowhoo, Ar.

κικλήσκω, poët. redupl. form of καλέω, only in pres. and impf. : Ep. inf. κικλήσκέμεν : Ep. impf. κίκλησκον : —to call, summon, Hom. 2. to call on, invoke, implore, Il., Aesch., etc. II. to accost, address, Il. III. to name, call by name, Ib., Aesch., Eur. : —Pass., νῆσός τις Συρίη κικλήσκεται there is an island called Syros, Od. ; cf. κλήζω II.

Κικύννα, ἡ, Cicynna, an Attic deme : Κικυννεύς, ὁ, a Cicynnian, Att. ; pl. Κικυννῆς, Ar. ; Κικυννόθεν from Cicynna, Id.

ΚΙ'ΚΥΣ, ἡ, strength, vigour, Od., h. Hom.

*ΚΙ'ΚΩ, a verb only found in Dor. aor. 1 ἔκικα, = ἤνεγκα, Anth. :—in Ar. we have ἀπ-έκιξαν, sent away, shook off.

Κίλιξ [ῐ], ἴκος, ὁ, a Cilician, Il. : fem. Κίλισσα, Aesch. : —Adj. Κιλίκιος, α, ον, Cilician, Id. ; ἡ Κιλικία (sc. γῆ), Cilicia, Hdt.

κιλλί-βας, αντος, ὁ, in pl. κιλλίβαντες, a three-legged stand for supporting any thing, κιλλίβαντες ἀσπίδος a shield-stand, Ar. Hence

ΚΙ'ΛΛΟΣ, ὁ, an ass.

κίμβιξ, ῐκος, ὁ, a niggard, Arist. (Deriv. unknown.)

Κιμμέριοι, οἱ, the Cimmerians, a people dwelling beyond the Ocean in perpetual darkness, Od. : in later geography, a people about the Palus Maeotis, Hdt. :—Adj. Κιμμερικός, ή, όν, Cimmerian, Κ. ἰσθμός the Crimea, Aesch. ; Κιμμέριος, α, ον, Hdt.

Κιμωλία (sc. γῆ), ἡ, Cimolian earth, a white clay, from Cimolus in the Cyclades, which was used by way of soap in the baths, Ar.

κίναβρα, ἡ, the rank smell of a he-goat, Luc. Hence

κιναβράω, to smell like a goat, Ar.

κίναδος [ῐ], εος, τό, a fox : hence of a cunning rogue, Soph., Ar., etc. :—in Theocr. the voc. κίναδε implies a masc. form κίναδος, ου, ὁ. (Sicilian word.)

κινάθισμα [ᾰ], τό, motion, rustling, as of wings, Aesch.

κιναιδία, ἡ, = lust, Aeschin., Luc. From

κίναιδος [ῐ], ὁ, Lat. cinaedus, a lewd fellow, Plat.

κινδύνευμα [ῠ], ατος, τό, (κινδυνεύω) a risk, hazard, venture, bold enterprise, Soph., Eur.

κινδυνευτέον, verb. Adj. one must venture, Eur. ; and

κινδυνευτής, οῦ, ὁ, a daring, venturesome person, Thuc. ; and

κινδυνευτικός, ή, όν, adventurous, Arist. From

κινδυνεύω, f. σω :—Pass., f. κινδυνευθήσομαι or κεκινδυνεύσομαι :—to be daring, to make a venture, take the risk, do a daring thing, Hdt., Ar., etc. :—to be in danger, Thuc. : in respect of which danger is incurred in dat., κ. τῷ σώματι, τῇ ψυχῇ Hdt.; κ. πάσῃ τῇ Ἑλλάδι to run a risk with all Greece, i. e. endanger it all, Id., etc. ; so, κ. περὶ τῆς ψυχῆς Ar., etc. 3. c. acc. cogn. to venture, hazard, κινδύνευμα Plat. ; μάχην Aeschin. :—Pass. to be risked or hazarded, μεταβολὴ κινδυνεύεται there is risk of change, Thuc. ; τὰ μέγιστα κινδυνεύεται are endangered, Dem. 4. c. inf. to run the risk of doing or being, Hdt., Thuc., etc. :— then, implying a chance of success, κινδυνεύω (c. inf.) is used to express what may possibly or probably happen, κινδυνεύουσι οἱ ἄνθρωποι γόητες εἶναι they run a risk of being reputed conjurors, Hdt. ; κινδυνεύσεις ἐπιδεῖξαι χρηστὸς εἶναι you will have a chance of showing your worth, Xen. ; κινδυνεύει ἀγαθὸν γεγονέναι it is very likely to prove good, Plat. :—then impers., κινδυνεύει it may be, possibly, Id. 5. Pass. to be endangered or imperilled, Thuc., Dem. From

ΚΙ'ΝΔΥΝΟΣ, ὁ, a danger, risk, hazard, venture, enterprise, Lat. periculum, Pind., Ar., etc.; κίνδυνον ἀναρίπτειν to run a risk, Hdt., etc. ; κίνδυνον or κινδύνους ἀναλαβέσθαι, ὑποδύεσθαι, αἵρεσθαι, ὑπομεῖναι, etc., Att.

κινεῦ, Dor. for κινοῦ, imper. pass. of κινέω.

ΚΙ'ΝΕ'Ω, f. ήσω : aor. 1 ἐκίνησα, Ep. κίνησα : Med. and Pass., κινήσομαι and -ηθήσομαι : aor. 1 ἐκινήθην, Ep. 3 pl. ἐκίνηθεν : pf. κεκίνημαι :—to set in motion, to move, Hom., Att. 2. to move or remove a thing from its place, Hdt. ; κ. τὰ ἀκίνητα to meddle with things sacred, Id., Soph. ; κ. τὰ χρήματα ἐς ἄλλο τι to apply them to an alien purpose, Hdt. ;—κ. τὸ στρατόπεδον, Lat. castra movere, Xen. :—to change, innovate, τὰ νόμαια Hdt. II. to rouse, disturb, of a wasps' nest, Il. : to stir up, arouse, urge on, Trag., etc. III. to set agoing, cause, call forth, Soph., etc. :—proverb., κ. πᾶν χρῆμα to turn every stone, try every way, Hdt.

B. Pass. to be put in motion, to be moved, move, stir, Il., Hdt., Att. 2. to move forward, of soldiers, Soph., Xen., etc.

κινήθην, Ep. for ἐκιν-, aor. 1 pass. of foreg.

κινηθμός, ὁ, (κινέω) = κίνησις, motion, Pind.

κίνημα [ῐ], ατος, τό, (κινέω) a motion, movement, Plut.

κίνησις [ῐ], εως, ἡ, (κινέω) movement, motion, Plat., etc. : a dance, Luc. 2. movement, in a political sense, Thuc. ; of the Peloponn. war, Id.

κινητέος, α, ον, verb. Adj. of κινέω, to be moved, Plat.

κινητήρ, ῆρος, ὁ, = κινητής, h. Hom., Pind.

κινητής, οῦ, ὁ, (κινέω) one that sets agoing, an author, Ar.

κινητικός, ή, όν, (κινέω) of or for putting in motion, Xen.

κιννάμωμον, τό, *cinnamon*, a word borrowed from the Phoenicians, Hdt.

κίνυγμα [ῑ], ατος, τό, (κινύσσομαι) *anything moved about*, αἰθέριον κ. *a sport* for the winds of heaven, Aesch.

κινῦμαι [ῑ], Dep. = κινέομαι, only in pres. and impf., *to go, move*, ἐς πόλεμον κίνυντο (Ep. impf.) they *were marching* to battle, Il. ; κινυμένοιο as he *moved*, Ib.

κινύρομαι [ῠ], Dep., only in pres. and impf., *to utter a plaintive sound, lament, wail*, Ar. :—c. acc. cogn., χαλινοὶ κινύρονται φόνον the bridles *ring* or *clash* murderously, Aesch. From

ΚΙˊΝΥˉΡΟˊΣ, ά, όν, *wailing, plaintive*, Il.

κῑνύσσομαι, Pass. = κινέομαι, *to sway backwards and forwards*, Aesch.

κῑό-κρᾱνον, τό, (κίων, κράνιον) *the capital of a column*, Xen.

κίον, Ep. for ἔκιον, impf. of κίω.

κίοσι, dat. pl. of κίων.

Κίρκη, ἡ, *Circé*, an enchantress, dwelling in the island *Aea*, who changed Ulysses' companions into swine, Od.

ΚΙˊΡΚΟΣ, ὁ, a kind of *hawk* or *falcon*, so called from its *wheeling flight*, ἵρηξ κίρκος (where ἵρηξ is the generic term, κίρκος the specific, like βοῦς ταῦρος), Od.   **II.** *a ring, circle*, mostly in form κρίκος.   Hence

κιρκόω, f. ώσω, *to hoop round, secure with rings*, Aesch.

κιρνάω and –ημι, = κεράννυμι, only in pres. and impf. :— *to mix wine with water*, in 3 sing. impf. ἐκίρνα and κίρνη, part. κιρνάς, Od. ; in Hdt., 3 sing. pres. κιρνᾷ, 1 pl. κίρναμεν.

ΚΙˊΣ, ὁ, gen. κιός, acc. κίν, *a worm in wood* or *in corn, the weevil*, Lat. *curculio*, Pind.

κίσηρις [ῑ], εως and ιδος, ἡ, *the pumice-stone*, Lat. *pumex*, Arist., Luc. (Deriv. unknown.)

ΚΙˊΣΣΑˇ, Att. **κίττᾰ**, ἡ, a chattering, greedy bird, *the jay* or *magpie*, Ar.   **II.** *a false appetite*.   Hence

κισσάω, Att. **κιττ**–, f. ήσω, *to crave for strange food*, of pregnant women : metaph., κ. τῆς εἰρήνης Ar. ; c. inf. *to long* to do a thing, Id.

κισσ-ήρης, ες, (κισσός, *ἄρω) *ivy-clad*, Soph.

κίσσηρις, less correct form of κίσηρις.

κίσσῐνος, η, ον, (κισσός) *of ivy*, Eur.

Κίσσιος, α, ον, *of* or *from Cissia* in southern Persia, Hdt. ; Κισσία ληλεμίστρια *a Cissian* mourner, Aesch.

κισσο-κόμης, ου, ὁ, (κόμη) *ivy-crowned*, h. Hom.

κισσο-ποίητος, ον, (ποιέω) *made of ivy*, Luc.

ΚΙΣΣΟˊΣ, Att. **κιττός**, ὁ, *ivy*, Lat. *hedera*, Soph., Eur., etc.

κισσο-στέφανος, Anth.

κισσο-στεφής, ές, (στέφω) = foreg., Anacreont.

κισσοφορέω, Att. **κιττ**–, *to be decked with ivy*, Anth.

κισσο-φόρος, Att. **κιττ**–, ον, (φέρω) *ivy-wreathed*, Pind. : *luxuriant with ivy*, Eur.

κισσόω, f. ώσω, (κισσός) *to wreathe with ivy*, Eur.

κισσύβιον [ῠ], τό, (κισσός) *a rustic drinking-cup*, prob. with an *ivy-wreath* carved on it, Od.

κισσωτός, ή, όν, (κισσόω) *decked with ivy*, Anth.

ΚΙˊΣΤΗ, ἡ, *a box, chest*, Lat. *cista*, Od., Ar.   **2.** *a writing-case, desk*, Ar.

κιστίς, ίδος, ἡ, Dim. of κίστη, Ar.

κιστο-φόρος, ον, (κίστη, φέρω) *carrying a chest* in mystic processions, Dem.

κίττα, **κιττάω**, Att. for κίσσα, κισσάω.

κιττός, **κιττοφόρος**, Att. for κισσ-.

κιχάνω [ᾰ], impf. ἐκίχανον: the other moods are formed from *κίχημι, Ep. subj. κιχείω, κιχείομεν ; opt. κιχείην ; inf. κιχῆναι, part. κιχείς :—impf. ἐκίχην [ῑ], 2 sing. ἐκίχεις, Ep. 1 pl. κίχημεν ; 3 dual κιχήτην :—the Att. pres. is κιγχάνω [ᾰ] :—Med. (in act. sense), κιχάνομαι, part. κιχήμενος (from *κίχημι) : f. κιχήσομαι : Ep. 3 sing. aor. 1 κιχήσατο :—*to reach, hit*, or *light upon, meet with, find*, Hom. :—*to overtake*, Il. : *to reach, arrive at*, Ib. ; σε δουρὶ κιχήσομαι shall *reach* thee, Ib. ; τέλος θανάτοιο κιχήμενον death *that is sure to reach one*, inevitable, Ib.   **2.** rarely c. gen., like τυγχάνω, Soph.

κιχηλᾱ̂, ἡ, Dor. for κίχλη.

κίχημι, v. κιχάνω.

ΚΙˊΧΛΗ [ῑ by nature], ἡ, *a thrush*, Lat. *turdus*, Od., Ar.

κιχλίζω, Dor. 3 pl. κιχλίσδοντι : f. Att. ιῶ, *to chirp like a thrush* : hence, *to titter, giggle*, or *to eat* κίχλαι, *to live luxuriously*, Ar.

ΚΙˊΩ, imperat. κίε, 2 sing. subj. κίῃς, Ep. 1 pl. κίομεν (for κίωμεν) : opt. κίοιμι ; part. κιών, κιοῦσα : impf. ἔκιον, Ep. κίον :—*to go*, Hom., Aesch.

ΚΙˊΩΝ [ῑ], ονος, ὁ or ἡ, *a pillar*, Lat. *columna*, Od. : *a flogging-post*, Soph., Aeschin. ; proverb., ἔσθιε τοὺς Μεγακλέους κίονας eat *the pillars* of his hall, for being a spendthrift, he had nothing else left to give, Ar.   **2.** in pl. *the pillars guarded by Atlas*, which keep heaven and earth asunder, Od. ; whereas in Hdt. *Mount Atlas* is ὁ κίων τοῦ οὐρανοῦ.   **II.** *a columnar grave-stone*, Anth.

κλαγγαίνω or –άνω, (κλάζω) of hounds, *to give tongue*, only in pres., Aesch., Xen.   From

κλαγγή, ἡ, (κλάζω) *any sharp sound*, such as *the twang* of a bow, Il. ; *the scream* of cranes, Hom. ; *the grunting* of swine, Od. ; *the hissing* of serpents, Aesch. ; *the barking* of dogs, Xen. :—also of song, Soph. ; κλ. δύσφατος, of Cassandra-prophecies, Aesch.

κλαγγηδόν, Adv. *with a clang, noise, din*, Il.

κλᾰγερός, ά, όν, (κλάζω) *screaming*, of cranes, Anth.

κλάγξας, aor. 1 part. of κλάζω.

κλᾷδα, Dor. for κλῇδα, κλεῖδα, acc. of κλείς.

κλᾰδί, metaplast. dat. of κλάδος :—but   **II. κλᾳδί**, Dor. dat. of κλείς.

κλάδιον, τό, Dim. of κλάδος, Anth.

κλᾱδίσκος, ὁ, Dim. of sq., Anacreont.

κλάδος [ᾰ], ου, ὁ, (κλάω) *a young slip* or *shoot broken off*: esp. *an olive-branch* wound round with wool and presented by suppliants, Hdt., Aesch., Soph.

κλάδος, τό, = foreg., dat. sing. and pl. κλαδί, κλάδεσι, Ar.

ΚΛΑˊΖΩ, f. κλάγξω : aor. 1 ἔκλαγξα : aor. 2 ἔκλᾰγον : pf. κέκλαγγα, subj. κεκλάγγω, Ep. part. κεκληγώς, pl. κεκληγῶτες :—Pass., f. κεκλάγξομαι :—*to make a sharp piercing sound*, of birds, *to scream, screech*, Il., Soph., etc. ; of dogs, *to bark, bay*, Od., Ar. ; of things, as of arrows in the quiver, *to clash, rattle*, Il. ; of the wind, *to whistle*, Od. ; of wheels, *to creak*, Aesch. ; c. acc. cogn., κλάζουσι φόβον ring *forth* terror, Id.   **2.** of men, *to shout, scream*, Il. :—the nearest approach to articulate sound is in Aesch., μάντις ἔκλαγξεν ἄλλο μῆχαρ shrieked *forth* another remedy ; Ζῆνα ἐπινίκια κλάζων *sounding loudly* the victory-song of Zeus, Id.

κλάϊστρον, τό, Dor. for κλείστρον.

ΚΛΑΙˊΩ, Att. **κλάω** [ᾱ] ; Ep. 2 sing. opt. κλαίοισθα ;

Att. impf. ἔκλᾶον, Ep. κλαῖον, Ion. κλαίεσκον :—f. κλαύσομαι, Dor. κλαυσοῦμαι, Att. also κλαιήσω or κλαήσω : aor. 1 ἔκλαυσα, Ep. κλαῦσα :—Pass., f. κεκλαύσομαι : aor. 1 ἐκλαύσθην : pf. κέκλαυμαι : **I.** intr. *to weep, lament, wail,* Hom., etc. ; αὐτὸν κλαίοντα ἀφήσω I shall send him home *weeping,* i. e. *well beaten,* Il. ; hence κλαύσεται *he shall weep,* i. e. *he shall repent it,* Ar.; κλαύσει μακρά Id.; κλάων *to your sorrow, at your peril,* Soph., Eur. ; κλάειν σε λέγω or κελεύω, Lat. *plorare te jubeo,* Ar. **II.** trans. *to weep for, lament,* Hom. :—in Pass. *to be lamented,* Aesch. : impers., μάτην ἐμοὶ κεκλαύσεται I shall mourn in vain, Ar. **III.** Med. *to bewail oneself, weep aloud,* Aesch.; so pf. part. pass., κεκλαυμένος *bathed in tears, all tears,* Id., Soph. 2. trans. *to bewail to oneself,* Soph.

κλαι-ωμῖλία, ἡ, (ὁμιλία) *fellowship in tears,* Anth.

κλαμβός, ή, όν, *mutilated,* Hippiatr.

κλάξ, ᾶκος, ἡ, Dor. for κλείς.

κλαξῶ, Dor. fut. of κλείω, *to shut.*

κλᾶρος, κλᾱρόω, Dor. for κληρ-.

κλάσε, Ep. for ἔκλᾰσε, 3 sing. aor. 1 of κλάω.

κλᾱσῐ-βῶλαξ, ᾱκος, ὁ, ἡ, (κλάω) *breaking clods,* Anth.

κλάσις [ᾰ], εως, ἡ, (κλάω) *a breaking,* N. T.

κλάσμα, ατος, τό, (κλάω) *that which is broken off, a fragment, morsel,* N. T., Plut.

κλαστάζω, f. σω, (κλάω) *to dress vines* : metaph. κλ. τινά *to give him a dressing,* Ar.

κλαστός, ή, όν, (κλάω) *broken in pieces,* Anth.

κλαθμός, ὁ, (κλαίω) *a weeping,* Hom., Hdt., Aesch.

κλαθμυρίζω, f. σω, *to make to weep* :—Pass. *to weep,* Plat. Hence

κλαθμυρισμός, ὁ, *a crying like a child,* Plut.

κλαῦμα, ατος, τό, (κλαίω) *a weeping, wailing,* Aesch. **II.** *a trouble, misfortune,* Soph., Ar.

κλαυσάρα, crasis for κλαύσει ἄρα.

κλαῦσε, Ep. for ἔκλαυσε, 3 sing. aor. 1 of κλαίω.

κλαύσετάρα, crasis for κλαύσεται ἄρα.

κλαυσιάω, Desiderat. of κλαίω, *to wish to weep,* τὸ θύριον φθεγγόμενον ἄλλως κλαυσιᾷ *the door is like to weep* (i. e. *shall suffer*) *for creaking without cause,* Ar.

κλαυσί-γελως [ῐ], ὁ, *smiles mixed with tears,* Xen.

κλαυσί-μᾰχος, ον, (μάχη) *Rue-the-fight,* a parody on the name of La-machus (*Ready-for-fight*), Ar.

κλαύσομαι, Dor. κλαυσοῦμαι, f. of κλαίω.

κλαυστός or **κλαυτός**, ή, όν, (κλαίω) *wept, bewailed : to be bewailed, mournful,* Aesch., Soph.

ΚΛΑ'Ω [ᾰ] : impf. ἔκλων : f. κλάσω : aor. 1 ἔκλᾰσα, Ep. 3 sing. κλάσε, κλάσσε :—Med., Ep. 3 sing. aor. 1 κλάσσατο :—Pass., aor. 1 ἐκλάσθην : pf. κέκλασμαι :— *to break, break off,* Hom., etc.

κλάω [ᾱ], Att. for κλαίω, *to weep,* as κάω for καίω.

κλέα, Ep. for κλέεα, pl. of κλέος.

κλεεννός or **κλεεινός**, ή, όν, lyr. form of κλεινός, Pind.

κληηδών, όνος, ὁ, Ion. and Ep. for κληδών.

κλεία, Ep. contr. from κλέεα, pl. of κλέος.

κλειδίον, τό, Dim. of κλείς, *a little key,* Ar.

κλειδουχέω, Att. κληδ-, f. ήσω, *to have charge of the keys,* κλ. θεᾶς *to be her priestess,* Eur. **II.** Pass. *to be closely watched, kept in check,* Id. From

κλειδ-οῦχος, Att. κληδ-, ον, (κλείς, ἔχω) *holding the*

keys, having charge of a place, Eur. ; of Aeacus, as *judge* of the dead, Anth.

κλείζω, f. κλείξω, Dor. for κλήζω, κλήσω.

κλειθρία, ἡ, *a keyhole* ; or, generally, *a cleft, chink,* Luc.

κλεῖθρον, Ion. κλήϊθρον, Att. κλῆθρον, τό, (κλείω) *a bar for closing a door,* h. Hom. :—mostly in pl., like Lat. *claustra,* Trag., etc.

κλεινός, ή, όν, (κλέος) *famous, renowned, illustrious,* Solon, Pind., Trag. ; καὶ τοῦτο κλεινὸν αὐτοῦ is *well-known* of him, Luc.

κλεῖξαι, Dor. for κλῆσαι, aor. 1 inf. of κλήζω.

κλείς, ἡ, gen. κλειδός : Att. acc. κλεῖν, later κλεῖδα ; pl. κλεῖδες, κλεῖδας, contr. κλεῖς, dat. κλεισίν :—Ion. κληίς, κληῖδος, κληῖδα, etc. : Dor. κλᾱΐς, κλαῖδος : —old Att. κλῄς, κληδός, acc. κλῇδα : (κλείω) :—*that which serves for closing :* 1. *a bar or bolt,* drawn or undrawn by a latch or thong (ἱμάς), Hom. 2. *a key,* or rather a kind of *catch* or *hook,* by which the bar (ὀχεύς) was shot or unshot from the outside, Id. 3. *a key* (unknown to Hom.), Aesch., Eur. 4. metaph., Ἀσυχία βουλᾶν τε καὶ πολέμων κλαῖδας ἔχοισα Pind. ; κλῇς ἐπὶ γλώσσᾳ βέβηκε, of enforced silence, Soph. ; so, καθαρὰν ἀνοῖξαι κλῇδα φρενῶν Eur. **II.** *the hook* or *tongue* of a clasp, Od. **III.** *the collar-bone,* so called because it *locks* the neck and breast *together* Il., Soph., etc. **IV.** *a rowing bench,* which *locked* the sides of the ship together, Od. **V.** *a narrow pass,* '*the key*' of a country, Hdt. ; *a strait,* Eur.

κλεῖσις, εως, ἡ, (κλείω) = κλῆσις.

κλειστός, Ion. κληϊστός, Att. **κληστός**, ή, όν, *that can be shut or closed,* Od., Thuc.

κλεῖστρον, τό, = κλεῖθρον, Lat. *claustrum,* Luc.

κλειτός, ή, όν, (κλείω B) = κλεινός, Hom., Pind.

κλείω (A) : f. κλείσω : aor. 1 ἔκλεισα :—Pass., f. κλεισθήσομαι and κεκλείσομαι : aor. 1 ἐκλείσθην : pf. κέκλειμαι or κέκλεισμαι :—Ion., κληίω : aor. 1 ἐκλήϊσα, Ep. κλήϊσα, inf. κληῖσαι :—Pass., aor. 1 ἀπ-εκλήϊσθην ; pf. κεκλήϊμαι : 3 pl. plqpf. ἐκεκλήϊντο :—old Att. κλῄω : f. κλῄσω : aor. 1 ἔκλῃσα : pf. κέκλῃκα :—Med., aor. 1 inf. κλῄσασθαι :—Pass., aor. 1 ἐκλῄσθην : pf. κέκλῃμαι :—Dor., f. κλαξῶ : aor. imper. and part. ἀπο-κλάξον, —κλάξας : *to shut, close,* door, κλήισεν δὲ θύρας *barred the doors,* Od. ; ἐκλήισεν ὀχῆας *shot the bars,* so as to *close the door,* Ib. ; κλήειν στόμα Eur. 2. *to shut up, close, block,* Βόσπορον κλῆσαι Aesch. ; κλήισειν τοὺς ἔσπλους ναυσί Thuc. :—Pass. *to be shut up,* Hdt. **II.** *to confine,* Eur.

κλείω (B), Ep. for κλέω, *to celebrate.*

Κλειώ, οῦς, ἡ, *Clio,* one of the Muses, Hes., etc. ; esp. the Muse of Ep. Poetry and History. (From κλέω, κλείω, *to celebrate.*)

κλέμμα, ατος, τό, (κλέπτω) *a theft,* Eur., Ar. **II.** *a stratagem in war,* Thuc. : *a fraud,* Dem., Aeschin.

κλέος, τό, only in nom. and acc. sing. and pl. : Ep. pl. κλέᾰ, κλεῖα (κλέω) :—*a rumour, report, news,* Lat. *fama,* Hom. ; σὸν κλέος *news of thee,* Od. ; c. gen., κλέος Ἀχαιῶν *the report* of their coming, Il. :—*a mere report,* to certainty, κλέος οἷον ἀκούομεν, οὐδέ τι ἴδμεν *we hear a rumour* only, but know naught, Ib. **II.** *good report, fame, glory,* Hom. ; κλέος οὐρανὸν ἵκει Od. ; κλ. ἑλέσθαι, εὑρέσθαι Pind. ; λαβεῖν

Soph.; κλ. καταθέσθαι to lay up store of *glory*, Hdt., etc.: —in pl., ἄειδε κλέα ἀνδρῶν (shortd. from κλέεα), was singing *the lays* of their achievements, Il. 2. in bad sense, δύσφημον κλέος ill *repute*, Pind. ; αἰσχρὸν κλ. Eur.;—both senses combined in Thuc., ἧς ἂν ἐπ' ἐλάχιστον ἀρετῆς πέρι ἢ ψόγου κλέος ᾖ of whom there is least *talk* either for praise or blame.

κλεπτέον, verb. Adj. of κλέπτω, *one must conceal*, Soph.

κλέπτης, ου, ὁ, (κλέπτω) *a thief*, Il., Aesch., etc. : generally, *a cheat, knave*, Soph.

κλεπτικός, ή, όν, (κλέπτω) *thievish* :—ἡ -κή (sc. τέχνη) *thieving*, Plat.

κλεπτίστατος, η, ον, Sup. Adj. formed from κλέπτης, *the most arrant thief*, Ar.

κλέπτον, v. κλέπτω I. 2.

ΚΛΕ'ΠΤΩ : Ion. impf. **κλέπτεσκον :** f. **κλέψω** and **κλέψομαι :** aor. I ἔκλεψα : pf. **κέκλοφα :** Pass., aor. I ἐκλέφθην ; aor. 2 ἐκλάπην [ᾰ]: pf. **κέκλεμμαι** :—*to steal, filch, purloin*, Hom., etc. ; τῆς γενεῆς ἔκλεψε from that breed Anchises *stole*, i. e. stole foals of that breed, Il. ; σῶμα κλ. *to let it down secretly*, Eur. 2. in part. act. *thievish*, κλέπτον βλέπει he has a *thief's look*, Ar. II. *to cozen, cheat, deceive, beguile*, Il., Hes., etc. :—Pass., προβαίνει κλεπτόμενος he goes on *blindfold*, Hdt. III. like κρύπτω, *to conceal, keep secret, disguise*, Pind., Soph., Eur., etc. IV. *to do secretly* or *treacherously*, κλ. σφαγάς *to perpetrate* slaughter *secretly*, Soph. ; κλ. μύθους *to whisper malicious* rumours, Id.; κλέπτων ἢ βιαζόμενος *by fraud* or *force*, Plat. 2. *to seize* or *occupy secretly*, Xen.

κλεψί-φρων, ον, (φρήν) *deceiving, dissembling*, h. Hom.

κλεψ-ύδρα, Ion. -ύδρη, ἡ, (ὕδωρ) *a water-clock*, like our *sand-glasses*, used to time speeches in the law-courts, Ar. II. name of an ebbing well in the Acropolis at Athens, Id.

ΚΛΕ'Ω, Ep. **κλείω :** Pass., Ep. 2 sing. impf. ἔκλεο (for ἐκλέεο) :—*to tell of, celebrate*, Od., Hes., Eur. :—Pass. *to be famous*, Od., Pind. ; ἔνθ' ἀγοραὶ κλέονται where *are held the famous* meetings, Soph.

κλῆδες, Att. nom. pl. of κλείς.

κλήδην, Adv. (καλέω) *by name*, Il.

κληδουχέω, κληδοῦχος, old Att. for κλειδ-.

κληδών, όνος, ἡ, Ep. **κληηδών** and **κληηδών,** (καλέω) *an omen* or *presage contained in a word* or *sound*, Od., Hdt., Aesch. II. *a rumour, tidings, report*, Hdt., Trag. ; κληηδὼν πατρός *news of my father*, Od. 2. *glory, repute*, Trag. III. *a calling on, appeal*, πατρῷαι κληδόνες Aesch. 2. *a name, appellation*, Id.

κλήζω, Ion. **κληίζω :** f. **κλήσω,** Dor. **κλείξω :** aor. I ἔκλησα, Dor. εὐκλεΐξαι:—Pass., pf. **κέκλησμαι** (κλέω) : —*to make famous, to celebrate in song, laud*, Il. Hom., Pind., Eur. :—Pass. *to be spoken of, talked of*, Aesch., Eur. II. *to name, call*, Soph. :— Pass., ἔνθα κλήζεται οὖμος Κιθαιρών where *is* Cithaeron *called* mine, Id. ; cf. κικλήσκω fin.

κλήζω, in late writers for κλείω, κλήω, *to shut*.

κληηδών, όνος, ἡ, Ep. for κληδών.

κληθῆναι, aor. I pass. inf. of κλέω.

ΚΛΗ'ΘΡΑ, Ion. -ρη, ἡ, *the alder*, prob. *alnus*, still called κλέθρα in Greece, Od.

κληθρον, Att. for κλεῖθρον.

κληίζω, Ion. for κλήζω.

κλήιθρον, τό, Ion. for κλῆθρον, h. Hom.

κληίς, ῖδος, ἡ, Ion. for κλείς : Ep. dat. pl. κληίδεσσι.

κλ:ηιστός, Ion. for κλειστός.

κληίω, Ion. for κλείω (A), *to shut*.

κλῆμα, ατος, τό, (κλάω) *a vine-twig, vine-branch*, Lat. *palmes*, Ar., Plat. : generally, *a cutting, slip*, Xen. : —metaph., ἀνατέμνειν τὰ κλ. τὰ τοῦ δήμου Dem. :— *the vine-switch* of the Roman centurions, Lat. *vitis*, Plut. Hence

κλημάτινος, η, ον, *of vine-twigs*, Theogn.

κληματίς, ίδος, ἡ, Dim. of κλῆμα : in pl. *brush-wood, fagot-wood*, Thuc.

κληρίον, τό, Dim. of κλῆρος, Anth.

κληρονομέω, f. ήσω, (κληρονόμος) *to receive a share of an inheritance, to inherit a portion* of property, c. gen., Dem. :—also c. acc. rei, *to inherit*, Luc. II. *to be an inheritor* or *heir*, τινός of a person, Id. : also c. acc. *to succeed* one, Plut., Anth. Hence

κληρονόμημα, ατος, τό, *an inheritance*, Luc. ; and

κληρονομία, ἡ, *an inheritance*, Dem. :—generally, κλ. λαμβάνειν τινός *to take possession of* . . , Arist. From

κληρο-νόμος, ὁ, (νέμομαι) *one who receives a portion of an inheritance, an inheritor, heir*, Dem., etc.

κληρο-πᾰλής, ές, (πάλη) *distributed by shaking the lots*, h. Hom.

κλῆρος, Dor. **κλᾶρος, ου, ὁ,** *a lot ;* in Hom., each man marks his own lot, and they are thrown into a helmet, and the first which came out was the winning lot. 2. *a casting lots, drawing lots*, Eur. ; many officers at Athens obtained their offices *by lot*, as opp. to election (χειροτονία, αἵρεσις), Xen., Arist.; cf. κύαμος II. II. *an allotment* of land assigned to citizens (cf. κληρουχία), Hdt., Thuc., etc. 2. *any piece of land, a portion, farm*, Hom., etc. III. in Eccl. *the clergy*, as opp. *to the laity*.

κληρουχέω, f. ήσω, (κληροῦχος) *to obtain by allotment, to have allotted to one*, esp. of lands divided among conquerors, Hdt., etc. Hence

κληρουχία, ἡ, *the allotment of land to citizens in a foreign country*, Arist. 2. collectively, = οἱ κληροῦχοι, *the body of citizens who receive such allotments*, Thuc., Plut.—An Athenian κληρουχία differed from a colony (ἀποικία), in that the κληροῦχοι were still citizens of the mother country, instead of forming an independent state ; and

κληρουχικός, ή, όν, of or for a κληρουχία, γῆ κλ. land for allotment, Ar. ; τὰ κληρουχικά (sc. χρήματα) Dem.

κληρ-οῦχος, ὁ, (κλῆρος, ἔχω) *one who held an allotment of land*, esp. *to citizens in a foreign country* (v. κληρουχία), *an allottee*, Hdt., Thuc., etc. :—metaph., μητέρα πολλῶν ἐτῶν κληρουχον having old age *for her lot*, Soph.

κληρόω, Dor. **κλᾱρόω,** f. ώσω, (κλῆρος) *to appoint to* an office *by lot*, opp. to αἱρεῖσθαι or χειροτονεῖν, Hdt., Att. :—of the lot, *to fall on*, Lat. *designare*, Eur. :— Pass. *to be appointed by lot*, Dem., etc. 2. *to cast lots, draw lots*, Plat. ;—so in Med., Aesch., Dem. 3. in Med. also, κληροῦσθαί τι *to have allotted one, obtain by lot*, Eur., Aeschin. ; also c. gen., Dem. II. *to allot, assign*, Pind., Thuc. 2. κλ. ὀμφάν τᾳ *deliver* an oracle, Eur. Hence

κλήρωσις, εως, ἡ, a choosing by lot, Plat.; πικρὰ κλ. of a choice of evils, Eur.; and

κληρωτός, ή, όν, appointed by lot, opp. to αἱρετός and κεχειροτονημένος (elected), Plat., etc.

κλής, ηδός, ἡ, old Att. for κλείς.

κλῆσις, εως, ἡ, (καλέω) a calling, call, Xen., etc. 2. a calling into court, legal summons, prosecution, Ar., Xen., etc. 3. an invitation to a feast, Xen., Dem. II. a name, appellation, Plat.

κλῆσις, εως, ἡ, (κλήω) a shutting up, closing, Thuc.

κληστός, old Att. for κλειστός.

κλήσω, Att. fut. of κλήω, κλείω. II. fut. of κλήζω.

κλητέος, α, ον, verb. Adj. of καλέω, to be called, named, Plat. II. κλητέον, one must call, Id.

κλητεύω, f. σω, to summon into court or give evidence that a summons has been served (v. κλητήρ), Ar.

κλητήρ, ῆρος, ὁ, (καλέω) one who calls, a summoner, or rather a witness who gave evidence that the legal summons had been served (cf. Horace's licet antestari), Ar., Dem. II. generally, = κῆρυξ, Aesch.

κλητός, ή, όν, (καλέω) called, invited, welcome, Od. 2. called out, chosen, Il.

κλήτωρ, ορος, ὁ, = κλητήρ, Dem.

κλήω, old Att. for κλείω (A).

κλιβᾰνίτης, κλίβανος, v. sub κριβαν-.

κλιθῆναι, aor. 1 pass. inf. of κλίνω.

κλίμα [ῐ], ατος, τό, (κλίνω) an inclination, slope:—esp. the supposed slope of the earth towards the pole: hence a region or zone of the earth, clime, Plut., Anth.

κλιμάκιον [ᾰ], τό, Dim. of κλῖμαξ, Ar.

κλιμακτήρ, ῆρος, ὁ, the round of a ladder, Eur. From

κλῖμαξ, ᾰκος, ἡ, (κλίνω) a ladder or staircase (because of its leaning aslant), Od., etc.:—a scaling-ladder, Thuc., Xen.; κλίμακος προσαμβάσεις Aesch.:—a ship's ladder, Eur., Theocr. II. a frame with cross-bars, on which persons to be tortured were tied, Ar. III. in Soph., κλίμακες ἀμφίπλεκτοι intertwining ladders, to express the entanglement of the limbs of wrestlers. IV. a climax, i. e. a gradual ascent from weaker expressions to stronger, Lat. gradatio, as Cicero's abiit, evasit, erupit.

κλίνα, Ep. for ἔκλινα, aor. 1 of κλίνω.

κλίνειος, α, ον, of or for beds, Dem. From

κλίνη [ῐ], ἡ, (κλίνω) that on which one lies, a couch or bed, Hdt., Ar., etc.:—also, a bier, Thuc.

κλῖνῆναι, aor. 2 pass. inf. of κλίνω.

κλῖν-ήρης, ες, (*ἄρω) bed-ridden, Lat. lecto affixus, Plut.

κλίνθην, Ep. for ἐκλίνθην, aor. 1 pass. of κλίνω.

κλῖνίδιον, τό, Dim. of κλίνη, Plut.

κλινικός, ή, όν, (κλίνη) ὁ, Lat. clinicus, a physician that visits his patients in their beds, Anth.

κλῖνο-πετής, ές, (πίπτω) bed-ridden, Xen.

κλῖνο-ποιός, ὁ, (ποιέω) making beds or bedsteads, an upholsterer, Plat., Dem.

κλῖν-ουργός, ὁ, (*ἔργω) = κλινοποιός, Plat.

κλιντήρ, ῆρος, ὁ, (κλίνω) a couch, sofa, Od., Theocr.

ΚΛΙΝΩ [ῐ], f. κλῖνῶ: aor. 1 ἔκλῑνα: pf. κέκλῐκα:—Med., f. κλῖνοῦμαι: aor. 1 ἐκλῖνάμην:—Pass., f. κλῑθήσομαι or κλῐνήσομαι:—aor. 1 ἐκλίθην [ῐ] or ἐκλίνθην: aor. 2 ἐκλίνην [ῐ], to make to bend, slope, or slant, Lat. inclinare, κλίνειν τάλαντα to incline or turn the scale, Il.; Τρῶας ἔκλιναν made them give way, Ib.; ἔκλινε

μάχην turned the tide of war, Ib. 2. to make one thing lean against another, i. e. σάκε' ὤμοισι κλίναντες, i. e. raising their shields so that the upper rim rested on their shoulders, Ib. 3. to turn aside, ὄσσε πάλιν κλίνασα having turned back her eyes, Ib. 4. to make to recline, ἐν κλίνῃ κλ. τινά to make him lie down at table, Hdt. :—metaph. ἡμέρα κλίνει ἄπαντα puts to rest, lays low all things, Soph. II. Pass. to be bent, bend, ἐκλίνθη he bent aside, swerved, Il.; of a pan, ἂψ ἑτέρωσ' ἐκλίθη it was tipped over to the other side, Od. 2. to lean or stay oneself upon or against a thing, c. dat., Hom.; so in Med., κλινάμενος Od.:—also, κεκλιμένος ἐπάλξεσιν seeking safety in them, Il. 3. to lie down, lie, Hom., etc.; to lie on a couch at meals, Hdt., etc. 4. of Places (in pf.), to lie sloping towards the sea, ἁλὶ κεκλιμένη Od.; νῆσοι, αἵθ' ἁλὶ κεκλίαται (Ep. for κέκλινται), Ib. 5. to wander from the right course, Theogn. III. Med. to decline, of the day, Hdt.; so, intr. in Act., ἡ ἡμέρα ἤρξατο κλίνειν N. T. :—metaph., κλ. ἐπὶ τὸ χεῖρον to fall off, degenerate, Xen.

κλισία, Ion. -ίη, ἡ, (κλίνω) a place for lying down: hence, I. a hut, cot, cabin, such as besiegers lived in during long sieges, Il.:—that they were not tents, but wooden huts, appears from Il. 24. 448 sq.; and when an army broke up, it burnt them on the spot, Od. 8. 501. II. a couch or easy chair, Od., Pind. 2. a bed, nuptial bed, Eur. III. a company of people sitting at meals, N. T. IV. a reclining or lying, Plut.

κλισιάδες, αἱ, (κλίνω) folding doors or gates, Plut.:—metaph. a means of entrance, access, Hdt.

κλισίηθεν, Adv. out of or from a hut, Il.

κλισίηνδε, Adv. into or to the hut, Il.

κλίσιον [κλῐ], τό, (κλίνω) the outbuildings round a herdman's cot, Od.

κλίσις [ῐ], εως, ἡ, (κλίνω) a bending, inclination, τοῦ τραχήλου Plut. II. a lying down, lying, Eur.

κλισμός, ὁ, (κλίνω) a couch, Hom.

κλίτος [ῐ], τό, = κλίμα II, a clime, Anth.

κλῑτύς, ύος, ἡ, acc. pl. κλῑτῦς, (κλίνω) a slope, hill-side, Lat. clivus, Hom., Soph.

κλοιός, ὁ, old Att. κλῳός, (κλείω) a dog-collar, esp. a large wooden collar, put on mischievous dogs, Ar., Xen. 2. a sort of pillory, Eur. 3. χρύσεος κλ. a collar of gold, Id., Anth.

κλονέω, f. ήσω, (κλόνος) to drive in confusion, drive before one, Il., Hes. 2. generally, to ruffle, Soph., Ar. II. Pass. to be driven in confusion, rush wildly, Il., Pind. 2. to be beaten by the waves, Soph.

ΚΛΟΝΟΣ, ὁ, any confused motion, the press of battle, battle-rout, turmoil, Il.; κλόνοι ἱππιοχάρμαι throngs of fighting horsemen, Aesch.

κλοπαῖος, α, ον, (κλέπ-τω) stolen, Aesch., Eur.

κλοπεύς, έως, ὁ, = κλώψ, a thief, stealer, Soph. 2. generally, a secret doer, perpetrator, Id.

κλοπή, ἡ, (κλέπ-τω) theft, Lat. furtum, Aesch., Eur. II. a secret act, fraud, Eur., Aeschin.; κλοπῇ by stealth or fraud, Soph.; ποδοῖν κλοπὰν ἀρέσθαι, i. e. to steal away, Id. III. the surprise of a military post, Xen.

κλοπῐμαῖος, α, ον, = κλόπιος, Luc.
κλόπιος, α, ον, (κλέπ-τω) thievish, artful, μῦθοι Od.
κλοπός, ὁ, = κλώψ, a thief, h. Hom.
κλοτοπεύω, to deal subtly, to spin out time by false pretences, Il. ; —it seems to be a lengthd. form of κλέπτω, κλωπεύω.
κλύδων [ῠ], ωνος, ὁ, (κλύζω) a wave, billow, and collectively surf, Od., Trag.   II. metaph., κλ. κακῶν a sea of troubles, Aesch. ; κλ. ξυμφορᾶς Soph. ; κλ. ἔφιππος a flood of horsemen, Id., etc.
κλυδωνίζομαι, Pass. to be tossed like waves, N. T.
κλυδώνιον, τό, Dim. of κλύδων, a little wave, ripple, Eur. ; generally, a wave, Aesch. : —as collective noun, the surf, Thuc.   II. metaph., κλ. χολῆς Aesch.
ΚΛΥΖΩ, f. κλύσω [ῠ], Ep. κλύσσω :—Pass., aor. 1 ἐκλύσθην ; pf. κέκλυσμαι :—to dash over, of a wave, h. Hom. : to dash like a wave, Aesch. :—Pass. to be dashed up, of the sea, Hom. ; to rise in waves, Hes.   II. to wash off or away, Eur.   2. to wash or rinse out, Xen.   3. εἰς ὦτα κλ. to put water into the ears and so cleanse them, Eur.   4. κεκλυσμένος καρῷ washed over or coated with wax, Theocr.
κλῦθι, aor. 2 imper. of κλύω.
κλύμενος [ῠ], η, ον, = κλυτός, famous, Theocr.
κλύσμα, ατος, τό, (κλύζω) a liquid used for washing out : esp. a clyster, drench, Hdt.   II. a place washed by the waves, the sea-beach, Plut., Luc.
κλυστήρ, ῆρος, ὁ, a clyster-pipe, syringe, Hdt.
Κλυται-μνήστρα, ἡ, (κλυτός, μνάομαι) the queen of Agamemnon, Il.
κλῦτε, 2 pl. aor. 2 imper. of κλύω.
κλῠτό-δενδρος, ον, (δένδρον) famous for trees, Anth.
κλῠτο-εργός, όν, (*ἔργω) famous for work, Od., Anth.
κλῠτό-καρπος, ον, glorious with fruit, Pind.
κλῠτό-μητις, ι, gen. ιος, famous for skill, h. Hom.
κλῠτό-μοχθος, ον, famous for toils, Anth.
κλῠτό-νοος, ον, famous for wisdom, Anth.
κλῠτό-παις, ὁ, ἡ, with famous children, Anth.
κλῠτό-πωλος, ον, with noble steeds, Il.
κλῠτός, ή, όν, and ός, όν, (κλύω) :—heard of, i. e. famous, renowned, glorious, of persons, Hom.   2. of things, noble, splendid, beauteous, Id., etc.
κλῠτο-τέχνης, ου, ὁ, (τέχνη) famous for his art, renowned artist, Hom.
κλῠτό-τοξος, ον, (τόξον) famous for the bow, renowned archer, Hom.
ΚΛΥΩ, aor. 2 ἔκλυον, Ep. κλύον ; imper. (as if from κλύμι) κλῦθι, κλῦτε, Ep. redupl. κέκλῠτε :—to hear, Hom., etc. ; κλύειν τί τινος to hear a thing from a person, Il., εἰc. ; then, κλύειν τινος to hear him, Ib. ; κλ. τι to hear it, Od., etc. :—c. gen. objecti, to hear of a person or thing, Soph.   II. to perceive generally, know, Od., Hes.   II. to give ear to, attend to, τινός Hom., etc. ; the imperat. is esp. used in prayers, give ear to me, hear me, κλῦθί μευ, Ἀργυρότοξε Il. ; κέκλυτέ μευ, θεοί Ib. :—also c. dat. to listen to, obey, Hes., etc.   III. in Trag. like ἀκούω v, to be called or spoken of so and so, with an Adv., εὖ or κακῶς κλύειν.
κλωβός, ὁ, a bird-cage, Anth.
κλωγμός or κλωσμός, ὁ, (κλώσσω) the clucking of hens : the clucking sound by which we urge on a horse, Xen.

ΚΛΩ΄ΖΩ, f. -ξω, to croak, of jackdaws :—then, in sign of disapprobation, to hoot, Dem.
Κλῶθες, ων, αἱ, the Spinners, a name of the Parcae or Goddesses of fate, Od.
ΚΛΩ΄ΘΩ, f. κλώσω, to twist by spinning, spin, Hdt., Luc. :—Pass., τὰ κλωσθέντα one's destiny, Plat.
Κλωθώ, οῦς, ἡ, Spinster, one of the three Μοῖραι or Parcae, who spins the thread of life, Hes. ; Lachesis had charge of the past, Clotho of the present, Atropos of the future, Plat., Luc.
κλωμᾰκόεις, εσσα, εν, stony, rocky, Il.   From
κλῶμαξ, ᾰκος, ὁ, a heap of stones.   (Deriv. unknown.)
κλών, gen. κλωνός, ὁ, (κλάω) a twig, spray, Soph., Eur.
κλωνίον, τό, Dim. of κλών, Anth.
κλῳός, ὁ, old Att. for κλοιός.
κλωπεύω, f. σω, (κλώψ) to steal, Xen.
κλωπικός, ή, όν, (κλώψ) thievish, clandestine, Eur.
ΚΛΩ΄ΣΣΩ, to cluck like a hen.
κλωστήρ, ῆρος, ὁ, (κλώθω) a spindle, Theocr.   II. a thread, yarn, line, Ar. ; λίνου κλ. the flaxen thread, i. e. the net, Aesch.
κλωστής, οῦ, ὁ, a web, Eur.
κλώψ, κλωπός, ὁ, (κλέπ-τω) a thief, Hdt., Eur., Xen.
κνᾱκός, κνάκος, Dor. for κνηκός, κνήκων.
κνάμα, ἡ, Dor. for κνήμη.
κνᾱμός, Dor. for κνημός.
κνάμπτω, v. γνάμπτω.
κνάπτω, (κνάω) to card or dress cloth, (which was done either with a prickly plant, the teasel, or with a comb) :—of torture, to card, lacerate, Aesch., Soph.
κνάσω, κνᾶσαι, Dor. for κνήσω, κνῆσαι, fut. and aor. 1 inf. of κνάω.
κνάφαλλον [ᾰ], τό, κνέφαλλον.
κνᾰφεῖον, Ion. -ήιον, τό, a fuller's shop, Hdt.   From
κνᾰφεύς, έως, ὁ, Att. pl. κναφῆς, (κνάπτω) a fuller, i. e. a cloth-dresser, clothes-cleaner, Hdt., Ar.
κνᾰφεύω, f. σω, = κνάπτω, to clean cloth, Ar.
κνᾰφήιον, τό, Ion. for κναφεῖον.
κνάφος, ὁ, (κνάω) the prickly teasel, a plant used by fullers to dress cloth.   II. a carding-comb, also used as an instrument of torture, Hdt.
ΚΝΑ΄Ω, Att. 2 and 3 sing. κνῆς, κνῆ, inf. κνῆν, Ion. κνᾶν : f. κνήσω : aor. 1 ἔκνησα : 3 sing. Ep. aor. 2 κνῆ (as if from κνῆμι) :—Med., Att. inf. κνῆσθαι : aor. 1 ἐκνησάμην :—to scrape or grate, Lat. radere, Il. ; τὸν κηρὸν κνᾶν to scrape it off, Hdt.   II. to scratch :—Med. to scratch oneself, Plat.   III. to tickle, Id. ; Med., κνᾶσθαι τὰ ὦτα to tickle one's ears, Luc.
κνεφάζω, f. άσω, (κνέφας) to cloud over, obscure, Aesch.
κνεφαῖος, α, ον, and ος, ον, (κνέφας) dark, dusky, Aesch., Eur.   2. in the dark, early in the morning, Ar.
ΚΝΕ΄ΦΑΣ, τό, dat. κνέφα, but also gen. κνέφους : dat. κνέφεῖ (as if from κνέφος) :—darkness, evening dusk, twilight, Il., Aesch. ; also, τὸ κατὰ γῆς κν. Eur.   2. later, the morning twilight or dawn, Lat. diluculum, κνέφα at dawn, Xen.
κνῇ, Att. 3 sing. of κνάω.
κνήθω, f. κνήσω, (κνάω) later form of κνάω, to scratch, tickle :—Pass. to itch, N. T.
κνηκίας, ὁ, v. κνηκός.
ΚΝΗΚΟ΄Σ, ή, όν, Dor. κνᾱκός, ά, όν, pale yellow,

tawny, Theocr., Anth. : hence the goat is called **κνάκων,** ὁ, Theocr. ; and the wolf **κνηκίας,** Babr.

κνήμ-αργος, ον, *white-legged,* Theocr.

ΚΝΗ'ΜΗ, ἡ, *the part between the knee and ankle, the leg,* Lat. *tibia,* Hom., Hdt., Eur., etc.

κνημῖδο-φόρος, ον, (φέρω) *wearing greaves,* Hdt.

κνημίς, ῖδος, ἡ, (κνήμη) *a greave* or *piece of armour from knee to ankle,* Lat. *ocrea,* περὶ κνήμῃσιν ἔθηκεν Il. ; the κνημῖδες were fastened at the ankle with clasps (ἐπισφύρια) : βόειαι κνημῖδες are *ox-hide leggings,* used by labourers, Od.

κνημός, ὁ, *the projecting limb* or (as we say) *shoulder* of a mountain, Hom.

κνησιάω, Desiderat. of κνάω, *to wish to scratch, to feel an itching, to itch,* Plat.

κνησί-χρῦσος, ον, *scraping* or *gnawing gold,* Anth.

κνῆσμα, ατος, τό, *a sting, bite,* Xen.

κνησμονή, ἡ, = κνησμός, ὁ, Anth.

κνησμός, ὁ, (κνάω) *an itching, irritation,* Plut.

κνῆστις, εως and ιος, ἡ, (κνάω) *a knife for scraping* cheese, Il. (in contr. dat. κνήστι).

κνίδη [ῐ], ἡ, (κνίζω) *a nettle,* Lat. *urtica,* Theocr., Anth.

Κνίδιος [ῐ], α, ον, (Κνίδος) *of* or *from Cnidos;* οἱ Κνίδιοι *the Cnidians,* Hdt.

ΚΝΙ'ΖΩ, Dor. **κνίσδω :** f. κνίσω [ῐ] : aor. 1 ἔκνισα, Dor. ἔκνιξα :—Pass., aor. 1 ἐκνίσθην :—*to scrape* or *grate* : *to tickle* : metaph., of love, *to nettle, chafe, irritate,* Hdt., Eur. ; of satiety, Pind. ; of anxiety, Hdt., etc. ; οὐ κνίσω τὸ ῥῆμ᾽ ἕκαστον *will not attack* every word, Ar. :—Pass., κνίζεσθαί τινος *to be stung* (with love) *for* one, Theocr.   **II.** κν. ὀργάν *to provoke* anger, Pind.

κνῖπός, όν, *niggardly,* Anth. (Deriv. uncertain.)

κνῖσα, Ep. **κνίση,** ης, ἡ, Lat. *nidor, the steam and odour* which exhales from roasting meat, *the savour and steam of burnt sacrifice,* which ascends up to heaven as a gift to the gods, Hom.   **II.** *that which caused this smell and steam,* i. e. *the fat,* in which the flesh of the victim was wrapped and burnt, μηρούς τ᾽ ἐξέταμον κατά τε κνίσῃ ἐκάλυψαν Il.

κνισάεις, Dor. for κνισήεις : contr. dat. κνισᾶντι.

κνισάω, f. ήσω, (κνῖσα) *to fill with the steam* or *savour of burnt sacrifice,* Eur., Ar.

κνισήεις, εσσα, εν, (κνῖσα) *full of the steam of burnt sacrifice, steamy,* Od.

κνίσμα, ατος, τό, (κνίζω) in pl. *scrapings,* Plat.   **II.** *scratches,* Anth. : *quarrels,* Id.

κνισμός, ὁ, *an itching of the skin, tickling,* Ar.

κνῖσόω, f. ώσω, (κνῖσα) *to reduce to vapour,* Luc.

κνίσσα, κνισσάω, κνισσήεις, incorrect forms of κνῖσα, etc.

κνίσσῃ, 3 sing. poët. subj. of κνίζω.

κνισωτός, ή, όν, (κνισόω) *steaming,* of a sacrifice, Aesch.

ΚΝΙ'Ψ, ὁ, gen. κνιπός, nom. pl. κνῖπες, like σκνίψ, a small *insect which gnaws* figs, Ar.

κνύζα, ἡ, poët. for κόνυζα, Theocr.

κνυζάομαι and **-έομαι,** Dep. (κνῦ) properly of a dog, *to whine, whimper,* Soph., Ar.

κνυζεῦνται, Dor. for -οῦνται, 3 pl. of κνυζέομαι.

κνυζηθμός, ὁ, (κνυζάομαι) *a whining, whimpering,* Od.

κνύζημα, τό, = κνυζηθμός, of infants, Lat. *vagitus,* Hdt.

κνυζόω, f. ώσω, *to disfigure* the eyes, *make dim and dark* Od. (Deriv. uncertain.)

κνώδαλον, τό, *any dangerous animal,* from a lion to a serpent or worm, *a monster, beast,* Od., Hes., Trag. : —of persons, as a term of reproach, ὦ παντομίση κνώδαλα Aesch. (Deriv. uncertain.)

κνώδων, οντος, ὁ, (ὀδούς) in pl. κνώδοντες, *two projecting teeth* on the blade of a hunting spear, Xen. ; ξίφους διπλοῖ κνώδοντες, i. e. *a two-edged sword,* Soph. : also **κνώδων** alone for *a sword,* Id.

ΚΝΩ'ΣΣΩ, *to slumber, sleep,* Od., Pind.

κοάλεμος [ᾰ], ὁ, *a stupid fellow, booby,* Ar. (Deriv. uncertain.)

κοάξ, Comic word, to express the croaking of frogs, βρεκεκεκὲξ κοὰξ κοάξ Ar.

κοβᾰλίκευμα, τό, *a knavish trick,* Ar. From

κόβᾰλος, ὁ, *an impudent rogue, arrant knave,* Ar. : —Κόβαλοι were *mischievous goblins,* invoked by rogues, Id.   **II.** as Adj. κόβαλα, *knavish tricks, rogueries,* Id. (Deriv. uncertain.)

ΚΟ'ΓΧΗ, ἡ, *a muscle* or *cockle,* Lat. *concha,* Xen.   **II.** *the case round a seal* attached to diplomas or documents, Ar.

κογχύλη [ῠ], ἡ, = κόγχη, Anth.

κογχῠλιάτης [ᾱ], ου, ὁ, *full of shells,* λίθος κογχ. *shelly marble,* Xen.

κογχύλιον, τό, Dim. of κογχύλη, *a small kind of muscle* or *cockle,* Arist.   **2.** *its shell, any bivalve-shell,* Hdt.

κοδράντης, ου, ὁ, the Lat. *quadrans,* = ¼ *of an as,* N. T.

ΚΟΕ'Ω, contr. κοῶ, *to mark, perceive, hear,* Anacr.

κόθεν, Ion. for πόθεν.

κόθορνος, ὁ, Lat. *cothurnus, a buskin* or *high boot,* reaching to the middle of the leg, Hdt., etc. The κόθορνος was worn by tragic actors, its heels serving to add height to the figure : thus it became the emblem of Tragedy, as the *soccus* of Comedy.   **2.** since the buskins might be worn on either foot, ὁ Κόθορνος was a nickname for *a trimmer* or *timeserver,* such as Theramenes, Xen.

κόθ-ουρος, ον, of drones, *dock-tailed,* i. e. *without a sting,* Hes. (Prob. from **κοθώ,** οῦς, ἡ, an old word for **βλάβη,** and **οὐρά** *tail.*)

κοΐ, Comic word, to express the *squeaking* of young pigs, Ar.

κοΐζω, *to cry* κοΐ, *squeak like a young pig,* Ar.

κοίη, Ion. for ποίᾳ, dat. sing. of ποῖος, Ion. κοῖος, used as Adv., *how ? in what way ? in what respect ?* Hdt.

κοιλαίνω, f. ᾰνῶ : aor. 1 ἐκοίληνα, Att. ἐκοίλᾱνα : (κοῖλος) :—*to make hollow, scoop out,* Hdt. ; κ. χῶμα, i. e. *to dig a grave,* Theocr.

κοιλάς, άδος, ἡ, (κοῖλος) *a hollow, deep valley,* Anth.

Κοίλη, ἡ, fem. of κοῖλος, name of a δῆμος in Attica, Hdt.

κοιλία, Ion. -ίη, ἡ, (κοῖλος) *the large cavity of the body, the belly,* Lat. *venter,* Hdt., Ar., etc.   **2.** *the intestines, bowels,* Hdt. ; κ. ὑεία *pig's tripe,* Ar. ; in pl. *tripe and puddings,* Id.   Hence

κοιλιο-πώλης, ου, ὁ, (πωλέω) *a tripe-seller,* Ar.

κοιλιο-γάστωρ, ορος, ὁ, (γαστήρ) *hollow-bellied, hungry,* Aesch. : metaph. *a hollow* shield, Id.

κοιλό-πεδος, ον, (πέδον) *lying in a hollow,* Pind.

ΚΟΙ͂ΛΟΣ, η, ον, *hollow, hollowed,* epith. of ships, which

in early times were hollowed out of trees, Hom.; later, κοίλη ναῦς was the hold of the ship, Hdt., Xen.; so, ἡ κοίλη alone, Theocr.:—of the Trojan horse, κ. λόχος, κ. δόρυ Od.; κ. κάπετος, of a grave, Il.; κ. δέμνια, of the bed when no one is in it, Soph. 2. of Places, lying in a hollow or forming a hollow, κοίλη Λακεδαίμων the vale of L., Od.; κ. Θεσσαλία Hdt.; κ. Ἄργος Soph.; τὰ Κοῖλα τῆς Εὐβοίας Hdt.; ἡ Κοιλή the valley of the Ilissus, Id.:—κ. λιμήν of a harbour lying between high cliffs, Od.; κ. αἰγιαλός an embayed beach, Ib.:—κ. ὁδός a hollow way, Il.:—κ. ποταμός a river nearly empty of water, Thuc. (so Virgil, cava flumina): metaph. of the voice, hollow, μυκάσατο κοῖλον Theocr.; φθέγγεσθαι κοῖλον Luc. II. as Subst. κοῖλον, τό, a hollow, cavity, ravine, Plat.; like κοιλία, of the cavities in the body, τὰ κ. γαστρός Eur.; also, ἐν τῷ κοίλῳ καὶ μυχῷ τοῦ λιμένος Thuc.

κοιλ-όφθαλμος, ον, hollow-eyed, Xen.

κοιλο-χείλης, ες, (χεῖλος) hollow-rimmed, Anth.

κοιλ-ώδης, ες, (εἶδος) hollow-like, cavernous, φάραγξ Babr.

κοίλωμα, ατος, τό, a hollow, cavity, Babr., etc.

κοιλ-ωπής, ές, (ὤψ) hollow-eyed: fem. -ῶπις, ιδος, Anth.

κοιλ-ωπός, όν, (ὤψ) hollow to look at: hollow, Eur.

κοιμάω, Ion. -έω: f. ἥσω, Dor. ἅσω [ᾱ]: aor. 1 ἐκοίμησα, Ep. κοίμησα:—Med., 3 sing. Ep. aor. 1 κοιμήσατο:—Pass., aor. 1 ἐκοιμήθην: (κεῖμαι):—to lull or hush to sleep, put to sleep, Hom. 2. metaph. to lull to rest, still, calm, ἀνέμους, κύματα Id.; ὀδύνας Il.; κοίμησον εὔφημον στόμα lay thy tongue asleep in silence, Aesch. II. Med. and Pass. to fall asleep, go or lie abed, Hom., Hdt., etc. 2. of the sleep of death, κοιμήσατο χάλκεον ὕπνον he slept an iron sleep, Il.: absol. to fall asleep, die, Soph., N.T. 3. to keep watch at night, Lat. excubare, Aesch., Xen.

κοίμημα, τό, (κοιμάω) sleep, κοιμήματα αὐτογέννητα intercourse of the mother with her own child, Soph.

κοίμησις, εως, ἡ, a lying down to sleep, Plat., N.T.

κοιμίζω, f. Att. ιῶ, = κοιμάω, to put to sleep, Eur.; ἅπμα ἐκοίμισε πόντον, i. e. the winds suffer the sea to rest—by ceasing (cf. Virg. straverunt aequora venti), Soph.:—metaph. μεγαληγορίαν κ. to lay pride asleep, Eur.; so, κ. τὰς λύπας Xen.:—Pass., παῖς κοιμίζεται Eur. 2. of the sleep of death, Soph., Eur.; also in Med., Eur. Hence

κοιμιστής, οῦ, ὁ, one who puts to bed, Anth.

κοινάν, ᾶνος, ὁ, Dor. for κοινών.

κοινάνέω, Dor. for κοινωνέω.

κοινάσομαι, κοινάσας, Dor. for κοινώσ-.

κοινῇ, dat. fem. of κοινός, used as Adv., v. κοινός B. II.

κοινο-βουλέω, (βουλή) to deliberate in common, Xen.

κοινό-λεκτρος, ον, (λέκτρον) having a common bed, a bedfellow, consort, Aesch.

κοινο-λεχής, ές, = κοινόλεκτρος, a paramour, Soph.

κοινο-λογέομαι, f. -ήσομαι: aor. 1 ἐκοινολογησάμην: pf. κεκοινολόγημαι: (λόγος):—to commune or take counsel with, τινι Hdt., Att.; πρός τινα Thuc.

κοινό-πλοος, ον, contr. -πλους, ουν, (πλέω) sailing in common, Soph.

κοινό-πους, ὁ, ἡ, πουν, τό, of common foot, κ. παρουσία, i. e. the arrival of persons all together, Soph.

κοινός, ή, όν, rarely ός, όν: (from ξύν = σύν, cf. ξυνός):

—common, shared in common, opp. to ἴδιος, Hes., Att.; proverb., κοινὸν τύχη Aesch.; κοινὰ τὰ τῶν φίλων Eur. 2. c. dat., κ. τινι common to or with another, Aesch.; also c. gen., πάντων κ. φάος Id. II. common to all the people, common, public, general, Hdt., Thuc., etc. III. τὸ κοινόν the state, Lat. respublica, Hdt., Att. 2. the government, public authorities, Thuc., Xen.; ἀπὸ τοῦ κοινοῦ by public authority, Hdt.; ἄνευ τοῦ τῶν πάντων κοινοῦ without consent of the league, Thuc. 3. the public treasury, Hdt., Thuc. 4. τὰ κοινά public affairs, Oratt.; πρὸς τὰ κοινὰ προσελθεῖν, προσιέναι to enter public life, Dem., etc.; also the public money, Ar. IV. common, ordinary, usual, Plat., etc. V. of Persons, of common origin or kindred, esp. of brothers and sisters, Pind., Soph. 2. like κοινωνός, a partner, Soph., Ar. 3. lending a ready ear to all, impartial, Thuc., Plat.:—courteous, affable, Xen. 4. of events, κοινότεραι τύχαι more impartial (i. e. more equal) chances, Thuc. VI. of meats, common, profane, N.T.

B. Adv. κοινῶς, in common, jointly, opp. to ἰδίᾳ, Eur., etc. 2. publicly, Thuc., etc. 3. sociably, like other citizens, Arist., Plut. 4. in common language or fashion, Plut. II. so fem. dat. κοινῇ, in common, by common consent, in concert, Hdt., Soph., Eur. 2. publicly, Xen. III. so with Preps., ἐς κοινόν in common, Aesch.; εἰς τὸ κ. for common use, Plat.

κοινότης, ητος, ἡ, a sharing in common, community, partnership, Plat., etc. II. affability, Xen.

κοινό-τοκος, ον, (τίκτω) of or from common parents, ἐλπίδες κ. hopes in one born of the same parents, i. e. a brother, Soph.

κοινο-φιλής, ές, (φιλέω) loving in common, Aesch.

κοινό-φρων, ον, (φρήν) like-minded with, τινί Eur.

κοινόω, f. κοινώσω: aor. 1 ἐκοίνωσα:—Med., f. κοινώσομαι, Dor. -άσομαι:—aor. 1 ἐκοινωσάμην:—Pass., aor. 1 ἐκοινώθην:—to make common, communicate, impart a thing to another, κ. τί τινι Aesch., Eur., etc.; τι ἔς τινα Eur. 2. to make common, to defile, profane, N.T.:—Med. to deem or pronounce profane, Ib. II. Med. to communicate one to another, Aesch., Soph. b. to cause to be communicated, τί τινι Plat. 2. to take counsel with, τινι Xen. 3. to be partner or partaker, τινος of a thing, Eur. 4. c. acc. rei, to take part or share in, Id., Thuc. III. Pass. to have intercourse with, Eur.

κοινών, ῶνος, Dor. κοινάν, ᾶνος, ὁ, = κοινωνός, Pind., Xen.

κοινωνέω, f. ήσω: pf. κεκοινώνηκα: (κοινωνός):—to have or do in common with, have a share of or take part in a thing with another, τινός τινι Xen. 2. κ. τινός to have a share of or take part in a thing, Trag., Xen. 3. κ. τινι to have dealings with or intercourse, Ar., Plat. 4. rarely c. acc. rei, κ. φόνον τινι to commit murder in common with him, Eur. 5. absol. to share in an opinion, to agree, Plat.:—to form a community, Arist. Hence

κοινώνημα, ατος, τό, in pl. acts of communion, communications, dealings between man and man, Plat.

κοινωνητέον, verb. Adj. one must give a share, Plat.

κοινωνία, ἡ, (κοινωνέω) communion, association, part-

nership, fellowship, Pind., Thuc., etc.　　2. c. gen. objecti, communion with, partnership in, Eur., etc.; τίς θαλάσσης βουκόλοις κ.; what communion have herdsmen with the sea? Id.　　II. a common gift, contribution, alms, N. T.

κοινωνικός, ή, όν, held in common, social, Arist.　　II. giving a share, τινος of a thing, Luc.　　From

κοινωνός, ὁ and ἡ, (κοινός) a companion, partner, τινος in a thing, Aesch., etc.; ὁ τοῦ κακοῦ κ. accomplice in the evil, Soph.; also, τινι in a thing, Eur.　　2. absol. a partner, fellow, Plat., Dem.　　II. as Adj. = κοινός, Eur.

κοινῶς, Adv. of κοινός, v. κοινός B.

κοῖος, η, ον, Ion. for ποῖος, α, ον.

κοιρᾰνέω, f. ήσω, (κοίρανος) to be lord or master, to rule, command, Hom.　　II. c. gen. to be lord of, Hes., Aesch.; also, c. dat., Aesch.

κοιρᾰνία, Ion. -ίη, ἡ, sovereignty, Anth.

κοιρᾰνίδης [νῐ], ου, ὁ, = κοίρανος, Soph.

κοίρᾰνος, ὁ, (κῦρος) a ruler, commander, Hom., Trag.

κοιτάζω, (κοίτη) to put to bed:—Med., Dor. aor. 1 ἐκοιταξάμην, to go to bed, sleep, Pind.

κοιταῖος, α, ον, (κοίτη) in bed, ap. Dem.　　2. as Subst., κοιταῖον, τό, the lair of a wild beast, Plut.

κοίτη, ἡ, (κεῖμαι) = κοῖτος, Hdt., Att.; the marriage-bed, Soph., Eur.　　2. the lair of a beast, nest of a bird, Eur.　　II. the act of going to bed, τῆς κοίτης ὥρη bed-time, Hdt.; τραπέζῃ καὶ κοίτῃ δέκεσθαι to entertain 'at bed and board,' Id.　　III. ἔχειν κοίτην ἔκ τινος to be pregnant by a man, N. T.:—in bad sense, chambering, lasciviousness, Ib.

κοῖτος, ὁ, (κεῖμαι) a place to lie on, bed, Od.　　II. sleep, Ib., Hes.

κοιτών, ῶνος, ὁ, (κοίτη) a bed-chamber, ὁ ἐπὶ τοῦ κοιτῶνος a chamberlain, praefectus cubiculi, N. T.

κόκκῐνος, η, ον, scarlet, Lat. coccineus, Plut., N. T.

ΚΟ'ΚΚΟΣ, ὁ, a grain, seed, h. Hom., Hdt.　　II. the kermesberry, used to dye scarlet, Theophr.

κόκκῠ, properly cuckoo! the bird's cry, used as an exclamation, now! quick! κόκκυ, πεδίονδε Ar.; κόκκυ, μεθεῖτε quick—let go, Id.

κοκκύζω, Dor. -ύσδω, f. ύσω: pf. κεκόκκῠκα: (κόκκυξ):—to cry cuckoo, Hes.; of the cock, to crow, Theocr.　　II. to cry like a cuckoo, give a signal by such cry, Ar.

κόκκυξ, ῡγος, ὁ, a cuckoo, so called from its cry κόκκυ, Lat. cuculus, Hes., Ar., etc.; ἐχειροτόνησάν με κόκκυγές γε τρεῖς I was elected by three cuckoo-voices, i. e. by three who gave their votes over and over again, Ar.

κοκκύσδω, Dor. for κοκκύζω.

κόκκων, ὁ, a pomegranate-seed, Solon.

κοκύαι, οἱ, ancestors, Anth. (Deriv. unknown.)

κολάζω, f. κολάσω: aor. 1 ἐκόλασα:—Med., f. κολάσομαι, Att. 2 sing. κολᾷ, pl. κολώμενος: aor. 1 ἐκολασάμην:—Pass., f. -ασθήσομαι: aor. 1 ἐκολάσθην: pf. κεκόλασμαι. (Prob. from κόλος, akin to κολούω.)　Properly, to curtail, dock, prune: then, like Lat. castigare, to keep within bounds, check, correct, Plat.:—pf. pass. part. chastened, Arist.　　2. to chastise, punish, Soph., Eur., etc.:—Med. to get a person punished, Ar., Plat.:— Pass. to be punished, Xen.

Κολαινίς, ίδος, ἡ, obscure epith. of Artemis, Ar.

κολᾰκεία, ἡ, flattery, fawning, Plat., Aeschin.

κολάκευμα, ατος, τό, a piece of flattery, Xen.

κολᾰκευτέος, α, ον, verb. Adj. to be flattered, Luc.; and

κολᾰκευτικός, ή, όν, disposed to flatter, flattering, fawning, Luc.: ἡ -κή (sc. τέχνη) = κολακεία, Plat.

κολᾰκεύω, f. σω, (κόλαξ) to flatter, Ar., Xen., etc.:— Pass. to be flattered, be open to flattery, Dem.

κολᾰκικός, ή, όν, = κολακευτικός, Plat.

Κολᾰκ-ώνῠμος, ὁ, (ὄνομα) parasite-named, Comic distortion of the name Κλε-ώνυμος, Ar.

ΚΟ'ΛΑΞ, ᾰκος, ὁ, a flatterer, fawner, Ar., Plat., etc.

κολαπτήρ, ῆρος, ὁ, a chisel, Luc.

ΚΟΛΑ'ΠΤΩ, f. ψω, of birds, to peck at, Luc., Anth.:—of Pegasus, to strike the ground with his hoof, Anth.　　2. to carve or chisel, Id.

κόλᾰσις, εως, ἡ, (κολάζω) chastisement, correction, punishment, Plat., etc.

κόλασμα, ατος, τό, (κολάζω) chastisement, Xen.

κολασμός, ὁ, = κόλασις, Plut.

κολάστειρα, ἡ, fem. of κολαστήρ, Anth.

κολαστέος, α, ον, verb. Adj. of κολάζω, to be chastised, Plat.　　II. κολαστέον, one must chastise, Id.

κολαστήριον, τό, (κολάζω) a house of correction, Luc.　　II. = κόλασμα, κόλασις, Xen.

κολαστής, οῦ, ὁ, (κολάζω) a chastiser, punisher, Trag.

κολαστικός, ή, όν, (κολάζω) corrective, Plat.

κολᾰφίζω, f. σω, to buffet, N. T.　　From

κόλαφος, ὁ, (κολάπτω) a buffet.

κολεόν, Ion. κουλεόν, τό, a sheath, scabbard of a sword, Lat. culeus, Hom., Att.

κολετράω, to trample on, τινα Ar. (Deriv. unknown.)

κόλλᾰ, ης, ἡ, glue, Lat. gluten, Hdt.

κόλλᾰβος, ὁ, = κόλλοψ, Luc.　　II. a kind of cake or roll, Ar.

κολλάω, f. ήσω, (κόλλα) to glue, cement, Ar., Plat.　　2. to join one metal to another, κ. χρυσὸν ἐλέφαντά τε, i. e. to make [a crown] inlaid with gold and ivory, Pind.　　II. generally, to join fast together:— Pass. to cleave to, κεκόλληται πρὸς ἄτᾳ is indissolubly bound to woe, Aesch.; so, of persons, κ. τινι to cleave to another, N. T.; and of things, ὁ κονιορτὸς ὁ κολληθείς τινι Ib.　　III. to put together, build, Pind.

κολλήεις, εσσα, εν, (κόλλα) = κολλητός, Il., Hes.

κόλλησις, εως, ἡ, (κολλάω) a glueing or welding, κ. σιδήρου a welding of iron, Lat. ferruminatio, or perhaps the art of inlaying or damasking iron, Hdt., Theophr.

κολλητός, ή, όν, (κολλάω) glued together, closely joined, well-framed, Hom., Eur., etc.　　II. ὑποκρητηρίδιον κολλητὸν a base welded to the κρητήρ, Hdt.

κολλῐκο-φάγος, ον, (φαγεῖν) roll-eating, Ar.　　From

ΚΟ'ΛΛΙΞ, ῖκος, ὁ, a roll or loaf of coarse bread.

ΚΟ'ΛΛΟΨ, οπος, ὁ, the peg or screw by which the strings of the lyre were tightened, Od., Plat.:—metaph. τῆς ὀργῆς τὸν κόλλοπ' ἀνιέναι to let down the strings of your passion, Ar.

κολλῠβιστής, οῦ, ὁ, (κόλλυβος) a small money-changer, N. T.　　From

κόλλῠβος, ὁ, a small coin, κολλύβου for a doit, Ar.　　2. in pl. κόλλυβα, τά, small round cakes, Id.

κολλύρα [ῠ], ἡ, = κόλλιξ, Ar.

κολλύριον [ῠ], τό, Dim. of κολλύρα, pl. eye-salve, Lat.

collyrium.　**II.** *a fine clay, in which a seal can be impressed*, Luc.

κολοβός, όν, (κόλος) *docked, curtailed*, c. gen., κολοβὸς κεράτων, Lat. *truncus pedum*, Plat.; κ. χειρῶν Anth.　**2.** absol. *maimed, mutilated*, Xen.

κολοβόω, f. ώσω, *to dock, curtail, shorten*, N. T.

κολοί-αρχος, ον, ὁ, *a chief of jackdaws, jackdaw-general*, Ar.　From

ΚΟΛΟΙΟ'Σ, ὁ, *a jackdaw, daw*, Lat. *graculus*, Il., Pind., Ar.: proverbs: κολοιὸς ποτὶ κολοιόν 'birds of a feather flock together,' Arist.; κολοιὸς ἀλλοτρίοις πτεροῖς ἀγάλλεται a jackdaw 'in borrowed plumes,' Luc.

κολόκῡμα, ατος, τό, *a large heavy wave* before it breaks (κόλον κῦμα), *the swell* that foreruns a storm, Ar.

κολοκύνθη or **-τη, ης, ἡ,** *a pumpkin*, Lat. *cucurbita.*

κολοκυνθιάς, ἡ, *made from pumpkins*, Anth.; and **κολοκύνθινος, η, ον,** *made from pumpkins*, πλοῖα Luc.

κόλον, τό, *the colon* or *lower intestine*, Ar.　From

ΚΟ'ΛΟΣ, ον, *docked, curtal*, Lat. *curtus*, Il.; of oxen, *stump-horned* or *hornless*, Hdt.; so, ὦ κόλε, addressed to a he-goat, Theocr.

κολοσσός, ὁ, *a colossus*, of the huge statues in the Egypt. temples, Hdt.: generally *a statue*, Aesch., Theocr.　The most famous Colossus was that of Apollo at Rhodes, 70 cubits high, made in the time of Demetrius Poliorcetes, Luc.　(Deriv. uncertain.)

κολοσυρτός, ὁ, poët. word, *a noisy rabble*, Il., Ar. (Deriv. uncertain.)

κόλ-ουρος, ον, (κόλος, οὐρά) *dock-tailed*, Plut.

κόλουσις, εως, ἡ, *a docking, cutting short*, Arist.　From

κολούω, f. -ούσω : aor. 1 ἐκόλουσα : Pass., aor. 1 ἐκολούθην or -ύσθην : pf. κεκόλουμαι : (κόλος) :—*to cut short, dock, curtail*, Hdt.　**II.** metaph. *to cut off, disappoint*, τὸ μὲν τελέει, τὸ δὲ κολούει part he brings to pass, part he *cuts off*, of the threats of Achilles, Il.; μηδὲ τὰ δῶρα κολούετε *curtail* them not, Od. :—of persons, τὰ ὑπερέχοντα κ. *to cut down, degrade*, those who are exalted above others, Hdt. :—Pass. *to be cut short* or *abridged*, Aesch.; ἐπειδὰν κολουθῶσι when *they suffer abatement*, Thuc.

κολοφών, ῶνος, ὁ, *a summit, top, finishing*, κολοφῶνα ἐπιτιθέναι, to put *the finishing stroke* to a thing, Plat. (Deriv. uncertain.)

κολπίας, ου, ὁ, *swelling in folds*, Aesch.　From

ΚΟ'ΛΠΟΣ, ὁ, Lat. *sinus*:　**I.** *the bosom*, Il.　**2.** *the womb*, Eur.　**II.** *the fold formed by a loose garment*, as it fell over the girdle, Il. :—this fold sometimes served for *a pocket*, Od., Hdt.; κόλπον ἀνιεμένη letting down *her robe so as to form a fold*, i. e. baring her breast, Il.; κόλπῳ πεπλώματος under the *deep-folded* robe, Aesch.; ἐπὶ σφυρὰ κόλπον ἀνεῖσαι having let *their folded robes* fall down to their ankles, Theocr.　**III.** *any hollow*, as　**1.** of the sea, first, in a half-literal sense, Θέτις ὑπεδέξατο κόλπῳ received him *in her bosom*, Il.; then, of *the deep hollow between waves*, Hom.　**2.** *a bay* or *gulf of the sea*, Il., Aesch.　**3.** *a vale*, κ. Ἀργεῖος Pind.; Ἐλευσινίας Δηοῦς ἐν κόλποις Soph.

κολπόω, f. ώσω, *to form into a swelling fold*, κ. to make a sail *belly* or *swell*, Lat. *sinuare*, ἄνεμος κ. τὴν ὀθόνην Luc.; χιτῶνας κολπώσαντες τῷ ἀνέμῳ, καθάπερ ἱστία Id. :—Pass. *to bosom* or *swell out*, of a sail,

Mosch.; κολποῦται Ζέφυρος εἰς ὀθόνας Anth.; of a bay, *to curve*, Polyb.

κολπ-ώδης, ες, (εἶδος) *embosomed, embayed*, Eur.

κόλπωμα, ατος, τό, *a folded garment*, Plut.

κολυμβάω, f. ήσω, *to plunge into the sea*, N. T.

κολυμβήθρα, ἡ, *a swimming-bath*, Plat.; and

κολυμβητής, οῦ, ὁ, *a diver*, Thuc., Plat., etc.; and

κολυμβίς, ίδος, ἡ, *a sea-bird, a diver*, Ar.　From

ΚΟ'ΛΥΜΒΟΣ, ὁ, *a diver*, Ar.

Κόλχος, ὁ, *a Colchian*, Hdt., etc. :—Adj. **Κολχικός, ή, όν,** *Colchian*, Id. :—fem. **Κολχίς, ίδος,** and as Subst. Κολχίς (sub. γῆ), *Colchis*, Id.; (sub. γυνή), Eur.

κολῳάω, (κολῳός) *to brawl, scold*, Il.

κολῶμαι, Att. for κολάσομαι, fut. med. of κολάζω.

ΚΟΛΩ'ΝΗ, ἡ, *a hill, mound*, Il.: esp. *a sepulchral mound, barrow*, Lat. *tumulus*, Soph.

Κολωνῆθεν, Adv. *from the deme* Κολωνός (q.v.), Dem.

κολωνία, ἡ, the Lat. *colonia*, N. T.

κολωνός, ὁ, = κολώνη, *a hill*, h. Hom., Hdt.; κ. λίθων *a heap* of stones, Hdt.　**II.** *Colonus*, a deme of Attica *lying on a hill*, about a mile NW. of Athens, immortalised by Sophocles, who was a native of it, in his Oed. Col.

κολῳός, οῦ, ὁ, *a brawling, wrangling*, Il.

κόμαρος, ἡ, *the strawberry-tree, arbūtus*, Ar.　Hence

κομαρο-φάγος, ον, (φαγεῖν) *eating the fruit of the arbūtus*, Ar.

κομάω, Ion. -έω, Ep. part. κομόων: f. ήσω: (κόμη) :—*to let the hair grow long, wear long hair*, Il.; κομέειν τὴν κεφαλήν Hdt.　In early times the Greeks wore their hair long, whence κάρη κομόωντες Ἀχαιοί in Hom.　At Sparta the fashion continued.　At Athens it was so worn by youths up to the 18th year, when they offered their long locks to some deity; and to wear long hair was considered as a sign of aristocratic habits: hence　**2.** κομᾶν meant *to plume oneself, give oneself airs, be proud* or *haughty*, like Lat. *cristam tollere*, Ar.; οὗτος ἐκόμησε ἐπὶ τυραννίδι he aimed at the monarchy, Hdt.; ἐπὶ τῷ κομᾷς; on what do you plume yourself? Ar.　**II.** of horses, χρυσέῃσιν ἐθείρῃσιν κομόωντε *decked* with golden manes, Il.　**III.** metaph. of trees, plants, foliage, h. Hom., etc.

κομέω, Ion. impf. κομέεσκον, *to take care of, attend to, tend*, Hom.

ΚΟ'ΜΗ, ἡ, *the hair, hair of the head*, Lat. *coma*, Hom., etc.; also in pl., Id. :—κόμην τρέφειν to let *the hair* grow long, Hdt.; κόμην κείρεσθαι to shave off *the hair*, in mourning, Od., etc.; κόμαι πρόσθετοι false *hair*, a *wig*, Xen.　**II.** metaph. *the foliage, leaves* of trees, Od.

Κομητ-αμυνίας, ου, ὁ, Comic adaptation of the name Amynias, *Coxcomb-amynias* (cf. κομάω), Ar.

κομήτης, ου, ὁ, (κομάω) *wearing long hair, long-haired*, ap. Hdt., Ar.　**2.** metaph. ἰὸς κ. *a feathered* arrow, Soph.; λειμὼν κ. *a grassy* meadow, Eur.　**II.** as Subst. *a comet*, Arist.

κομιδή, ἡ, (κομίζω) *attendance, care*, in Il., always of care *bestowed* on horses; in Od., of care *bestowed* on men, by means of baths, etc.; also, *care bestowed* on a garden, Od.　**2.** *provision, supplies*, Ib.　**II.** *carriage, conveyance, importation*, Thuc.: *a gather-*

ing in of harvest, Xen. **2.** (from Med. also) *a carrying away for oneself, a recovery*, Hdt.:—*the recovery* of a debt, *payment*, Dem. **3.** (from Pass.) *a going* or *coming*, Hdt.: *an escape, safe return*, Id.

κομῑδή or **κομῐδή**, Adv. (dat. of κομιδή) *exactly, just*, Plat., Dem. **2.** like πάνυ, *absolutely, altogether, quite*, Plat.; οὐ κομιδῆ *not at all*, Plut. **3.** in answers, κομιδῆ μὲν οὖν *just so, yes certainly*, Ar., Plat.

ΚΟΜΙ'ΖΩ, f. κομιῶ, later κομίσω: aor. 1 ἐκόμισα, Ep. ἐκόμισσα or κόμισσα, Dor. ἐκόμιξα:—pf. κεκόμικα:—Med., f. κομιοῦμαι, Ion. -ιεῦμαι: aor. 1 ἐκομισάμην, Ep. ἐκομισσ- or κομισσ-:—Pass., f. -ισθήσομαι: aor. 1 ἐκομίσθην: pf. κεκόμισμαι (often in med. sense):—*to take care of, provide for*, Hom.:—*to receive hospitably, to entertain*, Thuc.; more commonly in Med., Hom. **2.** of things, *to mind, attend to, give heed to*, Id., etc.; ἔξω κομίζειν πηλοῦ πόδα *to keep one's foot out of the mud*, Aesch. **II.** *to carry away so as to preserve, carry home, carry safe away*, Il., etc.; simply, *to save, rescue*, τινὰ ἐκ θανάτου Pind.; but, νέκρον κ. *to carry out to burial*, Soph., Eur. **2.** *to carry off as a prize* or *as booty*, Il., Pind.:—Med. *to get for oneself, receive in full, acquire, gain*, Soph., etc. **3.** *to carry, convey, bear*, Hom., etc.:—Pass. *to be conveyed, to journey, travel*, Hdt.; εἴσω κομίζου *get thee in*, Aesch.; so in fut. and aor. 1 med., κομιεύμεθα ἐς Σίριν Hdt., etc. **4.** *to bring to* a place, *bring hither, bring in*, καρπὸν κ. *to gather in* corn, Id., etc.:—so in Med., Id., Soph.; and pf. pass. in med. sense, τοὺς καρποὺς κεκόμισθε *you have reaped the fruits*, Dem. **5.** *to conduct, escort*, Soph., Plat., etc.; κ. ναῦς Thuc. **6.** *to get back, recover*, Pind., Eur., Plat., etc.:—Med. *to get back for oneself, recover*, Eur., Thuc.; κομίζεσθαι χρήματα *to recover a debt*, Dem.:—Pass. *to come* or *go back, return*, Hdt., Att. **7.** like Lat. *affero, to bring, give*, Aesch. Hence

κομιστέος, α, ον, verb. Adj. *to be taken care of, to be gathered in*, Aesch. **II.** κομιστέον, *one must bring*, Plat.

κομιστήρ, ῆρος, ὁ, = sq., Eur., Plut.

κομιστής, οῦ, ὁ, (κομίζω) *one who takes care of*, Eur. **II.** *a bringer, conductor*, Id.

κόμιστρον, τό, (κομίζω) in pl., like σῶστρα, *reward for saving*, Aesch. **II.** *reward for bringing*, Eur.

κομιῶ, Att. fut. of κομίζω.

κόμμα, ατος, τό, (κόπτω) *the stamp* or *impression of a coin*, Ar.: proverb., πονηροῦ κόμματος *of bad stamp*, Id. **2.** = νόμισμα, *coin, coinage*, Id. **II.** *a short clause* of a sentence, Lat. *comma*, Cic.

κομμάτικός, ή, όν, (κόμμα II) *consisting of short clauses*, μικρὰ καὶ κ. ἐρωτήματα Luc.

κόμμῑ, τό, *gum*, Lat. *gummi*, Hdt. (A foreign word.)

κομμός, οῦ, ὁ, (κόπτω) *a striking*: esp. like Lat. *planctus* (from *plango*), *a beating of the breast in lamentation*, ἔκοψα κομμὸν Ἄριον Ι *lamented with Median lamentation*, Aesch. **2.** in Att. Drama, *a wild lament*, sung alternately by an actor and the chorus, such as Aesch. Ag. 1072–1185.

κομμόω, *to beautify*, Arist. (Deriv. uncertain.) Hence

κομμωτής, οῦ, ὁ, *a beautifier, embellisher*, Luc.

κομμωτικός, ή, όν, *of* or *for embellishment*:—ἡ -κή (sc. τέχνη), *the art of embellishment*, Plat.

κομμώτρια, ή, fem. of κομμωτής, *a dresser, tirewoman*, Ar., Plat.

κομόωντες, Ep. part. pl. of κομάω.

κομόωντι, Dor. for κομῶσι, 3 pl. of κομάω.

κομπάζω, f. άσω, = κομπέω, *to vaunt, boast, brag*, Trag.; c. acc. cogn., κ. λόγον *to speak big* words, Aesch. **2.** *to boast of*, κ. γέρας *to boast* one's office, Id.:—Pass. *to be renowned*, Eur.; φόβος κομπάζεται *fear is loudly spoken*, Aesch.; τινὸς δὲ παῖς πατρὸς κομπάζεται; *of what father is he said to be the son?* Eur.

Κομπᾱσεύς, ὁ, Com. word, *one of the* Κόμπος-*deme, a Bragsman*, Ar.

κόμπασμα, τό, in pl. *boasts, braggart words*, Aesch., Ar.

κομπασμός, ὁ, = κόμπασμα, Plut.

κομπαστής, οῦ, ὁ, (κομπάζω) *a braggart*, Plut.

κομπέω, (κόμπος) *to ring, clash*, κόμπει χαλκός Il. **II.** metaph., like κομπάζω, *to speak big, boast, brag, vaunt*, Hdt., Eur.; c. acc. cogn., κ. μῦθον *to speak a boastful speech*, Soph. **2.** c. acc. *to boast of*, Aesch.:—Pass., *to be boasted of*, Thuc.

κομπο-λᾱκέω, *to talk big, be an empty braggart*, Ar.

ΚΟ'ΜΠΟΣ, ὁ, *a noise, din, clash*, as of a boar's tusks when he whets them, Il.; *the stamping* of dancers' feet, Od. **II.** metaph. *a boast, vaunt*, Hdt., Aesch., etc. **2.** rarely in good sense, *praise*, Pind.

κομπός, ὁ, = κομπαστής, Eur.

κομπο-φᾰκελορ-ρήμων, ον, *pomp-bundle-worded*, derisive epith. of Aeschylus in Ar.

κομπ-ώδης, ες, (εἶδος) *boastful, vainglorious*, Thuc.; τὸ κομπῶδες *boastfulness*, Id.

κομψεία, ή, *refinement*, esp. of language, Plat.

κομψ-εὐρῑπικῶς, Adv. *with Euripides-prettinesses* (shortened from κομψευριπιδικῶς), Ar.

κομψεύω, (κομψός) *to refine upon, quibble upon*, κόμψευε νῦν τὴν δόξαν aye, *quibble on the word* δόξα (referring to the previous line), Soph.:—Med. *to deal in refinements* or *subtleties*, Plat.

κομψο-πρεπής, ές, (πρέπω) *dainty-seeming*, Ar.

κομψός, ή, όν, (κομέω) *well-dressed*, Lat. *comptus*; hence, *a pretty fellow*, Lat. *bellus homo*, Ar. **2.** *accomplished, elegant, exquisite, refined, dainty, clever, witty*, of persons or their words and acts, Id.; κ. περί τι *clever about a thing*, Plat.; of a dog's instinct, *exquisite, acute*, Id.; in a sneering sense, of Sophists *who refine overmuch, studied, affected*, Eur., etc. **II.** Adv. κομψῶς, *elegantly, prettily, daintily*, Ar., Plat., etc. **2.** κομψότερον ἔχειν *to be better in health*, N. T.

κονᾰβέω, f. ήσω, (κόναβος) *to resound, clash, ring, re-echo*, Hom., Hes. Hence

κονᾰβηδόν, Adv. *with a noise, clash, din*, Anth.

κονᾰβίζω, = κοναβέω, Il.

ΚΟ'ΝΑΒΟΣ, ὁ, *a ringing, clashing, din*, Od., Hes.

ΚΟ'ΝΔΥ῭ΛΟΣ, ὁ, *a knuckle*, κονδύλοις πατάξαι, opp. to ἐπὶ κόρρης (a slap in the face), Dem.: proverb., κολλύραν καὶ κόνδυλον ὄψον ἐπ' αὐτῇ *a roll and knuckle-sauce to it, i. e. a good thrashing*, Ar.

κονέω, f. ήσω, (κόνις) *to raise dust*: *to hasten*, Anth.

κονία, Ion. and Ep. -ίη, ή, (κόνις): **1.** *dust, a cloud of dust*, stirred up by men's feet, Il.; also in pl., like Lat. *arenae*, Hom., etc. **2.** *sand* or *soil* (v. ὑπερέπτω) Il. **3.** *ashes*, in pl. like Lat. *cineres*,

Od. **II.** *a fine powder*, sprinkled over wrestlers' bodies after being oiled, to make them more easily grasped by the opponent:—this powder was also used in the bath, Ar. [ῐ in κονίησιν, in other cases ῐ usually.]

κονιᾱτός, ή, όν, *plastered* or *pitched*, Xen.

κονιάω, (κονία 11) *to plaster* or *whiten over*, Lat. *dealbare*, Dem. :—Pass. *to be whitened*, N. T.

κονι-ορτός, ό, (κόνις, ὄρνυμι) *dust stirred up, a cloud of dust*, such as is made by troops, Hdt., Ar., etc.; κ. τῆς ὕλης νεωστὶ κεκαυμένης, i. e. *a cloud* of wood-ashes, Thuc. **II.** metaph. *a dirty fellow*, Dem.

ΚΟΝΙΣ, ιος, Att. εως or εος, ἡ, Ep. dat. κόνι for κόνιι —Lat. *cinis, dust*, Il., etc.;—of the grave, Pind., Soph. **2.** *ashes*, Hom. **II.** = κονία 11, Luc.: metaph. of toil, Id. [ῐ in Hom., ῑ Att.]

κονίσᾰλος [ῐ], (κόνις) *a cloud of dust*, Il.

κονίω [ῑ], f. κονίσω [ῑ], aor. 1 ἐκόνῑσα: Pass., pf. κεκόνῑμαι, 3 sing. plqpf. κεκόνῑτο:—*to make dusty, cover with clouds of dust*, Il.:—Pass., φεύγον κεκονιμένοι *all dusty* fled they, Virgil's *pulverulenta fuga dant terga*, Ib.; hence, *to be in great haste*, Ar., etc. **2.** Pass. *to be sprinkled as with dust*, Theocr. **II.** intr., κονίοντες πεδίοιο *galloping o'er the dusty plain*, Hom.

Κοννᾶς or **Κόννας, ό,** a drunken flute-player; Κόννου ψῆφος, proverb. of *a worthless opinion*, Ar.

ΚΟΝΤΟΣ, οῦ, ό, *a pole, punting-pole, boat-hook*, Lat. *contus*, Od., Hdt., Att.: *the shaft* of a pike, Luc.

κοντο-φόρος, ον, (φέρω) *carrying a pole* or *pike*, Luc.

ΚΟΝΥΖΑ, ης, ἡ, a strong-smelling plant, *fleabane, pulicaria*, poët. κνύζα, Theocr.

κοπάζω, f. άσω, *to grow weary*: of the wind, *to abate*, Hdt., N. T.

κοπετός, ό, = κομμός, Plut., Anth.

κοπεύς, έως, ό, (κόπτω) *a chisel*, Luc.

κοπή, ή, (κόπτω) *a cutting in pieces, slaughter*, N. T.

κοπιάω, f. άσω [ᾱ]: aor. 1 ἐκοπίασα, pf. κεκοπίακα: (κόπος):—*to be tired, grow weary*, Ar., N. T. **II.** *to work hard, toil*, N. T.

κόπις, εως, ό, (κόπτω) *a prater, liar, wrangler*, Eur.

κοπίς, ίδος, ἡ, (κόπτω) *a chopper, cleaver, a broad curved knife*, somewhat like our *bill*, Eur., Xen.

κόπος, ου, ό, (κόπτω) *a striking, beating*, Aesch., Eur. **II.** *toil, trouble, suffering*, Aesch., Soph. **2.** *weariness, fatigue*, Eur., Ar.

κόππα, τό, a letter of the ancient Greek alphabet (Ϙ) retained as a numeral = 90, between π (80), and ρ (100); and this shews that it was the same as the Hebr. ף (*Koph*) and Lat. Q; cf. σταῦ, σάμπι.

κοππᾰτίας, ό, *branded with the letter Koppa* (Ϙ) *as a mark*, ἵππος κ. Ar.; cf. σαμφόρας.

κοππα-φόρος, ον, (φέρω) = κοππατίας, Luc.

κόπρειος, α, ον, (κόπρος) *full of dung, filthy*, Ar.

κοπρία, ἡ, *a dunghill*: also = κόπρος, Hdt.

κοπρίζω, f. ίσω, Ep. ίσσω, *to dung, manure*, Od.

κοπρο-λόγος, ό, (λέγω) *a dung-gatherer, a dirty fellow*, Ar.

ΚΟΠΡΟΣ, ή, *dung, ordure, manure*, Hom., Hdt., etc. **II.** *a farm-yard, home-stead*, Hom.

κοπροφορέω, f. ήσω, *to cover with dung* or *dirt*, Ar.

κοπρο-φόρος, ον, (φέρω) *carrying dung*; κόφινος κ. a *dung*-basket, Xen.

κοπρών, ῶνος, ό, (κόπρος) *a place for dung, privy*, Dem.

κοπτός, ή, όν, *chopped small*: κοπτή, ή, *a cake of pounded* sesame, Anth. From

κόπτω (from Root ΚΟΠ): f. κόψω: aor. 1 ἔκοψα: pf. κέκοφα, Ep. part. κεκοπώς: Pass., f. κεκόψομαι: aor. 2 ἐκόπην: pf. κέκομμαι:—*to strike, smite, knock down*, Od.; κόψε μιν παρήϊον smote him *on the cheek*, Il. **2.** *to cut off, chop off*, Hom., etc.; κ. δένδρα *to fell* trees, Thuc., etc.; κ. τὴν χώραν *to cut down the trees in it, to lay it waste*, Xen. :—Pass., of ships, *to be shattered* or *disabled* by the enemy, Thuc. :—metaph., φρενῶν κεκομμένος *stricken* in mind, Aesch. **3.** *to hammer, forge*, Hom.: *to stamp* metal, *coin* money, Hdt. :—Med. *to coin oneself* money, *order to be coined*, Id. : Pass., of the money, *to be stamped* or *coined*, Ar. **4.** *to knock at* the door, Lat. *pulsare*, Id., etc. **5.** *to cut small, chop up* or *pound* in a mortar, Hdt. **6.** of a horse, *to jolt* or *shake* his rider, Xen. **7.** metaph. *to tire out, weary*, Dem. **II.** Med. κόπτομαι, *to beat one's breast* through grief, Lat. *plangere*, Il., Hdt., Plat. **2.** κόπτεσθαί τινα *to mourn for* any one, Lat. *plangere aliquem*, Eur., etc.

Κόρα, ή, v. κόρη Β.

κορᾰκῖνος, ό, (κόραξ) *a young raven*, Ar.

ΚΟΡΑΞ, ᾰκος, ό, Lat. *corvus*, *a raven* or *carrion-crow*, Aesch., etc.; in imprecations, ἐς κόρακας ' *pasce corvos,*' ' go to the dogs,' ' go and be hanged,' Ar.; βάλλ' ἐς κόρακας Id.; οὐκ ἐς κόρακας ἀποφθερεῖ; Id.; ἐς κόρακας οἰχήσεται Id. **II.** *anything like a raven's beak, an engine for grappling ships*, Polyb. **2.** *a hooked handle of a door*, Anth. **3.** *an instrument of torture*, Luc.

κοράσιον, τό, Dim. of κόρη, *a girl, maiden*, Anth., N. T.

κόρανna, ἡ, a barbarism for κόρη, Ar.

κορβᾶν (indecl.) Hebrew word, *a gift* or *votive offering for the service of God*, N. T. :—hence **κορβανᾶς, ό,** *the treasury of the temple* at Jerusalem, Ib.

κορδᾰκίζω, f. σω, *to dance the* κόρδαξ.

κορδᾰκικός, ή, όν, *like the dance* κόρδαξ: hence, *tripping, running*, ῥυθμὸς κ., of trochaic metres, Arist.

κορδᾰκισμός, ό, *the dancing of the* κόρδαξ, Dem.

κόρδαξ, ᾰκος, ό, *the cordax, a dance* of the old Comedy, κόρδακα ἑλκύσαι *to dance the* κόρδαξ, prob. from its slow, trailing movement, Ar.

ΚΟΡΕΝΝΥΜΙ, f. κορέσω, Ep. 2 and 3 sing. κορέεις, κορέει: aor. 1 ἐκόρεσα, poët. κόρεσσα :—Med., aor. 1 ἐκορεσάμην, Ep. ἐκορεσσ-, κορεσσ-:—Pass., f. κορεσθήσομαι: aor. 1 ἐκορέσθην; pf. κεκόρεσμαι, Ion. κεκόρημαι:—Ep. part. pf. act. (with pass. sense) κεκορηώς, ότος :—*to sate, satiate, satisfy*, τινα Theogn., Aesch. : *to fill* one *with* a thing, c. dat., Il. ; also c. gen. rei, *to fill full of*, Soph. :—Med. *to satisfy oneself, have one's fill*, c. gen., ἐκορέσσατο φορβῆς Il., etc.; c. part., κλαίουσα κορέσσατο she had her *fill* of weeping, Il. :—Pass. *to be satiated*, Hes. ; rarely c. dat. rei, πλούτῳ κεκορημένος Theogn.; ὕβρι Hdt.

κόρεμα, τό, = κορεία, *maidenhood*, Eur., in pl. From

κορεύομαι, f. κορευθήσομαι, Pass. (κόρη) *to be a maid, grow up to maidenhood*, Eur.

ΚΟΡΕΩ, f. ήσω, *to sweep, sweep out*, Od.; κ. τὴν Ἑλλάδα *to sweep* Greece *clean*, depopulate her, Ar.

κορέω, Ion. fut. of κορέννυμι.

κόρη, ἡ, rarely κόρᾱ, even in Att.: Ion. κούρη, Dor. κώρα:—fem. of κόρος, κοῦρος, 1. *a maiden, maid, damsel*, Lat. *puella*, Il., Soph., etc. 2. *a bride, young wife*, Hom., Eur. 3. *a daughter*, κοῦραι Διός Il.; κ. Διός, of Athené, Aesch.:—in voc., κούρα *my daughter*, Id., Soph. II. *the pupil* of the eye, Lat. *pupula*, because a little image appears therein, Eur., Ar. III. *a long sleeve* reaching over the hand, Xen.

B. Κόρη, Dor. Κόρα, Ion. Κούρη, ἡ, *Cora, the Daughter* (of Demeter), name under which Persephoné (Proserpine) was worshipped in Attica, τῇ Μητρὶ καὶ τῇ Κούρῃ Hdt., etc.; Δημήτηρ καὶ Κόρη Xen., etc.

κόρημα, ατος, τό, (κορέω) *a besom, broom*, Ar.

κορθύνω and κορθύω [ῡ], (κόρθυς) *to lift up, raise*, Ζεὺς κόρθυνεν ἐὸν μένος *raised high* his wrath, Hes. :—Pass., κῦμα κορθύεται *waxes high, rears* its crest, Il.

κόρθῡς, υος, ἡ, lengthd. form of κόρυς: in Theocr., κόρθυος ἀ τομά *the swathe* of mown corn.

κορθύω, v. κορθύνω.

κορίαννον, τό, *coriander*, Ar. (Deriv. unknown.)

κορίζομαι, (κόρη) Dep. *to fondle, caress, coax*, Ar.

Κορίνθιος, α, ον, *Corinthian*, Hdt., etc.—also Κορινθιακός, ή, όν, Xen.; Κορινθικός, Anth.

Κόρινθος, ἡ, *Corinth*, the city and country, Il., Hdt., Att.; famed for its luxury, whence the proverb οὐ παντὸς ἀνδρὸς εἰς Κόρινθον ἐσθ᾽ ὁ πλοῦς;—with a masc. Adj., ὀφρυόεντα Κ. Orac. ap. Hdt.:—proverb., Διὸς Κόρινθος, used of persons who are always repeating the same old story, Ar., etc. II. Adv. Κορινθόθι, *at Corinth*, Il.

κόριον, τό, Dim. of κόρη, Theocr.: Dor. κώριον, Ar.

ΚΟΡΙΣ, ιος, Att. εως, ὁ, pl. κόρεις, *a bug*, Lat. *cimex*, Ar.

κορκορυγή, ἡ, the *rumbling* of the empty bowels: generally, *any hollow noise, a din, tumult*, Aesch., Ar. (Formed from the sound.)

κορμός, ὁ, (κείρω) *the trunk* of a tree (with the boughs lopped off), Od., Eur.; κορμοὶ ξύλων *logs* of timber, Hdt.; κ. ναυτικοί, i. e. oars, Eur.

ΚΟΡΟΣ (A), ου, ὁ, *one's fill, satiety, surfeit*, Hom., etc.; πάντων μὲν κόρος ἐστί, καὶ ὕπνου *one* may have *one's fill* of all things, even of sleep, etc., Il.; κ. ἔχειν τινός *to have one's fill* of a thing, Eur. 2. *the consequence of satiety, insolence*, Pind.; πρὸς κόρον *insolently*, Aesch.

κόρος (B), ου, ὁ, Ion. κοῦρος, Dor. κῶρος :—*a boy, lad, stripling*, Hom., etc.: κοῦροι *young men, warriors*, Il.; also *servants*, like Lat. *pueri*, Hom. 2. with gen. of prop. names, *a son*, Od.; Θησέως κ. Soph., etc. (Prob. from κείρω, *one who has* cut *his hair short on emerging from boyhood*.)

κόρος (C), ὁ, the Hebrew *cor*, *a dry measure* containing 10 Att. medimni, about 120 gallons, N. T.

κόρρη, new Att. for κόρση.

κόρση, ἡ, in new Att. κόρρη, Dor. κόρρα: (κάρα) :—*one of the temples, the side of the forehead*, Il. :—so in Att., ἐπὶ κόρρης πατάσσειν *to box on the ear*, Dem.; cf. κόνδυλος. 2. *the hair on the temples*, which is the first to turn gray, Aesch.

Κορυβάντειος, α, ον, (Κορύβας) *Corybantian*, Anth.

Κορῠβαντιάω, f. άσω, *to be filled with* Corybantic *frenzy*, Plat. :—in Ar., comically, of a drowsy person suddenly starting up ; and

Κορῠβαντίζω, f. Att. ιῶ, *to purify* or *consecrate by* Corybantic *rites*, Ar. From

Κορῠβας [ῠ], αντος, ὁ, *a Corybant, priest of Cybelé in Phrygia*; in pl. Κορύβαντες, Eur., etc. II. *enthusiasm*, Luc.

κορῠδαλλίς, ίδος, ἡ, and κορῠδαλλός, ὁ, = sq., Theocr.

κορῠδός, ἡ, (κόρυς) *the crested lark*, Ar.

κόρυζα, ης, ἡ, *a running at the nose*, Lat. *pituita*, Luc.: —metaph. *drivelling, stupidity*, Id. Hence

κορυζάω, f. ήσω, *to run at the nose*, Plat.

κόρυνθα, -θας, acc. sing. and pl. of κόρυς.

κορυθ-άϊξ [ᾰ], ῑκος, ὁ, (ἀΐσσω) *helmet-shaking*, i. e. *with waving plume*, Il.

κορυθ-αίολος, ον, *with glancing helm*, Il.

κόρυμβος, ὁ, pl. κόρυμβοι and κόρυμβα: (κόρυς, κορυφή): —*the uppermost point, head, end*, νηῶν ἄκρα κόρυμβα *high-pointed sterns* of ships, Il.; in pl. of a single ship, Aesch. 2. *the top* of a hill, Hdt., Aesch. II. = κρωβύλος, Anth. III. *a cluster of fruit* or *flowers*, Mosch., Anth.

κορύνη, ἡ, (κόρυς) *a club, mace*, Il., Hdt.:—*a shepherd's staff*, Theocr. [ῠ in Hom.; ῡ in Eur.] Hence

κορυνήτης, ου, ὁ, *a club-bearer, mace-bearer*, Il.

κορυνη-φόρος, ον, (φέρω) *club-bearing*: κορυνηφόροι, οἱ, *club-bearers*, the body-guard of Peisistratus, Hdt.

κορυπτίλος [ῐ], ὁ, *one that butts with the head*, Theocr.

ΚΟΡΥΠΤΩ, f. ψω, *to butt with the head*, Theocr. From

κόρυς, ῠθος, ἡ: acc. κόρυθα and κόρυν: poët. dat. pl. κορύθεσσι: (κάρα) :—*a helmet, helm, casque*, Hom. II. *the head*, Eur. Hence

κορύσσω, poët. inf. -έμεν: Ep. impf. κόρυσσον :—Med., aor. 1 ἐκορυσσάμην :—Pass., pf. κεκόρυθμαι: (κόρυς): — *to furnish with a helmet*, and, generally, *to fit out, equip, marshal*, Il., Hes. :—Pass. and Med. *to equip* or *arm oneself*, Il. II. *to make crested*, κόρυσσε κῦμα *he reared* his *crested* wave, Ib. :—Pass. *to rear its head*, of a wave, Ib.; of Rumour, Ib.; of clouds, Theocr. Hence

κορυστής, οῦ, ὁ, *a helmed man, an armed warrior*, Il.

κορυφαία, ἡ, (κορυφή) *the head-stall of a bridle*, Xen.

κορυφαῖον, τό, *the upper rim of a hunting-net*, Xen. From

κορυφαῖος, ὁ, (κορυφή) *the head man, chief man, leader*, Hdt., etc.:—in the Att. Drama, *the leader of the chorus*, Dem.; κ. ἑστηκώς *standing at the head of the row*, Ar. II. as Adj. *at the top*, ὁ κ. πῖλος *the apex*, of the Roman *flamen*, Plut.

κορυφή, ἡ, (κόρυς) *the head, top, highest point*; hence, 1. *the crown* or *top of the head*, Il., Hdt., Att. 2. *the top* or *peak* of a mountain, Il., Hdt., Aesch. II. metaph. *the highest point*, Lat. *summa*; παντὸς ἔχει κορυφάν *is the best* of all, Pind.; κορυφὰ λόγων προτέρων *the sum and substance* of ancient legends, Id. 2. *the height* or *excellence* of a thing, i. e. *the choicest, noblest, best*, Id.

κορυφόω, f. ώσω, (κορυφή) *to bring to a head* :—Pass., [κῦμα] κορυφοῦται *rises with* arching *crest*, Il.; τὸ ἔσχατον κορυφοῦται βασιλεῦσι *kings are on the highest pinnacle*, Pind. II. *to bring to an end, finish*, Plut. :—Pass., κορυφούμενος *being summed up*, Anth.

κορων-εκάβη [ᾰ], ἡ, *old as a crow* or *Hecuba*, Anth.

κορώνεως συκῆ, ἡ, a fig *of raven-gray colour*, Ar. From

κορώνη, ἡ, Lat. *cornix*, *the chough* or *sea-crow*, a small kind with red legs and bill, Od. **2.** = κόραξ, *the carrion-crow*, Hes., Ar. **II.** *anything hooked* or *curved*, like a crow's bill, **1.** *the handle on a door*, Od. **2.** *the tip of a bow*, on which the bowstring was hooked, Hom. :—metaph., βιῷ κορώνην ἐπιθεῖναι to put *a finish* to life, Luc.

κορωνιάω, f. άσω, (κορωνός) *to arch the neck*, Anth.

κορωνίς, ίδος, ἡ, acc. -νίν, (κορωνός) *crook-beaked, curved*, of ships, from the outline of the prow and stern, Hom. **2.** of kine, *with crumpled horns*, Theocr. **II.** as Subst. *a curved line, a flourish with the pen* at the end of a book, Anth. :—metaph. *an end, finish*, ἐπιθεῖναι κορωνίδα τινί Luc.

κορωνο-βόλος, ον, (βάλλω) *shooting crows*: κορωνοβόλον, τό, *a sling* or *bow for crow-shooting*, etc., Anth.

ΚΟΡΩΝΟΣ, ή, όν, *curved, crooked*: *with crumpled horns*, Archil.

κοσκῐνηδόν, Adv. *like, as in a sieve*, Luc.

κοσκῐνό-μαντις, εως, ὁ, and ἡ, *a diviner by a sieve*, Theocr. From

ΚΟΣΚΙΝΟΝ, τό, *a sieve*, Ar., Plat.

κοσκυλμάτια, ων, τά, *shreds of leather*; in Ar., of the *scraps of flattery* offered by the tanner Cleon to his patron Δῆμος.

κοσμέω, f. ήσω, (κόσμος) *to order, arrange*, Hom., etc.: esp. *to set* an army *in array, marshal* it, Il. :—Med., κοσμησάμενος πολίτας having arranged his men, Ib. **2.** generally, *to arrange, prepare*, δόρπον Od. ; ἔργα Hes., etc. **II.** *to dispose, order, rule, govern*, Hdt., Soph., etc.; τὰ κοσμούμενα *orderly institutions, set order*, Soph. **2.** in Crete, *to be Cosmos* (κόσμος III), *rule as such*, Arist. **III.** *to deck, adorn, equip, furnish, dress*, esp. of women, h. Hom., Hes., etc.: Med., κοσμέεσθαι τὰς κεφαλάς *to adorn their* heads, Hdt., etc. **2.** metaph. *to adorn, embellish*, Eur., Thuc., etc. **3.** *to honour, pay honour to*, Soph., Eur., etc. **IV.** in Pass. *to be assigned* or *ascribed to*, ἐς τὸν Αἰγύπτιον νόμον αὗται [αἱ πόλεις] ἐκεκοσμέατο Hdt.

κόσμηθεν, Ep. for ᾔσαν, 3 pl. aor. 1 pass. of κοσμέω.

κόσμημα, τό, (κοσμέω) *an ornament, decoration*, Xen.

κοσμήν, Dor. for κοσμεῖν, inf. of κοσμέω.

κόσμησις, εως, ἡ, *an ordering, disposition, arrangement, adornment*, Plat.

κοσμητήρ, ῆρος, ὁ, = sq., Epigr. ap. Aeschin., Plut.

κοσμητής, οῦ, ὁ, (κοσμέω) *an orderer, director*, Epigr. ap. Aeschin. **II.** *an adorner*, Xen. Hence

κοσμητικός, ή, όν, *skilled in arranging*: ἡ -κή (sc. τέχνη), *the art of dress and ornament*, Plat.

κοσμητός, ή, όν, (κοσμέω) *well-ordered, trim*, Od.

κοσμήτωρ, ορος, ὁ, poët. for κοσμητής, *one who marshals an army, a commander*, Hom.

κοσμικός, ή, όν, (κόσμος IV) *of the world* or *universe*, Luc. **II.** *of this world, earthly*, N. T.

κόσμιος, α or ον, and ος, ον, (κόσμος) *well-ordered, regular, moderate*, δαπάνῃ Plat. :—κόσμιόν ἐστι, c. inf., 'tis *a regular practice*, Ar. **2.** of persons, *orderly, well-behaved, regular, discreet, quiet*, Id., Plat., etc. : —τὸ κ. *decorum, decency, order*, Soph. :—Adv. κοσ-

μίως, *regularly, decently*, Ar., etc. ; κοσμίως ἔχειν to be *orderly*, Plat. Hence

κοσμιότης, ητος, ἡ, *propriety, decorum, orderly behaviour*, Ar., Plat.

κοσμο-κόμης, ου, ὁ, (κόμη) *dressing the hair*, Anth.

κοσμο-κράτωρ, ορος, ὁ, (κρατέω) *lord of the world*, N. T.

κοσμο-πλόκος, ον, *holding the world together*, Anth.

ΚΟΣΜΟΣ, ου, ὁ, *order, κόσμῳ* and *κατὰ κόσμον in order, duly*, Il., etc. ; μὰψ ἀτὰρ οὐ κατὰ κόσμον Ib. ; οὐδενὶ κόσμῳ *in no sort of order*, Hdt., Att. **2.** *good order, good behaviour, decency*, Aesch., Dem. **3.** *the form, fashion* of a thing, Od., Hdt. **4.** of states, *order, government*, Hdt., Thuc. **II.** *an ornament, decoration, embellishment, dress*, Il., etc.; esp. of women, Lat. *mundus muliebris*, Ib., Hes., etc. :—in pl. *ornaments*, Aesch., etc. **2.** metaph. *honour, credit*, Hdt., Soph., etc. **III.** *a regulator*, title of the chief magistrate in Crete, Arist. **IV.** *the world* or *universe*, from its perfect *order*, Lat. *mundus*, Plat., etc. **2.** *mankind*, as we use 'the world,' N. T.

κοσμο-φθόρος, ον, (φθείρω) *destroying the world*, Anth.

κόσος, η, ον, Ion. and Aeol. for πόσος.

κόσσᾰβος, ὁ, Ion. and old Att. for κότταβος.

κοταίνω, = κοτέω, Aesch.

κότε, κοτέ, Ion. for πότε, ποτέ.

κότερον, κότερα, Ion. for πότερον, πότερα.

κοτέω, pf. part. κεκοτηώς : Med. κοτέομαι : Ep. fut. κοτέσσομαι, 3 sing. aor. 1 κοτέσσατο : (κότος) :—*to bear a grudge against*, c. gen., ἀπάτης κοτέων *angry at the trick*, Il. : absol. *to be angry*, Hom.

κοτήεις, εσσα, εν, *wrathful, jealous*, Il.

κοτίνη-φόρος, ον, (φέρω) *producing wild olive-trees*, Mosch. From

ΚΟΤΙΝΟΣ, ὁ and ἡ, *the wild olive-tree*, Lat. *oleaster*, Ar. Hence

κοτίνο-τράγος [ᾰ], ον, (τραγεῖν) *eating wild olive-berries*, Ar.

ΚΟΤΟΣ, ου, ὁ, *a grudge, rancour, wrath*, Hom., Aesch.

κοτταβίζω, f. Att. ιῶ, *to play at the cottabus*, Ar.

κοττάβιον, τό, *the prize of the game κότταβος*, Arist.

κόττᾰβος, ὁ, *the cottabus*, a Sicilian game, much in vogue at Athens. Each person threw the wine left in his cup, so as to fall in a metal basin ; if the whole fell with a clear sound, it was a good sign. But the game was played in various ways. (Deriv. unknown.)

ΚΟΤΥΛΗ [ῠ], ἡ, *a cup*, Hom. **2.** *the cup* or *socket* of a joint, esp. of the hip-joint, Il. **3.** *a liquid measure*, containing 6 κύαθοι, i. e. nearly *half a pint*, Ar., Thuc. Hence

κοτυληδών, όνος, ἡ, *any cup-shaped hollow*: **1.** in pl. *the suckers on the arms* (πλεκτάναι) *of the polypus*, Od., in Ep. dat. pl. κοτυληδονόφιν. **2.** = κοτύλη 2, *the socket of the hip-joint*, Ar.

κοτῠλ-ήρῠτος, ον, (ἀρύω) *that can be drawn in cups*, i. e. *flowing copiously, streaming*, Il.

κοτύλων, ωνος, ὁ, (κς ὕλη) *nickname of a toper*, Plut.

κοῦ, κου, Ion. for ποῦ, που.

κουλεόν, Ion. for κολεόν.

κουρά, ᾶς, Ion. κουρή, ἡ, (κείρω) *a shearing* or *cropping* of the hair, *tonsure*, Hdt., Eur. **II.** *a lock cut off*, Aesch.

κουρεῖον, τό, (κουρεύς) a barber's shop, Ar.

κουρεύς, έως, ὁ, (κείρω) a barber, hair-cutter, Lat. tonsor, Plat., Anth., etc.

κουρεύτρια, ἡ, fem. of κουρεύς, Plut.

κούρη, Ion. for κόρη. II. κουρή, Ion. for κουρά.

κουρήϊος, η, ον, Ion. for κόρειος, youthful, h. Hom.

κουρῆτες, ων, οἱ, (κόρος, κοῦρος) young men, esp. young warriors, Il. II. Κουρῆτες, οἱ, the Curetes, oldest inhabitants of Pleuron in Aetolia, Il.

κουρίας, ου, ὁ, (κουρά) one with short hair, Luc.

κουριάω, f. άσω, (κουρά) of hair, to need clipping, Luc.

κουρίδιος, α, ον, (κοῦρος, κούρη) wedded, of the husband (κουρίδιος πόσις) or the wife (κουριδίη ἄλοχος), Hom. : esp. a lawful, wedded wife, as opp. to a concubine, Id., Hdt. :—hence, λέχος κουρίδιον our lawful marriage bed, Il. ; κ. δῶμα a husband's house. II. later, nuptial, bridal, Ar., Anth.

κουρίζω, (κόρος, κοῦρος) intr. to be a youth, Od. II. trans. to bring up from boyhood, Hes.

κουρίμος, η, ον, (κουρά) of, for cutting hair, Eur. II. pass. shorn off, Aesch., Eur. 2. shorn, κρᾶτα Eur.

κουρίξ, Adv. (κουρά) by the hair, Od.

κουρο-βόρος, ον, (βι-βρώσκω) devouring children, Aesch.

κοῦρος, ὁ, Ion. for κόρος, a boy, youth, Hom.

κουροσύνη, Dor. κωρ-, ἡ, (κοῦρος) youth, youthful prime, Anth. : mirthfulness, Theocr.

κουρόσυνος, η, ον, (κοῦρος) youthful, Anth.

κουρότερος, α, ον, Comp. of κοῦρος, younger, more youthful, Hom.; used much like a positive.

κουρο-τόκος, ον, (τίκτω) bearing boy-children, Eur.

κουρο-τρόφος, ον, (τρέφω) rearing boys ; ἀγαθὴ κ. good nursing-mother, of Ithaca, Od. ; so, κ. Ἑλλάς Eur.

κουστωδία, ἡ, the Lat. custodia, N. T.

κουφίζω, f. Att. ιῶ· (κοῦφος): I. intr. to be light, Hes., Eur.: of pain, to be alleviated, assuaged, Soph. II. trans. to make light : hence to lift up, raise, Id. ; ἄλμα κουφιεῖν to make a light leap, Id. ; κ. πήδημα Eur.:—Pass. to be lifted up, soar, Plat. 2. c. gen., ὄχλου κ. χθόνα to lighten earth of a multitude, Eur. : —absol. to lighten ships of their cargo, Thuc. : to relieve persons from burthens, Xen. :—Pass. to be relieved, νόσου from disease, Id. ; κουφισθήσομαι ψυχὴν Id.; metaph. to feel one's burthens lightened, Thuc. 3. c. acc. rei, to lighten, assuage, συμφοράς Dem.; ἔρωτα Theocr. Hence

κούφισις, εως, ἡ, a lightening, alleviation, relief, Thuc.

κούφισμα, ατος, τό, = κούφισις, Eur.

κουφολογία, ἡ, light talking, Thuc. From

κουφο-λόγος, ον, (λέγω) lightly talking.

κουφό-νοος, ον, contr. -νους, ουν, light-minded, thoughtless, Aesch., Soph.

ΚΟΥ'ΦΟΣ, η, ον, light, nimble, Trag.; used by Hom. only in neut. pl. as Adv., κοῦφα προβιβάς stepping lightly on, Il. :—metaph., κουφότεραι φρένες too buoyant, Pind. 2. metaph. also light, easy, Aesch., Xen. 3. empty, unsubstantial, vain, Soph., Thuc. 4. light in point of weight, opp. to βαρύς, Plat., etc. ; κοῦφα σοι χθὼν ἐπάνωθε πέσοι may earth lie lightly on thee, sit tibi terra levis, Eur. ; of soldiers, ὡπλισμένοι κουφοτέροις ὅπλοις Xen. II. Adv. -φως, lightly, nimbly, Aesch. ; κ. ἐσκευασμένοι, of soldiers, Thuc., Xen. 2. metaph. lightly, with light heart, κουφό-

τερόν μετεφώνεε Od. ; κούφως φέρειν to bear lightly, Eur. ; ὡς κουφότατα φέρειν Hdt. 3. lightly, with ease, Aesch.

ΚΟ'ΦΙ'ΝΟΣ, ὁ, a basket, Ar., Xen. ; in later times used specially by Jews, N. T. ; being apparently smaller than the σπυρίς.

κοχλίας, ου, ὁ, (κόχλος) a snail with a spiral shell, Lat. cochlea, Theocr.

κοχλίον, τό, Dim. of κόχλος, a small snail, Batr.

κόχλος, ου, ὁ, a shell-fish with a spiral shell, used for dying purple, Lat. murex, Arist., Anth. ; used as a trumpet, like Lat. concha, Eur., Theocr., etc.

κοχυδέω, Ion. impf. κοχύδεσκον, to stream forth copiously, Theocr. (Reduplicated from χέω, χύδην.)

ΚΟΧΩ'ΝΗ, ἡ, the posteriors, dual τὰ κοχῶνᾱ Ar.

κόψατο, 3 sing. Ep. aor. 1 med. of κόπτω.

κόψιχος, ὁ, a blackbird, Ar.

Κῶνδε, v. sub Κῶς.

κρᾶ, shortened for κράνος (as δῶ for δῶμα), Anth.

κράατος, κράατι, κράατα, lengthd. forms of κρᾶτος, κρᾶτι, κρᾶτα : v. κρᾶς.

κράββατος or κράβατος, ὁ, a couch, bed, Lat. grăbātus, N. T. (A Macedonian word.)

κράγον, aor. 2 part. neut. of κράζω.

κραδαίνω, (κραδάω) to swing, wave, brandish, Eur., Ar. : to shake, agitate, Aesch. :—Pass., αἰχμὴ κραδαινομένη κατὰ γαίης quivering in the ground, Il. 2. metaph. to agitate, Plut.

κραδάω, to shake, brandish, only in part., κραδάων δολιχόσκιον ἔγχος Hom. From

ΚΡΑ'ΔΗ [ᾰ], ἡ, the quivering spray at the end of a branch, Hes., Ar. :—generally, a fig-tree, Ar.

κραδίᾱ, ἡ, Dor. for κραδίη, which is Ep. for καρδία.

κράζω, Att. f. κεκράξομαι, later κράξω : aor. 2 ἔκραγον :—pf. with pres. sense, κέκραγα, imper. κέκραχθι, pl. κεκράγετε : plqpf. ἐκεκράγειν : (the Root is ΚΡΑΓ, as in aor. 2) :—to croak, of frogs, Ar. : generally, to scream, shriek, cry aloud, Aesch., Ar. ; κέκραχθι Ar. ; κραγὸν κεκράξεται will bawl aloud, Id. (κραγόν being aor. 2 part. used adverbially). 2. c. acc. rei, to clamour for a thing, Id.

κραθείς, aor. 1 pass. part. of κεράννυμι.

ΚΡΑΙ'ΝΩ, f. κρᾰνῶ : aor. 1 ἔκρᾱνα, Ep. ἔκρηνα :—Med. fut. inf. in pass. sense κρᾰνέεσθαι :—Pass., fut. κρανθήσομαι : aor. 1 ἐκράνθην : κέκρανται 3 pf. pass. both sing. and pl.—Hom. mostly uses Ep. pres. κραιαίνω, impf. ἐκραίαινον, aor. 1 imperat. κρήηνον, κρηήνατε, inf. κρηῆναι ; 3 pf. pass. κεκράανται and plqpf. κεκράαντο ; so ἐκράανθην Theocr. :—to accomplish, fulfil, bring to pass, Hom., Trag. :—Pass., with fut. med., to be accomplished or brought to pass, Il., Eur. ; v. ἐπικραίνω. 2. to finish the tale of . . , c. acc., h. Hom. II. absol. to exercise sway, to reign, c. acc. cogn., κρ. σκῆπτρα to sway the staff of rule, Soph. 2. c. gen. to reign over, govern, τοῦ στρατοῦ, τῆς χώρας Id. III. intr. to fulfil one's course, Aesch.

κραιπᾰλάω, only in pres., to have a sick head-ache, consequent upon a debauch, Ar., Plat. From

ΚΡΑΙΠΑ'ΛΗ [ᾰ], ἡ, a drunken head-ache, Lat. crāpula, ἐκ κραιπάλης after a drunken bout, Ar.

κραιπᾰλό-κωμος, ον, rambling in drunken revelry, Ar.

ΚΡΑΙΠΝΟ'Σ, ή, όν, rapid, rushing, of strong winds,

Hom.; of *swift* feet, Id. :—metaph. *hasty, rash,* Il.　II. Adv., *quickly, hastily,* Hom.; also neut. pl. as Adv., Id.

κραιπνό-σῦτος, ον, (σεύομαι) *swift-rushing,* Aesch.

κραιπνο-φόρος, ον, (φέρω) *swift-bearing,* αὖραι Aesch.

ΚΡΑ'ΜΒΗ, ἡ, *cabbage, kail,* Eupol., etc.

ΚΡΑ'ΜΒΟΣ, η, ον, of the voice, like καπυρός, *loud, ringing,* Ar.

κραμβο-φάγος, ον, *Cabbage-eater,* Batr.

κράνα, Dor. for κρήνη.

κρᾰνᾰή-πεδος, ον, (πέδον) *with hard rocky soil,* h. Hom.

κρᾶναι, aor. 1 inf. of κραίνω.

ΚΡΑ'ΝΑΟ'Σ, ή, όν, *rocky, rugged,* of Ithaca, Hom.; of Athens, Pind.; hence Athens was called Κραναὰ πόλις or αἱ Κρανααί Id.; Κραναοί *the people of Attica,* Hdt.; and Κραναός a mythical king of Athens, Aesch.

κρᾰνέεσθαι, v. sub κραίνω.

κρᾰνείᾰ [ᾰ], ἡ, (κράνον) *the cornel-tree, dog-wood,* Lat. *cornus,* its wood was used for shafts and bows, Hom.

κρᾰνέϊνος, η, ον, (κράνον) *made of cornel-wood,* Lat. *corneus,* τόξα Hdt., Xen.

κρᾱνίον, τό, (κάρα) *the upper part of the head, the skull,* Il., Pind., Eur.

ΚΡΑ'ΝΟΝ [ᾱ], τό, = κράνεια, Lat. *cornus,* Theophr.

κρᾱνο-ποιέω, *to make helmets :* in Ar. of one who *talks big and warlike.*

κρᾱνο-ποιός, ὁ, (ποιέω) *a helmet-maker,* Ar.

κρᾱνος [ᾰ], εος, τό, (κάρα) *a helmet,* Hdt., Aesch.

κραντήρ, ῆρος, ὁ, (κραίνω) *one that accomplishes : a ruler, sovereign,* fem. κράντειρα, Id.

κράντωρ, ορος, ὁ, = κραντήρ, Eur., Anth.

ΚΡΑ'Σ, poët. form of κάρα, found in gen. τῆς κρᾱτός, dat. κρᾱτί, acc. κρᾶτα: pl., gen. κρᾱτῶν, dat. κρᾱσίν, Ep. κρᾱτεσφι, acc. κρᾶτας : also κρᾱτα, τό, as nom. and acc., Soph. In Hom. also we have a lengthd. gen. and dat., κρᾱᾱτος, κρᾱᾱτι, pl. nom. κρᾱᾱτα :—*the head,* Hom., Trag.; ἐπὶ κρατὸς λιμένος at *the head* or *far end* of the bay, Od.　II. an old pen. κρῆθεν is used in the phrase κατὰ κρῆθεν, *down from the head, from the top,* Ib., Hes.: hence, like *penitus, from head to foot, entirely,* Τρῶας κατὰ κρῆθεν λάβε πένθος Il.

κρᾶσις, εως, ἡ, (κεράννυμι) *a mixing, blending, compounding,* Aesch., Plat.　2. *the temperature* of the air, Lat. *temperies,* Plat.　3. metaph. *combination, union,* Id.　4. in Gramm. *crasis,* i. e. the combination of two syllables into one long vowel or diphthong, e. g. τοὔνομα for τὸ ὄνομα, ἁνήρ for ὁ ἀνήρ.

κράσπεδον, τό, *the edge, border, skirt* or *hem* of a thing, esp. of cloth, Theocr.; mostly in pl., Eur., Ar. : —metaph., also in pl., *the skirts* of a mountain, Xen.; πρὸς κρασπέδοισι στρατοπέδου on *the skirts* of the army, Eur. Hence

κρασπεδόομαι, Pass. *to be bordered* or *edged,* Eur.

κρᾱτα, τό, *the head :* v. κράς.

κρᾱται-βόλος, ον, (βάλλω) *hurled with violence,* Eur.

κρᾱται-γύᾰλος, ον, (γύαλον) *with strong plates,* Il.

κρᾱταιίς, ἡ, (κράτος) *mighty force,* Od.

κρᾱται-λεως, ων, gen. ω, (λεῦς, = λᾶς) *of hard stones, rocky,* Aesch., Eur.

κρᾱταιόομαι, Pass., = κρατύνομαι, N. T.

κρᾱταιός, ά, όν, poët. form of κρατερός, *strong, mighty, resistless,* Hom., Trag.

κρᾰταί-πεδος, ον, (πέδον) *with hard ground* or *soil,* Od.

κρᾰταί-πους, ὁ, ἡ, πουν, τό, *stout-footed,* Ep. :—καρταίπους is used absol. for ταῦρος in Pind.

κρᾰταί-ρῑνος, ον, *hard-shelled,* Orac. ap. Hdt.

κρᾰτερ-αίχμης, ον, (αἰχμή) *mighty with the spear,* poët. καρτ-, Pind.

κρᾰτερ-αύχην, ὁ, ἡ, *strong-necked,* Plat.

κρᾰτερός, ά, όν, Ep. form of κάρτερος, *strong, stout, mighty,* Hom.　2. of things, conditions, etc., *strong, mighty, cruel,* Id., Hes.　3. of passions, *strong, vehement, mighty,* Hom.; κρ. μῦθος *a harsh, rough speech,* Id.　II. Adv. -ρῶς, *strongly, stoutly, roughly,* Id.

κρᾰτερό-φρων, ον, gen. ονος, (φρήν) *stout-hearted, dauntless,* Hom., Hes.

κρᾰτερό-χειρ, ὁ, ἡ, *stout of hand,* Anth.

κρᾰτερῶνυξ, ῠχος, ὁ, ἡ, (ὄνυξ) *strong-hoofed, solid-hoofed,* Hom. :—*strong-clawed,* of wolves, Od.

κρᾰτεσφι [ᾰ], Ep. dat. pl. of κράς.

κρᾰτευταί, ῶν, οἱ, *the forked stand* or *frame on which a spit turns,* Il. (Deriv. uncertain.)

κρᾰτέω, f. ήσω :—Pass., f. κρατηθήσομαι: (κράτος) : —*to be strong, mighty, powerful :* hence,　I. absol. *to rule, hold sway, be sovereign,* Hom., Trag.; ἡ κρατοῦσα *the lady of the house,* Aesch.　2. c. dat. *to rule among,* κρατέεις νεκύεσσιν Od.　3. c. gen. *to be lord* or *master of, ruler over,* πάντων Hom.; δωμάτων Aesch., etc.　II. *to conquer, prevail, get the upper hand,* Hdt., Att.; κρ. γνώμῃ *to prevail* in *opinion,* Hdt.; τῇ μάχῃ Eur., etc.; —also c. acc. cogn., κρ. τὸν ἀγῶνα Dem.:—οἱ κρατοῦντες *the conquerors,* Xen.:—of reports, etc., *to prevail, become current,* Soph., Thuc.　2. impers., κατθανεῖν κρατεῖ 'tis *better* to die, Aesch.; κρατεῖ ἀπολέσθαι Eur.　3. c. gen. *to prevail over,* Aesch.; ὁ λόγος τοῦ ἔργου ἐκράτει *surpassed, went beyond* it, Thuc.　4. c. acc. *to conquer, master, outdo, surpass,* Pind., Att. :—Pass. *to be conquered,* Hdt., Att.　III. *to become master of, get possession of,* τῆς ἀρχῆς Hdt.; τῆς γῆς Thuc.　IV. *to lay hold of,* τῆς χειρός N. T.　2. c. acc. rei, *to seize, hold fast,* θρόνους Soph., Xen.　V. *to control, command,* Aesch.

κρᾱτήρ, Ion. and Ep. κρητήρ, ῆρος, ὁ : (κεράννυμι) :— *a mixing vessel,* esp. *a large bowl,* in which the wine was mixed with water, and from which the cups were filled, Hom., etc.; οἶνον δ' ἐκ κρητῆρος ἀφυσσάμενοι δεπάεσσιν ἔκχεον Il.; πίνοντες κρητῆρας *drinking bowls of wine,* Ib.; κρητῆρα στήσασθαι ἐλεύθερον *to give a bowl of wine to be drunk* in honour of the deliverance, Ib.; ἐπιστέψασθαι ποτοῖο, ν. ἐπιστέφω.　2. metaph., κρατῆρα πλήσας κακῶν *having filled a bowl full of woes,* Aesch.　II. *any cup-shaped hollow, a basin* in a rock, Soph., Plat.

κρᾱτηρίζω, f. ίσω, *to drink from a bowl of wine,* Dem.

κρᾱτησί-μᾰχος, ον, (μάχη) *conquering in the fight,* Pind.

κρᾱτησί-πους, ὁ, ἡ, *victorious in the foot-race,* Pind.

κρᾱτησί-ιππος, ον, *victorious in the race,* Pind.

κρᾱτί, dat. of κράς.

κρᾰτιστεύω, f. σω, *to be mightiest, best, most excellent,* Soph.　2. *to gain the upper hand,* τινί or ἔν τινι in a thing, Xen.

κράτιστος [ᾰ], η, ον, Ep. κάρτ-, a Superl. formed from

κρατύς: (κράτος):—strongest, mightiest, Il., etc.; Λημνίων τὸ κρ. the best of their men, Thuc.:—of things, καρτίστη μάχη the fiercest fight, Il. 2. generally, best, most excellent, as Sup. of ἀγαθός, Pind., Soph., etc. 3. οἱ κράτιστοι, like οἱ βέλτιστοι, of the aristocracy, Xen. 4. neut. pl. κράτιστα as Adv., best, Id. —The Comp. in use is κρείσσων, q. v.

ΚΡΑΤΟΣ [ᾰ], Ion. and Ep. κάρτος, εος, τό:—strength, might, Hom., Att.; κατὰ κράτος with all one's might or strength, by open force, by storm, Thuc., Xen., etc. 2. personified, Strength, Might, Aesch. II. generally, might, power, Hom.: rule, sway, sovereignty, Hdt., Att. 2. c. gen. power over, Hdt., Att.; in pl., ἀστραπᾶν κράτη νέμων Soph. 3. of persons, a power, an authority, Aesch. III. mastery, victory, Hom., Att.; κρ. ἀριστείας the meed of highest valour, Soph.

κρατός, gen. of κράς.

κρατύνω [ῡ], Ep. καρτ-, f. ῠνῶ, (κράτος) to strengthen, Hdt., Thuc.:—Med., ἐκαρτύναντο φάλαγγας they strengthened their ranks, Il., so in Thuc.:—Pass. to wax strong, Hdt. 2. to harden, τοὺς πόδας Xen. II.=κρατέω, to rule, govern, c. gen., Soph., Eur.; also c. acc., Aesch.; absol., Id., Soph., etc. 2. to become master, get possession of, c. gen., Soph.:— c. acc., βασιληΐδα τιμὰν κρ. to hold, exercise, Eur. III. καρτύνειν βέλεα to ply or throw them stoutly, Pind.

κρατύς [ῠ], like κρατερός, strong, mighty, Hom.

κραυγάζω, f. σω, (κραυγή) to bay, of dogs, Poëta ap. Plat.; of men, to cry aloud, scream, Dem., N. T.

Κραυγασίδης, ου, ὁ, (κραυγάζω) as a Patronym. son of a Croaker, Batr.

κραυγή, ἡ, (κράζω) a crying, screaming, shrieking, shouting, Lat. clamor, Eur., Xen.

κρε-άγρα, ἡ, (κρέας, ἀγρέω) a flesh-hook, to take meat out of the pot, Ar.

κρεαγρίς, ίδος, ἡ, = κρεάγρα, Anth.

κρεάδιον [ᾰ], τό, Dim. of κρέας, a morsel of meat, slice of meat, Ar., Xen.

κρεανομέω, f. ήσω: pf. κεκρεανόμηκα:—to distribute flesh, to divide the flesh of a victim among the guests, Luc.:—Med. to divide among themselves, Theocr.

κρεανομία, ἡ, a distribution of flesh, Luc., etc.

κρεα-νόμος, ὁ, (νέμω) one who distributes the flesh of victims, a carver, Eur.

ΚΡΕΑΣ, τό, Dor. κρῆς: Att. gen. κρέως:—pl. κρέᾰ, gen. κρεῶν, Ep. κρειῶν and κρεάων; dat. κρέασι, Ep. also:—flesh, meat, a piece of meat, Od., etc.; τρία κρέα ἢ καὶ πλέα Xen.; also in collective sense, dressed meat, meat, flesh, Hom., etc. 2. a body, person, ὦ δεξιώτατον κρέας Ar.

κρεη-δόκος and κρειο-δόκος, ον, (δέχομαι) containing flesh, Anth.

κρεῖον, τό, (κρέας) a meat-tray, dresser, Il.

κρείουσα, ἡ, v. κρείων.

κρεισσό-τεκνος, ον, (τέκνον) dearer than children, Aesch.

κρείσσων, later Att. κρείττων, ον, gen. ονος, later Ion. κρέσσων, Dor. κάρρων:—Comp. of κρατύς (v. κράτιστος), stronger, mightier, more powerful, Il., etc. 2. in sense often as Comp. of ἀγαθός, better, οἱ κρέσσονες

one's betters, Pind.; so, τὰ κρείσσω Eur.:—τὰ κρείσσονα one's advantages, Thuc. 3. c. inf., οὔτις κρείσσων δόμεναι no one has a better right to give, Od.:—κρεῖσσόν ἐστι, c. inf., 'tis better to.., κρεῖσσόν ἐστι θανεῖν ἢ πάσχειν κακῶς Aesch.:—also κρείσσων εἰμι, c. part., κρείσσων ἦσθα μηκέτ' ὢν ἢ ζῶν τυφλός thou wert better not alive, than living blind, Soph. II. too great for, ὕψος κρεῖσσον ἐκπηδήματος too great for leaping out of, Aesch.; κρείσσον' ἀγχόνης too bad for hanging, Soph.; ἐλπίδος κρ. worse than one expected, Thuc. III. having power over, master of, γαστρός Xen.; κρ. χρημάτων superior to bribes, Thuc. IV. in Att. Prose in moral sense, better, more excellent, Ar.

ΚΡΕΙΩΝ, οντος, ὁ, a ruler, lord, master, Hom.; ὕπατε κρειόντων, of Zeus, Il.; as a general title of honour, Od.:—fem. κρείουσα, lady, mistress, Il., Hes.:—after Hom. in the form κρέων, Pind.

κρειῶν, Ep., gen. pl. of κρέας.

κρεκάδια, ων, τά, (κρέκω) a kind of tapestry, Ar.

κρεκτός, ή, όν, struck so as to sound, of stringed instruments: generally, played, sung, Aesch. From

ΚΡΕΚΩ, f. ξω: aor. 1 ἔκρεξα:—to strike the web with the κερκίς, to weave, Eur. 2. to strike the lyre with the plectron, Anth.:—generally, to play on an instrument, Ar. 3. of any sharp noise, βοὴν πτεροῖς κρ. Id.

κρεμάθρα, ἡ, (κρεμάννυμι) a net or basket to hang things up in, Ar.

κρεμάννυμι, f. κρεμάσω [ᾰ]; Att. κρεμῶ, ᾷς, ᾷ, Ep. κρεμόω: aor. 1 ἐκρέμασα, Ep. κρέμασα:—Pass., in shortened form κρέμαμαι, subj. κρέμωμαι, opt. κρεμαίμην: impf. ἐκρεμάμην, ατο: f. κρεμήσομαι: aor. 1 ἐκρεμάσθην. (From Root ΚΡΕΜ:) I. to hang, hang up, Il.; κρεμόω ποτὶ ναὸν will bring them to the temple and hang them up there, Il.; κρ. τινά τινος to hang one up by a thing, Ar.; κρεμάσαι, in allusion to Socrates in his basket, Id.;—κρεμάσαι τὴν ἀσπίδα to hang up one's shield, i. e. have done with war, Id.:—so in Med. πηδάλιον κρεμάσασθαι to hang up one's rudder, i.e. give up the sea, Hes. II. Pass. to be hung up, suspended, ὅτε τ' ἐκρέματο (2 impf.) when thou wert hanging, Il.: to be hung up as a votive offering, Pind., Hdt.; εἴπερ ἐκ ποδῶν κρέμαιτο Ar.:—metaph., μώμος κρέματαί τινι censure hangs over him, Pind.; ὁ ἐκ τοῦ σώματος κρεμάμενος depending on the body, Xen. 2. to be hung, of persons, Eur. 3. metaph. to be in suspense, Arist. Hence

κρεμάσας, κρεμασθείς, aor. 1 part. act. and pass.

κρεμαστός, ή, όν, (κρεμάννυμι) hung, hung up, hanging, κρ. αὐχένος hung by the neck, Soph.; c. gen., also, hung from or on a thing, Eur.:—κρεμαστὴ ἀρτάνη, i. e. a halter, Soph.; so, βρόχοι κρ. Eur.

κρεμβάλα, τά, rattling instruments, like our castanets.

κρεμβάλιαστύς, ύος, ἡ, a rattling as with castanets, h. Hom.

κρεμόω, Ep. fut. of κρεμάννυμι; Att. κρεμῶ.

κρέξ, ἡ, gen. κρεκός, (κρέκω) Lat. crex, the corn-crake, land-rail, Ar.

κρεο-δαίτης, ου, ὁ, (δαίω) a distributor of flesh, carver at a public meal, Lat. dispensator, Plut.

κρεοκοπέω, f. ήσω, to cut in pieces, Aesch., Eur. From

κρεο-κόπος, ον, (κόπτω) a cutter up of flesh.

κρεουργέω, f. ήσω, to cut up meat like a butcher (κρεουργός), to butcher, Luc.　Hence

κρεουργηδόν, Adv. like a butcher, in pieces, Hdt.

κρεουργία, ή, a cutting up, butchering.　From

κρε-ουργός, όν, (*ἔργω) working, i. e. cutting up meat, κρεουργὸν ἦμαρ a day of feasting, Aesch.

κρεο-φάγος, ον, (φάγεῖν) eating flesh, carnivorous, Hdt.

κρέων, οντος, = the Homeric κρείων.

κρεῶν, gen. pl. of κρέας :—**κρέως**, gen. sing.

κρήγυος, ον, good, agreeable, Il. : of persons, good, serviceable, Plat.　II. true, real, εἴπατέ μοι τὸ κρήγυον, Theocr.: Adv. in good earnest, Anth.　(Deriv. unknown.)

κρή-δεμνον, Dor. κρᾱ-, τό, (κάρα, δέω) a veil or mantilla with lappets, passing over the head and hanging down on each side, Hom.　II. metaph. in pl. the battlements which crown a city's walls, Id., Eur.　2. the cover of a wine-jar, Od.

κρηῆναι, Ep. aor. 1 inf. of κραίνω ; –**κρήηνον**, imper.

κρήθεν, old gen. of κράς, v. κράς II.

κρήμνημι, = κρεμάννυμι, Pind. : — Pass. κρήμναμαι, to hang, be suspended, Eur.: to float in air, Aesch.

κρημνο-βάτης [ᾰ], ου, ὁ, a haunter of steeps, Anth.

κρημνο-ποιός, όν, (ποιέω) speaking crags, i. e. using big, rugged words, Ar.

κρημνός, ὁ, (κρήμναμαι) an overhanging bank, as the steep bank of a river, edge of a trench, Il. : later, a beetling cliff, crag, Hdt., Ar. ; κατὰ τῶν κρημνῶν down from the cliffs of Epipolae, Thuc.

κρημν-ώδης, ες, (εἶδος) precipitous, Thuc.

κρῆναι, Ion. for κρᾶναι, aor. 1 inf. of κραίνω.

κρηναῖος, α, ον, (κρήνη) of, from a spring or fountain, Νύμφαι κρηναῖαι = Κρηνιάδες, Od. ; κρ. ὕδωρ spring water, Hdt. ; κρ. ποτόν Soph., etc.

ΚΡΗΝΗ, Dor. κράνα, ή, a well, spring, fountain, Lat. fons, Hom., etc. ; opp. to φρέαρ (a tank), Hdt., Thuc. : —Poets use it in pl. for water, Soph.　Hence

κρήνηθεν, Adv. from a well or spring, Anth. ; and

κρήνηνδε, Adv. to a well or spring, Od.

κρηνιάς, άδος, ή, fem. of κρηναῖος, Aesch. ; Dor. Κρᾱνιάδες spring-nymphs, Theocr. ; so Κρᾱνίδες Mosch.

κρηνίς, ίδος, ή, Dim. of κρήνη, Eur.

ΚΡΗΠΙ'Σ, ίδος, ή, a half-boot, Xen. :—κρηπῖδες soldiers' boots, i. e. soldiers themselves, Theocr.　II. generally, a groundwork, foundation, basement of a temple or altar, Hdt., Soph., etc. :—metaph., κρηπὶς σοφῶν ἐπέων Pind. ; οὐδέπω κρηπὶς κακῶν ὕπεστι we have not yet got to the bottom of misery, Aesch. ; ἡ ἐγκράτεια ἀρετῆς κρηπίς self-control is the foundation of virtue, Xen.　2. the walled edge of a river, a quay, Lat. crepīdo, Thuc.

Κρής, ὁ, gen. Κρητός, pl. Κρῆτες, ῶν, a Cretan, Hom., etc. ; fem. **Κρῆσσα**, ης, Aesch.　II. as Adj. Cretan, Soph. ; also **Κρήσιος**, α, ον, Id., Eur.

κρής, Dor. for κρέας.

κρῆσαι, Ep. for κεράσαι, aor. 1 inf. of κεράννυμι.

Κρήσιος, α, ον, **Κρῆσσα**, v. Κρής.

κρησ-φύγετον [ῠ], τό, (φυγεῖν) a place of refuge, retreat, resort, Hdt.　(The first part of the word, κρησ-, is uncertain.)

Κρήτη, ή, Crete, now Candia, Hom. ; Ep. gen. pl. Κρη-

τάων εὐρειάων Od. :—**Κρήτηθεν** from Crete, Il. ; **Κρήτηνδε** to Crete, Od.

κρητήρ, ῆρος, ὁ, Ion. and Ep. for κρατήρ.

Κρητίζω, (Κρής) to play the Cretan, N. T., Plut.

Κρητικός, ή, όν, of or from the island of Crete, Cretan, Aesch., Thuc.　II. **Κρητικόν** (sc. ἱμάτιον), τό, a short garment, used at sacred rites, Ar.　2. **Κρητικός** (sc. πούς), ὁ, a Cretic, a metrical foot [-◡-], e. g. 'Αντιφῶν, called also amphimacer (ἀμφίμακρος).

Κρητισμός, ὁ, Cretan behaviour, i. e. lying, Plut.

κρῖ, τό, Ep. shortd. form for κριθή, barley, only in nom. and acc., Hom.

κρῑβᾰνίτης [ῑ], ου, ὁ, baked in a pan (κρίβανος), ὁ κρ. (sc. ἄρτος), a loaf so baked, Ar. ; hence, comically, βοῦς κρ. Id.

κρίβᾰνος [ῑ], Ion. **κλίβᾰνος**, ὁ, an earthen vessel, a pan, wider at bottom than at top, wherein bread was baked by putting hot embers round it, Hdt., Ar.

κρῑβᾰνωτός, ή, όν, = κριβανίτης, Ar.

κρίζω, aor. 2 ἔκρικον, Ep. κρίκον : pf. κέκρῑγα : (from Root ΚΡΙΓ) :—to creak, Lat. stridere, Il.　II. of persons, to screech, Ar.

κρῑθάω, of a horse, to be barley-fed, to wax wanton, Aesch.　From

κρῐθείς, aor. 1 part. pass. of κρίνω.

κρίθεν, poët. for ἐκρίθησαν, 3 pl. aor. 1 pass. of κρίνω.

ΚΡΙΘΗ', ή, mostly in pl., barley-corns, barley (cf. κρῖ, the meal being ἄλφιτα, Hom., Ar., etc. ; οἶνος ἐκ κριθέων πεποιημένος a kind of beer (cf. κρίθῐνος), Hdt.

κρῑθίᾱσις, εως, ή, a disease of horses, a kind of surfeit caused by over-feeding with barley, Xen.

κρῑθιάω, f. άσω, (κριθή) = κριθάω, Babr.

κρῑθίζω, f. ίσω, to feed with barley, Babr.

κρίθῐνος, η, ον, made of or from barley, Xen., etc.

κρῑθο-τράγος, ον, (τράγεῖν) barley-eating, Ar.

κρίκε, 3 sing. Ep. aor. 2 of κρίζω.

ΚΡΙ'ΚΟΣ [ῐ], ὁ, Homeric form of κίρκος, a ring on a horse's breast-band, to fasten it to the peg (ἕστωρ) at the end of the carriage-pole, Il.　2. an eyelet-hole in sails, through which the reefing-ropes were drawn, Il.

κρῖμα, ατος, τό, (κρίνω) a decision, judgment, N. T. ; sentence, condemnation, Ib.　2. a matter for judgment, law-suit, Ib.

κρίμνον, τό, (κρίνω) coarse meal or a coarse loaf, Anth.

κρίνας [ῐ], aor. 1 part. of κρίνω.

ΚΡΙ'ΝΟΝ [ῐ], τό, heterocl. pl. κρίνεα, dat. κρίνεσι :—a lily, Hdt., Ar., etc.

ΚΡΙ'ΝΩ [ῑ], Ep. 3 subj. κρίνησι : f. κρῐνῶ, Ep. κρῐνέω : aor. 1 ἔκρῑνα : pf. κέκρῑκα :—Med., f. κρῐνοῦμαι (in pass. sense) : aor. 1 ἐκρῑνάμην :—Pass., f. κρῐθήσομαι : aor. 1 ἐκρίθην [ῐ], Ep. ἐκρίνθην : pf. κέκρῐμαι, inf. κεκρίσθαι :—Lat. cerno, to separate, part, put asunder, distinguish, Il., Xen.　II. to pick out, choose, Hom., Hdt., Att.:—Med. to pick out for oneself, choose, Hom., etc.: —Pass. to be chosen, Il. ; pf. and aor. 1 part. κεκριμένος, κρινθείς picked out, chosen, Hom.　I. to decide disputes, Id., Hdt., etc. ; σκολιὰς κρίνειν θέμιστας to judge crooked judgments, i. e. to judge unjustly, Il. ; κρίνουσι βοῇ καὶ οὐ ψήφῳ they decide the question by shouting, not by vote, Thuc. ; to decide a contest for a prize, Soph., etc. ; κρ. τὰς θεάς to decide their contest, i. e. judge them, Eur. :—Pass. and Med., of persons, to

have a contest *decided, come to issue*, Hom., etc. **2.** *to adjudge*, κράτος τινί Soph. **3.** *to judge of, estimate*, πρὸς ἐμαυτὸν κρίνων [αὐτόν] *judging of* him by myself, Dem.:—Pass., ἴσον παρ' ἐμοὶ κέκριται Hdt. **4.** *to expound, interpret* dreams, Id., Aesch., etc.: so in Med., Il. **5.** c. acc. et inf. *to decide* or *judge that*, Hdt., Att. **6.** c. inf. only, *to determine* to do a thing, N. T. **IV.** *to question*, Soph. **2.** *to bring to trial, accuse*, Xen., etc.:—Pass. *to be brought to trial*, Thuc., etc. **3.** *to pass sentence upon, to condemn*, Soph., Dem.

κριο-βόλος, ον, (βάλλω) *ram-slaying*, Anth.

κριο-πρόσωπος, ον, (πρόσωπον) *ram-faced*, Hdt.

ΚΡΙΟ'Σ [ῑ], ὁ, *a ram*, Lat. *aries*, Hom., Hdt., etc. **2.** *a battering-ram*, Lat. *aries*, Xen.

Κρῖσα (not Κρίσσα), ης, ἡ, *Crisa*, a city in Phocis, near Delphi, Il.:—Adj. **Κρισαῖος**, α, ον, *Crisaean*, Ib., Hdt.

κρίσῐμος [ῐ], ον, (κρίσις) *decisive, critical*, Anth.

κρίσις [ῐ], εως, ἡ, (κρίνω) *a separating, power of distinguishing*, Arist.: *choice, selection*, Id. **II.** *a decision, judgment*, Hdt., Aesch.; κρ. οὐκ ἀληθής no *certain means of judging*, Soph. **2.** in legal sense, *a trial*, Ar., Thuc., etc.:—*the result of a trial, condemnation*, Xen. **3.** *a trial* of skill, τόξου in archery, Soph. **4.** *a dispute*, περί τινος Soph. **III.** *the event* or *issue* of a thing, κρίσιν ἔχειν *to be decided*, of a war, Thuc.

κρῐτέος, α, ον, verb. Adj. of κρίνω, *to be decided* or *judged* :—κριτέον *one must decide* or *judge*, Plat.

κρῐτήριον, τό, (κριτής) *a means for judging* or *trying, a criterion, standard, test*, Plat. **2.** *a court of judgment, tribunal*, Id.

κρῐτής, οῦ, ὁ, (κρίνω) *a decider, judge, umpire*, Hdt., Thuc.:—at Athens, of *the judges in the poetic contests*, Ar. **2.** κρ. ἐνυπνίων *an interpreter* of dreams, Aesch. Hence

κρῐτῐκός, ή, όν, *able to discern, critical*, Arist. **2.** *of* or *for judging*, Id.

κρῐτός, ή, όν, verb. Adj. of κρίνω, *picked out, chosen*, Hom. **2.** *choice, excellent*, Pind., Soph.

κροαίνω, only in part. pres., of a horse, *to stamp, strike with the hoof*, Il.

κρόκα, heterocl. acc. of κρόκη.

κροκάλη [ᾰ], ἡ, *a pebble, shingle*, Anth. (Deriv. unknown.)

κρόκεος, ον, (κρόκος) *saffron-coloured*, Pind., Eur.

κρόκη, ἡ : also (as if from a nom. *κρόξ) heterocl. acc. κρόκα, nom. pl. κρόκες Anth. : (κρέκω) :—*the thread which is passed between the threads of the warp* (στήμων, *tela*), *the woof* or *weft*, Lat. *subtemen*, Hes., Hdt., etc. **2.** κροκύς, *the flock* or *nap of woollen cloth, cloth with curly nap*, Ar. : in pl., μαλακαῖς κρόκαις *with cloths of* soft *wool*, Pind. ; κροκαῖσι *with flocks of wool*, Soph.

κροκήιος, η, ον, Ep. for κρόκεος, h. Hom.

κρόκῐνος, η, ον, (κρόκος) *of saffron*, Anth.

κροκό-βαπτος, ον, *saffron-dyed*, Aesch.

κροκο-βαφής, ές, = foreg. :—metaph., ἐπὶ δὲ καρδίαν ἔδραμε κρ. σταγών *to my heart ran the sallow, sickly blood-drop* (that precedes death), Aesch.

κροκόδειλος, ὁ, *a lizard*, properly an Ion. word, Hdt. **2.** *the Nile-lizard, crocodile*, Id.

κροκόεις, εσσα, εν, (κρόκος) *saffron-coloured*, Eur., etc.

κροκό-πεπλος, ον, *with yellow veil*, Il., Hes. From

ΚΡΟ'ΚΟΣ, ου, ὁ, *the crocus*, Il., Soph. **2.** *saffron* (which is made from its stigmas), Aesch., etc.

κροκόω, f. ώσω, (κρόκος) *to crown with yellow ivy*, Anth.

κροκύς [ῠ], ύδος, ἡ, (κρόκη) *the flock* or *nap on woollen cloth*, Hdt., Luc., etc.

κροκωτός, ή, όν, (κροκόω) *saffron-dyed, saffron-coloured*, Pind. **2.** as Subst., κροκωτός (sc. χιτών), ὁ, *a saffron-coloured frock*, worn by Bacchus, Ar.

κρόμμυον, τό, v. κρόμυον.

κρομμυ-οξυ-ρεγμία, ἡ, *a belch of onions and vinegar*, Ar.

κρόμυον, τό, *an onion*, Hom. :—later κρόμμυον, Hdt., Ar.

Κρόνια, ων, τά, v. Κρόνιος.

Κρονιάς, άδος, ἡ, v. Κρόνιος.

Κρονίδης [ῐ], ου, ὁ, patronym., *son of Cronus*, i.e. Zeus, Hom.

Κρονικός, ή, όν, = sq., Κρ. ἀστήρ the planet Saturn, Anth. **II.** in contemptuous sense, *old-fashioned, out of date*, Ar.

Κρόνιος, α, ον, (Κρόνος) *Saturnian, of Cronus* or *Saturn*, Aesch., etc. **2.** Κρόνια (sc. ἱερά), τά, his *festival* celebrated on the twelfth of Hecatombaeon, Dem. :—later, τὰ Κρόνια were the Roman *Saturnalia* ; hence, αἱ Κρονιάδες ἡμέραι the time of the *Saturnalia*, Plut. **3.** Κρόνιον (sc. ὄρος), τό, *the hill of Cronus* or *Saturn*, Pind. **II.** like Κρονικός, in contemptuous sense, Κρονίων ὄζειν *to smell of the dark ages*, Ar.

Κρόν-ιππος, ον, (Κρόνος) *an old dotard*, Ar.

Κρονίων [ῑ], ὁ, gen. Κρονίωνος [ῑ] or Κρονίονος [ῑ], patronym., *son of Cronus*, i.e. Zeus, Hom.

Κρόνος, ὁ, (κραίνω) *Cronus*, identified with the Lat. *Saturnus*, son of Uranos and Gaia, husband of Rhea, father of Zeus, Poseidon, Hades, Hera, Demeter and Hestia, Hes. : he reigned in heaven until his sons banished him to Tartarus, Il., Aesch. ; his time was the golden age, Hes. **II.** *a hame* at Athens, *a superannuated old dotard, old fool*, Ar.

ΚΡΟ'ΣΣΑΙ, ῶν, αἱ, *battlements* on walls, Il. ; of *the steps* by which the Pyramids rose to a point, Hdt.

κροτᾰλίζω, f. σω, (κρόταλον) *to use rattles* or *castanets*, Hdt. :—generally, ἵπποι ὄχεα κροτάλιζον were *rattling* them *along*, Il.

κρότᾰλον, τό, (κροτέω) *a rattle, castanet*, used in the worship of Cybelé, or Dionysus, Hdt., Eur. **II.** metaph. *a rattling fellow, a rattle*, Ar.

κρότᾰφος, ὁ, (κροτέω) *the side of the forehead* (v. κόρση), in pl. *the temples*, Lat. *tempora*, Il., etc. **II.** of a mountain, *its side*, Aesch., Anth.

κροτέω, f. ήσω, (κρότος) *to make to rattle*, of horses, ὄχεα κροτέοντες *rattling* them *along*, Il. **II.** *to knock, strike, smite*, Hdt., Eur. ; κροτεῖν τὰς χεῖρας or τὼ χεῖρε *to clap* the hands, Hdt., Xen. : absol. *to clap, applaud*, Xen., etc. **2.** of a smith, *to hammer* or *weld together*, Plat. :—Pass. *to be wrought by the hammer* ; metaph., ἐξ ἀπάτας κεκροταμένος *one mass* of trickery, Theocr. **III.** intr. *to make a rattling noise*, Arist., Luc.

κρότημα, ατος, τό, *work wrought by the hammer* :—metaph. of Ulysses, *a hardened knave*, Eur.

κρότησις, εως, ἡ, *a clapping*, τινὶ χειρῶν Plat. ; and

κροτησμός, ὁ, = κρότος, Aesch.

κροτητός, ή, όν, verb. Adj. of κροτέω, stricken, sounding with blows, Aesch. : rattling, Soph.

ΚΡΟ'ΤΟΣ, ου, ό, a striking, the sound made by striking, κρ. ποδῶν the beat of the feet in dancing, Eur. ; κρ. χειρῶν a clapping of hands, applause, Ar., Xen.

κροῦμα, ατος, τό, (κρούω) a stroke : a sound made by striking stringed instruments with the plectron, a note, Plat.

κρουματικός, ή, όν, of or for playing on a stringed instrument, Anth.

κρουνίζω, f. σω, (κρουνός) to send forth a stream. Hence

κρούνισμα, ατος, τό, a gush or stream, Anth.

ΚΡΟΥΝΟ'Σ, οῦ, ό, a spring, well-head, whence the streams (πηγαί) issue, Il., Soph. ; so, κρουνοὶ Ἡφαίστου streams of lava from Etna, Pind. : metaph. a torrent of words, Ar.

κρουνο-χυτρο-λήραιος, ό, (κρουνός, χύτρα, ληρέω) a pourer forth of washy twaddle, Ar.

κροῦσις, εως, ή, (κρούω) a striking, smiting, Plut.   2. a tapping of earthen vessels, to see whether they ring sound : metaph. deception, cheatery, Ar.   3. a playing on a stringed instrument, Plut.

κροῦσμα, ατος, τό, = κροῦμα, Anth.

κρουστικός, ή, όν, fit for striking the ears, impressive, Arist. :—metaph. of a speaker, Ar. From

ΚΡΟΥ'Ω, f. σω: pf. κέκρουκα:—Med., aor. 1 ἐκρουσάμην: —Pass., pf. κέκρουμαι and –ουσμαι :—to strike, smite : to strike one against another, κρ. χεῖρας to clap hands, Eur. ; κρ. τὰ ὅπλα πρὸς ἄλληλα Thuc., etc. :—κρ. τὸν πόδα (i. e. κρ. τὴν γῆν τῷ ποδί) in dancing, Eur.   2. κέραμον κρούειν to tap an earthen vessel, to try whether it rings sound : hence to examine, prove, Plat.   3. to strike a lyre with the plectron, Id.   4. κρούειν τὴν θύραν to knock at the door on the outside, Xen., etc.   5. as a nautical term, in Med., κρούεσθαι πρύμναν, like ἀνακρούεσθαι, to back a ship, Thuc.

κρύβδα, Adv. (κρύπ-τω) without the knowledge of, κρύβδα Διός, Lat. clam Jove, Il.   2. absol., like κρύβδην, secretly, Il.

κρύβδην, Dor. -δᾱν, Adv. (κρύπ-τω) secretly, Od., Ar.   2. c. gen., like κρύβδα, κρύβδαν πατρός Pind.

κρύβηναι, aor. 2 pass. inf. of κρύπτω.

κρυερός, ά, όν, and ός, όν, (κρύος) icy, chilling, in Hom. only metaph., κρυεροῖο γόοιο, κρυεροῖο φόβοιο ; so κρυερὰ πάθεα Ar.   2. icy-cold, Id.

κρῦμός, ό, (κρύος) icy cold, frost, Hdt., Eur.

κρυμ-ώδης, ες, (εἶδος) icy-cold, frozen, icy, Anth.

κρυόεις, εσσα, εν, = κρυερός, chilling, Il., Hes.   2. icy-cold, Anth.

ΚΡΥ'ΟΣ, τό, icy cold, chill, frost, Hes. : metaph. καρδίαν περιπίτνει κρύος Aesch.

κρυπτάδιος [ᾰ], α, ον, and ος, ον, (κρύπτω) secret, clandestine, Il., Aesch. : neut. pl. as Adv., Il.

κρύπτασκε, 3 sing. Ion. impf. of κρύπτω.

κρυπτεία, ή, (κρυπτεύω) a secret commission on which young Spartans were obliged to serve, watching the country and enduring hardships, Plat.

κρυπτέον, verb. Adj. of κρύπτω, Soph., Anth.

κρυπτεύω, f. σω, (κρύπ-τω) to conceal, hide, Eur.   II. intrans. to hide oneself, lie concealed, Xen.   III. Pass. to be ensnared, Eur.

κρυπτός, ή, όν, verb. Adj. of κρύπτω, hidden, secret, Il., Hdt., etc. ; κρυπτὴ τάφρος a trench covered and concealed by planks and earth, Hdt. ; τὸ κρ. τῆς πολιτείας the secret character of [the Spartan] institutions, Thuc.

ΚΡΥ'ΠΤΩ, Ion. impf. κρύπτασκε: f. κρύψω: aor. 1 ἔκρυψα, Ep. κρύψα: later aor. 2 ἔκρυβον, pf. κέκρυφα :—Med., f. κρύψομαι : aor. 1 ἐκρυψάμην :—Pass., f. κρυφθήσομαι and κεκρύψομαι : aor. 1 ἐκρύφθην, Ep. κρ–: aor. 2 part. κρύφείς: pf. κέκρυμμαι, Ion. 3 pl. κεκρύφαται :—to hide, cover, cloak, Hom., Att. :—Med., κάρα κρυψάμενος having cloaked his head, Soph., etc. :—Pass. to hide oneself, lie hidden, of setting stars, Hes., Eur.   2. to cover in the earth, bury, Hes., Hdt., Att.   3. to hide, conceal, keep secret, Od., Soph. : —Pass., pf. part. κεκρυμμένος secret, Od., Soph.   4. c. dupl. acc. to conceal something from one, μή με κρύψῃς τοῦτο Aesch., etc.   II. intr. (sub. ἑαυτόν) to hide oneself, lie hidden, Soph.

κρυσταλλίζω, f. σω, to be clear as crystal, N. T.

κρυστάλλἴνος, η, ον, of crystal, crystalline, Anth.

κρυσταλλό-πηκτος, ον, congealed to ice, frozen, Eur.

κρυσταλλοπήξ, ῆγος, ό, ή, = foreg., Aesch.

κρύσταλλος, ό, (κρύος) clear ice, ice, Lat. glacies, Hom., Hdt., Att.   II. ή, crystal, rock-crystal, Anth.

κρύφᾰ, Adv. = κρύβδα, without the knowledge of, c. gen., Thuc. : absol. secretly, Id.

κρυφᾷ, Adv. Dor. for κρυφῇ, Pind.

κρυφαῖος, α, ον, and ος, ον, hidden, Pind., Trag.   2. secret, clandestine, Aesch. :—Adv. -ως, Id.

κρυφῇ, Adv. (κρύπ-τω) = κρύβδην, Soph., Xen.

κρυφηδόν, Adv., = foreg., opp. to ἀμφαδόν, Od.

κρυφθῆναι, Ep. aor. 1 pass. of κρύπτω.

κρύφιος [ῠ], α, ον, and ος, ον, (κρύπ-τω) hidden, concealed, Soph., etc.   2. secret, clandestine, Hes., Soph., etc.

κρυφός, ό, (κρύπ-τω) κρυφὸν θέμεν to throw a cloud over, Pind.

κρύφω [ῠ], late form of κρύπτω, Anth.

κρύψαι, aor. 1 inf. of κρύπτω.

κρυψί-νοος, ον, contr. -νους, ουν, hiding one's thoughts, dissembling, Xen.

κρύψις, εως, ή, (κρύπ-τω) a hiding, concealment, Eur. : —the art of concealing, Arist.

κρωβύλος [ῠ], ό, a roll or knot of hair on the crown of the head, Thuc., Anth. :—also a tuft of hair on a helmet, Xen.   2. a nickname of the orator Hegesippus, Aeschin. (Deriv. unknown.)

κρωγμός, ό, the cawing of a crow, Anth.

ΚΡΩ'ΖΩ, f. κρώξω, to cry like a crow, caw, Lat. crocitare, Hes., Ar. :—also of other birds, as cranes, Ar. ; of young halcyons, Luc. :—of a wagon, to creak, groan, Babr. (Formed from the sound.)

κρωσσίον, τό, Dim. of sq., Anth.

ΚΡΩΣΣΟ'Σ, οῦ, ό, a water-pail, pitcher, jar, Eur.   2. a cinerary urn, Mosch., Anth.

κτᾶ, for ἔκτα, 3 sing. Ep. aor. 2 of κτείνω :—κταίην, Ep. aor. 2 opt. : — Ep. inf. κτάμεν, -έναι ; part. κτάς ; κτάμενος, Ep. aor. 2 med. part. (in pass. sense).

κτανέων, Ep. fut. part. of κτείνω.

κτάνον, Ep. for ἔκτανον, aor. 2 of κτείνω.

κτάντης, ό, (κτείνω) a murderer, Anth.

ΚΤΑ'ΟΜΑΙ, Ion. κτέομαι:—f. κτήσομαι and κεκτήσομαι:

—aor. I ἐκτησάμην, Ep. κτησάμην :—pf. κέκτημαι and ἔκτημαι, Ion. 3 pl. ἐκτέαται, opt. κεκτήμην or κεκτῴμην : plqpf. ἐκεκτήμην and κεκτήμην, Ion. 3 pl. ἔκτεατο : Dep.:   I. in pres., impf., fut. and aor. I,   1. *to procure for oneself, to get, gain, acquire,* Hom. ; κτήσασθαι βίον ἀπό τινος *to get one's living from a thing,* Hdt. ; κ. χάριν *to win favour,* Soph. ; κ. φίλους, ἑταίρους Id.   b. of evils, *to bring upon oneself, incur,* Id., Eur., etc. :—κ. τινὰ πολέμιον *to make him so,* Xen.   2. *to procure* or *get for another,* ἐμοὶ ἐκτήσατο κεῖνος Od.   II. in pf. and plqpf. with f. κεκτήσομαι, *to have acquired,* i. e. *to possess, have, hold,* Il., Hdt., etc. ; κεκτ. τινὰ σύμμαχον Eur. ; of evils, κεκτ. κακά Soph., Eur. ; ὁ κεκτημένος *an owner, master,* as a Subst., ὁ ἐμοῦ κ. Soph. ; of a woman's *lord and master,* Eur.   III. aor. I pass. ἐκτήθην in pass. sense, *to be gotten,* Id., Thuc.

κτέανον, τό, (κτάομαι) = κτῆμα, Pind.   2. mostly in pl. κτέανα, *possessions, property,* Hes., Aesch., etc.

κτέαρ, τό, = foreg., in Ep. dat. pl. κτεάτεσσι Hom.

κτεάτειρα, ἡ, (as if from κτεάτήρ), κόσμων κτ. *thou that hast put us in possession of* honours, Aesch.

κτεατίζω, f. ίσω : Ep. aor. I κτεάτισσα: (κτάομαι) :— *to get, gain, win,* Hom. :—Med., with pf. pass., *to get for oneself, acquire,* h. Hom., Theocr.

κτεάτιστός, ή, όν, *gotten, acquired,* Anth.

κτείνω (Root ΚΤΕΝ or ΚΤΑΝ): Ion. impf. κτείνεσκε :— f. κτενῶ, Ion. κτενέω:—aor. I ἔκτεινα: aor. 2 ἔκτανον :— pf. ἔκτονα, later ἔκταγκα :—Pass., Ep. 3 pl. aor. I ἔκτάθεν ; later ἐκτάνθην Anth. :—Ep. forms (as if from *κτῆμι) 3 sing. and pl. aor. 2 syncop. ἔκτἄ, ἔκτᾰν ; 1 pl. subj. κτέωμεν, inf. κτάμεν, κτάμεναι [ᾰ], part. κτάς ; also aor. 2 med. (in pass. sense) ἐκτάμην, inf. κτάσθαι, part. κτάμενος :—*to kill, slay,* Hom., etc. ; of animals, *to slaughter,* Id. ; Οὖτίς με κτείνει δόλῳ *seeks to kill me* (the force of the pres. tense), Od. ; κτανών *the slayer, murderer,* Aesch. ; οἱ κτανόντες Id. :—*to put to death* by law, Thuc., Plat.—In Att. θνήσκω or ἀπο-θνήσκω is used for the Pass.

κτείνωμι, Ep. subj. of κτείνω.

ΚΤΕΙΣ, κτενός, ὁ, *a comb,* Lat. *pecten* : esp.,   1. *the comb in the loom,* which separates the threads of the warp, Anth.   2. *a rake,* Id.   3. in pl. *the fingers,* which branch like *the teeth of a comb,* Aesch.

κτενεῖν, fut. inf. of κτείνω.

κτενίζω, f. σω, (κτείς) *to comb, curry* horses, Eur. :— Med., κτενίζεσθαι τὰς κόμας *to comb one's hair,* Hdt.

κτενίον, τό, Dim. of κτείς, *a small comb,* Luc.

κτενισμός, ὁ, *a combing,* Eur.

κτέομαι, Ion. for κτάομαι.

κτέρας, τό, = κτέανον, *a possession,* Il.

κτέρεα, τά, (no sing. κτέρος in use) *funeral gifts,* burnt with the dead, *funeral honours,* Hom. Hence

κτερείζω, f. ίξω : aor. I inf. κτερεΐξαι, c. acc. pers. *to bury with due honours,* Il.   2. c. acc. cogn., κτέρεα κτερεΐξαι *to pay* funeral honours, Od.

κτερίζω, f. κτεριῶ : aor. I ἐκτέρισα :— = foreg. I, Il., Soph.   2. c. acc. cogn., κτέρεα κτ., like κτερεΐζω 2, Hom.

κτερίσματα, τά, = κτέρεα, only used in pl., Soph., Eur.

κτέρος, τό, v. κτέρεα.

κτέω, κτέωμεν, I sing. and pl. Ep. aor. 2 subj. of κτείνω.

κτηθείς, aor. I pass. part. of κτάομαι.

κτῆμα, ατος, τό, (κτάομαι) *anything gotten, a piece of property, a possession,* Od., Att. :—of a slave, παλαιὸν οἴκων κτ. Eur.   2. in pl. *possessions, property, wealth,* Hom. ; ἔρως, ὃς ἐν κτήμασι πίπτει *who fallest on wealth,* i. e. *on the wealthy,* Soph.

κτηνηδόν, Adv. (κτῆνος) *like beasts,* Hdt.

κτῆνος, εος, τό, (κτάομαι) mostly in pl. κτήνεα, contr. κτήνη, *flocks and herds,* which in ancient times constituted *wealth,* h. Hom., Hdt.   2. in sing. *a single beast,* as *an ox* or *sheep,* Hdt., Xen.: *a beast for riding,* Lat. *jumentum,* N. T.

κτηνοτροφία, ἡ, *cattle-keeping,* Plut. From

κτηνο-τρόφος, ὁ, (τρέφω) *keeping cattle, pastoral.*

κτήσαιτο, 3 sing. aor. I of κτάομαι.

κτήσιος, α, ον, (κτάομαι) *belonging to property,* χρήματα κτ. *property,* Aesch. ; κτ. βοτόν *a sheep of one's own flock,* Soph.   II. *belonging to one's house,* Ζεὺς κτήσιος *the protector of property,* Aesch. ; κτ. βωμός *the altar of* Ζεὺς κτήσιος, Id.

κτῆσις, εως, ἡ, (κτάομαι) *acquisition,* Thuc., Plat. ; κατ᾽ ἔργου κτῆσιν *according to success* in the work, Soph.   II. (from pf.) *possession,* Id., Thuc., etc.   2. as collective, = κτήματα, *possessions, property,* Hom. ; in pl., Hdt., Plat., etc.

κτητέος, α, ον, verb. Adj. of κτάομαι, *to be gotten,* Plat.   II. neut. *one must get,* Id.

κτητικός, ή, όν, (κτάομαι) *acquisitive* :—ἡ -κή (sc. τέχνη) *the art of getting property,* Plat.

κτητός, ή, όν, verb. Adj. of κτάομαι, *that may be gotten,* Il., Eur.   2. *worth getting, desirable,* Plat.   II. *acquired* : κτητή *a female slave,* Hes.

κτήτωρ, ορος, ὁ, *a possessor, owner,* N. T., Anth.

κτίδεος [ῐ], α, ον, for ἰκτίδεος (from ἰκτίς), *of a marten-cat,* κτιδέη κυνέη *a marten-skin* helmet, Il.

ΚΤΙΖΩ, f. ίσω: aor. I ἔκτισα, Ep. also ἔκτισσα, κτίσσα : —Med., poët. 3 pl. aor. I ἔκτισσαντο :—Pass., aor. I ἐκτίσθην : pf. ἔκτισμαι :—*to people* a country, *build houses and cities* in it, *colonise,* Il., Hdt., etc.   2. of a city, *to found, plant, build,* Od., Hdt., etc. :—Pass. *to be founded,* Σμύρνην τὴν ἀπὸ Κολοφῶνος κτισθεῖσαν *founded by emigrants from* Colophon, Hdt.   3. κτ. ἄλσος *to plant a grove,* Pind. ; κτ. βωμόν *to set up* an altar, Id. ; τὸν Κύρνον κτίσαι *to establish* his worship, Hdt.   4. *to create, bring into being, bring about,* Aesch. ; τὸν χαλινὸν κτίσας *having invented* it, Soph.   5. *to make so and so,* ἐλεύθερον κτ. τινά Aesch., etc.   6. *to perpetrate* a deed, Soph.

ΚΤΙΛΟΣ [ῐ], ον, *tame, docile, gentle,* Pind.   II. as Subst., κτίλος, ὁ, *a ram,* Il. Hence

κτιλόω, f. ώσω, *to tame* :—Med., ἐκτιλώσαντο τὰς λοιπὰς τῶν Ἀμαζόνων *got* them *tamed,* Hdt.

κτίσις [ῐ], εως, ἡ, (κτίζω) *a founding, foundation,* ἀποικιῶν Isocr., etc.   2. loosely, = πρᾶξις, *a doing, an act,* Pind.   3. *a creating, the creation* of the universe, N. T.   II. *that which was created, the creation,* Ib.   2. *an authority created* or *ordained,* Ib.

κτίσμα, τό, (κτίζω) *anything created, a creature,* N. T.

κτίστης, ου, ὁ, (κτίζω) *a founder,* Lat. *conditor,* Luc. : *a restorer,* Plut.

κτιστύς, ύος, ὁ, Ion. for κτίσις, Hdt.

κτίστωρ, ορος, ὁ, = κτίστης, Eur.

κτίτης [ῐ], ὁ, =κτίστης : generally, *an inhabitant*, Eur.
κτῠπέω, f. ήσω : aor. 1 ἐκτύπησα, poët. κτύπησα : Ep.
aor. 2 ἔκτῠπον and κτύπον : (κτύπος) :—*to crash*, of
trees falling, Il. ; of thunder, Hom., Soph.   2. *to
ring, resound, echo*, Il., etc.   II. Causal, *to
make to ring* or *resound*, χθόνα ; c. dupl. acc., κτύπησε
κρᾶτα πλᾱγάν *made the head ring with a blow*, Eur. :
—hence again in Pass. *to ring, resound*, Ar.
κτύπημα [ῠ], ατος, τό, =κτύπος, χειρός Eur.
ΚΤΥ'ΠΟΣ [ῠ], ου, ὁ, *any loud noise, a crash* of thunder,
Il., Aesch. ; of the trampling of feet, Hom. ; of a
storm, Aesch. ; battle-*din, clash* of arms, Il.
κύᾰθος, ὁ, (κύω) *a cup*, for drawing wine out of the
κρᾱτήρ or bowl, Xen., etc.   II. *a cupping-glass*, Ar.
κυᾰμευτός, ή, όν, *chosen by beans*, i. e. *by lot*, Xen.
κυᾰμεύω, f. σω, (κύᾰμος) *to choose by lot* (not *by ballot*) :
—Pass. *to be so elected*, Dem.
ΚΥ'Α'ΜΟΣ, ὁ, *a bean*, Lat. *faba*, Il.   II. *the lot*
by which public officers were elected at Athens (because
those who drew *white beans* were chosen), ὁ τῷ κυάμῳ
λαχών *an officer chosen by lot*, Hdt. ; βουλή ἡ ἀπὸ τοῦ
κυάμου Thuc. ; ἄρχοντας ἀπὸ κυάμου καθιστάναι Xen.
κυᾰμο-τρώξ, ῶγος, ὁ, (τρώγω) *bean-eater*, Ar.
κυᾰμο-φᾰγία, ἡ, (φᾰγεῖν) *the eating of beans, bean-
diet*, Luc.
κυᾰν-αιγίς, ίδος, ἡ, *she of the dark Aegis*, Pind.
κυᾰν-άμπυξ, ῠκος, ὁ, ἡ, *with dark edge*, Theocr.
κυᾰν-αυγέτις, ιδος, pecul. fem. of sq., Orph.
κυᾰν-αυγής, ές, *dark-gleaming*, Eur., Ar.
Κυάνεαι (νῆσοι or πέτραι), αἱ, gen. Κυανεῶν :—*Dark-
rocks*, two islands at the entrance of the Euxine, Hdt. ;
—mythically supposed to close and crush passing ships,
hence called Συμπληγάδες ; the sea near being Κυάνεα
πελάγη, Soph. [ῠ metri grat. in Soph.]
κυᾰν-έμβολος, ον, (ἔμβολον) =κυανόπρῳρος, Eur., Ar.
κυάνεος, α, ον, contr. κυανοῦς, ῆ, οῦν :—
properly, *dark-blue, glossy-blue*, of a serpent's iridesc-
ent hues, Il., Hes. ; of the swallow, Simon. ; of the
deep sea, Eur.   2. generally, *dark, black*, of the
mourning veil of Thetis, Il. ; of clouds, Hom. ; of hair,
Il. ; κυανέη κάπετος *a deep dark* trench, Ib. ; κυάνεαι
φάλαγγες *dark* masses of warriors, Ib., etc.
κυᾰνο-βλέφᾰρος, ον, (βλέφᾰρον) *dark-eyed*, Anth.
κυᾰνο-ειδής, ές, (εἶδος) *dark-blue, deep-blue*, Eur.
κυᾰνό-θριξ, ὁ, ἡ, *dark-haired*, Anth.
κυᾰνό-πεζα, ἡ, *with feet of κύανος*, Il. [ῠ, metri grat.]
κυᾰνό-πεπλος, ον, *dark-veiled*, h. Hom. [ῠ, metri grat.]
κυᾰνο-πρῴρειος, ον, =sq., Od.
κυᾰνό-πρῳρος, ον, (πρῷρα) *with dark-blue prow, dark-
prowed*, of ships, Hom.
κυᾰνό-πτερος, ον, *with blue-black feathers, dark-winged*,
Hes., Eur.
ΚΥ'ΑΝΟΣ, ου, ὁ, *cyanus, a dark-blue substance*, used
in the Heroïc Age to adorn works in metal, perh. *blue
steel*, Hom.   2. as fem. *the blue corn-flower*,
Anth.   II. as Adj. =κυάνεος, with Comp. and
Sup. κυανώτερος, -ώτατος, Anacreon.
κυᾰνό-στολος, ον, (στολή) *dark-robed*, Bion.
κυᾰνοῦς, ῆ, οῦν, contr. for κυάνεος, Plat.
κυᾰν-όφρυς, υ, gen. υος, *dark-browed*, Theocr.
κυᾰνο-χαίτης, ου, ὁ, (χαίτη) *dark-haired*, of Poseidon,
perh. in reference to the *dark blue* of the sea, Hom. ;

of a horse, *dark-maned*, Il., Hes. :—Ep. nom. κυανοχαῖτα
(like ἱππότα for ἱππότης), Il. ; so in voc., h. Hom. [ῠ,
metri grat.]
κυᾰνό-χροος, ον, (χρόα) *dark-coloured, dark-looking*,
Eur. ; so κυᾰνό-χρως, ωτος, ὁ, ἡ, Id.
κυᾰν-ώπης, ου, ὁ, (ὤψ) *dark-eyed*, fem. -ῶπις, ιδος,
Od. : generally, *dark-looking*, νῆες κυανώπιδες Aesch.
κυᾰν-ωπός, όν, (ὤψ) *dark-looking*, Anth.
κυβεία, ἡ, (κυβεύω) *dice-playing, dicing*, Xen., etc. :
metaph. *sleight of hand, trickery*, N. T.
κυβεῖον, τό, (κυβεύω) *a gaming-house*, Aeschin.
Κυβέλη, ἡ, *Cybelé*, a Phrygian goddess, Eur., Ar. ; cf.
Κυβήβη.
κυβερνάω, f. ήσω, Lat. *gubernare, to steer*, Od., etc. :
absol. *to act as pilot* or *helmsman*, Ar.   2. metaph.
to guide, govern, Pind., Soph.   Hence
κυβερνήσια (sc. ἱερά), ων, τά, *a festival* at Athens in
memory of the steersman of Theseus, Plut. ; and
κυβέρνησις, Dor. -ᾱσις, εως, ἡ, *steering, pilotage*,
Plat.   2. metaph. *government*, Pind.
κυβερνήτειρα, ἡ, fem. of sq., Anth.
κυβερνητήρ, ῆρος, ὁ, =κυβερνήτης, Od. : metaph., Pind.
κυβερνητήριος, α, ον, =κυβερνητικός, Orac. ap. Plut.
κυβερνήτης, ου, ὁ, (κυβερνάω) *a steersman, helmsman,
pilot*, Lat. *gubernator*, Hom., etc. : Ion. acc. κυβερνή-
τεα Hdt.   2. metaph. *a guide, governor*, Eur.,
Plat.   Hence
κυβερνητικός, ή, όν, *good at steering*, Plat. ; Comp.
-ώτερος, Id. ; Sup. -ώτατος, Xen. :—ἡ -κή (sc. τέχνη)
the pilot's art, Plat.
κυβευτής, οῦ, ὁ, (κυβεύω) *a dicer, gambler*, Xen.   Hence
κυβευτικός, ή, όν, *of* or *for dice-playing*, Aeschin.   II.
skilled in dice-playing, Plat.
κυβεύω, f. σω, (κύβος) *to play at dice*, Ar., etc.   2.
metaph. *to run a risk* or *hazard*, Xen., etc. ; c. acc.
to hazard, venture on, Eur. :—Pass. *to be set upon a
stake*, Anth.
Κυβήβη, ἡ, =Κυβέλη, q. v.
κῠβιστάω, f. ήσω, (κύπτω) *to tumble head foremost,
tumble*, Il., Xen., etc.   Hence
κῠβίστημα, ατος, τό, *a summerset*, Luc. ; and
κῠβίστησις, εως, ἡ, *a summerset*, Luc. ; and
κῠβιστητήρ, ῆρος, ὁ, *a tumbler*, Hom.   2. *a diver*,
Il.   3. *one who pitches headlong*, Eur.
ΚΥ'ΒΟΣ [ῠ], ὁ, Lat. *cubus, a cube* : *a cubical die*,
marked on all 6 sides (whereas the ἀστράγαλος was
marked only on four sides), in pl., *dice*, Hdt., etc. ; the
Greeks threw with *three* dice, so that τρὶς ἕξ, three
sixes, was the highest throw, Aesch., Plat. ; κρίνειν τι
ἐν κύβοις *to decide it by the dice*, by *chance*, Aesch.   2.
also of the single *pips* on the dice, βέβληκ' Ἀχιλλεὺς
δύο κύβω καὶ τέσσαρα *he has thrown two aces* and a
four, Aesch. ap. Ar.   II. *a cubic number*, i. e. a
number multiplied twice into itself, as 27 is the cube of
3, Plat.
κῠδάζω, (κῦδος, ὁ) *to revile* :—Pass. *to be reviled*, Soph.
κῠδαίνω : f. κυδᾰνῶ : Ep. aor. 1 κύδηνα, Dor. ἐκύδᾱνα :
(κῦδος) :—*to give* or *do honour to, glorify*, Hom.   II.
to gladden by marks of honour, Id.   III. in bad
sense, *to flatter, fawn upon*, Hes.
κῡδάλιμος [ᾰ], ον, (κῦδος) *glorious, renowned, famous*,
Hom.

κῡδάνω [ᾰ], = κυδαίνω, only in pres. and impf., *to hold in honour*, Il. II. *to vaunt, boast*, Ib.

κῡδήεις, εσσα, εν, (κῦδος) *glorious*, Anth.

κύδηνα, Ep. aor. 1 of κυδαίνω.

κῡδι-άνειρα, ἡ, (κῦδος, ἀνήρ) *glorifying* or *ennobling men, bringing them glory* or *renown*, Il. II. pass. *famous for men*, Anth.

κῡδιάω, Ep. 3 pl. κυδιόωσιν, part. κυδιόων, (κῦδος) only in pres. and impf., *to bear oneself proudly, go proudly along, exult*, Il.

κύδῑμος [ῠ], ον, = κυδάλιμος, h. Hom., Hes., Pind.

κύδιστος [ῠ], η, ον, Sup. of κυδρός (formed from κῦδος, as αἴσχιστος, posit. of αἰσχρός, from αἶσχος), *most glorious, most honoured, noblest*, Hom. II. Comp. κυδίων [ῑ], *nobler:* τί μοι ζῆν δῆτα κύδιον; *what boots it me to live?* Eur.

κυδνός, ή, όν, = κυδρός, Hes.

κῠδοιδοπάω, *to make a hubbub*, Ar. (Formed from the sound.)

κῠδοιμέω, f. ήσω, *to make an uproar, spread alarm*, Il. II. trans. *to drive in confusion*, Ib. From

κῠδοιμός, ὁ, *the din of battle, uproar, hubbub*, Il., Ar. (Formed from the sound.)

ΚΥ͂ΔΟΣ, εος, τό, *glory, renown*, esp. in war, Il. : of a single person, κῦδος Ἀχαιῶν *glory of the Achaians*, like Lat. *decus*, Hom.

κῠδρός, ά, όν, (κῦδος) = κυδάλιμος, *glorious, illustrious, noble*, Hom., Hes.; of a horse, *proud, stately*, Xen. (For the irreg. Comp. and Sup., v. κύδιστος.)

Κῠδώνιος, α, ον, (Κύδων) *Cydonian:* μῆλον Κ. *a quince*, Stesich., etc. II. metaph. *swelling like a quince, round and plump*, Ar.

ΚΥΕ͂Ω : impf. ἐκύουν : f. κυήσω : aor. 1 ἐκύησα :—like κύω, *to bear in the womb, to be pregnant with* a child, Lat. *gestare*, Il., Plat. 2. absol. *to be pregnant, be with child*, Hdt.

Κύζικος, ἡ, an island and town on the coast of Mysia, Hdt. :—hence Κυζικηνός, ή, όν, *of* or *from Cyzicus:* ὁ Κυζικηνός (with or without στατήρ), a gold coin, Xen.

κύημα, ατος, τό, (κυέω) *that which is conceived, an embryo, foetus*, Plat.

κυηρός, ά, όν, *pregnant*, Hesych.

κύησις, εως, ἡ, *conception*, Plat.

κύθε, 3 sing. Ep. aor. 2 of κεύθω.

Κῠθέρεια, ἡ, *Cythereia*, surname of Aphrodité, Od. :—also Κυθέρη and Κυθηριάς, άδος, Anth. From

Κύθηρα [ῠ], τά, an island, now *Cerigo* to the south of Laconia, Hom. :—Κυθήροθεν, Adv. *from Cythera*, Il. :—Adj. Κυθήριος, α, ον, *Cytherean*, Ib., etc.; ἡ Κυθηρία (sc. γῆ) Xen.

Κυθηρο-δίκης, ου, ὁ, *a Spartan magistrate sent annually to govern the island of Cythera*, Thuc.

κύθρα, κύθρος, Ion. for χύτρα, χύτρος.

κυΐσκομαι, Pass., only in pres., *to conceive, become pregnant*, Hdt., Plat.

ΚΥ͂ΚΑ͂Ω, f. ήσω, *to stir up* and *mix, beat up*, Hom., Ar. : Med. in Act. sense, Ar. II. like ταράσσω, *to stir up, to throw into confusion* or *disorder, confound*, Aesch., Ar., Plat., etc. :—Pass. *to be confounded, panic-stricken*, Il.; of waves, Hom.; ὑπ' ἀνδρὸς τοξότου κυκώμενος *hustled* by him, Ar. Hence

κῠκεών, ῶνος, ὁ : acc. κυκεῶνα, Ep. shortd. κυκεῶ and

Ep. κυκειῶ : (κυκάω) :—*mixed drink, a potion, tankard*, made of barley-meal, grated cheese and wine, Hom. II. metaph. of *any mixture, medley*, Luc.

κυκήθην, Ep. aor. 1 of κυκάω.

κύκηθρον [ῠ], τό, *a ladle for stirring :* metaph. *an agitator*, Ar.

κύκησις [ῠ], εως, ἡ, *a stirring up, mixing up*, Plat.

κῠκησί-τεφρος, ον, (τέφρα) *mixed with ashes*, Ar.

κυκλάς, άδος, ἡ, (κύκλος) *round, circular ;* and of Time, *revolving*, Eur. ; αἱ Κυκλάδες (sc. νῆσοι), *the Cyclades*, islands in the Aegaean sea, which *encircle* Delos, Att.

κυκλέω [ῠ by nature], f. ήσω, (κύκλος fin.) *to move round and round, wheel along*, c. acc., Il. 2. *to move round* or *in a circle*, Soph. ; βάσιν κυκλεῖν, metaph. from dogs *questing about* for the scent, Id. ; κ. πρόσωπον *to turn* the face *round*, look *round*, Eur. II. Med. and Pass. *to form a circle round, to surround, encompass, encircle*, Hdt., Soph. 2. *to go round and round, revolve*, Plat.

κυκλιάς, ὁ, ἡ, (κύκλος) *round*, Anth.

κυκλικός, ή, όν, (κύκλος) *circular :* οἱ κυκλικοί, Epic poets whose writings formed a *cycle* or series of legends down to the death of Ulysses, Att.

κυκλιο-διδάσκαλος, ὁ, *a teacher of the dithyrambic chorus* (v. κύκλιος II), Ar.

κύκλιος, α, ον, also ος, ον, Eur. : (κύκλος) :—*round, circular*, ὕδωρ κύκλιον, of the Delian lake (cf. τροχοειδής), Eur. II. κύκλιος χορός, *a chorus danced in a ring round an altar, a dithyrambic chorus*, Ar., etc. :—κύκλια μέλη *dithyrambic songs*, Ar.

Κυκλοβορέω, f. ήσω, *to brawl like the torrent Cycloborus*, Ar. From

Κυκλο-βόρος, ου, ὁ, (βι-βρώσκω) *Cycloborus*, a torrent in Attica, Ar.

κυκλο-δίωκτος, ον, (διώκω) *driven in a circle*, Anth.

κυκλόεις, εσσα, εν, poët. for κυκλικός, Soph., Anth.

κυκλόθεν, Adv. *from all around*, N. T.

κυκλο-μόλιβδος, ὁ, *a round lead-pencil*, Anth.

ΚΥ͂ΚΛΟΣ [ῠ by nature], ὁ, also with heterog. pl. κύκλα :—*a ring, circle, round*, Hom. ; ἀσπίδος κύκλος the *round* shield, Aesch. 2. Adverbial usages, κύκλῳ *in a circle* or *ring, round about*, Od., Hdt., Att. ; c. gen., κ. τοῦ στρατοπέδου Xen., etc. II. *any circular body :* 1. *a wheel*, Il. 2. *a place of assembly*, the ἀγορά, Ib., Att. :—then, like Lat. *corona*, *a ring* or *circle of people*, Soph., Xen. 3. *the vault of the sky*, Hdt., Soph., etc. 4. *the orb* or *disk of the sun and moon*, Hdt., Trag. 5. *the wall round* a city, esp. round Athens, Hdt., Thuc., etc. 6. *a round shield*, v. suprl. 1. 1. 7. in pl. *the eye-balls, eyes*, Soph. :—rarely in sing., *the eye*, Id. III. *any circular motion, an orbit* of the heavenly bodies, *revolution* of the seasons, *cycle* of events, Hdt., Eur. 2. *a circular dance*, Ar. Hence

κυκλόσε, Adv. *in* or *into a circle* or *round*, Il.

κυκλο-σοβέω, f. ήσω, *to drive round in a circle, whirl round*, Ar.

κυκλο-τερής, ές, (τείρω) *made round by turning* (as in a lathe), Hdt. : then, generally, *round, circular*, Hom., etc. ; κυκλοτερὲς τόξον ἔτεινεν *stretched* it *into a circle*, Il.

κυκλόω, f. ώσω : pf. κεκύκλωκα :—Med., f. -ώσομαι :

aor. 1 ἐκυκλωσάμην:—Pass.,aor. 1 ἐκυκλώθην: (κύκλος): —to encircle, surround, Eur.:—so in Med., Hdt., Aesch., etc. :—Pass. to be surrounded, Aesch., Thuc.　　II. to move in a circle, whirl round, Pind., Eur. :—Pass. or Med. to go in a circle, go round, Xen.; metaph., Aesch.　　III. to form into a circle, τόξα Anth. :— Pass., of a bow, to form a circle, Eur.; cf. κυκλοτερής.

κύκλωμα, ατος, τό, that which is rounded into a circle, a wheel, Eur.; βυρσότονον κύκλωμα a hide-stretched circle, i. e. a drum, Id.

Κυκλώπειος, α, ον, (Κύκλωψ) Cyclopean, commonly used of the architecture attributed to the Cyclopes, (also called Πελασγικός), Eur.

Κυκλωπικῶς, Adv. like the Cyclopes, Κ. ζῆν to live a savage unsocial life, Arist.

Κυκλώπιον, τό, Dim. of Κύκλωψ, little Cyclops, Eur.

Κυκλώπιος, α, ον, = Κυκλώπειος, Eur.: ἡ Κ. γῆ, i. e. Mycenae, Id. :—fem. Κυκλωπίς, ίδος, Id.

κύκλωσις, εως, ἡ, (κυκλόω) a surrounding, in a battle, Xen.; τὴν πλέονα κύκλωσιν σφῶν the larger body that was endeavouring to surround them, Thuc.

κυκλωτός, ή, όν, (κυκλόω) rounded, round, Aesch.

Κύκλ-ωψ [ῠ by nature], ωπος, ὁ, a Cyclops, properly Round-eye.—The Cyclopes appear in Od. as savage giants, dwelling in Sicily ; in sing. of Polyphemus :— they were builders of the walls of Mycenae, etc., τὰ Κυκλώπων βάθρα, i.e. Mycenae, Eur.

κύκνειος, α, ον, of a swan, Anth.

κυκνό-μορφος, ον, (μορφή) swan-shaped, Aesch.

κυκνό-πτερος, ον, (πτερόν) swan-plumed, Eur.

ΚΥ'ΚΝΟΣ, ὁ, a swan, Il., etc.:—metaph., from the legends of the swan's dying song (Aesch., Plat.), a minstrel, Anth.

κύκν-οψις, εως, ὁ, ἡ, swan-like, Anth.

κῠλινδέω, f. ήσω, = κυλίνδω, Plat., Xen.

κῠλινδήθρα, ἡ, = ἀλινδήθρα, q. v.

κῠλίνδησις, εως, ἡ, a rolling, wallowing, Plut.

κύλινδρος [ῠ], ὁ, a roller, cylinder, Plut.　　From

ΚΥ'ΛΙ'ΝΔΩ: (tenses formed from κυλίω), aor. 1 ἐκύλισα: —Pass., f. κυλισθήσομαι: aor. 1 ἐκυλίσθην, Ep. κυλ—: pf. κεκύλισμαι:—to roll, roll along or down, Od., Soph., etc.: metaph., πῆμα θεὸς Δαναοῖσι κυλίνδει rolls down calamity upon one, Il.　　2. to roll away, Anth.　　II. Pass. to be rolled, roll along, roll, Hom.: to toss about like a ship at sea, Pind. : to be whirled round on a wheel, of Ixion, Id.　　2. of persons, κυλίνδεσθαι κατὰ κόπρον to roll or wallow in the dirt (in sign of grief), Hom. : to roam to and fro, wander about, Xen.　　3. of Time, to roll by, Pind.　　4. of words, to be tost from man to man, i. e. be much talked of, Lat. jactari, Ar.

κύλιξ [ῠ], ικος, ἡ, (κύω) a cup, drinking-cup, wine-cup, Lat. calix, Hdt., Pind., etc.; περιελαύνειν τὰς κ. to push round the cup, Xen.

κῠλίσθην, Ep. aor. 1 pass. of κυλίνδω.

κύλισμα, ατος, τό, a rolling, wallowing, or a wallowing place, N. T.

κῠλίστρα, ἡ, a place for horses to roll in, Xen.

κῠλίω, later form of κυλίνδω, to roll along, Theocr., Luc.

κυλλάστις, Ion. -ῆστις, ιος, ὁ, Aegyptian bread, Hdt.

κυλλή, ἡ, cf. κυλλός.

Κυλλήνη, ἡ, Cyllené, a mountain in Arcadia, Il. ; whence Hermes was called Κυλλήνιος, Hom.

Κυλλο-ποδίων [ῐ], ονος, ὁ, (πούς) crook-footed, halting, of Vulcan, Il. ; voc. Κυλλοπόδιον Ib.

ΚΥΛΛΟ'Σ, ή, όν, crooked, crippled, properly of legs bent outwards by disease, Ar. :—ἔμβαλε κυλλῇ (sc. χειρί) put into a crooked hand, i. e. with the fingers crooked like a beggar's, Id.

κῠλ-οιδιάω, (κύλα, οἰδάω) to have a swelling below the eye, from a blow or from sleepless nights, Ar., Theocr.

κῦμα, ατος, τό, (κύω) anything swoln (as if pregnant): —hence,　　I. the swell of the sea, a wave, billow, Hom., etc.; collectively, ὡς τὸ κῦμα ἔστρωτο when the swell abated, Hdt.　　b. metaph. of a flood of men, Aesch. :—metaph., κ. ἄτης, κακῶν, συμφορᾶς Id., Eur.　　II. the foetus in the womb, embryo, Aesch. ; of the earth, Id.

κῡμαίνω, f. ἀνῶ, (κῦμα) to rise in waves or billows, to swell, Hom., Plat.　　2. metaph. of passion, to swell, seethe, Pind., Aesch.　　3. trans. to agitate, Luc., Anth. :—Pass., Plut.

κῡμᾱτίας, Ion. -ίης, ου, ὁ, (κῦμα) surging, billowy, κ. ὁ ποταμὸς ἐγένετο Hdt.　　2. act. causing waves, stormy, ἄνεμος Id.

κῡμᾰτο-ᾱγής, ές, (ἄγνυμι) breaking like waves, Soph.

Κῡμᾰτο-λήγη, ἡ, (λήγω) Wave-stiller, a Nereïd, Hes.

κῡμᾰτο-πλήξ, ῆγος, ὁ, ἡ, (πλήσσω) wave-beaten, Soph.

κῡμᾰτόω, f. ώσω, (κῦμα) to cover with waves, Plut.　　II. Pass. to be raised or to rise in waves, of the sea, Thuc.

κῡμᾰτ-ωγή, ἡ, (ἄγνυμι) a place where the waves break, the beach, Hdt.

κῡμᾰτ-ώδης, ες, (εἶδος) on which the waves break, Plut.

ΚΥ'ΜΒΑ'ΛΟΝ, τό, a cymbal, Xen.

κύμβᾱχος, ον, (κύπτω) head-foremost, Lat. pronus, Il.　　II. as Subst. the crown of a helmet, Ib.

κύμινδις [ῠ], -δος, ὁ, a bird, perh. the night-jar, Il.

κῠμῑνεύω, f. σω, (κύμινον) to strew with cummin, Luc.

κύμῑνον, τό, cummin, Att., N. T.　　(Deriv. uncertain.)

κῠμῑνο-πρίστης, ου, ὁ, (πρίω) a cummin-splitter, i. e. a skinflint, niggard, Arist.

κῠμῑνο-πριστο-καρδᾰμο-γλύφος [ῠ], ον, (γλύφω) a cummin-splitting-cress-scraper, Ar.

κῡμο-δέγμων, ον, (δέχομαι) meeting the waves, Eur.

Κῡμο-δόκη, ἡ, (δέχομαι) Wave-receiver, a Nereïd, Il.

κῡμο-θόη, ἡ, (θοός) Wave-swift, a Nereïd, Il., Hes.

Κῡμο-πόλεια, ἡ, (πολέω) Wave-walker, Hes.

Κῡμώ, οῦς, ἡ, (κῦμα) Wavy, a Nereïd, Hes.

κύνα, acc. of κύων.

κῠνᾱγέσιον, κυνᾱγέτας, -έτις, κυνᾱγία, v. sub κυνηγ-.

κῠνάγκη, ἡ, (κύων, ἄγχω) a dog's collar, Anth.

κῠν-ᾱγός, ὁ, ἡ, Dor. and Att. for κυνηγός, (ἄγω) :—a hound-leader, i. e. a huntsman, Aesch., Soph.

κῠν-ᾰγωγός, ὁ, (ἄγω) a leader of hounds, huntsman, Xen.

κῠν-αλώπηξ, εκος, ἡ, a fox-dog, mongrel between dog and fox, nickname of Cleon, Ar.

κῠνά-μυια [ᾰ], ἡ, dog-fly, i. e. shameless fly, abusive epithet of impudent women, Il.

κῠνάριον, τό, Dim. of κύων, a little dog, whelp, Xen., etc.

κῠνάς, άδος, fem. Adj. of a dog: as Subst. (sub. θρίξ), dog's hair, of a bad fleece, Theocr.

κῠνάω, = κυνίζω, to play the Cynic, Luc.

κῠνέη, Att. contr. κυνῆ, (properly fem. of κύνεος, sub. δορά), ἡ :—a dog's skin : then, a leathern cap, not necessarily of dog's skin, for we find κ. ταυρείη, κτιδέη, etc., Hom.

κύνειος [ῠ], α, ον, and ος, ον, of, belonging to a dog, Ar. ; κ. θάνατος a dog's death, Id. ; τὰ κύνεια (sub. κρέα) dog's flesh, Id.

κύνεος [ῠ], α, ον, (κύων) = foreg., Anth. : metaph. shameless, unabashed, Il., Hes.

κυνέω [ῠ], Ep. impf. κύνεον : f. κῠνήσομαι, later, κύσω [ῠ], poët. κύσσω : aor. 1 ἐκύνησα, also ἔκῠσα, Ep. κύσα [ῠ], ἔκυσσα, κύσσα :—to kiss, Hom., Eur., etc. 2. = προσκυνέω, Eur.

κῠνηγεσία, Dor. κυνᾱγ-, ἡ, later form for sq. (signf. II), Plut. ; and

κῠνηγέσιον, τό, a hunting-establishment, huntsmen and hounds, a pack of hounds, Hdt., Xen. II. a hunt, chase, pursuit, Xen. ; so in pl., Eur. III. that which is taken in hunting, the game, Xen. From

κῠνηγετέω, Dor. κυνᾱγ-, f. ήσω, (κυνηγέτης) to hunt, Ar., Xen., etc. :—metaph. to persecute, harass, Aesch. II. to quest about, like a hound, Soph.

κῠν-ηγέτης, ου, ὁ, Dor. κυνᾱγ-, a hunter, huntsman, Od., Eur., etc. ; κυναγέτας ἀμφὶ πάλᾳ one who seeks the prize in wrestling, Pind. :—fem. κυνηγέτις, Dor. -αγέτις, ιδος, a huntress, Anth. Hence

κῠνηγετικός, ή, όν, of or for hunting, fond of the chase, Plat. :—ὁ κυνηγετικός [λόγος] name of Xenophon's work on Hunting.

κῠνηγέτις, ιδος, ἡ, fem. of κυνηγέτης.

κῠνηγέω, Dor. κυνᾱγέω, f. ήσω, (κυνηγός) to hunt, chase, later form of κυνηγετέω, Plut.

κῠνηγία, Dor. κυνᾱγία, ἡ, hunt, chase, hunting, Trag.

κῠνήγιον, τό, = κυνηγέσιον, the hunt, chase, Plut.

κῠνηγός, v. κυναγός.

κῠνηδόν, Adv. (κύων) like a dog, Ar.

Κύνθος [ῠ], ὁ, Cynthus, a mountain in Delos, birth-place of Apollo and Artemis, h. Hom. :—hence Apollo is called Κύνθιος and Κυνθο-γενής, born on Cynthus, Ar., Anth.

κῠνῐδεύς, έως, ὁ, a puppy (cf. λαγιδεύς, λυκιδεύς), Theocr.

κῠνίδιον, τό, Dim. of κύων, a little dog, whelp, puppy, Ar., Plat., etc.

κῠνίζω, (κύων) to play the dog : metaph. to live like a Cynic, belong to their sect, Luc.

κῠνικός, ή, όν, (κύων) dog-like, Lat. caninus, Xen. II. Κυνικός, ὁ, a Cynic, as the followers of the philosopher Antisthenes were called, Plut.

κῠνίσκη, ἡ, (κύων) a bitch-puppy, Ar.

κῠνίσκος, ὁ, (κύων) a young dog, puppy, Hdt. 2. metaph. a little Cynic, Luc.

κῠνισμός, ὁ, Cynical philosophy or conduct, Luc.

κῠν-όδους, οντος, ὁ, a canine tooth, Xen., etc.

κῠνο-δρομέω, f. ήσω, (δρόμος) to run with dogs, Xen.

κῠνο-θαρσής, ές, (θάρσος) impudent as a dog, Theocr.

κῠνο-κέφαλος, ον, (κεφαλή) dog-headed; οἱ Κυνοκέφαλοι, Dog-heads, the name of a people, Hdt. 2. the dog-faced baboon, Plat., Luc. [κυνοκεφάλλῳ in Ar.]

κῠνο-κλόπος, ον, (κλέπτω) dog-stealing, Ar.

κῠνο-κοπέω, f. ήσω, (κόπτω) to beat like a dog, Ar.

κῠνό-μυια, ἡ, = κυνάμυια, Anth., Luc.

κῠνο-πρόσωπος, ον, (πρόσωπον) dog-faced, Luc.

Κῠνόσαργες, εος, τό, Cynosarges, a gymnasium outside Athens, for the use of those who were not pure Athenians, Hdt., Dem., etc. (Deriv. unknown.)

κῠνόσ-βατος, ἡ and ὁ, dog-thorn or dog-rose, Theocr.

κῠνόσ-ουρα, ἡ, dog's-tail, the Cynosure, a name for the constellation Ursa Minor, Arat.

κῠνο-σπάρακτος, ον, (σπαράσσω) torn by dogs, Soph.

κυν-οῦχος, ὁ, (ἔχω) a dog-holder, dog-leash, Anth. II. a dog-skin sack, used in hunting, Xen.

κῠνό-φρων, ον, (φρήν) dog-minded, shameless, Aesch.

κύντερος, α, ον, Comp. Adj. formed from κύων, more dog-like, i. e. more shameless, more audacious, Hom. ; more horrible, κύντερον ἄλλο ποτ' ἔτλης Od. II. Sup. κύντατος, η, ον, most audacious, Il., h. Hom.

κυνώ, οῦς, ἡ, a she-dog :—as prop. n. Κυνώ, Hdt.

κῠν-ώπης, ου, ὁ, (ὤψ) the dog-eyed, i. e. shameless one, Il. :—so fem. κῠνῶπις, ιδος, ἡ, Hom.

κυο-φορέω, (κύω, φέρω) to be pregnant, Luc.

κῠπᾰρίσσῐνος, Att. -ἰττῐνος, η, ον, of cypress-wood, Od., Thuc. From

ΚΥΠΑΡΙΣΣΟΣ, Att. -ιττος, ἡ, a cypress, Od., Hdt., etc.

κῠπασσίς, ίδος, or κύπασσις, ιδος, ὁ and ἡ, a short frock, Anth. (Deriv. uncertain.)

ΚΥΠΕΙΡΟΝ [ῠ], τό, a sweet-smelling marsh-plant, perh. galingale, used to feed horses, Hom.

κύπειρος [ῠ], ὁ, = foreg., h. Hom.

κῠπελλο-μάχος, ον, (μάχομαι) at which they fight with cups (cf. Horace pugnare scyphis), Anth.

κύπελλον [ῠ], τό, a big-bellied drinking vessel, a beaker, goblet, cup, Hom. (Deriv. uncertain.)

κῠπελλο-φόρος, ον, (φέρω) carrying cups, Anth.

ΚΥΠΕΡΟΣ, ὁ, prob. Ion. for κύπειρος, Hdt.

Κυπρίδιος, α, ον, (Κύπρις) like Cypris, i. e. lovely, tender, Anth.

Κύπριος, α, ον, of Cyprus, Cyprian, Hdt., etc. II. Κύπρια, τά, an Epic poem introductory to the Il., Id.

Κύπρις [ῠ by nature], ιδος, ἡ, acc. Κύπριν or Κύπριδα, Cypris, a name of Aphrodité, from the island of Cyprus, where she was most worshipped, Il., Trag., etc. II. as appellat. love, passion, Eur., etc.

Κυπρο-γενής, ές, (γίγνομαι) Cyprus-born, of Aphrodité, h. Hom., etc. :—fem. Κυπρο-γένεια, ἡ, Pind.

Κυπρόθεν, Adv. from Cyprus, Anth. ; and

Κύπρονδε, Adv. to Cyprus, Il. From

Κύπρος, ἡ, Cyprus, a Greek island on the S. coast of Asia Minor, Hom., etc. :—the Romans got from it the best copper, Lat. cyprium.

κυπτάζω, f. άσω, Frequent. of κύπτω, to keep stooping, to go poking about, potter about a thing, Ar., Plat.

κύπτω (Root ΚΥΠ), f. κύψω: aor. 1 ἔκυψα: pf. κέκυφα :— to bend forward, stoop down, Hom., Hdt., etc. ; θέει κύψας runs with the head down, i.e. at full speed, Ar. ; κύψας ἐσθίει eats greedily, Id. ; κέρεα κεκυφότα ἐς τὸ ἔμπροσθεν horns bent forward, of certain African oxen, Hdt. 2. to hang the head from shame, Ar. 3. to bow down under a burden, Dem.

Κύρβας, αντος, ὁ, shortd. form of Κορύβας, q. v.

κυρβᾱσία, ἡ, a Persian bonnet or hat, with a peaked crown, prob. much like the τιάρα, Hdt. : the King alone wore it upright, Ar.

κύρβεις, εων, αἱ, dat. κύρβεσιν :—triangular tablets,

fitted at the angles so as to form a pyramid of three sides, and having the earliest laws written on the sides, Ar., Plat. **II.** in sing. metaph. of *a pettifogging lawyer*, Ar.

Κύρειος, α, ον, *of Cyrus*, Xen.

ΚΥ´ΡΕΩ: impf. ἐκύρουν [ῠ]: f. κυρήσω: aor. 1 ἐκύρησα: pf. κεκύρηκα:—also **ΚΥ´ΡΩ** [ῠ]: impf. ἔκυρον, Ep. κῦρον: f. κύρσω: aor. 1 ἔκυρσα, part. κύρσας:—Med. κύρομαι [ῠ] in act. sense: **I.** followed by a case, *to hit, light upon:* **1.** c. dat. *to light upon, meet with, fall in with, strike against,* Il., Hes. :—of things, κυρεῖν τινι *to befall* or *be granted to* him, Soph., Eur. **2.** c. gen. *to hit* the mark, like τυγχάνω, Aesch. :—*to reach to* or *as far as,* h. Hom. : *to meet with, find,* Aesch., Soph. **b.** *to attain to, be master of, obtain,* Lat. *potiri,* Hdt., Trag. **3.** c. acc., like Lat. *potiri, to obtain, reach, find,* Aesch., Eur. **II.** *without a case, to happen, come to pass,* Trag. **2.** *to be right, hit the exact truth,* Soph. **3.** as auxil. Verb, like τυγχάνω with partic., *to turn out, prove to be* so and so, σεσωσμένος κυρεῖ Aesch.; ζῶν κυρεῖ Soph.; ἐχθρὸς ὢν κυρεῖ Eur.; with partic. omitted, it acts merely as the copula, *to be,* Trag.

κυρηβάζω, f. άσω, *to butt with the horns:* metaph., τὸ σκέλος κυρηβάσει *he shall come butt against* my leg, or my leg *shall butt* him, *kick* him, Ar. (Perh. akin to κυρίσσω.)

κυρήβια, ων, τά, *husks, bran :—a bran-shop,* Ar. (Deriv. unknown.)

Κυρήνη [ῠ], ή, *Cyrené,* a Greek colony in Africa, Hdt. :—the people were called Κυρηναῖοι, and the country ή Κυρηναία, Id.

κῡρία, ή, fem. of κύριος (signf. B. I. 2.)

κυριάζω, = κυριεύω, Hesych.

κῡριακός, ή, όν, (κύριος) *of* or *for a lord* or *master :* esp. *belonging to the* LORD (CHRIST); **Κ.** δεῖπνον *the* LORD'S Supper, ή κυριακή ήμέρα *the* LORD'S day, dies Dominica, N. T. (Assumed to be original of the Teutonic *kirk, kirche, church;* but how this Greek name came to be adopted by the Northern nations, rather than the Roman name *ecclesia,* has not been satisfactorily explained.)

κῡριεύω, f. σω, *to be lord* or *master of* people or of a country, c. gen., Xen. **2.** *to have legal power to* do, c. inf., ap. Aeschin. **From**

κῡριος [ῠ], α, ον, and ος, ον : (κύρος) : **I.** *of persons, having power* or *authority over, lord* or *master of,* c. gen., Pind., Att. :—κύριός εἰμι, c. inf., *I have authority* to do, *am entitled* to do, Aesch., etc.; κυριώτεροι δοῦναι *better able* to give, Thuc. **2.** absol. *having authority, authoritative, supreme,* κ. εἶναι to have authority, Plat.; τὸ κύριον *the ruling power* in a state, τὰ κύρια *the authorities,* Soph., Dem. **II.** not of persons, *authoritative, decisive, dominant, supreme,* δίκαι Eur.; μῦθος κυριώτερος *of more authority,* Id., etc. **2.** opp. to ἄκυρος, *authorised, ratified, valid,* νόμοι, δόγματα Dem.; κ. θέσθαι or ποιεῖσθαί τι to appoint *by authority,* Soph., Dem. **3.** of times, etc., *fixed, ordained, appointed,* Hdt., Eur., etc.; so, τὸ κύριον *the appointed* time, Aesch. :—at Athens, κυρία ἐκκλησία *a regular* or *ordinary* assembly,

opp. τὸ σύγκλητος ἐκκλησία (one specially summoned), Ar. **4.** *legitimate, regular, proper,* Aesch. **5.** of words, *authorised, vernacular,* Lat. *proprius,* Arist.

B. as Subst., κύριος, ὁ, *a lord, master,* Lat. *dominus,* of gods, Pind., Soph., etc. : *the head* of a family, *master* of a house, Aesch., etc. :—later, κύριε was a form of respectful address, like our *sir,* N. T. **2.** κυρία, ή, *mistress* or *lady of the house,* Lat. *domina,* Menand., etc. **II.** ὁ Κύριος, *the* LORD, = Hebr. *JEHOVAH,* LXX.; in N. T. esp. of CHRIST. Hence

κῡριότης, ητος, ή, *dominion,* N. T.

κῡρίσσω, Att. -ττω, f. ίξω, (κόρυς) *to butt with the horns,* Plat. :—metaph. of floating corpses *knocking against* the shore, Aesch.

κῡρίως, Adv. of κύριος, *like a lord* or *master, authoritatively,* Aesch. **II.** *regularly, legitimately, properly,* κ. ἔχειν to be fixed, hold good, Id.; κ. αἰτεῖσθαι, *suo jure,* Soph., etc. **III.** of words, *in their proper sense,* Arist.

κῦρμα, ατος, τό, (κύρω) *that which one meets with* or *finds,* i. e. *booty, prey, spoil,* Hom. **II.** of a person, *one who gets booty, a swindler,* Aesch.

Κύρνος, ή, *Cyrnus,* old name of Corsica, Hdt. : οἱ Κύρνιοι Id.

Κῦρος, ὁ, *Cyrus :* **1.** ὁ πρότερος, *the elder Cyrus,* Hdt. **2.** ὁ νεώτερος, *the brother of Artaxerxes,* Xen.

ΚΥ´ΡΟΣ, εος, τό, *supreme power, authority,* Hdt., Thuc., etc. **II.** *confirmation, validity, certainty,* Soph. Hence

κῡρόω, f. ώσω, *to make valid, confirm, ratify, determine,* Lat. *ratum facere,* Hdt., Aesch., etc. :—Med. *to accomplish one's end,* Plat. :—Pass. *to be ratified,* Hdt., Att. :—generally, κεκύρωται τέλος the end hath been *fixed* or *determined,* Aesch.; πρὶν κεκυρῶσθαι σφαγάς before *it has been accomplished,* Eur. :—impers. c. inf., ἐκεκύρωτο συμβάλλειν it had been *decided* to fight, Hdt.; ἐκυρώθη ναυμαχέειν Id. **2.** κ. δίκην *to decide* it, Aesch.

κύρσαι, aor. 1 inf. of κύρω, (v. κυρέω) : κύρσω, fut.

κυρτευτής, οῦ, ὁ, *one that fishes with the* κύρτη, Anth.

κύρτη, ή, *a fishing-basket,* Lat. *nassa,* Hdt.; and

κύρτος, ὁ, = foreg., Plat. **2.** *a bird-cage,* Lat. *cavea,* Anth. **From**

ΚΥΡΤΟ´Σ, ή, όν, *curved, arched,* of a wave breaking, Il.; ὤμω κυρτώ *round, humped,* Ib.; κ. τροχός Eur.

κυρτόω, f. ώσω, *to curve* or *bend into an arch,* κυρτῶν νῶτα, of a bull preparing to charge, Eur.; κ. λαίφεα Anth. :—Pass. *to form a curve* or *arch,* of a wave breaking, Od., Xen.

κύρω, v. κυρέω.

κύρωσις [ῠ], εως, ή, (κυρόω) *a ratification,* Thuc., Plat.

κύσαι [ῠ], Ep. κύσσαι, aor. 1 inf. of κυνέω; but **II.** κῦσαι of κύω.

κῡσαμένη, aor. 1 med. part. fem. of κύω II.

κύσσαι, Ep. for κύσαι [ῠ], aor. 1 inf. of κυνέω.

κύστις, εως and ιος, ή, (κύω) *the bladder,* Il., Ar.

κύσω [ῠ], fut. of κυνέω.

κύτισος [ῠ], ὁ, *cytisus,* a kind of clover, Theocr.

κυτίς, ίδος, ή, *a kind of plaster,* Luc.

κῡτο-γάστωρ, opos, ὁ, ή, *with capacious belly,* Anth.

κύτος [ῠ], εος, τό, (κύω) *the hollow* of a shield or breast-plate, Aesch., Ar. **2.** *any vessel, a vase, jar,*

urn, Aesch., Soph., etc.; πλεκτὸν κ. a basket, Eur. 3. anything that contains the body, Soph.

κύτταρος, ὁ, (κύτος) the cell of a comb of bees or wasps, Ar. 2. metaph., τοὐρανοῦ τὸν κ. the concave vault of heaven, Id.

κῦφ-ἄγωγός, ὁ, with neck arched and head low, of a horse, Xen.

κῠφᾰλέος, α, ον, poët. for κυφός, Anth.

κῡφός, ή, όν, (κύπτω) bent forwards, bent, stooping, hump-backed, Od., Ar.

κύφων, ωνος, ὁ, (κῦφός) the bent yoke of the plough, Theogn. II. a sort of pillory in which criminals were fastened by the neck, Ar. 2. one who has had his neck in the pillory, a knave, Lat. furcifer, Luc.

κυψέλη, ή, any hollow vessel : a chest, box, Hdt., Ar.

Κυψελίδαι, οἱ, descendants of Cypselus, Theogn.

ΚΥ῾Ω : I. in pres. and impf., of females, to conceive, Orac. ap. Hdt., Theogn., etc. 2. rarely c. acc. to be pregnant with a child, Xen. II. in aor. 1 ἔκῡσα, Causal, of the male, to impregnate, and med. ἐκῡσάμην, of the female, to conceive, Hes.

ΚΥ῾ΩΝ, ὁ and ἡ, gen. κῠνός, dat. κῠνί, acc. κύνα, voc. κύον:—pl., nom. κύνες, gen. κυνῶν, dat. κυσί, Ep. κύνεσσι, acc. κύνας:—a dog or bitch, Hom., etc.; most commonly of hounds, Id., etc.; the Laconian breed was famous, Soph.;—νή or μὰ τὸν κύνα was the favourite oath of Socrates, Plat.: cf. τραπεζεύς. II. as a word of reproach, to denote shamelessness or audacity in women, rashness, recklessness in men, Hom. 2. at Athens a nickname of the Cynics, Arist., Anth. III. the Trag. apply the term to the ministers of the gods; the eagle is Διὸς πτηνὸς κύων Aesch.; the griffins Ζηνὸς ἀκραγεῖς κύνες Id.; the Bacchantes Λύσσης κ. Eur., etc. IV. a sea-dog, mentioned as a fish in Od. V. the dog-star, i. e. the dog of Orion, placed among the stars with its master, Il.

κω, Ion. for πω.

κῶας, τό, irreg. pl. κώεα, dat. κώεσιν, a fleece, used as bedding, Hom., Hdt. (Deriv. uncertain.)

κωβιός, ὁ, a fish of the gudgeon kind, Plat., etc.

κωδάριον [ᾰ], τό, Dim. of κώδιον, Ar.

κώδεια, ή, the head, Il. (Deriv. uncertain.)

κώδιον, τό, Dim. of κῶας, a sheepskin, fleece, used for bedding, Ar., Plat.

ΚΩ῾ΔΩΝ, ωνος, ὁ and ἡ, a bell, Aesch., Eur.:—in fortified towns an officer went round at night with a bell to challenge the sentries, and see that they were awake, Thuc.; ὡς κώδωνα ἐξαψάμενος like one with an alarm-bell in his hand, Dem. Hence

κωδωνίζω, f. Att. ιῶ, to prove by ringing, of money, Ar.

κωδωνό-κροτος, ον, ringing, jingling, as with bells, Eur.

κωδωνο-φᾰλᾰρό-πωλος, ον, with bells on his horses' trappings, Ar.

κωδωνο-φορέω, f. ήσω, to carry the bell round, to visit the sentinels, Ar.:—Pass., ἅπαντα κωδωνοφορεῖται everywhere the bell goes round, i. e. the sentinels are being visited, Id.

κώεα, κώεσσι, nom. and dat. pl. of κῶας.

ΚΩ῾ΘΩΝ, ωνος, ὁ, a Laconian drinking-vessel, Ar.

Κῶιος, α, ον, contr. Κῷος.

κώκῡμα, ατος, τό, a shriek, wail, Aesch., Soph.; and

κωκῡτός, ὁ, a shrieking, wailing, Il., Trag. II. Κωκῡτός, ὁ, Cocytus, River of Wailing (cf. Ἀχέρων), one of the rivers of hell, Od., etc. From

ΚΩΚΥ῾Ω, f. ύσω [ῡ], -ύσομαι : aor. 1 ἐκώκῡσα, Ep. κώκῡσα:—to shriek, cry, wail, mostly of women, Hom. 2. c. acc. to wail over one dead, Od., Aesch., Soph.

κωλ-αγρέτης or -ακρέτης, ου, ὁ, (κωλῆ, ἀγρέω) collector of the pieces at a sacrifice, name of a magistrate at Athens, who had charge of the public table in the Prytaneion, and paid the dicasts, Ar.; κωλαγρέτου γάλα, comically for the μισθὸς δικαστικός, Id.

κωλῆ, ή, (κῶλον) the thigh-bone with the flesh on it, the ham, esp. of a swine, Ar., Xen. Hence

κώληψ, ηπος, ή, the hollow of the knees, Lat. poples, Il.

Κωλιάς (sub. ἄκρα), άδος, ή, Colias, a promontory of Attica, with a temple of Aphroditê there, Hdt., Ar.

ΚΩ῾ΛΟΝ, τό, a limb, esp. the leg, Trag. 2. of plants, a limb or arm, Anth. II. a member of anything, as, 1. a member of a building, as the side or front, Hdt. 2. one limb or half of the race-course (δίαυλος), Aesch. 3. a member or clause of a sentence, Lat. membrum, Arist.

κώλῡμα, ατος, τό, (κωλύω) a hindrance, impediment, Eur., Thuc. II. a defence against a thing, precaution, Thuc.

κωλύμη [ῡ], ή, = κώλυμα, ἐπὶ κωλύμῃ for the purpose of hindering, Thuc.

κωλυτέον, verb. Adj. of κωλύω, one must hinder, Xen.

κωλυτής, οῦ, ὁ, (κωλύω) a hinderer, Thuc.

κωλυτικός, ή, όν, preventive, Xen. From

κωλύω [ῠ], f. ύσω [ῡ]: aor. 1 ἐκώλῡσα: pf. κεκώλῡκα:—Pass., f. κωλῡθήσομαι and in med. form κωλύσομαι: aor. 1 ἐκωλύθην [ῡ]: pf. κεκώλῡμαι:—to let, hinder, check, prevent: 1. c. acc. et inf. to hinder or prevent one from doing, Hdt., Soph., etc.; with a negative added, κ. τινὰ μὴ θανεῖν Eur., etc. :—Pass. to be hindered, τοῦ ὕδατος πιεῖν from drinking of the water, Plat.; κωλυόμεσθα μὴ μαθεῖν Eur.; rarely with part., μὴ κωλύωνται περαιούμενοι Thuc. 2. c. gen. rei, κ. τινά τινος to let or hinder one from a thing, Xen.; so, κ. τινα ἀπό τινος Id. 3. c. acc. rei, to hinder, prevent, impede, Eur., Thuc.:—Pass., μηδὲ δαπάνη κεκωλύσθω and let there be no hindrance by reason of expense, Thuc. 4. absol., ὁ κωλύσων one to hinder, Soph.; τὸ κωλῦον a hindrance, Xen. 5. often in 3 pers., οὐδὲν κωλύει there is nothing to hinder, c. acc. et inf. Hdt.; Ar.:—οὐδὲν κωλύει, absol., as a form of assent, nothing hinders, be it so, Id.

κωλώτης, ου, ὁ, prob. = ἀσκαλαβώτης, Babr.

κῶμα, ατος, τό, (κεῖμαι) deep sleep, slumber, Lat. sopor, Hom., Hes. Hence

κωμάζω, f. άσω and άσομαι: aor. 1 ἐκώμασα, poët. κώμ-: pf. κεκώμακα:—Dor. κωμάσδω, fut. άξομαι: aor. 1 imper. κωμάξατε: (κῶμος):—to go about with a party of revellers, to revel, make merry, Lat. comissari, Hes., Theogn., Eur., etc. 2. to go in festal procession, Pind., Dem. II. to celebrate a κῶμος in honour of the victor at the games, to join in festivities, Pind.; c. acc. cogn., κῶμον ἐορτάν κ. Id. 2. c. dat. pers. to approach with a κῶμος, sing in his honour, Id. 3. c. acc. pers. to honour or celebrate him in or with the κῶμος, Id. III. to break in upon in the manner

of revellers, κ. ποτὶ τὰν Ἀμαρυλλίδα Theocr. :—generally, *to burst in,* Anth.

κωμ-άρχης, ου, ὁ, (κώμη, ἄρχω) *the head man of a village,* Xen.

κωμάσδω, Dor. for κωμάζω.

κωμαστής, οῦ, ὁ, (κωμάζω) *a reveller,* Plat., Xen. 2. epith. of Bacchus, *the jolly god,* Ar.

ΚΩ'ΜΗ, ἡ, = Lat. *vicus, a village* or *country town,* opp. to a fortified city; properly a Dor. word, = Att. δῆμος, Hes., Hdt.; κατοικῆσθαι κατὰ κώμας to live *in* separate *villages* (not in walled towns), of the Medes, Hdt.; so, of a country, κατὰ κώμας οἰκεῖσθαι to have its people distributed into *villages,* Thuc.

κωμήτης, ου, ὁ, (κώμη) *a villager, countryman,* Plat., Xen. II. in a city, *one of the same quarter,* Lat. *vicinus,* Ar.; more loosely, χθονὸς κωμῆται *dwellers in* a land, Eur.

κωμῐκός, ή, όν, Lat. *comicus,* = κωμῳδικός, Aeschin.

κωμό-πολις, εως, ὁ, (κώμη) *a village-town,* i. e. a place not entitled to be called a πόλις, N. T.

κῶμος, ου, ὁ, (κώμη) properly *a village festival : a revel, carousal, merry-making,* Lat. *comissatio,* h. Hom., Theogn., etc.: it ended in the party parading the streets crowned, bearing torches, singing, dancing, and playing frolics, Ar. II. *a band of revellers, a jovial troop,* Eur. :—metaph. *a rout, band,* κ. Ἐρινύων Aesch.; of an army, Eur., etc. III. *the Ode sung* at one of these festive processions, Pind.

κῶμῦς, ῦθος, ἡ, *a bundle* of hay, Lat. *manipulus,* Theocr. (Deriv. uncertain.)

κωμῳδέω, f. ήσω, (κωμῳδός) *to represent in a comedy, to satirise, lampoon, libel,* Ar., Plat.:—Pass. *to be so satirised,* Ar. 2. κωμῳδεῖν τὰ δίκαια = κωμῳδοῦντα εἰπεῖν τὰ δ., Id. II. *to write comedies,* Luc.

κωμ-ῳδία, ἡ, *a comedy,* Ar., etc. :—Two derivs. are suggested : one from κῶμος, ᾠδή, *the revel-song ;* the other from κώμη, ᾠδή, *the village-song.* There were three periods of Attic Comedy, Old, Middle, New,— παλαιά, μέση, νέα. The Old Comedy was used to attack by name the most powerful persons of the day, ending B. C. 393 ; the Middle Comedy lost the Chorus, but still attacked notabilities under assumed characters, ending B. C. 337 ; the New was our Comedy of Manners, and may be best understood from Plautus and Terence. Hence

κωμῳδικός, ή, όν, *of comedy, comic,* Ar.

κωμῳδό-γελως, ωτος, ὁ, = κωμῳδός, Anth.

κωμῳδο-γράφος [ᾰ], ὁ, = κωμῳδιογράφος, Anth.

κωμῳδοδῐδασκᾰλία, ἡ, *the comic poet's art,* Ar. From

κωμῳδο-δῐδάσκᾰλος, ὁ, *a comic poet,* because he had to train the actors and chorus, Ar.

κωμῳδο-λοιχέω, (λείχω) *to play the parasite and buffoon,* Ar.

κωμῳδο-ποιητής, οῦ, ὁ, = κωμῳδοποιός, Ar.

κωμῳδο-ποιός, ὁ, *a maker of comedies, comic poet,* Plat.

κωμ-ῳδός, ὁ, (v. κωμῳδία) :—*a comedian,* i. e., 1. *a comic actor,* Xen., Aeschin. 2. *a comic poet,* Plat.

κώνειον, τό, *hemlock,* Lat. *cicuta* :—*hemlock-juice,* by which criminals were put to death at Athens, Ar., etc.

κωνίον, τό, Dim. of κῶνος, *a small cone,* Anth.

κωνῖτις, ιδος, ἡ, (κῶνος 1) *extracted from pine-cones,* Anth.

ΚΩ'ΝΟΣ, ου, ὁ, *the fruit of the* πεύκη, *a pine-cone,* Theocr., etc. II. *a cone,* Lat. *conus,* in Mathematics, Arist. 2. *the cone* of a helmet, Anth.

κωνο-τομέω, f. ήσω, *to make a conic section,* Anth.

κωνο-φόρος, ον, (φέρω) *bearing a cone,* Anth.

κωνωπεῖον, τό, (κώνωψ) *an Egyptian couch with mosquito-curtains ; conopium* in Horat.

κωνωπεών, ῶνος, ὁ, = foreg., Anth.

ΚΩ'ΝΩΨ, ωπος, ὁ, *a gnat, mosquito,* Lat. *culex,* Hdt., Aesch., etc.

Κῷος, α, ον, (Κῶς) *of, from the island Cos, Coan,* Hdt. II. as Subst., Κῷος (sc. βόλος), ὁ, *the highest throw with the* ἀστράγαλοι, v. Χῖος.

Κωπαΐς, αΐδος, contr. Κωπᾷς, ᾷδος, ἡ, *of* or *near Copae* (in Boeotia), ἡ Κ. λίμνη *lake Copaïs,* Strab. 2. ἐγχέλεις Κωπαΐδες *eels from lake Copaïs,* Ar.

κωπεύς, έως, ὁ, only in pl. κωπέες, Att. κωπῆς, *pieces of wood fit for making oars, oar-spars,* Hdt., Ar., etc.

κωπεύω, f. σω, (κώπη) *to propel with oars,* Anth.

κώπη, ή, (from Root ΚΑΠ, Lat. *cap-io*) *any handle :* 1. *the handle of an oar,* and generally *an oar,* Od., Pind., Att.; νερτέρᾳ προσήμενος κώπη, = θαλαμίτης, metaph. of a man of low rank, Aesch.; παραπέμπειν ἐφ' ἕνδεκα κώπαις, a proverb of dub. origin, meaning 'to escort with all the honours,' Ar. :—poët. to express ships, σὺν κώπᾳ χιλιοναύτᾳ, of Agamemnon's fleet, Eur. 2. *the handle of a sword, the haft, hilt,* Lat. *capulus,* Hom., Soph. 3. *the handle of a key,* Od. 4. *the haft of a torch,* Eur.

κωπήεις, εσσα, εν, *hilted,* Il.

κωπηλᾰτέω, f. ήσω, *to pull an oar :* metaph. *of any similar motion forwards and backwards,* as of a carpenter using an auger, Eur. From

κωπ-ηλάτης [ᾰ], ου, ὁ, (ἐλαύνω) *a rower,* Polyb.

κωπ-ήρης, ες, (*ἄρω) *furnished with oars,* Aesch., Eur., Thuc. II. *holding the oar,* χείρ Eur.

κωπίον, τό, Dim. of κώπη, Ar.

κώρα, ἡ, Dor. for κούρη.

κώριον, τό, Dor. Dim. of κούρα, *a little girl,* Ar.

κῶρος, ὁ, Dor. for κοῦρος.

κωροσύνα, ἡ, Dor. for κουροσύνη, Theocr.

Κωρύκιος [ῠ], α, ον, *Corycian* (from the Corycian cave in Mt. Parnassus), Soph.; κορυφαὶ Κ. *the peaks of* Parnassus, Eur.; also **Κωρυκὶς πέτρα** Aesch.

ΚΩ'ΡΥΚΟΣ, ὁ, *a leathern sack* or *wallet for provisions,* Od. 2. in the gymnasium, *a large leathern sack hung up,* filled with fig-grains (κεγχραμίδες), *flour,* or *sand, for the athletes to strike,* Arist.

Κώρυκος, ὁ, *a promontory of Cilicia,* h. Hom., Thuc.

Κῶς, Ep. **Κόως,** ἡ, gen. Κῶ, *the island Cos,* opposite Caria, Hom. :—Κόωνδε *to Cos,* Il.

κῶς, Ion. for πῶς. II. enclit. **κως,** Ion. for πως.

κωτίλλοισαι, Dor. for -οῦσαι, part. pl. fem. of sq.

κωτίλλω, only in pres., *to prattle, chatter,* Lat. *garrire,* mostly with notion of *wheedling,* Hes., Theogn., etc. II. trans. *to talk over, attempt to wheedle,* Theogn., Soph. (Deriv. unknown.) Hence

κωτίλος, η, ον, of a swallow, *twittering,* Anacr., etc. : of persons, *chattering, prattling, babbling,* Lat. *garrulus,* Theogn., Theocr. II. metaph. *lively, expressive,* Theocr., Anth.

κωφός, ή, όν, (κόπ-τω) radical sense, *blunt, dull, obtuse.*

κωφὸν βέλος the blunt, dull shaft, opp. to ὀξύ, Il. II. metaph. : 1. dumb, mute, κύματι κωφῷ with dumb wave, before it breaks, Ib.; κωφὴν γαῖαν ἀεικίζει dishonours the dumb, senseless earth, Ib.; τὰ μὲν ἄλλα ἔσκε κωφά the other parts of the ground sounded dull, opp. to the ringing of the hollow parts, Hdt.; ὁ κ. λιμήν, prob. the bay of Munychia, as opp. to the noisy Peiræus, Xen. 2. after Hom., of men, dumb, Orac. ap. Hdt. : deaf and dumb, Id. 3. deaf, Lat. surdus, h. Hom., Aesch., etc. 4. of the mind, dull, stupid, Lat. fatuus, Soph.; also senseless, unmeaning, κ. καὶ παλαί ἔπη Id. Hence

κωφότης, ητος, ἡ, deafness, Plat., Dem., etc.

κῴχετο, crasis for καὶ ᾤχετο, 3 sing. impf. of οἴχομαι.

κῶψον, crasis for καὶ ὕψον.

Λ

Λ λ, λάμβδα or λάβδα, τό, indecl., eleventh letter of the Gr. Alphabet: as a numeral λ′ = 30, but λ = 30,000. 1. Att. λ is sometimes represented by ρ, as κλίβανος κρίβανος, γλώσσαλγος γλώσσαργος, ναύκραρος ναύκληρος, ἀλκ-ή ἀρκ-εῖν : so, ὁλᾶς Θέωλος κόλαξ were lisping pronunc. for ὁρᾶς Θέωρος κόραξ, Ar. 2. Dor. λ becomes ν, as, ἦνθον φίλτατος for ἦλθον φίλτατος ; whereas Att. λ sometimes replaces ν, as, λίτρον πλεύμων for νίτρον πνεύμων. 3. initial λ is dropt, as εἴβω for λείβω, αἴψηρὸς ἀφύσσω ἄχνη for λαιψηρὸς λαφύσσω λάχνη. 4. Ep. Poets double λ, metri grat., esp. after the augment, as, ἔλλαβε ἐλλιτάνευε ; and in compds., as in τρίλλιστος :—and Homer omits λ, where two come together, metri grat., as Ἀχιλεύς. 5. δ sometimes becomes λ, cf. Δ δ, II. 5. 6. γ and λ are interchanged in μόγις μόλις. 7. ν before λ becomes λ, as in συλλαμβάνω ἐλλείπω.

λᾶ-, insep. Prefix with intensive force, as in λά-μαχος very warlike, λα-κατάρατος much accursed.

ΛΑ͂ΑΣ, ὁ, acc. λᾶαν, gen. and dat. λᾶος, λᾶι ; dual λᾶε ; pl., gen. λάων, dat. λάεσσι Ep. λάεσσι :—in Att. also contr. λᾶς, acc. λᾶν : a gen. λάου in Soph. (as if λᾶας was of first decl.) :—Lat. lapis, a stone, Hom., etc.

λάβδα, τό, indecl., v. λάμβδα, Ar., etc.

λαβεῖν, aor. 2 inf. of λαμβάνω.

λαβή, ἡ, (λαβεῖν) the part intended for grasping, a handle, haft, Dem. ; λαβαὶ ἀμφίστομοι of a cup, Soph. II. as a pugilistic term, a grip or hold, ὥσπερ ἀθλητὴς λαβὴν ζητεῖν Plut. :—metaph. a handle, occasion, opportunity, λαβὴν διδόναι, Lat. ausam praebere, Ar. ; so, λ. παραδιδόναι, παρέχειν Id., Plat.

λαβῆν, Dor. for λαβεῖν, aor. 2 inf. of λαμβάνω.

λάβῃσι, Ep. for λαβῇ, 3 sing. aor. 2 subj. of λαμβάνω.

λαβοῖσα, Dor. for -οῦσα, aor. 2 part. fem. of λαμβάνω.

λαβρ-ᾱγόρης, ου, ὁ, (ἀγορεύω) a bold, rash talker, braggart, Il.

λάβραξ, ᾱκος, ὁ, (λάβρος) a ravenous sea-fish, perh. the bass, Ar.

λαβρεύομαι, Dep. (λάβρος) to talk rashly, brag, Il.

λαβρο-πόδης, ου, ὁ, (πούς) rapid of foot, rushing, Anth.

λαβρο-ποτέω, f. ήσω, (πότος) to drink hard, Anth.

ΛΑ͂ΒΡΟΣ [ᾰ by nature], ον, I. Hom. of wind, rain, etc., furious, boisterous, Hdt. ; λ. πῦρ, κύματα, πόντος, etc., Eur. II. after Hom., of men, boisterous, turbulent, violent, Theogn., Soph., etc. 2. greedy, Pind., Eur. III. Adv. λάβρως, violently, furiously, Theogn. 2. greedily, Aesch.

λαβροσύνη, ἡ, (λάβρος) violence, greed, Anth.

λαβρό-σῠτος, ον, (σεύω) rushing furiously, Aesch.

λαβύρινθος [ῠ], ὁ, a labyrinth or maze, a building consisting of halls connected by tortuous passages, Hdt. II. any spiral body, as a snail, Anth. ; ἐκ σχοίνων λαβ. a bow-net of rushes, Theocr. (Origin uncertain.)

λάβω, aor. 2 subj. of λαμβάνω :—λαβών, part.

λᾰγᾱρίζομαι, Pass. to be slack or gaunt through hunger, to starve, Ar. ; and

λᾰγᾱρόομαι, Pass. to be or become slack : of frozen water, to be in the act of thawing, Anth. From

ΛΑΓᾰΡΟ͂Σ, ά, όν, slack, hollow, sunken, of the flanks, Xen. :—κατὰ τὸ λαγαρώτατον in the least defensible part, Plut. 2. slack, loose, pliant, Xen.

λᾱ-γέτης, ου, Dor. λᾱ-γέτας, α, ὁ, (λαός, ἁγέομαι) leader of the people, Pind.

λάγῑνος [ᾰ], η, ον, of the hare, Aesch.

λάγιον, τό, Dim. of λαγώς, a leveret, Xen.

λαγνεία, ἡ, lasciviousness, lust, Xen. From

ΛΑΓΝΟΣ, η, ον, lascivious, lustful, Arist.

λᾰγω-δαίτης, ου, ὁ, (δαίω) hare-devouring, Aesch.

λάγο-θήρας, ου, ὁ, (θηράω) a hare-hunter, Anth.

λᾱγο-κτονέω, f. ήσω, (κτείνω) to kill hares, Anth.

λᾱγός, οῦ, ὁ, collat. form of λαγώς, q. v.

λάγῡνος, ὁ, a flask, flagon, Lat. lagēna, Anth., etc.

λαγχάνω (from Root ΛΑΧ), f. λήξομαι, Ion. λάξομαι :—aor. 2 ἔλαχον, Ep. ἔλλαχον, λάχον (for λέλαχον v. infr. IV) : pf. εἴληχα : plqpf. εἰλήχειν ; poët. and Ion. pf. λέλογχα : 3 sing. plqpf. ἐλελόγχη, Dor. λελόγχη :—Pass., aor. 1 ἐλήχθην : pf. εἴλημμαι. I. c. acc. rei, to obtain by lot, by fate, by the will of the gods, Hom. ; with inf. added, ἔλαχον πολιὴν ἅλα ναιέμεν I had the sea for my portion to dwell in, says Poseidon, Il. ; ἔλαχ' ἄναξ δούλην σ' ἔχειν Eur. :—of the genius presiding over one's life, ἐμὲ μὲν Κὴρ λάχε Il. ; esp. in pf. to be the tutelary deity of a place, to protect it, θεοῖσιν, οἳ Περσίδα γῆν λελόγχασι Hdt. :—absol., πρὸς Θύμβρης ἔλαχον Λύκιοι had their post assigned near Thymbra, Il. 2. of public officers, to obtain an office by lot, (v. κύαμος II) ; ἀρχὴν λαχεῖν, opp. to χειροτονηθῆναι to be elected), Ar. ; so, c. inf. ὃ λαχὼν πολεμαρχέειν he who had the lot to be polemarch, Hdt. ; οἱ λαχόντες βουλευταὶ (sc. εἶναι), Oratt. ; and absol., οἱ λαχόντες those on whom the lot fell, Thuc. 3. as Att. law-term, λαγχάνειν δίκην to obtain leave to bring on a suit, Plat., Oratt. ; and (without δίκην) λαγχάνειν τινι to bring an action against one, Oratt. II. c. gen. partit. to get one's share of, become possessed of, Hom., Att. III. absol. to draw (i. e. obtain) the lot, Od. : cast lots, N. T. IV. Causal Ep. redupl. aor. λέλαχον, to put in possession of a thing, πυρὸς λελαχεῖν τινα to grant one the right of funeral fire, Il. V. intr. to fall to one's lot or share, Od., Eur.

λἄγω-βόλον, τό, (βάλλω) a staff for flinging at hares, used as a shepherd's staff, Lat. pedum, Theocr.

λᾰγῴδιον, τό, Dim. of λαγώς, a leveret, Ar.

λᾰγών, όνος, ἡ, (λαγαρός) the hollow on each side below the ribs, the flank, Eur.; in pl. the flanks, Id., Ar. II. metaph. any hollow, Anth., Plut.

λᾰγωο-βόλον, τό, = λαγωβόλον, Anth.

λᾰγωός, οῦ, ὁ, Ep. for λαγώς.

λᾰγῴος, α, ον, contr. for λαγώιος, of the hare, Ar.:— τὰ λαγῷα (sc. κρέα), hare's flesh, and, generally, dainties, delicacies, ζῆν ἐν πᾶσι λαγώοις Id. From

ΛΑ͂ΓΩ͂Σ, ὁ, gen. λαγώ or λαγῶ; acc. λαγών, λαγώ or λαγῶ: pl., nom. λαγῴ, acc. λαγώς:—Ion. and poët. λαγός, οῦ:—Ep. λᾰγωός, οῦ:—a hare, Lat. lepus, Hom., Aesch., etc.

λᾰγω-σφᾰγία, ἡ, (σφαγή) a killing of hares, Anth.

λάδᾰνον, Ion. λήδανον, τό, an aromatic gum, gummastich, Hdt. (Foreign word.)

λαέρτης, ου, ὁ, a kind of ant: as pr. n. the father of Ulysses, Od.; also Λαέρτιος, ου, and Λάρτιος, Soph.

λάζομαι, Dep., poët. for λαμβάνω: Ep. 3 sing. impf. λάζε-το, 3 pl. opt. λαζοίατο (for -οιντο): Dor. imper. λάζεο or λάσθεο:—to take, seize, grasp, Il.; ὀδὰξ λαζοίατο γαῖαν may they bite the dust, Ib.; metaph., πάλιν δ' ὅ γε λάζετο μῦθον he took back, i. e. altered his speech, Hom. II. the form λάζυμαι occurs in h. Hom. and Eur.

λάθα, ἡ, Dor. for λήθη.

λάθε, Ep. for ἔλαθε, 3 sing. aor. 2 of λανθάνω.

λᾰθεῖν, Ep. λᾰθέμεν, aor. 2 inf. of λανθάνω. Hence

λᾰθητικός, ή, όν, likely to escape notice, Arist.

λᾰθῐ-κηδής, ές, (κῆδος) banishing care, Il., Anth.

λᾰθί-πονος, ον, (λήθη) forgetful of sorrow, Soph.; βίοτος ὀδυνᾶν λ. a life forgetful of pain, Id.

λᾰθί-φθογγος, ον, robbing of voice, Hes.

λᾰθοίατο, Ep. for -οιντο, aor. 2 med. opt. of λανθάνω.

λᾶθος, εως, τό, Dor. for λῆθος.

λάθρα, λάθρᾳ, v. sub λάθρη.

λαθραῖος, ον, secret, covert, clandestine, furtive, Aesch., Soph.; λ. ὠδίς one born in secret child-birth, Eur.:— Adv. -ως, Aesch., etc.

λάθρη, Att. λάθρᾳ, Adv. (λᾰθεῖν) secretly, covertly, by stealth, treacherously, Hom.; λάθρη γυῖα βαρύνεται imperceptibly, Il.; so in Att., Soph., etc. 2. c. gen. without the knowledge of, unknown to, λάθρη Λαομέδοντος Il.; λάθρη τῶν στρατηγῶν Hdt.; so in Att.

λᾰθρηδόν, Adv. = foreg., Anth.

λᾰθρίδιος [ῑ], α, ον, poët. for λάθριος: Adv. -ως, Anth.

λάθριος, ον, later form of λαθραῖος, Theocr.:—neut. pl. as Adv., treacherously, Id.

λαθρο-βόλος, ον, (βάλλω) hitting secretly, δόναξ Anth.

λαθρο-δάκνης, ου, ὁ, (δάκνω) biting secretly, Anth.

λαθρο-πόδης, ου, ὁ, (πούς) stealthy-paced, Anth.

λάθυρος, ὁ, a kind of pulse: pl. λάθυρα Babr.

λάθω [ᾰ], aor. 2 subj., and λάθων, part., of λανθάνω.

λαι-, λαισ-, insep. prefix, = λα- in λαίμαργος, etc.

λαία, ἡ, Dor. for λεία.

λαῖγξ, γγος, ἡ, Dim. of λᾶας, a small stone, pebble, Od.

λαίθ-αργος, ον, (λᾰθεῖν) biting secretly, i. e. without barking, of a dog, Ar.

λαικάζω, f. άσομαι, to wench, Ar. Hence

λαικαστής, οῦ, ὁ, a wencher, Ar.:—fem. λαικάστρια, a wench, harlot, Id.

λαῖλαψ, απος, ἡ, (from λα-, λαι- intensive):—a tempest, furious storm, hurricane, Hom.

λαῖμα, ατος, τό, perh. the same as λαιμός, Ar.

λαιμαργία, ἡ, gluttony, Plat. From

λαί-μαργος, ον, very greedy, gluttonous, Arist.

λαιμη-τόμος, ον, poët. for λαιμοτόμος, Anth.

λαιμο-δακής, ές, (δᾰκεῖν) throat-biting, Anth.

λαιμο-πέδη, ἡ, a dog-collar, Anth. II. a springe for catching birds, Id.

λαιμό-ρῠτος, ον, (ῥέω) gushing from the throat, Eur.

ΛΑΙΜΟ͂Σ, οῦ, ὁ, the throat, gullet, Hom., Eur. Hence

λαιμό-τμητος, ον, (τέμνω) with the throat severed, Eur.

λαιμο-τόμος, ον, (τέμνω) throat-cutting, Eur., Anth. II. proparox. λαιμότομος, ον, with the throat cut, severed by the throat, Eur.; Γοργοῦς λαιμότομοι σταλαγμοί the blood dripping from the Gorgon's severed head, Id.

λαῖνα, ἡ, = χλαῖνα, Lat. laena, Strab.

λαῖνεος, α, ον, = sq., Il., Eur.

λάϊνος [ᾰ], η, ον, (λᾶας) of stone or marble, Hom., etc.; λάϊνον ἕσσο χιτῶνα thou hadst put on a coat of stone, i. e. thou hadst been stoned to death, Il. 2. metaph. stony-hearted, Theocr.

λαῖον, Dor. for λήιον.

ΛΑΙΟ͂Σ, ά, όν, Lat. laevus, left, λαιᾶς χειρός on the left hand, Aesch.; πρὸς λαιᾷ χερί Eur.

λαιο-τομέω, f. ήσω, (λαῖον, τέμνω) to reap corn, Theocr.

λαῖς, Dor. for ληῖς.

λαισήιον, τό, (λάσιος) a kind of shield or target, lighter than the ἀσπίς, covered with raw hides, Il., Hdt.

λαῖτμα, ατος, τό, (λαιμός) the depth or gulf of the sea, μέγα λαῖτμα θαλάσσης, ἁλὸς λ. Hom.; alone, λαῖτμα μέγ' ἐκπερόωσι Od.

ΛΑ͂ΙΦΟΣ, εος, τό, a tattered garment, rags, in sing. and pl., Od. II. a piece of cloth or canvas, a sail, Aesch.; in pl., Soph.

λαιψηρός, ά, όν, = αἰψηρός, light, nimble, swift, Il., Pind., Eur.:—neut. pl. as Adv. swiftly, Eur.

λᾰκάζω, = λάσκω, to shout, howl, Aesch.

Λάκαινα [λᾰ], ἡ, fem. of Λάκων, Lat. Lacaena, a Laconian woman, Theogn., etc. II. as fem. Adj. = Λακωνική, Hdt., Eur. etc.

λᾰκαταπύγων [ῠ], ον, = καταπύγων with prefix λα-, very lascivious, Ar.

λάκε [ᾰ], Ep. for ἔλακε, 3 sing. aor. 2 of λάσκω.

Λᾰκεδαίμων, ονος, ἡ, voc. -ον, Lacedaemon, the capital of Laconia, and Laconia itself, Hom., Hdt., etc. II. as Adj., Hdt., Eur.; but regul. Adj. Λᾰκεδαιμόνιος, α, ον, of persons, Hdt., etc.

λᾰκεῖν, aor. 2 inf. of λάσκω. Hence

λᾰκέρυζα, ἡ, one that screams or cries, λ. κορώνη a cawing crow, Hes.; λ. κύων a yelping dog, ap. Plat.

λᾰκέω, Dor. for ληκέω.

λᾰκίζω, to tear, Anth. From

λᾰκίς, ίδος, ἡ, (λάσκω) a rent, rending, Aesch.; in pl., Id.; λακίδες πέπλων tatters, Ar.

λάκισμα, τό, (λᾰκίζω) in pl. tatters, Eur.

λᾰκιστός, ή, όν, (λᾰκίζω) torn, μόρος λ. death by rending, Luc.

λακκό-πλουτος, ὁ, *pit-wealth*, Comic nickname of Callias, who found a *buried* treasure, Plut.

ΛΑ'ΚΚΟΣ, ὁ, *a pond* for water-fowl, Lat. *vivarium*, Hdt., Dem. **2.** *a pit, reservoir*, Hdt., Xen.

λακ-πάτητος [πᾰ], *ον*, (λάξ) *trampled on*, Soph.

λακτίζω, f. Att. ιῶ: pf. λελάκτικα: (λάξ):—*to kick with the heel* or *foot, kick at, spurn*, Od. ; φλὸξ αἰθέρα λακτίζοισα *flames lashing* heaven, Pind. ; κραδία φόβῳ φρένα λακτίζει my heart 'knocks at my ribs' for fear, Aesch. ; τὸν πεσόντα λακτίσαι *to trample on* the fallen, Id. ; τὴν θύραν λ. *to kick at* the door, Ar. :—Pass., ὑπὸ ἵππου λακτισθείς Xen. **2.** absol. *to kick, struggle*, of one dying, Od. : proverb., λ. πρὸς κέντρα *to kick* against the pricks, Pind., Aesch., etc.

λάκτισμα, τό, *a trampling on*, c. gen., Aesch. ; and

λακτιστής, οῦ, ὁ, *one who kicks*, ἵπποι λ. *kicking* horses, Xen. ; λ. ληνοῦ *a treader* of the wine-press, Anth.

Λάκων [ᾱ], ωνος, ὁ, *a Laconian* or *Lacedaemonian*, of men, as Λάκαινα of women, Pind., Ar., etc. **II.** as Adj. *Laconian*, Anth.

Λακωνίζω, *to imitate the Lacedaemonians*, Plat., Xen. etc. **II.** *to be in the Lacedaemonian interest*, *to Laconise*, Xen. ; and

Λακωνικός, ή, όν, *Laconian*, Ar., etc. **II.** as Subst. **1.** ἡ Λακωνική (sub. γῆ), *Laconia*, Ar., etc. **2.** Λακωνικαί (sub. ἐμβάδες), αἱ, *Laconian shoes*, used by men, Id. **3.** τὸ Λακωνικόν *the state of Lacedaemon*, Hdt.

Λακωνίς, ίδος, pecul. fem. of foreg., h. Hom.

Λακωνισμός, ὁ, (Λακωνίζω) *imitation of Lacedaemonian manners*, Cic. **II.** *a being in the Lacedaemonian interest*, *Laconism*, Xen.

Λακωνιστής, οῦ, ὁ, (Λακωνίζω) *one who imitates the Lacedaemonians*, Plut. **II.** *one who takes part with them, a Laconiser*, Xen.

Λακωνο-μᾰνέω, f. ήσω, (μαίνομαι) *to have a Lacono-mania*, Ar.

λᾰλᾰγέω, f. ήσω, (λαλέω) *to prattle, to babble*, Pind. : of birds and grasshoppers, *to chirrup, chirp*, Theocr.

λᾰλάγημα, ατος, τό, *prattle, babbling*, Anth.

λᾰλέω, f. ήσω, (λαλός) *to talk, chat, prattle, babble*, Ar., etc. :—generally, *to talk, say*, Soph. **2.** c. acc. *to talk of*, Theocr. **3.** in late Gr., just like λέγω, *to speak*, N. T., Thuc. :—Pass., λαληθήσεται σοι *it shall be told* thee, N. T. **II.** the proper sense, *to chatter*, is sometimes opp. to articulate speech, as of monkeys, λαλοῦσι μὲν φράζουσι δὲ οὔ Plut. ; of locusts, *to chirp*, Theocr. **III.** of musical sounds, αὐλῷ λαλεῖν Id. Hence

λάληθρος, ον, *talkative*, Anth. ; and

λάλημα [λᾰ], ατος, τό, *talk, prattle*, Mosch. **II.** *a prater*, Soph., Eur.

λᾰλητέος, α, ον, verb. Adj., *to be talked of*, Anth.

λᾰλητικός, ή, όν, (λαλέω) *given to babbling*, Ar.

λᾰλήτρίς, ίδος, ἡ, (λαλέω) *a talker, prattler*, Anth.

λᾰλιά, ή, (λαλέω) *talking, talk, chat*, Ar., Anth. **2.** *speech, conversation*, N. T. ; *talkativeness, loquacity*, Aeschin. **II.** *a form of speech, dialect*, N. T.

λᾰλιός, ά, όν, poët. for λάλος, Anth.

λάλλαι, αἱ, (λαλέω) *pebbles*, from their *prattling* in the stream, Theocr.

λᾰλόεις, εσσα, εν, poët. for sq., Anth.

ΛΑ'ΛΟΣ [ᾰ], ον, *talkative, babbling, loquacious*, Eur., Plat., etc. :—metaph., λάλοι πτέρυγες Anth. :—irr. Comp. λαλίστερος Ar. : Sup. λαλίστατος Eur.

λᾶμα, Dor. for λῆμα.

λαμά, Hebr. words, *what ? why ?* N. T.

Λᾱμαχ-ίππιον, τό, *little jockey-Lamachus*, Ar.

Λά-μᾰχος [ᾰ], ον, (λα-, μάχομαι) *Eager-for-fight*, a well-known Athenian general, Ar., Thuc.

λαμβάνω (from Root ΛΑΒ): f. λήψομαι, Ion. λάμψομαι, Dor. λαψεῦμαι or –οῦμαι :— aor. 2 ἔλαβον, Ep. ἔλλᾰβον; Ion. λάβεσκον; imper. λαβέ :—pf. εἴληφα, Ion. λελάβηκα: plqpf. εἰλήφειν, Ion. ;ing. λελάβηκεε : —Med., aor. ; ἐλαβόμην, Ep. ἐλλ , Ep. redupl. inf. λελαβέσθαι :—Pass., f. ληφθήσομαι :—aor. 1 ἐλήφθην, Ion. ἐλάμφθην :—pf. εἴλημμαι, in Trag. λέλημμαι; Ion. λέλαμμαι. The orig. sense of the word is twofold, one (more active) *to take ;* the other (more passive) *to receive :* **I.** *to take*, **1.** *to take hold of, grasp, seize*, Hom., etc. ; the part *seized* in gen., the *whole* in acc., τὴν πτέρυγος λάβεν *caught her by* the wing, Il. ; γούνων λάβε κούρην Od., etc. :—then, with gen. of *part* only, ποδῶν, γούνων, κόρυθος λάβεν *took hold of* the feet, etc., Il. **2.** *to take by violence, seize, carry off as prize* or ὥ ;τῃ, Hom. **3.** λ. δίκην, ποινάς, Lat. *sumere poenas, to exact* punishment, Eur., etc. ; v. infr. II. 3. **4.** of passions, feelings, etc., *to seize*, Hom., etc. ; of fever/ and sudden illnesses, *to attack*, Att. **5.** of a deity, *to seize, possess*, τινά Hdt. : of darkness, and the like, *to occupy, possess*, Aesch. **6.** *to catch, come upon, overtake*, as an enemy, Hom., Hdt. : *to catch, find, come upon*, λ. τινὰ μοῦνον Hdt., etc. : also, *to catch, find out, detect*, Lat. *deprehendo*, Id. : so Pass., ἐπ' αὐτοφώρῳ εἰλημμένος *caught in* the act, Ar. **7.** λ. τινὰ ὁρκίοισι *to bind* him by oaths, Hdt. **8.** *to take as an assistant*, Soph. **9.** τὴν Ἴδην λαβὼν ἐς ἀριστερὴν χέρα *taking, keeping* Ida to your left ; so, λ. ἐν δεξιᾷ Thuc. **10.** λ. Ἑλληνίδα ἐσθῆτα *to assume* it, Hdt. **11.** *to apprehend by the senses*, Soph., Plat. :—*to seize with the mind, apprehend, comprehend*, Hdt., etc. :—*to take*, i.e. *understand*, a thing *so and so*, e.g. a passage of an author, Lat. *accipere*, Hdt., Thuc., etc. **12.** *to take in hand, undertake*, Hdt. **13.** the part. λαβών is almost pleon., as, λαβὼν κύσε χεῖρα *took and* kissed, Od. ; so in Att. **II.** *to receive :* **1.** *to have given one, to get, gain, win*, Hom., etc. :—also in bad sense, ὄνειδος Soph. ; θάνατον Eur., etc. **2.** *to receive in marriage*, Hdt., Xen. **3.** λ. δίκην *to receive*, i. e. *suffer*, punishment, as we say, *to catch it*, Lat. *dare poenas*, Hdt., Eur. : —an unusual sense, v. supr. 11. 3. **4.** λ. ὅρκον *to accept* an oath as a test, Arist. ; λ. λόγον *to demand* an account, Xen. **5.** *to conceive*, Aesch. **6.** *to receive as produce* or *profit*, Ar., Plat. ; *to purchase*, Ar. **7.** *to admit of*, Pind. **8.** of persons subject to feelings, passions, and the like, λ. θυμόν *to take heart*, Od. ; so, periphr. λ. φόβον = φοβεῖσθαι, Soph., etc. ; so, λ. ὕψος = ὑψοῦσθαι, Thuc. ; λ. νόσον (as we say) *'to take* a cold,' Plat. ; so, αἱ οἰκίαι ἐπάλξεις λαμβάνουσι *receiving* battlements, *having* battlements *added*, Thuc.

B. Med. *to take hold of, lay hold on*, c. gen., σχεδίης Od., Hdt., etc.   2. of place, λ. τῶν ὁρῶν *to take to* the mountains, *reach, gain* them, Thuc.

λάμβδα, λαμβδᾱκίζω, λαμβδᾱκισμός, v. sub Λ λ. init.

Λάμιᾶ, ἡ, (λαμός = λαιμός) *a monster said to feed on man's flesh, a bugbear* to frighten children with, Ar.

Λάμνος, Λαμνόθεν, Λαμνιάς, Dor. for Λημν-.

λαμπᾰδ-αρχία, ἡ, (ἄρχος) *the superintendence of the* λαμπαδηδρομία, a branch of the Gymnasiarchia, Arist.

λαμπᾰδη-δρομία, ἡ, (δρόμος) *the torch-race*, an Athenian ceremony at the festivals of the fire-gods Prometheus, Hephaestus, and Athena, in which the runners carried lighted torches, from the joint altar of these gods in the outer Cerameicus to the Acropolis; after the Persian war Pan received a like honour, Hdt.

λαμπᾰδηφορία, Ion. -ίη, ἡ, = λαμπαδηδρομία, Hdt.

λαμπᾰδη-φόρος, ὁ, (φέρω) *a torch-bearer*, Aesch.

λαμπάδιον [ᾰδ], τό, Dim. of λαμπάς, *a small torch*, Plat.   II. *a bandage* for wounds, Ar.

λαμπᾰδ-οῦχος, ον, (ἔχω) *torch-carrying, bright-beaming*, Eur.

λαμπάς, άδος, ἡ, (λάμπω) *a torch*, Aesch., Soph., etc.: *a beacon-light*, Aesch.:—later, *an oil-lamp*, N. T., Anth.   2. metaph. of the sun, Soph., Eur., etc.; ἡ ἐπιοῦσα λ. the coming *light*, i. e. the next day, Eur.   II. *the torch-race*, like λαμπαδηδρομία, Hdt.; λαμπάδα δραμεῖν to run *the race*, Ar.

λαμπάς, Adj., poët. fem. of λαμπρός, *gleaming with torches*, Soph.

λάμπεσκε, 3 sing. Ion. impf. of λάμπω.

λαμπετάω, = λάμπω, *to shine*, only in Ep. part. λαμπετόων, *shining*, ὄσσε δέ οἱ πυρὶ λαμπετόωντι ἐΐκτην Hom.

λάμπη, ἡ, = λαμπάς, *a torch*, Aesch.: *light*, Id.

λαμπηδών, ἡ, (λάμπω) *lustre*, Plut.

Λάμπος, ὁ, one of the horses of Aurora, *Bright*, Od.

λάμπ-ουρος, ον, (οὐρά) as a dog's name, *Firetail*, Theocr.

λαμπρός, ά, όν, (λάμπω) *bright, brilliant, radiant*, of the sun and stars, the eyes, etc., Il., Att.   2. of white objects, *bright*, Od., Hdt.   3. of water, *bright, limpid*, Aesch., etc.; of the air, Eur.   4. of the voice, *clear, sonorous, distinct*, Lat. *clarus*, Dem.; so, λαμπρὰ κηρύσσειν Eur.   5. metaph. of vigorous action, λ. ἄνεμος *a fresh keen* wind, Hdt.; λ. καὶ μέγας καθιεὶς swooping down like *a fresh* and mighty breeze, Ar.; λαμπρὸς φανήσεται he will come *vigorously* forth, Eur.:—so Adv., λαμπρῶς *vigorously*, Thuc.   6. metaph. also, *clear, manifest, decisive*, Aesch., Thuc.: —so Adv., λαμπρῶς κοὐδὲν αἰνικτηρίως λελυμένων λ. τῶν σπονδῶν Thuc.; λαμπρῶς ἐλέγετο it was said *without concealment*, Id.   II. of persons, *well-known, illustrious*, Hdt., Dem.: also *magnificent, munificent*, Lat. *splendidus, clarus*, Dem., etc.   2. *bright, joyous*, Soph.   III. of outward appearance, *splendid, brilliant*, Xen.; of youthful bloom, Thuc.: —so of dress, etc., Ar., etc.:—Adv., λαμπρότατα *most splendidly*, Xen. Hence

λαμπρότης, ητος, ἡ, *brilliancy, splendour*, Hdt., Att.: —in pl. *distinctions*, Thuc.   2. *splendid conduct, munificence*, Dem.

λαμπροφωνία, Ion. -ίη, ἡ, *clearness and loudness of voice*, Hdt. From

λαμπρό-φωνος, ον, (φωνή) *clear-voiced*, Dem.

λαμπρύνω [ῡ]; 3 sing. pf. pass. λελάμπρυνται: (λαμπρός): —*to make bright* or *brilliant*, Xen.:—Med., ἐλαμπρύνοντο τὰς ἀσπίδας *polished their* shields, Id.:— Pass., ὄμμασιν λαμπρύνεται is *made clear*-sighted, Aesch.; λελάμπρυνται κόρας Soph. ap. Ar.:—also *to be* or *become clear* or *notorious*, Eur.   II. Med. *to make oneself splendid, pride oneself on* a thing, *distinguish oneself in*, c. dat., Id., Thuc.

λαμπτήρ, ῆρος, ὁ, (λάμπω) *a stand* or *grate* for pine and other wood used *for lighting rooms*, Od.; ὦ χαῖρε, λ. νυκτός thou that lightest up the night, of the beacon-fire, Aesch.; ἕσπεροι λαμπτῆρες the evening *watch-fires*, Soph.   2. generally, = λαμπάς, Eur., Xen.

λαμπτηρ-ουχία, ἡ, (ἔχω) *a holding of torches, watchfire*, Aesch.

ΛΑ'ΜΠΩ, f. ψω: aor. 1 ἔλαμψα: pf. λέλαμπα (in pres. sense): Med., f. λάμψομαι:—*to give light, shine, beam, be bright, brilliant, radiant*, of the gleam of arms, Il.; of the eyes, Ib.; of fire, Soph.:—Med. or Pass., λαμπομένης κόρυθος Il., etc.   2. of sound, *to be clear, ring loud and clear*, Soph.   3. metaph. *to shine forth, to be famous* or *conspicuous*, Aesch., Eur., etc.   4. of persons, φαιδρὸς λάμποντι μετώπῳ with *beaming* face, Ar.: *to shine, gain glory*, Id.   II. trans. *to make to shine, light up*, Eur., Anth.

λαμῡρία, ἡ, *audacity, impudence*, Plut. From

λᾰμῠρός, ά, όν, (λαμός, = λαιμός) *gluttonous, greedy*, Theocr.   II. metaph. *bold, wanton, impudent*, Xen., Plut.

λαμφθῆναι, Ion. aor. 1 pass. inf. of λαμβάνω.

λάμψομαι, Ion. for λήψομαι, f. med. of λαμβάνω.

λανθάνω and **λήθω** (from Root ΛΑΘ): impf. ἐλάνθανον, ἐλάνθασκε, Ep. λῆθον, 3 sing. Ion. λήθεσκεν: λήσω, Dor. λᾱσῶ:—aor. 2 ἔλαθον:—pf. λέληθα: plqpf. ἐλελήθειν, Att. 2 and 3 sing. ἐλελήθης, -θη, Ion. ἐλελήθεε.   B. Causal λήθω, aor. 2 λέλαθον, v. infr. B.   C. Med. and Pass. λανθάνομαι; λήθομαι Il., Trag., Dor. λάθομαι [ᾱ]: Ep. impf. λανθανόμην:— f. λήσομαι; Dor. λᾱσεῦμαι; also λελήσομαι:—aor. 1 ἐλησάμην; also λήσθην, Dor. inf. λασθῆναι:—aor. 2 ἐλᾰθόμην, Ep. λαθ-; also Ep. redupl. λελάθοντο, etc. (v. infr. C):—λέλησμαι; Ep. λέλασμαι, part. λελασμένος, etc.: cf. ἐπιλήθω.

A. in most of the act. tenses, *to escape notice, to be unknown, unseen, unnoticed:*   1. c. acc. pers., λ. τινά only, *to escape his notice*, Lat. *latere aliquem*, Hom., Att.; impers., σὲ λέληθε it *has escaped* your notice, Plat.   2. most often with a part. added, in which case we usually translate the part. by a Verb, and express λανθάνω by an Adverb, *unawares, without being observed, unseen, unknown;* and this, either,   **a.** with an acc. pers., ἄλλον τινὰ λήθω μαρνάμενος I *am unseen by* others while fighting, i. e. I fight *unseen by* them, Il.; μὴ λάθῃ με προσπεσών lest he come on *unseen* by me, Soph.   **b.** without an acc., μὴ διαφθαρεὶς λάθῃ lest he perish *without himself knowing it*, Id.; δουλεύων λέληθας you are a slave *without knowing it*, Ar.—This construct. is reversed, as in our idiom, ἀπὸ τείχεος ἆλτο λαθών (for ἔλαθεν ἁλόμενος) Il.; λήθουσά μ' ἐξέπινες Soph.

B. the compd. Verbs ἐκ-ληθάνω, ἐπι-λήθω (v. sub vocc.), take a Causal sense, *to make one forget* a thing,

λανός — Λατογενής.   465

c. gen. rei : so in redupl. aor. 2 λέλᾰθον, ὄφρα λελάθη ὀδυνάων that *he may cause* him *to forget* his pains, Il.
C. Med. and Pass. *to let* a thing *escape one, to forget* : **1.** *to forget*, absol. or c. gen. rei, Hom. ; so in redupl. aor., οὐδέ σεθεν θεοὶ λελάθοντο Il., etc. ; and in pf. pass., ἐμεῖο λελασμένος Ib. ; κείνου λελῆσθαι Soph.   **2.** *to forget purposely, to pass over,* ἢ λάθετ' ἢ οὐκ ἐνόησεν either *he chose to forget it* or *perceived it not,* Il.

λᾱνός, Dor. for ληνός.

ΛΑΞ, Adv. *with the foot,* Hom., Aesch. ; λὰξ πατεῖσσαι *to be trodden under foot,* Aesch.

λαξευτός, ή, όν, *hewn out of the rock,* N. T.   From **λαξεύω,** *to hew in stone,* Lxx.

λάξις, ιος, ἡ, (λᾰχεῖν) *an allotment of land,* Hdt.

λάξομαι, Ion. for λήξομαι, fut. of λαγχάνω.

λᾱο-δάμᾱς [δᾰ], αντος, ὁ, (δαμάω) *man-taming* : in Hom. as prop. name.

λαο-δόκος, ον, (δέχομαι) *receiving the people* : in Hom. as prop. name **Λαόδοκος.**

λᾱο-μέδων, οντος, ὁ, *ruler of the people* : in Hom. as prop. n.

λᾱο-πᾰθής, ές, (πάσχω) *suffered by the people,* Aesch.

λᾱο-πόρος, ον, *serving as a passage for the people, man-conveying,* λ. μηχαναί, i. e. a bridge, Aesch.

ΛΑΟΣ, οῦ, ὁ, Ion. ληός, Att. λεώς :—*the people,* both in sing. and plur., i. e.   **1.** in the warlike language of Il., *the people* or *men* of the army, *soldiers ;* also *a land-army,* opp. to a fleet ; *the common men,* opp. to their leaders.   **2.** in the peaceful Od., *men, people ;* so, ναυτικὸς λεώς seafaring *folk,* Aesch. ; ὁ γεωργικὸς λεώς Ar. ; ἀκούετε, λεῴ hear *o people !* the usual way of beginning proclamations at Athens, like our *Oyez !* Id.   **3.** in N. T. of *Jews,* and later of *Christians,* as opp. to heathens.

λᾱος, irreg. gen. of λᾶας.

λᾱο-σεβής, ές, (σέβω) *worshipped by the people,* Pind.

λᾱοσ-σόος, ον, (σεύω) *rousing* or *stirring nations,* Hom.   **2.** λαοσσόοι ἀγῶνες *assemblies to which the people flock,* Pind.   **II.** (σώζω) *preserving the people* or *nations,* Anth.

λᾱο-τέκτων, ονος, ὁ, *a stone-worker,* Anth.

λᾱο-τίνακτος, ον, *stirred by a stone,* Anth.

λᾱο-τρόφος, ον, (τρέφω) *nourishing* or *tending the people,* Pind. ; τιμὴ λ. an office *useful to the people,* Id.

λᾱο-τύπος [ῠ], ον, (τύπτω) *cutting stones,* σμίλη Anth.   **II.** as Subst. *a stone-cutter, statuary,* Id.

λᾱο-φθόρος, (φθείρω) ον, *ruining the people, destructive,* c. gen., Theogn.

λᾱο-φόνος, ον, (*φένω) *slaying the people,* Theocr.

λᾱο-φόρος and **λεωφόρος,** ον, (φέρω) *bearing people,* λαοφόρος ὁδός *a highway, thoroughfare,* Il. ; ὑπὲρ τῶν μάλιστα λεωφόρων πυλέων *over the gates of greatest thoroughfare,* Hdt.

λᾰπαδνός, όν, poët. for ἀλαπαδνός.

λᾰπάζω, poët. for ἀλαπάζω.

λᾰπάρᾱ [πᾰ], Ion. -ρη, ἡ, (λαπαρός) *the soft part of the body* between the ribs and hip, *the flank,* Il., Hdt., etc. ; in pl. *the flanks,* Lat. *ilia,* Hdt.

ΛΑΠᾰΡΟΣ, ά, όν, *slack, loose,* Arist.

ΛΑΠΗ [ᾰ], ἡ, *the scum, filth,* Aesch. (?)

λάπτω (from Root ΛΑΠ), f. ψω : aor. 1 ἔλαψα : pf.

λέλᾰφα :—Med., f. λάψομαι :—*to lap with the tongue,* of wolves, Il.   **2.** *to drink greedily, suck in,* Luc.

λᾱρῑνός, ή, όν, (λᾱρός) *fatted, fat,* Ar. ; metaph., Id.

λᾰρίς, ίδος, ἡ, =λάρος, Anth.

Λάρῑσα [ᾱρ], ἡ, *Larissa,* a name of many old Greek cities, Il., etc. :—orig. it denoted *a citadel,* such as *the Larissa* of Argos.   **II.** Adj. **Λᾱρῑσαῖος,** α, ον, *Larissaean, of* or *from Larissa,* Thuc., etc. ; Ion. Ληρισσ– Hdt.   **2.** as Subst., *a kind of kettle* or *pot, first made at Larissa,* Arist.

λαρκίδιον, τό, Dim. of λάρκος, Ar.

ΛΑΡΚΟΣ, ὁ, *a charcoal-basket,* Ar.

ΛΑΡΝΑΞ, ᾰκος, ἡ, *a coffer, box, chest,* Il., Hdt.   **2.** *a cinerary urn* or *coffin,* Il., Thuc.   **3.** *an ark,* in which children were exposed, Simon.

ΛΑΡΟΣ [ᾰ], ὁ, *a ravenous sea-bird,* perh. *a cormorant,* described as dashing down into the sea and then floating on the waves, Od. : metaph. of demagogues, Ar.   **II.** *a singing bird,* Anth.

ΛΑΡΟΣ, όν, *pleasant to the taste, dainty, sweet,* Hom. : —Ep. Sup. λᾰρώτατος οἶνος (metri grat. for λᾱρότατος) Od. : Comp. λᾱρότερον as Adv., Anth.   **2.** *pleasant to the smell,* Mosch., Anth.   **3.** *pleasant to the eye, lovely,* Anth.   **4.** *pleasant to the ear, sweet to hear,* Id.

Λάρτιος, ὁ, Trag. form of Λαέρτης.

λᾰρυγγιάω, =λαρυγγίζω, Anth.

λᾰρυγγίζω, Att. f. -ιῶ, *to shout lustily, bellow, bawl,* Dem.   **II.** trans. *to outdo in shouting,* λαρυγγιῶ τοὺς ῥήτορας Ar.

ΛΑΡΥΓΞ [ᾰ], υγγος, ὁ, *the larynx* or *upper part of the windpipe,* Arist. :—in Poets *the throat,* Eur., Ar.

λᾶς, λᾶος, ὁ, *a stone,* Att. contr. for λᾶας, q. v.

λάσανα [ᾰσ], τά, always in pl., *a trivet* or *stand for a pot ;* also *a gridiron,* Ar.

λάσδομαι, Dor. for λάζομαι : imper. λάσσεο.

λάσευμαι, Dor. for λήσομαι, fut. med. of λανθάνω.

ΛΑΣΘΗ, ἡ, *mockery, insult,* Hdt.

λασθῆμεν, Dor. for λασθῆναι, aor. 1 pass. inf. of λανθάνω.

λᾰσι-αύχην, ενος, (λάσιος) *with rough, shaggy neck,* Hom., Ar., etc.

ΛΑΣΙΟΣ [ᾰ], α, ον, and ος, ον, (akin to δασύς) *hairy, rough, shaggy, woolly,* Hom., Soph., etc.   **II.** *shaggy with brushwood, bushy,* Xen., Theocr. ; τὰ λάσια *bushes,* Xen.

λασιό-στερνος, ον, (στέρνον) *hairy-breasted,* Anth.

λάσκω (from Root ΛΑΚ) : f. λᾰκήσομαι : aor. 1 ἐλάκησα [ᾰ] :—aor. 2 ἔλᾰκον, Ep. λάκον :—pf. λέλᾱκα, Ion. λέληκα, Ep. part. fem. λελᾱκυῖα : 3 pl. redupl. aor. 2 λελάκοντο :—*to ring, rattle, crash,* λάκε χαλκός Il. ; λάκε δ' ὀστέα the bones *cracked, broke with a crash,* Ib.   **II.** of animals, *to shriek, scream,* of the falcon, ὀξὺ λεληκώς Ib. ; of the nightingale in the falcon's talons, τί λέληκας ; Hes. ; also of dogs, *to howl, bay,* Eur.   **III.** of men, *to shout, scream, cry aloud,* Aesch., Soph., etc. ; τί λέλᾱκας ; Ar. ; μή νυν λακήσῃς Id. :—hence of Oracles, *to noise abroad,* Aesch., etc. : also, *to sing,* πρὸς αὐλόν Eur.   **2.** c. acc. cogn. *to shriek forth, utter aloud,* Trag.   **IV.** *to crack* or *burst asunder,* N. T.

λᾱσῶ, Dor. for λήσω, fut. of λανθάνω.

Λᾱτο-γενής, ές, Dor. for Λητογενής.

λᾱτομία, ἡ, in pl., like Lat. *lautumiae, quarries*, Anth.
λᾱ-τόμος, ὁ, (λᾶς, τέμνω) *a stone-cutter.*
λατρεία, ἡ, (λατρεύω) *the state of a hired workman, service, servitude*, Trag.   2. λ. τοῦ θεοῦ, θεῶν *service to* the gods, *divine worship*, Plat.; absol., N. T.
λάτρευμα, ατος, τό, in pl. *service for hire*, πόνων λατρεύματα *painful service*, Soph.   2. *service paid to the gods, worship*, Eur.   II. = λάτρις, *a slave*, Id. From
λατρεύω, f. σω, (λάτρις) *to work for hire* or *pay, to be in servitude, serve*, Xen.   2. λ. τινί *to be bound* or *enslaved to*, Soph., Eur., etc.; c. acc. pers. *to serve*, Eur.:—metaph., λατρ. πέτρᾳ, of Prometheus, Aesch.; μόχθοις λατρ. Soph.; λ. νόμοις *to obey*, Xen.   3. *to serve* the gods, λ. Φοίβῳ Eur.: c. acc. cogn., πόνον λ. *to render* them *due service*, Id.
λάτριος, α, ον, *of a servant* or *service*, Pind.; παραδιδόναι τινὰ λάτριον *to give him into slavery*, Id. From
λάτρις, ιος, ὁ and ἡ, *a workman for hire, hired servant*, and in fem. *a handmaid*, Theogn., Soph.   From
ΛΑ´ΤΡΟΝ, τό, *pay, hire*, Aesch. in pl.
Λᾱτώ, Dor. for Λητώ.
λαυκάνίη, ἡ, = λαιμός, *the throat*, Il.
ΛΑΥ´ΡΑ, Ion. -ρη, ἡ, *an alley, lane, passage*, Lat. *angiportus*, Od., Hdt.: *a sewer, drain, privy*, Ar.
Λαύρειον, τό, *a mountain* in the S. of Attica, famous for its silver-mines, Hdt., Thuc.:—**Λαυριωτικός, ή, όν,** *of Mt. Laurium*, Ar.
λᾰφυγμός, ὁ, (λαφύσσω) *gluttony*, Ar.
λάφῡρα [λᾰ], τά, (λαμβάνω) *spoils taken in war*, Lat. *spolia*, Trag., Xen.
λᾰφῡροπωλέω, f. ήσω, *to sell booty*, Xen.   From
λᾰφῡρο-πώλης, ου, ὁ, (πωλέω) *a seller of booty, one who has bought up booty to retail*, Lat. *sector*, Xen.
λᾰφύσσω, Att. -ττω, f. ξω, (λάπτω) *to swallow greedily, gulp down, devour*, Il.; metaph. of fire, *to consume*, Anth.   Hence
λᾰφύστιος, α, ον, *gluttonous*, Hdt., Anth.
λᾰχαίνω, f. ἄνω: aor. 1 ἐλάχηνα: (from Root ΛΑΧΑΝ) :—*to dig*, Mosch.
λᾰχάνη-λόγος, ον, (λέγω) *gathering vegetables*, Anth.
λᾰχᾰνισμός, ὁ, *a gathering of vegetables*, Thuc.   From
λάχανον, τό, (λᾰχαίνω) mostly in pl. *garden-herbs, potherbs, vegetables, greens*, Lat. *olera*, Plat., etc.   2. in pl. also, *the vegetable-market, green-market*, Ar.
λᾰχᾰνό-πτερος, ον, (πτερόν) *vegetable-winged*, Luc.
λᾰχᾰνο-πώλης, ου, ὁ, (πωλέω) *one who sells vegetables, a green-grocer;* fem. λᾰχᾰνόπωλις, ιδος, Ar.
λάχε, Ep. for ἔλαχε, 3 sing. aor. 2 of λαγχάνω.
λάχεια [ᾰ], (λαχαίνω) fem. Adj. *well-tilled, fertile*, Od. :—others read ἐλάχεια, from ἐλαχύς, *small.*
Λάχεσις, εως, Ion. ιος, ἡ, (λᾰχεῖν) *Lachesis, Disposer of lots*, one of the three Fates, Hes., Pind.; v. Κλωθώ.   II. λάχεσις, ἡ, as appellative, *lot, destiny*, ap. Hdt.
λᾰχή, ή, = λῆξις, *allotment*, τάφων πατρῷων λάχαι *a share* in their fathers' tombs, Aesch.
λαχναῖος, α, ον, = λαχνήεις, Anth.   From
ΛΑ´ΧΝΗ, ή, *soft hair, down*, Lat. *lanugo*, of a young man's beard, Od., Pind.; of the *thin hair* on Thersites' head, Il.; of the *nap* or *pile* on cloth, Ib.; of *sheep's-wool*, Soph.   Hence
λαχνήεις, Dor. -άεις, εσσα, εν, *hairy, shaggy*, Il., Pind.
λαχνό-γυιος, ον, (γυῖον) *with shaggy limbs*, Eur.

λαχνόομαι, Pass. *to grow downy*, of a youth's chin, Solon, Anth.   From
λάχνος, ὁ, = λάχνη, *wool*, Od.
λαχνώδης, ες, (εἶδος) = λαχνήεις, *downy*, Eur.
λάχοιην, Att. for λάχοιμι, aor. 2 opt. of λαγχάνω.
λάχος, τό, (λαγχάνω) *an allotted portion*, Lat. *sors*:   I. one's *special lot, portion, destiny*, Theogn., Soph.: one's *appointed office*, Aesch.   II. *a portion obtained by lot, a lot, share, portion*, Id., Xen.
λᾰχών, aor. 2 part. of λαγχάνω.
λαψεῦμαι or -οῦμαι, Dor. for λήψομαι, fut. of λαμβάνω.
ΛΑ´Ω (A), = βλέπω, *to behold, look upon*, c. acc., Od.; ὀξὺ λάων *quick of sight*, h. Hom.
ΛΑ´Ω (B), an old Doric Verb, found only in pres. = θέλω, *to wish, desire*; λῶ, λῇς, λῇ, λῶμες, λῆτε, λῶντι :—subj., 2 and 3 sing. λῇς, λῇ : opt. 3 sing. λῴη : inf. λῆν : part. τῷ λῶντι.
λᾱ-ώδης, ες, (εἶδος) *popular*, Lat. *popularis*, Plut.
λέαινα, ή, fem. of λέων, *a lioness*, Hdt., Aesch.
λεαίνω, Ep. λειαίνω : f. λεᾰνῶ, Ep. λειανέω :—aor. 1 ἐλέηνα, Ep. λείηνα : (λεῖος) :—*to smooth* or *polish*, Hom.; Ἵπποισι κέλευθον λειανέω *I will smooth* the way, Il.   2. *to rub smooth, pound in a mortar*, Lat. *levigare*, Hdt.; *to grind with the teeth*, Xen. :—generally, *to crush, extirpate*, Hdt.   3. *to smooth away* wrinkles, Plat. :—metaph. *to smooth* or *soften down* harsh words, Hdt.
λεάντειρα, fem. Adj. *smoothing, polishing*, Anth.
λέβης, ητος, ὁ, (λείβω) *a kettle* or *caldron* of copper, Hom., etc.   II. *a basin* in which the purifying water (χέρνιψ) was handed to the guests before meals, Od.; also *a pan* for washing the feet, Ib. : *a bath*, Aesch.   III. *a cymbal*, Hdt.   IV. *a cinerary urn*, Aesch., Soph. :—generally, *a casket*, Soph.
λεγεών, ῶνος, ή, the Lat. *legio*, N. T., Plut.
ΛΕ´ΓΩ (A), *to lay*, f. ξω :—1 ἔλεξα, Ep. λέξα :—Med., f. λέξομαι: aor. 1 ἐλεξάμην, Ep. λεξάμην :—Pass., only in 3 sing. Ep. aor. 2 ἔλεκτο, λέκτο, imper. λέξο, λέξαι, inf. λέχθαι, part. λέγμενος. (In this sense, the Root is ΛΕΧ, as in λέχ-ος, λόχ-ος.)   *To lay asleep, lull to sleep*, λέξον με Il.; ἔλεξα Διὸς νόον Ib. :—Pass. and Med. *to lie asleep, to lie*, Hom.
ΛΕ´ΓΩ (B), *to pick out*, f. ξω : aor. 1 ἔλεξα : pf. εἴλοχα :—Med., aor. 1 ἐλεξάμην : Ep. aor. 2 ἐλέγμην, 3 sing. λέκτο :—Pass., f. λέξομαι in pass. sense : aor. 1 ἐλέχθην : pf. εἴλεγμαι :—*to gather, pick up*, Lat. *lego, colligo*, Hom., Pind.; αἱμασιὰς λέγων *picking out stones for building* walls, Od. :—Med. *to gather for oneself*, Il.   2. Med. *to choose for oneself, pick out*, Hom. :—Pass. *to be chosen*, Il.   II. *to count, tell, reckon up*, Od.; μετὰ τοῖσιν ἐλέγμην *I reckoned myself among them*, Ib.; λέκτο δ' ἀριθμόν *he told over the number*, Ib. :—Pass., μετὰ τοῖσιν ἐλέχθην *I was counted among these*, Il.   2. so in Att., λ. ἐν ἐχθροῖς *to count among one's enemies, count* as a foe, Aesch.; λ. τινὰ οὐδαμοῦ *to count* him as naught, *nullo in numero habere*, Soph.   3. *to recount, tell over*, Od., Aesch., etc. :—Med., τί σὲ χρὴ ταῦτα λέγεσθαι; *why need'st thou tell the tale* thereof? Il.; μηκέτι ταῦτα λεγώμεθα Ib.
ΛΕ´ΓΩ (C), *to say*: f. λέξω: aor. 1 ἔλεξα :—Pass., f. λεχθήσομαι, so fut. med. in pass. sense, and λελέξομαι :

aor. 1 ἐλέχθην : pf. λέλεγμαι : **1.** *to say, speak,* Hdt., Trag., etc. ; λέγε *say on,* Hdt. ; so, λέγοις ἄν Plat. : of oracles, *to say, declare,* Hdt. **2.** λέγειν τινά τι *to say something of* another, esp., κακὰ λ. τινά *to speak ill* of him, *abuse, revile* him, Id. ; ἀγαθὰ λ. τινά Ar. ;—also, εὖ or κακῶς λ. τινά Aesch., etc. **3.** *to call by name,* Soph. :—*to call so and so,* οὗτοι γυναῖκας ἀλλὰ Γοργόνας λέγω Aesch. **4.** λ. τινά or τινί ποιεῖν τι *to tell* one *to do,* Soph., Xen., etc. **5.** λ. τι *to say something,* i. e. *to speak to the point* or *purpose,* Soph. ; λέγω τι ; *am I right ?* Id. ; opp. to οὐδὲν λέγει, *has no meaning, no authority,* Ar. ; but οὐδὲν λέγειν, also, *to say what is not, to lie,* Id., Plat., etc. **6.** like Lat. *dicere, to mean,* τί τοῦτο λέγει; *what does this mean ?* Ar., Plat. ; πῶς λέγεις ; *how mean you ?* Plat. :—to explain more fully, εἴσω κομίζου σύ, Κασάνδραν λέγω get thee in—thou, *I mean* Cassandra, Aesch. ; ποταμός Ἀχελῷον λέγω Soph. **7.** Pass., λέγεται, like Lat. *dicitur, it is said, on dit,* Hdt., Att. ; also λέγονται εἶναι *they are said* to be, Xen. :—τὸ λεγόμενον, absol., *as the saying goes,* Thuc., etc. :—ὁ λεγόμενος *the so-called,* οἱ λ. αὐτόνομοι εἶναι Xen. **8.** of orators, *to speak* (emphatically), λέγειν δεινός Soph. ; λ. τε καὶ πράσσειν δυνατώτατος Thuc. **9.** *to boast, tell of,* Xen. : *to recite* what is written, λαβὲ τὸ βιβλίον καὶ λέγε Plat., etc. :—but the sense of Lat. *lego, to read,* only occurs in compds., ἀναλέγομαι, ἐπιλέγομαι.

λεηλᾰσία, ἡ, *a making of booty, robbery,* Xen. From

λε-ηλᾰτέω, f. ήσω, (λεία, ἐλαύνω) *to drive away cattle as booty, to make booty,* Soph., Xen. **2.** c. acc. loci, *to plunder, despoil,* Hdt.

ΛΕΙ'Α, Ion. ληΐη, Dor. λαία, ἡ, *booty, plunder,* Hdt., Soph., Eur., etc. :—generally, *pillageable property,* Thuc., Xen. ; λείαν ποιεῖσθαι χώραν = λεηλατεῖν χώραν, Thuc. :—Μυσῶν λεία, of anything that may be plundered with impunity, from the effeminate character of the Mysians, Dem. **2.** *plunder* (as an act), ζῆν ἀπὸ ληΐης Hdt.

λειαίνω, Ion. for λεαίνω.

λείβω (from Root ΛΙΒ) : aor. 1 inf. λεῖψαι, part. λείψας : —Med., aor. 1 ἐλειψάμην :—*to pour, pour forth,* οἶνον λείβειν *to make a libation of* wine, Hom. ; also λείβειν (without οἶνον) Il. ; λείβειν θεοῖς Od. **II.** like εἴβω, *to let flow, shed,* δάκρυα λ. Hom., Trag. :—Pass., of the tears, *to be shed, pour forth,* Eur., Xen. ; of persons, λείβεσθαι δακρύοις κόρας *to have one's* eyes *running* with tears, Eur. : metaph. of sound, Pind. **III.** in Pass., also, *to melt* or *pine away,* Ar.

λείζομαι, Ion. and poët. for ληΐζομαι.

λείηνα, Ep. for λέηνα, aor. 1 of λεαίνω.

λεῖμαξ, ἄκος, ἡ, = λειμών, *a meadow,* Eur., Anth.

λεῖμμα, ατος, τό, = λείψανον, Plut. ; τοῦ παῖδος τὰ λείμματα *what was left* of him, his *remains,* Hdt.

λειμών, ῶνος, ὁ, (λείβω) *any moist, grassy place, a meadow, mead, holm,* Lat. *pratum,* Hom., Aesch., etc.

λειμωνιάς, άδος, poët. fem. of sq., Soph.

λειμώνιος, α, ον, (λειμών) *of a meadow,* Lat. *pratensis,* Aesch., Theocr.

λειμωνόθεν, (λειμών) Adv. *from a meadow,* Il. ; also -θε, Theocr.

λειο-γένειος, ον, (γένειον) *smooth-chinned,* Hdt.

λειο-κύμων [ῡ], ον, (κῦμα) *having low waves,* Luc.

λειό-μῑτος, ον, *smoothing the warp,* Anth.

λειοντῆ, ἡ, poët. for λεοντῆ, *a lion's skin,* Anth.

λειοντο-μάχης [ᾰ], ου, ὁ, (μάχομαι) poët. for λεοντ-, *a lion-fighter,* Theocr.

λειοντο-πάλης [ᾰ], ου, ὁ, (πάλη) poët. for λεοντ-, *a wrestler with a lion,* Anth.

ΛΕΙ'ΟΣ, α, ον, Lat. *lēvis, smooth,* Il., Plat., etc. :—of cloths, *smooth, plain, not embroidered,* Thuc. **2.** *smooth, level, flat,* of land, Hom. ; λεῖα δ' ἐποίησεν [θεμείλια] levelled them with the ground, Il. :—c. gen., χῶρος λεῖος πετράων *smooth* (i. e. *free*) *from* rocks, Od. **3.** *smooth-skinned, beardless,* Theocr. **4.** metaph. *smooth, soft,* of wind, Ar. ; of words, Aesch.

λειότης, ητος, ἡ, *smoothness,* Aesch., Xen., etc.

λείουσι, poët. for λέουσι, dat. pl. of λέων.

λειπτέον, verb. Adj. of λείπω, *one must leave* or *abandon,* Eur., Plat., etc.

λείπω (from Root ΛΙΠ), f. λείψω : aor. 2 ἔλιπον :—pf. λέλοιπα : plqpf. ἐλελοίπειν :—Med., aor. 2 ἐλιπόμην : —Pass., fut. med. in pass. sense λείψομαι ; also λειφθήσομαι and λελείψομαι : aor. 1 ἐλείφθην, Ep. 3 pl. ἔλιφθεν :—pf. λέλειμμαι, plqpf. ἐλελείμμην, Ep. λελ- : **I.** trans. **1.** *to leave, quit,* Hom., etc. **2.** *to leave behind, leave at home,* Id., etc. ; esp. of dying men, *to leave* (as a legacy), Il., etc. :— so in Med. *to leave behind one,* as a memorial, Hdt., etc. **3.** *to leave, forsake, abandon, desert, leave in the lurch,* Il., etc. ; λ. ἑρδνους *to fail in paying* . . , Dem. ; so, λ. δασμόν, φοράν Xen. :—conversely, λίπον ἰοὶ ἄνακτα the arrows *failed* him, Od. **II.** intr. *to be gone, to be wanting, cease, be missing,* Lat. *deficio,* Soph., Eur., etc.

B. Pass. *to be left, left behind,* Hom., etc. **2.** *to remain, remain over and above,* Il., Hdt., etc. **3.** *to remain alive,* Od. **II.** c. gen. *to be left without, to be forsaken of,* σοῦ λελειμμένη Soph. ;— but, λελειμμένος δορός left by the spear, i. e. not slain, Aesch. **III.** *to be left behind in a race,* Il. ; λελειμμένος οἰῶν *lingering behind* the sheep, Od. ; ἐς δίσκουρα λέλειπτο *he had been left behind* as much as a quoit's throw, Il. ; τοῦ κήρυκος λείπεσθαι *not to be behind* the herald, Thuc. **2.** *to come short of, be inferior, worse, weaker* or *less than,* τινος Hdt. Att. ; λέλειψαι τῶν ἐμῶν βουλευμάτων *you come short of,* understand not my plans, Eur. **3.** λείπεσθαι ἀπό τινος *to keep aloof from* one, Il. ; λ. βασιλέος or ἀπὸ βασιλέος *to desert* the king, Hdt. :—absol. *to keep aloof, be absent,* Id. **4.** *to be wanting* or *lacking* in a thing, ὀδύρμασιν ἐλείπετ' οὐδέν Soph., etc.

λειριόεις, εσσα, εν, properly, *like a lily* : metaph. χρὼς λειριόεις lily skin, Il. ; of the cicadae, ὄψ λειριόεσσα their *delicate* voice, Ib. From

ΛΕΙ'ΡΙΟΝ, τό, *a lily,* esp. *the white lily,* h. Hom.

λείριος, ον, = λειριόεις, Pind.

λειστός, ή, όν, = ληϊστός, Il.

***λεῖτος,** ον, (λεώς) *of* or *for the people, public.*

λειτουργέω, f. ήσω : pf. λελειτούργηκα : (λειτουργός) : **I.** at Athens, *to serve public offices at one's own cost,* Oratt. ; τὰ λελειτουργημένα the services *performed,* Dem. **II.** generally, *to perform*

public duties, *to serve the people* or *state*, τῇ πόλει Xen.; so, λ. τοῖς σώμασι *to serve* in one's own person, Dem.　III. more generally, *to serve* a master, c. dat., Arist.　2. *to perform religious service*, *minister*, N. T.

λειτούργημα, τό, *the performance of a* λειτουργία, Plut.

λειτουργία, ἡ, (λειτουργέω) at Athens, *a liturgy*, i. e. *a public duty*, which the richer citizens discharged at their own expense.—The ordinary *liturgies* (ἐγκύκλιοι) were the γυμνασιαρχία, χορηγία, and ἑστίασις: the extraordinary, such as the τριηραρχία, were reserved for special occasions.　II. generally, *any service* or *ministration*, *help*, N. T.　III. *the public service* of the gods, Arist.:—*the service* or *ministry* of priests, N. T.: hence our word *Liturgy*.

λειτουργικός, ή, όν, *ministering*, N. T.

λειτ-ουργός, ὁ, (*λεῖτος, *ἔργω) at Athens, *one who performed a* λειτουργία (q. v.).　II. *a public servant*, the Roman *lictor*, Plut.: metaph., λ. τῆς χρείας ἐμῆς *ministering* to my need, N. T.　III. *in religious sense*, *a minister*, Ib.

ΛΕΙΧΗ'Ν, ῆνος, ὁ, *a tree-moss*, *lichen*, then, *a lichen-like eruption*, *canker*, *scurvy*, *blight*, Aesch.

λειχ-ήνωρ, ορος, ὁ, (ἀνήρ) *Lick-man*, name of a mouse, Batr.: so also **λειχο-μύλη** [ῠ], ἡ, *Lick-meal*, Id.: **λειχο-πίναξ** [ῐ], ακος, ὁ, *Lick-platter*, Id.

ΛΕΙ'ΧΩ, f. λείξω: aor. 1 ἔλειξα:—*to lick up*, Hdt., Aesch., Ar.　2. irreg. part. pf., γλώσσῃσι λελειχμότες *playing* with their tongues, Hes.

λεῖψαι, aor. 1 inf. of λείβω;—not of λείπω.

λειψᾰνη-λόγος, ον, (λέγω Β) *gathering remnants*, Anth.

λείψᾰνον, τό, (λείπω) *a piece left*, *wreck*, *remnant*, *relic*, Eur.　2. in pl., *remains*, *remnants*, Lat. *reliquiae*, of the dead, Soph., Plat.;—but, ἀγαθῶν ἀνδρῶν λ. are *their deeds*, *good name*, Eur.; λείψανα, *remnants* of youth, Ar.

λειψ-ύδριον, τό, (λείπομαι, ὕδωρ) *a waterless district* near mount Parnes in Attica, Hdt.

λει-ώδης, ες, (εἶδος) = λεῖος, *smooth*; as pr. n. in Homer.

λείων, ὁ, Ep. for λέων.

λεκάνη [ᾰ], ἡ, = λέκος, Ar.: *a hod*, Id.

λεκάνιον, τό, Dim., Ar., Xen.

λεκῐθο-πώλης, ου, ὁ, fem. -πῶλις, ιδος, (πωλέω) *a peasepudding-seller*, Ar.

ΛΕ'ΚΙΘΟΣ, ὁ, *pulse-porridge*, *peasepudding*, Ar.

ΛΕ'ΚΟΣ, εος, τό, *a dish*, *plate*, *pot*, *pan*, Hippon.

λεκτέος, α, ον, verb. Adj. of λέγω, *to be said* or *spoken*, Plat.　II. λεκτέον, *one must speak*, Id.

λεκτικός, ή, όν, (λέγω C) *able to speak*, Xen.　II. *suited for speaking*, Dem.

λέκτο, 3 sing. Ep. aor. 2 pass. of λέγω Α.　2. aor. 2 med. of λέγω Β.

λεκτός, ή, όν, (λέγω Β) *gathered*, *chosen*, *picked out*, Aesch., Soph., etc.　II. (λέγω C) *capable of being spoken*, *to be spoken*, Soph., Eur., etc.

λέκτρον, τό, (λέγω Α) like λέχος, *a couch*, *bed*, Lat. *lectus*, in sing. and pl., Hom.; λέκτρονδε *to bed*, Od.　II. pl. *the marriage-bed*, Pind., Trag.; ἀλλότρια, νόθα, λέκτρα, of illicit connexions, Eur.

λελᾰβέσθαι, Ep. redupl. aor. 2 med. inf. of λαμβάνω.

λελάβηκα, Ion. pf. of λαμβάνω.

λελάθῃ, 3 sing. Ep. redupl. aor. 2 subj. of λανθάνω:—

λελάθεσθε, -οντο, 2 and 3 pl. med.; -έσθω, 3 sing. imper.

λέλᾱκα, pf. of λάσκω:—**λελᾰκυῖα**, Ep. part. fem.

λέλαμμαι, Ion. pf. pass. of λαμβάνω.

λέλασμαι, Ep. for λέλησμαι, pf. pass. of λανθάνω.

λελάχητε, -ωσι, 2 and 3 pl. Ep. redupl. aor. 1 of λαγχάνω IV.

λέλειπτο, Ep. for ἐλέλειπτο, 3 sing. plqpf. pass. of λείπω:—**λελεῖφθαι**, inf.

λελειχμότες, v. λείχω 2.

λεληθότως, Adv. part. pf. of λανθάνω, *imperceptibly*, Plat.

λέληκα, pf. of λάσκω.

λέλησμαι, pf. pass. of λανθάνω.

λέλησμαι, pf. in pass. sense of ληΐζομαι.

λελίημαι, Ep. pf. (λίαν) *to strive eagerly*, in part. λελιημένος, ll.; as a mere Adj. *eager*, *in haste*, Ib.: later 3 sing. plqpf., Theocr.

λελιμμένος, pf. pass. part. of λίπτω.

λελογισμένως, Adv. *according to calculation*, Hdt., Eur.

λέλογχα, pf. of λαγχάνω.

λέλοιπα, pf. of λείπω.

λέλουμαι, pf. pass. of λούω.

λελύμανται, 3 pl. pf. pass. of λυμαίνομαι.

λέλυμαι, pf. pass. of λύω.

λέλῠται, **λέλυνται**, 3 sing. and pl. pf. pass. of λύω.

λέλῠτο, Ep. for λελύοιτο, 3 sing. plqpf. pass. opt. of λύω.

ΛΕ'ΜΒΟΣ, ὁ, *a boat*, Lat. *lembus*, a ship's *cock-boat*, Dem.　II. *a fishing-boat*, Theocr.

λέμμα, ατος, τό, (λέπω) *that which is peeled off*, *peel*, *husk*, *skin*, *scale*, Ar.

λέντιον, τό, Lat. *linteum*, *a cloth*, *napkin*, N. T.

λέξεο, Ep. imper. aor. 1 med. of λέγω Α.

λέξις, εως, ἡ, (λέγω) *a speaking*, *saying*, *speech*, Plat.　2. *a way of speaking*, *diction*, *style*, Id., etc.　II. κατὰ λέξιν *as the phrase goes*, Anth.

λέξο, Ep. imperat. aor. 1 pass. of λέγω Α.

λεοντέη, contr. -ῆ, poët. **λειοντῆ** (sub. δορά), ἡ, *a lion's skin*, Hdt., Ar.　From

λεόντεος, α, ον, **λεόντειος**, α, ον, *of a lion*, Theocr.

λεοντό-βοτος, ον, (βόσκω) *fed on by lions*, Strab.

λεοντό-διφρος, ον, *in chariot drawn by lions*, Anth.

λεοντο-κέφᾰλος, ον, (κεφαλή) *lion-headed*, Luc.

λεοντο-φόνος, ον, (*φένω) *lion-killing*, Anth.

λεοντο-φόρος, ον, *bearing the figure of a lion*, Luc.

λεοντο-φυής, ές, (φυή) *of lion nature*, Eur.

λεοντό-χλαινος, ον, (χλαῖνα) *clad in a lion's skin*, Anth.

λεοντ-ώδης, ες, (εἶδος) *lion-like*, Plat., etc.

λέπαδνον, τό, *a broad leather strap* fastening the yoke (ζυγόν) to the neck, and passing between the fore-legs to the girth (μασχαλιστήρ), mostly in pl., ll., Aesch.: so metaph., ἀνάγκης δῦναι λέπαδνον to put on *the halter* of necessity, Aesch.

λεπαῖος, α, ον, (λέπας) *rocky*, *rugged*, Eur.

λέπ-αργος, ον, (λεπίς) *with white coat*, Theocr.

λέπας, τό, only in nom. and acc., (λέπω) *a bare rock*, *scaur*, *crag*, Aesch., Eur., etc.

λεπάς, άδος, ἡ, *a limpet*, from its clinging to the rock (λέπας), Ar.　Hence

λεπαστή, ἡ, *a limpet-shaped drinking-cup*, Ar.

λεπῐδόομαι, (λεπίς) Pass. *to be covered with scales*, Ar.

λεπῐδωτός, ή, όν, scaly, covered with scales, of the crocodile, Hdt. ; of scale-armour, Id. II. as Subst., a fish of the Nile with large scales, Id.

λεπίς, ίδος, ή, (λέπω) a scale, husk, λ. ᾠοῦ an egg-shell, Ar. ; the cup of a filbert, Anth. 2. collectively, the scales of fish, Hdt.

λέπρα, Ion. -ρη, ή, (λεπρός) leprosy, Hdt.

λεπράς, άδος, ή, poët. fem. of λεπρός, Theocr.

λεπρός, ά, όν, (λέπω) scaly, scabby, rough, leprous, Ar.

λεπτᾰκῖνός, ή, όν, poët. for sq., Anth.

λεπτᾰλέος, a, ον, (λεπτός) fine, delicate, Il., Anth.

λεπτ-επί-λεπτος, ον, thin-upon-thin, i. e. thin as thin can be, Anth.

λεπτό-γειος, ον, or λεπτό-γεως, ων, (γαῖα, γῆ) of thin, poor soil, Thuc.

λεπτό-γραμμος, ον, (γράμμα) written small or neat, Luc.

λεπτό-γρᾰφος, ον, (γράφω) written small or neat, Luc.

λεπτό-δομος, ον, (δέμω) slightly framed, slight, Aesch.

λεπτολογέω, f. ήσω, to talk subtly, to chop logic, quibble, Ar. ; λ. τι to discuss in quibbling fashion, Luc. :—so as Dep. λεπτολογέομαι, Id. From

λεπτο-λόγος, ον, (λέγω c) speaking subtly, subtle, quibbling, Ar.

λεπτό-μῐτος, ον, of fine threads, Eur., Anth.

λεπτόν (sub. νόμισμα), τό, a very small coin, a mite, N.T.

λεπτός, ή, όν, (λέπω) peeled, husked, threshed out, Il. 2. fine, small, of dust, ashes, etc., Ib., Soph., Ar. 3. thin, fine, delicate, of cloth, thread, etc., Hom., Eur. 4. of the human figure, thin, lean, meagre, Ar., Xen. : also slender, taper, Plat. 5. of space, like στενός, strait, narrow, Od. ; ἐπὶ λεπτόν in a thin line, Xen. 6. generally, small, weak, impotent, μῆτις Il. ; ἐλπίς Ar. ; λ. ἴχνη faint traces, Xen. ; τὰ λεπτὰ τῶν προβάτων small cattle, i. e. sheep and goats, Hdt. ; λ. πλοῖα small craft, Id., etc. 7. light, slight, of sounds, Aesch. ; λ. πνοαί light breezes, Eur. 8. of wine, light, Luc. II. metaph. fine, subtle, refined, νοῦς, μῦθος Eur., etc. :—so Adv., λεπτῶς μεριμνᾶν Plat.

λεπτοσύνη, ή, = λεπτότης, Anth.

λεπτότης, ητος, ή, (λεπτός) thinness : fineness, delicacy, leanness, Plat. 2. metaph. subtlety, Ar.

λεπτο-τομέω, f. ήσω, (τέμνω) to cut small, mince, Strab.

λεπτουργέω, f. ήσω, to do fine work, of joiners and turners, Plut. 2. metaph. = λεπτολογέω, Eur.

λεπτ-ουργής, ές, (*ἔργω) finely worked, h. Hom.

λεπτύνω [ῡ], f. ῠνῶ, (λεπτός) to make small or fine : to thresh out, winnow, Arist. :—Pass. to be reduced, grow lean, Arist. ; τοὺς ὤμους λεπτύνεσθαι Xen.

λεπύριον [ῠ], τό, Dim. of λέπυρον, Theocr.

λεπῠρι-ώδης, ες, (εἶδος) consisting of coats or layers, like the onion, Arist.

λέπῠρον, τό, (λέπω) a shell, husk, rind.

ΛΕ'ΠΩ, f. λέψω : aor. 1 ἔλεψα :—Pass., aor. 2 inf. λᾰπῆναι : pf. λέλεμμαι :—to strip off the rind or husks, to peel, bark, περὶ γάρ ῥά ἑ χαλκὸς ἔλεψεν φύλλα τε καὶ φλοιόν Il. II. metaph. in Com. poets, to hide, i. e. thrash.

Λέρνα, ή, Lerna, in Argolis, the abode of the Hydra, Eur.:—Adj. Λερναῖος, a, ον or ος, ον, Hes., Eur.

Λεσβιάζω, f. σω, to imitate Sappho (the Lesbian poetry), Ar. From

Λέσβιος, α, ον, Lesbian, of Lesbos, Hdt., etc.

Λεσβίς, ίδος, ή, a Lesbian woman, Il. ; so Λεσβιάς, άδος, Anth.

Λέσβος, ή, Lesbos, an island on the W. coast of Asia Minor, Hom., etc. :—Adv. Λεσβόθεν, from Lesbos, Il. :

λεσχάζω, to prate, chatter, Theogn. From

λέσχη, ή, (λέγω c) a place where people assembled to talk and hear news, a lounge, club-room, Od., etc. : —also a council-hall, council, Aesch., Soph. II. talk or gossip, such as went on in the λέσχαι, Eur. :— in good sense, conversation, discussion, Hdt., Soph.

λεσχηνεία, ή, gossip, Plat. From

λεσχηνεύω, (λέσχη) to chat or converse with, τινί App. ; in Med. to chat, converse, cf. προ-λεσχηνεύομαι.

λευγᾰλέος, α, ον, (akin to λυγρός) in sad or sorry plight, wretched, pitiful, dismal, Od. :—Adv., so, λευγαλέως χωρεῖν to go in ill plight, Il.

Λευίτης, ου, ὁ, (Λευί, Levi) a Levite, N. T.

λευκαίνω, Ep. impf. λεύκαινον, (λευκός) to make white, whiten, Od., Eur., etc. 2. to make bright or light, ἠὼς λευκαίνει φῶς morn brightens up her light, Eur.

λευκ-ανθής, ές, (ἀνθέω) white-blossoming : generally, blanched, white, Pind. ; v. χνοάζω. Hence

λευκανθίζω, to have white blossoms : generally, to be white or made white, Hdt., Babr.

λευκάργῐλος, ον, of or with white clay, Strab.

λευκάς, άδος, poët. fem. of λευκός, Eur. II. name of a promontory of Epirus, Od.

λευκ-ασπις, ιδος, ὁ, ή, white-shielded, Il., Xen. :—in Trag. the Argives are λευκάσπιδες.

λεύκη, ή, (λευκός) white leprosy, Hdt., etc. II. the white poplar, Lat. populus alba, Ar., Dem.

λευκ-ήρετμος, ον, (ἐρετμός) with white oars, Eur.

λευκ-ήρης, ες, (*ἄρω) white, blanched, Aesch.

Λευκιππίδες, αἱ, daughters of Leucippus, nymphs worshipped at Sparta, Eur.

λεύκ-ιππος, ον, riding or driving white horses, Pind., Soph. ; λ. ἀγυιαί streets thronged with white horses, Pind.

λευκίτης [ῐ], ου, ὁ, = λευκός, Theocr.

λευκο-γρᾰφέω, f. ήσω, (γράφω) to paint in white on a coloured ground, Arist.

Λευκοθέα, ή, the white goddess, under which name Ino was worshipped as a sea-goddess, Od.

λευκό-θριξ, τρῐχος, ὁ, ή, or λευκότρῐχος, ον, white-haired, white, Eur., Ar.

λευκο-θώραξ, ᾱκος, ὁ, ή, with white cuirass, Xen.

λευκόϊνος [ῐ], η, ον, made of λευκόϊον, Anth.

λευκό-ϊον, τό, (for λευκὸν ἴον, literally white-violet, but used for I. the wall-flower, Theocr., etc. II. a bulbous plant, the snow-flake, Anth.

λευκο-κύμων [ῠ], ον, (κῦμα) white with surf, Eur.

λευκό-λῐνον, τό, white flax for ropes and rigging, Hdt.

λευκο-λόφας, ᾱ, ὁ, = sq., Eur.

λευκό-λοφος, ον, white-crested, Ar. :—as Subst. λευκό-λοφος, ον, a white hill, Anth.

λευκόν, τό, white, as a colour, τὸ λ. οἶδεν knows black from white, Ar. 2. a white dress, λευκὸν ἀμπέχει are dressed in white, Id.

λευκο-όπωρος, ον, (ὀπώρα) with white fruit, Anth.

λευκο-πάρειος, Ion.-ηος, ον,(παρειά) fair-cheeked,Anth.
λευκό-πετρον, τό, (πέτρα) a white rock, Polyb.
λευκό-πηχυς, υ, gen. εως, white-armed, Eur.
λευκό-πους,ὁ,ἡ,πουν, τό, white-footed,bare-footed,Eur.
λευκό-πτερος, ον, (πτερόν) white-winged, of a ship,
Eur. :—generally, white, Aesch., Eur.
λευκό-πωλος, ον, with white horses,Trag.
λευκός, ή, όν, (from Root ΛΥΚ), light, bright, brilliant, of sun light, Hom., Soph.; and of metallic
surfaces, λέβης Il.; also, λ. γαλήνη a glassy calm,
Od.; of water,generally, bright,limpid,Hom., Eur. 2.
metaph. clear, plain, distinct, of authors, Anth. II.
of colour, white, Hom., etc. ; λ. ἅρμα=λεύκιππον,
Eur. 2. of the skin, white, fair, Hom., Trag.; with
a notion of bare, πούς Eur., cf. λευκόπους :—later, as a
mark of effeminacy,blanched, white, pale, Ar., Xen. :—
λευκαί φρένες in Pind. may be pale with envy, envious. 3. λ. χρυσός, pale gold, i. e. gold alloyed
with silver (prob. the same as ἤλεκτρον), opp. to χρυσὸς
ἄπεφθος, Hdt. 4. λευκὸν ἦμαρ νυκτὸς ἐκ μελαγ-
χίμου a bright day after a night of mourning, Aesch.
λευκό-στικτος, ον, (στίζω) grizzled, Eur.
λευκό-σφυρος, ον, (σφυρόν) white-ankled, Theocr.
λευκό-τρῖχος, ον, v. λευκόθριξ.
λευκό-τροφος, ον, τρέφομαι) white-growing, Ar.
λευκο-φαής, ές, (φάος) white-gleaming, Eur.
λευκο-φόρος, ον, (φέρω) white-robed, Anth.
λεύκ-οφρυς, υ, gen. νος, white-browed, Orac. ap. Hdt.
λευκο-χίτων [ῐ], ωνος, ὁ, ἡ, white-coated, Batr.
λευκό-χροος, ον, contr. -χρους, ουν, (χρόα) of white
complexion : heterocl. acc. λευκόχροα κόμαν Eur.
λευκό-χρως, ωτος, ὁ, ἡ, white-skinned, Theocr.
λευκόω, f. ώσω, (λευκός) to make white : λ. πόδα to
bare the foot, Anth. :—Med., λευκοῦσθαι τὰ ὅπλα to
whiten their shields, Xen. :—Pass. to be or become
white, Pind.
λευκ-ώλενος, ον, (ὠλένη) white-armed, Hom., Hes.
λεύκωμα, ατος, τό, (λευκόω) a tablet covered with
gypsum to write on, a notice-board, register, Lat.
album, Oratt.
λευρός, ά, όν, (λεῖος) smooth, level, even, Od., Aesch.,
Eur. 2. smooth, polished, Pind.
λεύσιμος, ον, (λεύω) stoning, Eur.; λ. καταφθοραί or
θάνατος death by stoning, Id.; λ. ἀραί curses that
will end in stoning, Aesch.
λευσμός, οῦ, ὁ, (λεύω) a stoning, Aesch.
ΛΕΥ'ΣΣΩ, Ep. impf. λεῦσσον :—to look or gaze upon,
see, behold, Il., Trag. 2. absol. to look, gaze, Hom.,
Soph., etc. :—ὁ μὴ λεύσσων he that sees no more, i. e.
is dead, Soph. ; so, εἰ λεύσσει φάος if he still sees
the light, Eur. 3. c. acc. cogn., λεύσσειν δέργμα
δράκοντος to look the look of a dragon, Aesch. ; λ. φόνον
to look murder, Theocr.
λευστήρ, ῆρος, ὁ, (λεύω) one who stones, a stoner, Eur. :
—in Orac. ap. Hdt., λευστήρ is prob. one deserving to
be stoned. II. as Adj., λευστὴρ μόρος death by
stoning, Aesch.
λεύω, f. λεύσω: aor. 1 ἔλευσα: (λᾶας) :—to stone,
Thuc., Eur. :—Pass., λευσθῆναι πέτροις Soph.
λεχαῖος, α, ον, (λέχος) in bed, τέκνα λεχαῖα nestlings,
Aesch.
λεχε-ποίη, ἡ, (λέχος, ποία) grown with grass fit to

make a bed, i. e. grassy, meadowy, Il., h. Hom. :—the
masc. λεχεποίης, ον, of the river Asopus, from its
grassy banks, Il., Orac. ap. Hdt.
λε-χήρης, ες, (*ἄρω) bed-ridden, Eur.
λέχος, εος, τό, (λέγω λ) a couch, bed, Hom., etc. 2.
a kind of state-bed or bier, Il., etc. 3. a marriage-
bed, and generally marriage, Od., Trag. ; so in pl.
τὰ νυμφικὰ λ. Soph. ; γῆμαι μείζω λέχη to make a
great marriage, Eur., etc. :—also for the concrete, σὰ
λέχεα thy spouse, Id. 4. a bird's nest, Aesch., Soph.
Hence
λέχοσ-δε, Adv. to bed, Hom.
λέχριος, α, ον, slanting, slantwise, crosswise, Lat.
obliquus, Soph., Eur. :—metaph., πάντα γὰρ λ. τὰν
χεροῖν all the business in hand is cross, Soph. From
ΛΕ'ΧΡΙ'Σ, Adv. crosswise, Lat. obliqué.
λεχώ, όος, contr. οῦς, ἡ, (λέχος) a woman in child-
bed, or one who has just given birth, Lat. puerpera,
Eur. Hence
λεχώιος, ον, of or belonging to child-bed, δῶρα λεχ.
presents made at the birth, Anth.
λεω-κόριον, τό, (κόρη) the temple of the daughters of
Leos, Thuc.
ΛΕ'ΩΝ, οντος, ὁ, Ep. dat. pl. λείουσι, Lat. leo, a lion,
Hom.; of Artemis, Ζεύς σε λέοντα γυναιξὶ θῆκε Zeus
made thee a lion toward women, because she was supposed to cause their sudden death, Il. ; οἴκοι λέοντες,
ἐν μάχῃ δ' ἀλώπεκες Ar. 2=λεοντῆ,a lion's skin,Luc.
λε-ωργός, όν, (Adv. λέως, *ἔργω) one who will do anything, i. e. audacious, villainous, a knave, Aesch. ;
λεωργότατος Xen.
λεώς, εώ, ὁ, ἡ, Att. for λαός.
λέως, Ion. Adv. =λίαν, entirely, wholly, λ. οὐδέν nothing
at all, Archil.; cf. λεωργός.
λεω-σφέτερος, ον, one of their own people, a fellow-
citizen, Hdt.
λεω-φόρος, ον, Att. for λαοφόρος.
λῆ, 3 sing. of λάω B.
ΛΗ'ΓΩ, Dor. λάγω [ᾱ]: f. ξω :—to stay, abate, like
παύω, Il. :—c. gen., χεῖρας λήγειν φόνοιο to stay hands
from murder, Od. II. intr. to leave off, cease,
come to an end, Il., Hdt., Att.: c. gen. to stop or
cease from a thing, χόλοιο, φόνοιο, etc.,Il., Att.: c. part.
to cease doing, λήγειν ἀείδων Il., etc.
ληδανον, Ion. for λάδανον.
ληδάριον [ᾰ], τό, Dim. of λῆδος, Ar.
ΛΗ'ΔΟΝ, τό, a shrub, the mastich, on which the gum
λάδανον is found, Cistus Creticus.
ΛΗ'ΔΟΣ, Dor. λᾶδος, εος, τό, a light summer dress,
Alcman.
λήζομαι, Att. contr. for ληίζομαι.
ληθαιος or ληθαῖος, α, ον, (Λήθη) of or from Lethé,
Lethean, Anth.
ληθάνω, Causal of λανθάνω, v. λανθάνω B.
ληθαργικός, ή, όν, drowsy, Anth. From
λήθ-αργος ον, (λήθη) forgetful : c. gen. forgetful of,
Anth. II. as Subst. lethargy, Arist.
ληθεδανός, ή, όν, (λήθη) causing forgetfulness, Luc.
ληθεδών, όνος, ἡ, poët. for λήθη, Anth.
λήθη, Dor. λάθα, ἡ, (λανθάνω) a forgetting, forgetfulness, Lat. oblivio, Il., Att.; λ. παρέχειν, ἐμποιεῖν
Plat. ; εἰς λήθην ἐμβάλλειν τινά Aeschin., etc. II.

after Hom., *a place of oblivion* in the lower world, Simon., etc.

λῆθος, Dor. **λᾶθος,** τό, (λήθομαι) = λήθη, Theocr.

λήθω, λήθομαι, collat. forms of λανθάνω, λανθάνομαι.

ληιάς, poët. fem. of ληίδιος, *taken prisoner, captive,* Il.

ληι-βοτήρ, ῆρος, ὁ, (λήϊον) *crop-consuming, crop-destroying :* fem., σῦς **ληιβότειρα** Od.

ληίδιος, α, ον, (ληίς) *taken as booty, captive,* Anth.

ληίζομαι, Att. **λῄζομαι :** Att. impf. ἐληϊζόμην : f. ληίσομαι, Ep. -ίσσομαι : aor. 1 ἐληισάμην, Att. 3 sing. ἐλῄσατο, Ep. ληίσσατο : pf. in pass. sense λέλημαι : Dep. : (ληίς) :—*to seize as booty, to carry off as prey,* Hom., Hdt. : *generally, to get by force, to gain, get,* Hes. **2.** *to plunder, despoil,* esp. by raids or forays, ἀλλήλους Thuc., Xen. **3.** absol. *to plunder,* Hdt. **II.** pf. λέλημαι in pass. sense, *to be carried off, taken as booty,* Eur.

ληίη, ἡ, Ion. for λεία.

ληι-νόμος, ον, (νέμω) *dwelling in the country,* Anth.

λήιον, Dor. **λᾶιον,** τό, *a crop,* Lat. *seges,* ὡς δ᾽ ὅτε κινήσῃ Ζέφυρος βαθὺ λήιον Il. ; so Hes., Hdt. **2.** *a corn-field, field,* Theocr., Babr.

ΛΗΙΣ, Dor. **λᾶίς,** ίδος, ἡ, Ep. for λεία, *booty, spoil,* Hom., etc. : mostly of cattle, Il. ; and without notion of plunder, *cattle, stock,* Hes., Theocr.

ληιστήρ, ῆρος, ὁ, Ep. form of ληιστής, *a robber,* esp. *a pirate, rover,* Od.

ληιστής, οῦ, ὁ, = Att. λῃστής, h. Hom., Hdt.

ληιστός, ή, όν, *to be carried off as booty, to be won by force,* Il. ; also (with the vowel shortd.) λειστός Ib.

ληιστύς, ύος, ἡ, *plundering,* Ion. form in Hdt.

ληίστωρ, ορος, ὁ, = ληιστήρ, Od. **II.** as Adj. *plundering,* Anth.

ληῖτις, ιδος, ἡ, (ληίς) *she who makes* or *dispenses booty,* Il.

λήιτον, τό, (λαός, λεώς) Achaean name for *the town-hall* or *council-room,* = Athen. πρυτανεῖον, Hdt., Plut.

ληκέω, Dor. **λᾱκέω,** *to sound,* Theocr.

ληκυθίζω, (λήκυθος II) *to adorn rhetorically, amplify,* Strab.

ληκύθιον [ῠ], τό, Dim. of λήκυθος, *a small oil-flask,* Ar.

λήκῠθος, ἡ, *an oil-flask, oil-bottle,* Od., Ar. : *a casket for unguents,* Ar. **II.** in pl. *tropes, tragic phrases,* Lat. *ampullae,* Cicero. (Deriv. unknown.)

ληκύθ-ουργός, όν, (*ἔργω) *making oil-flasks,* Plut.

λῆμα, ατος, τό, (λάω B) *will, desire, resolve, purpose, mind,* Aesch., Eur. **II.** *temper of mind, spirit,* whether, **1.** good, *courage, resolution,* Hdt., Pind., Att. ; or, **2.** bad, *insolence, arrogance, audacity,* Soph.

λημᾱτιάω, (λῆμα) only in pres. *to be high-spirited, resolute,* Ar.

λημάω, only in pres., *to be blear-eyed* or *purblind,* λημᾶν κολοκύνταις *to have one's eyes running* pumpkins, Ar. : metaph., λημᾶν τὰς φρένας Id. : From

ΛΗΜΗ, ἡ, *a humour that gathers in the corner of the eye, gum, rheum :*—metaph., Pericles called Aegina ἡ τοῦ Πειραιέως λ. the *eyesore* of Peiraeus, Arist., Plut. ; λῆμαι Κρονικαί *old prejudices that dim the eye,* Ar.

λῆμμα, ατος, τό, (εἴλημ-μαι, pf. pass. of λαμβάνω) *anything received, income,* Aesch. ; λ. καὶ ἀνάλωμα *receipt* and expense, Plat. : generally, *gain, profit,* Lat. *lucrum,*

Soph., etc. ; παντὸς ἥττων λήμματος *unable to resist any temptation of gain,* Dem. ; often in pl., Id.

Λήμνιος, α, ον, *Lemnian,* v. Λῆμνος.

λημνίσκος, ὁ, (λῆνος) *a woollen fillet* or *riband,* Lat. *taenia,* Plut., etc.

Λημνόθεν, Adv. *from Lemnos,* Pind. From

Λῆμνος, ἡ, *Lemnos,* an island in the Aegaean sea, sacred to Hephaestus, Hom., etc. :—from the volcanic nature of the island, the Λήμνιον πῦρ became proverbial, Soph.

λῆν, inf. of λάω B.

Λῆναι, αἱ, (ληνός) *Bacchanals,* Theocr.

Ληναϊκός, ή, όν, *of* or *belonging to the* Λήναια, Anth.

ληναῖος, α, ον, (ληνός) *belonging to the wine-press :* **1.** epith. of Bacchus as *god of the wine-press,* Diod. **2.** Λήναια (sc. ἱερά), τά, *the Lenaea,* an Athenian festival held in the month Ληναιών in honour of Bacchus, at which there were contests of the Comic Poets, Ar. **3.** Λήναιον, τό, *the Lenaeum,* or place at Athens where the Lenaea were held, Id., Plat.

Ληναΐτης, ου, ὁ, = Ληναϊκός, Ar.

Ληναιών, ῶνος, ὁ, Ion. name of the seventh Att. month Γαμηλιών, in which the Lenaea were held (v. Διονύσια), the latter part of Jan. and former of Feb., Hes.

ΛΗΝΟΣ, Dor. **λᾱνός,** οῦ, ἡ, like Lat. *lacus, alveus, a tub* or *trough ;* esp., **1.** *a wine-vat,* Theocr. **2.** *a trough for watering cattle,* h. Hom.

ΛΗ͂ΝΟΣ, εος, τό, Lat. *lana, wool,* Aesch.

λήξαιμι, aor. 1 opt. of λήγω.

ληξιαρχικός, ή, όν, *belonging to the* ληξίαρχος :—τὸ λ. γραμματεῖον *the register* of each Athenian deme, Dem. From

ληξί-αρχος, ὁ, *the officer at Athens who entered young citizens on the list of their deme when they came of age.*

λῆξις (A), εως, ἡ, (λήξομαι, f. of λαγχάνω) *a portion assigned by lot, an allotment,* Plat. ; cf. λάξις. **II.** as law-term, λ. δίκης or λ. alone, *a written complaint lodged with the Archon, as the first step to a law-suit,* Id., Aeschin.

λῆξις (B), εως, ἡ, (λήγω) *cessation,* Aesch.

ληπτέος, α, ον, verb. Adj. of λαμβάνω, *to be taken* or *accepted,* Plat. **II.** neut. ληπτέον, *one must take hold,* Ar. : *one must undertake,* Xen. ; *one must take* or *choose,* Id. **2.** *one must take, receive,* Id.

ληπτικός, ή, όν, (λαμβάνω) *disposed to accept,* Arist.

ληπτός, ή, όν, verb. Adj. of λαμβάνω, *to be apprehended,* Plat., Anth.

ληρέω, f. ήσω, (λῆρος) *to be foolish* or *silly, speak* or *act foolishly,* Lat. *nugari,* Soph., Ar. Hence

λήρημα, ατος, τό, *silly talk, nonsense,* Plat.

ΛΗ͂ΡΟΣ, ὁ, *silly talk, nonsense, trumpery,* Ar. :—of persons, *nonsense, a trifler,* Plat. ; λῆροι λεπτότατοι, of sophists, Ar. ; as an exclamation, λῆρος, *nonsense ! humbug !* Id.

λῆρος, ὁ, *a poor trinket,* Anth.

ληρ-ώδης, ες, (εἶδος) *frivolous, silly,* Plat., Arist.

λῆς, 2 sing. of λάω B.

λήσειν, fut. inf. of λανθάνω.

λησί-μβροτος, ον, (λήθω, βροτός) *taking men unawares, a thief,* h. Hom.

λησμοσύνη, ἡ, = λήθη, *forgetfulness,* Hes., Soph.

ληστ-άρχης, ου, ὁ, (ἄρχω) *a captain of robbers,* Plut.

ληστεία, ἡ, a robber's life, robbery, piracy, buccaneering, Lat. latrocinium, Thuc., Xen. From

ληστεύω, f. εύσω, (ληστής) to be a robber: to carry on a piratical war, to practise piracy, Lat. latrocinari, Dem. 2. c. acc. to spoil, plunder, Thuc.

ληστήριον, τό, a band of robbers, Xen., Aeschin.:—a retreat or nest of robbers, Strab. II. robbery, in pl., Luc. From

ληστής, οῦ, ὁ, Ion. ληιστής, Dor. λᾳστής: (ληίζομαι): —a robber, plunderer, Soph., Eur., Xen.; esp. by sea, a pirate, rover, buccaneer, Hdt., Thuc., etc.

ληστικός, ή, όν, inclined to rob, piratical, buccaneering, Thuc., Dem.:—τὸ ληστικόν piracy, Thuc.; also a band of robbers, Id. 2. Adv. -κῶς, in the manner of pirates; Comp. -κώτερον, Id.

λῆστις, ἡ, only in nom. and acc., = λήθη, Eur.; λῆστιν ἴσχειν = ἐπιλανθάνεσθαι, to forget, Soph.

ληστο-κτόνος, ον, (κτείνω) slaying robbers, Anth.

ληστρικός, ή, όν, = ληστικός, piratical, Thuc., etc.

ληστρίς, ίδος, ἡ, pecul. fem. of foreg., ναῦς λ. a pirate-vessel, Dem., etc.

λήσω, **λήσομαι**, fut. act. and med. of λανθάνω.

Λητο-γενής, Dor. Λᾱτ-, ές, (γίγνομαι) born of Leto, epith. of Apollo and Artemis, Eur.: pecul. fem. **Λατο-γένεια**, Aesch.

Λητοΐδης [ῐ], Dor. Λᾱτοΐδας, ου, ὁ, son of Leto, i.e. Apollo, h. Hom., Hes.

Λητώ, Dor. Λᾱτώ, η, gen. όος, contr. οῦς, voc. Λητοῖ, Leto, Lat. Latona, mother of Apollo and Artemis, Hom. Hence

Λητῷος, α, ον, of or born from Leto, Soph.; Dor. **Λατῷα**, Anth.: fem. also **Λητωΐς**, ίδος, Id.

ληφθείς, aor. 1 pass. part. of λαμβάνω.

λῆψις, εως, ἡ, (λήψομαι) a taking hold, seizing, catching, seizure, Thuc. 2. an accepting, receiving, Plat.; in pl. receipts, Id.

λήψομαι, f. of λαμβάνω.

λῐ-, insep. Prefix with intens. force, appearing in λίαν, λι-λαί-ομαι, λε-λί-ημαι.

λιάζομαι, aor. 1 ἐλιάσθην, Ep. λιάσθην: 3 sing. plqpf. λελίαστο:—Ep. Dep. = κλίνω, to bend, incline: I. mostly of persons, to go aside, withdraw, recoil, shrink back, Ib.; δεῦρο λιάσθης hither has thou retired, Ib.; παρὰ κληῖδα λιάσθη, of a vision, slipped away by the key-hole, Od.; ἐλιάσθην πρός σε I came away to thee, Eur. 2. to sink, fall, πρηνὴς ἐλιάσθη, λιαζόμενος προτὶ γαίῃ Il. II. of things, λιάζετο κῦμα retired, drew back, Ib.; πτερὰ λίασθεν (for ἐλιάσθησαν) the dying bird's wings dropped, Ib. (Deriv. uncertain.)

λίαν [ῐ], Ion. and Ep. λίην, (λι-) very, exceedingly, Hom.; οὐδέ τι λ. οὕτω not so very much, Od.; with a Verb, very much, overmuch, exceedingly, Hom.; strengthd. καὶ λίην, as, aye truly, verily, Id.; λίην πιστεύειν to believe implicitly, Hdt.; κόμπος λίαν ἐρημένος verily, truly, Aesch.; ἡ λίαν φιλότης his too great love, Id.

λιαρός, ά, όν, like χλιαρός, warm, Hom.; οὖρος λ. a warm soft wind, Od.; ὕπνος λ. balmy sleep, Il.

λιάσθην, Ep. for ἐλιάσθην, aor. 1 of λιάζομαι: 3 pl. **λίασθεν**, for ἐλιάσθησαν.

λιβάδιον, τό, Dim. of λιβάς, a small stream, Strab.

λιβάζω, f. σω, (λιβάς) = λείβω, to let fall in drops:— Med. to run out in drops, trickle, Anth.

λίβανος [ῐ], ὁ, the frankincense-tree, producing λιβανωτός, Hdt., etc. II. = λιβανωτός, in which sense it is fem., Eur., etc. (A foreign word.)

λιβανό-χροος, ον, contr. -χρους, ουν, frankincense-coloured, Strab.

λιβανωτίζω, to fumigate with frankincense, Strab.

λιβανωτός, οῦ, ὁ, frankincense, the gum of the tree λίβανος, Hdt., Ar., etc. II. a censer, Lat. thuribulum, N.T.

λιβανωτο-φόρος, ον, (φέρω) bearing frankincense, Hdt.

λιβάς, άδος, ἡ, (λείβω), anything that drops or trickles, a spring, stream, Soph., Eur.: standing water, Babr.: —in pl. streams, pools, Aesch., Eur.

λιβερτῖνος, ὁ, the Lat. libertinus, a freedman, N.T.

λιβός, gen. of λίψ.

λίβος [ῐ], τό, = λιβάς: λ. αἵματος a drop or fleck of blood, Aesch.: pl. λίβη tears, Id.

λιβρός, ά, όν, (λείβω) dripping, wet, Anth.

Λιβύη, ἡ, Libya, the north part of Africa west of Egypt, Od., Hdt.; in later writers also for the whole Continent:—Adj. **Λιβύηθε**, Dor. -ᾶθε, from Libya, Theocr.:—Adj., **Λιβυκός**, ή, όν, Hdt., etc.

Λιβυρνοί, οἱ, the Liburnians, a people on the Adriatic below Istria, Strab.:—Adj. **Λιβυρνικός**, ή, όν, Liburnian; **Λιβυρνικόν** (sc. πλοῖον), τό, a light vessel like a galley or felucca, such as was used by the Λιβυρνοί, Plut.; also **Λιβυρνίς** (sc. ναῦς), ίδος, ἡ, Id.

Λίβυς [ῐ], υος, ὁ, a Libyan, Hdt., etc.; and as Adj. = Λιβυκός, Eur.; fem. **Λίβυσσα**, Pind.; also **Λιβυστικός**, ή, όν, Aesch.

Λῐβυ-φοῖνιξ, ὁ, a Liby-Phoenician, i. e. Carthaginian, Polyb.

ΛΙ'ΓΑ [ῐ], Adv. of λιγύς, in loud clear tone, Hom.

λιγαίνω, only in pres. and impf.: (λιγύς):—poët. Verb, to cry aloud, of heralds, Il.; of mourners, Aesch.; also, σύριγγι λ. to produce clear sounds on the pipe, to play on it, Anth.; c. acc. cogn., μέλος λ. Bion, Mosch. II. trans. to sing of, Anth.

λίγγω, only in Ep. aor. 1, λίγξε βιός the bow twanged, Il.

λίγδην, Adv. just scraping, grazing, Lat. strictim, Od. (Deriv. uncertain.)

λιγέων, poët. for -ειῶν, gen. pl. fem. of λιγύς.

λιγέως, Adv. of λιγύς.

ΛΙΓΝΥ'Σ, ύος, ἡ, thick smoke mixed with flame, a murky flame, Aesch., Soph., Ar.; λιγνὺς πρόσεδρος in Soph. is the smoky flame hanging round Hercules.

Λιγυαστάδης, ου, ὁ, (λιγύς) a name borne by Mimnermus, Solon.

λῐγυ-ηχής, ές, (ἦχος) clear-sounding, κιθάρη Anth.

λῐγύ-μολπος, ον, (μολπή) clear-singing, h. Hom.

λῐγύ-μῦθος, ον, clear-speaking, Anth.

λῐγυ-πνείων, οντος, (πνέω) shrill-blowing, whistling, Od.

λῐγύ-πνοιος, ον, (πνοιή) = foreg., h. Hom.

λῐγυ-πτέρυγος, ον, (πτέρυξ) chirping with the wings, of the cicada, Anth.

λῐγυρός, ά, όν, clear, whistling, of winds, Il.; of a whip, Ib.; λιγυρὰ ἄχεα griefs which vent themselves in shrill wailings, Eur.:—also clear-voiced, sweet-toned, Hom., etc.:—neut. pl. as Adv., λιγυρὰ ἀείδειν

Theogn.; λιγυρῶς Theocr.　**II.** *pliant, flexible,*
of dogs' tails, Xen.　From

ΛΙΓΥΣ, λίγεια, Dor. λιγέα, λιγύ, *clear, whistling,*
of winds, Hom.: of a *clear, sweet sound, clear-toned,*
Id.; of the nightingale, Aesch.　**II.** Adv. *shrilly,*
Hom.; *clearly,* Il.:—neut. as Adv., λιγὺ μέλπεσθαι
Hes., Aesch.

Λίγυς [ῐ], *υος, ὁ, ἡ, a Ligurian,* Hdt., Thuc., etc.:—
Adj. **Λιγυστικός**, ή, όν, *Ligurian,* Strab.

λῐγύ-φθογγος, ον, (φθογγή) *clear-voiced,* of heralds,
Hom.; of the nightingale, Ar.

λῐγύ-φωνος, ον, (φωνή) *clear-voiced, loud-voiced,*
screaming, Il.; also of *sweet sounds,* Hes., Theocr.

λίην, Ion. and Ep. for λίαν.

λῖθ', allipt. for λῖτα, v. λίς.

λῐθάδεσσιν, Ep. for λιθάσιν, dat. pl. of λιθάς.

λῐθάζω, (λίθος) *to fling stones,* Strab.　**II.** trans.
to stone a man, N. T.

λίθαξ [ῐ], ᾰκος, ὁ, ἡ, (λίθος) *stony,* Od.　**II.** as
fem. Subst., = λίθος, *a grave-stone,* Anth.; of the
pumice-stone, Id.

λῐθάς, άδος, ἡ, Ep. dat. pl. λῐθάδεσσιν, = λίθος, Od.:—
collectively in sing. *a shower of stones,* Aesch.

λιθάω, v. λιθιάω.

λῐθεία, ἡ, (λίθος) *a sort of fine stone* or *marble for*
building, Strab.　**II.** *a precious stone,* Id.

λίθεος [ῐ], α, ον, = λίθινος, *of stone,* Hom.

λῐθη-λογής, ές, (λέγω B) *built of stones,* Anth.

λιθιάω or **λιθάω**, only in pres., *to suffer from stone,* Plat.

λῐθίδιον, τό, Dim. of λίθος, *a pebble,* Plat.

λίθινος [λῐ], η, ον, and ος, ον, (λίθος) *of stone,* Hdt.,
Plat., etc.; λ. θάνατος *stony death,* caused by seeing the
Gorgon's head, Pind.; στῆναι λίθινος, of a statue, Hdt.

λῐθό-βλητος, ον, *stone-throwing, pelting,* Anth.　**II.**
set with stones, Id.

λιθοβολέω, *to pelt with stones, stone,* N. T.　From

λῐθο-βόλος, ον, (βάλλω) *throwing stones, pelting with*
stones: λιθοβόλοι, οἱ, *stone-throwers,* Thuc., etc.　**2.**
λιθοβόλος, ὁ, *an engine for hurling stones,* Polyb.,
etc.　**II.** proparox. λιθόβολος, ον, pass. *struck*
with stones, stoned, Eur.

λῐθο-γλύφος [ῠ], ὁ, (γλύφω) *a sculptor,* Luc.

λῐθο-δερκής, ές, *petrifying with a glance,* Anth.

λῐθό-δμητος, ον, *stone-built,* Anth.

λῐθο-δόμος, ὁ, (δέμω) *building with stones, a mason,*
Xen.

λῐθο-εργός, όν, (*ἔργω) *turning to stone,* Anth.

λῐθο-κόλλητος, ον, (κολλάω) *set with precious stones,*
Theophr., Plut.:—λ. στόμιον *a bit set with stones* (to
make it sharper), Soph.　**II.** τὸ λ. *inlaid work,*
mosaic, Strab.

λῐθο-κόπος, ὁ, (κόπτω) *a stone-cutter,* Dem.

λῐθο-κτονία, ἡ, (κτείνω) *death by stoning,* Anth.

λῐθό-λευστος, ον, (λεύω) *stoned with stones:* λ. Ἄρης
death by stoning, Soph.

λῐθολόγημα, ατος, τό, *a stone-building,* Xen.　From

λῐθο-λόγος, ὁ, (λέγω B) *one who builds with stones*
picked out to fit their places, not cut square; then,
generally = λιθοδόμος, *a mason,* Thuc., etc.

λῐθο-ξόος, ὁ, (ξέω) *a stone* or *marble-mason,* Anth., Luc.

λῐθο-ποιός, όν, (ποιέω) *turning to stone,* Luc.

λῐθόρ-ρινος, ον, *with stony skin,* h. Hom.

ΛΙΘΟΣ [ῐ], ου, ὁ, *a stone,* Hom., etc.: *a precious*
stone, Hdt.: *marble,* Id.:—proverb., λίθον ἕψειν
to boil a stone, i.e. 'to lose one's labour,' Ar.;—
of stupidity, λίθοι *blocks, stones,* Id.　**2.**
stone as a substance, opp. to wood, flesh, etc., Il.,
etc.　**II.** also fem., Hom., Theocr.;—but the
fem. was mostly used of *some special stone,* as the
magnet, Eur., Plat.; of a *touchstone,* Plat.; ἡ διαφα-
νὴς λ. *a piece of crystal* used for a burning glass,
Ar.　**III.** at Athens, λίθος (masc.) was a name
for various *blocks of stone used for rostra* or *tribunes,*
as, **1.** the Bema of the Pnyx, Ar.　**2.** another
in the ἀγορά used by the κήρυκες, Plut.　**3.** an altar
in the ἀγορά, Dem.　**IV.** *a piece on a draughtboard,*
Theocr.

λῐθο-σπᾰδής ἁρμός, ὁ, *a chasm made by tearing out*
stones, Soph.

λῐθό-στρωτος, ον, *paved with stones,* Soph.:—λιθό-
στρωτον, τό, *a tesselated pavement,* N. T.

λῐθοτομία, Ion. -ίη, ἡ, *a place where stone is cut, a*
quarry; mostly in pl., *quarries,* Hdt., Thuc., etc.　From

λῐθο-τόμος, ὁ, (τέμνω) *a stone-cutter,* Xen.

λῐθουργέω, *to turn into stone, petrify,* Anth.　From

λῐθ-ουργός, ὁ, (*ἔργω) *a worker in stone, stone-mason,*
Ar., Thuc.　**II.** as Adj., σιδήρια λιθουργά *a stone-*
mason's tools, Thuc.

λῐθοφορέω, f. ήσω, *to carry stones,* Thuc.　From

λῐθο-φόρος, ὁ, (φέρω) *carrying stones:*—as Subst., =
λιθοβόλος, Polyb.

λῐθώ-δης, ες, (εἶδος) *like stone, stony,* Hdt., Xen.

λικμαῖος, α, *presiding over winnowing,* Anth.

λικμάω, f. ήσω: aor. 1 ἐλίκμησα: (λικμός):—*to part*
the grain from the chaff, to winnow, Il., Xen.:—
metaph. *to scatter like chaff,* N. T.　Hence

λικμητήρ, ῆρος, ὁ, *a winnower of corn,* Il.; and

λικμητός, ὁ, *a winnowing,* Anth.

λικμός, οῦ, ὁ, = λίκνον.

ΛΙΚΝΟΝ, τό, *a winnowing-fan,* i.e. a broad basket,
in which the corn was placed after threshing, and then
thrown against the wind:—it was sacred to Bacchus,
cf. Virgil's *mystica vannus Iacchi,* Soph., Anth.　**II.**
the infant Bacchus was carried in it: hence *a cradle,*
h. Hom., etc.

λικνο-φόρος, ον, (φέρω) *carrying the sacred λίκνον in*
procession, Dem.

λικρῐφίς, Adv. *crosswise, sideways,* Hom.; cf. λέχριος.

λῐλαίομαι, (λι-) Dep., only in pres. and impf., *to long*
or *desire earnestly,* Il.; metaph. of a lance, λιλαιομένη
χροὸς ἆσαι *longing* to taste flesh, Ib.; λιλαιομένη
πόσιν εἶναι *longing for him* to be her husband, Od.
—also c. gen. *to long for,* λιλαιόμενοι πολέμοιο Il.,
etc.:—also, φόωσδε λιλαίεσθαι *to struggle* to the light
of day, Od.

λιμαίνω, aor. 1 ἐλίμηνα, (λιμός) *to suffer from hunger,*
Hdt.

λιμενίτης [ῐ], ου, ὁ, voc. λιμενῖτα, *god of the harbour,*
Anth.: fem. λιμενῖτις, ιδος, Id.

λῐμεν-ορμίτης [ῐ], ου, ὁ, (ὁρμίζω) *tarrying in the har-*
bour, Anth.

λῐμενο-σκόπος, ον, *watching the harbour,* Anth.

ΛΙΜΗΝ, ένος, ὁ, *a harbour, haven, creek,* whereas
ὅρμος is properly the inner part of the harbour, the

landing-place, Hom., etc.; in pl., Od., Soph., etc.; —also c. gen. objecti, λιμένες θαλάσσης havens of refuge from the sea, Od.   II. metaph. a haven, retreat, refuge, Theogn.; ἑταιρείας λ. a haven of friendship, Soph.; λ. τῶν ἐμῶν βουλευμάτων Eur.; c. gen. objecti, χείματος λ. a harbour of refuge from the storm, Id.   2. a place of resort, receptacle, πλούτου λ. Aesch.; παντὸς οἰωνοῦ λ. Soph.; in O. T. 420, the sense seems to be—how will Cithaeron not be filled with thy cries (λιμὴν ἔσται τῆς σῆς βοῆς)? how will it not reëcho them?

λιμήνειε, 3 sing. aor. 1 opt. of λιμαίνω.

λῑμηρός, ά, όν, (λιμός) hungry, causing hunger, Theocr., Anth.

λῐμηρός, ά, όν, (λιμήν) furnished with a good harbour, Thuc.

λιμναῖος, α, ον, (λίμνη) of or from the marsh or mere, ὄρνιθας χερσαίους τε καὶ λ. both land-fowl and water-fowl, Hdt., Ar.

λιμνάς, άδος, ἡ, poët. fem. of λιμναῖος, Theocr., Babr.

λίμνη, ἡ, (λείβω) a pool of standing water left by the sea or a river, Il.: then, a marshy lake, mere, Lat. palus, Ib., Hdt., Att.:—also, a large pool or basin (artificial), Hdt.   2. in Hom. and other Poets, the sea.   II. Λίμναι, αἱ, a quarter of Athens (once prob. marshy), near the Acropolis, in which stood the Lenaeum, Ar., Thuc., etc.

Λιμνήσιος, ὁ, Laker, name of a frog, Batr.

λιμνήτης, ου, ὁ, fem. -ῆτις Dor. -ᾶτις, ιδος, living in marshes, Theocr.   II. epith. of Artemis, dat. Λιμνᾶτι shortd. for Λιμνάτιδι, Anth.

λιμν-ουργός, ὁ, (*ἔργω) one who works in λίμναι, a fisherman, Plut.

λιμνό-φυής, ές, (φύομαι) marsh-born, Anth.

λιμνό-χᾰρις, ὁ, Grace of the marsh, or -χαρής, Love-marsh, name of a frog, Batr.

λιμν-ώδης, ες, (εἶδος) like a marsh, marshy: τὸ λιμνῶδες τοῦ Στρυμόνος the marshy ground at the mouth of the Strymon, Thuc.

λῑμο-θνής, ῆτος, ὁ, ἡ, (θνήσκω) dying of hunger, Aesch.

λῑμο-κτονέω, (κτείνω) to kill by hunger, starve, Plat. Hence

λῑμοκτονία, Ion. -ίη, ἡ, a killing by hunger or by abstinence from food, Plat.

ΛΙΜΟΣ, οῦ, ὁ, and ἡ, hunger, famine, Hom., etc.:— proverb. ἀπολεῖτε λιμῷ Μηλίῳ, referring to the siege of Melos, Ar.:—metaph., of the mind, Eur.

λῑμο-φορεύς, ὁ, (φέρω) causing hunger, Anth.

λῑμό-ψωρος, ὁ, (ψώρα) a cutaneous disease, scurvy, Polyb.

λῑμώσσω, Att. -ττω, (λιμός) to be famished, hungry, Strab., Anth.

λίνεος [ῐ], α, ον, contr. λινοῦς, ῆ, οῦν: (λίνον):—of flax, flaxen, linen, Lat. lineus, Hdt., Plat., etc.

λῑνό-δεσμος, ον, =sq., Aesch.

λῑνό-δετος, ον, (δέω) bound with flaxen cords, Eur.; λινόδετος τοῦ ποδὸς tied by the foot, Ar.

λῑνο-θήρας, ου, ὁ, (θηράω) one who uses nets, Anth.

λῑνο-θώρηξ, ηκος, ὁ, ἡ, Att. -θώραξ, wearing a linen cuirass, Il., Xen.

λῑνό-κλωστος, ον, spinning flax, Anth.

λῑνό-κροκος, ον, (κρέκω) flax-woven, Eur.

ΛΙ'ΝΟΝ [ῐ], τό, anything made of flax: 1. a cord, fishing-line, Il.: the thread spun from a distaff, Eur., etc.; and in pl., Id.:—metaph. the thread of destiny spun by the Fates, Hom., Theocr.:—proverb., λίνον λίνῳ συνάπτειν, i. e. to join like with like, to deal with matters of like kind, Plat.   2. a fishing-net, Il.:— a hunting-net, Theocr.   3. linen, linen-cloth, Hom.: sail-cloth, Ar.   4. flax for spinning, Id.   II. the plant that produces flax, Lat. linum, Hdt., etc.; λίνου σπέρμα lint-seed, Thuc.   III. on λίνον ἄειδεν, v. Λίνος II.

λῑνό-πεπλος, ον, with linen robe, Anth.

λῑνό-πορος, ον, sail-wafting, Eur.

λῑνοπτάομαι, Dep. (λινόπτης) to watch nets, see whether anything is caught, Ar.

λῑνό-πτερος, ον, (πτερόν) sail-winged, of ships, Aesch.

λῑν-όπτης, ου, ὁ, (ὄψομαι, f. of ὁράω) one who watches nets to see whether anything is caught, Arist.

Λίνος [ῐ], ου, ὁ, Linos, a mythical minstrel, son of Apollo and Urania (Calliopé), teacher of Orpheus, Theocr., etc.   II. as appellat., the song or lay of Linos, sung by a boy to the cithara while the vintagers are at work, Λίνον ὑπὸ καλὸν ἄειδεν sang the lovely lay of Linos in accompaniment, Il.:—cf. αἴλινος which is a mournful song.

λῑνο-στᾰσία, ἡ, a laying of nets: the nets laid, Anth.

λῑν-ουργός, ὁ, (*ἔργω) a weaver, Strab.

λῑνοῦς, ῆ, οῦν, contr. for λίνεος.

λῑνο-φθόρος, ον, (φθείρω) linen-wasting, Aesch.

λίντεον, v. λέντιον.

λῐπᾰ [ῐ], (λίπος) Adv. unctuously, richly, ἀλεῖψαι or ἀλείψασθαι λίπ' ἐλαίῳ to anoint or cause to be anointed richly with oil, Il.; so, χρῖσαι or χρίσασθαι λίπ' ἐλαίῳ Ib.; only once without ἐλαίῳ, λοέσσατο καὶ λίπ' ἄλειψεν Od. In all these places, the final vowel is uncertain; but we have λίπα ἀλείψασθαι, -εσθαι in Thuc., etc.

λῐπαίνω, aor. 1 ἐλίπηνα, (λίπος) to oil, anoint: Med. to anoint oneself, Anth.   2. of rivers, to make fat, enrich, Eur.

λῐπ-ανδρέω, (λείπομαι, ἀνήρ) to be in want of men, Strab.; and λῐπ-ανδρία, ἡ, want of men, Id.

Λῐπάρα [πᾰ], ἡ, the largest of the Aeolian islands, Thuc., etc.:—Adj. Λῐπᾰραῖος, α, ον, of Lipara, αἱ Λ. νῆσοι the group of these islands, Polyb.

λῐπᾰρ-άμπυξ, ῠκος, ὁ, ἡ, with bright tiara, Pind.

λῐπᾰρέω, f. ήσω, to persist, persevere, hold out, Hdt.; so in part., διάγειν λιπαρέοντας to continue to hold out, Id.; also, reversely, λιπαρέετε μένοντες persist in holding your ground, Id.; so, c. dat., λ. τῇ πόσει to keep on drinking, Id.   II. of persistent entreaty,   1. absol. to persist in intreating, to be importunate, Id., Aesch., etc.   2. c. acc. et inf. to importune one to do a thing, Aesch., Soph.   3. c. acc., λιπαρεῖν αὐτόν entreat earnestly for him, Dem.   From

λῐπᾰρής, ές, persisting or persevering in a thing, earnest, indefatigable, Plat.   2. of things, Ar., Luc.   II. earnest in begging or praying, importunate, λ. χείρ a hand instant in prayer, Soph.:— τὸ λιπαρές importunity, Luc.; πρὸς τὸ λ. = λιπαρῶς, Soph.   III. Adv. -ρῶς, earnestly, importunately,

Plat. (Deriv. uncertain: the first syll. seems to be from λι-, λίαν.)

λῐπᾰρητέον, verb. Adj. of λιπαρέω, one must be importunate, Xen.

λῐπᾰρία, Ion. -ίη, ἡ, importunity, persistence, Hdt.

λῐπᾰρό-ζωνος, ον, (ζώνη) bright-girdled, Eur.

λῐπᾰρό-θρονος, ον, bright-throned, Aesch.

λῐπᾰρο-κρήδεμνος, ον, with bright head-band, Il.

λῐπᾰρο-πλόκᾰμος, ον, with glossy locks, Il.

λῐπᾰρός, ά, όν, (λίπος) oily, shiny with oil, acc. to the custom of oiling the skin in the palaestra, Od., Ar., etc. 2. oily, greasy, Ar. II. of the skin, shining, sleek, Lat. nitidus, λιπαροὶ πόδες bright, smooth feet, without a wrinkle, Il.; λιπαρώτεροι ἐγένοντο Hdt.; λ. στῆθος Ar., etc. III. of condition, rich, comfortable, easy, Lat. nitidus, lautus, Od., Pind.; so, λιπαρῶς γηράσκειν Od. IV. of things, bright, brilliant, costly, splendid, Hom. V. of soil, fat, rich, fruitful, Lat. pinguis, h. Hom., Theogn.; λιπαραὶ Ἀθῆναι, a favourite epith. with the Athenians, prob. with allusion to the Attic olive, Pind., Ar.

λῐπᾰρό-χροος, ον, (χρόα) with shining skin, Theocr.

λῐπᾰρό-χρως, ωτος, ὁ, ἡ, = foreg., Theocr.

λῐπ-αυγής, ές, (αὐγή) deserted by light, blind, Anth.

λῐπάω, (λίπας, λίπος) to be fat and sleek, Ep. part. λιπόων Anth.

λῐπέ, Ep. for ἔλιπε, 3 sing. aor. 2 of λείπω.

λῐπεῖν, aor. 2 inf. of λείπω.

λῐπερνής, ές, gen. έος, also ῆτος, desolate, forlorn, homeless, outcast, Archil.: —so λῐπερνήτης, ου, ὁ, fem. -ῆτις, ιδος, Anth., etc. (Deriv. unknown.)

λῐπό-γᾰμος, ον, having abandoned her marriage ties, of Helen, Eur.

λῐπό-γυιος, ον, (γυῖον) wanting a limb, maimed, Anth.

λῐποῖσα, Dor. for -οῦσα, aor. 2 part. fem. of λείπω.

λῐπο-μαρτῠρίου δίκη, (λείπω, μαρτύριον) an action against a witness for non-appearance, Dem.

λῐπο-μήτωρ, ορος, ὁ, ἡ, (μήτηρ) motherless, Anth.

λῐπό-ναυς, ὁ, ἡ, deserting the fleet, Aesch.

λῐπο-ναύτης, ου, ὁ, leaving the sailors, Theocr.

λῐπό-νεως, ων, = λιπόναυς, Dem.

λῐπό-πατρις, ιδος, ὁ, ἡ, causing to forget one's country, of the lotos, Anth.

λῐπο-πάτωρ [ᾰ], ορος, ὁ, ἡ, (πατήρ) deserter of one's father, Eur.

λῐπό-πνοος, ον, contr. -πνους, ουν, (πνοή) left by breath, breathless, dead, Anth.

ΛΙ'ΠΟΣ [ῐ], τό, fat, βεβρῶτες αἵματος λίπος gorged with fat and blood, Soph.

λῐπο-σαρκής, ές, (σάρξ) wanting flesh, Anth.

λῐπο-στέφᾰνος, ον, falling from the wreath, Anth.

λῐπο-στρᾰτία, ἡ, desertion of the army, refusal to serve, Hdt., Thuc.

λῐπο-στρᾰτίου, τό, = foreg., Thuc.

λῐπο-ταξία, ἡ, a leaving one's post, desertion, Dem.

λῐπο-ταξίου γραφή, ἡ, an indictment for desertion, Plat., Dem.

λῐπο-τρῐχής, ές, (θρίξ) having lost one's hair, Anth.

λῐπο-ψῠχέω, f. ήσω, (ψυχή) to leave life, swoon, Thuc., Xen. II. to lack spirit, fail in courage, Hdt.

λῐπόων, Ep. part. of λιπάω.

ΛΙ'ΠΤΟΜΑΙ, Dep., with pf. pass. λέλιμμαι, to be eager, Aesch.:—c. gen. to be eager for, long for, Id.

λῐπών, aor. 2 part. of λείπω.

λίς or λῖς [ῑ], ὁ, Ep. for λέων, a lion, only in nom. and acc., Il., Hes., Theocr.

λίς, ἡ, Ep. form for λισσή, smooth, Od. II. as masc. Subst., only in dat. λιτί and acc. λῖτα, smooth cloth, linen cloth: others take λῖτα to be acc. pl. neut. linen cloths:—in Anth., we have λίτα [ῐ] πολυδαίδαλα, embroidered stuffs.

λίσαι, aor. 1 imper. of λίσσομαι:—λίσῃ, 2 sing. subj.

λίσπος, η, ον, (λίς, ἡ) smooth, polished, Ar. II. as Subst. λίσπαι, αἱ, dice cut in two by friends (ξένοι), each of whom kept half as tallies (σύμβολα), Plat.

λισσάς, άδος, pecul. fem. of λισσός, smooth, bare, Eur., Theocr. II. as Subst. a bare, smooth cliff, Plut.

ΛΙ'ΣΣΟΜΑΙ, 3 sing. Ion. impf. λισσέσκετο: aor. 1 ἐλισάμην, Ep. λλ-, imper. λίσαι [ῐ], 2 sing. subj. λίσῃ; aor. 2 inf. λιτέσθαι, opt. λιτοίμην:—to beg, pray, entreat, beseech, either absol. or c. acc. pers., Hom.; that by which one prays, in gen., λ. τινα γούνων Il.; λ. Ζηνός Od.:—an inf. is often added, οὐδέ σ' ἔγωγε λίσσομαι μένειν I do not pray thee to remain, Il. 2. c. acc. rei, to beg or pray for, οἳ αὐτῷ θάνατον λιτέσθαι Ib.: c. dupl. acc. pers. et rei, ταῦτα μὲν οὐχ ὑμέας ἔτι λίσσομαι this I beg of you no more, Od.

λισσός, ή, όν, (λίς, ἡ) smooth, λισσὴ αἰπειά τε εἰς ἅλα πέτρα a smooth rock running sheer into the sea, Od.; λισσὴ δ' ἀναδέδρομε πέτρη Ib.

λιστός, ή, όν, (λίσσομαι) to be moved by prayer, ap. Plat.

λιστρεύω, to dig round a plant, Od. From

λίστρον, τό, a tool for levelling or smoothing, a spade, a kind of shovel, Od., Mosch. (Deriv. uncertain.)

λῖτα, v. λίς, ἡ, II.

λιταίνω, (λιτή) rare form for λιτανεύω, Eur.

λῑτᾰνεύω, f. σω: in the augm. tenses λ is doubled metri grat., ἐλλιτάνευε, ἐλλιτάνευσα: (λίτομαι):—to pray, entreat, esp. for protection, either absol. or c. acc. pers., Hom.; that by which one prays in genit. γούνων λιτανεύειν Od.; also, γούνων ἁψάμενοι λιτανεύσομεν (Ep. for -ωμεν), Il.; c. inf., Ib.

λῑτᾰνός, ή, όν, (λιτή) praying, suppliant, μέλη Aesch.:—as Subst., λιτανά, τά, = λιταί, ἀμφὶ λιτανὰ ἔχεσθαι to be engaged in prayer, Id.

λιτᾰργίζω, f. Att. ιῶ, to slip away, Ar.

λίτ-αργος [ῐ], ον, (λι-) running quick.

λιτέσθαι, aor. 2 inf. of λίσσομαι.

λιτή, ἡ, (λίτομαι) a prayer, entreaty, mostly in pl., Od., Hdt., Trag. II. Λιταί, Prayers of sorrow and repentance, personified in Il. 9. 502 sq.

λιτί, v. λίς, ἡ, II.

λῐτό-βιος, ον, (λιτός) living plainly or sparingly, Strab.

λιτοίμην, aor. 2 opt. of λίσσομαι.

λίτομαι [ῐ], = λίσσομαι, h. Hom., Anth.

λῑτός, ή, όν, (v. λίς, ἡ) smooth, plain: of style, simple, unadorned, Arist.: of persons, simple, frugal, Polyb.: Adv. λιτῶς, Anth. 2. paltry, petty, Lat.

λιτός, ή, όν, (λίτομαι) suppliant, supplicatory, Pind.

λιτότης, ητος, ἡ, (λιτός) plainness, simplicity, Plut.

λίτρα, ἡ, a silver coin of Sicily, Lat. libra:—as a weight, 12 ounces, a pound, Anth.:—metaph., λίτρᾰν

ἐτῶν ζήσας having lived *a pound* of years, i. e. 72 (for a pound of gold was coined into 72 pieces), Id.

λιτραῖος, α, ον, *weighing* or *worth a λίτρα,* Anth.

λίτρον, τό, older form for νίτρον, Hdt., Plat.

Λιτυέρσης, Dor. -έρσας, ὁ, *Lityerses,* a son of Midas: *a reaper's song named after him,* Theocr.

λίτυον, τό, the Roman *lituus,* Plut.

λιχἄνός, όν, (λείχω) *licking : ὁ λ.* (sc. δάκτυλος) the *fore-finger,* from its use *in licking up,* Luc.

λιχμάζω, (λείχω) = λιχμάω, Hes. II. trans. *to lick,* Ion. 3 sing. impf. λιχμάζεσκε Mosch.

λιχμάω, f. ήσω, (λείχω) *to lick with the tongue,* of snakes, Eur. :—Med., ἐλιχμῶντο περὶ τὴν κεφαλὴν *played like serpents* round the head, Ar.

λιχνεία, ἡ, *daintiness, greediness,* Xen., Plat. From

λιχνεύω, (λίχνος) *to lick,* Luc. II. *to lick up :—* metaph. *to desire greedily, covet,* δόξαν Plut.

λιχνο-βόρος, ον, (βι-βρώσκω) *nice in eating, dainty,* Anth.

λίχνος, η, ον, also *ος, ον,* (λείχω) *dainty, lickerish, greedy,* Xen., Plat. 2. metaph. *curious,* Eur.

λίψ, ὁ, gen. λῐβός, the SW. *wind,* Lat. *Africus,* Hdt., Theocr. (From λείβω, because *it brought wet.*)

λίψ, ἡ, (λείβω) only in gen. and acc. (λιβάς or λίβος being used as nom.), *a stream,* Aesch. : *a draught,* Id.

λιψ-ουρία, ἡ, (οὖρον) *desire of making water, natural needs,* Aesch.

λό', Ep. for λοῦ', i. e. λοῦε, imper. of λούω : also Ep. 3 sing. impf.

λοβός, οῦ, ὁ, (λέπω) *the lobe of the ear,* Il. 2. *the lobe of the liver,* Aesch., Eur. : generally, *the liver,* Aesch.

λογάδην [ᾰ], Adv. (λογάς) *by picking out,* of stones for building, Thuc.; of soldiers, Plut.

λογάριον [ᾰ], τό, Dim. of λόγος, λ. δύστηνα wretched *petty speeches,* Dem.

λογάς, άδος, ὁ and ἡ, (λέγω B) *gathered, picked, chosen,* of *picked men,* Hdt., Eur., etc. 2. λ. λίθοι *unhewn stones, taken just as they were picked,* cf. λογάδην.

λογεῖον, τό, (λόγος) properly *a speaking-place :* in the Att. theatre, the *part* of the stage occupied by the *speakers,* Lat. *pulpitum,* Plut., etc.

λογία, ἡ, (λέγω B) *a collection for the poor,* N. T.

λογίδιον, τό, Dim. of λόγος : *a little fable* or *story,* Ar.

λογίζομαι, Dep. : f. Att. -ιοῦμαι : aor. 1 ἐλογισάμην : pf. λελόγισμαι :—aor. 1 ἐλογίσθην and sometimes pf. λελόγισμαι in pass. sense : (λόγος) —*to count, reckon, calculate, compute,* Hdt.; λ. ἀπὸ χειρός *to calculate off hand,* Ar. :—c. acc. rei, λ. τοὺς τόκους *to calculate* the interest, Id.; τρεῖς μνᾶς ἀναλώσας λογίσασθαι δώδεκα *to spend 3 minae and set down 12,* Id. 2. c. acc. et inf. *to reckon* or *calculate that,* Hdt., Dem. 3. λ. τί τινι *to set down to one's account, charge* to one, Lat. *imputare,* Dem., N.T. 4. λογ. ἀπό .. *to deduct from* .., Dem. II. without reference to numbers, *to take into account, calculate, consider,* Hdt., Att.; λ. περί τινος *to form calculations* about .., Hdt., Xen. 2. c. acc. et inf. *to count, deem, consider that* .., Hdt., Att.; with the inf. omitted, *to reckon* or *account* so and so, τὸν καθ' ἡμέραν βίον λογίζου σόν Eur.; μίαν ἄμφω τὰς ἡμέρας λ. *to count both days as one,* Xen. 3. c. inf. fut. *to*

count or *reckon upon* doing, *to calculate* or *expect that* .., Hdt., Xen. ;—c. acc. only, *to count upon,* Soph. 4. *to conclude by reasoning, infer that* a thing is, Plat., Xen. III. the aor. 1 ἐλογίσθην and sometimes pf. λελόγισμαι are used in pass. sense, *to be counted* or *calculated,* Xen.

λογικός, ή, όν, (λόγος) *of* or *for speaking* or *speech,* Plut. II. *of* or *belonging to the reason,* Arist. : *logical,* Id. :—ἡ λογική (sub. τέχνη) *logic,* Cic.

λόγιμος, η, ον, and *ος, ον,* (λόγος) *worth mention, notable, remarkable, famous,* Hdt.

λόγιον, τό, (λόγος) *an announcement, oracle,* Hdt. ; in pl. *oracles,* Id., Eur., etc.

λόγιος, α, ον, (λόγος) *versed in tales* or *stories* (λόγος IV): as Subst. *a chronicler, annalist,* Hdt. 2. generally *learned, erudite,* Arist., etc. II. *skilled in words, eloquent,* Eur., Plut.

λογισμός, ὁ, (λογίζομαι) *a counting, reckoning, calculation, computation,* Thuc.:—in pl. *arithmetic,* Xen., Plat. 2. *an account, bill,* Dem. II. without reference to number, *calculation, consideration, reasoning,* Thuc., Dem. 2. *an argument, conclusion,* Xen. III. *reasoning power, reason,* Id.

λογιστέον, verb. Adj. of λογίζομαι, *one must calculate* or *subtract,* Dem.

λογιστήριον, τό, the place at Athens *where the λογισταί met,* Oratt.

λογιστής, οῦ, ὁ, (λογίζομαι) *a calculator, teacher of arithmetic,* Plat. 2. *a calculator, reasoner,* Ar., Dem. II. in pl. *auditors,* at Athens, ten members of the βουλή, to whom magistrates going out of office submitted their accounts, Dem., etc. Hence

λογιστικός, ή, όν, *skilled* or *practised in calculating,* Xen., Plat. :—ἡ λογιστική (sc. τέχνη), *arithmetic,* Plat. II. *endued with reason, rational,* Arist. :— τὸ λ. *the reasoning faculty,* Plat. 2. *using one's reason, reasonable,* Xen.

λογογράφέω, f. ήσω, *to write speeches,* Plut.

λογογραφία, ἡ, *a writing of speeches,* and, generally, *of prose,* Plat. ; and

λογογράφικός, ή, όν, *of* or *for writing speeches* or *prose,* Plat. From

λογο-γράφος [ᾰ], ὁ, (γράφω) *a prose-writer* :—the early Greek *chroniclers* are so called by Thuc. II. like λογοποιός II, *a speech-writer, one who lived by writing speeches* for others to deliver, Plat., etc.

λογο-λέσχης, ου, ὁ, (λέσχη) *a prater,* Anth.

λογομάχέω, f. ήσω, *to war about words,* N. T.; and

λογομαχία, ἡ, *a war about words,* N. T. From

λογο-μάχος, ον, (μάχομαι) *warring about words.*

λογοποιέω, f. ήσω, *to invent stories, to write, compose,* Plat. 2. *to fabricate* tales, of newsmongers, Thuc., Dem., etc. II. *to write speeches* (v. λογοποιός II), Plat. Hence

λογοποιία, ἡ, *tale-telling, news-mongering,* Theophr.

λογοποιικός, ή, όν, *of* or *like a λογοποιός : ἡ - κὴ τέχνη,* = λογογραφική, Plat.

λογο-ποιός, ὁ, (ποιέω) *a prose-writer,* esp. *an historian, chronicler,* Plat., etc. 2. *a writer of fables,* Hdt., Plut. II. = λογογράφος II, Plat. 2. *a tale-teller, newsmonger,* Dem.

λόγος, ὁ, (λέγω C), (A) *the word* or *that by which*

the inward thought is expressed, Lat. oratio; and, (B) the inward thought itself, Lat. ratio. **A.** Lat. vox, oratio, that which is said or spoken : I. a word, pl. words, i. e. language, talk, Hom., etc. ; λόγου ἕνεκα, Lat. dicis causa, merely for talking's sake, Plat. ; λόγῳ in word, in pretence, opp. to ἔργῳ (in deed, in reality), Hdt., Att. II. a word, saying, statement, Thuc. : an oracle, Pind., Plat. :—a saying, maxim, proverb, Pind., Aesch. 2. an assertion, promise, Soph. 3. a resolution, κοινῷ λ. by common consent, Hdt. 4. a condition, ἐπὶ λόγῳ τοιῷδε Id. 5. a command, Aesch. III. speech, discourse, conversation, εἰς λόγους ἐλθεῖν, συνελθεῖν, ἀφικέσθαι τινί Hdt., Att. ; λόγου μεῖζον, κρεῖσσον beyond expression, Hdt., Thuc.; λόγου ἄξιον worth mention, Hdt. 2. right of speech, power to speak, λόγον αἰτεῖσθαι Thuc. ; διδόναι Xen. 3. talk about one, report, repute, Lat. fama, λόγος Hdt., Att. ; λόγος ἐστί, λόγος ἔχει, κατέχει, φέρεται, c. acc. et inf., so the story goes, Lat. fama fert, Hdt., Att. 4. speech, language, Plat. IV. a saying, tale, story, opp. on the one hand to mere fable (μῦθος), on the other, to regular history (ἱστορία), Thuc., etc. : then, a fictitious story, fable, like those of Aesop, Hdt., Plat. 2. a narrative, and in pl. histories, history, Hdt. : in sing. one part of such a work, Id. V. generally, prose-writing, prose, Xen., etc. VI. a speech, oration, Oratt. VII. like ῥῆμα, the thing spoken of, the subject or matter of the λόγος, Hdt., Att. VIII. that which is stated, a proposition, position, principle, Plat. : also = ὁρισμός, a definition, Id. **B.** Lat. ratio, thought, reason, οὐκ ἔχει λόγον admits not of reason, Soph. ; ὀρθὸς λ. Plat. ; ὡς ἔχει λόγον, = ὡς ἔοικεν, Dem. :—κατὰ λόγον agreeably to reason, Plat. ; μετὰ λόγον Id. 2. an opinion, expectation, Hdt. 3. a reason, ground, plea, Soph., etc. ; ἐκ τίνος λόγου; on what ground? Aesch. ; ἐξ οὐδενὸς λ. Soph., etc. 4. ὁ λόγος αἱρέει, c. acc. et inf., it stands to reason that . . , Lat. ratio evincit, Hdt. II. account, consideration, esteem, regard, λόγον βροτῶν οὐκ ἔσχεν οὐδένα Aesch. ; Μαρδονίου λόγος ἐγίγνεται Hdt. ; λόγου οὐδενὸς γενέσθαι to be of no account, Id. ; λόγου ποιεῖσθαί τινα or τι, to make account of a person or thing, Id. ;—so, ἐν οὐδενὶ λόγῳ ποιεῖσθαι Id. ; ἐν ἀνδρὸς λόγῳ εἶναι to be reckoned as a man, Id. 2. an account, λόγον διδόναι τινός to give an account of a thing, Id., Att. ; so, λόγον παρέχειν Plat. ; λ. λαμβάνειν παρά τινος Dem. ; λ. ἀπαιτεῖν Id. ; ὑπέχειν Plat., Dem., etc. ; ἐγγράφειν Dem., etc. ; ἀποφέρειν Aeschin. ; cf. λογιστής. III. due relation, proportion, analogy, κατὰ λόγον τινός or τινί Hdt., Att. **C.** Ὁ ΛΟΓΟΣ, the LOGOS or WORD, comprising both senses of Thought and Word, N. T.

λογχεύω, to pierce with a spear, Anth. From

ΛΟΓΧΗ, ἡ, a spear-head, javelin-head, Lat. spiculum, Hdt., Att. ; in pl. of a single spear, the point with its barbs, τὸ ξυστὸν τῇσι λόγχῃσι ὁμοίως the shaft alike with the spear-head, Hdt. II. a lance, spear, javelin, Lat. lancea, Pind., Soph., etc. III. a troop of spearmen, 'a plump of spears,' Soph., Eur.

λογχ-ήρης, ες, (*ἄρω) armed with a spear, Eur.

λόγχῖμος, ον, (λόγχη) of a spear, κλόνοι λ. the clash of spears, Aesch.

λογχόομαι, Pass. to be furnished with a point, Arist.

λογχο-ποιός, όν, (ποιέω) making spears, Eur.

λογχο-φόρος, ον, (φέρω) spear-bearing, Eur.: as Subst. a spear-man, pike-man, Ar., Xen., etc.

λογχωτός, ή, όν, lance-headed, Eur., Anth.

λόγως, Dor. for λόγους, acc. pl. of λόγος.

λόε, Ep. for ἔλουε, 3 sing. impf. of λούω.

λοέσσας, λοεσσάμενος, Ep. aor. 1 part. act. and med. of λούω :—fut. med. **λοέσσομαι.**

λοετρόν, λοετροχόος, Ep. for λουτρ-, Hom.

λοέω, Ep. for λούω.

λοιβεῖον, τό, a cup for pouring libations, Plut. From

λοιβή, ἡ, (λείβω) a drink-offering, Lat. libatio, Hom. ; opt. in pl., Pind., Soph

λοίγιος, ον, (λοιγός) pestilent, deadly, fatal, Il.

ΛΟΙΓΟΣ, οῦ, ὁ, ruin, havoc, of death by plague, Il. ; by war, Ib. ; of the destruction of the ships, Ib.

λοιδορέω, f. ήσω : aor. 1 ἐλοιδόρησα : pf. λελοιδόρηκα : —Med., f. -ήσομαι : aor. 1 ἐλοιδορησάμην :—Pass., aor. 1 ἐλοιδορήθην : pf. λελοιδόρημαι : (λοίδορος) :—to abuse, revile, Hdt., Att. ; to rebuke, Xen. :—Med. to rail at one another, Ar. II. λοιδορούμαι is also used as Dep., c. dat., to rail at, Id., Xen. :—c. acc. cogn., πάντα τὰ αἰσχρὰ λοιδορέονται they use all kind of foul reproaches, Hdt. Hence

λοιδόρημα, ατος, τό, railing, abuse, an affront, Arist.

λοιδορησμός, οῦ, ὁ, = λοιδορία, Ar.

λοιδορία, ἡ, (λοιδορέω), railing, abuse, Thuc., Plat.

λοίδορος, ον, railing, abusive, Eur. :—Adv. -ρως, Strab. (Deriv. uncertain.)

ΛΟΙΜΟΣ, οῦ, ὁ, a plague, pestilence, Il., Hdt., Att. ; of the plague at Athens, Thuc. 2. of persons, a plague, pest, Dem. (Prob. akin to λύμη, Lat. lues.)

λοιμ-ώδης, ες, (εἶδος) like plague, pestilential, ἡ λ. νόσος the plague, Thuc.

λοιμώσσω, Att. -ττω, f. ξω, to have the plague, Luc.

λοιπός, ή, όν, (λείπω) remaining, the rest, Lat. reliquus, Hdt., etc. ; in Att. the Art. may either be in the same case as the Noun or have the Noun in gen. dependent on it, τὴν λοιπὴν ὁδὸν πορεύεσθαι Xen. ; αἱ λοιπαὶ τῶν νεῶν the rest, τὸ λοιπὸν τῆς ἡμέρας Xen. 2. λοιπόν [ἐστι], c. inf., it remains to shew, etc., Plat., Xen. ; with Art., τὸ λ. ἐστι σκέψασθαι what remains is to consider, Plat ; —ὃ δὲ λοιπόν, quod superest, Aesch., etc. 3. often of Time, ὁ λ. χρόνος the future, Pind., Att. ; πρὸς τὸν λοιπὸν τοῦ χρόνου Dem. ; τὸν λ. χρόνον for the future, Soph ; τοῦ λ. χρόνου Id.;—so in neut., τὸ λοιπόν henceforward, hereafter, Trag. ; so, τὰ λοιπά Ib. 4. τὸ λοιπόν and τὰ λοιπά the rest, Aesch. ; also λοιπόν as Adv., further, besides, Plat.

λοισθήϊος, ον, Ep. for λοίσθιος, λοισθήϊον ἄεθλον the prize for the last in the race, Il.

λοίσθιος, ον, also α, ον, = λοῖσθος, Pind., Trag. :—neut. λοίσθιον, as Adv. last, Soph., Eur.

λοῖσθος, ον, = λοῖπος, left behind, last, Il., Eur. ; Sup. λοισθότατος last of all, Hes.

λόκκη, ἡ, ἁ cloak, Anth. (Deriv. unknown.)

Λοκροί, οἱ, the Locrians, of which there were three tribes, the Opuntian, opposite Euboea, Il. ; the Epicne-

midian, on Mount Cnemis on the Maliac Gulf, Thuc.; and *the Ozolian*, on the Corinthian Gulf, Id.:—*the Epizephyrian* or *Zephyrian* were a colony of the last on Mount Zephyrium in lower Italy, Pind., Thuc. **II.** Adj. **Λοκρός, ά, όν,** *Locrian*, fem. **Λοκρίς, ίδος,** Pind.; ἡ Λοκρίς (sc. **γῆ**) Ar.

Λοξίας, Ion. -ίης, εω, ου, ὁ, epith. of Apollo, Hdt., Trag. ;—either from λοξός, *the Ambiguous*, or from λέγω, λόγος, *the Speaker*.

λοξο-βάτης [ἄ], ου, ὁ, (βῆμα) *going side-ways*, Batr.

ΛΟΞΟ'Σ, ή, όν, *slanting, crosswise, aslant,* Lat. *obliquus,* Eur.; λοξὰ βαίνειν, of a crab, Babr.; ὁ λοξὸς κυκλός *the ecliptic,* Arist. **2.** of suspicious looks, λοξὸν ὁρᾶν to look *askance,* Lat. *limis oculis,* Solon; λοξὰ βλ. Theocr.; αὐχένα λοξὸν ἔχειν to turn the neck *aside,* i. e. withdraw his favour, Tyrtae.; also = Horace's *stare capite obstipo,* Theogn. **3.** of language, *indirect, ambiguous,* of oracles, Luc. Hence

λοξότης, ητος, ἡ, *slanting direction, obliquity,* Strab.

λοξο-τρόχις, ή, (τρέχω) *oblique-running,* Anth.

λόξωσις, ή, *obliquity,* of the ecliptic, Anth.; Strab.

λοπάδ-αρπαγίδης, ου, ὁ, (ἁρπάζω) *dish-snatcher,* Anth.

λοπάδιον [ἄ], τό, Dim. of λοπάς, *a platter,* Ar.

ΛΟΠΑ'Σ, άδος, ή, *a flat dish,* Ar.

λοπίς, ίδος, ή, = λεπίς, Ar.

λοπός, οῦ, or **λόπος, ου, ὁ,** (λέπω) *the shell, husk, pee!,* λοπὸς κρομύοιο *the peel* of an onion, Od.

λουέω, Ep. for λούω : impf. ἐλούεον.

λοῦσα, Ep. for ἔλουσα, aor. 1 of λούω.

λοῦσθαι, contr. for λούεσθαι, inf. med. of λούω.

λουσῶ, Dor. fut. of λούω.

λουτρο-δάϊκτος, ον, (δαΐζω) *slain in the bath,* Aesch.

λουτρόν, τό, Ep. **λοετρόν,** (λούω) *a bath, bathing-place,* Hom.; mostly in pl., θερμὰ λοετρά hot *baths,* Il.; Att. θερμὰ λουτρά Aesch., etc.; also called λουτρὰ 'Ηράκλεια Ar.; ὑδάτων λοῦτρα *water for bathing* or *washing,* Soph.; λοῦσαι τινα λουτρόν to give one a *bath,* Id. **II.** in Poets, = σπονδαί or χοαί *libations to the dead,* Id., Eur.

λουτρο-φόρος, ὁ, (φέρω) *bringing water for bathing* or *washing,* esp. from the fountain Callirrhoé on the wedding-day: hence, λ. χλιδή *the marriage-ceremony,* Eur. **2.** as Subst., λουτροφόρος, ή, *the black urn* placed on the tomb of unmarried persons, Dem., Anth.

λουτροχοέω, f. ήσω, *to pour water into the bath,* Anth.

λουτρο-χόος, ον, Ep. **λοετρό-,** (χέω) *pouring water into the bath,* the slave who did this, Od., Xen.; λ. τρίπους a three-legged kettle, *in which water was warmed for bathing,* Hom.

λουτρών, ῶνος, ὁ, (λουτρόν) *a bathing-room, bath-house,* Aesch., Xen.

ΛΟΥ'Ω, contr. from λοέω, of which we have in Hom., impf. λόεον, aor. 1 inf. λοέσσαι, part. λοέσσας;—fut. med. λοέσσομαι, 3 sing. aor. 1 λοέσσατο, part. λοεσσάμενος:— also Ep. impf. ἐλούεον:—later forms, f. λούσω, Dor. λουσῶ, aor. 1 ἔλουσα, Ep. λοῦσα:—Med., f. λούσομαι:—aor. 1 ἐλουσάμην, Ep. 3 pl. λούσαντο:—Pass., pf. λέλουμαι, 3 sing. λέλουται, part. λελουμένος :—the orig. form of the pres. was λόω, whence 3 sing. λόει, Ep. 3 sing. impf. λόε, 3 pl. λόον; inf. λόεσθαι; also Att. contr. forms, 3 sing. and 1 pl. impf. ἔλου, ἐλούμεν : pres. pass. λοῦται, λοῦνται, 3 pl. impf. ἐλοῦντο, Ion. λοῦντο, inf. λοῦσθαι, part. λούμενος. *To wash* another, properly, *to wash* his *body* (νίζω being used of the *hands and feet,* πλύνω of *clothes),* Hom.; λούσατε ἐν ποταμῷ *bathe* him, i. e. *let him bathe,* Od. :—also, λό' ἐκ τρίποδος *washed* me [with water] from a caldron, Ib. **II.** Med. and Pass. *to bathe,* c. gen., λελουμένος 'Ωκεανοῖο (of a star just risen), *fresh from* Ocean's *bath,* Il.; so, λούεσθαι ποταμοῖο *to bathe* [in water] of the river, Ib.; so, ἀπὸ κρήνης λούμενος Hdt. :—absol., λούσαντο Od., etc.; λελουμένος *fresh-bathed, after bathing,* Hdt.; ἦλθε λουσόμενος (Horat., *ire lavatum*), Ar. **2.** in strict pass. sense, λοῦσθαι ὑπὸ τοῦ Διός, i. e. *to be washed* by the rain from heaven, Hdt. **3.** in strict med. sense, λοέσσασθαι χρόα *to wash one's body,* Hes.

λοφάω, f. ήσω, *to have a crest* (λόφος), of larks, Babr. **2.** *to be ill of a crest* (i. e. *to have more crest than enough),* Ar.

λοφεῖον, τό, (λόφος) *a crest-case,* Ar.: *any case,* Id.

λοφη-φόρος, ον, (φέρω) *crested,* of a lark, Babr.

λοφιά, Ion. -ιή, ή, (λόφος) *the mane* on the neck and back of certain animals, *the mane* of horses, *the bristly back* of boars and hyaenas, Od., Hdt. **2.** *the back-fin* of fishes, Anth. Hence

λοφιήτης, ου, ὁ, *a dweller on the hills,* of Pan, Anth.

λοφνίς, ίδος, ή, (λέπω) *a torch of vine bark,* Anth.

λοφόομαι, (λόφος) Pass. *to be crested.*

λοφο-ποιός, ὁ, (ποιέω) *a crest-maker,* Ar.

λόφος, ου, ὁ, properly *the back of the neck* of draught-cattle, because the yoke *rubs it* (λέπει); of a horse, *the mane,* Il.; of a man, *the nape of the neck,* Ib.; ὑπὸ ζυγῷ λόφον ἔχειν to have *the neck* under the yoke, i.e. *to obey patiently,* Soph. **II.** *the crest of a hill,* a ridge, Od., Hdt., etc. **III.** *the crest* of a helmet, Lat. *crista,* Hom., etc. **2.** *the crest on the head* of birds, Lat. *crista,* as of the lark, Simon.; the cock's *comb,* Ar. **3.** of men, *the tuft of hair* upon the crown, λόφους κείρεσθαι to shave so as to leave tufts, Hdt.

λόφωσις, ή, (λοφόομαι) *a being crested,* ἡ λ. ἡ τῶν ὀρνέων their *crests,* Ar.

λοχᾱγέτης, ου, ὁ, Dor. and Att. for λοχηγέτης, = λοχαγός, Aesch., Eur.

λοχᾱγέω, Dor. and Att. for λοχηγέω, *to lead a λόχος* or *company* (commonly of 100 men), Xen.; c. gen., λόχου λοχηγεῖν Hdt.

λοχᾱγία, ή, Dor. and Att. for λοχηγία, *the rank* or *office of λοχαγός,* Xen.

λοχ-ᾱγός, οῦ, ὁ, (λόχος, ἡγέομαι = ἄγω) Dor. and Att. for λοχηγός, *the leader of an armed band,* Soph. **II.** esp. *the captain of a company* (100 men), Xen.: —but, in the Spartan army, *the commander* of a λόχος, Id.; in the Persian, of 24 men, Id.

λοχάζομαι, = λοχάω, Anth.

λοχαῖος, α, ον, = λόχιος, *clandestine,* Anth.

λοχάω, f. ήσω, Ep. also ήσομαι: aor. 1 ἐλόχησα:—Ep. 3 pl. λοχόωσι, part. λοχόων: (λόχος) :—*to lie in wait for, to watch, waylay, entrap,* Od., Hdt. **2.** absol. *to lie in wait* or *ambush,* Il., Hdt.; in aor. 1 part. with another Verb, λοχήσας πολλοὺς διέφθειρεν Thuc.; Med., λοχησάμενος Od. **3.** c. acc. loci, *to occupy with an ambuscade,* ἐλόχησαν τὴν ὁδὸν Hdt.

λοχεία, ή, (λοχεύω) *childbirth, childbed,* Eur., Plat. **II.** = λόχευμα 1, Anth.

λοχεῖος, α, ον, and ος, ον, = λόχιος, λοχεῖα (sub. χωρία) the place of childbirth, Eur.

λοχέος, οῖο, ὁ, = λόχος, an ambush, Hes.

λόχευμα, ατος, τό, (λοχεύω) that which is born, a child, Eur. II. in pl., childbirth, Id.: metaph., κάλυκος ἐν λοχεύμασιν in the bursting of the bud, Aesch.

λοχεύω, (λόχος II) to bring forth, bear, h. Hom., Anth. 2. of the midwife, to bring to the birth. attend in childbirth, deliver, τινά Eur.:—Pass. to be delivered, bear children, Id.; λοχευθεῖσα πυρί, of Semelé, Id. II. Med., just like Act., of the mother, Eur.; of the birthplace, Anth. III. Pass., of the child, to be brought forth, born, Soph.; Προμᾱθεῖ λοχευθεῖσα brought to birth by Prometheus, Eur.: —metaph., generally, to lie embedded, ἐν τεύτλοισι Ar.

λοχηγέτης, λοχηγέω, λοχηγός, ὁ, Ion. for λοχαγ-.

λόχια, τά, and Λοχία, ἡ, v. λόχιος.

λοχίζω, f. σω, = λοχάω, to lie in wait for, τινά: Pass., λοχισθέντες διεφθάρησαν they were cut to pieces by falling into an ambuscade, Thuc. 2. to place in ambush, Id. II. to distribute men in companies (λόχοι), to put them in order of battle, Hdt., Plut.

λόχιος, α, ον, of or belonging to childbirth, λ. νοσήματα childbed, Eur.; ὠδίνων λοχίαις ἀνάγκαις Id. II. Λοχία, ἡ, epith. of Artemis Εἰλείθυια, Id. III. λόχια, τά, childbirth, Anth.

λοχισμός, ὁ, (λοχίζω) a placing in ambush, Plut.

λοχίτης [ῑ], ου, ὁ, (λόχος) one of the same company, a fellow-soldier, comrade, Aesch., Xen.

λοχμαῖος, α, ον, of the coppice, Μοῦσα λ., of the nightingale, Ar.

λόχμη, ἡ, (λόχος) a thicket, coppice, copse, Od., Pind.

λόχμιος, ον, = λοχμαῖος, Anth.

λοχμ-ώδης, ες, (εἶδος) overgrown with bushes, Thuc.

λόχονδε, Adv. to ambush, for an ambuscade, Hom.

λόχος, ὁ, (λέγω A): I. an ambush, i. e. 1. a place of ambush, place for lying in wait, Hom., Eur. 2. the act of lying in wait, λόχον εἷσαι to place an ambuscade, Hom.; λέγεσθαι ἐς λόχον to lie in ambush, Il.:—c. gen. objecti, λόχος θέοιο γέροντος the way to watch him, Od. 3. the men that form the ambush, Il., Eur. 4. any armed band, a body of troops, Od., Trag.:—a body of soldiers, a company, regiment, Xen.:—among the Spartans a λόχος was the fourth or fifth part of a μόρα Hdt.:—ὁ ἱερὸς λ. the sacred company at Thebes, Plut. 5. any body of people, a union for civil purposes, Xen., etc.:—used to transl. the Rom. centuria, Plut., etc. II. a lying-in, childbirth, parturition, Aesch.

λοχόων, Ep. for λοχῶν, part. of λοχάω.

λοχόωσι, Ep. for λοχῶσι, 3 pl. of λοχάω.

λόω, v. λούω.

λύᾱ, ἡ, Dor. for λύη.

Λυαῖος, ὁ, (λύω) Deliverer, of Bacchus, Anacreont.

λῠγαῖος, ον, (λύγη) shadowy, murky, gloomy, Eur.

λύγδην, Adv. (λύζω) with sobs, Soph., Anth.

λύγδῐνος [ῐ], α, ον, = λύγδινος, Anth.

λύγδῐνος, η, ον, of white marble, Babr., Anth. 2. marble-white, Anth. From

ΛΥΓΔΟΣ, ἡ, white marble, Anth.

λῠγίζω, Dor. f. λυγιξῶ: pf. λελύγισμαι:—Pass., Dor. aor.

ι ἐλυγίχθην: (λύγος):—to bend or twist as one does a withe, πλευρὰν λ. of a dancer, Ar.; λ. ἀλλήλους, of wrestlers, Luc. 2. to throw, master, Theocr. II. Pass. to bend or twist oneself like a withe, to bend aside or writhe, so as to avoid a blow, Plat., Luc.:—metaph., in pf. part. λελυγισμένος, broken, effeminate, Anth. 2. to turn, play, as a joint in the socket, Soph. 3. metaph. to be thrown or mastered, Theocr. Hence

λῠγισμός, οῦ, ὁ, a bending, twisting, of wrestlers, Luc.: metaph., of the windings and twistings of a sophist, Ar.

λύγκειος, α, ον, (λύγξ, ὁ) lynx-like, Anth.

ΛΥΓΞ, ὁ, ἡ, gen. λυγκός, a lynx, Eur., etc.

λύγξ, ἡ, gen. λυγγός, (λύζω) a spasmodic affection of the throat, hiccough, hiccup, λ. κενή an ineffectual retching, nothing being thrown off the stomach, Thuc.

ΛΥΓΟΣ [ῠ], ἡ, vitex agnus castus, a willow-like tree, withy; in pl. its withes, Lat. vimina, Hom., Eur.

λῠγο-τευχής, ές, (τεύχω) made of withes, Anth.

λῠγόω, f. ώσω, to tie fast, Anth.

ΛΥΓΡΟΣ, ά, όν, sore, baneful, mournful, Hom., Trag.: —τὰ λυγρά bane, misery, ruin, Hom., Hes. 2. baneful, with an act. force, φάρμακα λυγρά Od.; γαστὴρ λυγρή the stomach that cause of bane, Ib. 3. εἵματα λυγρά sorry garments, Ib. II. of persons, baneful, mischievous, Ib.: sorry, i. e. weak, cowardly, Hom., Soph. III. Adv. -ρῶς, sorely, Il.

Λῡδία, ἡ, Lydia, in Asia Minor, Hdt.:—τὰ Λυδιακά, a history of Lydia by Xanthus.

Λῡδίζω, to play the Lydian, of Magnes, in reference to his play called Λυδοί, Ar.

Λύδιος, α, ον, and ος, ον, of Lydia, Lydian, Pind., etc.: —Λυδία λίθος, ἡ, a stone used to assay gold, Soph.; also, Λ. πέτρα Theocr.

Λῡδιστί [ῑ], Adv. in the Lydian tongue, after the Lydian fashion, Plat.: of Music, in the Lydian mode, ἡ Λ. ἁρμονία Id.

Λῡδός, οῦ, ὁ, a Lydian, Pind., Hdt., etc.

ΛΥΖΩ, f. ξω, to have the hiccough or hiccup, to sob violently, Ar., Anth. (Formed from the sound.)

λύη, Dor. λύα, ἡ, (λύω) dissolution: hence, faction, sedition, Pind.

λύθεν, Ep. for ἐλύθησαν, 3 pl. aor. 1 pass. of λύω. II. λυθέν, neut. part. aor. 1 pass.

λυθῆναι, aor. 1 pass. inf. of λύω.

λύθρον, τό, or λύθρος, ὁ, (λούω) defilement from blood, gore, Hom., Anth.

λυθρ-ώδης, ες, (εἶδος) defiled with gore, Anth.

λῠκά-βας [κᾰ], αντος, ὁ, a year, Od., Bion. II. λῠκᾰβαντίδες ὧραι, αἱ, the hours that make up the year, Anth. (Prob. from *λύκη, βαίνω, the path of light, the sun's course.)

Λύκαια, τά, v. Λυκαῖος.

λύκαινα [ῠ], ἡ, fem. of λύκος, a she-wolf, Babr., Plut.

λύκαινίς, ίδος, ἡ, = foreg., Anth.

Λυκαῖος, α, ον, Lycaean, Arcadian, epith. of Zeus, Hdt., Pind., etc. II. Λύκαιον, τό, his temple, Plut.; so, Λ. σήκωμα Eur. 2. Mount Lycaeus in Arcadia, Theocr. III. Λύκαια (sc. ἱερά), τά, the festival of Lycaean Zeus, Xen.:—also = Roman Lupercalia, Plut.

Λυκαονία, ἡ, a district in the S. of Asia Minor, Xen.,

etc. : the people were **Λυκάονες**, οἱ, Id. :—Adv. **-ιστί**, in *Lycaonian*, N. T.

λῠκ-αυγής, ές, (*λύκη, αὐγή) *of* or *at twilight :* τὸ λυκαυγές *early dawn*, Luc.

λῠκέη (sub. δορά), ἡ, *a wolf-skin*, Il.

Λύκειον [ῠ], τό, *the Lyceum*, a gymnasium with covered walks in the Eastern suburb of Athens, named after the neighbouring temple of Apollo Λύκειος, Ar., Plat., etc.

λύκειος [ῠ], ον, *of* or *belonging to a wolf*, Eur. **II.** *Λύκειος*, as epith. of Apollo, either as λυκοκτόνος (q. v.), or as *the Lycian god* (v. Λυκηγενής), or (from *λύκη) as *the god of light*, Aesch. ; there is a play upon the doubtful meanings, Λύκει᾽ ἄναξ, λύκειος γενοῦ στρατῷ δαΐῳ, *Lycean lord*, be *a very wolf* to the enemy, Id.

***λύκη**, *light*, a Root, whence come λυκά-βας, λύχνος, etc.

Λῠκη-γενής, ές, (γίγνομαι) of Apollo, commonly explained *Lycian-born*, Il.

Λῠκία, ἡ, *Lycia :* **Λυκίηθεν** *from Lycia*, Il. ; **Λυκίηνδε** *to Lycia*, Ib.

Λῠκι-άρχης, ου, ὁ, (ἄρχω) *president of the Lycians*, Strab.

λῠκῐδεύς, έως, ὁ, (λύκος) *a wolf's whelp*, Solon, Theocr.

Λύκιο-εργής, contr. **-ουργής**, ές, *of Lycian workmanship*, Hdt., Dem.

Λύκιος, α, ον, *Lycian :* **Λύκιοι**, οἱ, *the Lycians*, Il., etc. **II.** epith. of Apollo (cf. Λύκειος), Pind., Eur.

Λυκιουργής, ές, contr. for Λυκιοεργής, Dem.

λῠκο-θαρσής, ές, (θάρσος) *bold as a wolf*, Anth.

λῠκο-κτόνος, ὁ, (κτείνω) epith. of Apollo, *wolf-slayer*, Soph.

λῠκορ-ραίστης, ὁ, (ῥαίω) *wolf-worrier*, Anth.

ΛΥ'ΚΟΣ [ῠ], ὁ, Lat. *lupus*, *a wolf*, Hom. ;—proverb., λύκον ἰδεῖν *to see a wolf*, i. e. *to be struck dumb*, as was vulgarly believed of any one of whom a wolf got the first look, Plat., Theocr. (so Virg., *Moerim lupi videre priores*) ; λύκος οὖν ὑμεναιοῖ, of an impossibility, Ar.

λῠκό-φως, ωτος, τό, (*λύκη) *twilight*, *the gloaming*, Lat. *diluculum*.

λῠκόω, (λύκος) *to tear like a wolf :*—Pass. *to be torn by wolves*, πρόβατα λελυκωμένα Xen.

λῠκ-ώδης, ες, = λυκοειδής, Arist.

λῦμα, ατος, τό, (λούω) mostly in pl. *the water used in washing*, *washings*, *off-scourings*, *filth*, Il. ; λύμαθ᾽ ἁγνίσας ἐμά, of blood on the hands, Soph. **II.** *moral filth*, *defilement*, in sing., Id. **III.** = λύμη, *ruin*, *bane*, Aesch. ; of a person, λῦμα Ἀχαιῶν, i. e. Hector, Eur.

λῡμαίνομαι, Dep. ; partly in med. forms, f. λυμᾰνοῦμαι, aor. 1 ἐλυμηνάμην :—partly in pass., aor. 1 part. λυμανθείς : pf. λελύμασμαι, 3 sing. λελύμανται, part. -ασμένος : (λύμη) :—*to treat with indignity*, *to outrage*, *to maltreat*, c. acc., Hdt., Soph., etc. ; c. acc. cogn., λύμης, ἥν με ἐλυμήνω Eur. :—of things, τὰς ῥήσεις ἃς ἐλυμαίνου the speeches you *used to murder* (as an actor), Dem.; ὀψοποιία λ. τὰ ὄψα *spoils*, Xen. **2.** c. dat. *to inflict indignities* or *outrages upon*, Hdt., Ar., etc. **3.** absol. *to cause ruin*, Thuc., Xen. **II.** sometimes as Pass., λυμανθὲν δέμας Aesch. ; λελυμάνθαι Dem. Hence

λῡμαντήρ, ῆρος, ὁ, *a spoiler*, *destroyer*, Xen. ; and

λῡμαντήριος, α, ον, *injurious*, *destructive*, Aesch. : c. gen. *destroying*, *ruining*, Id. ; and

λῡμαντής, οῦ, ὁ, as Adj. *ruining*, c. gen., Soph.

λῠμεών, ῶνος, ὁ, (λύμη) *a destroyer*, *spoiler*, *corrupter*, Soph., Eur.

ΛΥ'ΜΗ [ῠ], ἡ, *brutal outrage*, *maltreatment*, *maiming*, Hdt., Aesch., etc. :—in pl. *outrages*, *indignities*, Hdt., Aesch. **II.** = λῦμα, *defilement*, Polyb.

λύμην, Ep. aor. 2 pass. of λύω.

λῡμηνάμενος, aor. 1 med. part. of λυμαίνομαι.

λύντο, 3 pl. Ep. aor. 2 pass. of λύω.

λῡπέω, f. ήσω, *to give pain to*, *to pain*, *distress*, *grieve*, *vex*, *annoy*, Hdt., Trag., etc. ; ἡ θώραξ λ. *distresses* by its weight, Xen. :—absol. *to cause pain* or *grief*, Soph. **2.** of marauders, *to harass*, *annoy* by constant attacks, Hdt., Thuc., etc. **II.** Pass. with fut. med. *to be pained*, *grieved*, *distressed*, Theogn., etc. ; μὴ λυπέεο *be not distressed*, Hdt. :—c. acc. cogn., λύπας λυπεῖσθαι Plat. :—also c. acc. rei, *to grieve about* a thing, Soph. :—absol. *to feel pain*, Eur., etc. From

ΛΥ'ΠΗ [ῠ], ἡ, *pain of body*, Lat. *dolor*, Plat. : *distress*, *sad plight* or *condition*, Hdt. **2.** *pain of mind*, *grief*, Id., Att.

λύπημα, ατος, τό, (λυπέω) *pain*, Soph.

λυπῆν, Dor. for λυπεῖν, inf. of λυπέω.

λῡπηρός, ά, όν, (λυπέω) **I.** of things, *painful*, *distressing*, Lat. *molestus*, Hdt., Att. **II.** of persons, **1.** in good sense, *causing sorrow* by one's departure, Eur. **2.** in bad sense, *causing pain*, *troublesome*, *vexatious*, Soph., Thuc., etc. **III.** Adv. λυπηρῶς, *painfully*, so as to *cause pain*, Soph. ; λυπηρῶς ἔχει it is *painful*, Id.

λυπητέον, verb. Adj. *one must feel pain*, Xen.

λῡπρό-βιος, ον, *leading a wretched life*.

λῡπρός, ά, όν, (λυπέω) *wretched*, *poor*, *sorry*, of land, Od., Hdt. **II.** of persons, *causing pain*, *offensive*, *troublesome*, Aesch., Eur. **2.** of states and conditions, *painful*, *distressing*, Aesch., Eur. **III.** Adv., λυπρῶς ἔφερεν, *aegre ferebat*, Eur.

λῡπρότης, ητος, ἡ, *poverty*, of land, Strab.

λῡπρό-χωρος, ον, (χώρα) *with poor land*, Strab.

ΛΥ'ΡΑ [ῠ], ἡ, Lat. *lyra*, *a lyre*, a Greek musical instrument like the κιθάρα, invented by Hermes, with seven strings, h. Hom., Eur.

λῠρ-αοιδός, ὁ, ἡ, *one who sings to the lyre*, Anth. :—contr. **λυρῳδός**, Id., Plut. Hence

λῠρίζω, (λύρα) *to play the lyre*, Anacreon.

λῠρικός, ή, όν, *of* or *for the lyre*, *lyric*, Anacreon. **II.** as Subst., *a lyrist*, Anth., Plut.

λύριον, τό, Dim. of λύρα, Ar.

λῠρο-γηθής, ές, (γηθέω) *delighting in the lyre*, Anth.

λῠρόεις, εσσα, εν, (λύρα) *fitted for the lyre*, *lyric*, Anth.

λῠρο-θελγής, ές, (θέλγω) *charmed by the lyre*, Anth.

λῠροκτῠπία, ή, *a striking the lyre*, Anth. From

λῠρο-κτύπος, ον, (κτυπέω) *striking the lyre*.

λῠροποιικός, ή, όν, = λυροποιητικός :—ἡ -κή (sc. τέχνη), *the art* or *craft of lyre-making*, Plat. From

λῠρο-ποιός, ὁ, (ποιέω) *a lyre-maker*, Plat.

λῠρ-ώδης, ες, (εἶδος) = λυρόεις, Anth.

λῠρ-ῳδός, contr. for λυρ-αοιδός.

Λυσάνδρια, τά, *a festival in honour of Lysander*, Plut.

λῡσ-ανίας, ου, ὁ, (ἀνία) *ending sorrow*, Ar.

λύσειαν, 3 pl. aor. 1 opt. of λύω.

λῡσί-γαμος, ον, *dissolving marriage*, Anth.

λῡσί-ζωνος, ον, (ζώνη) loosing the zone, epith. of Eileithyia, who assisted women in travail, Theocr.
λῡσί-κᾰκος, ον, (κακόν) ending evil, Theogn.
λῡσί-μᾰχος, ον, (μάχη) ending strife, Anth. : fem. λυσιμάχη, Ar.
λῡσι-μελής, ές, (μέλος) limb-relaxing, of sleep, etc., Od., Hes., etc.
λῡσι-μέριμνος, ον, (μέριμνα) driving care away, Anth.
λύσῐμος [ῠ], ον, able to loose or relieve, Aesch.　II. pass. that can be redeemed, redeemable, Plat.
λύσιος [ῠ], α, ον, (λύσις) releasing, delivering, Plat.
λῡσί-παιγμος, ον, (παῖγμα) giving a loose to play or sport, Anacreon.
λῡσί-ποθος, ον, delivering from love, Anth.
λῡσί-πονος, ον, releasing from toil, Pind.
λύσις [ῠ], gen. εως Ion. ιος, ἡ, (λύω) a loosing, setting free, releasing, ransoming, of a slain man, Il. ; λ. θανάτου deliverance from death, Od. ; πενίης Theogn., etc.　2. absol. a means of letting loose, Soph. :— deliverance from guilt by expiatory rites, Id. ; οὐδ᾽ ἔχει λύσιν [τὰ πήματα] admit not of atonement, Id.　II. a loosing, parting, λ. ψυχῆς ἀπὸ σώματος Plat. : —dissolution, πολιτείας Arist.　III. = δόρπου λ. a place for banqueting, Pind.
λῡσῐτελέω, f. ήσω, = λύω τέλη (v. λύω v), to pay what is due, and then ‘ to pay,’ i. e. to profit, avail, c. dat., λυσιτελεῖ τί τινι Ar., Plat. : —impers., λυσιτελεῖ μοι it profits me, is better for me, τεθνάναι λυσιτελεῖ ἢ ζῆν 'tis better to be dead than alive, Andoc.; λυσιτελεῖ μοι ὥσπερ ἔχω ἔχειν it is expedient for me to be as I am, Plat.　II. neut. part. as Subst., τὸ λυσιτελοῦν, profit, gain, advantage, Id., Dem. ; τὰ λυσιτελοῦντα Thuc. From
λῡσῐ-τελής, ές, (λύω v, τέλος) paying what is due: hence, useful, profitable, advantageous, Plat.; τὸ λυσιτελέστατον πρὸς ἀργύριον what was most profitable in point of money, Dem.　2. cheap, Xen.
λῡσῐτελούντως, Adv. part. pres. of λυσιτελέω, usefully, profitably, Xen.
λῡσί-φλεβής, ές, (φλέψ) opening the veins, Anth.
λῡσί-φρων, ονος, ὁ, ἡ, (φρήν) releasing from care, Anacreon.
λυσι-ῳδός, ὁ, one who played women's characters in male attire, Plut.
ΛΥΣΣΑʹ, Att. λύττα, ἡ, rage, fury, esp. martial rage, Il.　2. after Hom. raging madness, raving, frenzy, Trag.　II. canine madness, rabies, Xen.
λυσσαίνω, to rave, τινί against one, Soph.
λυσσάς, ή, raging mad, Eur.
λυσσάω, Att. λυττάω, (λύσσα) to be raging in battle, Hdt.　2. to rave, be mad, Soph., Plat.　II. of dogs, Ar. ; of wolves, Theocr. Hence
λύσσημα, ατος, τό, a fit of madness : in pl. ravings, Eur.; and
λυσσητήρ, ῆρος, ὁ, one that is raging or raving mad, Il., Anth. ; and
λυσσητής, οῦ, ὁ, = foreg., Anth.
λυσσο-μᾰνής, ές, (μαίνομαι) raging mad, Anth.
λυσσόω, (λύσσα) to enrage, madden, Ep. part. λυσσώων, Anth.
λυσσ-ώδης, ες, (εἶδος) like one raging, frantic, of martial rage, Il.　2. of madness, Soph., Eur.
λῠτέον, verb. Adj. of λύω, one must solve, Plat.

λῠτήρ, ῆρος, ὁ, (λύω) one who looses, a deliverer, Eur.　II. an arbitrator, decider, νεικέων Aesch.
λῠτήριος, ον, (λύω) loosing, releasing, delivering, Aesch. : —c. gen., τῶνδ᾽ ἐμοὶ λυτήριος my deliverer from these things, Id. ; ἐκ θανάτου λ. Eur.　II. = λύτρον, recompense, Pind.
λῠτικός, ή, όν, (λύω) refutative, of arguments, Arist.
λῠτός, ή, όν, (λύω) that may be loosed or dissolved, Plat.　II. of arguments, refutable, Arist.
λύτρον, τό, (λύω) a price paid, 　1. for ransom, a ransom, mostly in pl. ransom-money, Hdt. ; λύτρα λαβεῖν τινος to receive as ransom for . . , Thuc. ; λύτρα ἀποδιδόναι, καταθεῖναι to pay ransom, Dem.　2. an atonement, συμφορᾶς for calamity, Pind. ; in pl., Plat. ; so also, λύτρον ἀντὶ πολλῶν N.T.　3. generally, a recompense, Pind.
λυτρόω, f. ώσω, (λύτρον) to release on receipt of ransom, to hold to ransom, Plat. : —Pass. to be ransomed, Dem. Hence
λύτρωσις, ή, ransoming, Plut.　II. Redemption.
λυτρωτέον, verb. Adj. of λυτρόω, one must ransom, Arist.
λυτρωτής, οῦ, ὁ, (λυτρόω) a ransomer, redeemer, N. T.
λύττα, λυττάω, v. λύσσα, λυσσάω.
λυχνεών, ῶνος, ὁ, (λύχνος) a place to keep lamps in, Luc.
λυχνίον, τό, (λύχνος) a lamp-stand, Theocr., Luc.
λυχνίς, ίδος, ή, (λύχνος) lychnis, a plant with a scarlet flower, Anth.　II. a precious stone that emits light, prob. the ruby, Luc.
λυχνίσκος, ὁ, a kind of fish, Luc.
λυχνίτης [ῑ], ου, ὁ, (λύχνος) a precious stone of a red colour, Strab.
λυχνο-καΐα, Ion. -ίη, ή, (καίω) a lighting of lamps, feast of Lanterns, Hdt.
λυχνο-ποιός, όν, (ποιέω) making lamps or lanterns, Ar.
λυχνό-πολις, ή, city of lamps, Luc.
λυχνο-πώλης, ου, ὁ, (πωλέω) a dealer in lamps or lanterns, Luc.
ΛΥΧΝΟΣ, ὁ, pl. λύχνοι and λύχνα :—a portable light, a lamp, carried in the hand or set on a lamp-stand (λύχνιον), Od., Hdt., Att. ; περὶ λύχνων ἁφάς about lamplighting time, Hdt.　2. in pl. the lamp-market, Ar.
λυχνο-φόρος, ον, (φέρω) carrying a lamp, Plut.
ΛΥΏ, f. λύσω [ῠ]: aor. 1 ἔλῡσα: pf. λέλῠκα: -Pass., pf. λέλῠμαι: plqpf. ἐλελύμην [ῠ]: aor. 1 ἐλύθην, Ep. λύθην [ῠ] : f. λῠθήσομαι and λελύσομαι [ῠ]: also, Ep. aor. 2 pass. ἐλύμην or λύμην [ῠ], 3 sing. λύτο [ῠ] and λῦτο, 3 pl. λύντο: 3 opt. plqpf. λελῦτο, for λελύοιτο : Med., f. λύσομαι: aor. 1 ἐλυσάμην. [In pres. and impf. ῡ Att., ῠ mostly in fut. and aor. 1 υ long always :—in other tenses ῠ.]
　　Orig. sense, to loose : 　I. of things, to loosen, unbind, unfasten, ζωστῆρα, θώρηκα Il. ; ἀσκὸν λ. to untie a skin (used as a bottle), Od. ; λ. ἡνίαν to slack the rein, Soph. ; λ. γράμματα to open a letter, Eur. ; στόμα λ. to open the mouth, Id. ; λ. ὀφρὺν to unfold the brow, Id. :—Med., ἐλύσατο ἱμάντα undid her belt, Il. ; λύσασθαι τρίχα to unbind one's hair, Bion.　2. of living beings, a. of horses, etc., to undo, unyoke, unharness, Hom. ; Med., λύεσθαι ἵππους ὑπ᾽ ὄχεσφι to unyoke one's horses, Il.　b. of men, to loose, release from bonds or prison, from difficulty

or danger, Hom., Att :—Med. *to get* one *loosed* or *set free*, Hes.   c. of prisoners, *to release on receipt of ransom* (ἄποινα), *hold to ransom, release*, Hom.; λύειν τινὰ ἀποίνων *on payment of* ransom, Il. :—Med. *to release by payment of ransom, to get a person released, to ransom, redeem*, Hom., Att.   3. *to give up*, [θρόνον] λῦσον ἄμμιν Pind.   II. *to resolve a whole into its parts, to dissolve, break up*, λ. ἀγορήν *to dissolve* the assembly, Hom.; also *to break up* the market, Xen.: — Pass., λῦτο ἀγών Il.; ἐλύθη ἡ στρατιά Xen.   2. *to loosen, slacken*, σπάρτα λέλυνται, i. e. have *rotted*, Il.   3. *to loosen*, i. e. *weaken, relax*, λῦσέ οἱ γυῖα made his limbs *slack* or *loose*, i. e. *killed* him, Ib.; λ. μένος τινί Ib.; but, καμάτῳ γούνατ' ἔλυσαν made the knees *weak* with toil, Od. :—so in Pass., λύντο δὲ γυῖα, as the effect of death, sleep, weariness, fear, etc., Il., etc.; γυῖα λέλυντο Hom., etc.   4. *to undo, bring to naught, break down, destroy*, Hom.: and generally, *to undo, do away with, put an end to*, Lat. *dissolvere*, Id., Att.; λ. βίον, i. e. *to die*, Eur.   b. *to repeal, annul, do away with*, Hdt., etc.; λ. ψῆφον *to rescind* a vote, Dem. :— Pass., λέλυνται πάντα all *ties are broken*, Id.   c. *to solve* a problem or difficulty, Plat.   d. *to refute* an argument, Arist.   e. *to unravel* the plot of a tragedy, Id.   5. *to break* a law or treaty, Hdt., Thuc.   III. *to solve, fulfil, accomplish*, τὰ μαντεῖα Soph.   IV. *to atone for, make up for*, Lat. *luere*, Id., Eur.   V. μισθοὺς λύειν *to pay* wages in full, Xen.   2. τέλη λύειν = λυσιτελεῖν, *to pay, profit, avail*, ἔνθα μὴ τέλη λύει φρονοῦντι where *it boots not* to be wise, Soph.; also λύει alone, much like λυσιτελεῖ, λύει ἄλγος Eur.; φημὶ τοιούτους γάμους λύειν βροτοῖς Id.

λῶ, *I will*, v. λάω (B).

λωβάομαι, f. -ήσομαι, Dor. 2 pl. λωβᾶσεῖσθε: aor. 1 ἐλωβησάμην: Dep.: (λώβη) :—*to treat despitefully, to outrage, maltreat*, λώβην λωβᾶσθαί τινα *to do* one *despite*, Il.: esp. *to maim, mutilate*, Hdt.; λ. βίον *to make ruin of* one's life, Soph.; λ. τοὺς νέους *to corrupt* the youth, Plat. :—sometimes, like λυμαίνομαι, c. dat., Ar., Plat. :—absol. *to do despite, act outrageously*, Il.   II. the pf. is used in pass. sense, λελωβημένος *mutilated*, Hdt., Plat.; also aor. 1 pass., μεγάλας λώβας λωβηθείς Plat.

λωβεύω, *to mock, make a mock of*, τινά Od.   From

ΛΩ'ΒΗ, ἡ, *despiteful treatment, outrage, dishonour*, Hom., Hdt., Att. :— esp. *mutilation, maiming*, Hdt.   2. of persons, *a disgrace*, Lat. *opprobrium*, λώβην εἶναι Il.

λωβήτειρα, fem. of λωβητήρ, Anth.

λωβητήρ, ῆρος, ὁ, *one who treats despitefully, a foul slanderer*, Il.; *a destroyer*, of the Furies, Soph.   II. pass. *a worthless wretch*, Il.

λωβητής, οῦ, ὁ, = foreg.: λ. τέχνης *one who disgraces* his trade, Ar.

λωβητός, ή, όν, (λωβάομαι) *despitefully treated, outraged*, Il., Soph.   II. act. *insulting, abusive*, Soph.

λωβήτωρ, ορος, ὁ, = λωβητήρ, Anth.

λωίτερος, v. sqq.

λωίων, ὁ, ἡ, λώιον, τό; Att. λῴων, λῷον, acc. sing. and neut. pl. λῴω (for λῴονα); acc. pl. λῴους (for λῴονας), neut. λώια: (from λάω B, λῶ) :—*more desirable, more*

agreeable, and (generally) *better*, τόδε λώιόν ἐστι Hom.; and as Adv. *better*, Od. :—we also find a Comp. λωίτερος, ον, in neut., λωίτερον καὶ ἄμεινον Ib.—In Att. λῴων was used as Comp. of ἀγαθός.   II. Sup. λῷστος, η, ον, Theogn., Att.; τὰ λῷστα βουλεύειν Aesch.; ὦ λῷστε *my good friend*, Plat.

λῶμα, ατος, τό, *the border of a robe* :—Dim. λωμάτιον, τό, Anth.

λῶντι, v. *λάω (B).

λῶος, ὁ, a Macedon. month, answering to the Att. βοηδρομιών, Philipp. ap. Dem.

λώπη, ἡ, (λέπω) *a covering, robe, mantle*, Od., Theocr.

λωπίζω, f. ίσω, (λῶπος) *to cover, cloak*, Soph.

λωποδῦτέω, f. ήσω, *to steal clothes*, esp. from bathers or travellers, Plat., Xen.   II. generally, *to rob, plunder*, Ar.   From

λωπο-δύτης [ῠ], ου, ὁ, (λῶπος, δύω) *one who slips into another's clothes, a clothes-stealer*, esp. one who steals the clothes of bathers, or strips travellers, Soph.   II. generally, *a thief, robber, footpad*, Ar., Dem.

λῶπος, τό, = λώπη, Theocr.

λῷστος, η, ον, Sup. Adj., v. λωίων.

λωτίζομαι, (λωτός) Med. *to choose for oneself, cull the best*, Aesch.

λώτινος, η, ον, (λωτός) *made of lotus-wood*, Theocr.

λώτισμα, ατος, τό, *a flower*: metaph. *the fairest, choicest, best*, Eur.

λωτόεις, εσσα, εν, *overgrown with lotus*, πεδία λωτεῦντα (Ion. for -όεντα) *lotus-plains*, Il.

ΛΩΤΟ'Σ, οῦ, ὁ, *the lotus*, name of several plants.   I. *the Greek lotus*, a plant on which horses fed, a kind of *clover* or *trefoil*, Hom.   II. *the Cyrenean lotus*, an African shrub, whose fruit was the food of certain tribes on the coast, hence called *Lotophagi*, Od., Hdt.   III. *the Egyptian lotus, the lily of the Nile*, Hdt.   IV. *a North-African tree;* from its hard black wood flutes were made :—hence Λιβὺς λωτός is used in Poets for *a flute*, Eur.

λωτο-τρόφος, ον, (λωτός I) *producing lotus*, Eur.

λωτο-φάγοι, οἱ, (λωτός II) *the Lotus-eaters*, a peaceful people on the coast of Cyrenaïca, Od., Hdt.

λωφάω, f. ήσω, *to rest from toil, take rest*, Il.   2. c. gen. *to take rest* or *abate from, recover from*, χόλου Aesch.; πόνου Soph.; λ. ἀπὸ νόσου καὶ πολέμου Thuc.   3. *to abate*, of a disease, Id.   II. trans. *to lighten, relieve*, ὁ λωφήσων γὰρ οὐ πέφυκέ πω Aesch. (Deriv. uncertain.)   Hence

λωφήιος, α, ον, *relieving*, λ. ἱερά *expiatory* offerings, Ap.

λωφήσειε, 3 sing. aor. 1 opt. of λωφάω.

λώφησις, ἡ, *abatement, cessation*, Thuc.

λώων, neut. λῷον, Att. contr. for λωίων, λώιον.

Μ.

Μ μ, μῦ, τό :—indecl., twelfth letter in the Gr. alphabet: as numerals, μ' = 40, but ͵μ = 40,000.

I. μ is the labial liquid, corresponding to β: II. changes: 1. Aeol. and Lacon. into π, as πεδά for μετά.   2. Att. and Dor. into ν, as νιν for μιν; so Lat. *ne, num* = μή, μῶν.   3. μ is doubled,   a.

poët. in compds., as ἄμμορος, φιλομμειδής; and after the augm., as ἔλλαβον. b. Aeol., as ἄμμες ὔμμες ἐμμί, for ἡμεῖς ὑμεῖς εἰμί. 4. μ is added, a. at the beginning of a word, as ἴα μία, ὄσχος μόσχος. b. in the middle of a word to facilitate pronunciation, as ὄμβριμος ὄβριμος, τύμπανον τύπανον, etc., esp. after redupl., as πίμπλημι for πίπλημι; after a- privat., as ἄμβροτος, ἄβροτος.

μ' apostr. for με. II. rarely for μοι, Hom.

μά [ᾰ], a Particle used in strong protestations and oaths, followed by acc. of the deity or thing appealed to; in itself neither affirmative nor negative, but made so by prefixing ναί or οὔ, or by the context :—thus, I. ναὶ μὰ .., in affirmation, ναὶ μὰ τόδε σκῆπτρον yea by this sceptre, Il.; ναὶ μὰ Δία, ναὶ μὰ τὸν Δία Ar., Plat. II. οὐ μὰ .., in negation, οὐ μὰ Ζῆνα, nay, by .., Il.; οὔ τοι μὰ τοὺς δώδεκα θεούς Ar. III. in Att. μά is often used alone, mostly in negat. sense μὰ τὸν Ποσειδῶ Eur.:—in answers, when the negation is expressed in the question, οὐκ αὖ μ' ἐάσεις; Answ. μὰ Δί' (sc. οὐκ ἐάσω) Ar. IV. the name of the deity was often suppressed, ναὶ μὰ τόν, οὐ μὰ τόν Plat.

μᾶ, shortd. Dor. form for μάτηρ, μᾶ γᾶ for μῆτερ γῆ, Aesch.; μᾶ, πόθεν ἄνθρωπος; Theocr.

μαγάδιον, τό, Dim. of μαγάς, Luc.

μάγαδις, ἡ, gen. μαγάδιδος, dat. μαγάδει or μαγάδι; acc. μάγαδιν:—the magadis, a kind of harp, with twenty strings, Comici. (A foreign word.)

ΜΑ'ΓΑ'Σ, άδος [ᾰ], ἡ, the bridge of the cithara, Lat. pons.

μαγγάνευμα, ατος, τό, a piece of jugglery; in pl. juggleries, deceptions, Plat. From

μαγγανεύω, f. σω, (μάγγανον) to use charms or philtres, of Circé, Ar. :—to play tricks, Dem. From

μάγγανον, τό, any means for charming or bewitching, a philtre. (Deriv. unknown.)

μαγεία, ἡ, (μαγεύω) the theology of the Magians, Plat.

μαγειρεῖον, τό, (μάγειρος) a cook-shop, Lat. popina, Arist., Babr. 2. the place where the public cooks lived, the cooks' quarter, Theophr.

μαγειρεύω, f. σω, to be a cook, to cook meat, Theophr. II. to be a butcher, Babr.

μαγειρικός, ή, όν, (μάγειρος) fit for a cook or cookery, Ar., etc. :—ἡ μαγειρικὴ τέχνη cookery, Plat. :—Adv. -κῶς, in a cook-like way, like a true 'artist,' Ar.

μάγειρος [ᾰ], ὁ, a cook, Hdt., Att. II. a butcher, Eur. (From ΜΑΓ, Root of μάσσω (q. v.), because baking bread was the business of the ancient cook.)

μάγευμα, ατος, τό, (μαγεύω) a piece of magic art; in pl. charms, spells, Eur.

μάγευς, έως, ὁ, (μάσσω) one who wipes, Anth.

μαγεύω, f. σω, (Μάγος) to be a Magus, use magic arts, Plut.: c. acc. cogn., μέλη μ. to sing incantations, Eur. II. trans. to call forth by magic arts, Anth.

μάγικός, ή, όν, fit for the Magians, Magian, Plut.

Μάγνης, ητος, ὁ, a Magnesian, a dweller in Magnesia in Thessaly, Il., etc.; or Magnesia in Lydia, Hdt., etc. : fem. Μάγνησσα, Theocr. :—Adj. Μαγνητικός, ή, όν, Magnesian, Aesch.; fem. Μαγνῆτις, ιδος, Pind. II. Μαγνῆτις λίθος, ἡ, the magnet, Plat.

Μάγος [ᾰ], ου, ὁ, a Magus, Magian, one of a Median tribe, Hdt. 2. one of the wise men in Persia who interpreted dreams, Id. 3. any enchanter or wizard, and in bad sense, a juggler, impostor, Soph., Eur., etc. ;—fem., Anth. (A Persian word.)

μάγο-φόνια, τά, (*φένω) the slaughter of the Magians, a Persian festival, Hdt.

μᾰδᾰρός, ά, όν, (μαδάω) wet, flaccid : bald, Anth.

μᾰδάω, f. ήσω, to be flaccid : to be bald, Ar.

μάδδα, ἡ, Dor. for μᾶζα.

μᾰδικεῖν [ᾰ], crasis for μὴ ἀδικεῖν.

*μαδός, ή, όν, the Root of μαδάω, μαδαρός.

μᾶζα, ἡ, (μάσσω) a barley-cake, Hdt., Hes., Att.

μαζίσκη, ἡ, Dim. of μᾶζα, a barley-scone, Ar.

μαζο-νόμος, (νέμω) ὁ, a trencher for serving barley cakes on, Horat.

μαθεῖν, aor. 2 inf. of μανθάνω.

μάθημα, ατος, τό, (μανθάνω) that which is learnt, a lesson, Hdt., Soph., etc. II. learning, knowledge, science, oft. in pl., Ar., Thuc., etc. : esp. the mathematical sciences, Plat., etc. Hence

μᾰθηματικός, ή, όν, disposed to learn, Plat. II. mathematical :—μαθηματικός, ὁ, a mathematician, Arist.; τὰ μαθηματικά mathematics, Id. 2. astronomical, mathematici = Chaldaei, Juven.

μάθησις, ἡ, (μανθάνω) learning, the getting of knowledge, Soph., Thuc., etc. 2. desire of learning, Soph. 3. education, instruction, Plat., Xen.

μᾰθητέος, ή, ον, verb. Adj of μανθάνω, to be learnt, Hdt. II. μαθητέον, one must learn, Ar., Xen.

μᾰθητεύω, f. σω, to be pupil, τινί to one, Plut. II. trans. to make a disciple of, instruct, N. T. From

μᾰθητής, οῦ, ὁ, (μανθάνω) a learner, pupil, Lat. discipulus, Hdt., Plat.

μᾰθητιάω, Desiderat. of μανθάνω, to wish to become a disciple, Ar. II. = μαθητεύω, Anth.

μᾰθητικός, ή, όν, disposed to learn, τινος Plat.

μᾰθητός, ή, όν, learnt, that may be learnt, Xen., Plat.

μάθοισα, Dor. for -οῦσα, aor. 2 part. fem. of μανθάνω.

μάθον, Ep. for ἔμαθον, aor. 2 of μανθάνω.

μάθος, ὁ, poët. for μάθησις, Aesch.

ΜΑΓΑ, ἡ, good mother, dame, Od. 2. a foster-mother, nurse, Eur. :—also a true mother, Aesch., Eur. 3. a midwife, Plat.

Μαῖα, Ion. Μαίη, ἡ, Maia, daughter of Atlas, mother of Hermes, h. Hom., Hes.

Μαίανδρος, ὁ, Maeander, a river of Caria, Il., Hdt. II. metaph. a winding pattern, Strab.

Μαιάς, άδος, ἡ, = Μαῖα, Od.

μαίευμα, ατος, τό, the product of a midwife's art, a delivery, σὸν μὲν παιδίον, ἐμὸν δὲ μαίευμα Plat. From

μαιεύομαι, f. σομαι, Dep. to serve as a midwife, Luc. 2. c. acc. pers. to deliver a woman, Plat.

μαίευσις, ἡ, delivery of a woman in childbirth, Plat.

μαιευτικός, ή, όν, of or for midwifery, obstetric, Plat. : —ἡ μαιευτικὴ τέχνη or ἡ -κή alone, midwifery,—the name given by Socrates to his art of eliciting from others what was in their minds, Plat.

Μαιῆτις, Ion. for Μαιῶτις.

Μαιμακτηριών, ῶνος, ὁ, the fifth Attic month, the end of November and beginning of December, Dem. From

Μαιμάκτης, ου, ὁ, (μαιμάσσω) epith. of Zeus, the boisterous, stormy, in whose honour a festival was held at Athens in the month Μαιμακτηριών, Plut.

μαιμάσσω, = sq., Anth.

μαιμάω (redupl. from *μάω): Ep. 3 pl. μαιμώωσι, part. μαιμώων, -ώωσα: Ep. aor. 1 μαίμησα:—to be very eager, pant or quiver with eagerness, Il.; c. gen., χεῖρα μαιμῶσαν φόνου a hand eager for murder, Soph.

Μαίναλον, τό, Mount Maenalus in Arcadia, sacred to Pan, Theocr.:—Adj. Μαινάλιος, α, ον, Pind.; ἡ Μαιναλία (sc. χώρα) Thuc.

μαινάς, άδος, ἡ, (μαίνομαι) raving, frantic, Eur. 2. as Subst. a mad woman, Il.: esp. a Bacchante, Bacchanal, Maenad, Soph.; of the Furies, Aesch.; of Cassandra, Eur. II. act. causing madness, Pind.

ΜΑΙ'ΝΗ, ἡ, maena, a small sea-fish, which, like our herring, was salted, Anth.

μαινίς, ἡ, gen. ίδος [ἵ], Dim. of μαίνη, a sprat, Ar., etc.

μαινόλης, ου, ὁ, (μαίνομαι) raving, frenzied, Sappho.

μαινόλιος, α, ον, = foreg., Anth.

μαινόλις, fem. of μαινόλης, Eur.

μαίνομαι (from Root ΜΑΝ), f. μανοῦμαι and μανήσομαι: pf. with pres. sense μέμηνα, also in pass. form μεμάνημαι [ᾰ]: aor. 2 pass. ἐμάνην, part. μανείς, inf. μανῆναι: also aor. 1 med. ἐμήναο, μήνατο, μηνάμενος:—to rage, be furious, Hom.; ὁ μανείς the madman, Soph.: to be mad with wine, Soph.:—of Bacchic frenzy, Il., Soph.; ὑπὸ τοῦ θεοῦ μ. to be driven mad by the god, Hdt.; τὸ μαίνεσθαι madness, Soph.; πλεῖν ἢ μαίνομαι more than madness, Ar.:—c. acc. cogn., μεμηνὼς οὐ σμικρὰν νόσον mad with no slight disease, Aesch. 2. of fire, to rage, riot, Il.; so, μαινομένη ἐλπίς Orac. ap. Hdt.; ἔρις Aesch., etc. II. the aor. 1 act. ἔμηνα, in Causal sense, to madden, enrage, Eur., Xen.

μαίομαι, Dep. (*μάω) to seek: 1. absol. to endeavour, strive, Od., Pind., Aesch. II. c. acc. to search, examine, Od. 2. to seek after, seek for, τι Pind.: c. inf. to seek to do, Id., Soph.

μαιόομαι, f. ώσομαι, Dep., = μαιεύομαι, to deliver a woman, Luc., Anth.

Μάϊος (with or without μήν), ὁ, the Lat. Maius, May, Plut., etc.:—as Adj., Μάϊαι Καλάνδαι the Calends of May, Id.

Μαῖρα, ἡ, (μαρμαίρω) the Sparkler, i.e. the dog-star, Anth.

μαίωσις, ἡ, (μαιόομαι) = μαίευσις, Plut.

Μαιῶται, Ion. Μαιῆται, οἱ, the Maeotians, a Scythian tribe to the North of the Black Sea, Hdt., Xen. II. as Adj. Μαιώτης, ου, Maeotian, ποταμὸς Μ. the Tanaïs, Hdt.:—Μαιῶτις λίμνη the Palus Maeotis, Sea of Azof, Aesch., etc.; ἡ λίμνη ἡ Μαιῆτις (Ion.) Hdt. 2. Μαιωτικός, ή, όν, αὐλὼν Μ., i.e. the Cimmerian Bosporus, Aesch. Hence

Μαιωτιστί, Adv. in Scythian fashion, Theocr.

μαίωτρα, τά, (μαιόομαι) a midwife's wages, Luc.

ΜΑ'ΚΑΡ, ᾰρος, ὁ; the fem. is μάκαιρα, but also μάκαρ: —blessed, happy, of the gods, as opp. to mortal men, Il.; absol., μάκαρες the blessed ones, Od., Hes., Pind., Trag. II. of men, blest, fortunate, ὦ μάκαρ Ἀτρείδη Il.; so, μάκαιρα ἑστία, etc., Pind.:— esp. wealthy, ἀνδρὸς μάκαρος κατ' ἄρουραν Il. III. μάκαρες also meant the dead, as secure from the ills of life, Hes.:—μακάρων νῆσοι the Islands of the Blest (in the ocean at the extreme West) where heroes and demi-gods enjoyed rest for ever, Id., Pind. IV. Comp. μακάρτερος, Sup. μακάρτατος Od. Hence

μᾰκᾰρία, ἡ, happiness, bliss, κενὴ μ. Luc.:—euphem. for ἐς κόρακας, ἄπαγ' ἐς μακαρίαν Ar.

μᾰκᾰρίζω, f. Att. ιῶ, (μάκαρ) to bless, to deem or pronounce happy, Lat. gratulari, Od., Hdt., Att.; ironically, μακαρίσαντες ὑμῶν τὸ ἀπειρόκακον while we bless your simplicity, Thuc.

μᾰκάριος [κᾰ], α, ον, and ος, ον, longer form of μάκαρ: 1. of men, blessed, happy, Pind., Eur., etc.:—in addresses, ὦ μακάριε, like ὦ θαυμάσιε, my good sir, my dear sir, Plat.:—c. gen., ὦ μ. τῆς τύχης happy you for your good fortune! Ar. 2. οἱ μακάριοι, like οἱ ὄλβιοι, the rich and better educated, Plat., Arist. II. Adv. -ίως, Eur., Ar. Hence

μᾰκᾰριότης, ητος, ἡ, happiness, bliss, Plat., Arist.; and

μᾰκᾰρισμός, οῦ, ὁ, a pronouncing happy, blessing, Plat., Arist.; and

μᾰκάριστός, ή, όν, verb. Adj. deemed or to be deemed happy, enviable, Hdt., Att.

μᾰκᾰρίτης [ῑ], ου, ὁ, like μάκαρ III, one blessed, i. e. dead, Aesch., etc. II. as Adj., μ. βίος, with a double meaning, Ar.

μᾰκαρτός, ή, όν, = μακαριστός, Anth.

μᾰκεδνός, ή, όν, = μηκεδανός, μακρός, tall, taper, Od.

Μᾰκεδονίζω, to be on the Macedonian side, Plut. II. to speak Macedonian, Id.:—hence Μᾰκεδονιστί, in Macedonian, Id.

Μᾰκεδών, όνος, ὁ, ἡ, a Macedonian, οἱ Μακεδόνες, the Macedonians, Hdt.:—Adj. Μακεδόνιος, α, ον, and -ονικός, ή, όν, Id., etc.; ἡ Μακεδονία, Macedon, Id.; so, ἡ Μακεδονὶς γῆ Id.; γῆ Μακεδών Anth.

μᾰκέλη, ἡ, = sq., Hes., Theocr.

μά-κελλα [μᾰ], ης, ἡ, (μία, κέλλω, as δί-κελλα from δίς, κέλλω) a pick-axe with one point, Il., Aesch.

μάκελλον, τό, the meat-market, shambles, N. T.

Μᾰκέτης, ου, ὁ, = Μακεδών: fem. Μᾰκέτις, ιδος, Anth.

μᾰκιστήρ, ῆρος, ὁ, long and tedious, Aesch.

μάκιστος, Dor. for μήκιστος.

μακκοάω, f. άσω [ᾱ], to be stupid, Ar.; part. pf. μεμακκοηκώς sitting mooning, Id. (Deriv. uncertain.)

μᾶκος, τό, Dor. for μῆκος: acc. μᾶκος as Adv., = μακράν, Pind.

μακρά (sub. γραμμή), v. τιμάω III.

μακρ-αίων, ωνος, ὁ, ἡ, (μακρός) lasting long, Soph. 2. of persons, long-lived, aged, Id.; οἱ μακραίωνες the immortals, Id.

μακράν, Ion. μακρήν, acc. fem. of μακρός used as Adv., a long way, far, far away, Aesch., Soph., etc.; τοὔργον οὐ μ. λέγεις the business you speak of is not far to seek, Soph.:—c. gen. far from, Eur.:—Comp., μακροτέραν to a greater distance, Thuc., Xen.; Sup., ὅτι μακροτάτην as far as possible, c. gen. loci, Xen. 2. μακρὰν λέγειν to speak at length, Aesch., Soph. II. of Time, long, μ. ζῆν, ἀναμένειν Soph.; οὐ μ. Lat. brevi, Eur.; so, οὐκ ἐς μακρήν Hdt., etc.

μακρ-αύχην, ὁ, ἡ, long-necked, long, Eur.

μακρηγορέω, f. ήσω, to speak at great length, Aesch., Eur., etc.; and

μακρηγορία, Dor. μακρᾱγ-, ἡ, tediousness, Pind. From

μακρ-ήγορος, ον, (ἀγορεύω) speaking at great length.

μακρ-ημερία, Ion. -ίη, ἡ, (ἡμέρα) the season of long days, Hdt.

μακρό-βιος, ον, (βίος) long-lived, Arist. ; μακροβιώτατος Hdt. :—οἱ M., an Ethiopian people, Id. Hence

μακροβιότης, ητος, ἡ, longevity, Arist.

μακρο-βίοτος, ον, = μακρόβιος, long, Aesch.

μακρό-γηρως, ων, gen. ω, very old, Anth.

μακρο-δρόμος, ον, running long or far, Xen.

μακρόθεν, Adv. from afar, Strab. ; of Time, from long since, Polyb.

μακροθῡμέω, to be longsuffering, N. T. ; and

μακροθῡμία, ἡ, longsuffering, forbearance, N. T. From

μακρό-θῡμος, ον, longsuffering, patient, Anth. : Adv. -μως, N. T.

μακρο-κέφᾰλος, ον, (κεφαλή) long-headed, of the Scythians, Strab.

μακρο-κομέω, f. ήσω, (κόμη) to have long hair, Strab.

μακρό-κωλος, ον, (κῶλον) long-limbed : ἡ μ. a kind of sling, Strab. 2. of sentences, with long clauses, Arist.

μακρολογέω, f. ήσω, to speak at length, use many words, Plat. ; c. acc. rei, to speak long on a subject, Xen. ; and

μακρολογία, ἡ, length of speech, Plat. From

μακρο-λόγος, ον, (λέγω) speaking at length, Plat.

μακρό-μαλλος, ον, with long wool, Strab.

μακρόν, τό, neut. of μακρός : v. μακρός III, παράβασις III.

μακρό-πνοος, ον, contr. -πνους, ουν, long-breathed, long-protracted, wearisome, Eur.

μακρο-πορέω, f. ήσω, (πόρος) to go or travel far, Strab.

μακροπορία, ἡ, a long way or journey, Strab.

μακρο-πώγων, ωνος, ὁ, ἡ, long-bearded, Strab.

μακρός [ᾰ by nature], ά, όν, (from MAK, Root of μῆκος) : I. of Space, 1. in point of length, long, Hom., etc. ; ἐπὶ τὰ μακρότερα towards the longer sides, i. e. lengthwise, Hdt. 2. in point of height, tall, Hom., e. g. μακρὸς Ὄλυμπος, μ. δένδρεα, τείχεα, etc. :—also reversely, like Lat. altus, deep, Il. 3. in point of distance, long, far, far distant, Ib., Hdt. ; τὰ μακρότατα the remotest parts, Hdt. :—often in neut. as Adv., μακρὰ βιβάς far-striding, Il. ; also, μακρὸν ἀΰτειν, βοᾶν to shout so as to be heard afar, Hom. ; so, μακρότερον σφενδονᾶν to sling to a greater distance, Xen. 4. generally, large in size or in degree, large, great, Aesch., Soph. 5. dat. μακρῷ is used to strengthen the Comp. and Sup. by far, Lat. longe, μακρῷ πρῶτος, μ. μάλιστα Hdt. ; ἀσθενεστέρα μ. Aesch., etc. II. of Time, long, long-lasting, long, Od., Hdt., etc. ; οὐ μακροῦ χρόνου for no long time, Soph. ; τὸν μ. βίον Aesch. ; μακρότερος μηνί by a month, Hdt. :—so, μακρὸν ἐέλδωρ a long-cherished wish, Od. 2. long, tedious, Pind., Soph. III. neut. with Preps. in adverb. sense, διὰ μακροῦ (sc. χρόνου) after a long time, long delayed, Eur. ; οὐ διὰ μακροῦ not long after, Thuc. :—but, διὰ μακρῶν at great length, Plat. :—οὐκ ἐς μακρόν for no long time, Pind. :—ἐπὶ μακρόν far, a long way, Xen. ; ὅσον ἐπὶ μακρότατον or ὅσον μ. as far as possible, Hdt. ; ἐπὶ μακρότερον yet more, Thuc. IV. regul. Comp. μακρότερος Od., Hdt., etc. ; Sup. μακρότατος Il., etc. :—irreg. Comp. μάσσων, Sup. μήκιστος, v. sub vocc. V. Adv. μακρῶς, at great length, slowly, Polyb.

μάκρος, ους, τό, = μῆκος, length, Ar.

μακρο-τένων, οντος, ὁ, ἡ, far-stretching, Anth.

μακροτέρως, Adv. Comp. of μακρός, beyond, further, Plat., etc.

μακρό-τονος, ον, (τείνω) far-stretching, long drawn out, σχοῖνοι Anth.

μακρο-τράχηλος, ον, long-necked, Anth.

μακρο-φάρυγξ, ὁ, ἡ, long-necked, of a bottle, Anth.

μακρο-φλυαρήτης, ου, ὁ, a tedious prater, Anth.

μακρό-χειρ, ὁ, ἡ, long-armed, Lat. longimanus, name of Artaxerxes I, Strab., Plut.

μακρό-χηλος, ον, (χηλή) with long hoofs, Strab.

μάκρων, ωνος, ὁ, (μακρός) a longhead ; Μάκρωνες, οἱ, a people of Pontus, Hdt.

μάκτρα, ἡ, (μάσσω) a kneading-trough, Ar., Xen.

μᾰκών [ᾱ], poët. aor. 2 part. of μηκάομαι.

μάκων [ᾱ], Dor. for μήκων.

μάλα [μᾰλᾰ], Adv. very, very much, exceedingly, Hom., etc. 1. strengthening the word with which it stands, μάλα πολλά very many, Id. ; μάλα πάντες, μ. πᾶσαι, μ. πάντα, all together, every one, Id. ; μάλ' ἀσκηθής all unhurt, Od. ; ἀβληχρὸς μάλα τοῖος so very weak, Ib. :—so in Att., μάλα δὴ πρεσβύτης very old, Xen. ; μ. γέ τινες ὀλίγοι Plat. :—so with Advs., πάγχυ μάλα and μάλα πάγχυ quite utterly, Il. ; εὖ μάλα right well, Od. ; μάλ' αἰεί for ever and aye, Il. ; ἄχρι μάλα κνέφαος until quite dark, Od. ; μάλα διαμπερές right through, Il. :—so in Att., to express repeated action, μάλ' αὖθις, μάλ' αὖ Aesch., etc. :—with Verbs, μή με μάλ' αἴνεε praise me not greatly, Il. ; ἡ δὲ μάλ' ἡνιόχευεν she drove carefully, Od., etc. 2. strengthening an assertion, εἰ μάλα μιν χόλος ἵκοι if wrath come on him ever so much, Hom. ; so μάλα περ with a partic., μάλα περ μεμαώς though desiring never so much, Il. 3. in Att. in answers, yes, certainly, exactly so, μάλα γε Plat., etc. ; μ. τοι Xen., etc. ; καὶ μ. δή Id. II. Comp. μᾶλλον, more, Hom. ; μᾶλλον τοῦ δέοντος more than is right, Plat., Xen., etc. ; παντὸς μᾶλλον more than anything, i. e. most certainly, Plat. 2. denoting increase, more and more, still more, Od. ; μᾶλλον μᾶλλον, Lat. magis magisque, Eur., Ar. 3. sometimes joined to a second Comp., ῥηΐτεροι μᾶλλον Il. ; μᾶλλον ἄσσον Soph., etc. 4. μᾶλλον δέ, much more, but rather, πολλοί, μᾶλλον δὲ πάντες Dem. 5. in μᾶλλον ἤ οὐ, οὐ seems redundant, ἥκει ὁ Πέρσης οὐδὲν μᾶλλον ἐπ' ἡμέας ἤ οὐ ἐπ' ὑμέας the Persians have come not more against us, than against you, Hdt. ; in this case μᾶλλον ἤ οὐ is preceded by another negat. 6. τὸ μ. καὶ ἧττον, a form of argument, which we call a fortiori, Arist. III. Sup. μάλιστα, most, most of all, Hom., etc. ; μάλιστα μέν . ., ἔπειτα δέ . ., first and above all . ., next . ., Soph. :—τί μάλιστα ; what is the precise thing that you want? Plat. ; ὡς or ὅτι μ., Lat. quam maxime, Id. ; ὅσον μ. Aesch. ; ὡς μ. certainly, in answers, Plat. ; ὡς δύναμαι μ. Id. ; μακρῷ μ. Hdt. 2. ἐς τὰ μάλιστα for the most part, mostly, Id. ; so, τὰ μάλιστα Thuc., etc. ; also, ἀνὴρ δόκιμος ὁμοῖα τῷ μ. as famous as he that is most [famous], Hdt. b. ἐν τοῖς μ. especially, as much as any, Thuc., Plat. 3. μάλιστα may be added to a Sup., ἔχθιστος μάλιστα, μάλιστα φίλτατος Il. ; μ. φίλτατος Eur. 4. with numbers, μάλιστα means

about, Thuc., Xen., etc. ; so, ἐς μέσον μάλιστα about the middle, Hdt. ; ἥμισυ μ. Thuc., etc.   5. καὶ μάλιστα is used in answers, most certainly, Lat. vel maxime, Ar. ; so, μ γε Soph. ; μ. πάντων Ar.

μᾰλᾰκαί-πους, ὁ, ἡ, πουν, τό, poët. for μαλακόπους, soft-footed, treading softly, Theocr.

μᾰλᾰκία, Ion. -ίη, ἡ, (μαλακός) softness, delicacy, effeminacy, Hdt., Thuc.   2. want of patience, weakness, Arist.   II. calmness of the sea, Caesar.

μᾰλᾰκιάω, = sq., Xen., Plut.

μᾰλᾰκίζομαι : f. μαλακισθήσομαι : aor. 1 ἐμαλακίσθην, and in med. form ἐμαλακισάμην: (μαλακός) :—to be softened or made effeminate, shew weakness or cowardice, Thuc., Xen.   2. to be softened or appeased, Thuc.

μᾰλᾰκό-γειος, ον, (γῆ) with or of soft soil, Strab.

μᾰλᾰκο-γνώμων, ον, (γνώμη) mild of mood, Aesch.

ΜΑ´ΛᾰΚΟ´Σ, ἡ, όν, Lat. mollis, soft, Hom., etc. ; μ. νειός a fresh-ploughed fallow, Il. ; μ. λειμών a soft grassy meadow, Od. ; μ. παρειαί Soph. ; σώματα Xen. : —Adv., καθίζου μαλακῶς sit softly, i. e. on a cushion, Ar.   II. of things not subject to touch, soft, gentle, θάνατος, ὕπνος Hom. ; μαλακῶς εὕδειν to sleep softly, Od. ; μαλακὰ ἔπεα, μ. λόγοι soft, fair words, Hom. ; μ. βλέμμα tender, youthful looks, Ar. ; light, mild, ζημία Thuc.   III. in bad sense, of persons, soft, yielding, remiss, Id., Xen. :—Adv., μαλακωτέρως ἀνθήπτετο attacked him somewhat feebly, Thuc. : — also faint-hearted, effeminate, cowardly, Id., Xen. ; μαλακὸν οὐδὲν ἐνδιδόναι not to give in from want of spirit, not to flag a whit, Hdt., Ar.   Hence

μᾰλᾰκότης, ητος, ἡ, = μαλακία, softness, Plat., etc.   II. weakness, effeminacy, Plut.

μᾰλᾰκό-χειρ, ὁ, ἡ, soft-handed, Pind.

μᾰλακτήρ, ῆρος, ὁ, one that melts and moulds, Plut.

μᾰλακύνομαι, Pass., like μαλακίζομαι, to flag, Xen.

μᾰλάσσω, Att. -ττω, f. ξω, (μαλακός) to make soft, of dressing leather, to make it soft and supple ;—hence, with reference to Cleon's trade of tanner, μαλ. τινά to give one a dressing, hide him, Ar. : Pass., ἐν παγκρατίῳ μαλαχθείς worsted in it, Pind.   2. to soften metal or other material for working, Plat.   II. metaph. to soften, appease, make to relent, Eur. :—Pass. to be softened, to relent, Soph., Ar. ; μ. νόσου to be relieved from disease, Soph.   Hence

μᾰλάχη [λᾰ], ἡ, mallow, Lat. malva, Hes., Ar., etc.

μάλβαξ, ακος, ὁ, = μαλάχη, Luc.

μᾰλερός, ά, όν, (μάλα) mighty, fierce, devouring, ravening, of fire, Il., etc.   2. metaph. fiery, glowing, vehement, furious, Pind., Trag.

ΜΑ´ΛΗ [ᾰ], ἡ, the arm-pit, Lat. ala, only in phrase ὑπὸ μάλης, under the arm, as the place for carrying concealed weapons, Xen., Plat. :—hence ὑπὸ μάλης underhand, secretly, Lat. furtim, Dem.

ΜΑ´ΛΘᾰ or μάλθη, ἡ, a mixture of wax and pitch for laying over writing-tablets, Dem.

μαλθᾰκία, ἡ, = μαλακία, Plat.

μαλθᾰκίζομαι, Pass. to be softened, of persons, Aesch., Eur. :—to relax, give in, Plat.

μαλθᾰκινος, η, ον, poët. for μαλθακός, Anth.

μαλθακιστέον, verb. Adj. of μαλθακίζομαι, one must be remiss, Plat. :—so μαλθακιστέα, Ar.

μαλθᾱκός, ή, όν, (μαλακός with θ inserted), soft, Pind., Att. :—Adv., μαλθακῶς κατακεῖσθαι to recline on soft cushions, Ar.   II. metaph. faint-hearted, remiss, cowardly, Il., Att. :—also weak, feeble, Ar.   2. in good sense, soft, gentle, mild, Theogn., Att. :—Adv. gently, Aesch., Soph. ; neut. as Adv., Aesch.

μαλθᾱκό-φωνος, ον, (φωνή) soft-voiced, Pind.

μαλθάσσω, = μαλάσσω, to soften, soothe, Trag. :—Pass., μαλθαχθεῖσ' ὕπνῳ unnerved by sleep, Aesch.

μάλιον [ᾰ], τό, Dim. of μαλλός, a lock of hair, Anth.

Μᾱλίς, ίδος, ἡ, Dor. for Μηλίς, cf. Μηλιάδες.

μᾱλίς, Dor. for μηλίς, = μηλέα.

μάλιστα, Adv., Sup. of μάλα, v. μάλα III.

ΜΑ´ΛΚΗ, ἡ, numbness from cold.   Hence

μαλκίω [ι], to become numb with cold, to be torpid, Hes., Xen.

μαλλά, crasis for μὴ ἀλλά.

μᾶλλον, Adv., Comp. of μάλα ; v. μάλα II.

ΜΑΛΛΟ´Σ, ὁ, a lock of wool, wool, Hes., Aesch., etc. : —a lock of hair, Eur.

μᾶλον, τό, Dor. for μῆλον.

μᾰλοπάρῃος, ον, Dor. for μηλοπάρῃος.

μᾱλός, ή, όν, white, Theocr.   (Akin to μαλλός ?)

μᾱλοφόρος, μᾱλοφύλαξ, Dor. for μηλοφ-.

μάμελεῖν, crasis for μὴ ἀμελεῖν.

Μαμμάκῦθος [ᾰκ], ὁ, Comic word for a blockhead, simpleton, Ar.

μαμμᾶν αἰτεῖν, to cry for the breast, to suck the breast, of babies, Ar.   From

μάμμη, ἡ, mamma, mammy, a child's attempt to articulate mother, Anth. :—so ἄττα, πάππας, τάτα, τέττα, papa, for father.   II. a grandmother, Plut.

Μαμμωνᾶς or Μαμωνᾶς, ᾶ, ὁ, a Syrian deity, god of riches ; hence riches, wealth, N. T.

μάν, Dor. and old Ep. for μήν.

μάναμίγνυσθαι, crasis for μὴ ἀναμίγνυσθαι.

μάνατραπῆναι, crasis for μὴ ἀνατραπῆναι.

ΜΑ´ΝΔΡΑ, ἡ, an inclosed space :   1. for cattle, a fold, byre, stable, Theocr., etc.   2. the setting of a ring, Anth.

μανδρᾰγόρας, ου or α, ὁ, mandrake, a narcotic plant, Xen., Dem.

Μανέρως, ὁ, Maneros, only son of the first king of Egypt : a national dirge named after him, Hdt.

μᾰνῆναι, aor. 2 pass. inf. of μαίνομαι.

μανθάνω (from Root ΜΑΘ), f. μᾰθήσομαι, Dor. μᾰθεῦμαι :—aor. 2 ἔμᾰθον, Ep. μέμᾰθον :—pf. μεμάθηκα, plqpf. ἐμεμᾰθήκη, 3 sing. μεμᾰθήκει :—to learn, esp. by inquiry ; and in aor. to have learnt, i. e. to understand, know, Od., Att. ; ἀεὶ γὰρ ἡβᾷ τοῖς γέρουσιν εὖ μαθεῖν Aesch. ; οἱ μανθάνοντες, learners, pupils, Xen. : —c. inf. to learn to do, learn how to do, Il., Aesch. etc.   II. to perceive by the senses, remark, notice, Hdt., Xen. :—with a part., μάνθανε ὤν, like ἴσθι ὤν, know that you are, Soph., etc.   III. to understand, comprehend, Aesch., etc. :—often in Dialogue, μανθάνεις ; Lat. tenes? d'ye see? —Answ. πάνυ μανθάνω, perfectly ! Ar.   IV. in Att., τί μαθών ; often begins a question, having learnt what? for what new reason? wherefore? Id., etc.

μανία, Ion. -ίη, ἡ, (μαίνομαι) madness, frenzy, Hdt.,

Trag., etc. **II.** enthusiasm, inspired frenzy, Eur., Plat. **III.** mad passion, fury, Trag.

μᾰνιάκης, ου, ὁ, an armlet, worn of gold used by Persians and Gauls, Polyb.

μᾰνιάς, άδος, (μανία) raging, frantic, mad, Soph. ; with a neut. Subst., μανιάσιν λυσσήμασι with mad ravings, Eur.

μᾰνῐκός, ή, όν, (μανία) of or for madness, mad, Ar. ; μανικόν τι βλέπειν to look mad, Id. **II.** of persons, frenzied, frantic, Plat. :—mad, extravagant, Xen. : —Adv., μανικῶς διακεῖσθαι Plat.

μᾶνις, Dor. for μῆνις.

μᾰνι-ώδης, ες, (εἶδος) like madness, mad, Xen. **2.** like a madman, crazy, Thuc. ; τὸ μ. madness, Eur.

μάννᾰ, ἡ, a Hebr. word, manna, a morsel, grain, the gum of the tamarisk ; generally, food, N. T.

ΜΑ'ΝΝΟΣ, ὁ, Lat. monile, a collar. Hence

μαννο-φόρος, ον, (φέρω) wearing a collar, Theocr.

ΜΑΝΟ'Σ, ή, όν, Lat. rarus, loose in texture, porous, Plat., etc. **II.** few, scanty, Xen., etc. :—Adv. -νῶς, τοσούτῳ μανότερον so much the less often, Id.

μανότης, ητος, ἡ, looseness of texture, porousness, Arist. **II.** fewness, scantiness, Plat.

μαντεία, Ion. -ηΐη, ἡ, (μαντεύομαι) prophesying, prophetic power, h. Hom. : mode of divination, Hdt. ; αἴνιγμα μαντείας ἔδει the riddle stood in need of divination, Soph. **II.** = μαντεῖον II, Tyrtae., Soph.

μαντεῖον, Ion. and Ep. -ήϊον, τό, an oracle, i. e., **I.** an oracular response, Od., Hdt., Att. **II.** the seat of an oracle, Hdt., Aesch., etc.

μαντεῖος, α, ον, and ος, ον, Ion. -ήϊος, η, ον :—poët. for μαντικός, oracular, prophetic, Pind., Aesch., etc. ; μ. ἄναξ, i. e. Apollo, Eur.

μάντευμα, ατος, τό, an oracle, Pind., Trag.

μαντεύομαι, Dep. : f. -εύσομαι : aor. 1 ἐμαντευσάμην, poët. μαντευσάμην, as Pass., v. infr. III : (μάντις) :— to divine, prophesy, presage, Hom., etc. ; c. acc. cogn., μαντεία μ. Aesch. **2.** generally, to divine, presage, augur, forbode, surmise, of any presentiment, Plat., etc. ; c. gen., μαντευσόμεσθα τἀνδρὸς ὡς ὀλωλότος Aesch. **3.** of animals, to get scent of a thing, Theocr. **II.** to consult an oracle, seek divinations, Hdt., Att. ; ταῦτα καὶ μ. this is the question I ask the oracle, Eur. **III.** aor. 1 and pf. pass. in pass. sense, ἐμαντεύθη an oracle was given, Hdt. ; τὰ μεμαντευμένα the words of the oracles, Id.

μαντευτέον, verb. Adj. one must divine, Eur. ; and

μαντευτός, ή, όν, foretold by an oracle, Eur. : prescribed by an oracle, Xen.

μαντηΐη, **μαντήϊον**, **μαντήϊος**, Ion. for μαντεία, etc.

μαντιδουλεύει, crasis for μὴ ἀντιδουλεύει.

μαντικός, ή, όν, of or for a soothsayer or his art, prophetic, oracular, Trag. **2.** ἡ μαντικὴ τέχνη, = μαντεία, the faculty of divination, prophecy, Soph. ; so, ἡ μαντική alone, Hdt., Plat. **II.** of persons, like a prophet, oracular, Plat. :—Adv. -κῶς, Ar.

μαντιπολέω, f. ήσω, to prophesy, Aesch. From

μαντῐ-πόλος, ον, (πολέω) frenzied, inspired, Eur.

μάντῐς, ὁ, gen. εως, Ion. ιος and ηος, voc. μάντῐ : dat. pl., μάντεσι : (μαίνομαι) :—one who divines, a seer, prophet, Hom., etc. :—as fem. a prophetess, Trag., Thuc. **2.**

metaph. a diviner, foreboder, Soph. **II.** a kind of grasshopper, Theocr.

μαντοσύνη, ἡ, (μάντις) the art of divination, Il., Pind.

μαντόσῠνος, η, ον, (μάντις) oracular, Eur.

μαντῷος, α, ον, = μαντεῖος, Anth.

μᾱνύω, Dor. for μηνύω.

μάομαι, contr. μῶμαι, v. *μάω II.

μᾱπέειν, Ep. aor. 2 inf. of μάρπτω.

μᾱπολακτίσῃς, crasis for μὴ ἀπολακτίσῃς.

μᾱπολείπεσθαι, crasis for μὴ ἀπολείπεσθαι.

μάραγνα [ᾰ], ἡ, a whip, scourge, Aesch., Eur. (Deriv. unknown.)

ΜΑ'ΡΑΘΟΝ [ᾰ], τό, fennel, Lat. marathrum, Dem.

Μᾰρᾰθών, ῶνος, ὁ, Marathon, a deme on the East of Attica, prob. so called from its being overgrown with fennel, Od., Hdt., etc.

Μᾰρᾰθωνο-μάχης [ᾰ], ου, ὁ, (μάχομαι) a Marathon fighter, a Marathon-man, proverb. of a brave veteran, Ar.

ΜΑ'ΡΑΙ'ΝΩ, f. μᾰρᾰνῶ : aor. 1 ἐμάρᾱνα :—Pass., f. μᾰρανθήσομαι : aor. 1 ἐμᾱράνθην : pf. μεμάρασμαι or -αμμαι :—to put out or quench fire, h. Hom. :—Pass. to die away, go slowly out, of fire, Il. **II.** metaph., ὄψεις μ. to quench the orbs of sight, Soph. ; νόσος μαραίνει με makes me waste away, wears me out, Aesch. ; of time, πάντα χρόνος μαραίνει Soph. : —Pass. to die away, waste away, decay, wither, Eur., Thuc. ; αἷμα μαραίνεται χερός blood dies away from my hand, Aesch. ; of a river, to dry up, Hdt.

μαρὰν ἀθά, Syriac phrase, = ὁ Κύριος ἥκει, N. T.

μαργαίνω, only in pres., (μάργος) to rage furiously, Il.

μαργαρίτης [ῐ], ου, ὁ, a pearl, Theophr., etc. (A Persian word.)

μάργαρον, τό, = μαργαρίτης, Anacreont.

μαργάω, (μάργος) only used in part. μαργῶν, raging, Aesch. ; c. inf. μαργῶν ἱέναι madly eager to go, Eur.

Μαργίτης [ῑ], ου, ὁ, (μάργος) Margites, i. e. a mad fellow, hero of a mock-heroic poem ascribed to Homer.

μαργόομαι, Pass., = μαργαίνω, Pind., Aesch.

ΜΑ'ΡΓΟΣ, η, ον, and ος, ον, raging mad, Lat. furiosus, μάργε, madman ! Od. ; then in Pind., Aesch., etc. **2.** of appetite, greedy, gluttonous, Od., Eur. **3.** lewd, lustful, Theogn., Eur.

μαργοσύνη, ἡ, = sq., Theogn.

μαργότης, ητος, ἡ, (μάργος) raging passion, Soph. **2.** gluttony, Plat. **3.** lust, Eur.

Μαρέη, Att. **Μάρεα**, ἡ, Marea, a town in Lower Egypt, Hdt., Thuc. **II.** a lake near it, Strab. ; more commonly called ἡ Μαρεῶτις (sc. λίμνη) Id. :—also ὁ **Μαρεώτης** (sc. οἶνος) Id.

ΜΑ'ΡΗ, ἡ, a hand, Pind.

Μαρῐανδῡνοί, οἱ, a people of Bithynia, Hdt., etc. :— **Μαριανδυνὸς θρηνητήρ** one who utters a wild, barbaric lament, Aesch. ; cf. Κίσσιος.

μάριλη [ῐ], ἡ, the embers of charcoal, Ar. :—hence, ὦ **Μαρῑλάδη** O son of Coal-dust ! comic name of an Acharnian collier, Id. (Deriv. unknown.)

μαρῑλο-πότης, ου, ὁ, (**ΠΟ**, Root of some tenses of πίνω) coal-dust-gulper, of a blacksmith, Anth.

ΜΑΡΜΑΙ'ΡΩ, only in pres. and impf., to flash, sparkle, of arms, Il. ; ὄμματα μαρμαίροντα the sparkling eyes

of Aphrodité, Il.; νύκτα ἄστροισι μαρμαίρουσαν Aesch.
Hence

μαρμάρεος [μᾰ], α, ον, *flashing, sparkling, glistening, gleaming*, of metals, Il., Hes.; also, ἅλς μαρμαρέη the *many-twinkling* sea, Il. **II.** *of marble*, Anth.

μαρμάρῐνος [μᾰ], η, ον, (μάρμᾰρος) *of marble*, Theocr.

μαρμᾰρο-γλῠφία, ἡ, *sculpture in marble*, Strab.

μαρμάροεις, εσσα, εν, = μαρμάρεος, Soph.

μάρμᾰρος, ου, ὁ, any *stone* or *rock* of crystalline structure, which sparkles (μαρμαίρει) in the light, Hom., etc.; also, πέτρος μάρμαρος Il. **II.** *marble*, Strab.: —*a marble tombstone*, Theocr.

μαρμᾰρῠγή, ἡ, (μαρμαίρω) *a flashing, sparkling*, of light, Plat.: of any quick motion, μαρμαρυγαὶ ποδῶν *the quick twinkling* of dancers' feet, Od.

μαρμᾰρ-ωπός, όν, (ὤψ) *with sparkling eyes*, Eur.

ΜΑ'ΡΝᾰΜΑΙ, Ep. imper. μάρναο, inf. μάρνασθαι, impf. ἐμαρνάμην, αο, ατο, Ep. μάρνατο, 3 dual ἐμαρνάσθην, pl. ἐμαρνάμεσθα, Ep. μαρνάμεθα, 3 pl. μάρναντο:—Dep., only in pres. and impf.:—*to fight, do battle*, τινί *with* or *against* another, Il.; ἐπί τινι Ib.; πρός τινα Eur. **2.** *to quarrel, wrangle* with words, Il. **3.** in Pind. *to contend, struggle, strive to one's uttermost*, Pind.

ΜΑ'ΡΠΤΩ, impf. ἔμαρπτον: f. μάρψω: aor. 1 ἔμαρψα: —also Ep. forms, 3 sing. subj. μάρπτῃσι: aor. 2 opt. μεμάποιεν, inf. μᾰπέειν: pf. part. μεμαρπώς, 3 sing. plqpf. μεμάρπει:—*to catch, lay hold of, seise*, τινά Hom., etc.: c. gen. partis, μ. τινὰ ποδός *to catch* one by the foot, Soph., Il.; ποσὶ μ. τινά *to overtake, catch* a fugitive, Il.: but, χθόνα μάρπτε ποδοῖιν *reached* ground with his feet, Ib.: metaph., τὸν ὕπνος ἔμαρψε him sleep *overtook*, Ib.; γῆρας ἔμαρψε old age *got hold of* him, Od.; εἴ σε μάρψει ψῆφος if the votes *shall convict* thee, Aesch.; ἄσκοποι πλάκες ἔμαρψαν the unseen land *engulphed* him, Soph.

ΜΑ'ΡΣῙΠΟΣ, ὁ, *a bag, pouch*, Lat. *marsupium*, Xen.

Μάρτιος (sc. μήν), ὁ, Lat. *Martius, the month of March*, Plut.

μάρτῠρ, ῠρος, ὁ and ἡ, Aeol. for the Att. μάρτυς.

μαρτῠρέω, aor. 1 ἐμαρτύρησα: pf. μεμαρτύρηκα:—Pass., f. μαρτυρηθήσομαι, also μαρτυρήσομαι in pass. sense: aor. 1 ἐμαρτυρήθην: pf. μεμαρτύρημαι: (μάρτυς):—*to be a witness, to bear witness, give evidence, bear testimony*, Simon., etc.: c. dat. pers. *to bear witness* to or *in favour of* another, Hdt., Att.; μαρτυρέει μοι τῇ γνώμῃ bears *witness to* my opinion, Hdt. **2.** c. acc. rei, *to bear witness to* a thing, *testify* it, Soph., etc. **3.** c. inf. *to testify that* a thing is, Id.; τίς σοι μαρτυρήσει κλύειν; who *will bear* thee *witness that* he heard . . ? Id. **4.** c. acc. cogn., μ. ἀκοήν *to give* hearsay *evidence*, Dem.:—so in Pass., μαρτυρίαι μαρτυρηθεῖσαι Id. **5.** Pass. also impers., μαρτυρεῖταί *testimony is borne*, Plat.; οἶδα μαρτυρήσεσθαι I know *that testimony will be given*, Xen. Hence

μαρτύρημα [ῠ], ατος, τό, *testimony*, Eur.; and

μαρτῠρία, ἡ, *witness, testimony, evidence*, often in pl., Od.; μαρτυριῶν ἀπέχεσθαι to refuse to give *evidence*, Ar.

μαρτύριον [ῠ], τό, *a testimony, proof*, Hdt., etc.; μαρτύρια παρέχεσθαι to bring forward *evidence*, Id.: —μαρτύριον δέ . . , followed by γάρ, here is a proof, *namely* . . , Id., Thuc., etc.

μαρτύρομαι [ῠ], f. μαρτῠροῦμαι: aor. 1 ἐμαρτῡράμην:

Dep.: (μάρτυς):—*to call to witness, attest, invoke*, Soph., Eur., etc.; c. part., μαρτύρομαι τυπτόμενος *I call you to witness that* I am being beaten, Ar. **2.** c. acc. rei, *to call* one *to witness* a thing, Hdt., Ar. **3.** *to protest, asseverate*, μ. ὅτι . . Ar., etc.; absol., μαρτύρομαι *I protest*, Id., Thuc.

μάρτῠρος, ὁ, old Ep. form for μάρτυς, Hom.

ΜΑ'ΡΤΥ'Σ, ὁ, also ἡ; gen. μάρτῠρος, acc. -ῠρα, etc., formed from μάρτυρ, but also acc. μάρτῠν, with dat. pl. μάρτῠσι:—*a witness*, Hes., Theogn.; μάρτυρα θέσθαι τινά Eur.; μ. θεοὺς ποιεῖσθαι Thuc.; μάρτυρι χρῆσθαί τινι Arist.; μάρτυρας παρέχεσθαι to produce *witnesses*, Plat., etc.; so, μ. παριστάναι Xen.

μᾰρῠκάομαι, μᾰρύκημα, τό, Dor. for μηρυκ-.

μᾰρύομαι, Dor. for μηρύομαι.

μάρψαι, aor. 1 inf. of μάρπτω.

μᾰσάομαι, f. ἥσομαι, (μάσσω) Dep. *to chew*, Ar.

μάσασθαι, v. ἐπι-μαίομαι.

μάσδα, μασδός, Dor. for μᾶζα, μαζός.

μάσθλης, ητος, ὁ, = ἱμάσθλη, *a leather strap, thong*, Soph.:—metaph. *a supple knave*, Ar.

μασθός, late form of μαστός.

μασί, Dor. for μησί, dat. pl. of μήν.

μάσομαι, *I shall touch*, fut. of *μάω Il.

Μασσαλία, ἡ, Lat. *Massilia, Marseilles*, Thuc., etc.: the *Marseillais* were Μασσαλιῶται or -ῆται, οἱ, Dem., etc.

μάσσω, Att. μάττω: f. μάξω: aor. 1 ἔμαξα: pf. μέμαχα: —Pass., aor. 2 ἐμάγην: pf. μέμαγμαι: (from ΜΑΓ, for μάγ-σω):—properly, *to handle, touch*, in Med., Anth.: cf. ἐπιμαίομαι. **II.** *to work with the hands, to knead dough*, Lat. *pinso*, Ar.; also in Med., Hdt., Ar.; metaph., μάττειν ἐπινοίας Ar.:—Pass., μᾶζα ὑπ' ἐμοῦ μεμαγμένη Id.; σῖτος μεμαγμένος dough *ready kneaded*, Thuc.

μάσσων, ον, neut. μᾶσσον, gen. μάσσονος, irreg. Comp. of μακρός or μέγας, *longer, greater*, Od.; μάσσον' ἢ ὡς ἰδέμεν *greater* than one could see, Pind.; τὰ μάσσω *anything more*, Aesch.

μάσταξ, ᾰκος, ἡ, (μασάομαι) *that with which one chews, the mouth*, Od. **II.** *that which is chewed, a mouthful, morsel*, Il., Theocr.

μαστᾰρύζω, only in pres., *to mumble*, of an old man, Ar. (Formed from the sound.)

μαστευτής, οῦ, ὁ, = μαστήρ, Xen. From

μαστεύω, poët. inf. μαστευέμεν: poët. aor. 1 μάστευσα: (*μάω):—like ματεύω, *to seek, search*, Eur. **2.** c. acc. *to seek* or *search after*:—*to crave, need*, Pind., Aesch., Xen. **3.** c. inf. *to seek* or *strive to do*, Pind., Eur., Xen.

μαστήρ, ῆρος, ὁ, (*μάω) *a seeker, searcher, one who looks for*, τινος Soph., Eur.

μαστίάω, = μαστίζω, only in Ep. part. μαστιόων, Hes.

μαστιγίας, ου, ὁ, (μάστιξ) *one that always wants whipping, a worthless slave, a sorry knave*, Lat. *verbero*, Ar., Plat.

μαστῑγο-φόρος, ὁ, (φέρω) *a scourge-bearer, a sort of policeman*, Thuc.

μαστῑγόω, opt. μαστιγοίην: f. ώσω: aor. 1 ἐμαστίγωσα: —Med., f. μαστιγώσομαι in pass. sense:—*to whip, flog*, Hdt., Plat. Hence

μαστιγώσῐμος, ον, *that deserves whipping*, Luc.

μαστῑγωτέος, α, ον, verb. Adj. of μαστιγόω, deserving a whipping, Ar.

μαστίζω, Dor. -ίσδω : Ep. aor. 1 μάστιξα: part. aor. 1 pass. μαστιχθείς : (μάστιξ) :—to whip, flog, Il., Theocr.: c. inf., μάστιξεν δ᾽ ἐλάαν (v. ἐλαύνω I. 2), Hom. Hence

μαστίκτωρ, ορος, ὁ, a scourger, Aesch.

μάστιξ, ῑγος, ἡ (from same Root as ἱ-μάς, μάσθλης) :— a whip, scourge, Hom., Hdt., etc. ; ἵππου μ. a horse-whip, Hdt. ; ὑπὸ μαστίγων βαίνειν to advance under the lash, of soldiers flogged on, Id. ; so, τοξεύειν ὑπὸ μ. Xen. II. metaph. a scourge, plague, Il., Aesch. ; διπλῆ μ., τὴν Ἄρης φιλεῖ, i. e. fire and sword, Aesch. ; μ. Θεοῦ of sickness, N. T.

μάστῑς, ιος, ἡ, Ion. for μάστιξ, dat. μάστῑ Il. ; acc. μάστιν Od.

μαστῑχάω, (μαστάξ?) to gnash the teeth, Ep. part. μαστιχόων, Hes.

μαστίω, only in pres., to whip, scourge, Il. :—Med., οὐρῇ πλευρὰς μαστίεται [the lion] lashing his sides with his tail, Il.

μαστό-δετον, τό, (δέω) a breast-band, Anth.

μαστός, ὁ, Ion. and Ep. μαζός, Dor. μασδός :—one of the breasts, δεξιτερὸν παρὰ μαζόν Il. ; βάλε στέρνον ὑπὲρ μαζοῖο struck his chest above the breast, Ib. ; βάλε στῆθος παρὰ μαζόν Ib. 2. esp. a woman's breast, μαζὸν ἄνεσχε, of Hecuba mourning over Hector, Ib. ; παῖς δέ οἱ ἦν ἐπὶ μαζῷ Od. ; πρόσεσχε μαστόν, of the mother, Aesch. ; of animals, the udder, Eur. II. metaph. a round hill, knoll (French mamelon), Pind., Xen. 2. a piece of wool fastened to the edge of nets, Xen.

μαστροπεία, ἡ, a pandaring, Xen. From

μαστροπεύω, f. σω, to play the pandar, Xen. ; μ. τινὰ πρὸς τὴν πόλιν to seduce one into public life, Id. From

μαστροπός, ὁ and ἡ (μαστήρ) a pandar, Lat. leno, lena, Ar. ; metaph., Xen.

μασχάλη [ᾰ], ἡ, (μάλη) the armpit, Lat. ala, axilla, Ar., etc. II. a bay, Strab.

μασχᾱλίζω, f. σω, (μασχάλη) to put under the arm-pits : hence, to mutilate a corpse, since murderers had a fancy, that by cutting off the extremities and placing them under the arm-pits, they would avert vengeance, Aesch., Soph. Hence

μασχᾱλιστήρ, ῆρος, ὁ, a broad strap passing round the horse and fastened to the yoke by the λέπαδνον : generally, a girth, girdle, band, Hdt., Aesch.

μᾰτάζω, (μάταιος) to speak or work folly, Soph.; σπλάγχνα δ᾽ οὐ ματάζει my heart is not deceived, Aesch.

μᾰταιολογέω, f. ήσω, to talk idly, at random, Strab.

μᾰταιο-λόγος, ον, (λέγω) talking idly, at random, N. T.

μᾰταιοπονία, ἡ, labour in vain, Strab., Luc. From

μάταιος, a, ον, and ος, ον, (μάτη) vain, empty, idle, trifling, frivolous, Theogn., Hdt., Att. II. thoughtless, rash, irreverent, profane, impious, Aesch. ; τὸ μὴ μάταιον seriousness, gravity, Id. III. Adv. -ως, idly, without ground, Soph.

μάταν, Dor. for μάτην.

μᾰτάω, f. ήσω: aor. 1 ἐμάτησα, Ep. μάτησα : (μάτη) :— to be idle, to dally, loiter, linger, Il. ; οὐ ματᾷ τοὔργον the work lags not, Aesch. ; ματᾶν ὁδῷ to loiter by the way, Id. ; φροίμιον ματᾷ is in vain, Id.

μᾰτεύω, f. σω : aor. 1 ἐμάτευσα: (*μάω) :—like μαστεύω, to seek, search, Il., Soph. 2. c. acc. pers. to seek after, seek for, search after, properly of hounds casting for the scent, Aesch. ; then generally, Id., Soph., etc. 3. c. inf. to seek or strive to do, Pind., Soph. 4. c. acc. loci, to search, explore, Theocr.

μᾰτέω, rarer form for ματεύω, Theocr.

ΜΑ´ΤΗ [ᾰ], ἡ, = ματία, a folly, a fault, Aesch. Hence

μάτην, Dor. μάταν, Adv. in vain, idly, fruitlessly, Lat. frustra, h. Hom., Pind., Att. ; μ. ὁ μόχθος in vain the labour, Aesch. ; with a Noun, τὸ μ. ἄχθος the fruitless burthen, Id. 2. at random, without reason, Lat. temere, Theogn., Hdt., Att. ; ὁ νοσῶν μ., of a madman, Soph. 3. idly, falsely, Lat. falso, Id. ; μ. βέβακεν of a dream, Aesch.

μᾰτία, Ion. -ίη, ἡ, (μάτη) a vain attempt, Od.

μᾱτιο-λοιχός, ὁ, a devourer of meal, Ar. (A dubious word, said to be derived from μάτιον a measure of meal. Others read ματτυό-λοιχος, a licker up of dainties.)

μᾱτρᾰδελφεός, ματροδόκος, ματρόθεν, μάτρῳος, μάτρως, Dor. for μητρ-.

ματτύη, ἡ, and ματτύης, ου, ὁ, a dainty dish, Menand. : v. ματιολοιχός.

μάττω, Att. for μάσσω.

μαυρόω, f. ώσω, for ἀμαυρόω, metri gratia, to darken, to blind, make powerless, Pind., Aesch. 2. metaph. to make dim or obscure, or forgotten, Hes. :—Pass. to become dim or obscure, Theogn., Aesch.

Μαύσωλος, ὁ, a king of Halicarnassus, husband of Artemisia, Hdt. :—Μαυσωλεῖον, τό, his tomb at Halicarnassus, and, as appellat. a mausoleum, Strab.

μᾰφελής, crasis for μὴ ἀφελῇς.

μάχαιρα, ἡ, (μάχομαι) a large knife or dirk, worn by the heroes of the Iliad next the sword-sheath, Il. : generally, a knife for cutting up meat, Hdt., Att. 2. as a weapon, a short sword or dagger, Hdt., etc.: a sabre or bent sword, opp. to the straight sword (ξίφος), Xen. 3. a kind of rasor, μιᾷ μαχαίρᾳ with the rasor's single blade, opp. to διπλῆ μ. scissars, Ar.

μᾰχαιρίδιον [ῐ], τό, Dim. of μάχαιρα, Luc.

μᾰχαίριον, τό, Dim. of μάχαιρα, Xen.

μᾰχαιρίς, ίδος, ἡ, Dim. of μάχαιρα, a rasor, Ar., Luc.

μᾰχαιρο-ποιεῖον, τό, a cutler's factory, Dem. From

μᾰχαιρο-ποιός, όν, (ποιέω) a cutler, Ar., Dem.

μᾰχαιρο-πώλης, ου, ὁ, hence :—μᾰχαιρο-πώλιον, τό, a cutler's shop, Plut.

μᾰχαιρο-φόρος, ον, (φέρω) wearing a sabre, Hdt., Aesch., etc.

μᾰχᾱτάς, Dor. for μαχητής.

Μᾱχάων [ᾰ], ονος, ὁ, Machaon, son of Aesculapius, the first surgeon that we hear of, Il. (Perh. akin to μάχαιρα.)

μᾰχειόμενος, Ep. for μαχόμενος, pres. part. of μάχομαι.

μᾰχέοιτο, Ion. pres. opt. for μάχοιτο.

μᾰχεούμενος, Ep. for μαχόμενος, pres. part. of μάχομαι.

μᾰχετέον, verb. Adj. of μάχομαι, one must fight, Arist.

μάχευ, Dor. for μάχου, imper. of μάχομαι.

μάχη [ᾰ], ἡ, (μάχομαι) battle, fight, combat, Hom., etc. ; μάχαι νεῶν sea fights, Pind. :—with Verbs, μάχην μάχεσθαι to fight a battle, Il., Att. ; μάχην ἀρτύνειν, ἐγείρειν, ὀρνύμεν, ὀτρύνειν Il. : μάχην συνάπτειν or συμ-

βάλλειν τινί to engage *battle* with one, Aesch., Eur. ; also,διὰ μάχης·τινὶ ἀπικέσθαι,ἔρχεσθαι,ἥκειν,μολεῖν Hdt., Att. ; μάχην νικᾶν to win *a battle*, Xen. :—μάχη τινός *battle with* an enemy, Il., etc.   **2.** in pl. *quarrels, strifes, wranglings,* Ib., Plat.   **3.**=ἀγών, *a contest for a prize* in the games, Pind. : *generally a struggle,* Xen.   **II.** *a mode of fighting, way of battle,* Hdt., Xen.   **III.** *a field of battle,* Xen.

μάχήμων, ον, gen. ονος, *warlike,* Il., Anth.

μάχητής, οῦ, ὁ, (μάχομαι) *a fighter, warrior,* Hom. : Dor. Adj., μαχᾱτάς, *warlike,* Pind.

μάχητικός, ή, όν, *inclined to battle* or *war, quarrelsome,* Arist. :—μ. ἵπποι *restive horses,* Plat.

μάχητός, ή, όν, *to be fought with,* Od.

μάχῐμος [ᾰ], η, ον, also ος, ον, (μάχομαι) *fit for battle, warlike,* Hdt., Att. ; οἱ μ. *the fighting men, soldiery,* and in Egypt *the warrior-caste,* Hdt. ; τὸ μ. *the effective force,* Thuc.

μάχῐμ-ώδης, ες, (εἶδος) *warlike, quarrelsome,* Anth.

μαχλάς, άδος, fem. of μάχλος, Anth.

ΜΑ΄ΧΛΟΣ, ον, *lewd, lustful,* Hes., Luc.   **2.** metaph. *wanton, luxuriant, insolent,* Aesch. Hence

μαχλοσύνη, ἡ, *lewdness, lust, wantonness,* Il., Hdt.

ΜΑ΄ΧΟΜΑΙ [ᾰ], Ion. μαχέομαι, Dep. ; Ion. pres. opt. μαχέοιτο μαχέοιντο ; Ion. part. μαχεόμενος Ep. μαχειόμενος, μαχεούμενος :—Ion. impf. μαχέσκετο :—f. μαχέσομαι, Att. μαχοῦμαι, Ep. 3 pl. μαχέονται ; Ep. μαχήσομαι ; Dor. μαχησεῦμαι : aor. 1 ἐμαχεσάμην, Ep. inf. μαχήσασθαι :—*to fight,* Hom., etc. ; c. dat. pers. *to fight with,* i. e. *against,* one, Id., etc. ; μ. ἀντία and ἐναντίον τινός Il. ; ἐπί τινι, πρός τινα Ib. ; but, μ. σύν τινι *with the sanction, under the auspices* of a deity, Od., Xen. ; κατὰ σφέας μαχέονται *will fight* by themselves, Il. ; καθ᾽ ἕνα μ. *to fight* one against one, in single combat, Hdt. :—τὸ μήπω μεμαχημένον *the force that had* not yet *come into action,* Thuc.   **II.** generally, *to quarrel, wrangle, dispute* with one, *to oppose, gainsay,* τινι Il., Plat.   **III.** *to contend for the mastery* in games, πὺξ μάχεσθαι Il. ; παγκράτιον μ. Ar.

μαχομένως, Adv. pres. part. *pugnaciously,* Strab.

ΜΑ΄Ψ, Adv. *in vain, idly, fruitlessly,* Il. ; μὰψ ὀμόσαι *to swear lightly,* i. e. *without meaning to perform,* Ib.   **II.** *vainly, idly, foolishly, thoughtlessly,* μὰψ αὔτως Hom. ; μάψ, ἀτὰρ οὐ κατὰ κόσμον Id.

μαψ-αῦραι, ῶν, αἱ, (αὔρα) *random breezes, squalls, gusts* or *flaws of wind,* Hes.

μαψίδιος, ον, (μάψ) *vain, false,* Eur., Theocr. : *useless, worthless,* Anth. :—Adv. μαψιδίως, = μάψ, Hom.

μαψῐ-λόγος, ον, (λέγω) *idly talking,* μ. οἰωνοί *birds whose cries convey no sure omen,* h. Hom.

μαψι-τόκος, ον, (τεκεῖν) *bringing forth in vain,* Anth.

μαψ-υλάκᾱς, ου, ὁ, (ὑλάω, ὑλακή) *idly barking,* i. e. *repeating* a thing *again and again,* Pind.

*ΜΑ΄Ω, found only in pf. μέμαα with pres. sense, 3 pl. μεμάασι ; and in syncop. forms, dual μέμᾰτον, pl. μέμᾰμεν ; 3 sing. imperat. μεμάτω ; 3 pl. plqpf. μέμᾰσαν ; part. μεμαώς μεμαυῖα, gen. μεμαότος, Ep. also μεμαῶτος :—to wish eagerly, strive, yearn, desire, c. inf., Hom., etc. : c. gen. to long for, be eager for :—often also with an Adv., πῆ μέματον ; *whither so fast?* Il. ; πρόσσω μεμαυῖαι *pressing forward,* Ib. : absol. in part.,

ἔβη μεμαώς *he strode on hastily, eagerly,* Ib. ; ἐν πέτρᾳ μεμαώς, *of a fisher, expectant,* Theocr.   **2.** *to be bent on* doing, *to purpose,* μεμάασιν αὖθι μένειν Il., etc.   **II.** Med. in Dor. inf. μῶσθαι, part. μώμενος : —*to seek after, covet,* c. acc., Theogn., etc. ; c. inf. or absol., Aesch.

μεγά-θαρσής, ές, (θαρσέω) *very bold,* Hes.

μέγᾰθος, τό, Ion. for μέγεθος.

μεγά-θῡμος, ον, *high-minded,* Hom., Hes.

μεγαίρω, aor. 1 ἐμέγηρα, (μέγας) *to look on* a thing *as too great, to grudge* one a thing *as too great* for him, Il. ; so c. inf., μηδὲ μεγήρῃς ἡμῖν τελευτῆσαι τάδε ἔργα *grudge* us not the accomplishment of these works, Od. ; c. acc. et inf., μνηστῆρας οὔτι μεγαίρω ἔρδειν *I complain* not that the suitors should do, Ib.   **2.** c. dat. pers. *to feel a grudge towards,* Il.   **3.** absol., ἢ πύξ, ἠὲ πάλῃ, ἢ καὶ ποσίν, οὔτι μεγαίρω *I care* not (which), Od.   **4.** c. gen. rei, βιότοιο μεγήρας *grudging* him the life [of Antilochus], Il. ; οὐ μ. τοῦδέ σοι δωρήματος Aesch.   **5.** Pass. *to be envied,* Anth.

μεγα-κήτης, ες, (κῆτος II) *with great hollows, cavernous,* of the sea, Od. ; (cf. βαθυκήτης) : of a ship, *with large hull,* Il. ; of a dolphin, *with huge maw,* Ib.

μεγα-κλεής, ές, *very famous,* declined (as if from μεγα-κλῆς) μεγακλέος, εἴ, εα, έες, έα, Anth.

μεγάλ-άδῐκος, ον, *unjust in great matters,* Arist.

μεγάλ-αλκής, ές, (ἀλκή) *of great strength,* ap. Plut.

μεγάλ-ᾱνορία, μεγάλ-ᾱνωρ, Dor. for μεγαλ-ην-.

μεγάλ-αυχέω, f. ήσω, *to boast highly, talk big,* Aesch. : —Med. *to boast oneself,* Plat. ; and

μεγάλαυχία, ἡ, *great boasting, arrogance,* Plat. From

μεγάλ-αυχος, ον, (αὐχέω) *greatly boasting, very glorious,* Pind., Aesch., etc.

μεγαλεῖος, α, ον, (μέγας) *magnificent, splendid,* Xen. ; τὰ μεγαλεῖα *mighty works,* N. T. :—Adv. -ως, *splendidly,* Xen.   **2.** of persons, *stately, haughty,* Id.

μεγάλειότης, ητος, ἡ, *majesty,* N. T.

μεγάληγορέω, f. ήσω, *to talk big, boast,* Xen. ; and

μεγάληγορία, ἡ, *big talking,* Eur., Xen. From

μεγάλ-ήγορος, ον, (ἀγορεύω) *talking big, vaunting, boastful,* Aesch., Xen.

μεγάληνορία, ἡ, *great manliness, proud self-confidence, haughtiness,* Pind., Eur. From

μεγάλ-ήνωρ, ορος, ὁ, ἡ, (ἀνήρ) *very manly, heroic : self-confident, haughty,* Pind.

μεγάλ-ήτωρ, ορος, ὁ, ἡ, (ἦτορ) *great-hearted, heroic,* Hom.

μεγαλίζομαι, Pass. only in pres., *to be exalted, to bear oneself proudly,* Hom.

μεγ-αλκής, ές, =μεγαλαλκής, Anth.

μεγαλογνωμοσύνη, ἡ, *high-mindedness,* Xen. From

μεγαλο-γνώμων, ον, *high-minded,* Xen.

μεγάλο-δενδρος, ον, *full of large trees,* Strab.

μεγάλό-δοξος, ον, (δόξα) *very glorious,* Pind., Plut.

μεγαλοδωρία, ἡ, *munificence,* Luc. From

μεγάλό-δωρος, ον, (δῶρον) *making great presents, munificent,* Ar.

μεγάλοεργής, contr. -ουργής, ές, (*ἔργω) *performing great deeds, magnificent,* Luc. Hence

μεγάλοεργία, ἡ, contr. -ουργία, *magnificence,* Luc.

μεγάλοεργός, contr. -ουργός, όν, =μεγαλοεργής, Plut.

μεγάλό-θυμος, ον, =μεγάθυμος, Plat.

μεγάλ-οιτος, ον, very wretched, Theocr.
μεγᾰλοκευθής, ές, concealing much : capacious, Pind.
μεγᾰλο-κίνδῠνος, ον, braving great dangers, Arist.
μεγᾰλοκόρῠφος, ον, with lofty summits, ap. Arist.
μεγᾰλο-κρᾰτής, ές, (κρατέιν) far-ruling, Anth.
μεγᾰλό-μητις, τι, of high design, ambitious, Aesch.
μεγᾰλό-μισθος, ον, receiving high pay, Luc.
μεγᾰλόνοια, ἡ, greatness of intellect, Plat., Luc. From
μεγᾰλό-νοος, ον, contr. -νους, ουν, greatminded, Luc.
μεγᾰλό-πολις, poët. -πτολις, ι, epith. of great cities, αἱ μεγαλοπτόλιες Ἀθᾶναι Athens that mighty city, Pind. ; ἁ μ. Τροία Eur.
μεγᾰλοπραγμοσύνη, ἡ, the disposition to do great things, magnificence, Plut. From
μεγᾰλο-πράγμων, ον, (πράσσω) disposed to do great deeds, forming great designs, Xen.
μεγᾰλοπρέπεια, Ion. -είη, ἡ, the character of a μεγαλοπρεπής, magnificence, Hdt., Plat.
μεγᾰλο-πρεπής, ές, (πρέπω) befitting a great man, magnificent, Hdt., Att. :—τὸ μεγαλοπρεπές, = μεγαλοπρέπεια, Xen. II. Adv. -ῶς, Ion. -έως, Hdt., Xen. : Comp. -έστερον Plat., Sup. -έστατα Hdt.
μεγᾰλόπτολις, v. μεγαλόπολις.
μεγᾰλος, v. μέγας.
μεγᾰλο-σθενής, ές, exceeding strong, Pind.
μεγᾰλό-σπλαγχνος, ον, (σπλάγχνον) with large heart: high-spirited, Eur.
μεγᾰλό-στονος, ον, very lamentable, most piteous, Aesch.
μεγᾰλο-σχήμων, ον, (σχῆμα) magnificent, Aesch.
μεγᾰλό-τολμος, ον, (τόλμα) greatly adventurous, Luc.
μεγᾰλ-ουργός, -γία, -γός, v. μεγαλο-εργ-
μεγᾰλοφρονέω, to be high-minded, μ. ἐφ' ἑαυτῷ to be confident in oneself, Xen. :—Med., in bad sense, to be arrogant, Plat. ; and
μεγᾰλοφροσύνη, ἡ, greatness of mind, Plat. ; ὑπὸ μεγαλοφροσύνης magnanimously, Hdt. 2. in bad sense, pride, arrogance, Id. From
μεγᾰλό-φρων, ονος, ὁ, ἡ, (φρήν) high-minded, noble, generous, Xen. 2. in bad sense, arrogant : Adv. -όνως, Plat., Xen.
μεγᾰλοφωνία, ἡ, grandiloquence, Luc.
μεγᾰλό-φωνος, ον, (φωνή) loud-voiced, Dem.
μεγᾰλοψῡχία, ἡ, greatness of soul, magnanimity, Arist. :—in bad sense, arrogance, Dem. 2. of things, magnificence, Id. From
μεγᾰλό-ψῡχος, ον, (ψυχή) high-souled, magnanimous, Dem. :—Adv. -χως, Id.
μεγᾰλύνω [ῡ], only in pres. and impf., (μέγας) to make great or powerful, to exalt, strengthen, Thuc. :—Pass., μεγαλύνεσθαι ἔκ τινος to gain great glory from . . , Xen. II. to make great by word, to extol, magnify, Eur., Thuc., etc. :—Med. to boast oneself, Aesch., Xen. 2. to aggravate a crime, Thuc.
μεγᾰλ-ώνῠμος, ον, (ὄνομα) with a great name, giving glory, Soph., Ar.
μεγᾰλως, Adv. of μέγας, v. μέγας B.
μεγᾰλωστί [ῐ], Ep. and Ion. Adv. of μέγας, far and wide, over a vast space, Hom. II. = μεγάλως, Hdt. 2. also = μεγαλοπρεπῶς, Id.
μεγᾰλωσύνη, ἡ, (μέγας) greatness, majesty, N. T.

μεγ-άνωρ [ᾰ], ορος, ὁ, ἡ, (ἀνήρ) man-exalting, Pind.
Μέγᾰρα, τά, Megara, Hdt., etc. ; Μέγαράδε to Megara, Ar. Hence
Μεγᾰρεύς, έως, ὁ, a citizen of Megara, pl. Μεγαρεῖς or -ῆς, Hdt., etc. Hence
Μεγᾰρίζω, f. ίω, to side with the Megarians or speak their dialect, Ar. ; and
Μεγᾰρικός, ή, όν, Megarian, Ar., etc. :—fem. Μεγαρίς (sc. γῆ), the Megarian territory, Megarid, Thuc.
Μεγᾰρόθεν, Adv. from Megara, Ar.
Μεγᾰροῖ, Adv. at Megara, Ar.
μέγᾰρον, τό, a large room or chamber, esp. the hall, Od. 2. the women's apartment, Ib. II. in pl. a house, palace, like Lat. aedes, because the house consisted of many rooms, Hom. ; ἐν μεγάροις at home, Id. III. the oracular chamber in the temple, the sanctuary, shrine, Hdt. ; in this sense always, like Lat. aedes, in sing. Hence
μέγᾰρόνδε, Adv. homewards, home, Od.
ΜΕΓΑΣ, μεγάλη [ᾰ], μέγᾰ, gen. μεγάλου, ης ου, dat. μεγάλῳ, ῃ, ῳ, acc. μέγαν, μεγάλην, μέγᾰ, voc. μέγαλε : dual. μεγάλω, α, ω, pl. μεγάλοι, αι, α, etc. I. Radic. sense, opp. to μικρός, σμικρός, big, great, of men's stature, tall, Hom. ; of women, καλή τε μεγάλη τε Od. :—also, great, full-grown, of age as shewn by stature, Ib., Aesch. 2. vast, high, οὐρανός, ὄρος, πύργος Hom. 3. vast, spacious, wide, πέλαγός, αἰγιαλός, etc., Id. II. of Degree, great, strong, mighty, of gods, Id., etc. ; μεγάλα θεά, of Demeter and Proserpine, Soph. ; μέγας ηὐξήθη rose to greatness, Dem. ; βασιλεὺς ὁ μέγας, i. e. the King of Persia, le grand Monarque, Hdt. ; βασιλεὺς μέγας Aesch. ; ὁ μ. ἐπικληθεὶς Ἀντίοχος the Great, Polyb. 2. great, strong, violent, etc., ἄνεμος, λαῖλαψ Hom. ; of properties, passions, etc., Id., etc. 3. of sounds, great, loud, Id., etc. ; μὴ φώνει μέγα Soph. ;—but, μέγας λόγος a prevailing rumour, Aesch. 4. great, mighty, weighty, important, μέγα ἔργον Od. ; μέγα ποιεῖσθαί τι to esteem of great importance, Hdt. ; καὶ τὸ μέγιστον and what is most important, Thuc. 5. in bad sense, over-great, μέγα εἰπεῖν to speak big, λίην μέγα εἰπεῖν Od. ; μέγα, μεγάλα φρονεῖν to have high thoughts, be presumptuous, Soph., Eur. ; μεγάλα πνεῖν Eur.
B. Adv. μεγάλως [ᾰ], greatly, mightily, exceedingly, Lat. magnopere, Hom., Aesch. II. neut. sing. and pl. μέγα and μεγάλα as Adv., very much, exceedingly, Hom. ; with verbs of sound, aloud, loudly, Id. ; so in Att. 2. of Space, far, μέγα ἄνευθε far away, Il., etc. :—with Comp. and Sup. by far, μέγ' ἀμείνων, ἄριστος, φέρτατος Hom.
C. degrees of Comparison : 1. Comp. μείζων (for μεγίων) -ον, gen. -ονος, Hom., Att. ; Ion. μέζων, ον, Hdt. ; later also μειζότερος, N. T. :—greater, Hom., etc. ; also, too great, too much, more than enough, Plat. :—neut. μεῖζον Eur. ; Ion. μέζονᾰ Hdt., etc. ; also neut. as Adv. μεῖζον σθένειν Soph., etc. 2. Sup. μέγιστος, η, ον, Hom. :—neut. as Adv., μέγιστον ἰσχύειν Soph. ; with another Sup. μέγιστον ἔχθιστος Eur. :—also in pl., χαῖρ' ὡς μέγιστα Soph.
μεγα-σθενής, ές, = μεγαλοσθενής, Pind., Aesch.
μεγ-αυχής, ές, = μεγάλαυχος, Pind., Aesch.

μέγεθος, Ion. **μέγαθος,** εος, τό, (μέγας) *greatness, magnitude, size, height, stature,* Hom., Hdt., etc. :—of sound, *loudness,* βοῆς μ. Thuc. :—dat. and acc. are used adverbially, *μεγάθεϊ μέγας* great *in size,* Hdt. ; *μεγάθεϊ μικρός* Id.; so, ποταμοὶ οὐ κατὰ τὸν Νεῖλον ἐόντες μεγάθεα rivers not bearing any proportion to the Nile *in size,* Id.　　**II.** of Degree, *greatness, magnitude,* Eur., Thuc., etc.　　**2.** *greatness,* i. e. *might, power,* Eur., Xen.　　**3.** *greatness, magnanimity,* Plut.

μεγ-ήρᾰτος, ον, (ἐρατός) *passing lovely,* Hes.

μεγιστᾶνες, οἱ, (μέγιστος) *great men, grandees,* N. T.

μεγιστό-πολις, ι, *making cities greatest,* Pind.

μεδέων, οντος, ὁ, like **μέδων** (v. μέδω), participial Subst. *a guardian,* Ζεὺς Ἴδηθεν μεδέων guardian of Ida, Il. ; δελφίνων μ., of Poseidon, Ar.　　**2.** fem. **μεδέουσα,** of Aphrodité, h. Hom. ; of Mnemosyné, Hes., etc.

μέδιμνος, ὁ, *the medimnus,* an Attic corn-measure, containing 6 ἑκτεῖς, 48 χοίνικες, 192 κοτύλαι = 6 Roman modii, i. e. very nearly 12 gallons, Hes., Att.

ΜΕΔΩ, only in pres., and mostly in participial Subst. **μέδων,** οντος, ὁ, like **μεδέων, μεδέουσα,** *a guardian, lord,* Ἀργείων ἡγήτορες ἠδὲ μέδοντες leaders and *guardians* of the Argives, Hom. ; μέδων ἁλός *lord of the sea,* Od.; of Bacchus, ὃ μέδεις Δηοῦς ἐν κόλποις Soph.　　**II.** as Dep. **μέδομαι,** f. μεδήσομαι, *to provide for, think on, be mindful of, bethink one of,* c. gen., πολέμοιο μεδέσθω Il. ; ὡς δείπνοιο μέδηται Od., etc.　　**2.** *to plan, contrive, devise* something for one, κακὰ Τρώεσσι μέδεσθαι Il.

μέζεα, ων, τά, = μήδεα (v. μῆδος Β), Hes.

μέζων, μεζόνως, Ion. for μείζων, μειζόνως, v. μέγας.

μεθ-αιρέω : aor. 2 μεθεῖλον, Ion. μεθέλεσκον :—*to catch in turn,* of a game at ball, Od.

μεθ-άλλομαι, Dep., syncop. aor. 2 part. μετάλμενος, *to leap* or *rush upon,* c. dat., Il.　　**2.** *to rush after,* in a race, Ib.

μεθᾱμέριος, Dor. for μεθημέριος.

μεθ-αρμόζω, late Att. -όττω, f. όσω, *to dispose differently,* i. e. *to correct,* Soph. :—Med., aor. 1 μεθηρμοσάμην, with pf. pass. -ήρμοσμαι, *to dispose for oneself,* μεθάρμοσαι νέους τρόπους *adopt new* habits, Aesch. ; μεθηρμόσμεσθα βελτίω βίον Eur.

μεθέηκα, Ion. for μεθῆκα, aor. 1 of μεθίημι.

μεθείην, aor. 2 opt. of μεθίημι :—**μεθεῖναι,** inf.

μεθεῖλον, aor. 2 of μεθαιρέω.

μεθείς, aor. 2 part. of μεθίημι.

μεθείω, Ep. for μεθῶ, aor. 2 subj. of μεθίημι.

μεθεκτέον, verb. Adj. of μετέχω, *one must have a share of,* τινός Thuc.

μεθέλεσκε, Ion. for μεθεῖλε, 3 sing. aor. 2 of μεθαιρέω.

μεθ-έλκω, *to draw to the other side,* ἡνίας Anth.

μέθεν, Dor. and poët. for ἐμέθεν.

μέθεξις, ἡ, (μετέχω) *participation,* Plat.

μεθέξομαι, f. of μετ-έχω.

μεθ-έπω, impf. μεθεῖπον, Ep. -επον : f. -έψω : aor. 2 μετ-έσπον, inf. μετασπεῖν, part. -σπών, med. -σπόμενος :—*to follow after, follow closely,* Hom. ; so in Med., μετασπόμενος Il. ; c. dat., μεθέπομαί σοι Soph.　　**2.** c. acc. *to follow with the eyes, to seek after,* Il.　　**3.** *to visit,* νέον μεθέπεις ; *dost thou come* but now *to visit us ?* Od.　　**4.** metaph. *to pursue, attend to,*

Pind. ; ἄχθος μεθέπων *carrying* a burden, Id.　　**II.** Causal, c. dupl. acc., Τυδείδην μέθεπε ἵππους he *turned* the horses *in pursuit of* Tydeides, Il.

μέθες, aor. 2 imper. of μεθίημι.

μεθέστηκα, pf. of μεθίστημι.

μέθη, ἡ, = μέθυ, *strong drink,* καλῶς ἔχειν μέθης *to be pretty well drunk,* Hdt. ; ὑπερπλησθεὶς μέθης Soph. ; μέθῃ βρεχθεὶς Eur.　　**II.** *drunkenness,* Plat.

μεθῆκα, aor. 1 of μεθίημι.

μεθ-ήκω, *to be come in quest of,* τινά Eur., Ar.

μέθ-ημαι, Pass. *to sit among,* c. dat., Od.

μεθ-ημερῖνός, ή, όν, (ἡμέρα) *happening by day, in open day,* Xen., Dem.

μεθ-ημέριος, ον, = foreg., Eur.

μεθημοσύνη, ἡ, *remissness, carelessness,* Il.　　From

μεθήμων, ον, gen. ονος, Ep. μεθίημι) *remiss, careless,* Hom.

μεθησέμεν, -έμεναι, Ep. for μεθήσειν, f. inf. of μεθίημι.

μεθίδρυσις, ἡ, *migration,* Strab.　　From

μεθ-ιδρύω, f. ύσω, *to place differently, transpose,* Plat. :—Pass. *to keep moving,* Plut.

μεθ-ίημι, 2 and 3 pers. μεθιεῖς, μεθιεῖ (as if from μεθιέω), Ion. μετιεῖ or μετίει ; 3 pl. μεθιᾶσι, Ion. μετιεῖσι : imperat. μεθίει : Ep. 3 sing. subj. μεθίῃσι : inf. μεθιέναι, Ep. -ιέμεναι, -ιέμεν :—impf. 3 sing., μεθίει, Ion. μετίει (for μεθίεσαν) :—f. μεθήσω, Ep. inf. μεθησέμεναι, -έμεν :—aor. 1 μεθῆκα, Ep. μεθέηκα, other moods being supplied by aor. 2, imper. μέθες ; subj. μεθῶ, Ep. μεθείω ; opt. μεθείην ; inf. μεθεῖναι, Ep. μεθέμεν, part. μεθείς :—Med., f. μεθήσομαι, Ion. μετήσομαι (in pass. sense) : 3 sing. aor. 2 μεθεῖτο, 2 pl. μέθεσθε ; 2 dual and pl. subj. μεθήσθον, μεθῆσθε ; inf. μεθέσθαι :—Pass., 3 sing. Ion. impf. μετίετο : 3 pl. pf. μεθεῖνται, Ion. imper. μετεῖσθαι ; Ion. part. μεμετιμένος : Ion. aor. 1 μετείθην. [Generally, ῐ Ep., ῑ Att.]　　**I.** trans. *to let go, let loose, release* a prisoner, Il., etc. : *to let* a visitor *depart,* Od. : *to dismiss* a wife, Hdt. :—c. inf. *to let one free to do as* he will, *allow* one to do, Id.; so, ἐλεύθερον μ. τινά Eur. :—Pass. *to be let go, dismissed,* Hdt.　　**b.** *to give up, abandon,* Il. :—metaph., εἴ με μεθείη ῥῖγος if the cold *would but leave* me, Od.　　**2.** c. acc. rei, *to let* a thing go, *let it fall, throw,* τι ἐς ποταμόν Ib., etc. :—also, μ. χόλον *to let go, give up* one's *wrath,* Hom.; so, Ἀχιλῆϊ μεθέμεν χόλον *to put away* anger in favour of Achilles, Il. ; so, μ. καρδίας χόλον *to put away* anger *from* one's *heart,* Eur. ; μ. ψυχήν *to give up* the ghost, Id. :—of liquids, *to let flow, let drop,* Hdt., Att. :—so, γλώσσαν Περσίδα μ. *to let drop,* i. e. *utter,* Persian words, Hdt. :—μ. βλαστόν *to let* it *shoot forth,* Id. :—μ. βέλος *to let* it *fly, discharge* it, Soph. ; μ. ξίφος ἐς γυναῖκα *to plunge* it into her, Eur. ; ναῒ μεθεῖναι (sc. ἱστία) *to give* the ship her way, Soph.　　**b.** *to relieve,* κῆρ ἄχεος the heart *from* grief, Il.　　**c.** *to give up, resign, throw aside,* Ib., Att.　　**d.** *to forgive* one a fault, *remit* a debt, Hdt. ; τόνδε κίνδυνον μεθεὶς *excusing* thee this peril, Eur.　　**II.** intr. *to relax* one's energies (where ἑαυτόν may be supplied), *to be slack, remiss, lukewarm, dally,* Hom. : c. inf. *to neglect* to do, Il., Hdt., Att.　　**b.** *to let, permit,* μεθεῖσά μοι λέγειν *having* left it for me to speak, *having allowed* me, Soph.　　**2.** c. gen. rei, *to relax* or *cease from,* πολέμου, μάχης Il., etc. ; μέθιεν χόλοιο Τηλεμάχῳ [the suitors] *ceased from* wrath in

deference to Telemachus, Od. **b.** c. gen. pers. *to abandon, neglect*, Il. **3.** c. part., κλαύσας μεθέηκε having wept *he left off*, Ib. **III.** the Med. agrees in construction with the intr. Act., *to free oneself from, let go one's hold of*, c. gen., παιδὸς οὐ μεθήσομαι Eur., etc. ;—the act. would be παῖδα οὐ μεθήσω.

μεθ-ίστημι : **A.** Causal, in pres. and impf., fut. and aor. 1, *to place in another way, to change,* μεταστήσω τοι ταῦτα *I will give* thee *another present instead of* this, Od.; μ. τὰ νόμιμα πάντα Hdt.; ὄνομα etc., Eur. **2.** c. gen. partit., οὐ μεθίστησι τοῦ χρώματος he changes *nothing* of his colour, Ar. **II.** of persons, *to set free,* νόσου from disease, Soph.; κακῶν, ὕπνου Eur. **2.** *to remove,* Id., Thuc. :—so in aor. 1 med., μεταστήσασθαι *to remove from oneself* or *from one's presence,* Hdt., Thuc., etc. **B.** Pass., aor. 1 μετεστάθην [ᾰ], with aor. 2, pf., and plqpf. act. : **I.** *to stand among* or *in the midst of,* ἑτάροισι μεθίστατο Il. **2.** *to change one's position, remove, depart,* Hdt., Att. ; μ. τυράννοις ἐκπόδων *to make way* for them, Eur. **3.** c. gen. rei, *to change* or *cease from,* κότου Aesch. ; λύπης, κακῶν Eur. ; μ. βίου to die, Id.; μ. φρενῶν to go mad, Id. **4.** *to go over to another party, to revolt,* Thuc. **II.** of things, *to change, alter,* sometimes *for the better,* τῆς τύχης εὖ μετεστεώσης Hdt. ; or *for the worse,* δαίμων μεθέστηκε στρατῷ fortune *hath changed* for the army, Aesch.

μεθό, for μεθ' ὅ, *after that.*

μεθοδεία, ἡ, *craft, wiliness,* N. T. From

μεθοδεύω, f. σω, (μέθοδος) *to treat by method : to use cunning devices, employ craft,* Lxx.

μεθ-οδηγέω, f. ήσω, *to lead another way,* Anth.

μέθ-οδος, ἡ, (μετά) *a following after, pursuit :* esp. *pursuit of knowledge, scientific inquiry, investigation, method of inquiry, method,* Plat., etc.

μεθ-ομῑλέω, f. ήσω, *to hold converse with,* τινί Il.

μεθ-όριος, α, ον, (ὅρος) *lying between as a boundary,* γῆ μεθορία τῆς Ἀργείας καὶ Λακωνικῆς the border country *between* Argolis and Laconia, Thuc. : in pl. *the borders, marches, frontier,* Id., Xen., etc. :—also, ἡ μεθορία (sub. χώρα) Plut.

μεθ-ορμάομαι, aor. 1 μεθωρμήθην, Pass. *to rush in pursuit of, make a dash at,* Hom.

μεθ-ορμίζω, f. Att. ιῶ, *to remove from one anchorage to another,* intr. (sub. νέας), μ. εἰς Σηστόν Xen. : metaph., τοῦ νῦν σκυθρωποῦ μεθορμιεῖ σε will unmoor, i. e. will remove, thee from thy sternness, Eur. :—Med., μεθορμίσασθαι *to seek a refuge,* Id. :—Pass. *to sail from one place to another, put out from,* Hdt.

ΜΕΘΥ͂, τό, only in nom. and acc. *wine, mead,* Hom.

μεθ-υδριάς, άδος, ἡ, (ὕδωρ) *a water-nymph,* Anth.

Μεθ-ύδριον, τό, (ὕδωρ) *Between-waters,* a place in Arcadia, whence the waters *ran* some north some south (cf. Ital. *Inter-amnia*), Thuc.

μεθυ-δώτης, ου, ὁ, *giver of wine,* Anth.

μεθυ-πίδαξ, ὁ, ἡ, *gushing with wine,* Anth.

μεθυ-πλήξ, ῆγος, ὁ, ἡ, *wine-stricken,* Anth.

μέθυσις, ἡ, (μεθύω) *drunkenness,* Theogn.

μεθύσκω, f. ύσω [ῠ] : aor. 1 ἐμέθυσα :—Pass., f. μεθυσθήσομαι : aor. 1 ἐμεθύσθην :—Causal of μεθύω, *to make drunk, intoxicate, inebriate,* Plat., Luc., etc. **2.** *to give to drink : to water, moisten,* Anth. **II.** Pass. = μεθύω, *to drink freely, to get drunk,* Hdt., Xen. ; aor. 1 ἐμεθύσθην, *to be drunk,* Eur., Dem. ; νέκταρος with nectar, Plat.

μεθυσο-κόττᾰβος, ον, drunk with cottabus-playing, Ar.

μέθυσος, η, ον, (μεθύω) *drunken,* Ar., etc.

μεθ-ύστερος, α, ον, *living after,* μεθύστεροι posterity, Aesch. **II.** neut. as Adv. *afterwards, hereafter,* h. Hom., Soph. ; *so long after, so late,* Aesch. ; οὐ μ. *in a moment,* Id. : *too late,* Soph.

μεθυστικός, ή, όν, (μεθύσκω) *intoxicating,* Arist. **II.** of men, *given to wine,* Plat.

μεθυ-σφᾰλής, ές, (σφάλλω) *reeling-drunk,* Anth.

μεθύω, (μέθυ) only in pres. and impf. ; the fut. and aor. act. belong to μεθύσκω :—*to be drunken with wine,* Od., etc. ; μ. ὑπὸ τοῦ οἴνου Xen. **II.** metaph. of things, βοείη μεθύουσα ἀλοιφῇ an ox-hide *soaked* in oil, Il. **2.** of persons, *to be drunken* or *intoxicated* with passion, pride, etc., Xen., Plat.

μεθῶμεν, 1 pl. aor. 2 subj. of μεθίημι.

μειαγωγέω, f. ήσω, *to bring the lamb to the scale,* and metaph. μ. τὴν τραγῳδίαν *to weigh* tragedy as you *would a lamb,* Ar. From

μει-ᾰγωγός, όν, (μεῖον, ἄγω) *bringing the sacrificial lamb* (μεῖον) *to be weighed,* Eupol.

ΜΕΙΔΑ͂Ω, only used in Ep. 3 sing. aor. 1 μείδησε, part. μειδήσας, -σασα :—*to smile,* Hom. : *to grin,* v. σαρδάνιος. Cf. μειδιάω. Hence

μείδημα, ατος, τό, *a smile, smiling,* Hes.

μειδίαμα, ατος, τό, *a smile,* Plut., Luc. From

μειδιάω, = μειδάω, only in Ep. part. μειδιόων, Hom.

μείζων, Compar. of μέγας.

μείλᾰνι, Ep. for μέλανι, dat. of μέλας.

ΜΕΙΛΙΑ, ων, τά, *soothing things, pleasing gifts,* Il. **II.** in sing., *a charm,* Anth.

μείλιγμα, ατος, τό, (μειλίσσω) *anything that serves to soothe,* μειλίγματα θυμοῦ scraps to appease the hunger of dogs, Od. :—metaph., γλώσσης μείλιγμα Aesch. **2.** in pl. *propitiations, atonements* made to the dead, Lat. *inferiae,* Id. **3.** of a person, *a fondling, darling,* Id. **II.** *a soothing song,* Theocr.

μειλικτήριος, ον, (μειλίσσω) *able to soothe :* μειλικτήρια (sc. ἱερά), τά, *propitiations,* Aesch.

μείλῐνος, Ep. for μέλινος.

μείλιον, τό, v. μείλια.

μειλίσσω, Ep. inf. μειλισσέμεν : f. ξω : (μείλια) :—*to make mild, to appease, propitiate,* πυρὸς μειλισσέμεν *to appease* [the dead] *by* fire, i. e. by funeral rites, Il. ; ὀργὰς μ. Eur. :—Med. *to use soothing words,* μηδέ τί μ' αἰδόμενος μειλίσσεο μηδ' ἐλεαίρων extenuate not aught from respect or pity to me, Od. Hence

μειλῐχία, Ion. -ίη, ἡ, *gentleness, softness,* μειλιχίη πολέμοιο lukewarmness in battle, Il.

μειλίχιος, α, ον, (μειλίσσω) *gentle, mild, soothing,* μειλιχίοις ἐπέεσσι, μ. μύθοις Hom.; and without Subst., προσαυδᾶν μειλιχίοισι to address with gentle words, Il. ; αἰδοῖ μειλιχίῃ Od., Hes.; neut. as Adv., *gently,* Mosch. **II.** *gracious,* Ζεὺς Μειλίχιος the protector of *those who invoked him with propitiatory offerings,* Thuc., Xen. **III.** μειλίχια ποτά *propitiatory* drink-offerings, or (as others) *honied* drinks, *honey* being mixed in the drink-offerings, Soph.

μειλῐχό-γηρυς, v, gen. vos, soft-voiced, Tyrtae.

μείλῐχος, ον, gentle, kind, like μειλίχιος, Hom., etc.; c. gen., Ἄρτεμις μ. ὠδίνων soother of pangs, Anth.; τὸ μείλιχον gentleness, Theogn.; τὰ μείλιχα joys, Pind.

μεῖναι, aor. 1 inf. of μένω.

μεῖναν, μεῖνε, Ep. for ἔμειναν, ἔμεινε, 3 pl. and sing. aor. 1 of μένω.

μεῖον, ονος, τό, neut. of μείων, less. II. μεῖον, τό, the lamb which was offered at the Apaturia, when a boy was enrolled in his φρατρία. It was to be of a certain weight; and the φράτερες, whose perquisite it was, used to cry out μεῖον, μεῖον, too light! cf. μειαγωγέω.

μειον-εκτέω, f. ήσω, (ἔχω) to have too little, to be poor, Xen.: to be worse off, come short, Id.; c. gen. rei, to be short of a thing, Id.

μειονεξία, ἡ, disadvantage, Xen.

μειόνως, μειότερος, v. μείων.

μειόω, f. ώσω, (μείων) to make smaller, to lessen, moderate, Xen. 2. to lessen in honour, degrade, Id. 3. to lessen by word, extenuate, disparage, Id. II. Pass. to become worse or weaker, Id.: c. gen. to fall short of, Id.

μειράκι-εξαπάτης, ου, ὁ, a boy-cheater, Anth.

μειρακιεύομαι, Dep. to play the boy, Plut., Luc.

μειράκιον [ἄ], τό, (μεῖραξ) a boy, lad, stripling, Plat.

μειρακιόομαι, Dep., = μειρακίζομαι, Xen.

μειρακίσκη, ἡ, Dim. of μεῖραξ, a little girl, Ar.

μειρακίσκος, ὁ, Dim. of μειράκιον, a lad, stripling, Plat.

μειρακῐ-ώδης, ες, (εἶδος) becoming a youth, youthful, Plat. II. puerile, Id.

μειρακύλλιον, τό, Dim. of μειράκιον, a mere lad, Ar.

ΜΕΙ͂ΡΑΞ, ἄκος, ἡ, a young girl, lass, (μειράκιον being used of boys), Ar., etc.

ΜΕΙ͂ΡΟΜΑΙ, Dep., with 3 sing. pf. ἔμμορε:—to receive as one's portion or due, καὶ ἥμισυ μείρεο τιμῆς take half the honour as thy due, Il. II. in pf. to have one's share of, c. gen., ἔμμορε τιμῆς he has gotten his share of honour, Hom. III. in 3 sing. pf. pass. εἵμαρται, impers. it is allotted, decreed by fate, Plat.; plqpf. εἵμαρτο it was decreed, Hom.; εἵμαρτο Dem., etc.:—part., εἱμαρμένος, η, ον, ordained, destined, allotted, Theogn., Aesch., etc.; ἡ εἱμαρμένη (sc. μοῖρα), that which is allotted, destiny, Plat.

μείς, ἡ, Ion. and Aeol. nom. for μήν (Dor. μής), a month, Il., Hes., Hdt.

μεῖστος, η, ον, Sup. of μείων, most, Bion.

μείωμα, ατος, τό, (μειόω) curtailment:—a fine, Xen.

μείων, irr. Comp. of μικρός, less, Aesch., etc.: older, Soph.:—neut. μεῖον, as Adv., less, μ. ἰσχύειν Διός Aesch.:—μειόνως ἔχειν to be of less value, Soph.

μελάγ-γαιος, ον, (γαῖα = γῆ) with black soil, loamy, Hdt.

μελάγ-κερως, ων, (κέρας) black-horned, black, Aesch.

μελαγ-κόρυφος, ὁ, (κορυφή) the blackcap, Ar.

μελάγ-κροκος, ον, (κρόκη) with black woof: of a ship, with black sails, Aesch.

μελαγ-χαίτης, ου, ὁ, (χαίτη) black-haired, of Centaurs, Hes., Soph., Eur.

μελάγχῐμος, ον, black, dark, Aesch., Eur. (Formed from μέλας, with termin. -χιμος, as δύσ-χιμος from δυσ-).

μελαγ-χίτων [ῐ], ωνος, ὁ, ἡ, with black raiment, darksome, gloomy, Aesch.

μελάγ-χλαινος, ον, black-cloaked, Mosch. II. οἱ M., a Scythian nation, Hdt.

μελαγχολάω, to be atrabilious, Ar., Plat.; and

μελαγχολικός, ή, όν, atrabilious, choleric, Plat. From

μελάγ-χολος, ον, (χολή) dipped in black bile, Soph.

μελαγ-χροιής, ές, (χροιά) black-skinned, swarthy, Od.

μελάγχροος, ον, contr. -χρους, ουν, (χρόα) swarthy, Plut., etc.; a heterocl. nom. pl. μελάγχροες, Hdt.

μελάγ-χρως, ωτος, ὁ, ἡ, = foreg., Eur., Plat.

μέλαθρον, τό, Ep. gen. μελαθρόφιν:—the ceiling of a room, or (rather) the main beam which bears the ceiling, Od.; in Od. 19. 544, the end of this beam outside the house. 2. generally, a roof, Hom. II. a house, hall, Pind., Eur.; mostly in pl., like Lat. tecta, Trag. (Deriv. uncertain.)

μελαίνω, f. ανῶ: pf. pass. μεμέλασμαι: aor. 1 ἐμελάνθην: (μέλας):—to blacken: Pass., μελαίνετο χρόα he had his skin stained black (with blood), Il.; of earth just turned up, Ib.; of ripening grapes, Hes.; of a newly-bearded chin, Id. II. intr., = Pass., to grow black, Plat., Anth.

μελαμ-βᾰθής, ές, (βάθος) darkly deep, Aesch., Eur.

μελάμ-βωλος, ον, with black soil, Anth.

μελαμ-πᾰγής, ές, Dor. for -πηγής, (πήγνυμι) blackclotted, Aesch.: generally, discoloured, Id.

μελάμ-πεπλος, ον, black-robed, Eur.: generally, black, Id.

μελάμ-πετᾰλος, ον, (πέταλον) dark-leaved, Anth.

μελάμ-πτερος, ον, (πτερόν) black-winged, Anth.

μελάμ-φαής, ές, (φάος) whose light is blackness, Eur.

μελάμ-φυλλος, ον, (φύλλον) dark-leaved, Anacr.: of places, dark with leaves, Pind., Soph.

μέλᾰν, ᾰνος, τό, (μέλας) black pigment, ink, Dem.

μελάν-αιγίς, ιδος, ἡ, and ἡ, with dark aegis, Aesch.

μελάν-αυγής, ές, (αὐγή) dark-gleaming, Eur.

μελάν-δετος, ον, bound or mounted with black, of swords with black scabbards, Il., Eur.; σάκος μ. an iron-rimmed shield, Aesch.

μελαν-δόκος, ον, (δέχομαι) holding ink, Anth.

μελάν-είμων, ον, (εἷμα) black-clad, μ. ἔφοδοι the assaults of the black-robed ones (the Furies), Aesch.

μελανέω, = μελαίνω, Anth.

μελανία, ἡ, (μέλας) blackness: a black cloud, Xen.

μελανο-κάρδιος, ον, (καρδία) black-hearted, Ar.

μελανό-ομμάτος, ον, (ὄμμα) black-eyed, Plat.

μελάνο-νεκυο-είμων, ον, gen. ονος, (εἷμα) clad in black death-clothes, Ar.

μελανό-πτερος, ον, (πτερόν) black-winged, Eur., Ar.

μελανό-πτέρυξ, ῠγος, ὁ, ἡ, = foreg., Eur.

μελάν-οσσος, ον, (ὄσσε) black-eyed, Il.

μελάν-οστος, ον, for μελάν-όστεος, black-boned, Il.

μελάν-ουρος, ὁ, (οὐρά) a sea-fish, the black-tail: fem. μελαν-ουρίς, ίδος, Anth.

μελᾰνό-χροος, ον, = μελάγ-χροος, Od.; heterocl. nom. pl., μελανόχροες, Il.

μελανό-χρως, ωτος, ὁ, ἡ, = μελάγ-χρως, Eur.

μελάν-τειχής, ές, (τεῖχος) black-walled, Pind.

μελάντερος, α, ον, Comp. of μέλας.

μελαντηρία, ἡ, a black dye, Luc.

μελάν-τρᾰγής, ές, black when eaten, Anth.

μελάν-υδρος, ον, with black water, κρήνη μελάνυδρος of water which looks black from its depth, Il., Od.

μελάνω, (μέλας) intr. to grow black, Il.

ΜΕ'ΛΑ¯Σ, μέλαινα, μέλᾰν ; gen. μέλᾰνος, μελαίνης, μέλανος, etc. : (cf. τάλας, the only word like it in form) : Ep. dat. μείλανι :—black, swart, Hom., etc. ; μέλαν ὕδωρ of water drawn from a deep well (cf. μελάνυδρος), Od. II. black, dark, murky, ἕσπερος, νύξ Hom., etc. III. metaph. black, dark, θάνατος, Κήρ, the origin of the metaphor being seen in such phrases as μέλαν νέφος θανάτοιο, Hom. 2. dark, obscure, Anth. IV. Comp. μελάντερος, α, ον, blacker, very black, Il. ; cf. ἠΰτε. V. μέλαν, τό, v. sub voc.

μέλασμα, ατος, τό, (μέλας) anything black, μ. γραμμοτόκον a black lead pencil, Anth.

ΜΕ'ΛΔΟΜΑΙ, Pass., only in pres., to melt, λέβης κνίσην μελδόμενος a pot filled with melting fat, Il.

μέλε, Ep. for ἔμελε, 3 sing. impf. of μέλω.

μέλε, and ὦ μέλε, only in voc., ὦ μέλε, dear! good friend! Ar. (Deriv. uncertain.)

μελεδαίνω, (μέλω) to care for, be cumbered about a thing, c. gen., Theogn., Theocr. 2. c. acc. to tend, attend to, Hdt., Theocr. 3. c. inf., γῆμαι οὐ μελεδαίνει cares not to marry, Theogn.

μελέδημα, ατος, τό, (μελεδαίνω) care, anxiety, Il. ; μελεδήματα πατρός anxieties about one's father, Od. :— μελεδήματα θεῶν the care of gods [for men], Eur.

μελεδήμων, ον, (μελεδαίνω) careful, busy, Anth.

μελεδών, ή, = μελεδώνη, Hes., etc.

μελεδωνεύς, ό, = μελεδωνός, Theocr.

μελεδώνη, ή, (μελεδαίνω) care, sorrow, Od., Theocr.

μελεδωνός, ό and ή, (μελεδαίνω) one who takes care of anything, a manager, keeper, μ. τῶν οἰκιῶν a house-steward, Hdt. ; ὁ μ. τῶν θηρίων the keeper of the crocodiles, Id. ; μ. τῆς τροφῆς one who provides their food, Id.

μέλει, impers., v. μέλω A. II. 2.

μελεϊστί, Adv. (μελεΐζω) limb from limb, Shaksp. ' limb-meal,' μελεϊστὶ ταμεῖν Hom.

μελεο-πᾰθής, ές, (πάσχω) sadly suffering, Aesch.

μελεό-πονος, ον, having laboured wretchedly, Aesch.

μέλεος, α, ον, and ος, ον, idle, useless, Lat. irritus, Hom. : neut. as Adv. in vain, Il. II. unhappy, miserable, ὦ μέλεοι, τί κάθησθε; Orac. ap. Hdt. ; μέλεος γάμων unhappy in marriage, Aesch., etc. ; μ. ἔργα, μ. θάνατος Id. (Deriv. uncertain.)

μελεό-φρων, ό, ή, (φρήν) miserable-minded, Eur.

μελεσί-πτερος, ον, (μέλος II, πτερόν) singing with its wings, of the cicada, Anth.

μελετάω, f. ήσω and ήσομαι, to care for, attend to a thing, c. gen., Hes. II. c. acc. rei, to attend to, study, Hdt., Soph. ; μ. δόξαν to study, court reputation, Thuc. 2. to practise an art, Lat. meditari, μαντείαν h. Hom. ; μ. τοῦτο (sc. κήρυκα εἶναι) Hdt. ; μ. σοφίαν Ar. ; ῥητορικήν Plat. :—in Att. also, to practise speaking, to con over a speech, Dem. :—Pass., τὸ ναυτικὸν οὐκ ἐνδέχεται ἐκ παρέργου μελετᾶσθαι nautical skill cannot be acquired by occasional practice, Thuc. ; εὐταξία μετὰ κινδύνων μελετωμένη discipline won by practice on the battle-field, Id. III. c. inf. to practise doing a thing, μ. τοξεύειν καὶ ἀκοντίζειν Xen. ; μ. ἀποθνήσκειν Plat. IV. absol. to practise, exercise oneself, the acc. rei being omitted, Thuc., Xen. ; ἐν τῷ μὴ μελετῶντι (= μελετᾶν) by want of practice, Thuc. : —esp. to rehearse a speech, declaim, Plat., etc. V. c. acc. pers. to exercise or train persons, Xen. From

μελέτη, ή, (μέλω) care, attention, Hes. ; μ. πλεόνων care for many things, Id. ; ἔργων μ. attention to action, Thuc. :—but c. gen. subjecti, care paid by one, θεῶν του μελέτῃ Soph. 2. practice, exercise, Lat. meditatio, Pind. ; ἡ δι' ὀλίγου μ. their short practice, Thuc. ; πόνων μελέται painful exercises, of the Spartan discipline, Id. b. in a military sense, exercise, practice, drill, Id. c. of an orator, rehearsal, Dem. II. care, pursuit, Pind. II. care, anxiety, μελέτῃ κατατρύχεσθαι Eur.

μελέτημα, ατος, τό, (μελετάω) a practice, exercise, study, Plat., Xen.

μελετηρός, ά, όν, (μελετάω) practising diligently, Xen.

μελετητέον, verb. Adj. of μελετάω, one must study, Plat.

μελετητήριον, τό, (μελετάω) a place for practice, Plut.

μελέτωρ, ορος, ό, (μέλω) one who cares for, an avenger, ἀμφί τινα Soph.

μεληδών, ή, = μελεδώνη, Simon., Anth.

μέλημα, ατος, τό, (μέλω) the object of care, a darling, of persons, τοὐμὸν μέλ., like Virgil's mea cura, Pind. ; ὦ φίλτατον μ. Aesch. II. a charge, duty, Id., Soph. 2. care, anxiety, Aesch., Theocr.

μελησί-μβροτος, ον, (μέλω, βρότος) with μ inserted, an object of care or love to men, Pind.

μελήσω, fut. of μέλω.

μελητέον, verb. Adj. of μέλω, one must take thought for, τινός Plat.

Μελητίδης, ου, ό, proverbial at Athens for a blockhead (in form a patronymic from Μέλητος), Ar.

ΜΕ'ΛΙ˘, τό : gen. ιτος, etc., Lat. mel, honey, Hom., etc.

ΜΕΛΙ'Α, Ion. -ίη, ή. the ash, Lat. fraxinus, Il., etc. II. an ashen spear, Ib.

μελί-βρομος, ον, (βρέμω) sweet-toned, Anth.

μελί-γδουπος, ον, sweet-sounding, Pind.

μελί-γηρυς, Dor. -γᾱρυς, νος, ό, ή, sweet-voiced, melodious, Od., Pind.

μελί-γλωσσος, ον, (γλῶσσα) honey-tongued, Aesch., Ar.

μέλιγμα, τό, a song, Mosch. II. a pitch-pipe, Id.

μελίζω, Dor. μελίσδω : Dor. f. med. μελίξομαι : (μέλος II) :—to modulate, sing, warble, Theocr. : mostly in Med., Id., Anth. II. trans. to sing of, celebrate in song, Pind., Aesch.

μελι-ηδής, ές, (ἡδύς) honey-sweet, of wine, Hom. :— metaph., μελιηδέα θυμὸν ἀπηύρα Il. ; μ. ὕπνος Od.

μελί-θρεπτος, ον, (τρέφω) honey-fed, Anth.

μελί-κηρον, τό, a honey-comb, Theocr.

μελί-κομπος, ον, sweet-sounding, Pind.

μελί-κρητον, Att. -κρᾶτον, τό, (κεράννυμι) a drink of honey and milk offered to the powers below, Od.

μελικτής, οῦ, ό, Dor. -κτάς, (μελίζω) a singer, player, Theocr., Mosch.

μελί-λωτον, τό, also μελί-λωτος, ό, melilot, a kind of clover, rich in honey, Cratin., etc.

ΜΕΛΙ'ΝΗ [ῐ], ή, millet, Lat. panicum, Hdt. : in pl. millet-fields, Xen., Dem.

μέλινος, Ep. μείλινος, η, ον, (μελία) ashen, Lat. fraxineus, Hom.

Μελινο-φάγοι, οἱ, (φαγεῖν) Millet-eaters, a Thracian tribe, Xen.

μελίπαις, ό, with honey-children, of a bee-hive, Anth.

μελί-πνοος, ον, contr. -πνους, ουν, honey-breathing, sweet-breathing, Theocr., Anth.

μελίρ-ρῠτος, ον, (ῥέω) honey-flowing, Plat.
μελίσδω, Dor. for μελίζω.
μελίσκιον, τό, Dim. of μέλος ΙΙ, Alcman, Antiph.
μέλισμα, τό, (μελίζω) a song, Theocr. : a tune, Anth.
μελισμάτιον, τό, Dim. of μέλισμα, Anth.
μέλισσᾰ, Att. -ττα, ης, ἡ, (μέλι) a bee, Lat. apis, Hom., etc. 2. one of the priestesses of Delphi, Pind. II. = μέλι, honey, Soph. Hence
μελίσσειος, α, ον, of bees, κηρίον μ. a honeycomb, N. T.
μελισσό-βοτος, ον, (βόσκω) fed on by bees, Anth.
μελισσο-νόμος, ον, (νέμω) keeping bees :—in Aesch. ap. Ar., the Μελισσονόμοι are priestesses of Artemis.
μελισσο-πόνος, ον, = μελιττουργός, Anth.
μελισσο-σόος, ον, guardian of bees, Anth.
μελισσό-τοκος, ον, (τεκεῖν) produced by bees, honied, Anth.
μελισσο-τρόφος, Att. μελιττ-, ον, feeding bees, Eur.
μελι-στᾰγής, ές, (στάζω) dropping honey, Anth.
μελί-στακτος, ον, = foreg., Anth.
μελίτεια, ἡ, (μέλι) baulm, Lat. apiastrum, Theocr.
μελίτειον [ῐ], τό, (μέλι) mead, Plut., etc.
μελῐτόεις, εσσα, εν, (μέλι) honied, i. e. sweet, delicious, Pind. II. sweetened with honey, μελιτόεσσα (sc. μᾶζα), ἡ, a honey-cake, as a sacred offering, Hdt. ; Att. contr. μελιτοῦττα, Ar.
μελῐτόομαι, pf. μεμελίτωμαι, (μέλι) Pass. to be sweetened with honey, Thuc.
μελῐτο-πώλης, ου, ὁ, (πωλέω) a dealer in honey, Ar.
μελῐτοῦττα, v. μελιτόεις ΙΙ.
μέλιττα, ἡ, Att. for μέλισσα :—Dim. μελίττιον, τό, Ar.
μελιττ-ουργός, ὁ, (*ἔργω) a bee-keeper, Plat.
μελῐτ-ώδης, ες, (*εἶδος) like honey : a name of Persephonê, Lat. Mellita, Theocr.
μελίτωμα, ατος, τό, (μελιτόομαι) a honey-cake, Batr.
μελί-φθογγος, ον, (φθογγή) honey-voiced, Pind.
μελί-φρων, ονος, ὁ, ἡ, (φρήν) sweet to the mind, delicious, Hom., Hes.
μελί-χλωρος, ον, honey-pale, Plat., Theocr.
μελί-χροος, ον, contr. -χρους, ουν, (χρόα) = foreg., Anth.
μελιχρός, ά, όν, (μέλι) honey-sweet, Theocr. :—metaph., of Sophocles, Anth. :—Comp. Adv. μελιχρότερον, Id.
μελιχρ-ώδης, ες, (*εἶδος) ὁ, ἡ, yellow as honey, Anth.
μελί-χρως, ωτος, ον, = μελίχροος, Anth.
μελλ-είρην, ὁ, a Spartan youth before the age of 20, Plut.
μέλλημα, ατος, τό, (μέλλω) a delay, Eur., Aeschin.
μελλησέμεν, Ep. for μελλήσειν, f. inf. of μέλλω.
μέλλησις, ἡ, (μέλλω) a being about to do, threatening to do, Thuc. II. an intention not carried into effect, delay, Id. ; διὰ βραχείας μελλήσεως at short notice, Id. 2. c. gen. rei, a putting off, a delaying to execute, Id.
μελλητέον, verb. Adj. of μέλλω, one must delay, Eur.
μελλητής, οῦ, ὁ, (μέλλω) a delayer, loiterer, Thuc., Arist.
μελλό-γαμος, ον, betrothed, Soph., Theocr.
μελλο-νῑκιάω, to be going to conquer, with a play on the name of Νικίας, the Athenian Cunctator, Ar.
μελλό-νυμφος, ον, (νύμφη) of girls, about to be betrothed or wedded, Lat. nubilis, Soph. :—in Soph. Tr. 207, ἀνολολύξατε ὁ μελλόνυμφος ὁ μ. (sc. χόρος) must be taken collectively for αἱ μελλόνυμφοι, the maidens of the house.
ΜΕ'ΛΛΩ : impf. ἔμελλον or ἤμελλον, Ep. μέλλον, Ion.

μέλλεσκον : f. μελλήσω : aor. ι ἐμέλλησα :—Pass., v. infr. ΙΙΙ :—to think of doing, intend to do, to be about to do, with inf., mostly inf. fut., τάχ᾽ ἔμελλε δώσειν he was just going to give, Il. ; μέλλεις ἀφαιρήσεσθαι ἄεθλον thou thinkest to strip me of the prize, Ib.; often with οὐκ ἄρα, as, οὐκ ἄρ᾽ ἔμελλες λήξειν ; did you not think you might stop ? could you not stop ? Od., etc. ; to be about to do (on compulsion), to be destined to do or to be, τὰ οὐ τελέεσθαι ἔμελλον which were not to be accomplished, Il. ; μέλλεν οἶκος ἀφνειὸς ἔμμεναι the house was destined to be wealthy, Od. ; εἰ ἐμέλλομεν ἀνοίσειν if we were able to refer, Plat. 2. to express a certainty, μέλλω ἀπέχθεσθαι Διί it must be that I am hated by Zeus, Il. ; μέλλω ἀθανάτους ἀλιτέσθαι I must have sinned against the immortals, Od. 3. to mark a probability, when it may be rendered to be like to do or be, or expressed by an Adv., τὰ δὲ μέλλετ᾽ ἀκουέμεν belike ye have heard it, Hom. ; μέλλεις ἴδμεναι thou art like to know of it, Od. ; ἐμέλλετ᾽ ἄρα πάντες ἀνασείειν βοήν aye, all of you were like to raise (i. e. I thought you would raise) a cry of submission, Ar. II. to mark mere intention, to be always going to do without ever doing, and so to delay, put off, hesitate, scruple, mostly with inf. pres., τί μέλλομεν χωρεῖν ; Soph. ; often followed by μὴ οὐ or μή, τί μέλλομεν μὴ πράσσειν ; Eur. 2. μέλλω often stands without its inf., τὸν υἱὸν ἑόρακας αὐτοῦ ; Answ. τί δ᾽ οὐ μέλλειν ; why shouldn't I have seen him ? i. e. be sure I have, Xen. ; οὐδὲν ἐπάθετε οὐδὲ ἐμελλήσατε (sc. παθεῖν) Thuc. :—so, when μέλλω seems to govern an acc., an inf. is omitted, τὸ μέλλειν ἀγαθά (sc. πράσσειν) the expectation of good things, Eur. : hence 3. the part. μέλλων without an inf. (where εἶναι or γίγνεσθαι may be supplied), ὁ μ. χρόνος the future time, Pind., Aesch. ; esp. in neut., τὸ μέλλον, τὰ μέλλοντα things to come, the event, issue, future, Aesch., etc. :—so in Med., τὰ ἰσχυρότατα ἐλπιζόμενα μέλλεται your strongest pleas are hopes in futurity, Thuc. III. μέλλομαι as Pass., ὡς μὴ μέλλοιτο τὰ δέοντα the necessary steps might not be delayed, Xen. ; ἐν ὅσῳ ταῦτα μέλλεται while these delays are going on, Dem.
μελλώ, οῦς, ἡ, poët. for μέλλησις, Aesch.
μελλογρᾰφία, ἡ, song-writing, Anth. From
μελο-γράφος, ον, (μέλος ΙΙ) writing songs, Anth.
μελοποιέω, f. ήσω, to make lyric poems, Ar. ; and
μελοποιητής, οῦ, ὁ, = μελοποιός, Anth. ; and
μελοποιία, ἡ, a making of lyric poems or music : the theory of music, as opposed to its practice, Plat. From
μελο-ποιός, ὁ, (μέλος ΙΙ, ποιέω) a maker of songs, a lyric poet, Ar., Plat. II. as Adj. tuneful, Id.
ΜΕ'ΛΟΣ, εος, τό, a limb, Hom., etc. ; μελέων ἔντοσθε within my bodily frame, Aesch. ; κατὰ μέλεα limb by limb, like μελεϊστί, Hdt. II. τό, a song, strain, h. Hom., etc. :—esp. of lyric poetry, ἐν μέλεϊ ποιέειν to write in lyric strain, Hdt. ; μέλη, τά, lyric poetry, the choral songs, opp. to the dialogue, Plat. 2. the music to which a song is set, the tune, Id. ; ἐν μέλει in tune, Id. ; παρὰ μέλος, out of tune, Id.
μελο-τῠπέω, (μέλος ΙΙ) to strike up a strain, chant, Aesch.
μέλπηθρον, τό, (μέλπω) the song with the dance, festive

sport, κυνῶν μέλπηθρα a sport for dogs, of a corpse, κυσὶ μέλπηθρα γενέσθαι Il.

Μελπομένη, ἡ, Melpomené, a Muse, properly the Songstress, Hes.: later the Muse of Tragedy. From

μέλπω, f. μέλψω: aor. 1 ἔμελψα: (μέλος):—to sing of, celebrate with song and dance, Il., Eur.; μ. τινὰ κατὰ χέλυν Eur. 2. intr. to sing, Aesch., Eur.;— c. acc. cogn., μ. θανάσιμον γόον Aesch.; ἰαχάν, βοάν Eur. II. also as Dep. **μέλπομαι:** aor. 1 part. μελψάμενος: f. μέλψομαι in pass. sense:—to sing to the lyre or harp, Od.; to dance and sing, as a chorus, μετὰ μελπομένῃσιν ἐν χορῷ Il.; μέλπεσθαι Ἄρηι to dance a war-dance in honour of Ares, i. e. to fight, Ib. 2. c. acc., as in Act. to sing, celebrate, Hes., Eur.

μελύδριον, τό, Dim. of μέλος II, a ditty, Theocr., Bion.

ΜΕ'ΛΩ, A. neut. to be an object of care, B. trans., c. gen. to care for.

A. neuter, with pf. μέμηλα, to be an object of care or thought to anyone, c. dat. pers., ἀνθρώποισι μέλω I am a source of care to men, i. e. am well known to them, Od.; so, Ἀργὼ πᾶσι μέλουσα Ib.; νερτέροισι μέλω Eur., etc. II. most usual in 3 sing. and pl. of act. pres. μέλει, μέλουσι; impf. ἔμελε Ep. μέλε; f. μελήσει; inf. pres. and fut. μέλειν and μελήσειν: aor. ἐμέλησε: pf. μεμέληκε; plqpf. ἐμεμελήκει; Ep. pf. μέμηλε, plqpf. μεμήλει:—μή τοι ταῦτα μελόντων let not these things be a care to thee, Hom.; πόλεμος ἄνδρεσσι μελήσει Il.; ᾧ τόσσα μέμηλε to whom so great things are a care, Od., etc.:—an inf. often stands as nom., οὐκ ἔμελέν μοι ταῦτα μεταλλῆσαι Ib. 2. in Att. 3 sing. is commonly used impers. with the object in gen., and pers. in dat., ᾧ μέλει μάχας to whom there is care for the battle, who careth for it, Aesch.; Ζηνὶ τῶν σῶν μέλει πόνων Eur., etc.;—also, μέλει μοι περί τινος Hdt., Att.; ὑπέρ τινος Dem. 3. absol., with a neg., οὐδέν μοι μέλει I care not, Ar. 4. μέλον ἔστι periphr. for μέλει, as, ἐστί τι μέλον τινί Soph.; τοῦτο ἴσασιν ἐμοὶ μεμεληκός Xen. :—also absol., μέλον γέ σοι since you have thought about it, Plat. III. Med. is used by Poets like Act., to be an object of care, ἐμοὶ δέ κε ταῦτα μελήσεται Il.; τἀνθάδ' ἂν μέλοιτό μοι what remains should be a care to you, Soph., etc.; rarely impers., μέλεταί μοί τινος Theocr. 2. in Ep. Poets are found pf. and plqpf. pass. μέμβλεται, μέμβλετο, shortd. for μεμέληται, μεμέλητο, with pres. and impf. sense, οὐκέτι μέμβλετ' Ἀχιλλεύς (for μέλει) Achilles cares no longer for it, Il.; μέμβλετο οἱ τεῖχος (for ἔμελε) the wall was a care to him, Ib. :—the regul. pf. occurs in later Poets, Φοίβῳ μεμελήμεθα Anth.; 2 and 3 sing. plqpf. μεμέλησο, -ητο, Id., Theocr.

B. trans., c. gen. of persons, to care for, take care of, take an interest in a thing, πλούτοιο μεμηλώς busied with riches, Il.; πολέμοιο μεμηλώς Ib.; θεοὶ τῶν ἀδίκων μέλουσιν Eur.:—absol. to be anxious, μέλει κέαρ Aesch., etc. II. Med. μέλομαι, to care for, take care of, c. gen., Trag.; so in aor. 1 pass., τάφου μεληθείς having provided for the burial, Soph.:—also μεληθέν, as Pass. cared for, Anth.; and pf. part. μεμελημένος, Id.

μελῳδέω, to sing, chant, Ar.; and

μελῳδία, ἡ, a singing, chanting, Eur. II. a chant, choral song, Plat. From

μελ-ῳδός, όν, (μέλος II, ᾄδω) singing, musical, melodious, Eur.

μέμαα, 3 pl. μεμάασι, pf. of *μάω.

μεμάθηκα [ᾰ], pf. of μανθάνω.

μεμᾰκυῖα, Ep. for μεμηκυῖα, pf. part. fem. of μηκάομαι.

μεμᾱλώς, Dor. for μεμηλώς, pf. part. of μέλω.

μέμᾰμεν, Ep. for μεμάομεν, 1 pl. pf. of *μάω.

μεμάνημαι [ᾰ], pf. of μαίνομαι.

μεμᾱότες, pf. part. pl. of *μάω.

μεμάποιεν [ᾰ], 3 pl. Ep. pf. opt. of μάρπτω.

μέμαρπον, Ep. redupl. aor. 2 of μάρπτω.

μεμαρπώς, pf. part. of μάρπτω.

μεμάτε, Ep. for μεμάετε, 2 pl. pf. of *μάω.

μεμάχα, pf. of μάσσω.

μέμβλεται, μέμβλετο, v. μέλω A. III. 2.

μέμβλωκα, pf. of βλώσκω.

μεμβράνα, ἡ, the Lat. membrāna, parchment, N. T.

ΜΕΜΒΡΑ'Σ, άδος, ἡ, a small kind of anchovy, Ar.

μεμέληκα, pf. of μέλω.

μεμελημένως, Adv. pf. pass. part. (μέλω), carefully, Plat.

μεμένηκα, pf. of μένω.

μεμετιμένος, Ion. for μεθειμένος, pf. pass. part. of μεθίημι.

μεμετρημένως, Adv. pf. pass. part. of μετρέω, according to a stated measure, Luc.

μεμηκώς, pf. part. of μηκάομαι.

μέμηλε, 3 sing. Ep. pf. of μέλω.

μεμήλει, 3 sing. Ep. plqpf. of μέλω.

μέμηνα, pf. of μαίνομαι.

μεμηχανημένως, Adv. pf. part. of μηχανάομαι, by stratagem, Eur.

μεμίασμαι, pf. pass. of μιαίνω.

μέμιγμαι, pf. pass. of μίγνυμι: inf. μεμῖχθαι.

μέμναμαι, Dor. for μέμνημαι, pf. pass. of μιμνήσκω.

μεμνέο, Ion. for μέμνησο, pf. pass. imper. of μιμνήσκω.

μεμνέωτο, Ep. for μεμνῷτο, 3 sing. pf. pass. opt. of μιμνήσκω.

μέμνημαι, pf. pass. of μιμνήσκω:—μεμνῄμην, optat.

μεμνήστευμαι, pf. pass. of μνηστεύω.

μέμνωμαι, pf. pass. subj. of μιμνήσκω.

Μέμνων, ονος, ὁ, (μένω) the Steadfast or Resolute (cf. Ἀγαμέμνων), Memnon, son of Eôs and Tithonus, killed by Achilles, Od., Hes.:—hence **Μεμνόνειος, α, ον,** of Memnon; **Μεμνόνειον, τό,** the temple of M., in Egypt, Luc.; τὰ βασίληια τὰ Μεμνόνεια (or Μεμνόνια) Hdt.

μεμόλυγκα, pf. of μολύνω.

μέμονα, pf. used as pres., but only in sing., the pl. being supplied by μέμαα, to wish eagerly, to yearn, strive, be fain, to do a thing, c. inf., Hom.:—absol., διχθὰ δέ μοι κραδίη μέμονε my heart yearneth with a twofold wish, Il.; μέμονεν ὅγε ἶσα θεοῖσι he puts forth spirit equal with the gods, Ib.; τί μέμονας; what wishest thou? Aesch.

μεμόρηται, 3 sing. pf. pass. of μείρομαι:—part. **μεμορημένος.**

μεμορυγμένος, pf. pass. part. of μορύσσω.

μεμουνωμένος, Ion. for μεμονωμένος, pf. pass. part. of μονόω.

μεμπτός, ή, όν, to be blamed, blameworthy, Hdt., Eur.; Comp. μεμπτότερος Thuc.; οὐ μ. not contemptible, Id.:—Adv. μεμπτῶς Plut. II. act. throwing blame upon, τινι Soph.; where μεμπτός is fem. for -τή.

μέμῦκα, pf. both of μυκάομαι and μύω.

ΜΕ'ΜΦΟΜΑΙ, f. μέμψομαι: aor. 1 ἐμεμψάμην, also in pass. form ἐμέμφθην:—*to blame, censure, find fault with* a person or thing, c. acc., Hes., Hdt., Att. **2.** c. dat. pers. et acc. rei, *to impute as blameworthy, cast* it *in his teeth*, Lat. *exprobrare* or *objicere alicui*, Hdt., Att. **3.** c. dat. pers. only, *to find fault with*, Trag.;—c. gen. rei only, *to complain of* a thing, Eur., Thuc.; and with both these cases, τοῦδ' ἂν οὐδεὶς μέμψαιτό μοι no one *would find fault with* me *for* this, Aesch. **4.** c. inf. with μή pleonastic, μ. μὴ πολλάκις βουλεύεσθαι to *impute blame for* doing, Thuc.

μεμψίμοιρέω, f. ήσω, *to complain of fate*, Luc. **II.** *to impute as blameworthy*, τί τινι ap. Dem.

μεμψί-μοιρος, ον, (μοῖρα) *complaining of one's fate, repining, querulous*, Isocr., Luc.

μέμψις, εως, ἡ, (μέμφομαι) *blame, censure, reproof*, μ. ἐπιφέρειν τινί Ar.; ἔχειν μ. *to incur blame*, Eur. **2.** act. *cause for complaint*, Aesch., Soph.

μέν, Particle, used to shew that the word or clause with which it stands answers to a following word or clause, which is introduced by δέ. Generally, μέν and δέ may be rendered *on the one hand, on the other hand*, or *as well .., as, while* or *whereas*, but it is often necessary to leave μέν untranslated. **2.** μέν is not always answered by δέ, but by other equiv. Particles, as ἀλλά, ἀτάρ or αὐτάρ, αὖ, αὖθις, αὖτε; also πρῶτον μέν, εἶτα Soph.; πρῶτον μέν, ἔπειτα Id.; πρῶτον μέν, μετὰ τοῦτο Xen. **3.** The answering clause with δέ is sometimes left to be supplied, ὡς μὲν λέγουσι as *indeed* they say, (but as I believe not), Eur.; this isolated μέν is often a Pron., ἐγὼ μὲν οὐκ οἶδα I *for my part*, (whatever others may say), Xen.; οὗτος μέν Plat. **4.** μέν was orig. the same as μήν, and like it is used in protestations, καί μοι ὄμοσσον, ἦ μέν μοι ἀρήξειν and swear to me, that *surely* thou wilt assist me, Il. **II.** μέν before other Particles: μὲν ἄρα, μέν ῥα *accordingly, and so*, Hom., etc. **2.** μέν γε, used much like γοῦν, *at all events, at any rate*, Ar., etc. **3.** μὲν δή to express certainty, Soph., etc. **4.** μὲν οὖν or μενοῦν, a strengthd. form of οὖν, *so then*, Id.; in replies, it affirms strongly, πάνυ μὲν οὖν Plat., etc.; also it corrects a statement, *nay rather*, like Lat. *imo, imo vero*, μου πρὸς τὴν κεφαλὴν ἀποψῶ wipe your nose on my head, Answ. ἐμοῦ μὲν οὖν . ., *nay* on mine, Ar., etc.; μὲν οὖν δή Soph.:—so in N. T., μενοῦνγε, to *begin* a sentence, *yea rather*, Lat. *quin imo*. **5.** μέν τοι or μέντοι, a. conjunctive, *yet, but however, nevertheless, tamen, vero*, Aesch., etc. b. Adverbial, *of course, certainly*, Plat., etc.; with an imperat., to enforce the command, τουτὶ μέντοι σὺ φυλάττου *only* take heed .., Ar.; strengthd. μέντοι γε Xen.:—in narrative, etc., to add something, καὶ φυλάξασθαι μέντοι .., and *of course* to take care .., Id.

μεν-αίχμης, ου, Dor. -αίχμας, α, ὁ, (αἰχμή) *abiding the spear, staunch in battle*, Anth.

μενεαίνω, only in pres., (μένος) *to desire earnestly* or *eagerly, to be bent on doing*, c. inf., Hom.; also, c. gen., μ. μάχης *to long for* battle, Hes. **II.** absol. *to be angry, rage*, Hom.; but, κτεινόμενος μενέαινε he *struggled* as he was dying, Il.

μεν-έγχης, ες, (ἔγχος) =μεναίχμης, Anth.

μενε-δήϊος, ον, *standing against the enemy, staunch, steadfast*, Il.; Dor. -δάϊος, Anth.

Μενέ-λᾱος, ὁ, pr. n. *Withstanding-men*, Hom.: Att. **Μενέλεως**, gen. εω, Trag.; Dor. dat. Μενέλᾳ, Pind., acc. Μενέλαν Eur.

μενε-πτόλεμος, ον, *staunch in battle, steadfast*, Il.

Μενεσθεύς, έως, Ion. ῆος, ὁ, pr. n., *Abider*, Il.

μενετέον, verb. Adj. *one must remain*, Plat., Xen.

μενετός, ή, όν, (μένω) *inclined to wait, patient*, Ar.: οἱ καιροὶ οὐ μενετοί *opportunities will* not *wait*, Thuc.

μενε-φύλοπις [ῡ], ιος, ὁ, ἡ, =μενεπτόλεμος, Anth.

μενε-χάρμης, ου, ὁ, (χάρμη) *staunch in battle*, of heroes, Il.:—also **μενέχαρμος**, ον, Ib.

μενο-εικής, ές, (εἶκος, ἔοικα) *suited to the desires, satisfying, sufficient, plentiful, agreeable to one's taste*, Hom.; τάφος μ. a *plentiful* funeral feast, Il.; μενοεικέα ὕλην *great store* of wood, Ib.

μενοινάω, Ep. **μενοινώω**, Ep. 3 sing. μενοινᾷ: Ep. impf. μενοίνεον, 3 sing. μενοίνα: Ep. aor. 1 μενοίνησα, opt. μενοινήσειε: (μένος):—*to desire eagerly, to be bent on* a thing, c. acc., Hom.: also c. inf. *to be eager to do*, Id.:—absol., ὧδε μενοινῶν *so eager*, Il.:—μ. τί τινι *to design* or *purpose* something against one, κακὰ Τρώεσσι μενοίνα Od.; c. dat. rei, *to strive for* a thing, Theogn. From

μενοινή, ἡ, *eager desire*, Anth. From

μένος, εος, τό, (*μάω) *might, force, strength, prowess, courage*, Hom., etc. **2.** *strength*, as implying life, *life itself*, Il.: *life-blood*, Soph. **3.** *rage, passion*, μένος ἔλλαβε θυμόν Il.; μένεος φρένες πίμπλαντο Ib.; μένεα πνείοντες Ib.:—μένει in dat. *violently, furiously*, Aesch. **4.** *the bent, intent, purpose* of any one, Τρώων μ. αἰὲν ἀτάσθαλον their *bent* is aye to folly, Il. **II.** μένος is also used in periphr., ἱερὸν μένος Ἀλκινόοιο, i. e. *Alcinoüs* himself, Od.; μένος Ἀτρείδαο, Ἕκτορος, etc., Il.

μὲν οὖν, μέν ῥα, μέντοι, v. μέν II.

μεντἄν, crasis for μέντοι ἄν.

Μεντορ-ουργής, ές, *wrought by Mentor*, Luc.

ΜΕ'ΝΩ, Ion. impf. μένεσκον: f. μενέω, Att. μενῶ: aor. 1 ἔμεινα: pf. μεμένηκα:—Lat. *maneo, to stay, stand fast, abide*, in battle, Hom., Aesch.; μ. κατὰ χώραν, of soldiers, Thuc. **2.** *to stay at home, stay where one is*, not stir, Il.; μ. εἴσω δόμων Aesch.; κατ' οἶκον Eur., etc.:—but, μ. ἀπό τινος *to stay away from*, Il. **3.** *to stay, tarry*, Hom., etc. **4.** of things, *to be lasting, remain, last, stand*, στήλη μένει ἔμπεδον Il., etc. **5.** of condition, *to remain as one was*, of a maiden, Il.; ἢν μείνωσιν ὅρκοι if oaths *hold good*, Eur.; μ. ἐπὶ τούτων *to remain contented* with . ., Dem. **6.** *to abide by* an opinion, conviction, etc., ἐπὶ τῷ ἀληθεῖ Plat. **7.** impers. c. inf., *it remains* for one to do, ἀνθρώποισι κατθανεῖν μένει Eur. **II.** trans. *to await, expect, wait for*, c. acc., Il.; so, like Lat. *manere hostem*, Hom., etc.:—so, also c. acc. et inf., ἦ μένετε Τρῶας σχεδὸν ἐλθέμεν; *wait ye for* the Trojans to come nigh? Il.; μένον δ' ἐπὶ ἕσπερον ἐλθεῖν *they waited for* evening's coming on, Od.; μένω δ' ἀκοῦσαι I *wait*, i. e. *long*, to hear, Aesch.

Μεριδ-άρπαξ, ὁ, *Bit-stealer*, a mouse in Batr.

μερίζω, Dor. -ίσδω: f. Att. ιῶ:—Pass., aor. 1 ἐμερίσ-

θην : pf. μεμέρισμαι : (μερίς) :—to divide, distribute, Plat., etc.　II. Med., μερίζεσθαί τι to divide among themselves, Theocr., Dem. :—c. gen. rei, to take part in, Arist.　III. Pass. to be divided, Xen.　2. to be reckoned as part, Dem.

μέριμνα, ἡ, care, thought, esp. anxious thought, solicitude, Hes., Trag.; μ. τινος care for, Aesch., Soph. : —pl. cares, anxieties, Aesch., Ar.　II. the thought, mind, Aesch. (Deriv. uncertain.) Hence

μεριμνάω, f. ήσω, to care for, be anxious about, think earnestly upon, scan minutely, Lat. meditari, Soph., Xen.; πολλὰ μ. to be cumbered with many cares, Xen. :—c. inf. to be careful to do, Dem. Hence

μερίμνημα, ατος, τό, anxiety, Soph. ; and

μεριμνητής, οῦ, ὁ, one who is anxious about a thing, c. gen., Eur.

μεριμνο-τόκος, ον, (τίκτω) mother of cares, Anth.

μεριμνο-φροντιστής, ὁ, an anxious thinker, 'minute philosopher,' Ar.

μερίς, ίδος, ἡ, (μέρος) a part, portion, share, parcel, Plat.　2. a contribution, Dem.　II. a part, division, class, Eur., Dem.

μερισμός, ὁ, a dividing, division, Plat.

μεριστής, οῦ, ὁ, (μερίζω) a divider, N. T.

μεριστός, ή, όν, divided, divisible, Plat., Arist.

μερίτης [ῐ], ου, ὁ, (μερίς) a partaker in, τινός Dem.

μέρμερος, ον, causing anxiety, mischievous, baneful, μέρμερα μητίσασθαι to meditate mischief, Il.; μέρμερα ῥέξειν Ib.; πολέμοιο μ. ἔργα Ib.　II. of persons, anxious, peevish, morose, Plat.

μερμηρά, ἡ, Ep. gen. pl. -άων, poët. form of μέριμνα, care, trouble, Hes., Theogn. Hence

μερμηρίζω, f. ἴξω: Ep. aor. 1 μερμήριξα: (μέρμερος):　I. intr. to be full of cares, to be anxious or thoughtful, to be in doubt, Hom.; δίχα or διάνδιχα μερμηρίζειν to halt between two opinions, Id.　II. trans. to devise, contrive, δόλον ἐνὶ φρεσὶ μερμ. Od.; φόνον ἡμῖν μερμηρίζει Ib.

μέρμις, ῖθος, ἡ, a cord, string, rope, Od. (Deriv. unknown.)

ΜΕ′ΡΟΣ, έος, τό, a part, share, Hdt., etc.　2. one's portion, heritage, lot, Aesch.; ἀπὸ μέρους from considerations of rank, Thuc.　II. one's turn, Hdt., etc.; ἀγγέλου μ. his turn of duty as messenger, Aesch. :—ἀνὰ μέρος in turn, by turns, Eur.; so, κατὰ μέρος Thuc.; ἐν μέρει in turn, Hdt., etc.; ἐν τῷ μέρει in one's turn, Id.; παρὰ τὸ μ. out of one's turn, Xen.; πρὸς μέρος in proportion, Thuc.; τὸ μέρος in part, Hdt.　III. the part one takes in a thing, or the part assigned one, τοὐμὸν μέρος, τὸ σὸν μ. my or thy part, i. e. simply I or me, thou or thee, Soph.; and absol. as Adv., τοὐμὸν μ. as to me, Lat. quod ad me attinet, Id.　IV. a part, as opp. to the whole, ἡμέρας μ. Aesch. : a division of an army, Xen.; τὰ πέντε μ. five-sixths, τὰ ὀκτὼ μ. eight-ninths, etc.　2. ἐν μέρει τινὸς τιθέναι, ποιεῖσθαι to put in the class of .. , consider as so and so, Plat.; ἐν οὐδενὸς εἶναι μέρει to be as no one, Dem.; ἐν προσθήκης μέρει as an appendage, Id.

μέρ-οψ, οπος, ὁ, (μείρομαι, ὄψ) only in pl. as epithet of men, dividing the voice, i. e. articulate-speaking, endowed with speech, Hom., Hes. :—hence μέροπες as Subst. = ἄνθρωποι, Aesch., Eur.

μέσᾰ-βον, τό, (μέσος, βοῦς) a leathern strap, by which the yoke was fastened to the pole, Hes.

μεσ-άγκυλον, τό, a javelin with a strap (ἀγκύλη) for throwing it by, Eur.

μεσαι-πόλιος, ον, poët. for μεσοπόλιος, half-gray, grizzled, i. e. middle-aged, Il.

μεσαίτατος, -τερος, v. μέσος.

μέσ-ακτος, ον, (ἀκτή) between shores, in mid-sea, Aesch.

μεσαμβρίη, Dor. for μεσημβρία.

μεσ-αμβρῖνός, μεσ-αμέριος, Dor. for μεσ-ημ-.

μέσᾰτος, η, ον, v. μέσσατος.

μέσ-αυλος, Ep. μέσσ-αυλος, ὁ, or μέσσ-αυλον, τό, the inner court, behind the αὐλή, where the cattle were put at night, Il.; of the cave of the Cyclops, Od.　II. in Att., μέταυλος (with or without θύρα), ἡ, the door between the αὐλή and the inner part of the house, Ar.; θύραι μέσαυλοι Eur.

μεσ-εγγυάω, aor. 1 pass. part. μεσ-εγγυηθείς, to deposit a pledge in the hands of a third party, Plat. : —Med., μεσεγγυᾶσθαι ἀργύριον to have one's money deposited in the hands of a third party, Dem. Hence

μεσεγγύημα, ατος, τό, money or a pledge deposited with a third party, Aeschin.

μεσεύω, like μεσόω, to keep the middle or mean between two, c. gen., Plat. : absol. to stand mid-way, to be neutral, Xen.

μεσηγύ, Ep. μεσσηγύ, Ep. also μεσσηγύς, (μέσος) Adv.,　I. of Space, absol. in the middle, between, οὐδέ τι πολλὴ χώρη μεσσηγύς Il.　2. c. gen. between, betwixt, μ. γαίης τε καὶ οὐρανοῦ Ib., etc.　3. of Time, meanwhile, meantime, Od.　II. as Subst., τὸ μεσηγύ the part between, h. Hom.; τὸ μεσηγὺ ἤματος mid-day, Theocr.

μεσήεις, εσσα, εν, (μέσος) middle, middling, Il.

μεσ-ημβρία (for μεσ-ημερία), Ion. μεσ-αμβρίη, ἡ :— mid-day, noon, Hdt.; μεσαμβρίης at noon, Id.; τῆς μεσημβρίας Ar.; so, τῇ μεσαμβρίῃ Hdt.; ἐν μεσημβρίᾳ Thuc.; μ. ἵσταται 'tis high noon, Plat.　II. the parts towards noon, the South, Hdt. Hence

μεσημβριάζω, to pass the noon, Lat. meridiari, μεσημβριάζοντα εὕδειν to sleep at noon, Plat.

μεσημβριάω, poët. for μεσημβριάζω, Anth.

μεσημβρίζω, = μεσημβριάζω, Strab.

μεσ-ημβρῖνός, ή, όν, for μεσημερινός, Dor. μεσαμβρῖνός, ά, όν :—belonging to noon, about noon, noontide, ὥτε πόντος ἐν μεσημβριναῖς κοίταις εὕδοι Aesch.; μεσημβρινοῖσι θάλπεσι in the noon-day heats, Id.; ὁ μ. ᾠδός, of the cicada, Anth. :—τὸ μεσαμβρινόν noon, Theocr.　II. southern, Aesch., Thuc.

μεσ-ημέριος, ον, = foreg., μεσαμέριον at mid-day, Theocr.

μεσ-ήρης, poët. μεσσ-, ες, (*ἄρω) in the middle, midmost, Eur.; Σείριος ἔτι μ. Sirius is still in mid-heaven, Id.

μεσίδιος [σῐδ], poët. μεσσ-, α, ον, = μέσος, δικαστὴς μ. = μεσίτης, Arist.

μεσῑτεία, ἡ, mediation, negotiation, Babr.; and

μεσῑτεύω, to act as mediator, Babr., N. T. From

μεσίτης [ῑ], ου, ὁ, (μέσος) a mediator, umpire, arbitrator, Polyb., N. T.

μεσο-βασίλεια, ἡ, an interregnum, Plut.

μεσο-βᾰσῐλεύς, έως, ὁ, the Roman interrex, one who

holds kingly power between the death of one king and the accession of another, Plut.

μεσό-γαιος, ον, also **α, ον,** (γαῖα, = γῆ) *inland, in the heart of a country,* Hdt.; τὴν μ. τῆς ὁδοῦ the *inland* road, Id. :—Att. also **μεσόγεως, ων,** Plat.   **II.** as Subst., **μεσογαία, ἡ,** *the inland parts, interior,* Lat. *loca mediterranea,* Hdt.; so, **μεσογεία, ἡ,** Thuc., Dem.

μεσό-γράφος, ον, (γράφω) *drawn in the middle :* τὸ μ. a *mean proportional* found by the μεσόλαβος, Anth.

μεσό-δμη, ἡ, (δέμω, for μεσο-δόμη) *something built between :* in pl., prob., the *bays* or *compartments between* the pillars that supported the roof, Od.   **2.** *a box amidships* in which the mast was stepped, Ib.

μεσόθι, v. μεσσόθι.

μεσο-λᾰβής, ές, (λαβεῖν) *held by the middle,* Aesch.

μεσό-λευκος, ον, *middling white,* χιτὼν πορφυρᾶ μ. a tunic of purple *shot with white,* Xen.

μεσ-όμφᾰλος, ον, *in mid-navel, central,* of Apollo's shrine at Delphi (cf. ὀμφαλός), Aesch., Eur.; τὰ μ. γῆς μαντεῖα Soph.

μεσο-νύκτιος, ον, (νύξ) *of* or *at midnight,* Pind., Eur.:—neut. as Adv., Theocr.

μεσο-πᾰγής, ές, Ep. **μεσσο-,** (πήγνυμι) *fixed up to the middle,* μεσσοπαγὲς δ' ἄρ' ἔθηκε ἔγχος drove the spear in *up to the middle,* Il.

μεσο-πόλιος, ον, regular form for μεσαιπόλιος, Aesop.

μεσοπορέω, *to be half-way,* Theophr.   From

μεσό-πορος, Ep. **μεσσο-, ον,** *going in the middle,* μ. δι' αἰθέρος through *mid-air,* Eur.

μεσο-ποτάμιος, α, ον, *between rivers :* **Μεσοποταμία** (sc. χώρα), **ἡ,** a land *between two rivers,* esp. that between the Tigris and Euphrates, *Mesopotamia,* Polyb., Strab. :—**Μεσοποταμίτης [ῑ], ου, ὁ,** Luc.

ΜΕ'ΣΟΣ, Ep. in Poets also **μέσσος, η, ον** :—*middle, in the middle,* Lat. *medius,* Hom., etc. ; μέσον σάκος the *middle* or *centre* of the shield, Il. ; ἐν αἰθέρι μέσῳ in *mid* air, Soph. ; with the Art. following, διὰ μέσης τῆς πόλεως, ἐν μ. τῇ χώρᾳ Xen.   **2.** with a Verb, ἔχεται μέσος *by the middle, by the waist,* proverb. from wrestling-ring, Ar.   **3.** μ. δικαστής = μεσίτης, a judge *between two,* an umpire, Thuc.   **4.** ὁ μέσος (sc. δάκτυλος) Plat.   **5.** of Time, μέσον ἦμαρ *mid*-day, Hom. ; μέσαι νύκτες Hdt. ; also, μέσον τῆς ἡμέρας Id.   **II.** *middling, moderate,* μέσος ἀνήρ a man *of middle rank,* Id.; μ. πολίτης Thuc.; also οἱ διὰ μέσου the *moderate* or *neutral* party, Id.   **2.** *middling,* i.e. *middling good,* Plat.   **III.** μέσον, Ep. μέσσον, τό, as Subst. *the middle, the space between,* ἐν μέσσῳ, for ἐν μεταιχμίῳ, Il. ; or without ἐν, ἔνθορε μέσσῳ he leaped *into the middle,* Ib. ; οἱ ἐν μ. λόγοι the *intervening* words, Soph. ; τὰ ἐν μ. what *went between,* Id. ; ἐν μ. ἡμῶν καὶ βασιλέως *between* us and him, Xen. ; ἐν μ. νυκτῶν at *midnight,* Id. ; ἆθλα κείμενα ἐν μέσῳ prizes set up *for all to contend for,* Dem. ;—so in pl., κεῖτο δ' ἄρ' ἐν μέσσοισι Il.   **b.** ἐς μέσον, ἐς μ. ἀμφοτέρων Hom. ; ἐς μ. τιθέναι τισί τι to set a prize *before all,* for all to contest, Lat. *in medio ponere,* Il. ; ἐς τὸ μ. τιθέναι to propose, bring forward in *public,* Hdt. ; ἐς τὸ μ. λέγειν to speak *before all,* Id. ; ἐς μ. Πέρσῃσι καταθεῖναι τὰ πρήγματα to give up the power *in common to all,* Id.   **c.** ἐκ τοῦ μέσου καθέζεσθαι to keep *clear of*

a contest, i.e. remain neutral, Id.   **d.** διὰ μέσου = μεταξύ, *between,* Id., Thuc. ; and of Time, *meanwhile,* Hdt., Thuc.   **e.** ἀνὰ μέσον *midway between,* Theocr.   **f.** κατὰ μέσον, = ἐν μέσῳ, Il.   **2.** τὸ μέσον, also, *the difference, average,* Hdt., Thuc.   **3.** *the middle state* or *mean,* Lat. *mediocritas,* Arist. ; παντὶ μέσῳ τὸ κράτος θεὸς ὤπασεν Aesch.   **IV.** Adv. μέσον, Ep. μέσσον, *in the middle,* Hom. : c. gen. *between,* οὐρανοῦ μ. χθονός τε Eur.   **2.** in Att. **μέσως,** *moderately,* Id. ; καὶ μέσως *even a little,* Thuc. ; μέσως βεβιωκέναι *in a middle way,* i.e. *neither well nor ill,* Plat.   **V.** irreg. Comp. **μεσαίτερος** (cf. μεσαῖος) Id. ; Sup. **μεσαίτατος** Hdt., etc.

μεσο-σχῐδής, ές, (σχίζω) *split in two,* Anth.

μεσότης, ητος, ἡ, (μέσος) *a middle* or *central position,* Plat.   **II.** *a mean between two extremes,* Arist.

μεσό-τοιχος, τό, (τοῖχος) *a partition-wall,* N. T.

μεσοτομέω, f. ήσω, *to cut through the middle, cut in twain, bisect,* Plat., Xen.   From

μεσό-τομος, poët. **μεσσο-, ον,** (τέμνω) *cut through the middle,* Anth.

μεσ-ουράνημα, τό, (οὐρανός) *mid-heaven, mid-air,* N. T.

μεσ-ουράνησις, ἡ, (οὐρανός) *the sun's place in meridian,* Strab.

μεσόω, f. ώσω, (μέσος) *to form the middle, be in* or *at the middle,* Aesch., Eur. :—of time, ἡμέρα μεσοῦσα *mid*-day, Hdt. ; θέρους μεσοῦντος *in midsummer,* Thuc.   **2.** c. gen. *to be in the middle of,* τῆς ἀναβάσιος Hdt. ; so, c. acc., μεσῶν τὴν ἀρχήν *in the middle of* his time of office, Aeschin.

μέσσᾰτος, η, ον, irreg. Sup. of μέσσος, μέσος, *midmost,* Il. ; Att. μέσατος, Ar.

μέσσ-αυλος, μεσσηγύ, v. μέσ-αυλος, μεσηγύ.

μεσσ-ήρης, v. μεσ-ήρης.

μεσσόθεν, poët. for μεσόθεν, Adv. *from the middle,* Anth.

μεσσόθῐ, Adv. for μεσόθι, *in the middle,* Hes.

μεσσοπαγής, -πορος, v. μεσο-.

μέσσος, ον, Ep. for μέσος.

μεστός, ή, όν, *full, filled, filled full,* Ar., etc.   **II.** c. gen. *full of, filled with* a thing, Hdt., Ar. :—metaph., ἀπάτης, ἀπορίας μ. Plat. :—metaph. also, *sated with* a thing, Eur. ; so c. part., μεστὸς ἦν θυμούμενος i. e. had had my *fill* of anger, Soph.

μεστόω, f. ώσω, (μεστός) *to fill full of* a thing, c. gen., Soph. :—Pass. *to be filled* or *full of,* Id.

μέσφᾰ, Adv., poët. for μέχρι, *until,* c. gen., μέσφ' ἠοῦς Il. ; with Adv., μ. ἐχθές *till to-morrow,* Theocr.

ΜΕΤΑ', poët. **μεταί,** Aeol. and Dor. **πεδά** (q. v.) :—Prep. with gen., dat., and acc.

A. WITH GEN. *in the midst of, among* a number, μετ' ἄλλων ἑταίρων Od. ; πολλῶν μετὰ δούλων Aesch.   **II.** *in common, along with,* μετὰ Βοιωτῶν ἐμάχοντο Il. ; μ. ξυμμάχων κινδυνεύειν Thuc. ; μετά τινος πάσχειν, στῆναι Aesch., Soph.   **III.** *with, by means of,* ἱκετεύειν μετὰ δακρύων Plat. ; μετ' ἀρετῆς πρωτεύειν Xen. :—as a periphr. for Adverbs, ὁσίως καὶ μετ' ἀληθείας Plat.

B. WITH DAT., only poët., mostly Ep.,   **1.** properly of persons, *among, in company with,* μετὰ τριτάτοισιν ἄνασσεν *in* or *among* the third generation Nestor reigned, Il.   **2.** of things, μετὰ νηυσί, ἀστράσι *among,*

in the midst of, Hom.; μετὰ πνοιῆς ἀνέμοιο in company with the winds, as swift as they, Id. 3. between, μετὰ χερσὶν ἔχειν to hold between, i. e. in, the hands, Il.; μετὰ φρεσίν Ib. II. to complete a number, with, besides, πέμπτος μετὰ τοῖσιν a fifth with them, Hom.;—N.B., μετά is never used with dat. sing., unless of collective Nouns, μετὰ στρατῷ Il. C. WITH ACCUS., I. of motion, into the middle of, coming among a number, μετὰ φῦλα θεῶν Hom.; μετὰ λαὸν Ἀχαιῶν Il. II. in pursuit or quest of, βῆναι μετὰ Νέστορα Ib.; in hostile sense, βῆναι μετά τινα to go after, pursue him, Ib.;—also, βῆναι μετὰ πατρὸς ἀκονήν to go in search of news of thy father, Od.; πόλεμον μέτα θωρήσσοντο they were arming for the battle, Il. III. of mere sequence or succession, 1. of Place, after, next after, behind, λαοὶ ἔπονθ᾽, ὡσεὶ μετὰ κτίλον ἕσπετο μῆλα as sheep follow after the bell-wether, Il. 2. of Time, after, next to, μεθ᾽ Ἕκτορα πότμος ἑτοῖμος after Hector thy death is at the door, Ib.; μετὰ ταῦτα thereupon, thereafter, Att.; μεθ᾽ ἡμέραν in the course of the day, Hdt. 3. of Worth, Rank, next to, next after, following a Sup., κάλλιστος ἀνὴρ μετ᾽ ἀμύμονα Πηλείωνα Il. IV. after, according to, μετὰ σὸν καὶ ἐμὸν κῆρ as you and I wish, Ib.; μετ᾽ ὄγμον by the line of the furrow, Ib. V. generally, among, between, as with dat., μετὰ πάντας ἄριστος best among all, Il.; μετὰ χεῖρας ἔχειν Hdt. D. absol. as ADV. among them, with them, Il. II. and then, next afterwards, thereafter, Hom., Hdt. E. μέτα for μέτεστι, Od., etc. F. IN COMPOS.: I. of community or participation, as μεταδίδωμι, μετέχω, c. gen. rei. 2. of action in common with another, as μεταδαίνυμαι, c. dat. pers. II. of an interval, as μεταίχμιον. III. of succession, as μεταδόρπιος. IV. of pursuit, as μετέρχομαι. V. of letting go, as μεθίημι. VI. after, behind, as μετάφρενον. VII. back again, reversely, as μετατρέπω, μεταστρέφω. VIII. most often of change of place, condition, plan, etc., as μεταβαίνω, μεταβουλεύω, etc.

μετα-βαίνω, f. -βήσομαι: aor. 2 μετέβην: pf. μεταβέβηκα:—to pass over from one place to another, μετὰ δ᾽ ἄστρα βεβήκει (for μετεβεβήκει) the stars had passed over the meridian, Od.; μ. ἐς τὴν Ἀσίην Hdt.: to go over to the other side, Aesch. 2. to pass from one point to another, μετάβηθι change thy theme, Od.; μεταβάντες changing their course, turning round, Hdt.; μ. ἐκ μείζονος εἰς ἔλαττον Plat. 3. c. acc., μεταβὰς βίοτον having passed to another life, Eur. II. Causal in aor. 1 μεταβῆσαι, to carry over, to change, Id.

μετα-βαλεῖν, aor. 2 inf. of μεταβάλλω.

μετα-βάλλω, f. -βαλῶ: aor. 2 μετέβαλον:—to throw into a different position, to turn quickly, μετὰ νῶτα βαλών Il.; μ. θοιμάτιον ἐπὶ δεξιάν to throw one's mantle over to the right, Ar. II. to turn about, change, alter, Hdt., Att.; μ. ὕδατα to drink different water, Hdt.:—μ. ὀργάς to change, i. e. give up, anger, Eur. 2. intr. to undergo a change, change one's condition, Hdt., Plat. 3. to change one's course, μεταβαλὼν πρὸς Ἀθηναίους changing his course and

turning to the Athenians, Hdt.:—the part. μεταβάλλων or μεταβαλών is used absol., almost like an Adv. instead, in turn, Id., Eur. B. Med. to change what is one's own, etc., μ. ἱμάτια to change one's clothes, Xen.; μ. τοὺς τρόπους Ar., etc. 2. to change one with another, exchange, μ. σιγὰν λόγων to exchange silence for words, Soph.: —to barter, traffic, Xen. II. to turn oneself, turn about, Plat.:—to change one's purpose, change sides, Hdt., Thuc. 2. to turn or wheel about, Xen.

μετα-βάπτω, f. ψω, to change by dipping, Plut., Luc.

μετα-βάς, aor. 2 part. of μεταβαίνω.

μετάβασις, ἡ, (μεταβαίνω) a passing over, migration, Plut. II. change, revolution in government, Plat. III. transition from one to another, Luc.

μετα-βέβηκα, pf. of μεταβαίνω.

μετά-βηθι, aor. 2 imper. of μεταβαίνω.

μετα-βήσομαι, fut. of μεταβαίνω.

μεταβιβάζω, Att. f. -βιβῶ, Causal of μεταβαίνω, to carry over, shift, bring into another place or state, Ar., Xen. 2. to lead in a different direction, Plat.

μεταβλητέον, verb. Adj. of μεταβάλλω, one must change, trans., τινὰ εἴς τι Plat. II. intr., ld.

μεταβλητικός, ή, όν, by way of exchange, Arist.: ἡ μεταβλητική (sub. τέχνη) exchange, barter, Plat.

μεταβολή, ἡ, (μεταβάλλω) a change, changing, Pind. 2. exchange, barter, traffic, Thuc. II. (from Med.) a transition, change, and in pl. changes, vicissitudes, Hdt., Eur.:—c. gen. change from a thing, μ. κακῶν Eur.; rarely change to . . , μ. ἀπραγμοσύνης Thuc.; but this is generally expressed by a Prep., ἅμα τῇ μ. ἐς Ἕλληνας their going over to the Greeks, Hdt.; ἡ ἐναντία μ. change to the contrary, Thuc. 2. μ. τῆς ἡμέρης an eclipse, Hdt. 3. μ. πολιτείας change of government, a revolution, Thuc. 4. as military term, a wheeling about, Polyb.; metaph. of a speaker, Aeschin.

μετα-βουλεύω, f. σω, to alter one's plans, change one's mind, Od.; but commonly as Dep. μεταβουλεύομαι, Hdt., Eur.; μετ. στράτευμα μὴ ἄγειν ἐπὶ τὴν Ἑλλάδα to change one's mind and not march, Hdt.

μετα-βουλος, ον, (βουλή) changing one's mind, changeful, Ar.

μετα-βῶ, aor. 2 subj. of μεταβαίνω.

μετ-άγγελος, ου, ὁ and ἡ, a messenger between two parties, Lat. internuncius, -cia, of Iris, Il.

Μετα-γειτνιών, ῶνος, ὁ, (γείτων) the second month of the Athen. year, the latter half of August and first of September, so called because then people flitted and changed their neighbours.

μετα-γιγνώσκω, Ion. and later -γινώσκω: f. -γνώσομαι: aor. 2 μετέγνων:—to change one's mind, to repent, Hdt., Att. 2. c. acc. rei, to change one's mind about a thing, to repent of, μετέγνων τὰ πρόσθ᾽ εἰρημένα Eur.; μ. τὰ προδεδογμένα to alter or repeal a previous decree, Thuc. 3. c. inf. to change one's mind so as to do something different, Id.; μετ. ὡς . . , to change one's mind and think that . . , Xen.

μετά-γνοια, ἡ, = μετάνοια, repentance, remorse, Soph.

μετά-γνωσις, ἡ, change of mind or purpose, Hdt., Dem.

μετα-γράφω [ᾰ], f. ψω, to write differently, to alter or correct what one has written, Eur., Thuc.; in a trial,

to alter the record, Dem.   2. to translate, Luc.:
Med., τὰς ἐπιστολὰς μεταγραψάμενοι having got them
translated, Thuc.   3. to transcribe, Luc.

μετ-άγω [ᾰ], f. άξω, to convey from one place to another: metaph., τὴν ψυχὴν ἐς εὐφροσύνην Anth.   II.
intr. to go by another route, change one's course, Xen.

μετα-δαίνυμαι, f. -δαίσομαι, Dep. to share the feast
with another, c. dat., Hom.:—to partake of a thing,
c. gen., Il.

μετα-δετέον, verb. Adj. (δέω A) one must untie, Xen.

μετα-δήμιος, ον, (δῆμος) in the midst of or among the
people, in the country, Od.

μετα-διαιτάω, f. ήσω, to change one's way of life, Luc.

μετα-δίδωμι [ῐ], f. -δώσω, to give part of, give a share
of a thing, c. gen., Theogn., Hdt., Att.   2. the part
given is sometimes expressed, μ. τὸ τριτημόριόν τινι
Hdt.; μ. τὸ μέρος Xen.

μεταδίωκτος, ον, pursued, overtaken, Hdt.   From
μετα-διώκω, f. ξομαι, rarely ξω, to follow closely after,
pursue, c. acc., Hdt., Xen.

μετα-δοκέω, f. -δόξω: pf. pass. -δέδογμαι:—to change
one's opinion:—mostly impers., δείσασα μὴ σφι μετα-
δόξῃ in fear lest they should change their mind, Hdt.;
c. acc. et inf., μετέδοξέ σοι ταῦτα βελτίω εἶναι you
changed your mind and thought that this was better,
Luc.:—part., μεταδόξαν when they changed their
mind, Dem.; and in Pass., μεταδεδογμένον μοι μὴ
στρατεύεσθαι since I have changed my mind and resolved not to march, Hdt.

μετα-δοξάζω, f. σω, to change one's opinion, Plat.

μετα-δόρπιος, ον, (δόρπον) in the middle of supper,
during supper, Od.   II. after supper, Anth.

μεταδός, aor. 2 imper. of μεταδίδωμι.

μετά-δοσις, ἡ, the giving a share, imparting, Xen.   2.
exchange of commodities, Arist.   3. a contribution,
Plut.

μετα-δοτέον, verb. Adj. one must give a share, τινί
τινος Plat., Xen.

μεταδοῦναι, aor. 2 imp. of μεταδίδωμι:—μεταδούς, part.

μετά-δουπος, ον, falling at haphazard, Hes.

μετα-δρομάδην, (δρόμος) Adv. running after, following close upon, Il.

μετα-δρομή, ἡ, a running after, pursuit, Eur., Xen.

μετά-δρομος, ον, running after, taking vengeance for
a thing, c. gen., Soph.

μέταζε, Adv. (μετά) afterwards, in the rear, Hes.

μετα-ζεύγνυμι, to put to another carriage, Xen.

μετά-θεσις, ἡ, transposition, Dem.   2. change of
sides or opinions, amendment, Polyb.   II. a
power of changing, Thuc.

μετα-θέω, f. -θεύσομαι, to run after, chase, Xen.,
etc.   II. to hunt or range over, τὰ ὄρη Id.:
absol. to hunt about, range, Id.

μεταί, poët. for μετά.

μετα-ΐζω, poët. for μεθ-ίζω, to seat oneself with or beside, Od.

μετ-αίρω, Aeol. πεδ-, to lift up and remove, to shift,
Eur.; ψήφισμα μ. to repeal a decree, Dem.   II.
intr. to depart, N. T.

μετ-αΐσσω, f. ξω, to rush after, rush upon an enemy,
Hom.   II. μ. τινά to follow him closely, Pind.

μετ-αιτέω, f. ήσω, to demand one's share of a thing,

c. gen., Hdt.: also μεταιτεῖν μέρος τινός Ar.:—absol.,
μ. παρά τινος Dem.   II. to beg of, ask alms of, c.
acc. pers., Ar.   III. to beg, solicit, Luc.   Hence
μεταίτης, ου, ὁ, a beggar, Luc.

μετ-αίτιος, ον, and α, ον, c. gen. rei, being in part the
cause of a thing, accessory to it, c. gen., Hdt., Att.:
—c. dat. pers., θεοὺς τοὺς ἐμοὶ μεταιτίους νόστου who
were accessory to my return, Aesch.

μετ-αίχμιος, ον, Aeol. πεδ-, (αἰχμή) between two
armies:—as Subst. μεταίχμιον, τό, the space between
two armies, Hdt., Eur.; ἐν μεταιχμίοις δορός Eur.   2.
a disputed frontier, Debateable Land, Hdt.:—metaph.,
ἐν μεταιχμίῳ σκότου in the border-land between light
and darkness, Aesch.   II. what is midway between, c. gen., ἀνὴρ γυνή τε χὥτι τῶν μεταίχμιον
Id.; πεδαίχμιοι λαμπάδες hanging in mid air, Id.

μετα-καθέζομαι, Med. to change one's seat, Luc.

μετα-καινίζω, to model anew, Anth.

μετα-κάλέω, f. έσω, to call away to another place,
Aeschin.: to call back, recall, Thuc.   II. in Med.
to call in a physician, Luc.

μετἄ-κῑάθω, only in impf. μετεκίαθον, to follow after,
absol., Il.:   c. acc. to come, Τρῶας μετεκίαθε
Ib.   II. to go to visit, Αἰθίοπας μετεκίαθε Od.

μετα-κῑνέω, f. ήσω, to transpose, shift, remove, Hdt.:—
Med. to go from one place to another, Id.   2. to
change, alter, τὴν πολιτείαν Dem.   Hence
μετακινητέος, α, ον, verb. Adj. to be removed, Luc.; and
μετακινητός, ή, όν, to be disturbed, Thuc.

μετα-κλαίω, f. -κλαύσομαι, to weep afterwards or too
late, Il.:—Med. to lament after or next, Eur.

μετα-κλίνομαι [ῐ], aor. 1 μετ-εκλίνθην, Pass. to shift
to the other side, Il.

μετα-κοιμίζομαι, aor. 1 μετ-εκοιμίσθην, Pass. to change
to a state of sleep, to be lulled to sleep, Aesch.

μετά-κοινος, ον, sharing in common, partaking, Aesch.;
τινι with another, Id.

μετα-κομίζω, f. σω, to transport, Plat.:—Med. to cause
to be carried over, Lycurg.

μετα-κῠλινδέω, to roll to another place, to roll over, Ar.

μετα-κύμιος, ον, (κῦμα) between the waves, ἄτας μ. between two waves of misery, i. e. bringing a short lull
or pause from misery, Eur.

μετα-λαγχάνω, f. -λήξομαι, to have a share of a thing
allotted one, c. gen., Plat.; also, μ. μέρος τινός Eur.

μετα-λαμβάνω, f. -λήψομαι, to have or get a share of,
to partake of a thing, c. gen., Hdt., etc.:—Med., μετα-
λαμβάνεσθαί τινος to get possession of, lay claim to,
Id.   2. the part received is sometimes added in
acc., μ. μοῖραν or μέρος τινός Eur., etc.; μ. τὸ πέμπτον μέρος τῶν ψήφων Plat.   3. c. gen. pers. to
share his society, Xen.: in bad sense, to lay hold
of, accuse, Ar.   II. to take after another, to
succeed to, c. acc., Xen.   III. to take in exchange, substitute, πόλεμον ἀντ' εἰρήνης Thuc.; μ. τὰ
ἐπιτηδεύματα to adopt new customs, Id.; ἱμάτια μ.
Xen.   2. to interchange, Plat.

μετα-λήγω, Ep. μεταλ-λήγω, f. ξω, to leave off, cease
from, c. gen., Il.

μετά-ληψις, ἡ, participation, Plat.; τινος in a thing, Id.

μεταλλάγή, ἡ, (μεταλλάσσω) change, μ. τῆς ἡμέρης an
eclipse, Hdt.; ἐν μεταλλαγῇ πολυμηχάνου ἀνδρός by

having a crafty man for thy master instead [of me], Soph. 2. c. gen. objecti, μ. πολέμου a change from war, Xen.

μεταλλακτός, όν, verb. Adj. changed, altered, Aesch.

μετάλλαξις, ή, =μεταλλαγή, Xen. From

μετ-αλλάσσω, Att. -ττω, f. ξω, to change, alter, Hdt. II. to exchange, 1. to take in exchange, adopt, assume, ὀρνίθων φύσιν Ar.; so, μ. τόπον, χώραν to go into a new country, Plat. 2. to exchange by leaving, to quit, μ. τὸν βίον Isocr.; so, μεταλλάσσειν alone, Plat. III. intr. to undergo a change, Hdt.

μετάλλᾱτος, Dor. for μετάλλητος, to be searched out, Pind.

μεταλλάω, f. ήσω, properly, to search after other things (μετὰ ἄλλα, cf. μέταλλον), to search carefully, to inquire diligently, Od. 2. c. acc. pers. to inquire of, question, Hom. 3. c. acc. objecti, to ask about or after, Id.; so, μεταλλῆσαι ἀμφὶ πόσει Od. 4. c. dupl. acc. to ask one about a thing, ask him a thing, Id.

μεταλλεία, ή, a searching for metals and the like, mining, Plat.; and

μεταλλευτής, οῦ, ὁ, one who searches for metals, a miner, Strab.; and

μεταλλευτικός, ή, όν, skilled in searching for metals: ἡ -κή (sc. τέχνη) the art of mining, Arist. From

μεταλλεύω, f. σω, (μέταλλον) to get by mining :—Pass. to be got by mining, of metals, Plat., etc. 2. generally, to explore, Anth.

μεταλλήγω, Ep. for μεταλήγω.

μεταλλικός, ή, όν, of or for mines, Dem. From

μέταλλον, τό, a mine or quarry, ἁλὸς μέταλλον a salt-pit, salt-mine, Hdt.; χρύσεα καὶ ἀργύρεα μέταλλα gold and silver mines, Id.; μέταλλα (alone) silver mines, Xen.; μαρμάρου μ. marble quarries, Strab. II. the sense of metal, Lat. metallum, does not occur in classical Greek. (Prob., like μεταλλάω, from μετ' ἄλλα, a search for other things.)

μετάλμενος, Ep. aor. 2 part. of μεθάλλομαι.

μετα-μαίομαι, Dep. to search after, chase, Pind.

μετα-μανθάνω, f. -μαθήσομαι, to learn differently, μετ. γλῶσσαν to unlearn one language and learn another instead, Hdt.; μ. ὕμνον to learn a new strain, Aesch. 2. to learn to forget, unlearn, Lat. dediscere, Aeschin. 3. absol. to learn better, Ar.

μετ-ἀμείβω, Dor. πεδ-, f. ψω, to exchange, ἐσθλὸν πήματος good for ill, Pind. 2. to change to another form, ἐκ βοὸς μεταμείβε γυναῖκα Mosch. 3. γᾶν τέκνοις μ. to hand down land to children, Eur. II. Med. to change one's condition, to escape, Pind.; μεταμειβόμενοι in turns, Id. 2. c. acc., μ. τί τινι to change one thing for another, Eur.

μετα-μέλει, impf. μετ-έμελε: f. -μελήσει: aor. 1 μετε-μέλησε: (μέλω): I. impers. it repents me, rues me, Lat. poenitet me :—Construction : 1. c. dat. pers. et gen. rei, μεταμέλει σοι τῆς δωρεᾶς Xen. 2. oftener, the thing one repents of is in part. agreeing with the dat., μεταμέλει μοι οὕτως ἀπολογησαμένῳ I repent of having so defended myself, Plat. 3. absol., μ. μοι it repents me, Ar.; ξυνέβη ὑμῖν πεισθῆναι μὲν ἀκεραίοις μεταμέλειν δὲ κακουμένοις to adopt a measure when your forces are unbroken, and to repent when in distress, Thuc. 4. part. neut. μεταμέλον absol.,

since it repented him, Plat. II. seldom with a nom., to cause repentance or sorrow, τῷ Ἀρίστωνι μετέμελε τὸ εἰρημένον (for τοῦ εἰρημένου) Hdt.; οἶμαί σοι ταῦτα μεταμελήσει (for τούτων) Ar. Hence

μεταμέλεια, ή, change of purpose, regret, repentance, Thuc.; μ. ἔχει με = μεταμέλει μοι, Xen.

μεταμελητικός, ή, όν, full of regrets, Arist. From

μετα-μέλομαι, f. -μελήσομαι : aor. 1 -εμελήθην : Dep. : (μεταμέλει) :—to feel repentance, to rue, regret, c. part., μετεμέλοντο οὐ δεξάμενοι they repented that they had not received, Thuc. : absol. to change one's purpose or line of conduct, Xen. II. Causal in part. fut. τὸ μεταμελησόμενον that which will cause regret, matter for future repentance, Id.

μετάμελος, ὁ, repentance, regret, Thuc.

μεταμέλπομαι, Dep. to sing or dance among others, c. dat., h. Hom.

μεταμέλω, v. μεταμέλει.

μετα-μίγνυμι, f. -μίξω, to mix among, confound with, τί τινι Od.

μετα-μίσγω, =μεταμίγνυμι, Od.

μετα-μορφόω, f. ώσω, to transform : Pass. to be transfigured, N. T. Hence

μεταμόρφωσις, ή, a transformation, Luc.

μετ-αμπέχομαι or -ίσχομαι : aor. 2 -ημπισχόμην : Med. :—to put on a different dress, μ. δουλείαν to put on the new dress of slavery, Plat.

μετ-αμφιάζω and -έζω, f. άσω, to change the dress of another, strip off his dress, τινά Plut., Luc. :—metaph. to change, τι εἴς τι Anth.; ἀποδυσάμενος τὸν Πυθαγόραν τίνα μετημφιάσω μετ' αὐτόν; what body didst thou assume after him? Luc.

μετ-ἀμώνιος, ον, (ἄνεμος) borne by the wind, τὰ δὲ παντὰ θεοὶ μετ. θεῖεν may the gods give all that to the winds, Il.; ἐς κόρακας βαδιεῖ μεταμώνιος Ar. II. bootless, vain, idle, μεταμώνια νήματα vainly-woven webs, Od.; μεταμώνια βάζειν to talk idly, Ib.

μετ-αναγιγνώσκομαι, Pass. to repent of a thing, c. gen., Soph.

μετα-ναιετάω, to dwell with, τινί h. Hom. From

μετα-ναιέτης, ου, ὁ, one who dwells with, Hes.

μετ-ανάστασις, ή, migration, Thuc.

μετα-νάστης, ου, ὁ, (ναίω) one who has changed his home, a wanderer, immigrant, commonly as a term of reproach, like Scottish land-louper, Il. Hence

μετανάστιος, ον, wandering, Anth.

μετα-νάστρια, ή, a wanderer, Anth.; and

μετα-νίσσομαι, Dep. to pass over to the other side, Ἥλιος μετενίσσετο the sun was passing over the meridian, Hom. II. c. acc. to go after, pursue, Eur. : also to win, get possession of, Pind.

μετ-ανίστημι, f. -αναστήσω, to remove one from his country, Polyb. II. Pass. c. aor. 2 et pf. act. to move off and go elsewhere, to migrate, Hdt., Soph.

μετα-νοέω, f. ήσω, to change one's mind or purpose, Plat., Xen. 2. to repent, Antipho, etc. Hence

μετάνοια, ή, after-thought, repentance, Thuc., etc.

μετ-αντλέω, f. ήσω, to draw from one vessel into another, Anth.

μετα-ξύ, Adv. (μετά, ξύν) Adv., 1. of Place, betwixt, between, Il., etc.; with the Art., τὸ μεταξύ Hdt.; ἐν τῷ μ. Thuc. 2. of Time, between-whiles,

meanwhile, Hdt., etc.; with pres. part., μεταξὺ ὀρύσσων *in the midst of* his digging, Lat. *inter fodiendum*, Id.; μ. θύων Ar.; λέγοντα μ. *in the middle of* his discourse, Plat.   b. *after, afterwards*, N. T.   3. of Qualities, τὰ μ. *intermediate*, i. e. *neither good nor bad*, Plat.   II. as Prep. with gen. *between*, Hdt., etc.   2. of Time, ὁ μ. τῆς δίκης τε καὶ τοῦ θανάτου [χρόνος] Plat.; τὰ μ. *tούτου meanwhile*, Soph.

μετα-παιδεύω, f. σω, *to educate differently*, Luc.

μετα-παύομαι, Med. *to rest between-whiles*, Il.

μετα-παυσωλή, ή, *rest between-whiles*, πολέμοιο *from war*, Il.

μετα-πείθω, f. σω, *to change a man's persuasion*, Ar., Dem. :—Pass. *to be persuaded to change*, Plat., etc.

μεταπεμπτέος, α, ον, verb. Adj. *to be sent for*, Thuc.; and

μετάπεμπτος, ον, *sent for*, Hdt., Thuc. From

μετα-πέμπω, f. ψω, *to send after*, Eur., Ar. :—*to send for, summon*, Lat. *arcessere*, Hdt., etc.; so in Med.: —Pass., aor. 1 μεταπεμφθῆναι *to be sent for*, Dem.

μεταπέταμαι or **-πέτομαι**, f. -πτήσομαι, aor. 2 -επτά-μην, Dep. *to fly to another place, fly away*, Luc.

μετα-πηδάω, f. ήσομαι, *to leap from one place to another, jump about*, Luc.

μετα-πίπτω, f. -πεσοῦμαι, *to fall differently, undergo a change*, μ. τὸ εἶδος Hdt., or εἰς ἄλλο εἶδος Plat.: also, *to change one's opinion suddenly*, Eur., Ar.; εἰ τρεῖς μόναι μετέπεσον τῶν ψήφων Plat.   2. *to change*, esp. *for the worse*, μεταπίπτοντος δαίμονος if fortune *changes*, Eur.; rarely *for the better*, Id. :—of political changes, *to undergo change* or *revolution*, Thuc.

μετα-πλάσσω, Att. -ττω, f. -πλάσω [ἄ], *to mould differently, remodel*, Plat.; so in Med., Anth.

μετα-ποιέω, f. ήσω, *to alter the make of* a thing, *remodel, alter*, Solon, Dem.   II. Med. *to make a pretence of, lay claim to, pretend to*, c. gen., ἀρετῆς Plat.

μετα-πορεύομαι, f. -εύσομαι, aor. 1 -επορεύθην : Dep. : —*to go after, follow up*, ἔχθραν Lys.   II. *to pursue, punish*, Polyb.

μετά-πρᾶσις, ή, *a selling by retail, retail-trade*, Strab.

μετα-πρεπής, ές, (πρέπω) *distinguished among* others, c. dat. pl., Il.

μετα-πρέπω, only in pres. and impf., *to distinguish oneself* or *be distinguished among* others, c. dat. pl., Hom.

μετα-πτάμενος, aor. 2 part. of μεταπέταμαι.

μετάπτωσις, ή, *change*, Plat. : *change of party*, Polyb.

μετα-πύργιον, τό, (πύργος) *the wall between two towers, the curtain*, Thuc.

μετ-ἄρίθμιος, ον, (ἀριθμός) *counted among* others, c. dat. pl., h. Hom.

μεταρ-ρέω, f. -ρεύσομαι, *to flow differently, to change to and fro, ebb and flow*, Arist.

μεταρ-ρίπτω, f. ψω, *to turn upside down*, Dem.

μεταρ-ρυθμίζω, f. σω, *to change the fashion of* a thing, *to remodel*, Hdt., Aesch. :—*to reform, amend*, Xen.

μεταρσιο-λεσχία, ή, (λέσχης) = μετεωρολογία, Plut.

μεταρσιόομαι, Pass. *to rise high into the air*, νέφος μεταρσιωθέν From

μετάρσιος, Dor. **πεδάρσιος**, ον, and α, ον, (μεταίρω) *raised from the ground, high in air*, Lat. *sublimis*, Trag.; λόγοι πεδάρσιοι *scattered to the winds*, Aesch.;

ναῦς ἄρμεν᾽ ἔχοισα μετάρσια *a ship having her sails hoisted*, Theocr.   2. like μετέωρος II. 2, *on the high sea, out at sea*, Hdt.   II. metaph. *in air, high above this world*, Eur.   2. *of things, airy, empty*, Id.   III. in Medic., *of the breath, high, quick*.

μετα-σεύομαι, Ep. μετασσεύομαι : 3 sing. Ep. aor. 2 μετέσσυτο : Pass. :—*to rush towards* or *after*, Il. :— c. acc. *to rush upon*, μετέσσυτο ποιμένα λαῶν Ib.

μετα-σκευάζω, f. άσω, *to put into another dress* (σκευή), *to change the fashion of, transform*, Xen.   II. Med. *to pack up so as to shift one's quarters*, Luc.

μετα-σπάω, f. άσω, *to draw over from one side to another*, Soph.

μετασπόμενος, μετασπών, aor. 2 med. and act. part. of μεθέπω.

μέτασσαι, αἱ, (μετά) lambs *born midway* between the πρόγονοι (early-born) and the ἕρσαι (freshlings or late-born).

μετασσεύομαι, Ep. for μετασεύομαι.

μετασταθῶ, aor. 1 pass. subj. of μεθίστημι.

μεταστάς, aor. 2 part. of μεθίστημι.

μετάστασις, ή, (μεθίστημι) *a removing, removal*, κακοῦ Andoc.   II. (μεθίσταμαι) *a being put into a different place, removal, migration*, Plat.; μ. ἡλίου *an eclipse*, Eur.   2. *a changing, change*, Id.; θυμῷ μετάστασιν διδόναι *to allow a change to one's wrath*, i. e. *suffer it to cease*, Soph.   3. *a change of political constitution, revolution*, Thuc.

μετα-στᾰτέον, verb. Adj. *one must alter*, Isocr.

μετα-στείχω, f. ξω, *to go in quest of*, τινά Eur.

μεταστέλλομαι, Med., *to send for, summon*, Luc.

μετα-στένω, only in pres. and impf., *to lament afterwards*, Od., Aesch.   II. *to lament after this* or *next*, Eur.

μετα-στοιχεί or **-ί**, (στοῖχος) Adv. *all in a row*, Il.

μετα-στονᾰχίζω, *to sigh* or *lament afterwards*, Hes.

μετα-στρᾰτοπεδεύω, f. σω, *to shift one's ground* or *camp*, Polyb. :—so in Med., Xen.

μεταστρεπτικός, ή, όν, *fit for turning another way, fit for directing*, Plat. From

μετα-στρέφω, f. ψω, Pass., aor. 1 -εστρέφθην, aor. 2 -εστράφην [ἄ] :—*to turn about, turn round, turn*, Il., Ar. :—Pass. *to turn oneself about, turn about*, whether *to face the enemy* or *to flee*, Il.; then, simply, *to turn round*, Hdt., Plat.   2. *to pervert, change, alter*, Plat., etc. :—Pass., τἀμὰ μετεστράφη *my fortunes are changed*, Eur.; τὸ ψήφισμ᾽ ὅπως μεταστραφείη Ar.   II. intr. *to turn another way, change one's ways*, Il.; μεταστρέψας *contrariwise*, Plat.   2. c. gen. *to care for, regard*, Eur. Hence

μεταστροφή, ή, *a turning from* one thing *to another*, Plat.

μετασχεῖν, aor. 2 inf. of μετέχω.

μετά-σχεσις, εως, ή, *participation*, τινος *in the nature* of a thing, Plat.

μετα-σχημᾰτίζω, f. Att. ιῶ, *to change the form of* a person or thing, Plat.   II. *to transfer as in a figure*, N. T.

μετα-τάσσω, Att. -ττω, f. ξω, *to transpose* : Med. *to change one's order of battle*, Xen.; μετατάσσεσθαι παρ᾽ Ἀθηναίους *to go over and join them*, Thuc.

μετα-τίθημι, f. -θήσω : aor. 1 μετ-έθηκα, aor. 2 -έθην :

—to place among, τῷ κ' οὔτι τόσον κέλαδον μετέθηκεν (v. l. μεθῆκεν) then he would not have caused so much noise among us, Od. II. to place differently, 1. in local sense, to transpose, Plat. 2. to change, alter, of a treaty, Thuc., Xen.; μ. τὰς ἐπωνυμίας ἐπὶ ὑός to change their names and call them after swine, Hdt.; μ. τι ἀντί τινος to put one thing in place of another, substitute, Dem. 3. Med. to change what is one's own or for oneself, τοὺς νόμους Xen.; μετατίθεσθαι τὴν γνώμην to adopt a new opinion, Hdt.; so, absol., Plat. b. μ. [τὸν φόβον] to get rid of, transfer one's fear, Dem. c. c. dupl. acc., τὸ κεῖνων κακὸν τῷδε κέρδος μ. to alter their evil designs into gain for him, Soph. 4. Pass. to be changed, to alter, Eur.

μετα-τίκτω, to bring forth afterwards, Aesch.

μετα-τρέπομαι, 3 sing. aor. 2 μετ-ετράπετο: Med.:— to turn oneself round, turn round, Il. 2. to look back to, shew regard for, c. gen., Ib.

μετα-τρέχω, f. -θρέξομαι: aor. 2 -έδραμον:—to run after, οὔκουν παρ' Ἀθηναίων σὺ μεταθρέξει; you run and get it from the Athenians, Ar.

μετα-τροπαλίζομαι, Pass. to turn about, Il.

μετατροπή, ἡ, (μετατρέπω) retribution, vengeance for a thing, c. gen., Eur.

μετατροπία, ἡ, a turn of fortune, a reverse, Pind. From

μετά-τροπος, ον, (μετατρέπω) turning about, returning, Anth. 2. turning round upon, Aesch.; ἔργα μετάτροπα deeds that turn upon their author or are visited with vengeance, Hes.; so, μ. αὖραι Eur.; πολέμου μετάτροπος αὖρα Ar.

μετ-αυγάζω, to look keenly about for, τινά Pind.

μετ-αυδάω, impf. μετ-ηύδων: to speak among others, to address them, c. dat. pl., Hom. 2. c. acc. pers. to accost, address, Mosch.

μετ-αῦθις, Ion. -αῦτις, Adv. afterwards, Hdt., Aesch.

μέτ-αυλος, ον, Att. for μέσαυλος.

μετ-αυτίκα [ῐ], Adv. just after, presently after, Hdt.

μετ-αῦτις, Ion. for μεταῦθις.

μετα-φέρω, f. μετ-οίσω: aor. 1 -ήνεγκα: pf. -ενήνοχα:—to carry over, transfer, Dem.; μ. κέντρα πώλοις to apply the goad to the horses in turn, Eur. 2. to change, alter, Soph., Dem.; μ. τὰ δίκαια to change, confound, Aeschin. 3. in Rhetoric, to use a word in a changed sense, to employ a metaphor, Arist.

μετά-φημι, impf. μετ-έφην, (cf. μετ-εῖπον):—to speak among others, to address them, c. dat. pl., Hom. 2. c. acc. pers. to accost, Il.

μετα-φορέω, =μεταφέρω 1, Hdt.

μεταφορικός, ή, όν, apt at metaphors, Arist. II. metaphorical: Adv. -κῶς, Plut.

μετα-φράζω, f. σω, to paraphrase, to translate, Plut. II. Med. to consider after, ταῦτα μεταφρασόμεσθα καὶ αὖτις Il. Hence

μετάφρασις, ἡ, a paraphrasing, Plut.

μετά-φρενον, τό, properly, the part behind the midriff (μετὰ τὰς φρένας), the back, Il., Plat.

μετα-φωνέω, to speak among others, c. dat. pl., Il.

μετα-χειρίζω, f. Att. ιῶ: aor. 1 -εχείρισα:—more commonly as Dep., f. Att. -ιοῦμαι: aor. 1 -εχειρισάμην and -εχειρίσθην: pf. -κεχείρισμαι:—to have or take in hand, handle, administer, manage, Hdt. 2. to

manage, arrange, conduct, Thuc. :—so as Dep., Ar., Xen. 3. to practise, pursue an art or study, Plat.; c. inf. to study to do, Id. 4. c. acc. pers. to handle, treat, or deal with in a certain way, χαλεπῶς τινὰ μεταχειρίζειν Thuc. :—of a physician, Plat.

μετα-χρόνιος, ον, and α, ον, (χρόνος) happening afterwards, Luc. II. in Hes. =μετάρσιος.

μετά-χρονος, ον, after the time, done later, Luc.

μετα-χωρέω, f. ήσω, to go to another place, to withdraw, migrate, emigrate, Aesch., Thuc.

μετα-ψαίρω, to brush against a thing, c. acc., Eur.

μετέασι, Ep. for μέτεισι, 3 pl. of μέτειμι (εἰμὶ sum).

μετ-εγγράφω, f. ψω, to put upon a new register: 3 sing. fut. 2 pass. μετεγγραφήσεται he will be put on a new register, Ar.

μετέειπον, Ep. for μετεῖπον (q. v.).

μετέῃσι, Ion. for μετῇ, 3 sing. subj. of μέτειμι.

μετέθηκα, aor. 1 of μετατίθημι.

μετείθη, Ion. for μεθείθη, 3 sing. aor. 1 pass. of μεθίημι.

μέτ-ειμι, (εἰμὶ sum) to be among, c. dat. pl., Hom.; absol., οὐ παυσωλὴ μετέσσεται no interval of rest will be mine, Il. II. impers., μέτεστί μοί τινος I have a share in or claim to a thing, Hdt., Att. :—so part. neut. used absol., οὐδὲν Αἰολεῦσι μετεὸν τῆς χώρης since the Aeolians had no share in the land, Hdt. 2. sometimes the share is added in nom., μέτεστι πᾶσι τὸ ἴσον Thuc.; ἐμοὶ τούτων οὐδὲν μ. Plat.

μέτ-ειμι, Att. fut. of μετέρχομαι: impf. μετῄειν: Ep. aor. 1 part. μετεισάμενος:—to go between or among others, Il. II. to go after or behind, follow, Ib., Xen. 2. c. acc. to go after, go in quest of, pursue, Hdt., Att. 3. to pursue with vengeance, Aesch., Thuc.; δίκας μ. τινα (where δίκας is acc. cogn.), to execute judgment upon one, Aesch. 4. to pursue, go about a business, Eur. 5. μ. τινὰ θυσίαις to approach one with sacrifices, Hdt.: c. acc. et inf., ἕνα ἕκαστον μετῄεσαν μὴ ἐπιτρέπειν besought each one not to permit, Thuc. III. to pass over to another, Eur.

μετ-εῖπον, Ep. μετ-έειπον, serving as aor. 2 of μετάφημι, to speak among others, address them, c. dat. pl., Hom. 2. absol. to speak thereafter, afterwards, Id.

μετείθην, aor. 1 pass. of μεθίημι.

μετείσθω, 3 sing. Ion. pf. pass. imper. of μεθίημι.

μετείς, Ion. for μεθ-είς, aor. 2 part. of μεθίημι.

μετεισάμενος, Ep. aor. 1 med. part. of μέτειμι (εἶμι ibo).

μετείω, Ep. for μετῶ, pres. subj. of μέτειμι (εἰμὶ sum).

μετ-εκβαίνω, f. -βήσομαι, to go from one place into another, Hdt.; c. acc., μ. φθόγγον to pass from one note to another, Anth.

μετ-εκδίδωμι, to lend out, Plut.

μετ-εκδύομαι, Med. to pull off one's own clothes and put on others, to assume, Plut.

μετελεύσομαι, fut. of μετέρχομαι.

μετελθών, aor. 2 part. of μετέρχομαι.

μετ-ελευστέον, verb. Adj., one must punish, Luc.

μετ-εμβαίνω, to go on board another ship, Plut.

μετ-εμβιβάζω, Causal of foreg., to put on board another ship, Thuc.

μετέμμεναι, Ep. for μετεῖναι, inf. of μέτειμι (εἰμὶ sum).

μετ-έμφυτος, ον, engrafted afresh, Anth.

μετενδύω, I. Causal in aor. 1 μετ-ενέδυσα, to put other clothes on a person, invest with new power, τινά

τι Luc.　　II. Pass. μετενδύομαι, with aor. 2 act. μετενέδῦν, to put on other clothes, Strab.

μετ-ενεκτέον, verb. Adj. of μεταφέρω, Strab.

μετενήνοχα, pf. of μεταφέρω.

μετ-εννέπω, to speak among, τινί Mosch.

μετ-εντίθημι, to put into another place: Med., μετεντίθεσθαι τὸν γόμον to shift a ship's cargo, Dem.

μετ-εξαιρέομαι, Med. to take out of and put elsewhere, Dem.

μετ-εξανίσταμαι, Pass. to move from one place to another, Luc.

μετ-εξέτεροι, αι, α, Ion. Pron., = ἔνιοι, some among many, certain persons, Hdt.

μετ-έπειτα, Adv. afterwards, thereafter, Hom.: Ion. μετ-έπειτεν, Hdt.

μετ-έρχομαι, Aeol. and Dor. πεδ-έρχομαι: f. μετελεύσομαι (in Att., the impf. and fut. are borrowed from μέτειμι, q. v.): Dep., with aor. 2 μετ-ῆλθον, pf. -ελήλυθα:—to come or go among others, c. dat. pl. or absol., Hom.; μετελθών having gone between the ranks, Il.　II. to go to another place, Ib.: simply to come next, follow, Pind.　III. c. acc. to go after, to go to seek, go in quest of, Il., Att.: generally, to seek for, aim at, Eur., Thuc.　2. in hostile sense, to pursue, Il., Hdt., Att.: c. acc. rei, to seek to avenge, Aesch., Eur. :—then c. dupl. acc. pers. et rei, μ. τι τινά to visit a crime upon a person, Eur.　3. of things, to go after, attend to, to pursue a business, Hom., Att.　4. to approach with prayers, Lat. adire, prosequi, τινα Hdt., Eur.: to court or woo, Pind.

μετέσσῦτο, 3 sing. Ep. aor. 2 of μετασεύομαι.

μετ-εύχομαι, f. -εύξομαι, Dep. to change one's wish, to wish something else, Eur.

μετέφην, impf. of μετάφημι.

μετ-έχω, Aeol. πεδ-έχω: f. μεθ-έξω: pf. μετ-έσχηκα: —to partake of, enjoy a share of, share in, take part in, c. gen. rei, Theogn., Aesch.; c. gen. pers. to partake of a person's friendship, Xen.; μ. τῶν πεντακισχιλίων to be members of the 5000 in turn, Thuc. :— with dat. pers. added, μετ. τινός τινι to partake of something in common with another, Pind., Eur. :— often the part or share is added, μ. τάφου μέρος Aesch., etc.　2. rarely with the acc. only, ἀκερδῆ χάριν μ. Soph.　3. absol., οἱ μετέχοντες the partners, Hdt.

μετέω, Ion. for μετῶ, subj. of μέτειμι (εἰμί sum).

μετεωρίζω, f. σω, (μετέωρος) to raise to a height, raise, Thuc. :—Med., δελφῖνας μετεωρίζου heave up your dolphins (v. δελφίς II), Ar. :—Pass. to be raised up, to float in mid-air, Lat. suspendi, Id., etc.: of ships, to keep out on the high sea, Thuc.　II. metaph. to lift up, buoy up with false hopes, Dem. :—Pass. to be elevated, excited, Ar.

μετεωρο-κοπέω, f. ήσω, (κόπτω) to prate about high things, Ar.

μετεωρο-λέσχης, ου, one who prates on things above, a star-gazer, visionary, Plat.

μετεωρολογέω, f. ήσω, to talk of high things, Plat.; and

μετεωρολογία, ἡ, discussion of high things, Plat.

μετεωρο-λόγος, ὁ, (λέγω) one who talks of the heavenly bodies, an astronomer, Plat.

μετέωρος, ον, Ep. μετήορος, q. v., (ἑώρα, ἀείρω) raised from the ground, hanging, Lat. suspensus, Hdt. ;—of

high ground, Thuc.　II. like μετάρσιος, in mid-air, high in air, Lat. sublimis, Hdt., Ar.; Ἀήρ, ὃς ἔχεις τὴν γῆν μ. poised on high, Ar.; τὰ μ. χωρία the regions of air, Id.; τὰ μ. things in heaven above, astronomical phenomena, Id., Plat.　2. on the high sea, out at sea, of ships, Thuc.　III. metaph. of the mind, lifted up, buoyed up, on the tiptoe of expectation, in suspense, Lat. spe erectus, Id.　2. wavering, uncertain, Dem.: —Adv., μετεώρως ἔχειν to be in uncertainty, Plut.

μετεωρο-σκόπος, ὁ, a star-gazer, Plat.

μετεωρο-σοφιστής, ὁ, an astrological sophist, Ar.

μετεωρο-φέναξ, ακος, ὁ, an astrological quack, Ar.

μετηΐσαν, Ion. 3 pl. impf. of μέτειμι (εἶμι ibo).

μετῆλθον, aor. 2 of μετέρχομαι.

μετ-ηνέμιος, ον, (ἄνεμος) swift as wind, Anth.

μετ-ήορος, ον, Ep. form of μετέωρος, lifted off the ground, hanging, Il. :—Dor. πεδάορος Aesch.　II. metaph. wavering, thoughtless, h. Hom.

μετῆρα, aor. 1 of μεταίρω.

μετήσεσθαι, Ion. f. med. inf. of μεθίημι.

μετίει, v. μεθίημι.

μετίετο, Ion. for μεθίετο, 3 sing. impf. med. of μεθίημι.

μετ-ίημι, μετ-ίστημι, Ion. for μεθ-.

μετ-ίσχω, = μετέχω, c. gen. rei, Hdt.

μετοικεσία, ἡ, = μετοικία, Anth. :—the Removal or Captivity of the Jews, N. T.

μετ-οικέω, f. ήσω, to change one's abode, remove to a place, c. acc. loci, Eur. :—c. dat. loci, to settle in, Pind.　II. absol. to be μέτοικος or settler, reside in a foreign city, Eur., Ar., etc.　Hence

μετοίκησις, ἡ, = sq. 1, Plat.; and

μετοικία, ἡ, change of abode, removal, migration, Thuc.　II. a settling as μέτοικος, settlement or residence in a foreign city, Aesch., etc.; and

μετοικίζω, to lead settlers to another abode, Plut.

μετοικικός, ή, όν, in the condition of a μέτοικος, Plut.: —τὸ μ. the list of μέτοικοι, Luc.

μετοίκιον, τό, the tax paid by the μέτοικοι, Plat.　II. μετοίκια, τά, the feast of migration, Plut.

μετοικισμός, οῦ, ὁ, (μετοικίζω) emigration, Plut.

μετοικιστής, οῦ, ὁ, (μετοικίζω) an emigrant, Plut.

μετ-οικοδομέω, f. ήσω, to build differently, Plut.

μέτ-οικος, ον, changing one's abode, emigrating and settling elsewhere, Hdt.　II. as Subst. μέτοικος, ὁ, ἡ, an alien settled in a foreign city, a settler, emigrant, sojourner, Aesch., etc.; μ. γῆς one who has settled in a country, Id.　2. at Athens, a resident alien, who paid a tax (μετοίκιον), but enjoyed no civic rights, Thuc., etc.

μετοικο-φύλαξ, ὁ, ἡ, guardian of the μέτοικοι, Xen.

μετ-οίχομαι, f. -οιχήσομαι, Dep. to have gone after, to have gone in quest of, c. acc. pers., Hom.: c. acc. rei, to seek for, Eur.　2. with hostile intent, to pursue, Il.　3. to have gone among or through, Od.　4. to have gone with, Ib.

μετ-οκλάζω, f. σω, to keep changing from one knee to another, said of a coward crouching in ambush, Il.

μετ-ονομάζω, f. σω, to call by a new name, αἰγίδας μετωνόμασαν called them by a new name—αἰγίδες, Hdt. :—Pass. to take or receive a new name, Id., Thuc.

μετ-οπῖν, Adv., = μετόπισθε, Soph.

μετ-όπισθε, before a vowel, -θεν: Adv.,　1. of

Place, *from behind, backwards, back*, Hom., Hes. 2. *of Time, after, afterwards*, Hom. II. Prep. with gen. *behind*, Id.

μετοπωρῐνός, ή, όν, *autumnal*, Thuc., Xen. :—neut. as Adv., Hes. [Cf. ὀπωρινός.] From

μετ-όπωρον, τό, (ὀπώρα) *late autumn*, Thuc.

μετ-ορμίζω, Ion. for μεθορμίζω.

μετ-όρχιον, τό, *the space between rows of vines*, Ar.

μετουσία, ἡ, *participation, partnership, communion*, τινός in a thing, Ar., Dem.

μετοχή, ἡ, (μετέχω) *participation, communion*, Hdt.

μετ-οχλίζω, f. ίσω: 3 sing. Ep. aor. 1 opt. μετοχλίσσειε :—*to remove by a lever, hoist* a heavy body *out of the way*, Od. II. *to push back the bar*, Il.

μέτοχος, ον, (μετέχω) *sharing in, partaking of*, c. gen., Hdt., Eur. II. as Subst. *a partner, accomplice in*, τοῦ φόνου Eur. ; absol., Thuc.

μετρέω, f. ήσω, (μέτρον) *to measure in any way* : I. of Space, *to measure*, i. e. *pass over, traverse*, πέλαγος μέγα μετρήσασαν Od. :—Med., ἅλα μετρήσασθαι Mosch. II. in the common sense, *to measure*, Lat. *metiri*, τὴν γῆν σταδίοισι Hdt.; τῇ γαστρὶ μ. τὴν εὐδαιμονίαν *to measure* happiness by sensual enjoyments, Dem. :—Med., μετρεῖσθαι ἴχνη *to measure* his steps *by the eye*, Soph. :—Pass. *to be measured*, Hdt., Aesch. 2. *to count*, Theocr. 3. *to measure out, dole out*, Ar., Dem. :—Med. *to have measured out to one*, εὖ μετρεῖσθαι *to get* good *measure*, Hes.; τὰ ἄλφιτα μετρούμενοι Dem. Hence

μέτρημα, ατος, τό, *a measured distance*, Eur. 2. *a measure, allowance, dole*, Id. ; and

μέτρησις, ἡ, *measuring, measurement*, Hdt., Xen.

μετρητέον, verb. Adj., *one must measure*, Plat.

μετρητής, οῦ, ὁ, (μετρέω) *a measurer*, Plat. II. = ἀμφορεύς, *a liquid measure*, holding 12 χόες or 144 κοτύλαι, about 9 gallons Engl., Dem.

μετρητικός, ή, όν, (μετρέω) *of* or *for measuring*, Plat. : ἡ -κή (sc. τέχνη) *mensuration*, Id.

μετρητός, ή, όν, (μετρέω) *measurable*, Eur., Plat.

μετριάζω, f. σω, (μέτριος) *to be moderate, keep measure*, Soph., Thuc., etc. II. trans. *to moderate, regulate, control*, Lat. *moderari*, Plat., etc.

μετρικός, ή, όν, (μέτρον) *of* or *for metre, metrical*, Arist. : τὰ -κά and ἡ -κή (sc. τέχνη), *prosody*, Id.

μετριοπᾰθέω, *to bear reasonably with*, τινί N.T. From

μετριο-πᾰθής, ές, (πάθος) *moderating one's passions*, a Peripatetic word.

μετριο-πότης, ου, ὁ, *a moderate drinker*, Xen.

μέτριος, α, ον, and ος, ον, (μέτρον) *within measure*, and so, I. of Size, *of average height*, Hdt. ; μ. πῆχυς the common cubit, Id. ; so of Time, *moderate*, Plat. II. of Number, *few*, Xen. III. of Degree, *holding to the mean, moderate*, Hes., Eur., etc. :—of a *mean* or *middle* state, opp. to a high or low estate, Trag., etc. ; τὸ μέτριον *the mean*, Lat. *aurea mediocritas*, Soph. ; so, τὰ μέτρια Eur., etc. ; —so, μ. φιλία a friendship *not too great*, Id.; μ. ἐσθῆτι χρῆσθαι *common dress*, Thuc. ; μετρίᾳ φυλακῇ *not in strict* custody, Id. ; οἱ μέτριοι *common men, the common* sort, Dem. :—also, ὅσον οἰόμεθα μέτριον εἶναι *just sufficient*, Plat. 2. *moderate, tolerable*, Hdt., Soph., etc. ; τὰ μ. *moderate terms*, Thuc. 3.

of Persons, *moderate, temperate, virtuous*, Theogn., Eur. ; μετριώτεροι ἐς τὰ πολιτικά Thuc. ; μέτρ. πρὸς δίαιταν Aeschin. 4. *proportionate, fitting*, Xen. B. Adv. μετρίως, *moderately, within due limits, in due measure, fairly*, Hdt., Thuc., etc. ; μ. ἔχειν τοῦ βίου *to be moderately* well off, Hdt. :—Comp. μετριώτερον, Sup. -ώτατα, Thuc. 2. *enough, sufficiently*, Eur., etc. 3. *modestly, temperately*, Eur., Xen. :—*on fair terms*, Thuc. II. the neut. μέτριον and μέτρια are also used as Adv., Plat. :—with Art., τὸ μέτριον Xen. ; τὰ μέτρια Thuc. Hence

μετριότης, ητος, ἡ, *moderation*, Thuc., Plat. ; μ. τῶν σίτων *moderation* in food, Xen. II. *a middle condition*, Lat. *mediocritas*, Arist.

ΜΕ΄ΤΡΟΝ, τό, *that by which anything is measured* : 1. *a measure* or *rule*, Il. ; ἄνδρα πάντων χρημάτων μ. εἶναι is *a measure* of all things, Plat. 2. *a measure of content*, whether solid or liquid, δῶκεν μέθυ, χίλια μέτρα Il. ; εἴκοσι μέτρα ἀλφίτου Od. 3. *measure, length, size*, μέτρα κελεύθου *the length* of the way, Od. ; μέτρον ἑξήκοντα σταδίους Thuc. ; μέτρον ἥβης *full measure*, i. e. *the prime*, of youth, Il. ; μέτρα μορφῆς one's size and shape, Eur. 4. *due measure* or *limit, proportion*, μέτρα φυλάσσεσθαι Hes. ; κατὰ μέτρον Id. ; ὑπὲρ μέτρον Theogn. ; πλέον μέτρου Plat. ;—μέτρῳ = μετρίως, Pind. II. *metre*, opp. to μέλος (tune) and ῥυθμός (time), Ar., Plat. 2. *a verse*, Plat.

μετωπηδόν, (μέτωπον) Adv. *with front-foremost* ; of ships, *forming a close front, in line*, Hdt. ; opp. to ἐπὶ κέρως (in column), Thuc.

μετωπίδιος, ον, (μέτωπον) *on the forehead*, Anth.

μετ-ώπιον, τό, = μέτωπον, *the forehead*, Il.

μέτ-ωπον, τό, (μετά, ὤψ) *the space between the eyes, the brow, forehead*, Hom., etc. II. *the front* or *face* of a wall or building, Hdt. : *the front* of an army or fleet, Aesch., Xen. ; ἐπὶ μετώπου or ἐν μετώπῳ *in line*, opp. to ἐπὶ κέρως or κέρας (in column), Xen.

μεῦ, Ep. and Ion. for μοῦ, gen. of ἐγώ.

ΜΕ΄ΧΡΙ, and μέχρις, Adv. *to a given point, even so far*, I. before a Prep. μέχρι πρός, Lat. *usque ad*, Plat. :—so before Advs., μ. δεῦρο τοῦ λόγου Id. ; μ. τότε Thuc. II. serving as a Prep. c. gen. *even to, as far as*, 1. of Place, μεχρὶ θαλάσσης Il. ; μ. τῆς πόλεως Thuc. 2. of Time, τέο μέχρις ; i. e. τινὸς μέχρι χρόνου ; Lat. *quousque?* how long? Il. ; so, μέχρι οὗ ; μέχρι ὅσου ; Hdt. ; with the Art., τὸ μ. ἐμεῦ *up to* my time, Id. 3. of Measure or Degree, μ. σοῦ δικαίου *so far as* consists with right, Thuc. ; μ. τοῦ δυνατοῦ Plat. 4. with Numbers, *up to, about, nearly*, sometimes without altering the case of the Subst., μέχρι τριάκοντα ἔτη Aeschin. 5. in Ion., μέχρι οὗ is sometimes used like the simple μέχρι, μέχρι οὗ ὀκτὼ πύργων Hdt. III. as a Conjunct. *so long as, until*, μέχρι μὲν ὤρεον, with δέ in apodosi, Id. ; μ. σκότος ἐγένετο Xen. 2. μέχρι ἄν foll. by the subj., Id. ; so without ἄν, μ. τοῦτο ἴδωμεν Hdt.

ΜΗ΄, *not*, is the negative of *thought*, as οὐ of *statement*, i. e. μή says *that one thinks a thing is not*, οὐ *that it is not*. The same differences hold for all compds. of μή and οὐ. A. μή in INDEPENDENT sentences, 1. with Imperat., μή μ᾽ ἐρέθιζε *do not provoke me*, Il. ; μή τις

ἀκουσάτω let *not* any one hear, Od.　2. with Subj., μὴ δή μ᾽ ἐάσῃς Il.; μὴ ἴομεν (Ep. for ἴωμεν) Ib.; μὴ πάθωμεν Xen.　3. with Opt. to express a wish that a thing may not happen, ἃ μὴ κραίνοι τύχη which may fortune *not* bring to pass, Aesch.:—also in wishes that refer to past time and therefore cannot be fulfilled, μή ποτ᾽ ὤφελον λιπεῖν Soph.　4. in vows and oaths, where οὐ might be expected, ἴστω Ζεὺς μὴ μὲν τοῖς ἵπποισιν ἀνὴρ ἐποχήσεται ἄλλος Zeus be my witness, *not* another man shall ride on these horses, Il.; μὰ τὴν Ἀφροδίτην, μὴ ἐγώ σ᾽ ἀφήσω Ar.　5. with Infin., used as Imperat., μὴ δή μοι ἀπόπροθεν ἰσχέμεν ἵππους Il.
B. In DEPENDENT clauses:　1. with Final Conjunctions, ἵνα μή, ὅπως μή, ὡς μή, ὄφρα, *that not*, Lat. *ne*, Il., Att.:—μή often stands alone = ἵνα μή, Hom., Att.　2. in the protasis of conditional sentences, after εἰ (Ep. αἰ), εἴ κε (αἴ κε), εἰ ἄν, ἤν, ἐάν, ἄν, Lat. *nisi*, Hom., etc.;—so, ὅτε μή = εἰμή; etc.　3. in relat. clauses, when they imply a condition or supposition, λέγονθ᾽ ἃ μὴ δεῖ *such things as one ought not*, Soph.; λόγοις τοιούτοις οἷς σὺ μὴ τέρψει κλύων Id.　4. with Infin., always except when the Inf. represents Indic. or Opt., as in *oratio obliqua*.　5. with Participle, when it can be resolved into a conditional clause, μὴ ἀπενείκας = εἰ μὴ ἀπήνεικε Hdt.; μὴ θέλων = εἰ μὴ θέλεις, Aesch.; so in a general sense, δίδασκέ μ᾽ ὡς μὴ εἰδότα = ut qui nihil sciam, Soph.　6. with abstract Nouns as with Partic., τὰ μὴ δίκαια = ἃ ἂν μὴ ᾖ δίκαια, Aesch.; τὸ μὴ καλόν Soph.; ἡ μὴ ᾽μπειρία = τὸ μὴ ἔχειν ἐμπειρίαν, want of experience, Ar.　7. after Verbs expressing *fear* or *apprehension* (cf. μὴ οὐ):　a. when the thing feared is fut., with pres. Subj., I fear he may persuade me, Il.　b. with Opt. for Subj., according to the sequence of moods and tenses, Hom., etc.　c. when the action is present or past, the Indic. is used, φοβούμεθα μὴ ἡμαρτήκαμεν we fear we have made a mistake, Thuc.　8. without a Verb to express hesitation, *perhaps*, μὴ ἀγροικότερον ᾖ τὸ ἀληθὲς εἰπεῖν Plat.
C. In QUESTIONS:　I. Direct questions,　a. with Ind., implying a negat. answer, *surely not, you don't mean to say that*, Lat. *num?* whereas with οὐ an affirm. answer is expected, Lat. *nonne? ἆρ᾽ οὐ τέθνηκε; surely he is dead, is he not? ἆρα μὴ τέθνηκε; surely he is not dead, is he?*:—when οὐ and μή appear in consecutive clauses, each negat. retains its proper force, οὐ σῖγ᾽ ἀνέξει μηδὲ δειλίαν ἀρεῖς; *will you not be silent, and will you be* cowardly? i. e. be silent and be not cowardly, Soph.　b. with the Subj., when the answer is somewhat doubtful, μὴ οὕτω φῶμεν; can we say so? Plat.:—so also with Opt. and ἄν, πῶς ἄν τις μὴ λέγοι; *how can a man help* speaking? Id.　II. indirect questions, where μή belong in fact to μή with Verbs of *fear* and *apprehension*, περισκόπω μή πού τις ἐγχρίμπτῃ Soph.
μὴ ἀλλά, an elliptic phrase for μὴ γένοιτο, ἀλλά.., in answers, *nay but, not so but*, σὺ δὲ ταῦτ᾽ ἀρέσκει; Answ. μἀλλὰ πλεῖν ἢ μαίνομαι Ar.
μὴ γάρ, an elliptic phrase, used in emphatic denial, *certainly not*, where a Verb must be supplied from the foregoing passage, μὴ λεγέτω τὸ ὄνομα, Answ. μὴ γάρ

(sc. λεγέτω) Plat.:—also in parenthesis, where it may be translated *much less*, like μὴ ὅτι, Aeschin.
μηδάμῃ or **μηδάμά** (v. οὐδαμῆ), Adv. of μηδαμός, *in no wise, not at all*, Hdt., Aesch., etc.
μηδᾰμόθεν, Adv. of μηδαμός, *from no place*, Xen.; μ. ἄλλοθεν *from no other place*, Plat.
μηδᾰμοῖ, Adv. *nowhere*, Luc.
μηδᾰμοῖ, Adv. *nowhither*, Plat.
μηδᾰμός, ή, όν, for μηδὲ ἀμός, only in pl. μηδαμοί (in Ion. writers), *none*, Hdt.
μηδᾰμόσε Plat.
μηδᾰμοῦ, Adv. *nowhere*, μ. ἄλλοσε Plat.:—metaph., μ. νομίζεται *nullo in numero habetur*, Aesch.
μηδᾰμῶς, Adv. of μηδαμός, = μηδαμῆ, Hdt., Aesch., etc.
μηδέ, (μή, δέ), Negat. Particle, (related to οὐδέ as μή to οὐ):　I. as Conjunct. *but not* or *and not*, nor, μή τι σὺ ταῦτα διείρεο μηδὲ μετάλλα Il.:—more rarely without a negative preceding, τεκνοῦσθαι, μηδ᾽ ἄπαιδα θνήσκειν Aesch.　2. doubled, μηδέ.. μηδέ.., opposing the two clauses of a sentence, Il.:—μηδέ also follows μήτε, Soph., Plat.　II. as Adv., joined with a single word or phrase, *not even*, Lat. *ne.. quidem*, Hom., etc.
μηδ-είς, μηδε-μία, μηδ-έν, (i. e. μηδὲ εἷς, μηδὲ μία, μηδὲ ἕν):—*and not one*, related to οὐδείς as μή to οὐ, Il., etc.;—rare in pl., Xen.　2. μηδὲ εἷς, which (so written) is never elided even in Att., retained the first emphatic sense *not even one*, and often had a Particle between, as, μηδ᾽ ἂν εἷς, or a Prep. μηδ᾽ ἐξ ἑνός, μηδὲ περὶ ἑνός etc., Plat.　II. *nobody, naught, good for naught*, ὁ μηδεὶς Soph.; pl., οὐ γὰρ ἠξίου τοὺς μηδένας Id.:—so, μηδέν or τὸ μηδέν often as Subst., *naught, nothing*, Id.; μηδὲν λέγειν to say *what is naught*, Xen.; τοῦ μηδενὸς ἄξιος Hdt.; ἐς τὸ μηδὲν ἥκειν Eur.;—and of persons, τὸ μηδέν *a good for naught*, τὸ μηδὲν εἶναι of an eunuch, Hdt.; τὸ μ. ὄντας Soph.　III. neut. μηδέν as Adv. *not at all, by no means*, Aesch., etc.
μηδέ-ποτε, Adv. *never*, Ar., Plat., etc.　II. μηδέ ποτε *and never*, Hes.
μηδέ-πω, Adv. *nor as yet, not as yet*, Aesch., etc.
μηδε-πώποτε, Adv. *never yet*, Dem.
Μηδεσῐ-κάστη, ή, fem. prop. n., *Adorned-with-prudence*, from μήδεσι (dat. pl. of μῆδος) and κέκασμαι, Il.
μηδ-έτερος or **μηδ᾽ ἕτερος**, α, ον, *neither of the two*, Thuc., Plat.: Adv. -ρως, *in neither of two ways*, Arist.
μηδ-ετέρωσε, Adv. *to neither side*, Thuc.
μὴ δή, *nay do not.*., Il., etc.; so, μὴ δῆτα Aesch., etc.
Μηδίζω, f. σω, *to be a Mede in language* or *habits: to side with the Medes, to Medize*, Hdt., Thuc.
Μηδικός, ή, όν, (Μῆδος) *Median:* τὰ Μηδικά (sc. πράγματα) *the war with the Medes*, the name given to the great Persian war, Thuc.; ὁ Μ. πόλεμος Id.　II. Μηδικὴ πόα *medick*, a kind of clover, Ar.
Μηδίς (sub. γυνή), ή, *a Median woman*, Hdt.
Μηδισμός, ὁ, *a leaning towards the Medes, being in their interest, Medism*, Hdt., Thuc.
Μηδο-κτόνος, ον, (κτείνω) *Mede-slaying*, Anth.
μήδομαι: Ep. 3 sing. impf.: f. μήσομαι, Ep. 2 sing. μήσεαι: 3 sing. aor. 1 ἐμήσατο, Ep. μήσατο: Dep.: (μῆδος):—*to be minded, to intend, resolve*, Il.; ἅσσ᾽ ἂν μηδοίμην *what counsels I should take*, Od.　2. c. acc. rei, *to plan, plot, contrive*, κακὰ

μηδεσθαί τινι to scheme misery for him, Il.; λήσατό μοι ὄλεθρον Od. :—also c. acc. pers. et rei, κακὰ μήσατ' Ἀχαιούς he wrought them mischief, Hom.; so ἐπ' ἀνδρὶ τοῦτ' ἐμήσατο στύγος Aesch. 3. to invent, τέχνας Id.; τί δὲ μήσωμαι; what shall I attempt? Id.

μηδ-οπότερος, α, ον, = μηδέτερος, Anth.

μῆδος (A), εος, τό, (μέδω) only in pl. μήδεα, counsels, plans, arts, schemes, Hom.; μάχης μ. plans of fight, Il.

ΜΗ͂ΔΟΣ (B), εος, τό, only in pl. μήδεα, the genitals, Od.

Μῆδος, ὁ, a Mede, Median, Hdt., etc.

μηδοσύνη, ἡ, (μῆδος) counsel, prudence, Anth.

Μηδο-φόνος, ον, (*φένω) = Μηδοκτόνος, Anth.

μηθ-είς, neut. μηθ-έν, later form of μηδ-είς, μηδ-έν.

μηκάομαι, Dep. with aor. 2 act. part. μᾰκών, pf. μεμηκώς, shortd. fem. μεμᾰκυῖα; and an impf. (formed from pf.) ἐμέμηκον :—to bleat, of sheep, Hom.; of a hunted fawn or hare, to scream, shriek, Il.; of a wounded horse, Ib. (Formed from the sound.) Hence

μηκάς, άδος, ἡ, the bleating one, of she-goats, Hom.: —later, μ. ἄρνες, = βληχάδες, Eur.; and

μηκασμός, ὁ, a bleating, Lat. balatus, Plut.

μηκεδᾰνός, ή, όν, (μῆκος) long, Anth.

μηκ-έτι, Adv. (formed from μή, ἔτι, with κ inserted) no more, no longer, no further, Hom., etc.

μήκιστος, η, ον, Dor. and Trag. μάκιστος [ᾰ], irr. Sup. of μακρός (formed from μῆκος, as αἴσχιστος from αἴσχος), tallest, Hom. 2. greatest, Soph., Eur. 3. longest, in point of Time, Xen. :—neut. μήκιστον as Adv., in the highest degree, h. Hom.; also, τί νύ μοι μήκιστα γένηται; what is to become of me in the long run, at last? Od. 4. farthest, ὅτι δυνᾷ μάκιστον as far as possible, Soph.; μήκιστον ἀπελαύνειν to drive as far off as possible, Xen.

μῆκος, Dor. μᾶκος, εος, τό, (μακρός) length, Od.; ἐν μήκει καὶ πλάτει καὶ βάθει Plat.; μ. ὁδοῦ Hdt.; πλοῦ Thuc. : —in pl. τὰ μέγαλα μ. great distances, Plat. b. of persons, height, tallness, stature, Od. 2. of Time, Aesch., etc. :—also μ. λόγου, μ. τῶν λόγων a long speech, Id.; ἐν μήκει λόγων Thuc. II. τὸ μῆκος or μῆκος absol. as Adv. in length, Hdt., etc.:— at length, in full, οὐ μῆκος ἀλλὰ σύντομα Soph. 2. μῆκος in height, Od.

μή-κοτε, Adv., Ion. for μή-ποτε.

μηκύνω [ῡ], f. ῠνῶ, Ion. ῠνέω: Dor. μᾱκ-: (μῆκος) :—to lengthen, prolong, extend, Xen. :—of Time, μ. χρόνον, βίον Eur. 2. μ. λόγον, λόγους to spin out a speech, speak at length, Hdt., Soph., etc. :—also without λόγον, to be lengthy or tedious, Hdt.: c. acc., μ. τὰ περὶ τῆς πόλεως to talk at length about them, Thuc. 3. μ. βοήν to raise a loud cry, Soph. 4. Med., ἐμακύναντο κολοσσόν reared a tall statue, Anth.

ΜΗ'ΚΩΝ, Dor. μάκων [ᾱ], ωνος, ἡ, the poppy, Il., etc.

μηλέα, ἡ, (μῆλον) an apple-tree, Lat. malus, Od.

μήλειος, ον, also α, ον, (μῆλον A) of a sheep, κρέα Hdt.; μ. φόνος slaughter of sheep, Eur.

μήλη, ἡ, a probe, etc., Lat. specillum, Hipp., etc.

Μηλιάδες, αἱ, nymphs of Malis in Trachis, Soph.

Μηλιεύς, an inhabitant of Malis (Μῆλις), a Malian, pl. Μηλιέες, Hdt.; in old Att. Μηλιῆς, Soph., Thuc. II. as Adj., Μηλιεὺς κόλπος the Sinus Maliacus, Hdt.;—Μηλιακός, ή, όν, Thuc. :—fem. Μηλὶς λίμνη = Μηλιεὺς κόλπος, Soph.

Μήλιος, α, ον, from the island of Melos, Melian, Theogn., Thuc.; λιμὸς Μ., proverb. of famine, because of the sufferings during the siege of Melos, Ar.

μηλίς, ίδος, ἡ, (μῆλον B) = μηλέα, Dor. μᾱλίς, Theocr.

Μηλίς, ίδος, ἡ, Ion. for Μᾱλίς, with or without γῆ, Malis in Trachis, Hdt.; cf. Μηλιεύς.

μηλο-βοτήρ, ῆρος, ὁ, a shepherd, Il.

μηλο-βότης, ου, ὁ, Dor. -τας, = foreg., Pind., Eur.

μηλό-βοτος, ον, grazed by sheep, epith. of pastoral districts, Pind.

μηλο-δόκος, ον, (δέχομαι) sheep-receiving, in sacrifice, of Apollo, Pind.

μηλο-θύτης [ῠ], ου, ὁ, (θύω A) one who sacrifices sheep, a priest, Eur.; βωμὸς μ. a sacrificial altar, Id.

μηλολόνθη, ἡ, the cockchafer, Ar. (Deriv. unknown.)

ΜΗ'ΛΟΝ (A), ου, τό, a sheep or goat, Od.; in pl. sheep and goats, small cattle, Lat. pecudes, opp. to βόες, Il.; with an Adj. added to distinguish the gender, ἄρσενα μ. rams, wethers, Od.

ΜΗ'ΛΟΝ (B), Dor. μᾶλον, ου, τό, Lat. mālum, an apple or (generally) any tree-fruit, Hom., Hes., Hdt., Att. II. pl., metaph. of a girl's breasts, Theocr.:—also, the cheeks, Lat. malae, Anth., Luc.; cf. μηλοπάρηος :—but in Theocr., τὰ σὰ δάκρυα μᾶλα ῥέοντι thy tears run sweet or round as apples.

μηλο-νόμης, ου, ὁ, Dor. -μας, (νέμω) a shepherd or goatherd, Eur.; —so μηλο-νομεύς, έως, ὁ, Anth.

μηλο-νόμος, ον, (νέμω) tending sheep or goats, Eur.

μηλο-πάρηος, ον, Dor. -ρος, (παρειά) apple-cheeked, Theocr.

μηλο-σκόπος κορυφή, the top of a hill from which sheep or goats (μῆλα) are watched, h. Hom.

μηλό-σπορος, ον, (σπείρω) set with fruit-trees, Eur.

μηλο-σσόος, ον, sheep-protecting, Anth.

μηλο-σφᾰγέω, f. ήσω, (σφάζω) to slay sheep, ἱερὰ μ. to offer sheep in sacrifice, Soph.; absol., Ar.

μηλο-τρόφος, ον, sheep-feeding, Orac. ap. Hdt., Aesch.

μηλ-οῦχος, ὁ, (μῆλον B. II, ἔχω) a girdle that confines the breasts, Anth.

μηλο-φόνος, ον, (*φένω) sheep-slaying, Aesch.

μηλοφορέω, to carry apples, Theocr. From

μηλο-φόρος, ον, (φέρω) bearing apples, Eur.

μηλο-φύλαξ [ῠ], ᾰκος, ὁ and ἡ, a sheep-watcher, Anth.

μηλ-ωψ, οπος, ὁ, ἡ, (μῆλον B, ὤψ) looking like an apple, yellow, ripe, Od. :—with the gen. cf. αἴθων, -ονος.

μήν, in Dor. and Ep. μάν, a Particle used to strengthen asseverations, Lat. vero, verily, truly, Hom., etc. II. after other Particles, 1. ἦ μήν, like ἦ μέν (μήν being only a stronger form), now verily, full surely, ἦ μὴν καὶ πόνος ἐστίν Il. :—so in Att., to introduce an oath, c. inf., ὄμνυσι δ' ἦ μὴν λαπάξειν Aesch., etc. 2. καὶ μήν, to introduce something new or special, καὶ μὴν Τάνταλον εἰσεῖδον Od.: in dramatic Poets to mark the entrance of a person on the stage, and see . . , here comes . . ; so of new facts or arguments, Trag., Dem. 3. ἀλλὰ μήν, yet truly, Lat. verum enimvero, Aesch., Ar. 4. οὐ μήν, of a truth not, Il., Att. III. after interrogatives, it mostly takes somewhat of an objective force, τί μήν; quid vero? what then? i.e. of course, naturally so, Aesch., etc.; τί μὴν οὔ; well, why not? Eur.; πῶς μήν; well, but how . . ? Xen. IV. much like μέντοι, Lat. tamen, οὐ μὴν ἄτιμοι τεθνήξομεν Aesch.

ΜΗ'Ν, ὁ, gen. μηνός, dat. pl. μησί: Ion. or Aeol. **μείς**, q. v.: — *a month*, Hom., etc. In early times the month was divided into two parts, *the beginning* and *the waning* (μὴν ἱστάμενος and μὴν φθίνων), Od.: the Attic division was into three decads, μὴν ἱστάμενος (also ἀρχόμενος or εἰσιών), μεσῶν, and φθίνων (or ἀπιών): the last division was reckoned backwards, μηνὸς τετάρτῃ φθίνοντος on the fourth day *from the end of the month*, Thuc.; Μαιμακτηριῶνος δεκάτῃ ἀπιόντος, i. e. on the 21st, ap. Dem.; but sometimes forwards, as, τῇ τρίτῃ ἐπ' εἰκάδι the three-and-twentieth, etc.: — ἐκείνου τοῦ μηνός in the course of that month, Xen.: — κατὰ μῆνα *monthly*, Ar.; so τοῦ μηνὸς ἑκάτου Id.; or τοῦ μηνός alone, *by the month*, Id. 2. = μηνίσκος, Id.

μηνάς, άδος, ἡ, = μήνη, *the moon*, Eur.

μήνατο, Ep. for ἐμήνατο, 3 sing. aor. 1 of μαίνομαι.

μήνη, ἡ, (μήν) *the moon*, Il., Aesch.

μηνιαῖος, α, ον, *monthly*, Strab.

μηνιθμός, οῦ, ὁ, (μηνίω) *wrath*, Il.

μήνῑμα, ατος, τό, (μηνίω) *a cause of wrath*, μή τοί τι θεῶν μήνιμα γένωμαι lest I be *the cause of bringing wrath* upon thee, Hom. 2. *guilt, blood-guiltiness*, Plat.

μῆνις, Dor. **μᾶνις**, ιος, ἡ, (*μάω) *wrath, anger*, of the gods, Hom., Hdt., Att.

μηνίσκος, ὁ, Dim. of μήνη, *a crescent*, Lat. *lunula: a covering to protect the head of statues* (like the *nimbus* or *glory* of Christian Saints), Ar. Hence

μηνίω [ῑ], Dor. **μᾱνίω**: aor. 1 ἐμήνῑσα: — *to be wroth with* another, vent *one's wrath on* him, c. dat. pers., Il.; c. gen. rei, ἱρῶν μηνίσας *wrathful because of sacred rites*, Ib.; πατρὶ μηνίσας φόνου Soph.; absol. *to be wrathful*, Hom.: so in Med., Aesch.

μηνο-ειδής, ές, (μήνη, εἶδος) *crescent-shaped*, Lat. *lunatus*, Hdt., Thuc., etc.; μηνοειδὲς ποιήσαντες τῶν νεῶν having formed them in a *crescent*, Hdt.: — of the sun and moon *when partially eclipsed*, Thuc., Xen.

μήνῡμα, ατος, τό, (μηνύω) *an information*, Thuc.

μηνυτήρ, ῆρος, (μηνύω) ὁ, *an informer, guide*, Aesch.

μηνυτής, οῦ, Dor. **μᾱνῠτάς**, ᾶ, ὁ, (μηνύω) *bringing to light*, μ. χρόνος Eur. II. Subst. *an informer*, Lat. *delator*, Thuc.; κατά τινος against a person, Dem.

μήνῡτρον, τό, *the price of information, reward*, h. Hom.: — in Att. only pl. μήνυτρα, Thuc., etc.; and

μηνύτωρ [ῡ], ορος, ὁ, = μηνυτήρ, Anth. From

ΜΗΝΥ'Ω, Dor. **μᾱνύω**: f. ύσω [ῡ]: aor. 1 ἐμήνῡσα: pf. μεμήνῡκα: — Pass., 3 sing. pf. μεμήνῡται: aor. 1 ἐμηνύθην: — *to disclose what is secret, reveal, betray*, generally, *to make known, declare, indicate*, h. Hom., Hdt., Att.: — with acc. and part., μ. τινὰ ἔχοντα *to shew* that he has, Hdt.; the part. is sometimes omitted, τόδ' ἔργον σε μηνύει κακόν (sc. ὄντα) Eur. II. at Athens *to inform, lay public information against* another, κατά τινος Oratt.: — impers. in Pass., μηνύεται *information is laid*, μεμήνυται it has been laid, Thuc. 2. in Pass. also of persons, *to be informed against, to be denounced*, Xen.: — also of things, μηνυθέντος τοῦ ἐπιβουλεύματος Thuc.

μὴ ὅπως, an elliptic phrase, μὴ [λέγε] ὅπως, followed by ἀλλ' οὐδέ, as μὴ ὅπως ὀρχεῖσθαι, ἀλλ' οὐδ' ὀρθοῦσθαι ἐδύνασθε *not only* could you *not* dance, but not even stand upright, Xen.

μὴ ὅτι, = μὴ ὅπως, foll. by ἀλλά, Lat. *ne dicam*, as, μὴ

ὅτι ἰδιώτην τινά, ἀλλὰ τὸν μέγαν βασιλέα *not to say* a private person, but the great king, Plat.; μὴ ὅτι θεός, ἀλλὰ καὶ ἄνθρωποι οὐ φιλοῦσιν Xen. 2. οὐδέ or καὶ οὐ followed by μὴ ὅτι, as οὐδὲ ἀναπνεῖν, μὴ ὅτι λέγειν τι δυνησόμεθα we shall not be able to breathe, *much less* to speak, Id.

μὴ οὐ, after Verbs expressing *fear* or *apprehension*, = Lat. *vereor ut*, δέδοικα μὴ οὐ γένηταί τι I fear *it will not* be; whereas δέδοικα μὴ γένηται mean, I fear it *will* be. Here, μή and οὐ each retain their proper force. II. with Infin., 1. after Verbs of *hindering, denying, avoiding, needing*, when μὴ οὐ resembles Lat. *quin* or *quominus*, οὐδὲν κωλύει μὴ οὐκ ἀληθὲς εἶναι τοῦτο nihil impedit quin hoc verum sit; or with the Art., οὐδὲν ἐλλείψω τὸ μὴ οὐ πυθέσθαι *nihil praetermittam quominus reperiam*, Soph. 2. after Verbs signifying *impossibility, impropriety, reluctance*, μὴ οὐ has a negative translation, δεινῶν ἐδόκεε εἶναι μὴ οὐ λαβεῖν Hdt.; αἰσχύνη ἦν μὴ οὐ συσπουδάζειν Xen. 3. μὴ οὐ with the Partic., only after a negat., expressed or implied, δυσάλγητος γὰρ ἂν εἴην μὴ οὐ κατοικτείρων I should be hard-hearted if I did *not* pity, Soph. 4. = εἰ μή, *except*, πόλεις χαλεπαὶ λαβεῖν, μὴ οὐ πολιορκίᾳ Dem.

μὴ πολλάκις, *lest perchance*, Lat. *ne forte*, Plat.

μή-ποτε or **μή ποτε**, I. as Adv. *never, on no account*, after ὡς, εἰ, etc., Aesch., etc.; — also with inf., in oaths, ὀμοῦμαι, μήποτε τῆς εὐνῆς ἐπιβήμεναι Il. 2. in prohibition or strong denial, with aor. subj., μήποτε καὶ σὺ ὀλέσσῃς Od. 3. *perhaps*, like *nescio an*, Arist. II. as Conj. *that at no time, lest ever*, Lat. *ne quando*, Od.

μή που, *lest anywhere, that nowhere*, Lat. *necubi*, Od.: *lest perchance*, Hom., etc.

μή-πω or **μή πω**, I. as Adv. *not yet*, Lat. *nondum*, Od., Att. II. as Conj. *that not yet, lest yet*, Od., etc.

μὴ πώποτε, of past time, *never yet*, Soph.

μή-πως or **μή πως**, *lest in any way, lest any how, lest perchance*, Hom. II. in case of doubt, or in indirect questions, *whether or no*, Il.

μῆρα, τά, = μηρία, Il., Ar.

μηρῐά, τά, (μηρός) *slices cut from the thighs*, Hom. It was the custom to cut out the μηρία (ἐκ μηρία τάμνον), wrap them in two folds of fat (κνίσῃ ἐκάλυψαν, δίπτυχα ποιήσαντες), and burn them upon the altar. II. = μηροί, *the thighs*, Bion.

μηριαῖος, α, ον, (μηρός) *of* or *belonging to the thigh*, Lat. *femoralis*, αἱ μ. the *thighs*, Xen.

μήρινθος, ἡ, gen. ον, (μηρύομαι) *a cord, line, string*, Il.: *a fishing-line*, Theocr.

ΜΗΡΟ'Σ, οῦ, ὁ, *the thigh*, Lat. *femur*, in Hom. 2. in pl. = μηρία, Hom., Soph. 3. in pl. also, generally, *the leg-bones*, Hdt.

μηρο-τρᾰφής, ές, (τρέφω) *thigh-bred*, of Bacchus, Anth.

μηρο-τῠπής, ές, (τύπτω) *striking the thigh*, Anth.

μηρύομαι, Dor. **μᾱρ**—: aor. 1 ἐμηρῡσάμην. Dep.: — *to draw up, furl* sails, Od.: *to draw up* cables, etc., Anth.: — κρόκα ἐν στήμονι μηρύσασθαι *to weave* the woof into the warp, Hes. II. Pass., κισσὸς μαρύεται περὶ χείλη ivy *winds* round the edge, Theocr.

μήσαο, **μήσατο**, 2 and 3 sing. Ep. aor. 1 of μήδομαι.

μήσεαι, Ep. 2 sing. fut. of μήδομαι.

μήστωρ, ωρος, ὁ, (μήδομαι) an adviser, counsellor, Hom.; Ἀθηναῖοι μήστωρες ἀϋτῆς authors of the battle-din, Il.; κρατερὸν μήστωρα φόβοιο, of Diomede, Ib.

μήτε, and not, mostly doubled, μήτε . . μήτε . . , neither . . nor, Hom., etc.

ΜΗ'ΤΗΡ, Dor. μάτηρ, ἡ, voc. μῆτερ: but it follows πατήρ in the accent of the other cases, — gen. μητέρος μητρός, dat. μητέρι μητρί, etc. :—a mother, Hom., etc.; of animals, a dam, Id.; ἀπό or ἐκ μητρός from one's mother's womb, Pind., Aesch. 2. also of lands, μήτηρ μήλων, θηρῶν mother of flocks, of game, Il.; of Earth, γῆ πάντων μ. Hes.; γῆ μήτηρ Aesch.; ὦ γαῖα μῆτερ Eur.: — also ἡ Μάτηρ alone for Δημήτηρ, Hdt. 3. of one's native land, μᾶτερ ἐμά, Θήβα Pind., etc. 4. poët. as the source of events, μ. ἀέθλων of Olympia, Id.; night is the mother of day, Aesch.; the grape of wine, Id.

μήτῐ, neut. of μῆτις, q. v.

μήτῑ, contr. for μήτιϊ, dat. of μῆτις.

μητιάω, Ep. 3 pl. μητιόωσι and part. μητιόων, όωσα: also as Dep., 2 pl. μητιάασθε, 3 pl. impf. μητιόωντο, inf. μητιάασθαι: (μῆτις) :—to meditate, deliberate, de-bate, Il.: Med., μητιάασθε consider among you, Ib. 2. c. acc. rei, =μητίομαι, Hom.

μητίετα, ὁ, (μῆτις) Ep. for μητιέτης, a counsellor, as epith. of Ζεύς, all-wise! Hom.

μητιόεις, εσσα, εν, (μῆτις) wise in counsel, all-wise, h. Hom., Hes. 2. φάρμακα μητιόεντα wise, i. e. well-chosen, helpful, remedies, Od.

μητίομαι, f. ἴσομαι [ῐ] : aor. 1 ἐμητῑσάμην : Dep. :—to devise, contrive, plan, Hom.: c. dupl. acc. to plan evil against one, Od. From

μητιόων, Ep. part. of μητιάω: μητιόωσι, Ep. 3 pl.

μῆτις, ἡ, gen. ιος, Att. ιδος; dat. μήτιδι, Ep. μήτῑ for μήτιι, pl. μητίεσσι: acc. μῆτιν: (*μάω):—the faculty of advising, wisdom, counsel, cunning, craft, Hom., Aesch.; μῆτιν ἀλώπηξ a fox for craft, Pind. :—of a poet's skill or craft, Id. II. advice, counsel, a plan, undertaking, Hom. ὑφαίνειν Hom.

μή-τῐς or μή τις, ὁ, ἡ, neut. μή-τῐ, gen. μή-τῐνος : (τίς) :—lest any one, lest anything; that no one, that nothing, Lat. ne quis, ne quid, constructed like the Adv. μή, Hom., etc. :—μήτι or μή τι, Adv., used imperatively, Il. ;—with Opt. to express a wish, ὄλοιτο μή τι πάντες Soph. 2. after Verbs of fear or doubt, Hom., etc. 3. in questions, μή τί σοι δοκῶ ταρβεῖν; do I seem to thee to fear? (i. e. I do not), Aesch. 4. μή τί γε, let alone, much less, Lat. nedum, ne dicam, Dem.

μή-τοι or μή τοι, stronger form of μή, with Imper. and Subj., μή τοι δοκεῖτε Aesch., etc. : in an oath, with Inf., Id. 2. after Verbs implying negation, Soph.

μήτρα, Ion. -τρη, ἡ, (μήτηρ) Lat. matrix, the womb, Hdt., Plat., etc.

μητρ-ἀγύρτης, ου, ὁ,. a begging priest of Cybelé, the Mother of the gods :—Iphicrates gave this name to Callias, who was really her Δαδοῦχος, Arist.

μητρ-άδελφος, ὁ and ἡ, a mother's brother or sister, uncle or aunt :—in Pind., ματραδελφεός.

μητρ-ᾰλοίας, ου, ὁ, (ἀλοιάω) striking one's mother, a matricide, Aesch., Plat., etc.

μήτρη, ἡ, Ion. for μήτρα.

μητριάς, άδος, ἡ, fem. of μήτριος, Anth.

μητρικός, ή, όν, of a mother, Lat. maternus, Arist.

μητρίς (sc. γῆ) one's mother country (cf. πατρίς), Cretan word in Plat.

μητρό-δοκος, Dor. ματρ-, ον, (δέχομαι) received by the mother, Pind.

μητρο-ήθης, ες, (ἦθος) with a mother's mind, Anth.

μητρόθεν, Dor. ματρ-, Adv. (μήτηρ) from the mother, by the mother's side, Hdt., Pind. 2. from one's mother, from one's mother's hand, Aesch., Ar. 3. from one's mother's womb, Aesch.

μητρο-κᾰσιγνήτη, ἡ, a sister by the same mother, Lat. soror uterina, Aesch.

μητροκτονέω, to kill one's mother, Aesch., Eur. From

μητρο-κτόνος, ον, (κτείνω) killing one's mother, ma-tricidal, Aesch.; μ. μίασμα the stain of a mother's murder, Id.; so, μ. κηλίς, αἷμα Eur. 2. as Subst. a matricide, Aesch., Eur.

μητρο-μήτωρ, Dor. ματρομάτωρ, ορος, ἡ, one's mother's mother, Pind.

μητρο-πάτωρ [ᾰ], ορος, ὁ, one's mother's father, Il., Hdt.

μητρό-πολις, Dor. ματρ-, εως, ἡ, the mother-state, in relation to colonies, as of Athens to the Ionians, Hdt., Thuc.; of Doris to the Peloponn. Dorians, Hdt., Thuc. II. one's mother-city, mother-country, home, Pind., Soph. III. a metropolis in our sense, capital city, Xen.

μητρο-πόλος, ον, (πολέω) tending mothers, epith. of Eileithyia, Pind.

μητρόρ-ριπτος, ον, rejected by one's mother, Anth.

μητρο-φθόρος, ον, (φθείρω) mother-murdering, Anth.

μητρο-φόνος, ον, (*φένω) murdering one's mother, ma-tricidal, Aesch. 2. as Subst. a matricide, Id.

μητρο-φόντης, ου, ὁ, = μητροφόνος, Eur.

μητρυιά, Dor. ματρ-, ᾶς, Ion. μητρυιή, ῆς, ἡ :—a step-mother, Il., etc.: the unkindness of step-mothers was proverbial (cf. Lat. injusta noverca); hence me-taph., μ. νεῶν, of a dangerous coast, Aesch.

μητρῷος, Dor. μάτρ-, α, ον, contr. for μητρώιος (which occurs in Od.) :—of a mother, a mother's, maternal, Od., Att.; μ. δέμας, periphr. for τὴν μητέρα, Aesch. : —τὰ μ. a mother's right, Hdt. II. Μητρῷον (sc. ἱερόν), τό, the temple of Cybelé at Athens, which was the depository of the state-archives, Dem., Aeschin.

μήτρως, Dor. μάτρ-, ὁ : gen. ωος and ω, acc. ωα and ων ; pl. always of the third decl., like πάτρως :—a ma-ternal uncle, Il., Hdt., etc. 2. any relation by the mother's side, Pind., Eur. 3. = μητροπάτωρ, Pind.

μηχᾰνάομαι, Ion. -έομαι: f. ήσομαι: aor. 1 ἐμηχανη-σάμην : pf. μεμηχάνημαι : Ep. forms, 2 pl. μηχανάασθε, 3 pl. pres. and impf. μηχανόωνται, -ωντο ; 3 sing. opt. μηχανόῳτο; inf. -άασθαι: Dep. (μηχανή) :—like Lat. machinari, to make by art, put together, construct, build, Il., Hdt., etc.; generally to prepare, make ready, Hdt., Aesch., etc. 2. to contrive, devise, by art or cunning, Hom., etc.; to also simply to cause, effect, Hdt., Att. :—absol. to form designs, Od. :—c. acc. et inf. to contrive to do or that a thing may be, Xen. II. Med. to procure for oneself, Soph., Xen.

B. the Act. μηχανάω is used by Hom. only in Ep. part., ἀτάσθαλα μηχανόωντας contriving dire effects,

Od., and by Soph. in inf. μηχανᾶν: but pf. μεμηχάνημαι is used in pass. sense by Hdt. and in Att.; but also in act. sense, Plat., Xen.

μηχᾰνή, Dor. **μᾱχᾰνά, ἡ, (μῆχος)** – Lat. *machina*: I. *an instrument, machine* for lifting weights and the like, Hdt.; μ. Ποσειδῶνος, of the trident, Aesch.; λαοπόροις μ., of Xerxes' bridge of boats, Id.   2. *an engine* of war, Thuc.   3. *a theatrical machine*, by which gods were made to appear in the air, Plat.: hence proverb. of any sudden appearance, ὥσπερ ἀπὸ μηχανῆς (cf. Lat. *deus ex machina*), Dem.   II. *any contrivance* for doing a thing, Hdt., etc.: in pl. μηχαναί, *shifts, devices, arts, wiles,* Hes., Att.; μηχαναῖς Διός *by the arts* of Zeus, Aesch.; proverb., μηχαναὶ Σισύφου Ar.:—Phrases, μηχανήν or μηχανὰς προσφέρειν Eur.; εὑρίσκειν Aesch., etc.:—c. gen., μ. κακῶν *a contrivance against* ills, Eur.; but, μ. σωτηρίας *a way of providing* safety, Aesch.   2. οὐδεμία μηχανή [ἐστι] ὅπως οὐ, c. fut., Hdt.; also, μὴ οὐ, c. inf., Id.   3. in adverb. phrases, ἐκ μηχανῆς τινος in some *way* or other, Id.; μηδεμιῇ μηχανῇ by no *means* whatsoever, Id.

μηχάνημα, ατος, τό, = μηχανή, *an engine*, used in sieges, Dem.   II. *a subtle contrivance, cunning work*, Trag.; of the robe in which Agamemnon was entangled, Aesch.

μηχάνητέον, verb. Adj. of μηχανάομαι, *one must contrive*, Plat.

μηχάνητικός, ή, όν, = μηχανικός, Xen.

μηχᾰνικός, ή, όν, *full of resources, inventive, ingenious, clever*, Xen.   2. c. gen. rei, *able to procure*, Id.   3. *of* or *for machines, mechanical*, Arist.:—ὁ μηχανικός *an engineer*, Plut.

μηχανιώτης, ου, ὁ, h. Hom.

μηχᾰνο-δίφης, ου, ὁ, (δίφάω) *inventing artifices*, Ar.

μηχᾰνόεις, εσσα, εν, (μηχανή) *ingenious*, Soph.

μηχᾰνο-ποιός, ὁ, (ποιέω) *an engineer, maker of war-engines*, Plat., Xen.: *a theatrical machinist*, Ar.

μηχᾰνορρᾰφέω, *to form crafty plans*, Aesch. From

μηχᾰνορ-ράφος, ον, (ῥάπτω) *craftily-dealing*, Soph.: c. gen., μ. κακῶν *crafty workers* of ill, Eur.

μηχᾰν-ουργός, όν, (*ἔργω) = μηχανοποιός, Anth.

μηχᾰνο-φόρος, ον, *conveying military machines*, Plut.

μῆχαρ, τό, = μῆχος, Aesch.

ΜΗ'ΧΟΣ, τό, *a means, expedient, remedy*, Il.; μῆχος κακοῦ *a remedy for* ill, Od., Hdt.; κακῶν Eur.

μίᾰ, ἡ, gen. μιᾶς, Ep. and Ion. μιῆς, dat. μιᾷ, μιῇ, acc. μίαν, fem. of εἷς, *one*.

ΜΙΑΙ'ΝΩ, f. μιᾰνῶ: aor. 1 ἐμίηνα; Dor. and Att. ἐμίᾱνα: pf. μεμίαγκα:—Med. aor. 1 ἐμιάνατο:—Pass., f. μιανθήσομαι: aor. 1 ἐμιάνθην, Ep. μιάνθην: pf. μεμίασμαι:—properly, *to stain, dye*, ἐλέφαντα φοίνικι μιαίνειν (cf. Virgil's *violaverit ostro si quis ebur*), Il.   2. *to stain, defile, sully*, esp. with blood, μιάνθην (Ep. 3 dual for μιανθήτην) αἵματι μηροί Ib.; αἵματι πεσεῖ μιανθείς Soph.; μ. τοὺς θεῶν βωμοὺς αἵματι Plat.; βορβόρῳ ὕδωρ μιαίνειν Aesch.   3. of moral stains, *to taint, defile*, Pind., Trag.; hence Soph. says, θεοὺς μιαίνειν οὔ τις ἀνθρώπων σθένει:—Pass. *to incur such defilement*, Aesch., etc.; μιαίνεσθαι τὴν ψυχήν Plat.; τῆς ἄλλης [γῆς] αὐτῷ μεμιασμένης Thuc.

μιαιφονέω, *to be* or *become blood-stained*, Eur.   2. c. acc. *to murder*, Isocr., Plat.

μιαιφονία, ἡ, *bloodguiltiness*, Dem., Diod.   II. *pollution from eating blood*, Plut.

μιαι-φόνος, ον, *blood-stained, bloody*, Il.: *defiled with blood, blood-guilty*, Trag.; c. gen., μ. τέκνων *stained with thy children's blood*, Eur.:—Comp. -ώτερος Hdt., Eur.; Sup. -ώτατος Id.

μιάνθην, Ep. for ἐμιάνθην, aor. 1 pass. of μιαίνω.   2. 3 dual for μιανθήτην.

μιᾰρία, ἡ, (μιαρός) *brutality*, Xen., Dem.

μιᾰρό-γλωσσος, ον, (γλῶσσα) *foul-tongued*, Anth.

μιᾰρός, ά, όν, (μιαίνω) *stained* with blood, Il.: *defiled with blood*, Eur.   2. generally, *defiled, polluted, unclean*, Hdt.: in moral sense, Soph.; as a term of foul reproach, *brutal, coarse, disgusting*, Ar.; μ. φωνή *a coarse, brutal* voice, Id.:—Adv. μιαρῶς, Id.

μίασμα, ατος, τό, (μιαίνω) *stain, defilement, the taint of guilt*, Lat. *piaculum*, Trag., etc.   II. of persons, *a defilement, pollution*, Aesch., Soph.

μιάστωρ, ορος, ὁ, (μιαίνω) *a wretch stained with crime, a guilty wretch, a pollution*, Lat. *homo piacularis*, Trag.   II. = ἀλάστωρ, *an avenger*, Ib.

μίγα [ῐ], Adv. *mixed with*, c. dat., Pind.

μῑγάζομαι, Ep. for μίγνυμαι, *to have intercourse*, Od.

μῑγάς, άδος, ὁ and **ἡ, (μίγα)** *mixed pell-mell*, Eur.

μίγδᾰ, Adv., = μίγα, *promiscuously, confusedly*, Od.; c. dat., μίγδα θεοῖς *among the gods*, Il.

μίγδην, Adv., = μίγδα, h. Hom.

μῖγμα, ατος, τό, (μίγνυμι) *a mixture*: μίγματα *mixtures, medicines*, N. T.

ΜΙ'ΓΝΥΜΙ, imper. μίγνυ: impf. ἐμίγνυν, poët. μίγνυον: —f. μίξω:—aor. 1 ἔμιξα, inf. μῖξαι:—Pass., 3 pl. impf. ἐμίγνυντο:—f. μεμίξομαι, and μιγήσομαι, also f. med. μίξομαι:—aor. 1 ἐμίχθην: aor. 2 ἐμίγην [ῐ], Ep. μίγην:—Ep. 3 sing. aor. pass. μίκτο or μῖκτο:—pf. μέμιγμαι: Ep. 3 sing. plqpf. μέμικτο:—there is also a pres. **ΜΙ'ΣΓΩ**, pass. μίσγομαι:—like Lat. *misceo*, *to mix, mix up, mingle*, properly of liquids, οἶνον καὶ ὕδωρ Hom.; μ. τί τινι *to mix* one thing *with* another, Id., etc.   II. generally, *to join, bring together*,   1. in hostile sense, μῖξαι χεῖράς τε μένος τε *to join* battle hand to hand, Il.; Ἄρη μίξουσιν Soph.   2. *to bring into connexion with, make acquainted with*, ἄνδρας μισγέμεναι κακότητι *to bring men to misery*, Od.; reversely, πότμον μῖξαί τινι *to bring death upon* him, Pind.

B. Pass. *to be mixed up with, mingled among*, προμάχοισιν ἐμίχθη Il.; ἐώλπει μίξεσθαι ξενίῃ hoped *to be bound by hospitable ties*, Od.:—also, *to mingle with, hold intercourse with, live with*, Ib., Aesch.: absol. in pl., of several persons, *to hold intercourse*, Od.   2. *to be brought into contact with*, κάρη κονίησιν ἐμίχθη his *head was rolled* in the dust, Hom.; ἐν κονίῃσι μιγῆναι Il.; κλισίηισι μιγῆναι *to reach, get at* them, Ib.; μίσγεσθαι ἐς Ἀχαιοὺς *to go to join* them, Ib.; μίσγεσθαι ὑπὲρ ποταμοῖο *to cross the river*, Ib.; μίσγεσθαι φύλλοις, στεφάνοις *to come to, i.e. win*, the crown of victory, Pind.   3. in hostile sense, *to mix in fight*, Il.   4. *to have intercourse with, to be united to*, of men and women, Hom.; φιλότητι and ἐν φιλότητι μιγῆναι Id.; εὐνῇ ἔμικτο Od.

Μίδας [ῐ], gen. ου or α, Ion. **Μίδης**, εω, ὁ, *Midas, a king of Phrygia proverbial for his wealth*, Tyrtae., Plat.

μιήνῃ, 3 sing. aor. 1 subj. of μιαίνω.

Μίθρας, ου, ὁ, *Mithras, the Persian Sun-god*, Xen.

μικκός, ά, όν, Dor. for μικρός, Ar., Theocr.

μικκύλος [ῠ], Dim. of μικρός, Mosch.

μῑκρ-ᾰδῐκητής, οῦ, ὁ, *doing petty wrongs*, Arist.

μῖκρ-αίτιος, ον, *complaining of trifles*, Luc.

μῖκρ-αῦλαξ, ᾰκος, ὁ, ἡ, *with small furrows : χῶρος μ. a little field*, Anth.

μῑκρ-έμπορος, ὁ, *a pedlar, huckster*, Babr.

μῑκρο-κίνδῡνος, ον, *exposing oneself to danger for trifles*, Arist.

μῑκρολογέομαι, f. ήσομαι, Dep. *to examine minutely, treat* or *tell with painful minuteness*, Xen. **2.** *to deal meanly* or *shabbily*, Luc. ; and

μῑκρολογία or σμικρ-, ἡ, *the character of a μικρολόγος, frivolity : pettiness, meanness*, Plat., etc. From

μῑκρο-λόγος or σμικρο-, ον, *reckoning trifles ;* and so, **1.** *caring about petty expenses, penurious*, Dem. **2.** *cavilling about trifles, captious*, Plat.

μῑκρο-πολίτης [ῑ], ου, ὁ, *a citizen of a petty town*, German *Kleinstädter*, Ar., Xen.

μῑκρο-πόνηρος, ον, *wicked in small things*, Arist.

μῑκροπρέπεια, ἡ, *the character of a μικροπρεπής, meanness, shabbiness*, Arist.

μῑκρο-πρεπής, ές, (πρέπω) *petty in one's notions, mean, shabby*, Arist.

ΜΙΚΡΟΣ and σμικρός, ά, όν, Dor. **μικκός** (q. v.), *small, little*, in point of Size, Hom., etc. ; also in point of Quantity, Hes., Ar., etc. **2.** in Amount or Importance, *little, petty, trivial, slight*, Theogn., Soph., etc. ; σμ. τίθησί με makes me *of small account*, Soph. ; οὐ σμικρὸν φρονεῖ Id. **II.** of Time, *little, short*, Pind., Ar., etc. ; ἐν σμικρῷ (sc. χρόνῳ) *shortly*, Xen. **III.** Adverbial usages. **1.** regul. Adv., σμικρῶς, *but little*, Sup. σμικρότατα, Id. **2.** σμικροῦ or μικροῦ *within a little, almost*, Id., Dem. ; in full, μικροῦ δεῖ or δεῖν, v. δεῖ II :—but μικροῦ πρίασθαι to buy *for a little, cheap*, Xen. **3.** μικρῷ *by a little*, with the Comp., Plat. **4.** μικρόν and μικρά, *a little*, Xen., Plat. **5.** with Preps., **a.** ἐπὶ σμικρόν *but a little*, Soph. **b.** κατὰ μικρόν *into small pieces*, Xen. ; so, κατὰ μικρὰ γενόμενοι Id. :— also *little by little*, κατὰ μικρὸν ἀεί Ar. **c.** παρὰ μικρόν *within a little*, παρὰ μ. ἐλθεῖν, c. inf., to be *within an ace of doing*, Eur. **d.** μετὰ μικρόν *a little after*, N. T. **IV.** besides the regul. Comp. and Sup. μικρότερος, -ότατος, there are the irreg. ἐλάσσων, ἐλάχιστος, from ἐλαχύς, and μείων or μειότερος, μειότατος. Hence

μῑκρότης or σμικρ-, ητος, ἡ, *smallness : littleness, meanness, pettiness*, Arist.

μῑκροφῐλοτῑμία, ἡ, *petty ambition*, Theophr. From

μῑκρο-φῐλότῑμος, ον, *seeking petty distinctions*, Theophr.

μῑκρό-χωρος, ον, (χώρα) *with little land* or *soil*, Strab.

μῑκροψῡχία, ἡ, *littleness of soul, meanness of spirit*, Dem., Arist. From

μῑκρο-ψῡχος, ον, (ψυχή) *little of soul, mean-spirited*, Dem., Arist.

μίκτο or μῖκτο, 3 sing. Ep. aor. 2 pass. of μίγνυμι.

μικτός, ή, όν, (μίγνυμι) *mixed, blended, compound*, Plat., etc.

μῖλαξ, ᾰκος, ἡ, Att. for σμῖλαξ.

Μῑλήσιος, α, ον, *Milesian*, Μιλήσιοι, οἱ, *the Milesians*, Hdt. ; Μιλησίη (sc. χώρα), ἡ, Id.

Μίλητος [ῑ], ἡ, *Miletus, a Greek city in Caria*, Il.

μιλιάριον, τό, = Lat. *milliarium, a mile-stone*. **II.** *a copper vessel*, pointed at the top and furnished with winding tubes, to boil water in, Anth. [where μῑλῐάριον].

μῑλιασμός, ὁ, *a marking by milestones*, Strab. From

μίλιον, τό, *a Roman mile, milliarium*, = 1000 paces, = 8 stades, = 1680 yards, i. e. 80 yards less than our mile, Polyb., etc.

μιλτεῖον, τό, *a vessel for keeping μίλτος in*, Anth.

μίλτειος, α, ον, (μίλτος) *red, μ. στάγμα* the *red mark* made by the carpenter's line, Anth.

μιλτ-ηλῐφής, ές, (ἀλ-ήλῐφα, pf. of ἀλείφω) *painted with μίλτος, painted red*, of ships, Hdt.

μιλτο-πάρῃος, ον, (πᾰρειά) *red-cheeked*, of ships which had their bows painted red, Hom.

ΜΙΛΤΟΣ, ή, *red chalk, ruddle*, Lat. *rubrīca*, Hdt.

μιλτο-φῠρής, ές, (φύρω) *daubed with red*, Anth.

μιλτόω, f. ώσω, (μίλτος) *to paint red* :—Pass. *to paint oneself red* or *be painted red*, Hdt. ; σχοινίον μεμιλτωμένον the rope *covered with red chalk* with which they swept loiterers out of the Agora to the Pnyx, Ar.

μίμαρκυς [ῑ], ἡ, *hare-soup* or *jugged hare*, with the blood of the animal in it, Ar. (A foreign word.)

μιμέομαι, f. ήσομαι : aor. 1 ἐμιμησάμην : pf. μεμίμημαι : (μῖμος) : Dep. :—*to mimic, imitate, represent, portray*, h. Hom., Aesch., etc. ; μ. τινά τι one *in a thing*, Hdt. ; τινα κατά τι Id. ; pf. part. in act. sense, στύλοισι φοίνικας μεμιμημένοισι pillars *made to represent* palms, Id. ; but also in pass. *made exactly like, portrayed*, Id., Plat. **II.** of the fine arts, *to represent, express by means of imitation*, of an actor, Ar., Plat. ; of painting and music, Plat. ; of sculpture and poetry, Arist. Hence

μῑμηλός, ή, όν, *imitative*, c. gen., Luc., Anth. **II.** pass. *imitated, copied*, Plut. ; and

μίμημα [ῑ], ατος, τό, *anything imitated, a counterfeit, copy*, Eur., Plat. ; and

μίμησις [ῑ], ἡ, *imitation*, Thuc., Plat., etc. ; κατὰ σὴν μ. *to imitate you*, Ar. **II.** *representation by means of art*, Plat. : *a representation, portrait*, Hdt.

μῑμητέος, α, ον, verb. Adj. of μιμέομαι, *to be imitated*, Xen. **II.** μιμητέον, *one must imitate*, Eur., Xen.

μῑμητής, οῦ, ὁ, (μιμέομαι) *an imitator, copyist*, Plat., etc. **II.** *one who represents* characters, Arist. **2.** *a mere actor, an impostor* (cf. ὑποκριτής), Plat.

μῑμητικός, ή, όν, (μιμέομαι) *imitating, imitative*, of the fine arts, Plat., etc. :—ἡ -κή (with or without τέχνη) *the power of imitating*, Id.

μῑμητός, ή, όν, (μιμέομαι) *to be imitated* or *copied*, Xen.

μιμνάζω, Ep. form of μίμνω, *to wait, stay*, Il. **II.** *to await, expect*, c. acc., h. Hom.

μιμνήσκω (tenses formed from ΜΝΑΩ) : f. μνήσω : aor. 1 ἔμνησα :—Causal of μνάομαι, *to remind, put one in mind*, Od. ; τινός *of a thing*, Hom., etc. **II.** *to recall to memory, make famous*, Pind.

B. Med. and Pass. **μιμνήσκομαι**, Ep. imper.

-ήσκεο, impf. μιμνήσκοντο: f. μνήσομαι, μνησθήσομαι and μεμνήσομαι:—aor. 1 ἐμνησάμην and ἐμνήσθην:—pf. μέμνημαι (used in pres. sense like Lat. *memini*), Ep. 2 sing. μέμνηαι or μέμνῃ, Ion. 3 pl. ἐμεμνέατο; imper. μέμνησο, Ion. μέμνεο; subj. μέμνωμαι, Ion. 1 pl. -ἐώμεθα; opt. μεμνήμην, -ῆτο, also 2 and 3 sing. μεμνῷο, -ῷτο; Ep. 3 sing. μεμνέῳτο: plqpf. ἐμεμνήμην, Ion. 3 pl. ἐμεμνέατο:—*to remind oneself of a thing, call to mind, remember,* c. acc., Hom., etc.:—c. gen., ἀλκῆς μνήσασθαι *to bethink one of one's strength,* Hom., etc.; also, περὶ πομπῆς μνησόμεθα Od. 2. c. inf. *to remember* or *be minded* to do a thing, Il., Ar., etc. 3. c. part., μέμνημαι κλύων *I remember* hearing, Aesch.; μ. ἐλθών *I remember having come,* i. e. *to have come,* Eur. 4. absol. μεμνήσομαι *I will bear in mind, not forget,* Hom.; pf. part., ὧδέ τις μεμνημένος μαχέσθω *let him fight with good heed, let him remember* to fight, Il. II. *to remember* a thing *aloud,* i. e. *to mention, make mention of,* c. gen., Hom.; περί τινος Hdt., etc.; ὑπέρ τινος Dem.

μίμνω, formed by redupl. from μένω (i. e. μι-μένω, cf. γί-γνομαι, πί-πτω), and used for μένω when the first syll. was to be long; μιμνόντεσσι, Ep. dat. pl. part. for μίμνουσι:—*to stay, stand fast,* in battle, Il. 2. *to stay, tarry,* Ib. 3. of things, *to remain,* Od.: also *to be left* for one, Aesch. II. c. acc. *to await, wait for,* Il., etc.:—impers., μίμνει παθεῖν τὸν ἔρξαντα *it awaits* the doer to suffer, Aesch.

μιμολογέομαι, Pass. *to be recited like mimes,* Strab.

μῑμο-λόγος, ον, *composing* or *reciting μῖμοι,* Anth.

ΜΙ͂ΜΟΣ, ου, ὁ, *an imitator, mimic: an actor, mime,* Dem., Plut. II. *a mime,* a kind of prose drama, such as Sophron wrote, Arist.

μιμ-ῳδός, ὁ, *a singer of μῖμοι,* Plut.

μίν [ῐ], Ion. acc. sing. of the pron. of the 3rd pers. (v. ἷ) through all genders, for αὐτόν, αὐτήν, αὐτό: always enclitic, Hom., Hdt.; Dor. and Att. νιν:—Hom. joins μίν αὐτόν *himself,* as a stronger form; but αὐτόν μιν is reflexive, *oneself,* for ἑαυτόν, Od. II. rarely as 3 pers. pl. for αὐτούς, αὐτάς, αὐτά.

μίνθος, ὁ, *human ordure.* Hence

μινθόω, f. ώσω, *to besmear with dung, befoul,* Ar.

Μινύαι, οἱ, *the Minyans,* a race of nobles in Orchomenos, Hdt., etc.:—Adj. **Μινύειος,** α, ον, *Minyan,* Il.; Ep. also **Μινυήϊος,** Hom.

ΜΙΝΥΘΩ [ῠ], only used in pres. and Ion. impf. μινύθεσκον:—*to make smaller* or *less, lessen, curtail,* Il., Hes. 2. *to diminish in number,* Od. II. intr. *to become smaller* or *less, decrease, decay, come to naught, perish,* Hom., Hes. Hence

μίνυνθα, Adv., *a little, very little,* Hom.; of Time, *a short time,* Id.; μίνυνθα δέ οἱ γένεθ' ὁρμή but *short-lived* was his effort, Il. Hence

μῐνυνθάδιος, α, ον, *shortlived,* Hom.:—Comp. μινυνθαδιώτερος Il.

μῐνυρίζω, mostly in pres. and impf.: (μινυρός):—*to complain in a low tone, to whimper, whine,* Hom.: generally, *to sing in a low soft tone, to warble, hum,* Ar., Plut. Hence

μῐνύρισμα [ῠ], ατος, τό, *a warbling,* Theocr.

μῐνύρομαι, Dep., = μινυρίζω, of the nightingale, *to warble,* Soph.: *to hum a tune,* Aesch.

ΜΙ͂ΝΥ͂ΡΟ͂Σ, ά, όν, *complaining in a low tone, whining, whimpering,* Theocr.; μινυρὰ θρέεσθαι = μινυρίζειν, Aesch.

μῐνύ-ώριος and **μῐνύ-ωρος,** ον, (ὥρα) *shortlived,* Anth.

Μίνως [ῑ], ὁ, *Minos,* son of Zeus and Europa, king of Crete, Hom., Hes., etc.:—gen. Μίνωος Od.; acc. Μίνωα Hom.;—also gen. Μίνω Hdt.; acc. Μίνων Il., or Μίνω Hdt., etc.; dat. Μίνῳ Plat.:—Adj. **Μινώιος,** α, ον, Att. -ῷος, *of Minos,* h. Hom.

μῖξις, εως, ἡ, (μίγνυμι) *a mixing, mingling,* Plat.; v. κρᾶσις. II. *intercourse with* others, esp. *sexual intercourse,* Hdt.

μιξο-βάρβαρος, *half barbarian half Greek,* Eur., Xen.

μιξό-θηρ, ὁ, *half-beast,* Eur.

μιξό-θροος, ον, *with mingled cries,* Aesch.

μιξό-λευκος, ον, *mixed with white,* Luc.

μιξο-λύδιος [ῠ], ον, *half-Lydian,* Strab.:—**μιξο-λυδιστί,** Adv. *in the mixed-Lydian measure,* Plat.

μιξο-πάρθενος, ον, *half-woman,* Hdt., Eur.

μιξο-φρύγιος [ῠ], ον, *half-Phrygian,* Strab.

μῑσᾰγᾰθία, ἡ, *a hatred of good* or *goodness,* Plut. From

μῑσ-ἀγᾰθος, ον, *hating good* or *goodness.*

μῑσ-ᾰθήναιος, ον, *hating the Athenians:* Sup. μισαθηναιότατος Dem.

μῑσ-ᾰλάζων, ον, gen. ονος, *hating boasters,* Luc.

μῑσ-ᾰλέξανδρος, ον, *hating Alexander,* Aeschin.

μῑσ-άμπελος, ον, *hating the vine,* Anth.

μῑσανθρωπία, ἡ, *hatred of mankind,* Plat., Dem. From

μῑσ-άνθρωπος, ον, *hating mankind, misanthropic,* Plat.

μισγ-άγκεια, ἡ, (μίσγω, ἄγκος) *a place where mountain glens and their streams meet, a meeting of glens,* Il.

μίσγω, v. μίγνυμι.

μῑσ-έλλην, ηνος, ὁ, *a hater of the Greeks,* Xen.

μῑσέω, f. ήσω: aor. 1 ἐμίσησα: pf. μεμίσηκα:—Pass., fut. med. in pass. sense, μισήσομαι: aor. 1 ἐμισήθην: (μῖσος):—*to hate,* Pind., Att.:—c. acc. et inf., μίσησεν δ' ἄρα μιν κυσὶ κύρμα γενέσθαι Zeus hated (would not suffer) that he should become a prey to dogs, Il.; οὐ μισοῦντα τὴν πόλιν, τὸ μὴ οὐ μεγάλην εἶναι *not grudging* that the city should be great, Ar.:—Pass. *to be hated,* Hdt., Att. Hence

μίσημα [ῑ], ατος, τό, *an object of hate,* of persons, μ. ἀνδρῶν καὶ θεῶν Aesch.; c. dat., μ. πᾶσιν Eur.

μισητέος, α, ον, verb. Adj. of μισέω, *to be hated,* Xen. II. μισητέον, *one must hate,* Luc.

μισητία, ἡ, (μισητός) *hateful lust, lewdness,* Ar. 2. generally, *greediness, greed,* Id.

μισητός, ή, όν, *hateful,* Aesch., Att.

μισθᾰποδοσία, ἡ, *payment of wages, recompense,* N. T. From

μισθ-ᾰποδότης, ου, ὁ, *one who pays wages, a rewarder,* N. T.

μισθάριον [ᾰ], τό, Dim. of μισθός, *a little fee,* Ar.

μισθαρνέω, f. ήσω, *to work* or *serve for hire,* Plat., Dem.; μισθαρνεῖν ἀνύειν τι *to do a thing for pay,* Soph.

μισθ-άρνης, ὁ, (ἄρνυμαι) *a hired workman,* Plut. Hence

μισθαρνητικός, ή, όν, *of* or *for hired work, mercenary:* ἡ -κή (sc. τέχνη) *the trade of one who takes wages* or *pay,* Plat.; and

μισθαρνία, ἡ, *an earning of wages,* Dem.

μισθαρνικός, ή, όν, (μισθάρνης) of or for hired work, mercenary, Arist.

μισθ-αρχίδης, ου, ό, (ἀρχή) Comic Patron., Son of a Placeman, Ar.

μίσθιος, α, ον, (μισθός) salaried, hired, Plut., N. T.

μισθοδοσία, ή, payment of wages, Thuc., Xen. From

μισθοδοτέω, f. ήσω, to pay wages, absol., Xen., Dem. : —c. acc. to furnish with pay, Decret. ap. Dem. From

μισθο-δότης, ου, ό, one who pays wages, a paymaster, Plat., Xen.

ΜΙΣΘΟ'Σ, οῦ, ὁ, wages, pay, hire, Hom., etc. ; μισθῷ ἐπὶ ῥητῷ for fixed wages, Il. ; μισθοῖο τέλος the end of our hired service, Ib. ; θητεύειν ἐπὶ μισθῷ Hdt. ; μισθοῦ ἕνεκα for pay or wages, Xen. ; so in gen., μισθοῦ Soph., Xen. ; μηνὸς μισθόν as a month's pay, Thuc. 2. at Athens, the pay of the soldiers and sailors, Id., etc. :—also, μ. βουλευτικός the pay of the council of 500, a drachma to each for each day of sitting ; μ. δικαστικός or ἡλιαστικός the pay of a dicast (at first one obol, but from the time of Cleon three) for each day he sat on a jury ; μ. συνηγορικός the fee of a public advocate, one drachma for each court-day ; μ. ἐκκλησιαστικός the fee for attending the popular assembly. 3. a physician's fee, Arist. II. generally, recompense, reward, Hom., etc. 2. in bad sense, payment, requital, Trag.

μισθο-φορά, ή, =ἡ τοῦ μισθοῦ φορά, receipt of wages or wages received, hire, pay, Ar., Thuc., etc.

μισθοφορέω, f. ήσω, to be a μισθοφόρος, to receive wages or pay in the public service, to serve for hire, Ar., Xen., etc. ;—also c. acc. rei, to receive as pay, τρεῖς δραχμάς Ar. b. of mercenary soldiers, Id., Thuc.; μισθ. τινί Xen. ; μ. ἐν τοῖς ἀδυνάτοις, as if he were a pauper, Aeschin. 2. to bring in rent or profit, μισθοφοροῦσα οἰκία Isae. ; ζεῦγος ἢ ἀνδράποδον μισθοφοροῦν Xen. :— Pass. to be let for hire, Id.

μισθοφορητέον, verb. Adj. of foreg., one must receive pay, Thuc.

μισθοφορία, ή, service as a mercenary, Dem.

μισθο-φόρος, ον, (φέρω) receiving wages or pay, serving for hire, mercenary, Plat., Dem. II. as Subst., μισθοφόροι, οἱ, mercenaries, Thuc., Xen., etc. ; —also, μ. τριήρεις galleys manned with mercenaries, Ar.

μισθόω, f. ώσω : aor. 1 ἐμίσθωσα : pf. μεμίσθωκα : (μισθός) :—to let out for hire, farm out, let, Lat. locare, τί τινι Ar. : in pres. and impf. to offer to let, μισθοῖ αὐτὸν Ὀλυνθίοις offers his services for pay to them, Dem. :—c. inf., μ. τὸν νηὸν τριηκοσίων ταλάντων ἐξεργάσασθαι to let out the building of it for 300 talents, Lat. locare aedem exstruendam, Id. II. Med., f. μισθώσομαι : aor. 1 ἐμισθωσάμην : pf. μεμίσθωμαι :—to have let to one, to hire, Lat. conducere, Hdt., Att. ; μ. τινα ταλάντου to engage his services at a talent a year, Hdt. ; c. inf., μ. νηὸν ἐξοικοδομῆσαι to contract for the building of the temple, Lat. conducere aedem aedificandam, Id. III. Pass., aor. 1 ἐμισθώθην : pf. μεμίσθωμαι (v. supr. II) :—to be hired for pay, Id. ; ἐκ τοῦ μισθωθῆναι from the hire, Dem. : of a house, to be let on contract, Id. Hence

μίσθωμα, ατος, τό, the price agreed on in hiring, the contract-price, Hdt., Dem. II. that which is let for hire, a hired house, N. T. ; and

μίσθωσις, ή, a letting for hire, δίκη μισθώσεως or δ. ϟμισθώσεως οἴκου an action against a guardian who neglected to let his ward's house. II. rent, Dem.

μισθωτής, οῦ, ὁ, one who pays rent, a tenant, Dem.

μισθωτικός, ή, όν, of or for letting out :—ἡ μισθωτική, =μισθαρνική, a mercenary trade, Plat. ; and

μισθωτός, ή, όν, hired, Hdt., Plat. II. as Subst. an hireling, hired servant, Ar. : of soldiers, in pl., mercenaries, Hdt., Thuc.

μῑσο-γόης, ου, ό, hating fraud or jugglery, Luc.

μῑσο-γύνης [ῠ], ου, ό, woman-hater, Strab.

μῑσοδημία, ή, hatred of democracy, Oratt. From

μῑσό-δημος, ον, hating the commons, Ar., Xen.

μῑσό-θεος, ον, hating the gods, godless, Aesch.

μῑσό-θηρος, ον, hating the hunt, Xen.

μῑσο-καῖσαρ, ἄρος, ό, hating Caesar, Plut.

μῑσο-λάκων [ἄ], ωνος, ό, a Laconian-hater, Ar.

μῑσο-λάμᾱχος [λᾱ], ον, hating Lamachus, Ar.

μῑσολογία, ή, hatred of argument, Plat. From

μῑσό-λογος, ον, hating argument or dialectic, Plat.

μῑσό-νοθος, ον, hating bastards, Anth.

μῑσό-παις, ό, ή, hating boys or children, Luc.

μῑσο-πέρσης, ου, ό, an enemy to the Persians, Xen.

μῑσό-πολις, ιος, ό, ή, hating the commonwealth, Ar.

μῑσο-πονέω, f. ήσω, (πόνος) to hate work, Plat.

μῑσο-πόνηρος, ον, hating knaves, Dem., Aeschin.

μῑσοπονία, ή, (μισοπονέω) hatred of work, Luc.

μῑσο-πόρπαξ, ᾱκος, ό, ή, hating the shield-handle (πόρπαξ), i. e. hating war, Ar., in Com. Sup. μισοπορπᾱκίστατος.

μῑσό-πτωχος, ον, hating the poor, of the gout, Anth.

μῑσο-ρώμαιος, ον, a Roman-hater, Plut.

ΜΙ^ΣΟΣ, τό, hate, hatred : and so, I. pass. hate borne one, a being hated, Trag., Plat. 2. act. hate felt against another, a grudge, Soph., etc.; μ. τινός τινι felt by one against another, Eur. II. of persons, a hateful object, =μίσημα, Trag.

μῑσό-σοφος, ον, hating philosophy, Plat.

μῑσο-σύλλας, ου, ό, an enemy of Sulla, Plut.

μῑσό-τεκνος, ον, (τέκνον) hating children, Aeschin.

μῑσο-τύραννος, ον, a tyrant-hater, Hdt., Aeschin.

μῑσό-τῦφος, ον, hating arrogance, Luc.

μῑσο-φίλιππος, ον, hating Philip, Aeschin.

μῑσό-χρηστος, ον, hating the better sort, Xen.

μῑσο-ψευδής, ές, (ψεῦδος) hating lies, Luc.

μῑστύλλω, aor. 1 ἐμίστῡλα, to cut up meat, Hom. (Deriv. uncertain.)

μῑτο-εργός, όν, (*ἔργω) working the thread, Anth.

μῑτόομαι, Med. to ply the woof, Anth. :—φθόγγον μιτώσασθαι to let one's voice sound like a string, Id.

μῑτορ-ραφής, ές, (ῥάπτω) composed of threads, Anth.

ΜΙ'ΤΟΣ [ῐ], ου, ό, a thread of the warp, Lat. tela, Il. ;—κατὰ μίτον thread by thread, i. e. in an unbroken series, Polyb. II. the string of a lyre, Anth.

μίτρα [ῐ], Ep. and Ion. μίτρη, ή, a belt or girdle, worn round the waist beneath the cuirass (whereas the ζωστήρ went over it), Il. 2. = ζώνη, the maidenzone, Theocr., Mosch., etc. 3. a girdle worn by wrestlers, Anth. II. a head-band worn by Greek women to tie up their hair, a snood, Eur. 2. the victor's chaplet at the games, Pind. ; Λυδία μίτρα a

Lydian *garland* (i. e. an ode in Lydian measure), Id.   **3.** *a Persian head-dress, turban,* Hdt.

Μίτρα, ης, ἡ, the Persian Aphrodité, Hdt.

μιτρη-φόρος, μιτροφόρος, ον, *wearing a μίτρα or turban,* Hdt.

μιτρό-δετος, ον, *bound with a μίτρα,* Anth.

μίτυλος [ῐ] or **μύτῐλος,** η, ον, Lat. *mutilus, curtailed,* esp. *hornless,* Theocr.   (Deriv. uncertain.)

μῑτ-ώδης, ες, (εἶδος) *like threads, of threads,* βρόχος μ. σινδόνος a halter *of threads or linen,* Soph.

μίχθη, Ep. for ἐμίχθη, 3 sing. aor. 1 pass. of μίγνυμι.

μιχθήμεναι, Ep. for μιχθῆναι, aor. 1 pass. inf. of μίγνυμι.

ΜΝΑˆ, ἡ, gen. μνᾶς: nom. pl. μναῖ: Ion. nom. sing. **μνέα:**—the Lat. *mina,*   **I.** as *a weight,* = 100 drachmae, = about 15·2 oz. troy.   **II.** as *a sum of money,* also = 100 drachmae, i. e. 4*l.* 1*s.* 3*d.*:—60 μναῖ made a talent.   Hence

μναῖος, α, ον, *of the weight of a μνᾶ,* Xen., etc.

μνᾶμα, μνάμειον, μναμοσύνα, μνάμων, Dor. for μνημ-.

ΜΝΑ΄ΟΜΑΙ, contr. **μνῶμαι,** Dep.: Ep. forms 2 sing. pres. μνάᾳ, inf. μνάασθαι [μνᾱ-], part. μνωόμενος, Ion. **μνέωμενος:** 3 pl. impf. μνώοντο; 3 sing. Ion. impf. **μνάσκετο:**—only in pres. and impf.:   **I.** like μιμνήσκομαι, *to be mindful of* a person or thing, c. gen., Il.:—*to turn one's mind* to a thing, φύγαδε μνώοντο Ib.   **II.** *to woo for one's bride, to court,* c. acc. pers., Od.   **2.** *to sue for, solicit* a favour or office, Lat. *ambire,* Hdt.

μνάσθω, 3 sing. imper. of μνάομαι.

μνασῐδωρέω, Dor. for μνησιδωρέω.

μνάσομαι [ᾱ], Dor. for μνήσομαι, fut. med. of μιμνήσκω.

μναστήρ, ὁ, fem. **μνάστειρα, μνᾶστις,** Dor. for μνηστ-.

μνέα, ἡ, Ion. for μνᾶ.

μνεία, ἡ, (μνάομαι) = μνήμη, *remembrance, memory,* Soph., Eur.   **II.** *mention,* μνείαν ποιεῖσθαί τινος or περί τινος Plat., Aeschin.

μνῆμα, Dor. **μνᾶμα,** τό, (μνάομαι) Lat. *monimentum:*   **I.** *a memorial, remembrance, record* of a person or thing, Od., Soph., etc.   **2.** *a mound or building* in honour of the dead, *a monument,* Il., Hdt., Att.   **3.** *a memorial* dedicated to a god, Simon. ap. Thuc.   **II.** = μνήμη, *memory,* Theogn.

μνημεῖον, Dor. **μνᾱμεῖον,** Ion. **μνημήϊον,** τό, like μνῆμα, Lat. *monimentum, any memorial, remembrance, record* of a person or thing, Hdt., Att.   **2.** of one dead, *a monument,* Soph., etc.

μνήμενος, *remembering,* Od., as cited by Arist.

μνήμη, ἡ, (μνάομαι) *a remembrance, memory, record* of a person or thing, Theogn., Hdt., etc.; πρὸς ἃ ἔπασχον τὴν μνήμην ἐποιοῦντο made their *recollection* suit their sufferings, Thuc.   **2.** *memory* as a power of the mind, Att.:—εἰπεῖν τι μνήμης ὕπο (or ἄπο) from *memory,* Soph.   **3.** = μνημεῖον *a monument,* Plat.; *an epitaph,* Arist.   **II.** *mention* of a thing, Hdt.

μνημήϊον, τό, Ion. for μνημεῖον.

μνημόνευμα, ατος, τό, *a record* of the past, Arist.; and

μνημονευτέον, verb. Adj. *one must remember,* Plat.; and

μνημονευτικός, ή, όν, *of* or *for reminding,* Plotin.

μνημονευτός, ή, όν, *that can be* or *ought to be remembered,* Arist.   From

μνημονεύω, f. σω:—Pass., f. **μνημονευθήσομαι,** also med. **μνημονεύσομαι** in pass. sense: aor. 1 ἐμνημονεύθην:

(μνήμων) :—*to call to mind, remember,* c. acc., Hdt., Trag.; c. gen., Plat.   **II.** *to call to* another's *mind, mention,* Lat. *memorare,* c. acc., Id.

   B. Pass. *to be remembered, had in memory,* μνημονεύσεται χάρις Eur.; μνημονευθήσεται Dem.

μνημονικός, ή, όν, (μνήμων) *of* or *for remembrance* or *memory,* τὸ μνημονικόν = μνήμη, *memory,* Xen.; but, also, *memoria technica,* Plat.   **II.** *of persons, having a good memory,* Ar.; μνημονικώτατος Dem.   **III.** Adv. -κῶς, *from* or *by memory,* Aeschin.

μνημοσύνη, Dor. **μναμοσύνα,** ἡ, *remembrance, memory,* μνημοσύνη πυρὸς γενέσθω let us be mindful of the fire, Il.   **II.** as prop. n. *Mnemosyné,* mother of the Muses, h. Hom., Hes., etc.

μνημόσυνον, τό, = μνημεῖον, *a remembrance, memorial, record* of a person or thing, Hdt.   **2.** *a memorandum, reminder,* μνημόσυνα γράψομαι Ar.

μνήμων, Dor. **μνάμων,** ὁ, ἡ, μνῆμον, τό, gen. ονος: (μνάομαι) :—*mindful, καὶ γὰρ* μνήμων εἰμί I remember it well, Od.; μνήμοσιν δέλτοις φρενῶν Aesch.: c. gen. *mindful of, giving heed to,* Od.   **2.** *ever-mindful, unforgetting,* Aesch.   **3.** *having a good memory,* Ar., Plat.   **II.** as Subst., μνήμονες, οἱ, municipal officers, *Recorders,* Arist.

μνῆσαι, aor. 1 act. inf., and med. imper. of μιμνήσκω.

μνησαίατο, Ion. for -αιντο, 3 pl. aor. 1 med. opt. of μιμνήσκω.

μνησάσκετο, 3 sing. Ion. aor. 1 med. of μιμνήσκω.

μνησθῆναι, aor. 1 pass. inf. of μιμνήσκω.

μνήσθητι, aor. 1 pass. imper. of μιμνήσκω.

μνησῐ-δωρέω, Dor. **μνᾱσ-,** ἡ, (δῶρον) *to offer public thanksgiving,* Orac. ap. Dem.

μνησῐκᾰκέω, f. ήσω, *to remember wrongs done one, remember past injuries,* Hdt., Dem.; οὐ μν. *to bear no malice, pass an act of amnesty,* Ar., Thuc., etc.: c. dat. pers. et gen. rei, μ. τινί τινος *to bear* one a *grudge for* a thing, Xen.   **II.** c. acc. rei, τὴν ἡλικίαν μν. *to remind* one *of the ills* of age, Ar.   From

μνησί-κακος, ον, (κακόν) *bearing malice,* Arist.

μνησῐ-πήμων, ον, *reminding of misery,* μν. πόνος the *painful memory* of woe, Aesch.

μνήσομαι, f. of μιμνήσκομαι.

μνηστεία, ἡ, *a wooing, courting,* Plat.

μνήστειρα, ἡ, fem. of μνηστήρ, *mindful of,* c. gen., Pind.

μνήστευμα, ατος, τό, *courtship, wooing,* in pl., *espousals,* Eur.   From

μνηστεύω, Dor. **μναστεύω,** f. σω: **μεμνήστευκα:** (μνάομαι):—*to woo, court, seek in marriage,* Od., Eur.: *to woo and win, espouse,* Theogn., Theocr.:—Pass., μναστευθεῖσ' ἐξ Ἑλλάνων Eur.   **II.** *to promise in marriage, betroth,* τὴν θυγατέρα τινί Id.:—Pass., τῇ μεμνηστευμένῃ αὐτῷ γυναικί to his *betrothed* wife, N. T.   **III.** *to sue* or *canvass for* a thing, Plut.

μνηστήρ, Dor. **μναστήρ,** ηρος, ὁ, Ep. dat. pl. μνηστήρεσσι: (μνάομαι) :—*a wooer, suitor,* Od.; c. gen., παιδὸς ἐμῆς μν. Hdt.; γάμων μν. Aesch.   **II.** *calling to mind, mindful of,* c. gen., Pind.

μνῆστις, Dor. **μνᾶστις,** ιος, ἡ, (μνάομαι) *remembrance, heed,* οὐδέ τις ἡμῖν δόρπου μνῆστις ἔην Od.; ἴσχε κἀμοῦ μνῆστιν Soph. :—οὕτω δὴ Γέλωνος μνῆστις γέγονεν then you bethought yourselves of Gelon, Hdt.

μνηστός, ή, όν, (μνάομαι) wooed and won, wedded, ἄλοχος μνηστή a wedded wife, Hom.

μνηστύς, ύος, ἡ, Ion. for μνηστεία, Od.

μνήστωρ, ορος, ὁ, (μνάομαι) mindful of, τινός Aesch.

μνιᾱρός, ά, όν, mossy, soft as moss, Anth. From

ΜΝΙ'ΟΝ, τό, moss, sea-weed.

μνώομενος, Ep. for μνώμενος, part. of μνάομαι :—μνώοντο, for ἐμνῶντο.

μογερός, ά, όν, (μόγος) of persons, toiling, wretched, Trag. II. of things, toilsome, grievous, Eur.

μογέω, aor. 1 ἐμόγησα, Ep. μόγησα : (μόγος) :—to toil, suffer, Hom.; ἐξ ἔργων μογέοντες tired after work, Od. : the part. is nearly = μόγις, with pain or trouble, hardly, μογέων ἀποκινήσασκε Il. 2. in Trag. to suffer pain, be distressed, Aesch. II. trans. to labour at, τι Anth.

μογιλάλος, ον, hardly-speaking, dumb, N. T.

μόγις, Adv., (μόγος) with toil and pain, i. e. hardly, scarcely, Hom., Hdt., Att. :—cf. the post-Hom. μόλις.

ΜΟ'ΓΟΣ, ου, ὁ, toil, trouble, Il. 2. trouble, distress, Lat. labor, Soph.

μογοσ-τόκος, ον, (τίκτω) helping women in hard childbirth, of Eileithyia, Il. ; of Artemis, Theocr.

μόδιος, ὁ, a dry measure, Lat. modius, = the sixth of a medimnus, about 2 gallons, N. T.

ΜΟ'ΘΟΣ, ὁ, battle, battle-din, Il.

μόθων, ωνος, ὁ : at Lacedaemon, the child of an Helot, brought up as foster-brother of a young Spartan :—since such young Helots were likely to presume, μόθων came to mean an impudent fellow, Ar. II. a rude, licentious dance, Eur., Ar.

μοθωνικός, ή, όν, like a μόθων, Ion ap. Plut.

μοῖρα, gen. ας, Ion. ης : (μείρομαι) :—a part, portion, Hom. 2. a division of a people, Hdt. 3. a political party, Lat. partes, Id., Eur. II. the part, portion, share which falls to one, in the distribution of booty, Hom. ; or of a meal, Od. ; ἡ τοῦ πατρὸς μοῖρα one's patrimony, ap. Dem. 2. in various phrases, οὐδ' αἰδοῦς μοῖραν ἔχουσιν has no part in shame, Od.; τέσσαρας μοίρας ἔχον ἐμοί filling the place of four relations to me, Aesch. III. one's portion in life, lot, fate, destiny, Hom., etc. ; ἡ πεπρωμένη μ. Hdt. ; μοῖρ' ἐστι, c. inf., 'tis one's fate, Hom. ; ἔσχε μοῖρ' Ἀχιλλέα θανεῖν 'twas his fate to die, Soph. ;—μ. βιότοιο one's portion or measure of life, Il. ; ὑπὲρ μοῖραν (v. μόρος) Ib. ; ἀγαθῇ μοίρᾳ by good luck, Eur. ; θείᾳ μοίρᾳ by divine providence, Xen. 2. like μόρος, man's appointed doom, i. e. death, Hom., Aesch. :—also the cause of death, Od. IV. that which is one's due, Lat. quod fas est, κατὰ μοῖραν is is meet, rightly, Hom. ; opp. to παρὰ μοῖραν, Od. ; μοῖραν νέμειν τινί to give one his due, Soph. 2. respect, esteem, ἐν οὐδεμίᾳ μοίρῃ μεγάλῃ ἄγειν to hold one in no great respect, Hdt. ; ἐν μείζονι μ. εἶναι Plat. V. with a gen. almost periphr., μ. φρενῶν, for φρένες, Aesch. ; ἀνδρὸς μοῖρα προσετέθη it was accounted manly, Thuc. ; ἐν πολεμίου μοίρᾳ as if he were an enemy, Dem.

B. Μοῖρα, as prop. n., the goddess of fate, the Roman Parca, Hom. ; later, there were three, Clotho, Lachesis, Atropos, Hes. II. Μοῖραι, of the Furies, Aesch.

μοιράω, f. άσω [ᾱ], Ion. ήσω : (μοῖρα) :—to share, divide, distribute, Luc.; Med. to divide among themselves, Aesch. :—Pass. to be allotted, Luc.

μοιρη-γενής, ές, (γίγνομαι) child of Destiny, Il.

μοιρίδιος, α, ον, and ος, ον, (μοῖρα) allotted by destiny, destined, doomed, Lat. fatalis, μ. ἆμαρ etc., the day of doom, Pind. ; μοιριδία τίσις Soph. ; ἁ μοιριδία δύνασις the power of fate, Id.

μοιρό-κραντος, ὁ, (κραίνω) ordained by destiny, Aesch.

Μοῖσα, ἡ, Aeol. for Μοῦσα : gen. pl. Μοισᾶν.

μοιχ-άγρια, τά, (ἄγρα) a fine imposed on one taken in adultery, Od.

μοιχᾰλίς, ίδος, ἡ, = sq., an adulteress, N. T. : as Adj. adulterous, Ib. II. as Subst. = μοιχεία, Ib.

μοιχάω, trans., = μοιχεύω : metaph. μοιχᾶν τὴν θάλατταν to have dalliance with the sea, Xen. :—Pass., like μοιχεύομαι, to commit adultery, N. T.

μοιχεία, ἡ, adultery, Plat. ; and

μοιχεύτρια, ἡ, an adulteress, Plat. From

μοιχεύω, f. σω, to commit adultery with a woman, to debauch her, c. acc., Ar., Plat. :—Pass., of the woman, Ar. II. intr. to commit adultery, Lat. moechari, Id., Xen.

μοιχίδιος [ῐ], α, ον, born in adultery, Luc.

μοιχικός, ή, όν, adulterous, μ. διαβολαί accusations of adultery, Luc.

ΜΟΙΧΟ'Σ, ὁ, an adulterer, paramour, debaucher, Lat. moechus, Ar., Plat. :—κεκάρθαι μοιχόν to have the head shaven, as was done to adulterers, Ar.

μολεῖν, aor. 2 inf. of βλώσκω.

μολιβ-αχθής, ές, (ἄχθος) heavy with lead, leaded, Anth.

μόλιβδος, etc., v. μόλυβδος.

ΜΟ'ΛΙΒΟΣ, ου, ὁ, older form of μόλυβδος, lead, Hom. ; fem. in Anth.

μόλῑς, Adv., later form for μόγις, Trag., Thuc., etc. ; with a negat., οὐ μόλις not scarcely, i. e. quite, utterly, Aesch., Eur.

μολοβρός, ὁ, a greedy fellow, applied to a beggar, Od. (Deriv. uncertain.)

Μολοσσός, Att. -ττός, όν, Molossian, Hdt., Aesch., etc. :—fem. Μολοσσία (sc. γῆ) Pind.

μολοῦμαι, fut. of βλώσκω.

μολπάζω, only in pres. to sing of, Lat. canere, Ar. Hence

μολπαστής, οῦ, ὁ, a minstrel or dancer, Anth.

μολπή, ἡ, (μέλπω) the song and dance, a chant or song accompanied by measured movements, in honour of a god, or as an amusement, Hom. :—then, generally, play, sport, of a game at ball, Od. 2. singing, song, as opp. to dancing, Hom., Trag. Hence

μολπηδόν, Adv. like a song, Aesch. ; and

μολπῆτις, Dor. -ᾶτις, ιδος, ἡ, she who sings and dances, Anth.

μολύβδαινα, Ep. -αινη, ἡ, μολυβδίς, a piece of lead, used as the sink of a fishing-line, Il.

μολύβδῐνος, η, ον, leaden, of lead, μ. κανών, a flexible rule that could be moulded to curves, Arist.

μολυβδίς, ίδος, ἡ, like μολύβδαινα, a leaden weight on a net, Plat. 2. a leaden ball, Xen. From

μόλυβδος, ου, ὁ, = μόλιβος, lead, Hdt., Eur. II. plumbago, vulgarly called black lead, used as a test of gold, Theogn. :—a black-lead pencil, Anth.

μολῦνο-πραγμονέομαι, (πρᾶγμα) Pass. *to get into dirty quarrels*, Ar.

ΜΟΛΥ'ΝΩ [ῠ], f. ῠνῶ : pf. pass. μεμόλυσμαι :—*to stain, sully, defile*, Ar. ; μ. τινά *to make a beast of* him, Id. ; also *to defile* a woman, Theocr. :—Pass. *to become vile*, ἐν ἀμαθίᾳ μολύνεσθαι *to wallow in* ignorance, Plat. Hence

μολυσμός, ὁ, *defilement*, N. T.

μομφή, ἡ, (μέμφομαι) *blame, censure*, Pind., Aesch. :— *cause* or *ground of complaint*, μομφὴν ἔχειν τινί Pind. ; ἔν σοι μομφὴν ἔχω in one thing I blame thee, Eur. ; μ. ξυνοῦ δορός *blame as to helping spear*, Soph.

μόνα, Dor. for μόνη.

μονᾰδικός, ή, όν, (μονάς) *consisting of units*, μ. ἀριθμός *abstract* number, Arist.

μον-αμπῠκία, ἡ, = sq., abstract for concrete, Pind.

μον-άμπῠκος, ον, and μον-άμπυξ, ῠκος, ὁ, ἡ, *of horses, having one frontlet*, μονάμπυκες πῶλοι horses *that run single*, race-horses, opp. to chariots, Eur. ; so, μονάμπυκες *alone*, Id. ; of a bull, *having no yokefellow*, Id.

μοναρχέω, Ion. μουν-, f. ήσω, (μόναρχος) *to be sovereign*, Pind., Plat. ; ἐπὶ τούτου μουναρχέοντος in this *monarch's* time, Hdt. ; c. gen., ἐκόντων μ. Arist. Hence

μοναρχία, Ion. μουναρχίη, ἡ, *the rule of one, monarchy, sovereignty*, Hdt., Trag., etc. :—*of a general in chief*, Xen. ; of the Roman Dictator, Plut.

μοναρχικός, ή, όν, *monarchical*, Plat. 2. of persons, *inclined to monarchy* :—Adv. -κῶς, Plut. From

μόν-αρχος, Ion. μουν-, ὁ, *one who rules alone, a monarch, sovereign*, Theogn., Aesch., etc. 2. as Adj., σκᾶπτον μ. the *sovereign* sceptre, Pind. II. for the Roman *Dictator*, Plut.

μονάς, Ion. μουνάς, άδος, special fem. of μόνος, *alone, solitary*, Eur. ; as masc. of a man, Aesch. II. as Subst., μονάς, ἡ, *a unit*, Plat.

μοναυλέω, f. ήσω, *to play a solo on the flute*, Plut. From

μοναυλία, ἡ, (αὐλή) *a living alone, celibacy*, Plat.

μόν-αυλος, ὁ, *a player on the single flute*, Ath.

μονᾰχῆ or -χῇ, Adv., *in one way only*, Plat. ; ᾗπερ μοναχῇ in which way only, Xen.

μονᾰχός, ή, όν, (μόνος) *single, solitary* : as Subst. *a monk*, Anth. Hence

μονᾰχοῦ, Adv. *alone, only*, μ. ἐνταῦθα Plat. ; and

μονᾰχῶς, Adv. *in one way only*, Arist.

μον-ερέτης, Ion. μουν-, ου, ὁ, *one who rows singly*, Anth.

μονή, ἡ, (μένω) *a staying, abiding, tarrying, stay*, Hdt., Eur., etc. ; μονὴν ποιεῖσθαι *to make delay, tarry*, Thuc. : *a stopping place, station, mansion*, N. T.

μον-ήρης, ες, (*ἄρω) *single, solitary*, Luc.

μόνιμος, ον, and η, ον, (μονή) *staying in one's place, stable, steadfast*, Soph., Plat. ; of soldiers, Lat. *statarius*, Xen. 2. of things, conditions, and the like, *abiding, lasting, stable*, Lat. *stabilis*, Eur., Thuc., etc.

μόν-ιππος, ον, *one who uses a single horse, a horseman, rider*, Xen., etc.

μονο-βάμων [ᾰ], ον, (βῆμα) gen. ονος, *walking alone* : μέτρον μ. metre *of but one foot*, Anth.

μονο-γενής, Ep. and Ion. μουνο-γενής, ές, (γίγνομαι) *only-begotten, single*, Hes., Hdt., etc. ; μ. αἷμα *one and the same* blood, Eur.

μονό-γληνος, ον, (γλήνη) *one-eyed*, Anth.

μονο-δάκτῠλος, ον, *one-fingered*, Luc.

μονο-δέρκτης, ου, ὁ, (δέρκομαι) *one-eyed*, Eur.

μονό-δουπος, ον, *uniform in sound*, Anth.

μον-όδους, -όδοντος, ὁ, ἡ, *one-toothed*, Aesch.

μονό-δρομος, ον, (δρέμω) *plucked from one stem, cut from one block*, of a statue, Pind.

μονο-ειδής, ές, (εἶδος) *of one form* or *kind, uniform*, Plat.

μονό-ζυξ, ῠγος, ὁ, ἡ, (ζεύγνυμι) *yoked alone*, i. e. *single, solitary*, Aesch. :—so μονοζῠγής, ές, Anth.

μονο-ήμερος, ον, *lasting one day only*, Batr.

μονόθεν, Ion. μουν-, Adv. *alone, singly*, Hdt.

μονο-κέλης, Ion. μουνο-, ὁ, *a single horse*, Anth.

μονό-κερως, ων, *with but one horn*, Plut.

μονό-κλαυτος θρῆνος, ὁ, *a lament by one only*, Aesch.

μονό-κλῖνον, τό, (κλίνη) *a bed for one only*, i. e. *a coffin*, Anth.

μονο-κρηπῖς, ῖδος, ὁ, ἡ, *with but one sandal*, Pind.

μονό-κροτος, ον, (κροτέω) *with one bank of oars*, Xen.

μονό-κωλος, Ion. μουνο-, ον, (κῶλον) *with but one leg* : of buildings, *of one story*, Hdt. :—of sentences, *consisting of one clause*, Arist. :—generally, *of one kind, one-sided*, Id.

μονό-κωπος, ον, (κώπη) *with one oar* or *one ship*, Eur.

μονο-λέων, Ion. μουνο-, ὁ, *a singularly huge lion*, Anth.

μονό-λῖθος, Ion. μουνο-, ον, *made out of one stone*, Hdt.

μονό-λῠκος, ὁ, *a singularly huge wolf*, Plut.

μονομάτωρ [ᾱ], opos, Dor. for μονομήτωρ.

μονο-μᾰχέω, Ion. μουνο-, f. ήσω, *to fight in single combat*, Eur. ; τινι *with* one, Hdt. ; of the Athenians at Marathon, μοῦνοι μουνομαχήσαντες τῷ Πέρσῃ *having fought single-handed* with the Persians, Id.

μονομᾰχία, Ion. μουνομαχίη, ἡ, *single combat*, Hdt.

μονομᾰχικός, ή, όν, *of* or *in single combat*, Polyb. From

μονο-μάχος [ᾰ], ον, (μάχομαι) *fighting in single combat*, Aesch., Eur. II. μονόμαχος, ὁ, *a gladiator*, Luc.

μονο-μερής, ές, (μέρος) *consisting of one part*, Luc.

μονο-μήτωρ, Dor. -μάτωρ, opos, ὁ, ἡ, (μήτηρ) *reft of mother*, Eur.

μονον-ού, μονον-ουχί, v. μόνος B. II. 5.

μονο-νυχί, Ion. μουν-, Adv. *in a single night*, Anth.

μονό-ξῠλος, ον, (ξύλον) *made from a solid trunk*, Xen. II. *made of wood only*, Plat.

μονό-παις, παιδος, ὁ, ἡ, *an only child*, Eur.

μονό-πελμος, ον, (πέλμα) *with but one sole*, Anth.

μονό-πεπλος, ον, *wearing the tunic only*, Eur.

μονό-πους, Ion. μουνο-, ὁ, ἡ, -πουν, τό, *one-footed*, Anth.

μονο-πραγμᾰτέω, f. ήσω, *to be engaged in one thing*, Arist.

μονο-πωλία, ἡ, (πωλέω) *exclusive sale, monopoly*, Arist.

μονό-πωλος, ον, *with one horse*, Eur.

μον-ορύχης [ῠ], ου, ὁ, (ὀρύσσω) *digging with one point*, Anth.

ΜΟ'ΝΟΣ, Ep. and Ion. μοῦνος, η, ον, Dor. μῶνος, α, ον, *alone, left alone, forsaken, solitary*, Lat. *solus*, Hom., etc. ; μοῦνος ἐών Id. ; μούνῳ ἄνευθ' ἄλλων Od. 2. c. gen., μόνος σοῦ *without* thee, Soph. ; also, μοῦνος ἀπό τινος h. Hom., Soph. II. *alone, only*, μοῦνος παῖς υἱός an *only* son, Hom. ; εἷς μόνος, μόνος εἷς Hdt., Soph. 2. c. gen., μοῦνος πάντων ἀνθρώπων *alone* of all men, Hdt. ; μόνος ἀνδρῶν Soph., etc. III. Sup. μονώτατος, *the one only person, one above all others*, Ar., Theocr.

B. Adv. μόνως, *only*, Thuc., Xen. II. the common Adv. is μόνον, *alone, only*, Lat. *solum*, Hdt., Att.; οὐχ ἅπαξ μ. Aesch. 2. *only*, Lat. *modo*, with an imperat., ἀποκρίνου μ. Plat.; μή με καταπίης μ. Eur. 3. the Adj. often stands as an Adv., χοίνικος μόνης ἁλῶν for a gallon of salt *only*, Ar. 4. οὐ μόνον .. , ἀλλὰ καί .. , Id., etc. :—μόνον, like Lat. *solum*, is sometimes omitted in these phrases, μὴ τοὺς ἐγγύς, ἀλλὰ καὶ τοὺς ἀπόθεν Thuc. 5. μόνον οὐ, like Lat. *tantum non, all but*, Ar., Dem.; μονονουχί Dem. III. κατὰ μόνας, as Adv. *alone*, Thuc.

μονο-σῑτέω, f. ήσω, (σῖτος) *to eat once in the day*, Xen.
μονο-στῐβής, ές, (στείβω) *walking alone*, Aesch.
μονό-στῐχος, ον, *consisting of one verse*, Anth.; τὰ μ. *single verses*, Plut.
μονόστολος, ον, *going alone, alone, single*, Eur.
μονο-στόρθυγξ, ὁ, ἡ, *carved out of a single block*, Anth.
μονο-σύλλᾰβος, ον, (συλλαβή) *of one syllable, dealing in monosyllables*, of grammarians, Anth.
μονό-τεκνος, ον, (τέκνον) *with but one child*, Eur.
μονο-τράπεζος, ον, (τράπεζα) *at a solitary table*, Eur.
μονό-τροπος, ον, *living alone, solitary*, Eur.
μονο-τροφέω, f. ήσω, (τρέφω) *to eat but one kind of food*, Strab.
μονο-τροφία, ἡ, (τρέφω) *a rearing singly*, Plat.
μονο-φάγος, ον, (φᾰγεῖν) = μονόσιτος, irreg. Sup. μονοφαγίστατος, Ar.
μον-όφθαλμος, Ion. μουν-, ον, *one-eyed*, Hdt.
μονό-φρουρος, ον, (φρουρά) *watching alone, sole guardian*, Aesch.
μονό-φρων, ον, (φρήν) *single in one's opinion*, Aesch.
μονο-φυής, Ion. μουν-, ές, (φυή) *of single nature, single*, Hdt.
μονό-χηλος, Dor. -χᾱλος, ον, (χηλή) *solid-hoofed*, Eur.
μονο-χίτων [ῐ], ωνος, ὁ, ἡ, *wearing only the tunic*, Luc.
μονό-ψηφος, Dor. -ψᾱφος, ον, *voting alone*, μονόψαφον κατασχοῖσα ξίφος *keeping her sword solitary of purpose*, of Hypermnestra, Pind.
μονόω, Ion. μουνόω, f. ώσω, (μόνος) *to make single or solitary*, ἡμετέρην γενεὴν μούνωσε *isolated* our house, i. e. *allowed but one son* in each generation, Od. II. Pass. *to be left alone* or *forsaken*, Hom.; ἐμουνοῦντο *they were left* each man by himself, Hdt.; μουνωθέντα *taken apart, without witnesses*, Id. 2. c. gen., μεμουνωμένοι συμμάχων *deserted* by allies, Id.; μονωθεὶς δάμαρτος Eur.; μονωθεῖσα ἀπὸ πατρός Id.
μονῳδέω, f. ήσω, *to sing a monody* or *solo*, Ar.; and
μονῳδία, ἡ, *a monody* or *solo*, opp. to the song of the chorus, Ar. From
μον-ῳδός, όν, *singing alone, not in chorus*.
μόνως, Adv., v. μόνος B.
μόνωσις, ἡ, (μονόω) *separation from*, τινος, Plut.
μονώτης, ου, ὁ, (μονόω) *solitary*, Arist.
μον-ώψ, Ion. μουνώψ, ῶπος, ὁ, ἡ, *one-eyed*, Aesch., Eur.
μόρα, ἡ, (μείρομαι) *a mora, one of the six regiments* in which all Spartans of military age were enrolled, Xen.
μορέω, f. ήσω, (μόρος) *to make with pain and toil*, Anth.
μορίαι (sc. ἐλαῖαι), αἱ, *the sacred olives* in the Academy, prob. so called, because *parted* (μειρόμεναι) from the original olive-stock in the Acropolis, Ar. :—Ζεὺς Μόριος was *the guardian of these sacred olives*, Soph.
μόρῐμος, ον, poët. for μόρσιμος. Il., Aesch.

μόριον, τό, Dim. of μόρος, *a piece, portion, section*, Hdt., Plat., etc.; of quarters of the globe, Hdt.; of parts of a country, Thuc.; of an army, Id. 2. *a member* of a council, Arist.
μόριος, α, ον, = μόρσιμος, Anth. II. v. μορίαι.
μορμολῠκεῖον, τό, = μορμώ, Plat. From
μορμολύττομαι, Dep. only in pres. and impf., (μορμώ) *to frighten, scare*, Ar., Plat. II. *to be afraid of*, τι Plat.
μορμορ-ωπός, όν, (μορμώ, ὤψ) *hideous to behold*, Ar.
μορμύρω [ῠ], of water, *to roar and boil*, Il. (Formed from the sound, Lat. *murmur*.)
ΜΟΡΜΩ′ and Μορμών, όνος, ἡ, *a hideous she-monster*, used by nurses to frighten children with, Luc. : generally, *a bugbear*, Ar., Xen. II. as an exclamation to frighten children with, *boh!* μορμώ, δάκνει ἵππος Theocr.; μορμὼ τοῦ θράσους *a fig* for his courage! Ar.
μορόεις, εσσα, εν, (ΜΕΡ, Root of μέριμνα) *of earrings, wrought with much pains, skilfully wrought*, Hom.
μόρος, ὁ, (μείρομαι) = μοῖρα III, *man's appointed doom, fate, destiny*, μόρος [ἐστὶν] ὀλέσθαι 'tis one's *doom to die*, Il.; ὑπὲρ μόρον *beyond* one's *destiny*, Hom. II. *doom, death*, Lat. *fatum*, Il., Hdt., Trag. 2. = νεκρός, *a corpse*, Anth. III. the son of Night, Hes.
μόρσῐμος, ον, (μόρος) *appointed by fate, destined*, Lat. *fatalis*, Hom., Hdt., Aesch.; τὸ μόρσιμον *destiny, doom*, Pind., Trag.; τὰ μόρσιμα Solon. II. *fore-doomed to die*, Hom.
μορύσσω, = μολύνω, *to soil, stain, defile* : pf. pass. part. μεμορυγμένα καπνῷ Od.
μορφάζω, (μορφή) *to use gesticulations*, Xen.
μορφάω, (μορφή) *to shape, fashion, mould*, Anth.
Μορφεύς, έως, ἡ, *Morpheus, god of dreams*, because of the *forms* he calls up before the sleeper, Ovid.
ΜΟΡΦΗ′, ἡ, *form, shape*, Lat. *forma*, σοὶ δ' ἐπὶ μὲν μορφὴ ἐπέων thou hast *power to give shape* to words, i. e. to give a colour of truth to lies, Od.; θεὸς μορφὴν ἔπεσι στέφει God adds a crown of *shapeliness* to his words, Ib. 2. *form, shape, figure*, esp. like Lat. *forma, a fine* or *beautiful form*, Pind., Trag. 3. generally, *form, fashion, appearance*, Soph., Xen. 4. *a form, kind, sort*, Eur., Plat. Hence
μορφήεις, εσσα, εν, *formed*, λίθου μ. of stone, Anth. : esp. *well-formed, shapely*, Lat. *formosus*, Pind.
μόρφνος, ὁ, epith. of an eagle, prob. *dusky, dark*, Lat. *furvus*, (from ὄρφνη with μ prefixed), Il., Hes.
μορφόω, f. ώσω, (μορφή) *to give form* or *shape to*, Anth.
μόρφωμα, ατος, τό, *form, shape*, Aesch., Eur.
μόρφωσις, ἡ, *form, semblance*, N. T.
μορφώτρια, ἡ, (μορφόω) συῶν μ. *changing men into swine*, Eur.
μόσσυν, υνος, ὁ, *a wooden house* or *tower*, Xen. (Prob. a foreign word.) Hence
Μοσσύν-οικοι, οἱ, *dwellers-in-wooden-houses*, a people on the Black Sea, near Colchis, Xen., etc.
μόσχειος, ον, (μόσχος B) *of a calf*, κρέα μόσχεια *veal*, Xen.; μόσχεια alone, Anth.; μ. αἷμα Id.; μ. κυνούχος a *calf-skin leash*, Xen.; μόσχειον (sc. δέρμα), τό, a *calf-skin*, Id.
μοσχεύω, f. σω, (μόσχος A) *to plant a sucker* : metaph. *to plant* or *propagate* men, Dem.

μοσχίδιον [ῐ], τό, Dim. of μόσχος A, *a young shoot*, συκίδων from fig-trees, Ar.

μοσχίον, τό, Dim. of μόσχος B, *a young calf*, Theocr.

μόσχιος, α, ον, (μόσχος B)=μόσχειος, Eur.

μοσχο-ποιέω, f. ήσω, *to make a calf*, N. T.

ΜΟ'ΣΧΟΣ (A), ὁ, *a young shoot* or *twig*, Il. : cf. ὄσχος, ὄζος.

ΜΟ'ΣΧΟΣ (B), ὁ, ἡ, *a calf*, Eur. : *a young bull*, which form the god Apis was believed to assume, Hdt. : and as fem. *a heifer, young cow*, Eur. :—a calf was the prize of Lyric Poets, ᾄδειν ἐπὶ μόσχῳ Ar. 2. metaph. *a boy*, or as fem. *a girl, maid*, Lat. *juvenca*, Eur. 3. *any young animal*, Id.

ΜΟΤΟ'Σ, ὁ, *shredded linen, lint*, cf. ἔμμοτος.

μουνάξ, Adv. (μοῦνος) *singly, in single combat*, Od.

μουναρχέω, -ίη, Ion. for μοναρχέω, -ία.

μουνο-γενής, -γονος, -λιθος, -μήτωρ, -τόκος, μουνόω, Ion. for μον-.

Μουνῠχία, ἡ, *Munychia*, a harbour at Athens between Phalerum and Peiræeus, Hdt., Thuc.

Μουνυχίᾱσι, Adv. *at Munychia*, Thuc.

Μουνῠχιών, ῶνος, ὁ, the 10th Attic month, in which was held the festival of Munychian Artemis, = the latter part of April and beginning of May, Ar., Aeschin.

μουνώψ, Ion. for μονώψ.

Μοῦσα, ης, ἡ, Aeol. Μοῖσα, Dor. Μῶσα, (*μάω) *the Muse*, in pl. *the Muses*, goddesses of song, music, poetry, dancing, the drama, and all fine arts, Hom. : the names of the nine were Clio, Euterpé, Thalia, Melpomené, Terpsichoré, Erato, Polymnia or Polyhymnia, Urania, and Calliopé, Hes. II. μοῦσα, as appellat., *music, song*, Pind., Trag. :—also *eloquence*, Eur. :—in pl. *arts, accomplishments*, Ar., Plat.

Μουσ-ᾱγέτης, ου, ὁ, Dor. for Μουσ-ηγέτης, *leader of the Muses*, Lat. *Musagetes*, of Apollo, Plat.

Μουσεῖον, τό, (Μοῦσα) *a temple of the Muses, seat* or *haunt of the Muses*, Aeschin. 2. generally, *a school of art* and *poetry*, Id. : metaph., μουσεῖα θρηνήμασι ξυνῳδά *choirs* chiming in with dirges, Eur. ; χελιδόνων μουσεῖα *choirs* of swallows (whose twittering was a type of barbarous tongues), Ar.

Μούσειος, ον, Aeol. Μοισαῖος, α, ον, (Μοῦσα) *of* or *belonging to the Muses*, Eur. ; ἅρμα Μοισαῖον the car *of Poesy*, Pind. ; λίθος Μ. a monument *of song*, Id. II. *musical*, Anth.

μουσίζω, Dor. μουσίσδω, (μοῦσα) only in pres., *to sing of, chant*, Theocr. :—Med. in act. sense, Eur.

μουσϊκή (sc. τέχνη), ἡ, *any art over which the Muses presided*, esp. *music* or *lyric poetry*, Hdt., Att. II. generally, *art, letters, accomplishment*, Hdt., Plat. ; young Athenians were taught μουσική, γράμματα, γυμναστική, Plat., Arist.

μουσϊκός, ή, όν, Dor. -ά, όν, *of* or *for music, musical*, Ar., Thuc., etc. ; τὰ μουσικά *music*, Xen. ; v. μουσική. II. *of persons, skilled in music, musical*, Id., Plat. 2. generally, *a votary of the Muses, a man of letters and accomplishment, a scholar*, Ar., Plat. :—c. inf., μουσικώτεροι λέγειν *more accomplished in* speaking, Eur. III. Adv. -κῶς, *harmoniously, suitably*, Plat. : Sup. μουσικώτατα Ar.

μουσίσδω, Dor. for μουσίζω.

μουσό-δομος, ον, (δέμω) *built by song*, of the walls of Thebes, Anth.

μουσό-ληπτος, ον, *Muse-inspired*, Plut.

μουσομᾰνέω, *to be Muse-mad*, Luc. ʹFrom

μουσο-μᾰνής, ές, *devoted to the Muses*, Anth.

μουσο-μήτωρ, opos, ἡ, *the mother of Muses and all arts*, of Memory, Aesch.

μουσόομαι, Pass. *to be trained in the ways of the Muses, to be educated* or *accomplished*, Ar., Pericl.

μουσοποιέω, *to write poetry* : *to sing of*, τινά Ar.

μουσο-ποιός, όν, (ποιέω) *making poetry, a poet, poetess*, Hdt. II. *singing* or *playing*, Eur.

μουσο-πόλος, ον, (πολέω) *serving the Muses*; μ. στοναχά *a tuneful lament*, Eur. II. as Subst. *a bard, minstrel, poet*, Id.

μουσο-πρόσωπος, ον, *musical-looking*, Anth.

μουσουργία, ἡ, *a singing, making poetry*, Luc. From

μουσο-ουργός, όν, (*ἔργω) *cultivating music* : as Subst. *a singing girl*, Xen.

μουσο-φῐλής, ές, (φιλέω) *loving the Muses*, Anth.

μουσο-χᾰρής, ές, *delighting in the Muses*, Anth.

μουσόω, v. μουσόομαι.

μοχθέω, f. ήσω, (μόχθος) *to be weary with toil, to be sore distressed*, Il., Soph. :—*to work hard, labour*, Eur., etc. ; c. acc. cogn., μ. μόχθους, πόνους *to undergo* hardships, or *to execute painful* tasks, Id. ; μ. μαθήματα *to toil at* learning, Id. 2. c. acc. objecti, τέκνα ἀμόχθησα the children whom *I toiled for*, Id. ; μ. τινά θεραπεύμασι = θεραπεύειν, Id. ; cf. μόχθος. Hence

μόχθημα, ατος, τό, always in pl. *toils, hardships*, Trag.

μοχθηρία, ἡ, *bad condition, badness*, Plat. II. in moral sense, *badness, wickedness, depravity*, Ar., Plat. ; τὰ πρῶτα τῆς ἐκεῖ μ. *chief of the rascaldom* down there (in Hades), Ar.

μοχθηρός, ά, όν, voc. μόχθηρε (not μοχθηρέ) : (μοχθέω): —*suffering hardship, in sore distress, miserable, wretched*, Aesch., Ar., etc. ; μοχθηρὰ τλῆναι to suffer *hardships*, Aesch. 2. in *a bad state, in sorry plight, worthless*, Ar., Plat., etc. :—Adv., μοχθηρῶς διακεῖσθαι to be in *a sorry plight*, Plat. ; so in Comp., μοχθηροτέρως ἔχειν Id. ; -ότερον Xen. :—Sup. -ότατα Plat. II. in moral sense, *wicked, knavish, rascally*, Lat. *pravus*, Thuc., Ar., etc.

μοχθητέον, verb. Adj. of μοχθέω, *one must labour*, Eur.

μοχθίζω, =μοχθέω, *to suffer*, ἕλκει μοχθίζοντα ὕδρου *suffering* by its sting, Il. ; μ. δαίμονι φαύλῳ Theogn.

μόχθος, ὁ, =μόγος, *toil, hard work, hardship, distress, trouble*, Hes., Trag. : pl. *toils, troubles, hardships*, Trag. ; τέκνων for *children*, Eur.—μόχθος and πόνος are both used in the sense of *hardship, distress*; yet this notion belongs properly to μόχθος, while πόνος is properly *work*, Lat. *labor* (from πένομαι, πένης, the *poor man's toil*).

μοχλευτής, οῦ, ὁ, *one who heaves by a lever*, γῆς καὶ θαλάσσης μ. he who makes earth and sea *to heave*, Ar. ; καινῶν ἐπῶν μ. one who heaves up new words, Id. From

μοχλεύω, f. σω, (μοχλός) *to prise up, heave up by a lever*, Hdt., Eur.

μοχλέω, Ion. for foreg., στήλας ἐμόχλεον they strove to *heave* them *up* with levers, Il.

μοχλίον, τό, Dim. of μοχλός, Luc.

ΜΟΧΛΟ'Σ, ὁ, *a bar* used as *a lever, a crowbar, hand-*

spike, Lat. *vectis*, used for moving ships, Od.; for forcing doors and gates, Eur. **II.** the *stake* which Ulysses ran into the Cyclops' eye, Od. **III.** *a wooden bar*, placed across gates on the inside and secured by the βάλανος, Aesch., Thuc.

μύ or μῦ, *a muttering sound* made with the lips, μῦ λαλεῖν *to mutter*, Hippon. :—to imitate the sound of *sobbing*, μὺ μῦ, μὺ μῦ, or rather μυμῦ, μυμῦ, Ar.

μυ-άγρα, ή, (μῦς) *a mouse-trap*, Anth.

μῦ-γἄλῆ, ή, (μῦς, γαλέη) *the shrew-mouse, field-mouse*, Lat. *mus araneus*, Hdt.

μυγμός, οῦ, ό, (μύζω) *a moaning, muttering*, Aesch.

μυδᾰλέος [ŭ], a, ον, *wet, dripping*, Il., Hes., Soph.

μῦδᾰλόεις, εσσα, εν, = μυδαλέος, Anth.

μυδάω, f. ήσω, (μύδος) *to ooze with damp, be clammy* from decay, of a corpse, Soph.; μυδῶσα κηκίς *clammy moisture*, Id.; μυδῶσαι σταγόνες *oozing drops*, Id.

ΜΥΔΟΣ [ŭ], ό, *damp, clamminess, decay*.

μυδρο-κτῠπέω, f. ήσω, *to forge red-hot iron*, Aesch. From

μυδρο-κτῠπος, ον, *forging red-hot iron*, μ. μίμημα the manner *of a smith smiting iron*, Eur.

ΜΥΔΡΟΣ, ό, *a mass of red-hot metal*, Hdt.; μύδρους αἴρειν χεροῖν *to hold red-hot iron in the hands, as an ordeal*, Soph.

μυελῖνος, η, ον, *of marrow* ; = sq., Anth.; and

μυελόεις, εσσα, εν, *full of marrow*, Od. From

ΜΥΕΛΟΣ [ŭ], ό, *marrow*, Lat. *medulla*, Il., Hom., etc. :—*the brain*, Soph. : metaph. of *strengthening food*, οἶνον καὶ ἄλφιτα, μυελὸν ἀνδρῶν Od.; πρὸς ἄκρον μ. ψυχῆς *the marrow* or *inmost part*, Eur.; Τρινακρίας μ., of Syracuse, Theocr.

μυέω, f. ήσω : aor. ι ἐμύησα : Pass., pf. μεμύημαι : aor. ι ἐμυήθην : (μύω) :—*to initiate into the mysteries*, μνῆσαι Dem. :—in Pass. *to be initiated*, Hdt., Ar.; οἱ μεμυημένοι *the initiated*, Ar.; c. acc. cogn. *to be initiated in a thing*, τὰ Καβείρων ὄργια μεμύηται in the mysteries of the Cabiri, Hdt.; τὰ μέγαλα (sc. μυστήρια) μεμύησαι Plat. **II.** generally, *to teach, instruct*, c. inf., ἐμύησάς τινα ἰδεῖν Anth.

μύζω, f. μύξω : aor. ι ἔμυξα : (μύ, μῦ) :—*to murmur with closed lips, to mutter, moan*, Aesch.; οἰκτισμὸν μ. *to make a piteous moaning*, Id. **II.** *to drink with closed lips, to suck in*, Xen.

μυθέομαι, Ep. 2 sing. μυθεῖαι (for μυθέεαι) and μύθεαι : 3 pl. Ion. impf. μυθέσκοντο : f. μυθήσομαι : Ep. 3 sing. aor. ι μυθήσατο : Dep. : (μῦθος) : **I.** *to say, speak*, absol., Il. :—c. acc. et inf. *to say that*, Il. : c. inf. only, *to order*, Aesch. :—c. acc. *to tell, recount*, Hom.; also, *to tell of*, Il. :—c. acc. cogn. *to say, speak, utter*, Hom.; πόλιν μ. πολύχρυσον *to speak of the city as rich in gold*, Il. **II.** *to say over to oneself, con over, consider*, Hom.

μύθευμα, ατος, τό, *a story told, tale*, Arist., Plut. From

μυθεύω, later form of μυθέομαι, Eur. :—Pass. *to be spoken of*, Id.; ὡς μεμύθευται βροτοῖς *as is related by mortals*, Id.

μυθέω, v. μυθέομαι.

μυθιάζομαι, (μῦθος II) Dep. *to recount fables*, Babr.

μυθ-ίαμβοι, οἱ, a collection of Fables, like those of Babr.

μυθίδιον, τό, Dim. of μῦθος, Luc.

μυθίζω, later form for μυθέομαι, Dor. μυθίσδω, Theocr.

μυθικός, ή, όν, *mythic, legendary*, Plat.

μυθίσδω, Dor. for μυθίζω.

μυθογρᾰφέω, f. ήσω, *to write fabulous accounts*, Strab.

μυθογρᾰφία, ή, *a writing of fables*, Strab. From

μῦθο-γράφος [ᾰ], ό, (γράφω) *a writer of legends*, Polyb., Plut.

μῦθο-λογέω, only in pres., *to tell word for word*, Od.

μυθολογέω, f. ήσω, (μυθολόγος) *to tell mythic tales* or *legends*, Plat., Xen. **2.** c. acc. *to tell as a legend* or *mythic tale*, Plat. :—Pass., οἷα μυθολογοῦνται παλαιαὶ γενέσθαι φύσεις such as *they are fabled* to have been, Id. : impers., μυθολογεῖται *the legend goes*, Arist. **II.** *to invent like a mythical tale*, μ. πολιτείαν *to frame an imaginary constitution*, Plat. **III.** *to tell stories, converse*, Lat. *confabulari*, Id. Hence

μυθολόγημα, ατος, τό, *a mythical narrative*, Plat., Plut.

μυθολογητέον, verb. Adj. of μυθολογέω ι, Plat.

μυθολογία, ή, *a telling of mythic legends, legendary lore, mythology*, Plat. **2.** *a legend, story, tale*, Id.; and

μυθολογικός, ή, όν, *versed in legendary lore*, Plat.

μῦθο-λόγος, ό, (λέγω) *a teller of legends, romancer*, Plat.

μυθέομαι, = μυθέομαι ι, Aesch.

μῦθο-ποιός, όν, (ποιέω) *making mythic legends*, Plat.

ΜΥΘΟΣ, ό, *anything delivered by word of mouth, word, speech*, opp. to ἔργον, Hom., etc. **2.** *a speech in the public assembly*, Od., Ar. **3.** *talk, conversation*, mostly in pl., Od. **4.** *counsel, advice, a command, order*, also *a promise*, Il. **5.** *the subject of speech, the thing* or *matter* itself, Od., Eur. **6.** *a resolve, purpose, design, plan*, Hom. **7.** *a saying, saw, proverb*, Aesch. **8.** *the talk of men, rumour*, Soph., Eur. **II.** *a tale, story, narrative*, Hom.; μ. παιδός *of* or *about him*, Od. :—after Hom., μῦθος, like Lat. *fabula*, is *a tale, legend, myth*, opp. to λόγος *the historic tale*, Hdt., Plat., etc. : *a fable*, such as those of Aesop, Plat.

μῦθ-ώδης, ες, (εἶδος) *legendary, fabulous*, Plat. : τὸ μ. *the domain of fable*, Thuc.; τὸ μὴ μ. αὐτῶν such part of them *as is not fabulous*, Id.

ΜΥΙΑ, ή, *a fly*, Lat. *musca*, Il. :—proverb., μυίης θάρσος, *of excessive boldness*, Ib.

μυιο-σόβη, ή, (σοβέω) *a fly-flap*, of a long beard, Anth.

μυιο-σόβος, ον, (σοβέω) *flapping away flies*, Anth.

ΜΥΚΑΟΜΑΙ, f. ήσομαι : aor. ι ἐμυκησάμην :—to this belong Ep. aor. 2 act. ἔμῡκον, pf. μέμῡκα, plqpf. ἐμεμύκειν or μεμύκειν :—Lat. *mugire*, *to low, bellow, roar*, of oxen, Il.; of calves, Od.; of Hercules in agony, Eur., etc. **2.** of things, as of heavy gates, *to grate, creak*, Il.; of a shield, *to ring*, Ib.; of meat roasting, *to hiss* upon the spits, Od.; of thunder, Ar. (Formed from the sound, cf. βληχάομαι, μηκάομαι, βρυχάομαι, βρωμάομαι.) Hence

μυκηθμός, ό, *a lowing, bellowing*, of oxen, Hom.; and

μύκημα [ŭ], τό, *a lowing, bellowing, roaring*, of oxen, Eur.; of a lioness, Theocr.; *the roar* of thunder, Aesch.

Μυκήνη, ή, and Μυκῆναι, αἱ, *Mycené, Mycenae*, an ancient Pelasgic or Achaean city, superseded by the Dorian Argos, Hom., etc. :—Adj. Μυκηναῖος, a, ον, *Mycenaean*, Id. : fem. Μυκηνίς, ίδος, Eur. :—Adv. Μυκήνηθεν, *from Mycené*, Il.

ΜΥΚΗΣ [ŭ], ητος, ό, *a mushroom*, Lat. *fungus*. **II.**

any thing shaped like a mushroom,   1. *the chape* or *cap at the end of a scabbard*, Hdt.   2. *the snuff of a lamp-wick*, supposed to forbode rain, Ar.

μύκητής, οῦ, Dor. **μῡκᾱτάς, ᾶ, ὁ**, (μυκάομαι) *a bellower*, of oxen, Theocr.

μῡκήτῐνος, η, ον, (μύκης) *made of mushrooms*, Luc.

μύκον [ῠ], Ep. aor. 2 of μυκάομαι.

Μύκονος [ῠ], **ἡ**, one of the Cyclades, Hdt.

μυκτήρ, ῆρος, ὁ, (μύσσομαι) *the nose, snout*, Ar. : in pl. *the nostrils*, Hdt., Ar.   2. from the use of the nose to express ridicule, *a sneerer*, Anth. Hence

μυκτηρίζω, *to turn up the nose* or *sneer at* :—Pass. *to be mocked*, N.T.

μυκτρόθεν, Adv. *out of the nose*, Anth.

μυκτρό-κομπος, ον, *sounding from the nostril*, Aesch.

μύλαῖος, ον, (μύλη) *of* or *working in a mill*, Anth.

μύλαξ [ῠ], **ἄκος, ὁ**, Ep. dat. pl. μυλάκεσσι, (μύλη) *a mill-stone, a large round stone*, Il.

μυλ-εργάτης, ου, ὁ, *a miller*, Anth.

ΜΥ΄ΛΗ [ῠ], **ἡ**, Lat. *mola, a mill, a handmill* turned by women, Od.   II. *the nether millstone*, Ar. ; the upper being ὄνος, Id.

μύλή-φᾰτος, ον, (πέφαμαι, pf. pass. of *φένω) *bruised in a mill*, Od.

μυλίας, ου, masc. Adj. *of* or *for a mill*, λίθος μ. *a mill-stone*, Plat.   2. *rock for millstones*, Strab.

μυλῐάω, (μύλη) *to grind the teeth*, Hes., in Ep. part. μυλιόωντες.

μυλικός, ή, όν, (μύλη) *of* or *for a mill*, λίθος N. T.

μυλο-ειδής, ές, (εἶδος) *like a millstone*, Lat. *molaris*, Il.

μύλος [ῠ], **ὁ**, (μύλη) *a millstone*, Strab.

μυλωθρός, ὁ, (μύλη) *a miller* who keeps slaves to work his mill, Dem.

μυλών, ῶνος, ὁ, (μύλη) *a mill-house*, Thuc. ; εἰς μ. καταβαλεῖν, Lat. *detrudere in pistrinum, to condemn* [a slave] *to work the mill*, Eur.

μύνη, ἡ, (ἀ-μύνω) *an excuse, pretence*, Od.

μύξα, ἡ, (μύσσομαι) *the discharge from the nose*, Lat. *pituita*, Hes., etc.

μυξωτῆρες, οἱ, *the nostrils*, Lat. *nares*, Hdt.

μυο-θηρέω, (θηράω) *to catch mice*, Strab.

μυο-κτόνος, ον, (κτείνω) *mouse-killing*, Batr.

μυο-μάχία, ἡ, (μάχη) *a battle of mice*, Plut.

μυοπάρων, ωνος, ὁ, *a light vessel*, chiefly used by pirates, Plut. (Deriv. unknown.)

μύ-ουρος, ον, (οὐρά) *mouse-tailed : curtailed*, Arist.

ΜΥ΄ΡΑΙΝΑ [ῠ], **ἡ**, Lat. *muraena, a sea-eel, lamprey*, Ar. ; *a sea-serpent*, Aesch.

μυρεψέω, f. ήσω, *to prepare unguents*, Aesop. From

μύρ-εψός, ὁ, (μύρον, ἕψω) *one who prepares unguents. a perfumer.*

μυριάκις [ᾰ], Adv. (μυρίος) *ten thousand times*, Ar.

μυρι-άμφορος, ον, (ἀμφορεύς) *holding* 10,000 *measures* : metaph. *of prodigious size*, Ar.

μυρί-ανδρος, ον, (ἀνήρ) *containing* 10,000 *inhabitants*, Arist.

μῡρι-άρχης, ου, ὁ, *commander of* 10,000 *men*, Hdt. : so **μῡρί-αρχος, ου, ὁ**, Xen.

μυριάς, άδος, ἡ, *a number of* 10,000, *a myriad*, Hdt., etc. ; indefinitely of *countless numbers*, Eur. :—when μυριάς, μυριάδες are used absol. of money, δραχμῶν

must be supplied, Ar. ; when of corn, μεδίμνων, Dem.   II. Adj. *consisting of* 10,000, Aesch., Eur.

μῡρι-ετής, ές, (ἔτος) *of* 10,000 *years : of countless years*, Aesch.

μῡρίζω, *to rub with ointment* or *unguent, anoint*, Ar. :—Pass., μεμυρισμένοι τὸ σῶμα *having the body anointed*, Hdt.

μῡρίκη [ῐ], **ἡ**, Lat. *myrīca*, a shrub esp. thriving in marshy ground and near the sea, *the tamarisk*, Il. Hence

μῡρίκῐνος θάμνος, ὁ, *a tamarisk bush*, Anth.

μῡρίκῐνος ὄζος [ρῐ], **ὁ**, *a tamarisk bough*, Il.

μῡριό-βοιος, ον, (βοῦς) *with ten thousand oxen*, Anth.

μῡριό-δους, -όδοντος, ὁ, ἡ, *with immense teeth*, Anth.

μῡριό-καρπος, ον, *with countless fruit*, Soph.

μῡριό-κρανος, ον, *many-headed*, Eur.

μῡριό-λεκτος, ον, *said ten thousand times*, Xen.

μῡριό-μορφος, ον, (μορφή) *of countless shapes*, Anth.

μῡριό-μοχθος, ον, *of countless labours*, Anth.

μῡριό-ναυς, αος, ὁ, ἡ, *with countless ships*, Anth.

μῡριό-νεκρος, ον, *where tens of thousands die*, Plut.

μῡριόνταρχος, ὁ, = μυρίαρχος, Aesch.

μῡριο-πλάσιος [ᾰ], **ον**, 10,000 *times as many as*, c. gen., Xen., Arist.

μῡριο-πληθής, ές, (πλῆθος) *infinite in number*, Eur.

ΜΥ΄ΡΙΟΣ, α, ον, *numberless, countless, infinite*, properly of Number, and commonly in pl., Hom. ; in sing. with collective Nouns, μυρίον χέραδος Il. ; χαλκός Pind.   2. of Size, *measureless, immense, infinite*, πένθος, ἄχος Il. ; μ. κέλευθος *an endless* journey, Pind. ; μ. χρόνος Id. ; μυρίη ὄψις *all kinds* of sights, Hdt., etc.   3. neut. pl. μυρία as Adv., *much, immensely, incessantly*, κλαίειν Anth.   4. dat. as Adv., μυρίῳ σοφώτερος *infinitely* wiser, Eur. ; μυρίῳ βέλτιον, μ. κάλλιον Plat.   II. as a definite numeral, in pl. μύριοι, αι, α, *ten thousand*, the greatest number in Greek expressed by one word, Hes., etc. :—in sing. with collective nouns, ἵππος μυρίη 10,000 *horse*, Hdt. ; ἀσπὶς μυρία Xen.

μῡριοστός, ή, όν, *the* 10,000*th*, Ar. ; μ. ἔτος 10,000 *years hence*, Plat.

μῡριοστύς, ύος, ἡ, *a body of ten thousand*, Xen.

μῡριο-τευχής, ές, (τεῦχος) *with ten thousand armed men*, Eur.

μῡριο-φόρος, ον, (φέρω) *carrying* 10,000 *measures*, to designate *a merchant-ship of large tonnage*, Thuc.

μῡριό-φορτος, ον, = foreg., Anth.

μῡριό-φωνος, ον, (φωνή) *with ten thousand voices*, Anth.

μῡρί-πνοος, ον, contr. -πνους, ουν, = μυρόπνοος, Anth.

μῡρί-ωπός, όν, (ὤψ) *with countless eyes*, Aesch.

ΜΥ΄ΡΜΗΞ, ηκος, ὁ, Lat. *formica, the ant*, Hes., etc.   II. *a beast of prey* in India, Hdt.

Μυρμῐδόνες, οἱ, *the Myrmidons*, a warlike people of Thessaly; subjects of Achilles, Hom.

μῡρόεις, εσσα, εν, *anointed*, Anth. From

ΜΥ΄ΡΟΝ [ῠ], **τό**, *sweet juice extracted from plants, sweet-oil, unguent, balsam*, Hdt., etc.   2. *a place where unguents were sold, the perfume-market*, Ar.

μῡρό-πνοος, ον, contr. -πνους, ουν, *breathing sweet unguents*, Anth.

μῡρο-πώλης, ου, ὁ, (πωλέω) *a dealer in unguents* or *scented oils, a perfumer*, Xen.

μῦροπώλιον, τό, a perfumer's shop, Dem.

μῦρο-φεγγής, ές, (φέγγος) shining with unguent, Anth.

μῦρό-χριστος, ον, anointed with unguent, Eur.

μῦρό-χροος, ον, (χρόα) with anointed skin, Anth.

ΜΥΡΡΑ, ἡ, Aeol. for σμύρνα.

μυρρίνη, Att. for μυρσίνη.

μυρρῖνών, ῶνος, ὁ, Att. for μυρσινών.

μυρσίνη [ῐ], later Att. μυρρίνη, ἡ, = μύρτος, Pind., Eur. II. a branch or wreath of myrtle, Hdt., Ar.

μυρσῖνο-ειδής, ές, (εἶδος) myrtle-like, h. Hom.

μυρσῖνών, Att. μυρρινών, ῶνος, ὁ, a myrtle-grove, Lat. myrtetum, Ar.

μύρτον, ου, τό, a myrtle-berry, Lat. myrtum, Ar. From

ΜΥΡΤΟΣ, ἡ, the myrtle, Lat. myrtus, Simon., etc. II. a twig or spray of myrtle, Pind., Ar.

ΜΥΡΩ [ῠ], Ep. Verb, only in pres. and impf., to flow, run, trickle, δάκρυσι μῦρον (Ep. impf.) were melting into tears, Hes. II. Med. μύρομαι, to melt into tears, to shed tears, weep, Hom., Hes. 2. c. acc. to weep for, bewail, Bion, Mosch.

ΜΥ͂Σ, ὁ, gen. μυός, acc. μῦν, voc. μῦ :—Lat. mus, a mouse, Batr.; μ. ἀρουραῖος the field-mouse, or the hamster, Hdt.; μῦς πίσσας γεύεται, proverb. of one who is tempted to eat and finds himself caught, Theocr. II. a muscle of the body, Lat. musculus, Id.

μῦσαρός, ά, όν, (μύσος) foul, dirty: hence, loathsome, abominable, Eur.; τὸ μ. an abomination, Hdt. 2. of persons, defiled, polluted, Eur.

μῦσάττομαι, f. μυσαχθήσομαι: aor. 1 ἐμυσάχθην = Dep.: (μύσος) :—to feel disgust at anything loathsome, to loathe, abominate, c. acc., Eur., Xen. Hence

μῦσαχθής, ές, poët. for μυσαρός, Anth.

Μύσιος [ῠ], α, ον, (Μυσός) Mysian: Μύσιον (sc. θρήνημα), τό, a Mysian dirge, Aesch.; cf. Κίσσιος.

ΜΥΣΟΣ [ῠ], τό, uncleanness of body or mind: metaph. an abomination, defilement, Lat. piaculum, Trag.

Μυσός, ὁ, a Mysian, Aesch.:—from their effeminate character, Μυσῶν λεία came to mean a prey to all, of anything that can be plundered with impunity, Dem.

μῦσ-πολέω, (μῦς) to run about like a mouse, Ar.

μυστἄγωγία, ἡ, initiation into the mysteries, Plut.

μυστ-ἄγωγός, ὁ, (μύστης, ἄγω) one who initiates into mysteries, a mystagogue, Plut.

ΜΥΣΤΑΞ, ἄκος, ὁ, Dor. and Lacon. word, the upper lip, the moustache, Theocr.: cf. μάσταξ.

μυστηρικός, ή, όν, of or for mysteries, mystic, Ar.

μυστήριον, τό, (μύστης) a mystery or secret doctrine; in pl., τὰ μ. the mysteries of the Cabiri in Samothrace, Hdt.; of Demeter at Eleusis, Aesch., etc. 2. any mystery or secret, Plat. 3. mystic implements, Eur., Ar. 4. in N.T. a mystery, a divine secret, something above human intelligence.

μυστηρίς, ίδος, pecul. fem. of μυστηρικός, Anth.

μυστηριῶτις, ιδος, ἡ, (μυστήριον) of or for the mysteries: μ. σπονδή an armistice during the Eleusinian mysteries, Aeschin.

μύστης, ου, ὁ, (μυέω) one initiated, Eur. 2. as Adj. mystic, Ar., Anth. Hence

μυστικός, ή, όν, mystic, connected with the mysteries, μ. Ἴακχος the mystic chant Iacchus, Hdt.; τὰ μ. the mysteries, Thuc.:—χοιρία μ., in Ar., are prob. wretched lean pigs, such as the μύσται were wont to offer.

μυστῑλάομαι, pf. μεμυστῑλήμαι, Dep. to sop bread in soup or gravy and eat it, Ar.: metaph., μυστιλᾶται τῶν δημοσίων he ladles out public money, Id.:—pf. part. in pass. sense, scooped out, Id. From

μυστίλη [ῐ], ἡ, a piece of bread used to sup up soup or gravy with, Ar. (Deriv. unknown.)

μυστῐ-πόλος, ον, (μύστης, πολέω) solemnising mysteries, performing mystic rites, Anth.

μύστῐς, ῐδος, fem. of μύστης, as Adj. mystic, Anth. II. a mystagogue, Anacreon.

μυστο-δόκος, ον, (μύστης, δέχομαι) receiving the initiated, δόμος μ., i.e. Eleusis, Ar.

Μυτιλήνη, ἡ, Mytilené, the chief city of Lesbos, Thuc.

μυττωτεύω, to hash up, make mince-meat of, τινά Ar.

μυττωτός, ὁ, a savoury dish of cheese, honey, garlic, mashed up into a sort of paste, Lat. moretum, Ar. (Deriv. unknown.)

μυχθίζω, (μύζω) to snort, jeer, Theocr.

μυχθισμός, ὁ, a snorting, moaning, Eur.

μύχιος, α, ον, (μυχός) inward, inmost, retired, embayed, Aesch., Luc.

μυχμός, ὁ, (μύζω) = μυγμός, moaning, groaning, Od.

μυχόθεν, (μυχός) Adv. from the inmost part of the house, from the women's chambers, Aesch.

μυχοίτατος, η, ον, irreg. Sup. of μύχιος, in the farthest corner, Od.

μυχόνδε, (μυχός) Adv. to the far corner, Od.

μυχός, ὁ, (μύω) the innermost place, inmost nook or corner, Lat. sinus, recessus, Hom., etc. 2. the inmost part of a house, the women's apartments, Lat. penetralia, Od., Trag. 3. a bay or creek running far inland, Hdt.; πόντιος μ., i.e. the Adriatic, Aesch.

μυχ-ώδης, ες, (εἶδος) full of recesses, cavernous, Eur.

ΜΥΩ, f. σω: aor. 1 ἔμυσα, Ep. 3 pl. μύσαν: pf. μέμῦκα :—intr. to close, be shut, of the eyes, Il., Eur.; so, χείλεα μεμυκώς having the lips closed, Anth. 2. of persons, μύσας with one's eyes shut, Soph., Ar. 3. metaph. to be lulled to rest, to abate, of pain, Soph.; of storms, Anth. II. trans. to close, shut, Id.

μυῶν, ῶνος, ὁ, (μῦς II) a cluster of muscles, a muscle, Il.

μυωπάζω, (μύωψ) to be shortsighted, see dimly, N.T.

μυωπίζω, (μύωψ II. 2) to spur, prick with a spur, Xen. II. Pass. (μύωψ II. 1) to be teased by flies, of a horse, Id.

μυωπός, όν, = μύωψ I, Xen.

μύ-ωψ, ωπος, ὁ, ἡ, (μύω, ὤψ) contracting the eyes, as shortsighted people do, shortsighted, Arist. II. as Subst., μύωψ, ωπος, ὁ, the horsefly or gadfly, Lat. tabānus, Aesch., Plat. 2. a goad, spur, Xen., Theophr. :—metaph. a stimulant, Luc., Anth.

ΜΩΛΟΣ, ὁ, the toil and moil of war, Il.; ξείνου καὶ Ἴρου μ. the struggle between Irus and the stranger, Od.

ΜΩΛΥ, τό, moly, mandrake, a fabulous herb of magic power, having a black root and white blossom, given by Hermes to Ulysses, as a counter-charm to the charms of Circé, Od.

μῶμαι, v. sub *μάω II.

μωμάομαι, Ion. -έομαι, 3 pl. -εῦνται: f. ἥσομαι: aor. 1 ἐμωμησάμην, Dor. sing. μωμάσατο: Dep.: (μῶμος) :—to find fault with, blame, c. acc., Il., Aesch. :—an aor. 1 inf. μωμηθῆναι in pass. sense, N.T.

μωμεύω, = μωμάομαι, Od., Hes.

μωμητός, ή, όν, (μωμάομαι) to be blamed, Aesch.

ΜΩ͂ΜΟΣ, ό, blame, ridicule, disgrace, μῶμον ἀνάψαι to set a brand upon one, Od.   II. personified Momus, the critic God, Hes.   (Akin to μέμφομαι?)

μῶν, Adv., contr. for μὴ οὖν, used like μή; in questions to which a negative answer is expected, but surely not? is it so? Lat. num? μῶν ἐστι . . ; Answ. οὐ δῆτα, Eur. : sometimes it asks doubtingly like Lat. num forte? and answered in the affirm., Id. : —μῶν οὐ . . ; requires an affirm. answer, Lat. nonne? Trag.

μῶνος, α, ον, Dor. for μοῦνος, μόνος.

μῶ-νυξ, ὔχος, ὁ, ἡ, (μόνος, ὄνυξ) with a single, i. e. uncloven, hoof, Lat. solipes, of the horse, Hom., Eur.

μώομαι, Ep. lengthd. form for μάομαι.

μωραίνω, f. ἀνῶ, aor. 1 ἐμώρᾱνα : (μῶρος) :—to be silly, foolish, Eur., Xen., etc. :—c. acc. rei, πεῖραν μωραίνειν to make a mad attempt, Aesch.   II. Causal, to make foolish, convict of folly, N. T. :—Pass., of salt, to become insipid, lose its savour, Ib.

μωρία, Ion. -ίη, ἡ, (μῶρος) silliness, folly, μωρίην ἐπιφέρειν τινι to impute folly to him, Hdt.; μωρίαν ὀφλισκάνειν to be charged with it, Soph. ; ἐδόκει μωρία εἶναι ταῦτα Thuc. ; τῆς μωρίας! what folly! Ar.

μωρολογία, ή, silly talking, N. T. From

μωρο-λόγος, ον, speaking foolishly, Arist.

ΜΩΡΟ͂Σ, ά, όν, rarely ος, ον, dull, sluggish, stupid, Soph., etc. ; τὸ·μ. folly, Eur. ; μῶρα φρονεῖν, δρᾶν, λέγειν Soph., Eur. :—Adv. -ρως, Xen.

μωρό-σοφος, ον, foolishly wise, a sapient fool, Luc.

Μῶσα, Dor. for Μοῦσα.

μῶσθαι, inf. of μῶμαι, v. *μάω II.

N.

N, ν, νῦ, τό, indecl., thirteenth letter of Greek alphabet; as numeral, ν´ = 50, but ,ν = 50,000.   ν is the dental or palatal liquid, corresponding with the mute δ.
    Dialectic changes,   1. Dor., ν represents λ, v. Λ λ. 2.   2. Att. and Dor. for μ, v. Μ μ. II. 2.   II. Euphonic changes :   1. into γ before the palatals γ κ χ, and before ξ, as ἔγγονος ἔγκαιρος ἐγχώριος ἐγξέω etc.   2. into μ before the labials β π φ, and before ψ, as σύμβιος συμπότης συμφυής ἔμψυχος ; likewise before λ, ρ, as ἔμμανής.   3. into λ, before λ, as ἐλλείπω συλλαμβάνω.   4. into ρ before ρ, as συρράπτω : in compds. of ἐν ν sometimes remains, as ἔνρυθμος.   5. into σ before σ, as σύσσιτος πάσσοφος.   III. the so-called νῦ ἐφελκυστικόν is found with dat. pl. in σι, as ἀνδράσιν ; 3 pl. of verbs in σι, as εἰλήφασιν ; 3 sing. in -ε, -ι, as ἔκτανεν δείκνυσιν : the local termin. -σι, as Ἀθήνησι Ὀλυμπίασι ; the Epic. termin. φι, as ὀστεόφιν ; the numeral εἴκοσι ; the Advs. νόσφι, πέρυσι ; the enclit. Particles κέ and νύ.   This ν was mostly used to avoid a hiatus where a vowel follows.

νᾶας, Dor. acc. pl. of ναῦς.

ναετήρ, ῆρος, ὁ, = sq., Anth.

ναέτης, ου, ὁ, an inhabitant, Simon. ; as fem., Anth.

ναί, Adv., used in strong affirmation, yea, verily, Lat.

nae, Hom., Att. ; in Hom. mostly followed by δή.   2. ναὶ μά in oaths, yea by . . , ναὶ μὰ τόδε σκῆπτρον Il. ; μά is sometimes omitted, ναὶ τὰν κόραν Ar. ; ναὶ πρὸς θεῶν Eur.   II. in answers, alone, aye, yes, τοῦτ' ἐτήτυμον ; Answ. ναί Aesch.; ναί, ναί Ar.

ναῖ, poët. dat. of ναῦς.

Ναϊᾱκός, ή, όν, of or for the Naiads, Anth.

Ναϊάς, Ion. Νηϊάς, άδος, ἡ, (νάω) a Naiad, a river-nymph, (as Νηρηίς a sea-nymph), mostly in pl. Ναϊάδες, Ion. Νηϊάδες, Od., Eur. :—so also Ion. Νηΐς, ΐδος, ἡ, in sing., Il., Eur.

ναΐδιον [ῐδ], τό, Dim. of ναός, Polyb.

ναίεσκον, Ion. impf. of ναίω.

ναιετάω, Ep. part. ναιετάωσα ; Ion. impf. ναιετάασκον : (ναίω) :   1. of persons, to dwell, often in Hom. and Hes.   2. c. acc. loci, to dwell in, inhabit, Hom., Hes.   II. of places, to be situated, lie, Hom. : hence to exist, Ἰθάκης ἔτι ναιεταούσης Il.

ναίοισα, Dor. for ναίουσα, part. fem. of ναίω.

νάϊος, α, ον, Dor. for νήϊος.

ναίχι, Adv. for ναί, like οὐχί for οὐ, Soph.

ΝΑΙ͂Ω (Α).   I. of persons, to dwell, abide, Il., Hes., Trag. :—c. acc loci, to dwell in, inhabit, οἶκον, δῶμα, ἅλα, etc., Hom., etc. :—Pass. to be inhabited, Theocr.   2. of places, to lie, be situated, Soph.   II. Causal, in Ep. aor. 1 ἔνασσα or νάσσα,   1. c. acc. loci, to give one to dwell in, νάσσα πόλιν I would have given him a town for his home, Od. : also to make habitable, to build, νηὸν ἔνασσαν h. Hom. :—Pass., v. εὐναιόμενος.   2. c. acc. pers. to let one dwell, settle him, Pind. ; Pass., Ep. aor. 1 νάσθην, to be settled, to dwell, Il. ; so, aor. 1 med., νάσσατο ἄγχι Ἑλικῶνος Hes. ; pf. νέναστat Anth.

ΝΑΙ͂Ω (Β), = νάω, to run over, to be full, Od.

ΝΑ͂ΚΗ [ᾰ], ἡ, a woolly or hairy skin, a goatskin, Od.

ΝΑ͂ΚΟΣ [ᾰ], τό, a fleece, Lat. vellus, Hdt., Pind., etc.

νακτός, ή, όν, (νάσσω) close-pressed, solid.

νᾶμα, ατος, τό, (νάω) anything flowing, running water, a river, stream, Trag., Plat.

νᾱμέρτής, νᾱμέρτεια, Dor. for νημ-.

νᾶν, Dor. for ναῦν, acc. of ναῦς.

ΝΑ͂ΝΟΣ, ὁ, a dwarf, Ar.

νανο-φυής, ές, (φυή) of dwarfish stature, Ar.

Ναξι-ουργής, ές, (*ἔργω) of Naxian work, Ar.

Νάξος, ἡ, Naxos, one of the Cyclades, h. Hom. :—Adj. Νάξιος, α, ον, Naxian ; οἱ Ν. the Naxians, Hdt. ; Ναξία ἀκόνα a Naxian whetstone, Pind.

νᾱο-πόλος, Ion. νηοπ-, ὁ, (πολέω) the overseer of a temple, Hes.

νᾱός, Ion. νηός, Att. νεώς, ὁ, (ναίω) the dwelling of a god, a temple, Hom., Hdt., etc.   II. the inmost part of a temple, the cell, in which the image of the god was placed, Hdt., Xen.

νᾱο-φύλαξ [ῠ], ᾰκος, ὁ, (ναός) the keeper of a temple, Lat. aedituus, Eur., Arist.

νάπᾰ, α, ον, of a wooded vale or dell, Soph., Eur.

ΝΑ͂ΠΗ [ᾰ], ἡ, a wooded vale, dell, or glen, Il., Soph.

νάπος, τό, later form of νάπη, Soph., Eur., Xen.

νᾶπυ, τό, = σίναπι, v. βλέπειν Ar. ; cf. κάρδαμον.

ναρδο-λῐπής, ές, (λίπος) anointed with nard-oil, Anth.

νάρδος, ή, a plant, nard, spikenard, nard-oil, Anth. (Prob. a foreign word.)

ναρθηκο-φόρος, ον, (φέρω) carrying a νάρθηξ, a wand-bearer, πολλοί τοι ναρθηκοφόροι, Βάκχοι δέ τε παῦροι, i. e. there are many officials, but few inspired, Plat.

νάρθηξ, ηκος, ὁ, a tall umbelliferous plant, Lat. ferula, with a hollow, pithy stalk, in which Prometheus conveyed fire from heaven to earth, Hes. The stalks furnished the Bacchanalian wands (θύρσοι), Eur., (cf. foreg.); they were also used for canes by schoolmasters, Xen. II. a casket for unguents, Luc.

ναρκάω, f. ήσω: Ep. aor. 1 νάρκησα: to grow stiff or numb, Lat. torpere, Il., Plat. From

ΝΑ´ΡΚΗ, ἡ, numbness, deadness, Lat. torpor, Ar. II. a flat fish, the torpedo or electric ray, Plat.

νάρκισσος, ὁ, rarely ἡ, the narcissus, h. Hom., Soph., etc. (From ναρκάω, because of its narcotic properties.)

νᾶς, ἡ, Dor. for ναῦς.

νάσθην, Ep. for ἐνάσθην, aor. 1 pass. of ναίω A.

νασιώτας, α, ὁ, Aeol. and Dor. for νησιώτης.

νασμός, ὁ, (νάω) a flowing stream, a stream, Eur.

νάσσα, Ep. for ἔνασσα, aor. 1 of ναίω A. II :—νάσσατο, 3 sing. aor. 1 med.

νᾶσσα, Dor. for νῆσσα, νῆττα.

ΝΑ´ΣΣΩ, Att. νάττω: aor. 1 ἔναξα: pf. pass. νένασμαι and νέναγμαι :—to press or squeeze close, stamp down, Od., Theocr. Hence

ναστός, ή, όν, close-pressed: ναστός (sc. πλακοῦς), ὁ, a well-kneaded cake, cheese-cake, Ar.

ναυαγέω, Ion. **ναυηγ-, f. ήσω,** to suffer shipwreck, be shipwrecked, Hdt., Xen., etc. :—metaph. of chariots, to be wrecked, Dem.; and

ναυαγία, Ion. **-ηγίη, ἡ,** shipwreck, Hdt., Eur.; and

ναυάγιον [ᾰ], Ion. **ναυήγιον, τό,** a piece of wreck, Hdt., Aesch., Thuc.: metaph., ναυάγια ἱππικά the wreck of a chariot, Soph. II. = ναυαγία, ἡ, Strab. From

ναυ-αγός, όν, Ion. **ναυ-ηγός, (ἔ-αγα** pf. of ἄγνυμι) ship-wrecked, stranded, Lat. naufragus, Hdt., Eur.; ναυα-γοὺς ἀναιρεῖσθαι to pick up the shipwrecked men, Xen.; ν. τάφος the grave of the shipwrecked, i. e. the sea, Anth. 2. act. causing shipwreck, ἄνεμοι Id.

ναυαρχέω, f. ήσω, to command a fleet, Hdt., Xen.; and

ναυαρχία, ἡ, the command of a fleet, office of ναύαρχος, Thuc.: the period of his command, Xen.; and

ναυαρχίς, ίδος, ἡ, the ship of the ναύαρχος, Polyb. From

ναύ-αρχος, ὁ, the commander of a fleet, an admiral, Hdt., Aesch., Soph. :—esp. the Spartan admiral-in-chief, whereas the Athen. admirals retained the name of στρατηγοί (generals), Thuc., Aesch.

ναυ-βάτης [ᾰ], ου, ὁ, (βαίνω) a 'ship-goer,' a seaman, Hdt., Aesch., Soph., etc. II. as Adj., ν. στρατός Aesch.; στόλος Soph., etc.

ναύ-δετον, τό, (δέω) a ship's cable, Eur.

ναυηγός, ναυηγέω, ναυηγία, etc., Ion. for ναυαγ-.

ναυκληρέω, f. ήσω, to be a shipowner, Ar., Xen. 2. metaph., ν. πόλιν to manage, govern, Aesch., Soph.; and

ναυκληρία, ἡ, a seafaring life, ship-owning, Arist. 2. poët. a voyage, Eur. :—an adventure, enterprise, Id. II. a ship, Id.; and

ναυκλήριον, τό, the ship of a ναύκληρος, Dem. II. = ναύσταθμος, Eur. From

ναύ-κληρος, ὁ, a shipowner, ship-master, Hdt., Soph., etc. 2. as Adj., ν. χείρ the master's hand, of a charioteer (cf. ἡνίοχος I. 3), Eur.

ναύ-κρᾱρος, ὁ, at Athens, one of a division, of the citizens, made for financial purposes before Solon's time. There were 4 in each φρατρία, 12 in each of the 4 old φυλαί, in all 48, afterwards increased to 50. (Apparently an old form of ναύ-κληρος: but the connexion of the word with ναῦς ship is not explained.)

ναυκρατέω, f. ήσω, to be master of the sea, Thuc. :—Pass. to be mastered at sea, Xen. From

ναυ-κράτης [ᾰ], εως, ὁ, ἡ, (κρατέω) master or mistress of the seas, Hdt.

Ναύκρᾱτις, ιος or εως, ἡ, Naucratis in Egypt, Hdt.

ναυ-κράτωρ [ᾰ], ορος, ὁ, ἡ, = ναυκράτης, Hdt., Thuc. II. the master of a ship, Soph.

ναῦλος, ὁ, and **ναῦλον, τό,** (ναῦς) passage-money, the fare or freight, Xen. II. the freight or cargo of ships, Dem.

ναυλοχέω, f. ήσω, to lie in a harbour or creek, esp. to lie in wait there in order to sally out on passing ships, Hdt., Eur. 2. c. acc. to lie in wait for, Thuc. From

ναύ-λοχος, ον, affording safe anchorage, of a harbour, Od., Soph.; ἃ ναύλοχα καὶ πετραῖα λουτρά ye springs by the haven and from the rock (where some take ναύλοχα as Subst.) Soph.

ναυμᾰχέω, f. ήσω, (ναύμαχος) to fight in a ship or by sea, engage in a naval battle, Hdt., Xen.; ν. τὴν περὶ τῶν κρεῶν to be in the battle for the carcases (i.e. Arginusae), Ar. 2. metaph. to do battle with, κακοῖς Id. Hence

ναυμᾰχησείω, Desid., to wish to fight by sea, Thuc.

ναυμᾰχητέον, verb. Adj. one must fight by sea, Arist.

ναυ-μᾰχία, Ion. **-ίη, ἡ,** a sea-fight, Hdt., Thuc.

ναύ-μᾰχος, ον, (μάχομαι) of or for a sea-fight, ξυστὰ ναύμαχα boarding pikes, Il.; δόρατα Hdt. II. parox. ναυμάχος, ον, act. fighting at sea, Anth.

Ναύ-πακτος, ἡ, (ναῦς, πήγνυμι) a city on the north of the gulf of Corinth.

ναυπηγέω, f. ήσω, (ναυπηγός) to build ships, Ar., Plat.: —Med., ναῦς ναυπηγέεσθαι to build oneself ships, get them built, Hdt., Att. :—Pass., of ships, to be built, Thuc., Xen. Hence

ναυπηγήσιμος, ον, and **η, ον,** useful in shipbuilding, of wood, Hdt., Thuc.; and

ναυπηγία, Ion. **-ίη, ἡ,** shipbuilding, Hdt., Thuc.; and

ναυπηγικός, ή, όν, skilled in shipbuilding, Luc.: ἡ ναυπηγική (sc. τέχνη) the art of shipbuilding, Arist.; and

ναυπήγιον, τό, a shipbuilder's-yard, dockyard, Ar.

ναυ-πηγός, ὁ, (πήγνυμι) a shipwright, Plat.

Ναυπλία, ἡ, Nauplia in Argolis, Hdt., etc.: **Ναυ-πλιεύς, έως, ὁ,** a Nauplian, Strab. :—Adj. **Ναύπλιος** or **-ίειος, α, ον,** Eur.

ναύ-πορος, ον, of a country, ship-frequented, Aesch. II. parox., ναυπόρος, ον, = ναυσίπορος II. 2, ship-speeding, of oars, Eur.

ΝΑΥ˜Σ, ἡ, (v. infr.) a ship, Hom., etc.; ἐν νήεσσι or ἐν νηυσίν at the ships, i. e. in the camp formed by the ships drawn up on shore, Il.; ναῦς μακραί, Lat. naves longae, ships of war, which were built long for speed, while the merchant-vessels (ναῦς στρογγύλαι, γαῦλοι, ὁλκάδες) were round-built, Hdt., etc.—Att. declens., **ναῦς, νεώς, νηΐ, ναῦν,** dual gen. and dat. νεοῖν, pl. **νῆες, νεῶν, ναυσί, ναῦς;**—Ep. declens., **νηῦς, νηός, νηΐ, νῆα,** pl. **νῆες, νηῶν, νηυσί** or **νήεσσι, νῆας,** with a special

gen. and dat. pl. ναῦφι, -φιν; in late Ep., nom. νηύς:
—Ion. declens., νηῦς, νεός, νηί, νέα, pl. νέες, νεῶν,
νηυσί, νέας:—Dor. declens., ναῦς, νᾱός, νᾱΐ, ναῦν, pl.
νᾶες, ναῶν, ναυσί (poët. νέεσσι), νᾶας:—Trag. declens.,
ναῦς, ναός or νεώς, ναΐ, ναῦν, pl. νᾶες, ναῶν or νεῶν,
ναυσί, ναῦς.

ναυσθλόω, f. ώσω, contr. for ναυστολέω, *to carry by
sea*, Eur.:—Med. *to take with one by sea*, Id.:—Pass.
to go by sea, Id.

ναυσι-κλειτός, ή, όν, *famed for ships*, Od.

ναυσι-κλῠτός, όν, = foreg., epith. of the Phaeacians, Od.

ναυσῐ-πέρᾱτος, Ion. νηυσι-πέρητος, ον, = ναυσίπορος,
navigable or (perhaps) *to be crossed by a ferry*, Hdt.

ναυσί-πομπος [ῐ], ον, act. *shipwafting*, Eur.

ναυσί-πορος [ῐ], ον, *traversed by ships, navigable*, of
a river, Xen. II. parox. ναυσιπόρος, ον, act. *passing
in a ship, seafaring*, Eur. 2. *causing a ship to
pass*, of oars, Id.

ναυσί-στονος, ον, *lamentable to ships*, Pind.

ναυσί-φόρητος, ον, *carried by ship, seafaring*, Pind.

ναύ-σταθμον, τό, (σταθμός) *a harbour, anchorage,
roadstead*, Lat. *statio navium*, Eur., Thuc.

ναύ-σταθμος, ὁ, = foreg., Plut.

ναυστολέω, f. ήσω, (ναύστολος): I. trans. *to carry
or convey by sea*, Eur.:—Pass., with f. med. -ήσομαι,
to go by sea, Id. 2. *to guide, steer*, Aesch., Eur.:
metaph., τὼ πτέρυγε ποῖ ναυστολεῖς; whither *pliest thou
thy wings?* Ar. II. intr. like Pass. *to go by ship,
sail*, Soph., Eur. 2. generally, c. acc. loci, *to travel
over*, Eur. Hence

ναυστόλημα, ατος, τό, *anything conveyed by ship*: in
pl. also = ναυστολία, πόντου ναυστολήματα Eur.

ναυστολία, ή, *a going by sea, naval expedition*, Eur.

ναύ-στολος, ον, (στέλλω) *crossing the water*, Aesch.

ναύτης, ου, ὁ, (ναῦς) Lat. *nauta, a seaman, sailor*,
Hom., Hes., etc.; as Adj., ν. ὅμιλος Eur. II. *a
mate or companion by sea*, ναύτην ἄγειν τινά Soph.

ναυτία, ή, (ναῦς) *seasickness, qualmishness, disgust*,
Lat. *nausea*, Simon.

ναυτιάω, only in pres. and impf., *to be qualmish, suffer
from seasickness* or *nausea*, Ar., Plat.

ναυτικός, ή, όν, (ναύτης) *seafaring, naval*, ὁ ν. στρατός
opp. to ὁ πεζός, Hdt.; ν. λεώς Aesch.; στόλος Soph.;
ν. ἐρείπια *wrecks of ships*, Aesch.; ν. ἀναρχία *among
the seamen*, Eur.:—τὸ ναυτικόν *a navy, fleet*, Hdt.,
Ar., etc. 2. of persons, *skilled in seamanship,
nautical*, ναυτικοὶ ἐγένοντο became *a naval power*,
Thuc. 3. ἡ ναυτική (sc. τέχνη) *navigation, seamanship*, Hdt.; so, τὰ ναυτικά Plat.;—but, τὰ ναυτικά,
also, *naval affairs, naval power*, Thuc., Xen. II.
at Athens, ναυτικόν technically meant *money borrowed
or lent on bottomry*, Xen., etc.

ναυτιλία, Ion. -ίη, ή, *sailing, seamanship*, Od., Hes. 2.
a voyage, Pind., Hdt. II. *a ship*, Anth.

ναυτίλλομαι, Dep., only in pres. and impf., *to sail, go
by sea*, Hdt.; rare in Att. From

ναυτίλος [ῐ], ὁ, (ναύτης) *a seaman, sailor*, Hdt., Aesch.,
etc. 2. as Adj., ναυτίλος, ον, *of a ship*, Aesch. II.
the nautilus, a shell-fish, furnished with a membrane
which serves it for a sail, Arist.

ναυτολογέω, *to take on board*; metaph., Anth. From

ναυτο-λόγος, ον, *collecting seamen*, Strab.

ναύφαρκτος, v. ναύφρακτος.

ναυφθορία, ή, *shipwreck, loss of ships*, Anth. From

ναύ-φθορος, ον, (φθείρω) *shipwrecked*, ν. στολή, πέπλοι
the garb *of shipwrecked men*, Eur.

ναύφρακτος, -ιν, Ep. gen. and dat. pl. of ναῦς.

ναύ-φρακτος, Att. **ναύ-φαρκτος**, ον, (φράσσω) *ship-
fenced*, Aesch., Eur.; στρατός Ar.:—ναύφρακτον βλέπειν *to look like a ship of war*, Id.

ΝΑ'Ω, prob. only in pres. and impf. *to flow*, Hom.

νέα, Ion. acc. of ναῦς.

νε-άγγελτος, ον, (ἀγγέλλω) *newly* or *lately told*,
Aesch.

νεάζω, only in pres., (νέος) intr. *to be young* or *new*,
Aesch.; τὸ νεάζον *youth*, Soph.; νεάζων *thinking* or
acting like a youth, Eur. 2. *to be the younger of
two*, ὁ μὲν νεάζων Soph. 3. *to grow young*, Anth.

νε-αίρετος, ον, *newly taken*, Aesch.

νε-ᾱκόνητος, ον, (ἀκονάω) *newly-whetted*, Soph.

νεᾱλής, ές, = νέος, *young, fresh*, Xen., Plat. 2. of
fish, *fresh*, Hdt.

νε-άλωτος [ᾰ], ον, *newly caught*, Hdt.

νε-ανθής, ές, (ἄνθος) *new-blown*, Anth.

νεᾱνίας, ου, Ep. and Ion. **νεηνίης**, εω, ὁ, (νέος) *a young
man, youth*, with ἀνήρ, Od.; so, παῖς νεηνίης Hdt.;
alone, like νεανίσκος, Soph., Eur., etc. 2. *youthful*,
i. e. in good sense, *impetuous, brave, active*, Eur., Ar.,
etc.; or in bad sense, *hot-headed, headstrong*, Eur.,
Dem. II. of things, *new, young, fresh*, Eur.

νεᾱνίευμα, ατος, τό, *a youthful*, i. e. *a spirited* or (in
bad sense) *a wanton act or word*, Plat., etc. From

νεᾱνιεύομαι, Dep., with fut. med. -εύσομαι: aor. 1
ἐνεανιευσάμην: pf. pass. νενεανίευμαι:—Pass. (νεανίας) *to act like a hot-headed youth, to act wantonly, to brawl, swagger*, Plat.; τοιοῦτον ν. *to make
such youthful promises*, Dem.:—c. inf. *to undertake
with youthful spirit*, Plut.:—Pass., ἐφ᾽ ἅπασι τοῖς
ἑαυτῷ νενεανιευμένοις *to all his wanton acts*, Dem.

νεᾱνικός, ή, όν, (νεανίας) *youthful, fresh, active, vigorous*, Ar.; ν. κρέας *a fine large piece*, Id. 2.
high-spirited, impetuous, dashing, generous, gay, τὸ
νεανικώτατον *the gayest, most dashing* feat, Id.; so, ν.
καὶ μεγαλοπρεπεῖς τὰς διανοίας Plat.; μέγα καὶ νεανικὸν
φρόνημα Dem. 3. in bad sense, *headstrong, wanton,
insolent*, Plat. 4. of things, *vehement, mighty*,
Eur., Arist. II. Adv. νεανικῶς, *vigorously*, Ar. 2.
violently, wantonly, τύπτειν, τωθάζειν Id.

νεᾶνις, Ep. and Ion. **νεῆνις**, ἴδος, ἡ, acc. -ιδα and -ιν:
—*a young woman, girl, maiden*, Il., Trag.; of a
young married woman, Eur. II. as Adj. *youthful*,
Id. 2. *new*, Anth.

νεᾱνισκεύομαι, Dep. *to be in one's youth*, Xen. From

νεᾱνίσκος, Ion. νεην-, ὁ, (νέος) *a youth*, Hdt., Att.

νε-ᾱοιδός, όν, *singing youthfully*, Anth.

νεά-πολις [ᾱ], εως, ἡ, *a new city*, prop. n. of several
cities (like our *Newtown*), esp. *Neapolis, Naples*.

νεᾱρός, ά, όν, poët. for νέος, *young, youthful*, Il.,
Trag.; νεαροί *youths*, Aesch.;—τὸ ν. *youthful spirit*,
Xen. 2. of things, *new, fresh*, νεαρὰ ἐξευρεῖν Pind.;
ν. μυελός Aesch. 3. of events, *new, recent*, Soph. II.
Adv. -ρῶς, *youthfully, rawly*, Luc.

νέας, Ion. acc. pl. from ναῦς.

νεάτη [ᾰ] (sc. χορδή) ἡ, *the lowest of the three strings*

which formed the old musical scale (the other two being ἡ μέση and ἡ ὑπάτη), Plat. From

νέατος, Ep. **νείᾰτος**, η, ον, a poët. Sup. of νέος, as μέσατος of μέσος, the last, uttermost, lowest, Hom.; ὑπαὶ πόδα νείατον Ἴδης at the lowest slope of Ida, Il. :—c. gen., πόλις νεάτη Πύλου a city on the border of Pylos, Ib. II. of Time, latest, last, Soph.; τίς ἄρα νέατος λήξει; i.e. ὥστε νέατος γενέσθαι, Id.; νέατον as Adv. for the last time, Eur.

νεᾱτός, ὁ, a ploughing up of fallow land, Xen. From

νεάω, f. άσω, (νέος) to plough up anew, of fallow land, Lat. agros novare, Ar. :—Pass., νεωμένη (sc. γῆ) land new-ploughed, Lat. novale, Hes.

νέβρειος, ον, (νεβρός) of a fawn, Anth.

νεβρῐδό-πεπλος, ον, clad in fawnskin, Anth.

νεβρίζω, f. σω, to wear a fawnskin at the feast of Bacchus, or, as trans., to robe in fawnskins, Dem. From

νεβρίς, ίδος, ἡ, a fawnskin, esp. as the dress of Bacchus and the Bacchantés, Eur.

ΝΕΒΡΟ'Σ, ὁ and ἡ, the young of the deer, a fawn, Hom., etc.; πέδιλα νεβρῶν fawnskin brogues, Hdt.

νεβρ-ώδης, ες, (εἶδος) fawn-like, of Bacchus, Anth.

νέες, Ion. nom. pl. of ναῦς: Ep. dat. **νέεσσι**.

νέηαι, Ep. for νέῃ, 2 sing. of νέομαι.

νεη-γενής, ές, (γίγνομαι) Ion. for νεᾱγενής, new-born, just born, Od.

νεη-θᾰλής, ές,=νεοθαλής, fresh-blown, young, Eur.

νεηκής, ές, (ἀκή) newly whetted or sharpened, Il.

νε-ηκονής, ές, (ἀκόνη)=νεηκής, Soph.

νε-ηλᾰτος, ον, (νέος, ἐλαύνω III) newly kneaded: νεήλατα, τά, new cakes, Dem.

νέ-ηλυς, υδος, ὁ, ἡ, (ἤλυθον, aor. 2 of ἔρχομαι) newly come, a new-comer, Il., Hdt.

νεηνίης, **νεῆνις**, **νεηνίσκος**, Ion. for νεᾱν-.

νεή-τομος, ον, (τέμνω) castrated when young, Anth.

νεή-φᾰτος, ον, poët. word, new-sounding, h. Hom.

νεῖαι, Ep. for νέῃ, 2 sing. of νέομαι.

νείαιρᾱ, Ep. -ρη, irreg. fem. Comp. (cf. πρέσβειρα) of νέος, as νέατος, νείατος is Sup., lower, νειαίρῃ δ' ἐν γαστρί in the lower part of the belly, Il.

νείατος, η, ον, Ep. for νέατος.

νεικείω, Ion. for νεικέω, q. v.

νεικεστήρ, ῆρος, ὁ, one who wrangles with another, c. gen., Hes. From

νεικέω, f. έσω: aor. 1 ἐνείκεσα, Ep. νείκεσα and νείκεσσα:—Ep. forms, pres. νεικείω, 3 sing. subj. νεικείῃσι, impf. νείκειον, Ion. νεικέεσκον: (νεῖκος) :— to quarrel or wrangle with one, c. dat., Il. :—absol., Hom.; part. νεικέων, obstinately, Il. II. trans. to rail at, abuse, upbraid, revile, c. acc. pers., Hom.

νείκη, ἡ,=νεῖκος, Aesch.

ΝΕΙ'ΚΟΣ, τό, a quarrel, wrangle, strife, Hom., Hdt., etc. 2. strife of words, railing, abuse, a taunt, reproach, Il., Hdt. 3. a strife at law, dispute before a judge, Od. 4. battle, fight, Hom.; ν. φυλόπιδος Od.; of dissensions between whole nations, νεῖκος πρὸς Καρχηδονίους Hdt. II. cause of strife, matter of quarrel, Soph.

Νειλαιεύς, ὁ, and **Νειλαῖος**, α, ον, from the Nile, Anth.

Νειλο-γενής, ές, (γίγνομαι) Nile-born, Anth.

Νειλο-μέτριον, τό, a Nilometer, a rod graduated to shew the rise and fall of the Nile, Strab.

Νειλό-ρῠτος, ον, (ῥέω) watered by the Nile, Anth.

Νεῖλος, ὁ, the Nile, first in Hes. ;—in Hom. the river is called Αἴγυπτος. Hence

Νειλωΐς, ΐδος, ἡ, situate on the Nile, Anth.; and

Νειλῷος, α, ον,=Νειλαῖος, Anth.

Νειλώτης, ου, ὁ, in or on the Nile :—fem., **Νειλῶτις** χθών the land of Nile, Aesch.

νεῖμεν, Ion. for ἔνειμεν, 3 sing. aor. 1 of νέμω.

νειόθεν, Ion. for νεόθεν, Adv., (νέος) from the bottom, νειόθεν ἐκ κραδίης from the bottom of his heart, Il.

νειόθῐ, Ion. for νεόθι, Adv. (νέος) at the bottom, δάκε νειόθι θυμόν it stung him to his heart's core, Hes. : c. gen., νειόθι λίμνης Il.

νειο-κόρος, ὁ, ἡ, Ion. for νεωκόρος, Anth.

νειο-ποιέω, f. ήσω, to take a green crop off a field, by which it is freshened and prepared for corn, Xen.

νειός, ἡ, Lat. novāle, new land, i. e. land ploughed up anew after being left fallow, fallow-land, Il.; νειὸς τρίπολος a thrice-ploughed fallow, Hom. : in Att. also **νεός**, ἡ, Xen.

νειο-τομεύς, ὁ, (τέμνω) one who breaks up a fallow, Anth.

νεῖρα or **νείρα**, ἡ, contr. for νείαιρα, Aesch.

νεῖται, contr. for νέεται, 3 sing. of νέομαι.

νεκάς, άδος, ἡ, (νέκυς) a heap of slain, ἐν αἰνῇσιν νεκάδεσσιν (Ep. dat. pl.) Il.

νεκρ-άγγελος, ον, messenger of the dead, Luc.

νεκρᾰγωγέω, f. ήσω, to conduct the dead, Luc. From

νεκρ-ᾰγωγός, όν, conducting the dead.

νεκρ-ᾰκᾰδήμεια, ἡ, a school of the dead, Luc.

νεκρικός, ή, όν, (νεκρός) of or for the dead, Luc. Adv. -κῶς, Id.

νεκρο-βᾰρής, ές, (βαρύς) laden with the dead, Anth.

νεκρο-δέγμων, ον, (δέχομαι) receiving the dead, Aesch.

νεκρο-δόκος, ον,=νεκροδέγμων, Anth. Hence

νεκροδοχεῖον, τό, a cemetery, mausoleum, Luc.

νεκρο-κορίνθια, τά, the cinerary urns dug out of the tombs of Corinth, Strab.

νεκρο-μαντεῖον, τό,=νεκυομαντεῖον, Cic.

νεκρό-πολις, εως, ἡ, city of the dead, a suburb of Alexandria used as a burial place, Strab.

νεκρο-πομπός, όν, conducting the dead, of Charon, Eur., Luc.

ΝΕΚΡΟ'Σ, ὁ,=νέκυς, a dead body, corpse, Hom., etc. : —in pl. the dead, as dwellers in the nether world, Od.; τοὺς ἑαυτῶν ν. their own dead, of those killed in battle, Thuc. II. as Adj., νεκρός, ά, όν, dead, Pind. :— Comp. -ότερος Anth.

νεκροστολέω, to ferry the dead, of Charon, Luc. From

νεκρο-στόλος, ον, (στέλλω) a corpse-bearer.

νεκρο-σῡλία, ἡ, robbery of the dead, Plat.

νεκρο-φόνος, ον, (*φένω) murderer of the dead, Anth.

νεκρο-φόρος, ον, (φέρω) burying the dead, Polyb.

νεκρόω, f. ώσω, to make dead :—Pass. to be dead, νεκρωθείς Anth.; νενεκρωμένος N. T. II. to mortify, N. T.

νεκρ-ώδης, ες, (εἶδος) corpse-like, Luc.

νεκρών, ῶνος, ὁ, (νεκρός) a burial-place, Anth.

νέκρωσις, ἡ, a state of death, deadness : death, N. T.

ΝΕ'ΚΤΑΡ, ᾰρος, τό, nectar, the drink of the gods, as ambrosia was their food, Hom., etc. ; poured like wine by Hebé, and mixed with water, Id. II. metaph.,

νέκταρ μελισσᾶν, i. e. honey, Eur.: of *perfumed unguent*, Anth. :—Pind. calls his Ode ν. χυτόν. Hence

νεκτάρεος, έα, Ion. έη, εον, *nectarous*, of garments, prob., *scented, fragrant*, or generally, *divine, beautiful*, Il. :—literally, ν. σπονδαί libations *of nectar*, Pind.

νεκυ-ηγός, όν, (ἄγω) = νεκραγωγός, Anth.

νέκυια, ἡ, (νέκυς) a rite *by which ghosts were called up and questioned*, name for Od. 11.

νεκυο-μαντεῖον, Ion. -ήιον, τό, *an oracle of the dead*, a place where ghosts were called up and questioned, Hdt.

νεκυο-στόλος, ον, (στέλλω) *ferrying the dead*, of Charon, Anth.   2. *bearing the dead*, of a bier, Id.

ΝΕ'ΚΥΣ [ῠ], υος, ὁ, Ep. dat. sing. νέκυϊ, pl. νεκύεσσι, νέκυσσι: acc. pl. νέκυας, contr. νέκῡς :—like νεκρός, *a dead body, a corpse, corse*, Hom., Hdt., Soph., etc. :—in pl. *the spirits of the dead*, Lat. *Manes, inferi*, in Od., Il.   II. as Adj. *dead*, Soph., Anth.

'νεμάττετο, for ἐνεμάττετο, 3 sing. impf. of ἐμμάττομαι.

Νεμέα, Ion. -έη, Ep. -είη, ἡ, (νέμος, *nemus*) *a wooded district* between Argos and Corinth, Pind., etc. :—Adj. Νέμειος, α, ον, *Nemean*, Eur., etc.; also Νέμεος, Theocr.; Νεμεαῖος, Hes.; Νεμεαῖος, Pind.: fem. Adj. Νεμεάς, άδος, Id.   II. Νέμεα, poët. Νέμεια (sc. ἱερά), τά, *the Nemean games*, celebrated in the second and fourth years of each Olympiad, Id., Thuc.

νεμέθω, Ep. for νέμω :—Med., νεμέθοντο the cattle *were grazing, feeding*, Il.

νεμεσάω, Ep. 3 sing. νεμεσσᾷ, imper. νέμεσσα :—aor. 1 ἐνεμέσησα, poët. νεμέσσα, Dor.-ᾱσα :—Med. and Pass., f. νεμεσήσομαι: Ep. 3 sing. aor. 1 opt. νεμεσήσαιτο: Ep. aor. 1 also νεμεσσήθην: (νέμεσις) :—*to feel just resentment, to be wroth at* undeserved good or bad fortune (cf. νέμεσις), properly of the gods, Il., Hes.; ν. τινι *to be wroth with* a person or *at* a thing, Hom.   II. Med. and Pass., properly, *to be displeased with oneself : to take shame to oneself, feel shame*, Hom.   2. Med. very much like the Act., c. dat. pers., Id.; c. acc. et inf. *to be indignant* at seeing, Od.; c. acc. rei, νεμεσσᾶται κακὰ ἔργα visits evil deeds *upon* the doers, Ib.   Hence

νεμεσητικός, ή, όν, *disposed to just indignation*, Arist.

νεμεσητός, Ep. νεμεσσητός, ή, όν, *causing indignation or wrath*, νεμεσσητὸν δέ κεν εἴη 'twere *enough to make* one *wroth*, Il., etc.; so Soph., etc.   II. *to be regarded with awe, awful*, Il., Theocr.

νεμεσίζομαι, Ep. Dep., only in pres. and impf., *to be wroth with* another, c. dat., Hom.; c. acc. rei, *to be wroth with* one *for* a thing, Il.; c. acc. et inf. *to be angry* or *amazed that* .., Ib.   II. like νεμεσάομαι, *to feel shame*, c. acc. et inf., Ib.   III. *to dread*, θεοὺς νεμεσίζετο he stood in awe of the gods, Od.

νέμεσις, εως, ἡ, Ep. dat. νεμέσσει : (νέμω) :—properly, *distribution of what is due* ; hence *a righteous assignment of anger, wrath at anything unjust, just resentment*, Hom.: *indignation at undeserved good fortune*, Arist.   2. of the gods, *indignation, wrath*, ἐκ θεοῦ ν. Hdt., Soph.   II. *the object of just resentment*, Hom.; οὐ νέμεσις [ἐστί] 'tis *no cause for wrath* that . ., c. inf., Id., Soph.   III. *indignation at one's own misdeed, a sense of sin*, Il.

     B. Νέμεσις, ἡ, as prop. n., voc. Νέμεσι, *Nemesis*,

the impersonation of *divine wrath*, Hes.: in Trag., *the goddess of Retribution*.

νεμεσσάω, νεμεσσητός, νέμεσσις, Ep. for νεμεσ- (with single σ).

νεμεσσηθῶμεν, Ep. for νεμεσηθῶμεν, 1 pl. aor. 1 pass. subj. of νεμεσάω.

νεμέτωρ, ορος, ὁ, (νέμω) *an avenger*, Aesch.

νέμος, εος, τό, (νέμω Β) *a wooded pasture, glade*, Lat. *nemus*, Il., Soph.

ΝΕ'ΜΩ, f. νεμῶ: aor. 1 ἔνειμα, Ep. νεῖμα: pf. νενέμηκα: —Med., f. νεμοῦμαι, Ion. νεμέομαι: aor. 1 ἐνειμάμην: —Pass., f. νεμηθήσομαι: aor. 1 ἐνεμήθην: pf. νενέμημαι.

     A. *to deal out, distribute, dispense*, of meat and drink, Hom., etc.; of the gods, νέμει ὄλβον Ὀλύμπιος ἀνθρώποισιν Od.; μοῖραν ν. τινί *to pay* one *due* respect, Aesch., etc. :—Pass., ἐπὶ τοὺς Ἕλληνας νέμεται *is freely bestowed* upon them, Hdt.; κρέα νενεμημένα portions of meat, Xen.   II. Med. *to distribute among themselves*, and so, *to have as one's portion, possess, enjoy*, Hom., etc.   2. *to dwell in, inhabit*, Id.: absol. *to dwell*, Hdt.   3. *to spend, pass*, αἰῶνα, ἡμέραν Pind.   III. Act. much like Med. *to hold, possess*, γῆν, χώραν, πόλιν Hdt., Att. :—Pass., of places, *to be inhabited*, Hdt.; of a country, *to maintain itself, be constituted*, Thuc.   2. *to hold sway, manage*, Hdt., Aesch. :—ν. οἴακα *to manage the helm*, Aesch.; ν. ἰσχὺν ἐπὶ σκήπτροισι *to support* one's strength on staves, Id.; ν. γλῶσσαν *to use the tongue*, Id.   3. like νομίζω, *to hold, consider as* so and so, σὲ νέμω θεόν Soph.; προστάτην ν. τινά *to take as* one's patron, Arist.

     B. of herdsmen, *to pasture* or *graze* their flocks, *drive to pasture, tend*, Lat. *pascere, to feed*, Od., Hdt., Att., etc. :—metaph. ν. χόλον Soph.   2. Med., of cattle, *to feed*, i. e. *go to pasture, graze*, Lat. *pasci*, Hom., etc.: c. acc. cogn. *to feed on*, Hdt., etc.; of men, *to eat*, Soph.; of fire, *to consume, devour*, Il., etc.; of cancerous sores, *to spread*, ἐνέμετο πρόσω Hdt.   II. c. acc. loci, ὄρη νέμειν *to graze* the hills [with cattle], Xen. :—Pass.; [τὸ ὄρος] νέμεται βουσί Xen.   2. metaph., πυρὶ νέμειν πόλιν *to give* a city to the flames, Hdt.: Pass., πυρὶ χθὼν νέμεται the land *is devoured by fire*, Il.

νένασμαι, pf. pass. of ναίω.   II. also of νάσσω.

νενέαται, Ion. for νένηνται, 3 pl. pf. pass. of νέω, *to heap*.

νενέμηκα, pf. of νέμω.

νένηκα, pf. of νέω, *to spin*.

νένιπται, 3 sing. pf. pass. of νίζω.

νενόμισμαι, pf. pass. of νομίζω.

νένοφα, v. συν-νέφω.

νένωμαι, Ion. and Dor. for νενόημαι, pf. pass. of νοέω.

νεο-άλωτος [ᾰ], ον, = νεάλωτος, Hdt.

νεο-αρδής, ές, (ἄρδω) *newly watered*, Il.

νεό-γαμος, ον, *newly married, a young husband* or *wife*, Hdt.; ν. νύμφη, κόρη Aesch., Eur.

νεο-γενής, ές, (γίγνομαι) *new-born*, Aesch., Plat.

νεο-γιλός, ή, όν, *new-born, young*, Od., Theocr. (Deriv. uncertain.)

νεογνός, όν, contr. for νεόγονος, Hdt., Aesch., etc.

νεό-γονος, ον, = νεογενής, Eur.

νεό-γραπτος, ον, = sq., Theocr.

νεό-γραφος, ον, (γράφω) *newly painted* or *written*, Anth.

νεό-γυιος, ον, (γυῖον) with young limbs, Pind.

νεο-δᾱμώδης, ες, (νέος, δᾱμος = δῆμος) a Spartan word, newly enfranchised, Thuc.; Helots were called Νεοδαμώδεις when set free for service in war, Xen.

νεό-δαρτος, ον, (δείρω) newly stripped off, Od. 2. newly flayed, βοῦς Xen.

νεο-δίδακτος, ον, of dramas, newly brought out, Luc.

νεο-δμής, ῆτος, ὁ, ἡ, = sq., newly tamed, πῶλος h. Hom.; γάμοι a newly formed marriage, Eur.

νεό-δμητος, ον, (δαμάω) newly tamed, of horses: metaph. new-wedded, Eur.

νεό-δμητος, Dor. -δμᾱτος, ον, (δέμω) new-built, Pind., Anth.

νεό-δρεπτος, ον, (δρέπω) fresh-plucked, βωμοὶ ν. altars wreathed with fresh-plucked leaves, Theocr.

νεό-δρομος, ον, (δραμεῖν) just having run, Babr.

νεό-ζευκτος, ον, (ζεύγνυμι) = νεόζυγος, Anth.

νεο-ζυγής, ές, = νεόζυγος, Aesch.

νεό-ζυγος, ον, (ζεύγνυμι) newly yoked: metaph. new-married, Eur.

νεο-θᾱλής, Dor. for νεοθηλής.

νεόθεν, Adv., like νεωστί, newly, lately, Soph.

νεο-θηγής, ές, (θήγω) = sq., Anth.

νεο-θηλής, Dor. -θᾱλής, ές, (θάλλω) fresh budding or sprouting, Il., Hes. 2. of animals, new-born, Anth. 3. metaph. fresh, εὐφροσύνη h. Hom.; ν. αὔξεται grows with youthful vigour, Pind.

νεό-θηλος, ον, (θηλή) just giving milk, Aesch.

νεο-θήξ, ῆγος, ὁ, ἡ, = νεοθηγής, Anth.

νεο-θλῑβής, ές, (θλίβω) = sq., Anth.

νεοίη, ἡ, Ep. for νεότης, youthful passion, Il.

νέ-οικος, ον, newly built, Pind.

νεο-κατάστᾰτος, ον, (καταστῆναι, aor. 2 of καθίστημι) newly settled, Thuc.

νεο-κηδής, ές, (κῆδος) whose grief is fresh, fresh-grieving, Hes.

νεο-κληρόνομος, ον, having lately inherited, Anth.

νεό-κλωστος, ον, fresh spun, Theocr.

νεό-κμητος, ον, (κάμνω) just slain, Eur.

νεό-κοπτος, ον, (κόπτω) fresh-chiselled, Ar.

νεό-κοτος, ον, new and strange, unheard of, Aesch. (-κοτος seems to be a mere termin.)

νεο-κράς, ᾱτος, ὁ, ἡ, (κεράννυμι) newly mixed: metaph. newly made, νεοκράτα φίλον Aesch.

νεό-κτιστος, ον, and η, ον, (κτίζω) newly founded or built, Hdt., Thuc.

νεό-κτονος, ον, (κτείνω) lately or just killed, Pind.

νεο-λαία, ἡ, (λαός) a band of youths, the youth of a nation, Lat. juventus, Aesch., Theocr.

νεό-λουτος, Ep. νοέλ-λουτος, ον, just bathed, h. Hom.

ΝΕ'ΟΜΑΙ, contr. νεῦμαι, Ep. 2 sing. νεῖαι, 1 pl. νεύμεθα: imperat. νεῖο: subj. 2 sing. νέηαι, 1 pl. νεώμεθα; opt. νεοίμην: inf. νέεσθαι, contr. νεῖσθαι; part. νεόμενος, νεύμενος: Ep. impf. νεόμην, 3 pl. νέοντο: Dep.: only in pres. and impf.:—to go or come (mostly with fut. sense), πάλιν ν. to go away or back, return, Hom.; οἴκόνδε νέεσθαι Id.; of streams, to flow back, Il.

νεο-πᾰθής, ές, (πάθος) = sq., Aesch.

νεο-παθής, ές, (πένθος) fresh-mourning, Od.

νεο-πηγής, ές, (πήγνυμι) lately built or made, Anth.

νεό-πηκτος, ον, fresh curdled, fresh made, Babr.

νεό-πλουτος, ον, newly become rich, upstart (cf. Fr. nouveau riche), Dem., Arist.

νεό-πλῠτος, ον, (πλύνω) newly washen, Od.

νεό-ποκος, ον, newly shorn, Soph.

νεο-πρεπής, ές, (πρέπω) befitting young people, youthful, extravagant, Plut.

νεό-πριστος, ον, (πρίω) fresh-sawn, Od.

Νεο-πτόλεμος, ὁ, surname of Pyrrhus, son of Achilles, New-warrior, because he came late to Troy, Soph., Eur.

νεόπτολις, ἡ, poët. for νεόπολις, newly-founded, Aesch.

νεόρ-ραντος, ον, (ῥαίνω) fresh-reeking, Soph.

νεόρ-ρῠτος, ον, (ῥέω) fresh-flowing, Soph., Anth.

νεόρ-ρῠτος, ον, (ῥύω) newly drawn, Aesch.

νέ-ορτος, ον, (ὄρνυμι) newly arisen, new, Soph.

ΝΕ'ΟΣ, νέα Ion. νέη, νέον, Att. also νέος, ον: Ion. νεῖος: 1. young, youthful, Hom.; or alone, νέοι youths, Il., Hes., etc.; in Att. with Art., ὁ νέος, οἱ νέοι, Ar., etc.:—τὸ νέον, = νεότης, Soph.; ἐκ νέου from a youth, from youth upwards, Plat., etc.; ἐκ νέων Arist. 2. suited to a youth, youthful, Lat. juvenilis, Aesch., Eur. II. of things, new, fresh, Il., Att. 2. of events, new, strange, τί νέον; Aesch.; μῶν τι βουλεύειν νέον; Soph. III. neut. νέον as Adv. of Time, newly, lately, just, just now, Hom., Att.; also with the Art., καὶ τὸ παλαιὸν καὶ τὸ νέον Hdt.: Comp. Adv. νεωτέρως Plat.; Sup. νεώτατα most recently, Thuc.;—also, ἐκ νέας, Ion. ἐκ νέης, anew, afresh, Lat. denuo, Hdt. IV. for νεώτερος, νεώτατος, v. νεώτερος: the orig. Comp. and Sup. were νεαρός, νέατος.

νεός, Ion. gen. of ναῦς.

νεο-σίγᾰλος [ῐ], ον, (σιγαλόεις) new and sparkling, with all the gloss on, Pind.

νεο-σκύλευτος [ῠ], ον, newly taken as booty, Anth.

νεό-σμηκτος, ον, (σμήχω) newly cleaned, Il., Plut.

νεο-σμίλευτος [ῐ], ον, new-carved, Anth.

νεο-σπᾰδής, ές, (σπάω) newly drawn, Aesch.

νεοσ-πάς, άδος, ὁ, ἡ, fresh-plucked, Soph.

νεό-σπορος, ον, (σπείρω) newly sown, fresh-sown, Aesch.

νεοσσεύω, Att. νεοττεύω, f. σω, (νεοσσός) to hatch, Ar. 2. to build a nest:—Pass., ὅσα ἦν νενεοσσευμένα ὀρνίθων γένεα as many as had their nests built, Hdt.

νεοσσιά, Ion. -ιή, Att. νεοττιά, ἡ, (νεοσσός) a nest of young birds, a nest, Hdt., Att.

νεόσσιον, Att. νεόττιον, τό, Dim. of νεοσσός, νεοττός, a young bird, nestling, chick, Ar.

νεοσσίς, Att. νεοττίς, ίδος, ἡ, = foreg., of a girl, Anth.

νεοσσο-κόμος, Att. νεοττ-, ον, rearing chickens, Anth.

νεοσσός, Att. νεοττός, ὁ, (νέος) a young bird, nestling, chick, Il., Soph., etc. 2. any young animal, as a young crocodile, Hdt.; of young children, Aesch., Eur.

νεοσσο-τροφέομαι, Att. νεοττ-, Pass. to be reared as in the nest, of a child, Ar.

νεοσσώς, Dor. for -ούς, acc. pl. of νεοσσός.

νεό-στροφος, ον, (στρέφω) newly twisted, νευρῆ Il.

νεο-σφᾰγής, ές, (σφάζω) fresh-slain, Soph., Eur.

νεο-τελής, ές, (τέλος) newly initiated, Plat.

νεό-τευκτος, ον, (τεύχω) newly wrought, Il.

νεο-τευχής, ές, (τεύχω) newly made, Il.

νεότης, ητος, ἡ, (νέος) youth, Lat. juventa, Il., Eur., etc. 2. youthful spirit, impetuosity, Hdt.: in

bad sense, *rashness, petulance*, Plat., etc.   **II.** collective, like νεολαία, *a body of youth, the youth,* Lat. *juventus,* Hdt., Thuc., etc.

νεό-τμητος, Dor. -τμᾶτος, ον, *newly cut,* Theocr.

νεο-τόκος, ον, (τίκτω) *having just brought forth,* Eur.

νεό-τομος, ον, (τέμνω) *fresh cut* or *ploughed,* Aesch.; ν. πλήγματα *newly inflicted,* Soph.   **II.** *fresh cut off, fresh cut,* ἕλιξ Eur.

νεό-τροφος, ον, (τρέφω)=νεοτρεφής, Aesch.

νεοττεύω, νεοττιά, νεόττιον, νεοττίς, νεοττός, νεοττοτροφέομαι, v. νεοσσ-.

νεουργέω, *to make new, renew,* Anth. From

νε-ουργής, ές, =sq., Plut.

νε-ουργός, όν, (*ἔργω) *new-made,* Plat.

νε-ούτατος, ον, (οὐτάω) *lately wounded,* Il., Hes.

νεό-φοιτος, ον, (φοιτάω) *newly trodden,* Anth.

νεό-φονος, ον, *of blood, fresh-shed,* Eur.

νεό-φυτος, ον, *newly planted :* metaph. *a new convert, neophyte,* N. T.

νεο-χάρακτος, ον, (χαράσσω) *newly imprinted,* Soph.

νεοχμός, όν, =νέος, *new,* Aesch., Eur., Ar.   **II.** of political innovations, νεοχμόν τι ποιέειν, = sq., Hdt. Hence

νεοχμόω, =νεωτερίζω, esp. *to make political innovations,* Lat. *res novas tentare,* πολλὰ νεόχμωσε *caused* many *innovations,* Thuc.

νεό-χνοος, ον, *with the first down* or *beard,* Anth.

νεόω, only used in aor. 1, (νέος) *to renovate, renew,* νέωσον Aesch. :—Med., τάφους ἐνεώσατο *had them renewed,* Anth.

νέποδες, οἱ, *young ones, children,* Od., Theocr. (An old word of uncertain deriv.)

νέρθε, and before a vowel or metri grat. **νέρθεν**=ἔνερθε.

νερτέριος, α, ον, (νέρτερος) *underground,* Anth.

νερτερο-δρόμος, ον, ὁ, *the courier of the dead,* Luc.

νέρτερος, α, ον, and ος, ον,=ἐνέρτερος, *lower, nether,* Lat. *inferior,* a Comp. without any Posit. in use (νέρθε, ἔνερθε), Aesch.   **2.** mostly of the world below, Trag. ; ἡ νερτέρα θεός Soph.; νέρτεροι, Lat. *inferi, the dead,* Aesch., etc. ; also, ν. πλάκες, χθών, δώματα, *of the realms below,* Soph., Eur.

νέρτος, ὁ, *an unknown bird of prey,* Ar.

νεῦμα, ατος, τό, (νεύω) *a nod* or *sign,* Thuc. ; νεύματος ἕνεκα *for a mere nod, i. e. without cause,* Xen.

νεῦμαι, Ep. contr. for νέομαι.

νευρά, Ion. -ρή, ἡ, =νεῦρον II, *a string* or *cord of sinew, a bowstring,* Hom., Hes., etc.

νευρειή, ἡ, Ep. for νευρά, Theocr.

νευρή, ἡ, Ion. for νευρά :—νευρῆφι, -φιν, Ep. gen. and dat.

νευρο-λάλος [ἄ], ον, *with sounding strings,* Anth.

ΝΕΥ͂ΡΟΝ, τό, *a sinew, tendon ;* in pl., *the tendons of the feet,* Il., Plat.   **2.** metaph. in pl., τὰ νεῦρα τῆς τραγῳδίας, *of lyric odes, their sinews, vigour,* Ar. ; τὰ νεῦρα τῶν πραγμάτων Aeschin.   **II.** *gut, cord made of sinew,* for fastening the head of the arrow to the shaft, Il. : *the cord of a sling,* Xen.

νευρο-πλεκής, ές, (πλέκω) *plaited with sinews,* Anth.

νευρορράφέω, *to stitch* or *mend shoes,* Xen. From

νευρορ-ράφος, ον, (νεῦρον II, ῥάπτω) *one who stitches with sinews, a mender of shoes, cobbler,* Ar., Plat.

νευρο-σπᾰδής, ές, (νεῦρον II, σπάω) *drawn by the*

string, ν. ἄτρακτος *the arrow drawn and just ready to fly,* Soph.

νευρό-σπαστος, ον, (σπάω) *drawn by strings, moved by strings,* of puppets, Hdt., Xen.

νευρο-τενής, ές, (τείνω) *stretched by sinews, made of gut,* Anth.

νευρο-χᾰρής, ές, (χαίρω) *delighting in the bowstring* or *in the lyre,* Anth.

νευστάζω, only in pres., (νεύω) *to nod,* of a warrior threatening his foe, Il. ; of one making signs, Od. ; of one fainting, Ib.

νευστέον, verb. Adj. of νέω B, *one must swim,* Plat.

νευστικός, ή, όν, (νέω B) *able to swim,* Plat.

ΝΕΥ'Ω, f. -σω : aor. 1 ἔνευσα, Ep. νεῦσα : pf. νένευκα :— *to nod* or *beckon,* as a sign, Hom. : c. inf. *to beckon* to one *to do* a thing, in token of command, Hom., Eur.   **2.** *to nod* or *bow in token of assent,* Hom., Soph. :—c. acc. et inf. *to promise that,* Il. :—c. acc. rei, *to grant, promise,* Soph., Eur.   **3.** generally, *to bow the head, bend forward,* of warriors charging, Il. ; of ears of corn, Hes. ; ν. κάτω *to stoop,* Eur. :—c. acc. cogn., ν. κεφαλήν Od.   **4.** *to incline* in any way, ν. εἴς τι *to incline* towards, Thuc. :—of countries, like Lat. *vergere, to slope,* ν. εἰς δύσιν Polyb.

νεφέλη, ἡ, (νέφος) *a cloud,* Hom., etc.   **2.** metaph., νεφέλη δέ μιν ἀμφεκάλυψεν κυανέη, of death, Il. ; ἄχεος ν. *a cloud* of sorrow, Hom. ; Κενταύρου φονίᾳ νεφέλᾳ, i. e. with his blood, Soph.   **II.** *a bird-net,* Ar.

νεφελ-ηγερέτᾰ, Ep. for -της, ὁ, (ἀγείρω) only in nom. and in Ep. gen. νεφεληγερέταο, *cloud-gatherer, cloud-compeller,* of Zeus, Hom.

Νεφελο-κένταυρος, ὁ, *a cloud-centaur,* Luc.

Νεφελο-κοκκῡγία, ἡ, (κόκκυξ) *Cloud-cuckoo-town,* built by the birds in Ar. :—**Νεφελοκοκκῡγιεύς,** ὁ, *a Cloud-cuckoo-man,* Id.

νεφελωτός, ή, όν, (as if from νεφελόω *to form clouds*) *clouded : made of clouds,* Luc.

νεφο-ειδής, ές, (εἶδος) *cloud-like,* Anth.

ΝΕ'ΦΟΣ, εος, τό, *a cloud, mass* or *pile of clouds,* Hom., etc.   **2.** metaph., θανάτου νέφος *the cloud* of death, Id. ; so, σκότου ν., *of blindness,* Soph. ; ν. οἰμωγῆς, στεναγμῶν Eur. ; ν. ὀφρύων *a cloud* upon the brows, Id.   **II.** metaph. also *a cloud* of men or birds, Il., Hdt. ; ν. πολέμοιο *the cloud* of battle, Il.

νεφρῖτις (sc. νόσος), ἡ, *nephritis, a disease of the kidneys,* Thuc.

ΝΕΦΡΟ'Σ, ὁ, in pl. *the kidneys,* Plat., etc. ; so in dual, Ar.

νεφ-ώδης, ες, (νέφος)=νεφοειδής, Strab.

ΝΕ'Ω (A), *to go,* v. νέομαι.

ΝΕ'Ω (B) : impf. ἔνεον, Ep. ἔννεον : f. νευσοῦμαι : aor. 1 ἔνευσα : pf. νένευκα :—*to swim,* Od., Hdt., etc. :— metaph. of shoes that are too large, ἔνεον ἐν ταῖς ἐμβάσιν *I was floating* in my shoes, as if they were boats, Ar.

ΝΕ'Ω (C), f. νήσω : aor. 1 ἔνησα :—Pass., aor. 1 ἐνήθην : pf. νένησμαι :—*to spin,* of a spider, νεῖ νήματα Hes. : Med., ἅσσα οἱ νήσαντο *the threads which* [the Fates] *spun* out to him, Od. :—Pass., τὰ νηθέντα Plat.

ΝΕ'Ω (D), f. νήσω : aor. 1 ἔνησα :—Pass., pf. νένησμαι or -ημαι, Ion. 3 pl. νενέαται :—*to heap, pile, heap up,* πυρὰν νῆσαι *to pile* a funeral pyre, Hdt. ; νήσαντες

ξύλα Eur. :—Pass., ἀμφορῆς νενησμένοι Ar. ; ἄρτοι νενημένοι Xen.

νεώ, Att. acc. of νεώς (ναός), *a temple* :—νεῷ dat.

νεωκορέω, (νεωκόρος) *to serve a temple* : ironically, *to sweep clean, clean out, plunder a temple*, Plat. ; and

νεωκορία, Ion. -ίη, ἡ, *the office of a νεωκόρος*, Anth.

νεω-κόρος, ὁ, *the custodian of a temple*, Lat. *aedituus*, Plat., Xen. II. a title of Asiatic towns, which *had* built a temple in honour of their patron-god, as Ephesus was, ν. Ἀρτέμιδος N. T. (Deriv. uncertain.)

νεωλκέω, f. ήσω, *to haul a ship up on land*, Lat. *subducere navem*, Polyb. From

νε-ωλκός, ὁ, (ναῦς, ἕλκω) *a ship-hauler*, Arist.

νε-ώνητος, ον, *newly bought*, of slaves, Ar.

νε-ώρης, ες, (ὥρα) *new, fresh, late*, Lat. *recens*, νεώρη βόστρυχον τετμημένον *a lock of hair but just cut off*, Soph. ; φόβος νεώρης Id.

νεώριον, τό, (νεωρός) *a place were ships are taken care of, a dockyard*, Ar., Thuc. ; also in pl., like Lat. *navalia*, Eur., Thuc., etc. Cf. νεώσοικος.

νεωρίς, ίδος, ἡ, = νεώριον, Strab.

νεωρός, ὁ, (ναῦς, ὥρα) *superintendent of the dockyard*.

νεώς, ώ, ὁ, Att. for ναός, (as λεώς for λαός) *a temple*, Aesch., etc. : gen. νεώ, dat. νεῴ, acc. νεών :—pl. nom. νεῴ, acc. νεώς.

νεώς, Adv. of νέος.

νεώς, Att. gen. of ναῦς.

νεώσ-οικος, ὁ, (ναῦς, οἶκος) *a dock*, Ar. :—in pl. *sheds, slips, docks*, in which ships might be built, repaired, or laid up, being parts of the νεώριον, Hdt., Thuc.

νεωστί, Adv. of νέος, for νέως, as μεγαλωστί for μεγάλως, *lately, just now*, Hdt., Soph.

νέ-ωτα, (νέος, ἔτος) Adv. *next year, for next year*, εἰς νέωτα Xen., Theocr.

νεώτατος, η, ον, Sup. of νέος, *youngest*, Il. 2. *most recent*, Arist.

νεωτερίζω, f. Att. ιῶ, (νεώτερος II) *to attempt anything new, make a violent* change, Thuc., Xen., etc. : ν. ἐς τὴν ἀσθένειαν *to change* [health] into sickness, Thuc. II. *to attempt political changes, make innovations* or *revolutionary movements*, Lat. *res novas tentare*, Id., etc. 2. c. acc., ν. τὴν πολιτείαν *to revolutionise* the state, Id. :—Pass., ἐνεωτερίζετο τὰ περὶ τὴν ὀλιγαρχίαν Id. Hence

νεωτερισμός, ὁ, *innovation, revolutionary movement*, Plat., etc. ; and

νεωτεριστής, οῦ, ὁ, *an innovator*, Plut.

νεωτεροποιία, ἡ, *innovation, revolution*, Thuc. From

νεωτερο-ποιός, όν, (ποιέω) *innovating, revolutionary*, Thuc., Arist.

νεώτερος, α, ον, Comp. of νέος, *younger*, Il., Soph. :— οἱ νεώτεροι *the younger sort, men of military age*, Thuc. 2. *too young*, Od. :—c. gen., οἱ νεώτεροι τῶν πραγμάτων *those who are too young to remember* the events, Dem. II. of events, *newer, later*, Pind. : metaph. *later, worse*, Soph. ; νεώτερα alone, Lat. *gravius quid*, Hdt., Att. ; μῶν τι ν. ἀγγέλλεις ; Plat. ; νεώτερα βουλεύειν or ποιεῖν περί τινος Hdt., Thuc. 2. of political changes, νεώτερόν τι, *an innovation, revolutionary movement*, Hdt., Xen.

νη-, negat. Prefix, being a stronger form of ἀνα- privat., combined with short vowels, as in νηλεής, νήριθμος,

νήκεστος, νήνεμος, or before consonants, as in νηκερδής, νηπενθής, νήποινος.

νή, Att. Particle of strong affirmation, like Ep. ναί ; with acc. of the Divinity invoked, νὴ Δία (in familiar Att., νὴ Δί᾽ or νηδί), Ar. ; also with the Art., νὴ τὸν Δία Id. ; νὴ τὴν Ἀθηνᾶν, νὴ τὴν Ἄρτεμιν, νὴ τὸν Ποσειδῶ Id.

νῆα, **νῆας**, Ion. acc. sing. and pl. of ναῦς.

νη-γάτεος [ᾰ], η, ον, *new-made*, Il. (Perh. from νέος, γέ-γαα.)

νή-γρετος, ον, (νη-, ἐγείρω) *unwaking*, νήγρετος ὕπνος a sleep *that knows no waking, deep sleep*, Od. ; neut. as Adv., νήγρετον εὕδειν *without waking*, Ib.

νήδυια, ων, τά, (νηδύς) *the bowels, entrails*, Il.

νήδῠμος, ον, epith. of ὕπνος, either = ἡδύς, *sweet, delightful ;* or 2. from νη-, δύνω, *sleep from which one rises not, sound* sleep, much like νήγρετος, Hom.

ΝΗΔΥ´Σ [ῠ], ύος [ῠ], ἡ, *the stomach*, Od., Hes., Aesch., etc. 2. *the belly, paunch*, Il., Hdt. ; *the womb*, Il. : metaph., *of earth, gremium telluris*, Eur.

νῆες, nom. pl. of ναῦς :—**νήεσσι**, Ep. dat. pl.

νηέω, Ep. longer form of νέω D : Ep. aor. 1 νήησα :— *to heap, heap* or *pile up*, Hom. II. *to pile, load*, [νῆας] νηήσας εὖ Il. : Med., νῆα χρυσοῦ νηησάσθω *let him pile his* ship with gold, Ib.

νήθω, (νέω C) *to spin*, Plat. ; 2 sing. Ion. impf. νήθεσκες, Anth.

νηί, Ion. dat. of ναῦς.

Νηιάς, άδος, ἡ, Ion. for Ναϊάς.

νήιος, η, ον, Dor. and Trag. νάϊος, α, ον, also ος, ον : (ναῦς) :—*of* or *for a ship*, δόρυ νήιον or νήιον alone, *ship-timber*, Hom.

Νηίς, ίδος, ἡ, Ion. for Ναΐς.

νῆ-ις, ιδος, ὁ, ἡ : acc. νήιδα, (νη-, εἰδέναι) *unknowing of, unpractised in* a thing, c. gen., Od. ; absol., Il.

νηίτης [ῑ], ου, ὁ, (ναῦς) *consisting of ships*, στρατὸς ν. a fleet, Thuc.

νη-κερδής, ές, (νη-, κέρδος) *unprofitable*, Hom.

νή-κερως, ων, (νη-, κέρας) *not horned*, Ep. nom. pl. νήκεροι Hes.

νή-κεστος, ον, (νη-, ἀκέομαι) *incurable*, neut. as Adv. *incurably*, Hes.

νη-κουστέω, (νη-, ἀκούω) *not to hear, to give no heed to, disobey* one, c. gen., Il.

νηκτός, ή, όν, (νήχω) *swimming*, Anth.

νηλεής, ές, v. νηλής.

νηλεό-ποινος, ον, (ποινή) *punishing without pity, ruthlessly punishing*, Hes.

Νηλεύς, έως, ἡ, father of Nestor, Hom. :—Ep. Adj. **Νηλήιος**, Il., etc. :—Patr., **Νηληΐδης**, ου, ὁ, and **Νηληιάδης**, εω, or ἀο, Hom.

νη-λής, ές, Ep. neut. νηλεές (as if from νηλής), Ep. also **νηλειής**, ές, (νη-, ἔλεος), *pitiless, ruthless*, Il. ; νηλέϊ χαλκῷ with *ruthless* steel, Hom. ; νηλέϊ ὕπνῳ *relentless* sleep, which exposes men without defence to ill, Od. ; νηλεὲς ἦμαρ, i. e. the day of death, Hom. :— Adv. νηλεῶς Aesch. II. pass. *unpitied*, Soph.

νηλιπο-και-βλεπ-έλαιοι, ον, nickname of philosophers, *barefoot and looking after oil*, Anth.

νηλίπους, ὁ, ἡ, *unshod, barefooted*, Soph. (Commonly deriv. from νη-, ἤλιψ *without shoe*.)

νη-λῑτής, ές, (νη-, ἀλιτεῖν) *guiltless, harmless*, Od.

νῆμα, ατος, τό, (νέω *to spin*) *that which is spun, a thread, yarn*, Od., Hes., Eur.

νημέρτεια, ἡ, *certainty, truth*, Dor. **νᾱμέρτεια** Soph.

νη-μερτής, ές, Dor. and Trag. **νᾱμερτής**, (νη-, ἁμαρτεῖν) *unerring, infallible*, Od., Hes.; **νημερτέα βουλήν** *a sure decree*, i. e. one *that will infallibly be enforced*, Od.; **νημερτέα εἰπεῖν** or **μυθήσασθαι** to speak *sure truths*, Hom.; Ion. Adv. **νημερτέως** as trisyll., Od.

νηνεμία, Ion. -ίη, ἡ, *stillness in the air, a calm*, **νηνεμίης** *in a calm*, Il.; **γαλήνη ἔπλετο νηνεμίη** *there was a calm, a ceasing of all winds*, Od.; **ἐξ αἰθρίης τε καὶ νηνεμίης** Hdt. From

νή-νεμος, ον, (νη-, ἄνεμος) *without wind, breezeless, calm, hushed*, Il., Aesch., Eur.:—metaph., ν. **ἔστησ' ὄχλον** Eur.

νῆξις, εως, ἡ, (νήχω) *a swimming*, Batr.

νηο-βάτης [ᾰ], ου, ὁ, poët. for **ναυβάτης**, Anth.

νηο-κόρος, ον, (νηός) poët. for **νεωκόρος**, Anth.

νηο-πόλος, Att. **νᾱοπ-**, ὁ, ἡ, (νηός, πολέω) *busying oneself in a temple: a temple-keeper*, Hes., Anth.

νηο-πορέω, f. ήσω, poët. for **ναυπορέω**, *to go by sea*, Anth.

νηός, ὁ, Ion. for **ναός**, *a temple*.　　II. Ion. gen. of **ναῦς**.

νηο-φόρος, ον, (φέρω) *bearing ships*, Anth.

νηοχος, ον, = **νηοῦχος**, Anth.

νη-πενθής, ές, (πένθος) *banishing pain*, **φάρμακον νηπενθές** *an opiate*, Od.:—**νηπενθής**, as epith. of Apollo, Anth.

νηπιάα, **νηπιέη**, ἡ, Ep. forms of **νηπία**, *childhood*, **ἐν νηπιέῃ** Il.:—in pl. *childish tricks* or *follies*, **νηπιέῃσιν** *in childish fashion, in folly*, Hom.

νηπιαχεύω, *to be childish, play like a child*, Il. From

νηπίαχος, ον, Ep. Dim. of **νήπιος**, *infantine, childish*, Il.

νηπιάχω, = **νηπιαχεύω**, Mosch.

νηπιέη, v. **νηπιάα**.

νήπιος, α Ion. η, ον, (νη-, ἔπος) *not yet speaking*, Lat. *infans*, Hom.; **νήπια τέκνα, βρέφος ν.** Eur.:—also **νήπια** *young animals*, Il.　　II. metaph. *like a child, childish, silly*, Hom., Hes.; *without forethought*, Hom., Aesch. Hence

νηπιότης, ητος, ἡ, *childhood, childishness*, Plat.

νηπιό-φρων, ονος, ὁ, ἡ, *of childish mind, silly*, Strab.

νή-πλεκτος, ον, *with unbraided hair*, Bion.

νη-ποινεί or -ί, Adv., Lat. *impune*, Plat. From

νή-ποινος, ον, (νη-, ποινή) *unavenged*, Hom.:—neut. **νήποινον** as Adv., Od.　　II. **φυτῶν νήποινος** *without share of fruitful trees*, Pind.

νηπυτιεύομαι, Dep. *to play child's tricks*, Anth. From

νηπύτιος [ῠ], ὁ, ἡ, (νήπιος) *a little child*, Il., Ar.　　II. as Adj. *like a child, childish*, Il.

Νηρεύς, έως, Ion. ῆος, ὁ, *Nereus, a sea-god, son of* **Πόντος** (*the sea*), *father of the Nereïds*, Hes. Hence

Νηρηΐς or **Νηρεΐς**, ῖδος, ἡ, *a daughter of Nereus, a Nereïd* or *Nymph of the sea*, mostly in pl., **Νηρηΐδες**, Hom.; **Νηρεΐδες** Hes.; Att. **Νηρῇδες** Soph., Eur.

νήριθμος, ον, = **ἀνάριθμος**, *countless*, Theocr.

νήριτος, ον, = **νήριθμος**, *countless, immense*, Hes.:—hence the name of the Ithacan mountain, **Νήριτον εἰνοσίφυλλον** Hom.

νησαῖος, α Ion. η, ον, *of an island, insular*, Eur.

νήσαντο, Ep. for **ἐνήσαντο**, 3 pl. aor. 1 of **νέω** *to spin*.

νησιάζω, = **νησίζω**, Strab.

νησίδιον [σῐ], τό, Dim. of **νῆσος**, *an islet*, Thuc.

νησίζω, (νῆσος) *to be* or *form an island*, Polyb.

νησίον, τό, Dim. of **νῆσος**, *an islet*, Strab.

νῆσις, εως, ἡ, (νέω C) *spinning*, Plat.

νησίς, ῖδος, ἡ, Dim. of **νῆσος**, *an islet*, Hdt., Thuc.

νησίτης [ῑ], ου, ὁ, (νῆσος) *of* or *belonging to an island*: Dor. fem. **νᾱσῖτις**, ιδος, Anth.

νησιώτης, ου, ὁ, fem. -ῶτις, ιδος: Dor. **νᾱσ-**, (νῆσος) *an islander*, Hdt., Ar., etc.　　II. as Adj. *of* or *in an island, insular*, Hdt., Eur.; **νησιῶτις πέτρα** *an island rock*, Aesch. Hence

νησιωτικός, ή, όν, *of* or *from an island*, Hdt., Eur.; **ὄνομα νησιωτικὸν Σαλαμῖνα θέμενον** *having given it the island name of Salamis*, Eur.:—**τὸ ν.** *insular situation*, Thuc.

νησο-ειδής, ές, (εἶδος) *like an island*, Strab.

νησο-μαχία, ἡ, (μάχη) *an island-fight*, Luc.

νῆσος, Dor. **νᾶσος**, ἡ, *an island*, Lat. *insula*, Hom., Hes., etc.; **ἐν τᾷ μεγάλᾳ Δωρίδι νάσῳ Πέλοπος**, i. e. *in Peloponnese*, Soph.; **μακάρων νῆσοι**, v. sub **μάκαρ**. (Perhaps from **νέω** *to swim*, as if *floating land*.)

νῆσσα, v. **νῆττα**.

νηστεία, ἡ, *a fast*, Hdt. From

νηστεύω, f. σω, *to fast*, Ar.

νῆστις, ιος, ὁ, and ἡ, gen. ιος or ιδος, pl. **νήστιες** or **νήστεις**: (νη-, ἐσθίω):—*not eating, fasting*, of persons, Hom.; c. gen., **νῆστις βορᾶς** Eur.:—metaph., **νῆστιν ἀνὰ ψάμμον** *over the hungry sand*, Aesch.　　2. **νῆστις νόσος, λιμός** *hungry famine*, Id.; **νήστισιν αἰκίαις** *the pains of hunger*, Id.; **νήστιδες δύαι** Id.　　3. act. *causing hunger, starving*, **πνοιαὶ νήστιδες** Id.

νησύδριον, τό, Dim. of **νῆσος**, Xen., etc.

νή-τιτος, ον, (νη-, τίνω) *unavenged*, Anth.

νητός, ή, όν, (νέω D) *heaped, piled up*, Od.

ΝΗ΄ΤΤΑ, Ion. **νῆσσα**, Boeot. **νᾶσσα**, *a duck*, Lat. *anas* (gen. *a-nat-is*), Hdt., Ar., etc.

νηττάριον [ᾰ], Dim. of **νῆττα**, *a little duck*, Ar.

νηῦς, Ion. for **ναῦς**.

νηυσιπέρητος, ον, v. **ναυσιπέρατος**.

νή-ϋτμος, ον, (νη-, ἀϋτμή) *breathless*, Hes.

νηφαλιεύς, ὁ, = **νηφάλιος**, Anth.

νηφάλιος [ᾰ], α, ον, (νήφω) *unmixed with wine, wineless*, νηφ. **μειλίγματα** *the offerings to the Eumenides, composed of water, milk, and honey*, Aesch.　　II. *of persons, sober*, N. T.

ΝΗ΄ΦΩ, aor. 1 **ἔνηψα**:—*to drink no wine*, Theogn., Plat.; part. **νήφων** act. Adj. = **νηφάλιος**, Hdt., Plat.　　II. metaph. *to be sober, dispassionate*, Xen.

νήφων, ονος, ὁ, ἡ, dat. pl. **νήφοσι** *sober*, Theogn., Soph.

νήχω, Dor. **νάχω**: Ep. impf. **νῆχον**, inf. **νηχέμεναι**: f. **νήξω**: (νέω B):—*to swim*, Od., Hes.:—also as Dep. **νήχομαι**, part. **νηχόμενος**: f. **νήξομαι**: aor. 1 part. **νηξάμενος** Anth.: = Act., Od., Anth.

νῆψις, ἡ, (νήφω) *soberness*, Strab.

νίγλαρος, ὁ, *a pipe* or *whistle*, used by the **κελευστής** *to give the time in rowing*, Ar. (Deriv. unknown.)

ΝΙ΄ΖΩ, Ep. impf. **νίζον**: (the pres. **νίπτω**, from which the tenses are formed, only in late writers): f. **νίψω**: aor. 1 **ἔνιψα**, Ep. **νίψα**:—Med., f. **νίψομαι**: Ep. 3 sing. aor. 1 **νίψατο**:—Pass., pf. **νένιμμαι**:—*to wash the hands* or *feet of another*, Od.:—Med., **χεῖρας νίψασθαι**

to wash one's hands, Il., Hes. ; so, νίψασθαι, absol., to wash one's hands, Od., etc. ; νίψασθαι ἁλός to wash [with water] from the sea, Ib. 2. generally to purge, cleanse, Soph., Eur. II. to wash off, ἱδρῶ νίψεν ἀπὸ χρωτός washed off the sweat from the skin, Il. ; αἷμα νίζ' ὕδατι Ib. :—Med., χρόα νίζετο ἅλμην he washed the brine off his skin, Od. :—Pass., αἷμα νένιπται Il.—The word is commonly said of persons washing part of the person, while λούομαι is used of bathing, πλύνω of washing clothes.

νικαξῶ, Dor. for νικήσω, fut. of νικάω.

νῑκάτωρ, ορος, ὁ, Dor. for νικήτωρ, a conqueror, Plut.

νικαφορία, -φόρος, Dor. for νικηφ-.

νῑκάω, f. ήσω : aor. 1 ἐνίκησα, Ep. νίκησα : pf. νενίκηκα : (νίκη) : I. absol. to conquer, prevail, vanquish, Hom., etc. ; ὁ νικήσας the conqueror, ὁ νικηθείς the conquered, Il. ; ἐνίκησα καὶ δεύτερος καὶ τέταρτος ἐγενόμην I won the first prize, Thuc. ; νικᾶν ἐπὶ πᾶσι κριταῖς in the opinion of all the judges, Ar. ; c. acc. cogn., πάντα ἐνίκα he won all the bouts, Il. ; παγκράτιον Thuc. ; ν. Ὀλύμπια to be conqueror in the Ol. games, Id., etc. 2. of opinions, to prevail, carry the day, Hom., etc. ; ἐκ τῆς νικώσης [γνώμης] according to the prevailing opinion, vote of the majority, Xen. :—impers. ἐνίκα (sc. ἡ γνώμη) it was resolved, Lat. visum est, c. inf. ; ἐνίκα μὴ ἐκλιπεῖν τὴν πόλιν it was carried not to leave the city, Hdt. ; ἐνίκησε λοιμὸν εἰρῆσθαι it was the general opinion that λοιμός was the word, Thuc. 3. as law-term, ν. τὴν δίκην to win one's cause, Eur., Ar. II. c. acc. pers. to conquer, vanquish, Hom., etc. ; μὴ φῦναι τὸν ἅπαντα νικᾷ λόγον not to be born is best, Soph. ; νικᾶν τινα to win victory over one, Od. 2. generally of passions, etc., to conquer, to overpower, Il. ; βαρεῖαν ἡδονὴν νικᾶτέ με ye force me to grant you pleasure against my will, Soph. ; c. inf. ἤ ᾗ βία σε νικησάτω μισεῖν let not force prevail on thee to hate, Id. 3. Pass., νικᾶσθαί τινος, like ἡττᾶσθαι, to be inferior to, give way, yield to, Id., Eur. ; ἢν τοῦτο νικηθῇς ἐμοῦ Ar.

νίκη, poët. 3 sing. impf. of νίκημι.

ΝΙ'ΚΗ [ῑ], ἡ, victory in battle, Il., etc. ; in the games, Pind., etc. :—c. gen. subjecti, νίκη φαίνεται Μενελάου plainly belongs to Menelaus, Il. ; but c. gen. objecti, νίκη ἀντιπάλων victory over opponents, Ar. 2. generally, the upper hand, ascendancy, νίκην διασώζεσθαι to keep the fruits of victory, Xen. II. as prop. n. Νίκη, the goddess of victory, Hes. Hence

νικήεις, Dor. νικάεις, εσσα, εν, victorious, Anth.

νίκημα [ῑ], ατος, τό, (νικάω) victory, Polyb.

νίκημι, Aeol. for νικάω, Theocr. ; poët. 3 sing. impf. νίκη, Theocr.

νικησέμεν, Ep. fut. inf. of νικάω.

νῑκητέον, verb. Adj. of νικάω, one must conquer, Eur.

νῑκητήριος, α, ον, (νικάω) belonging to a conqueror or to victory ; ν. φίλημα a kiss as the conqueror's reward, Xen. II. as Subst., νικητήριον (sc. ἄθλον), τό, the prize of victory, Ar., Xen. ; mostly in pl., Eur., Plat. 2. νικητήρια (sc. ἱερά), τά, the festival of victory, Xen.

νῑκητικός, ή, όν, (νικάω) likely to conquer, conducing

to victory, Xen. ; τὸ νικητικώτατον the most likely way to conquer, Plut.

νικηφορέω, f. ήσω, to carry off as a prize, δάκρυα ν. to win naught but tears, Eur. ; and

νικηφορία, Dor. νικᾱφ-, ἡ, a conquering, victory, Pind.

νίκη-φόρος, Dor. νικᾱφ-, ον, (φέρω) bringing victory, Aesch. II. (φέρομαι) bearing off the prize, conquering, victorious, Pind., Soph., etc.

νικό-βουλος, ον, (βουλή) prevailing in the council, Ar.

νῖκος, τό, later form for νίκη, Anth.

νικῷεν, Att. for -άοιεν, 3 pl. opt. of νικάω.

νίν, Dor. and Trag. enclit. acc. of 3rd pers. Pron., like Ep. and Ion. μιν, for αὐτόν, αὐτήν, him, her, Pind., Trag. ;—rarely for αὐτό, it, Pind., Aesch. ; and for αὐτούς, -τάς (in pl.), Pind. 2. for dat. αὐτῷ, Id.

νιπτήρ, ῆρος, ὁ, (νίζω) a washing vessel, basin, N. T.

νίπτρον, τό, (νίζω) water for washing, mostly in pl., Eur., Anth.

νίπτω, later form of νίζω.

νίσσομαι, Ep. 3 pl. impf. νίσσοντο :—f. νίσομαι [ῑ] :—like νέομαι, to go, go away, Hom., Pind. ; c. acc. loci, to go to a place, Eur.

νίτρον, τό, in Hdt. and Att. λίτρον, carbonate of soda, Hdt. (Prob. a foreign word.)

νίφα [ῑ], τήν, snow, acc. formed from a nom. νίψ, which is not found, Hes.

νιφάς, άδος, ἡ, (νίφω) a snowflake, in pl. snowflakes, Il., Hdt. ; as a simile for persuasive eloquence, ἔπεα νιφάδεσσι ἐοικότα χειμερίησιν Il. :—the sing. in collective sense, a snowstorm, snow, Ib., Pind. 2. generally, a shower of stones, Aesch., Eur. ; ν. πολέμου the sleet of war, Pind. II. as fem. Adj., = νιφόεσσα, Soph.

νιφετός, οῦ, ὁ, (νίφω) falling snow, a snowstorm, Hom., etc.

νιφετ-ώδης, ες, (εἶδος) like snow, snowy, Polyb.

νιφο-βλής, ῆτος, ὁ, ἡ, = νιφόβολος, Ἄλπεις Anth.

νιφό-βολος, ον, (βάλλω) snow-stricken, snowclad, of mountains, Eur., Ar.

νιφόεις, εσσα, εν, (νίφα) snowy, snowclad, snowcapt, Hom., Hes., etc.

νιφο-στιβής, ές, (στείβω) piled with snow, Soph.

ΝΙ'ΦΩ [ῑ], aor. 1 ἔνιψα :—to snow, pers., ὅτε ὤρετο Ζεὺς νιφέμεν (Ep. inf.) when Zeus started to snow, Il. ; ὅταν νίφῃ ὁ θεός Xen. :—metaph., χρυσῷ νίφων falling in a shower of gold, Pind. 2. impers., νίφει it snows (cf. ὕω, συσκοτάζω), Ar. :—so in Med., νιφάδος νιφομένας when the snow is snowing, Aesch. 3. Pass. to be snowed on, Hdt., Ar., etc.

νίψαι, aor. 1 inf. of νίζω ; νίψω, fut.

νόα, heterocl. acc. of νοῦς.

νοερός, ά, όν, (νόος) intellectual, Plat., etc.

νοέω, f. ήσω : aor. 1 ἐνόησα, Ep. νόησα, Ion. ἔνωσα : pf. νενόηκα, Ion. νένωκα :—Med., Ep. 3 sing. aor. 1 νοήσατο, Ion. part. νωσάμενος :—Pass., aor. 1 ἐνοήθην, Ion. ἐνώθην : pf. νενόημαι, Ion. νένωμαι : 3 pl. plqpf. ἐνένωτο :—to perceive by the eyes, observe, notice, ὀφθαλμοῖς or ἐν ὀφθαλμοῖς νοέειν Il. ; distinguished from mere sight, τὸν δὲ ἰδὼν ἐνόησε Ib. ; οὐκ ἴδεν οὐδ' ἐνόησε Hom. :—hence, θυμῷ νοέω καὶ οἶδα ἕκαστα Od., etc. :—so in Med., Theogn., Soph. II. absol. to think, suppose, Hom., Hdt., etc. ; ἄλλα ν. to be of another mind, Hdt. :—part. νοέων, ἔουσα thoughtful,

wary, discreet, Hom.　　　**III.** *to think out, devise, contrive, purpose, intend*, Od., Hdt.　　**2.** c. inf. *to be minded to do* a thing, Il., Soph., etc. :—so in Med., Il., Hdt.　　**IV.** *to conceive of* or *deem* to be so and so, ὡς μηκέτ' ὄντα κεῖνον νόει Soph.　　**V.** *of words, to bear a certain sense, to mean* so and so, πυθοίμεθ' ἂν τὸν χρησμὸν ὅ τι νοεῖ Ar., Plat.　Hence

νόημα, ατος, τό, (νοέω) *that which is perceived, a perception, thought*, Hom., Hes., Att. : as an emblem of swiftness, ὡσεὶ πτερὸν ἠὲ νόημα Od.　**2.** *a thought, purpose, design*, Hom., Ar.　**II.** like νόησις, *understanding, mind*, Hom. : *disposition*, Pind.

νοήμων, ον, gen. ονος, (νοέω) *thoughtful, intelligent*, Od.　**II.** *in one's right mind*, Hdt.

νόησις, Ion. νώσις, εως, ἡ, *intelligence, thought*, Plat.

νοητικός, ή, όν, (νοέω) *intelligent*, Arist.

νοητός, ή, όν, (νοέω) *perceptible to the mind, thinkable*, opp. to visible (ὁρατός), Plat.

νοθᾰ-γενής, ές, Dor. and poët. for νοθηγενής, (γίγνομαι) *base-born*, Eur.

νοθεία, ἡ, *birth out of wedlock*, Plut.　From

νοθεύω, *to adulterate* : Pass., aor. 1 inf. νοθευθῆναι Luc.

νοθο-καλλοσύνη, ἡ, *counterfeit charms*, Anth.

ΝΟΘΟΣ, η, ον, and ος, ον, *a bastard, baseborn child*, i. e. one born of a slave or concubine, opp. to γνήσιος, Lat. *legitimus*, Il., Hdt., Att. ; νόθη κούρη Il.　**II.** generally, *spurious, counterfeit, suppositicious*, Plat.

νοίδιον, τό, Dim. of νόος, νοῦς, Ar.

νομᾰδικός, ή, όν, (νομάς) *of* or *for a herdsman's life, nomadic, pastoral*, Arist. :—Adv. -κῶς, *like Nomads*, Strab.　**2.** *Numidian*, Polyb.

νομαῖος, α, ον, = νομαδικός, Anth.

νόμαιος, α, ον, (νόμος) *customary* : νόμαια, τά, like νόμιμα, *customs, usages*, Hdt.

νομ-άρχης, ου, ὁ, *the chief of an Egyptian province* (νομός), Hdt.

νομάς, άδος, ὁ, ἡ, (νομός) *roaming about for pasture* : οἱ Νομάδες *roaming, pastoral tribes, Nomads*, Hdt., Att. ; and as prop. n., *Numidians*, Polyb.　**II.** fem. Adj. *grazing, feeding, at pasture*, Soph.　**2.** metaph. κρῆναι νομάδες *wandering streams*, Id.

νομέας, ου, ὁ, later form for νομεύς, Anth.

νόμευμα, ατος, τό, (νομεύω) *that which is put to graze*, i. e. *a flock*, Aesch.

νομεύς, έως, Ep. ῆος, ὁ, (νέμω) *a shepherd, herdsman*, Hom., etc.　**II.** *a dealer out, distributer*, ἀγαθῶν Plat.　**III.** pl. νομέες, *the ribs of a ship*, Hdt.　Hence

νομεύω, f. σω, (νομεύς) *to put to graze, drive afield*, of the shepherd, Od. :—in Pass. of the flocks, *to go to pasture*, Plat.　**2.** βουσὶ νομοὺς ν. *to eat down the pastures* with oxen, Lat. *depascere*, h. Hom.　**3.** absol. *to be a shepherd, tend flocks*, Theocr.

νομή, ἡ, (νέμω) *a pasture, pasturage*, Hdt., Soph.　**2.** *fodder, food*, Plat.　**3.** *a feeding, grazing*, of herds : metaph., νομὴ πυρός *a spreading of fire*, Polyb. ; νομὴν ἔχειν, of a cancerous sore, *to spread*, N. T.　**II.** *division, distribution*, Hdt., Plat., etc.

νομίζω, f. Att. νομιῶ, Ion. 1 pl. νομιέομεν : aor. 1 ἐνόμισα, poët. νόμιξα : pf. νενόμικα :—Pass., f. νομισθήσομαι : aor. 1 ἐνομίσθην : pf. νενόμισμαι : 3 sing. plqpf. νενόμιστο : (νόμος) :—*to hold* or *own as a custom* or *usage, to use customarily, practise*, Hdt. ; ν. γλῶσσαν *to have* a language *in common use*, Id. ; ν. οὔτε ἀσπίδα οὔτε δόρυ Id. :—Pass. *to be the custom, be customary*, Aesch. ; σωφροσύνη νενόμιστο *was the fashion*, Ar. ; —impers., ὡς νομίζεται *as is the custom*, Trag. :—part. νομιζόμενος, η, ον, *customary, usual*, Thuc. ; τὰ νομιζόμενα *customs, usages*, Lat. *instituta*, Hdt., Att. ; τὰ νομισθέντα Eur.　**2.** *to adopt a custom* or *usage*, Ἕλληνες ἀπ' Αἰγυπτίων ταῦτα νενομίκασι Hdt.　**3.** c. dat. *to be used to* a thing, νομίζουσιν Αἰγύπτιοι οὐδ' ἥρωσιν οὐδέν, i. e. *do not worship* heroes, Id. : hence *to make common use of, use*, φωνῇ Id. ; ἀγῶσι καὶ θυσίαις Thuc.　**4.** c. inf. *to have a custom of* doing, *to be accustomed to* do, Hdt. :—Pass. impers., γυμνοὺς εἰσιέναι νομίζεται *it is customary* for them . . , Ar. ; νενόμισται καλέεσθαι *it has been usual* to be called, Hdt.　**5.** Pass. *to be ordered and governed after old laws and customs*, Id.　**II.** *to own, acknowledge, consider as*, τοὺς κακοὺς χρηστοὺς ν. Soph. ; νομίσαι χρὴ ταῦτα μυστήρια Ar. : θεὸν ν. τινά *to hold* or *believe in* one as a god, Plat., Xen. :—hence, νομίζειν τούτους [θεούς] *to believe in* these [as gods], Hdt. ; οὓς ἡ πόλις νομίζει θεοὺς οὐ νομίζων *not believing in* the gods in which the State *believes*, Xen., Plat. : —but, νομίζειν θεοὺς εἶναι *to believe* that there are gods, Plat. ; θεοὺς ν. οὐδαμοῦ Aesch. ;—so that ν. τοὺς θεούς and ν. θεούς differ, the one being *to believe in* certain gods, the other *to believe in gods generally*, cf. ἡγέομαι III. 2 :—Pass., Ἕλληνες ἤρξαντο νομισθῆναι *to be considered* as . . , Hdt.　**2.** *to esteem* or *hold in honour*, Pind. :—Pass. *to be in esteem*, Plat.　**3.** c. acc. rei, *to deem, hold, believe*, τι *περὶ τινος* Id.　**4.** c. acc. et inf. *to deem, hold, believe that*, Soph., Xen. ;—also, like δοκέω, c. inf. fut. *to expect that* . . , Soph.　**5.** Pass., with gen. of the person in possession, τοῦ θεῶν νομίζεται ; *whose sanctuary is it held to be?* Id.　**6.** absol., νομίζοντα λέγειν *to speak with full belief*, Plat.

νομικός, ή, όν, (νόμος) *resting on law, conventional*, Arist. :—Adv. -κῶς, Id.　**2.** *relating to the law*, N.T., Plut.　**II.** *learned in the law, a lawyer*, N. T.

νόμιμος, η, ον, (νόμος) *conformable to custom, usage*, or *law, customary, prescriptive, established, lawful, rightful*, Eur. :—νόμιμόν [ἐστί] *it is* or *one may* ποιεῖν τι Xen.　**II.** νόμιμα, τά, *usages, customs*, Hdt., Att.　**2.** *funeral rites*, Lat. *justa*, Thuc.　**III.** Adv. -μως, Plat. : Comp. -ώτερον Xen.

νόμιος, α, ον, also ος, ον, (νομεύς) *of shepherds, pastoral*, ν. θεός, i. e. Pan, h. Hom. ; *of Apollo, as shepherd of* Admetus, Theocr.

νόμισις, ὁ, (νομίζω) *usage, prescription, custom*, ἡ ἀνθρωπεία ἐς τὸ θεῖον νόμισις *the established belief* about the Deity, Thuc.

νόμισμα, ατος, τό, (νομίζω) *anything sanctioned by usage, a custom, institution*, Trag., Ar.　**II.** *the current coin* of a state, Hdt.

νομιστέος, α, ον, verb. Adj., *to be accounted*, Plat.

νομιστεύομαι, Pass. *to be current*, Polyb.

νομογραφία, ἡ, *written legislation*, Strab.　From

νομο-γράφος, ὁ, (γράφω) *one who draws up laws*, Hdt.　**II.** (νόμος II) *a composer of music*, Plat.

νομο-δείκτης, ου, ὁ, *one who explains laws*, Plut.

νομο-δῐδάκτης, ου, ὁ, = sq., Plut.

νομο-διδάσκᾰλος, ὁ, *a teacher of the law*, N. T.
νομοθεσία, ἡ, *lawgiving, legislation*, Plat. From
νομοθετέω, f. ήσω, *to make laws*, Plat., Xen., etc. :—Med. *to make laws for oneself, frame laws*, Plat.   **II.** trans. *to ordain by law*, τι Id., etc. :—Pass., impers., περὶ ταῦτα οὕτω σφι νενομοθέτηται *it hath been so ordained by law*, Hdt. Hence
νομοθέτημα, ατος, τό, *a law, ordinance*, Plat.
νομο-θέτης, ου, ὁ, (τίθημι) *a lawgiver*, Thuc., Plat., etc.   **II.** at Athens, *the Nomothetae* were a committee of the dicasts charged with the revision of the laws, Dem.
νομοθετητέος, α, ον, verb. Adj., *to be settled by law*, Plat.   2. trans. *one must ordain by law*, Arist.
νομοθετικός, ή, όν, *of* or *for a lawgiver* or *legislation*, Plat. : ἡ -κή (sc. τέχνη) *legislation*, Id.   **II.** of persons, *fitted for legislation*, Arist.
νομόνδε, Adv. (νομός) *to pasture*, Hom.
νομός, ὁ, (νέμω) *a feeding-place* for cattle, *pasture*, Hom. ; ν. ὕλης *a woodland pasture*, Od.   2. *herbage*, h. Hom. :—generally, *food*, Hes., Ar.   3. metaph., ἐπέων πολὺς νομός *a wide range* for words, Il.   **II.** *an abode allotted* or *assigned* to one, *a district, province*, Pind., Soph., etc. ; νομὸν ἔχειν *to have one's dwelling-place*, Hdt., Ar.   2. *one of the districts* into which Egypt was divided, Hdt., etc. ; applied also to other *provinces*, Id.   **III.** *anything assigned, a usage, custom, law, ordinance*, Lat. *institutum*, Hes. ; νόμος πάντων βασιλεύς *custom is lord of all*, Pind. ap. Hdt. ; κατὰ νόμον *according to custom* or *law*, Hes., Hdt., Att. ; poët. κὰν νόμον Pind. :—παρὰ νόμον *contrary to law*, Aesch. :—dat. νόμῳ *by custom, conventionally*, opp. to φύσει, Hdt., Arist. :—at Athens νόμοι were *Solon's laws*, those of Draco being called θεσμοί.   **2.** ἐν χειρῶν νόμῳ *by the law of force, in the fight* or *scuffle*, Hdt. ; ἐν χειρὸς νόμῳ *in actual warfare*, Arist. ; also, ἐς χειρῶν νόμον ἀπικέσθαι *to come to blows*, Hdt.   **IV.** *a musical mode* or *strain*, Aesch., Plat., etc. ; νόμοι κιθαρῳδικοί Ar.   **2.** *a song* sung in honour of some god, Hdt. ; νόμοι πολεμικοί *war-tunes*, Thuc.
νομο-φύλαξ [ῠ], ᾰκος, ὁ, *a guardian of the laws*, Plat.
νοό-πληκτος, ον, (πλήσσω) *palsying the mind*, Anth.
ΝΟ′ΟΣ, νόου, Att. contr. **νοῦς**, νοῦ, ὁ : in late writers are found cases of the third decl., gen. νοός, dat. νοΐ, acc. νόα :   **1.** *mind, perception*, Hom., etc. ; νόῳ *heedfully*, Od. ; παρὲκ νόον *senselessly*, Il. ; σὺν νόῳ *wisely*, Hdt. ; νόῳ λαβεῖν τι *to apprehend it*, Id. ; νόῳ ἔχειν *to keep in mind*, Id.   **2.** νοῦν ἔχειν means   **a.** *to have sense, be sensible*, Soph., Ar., etc. ; περισσὰ πράσσειν οὐκ ἔχει νοῦν οὐδένα *to aim too high has no sense*, Soph.   **b.** *to have one's mind* directed to something, ἄλλοσ' ὄμμα, θατέρᾳ δὲ νοῦν ἔχειν Id. ; δεῦρο νοῦν ἔχε Eur.   **3.** *the mind, heart*, χαῖρε νόῳ Od. ; so, νόος ἔμπεδος, ἀπηνής Hom. ; ἐκ παντὸς νόου *with all his heart and soul*, Hdt., etc.   **4.** one's *mind, purpose*, τί σοι ἐν νόῳ ἐστὶ ποιεῖν *what do you intend to do?* Id. ; ἐν νόῳ ἔχειν, c. inf., *to intend*, Id. ; νόον τελεῖν Il.   **II.** *the sense* or *meaning* of a word or speech, Hdt., Ar.
νοσᾰκερός, ά, όν, (νόσος) *liable to sickness, sickly*, Arist.

νοσερός, ά, όν, = νοσηρός, Eur. ; ν. κοίτη *a bed of sickness*, Id. :—Adv., νοσερῶς ἔχειν τὸ σῶμα Arist.
νοσέω, f. ήσω : pf. νενόσηκα : (νόσος) :—*to be sick, ill, to ail*, whether in body or mind, Hdt., Att. ; τῆς πόλεως οὔπω νενοσηκυίας *not yet having suffered from the plague*, Thuc. ; ν. ὀφθαλμούς *to be affected in the eyes*, Plat. ; τὸ νοσοῦν, = νόσος, Soph. :—also of things, γῆ νοσεῖ Xen.   **2.** of passion, ν. μάτην *to be mad*, Soph. ; θολερῷ χειμῶνι νοσήσας Id.   **3.** generally, *to be in an unsound state, to suffer*, νοσεῖ τὰ τῶν θεῶν Eur. ; ν. τι τῶν ἀπορρήτων κακῶν Id. :—of states, *to suffer* from faction, *be in disorder*, Hdt.
νοσηλεία, ἡ, *care of the sick, nursing*, Plut.   **II.** (from Pass.) *matter discharged* from a sore, Soph. From
νοσηλεύω, only in pres., *to tend a sick person*, Babr.
νόσημα, ατος, τό, (νοσέω) *a sickness, disease, plague*, Soph., etc.   **2.** metaph. *disease, affliction*, Aesch., Plat.   **3.** of *disorder* in a state, Plat., etc. Hence
νοσημᾰτ-ώδης, ες, = νοσώδης, Arist.
νοσηρός, ά, όν, like νοσερός, *diseased, unhealthy*, Xen.
ΝΟ′ΣΟΣ, Ion. νοῦσος, ἡ, *sickness, disease, malady*, Hom., etc.   **II.** generally, *distress, misery, suffering, sorrow, evil*, Hes., Trag.   **2.** *disease of mind*, Trag. ; θεία ν., i. e. *madness*, Soph.   **3.** of states, *disorder, sedition*, Plat.   **4.** *a plague, bane*, of a whirlwind, Soph.
νοσο-τροφία, ἡ, (τρέφω) *care of the sick*, Plat.
νοσσεύω, v. νεοσσεύω.
νοσσο-τροφέω, f. ήσω, contr. for νεοσσοτροφέω, Anth.
νοστέω, f. ήσω, *to come* or *go back, return*, esp. to one's home or country, Hom., Soph., etc.   **2.** *to return safe, to escape*, Il., etc.
νόστιμος, ον, (νόστος) *belonging to a return*, ν. ἦμαρ *the day of return*, i. e. *the return* itself, Od. ; so, ν. φάος Aesch.   **2.** *able* or *likely to return, alive, safe*, Lat. *salvus*, Od.   **II.** of plants, *yielding a return, productive*, τὸ ἐν σοι νοστιμώτατον *what was most flourishing* in you, Luc.
νόστος, ου, ὁ, (νέομαι) *a return home* or *homeward*, Hom. ; c. gen. objecti, νόστος Ἀχαιΐδος *his chance of returning* to Greece, Od. ; νόστον γαίης Φαιήκων *thy way to* the land of the Phaeacians, Ib.   **2.** generally, *travel, journey*, ἐπὶ φορβῆς ν. *a journey after* (i. e. *in search* of) *food*, Soph. ; ν. πρὸς Ἴλιον Eur.
νόσφῐ, before a vowel or metri grat. -φῐν, though ι may also be elided :   **I.** as Adv. of Place, *aloof, apart, afar, away*, Hom. ; ν. ἰδών *having looked aside*, Od. ; νόσφιν ἀπ' aloof *from*, Il. ; νόσφιν ἤ . . , like πλὴν ἤ . . , *besides, except*, Theocr.   **II.** as Prep. *aloof* or *away from, far from*, Hom., Hes.   **2.** *without, forsaken* or *unaided by*, Hom.   **3.** of mind or disposition, νόσφιν Ἀχαιῶν βουλεύειν *apart from* the Achaians, i. e. of a *different way of thinking*, Il. ; ν. Δήμητρος, Lat. *clam Cerere, without* her *knowledge*, h. Hom.   **4.** *beside, except*, νόσφι Ποσειδάωνος Od. ; νόσφ' Ὠκεανοῖο Il.
νοσφίζομαι, Dep., with aor. 1 med. and pass. ἐνοσφισάμην (Ep. νοσφισάμην, part. νοσφισσάμενος), ἐνοσφίσθην :—*to turn one's back upon* a person, *to turn away, shrink back*, Hom.   **2.** *to turn away from* a person, c. gen., Od.   **3.** c. acc. *to forsake, abandon*, Hom., Soph.   **II.** after Hom., in Act.,

Att. fut. νοσφιῶ: aor. 1 ἐνόσφισα:—*to set apart* or *aloof*, *to separate*, *remove*, Eur.:—metaph., *v. τινὰ βίου to separate* him from life, i. e. kill him, Soph.; so, *v. τινά* alone, Aesch.　　2. *to deprive*, *rob*, *τινά τι* one of a thing, Pind.; also, *τινά τινος* Aesch., Eur.　　3.·Med. *to put aside for oneself*, *to appropriate*, *purloin*, Xen.:—*v. ἀπὸ τῆς τιμῆς to appropriate part of* the price, N. T.　　b. but the Med. is also just like the Act., *to deprive*, *rob*, Eur.

νοσ-ώδης, ες, (εἶδος) *sickly*, *diseased*, *ailing*, Plat., etc.　　II. act. *pestilential*, *baneful*, Eur.

νοτερός, ά, όν, (νότος) *wet*, *damp*, *moist*, Eur.; χειμὼν *v.* a storm *of rain*, Thuc.

νοτία, ἡ, (νότος) *wet*, νοτίαι εἰαριναί spring *rains*, Il.

νοτίζω, f. ίσω, (νότος) *to wet* :—Pass. *to be wetted* or *wet*, Plat., Anth.

νότιος, α, ον, and ος, ον: (νότος) :—*wet*, *moist*, *damp*, Il., Aesch. :—ἐν νοτίῳ, i. e. *the open sea*, Od.　　II. *southern*, *v. θάλασσα*, i. e. the Indian ocean, Hdt.

νοτίς, ίδος, ἡ, (νότος) *moisture*, *wet*, Eur.

ΝΟ'ΤΟΣ, ὁ, *the south* or *south-west wind*, Lat. *Auster*, Od., Hdt., etc.　　2. *Notus* is personified as god of the S. wind, Hes.　　II. *the south* or *south-west quarter*, πρὸς νότον τῆς Λήμνου Hdt.; τὸ πρὸς ν. τῆς πόλεως Thuc.

νοττίον, contr. for νεοττίον.

νου-βυστικός, ή, όν, (νοῦς, βύω) *choke-full of sense*, *clever* : Adv. -κῶς, Ar.

νουθεσία, ἡ, = νουθέτησις, Ar.

νου-θετέω, f. ήσω, (τίθημι) *to put in mind*, *to admonish*, *warn*, *advise*, Hdt., Aesch., etc. ;—c. dupl. acc., τοιαῦτ᾽ ἄνολβον ἄνδρ᾽ ἐνουθέτει Soph. :—Pass., Id., etc.　　2. *ν. τινα κονδύλοις*, *πληγαῖς* Ar. Hence

νουθέτημα, ατος, τό, *admonition*, *warning*, Aesch., Eur., etc. ; τἀμὰ νουθετήματα given to me, Soph.

νουθέτησις, ἡ, *admonition*, *warning*, Eur., Plat., etc.

νουθετητέος, α, ον, verb. Adj. *to be admonished*, Eur.　　2. νουθετητέον, one must warn, Arist.

νουθετητικός, ή, όν, *monitory*, Plat.

νουθετικός, ή, όν, = foreg., Xen.

νου-μηνία, ἡ, Att. contr. for νεο-μηνία, (νέος, μήν) *the new moon*, *the first of the month*, Pind., Ar. ; *ν. κατὰ σελήνην*, to denote the *true new moon*, as opp. to the νουμηνία of the calendars, Hdt., Ar., etc.

νουνέχεια, ἡ, *good sense*, *discretion*, Polyb. From

νουν-εχής, ές, (ἔχω) *with understanding*, *sensible*, *discreet*, Polyb. Adv. -χῶς, Id.

νοῦς, ὁ, Att. contr. for νόος.

νοῦσος, ἡ, Ion. for νόσος.

νουσο-φόρος, ον, Ion. for νοσοφόρος, Anth.

νύ, νυ, v. νῦν II.

νῠγείς, aor. 2 pass. part. of νύσσω:—νῠγῆναι, inf.

νυγμή, ἡ, (νύσσω) *a pricking*, *puncture*, Plut.

νυκτ-εγερτέω, f. ήσω, (ἐγείρω) *to watch by night*, Plut.

νυκτέλιος, ον, (νύξ) *nightly*, name of Bacchus, from *his nightly festivals*, Anth.

νυκτ-ερέτης, ου, ὁ, *one who rows by night*, Anth.

νυκτερευτικός, ή, όν, *fit for hunting by night*, Xen.

νυκτερεύω, f. σω, (νύκτερος) *to pass the night*, Xen. : of soldiers, *to keep watch by night*, *bivouac*, Id.

νυκτερήσιος, ον, (νύκτερος) *nightly*, Ar.

νυκτερινός, ή, όν, (νύξ) *by night*, *nightly*, Lat. *nocturnus*, Ar.; *ν. γενέσθαι* to happen *by night*, Id.

νυκτέριος, α, ον, and ος, ον, = foreg., Luc., Anth.

νυκτερίς, ίδος, ἡ, (νύκτερος) *a bat*, Lat. *vespertilio*, Od., Hdt., Ar.

νύκτερος, ον, = νυκτερινός, Aesch., Soph.

νυκτερ-ωπός, όν, (ὤψ) *appearing by night*, Eur.

νυκτ-ηγορέω, f. ήσω, (ἀγορά) *to summon by night*, Eur. ; so in Med., Aesch.　Hence

νυκτηγορία, ἡ, *a nightly summons*, Eur.

νυκτ-ηρεφής, ές, (ἐρέφω) *covered by night*, *murky*, Aesch.

νυκτί-βρομος, ον, (βρέμω) *roaring by night*, Eur.

νυκτι-κλέπτης, ου, ὁ, *thief of the night*, Anth.

νυκτῐ-κόραξ, ἄκος, ὁ, *the night-raven*, Anth.

νυκτῐ-λαθραιο-φάγος, ον, (φαγεῖν) *eating secretly by night*, Anth.

νυκτῐ-λάλος [ᾰ], ον, *nightly-sounding*, Anth.

νυκτῐ-λαμπής, ές, (λάμπω) *illumined by night* alone, i. e. *murky*, *dark*, Simon.

νύκτιος, α, ον, (νύξ) *nightly*, Anth.

νυκτῐ-πάται-πλάγιος, ον, (πατέω) *nightly-roaming-to-and-fro*, Anth.

νυκτί-πλαγκτος, ον, *making to wander by night*, *rousing from bed*, Aesch.; *ν. εὐνή* a restless, uneasy bed, Id.

νυκτῐ-πλάνος, ον, *roaming by night*, Luc.

νυκτῐ-πόλος, ον, (πολέω) *roaming by night*, Eur.

νυκτί-σεμνος, *solemnised by night*, Aesch.

νυκτῐ-φᾰής, ές, (φαίνομαι) *shining by night*, Anth.　　II. *with shades dark as night*, Id.

νυκτί-φαντος, ον, *appearing by night*, Aesch., Eur.

νυκτί-φοιτος, ον, (φοιτάω) *night-roaming*, Aesch.

νυκτι-φρούρητος, ον, *watching by night*, Aesch.

νυκτο-θήρας, ου, ὁ, (θηράω) *a night-hunter*, Xen.

νυκτο-μᾰχέω, f. ήσω, (μάχομαι) *to fight by night*, Plut.

νυκτομᾰχία, Ion. -ίη, ἡ, *a night-battle*, Hdt., Thuc.

νυκτο-περι-πλάνητος, ον, (πλανάομαι) *roaming about by night*, Id.

νυκτο-πορέω, f. ήσω, (πόρος) *to travel by night*, Xen.

νυκτοπορία, ἡ, *a night-journey*, *night-march*, Polyb.

νυκτοφῠλᾰκέω, f. ήσω, *to keep guard by night*, *v. τὰ ἔξω to watch* the outer parts *by night*, Xen. From

νυκτο-φύλαξ [ῠ], ἄκος, ὁ, ἡ, *a night-watcher*, *warder*, Lat. *excubitor*, Xen.

νυκτῷον, τό, (Νύξ) *a temple of Night*, Luc.

νυκτ-ωπός, όν, = νυκτερωπός, Eur.

νύκτωρ, Adv., (νύξ) = *by night*, Hes., Soph., etc.

νύμφᾱ, Ep. voc. for νύμφη.　　II. νύμφᾱ, Dor. for νύμφη.

νυμφ-ᾱγωγέω, *to lead the bride to the bridegroom's house*, γάμους *v. to co. rt* a marriage, Plut. From

νυμφ-ᾱγωγός, ὁ, *leader of the bride*, Eur.

νύμφαιον, τό, (νύμφη) *a temple of the nymphs*, Plut.

νυμφαῖος, α, ον, (νύμφη) *of* or *sacred to the nymphs*, Eur., Anth.

νυμφεῖος, α, ον, and ος, ον (νύμφη) *of a bride*, *bridal*, *nuptial*, Pind., Eur.　　II. as Subst., 1. νυμφεῖον (sc. δῶμα), τό, *the bridechamber*, Soph.　　2. νυμφεῖα (sc. ἱερά), τά, *nuptial rites*, *marriage*, Id.　　3. νυμφεῖα τοῦ σαυτοῦ τέκνου *thine own son's bride*, Id.

νύμφευμα, ατος, τό, (νυμφεύω) *marriage*, *espousal*, Soph., Eur.　　II. in sing. *the person married*, καλὸν ν. τινι 'a good *match* for him,' Eur.

νυμφευτήριος, α, ον, nuptial, Eur.　From
νυμφευτής, οῦ, ὁ, (νυμφεύω) one who escorts the bride to the bridegroom's house, negotiator of a marriage, Plat.　II. a bridegroom, husband, Eur.　Hence
νυμφεύτρια, ἡ, a bride's-maid, Ar.
νυμφεύω, f. σω, (νύμφη) to lead the bride, to give in marriage, betroth, Eur.　2. to marry, of the woman, Lat. nubere, Soph.; but also of the man, Lat. ducere, Eur.; of both parties, νυμφεύετ', εὖ πράσσοιτε Id.　II. Pass. c. fut. med. νυμφεύσομαι; aor. 1 med. et pass. ἐνυμφευσάμην, ἐνυμφεύθην:—to be given in marriage, marry, of the woman, Id.; ν. ἔκ τινος to be wedded by him, Id.　III. in Med. of the man, to take to wife, Id.
ΝΥ'ΜΦΗ, ἡ, Ep. voc. νύμφᾱ: Dor. νύμφᾱ:—a young wife, bride, Lat. nupta, Il., Trag.　2. any married woman, Od., Eur.　3. a marriageable maiden, Il., Hes.　4. = Lat. nurus, daughter-in-law, N. T.　II. as prop. name, a Nymph, Hom.; θεαὶ Νύμφαι Il.; distinguished by special names, spring-nymphs being Ναϊάδες, sea-nymphs Νηρηΐδες, tree-nymphs Δρυάδες, Ἁμαδρυάδες, mountain-nymphs ὀρεστιάδες, ὀρεάδες, meadow-nymphs λειμωνιάδες.　2. persons in a state of rapture, as seers and poets, were said to be caught by the Nymphs, νυμφόληπτοι, Lat. lymphatici.　III. the chrysalis, or pupa of moths, Anth.　Hence
νυμφίδιος [ῐ], α, ον, and ος, ον, of a bride, bridal, Eur., Ar.
νυμφικός, ή, όν, = foreg., Trag., etc.
νυμφίος, ὁ, (νύμφη) a bridegroom, one lately married, Hom., etc.; in pl., τοῖς νεωστὶ νυμφίοις to the bridal pair, Eur.　II. as Adj. νύμφιος, α, ον, bridal, Pind.
νυμφο-γενής, ές, (γίγνομαι) nymph-born, Anth.
νυμφό-κλαντος, ον, to be deplored by wives, Aesch.
νυμφοκομέω, f. ήσω, to dress a bride, Anth.　II. intr. to dress oneself as a bride, Eur.　From
νυμφο-κόμος, ον, (κομέω) dressing a bride:—generally, bridal, Eur.
νυμφό-ληπτος, ον, caught by nymphs, Plat.
νυμφοστολέω, to escort the bride, Anth.
νυμφο-στόλος, ον, (στέλλω) escorting the bride.
νυμφό-τιμος, ον, (τιμή) honouring the bride: μέλος ν. the bridal song, Aesch.
νυμφών, ῶνος, ὁ, (νύμφη) the bridechamber, N. T.
νῦν, Adv. now, at this very time, Lat. nunc, οἱ νῦν βροτοί εἰσι mortals who now live, such as they are now, Il.; so in Att., οἱ νῦν ἄνθρωποι men of the present day; τὸ νῦν the present time, Plat.; —τὰ νῦν (often written τανῦν) used simply like νῦν, Hdt., Att.　2. also of what is just past, just now, but now, Hom., Soph.　3. now, i.e. as it is, as the case now stands, Thuc.; so, καὶ νῦν even in this case, Xen.　II. besides the sense of Time, the enclit. νυν, νυ denotes 1. immediate sequence of one thing upon another, then, thereupon, thereafter, Hom.　2. also by way of Inference, then, therefore, Il., etc.　3. used to strengthen a command, δεῦρό νυν quick then! Il.; εἶά νυν, etc.; φέρε νυν, ἄγε νυν, σπεῦδέ νυν, σίγα νυν, etc., Xen.:—also to strengthen a question, τίς νυν; τί νυν; who then? what then? Id.
νῦν δή, stronger form of νῦν, with pres. now, even now, Plat.　2. with past tenses, just now, ἃ νῦν δὴ ἐγὼ ἔλεγον Id.

νυνί, Att. form of νῦν, strengthd. by -ῑ demonstr., now, at this moment, Dem., Aeschin.　So in familiar Att., νυνμενί, for νυνὶ μέν, Ar.; νυνδί, for νυνὶ δέ, Id.
ΝΥ'Ξ, νυκτός, ἡ, Lat. nox, night, i. e. either the night-season or a night, Hom., Hes., etc.; νυκτός by night, Lat. noctu, Od., Att.; νυκτὸς ἔτι while it was still night, Hdt.; ν. τῆσδε Soph.; ἄκρας ν. at dead of night, Id.; also, νυκτί Hdt., Soph.;—νύκτα through night long, the livelong night, Hom.; νύκτας by nights, Id.;—μέσαι νύκτες midnight, Plat.　2. with Preps., ἀνὰ νύκτα by night, Il.; διὰ νύκτα by night, εἰς νύκτα, εἰς τὴν ν. towards night, Xen.; ὑπὸ νύκτα just at night-fall, Thuc., Xen.; διὰ νυκτός in the course of the night, Plat.; ἐκ νυκτός just after night-fall, Xen.; πόρρω τῶν νυκτῶν far into the night, Id.:— ἐπὶ νυκτί by night, Il.; ἐν νυκτί, ἐν τῇ ν. Aesch., etc.　3. in pl. also, the watches of the night, Pind., Plat.:—the Greeks divided the night into three watches, Hom., etc.　II. the dark of night, Hom.　2. the night of death, Id.; ν. Ἄϊδής τε Soph.　III. Νύξ as prop. n., the goddess of Night, daughter of Chaos, Il., Hes.　IV. the quarter of night, i. e. the West, Hes.
νύξα, Ep. for ἔνυξα, aor. 1 of νύσσω.
ΝΥΟ'Σ [ῠ], οῦ, ἡ, a daughter-in-law, Hom.; in wider sense, any female connected by marriage, Il.　II. a bride, wife, Theocr., Anth.
Νῦσα, ης, ἡ, name of several hills sacred to Bacchus, h. Hom., etc.;—Adj. Νύσιος, α, ον, Id.; Νυσήιος, Ar.
νύσσα, ης, ἡ, (νύσσω) like Lat. meta, the name of two posts in the ἱππόδρομος: 1. the turning-post, so placed that the chariots driving up the right side of the course, turned round it, and returned by the left side (cf. καμπτήρ), Il.　2. the starting post, which was also the winning post, Hom.
ΝΥ'ΣΣΩ, Att. νύττω, f. ξω, to touch with a sharp point, to prick, spur, pierce, Il., Hes.; ἀγκῶνι νύξας having nudged him with the elbow, Od.; ν. γνώμην to prick it (and see what is in it), Ar.
νυστάζω, aor. 1 ἐνύσταξα and ἐνύστασα:—to nod in sleep, to nap, slumber, Xen., Plat.　2. to be sleepy, napping, Lat. dormito, Ar., Plat.　3. to hang the head, Anth.　Hence
νυστακτής, οῦ, ὁ, one that nods, nodding, Ar.
νύττω, Att. for νύσσω.
νύχευμα [ῠ], ατος, τό, a nightly watch, Lat. pervigilium, Eur.　From
νῠχεύω, f. σω, (νύξ) to watch the night through, to pass the night, Eur.
νυχθ-ήμερον, τό, (ἡμέρα) a night and a day, N. T.
νύχιος [ῠ], α, ον, and ος, ον, nightly, i. e., 1. of persons, doing a thing by night, Hes., Aesch., etc.　2. of things, happening by night, Soph., Eur.　3. of places, dark as night, gloomy, Aesch., Eur.
νώ, v. ἐγώ III.
νωδός, ή, όν, (νη-, ὀδούς) toothless, Ar., Theocr.
νωδυνία, ἡ, ease from pain, Pind.　II. an ano-dyne, Pind.　From
νώ-δῠνος, ον, (νη-, ὀδύνη) = ἀνώδυνος, q.v., without pain, Pind.　II. act. soothing pain, anodyne, Soph.
νώθεια, ἡ, sluggishness, dulness, Plat., etc.　From
ΝΩΘΗ'Σ, ές, gen. έος, sluggish, slothful, torpid, epith.

of the ass, Il., Eur., etc.   2. of the understanding, *dull, stupid*, **νωθέστερος** *somewhat dull*, Hdt.

νώθητι, Ion. for **νοήθητι**, aor. 1 pass. imper. of **νοέω**.

ΝΩΘΡΟ'Σ, ά, όν, = **νωθής**, *sluggish, slothful, torpid*, Plat.

νῶι, *we two*, v. **ἐγώ** III. Hence

νωίτερος [ῐ], α, ον, *of* or *from us two*, Hom.

νωλεμές, Adv. *without pause, unceasingly, continually*, Hom. :—so, **νωλεμέως**, Il. ; *v.* **ἐχέμεν** to *persevere*, Ib.; but, *v.* **κτείνοντο** they were murdered *without pause*, i. e. one after the other, Od. (Deriv. unknown.)

νωμάω, f. **ήσω**, (**νέμω** I) *to deal out, distribute*, esp. food and drink at festivals, Hom.   II. (**νέμω** III. 2) *to direct, guide, control*,   1. of weapons, *to handle, wield, sway* the lance, shield, rudder, Hom.; so metaph., **νῶμα πηδαλίῳ πόλιν** *was steering it*, Lat. *gubernabat*, Pind. ; **πᾶν** *v.* **ἐπὶ τέρμα** Aesch.   2. of the limbs, *to ply nimbly*, **γούνατα νωμᾶν** Il. ; **πόδα** *v.* Soph. ; *v.* **ὀφρύν** *to move the brow*, Aesch.   3. *to revolve* in the mind, Od.: *to observe, watch*, Hdt., Trag.

νῷν, Att. for **νῶιν**, v. **νῶι**.

νώνυμος, ον, Ep. for **νώνυμος**, used when the penult. is to be long, Hom., Hes.

νώνυμος, ον, (νη-, ὄνυμα, Aeol. for ὄνομα) *nameless, unknown, inglorious*, Od., Aesch., Soph.   II. c. gen., **Σαπφοῦς νώνυμος** *without the name of* Sappho, i. e. *without knowledge of* her, Anth.

νῶροψ, οπος, ὁ, ἡ, *flashing, gleaming*, of metal, Il. (Deriv. uncertain.)

νωσάμενος, **νώσασθαι**, Ion. and Dor. for νοη-, aor. 1 med. part. and inf. of **νοέω**.

νωτ-άκμων, ονος, ὁ, ἡ, *with mailed back*, Batr.

νωτιαῖος, α, ον, (**νῶτον**) *of the back* or *spine*, *v.* **ἄρθρα** the *spinal* vertebrae, Eur.

νωτίζω, (**νῶτον**) only in aor. 1 **ἐνώτισα**, *to turn one's back*, Lat. *terga dare*, Eur.; c. acc. cogn., **παλίσσυτον δράμημα νωτίσαι** *to turn about* in backward course, Soph.   II. *to cover the back of*, **τινά** Eur.; **πόντον νωτίσαι** *to skim* the sea, Aesch.

νώτισμα, ατος, τό, (**νωτίζω**) *that which covers the back*, of wings, Eur.

νῶτον, τό, or **νῶτος**, ὁ, pl. always **νῶτα**, τά :—*the back*, Lat. *tergum*, Il.; often in pl., like Lat. *terga*, Hom.; **τὰ νῶτα ἐντρέπειν**, **ἐπιστρέφειν** *to turn the back*, i. e. flee, Hdt.; **νῶτα δεῖξαι** Plut.; **κατὰ νώτου** from *behind*, in *rear*, Hdt., Thuc.   II. metaph. *any wide surface*, **ἐπ' εὐρέα νῶτα θαλάσσης** Hom.; of plains, Pind., Eur.   2. *the back* or *ridge* of a hill, Pind., Eur.; of a chariot, Eur.

νωτο-φόρος, ον, (**φέρω**) *carrying on the back* : as Subst. *a beast of burthen*, Xen.

νωχελής, ές, *moving slowly and heavily, sluggish*, Eur. (Deriv. uncertain.) Hence

νωχελία, Ep. -**ίη**, ἡ, *laziness, sluggishness*, Il.

Ξ.

Ξ, **ξ**, **ξῖ**, τό, indecl., fourteenth letter of the Gk. alphabet : as numeral **ξ'** = 60, but **͵ξ** = 60,000 : introduced in the archonship of Euclides, 403 B.C.—It is a double consonant, compounded of γσ, κσ, or χσ. Changes   1.

ξ in Aeol. and Att. appears as an aspirated form of **κ**, cf. **ξυνός** with **κοινός**, **ξύν** with *cum ;*—or of **σ**, cf. **ξύν** with **σύν**, **ξέστης** with Lat. *sextarius* ; and so in Dor. fut. of Verbs in -**ζω**, **κομίξω κλαξῶ παιξῶ** for **κομίσω κλήσω παίσω**.   2. interchanged with σσ, Ion. **διξός**, **τριξός** for **δισσός**, **τρισσός**.

ΞΑΙ'ΝΩ, f. **ξἄνῶ** : aor. 1 **ἔξηνα** :—Pass., aor. 1 **ἐξάνθην** :—*to comb* or *card* wool, so as to make it fit for spinning, Od., etc.   2. of cloth, *to full* or *dress* it, Ar.   II. metaph. *to dress, thrash, beat*, **ῥάβδοις ἔξαινόν τὰ σώματα** Plut. :—Pass., **ξανθέν** *mangled*, Anth. ;—c. acc. cogn., **ξαίνειν κατὰ τοῦ νώτου πολλὰς** (sc. **πληγάς**) Dem.

Ξανθίας, ου, ὁ, *Xanthias*, name of a slave in Comedy, Ar.;—no doubt he had yellow hair; cf. **πυρρίας**.

ξανθίζω, f. Att. **ιῶ**, (**ξανθός**) *to make yellow* or *brown*, by roasting or frying, Ar.

ξανθό-θριξ, ὁ, ἡ, *yellow-haired*, Solon, Theocr.

ξανθο-κάρηνος [ᾰ], ον, (**κάρηνον**) *with yellow head*, Anth.

ξανθο-κόμης, ου, ὁ, (**κόμη**) = **ξανθόθριξ**, Pind., Theocr.

ΞΑΝΘΟ'Σ, ή, όν, *yellow*, of various shades ; of *golden hair*, Hom.; so, **ξανθαὶ ἵπποι** *bay* or *chestnut* mares, Il.   II. **Ξάνθος** paroxyt., as prop. n.   1. a stream of the Troad, so called by gods, by men Scamander, Ib.   2. a horse of Achilles, *Bayard*, the other being **Βαλίος**, *Dapple*, Ib. Hence

ξανθότης, ητος, ἡ, *yellowness*, esp. of hair, Strab.

ξανθοτρῐχέω, (**ξανθόθριξ**) *to have yellow hair*, Strab.

ξανθο-φυής, ές, (**φυή**) *yellow by nature*, **ἕλικες** Anth.

ξανθό-χίτων, ωνος, ὁ, ἡ, *with yellow coat*, Anth.

ξανθό-χροος, ον, (**χρόα**) *with yellow skin*, Mosch.

ξειν-ἀπάτης, **ξείνη**, Ion. for ξεν-.

ξεινήιον, τό, (**ξεῖνος**) Ion. for **ξενεῖον** which is not used, *a host's gift*, given to a departing guest, Hom.; **δῶρα ξεινήια** Od.

ξεινίζω, **ξεινίη**, **ξεινικός**, **ξείνιος**, Ion. for ξεν-.

ξεινοδοκέω, **ξεινοδόκος**, **ξεινοκτονέω**, Ion. for ξεν-.

ξεῖνος, **ξεινοσύνη**, **ξεινόω**, Ion. for ξεν-.

ξεν-ἀγέτης, ου, ὁ, *one who takes charge of guests*, Pind.

ξεναγέω, f. **ήσω**, *to be a* **ξεναγός**, Xen., Dem.   II. *to guide strangers, shew them the sights*, Luc. :—Pass., impers., **ἄριστά σοι ξενάγηται** *your work as a guide has been done* excellently, Plat.

ξεν-αγός, ὁ, (**ἡγέομαι**) *a commander of auxiliary* or *mercenary troops* (**ξένοι**), Thuc., Xen., etc. (The form is Dor. ; but like many military terms, it was adopted in Att.)   II. *a stranger's guide*, Plut.

ξεν-ἀπάτης, ου, ὁ, poët. **ξειν-**, (**ἀπατάω**) *one who cheats strangers*, or, *who cheats his host*, Eur.

ξεν-αρκής, ές, (**ἀρκέω**) *aiding strangers*, Pind.

ξένη, ἡ, fem. of **ξένος** :   1. (sub. **γυνή**) *a female guest* : *a foreign woman*, Aesch., etc.   2. (sub. **γῆ**), *a foreign country*, Soph., Xen.

ξενηλᾰσία, ἡ, at Sparta, *expulsion of foreigners, an alien act*, Thuc., Plat., etc. From

ξεν-ηλᾰτέω, f. **ήσω**, (**ἐλαύνω**) *to banish foreigners*, Ar.

ξενία, ἡ, Ep. **ξενίη**, Ion. **ξεινίη** : (**ξένος**) :—*the rights of a guest, hospitality, friendly entertainment* or *reception*, Lat. *hospitium*, Od., Hdt., etc.   2. *a friendly relation* between two foreigners, or between an individual and a foreign state (cf. **πρόξενος**), **ξεινίην τινὶ συντίθεσθαι**, Lat. *hospitium facere cum aliquo*, Hdt.; **κατὰ τὴν ξ.** because of their *friendly relations*, Thuc. ;

πρὸς ξενίας τὰς σὰς by *thy friendship with* us, Soph. 3. *the state* or *disabilities of an alien*, ξενίας φεύγειν (sc. γραφήν) to be indicted *as an alien*, Ar.

ξενίζω, Ion. and Ep. **ξεινίζω**, f. ίσω, Ep. ίσσω, Att. ιῶ: Ep. aor. 1 ἐξείνισσα or ξείνισσα: (ξένος):—*to receive* or *entertain strangers*, *to receive as a guest*, Lat. *hospitio excipere*, Hom., Hdt., etc.; ξ. τινὰ πολλοῖς ἀγαθοῖς *to present with* hospitable *gifts*, Xen.:—metaph., ὃν ῎Αρης οὐκ ἐξένισεν, i. e. who fell not in battle, Soph. :—Pass. *to be entertained as a guest*, Hdt., Att. II. *to astonish by some strange sight*, Polyb. :—Pass. *to be astonished*, Id. III. intr. *to be a stranger*, *speak with a foreign accent*, Luc.: *to be strange* or *unusual*, Id.

ξενικός, ή, όν, and ός, όν; Ion. **ξεινικός** :—*of* or *for a stranger*, *of foreign kind*, opp. to ἀστικός, Dem.;—τὸ ξ. the *taxes paid by aliens* at Athens, Dem.;—τὸ ξ. *the class of aliens*, Arist.; τὸ ξ. (sc. δικαστήριον) the court *in which aliens sued* or *were sued*, Id. 2. of soldiers, *hired for service*, *mercenary*, Hdt., Xen.; τὸ ξενικόν = οἱ ξένοι, *a body of mercenaries*, Ar., Thuc., etc. 3. = ξένιος, *hospitable*, *friendly*, Aeschin. :— ἡ ξενικὴ *friendly relation*, as between host and guest, Arist. II. *foreign*, *alien*, Hdt.; ξ. ὀνόματα *foreign* names, Plat.; of style, *foreign*, i. e. *abounding in unusual words*, Arist.

ξένιος, α, ον, Att. also ος, ον, Ion. **ξείνιος** :—*belonging to a friend and guest*, *hospitable*, Ζεὺς ξένιος as *protector of the rights of hospitality*, Il., Aesch. :—τράπεζα ξ. the *guests' table*, Od.; ξένιός τινι *bound to him by ties of hospitality*, Hdt. 2. ξένια, Att. ξένια, τά, *friendly gifts*, *meat and drink*, given to the guest by his host, Hom.; ξένια πάρεσχε δαῖτα as a *friendly gift*, Aesch.; βοῦν ξένια ἔπεμψεν Xen.; ἐπὶ ξένια καλεῖν *to invite any one to eat with you*, Hdt., etc.; metaph., θάνατος ξένιά σοι γενήσεται Eur. II. *foreign*, Pind., Att.

ξένισις, ἡ, (ξενίζω) *the entertainment of guests*, Thuc.

ξενισμός, ὁ, = ξένισις, Plat.

ξενιτεία, ἡ, *a living abroad*, Luc. From

ξενιτεύω, f. σω, (ξένος) *to live abroad*, Luc. II. Dep. ξενιτεύομαι, *to be in foreign service*, Isocr.

ξενο-δαίκτης, ου, ὁ, *one who murders guests*, Eur.

ξενο-δαίτης, ου, ἡ, (δαίς) *one that devours guests* or *strangers*, of the Cyclops, Eur.

ξενοδοκέω, Ion. **ξεινο-**, *to entertain guests* or *strangers*, Hdt., Eur., etc. :—in late Gr. **ξενοδοχέω**, N.T. From

ξενο-δόκος, Ion. and Ep. **ξεινοδόκος**, ὁ, (δέχομαι) *one who receives strangers*, *a host*, Od. Hence

ξενοδοχία, ἡ, *entertainment of a stranger*, Xen.

ξενο-δώτης, ου, ὁ, *a host*, epith. of Bacchus, Anth.

ξένοεις, εσσα, εν, (ξένος) *full of strangers*, Eur.

ξενο-θῦτέω, f. ήσω, (θύω) *to sacrifice strangers*, Strab.

ξενοκτονέω, Ion. **ξεινοκτ-**, *to slay guests* or *strangers*, Hdt., Eur. II. *to slay one's host*, Eur. From

ξενο-κτόνος, ον, (κτείνω) *slaying guests* or *strangers*, Eur., Aeschin.

ξενολογέω, f. ήσω, *to enlist strangers*, *levy mercenaries*, Dem., etc. From

ξενο-λόγος, ον, (λέγω) *levying mercenaries*, Polyb.

ξενο-πᾰθέω, f. ήσω, (πάθος) *to have a strange feeling*, *feel strange* or *shy*, Plut.

ΞΕ΄ΝΟΣ, ὁ, Ion. **ξεῖνος** (used also by Trag.) : I. *a guest-friend*, i. e. any citizen of a foreign state, with whom one has a treaty of hospitality for self and heirs, confirmed by mutual presents (ξένια) and an appeal to Ζεὺς ξένιος, Hom. 2. of one of the parties bound by ties of hospitality, i. e. either *the guest*, or = ξεινοδόκος, *the host*, Id., Hdt., etc. 3. any one entitled to hospitality, *a stranger*, *refugee*, Od. 4. *any stranger* or *foreigner*, Hes., Att. :—the term was politely used of any one whose name was unknown, and the address ὦ ξένε came to mean little more than *friend*, Soph. II. *a foreign soldier*, *hireling*, *mercenary*, Thuc., Xen.
B. as Adj. **ξένος**, η, ον, and ος, ον, Ion. **ξεῖνος**, η, ον, *foreign*, Soph., Eur., etc. II. c. gen. rei, *strange to* a thing, *ignorant of* it, Soph. :—Adv., ξένως ἔχω τῆς λέξεως I am *a stranger to* the language, Plat. III. *alien*, *strange*, *unusual*, Aesch.

ξενό-στασις, ἡ, *a lodging for guests* or *strangers*, Soph.

ξενοσύνη, Ion. **ξεῖν-**, ἡ, *hospitality*, Od.

ξενό-τῑμος, ον, (τιμή) *honouring strangers*, Aesch.

ξενοτροφέω, f. ήσω, (τρέφω) *to entertain strangers*, *to maintain mercenary troops*, Thuc., Dem.

ξενοφονέω, f. ήσω, *to murder strangers*, Eur. From

ξενο-φόνος, ον, (*φένω) *murdering strangers*, Eur.

ξενόω, Ion. **ξεινόω**, f. ώσω, (ξένος) *to make one's friend and guest*, Aesch. II. mostly in Pass., with fut. med. ξενώσομαι: pf. ἐξένωμαι: aor. 1 ἐξενώθην : 1. *to enter into a treaty of hospitality with* one, Lat. *hospitio jungi*, c. dat., Hdt., Xen.; absol., Xen. 2. *to take up* his *abode with* one *as a guest*, *to be entertained*, Trag., Xen. 3. *to be in foreign parts*, *to be abroad*, Soph., Eur. : *to go into banishment*, Eur.

ξενών, ῶνος, ὁ, (ξένος) *a guest-chamber*, Eur.

ξένωσις, ἡ, (ξενόω II. 3) *a being abroad*, Eur.

ξερός, ά, όν, Ion. for ξηρός, *dry*, ποτὶ ξερόν *to the dry land*, Od., Anth.

ξέσμα, ατος, τό, (ξέω) = ξόανον, Anth.

ξέσσε, Ep. 3 sing. aor. 1 of ξέω.

ξέστης, ου, ὁ, = Lat. *sextarius*, nearly *a pint*, N.T.

ξεστός, ή, όν, *smoothed*, *polished*, *wrought*, Hom., Hdt., Att.; ξ. αἴθουσαι halls *of polished stone*, Il. From

ΞΕ΄Ω, impf. ἔξεον: aor. 1 ἔξεσα, Ep. ἔξεσσα : — Pass., pf. ἔξεσμαι :—*to smooth* or *polish by scraping*, *planing*, *filing*, of a carpenter, Od., etc.

ξηρά (sc. γῆ), ἡ, *dry land*, v. ξηρός III.

ξηραίνω, f. ἄνῶ: aor. 1 ἐξήρᾱνα:—Pass., aor. 1 ἐξηράνθην : pf. ἐξήρασμαι: (ξηρός) :—*to parch up*, *dry up*, Eur., Xen. :—Pass. *to become* or *be dry*, *parched*, Il., etc. 2. *to lay dry*, Lat. *siccare*, Thuc.

ξηρ-ἀλοιφέω, (ἀλείφω) properly *to rub dry with oil*, without the use of the bath, Lex ap. Plut., Aeschin.

ξηρ-αμπέλινος, η, ον, *of the colour of withered vine-leaves*, *bright red*, Juven.

ΞΗΡΟ΄Σ, ά, όν, *dry*, Lat. *siccus*, opp. to ὑγρός, Hdt., Ar.; ξηροῖς ὄμμασι, Horace's *siccis oculis*, Aesch. 2. of bodily condition, *withered*, *lean*, *haggard*, δέμας Eur., Theocr. II. like Lat. *siccus*, *fasting*, *austere*, *harsh*, Eur., Ar.; ἐν ξηροῖσιν ἐκτρέφειν Eur. III. as Subst., ἡ ξηρά (sc. γῆ), *dry land*, Xen.; so, τὸ ξηρόν Hdt.; ναῦς ἐπὶ τοῦ ξηροῦ ποιεῖν *to leave the ships aground*, Thuc.

ξηρότης, ητος, ἡ, (ξηρός) *dryness*, Plat., Xen.: ἡ ξ.

τῶν νεῶν the *dryness*, i. e. *soundness*, of their timbers, Thuc.

ξηρο-φᾰγέω, f. ήσω, (φαγεῖν) *to eat dry food*, Anth., etc.

ξῐφ-ήρης, ες, (*ἄρω) *sword in hand*, Eur.

ξιφη-φόρος, ον, (φέρω) *sword in hand*, Aesch., Eur.

ξῐφίδιον, τό, Dim. of ξίφος, *a dagger*, Thuc., etc.

ξῐφιστήρ, ῆρος, ὁ, (ξίφος) *a sword-belt*, Plut.

ξῐφο-δήλητος, ον, (δηλέομαι) *slain by the sword*, ξ. θάνατος *death by the sword*, Aesch.

ξῐφο-κτόνος, ον, (κτείνω) *slaying with the sword*, Soph.

ΞΙ΄ΦΟΣ [ῐ], Aeol. **σκίφος**, εος, τό, *a sword*, Hom.; distinguished from μάχαιρα, q. v.

ξῐφουλκία, ἡ, *the drawing of a sword*, Plut. From

ξῐφ-ουλκός, όν, (ἕλκω) *drawing a sword*, Aesch.

ξῐφ-ουργός, (*ἔργω) *a sword-cutler*, Ar.

ξόᾰνον, τό, (ξέω) *an image carved* of wood, Xen.: generally, *an image, statue*, Eur.

ξοᾰν-ουργία, ἡ, (*ἔργω) *a carving of images*, Luc.

ξοῖς, ῖδος, ἡ, (ξέω) *a sculptor's chisel*, Anth.

ξουθό-πτερος, ον, (πτερόν) *with tawny wings*, Eur.

ΞΟΥΘΟ΄Σ, ή, όν, of a colour, between ξανθός and πυρρός, *yellowish, brown-yellow, tawny*, epith. of the bee, Eur.; of the nightingale, Aesch., Eur., etc.   **II.** later of sound, *shrill, thrilling*, Babr., Anth.

ξυγγ-, for all words so beginning, v. sub συγγ-.

ξυήλη, ἡ, (ξύω) *a tool for scraping wood, a plane* or *rasp*, Xen.   **II.** *a sickle-shaped dagger*, Id.

ξυληγέω, f. ήσω, (ἄγω) *to carry wood*, Dem. From

ξυλ-ηγός, όν, (ἄγω) *carrying wood*.

ξυλήφιον, τό, Dim. of ξύλον, *a piece of wood, a stick*, Polyb.

ξυλίζομαι, (ξύλον) Med. *to gather wood*, Xen.

ξύλῐνος [ῠ], η, ον, (ξύλον) *of wood, wooden*, Hdt., Att.   **2.** metaph. *wooden*, νοῦς Anth.

ξυλλ-, for all words so beginning, v. sub συλλ-.

ξῠλοκοπέω, *to beat with a stick, cudgel*, Polyb.

ξῠλοκοπία, ἡ, *a cudgelling*, Lat. *fustuarium*, Polyb.

ξῠλοκόπος, ον, (κόπτω) *hewing* or *felling wood*, Xen.

ξύλον [ῠ], τό, (perh. from ξύω) *wood* cut and ready for use, *firewood, timber*, Hom.; ξύλα νήϊα *ship-timber*, Hes.; ξ. ναυπηγήσιμα Thuc.   **II.** in sing. *a piece of wood, a post*, Hom.: *a perch*, Ar.: *a stick, cudgel, club*, Hdt., Ar.   **2.** *a collar of wood*, put on the neck of the prisoner, Ar.:—also *stocks*, for the feet, Hdt., Ar.; cf. πεντεσύριγγος.   **3.** *a plank or beam to which malefactors were bound, the Cross*, N. T.   **4.** *a money-changer's table*, Dem.   **5.** πρῶτον ξύλον *the front bench* of the Athenian theatre, Ar.   **III.** of live wood, *a tree*, Xen.

ξῠλο-πᾰγής, ές, (πήγνυμι) *built of wood*, Strab.

ξῠλ-ουργέω, (*ἔργω) *to work wood*, Hdt. Hence

ξῠλουργία, ἡ, *a working of wood, carpentry*, Aesch.

ξῠλο-φάγος, ον, (φαγεῖν) *eating wood*, Strab.

ξῠλοφορέω, *to carry a stick*, as the Cynics did, Luc.

ξῠλο-φόρος, ον, (φέρω) *carrying wood*.

ξῠλοχίζομαι, Dor. **-ίσδομαι**, = ξυλίζομαι, Theocr.

ξύλ-οχος [ῠ], ἡ, (perh. from ξύλον, ἔχω) *a thicket, copse*, Il.

ξῠλόω, f. ώσω, *to make of wood*. Hence

ξύλωσις, ἡ, *the woodwork of a house, frame-work*, Thuc.

ξυμμ-, for all words so beginning, v. sub συμμ-.

ξύν, harsher pronunciation of σύν, v. σύν init. :—for compds. of ξυν-, v. sub συν-.

ξῠνάν, ξῠνάων, v. ξυνήων.

ξῠν-εείκοσι, Ep. for συν-είκοσι, *twenty together*, Od.

ξυνεών, v. ξυνήων.

ξῠνήϊος, η, ον, Ep. and Ion. for ξύνειος, which does not occur : ξυνήϊα *common property, common stock*, Il.

ξῠνήων, ονος, ὁ, Dor. **ξῠνάων** [ᾱ], **ξῠνάν** : (ξυνός) :—*a joint-owner, partner* in a thing, c. gen., Hes.; ξυνάονες ἑλκέων, i. e. *afflicted* by sores, Pind. :—absol., ξυνάν *a friend*, Id.

ξύνηκα, aor. 1 of συν-ίημι.

ξύνῑε, imper. of ξυν-ίω, = συν-ίημι.

ξυνίει, imper. of συν-ίημι.

ξύνιον, Ep. 3 pl. impf. of συν-ίημι.

ξῠνο-δοτήρ, ῆρος, ὁ, *the free, bounteous giver*, Anth.

ξῠνός, ή, όν, (ξύν) older form of κοινός, *common, public, general, concerning* or *belonging to all in common*, Il.; γαῖα ξυνὴ πάντων *earth the common property* of all, Ib.; ξ. Ἐνυάλιος, i. e. *war hath an even hand, is uncertain*, Ib.; ξ. πᾶσι ἀγαθόν Hdt.; ξυνὰ λέγειν *to speak for the common good*, Aesch.

ξῠνό-φρων, ονος, ὁ, ἡ, (φρήν) *friendly-minded*, Anth.

ξῠνο-χᾰρής, ές, (χαίρω) *rejoicing in common*, Anth.

ξῠνωρίς, ίδος, ἡ, v. συνωρίς.

ξυρεῦντες, Ion. for -οῦντες, part. of sq.

ξῠρέω, f. ήσω: aor. 1 ἐξύρησα :—Pass., pf. ἐξύρημαι: (ξυρόν) :—*to shave*, Il.: proverb. of great danger or sharp pain, ξυρεῖ ἐν χρῷ *it shaves close, touches* the quick, Soph. :—Med. and Pass. *to shave oneself* or *have oneself shaved*, Hdt.; ξυρεῦνται πᾶν τὸ σῶμα *they have their whole body shaved*, Id.

ξῠρ-ήκης, ες, (ἀκή) *keen as a rasor*, Xen.   **II.** pass. *close-shaven*, Eur.; κουρᾷ ξυρήκει with *close* tonsure, Id.

ξῠρόν, τό, (ξύω) *a rasor*, Hom., etc. :—proverb., ἐπὶ ξυροῦ ἵσταται ἀκμῆς ὄλεθρος ἠὲ βιῶναι *death or life is balanced on a rasor's edge*, Il.; ἐπὶ ξυροῦ τῆς ἀκμῆς ἔχεται ἡμῖν τὰ πράγματα Hdt.; βεβὼς ἐπὶ ξυρῷ τύχης Soph.

ξυρρ-, for words so beginning, v. sub συρρ-.

ξυσμή, ἡ, (ξύω) in pl., *scrapings*, Anth.

ξυσσ-, for words so beginning, v. sub συσσ-, cf. ξύν.

ξυστήρ, ῆρος, ὁ, (ξύω) *a graving tool*, Lat. *scalprum*, Anth.

ξυστίς, Att. **ξύστις**, ίδος, ἡ, (ξύω) *a xystis, a robe of fine material, a robe of state*, Ar., Plat., etc.

ξυστο-βόλος, ον, (βάλλω) *spear-darting*, Anth.

ξυστόν, τό, (ξύω) *the polished shaft* of a spear, Il., Hdt.   **2.** generally, *a spear, lance*, Il., Eur.

ξυστός, όν, (ξύω) *scraped, polished*, Hdt.

ξυστός, ὁ, (ξύω) *a covered colonnade* on the S. side of the gymnasium, where athletes exercised in winter, Xen., etc. : so called from its smooth and polished floor.

ξυστο-φόρος, ον, (φέρω) *carrying a spear*, Xen.

ΞΥ΄Ω, Ep. impf. ξῦον, aor. 1 ἔξυσα :—Pass., aor. 1 ἐξυσάμην Xen. : pf. ἔξυσμαι : (akin to ξέω) :—*to scrape, plane, smooth* or *polish*, Od.: metaph., ξῦσαι ἀπὸ γήρας *to scrape off, get rid* of old age, h. Hom. :—Med., παλτὸν ξύσασθαι *to shape oneself* a javelin-shaft, Xen.   **II.** *to make smooth, work delicately*, Il.

O.

O, o, ὃ μικρόν, *little* or *short o*, as opp. to ὃ μέγα *great* or *long o*, i. e. *double o* (for ω was orig. written ∞, i. e. *oo*): fifteenth letter in the Greek alphabet: as numeral ο´ = 70, but ͵ο = 70,000.

In early times o r⋯esents both o and ω; and in many words must hav⋯ ⋯unded like ου, as in βόλομαι for βούλομαι; while r⋯rsely, in Ion. μοῦνος νοῦσος κοῦρος οὔνομα stand fo⋯ ⋯νος νόσος κόρος ὄνομα.

Dialect. changes: ⋯ ⋯l. for α, as στροτός for στρατός;—for ε, Ἐρχόμενος ⋯Ορχόμενος (Boeot.);—for ῠ, as ὔνυμα στύμα for ὄνομ⋯ ⋯μα. 2. Dor. often into οι, ἀγνοιέω πτοιέω πνοιά f⋯ ⋯γνοέω ἀλοάω πτοέω. 3. like α, o is often reject⋯ ⋯r prefixed for euphony, as κέλλω ὀκέλλω, δύρομαι ⋯ύρομαι. 4. in compd. Adjectives, o is changed ⋯etri grat. into η, θεογενής ξιφοφόρος into θεηγενής ⋯φόρος.

ὁ, ἡ, τό, is A. dem⋯tr. Pronoun. B. the definite Article. C. ⋯ Ep., the relative Pronoun, when it is written with th⋯ ⋯cent ὅ, ἥ, τό = ὅς, ἥ, ὅ.

Besides the common ⋯ms, note Ep. gen. sing. τοῖο for τοῦ; pl. nom. τ⋯ ⋯ραί; gen. fem. τάων [ᾰ], dat. τοῖσι, τῆς and τῇσι; ⋯al gen. and dat. τοῖιν:— in Trag. we find τοὶ μέν . ⋯ τοὶ δέ . ., for οἱ μέν . ., οἱ δέ . .; dat. pl. also τοῖ⋯ ⋯ραῖσι: the dual has commonly but one gender, τώ ⋯ ⋯τά, τοῖν for ταῖν.

A. ὁ, ἡ, τό, DEMONSTR⋯ PRONOUN: **I.** joined with a Subst., not as the ⋯., but like Lat. *ille*, ὁ Τυδείδης Tydeus' *famous* ⋯, Il.; Νέστωρ ὁ γέρων Nestor—*that aged man*, Il⋯ τιμῆς τῆς Πριάμου for honour, *namely that* of Pria⋯ Ib. **II.** without a Subst., *he, she, it,* ὁ γὰρ ἦλθ⋯ ⋯b., etc. **III.** pecul. usages, **1.** before Relat. ⋯nouns, to call attention to the foregoing noun, ἐφάμ⋯ ⋯σε περὶ φρένας ἔμμεναι ἄλλων, τῶν ὅσσοι Λυκίην ναιε⋯ ⋯υσιν far above the rest, *namely* above *those who* . ., **2.** ὁ μέν . ., ὁ δέ . ., either in Opposition, ⋯ ⋯ *the former, ὁ δέ the latter*), or in Partition, *the on⋯ . ., the other* . ., Lat. *hic* . ., *ille* . . . **IV.** a⋯olute usages of single cases, **1.** fem. dat. τῇ, *the⋯, on that spot*, Hom.; τὸ μὲν τῇ, τὸ δὲ τῇ Xen. ⋯—w⋯h a notion of motion towards, *thither*, Il. **b.** of ⋯lanner, τῇπερ *in this way, thus*, Od.; τῇ μέν . ., τῇ δέ . ., *in one way* . ., *in another* . ., or *partly* . ., *partly*, Eur., etc. **c.** relative, *where*, for ᾗ, Hom. **2.** neut. gen. τοῦ, *therefore*, Id. **3.** neut. dat. τῷ, *therefore*, Id., Soph. **b.** *thus, in this wise, then, if this be so*, on this condition, Hom. **4.** neut. acc. τό, *wherefore*, Id., Soph.; τὸ δέ, absol., *but as to this* . ., Plat. **5.** τὸ μέν . ., τὸ δέ . ., *partly* . ., *partly* . ., or *on the one hand* . ., *on the other* . ., Od., Att.; τὰ μέν . ., τὰ δέ . ., Hdt., Soph., Thuc.; also, τὰ μέν τι . ., τὰ δέ τι . ., Xen. **6.** with Prepositions, of Time, ἐκ τοῦ, Ep. τοῖο, *ever since*, Il. **b.** πρὸ τοῦ, sometimes written προτοῦ, *before this, aforetime*, Hdt., Aesch.; so, ἐν τῷ προτοῦ χρόνῳ Thuc. **7.** ἐν τοῖς is often used in Prose with Superlatives, ἐν τοῖς θειότατον one of the most marvellous things, Hdt.; ἐν τοῖς πρῶτοι among the first, Thuc.

B. ὁ, ἡ, τό, THE DEFINITE ARTICLE, *the*, the indefin. being τὶς, τὶ, *a* or *an*. The use of ὁ, ἡ, τό, as the Article sprung from its use as demonstr. Pron., τὸν ὀπίστατον him that was hindmost, i. e. *the hindmost man*, Il.; τὸν ἄριστον him that was bravest, etc.;— also with Advs. τὸ πρίν, τὸ πάρος περ, τὸ πρόσθεν, τὸ τρίτον, τὰ πρῶτα all in Il. **II.** the true Article is first fully established in Att.: it is omitted with prop. names and with appellatives which require no specification, as θεός, βασιλεύς:—but it is added to Prop. Names, when there has been previous mention of the person, as Thuc. speaks first of Πειθίας, and then refers to him as ὁ Π.; or to give pecul. emphasis, like Lat. *ille*, ὁ Λάϊος, ὁ Φοῖβος Soph. **2.** with Infinitives, which thereby become Substantives, τὸ εἶναι *the being*; τὸ φρονεῖν good sense, etc. **3.** in neuter, to specify any word or expression, τὸ ἄνθρωπος *the word* man; τὸ λέγω *the word* λέγω; τὸ μηδὲν ἄγαν *the sentiment* 'ne quid nimis.' **4.** before Pronouns, **a.** before the pers. Pron., to give them greater emphasis, but only in acc., τὸν ἐμέ, τὸν σὲ καὶ ἐμέ Plat. **5.** before the interrog., to make the question more precise, τὸ τί; Aesch., etc.; τὰ ποῖα; Eur. **III.** Elliptic expressions: **1.** before the gen. of a prop. n., to express descent, ὁ Διός (sc. παῖς), ἡ Λητοῦς (sc. θυγάτηρ) often in Att.; but sometimes, as appears from the context, to denote *husband, brother, friend, wife*:— then before a gen. it indicates all general relations, as, τὰ τῆς πόλεως all that concerns the state; τὰ τῶν Ἀθηναίων φρονεῖν to hold with the Athenians, be on their side, Hdt.:—so with neut. of possess. Pron., τὸ ἐμόν, τὸ σόν what regards me or thee, my or thy business. But τό τινος is often also, *a man's saying*, as, τὸ τοῦ Σόλωνος Hdt. **2.** with cases governed by Preps., οἱ ἐν τῇ πόλει, οἱ ἀπὸ (or ἐκ) τῆς πόλεως the men of the city; οἱ ἀμφί τινα, οἱ περί τινα such an one and his followers, but also periphr. for the person himself. **3.** on μὰ τόν, v. μά IV. **4.** πορεύεσθαι τὴν ἔξω τείχους (sc. ὁδόν), Plat.; κρίνασθαι τὴν ἐπὶ θάνατον, v. θάνατος I. 2; ἡ αὔριον (sc. ἡμέρα) the morrow:—also with Advs., which thus take an Adject. sense, as, ὁ, ἡ, τὸ νῦν the present; οἱ τότε ἄνθρωποι the men of that time, also οἱ τότε, οἱ νῦν, etc.; τὸ πρὶν formerly; τὸ πρόσθεν, τὸ πρῶτον, etc.; τὸ ἀπὸ τούτου, τὸ ἀπὸ τοῦδε from the present time, etc.

C. CRASIS OF ART.:— in Trag. ὁ, ἡ, τό, with ᾰ make ᾱ, as ἁνήρ, ἅνθρωπος, ἁλήθεια, ἁρετή, τἀγαθόν, τἀδικεῖν, τἄτιον; so, οἱ, αἱ, τά, as ἅνδρες, ἅνθρωποι, τἀγαθά, τἀκίνητα; also τοῦ, τῷ, as τἀγαθοῦ, τἀγαθῷ: —ὁ, τό, οἱ, with ε become ου, οὐξ, οὑπί, οὑμός, τοὔργον, οὑπιχώριοι, etc.; also τοῦ, as τοὐμοῦ, τοὐπιόντος; but in one case ᾰ, ἅτερος, θάτερον, for οὕτερος (which is Ion.); τῷ remains unchanged, τὡμῷ, τὡπιόντι:—ἡ with ε becomes ᾱ, ἁτέρα:—ὁ, τό before ο becomes ου, as Οὑλύμπιος, τοὐνομα:—ὁ, τό, etc., before αυ do not change the diphthong, αὑτός, ταὐτό, ταὐτῷ; so, τὰ αὐτά = ταὐτά, αἱ αὐταί = αὑταί:—ἡ before ευ becomes ηὑ, as ηὑλάβεια:—τῇ before ἡ becomes θη, as θἠμέρα: —τό before ὕ becomes θου-, as θοὔδωρ for τὸ ὕδωρ.

ὅ, Ion. and Dor. masc. for relat. pron. ὅς. **II.** generally, neut. of the same.

ὀά [ᾰ], *woe, woe!* Lat. *vae!* Aesch.

ᾍΟΑΡ, ὄαρος, ἡ, *a wife*, in gen. pl., ὀάρων ἕνεκα σφετεράων Il. ; contr. dat. pl., ἀμυννέμεναι ὤρεσσιν Ib.

ὀαρίζω (ὄαρος), used in pres. and impf. *to converse or chat with* one, c. dat., Il. ; ὀαριζέμεναι (Ep. inf.) Ib.

ὀάρισμός, οῦ, ὁ, = ὄαρος, Hes. ; and

ὀάριστής, οῦ, ὁ, *a familiar friend*, Od. ; and

ὀάριστύς, ύος, ἡ, *familiar converse, fond discourse*, Il., Theocr. :—generally, ἡ γὰρ πολέμου ὀαριστύς such is war's *intercourse*, Il. II. as concrete, προμάχων ὀαριστύς the *company* of out-fighters, Ib. From

᾽ΟΑΡΟΣ, ὁ, *familiar converse, fond discourse, chat, talk*, h. Hom., Hes. 2. *a song, lay, ditty*, Pind.

ᾍΟασις, εως, ἡ, a name of the fertile islets in the Libyan desert, Hdt. (The name is prob. Egyptian.)

ὀβελίσκος, ὁ, Dim. of ὀβελός, *a small spit*, Ar., Xen., etc. 2. *a coin stamped with a spit*, Plut. II. *the leg of a compass*, Ar.

ὀβελός, Dor. ὀδελός, ὁ, *a spit*, Il., Hdt., Att. 2. ὀβ. λίθινος *a pointed square pillar, obelisk*, Hdt. (ὀβελός is prob. βέλος with ο prefixed.)

᾽ΟΒΟΛΟΣ, ὁ, *an obol*, as a weight, = ⅙th part of a δραχμή, worth rather more than three halfpence, Ar. ; ἐν δυοῖν ὀβολοῖν θεωρεῖν, as we might say ' to sit in the shilling gallery,' Dem.

ὀβολοστατέω, f. ήσω, *to weigh obols : practise petty usury*, Luc. From

ὀβολο-στάτης [ᾰ], ου, ὁ, (ἵστημι) *a weigher of obols*, i. e. *a petty usurer*, Ar. :—hence ὀβολοστατική (sc. τέχνη), ἡ, *the trade of a petty usurer, usury*, Arist.

ᾍΟΒΡΙΑ, τά, *the young of animals*, Aesch., Eur. Hence

ὀβρίκάλα [ῐ], τά, = foreg., Aesch.

ὀβρῐμο-εργός, όν, (*ἔργω) *doing deeds of violence*, Il.

ὀβρῐμό-θυμος, ον, *strong-minded*, Hes.

ὀβρῐμο-πάτρη, ἡ, (πατήρ) *daughter of a mighty sire*, Il., Solon, etc.

ὄβρῐμος, ον, and η, ον, *strong, mighty*, Il. :—neut. as Adv., ὄβριμον ἐβρόντησε he thundered *mightily*, Hes. (From βρι–, βριαρός, with ο prefixed.)

ὀγδόατος, η, ον, poët. for ὄγδοος, as τρίτατος for τρίτος, *the eighth*, Hom.

ὀγδοήκοντα, οἱ, αἱ, τά, indecl. *eighty*, Lat. *octoginta*, Thuc., etc. :—Ion. and Dor. ὀγδώκοντα, Il., Theocr.

ὀγδοηκοντα-τέσσαρες, α, *eighty-four*, N. T.

ὀγδοηκοντ-ούτης, ες, (ἔτος) *eighty years old*, Luc. :—Ion. and Dor. ὀγδωκοντα-έτης, ες, Solon.

ὀγδοηκοστός, ή, όν, (ὀγδοήκοντα) *eightieth*, Thuc., etc.

ὄγδοος, η, ον, (ὀκτώ) *eighth*, Lat. *octavus*, Hom., etc.

ὀγδώκοντα, ὀγδωκοντούτης, v. ὀγδοήκ–.

ὅγε, ἥγε, τόγε, the demonstr. Pron. ὁ, ἡ, τό, made more emphatic by the addition of γε, like Lat. *hicce, haecce, hocce, he, she, it*, Hom., Hes., etc. :—γε may be rendered sometimes by *indeed* or *at least*, Lat. *quidem*. II. Adverbial usages : 1. dat. τῆγε, of place, *here, on this very spot*, Il. 2. acc. neut. τόγε, *on this account, for this very reason*, Hom.

ᾍΟγκα, ἡ, a name of Athena at Thebes, Aesch.

ὀγκάομαι, Dep. *to bray*, of the ass, Luc. (Formed from the sound.)

ὀγκηρός, ά, όν, (ὄγκος Β) *bulky, swollen* :—metaph. *stately, pompous*, Xen. ; τὸ ὀγκηρόν *trouble*, Arist.

ὀγκητής, οῦ, ὁ, (ὀγκάομαι) *a brayer*, i. e. *an ass*, Anth.

ὄγκιον or ὀγκίον, τό, *a case for arrows and other implements*, Od. From

ὄγκος (Α), ὁ, *the barb* of an arrow, in pl. *the barbed points*, Il. (From same Root as Lat. *uncus*.)

ὄγκος (Β), ὁ, *bulk, size, mass*, Lat. *moles*, Plat., etc. 2. *a bulk, mass, heap*, ὄ. φρυγάνων *a heap* of fagots, Hdt. ; σμικρὸς ὄ. ἐν σμικρῷ κύτει, of a dead man's ashes, Soph. ; ὄ. γαστρός, of a child in the womb, Eur. II. metaph. *weight, trouble*, Soph. 2. *weight, importance, dignity, pride*, and in bad sense *self-importance, pretension*, Id., Eur., etc. (From Root ΕΓΚ in ἐν-εγκ-εῖν *to bear*.) Hence

ὀγκόω, aor. 1 ὤγκωσα :—Med., f. –ώσομαι :—Pass., aor. 1 ὠγκώθην, pf. ὤγκωμαι :—*to heap up* a mound : —Pass., Anth. II. metaph. *to bring to honour and dignity, exalt, extol*, Eur. ; ὀγκῶσαι τὸ φρόνημα *to puff up* one's conceit, Ar. ; so in Med., Id. :—Pass. *to be puffed up, inflated*, Eur.: in good sense, *to be honoured*, Id.

ὀγκύλλομαι, Pass., = ὀγκόομαι, *to be puffed up*, Ar.

ὀγκ-ώδης, ες, (ὄγκος Β, εἶδος) *swelling, rounded*, Xen. II. metaph. *swollen, inflated*, Plat.

ὀγκωτός, ή, όν, (ὀγκόω) *heaped up*, Anth.

ὀγμεύω, only in pres. and impf. *to move in a straight line*, properly of ploughers or mowers; metaph., ὀγμ. στίβον *to trail one's weary way*, of a lame man, Soph. ; ὤγμευον αὐτῷ *they were marching in file before* him, Xen. From

ὄγμος, ὁ, (ἄγω) *any straight line, a furrow* in ploughing, Il. : *a swathe* in reaping, Ib. 2. metaph. *the path* of the heavenly bodies, h. Hom. ; ὄγμος ὀδόντων *a row* of teeth, Anth.

ᾍΟΓΧΝΗ, ἡ, *a pear-tree*, Od.

ὀδαγμός, ὁ, (ὀδάξομαι) = ἀδαγμός, Soph.

ὀδαῖος, α, ον, (ὁδός) = ἐνόδιος :—ὀδαῖα, τά, *goods with which a merchant travels*, his *freight*, Od.

ὀδάξ, Adv. *by biting with the teeth*, Lat. *mordicus*, Hom. ; ὀδὰξ ἕλον οὖδας *they bit the ground*, of men in the agonies of death, Il. ; so, γαῖαν ὀδὰξ ἑλόντες Eur. ; ὀδὰξ ἐν χείλεσι φύντες *biting the lips* in smothered rage, Od. ; διατρώξομαι ὀδὰξ τὸ δίκτυον Ar. (From δακ-εῖν with ο prefixed.)

ὀδάξω, impf. ὤδαξον, (ὀδάξ) *to feel a biting, stinging pain, feel irritation*, Xen.

ὀδάω, aor. 1 ὤδησα, pass. ὠδήθην :– (ὁδός) :—*to export and sell* ; generally, *to sell*, Eur. :—Pass. *to be carried away and sold*, Id.

ὅ-δε, ἥ-δε, τό-δε, demonstr. Pron., *this*, formed by adding the enclit. -δε to the old demonstr. Pron. ὁ, ἡ, τό, and declined like it : Ep. dat. pl. τοῖσδεσσι, τοῖσδεσσιν and τοῖσδεσι ; Ion. τοισίδε :—ὅδε, like οὗτος opp. to ἐκεῖνος, to designate the *nearer* as opp. to the *more remote ;* but ὅδε is also deictic, i.e. refers to *what can be pointed out*. This *deictic* force is more emphat. in the forms ὀδί, ἡδί, etc. [ῑ], which belong to Com. and Oratt., and are never used in Trag. : I. of Place, like French *voici*, to point out *what is before* one, Ἕκτορος ἥδε γυνή *here is* the wife of Hector, Il., etc. :—also with Verbs, *here*, ὅστις ὅδε κρατέει *who holds sway here*, Ib. ; ἔγχος μὲν τόδε κεῖται *here it lies*, Ib. :—in Trag., to indicate the entrance of a person on the stage, καὶ μὴν Ἐτεοκλῆς ὅδε χωρεῖ *and see here comes ..*, Eur. ; ὅδ' εἰμ'

Ὀρέστης here I am—Orestes, Id. 2. so also with τίς interrog., τίς ὅδε Ναυσικάᾳ ἕπεται; who is this following her? Od. 3. in Trag., ὅδε and ὅδ' ἀνήρ, emphatic for ἐγώ; so, τῇδε χερί with this hand of mine, Soph. II. of Time, to indicate the immediate present, ἥδ' ἡμέρα Id., etc.; τοῦδ' αὐτοῦ λυκάβαντος on this very day, Od.; νυκτὸς τῆσδε in the night just past, Soph. 2. ἐς τόδε, elliptic c. gen., ἐς τόδ' ἡμέρας Eur.; ἐς τόδε ἡλικίης Hdt. III. in a more general sense, to indicate something before one, οὐκ ἔρανος τάδε γ' ἐστίν these preparations which I see are not an ἔρανος, Od.; Ἀπόλλων τάδ' ἦν this was Apollo, Soph. 2. to indicate something immediately to come, ταῦτα μὲν Λακεδαιμόνιοι λέγουσι, τάδε δὲ ἐγὼ γράφω Hdt. IV. Adverbial usage of some cases: 1. fem. dat. τῇδε, of Place, here, on the spot, Lat. hac, Hom., etc.:—of Way or Manner, thus, Il., Att. 2. acc. neut. τόδε, hither, to this spot, Hom.; δεῦρο τόδε Id. b. therefore, on this account, Od.; acc. neut. pl., τάδε Ib. 3. neut. dat. pl. τοῖσδε and τοισίδε, in or with these words, Hdt.

ὁδεύω, f. σω, (ὁδός) to go, travel, Il., Xen. 2. Pass. to be provided with thoroughfares, Strab.

ὁδηγέω, f. ήσω, (ὁδηγός) to lead one upon his way, c. acc. pers., Aesch.; absol. to lead the way, Eur.

ὁδ-ηγός, ὁ, (ὁδός, ἡγέομαι) a guide, Plut.

ὁδί, ἡδί, τοδί [ῐ], Att. for ὅδε, ἥδε, τόδε, q. v.

ὅδιος, ον, (ὁδός) belonging to a way, ὄρνις ὅδ. a bird of omen for the journey (or seen by the way), Aesch.

ὅδισμα, ατος, τό, (as if from ὁδίζω) a road-way, Aesch.

ὁδίτης [ῑ], ου, ὁ, a wayfarer, traveller, Od., Soph.; Dor. ὁδίτας, Theocr.

ὁδμάομαι, older form of ὀσμάομαι.

ὀδμή, ἡ, older Ep. and Ion. form of ὀσμή.

ὁδοιπλανέω, f. ήσω, to stray from the road, wander or roam about, Anth.

ὁδοι-πλανής, ές, (πλανάομαι) straying from one road into another, wandering about, Anth.

ὁδοιπορέω, impf. ὡδοιπόρεον,-ουν: f. ήσω: pf. ὡδοιπόρηκα: pf. pass. ὡδοιπόρημαι Luc.: (ὁδοιπόρος):—to travel, walk, Hdt., Soph., etc.; ὁδ. τοὺς τόπους to walk over this ground, Soph. Hence

ὁδοιπορία, Ion. -ίη, ἡ, a journey, way, Hdt., etc.

ὁδοιπόριον, τό, provisions for the voyage, Lat. viaticum, Od. From

ὁδοι-πόρος, ὁ, a wayfarer, traveller, Aesch., Soph., Ar.;—in Il., a fellow-traveller or guide.

ὀδοντο-φόρος, ον, (φέρω) bearing teeth, κόσμος ὀδ. an ornament formed of strings of teeth, Anth.

ὀδοντο-φυής, ές, (φύομαι) sprung from the dragon's teeth, Eur.

ὁδοποιέω, impf. ὡδοποίουν: f. ήσω: Pass., pf. ὡδοποίημαι: (ὁδοποιός):—to make or level a road, Xen.:—Pass., of roads, to be made fit for use, Id.: 2. metaph. to reduce to a system, τι Arist. II. c. dat. pers. to act as pioneer, serve as guide, Xen.:—Pass. to make one's way, advance, Lat. progredi, Plat. Hence

ὁδοποίησις, ἡ, a making of roads:—hence, a pioneering, preparation, Arist.

ὁδοποιΐα, ἡ, the work of a pioneer, Xen. From

ὁδο-ποιός, ὁ, (ποιέω) one who opens the way, a pioneer, Xen. 2. a road-surveyor, Aeschin.

ὀδός, ὁ, Att. for οὐδός, a threshold, Soph., etc.

ΟΔΟΣ, ἡ: I. a way, path, track, road, highway: ποταμοῦ ὁδός the course of a river, Xen.; the path of the heavenly bodies, Eur. 2. with Preps., πρὸ ὁδοῦ further on the way, forwards, Il. (cf. φροῦδος):—κατ' ὁδόν by the way, Hdt.;—ἐκ τῆς ὁδοῦ on his road, Id. II. a travelling, journeying, whether by land or water, a journey or voyage, Hom., etc.:—also an expedition, foray, Il.:—c. gen., τὴν εὐθὺς Ἀργοῦς ὁδόν the way leading straight to Argos, Eur. III. metaph. a way or manner, θεσπεσία ὁδός the way or course of divination, Aesch.; ὀδ. μαντικῆς Soph.; λογίων ὁ. the way, intent of the oracles, Eur. 2. a way of doing, speaking, etc., τριφασίας ἄλλας ὁδοὺς λόγων three other ways of telling the story, Hdt.; ὁδὸν ἥντιν' ἰών by what course of action, Ar., etc. 3. a way, method, system; ὁδῷ methodically, systematically, Plat. 4. the Way, i.e. the Christian Faith, N.T.

ὁδ-ουρός, ὁ or ἡ, a conductor, conductress, Eur.

ΟΔΟΥΣ, Ion. ὀδών, ὀδόντος, ὁ, Lat. dens, dentis, a tooth, Hom., Hes., etc.; ἕρκος ὀδόντων, v. ἕρκος I; πρίειν ὀδόντας, v. πρίω.

ὀδο-φύλαξ [ῠ], ἄκος, ὁ, a watcher of the roads, Hdt.

ὀδόω, f. ώσω: aor. 1 ὥδωσα: (ὀδός):—to lead by the right way, Aesch.; c. inf., τὸν φρονεῖν βροτοὺς ὁδώσαντα who put mortals on the way to wisdom, Id.: of things, to direct, ordain, Eur.:—Pass. to be on the right way, be conducted, Hdt.

ὀδυνᾱρός, Dor. for ὀδυνηρός.

ὀδυνάω, f. ήσω: Pass., 2 sing. ὀδυνᾶσαι in N.T.: aor. 1 ὠδυνήθην:—to cause one pain or suffering, to distress, Eur., etc.:—Pass. to feel pain, suffer pain, Soph., Ar.; ἃ ὠδυνήθην the pains I suffered, Ar. From

ΟΔΥΝΗ [ῠ], ἡ, pain of body, Lat. dolor, Hom., Att. 2. pain of mind, grief, distress, Hom., etc.; ὀδύνη τινὸς grief for him, Il. Hence

ὀδυνηρός, Dor. -ᾱρός, ά, όν, painful, Pind., Ar. 2. painful, distressing, Eur., Ar.

ὀδυνή-φατος, ον, (πέ-φαται, 3 sing. pf. pass. of *φένω) killing, i.e. stilling, pain, Il.

ὄδυρμα, ατος, τό, a complaint, wailing, Trag.; and

ὀδυρμός, ὁ, a complaining, lamentation, Aesch., Eur. etc. From

ΟΔΥΡΟΜΑΙ [ῠ], Dep., mostly in pres. and impf., Ep. impf. ὀδύρετο, ὀδύροντο (without augm.), Ion. ὀδυρέσκετο: f. ὀδυροῦμαι: aor. 1 ὠδυράμην: (the Trag. use a form δύρομαι when required by the metre):—to lament, bewail, mourn for: 1. c. acc. pers., Hom., Soph.: c. acc. rei, ὁ δ' ὀδύρετο πατρίδα γαῖαν mourned for it, i.e. for the want of it, Od.; so, νόστον ὀδυρομένη Ib. 2. c. gen. pers. to mourn for, for the sake of, Hom. 3. c. dat. pers. to wail or lament to or before others, Id. 4. absol. to wail, mourn, Id., Eur. Hence

ὀδυρτικός, ή, όν, disposed to complain, querulous, Arist. Adv. -κῶς, Comp. -κωτέρως, Id.

ὀδυρτός, ή, όν, (ὀδύρομαι) mourned for, lamentable: neut. pl. ὀδυρτά, as Adv., painfully, Ar.

Ὀδύσσεια, ἡ, the Odyssey, Arist. From

Ὀδυσσεύς, έως, ὁ, Ion. ἦος, ὁ, Lat. Ulysses, Ulixes, king of Ithaca, whose adventures after the fall of Troy are told in the Odyssey: Ep. Ὀδῠσεύς, Aeol. gen. Ὀδῠσεῦς

acc. 'Οδυσσέᾱ, but the two last syll. form. one in Soph. Cf. ὀδύσσομαι. Hence

'Οδύσσειος, Ep. 'Οδυσήϊος, η, ον, of Ulysses, Od.

ὀδύσσομαι, Ep. Verb, only in aor. 1 med. 2 and 3 sing. ὠδύσαο, -ατο, 3 pl. ὀδύσαντο, part. ὀδυσσάμενος :—to be wroth against, to hate another, c. dat., Hom., Hes. (Prob. from the Root δυσ- with ὁ prefixed. 'Οδυσσεύς is derived from it, v. Od. 19. 407 sq.)

ὄδωδα, ὀδώδει, pf. and 3 sing. plqpf. of ὄζω.

ὀδωδή, ἡ, (ὄζω) smell, scent, Anth.

ὀδών, όντος, ὁ, Ion. for ὀδούς.

ὀδωτός, ή, όν, (ὀδόω) passable : practicable, Soph.

ὄεσσι, Ep. for ὄϊσι, dat. pl. of ὄϊς, οἶς.

ὀξαλέος, α, ον, (ὄζος) branching, Anth.

'Οξόλαι, οἱ, the Ozolae, a tribe of the Locrians, perhaps from the strong-smelling sulphur-springs in their country, Strab.

'ΟΖΟΣ, Aeol. ὔσδος, ὁ, a bough, branch, twig, shoot, Il., Hes., etc. II. metaph. an offshoot, scion, ὄζος Ἄρηος, of a famous warrior, Il. ; so, τὼ Θησείδα ὄζω 'Αθηνῶν Eur.

ὀξό-στομος, ον, (ὄζω, στόμα) with bad breath, Anth.

'ΟΖΩ, Dor. ὄσδω : f. ὀξήσω : aor. 1 ὤζησα : pf. with pres. sense ὄδωδα, and plqpf. as impf. ὀδώδειν, Ep. ὀδώδειν :—to smell, whether to smell sweet or to stink, used by Hom. only in 3 sing. plqpf. :—c. gen. rei, to smell of a thing, ὄζων τρυγός smelling of wine-lees, Ar. ; metaph. to smell or savour of a thing, Lat. sapere aliquid, Κρονίων ὄζων smelling of musty antiquity, Id. II. impers., ὄζει ἀπ' αὐτῆς ὡσεὶ ἴων there is a smell from it as of violets, Hdt. ; ὄζει ἡδὺ τῆς χρόας there is a sweet smell from the skin, Ar. ;—so c. dupl. gen., ἱματίων ὀξήσει δεξιότητος there will be an odour of cleverness from your clothes, Id.

ὅθεν, relat. Adv., answering to demonstr. τόθεν and interr. πόθεν, Lat. unde, whence, from which, Hom., etc. :—also from whom, ὅθεν περ αὐτὸς ἐσπάρη from whom himself was born, Soph. b. ὅθεν δή from whatever source, in what manner soever, Plat. 2. = ὅθι, οὗ, ὅπου, where, Il., Soph. II. whence, wherefore, Eur., Plat.

ὅθῐ, relat. Adv., answering to demonstr. τόθι and interr. πόθι, poët. for οὗ, Lat. ubi, where, Hom., Trag.

ὀθνεῖος, α, ον, and ος, ον, strange, foreign, Lat. alienus, Eur., Plat. (Deriv. uncertain.)

"ΟΘΟΜΑΙ, Dep. only in pres. and impf. to care for, take heed, regard, reck, always with a negat., Hom.

ὀθόνη, ἡ, fine linen, in pl., fine linen cloths, Hom. 2. sails, Anth. : in sing. a sail, Luc. (Deriv. unknown.)

ὀθόνιον, τό, Dim. of ὀθόνη, a piece of fine linen :—in pl. linen cloths, bandages, N.

ὀθ-ούνεκα, for ὅτου ἕνεκα (as οὕ-νεκα for οὗ ἕνεκα), because, Soph. II. like οὕνεκα, simply for ὡς or ὅτι, that, Lat. quod, Trag.

ὅ-θριξ, gen. ὑτρῐχος, poët. for ὁμό-θριξ, ὁ, ἡ, with like hair, Il.

"Οθρυς, υος, ὁ, Mount Othrys in Thessaly, Hdt.

ΟΙ´, exclam. of pain, grief, pity, astonishment, ah! woe! Lat. heu! vae! sometimes with nom., οἶ 'γὼ Soph. ; mostly c. dat., v. οἴμοι ; c. acc., οἶ ἐμὲ δειλήν Anth.

οἱ, nom. pl. masc. of Art. ὁ, II. οἵ, of relat. Pron. ὅς.

оἱ, enclit. οἱ, dat. sing. of pron. of 3rd pers. masc. and fem. ; v. οὗ.

οἷ, relat. Adv. (from ὅς) whither, Lat. quo, Trag.; οὐκ ἤκουσας οἷ προβαίνει τὸ πρᾶγμα Ar. :—c. gen., οἷ μ' ἀτιμίας ἄγεις to what a height of dishonour you lead me, Soph. 2. with Verbs of rest, οἷ φθίνει τύχα where, i. e. how, in what, it ends, Eur. ; so, οἷ κακίας τελευτᾷ in what state of vice he ends, Plat.

οἰακίζω, Ion. οἰηκ-, f. σω, (οἴαξ) to steer, and so to guide, manage, Hdt., Arist.

οἰακο-νόμος, ὁ, (νέμω) a helmsman : metaph. a pilot, ruler, Aesch.

οἰακοστροφέω, f. ήσω, to steer, direct, Aesch. From

οἰακο-στρόφος, ὁ, (στρέφω) = οἰακονόμος, Aesch., Eur.

ΟΙ´ΑΞ, ᾱκος, Ion. οἴηξ, ηκος, ὁ, the handle of the rudder, the tiller, and generally, the helm, Aesch., Eur., etc. :—metaph. the helm of government, Aesch. II. in Il., οἴηκες are the rings of the yoke, through which pass the reins for guiding the mules.

οἰάτης [ᾱ], ου, ὁ, a villager : Οἰᾶτις νομός is a pasture in the Attic deme Οἴα, Soph.

ΟΙ´ΓΩ, οἴγνυμι Anth. : f. οἴξω : aor. 1 ᾦξα, Ep. also ὤϊξα :—Pass., Ep. 3 pl. impf. ὠΐγνυντο : aor. 1 ὠΐχθην : —to open, ὤϊξα θύρας Il. : absol., ᾦξε γέροντι he opened the door to the old man, Ib. ; [οἶνον] ᾤξεν ταμίη she broached the wine, Od.; πρὸς φίλους οἴγειν στόμα Aesch.

οἶδα, Aeol. οἶδα, pf. in pres. sense of *εἴδω B.

οἰδάνω [ᾰ], to make to swell, Lat. tumefacere, Il. :— Pass. to swell, Lat. tumere, Ib. II. = οἰδέω, Ar.

οἶδας, 2 sing. pf. of *εἴδω B.

οἰδέω, Ep. impf. ᾤδεον : aor. 1 ᾤδησα : pf. ᾤδηκα, Dor. 3 pl. -αντι : (οἶδος) :—to swell, become swollen, Lat. tumere, ᾤδεε δὲ χρόα he had his body swollen, Od. ; οἰδεῖν τὼ πόδε to have swollen feet, Ar. II. metaph. of inflated style, Id. ; also, οἰδεόντων πρηγμάτων when times were troublous (like tument negotia in Cic.), Hdt. Hence

οἴδημα, ατος, τό, a swelling, tumour, Dem.

Οἰδιπόδειος, α, ον, or ος, ον, of Oedipus, Plut.

Οἰδι-πόδης, ὁ, = Οἰδίπους : Ep. gen. Οἰδιπόδαο Hom., Dor. Οἰδιπόδα Pind., Trag., Ion. Οἰδιπόδεω Hdt. ; acc. Οἰδιπόδαν Soph. ; voc. Οἰδιπόδα Id.

Οἰδί-πους [ῐ], ὁ, (οἰδέω, πούς) Oedipus, i. e. the swoln-footed (v. Soph. O. T. 718, Eur. Phoen. 25) :—gen. Οἰδίποδος, but in Trag. Οἰδίπου (as if from Οἰδίπος), acc. Οἰδίπουν : voc. Οἰδίπους.

οἶδμα, ατος, τό, (οἰδέω) a swelling, swell, οἴδματι θύων raging with swollen waves, Il. ; in pl., Soph. :—generally, the sea, Id., Eur.

ΟΙ´ΔΟΣ, τό, a swelling, tumour.

οἴεος, α, ον, (οἶς) of or from a sheep, Hdt.

ὄτεσσι, Ep. for οἴεσι, dat. pl. of ὄϊς.

οἰ-έτης, ες, (ἔτος) poët. for ὁμο-έτης, of the same age, Il.

ὄϊζνος, ον, = sq., sorry, wretched, Theocr.

ὀϊζυρός, Att. οἰζυρός (as trisyll.), ά, όν, woful, pitiable, miserable, Hom. ; of conditions, toilsome, dreary, Id. ; also sorry, poor, Hdt. [Though Hom. makes ῠ, he forms the Comp. and Sup., metri grat., ὀϊζῠρώτερος, -ώτατος, for -ότερος, -ότατος.] From

ὀϊζύς, Att. οἰζύς, dissyll., ή, gen. ὀϊζύος, contr. dat. ὀϊζυῖ (οἶ oh !) :—woe, misery, distress, hardship, suffering, Hom. [ῡ in nom. and acc.; ῠ in trisyll. cases.] Hence

ὀϊζύω, aor. 1 ὀΐζ-υσα:—to wail, mourn, lament, περὶ κεῖνον ὀΐζυε (imperat.) Il. II. c. acc. rei, to suffer, ὀϊζύομεν κακὰ πολλά Il.: absol. to suffer greatly, Od.

οἰηθῆναι, aor. 1 inf. of οἴομαι.

οἰήϊον, τό, Ep. for οἴηξ, οἴαξ, a rudder, helm, Hom.

οἰηκίζω, Ion. for οἰακίζω:—οἴηξ, for οἴαξ.

οἴησις, εως, ἡ, (οἴομαι) opinion, an opinion, Plat.: self-conceit, Bion.

οἰήσομαι, f. of οἴομαι.

οἰητέον, verb. Adj. of οἴομαι, one must suppose, Arist.

οἶϊς, ἡ, acc. οἶϊδα, Ep. for ὄϊς, a sheep, Theocr.

οἶκα, Ion. for ἔοικα.

οἴκᾱδε, Adv. = οἴκόνδε, to one's home, home, home-wards, Hom., etc. II. = οἴκοι, at home, Xen.

οἴκαδις, Doric for οἴκαδε, Ar.

οἰκειᾱκός, ἡ, όν, = οἰκεῖος III, one's own, Plut.

οἰκειο-πρᾱγία, ἡ, a minding one's own affairs, Plat.

οἰκεῖος, α, ον, and ος, ον, Ion. οἰκήϊος, η, ον:—in or of the house, domestic, Hes., etc.; τὰ οἰκεῖα household affairs, property, Lat. res familiaris, Hdt., Thuc., etc. II. of persons, of the same family or kin, related, Lat. cognatus, Hdt., Att.; οἱ ἑωυτοῦ οἰκηϊότατοι his own nearest kinsmen, Hdt.; κατὰ τὸ οἰκεῖον Ἀτρεῖ because of his relationship to Atreus, Thuc. 2. friendly, Dem. III. of things, belonging to one's house or family, one's own, Aesch., etc.; ἡ οἰκεία (sc. γῆ), Ion. ἡ οἰκηΐη, Hdt.; τὰ οἰκήϊα one's own property, Id.; οἰκεῖοι πόλεμοι wars in one's own country, Thuc.; of corn, home-grown, Id. 2. personal, private, opp. to δημόσιος, κοινός, Theogn., Hdt., Att.; μηδὲν οἰκειοτέρα τῇ ἀπολαύσει with enjoyment not more our own, Thuc.; οἰκεία ξύνεσις mother wit, Id. IV. proper to a thing, fitting, suit-able, becoming, Hdt., Dem. 2. c. dat. rei, belonging to, conformable to the nature of a thing, Plat. 3. οἰκ. ὄνομα a word in its proper, literal sense, Arist. B. the Adv. οἰκείως has the same senses as the Adj., familiarly, Thuc., Xen. II. affectionately, dutifully, Id. Hence

οἰκειότης, Ion. οἰκηϊότης, ητος, ἡ, kindred, relation-ship, Hdt., Att.: intimacy, friendliness, kindness, Thuc.:—in pl. friendly relations, Dem. II. of words, the proper sense, Plat.

οἰκειόω, Ion. οἰκηϊόω, f. ώσω, (οἰκεῖος) to make one's own: 1. to make a person one's friend, Thuc.; so in Med. to win his favour or affection, conciliate, Hdt.:—Pass. to be made friendly, Thuc.: to be closely united, Plat. 2. Med. also, c. acc. rei, to make one's own, claim as one's own, appropriate, Hdt., Plat. Hence

οἰκείωμα, Ep. for οἰκέω, Hes.

οἰκείωμα, ατος, τό, kindred, relationship, Strab.

οἰκείως, v. οἰκεῖος B.

οἰκείωσις, ἡ, (οἰκειόω) a taking as one's own, appro-priation, Thuc.

οἰκετεία, ἡ, the household, Lat. familia, Strab., Luc.

οἰκετεύω, to inhabit, Eur. From

οἰκέτης, ου, ὁ, (οἰκέω) a house-slave, menial, Hdt., Att.; οἱ οἰκέται, Lat. familia, one's household, the women and children, Hdt., Att.; opp. to οἱ δοῦλοι, Plat.

οἰκετικός, ἡ, όν, (οἰκέτης) of or for the menials or household, Plat., Arist.

οἰκετίς, ἴδος, ἡ, fem. of οἰκέτης, Eur. II. the mis-tress of the house, Lat. matrona, Theocr.

οἰκεύς, έως Ion. ῆος, ὁ, = οἰκέτης, an inmate of one's house, Hom. II. a menial, servant, Od., Soph.

οἰκέω, Ep. οἰκείω: impf. ᾤκεον, Att. ᾤκουν, Ion. οἴκεον: f. οἰκήσω: aor. 1 ᾤκησα: pf. ᾤκηκα:—Pass. and Med., f. οἰκήσομαι: aor. 1 ᾠκήθην: pf. ᾤκημαι, Ion. 3 pl. οἰκέαται: (οἶκος): A. trans. to inhabit, occupy, Il., Hdt., Att.:—Pass. to be inhabited, Il., Hdt., etc.; cf. οἰκουμένη. 2. Pass. to be settled, of those to whom new abodes are assigned, Il.; οἱ ἐν τῇ ἠπείρῳ οἰκημένοι those who have been settled, Id.; to be those who dwell on the mainland, Hdt.; of cities, to be situate, to lie, Id. II. to manage, direct, govern, like διοικέω, Soph., etc. B. intr. to dwell, live, be settled, Hom., etc.; ἔξω τῶν κακῶν οἰκεῖν γλυκύ sweet is it to live free from cares, Soph. II. of cities, in a pass. sense, to be settled, be situated, Hdt., Xen. 2. to conduct oneself or be conducted so and so, σωφρόνως γε οἰκοῦσα [πόλις] εὖ ἂν οἰκοῖτο a state with habits of self-control would be well governed, Plat.

οἰκήϊος, οἰκηϊότης, οἰκηϊόω, Ion. for οἰκει-.

οἴκημα, ατος, τό, (οἰκέω) any inhabited place, a dwelling-place, Pind., Att.: a chamber, and in pl. a house, Hdt. II. special senses, 1. a brothel, Hdt.: a tavern, Isae. 2. a cage or pen for animals, Hdt. 3. a temple, fane, chapel, Id. 4. a prison, Dem. 5. a storeroom, Plat., Dem. 6. a workshop, Plat. 7. a story, Lat. tabulatum, Xen.

οἰκήσιμος, ον, (οἰκέω) habitable, Polyb.

οἴκησις, ἡ, (οἰκέω) the act of dwelling, habitation, Hdt., Att. 2. management, administration, Plat. II. a house, dwelling, residence, Hdt., Soph., etc.; κατασκαφὴς οἴκ. of the grave, Soph.

οἰκητήρ, ῆρος, ὁ, poët. for οἰκητής, Soph. Hence

οἰκητήριον, τό, a dwelling-place, habitation, Eur.

οἰκητής, οῦ, ὁ, = οἰκήτωρ, Soph., Plat.

οἰκητός, ἡ, όν, (οἰκέω) inhabited, Soph.

οἰκήτωρ, ορος, ὁ, (οἰκέω) an inhabitant, Hdt., Att.; οἰκ. θεοῦ one who dwells in the temple of the god, Eur.; Ἅιδου οἰκ., of one dead, Soph. 2. a colonist, Thuc.

οἰκία, Ion. -ίη, ἡ, (οἶκος) a building, house, dwelling, Hdt. II. a household, domestic establishment, Plat.; οἰκίας δύο ᾤκει, i.e. he kept two establishments, Dem. 2. the household, i.e. inmates of the house, Lat. familia, Plat. III. the house or family from which one is descended, Hdt., Att.

οἰκιᾱκός, ἡ, όν, of or belonging to a house, οἱ οἰκ. one's domestics, N.T.

οἰκίδιον, τό, Dim. of οἶκος, a chamber, Ar.

οἰκίζω, f. Att. οἰκιῶ: aor. 1 ᾤκισα, Ion. οἴκισα, poët. ᾤκισσα: pf. ᾤκικα:—Med., f. οἰκιοῦμαι: aor. 1 ᾠκι-σάμην:—Pass., f. οἰκισθήσομαι: aor. 1 ᾠκίσθην: pf. ᾤκισμαι, Ion. οἴκισμαι: I. c. acc. rei, to found as a colony or new settlement, πόλιν Hdt., Ar., etc.:—Pass., πόλις οἴκισται Hdt. 2. to people with new settlers, colonise, χώρην Id.; νήσους Thuc.:—Med., ὅπη γῆς πύργον οἰκιούμεθα in what part of the world we shall make ourselves a fenced home, Eur. II. c. acc. pers. to remove, transplant, Id.; metaph., τὸν μὲν ἀφ᾽ ὑψηλῶν βραχὺν ᾤκισεν brought him from high to

low estate, Eur. :—Pass. *to settle* in a place, Id., Plat.

οἰκίον, τό, in form a Dim. of οἶκος : only in pl. like Lat. *aedes*, *a house, dwelling, abode*, Hom., Hdt.

οἴκισις, ἡ, (οἰκίζω) *a peopling, colonisation*, Thuc.

οἰκίσκος, ὁ, Dim. of οἶκος, *a small room*, Dem.

οἰκισμός, ὁ, = οἴκισις, Solon, Plat.

οἰκιστήρ, ῆρος, poët. for sq., Pind., Orac. ap. Hdt.

οἰκιστής, οῦ, ὁ, (οἰκίζω) *a coloniser, founder of a city*, Hdt., Thuc.

οἰκο-γενής, ές, (γίγνομαι) *born in the house, homebred*, of slaves, Lat. *verna*, Plat. ; of quails, Ar.

οἰκοδεσποτέω, *to be master of the house, to rule the household*, N. T. From

οἰκο-δεσπότης, ου, ὁ, *the master of the house, the good man of the house*, N. T.

οἰκοδομέω, f. ήσω : aor. 1 ᾠκοδόμησα : (οἰκοδόμος) :— *to build a house* : generally, *to build*, οἰκίαν, γέφυραν, τεῖχος Hdt. :—Med., οἰκοδομεῖσθαι οἴκημα *to build oneself* a house, *have it built*, Id. :—Pass. *to be built*, Id. 2. metaph. *to build* or *found upon*, ἔργα ἐπί τι Xen. ; οἰκ. τέχνην ἔπεσιν Ar. 3. metaph., also, *to build up, edify*, N. T. :—Pass., οἰκοδομηθήσεται εἰς τὸ ἐσθίειν *will be emboldened* to eat, Ib.

οἰκοδομή, ἡ, a late form for οἰκοδόμημα, Plut., N. T.

οἰκοδόμημα, ατος, τό, *a building, structure*, Hdt., Thuc.

οἰκοδόμησις, ἡ, *the act* or *manner of building*, Thuc. II. = οἰκοδόμημα, Plat.

οἰκοδομητέον, verb. Adj. *one must build*, Plat.

οἰκοδομητικός, ή, όν, *fitted for building* : ἡ -κή (sc. τέχνη) *architecture*, Luc.

οἰκο-δομητός, ή, όν, *built*, Strab.

οἰκοδομία, ἡ, = οἰκοδόμησις, Thuc. 2. *a building, edifice*, Plat.

οἰκοδομικός, ή, όν, (οἰκοδόμος) *practised* or *skilful in building*, Plat. : ἡ -κή (sc. τέχνη), *the art of building, architecture*, Id. ; so, τὰ οἰκοδομικά Id.

οἰκο-δόμος, ὁ, (δέμω) *a builder, an architect*, Hdt., Plat.

οἴκοθεν, Adv. *from one's house, from home*, Il., Thuc. ; οἴκοθεν οἴκαδε *from house to house*, proverb. of one who has two homes, Pind. ; εὐθὺς οἴκ., i. e. *from childhood*, Arist. :—often without any sense of motion, τὰ οἴκ. *domestic affairs*, Eur. ; στρατηγοὺς εἵλοντο ἐκ τῶν οἴκ. Xen. 2. *from one's household stores*, Il. 3. *from one's own resources, by one's own virtues, by nature*, Pind., Eur. 4. *wholly, absolutely*, Aeschin.

οἴκοθι, Ep. for οἴκοι, Adv. *at home*, Hom.

οἴκοι, (οἶκος) Adv. *at home, in the house*, Lat. *domi*, Il., Hes., etc. ; τὰ οἴκοι *one's domestic affairs*, Xen., Plat. ; so, ἡ οἴκοι δίαιτα Soph. ; ἡ οἴκοι (sc. πόλις) *one's own country*, Id.

οἴκόνδε, Ep. Adv., = οἴκαδε, Hom., Hes.

οἰκονομέω, f. ήσω, (οἰκονόμος) *to manage as a housesteward, to manage, order, regulate*, Soph., Xen. 2. metaph. of an artist, *to treat, handle* a subject, Arist., Luc. II. intr. *to be a house-steward*, N. T.

οἰκονομία, ἡ, *the management of a household* or *family, husbandry, thrift*, Plat., etc. ; and

οἰκονομικός, ή, όν, *practised in the management of a household* or *family*, Plat., etc. : hence, *thrifty, frugal, economical*, Xen. :—ὁ οἰκ. title of *a treatise*

on the duties of domestic life, by Xen. ; and τὰ οἰκονομικά, a similar treatise by Arist. : ἡ -κή (sc. τέχνη), *domestic economy*, Plat., Xen., etc. From

οἰκο-νόμος, ὁ, (νέμω) *one who manages a household*, Xen., Plat. 2. generally, *a manager, administrator*, Arist. : οἱ Καίσαρος οἰκ. the Roman *procuratores*, Luc. II. as fem. *a housekeeper, housewife*, Aesch.

οἰκό-πεδον, τό, *the site of a house*, Xen., Aeschin., etc. 2. *the house itself, a building*, Thuc.

οἰκο-ποιός, όν, (ποιέω) *constituting a house*, οἰκ. τροφή *the comforts of a house*, Soph.

οἰκ-όριος, poët. for οἰκ-ούριος.

ΟΙ'ΚΟΣ, ὁ, *a house, abode, dwelling*, Hom., Hes., etc. :— acc. οἶκον, = οἴκονδε, οἴκαδε, *homeward, home*, Od. ; κατ' οἶκος *at home, within*, Hdt. ; κατ' οἶκον Soph., etc. : — ἐπ' οἶκον ἀποχωρεῖν *to go homewards*, Thuc., etc. : ἀπ' οἶκου *from home*, Id. 2. *part of a house, a room, chamber*, Od. : pl. οἶκοι *for a single house*, Lat. *aedes, tecta*, Ib., Att. 3. *the house of a god, a temple*, Hdt., Eur. II. *one's house, household goods, substance*, Hom., etc. III. *a house, household, family*, Od., etc.

οἰκός, Ion. for ἐοικός, part. neut. of ἔοικα.

οἰκό-σιτος, ον, *taking one's meals at home, living at one's own expense, unpaid*, Menand.

οἰκο-τρίβής, ές, (τρίβω) *ruining a family*, Critias.

οἰκό-τριψ, ῐβος, ὁ, (τρίβω) *a slave born and bred in the house*, Dem.

οἰκο-τύραννος [ῠ], ὁ, *a domestic tyrant*, Anth.

οἰκότως, Ion. Adv. part. pf. of οἰκώς (for ἐοικώς), *reasonably, probably*, Hdt.

οἰκουμένη (sc. γῆ), ἡ, *the inhabited world*, a term used to designate *the Greek world*, as opp. to barbarian lands, Hdt., Dem., etc. :—so in Roman times, *the Roman world*, N. T. : metaph. ἡ οἰκ. ἡ μέλλουσα *the world to come*, i. e. the kingdom of Christ, Ib.

οἰκουμενικός, ή, όν, *of* or *from the whole world* (ἡ οἰκουμένη) ; of Eccl. Councils, *oecumenical*.

οἰκ-ουργός, ὁ, (οἶκος, *ἔργω) *a house-steward*, N. T.

οἰκουρέω, (οἰκουρός) mostly in pres., *to watch* or *keep the house*, Aesch., Soph. : generally *to keep safe, guard*, Ar. II. *to keep at home*, as women, Soph., Plat. 2. ἑβδομον οἰκ. μῆνα πολιορκοῦντες *they idled away* seven months in the siege, Plut. Hence

οἰκούρημα, ατος, τό, *the watch* or *keeping of a house*, Eur.; οἰκ. τῶν ξένων = οἱ οἰκουροῦντες ξένοι, Soph. II. *a keeping the house, staying at home*, Eur. 2. in concrete sense, of persons, οἰκουρήματα φθείρειν *to corrupt the stay-at-homes*, i. e. the women, Eur.

οἰκουρία, ἡ, *housekeeping, the cares of housekeeping*, Eur. II. *a staying at home, of women*, Plut.

οἰκουρικός, ή, όν, (οἰκουρέω) *inclined to keep at home* : —τὸ -κόν, = οἰκουρία, Luc.

οἰκούριος, ον, and α, ον, *of* or *for housekeeping* : hence οἰκούρια (sc. δῶρα), τά, *wages, reward for keeping the house*, Soph. II. *keeping within doors*, ἑταῖραι οἰκούριαι (Dor. for οἰκούριαι) *female house-mates*, Pind.

οἰκ-ουρός, όν, (οὖρος) *watching the house*, of a watchdog, Ar. II. as Subst., οἰκουρός, ἡ, *the mistress of the house, housekeeper*, Eur. :—contemptuously of a man, *a stay-at-home*, opp. to one who goes forth to war, Aesch. ; so, δίαιτα οἰκ. Plut.

οἰκοφθορέω, f. ήσω, (οἰκοφθόρος) *to ruin a house, squander one's substance,* Plat. :—Pass., aor. 1 οἰκοφθόρην, pf. οἰκοφθόρημαι, *to be ruined, undone,* Hdt.

οἰκοφθορία, ἡ, *a squandering one's substance,* Plat.

οἰκο-φθόρος, ὁ, (φθείρω) *one who ruins a house, a prodigal,* Plat.

οἰκο-φύλαξ [ῠ], ὁ, ἡ, *a house-guard,* Anth.

οἰκτείρέω, f. ήσω, later form of οἰκτείρω, N. T.

οἰκτείρω: impf. ᾤκτειρον: f. οἰκτερῶ: aor. 1 ᾤκτειρα, Ion. οἴκτειρα: Pass., only in pres. and impf. : (οἶκτος): —*to pity, feel pity for, have pity upon,* c. acc., Il., Hdt., Att. :—οἰκτ. τινά τινος *to pity* one *for* or *because of* a thing, Aesch. :—also c. acc. rei, Ar. 2. c. inf., οἰκτ. νιν λιπεῖν *I am sorry* to leave her, Soph.

οἰκτίζω, f. Att. οἰκτιῶ: aor. 1 ᾤκτισα: (οἶκτος): —*to pity, have pity upon,* c. acc., Aesch., Soph., etc. :—Med. in same sense, Eur., Thuc. 2. in Med. also, *to bewail, lament,* Eur. : absol. *to express one's pity,* Id. ; οἶκτον οἰκτίζεσθαι *to utter a wail,* Aesch.

οἰκτιρμός, οῦ, ὁ, *pity, compassion,* Pind. :—in pl. *compassionate feelings, mercies,* N. T.

οἰκτίρμων, ον, gen. ονος, *merciful,* Theocr., N. T

οἰκτίρω [ῐ], late form of οἰκτείρω, Anth.

οἴκτισμα, ατος, τό, (οἰκτίζω) *lamentation,* Eur.

οἰκτισμός, οῦ, ὁ, (οἰκτίζω) *lamentation,* Aesch., Xen., etc.

οἴκτιστος, η, ον, irreg. Sup. of οἰκτρός (cf. αἰσχρός, αἴσχιστος) *most pitiable, lamentable,* Hom. :—neut. pl. οἴκτιστα as Adv., Od.

οἶκτος, ὁ, (οἲ oh!) *pity, compassion,* Od., Hdt., Att. :—c. gen. objecti, *compassion for,* οἶκτος τῆς πόλιος Hdt. 2. *the expression of pity, lamentation, piteous wailing,* Aesch., Soph. ;—and in pl., Plat., Eur.

οἰκτρό-γοος, ον, *wailing piteously, piteous,* Plat.

οἰκτρός, ά, όν, (οἶκτος) *pitiable, in piteous plight,* Il., Soph., etc. 2. of things, *pitiable, piteous, lamentable,* Hdt., Aesch., etc. II. in act. sense, *piteous,* Od., Soph. ; οἰκτρᾶς γόον ὄρνιθος, of the nightingale, Soph. ;—neut. pl. as regul. Adv. οἰκτρῶς, Aesch., Soph. —Besides Comp. and Sup. οἰκτρότερος, -τατος, Hom. has an irreg. Sup. οἴκτιστος (q. v.).

οἰκτρο-χοέω, f. ήσω, (χέω) *to pour forth piteously,* Ar.

οἰκώς, υῖα, ός, Ion. for ἐοικώς, part. of ἔοικα.

οἰκ-ωφελής, ές, (ὀφέλλω) *profitable to a house,* γυνὴ οἰκ. a wife *whose prudence makes the house thrive,* Theocr. Hence

οἰκωφελία, Ion.-ίη, ἡ, *profit to a house, housewifery,* Od.

Ὀϊλεύς, έως, ὁ, Oïleus, a Locrian chief, father of Ajax the Less, Il. (The orig. form was Ϝῑλεύς, from Ϝίλη (ἴλη), *a troop.*)

οἶμα, ατος, τό, = ὅρμημα, Lat. *impetus,* οἶμα λέοντος ἔχων *with the spring* of a lion, Il. ; αἰετοῦ οἴματ᾽ ἔχων *with the swoop* of an eagle, Ib.

οἶμαι, contr. from οἴομαι, q. v.

οἰμάω, f. ήσω: Ep. aor. 1 οἴμησα:—*to swoop* or *pounce upon* its prey, of an eagle, Hom. ; κίρκος οἴμησε μετὰ τρήρωνα πέλειαν *swooped after* a dove, Il. 2. absol. *to dart along,* Orac. ap. Hdt.

οἴμη, ἡ, = οἶμος: metaph. *a song, lay,* Od.

οἴ-μοι, exclam. of pain, fright, pity, anger, grief, also of surprise, properly οἴ μοι ah me! *woe's me!* Theogn., Trag. :—οἴμοι is mostly absol., or is used with a nom., οἴμοι ἐγὼ τλάμων, οἴμοι τάλας etc., Soph. ;—c. gen.

causae, οἴμοι τῶν κακῶν, οἴμοι γέλωτος ah me for my misfortunes, for the laughter, Trag. [The last syll. in οἴμοι may be elided before ὡς.]

ΟἸ'ΜΟΣ, ὁ and ἡ, *a way, road, path,* Hes., Aesch., etc. 2. *a stripe, layer,* Il. 3. *a strip of land, tract, country,* Σκύθην ἐς οἶμον Aesch. 4. metaph. *the course* or *strain* of song, h. Hom., Pind.

οἰμωγή, ἡ, *loud wailing, lamentation,* Il., Hdt., Trag., etc. ; and

οἴμωγμα, ατος, τό, *a cry of lamentation, wail,* Aesch., Eur.

οἰμώζω, f. οἰμώξομαι; later οἰμώξω: aor. 1 ᾤμωξα: (οἴμοι):—*to wail aloud, lament,* Hom., Trag. 2. in familiar Att., οἴμωζε is a curse, *plague take you, go howl!* Lat. *abeas in malam rem,* Ar. ; οἰμώξετε Id. ; οἰμώξεσθ᾽ ἄρα Id. ; οἰμώζειν λέγω σοι Id. ; so, οὐκ οἰμώξεται ; Id. II. trans. *to pity, bewail,* c. acc., Tyrtae., Trag. : Pass., οἰμωχθείς *bewailed,* Theogn. ; ᾠμωγμένος Eur.

οἰμωκτός, ή, όν, *pitiable,* Ar.

οἰμώξάρα, v. sub κλαύσάρα.

οἰν-άνθη, ἡ, (ἄνθος) *the first shoot of the vine:* generally, *the vine,* Eur., Ar. 2. *the soft down of the young vine-leaves,* Pind.

οἰνάρεον, τό, poët. for οἴναρον, *a vine-leaf,* Theocr.

οἰναρίζω, f. σω, (οἴναρον) *to strip off vine-leaves,* as is done when the grapes are ripening, Ar.

οἰνάριον [ᾰ], τό, Dim. of οἶνος, *weak* or *bad wine,* Dem.

οἴναρον, τό, *a vine-leaf,* Xen.

οἰνάς, άδος, ἡ, = οἴνη, *the vine,* Babr. II. Adj. of *wine, vinous,* Anth.

οἴνη, Dor. οἴνα, ἡ, (οἶνος) *the vine,* Hes., Eur. 2.= οἶνος, *wine,* Anth.

οἰνηρός, ή, όν, *of wine,* Eur. II. *containing wine,* Hdt., Pind. III. of countries, *rich in wine,* Anth.

οἰν-ήρυσις, ἡ, (ἀρύω) *a vessel for drawing wine,* Ar.

οἰνίζομαι, Med. *to procure wine by barter, buy wine,* Il.

οἰνο-βαρείων, ὁ, = οἰνοβαρής, Od.

οἰνοβαρέω, *to be heavy with wine,* Theogn.

οἰνο-βαρής, ές, (βαρύς) *heavy with wine,* Lat. *vino gravis,* Il., Anth.

οἰνο-βρεχής, ές, (βρέχω) *wine-soaked, drunken,* Anth.

οἰνο-δόκος, ον, (δέχομαι) *holding wine,* Pind.

οἰνο-δότης, ου, (δίδωμι) *giver of wine,* of Bacchus, Eur.

οἰνόεις, εσσα, εν, (οἶνος) *of* or *with wine.*

Οἰνόη, ἡ, (οἶνος) Oenoë, name of an Attic deme, Hdt., etc.

οἰνό-μελι, ιτος, τό, *honey mixed with wine, mead,* Anth.

οἰνό-πεδον, ον, (πέδον) *with soil fit to produce wine, wine-producing,* Od. II. οἰνόπεδον, τό, as Subst. *a vineyard,* Il., Theogn.:—also οἰνοπέδη, ἡ, Anth.

οἰνο-πέπαντος, (πεπαίνω) *ripe for wine-making,* Anth.

οἰνο-πλάνητος, ον, (πλανάομαι) *wine-bewildered,* Eur.

οἰνο-πληθής, ές, (πλήθω) *abounding in wine,* Od.

οἰνο-πλήξ, ῆγος, ὁ, ἡ, (πλήσσω) *wine-stricken,* Anth.

οἰνο-ποτάζω, (ποτόν) only in pres., *to drink wine,* Hom.

οἰνο-ποτήρ, ῆρος, ὁ, (ποτόν) *a wine-drinker,* Od.

ΟἸ'ΝΟΣ, ὁ, Lat. *vinum, wine,* Hom., etc.; παρ᾽ οἴνῳ *over* one's *wine,* Lat. *inter pocula,* Soph. ; οἶνος ἐκ κριθῶν *barley-wine,* a kind of *beer,* Hdt.

οἰνο-τρόφος, ον, (τρέφω) *rearing* or *bearing wine,* Anth.

οἰνοῦττα, ἡ, (οἰνόεις) *a cake* or *porridge of wine mixed with barley, water and oil,* eaten by rowers, Ar.

οἰνο-φάγία, ἡ, *meat full of wine,* Luc.

οἰνοφλῠγία, ἡ, drunkenness, Xen. From
οἰνό-φλυξ, ῠγος, ὁ, ἡ, (φλύω) given to drinking, drunken, Xen., etc.
οἰνο-φόρος, ον, (φέρω) holding wine, Critias; οἰνοφόρον (sc. σκεῦος) a wine-jar, oenophorus in Horace.
οἰνό-φῠτος, ον, planted or grown with vines, Strab.: —hence Οἰνόφυτα, τά, in Boeotia, Thuc.
οἰνο-χᾰρής, ές, (χαίρω) rejoicing in wine, Anth.
οἰνο-χάρων [ἄ], οντος, ὁ, Wine Charon, nickname of Philip of Macedon, because he put poison in his enemies' wine, and so sent them over the Styx, Anth.
οἰνοχοεύω, only in pres., = οἰνοχοέω, Hom.
οἰνοχοέω, 3 sing. Ep. impf. οἰνοχόει, ἐῳνοχόει: f. ήσω: aor. 1 inf. οἰνοχοῆσαι: (οἰνοχόος): —to pour out wine for drinking, Hom. 2. c. acc., νέκταρ ἐῳνοχόει she was pouring out nectar for wine, Il.
οἰνο-χόη, ἡ, (χέω) a can for ladling wine from the mixing bowl (κρατήρ) into the cups, Hes., Eur.
οἰνοχόημα, ατος, τό, (οἰνοχοέω) a festival at which wine is offered, Plut.
οἰνο-χόος, ὁ, (χέω) a wine-pourer, cupbearer, Hom., etc.
οἰνό-χῠτος, ον, of poured wine, πῶμα οἰν. a draught of wine, Soph.
οἰν-οψ, οπος, ὁ, (ὤψ) wine-coloured, wine-dark (never in nom.), ἐπὶ οἴνοπι πόντῳ Hom.; of oxen, wine-red, Id.
οἰνόω, to intoxicate, οἰνῶσαι σῶμα ποτοῖς Critias. II. Pass. οἰνόομαι, to get drunk, be drunken, οἰνωθέντες Od.; pf. part., ᾠνωμένος, Ion. οἰνωμένος, Hdt., Soph.
οἰνών, ῶνος, ὁ, (οἶνος) a wine-cellar, Xen.
οἰν-ωπός, ή, όν, and ός, όν, = οἶνοψ, Eur.; of a fresh, ruddy complexion, Id., Theocr.
οἰν-ώψ, ῶπος, ὁ, ἡ, = οἰνωπός, of Bacchus, Soph.: generally, dark, Id.
οἴξας, aor. 1 part. of οἴγω.
οἷο, Ep. for οὗ, gen. of Pron. possess. ὅς, ἥ, ὅν, his, her.
οἰό-βᾰτος, ὁ, lonesome, Anth.
οἰο-βώτας, ὁ, (βόσκω) feeding alone, of cattle: metaph. of Ajax, φρενὸς οἰοβώτας = μονόφρων, Soph.
οἰό-γᾰμος, ὁ, = μονόγαμος, Anth.
οἰό-ζωνος, ον, (ζωνή) = μονόζωνος, Soph.
οἰόθεν, Adv. (οἶος) from one only, i. e. by oneself, alone, in phrase οἰόθεν οἶος all alone, Il.
ΟΙ'ΟΜΑΙ, Ep. also ὀίομαι, Att. usually οἶμαι: —impf. ᾠόμην, Att. ᾤμην: f. οἰήσομαι: Ep. aor. 1 ᾠισάμην; also in pass. form ᾠίσθην, part. ὀϊσθείς, Att. ᾠήθην.— An act. pres. οἴω, Ep. ὀΐω, is also used but only in 1 pers. sing. [In the resolved diphthong, ι in all tenses, ὀΐομαι, ὀΐεαι, ὀΐεται, ὀΐσατο, etc.; ὀΐω.] To suppose, think, deem, imagine, c. acc. et inf., mostly inf. fut., Hom., etc. 2. c. inf. alone, when both Verbs have the same subject, as, κιχήσεσθαί σε ὀΐω I think to catch, i. e. I think I shall . . , Il.; οὐ γὰρ ὀΐω πολεμίζειν I do not think, i. e. mean, to fight, Ib.; ἐν πρώτοισιν ὀΐω ἔμμεναι I expect to be, Od. 3. sometimes the subject of the inf. is to be supplied from the context (as in 1), τρώσεσθαι ὀΐω I fear [that many] will be wounded, Il.; διωκέμεναι γὰρ ὀΐω I fear [they] are pursuing me, Od. 4. absol., αἰεὶ ὀΐεαι thou art ever suspecting, Il.: also, to deem, forebode, θυμὸς ὀΐσατό μοι my heart foreboded it, Od.; ὀΐσατο κατὰ θυμόν he had a presage of it in his soul, Ib.:—impers., ὀΐεταί μοι ἀνὰ θυμόν there comes a boding into my heart, Ib. II.

trans. to wait for, look for, κεῖνον ὀϊομένη looking for his return, Ib.; γόον δ' ὠίετο θυμός his soul was intent on grief, Ib. III. used by Hom. parenthetically, in first person, ἐν πρώτοισιν, ὀΐω, κείσεται among the first, I ween, will he be lying, Il.; ἔπειτά γ', ὀΐω, γνώσεαι Od. 2. in Att. this parenthetic use is confined to the contr. form οἶμαι, impf. ᾤμην, I think, I suppose, I believe; even between a Prep. and its case, ἐν οἶμαι πολλοῖς Dem. :—answering a question, expressive of positive certainty, I believe you, of course, no doubt, Ar., etc.; οἶμαι ἔγωγε yes I think so, yes certainly, Plat. :—also in a parenthetic question, πῶς οἴει; πῶς οἴεσθε; how think you? like πῶς δοκεῖς; also οἴει; alone, don't you think so? what think you? Id. IV. οἴομαι δεῖν I hold it necessary, think it my duty, like Fr. je crois devoir, Soph., Plat.
οἷον, neut. of οἷος, v. οἷος v.
οἰον-εί, for οἷον εἰ, as if, Lat. quasi, tanquam si, Arist.
οἰο-νόμος, ον, (οἷος, νέμω) feeding alone : hence, lone, lonely, of places, ἐπ' οἰονόμοιο (neut.) in solitude, Anth. II. (ὄϊς, οἶς) as Subst., a shepherd, Id.
οἰονπερεί, Adj. = οἷόν περ εἰ, as it were, Plat.
οἰόντε, possible; οὐχ οἰόντε impossible: v. οἷος III. 2.
οἴομαι, Pass. to be left alone, abandoned, forsaken, only in 3 sing. aor. 1 οἰώθη Il.
οἰοπολέω, f. ήσω, (οἰοπόλος), to tend sheep, to roam the mountains, Eur. :—c. acc. loci, to roam over, Anth.
οἰο-πόλος, ον, (οἶς, πολέω) traversed by sheep, Hom. 2. lonely, solitary, single, Pind. II. act. tending sheep, h. Hom.
οἰόρ-πατα, Scyth. for ἀνδρο-κτόνοι, οἰόρ being = ἀνήρ (vir), Hdt.
ΟΙ'ΟΣ, η, ον, like μόνος, alone, lone, lonely, though it can often only be rendered by an Adv. alone, only, Hom., Hes.; οἶος ἄνευθ' ἄλλων Il.;—with negat., οὐκ οἶος, ἄμα τῷγε . . , and some more, but . . , Ib.;—neut. οἶον as Adv., Ib. 2. strengthd., εἷς οἶος, μία οἴη one alone, one only, Hom.; in dual, δύο οἴω Id.; in pl., δύο οἴαι Od. :—rare in Att. 3. c. gen., οἴη θεῶν alone of the gods, Il.; so, οἶη ἐν ἀθανάτοισιν alone among the goddesses, Ib.; οἶος μετὰ τοῖσι Od.; but, οἶος ἀπ' ἄλλων alone from, apart from, Ib.; οἶος Ἀτρειδῶν δίχα, clam Atridis, Soph. II. single in its kind, unique, excellent, Il.
οἷος, οἵα Ion. οἵη, οἷον, (ὁ, ὅς) such as, what sort or manner of nature, kind, or temper, Lat. qualis, relat. Pronoun, correlative to the interrog. ποῖος, the indef. ποιός, and the demonstr. τοῖος, Hom., Hes., etc.; strengthd., ὅσσος ἔην οἷός τε, Lat. qualis erat quantusque, Il.: c. acc., οἶος ἀρετὴν what a man for virtue, Ib.; often only to be rendered by an Adv., οἶος μέτεισι πολεμόνδε how he rushes into war, Ib.
Usage: I. οἷος in an independent sentence expresses astonishment, strengthd. by δή, οἶον δὴ τὸν μῦθον ἐπεφράσθης ἀγορεῦσαι why, what a word it has come into thy mind to speak! Od.; so in neut., as Adv., v. infr. v. 2. so in indirect sentences, where no antec. can be supplied, ὁρῶν ἐν οἵοις ἐσμέν Xen. II. containing a Comparison, often without an antec., οἶος ἀστὴρ εἶσι like as a star wanders, Il.; οἶος καὶ Πάρις ᾔσχυνε like as Paris also dishonoured, Aesch. :—in this sense, οἶος is often attached to the case of its

antec., πρὸς ἄνδρας τολμηρούς, οἵους Ἀθηναίους (for οἷον Ἀθηναῖοι), Thuc. **2.** οἷος, οἵα, οἷον, esp. in Att., often stand for ὅτι τοῖος, τοία, τοῖον, so that the relat. introduces the *reason* for the preceding statement, ἄνακτα χόλος λάβεν, οἷον ἄκουσεν anger seized the king, *because of what* he heard, Il. **3.** but if the Comparison is general, Homer uses οἷον (which must be distinguished from οἷός τε c. inf., v. infr. III. 2), οἷός τε Ἄρης some such one as Ares, Il.; also, οἷός τις the sort of person who, Hom. **4.** when a Comparison involves Time, οἷος ὅ τε is used, *like as when . . ,* Od. **5.** οἷος is used in many brief Att. phrases, οὐδὲν γὰρ οἷον ἀκούειν αὐτοῦ τοῦ νόμου there's nothing *like* hearing the words of the law, Dem.;—it adds force to the Sup., χωρίον οἷον χαλεπώτατον, = τοιοῦτον οἷόν ἐστι χαλεπώτατον, Xen. **III.** οἷος with inf. implies Fitness or Ability to do, οἷος ἔην τελέσαι ἔργον τε ἔπος τε so ready was he to make good both deed and word, Od.; οἷος ἔην βουλευέμεν ἠδὲ μάχεσθαι so good both at counsel and in fight, Plat.; τὸ πρᾶγμα μέγα καὶ μὴ οἷον νεωτέρῳ βουλεύσασθαι the matter is great and not *such as* for a young man to advise upon, Thuc.; without an inf., ὃ δ' οἷός ἐστιν οἰκουρὸς μόνον *fit* only [to be] a house-dog, Ar. **2.** but this sense is commonly expressed by οἷός τε, c. inf., *fit* or *able* to do, λέγειν οἷός τε κἀγώ Id.; οἷός τε ἦν πείθειν Dem.: freq. in neut. sing. and pl., οἷόν τε ἐστί and οἷόν τε ἐστί, οἷόν τε γίγνεται it is *possible*, Hdt., Att.; without inf., οἷόν τε ἐστίν it is *possible*, οὐχ οἷόν τε ἐστίν it *cannot* be, Ar.; with a Sup., καλὸν ὡς οἷόν τε μάλιστα as beautiful as is possible, Plat.; ὡς οἷόν τε διὰ βραχυτάτων Id. **IV.** the relat. is in Att. often repeated in the same clause, οἳ ἔργα δράσας οἷα λαγχάνει κακά after *what* deeds *what* sufferings are his! Soph.; οἵαν ἀνθ' οἵων θυμάτων χάριν *what* thanks and *for what* offerings! Id. **V.** as Adv. in neut., to add force, οἷον ἐερσήεις *how* fresh, Il.; οἷα ἀτάσθαλα Od.:—the regul. Adv. οἵως is seldom used, οἷος ὢν οἵως ἔχεις *in what* a state art thou for such a man! Soph. **2.** in Comparisons, *as, like as, just as,* Hom., Trag.; οἷά τις ἀηδών Aesch.:—οἷον ὅτε *like as when,* cf. II. 4. **b.** *as,* οἷον τί λέγεις; *as for example,* what do you mean? Plat. **3.** *like* as with a partic., οἷα ἀπροσδοκήτου γενομένου *inasmuch as* it was unexpected, Thuc. **4.** with Numerals, *about,* οἷον δέκα σταδίους, etc.

οἷος, οἰός, of **ὄϊς,** οἷς, a sheep.

οἰοσ-δήποτε, of such and such a kind, Arist.

οἰο-χίτων [χῐ], ωνος, ὁ, ἡ, with only a tunic on, lightly clad, Od.

οἷπερ, Adv. *whither,* Lat. *quo,* v. οἷ.

ΟΙ'Σ [ῐ], ὁ and ἡ, gen. οἰός, acc. ὄϊν (οἶδα Theocr.): pl. ὄϊες, gen. ὀΐων; dat. οἴεσι, Ep. ὀΐεσσι, ὄεσσι; acc. ὄϊας, contr. ὄϊς [ῐ]:—the Att. contract all cases, οἶς, οἰός, οἶ, οἶν; pl. οἶες, οἰῶν, οἰσί, οἶας:—Lat. *ovis,* sheep, both *ram* and *ewe,* Hom., etc.; but the gender is sometimes marked by a word added, ὄϊν ἀρνειὸν ῥέξειν θῆλύν τε to sacrifice a male *sheep* and a female, Od.

ὄϊσατο, ὀϊσάμενος [ῐ], 3 sing. and part. aor. 1 of οἴομαι.

οἶσε, -έτω, -ετε, fut. imper. of φέρω.

οἰσέμεν, -έμεναι, fut. inf. of φέρω.

οἰσεῦμες, Dor. for οἴσομεν, 1 pl. fut. of φέρω.

οἶσθα, οἶσθας, 2 sing. pf. (in pres. sense) of *εἴδω Β.

ὀϊσθείς, aor. 1 pass. part. of οἴομαι.

οἰσπη, v. οἰσύπη.

οἰστέος, α, ον, verb. Adj. of φέρω, *to be borne,* Soph. **II.** οἰστέον *one must bear,* Eur. **2.** one must get, κέρδος Soph.

ὀϊστευτήρ, ῆρος, ὁ, an archer, Anth. From

ὀϊστεύω, f. σω, (ὀϊστός) *to shoot arrows,* Hom.: c. gen. *to shoot at,* ὀϊστευσον Μενελάου Il.

ὀϊστο-βόλος, ον, (βάλλω) arrow-shooting, Anth.

οἰστο-δέγμων, ὁ, ἡ, an arrow-holder, a quiver, Aesch.

οἰστός, ή, όν, verb. Adj. of φέρω, *that must be borne, endurable,* Thuc.

ὀϊστός, Att. **οἰστός,** an arrow, Hom., Hes., etc. (Deriv. uncertain.)

οἰστράω or **-έω,** f. ήσω: aor. 1 ᾤστρησα or οἴστρησα:—Pass., aor. 1 part. οἰστρηθείς: (οἶστρος):—*to sting,* properly of the gadfly; then metaph. *to sting to madness,* αὐτὰς ἐκ δόμων οἴστρησα *I drave* them *raging* out of the house, Eur.:—Pass., οἰστρηθείς *driven mad,* Soph. **II.** intr. like Pass. *to be driven by the gadfly, driven mad,* οἰστρήσασα *in frenzy, frantically,* Aesch.; of Menelaus, Eur.; ἡ ψυχὴ οἰστρᾷ Plat. Hence

οἰστρ-ήλατος, ον, (ἐλαύνω) driven by a gadfly, Aesch.

οἴστρημα, ατος, τό, the smart of a gadfly's sting: metaph. *frenzy,* Soph.

οἰστρο-βολέω, f. ήσω, to strike as with a sting, Anth.

οἰστρο-δίνητος [ῑ], ον, driven round and round by the gadfly, Aesch.

οἰστρο-πλήξ, ῆγος, ὁ, ἡ, (πλήσσω) stung by a gadfly, driven wild, Trag.

ΟΙ'ΣΤΡΟΣ, ὁ, the gadfly, breese, Lat. *asilus,* an insect which infests cattle, Od., Aesch. **II.** metaph. *a sting, anything that drives mad,* Eur.: absol. *the smart of pain, agony,* Soph. **2.** *mad desire, insane passion,* Hdt., Eur., etc.:—generally, *madness, frenzy,* Soph., Eur.

ΟΙ'ΣΥ'Α, ἡ, a tree of the *osier* kind. Hence

οἰσύϊνος [ῐ], η, ον, of osier, of wicker-work, Od., Thuc., etc.

ΟΙ'ΣΥ'ΠΗ [ῠ] or **οἴσπη, ἡ,** *the grease extracted from sheep's wool,* Hdt. Hence

οἰσυπηρός, ά, όν, with the grease in it, greasy, Ar.

οἴσω, fut. of φέρω.

Οἴτη, ἡ, Mount *Oeta* in Thessaly, Strab.:—Adj. **Οἰταῖος, α, ον,** of Oeta, Soph., etc.; οἱ Οἰταῖοι the men of Oeta, Thuc.

ΟΙ'ΤΟΣ, ὁ, fate, doom, Hom., Soph., Eur.

Οἰχαλία, Ion. -ίη, ἡ, name of a city in Thessaly, Il.:—**Οἰχαλιεύς, έως, ὁ,** an Oechalian, Ib.; Ep. Adv. -ίηθεν, from Oechalia, Ib.

οἰχέομαι, =οἴχομαι, Anth.

οἰχνέω, only in pres. and Ion. impf. οἴχνεσκον, *to go, come,* Od.; *to walk,* i. e. *to live,* Soph. **II.** like οἴχομαι, *to be gone,* Id. **III.** c. acc. pers., like προσέρχομαι, *to approach,* Pind.

ΟΙ'ΧΟΜΑΙ, impf. ᾠχόμην, Ion. οἰχόμην: f. οἰχήσομαι:—pf. ᾤχωκα, Ion. οἴχωκα: 3 sing. plqpf. ᾤχωκεε:—also pf. pass. ᾤχημαι, Ion. οἴχημαι:—Dep.: **I.** *to be gone, to have gone,* Lat. *abesse* (not *abire*), in pf. sense, and impf. ᾠχόμην in plqpf. sense, directly opp. to ἥκω, *to have come,* while ἔρχομαι, *to go* or *come,* serves as the

pres. to both, Hom., etc.;—often c. part., οἴχεται φεύγων is fled *and gone*, Il. ; ᾤχετ' ἀποπτάμενος he hath taken flight *and gone*, Ib.; οἴχεται θανών (v. infr. II. 1); also with an Adj., οἴχεται φροῦδος he's clean gone, Ar. :—c. acc. pers. *to have escaped from*, Id.　　II. Special usages, 1. euphem. for θνήσκω, *to be gone hence*, οἴχεται εἰς 'Αΐδαο Il. ; in Att., οἴχεται θανών Soph., etc. :—part. οἰχόμενος for θανών, *departed, dead*, Trag. ; but in Hom. simply *absent* or *away*, 'Οδυσῆος πόθος οἰχομένοιο desire of *the absent* Ulysses, Od.　　2. *to be undone, ruined*, Soph. ; esp. in ᾤχωκα or οἴχωκα, Lat. *perii*, Aesch., etc.　　3. of things, to denote any quick, violent motion, *to rush, sweep along*, Il.

οἴω, ὀΐω [ῑ], v. οἴομαι.

οἰωνίζομαι, f. Att. -ιοῦμαι: 3 sing. aor. 1 opt. οἰωνίσαιτο: Dep. :—*to take omens from the flight and cries of birds*, Lat. *augurium capere*, Xen.　　II. generally, *to divine from omens, augur*, c. acc. et inf., Id. Hence

οἰώνισμα, ατος, τό, *divination by the flight* or *cries of birds*, Lat. *augurium*, Eur. ; and

οἰωνισμός, ὁ, = foreg., Plut. ; and

οἰωνιστήριον, τό, *a place for watching the flight of birds* :—*an omen* or *token*, Xen. ; and

οἰωνιστής, οῦ, ὁ, *one who foretells from the flight and cries of birds, an augur*, Il., Hes. ; and

οἰωνιστικός, ή, όν, *of* or *for an omen* : ἡ -κή (sc. τέχνη), *augury*, Plat.

οἰωνο-θέτης, ου, ὁ, (τίθημι) *an interpreter of auguries*, Soph.

οἰωνό-θροος, ον, *of the cry of birds*, οἰ. γόος the wailing *cry of birds*, Aesch.

οἰωνο-κτόνος, ον, (κτείνω) *killing birds*, Aesch.

οἰωνό-μαντις, εως, ὁ and **ἡ**, *one who takes omens from the flight and cries of birds, an augur*, Eur.

οἰωνο-πόλος, ὁ, (πολέω) *one busied with the flight and cries of birds, an augur*, Il., etc.

οἰωνός, ὁ, (v. sub fin.) :—*a large bird, bird of prey*, such as *a vulture* or *eagle*, and so distinguished from a common bird (ὄρνις), Hom., etc.　　II. *a bird of omen* or *augury*, Hom., etc. :—the flight *to* (not *from*) the right, i.e. towards the East, was fortunate, and vice versa.　　2. *an omen, presage*, drawn from these birds, Lat. *auspicium* or *augurium*, according as taken from *seeing their flight* or *hearing their cry*, Il., etc.; δέκομαι τὸν οἰωνόν I accept *the omen*, hail it as favourable, Hdt. (Commonly deriv. from οἶος, — most birds of prey being *solitary*,—cf. κοινωνός from κοινός).

οἰωνοσκοπέω, f. ήσω, *to watch the flight of birds, to take auguries*, Eur. From

οἰωνο-σκόπος, ὁ, = οἰωνιστής, Eur.

οἴως, Adv., v. οἶος v. 1.

ὀκᾶ or **ὅκκᾶ**, Dor. for ὅτε, as πόκα for πότε, Ar., etc.

ὀκέλλω, = κέλλω : impf. ὤκελλον : aor. 1 ὤκειλα :—a nautical word, used, 　I. trans. of the seamen, *to run* [a ship] *aground* or *on shore*, Hdt., Thuc. 　II. intr. of the ship, *to run aground*, Thuc., Xen. ; so, metaph., Ar.

ὄκη, Ion. for ὅπη.

ὅκκα, v. ὀκα.

ὀκλαδίας, ὁ, (ὀκλάζω) *a folding-chair, camp-stool*, Ar.

ὀκλαδιστί, Adv., *squatting*, of a frog, Babr. From

ὀκλάζω, f. σω : aor. 1 ὤκλασα :—*to crouch down on one's hams, to squat*, Xen. : ἐς γόνυ ὀκλάσας δέχεται τῇ σαρίσσῃ τὴν ἐπέλασιν, of a soldier waiting an attack, Luc. ; of a weary traveller, Soph. :—c. acc., ὀκλ. τὰ ὀπίσθια, τοὺς προσθίους *to bend* their hind or fore legs, Xen.

ὀκνέω, Ep. ὀκνείω : impf. ὤκνεον : f. -ήσω : aor. 1 ὤκνησα : (ὄκνος) :—*to shrink from doing, to scruple, hesitate* to do a thing, c. inf., Il., etc. ; ὀκνῶ προδότης καλεῖσθαι I shrink from being called, *fear* to be called, Soph. ; ὀκνῶ ὀνομάσαι I shrink from naming, hesitate to name, Dem. ; rarely c. acc., ὃν ὀκνεῖτε Soph. ; ὀκνεῖν περί τινος Xen.　　II. absol. *to shrink, hesitate, hang back*, Hdt., Soph., etc.

ὀκνηρός, ά, όν, (ὄκνος) *shrinking, hesitating, backward, unready, timid*, Pind. ; ὀκνηρὸς ἐς τὰ πολεμικά Thuc. :—Adv. -ρῶς, Xen., etc.　　II. of things, *causing fear, vexatious, troublesome*, Soph.

ΟΚΝΟΣ, ὁ, *shrinking, hesitation, unreadiness, sluggishness*, Il., Aesch., Soph. ; ὄκνος καὶ μέλλησις Thuc.　　2. *alarm, fear*, Aesch., Soph.　　3. c. gen., τοῦ πόνου οὐκ ὄκνος [ἐστί] I *grudge* not labour, Soph.　　4. c. inf., πάρεσχεν ὄκνον μὴ ἐλθεῖν made them *hesitate* to go, Thuc. ; ὄκνος ἦν ἀνίστασθαι Xen.

ὁκοδαπός, ὁκόθεν, ὁκοῖος, ὁκόσος, ὁκότε, ὁκότερος, ὅκου, Ion. for ὁπ-.

ὀκριάομαι, Pass. (ὄκρις) *to be made rough* or *jagged* : metaph. *to be exasperated*, πανθυμαδὸν ὀκριόωντο Od.

ὀκρί-βας [ῑ], αντος, ὁ, (ὄκρις, βαίνω) *a kind of tribune on the stage*, from which the actors declaimed, Plat.

ὀκρίοεις, εσσα, εν, (ὄκρις) *having many points* or *roughnesses, rugged, jagged*, Il., Aesch.

ὄκρίς, ιος, ἡ, like ἄκρις, ἄκρα, *a jagged point* or *prominence*.　　II. as Adj. ὀκρίς, ίδος, ὁ, ἡ, = ὀκριόεις, *rugged*, Aesch.

ὀ-κρυόεις, εσσα, εν, for κρυόεις with ο euphon., = κρυερός, *chilling, horrible*, Il.

ὀκτά-βλωμος, ον, *consisting of eight pieces*, Hes.

ὀκτά-δραχμος, ον, (δραχμή) *weighing* or *worth eight drachmae*, Anth.

ὀκτα-ήμερος, ον, (ἡμέρα) *on the eighth day*, N. T.

ὀκτάκις [ᾰ], (ὀκτώ) Adv. *eight times*, Luc.

ὀκτᾰκισ-χίλιοι [ῑ], αι, α, *eight thousand*, Hdt., Xen. ; in sing., ἵππος ὀκτακισχιλίη '8000 horse,' Hdt.

ὀκτά-κνημος, ον, (κνήμη) *eight-spoked*, Il.

ὀκτᾰκόσιοι, αι, α, (ὀκτώ) *eight hundred*, Hdt.

ὀκτά-μηνος [ᾰ], ον, (μήν) *eight months old*, Xen.

ὀκτᾰ-πλάσιος [ᾰ], α, ον, *eightfold*, Lat. *octuplus*, Ar.

ὀκτά-πόδης, ου, ὁ, (πούς) *eight feet long*, Hes.

ὀκτά-πους [ᾰ], ὁ, ἡ, πουν, τό, *eight-footed*, Batr., Anth.

ὀκτάρ-ριζος, ον, (ῥίζα) *with eight roots* : of a stag's horns, *with eight points*, Anth.

ὀκτάρ-ρῦμος, ον, of chariots, *with eight poles*, i.e. drawn by eight pairs of oxen abreast, Xen.

ὀκτά-τονος [ᾰ], ον, *eight-stretched*, ἕλικες ὀκτ. the *eight arms* of the cuttlefish, Anth.

ΟΚΤΩ, οἱ, αἱ, τά, indecl. Lat. *octo, eight*, Hom., etc.

ὀκτω-καί-δεκα, οἱ, αἱ τά, indecl. *eighteen*, Hdt., etc.

ὀκτωκαιδεκά-δραχμος, ον, (δράχμη) *weighing* or *worth* 18 *drachmae*, Dem.

ὀκτωκαιδεκα-έτης, ες, (ἔτος) = ὀκτωκαιδεκέτης, Luc

ὀκτω-και-δέκᾰτος, η, ον, eighteenth: ὀκτωκαιδεκάτῃ (sc. ἡμέρᾳ) on the eighteenth day, Od.

ὀκτωκαιδεκ-έτης, ου, ὁ, (ἔτος) eighteen years old, Dem., Theocr. :—fem. ἔτις, ιδος, Luc.

ὀκτώ-πους, ὁ, ἡ, πουν, τό, eight feet long, broad or high, Plat.

ὀκχέω, v. ὀχέω.

ὅκως, Ion. for ὅπως.

ὄκωχα, Ep. pf. of ἔχω.

ὀλάω, a lisping way of pronouncing ὁράω, Ar.

ὀλβίζω, f. Att. ιῶ: aor. 1 ὤλβισα: (ὄλβιος):—to make happy, Eur. :—to deem or pronounce happy, Aesch., Soph., etc. :—Pass. to be or be deemed happy, pf. part. ὠλβισμένοι Eur. ; aor. 1 part. ὀλβισθείς Id.

ὀλβιο-δαίμων, ονος, ὁ and ἡ, of blessed lot, Il.

ὀλβιό-δωρος, ον, (δῶρον) bestowing bliss, Eur.

ὀλβιο-εργός, όν, (*ἔργω) making happy, Anth.

ὄλβιος, ον, and α, ον: (ὄλβος):   I. of persons, happy, blest, in Hom., always in reference to worldly goods, wealth, like Lat. beatus, Hom., etc.   II. of things, in neut. pl., θεοὶ δέ τοι ὄλβια δοῖεν may they give thee rich gifts, Od. ; neut. pl. as Adv., ὄλβια ζωέμεναι to live happily, Ib. :—Adv. -ίως, Soph. ; Sup. ὀλβιώτατος Hdt. ; in later Poets, ὄλβιστος.

ὀλβο-δότειρα, ἡ, fem. of sq., Eur.

ὀλβο-δότης, ου, Dor. -δότᾱς, α, ὁ, giver of bliss, of good or wealth, like ὀλβιοδώτης, Eur.

ΌΛΒΟΣ, ὁ, happiness, bliss, weal, wealth, Hom., etc.

ὀλβο-φόρος, ον, (φέρω) bringing bliss or wealth, Eur.

ὀλέσθαι, Ion. for ὀλεῖσθαι, fut. inf. of ὄλλυμι.

ὀλέεσκε, 3 sing. Ion. aor. 2 of ὄλλυμι.

ὀλέθριος, ον, and α, ον, destructive, deadly, ὀλ. ἦμαρ the day of destruction, Il. ; ψῆφος ὀλεθρία a vote of death, Aesch. :—ὀλέθριον as Adv. fatally, Soph.   2. c. gen., γάμοι ὀλέθριοι φίλων bringing ruin on his friends, Aesch.   II. of persons, ruined, lost, undone, Soph. :—rascally, worthless, Luc.

ὄλεθρος, ὁ, (ὄλλυμι) ruin, destruction, death, Hom., Trag., etc. ; ὀλέθρου πείρατα, like θανάτου τέλος, the consummation of death, Il. :—οὐκ εἰς ὄλεθρον ; as an imprecation, ruin seize thee! Soph. :—χρημάτων ὀλέθρῳ by loss of money, Thuc. ; ἐπ' ὀλέθρῳ Plat.   II. like Lat. pernicies and pestis, that which causes destruction, a pest, plague, curse, Hes. ; of persons, Hdt. ; so Oedipus calls himself τὸν ὄλεθρον μέγαν Soph. ; ὀλ. Μακεδών, of Philip, Dem., etc.

ὀλεῖ, ὀλεῖται, 2 and 3 sing. fut. of ὄλλυμι.

ὀλέκρανον, τό, Att. for ὠλέκρανον, Ar.

ὀλέκω, Ep. impf. ὄλεκον, Ion. ὀλέκεσκον, like ὄλλυμι, to ruin, destroy, kill, Hom., Trag. :—Pass. to perish, die, esp. a violent death, ὀλέκοντο δὲ λαοί Il.

ὀλέσαι, aor. 1 inf. of ὄλλυμι :—ὀλέσας, part.

ὀλέσειε, 3 sing. aor. 1 opt. of ὄλλυμι.

ὀλεσ-ήνωρ, ορος, ὁ, ἡ, (ἀνήρ) man-destroying, Theogn.

ὀλέσθαι, aor. 2 med. inf. of ὄλλυμι.

ὀλεσί-θηρ, ηρος, ὁ, ἡ, beast-slaying, Eur.

ὄλεσσα, Ep. aor. 1 of ὄλλυμι : inf. ὀλέσσαι, part. -σσας.

ὀλεσσι-τύραννος, ον, destroying tyrants, Anth.

ὀλέσω, f. of ὄλλυμι.

ὀλετήρ, ῆρος, ὁ, (ὄλλυμι), a destroyer, murderer, Il. :—fem. ὀλέτειρα, Babr., Anth.

ὀλέτης, ου, ὁ, = ὀλετήρ :—fem. ὀλέτις, Anth.

ὀλή, ἡ, v. οὐλαί.

ὄληαι, Ep. 2 sing. aor. 2 med. of ὄλλυμι.

ὀλῐγάκῐς [ᾰ], Adv. (ὀλίγος) but few times, seldom, Eur., Thuc., etc.

ὀλῐγ-άμπελος, ον, scant of vines, Anth.

ὀλῐγ-ανδρέω, (ἀνήρ) to be scant of men, Plut., etc.

ὀλῐγανδρία, ἡ, scantiness of men, Strab.

ὀλῐγανθρωπία, ἡ, scantiness of men, Thuc., Xen. From

ὀλῐγ-άνθρωπος, ον, scant of men, Xen.

ὀλῐγ-ᾰριστία, ἡ, (ἄριστον) a scanty meal, Plut.

ὀλῐγ-αρκής, ές, (ἀρκέω) contented with little, Luc.

ὀλῐγαρχέω, f. ήσω, to be member of an oligarchy, Arist. :—Pass. to be governed by the few, be under an oligarchy, Thuc., Plat. From

ὀλῐγ-άρχης, ου, ὁ, (ἄρχω) an oligarch. Hence

ὀλῐγαρχία, Ion. -ίη, ἡ, an oligarchy, government in the hands of a few families or persons, Hdt., Att.

ὀλῐγαρχικός, ή, όν, oligarchical, of, for or like oligarchy, ὀλ. κόσμος Thuc.; Arist. :—Adv. -χῶς, Plat., Dem.   2. of persons, inclined to oligarchy, Plat.

ὀλῐγ-αῦλαξ, ακος, ὁ, ἡ, having little arable land, Anth.

ὀλῐγᾰχόθεν, Adv. (ὀλίγος) from some few parts, Hdt.

ὀλῐγᾰχοῦ, Adv. (ὀλίγος) in few places, Plat.

ὀλῐγηπελέων, ουσα, part. with no pres. in use, having little power, in feeble case, powerless, Od. From

ὀλῐγη-πελής, ές, (πέλω) weak, powerless, Anth. Hence

ὀλῐγηπελίη, Ion. -ίη, ἡ, weakness, faintness, Od.

ὀλῐγήριος, ον, = ὀλίγος, Anth.

ὀλῐγ-ηροσίη, ἡ, (ἄροσις) want of arable land, Anth.

ὀλῐγη-σίπυος, ον, (σίπυα) with little corn, or with a small bread-basket, Anth.

ὀλίγιστος, η, ον, irreg. Sup. of ὀλίγος, (v. ὀλίγος VI).

ὀλῐγογονία, ἡ, production of few at a birth, Plat. From

ὀλῐγό-γονος, ον, producing few at a birth, Hdt.

ὀλῐγο-δρᾰνέων, έουσα, part. with no pres. in use, able to do little, feeble, powerless, Il. From

ὀλῐγο-δρᾰνής, ές, (δραίνω) of little might, feeble, Ar.

ὀλῐγοδρᾰνία, ἡ, weakness, feebleness, Aesch.

ὀλῐγο-ετίη, ἡ, (ἔτος) fewness of years, youth, Xen.

ὀλῐγό-ξῠλος, ον, (ξύλον) with little wood, Anth.

ὀλῐγό-πιστος, ον, of little faith, N. T.

'ΟΛΙΓΟΣ [ῐ], η, ον, of Number or Quantity, few, little, scanty, small, opp. to πολύς, Hom., etc. ; the governing body in Oligarchies was called οἱ ὀλίγοι, Thuc., etc.   2. c. inf. too few to do a thing, Hdt.; Thuc.   II. of Size, little, small, opp. to μέγας, Hom.; ὀλίγον ἢ οὐδέν little or nothing, Plat.   III. neut. ὀλίγον as Adv., little, a little, slightly, Hom., Eur.; with comp. Adjs., ὀλίγον προγενέστερος Il.; ὀλ. ἧσσον Od.; so, ὀλ. τι πρότερον Hdt.; but ὀλίγῳ is more common with the Comp. in Prose, Id., etc.   IV. special phrases: 1. ὀλίγου δεῖν almost, ὀλίγου ἐδέησε καταλαβεῖν wanted but little of overtaking, Id. :—hence ὀλίγου alone, all but, almost, Od., Att.; ὀλίγου ἐς χιλίους hard upon 1000, Thuc.   2. δι' ὀλίγου (sc. χώρου) at a short distance, Aesch., etc. : also, δι' ὀλίγου (sc. χρόνου) at short notice, suddenly, Thuc. :—δι' ὀλίγων in few words, Plat.   3. ἐν ὀλίγῳ (sc. χώρῳ) in a small space, within small compass, Thuc. :—also, ἐν ὀλίγῳ (sc. χρόνῳ) in a short time, suddenly, Plat., N. T.   4. ἐν ὀλίγοις one among few, i. e. exceedingly, remarkably, Hdt.   5.

ἐξ ὀλίγου = δι' ὀλίγου, of Time, Thuc. 6. ἐς ὀλίγον *within a little*, Id. 7. κατ' ὀλίγον *by little and little*, Id.; but the Adj. often takes the gender and number of its Subst., κατ' ὀλίγους *few at a time, in small parties*, Hdt., Thuc. 8. μετ' ὀλίγον τούτων *shortly* after these things, Xen. 9. παρ' ὀλίγον *within a little, almost*, Eur.:—but, παρ' ὀλ. ποιεῖσθαι *to hold of small account*, Xen. V. the Adv. ὀλίγως is rare, οὐκ ὀλίγως Anth. VI. Comparison: 1. the Comp. is commonly supplied by μείων, ἥσσων or ἐλάσσων: the form ὀλίζων, ον, gen. ονος, is rare. 2. Sup. ὀλίγιστος, η, ον, Il., Att.:—ὀλίγιστον or τὸ ὀλ., as Adv., Lat. *minime*, Plat.; ὡς ὀλίγιστα Id.

ὀλῐγό-σαρκος, ον, (σάρξ) *with little flesh*, Luc.

ὀλῐγοσῐτία, ἡ, *small eating, moderation in food*, Arist.

ὀλῐγό-σῑτος, ον, *eating little*.

ὀλῐγοστῐχία, ἡ, *the consisting of few lines*, Anth. From

ὀλῐγό-στῐχος, ον, *consisting of few lines*.

ὀλῐγοστός, ή, όν, (ὀλίγος) *one out of a few*, opp. to πολλοστός, Plut. II. ὀλ. χρόνον *for the smallest space* of Time, Soph.

ὀλῐγότης, ητος, ἡ, (ὀλίγος) *of Number, fewness*, Plat. II. *of Amount, smallness, scantiness* :—of Time, *shortness*, Id.

ὀλῐγο-φῐλία, ἡ, *fewness of friends*, Arist.

ὀλῐγο-χρόνιος, ον, and α, ον, (χρόνος) *lasting* or *living but little time, of short duration*, Theogn., Hdt., etc.

ὀλῐγό-ψῡχος, ον, (ψυχή) *faint-hearted*, N. T.

ὀλῐγωρέω, f. ήσω, *to esteem little* or *lightly, make small account of*, c. gen., Xen., Plat. :—absol. *to take no heed*, Thuc. :—Pass., pf. ὠλιγώρημαι, *to be lightly esteemed*, Dem. Hence

ὀλῐγωρία, Ion. -ίη, ἡ, *an esteeming lightly, slighting, contempt*, Hdt., Thuc., etc. 2. *negligence*, ap. Dem.

ὀλίγ-ωρος, ον, (ὥρα) *little-caring, lightly-esteeming, scornful, contemptuous*, Hdt., Dem. :—Adv. ὀλιγώρως ἔχειν *to be careless, negligent*, Plat., Xen.

ΟΛΙΣΘΑ΄ΝΩ, aor. 2 ὤλισθον, Ep. ὄλισθον : f. ὀλισθήσω, aor. 1 ὠλίσθησα, pf. -ηκα are late :—*to slip, slip and fall*, Il. ; ἐξ ἀντύγων ὤλισθε *he slipt* from the chariot, Soph. :—metaph. *to make a slip*, Ar. 2. *to slip* or *glide along*, Theocr. Hence

ὀλισθήεις, εσσα, εν, poët. for ὀλισθηρός, Anth. ; and

ὀλισθηρός, ά, όν, *slippery*, Lat. *lubricus*, Pind., Xen. II. *of persons, slippery, hard to catch and keep hold of*, Plat., Anth. 2. *liable to slip*, Plut.

ὄλισθος, ὁ, *slipperiness*, Luc. 2. = *a slip*, Id.

ὀλισθών, aor. 2 part. of ὀλισθάνω.

ὁλκάς, άδος, ἡ, (ἕλκω) *a ship which is towed, a ship of burthen, trading vessel, merchantman*, Hdt.

ὁλκή, ἡ, (ἕλκω) *a drawing, dragging, tugging : a drawing on* or *towards a thing, attraction, force of attraction*, Plat.

ὁλκίον, τό, (ἕλκω) *a bowl* or *basin*, Plut.

ὁλκός, ή, όν, (ἕλκω) *drawing to oneself, attractive*, Plat.

ὁλκός, ὁ, (ἕλκω) : I. *as an Instrument, a machine for hauling ships on land, a hauling-engine*, Hdt., Thuc. 2. *a strap, rein*, Soph. II. *as an Effect, a furrow*, Lat. *sulcus*, ὁλκὸς τοῦ ξύλου *the furrow made* by the wood, Xen. 2. periphr., ὁλκοὶ δάφνης *drawings* of laurels, i. e. laurel-boughs (or *brooms* made of them) *drawn along*, Eur.

ὄλλῡμι and **ὀλλύω** (from Root ΟΛ) :—impf. ὤλλυν, 3 pl. ὤλλυσαν :—f. ὀλέσω, Ep. also ὀλέσσω, Ion. ὀλέω, Att. ὀλῶ, εῖς, εῖ : aor. 1 ὤλεσα, Ep. ὄλεσα, ὄλεσσα :—Med. ὄλλῡμαι, impf. ὠλλύμην : f. ὀλοῦμαι, Ep. ὀλέομαι : aor. 2 ὠλόμην, Ion. 3 sing. ὀλέσκετο, part. ὀλόμενος, as Adj., v. οὐλόμενος : pf. ὄλωλα, ὀλώλειν (infr. B. III) A. Act. = Lat. *perdo*, I. *to destroy, make an end of*, Hom., Trag. :—also of *doing away with evil*, ὤλεσεν νόσον Aesch. II. *to lose*, θυμόν, ψυχήν, μένος, ἦτορ ὀλέσαι *to lose life*, Hom.; πόνον ὀλέσαντες *having lost* their labour, Aesch.

B. Med., = Lat. *pereo*, I. *to perish, come to an end*, Hom. ; also c. acc. cogn., κακὸν οἶτον, κακὸν μόρον ὀλέσθαι *to die* by an evil death, Il. :—ὄλοιο, ὄλοισθε *may'st thou, may ye, perish!* an imprecation, Trag. ; so, ὀλοίμην, ὄλοιτο, ὄλοιντο, Soph. 2. *to be ruined, undone*, Hom., Att. II. of things, *to be lost*, Hom. III. pf. ὄλωλα, in sense of Med., *to have perished, to be undone, ruined*, Il., Aesch., etc. ; τῶν ὀλωλότων *of the dead*, Aesch.

ὀλμο-ποιός, ὁ, (ποιέω) *a maker of mortars*, Arist.

ὅλμος, ὁ, (εἴλω, *volvo*) *a round smooth stone, a roller*, Il. II. *any round body : a mortar*, Hes., Hdt. : *a kneading-trough*, Ar.

ὀλοθρευτής, οῦ, ὁ, *a destroyer*, N. T.

ὀλοθρεύω, *to destroy utterly*, N. T. (Deriv. uncertain.)

ὀλοιός, όν, an Ep. form of ὀλοός, Il.

ὀλοί-τροχος or **ὀλοί-τροχος, ὁ,** (εἴλω, *volvo*, τροχός) *a rolling stone, a round stone*, such as besieged people rolled down upon their assailants, Hdt., Xen. ; ὀλοοί-τροχος in Il. and Orac. ap. Hdt. 2. as Adj., πέτροι ὀλοίτροχοι *round* stones, to which the muscles of an athlete's arm are compared, Theocr.

ὀλο-καυτέω, f. ήσω, (καίω) *to bring a burnt-offering, to offer whole*, Xen.

ὀλοκαυτόω, f. ώσω, = foreg., Xen. Hence

ὀλοκαύτωμα, τό, *a whole burnt-offering, holocaust*, N.T.

ὀλοκληρία, ἡ, *completeness* or *soundness in all its parts*, N. T. From

ὀλό-κληρος, ον, *complete in all parts, entire, perfect*, Lat. *integer*, Plat., etc.

ὀλολυγή, ἡ, (ὀλολύζω) *any loud cry*, mostly of a joyous kind (unlike Lat. *ululatus*), used by women invoking a god, Il., Hdt., etc.

ὀλόλυγμα, τό, (ὀλολύζω) *a loud cry*, mostly of joy, Eur.

ὀλολυγμός, ὁ, (ὀλολύζω) *a loud crying*, mostly *a joyous cry*, in honour of the gods, Aesch., Eur. ;—rarely of lamentation, Eur.

ὀλολυγών, όνος, ἡ, (ὀλολύζω) an unknown *animal*, named from its note : prob. a kind of *owl*, Theocr.

ὀλολύζω : f. -ύξομαι : aor. 1 Ep. ὀλόλυξα :—*to cry to the gods with a loud voice, cry aloud*, of women *crying aloud* to the gods in prayer or thanksgiving, Od., h. Hom. Apoll. ; so also in Aesch., Eur., etc.

ὀλόμενος, v. sub οὐλόμενος.

ὠλόμην, ὄλοντο, 1 sing. and 3 pl. aor. 2 med. of ὄλλυμι.

ὀλοοίτροχος, ὁ, lengthd. Ep. form of ὀλοίτροχος.

ὀλοός, ή, όν, (ὄλλυμι) *destroying, destructive, fatal, deadly, murderous*, Hom., Hes., Aesch., Eur. :—ὀλοὰ φρονεῖν *to be bent on ill, design ill*, Il. :—Comp. ὀλοώτερος Ib. ; Sup. ὀλοώτατος (used as fem.) Od. II. in pass. sense, *lost, dead*, Aesch.

ὀλοός, ὀλοόφρων, v. sub οὖλω.

ὀλοό-φρων, ονος, ὁ and ἡ, (ὀλοός, φρήν) meaning mischief, baleful, Il. :—in Od. always of crafty, shrewd, men, not Greeks ; such men being regarded as baneful.

ὀλο-πόρφῠρος, ον, (πορφύρα) all-purple, Xen.

ὀλόπτω, f. ψω, to pluck out, tear out, Anth. (From λέπω with ὀ- euphon.)

ὀλός, ὁ, = θολός, mud, muddy liquor, Anth.

ΌΛΟΣ, Ion. οὖλος, η, ον, whole, entire, complete, Lat. integer, οὖλος ἄρτος a whole loaf, Od. ; ὅλην πόλιν a whole city, Eur. ; ὅλους βοῦς Ar., etc. ; — πόλεις ὅλαι are whole, entire cities, opp. to ὅλη ἡ πόλις, the whole city, the city as a whole, Plat. :—with the Art. it may either precede or follow the Subst., τῆς ἡμέρας ὅλης the whole day, δι’ ὅλης τῆς νυκτός through the whole night, Xen., etc. 2. whole, i. e. safe and sound, Plat. 3. entire, utter, ὅλον ἁμάρτημα an utter blunder, Xen. ; of a person, ὅλος εἶναι πρός τινι = Lat. totus in illis, Dem. 4. neut. as Adv., ὅλον or τὸ ὅλον, wholly, entirely, Plat. ; ὅλῳ καὶ παντί Id., etc. ; τῷ ὅλῳ καὶ παντί Id. ;—so, κατὰ ὅλον on the whole, generally, Id. ; δι’ ὅλου, καθ’ ὅλου (v. sub διόλου, καθόλου). II. as Subst., τὸ ὅλον the universe, Id. ; τὰ ὅλα, one’s all, Dem. ; τοῖς ὅλοις = ὅλως, altogether, Philipp. ap. Dem. III. Adv. ὅλως, wholly, altogether, Plat., etc. 2. on the whole, speaking generally, in short, in a word, like ἐνὶ λόγῳ, Lat. denique, Dem. 3. often with a neg., οὐχ ὅλως not at all, Plat., Xen., etc.

ὀλο-σφύρητος [ῡ], Dor. -ᾱτος, ον, (σφῦρα) made of solid beaten metal, Anth.

ὀλοσχέρεια, ἡ, a general survey or estimate, Strab. From

ὀλο-σχερής, ές, like ὁλόκληρος, whole, entire, complete, Lat. integer, Theocr. 2. relating to the whole, important, considerable, Polyb.:—Adv. -ρῶς, entirely, utterly, Id. (The sense of -σχερής is uncertain.)

ὀλό-σχοινος, ὁ, a coarse rush, used in wicker-work : —hence the proverb, ἀπορράπτειν τὸ Φιλίππου στόμα ὀλοσχοίνῳ ἀβρόχῳ to stop Philip's mouth with an unsoaked rush, (for rushes were soaked to make them tough), i. e. without any trouble, Aeschin.

ὀλοφυγδών, όνος, ἡ, = ὀλοφυκτίς, Theocr.

ὀλοφυδνός, ή, όν, of lamentation, lamenting, Hom. : —ὀλοφυδνά, as Adv., Anth.

ὀλοφυρμός, οῦ, ὁ, lamentation, Ar., Thuc., etc. From

ΌΛΟΦΎΡΟΜΑΙ [ῡ], f. ὀλοφῠροῦμαι : aor. 1 ὠλοφῠράμην, Ep. 2 and 3 sing. ὀλοφύραο, ὀλοφύρατο: aor. 1 part. pass. ὀλοφυρθείς : I. intr. to lament, wail, moan, weep, Hom., etc. 2. to lament or mourn for the ills of others, to feel pity, Hom. : c. gen. to have pity upon one, Il. 3. to beg with tears and lamentations, καί μοι δὸς τὴν χεῖρ’, ὀλοφύρομαι Ib. 4. c. inf., πῶς ὀλοφύρεαι ἄλκιμος εἶναι ; why lament that thou must be brave ? Od. II. c. acc. to lament over, bewail, Ib., Hdt., Att. 2. to pity, Hom. Hence

ὀλόφυρσις, ἡ, = ὀλοφυρμός, Thuc. ; ὀλοφύρσεις τῶν ἀπογιγνομένων lamentations for the departed, Id. ; and

ὀλοφυρτικός, ή, όν, querulous, Arist.

ὀλο-φώιος, ον, Ep. Adj. destructive, deadly, pernicious, Od.; ὀλοφώια εἰδώς versed in pernicious arts, Ib.

(From ΟΛ, the Root of ὄλλυμι : the term. -φώιος has not been explained.)

ΌΛΠΗ, ἡ, a leathern oil-flask, Theocr., Anth.

ὄλπις, ιος and ιδος, ἡ, = ὄλπη, Theocr.

Ὀλυμπία (sc. χώρα), ἡ, Olympia, a district of Elis round the city of Pisa, where the Olympic games were held, Hdt., etc. ; or the city Pisa itself, Pind.; also Ὀλυμπίᾱ, Id.

Ὀλύμπια (sc. ἱερά), τά, the Olympic games, in honour of Olympian Zeus, established by Hercules in 776 B. C., and renewed by Iphitus, and held at intervals of four years at Olympia, Hdt. ; Ὀλ. ἀναιρεῖν, νικᾶν to win at the Olympic games, Id., etc.

Ὀλυμπίαζε, Adv. to Olympia, Thuc.

Ὀλυμπιακός, ή, όν, Olympian, Thuc., Xen.

Ὀλυμπιάς, άδος, ἡ, pecul. fem. of Ὀλύμπιος, Olympian as epith. of the Muses, Il., Hes. ; of the Graces, Ar. 2. Ὀλ. ἐλαία the olive-crown of the Olympic games, Pind. II. as Subst., 1. the Olympic games, Hdt., Pind. 2. (sub. νίκη), a victory at Olympia, Hdt. 3. an Olympiad, i. e. the space of four years between the celebrations of the Olympic games ; used as an historical date from about 300 B. C. The 1st Olympiad began 776 B. C. ; the 293rd and last in 393 A. D.

Ὀλυμπίᾱσι, Adv., at Olympia, Ar., etc. ; cf. θύρᾱσι; —but II. Ὀλυμπιάσι [ᾰ], dat. pl. of Ὀλυμπιάς.

Ὀλυμπιεῖον or Ὀλυμπίειον, τό, the temple of Olympian Zeus, Thuc. ;—wrongly written Ὀλύμπιον.

Ὀλυμπικός, ή, όν, of Olympus, Hdt. 2. of Olympia, Olympic, ὁ Ὀλ. ἀγών the Olympic games, Ar.

Ὀλυμπιο-νίκης [ῑ], ου, Dor. -νίκᾱς, ᾱ, ὁ, (νικάω) a conqueror in the Olympic games, Pind. II. as Adj., Ὀλ. ὕμνος Id.

Ὀλυμπιό-νῑκος, ον, (νικάω) = foreg., Pind.

Ὀλύμπιος, ον, Olympian, of Olympus, dwelling on Olympus, Hom., etc. ; Zeus is called simply Ὀλύμπιος in Hom. ; Ζεὺς πατὴρ Ὀλ. Soph. ; ὁ Ζεὺς ὁ Ὀλ. Thuc.

ΌΛΥΜΠΟΣ, Ion. Οὔλυμπος, ὁ, Olympus, a mountain on the Macedonian frontier of Thessaly.—Hom. makes it the seat of the gods, but distinguished from heaven (οὐρανός). II. the name was common to several other mountains, each apparently the highest in its own district, in Mysia, Polyb., etc. ; in Laconia, Polyb., etc. III. as Adv., Ὄλυμπόνδε, Ion. Οὔλυμπόνδε, to Olympus, Hom., etc. :—Οὐλυμπόθεν, from Ol., Pind.

Ὀλυνθιακός, ή, όν, of or relating to Olynthus (in Chalcidice), Dem.

ὄλυνθος, ὁ, a winter-fig which seldom ripens, an untimely fig, Lat. grossus, Hdt. (Deriv. unknown.)

ὀλῠρᾱ, ἡ, mostly in pl. ὄλυραι, a kind of grain, spelt or rye, Il., Hdt. ; cf. ζειά.

ὀλώιος, rare Ep. form of ὀλοός, ὀλοιός, Hes.

ὄλωλα, pf. in med. signf. of ὄλλυμι.

ὅλως, v. ὅλος III.

ὁμᾰδέω, f. ήσω, to make a noise or din, of a number of people speaking at once, Od. From

ὅμᾰδος, ὁ, (ὁμός) a noise, din, made by a number of people speaking together, Hom., Eur. ; of a tempest, Il. II. a noisy throng, Il.

ὁμ-αίμιος, ον, (αἷμα) related by blood, Pind.

ὅμ-αιμος, ον, (αἷμα) of the same blood, related by blood, Lat. consanguineus, Hdt., Aesch. ; φόνος ὅμ.

murder *by one near of kin*, Aesch.　　2. as Subst., **ὅμαιμος, ὁ** or **ἡ**, *a brother* or *sister*, Id., Soph. Hence

ὁμαιμοσύνη, ἡ, *blood-relationship*, Anth.

ὁμ-αίμων, ον, gen. ονος, = ὅμαιμος, Hdt., Aesch. : — Comp. ὁμαιμονέστερος *more near akin*, Soph.　　2. as Subst. *a brother* or *sister*, Id.　　3. = ὁμόγνιος (11), Aesch.

ὁμαιχμία, Ion. -ίη, ἡ, *union for battle, a defensive alliance, league*, Hdt., Thuc. From

ὅμ-αιχμος, ὁ, (αἰχμή) *a fellow-fighter, an ally*, Thuc.

ὁμᾰλής, ές, = ὁμαλός, *level*, τὰ ὁμαλῆ *level ground*, Xen.

ὁμᾰλίζω, f. Att. -ιῶ :—Pass., pf. ὡμάλισμαι : aor. 1 ὡμαλίσθην : f. ὁμαλισθήσομαι : f. med. ὁμαλιεῖται in pass. sense :—*to make even* or *level*, Xen.　　2. *to level, equalise*, Arist. From

ὁμᾰλός, ή, όν, (ὁμός): *of a surface, even, level*, Od., etc.; ἐν τῷ ὁμαλῷ on *level* ground, Thuc.; ὁμαλώτατον Id.　　2. *of circumstances, on a level, equal*, ὁμαλὸς ὁ γάμος *marriage with an equal*, Aesch.; ὁμαλοὶ ἔρωτες Theocr.; ἀλλάλοις ὁμαλοί *on a level with* one another, *equal*, Id.　　3. *of the average sort*, ὁμ. στρατιώτης *an ordinary sort of* soldier, Id.　　II. Adv. ὁμαλῶς, *evenly*, ὁμ. βαίνειν *to march in an even line*, Thuc.; ὁμ. προϊέναι Xen.　　2. *of all alike*, Plut.

ὁμᾰλότης, ητος, ἡ, *evenness* of surface, Arist.; *a level*, Id.　　II. *equality*, Plat., Arist.

ὁμαρτέω, impf. ὡμάρτουν, Ep. 3 dual ὁμαρτήτην : f. ήσω : aor. ὡμάρτησα, Ep. 3 sing. opt. ὁμαρτήσειεν : (ὁμός, ἀρτάω) :—*to meet*, 1. in hostile sense, *to meet in fight*, τὼ δ' ἄρ' ὁμαρτήτην Il.　　2. *to go together*, βῆσαν δ' ὁμαρτήσαντες *they walked together*, Od.; οὐδέ κεν Ἴρηξ κίρκος ὁμαρτήσειε *could* not *keep pace with* the ship, Ib.　　3. c. dat. *to walk beside, accompany, attend*, τινί Hes., Trag. :—also, *to pursue, chase*, Xen.　　4. *of things, to attend*, Id.　　II. in Med. c. acc. *to go after* or *attack jointly*, Il. Hence

ὁμαρτῇ or **ὁμαρτῆ**, Adv. *together*, Eur.　　II. **ὁμάρτη**, Dor. for ὁμάρτει, imper. of ὁμαρτέω.

ὁμ-ασπις, ιδος, ὁ, ἡ, *a fellow-soldier*, Anth.

ὁμ-αῦλαξ, Dor. -ῶλαξ, ἄκος, ὁ, ἡ, *with adjoining lands*, Anth.

ὁμαυλία, ἡ, *a dwelling together*, σύζυγοι ὁμ. *wedded unions*, Aesch. From

ὅμ-αυλος, ον, (αὐλή) *living together*.　　II. (αὐλός) *sounding together* or *in concert*, Soph.

ὀμβρέω, f. ήσω, (ὄμβρος) *to rain*, μετοπωρινὸν ὀμβρήσαντος Ζηνός *when Zeus sends* the autumn rains, Hes.　　II. trans. *to bedew*, Anth.

ὄμβριος, ον, (ὄμβρος) *rainy, of rain*, ὕδωρ ὄμβριον *rainwater*, Hdt.; ὀμβρία χάλαζα Soph.; νέφος Ar.

ὀμβρο-δόκος, ον, (δέχομαι) *receiving rain*, Anth.

ὀμβρο-κτύπος [ῠ], **ον**, *sounding with rain*, Aesch.

ΟΜΒΡΟΣ, ὁ, Lat. *imber*, *a storm of rain, a thunderstorm*, Il., Hdt.: *heavy rain*, Hdt., Soph., etc.　　2. generally, *water*, Soph.　　II. metaph. *a shower of* tears, blood, etc., Aesch., Soph.

ὀμβρο-φόρος, ον, (φέρω) *rain-bringing*, Lat. *imbrifer*, Aesch., Ar.

ὀμείρομαι, = ἱμείρομαι, N. T.

ὀμεῖται, 3 sing. fut. of ὄμνυμι.

ὀμ-ευνέτης, ου, ὁ, = ὅμευνος, Eur. :—fem. **ὀμευνέτις, ιδος**, Soph.

ὅμ-ευνος, ον, (εὐνή) *a partner of the bed, consort*, both of the man and woman, Anth.

ὀμ-έψιος, ον, (ἑψία) *playing together, a playmate*, Anth.

ὀμ-ηγερής, ές, (ὁμός, ἀγείρω) *assembled*, ὁμηγερέεσσι θεοῖσι (Ep. dat. pl.) Il.

ὀμ-ηγυρής, Dor. **ὁμ-ᾱγυρής, ές**, (ἄγυρις) = foreg., Pind.

ὁμηγῠρίζομαι, aor. 1 inf. ὁμηγυρίσασθαι, Dep. *to assemble, call together*, Od. From

ὁμ-ήγῠρις, Dor. **ὁμάγ-, ιος, ἡ**, (ἄγυρις) *an assembly, meeting, company*, Il., Aesch., Eur.

ὀμ-ηλῐκία, Ion. -ίη, ἡ, *sameness of age*, esp. of young persons; and as a collective, *those of the same age, one's friends, comrades*, Hom., Theogn.　　II. addressed to a female, = ὁμῆλιξ, ὁμιλικίη δέ μοι αὐτῷ *but thou art of the same age with* myself, Od.

ὀμ-ῆλιξ, ικος, ὁ, ἡ, *of the same age*, mostly of young persons, Od., Hdt., etc.　　2. as Subst. *an equal in age, comrade*, Lat. *aequalis*, Od., Eur.　　II. *of like stature*, Luc.

ὁμηρεία, ἡ, (ὁμηρεύω) *a giving of hostages* or *securities, a security*, Lat. *vadimonium*, Thuc.

Ὁμήρειον, τό, *a temple of Homer*, Strab.

Ὁμήρειος, ον, *Homeric*, Hdt.: τὸ Ὁμ. *the Homeric phrase*, Plat.

ὁμήρευμα, ατος, τό, *a hostage, pledge*, Plut. From

ὁμηρεύω, f. σω, (ὅμηρος) *to be* or *serve as a hostage*, Aeschin.　　II. trans. *to give as a hostage*, Eur.

ὁμηρέω, f. ήσω, aor. 1 ὡμήρησα: (ὅμηρος) :—*to meet*, Od.　　2. metaph. *to accord, agree*, φωνῇ ὁμηρεῦσαι (Ion. for ὁμηροῦσαι, part. pl. fem.) Hes.

Ὁμηρίδαι, οἱ, *the Homerids*, a family or guild of poets in Chios, who traced their descent from Homer and recited his poems, Pind. :—generally, *the imitators* or *the admirers of Homer*, Plat.

Ὁμηρικός, ή, όν, *Homeric, in Homeric manner*, Plat.

Ὅμηρος, ὁ, *Homer*; *the name* first occurs in a Fragm. of Hes.

ὅμηρος, ὁ, *a pledge for the maintenance of unity, a surety, a hostage*, Hdt., Att.　　2. *of things, a pledge, security*, τὴν γῆν ὅμηρον ἔχειν Thuc. (Deriv. uncertain.)

ὁμῑλᾰδόν, Adv. (ὅμιλος) *in groups* or *bands, in crowds*, Lat. *turmatim*, Il.

ὁμῑλέω, f. ήσω, (ὅμιλος) *to be in company with, consort with* others, c. dat. pl., Od., Att.; also, ὁμ. μετὰ Τρώεσσιν Il.; ἐνὶ πρώτοισιν ὁμιλεῖ *is in company* with the foremost, Ib.　　2. absol. *to join in company*, Od.; περὶ νεκρὸν ὁμ. *to throng* about the corpse, Hom.　　II. in hostile sense, *to join battle with*, ὁμιλέομεν Δαναοῖσιν Id. :—absol. *to join battle*, Il.　　III. *of social intercourse, to hold converse with, consort with, associate with* others, c. dat., Hdt., Aesch.; ἀλλήλοις, μετ' ἀλλήλων, πρὸς ἀλλήλους Plat. :—*of scholars*, ὁμ. τινι *to frequent* a teacher's lectures, *be his pupil*, Xen.　　2. absol. *to be friends*, Hdt.　　IV. *of marriage*, Soph., Xen.　　V. *of things* or *business which one has to do with, to attend to, busy oneself with*, ὁμιλεῖν πολέμῳ Thuc.; πράγμασι καινοῖς Ar.; φιλοσοφίᾳ Plat. :—then, much like χρῆσθαι, νομίζειν, Lat. *uti*, ὁμ. τύχαις *to be in good fortune*,

Pind.; εὐτυχίᾳ ὁμιλεῖν Eur.; ἐκτὸς ὁμιλεῖ (sc. τῶν ὀργῶν), i. e. wanders from his right mind, Soph. 2. of the things themselves, πλαγίαις φρένεσσιν ὄλβος οὐ . . ὁμ. does not consort with a crooked mind, Pind.; κυλίκων νεῖμεν ἐμοὶ τέρψιν ὁμιλεῖν gave me the delight of cups to keep me company, Soph. VI. to deal with a man, ταῦτα ἡ ἐμὴ νεότης ἐς τὴν Πελοποννησίων δύναμιν ὡμίλησε thus hath my youth wrought by intercourse with the power, Thuc. VII. of place, to come into, be in, visit, c. dat., Hdt., Aesch.

ὁμιληδόν, Adv., = ὁμιλαδόν, Hes.

ὁμίλημα [ῐ], ατος, τό, (ὁμιλέω) intercourse, Plat.

ὁμιλητέον, verb. Adj. of ὁμιλέω, Arist.

ὁμιλητής, οῦ, ὁ, (ὁμιλέω) a disciple, scholar, Xen.

ὁμιλητός, ή, όν, (ὁμιλέω) with whom one may consort, οὐχ ὁμιλητός unapproachable, Aesch.

ὁμιλία, Ion. -ίη, ἡ, (ὁμιλέω) a being together, communion, intercourse, converse, company, Lat. commercium, Aesch., etc. :—ὁμ. τινός communion or intercourse with one, Hdt.; πρός τινα Soph., etc.; τοὺς ἀξίους δὲ τῆς ἐμῆς ὁμιλίας those who are worthy of my society, Ar.; ὁμ. χθονός intercourse with a country, Eur.; πολιτεία καὶ ὁμ. public and private life, Thuc.:—also in pl., Ἑλληνικαὶ ὁμιλίαι association with Greeks, Hdt.; αἱ συγγενεῖς ὁμιλίαι intercourse with kinsfolk, Eur. 2. sexual intercourse, Hdt., Xen., etc. 3. instruction, Xen.:—later, a homily, sermon. II. an association, company, Hdt., Aesch.:—in collect. sense, fellow-sojourners, Aesch.; ναὸς ὁμ. ship-mates, Soph.

ὅμ-ῑλος, ὁ, (ὁμός, ἴλη) any assembled crowd, a throng of people, Hom., Hdt., Aesch.: the mass of the people, the crowd, opp. to the chiefs, Il.; ὁ ψιλὸς ὅμ. the crowd of irregulars, as opp. to the ὁπλῖται, Thuc. 2. the throng of battle, Il.; πρώτῳ ἐν ὁμ., Lat. in prima acie, Ib.: generally tumult, confusion, Hdt.

ΟΜΙΧΕΩ, Lat. mingo, to make water, Hes.

ΟΜΙΧΛΗ, Ion. ὀμίχλη, Dor. ὀμίχλα, a mist, fog, (not so thick as νέφος or νεφέλη), Il.; κονίης ὀμίχλη a cloud of dust, Ib. 2. metaph. a mist over the eyes, Aesch.: darkness, gloom, Anth.

ὄμμα, ατος, τό, (Root found in ὦμμαι, pf. pass. of ὁράω) :—the eye, Hom., etc.; κατὰ χθονὸς ὄμματα πήξας Il.; ὀρθοῖς ὄμμασιν ὁρᾶν τινα, Lat. rectis oculis aspicere, to look straight, Soph., etc.; οὐκ οἶδ' ὄμμασιν ποίοις βλέπων πατέρα ποτ' ἂν προσεῖδον how I could have looked him in the face, Id.; so, ὁρᾶν τινα ἐν ὄμμασι Id.; λαμπρὸς ὥσπερ ὄμματι to judge by his eyes or expression, Id.; ἐς ὄμμα τινὸς ἐλθεῖν to come within sight of him, Thuc.; —κατ' ὄμματα before one's eyes, Soph.; ἐλθεῖν κατ' ὄμμα face to face, Eur.; but κατ' ὄμμα, also, in point of eye-sight, Soph. :—ὡς ἀπ' ὀμμάτων to judge by the eye, Lat. ex obtutu, Id.; —ἐν ὄμμασι, Lat. in oculis, before one's eyes, Aesch., Thuc.; —ἐξ ὀμμάτων out of sight, Eur. II. that which one sees, a sight, vision, Soph. III. the eye of heaven, i. e. the sun, Id., Eur.; but, ὄμμα νυκτὸς periphr. for νύξ (v. infr. v), Aesch., Eur. IV. generally, light, that which brings light, ὄμμα δόμων νομίζω δεσπότου παρουσίαν Aesch.; ὄμμα φήμης the light of glad tidings, Soph. :—hence, anything dear or precious, Aesch. V. periphr. of the person, ὄμμα πελείας for πελεία, Soph.; ὄμμα νύμφας for νύμφα, Eur.

Soph.; ξύναιμον ὄμμα for ξυναίμων, Id.; ὦ ταυρόμορφον ὄμμα Κηφισοῦ for ὦ ταυρόμορφε Κηφισέ, Eur.

ὀμμάτο-στερής, ές, (στερέω) bereft of eyes, Soph., Eur. II. act. depriving of eyes, φλογμὸς ὀμμ. φυτῶν heat that robs plants of their eyes or buds, Aesch.

ὀμμάτόω, f. ώσω, (ὄμμα) to furnish with eyes :—Pass., φρὴν ὠμματωμένη a mind furnished with eyes, quick of sight, Aesch.

ΟΜΝΥΜΙ and ὀμνύω: imper. ὄμνυθι and ὄμνῡ: 3 pl. ὀμνύντων, 3 sing. (from pres. ὀμνύω) ὀμνυέτω: impf. ὤμνυν :—f. ὀμοῦμαι, εῖ, εῖται, later ὀμόσω: aor. 1 ὤμοσα, Ep. ὄμοσσα, ὄμοσα, -οσσα: pf. ὀμώμοκα: plqpf. ὀμωμόκειν :—Pass., f. ὀμοσθήσομαι: aor. 1 ὠμόσθην Il.; 3 sing. pf. ὀμώμοται or ὀμόμοσται, part. ὀμωμοσμένος :—to swear, Hom.; c. acc. cogn., ὀμνύετω δέ τοι ὅρκον Il.; ὅ τις κ' ἐπίορκον ὀμόσσῃ whosoever swears a false oath, Ib. II. to swear to a thing, affirm or confirm by oath, ταῦτα δ' ἐγὼν ἐθέλω ὀμόσαι Ib.; ὀμν. τὴν εἰρήνην Dem. 2. foll. by inf. fut. to swear that one will . . , Il., Soph.; —often with ἦ μέν or (in Att.) ἦ μήν preceding the inf., καί μοι ὀμόσσον ἦ μέν μοι ἀρήξειν Il.; so by inf. aor. and ἄν, Xen. :—foll. by inf. pres. to swear that one is doing a thing, Soph.; by inf. pf. to swear that one has done, Dem. 3. absol. εἰπεῖν ὀμόσας to say with an oath, Plat. II. with acc. of the person or thing sworn by, to swear by, ὀμόσαι Στυγὸς ὕδωρ Il.; ὀμωμοκὼς τοὺς θεούς Dem.;—rarely c. dat., τῷ δ' ἄρ' ὄμνυτ'; Ar. :—Pass., ὀμώμοσται Ζεὺς Zeus has been sworn by, adjured, Aesch.

ὁμο-βώμιος, ον, (βωμός) having a common altar, Thuc.

ὁμο-γάλακτες, οἱ, (γάλα) persons suckled with the same milk, foster-brothers or sisters, clansmen, Arist.

ὁμό-γαμος, ον, married to the same wife, Eur.; ὁμόγαμοι having married sisters, Id.

ὁμο-γάστριος, ον, (γαστήρ) from the same womb, born of the same mother, Il.

ὁμο-γενέτωρ, ορος, ἡ, (γίγνομαι) an own brother, Eur.

ὁμο-γενής, ές, (γίγνομαι) of the same race or family, Eur.; ὁμ. μιάσματα, of bloodshed in a family, Id. :—also as Subst., ὁμογενής τινος one's congener, Id. II. act. having the same wife, Soph.

ὁμο-γέρων, οντος, ὁ, one equally aged, Luc.

ὁμό-γλωσσος, ον, Att. -ττος, (γλῶσσα) speaking the same tongue, Hdt.; τινι with one, Id., Xen.

ὁμό-γνιος, ον, contr. for ὁμογένιος, (ὁμός, γένος) of the same race : ὁμόγ. θεοὶ gods who protect a race or family, Lat. Dii gentilitii, Soph.; Ζεὺς ὁμ. Eur., Ar.

ὁμογνωμονέω, f. ήσω, to be of one mind, to league together, Thuc., Xen.; ὁμ. τινι to consent to, Xen.; ὁμ. τινί τι to agree with one in a thing, Id. From

ὁμο-γνώμων, ον, gen. ονος, (γνώμη) of one's mind, like-minded, τινί with one, Thuc., Xen., etc.; ὁμ. τινα λαμβάνειν, ποιεῖν, ποιεῖσθαι to bring to one's own opinion, Xen.

ὁμό-γονος, ον, = ὁμο-γενής, Pind.; τινι with one, Xen.

ὁμό-δαμος, ον, Dor. for ὁμό-δημος.

ὁμοδέμνιος, ον, (δέμνιον) sharing one's bed, Aesch.

ὁμό-δημος, Dor. -δᾶμος, ον, of the same people or race, Pind.; τινι with one, Id.

ὁμο-δίαιτος, ον, (δίαιτα) living with others, Luc.; ὁμο-δίαιτα τοῖς πολλοῖς common to the generality, Id.

ὁμοδοξέω, f. ήσω, to be of the same opinion, agree per-

fectly, τινι *with* one, Plat. : absol. *to agree together,* Id. ; and

ὁμοδοξία, ἡ, *unanimity,* Plat.   From

ὁμό-δοξος, ον, (δόξα) *of the same opinion,* Luc.

ὁμό-δουλος, ὁ, ἡ, *a fellow-slave,* Eur., Plat., etc. ; ὁμ. τινος Plat. ; τινι Xen.

ὁμοδρομία, ἡ, *a running together, meeting,* Luc. From

ὁμό-δρομος, ον, (δραμεῖν) *running the same course with,* Plat.

ὁμο-εθνής, ές, (ἔθνος) *of the same people* or *race,* Hdt., Arist. :—generally, *of the same kind,* Arist.

ὁμο-εθνος, ον, = ὁμοεθνής, Polyb.

ὁμό-ζυξ, υγος, ὁ, ἡ, (ζεύγνυμι) *yoked together,* Plat.

ὁμο-ήθης, ες, (ἦθος) *of the same habits* or *character,* Plat., Arist.

ὁμο-ῆλιξ, ικος, ὁ, ἡ, = ὁμῆλιξ, Anth.

ὁμο-θάλαμος, ον, *living in the same chamber with* another, c. gen., Pind.

ὁμόθεν, (ὁμός) *from the same place,* properly a gen. (like ἐμέθεν, σέθεν, οὐρανόθεν), ἐξ ὁμόθεν Od.   **II.** as Adv. *from the same source,* h. Hom., Hes. ; τὸν ὁμόθεν *a brother,* Eur. ; so, τὸν ὁμ. πεφυκότα Id. ; ὁμ. εἶναί τινι *to be from the same parents with* him, Soph.   **III.** *from near, hand to hand,* ὁμ. μάχην ποιεῖσθαι, Lat. *cominus pugnare,* Xen. ; ὁμόθεν διώκειν *to follow close upon,* Id.

ὁμό-θρονος, ον, *sharing the same throne,* Pind.

ὁμο-θῡμᾱδόν, Adv. (θυμός) *with one accord,* Dem. ; mostly joined with πάντες, Ar., Xen.

ὁμοιάζω, (ὅμοιος) *to be like,* N. T.

ὁμοῖιος, ον, Ep. for ὅμοιος, ον, Il. [ῑ metri grat. before a long syll.]

ὁμοιο-κατάληκτος, ον, *ending alike, rhyming,* of verses.

ὁμοιοπᾰθέω, f. ήσω, *to have similar feelings* or *affections, to sympathise,* τινί with another, Arist.   **II.** of things, *to be subject to the same laws, to be homogeneous,* Strab.

ὁμοιο-πᾰθής, ές, (πάθος) *having like feelings* or *affections, sympathetic,* τινί with another, Plat.   **II.** generally, *of like nature,* Ib.

ὁμοιο-πρεπής, ές, (πρέπω) *of like appearance with,* τινι Aesch.

ὅμοιος or (Ion. and old Att.) **ὁμοῖος, α, ον,** or os, ον : Ep. also **ὁμοῖιος** (q. v.), Aeol. **ὕμοιος:** (ὁμός) :—*like, resembling,* Lat. *similis,* Hom., etc. ; proverb., τὸν ὁμοῖον ἄγει θεὸς ὡς τὸν ὁμοῖον 'birds of a feather flock together,' Od. ; so, ὁ ὅμοιος τῷ ὁμοίῳ Plat. :—Comp. ὁμοιότερος *more like,* Id. ; Sup. -ότατος *most like,* Hdt., Soph., etc.   **2.** = ὁ αὐτός, *the same,* Hom. ; ἐν καὶ ὁμ. one and *the same,* Plat. ; ὁμοῖον ἡμῖν ἔσται it will be *all one* to us, Lat. *perinde erit,* Hdt. ; σὺ δ' αἰνεῖν εἴτε με ψέγειν θέλεις, ὁμοῖον Aesch.   **3.** *shared alike by both, common,* ὁμ. πόλεμος war in which each takes part, Hom. ; γῆρας, θάνατος, μοῖρα *common to all,* Id.   **4.** *equal in force, a match for* one, Lat. *par,* Il., Hdt.   **5.** *like in mind, at one with, agreeing with,* τινι Hes. :—hence (sub. ἑαυτῷ) *always the same,* Id. ; ὅμοιος πρὸς τοὺς αὐτοὺς κινδύνους Thuc.   **6.** τὸ ὁμοῖον ἀνταποδιδόναι *to give* 'tit for tat,' Lat. *par pari referre,* Hdt. ; so, τὴν ὁμοίην (sc. χάριν) διδόναι or ἀποδιδόναι τινί Id. ; τὴν

ὁμοίην φέρεσθαι παρά τινος *to have a like return* made one, Id. ; ἐπ' ἴσῃ καὶ ὁμοίᾳ (v. ἴσος II. 2).   **7.** ἐν ὁμοίῳ ποιεῖσθαί τι *to hold a thing in like esteem,* Id.   **8.** ἐκ τοῦ ὁμοίου, *alike,* much like ὁμοίως, Thuc. ; ἐκ τῶν ὁμοίων *with equal advantages, in fair fight,* Aesch.   **II.** *of the same rank* or *station,* Hdt. : οἱ ὅμοιοι, *the peers,* Xen., Arist.

  B. Construction :   **1.** absol., as often in Hom., etc.   **2.** *the person* or *thing to which one is like* in dat., as with Lat. *similis,* Hom., etc. ; also in gen. : —ellipt., κόμαι Χαρίτεσσιν ὁμοῖαι, for κόμαι ταῖς τῶν Χαρίτων ὁμοῖαι, Il.   **3.** *that in which* a person or thing *is like* another is in acc., ἀθανάτῃσι φυὴν καὶ εἶδος ὁμοίη Od.   **4.** with inf., θείειν ἀνέμοισιν ὁμοῖοι *like* the winds *to run,* Il.   **5.** foll. by καί, like Lat. *perinde ac,* Hdt., etc.

  C. Adv., often in the neuters, ὅμοιον and ὅμοια, Ion. and old Att. ὁμοῖον, ὁμοῖα, *in like manner with,* ὁμοῖα τοῖς μάλιστα 'second to none,' Hdt. ; ὁμοῖα τοῖς πρώτοισι Id.   **2.** *alike,* Aesch.   **II.** regul. Adv. ὁμοίως, *in like manner with,* c. dat., Hdt., Att. ; ὁμ. καὶ .. Hdt.   **2.** *alike, equally,* Id., Aesch.

ὁμοιο-τέλευτος, ον, (τελευτή) *ending alike,* Arist. : τὸ ὁμοτέλευτον *the like ending of two verses.*

ὁμοιότης, ητος, ἡ, (ὅμοιος) *likeness, resemblance,* Plat.

ὁμοιοτροπία, ἡ, *likeness of manners and life,* Strab.

ὁμοιό-τροπος, ον, *of like manners and life,* Thuc. :— Adv. -πως, *in like manner with* another, c. dat., Id.

ὁμοιόω, f. -ώσω : aor. 1 ὡμοίωσα :—Pass., f. ὁμοιωθήσομαι, or in med. form ὁμοιώσομαι : aor. 1 ὡμοιώθην, Ep. inf. ὁμοιωθήμεναι : (ὅμοιος) :—*to make like,* Lat. *assimilare,* τί τινι Eur., Plat. ; πρὸς τὰ παρόντα τὰς ὀργὰς ὁμ. *to make their feelings suitable* to present circumstances, Thuc. :—Pass. *to be made like, become like,* Hom., Eur., etc. ; in pf. ὡμοίωμαι, *to be like,* Plat.   **2.** *to liken, compare,* τί τινι Hdt., etc. ; so in Med., Id. :— in N. T. of parables.   **3.** in Med. also *to make a like return,* Hdt.   Hence

ὁμοίωμα, ατος, τό, *a likeness, image, resemblance, counterfeit,* Plat. ; and

ὁμοίως, Adv. of ὅμοιος, v. ὅμοιος C.

ὁμοίωσις, ἡ, *a becoming like, assimilation,* Plat.   **2.** *likeness, resemblance,* N. T.

ὁμό-κάπος, ον, (κάπη) *eating together,* ap. Arist.

ὁμό-κεντρος, ον, (κέντρον) *concentric with,* Strab.

ὁμόκλαρος, Dor. for ὁμόκληρος.

ὁμοκλέω : impf. ὁμόκλεον, and 3 sing. ὁμόκλᾱ (as if from ὁμοκλάω) : aor. 1 ὁμόκλησα, 3 sing. Ep. ὁμοκλήσασκε :—*to call out together,* Od., Soph. ; ὁμ. τινι *to call* or *shout to,* whether *to encourage* or *upbraid, threaten,* Il. ;—c. inf. *to command loudly, call* one *to do,* Ib.   From

ὁμο-κλή, ἡ, (ὁμοῦ, καλέω) properly *of several persons, a joint call ;* but *of single persons,* μεῖναι ὁμοκλήν *to bide his call,* Il. ; with a sense of *reproof, rebuke,* Hom.   **II.** generally, *harmony.*

ὁμό-κληρος, Dor. -κλᾱρος, ὁ, *one who has an equal share* of an inheritance, *a coheir,* Pind.

ὁμοκλήσασκε, 3 sing. Ep. aor. 1 of ὁμοκλέω.

ὁμοκλητήρ, ηρος, ὁ, (ὁμοκλέω) *one who calls out to, an upbraider, threatener,* Il.

ὁμό-κλῖνος, ον, (κλίνη) reclining on the same couch, at table, Hdt.

ὁμό-λεκτρος, ον, (λέκτρον) sharing the same bed, Eur.; but, Ζηνὸς ὁμόλεκτρον κάρα, of Tyndarëus, as husband of Leda, Id.

ὁμολογέω, f. -ήσω: aor. 1 ὡμολόγησα: pf. ὡμολόγηκα:— Med. and Pass., f. ὁμολογήσομαι and ὁμολογηθήσομαι: aor. 1 ὡμολογησάμην and ὡμολογήθην: pf. ὡμολόγημαι: (ὁμόλογος):—to speak together; hence, I. to speak one language, τινί with one, Hdt.:—generally, οὐδὲν ὁμ. τινί to have naught to do with, Id. II. to hold the same language with, i. e. to agree with, τινί Id., Thuc. 2. to agree to a thing, allow, admit, confess, concede, grant, c. acc. rei, Hdt., Soph., etc.; ὁμ. τὴν εἰρήνην to agree to the terms of peace, Dem. :— without the acc. rei, ὁμολογῶ σοι I grant you, i. e. I admit it, Ar., Xen.:—c. inf. to allow, confess, grant that . . , Ar., Plat. 3. to agree or promise to do, c. inf., Plat. b. the inf. is often omitted, ὁμολογήσαντες (sc. ἀπαλλάξεσθαι) Hdt.:—hence simply to make an agreement, come to terms, τινί with another, Id.
B. Med., just like the Act., Plat., Xen.
C. Pass. to be agreed upon, allowed or granted by common consent, Xen.; c. inf. to be allowed or confessed to be, Plat., Xen. 2. absol., ὁμολογεῖται it is granted, allowed, Plat.; τὰ ὁμολογούμενα, τὰ ὡμολογημένα things granted, Lat. concessa, Id. Hence

ὁμολόγημα, ατος, τό, that which is agreed upon, taken for granted, a postulate, Plat.; and

ὁμολογία, Ion. -ίη, ἡ, agreement, Plat. 2. an assent, admission, concession, Id.: κατὰ τὴν ἐμὴν ὁμ. by my admission, Id. 3. an agreement made, compact, Id.; often in pl., Id.; esp. in war, terms of surrender, Hdt., Thuc.

ὁμό-λογος, ον, (ὁμοῦ, λέγω) agreeing, of one mind, ὁμ. γενέσθαι τινὶ περί τινος to be of one mind with one on a point, Xen.:—also of things, agreeing, correspondent, Arist. II. Adv. -γως, agreeably to, in unison with, Id.:—so, ἐξ ὁμολόγου confessedly, Polyb.

ὁμολογουμένως, Adv. part. pres. pass. of ὁμολογέω, conformably with, τοῖς εἰρημένοις Xen. 2. by common consent, confessedly, Thuc., Plat.

Ὁμολώϊος, ὁ, a name of Zeus in Boeotia and Thessaly: —hence one of the Gates of Thebes were called πύλαι Ὁμολωΐδες, Aesch., Eur.

ὁμο-μαστιγίας, ου, ὁ, a fellow-knave (cf. μαστιγίας), Ar.

ὁμομήτριος, α, ον, born of the same mother, Lat. frater uterinus, Hdt., Plat.; ὁμομήτρια ἀδελφή Ar.

ὁμό-νεκρος, ον, companion in death, Luc.

ὁμονοέω, f. ήσω, (ὁμόνοος) to be of one mind, agree together, live in harmony, Thuc.; ὁμονοοῦσα ὀλιγαρχία a united oligarchy, Arist. 2. c. dat. to live in harmony with others, c. dat.; Plat. Hence

ὁμονοητικός, ή, όν, conducing to agreement, in harmony, Plat. :—Adv. -ικῶς ἔχειν to be of one mind, Id.

ὁμόνοια, ή, oneness of mind or thought, unity, concord, Thuc., Plat., etc. From

ὁμό-νοος, ον, contr. -νους, ουν, of one mind, Lat. concors: Adv. -νόως, Xen.

ὁμο-παθής, ές, (πάθος) of like feelings or affections, sympathetic, Arist.; c. gen., ὁμ. λύπης καὶ ἡδονῆς affected alike by pain and pleasure, Plat.

ὁμο-πάτριος, α, ον, by the same father, Hdt., Aesch.

ὁμοπλοέω, f. ήσω, to sail together or in company, Polyb.; and

ὁμόπλοια, ἡ, a sailing in company, Cic. From

ὁμό-πλοος, ον, contr. -πλους, ουν, sailing together or in company, Anth.

ὁμό-πολις, εως, ὁ, ἡ, from or of the same city: poët.

ὁμό-πτολις, Soph.

ὁμό-πτερος, ον, (πτερόν) of or with the same plumage, Plat.; ὁμόπτεροι ἐμοί my fellow-birds, birds of my feather, Ar. 2. metaph. of like feather, closely resembling, Aesch., Eur.; νᾶες ὁμ. consort-ships (or equally swift), Aesch.; ἀπήνη ὁμ. i. e. the two brothers, Eteocles and Polynices, Eur.

ὁμόπτολις, εως, ὁ, ἡ, poët. for ὁμόπολις.

ὁμοργάζω, = ὁμόργνυμι, to wipe off, 3 sing. impf. ὠμόργαζε h. Hom.

ΟΜΟ'ΡΓΝῩΜΙ, to wipe:—Med., δάκρυα ὠμόργνυντο were wiping away their tears, Od.; παρειάων δάκρυ᾽ ὁμορξαμένη were wiping the tears from their cheeks, Il.

ὁμορέω, Ion. ὁμουρέω, f. ήσω, to border upon, march with, [οἱ Κελτοὶ] ὁμουρέουσι Κυνησίοισι Hdt. From

ὅμ-ορος, Ion. ὅμ-ουρος, ον, having the same borders with, marching with, bordering on, τοῖσι Δωριεῦσι, τῇ Λιβύῃ Hdt.; absol. bordering, Thuc.; πόλεμος ὅμορος a border war, Dem. 2. metaph. bordering on, closely resembling, Arist. 3. also as Subst., a neighbour, Hdt., Thuc.; κατὰ τὸ ὅμορον because of their neighbourhood, Thuc.

ὁμορροθέω, f. ήσω, to row together; metaph. to agree, consent, Soph.; ὁμ. τινι to agree with him, Eur.

ὁμόρ-ροθος, ον, properly, rowing together: hence side by side, Theocr.:—so, ὁμορρόθιος, ον, Anth.

ΟΜΟ'Σ, ή, όν, (akin to ἅμα) one and the same, common, joint, Lat. communis, Hom., Hes.; ὁμὰ φρονεῖν to be of one mind, Hes.

ὁμόσαι, aor. 1 inf. of ὄμνυμι :—ὁμόσας, part.

ὁμόσε, Adv. (ὁμός) to one and the same place, Il.; ὁμόσ᾽ ἦλθε μάχη the battle came to the same spot, i. e. the armies met, Ib.; ὁμόσε ἰέναι, like Lat. cominus pugnare, ὁμ. ἰέναι τοῖς ἐχθροῖς to close with the enemy, Thuc.; ὁμ. χωρεῖν; so, ὁμ. θεῖν, φέρεσθαι to run to meet, Xen. 2. metaph., ὁμ. ἰέναι τοῖς λόγοις to come to issue with the arguments, Eur.

ὁμο-σθενής, ές (σθένος) of equal might, Anth.

ὁμοσιτέω, f. ήσω, to eat with, take one's meals with others, c. dat.; Hdt. From

ὁμό-σιτος, ον, eating together, μετά τινος Hdt.

ὁμό-σκευος, ον, (σκευή) equipped in the same way, Thuc.

ὁμό-σκηνος, ον, (σκηνή) living in the same tent.

ὁμοσκηνόω, f. ώσω, to live in the same tent or house with others, c. dat., Xen.

ὁμό-σπλαγχνος, ον, = ὁμογάστριος, Aesch., Soph.

ὁμό-σπονδος, ον, (σπονδή) sharing in the drink-offering, sharing the same cup, Hdt., Dem.

ὁμό-σπορος, ον, (σπείρω) sown together: sprung from the same race, kindred, h. Hom., Trag. : as Subst. a brother or a sister, Trag. II. ὁμ. γυνή a wife common to two (Laius and Oedipus), Soph.; of Oedipus, τοῦ πατρὸς ὁμόσπορος having the same wife with his father, Id.

ὀμόσσαι, Ep. aor. 1 inf. of ὄμνυμι:—ὀμόσσας, part.

ὁμό-στολος, ον, (στέλλω) in company with others, c. gen., Soph.

ὁμό-τἄφος, ον, buried together, Aeschin.

ὁμό-τεχνος, ον, (τέχνη) practising the same craft with another, c. dat., Plat.:—as Subst., a fellow-workman, Hdt., Plat.

ὁμοτῑμία, ἡ, sameness of value or honour, Luc. From

ὁμό-τῑμος, ον, (τιμή) held in equal honour, Il.; μακάρεσσι with the gods, Theocr.; c. gen. rei, τῆς στρατηγίας ὁμ. having an equal share in the command, Plut.   II. οἱ ὁμότιμοι, among the Persians, nobles of equal rank, the peers of the realm, Xen.

ὁμότοιχος, ον, having one common wall, separated by a party-wall, contiguous, Plat.:—metaph., of disease, γείτων ὁμ. a next-door neighbour, Aesch.

ὁμο-τράπεζος, ον, (τράπεζα) eating at the same table with another, c. dat., Hdt.; συνέστιος καὶ ὁμ. Plat.; οἱ ὁμ., messmates, Persian name for certain courtiers, Xen.

ὁμό-τροπος, ον, of the same habits or life, Plat.:—as Subst., οἱ ὁμότροποί τινος one's messmates, Aeschin.   2. of like fashion, Hdt.

ὁμό-τροφος, ον, (τρέφω) reared or bred together with another, c. dat., h. Hom.; ὁμότροφα τοῖσι ἀνθρώποισι θηρία, of domestic animals, Hdt.   II. absol., ὁμότρ. πεδία plains where we fed in common, Ar.

ὁμοῦ, Adv., properly gen. neut. of ὁμός,   I. of Place, at the same place, together, Il., Soph., etc.   2. together, at once, ἄμφω ὁμοῦ Od.; δυοῖν ὁμοῦ Soph.; αἶγας ὁμοῦ καὶ ὄῑς both sheep and goats, Il.; λιμὸν ὁμοῦ καὶ λοιμόν Hes., etc.   3. c. dat. together with, along with, κεῖσθαι ὁμοῦ νεκύεσσι Il.; οἰμωγὴ ὁμοῦ κωκύμασιν Aesch.   II. close at hand, hard by, Soph., Ar.: c. dat. close to, Soph., Xen.   2. rarely c. gen., νεὼς ὁμοῦ στείχειν to go to join my ship, Soph.   3. of amount, in all, εἰσὶν ὁμοῦ δισμύριοι Dem., etc.   III. ὁμοῦ καί just like, Xen.

ὁμοῦμαι, f. of ὄμνυμι.

ὅμουρος, Ion. for ὅμορος.

ὁμό-φοιτος, ον, (φοιτάω) going by the side of another, c. gen., Pind.

ὁμοφρονέω, f. ήσω, to be of the same mind, have the same thoughts, Ib.; ὁμοφρονέοντε νοήμασιν in unity of purposes, Ib.; πόλεμος ὁμοφρονέων a war of common consent, Hdt.:—c. dat., οὐ γὰρ ἀλλήλοισι ὁμοφρόνεουσι are not agreed together, Id.; and

ὁμοφροσύνη, ἡ, = ὁμόνοια, Od.   From

ὁμό-φρων, ονος, ὁ, ἡ, (φρήν) = ὁμόνοος, Il., Hes.; ὁμ. λόγοι Ar.

ὁμο-φυής, ές, (φυή) of the same growth or nature, Plat.

ὁμοφῡλία, ἡ, sameness of race or tribe, Strab. From

ὁμό-φῡλος, ον, (φῦλον) of the same race or stock, Thuc., etc.; οἱ ὁμ. those of the same race, Xen.; φιλία ὁμόφ. friendship with those of the same stock, Eur.:—τὸ ὁμόφυλον, = ὁμοφυλία, Id.; τὸ μὴ ὁμ. a city peopled by different races, Arist.

ὁμοφωνέω, f. ήσω, to speak the same language with another, c. dat., Hdt.   II. to sound together, c. dat., σ. τῷ λόγῳ chimes in with the argument, Arist.

ὁμοφωνία, ἡ, in Music, unison, Arist. From

ὁμό-φωνος, ον, (φωνή) speaking the same language

with others, c. dat., Hdt., Thuc., etc.   II. of the same sound or tone, in unison with, τινι Aesch.

ὁμό-χροια, Ion.-χροίη, ἡ, sameness of colour, Xen.   II. the even surface of the body, the skin, Hdt.

ὁμοχρονέω, f. ήσω, to keep time with, τινί Luc.: absol. to keep time, Id.   From

ὁμό-χρονος, ον, contemporaneous.

ὁμό-ψηφος, ον, having an equal right to vote with others, c. dat., Hdt.; μετά τινων Id.

ὁμόω, f. ώσω, (ὁμός) to unite: aor. 1 pass. inf. ὁμωθῆναι Il.

῞ΟΜΠΝΗ, ἡ, food, corn.   Hence

ὄμπνιος, α, ον, of or relating to corn: hence bountiful, wealthy, ὀμπνιὰ Anth.

ὀμφᾰκίας, ὁ, (ὄμφαξ) made from unripe grapes: hence harsh, austere, crabbed, Ar.

ὀμφᾰκο-ράξ, ᾶγος, ὁ, ἡ, with sour grapes, Anth.

ὀμφάλιον, τό, Dim. of ὀμφᾰλός, Anth.

ὀμφάλιος, ον, (ὀμφᾰλός) having a boss, bossy, Anth.

ὀμφᾰλόεις, εσσα, εν, having a navel or boss, ἀσπίδος ὀμφαλοέσσης of the shield with a central boss, Il.; ζυγὸν ὀμφαλόεν a yoke with a knob on the top, Ib.

᾽ΟΜΦᾰΛΟΣ, ὁ, the navel, Lat. umbilicus, Il., Hdt., etc.   II. anything central (like a navel):   1. the knob or boss in the middle of the shield, Lat. umbo, Il.   2. a button or knob on the horse's yoke to fasten the reins to, Ib.   3. in pl. the knobs at each end of the stick round which books were rolled, Lat. umbilici, Luc.   III. the centre or middle point, as the island of Calypso is the ὀμφᾰλός of the sea, Od.; and Delphi (or rather a round stone in the Delphic temple) was called ὀμφᾰλός as marking the middle point of Earth, Pind., Aesch., etc.

ὄμφαξ, ᾰκος, ἡ, an unripe grape, πάροιθε δέ τ᾽ ὀμφακές εἰσιν Od.; ὅτ᾽ ὄμφακες αἰόλλονται Hes.; ὅταν δὲ τεύχῃ Ζεὺς ἀπ᾽ ὄμφακος οἶνον, i. e. autumn, when the unripe grapes become fit to make wine, Aesch.

᾽ΟΜΦΗ, ἡ, the voice of a god (opp. to αὐδή, the human voice), Hom.; θείη δέ μιν ἀμφέχυτ᾽ ὀμφή, of the voice of the dream sent by Zeus to Agamemnon, Il.; κατ᾽ ὀμφὴν σήν on hearing the sound of thy name (for the name of Oedipus had something awful in it), Soph.   2. a sweet voice, Pind.:—a voice, sound, Eur.

ὀμ-ώλαξ, ᾰκος, ὁ, ἡ, Dor. for ὁμ-αύλαξ.

ὁμωνῠμία, ἡ, a having the same name, identity, an equivocal word, Arist.; and

ὁμωνύμιος, α, ον, = sq., Anth.   From

ὁμ-ώνῠμος, ον, (ὄνομα) having the same name, Il., etc.; τινι with one, Thuc., etc.; τὸν ἐμαυτῷ my own namesake, Dem.:—as Subst., c. gen., ὁ σαυτοῦ or ὁ σὸς ὁμώνυμος your namesake, Plat.   II. of like kind, Il.

ὁμ-ωρόφιος, ον, (ὄροφος) lodging under the same roof with another, c. dat., Dem.

ὁμ-ώροφος, ον, = foreg., Babr.

ὁμῶς, Adv. of ὁμός, equally, likewise, alike, Lat. pariter, Hom., Trag.; πλήθεν ὁμῶς ἵππων τε καὶ ἀνδρῶν was filled full both of men and horses alike, Il.; πάντες ὁμῶς all alike, Hom.   II. c. dat. like as, equally with, ἐχθρὸς ὁμῶς ᾽Αΐδαο πύλῃσι hated like the gates of hell, Il.   2. together with, Theogn.

ὅμως, Conj. from ὁμός (but with changed accent), all

the same, nevertheless, notwithstanding, still, Lat. *tamen,* Il., Soph., etc. :—often strengthened by other words, ἀλλ᾽ ὅμως, Lat. *attamen, but still, but for all that,* Ar., etc. ; ὅμως μήν, ὅμως μέντοι Plat. ; ὅμως γε μήν, ὅμως γε μέντοι Ar. :—used elliptically, οἴσεις οὐδὲν ὑγιές, ἀλλ᾽ ὅμως (sc. οἰστέον) Id.   II. in apodosis after καὶ εἰ or καὶ ἐάν, as *tamen* after *etsi* or *quamquam,* κεἰ τὸ μηδὲν ἐξερῶ, φράσω δ᾽ ὅμως even if I shall say nothing plainly, *yet* I will speak, Soph. ;—so, κλῦθί μου νοσῶν ὅμως (i.e. εἰ νοσεῖς, ὅμως κλῦθι), Id.   III. to limit single words, Lat. *quamvis,* ἀπάλαμόν περ ὅμως *helpless though* he be, Hes., etc.

ὀμ-ωχέτης, ου, ὁ, Aeol. for ὁμοεχέτης, (ὁμοῦ, ἔχω) *holding* or *dwelling together,* τοὺς ὀμωχέτας δαίμονας *worshipped in the same temple,* Thuc.

ὄν-αγρος, ὁ, = ὄνος ἄγριος, *the wild ass,* Strab., Babr.

ὀναίμην, aor. 2 med. opt. of ὀνίνημι :—**ὄνασθαι,** inf.

ὌΝΑΡ, τό, only used in nom. and acc. sing. (the other cases being supplied by ὄνειρος), *a dream, vision in sleep,* opp. to a waking vision (ὕπαρ), Od., Soph., etc. ; ὥστε μηδ᾽ ὄναρ ἰδεῖν, to express profound sleep, Plat.   2. proverb. of anything fleeting or unreal, ὀλιγοχρόνιον ὥσπερ ὄναρ Theogn. ; παρέρχεται ὡς ὄναρ ἥβη Theocr.   II. ὄναρ as Adv., *in a dream, in sleep,* ὄναρ ὑμᾶς καλῶ Aesch. ; μηδ᾽ ἰδὼν ὄναρ *not even in my dreams,* Eur., etc. ; cf. ὕπαρ.

ὄνᾰσις, ὀνάτωρ, Dor. for ὄνησις, ὀνήτωρ.

ὀνεία (sc. δορά), ἡ, *ass's skin,* fem. of ὄνειος, Babr.

ὄνειαρ, ἄτος, τό, (ὀνίνημι) *anything that profits* or *helps,* Il. : *advantage, aid, succour,* Hes., etc.   2. a *means of strengthening, refreshment,* Od., Hes. ; στιβάδεσσιν ὄνειαρ *good* for beds, Theocr.   3. in pl. ὀνείατα, *food, victuals,* Hom. ; also of *rich presents,* Il.   4. of persons, πᾶσιν ὄνειαρ Ib.

ὀνείδειος, ον, (ὄνειδος) *reproachful,* Hom.   2. *dishonourable,* Anth.

ὀνειδίζω, f. Att. -ιῶ : aor. 1 ὠνείδισα : pf. ὠνείδικα : —Pass., with fut. med. ὀνειδιεῖσθε (in pass. sense) : aor. 1 ὠνειδίσθην :   I. c. acc. rei et dat. pers. *to throw a reproach upon* one, *cast* in one's teeth, *object* or *impute* to one, Lat. *objicere, exprobrare,* Hom., etc.; also, ὀνειδίζειν τινὶ ὅτι .. *to impute* it to him that .. , Il., Plat.   II. omitting the acc. rei, *to reproach, upbraid,* Il.   1. c. dat. pers., Il., Hdt.   2. c. acc. pers., ἐπεσίν μιν ὀνείδισον Il. ; τυφλόν μ᾽ ὠνείδισας (sc. ὄντα) *did'st reproach* me *with being blind,* Soph. Hence

ὀνείδισμα, ατος, τό, *insult, reproach, blame,* Hdt. ; and

ὀνειδιστήρ, ῆρος, ὁ, = sq., *full of reproach,* Eur. ; and

ὀνειδιστής, οῦ, ὁ, *one who reproaches with* a thing, c. gen. rei, Arist. ; and

ὀνειδιστικός, ή, όν, *reproachful, abusive,* Luc. From

ὌΝΕΙΔΟΣ, τό, *reproach, censure, blame,* Hom. ; ὄνειδος ἔχειν *to be in disgrace,* Hdt. ; ὀνειδός [ἐστι], c. inf., Eur. ; ὡς ἐν ὀνείδει *by way of reproach,* Plat. :—pl., ὀνείδη ἔχειν τὰ μέγιστα Id., etc.   2. *matter of reproach, a reproach, disgrace,* σοὶ μὲν δὴ κατηφείη καὶ ὄν., Il. ; c. gen., τὸ πόλεως ὄν. *the reproach* of the city, Aesch. ; ὄν. Ἑλλάνων Soph. ; so, Oedipus calls his daughters τοιαῦτ᾽ ὀνείδη Id.

ὄνειος, α, ον, (ὄνος) *of an ass,* Ar. ; ὄν. γάλα *ass's milk,* Dem.

ὄνειραρ, ατος, τό, v. ὄνειρος.

ὀνείρειος, α, ον, (ὄνειρος) *dreamy, of dreams,* ἐν ὀνειρείῃσι πύλῃσι *at the gates of dreams,* Od.

ὀνειρο-κρίτης [ῐ], ου, ὁ, *an interpreter of dreams,* Theocr., Theophr.   Hence

ὀνειροκρῐτικός, ή, όν, *for interpreting dreams,* πινάκιον Plut.

ὀνειρό-μαντις, εως, ὁ, ἡ, *an interpreter of dreams,* Aesch.

ὀνειροπολέω, f. ήσω, *to deal with dreams,* i. e. *to dream,* Plat. ; ὀν. τι *to dream of* a thing, Ar. ; πολλὰ ὀνειροπολεῖ ἐν τῇ γνώμῃ 'builds many such castles in the air,' Dem.   II. *to cheat by dreams,* Ar.

ὀνειρο-πόλος, ὁ, (πολέω) *one occupied with dreams, a dreamer,* or *an interpreter of dreams,* Il., Hdt.

ὄνειρος, ὁ, or **ὄνειρον,** τό, pl. ὄνειρα, but the metaph. form ὀνείρατα (as if from ὄνειαρ) was more common in nom. and acc. ; so, gen. ὀνειράτων, dat. -ασι ; also in sing., gen. ὀνείρατος, dat. ὀνείρατι : (ὄναρ) :—*a dream,* Hom., etc.   2. as prop. n. Ὄνειρος, *god of dreams,* Id., Hes. ; cf. ἐνύπνιον.

ὀνειρό-φαντος, ον, *appearing in dreams.*

ὀνειρό-φρων, ονος, ὁ, ἡ, (φρήν) *versed in dreams and their interpretations,* Eur.

ὀνεύω, *to draw up with a windlass* (ὄνος III. 1), impf. ὤνευον Thuc.

ὀν-ηλάτης [ᾰ], ου, ὁ, (ἐλαύνω) *a donkey-driver,* Dem.

ὀνήμενος, aor. 2 med. part. of ὀνίνημι :—ὄνησα, aor. 1 Ep. for ὤνησα ; ὤνησο, aor. 2 imper. :—ὄνησο, aor. 2, fut.

ὀνήσιμος, ον, (ὀνίνημι) *useful, profitable, beneficial,* Aesch., Soph. : *aiding, succouring,* Soph.

ὀνησί-πολις [ῐ], εως, ὁ, ἡ, *useful to the state,* Simon.

ὄνησις, Dor. ὄνᾰσις, ἡ, (ὀνίνημι) *use, profit, advantage, good luck,* Od., Soph. :—c. gen. rei, *enjoyment* of a thing, *profit* or *delight from* it, Aesch., etc. ; so, ὄν. ὀνεῖν ἀπό τινος Soph.

ὀνήτωρ, Dor. **ὀνάτωρ,** ορος, ὁ, = ὀνήσιμος, Pind.

ὌΝΘΟΣ, ὁ, *the dung* of animals, Il.

ὀνίδιον [ῐ], τό, Dim. of ὄνος, *a little ass, donkey,* Ar.

ὀνῐκός, ή, όν, *of* or *for an ass : ὀνικὸς μύλος,* v. ὄνος III. 2.

'ΟΝΙ'ΝΗΜΙ, ὀνίνης, ὀνίνησι, inf. ὀνῐνάναι, part. ὀνῐνάς, ᾶσα :—impf. supplied by ὠφέλουν :—f. ὀνήσω, Dor. 3 sing. ὀνασεῖ :—aor. 1 ὤνησα, Ep. ὄνησα :—Med., ὀνίνᾰμαι :—impf. ὠνινάμην :—f. ὀνήσομαι : aor. 2 ὠνήμην, imper. ὄνησο, part. ὀνήμενος ; also ὠνάμην, 2 pl. ὤνασθε ; opt. ὀναίμην, inf. ὄνασθαι :—Pass., aor. 1 ὠνήθην, Dor. ὠνάθην :   I. Act. *to profit, benefit, help, assist,* and, like Lat. *juvo, to gratify, delight ;* absol. and c. acc. pers., Il., etc. ; πολλὰ ὀν. τινα Od. ; ὡς ὤνησας ὅτι ἀπεκρίνω *how you pleased* me *by answering,* Plat.   II. Med. *to have profit* or *advantage, derive benefit, have enjoyment* or *delight,* Hom., etc. ; c. gen. *to have advantage from, have enjoyment of,* δαιτὸς ὄνησο Od. ; τί σευ ἄλλος ὀνήσεται ; *what good will* others *have* of thee, i. e. what good will you have done them ? Il. ; so, ὄνασθαί τι ἀπό τινος Plat.   2. aor. 2 part. ὀνήμενος, = *felix,* ἐσθλός μοι δοκεῖ εἶναι, ὀνήμενος he seems to me noble, *favoured by the gods,* Od.   3. aor. opt. ὀναίμην, in protestations and wishes, ὄναιο, Lat. *sis felix !* Eur., etc. ; and c. gen., ὄναιο τῶν φρενῶν *bless thee* for thy good sense, Id. ; μὴ νῦν ὀναίμην *may I not thrive* (where βίου must be

supplied), Soph. :—also in ironical sense, ὄναιο μέν-
ταν you'd be the better of it! Ar.; ἀλσὶν διασμηχθεὶς
ὄναιτ' ἂν οὑτοσί he'd be very nice if he were rubbed
down with salt, Id.

ὀνίς, ίδος, ἡ, ass's dung, in pl., Ar.

ὀνο-βᾰτέω, f. ήσω, (βαίνω) to have a mare covered by
an ass, Xen.

ὄνοιτο, 3 sing. opt. of ὄνομαι.

"ΟΝΟΜΑ, τό, Ion. and poët. οὔνομα, Aeol. ὄνῠμα,
Lat. nomen, a name, Hom., etc. :—absol., by name,
πόλις ὄνομα Καιναί Xen., etc.; also in dat., πόλις
Θάψακος ὀνόματι Id.   2. ὄν. θεῖναί τινα to give one
a name, Od.; but commonly in Med., ὄν. θέσθαι Ib.,
Att.; and for Pass., ὄν. κεῖταί τινι Ar., etc.; ὄν. ἔχειν
ἀπό τινος Hdt.   3. ὄνομα καλεῖν τινα to call one by
name, Od., Att.; so with pass. verbs, ὄν. ὠνομάζετο Ἕλενος Soph.; ὄν. κέκληται δημοκρατία Thuc.   II. name,
fame, Ἰθάκης γε καὶ ἐς Τροίην ὄνομ' ἵκει Od.; τὸ μέγα
ὄν. τῶν Ἀθηνῶν Thuc.; ὄνομα or τὸ ὄν. ἔχειν to have a
name for a thing (good or bad), 2 opt., Thuc.   III. a
mere name, opp. to the real person or thing, Od.;
opp. to ἔργον, Eur., etc.   2. a false name, pretence,
pretext, ὀνόματι or ἐπ' ὀνόματι under the pretence,
Thuc.   IV. phrase or name in periphr. phrases,
ὄνομα τῆς σωτηρίας, for σωτηρία, Eur.; ὦ φίλτατον ὄν.
Πολυνείκους Id.   V. a phrase, expression, Xen.:
generally, a saying, speech, Dem.   VI. in Grammar, a noun, Lat. nomen, opp. to ῥῆμα, verbum, Ar.,
Plat., etc. Hence

ὀνομάζω, Ion. οὐνομάζω :— impf. ὠνόμαζον, Ep. ὀν-: f.
ὀνομάσω :— aor. 1 ὠνόμασα, Ion. οὐν-: pf. ὠνόμακα:
—Pass., aor. 1 ὠνομάσθην: ὠνόμασμαι :—an Aeol. fut.
med. ὀνυμάξομαι, and aor. 1 act. ὀνύμαξα: (ὄνομα):—to
name or speak of by name, call or address by name, Il.,
Hdt., Xen.   2. of things, to name, specify, Il.   II.
ὀν. τινά τι to call one something, Hdt., Att.: in Med.,
παῖδά μ' ὠνομάζετο called me his son, Soph. :—Pass.,
ὄνομα δ' ὠνομάζετο Ἕλενος Id., etc.   2. εἶναι is
often added pleon., τὰς οὐνομάζουσι εἶναι Ὑπερόχην καί
. . whose names they say are Hyperoché and . . , Hdt.;
σοφιστὴν ὀνομάζουσιν τὸν ἄνδρα εἶναι Plat.   III. to
name or call after . . , ἐπί τινι Hdt., etc.; ἔκ τινος
Soph. :—Pass., ἀπὸ τούτου τοῦτο οὐνομάζεται hence
this saying has arisen, Hdt.   IV. to use names or
words, μάλα σεμνῶς ὀνομάζων Dem.

"ΟΝΟΜΑΙ, Ep. 2 sing. ὄνοσαι, 2 pl. οὔνεσθε, 3 pl. ὄνον-
ται, 3 sing. opt. ὄνοιτο: 3 pl. impf. ὤνοντο :—Ep. f. ὀνόσ-
σομαι: aor. 1 ὠνοσάμην, Ep. part. ὀνοσσάμενος: Ep. aor.
3 sing. ὤνατο; and pass. ὠνόσθην: Dep. :—to blame,
find fault with, throw a slur upon, treat scornfully,
τι Hom.; ἦ ὄνεσθ', ὅτι μοι Ζεὺς ἔδωκεν; do ye complain that Zeus has given? Il.; c. gen., οὐδ' σε ἔολπα
ὀνόσσεσθαι κακότητος I hope thou wilt not quarrel
with thy ill-luck (i. e. deem it too light), Od.; ὀν.
τινα to throw a slur upon, Hdt.

ὀνομαίνω, Ion. f. οὐνομανέω: aor. 1 ὠνόμηνα, Ep. ὀνόμηνα:—Ep. and Ion. for ὀνομάζω, to name or call by
name, and of things, to name, repeat, Hom.   2.
simply, to utter, speak, Od.: c. inf. fut. to promise to
do, Ib.   II. to nominate, appoint, Il.

ὀνομα-κλήδην, Adv. (καλέω) calling by name, by name,
Lat. nominatim, Od.

ὀνομα-κλήτωρ, ορος, ὁ, (καλέω) one who announces
guests by name, Lat. nomenclator, Luc.

ὀνομα-κλῠτός, όν, of famous name, Il.

ὀνομαστί, Adv. (ὀνομάζω) by name, Hdt., Thuc.

ὀνομαστός, Ion. οὐνομ-, ἡ, όν, (ὀνομάζω) named, to be
named, and οὐκ ὀνομαστός not to be named or mentioned, i. e. abominable, Lat. infandus, Od.   II.
of name or note, notable, famous, Theogn., Hdt., etc.

ὀνομᾱτο-λόγος, ον, (λέγω) telling people's names, Lat.
nomenclator, Plut.

ὀνομᾱτο-ποιέω, f. ήσω, to coin names, Arist.

ὀνόμηνα, Ep. for ὠν-, aor. 1 of ὀνομαίνω.

"ΟΝΟΣ, ὁ and ἡ, an ass, Il., Hdt., etc. :—proverb.,   1.
περὶ ὄνου σκιᾶς for an ass's shadow, i. e. for nothing
at all, Lat. de lana caprina, Ar., Plat.   2. ὄνου
πόκαι or πόκος, v. πόκος II.   3. ἀπ' ὄνου πεσεῖν,
of one who gets into a scrape by his own clumsiness,
with a pun on ἀπὸ νοῦ πεσεῖν, Ar.   4. ὄνος ἄγων
μυστήρια, of one heavily laden, Id.   5. ὄνου ὑβριστότερος, of brutality, Xen.   6. ὄνου ὦτα λαβεῖν, like
Midas, Ar.   II. ὄνων φάτνη a luminous appearance
between the ὄνοι (two stars in the breast of the Crab),
Lat. praesepe, Theocr.   III. from the ass as a
beast of burden,   1. a windlass, pulley, Hdt.   2.
the upper millstone, ὄνος ἀλέτης Xen. :—so, μύλος ὀνικός
N. T.   3. a beaker, wine-cup, Ar.

ὄνοσαι, Ep. 2 sing. of ὄνομαι.

ὀνοσσάμενος, Ep. aor. 1 part. of ὄνομαι:—ὀνόσσεσθαι,
Ep. fut. inf.

ὀνοστός, ή, όν, (ὄνομαι) to be blamed or scorned, Il.

ὀνοτάζω, = ὄνομαι, to blame, h. Hom., Hes.

ὀνοτός, ή, όν, = ὀνοστός, Pind.

ὀνο-φορβός, όν, (φέρβω) an ass-keeper, Hdt.

ὄντα, τά, pl. part. neut. of εἰμί (sum), existing things,
the present, opp. to the past and future; but also,
reality, truth, opp. to that which is not, Plat.   II.
that which one has, property, like οὐσία, Dem.

ὄντως, Adv. part. of εἰμί (sum), really, verily, Eur..
etc.; ὄντως τε καὶ ἀληθῶς really and truly, Plat.

ὄνῠμα, ὀνῠμάζω, Aeol. ὀνομαίνω, Aeol. and Dor. for ὄνομ-.

"ΟΝΥΞ, ὔχος, ὁ, Ep. dat. pl. ὀνύχεσσι :—Lat. unguis,
in Hom. only in pl. of the eagle's talons;—of human
beings, a nail, Hes., Hdt., Att. :—of horses and oxen,
a hoof, Xen.—Special phrases, ἐς ἄκρους τοὺς ὄνυχας
ἀφίκετο (sc. ὁ οἶνος) warmed me to my fingers' ends,
Eur.; ὄνυχας ἐπ' ἄκρους στάς on tiptoe, Lat. summis
digitis, Id.; ἐξ ἁπαλῶν ὀνύχων from childhood, Hor.
de tenero ungui, Anth.; ὀδοῦσι καὶ ὄνυξι, i. e. in every
possible way, Luc.   II. a veined gem, onyx, Id.

ὀνύχῐνος, η, ον, (ὄνυξ II) made of onyx, Plut.

ὀξ-άλμη, ἡ, (ὄξος) a sauce of vinegar and brine, Ar.

ὀξέα, fem. of ὀξύς: ὀξέσι, dat. pl.

ὀξέως, Adv. of ὀξύς.

ὀξηρός, ά, όν, (ὄξος) of or for vinegar, Anth.

ὀξίνης [ῐ], ου, ὁ, sharp, sour, tart, Ar.

ὀξίς, ίδος, ἡ, (ὄξος) a vinegar-cruet, Lat. acetabulum,
Ar.; applied to a diminutive person, Id.

ὄξος, εος, τό, (ὀξύς) poor wine, vin-de-pays, Ar.,
Xen.   2. vinegar made therefrom, Aesch., Ar.   3.
metaph. of a sour fellow, Theocr.

ὀξύα or ὀξύη, ἡ, a kind of beech: a spear-shaft made
from its wood, a spear, Eur.

ὀξύ-βᾰφον, τό, (βάπτω) a vinegar-saucer, then, generally, a shallow vessel, saucer, Ar.

ὀξῠ-βελής, ές, (βέλος) sharp-pointed, Il.

ὀξυ-βόας, ου, ὁ, (βοάω) shrill-screaming, Aesch.

ὀξύ-γᾰλα, ακτος, τό, sour milk, whey, Strab.

ὀξύ-γοος, ον, shrill-wailing, Aesch.

ὀξῠ-δερκής, ές, (δέρκομαι) quick-sighted, Hdt., Luc.

ὀξύ-δουπος, ον, sharp-sounding, Anth.

ὀξύ-θηκτος, ον, sharp-edged, sharp-pointed, Eur. II. of a person, goaded to passion, infuriated, Soph.

ὀξῠθῡμέω, f. ήσω, to be quick to anger, Eur. II. Pass. to be provoked, Ar.; and

ὀξῠθῡμία, ή, sudden anger, Eur. From

ὀξύ-θῡμος, ον, quick to anger, choleric, Eur., Ar., etc.: —sharp to punish, of the Areopagus, Aesch.: τὸ ὀξύθυμον, by crasis τοὐξύθυμον, = ὀξυθυμία.

ὀξῠ-κάρδιος, ον, (καρδία) = ὀξύθυμος, Aesch., Ar.

ὀξύ-κομος, ον, with pointed leaves, of a pine, Anth.

ὀξῠ-κώκῡτος, ον, (κωκύω) wailed with shrill cries, Soph.

ὀξῠ-λᾰβέω, f. ήσω, (λαμβάνω) to seize quickly : to seize an opportunity, Xen.

ὀξῠ-λάλος [ᾰ], ον, glib of tongue, Ar.

ὀξῠμάθεια, ή, quickness at learning, Strab. From

ὀξῠ-μᾰθής, ές, (μανθάνω) learning quickly, Ar.

ὀξῠ-μέριμνος, ον, (μέριμνα) keenly studied, Ar.

ὀξῠ-μήνῑτος, ον, (μηνίω) bringing down the quick anger (of the Erinyes), Aesch.

ὀξῠ-μολπος, ον, (μέλπω) clear-singing, Aesch.

ὀξυντήρ, ὁ, a sharpener, Anth. From

ὀξύνω [ῡ], f. ὀξυνῶ: aor. 1 ὤξυνα: pf. ὤξυγκα:—Pass., aor. 1 ὠξύνθην: pf. ὤξυμμαι and ὤξυσμαι: (ὀξύς):— to sharpen: metaph. to goad to anger, provoke, Soph.:—Pass., Hdt. 2. to sharpen, quicken, Anth.

ὀξυόεις, εσσα, εν, (ὀξύς) sharp-pointed, Il.

ὀξύ-πᾱγής, ές, (πήγνυμι) sharp-pointed, Anth.

ὀξύ-πεινος, ον, (πεῖνα) ravenously hungry, Cic.

ὀξῠ-πευκής, ές, (πεύκη) sharp-pointed, Aesch.

ὀξύ-πους, ὁ, ἡ, πουν, τό, swift-footed, Eur.

ὀξύ-πρωρος, ον, (πρῷρα) sharp-pointed, Aesch.

ὀξύ-πτερος, ον, (πτερόν) swift-winged :—τὰ ὀξύπτερα swift wings, Aesop.

ὀξῠ-ρεπής, ές, (ῥέπω) = ὀξύρροπος, Pind.

ὀξύρ-ροπος, ον, (ῥέπω) turning quickly, of a delicate balance : metaph., ὀξ. πρὸς τὰς ὀργάς sudden and quick to anger, Plat.; ὀξ. θυμός sudden anger, Id.

ΟΞΥ΄Σ, εῖα, ύ: Ion. fem. ὀξέα: ὀξεῖα, Ep. for neut. pl. ὀξέα: (akin to ὠκύς) :—sharp, keen, Hom., Hes., etc.; ἐς ὀξὺ ἀπηγμένος brought to a point, Hdt.; τὸ ὀξύ the vertex of a triangle, Id. II. of feeling, sharp, keen, ὀδύναι Il.; ὀξὺς ἠέλιος the piercing sun, h. Hom.; so, χιὼν ὀξεῖα, like Horace's gelu acutum, Pind.; μάχη ὀξέα keenly contested, Hdt. 2. of the sight, neut. as Adv., ὀξύτατον δέρκεσθαι to be keenest of sight, Il.; so, ὀξὺ νοεῖν to notice a thing sharply, Ib.; ὀξὺ ἀκούειν to be quick of hearing, Ib. b. of things that affect the sight, dazzling, bright, of the sun, Ib.; of colours, Ar. 3. of sound, sharp, shrill, piercing, Il.; and of the voice, ὀξὺ βοήσας, ὀξὺ λεληκώς Ib., etc. b. of musical tones, sharp, high, opp. to βαρύς, Plat. 4. of taste, sharp, pungent, acid, Xen., etc. 5. of smell, ὀξύτατον ὄζειν Ar. III. metaph. of mind, sharp,

keen : quick to anger, hasty, passionate, Il., Soph., etc. 2. sharp, quick, clever, Plat.; c. inf., ὀξ. ἐπινοῆσαι Thuc.; γνῶναι ὀξύτατοι Dem. IV. of motion, quick, swift, Ar.; [ἡ νόσος] ὀξεῖα φοιτᾷ καὶ ταχεῖ' ἀπέρχεται Soph.; ὀξὺς νότος Id. V. regul. Adv. ὀξέως, quickly, soon, Thuc., Plat.; but, 2. neut. ὀξύ and pl. ὀξέα as Adv., v. supr. :—Comp. ὀξύτερον Thuc., etc.; Sup. ὀξύτατον Il.; ὀξύτατα Plat.

ὀξύ-στομος, ον, (στόμα) sharp-toothed, sharp-fanged, Aesch.; of a gnat, Ar. :—of a sword, sharp-edged, Eur.

ὀξύτης, ητος, ἡ, (ὀξύς) sharpness, pointedness, Plat. II. of sound, sharpness, opp. to βαρύτης, Id. III. of the mind, sharpness, cleverness, Id. IV. of motion, quickness, Id., Dem.

ὀξῠ-τόμος, ον, (τέμνω) sharp-cutting, keen, Pind.

ὀξύτονος, ον, sharp-sounding, piercing, of sound, Soph. II. oxytone, having the acute accent, i. e. the accent on the last syllable.

ὀξῠ-τόρος, ον, piercing, pointed, πίτυς ὀξ. the pine with its sharp spines, Anth.

ὀξύ-φθογγος, ον, = ὀξύφωνος, Anth.

ὀξύ-φρων, ονος, ὁ, ἡ, (φρήν) = ὀξύθυμος, Eur.

ὀξῠφωνία, ἡ, sharpness of voice, Arist. From

ὀξύ-φωνος, ον, (φωνή) sharp-voiced, thrilling, Soph.

ὀξύ-χειρ, χειρος, ὁ, ἡ, quick with the hands, quick to strike, Theocr. 2. ὀξύχειρι σὺν κτύπῳ with quick beating of the hands in lamentation, Aesch.

ὀξύ-χολος, ον, quick to anger, Solon, Soph.

ὀξυ-ωπής, ές, (ὤψ) sharp-sighted, Arist., Luc.

ὄον, Ep. for οὗ, of whom, Hom.

ὀπᾱδέω, Dor. for Ion. ὀπηδέω: 3 sing. Ep. and impf. ὀπήδει :—to follow, accompany, attend, τινί Il., Pind. II. of things, ἀνεμώλια γάρ μοι ὀπηδεῖ [τόξα] useless do they go with me, Il.; ἀρετὴν σήν, ἥ σοι ὀπηδεῖ Od., etc. From

ὀπᾱδός, όν, Dor. and Att. for Ion. ὀπηδός, attendant, Soph., Eur.: metaph. ἀοιδὰ στεφάνων ὀπαδός Pind.; πυκνοστίκτων ὀπ. ἐλάφων pursuing them, of Artemis, Soph.; ἀστέρες νυκτὸς ὀπ. Theocr. II. as Adj. accompanying, attending, c. dat., h. Hom.

ὀπάζω, impf. ὤπαζον : Ep. f. ὀπάσσω: aor. 1 ὤπασα, Ep. also ὄπασσα :—Med., Ep. 2 sing. f. ὀπάσσεαι: aor. 1 ὠπασάμην, Ep. 3 sing. ὀπάσσατο :—Causal of ἕπομαι, to make to follow, send with one, give as a companion or follower, ἐπεί ῥά οἱ ὤπασα πομπόν Il.; πολὺν δέ μοι ὤπασε λαόν gave me many subjects, Ib. :—Med. to bid another follow one, take as a companion, Hom. II. of things, κῦδος ὀπάζει gives him glory to be with him, Il.; then, simply, to give, grant, Hom., Pind., Aesch. 2. to give besides, add, ἔργῳ δ' ἔργον ὄπαζε h. Hom.; ἔργον πρὸς ἀσπίδι ὤπασεν put a work of art on the shield, Aesch. III. like διώκω, to press hard, chase, Ἕκτωρ ὤπαζε Ἀχαιούς Il.; χαλεπὸν δέ σε γῆρας ὀπάζει Ib. :—Pass., χείμαρρους ὀπαζόμενος Διὸς ὄμβρῳ a torrent following, i. e. swollen with, rain, Ib.

ὀπαῖον, τό, (ὀπή) a hole in the roof, Plut.; cf. ἀνοπαῖα.

ὄ-πατρος, ον, (ὁμός, πατήρ) by the same father, Il.; so, ὁπάτωρ, ορος, ὁ, ἡ, Anth.

ὀπάων [ᾰ], ονος, ὁ, Ion. ὀπέων, ωνος: ὀπάζω :—a comrade in war, an esquire, such as was Meriones to Idomeneus, Phoenix to Peleus, Il. 2. generally, a

follower, attendant, Lat. famulus, Hdt., Aesch., etc.　　II. as Adj. following, Anth.

ὄπεᾰς, ᾰτος, τό, (ὀπή) an awl, Lat. subula, Hdt.

ὄπερ, Ep. for ὅσπερ.

ὀπέων, Ep. for ὀπάων.

ὈΠΉ, ἡ, an opening, hole, Ar.　　2. a hole in the roof, serving as a chimney, Id.

ὅπη, Ep. ὅππη, Dor. ὅπᾱ, Ion. ὅκη, Adv. (properly dat. from an old Pron. *ὅπός):　　I. of Place, by which way, Lat. qua; also = ὅπου, where, Lat. ubi, Hom.; sometimes much like ὅποι, whither, Lat. quo, Hom., Hdt., Aesch.　　2. c. gen., ὅπη γᾶς, Lat. ubi terrarum, where in the world, Eur.　　II. of Manner, in what way, how, Hom., Att.; ὅπη ἄν, with subjunct., like other Conjunctions, ὅπη ἄν δοκῇ ἀμφοτέροις Foed. ap. Thuc.:—ἔσθ᾽ ὅπη or ἔστιν ὅπη in any manner, in some way, Plat.

ὀπηδέω, ὀπηδός, Ion. for ὀπᾱδ-.

ὀπηνίκᾰ, Dor. ὀπᾱνίκα, Adv., correl. to πηνίκα, at what point of time, at what hour, on what day, Soph., etc.; ὀπ. ἄν at whatever hour or time, Id.　　2. in indirect questions, ἣν ὥραν προσήκει ἰέναι, καὶ ὀπ. ἀπιέναι Aeschin.; in answer to a direct question, πηνίκ᾽ ἐστὶ τῆς ἡμέρας;—ὀπηνίκα; what time of day is it?—what time, do you ask? Ar.: c. gen., ὀπ. τῆς ὥρας Xen.　　II. in a causal sense, supposing that, ὀπ. ἐφαίνετο ταῦτα πεποιηκώς Dem.

ὀπίας (sc. τυρός), ὁ, cheese from milk curdled with fig-juice (ὀπός), Ar. (with a pun on ὀπή); in full, τυρὸς ὀπίας Eur.

ὀπίζομαι, Dep., only in pres. and impf.: Ep. 2 sing. ὀπίζεο, 3 sing. ὠπίζετο: (ὄπις):—to regard with awe and dread, Lat. vereri, revereri, Hom.:—absol., ὀπιζόμενος a pious man, Pind.; χάρις ὀπιζομένα pious gratitude, Id.　　2. to care for, c. gen., Theogn.:—so in Act. σώματος ὀπίζων Anth.

ὀπῐθε and ὄπῐθεν, Ep. for ὄπισθε, ὄπισθεν.

ὀπῐθό-μβροτος, ον, poët. for ὀπισθό-μβροτος, following a mortal, ὀπιθ. αὔχημα glory that lives after men, Pind.

Ὀπῐκοί, οἱ, the Opici, an ancient people of Southern Italy, Arist.; also Ὄπικες, Thuc.:—Ὀπικία, ἡ, their country, Id.　　II. Ὀπῐκός, ἡ, όν, barbarous, Anth.

ὀπιπτεύω, f. σω, (redupl. from ὈΠ, Root of ὄπ-ωπα) to look around after, gaze curiously or anxiously at, c. acc., Hom.　　II. to lie in wait for, watch, οὐ λάθρη ἀνακτεύσας, ἀλλ᾽ ἀμφαδὸν Il.

ὄπῐς, ιδος, ἡ, acc. ὄπιν and ὄπιδα: poët. dat. ὀπῑ· (ὈΠ, Root of ὄψ):　　I. of the gods,　　1. in bad sense, ὄπις θεῶν the vengeance or visitation of the gods for transgressing divine laws, Hom., Hes.; without θεῶν, divine vengeance, Od.　　2. in good sense, the care or favour of the gods, Pind.　　II. of men, the regard which men pay to the gods, religious awe, veneration, reverence, οὐδὲ θεῶν ὄπιν ἔχοντας paying no regard to the gods, Hdt.; ὄπι ξένων in his reverence towards strangers, Pind.

ὄπισθεν, Ion. and poët. -θε before a conson.: poët. also ὄπῐθεν, -θε: (ὄπις): Adv.　　I. of Place, behind, at the back, Hom., etc.; οἱ ὄπιθεν those who are left behind, Od.; also, τοὺς ὄπισθεν ἐς τὸ πρόσθεν ἕξομεν shall bring the rear ranks to the front, Soph.;

τὰ ὄπ. the rear, back, Il., Xen.:—εἰς τοὔπισθεν back, backwards, Eur., etc.　　2. as Prep. with gen. behind, ὄπιθεν δίφροιο Il.; ὄπισθε τῆς θύρης Hdt., etc.　　II. of Time, in future, hereafter, Hom., etc.　　2. ἐν τοῖσι ὄπισθε λόγοισι in the following books, Hdt.　　Hence

ὀπίσθιος, α, ον, hinder, belonging to the hinder part, Lat. posticus, τὰ ὀπ. σκέλεα the hind-legs, Hdt.

ὀπισθο-βάμων [ᾱ], ον, walking backwards, Anth.

ὀπισθό-γραφος, ον, written on the back or cover, Luc.

ὀπισθο-δάκτῠλος, ον, with back-bent fingers, Strab.

ὀπισθό-δομος, ὁ, the back chamber or inner cell of the temple of Athena in the Acropolis at Athens, used as the Treasury, Ar., Dem.

ὀπισθο-νόμος, ον, (νέμω) grazing backwards, of certain cattle with large horns slanting forwards, Hdt.

ὀπισθο-νῠγής, ές, (νύσσω) pricking from behind, Anth.

ὀπισθό-πους, ὁ, ἡ, πουν, τό, walking behind, following, attendant, Eur.:—also ὀπίσθοπος (cf. Οἰδίπος), Aesch.

ὀπισθοφῠλᾰκέω, f. ἤσω, to guard the rear, form the rear-guard, Xen.　　II. to command the rear-guard, Id.

ὀπισθοφῠλᾰκία, ἡ, the command of the rear, Xen.

ὀπισθο-φύλαξ, ᾰκος, ὁ, ἡ, one who guards the rear: οἱ ὀπ. the rear-guard, Xen.

ὀπίσσω, Adv., Ep. for ὀπίσω.

ὀπίστατος, η, ον, (ὄπισθε) hindmost, Lat. postremus, Il.

ὀπίσω [ῐ], Ep. ὀπίσσω, Adv.: (ὄπις):　　I. of Place, backwards, opp. to πρόσω, Il.:—in Prose also τὸ ὀπίσω, contr. τοὐπίσω, Hdt., Att.　　2. back, back again, i.e. by the same way as one came, Od., Hdt.　　3. again, ἀνακτᾶσθαι ὀπ. Hdt., etc.　　4. c. gen., δεῦτε ὀπ. μου come after me, follow me, N.T.　　II. of Time, hereafter, since the future is unseen or behind us, whereas the past is known and before our eyes, Hom.; ἅμα πρόσσω καὶ ὀπ. λεύσσει Il.; οὔτ᾽ ἐνθάδ᾽ ὁρῶν οὔτ᾽ ὀπίσω neither present nor future, Soph.　　2. ἐν τοῖσι ὀπίσω λόγοις in the following books, Hdt.

ὀπλάριον [ᾰ], τό, Dim. of ὅπλον, Plut.

ὁπλέω, only in impf. to make ready, Od.

ὁπλή, ἡ, (ὅπλον) a hoof, the solid hoof of the horse and ass, Il., Att.:—after Hom., like χηλή, the cloven hoof of horned cattle, h. Hom., Hes., etc.

Ὅπλητες, οἱ, = ὁπλῖται, name of one of the four old tribes at Athens, Hdt., Eur.

ὁπλίζω, f. σω: aor. 1 ὥπλισα, Ep. ὥπλισσα:—Med., aor. 1 ὡπλισάμην, Ep. 3 sing. ὡπλίσσατο:—Pass., aor. 1 ὡπλίσθην, Ep. 3 pl. ὡπλίσθησαν: pf. ὥπλισμαι Eur.: (ὅπλον):—to make or get ready, of meats and drink, Hom., Eur.:—Med., δόρπον or δεῖπνον ὁπλίζεσθαι to prepare oneself a meal, Hom.; ὀπ. θυσίαν to cause a sacrifice to be prepared, Eur.　　2. of chariot-horses, to get ready, harness, Il.; Med. to get them ready for oneself, Ib.:—Pass., of ships, Od.; of any implements, ὡπλισμένη ready for use, Aesch.; ὡπλισμένος τινί furnished with a thing, Eur.　　3. of soldiers, to equip, arm, Hdt., etc.:—also, to train, exercise, Id.:—in Att. Prose, to arm or equip as ὁπλῖται, Thuc.:—Med. and Pass. to prepare or equip oneself, accoutre or arm oneself, get ready, Od.; ὥπλισθεν (for ὡπλίσθησαν) δὲ γυναῖκες the women got ready [for dancing], Ib., etc.;—c. inf. to

prepare oneself to do a thing, Il., Eur. :‑ in Med., also, c. acc., ὁπλίζεσθαι χέρα *to arm one's hand,* Eur.; ὁπλίζεσθαι θράσος *to arm oneself* with boldness, Soph. Hence

ὅπλισις, ἡ, *equipment, accoutrement, arming,* Ar., Thuc.

ὅπλισμα, ατος, τό, *an army, armament,* Eur. II. *a weapon,* Id.

ὁπλισμός, ὁ, = ὅπλισις, Aesch.

ὁπλιστέον, verb. Adj. of ὁπλίζω, *one must arm,* Xen.

ὁπλιστὴς κοσμός, ὁ, (ὁπλίζω) *a warrior*-dress, Anth.

ὁπλῑτ-ᾰγωγός, όν, *carrying the heavy-armed,* ναῦς ὁπλ. *troop*-ships, *transports,* Thuc.

ὁπλῑτεύω, f. σω, *to serve as a man-at-arms,* Thuc., Xen.; οἱ ὁπλιτεύοντες *men now serving,* opp. to οἱ ὠπλιτευκότες, Arist. From

ὁπλίτης [ῐ], ου, ὁ, (ὅπλον) *heavy-armed, armed,* δρόμος ὁπλ. *a race of men in armour,* opp. to the *naked* race, Pind.; ὁπλ. στρατός *an armed* host, Eur.; ὁπλ. κόσμος *warrior*-dress, *armour,* Id. II. *as Subst.* ὁπλίτης, ὁ, *a heavy-armed foot-soldier, man-at-arms,* who carried a large shield (ὅπλον), whence the name, as *the light-armed foot-soldier* (πελτάστης) had his from the light πέλτη, Hdt., Att.; ὁπλῖται are opp. to ψιλοί, Hdt., Thuc. Hence

ὁπλῑτικός, ή, όν, *of* or *for a man-at-arms,* Plat., Xen. 2. ἡ -κή (sc. τέχνη), *the art of using heavy arms, the soldier's art,* Plat.; τὰ ὁπλιτικὰ ἐπιτηδεύειν *to serve as a man-at-arms,* Id. II. *of persons, fit for service,* opp. to ἄνοπλος, Arist. :‑ τὸ ὁπλιτικόν *the soldiery,* = οἱ ὁπλῖται, Thuc., Xen.

ὁπλο-θήκη, ἡ, *an armoury,* Plut.

ὅπλομαι, poët. for ὁπλίζομαι, *to prepare,* Il.

ὁπλομᾰνέω, f. ήσω, *to be madly fond of war,* Anth.

ὁπλο-μᾰνής, ές, (μαίνομαι) *madly fond of war.*

ὁπλο-μᾰχέω, f. ήσω, ὁ, = ὁπλομάχος, Plat.

ὁπλομᾰχία, ἡ, *a fighting with heavy arms, the art of using them,* Plat. :‑ generally, *the art of war, tactics,* Xen. From

ὁπλο-μᾰχος [ᾰ], ον, (μάχομαι) *fighting in heavy arms,* Xen. II. ὁπλ., ὁ, *one who teaches the use of arms, a drill-sergeant,* Theophr.

ὍΠΛΟΝ, τό, *a tool, implement,* mostly in pl. : I. *a ship's tackle, tackling,* Od., Hes. : esp. *ropes,* Od., Hdt. :‑ in sing. *a rope,* Od. II. *tools,* of *smiths' tools,* Hom. :‑ in sing., ὅπλον ἀρούρης *a sickle,* Anth.; δείπνων ὅπλον, of a wine-flask, Id. III. in pl., also, *implements of war, arms,* Il., etc. :‑ rarely in sing., *a weapon,* Hdt., Eur. 2. in Att., ὅπλον was *the large shield,* from which the men-at-arms took their name of ὁπλῖται, Ar., Thuc., etc. :‑ then, in pl., *heavy arms,* Hdt., Att.; ὅπλων ἐπιστάτης = ὁπλίτης, Aesch.; whence, 3. ὅπλα, = ὁπλῖται, *men-at-arms,* Soph., Thuc., etc. 4. τὰ ὅπλα, also, *the place of arms, camp,* Hdt., Xen.; ἐκ τῶν ὅπλων προϊέναι Thuc. 5. *phrases,* ἐν ὅπλοισι εἶναι *to be in arms, under arms,* Hdt.; εἰς τὰ ὅπλα παραγγέλλειν Xen.; ἐφ' ὅπλοις or παρ' ὅπλοις ἧσθαι Eur.; μένειν ἐπὶ τοῖς ὅπλοις Xen.; ὅπλα τίθεσθαι, v. τίθημι A. I. 7.

ὁπλοποιΐα, ἡ, *a making of arms,* Il. 18, Strab.

ὁπλότερος, α, ον, Comp. without any Posit. in use, *the younger,* Hom.; ὁπλότερος γενεῇ *younger* by birth,

Lat. *minor natu,* Ib.; fem. gen. pl. ὁπλοτεράων Il. :‑ Sup. ὁπλότατος, η, ον, *youngest,* Hom., Hes.—The orig. sense was perhaps (from ὅπλον), *those capable of bearing arms,* opp. to the old men and children, Il. :‑ but it soon came to mean simply *younger* or *youngest;* then, as *the youngest* are *the last born,* ἄνδρες ὁπλότεροι also means *the latter generations, men of later days,* Theocr.

ὁπλοφορέω, *to bear arms, be armed,* Xen. II. Pass. *to have a body-guard,* Plut. From

ὁπλο-φόρος, ον, (φέρω) *bearing arms : a warrior, soldier,* Eur., Xen. II. = δορυφόρος, Xen.

ὁποδᾰπός, ή, όν, correlative to ποδαπός in indirect questions, *of what country, what countryman,* Lat. *cujas,* Hdt.; τίς καὶ ὁπόδαπος Plat.

ὁπόθεν, Ep. ὁππόθεν, Ion. ὁκόθεν, Adv., correlative to πόθεν : 1. chiefly in indirect questions, *whence, from what place,* Lat. *unde,* εἴρεαι ὁππόθεν εἰμέν thou askest *whence we are,* Od. 2. relat., γαμεῖν ὁπόθεν ἂν βούληται *to marry a wife from whatever family* he likes, Plat. :‑ also ὁποθενοῦν, Id.

ὁπόθῐ, Ep. ὁππόθῐ, Adv., correlative to πόθι, *where,* Il. 2. in indirect questions, εἰπέμεν ὁππόθ' ὅλωλεν Od.

ὅποι, Ion. ὅκοι, Adv. correlat. to ποῖ : 1. *to which place, whither,* Lat. *quo,* Soph., etc.; ὅποι ἄν, with subjunct., *whithersoever,* Plat. :‑ in pregnant sense with Verbs of rest, διδάξαι μ' ὅποι καθέσταμεν (i. e. ὅποι ἐλθόντες καθέσταμεν) Soph. 2. c. gen., ὅποι γῆς *whither in the world,* Lat. *quo terrarum,* Aesch., Ar. 3. in indirect questions, *to what place, whither,* ἀμηχανεῖν ὅποι τράποιντο Aesch.

ὁποῖος, α, ον, Ep. ὁπποῖος, η, ον, Ion. ὁκοῖος, η, ον :‑ correlat. to ποῖος : 1. as relat., *of what sort* or *quality,* Lat. *qualis,* ὁπποῖόν κ' εἴπῃσθα ἔπος, τοῖόν κ' ἐπακούσαις *as* is the word thou hast spoken, such shalt thou hear again, Il.; οὔθ' οἷ' ἔπασχεν οὔθ' ὁποῖ' ἔδρα κακά Soph. 2. in indirect questions, Od., etc. II. with indefinite words added, ὁποῖός τις Hdt., Att.; ὁπποῖ' ἄσσα *of what sort* was it, for ὁποῖά τινα, Od. ;‑ ὁποιοσοῦν *of what kind soever,* Lat. *qualiscunque,* ὁποῖος δή, δήποτε, δηποτοῦν, and οὖν δή, Att. III. neut. pl. used as Adv. *like as,* Lat. *qualiter,* Soph., Eur.

ὈΠΌΣ, ὁ, Lat. *sapor, sap* : esp. *the juice of the fig-tree,* used as rennet (τάμισος) for curdling milk, Il.

ὀπός, gen. of ὄψ.

ὁποσάκῐς [ᾰ], Adv. *as many times as,* Lat. *quoties,* Xen.

ὁποσά-πους, ὁ, ἡ, πουν, τό, *how many feet long,* Luc.

ὁποσᾰχῆ, (ὁπόσος) Adv. *at as many places as,* Xen.

ὁπόσε, Ep. ὁππόσε, poët. for ὅποι, Od.

ὁπόσος, η, ον, Ep. ὁππόσος, ὁπόσσος, Ion. ὁκόσος :‑ correlat. to πόσος, 1. like ὅσος, of Number, *as many as,* Lat. *quot, quotquot,* Hom., etc.; ὁπόσαι ψάμαθοι κλονέονται, καθορᾷς Pind.; πᾶσι θεοῖς, ὁπόσοι τὴν Διὸς αὐλήν εἰσοιχνεῦσιν Aesch.; τοσαῦτα, ὁπόσα σοι φίλον Plat.; ὁπόσους πλείστους ἐδυνάμην Xen. :‑ in Prose ὁπόσος ἄν with subj., ὁπόσοις ἄν δοκῇ Thuc. 2. of Quantity, *as much as,* of Size or Space, *as great as,* Lat. *quantus,* ὁπόσον ἔπεσχε *as far as* it spread, Il. 3. with indefin. Particles added, ὁποσοσοῦν, *how great* or *much soever,* Lat. *quantuscunque,* Thuc.; Ion. dat. pl. fem. ὁκοσῃσιῶν,

Hdt. ;—so, ὁποσῳδήποτε Dem.   II. in indirect questions, ἠρώτων τὸ στράτευμα, ὁπόσον εἴη Xen.

ὁπόστος, η, ον, *in what relation of number*, Lat. *quotus*, ὅποστος εἰλήχει *what number* he had drawn, Plat. :—ὁποστοσοῦν, Lat. *quotuscunque*, Dem.

ὁποτάν, i. e. ὁπότ' ἄν, Ep. ὁππότε κεν, Adv., related to ὅταν, as ὁπότε to ὅτε, *whensoever*, Lat. *quandocunque*, with Subj., Hom., etc. :—ὁπότ' ἂν τὸ πρῶτον, Lat. *quum primum*, h. Hom.

ὁπότε, Ep. ὁππότε, Ion. ὁκότε, Dor. ὁππόκᾰ :—Adv. of Time, correlat. to πότε, much like ὅτε :   I. with the indic., *when*, Lat. *quando*, Hom. :—εἰς ὁπότε, with fut., *when, by what time*, λέγειν εἰς ὁπότ' ἔσται Aeschin. 2. with the optat. in reference to the past, *whenever*, to express an event that has often occurred, ὁπότε Κρήτηθεν ἵκοιτο Il., etc. :—also in oratio obliqua, Soph., etc.   II. in indirect phrases, ἴδμεν, ὁππότε Τηλέμαχος νεῖται when he *is to return*, Od. ; with optat., δέγμενος ὁππότε ναυσὶν ἐφορμηθεῖεν Il.

B. in causal sense, *for that, because, since*, like Lat. *quando* for *quoniam*, Theogn., Hdt., etc. : so ὁπότε γε, Lat. *quandoquidem*, Soph., Xen.

ὁπότερος, α, ον, Ep. ὁππότερος, η, ον, Ion. ὁκότερος, correlat. to πότερος : 1. as relat. *which of two, whether of the twain*, Lat. *uter*, Il., etc. :—properly in sing., but in pl. when there are several on either side, e. g. of two armies, Ib., etc. :—also, ὁποτεροσοῦν Plat. 2. in indirect questions, Ζεὺς οἶδ' ὁπποτέρῳ θανάτοιο τέλος πεπρωμένον ἐστίν Il. ; ἀσαφῶς ὁποτέρων ἀρξάντων, for ἀσαφὲς ὂν ὁπότεροι ἂν ἄρξωσιν, Thuc. 3. *either of two*, Lat. *alteruter*, Plat., etc.   II. Adv. ὁποτέρως, *in which of two ways*, as relat., Thuc., etc. 2. also neut. ὁπότερον or -ερα as Adv., in indirect questions, Lat. *utrum*, Hdt., Ar., etc.

ὁποτέρωθε, -θεν, Ep. ὁππποτ-, Adv. *from which of the two, from whether of the twain*, Il.

ὁποτέρωθι, Adv. *on whether of the two sides*, Xen.

ὁποτέρωσε, Adv. *to whichever of two sides*, Thuc. 2. *in which of two ways*, ὁπ. βουληθείη Plat.

ὅπου, Ion. ὅκου, relat. Adv. of Place, properly gen. of an obsol. Pron. ὅπος, correlat. to ποῦ :   I. as a relat., Hdt., Att. ;—sometimes with gen. loci, ὅπου γῆς, Lat. *ubi terrarum*, Plat. :—ἔσθ' ὅπου *in some places*, Lat. *est ubi*, Aesch., Dem. :—with other Particles, ὅκου δή *somewhere or other*, Lat. *nescio ubi*, Hdt. :—ὅπου ἄν or ὅπουπερ ἄν, *wherever*, with Subjunct., Trag. :—ὁπουοῦν, Lat. *ubicunque*, Plat. 2. in indirect questions, ὄφρα πύθηαι πατρός, ὅπου κύθε γαῖα Od., etc. :—with Verbs of motion in pregnant sense, just as, reversely, ὅποι is used with Verbs of rest, κεῖνος δ' ὅπου βέβηκεν, οὐδεὶς οἶδε Soph. :—in repeating a question, ὴ Λακεδαίμων ποῦ 'στιν ; Answ. ὅκου δή you ask) *where* it is? Ar.   II. of Time or Occasion, like Lat. *ubi*, σιγᾶν ὅπου δεῖ Aesch., etc. 2. of Manner, οὐκ ἔσθ' ὅπου *there are no means by which*, it is impossible *that*, Soph., Eur. 3. of Cause, *whereas*, Lat. *quando, quoniam*, Hdt., Att. ;—ὅπουγε, Lat. *quandoquidem* Xen.

ὁππᾶ, Adv., poët. for ὅπα, ὅπη.

ὁππάτεσσι, Aeol. for ὄμμασι, Sappho.

ὅππη, Adv., Ep. for ὅπη.

ὅππόθεν, ὁππόθῐ, Ep. for ὁπόθεν, ὁπόθι.

ὁπποῖος, ὁππόσε, ὁππόσος, Ep. for ὁποῖος, etc.

ὁππόκα, Dor. for ὁπότε.

ὁππόταν, ὁππότε, Ep. for ὁπότ' ἄν, ὁπότε.

ὁππότερος, ὁπποτέρωθεν, Ep. for ὁποτ-.

ὅππως, Ep. for ὅπως.

ὀπτάζομαι or ὀπτάνομαι, (ὄψ) Pass. *to be seen*, N. T.

ὀπτᾰλέος, α, ον, (ὀπτάω) *roasted, broiled*, Hom.

ὀπτάνιον, τό, (ὀπτάω) *a place for roasting, a kitchen*, Ar.

ὀπτασία, ἡ. = ὄψις, *a vision*, N. T.

ὀπτάω, Ion. -έω, f. ήσω : aor. 1 ὤπτησα :—a part. pass. ὀπτεύμενος in Theocr. : (ὀπτός) :—*to roast, broil*, Hom., etc. ; c. gen. partit., ὀπτῆσαί τε κρεῶν *to roast some meat*, Od. :—ὀπτᾶν was used of *cooking by means of fire or dry heat*, opp. to ἕψω *to boil in water*, which never appears in Hom. ; and a Com. poet remarks that Homer's heroes ate only roast meat :—Pass., aor. 1 inf. ὀπτηθῆναι Od. 2. *to bake* bread, Hdt., Xen., Ar.:—also of bricks or pottery, *to bake, burn*, Hdt. 3. *to bake, harden*, of the sun, Bion. 4. metaph. in Pass. *to be burned* by love, Theocr., Anth.

ὀπτεύω, = ὁράω, *to see*, Ar.

ὀπτήρ, ῆρος, ὁ, (ὄψ) *one who looks* or *spies*, *a spy, scout*, Lat. *speculator*, Od., Soph.   II. in Prose, *an eyewitness*, Xen.

ὀπτήρια (sc. δῶρα), τά, (ὄψ) *presents made by the bridegroom on seeing the bride without the veil* : generally, *presents for seeing*, Eur.

ὀπτίλος [ῐ], ὁ, Dor. for ὀφθαλμός, Plut.

ὀπτίων, ονος, ὁ, Lat. *optio, an adjutant*, Plut.

ὈΠΤΌΣ, ή, όν, *roasted, broiled*, Od. ; ἑφθὰ καὶ ὀπτά *boiled meats and roast*, Eur. 2. *baked*, Hdt. 3. *of iron, forged, tempered*, Soph.

ὀπύίω or ὀπύω, f. ὀπύσω : 1. Act. of the man, *to marry, wed, take to wife*, Hom., Hes., etc. 2. Pass. of the woman, *to be married*, Il.

ὄπωπα, pf. 2 of ὁράω.

ὀπωπή, ἡ, (ὤπωπα) poët. for ὄψις, *a sight* or *view*, Od.   II. *sight, power of seeing*, Ib.

ὀπώπη, Dor. 3 sing. of ὄπωπα.

ὀπωπητήρ, ῆρος, ὁ, = ὀπτήρ, h. Hom.

ὈΠΏΡΑ, Ion. -ρη, ἡ, *the part of the year between the rising of Sirius and of Arcturus* (i. e. the end of July, all Aug., and part of Sept.), *the end of summer*, Od. : —later it was used for *autumn*, though φθινόπωρον or μετόπωρον were the proper terms for autumn, Ar., Xen.   II. since it was the *fruit-time*, it came to mean *the fruit itself*, Soph., Plat.   III. metaph. *summer-bloom*, i. e. *the bloom of youth*, Pind.

ὀπωρίζω, f. ιῶ, (Ion. part. pl. ὀπωριεῦντες) : (ὀπώρα II) :—*to gather fruits*, Plat.   II. *to gather fruit off* trees, c. acc., Hdt.

ὀπωρινός, ή, όν, (ὀπώρα) *at the time of late summer*, ἀστὴρ ὀπ., i. e. Sirius (cf. ὀπώρα 1), Hom. [ῐ Att., ῑ in Hom. before another long syll.]

ὀπωροφορέω, *to bear fruit*, Anth.   From

ὀπωρο-φόρος, ον, (φέρω) *bearing fruit*, Anth.

ὀπωρ-ώνης, ου, ὁ, (ὠνέομαι) *a fruiterer*, Dem.

ὅπως, Ep. and Aeol. ὅππως, Ion. ὅκως : (compd. of the relat. ὅ or ὅς, and the Adv. πῶς) :   A. Conj. ον MANNER, *as, in such manner as*, and with interrog.

force *how, in what manner*, Lat. *ut, quomodo.* **B.** FINAL CONJ., like ἵνα, *that, in order that.*

A. CONJ. OF MANNER, *how, as :* **I.** Relative to ὥς or οὕτως, *in such manner as, as,* Lat. *ut, sicut,* ἔρξον ὅπως ἐθέλεις Hom.; with fut. Indic., esp. after Verbs of seeing, providing, taking care that, *in what manner, how,* ἔπρασσον ὅπως τις βοηθεία ἥξει Thuc. **2.** with ἄν (Ep. κε) and Subj. in indefinite sentences, *just as, however,* ὅππως κεν ἐθέλησιν Il.; οὕτως ὅπως ἂν αὐτοὶ βούλωνται Xen. **3.** with opt. after historical tenses, οὕτως ὅπως βούλοιντο Id. **4.** οὐκ ἔστιν ὅπως there is no way *in which,* it cannot be *that,* οὐκ ἔσθ' ὅπως σιγήσομαι Ar.; so, οὐκ ἔστιν ὅπως οὐ, *fieri non potest quin,* οὐκ ἔσθ' ὅπως οὐ ναυτιᾷς Id. : —so in questions, ἔσθ' ὅπως ἔλθωμεν can we possibly come ? Id. **5.** like ὡς in comparisons, *as, like as,* κῦμ' ὅπως Aesch., etc. **6.** also like ὡς or ὅτι, Lat. *quam,* with Sup. of Advs., ὅπως ἄριστα Id.; ὅπως ἀνωτάτω as high up *as* possible, Ar. **7.** with a gen. added, σοῦσθε ὅπως ποδῶν (sc. ἔχετε) run *as you are off for feet,* i. e. as quick as you can, Aesch. **8.** sometimes of Time, *when,* ὅπως ἴδον αἷμ' Ὀδυσῆος Il., etc.; with opt., *whenever,* ὅπως μὲν εἴη καρπὸς ἀδρός Hdt.; with Sup. of Advs., ὅπως τάχιστα Aesch. **9.** οὐχ ὅπως . . , ἀλλὰ . . , *not only not . . but . .* (where there is an ellipsis of λέγω or ἐρῶ), οὐχ ὅπως κωλυταὶ γενήσεσθε, ἀλλὰ καὶ . . δύναμιν προσλαβεῖν περιόψεσθε, *not only* will you *not* become hinderers, *but* you will *also* . . , Thuc., etc. :—so sometimes μὴ ὅπως (where an imperat. must be supplied), μὴ ὅπως ὀρχεῖσθαι ἀλλ' οὐδὲ ὀρθοῦσθαι ἐδύνασθε do not [think] *that* you can dance, but not even could you stand upright (i. e. *so far from being able* to dance), Xen. **II.** in indirect questions, *how, in what way* or *manner,* οὐδὲ ἴδμεν ὅπως ἔσται τάδε ἔργα Il., etc. :—also λεύσσει ὅπως τι γένηται Ib. **2.** with Opt., after tenses of past time, μερμήριξεν ὅπως ἀπολοίατο νῆες Od. **3.** ὅπως ἄν (κεν) with the Subj. makes the manner indefinite, πείρα ὅπως κεν δὴ σὴν πατρίδα γαῖαν ἵκηαι try *how* or *that in some way or other,* Ib.; after Verbs of fear and caution, ὅπως and ὅπως μή are used with Fut. Indic. or Aor. Subj., δέδοιχ' ὅπως μὴ τευξόμαι Ar.; ὅπως λάθω δέδοικα Eur. :—this construction is most freq. in an imperative sense, ἄθρει, ὅπως μὴ ἐκδύσεται Ar. :—hence ὅπως or ὅπως μή are used with fut. or Subj. just like the imperat., ὅπως παρέσει μοι : = πάρισθι, be present, Id.; ὅπως μὴ ᾖ τοῦτο Plat. **4.** ὅπως is used as the echo to a preceding πῶς ; in dialogue : *A.* καὶ πῶς ; *B.* ὅπως ; [d'ye ask] *how* ? Ar. ; *A.* πῶς με χρὴ καλεῖν ; *B.* ὅπως ; Id. **B.** as FINAL CONJ. *that, in order that,* Lat. *quo* = *ut,* with Subj. after principal tenses, τὸν δὲ μνηστῆρες λοχῶσιν, ὅπως ὄληται Od. **2.** with Opt. after historical tenses, πὰρ δέ οἱ ἔστη, ὅπως κῆρας ἀλάλκοι Il. **3.** with Indic. of historical tenses, of consequence which has not followed or cannot follow, τί οὐκ ἔρριψ' ἐμαυτὸν τῆσδ' ἀπὸ πέτρας, ὅπως ἀπηλλάγην Aesch. ὅπως δή, *how possibly,* Il. **II.** = ὁπωσοῦν, Plat. : —so, ὅπως δήποτε Dem. ὁπωσοῦν or ὅπως οὖν, *in any way whatever, in some way or other,* Lat. *utcunque,* Thuc., etc. ;—so ὁπωστιοῦν Plat.

ὅπως περ, = ὥσπερ, Hdt., Soph.
ὅπως ποτέ, *how ever,* Dem.
ὁρᾷ, 3 sing. pres. of ὁράω :—but ὅρα, Ep. 3 sing. impf.
ὁράᾳς, Ep. 2 sing. of ὁράω.
ὅραμα, τό, *that which is seen, a sight, spectacle,* Xen.
ὁρανός, Aeol. for οὐρανός.
ὅρασις, εως, ἡ, *seeing, the act of sight,* Lat. *visus,* Arist. **II.** *a vision,* N. T. ; and
ὁρᾱτός, ή, όν, *to be seen, visible,* Plat., etc. From
ΌΡΆΩ, Ep. ὁρόω, ὁράας, Ion. ὁρέω : — Att. impf. ἑώρων, Ion. ὥρεον, Ep. 3 sing. ὅρα ;—pf. ἑόρᾱκα and ἑώρᾱκα : —Med., Ep. 2 sing. ὅρηαι, inf. ὁράασθαι : impf. ἑωρώμην, also ὡρώμην (προ-), Ep. 3 sing. ὁρᾶτο :—Pass., pf. ἑόραμαι and ἑώραμαι. Besides the forms from Root ΟΡ, we have **II.** from ΟΠ (v. ὄψ) f. ὄψομαι, Ep. 2 sing. ὄψεαι : aor. 1 ὠψάμην, 2 pl. subj. ὄψησθε : pf. ὄπωπα : 3 sing. plqpf. ὀπώπει, Ion. ὀπώπεε, 3 pl. ὀπώπεσαν :—Pass., aor. 1 ὤφθην, Ion. 3 pl. subj. ὀφθέωσι : f. ὀφθήσομαι :—pf. ὦμμαι, ὦψαι, ὦπται ;— and **III.** from Root ΙΔ, aor. 2 act. εἶδον, pf. οἶδα, for which tenses, v. *εἴδω.

To see : **I.** absol. *to see* or *look,* Hom., etc. ; κατ' αὐτοὺς αἰὲν ὅρα he kept *looking* down at them, Il.; ὁρόων ἐπὶ οἴνοπα πόντον *looking* over the sea, Ib. : — ὁρᾶν πρός τι, like Lat. *spectare ad, to look towards,* ἀκρωτήριον τὸ πρὸς Μέγαρα ὁρῶν Thuc. **2.** *to have sight,* Soph. : hence says Oedipus, ὅσ' ἂν λέγωμεν, πάνθ' ὁρῶντα λέξομεν [though I am blind], my words *shall have eyes,* i. e. shall be to the purpose, Id.; ἀμβλύτερον ὁρᾶν *to be* dim-sighted, Plat. **3.** *to see to, look to,* i. e. *take heed, beware,* ὅρα ὅπως . . , Ar.; ὅρα εἰ . . , *see* whether . . , Aesch., etc. **4.** ὁρᾷς ; ὁρᾶτε ; *see'st thou ? d'ye see ?* parenthetically, esp. in explanations, like Lat. *viden'?* Ar. **5.** c. acc. cogn. *to look* so and so, δεινὸν ὁρᾶν ὕσσοισι Hes.; ἔαρ ὁρόωσα Theocr. **II.** trans. *to see* an object, *look at, behold, perceive, observe,* c. acc., Hom., etc. ; αἰεὶ τέρμ' ὁρόων always *keeping* it *in sight,* Il. **2.** poët. for ζάω, ζώει καὶ ὁρᾷ φάος Ἡελίοιο Hom.; so, φῶς ὁρᾶν Soph.; and in Med., φέγγος ὁρᾶσθαι Eur. **III.** *to look out for, provide,* τί τινι Soph., Theocr. **2.** the inf. is used after an Adj., δεινὸς ἰδεῖν terrible *to behold,* Solon; ἔχθιστος ὁρᾶν Soph., etc. **IV.** the Med. is used by Poets just like the Act., Il., Aesch., etc. **V.** Pass. *to be seen,* Aesch., etc. : also like φαίνομαι *to let oneself be seen, appear,* Plat. : τὰ ὁρώμενα all *that is seen, things visible,* Id. **VI.** metaph., ὁρᾶν is used of mental sight, *to discern, perceive,* Soph., etc. ; so blind Oedipus says, φωνῇ γὰρ ὁρῶ, τὸ φατιζόμενον *I see* by sound, as the saying is, Id.

ὀργάζω, f. σω: aor. 1 ὤργᾰσα :—Pass., pf. ὤργασμαι : (ὀργάω) :—*to soften, knead, temper,* Lat. *subigere,* Ar. :—Pass., ὠργασμένος well *kneaded,* Plat.
ὀργαίνω, f. ᾰνῶ : aor. 1 ὤργᾱνα : (ὀργή) :—*to make angry, enrage,* Soph. **II.** intr. *to grow* or *be angry,* Id., Eur.
ὀργανικός, ή, όν, *serving as instruments* or *engines,* Plut. Adv. -κῶς, *by way of instruments,* Arist.
ὄργανον, τό, (*ἔργω) *an organ, instrument, tool, for making* or *doing* a thing, Soph., Eur., etc. :—of a person, ἁπάντων ἀεὶ κακῶν ὄργ. Soph. **2.** *an organ*

of sense, Plat. 3. *a musical instrument*, Id. 4. *a surgical instrument*, Xen. II. *a work, product*, λαίνεα 'Αμφίονος ὄργανα the stony *works* of Amphion, i. e. walls of Thebes, Eur.

ὄργανος, η, ον, (*ἔργω*) *working*, ὀργάνη χείρ Eur.

ὀργάς (sc. γῆ), άδος, ἡ, *any well-watered, fertile spot, meadow-land*, Eur., Xen.

ὀργάω, only in pres., (ὀργή) *to swell with moisture*: of fruit, *to swell and ripen*, Hdt.; of corn, ὀργᾷ ἀμᾶσθαι is *ripe* for cutting, Id. II. of persons, *to wax wanton*: then, generally, *to be eager* or *ready*, *to be excited*, Thuc.; ὀργῶν κρίνειν to judge *under the influence of passion*, Id. :—c. inf., ὄργα μαθεῖν be *eager* to learn, Aesch. III. trans., like ὀργάζω, *to soften, tan leather*, Hdt.

ὀργέων, ῶνος, ὁ, (perh. from ὄργια) at Athens, a *citizen* from every δῆμος, who had to perform certain sacrifices: then, generally, *a priest*, Aesch. :—an Ep. acc. pl. ὀργειόνας in h. Hom.

'ΟΡΓΗ', ἡ, *natural impulse* or *propension*: one's *temper, temperament, disposition, nature*, Hes., Theogn., etc.; ἀλωπέκων ὀργαῖς ἴκελοι Pind.; ὀργαὶ ἀστυνόμοι social *dispositions*, Soph.; πρὸς τὰ παρόντα τὰς ὀργὰς ὁμοιοῦν Thuc., etc. II. *passion, anger, wrath*, Hdt., Soph., etc.; ὀργῇ χάριν δοῦναι Soph.; ὀργῇ εἴκειν Eur.; δι' ὀργῆς ἔχειν τινά Thuc.; ἐν ὀργῇ ἔχειν or ποιεῖσθαί τινα Id., etc. 2. Adverbial usages, ὀργῇ, *in anger*, Hdt., etc.; so, δι' ὀργῆς, ἐξ ὀργῆς, κατ' ὀργήν Soph.; μετ' ὀργῆς Plat. 3. Πανὸς ὀργαί panic *fears* (i. e. terrors sent by Pan), Eur. :—but, ὀργή τινος *anger against* a person or *at* a thing, Soph.; ἱερῶν ὀργάς *wrath at* or *because of* the rites, Aesch.

ὄργια, ίων, τά, *orgies*, i. e. *secret rites, secret worship*, practised by the initiated alone, of the secret worship of Demeter at Eleusis, h. Hom., Ar.;—but, most commonly, of the *rites of Bacchus*, Hdt., Eur. II. *any worship, rites, sacrifices*, Aesch., Soph. (Prob. from *ἔργω = ἔρδω, ῥέζω*, in the sense of *performing* sacred rites, *sacra facere*.)

ὀργιάζω, f. άσω, *to celebrate orgies*, Eur. : c. acc. cogn., ὀργ. τελετήν, ὄργια Plat. II. *to honour* or *worship with orgies*, Strab. Hence

ὀργιασμός, ὁ, *celebration of orgies*, Strab.; and

ὀργιαστικός, ή, όν, *fit for orgies, exciting*, Arist.

ὀργίζω, aor. ὤργισα, (ὀργή II) *to make angry, provoke to anger, irritate*, Ar., Plat. II. more common in Pass., with fut. med. and pass. ὀργοῦμαι, ὀργισθήσομαι : aor. ὠργίσθην : pf. ὤργισμαι :—*to grow angry, be wroth*, Soph., etc.; τινι *with* a person or thing, Eur., Thuc., etc.; τὸ ὀργιζόμενον τῆς γνώμης their *angry feelings*, Thuc.

ὀργίλος [ῐ], η, ον, (ὀργή II) *prone to anger, irascible*, Xen., Dem. Adv., ὀργίλως ἔχειν to be *angry*, Dem.

ὀργιλότης, ητος, ἡ, *irascibility*, Arist.

ὄργιον, τό, v. ὄργια, τά.

ὀργιο-φάντης, ου, ὁ, (φαίνω) *a priest, one who initiates others into orgies*, Anth.

ὀργιστέον, verb. Adj., *one must be angry*, Dem.

ὀργυιᾰ or **ὀργυιά**, Ion. -ή, ῆς, ἡ, (ὀρέγω, cf. ἀγυιά) :—*the length of the outstretched arms*, about 6 *feet*, or 1 *fathom*, Hom., Hdt. (who says that 100 ὀργυιαί make one stadium). Hence

ὀργυιαῖος, α, ον, *six feet long* or *large*, Anth.

ὄρεγμα, ατος, τό, (ὀρέγω) *an outstretching*, Aesch. 2. *a holding out, offering*, Eur.

ὀρέγνυμι, = ὀρέγω, only in part., χεῖρας ὀρεγνύς Il.: Med., χεῖρας ὀρεγνύμενος Anth.

'ΟΡΕ'ΓΩ, impf. ὤρεγον : f. ὀρέξω : aor. 1 ὤρεξα :—Med. and Pass. f. ὀρέξομαι : aor. 1 ὠρεξάμην and ὠρέχθην : pf. ὤρεγμαι, redupl. 3 pl. ὀρωρέχαται, plqpf. -έχατο :—*to reach, stretch, stretch out*, Lat. *porrigo*, χεῖρ' ὀρέγων Od.; esp. in entreaty, Ib. 2. *to reach out, hold out, hand, give*, Hom., Hes., etc. II. Med. and Pass., 1. absol. *to stretch oneself out, stretch forth one's hand*, Hom.; ὀρέξασθαι ἀπὸ δίφρου *to reach* or *lean over* the chariot, Hes.; ὀρέξατ' ἰών let him *lunge* with the spear (from the chariot, instead of dismounting), Il.; ποσσὶν ὀρωρέχαται πολεμίζειν, of horses, *they stretched themselves, galloped*, to the fight, Ib.; ὀρέξατ' ἰών he *stretched himself* as he went, i. e. went *at full stride*, Ib.; ὀρωρέχατο προτὶ δειρήν *stretched themselves* with the neck (like Virgil's *irasci in cornua, in clipeum assurgere*), Ib.:—of fish, *to rise at the bait*, Theocr. 2. c. gen. *to reach at* or *to* a thing, *grasp at*, οὗ παιδὸς ὀρέξατο he *reached out to* his child, Il.; also in a hostile sense, τοῦ Θρασυμήδης ἔφθη ὀρεξάμενος ὦμον hit him first on the shoulder, Ib.; so, ἔφθη ὀρεξάμενος σκέλος (sc. αὐτοῦ) Ib. b. metaph. *to reach after, grasp at, yearn for* a thing, c. gen., Eur., Thuc., etc. :—c. inf., πόλιν ὠρέξατ' οἰκεῖν Eur. 3. c. acc. *to help oneself to*, σῖτον Ib.

ὀρει-άρχης, ου, ὁ, *mountain-king*, i. e. *Pan*, Anth.

ὀρειάς, άδος, ἡ, (ὄρος) *of* or *belonging to mountains*, πέτρα ὀρ. a *mountain crag*, Anth. II. as Subst. an *Oread, mountain-nymph*, Bion.

ὀρειβασία, ἡ, *a mountaineer's life*, Strab. II.

ὀρειβάσια (sc. ἱερά), τά, (βαίνω) *a festival in which persons traversed the mountains*, Id.; and

ὀρειβατέω, *to roam the mountains*, Anth., Plut. From

ὀρει-βάτης [ᾰ], ου, ὁ, *mountain-ranging*, Soph., Eur.

ὀρειδρομία, ἡ, *a running on the hills*, Anth. From

ὀρει-δρόμος, ον, (δραμεῖν) *running on the hills*, Eur.

ὀρει-νόμος, ον, (νέμω B) *mountain-ranging*, Eur.

ὀρεινός, ή, όν, (ὄρος) *mountainous, hilly*, Hdt., Xen. II. *dwelling on the mountains*, Thuc., Xen.

ὀρειο-νόμος, ον, = ὀρεινόμος, Anth.

ὄρειος, α, ον, and ος, ον, Ion. and Ep. οὔρειος, *of* or *from the mountains, mountain-haunting*, h. Hom., Trag.

ὀρειο-χαρής, ές, (χαίρω) *delighting in the hills*, Anth.

ὀρείτης, ου, ὁ, (ὄρος) *a mountaineer*, Polyb.

ὀρεί-φοιτος, ον, (φοιτάω) *mountain-roaming*, Babr.

ὀρεί-χαλκος, ὁ, Lat. *orichalcum, mountain-copper*, i. e. *copper ore*, or *copper made from it*, Hes., Plat.

ὀρειώτης, ου, ὁ, (ὄρος) = ὀρείτης, Anth.

ὀρεκτικός, ή, όν, (ὄρεξις) *of* or *for the desires, appetitive*, Arist.; τὸ ὀρεκτικόν, *the appetites*, Id.

ὀρεκτός, ή, όν, (ὀρέγω) *stretched out*, μελίαι ὀρ. pikes *to be presented* (not thrown), Il.

ὄρεξις, εως, ἡ, (ὀρέγω) *desire, appetite*, Arist. : c. gen. *a longing* or *yearning after* a thing, *desire for* it, Id.

ὀρέοντο, Ep. 3 pl. aor. 2 of ὄρνυμι.

ὀρεοπολέω, *to haunt mountains*, Luc. From

ὀρεο-πόλος, ον, (πολέω) *haunting mountains*.

ὀρεσι-τρόφος, ον, (τρέφω) *mountain-bred*, Hom.

ὀρέ-σκιος, ον, (σκιά) overshadowed by mountains, Anth.

ὀρεσκ-ῷος, ον, (κεῖμαι) lying on mountains, mountain-bred, of the Centaurs, Il.; of goats, Od.:—the Trag. form is ὀρέσκοος, ον, Aesch., Eur.

ὀρέσσ-αυλος, ον, (αὐλή) mountain-dwelling, Anth.

ὄρεσσι, Ep. for ὄρεσι, dat. pl. of ὄρος, a mountain.

ὀρεσσῖ-βάτης, ὁ, poët. for ὀρεσιβάτης, mountain-roaming, Soph.

ὀρεσσί-γονος, ον, poët. for ὀρεσι-, mountain-born, Ar.

ὀρεσσῐ-νόμος, ον, = ὀρεινόμος, Hes.

'Ορέστεια, ἡ, the tale of Orestes, the name of Aeschylus' Agamemnon, Choëphoroe and Eumenides, being the only certain Trilogy extant, Ar. II. 'Ορέστειον, τό, a temple of Orestes, Hdt.

'Ορέστειος, α, ον, of Orestes, Soph.

ὀρέστερος, α, ον, poët. for ὀρεινός II, Hom., Trag.

ὀρεστιάς, άδος, ἡ, (ὄρος) of the mountains, Νύμφαι ὀρεστιάδες = 'Ορεάδες, Il.

ὄρεσφι, -φιν, Ep. gen. and dat. sing. and pl. of ὄρος, a mountain.

ὀρεύς, Ion. οὐρεύς, έως, ὁ, a mule, Il., Ar. (From ὄρος a mountain, mules being much used in mountainous countries.)

ὀρεχθέω, only in pres. and Ep. impf. ὀρέχθεον, either to stretch oneself or struggle in the throes of death (from ὀρέγομαι), or (akin to ῥοχθέω), to gasp in the death-ruckle, Il.; of the heart, to palpitate, Ar.; of the sea, to stretch itself, i. e. roll up, to the beach, Theocr. (in Dor. inf. ὀρεχθῆν).

ὀρέω, Ion. for ὁράω, Hdt.

ὀρεω-κόμος, ὁ, (ὀρεύς, κομέω) a muleteer, Plat., Xen.

ὄρηαι, Ep. for ὁρᾷ, 2 sing. med. of ὁράω.

ὄρθαι, Ep. for ὀρέσθαι, aor. 2 med. inf. of ὄρνυμι.

ὀρθεύω, (ὀρθός) = ὀρθόω, impf. ὤρθευον Eur.

'Ορθία, ἡ, a name of Artemis in Laconia and Arcadia; at her altar the Spartan boys were whipped, Xen.

ὀρθιάδε, Adv. (ὄρθιος), uphill, Xen.

ὀρθιάζω, f. άσω, (ὄρθιος) to speak in a high tone, ὀρθ. γόοις to shriek with loud wailings, Aesch. II. trans., = ὀρθόω, to set upright, Anth. Hence

ὀρθίασμα, ατος, τό, a high pitch of voice: in pl. loud commanding tones, Aesch.

ὄρθιος, α, ον, and ος, ον, (ὀρθός) straight up, going upwards, steep, uphill, Hes., Eur.; ὄρθιον ἐτέραν (sc. ὁδόν) ἐπορεύοντο Thuc.; so, ὄρθιον or πρὸς ὄρθιον ἰέναι to march up-hill, Xen.; πρὸς ὄρθιον ἄγειν to lead by a steep path, Id.:—τὰ ὄρθια the country from the coast upwards, Hdt. 2. upright, standing, Id., Eur.:—esp. of hair, Trag.: of animals, rampant, Pind. II. of the voice, high-pitched, loud, shrill, Trag.; neut. as Adv., ὄρθια ἤϋσε she cried aloud, Il.; ὄρθιον φωνεῖν Pind. 2. νόμος ὄρθιος the orthian strain, a favourite air at Athens, Hdt., Ar.; ὄρθιος νόμος, Ar. III. in military language, ὄρθιοι λόχοι were companies formed in column, opp. to a line of battle, Xen. IV. generally, like ὀρθός, straight, Id.; ᾔδη ὄρθια straightforwardness, Plut.

ὀρθο-βατέω, to go straight on or upright, Anth.

ὀρθό-βουλος, ον, right-counselling, Pind., Aesch.

ὀρθο-δαής, ές, (δαῆναι) knowing rightly how to do a thing, c. inf., Aesch.

ὀρθο-δίκας [ι], Dor. for ὀρθοδίκης, ου, ὁ, δίκη, judging righteously, Pind.

ὀρθο-δίκαιος, ον, = foreg., Aesch.

ὀρθοδοξέω, to have a right opinion, Arist. From

ὀρθό-δοξος, ον, (δόξα) right in opinion.

ὀρθο-δρομέω, f. ήσω, to run straight forward, Xen.

ὀρθο-έπεια, ἡ, ἔπος) correctness of diction, Plat.

ὀρθό-θριξ, τρίχος, ὁ, ἡ, with hair up-standing, Aesch.

ὀρθό-κραιρος, α, ον, (Ep. gen. pl. fem. -κραιράων): (κραῖρα):—with straight horns, Hom.:—also of the two ends of a galley which turned up like horns, Il.

ὀρθό-κρᾱνος, ον, having a high head, lofty, Soph.

ὀρθομαντεία, ἡ, true prophecy, Aesch. From

ὀρθό-μαντις, εως, Ion. ιος, ὁ, ἡ, a true prophet, Pind.

ὀρθο-νόμος, ον, (νέμω) making right award, Aesch.

ὀρθο-ποδέω, f. ήσω, (πούς) to walk uprightly, N. T.

ὀρθό-πολις, εως, ὁ, ἡ, upholding the city, Pind.

ὀρθό-πους, ὁ, ἡ, πουν, τό, with straight feet: II. of a hill, steep, Soph.

'ΟΡΘΟ'Σ, ή, όν, straight, Lat. rectus: I. in height, upright, erect, Hom., Hdt., Att.; ὀρθὸν οὖς ἱστάναι, i. e. to give attentive ear, Soph.:—of buildings, standing with their walls entire, [τὸ Πάνακτον ὀρθὸν παραδοῦναι Thuc. II. in line, straight, right, ὀρθὸς ἀντ' ἠελίοιο right opposite the sun, Hes.; ὀρθὴ ὁδός Theogn.; ὀρθὴν κελεύεις, i. e. ὀρθὴν ὁδόν με κελεύεις ἱέναι, Ar.; δι' ὀρθῆς (sc. ὁδοῦ) Soph.:—also, ὀρθᾷ χερί, ὀρθῷ ποδί straight-way, Pind.; but ὀρθὸν πόδα τιθέναι is prob. to put the foot out, as in walking (cf. κατηρεφής 1), Aesch. 2. βλέπειν ὀρθά, to see straight, opp. to being blind, Soph.; so, ἐξ ὀμμάτων ὀρθῶν, ὀρθοῖς ὄμμασιν, Lat. rectis oculis, Id. III. metaph., 1. right, safe, happy, prosperous: a. from signf. 1, ὀρθὸν ἱστάναι τινά = ὀρθοῦν, to set up, restore, Pind., Eur.; so, στάντες τ' ἐς ὀρθὸν καὶ πεσόντες ὕστερον Soph.; πλεῖν ἐπ' ὀρθῆς (sc. νεώς, the state being represented as a ship), Id. b. from signf. 11, κατ' ὀρθὸν ἐξελθεῖν, of prophecies, Id.; κατ' ὀρθὸν οὐρίσαι to waft in straight course, Id. 2. right, true, correct, Pind., Aesch., etc.; ὀρθῷ ἀκούειν to be rightly called, Soph.; ὀρθῷ λόγῳ strictly speaking, in very truth, Hdt.:—so in Adv., ὀρθῶς λέγειν Id.; ὀ. φράσαι Aesch., etc.; ὀρθῶς ἔχει 'tis right, c. inf., Plat.:—Sup. ὀρθότατα Hdt. 3. real, genuine, Arist.:—ὀρθῶς, really, truly, Plat. 4. upright, righteous, just, Soph., etc.; κατὰ τὸ ὀρθὸν δικάζειν Hdt.:—Adv. ὀρθῶς, rightly, justly, Thuc. 5. of persons, steadfast, firm, Plat. IV. ἡ ὀρθή, 1. (sub. ὁδός), v. supr. II. 2. (sub. γωνία) a right angle, Id., etc. 3. (sub. πτῶσις) the nominative, Lat. casus rectus. V. Adv. ὀρθῶς, v. supr. III. 2-4.

ὀρθο-στάδην [ᾰ], Adv. standing upright, Aesch.

ὀρθο-στάτης [ᾰ], ου, ὁ, (στῆναι) one who stands upright: an upright shaft, pillar, Eur. II. a sort of cake used in funeral oblations, Id.

ὀρθό-στατος, ον, (στῆναι) upstanding, upright, Eur.

ὀρθότης, ητος, ἡ, (ὀρθός) upright posture, erectness, Xen. II. metaph. rightness, correctness, Ar., Plat.

ὀρθοτομέω, to cut in a straight line: metaph., ὀρ. τὸν λόγον to teach it aright, N. T.

ὀρθόω, f. ώσω, (ὀρθός) to set straight: I. in height, to set upright, set up one fallen or lying down, raise up, Il.; ὀρθοῦν κάρα, πρόσωπον Eur.:—of buildings, to

raise up, rebuild, or, generally, to erect, build up, Eur., Thuc.:—Pass. to be set upright, Il., etc.: simply to rise from one's seat, stand up, Aesch., Soph. **II.** in line, to make straight, Arist.:—Pass., ἢν τόδ' ὀρθωθῇ βέλος if this dart go straight, Soph. **III.** metaph. (from signf. 1) to raise up, restore to health, safety, happiness, Hdt., Aesch., etc.:—also to exalt, honour, Pind. 2. (from signf. 11) to guide aright, Aesch.; ὀρθ. ἀγῶνας to bring to a happy end, Id.; ὀ. βίον Soph.:—Pass. to succeed, prosper, Hdt., Soph., etc.; τὸ ὀρθούμενον success, Thuc.:—of words and opinions, to be right, true, Hdt., Eur.; ἐν ἀγγέλῳ κρυπτὸς ὀρθοῦται λόγος a secret message is rightly sent by messenger, not by letter, Aesch. 3. in Pass. also, to be upright, deal justly, Id.

ὀρθρεύω, f. σω, (ὄρθρος) to rise early, to be awake early, Eur., Theocr.:—also in Med., γόοισιν ὀρθρευομένα rising up early with groans, Eur.

ὀρθρίδιος [ῐ], α, ον, poët. for ὄρθριος, Anth.

ὀρθρίζω, = ὀρθρεύω, N. T.

ὀρθρῐνός, ή, όν, (ὄρθρος) = ὄρθριος, Anth., Luc.

ὄρθριος, α, ον, and ος, ον, (ὄρθρος) at day-break, in the morning, early, mostly with Verbs of motion, so as to agree with the person, ἀφίκετο ὄρθριος h. Hom.; ὄρθριος ἥκειν Plat.; also, ὄρθριον ᾄδειν (sc. ᾆσμα), of the cock, Ar.:—τὸ ὄρθριον as Adv., in the morning, early, Hdt.

ὀρθρο-βόας, ου, ὁ, the early caller, chanticleer, Anth.

ὀρθρο-γόη, ἡ, (γοάω) the early-wailing, Hes.

ὀρθρο-λάλος [ᾰ], ον, early-twittering, Anth.

ὌΡΘΡΟΣ, ὁ, day-break, dawn, cock-crow, h. Hom., Ar.; ὄρθρου at dawn, Hes.; ὄρθρου γενομένου Hdt.; ἅμα ὄρθρῳ Id., etc.; also, τὸν ὄρθρον, absol., in the morning, Id.; δι' ὄρθρων each morning early, Eur.:—ὄρθρος βαθύς early dawn, just before daybreak, Ar., Plat.

ὀρθρο - φοιτο - συκοφαντο - δῐκο - τᾰλαίπωροι τρόποι, early-prowling-base-informing-sad-litigious-plaguy ways, Ar.

ὀρθ-ώνυμος, ον, (ὄνομα) rightly named, Aesch.

Ὀρθωσία, Ion. -ίη, ἡ, = Ὀρθία, Hdt., Pind.

ὀρθωτήρ, ῆρος, ὁ, one who sets upright, a restorer, Pind.

ὀρίγανον [ῐ], τό, a bitter herb, marjoram, ὀρίγανον βλέπειν to look origanum, i.e. to look sour or crabbed, Ar.

ὀριγνάομαι, f. ήσομαι: (ὀρέγομαι):—to stretch oneself, ἔγχεσιν ὠριγνῶντο they fought with outstretched spears, Hes. 2. c. gen. to stretch oneself after a thing, reach at, grasp at, Eur., Theocr.

ὀρίζω, Ion. οὐρ-: Att. f. ὁριῶ: aor. 1 ὥρισα, Ion. οὔρισα: pf. ὥρικα:—Med., f. ὁριοῦμαι: aor. 1 ὡρισάμην:—Pass., f. ὁρισθήσομαι: aor. 1 ὡρίσθην:—pf. ὥρισμαι (also used in med. sense): (ὅρος):—to divide or separate from, as a boundary, c. acc. et gen., ὁ Νεῖλος τὴν Ἀσίην οὐρίζει τῆς Λιβύης Hdt.:—with two accs. joined by καί, to separate, be a boundary between, Τύρης ποταμὸς οὐρίζει τήν τε Σκυθικὴν καὶ τὴν Νευρίδα γῆν Id. 2. to bound, Thuc., Xen.:—Pass. to be bounded, Eur.; metaph., ὡρίσθω μέχρι τοῦδε so far let it go and no further, Thuc. 3. to pass between or through, διδύμους πέτρας Eur. 4. to part and drive away, banish, Id.:—Pass. to depart from, Id. **II.** to mark out by boundaries, mark out, Hdt., Soph.; so, ὀρ. θεόν to mark out his sanctuary,

Eur. **III.** to limit, determine, appoint, lay down, Trag., Xen.:—so, c. inf. to appoint, order, Eur.:—so, θάνατον ὥρισε τὴν ζημίαν determined the penalty to be death, Dem.:—Pass., pf. part. ὡρισμένος determinate, definite, Arist. 2. to define a word, mostly in Med., Xen., etc. **IV.** Med. to mark out for oneself, take possession of, Aesch., Eur.:—ὁρίζεσθαι βωμούς, στήλας to set them up, Soph., Xen. 2. to determine for oneself, to get a thing determined, Dem. 3. to define a word, Plat.;—c. acc. et inf., Xen., etc. **V.** intr. to border upon, Hdt. **VI.** as Att. law-term, δισχιλίων ὡρισμένος τὴν οἰκίαν having the house marked with ὅροι (cf. ὅρος 11), i.e. mortgaged to the amount of 2000 drachms, Dem.

ὀρῐκός, ή, όν, (ὀρεύς) of or for a mule, ὀρ. ζεῦγος a pair of mules, Plat., etc.

ὀρίνω [ῑ]: aor. 1 ὥρινα, Ep. ὄρῑνα: Pass., 3 sing. impf. ὠρίνετο: aor. 1 ὠρίνθην, Ep. ὀρ-: (ὄρ-νυμι):—to stir, raise, agitate, Hom.: metaph., θυμὸν ὀρίνειν Id.:—Pass., ὠρίνετο θυμός his heart was stirred within him, Od.

ὅριον, τό, = ὅρος, a boundary, limit, in pl. boundaries, the borders, frontier, Eur., Thuc., etc.

ὅριος, ον, (ὅρος) of boundaries, Ζεὺς ὅριος guardian of land-marks, Lat. Terminus.

ὅρισμα, ατος, Ion. οὔρ-, τό, (ὁρίζω) a boundary, limit, and in pl., boundaries, the borders, Hdt., Eur.

ὁρισμός, οῦ, ὁ, (ὁρίζω) a marking out by boundaries, limitation, Arist. **II.** the definition of a word, Id.

ὁριστέον, verb. Adj. one must determine, Plat., etc.

ὁριστής, οῦ, ὁ, (ὁρίζω) one who marks the boundaries; in pl. officers appointed to settle boundaries, Plut. **II.** one who determines, Dem.

ὀρι-τρόφος, ον, (τρέφω) mountain-bred, Babr.

ὁρκάνη, ἡ, = ἑρκάνη, ἕρκος (from ἔργω, εἴργω), an enclosure, fence, Aesch.: a net, trap, or pitfall, Eur.

ὁρκ-ἀπάτης, ου, ὁ, (ἀπατάω) an oath-breaker, Anth.

ὁρκίζω, f. σω, to make one swear, Xen., Dem.; ὁρκίζω σε τὸν Θεόν I adjure one by God, N. T.

ὅρκιον, τό, = ὅρκος, an oath, Hom., etc. **II.** mostly in pl., ὅρκια, τά, that which is sworn, the articles of a treaty, Hom., etc.; ὅρκια πιστὰ ταμεῖν (v. τέμνω 11), Il.:—on the other hand, ὅρκια δηλήσασθαι or ὑπὲρ ὅρκια δηλ. to violate a solemn treaty, Ib.; ὅρκια πατῆσαι to trample on the treaties, Ib.; so, ὅρκια συγχεῦαι, ψεύσασθαι Ib. 2. the victims sacrificed on taking these solemn oaths, Ib. 3. a surety resting on oath, in sing., Pind., Ar.

ὅρκιος, ον, rarely α, ον:—belonging to an oath, i.e. **1.** sworn, bound by oath, Aesch.; ὅρκιος λέγω I speak as if on oath, Soph. **2.** that which is sworn by, ὅρκιοι θεοί the gods invoked to witness an oath, Eur.; so, θεοὶ οἱ ὅρκ. Thuc.; esp., Ζεὺς ὅρκιος Soph., Eur.; ξίφος ὅρκιον a sword sworn by, Eur.

ὁρκισμός, ὁ, (ὁρκίζω) administration of an oath, Plut.

ὅρκος, ὁ, (v. fin.) the object by which one swears, the witness of an oath, as the Styx among the gods, Hom., etc.:—hence, **2.** an oath, Id., etc.; ὅρκος θεῶν an oath by the gods, Od.; ὅρκον ὀμόσαι to swear an oath, Hom., etc.; ὅρκον ἐπιορκεῖν to take a false oath, Aeschin.; ὅρκον διδόναι καὶ δέξασθαι to tender an oath to another and accept the tender from him, Hdt., Att.; ὅρκον ἀποδιδόναι to take an oath, ἀπολαμβάνειν to

tender it, Dem.; so, ὅρκον διδόναι καὶ λαμβάνειν Arist.; ὅρκοις τινὰ καταλαμβάνειν to bind one by oaths, Thuc.; ὅρκῳ ἐμμένειν to abide by it, Eur.; εἶπαι ἐπ᾽ ὅρκου to say on oath, Hdt. II. Ὅρκος, personified, son of Ἔρις, a divinity, who punishes the perjured, Hes., etc. (ὅρκος was orig. equiv. to ἕρκος, as ὁρκάνη to ἑρκάνη, from ἔργω, εἴργω, properly, that which restrains from doing a thing).

ὀρκ-οῦρος, ὁ, = ἑρκ-οῦρος, Anth.

ὀρκόω, f. ώσω, to bind by oath, Thuc., etc. Hence

ὅρκωμα, ατος, τό, an oath, Aesch.

ὀρκωμοσία, ἡ, a swearing, an oath, Ep.

ὀρκωμόσια, τά, asseverations on oath, Plat. II. the sacrifice on taking an oath, Id. III. ὀρκωμόσιον, τό, the place where a treaty has been sworn to, Plut.

ὀρκ-ωμοτέω, f. ήσω, (ὄμνυμι) to take an oath, Trag.:— foll. by inf. aor., ὀρκ. θεοὺς τὸ μὴ δρᾶσαι to swear by the gods that they did it not, Soph.; by inf. fut., Ἄρη ὠρκωμότησαν λαπάξειν made oath by Ares that they would destroy, Aesch.

ὀρκωτής, οῦ, ὁ, (ὀρκόω) the officer who administers the oath, Xen.

ὁρμᾰθός, ὁ, (ὅρμος) a string, chain, or cluster of things hanging one from the other, as of bats, Od.; so, ὁρμ. κριβανιτῶν, ἰσχάδων Ar.

ὁρμᾱθῶ, Dor. for ὁρμηθῶ, aor. 1 pass. subj. of ὁρμάω.

ὁρμαίνω, only in pres., impf. and aor. 1 ὥρμηνα: (ὁρμάω): I. to turn over or revolve anxiously in the mind, to debate, ponder, Lat. animo volvere, ὁρμαίνειν τι κατὰ φρένα or ἐνὶ φρεσί Hom.:—so also ὁρμαίνειν τι alone, to ponder over, meditate, πόλεμον, ὁδόν Id. 2. absol., ὣς ὥρμαινε thus he debated with himself, Il. 3. foll. by a relat. clause, ἤ .., ἤ .., to debate whether .., or .., Hom.; ὁρμ. ὅπως .., to debate, ponder how a thing is to be done, Il. 4. c. inf. to long, desire, wish, Theocr. II. after Hom., 1. to set in motion, θυμὸν ὁρμ. to gasp out one's life, Aesch.; to excite, urge, Pind. 2. intr. to be eager, to chafe, fret, Aesch.; part. ὁρμαίνων eagerly, Pind.

ὁρμάω, f. ήσω, Att.: aor. 1 ὥρμησα: pf. ὥρμηκα:— Med. and Pass., f. ὁρμήσομαι: aor. 1 ὡρμησάμην and ὡρμήθην:—Pass., Ion. 3 pl. pf. and plqpf. ὡρμέαται and -έατο: (ὁρμή): A. Act., I. Causal, to set in motion, urge or push on, spur on, cheer on, Il., Hdt., Att. :—Pass., ὁρμηθεὶς θεοῦ inspired by the god, Od.; so, πρὸς θεῶν ὡρμημένος Soph. 2. with a thing as the object, to stir up, πόλεμον Od. :— Pass., ὡρμάθη πλαγά was inflicted, Soph. II. intr. to make a start, hasten on, 1. c. inf., ὁ ὁρμήσῃ διώκειν who starts in chase, Il.; ὁσσάκι δ᾽ ὁρμήσειε πυλάων ἀντίον ἀΐξασθαι whenever he started to rush against the gates, Ib.: to begin to do, Hdt., Soph. 2. c. gen. to rush headlong at one, Il.; so, ὁρμᾶν ἐπί τινα Hdt., etc.; εἴς τινα, κατά τινα Xen.; ἐπὶ τὸ σκοπεῖν Id., etc.: also, ὁρμ. ἐς μάχην to hasten to battle, Aesch.; εἰς ἀγῶνα Eur. 3. absol. to start, begin, Plat.; αἱ μάλιστα ὁρμήσασαι [νῆες] the ships that had got the greatest start, Thuc. B. Med. and Pass., like intr. Act.: 1. c. inf., μὴ φεύγειν ὁρμήσωνται that they put not themselves in motion to flee, think of fleeing, Il.; so, διώκειν ὡρ-

μήθησαν Ib.; ὁ λόγος οὗτος ὡρμήθη λέγεσθαι this account began to be given, was taken in hand, Hdt.; but, λόγον, τὸν ὥρμητο λέγειν which he purposed to make, Id.; and with the inf. omitted, μενεήναμεν ὁρμηθέντε we eagerly desired, Od. 2. c. gen. to hasten after, Hom.; so, ὁρμᾶσθαι ἐπί τινι Od.; ἐπί τινα Soph., etc. :—rarely c. acc. loci, νερτέρας πλάκας Id. 3. to start from, begin from, ἐνθεῦτεν ὁρμώμενοι going out from thence to do one's daily work, Hdt.; so of a general, to make a place his headquarters or base of operations, Id., Thuc.; so, ὁρμ. ἀπὸ Σάρδεων Xen.; ἀπ᾽ ἐλασσόνων ὁρμώμενος setting out, beginning, with smaller means, Thuc. 4. absol. to rush on, Hom. :—generally, to hasten, be eager, Aesch.: to go forth, τὸ φέγγος ὁρμάσθω πυρός Id.; ὕβρις ἀτάρβητος ὁρμᾶται insult goes fearless forth, Soph. 5. in a really pass. sense, πρὸς θεῶν ὡρμημένος incited by the gods, Id.

ὁρμέαται, -το, Ion. 3 pl. pf. and plqpf. of ὁρμάω.

ὁρμειά, ἡ, = ὁρμιά, Theocr.

ὅρμενος, aor. 2 med. part. of ὄρνυμι.

ὁρμέω, f. ήσω, (ὅρμος II) to be moored, lie at anchor, of a ship, Hdt., Eur., etc. :—proverb. phrases, ἐπὶ δυοῖν ἀγκύραιν ὁρμεῖν, v. ἄγκυρα; μέγας ἐπὶ σμικροῖς ὁρμεῖν to be dependent on small matters, Soph.

ὁρμέμενος, Ion. for ὁρμώμενος, part. med. of ὁρμάω.

ΟΡΜΗ', ἡ, a violent movement onwards, an assault, attack, onset, Lat. impetus, Il., Hdt., Xen. 2. of things, πυρὸς ὁρμή the rage of fire, Il.; ὑπὸ κύματος ὁρμῆς by the shock of a wave, Il.; ἐς ὁρμὴν ἔγχεος ἐλθεῖν within reach of my spear, Il. II. the first stir or start in a thing, an effort or attempt to reach a thing, impulse to do it, Hom., Hdt., Att. :— μιᾷ ὁρμῇ with one impulse, Lat. uno impetu, Xen.; so, ἀπὸ μιᾶς ὁρμῆς Thuc. :—c. gen. objecti, eager desire of or for a thing, Id. 2. a start on a march, ἐν ὁρμῇ εἶναι to be on the point of starting, Xen.

ὅρμημα, ατος, τό, = ὁρμή, stir, impulse, Ἑλένης ὁρμήματά τε στοναχάς τε longings and sighs [of the Greeks] for Helen, or, their struggles and sighs for her recovery (Ἑλένης being an objective gen.), Il.

ὁρμητήριον, τό, (ὁρμάω) any means of stirring up or rousing, a stimulant, incentive, Xen. II. (from Med. ὁρμάομαι), a starting place, military position, base of operations, point d'appui, Dem., etc.

ὁρμιά, ἡ, (ὅρμος) a fishing-line of horsehair, Eur., Theocr. [ῑ Eur., ῐ Theocr.]

ὁρμίζω, f. ίσω, Ep. ίσσω: aor. 1 ὥρμισα:—Med. and Pass., f. -ιοῦμαι: aor. 1 med. ὡρμισάμην and pass. ὡρμίσθην: pf. ὥρμισμαι: (ὅρμος II):—to bring to a safe anchorage, bring into harbour, to moor, anchor, Od., etc.; οἴκαδε ὁρμ. πλάτην to bring the ship safe home, Eur.:—metaph. to put a child to sleep, Aesch. II. Med. and Pass. to come to anchor, lie at anchor, anchor, Hdt., Att. :—metaph., ὁρμίζεσθαι ἐκ τύχης to be dependent on fortune, Eur.

ὁρμῖνο-βόλος, ον, (βάλλω) throwing a line, Anth.

ὁρμο-δοτήρ, ῆρος, ὁ, harbour-giver, of a god, Anth.

ὅρμος, ὁ, (εἴρω) a cord, chain, esp. a necklace, collar, Hom., Att. 2. generally, anything strung like a necklace, a wreath, chaplet, Pind.; στεφάνων ὅρμος a string of crowns, i. e. of praises, Id. 3. a dance

performed in a ring, Luc.　　II. *a roadstead, anchorage, moorings*, Il., Hdt., Att.　　2. metaph. *a haven, place of shelter* or *refuge*, Eur., Anth.　III. =ἕρμα 1, Anth.

ὀρναπέτιον, τό, Boeot. for ὄρνεον.

ὄρνεον, τό, =ὄρνις, *a bird*, Il., Ar.　　II. τὰ ὄρνεα *the bird-market*, Ar.

ὀρνεό-φοιτος, ον, (φοιτάω) *frequented by birds*, Anth.

ὀρνίθ-αρχος [ῑ], ὁ, *king of birds*, Ar.

ὀρνίθειος, α, ον, and ος, ον, *of* or *belonging to a bird*, ὀρνίθεια (sc. κρέα) *fowl's flesh, chicken*, Ar.

ὀρνῑθευτής, οῦ, ὁ, *a fowler, bird-catcher*, Ar., Plat.; and **ὀρνῑθευτικός**, ή, όν, *of* or *for bird-catching* :—ἡ -κή (sc. τέχνη), *the art of bird-catching, fowling*, Plat.

ὀρνῑθεύω, f. σω, (ὄρνις) *to catch* or *trap birds*, Xen.

ὀρνῑθικός, ή, όν, *of* or *for birds*, Luc.

ὀρνίθιον [ῑ], τό, Dim. of ὄρνις, *a small bird*, Hdt.

ὀρνῑθό-γονος, ον, (γίγνομαι) *sprung from a bird*, Eur.

ὀρνῑθο-θήρας, ου, ὁ, (θηράω) *a bird-catcher, fowler*, Ar.; Dor. ὀρνῑχ-, ὁ, (λοχάω) =foreg., Pind.

ὀρνῑθομᾰνέω, *to be bird-mad*, Ar. From

ὀρνῑθο-μᾰνής, ές, (μαίνομαι) *bird-mad*, Ath.

ὀρνῑθο-πέδη, ἡ, *a snare for birds*, Anth.

ὀρνῑθο-σκόπος, ον, (σκοπέω) *observing and predicting by the flight and cries of birds* :—θᾶκος ὀρν. *an augur's seat*, Lat. *templum augurale*, Soph.

ὀρνῑθοτροφία, ἡ, *a keeping of birds*, Plut. From

ὀρνῑθο-τρόφος, ον, (τρέφω) *keeping birds*.

ὄρνιος, poët. for ὀρνίθειος, Anth.

ΌΡΝΙΣ [ῐ], ὁ and ἡ : gen. ὄρνῑθος ; acc. ὄρνῑθα and ὄρνιν :—plur., nom. and acc. ὄρνῑθες, -θας, but in acc. also ὄρνεις or ὄρνῑς :—Dor. acc. ὄρνῑχα ; gen. pl. ὀρνίχων ; dat. ὄρνιξι, ὀρνίχεσσι (as if from ὄρνιξ) :　I. *a bird*, Hom., etc. ; often added to the specific names, ὄρνισιν ἐοικότες αἰγυπιοῖσιν Il. ; λάρῳ ὄρνιθι ἐοικώς Od. ; ὁ. αἰδῶν, πέρδιξ Soph. ; ὁ. ἀλκυών, ὁ. κύκνος Eur.　II. like οἰωνός, *a bird of omen*, from the flight or cries of which the augur divined, Hom., Soph.　2. metaph., like Lat. *avis* for *augurium, the omen* or *prophecy taken from the flight* or *cries of birds*, Hom., etc. :—then, generally, *an omen, presage*, without direct reference to birds, Il.　III. in Att., ὄρνις, ὁ, is mostly *a cock*, ὄρνις, ἡ, *a hen*, Soph., Ar., etc.　IV. in pl. sometimes *the bird-market*, Ar., Dem.　V. Μοισᾶν ὄρνιθες *birds* of the Muses, i. e. *Poets*, Theocr. :—proverb., ὀρνίθων γάλα ' pigeon's milk,' i.e. any marvellous dainty or good fortune, Ar.

ὀρνῑχο-λόχος, **ὀρνῑχος**, **ὄρνῑχα**, Dor. for ὀρνιθ-.

ὄρνῡμι or -ύω, imperat. ὄρνῡθι, ὄρνῠτε ; 3 sing. and pl. impf. ὤρνῡεν, -υον ; f. ὄρσω : aor. 1 ὦρσα, Ion. 3 sing. ὄρσασκε : redupl. aor. 2 ὤρορα :—Med., ὄρνῠμαι ; impf. ὠρνύμην : f. ὀροῦμαι, 3 sing. : ὀρεῖται : aor. 2 ὠρόμην, 3 sing. ὤρετο, contr. ὦρτο, Ep. 3 pl. ὄροντο, ὀρέοντο ; imperat. ὄρσο or ὄρσεο, Ion. ὄρσευ ; 3 sing. subj. ὄρηται ; inf. ὄρθαι contr. for ὀρέσθαι ; part. ὀρόμενος, ὄρμενος :—to the Med. also belongs the pf. ὄρωρα (once ὤρορε), and 3 sing. plqpf. ὀρώρει, ὠρώρει :—in Hom. also a pass. form ὄρωρεται=ὄρωρε, subj. ὀρώρηται. (*ΌΡΩ is the Root from which most tenses are formed.) Radical sense, *to stir, stir up* : esp., 1. of bodily movement, *to set on, urge on, incite*, Il., Hes. :

—c. inf., Ζεὺς ὦρσε μάχεσθαι *urged* him *on to fight*, Il. :—Med., with pf. ὤρωρα, *to move, stir oneself*, εἰσόκε μοι φίλα γούνατ' ὀρώρῃ while my limbs *have power to move*, Hom. ; aor. 1 imper. ὄρσεο, ὄρσευ, ὄρσο *rouse thee! up! arise!* Id. :—in hostile sense, *to rush on, rush furiously*, Il., Aesch., etc.　2. *to make to arise, to awaken, call forth*, Il. ; of animals, *to rouse, start, chase*, Hom. :—Med. *to arise, start up*, esp. from bed, Id. ; in pf. med., ὤρορε θεῖος ἀοιδός Od. :—c. inf. *to rise to do* a thing, *set about* it, ὦρτο ἴμεν Ib. ; ὦρτο Ζεὺς νιφέμεν *started* or *began to* snow, Il.　3. *to call forth, excite*, Lat. *ciere*, of storms and the like, which the gods *call forth*, Hom., Aesch. ; so ὄρσαι ἵμερον, φόβον, μένος, πόλεμον, etc., Hom. :—Med. *to break forth, arise*, Lat. *orior*, Il. ; ὄρνυται πένθος, στόνος, etc., Ib. ; δοῦρα ὄρμενα πρόσσω the darts *flying* onwards, Ib.

ὀρόγυια, ἡ, poët. for ὀργυιά.

ὀροδαμνίς, ίδος, ἡ, Dim. of sq., *a sprig, spray*, Theocr.

ὀρόδαμνος, ὁ, *a branch*, Anth. (Deriv. uncertain.)

ὀροθύνω, chiefly in Ep. impf. ὀρόθῡνον : aor. 1 ὠρόθυνα, imper. ὀρόθῡνον : (ὄρνυμι, ὀρίνω) :—*to stir up, rouse, urge on, excite*, Hom., Aesch.

ΌΡΟΜΑΙ, Ep. 3 pl. impf. ὄροντο :—Dep. *to watch, keep watch and ward*, Il.

ὀρο-μᾰλίδες, αἱ, (μῆλον Β) Dor. for ὀρομηλίδες, *wild apples*, Theocr.

ΌΡΟΣ, Ion. οὖρος, εος, τό : gen. pl. ὀρέων, ὀρῶν, *a mountain, hill*, Hom., etc. ; pl. οὔρεα, Id.

ΌΡΟ'Σ, ὁ, Lat. *serum, the watery part of milk, whey*, Od.

ΌΡΟΣ, Ion. οὖρος, ὁ, *a boundary, landmark*, and in pl. *bounds, boundaries*, Il., etc. :—*the boundary between* two places is expressed by putting both in gen., οὖρος τῆς Μηδικῆς καὶ τῆς Λυδικῆς Hdt. : generally, *a boundary, limit*, ἑβδομήκοντα ἔτη ζόης ἀνθρώπῳ προτίθημι I set 70 years *as the limit* of human life, Id. ; metaph. of a woman's mind, Aesch.　II. in pl. *marking-stones* (στῆλαι, *cippi*), bearing inscriptions, Hdt. : in Att. Law, *stone tablets* set up on mortgaged lands as a register of the debt, Dem.　III. *a limit, rule, standard, measure*, Plat., Dem., etc.　2. *an end, aim*, Dem., etc.　IV. in Aristotle's Logic, *the term* of a proposition :—its *definition, species* : so, in Mathematics, ὅροι are *the terms* of a ratio or proportion, Arist.

Ὀροσάγγαι, οἱ, Persian word for *Benefactors*, Hdt.

ὀρο-τύπος [ῠ], ον, *driven from the mountain*, Aesch.

ὀρούω, impf. ὤρουον : f. ὀρούσω : aor. 1 ὤρουσα, Ep. ὄρουσα : (ὄρ-νυμι) :—*to rise and rush violently on, to move quickly, rush on, hasten, dart forward*, Hom., etc.　2. c. gen. objecti, *to rush at, strive after*, Pind.　3. c. inf. *to be eager to do*, Id.

ὀροφή, ἡ, (ἐρέφω) *the roof of a house*, or *the ceiling of a room*, Od., Hdt., etc.

ὀροφη-φάγος [ᾰ], ον, (φαγεῖν) *roof-destroying*, Anth.

ὀροφη-φόρος, ον, (φέρω) *bearing a roof*, Anth.

ὀροφίας, ου, ὁ, *living under a roof*, μῦς ὀρ. the common mouse, opp. to μ. ἀρουραῖος, Ar.

ὄροφος, ὁ, (ἐρέφω) in collective sense, *the reeds used for thatching houses*, Il.　II. =ὀροφή, *a roof*, Orac. ap. Hdt., Aesch., etc.

ὁρόω, Ep. for ὁράω.
ὅρπετον, τό, Aeol. for ἑρπετόν.
ΌΡΠΗΞ, Att. **ὅρπηξ**, ηκος, Dor. **ὅρπαξ**, ἄκος, ὁ, a sapling, young tree, Il., Theocr. 2. anything made of such trees, a goad, Hes. ; a lance, Eur.
ὀρρο-πύγιον [ῡ], τό, the rump of birds :—generally, the tail or rump of any animal, Ar.
ΌΡΡΟΣ, ὁ, the rump, Ar.
ὀρρωδέω, Ion. **ἀρρ-**, f. ήσω, to fear, dread, shrink from, c. acc., Hdt., Eur., etc.: c. gen. rei, to fear for or because of a thing, Hdt.; so, ὀρρ. περί τινος etc. (Formed so as to express the shuddering of fear.)
ὀρρωδία, Ion. **ἀρρωδίη**, ἡ, terror, affright, Hdt., Eur.
ὅρσας, aor. 1 part. of ὄρνυμι.
ὅρσασκε, Ion. 3 sing. aor. 1 of ὄρνυμι.
ὅρσεο, **ὅρσευ**, Ep. 2 sing. aor. 1 imper. med. of ὄρνυμι.
ὀρσί-κτῠπος, ον, stirring or making noise, Ζεὺς ὀρσ. the rouser of thunder, Pind.
ὀρσϊ-νεφής, ές, (νέφος) cloud-raising, Pind.
ὀρσί-πους [ῐ], ποδος, ὁ, ἡ, swift-footed, Anth.
ὅρσο, Ep. for ὅρσαι, aor. 1 imper. med. of ὄρνυμι.
ὀρσο-θύρη [ῠ], ἡ, prob. a door approached by steps, a side-door, Od.
ὀρσολοπεύω or **-έω**, to irritate, provoke, h. Hom. :—Pass., θυμὸς ὀρσολοπεῖται my heart is troubled, Aesch.
ὀρσόλοπος, ον, eager for the fray, of Ares, Anacr. (Deriv. unknown.)
ὀρσο-τρίαινᾰ, gen. ᾱ, acc. ᾱν, Dor. for -τριαίνης, ου, ην, wielder of the trident, Pind.
ὅρσω, fut. of ὄρνυμι.
ὀρτάζω, Ion. for ἑορτάζω.
ὀρτάλῐχος [ᾰ], ὁ, a chick, chicken, Ar., Theocr. :—generally, a young bird, Aesch. Boeot. word.
ὀρτή, ἡ, Ion. for ἑορτή.
Ὀρτῠγία, Ion. **-ίη**, ἡ, (ὅρτυξ) Quail-island, ancient name of Delos, whence Artemis is called Ὀρτυγία, Soph.
ὀρτῠγο-θήρας, ου, ὁ, (θηράω) a quail-catcher, Plat.
ὀρτῠγο-κόπος, ον, (κόπ-τω) a quail-striker.
ὀρτῠγο-μήτρα, ἡ, a bird which migrates with the quails, perh. the land-rail, ludicrously applied to Latona, the Ortygian mother (cf. Ὀρτυγία), Ar.
ὀρτῠγο-τρόφος, ον, (τρέφω) keeping quails, Plat.
ΌΡΤΥΞ, ῠγος, ὁ, the quail, Lat. coturnix, Hdt., etc.
ὅρυγμα, ατος, τό, (ὀρύσσω) a trench, ditch, moat, Lat. scrobs, Hdt., Thuc., etc.: a tunnel, mine, Hdt., Xen. :—ὅρ. τύμβου the grave, Eur. II. = ὅρυξις, Luc.
ὀρυκτός, ή, όν, (ὀρύσσω) formed by digging, opp. to a natural channel, Il., Hdt., Att.
ὀρῡμαγδός, ὁ, a loud noise, din, Hom. ; ὀρ. δρυτόμων the sound of wood-cutters, Il. ; the rattling made by throwing a bundle of wood on the ground, Od. ; of the roar of a torrent, Il. (Formed from the sound.)
ὅρυξ, ῠγος, ὁ, (ὀρύσσω) a pickaxe, Anth.
ὀρύξαι, aor. 1 inf. of ὀρύσσω.
ὅρυξις, ἡ, (ὀρύσσω) a digging, Plut.
ὅρυς, νος, ὁ, a Libyan animal, perh. an antelope, Hdt.
ΌΡΥΣΣΩ, Att. **-ττω** : f. ὀρύξω : aor. 1 ὤρυξα, Ep. ὅρυξα : pf. ὀρώρυχα : plqpf. ὠρώρυχειν :—Med., aor. 1 ὠρυξάμην :—Pass., f. ὀρυχθήσομαι and ὀρυχήσομαι : aor. 1 ὠρύχθην : pf. ὀρώρυγμαι : plqpf. ὀρωρύγμην :—to dig a trench, etc., Hom., Hdt., Att. ; τὸ ὀρυχθέν = ὅρυγμα, a trench, Hdt. II. to dig up a plant, Od. :

—Med., λίθους ὀρύξασθαι to have stones dug or quarried, Hdt. :—Pass., ὁ ὀρυσσόμενος χοῦς the soil that was dug up, Id. III. to dig through, i. e. make a canal through, (like διορύσσειν), τὸν ἰσθμὸν ὀρ. ap. Hdt. ; τὸ χωρίον ὀρώρυκτο Id. IV. to bury, ἔγχος ὀρύξας Soph. V. πὺξ ὀρ., of a pugilist, to give a dig or heavy blow, Ar.
ὀρῠχή, ἡ = ὅρυξις, Luc.
ὀρφάνευμα [ᾰ], ατος, τό, orphan state, orphanhood, Eur.
ὀρφανεύω, f. σω, to take care of, rear orphans, Eur. :—Pass. c. fut. med. to be an orphan, Id.
ὀρφᾰνία, ἡ, (ὀρφᾰνός) orphanhood, Plat. II. bereavement, want of, στεφάνων Pind.
ὀρφᾰνίζω, f. Att. ιῶ : aor. 1 ὠρφάνισα : (ὀρφανός) :—to make orphan, make destitute, Eur. :—c. gen. to bereave of a thing, Pind. :—Pass. to be bereaved of, Soph. : absol. to be left in orphanhood, Pind.
ὀρφᾰνικός, ή, όν, (ὀρφανός) orphaned, fatherless, Il. ; ἦμαρ ὀρφανικόν the day which makes one an orphan, i. e. orphanhood, Il. II. of or for orphans, Plat.
ὀρφάνιος, ον, = foreg., desolate, Anth.
ὀρφᾰνιστής, οῦ, ὁ, (ὀρφᾰνίζω) a tender of orphans, a guardian, Soph.
ὀρφᾰνόομαι, Pass. to be destitute of, c. gen., Anth.
ὈΡΦΑΝΟΣ, ή, όν, and ός, όν, Lat. orbus, orphan, without parents, fatherless, Od., Hes., Att. :—as Subst., an orphan, Plat. II. c. gen. bereaved or bereft, 1. of children, ὀρφ. πατρός reft of father, Eur. 2. of parents, ὀρφ. παίδων Id. ; νεοσσῶν ὀρφανὸν λέχος Soph. 3. generally, ὀρφ. ἑταίρων Pind. ; ἐπιστήμης Plat., etc.
ὀρφᾰνο-φύλαξ [ῠ], ἄκος, ὁ, guardian of an orphan who had lost the father in war, Xen.
Ὀρφεο-τελεστής, οῦ, ὁ, one who initiates into the mysteries of Orpheus : generally, a hierophant, Theophr.
Ὀρφεύς, έως, ὁ, Orpheus, a famous Thracian bard, Pind., etc. :—Adj. Ὅρφειος, α, ον, of Orpheus, Orphic, Eur. ; so, Ὀρφικός, ή, όν, Plat.
ὀρφναῖος, α, ον, dark, dusky, murky, Hom., Eur. etc. II. nightly, by night, Aesch. From
ὈΡΦΝΗ, Dor. **ὅρφνᾱ**, ἡ, the darkness of night, night, Theogn., Pind., Eur. Hence
ὀρφνῐνος, η, ον, brownish gray, Xen., etc.
ὀρφνίτης [ῐ], ου, ὁ, = foreg., Anth.
ὅρχᾰμος, ὁ, (ὅρχος) the first of a row, a file-leader : then, generally, a leader, chief, Hom., Hes.
ὅρχᾰτος, ὁ, (ὅρχος) a row of trees or plants, Il. :—as collective noun, a garden, Od.
ὀρχέομαι, impf. ὠρχούμην : f. ὀρχήσομαι : aor. 1 ὠρχησάμην : Dep. : (ὅρχος) :—to dance in a row, and generally, to dance, Hom., etc. ; δώσω τοι Τεγέην ὀρχήσασθαι will give thee Tegea to dance in or on, Orac. ap. Hdt. ; c. acc. sign., Λακωνικὰ σχήματα ὀρχεῖσθαι to dance Laconian figures, Hdt. 2. trans. to represent by pantomimic dancing, ὀρχεῖσθαι τὸν Αἴαντα (as Horace, Cyclopa moveri), Luc. II. metaph. to bound, ὀρχεῖται καρδία φόβῳ Aesch.
ὀρχηδόν, Adv. (ὅρχος) in a row, one after another, man by man, Lat. viritim, Hdt.
ὀρχηθμός, ὁ, (ὀρχέομαι) a dancing, the dance, Hom.
ὅρχημα, τό, in pl. dances, dancing, Soph., Xen., etc.

ὄρχησις, εως, ἡ, *dancing, the dance*, Hdt., Att. : esp. *pantomimic dancing*, Hdt., Att.

ὀρχησμός, ὁ, = ὀρχηθμός, Aesch.

ὀρχηστήρ, ῆρος, ὁ, = sq., Il.

ὀρχηστής, οῦ, ὁ, (ὀρχέομαι) *a dancer*, Il., Pind., etc.   II. *a dancing-master*, Plat.

ὀρχηστικός, ή, όν, *of* or *fit for dancing*, of the trochaïc verse, Arist.   II. *pantomimic*, Luc.

ὀρχηστο-διδάσκαλος, ὁ, *a dancing-master*, Xen.

ὀρχηστο-μᾰνέω, (μαίνομαι) *to be dancing-mad*, Luc.

ὀρχήστρα, ἡ, (ὀρχέομαι) *the orchestra*, in the Attic theatre *a semicircular space in which the chorus danced*, between the stage and the audience, Plat.

ὀρχηστρίς, ίδος, ἡ, = ὀρχήστρια, Ar., Plat.

ὀρχηστύς, ύος, ἡ, Ion. for ὄρχησις, *the dance*, Hom., Eur. ; contr. dat. ὀρχηστῦ Od. [ῠ in nom. and acc.]

ὀρχίλος [ῐ], ὁ, *the golden-crested wren*, Ar.

ὄρχις, ιος and εως, ὁ, Att. nom. pl. ὄρχεις, Ion. ὄρχιες, *the testicles*, Hdt.

Ὀρχομενός, ὁ or ἡ, the name of several Greek cities, the most famous being Ὀ. Μινύειος in Boeotia, Hom.

ΟΡΧΟΣ, ὁ, *a row of vines* or *fruit-trees*, Od., Ar., etc.

ὄρωρα, intr. pf. of ὄρνυμι :—ὀρώρει, 3 sing. plqpf.

ὀρώρεται, 3 sing. pass. of ὄρνυμι, = ὄρωρε.

ὀρωρέχαται, ἄτο, 3 pl. pf. and plqpf. pass. of ὀρέγω.

ὀρώρυκτο, 3 sing. plqpf. pass. of ὀρύσσω.

ὀρώρυχα, pf. of ὀρύσσω.

ΟΣ, ἥ, ὅ, gen. οὗ, ἧς, οὗ, etc. :—Ep. gen. ὅου, ἕης ; dat. pl. οἷσι, ᾗς, ᾗσι.—Pronoun, which in early Greek was used   A. as a Demonstr. = οὗτος, ὅδε.   B. as a Relat.

A. DEMONSTR., *this, that;* sometimes also for αὐτός, *he, she, it*, only in nom. :   I. in Hom., ἀλλὰ καὶ ὃς δείδοικε Il. ; ὁ γὰρ γέρας ἐστὶ θανόντων Od.   II. in later Greek,   1. at the beginning of a clause, καὶ ὅς and *he*, καὶ ἥ and *she*, καὶ οἱ and *they*, Hdt., Plat.   2. ὃς καὶ ὅς *such and such a person*, Hdt.   3. ἦ δ' ὅς, ἦ δ' ἥ said *he*, said *she*, Plat.   4. in oppositions, Λέριοι κακοί· οὐχ ὁ μέν, ὃς δ' οὐ Phocyl. ; ὃς μὲν . . , ὁ δὲ . . , Mosch., etc.

B. RELAT., *who, which*, Lat. *qui, quae, quod* : properly, the Relat. is governed by the Noun or Verb in its own clause, but it often takes the case of the Anteced. *by attraction*, τῆς γενεῆς, ἧς Τρωὶ Ζεὺς δῶκε (where the proper case would be ἥν) Il. ; οὐδὲν ὧν λέγω (for οὐδὲν τούτων ἃ λέγω) Soph. :—reversely the Anteced. passes into the case of the Relat., τὰς στήλας, ἃς ἵστα, αἱ πλεῦνες (for τῶν στηλῶν, ἃς ἵστα, αἱ πλεῦνες) Hdt.   2. the neut. was used in Att. without an Antecedent, ὃ δὲ δεινότατόν γ' ἐστὶν ἁπάντων, ὁ Ζεὺς γὰρ ἕστηκεν but *what* is the strangest thing of all is, that Zeus stands, Ar., etc.   3. in many instances the Gr. Relat. must be resolved into a Conjunction and Pron., ἄτοπα λέγεις, ὅς γε (for ὅτι σύ γε) Eur. ; συμφορὰ δ', ὃς ἂν τύχῃ κακῆς γυναικός (for ἐάν τις) Eur. :—it is also used, where we should use the Inf., ἄγγελον ἧκαν, ὃς ἀγγείλειε *nuncium miserunt, qui nunciaret*, sent a messenger *to tell*, Od. ; πέμψον τιν', ὅστις σημανεῖ Eur.

II. the Relat. Pron. joined with Particles or Conjunctions :   1. ὅς γε, v. ὅσγε.   2. ὃς δή, v. δή I. 5.   3. ὃς καί *who also, but* καὶ ὅς and *who*.   4.

ὅς κε or κεν, Att. ὃς ἄν, much like ὅστις, Lat. *quicunque, whosoever, who if any.*

III. absol. usages of certain Cases of the Relat. Pron. :   1. gen. sing. οὗ, of Place, like ὅπου, *where*, Aesch., Trag., etc. :—ἔστιν οὗ *in some places*, Eur. ; οὐκ εἶδεν οὗ γῆς *in what part* of the earth, Id. :—in pregnant phrases, μικρὸν προϊόντες, οὗ ἡ μάχη ἐγένετο (for ἐκεῖσε οὗ) having gone on *to the place where . .* , Xen.   2. ἐξ οὗ (sub. χρόνου) *from the time when*, Hom., etc.   3. dat. fem. ᾗ, Dor. ᾷ, of Place, like Lat. *qua, where :* also with Sup. Adv., ᾗ μάλιστα, ᾗ ῥᾷστα, ᾗ ἄριστον, etc., like ὡς μάλιστα, etc., and Lat. *quam celerrime*, Xen.   4. acc. sing. neut. ὅ for δι' ὅ or ὅτι, *that, how that*, also *because*, Lat. *quod*, Hom. :—also *wherefore*, Lat. *quapropter*, Eur.

ΟΣ, ἥ, ὅν : gen. οἷο, etc. : POSSESSIVE PRON. :   I. of 3rd person, for ἑός, *his, her*, Lat. *suus*, Hom., old Att.   II. of 2nd person, for σός, *thy, thine*, Hes.   III. of 1st person, for ἐμός, *my, mine*, Od.

ὁσάκις [ᾰ], Ep. ὁσσάκι, (ὅσος) *as many times as, as often as*, Lat. *quoties*, Il. ; relative to τοσσάκι, Od.

ὁσαχῇ, (ὅσος) Adv. *in as many ways*, Plat. :—ὁσᾰχοῦ, Adv. *in as many places as*, Dem.

ὅσγε, ἥγε, ὅγε, (ὅς, γε) *who* or *which at least*, Hdt., Soph.   II. = Lat. *qui quidem* or *quippe qui*, οἵγε ὑπῆρξαν *since it was they who began*, Hdt.

ὅσδος, ὅσδω, Dor. and Aeol. for ὄζος, ὄζω.

ὁσ-ημέραι, Adv. for ὅσαι ἡμέραι, *as many days as are*, i. e. *daily, day by day*, Lat. *quotidie*, Ar., Thuc., etc.

ὁσία, Ion. -ίη, ἡ, (fem. of ὅσιος) *divine law, natural law*, οὐκ ἔστι ὁσίη *it is not lawful, nefas est*, Od., Hdt. ; πολλὴν ὁσίαν τοῦ πράγματος νομίσαι *to hold a thing fully sanctioned*, Ar.   II. *the service owed by man to God*, ὁσίης ἐπιβῆναι *to undertake the due rites*, h. Hom.   III. proverb., ὁσίας ἕκατι ποιεῖσθαί τι *to do a thing for form's sake*, Lat. *dicis caussa*, Eur.

ΟΣΙΟΣ, α, ον, and ος, ον, *hallowed, sanctioned by the law of God*, Theogn., Trag. :—οὐχ ὅσιος *unhallowed*, Eur., etc. :   1. opp. to δίκαιος (sanctioned by *human* law), *sanctioned by divine law*, τὰ ὅσια καὶ δίκαια *things of divine* and *human ordinance*, Plat. ; θεοὺς ὁσίων τι δρᾶν *to discharge a duty men owe the gods*, Eur.   2. opp. to ἱερός (*sacred* to the gods), *permitted* or *not forbidden by divine law*, ἱερὰ καὶ ὅσια *things sacred and profane*, Thuc., etc. :—ὅσιόν *or* ὅσιά [ἐστί], foll. by inf., *it is lawful, fas est*, Hdt., etc. ; οὐκ ὅσιόν ἐστι *nefas est*, Id. ; ὅσιον χωρίον *a place which may be trodden without impiety*, and so = βέβηλος, Lat. *profanus*, Ar. ; so, ὅσια ποιεῖειν Hdt. ; φρονεῖν Eur.   II. of persons, *pious, devout, religious*, Aesch., Eur., etc.   2. *pure*, ἱερῶν πατρῴων ὅσιος *scrupulous in performing* the rites of his forefathers, Aesch. ; ὅσιαι χεῖρες *pure, clean hands*, Eur.   III. Adv. ὁσίως Eur., etc. ; οὐχ ὁσίως Thuc. :—ὁσίως ἔχει τινί, c. inf., *it is allowed for one to do*, Xen. :—also ὅσια as Adv., ἐξ ἐμοῦ οὐχ ὅσι' ἔθνησκες *in unholy manner*, Eur. :—Comp. ὁσιώτερον, Id. : Sup. ὡς ὁσιώτατα Plat. Hence

ὁσιότης, ητος, ὁ, *piety, holiness*, Plat., Xen. ; and

ὁσιόω, f. ώσω, *to make holy, purify, set free from guilt by offerings*, Lat. *expiare*, Eur. :—Med., στόμα

ὁσιοῦσθαι to keep one's tongue pure, not to speak profanely, Id. :—Pass. to be purified, Plut.

ὀσμάομαι, older form ὀδμ-, Dep. to smell at a thing : metaph. to perceive, remark, c. gen., Soph. From

ὀσμή, ἡ, Att. form of the older ὀδμή, a smell, scent, odour, good or bad, Hom., Aesch.

ὅσον-οὖν, Ion. ὅσον-ῶν, Adv. ever so little, Hdt.

ὅσος, Ep. also ὅσσος, η, ον, like Lat. quantus, of Size, as great as, how great; of Quantity, as much as, how much; of Space, as far as, how far; of Time, as long as, how long; of Number, as many as, how many ; of Sound, as loud as, how loud; in pl. as many as, Lat. quot :—its antecedent is τόσος, after which ὅσος is simply as; τόσσον χρόνον, ὅσσον ἄνωγας so long time as thou dost order, Il. :—often the antec. is omitted, φωνὴ ὅση σκύλακος Od. 2. with τις, to denote indefinite size or number, ὅσον τι δένδρον Hdt., etc. 3. with Adjs. expressing Quantity, ὄχλος ὑπερφυὴς ὅσος prodigiously large, Ar. ; θαυμαστὸν ὅσον διαφέρει differs amazingly, Plat. ;—so in Lat. mirum quantum, immane quantum. 4. with Sup., ὅσα πλεῖστα the most possible, Hdt., etc.; v. infr. IV. 4. 5. c. inf. so much as is enough, ὅσον ἀποζῆν enough to live off, Thuc. ; ὅσον δοκεῖν enough for appearance, Soph. 6. with indic., ὅσσον ἔγωγε γιγνώσκω so far as I know, Il. ; ὅσονπερ σθένω Soph., etc. II. followed by Particles : ὅσος ἄν how great soever, with Subjunct., Hom., etc. 2. with ὅση how much, ἐπὶ μισθῷ ὅσῳ δή for payment of a certain amount, Hdt. ;—ὁσοσοῦν, Ion. -ῶν, ever so small, Id. III. ὅσον and ὅσα as Adv. : 1. so far as, so much as, οὐ μέντοι ἐγὼ τόσον αἴτιός εἰμι, ὅσσον οἱ ἄλλοι Il. ; c. inf. ὅσον γ' ἔμ' εἰδέναι so far as I know, Ar. b. how far, how much, ἴστε ὅσσον περιβάλλετον ἵπποι ye know how much they excel, Il. ;—with Adjs. how, ὅσον μέγα Hes., etc. 2. only so far as, only just, ὅσον ἐς Σκαιάς τε πύλας καὶ φηγὸν ἵκανεν Il.; εἰ μὴ ὅσον γραφῇ except only by a picture, Hdt. 3. in reference to distances, ὅσον τε, about, nearly, ὅσον τ' ὄργυιαν Od. ; ὅσον τε δέκα στάδια Hdt. 4. with Adjs. ὅσσον βασιλεύτερός εἰμι so far as, inasmuch as I am a greater king, Il. ; ὅσον εἰμὶ κάρτιστος how I am far the strongest, Ib. : —so with Advs., ὅσον τάχιστα Att. ; ὅσον μάλιστα Aesch. 5. with negatives, ὅσον οὐ or ὀσονού, Lat. tantum non, only not, all but, Thuc. ; ὅσον οὐκ ἤδη immediately, Eur. : οὐχ ὅσον οὐκ ἠμύναντο, ἀλλ' not only did they not avenge themselves, Thuc. :—ὅσον μή so far as not, save or except so far as, ὅσον γε μὴ ποτιψαύων so far as I can without touching . . , Soph., etc. IV. ὅσῳ, ὅσῳ περ, by how much, ὅσῳ πλέον Hes. ; διέδεξε, ὅσῳ ἐστὶ τοῦτο ἄριστον Hdt. 2. ὅσῳ with Comp. when followed by another, Comp. with τοσούτῳ, like Lat. quo or quanto melior, eo magis, ὅσῳ μᾶλλον πιστεύω, τοσούτῳ μᾶλλον ἀπορῶ Plat. V. ὅσον, εἰς ὅσον σθένω Soph. ; ἐφ' ὅσον ἠδύνατο Thuc. 2. ἐν ὅσῳ, while, Ar., Thuc.

ὅσ-περ, (Ep. also ὅ-περ) ἥ-περ, ὅ-περ ; gen. οὗπερ : in Ion. writers and Poets the obl. cases are borrowed from the Art., gen. τοῦπερ, dat. τῇπερ, pl. τοίπερ, τάπερ, τῶνπερ :—the very man who, the very thing which,

but often simply for ὅς, Hom., etc. II. absol. ἅπερ, as, like καθάπερ (v. καθά), Aesch. 2. ἧπερ, which way, where, whither, Il., Xen., etc.; Ion. τῆπερ : —also as, Il., etc.

ὌΣΠΡΙΟΝ, τό, pulse of all kinds, Hdt. ; in pl., Xen.

ὌΣΣΑˇ, Att. ὄττα, ἡ, a rumour, Lat. fama, which, from its origin being unknown, was held divine, a word voiced abroad, ὄσσα ἐκ Διός Od. ; personified as messenger of Zeus, Hom. 2. generally, a voice, Hes. 3. still more generally, a sound, of the harp, h. Hom. ; the din of battle, Hes. 4. an ominous voice, prophecy, warning, Pind.

ὄσσα, Ion. and Ep. neut. pl. of ὅσα.

ὀσσάκι, Ion. and Ep. for ὁσάκις.

ὀσσάτιος [ᾰ], Ep. lengthd. form of ὅσος, Il.

ὌΣΣΕ, τώ, neut. dual, the two eyes, nom. and acc. with Adj. in the pl., ὄσσε φαεινά, αἱματόεντα Il. ; with Verb in sing., πυρὶ δ' ὄσσε δεδήει Ib. ; a gen. pl. ὄσσων Hes., Aesch. ; dat. ὄσσοις, ὄσσοισι Hes.

ὀσσίχος [ῐ], η, ον, Ep. Dim. of ὅσος, ὅσσος, as little, how little, Lat. quantulus, Theocr.

ὄσσομαι, (ὄσσε), Epic Dep., only in pres. and impf. without augm., to see, ὀσσόμενος πατέρ' ἐσθλὸν ἐνὶ φρεσίν (so Shaksp. 'in my mind's eye'), Od. 2. to presage, have foreboding of, κακά, ἄλγεα Hom. 3. to foretoken, Id.

ὄσσος, η, ον, Ep. and Ion. for ὅσος.

ὀστάριον [ᾰ], τό, Dim. of ὀστέον, a little bone, Anth.

ὅσ-τε, (Ep. also ὅ-τε) ἥ-τε, ὅ-τε, who, which, just like the simple ὅς or ὅστις, Hom., etc.; neut. τό τε Hes. ; pl. τά τε Il. ; pl. fem. τάς τε Ib. 2. ἐξ οὗτε from the time when, Aesch.

ὀστέϊνος, η, ον, made of bone, of bone, Hdt., Plat.

ὈΣΤΕΌΝ, τό, Att. contr. ὀστοῦν, poët. ὀστεῦν : pl. ὀστέα, Att. contr. ὀστᾶ:—Att. gen. pl. ὀστῶν, also ὀστέων (metri grat.) Soph., Ar. : Ep. gen. pl. ὀστεόφιν (v. infr.) :—Lat. os, ossis, a bone, Hom., Hdt., Att. ; λευκὰ ὀστέα the bleached bones of the dead, Od.

ὀστῖνος, η, ον, (ὀστέον) Att. form of ὀστέϊνος ; τὰ ὀστίνα, Lat. tibiae, bone-pipes, Ar.

ὅσ-τις, ἥ-τις, ὅ τι (often written ὅ, τι—to distinguish it from ὅτι, that), with double inflexions, gen. οὗτινος, ἧστινος, dat. ᾧτινι, ᾗτινι, etc. ; pl. οἵ-τινες, αἵ-τινες, ἅ-τινα, etc. : Hom. has also the masc. collat. form ὅτις and the neut. ὅ ττι. From ὅτις also come cases with a single inflexion, viz. gen. ὅτου, Ep. ὅττεο, contr. ὅττευ, ὅτευ ; dat. ᾧτῳ· Ep. ὅτεῳ :—Ep. acc. ὅτινα :—pl. nom. neut. ὅτινα ; gen. ὅτεων, Ep. ὀτέοισιν, Att. ὅτοισι ; fem. ὀτέῳσιν ; acc. ὅτινας.—For the Ion. and Ep. form ἅσσα, Att. ἅττα, v. sub ἄσσα. Any one who, anything which, i. e. whosoever, whichsoever, differing from ὅς, as Lat. quisquis, from qui, Hom., etc. ; ὅντινα κιχείη whomsoever he caught, Il., etc. :— ἔστιν ὅστις, Lat. est qui, often with a negat., οὐκ ἔστιν ὅτῳ μείζονα μοῖραν νείμαιμ' there is no one to whom I would give more, Aesch., etc. :—οὐδὲν ὅ τι οὐ everything, Hdt. II. hardly different from ὅς, who, βωμόν, ὅστις νῦν ἔξω τῆς πόλεώς ἐστι the altar, which . . , Thuc. III. in indirect questions, ξεῖνος ὅδ', οὐκ οἶδ' ὅστις Od. :—in dialogue, when the person questioned repeats the question asked by τίς, as οὗτος

τί ποιεῖς; Answ. ὅ τι ποιῶ; [you ask] *what* l'm *doing?* Ar.   IV. neut. ὅ τι used absol. as a Conjunction, v. ὅ τι.   V. ἐξ ὅτου *from which time*, Soph., etc.   2. *from what cause*, Id., Eur.

ὀστοῦν, τό, Att. contr. for ὀστέον.

ὀστο-φυής, ές, (φυή) *of bony nature* or *substance*, Batr.

ὀστρᾰκεύς, έως, ὁ, (ὄστρακον) *a potter*, Anth.

ὀστρᾰκίζω, f. ίσω, *to banish by potsherds, ostracize*, Thuc.—Ostracism (ὀστρᾰκισμός) was adopted at Athens to check the power of individuals, which had become too great for the liberties of the people.

ὀστρᾰκίνδα, Adv. *played with potsherds* or *oyster-shells*, παιδιὰ ὀστρ. a game in which an ὄστρακον, black on one side and white on the other, was thrown on a line, and according as the black or white turned up, one party was obliged to fly and the other pursued, ὀστρ. βλέπειν (with a reference to ὀστρᾰκισμός), Ar.

ὀστρᾰκῐνος [ᾰ], η, ον, *earthen, of clay*, Anth., N. T.

ὀστρᾰκισμός, ὁ, *ostracism*, v. ὀστρᾰκίζω.

ὀστρᾰκό-δερμος, ον, (δέρμα) *with a shell like a potsherd, hard-shelled*, Batr.

ὀστρᾰκόεις, εσσα, εν, poët. for ὀστράκινος, δόμος ὀστρ. Anth. From

ὄστρᾰκον, τό, *an earthen vessel*, Lat. *testa*, Ar.   2. *a tile* or *potsherd*, esp. *the tablet used in voting* (v. ὀστρᾰκίζω), Plat.   3. *a sort of earthenware castanet*, Ar.   II. *the hard shell of testaceous animals*, as snails, muscles, tortoises, h. Hom., Theocr.

ὀστρᾰκοφορία, ἡ, *a voting with ὄστρακα*, Plut.

ὀστρᾰκό-χροος, ον, (χρόα) *with metapl. acc.* ὀστρακό-χροα, *with a hard skin or shell*, Anth.

ὀστρειο-γρᾰφής, ές, (γράφω) *purple-painted*, Anth.

ΟΣΤΡΕΟΝ, Att. ὄστρειον, τό, *an oyster*, Lat. *ostrea*, Aesch., Plat.

ὀστ-ώδης, ες, (εἶδος) *like bone, bony*, Xen.

ὀσφραίνομαι, f. ὀσφρήσομαι: aor. 2 ὠσφρόμην, inf. ὀσφρέσθαι, part. ὀσφρόμενος: (ὄζω):—*to catch scent of, smell, scent, track*, c. gen., Hdt., Ar., etc.; absol., Plat. Hence

ὀσφραντήριος, α, ον, *smelling, able to smell, sharp-smelling*, Ar.

ὄσφραντο, Ion. 3 pl. plqpf. of ὀσφραίνομαι.

ὄσφρησις, ἡ, *the sense of smell, smell*, Plat.

ὀσφρόμενος, aor. 2 part. of ὀσφραίνομαι.

ΟΣΦΥΣ [ῡ], ἡ, gen. ὀσφύος [ῠ]: acc. ὀσφύν, also ὀσφύα:—*the loin* or *loins, the lower part of the back*, Hdt., Aesch., etc.:—ἀναζώννυσθαι τὴν ὀσφύν *to gird up one's loins*, N. T.; ὁ καρπὸς τῆς ὀσφύος *the fruit of the loins*, i. e. *a son*, Ib.

ΟΣΧΟΣ, ὁ, = μόσχος, *a vine-branch*, Ar.

ὀσχο-φόρια or ὠσχ-, τά, (φέρω) *one day of the Athen.* festival Σκίρα, on which boys, *carrying vine-branches loaded with grapes* (v. ὄσχος), went in procession from the temple of Bacchus to that of Ἀθηνᾶ Σκιράς, Plut.

ὅταν, for ὅτ' ἄν (ὅτε ἄν), Adv. of Time, *whenever*, Lat. *quandocunque*, foll. by Subjunct., Hom., etc.; in Ep. also ὅτε κεν Il. :—εἰς ὅτε κεν *until such time as* . . , Od. :—ὅταν τάχιστα, Lat. *quum primum*, Xen.

ὅτε, relat. Adv. of Time, formed from the relat. stem ὁ- and τε (v. τε B), answering to demonstr. τότε, and interrog. πότε :—*when*, Lat. *quum, quando*, foll. by In-

dic., Hom., etc. ;—by Optat. :—*of future events represented as uncertain*, Il. :—in Hom. sometimes for ὅταν, with Subj.   2. *elliptical in phrase* ἔστιν ὅτε or ἔσθ' ὅτε, like Lat. *est ubi, there are times when, sometimes, now and then*, Hdt., Att.   II. *in Causal sense*, like Lat. *quum, whereas*, Il., Att.   III. ὁτέ *absol. Adv.*, like ἔσθ' ὅτε, *sometimes*, ὁτὲ μὲν . . , ἄλλοτε . . , ὁτὲ μὲν . . , ἄλλοτε δ' αὖ . . , Il. ; ὅτε μὲν . . , ὅτε δὲ . . , Arist.

ὅ-τε, neut. of ὅσ-τε.   II. Ion. masc. for ὅσ-τε, Il.

ὀτέοισιν, Ep. and Ion. dat. pl. of ὅστις; ὅτευ, gen.; ὅτεῳ dat. ; ὅτεων, gen. pl.

ὅ τι, Ep. ὅ ττι, (often written ὅ, τι and ὅ, ττι—to distinguish them from ὅτι, ὅττι, *that*), neut. of ὅστις, used as an Adv. like διότι, in indirect questions, *for what, wherefore*, ὅς κ' εἴποι, ὅ τι τόσσον ἐχώσατο who might say, *wherefore he is so angry*, Il. ; ἢν μὴ φράσῃς ὅ τι . . *unless you tell me why* . . , Ar.   II. ὅ τι μή or ὅτι μή, after a negat. clause, *except*, Il. ; οὐδαμοί, ὅτι μὴ Χῖοι μοῦνοι Hdt.   III. with Sup. Adv., ὅ ττι τάχιστα, *as quick as possible*, Hom. ;—so, ὅ τι τάχος Hdt., etc. ; ὅ τι μάλιστα, ὅ τι ἐλάχιστα, etc., Thuc. ; also with Adjs., ὅ τι πλεῖστον ναυτικόν, ὅ τι πλεῖστον χρόνον Xen. ; ὅ τι πλείστη εὐδαιμονία Plat.

ὅτι, Ep. also ὅττι, Conjunction, *that*, Lat. *quod*, after Verbs of *seeing* or *knowing, thinking* or *saying*, used in quoting another person's words, ἠγγέλθη, ὅτι Μέγαρα ἀφέστηκε news *came that Megara has revolted* (where we say *had*), Thuc. ; ἀποκρινάμενοι ὅτι πέμψουσι (where we say *that they would* send), Id. ;—in orat. obliq., with opt., ἠπείλησ' ὅτι βαδιοίμην I threatened *that I would* go, Ar.   II. pleonast. before the very words of a speech (where in our idiom the Conjunction is left out, its place being supplied by inverted commas), καὶ ἐγὼ εἶπον, ὅτι ἡ αὐτή μοι ἀρχή ἐστι and I said : ' I will begin at the same point,' Plat.   III. ὅτι in Att. may represent a whole sentence, esp. in affirm. answers, οὐκοῦν τὸ ἀδικεῖν κάκιον ἂν εἴη τοῦ ἀδικεῖσθαι ; Answ. δῆλον δὴ ὅτι (i. e. ὅτι κάκιον ἂν εἴη), Id. ; so in the affirmations conveyed by οἶδ' ὅτι, οἶσθ' ὅτι, etc., and in δηλονότι (i. e. δῆλόν ἐστιν ὅτι) used as Adv.   IV. οὐχ ὅτι . . , ἀλλὰ or ἀλλὰ καί . . , *not only*, but also . . , Xen. ; οὐ μόνον ὅτι ἄνδρες, ἀλλὰ καὶ γυναῖκες Plat. :—οὐχ ὅτι, not followed by a second clause, means *although*, οὐχ ὅτι παίζει καί φησι Id.   2. for ὅτι μή, v. ὅ τι II.   V. as a Causal Particle *for that, because, seeing that, inasmuch as*, Lat. *quod*, Hom., etc.

ὀτιή, Conjunction, Comic form of ὅτι, *because*, Ar.   2. = ὅτι, *that*, Id.   II. = ὅ τι, *wherefore*, ὀτιὴ τί ; *why so ? wherefore so ?* Id.

ὀτι-οῦν, = ὅτι οὖν, neut. of ὅστις οὖν, *whatsoever*, Thuc.

ὅ-τις, ὅ-τινα, ὅ-τινας, Ep. for ὅσ-τις, ὅν-τινα, οὕσ-τινας.

ὀτλεύω, f. σω, *to suffer, endure*, Babr. From

ΟΤΛΟΣ, ὁ, *a burden, distress*, Aesch.

ΟΤΟΒΟΣ, ὁ, *any loud noise*, as *the din* of battle, Hes. ; *the rattling* of chariots, Aesch. ; *the crash* of thunder, Soph. ; also of the flute, γλυκὺν αὐλῶν ὄτ. Id. (Formed from the sound.)

ὀτοτοῖ, *an exclamation of pain and grief, ah! woe!* Trag. : so ὀτοτοτοῖ Aesch. ; ὀτοτοτοῖ τοτοῖ Id. ; ὀτοτοτοῖ τοτοῖ Soph. ; ὀτοτοτοτοτοτοῖ Eur. Hence

ὀτοτύζω, f. ξομαι, to wail aloud, Ar.; f. ὀτοτύξομαι, Id.:—Pass. to be bewailed, Aesch.

Ὀτοτύξιοι, οἱ, Com. pr. n., men of Wails, with a play on Ὀλοφύξιοι (men of Olophyxus near Mt. Athos), Ar.

ὀτρᾰλέος, α, ον, (v. ὀτρύνω) = sq.:—used by Hom. and Hes. only in Adv. ὀτρᾰλέως, quickly, readily.

ὀτρηρός, ά, όν, (ὀτρύνω) quick, nimble, busy, ready, Hom., Ar.:—Adv. - ρῶς, = ὀτραλέως, Od.

ὄτρῐχες, nom. pl. of ὄθριξ.

ὀτρυντύς [ῠ], ύος [ῠ], ἡ, a cheering on, exhortation, Il.

ΟΤΡΥ'ΝΩ [ῠ]: Ep. inf. ὀτρυνέμεν: impf. ὤτρυνον, Ion. ὀτρύνεσκον: Ep. f. ὀτρῠνέω: aor. 1 ὤτρῡνα:—to stir up, rouse, egg on, spur on, encourage, Il.; c. inf., ὀτρ. τινὰ πολεμίζειν Ib.; γήμασθαι Od., etc.; inf. omitted, ἦ τινα ὀτρύνεεις ἐπίσκοπον (sc. ἰέναι); wilt thou urge one (to go) as a spy? Il.:—Med. or Pass. to bestir oneself, hasten, Od., etc.; c. inf., ὀτρυνώμεθ᾽ ἀμυνέμεν ἀλλήλοισιν Il. 2. of things, to urge forward, quicken, speed, Hom., etc.

ὄττα, Att. for ὄσσα.

ὄτ-τεο, ὄτ-τευ, Ep. for οὗ-τινος, gen. of ὅστις.

ὄττῐ, Ep. for ὅτι (the Conjunction), that, because.

ὅ ττι, Ep. for ὅ τι, neut. of ὅστις, whatever.

ὄ-τῳ, Att. for ᾧ-τινι, dat. of ὅσ-τις.

ΟΥ', before a vowel with smooth breathing οὐκ, with rough breathing οὐχ, Att. also οὐχί, Ep. οὐκί: Adv. used in direct negation (cf. μή), not, Lat. non.

A. USAGE: I. adhering to single words so as to form a quasi-compd. with them, οὐ δίδωμι to withhold, οὐκ ἐῶ to refuse, οὐκ ἐθέλω nolo, οὔ φημι nego. II. as negativing the whole sentence, τὴν δ᾽ ἐγὼ οὐ λύσω Il., etc. 2. in dependent clauses οὐ is used, a. with ὅτι or ὡς, after Verbs of saying or knowing, ἔλεξε ὡς Ἕλληνες οὐ μενοῖεν Aesch. b. in Causal sentences, and in Temporal sentences that involve special times, ἄχθεται ὅτι οὐ κάρτα θεραπεύεται Hdt.; οὐκ ἔσθ᾽ ἐραστὴς ὅστις οὐκ ἀεὶ φιλεῖ Eur. 3. in a conditional clause μή is necessary, except, a. when οὐ is closely attached to the Verb (v. supr. 1), εἰ φθονέω τε καὶ οὐκ ἐῶ διαπέρσαι Il. b. when the subjoined clause is hypothetical in form only, μὴ θαυμάσῃς, εἰ πολλὰ οὐ πρέπει σοι (where εἰ = ὅ τι) Isocr.; δεινὸν γὰρ ἂν εἴη πρῆγμα, εἰ Ἕλληνας οὐ τιμωρησόμεθα Hdt. 4. οὐ is used with Inf. in oratio obl., when it represents the Indic. of oratio recta, λέγοντες οὐκ εἶναι αὐτόνομοι Thuc.; οἶμαι οὐκ ὀλίγον ἔργον αὐτὸ εἶναι Plat. 5. οὐ is used with the Participle, when it can be resolved into a finite sentence with οὐ, κατενόησαν οὐ πολλοὺς τοὺς Θηβαίους ὄντας = ὅ τι οὐ πολλοί εἰσι, Thuc. 6. Adjectives and abstract Substantives with the Article commonly take μή (v. μή B. 6), but οὐ is occasionally attached to them, τῶν γεφυρῶν οὐ διάλυσιν the non-dissolution of the bridge, the fact of its not being broken up, Thuc.; so, ἡ οὐ περιτείχισις Id.

B. ACCUMULATION: the negative is often repeated, so that two negatives do not make an affirmative, Att., οὐκ ἔστιν οὐδὲν κρεῖσσον φίλου Eur.; καθεύδων οὐδεὶς οὐδενὸς ἄξιος οὐδὲν μᾶλλον τοῦ μὴ ζῶντος Plat.; οὐδενὶ οὐδαμῇ οὐδαμῶς οὐδεμίαν κοινωνίαν ἔχει Id.

C. PLEONASM OF οὐ: after Verbs of denying, doubting, and disputing, followed by ὡς or ὅτι, οὐ is inserted, where in Engl. the negat. is not required,

ἀμφισβητεῖ ὡς οὐ δεῖ δίκην διδόναι Plat. Like this is the appearance of οὐ in the second member of a negative comparative sentence, ἥκει ὁ Πέρσης οὐδέν τι μᾶλλον ἐπ᾽ ἡμέας ἢ οὐ καὶ ἐπ᾽ ὑμέας Hdt.

D. in Poetry, if ἤ stands before οὐ, the two sounds coalesce into one syllable, as in ἢ οὐ, μὴ οὐ.

E. οὐ in connexion with other Particles will be found in alphabetical order, οὐ γάρ, οὐ μή, etc.

οὗ, gen. of relat. Pron. ὅς. II. as Adv. where, v. ὅς, ἥ, ὅ B. III.

οὗ, Lat. sui, gen. sing. of 3 pers. masc. and fem. for αὑτοῦ, αὑτῆς, but also for αὐτοῦ, αὐτῆς, Hom.; Ion. and Ep. forms, ἕο, εὗ, εἷο; Ep. also ἕθεν. II. dat. οἷ, sibi, = αὑτῷ, αὑτῇ, to himself, to herself, οἷ αὐτῷ and ἑοῖ αὐτῷ Hom.:—but οἱ enclit., = αὐτῷ, αὐτῇ, to him, to her, Id. III. acc. ἕ, se, ἓ αὐτόν, ἓ αὐτήν Hom.: which in Att. becomes ἑαυτόν, v. ἑαυτοῦ:—enclit. ἑ, ἑέ, him, her, Il. IV. other forms of the acc. are σφε, μιν, νιν, v. sub vv. V. the nom. was ἵ, v. sub v, etc. VI. for the dual and pl., v. σφωέ, σφεῖς.

οὐά, Lat. vah! exclam., ha! ah! N.T.

οὐαί, exclam., Lat. vae! ah! οὐαί σοι woe to thee! N. T.

οὐᾰτόεις, εσσα, εν, long-eared, Anth.

οὖς, τό, poët. for οὖς, ear. Hence

οὐ γάρ, for not, assigning a negative reason, Hom., etc.: οὐ γάρ, in answers, why no, Plat. II. elliptic, in interrogative replies, where yes must be supplied, τούτους ἀγαθοὺς ἐνόμισας; Answ. οὐ γάρ..; yes, for why shouldn't I? yes; why not? Ar. 2. in questions, after an affirm. answer is expected, οὐ γὰρ ὁ Παφλαγὼν ἀπέκρυπτε ταύτας; why, did he not keep them hidden? Id.

οὐ γὰρ ἀλλά, an ellipt. phrase, used in Att. to express a negation and give a reason for it, Lat. enimvero, οὐ σκῶπτέ μ᾽, οὐ γὰρ ἀλλ᾽ ἔχω κακῶς (i. e. μὴ σκῶπτέ με· οὐ γὰρ σκωπτικῶς, ἀλλὰ κακῶς ἔχω) Ar.

οὐ γὰρ οὖν, in answer to a negat. propos., where οὖν refers to a foregone proof as conclusive, why no,—certainly not, Plat.

οὐ γάρ που, for in no manner, Plat.

οὐ γάρ τοι, merely οὐ γάρ strengthd., Od., etc.:—so οὐ γάρ τοι ἀλλά Plat.

οὐγώ, Att. crasis for ὁ ἐγώ.

οὐδαῖος, α, ον, (οὖδας) infernal, of Pluto, Anth.

οὐδᾰμῆ or οὐδᾰμά (v. sub fin.), Adv. of οὐδαμός: I. of Place, nowhere, in no place, Hes., Aesch.; οὐδ. ἄλλη Hdt.; ἄλλη οὐδ. in no other place, Id.; c. gen., οὐδ. Αἰγύπτου in no part of Egypt, Id. 2. in no direction, no way, Id. II. of Manner, in no way, in no wise, Id., Aesch., etc.:—not at all, never, Hdt., Soph.—The Poets use either οὐδαμῇ Dor. -μᾶ [ᾱ], or οὐδαμά [-μᾰ], as the metre requires.

οὐδᾰμόθεν, Adv. of οὐδαμός, from no place, from no side, Plat., etc.

οὐδᾰμόθῐ, Ion. for οὐδαμοῦ, nowhere, in no place, Hdt.

οὐδᾰμοῖ, Adv. of οὐδαμός, no-whither, Ar., Xen.

οὐδ-ᾰμός, ή, όν, for οὐδὲ ἀμός, Ion. for οὐδ-είς, not even one, not one, only in pl., none, Hdt.

οὐδᾰμόσε, Adv. of οὐδαμός, = οὐδαμοῖ, Thuc., Plat.

οὐδᾰμοῦ, Adv. of οὐδαμός, = οὐδαμόθι, nowhere, answering to ποῦ; where? Hdt., Thuc., etc.; c. gen., οὐδά-

μοῦ γῆς Hdt.; οὐδαμοῦ ἦν φρενῶν Eur.   2. οὐδαμοῦ λέγειν τινά to esteem as naught, Lat. nullo in loco habere, Soph.; so, θεοὺς νομίζων οὐδ. Aesch.; οὐδ. (or μηδαμοῦ) εἶναι, φαίνεσθαι, like Cicero's ne apparere quidem, not to be taken into account, Plat.   II. of Manner, ἄλλοθι οὐδαμοῦ in no other way, Id.

οὐδαμῶς, Adv. of οὐδαμός, in no wise, Hdt., Att.; ἄλλως οὐδαμῶς Hdt.; οὐδέποτε οὐδαμῇ οὐδαμῶς Plat.

ΟΥ'ΔΑΣ, τό, gen. οὔδεος, dat. οὔδεϊ, οὔδει, the surface of the earth, the ground, earth, Hom.; πῖαρ οὖδας the rich soil, Od.; ὀδὰξ ἕλον οὖδας they bit the dust, of dying men, Hom.; οὔδει ἐρείσθη he propped himself on the ground, Il.; ἀπ' οὔδεος from the ground, οὐδάσδε to the ground, to earth, Hom.; πρὸς οὖδας φορεῖσθαι, πεσεῖν, βεβλῆσθαι Trag.   2. the floor or pavement of rooms and houses, Hom. :—proverb., ἐπ' οὔδεϊ καθίζειν τινά to bring a man to the pavement, i. e. to strip him of all he has, h. Hom.

οὐδέ (οὐ δέ), Negat. Particle, related to μηδέ as οὐ to μή:—   I. as Conjunct., but not, answering to μέν, ἄλλοις μὲν πᾶσιν ἑήνδανεν, οὐδέ ποθ' Ἥρῃ, οὐδὲ Ποσειδάων', οὐδὲ γλαυκώπιδι κούρῃ Il. :—and not, nor, Lat. neque, nec, τραχὺς μόναρχος οὐδ' ὑπεύθυνος Aesch.; ἄθικτος οὐδ' οἰκητός Soph.   2. with a simple negat. preceding, nor, οὐκέτι σοὶ μένος ἔμπεδον οὐδέ τις ἀλκή Od.   II. when οὐδέ is repeated at the beginning of two following clauses, the first οὐδέ is often adverbial (infr. III), not even .., nor yet .., marking a stronger opposition than οὔτε .., οὔτε, neither .., nor .., Ib., Att.   III. as Adv. not even, Lat. ne .. quidem, οὐδ' ἠβαιόν not even a little, οὐδέ τυτθόν, οὐδὲ μίνυνθα Il., Att. :—before ἕν (one) it is not elided, οὐδὲ ἕν Ar.   2. οὐδέ is often repeated with other negatives: ἀλλ' οὐ γὰρ οὐδὲ νουθετεῖν ἔξεστί σε Soph.; so, οὐδὲ γὰρ οὐδέ Il., etc.

οὐδ-είς, οὐδε-μία (never –μίη), οὐδ-έν, and not one, i. e. no one, none, as Lat. nullus, for ne ullus, Hom., etc. :—rare in pl. (οὐδαμοί being used instead), Xen.; πρὸς οὐδένας τῶν Ἑλλήνων Dem.; v. infr. II. 3.   2. οὐδεὶς ὅστις οὐ, Lat. nemo non, every one, Hdt., Att.; οὐδὲν ὅ τι οὐ, Lat. nihil non, every, Hdt.; this came to be regarded as one word, so that οὐδείς passed into the same case as the relative, οὐδένα ὅντινα οὐ κατέκλασε Plat.   II. naught, good for naught, Ar.   2. in neut. of persons, οὐδέν εἰμι Hdt.; πρὸς τὸν οὐδένα Eur.; οὐδὲν εἶναι to be good for nothing, Ar.   3. in pl., οὐδένες ἐόντες being nobodies, Hdt.; ὄντες οὐδένες Eur.; ὁ μηδὲν ὢν κἀξ οὐδένων κεκλήσομαι Id.   4. with Preps., παρ' οὐδὲν ἄγειν, θέσθαι to make of no account, Soph., Eur.; δι' οὐδενὸς ποιεῖσθαι Soph.; ἐν οὐδενὸς εἶναι μέρει Dem.   III. neut. οὐδέν as Adv. not at all, naught, Il., etc.   2. οὐδὲν ἄλλο ἤ, v. ἄλλος.

οὐδέκοτε, Ion. for οὐδέποτε.

οὐδένεια, ἡ, (οὐδείς) nothingness, worthlessness, Plat.

οὐδενόσ-ωρος, ον, (ὥρα) worth no notice or regard, Il.

οὐδέ πη or οὐδέ-πη, Adv. in no wise, Od.

οὐδέ-ποτε, Ion. -κοτε, Dor. -ποκα, Adv. and not ever or nor ever, not even ever, never, Lat. ne unquam quidem, nunquam, Hom., etc.

οὐδέ πω, Adv. and not yet, not as yet, Aesch., Plat. :— in Hom., with a word between, οὐδέ τί πω, οὐδ' ἄν πω.

οὐδε-πώποτε, Adv. nor yet at any time, never yet at any time, Soph., Plat.

οὐδ-έτερος, α, ον, not either, neither of the two, Lat. neuter for ne uter, Hdt.; in pl., when each party is pl., Hes., Hdt. :—Adv. οὐδετέρως, in neither of two ways, Plat.; also neut. pl. as Adv. = οὐδετέρως, Id.   II. neutral, τῶν μὲν αἱρετῶν οὐσῶν, τῶν δὲ φευκτῶν, τῶν δ' οὐδετέρων Arist.

οὐδ-ετέρωσε, Adv. to neither of two sides, neither way, Il., Theogn.

οὐδ' ἔτι, Adv. and no more, no longer, Hom.

οὐ δή, Adv. certainly not, Lat. non sane, Hom.

οὐδήεις, εσσα, εν, (οὖδας) terrestrial, v. l. Od.

οὐ δή που or οὐ δήπου, Adv. I suppose not, v. δήπου.

οὐ δῆτα, Adv. no truly, Aesch., etc.

ΟΥ'ΔΟ'Σ, Att. ὀδός, ὁ, a threshold, Hom., Hes. :—the threshold or entrance to any place, Hom., Soph.   2. metaph., ἐπὶ γήραος οὐδῷ on the threshold, i. e. the verge, of old age, Hom.

οὐδός, ἡ, Ion. for ὁδός, a way, Od.

Οὐδυσσεύς, crasis for ὁ Ὀδυσσεύς.

ΟΥ'ΘΑΡ, ατος, τό, the udder of animals, Od., Hdt.: rarely of women, the breast, Aesch.   II. metaph., οὔθαρ ἀρούρης the richest, most fertile land, like Virgil's uber arvi, Il.; of the vine, οὔθαρ βοτρύων Anth.

οὐθάτιος [ᾰ], α, ον, of the udder, Anth.

οὐθείς, οὐθέν, later form for οὐδείς, οὐδέν.

οὔ θην, Adv. surely not, certainly not, Hom.

οὐκ, for οὐ before a smooth breathing, and in Ion. for οὐχ before a rough breathing.

οὐκ ἄρα, Adv. so not, not then, surely not, Hom.   II. in questions, οὐκ ἄρ' ἔμελλες οὐδὲ θανὼν λήσεσθαι χόλου; so not even in death canst thou forget thine anger? Od.

οὐκ-έτι or οὐκ ἔτι, Adv. no more, no longer, no further, opp. to οὔπω (not yet), Hom., etc.

οὐκί, Ion. for οὐχί.

οὔκ-ουν Ion. οὔκ-ων, Adv. (οὐκ, οὖν):   I. in direct negation, not therefore, so not, Lat. non ergo, non igitur, itaque non, Hdt., Soph., etc.; rarely in apodosi :—but the inferential force is scarcely discernible, like Lat. non sane, in narrative, οὔκων δὴ ἔπειθε so he failed to persuade him, Hdt.   II. in interrog. not therefore? not then? and so not? like Lat. nonne ergo? Aesch.; cf. sq.

οὐκοῦν, Adv. orig. identical with οὔκουν, but losing all negat. force, therefore, then, accordingly, Lat. ergo, igitur, itaque, Soph., etc.   2. in questions, so then? mostly in irony, Xen.   3. in answers, why yes, doubtless, Ar., Plat.

οὔκω, Ion. for οὔπω.

οὔκων, οὐκῶν, Ion. for οὔκουν, οὐκοῦν.

οὔκως, Ion. for οὔπως.

οὐλαί, Att. ὀλαί, αἱ, barley-corns, barley-groats, which were sprinkled on the head of the victim before the sacrifice, Od., Hdt., Att. (Commonly derived from οὖλος, ὅλος, as if οὐλαί or ὀλαί were whole grains, unground barleycorns. Others from ἀλέω, to grind, as Lat. mola from molere).

οὐλαμός, οῦ, ὁ, (εἴλω) a throng of warriors, οὐλαμὸς ἀνδρῶν Il.   II. later, a troop of cavalry, Lat. turma, ala, Polyb., Plut.

οὖλε, imper. of οὖλω.

οὐλή, ἡ, v. οὐλαί.

οὐλή, ἡ, (οὖλος A) a wound scarred over (cf. ὕπουλος), a scar, Lat. cicatrix, Od., Eur., Xen.

οὖλιος, α, ον, (οὖλος C) = ὀλοός, baleful, baneful, οὖλιος ἀστήρ of the dog-star, Il.; of Ares, Hes.

οὐλό-θριξ, τρῖχος, ὁ, ἡ, (οὖλος B) with curly hair, Hdt.

οὐλο-κάρηνος [ᾰ], ον, (οὖλος B, κάρηνον) with crisp, curling hair, Od. II. οὐλόποδ', οὐλοκάρηνα, poët. for ὅλους πόδας, ὅλα κάρηνα, h. Hom.

οὐλό-κερως, ων, (οὖλος B) with twisted horns, Strab.

οὐλόμενος, η, ον, Att. ὀλόμενος, aor. 2 med. part. of ὄλλυμι, used as Adj. destructive, baneful, Lat. fatalis, Hom., Hes., etc. II. unhappy, undone, lost, Lat. perditus, Aesch., Eur.

οὖλον, τό, mostly in pl., οὖλα, τά, the gums, Aesch., Plat.

οὐλό-πους, ποδος, v. οὐλοκάρηνος II.

ΟΥ'ΛΟΣ, η, ον (A), Ion. form of ὅλος, whole, entire, v. ὅλος :—of sound, continuous, incessant, οὖλον κεκλήγοντες screaming incessant, Il.; so, οὖλον γεράνων νέφος Anth.

ΟΥ'ΛΟΣ, η, ον (B), woolly, woollen, Hom.; οὖλη λάχνη thick, fleecy wool, Il.; οὖλαι κόμαι crisp, close-curling hair, Od.; οὐλότατον τρίχωμα of the hair of negroes, Hdt. 2. of plants, twisted, curling, Anth. :—generally, twisted, crooked, οὖλα σκέλεα ap. Arist.

οὖλος, η, ον (C), = οὐλόμενος, destructive, baneful, Il.

οὐλοτρῐχέω, f. ήσω, (οὐλόθριξ) to have curly hair, Strab.

οὐλο-χύται [ῠ], αἱ, (οὐλαί, χέω) barley-groats or coarsely-ground barley sprinkled over the victim before a sacrifice, Hom.; cf. ἄρχω II. 2.

Οὔλυμπος, Οὔλυμπόνδε, Ion. for Ὄλυμπ-.

οὐλω, (οὖλος A) to be whole or sound, imper. οὖλε, Lat. salve, as a salutation, health to thee, οὖλέ τε καὶ μέγα χαῖρε health and joy be with thee, Od.

οὐ μά, v. μά.

οὐ μάν, assuredly not, Dor. and Ep. for οὐ μήν, Hom.

οὐ μέν, no truly, nay verily, Hom.

οὐ μὲν οὖν or οὐμενοῦν, verily and indeed not, Ar. II. in answers, ἐγώ σοι οὐκ ἂν δυναίμην ἀντιλέγειν; Answ. οὐμενοῦν τῇ ἀληθείᾳ δύνασαι ἀντιλέγειν nay it is not me, but rather truth, that thou canst not gainsay, Plat.

οὐ μέντοι, not surely, not verily, Il. 2. not however, Hdt., Thuc., etc.; οὐ μέντοι ἀλλά not but that, Plat. II. in interrog. οὐ μέντοι; is it not surely? where an affirm. answer is expected, Id.

οὐ μή, in independent sentences, is used either in Denial or in Prohibition. I. in Denial, with Subj., chiefly of aor., οὔ τι μὴ ληφθῶ I shall not be captured, Aesch.; οὐ μὴ ἐσβάλωσιν they shall not make an inroad, Thuc., etc. :—οὐ μή with Subj. is commonly explained by the ellipsis of words expressing fear, which indeed are sometimes expressed, οὐ γὰρ ἦν δεινὸν μὴ ἀλφ κοτε Hdt.; οὐχὶ δέος μή σε φιλήσῃ Ar. But οὐ μή are also used with fut. Indic., οὔ σοι μὴ μεθέψομαί ποτε Soph.; οὐ μὴ δυνήσεται εὑρεῖν he will not be able to find, Xen. II. in Prohibition, οὐ μή is used interrogatively with fut. Indic. (chiefly of the 2nd person), = οὐ μὴ προσοίσεις χεῖρα ; = μὴ πρόσφερε χεῖρα Eur.; οὐ μὴ πρόσει = μὴ πρόσιθι, Ar.

οὐ μήν, not however, Aesch., etc.; οὐ μὴν οὐδέ not at all however, Thuc., Xen., etc. 2. οὐ μήν .. γε after a negative, no nor even yet, Lat. nedum, Ar.

οὐ μὴν ἀλλά, οὐ μὴν ἀλλά .. γε; also, οὐ μὴν ἀλλὰ καί .. γε, nevertheless, notwithstanding, yet, still, Plat., Dem.

οὐμός, crasis for ὁ ἐμός :— οὐμοί for οἱ ἐμοί.

ΟΥ'Ν, Ion. and Dor. ὦν, Adv., really, at all events, used like γοῦν to dismiss a perplexing subject, οὔτ' οὖν ἀγγελίης ἔτι πείθομαι, οὔτε θεοπροπίης ἐμπάζομαι Od.; ἐλέχθησαν λόγοι ἄπιστοι μὲν ἐνίοισι Ἑλλήνων, ἐλέχθησαν δ' ὦν but they really were spoken, Hdt.; εἴτ' οὖν, εἴτε μὴ γενήσεται whether it shall be really so, or no, Eur.; εἴτ' οὖν ἀληθὲς εἴτ' οὖν ψεῦδος Plat.; εἰ δ' ἔστιν, ὥσπερ οὖν ἔστι, θεός if he is, as he surely is, a god, Id. 2. added to indef. Pronouns and Advs., like Lat. cunque, ὅστις whoever, ὁστισοῦν whosoever; ὅπως how, ὁπωσοῦν howsoever; ἄλλος ὁστισοῦν another, be he who he may; so, ὁποιοσοῦν, ὁποσοσοῦν, ὁπωσοῦν, ὁποθενοῦν, etc. II. to continue a narrative, οἱ δ' ἐπεὶ οὖν ἤγερθεν so when they were assembled, Il., etc. :—also to resume after an apodosis, I say, Hdt., etc.; Hdt. inserts it between the Prep. and its Verb, ἐπεὰν δὲ ταῦτα ποιήσωσι, ἀπ' ὦν ἔδωκαν. III. in Inferences, then, therefore, Lat. igitur, Hdt., etc.; so, δὴ οὖν, οὖν δή Plat.

οὖν, crasis for ὁ ἐν and οἱ ἐν.

οὕνεκα, in Poets before a vowel οὕνεκεν, relat. Conj. for οὗ ἕνεκα on which account, wherefore, Hom. 2. relative to τούνεκα, for that, because, Pind., Trag. 3. after certain Verbs, just like ὅτι, Lat. quod, that, i. e. the fact that, after εἰδέναι, νοεῖν, ἐρεῖν, Od.; after ἴσθι, μαθεῖν, Soph. :—cf. ὁθούνεκα. II. as Prep. c. gen., equiv. to ἕνεκα, εἵνεκα, on account of, because of, Aesch., Soph.

οὔνεσθε, Ion. 2 pl. aor. 2 of ὄνομαι.

οὔνομα, τό, Ion. for ὄνομα.

οὐνομάζω, οὐνομαίνω, οὐνομαστός, Ion. for ὀνομ-.

οὔ νυ, nearly like οὐ δή, surely not, Hom.

οὔξ, crasis for ὁ ἐξ.

οὐξιών, crasis for ὁ ἐξιών.

οὐπαρήξων, crasis for ὁ ἐπαρήξων.

οὔ περ or οὔπερ, strengthd. for οὐ, not at all, Il.

οὔπερ, Adv., v. ὅς, ἥ, ὅ B. II.

οὔ-πη, nowhere, Hom. II. in no wise, Id.

οὐπί, crasis for ὁ ἐπί.

οὐπίτριπτος, crasis for ὁ ἐπίτριπτος.

οὐπιχώριος, crasis for ὁ ἐπιχώριος.

οὔ ποθι, nowhere, Il. :—οὐδέ ποθι nor anywhere, Hom.

οὔ ποτε or οὔποτε, Dor. οὔποκα, Adv. not ever, never, Hom., Att.

οὔ που; Adv. surely you do not mean that . . ? Eur.

οὔποψ, crasis for ὁ ἔποψ.

οὔ πω or οὔπω, Ion. οὔκω, Adv. not yet, Lat. nondum, opp. to οὐκέτι (no longer, no more), Hom., Hes., etc. 2. as a stronger form of the negat., not, not at all, σοὶ δ' οὔ πω θεοὶ κοτέουσιν Il., etc.

οὔ πώποτε or οὐπώποτε, Adv. never yet at any time, Hom., Att.

οὔ πως or οὔπως, Ion. οὔκως, Adv. nohow, in nowise, not at all, Il., etc.

οὐρά, Ion. οὐρή, ἡ, (akin to ὄρρος) the tail, of a lion,

dog, etc., Hom., Hdt.   II. of an army marching, the rear-guard, rear, Xen.; κατ᾽ οὐράν τινος ἕπεσθαι to follow in his rear, Id.; ὁ κατ᾽ οὐράν the rear-rank man, Id.; ἐπί or κατ᾽ οὐράν to the rear, backwards, Id.; ἐπ᾽ οὐρᾷ in rear, Id.   2. ῥήματος οὐρή, i. e. its echo, Anth.

οὐραγία, ἡ, the rear, Polyb. From

οὐρ-ᾱγός, ὁ, (ἡγέομαι) leader of the rear-guard, Xen.

οὐραῖος, α, ον, (οὐρά) of the tail, τρίχες οὐραῖαι Il.: —generally, hindmost, οὐρ. πόδες the hind-feet, Theocr.; cf. οὐραία.   2. οὐραῖον, τό, the tail, in pl., οὐραῖα the hinder part, rear, Eur., Luc.

Οὐρανία, ἡ, Urania, the Heavenly One, one of the Muses, Hes.   II. name of Aphrodité, Plat.

Οὐρᾰνίδης, ου, ὁ, son of Uranus, Hes., Pind. :—Οὐρανίδαι the Titans, Hes.

οὐράνιος [ᾰ], α, ον, and ος, ον, heavenly, of or in heaven, dwelling in heaven, οὐρ. θεοί Aesch., Eur.; οὐράνιαι alone, the goddesses, Pind.   2. generally, in or of heaven, ἀστήρ Id.; πόλος Aesch.; οὐρ. βρέτας fallen from heaven, Eur.; οὐρ. ὕδατα, i. e. rain, Pind.; οὐρ. ἄχος, of a storm, Soph.   II. reaching to heaven, high as heaven, οὐρ. κίων, of Aetna, Pind.; ἐλάτης οὐράνιος κλάδος Eur.; σκέλος οὐράνιον ἐκλακτίζειν, ῥίπτειν to kick up sky-high, Ar.   2. metaph. enormous, awful, furious, οὐρ. ἄχη Aesch.; οὐράνιόν γ᾽ ὅσον, like θαυμάσιον ὅσον, Lat. immane quantum, Ar. :—οὐράνια, as Adv. vehemently, Eur.

οὐρᾰνίς, ίδος, ἡ, pecul. fem. of οὐράνιος, Anth.

οὐρανίσκος, ὁ, Dim. of οὐρανός: hence, the vault of a room or tent, a canopy, Plut.

Οὐρανίωνες, οἱ, (οὐρανός) the heavenly ones, the gods above, Lat. coelites, with or without θεοί, Il.;—also the Titans, as descendants of Uranus, Ib. :—fem., θεαὶ Οὐρανίωναι Anth.

οὐρανο-γνώμων, ον, skilled in the heavens, Luc.

οὐρανό-δεικτος, ον, shewn from heaven, shewing itself in heaven, h. Hom.

οὐρανόθεν, (οὐρανός) Adv. from heaven, down from heaven, Hom., Hes.; properly an old gen. of οὐρανός, and therefore joined with Preps., ἀπ᾽ οὐρανόθεν Il.; ἐξ οὐρανόθεν Ib.

οὐρανόθι, (οὐρανός) Adv. in the heavens: but οὐρανόθι πρό = πρὸ οὐρανοῦ, in the front of heaven (cf. foreg.), Il.

οὐρανο-μήκης, ες, (μῆκος) high as heaven, shooting up to heaven, exceeding high or tall, Od.; δένδρεα Hdt.; λαμπάς Aesch.   2. metaph. stupendous, Ar.

ΟΥ᾽ΡΑ᾽ΝΟ᾽Σ, ὁ, Dor. ὠρανός, Aeol. ὀρανός; only in sing.:   I. heaven: in Hom. and Hes.,   1. the vault or firmament of heaven, the sky, conceived as a concave hemisphere resting on the verge of earth, upborne by the pillars of Atlas, Od., Hes., etc.; conceived to be of solid metal, χάλκεος, πολύχαλκος, σιδήρεος, Hom.: on this vault the sun performed his course, Od.; the stars were fixed upon it, and moved with it, for it was supposed to be always revolving, Il.   2. heaven, as the seat of the gods, above this skyey vault, the portion of Zeus, Hom.; πύλαι οὐρανοῦ Heaven-gate, which the Hours lifted and put down like a trap-door, Il.   3. in common language, heaven, the sky, Hom., etc.; πρὸς οὐρανὸν βιβάζειν τινά to exalt to heaven, as Horace evehere ad Deos, Soph.; εἰς τὸν οὐρ.

ἥλλοντο leapt up on high, Xen.: a region of heaven, climate, Hdt.   II. as prop. n. Uranus, son of Erebus and Gaia, Hes.; or husband of Gaia, parent of the Titans, Id., Aesch.

οὐρᾰν-οῦχος, ον, (ἔχω) holding heaven, ἀρχὴ οὐρ. the rule of heaven, Aesch.

οὐργάτης, crasis for ὁ ἐργάτης.

οὔρεα, τά, Ion. nom. and acc. pl. of ὄρος, mountain.

οὔρειος, η, ον, Ion. and Ep. for ὄρειος.

οὐρεό-φοιτος, ον, poët. for ὀρεοφ-, (φοιτάω) mountain-haunting, Anth. : fem. -φοιτάς, άδος, Ib.

οὐρεσι-βώτης, ου, ὁ, poët. for ὀρεσιβ-, feeding on the mountains, Soph.

οὐρεσί-οικος, ον, poët. for ὀρεσίοικος, Anth.

οὐρεσι-φοίτης, ου, ὁ, = οὐρεόφοιτος, Anth.

οὐρεύς, ῆος, ὁ, Ion. for ὀρεύς, a mule, Il.   II. = οὖρος a guard, in Il. 10. 84 the sense is uncertain.

οὐρέω, impf. ἐούρουν : f. -ήσομαι : (οὖρον):—to make water, Hes., Hdt.

οὐρῆας, Ion. acc. pl. of οὐρεύς, a mule.

οὐρητιάω, Desiderat. of οὐρέω, to want to make water, Ar.

οὐρήων, Ep. gen. pl. of οὐρεύς.

οὐρῐάς, ὁ, (οὐρά) the hindmost part, bottom, ἔγχεος οὐρ. the butt-end of the spear, shod with iron, Il.

οὐρι-βάτας, ου, ὁ, poët. and Dor. for ὀρειβάτης, walking the mountains, Eur. : also ὀριβάτης, Ar.

οὐρίζω, Ion. for ὁρίζω.

οὐρίζω, f. Att. ιῶ, (οὖρος A) to carry with a fair wind, to waft on the way, of words and prayers, Aesch.; κατ᾽ ὀρθὸν οὐρ. to speed on the way, guide prosperously, Soph.   II. intr. to blow favourably, Aesch.

οὐρί-θρεπτος, η, ον, poët. for ὀρει-, mountain-bred, Eur.

οὔριος, α, ον, and ος, ον, (οὖρος A) with a fair wind, Lat. vento secundo, οὐρ. πλοῦς, δρόμος a prosperous voyage, Soph.   2. metaph. prosperous, successful, Aesch., Eur. :—neut. pl. οὔρια as Adv., Eur.   II. prospering, favouring, fair, of winds, Id., Thuc.; comically of the bellows, οὐρίᾳ ῥιπίδι Ar.   2. οὐρία (sc. πνοή), ἡ, = οὖρος, a fair wind, οὐρίᾳ ἐφιέναι (sc. ἑαυτόν) to run before the wind, Plat.; so, ἐξ οὐρίων δραμοῦσα (sc. δρόμων) after having run a fair course, Soph.; ἀφήσω ἐμαυτὸν οὔριον Ar.   III. Ζεὺς οὔριος, as sending fair winds, i. e. conducting things to a happy issue, Aesch., Anth.

οὐριο-στάτης, ου, ὁ, steady and prosperous, Aesch.

οὐριόω, f. ώσω, to give to the winds, Anth.

οὔρισμα, ατος, τό, Ion. for ὅρισμα, a boundary-line, Hdt.

οὖρνις, crasis for ὁ ὄρνις.

ΟΥ᾽ΡΟΝ, τό, urine, Hdt., etc.

οὖρον, τό, Ion. for ὅρος, boundary, used by Hom. in three places, viz., ὅσα δίσκου οὖρα πέλονται as far as is the limit or space of a quoit's throw (cf. δίσκουρα), Il.; ὅσσον τ᾽ ἐπὶ οὖρα πέλονται ἡμιόνων as far as is the range of mules (in ploughing), Ib.; and so, more fully ὅσσον τ᾽ οὖρον πέλει ἡμιόνοιϊν, τόσσον ὑπεκπροθέων Od.: —what the distance expressed by the range of mules may be is uncertain; the common explanation is the length by which mules would distance oxen in ploughing a given space in the same time.

ΟΥΡΟΣ, οὖ, ὁ, *a trench* or *channel* for hauling up ships and launching them again, Il.

ΟΥΡΟΣ (A), ὁ, *a fair wind*, Hom., etc.; ἡμῖν δ' αὖ κατόπισθε νεὼς οὖρον ἵει Od.; πέμψω δέ τοι οὖρον ὄπισθεν Ib.; ἂψ δὲ θεοὶ οὖρον στρέψαν the gods changed *the wind* again *to a fair one*, Ib.; πέμπειν κατ' οὖρον to send *down* (i.e. *with*) the wind, speed on its way, Orac. ap. Hdt.; so, metaph., ἴτω κατ' οὖρον let it be swept *before the wind* to ruin, Aesch.; ταῦτα μὲν ῥείτω κατ' οὖρον let these things drift with *the wind*, Soph. **2.** οὖρός [ἐστι], like καιρός, 'tis *a fair time*, Id.; ἐγένετο τις οὖρος ἐκ κακῶν Eur.

οὖρος (B), ου, ὁ, *a watcher, warder, guardian*, Hom., Pind. (From the same Root as ὁράω and ὤρα *cura*.)

οὖρος (C), ου, ὁ, Ion. for ὅρος, *a boundary*.

ΟΥΡΟΣ (D), ου, ὁ, Lat. *urus*, a buffalo, Anth.

ΟΥΣ, τό, gen. ὠτός, dat. ὠτί: pl. nom. and acc. ὦτα, gen. ὤτων, dat. ὠσί: Ep. gen. also οὔατος, pl. nom. and acc. οὔατα, dat. οὔασι:—Lat. *auris, the ear*, Hom.; ὀρθὰ ἱστάναι τὰ ὦτα, of horses, Hdt.; βοᾷ ἐν ὠσὶ κέλαδος rings *in the ear*, Aesch.; φθόγγος βάλλει δι' ὤτων Soph.; δι' ὤτων ἦν λόγος, i.e. heard generally, Eur.; εἰς οὖς into *the ear*, secretly, Id.; so, εἰς ὦτα φέρειν Soph.:—metaph. of spies, Xen.;—τὰ ὦτα ἐπὶ τῶν ὤμων ἔχοντες, of persons who slink away ashamed (hanging their ears like dogs), Plat.:—athletes are described as having their ears bruised and swollen, τεθλαγμένος οὔατα πυγμαῖς Theocr. **II.** *the ear* or *handle*, of pitchers, cups, etc., οὔατα δ' αὐτοῦ τέσσαρ' ἔσαν Il.

οὐσία, Ion. -ίη, ἡ, (οὖσα, part. fem. of εἰμί) *that which is one's own*, *one's substance, property*, Hdt., Eur. **II.** = τὸ εἶναι, *being, existence*, Plat.; τὰς ἄπαιδας οὐσίας her childless *state*, Soph. **III.** *the being, essence, nature* of a thing, Plat., etc.

οὐτάζω, f. σω: aor. 1 οὔτασα:—Pass., pf. οὔτασμαι: = οὐτάω, *to wound*, c. dupl. acc., Κυπρίδα οὔτασε χεῖρα *wounded* Venus on the hand, Il.; also, σάκος οὔτασε *pierced* the shield, Ib.; c. acc. cogn., ἕλκος, ὅ με βροτὸς οὔτασεν ἀνήρ the wound which a man *struck* me withal, Ib.

οὔ τᾶν, crasis for οὔ τοι ἄν.

οὐ τᾶρα or **οὔ τᾶρα**, crasis for οὔ τοι ἄρα.

ΟΥΤΑΩ, Ep. imperat. οὔτἄ: Ion. impf. οὔτασκον: aor. 1 οὔτησα, Ion. οὐτήσασκον:—Pass., aor. 1 part. οὐτηθείς:—(also, as if from οὔτημι) 3 sing. Ep. aor. οὖτἄ, inf. οὐτάμεναι, οὐτάμεν: part. (in pass. sense) οὐτάμενος:—*to wound, hurt, hit* with any kind of weapon, οὔτα δὲ δουρί, οὔτ. ἔγχεϊ, χαλκῷ, etc., Il.; properly opp. to βάλλω, *to wound by striking* or *thrusting*, Ib.; cf. οὐτάζω; κατ' οὐταμένην ὠτειλήν by the wound *inflicted*, Ib.; τὸ ξίφος διανταίαν [πληγήν] οὐτᾷ Aesch. **2.** sometimes, generally, *to wound*, like βάλλω, Eur.

οὔτε, Adv. (οὔ τε) *and not*, Il., Hdt. **II.** mostly repeated, οὔτε . . , οὔτε . . , *neither* . . , *nor* . . , Lat. *neque* . . , *neque* . . , Hom., etc.:—οὔτε may be foll. by a posit. clause with τε, Lat. *neque* . . , *et* . . , οὔτ' αὐτὸς κτενέει, σύν τ' ἄλλους πάντας ἐρύξει he will *both not* kill *and* will defend, Il.:—the former οὔτε is sometimes omitted, ναυσὶ δ' οὔτε πεζός [neither] by sea nor by land, Pind.

οὔτερος, crasis for ὁ ἕτερος.

ουτήσασκε, 3 sing. Ion. aor. of οὐτάω.

οὔτησις, ἡ, (οὐτάω) *a wounding*, Zonar.

οὐτήτειρα, ἡ, (οὐτάω) she who wounds, Anth.

οὐτϊδᾰνός, ή, όν, (οὔτις) *of no account, worthless*, Hom. **II.** *regardless, reckless*, Aesch.

οὔτι πη, Dor. **οὔτι πα**, Adv. *in no wise*, Hes., Theocr.

οὔτι που, Adv. *not, I suppose* . . , *surely you do not mean that* . . , Pind., Soph., etc.

οὔτι πω, Ion. **οὔτι κω**, Adv. *not at all yet*, Hdt.

οὔ-τις, neut. **οὔτι**, declined like τις :—*no one* or *nobody*, Lat. *nemo, nullus*, neut. *nothing*, Lat. *nihil*, Hom., etc. :—οὐδείς being used in Prose. **2.** neut. **οὔτι** as Adv. *not a whit, by no means, not at all*, Il., Hdt., Att. **II.** as prop. n. with changed accent, **Οὖτις**, ὁ, acc. **Οὖτιν**, *Nobody, Noman*, a name assumed by Ulysses to deceive Polyphemus, Od.

οὔ τοι or **οὔτοι**, Adv. *indeed not*, Lat. *non sane*, Hom., Hes., etc.; in Att. before oaths, οὔτοι μὰ τὴν Δήμητρα, μὰ τὸν Ἀπόλλω Ar., etc.

ΟΥΤΟΣ, αὕτη, τοῦτο, gen. τούτου, ταύτης, τούτου, etc. :—demonstr. Pron. *this*, Lat. *hic*, to designate *the nearer* of two things, opp. to ἐκεῖνος, *the more remote* (cf. ὅδε), Hom., etc. **2.** when, of two things, one precedes and the other follows, ὅδε generally refers to *what follows*, οὗτος to *what precedes*, Soph., etc. **3.** so also, οὗτος is used emphat., generally in contempt, while ἐκεῖνος (like Lat. *ille*) denotes praise, ὁ πάντ' ἄνακις οὗτος, i.e. Aegisthus, Id.; οὗτος ἀνήρ Plat.; τούτους τοὺς συκοφάντας Id. **4.** in Att. law-language, οὗτος is commonly applied to *the opponent*, whether plaintiff or defendant, whereas in Lat. *hic* was the client, *iste* the opponent, Dem. **5.** often much like an Adv., in local sense (cf. ὅδε init.), τίς δ' οὗτος κατὰ νῆας ἔρχεαι; who art thou *here* that comest . . ? Il.; often in Att., τίς οὑτοσί; who's this *here*? Ar. **6.** with Pron. of 2nd pers., οὗτος σύ, Lat. *heus tu! ho you!* you *there!* Soph., etc.; and then οὗτος alone like a Vocat., οὗτος, τί ποιεῖς; Aesch.; ὦ οὗτος οὗτος, Οἰδίπους Soph. **7.** this phrase mostly implies anger, impatience, or scorn:—so, οὗτος ἀνήρ for ἐγώ, Od. **II.** καὶ οὗτος is also added to heighten the force of a previous word, ναυτικῷ ἀγῶνι, καὶ τούτῳ πρὸς Ἀθηναίους Thuc.; v. infr. III. 5. **III.** neut. ταῦτα in various phrases, **1.** ταῦτ', ὦ δέσποτα yes Sir, (i.e. ταῦτα ἐστι, etc.), Ar.; so ταῦτα δή Id. **2.** ταῦτα μὲν δὴ ὑπάρξει so it shall be, Plat. **3.** καὶ ταῦτα μὲν δὴ ταῦτα, Lat. *haec hactenus*, Id. **4.** διὰ ταῦτα *therefore*, Att.; πρὸς ταῦτα *so then, therefore*, Trag.:—also ταῦτα absol., *therefore*, Il.; ταῦτ' ἄρα Ar.; ταῦτα τοῦν Soph. **5.** καὶ ταῦτα, adding a circumstance heightening the force of what has been said, *and that*, Lat. *et hoc*, ἀνδρὰ θανεῖν, καὶ ταῦτα πρὸς γυναικός to think that a man should die, *and that* by a woman's hand, Aesch., etc. **6.** τοῦτο μέν . . , τοῦτο δέ . . , *on the one hand* . . , *on the other* . . , *partly* . . , *partly* . . , Hdt. **IV.** dat. fem. ταύτῃ *on this spot, here*, Soph., etc. **2.** *in this point, herein*, Ar., etc. **3.** *in this way, thus*, Trag., etc. **V.** ἐκ τούτου or τούτων, *thereupon*, Xen.: *therefore*, Id. **VI.** ἐν τούτῳ *herein, so far*, Thuc., Plat., etc. **2.** *in the meantime*, Thuc., Xen. **VII.** πρὸς τούτοις *besides*, Hdt., Att.

οὑτοσ-ί, αὑτη-ΐ, τουτ-ί, etc., οὗτος strengthd. by the demonstr. affix -ί [ῐ], this man here, Lat. hic-ce, Ar. and Att. Prose: after a vowel, γ is often inserted, αὑτηγί for αὑτηΐ γε, ταυταγί for ταυταί γε, etc., Ar.

οὕτως, before a consonant οὕτω, Adv. of οὗτος, as Lat. sic of hic, in this way or manner, so, thus:—properly, οὕτως is antec. to ὡς, as Lat. sic to ut, Hom., etc.; οὕτω δὴ ἔσται so it shall be, ratifying what goes before, Od., etc.:—in Prose οὕτω alone in answers, even so, just so, Xen. 2. in wishes or prayers, οὕτω νῦν Ζεὺς θείη (as Horace sic te diva regat), Od.; οὕτως ὀναίμην τῶν τέκνων, μισῶ τὸν ἄνδρα (as in Engl., so help me God), Ar.; οὕτω νομιζοίμην σοφός .. Id. 3. beginning a story, οὕτω ποτ᾽ ἦν μῦς καὶ γαλῆ so once upon a time .., Id.; ἦν οὕτω δὴ παῖς Plat. 4. οὕτως ἔχειν, οὕτως ἔχειν τινός, v. ἔχω B. II. 2; ἔχειν is sometimes omitted, τούτων μὲν οὕτω so much for this, Aesch. 5.=εἰς τοῦτο, οὕτω τάρβους to such a pitch of terror, Eur. 6. οὕτω, or οὕτω δή, introduces the apodosis after a protasis, ἐπειδὴ περιελήλυθε ὁ πόλεμος, οὕτω δὴ Γέλωνος μνῆστις γέγονε Hdt.:—after participles, ἐν κλιβάνῳ πνίξαντες, οὕτω τρώγουσι, i. e. ἐπειδὴ ἔπνιξαν, οὕτω .., Id. II. inferential Lat. itaque, Soph., Plat. III. with an Adj. or Adv. so, so much, so very, καλὸς οὕτω Il.; πρυμνόθεν οὕτως so entirely, Aesch. IV. like αὕτως, with a diminishing power, so, merely so, simply, like Lat. sic, μὰψ οὕτως Il.; οὕτω πίνοντας πρὸς ἡδονὴν (as Horace jacentes sic temere), Plat.; also off-hand, at once, Id.; οὐ .. οὕτως ἄπει=impune, Eur.

οὑτωσ-ί [ῐ], strengthd. for οὕτως (v. οὑτοσί), Att. Prose.

οὔφις, crasis for ὁ ὄφις.

οὐχ ὅτι, v. sub ὅπως Α. I. 9.

οὐχί, Att. form of οὐ.

οὐχῖνος, crasis for ὁ ἐχῖνος.

ὀφειλέτης, ου, ὁ, (ὀφείλω) a debtor, τινί Plat.: ὀφ. εἰμί, c. inf., I am under bond to do a thing, Soph.:—fem. ὀφειλέτις, ιδος, Eur.

ὀφειλή, ή, (ὀφείλω) a debt, N. T.:—one's due, Ib.

ὀφείλημα, τό, that which is owed, a debt, Thuc., Plat.

ΟΦΕΙ´ΛΩ, impf. ὤφειλον, Ep. ὀφέλλω, impf. ὤφελλον or ὄφελλον: f. ὀφειλήσω: aor. 1 ὠφείλησα: pf. ὠφείληκα, plqpf. -ήκειν: aor. 2 ὤφελον, v. infr. II. 2, 3:—Pass., aor. 1 part. ὀφειληθείς :—to owe, have to pay or account for, Hom., etc.:—ὀφ. τινί to be debtor to another, Ar.; absol. to be in debt, Id.:—Pass. to be owed, to be due, Hom., Att.: of persons, to be liable to, θανάτῳ πάντες ὀφειλόμεθα (as Horace debemur morti), Anth. II. c. inf. to be bound, to be obliged to do a thing, Il., etc.:—Pass., σοι ταῦτ᾽ ὀφείλεται παθεῖν it is thy destiny to suffer this, Soph.; πᾶσιν κατθανεῖν ὀφείλεται Eur. 2. in this sense Ep. impf. ὤφελλον, ὄφελλον and aor. 2 ὤφελον, ὄφελον are used of that which one ought to have done (ought being the pret. of owe), ὤφελεν εὔχεσθαι Il., etc. 3. these tenses are also used, foll. by inf., to express a wish that cannot be accomplished, τὴν ὄφελε κατακτάμεν Ἄρτεμις would that Artemis had slain her! (but she had not), Lat. utinam interfecisset! Ib.; often preceded by εἴθε (Ep. αἴθε), αἴθ᾽ ὤφελες ἄγονός τ᾽ ἔμεναι O that thou hadst been unborn, Ib.; αἴθ᾽ ὤφελλ᾽ ὁ ξεῖνος ὀλέσθαι Od.; —so with ὡς, ὡς ὄφελον ὠλέσθαι O that I had taken!

II.; ὡς ὤφελες ὀλέσθαι Ib.; with negat., μηδ᾽ ὤφελες λίσσεσθαι would thou hadst never prayed! Ib.; so in Att.:—in late Greek with Indic., ὄφελον ἐβασιλεύσατε, for βασιλεῦσαι, would ye were kings, N. T. III. impers. ὀφείλει, Lat. oportet, c. acc. et inf., Pind.

ὀφέλλω (Α), Ep. for ὀφείλω.

ΟΦΕ´ΛΛΩ (Β), Ep. inf. -έμεν: impf. ὤφελλον, Ep. Aeol. aor. 1 opt. ὀφέλλειεν:—to increase, enlarge, strengthen, Hom.; ἲς ἀνέμου κύματ᾽ ὀφέλλει the force of the wind raises high the waves, Il.; μῦθον ὀφ. to multiply words, Ib.; ὄφρ᾽ ἂν Ἀχαιοὶ υἱὸν ἐμὸν τίσωσιν, ὀφέλλωσί τέ ἑ τιμῇ and may advance him in honour, Ib.: —Pass., οἶκος ὀφέλλεται it waxes great, prospers, Od.

ὄφελον, Ep. aor. 2 of ὀφείλω.

ὄφελος, τό, (ὀφέλλω Β) only in nom. furtherance, advantage, help, used often (like opus) as an indecl. Adj., αἴ κ᾽ ὄφελός τι γενώμεθα whether we can be of any use, Il.; τί δῆτ᾽ ἂν εἴης ὄφ. ἡμῖν; what good couldst thou be to us? Ar.; c. inf., τί ὄφ. σώματι κάμνοντι σιτία διδόναι; Plat.; c. gen., τῶν ὄφελός ἐστι οὐδέν of which there is no profit, Hdt.; ὄφ. οὐδὲν γεωργοῦ ἀργοῦ Xen.;—but, ὅ τι πέρ ὄφελος στρατεύματος the serviceable part of the army, Id.

ὀφε-ώδης, ες, (ὄφις, εἶδος) snake-like, Plat.

ὀφθαλμία, ή, (ὀφθαλμός) ophthalmia, Ar., Xen., etc.

ὀφθαλμιάω, to suffer from ophthalmia, Hdt., Ar.

ὀφθαλμίδιον [μῖ], τό, Dim. of ὀφθαλμός, Ar.

ὀφθαλμο-δουλεία, ή, eye-service, N. T.

ὀφθαλμός, οῦ, ὁ, (from ΟΠ, Root of ὄψ-ομαι, ὀφ-θῆναι) the eye, mostly in pl., Hom., etc.; ἐλθεῖν ἐς ὀφθαλμοὺς τινος to come before one's eyes, Il.; ἐν ὀφθαλμοῖσιν before one's eyes, Lat. in oculis, Hom., Att.; πρὸ τῶν ὀφθ. Aeschin.; ἐξ ὀφθαλμῶν out of one's sight, Hdt.; κατ᾽ ὀφθαλμούς to one's face, Ar. II. in sing. the eye of a master or ruler, πάντα ἰδὼν Διὸς ὀφθ. Hes.; as a king is called ὀφθ. οἴκων Aesch.; and in Persia ὀφθαλμὸς βασιλέως, the king's eye, was a confidential officer, through whom he beheld his subjects, Hdt., Ar., etc. III. ἑσπέρας ὀφθ., νυκτὸς ὀφθ., of the moon, Pind. IV. the dearest, best, as the eye is the most precious part of the body, ὀφθαλμὸς Σικελίας Id.; μέγας ὀφθαλμός a great comfort, Soph. V. the eye or bud of a plant or tree, Xen.

ὀφθαλμό-τεγκτος, ον, (τέγγω) wetting the eyes, Eur.

ὀφθαλμο-φᾰνής, ές, (φαίνομαι) apparent to the eye, Strab.

ὀφθαλμ-ωρύχος [ῠ], ον, tearing out the eyes, Aesch.

ὀφθῆναι, aor. 1 pass. inf. of ὁράω—ὀφθήσομαι, f. pass.

ὀφιό-πους, ποδος, with serpents for legs, Luc.

ΟΦΙΣ, ὁ: gen. ὄφεως, poët. also ὄφεος, Dor. and Ion. ὄφιος:—a serpent, snake, Il., Hdt., Trag.:—metaph. πτηνὸν ὄφιν, of an arrow, Aesch. [The first syll. is sometimes made long, when it was pronounced (and perh. ought to be written) ὄπφις, v. ὀχέω.]

ὀφλεῖν, aor. 2 inf. of ὀφλισκάνω.

ὄφλημα, τό, a fine incurred in a lawsuit, Dem. From

ὀφλισκάνω, f. ὀφλήσω: pf. ὤφληκα: aor. 2 ὦφλον, inf. ὀφλεῖν, part. ὀφλών: (ὀφείλω):—to owe, to be liable to pay a fine, Eur., etc. 2. δίκην ὀφλεῖν to be cast in a suit, lose one's cause, Ar.; so, ὀφλεῖν δίαιταν to lose in an arbitration, Dem.; τὰς εὐθύνας ὀφλεῖν to have one's accounts not passed, Aeschin. 3. absol. to

be cast, to be the losing party, Ar., Thuc. **4.** c. gen. criminis, ὀφλὼν κλοπῆς δίκην to be convicted in an action for theft, Aesch.; then, without δίκην, ὠφληκὼς φόνου found guilty of murder, Plat.: also c. gen. poenae, θανάτου δίκην ὀφλ. Id. **II.** generally, of anything which one deserves or brings on oneself, αἰσχύνην, βλάβην ὀφλ. to bring infamy, loss on oneself, incur them, Eur.; ὀφλ. γέλωτα to be laughed at, Id.; δειλίην ὤφλεε πρὸς βασιλῆος he drew upon himself the reproach of cowardice from the king, Hdt.; so, μωρίαν ὀφλισκάνω Soph.

"ΟΦΡΑ´, Final and Temporal Conj. in Ion. and Dor. Poets: **I.** Final Conj., like ἵνα, ὡς, that, in order that, to the end that, Hom., Pind. **II.** Temporal Conj., like ἕως, Lat. donec, so long as, while, mostly with impf., ὄφρα μὲν ἠὼς ἦν Od. **2.** with subj., it commonly has ἄν (κε or κεν) with it, Hom. **3.** until, ὄφρα καὶ αὐτὼ κατέκταθεν till they too were slain, Il.; with subj., of future time, ἔχει κότον, ὄφρα τελέσσῃ he bears malice till he have satisfied it, Ib.; —but in this case, ἄν (κε or κεν) is commonly added.

ὀφρυάω, (ὀφρύς ΙΙ) to have ridges, Strab.

ὀφρύη, ἡ, Ion. for ὀφρύς ΙΙ, Hdt., Eur.

ὀφρυόεις, εσσα, εν, (ὀφρύς ΙΙ) on the brow of a rock, beetling, Il., ap. Hdt. **2.** metaph. majestic, Anth.

'ΟΦΡΥ´Σ [ῠ], ἡ, gen. ύος [ῠ], ἡ, acc. ὀφρύν, pl. ὀφρύας, contr. ὀφρῦς:—the brow, eyebrow, Lat. supercilium, mostly in pl., the brows, Hom.: ἐπ' ὀφρύσι νεῦσε Κρονίων, i.e. ἐπένευσε ὀφρύσι, nodded assent, Il.; ἀνὰ δ' ὀφρύσι νεῦσεν ἑκάστῳ made a sign not to do, Od.: used in phrases to denote grief, scorn, pride, τὰς ὀφρῦς ἀνασπᾶν Lat. supercilium, scorn, pride, Anth. **II.** the ὀφρῦς ἐπαίρειν Eur., etc.; τὰς ὀφρῦς συνάγειν to knit the brows, frown, Ar.:—on the other hand, καταβάλλειν, λύειν, μεθιέναι τὰς ὀφρῦς to let down or unknit the brow, Eur. **2.** ὀφρύς alone, like Lat. supercilium, scorn, pride, Anth. **II.** the brow of a hill, a beetling crag, Il., etc.

ὀχά, (ἔχω) Adv., used to strengthen the Sup. ἄριστος, ὄχ' ἄριστος far the best, Il., etc.

ὄχανον [ᾰ], τό, (ἔχω) the holder of a shield, a bar across the hollow of the shield, through which the bearer passed his arm, Hdt.

ὀχέεσκον, Ion. impf. of ὀχέω.

ὀχεία, ἡ, (ὀχεύω) a covering or impregnating, of the male animal, Xen.

ὄχεσφι, -φιν, Ep. dat. pl. of ὄχος, a chariot.

ὀχετεύω, f. σω, (ὀχετός) to conduct water by a conduit or canal, Hdt.:—Pass. to be conducted, conveyed, Id.; metaph., ὠχετεύετο φάτις Aesch.

ὀχετ-ηγός, όν, (ὀχετός, ἄγω) conducting or drawing off water by a ditch or conduit, Il.: metaph., πνεῦμα ὀχ., of the flute, Anth.

ὀχετός, ὁ, (ὀχέω) a means for carrying water, a waterpipe, Hdt., Thuc., etc.: a conduit, channel, aqueduct, Arist. **II.** in pl. streams, Pind., Eur. **III.** metaph., ὀχετὸν παρεκτρέπειν to make a side channel or means of escape, Eur.

ὀχεύς, έως Ep. ῆος, ὁ, (ἔχω) anything for holding or fastening: **1.** a strap for fastening the helmet under the chin, Il. **2.** in pl. the fastenings of the belt, Ib. **3.** a bar to fasten the door inside, Hom.

ὀχεύω, of male animals, to cover, Plat.: Pass., of the female: Med. of both sexes, Hdt.

ὀχέω, impf. Ion. ὀχέεσκον: f. ὀχήσω:—Med., 3 sing. impf. ὠχέετο, -εῖτο: f. ὀχήσομαι: 3 sing. Ep. aor. 1 ὀχήσατο (ὄχος):—Frequent. of ἔχω, to uphold, sustain, endure, Od., Pind.; νηπίας ὀχέειν to keep playing childish tricks, Od.; φρουρὰν ὀχήσω will maintain a watch, Aesch. **2.** to carry, Eur., Xen. **3.** to let another ride, to mount him, αὐτὸς βαδίζω, τοῦτον δ' ὀχῶ Ar.; of a general, to let the men ride, Xen. **II.** Med. to have oneself carried, to be carried or borne, Hom., Hdt., Att. **2.** absol. (without the dat. ἵππῳ or νηΐ), to drive, ride, sail, [ἵπποι] ἀλεγεινοὶ ὀχέεσθαι difficult to use in a chariot, Il. **3.** of a ship, to ride at anchor, λεπτή τις ἐλπίς ἐστ' ἐφ' ἧς ὀχούμεθα 'tis but a slender hope on which we ride at anchor, Ar.; so, ὠχεῖσθ' Id.; cf. Plat.; so, ἐπ' ἀσθενοῦς ῥώμης ὀχεῖσθαι Eur. [In Pind. the first syll. is made long, when it was pronounced (and perh. ought to be written) ὀκχέω, v. ὄφις.] Hence

ὄχημα, ατος, τό, anything that bears or supports, γῆς ὄχημα, stay of earth, = γαιήοχος, Eur. **II.** a carriage, a chariot, Lat. vehiculum, Hdt., Soph., Eur. **2.** of ships, but mostly with some addition, λινόπτερα ναυτίλων ὄχ. Aesch.; ὄχ. ναός Soph. **3.** of animals that are ridden, ὄχημα κανθάρου a riding-beetle (as we say a riding-horse), Ar.

ὄχησις, ἡ, (ὀχέω) a bearing, carrying, Plat. **II.** (from Pass.) a being carried, ἵππων ὀχήσεις riding, Id.

ὀχθέω, f. ήσω: aor. 1 ὤχθησα:—to be sorely angered, to be vexed in spirit, Hom. (Deriv. uncertain.)

"ΟΧΘΗ, ἡ, older form of ὄχθος, a rising ground, a bank, dyke by the side of a river, Il.: mostly in pl. the raised banks of a river, Hom.; ὄχθαι καπέτοιο the banks of the trench, Il.; also the dunes or denes along the sea (cf. θίς), Od. Hence

ὀχθηρός, ά, όν, hilly, Anth. Hence

ὄχθος, ὁ, later form of ὄχθη, a bank, hill, h. Hom., Hdt., Att.: a barrow or mound, Lat. tumulus, Aesch.

ὀχλᾱγωγία, ἡ, mob-oratory, Plut. From

ὀχλ-ᾱγωγός, ὁ, a mob-leader.

ὀχλέω, f. ήσω, (ὄχλος) to move, disturb, ψηφῖδες ἅπασαι ὀχλεῦνται (Ion. for -οῦνται) all the pebbles are rolled or swept away by the water, Il. **II.** to trouble, importune, Hdt., Aesch.:—absol. to be troublesome or irksome, Soph. Hence

ὀχληρός, ά, όν, troublesome, irksome, importunate, Hdt., Eur., Plat.

ὀχλίζω, f. ίσω: Ep. aor. 1 opt. ὀχλίσσεια: (ὄχλος = μόχλος) to move by a lever, to heave up, τὸν [λᾶαν] οὔ κε δύ' ἀνέρε ὀχλίσσειαν Hom.

ὀχλο-κόπος, ὁ, a mob-courtier, Polyb.; cf. δημο-κόπος.

ὀχλο-κρᾱτία, ἡ, mob-rule, the lowest grade of democracy, Polyb.

ὀχλο-ποιέω, to make a riot, N. T.

"ΟΧΛΟΣ, ὁ, a moving crowd, a throng, mob, Pind., Aesch., etc.; ὁ ὄχλος τῶν στρατιωτῶν the mass of the soldiers, Xen.; τῷ ὄχλῳ in point of numbers, Thuc.; οἱ τοιοῦτοι ὄχλοι undisciplined masses like these, Id. **2.** in political sense, the populace, mob, Lat. turba, opp. to δῆμος, Id., Xen. **3.** generally, a mass, multitude, ὄχλος λόγων Aesch. **II.**

like Lat. *turba*, *annoyance*, *trouble*, ὄχλον παρέχειν τινί to give one *trouble*, Hdt.; δι' ὄχλου εἶναι, γενέσθαι to *be* or become *troublesome*, Ar., Thuc.

ὀχλ-ώδης, ες, (εἶδος) *like a mob*, and so, 1. *turbulent*, *unruly*, Plat.; τὸ ὀχλ. *troublesomeness*, Thuc. 2. *common*, *vulgar*, Plut.

ὀχμάζω, f. σω, to *grip fast*, Eur.; τὸν λεωργὸν ὀχμάσαι to *bind* him *fast*, Aesch.; ἵππον ὀχμάζει he makes the horse *obedient to the bit*, Eur.

ὄχνη, ἡ, later form of ὄγχνη, *a wild pear*, Theocr.

ὄχος, ὁ, (ἔχω) *anything which bears*, *a carriage*, Lat. *vehiculum*, Hdt., Aesch., etc.; by Hom. in heterocl. neut. pl. ὄχεα, τά, of *a single chariot*, ἐξ ὀχέων Il.; and in poët. dat. ὄχεσφι, -φιν, Ib.; later in masc. pl. ἐπ' εὐκύκλοις ὄχοις, of the Scythian waggons, Aesch. 2. τρόχαλοι ὄχοι ἀπήνης the swift-running *bearers* of the chariot, i. e. the *wheels*, Eur. II. *anything which holds*, νηῶν ὄχοι *steads* for ships, *harbours*, Od.

ὀχυρο-ποιέομαι, Dep. *to make secure*, *fortify*, Polyb.

ὀχυρός, ά, όν, (ἔχω) like ἐχυρός, *firm*, *lasting*, *stout*, Hes., Aesch. 2. of places, *strong*, *secure*, Eur.: esp. of a stronghold or position, *strong*, *tenable*, Xen. II. Adv. -ρῶς, Eur. Hence

ὀχυρόω, f. ώσω, to *make fast and sure*, *fortify*, Polyb.: —the Med. just like Act., Xen. Hence

ὀχύρωμα, ατος, τό, *a stronghold*, *fortress*, Xen.; and

ὀχυρωτέον, verb. Adj. *one must strengthen*, Plut.

ὄψ, ἡ, only used in obl. cases of sing. ὀπός, ὀπί, ὄπα: (εἰπεῖν):—*a voice*, Hom., Hes., Trag.; of flutes, Theogn. II. *a word*, Il., Soph.

ὀψ-αμάτης, voc. -ᾶτα, Dor. for -αμήτης, ὁ, (ὀψέ, ἀμάω) *one who mows till late at even*, Theocr.

ὄψανον, τό, (ὄψομαι) = ὄψις, Aesch.

ὀψ-ἀρότης, ου, ὁ, (ὀψέ) *one who ploughs late*, Hes.

ΟΨΈ, Adv. *after a long time*, *late*, Lat. *sero*, Hom., etc.; ὀψὲ διδάσκεσθαι or μανθάνειν to be *late* in learning, *learn too late*, Aesch., Soph. 2. *late in the day*, *at even*, opp. to πρωΐ, Hom., Thuc., etc.; ὀψὲ ἦν, ὀψὲ ἐγίγνετο it was, it was getting, *late*, Xen.; so, ἐς ὀψέ Thuc. 3. c. gen., ὀψὲ τῆς ἡμέρας *late* in the day, Livy's *serum diei*, Id.; so, τῆς ὥρας ἐγίγνετο ὀψέ Dem.; ὀψὲ τῆς ἡλικίας *late* in life, Luc.

ὀψείω, (ὄψομαι) Desiderat. of ὁράω, *to wish to see* a thing, c. gen., Il.

ὄψεσθαι, fut. inf. of ὁράω.

ὀψία, Ion. -ίη (sc. ὥρα), ἡ, *the latter part of day*, *evening*, opp. to ὄρθρος, often also joined with δείλη, δείλη ἦν ὀψίη Hdt.; περὶ δείλην ὀψίαν Thuc.; δείλης ὀψίας *late* in the evening, Dem. Cf. δείλη.

ὀψιαίτερος, ὀψιαίτατος, Att. Comp. and Sup. of ὄψιος.

ὀψί-γονος [ῐ], ον, (γίγνομαι) *late-born*, *after-born*, Hom. 2. of a son, *late-born*, *born in one's old age*, h. Hom. 3. *later-born*, i. e. *younger*, Hdt.: *young*, Theocr.

ὀψίζω, f. σω, (ὀψέ) *to do*, *go* or *come late*, Xen.:— Pass., ὀψισθέντες *belated*, *benighted*, Id.

ὀψί-κοιτος, ον, (κοίτη) *going late to bed*, Aesch.

ὀψῑμαθέω, *to learn late*, Luc. From

ὀψῐ-μαθής, ές, (μανθάνω) *late in learning*, *late to learn*, Horace's *serus studiorum*, Plat.:—*too old to learn*, c. gen., Xen. II. *vain of late-gotten learning*, *pedantic*, Theophr. Hence

ὀψῐμαθία, ἡ, *late-gotten learning*, Theophr.

ὄψιμος, ον, (ὀψέ) poët. for ὄψιος, *late*, *slow*, τέρας ὄψ. a prognostic *late of fulfilment*, Il.:—*late in the season*, Xen., N. T.

ὀψί-νοος, ον, *late-observing*, of Epimetheus, Pind.

ὄψιος, α, ον, (ὀψέ) *late*, Lat. *serus*, Pind.: Att. Comp. ὀψιαίτερος, α, ον, *earlier*; Sup. ὀψιαίτατος, η, ον, *earliest*, Xen.:—neut. ὀψιαίτερον as Adv., Comp. of ὀψέ, Plat.; Sup. ὀψιαίτατα Id., Xen.

ὄψις, ἡ, gen. εως Ion. ιος: (from ΟΠ, Root of ὄψομαι): I. *look*, *appearance*, *aspect* of a person or thing, Lat. *species oris*, *aspectus*, Il., Soph.; εἰκάζεσθαι ἀπὸ τῆς φανερᾶς ὄψεως Thuc.:—acc. absol. *in appearance*, Pind., Att. 2. *the countenance*, *face*, Eur., etc. 3. = θέαμα, *a sight*, Aesch., Eur., etc.; ἄλλην ὄψιν οἰκοδομημάτων other architectural *sights*, Hdt.; τῇ ὄψει *from what they saw*, opp. to τῇ γνώμῃ, Thuc. 4. *a vision*, *apparition*, Hdt., Trag. II. *eyesight*, *vision*, Hom., Hdt., Att.: in pl. *the organs of sight*, *the eyes*, Soph., Xen. 2. *view*, *sight*, Lat. *conspectus*, ἀπικέσθαι ἐς ὄψιν τινί to come into one's *sight*, i. e. *presence*, Hdt.; εἰς ὄψιν τινός or τινὶ ἥκειν, μολεῖν, ἐλθεῖν, περᾶν Aesch., Eur.

ὀψῐ-τέλεστος, ον, *to be late fulfilled*, Il.

ὄψομαι, fut. of ὁράω.

ὄψον, τό, (ἕψω) properly, *cooked meat*, or, generally, *meat*, opp. to bread and other provisions, Hom., Ar. 2. *anything eaten with bread* or *food*, to give it flavour and relish, κρόμυον, ποτῷ ὄψον onions, a *zest* or *relish* to wine, Il.; ἐσθίουσι ἐπὶ τῷ σίτῳ ὄψον Xen. 3. *seasoning*, *sauce*, Plat.; κολλύραν καὶ κόνδυλον ὄψον ἐπ' αὐτῇ *pudding and knuckle-sauce* withal, Ar.; λιμῷ ὅσαπερ ὄψῳ διαχρῆσθε, i. e. 'hunger is the best sauce,' Xen. 4. generally, *dainty fare*, in pl. *dainties*, Plat. II. at Athens, mostly, *fish*, the chief dainty of the Athenians, Ar. 2. *the fish-market*, Id., Aeschin.

ὀψοποιέομαι, *to eat meat* or *fish with bread*, Xen.

ὀψοποιητικός, ή, όν, *of* or *fit for cookery*: ἡ -κή (sc. τέχνη) *the art of cookery*, Arist.

ὀψοποιΐα, ἡ, *cookery*, esp. *fine cookery*, Xen., Plat.; and

ὀψοποιϊκός, ή, όν, = ὀψοποιητικός, Plat., Xen. From

ὀψο-ποιός, ὁ, (ποιέω) *one who cooks meat*, *a cook*, Hdt.; distinguished from ἀρτοποιός and σιτοποιός, Xen.; Plat.

ὀψο-πόνος, ον, *dressing food elaborately*, Anth.

ὀψοφάγέω, f. ήσω, *to eat things meant to be eaten only with bread*, *to live daintily*, Ar.; and

ὀψοφάγία, ἡ, *dainty living*, Aeschin. From

ὀψο-φάγος [ᾰ], ὁ, (φαγεῖν) *one who eats things meant to be only eaten with bread*, such as *fish* and *dainties*, *a dainty fellow*, *epicure*, *gourmand*, Ar., Xen.:— irreg. Sup. ὀψοφαγίστατος Xen.

ὀψωνέω, f. ήσω, *to buy fish and dainties*, Ar., Xen.

ὀψ-ώνης, ου, ὁ, (ὀψέ, ὠνέομαι) *one who buys fish* or *victuals*, *a purveyor*, Xen.

ὀψωνιάζω, (ὀψώνιον) *to furnish with provisions*. Hence

ὀψωνιασμός, ὁ, *a furnishing with provisions*, *the supplies and pay of an army*, Polyb.

ὀψώνιον, τό, (ὀψώνης) *provisions* or *provision-money*, Lat. *obsonium*, *supplies and pay for an army*, Polyb.: —metaph., ὀψώνια ἁμαρτίας *the wages* of sin, N. T.

Π.

Π, π, πῖ, indecl. : sixteenth letter of Gr. alphabet. As numeral π' = 80, but ͵π = 80,000.

π is the tenuis labial mute, related to the medial β and the aspirate φ. Changes of π in the Gr. dialects, etc. 1. π becomes φ, βλέπ-ω βλέφ-αρον, λάπ-τω λαφ-ύσσω. 2. in Aeol. and Ion., it stands for the asp. φ, ἀμφί for ἀμφί, πανός for φανός, ἀπικέσθαι for ἀφικ-: in Ion. it was retained in apostrophé before an aspirate, ἀπ᾽ ἡμῶν, ἐπ᾽ ἡμέρην, ὑπ᾽ ὑμῶν, etc. : on the contrary the aspirated form was preferred in Att., ἀσφάραγος for ἀσπάραγος, σφόνδυλος for σπόνδυλος. 3. in Ion. Prose, π becomes κ in relatives and interrogatives, κῶς ὅκως ὁκοῖος ὁκόσος for πῶς ὅπως ὁποῖος ὁπόσος. 4. in Aeol., π is used for μ, ὅππα for ὄμμα, πεδά for μετά. 5. in Aeol. and Dor., π for τ, πέτορες for τέσσαρες, πέμπε for πέντε. 6. sometimes interchanged with γ, as in λαπαρός λαγαρός, λαπάρα λαγών, λάγος lepus. 7. in Aeol. and Ep. Poetry, π is often doubled in relatives, as ὅππη ὅππως ὁπποῖος for ὅπη, etc. 8. in Poets, τ is inserted after π, as in πτόλις, πτόλεμος for πόλις, πόλεμος.

πᾶ; Dor. for **πῆ;** how? **II.** **πα** for **πη,** anywhere, anyhow.

πᾱγά, Dor. for **πηγή.**

παγ-γέλοιος, ον, (πᾶς) quite ridiculous, Plat.

παγ-γενέτης, ου, ὁ, father of all ;—fem. **παγγενέτειρα,** mother of all, Anth.

παγγλωσσία, ἡ, wordiness, garrulity, Pind. From **πάγ-γλωσσος** or **-ττος,** ον, speaking all tongues.

πᾱγείς, εῖσα, έν, aor. 2 pass. part. of **πήγνυμι.**

πᾱγεν, Ep. for ἐπάγησαν, 3 pl. aor. 2 pass. of **πήγνυμι.**

πᾱγετός, ὁ, frost, Xen. ; cf. **πάγος** II.

πᾱγετ-ώδης, ες, (εἶδος) frosty, ice-cold, Soph.

πάγη [ᾰ], ἡ, (πήγνυμι) anything that fixes or fastens, a snare, noose, trap, Hdt. : a fowling-net, Xen. 2. metaph. a trap, snare, Aesch.

πᾱγῆναι, aor. 2 pass. inf. of **πήγνυμι.**

πᾱγῑδεύω, (παγίς) to lay a snare for, entrap, N. T.

πάγιος [ᾰ], α, ον, (πήγνυμι) solid, Luc. :—Adv., παγίως λέγειν to say positively, without reservations, Plat.

πᾱγίς, ίδος, ἡ, (πήγνυμι) = **πάγη,** a trap, Ar. : metaph. a trap, snare, δουρατέα π. of the Trojan horse, Anth. **II.** ἄγκυρα παγὶς νεῶν the anchor which holds ships fast, Id.

παγ-καίνιστος, ον, ever renewed, ever fresh, Aesch.

πάγ-κᾰκος, ον, utterly bad, all-unlucky, Hes. : most noxious, Id., Plat.—Adv., παγκάκως ὀλέσθαι Aesch. ; π. ἔχει τινί Id. 2. of persons, utterly bad, most evil or wicked, Theogn. : Sup. ὦ παγκάκιστε, Soph., Eur.

πάγ-κᾰλος, ον, and η, ον, all beautiful, good or noble, Ar., Plat. : Adv. -λως, Plat., etc.

πάγ-καρπος, ον, of all kinds of fruit, Soph. : rich in every fruit, rich in fruit, Pind.

παγ-κευθής, ές, (κεύθω) all-concealing, Soph.

πάγκλαυστος or **-κλαυτος,** ον, (κλαίω) all-lamented, most lamentable, Aesch., Soph. **II.** act. alltearful, Soph.

παγκληρία, ἡ, a complete inheritance, Aesch., Eur.

πάγ-κληρος, ον, held in full possession, Eur.

πάγ-κοινος, ον, common to all, Soph. ; θεοῦ μάστιγι παγκοίνῳ, i. e. by death, Aesch. ; ἐν ἀπέχθημα π. βροτοῖς one object of hate common to all mankind, Eur. ; π. στάσις all the band together, Aesch.

παγ-κοίτης, ου, ὁ, (κοίτη) where all must sleep, θάλαμος παγκοίτας, i. e. the grave, Soph. ; π. ᾍδας Id.

παγ-κόνῑτος, ον, (κονίω) covered all over with dust, ἄεθλα παγκ. prizes gained in all the contests, Soph.

παγ-κρᾰτής, ές, (κράτος) all-powerful, all-mighty, Trag. ; π. ἕδραι the imperial throne of Zeus, Aesch. :—τοῖνδε π. φονεύς their victorious slayer, Id.

παγκρᾰτιάζω, to perform the exercises of the παγκράτιον, Plat. :—metaph. to sway one's arms about like a gymnast, to gesticulate violently, Aeschin. ; and

παγκρᾰτιαστής, οῦ, ὁ, one who practises the παγκράτιον, Plat. ; and

παγκρᾰτιαστικός, ή, όν, of or for the παγκράτιον, ἡ παγκ. τέχνη the pancratiast's art, Plat. **II.** skilled in the παγκράτιον, Arist. From

παγκρᾰτιον, τό, (παγκρᾰτής) a complete contest, an exercise which combined both wrestling and boxing (πάλη and πυγμή), Hdt., Pind., etc.

πάγος [ᾰ], ὁ, (πήγνυμι) that which is fixed or firmly set: **I.** a mountain-peak, a rocky hill, Od., Hes., Trag. ; ὁ Ἄρειος (Ion. Ἀρήιος) πάγος the Areopagus at Athens, v. Ἄρειος II. **II.** = παγετός, Soph.

πάγος, ὁ, Lat. pagus, a canton, district, Plut.

πάγουρος [ᾰ], ὁ, (παγῆναι, οὐρά) a kind of crab, Lat. pagurus, Ar.

παγ-χάλεπος [ᾰ], ον, most difficult to deal with, Xen., Plat. Adv., παγχαλέπως ἔχειν πρός τινα to be ill-affected towards him, Xen.

παγ-χάλκεος, ον, all-brasen, all-brass, Hom.

πάγ-χαλκος, ον, = foreg., Od., Trag.

πάγ-χρηστος, ον, good for all work, Ar., Xen.

πάγ-χριστος, ον, (χρίω) all-anointed : παγχριστόν (sc. φάρμακον) seems to mean full-anointing, Soph.

παγ-χρύσεος [ῡ], ον, all-golden, of solid gold, Il., Hes.

πάγ-χρῡσος, ον, = foreg., Pind., Soph., Eur.

πάγχῠ, Adv. (πᾶς, πᾶν) = πάνυ, quite, wholly, entirely, altogether, Hom., Pind. ; πάγχυ δοκέειν or ἐλπίζειν to think or hope fully, Hdt.

πᾱδάω, Dor. for πηδάω.

πάθε, Ep. for ἔπαθε, 3 sing. aor. 2 of πάσχω.

πᾰθεῖν, Ep. for παθέειν, aor. 2 inf. of πάσχω.

πάθη [ᾰ], ἡ, (παθεῖν) a passive state, Plat. ; τὰς ἐκεῖ πάθας what happened there, Soph. ; πᾶσαν τὴν ἑωυτοῦ π. all that had happened to him, Hdt. 2. = πάθημα, Pind., Soph. ; ἡ π. τῶν ὀφθαλμῶν blindness, Hdt.

πάθημα [ᾰ], ατος, τό, (παθεῖν) anything that befals one a suffering, calamity, misfortune, Soph., Thuc.: mostly in pl., Hdt., Att. ; proverb., τὰ δέ μοι παθήματα μαθήματα γέγονε my sufferings have been my lessons, Hdt. **II.** a passive emotion or condition, Xen., Plat. **III.** in pl. incidents, occurrences, Plat.

πάθησθα, Ep. for πάθῃς, 2 sing. aor. 2 subj. of πάσχω.

πᾰθητικός, ή, όν, (παθεῖν) subject to feeling, capable of feeling a thing, c. gen., Arist. 2. impassioned, pathetic, Id. :—Adv., παθητικῶς λέγειν Id.

πᾰθητός, ή, όν, (παθεῖν) one who has suffered : subject

to passion, Plut. **II.** of the Saviour, destined to suffer, N. T.

πάθος [ᾰ], εος, τό, (παθεῖν) anything that befalls one, an incident, accident, Hdt., Soph. 2. what one has suffered, one's experience, Aesch.; in pl., Plat.: —commonly in bad sense, a suffering, misfortune, calamity, Hdt., Aesch., etc.; ἀνήκεστον π. ἔρδειν to do an irreparable mischief, Hdt. **II.** of the soul, a passion, emotion, such as love, hate, etc., Thuc., Plat., etc. **III.** any passive state, a condition, state, Plat. : in pl. the incidents or changes to which things are liable, τὰ περὶ τὸν οὐρανὸν π. Id., etc. **IV.** a pathetic mode of expression, pathos, Arist.

πάθω [ᾰ], aor. 2 subj. of πάσχω :—παθών, part.

παῖ, voc. of παῖς.

Παιάν, ᾶνος, ὁ, Ep. **Παιήων, ονος**, Att. **Παιών, ῶνος**, Paean or Paeon, the physician of the gods, Il.; Παιήονος γενέθλη the sons of Paeon, i. e. physicians, Od. 2. after Hom., the name and office were transferred to Apollo, who was invoked by the cry ἰήιε Παιάν Aesch., Soph.; ἰὼ Παιάν Soph. 3. as appellat. a physician, healer, Aesch., Soph. : then, a saviour, deliverer, Eur. **II.** παιάν, Ep. παιήων, a paean, i. e. a choral song, a hymn or chant, addressed to Apollo, Il., Aesch., Soph. 2. a song of triumph after victory, properly to Apollo, Il., Aesch.; also a war-song, Aesch., Xen. :—the phrase was, ἐξάρχειν τὸν παιᾶνα Xen.; π. ἐξάρχεσθαι, ποιεῖσθαι Id. 3. any solemn song or chant, esp. on beginning an undertaking, in omen of success, Thuc.; a song sung at a feast, Xen. 4. Aesch., by an oxymoron, joins π. Ἐρινύων, π. τοῦ θανόντος; so, π. στυγνός, of a dirge, Eur. **III.** Κρητῶν παιήονες paean-singers, h. Hom. **IV.** in Prosody, a paeon, a foot consisting of three short and 1 long syll., –◡◡◡, ◡–◡◡, ◡◡–◡, or ◡◡◡–, Arist.

παιανίζω, f. σω, =παιωνίζω, Aesch. Hence

παιανισμός, ὁ, =παιωνισμός, Strab.

παῖγμα, τό, (παίζω) play, sport, sportive strain, Eur.

παιγνία, Ion. -ίη, ἡ, (παίζω) play, sport, a game, Hdt. Hence

παιγνιήμων, ον, fond of a joke, Hdt.

παίγνιον, τό, (παίζω) a plaything, toy, Plat. **II.** in Theocr., the Egyptians are called κακὰ παίγνια roguish playmates. **III.** a game, a sportive poem, Anth.; of the merry chirp of the cicada, Id.

παίγνιος, ον, (παίζω) sportive, droll, Anth.

παιγνι-ώδης, ες, (εἶδος) playful, sportive, Plut. : τὸ παιγνιῶδες playfulness, Xen.

παιδᾰγωγεῖον, τό, the room in which the παιδαγωγοί waited for their boys, Dem. : a school, Plut.

παιδᾰγωγέω, f. ήσω: Pass., f. παιδαγωγήσομαι in pass. sense: aor. 1 ἐπαιδαγωγήθην: pf. πεπαιδαγώγημαι :—to attend as a παιδαγωγός, to train and teach, educate, Plat. : to watch as one does a child, Eur. 2. generally, to educate, Plat.

παιδᾰγωγία, ἡ, the office of a παιδαγωγός, attendance on boys, education, Plat.: generally, attendance on the sick, Eur.

παιδᾰγωγικός, ή, όν, suitable to a παιδαγωγός :–ἡ -κή (sc. τέχνη) τῶν νοσημάτων =ἡ ἰατρική, the tending of diseases, Plat.

παιδ-ᾰγωγός, ὁ, = παιδὸς ἀγωγός, a boy-ward; at Athens, the slave who went with a boy from home to school and back again, a kind of tutor, Hdt., Eur., etc. : —hence Phoenix is called the παιδαγωγός of Achilles, Plat.; Fabius is jeeringly called the παιδαγωγός of Hannibal, because he always followed him about, Plut.

παιδάριον [ᾰ], τό, Dim. of παῖς, a young, little boy, Ar.; ἐκ παιδαρίου from a child, Plat. : in pl. young children, Ar. : a young slave, Id., Xen.

παιδᾰρι-ώδης, ες, (εἶδος) childish, puerile, Plat.

παιδεία, ἡ, the rearing of a child, Aesch. 2. training and teaching, education, Ar., Thuc., etc. 3. its result, culture, learning, accomplishments, Plat. 4. πλεκτὰ Αἰγύπτου παιδεία the twisted handiwork of Egypt, i. e. ropes of byblus, Eur. **II.** youth, childhood, Theogn., Eur.

παίδειος or **παιδεῖος, ον**, =παιδικός, of or for a boy, Aesch.; π. τροφή the care of rearing children, a mother's cares, Soph.

παιδεραστέω, f. ήσω, to be a παιδεραστής, Plat.

παιδ-εραστής, οῦ, ὁ, a lover of boys, Ar., Plat.

παίδευμα, ατος, τό, (παιδεύω) that which is reared up, taught, a nursling, scholar, pupil, Eur., etc.; μῆλα, φυλλάδος Παρνασίας παιδεύματ' Id. :—in pl. of a single object, Id. **II.** a thing taught, subject of instruction, lesson, Xen.

παίδευσις, εως, ἡ, (παιδεύω) education, a system of education, Hdt., Ar., etc.; τὴν ὑπ' ἀρετῆς Ἡρακλέους παίδευσιν his education by virtue, Xen. 2. its result, culture, learning, accomplishments, Ar., Plat. 3. an instructing or priming of witnesses, Dem. **II.** a means of educating, τὴν πόλιν τῆς Ἑλλάδος παίδευσιν εἶναι that our city is the school of Greece, Thuc.

παιδευτέος, α, ον, verb. Adj. of παιδεύω, to be educated, Plat. **II.** παιδευτέον, one must educate, Id.

παιδευτήριον, τό, (παιδεύω) a school, Strab.

παιδευτής, οῦ, ὁ, (παιδεύω) a teacher, instructor, preceptor, Plat. **II.** a corrector, chastiser, N. T.

παιδευτικός, ή, όν, of or for teaching :—ἡ -κή (sc. τέχνη), education, Plat.; so, τὸ παιδευτικόν Plut.; and

παιδευτός, ή, όν, to be gained by education, Plat. From

παιδεύω, f. -σω: aor. 1 ἐπαίδευσα: pf. πεπαίδευκα :— Med., f. παιδεύσομαι: aor. 1 ἐπαιδευσάμην :—Pass., f. παιδευθήσομαι, also med. παιδεύσομαι (in pass. sense): aor. 1 ἐπαιδεύθην: pf. πεπαίδευμαι: (παῖς) :—to bring up or rear a child, Soph. **II.** mostly, opp. to τρέφω, to train, teach, educate, Id., Eur., etc.; παιδεύειν τινα μουσικῇ καὶ γυμναστικῇ Plat.; ἐν μουσικῇ Id.; π. τινὰ εἰς πρὸς ἀρετήν Id.; c. dupl. acc., π. τινά τι to teach one a thing, Id.; c. acc. et inf., π. τινὰ κιθαρίζειν Hdt.; and without inf., π. γυναῖκας σώφρονας [εἶναι] Eur.:—hence in Pass., c. acc. rei, to be taught a thing, Plat. :—absol., ὁ πεπαιδευμένος a man of education, opp. to ἀπαίδευτος or ἰδιώτης, Xen., Plat. :—Med. to have any one taught, cause him to be educated, Plat. **III.** to correct, discipline, Soph., Xen. : to chastise, punish, N. T.

παιδιά, ᾶς, ἡ, (παίζω) childish play, sport, game, pastime, Xen., Plat.; π. παίζειν πρός τινα to play a game with him, Ar.; μετὰ παιδιᾶς in sport, Thuc.;

ὥστε σοι τὸν νῦν χόλον παιδιὰν εἶναι δοκεῖν will seem mere child's play, Aesch.

παιδικός, ή, όν, (παῖς) of, for or like a child, boyish, Lat. puerilis, Plat., etc. 2. playful, sportive, Id., Xen.; so, Adv. -κῶς, Plat. II. of or for a beloved youth, π. λόγος a love-tale, Xen. 2. as Subst., παιδικά, ῶν, τά, a darling, favourite, Lat. deliciae, Thuc., Plat., etc.

παιδιόθεν, Adv. from a child, N.T. From

παιδίον, τό, Dim. of παῖς, a little or young child, Hdt., Ar., Plat. II. a slave-lad, Ar.

παιδισκάριον, τό, Dim. of παιδίσκη, Luc.

παιδίσκη, ή, Dim. of παῖς (ή), a young girl, maiden, Xen. II. a young slave, courtesan, Hdt., Plut.

παιδίσκος, ὁ, Dim. of παῖς (ὁ), a young boy or son, Xen.

παιδι-ώδης, ες, (παιδιά) playful, Lat. ludibundus, Arist.

παιδνός, ή, όν, and ός, όν, childish, Aesch., Anth. II. παιδνός, ὁ, as Subst. a boy, lad, Od.

παιδο-βόρος, ον, (βι-βρώσκω) child-eating, μόχθοι π., said of Thyestes, Aesch.

παιδογονία, ή, a begetting of children, Plat. From

παιδο-γόνος, ον, (γονή) begetting children, Ζεῦ παιδο-γόνε πόριος Ἰνάχου father of a child by the daughter of Inachus, Eur. II. making fruitful, Theocr.

παιδοκομέω, f. ήσω, to take care of a child, Anth. From

παιδο-κόμος, ον, (κομέω) taking care of children.

παιδοκτονέω, f. ήσω, to murder children, Eur. From

παιδο-κτόνος, ον,(κτείνω) child-murdering, Soph., Eur.

παιδ-ολέτηρ, ήρος, ὁ, murderer of children: fem. παιδ-ολέτειρα, murderess of children, Eur.

παιδ-ολέτωρ, ορος, voc. -op, ὁ, ή, = foreg., Aesch., Eur.

παιδολέτις, ιδος, ή, = παιδολέτειρα, Anth.

παιδο-λύμας [ῠ], ου, ὁ, destroying children, Aesch.

παιδονομία, ή, the education of children, Arist. II. the office of παιδονόμος, Id. From

παιδο-νόμος, ὁ, (νέμω) one of a board of magistrates in Dorian States, who superintended the education of youths, Xen., Arist.

παιδοποιέω, f. ήσω, to beget children, Eur.; πεπαιδο-ποίηται has been begotten, Dem. 2. to bear children, of the woman, Soph. II. more commonly as Dep., f. -ήσομαι: aor. 1 ἐπαιδοποιησάμην: pf. πεπαιδοποίη-μαι, in same sense as Act., Eur., Xen., etc.

παιδοποιία, ή, procreation of children, Plat. From

παιδο-ποιός, όν, (ποιέω) begetting or bearing children, Eur. 2. generative, Hdt.

παιδο-πόρος, ον, through which a child passes, Anth.

παιδοσπορέω, f. ήσω, to beget children, Plat. From

παιδο-σπόρος, ον, (σπείρω) begetting children, Ar.

παιδοτρῐβέω, f. ήσω, to train as a gymnastic master: generally, to train, π. τινὰ πονηρὸν εἶναι Dem.

παιδο-τρίβης [ῐ], ου, ὁ, (τρίβω) one who teaches boys wrestling and other exercises, a gymnastic master, Ar., Plat., etc.; ἐν παιδοτρίβου at his school, Ar. Hence παιδοτριβικός, ή, όν, of or for a παιδοτρίβης: ή -κή (sc. τέχνη) his art, the art of wrestling, Arist.: Adv., παιδοτριβικῶς like a gymnastic master, Ar.

παιδοτροφία, ή, the rearing of children, Plat. From

παιδο-τρόφος, ον, (τρέφω) rearing boys, Simon.: παι-δοτρόφος ἐλάα Soph. 2. as fem. Subst. a mother, Eur.

παιδό-τρωτος, ον, (τι-τρώσκω) wounded by children, πάθεα π. wounds and death at children's hands, Aesch.

παιδουργέω, ή, = παιδοποιέω, Eur.; and

παιδουργία, ή, = παιδοποιία, Plat. II. in Soph. = γυνὴ παιδοποιός, a mother. From

παιδουργός, όν, (*ἔργω) = παιδοποιός.

παιδοφῐλέω, f. ήσω, to love boys, Theogn., Solon.

παιδο-φίλης [ῐ], ου, ὁ, = παιδεραστής, Theogn.

παιδο-φόνος, ον, (*φένω) killing children, Il., Eur.; π. συμφορή the accident or calamity of having killed a son, Hdt.; π. αἷμα the blood of slain children, Eur.

παιδο-φορέω, f. ήσω, (φέρω) to waft away a boy, Anth.

παίζω, Dor. παίσδω: f. παιξοῦμαι and παίξομαι: aor. 1 ἔπαισα: pf. πέπαικα, later πέπαιχα:—Pass., pf. πέ-παισμαι, later πέπαγμαι: (παῖς):—properly, to play like a child, to sport, play, Od., Hdt., etc. 2. to dance, Od., Pind.:—so in Med., Hes. 3. to play [a game], σφαίρῃ π. to play at ball, Od.; also, π. σφαῖραν Plut. 4. to play (on an instrument), h. Hom. II. to sport, play, jest, joke, Hdt., Xen., etc.; π. πρός τινα to make sport of one, mock him, Eur.; π. εἴς τι to jest upon a thing, Plat.: the part. παίζων is used absol. in jest, jest-ingly, Id.:—Pass., ὁ λόγος πέπαισται is jocularly told, Hdt.; ταῦτα πεπαίσθω ὑμῖν enough of jest, Plat. 2. c. acc. to play with, Anth., Luc.

Παιήόνιος, a, ον, healing, like Παιώνιος, Anth. From

παιήσω, f. of παίω.

Παιήων, ονος, ὁ, Ep. for Παιάν.

παιξοῦμαι or παίξομαι, f. of παίζω.

Παίονες, οἱ, the Paeonians, a people of Macedonia, Il.; Παιόνων στρατός Eur.:—Παιονία, Ion. -ίη, ἡ, their land, Il.:—Adj. Παιονικός, ή, όν, Paeonian, Thuc.; pecul. fem. Παιονίς, ίδος, Hdt.

παιόνιος, η, ον, poët. for παιώνιος, Anth.

παιπάλη [ἄ], ή, (redupl. from πάλη, pollen), the finest flour or meal, Lat. flos farinae, Ar.: metaph. of a subtle rogue, Id.

παιπάλημα, ατος, τό, like παιπάλη, a piece of subtlety, of a man, Ar., Aeschin.

παιπάλόεις, εσσα, εν, craggy, rugged, old Ep. word of uncertain origin, epith. of hills, mountain-paths, and rocky islands, Hom.

ΠΑΙ͂Σ, Ep. also παῖς, παιδός, ὁ, ή: plur. gen. παίδων, Dor. παιδῶν, dat. παισί, Ep. παίδεσσι: I. in rela-tion to Descent, a child, whether son or daughter, Il.:—παῖς παιδός a child's child, grandchild, Ib.; Ἀγή-νορος παῖδες ἐκ παίδων Eur.;—of animals, Aesch. 2. metaph., ἀμπέλου παῖς, i.e. wine, Pind. 3. periphr., δυστήνων παῖδες (v. sub δύστηνος); οἱ Λυδῶν παῖδες sons of the Lydians, i.e. the Lydians, Hdt.; π. Ἑλλή-νων Aesch.; οἱ Ἀσκληπιοῦ π. i.e. physicians, Plat., etc. II. in relation to Age, a child, either a boy, youth, lad, or a girl, maiden, Hom., etc.; with an-other Subst., παῖς συφορβός a boy-swineherd, Il.: —ἐκ παιδός from a child, Plat.; ἐκ παίδων or παίδων εὐθύς Id.; εὐθὺς ἐκ παίδων ἐξελθών Dem. III. in relation to Condition, a slave, servant, man or maid, Aesch., Ar., etc.

παίσατε, 2 pl. aor. 1 imper. of παίζω.

παίσδω, Dor. for παίζω.

παι-φάσσω, (redupl. from **ΦΑ,** Root of φαίνομαι) only in pres., *to dart* or *rush wildly about,* Il.

ΠΑΙ'Ω (A), f. παίσω and παιήσω: aor. 1 ἔπαισα: pf. πέπαικα:—Med., aor. 1 ἐπαισάμην:—Pass., aor. 1 ἐπαίσθην: pf. πέπαισμαι:—*to strike, smite,* Hdt., Trag.; π. τινὰ ἐς τὴν γῆν Hdt.; π. τινὰ ἐς τὴν γαστέρα Ar.; εἰς τὰ στέρνα or κατὰ τὸ στέρνον Xen.; c. dupl. acc., π. τινὰ τὸ νῶτον Ar.:—also c. acc. cogn., ὀλίγας π. (sc. πληγάς) Xen.;—π. ἄλμην, of rowers, Aesch.:—Med., ἐπαίσατο τὸν μηρόν *he smote his thigh,* Xen. 2. c. acc. instrumenti, *to strike, dash* one thing against another, ναῦς ἐν νηὶ στόλον ἔπαισε one ship *struck* its beak against another, ναῦν; metaph., ἐν δ' ἐμῷ κάρᾳ θεὸς μέγα βάρος ἔπαισεν the god *dashed* a great weight upon my head, i. e. smote me heavily, Soph.; ἔπαισας ἐπὶ νόσῳ νόσον Id. 3. *to drive away,* τοὺς σφῆκας ἀπὸ τῆς οἰκίας Ar. 4. *to hit hard in speaking,* Id. II. intr. *to strike* or *dash against,* Lat. *illido,* πρός τινι or τι Aesch., Xen.; c. acc., παίειν ἄφαντον ἕρμα strikes on a hidden reef, Aesch.; so, στήληι παίσας, of a charioteer, Soph.

παίω (B), = πατέομαι, *to eat,* Ar.

Παιών, παιών, another form of Παιάν, παιάν.

Παιωνιάς, άδος, ἡ, v. Παιώνιος.

παιωνίζω, f. σω, (παιών = παιάν) *to chant the paean* or *song of triumph,* Hdt., Ar., etc.; c. acc. cogn. *to sing in triumph,* Aesch.; of *an after-dinner song,* Xen.: Pass., 3 sing. impf. used impersonally, ἐπεπαιώνιστο αὐτοῖς the paean had been sung by them, Thuc.

Παιώνιος, α, ον, (Παιών) *belonging to Paeon, medicinal, healing,* Aesch., Soph., Ar.:—**Παιωνιὰς σοφία** *the healing art, medicine,* Anth. 2. as Subst., **Παιώνιος, ὁ,** *a healer, reliever,* c. gen., Soph. b. **Παιώνια, τά,** *a festival of Paeon,* Ar. II. like a *paean* or *song of victory,* Aesch.

παιωνισμός, ὁ, (παιωνίζω) *a chanting of the paean,* Thuc.

πακτός, Dor. for πηκτός.

πακτόω, f. ώσω, (πακτός) *to fasten, make fast,* δῶμα πάκτου *make fast* the house, Soph. 2. *to stop up, stop, caulk,* Ar. 3. *to bind fast,* Anth.

πᾰλάθη [λᾰ], ἡ, *a cake of preserved fruit,* Hdt., Luc.

πᾰλᾰθίς, ἡ, = foreg., Strab.

ΠΑ'ΛΑΙ [ᾰ], Adv. *long ago, in olden time, in days of yore, in time gone by* Il., Soph., etc.; **πάλαι ποτέ** *once upon a time,* Ar.:—often used with a pres. in the sense of a pf., ὁρῶ πάλαι, Lat. *dudum video,* I have *long* seen, Soph.; πάλαι ποτ' ὄντες ye who have *long ago* been, Ar.;—also with the Art., τὰ πάλαι Hdt., Thuc., etc. 2. πάλαι is often used like an Adj. with the Art. and a Noun, οἱ πάλαι φῶτες men *of old,* Pind.; Κάδμου τοῦ πάλαι Soph.; τὰ π. Dem. II. of time *just past,* ἡμὲν πάλαι ἠδ' ἔτι καὶ νῦν Il.: hence πάλαι comes to mean *not long ago, but now, just now,* much like ἄρτι, Aesch., Plat.

πάλαι-γενής, ές, (γίγνομαι) *born long ago, full of years, ancient,* Hom.; ἄνθρωποι Aesch., Eur.

πᾰλαί-γονος, ον, = παλαιγενής, Pind.

πᾰλαιμονέω, *to wrestle* or *fight,* Pind.; cf. Παλαίμων.

Πᾰλαίμων, ονος, ὁ, (παλαίω) *Palaemon,* i. e. *Wrestler,* masc. prop. n., a name of Melicertes, son of Ino, who was adored as a sea-god friendly to the shipwrecked, Eur.

πᾰλαιο-γενής, ές, = παλαιγενής, Ar.

πᾰλαιό-γονος, ον, = παλαίγονος, Anth.

πᾰλαιό-μάτωρ, ορος, ὁ, (μήτηρ) *ancient mother,* Eur.

πᾰλαιό-πλουτος, ον, *rich from early times,* Thuc.

πᾰλαιός, ά, όν, regul. Comp. and Sup. παλαιότερος, -ότατος, but the usual forms are παλαίτερος, -αίτατος (formed from πάλαι): I. *old in years,* a. of persons, *old, aged,* ἢ νέος ἠὲ παλαιός Hom.; π. γέρων, π. γρηῦς Od.; χρόνῳ π. Soph. 2. of things, οἶνος Od.; νῆες Ib. II. *of old date, ancient,* 1. of persons, Hom.; Μίνως παλαίτατος ὢν ἀκοῇ ἴσμεν Thuc.; οἱ π. *the ancients,* Lat. *veteres,* Id. 2. of things, Od., Hdt., etc.:—τὸ παλαιόν, as Adv. like τὸ πάλαι, *anciently, formerly,* Hdt., etc.; ἐκ παλαιοῦ *from of old,* Id.; ἐκ παλαιτέρου *from older time,* Id.; ἐκ παλαιτάτου Thuc. b. of things, also, *antiquated, obsolete,* Aesch., Soph. Hence

πᾰλαιότης, ητος, ἡ, *antiquity, obsoleteness,* Eur., Plat.

πᾰλαιό-φρων, ονος, ὁ, ἡ, (φρήν) *old in mind, with the wisdom of age,* Aesch.

πᾰλαιόω, f. ώσω: pf. πεπαλαίωκα: (παλαιός):—*to make old,* mostly in Pass. (pres.) *to be old* or *antiquated,* βραχίονος π. *is of long standing,* Hipp. II. in Pass. also, *to become old,* Plat. III. like Lat. *antiquare, to abrogate* a law, N. T.

πάλαισμα [ᾰ], ατος, τό, (παλαίω) *a bout* or *fall in wrestling,* Hdt.; ἐν μὲν τόδ' ἤδη τῶν τριῶν παλαισμάτων Aesch. 2. *any struggle,* Trag. 3. *any trick* or *artifice, subterfuge,* Ar.; π. δικαστηρίου *a trick* of the courts, Aeschin.

πᾰλαισμοσύνη, ἡ, poët. for πάλη, *wrestling, the wrestler's art,* Hom.

πᾰλαιστή, ἡ, later form of παλαστή, q. v.

πᾰλαιστής, οῦ, ὁ, (παλαίω) *a wrestler,* Hdt., Plat., etc. 2. generally, *a rival, adversary,* Aesch., Soph.: *a candidate, suitor,* Aesch.

πᾰλαιστιαῖος, α, ον, later form of παλαστιαῖος.

πᾰλαιστικός, ή, όν, *expert in wrestling,* Arist., Luc.

πᾰλαίστρα, ἡ, *a palaestra, wrestling-school,* wherein wrestlers (παλαισταί) were trained, Hdt., Eur.

πᾰλαιστρίτης [ῑ], ου, ὁ, *like a* παλαιστής, π. θεός god *of the palaestra,* Babr.

πᾰλαίτερος, -αίτατος, irr. Comp. and Sup. of παλαιός.

πᾰλαί-φᾰτος, ον, I. *spoken long ago,* Od., Pind., Aesch. II. *having a legend attached to it, legendary,* δρῦς π. an oak of *ancient story,* Od. 2. generally, *primeval, ancient, olden,* Pind., Soph.

πᾰλαί-χθων, ονος, ὁ, ἡ, *that has been long in a country, an ancient inhabitant, indigenous,* Aesch., Anth.

πᾰλαίω, f. παλαίσω: aor. 1 ἐπάλαισα: Pass., aor. 1 ἐπαλαίσθην: (πάλη):—*to wrestle,* Il., Plat.: π. τινί *to wrestle with* one, Od., Pind. :—Pass., παλαισθείς *beaten,* Eur.

πᾰλαίωσις, ἡ, (παλαιόομαι) *a growing old,* Strab.

πᾰλᾰμάομαι, f. ήσομαι, Dep. *to manage, execute,* Xen. II. like μηχανάομαι, *to manage adroitly, contrive cunningly,* Ar. From

ΠΑ'ΛΑ'ΜΗ [ᾰ], ἡ: Ep. gen. and dat. παλάμηφι, -φιν, *the palm of the hand, the hand,* Hom., Pind.; πάσχειν τι ὑπ' Ἄρηος παλαμάων by the hands of Ares, Il.:—hence *a deed of force,* Soph. 2. *the hand as used in works of art,* Hes. II. metaph. *cunning,*

art, a device, plan, method, Hdt., etc. ; π. βιότου a device for one's livelihood, Theogn. : of the gods, θεοῦ σὺν παλάμᾳ, θεῶν παλάμαι, παλάμαις Διός by their arts, Pind. ; παλάμας πλέκειν Ar. ; π. πυριγενής a fire-born instrument, i. e. a sword, Eur.

Παλαμήδης, ὁ, gen. -ovs, dat. -ει, acc. -εα or -ην, (παλάμη) name of a hero, the Inventor, Ar., etc.

πᾰλαμναῖος, ὁ, (παλάμη) one guilty of violence, a blood-guilty man, murderer, Aesch., Soph.:— ὦ παλαμναίη oh miscreant! of the fox, Babr. II.= ἀλάστωρ, the avenger of blood, Eur., Xen.

πᾰλαξέμεν, Ep. for παλάξειν, f. inf. of παλάσσω.

πᾰλάσιον, τό, = παλάθιον, Dim. of παλάθη, Ar.

πᾰλάσσω, f. ξω : pf. pass. πεπάλαγμαι : Ep. 3 sing. plqpf. πεπάλακτο: (πάλλω):—to besprinkle, sully, defile, Od. ; mostly in Pass., Hom. :—Med., παλάσσετο χεῖρας he defiled his hands, Il. 2. Pass. also of things, to be scattered abroad, Ib. II. pf. pass. of lots shaken in an urn, κλήρῳ πεπαλάχθαι to determine one's fate by lot, Hom. ; cf. πάλος.

πᾰλαστή, later παλαιστή, ἡ, = παλάμη, the palm of the hand : as a measure of length, a palm, four fingers' breadth, a little more than three inches. Hence πᾰλαστιαῖος, a, ον, later παλαιστιαῖος, a palm long or broad, Hdt.

πᾰλεύω, f. σω, to catch by decoy-birds, Ar. (Deriv. uncertain.)

πᾰλέω, 3 sing. aor. 2 opt. παλήσειε : to be disabled, Hdt.

πάλη [ᾰ], Dor. πᾰλᾱ, ἡ, (πάλλω) wrestling, Lat. lucta, Hom., Pind., etc. 2. generally, battle, Aesch., Eur.

πᾰλιγ-γενεσία, ἡ, (γένεσις) a being born again, new birth ; used by Cic. of his restoration after exile :— hence, in N. T., 1. the resurrection. 2. re-generation by baptism.

πᾰλίγ-γλωσσος, ον, (γλῶσσα) contradictory, false, Pind. II. of strange or foreign tongue, Id.

πᾰλιγ-κᾰπηλεύω, f. σω, to sell over again, sell wares by retail, Dem.

πᾰλιγ-κᾰπηλος, ὁ, one who buys and sells again, a petty retailer, huckster, Ar., Dem.

πᾰλίγ-κοτος, ον, of wounds, breaking out afresh : metaph. in Adv., αὐτῷ παλιγκότως συνεφέρετο according to his old ill-luck fared it with him, Hdt. II. of fresh outbreaks of passion, κληδόνες π. injurious, untoward reports, Aesch. ; π. τύχη adverse fortune, Id. 2. of persons, hostile, malignant, Ar., Theocr. ; παλίγκοτοι adversaries, Pind. (-κοτος seems to be a termin., as in ἀλλόκοτος.)

πᾰλίγ-κραιπνος, ον, very swift, Anth.

πᾰλιλλογέω, to say again, repeat, recapitulate, 3 sing. plqpf. ἐπαλιλλόγητο Hdt. ; and

πᾰλιλλογία, ἡ, recapitulation, Arist. II. retracta-tion, recantation, Theophr. From

πᾰλίλ-λογος, ον, (λέγω to gather), collected again, Il. II. (λέγω to say) repeated.

πᾰλίμ-βᾰμος, ον, (βαίνω) walking back, ἱστῶν παλίμ-βαμοι ὁδοί, of women working at the loom, Pind.

πᾰλιμ-βλαστής, ές, (βλαστάνω) growing again, Eur.

πᾰλίμ-βολος, ον, (βάλλω) thrown back, reversed : hence, untrustworthy, uncertain, unstable, Plat. : τὸ παλίμβολον instability, Aeschin.

πᾰλιμ-μήκης, ες, (μῆκος) doubly long, Aesch.

πᾰλιμ-πετής, ές, (πίπτω) falling back :—in neut. as Adv., back, back again, Hom.

πᾰλίμ-πηξις, ἡ, (πήγνυμι) a patching up or cobbling of shoes, Theophr.

πᾰλίμ-πλαγκτος, ον, back-wandering, Aesch.

πᾰλίμ-πλάζομαι, Pass. to wander back, only in aor. I part. παλιμπλαγχθείς wandering homewards, Hom.

πᾰλίμ-πλᾰνής, ές, wandering to and fro, Anth.

πᾰλίμ-πλῠτος, ον, washed up again, vamped up ; metaph. of a plagiarist, Anth.

πᾰλίμ-ποινος, ον, (ποινή) retributive : παλίμποινα, τά, retribution, repayment, Aesch.

πᾰλιμ-πρυμνηδόν, (πρύμνα) Adv. stern-foremost, Eur.

πᾰλίμ-φημος, Dor. -φᾱμος, ον, (φήμη) back-speaking, recanting, π. ἀοιδά = παλινῳδία, Eur.

πᾰλίμ-ψηστος, ον, (ψάω) scraped again, βιβλίον παλ. a palimpsest, i. e. a parchment from which one writing has been erased to make room for another, Plut.

ΠΑΛΙΝ [ᾰ], Adv., 1. of Place, back, backwards, Hom., Hes., etc. ; π. χωρέειν Hdt. ; π. ἔρχεσθαι Aesch., etc. ; also, πάλιν δοῦναι to give back, restore, Il. :—c. gen., πάλιν τράπεθ' υἷος ἑοῖο she turned back from her son, Ib. ; πάλιν κίε θυγατέρος ἧς Ib. ;—also πάλιν αὖτις back again, αὖτε πάλιν, ἀψ π., π. ὀπίσσω, etc. 2. with a notion of contradiction, πάλιν ἐρεῖν to gainsay (i. e. say against), Il. ; but, μῦθον πάλιν λάζεσθαι to take back one's word, unsay it, Ib. ; opp. to ἀληθέα εἰπεῖν, Od. : in Prose, contrariwise, Plat. : —c. gen., τὸ πάλιν νεότητος youth's opposite, Pind. ; χρόνου τὸ πάλιν the change of time, Eur. II. of Time, again, once more, anew, Soph., etc. ; so, αὖθις πάλιν, πάλιν αὖθις, αὖ πάλιν, πάλιν αὖ, αὖ πάλιν αὖθις, αὖθις αὖ πάλιν, Att. III. again, in turn, Soph.

πᾰλίν-άγρετος, ον, (ἀγρέω) to be taken back or recalled, ἔπος οὐ παλινάγρετον an irrevocable word, Il.

πᾰλίν-αυξής, ές, (αὔξω) growing again, Anth.

πᾰλίν-αυτόμολος, ὁ, a double deserter, Xen.

πᾰλιν-δῐκία, a second action, a new trial, Plut.

πᾰλίν-δίνητος [ῐ], ον, whirling round and round, Anth.

πᾰλινδρομέω, to run back again, of a ship, Plut.

πᾰλινδρομία, ἡ, a running back or backwards, Anth.

πᾰλινδρομικός, ή, όν, recurring, of the tide, Strab.

πᾰλίν-δρομος, ον, (δραμεῖν) running back again, Luc.

πᾰλῐ-νηνεμία, ἡ, a returning calm, Anth.

πᾰλίν-ορμενος, η, ον, rushing back, Il.

πᾰλίν-ορσος, ον, (ὄρνυμι) starting back, Il. :—neut. as Adv. back again, Anth. ; Att. παλίνορρον, with a backward wrench, Ar.

πᾰλίν-ορτος, ον, = παλίνορσος, recurring, inveterate, much like παλίγ-κοτος, Anth.

πᾰλίν-σκιος or παλί-σκιος, ον, shaded over again, thick-shaded, h. Hom., etc.

πᾰλιν-σκοπιά, ἡ, a looking back again ; acc. as Adv. in the opposite direction, Eur.

πᾰλίν-σοος, ον, safe again, recovered, Anth.

πᾰλιν-στομέω, to speak words of ill omen, Aesch.

πᾰλίν-τιτος, ον, (τίνω) like ἄντιτος, requited, avenged, Od.

πᾰλίν-τονος, ον, (τείνω) back-stretched, back-bending, epith. of the bow, Hom. It denotes the form of the Homeric bow, which when unstrung bent in a direction

contrary to that which it took when strung.   2.
ἡνίαι π. *back-stretched* reins, Ar.

πᾰλιν-τρᾰπελος, ον, = παλίντροπος, Pind.

πᾰλιν-τρῐβής, ές, (τρίβω) *rubbed again and again*:
hence *hardened, knavish*, Soph.

πᾰλίν-τροπος, ον, *turned back, averted*, Lat. *retortus*,
π. ὄμματα Aesch.   II. *turning back*, Soph., Eur.

πᾰλιν-τῠχής, ές, (τύχη) *with a reverse of fortune*, Aesch.

πᾰλῐνῳδέω, f. ήσω, *to recant an ode* and so, generally,
to revoke, recant, Plat.   From

πᾰλῐν-ῳδία, ἡ, (ᾠδή) *a palinode* or *recantation*, a
name first given to an ode by Stesichorus, in which he
recants his attack upon Helen, Plat.

πᾰλίουρος, ὁ or ἡ, a thorny shrub, *Rhamnus paliurus*,
Eur., Theocr.

πᾰλίουρο-φόρος, (φέρω) ὁ, *made of the wood of the*
παλίουρος, Anth.

πᾰλιρροέω, f. ήσω, (παλίρροος) *to ebb and flow*, Lat.
reciprocare, Strab., Theophr.

πᾰλιρ-ρόθιος, η, ον, *back-rushing, refluent*, Od.

πᾰλίρροθος, ον, = παλιρρόθιος, Aesch.

πᾰλίρροια, ἡ, *the reflux of water, back-water*, Hdt.:—
metaph. of fortune, Polyb.   From

πᾰλίρ-ροος, ον, contr. -ρους, ρουν, *back-flowing*,
refluent, Eur.   II. metaph. *recurring, returning upon one's head*, Id.

πᾰλίρ-ροπος, ον, (ῥέπω) *inclining backwards*, π. γόνυ
backward-sinking knee, Eur.

πᾰλιρ-ροχθος, ον, *roaring with ebb and flow*, Aesch.

πᾰλίρ-ρύμη [ῠ], ἡ, *a rush backwards, back-flow*, Plut.

πᾰλίρ-ρῠτος, ον, = παλίρροος: *in retribution*, Soph.

πᾰλί-σκιος, v. παλίνσκιος.

πᾰλίσ-σῦτος, ον, (σεύω) *rushing hurriedly back*,
δρόμημα π. *hurried flight*, Soph.; πᾰλ. στείχειν Eur.

πᾰλί-ωξις [ῐ], ἡ, (παλίν, ἰωκή) *pursuit back again* or
in turn, as when fugitives rally and turn on their pur-
suers, Il., Hes.

Παλλάδιον [ᾰ], τό, *a statue of Pallas*, Hdt., Ar.

παλλᾰκεύομαι,   I. as Dep., π. τινα *to keep as a*
concubine, Hdt.   II. as Pass. *to be a concubine*,
Plut.   From

παλλᾰκή, ἡ, = παλλακίς, Hdt., Ar., etc.

παλλᾰκίδιον, τό, Dim. of παλλακίς, Plut.

παλλᾰκίς, ίδος, ἡ, *a concubine, mistress*, Lat. *pellex*,
opp. to a lawful wife (κουριδίη ἄλοχος), Hom.   (Prob.
from same Root as παλλάς - νεᾶνις.)

Παλλάς, άδος, ἡ, *Pallas*, in Hom. always Παλλὰς
Ἀθήνη or Παλλὰς Ἀθηναίη. (Commonly deriv. from
πάλλω, either as *Brandisher* of the spear:—but prob.
it is an old word παλλάς = νεᾶνις.)

πάλ-λευκος, ον, *all-white*, Aesch., Eur.

Παλλήνη, ἡ, a peninsula and town of Chalcidice, Hdt.,
etc.   II. an Attic deme: Παλληνεύς, ὁ, *an*
inhabitant thereof; fem. Παλληνίς, ίδος, Id.

ΠΑ'ΛΛΩ, impf. ἔπαλλον, Ep. πάλλον: aor. 1 ἔπηλα:
Ep. aor. 2 part. πεπαλών:—Pass., pf. πέπαλμαι: 3
sing. Ep. aor. 2 πάλτο:—*to poise* or *sway* a missile
before it is thrown, Eur., Ar.   2. *to sway* other
arms, not missiles, σάκος Hes.; πέλτας Eur.:—then, *to*
toss a child, Il.; Νὺξ ὄχημ' ἔπαλλε she *drave* it
furiously, Eur.   3. κλήρους ἐν κυνέῃ πάλλον they
shook the lots together in a helmet, till one *leapt forth*,

Hom.: absol. *to cast lots*, Il.; ὅθ' αὐτοὺς οἱ βραβεῖς
κλήροις ἔπηλαν where the stewards *ranged* them *by*
casting lots, Soph.:—Med. *to draw lots*, ἔλαχον ἅλα
παλλομένων I obtained the sea *when we cast lots*, Il.;
so in Hdt., Soph.   II. Pass. *to swing* or *dash*
oneself, ἐν ἄντυγι πάλτο he *dashed himself* upon the
shield-rim, Il. : *to quiver, leap*, esp. in fear, πάλλεται
ἦτορ Ib. ; also of the person, παλλομένη κραδίην Ib. ; of
dying fish, *to quiver, leap*, Hdt.   III. intr., like
the Pass., *to leap, bound*, Eur.: *to quiver*, Soph.,
Eur.

πάλος [ᾰ], ὁ, (πάλλω I. 3) *the lot cast from a shaken*
helmet, ἂμ πάλον θέμεν to cast *the lot* again, Pind. ;
πάλῳ λαχεῖν to obtain *by lot*, Hdt., Aesch. ; ἀρχὰς
πάλῳ ἄρχειν to hold public offices *by lot*, Hdt. ; οὓς
ἐκλήρωσεν πάλος Eur.

πάλτο, 3 sing. Ep. aor. 2 pass. of πάλλω.

παλτός, ή, όν, (πάλλω) *brandished, hurled*, Soph.   II.
as Subst., παλτόν, τό, *a light spear* used by the
Persian cavalry, like the Moorish *jereed*, Xen.

πᾰλύνω [ῠ], Ep. impf. πάλῡνον, (πάλλω) *to strew* or
sprinkle, ἄλφιτα παλύνειν Hom.   II. *to bestrew*,
besprinkle, with dat. of the thing sprinkled, παλύνας
ἀλφίτου ἀκτῇ Od.   2. of liquids, ἃ σύριγξ εὑρῶτι
παλύνεται Theocr.   III. *to sprinkle, cover*
lightly, χιὼν ἐπάλυνεν ἀρούρας Il.

πάμα, ατος, τό, (πάομαι) *property*, Anth.

παμ-βᾰσῐλεία, ἡ, *absolute monarchy*, Arist.

παμ-βᾰσίλεια, ἡ, *queen of all*, Ar.

παμ-βᾰσῐλεύς, έως, ὁ, *an absolute monarch*, Arist.

παμ-βίας, ου, ὁ, (βιάω) *all-subduing*, Pind.

παμ-μάταιος, ον, *all-vain, all-useless*, Aesch.

παμ-μάχος [ᾰ], ον, (μάχομαι) *fighting with all*, Aesch. :
esp. = παγκρατιαστής, *ready for every kind of contest*, Plat., Theocr.

πάμ-μεγας, άλη, α, *very great, immense*, Plat.

παμ-μεγέθης, ες, = foreg., Xen., Dem. :—neut. as Adv.,
παμμέγεθες ἀναβοᾶν Aeschin.

παμ-μέλας, αινα, ἄν, *all-black*, Od.

παμ-μήκης, ες, (μῆκος) *very long, prolonged*, Soph.,
Plat.

πάμ-μηνος, ον, (μήν) *through all months, the live-long*
year, Soph.

παμμήτειρα, ἡ, = παμμήτωρ, h. Hom., Anth.

παμ-μήτωρ, ορος, ἡ, (μήτηρ) *mother of all*, Aesch.   II.
a very mother, mother indeed, τοῦδε π. νεκροῦ Soph.

παμ-μίαρος, ον, *all-abominable*, Ar.

παμ-μῐγής, ές, *all-mingled, promiscuous*, Aesch.

πάμμικτος, ον, = foreg., Aesch.

πάμ-μορος, ον, = all-hapless*, Soph.

παμ-πάλαιος, ον, *very old*, Plat., etc.

πάμ-πᾰν, Adv., (πᾶς) like πάντη, *quite, wholly, altogether*, Hom., Hes., Eur.; οὐδέ τι πάμπαν *not at all*,
by no means, Il.: with the Art., τὸ π. Eur.

παμ-πειθής, ές, (πείθω) *all-persuasive*, Pind.

παμπήδην, Adv., (πᾶς) like πάμπαν, *entirely*, Theogn.,
Aesch., Soph.

παμ-πησία, ἡ, (πάομαι) *entire possession, the full*
property, Aesch., Eur.

παμπληθεί, Adv. *with the whole multitude*, N.T. From

παμ-πληθής, ές, (πλῆθος) *of* or *with the whole multitude*, Xen.   II. = πάμπολυς, *very numerous*.

multitudinous, Plat., Dem. III. neut. as Adv. entirely, Dem.

πάμ-πληκτος, ον, (πλήσσω) in which all sorts of blows are given and received, ἄεθλα Soph.

παμ-ποίκῐλος, ον, all-variegated, of rich and varied work, Hom. : all-spotted, of fawn-skins, Eur.

πάμ-πολις, εως, ὁ, ἡ, prevailing in all cities, universal, Soph.

πάμ-πολυς, -πόλλη, -πολυ, very much, great, large or numerous, Ar., Xen. :—in pl. very many, Ar.

παμ-πόνηρος, ον, all-depraved, thoroughly knavish, Ar., Plat. : Adv., παμπονήρως ἔχειν to be very ill, Luc.

παμ-πόρφῠρος, ον, (πορφύρω) all-purple, Pind.

πάμ-πότνια, ἡ, all-venerable, Anth.

πάμπρεπτος, ον, (πρέπω) all-conspicuous, Aesch.

παμπρόσθη, corrupt in Aesch. Ag.

πάμ-πρωτος, η, ον, first of all, the very first, Il. : in neut. πάμπρωτον and -τα as Adv., Hom.

παμ-φάγος [ᾰ], ον, all-devouring, voracious, Eur.

παμ-φαής, ές, (φάος) all-shining, all-brilliant, radiant, Soph., Eur., etc. ; of honey, bright, pure, Aesch.

παμ-φαίνω, Ep. 3 sing. subj. παμφαίνῃσι : Ep. impf. παμφαῖνω : not used in other tenses :—redupl. from φαίνω, to shine or beam brightly, of burnished metal, Il.; of a star, Ib.; στήθεσι παμφαίνοντες with their breasts white-gleaming, i. e. naked, Ib.

παμ-φᾰνόων, gen. ωντος, fem. παμφᾰνόωσα, Ep. part. as if from παμφᾰνάω (= παμφαίνω), bright-shining, beaming, of burnished metal, Il.; of the Sun, Od.

παμ-φάρμᾰκος, ον, skilled in all charms or drugs, Pind.

πάμ-φεγγής, ές, = παμφαής, Soph.

πάμ-φθαρτος, ον, (φθείρω) all-destroying, Aesch.

πάμφλεκτος, ον, (φλέγω) all-blazing, Soph.

πάμ-φορβος, η, ον, (φέρβω) all-feeding, Anth.

πάμ-φορος, ον, (φέρω) all-bearing, all-productive, Lat. omnium ferax, χώρη παμφορωτάτη Hdt. ; a friend is called παμφορώτατον κτῆμα by Xen. II. bearing all things with it, π. χέραδος a mixed mass of rubbish, Pind.

πάμ-φῡλος, ον, of mingled tribes, of all sorts, Ar.

πάμ-φωνος, ον, (φωνή) with all tones, full-toned or many-toned, Pind. : generally, expressive, Anth.

πάμ-ψηφεί, (ψῆφος) Adv. by all the votes, Anth.

πάμ-ψῡχος, ον, (ψυχή) with all his soul, or = πασῶν τῶν ψυχῶν, Soph.

Πάν, gen. Πᾰνός, ὁ, Pan, god of Arcadia, son of Hermes, h. Hom. ; represented with goat's feet, horns, and shaggy hair. At Athens his worship began after the battle of Marathon, Hdt. :—pl. Πᾶνες in Ar., Theocr.

πάν-αβρος, ον, quite or very soft, Luc.

πᾰν-ᾰγής, ές, all-hallowed, Lat. sacrosanctus, Plut.

πάν-ᾰγρος, ὁ, one who catches everything, Anth.

πάν-ᾰγρος, ον, (ἄγρα) catching all, Il.

πάν-άγρυπνος, ον, all-wakeful, Anth.

πανάγυρις, Dor. for πανήγυρις.

Πᾰν-ᾰθήναια (sc. ἱερά), τά, the Panathenaea, two festivals of the Athenians, τὰ μεγάλα and τὰ μικρά, in honour of Athena, Ar., etc. The greater was celebrated in the third year of each Olympiad, the latter annually.

Πᾰνᾰθηναϊκός, ή, όν, of or at the Panathenaea, Thuc.

πᾰν-άθλιος, α, ον, all-wretched, Trag.

πᾰν-αιγλήεις, εσσα, εν, all-shining, Anth.

πάν-αιθος [πᾰν-], η, ον, all-blazing, Il.

πᾰν-αίολος, ον, epith. of armour, either all-variegated, sparkling, or, quite light, easily-moved, Il. II. metaph. manifold, Aesch.

πᾰν-αισχής, ές, (αἶσχος) utterly ugly, ugliest, Arist.

πάν-αισχρος, ον, = παναισχής ; Sup. -αίσχιστος Anth.

πάν-αίτιος, ον, (αἰτία) the cause of all, Aesch. 2. to whom all the guilt belongs, Id.

πᾰν-ἀλάστωρ, ορος, ὁ, all-avenging, Anth.

πάν-ἀληθής, ές, all true, all too true, of a person, Aesch. 2. of things, absolutely true or real, Plat.

πᾰν-αλκής, ές, (ἀλκή) all-powerful, Aesch.

πάν-ἀλωτος [ᾰλ], ον, all-embracing, Aesch.

πᾰνάμερος, ον, Dor. for πανήμερος.

πάν-άμμορος, ον, without any share in a thing, c. gen., Anth.

πᾰν-άμωμος, ον, all-blameless, Simon.

πᾰν-αοίδιμος, ον, sung by all, Anth.

πᾰν-άπᾰλος, ον, all-tender, all-delicate, Od.

πᾰν-ἀπήμων, ον, all-harmless, Hes., Anth.

πάν-άποτμος, ον, all-hapless, Il.

πᾰν-άργυρος, ον, all-silver, Od.

πᾰν-άρετος [ᾰρ], ον, (ἀρετή) all virtuous, Luc.

πᾰν-άριστος, ον, best of all, Hes., Anth.

πᾰν-αρκής, ές, (ἀρκέω) all-sufficing :—the gen. fem. πᾰναρκέτας in Aesch. is prob. corrupt.

πᾰν-αρμόνιος, α, ον, (ἁρμονία) in Music, suited to all modes ; τὸ π. (sc. ὄργανον) an instrument on which all modes can be played, Plat. 2. metaph. all-harmonious, Id.

πάν-αρχος, ον, all-powerful, ruling all, Soph.

πᾰν-ἀτρεκής, ές, all-exact, infallible, Anth.

πᾰν-άφηλιξ, ικος, ὁ, ἡ, all-away from the friends of one's youth, Il.

πᾰν-άφθιτος, ον, all-imperishable, Anth.

πάν-άφυκτος, ον, all-inevitable, Anth.

πάν-άφυλλος, ον, all-leafless, h. Hom.

Πάν-ἄχαιοί, οἱ, all the Achaians, Hom.

πάν-αώριος, ον, (ἄωρος) all-untimely, doomed to an untimely end, Il., Anth.

πᾰν-δαισία, Ion. -ίη, ἡ, (δαίς) a complete banquet, a banquet at which nothing is wanting, Hdt., Ar.

πᾰν-δάκρῠτος, ον, all-tearful, Soph. II. all-bewept, most miserable, Trag.

πᾰν-δᾰμάτωρ [μᾰ], ορος, ὁ, (δαμάω) the all-subduer, all-tamer, Hom., Soph.

πανδαμεί, πάνδαμος, Dor. for πανδημεί, πάνδημος.

πάν-δεινος, ον, all-dreadful, terrible, Plat. :—πάνδεινόν ἐστι it is outrageous, Dem. II. clever at all things, Plat., Dem.

πᾰνδελέτειος, ον, knavish like Pandeletus (a sycophant), Ar.

πᾰν-δερκέτης, ου, ὁ, = sq., Eur.

πᾰν-δερκής, ές, (δέρκομαι) all-seeing, Anth.

πανδημεί or -μί, Dor. πανδᾱμί, Adv. of πάνδημος, with the whole people, in a mass or body, Hdt., Aesch.; π. βοηθεῖν, στρατεύειν, of a whole people going out to war, a levée en masse, Thuc.

πανδημία, ἡ, the whole people, Plat. ; and

πανδήμιος, ον, = sq., πτωχὸς πανδήμιος one who begs of all people, a public beggar, Od. ; π. πόλις the city with all its people, Soph. From

πάν-δημος, Dor. πάν-δᾱμος, ον, *of or belonging to all the* people, *public, common,* Soph., Eur.; π. πόλις, στρατός *the whole body of* the city, *of* the army, Soph.　　II. π. Ἔρως, *common, vulgar* love, as opp. to the spiritual sort (οὐράνιος), Plat., Xen.

Πάν-δια (sc. ἱερά), τά, (Διός) *a feast of Zeus,* Dem.

πάν-δῐκος, ον, (δίκη) *all righteous,* Soph.　Adv. -κως, *most justly,* Aesch.; but simply = πάντως, Soph.

Πανδιονίδης, ου, ὁ, *son of Pandion,* fem. Πανδιονίς, ίδος, *daughter of Pandion,* i.e. the swallow, Hes.　II. Πανδιονίς, ή, one of the Attic tribes, Aeschin.

πανδοκεῖον, τό, *a house for the reception of strangers, an inn, hotel,* Ar., Dem., etc.　From

πανδοκεύς, έως, ὁ, (πάνδοκος) *one who receives all comers, an innkeeper, host,* Plat., etc.: metaph., πάσης κακίας π. Id.

πανδοκεύτρια, ή, *a hostess,* Ar.; metaph. φάλαινα π. *a sea-monster ready to take all in,* Id.

πανδοκεύω, f. σω, (πάνδοκος) *to receive and entertain as a host,* Hdt., Plat.: absol. *to keep an inn,* Theophr. πανδοκέω, = foreg.:—metaph. *to take upon oneself, assume,* Aesch.

πάν-δοκος, ον, (δέχομαι) *all-receiving, common to all,* Pind., Aesch.: c. gen., δόμοι π. ξένων Aesch.

παν-δοξία, ή, (δόξα) *absolute fame, perfect glory,* Pind.

πάν-δυρτος, ον, poët. for παν-όδυρτος, *all-lamentable, all-plaintive,* Trag.

παν-δῠσία, ή, (δύω) *the total setting of a star,* Anth.

παν-δώρα, ή, (δῶρον) *giver of all,* Ar.　　II. pass. as fem. prop. n., *Pandora,* i.e. *the All-endowed,* a beautiful female, made by Hephaestus, *who received presents from all the gods,* in order to win the heart of Epimetheus, Hes.

πάν-δωρος, ον, (δῶρον) *giver of all,* Ep. Hom.

πᾰν-εθνεί, Adv. (ἔθνος) *with the whole nation,* Strab.

παν-είκελος, ον, *like in all points,* Anth.

Πανεῖον, τό, (Πάν) *a temple of Pan,* Strabo.

πάν-ελεύθερος, ον, *entirely free,* Anth.

Πάν-ελληνες, οἱ, *all the Hellenes,* Il., Hes., Eur.

Πάνεμος, ὁ, Boeotian name of the month Μεταγειτνιών, Philipp. ap. Dem.

πάν-επήρᾱτος, ον, *all-lovely,* Anth.

πάν-επίσκοπος, ον, *all-surveying,* Anth.

πάν-εργέτης, ον, ὁ, (*ἔργω) *all-effecting,* Dor. gen. -εργέτα Aesch.

πάν-έρημος, ον, *all-desolate,* Luc.

πάν-έσπερος, ον, *lasting the whole evening,* Anth.

πάν-έστιος, ον, (ἑστία) *with all the household,* Plut.

πάν-ετες, Adv. (ἔτος) *all the year long,* Pind.

πάν-ευδαίμων, ον, *quite happy,* Luc.

πάν-εύτονος, ον, *much strained, very active,* Anth.

πάν-εφθος [ᾰ], ον, of metals, *quite purified,* Hes.

πᾰνηγῠρίζω, f. σω, *to celebrate* or *attend a festival,* πανηγύρις π. *to keep holy-days,* Hdt.; and

πᾰνηγῠρικός, ή, όν, *fit for a public festival,* ὁ λόγος ὁ π., or ὁ π. alone, *a panegyric, eulogy,* Isocr. Arist.　2. *ostentatious, pompous,* Plut.　From

πᾰν-ήγῠρις, Dor. παν-ᾱγ-, εως, ή, (πᾶς, ἄγυρις = ἀγορά) *a general* or *national assembly,* esp. *a festal assembly* in honour of a national god, Pind., Aesch., etc.; πανηγύρις πανηγυρίζειν, ἀνάγειν, ποιεῖσθαι *to hold such festivals, keep holy-days,* Hdt.　2. *any assembly,*

θεῶν Aesch.; φίλων Eur.:—*the assembly, people assembled,* Thuc.

πᾰνηγῠριστής, οῦ, ὁ, *one who attends a* πανήγυρις, Luc.

πᾰν-ῆμαρ, Adv. *all day, the livelong day,* Od.

πᾰνημερεύω, *to spend the whole day* in a thing, c. acc., Eur.　From

πᾰν-ημέριος, Dor. παν-ᾱμ-, α, ον, *all day long,* πανημέριοι θεὸν ἱλάσκοντο *continued to appease the god all day long,* Il.; ὅσσον τε πανημερίη νηῦς ἤνυσεν *as much as a ship sails in a whole day,* Od.:—neut. πανημέριον, as Adv. = πάνημαρ, Il.　2. *of the whole day,* Eur.

πᾰν-ήμερος, ον, = foreg., Aesch.:—neut. πανημερόν (oxyt.) as Adv., Hdt.　　II. Dor. πανάμερος = πάντως τῇδε τῇ ἡμέρᾳ, Soph.

παν-θηλής, ές, (θάλλω) *with all manner of trees,* Anth.

πάνθηρ, ηρος, ὁ, *the panther* or *leopard,* Hdt., Xen.

παν-θῠμᾰδόν, (θυμός) Adv. *in high wrath,* Od.

πάν-θῠτος, ον, (θύω) *celebrated with all kinds of sacrifices,* Soph.

Πᾰνῐκός, ή, όν, (Πάν) *of* or *for Pan,* Luc.　　II. of fears, *panic,* such fears being attributed to Pan, Plut.

πάν-ίμερος [ῐ], ον, *all-lovely,* Anth.　　II. *burning with desire,* Soph.

πᾰνίσδομαι, Dor. for πηνίζομαι.

Πᾰν-ίωνες, οἱ, *the whole body of Ionians:*—Πᾰνιώνιον, τό, *their place of meeting* at Mycalé, and *the common temple* there built, Hdt.　2. Πᾰνιώνια (sc. ἱερά), τά, *the festival of the united Ionians,* Id.

παν-λώβητος, ον, *grievously disfigured, hideous,* Luc.

πάννῠχα, v. πάννυχος.

πᾰννῠχίζω, f. σω, (παννυχίς) *to celebrate a night-festival, keep vigil,* τῇ θεᾷ Ar.　　II. generally, *to do anything the livelong night,* φλὸξ συνεχὲς π. *it lasts all night long,* Pind.; c. acc., π. τὴν νύκτα *to spend the livelong night,* Ar.

πᾰννῠχικός, ή, όν, *fit for a night-reveller,* Anth.

πᾰν-νύχιος [ῠ], η, ον, and ος, ον, *all night long,* εὗδον παννύχιοι Il.; π. χοροί Soph.; τὸ ἐλλύχνιον καίεται παννύχιον Hdt.:—neut. as Adv., Il.

παν-νῠχίς, ίδος, ή, (νύξ) *a night-festival, vigil,* Hdt., Eur., etc.　　II. *a night-watch, vigil,* Soph.

πάν-νῠχος, ον, = παννύχιος, Od., Hdt., Att.　2. *lasting all the night,* τί πάννυχον ὕπνον ἀωτεῖς; Il.; π. σελάνα Eur.:—neut. pl. as Adv., πάννυχα *the livelong night,* Soph.

πάν-όδυρτος, ον, *most lamentable,* Anth.

πάν-οιζυς, υ, gen. υος, *all-unhappy,* Aesch.

πανοικησία, dat., = πανοικία, Thuc.

πάν-οικία, Ion. -ίη, Adv. (nom. πανοικία is not used) *with all the house, household and all,* Hdt.

πάν-οίκιος, ον, (οἶκος) *with all one's house,* Strab.

παν-οίμοι, Exclam. *oh utter woe!* Aesch.

πάν-όλβιος, ον, *truly happy,* h. Hom., Theogn.

πᾰν-ομῑλεί, (ὅμιλος) Adv. *in whole troops,* Aesch.

πάν-ομμᾰτος, ον, (ὄμμα) *all-eyed,* Anth.

πάν-ομοιος, Ep. -ομοῖιος, ον, *just like,* Anth.

πάν-ομφαῖος, ὁ, (ὀμφή) *sender of all ominous voices, author of all divination,* Il., Anth.

πάν-οπλία, Ion. -ίη, ή, *the full armour of an* ὁπλίτης, i.e. shield, helmet, breastplate, greaves, sword, and lance, *a full suit of armour, panoply,* Thuc., etc.; πανοπλίᾳ, Ion. -ίῃ, *in full armour, cap-à-pie,* Hdt.;

so, πανοπλίαν ἔχων στῆναι Ar. ; τὴν π. λαβεῖν Id. :— metaph., ἡ π. τοῦ θεοῦ N. T.

πᾰν-οπλίτης [ῑ], ου, ὁ, *a man in full armour*, Tyrtae.

πάν-οπλος [ᾰ], ον, (ὅπλον) *in full armour*, *full-armed*, Aesch., Eur.; πάνοπλα ἀμφιβλήματα *suits of full armour*, Eur.

πᾰν-όπτης, ου, ὁ, (ὄψομαι) *the all-seeing*, of the sun, Aesch.; of the herdsman Argus, Eur.

πάν-ορμος, ον, *always fit for landing in*, Od. II. Πάνορμος, ὁ, *the ancient name of Palermo*, Thuc.; Πανορμῖτις, ιδος, ἡ, *its territory*, Polyb.

πᾱνός, ὁ, *a torch*, = φανός, Aesch.

πᾰνουργέω, f. ήσω: pf. πεπανούργηκα :—*to play the knave or villain*, Eur., Ar.; ἃ πανουργεῖς *the rogueries you are playing*, Ar.; ὅσια πανουργήσασα, an oxymoron, *having dared a righteous crime*, Soph.

πᾰνούργημα, ατος, τό, *a knavish trick, villany*, Soph.

πᾰνουργία, ἡ, *knavery, roguery, villany*, Lat. *malitia*, Aesch., Soph.: in pl. *knaveries, villanies*, Soph., etc.

πᾰνουργ-ιππαρχίδας, ου, ὁ, *knave-Hipparchides*, Ar.

πᾰν-οῦργος, ον, (*ἔργω) *ready to do anything wicked, knavish, villanous*, Aesch., etc. :—as Subst. *a knave, rogue, villain*, Eur., Ar.; τὰ π. *the knavish sort*, Soph.; but also = πανουργία, Id. :— Comp. -ότερος, Sup. -ότατος, Ar. II. Adv. -γως, Sup. -ότατα, Id. II. in a less positively bad sense, *cunning, crafty, clever, smart*, Plat., etc.

πᾰν-όψιος, ον, (ὄψις) *all-seen, in the sight of all*, Il.

πᾰν-σᾰγία, ἡ, (σάγη) = πανοπλία, dat. πανσαγίᾳ *in full armour*, Soph.

πᾰν-σέληνος or πᾰσ-σέληνος, ον, (σελήνη) *of the moon*, *at the full*, ἡ πανσέλ. ἐτύγχανε οὖσα π. Thuc.; π. κύκλος *the moon's full orb*, Eur. 2. ἡ πανσέληνος (sc. ὥρα) *the time of full moon*, Hdt., Ar.; τὰν αὔριον π. *at the next full moon*, Soph.; *without the Art.*, Aesch.

πάν-σεμνος, ον, *all-majestic*, Luc.

πάν-σκοπος, ον, *all-seeing*, Anth.

πάν-σοφος and πᾱσ-σοφος, ον, *all-wise*, Eur., Plat.

πᾰν-σπερμία, ἡ, *a mixture of all seeds*, Luc. From

πάν-σπερμος, ον, (σπέρμα) *composed of all sorts of seeds*, Anth.

πᾰν-στρατιά, Ion. -ιή, ἡ, *a levy of the whole army*, πανστρατιᾶς γενομένης Thuc.: elsewhere only in dat. πανστρατιᾷ *as Adv.*, *with the whole army*, Hdt., Thuc.; cf. πανσυδίῃ.

πᾰν-συδί or πᾰσ-συδί, Adv. (σεύομαι) *with all one's force*; π. διεφθάρθαι *utterly*, Thuc.

πᾰν-συδίῃ, Adv. (σεύομαι) *with all speed*, = πάσῃ τῇ σπουδῇ, Il.; Att. πανσυδίᾳ or πασσυδίᾳ, Eur.—No nom. πανσυδία occurs, cf. πανστρατιά.

πάν-συρτος, ον, (σύρω) *swept all together*, αἰὼν πάνσυρτος ἀχέων *a life of accumulated woes*, Soph.

παντᾷ, Dor. for πάντῃ.

πᾰν-τάλᾱς, αινα, αν, *all-wretched*, Aesch., Eur.

παντά-πᾱσι or (before a vowel) -ιν, Adv. *all in all, altogether, wholly, absolutely*, Hdt., Att.; οὐ π. οὕτως ἀλόγως *not so absolutely without reason*, Thuc. :—with the Art., τὸ π. Id. 2. in replying, it affirms strongly, *by all means, quite so, undoubtedly*, Plat., Xen.

παντ-αρκής, ές, (ἀρκέω) *all-powerful*, Aesch.

παντ-άρχας, ου, ὁ, Dor. for -άρχης, *lord of all*, Ar.

πάντ-αρχος, ον, *all-ruling*, Soph.

πανταχῇ or -χῆ, (πᾶς) Adv. of Place, *everywhere*, Lat. *ubique, ubivis*, Thuc., Plat., etc. :—c. gen. loci, *in every part of*, π. τοῦ Ἑλλησπόντου Hdt.; π. ἄστεως Eur. 2. *on every side, in every direction, every way*, Hdt., Att. II. *by all means, absolutely*, Hdt.; οὐ κατ᾽ ἓν μόνον, ἀλλὰ π. *in all respects*, Id.; π. δρῶντες, i. e. *whatever we do*, Soph.

πανταχόθεν, (πᾶς) Adv. *from all places, from all quarters, on every side*, Lat. *undique*, Hdt., Att. II. *from every side*, i. e. *in every way*, Thuc., Xen.

πανταχόθι, (πᾶς) Adv. = πανταχοῦ, c. gen., Luc.

πανταχοῖ, (πᾶς) Adv. *in every direction, any whither, every way*, Lat. *quovis, quoquoversus*, Ar., Dem.

πανταχόσε, (πᾶς) Adv., = foreg., Thuc., Plat.

πανταχοῦ, (πᾶς) Adv. *everywhere*, Lat. *ubique, ubivis*, Hdt., Att. :—c. gen., π. τῆς γῆς Plat. II. *altogether, always, absolutely*, Id.

πανταχῶς, (πᾶς) Adv. *in all ways, altogether*, Lat. *omnino*, Plat.

παντέλεια, ἡ, *consummation*, Polyb. From

πᾰν-τελής, ές, (τέλος) *all-complete, absolute, complete, entire*, Aesch., etc.; π. δάμαρ *uxor legitima*, the mistress of the house, Soph.; π. ἐσχάραι *the whole number* of sacrificial hearths, their *complete tale*, Id. II. act. *all-accomplishing, all-achieving*, Aesch. III. Adv. παντελῶς, Ion. -έως, *altogether, utterly, absolutely, entirely, completely*, Hdt., Att.; παντελέως εἶχε *it was quite finished*, Hdt.; π. θανεῖν *to die outright*, Soph. 2. in answers, *most certainly*, παντελῶς γε, π. μὲν οὖν Id., Plat. 3. later, εἰς τὸ παντελές = παντελῶς, N. T.

πᾰν-τευχία, ἡ, (τεῦχος) = πανοπλία, Eur.; ὅπλων πολέμιος παντευχία *enemies in full array*, Id.; ξὺν παντευχίᾳ *in full armour*, Aesch.

πάν-τεχνος, ον, (τέχνη) *assistant of all arts*, Aesch.

πάντη, Dor. πάντᾱ, (πᾶς) Adv. *every way, on every side*, Hom., Hdt., Ar. II. *in every way, by all means, altogether, entirely*, Plat., etc.

πάν-τῑμος, ον, (τιμή) *all-honourable*, Soph.

πᾰν-τλήμων, Dor. -τλάμων, ον, gen. ονος, = παντάλας, Soph., Eur.

παντο-βίης, ου, ὁ, (βιάω) *all-overpowering*, Anth.

παντο-γήρως, ων, gen. ω, (γῆρας) *making all old*, i. e. *subduing all*, Soph.

παντοδᾰπός, ή, όν, (πᾶς, with term. -δᾰπός, cf. ποδαπός) *of every kind, of all sorts, manifold*, h. Hom., Aesch., etc. :—in pl. πολλοὶ καὶ π. Hdt. :—Adv. -πῶς, *in all kinds of ways*, Poëta ap. Arist. 2. παντοδαπὸς γίγνεται, = παντοῖος γίγνεται, *assumes every shape*, Ar.

πάντοθε, = sq., h. Hom., Theocr.

πάντοθεν, Adv. (πᾶς) *from all quarters, from every side*, Lat. *undique*, Il., Hdt., Trag.

πάντοθι, (πᾶς) Adv. *everywhere*, Anth.

παντοῖος, α, ον, (πᾶς) *of all sorts or kinds, manifold*, Hom., Hdt., Soph. 2. παντοῖος γίγνεται *he takes all shapes*, i. e. *tries every shift, turns every stone*, Hdt. II. Adv. -ως, *in all kinds of ways*, Id., Plat.

παντοκράτωρ, ορος, ὁ, (κρατέω) *almighty*, N. T., Anth.

παντ-ολῐγο-χρόνιος, ον, *utterly shortlived*, Anth.

πάν-τολμος, ον, *all-daring, shameless*, Aesch., Eur.

παντό-μιμος, ὁ, *a pantomimic actor*, Luc.

παντομῑσής, ές, (μῖσος) all-hateful, Aesch.

παντο-ποιός, όν, ready for all, reckless, Theophr.

παντο-πόρος, ον, all-inventive, opp. to ἄπορος, Soph.

παντ-όπτης, ου, Dor. **-τας**, α, ό, = πανόπτης, Soph., Ar.

παντο-πώλιον, τό, a place where all things are for sale, a general market, bazaar, Plat.

πάντοσε, Adv. every way, in all directions, Il., Xen.

παντό-σεμνος, ον, = πάνσεμνος, Aesch.

πάντοτε, (πᾶς) Adv. at all times, always, N. T.

παντό-τολμος, ον, = πάντολμος, Aesch.

παντ-ουργός, όν, = παν-οῦργος, Soph.

παντο-φάγος, ον, (φαγεῖν) all-devouring, Anth.

παντό-φυρτος, ον, (φύρω) mixed all together, Aesch.

πάν-τρομος, ον, (τρέμω) all-trembling, Aesch.

πάν-τροπος, ον, (τρέπω) all-routed, tumultuous, Aesch.

πάν-τροφος, ον, (τρέφω) all-nourishing, Anth.; π. πελειάς a dove that rears all her nestlings, Aesch.

πάντως, Adv. (πᾶς) altogether; in Hom. always πάντως οὐ, in nowise, by no means, not at all, Lat. omnino non : ἔδεε πάντως it was altogether necessary, Hdt. ; εἰ π. ἐλεύσεσθε if ye positively will go, Id. **II.** in affirmations, at all events, at any rate, Id., Att. ; ἄλλως τε πάντως καί above all . . , Aesch. **2.** with the imperat., in command or entreaty, π. παρατίθετε only put on table, Plat. **3.** in answers, yes by all means, Id. ; so, πάντως γάρ . . Ar. ; π. δήπου Plat. **πάνυ** [ᾰ], Adv. (πᾶς) altogether, entirely, Aesch., etc. ; π. μανθάνω perfectly, Ar. :—with Adjs. very, exceedingly, π. πολλοί; ὀλίγοι, π. μικρός, μέγας Aesch., etc. :— with Advs., π. σφόδρα Ar. ; μόλις or μόγις π. Plat. ; with Nouns in Adv. sense, π. σπουδῇ in very great haste, Dem. ; π. ἐξ εἰκότος λόγου Plat. :—with a Part., π. ἀδικῶν if ever so criminal, Thuc. **2.** strengthd., καί πάνυ Id., Xen. **3.** οὐ πάνυ, like οὐ πάντως, Lat. omnino non, not at all, Soph., etc. **4.** in answers, yes by all means, no doubt, certainly, Ar. ; πάνυ γε, πάνυ μὲν οὖν Id., Plat. :—πάνυ καλῶς, Lat. benigne, no I thank you, Ar. **II.** ὁ πάνυ (where κλεινός may be supplied), the excellent, the famous, οἱ πάνυ τῶν στρατιωτῶν Thuc.; ὁ πάνυ Περικλῆς Xen.

πᾰν-υπείροχος, ον, eminent above all, Anth.

πᾰν-ὑπέρτατος, η, ον, highest of all, Od.

πᾰν-υστάτιος, α, ον, later for sq., Anth.

πᾰν-ύστᾰτος, η, ον, last of all, Hom., Soph., Eur. :— neut. πανύστατον, Adv., for the very last time, Soph., Eur. ; so πανύστατα Eur.

πᾰνωλεθρία, ή, utter destruction, utter ruin : in dat., πανωλεθρίῃ ὀλλυσθαι Il. ; πανωλεθρία ἀπώλετο Thuc.

πᾰν-ώλεθρος, ον, (ὄλεθρος) utterly ruined, utterly destroyed, Hdt. ; πανωλέθρους ὀλέσθαι Soph. ; π. πίπτειν Aesch., etc. **2.** in moral sense, utterly abandoned, Lat. perditissimus, Soph., Eur. **II.** act. all-destructive, all-ruinous, Hdt., Aesch.

πᾰν-ώλης, ες, (ὄλλυμι) = πανώλεθρος, Aesch. **2.** in moral sense, like πανώλεθρος I. 2, Soph., Eur. **II.** act. all-destructive, Soph.

πᾰν-ωπήεις, εσσα, εν, = πανόψιος, visible to all, Anth.

πάξαις, Dor. for πήξας, aor. 1 part. of πήγνυμι :—πάξαιτο, Dor. 3 sing. aor. 1 med.

πάξω, Dor. for πήξω, f. of πήγνυμι.

***ΠΑ'ΟΜΑΙ**, f. πάσομαι [ᾱ] : aor. 1 ἐπᾰσάμην : Dep. :— to get, acquire, Lat. potior, πᾱσάμενος ἐπίτασσε when

you've got slaves order them, Theocr. : chiefly in pf. πέπᾱμαι, = κέκτημαι, to possess, Pind., Eur., Ar., 3 pl. πέπανται Xen. ; inf. πεπᾶσθαι Solon, Eur. ; part. πεπᾱμένος Aesch., Xen. ; plqpf. ἐπεπάμην Xen. (The forms ἐπᾱσάμην, πέπᾱμαι must not be confounded with ἐπᾱσάμην, πέπασμαι from πατέομαι, to eat.)

πᾰπαῖ, Exclam. of suffering, Lat. vae, oh! Trag. ; φεῦ παπαῖ, παπαῖ μάλ' αὖθις Soph. ; also, παππαπαππαπαῖ Id. ; παπαῖ, ἀπαππαπαῖ, παπαπαππαπαππαπαππαπαῖ Id. **II.** of surprise, like Lat. papae, vah, atat, Hdt.

πᾰπαιάξ, Comic exaggeration of παπαῖ, ἀππαπαῖ παπαιάξ Ar. **II.** as exclam. of surprise, Eur.

πά-ποκα, Dor. for πῇ ποτε, Theocr.

παππάζω, only in pres., to call any one papa, Il.

παππα-παππα-παῖ, v. παπαῖ.

πάππας, ου, ό, papa, a child's word for πατήρ, father, (as μάμμα for μήτηρ) in voc., πάππᾰ φίλε Od. ; in acc., πάππαν καλεῖν, like παππάζειν, Ar.

παππίας, ου, ό, Dim. of πάππας, dear little papa, Ar.

παππίδιον [πῐ], τό, = foreg., Ar.

παππίζω, = παππάζω, to wheedle one's father, Ar.

πάππος, ό, (akin to πάππας) a grandfather, Hdt., Ar. : —in pl. one's grand-parents, ancestors, Arist. **II.** a little bird, Ar.

παππῷος, α, ον, of or from one's grand-fathers, Ar.

πάππαξ, ακος, ό, a Thracian lake-fish, Hdt.

ΠΑΠΤΑΙΝΩ, f. ᾰνῶ : aor. 1 ἐπάπτηνα, Ep. πάπτηνα :— to look earnestly, gaze, Hom. ; mostly with notion of alarm or caution, to look or peer around, Il. **II.** c. acc. to look round for, look after, Il., Pind. ; παπτήναις (Dor. aor. 1 part.) having set eyes on a thing, Pind. : to glare at, τινά Soph.

πάπῡρος, ό and ή, the papyrus, an Egyptian rush with triangular stalks: paper was made by peeling off its outer coat (βύβλος), and gluing the slips together. **2.** anything made of it, linen, cord, etc., Anth.

ΠΑ'ΡΑ' [ρᾱ], Ep. and Lyr. **παραί** and shortened **παρ**, Prep. with gen., dat., and acc. : Radical sense beside : **A. WITH GENIT.** from the side of, from beside, from, φάσγανον ὀξὺ ἐρυσσάμενος παρὰ μηροῦ Il. **II.** commonly of Persons, ἦλθε πὰρ Διός Ib. ; ἀγγελίη ἥκει παρὰ βασιλῆος Hdt. ; ὁ παρά τινος ἥκων his messenger, Xen. **2.** issuing from a person, γίγνεσθαι παρά τινος to be born from him, Plat.; when it follows a Noun, a particip. may be supplied, ἡ παρὰ τῶν ἀνθρώπων δόξα glory from (given by) men, Id. ; τὸ παρ' ἐμοῦ ἀδίκημα done by me, Xen. ; παρ' ἑαυτοῦ διδόναι to give from oneself, i. e. from one's own means, Hdt. **3.** with Verbs of receiving and obtaining, τυχεῖν τινος παρά τινος Od. ; εὑρέσθαι τι παρά τινος Isocr. ; δέχεσθαι, λαμβάνειν τι παρά τινος Thuc. ; μανθάνειν, ἀκούειν παρά τινος Hdt. **4.** with Pass. Verbs, on the part of (not, like ὑπό, of the direct agent), παρὰ θεῶν δίδοταί τι Plat. ; τὰ παρά τινος λεγόμενα or συμβουλευόμενα Xen. ; φάρμακον πιεῖν παρὰ τοῦ ἰατροῦ by his prescription, Plat. **III.** in poetic passages, for παρά c. dat., near, πὰρ Σαλαμῖνος Pind. ; πὰρ Κυανέαν σπιλάδων Soph. ; παρ' Ἰσμηνοῦ ῥείθρων Id.

B. WITH DAT. beside, alongside of, by, with Verbs implying rest, used to answer the question where? **I.** of Places, ἧσθαι πὰρ πυρί Od. ; ἑστάναι παρ' ὄχεσφιν Il. ; πὰρ ποσσί at one's feet, Ib. ; παρὰ ῥηγμῖνι θαλάσ-

σης Ib.　　II. of persons, κεῖτο παρὰ μνηστῇ ἀλόχῳ Ib.; στῆναι παρά τινι to stand *by* him, Ib.　2. like Lat. *apud*, French *chez*, at one's *house*, μένειν παρά τινι Ib.; οἱ παρ' ἡμῖν ἄνθρωποι the people *here*, Plat.; ἡ παρ' ἡμῖν πολιτεία Dem. :—like Lat. *apud* for *penes*, in one's *own hands*, ἔχειν παρ' ἑωυτῷ Hdt.　3. Lat. *coram*, *before*, in the *presence of*, ἥειδε παρὰ μνηστῆρσιν Od. : *before* a judge, Hdt., Att.; παρ' ἐμοί, Lat. *me judice*, Hdt.; εὐδοκιμεῖν, μέγα δύνασθαι, τιμᾶσθαι παρά τινι *with* one, Plat.
C. WITH ACCUS. *to the side* of an object, or *motion alongside* of it :　I. of Place,　1. with Verbs of coming and going, βῆ παρὰ θῖνα Il.; παρ' Ἥφαιστον to his *chamber*, Ib.; εἰσιέναι παρά τινα to go *into* his *house*, Thuc., Plat.　2. with Verbs of rest, *beside*, *near*, *by*, κεῖται ποταμοῖο παρ' ὄχθας lies stretched *beside* the river banks, Il.; παρ' ἔμ' ἵστασο come and stand *by* me, Ib.　3. with Verbs of striking, wounding, βάλε στῆθος παρὰ μαζόν Il.; αἰχμὴ δ' ἐξεσύθη παρὰ ἀνθερεῶνα Ib.　4. with Verbs of *passing by*, leaving on one side, Hom.; παρὰ τὴν Βαβυλῶνα παριέναι Xen.　b. *by* or *beside* the mark, πὰρ δύναμιν *beyond* one's *strength*, Il.　c. *contrary to*, *against*, παρὰ μοῖραν *contrary* to destiny, Hom.; παρ' αἶσαν, παρὰ τὰς σπονδάς Thuc.; παρὰ δόξαν *contrary to* opinion, Id.; παρ' ἐλπίδας Soph.　5. *beside*, *except*, οὐκ ἔστι παρὰ ταῦτ' ἄλλα *beside* this there is nothing else, Ar.; παρὰ ἓν πάλαισμα ἔδραμε νικᾶν 'Ολυμπιάδα he won the Olympic prize *save in* one conflict, he was *within* one of winning it, Hdt.; so, παρὰ ὀλίγον *only just*, Eur.; παρ' ἐλάχιστον ἦλθε ἀφελέσθαι was *within* an ace *of* taking away, Thuc.; παρὰ τοσοῦτον ἦλθε κινδύνου came *within* such a degree of peril, i. e. was in such imminent peril, Id.; —opp. to these phrases is παρὰ πολύ *by far*, δεινότατον παρὰ πολύ Ar.; παρὰ πολὺ νικᾶν Thuc. :—but　6. παρὰ ὀλίγον ποιεῖσθαι, ἡγεῖσθαι to hold *of* small account, Xen.; παρ' οὐδέν ἐστι are *as nothing*, Soph.　7. with a sense of alternation, παρ' ἡμέραν or παρ' ἦμαρ, Dor. παρ' ἆμαρ, *day by day*, Pind., Soph.; πληγὴ παρὰ πληγήν *blow for blow*, Ar.　8. with a sense of Comparison, παρὰ τὰ ἄλλα ζῷα ὥσπερ θεοὶ οἱ ἄνθρωποι βιοτεύουσι men *beyond* all other animals live like gods, Xen.; χειμὼν μείζω παρὰ τὴν καθεστηκυῖαν ὥραν Thuc.　9. metaph. to denote dependence, *on account of*, *because of*, *by means of*, παρὰ τὴν ἑαυτοῦ ἀμέλειαν Id.; παρὰ τοῦτο γέγονε Dem.　II. of Time, along the *whole course of*, *during*, παρὰ τὴν ζόην Hdt.; παρὰ πάντα τὸν χρόνον Dem.; παρὰ ποτὸν while they were *at wine*, Aeschin.　2. *at* the *moment of*, παρ' αὐτὰ τἀδικήματα, *flagrante delicto*, Dem.
D. POSITION :—παρά may follow its Subst. in all cases, but then becomes by anastrophé πάρα.
E. πάρα (with anastrophé) also stands for πάρεστι and πάρεισι.
F. παρά absol., as ADV., *near*, *together*, *at once*, in Hom.
G. IN COMPOS.,　I. *alongside of*, *beside*, παραλίσκοι, παραπλέω.　II. *to the side of*, *to*, παραδίδωμι, παρέχω.　III. *to one side of*, *by*, *past*, παρέρχομαι, παρατρέχω.　IV. metaph.:　1. *aside*, i.e. *amiss*, *wrong*, παραβαίνω, παρακούω.　2. of com-

parison, παραβάλλω, παρατίθημι.　3. of change, παραλλάσσω, παράφημι.
παρα-βαίνω, f. -βήσομαι : pf. -βέβηκα, -βέβαα, part. -βεβώς, Ep. -βεβαώς : aor. 2 παρέβην :—Pass., aor. 1 pass. παρεβάθην [ἄ] : pf. παραβέβασμαι :—*to go by the side of*, c. dat., 'Έκτορι παρβεβαώς *standing beside* Hector in the chariot, Il.; παρβεβαῶτε ἀλλήλοιιν Ib.; so impf. παρέβασκε is used as = ἦν παραβάτης, Ib.　II. *to pass beside* or *beyond*, *to overstep*, *transgress*, τὰ νόμιμα Hdt.; δίκην Aesch.; τὰς σπονδάς Ar., Thuc. :—absol., παραβάντες the *transgressors*, Aesch. :—Pass. *to be transgressed*, σπονδὰς ἅς γε ὁ θεὸς νομίζει παραβεβάσθαι Thuc.; νόμῳ παραβαθέντι Id.; παραβαινομένων, absol., *though offences are committed*, Id.　2. *to pass over*, *omit*, Soph., Dem. : οὔ με παρέβα φάσμα *it escaped* me not, Eur.　III. *to come forward*, π. πρὸς τὸ θέατρον *to step forward* to address the spectators, Ar.; cf. παράβασις III.
παρα-βάκτρος, ον, (βάκτρον) *like a staff*, π. θεραπεύμασι *with service as of a staff*, Eur.
παρά-βακχος, ον, *like a Bacchanal*, *theatrical*, Plut.
παρα-βάλλω, f. -βαλῶ : aor. 2 παρέβαλον : pf. παραβέβληκα :—Pass., pf. -βέβλημαι :—*to throw beside* or *by*, *throw* to one, as *fodder* for horses, Hom. : *to hold out as a bait*, Xen.　2. *to cast* in one's *teeth*, Lat. *objicere*, τί τινι Aeschin.　II. *to expose*, παρέβαλεν ἐμὲ *exposed* me to them, Ar. :—Med. *to expose oneself* or *what is one's own to danger*, αἰὲν ἐμὴν ψυχὴν παραβαλλόμενος πολεμίζειν *risking* it in war, Il.; so, παραβάλλεσθαι τὰ τέκνα Hdt. :—Pass., κύβοισι παραβεβλημένος *given up* to dice, Ar.　2. Med. also *to set what one values upon a chance*, *to hazard* it as at play, πλείω παραβαλλόμενοι having greater *interests at stake*, Thuc.; so in pf. pass., Λακεδαιμονίοις πλεῖστον δὴ παραβεβλημένοι having *risked* far the most upon them, Id. ;—also, τὸν κίνδυνον τῶν σωμάτων παραβαλλομένους Id.　III. *to lay beside*, *to compare* one with another, τί τινι Hdt.; τι πρός τι Xen.; τι παρά τι Plat. :—so in Med., absol., παραβάλλεσθαι *vying with* one another, Eur. ;—and in Pass., ἀπάτα δ' ἀπάταις παραβαλλομένα one piece of treachery *set against* others, Soph.　2. Med. *to bring alongside*, τὴν ἄκατον παραβάλλου *bring your boat alongside*, Ar.; and absol. παραβαλοῦ Id.　IV. *to throw*, *turn*, *bend sideways*, παραβάλλειν τὸν ὀφθαλμόν or τὼ ὀφθαλμώ *to cast the eyes askance*, like a timid animal, Id., Plat.; so, π. τὸ ἕτερον οὖς πλάγιον *to turn* one's ears *to listen*, Xen.; π. τοὺς γομφίους *to lay* to one's *grinders*, Ar.　V. *to deposit with* one, *entrust* to him, Lat. *committere*, τί τινι Hdt.　VI. in Med. *to deceive*, *betray*, Id., Eur., etc.
B. intr. *to come near*, *approach*, Plat., Arist.; π. ἀλλήλοις *to meet* one another, Plat.　II. *to go by sea*, *to cross over*, Lat. *trajicere*, παρέβαλε νηυσί Hdt.; so of the ships, ναῦς Πελοποννησίων παρέβαλον εἰς 'Ιωνίαν Thuc.　III. *to turn aside*, *pass over*, Arist.
παρα-βάπτω, f. ψω, *to dye at the same time*, Plut.
παραβασία, ἡ, Ep. παραιβασίη, = παράβασις II, Hes.; poët. παρβασία Aesch.
παρά-βασις, Ep. παραί-β-, ἡ, *a going aside*, *deviation*, Arist.　II. *an overstepping*, τῶν δικαίων

Plut. :—absol. *a transgression*, Id.   **III.** *the parabasis*, a part of the old Comedy, *in which the Chorus came forward* and addressed the audience in the Poet's name.

παραβάτης, poët. **παραιβάτης** and **παρβάτης**, ου, ὁ, (παραβαίνω 1) *one who stands beside*: properly *the warrior who stood beside the charioteer*, Il., Eur., Xen.   **2.** in pl. *light troops* (*velites*) *who ran beside the horsemen*, Plut.   **II.** (παραβαίνω 11. 1) *a transgressor*, Aesch.

παραβάτις, poët. **παραιβάτις**, ιδος, fem. of παραβάτης: *a woman who follows the reapers*, Theocr.

παρα-βᾰτός, poët. **παρ-βᾰτός**, όν, *to be overcome* or *overreached*, Aesch., Soph.

παραβεβάσθαι, pf. pass. inf. of παραβαίνω.

παρα-βιάζομαι, f. άσομαι. Dep. *to use violence to one, to constrain, compel* him, N. T.

παρα-βλαστάνω, f. -βλαστήσω, aor. 2 -έβλαστον, *to grow up beside* or *by*, Plat.

παρα-βλέπω, f. ψω, *to look aside, take a side look*, Ar. ; π. θατέρῳ (sc. ὀφθαλμῷ) *to look suspiciously* with one eye, Id.   **2.** *to see wrong*, Luc.

παραβλήδην, Adv. (παραβάλλω) *thrown in by the way*, παραβλήδην ἀγορεύων *speaking with a side-meaning*, i. e. *maliciously, deceitfully*, Il.; cf. παράβολος 1.

παράβλημα, ατος, τό, (παραβάλλω) *that which is thrown beside* or *before, a curtain* or *screen used to cover* the sides of ships, Xen.

παραβλητέος, α, ον, verb. Adj. of παραβάλλω, *to be compared*, τινί to one, Plut.

παραβλητός, ή, όν, (παραβάλλω) *comparable*, Plut.

παρα-βλώσκω, Ep. pf. παρ-μέμβλωκα, *to go beside*, for the purpose of protecting, c. dat., Il.

παραβλώψ, ῶπος, ὁ, ἡ, (παραβλέπω) *looking askance, squinting*, Il.

παραβοήθεια, ἡ, *help, aid, succour*, Plat. From

παρα-βοηθέω, f. ήσω, *to come up to help*, τινί Thuc. : —absol. *to come to the rescue*, Ar., Thuc.

παραβολεύομαι, (παράβολος) Dep. *to run hazard*, N.T.

παραβολή, ἡ, (παραβάλλω) *juxta-position, comparison*, Plat.   **2.** *a comparison, illustration, analogy*, Arist.   **3.** *a parable*, i. e. *a fictitious narrative by which some religious* or *moral lesson is conveyed*, N. T.   **4.** *a by-word, proverb*, Ib.

παράβολος, poët. **παραιβ-**, ον, (παραβάλλω) :   **I.** *thrown in by the way, deceitful*, παραίβολα = παραβλήδην, h. Hom.   **II.** *exposing oneself*: hence, **1.** of persons, *venturesome, reckless*, Ar.   **2.** of things and actions, *hazardous, perilous*, Hdt.

παράβυστος, ον, *stuffed in*: *pushed aside* or *into a corner*, ἐν παραβύστῳ in a corner, Dem. From

παρα-βύω, f. -βύσω [ῠ], *to stuff in, insert*, Luc.

παρ-αγγελία, ἡ, *a command* or *order* issued to soldiers, *a charge*, Xen., N. T.   **II.** *the summoning one's partisans* to support one in a law-suit, *exertion of influence*, Dem.   **2.** *canvassing for public office*, Lat. *ambitus*, Plut.   **III.** *a set of rules*, Arist.

παρ-αγγέλλω, f. ελῶ: aor. 1 -ήγγειλα: pf. -ήγγελκα: —*to transmit as a message*, as by telegraph, παραγγείλασα σέλας Aesch. ; μνήμην παραγγέλλοντες ὧν ἐκύρσατε Eur. ; π. τὸ σύνθημα *to pass on the watchword*, Xen.   **II.** generally, *to give the word, give orders*,

of the general, Hdt., Aesch., etc. ; π. τινὶ ποιεῖν τι Hdt., Xen., etc. :—Pass., τὰ παραγγελλόμενα military *orders*, Thuc. ; so, τὰ παρηγγελμένα Xen.   **2.** *to order, recommend, exhort*, π. τινὶ ποιεῖν τι Soph., etc.; τί τινι Eur. ; ὅπως ἂν . . , *to give orders* to the end that . . , Plat. :—c. acc. rei only, *to order*, π. παρασκευὴν σίτου *to order* corn *to be prepared*, Lat. *imperare frumentum*, Hdt. ; π. σιτία Thuc. ; στρατείαν Aeschin.   **III.** *to encourage, cheer on*, ἵππους Theogn.; π. εἰς ὅπλα *to call* to arms, Xen.   **IV.** *to summon to one's help, summon one's partisans, form a cabal*, Dem.   **2.** π. τὴν ἀρχὴν *to canvass for* office, Lat. *magistratum ambire*, Plut. ; π. εἰς ὑπατείαν *to be candidate* for the consulship, Id.   Hence

παρ-άγγελμα, ατος, τό, *a message transmitted* by beacons, Aesch.   **II.** *an order, command*, ἀπὸ παραγγέλματος *by word of command*, Thuc.   **III.** *an instruction, precept*, Xen. ; and

παρ-άγγελσις, ἡ, in war, *a giving the word of command*, Thuc. ; ἀπὸ παραγγέλσεως πορεύεσθαι Xen.

παρα-γεύω, *to give just a taste of*, τινός Plut.

παρα-γηράω, f. άσομαι, *to be superannuated*, Aeschin.

παρα-γίγνομαι, Ion. and later -γίνομαι [ῑ]; f. γενήσομαι: aor. 2 παρεγενόμην :—*to be beside, to be by* or *near, attend upon* one, c. dat., Od., Plat. : c. dat. rei, π. τῇ μάχῃ *to be present at* . . , Plat.   **2.** π. τινι *to come to one's side, come to aid, stand by, second, support*, Hes., Hdt., Att.   **3.** of things, *to be at hand, to be gained, to accrue to* one, π. τινι, Lat. *contingere alicui*, Thuc., Xen. :—impers., σῷ τρόπῳ παραγίγνεται εἰδέναι Plat.   **II.** *to come to*, τινι Theogn., Hdt. ; π. ἐς τὠυτό *to come to the same point*, Hdt. :—absol. *to arrive, come up*, Id.   **2.** *to come to maturity*, of corn, Id. ; of the horns of oxen, *to be fully grown*, Id.

παρα-γιγνώσκω, later -γῑνώσκω : f. -γνώσομαι : aor. 2 -έγνων :—*to decide wrongly, err in their judgment*, Xen.

παρ-αγκάλισμα, ατος, τό, (ἀγκαλίζομαι) *that which is taken into the arms, a beloved one*, Soph.

παρ-αγκωνίζω, f. σω, *to set the arms a-kimbo* :—Med. *to push aside with the elbows, elbow*, Luc.

παρα-γνᾰθίς, ίδος, ἡ, (γνάθος) *the cheekpiece* of a helmet or tiara, Strab.

παρα-γνούς, aor. 2 part. of παραγιγνώσκω :—**παραγνῶναι**, inf.

παρ-αγορέομαι, Dor. for παρ-ηγ-.

παράγραμμα, ατος, τό, (παραγράφω) *that which one writes beside, an additional clause*, Dem.

παραγρᾰφή, ἡ, (παραγράφω) *anything written beside*: *an exception taken* by the defendant *to the admissibility of a suit* (γραφή), *a demurrer*, Dem.

παρα-γράφω, f. ψω, *to write by the side*, Ar. :—generally, *to add a clause* to a law or contract, Plat., Dem. : esp. by fraud, ἄλλου πατρὸς ἑαυτὸν παραγράφειν *to enroll oneself with a wrong* father's name, Dem.   **II.** Med., with pf. pass., **1.** παραγράφεσθαι τὸν νόμον *to have the law written in parallel columns with a decree* charged with illegality, Id. ; Pass., οἱ παραγεγραμμένοι νόμοι Id., Aeschin.   **2.** παραγραφὴν παραγράφεσθαι *to demur to the admissibility of a suit* (v. παραγραφή), Dem.

παρα-γυμνόω, f. ώσω, *to lay bare at the side :* metaph. *to lay bare, disclose,* τὸν πάντα λόγον Hdt.

παρ-άγω, f. -άξω : aor. 2 παρήγαγον :—*to lead by* or *past* a place, c. acc. loci, Hdt. **2.** as military term, *to march* the men *up from the side, to bring them from column into line,* Xen. **II.** *to lead aside from the way, mislead,* Lat. seducere, Pind., Att. :—Pass., φόβῳ παρηγόμην Soph. ; ἀπάτῃ Thuc. **2.** generally, *to lead to* or *into* a thing, ἔς τι Eur. ; mostly of something bad, Theogn., etc. :—Pass. *to be induced,* c. inf., παρηγμένος εἰργάσθαι τι Soph. **3.** of things, *to lead aside, alter the course of* a thing, Hdt., Plat. **III.** *to bring and set beside* others, *to bring forward, introduce,* ἐς μέσον Hdt. ; π. εἰς τὸ δικαστήριον *to bring* a matter *before the court,* Dem. :—also *to bring forward* as a witness, Id. **2.** *to bring in,* with a notion of secrecy, Hdt. :—Pass. *to come in stealthily, slip in,* Soph. **B.** intr. *to pass by, pass on* one's *way,* Xen. **2.** *to pass away,* N. T. ; so in Pass., Ib., Plut. Hence

παραγωγή, ἡ, (παράγω) *a leading by* or *past, carrying across,* Xen. **2.** as military term, *a wheeling from column into line,* Id. **3.** π. τῶν κωπῶν *a sliding motion* of the oars, so that they made no dash (πίτυλος) in coming out of the water, Id. **II.** *a misleading, seduction,* Hdt. :—*a false argument, fallacy, quibble,* Dem. :—also *delay,* Plut. **2.** *a variation,* as of language, Plat. **3.** *a persuading,* Plat.

παρα-δακρύω, f. σω, *to weep beside* or *with,* τινί Luc.

παρα-δαρθάνω, f. -δαρθήσομαι : aor. 2 παρέδαρθον, Ep. παρέδραθον, inf. παραδραθεῖν :—*to sleep beside* another, c. dat., Hom.

παράδειγμα, ατος, τό, (παραδείκνυμι) *a pattern* or *model* of the thing to be executed, Lat. exemplar, an architect's *plan,* Hdt. ; a sculptor's or painter's *model,* Plat. **2.** *a precedent, example,* Thuc., Plat. ; ἐπὶ παραδείγματος by way of *example,* Aeschin. **3.** *an example,* i. e. *a lesson* or *warning,* π. ἔχειν τινός to take *a lesson* from another, Thuc. ; τὸ σὸν π. ἔχων Soph. ; ζῶντά τινα τοῖς λοιποῖς π. ποιεῖν Dem. **4.** *an argument, proof from example,* Thuc. **II.** *the model* or *copy* of an existing thing, Hdt. Hence

παραδειγμᾰτίζω, f. σω, *to make an example of* one, c. acc., Polyb., N. T.

παραδειγμᾰτ-ώδης, ες, (εἶδος) *characterised by examples,* Arist.

παραδείκνυμι and -ύω, f. -δείξω :—*to exhibit side by side :* generally, *to exhibit, bring forward,* in Med., Dem. **2.** *to represent* as so and so, π. τινὰ οὐκ ὄντα Polyb. : also in bad sense, like παραδειγματίζω, Plut. **3.** *to exhibit and hand over,* τί τινι Xen.

παρα-δειπνέομαι, (δεῖπνον) Pass. *to go without* one's *dinner,* Theophr.

παράδεισος, ὁ, *a park,* a Persian word brought in by Xen. ; used for *the garden of Eden, Paradise,* N. T.

παραδέκομαι, Ion. for παραδέχομαι.

παραδεκτέον, verb. Adj. of παραδέχομαι, *one must admit,* Plat. **II.** παραδεκτέος, α, ον, *to be admitted,* Id.

παρα-δέχομαι, Ion. -δέκομαι, f. ξομαι : pf. -δέδεγμαι : Dep. :—*to receive from* another, Il., Xen., etc. :—of children, *to receive as inheritance, succeed to,* τὴν

ἀρχήν Hdt. ; so, τὴν μάχην π. *to take up and continue* the battle, Id. **2.** c. inf., π. τινι πράττειν τι *to take upon oneself, engage* to do a thing, Lat. recipere se facturum, Dem. **3.** *to admit,* Plat.

παρα-δηλόω, f. ώσω, *to make known by a side-wind, to intimate* or *insinuate,* Dem., Plut. **2.** *to accuse underhand,* Plut.

παρα-διᾱκονέω, f. ήσω, *to live with and serve* another, c. dat., Ar.

παρα-δίδωμι, f. -δώσω, *to give* or *hand over to another, transmit,* τί τινι, Lat. tradere, Hdt. ; of *transmission* to one's *successor,* Id. ; π. τὴν ἀρετήν *to transmit, impart* as a teacher, Plat. :—c. inf., π. τινὶ τοὺς νέους διδάσκειν Id. **2.** *to give* a city or person *into another's hands,* Hdt. ; esp. as an hostage, *to deliver, surrender,* Lat. dedere, Id., Thuc., etc. ; also, with notion of treachery, *to betray,* Xen. : τύχῃ αὑτὸν π. *to commit* oneself to fortune, Thuc. **3.** *to give up* to justice, ἑωυτὸν Κροίσῳ Hdt. ; τινὰ εἰς τὸν δῆμον Xen. **4.** *to hand down* legends, opinions, and the like, Lat. memoriae prodere, Dem. **II.** *to grant, bestow,* κῦδός τινι Pind. :—in pres. and impf. *to offer, allow,* αἵρεσίν Id. : c. inf. *to allow* one to do, Hdt. ; so, c. acc. rei, ὁ θεὸς τοῦτό γε οὐ παρεδίδου Id. :—absol., τοῦ θεοῦ παραδιδόντος if he *permits,* Id.

παρα-διηγέομαι, Dep. *to relate by the way,* Arist.

παραδιδῶ, aor. 1 pass. subj. of παραδίδωμι.

παρα-δοξία, ἡ, (παράδοξος) *marvellousness,* Strab.

παρα-δοξολογέω, *to tell marvels,* Strab. :—Pass., πολλὰ παραδοξολογεῖται many *marvels are told,* Id. ; and

παραδοξολογία, ἡ, *a tale of wonder, marvel,* Aeschin.

παραδοξο-λόγος, ον, (λέγω) *telling of marvels.*

παρά-δοξος, ον, (δόξα) *contrary to opinion, incredible, paradoxical,* Plat., Xen., etc. ; ἐκ τοῦ παραδόξου *contrary to expectation,* Dem. :—Adv. -ξως, Aeschin.

παραδόσιμος, ον, *handed down, hereditary,* Polyb.

παράδοσις, ἡ, (παραδίδωμι) *a handing down, transmission,* Thuc. **2.** *the transmission* of legends and doctrines, *tradition,* Plat., etc. :—also *that which is so handed down, a tradition,* N. T. **II.** *a giving up, surrender,* Thuc.

παραδοτέος, α, ον, verb. Adj. of παραδίδωμι, *to be handed down,* Plat. : παραδοτέον *one must hand over,* τί τινι Id. **II.** *to be given up,* Id. **2.** παραδοτέα *one must give up,* Thuc.

παραδοτός, ή, όν, *capable of being taught,* Plat.

παραδοῦναι, aor. 2 inf. of παραδίδωμι :—παραδούς, part.

παραδοχή, ἡ, (παραδέχομαι) *a receiving from another :* also *that which has been received, a hereditary custom,* Eur. **II.** *acceptance, approval,* Polyb.

παραδρᾰθέειν, Ep. for -δρᾰθεῖν, aor. 2 inf. of -δαρθάνω.

παραδρᾰμεῖν, aor. 2 inf. of παρατρέχω.

παρα-δράω, Ep. 3 pl. παραδρώωσι, *to be at hand, to serve* another, c. dat., Od.

παραδρομή, ἡ, (παραδραμεῖν) *a running beside* or *over, traversing,* Plut. ; ἐν παραδρομῇ *cursorily,* Arist.

παράδρομος, ον, *that may be run through,* παράδρομα *gaps,* Xen.

παρα-δρώωσι, Ep. for -δρῶσι, 3 pl. of παραδράω.

παρα-δυναστεύω, f. σω, *to reign with* another, Thuc.

παρα-δύομαι, Med., with intr. aor. 2 act. παρέδυν, Ep.

inf. παραδύμεναι [ῠ]:—to creep past, slink or steal past, Il.   2. to creep or steal in, Plat., Dem. Hence

παράδυσις, ἡ, a creeping in beside, encroachment, Dem.

παρα-δυσείω, Desiderat. of παραδίδωμι, to be disposed to deliver up, Thuc.

παρ-αείδω, to sing beside or to one, c. dat., Od.

παρ-αείρω, contr. -αίρω, to lift up beside :—Pass., aor. 1 παρ-ηέρθην, to hang on one side, Il.

παρα-ζεύγνυμι and -ύω, f. -ζεύξω, to yoke beside, set beside, Eur. :—Pass. to be joined, coupled with another, c. dat., Dem.

παράζυξ, ῠγος, ὁ, ἡ, yoked beside: pl. παράζυγες supernumeraries, Arist.

παρα-ζώννυμι and -ύω, f. -ζώσω, to gird to the side, Plat. :—Med. to wear at the girdle, Plut.

παρα-θαλασσίδιος, ον, = sq., Thuc.

παρα-θαλάσσιος, Att. -ττιος, α, ον, beside the sea, lying on the sea-side, maritime, Hdt., Xen.

παρα-θάλπω, f. ψω, to comfort, cheer;—Pass., Eur.

παρα-θαρσύνω [ῠ], Att. -θαρρύνω, to embolden, cheer on, encourage, Thuc., Xen.

παρα-θεάομαι, Dep. to compare, Theophr.

παραθεῖεν, 3 pl. aor. 2 opt. of παρατίθημι.

παρα-θέλγω, f. ξω, to assuage, Aesch.

παρα-θερμαίνω, to heat to excess :—Pass., aor. 1 part. παραθερμανθείς, of a man become quarrelsome in his cups, Aeschin.

παρά-θερμος, ον, over-hot, Plut.

παράθεσις, εως, ἡ, juxta-position, neighbourhood, Polyb. ; ἐκ παραθέσεως on comparison, Id.

παρα-θέω, f. -θεύσομαι, to run beside or alongside, Plat., Xen.   II. to run beyond, outrun, τινά Xen. : to run past, Id.   III. to touch on cursorily, Luc.

παρα-θεωρέω, f. ήσω, to examine a thing beside another, compare, τινὰ πρός τινα Xen.   II. to look slightly at, overlook, neglect, Dem. :—Pass., N. T.

παρα-θήκη, ἡ, anything entrusted to one, a deposit, Hdt. : of persons, a hostage, Id.

παρα-θήσομαι, f. med. of παρατίθημι.

πᾰραί, poët. for παρά.

παραιβάσίη, -βᾰσις, = παρα-βασία, -βασις.

παραι-βάτης, -βάτις, poët. for παρα-βάτης, -βάτις.

παραίβολος, ον, poët. for παράβολος.

παρ-αιθύσσω, f. ξω : poët. aor. 1 -αίθυξα :—to move or stir in passing, Anth. :—metaph., θόρυβον π. to raise a shout in applause, Pind.   II. intr., of words, to fall by chance from a person, Id.

παραίνεσις, ἡ, an exhortation, address, Hdt., Att. ; c. gen. pers. advice or counsel given by a person, Hdt. ; c. gen. rei, advice given for or towards a thing, Thuc. ; ἐπὶ γνώμης παραινέσει to recommend an opinion, Id.

παρ-αινέω, 3 sing. impf. παρῄνει, Ion. παραίνεε : f. -έσω and -έσομαι : aor. 1 παρῄνησα : pf. παρῄνεκα :—Pass., pf. inf. παρῃνῆσθαι :—to exhort, recommend, advise, π. τινὶ ποιεῖν τι Hdt., Ar., etc. ; π. τί τινι Aesch. ; π. τινί to advise a person, Id.   2. to advise or recommend publicly, παρῄνει τοιάδε Thuc. ; οὐ π. to advise not to do, Id.

παραι-πεπίθησιν, Ep. for παρα-πίθῃ, 3 sing. aor. 2 subj. of παραπείθω :—παραι-πεπιθών, Ep. part.

παραίρεσις, ἡ, a taking away from beside, curtailing, τῶν προσόδων Thuc. From

παρ-αιρέω, f. ήσω : aor. 2 παρεῖλον : pf. παρῄρηκα :— to take away from beside, withdraw, remove, Eur. :— c. gen. partit. to take away part of a thing, Id., Thuc. :—Pass., παρῃρημένοι τὰ ὅπλα having their arms taken from them, Thuc.   2. π. ἀρὰν εἰς παῖδα to draw aside the curse on thy son's head, Eur.   II. Med. to draw over to one's own side, seduce, detach, Xen., Dem.   2. to take away, Xen. : Med., παραιρεῖσθαι τὴν θρασύτητα to lessen, damp it, Dem.   3. generally, to take away from, steal away from, τί τινος Hdt., Eur. Hence

παραίρημα, ατος, τό, the edge or selvage of cloth (cut off by the tailor) : generally, a band, strip, Thuc.

παρ-αίρω, contr. for poët. παρ-αείρω.

παρ-αισθάνομαι, f. -αισθήσομαι : aor. 2 -ησθόμην : Dep. :—to remark or hear of by the way, τινος Xen. ; absol., οὐχὶ παρήσθεν (Dor. for παρῄσθου), Theocr.

παρ-αίσιος, ον, of ill omen, ominous, Il.

παρ-αΐσσω, f. ξω : aor. 1 -ήϊξα :—to dart past, Il. ; c. acc., ἵπποι γάρ με παρήϊξαν Ib.

παρ-αιτέομαι, f. ήσομαι : pf. -ῄτημαι : Dep. :—to beg from another, ask as a favour of him, Lat. exorare, τί τινα Eur., Plat., etc. : to obtain by entreaty, τι Hdt.   2. π. τινα to move by entreaty, obtain leave from, Id. : to intercede with a person, prevail upon him by supplications, Id., Eur.   3. c. acc. et inf. to entreat one to do or be so and so, Hdt., Xen., etc. :—also c. gen. pers. et inf. to beg of a person to do a thing, Eur. :—c. inf. only, to obtain leave to do, Hdt.   II. c. acc. rei, Lat. deprecari, to avert by entreaty, deprecate, τὴν ὀργήν, τὰς ζημίας Aeschin.   2. to decline, deprecate, χάριν Pind.   3. c. acc. pers. to ask him to excuse one, decline his invitation, Polyb. ; absol., N. T. :—Pass., ἔχε με παρῃτημένον have me excused, Ib.   4. π. γυναῖκα to divorce her, Luc.   III. c. acc. pers. to intercede for, beg off, esp. from punishment, Hdt. ; π. περί τινος Xen. Hence

παραίτησις, ἡ, earnest prayer, Plat.   II. a deprecating, Thuc.   III. an interceding for, begging off, Dem.

παραιτητής, οῦ, ὁ, an intercessor, Plut.

παρ-αίτιος, ον and α, ον, being in part the cause of a thing, c. gen., ap. Dem.

παραι-φάμενος, η, ον, Ep. part. med. of παράφημι, exhorting, encouraging, h. Hom., Hes.   II. rebuking, Il.

παραίφάσις, ἡ, poët. for παράφασις, persuasion, Il.

παραιφρονέω, poët. for παραφρονέω.

παρ-αιωρέω, f. ήσω, to hang up beside :—Pass. to be hung or hang beside, Hdt. :—absol., of a suppliant, to hang upon another, Thuc.

παρακάββαλε, Ep. for παρακατέβαλε, 3 sing. aor. 2 of παρακαταβάλλω.

παρα-κάθημαι, inf. -καθῆσθαι, Dep. to be seated beside or near another, c. dat., Ar., Thuc., etc.

παρα-καθιδρύομαι, Pass. to be placed by or near, Plut.

παρα-καθίζω, f. -καθιζήσω, Att. -καθιῶ :—to set beside or near, Plat.   2. aor. 1. med. παρεκαθισάμην : τινά to make him assessor or coarbiter, Dem.   II. Pass. and Med. : f. -καθιζήσομαι : impf. -καθιζόμην : aor. 1 παρεκαθισάμην :—to seat oneself or sit down beside another, c. dat., Ar., Xen.

παρα-καθίημι, f. -καθήσω, to let down beside: in Med., πηδάλια ζεύγλαισι παρακαθίετο caused the rudder to be let down beside the rudder-bars, Eur.

παρα-καθίστημι, f. -καταστήσω, to station or establish beside, Dem.

παρα-καίομαι, Pass. to be kept lighted beside, Hdt.

παρα-καίριος, ον, = sq., Hes.

παρά-καιρος, ον, unseasonable, ill-timed, Luc.

παρακᾰλέω, Att. f. -καλῶ, later -καλέσω :—to call to one, Xen. II. to call to aid, call in, send for, Lat. arcessere, Hdt., Ar., etc. ; π. τινα σύμβουλον Xen. :—to call on, invoke the Gods, Id., etc. :—Pass., παρακαλούμενος καὶ ἄκλητος, 'vocatus atque non vocatus,' Thuc. 2. to summon one's friends to attend one in a trial (cf. παράκλησις I. 1) :—Pass., παρακεκλημένοι summoned to attend at a trial, Aeschin. 3. to invite, ἐπὶ δαῖτα Eur. ; ἐπὶ θήραν Xen. ; π. τινὰ ἐπὶ τὸ βῆμα to invite him to mount the tribune, Aeschin. III. to call to, exhort, cheer, encourage, τινά Aesch., Xen. 2. to comfort, console : in Pass., N. T. 3. to excite, τινὰ ἐς φόβον, ἐς δάκρυα Eur. : —of things, to foment, φλόγα Xen. 4. π. τινά, c. inf., to exhort one to do, Eur., Xen. IV. to demand, require, ὁ θάλαμος σκεύη π. Xen.

παρακάλυμμα, ατος, τό, anything hung up beside or before, a covering, curtain, Plut. :—metaph. an excuse, τινος for a thing, Id. From

παρα-κᾰλύπτω, f. ψω, to cover by hanging something beside, to cloak, disguise, Plut. :—Med. to cover one's face, Plat.

παρα-καταβαίνω, f. -βήσομαι, to dismount beside, of horsemen who dismount to fight on foot, Polyb.

παρα-καταβάλλω, f. -καταβᾰλῶ, aor. 2 -κατέβᾰλον, Ep. -κάββαλον :—to throw down beside, Il. ; ζῶμα δέ οἱ παρακάββαλεν put a waistband on him, Ib. II. as Att. law-term, to make a special claim to property, when the claimant deposited a sum of money called παρακαταβολή, Dem. Hence

παρα-καταβολή, ή, money deposited in court by claimants, and forfeited in case of failure (v. παρακαταβάλλω II), Dem.

παρα-καταθήκη, ή, a deposit entrusted to one's care, Lat. fideicommissum, Hdt., Thuc., etc. 2. of persons entrusted to guardians, Ἀπόλλωνα παρακαταθήκην δεξαμένη Hdt. ; of children, Dem.

παρα-καταθνήσκω, to die beside, poët. aor. 2 παρακάτθανε Anth.

παρα-κατάκειμαι, Pass. to lie beside another at meals, Lat. accumbere, c. dat., Xen.

παρα-κατακλίνω [ῑ], to lay down beside, to put to bed with, τινά τινι Aeschin., Luc.

παρα-καταλέγομαι, 3 sing. Ep. aor. 2 παρκατέλεκτο, Pass. to sleep beside another, c. dat., Il.

παρα-καταλείπω, to leave with one, τινά τινι Thuc.

παρα-καταπήγνυμι, f. -καταπήξω, to drive in alongside, Thuc.

παρα-κατατίθεμαι, Med. to deposit one's own property with another, entrust it to his keeping, give it him in trust, Hdt., Xen., etc.

παρα-κατέχω, f. -καθέξω, to keep back, restrain, detain, Thuc.

παρα-κατοικίζω, f. Att. -ιῶ, to make to dwell or settle

beside, π. φόβον τινι to make fear his companion, Plut.

παρα-καττύω [ῠ], to sew on beside, patch up :—in Med., generally, to put all in order, set straight, Ar.

παρά-κειμαι, poët. **πάρ-κειμαι** : Ep. 3 sing. impf. παρεκέσκετο :—used as Pass. to παρατίθημι, to lie beside or before, Hom. :—metaph., ὑμῖν παράκειται ἐναντίον ἠὲ μάχεσθαι ἠ φεύγειν the choice lies before you, to fight or to flee, Od. :—in part. close at hand, present, Pind.

παρακέλευμα or -ενσμα, ατος, τό, an exhortation, cheering address, Eur. 2. a precept, maxim, Plat.

παρακελεύομαι, Dep. to order one to do a thing, advise, prescribe, τί τινι Hdt., Thuc., etc. ; π. ταῦτα to give this advice, Plat. ;—also, π. τινι, c. inf., Id., Xen. II. to exhort, τοιαῦτα παρακελευσάμενος having delivered this address, Thuc. :—absol. to encourage one another by shouting, Hdt. III. παρακεκέλευστο in pass. sense, orders had been given, Id.

παρακέλευσις, εως, ή, a calling out to, cheering on, exhorting, addressing, Thuc., Xen.

παρακέλευσμα, v. παρακέλευμα.

παρακελευσμός, ὁ, = παρακέλευσις, Thuc., Xen.

παρακελευστικός, ή, όν, calling out to, cheering on, Plat.

παρακελευστός, ή, όν, summoned, of a packed audience, Thuc.

παρα-κελεύω, v. παρακελεύομαι.

παρα-κελητίζω, to ride by or past, τινά Ar.

παρα-κινδύνευσις, ή, a desperate venture, Thuc. ; and

παρακινδῡνευτικός, ή, όν, venturesome, audacious, Plat., Dem. : Adv., παρακινδυνευτικῶς λέγειν Plat.

παρα-κινδῡνεύω, f. σω, to make a rash venture, to venture, run the risk, Ar., Thuc., etc. ; π. εἰς Ἰωνίαν to venture to Ionia, Thuc. 2. c. acc. rei, to venture, risk a thing, Ar., Plat. ; τοιουτονί τι παρακεκινδυνευμένον a bold, venturous phrase, Ar. 3. c. inf. to have the hardihood to do a thing, Id., Xen.

παρα-κῑνέω, f. ήσω, to move aside, disturb, Plat. : absol. to raise troubles, enter into plots, Dem. :—Pass. to be violently incited, Luc. II. intr. to be disturbed, to shift one's ground, Plat. 2. to be highly excited, θεῷ τινι Xen. ; παρακινῶν out of his senses, Plat. Hence

παρακῑνητικός, ή, όν, inclined to insanity : Adv., παρακινητικῶς ἔχειν to shew symptoms of insanity, Plut.

παρακίω [ῐ], to pass by, τινά Il.

παρα-κλείω, Ion. -κλήω, to shut out, exclude, Hdt.

παρα-κλέπτω, f. ψω, to steal from the side, filch underhand, Ar.

παρακληίω, Ion. for παρακλείω.

παράκλησις, ή, (παρακαλέω) a calling to one's aid, summons, οἱ ἐκ παρακλήσεως συγκαθήμενοι a packed party in the jury, Dem. 2. a calling upon, appealing, τινος to one, Thuc. : intreaty, deprecation, Strab. II. an exhortation, address, Thuc., Aeschin. : encouragement, N. T.

παρακλητέον, verb. Adj. of παρακαλέω, one must call on, summon, Arist.

παρακλητικός, ή, όν, hortatory, Plat.

παρά-κλητος, ον, called to one's aid, Lat. advocatus : as Subst. a legal assistant, advocate, Dem. II. in N. T., ὁ Παράκλητος, the Intercessor or the Comforter.

παρακλῖδόν, Adv. (παρακλίνω) *bending sideways, turning aside, swerving,* οὐκ ἂν ἔγωγε ἄλλα παρὲξ εἴποιμι **παρακλιδόν** I would not tell you another tale beside the mark, *swerving from the truth,* Od.

παρακλίντωρ, ορος, ὁ, = παρακλίτης, Anth.

παρα-κλίνω [ῑ]: f. -κλῖνῶ: Pass., pf. -κέκλῖμαι: aor. 1 -εκλίθην [ῑ]:—*to bend* or *turn aside, turn* the head Od.; π. τὴν θύραν, τὴν πύλην *to set* it *ajar,* Hdt.   **2.** metaph., ἄλλη παρκλίνουσι δίκας *they turn* justice *from her path,* Hes.   **3.** *to lay beside* another:—Pass. *to lie down beside,* at meals, Lat. *accumbere,* τινι Theocr.   **II.** intr. *to turn aside,* Il.; **παρακλίνασα** *having swerved from the course,* Aesch.

παρακλίτης [ῑ], ου, ὁ, *one who lies beside* at meals, Xen.

παρακλύω, = παρακούω IV, Anth.

παρ-ακμάζω, f. άσω: pf. -ήκμᾶκα:—*to be past the prime,* Xen.

παρ-ακμή, ἡ, *the point at which the prime is past, abatement,* Plut.

παρ-ἀκοή, ἡ, *unwillingness to hear, disobedience,* N. T.

παρα-κοινάομαι, Med. *to communicate,* τί τινι Pind.

παρακοιτέω, f. ήσω, *to keep watch beside,* Polyb. From

παρακοίτης, ου, ὁ, (κοίτη) *one who sleeps beside, a bedfellow, husband, spouse,* Il., Hes.

παράκοιτῖς, ιος, ἡ, acc. ῐν, fem. of foreg. *a wife, spouse,* Il.; Ep. dat. παρακοίτῑ Od.

παρ-ἀκολουθέω, f. ήσω, *to follow beside, follow closely,* c. dat., Dem.: of a physician, π. νοσήματι Plat.; so, π. τοῖς πράγμασιν ἐξ ἀρχῆς Dem.: of an audience, *to follow with the mind,* Aeschin.

παρακομῖδή, ἡ, *a carrying across, transporting,* Thuc.   **II.** (from Pass.) *a going* or *sailing across, passage, transit,* Id. From

παρα-κομίζω, f. Att. ιῶ, *to carry along with one, escort, convoy,* Eur.   **2.** *to carry* or *convey over, to transport,* Xen.: generally, *to convey, carry,* Hdt.: —Med. *to have a thing brought one,* Xen.   **II.** Pass. *to go* or *sail beside, coast along,* τὴν Ἰταλίαν Thuc.   **2.** *to go* or *sail across, pass over,* Polyb.

παρ-ακονάω, f. ήσω, *to sharpen besides, sharpen also,* Xen.:—Pass. *to be so sharpened,* 3 pl. pf. pass. **παρηκόνηνται** Ar.

παρ-ακοντίζω, *to throw the dart with others,* Luc.

παρακοπή, ἡ, metaph. (παρακόπτω II) *infatuation, insanity, frenzy,* Aesch.

παράκοπος, ον, (παρακόπτω II) *frenzied, frantic,* Aesch.; also, παράκοπος φρενῶν Eur.

παρα-κόπτω, f. ψω, *to strike falsely:* Pass., pf. part. **παρακεκομμένος,** of coin, *counterfeit;* metaph. of men, ἀνδράρια μοχθηρά, παρακεκομμένα *knavish mannikins, base coin,* Ar.   **2.** Med. *to cheat* or *swindle out of* a thing, π. τινὰ ἀγαθῶν Id.; simply, *to cheat,* τινά Id.:—Pass. *to be cheated,* τινι in a thing, Id.   **II.** metaph. *to strike the mind awry, drive mad,* Eur.

παράκουσμα, ατος, τό, *a false story,* Strab. From

παρακουστέον, verb. Adj. *one must disobey,* τινός Muson. ap. Stob.

παρ-ακούω, f. -ακούσομαι: pf. -ακήκοα:—*to hear beside,* esp. *to hear accidentally, to hear talk of,* c. acc., Hdt.   **II.** *to hear underhand, overhear from,* τί τινος Ar.; τι παρά τινος Plat.   **III.** *to*

hear imperfectly or *wrongly, misunderstand,* Id.   **IV.** *to hear carelessly, take no heed to,* c. gen., N. T.

παρα-κρεμάννυμι, f. -κρεμάσω, *to hang beside,* χεῖρα **παρακρεμάσας** *letting* the hand *hang down,* Il.

παρά-κρημνος, ον, *on the edge of a precipice,* Strab.

παρα-κρίνω [ῑ], f. -κρῖνῶ, *to draw up in line opposite:* Pass., πεζὸς παρακεκριμένος παρὰ τὸν αἰγιαλόν the land force *drawn up* along the shore, Hdt.; **παρεκρίθησαν διαταχθέντες** Id.

παρα-κροτέω, f. ήσω, *to pat* or *clap* one, Luc.

παράκρουσις, ἡ, *a striking falsely:* metaph. *a cheating, deception,* Dem.:—*a fallacy,* Arist. From

παρα-κρούω, f. σω, *to strike aside: to disappoint, mislead,* Plat.:—Pass. *to be led astray, go wrong,* Id., Dem.:—so also in Med., Isocr.   **II.** in Med. also, *to strike away from oneself, parry,* Plut.

παρα-κτάομαι, f. -κτήσομαι, Dep. *to get over and above:* in pf. -κέκτημαι, *to have over and above,* Hdt.

παρ-ακτίδιος, ον, = sq., Anth.

παρ-άκτιος, α, ον, *on the sea-side, by the shore,* Trag.

παρα-κύπτω, poët. **παρ-κύπτω,** f. ψω, *to stoop sideways,* of the attitude of a bad harp-player, Ar.   **II.** *to stoop for the purpose of looking at,* and so, **1.** *to look sideways at, cast a careless glance on* a thing, Dem.   **2.** *to peep out of* a door or window, Ar.:— or, of persons outside, *to peep in, look in,* κατ' ἄντρον **παρκύπτοισα** Theocr.; **παρέκυψεν εἰς τὸ μνημεῖον** N. T.

παρα-λαμβάνω, f. -λήψομαι, Ion. -λάμψομαι: pf. -είληφα:—*to receive from* another, of persons succeeding to an office, π. τὴν βασιληίην Hdt.; τὴν ἀρχήν Plat., etc.:—also of persons succeeding *by inheritance,* Eur., Dem.; π. ἀράς *to inherit* curses, Eur.   **2.** *to take upon oneself, undertake,* πρᾶγμά τι Ar.: Pass., τὰ **παραλαμβανόμενα** *undertakings,* Hdt.   **3.** *to take in pledge,* Id.: also, *to take by force* or *treachery, get possession of,* Id., Thuc.   **4.** *to receive by hearsay* or *report, to ascertain,* π. τὴν ἀλήθειαν Hdt., etc.   **5.** *to take up, catch up,* τὸ οὔνομα τοῦτο Id.   **II.** c. acc. pers. *to take to oneself, associate with oneself,* as a wife or mistress, an adopted son, a partner or ally, Id., Thuc., etc.; as a pupil, Plat.   **2.** *to invite,* Hdt.   **3.** *to wait for, intercept,* Lat. *excipere,* Id., Xen.: *to take prisoner,* Polyb.

παρα-λανθάνω, *to escape the notice of,* τινά Plat.

παρα-λέγω, f. ξω, *to lay beside:* Med. *to lie beside* or *with* another, c. dat.; ὁ δέ οἱ παρελέξατο λάθρη Il.; Ep. aor. 2 παρέλεκτο h. Ven.   **2.** **παραλέγεσθαι τὴν γῆν** *to sail* or *coast along,* Lat. *legere oram,* N. T.

παραλειπτέον, verb. Adj. *one must pass over,* τι Xen.

παρα-λείπω, f. ψω: pf. -λέλοιπα:—*to leave on one side, leave remaining,* Thuc., Xen.:—τοῖς ἐχθροῖς **παραλείπεται** *is reserved* for enemies, Dem.   **II.** *to leave to* another, λόγον τινί π. *to leave* him time for speaking, Aeschin.   **III.** *to leave on one side, pass by, neglect,* Eur., Ar., etc.: Pass., εἴ τις **παραλείπεται** [πρόσοδος] if the revenue is *insufficient,* Arist.   **2.** *to pass over, leave untold, omit,* Eur., Thuc., etc.: Pass., τὰ **παραλειπόμενα** *omissions,* Plat.

παρ-αλείφω, f. ψω, *to bedaub as with ointment,* Arist.

παραληπτέον, verb. Adj. of παραλαμβάνω, *one must produce,* μάρτυρας Dem.

παρα-ληπτός, ή, όν, *to be accepted,* Plat.

παρα-ληρέω, f. ήσω, *to talk like a dotard, talk nonsense*, Lat. *delirare*, Ar., etc.

παραληφθήσομαι, fut. pass. of παραλαμβάνω.

παράληψις, ή, (παραλαμβάνω) *a receiving from another, succession to,* τῆς ἀρχῆς Polyb. 2. *the taking of a town,* Id.

παραλήψομαι, fut. med. of παραλαμβάνω.

Παράλιον, τό, *a chapel of the hero Paralus*, Dem.

παρ-άλιος, α, ον, and **ος, ον,** =πάραλος, *by the sea,* Trag. II. ή **παραλία,** Ion. -ίη (sc. γῆ or χώρα), *the seacoast, sea-board,* Hdt., Arist. 2. *the Eastern coast of Attica,* between Hymettus and the sea, Hdt., Thuc.

παραλλαγή, ή, *a passing from hand to hand, transmission,* Aesch. 2. *variation, change,* N.T.

παράλλαγμα, ατος, τό, *an interchange, variation,* Strab.

παραλλάξ, Adv. *alternately, in turn,* Lat. *vicissim,* Soph. 2. *in alternating rows,* Lat. *ad quincuncem dispositi,* Thuc.; and

παρ-άλλαξις, ή, *alternation, alternating motion,* τῶν σκελῶν Plut. II. *a change for the worse, alteration,* Plat. From

παρ-αλλάσσω, Att. -ττω, f. -ξω : aor. 1 -ήλλαξα :— Pass., aor. 1 -ηλλάχθην, aor. 2 -ηλλάγην [ἄ] : pf. -ήλλαγμαι :—*to make things alternate, to transpose,* Plat. 2. *to change* or *alter a little,* Hdt., Soph. 3. of Place, *to pass by, go past, elude,* Xen. :—*to get rid of,* Plut. 4. *to go beyond, exceed* in point of time, Id. II. intr. *to pass by* one another, *to overlap,* Hdt. 2. *to differ, vary,* Id. :—impers., οὐ σμικρὸν παραλλάττει *it makes no small difference,* Plat. 3. π. τοῦ σκοποῦ *to go aside from the mark,* Id. 4. *to deviate from the course, to be liable to deviation,* Id.; λόγοι παραλλάσσοντες *delirious,* Eur. 5. *to slip aside* or *away,* Aesch.

παρ-άλληλος, ον, *beside one another, side by side,* αἱ παράλληλοι (sc. γραμμαί) *parallel lines,* Arist.; π. (sub. κύκλος) *a parallel of latitude,* Strab.; οἱ βίοι οἱ π. *the parallel lives* of Plutarch, Plut.; ἐκ παραλλήλου *parallelwise,* Id. 2. c. dat. *parallel to,* Polyb.

παρα-λογίζομαι, f. ίσομαι, Dep.: I. *in keeping accounts, to misreckon, miscalculate,* Dem. 2. *to cheat out* of a thing, *to defraud of,* c. dupl. acc., Arist. II. *to mislead by fallacious reasoning,* Aeschin. :—Pass. *to be so misled,* Arist.

παραλογισμός, ὁ, *false reasoning, deception,* Polyb.; and

παραλογιστικός, ή, όν, *fallacious,* Arist.

παρά-λογος, ον, *beyond calculation, unexpected, casual, uncertain,* Arist., etc.—παράλογον, τό, *an unexpected event* ; but, τὰ παράλογα *the portions of food* given to *unexpected* guests, Xen. :—Adv. παραλόγως Dem. II. **παράλογος, ὁ,** as Subst., *an unexpected issue,* Thuc.; πολύς, μέγας ὁ π. *the event is greatly contrary to calculation* ; so, τὸν π. τοσοῦτον ποιῆσαι τοῖς Ἕλλησι *caused so great a miscalculation to the Greeks,* Id.; ἐν τοῖς ἀνθρωπείοις παραλόγοις *by miscalculations* such as men make, Id.

πάρ-αλος, ον, (ἅλς) *by* or *near the sea,* Soph., Eur. : *near the salt,* (with a pun on ή Πάραλος), Ar. 2. generally, *concerned with the sea, naval,* Hdt. II. ή πάραλος γῆ *the coast-land* of Attica (cf. παράλιος II),

Thuc. ;—hence οἱ Πάραλοι *the people of the coast-land,* Hdt., Eur. III. ή Πάραλος ναῦς, or ή Π. alone, *the Paralus,* one of the Athenian sacred galleys, reserved for state-service, Thuc., Dem. ; also Πάραλος (without Art.), Ar. 2. οἱ Πάραλοι, *the crew of the Paralus,* Id., Thuc.

παρ-άλπιος, ον, *dwelling near the Alps,* Plut.

παρα-λῡπέω, f. ήσω, *to grieve* or *trouble besides,* ἄλλο παρελύπει οὐδέν *no disease attacked them besides the plague,* Thuc.; ὅταν μηδὲν αὐτὴν παραλυπῇ Plat.; οἱ παραλυποῦντες *the troublesome, the refractory,* Xen.

παρά-λυπρος, ον, of soil, *rather poor,* Strab.

παράλυσις, ή, *a loosening by the side : paralysis, palsy,* Theophr. Hence

παραλῠτικός, ή, όν, *paralytic,* N.T.

παρα-λύω, f. -λύσω [ῠ] : aor. 1 -έλῡσα : pf. -λέλῠκα : Pass., aor. 1 -ελύθην [ῠ] : pf. -λέλῠμαι : I. c. acc. rei, *to loose from the side, take off, detach,* Hdt., etc. 2. *to undo, put an end to,* Eur. II. c. acc. pers. et gen. rei, *to unyoke* or *part from,* πολλοὺς παρέλυσεν θάνατος δάμαρτος Id.; π. τινὰ τῆς στρατηίης *to set free from* military service, Hdt.; π. τινὰ τῆς στρατηγίης *to dismiss from* the command, Id. : —τοὺς Ἀθηναίους π. τῆς ὀργῆς *to set them free from* .. , Thuc. : c. acc. only, *to set free,* Eur. :—Pass. *to be parted from,* τινος Hdt. : *to be exempt* from service, Id. III. in Pass. *to loose beside,* i.e. *one beside another,* Xen. IV. in Pass. *to be disabled at the side, to be paralysed,* Arist. : generally, *to be exhausted, to flag,* of camels, Hdt.

παρ-αμείβω, f. -αμείψω, *to leave on one side, pass by,* c. acc. loci, Plut. 2. *to outrun, exceed, excel,* σοφίᾳ σοφίαν Soph. II. *to pass,* βίον Anth. B. mostly in Med. *to go past, pass by, leave on one side,* Od., Hdt., etc.; τὸν παραμειψάμενος Od.; παραμείβεσθαι ἔθνεα πολλά Hdt. ;—but, πύλας παραμείψεται *shall pass through* the gates, Theogn. 2. *to pass over, make no mention of,* Lat. *praetermitto,* Hdt. 3. *to outrun, outstrip,* Pind., Eur. 4. of Time, *to pass, go by,* Hes. II. in a causal sense, *to turn aside, divert,* Pind.

παρ-αμελέω, f. ήσω, *to pass by and disregard, to be disregardful of,* τινός Thuc., Xen., etc. : absol. παρημελήκεε *he recked little,* Hdt.; παραμελοῦντες *being negligent,* Plat. : —Pass. *to be abandoned,* Aesch.

παρα-μένω, poët. **παρ-μένω,** f. -μενῶ : aor. 1 -έμεινα : —*to stay beside* or *near, stand by* another, c. dat., Il., Ar.; παρά τινι Aeschin. :—of slaves, *to remain faithful,* Plat.; hence Παρμένων, *Trusty,* as a slave's name, Menand. II. absol. *to stand one's ground, stand fast,* Il., Hdt., Att.; *to remain with* the army, Thuc. 2. *to stay* at a place, *stay behind* or *at home,* Hdt. 3. *to survive, remain alive,* Id. 4. of things, *to endure, last,* Eur., Xen.

παρ-άμερος, ον, Dor. for παρ-ήμερος.

παρα-μετρέω, f. ήσω, *to measure one thing by* another, *to compare,* Plat.

παρ-ἀμεύομαι, Dor. for παραμείβομαι, παραμενέσθαι τινος μορφάν *to surpass,* Pind.

παρα-μήκης, ες, (μῆκος) *oblong* or *oval,* Polyb. II. *extending parallel to* the mainland, Strab.

παρα-μηρίδιος, ον, (μηρός) along the thighs; τὰ παραμ. armour for the thighs, cuisses, Xen.

παραμίγνυμι and –ύω, Ion. –μίσγω, f. –μίξω:—to intermix with, τί τινι Ar. :—Pass., ἡδονὴν παραμεμίχθαι τῇ εὐδαιμονίᾳ Arist. II. to add by mixing, Lat. admiscere, ὕδωρ παραμίσγειν Hdt. :—Pass., ὅ τι αὐτοῖς παραμέμικται Plat.

παρα-μιμνήσκομαι, f. –μνήσομαι: pf. –μέμνημαι: Dep.:—to mention besides, to make mention of a thing along with another, c. gen. rei, Hdt., Soph.

παρα-μίμνω, poët. for παραμένω, to abide, tarry, Od.

παραμίσγω, v. παραμίγνυμι.

παραμόνιμος, ον, poët. fem. παρμονίμα, (παραμένω) staying beside, i. e. steadfast, permanent, Theogn., Pind. 2. of slaves, trusty, Xen.

παράμονος, poët. πάρμονος, ον, =foreg., Pind.

παρά-μουσος, ον, (Μοῦσα) out of tune with, discordant with, c. dat., Eur.: absol. harsh, horrid, Aesch.

παρ-αμπέχω or –αμπίσχω, f. –αμπέξω: aor. 2 –ήμπισχον:—to wrap a thing round as a cloak : metaph., π. λόγους to use a cloak of words, Eur.

παρα-μῡθέομαι, f. ήσομαι, Dep. to encourage or exhort one to do a thing, c. dat. pers. et inf., τοῖς ἄλλοισιν ἔφη παραμυθήσασθαι οἴκαδ' ἀποπλείειν Il. ; c. acc. pers., παραμυθοῦ με (sc. ποιεῖν) ὅ τι καὶ πείσεις Aesch. :—c. acc. pers. only, to encourage, exhort, advise, Plat., Xen. 2. to console, comfort, τινα Hdt., Att. 3. to pacify, παρεμυθεῖτο attempted to pacify them, Thuc. 4. to assuage, abate, Plut. : to soften down, explain away, Strab. Hence

παραμῡθητικός, ή, όν, consolatory, Arist. ; and

παραμῡθία, ἡ, encouragement, exhortation, persuasion, Plat. 2. consolation, diversion, Id. 3. relief from, abatement of, φθόνου Plut. ; and

παραμύθιον [ῠ], τό, an address, exhortation, Plat. 2. an assuagement, abatement, καμάτων Soph. ; πυρσῶν of the fires of love, Theocr. ; ἐλπὶς κινδύνῳ π. οὖσα Thuc.

παρα-μῡκάομαι, Dep. to bellow beside or in answer, of thunder following on earthquake, Aesch.

παρ-αναγιγνώσκω, later –γῑνώσκω, f. –αναγνώσομαι :— to read beside, so as to compare one document with another, π. τῷ ψηφίσματι τοὺς νόμους Aeschin. ; π. παρὰ μαρτυρίας τὰς ῥήσεις Dem. II. to read publicly, Polyb.

παρ-αναδύομαι, Med., with aor. 2 and pf. act., to come forth and appear beside or near, Plut.

παρ-αναιετάω, to dwell near, c. acc. loci, Soph.

παρ-ᾰναλίσκω, f. –αναλώσω, to spend amiss, to waste, squander, Dem. :—Pass., of persons, to be sacrificed uselessly, 3 pl. aor. 1 παραναλώθησαν Plut. Hence

παρανάλωμα, ατος, τό, useless expense, Plut.

παρα-νηνέω, Ep. for παρανέω (νέω D) to heap or pile up beside, only in impf., σῖτον παρενήνεον ἐν κανέοισιν Od.

παρα-νήχομαι, f. –ξομαι, Dep. to swim along the shore, Od. : to swim beside, τῇ τριήρει Plut.

παρα-νῑκάω, f. ήσω, to subdue to evil, pervert, Aesch.

παρανίσσομαι, Dep. to go past, c. acc., h. Hom.

παρ-ανίστημι, f. –αναστήσω, to set up beside : Med. with aor. 2 act. to stand up beside, Plut.

παρ-ανίσχω, trans. to raise in answer, Thuc. II. intr. to stand forth beside, Plut.

παρα-νοέω, f. ήσω, to think amiss, to be deranged, lose one's wits, Eur., Ar. Hence

παράνοιᾰ, ἡ, derangement, madness, Aesch., Eur., Ar.

παρ-ανοίγνυμι and –οίγω, to open at the side or a little, set ajar, θύραν Dem.

παρα-νομέω, impf. παρενόμουν : f. ήσω : aor. 1 παρενόμησα : pf. παρανενόμηκα :—Pass., aor. 1 παρενομήθην : pf. παρανενόμημαι : later with double augm., παρηνόμουν, παρηνόμησα, etc. : (παράνομος) :—to transgress the law, act unlawfully, Thuc., Plat. :—Pass., κάθοδος παρηνομηθεῖσα a return illegally procured, Thuc. 2. to commit an outrage, ἐς τὸν νεκρὸν ταῦτα παρενόμησε Hdt. ; περί τινα Thuc. :—Pass. to be outraged, ill-used, Dem. Hence

παρανόμημα, τό, an illegal act, transgression, Thuc.

παρανομία, ἡ, transgression of law, decency or order, Thuc., Plat. ; ἡ κατὰ τὸ σῶμα π. εἰς τὴν δίαιταν loose and disorderly habits of life, Thuc. From

παρά-νομος, ον, acting contrary to law, lawless, Eur., Plat. II. of things, contrary to law, unlawful, Ar., Thuc., etc. :—Adv., παρανόμως, illegally, Thuc. 2. in Att. law, παράνομα γράφειν, εἰπεῖν to propose an illegal measure, Dem. ; παρανόμων γράφεσθαί τινα to indict one for proposing such a measure, Id. : the indictment itself was παρανόμων γραφή Aeschin. :—in Superl., παρανομώτατα γεγραφότα Id.

παρά-νοος, ον, contr. –νους, ουν, distraught, Aesch.

πάρ-αντα, Adv. sideways, sidewards, Il.

παρ-αντέλλω, poët. for παρανατέλλω, Anth.

παρα-νυκτερεύω, to pass the night beside, Plut.

παρά-νυμφος, ὁ, (νύμφη) the bridegroom's friend or best man, who went beside him in his chariot to fetch his bride :—as fem. the bride's-maid, Ar.

παρά-ξενος, ον, half-foreign, counterfeit, Ar.

παραξέω, f. έσω, to graze or rub in passing, Anth.

παρα-ξῐφίς, ίδος, ἡ, (ξίφος) a knife worn beside the sword, a dirk, Strab.

παρ-αξόνιος, ον, (ἄξων) beside the axle : τὸ π. a linch-pin :—παραξόνια, in Ar. Ran., perh., rapid whirlings.

παρ-άορος, Dor. for παρ-ήορος.

παρα-παιδᾰγωγέω, f. ήσω, to help to train : to reform gradually, Luc.

παρα-παίω, f. σω, to strike on one side : to strike a false note, and metaph. to be infatuated, lose one's wits, Aesch. :—π. τι to commit a folly, Luc. 2. to fall away from, Lat. aberrare, τῆς ἀληθείας Polyb.

παρα-πάλλομαι, Pass. to bound beside, τινι Eur.

παρά-πᾶν, Adv. for παρὰ πᾶν, altogether, absolutely, generally with Art., τὸ π. Hdt., Thuc., etc. :—with a negat., τὸ π. οὐδέν not at all, Hdt. ; οὐκ εἰμὶ τὸ π. ἄθεος Plat. 2. in reckoning, ἐπὶ διηκόσια τὸ παράπαν up to two hundred altogether, Hdt.

παρ-ᾰπᾰτάω, f. ήσω, to deceive, cajole, Aesch.

παρ-ᾰπᾰφίσκω, only in aor. 2 παρήπαφον, to mislead, beguile, Od. :—c. inf. to induce one to do a thing by craft or fraud, Il.

παρα-πείθω, f. –πείσω, to persuade gradually, win over, beguile, Hom., in Ep. aor. 2, 3 sing. παραιπεπίθῃσιν, part. παρ-πεπίθών.

παρα-πέμπω, f. ψω, to send past, convey past or through, c. acc. loci, Od. 2. to send by or along the coast, Thuc. 3. to escort, convoy, of ships of war convoy-

ing merchant vessels, Dem.; so in Med., Id.　4. *to convoy* supplies to an army, Xen.　5. *to send* troops *to the flank*, in support, Id.　II. *to pass on to*, of an echo, π. στόνον τινί Soph.; θόρυβον π. *to waft* him applause, Ar.　III. *to send away, dismiss*, Philipp. ap. Dem.

παρα-πέτασμα, ατος, τό, *that which is spread before* a thing, *a hanging curtain*, Hdt., Ar.: — metaph. *a screen, cover*, Plat., Dem.

παρα-πέτομαι, f. -πτήσομαι: aor. 2 παρ-επτόμην or -επτάμην: Dep.: — *to fly alongside*, Arist.　2. *to fly past, to escape*, Anth.

παρα-πήγνῡμι and -ύω, f. -πήξω, *to fix* or *plant beside*, Hdt.: —Pass., with pf. 2 πέπηγα, *to be fixed in the ground beside*, Il.: *to be closely annexed to* a thing, c. dat., Isocr.

παρα-πηδάω, f. ήσομαι, *to spring beyond, transgress*, τοὺς νόμους Aeschin.

παρα-πικραίνω, *to embitter, provoke*, N. T.　Hence
παραπικρασμός, ὁ, *provocation*, N. T.

παρα-πίμπραμαι, Pass. *to be inflamed*, Xen.

παρα-πίπτω, f. -πεσοῦμαι, *to fall beside*, Plut.　II. *to fall in one's way*, Hdt., Xen.: —καιρὸς παραπίπτει an opportunity *offers*, Thuc.: —ὁ παραπεσών, like ὁ παρατυχών, *the first that comes*, Plat.　2. c. dat. *to befall*, Id.　III. *to fall aside* or *away from*, c. gen., Polyb.: —absol. *to fall away*, N. T.

παρα-πλάζω, f. -πλάγξω: aor. 1 παρ-έπλαγξα, pass. -επλάγχθην: —*to make to wander from the right way*, *to drive* seamen *from their course*, Od.: —metaph. *to lead astray, perplex*, Ib.; παρεπλάγχθη ἰός the arrow *went aside*, Il.; παραπλαγχθῆναι γνώμης *to wander from* reason, Eur.

παρά-πλειος, α, ον, *almost full*, Plat.

παρα-πλέκω, f. ξω, *to braid* or *weave in*, Strab.

παρα-πλευρίδια, τά, (πλευρά) *covers for the sides of horses*, Xen.

παραπλευστέος, α, ον, *that must be sailed past*, Strab.

παρα-πλέω, Ion. -πλώω: f. -πλεύσομαι and -οῦμαι: Ep. aor. 2 παρέπλων (as if from a Verb in μι): —*to sail by* or *past*, absol., οἴη δὴ κείνη γε παρέπλω Ἀργώ was the only ship that *sailed past* or *through* that way, Od.; ἐν χρῷ παραπλέοντες *sailing past* so as to shave closely, Thuc.　2. *to sail along the coast*, c. acc. loci, of persons making a *coasting* voyage, Hdt.

παρά-πληκτος, ον, (πλήσσω) *frenzy-stricken*, Soph.

παρα-πλήξ, ῆγος, ὁ, ἡ, *stricken sideways*, ἠιόνες π. spits on which the waves *break obliquely*, Od.　II. metaph. = παράπληκτος, *mad*, Hdt., Eur.

παρα-πλησιάζω, *to be a neighbour*, Aesop.

παρα-πλήσιος, α, ον, and ος, ον, *coming near, nearly resembling, such-like*, τοιαῦτα καὶ παραπλήσια *such and such-like*, Thuc.; ναυσὶ παραπλησίαις τὸν ἀριθμόν *with ships nearly equal* in number, Id.: —with dat., παραπλήσιοι ἀλλήλοις *about equal*, Hdt.; ὅμοια ἢ π. τούτοις Dem.　2. foll. by a relat., παρ. ὡς . . , Id.; π. ὥσπερ ἂν εἰ . . , Isocr. : —Neut. παραπλήσια as Adv., π. ὡς εἰ . . , Hdt.; so Adv. -ίως, Plat.; παραπλησίως ἀγωνίζεσθαι, Lat. *aequo Marte contendere*, Hdt.

παρα-πλήσσω, Att. -ττω: f. ξω, *to strike at the side*:

—Pass. *to be stricken on one side*: *to be deranged, frantic*, γέλως παραπεπληγμένος Eur.

παρά-πλοος, contr. -πλους, ὁ, *a sailing beside*, *a coasting voyage*, τῆς Ἰταλίας *towards* Italy, Thuc.　II. *a point sailed by* or *doubled*, Strab.

παραπλώω, Ion. for παραπλέω.

παρα-πνέω, f. -πνεύσομαι: aor. 1 παρ-έπνευσα :—*to blow by the side, to escape by a sideway*, of the winds confined by Aeolus, Od.

παρα-ποδίζω, f. Att. ιῶ, *to entangle the feet; generally, to impede*, Polyb. : —Pass. *to be ensnared*, Plat.

παρα-πόδιος, poët. παρπ-, ον, (πούς) *at the feet*, i. e. *present*, Pind.

παρα-ποιέω, f. ήσω, *to make falsely*: Med., παραποιησάμενος σφραγῖδα *having got a false seal made*, Thuc.　2. *to alter slightly*, Arist.

παρ-απολαύω, *to have the benefit of besides*, τινός Luc.

παρ-απόλλυμι, *to destroy besides* : —Med., with pf. 2 παραπόλωλα, *to perish besides*, παραπολεῖ (2 sing. fut.) Ar.　2. *to be ruined undeservedly*, Dem.

παραπομπή, ἡ, (παραπέμπω) *a convoying*, σίτου Decret. ap. Dem.　II. *a procuring, providing*, Arist.　2. *that which is procured, supplies*, Lat. *commeatus*, Xen.

παραπομπός, όν, (παραπέμπω) *escorting*, Polyb.

παρα-πόντιος, ον, *beside* or *near the sea*, Anth.

παρα-πορεύομαι, Dep., with fut. med. and aor. 1 pass. *to go beside* or *alongside*, Polyb.　II. *to go past*, c. acc. loci, Id.: *to pass*, διὰ τῶν σπορίμων N. T.

παρα-ποτάμιος, α, ον, *beside a river, lying on a river*, Hdt., Eur.: οἱ π. *people who live on a river*, Hdt.

παρα-πράσσω, Att. -ττω, Ion. -πρήσσω, f. ξω, *to do* a thing *beside* or *beyond* the main purpose, Hdt.　II. *to help in doing*, Soph.

παρα-πρεσβεία, ἡ, *a dishonest embassage*, Dem.

παρα-πρεσβεύω, *to execute an embassy dishonestly*, Dem., Aeschin. : —so Dep. παραπρεσβεύομαι, Dem.

παρά-πρισμα, ατος, τό, (πρίω) *saw-dust*, metaph., *of poetic phrases*, Ar.

παρ-άπτω, f. ψω, *to fasten beside* :—Pass., χερσὶ παραπτομένα πλάτα *fitted* to the hands, *plied* by the hands, Soph.; others take it as contr. for παραπετομένα, *flying*.

παρά-πτωμα, ατος, τό, (παραπίπτω) *a false step, a transgression, trespass*, N. T.

παράπτωσις, ἡ, (παραπίπτω) *a falling beside*; κατὰ τὴν π. τινος *in the course* of an action, Polyb.

παρα-πύθια, τά, Comic word, *a sickness which prevented one from being victor at the* Πύθια, Anth.

πάραρος, ον, Dor. for παρήορος III, Theocr.

παρ-αρπάζω, *to filch away*, Anth.

παραρ-ράπτομαι, Pass. *to be sewn as a fringe along*, Hdt.

παραρ-ρέω, f. -ρεύσομαι: aor. 2 -ερρύην: pf. act. -ερρύηκα :—*to flow beside* or *past*, τόπον or παρὰ τόπον Hdt. : *to drift away*, N. T.　II. *to slip out* or *off*, Soph., Xen.　III. *to slip in unawares*, Dem.

παραρ-ρήγνῡμι or -ύω, f. -ρήξω, *to break at the side*, esp. *to break* a line of battle, Thuc.; and in Pass. *to be broken*, Id.　II. Pass., aor. 2 παερράγην [ᾰ], with pf. 2 act. παέρρωγα, *to break* or *burst at the side*, Soph., Plut.　2. φωνὴ παερρωγυῖα a voice *broken* (by passion), Theophr.

παραρ-ρητός, ή, όν, of persons, *that may be moved by words*, Il.   II. of words, *persuasive*, Ib.

παραρ-ρίπτω, later -έω, *to throw beside*: metaph. *to run the risk* of doing a thing, c. part., π. λαμβάνων Soph. : *to throw aside, reject*, Anth.

παράρ-ρυμα, ατος, τό, *anything drawn along the side*: *a leathern* or *hair curtain, stretched along* the sides of ships to protect the men, Xen.

παρ-αρτάομαι, Pass. *to be hung by one's side*, Plut.

παραρτέομαι, Ion. Verb (cf. ἀρτέομαι), Med. :   I. trans. *to fit out for oneself*, παραρτέετο στρατιήν *was engaged in preparing his* army, Hdt.   II. in pass. sense, *to hold oneself in readiness*, Id.

παρ-αρτύω, of food, *to season by additions*.

παρασάγγης, ου, ὁ, *a parasang* (the Persian *farsang*), containing thirty stades, Hdt., Xen.

παρα-σάττω, f. ξω, *to stuff in beside*, τι παρά τι Hdt.

παρά-σειον, τό, *a topsail*, Luc. (Deriv. uncertain.)

παρά-σειρος, ον, (σειρά) *fastened alongside*, π. ἵππος *a horse harnessed alongside of the regular pair, an outrigger*:—metaph. *a yoke-fellow, true associate*, Eur.

παρα-σείω, f. σω, *to shake at the side*, π. τὰς χεῖρας *to swing one's arms* in running ; then (without χεῖρας) φεύγειν παρασείσας, like *demissis manibus fugere*, i. e. *celerrimè*, Arist.

παρα-σημαίνομαι, Med. *to set one's seal beside, to counterseal, seal up*, Dem. :—pf. part. παρασεσημασμένος in pass. sense, Id.   2. *to note in passing, to notice besides*, Arist.

παρά-σημον, τό, (σῆμα) *a side-mark*: *a mark of distinction, the ensign of a ship*, Lat. *insigne*, N. T. : *the badge of* a soldier, Plut.

παρά-σημος, ον, (σῆμα) *marked amiss, falsely struck, counterfeit*, of coin, Dem. ; metaph. of men, Ar. ; so, π. δόξα Eur. ; παράσημος αἴνῳ *falsely stamped with praise*, i. e. *praised by a wrong standard*, Aesch.   2. of words, *false, incorrect*, Anth.   II. *noted*, Plut.

παρα-σιγάω, f. ήσομαι, *to pass by in silence*, Strab.

παρασῑτέω, f. ήσω, *to play the parasite* or *toad-eater*, Luc.   II. *to be honoured with a seat at the public table*, Plut. ; and

παρασῑτικός, ή, όν, of a παράσιτος: ἡ -κή (sc. τέχνη), *the trade of a* παράσιτος, *toad-eating*, Luc. From

παρά-σῑτος, ὁ, *one who eats at another's table, one who lives at another's expense, a parasite, toad-eater*, Comici, Luc.

παρα-σιωπάω, f. ήσομαι, *to pass over in silence*, Polyb.

παρα-σκευάζω, f. άσω :—Pass., pf. παρεσκεύασμαι, Ion. 3 pl. plqpf. παρεσκευάδατο :—*to get ready, prepare*, Hdt., Att.   2. *to provide, procure, to get up*, Dem.   3. *to make* or *render* so and so, with a Part. or Adj., π. τινὰ εὖ ἔχοντα, π. τινα ὅτι βέλτιστον Xen. ; c. inf., π. τινὰ ὡς μὴ ποιεῖν *to accustom* him not to do, Id. ;—so, π. ὅπως ὡς βέλτισται ἔσονται αἱ ψυχαί Plat.   4. absol. *to make one's friend*, Dem.   B. Med. and Pass. :   I. in proper sense of Med., *to get ready* or *prepare for oneself*, Hdt., Att.   2. in Oratt. *to procure* witnesses and partisans, so as to obtain a false verdict (cf. παρασκευή I. 3) :—absol. *to form a party, intrigue*, Dem.:—so in Act., Xen.   II. in Med., absol. *to prepare oneself, make preparations*, Hdt., Att.   2. pf. παρεσκεύασμαι is mostly pass. *to*

be ready, be prepared, Hdt., Att. ; παρεσκευάσθαι τί *to be provided with* a thing, Plat. :—impers., ὡς παρεσκεύαστο when *preparations had been made*, Thuc. Hence

παρασκεύασμα, ατος, τό, *anything prepared, apparatus*, Xen. ; and

παρασκευαστέον, verb. Adj. *one must prepare* or *provide*, Plat., Xen.   2. (from Pass.) *one must prepare oneself, be ready*, Plat. ; and

παρασκευαστής, οῦ, ὁ, *a provider*, τινος Plat. ; and

παρασκευαστικός, ή, όν, *skilled in providing*, τινος Xen.

παρασκευαστός, όν, *that can be provided*, Plat.

παρα-σκευή, ἡ, *preparation*, Hdt., Att. ; ἐν τούτῳ παρασκευῆς in this state of *preparation*, Thuc. :—*preparation* of a speech, Xen. :—with Preps., ἐκ παρασκευῆς *of set purpose*, μάχη ἐγένετο ἐκ π. a *pitched battle*, Thuc. ; so, ἀπὸ παρασκευῆς Id. ; δι' ὀλίγης παρασκευῆς at short *notice, offhand*, Id. ; ἐν παρασκευῇ in course of preparation, Id.   2. *a providing, procuring*, π. φίλων καὶ οὐσίας Plat.   3. *an intrigue* or *cabal*, for the purpose of gaining a verdict or carrying a measure, Dem., etc.   II. *that which is prepared, equipage*, Lat. *apparatus*, Plat., Xen. : *an armament*, Thuc., Dem.   2. generally, *power, means*, Thuc.   III. among the Jews, *the day of Preparation*, the day before the sabbath of the Passover, N. T.

παρα-σκηνάω or -έω, f. ήσω, *to pitch one's tent beside* or *near*, Xen.

παρα-σκήνια, τά, (σκηνή) *the side-scenes*, Dem.

παρα-σκηνόω, f. ώσω, *to throw over* one *like a tent* or *curtain*, Aesch.

παρα-σκήπτω, f. ψω, *to fall beside*, εἴς τι Luc.

παρα-σκιρτάω, f. ήσω, *to leap upon*, Plut.

παρα-σκοπέω, f. ήσω, *to give a sidelong glance at*, τινά Plat.   II. c. gen. *to miss seeing the force of* a thing, Aesch.

παρα-σκώπτω, f. ψω, *to jeer indirectly*, h. Hom.

παρα-σοβέω, f. ήσω, *to scare away* birds : intr. *to stalk haughtily past*, Plut.

παρα-σοφίζομαι, Dep. *to out-do in skill*, τινα Arist.

παρα-σπάω, f. άσω [ᾰ], *to draw forcibly aside, wrest aside*, Soph. : metaph., παρασπᾶν τινα γνώμης Id. ; ἀδίκους φρένας παρασπᾷς, i. e. ὥστε εἶναι ἀδίκους, Id. : —Med., παρασπᾶσθαί τινά τινος *to detach* him *from another's side*, Xen.

παρ-ασπίζω, f. σω, *to bear a shield beside*, i. e. *to fight beside, stand by*, Eur. :—metaph., [τόξα] παρασπίζοντ' ἐμοῖς βραχίοσι Id. Hence

παρ-ασπιστής, οῦ, ὁ, *a companion in arms*, Eur.

παρα-σπονδέω, f. ήσω, *to act contrary to an alliance* or *compact, break a treaty*, Dem.   II. trans. *to break faith with* one, Polyb. :—Pass. *to suffer by a breach of faith*, Id.

παρασπόνδημα, ατος, τό, *a breach of faith*, Polyb. ; and

παρασπόνδησις, ἡ, *a breaking of faith*, Polyb. From

παρά-σπονδος, ον, *contrary to a treaty*, Thuc., Xen.

παρασταδόν, Adv. *at one's side*, Hom., Theogn.

παρασταίην, aor. 2 opt. of παρίστημι :— -στάς, part.

παραστάς, άδος, ἡ, (παρίσταμαι) *anything that stands beside*: pl. παραστάδες, *doorposts, pilasters*, Lat.

antae:—also, *the space enclosed between the antae, the vestibule*, Eur. :—sometimes in sing., Id.

παράστᾰσις, εως, ἡ, I. (παρίστημι) *a putting aside* or *away, banishing, relegatio*, Plat., etc. 2. *a setting out* things *for sale, retail-trade*, Arist. II. (παρίσταμαι) intr. *a being beside:* 1. *a position* or *post near* a king, Xen. 2. *presence of mind, courage*, Polyb. : also, *desperation*, Id. III. as law-term, *a small money deposit* on entering law-suits, Oratt.

παραστᾰτέω, f. ήσω, *to stand by* or *near*, Trag. 2. *to stand by, to support, succour,* τινί Aesch., Soph.

παραστᾰτης [ᾰ], ου, ὁ, (παρίσταμαι) *one who stands by, a defender*, Eur. II. *one's comrade on the flank* (as προστάτης is one's *front-rank-man,* ἐπιστάτης one's *rear-rank-man*), Hdt., Xen. : generally, *a comrade, supporter*, Hdt., etc. 2. *one's right* or *left-hand-man* in a chorus, Arist. Hence

παραστᾰτικός, ή, όν, *fit for standing by* : 2. *able to exhort* or *rouse*, c. gen., Polyb., Plut. II. *having presence of mind, courageous, desperate,* Polyb.

παραστᾰτίς, ίδος, fem. of παραστάτης, *a helper, assistant*, Soph., Xen.

παρα-στείχω, aor. 2 παρέστιχον, *to go past, pass by,* c. acc. loci, h. Hom., Aesch. : absol., Soph. II. *to pass into, enter,* δόμους Id.

παρα-στῆναι, -στῆσαι, aor. 2 and 1 inf. of -ίστημι.

παρα-στορέννυμι, *to lay flat, lay low,* ἐγώ σε παραστορῶ (Att. fut.) Ar.

παρα-στρᾱτηγέω, f. ήσω, *to be at the general's side, interfere with him*, Plut.

παρα-στρᾰτοπεδεύω, *to encamp opposite to,* τινί Polyb.

παρα-στρέφω, f. ψω, *to turn aside* : metaph., pf. pass. part. παρεστραμμένος, *perverted*, Arist. 2. π. τὸν τριβῶνα, *to wear it crooked*, Theophr.

παρα-συγγρᾰφέω, *to break contract with,* τινα Dem.

παρασυλλέγομαι, Pass. *to assemble with others,* Andoc.

παρα-σύρω [ῠ], f. -σῠρῶ, *to sweep away, carry away,* of a rapid stream, Ar. II. π. ἔπος *to drag a word in, use it out of time and place,* Aesch.

παρα-σφάλλω, f. -σφᾰλῶ : aor. 1 παρ-έσφηλα :—*to make an arrow glance aside,* Il.; π. τινά τινος *to foil one of* [obtaining] *a thing,* Pind.

παρασχέ, aor. 2 imper. of παρέχω.

παρασχεθεῖν, poët. aor. 2 inf. of παρέχω.

παρασχεῖν, Ep. -χέμεν, aor. 2 inf. of παρέχω.

παρα-σχίζω, f. -σχῐῶ, *to rip up lengthwise, slit up,* Hdt.

παράταξις, ἡ, *a placing in line of battle,* ἐκ παρατάξεως *in regular battle*, Thuc., etc. II. of *marshalling* a political party, *arrangement*, Aeschin., Dem. From

παρα-τάσσω, Att. -ττω, f. ξω, *to place side by side, draw up in battle-order,* Hdt., Thuc., etc. :—Med. *to draw up one's men in battle-order,* Xen. ; so of ships, Thuc. :—Med. and Pass. *to be drawn up along,* παρα-τετάχατο παρὰ τὴν ἀκτήν Hdt. ; ἑκατέρωθεν παρατεταγ-μένοι Thuc. ; so, παρετάξαντο ἀλλήλοις Xen. : absol., παρατεταγμένοι or παραταξάμενοι *in order of battle,* Thuc., Dem. 2. in Med. and Pass., also, *to stand prepared,* παρατετάχθαι πρὸς τὸ ἀποκρίνεσθαι Plat.

παρα-τείνω, f. -τενῶ : aor. 1 -έτεινα : pf. -τέτᾰκα :—*to stretch out along* or *beside, to extend the line of* battle, Lat. *ordines explicare*, Xen. ; π. τάφρον *to draw a long trench*, Id. : — Pass. *to be stretched along* (v. infr. II. 1) : *to be stretched at length, laid low*, Ar. 2. *to stretch on the rack, torture*, Xen. : —Pass. *to be half-dead, worn out*, Plat. 3. Pass., παρατείνεσθαι εἰς τοὔσχατον *to strain themselves* to the uttermost, *hold out* to the last, Thuc. 4. *to prolong, protract*, Arist., Luc. 5. *to apply* a figure to a right line, Plat. 6. of pronunciation, *to lengthen in pronunciation*, Lat. *producere*, Luc. II. intr. *to stretch along*, of a wall, a tract of country, Hdt. :— so also in Pass., παρατέταται τὸ ὄρος Id., etc. 2. of Time, *to continue* one's life, Luc.

παρα-τείχισμα, τό, *a wall built beside* or *across*, Thuc.

παρα-τεκταίνομαι, Ep. aor. 1 -ετεκτηνάμην : Med. :—of timber, *to work into another form* ; then, generally, *to transform, alter*, οὐδέ κεν ἄλλως Ζεὺς παρατεκτή-ναιτο *not even Zeus could make it any way else*, Il. ; αἶψά κε ἔπος παρατεκτήναιο *soon couldst thou dress up some other* tale, Od. II. Act. *to build besides*, Plut.

παρατεταγμένως, Adv. part. pf. pass. of παρατάσσω, *as in battle-array, steadily*, Plat.

παρα-τηρέω, f. ήσω, *to watch closely, observe narrowly, to watch one's opportunity*, Xen. : — so in Med., N. T. 2. *to take care,* ὅπως μὴ . . Dem.

παρατήρησις, ἡ, *observation,* μετὰ παρατηρήσεως so that *it can be observed*, N. T.

παρα-τίθημι, poët. παρ-τίθημι : 2 and 3 sing. -τιθεῖς, -τιθεῖ : impf. -ετίθεις, -ετίθει : aor. 1 act. παρέθηκα : pf. παρατέθεικα :—Med., aor. 2 παρεθέμην, Ep. part. παρθέμενος :—in Att. παράκειμαι generally serves as the Pass. :—*to place beside*, Od., Att. :—of meals, *to set before, serve up,* τί τινι Hom.; οἱ παρατιθέντες *the serving-men*, Xen. :—Pass., τὰ παρατιθέμενα *meats set before one*, Id. 2. generally, *to offer, provide,* Od., Plat. 3. *to place upon,* στεφάνους παρέθηκε καρήατι Hes. 4. *to lay before* one, *explain,* τί τινι Xen., N. T. 5. *to compare,* τί τινι Plut.

B. Med. *to set before oneself, have set before one,* Od., Thuc., etc. 2. *to deposit what belongs to one* in another's hands, *give in charge, commit*, Hdt., Xen. ; τι εἴς τινα or τινά τινι N. T. 3. *to venture, stake, hazard*, παρθέμενοι κεφαλάς, ψυχάς Od. 4. *to employ* something *of one's own,* τι ἔν τινι Plat.

παρα-τίλλω, f. -τῐλῶ, *to pluck the hair off*, Ar. :— Med. *to pluck out one's hairs,* Id. : pf. pass. part. παρατετιλμένος, η, *clean-plucked*, Id.

παρά-τολμος, ον, *foolhardy*, Plut.

παράτονος, ον, (παρατείνω) *stretched beside, hanging down by the side*, Eur.

παρα-τρᾰγεῖν, aor. 2 inf. of παρατρώγω.

παρα-τρέπω, f. -τρέψω, *to turn aside*, Il. ; ποταμὸν π. *to turn* a river *from* its channel, Lat. *derivare*, Hdt. ; π. ἄλλῃ τὸ ὕδωρ Thuc. :—Pass., παρατρεπόμενος εἰς Τένεδον *turning aside to* . . , Xen. 2. *to turn* one *from* his *opinion, change* his *mind*, Hes. : so in Med., Theocr. 3. of things, π. λόγον *to pervert* or *falsify* a story, Hdt. 4. *to alter* or *revoke* a decree, Id.

παρα-τρέφω, f. -θρέψω, *to feed beside* another :—Pass., of men not worth their keep, *to feed at another's expense*, Dem.

παρα-τρέχω, f. -θρέξομαι and -δρᾰμοῦμαι : aor. 2 πηρ-

ἔδραμον; 3 pl. plqpf. -δεδραμήκεσαν:—to run by or past, Il., Ar.   2. to outrun, overtake, Il. : π. τὰ τότε κακά to go beyond, exceed them, Eur.   3. to run through or over, run across (a space of ground expressed or implied), Xen.   4. to run over, i. e. treat in a cursory way, Isocr.:—to slight, neglect, Theocr.   5. to escape unnoticed, τινά Polyb.

παρα-τρέω, aor. 1 παρ-έτρεσα, Ep. -έτρεσσα:—to start aside from fear, Il.

παρα-τρίβω [ῐ], f. ψω, to rub beside or alongside, π. χρυσὸν ἀκήρατον ἄλλῳ χρυσῷ (sc. εἰς βάσανον) to rub pure gold by the side of other gold on the lapis Lydius and see the difference of the marks they leave, Hdt.   II. παρατρίψασθαι τὸ μέτωπον, Lat. frontem perfricare, to harden the forehead by rubbing, i. e. to be hardened, dead to shame, Strab.

παρα-τροπέω, = παρατρέπω, τί με ταῦτα παρατροπέων ἀγορεύεις; why tell me this, leading me astray? Od.

παρατροπή, ἡ, a turning away, means of averting, θανάτου Eur.   II. intr. a digression, Luc.

παράτροπος, ον, turned aside, lawless, strange, unusual, Plut.   II. act. averting a thing, c. gen., Eur.

παρα-τροχάζω, poët. for παρατρέχω, to run past, τινά Anth. : to pass by or over, to leave unnoticed, Id.

παρα-τρώγω, f. -τρώξομαι : aor. 2 -έτραγον :—to gnaw at the side, nibble at, take a bite of, c. gen., Ar.

παρα-τρωπάω, poët. for παρατρέπω, θεοὺς θυέεσσι παρατρωπῶσ' ἄνθρωποι turn away the anger of the gods by sacrifices, Il.

παρα-τυγχάνω, f. -τεύξομαι : aor. 2 παρ-έτυχον :—to happen to be near, be among others, c. dat., Il. ; π. τῷ λόγῳ, τῷ πάθεῖ to be present at. . , Lat. interesse, Hdt.   2. absol. to happen to be present, Id. : of a thing, to offer itself, παρατυχούσης τινὸς σωτηρίας Thuc.   3. often in partic. παρατυχών, whoever chanced to be by, i. e. the first comer, any chance person, Id. ;—so, τὸ παρατυγχάνον or παρατυχόν whatever turns up or chances, πρὸς τὸ παρατυγχάνον as circumstances required, Id. : nom. absol., ἐν τῷ παρατυχόντι Id. :—παρατυχόν, it being in one's power, since it was in one's power to do, c. inf., Id.

παρ-αυγάζω, f. σω, to illumine slightly :—Pass. to be illumined, Strab. ; and of the sun, to shine, Id.

παρ-αυδάω, f. ήσω, to address so as to console or encourage, Od. ; μὴ ταῦτα παραύδα do not talk me into this, Ib.   II. c. acc. rei, to speak lightly of, μὴ δή μοι θάνατόν γε παραύδα Ib.

παρ-αυλίζω, to lie near a place, c. dat., Eur.

πάρ-αυλος, ον, (αὐλή) dwelling beside, πάραυλον οἰκίζειν τινά to place one on the borders (of a land), Soph. ; βοὴ πάραυλος a cry close at hand, Id.

παραυτᾶ, Adv. for παρ' αὐτά (sc. τὰ πράγματα), in like manner, Lat. perinde or (as others) = παραυτίκα, at first, Aesch., Dem.

παρ-αυτίκα, Adv. immediately, forthwith, straightway, Lat. illico, Hdt. ; also, τὸ π. Id. ; ἐν τῷ π. Thuc.   2. with Substantives, to express brief duration, Ἅιδην τὸν π. present death, Eur. ; ἡ π. λαμπρότης momentary splendour, Thuc. ; ἡ π. ἐλπίς Id.

παρ-αυχένιος, η, ον, hanging from the neck, Anth.

παρα-φᾰγεῖν, aor. 2 inf. of παρεσθίω.

παρα-φαίνω, poët. παρ-φ-, to shew beside or by un-

covering, Hes.   2. to walk beside and light, light one to a place, Ar.   II. Pass. to appear by the side, disclose itself, Plat.

παράφᾰσις, ἡ, (παράφημι) only in poët. forms παραίφᾰσις, πάρφᾰσις :—an address, encouragement, consolation, Il.   2. allurement, persuasion, said of the cestus of Aphrodité, Ib. : deceit, Pind.

παρα-φέρω, poët. παρ-φέρω, f. -οίσω :—to bring to one's side, to hand to, set before one, Hdt., Xen. ; π. τὰς κεφαλὰς to exhibit them, Hdt. :—Pass. to be set on table, Id.   2. to bring forward, by way of argument, π. ἐς μέσον Id. : to bring forward, allege, cite, Id., Eur., etc.   3. to hand over, transmit, Eur.   II. to carry beside, τί τινι Id.   III. to carry past or beyond, Plat. ; π. τὴν χεῖρα to wave the hand, Dem. :—Pass. to be carried past or beyond, Thuc. ; τοῦ χειμῶνος παραφερομένου while the winter was passing, Plut.   2. to turn aside or away, τὴν ὄψιν π. τινός Xen. : to put away, remove, N. T.   3. to turn in a wrong direction, Dem. :—Pass. to move in a wrong direction, of paralysed limbs, Arist.   4. to lead aside, mislead :—Pass. to be misled, err, go wrong, Plat.   IV. to sweep away, of a river, Plut. : —Pass. to be carried away, Anth.   V. to let pass, Lat. praetermittere, τὰς ὥρας παρηνέγκατε τῆς θυσίας Orac. ap. Dem. :—Pass. to slip away, escape, Xen.   B. intr. to be beyond or over, ἡμερῶν ὀλίγων παρενεγκουσῶν, ἡμέρας οὐ πολλὰς παρενεγκούσας a few days over, more or less, Thuc.

παρα-φεύγω, to flee close past or beyond, παρφυγέειν (Ep. aor. 2 inf.) Od.

παρά-φημι, poët. παραί-φημι and πάρ-φημι, to speak gently to, to advise, c. dat., Il. :—Med. to persuade, appease, c. acc., Hom.   2. to speak deceitfully or insincerely, Pind. ; and, in Med., Id.

παρα-φθάνω [ᾰ], aor. 2 παρέφθην, part. act. and med. παραφθάς, -φθάμενος :—to overtake, outstrip, Il. ; εἰ δ' ἄμμε παραφθαίησι πόδεσσι (Ep. 3 sing. opt.) Ib.

παρα-φθέγγομαι, f. -φθέγξομαι, Dep. to add a qualification, Plat.   2. to interrupt, Plut.   Hence

παραφορά, ἡ, (παραφέρομαι) a going aside : of the mind, derangement, Aesch.

παρα-φορέω, f. ήσω, = παραφέρω, to set before, τί τινι Ar. :—Pass., Hdt.

παράφορος, ον, (παραφέρομαι) borne aside, carried away, Plut.   2. wandering, reeling, staggering, Eur., Luc.   3. mad, frenzied, Plut., Luc.

παράφραγμα, τό, a breastwork on the top of a mound, only in pl., Thuc. ; in a ship, the bulwarks, Id. : a low screen, Plat.   From

παρα-φράσσω, Att. -ττω, f. ξω, to enclose with a breastwork, Polyb.

παρα-φρονέω, (παράφρων) to be beside oneself, be deranged or mad, Hdt., Aesch., etc. ; poët. παραιφρ-, Theocr.

παραφρονία, ἡ, = παραφροσύνη, N. T.

παραφρόνιμος, ον, = παράφρων, Soph.

παρα-φροσύνη, ἡ, (παράφρων) derangement, Plat.

παρα-φρουρέω, f. ήσω, to keep guard beside, c. acc., Strab.

παρά-φρων, ον, (φρήν) wandering from reason, out of one's wits, deranged, Soph., Eur., etc.

παραφυάς, άδος, ή, (παραφύομαι) an offshoot, Arist.

παραφυής, ές, growing beside : παραφυές, τό, = παραφυάς, Arist.

παραφυλᾰκή, ή, a guard, watch, garrison, Polyb. From

παρα-φῠλάσσω, Att. -ττω, f. ξω, to watch beside, to guard closely, watch narrowly, Xen., etc. 2. Med. to be on one's guard, Plat.

παρα-φύομαι, Pass., with pf. act. -πέφῡκα, and aor. 2 -έφυν, to grow beside or at the side, Hdt.

παρα-χᾰλάω, f. άσω [ᾰ], to slacken at the side : of a ship, to let in water, leak, Ar.

παρα-χᾰράσσω, Att. -ττω, to mark with a false stamp, falsify, Luc.

παρα-χειμάζω, pf. part. -κεχειμακώς, to winter in or at a place, Dem., etc. Hence

παραχειμᾰσία, ή, a wintering in a place, Polyb.

παρ-αχελωίτης, ό, a dweller by the Acheloüs, Strab. : —fem. παραχελωῖτις, ιδος, (sc. χώρα) the country along the Acheloüs, Id.

παρα-χέω, f. -χεῶ : aor. 1 -έχεα : pf. -κέχῠκα :—to pour in beside, pour in, Hdt. II. of solids, to heap up on the side, Id. 2. Pass. to lie spread out near, of a country, Plut.

παρα-χράομαι, f. ήσομαι, Dep. to use improperly, misuse, abuse, c. dat., Polyb. 2. π. ἔς τινα to deal wrongly or unworthily with him, Hdt. II. = ἐκ παρέργου χράομαι, to treat with contempt, disregard, c. acc., Id. : Ion. part. παραχρεώμενοι, of furious combatants, setting nothing by their life, Id.

παραχρῆμα, Adv. for παρὰ τὸ χρῆμα, on the spot, forthwith, straightway, Hdt., Thuc., etc. :—with the Art., τὸ π. Hdt., Att. ; ἐκ or ἀπὸ τοῦ παραχρῆμα off-hand, immediate, Xen., etc. ;—ἐς τὸ π. Plat., etc. ;—ἐς τὸ π. ἀκούειν Thuc.

παρα-χρηστηριάζω, f. σω, to give a false oracle, Strab.

παρά-χροος, ον, contr. -χρους, ουν, (χρόα) of false or altered colour, colourless, faded, Luc.

παρα-χρώννῡμι, f. -χρώσω, to corrupt music by the ἁρμονία χρωματική, Arist.

παράχωμα, τό, a side embankment, a dyke, Strab. From

παρα-χώννῡμι, f. -χώσω, to throw up beside, Hdt.

παρα-χωρέω, f. ήσομαι, later -ήσω, to go aside, make room, give place, retire, etc. : π. τινί to give way, yield, submit, Plat., etc. :—π. τινός to retire from, Dem. 2. to step aside out of the way for another, as a mark of respect, ὁδοῦ π. πρεσβυτέρῳ Xen. ; π. τινί τοῦ βήματος Aeschin. ; τῇ πόλει παραχωρῶ τῆς τιμωρίας I leave the task of punishment to the state, Dem. 3. to concede a thing, c. acc., Plat. Hence

παραχώρησις, ή, a giving way : c. gen. a retiring from, τῆς ἀρχῆς Plut. ; and

παραχωρητέον, verb. Adj. one must give way, Xen.

παρα-ψάλλω, to touch lightly, Plut.

παρα-ψελλίζω, f. σω, to stammer out somewhat of the truth, Strab.

παραψῡχή, ή, cooling, refreshment, consolation, Eur. ; ἀλγέων π. Id. ; π. τᾷ πένθει Dem. From

παραψύχω [ῠ], to cool gently : metaph. to console, soothe, Theocr.

παρ-βασία, -βάτης, -βεβαώς, poët. for παρα-βασία, etc.

παρδᾰκός, όν, wet, damp, Ar. (Deriv. unknown.)

'παρδᾰλέη (sc. δορά), ή, a leopard-skin, Il., Hdt.; Dor. παρδαλέα, Pind. From

παρδᾰλεος, α, ον, (πάρδᾰλις) of a leopard.

παρδᾰλιο-κτόνος, ον, (κτείνω) leopard-killing, Anth.

πάρδᾰλις, ή, gen. εως Ion. ιος ; dat. ει, the pard, whether leopard, panther, or ounce, Hom., Att.

παρδᾰλωτός, ή, όν, (as if from παρδαλόω) spotted like the pard, Luc.

παρδεῖν, aor. 2 inf. of πέρδομαι.

παρέᾱσι, 3 pl. of πάρειμι (εἰμί sum).

παρεβάθην [ᾰ], aor. 1 pass. of παραβαίνω.

παρέβᾰλον, aor. 1 of παραβάλλω.

παρέβασκε, Ep. for παρέβη, 3 sing. aor. 2 of παραβαίνω.

παρέβην, aor. 2 of παραβαίνω.

παρ-έγγρᾰπτος, ον, illegally registered, π. πολίτης an intrusive citizen, Aeschin.

παρ-εγγράφω, f. ψω, to interpolate, Aeschin. ; παρεγγραφεὶς πολίτης = παρέγγραπτος, Id.

παρ-εγγυάω, f. ήσω, to hand over to another, to entrust or commend to his care, Hdt. II. as a military term, to pass on the word of command along the line, Lat. imperium tradere per manus, Eur., Xen. 2. of a general, to give the word to do a thing, command suddenly, π. τινι ποιεῖν τι Xen. 3. of a general also, to deliver an address before battle, Id. 4. to pledge one's word, promise, c. acc. et inf. fut., Soph.

παρ-εγγύη, ή, a word of command passed on, Xen.

παρεγγύησις, ή, (παρεγγυάω) a passing on the word of command, Xen.

παρ-εγείρω, f. -εγερῶ, to raise partly, Plut.

παρ-εγκλίνω [ῑ], f. -κλῑνῶ, to make to incline sideways :—Pass. to incline sideways, Plut.

παρεδόθην, aor. 1 pass. of παραδίδωμι.

παρέδρᾰθον, aor. 2 of παραδαρθάνω.

παρέδρᾰμον, aor. 2 of παρατρέχω.

παρεδρεύω, f. σω, (πάρεδρος) to sit constantly beside, attend constantly, be always near, Lat. assidere, c. dat., Eur. 2. of judges, to be an assessor, Dem.

πάρ-εδρος, ον, (ἕδρα) sitting beside, as at table, Hdt. : generally, sitting beside, near, τινι Eur. II. as Subst. an assessor, coadjutor, associate, foll. by dat. or gen., Pind., Eur. 2. in Prose, the assessor or coadjutor of a king or magistrate, Hdt.

παρέδωκα, aor. 1 of παραδίδωμι.

παρ-έζομαι, Dep. to sit beside, Theogn. ; cf. παρίζω.

παρεζόμην, aor. 2 med. of παρίζω.

παρέθηκα, aor. 1 of παρίημι.

παρεῖθεν, aor. 1 pass. inf. of παρίημι.

πᾰρειά, ή, the cheek, mostly in pl., (παρήιον being used by Hom. for sing.), Hom., Trag. (Prob. from παρά, being literally the side of the face.)

πᾰρείας, ου, ό, a reddish-brown snake, sacred to Aesculapius, Ar., Dem. (Deriv. unknown.)

παρ-εῖδον, aor. 2, παροράω being used as the pres. :—to observe by the way, notice, τί τινι something in one, Hdt. II. to look past, overlook, disregard, Dem.

παρείθην, aor. 1 pass. of παρίημι.

παρ-εικάζω, f. σω, to compare, τινί τι Plat.

παρείκω, f. ξω : poët. aor. 2 παρείκαθον, inf. -αθεῖν :—to give way, τινί τι, use, Soph. ; absol. to permit, allow, Plat. ; κατὰ τὸ παρεῖκον by such ways as were practicable, Thuc. II. impers., παρείκει μοι it is compe-

tent, allowable for me, εἴ μοι παρείκοι Soph.; ὅπη παρείκοι *wherever it was practicable,* Thuc.

παρείμενος, pf. pass. part. of παρίημι.

παρείμην, aor. 2 med. of παρίημι.

πάρ-ειμι (εἰμί *sum*), Ep. 3 pl. παρέᾱσι, subj. παρῶ, Ep. παρέω, inf. παρεῖναι, Ep. παρέμμεναι, part. παρών, Ep. παρέων: impf. παρῆν, Ep. παρέην, 3 pl. πάρεσαν: Ep. f. παρέσσομαι:—*to be by* or *present,* Hom.   **2.** *to be by* or *near one,* c. dat., Od., Soph., etc.: *to be present in* or *at a thing,* Hom., Att.   **3.** *to be present so as to help, stand by,* Lat. *adesse,* τινι Il.   **4.** παρεῖναι εἰς . . , *to arrive at, to have come to, a place,* Hdt.; π. ἐπὶ δεῖπνον Id., Att.   **II.** *of things, to be by, to be ready* or *at hand,* Lat. *praesto esse,* Od., etc.; εἴ μοι δύναμίς γε παρείη *if power were at my command,* Ib.:—so of feelings, φόβος βαρβάροις παρῆν Aesch.; θαῦμα παρῆν Soph.   **2.** *of Time,* ὁ παρὼν νῦν χρόνος Id.; τὰ παρόντα (Ion. παρεόντα) *the present state of affairs, present circumstances,* Hdt.; ἐκ τῶν παρόντων *according to present circumstances,* Thuc.; ἐν τῷ παρόντι, opp. to ἐν τῷ ἔπειτα, Id.; πρὸς τὸ π. αὐτίκα Id.   **III.** impers., πάρεστί μοι *it is in my power* to do, c. inf., Hdt., Aesch., etc.; and without dat., παρῆν κλύειν *one might bear,* Aesch.   **2.** part. παρόν, Ion. παρεόν, *it being possible since it is allowed,* Lat. *quum liceret,* παρεὸν αὐτῷ βασιλέα γενέσθαι Hdt.

πάρ-ειμι (εἶμι *ibo*), inf. -ιέναι, used as f. of παρέρχομαι, and παρῄειν as impf.:—*to go by, beside* or *past, to pass by, pass,* Od., Plat., etc.:—*to go alongside,* Thuc.: *to march along the coast, of an army,* as παραπλέω *of a fleet,* Id., Xen.   **2.** c. acc. loci, *to pass by,* Hdt.; absol., Id.   **3.** *of Time, to pass on, pass,* Id.   **II.** *to pass by, overtake, surpass,* Xen.   **III.** *to pass into, enter,* Hdt., Eur.   **2.** *in discourse, to pass on* from one part of a subject to another, Ar.   **IV.** *in Att. Prose, to come forward,* Xen.; πάριτ' ἐς τὸ πρόσθεν Ar.   **2.** *to come forward to speak,* Plat., Dem.; οἱ παριόντες *orators,* Dem.   **V.** *to pass from man to man,* Xen.

παρεῖναι, inf. of πάρειμι (*adsum*).

παρ-εῖπον, aor. 2, with no pres. in use, παρά-φημι or παρ-αγορεύω being used instead, *to persuade by indirect means, to talk over, win over,* Il., Aesch.; παρειπών *by thy persuasions,* Il.:—c. acc. cogn. *to give such and such advice,* αἴσιμα παρειπών Ib.   [In Il. the first syll. is long, παρειπών, πάρειπ0ῦσα, the orig. form having been παρϜειπών.]

παρ-ειρύω, poët. and Ion. for παρερύω.

παρ-είρω, only in pres., *to fasten in beside, insert,* Xen.; νόμους παρείρων *if he adds observance* of laws, Soph.

πάρεις, aor. 2 part. of παρίημι.   **II.** aor. 2 pass. part. of πείρω.

παρεῖσα, v. παρίζω.

παρ-εισάγω, f. ξω, *to lead in by one's side, bring forward, introduce,* Isocr., N. T.   Hence

παρείσακτος, ον, *introduced privily,* N. T.

παρ-εισέρχομαι, Dep. with aor. and pf. act. *to come or go in beside or secretly,* Polyb.

παρ-εισπίπτω, aor. 2 -εισέπεσον, *to get in by the side, steal in,* Polyb.

παρ-εισρέω, f. -εισρεύσομαι, *to flow on beside,* Plut.

παρ-εισφέρω, *to bring in beside,* π. νόμον *to propose a new law to amend another,* Lat. *subrogare,* Dem.   **II.** *to apply besides,* N. T.

πάρ-εκ, before a vowel **πάρ-εξ:** (παρά, ἐκ):—**A.** as Prep., **1.** c. gen. loci, *outside, before,* παρὲκ λιμένος Od.; παρὲξ ὁδοῦ *out of* the road, Il.   **2.** like χωρίς, *besides, except, exclusive of,* παρὲξ τοῦ ἀργύρου Hdt.   **II.** c. acc. *out by the side of, along side of,* παρὲξ ἅλα Il.; παρὲξ τὴν νῆσον *away from* the island, Od.; παρὲξ δοῦρα *out of the way of* spears, Ib.; παρὲκ νόον *out of* sense and reason, *foolishly,* Il.; παρὲξ Ἀχιλῆα *without the knowledge of* Achilles, Ib.

B. as Adv., **1.** of Place, *out beside,* στῆ δὲ παρὲξ *hard by,* Il.; νῆχε παρὲξ *was swimming out along shore,* Od.   **2.** metaph. *beside the mark,* παρὲξ ἀγορεύειν Il.   **3.** ἄλλα παρὲξ μεμνώμεθα *let us talk of something else,* Od.; παρὲξ ἢ ὅσον *except so long as,* Hdt.

παρ-εκβαίνω, f. -βήσομαι: aor. 2 παρεξέβην:—c. gen. *to step out aside from, deviate from,* Hes., Arist.   **2.** c. acc. *to overstep, transgress,* Aesch., Arist.   **3.** absol. *to deviate,* Arist.: *to make a digression,* Id.

παρέκβασις, εως, ἡ, *a deviation from,* c. gen., Arist.; *of constitutional forms,* τυραννίς is a παρέκβασις from monarchy, oligarchy from aristocracy, Id.

παρεκέσκετο, Ion. for -έκειτο, 3 sing. impf. of παράκειμαι.

παρ-εκκλίνω [ῑ], f. -κλῐνῶ, *to deviate,* Aeschin.

παρ-εκλέγω, f. ξω, *to collect covertly,* π. τὰ κοινά *to embezzle* the public moneys, Dem.

παρ-εκπροφεύγω, *to flee forth from, elude,* ἵνα μή σε παρεκπροφύγῃσιν ἄεθλα (Ep. 3 sing. aor. 2 subj.), Il.

παρ-εκτείνω, f. -τενῶ, *to stretch out in line,* Polyb.

παρ-εκτελέω, f. -έσω, *to accomplish otherwise,* Mosch.

παρ-εκτέον, verb. Adj. of παρέχω, *one must cause,* Xen.

παρ-εκτός, Adv. *besides* or *except for,* c. gen., N. T.: —absol. τὰ παρεκτός *things external,* Ib.

παρ-εκτρέπω, f. ψω, *to turn aside, divert,* Eur.

παρ-εκτρέχω, f. -δραμοῦμαι, *to run out past,* Plut.

παρ-εκχέω, f. -χεῶ, *to pour out by degrees* :—Pass., *of rivers and lakes, to overflow,* Strab.   Hence

παρέκχῠσις, ἡ, *an overflowing,* of rivers, Strab.

παρέλαβον, aor. 2 of παραλαμβάνω.

παρέλασσα, Ep. for -ήλασα, aor. 1 of παρελαύνω.

παρ-ελαύνω or **-ελάω:** f. -ελάσω, Att. -ελῶ: aor. -ήλᾰσα, Ep. -έλᾰσα· -έλασσα:—*to drive by* or *past,* ἐναντίω δι' ἄρματε π. *to drive them past* one another, Ar.; τὰς αἶγας παρελάντα (Dor. pres. part. acc.) Theocr.   **II.** intr., **1.** *to drive by,* Il.:—then c. acc. pers. *to drive past, overtake,* Ib., Xen.   **2.** *to row* or *sail past,* Od.; c. acc. pers., Σειρῆνας παρήλασε Ib.   **3.** *to ride by, run by,* c. acc., Xen.   **4.** more rarely *to ride up to, rush towards,* Id.: *to ride on one's way,* Id.

παρέλεκτο, 3 sing. Ep. aor. 2 pass. of παραλέγω.

παρελεύσομαι, f. of παρέρχομαι.

παρ-έλκω: f. ξω, also -ελκύσω [ῠ]: aor. 1 παρείλκῠσα: pf. pass. παρείλκυσμαι:—*to draw aside,* Pind.: —Med. *to draw aside to oneself, draw away from,* τὶ τινος Od.   **2.** *to lead alongside,* as one does a led horse, Hdt.; παρέλκειν ἐκ γῆς *to tow* [boats] from the bank, Id.; κενὰς παρέλκειν (sc. τὰς κώπας) *to pull* them through the air without dipping them, i. e. *to make a mere show of working,* Ar.   **II.** *to drag to one side, put off,* μὴ μυνῆσι παρέλκετε *put not*

things *off* by excuses, Od.   **III.** intr. *to be prolonged, to continue*, Luc.

παρ-εμβάλλω, f. -βᾰλῶ, *to put in beside, insert, interpolate, interpose*, τι Ar., Dem.; π. ὑποψίας *to insinuate* suspicions, Aeschin.   **2.** *to put* the auxiliaries *in line with* the legionaries, Polyb.   **II.** intr. *to fall into line, to encamp*, Id.

παρ-εμβλέπω, f. ψω, *to look askance*, Eur.

παρεμβολή, ἡ, (παρεμβάλλω) *insertion, interpolation*, Aeschin.   **II.** *an encampment, fortress*, N. T.

παρ-εμβύω [ῠ], f. -βύσω, *to stuff in*, Luc.

παρέμμεναι, Ep. for -εῖναι, inf. of πάρειμι (εἰμί sum).

παρ-εμπίπλημι, *to fill secretly with*, c. gen., Plut.

παρ-εμπίπραμαι, Pass. *to be inflamed by rubbing*, Strab.

παρ-εμπίπτω, f. -πεσοῦμαι : aor. 2 -ενέπεσον :—*to fall in by the way, creep* or *steal in*, Plat., Aeschin.

παρ-εμπολάω, f. ήσω, *to traffic underhand in* a thing, *to smuggle* a thing in, Eur.

παρ-εμπόρευμα, ατος, τό, *of small wares* : metaph. *an appendix*, Luc.   From

παρ-εμπορεύομαι, Dep. *to traffic in besides* :—metaph., τὸ τερπνὸν π. *to yield* delight *besides* instruction, Luc.

παρενεγκεῖν, aor. 2 inf. of παραφέρω.

παρενήνεον, impf. of παρανηνέω.

παρενήνοθε, v. ἐνήνοθε.

παρενθεῖν, Dor. for παρελθεῖν, aor. 2 inf. of παρέρχομαι.

παρ-ενθήκη, ἡ, *something put in beside, an addition, appendix*, Hdt.; παρενθήκην ἔχρησε ἐς Μιλησίους delivered an oracle *by way of parenthesis*, Id.

παρ-ενοχλέω, f. ήσω, *to trouble greatly*, N. T. :—Pass., καὶ ὑμεῖς παρηνωχλήσθε (2 pl. pf. pass.) Dem.

παρ-ενσαλεύω, f. σω, *to swing to and fro*, Ar.

παρ-εντείνω, f. -τενῶ, *to rouse to exertion*, Plut.

πᾰρέξ, v. παρέκ.

παρ-εξαίρω, f. -ἄρῶ, *to lift up beside*, Strab.

παρ-εξαυλέω, f. ήσω, whence part. pass. pf. **παρεξηυλημένοι**, of musical instruments, *worn out by being played upon*, and so, generally, *worn out*, Ar.

παρ-έξειμι (εἶμι ibo), inf. -εξιέναι, *to go out beside, pass by* or *alongside of*, c. acc. loci, Hdt.; absol., Id., Eur., etc.   **2.** *to turn aside out of the path*, Plat.   **II.** *to overstep, transgress*, Aesch., Soph.

παρεξ-ειρεσία, ἡ, *the part of the ship beyond the rowers*, at either end, Thuc.

παρ-εξελαύνω, f. -ελάσω, *to drive out past, to pass* in a race, Il. : *to row past*, c. acc., Od. : *to march by*, Hdt.   **II.** *to march out to meet*, ἀλλήλοις Plut.

παρεξελθεῖν, aor. 2 inf. of παρεξέρχομαι.

παρεξέμεν, Ep. for -εξιέναι, aor. 2 inf. of παρεξίημι.

παρ-εξέρχομαι, Dep. with aor. 2 -εξῆλθον, pf. -εξελήλῠθα :—*to go out beside, slip past*, Od.; π. ὁδοῦ Hdt.   **2.** παρεξελθεῖν πεδίον τυτθόν *to pass over* a little of it, Il.   **II.** *to overstep, transgress*, Διὸς νόον Od.; δίκην Soph.

παρ-εξετάζω, f. σω, *to examine by comparing*, Dem.

παρ-εξευρίσκω, -εξευρήσω, *to find out besides*, π. ἄλλον νόμον *to find out* another *different* law, Hdt.

παρ-εξίημι, *to let out beside* : of Time, *to let pass*, Hdt.

παρεξίμεν, Ep. for -εξιέναι, inf. of παρέξειμι (εἶμι ibo).

παρεοῦσα, Dor. part. fem. of πάρειμι (εἰμί sum).

παρ-έπαινος, ὁ, *subordinate* or *incidental praise*, Plat.

παρ-επάλλομαι, Ion. for παρ-εφάλλομαι.

παρέπεισα, aor. 1 of παραπείθω.

παρ-επιγράφω, f. ψω, *to correct an inscription*, Strab.

παρ-επιδείκνῠμαι, Med. *to exhibit out of season, make a display*, Luc.

παρ-επιστροφή, ἡ, *a turning round in passing*, Plut.

παρεπλάγχθην, aor. 1 of παραπλάζω.

παρέπλω, 3 sing. Ep. aor. 2 of παραπλέω.

παρ-έπομαι, f. -έψομαι, Dep. *to follow along side, follow close*, c. dat., Xen.; absol., Plat.

παρ-εργάτης, ου, ὁ, *a pottering workman*, Eur.

πάρ-εργον, τό, *a bye-work, subordinate* or *secondary business, appendage, appendix*, Eur.; πάρεργ' ὁδοῦ a *secondary purpose* of my journey, Id.   **II.** π. τύχης an unhappy addition to my fortune, Id.; πάρεργα κακῶν things useless to remedy my ills, Id. :—ἐν παρέργῳ as a *bye-work*, as subordinate or secondary, Lat. obiter, ἐν π. θέσθαι *to treat* as a *bye-work*, Soph.; ὡς ἐν π. Eur.; ἐκ παρέργου Thuc.

παρ-έρπω, f. ψω, *to creep secretly up to*, Theocr.   **II.** *to pass by*, Anth.

παρ-ερύω, -ειρύω, *to draw along the side*, φραγμόν Hdt.

παρ-έρχομαι, aor. 2 -ῆλθον, inf. -ελθεῖν, rarely -ήλῠθον : Dep. :—*to go by, beside* or *past, to pass by, pass*, Od.; παρῆλθεν ὁ κίνδυνος ὥσπερ νέφος passed away, Dem.   **2.** of Time, *to pass*, Hdt.; ὁ παρελθὼν ἄροτος the past season, Soph.; π. ὁδοί wanderings *now gone by*, Id.; ἐν τῷ παρελθόντι in time past, of old, Xen.; τὰ παρεληλυθότα past events, Dem.   **II.** *to pass by, outstrip*, Hom., Theogn., Att.; τοὺς λόγους τὰ ἔργα παρέρχεται Dem.   **2.** *to outwit, escape, elude*, Il., Hdt., Eur.   **III.** *to arrive at*, π. εἰς . . Hes.   **2.** *to pass in, εἰς τὴν αὐλήν* Hdt.; π. ἔσω or εἴσω *to go into* a house, etc., Trag.; c. acc., π. δόμους Eur.   **IV.** *to pass without heeding*, τεὸν βωμόν Il. : *to pass by, pass over, disregard, slight*, θεούς Eur.   **2.** *to overstep, transgress*, τοὺς νόμους Dem.   **V.** *to pass unnoticed, escape the notice of*, τουτὶ παρῆλθέ με εἰπεῖν Id.   **VI.** in Att. *to come forward* to speak, π. εἰς τὸν δῆμον Thuc.; absol., παρελθὼν ἔλεξε τοιάδε Id.

πάρεσαν, Ep. 3 pl. impf. of πάρειμι (εἰμί sum).

παρ-εσθίω, f. -έδομαι : aor. 2 -έφαγον, inf. -φάγεῖν :—*to gnaw* or *nibble at* a thing, c. gen., Ar.

πάρεσις, ἡ, (παρίημι) *a letting go, remission*, N. T.

παρ-εσκευάδαται, -άδατο, 3 pl. pf. and plqpf. pass. of παρασκευάζω.

παρεστάμεν, -άμεναι, Ep. for -εστάναι, pf. inf. of παρίστημι.

παρέστηκα, pf. of παρίστημι :—**παρέστην**, aor. 2.

παρ-έστιος, ον, (ἑστία) *by* or *at the hearth*, Soph. :—generally, = ἐφέστιος, Id., Eur.

πάρεσχον, aor. 2 of παρέχω.

παρ-έτρεσσα, Ep. for -έτρεσα, aor. 1 of παρατρέω.

παρ-ευδοκῐμέω, f. ήσω, *to surpass in reputation*, τινα Plut.

παρ-ευθύνω, *to direct, constrain*, Soph.

παρ-ευκηλέω, f. ήσω, *to calm, soothe*, Eur.

παρ-ευνάζομαι, Pass. *to lie beside* another, c. dat., Od.

πάρ-ευνος, ον, (εὐνή) *lying beside* or *with* :—metaph., πῆμα πατρὶ πάρευνον Aesch.

παρεύρεσις, ἡ, *the invention of a false pretext, a pretence*, Decret. ap. Dem.   From

παρ-ευρίσκω, f. -ευρήσω, aor. 2 -εῦρον :—*to discover*

besides, invent, Hdt.   2. Pass. *to be discovered besides,* aor. 1 παρευρέθην Id.

παρ-ευτακτέω, f. ήσω, (εὔτακτος) *to perform one's duty regularly,* Polyb.

παρ-εντρεπίζω, f. σω, *to put in order, arrange, make ready,* Eur.   2. *to arrange badly, neglect,* Id.

παρ-εφεδρεύω, f. σω, *to lie near to guard, to keep guard,* Polyb.

παρ-έχω: f. παρέξω or παρασχήσω: pf. παρέσχηκα:— aor. 2 παρέσχον, Ep. inf. παρασχέμεν, imper. παράσχες; poët. also παρέσχεθον, inf. παρασχεθεῖν.
    A. Act. *to hold beside, hold in readiness, to furnish, provide, supply,* Hom., etc.:—absol., πᾶσι παρέξω *I will provide* for all, Od.   2. *to afford, cause, grant, give,* φιλότητα, εὐφροσύνην Hom.; ὄχλον Hdt.; χάριν, εὔνοιαν Soph., etc.   II. *to present* or *offer* for a purpose, c. inf., [ὀῖες] παρέχουσι γάλα θῆσθαι Od.; π. τὸ σῶμα τύπτειν Ar.; π. ἑαυτόν τινι ἐρωτᾶν Plat.:—hence, absol., *to submit oneself,* ἰατροῖς παρέχουσι ἀποτέμνειν Xen.; πάρεχε ἐκποδών *make yourself* scarce, Ar.   2. with reflex. Pron. and a predicative, *to shew* or *exhibit* oneself so and so, π. ἑαυτὸν σοφιστήν Plat.; εὐπειθῆ Xen.; π. γῆν ἄσυλον *to offer* the country as an asylum, Eur.   III. *to allow, grant,* σιγὴν παρασχών Soph.;—c. inf. *to allow* one to do a thing, Id.   2. impers., παρέχει τινί c. inf. (where ὁ καιρός may be supplied), *it is allowed, easy, in one's power* to do so and so, Hdt., Eur., etc.:—so neut. part. used absol., παρέχον *it being in one's power, since one can,* Hdt., Thuc.   IV. in Att. *to produce* a person *on demand,* Xen., etc.   B. Med. παρέχομαι, f. -έξομαι and -σχήσομαι: pf. pass. (in med. sense) -έσχημαι:—*to supply of oneself* or *from one's own means,* Hdt., etc.   2. *to furnish, produce,* κροκοδείλους Id.   3. *to display* on one's *own part, exhibit,* προθυμίαν Id., etc.   II. in Att. law, παρέχεσθαί τινα μάρτυρα *to bring forward* as a witness, Plat.   III. *to produce* as one's own, ἄρχοντα παρέχεσθαί τινα *to acknowledge* as one's general, Hdt.; π. πόλιν, of an ambassador, *to represent* a city *in one's own person,* Thuc.   IV. *to offer, promise,* Hdt., etc.   V. *to make* so and so *for* or *towards* oneself, παρασχέσθαι θεὸν εὐμενῆ Eur.   VI. in Arithmetic, *to make up, amount to,* παρέχονται ἡμέρας διηκοσίας Hdt.

παρ-ηβάω, f. ήσω: pf. -ήβηκα:— *to be past one's prime, to be growing old,* Hdt., Thuc.

πάρ-ηβος, ον, (ἥβη) *past one's prime,* Anth.

παρηγάγον, aor. 2 of παράγω:—**παρῆγον,** impf.

παρηγορέω: impf. παρηγόρουν: f. -ήσω: aor. 1 -ησα:—Pass., aor. 1 -ήθην: (παρήγορος):—*to address, exhort,* Hdt., Aesch., etc.; c. inf. *to advise,* Eur.; so in Med., Hdt.   II. *to console, appease,* Aesch.

παρηγορία, Ion. -ίη, ή, *exhortation, persuasion,* Aesch.   II. *consolation,* Plut.

παρ-ήγορος, Dor. **παρ-ᾱγ-,** ον, (ἀγορεύω) *consoling,* and as Subst. *a comforter,* Soph.

παρήερθην, aor. 1 pass. of παραείρω.

παρήιξα, aor. 1 of παραΐσσω.

πάρηιον, τό, (Ion. for παρεῖον, which is not in use), *the cheek, jaw,* Hom.   II. παρήιον *the cheek-ornament* of a bridle, Il. Cf. παρειά.

πάρηίς, ίδος, ή, later form of foreg., Aesch., Eur.:—contr. **παρῆς,** ῆδος, Eur.; pl. παρῇδες Id.

παρῆκα, aor. 1 of παρίημι.

παρ-ήκω, f. ξω, *to have come alongside,* i.e. *to lie beside, stretch along,* Hdt., Thuc.   II. *to pass forth,* Soph.

παρήλᾰσα, aor. 1 of παρελαύνω.

παρῆλθον, aor. 2 of παρέρχομαι.

παρ-ῆλιξ, ικος, ὁ, ή, *past one's prime,* Plut., Anth.

πάρ-ημαι, properly pf. pass. of παρίζω, *to be seated beside* or *by,* c. dat., Il., Eur.; ἀλλοτρίοισι παρήμενος *seated* at other men's tables, Od.: generally, *to dwell with,* σύεσσι π. Ib.:—absol. *to sit beside* or *near,* Hom.

παρ-ήμερος, Dor. **-άμερος,** ον, *day by day, daily,* Pind.

παρήνουν, impf. of παραινέω.

παρηνώχλημαι, pf. pass. of παρ-ενοχλέω.

πάρ-ηξις, ή, (παρήκω) *a coming to shore: a landing-place,* Aesch.

παρ-ηονῖτις, ιδος, (ἠών) fem. Adj. *on the shore,* Anth.

παρηορία, ή, in pl. *side-traces,* i.e. *the traces by which the outside horse* (παρήορος) *was harnessed beside the regular pair,* Il.; ἐν δὲ παρηορίῃσι Πήδασον ἵει he harnessed Pedasus *with side-traces,* Ib.

παρ-ηόριος, α, ον, = sq. III, Anth.

παρ-ήορος, Dor. **-ᾱορος,** ον, (παραείρω) *hanging* or *hung beside:* παρήορος (sc. ἵππος) *a horse which draws by the side of the regular pair* (ξυνωρίς), *an outrigger,* elsewhere παράσειρος, σειραφόρος, Il.   II. *lying along, outstretched, sprawling,* Ib., Aesch.   III. metaph. (from the fact that the ἵππος π. was given to prancing), *reckless, distraught, senseless,* Il.

παρήπᾰφον, aor. 2 of παραπαφίσκω.

παρήρτητο, 3 sing. plqpf. of παραρτέομαι.

παρῆς, ῆδος, ή, contr. for παρηΐς, Eur.

παρθέμενος, aor. 2 med. part. of παρατίθημι.

παρθενεία, ή, (παρθένος) *maidenhood, virginity,* Eur.

παρθένεια, τά, v. παρθένια, τά.

παρθένειος, Ion. and poët. **-ήιος,** ον, *of* or *belonging to a maiden,* Pind., Aesch., Eur.

παρθένευμα, τό, in pl. *the pursuits* or *amusements of maidens,* Eur.; so in sing., *a maiden's work,* Id.   2. νοῦδν π. *the child of an unmarried woman,* Id.; and

παρθένευσις, ή, = παρθενεία, Luc. From

παρθενεύω, f. σω, (παρθένος) *to bring up as a maid,* Eur.:—Pass. *to lead a maiden life, remain a maid,* Hdt., Aesch.; πολιὰ (neut. pl.) παρθενεύεται *grows gray in maidenhood,* Eur.

παρθενεών, ῶνος, ὁ, Ion. for παρθενών, Anth.

παρθενία, ή, = παρθενεία, Pind., Aesch., Eur.

παρθένια (sc. μέλη), τά, *songs sung by maidens to the flute* (αὐλὸς παρθένιος) Pind.; so **παρθένεια,** τά, Ar.

παρθενίας, ου, ὁ, (παρθένος) *the son of a concubine:* Παρθένιαι *the youths* born at Sparta during the Messenian War, Arist.

παρθενική, ή, poët. for παρθένος, Hom., Eur.

παρθενικός, ή, όν, *of* or *for a maiden,* Plut.

παρθένιος, α, ον, and ος, ον, (παρθένος) like παρθένειος, *of a maiden* or *virgin, maiden, maidenly,* Od., Hes., Aesch., etc.   2. παρθένιος, ὁ, *the son of an unmarried girl,* Il.:—but, π. ἀνήρ *the husband of maidenhood, first husband,* Plut.   II. metaph.

pure, undefiled, h. Hom.; π. μύρτα, of *white* myrtle-berries, Ar.

Παρθενοπαῖος, ὁ, (παρθένος) *the Maiden-hero* or *Son of the Maiden* (Atalanta), one of the Seven against Thebes: [to be pronounced Παρθενοπαῖος in Aesch.].

παρθεν-οπίπης [ῐ], ου, ὁ, (ὀπιπτεύω) *one who looks after maidens, a seducer*, Il.

παρθένος, ἡ, *a maid, maiden, virgin, girl*, Hom., etc. **2.** Παρθένος, as a name of Athena at Athens, of Artemis, etc. **II.** as Adj. *maiden, virgin, chaste*, πάρθενον ψυχὴν ἔχων Eur.: metaph., π. πηγή Aesch.; παρθένοι τριήρεις *maiden*, i. e. *new*, ships, Ar. **III.** as masc., **παρθένος, ὁ,** *an unmarried man*, N. T. (Deriv. unknown.)

παρθενό-σφαγος, ον, (σφάζω) *of a slaughtered maiden's blood*, Aesch.

παρθενών, ῶνος, ὁ, (παρθένος) *the maidens' apartments, young women's chambers* in a house, mostly in pl., Aesch., Eur., etc. **II.** in sing. *the Parthenon* or *temple of Athena Parthenos* in the citadel at Athens, rebuilt under Pericles, Dem.

παρθεν-ωπός, όν, (ὤψ) *of maiden aspect*, Eur.

πάρθεσαν, Ep. for παρέθεσαν, 3 pl. aor. 2 of παρατίθημι.

παρθεσίη, ἡ, (παρατίθημι) *a deposit, pledge*, Anth.

Παρθιστί, Adv. *in the Parthian tongue*, Plut.

Πάρθοι, οἱ, *the Parthians*, Hdt.:—**Παρθυαία, ἡ,** *Parthia*, Strab.:—Adj. **Παρθικός, ή, όν,** Id.; **Παρθικά, τά,** *a history of Parthia*, Id.; so **Παρθίς, ίδος, ἡ,** Luc.

παρ-ιαύω, only in pres., *to sleep beside*, c. dat., Hom.

παρϊδεῖν, inf. of παρείδον.

παρ-ιδρύω, *to set up beside* :—in Med., Anth.

παρ-ίζω, *to sit beside* another, c. dat., Od., Hdt. **II.** Causal, *to seat* or *make to sit beside*, τινά τινι Hdt. :—Med. **παρίζομαι** *to seat oneself* or *sit beside*, Id., Bion; aor. 2 παρ-εζόμην, Ep. imper. -εζεο, Hom.

παρ-ίημι, 2 sing. παριεῖς : f. παρήσω : aor. 1 παρῆκα : 3 pl. aor. 2 παρεῖσαν, part. παρείς : pf. παρεῖκα :—Pass., aor. παρείθην, inf. παρεθῆναι : aor. παρείμην : pf. παρεῖμαι :—*to let drop beside* or *at the side, let fall*, Soph., Eur. :—Pass., παρείθη ποτὶ γαῖαν it *hung down* to earth, Il. **II.** *to pass by, pass over, leave out*, Lat. *omitto*, Hdt., Soph. **2.** *to pass unnoticed, disregard, let alone*, Lat. *praetermittere*, Hdt., Aesch.; τὰ παθήματα παρεῖσ᾽ ἐάσω Soph.; so in Pass., πόθος παρεῖτο Id.; παρεθῆναι Dem. **3.** c. inf. *to omit to do*, Plat., etc.; and with a negat. repeated, μὴ παρῇς τὸ μὴ οὐ φράσαι Soph. **4.** of Time, *to let pass*, τὸν χειμῶνα Hdt.; τὸν καιρόν Thuc. **III.** *to relax, slacken, remit, γόον, χόλον* Eur. :—Pass. *to be relaxed, weakened, exhausted*, Id., τοῦ ποδὸς παριέναι *to slack away* the sheet, v. πούς II. 2 ; so metaph., τοῦ μετρίου παρείς *letting go one's hold of* moderation, i. e. *giving it up*, Soph. **3.** *to remit* punishment, *to forgive, pardon*, Ar. **IV.** *to yield, give up*, Lat. *concedere*, νίκην τινί Hdt., Att. :—*to leave* a thing to another, σοὶ παρεὶς τάδε Soph. ; παρῆκεν, ὥστε βραχέα μοι δεῖσθαι φράσαι *left* it so that there is need for me to say but little, Id. **2.** *to permit, allow*, c. dat. pers. et inf., ἄλλῳ παρήσομεν ναυμαχήσειν Hdt.; absol., the inf. being understood,

Soph. **V.** *to allow to pass, let pass, let in, admit*, Hdt., Eur., etc.; so pf. pass. in med. sense, βαρβάρους εἰς τὰς ἀκροπόλεις παρεῖνται *have admitted* them into *their* citadels, Dem. **VI.** Med. **παρίεσθαί τινα** *to obtain leave from* him, *obtain* his *consent*, Soph., Plat. **2.** *to beg to be let off* something, οὐδέν σου παρίεμαι *I ask no quarter*, Plat. : *to beg a favour*, Id. ; παριέμεσθα *we ask pardon*, Eur.

παρ-ίκω [ῑ], poët. for παρήκω, of Time, *to be gone by*, Pind.

παρ-ιππεύω, f. σω, *to ride along* or *over*, πόντον Eur. : *to ride alongside*, Thuc.

παρ-ισόομαι, aor. 1 -ισώθην : (ἴσος) :—Pass. *to make oneself equal to, measure oneself with*, c. dat., Hdt., Theocr. **2.** *to be made equal* or *like to*, τινι Plat.

πάρ-ῐσος, ον, *almost equal, evenly balanced*, Polyb. : *of the clauses of a sentence*, Arist.

παρ-ιστάνω, late form of παρίστημι, Polyb.

παρ-ίστημι, A. Causal in pres., impf., fut. and aor. 1 *to make to stand* or *to place beside*, Polyb.; παραστήσας τὰ ὅπλα *having brought* his arms *into view*, Dem. **II.** *to set before the mind, present, offer, bring home to the mind*, c. inf., Id. ; π. τινι θαρρεῖν *to give* one confidence, Aeschin. **2.** *to make good, prove, shew*, Lys., N. T. **III.** *to set side by side, compare*, Isocr.

B. Pass., with aor. 2, pf. and plqpf. act., intr., *to stand by, beside* or *near*, Hom. ; so aor. 1 pass. part. παρασταθείς, Eur. **2.** *to stand by*, i. e. *to help* or *defend*, τινι Il., Hdt., Trag. **II.** in past tenses, *to have come, be at hand, be present*, Il. **2.** of events, *to be near, be at hand*, Hom. ; pf. part., Lat. *praesens*, τὸ χρῶμα τὸ παρεστηκός Ar. ; Att. also παρεστώς, ῶσα, ός, Trag. ; τὰ παρεστῶτα *present circumstances*, Aesch. ; πρὸς τὸ παρεστός Ar. **III.** *to come to the side* of another, *come over to* his *opinion*, Hdt. : absol. *to come to terms, surrender, submit*, Id., Dem. **IV.** *to happen to* one, Hdt. : *to come into one's head, occur to* one, δόξα μοι παρεστάθη Soph. :—impers., παρίσταταί μοι it *occurs to me*, Hdt., Thuc. **V.** absol., παρεστηκός = παρόν, *since it was in their power, since the opportunity offered*, Thuc.

C. Some tenses of Med., esp. fut. and aor. 1, are used in causal sense : **I.** *to bring forward, produce*, Xen. ; esp. *in a court of justice*, Dem. **II.** *to bring to one's side*, and so, **1.** *to bring over by force, bring to terms*, Hdt., Soph., etc. **2.** *to gain by kindness, win over*, Thuc., Dem. **3.** generally, *to dispose for one's own views* or *purposes*, Hdt.

παρ-ιστίδιος, α, ον, (ἱστός) *at the loom*, Anth.

παρ-ίσχω, collat. form of παρέχω, *to hold in readiness*, Il. : *to present, offer*, Ib.

παρίσωσις, ἡ, (παρισόω) *an even balancing of the clauses* in a sentence, Isocr.

παριτητέα, verb. Adj. of πάρειμι (εἶμι *ibo*), *one must come forward*, Thuc.

παρ-κατέλεκτο, 3 sing. Ep. aor. 2 pass. of παρακατα-λέγω.

παρκείμενος, poët. for παρακείμενος.

παρκύπτοισα, Dor. poët. for παρακύπτουσα.

παρμέμβλωκε, Ep. 3 sing. pf. of παραβλώσκω.

παρμένω, poët. for παραμένω.

παρμόνιμος, πάρμονος, poët. for παραμ-.

Παρνᾱσός, Ion. Παρνησός, ὁ, Parnassus, a mountain of Phocis, Od. :—Adj. Παρνάσιος, α, ον, and ος, ον, Parnassian, Pind. ; fem. Παρνᾱσιάς, άδος, Ion. Παρνησιάς, Eur. ; also Παρνησίς, ίδος, Aesch.

Πάρνης, ηθος, ἡ, (rarely ὁ) Parnes, a mountain of Attica, Ar. :—Adj. Παρνήθιος, α, ον, Id.

πάρνοψ, οπος, ὁ, a locust, Ar. (Deriv. unknown.)

παρ-οδεύω, f. σω, to pass by, Theocr. 2. c. acc. to go past, Luc.

παροδίτης [ῑ], ου, ὁ, a passer-by, wayfarer, Anth. :— fem. παροδῖτις, ιδος, Id.

παρ-οδοιπόρος, ὁ, = παροδίτης, Anth.

πάρ-οδος, ἡ, a by-way, passage, Thuc. 2. a going by, passing, Id. ; ἐν τῇ παρόδῳ as they passed by, Id. II. a side-entrance, a narrow entrance or approach, Xen.; λαβεῖν τὰς παρόδους (of Thermopylae), Dem. III. a coming forward, esp. before the assembly to speak, Id. 2. the first entrance of the chorus, their first song, Arist.

παρ-οίγνυμι or -οίγω, f. -οίξω, to open at the side or a little, half-open, h. Hom., Eur. ; παροίξας τῆς θύρας having opened a bit of the door, put it ajar, Ar.

πάροιθε [ᾰ], before a vowel -θεν: (πάρος): I. Prep. c. gen. before, in the presence of, Hom. 2. of Time, π. ἐμοῦ before me, Aesch. II. Adv., 1. of Place, before, in front, Il. 2. of Time, before this, formerly, Hom., Trag.; οἱ π. men bygone, Pind.; τῆς π. ἡμέρας Eur. 3. πάροιθεν πρὶν . ., Lat. priusquam, Soph.

παρ-οικέω, f. ήσω, to dwell beside, c. acc., π. τὴν Ἀσίαν dwell along the coast of Asia, Isocr. : c. dat. to live near, Thuc. : to dwell among, τισίν Id. ; of places, to lie near, Xen. II. (πάροικος II) to live in a place, sojourn, N. T. Hence

παροίκησις, ἡ, a neighbourhood, Thuc.

παροικία, ἡ, (πάροικος II) a sojourning in a foreign land, N. T.

παρ-οικίζω, f. σω, to place near :—Pass. to settle near, dwell among, τισίν Hdt.

παροικίς, ίδος, fem. of πάροικος, Strab.

παρ-οικοδομέω, f. ήσω, to build beside or across, Thuc.

πάρ-οικος, ον, dwelling beside or near, c. gen., Aesch., Soph. ; c. dat., Thuc. :—absol. a neighbour, Arist. 2. πάροικος πόλεμος a war with neighbours, Hdt. II. as Subst. a sojourner, alien, N. T.

παρ-οιμία, ἡ, (οἶμος) a by-word, common saying, proverb, maxim, saw, Aesch., Soph., etc.; κατὰ τὴν π. as the saying goes, Plat. 2. a parable, N. T.

παροιμιάζω, f. σω, to make proverbial :—Pass. to pass into a proverb, become proverbial, Plat. II. Med. to speak in proverbs, Id.

παροιμιακός, ή, όν, proverbial : Adv. -κῶς, Anth. II. παροιμιακόν (sub. μέτρον), τό, a paroemiac, i. e. an Anapaestic dimeter catalectic, used at the end of an Anapaestic system.

παροινέω : with double augm., impf. ἐπαρώνουν, ἐπαρώνησα; pf. πεπαρώνηκα:—Pass., ἐπαρωνήθην: pf. πεπαρώνημαι : (πάροινος):—to behave ill at wine, play drunken tricks, Oratt. 2. to act like a drunken man, Plat.; παροινήσας in a drunken fit, Plat. II. trans.

to treat with drunken violence :—Pass. to be so treated, Dem. Hence

παροινία, ἡ, drunken behaviour, drunken violence, a drunken frolic, Xen., etc.

παροινικός, ή, όν, addicted to wine, Ar.

πάροινος, ον, (οἶνος) = παροινικός, Ar. II. befitting a drinking party, Luc.; παροίνια drinking songs, Plut.

πάρ-οινος, ον, = παροινικός, Lysias, etc.

πάροίτερος, α, ον, Comp. of πάροιθε, the one before or in front, Il.

παρ-οίχομαι, f. -οιχήσομαι : pf. -ῴχηκα, Ion. -οίχωκα, and in late writers -ῴχημαι : 3 sing. Ion. plqpf. -οιχώκεε :—to have passed by, παρῴχετο γηθόσυνος κῆρ he passed on, went on his way, Il. 2. of Time, to be gone by, Ib.; ἡ παροιχομένη νύξ the by-gone night, Pind. ; τὰ παροιχόμενα the past, Hdt. II. c. gen., ὅσον μοίρας παροίχῃ how art thou fallen from thine high estate, Eur.

παρ-οκωχή, ἡ, redupl. form of παροχή, a supplying, furnishing, Thuc.

παρ-ολῑγωρέω, f. ήσω, to neglect a little, Xen.

παρ-ομαρτέω, f. ήσω, to accompany, Plut., Luc.

παρ-ομοιάζω, to be much like, τινί N. T.

παρ-όμοιος, ον, and α, ον, much like, nearly like, closely resembling, τινί Hdt., Thuc. :—absol., Hdt. 2. of numbers, nearly equal, Xen.

πάρόν, part. neut. of πάρειμι (εἰμί sum), q. v.

παρ-ονομάζω, f. σω, to alter slightly, Strab.

παροξυντικός, ή, όν, fit for inciting or urging on, Xen., Dem. 2. exasperating, provoking, Isocr.

παρ-οξύνω [ῡ], f. ὔνῶ, to urge, prick or spur on, stimulate, Xen., Dem. 2. to anger, provoke, irritate, exasperate, πατρὸς μὴ π. φρένα Eur., Thuc. :—Pass. to be provoked, Thuc., etc. Hence

παροξυσμός, ὁ, irritation, exasperation, Dem., N. T. : a provoking, N. T.

παρ-οπλίζω, f. ίσω, to disarm, Polyb. :—Pass., Plut.

παροπτέος, α, ον, (παρ-ψομαι) to be overlooked, Luc. II. παροπτέον, one must overlook, Dem.

παρόρᾱσις, ἡ, overlooking, negligence, Plut., Luc.

παρ-οράω, f. -όψομαι : aor. 2 παρεῖδον : aor. 1 pass. -ὤφθην : pf. pass. -ῶμμαι :—to look at by the way, notice, remark, Xen. ; τί τινι something in one, Hdt., Ar. II. to overlook, disregard, neglect, Xen., etc. III. to see amiss, see wrong, Plat. IV. to look sideways, Xen.

παρ-οργίζω, f. ιῶ, to provoke to anger, N. T. :—Pass., Dem. Hence

παροργισμός, ὁ, provocation ; anger, N. T.

παρ-όρειος, ον, (ὄρος) along a mountain, Strab.

παρ-ορίζω, f. σω, to outstep one's boundaries, encroach on a neighbour's property, Anth. Hence

παροριστής, οῦ, ὁ, an encroacher, Anth.

παρ-ορμάω, f. ήσω, to urge on, stimulate, Xen.

παρ-ορμέω, f. ήσω, to lie at anchor beside or near, Plut.

παρόρμησις, ἡ, (παρορμάω) incitement, Xen.

παρορμητικός, ή, όν, (παρορμάω) stimulative, Plut.

παρ-ορμίζω, f. Att. ιῶ, to anchor side by side, Lys.

πάρ-ορνῑς, ῑθος, ὁ, ἡ, ill-omened, Aesch.

παρ-ορύσσω, Att. -ττω, f. ξω, to dig alongside or parallel, Thuc. II. to dig one against another,

as was done by men in training for a preparatory exercise as the Olympic games.

παρ-ορχέομαι, Dep. *to represent by vulgar dancing*, Luc.

ΠΑ͂ΡΟΣ: **A.** Adv., **1.** of Time, *beforetime, formerly, erst*, Hom., Trag. ; θεοὶ οἱ πάρος Aesch. ; τά τε πάρος τά τ᾽ εἰσέπειτα Soph., etc. **2.** like πρίν, *before*, Lat. *priusquam*, c. inf., πάρος τάδε ἔργα γενέσθαι Il. **3.** anteced. to πρίν γε, πάρος δ᾽ οὐκ ἔσσεται ἄλλως, πρίν γε . . *not until*, Ib. **4.** *before the time, too soon*, Ib. **5.** *rather, sooner*, Ib. **II.** rarely of Place, *first*, σοι βαδιστέον π. Soph. **B.** Prep., poët. = πρό, **I.** of Place, *before*, Il., Soph., Eur. **II.** of Time, θανεῖν πάρος τέκνων Eur. **III.** Causal, *before, above, in preference to*, Id. **2.** *for, instead of*, ἀδελφῶν πάρος θανεῖν Id.

Πάρος [ᾰ], ἡ, *Paros*, one of the Cyclades, famous for its white marble, h. Hom. :—Adj. **Πάριος, α, ον**, Πάριος λίθος *Parian* marble, Pind., Hdt.

παρ-οτρύνω, f. ῠνῶ, *to urge* one *on* to do a thing, Pind.

παρουσία, ἡ, (πάρειμι) *a being present, presence*, Aesch., Eur., etc. ; so, πόλις μείζων τῆς ἡμετέρας παρουσίας = ἡμῶν τῶν παρόντων, Thuc. :—of things, κακῶν π. Eur. :—παρουσίαν ἔχειν for παρεῖναι, Soph. **2.** *arrival*, Id., Eur. :—*the Advent*, N. T.

παρ-οχέομαι, Pass. *to sit beside in a chariot*, τινι Xen.

παρ-οχετεύω, f. σω, *to turn from its course, divert*, Plut. :—metaph., τοῦτ᾽ αὖ παρωχέτευσα εὖ Eur.

παροχή, ἡ, (παρέχω) *a supplying, furnishing*, νεῶν παροχῇ *with liability to furnish* ships, Thuc.

παρ-οχλίζω, f. σω, *to move as with a lever*, Anth.

πάρ-οχος, ὁ, one who goes beside another *in a chariot*, one who attends the bridegroom (v. παράνυμφος), Ar.

παρ-οψάομαι, Dep. *to eat dainties*, Luc.

παρ-οψίς, ίδος, ἡ, (ὄψον) *a dainty sidedish*, Xen.

παρόψομαι, f. of παροράω.

παρ-οψώνημα, ατος, τό, (ὀψωνέω) *an addition to the regular fare, a dainty*, metaph., π. χλιδῆς *a new relish to* luxury, Aesch.

παρπεπῐθών, Ep. redupl. aor. 2 part. of παραπείθω.

παρπόδιος, poët. for παρα-πόδιος.

παρ-ρησία, ἡ, (πᾶς, ῥῆσις) *freespokenness, openness, frankness*, Eur. ; μετὰ παρρησίας Dem. **2.** in bad sense, *licence of tongue*, Isocr.

παρρησιάζομαι, f. άσομαι : aor. 1 ἐπαρρησιασάμην : pf. πεπαρρησίασμαι (in act. and pass. sense) : Dep. : —*to speak freely, openly, boldly*, Plat., etc. Hence

παρρησιαστής, οῦ, ὁ, *a free speaker*, Arist. ; and

παρρησιαστικός, ή, όν, *freespoken*, Arist.

παρσένος, Lacon. for παρθένος.

παρσταίην, Ep. for παρασταίην, aor. 2 opt. of παρίστημι :—**παρστάς**, part.

παρστήετον, Ep. for παραστῆτον, 2 dual aor. 2 subj. of παρίστημι.

παρτέμνω, Ep. for παρατέμνω :—**παρταμών**, for παρα-ταμών, aor. 2 part.

παρτιθεῖ, poët. for παρατιθεῖ, 3 sing. of παρατίθημι.

παρ-υφαίνω, f. ᾰνῶ : Pass., pf. παρύφασμαι : —*to furnish with a hem* or border (παρυφή) :—ὅπλα παρυφασμένα *armed men hemming in* an unarmed crowd, Xen.

παρ-υφή, ἡ, *a border woven along* a robe, Lat. *clavus*.

πάρφαινε, poët. for παρέφαινε, 3 sing. impf. of παραφαίνω.

παρφάμενος, poët. for παραφάμενος, aor. 2 med. part. of παράφημι :—**παρφάσθαι**, inf.

πάρφασις, -φασία, poët. for παράφασις, -φασία.

παρφέρω, poët. for παραφέρω.

παρφύγέειν, Ep. for -φυγεῖν, aor. 2 inf. of παραφεύγω.

πάρ-φυκτος, poët. for παράφυκτος, *to be avoided*, Pind.

παρῳδία, ἡ, *a song* or *poem in which serious words become burlesque, a burlesque, parody*, Arist. From

παρ-ῳδός, όν, (ᾠδή) *singing indirectly, obscurely hinting*, Eur.

παρ-ωθέω, f. -ώσω and -ωθήσω, *to push aside, reject, slight*, Soph., Eur. :—Pass. *to be set aside, slighted*, Xen., Dem. **2.** Med. *to push away from oneself, reject, renounce*, Eur., Aeschin. **3.** of Time, *to put off*, Plat.

παρ-ωκεάνιος, ον, *near* or *on the ocean*, Plut.

παρ-ώμᾰλος, ον, (ὁμαλός) *nearly even* or *equal*, Strab.

παρ-ωνύμιος [ῠ], ον, = sq., Plat. **II.** as Subst., παρωνύμιον, τό, *a derivative*, Id. **2.** *a surname*, Plut.

παρ-ώνυμος, ον, (ὄνομα) *formed by a slight change, derivative*, Aesch.

παρ-ώρεια, ἡ, (ὄρος) *a district on the side of a mountain*, Polyb.

παρ-ωρείτης, ου, ὁ, (ὄρος mons) *a mountaineer*, Anth.

πάρ-ωρος, ον, (ὥρα) *out of season, untimely* : neut. πάρωρα as Adv., Anth.

παρ-ωροφίς, ίδος, ἡ, (ὀροφή) *the projecting eaves* or *cornice* of a roof, Hdt.

ΠΑ͂Σ, πᾶσα, πᾶν: gen. παντός, πάσης, παντός: gen. pl. masc. and neut. πάντων, fem. πασῶν, Ion. πασέων, Ep. πασάων [σᾰ]: dat. pl. masc. and neut. πᾶσι, Ep. πάντεσσι :—Lat. *omnis, all*, when used of many; when of one only, *all, the whole*: **I.** in pl. *all*, πάντες τε θεοὶ πᾶσαί τε θέαιναι Il. ; τῶν Σαμίων πάντες Thuc. ; ἅμα πάντες, πάντες ἅμα all *together*, Il., etc. **2.** with a Sup., πάντες ἄριστοι all *the* noblest, Lat. *optimus quisque*, Hom. **II.** *all, the whole*, πᾶσα ἀλήθεια all *the truth*, Il. ; χαλκέη πᾶσα all of bronze, Hdt. ; ἣν ἡ μάχη ἐν χερσὶ πᾶσα all *hand to hand*, Thuc. ; ἡ πᾶσα βλάβη *nothing but* mischief, Soph. **III.** = ἕκαστος, *every*, Hom., etc. ; πᾶς χώρος *let everyone go*, Ar. :—also, πᾶς ἀνήρ Soph., etc. ; πᾶς τις *every single* one, Hdt., etc. ; πᾶς ὅστις . . Soph. ; πᾶν ὅσον Aesch., etc.

B. When the Art. is used, it is generally put after πᾶς, πᾶσαν τὴν δύναμιν all his force, Hdt. ; πᾶσαν τὴν ἀλήθειαν Thuc. **II.** πᾶς is put *between* the Art. and Subst., to denote *totality*, ὁ πᾶς ἀριθμός Aesch. ; τὸ πᾶν πλῆθος Thuc. **III.** as a Subst., τὸ πᾶν *the whole*, Aesch. ; τὰ πάντα *the whole*, Id.

C. With Numerals it marks an exact number, ἐννέα πάντες *quite nine, full* nine, no less, Od. ; δέκα πάντα τάλαντα Il. ; but, κτήνεα τὰ θύσιμα πάντα τρισχίλια ἔθυσε 3000 *of all kinds*, Hdt. **II.** with the Article, *in all*, οἱ πάντες εἷς καὶ ἐννενήκοντα Id.

D. Special Usages :—in dat. pl. masc. πᾶσι, *with* or *in the judgment of all*, Il., Soph. **2.** πᾶσι as neut., *in all things, altogether*, Soph. **II.** πάντα γίγνεσθαι *to become all things*, i. e. assume every shape, Od. ; εἰς πᾶν ἀφικνεῖσθαι *to venture everything*, Xen. **2.** πάντα εἶναί τινι *to be everything* to one, Hdt., Thuc.,

etc. 3. πάντα as Adv. for πάντως, *in all points, entirely, wholly,* Od., Soph., etc. :—but, τὰ πάντα *in every way, by all means, altogether,* Hdt. III. neut. sing. τὸ πᾶν *the whole, one's all,* περὶ τοῦ παντὸς δρόμον θέειν Id.; τοῦ π. ἐλλείπειν Aesch. : —τὸ πᾶν as Adv., *on the whole, altogether,* Soph., etc.; with a negat. *at all,* Aesch. 2. πᾶν *every-thing, anything,* πᾶν μᾶλλον ἢ στρατιήν *anything rather than an army,* Hdt.; πᾶν ποιῶν *by any means whatever,* Plat.; so, πάντα ποιῶν Dem. 3. ἐπὶ πᾶν *on the whole, in general, generally,* Plat. 4. παντὸς μᾶλλον *above all, absolutely, necessarily,* Lat. *ita ut nihil supra,* Id. :—in answers, π. γε μᾶλλον *yes, absolutely so,* Id. 5. with Preps., ἐς πᾶν κακοῦ ἀπικέσθαι *to all extremity* of ill, Hdt.; so, εἰς πᾶν ἀφικέσθαι Xen.; ἐς τὸ πᾶν *altogether,* Aesch. :—ἐν παντὶ ἀθυμίας εἶναι *in all extremity* of despair, Thuc. :—περὶ παντὸς ποιεῖσθαι *to esteem above all,* Lat. *maximi facere,* Xen. :—διὰ παντός (sc. χρόνου), or as one word διάπαντος, *for ever, continually,* Soph., Thuc., etc. : but also, *altogether,* Thuc., Plat.

πάσασθαι [ᾰ], aor. 1 inf. of πατέομαι : but II. πάσασθαι [ᾱ], of πάομαι.

πᾱσῐ-μέλουσα, ἡ, (μέλω) of the ship Argo, *a care to all,* i. e. *known to all,* Od.

πάσομαι [ᾰ], f. of πατέομαι : but II. πάσομαι [ᾱ], of πάομαι.

πασπάλη [ᾰ], ἡ, =παιπάλη, *the finest meal* : metaph., ὕπνου οὐδὲ πασπάλη *not a morsel of sleep,* Ar.

πασσᾱγία, ἡ, =πανσαγία.

πασσάλευτός, ή, όν, *pinned down,* Aesch. From

πασσᾱλεύω, Att. παττ-, f. σω, *to pin or fasten to,* τί τινι Aesch., Eur. 2. *to drive in like a peg,* Aesch.

πάσσᾱλος, Att. πάττ-, ὁ : Ep. gen. πασσαλόφι : (πήγνυμι) :—*a peg on which to hang clothes, arms,* etc., Hom., etc.; ἀπὸ πασσαλόφι ζυγὸν ᾕρεον Il.; ἀπὸ πασσάλου αἴνυτο τόξον Od.; ἐκ πασσαλόφι κρέμασεν φόρμιγγα Ib. II. *a gag,* Ar.

πασσάμενος, Ep. for πᾰσάμενος, aor. 1 part. of πατέομαι :—πάσσασθαι, inf.

πάσσαξ, ᾰκος, ὁ, =πάσσαλος, Ar.

πασ-σέληνος, ον, =παν-σέληνος.

πάσσος οἶνος, Lat. *vinum passum, raisin wine,* Polyb.

πάσ-σοφος, ον, πάν-σοφος.

πασ-σῠδεί, -δί, -δίῃ, -δίην, =πανσ-.

ΠΑ'ΣΣΩ, Att. πάττω : f. πάσω [ᾰ] : aor. 1 ἔπᾱσα : —Pass., aor. 1 ἐπάσθην : pf. πέπασμαι :—*to sprinkle,* φάρμακα πάσσων *laying* salves *upon* a wound, Il. : —c. gen. partit., πάσσε ἁλός *sprinkle some* salt, Ib. 2. *to besprinkle,* χρυσῷ, ῥόδοις π. τινά Ar. II. metaph. *to embroider, broider,* Il.; π. ἀέθλους *to work battles in embroidery,* Ib.

πάσσων, ον, gen. ονος, irreg. Ep. Comp. of παχύς, for παχύτερος or παχίων, *thicker, stouter,* Od.

παστάς, άδος, ἡ, =παραστάς, *a porch,* Hdt.: also, *a colonnade, piazza, corridor,* Xen. II. like θάλαμος, *an inner room, bridal chamber,* Eur., Theocr.; of the cave in which Antigoné was immured, Soph.

παστέος, ον, verb. Adj. of πάσσω, *to be besprinkled,* Ar.

παστός, ὁ, =παστάς II, *a bridal chamber,* Luc.

πάσχα, τό, indecl., the Hebrew *Passover* (from *pâsach to pass over*), *the paschal supper,* N.T.

ΠΑ'ΣΧΩ, f. πείσομαι : aor. 2 ἔπᾰθον : pf. πέπονθα : plqpf. ἐπεπόνθειν : all these tenses occur in Hom., and Att. :—Ep. forms, pf. πέποσθε for πεπόνθατε, pf. part. fem. πεπᾰθυῖα for πεπονθυῖα. Radical .sense, *to receive an impression from without, to suffer,* as opp. to *doing,* ἔρξαν τ' ἔπαθόν τε Od.; δρᾶν καὶ πάσχειν, etc.; ὁμοίως π. τινί *to be in* the same *case with* . . , Hdt. II. the sense is often limited by some word expressing good or evil : 1. κακῶς πάσχειν *to be ill off, in evil plight, unlucky,* Od., etc.; κακῶς π. ὑπό τινος *to be ill used, ill treated by* . . , Aesch.; often with an Adj., κακά, λυγρά π. Il., etc.; δεινὰ π. Dem.; also with a Subst., ἄλγεα π. etc., Hom. 2. εὖ πάσχειν *to be well off, in good case, lucky,* Theogn., etc.; also, *to receive benefits,* opp. to εὖ δρᾶν, Aesch., etc.; so, ἀγαθὰ π. Hdt., etc. 3. without a limiting word, it always refers to *evil,* being used for κακῶς or κακὰ π., μάλα πολλ' ἔπαθον Od., etc.; μή τι πάθῃς *lest thou suffer any ill,* Hom.; εἴ τι πάθοιμι or ἤν τι πάθω, a euphemism, *if aught were to happen to me,* i. e. if I were to die, Hdt., Att. 4. τί πάθω; *to express the extreme of perplexity, what is to become of me ? what can I do ?* Hom., etc.; τί πάσχεις; *what are you about ?* Ar. 5. the interrog. τί παθών; *expresses something amiss,* τί παθόντες γαῖαν ἔδυτε; *what ailed you that you died ?* Od. III. *to be affected* in a certain way, *be in a certain state of mind, entertain* certain feelings, Thuc., Plat.; ὅπερ ἂν οἱ πολλοὶ πάθοιεν *as would be the case with* most men, Thuc.; ἵνα μὴ ταὐτὸ πάθητε τῷ ἵππῳ *that it be not with you as with the horse in the fable,* Arist.; ὑῖκόν πάσχει *he is swinishly disposed,* Xen.; so of things, πάσχει τοῦτο καὶ κάρδαμα *this is just the way with cress,* Ar. IV. τὰ εὖ πεπονθότα *benefits received,* Aeschin.; cf. δράω.

πατά, Scythian word, =κτείνω, Hdt.

πᾰτᾰγέω, f. ήσω, (πάταγος) *to clatter, clash, clap,* of the sharp noise caused by the collision of two bodies, Ar.; of waves, *to dash, plash,* Theocr. : *to chatter,* as birds, Soph. II. trans., τύμπανα π. *to beat drums,* Luc.

ΠΑ'ΤᾹΓΟΣ, ὁ, *a clatter, crash,* of trees falling, Il.; *a chattering* of teeth, Ib.; *the plash* of a body falling into water, Ib.; *the rattling* or *crash* of thunder, Ar. : *a clashing* of arms, Hdt., Trag. (Formed from the sound.)

Πᾰταικίων, ωνος, ὁ, the name of *a notorious impostor,* Aeschin. :—from Πάταικοι, οἱ, Phoenician deities of dwarfish shape, forming the figure-heads of ships, Hdt.

πατάξ, v. εὐράξ.

ΠΑ'ΤΑ'ΣΣΩ, Ep. impf. πάτασσον : f. άξω : aor. 1 ἐπάταξα :—Pass., f. παταχθήσομαι : aor. 1 ἐπατάχθην : pf. πεπάταγμαι : I. intr. *to beat, knock,* Lat. *palpito,* θυμὸς ἐνὶ στήθεσσι πάτασσεν Il.; κραδίη στέρνοισι πατάσσει (as Shaksp., 'my heart *knocks* at my ribs') Ib. II. like πλήσσω, *to strike, smite,* π. τινὰ δορί Eur.; absol., Soph., etc.; of a deadly blow, ἐὰν λίθος ἢ σίδηρος πατάξῃ Dem. 2. πατάξαι θύραν *to knock at the door,* Ar. 3. metaph., πατάξαι θυμόν Soph.; π. καρδίαν Ar.

ΠΑΤΕ'ΟΜΑΙ : aor. 1 ἐπᾰσάμην, Ep. part. πασσάμενος : pf. πέπασμαι : Ep. plqpf. πεπάσμην :—*to eat,* σπλάγχν' ἐπάσαντο Il.; c. gen. partit. *to eat of, partake of,*

σίτοιό τ' ἐπασσάμεθ' ἠδὲ ποτῆτος Od. ; δείπνου πασσάμενος, etc., Ib. : absol. *to taste food*, οὔτι πεπάσμην Ib.

πᾰτερίζω, f. Att. ιῶ, (πατήρ) *to say* or *call father*, Ar.

πᾰτέριον, τό, Dim. of πατήρ, *little father*, Luc.

πᾰτέω, f. ήσω, (πάτος) *to tread, walk*, Pind., Aesch.   II. trans. *to tread on, tread*, πορφύρας πατεῖν Aesch. ; χῶρος οὐχ ἁγνὸς πατεῖν, i. e. *it is holy ground*, Soph. ; πατεῖν πύλας *to pass the gates*, Aesch.   2. *to walk in*, i. e. *to dwell in, frequent*, Soph., Theocr. :—metaph., like Lat. *terere*, εὐνὰς π. *to frequent, use, misuse*, Aesch. ; π. Αἴσωπον *to be always thumbing Aesop*, Ar.   3. *to tread under foot, trample on*, Aesch., Soph., etc.

ΠΑ·ΤΗ·Ρ, ὁ, gen. and dat. πατέρος, πατέρι, contr. Att. πατρός, πατρί : acc. always πατέρα : voc. πάτερ :—pl., πατέρες, πατέρας, πατέρων (rarely πατρῶν) : dat. πατράσι [ᾰ] :—*a father*, Hom., etc. ; πατρὸς πατήρ *a grandfather*, Il. ; τὰ πρὸς πατρός = πατρόθεν, *by the father's side*, Hdt.   II. among the gods *Zeus* is called πατήρ, πατὴρ Ζεύς, π. ἀνδρῶν τε θεῶν τε Hom., Hes.; so Ζεὺς π. Aesch.; Ζεῦ πάτερ καὶ θεοί Ar.   III. a respectful mode of addressing elderly persons, Od.   IV. metaph. *the father* of anything, Lat. *auctor*, π. ἀοιδᾶν Pind., etc.   V. in pl. *fathers*, i. e. *forefathers*, Hom. ; ἐξ ἔτι πατρῶν *as an inheritance from one's fathers*, Od.

πατησεῖς, Dor. for πατήσεις, 2 sing. fut. of πατέω.

πάτησμός, ὁ, (πατέω) *a treading on*, εἱμάτων Aesch.

ΠΑ·ΤΟΣ, ὁ, *a trodden* or *beaten way, path*, Hom. : —metaph., ἔξω πάτου *out-of-the-way*, Luc.

πάτρᾱ, Ion. πάτρη, ἡ, (πατήρ) :—*one's fatherland, native land, country, home*, Il., Trag. :—πατρίς was the common prose form.   II. *fatherhood, descent from a common father*, ὁμὸν γένος ἠδ' ἴα πάτρη Il. : then, like πατριά II, *a house, clan*, Lat. *gens*, Pind.

πατρ-άδελφος, ὁ, =πάτρως, Dem.

πάτρᾱθε, Adv., Dor. for πάτρηθε.

Πάτραι, ῶν, αἱ, *a city of Achaia*, now *Patras*, Thuc., etc. : Πατρέες, οἱ, *its citizens*, Hdt.

πατρ-ᾰλοίας, gen. α and ου, ὁ, voc. -αλοῖα : (ἀλοιάω) : —*one who slays his father, a parricide*, Ar., etc.

πάτρη, ἡ, Ion. for πάτρα.

πάτρηθε, Dor. -αθε, Adv. *from a race* or *family*, Pind.

πατριά, Ion. -ιή, ἡ, (πατήρ) *lineage, pedigree, by the father's side*, Hdt.   II. = πάτρα II, *a clan, house, family*, Id., N. T.

πατρι-άρχης, ου, ὁ, (πατριά II) *the father* or *chief of a race, a patriarch*, N. T.

πατρίδιον, τό, Comic Dim. of πατήρ, *daddy*, Ar.

πατρικός, ή, όν, (πατήρ) *derived from one's fathers, paternal, hereditary*, Ar., Thuc., etc.   II. *of* or *belonging to one's father*, ἡ πατρική (sc. οὐσία) *patrimony*, Eur. ; τὰ πατρικά Anth.   2. *like a father, paternal*, Arist.

πάτριος, α, ον, and ος, ον, (πατήρ) *of* or *belonging to one's father*, Lat. *patrius*, Pind., Soph., etc.   II. = πατρικός, *derived from one's fathers, hereditary*, οἱ π. θεοί Hdt., Ar., etc. :—τὰ πάτρια, Lat. *instituta majorum*, κατὰ τὰ πάτρια Ar., Thuc., etc.; rarely in sing., τὸ πάτριον παρεὶς *neglecting the rule of our fathers*, Thuc.   Cf. πατρῷος.

πατρίς, ίδος, poët. fem. of πάτριος, *of one's fathers*,

πατρὶς γαῖα, αἶα, ἄρουρα *one's fatherland, country*, Hom.   II. as Subst., like πάτρα, Il., Att.

πατριώτης, ου, ὁ, (πάτριος) *one of the same country, a fellow-countryman*, applied to barbarians who had only a common πατρίς, πολῖται being used of Greeks who had a common πόλις (or *free state*), Plat.; ἵπποι πατρ. Xen. ; by a metaph., *Mount Cithaeron is the* πατριώτης *of Oedipus*, Soph.

πατριῶτις, ιδος, fem. of πατριώτης, π. γῆ = πατρίς, Eur.

πατρόθεν, Adv. (πατήρ) *from* or *after a father*, πατρόθεν ἐκ γενεῆς ὀνομάζων *naming him by descent by his father's name*, Il. ; ἐμὸς τὰ πατρόθεν *mine by the father's side*, Soph. ; ἀναγραφῆναι π. *to have one's name inscribed as the son of one's father*, Hdt.   2. *coming from, sent by one's father*, π. ἀλάστωρ Aesch. ; π. εὐκταία φάτις *a father's curse*, Id.

πατρο-κᾰσίγνητος, ὁ, *a father's brother*, Hom., Hes.

Πάτροκλος, ον, *Patroclus the friend of Achilles*, the obl. cases as if from *Πατροκλεύς, gen. Πατροκλῆος, acc. Πατροκλῆα, voc. Πατρόκλεις, Il.; nom. pl. Πάτροκλοι, Ar. ;—a nom. Πατροκλῆς, Theocr.

πατροκτονέω, f. ήσω, *to murder one's father*, Aesch.

πατροκτονία, ἡ, *murder of a father, parricide*, Plut.

πατρο-κτόνος, ον, (κτείνω) *murdering one's father, parricidal*, Trag. ; π. μίασμα *the pollution of parricide*, Aesch. :—but χεὶρ πατροκτόνος *a father's murdering hand*, Eur.

πατρ-ολέτωρ, ορος, ὁ, (ὄλλυμι) *a parricide*, Anth.

πατρο-μήτωρ, ορος, ὁ, (μήτηρ) *a mother's father*, Luc.

πατρονομέομαι, Pass. *to be under a patriarchal government*, Plat.

πατρονομία, ἡ, *paternal government*, Luc.

πατρονομικός, ή, όν, *of* or *like a* πατρονόμος : ἡ -κή (sc. ἀρχή or τροφή) *the rule of a father*, Plat.

πατρο-νόμος, ον, (νέμω) *ruling as a father*.

πατρο-πάτωρ, ὁ, *a father's father*, Pind.

πατρο-στερής, ές, (στέρομαι) *reft of father*, Aesch.

πατρ-οῦχος, ή, *holding from the father* : π. πάρθενος *a sole-heiress*, Hdt.

πατρο-φονεύς, έως Ep. ῆος, ὁ, (*φένω) *murderer of one's father*, Od.

πατρο-φόνος, ον, (*φένω) *parricidal*, Aesch., Eur. :—as Subst. *a parricide*, Plat.

πατρο-φόντης, ου, ὁ, ἡ, =foreg., Soph.

πατρ-ωνύμιος, ον, (ὄνομα) *named after his father*, Aesch.

πατρῷος, α, ον, and ος, ον ; Ion. πατρώϊος, η, ον : (πατήρ) :—*of* or *from one's father, coming* or *inherited from him*, Lat. *paternus*, Hom., etc. ; ξεῖνος πατρώϊος *my hereditary friend*, Il. ; γαῖα πατρωΐη =*one's fatherland*, Ib.; πατρώϊα *one's patrimony*, Ib., etc. ; π. δόξα *hereditary glory*, Xen. ; Ζεὺς π. *also the god who protects a parent's rights*, Ar.   II. like πάτριος, *of* or *belonging to one's father*, Pind., Soph. ; τὰ πατρῷα *the cause of one's father*, opp. to τὰ μητρῷα, Hdt.

πάτρως, ὁ, gen. ωος and ω ; dat. πάτρῳ, acc. πάτρων : (πατήρ) :—*a father's brother, uncle by the father's side*, Lat. *patruus*, Hdt., Pind.

παττᾰλεύω, πάττᾰλος, πάττω, Att. for πασσ-.

παῦλα, ἡ, (παύω) *rest, a resting-point, stop, end, pause*, Soph. ; οὐκ ἐν παύλῃ ἐφαίνετο *there seemed to be no*

end of it, Thuc. *2.* c. gen., π. *νόσου cessation of disease* or *rest from* it, Soph. ; **παυλάν τιν' αὐτῶν** some *means of stopping* them, Xen.

παυράκι [ᾰ], Adv., like ὀλιγάκις, *seldom*, Theogn.

παυρίδιος, α, ον, = παῦρος, Hes.

παυρο-επής, ές, (ἔπος) *of few words*, Anth.

ΠΑΥ῀ΡΟΣ, ον, (παύω) *little, small*, of Time, *short*, Hes., Pind. 2. of number, *few*, Hom., Hes., etc. : Comp. **παυρότερος**, *fewer*, Il. ; —neut. pl. **παῦρα** as Adv. *few times, seldom*, Hes., Ar.

παυσ-άνεμος, ον, *stilling the wind*, θυσία Aesch.

παύσειεν, 3 pl. aor. 1 opt. of παύω.

παυσί-λῡπος, ον, (λύπη) *ending pain*, Eur.

παυσί-νοσος, ον, *curing sickness*, Anth.

παυσί-πονος, ον, *ending toil* or *hardship*, c. gen., Eur.

παυστέον, verb. Adj. of παύω, *one must stop*, Plat.

παυστήρ, ῆρος, ὁ, (παύω) *one who stops, calms, a reliever*, νόσου Soph.

παυστήριος, ον, *fit for ending* or *relieving*, νόσου Soph.

παυσωλή, ή, like παῦλα, *rest*, Il.

ΠΑΥ῀Ω, Ion. impf. παύεσκον : f. παύσω : aor. 1 ἔπαυσα : pf. πέπαυκα : —Med. and Pass., 3 sing. Ion. impf. παυέσκετο : f. παύσομαι, πεπαύσομαι, παυθήσομαι : aor. 1 ἐπαυσάμην, ἐπαύθην : pf. πέπαυμαι : I. Causal, *to make to cease* : 1. of persons, *to bring to an end, check, make an end of* (by death), Hom., etc. : —Pass. and Med. *to take one's rest, rest, cease, have done*, Il. : —also of things, *to make an end of, stop, abate*, Ib., etc. ; π. τόξον *to let* one's bow *rest*, Od. ; π. τὸν νόμον *to annul* it, Eur. ; π. τυραννίδα *to put* it *down*, Dem. 2. c. acc. pers. et gen. rei, *to make to rest, stop, hinder, keep back from* a thing, π. Ἕκτορα μάχης, etc., Hom., etc. : —π. τινὰ τῆς βασιλείας *to depose* one *from being king*, Hdt., etc. : —Pass. and Med. *to leave off from, rest* or *cease from*, πολέμου Hom., etc. ; τῆς μάχης Hdt., etc. ; ἐκ τρόχων πεπαυμένοι *at rest* from play, Eur. 3. rarely c. gen. rei only, αἴ κέ ποθι Ζεὺς παύῃ ὀϊζύος oh that Zeus *would make an end* of woe! Od. ; φάρμαχ', ἅ κεν παύῃσι ὀδυνάων Il. 4. c. part. praes. *to stop* a person from *doing* or *being*, π. τινὰ ἀριστεύοντα *to stop* him *from being* first, Il., Att. : —Pass. and Med. *to leave off doing* or *being*, ἄνεμος μὲν ἐπαύσατο θύων *left off* blowing, Od. ; the partic. omitted, αἷμα ἐπαύσατο the blood *stopt* [*flowing*], Il., etc. 5. inf. for part., ἔμ' ἔπαυσας μάχεσθαι Ib. ; with μή inserted, θνητούς γ' ἔπαυσα μὴ προδέρκεσθαι Aesch. II. intr. in imperat. *cease, leave off*, Soph., Ar. ; so, παῦε, παῦε τοῦ λόγου Ar.

Παφλᾱγών, όνος, ὁ, *a Paphlagonian*, Il. : —Adj. **Παφλαγονικός**, ή, όν, Xen.

παφλάζω, f. άσω, *to boil, bluster*, of the sea, Il. : — metaph. *to splutter, bluster*, of the angry Cleon (hence called Παφλαγών), Ar. (Formed from the sound.) Hence

πάφλασμα, ατος, τό, *a boiling*, of the sea : —metaph., **παφλάσματα** *blusterings*, Ar.

Πάφος [ᾰ], ή, *Paphos*, a town in Cyprus celebrated for its temple of Aphrodité, Od. : —Adj. **Πάφιος**, α, ον, of Aphrodité, Ar.

πάχετος, ον, seemingly a poët. form of παχύς, *massive*, as περιμήκετος of περιμήκης, Od.

παχθῇ, Dor. for πηχθῇ, aor. 1 pass. subj. of πήγνυμι.

πάχίων [ῐ], **πάχιστος**, irreg. Comp. and Sup. of παχύς.

πάχνη, ή, (πάγῆναι) *hoar-frost, rime*, Lat. *pruina*, Od., Aesch. : metaph., κουροβόρος π. *the clotted blood* of the eaten children, Aesch.

παχνόω, f. ώσω, (πάχνη) *to congeal, make solid* : metaph., ἐπάχνωσεν φίλον ἦτορ he *made* his blood *run cold, made* it *curdle*, Hes. ; Pass., ἦτορ παχνοῦται his *heart is cold and stiff* [with grief], Il. ; παχνοῦσθαι πένθεσιν, λύπῃ Aesch., Eur.

πάχος [ᾰ], εος, τό, (παχύς) *thickness*, Od., Thuc. : — absol., πάχος *in thickness*, Hdt. 2. π. σαρκός *stoutness*, Eur.

παχύ-κνημος, ον, (κνήμη) *with stout calves*, Ar.

πάχῡλός, ή, όν, (παχύς) *thickish* : Adv. -λῶς, *coarsely, roughly*, Arist.

πάχυ-μερής, ές, *consisting of thick* or *coarse parts* : metaph. in Adv. *roughly*, Strab.

πάχύνω [ῡ], f. ῠνῶ : pf. pass. πεπάχυσμαι : (παχύς) : — *to thicken, fatten*, Plat., Xen. : —Pass. *to grow fat*, Ar. : *to become thick*, of the skull, Hdt. 2. metaph. *to increase* : —Pass., ὄλβος ἄγαν παχυνθείς Aesch. 3. metaph. also *to make gross* or *stupid* : —Pass., N. T.

παχύς, εῖα, ύ, (πάγῆναι) *thick, stout*, Hom., Hes. : — later, *stout, fat*, Ar. 2. of things, *thick, massive*, Hom., Ar. : —Adv. -έως, *roughly*, of stating or arguing, Arist. ; παχύτερον or -έρως, Plat. 3. of liquids, *thick, curdled, clotted*, Il., Hdt. II. οἱ παχέες *the men of substance, the wealthy class*, Hdt. ; τοὺς παχεῖς καὶ πλουσίους Ar. III. in Com. and Prose, *thick-witted, gross, dull, stupid*, like Lat. *pinguis, crassus*, Id. IV. Comp. **παχύτερος**, Sup. -ύτατος : —irreg. Comp. **πάσσων**, ον, Od. : —Sup. **πάχιστος**, Il.

παχύ-στομος, ον, *speaking broad* or *roughly*, Strab.

πάχύτης, ητος, ή, (παχύς) *thickness, stoutness*, Hdt. 2. *the thickness* or *sediment* of liquor, Id.

πεδά, Aeol. and Dor. for μετά.

πεδάᾳ, Ep. 3 sing. of πεδάω : —**πεδάασκον**, Ion. impf.

πεδ-αίρω, Aeol. or Dor. for μετ-αίρω.

πεδ-αίχμιος, ον, Aeol. or Dor. for μετ-αίχμιος.

πεδ-ᾰμείβω, Aeol. or Dor. for μετ-αμείβω.

πεδ-άορος, ον, Aeol. and Dor. for μετ-ήορος.

πεδ-άρσιος, ον, Aeol. or Dor. for μετ-άρσιος.

πεδ-αυγάζω, Aeol. for μετ-αυγάζω.

πεδάω, Ep. 3 sing. πεδάᾳ : Ion. impf. πεδάασκον : f. ήσω : (πέδη) : —*to bind with fetters, to bind fast, make fast*, Od., Hdt., Aesch. 2. *to shackle, trammel, constrain*, Hom., Soph. ; c. inf. *to constrain* one to do a thing, Hom.

πεδ-έρχομαι, Aeol. and Dor. for μετ-έρχομαι, *to chase*.

πεδ-έχω, Aeol. for μετ-έχω.

πέδη, ή, (πέζα) *a fetter*, Lat. *pedica, compes*, mostly in pl. *fetters, shackles*, Il., etc. ; πεδέων (Ion.) ζεῦγος a pair *of fetters*, Hdt. ; metaph., πέδαι ἀχάλκευτοι *fetters* not forged by smiths, of the robe in which Agamemnon was entangled, Aesch. II. *a mode of breaking in* a horse, Xen.

πεδητής, οῦ, ὁ, (πεδάω) *a hinderer*, Anth.

πεδήτης, ου, ὁ, (πεδάομαι), *one fettered, a prisoner*, Luc.

πεδῐακός, ή, όν, (πεδίον) of or on the plain : —οἱ πεδιακοί *the party of the plain*, i. e. those who opposed Peisistratus, Arist. ; called οἱ ἐκ τοῦ πεδίου by Hdt. ; οἱ πεδιεῖς by Plut.

πεδιάς, άδος, poët. fem. of πέδιος, = πεδινός, *flat, level*, Hdt. : ἡ πεδιάς (sc. γῆ) *the level country*, Id. II. *on* or *of the plain*, Soph. ; λόγχη πεδιάς spearmen *on the plain*, Id.

πεδιάσιος, ον, (πεδίον) *of the plain*, Strab.

πεδιεύς, έως, ὁ, v. πεδιακός.

πεδι-ήρης, ες, (*ἄρω) *abounding in plains, level*, Aesch.

πέδῑλον, τό, (πέδη) mostly in pl. *sandals*, Hom., Hes., Eur. II. *any covering for the foot, shoes* or *boots*, Hdt. III. metaph., Δωρίῳ πεδίλῳ φωνὰν ἐναρμόξαι, i. e. to adapt the song to Doric *rhythm*, Pind. ; also, ἐν τούτῳ πεδίλῳ πόδ' ἔχειν to have one's foot in this *shoe*, i. e. to be in this condition or fortune, Id.

πεδῑνός, ή, όν, (πεδίον) *flat, level*, Hdt. : Comp. πεδινώτερος Plat. II. *of* or *on the plain*, Xen.

πεδίον, τό, (πέδον) *a plain* or *flat*, and collectively *a plain flat open country*, Hom., Hes., etc.

πεδίονδε, Adv. *to the plain*, Hom., Ar.

πεδιο-νόμος, ον, (νέμομαι) *dwelling in plains*, π. θεοί *gods of the country*, Aesch.

πεδο-βάμων [ᾰ], ον, (βαίνω) *earth-walking*, Aesch.

πεδόθεν, Adv. (πέδον) *from the ground*, Hes., Eur. II. *from the bottom*, Pind. : metaph. *from the bottom of the heart*, Od. 2. *from the beginning*, Pind.

πέδοι, Adv. *on the ground, on earth*, Aesch.

πεδο-κοίτης, ου, ὁ, (κοίτη) *lying on the ground*, Anth.

πέδον, ου, τό, (πούς) *the ground, earth*, h. Hom., Att. ; πέδῳ πεσεῖν *to fall on the ground, to earth*, Aesch. ; so, ῥίπτειν πέδῳ Eur. 2. = πεδίον, Soph., Ar.

πέδονδε, Adv. *to the ground, earthwards*, Il., Soph. 2. *to the plain*, Od.

πεδόσε, Adv. = foreg., Eur.

πεδο-στῐβής, ές, (στιβεῖν) *earth-treading*, Eur. :—*on foot*, opp. to ἱππηλάτης, Aesch.

πεδ-ώρυχος [ῠ], ον, (ὀρύσσω) *digging the soil*, Anth.

πέζᾰ, ης, ἡ, = πούς, Anth. II. metaph. the *bottom* or *end* of a body, πέζῃ ἐπὶ πρώτῃ at the far end, Il. 2. the *edge* or *border* of anything, of a garment, Anth.

πέζ-αρχος, ὁ, *a leader of foot*, Xen.

πεζ-έμπορος, ον, *trafficking by land*, Strab.

πεζ-έταιροι, οἱ, the *foot-guards* in the Macedon. army, the *horse-guards* being ἑταῖροι, Dem.

πεζεύω, f. σω, (πεζός) *to go* or *travel on foot, walk*, opp. to riding, Eur. 2. *to go by land*, opp. to going by sea, Xen. ; οἱ πεζεύοντες *land-forces*, Arist.

πεζῇ, v. πεζός III.

πεζῐκός, ή, όν, (πεζός) *on foot, of* or *for a foot-soldier*, τὸ πεζικόν *the foot, the infantry*, Xen. ; τὰ π. the *evolutions of infantry*, Id. 2. like πεζός, *of a land force*, opp. to a fleet, Id., Aeschin., etc.

πεζο-βᾰτέω, f. ήσω, *to walk over*, Anth.

πεζο-βόας, Dor. for -βόης, ου, ὁ, (βοάω) *one who shouts the battle-cry on foot, a foot-soldier*, Pind.

πεζομᾰχέω, f. ήσω, *to fight by land*, opp. to ναυμαχέω, Hdt., Ar. ; τισί with others, Thuc. ; π. ἀπὸ τῶν νεῶν *to fight like soldiers* from ship-board, Id.

πεζο-μάχης, ου, ὁ, = πεζομάχος, Pind.

πεζομᾰχία, Ion. -ίη, ἡ, *a battle by land*, opp. to ναυμαχία, Hdt., Thuc., etc. From

πεζο-μάχος [ᾰ], ον, (μάχομαι) *fighting on foot*, Luc. II. *fighting as a soldier*, opp. to ναυμάχος, Plut.

πεζο-νόμος, ον, (νέμω) *commanding by land*, Aesch.

πεζο-πορέω, *to go on foot*, Xen. II. *to go by land, to march*, Polyb. From

πεζο-πόρος, ον, *going by land*, Anth. ; ναύτης ἠπείρου, π. πελάγους, of Xerxes, Id.

πεζός, ή, όν, (πούς) : 1. *on foot*, πεζοί *fighters on foot*, opp. to horsemen, Hom. :—also *on land, going by land*, opp. to sea-faring, Id. :—so, ὁ πεζὸς στρατός, or ὁ πεζός alone, sometimes *foot-soldiery, infantry*, opp. to cavalry (ἡ ἵππος), Hdt., Xen. 2. ὁ πεζός, also, *a land-force* or *army*, opp. to a naval force, Hdt., Thuc. ; so, τὸ πεζόν Hdt. ; στρατιὰ καὶ ναυτικὴ καὶ πεζῇ Thuc. ; τὰ πεζὰ κράτιστοι strongest *by land*, Id. 3. *of animals, land*, as opp. to birds and fishes, τὰ π. καὶ τὰ πτηνά *beasts* and birds, Plat. II. metaph. of language, *not rising above the ground, prosaïc*, Luc. III. dat. fem. πεζῇ (sub. ὁδῷ) as Adv., *on foot*, Xen. 2. *by land*, Thuc.

πειθ-άνωρ [ᾱ], ορος, ὁ, ἡ, *obeying men, obedient*, Aesch.

πειθαρχέω, f. ήσω, *to obey one in authority*, c. dat., π. πατρί Soph. ; τοῖς νόμοις Ar. : absol. *to be obedient*, Arist. :—so in Med., Hdt.

πειθαρχία, ἡ, *obedience to command*, Aesch., Soph.

πειθαρχικός, ή, όν, *obeying readily*, Arist.

πειθ-αρχος, ον, (ἀρχή) *obedient*, Aesch.

πειθός, ή, όν, late form of πιθανός, N. T.

ΠΕΙ'ΘΩ, f. πείσω :—aor. 1 ἔπεισα : aor. 2 ἔπῐθον, Ep. redupl. 1 pl. subj. aor. πεπίθωμεν, πεπίθοιμεν, inf. πεπῐθεῖν, part. πεπῐθών: pf. πέπεικα :—Med. and Pass., f. πείσομαι : aor. 2 ἐπῐθόμην, Ep. πιθόμην, 3 sing. redupl. πεπίθοιτο : f. πεισθήσομαι : aor. 1 ἐπείσθην:—pf. πέπεισμαι. II. intr. tenses of act., in pass. sense, pf. 2 πέποιθα ; imperat. πέπεισθι, subj. πεποίθω, Ep. 1 pl. πεποίθομεν (for -ωμεν) ; opt. πεποιθοίην (for -θοι) ; plqpf. ἐπεποίθειν, Ep. πεποίθεα, syncop. 1 pl. ἐπέπιθμεν. III. as if from a collat. form πῑθω, Hom. has f. πῑθήσω and part. aor. 2 πῐθήσας, both intr. ; but the redupl. aor. 1 subj. πεπῐθήσω trans., Il.

I. Act. *to prevail upon, win over, persuade*, τινά Hom., etc. :—c. acc. pers. et inf. *to persuade one to do*, Il., etc. ; also, π. τινὰ ὥστε δοῦναι, etc., Hdt. ; π. τινα ὡς χρή Plat. ; π. τινὰ εἴς τι Thuc. ; in part., πείσας *by persuasion, by fair means*, Soph. II. Special usages : 1. *to talk over, mislead*, ἔλπετε δόλῳ καὶ ἔπεισεν Ἀχαιούς Od. 2. *to prevail on by entreaty*, Hom. 3. π. τινὰ χρήμασι *to bribe*, Hdt. ; so, π. ἐπὶ μισθῷ or μισθῷ Id., Thuc. : so, πείθειν τινά alone, Xen., N. T. 4. c. dupl. acc. πείθειν τινά τι *to persuade* one of a thing, Hdt., Aesch., etc.

B. Pass. and Med. *to be prevailed on, won over, persuaded*, absol., Hom., Att. ; the imperat. πείθου or πιθοῦ *listen, comply*, Trag. ; c. inf. *to be persuaded to do*, Soph. ; also, πείθεσθαι ὥστε . . Thuc. 2. πείθεσθαί τινι *to listen to* one, *obey* him, Hom., etc. ; νῦν μὲν πειθώμεθα νυκτὶ μελαίνῃ, of leaving off the labours of the day, Il. ;—πάντα πείθεσθαί τινι *to obey* him in all things, Od. ; etc. 3. πείθεσθαί τινι, also, *to believe* or *trust in* a person or thing, Hom., etc. : —c. acc. et inf. *to believe that*, Od., etc. : with an Adj. neut. π. τὰ περὶ Αἴγυπτον Hdt. ; ταῦτ' ἐγώ σοι οὐ πείθομαι *I do* not *take* this *on your word*, Plat. II. pf. 2 πέποιθα, like the Pass., *to trust, rely on, have*

confidence in a person or thing, Hom., etc.; c. inf., πέποιθα τοῦτ' ἐπισπάσειν κλέος *I trust to win this fame*, Soph.; πέποιθα τὸν πυρφόρον ἥξειν Aesch.;— πεπ. εἴς τινα, ἐπί τινα N. T.   III. pf. pass. πέπεισμαι *to believe, trust*, c. dat., Aesch., Eur.: c. acc. et inf., πεπ. ταῦτα συνοίσειν Dem.   Hence

Πειθώ, gen. όος contr. οῦς, ἡ, *Peitho, Persuasion* as a goddess, Lat. *Suada, Suadela*, Hes., Hdt., Trag.   II. as appellat., *the faculty of persuasion, winning eloquence, persuasiveness*, Aesch., Plat., etc.   2. *a persuasion in the mind*, Aesch.   3. *a means of persuasion, inducement, argument*, Eur., Ar.   4. *obedience*, Xen.

ΠΕΙΝΑ, Ion. πείνη, ης, ἡ, *hunger, famine*, Od., Plat.   2. metaph. *hunger* or *longing for* a thing, Plat.

πειναλέος, α, ον, also ος, ον, *hungry*, Anth.; π. πίνακες *empty dishes*, Id.

πεινάω (forms in αε contr. into η not ᾱ, as in διψάω), 2 and 3 sing. πεινῇς, ῇ, inf. πεινῆν, Ep. πεινήμεναι: impf. ἐπείνων: f. πεινήσω, later -άσω [ᾱ]: aor. 1 ἐπείνησα, ἐπείνᾱσα: pf. πεπείνηκα: (πεῖνα):—*to be hungry, suffer hunger, be famished*, Lat. *esurio*, Hom., etc.: πεινῶντι (Dor. for -ῶντι) μὴ προσενθῇς *don't go near a hungry man*, Theocr.   II. c. gen. *to hunger after*, Od.: —metaph., π. χρημάτων, ἐπαίνου Xen., N. T.

ΠΕΙΡΑ, ἡ, *a trial, attempt, essay, experiment*, Theogn., Soph., etc.; — πεῖραν ἔχειν *to be proved*, Pind.; but, πεῖραν ἔχειν τινός *to have experience of a thing*, Xen.; π. ἔχει τῆς γνώμης *involves a trial of your resolution*, Thuc.;— πεῖράν τινος λαμβάνειν *to make trial or proof of* . . , Xen., etc.:—πεῖράν τινος διδόναι, Lat. *specimen sui edere*, Thuc.   2. with Preps., ἀπὸ πείρης *experiment*, Hdt.:—εἰς πεῖράν τινος ἔρχεσθαι, ἰέναι Eur., Thuc.:—ἐν πείρᾳ τινὸς γίγνεσθαι *to be acquainted with, associate with* one, Xen.:—ἐπὶ πείρᾳ *by way of test or trial*, Ar.   II. *an attempt on or against* one, c. gen., Soph.   III. *generally, an attempt, enterprise*, Aesch., Soph.

πειράζω: Pass., aor. 1 ἐπειράσθην, pf. πεπείρασμαι:— like πειράω, *to make proof or trial of*, τινός Od.:—c. inf. *to attempt* to do, N. T.:—Pass., πεπειράσθω *let trial be made*, Plat.   II. c. acc. pers. *to try or tempt* a person, *put him to the test*, N. T.: absl., ὁ πειράζων *the Tempter*, Ib.:—Pass. *to be sorely tempted, to be tempted to sin*, Ib.

Πειραιεύς or **Πειραεύς,** ὁ, *Peiræeus*, the most noted harbour of Athens; gen. Πειραιέως, Att. Πειραιῶς, dat. Πειραιεῖ, acc. Πειραιᾶ, Ion. Πειραιέα.—Adj. **Πειραϊκός,** ή, όν, Plut.

πειραϊκός, ή, όν, *over the border*, γῆ π. *border-country, the March*, Thuc.

πειραίνω, aor. 1 ἐπείρηνα, (πεῖραρ) *to fasten by the two ends, to tie fast*, σειρὴν ἐξ αὐτοῦ πειρήναντε *having tied* a rope to him, Od.

πεῖραρ, ατος, τό, poët. for πέρας, *an end*, mostly in pl., πείρατα γαίης *the ends of the earth*, Hom.:—absol., πείρατα *the ends or ties of ropes*, Od.; cf. ἐπαλλάσσω.   II. *the end or issue of a thing*, Ib.; ἑκάστου πείρατ' ἔειπεν *of the issues or chief points*, Il.:—pleonastic, πείρατα νίκης = νίκη, πείρατ' ὀλέθρου = ὄλεθρος, Hom.   III. act. *that which gives the*

finish to a thing, πείρατα τέχνης, *the finishers of his art* (of tools), Od.

πειρασμός, ὁ, (πειράζω) *trial, temptation*, N. T.

πειραστικός, ή, όν, (πειράζω) *tentative*, Arist.

πειρατέον, verb. Adj. of πειράω, *one must attempt*, Plat.

πειρατεύω, (πειρατής) *to be a pirate*, Strab.

πειρατήριον, Ion. πειρητ-, τό, = πεῖρα, φόνια πειρατήρια *the murderous ordeal*, Eur.   II. *a pirate's nest*, Strab., Plut.   From

πειρατής, οῦ, ὁ, (πειράω) *a pirate*, Lat. *pirata*, i. e. *one who attacks ships*, Polyb., Plut.   Hence

πειρατικός, ή, όν, *piratical*, Plut.: τὰ π. *gangs of pirates*, Strab.

πειράω, f. άσω [ᾱ]: aor. 1 ἐπείρᾱσα: pf. πεπείρᾱκα: —Pass., aor. 1 ἐπειράθην [ᾱ].   B. Dep. πειράομαι, f. άσομαι, Dor. 2 pl. πειράσεῖσθε: aor. 1 med. ἐπειρᾱσάμην, Ion. -ησάμην, pass. ἐπειρήθην, Att. -άθην [ᾱ]: pf. πεπείρᾱμαι, Ion. -ημαι: Ion. 3 pl. plqpf. ἐπεπειρέατο: (πεῖρα).

A. Act. *to attempt, endeavour, try* to do, c. inf., Il., Hdt., etc.   II. c. gen. pers. *to make trial of* one, Il.: in hostile sense, *to make an attempt on*, Hom., Hdt.   III. absol. *to try one's fortune, try one's skill in thieving*, h. Hom.; ναυσὶ π. *to make an attempt* by sea, Thuc.; cf. πειρατής.   IV. c. acc. pers. *to make an attempt on*, Ar.

B. Dep. in the same sense, c. inf. *to try* to do, Il., Hdt.;—also foll. by εἰ, *to try whether*, Il.; by μή, Od.   II. most commonly, c. gen.,   1. c. gen. pers. *to make trial of* one, *to see whether* he is trustworthy, Hom., Hdt.:—also in hostile sense, *to make trial of the strength* of an enemy, Il.; π. τῆς Πελοποννήσου *to make an attempt* on it, Hdt.; τοῦ τείχους Thuc.   2. c. gen. rei, *to make proof or trial of* one's strength, Hom.:—*to try one's chance at* or *in* a work or contest, Id.:—also *to make proof of a thing, to see what it is good for*, τόξου, νευρῆς Od.:—*to make proof of, have experience of, make acquaintance with* others, Hdt., Thuc.   3. absol. *to try one's fortune, try the chances of war*, Il.   III. c. dat. modi, *to make a trial* or *attempt with*, ἐπειρήσαντο πόδεσσι *tried their luck* in the foot-race, Od.; σφαίρῃ πειρήσαντο Ib.; also, π. σὺν ἔντεσι, σὺν τεύχεσι πειρηθῆναι Il.   IV. c. acc. rei, ἣ ἕκαστα πειρήσαιτο or *should examine into* each particular, Od.   2. c. acc. pers. *to make an attempt on*, Pind.

πειρητίζω, Ep. form of πειράω, only in pres. and impf., *to attempt, try, prove*, c. inf., or absol., Hom.   II. c. gen. pers. *to make trial of*, Id.: c. gen. rei, σθένεος καὶ ἀλκῆς Id.   III. c. acc., π. στίχας ἀνδρῶν *to attempt*, i. e. *attack*, the lines, Il.

πεῖρινς, ινθος, ἡ, *a wicker-basket* fixed upon the ἅμαξα or carriage, being in fact *the body of the cart*, Hom.

ΠΕΙΡΩ: aor. 1 ἔπειρα, Ep. πεῖρα, Hom.:—Pass., pf. πέπαρμαι: aor. 2 ἐπάρην [ᾱ]:—*to pierce quite through, fix meat on spits*, for roasting, Il.; κρέα ἀμφ' ὀβελοῖσιν ἔπειραν Ib.:—also, διὰ πεῖρεν ὀδόντων ἔγχεῖ *he ran* him *through the teeth with a spear*, Ib.:— Pass., ἥλοισι πεπαρμένον *studded* with golden nails, Ib.; but, ὀδύνῃσι πεπαρμένος *pierced* with pain, Ib.; also, πεπαρμένη περὶ δουρί Ib.   II. metaph., κύματα

πείρειν to cleave the waves, Hom. ; πεῖρε κέλευθον clave her way [through the sea], Od.

πεῖσα, ης, ἡ, poët. for πειθώ, obedience, ἐν πείσῃ κραδίη μένε, i. e. it remained calm, Od.

πείσαις, Dor. for πείσας, aor. 1 part. of πείθω.

πείσειε, Aeol. for πείσαι, 3 sing. aor. 1 opt. of πείθω.

πεισέμεν, Ep. for πείσειν, fut. inf. of πείθω.

πεισί-βροτος, ον, persuading or controlling mortals, of a king's sceptre, Aesch.

πεισῐ-χάλινος, ον, obeying the rein, Pind.

πεῖσμα, ατος, τό, (πείθω) a ship's cable, Od., Aesch. :— generally, a rope, Od. (Properly, that which holds in obedience.)

πεισμονή, ἡ, = πειθώ, persuasion, N. T.

πείσομαι, f. med. of πείθω. II. irr. f. of πάσχω.

πεῖσος, τό, v. πίσεα.

πειστέον, verb. Adj. of πείθω, one must persuade, Plat. II. (from Pass.) one must obey, Soph., Eur.

πειστήρ, ῆρος, ὁ, = πεῖσμα, a rope, Theocr.

πειστήριος, α, ον, = sq., persuasive, Eur.

πειστικός, ἡ, όν, (πείθω) persuasive, Plat.

πείσω, fut. of πείθω.

πεκτέω, to shear, clip, Ar. From

ΠΕΚΩ, Ep. πείκω : Dor. f. πεξῶ: aor. 1 ἔπεξα :— Med., aor. 1 ἐπεξάμην :—Pass., aor. 1 ἐπέχθην :—to comb or card wool, Od. : Med., χαίτας πεξαμένη when she combed her hair, Il. 2. to shear sheep, Hes., Theocr. : Med., πόκως πέξασθαι to have their wool shorn, Simon. ap. Ar.

πελαγίζω, f. ίσω, (πέλαγος) to form a sea or lake, of a river that has overflowed, Hdt. :—of places, to be flooded, Id. II. to keep the sea, cross the sea, Xen.

πελάγιος, α, ον, and also ος, ον, (πέλαγος) :—of the sea, Lat. marinus, Eur. :—of animals, living in the sea, Id. 2. out at sea, on the open sea, Soph. ; of seamen or ships, Thuc., Xen.

πελᾰγῖτις, ιδος, fem. Adj. of or on the sea, Anth.

ΠΕΛΑΓΟΣ, εος, τό, gen. pl. πελαγέων, πελαγῶν : Ep. dat. πελάγεσσι :—the sea, esp. the high sea, open sea, the main, Lat. pelagus, Hom., etc. ; joined with other words denoting sea, ἁλὸς ἐν πελάγεσσιν (cf. aequora ponti), Od. ; πόντιον π. or πόντου π., Pind. ; ἁλς πελαγία Aesch. ; ἅλιον π. Eur. : often of parts of the sea (θάλασσα), Αἰγαῖον π. Aesch. ; ἐκ μεγάλων πελαγῶν, τοῦ τε Τυρσηνικοῦ καὶ τοῦ Σικελιοῦ Thuc. II. metaph., of any vast quantity, π. κακῶν a 'sea of troubles,' Aesch. ; π. δύης Id. ; εἰς τὸ π. τῶν λόγων Plat. ; also of great difficulties, Soph.

πελάζω, f. άσω, Att. πελῶ, poët. πελάσσω: aor. 1 ἐπέλασα, Ep. πέλασα, ἐπέλασσα, πέλασσα :—Med., 3 pl. aor. 1 opt. πελασαίατο :—Pass., aor. 1 ἐπελάσθην, also ἐπλάθην [ἄ]: Ep. 3 sing. and pl. syncop. aor. 2 pass. ἔπληντο πλῆντο πλῆντο : pf. πέπλημαι, part. ἐπεπλημένος : (πέλας) :

A. intr. to approach, come near, draw near or nigh, c. dat., πελάσειν νήεσσι Il. ; τούτοις σὺ μὴ π. Aesch., etc. 2. rarely c. gen., πελάσαι νεῶν to come near the ships, Soph. ; πελάζειν σῆς πάτρας Id. 3. with a Prep., π. πρὸς τοῖχον Hes. ; εἰς ὄψιν τινός Eur. ; c. acc. loci, δῶμα πελάζειν Id. ; οὐκέτι πελᾶτε will no more approach me, Soph. 4. absol., Xen.

B. Causal, to bring near or to, make to approach,

Κρήτῃ ἐπέλασσεν (sc. τὰς νέας) Od. ; νευρὴν μαζῷ πέλασεν brought the string up to his breast, in drawing a bow, Ib. ; ἐπέλασσα θαλάσσῃ στῆθος,in swimming, Ib. ; πέλασε χθονί brought them to earth, Il. ; π. τινὰ δεσμοῖς Aesch. :—metaph., π. τινὰ ὀδύνῃσι to bring him into pain, Il. ; ἔπος ἐρέω, ἀδάμαντι πελάσσας having made it firm as adamant, Orac. ap. Hdt. 2. followed by a Prep., με νῆσον ἐς Ὠγυγίην πέλασσαν θεοί Od.

C. in Pass., like the intr. Act. to come nigh, approach, etc., c. dat., Il. ; πλῆτο χθονί he came near (i. e. sank to) earth, Ib. 2. rarely c. gen., Soph. 3. foll. by a Prep., πελασθῆναι ἐπὶ τὸν θεόν Id. II. to approach or wed, of a woman, Aesch.

πελάθω [ἄ], collat. form of πελάζω (intr.), only in pres., Aesch. ap. Ar., Eur.

πέλανος, ὁ, any half-liquid substance, of various consistency, as oil, Aesch. ; clotted blood, Id. ; foam at the mouth, Eur. II. a mixture offered to the gods, of meal, honey, and oil, Aesch., Eur. (Deriv. unknown.)

πελαργῐδεύς, ὁ, a young stork, Ar.

Πελαργικός, ἡ, όν, = Πελασγικός : τὸ Πελαργικόν the northern slope of the Acropolis at Athens, Ar. ; written Πελασγικόν in Hdt., Thuc.

πελ-αργός, ὁ, the stork, Lat. ciconia, Ar., etc. (From πελός, ἀργός, properly, the black-and-white.)

πελαργ-ώδης, ες, (εἶδος) like a stork, Strab.

ΠΕΛΑΣ, Adv. near, hard by, close, c. gen., Od., Hdt., Trag. 2. like ἐγγύς, c. dat., Pind., Aesch. 3. absol., χριμφθεὶς πέλας Od. ; π. στείχειν, παρεῖναι, στῆναι Trag. II. οἱ πέλας (sc. ὄντες) one's neighbours, Thuc., etc. : hence one's fellow-creatures, all men, Hdt., Trag. : in sing., ὁ πέλας one's neighbour, any man, Hdt., Eur.

πελᾰσαίατο, Ep. 3 pl. aor. 1 med. opt. of πελάζω.

Πελασγός, ὁ, a Pelasgian ; in Il., the Pelasgians appear among the allies of the Trojans ; in Od. we hear of them in Crete ; but in Il., Achilles prays to Dodonaean Zeus as Pelasgian, and τὸ Πελασγικὸν Ἄργος was Thessalian Argos, the original seat of the Hellenes ; Hdt. contrasts them with the Hellenes ; but Πελασγοί is used for Greeks in Eur., as in Virg. Hence Adj. Πελασγικός, ἡ, όν, Thessalian, but later for Argive, Eur. :—so Πελάσγιος, α, ον, Aesch., Eur. :—Πελασγιῶται, οἱ, Pelasgiotes (in Thessaly), Strab. :—fem. Adj. Πελασγίς, ίδος, Hdt. (Deriv. uncertain.)

πελάτης [ἄ], ου, ὁ, (πελάζω) one who approaches or comes near, Soph. : a neighbour, Lat. accola, Aesch. II. esp. of one who approaches a woman, τὸν πελάταν λέκτρων Διός, of Ixion, Soph. III. one who approaches to seek protection, a dependant, Plat. ; the Rom. cliens, Plut.

πελάτις [ἄ], ιδος, ἡ, fem. of πελάτης, Plut.

πελάω, poët. form for the pres. πελάζω, inf. πελᾶν Soph. ; imperat. πέλα h. Hom.

ΠΕΛΕΘΟΣ, ὁ, ordure, Ar.

πέλεθρον,τό, older form of πλέθρον, Hom.

πέλεια, ἡ, (πελός) the wild-pigeon, rock-pigeon, stock-dove, so called from its dark colour, Hom., Soph. II. πέλειαι, αἱ, name of prophetic priestesses, prob. borrowed from the prophetic doves of Dodona, Hdt.

πελειάς, άδος, ἡ, = πέλεια, Il., Hdt., Trag. II. = foreg. II, Soph.

πελειο-θρέμμων, ον, (τρέφω) dove-nurturing, Aesch.

πελεκᾶς, ᾶντος, ὁ, the woodpecker, as if joiner-bird (from πελεκάω), Ar.

πελεκάω, f. ήσω, (πέλεκυς) to hew or shape with an axe, Lat. dolare, Od. (in Ep. aor. 1 πελέκκησε), Ar.

πελεκίζω, f. ίσω, (πέλεκυς) to cut off with an axe, esp. to behead, Polyb.

πελεκῖνος, ὁ, a water-bird of the pelican kind, Ar.

πελέκκησε, Ep. 3 sing. aor. 1 of πελεκάω.

πέλεκκον, τό, or **πέλεκκος**, ὁ, (πέλεκυς) an axe-handle, Il.

ΠΕ'ΛΕΚΥ-Σ, εως Ion. εος, ὁ: dat. pl. πελέκεσι, Ep. πελέκεσσι :—an axe for felling trees, with two edges, opp. to the ἡμιπέλεκκον, Hom., Xen. 2. a sacrificial axe, Hom.—That it was not, properly, a battle-axe appears from the phrase, οὐ δόρασι μάχεσθαι, ἀλλὰ καὶ πελέκεσι to fight not with spears only, but with common axes, i. e. to the last, Hdt. 3. in Theophr. Char., πέλεκυς as a child's nickname seems to mean a sharp blade.

πελεκυ-φόρος, ὁ, an axe-bearer, Lat. consul or praetor, before whom axes are carried, Polyb.

πελεμίζω, Ep. inf. -έμεν : Ep. aor. 2 πελέμιξα :—Pass., Ep. impf. πελεμίζετο : aor. 1 πελεμίχθην : (πάλλω) :—to shake, to make to quiver or tremble, Il.; π. [τόξον] to struggle at the bow, in order to bend it, Od. :—Pass. to be shaken, to tremble, quiver, quake, Il. 2. to shake or drive from his post, Ib. : Pass., χασσάμενος πελεμίχθη Ib.

πελέσκεο, Ion. and Ep. 2 sing. impf. of πέλομαι :— **πέλευ**, for πέλου, imper.

πελιδνός or **πελιτνός**, ή, όν, = πελιός, livid, Thuc.

πελιός, ά, όν, (πελός) livid, Dem.

πελιτνός, ή, όν, v. πελιδνός.

ΠΕ'ΛΛΑ, Ion. **πέλλη**, ης, ἡ, Lat. pelvis, a wooden bowl, milk-pail, Il., Theocr.

πελλός, ή, όν, v. πελός.

πέλομαι, v. πέλω.

Πελοπόννησος, ἡ, for Πέλοπος νῆσος, the Peloponnesus, now the Morea, h. Hom., etc. :—οἱ Πελοποννήσιοι, Hdt., etc. : Adj., **Πελοποννησιακός**, ή, όν, Strab. :— Adv., **Πελοποννᾱσιστί** in the Peloponnesian (i. e. Dorian) dialect, Theocr.

ΠΕΛΟ'Σ or **πελός**, ή, όν, Lat. pullus, dark-coloured, dusky, ash-coloured, Theocr.

Πέλ-οψ, οπος, ὁ, (πελός ὄψ) Pelops, i. e. Dark-face, son of Tantalus, who migrated from Lydia, and gave his name to Peloponnesus, Il.

πελτάζω, f. σω, (πέλτη) to serve as a targeteer, Xen.

πελταστής, οῦ, ὁ, (πελτάζω) one who bears a light shield (πέλτη) instead of the heavy ὅπλον, a targeteer, Lat. cetratus, Eur., Thuc., etc. The peltasts held a place between the ὁπλῖται and ψιλοί. Hence

πελταστικός, ή, όν, skilled in the use of the πέλτη, like a targeteer, Plat. :—ἡ -κή (sc. τέχνη) the art or skill of a targeteer, Id. ; τὸ -κόν, = οἱ πελτασταί, Xen. —Sup. Adv., **πελταστικώτατα** quite in the manner of πελτασταί, in the best style, Id.

ΠΕ'ΛΤΗ, ἡ, a small light shield of leather without a rim (ἴτυς), a target, Lat. cetra, orig. used by the Thracians, Hdt., Eur., etc. 2. a body of πελτασταί, Eur. 3. a horse's ornament, Id. II. = παλτόν, a shaft, pole, Xen.

πελτο-φόρος, ον, (φέρω) bearing a target, Xen.

πέλυξ, υκος, ὁ, a kind of axe, Babr.

πελῶ, Att. fut. of πελάζω.

ΠΕ'ΛΩ and **ΠΕ'ΛΟΜΑΙ**, only in pres. and impf. :—Act., mostly in 3 sing. pres. πέλει, Ep. impf. πέλεν, sync. with the augm. ἔπλεν : rare in other persons, ἔπελες, πέλες ; Dor. 1 pl. πέλομες, 3 pl. πέλοντι ; fem. part. πέλουσα. Much more common as Dep., in the same sense, πέλομαι, πέλει, πέλεται, πελόμεσθα, πέλονται : impf. syncop. 2 sing. ἔπλεο, contr. ἔπλευ, ἔπλετο, πέλοντο ; Ion. 2 sing. πελέσκεο : imperat. πέλευ : subj. πέληται, -ώμεθα, -ωνται : opt. πέλοιτο. The orig. sense, to be in motion, appears in Hom., κλαγγὴ πέλει οὐρανόθι πρό the cry goes, rises to heaven, Il. ; τῷ δεκάτῃ πέλεν ἠώς to him came the tenth morn, Od. ; γῆρας καὶ θάνατος ἐπ' ἀνθρώποισι πέλονται old age and death come upon men, Ib. :—this sense of motion is plain in the compd. participles ἐπιπλόμενος, περιπλόμενος. II. commonly to be, Hom. ; but generally implying continuance, to be used or wont to be, Il. :—the impf. in pres. sense, ὀϊζυρὸς ἔπλεο thou wast doomed to be, i. e. thou art, Ib.

ΠΕ'ΛΩΡ, τό, a portent, prodigy, monster, only in nom. and acc., of the Cyclops, Od. ; of Scylla, Ib. ; even of Hephaestus, Il.

πελώριος, ον, like πέλωρος, gigantic, Hom. : of things, huge, ἔγχος, λᾶας, κύματα Id. ; τὰ πρὶν πελώρια the mighty things, or mighty ones, of old, Aesch.

πέλωρον, τό, = πέλωρ, a monster, prodigy, of the Gorgon, Hom. ; of a large stag, Od. ; of the animals transformed by Circé, Ib. ; πέλωρα θεῶν portents sent by the gods, Il.

πέλωρος, η, ον, and ος, ον, (πέλωρ) monstrous, prodigious, huge, gigantic, with collat. notion of terrible, like πελώριος, Hom., Hes. :—neut. pl. as Adv., πέλωρα βιβᾷ he strides gigantic, h. Merc.

πέμμα, ατος, τό, (πέσσω) any kind of dressed food; but mostly in pl., pastry, cakes, sweetmeats, Hdt.

πεμπάδ-αρχος, ὁ, a commander of a body of five, Xen.

πεμπάζω, f. άσω, (πέμπε) properly to count on the five fingers, i. e. to count by fives, and then, generally, to count, Aesch. :—so in Med., ἐπὴν πάσας πεμπάσσεται (Ep. for πεμπάσηται aor. 1 subj.) when he has done counting them all, Od.

πεμπάς, άδος, ἡ, (πέμπε) a body of five, Plat., Xen.

πεμπαστής, οῦ, ὁ, (πεμπάζω) one who counts : used as a Verbal c. acc., μύρια π. reviewing by tens of thousands, Aesch.

πέμπε, Aeol. for πέντε.

πεμπταῖος, α, ον, (πέμπτος) on the fifth day, agreeing with the Subject, πεμπταῖοι ἱκόμεθα on the fifth day we came, Od. ; πεμπταῖον ἐγένετο it was on the fifth day, Dem. ; π. προκεῖσθαι to have been five days laid out as dead, Ar.

πεμπτέος, α, ον, verb. Adj. of πέμπω, to be sent, Luc. II. πεμπτέον, one must send, Xen.

πέμπτος, η, ον, (πέντε) the fifth, oneself with four others, πέμπτος μετὰ τοῖσιν Od. ; πέμπτος αὐτός Thuc. ; π. σπιθαμή, i. e. 4 cubits and a span, Hdt. ; τὸ πέμπτον μέρος a fifth, Plat. II. ἡ πέμπτη (sc. ἡμέρα) the fifth day, Hes., Ar.

πεμπτός, ή, όν, verb. Adj. sent, Thuc. From

ΠΕ'ΜΠΩ, Ep. inf. -έμεναι, -έμεν : Ion. impf. πέμπεσκε : f. πέμψω, Dor. πεμψῶ, Ep. inf. πεμψέμεναι : aor. 1 ἔπεμψα, Ep. πέμψα : pf. πέπομφα : 3 sing. plqpf. ἐπεμπόμφει, Ion. -εε :—Med., f. πέμψομαι : aor. 1 ἐπεμψάμην :—Pass., f. πεμφθήσομαι : aor. 1 ἐπέμφθην : 3 sing. pf. πέπεμπται, part. πεπεμμένος :—to send, despatch, Il., etc.; of a ship, to convey, carry, Od.; c. dupl. acc., ὁδὸν π. τινά to conduct one on his way, Soph. **II.** to send forth or away, dismiss, like ἀποπέμπω, to send home, Hom.; χρὴ ξεῖνον παρεόντα φιλεῖν, ἐθέλοντα δὲ πέμπειν, 'welcome the coming, speed the parting guest,' Od. **2.** of missiles, to discharge, shoot forth, Hes. **3.** of words, to send forth, utter, Aesch., Soph. **III.** to conduct, convoy, escort, Lat. deduco, Hom., etc.; ὁ πέμπων absol., of Hermes, Soph. :—πομπὴν πέμπειν to conduct a procession, Hdt., Thuc.; π. χορούς Eur., Xen. : in Pass., πέμπεσθαι Διονύσῳ to be carried in procession in his honour, Hdt. **IV.** to send with one, give as provision for a journey, Od., Hdt., etc. **V.** like ἀναπέμπω, to send up, produce, Soph. **B.** in Med., πέμπεσθαί τινα, = μεταπέμπεσθαι, to send for one, Soph., Eur. **II.** to send for one-self, to send in one's own service or cause some one to be sent, Soph.

πεμπ-ώβολον, τό, (πέμπε, ὀβελός) a five-pronged fork, for stirring the sacrificial fire, Hom.

πέμψειας, 2 sing. Aeol. aor. 1 opt. of πέμπω.

πεμψέμεναι, Ep. for πέμψειν, fut. inf. of πέμπω.

πέμψις, εως, ἡ, (πέμπω) a sending, mission, dispatch, Hdt., Thuc.

πεμψῶ, εῖς, εῖ, Dor. fut. of πέμπω.

πενεστεία, ἡ, = οἱ πενέσται, the class of Penestae, Arist.

πενέστατος, -τατος, Comp. and Sup. of πένης.

πενέστης, ου, ὁ, (πένομαι) a labourer, workman :—the πενέσται were the Thessalian serfs, ascripti glebae, Ar., Xen., etc. Like the Εἵλωτες in Laconia, they were orig. a conquered tribe, afterwards increased by prisoners of war, and formed a link between the free-men and the born slaves. **II.** generally, any slave or bondsman, Eur. :—a poor man, Ar.

πένης, ητος, ὁ, (πένομαι) one who works for his daily bread, a day-labourer, a poor man, distinguished from πτωχός (beggar), Hdt., Soph., etc. **II.** as Adj. of a poor man, δόμος Eur.; ἐν πένητι σώματι Id. : c. gen., π. χρημάτων poor in money, Id.; π. φίλων Plat. :—Comp. πενέστερος Xen.; Sup. πενέστατος Dem.

πενητο-κόμος, ον, (κομέω) tending the poor, Anth.

πενθάλεος, α, ον, sad, mourning, Anth.

πένθεια, ἡ, poët. form of πένθος, Aesch.

πενθείετον, Ep. for πενθεῖτον, 3 dual of πενθέω.

πενθερά, Ion. -ρη, ἡ, fem. of πενθερός, a mother-in-law, Lat. socrus, Eur.

ΠΕΝΘΕΡΟ'Σ, ὁ, a father-in-law, Lat. socer, Hom., etc. :—in pl. parents-in-law, Eur. **II.** generally, a connexion by marriage, e. g. brother-in-law, Id.

πενθέω, Ep. 3 dual πενθείετον, inf. πενθήμεναι : aor. 1 ἐπένθησα : pf. πεπένθηκα (πένθος) :—to bewail, lament, mourn for, Il.; πενθεῖν τινα ὡς τεθνεῶτα Hdt., etc. :—Pass. to be mourned for, Isocr. Hence

πένθημα, ατος, τό, lamentation, mourning, Aesch., Eur.

πενθήμεναι, Ep. inf. of πενθέω.

πενθ-ήμερος, ον, of five days, κατὰ πενθήμερον for alternate spaces of five days, Xen.

πενθ-ημι-μερής, ές, consisting of five halves, or two and a half :—in Prosody, τομὴ π. the caesura after two feet and a half, as in hexam. and iamb. verses.

πενθ-ημι-πόδιος, α, ον, (πούς) consisting of five half feet, i. e. of 2½ feet, Xen.

πενθ-ήρης, ες, (*ἄρω) lamenting, mourning, Eur.

πενθητήρ, ῆρος, ὁ, ἡ, (πενθέω) a mourner, Aesch. :—fem., κακῶν πενθητριά she who mourns for evils, Eur.

πενθητήριος, α, ον, (πενθέω) of or in sign of mourning, Aesch.

πενθικός, ή, όν, (πένθος) of or for mourning, mournful :—Adv. πενθικῶς ἔχειν τινός to be in mourning for a person, Xen.

πένθιμος, ον, mournful, mourning, sorrowful, Aesch., Eur. **II.** mournful, sorry, wretched, γῆρας Eur.

ΠΕ'ΝΘΟΣ, εος, τό, grief, sadness, sorrow, Hom., etc.; τινός for one, Od. :—esp. of the outward signs of grief, mourning for the dead, Hom., etc.; π. ποιήσασθαι to make a public mourning, Hdt. **II.** a misfortune, Hdt., Pind. **III.** of persons, a misery, Soph. (Related to πάθος, as βένθος to βάθος.)

πενία, Ion. -ίη, ἡ, (πένομαι) poverty, need, Od., etc.

πενιχραλέος, α, ον, collat. form of πενιχρός, Anth.

πενιχρός, ά, όν, like πένης, poor, needy, Od., Theogn.

ΠΕ'ΝΟΜΑΙ, Dep., used in pres. and impf. : **I.** intr. to work for one's daily bread; generally, to toil, work, labour, Hom. **2.** to be poor or needy, Solon, Eur., etc. **3.** c. gen. to be poor in, have need of, Aesch., Eur. **II.** trans. to work at, prepare, get ready, δαῖτα πένοντο Od.; τί σε χρὴ ταῦτα πένεσθαι; Ib.

πεντα-δραχμία, ἡ, five drachmae, Xen. From

πεντά-δραχμος, ον, (δραχμή) of the weight or value of five drachmae, Hdt.

πεντάεθλος, -άεθλον, poët. and Ion. for πένταθλος, -ον.

πενταετηρίς, ίδος, ἡ, (ἔτος) = πεντετηρίς, Arist. **II.** as Adj. coming every fifth year, Pind.

πεντα-έτηρος, ον, (ἔτος) poët. for πενταετής, five years old, Hom.

πεντα-ετής, ές, or πεντα-έτης, ες, five years old, Hdt. **II.** of Time, lasting five years, Thuc. :—neut. Adv. πεντάετες, for five years, Od.

πεντaετία, ἡ, = πεντετηρίς, Plut.

πεντά-ζωνος, ον, (ζώνη) with five zones, Strab.

πενταθλία, ἡ, = πένταθλον ;—so πεντάθλιον, τό, Pind.

πέντ-αθλον, Ion. -άεθλον, τό, the contest of the five exercises, Lat. quinquertium, Pind.; πεντάεθλον ἀσκεῖν or ἐπασκεῖν Hdt. :—These exercises were ἅλμα, δίσκος, δρόμος, πάλη, πυγμή, the last being exchanged for the ἀκόντισις or ἀκών; they are summed in one pentam., ἅλμα, ποδωκείην, δίσκον, ἄκοντα, πάλην.

πέντ-αθλος, Ion. -άεθλος, ὁ, one who practises the πένταθλον or conquers therein, Arist. : metaph. of 'a jack of all trades,' Xen.

πέντ-αιχμος, ον, (αἰχμή) five-pointed, Anth.

πεντάκις [ᾰ], (πέντε) Adv. five times, Pind., Aesch., etc. :—in late Poets πεντάκι, Anth.

πεντάκις-μύριοι [ῠ], αι, α, five times ten thousand, 50,000, Hdt.

πεντάκις-χίλιοι [ῐ], αι, α, five thousand, Hdt.

πεντάκοσι-άρχης or -άρχος, ὁ, the commander of 500 men, Plut.

πεντάκόσιοι, Ep. πεντηκόσιοι, αι, α, five hundred, Od., Hdt.   II. at Athens, οἱ πεντακόσιοι the senate of 500 (ἡ βουλή), chosen by lot (ἀπὸ κυάμου), 50 from each tribe, Dem., etc.

πεντάκοσιο-μέδιμνος, ὁ, possessing land which produced 500 medimni yearly, Thuc., Arist. :—acc. to Solon's distribution of the Athen. citizens, the πεντακοσιομέδιμνοι formed the first class.

πεντάκοσιοστός, ή, όν,the five-hundredth,one of 500,Ar.

πεντάκῦμία, ἡ, the fifth wave, supposed to be larger than the four preceding, Luc.

πεντά-μερής, ές, (μέρος) in five parts, Strab.

πεντά-πάλαστος or -πάλαιστος, ον, five handbreadths wide, long, Xen.

πεντά-πηχυς, υ, gen. εος, five cubits long or broad, Hdt.

πεντα-πλάσιος, α, ον, Ion. -πλήσιος, η, ον, five-fold, Hdt.; π. τινος five times as large as . . , Arist.

πεντάρ-ρᾱγος, ον, (ῥάξ) with five berries, Anth.

πεντ-αρχία, ἡ, a magistracy of Five, Arist.

πεντάς, άδος, ἡ, later form of πεμπάς.

πεντα-σπίθαμος, ον, five spans long or broad, Xen.

πεντα-στάδιος, ον, (στάδιον) of five stades, Strab. :— also πεντα-σταδιαῖος, ον.

πεντά-στίχος, ον, of five lines or verses, Anth.

πεντά-στομος, ον, (στόμα) with five mouths or openings, of rivers, Hdt.

πεντά-τευχος, ον, consisting of five books : as Subst., ἡ π. (sc. βίβλος) the five books of Moses, Pentateuch.

πεντάφυής, ές, (φυή) of five-fold nature, five, Anth.

πένταχά, (πέντε) Adv. five-fold, in five divisions, Il.

πενταχοῦ, (πέντε) Adv. in five places, Hdt.

ΠΕ'ΝΤΕ, Aeol. πέμπε, οἱ, αἱ, τά, indecl. five, Hom., etc.

πεντε-καί-δεκα, οἱ, αἱ, τά, indecl. fifteen, Hdt., etc.

πεντεκαιδεκά-ναϊα,ἡ,(ναῦς)a squadron of 15 ships,Dem.

πεντεκαιδεκά-τάλαντος, ον, worth fifteen talents, Dem.

πεντε-και-δέκατος, η, ον, the fifteenth, N. T.

πεντεκαιπεντηκοντα-ετής, ές, or -έτης, ες, twenty-five years old, Plat.

πεντ-επι-και-δέκατος, η, ον, poët. for πεντεκαιδέκατος, Anth.

πεντε-σύριγγος [ῠ], ον, (σύριγξ) with five holes, ξύλον π. a pillory, furnished with five holes, through which the head, arms, and legs of criminals were passed, Ar.

πεντε-τάλαντος [ᾰ], ον, (τάλαντον) worth or consisting of five talents, Dem. ; π. δίκη an action for the recovery of five talents, Ar.

πεντ-ετηρικός, ή, όν, happening every five years, quinquennial, Strab.   From

πεντ-ετηρίς, ίδος, ἡ, (ἔτος) a term of five years, Lat. quinquennium, διὰ πεντετηρίδος every five years, Hdt.   II. a festival celebrated every five years, Id., Thuc.

πεντ-έτης, ες, (ἔτος) of five years, σπονδαί Ar.

πεντε-τριάζομαι, Dep. to conquer five times, Anth.

πεντήκοντα, οἱ, αἱ, τά, indecl. fifty, Lat. quinquaginta, Il., etc.

πεντηκοντά-δραχμος, ον, worth fifty drachmae, Plat.

πεντηκοντα-ετής, ές, or -έτης, ες, (ἔτος) fifty years old, Plat.   II. of or lasting fifty years ; fem., πεντηκονταέτιδες σπονδαί Thuc.

πεντηκοντά-και-τρίετης, ες, of fifty-three years, Polyb.

πεντηκοντά-κάρηνος, ον, (κάρηνον) fifty-headed, Hes.

πεντηκοντά-παις, παιδος, ὁ, ἡ, consisting of fifty children, Aesch.   II. having fifty children, Id.

πεντηκονταρχέω, f. ήσω, to be a πεντηκόνταρχος, Dem.

πεντηκόντ-αρχος, ὁ, the commander of fifty men, Xen., Dem.

πεντηκόντερος, ἡ, πεντηκόντορος, Hdt.

πεντηκοντήρ, ῆρος, ὁ, the commander of fifty men, an officer in the Spartan army, Thuc., Xen.

πεντηκοντό-γυος, ον, (γύα) of fifty acres of corn-land, Il.

πεντηκοντ-όργυιος, ον, (ὄργυια) fifty fathoms deep, high, long, Hdt.

πεντηκόντορος (sc. ναῦς), ἡ, a ship of burden with fifty oars, Pind., Eur., Thuc.

πεντηκοντ-ούτης, ες, contr. for πεντηκοντα-έτης, fifty years old, Plat.

πεντηκόσιοι, αι, α, Ep. for πεντάκόσιοι, five hundred, Od.

πεντηκοστεύομαι, Pass. to be charged with the tax πεντηκοστή on any articles, Dem.

πεντηκοστο-λόγος, ὁ, (λέγω) a collector of the tax πεντηκοστή, Dem.

πεντηκοστός, ή, όν, (πεντήκοντα) fiftieth, Plat.   II. as Subst., ἡ πεντηκοστή,   1. (sub. μερίς), at Athens the duty of one-fiftieth, or two per cent., on all exports and imports, Oratt. ; εὕρηκε καινὴν ἱππικῆς τινα πεντηκοστήν he invented a new two per cent. duty, in lieu of his cavalry service, i. e. paid this instead of it, Dem.   2. (sub. ἡμέρα), the fiftieth day (after the Passover), Pentecost, N. T.

πεντηκοστύς, ύος, ἡ, (πεντήκοντα) a number of fifty, esp. as a division of the Spartan army, Thuc. ; κατὰ πεντηκοστῦς (acc. pl.) Xen.

πεντ-ήρης (sc. ναῦς), ἡ, a quinquereme, Hdt. :—so, πεντηρικὸν πλοῖον, σκάφος Polyb. :—v. τριήρης.

πέντ-οζος, ον, like πεντάοζος, with five branches : Hes. calls the hand πέντοζον, the five-branch.

πεντ-όργυιος, ον, (ὄργυια) of five fathoms, Anth.

πεντ-ώργυος, ον, Att. form of πεντόργυιος, Xen.

*πένω, v. πένομαι.

πεξάμενος, aor. 1 med. part. of πέκω.

πεξῶ, Dor. for πέξω, fut. of πέκω.

πέος, εος, τό, membrum virile, Ar., etc.

πεπᾰθυῖα, Ep. for πεπονθυῖα, pf. part. fem. of πάσχω.

πεπαίνω : aor. 1 ἐπέπᾱνα :—Pass., f. πεπανθήσομαι, aor. 1 ἐπεπάνθην : (πέπων) :—to ripen, make ripe, Hdt. ; absol., διασκοπῶν τὰς ἀμπέλους, εἰ πεπαίνουσιν ἤδη, i. e. if the grapes are ripening, Ar. :—Pass. to become ripe, Hdt., etc.   2. metaph. to soften, assuage anger, Ar., Xen. ; of a person, ἢν πεπανθῇς Eur.

πεπαίτερος and -τατος, irreg. Comp. and Sup. of πέπων.

πεπαλαγμένος, pf. part. pass. of παλάσσω :—πεπάλακτο, 3 sing. plqpf.

πέπαλμαι, pf. pass. of πάλλω.

πεπᾱλών, redupl. aor. 2 part. of πάλλω.

πέπάμαι, pf. of πάομαι : 3 pl. πέπανται.

πέπᾱνος, ον, rarer collat. form of πέπων, Anth.

πεπάρεῖν, aor. 2 inf., only in Pind., to display, manifest. (Origin uncertain.)

πέπαρμαι, pf. pass. of πείρω.

πεπάσθαι, pf. inf. of πατέομαι : but   II. πεπᾶσθαι, of πάομαι.

πεπάσμαι, pf. pass. of πατέομαι :—πεπάσμην, Ep. plqpf.

πέπειρος, ον, and α, ον, like πέπων, ripe, Lat. maturus, Anth. 2. metaph. softened, ὀργή Soph.

πέπεισθι, for πέποιθε, pf. imper. intr. of πείθω.

πέπεισμαι, pf. pass. of πείθω.

πεπέρασμαι, pf. pass. of περαίνω :—3 pl. πεπέρανται.

πεπερημένος, pf. pass. part. of περάω (B).

πέπερι, τό, pepper, the pepper-tree, Lat. piper :—gen. πεπέρεως, πέπεριος, πεπέριδος.

πεπέτασμαι, pf. pass. of πετάννυμι.

πέπηγα, intr. pf. of πήγνυμι.

πεπίθεῖν, Ep. redupl. aor. 2 of πείθω :—πεπίθοιμεν, -οῖεν, 1 and 3 pl. opt. :—πεπίθωμεν, 1 pl. subj.

πεπιθήσω, Ep. redupl. aor. 1 subj. of πείθω.

πέπλασμαι, pf. pass. of πλάσσω. Hence

πεπλασμένως, Adv. artificially, by pretence, Plat., Arist.

πέπλευσμαι, pf. pass. of πλέω.

πέπληγον, Ep. redupl. aor. 2 of πλήσσω :—πεπληγέμεν, inf. πεπληγώς, part. :—πεπλήγετο, 3 sing. med.

πεπλημένος, pf. pass. part. of πελάζω.

ΠΕ'ΠΛΟΣ, ὁ, in late Poets with heterog. pl. πέπλα, any woven cloth used for a covering, a sheet, carpet, curtain, veil, Il., Eur. II. a robe, worn by women over the common dress, and falling in folds about the person, answering to the man's ἱμάτιον or χλαῖνα, Hom., etc. 2. esp. of the πέπλος of Athena, embroidered with mythol. subjects, which was carried like the sail of a galley in public procession at the Panathenaea, Eur., Plat. 3. a man's robe, Trag.; esp. of the long Persian dresses, Aesch.

πέπλυμαι, pf. pass. of πλύνω.

πέπλωμα, ατος, τό, (as if from πεπλόω) a robe, Trag.

πέπνυμαι, old Ep. pf. pass. of πνέω, with pres. sense, to have breath or soul, and metaph. to be wise, discreet, prudent, πέπνῦσαι νόῳ Il.; inf. πεπνῦσθαι Hom.; 2 sing. plqpf. with impf. sense, πέπνῦσο Od.; part. πεπνῦμένος, as Adj., sage, wise, sagacious, Hom., Hes.

πέποιθα, pf. intr. of πείθω. Hence

πεποίθησις, ἡ, trust, confidence, boldness, N. T.

πεποίθομεν, Ep. for πεποίθωμεν, 1 pl. pf. subj. of πείθω.

πεπόλισμαι, pf. pass. of πολίζω :—πεπόλιστο, Ep. 3 sing. plqpf.

πεποτήαται, pf. of ποτάομαι : Ep. 3 pl. πεποτήαται.

πέπονθα, pf. of πάσχω.

πεπόσθαι, pf. pass. inf. of πίνω.

πέποσθε, Ep. for πεπόνθατε, 2 pl. pf. of πάσχω.

πέπρᾱγα and πέπρᾱχα, pf. of πράσσω :—πέπραγμαι, pf. pass.

πέπρᾱκα, pf. of πιπράσκω.

πέπρωται, πέπρωτο, 3 sing. pf. and plqpf. of *πόρω :— πεπρωμένος, part.

πέπτᾱμαι, pf. pass. of πετάννυμι.

πεπτεώς, Ep. pf. part. of πίπτω.

πεπτηώς, Ep. for -ηκώς, pf. part. both of πτήσσω and of πίπτω.

πέπτω, v. πέσσω.

πέπτωκα, pf. of πίπτω.

πεπύθοιτο, 3 sing. Ep. redupl. aor. 2 opt. of πυνθάνομαι.

πεπυκασμένος, pf. pass. part. of πυκάζω.

πέπυσμαι, pf. of πυνθάνομαι :—πέπυστο, Ep. 3 sing. plqpf.

ΠΕ'ΠΩΝ, ον, gen. ονος : Comp. and Sup. πεπαίτερος,

-τατος :—of fruit, cooked by the sun, ripe, mellow, Lat. mitis, Hdt., Ar., etc. II. metaph. in voc., mostly as a term of endearment, kind, gentle, ὦ πέπον my good friend, Il.; κριὲ πέπον my pet ram, Od.;— in bad sense, soft, weak, Il.; ὦ πέπονες ye weaklings, Ib. :—μόχθος πέπων softened pain, Soph., etc.: c. dat., ἐχθροῖς π. gentle to one's foes, Aesch.

ΠΕ'Ρ, encl. Particle, adding force to the word to which it is added: when this is a Noun, the part. ὤν or ἐών is added, μινυνθάδιόν περ ἐόντα all shortlived as I am, Il.; ἀγαθός περ ἐών however brave he be, Lat. quamvis fortis, Ib.; ἀλόχῳ περ ἐούσῃ though she be my wife, Ib.; the part. ὤν is often omitted, φράδμων περ ἀνήρ however shrewd, Ib.; κρατερός περ, θεοί περ Hom.; also subjoined to other participles, ἱεμένων περ however eager, Il.; ἀχνύμενός περ grieved though he be, etc. 2. sometimes it simply adds force, ἐλεεινότερός περ more pitiable by far, Ib.; μίνυνθά περ for a very little, ὀλίγον περ Ib. :—also to strengthen a negation, οὐδέ περ no, not even, not at all, οὐδ' ὑμῖν ποταμός περ εὔρροος ἀρκέσει Ib. 3. to call attention to one or more things of a number, however, at any rate, τιμήν πέρ μοι ὄφελλεν ἐγγυαλίξαι honour however (whatever else) he owed me, Ib.; τόδε πέρ μοι ἐπικρήηνον ἐέλδωρ this vow at all events, Ib. II. added to various Conjunctions and Relative words, with which it may form one word: 1. after hypothetical Conjs., v. εἴπερ. 2. after temporal Conjs., ὅτε περ just when, Il.; ὅταν περ Soph. 3. after Causal Conjs., v. ἐπεί-περ, ἐπειδήπερ. 4. after Relatives, v. ὅσπερ, οἷός περ, ὥσπερ. 5. after καί, v. καίπερ.

πέρα, Adv. beyond, across or over, further, Lat. ultra, Plat. 2. c. gen. Ἀτλαντικῶν πέρα ὅρων Eur. II. of Time, beyond, longer, Xen. 2. c. gen., π. μεσούσης ἡμέρας Id. III. beyond measure, excessively, extravagantly, πέρα λέγειν, φράζειν Soph., etc. 2. c. gen. more than, beyond, exceeding, π. δίκης, καιροῦ Aesch.; π. τῶν νῦν εἰρημένων Soph.; θαυμάτων π. more than marvels, Eur. :—sometimes the gen. is omitted, ἄπιστα καὶ πέρα things incredible, and more than that, Ar. 3. also as Comp., foll. by ἤ, Soph. IV. above, higher than, τῶν ἐχθρῶν πέρα Id.

πέρα, ἡ, v. πέραν sub fin.

περάαν, Ep. for περᾶν, inf. of περάω :—περάασκε, 3 sing. Ion. impf.

πέρᾱθεν, Ion. -ηθεν, Adv. (πέρα) from beyond, from the far side, Hdt., Eur.

περαίη, ἡ, v. περαῖος.

περαίνω, poët. πειραίνω : f. περανῶ : aor. 1 ἐπέρᾱνα :— Med., f. περανοῦμαι : aor. 1 ἐπερᾱνάμην :—Pass., aor. 1 ἐπεράνθην : 3 sing. pf. πεπέρανται, pf. pass. πεπείρανται (πέρας) :—to bring to an end, finish, accomplish, execute, Trag., etc. :—Pass. to be brought to an end, be finished, πάντα πεπείρανται Od. : to be fulfilled, accomplished, Eur., etc. 2. in speaking, to end a discourse, finish speaking, Aesch., etc. 3. to repeat from beginning to end, Ar. :—to relate, Eur. 4. absol. to effect one's purpose, esp. with a neg., οὐδὲν π. to come to no issue, do no good, make no progress, Eur., Thuc. II. intr. to make way, reach or penetrate, Aesch., Plat. III. intr. to come to an end, end, Plut.

περαῖος, ον, (πέραν) on the other side :—as Subst., ἡ

περαίη (sc. γῆ, χώρα) the opposite country, the country on the other side of a strait, Strab.; ἡ π. τῆς Βοιωτίης χώρης the part of Boeotia over against [Chalcis], Hdt.; ἡ π. τῶν Τενεδίων the coast [of Mysia] opposite Tenedos, Strab. Hence

περαιόω, f. ώσω, to carry to the opposite side, carry over or across, στρατιὰν ἐπεραίωσε, Lat. trajecit exercitum, Thuc. :—Pass., with fut. med., to pass over, cross, pass, Od., Ar., Thuc.;—also c. acc. loci, ἐπεραιώθη τὸν Ἀραξέα Hdt.; τὸ πέλαγος Thuc.

περαίτερος, α, ον, Comp. Adj., (πέρα) beyond, ὁδοὶ περαίτεραι roads leading further, Pind. II. Adv. περαιτέρω, further, Eur.; καὶ ἔτι π. Thuc. 2. c. gen., τῶνδε καὶ π. Aesch.; π. τοῦ μετρίου Xen.; and absol., π. (sc. τοῦ δέοντος) πεπραγμένα beyond what is fit, too far, Soph.

περαίωσις, ἡ, (περαιόω) a carrying over, Strab.

πέρᾱν, Ion. and Ep. πέρην, Adv. on the other side, across, beyond, Lat. trans, c. gen., πέρην ἁλός Il.; τὰ πέρην τοῦ Ἴστρου Hdt.; πόντου πέραν Aesch. 2. absol. on the other side, Hdt., Xen. 3. with Verbs of motion, foll. by εἰς, over or across to, πέρην ἐς τὴν Ἀχαιίην διέπεμψα Hdt.; πέραν εἰς τὴν Ἀσίαν διαβῆναι Xen. : also without εἰς, διαβαλόντες πέρην having crossed over to the main land, Hdt. 4. with the Art., διαβιβάζειν εἰς τὸ πέραν τοῦ ποταμοῦ Xen.; τὰ πέραν things done on the opposite side, Id. :—ἡ πέραν γῆ the country just over the border, the border-country, Thuc. II. over against, opposite, c. gen., πέρην Εὐβοίης Il. III. = πέρα, beyond, c. gen., π. γε πόντου τερμόνων τ' Ἀτλαντικῶν Eur.

περαντικός, ή, όν, (περαίνω) conclusive, logical, Ar.

περάπτων, Aeol. for περιάπτων.

πέρᾱς, ᾱτος, τό, (πέρα) an end, limit, boundary, ἐκ περάτων γῆς Thuc. II. an end, finish, οὐ π. ἔχων κακῶν Eur.; πέρας ἐστὶ τοῦ βίου θάνατος Dem. an end, completion, Luc. III. as Adv., ïike τέλος, at length, at last, Aeschin., etc.

περάσιμος [ᾰ], ον, (περάω) passable, Plut.

πέρασις, ἡ, (περάω) a crossing, βίου πέρασις passage from life to death, Soph.

πέρασσα, Ep. for ἐπέρασα, aor. 1 of περάω B.

πέρᾱτος, η, ον, (πέρα) on the opposite side :—as Subst., περάτη (sc. χώρα) an opposite land or quarter, esp. of the west, as opp. to the east, ἐν περάτῃ Od.

περᾱτός, Ion. -ητός, ή, όν, = περάσιμος, Pind., Hdt.

περάω (A), Ep. inf. περάαν: Ion. 3 sing. impf. περάασκε: f. περάσω [ᾱ], Ion. περήσω: aor. ἐπέρασα, Ion. ἐπέρησα: pf. πεπέρακα: (πέρα) :—to drive right through, λευκοὺς ἐπέρησεν ὀδόντας Il. 2. commonly, to pass across or through a space, to pass over, pass, cross, traverse, περᾶν θάλασσαν, πόντον Od.; πύλας πέρησεν passed through the gates, Il.; τάφρος ἀργαλέη περᾶν hard to pass, Ib.; τὰς φυλακὰς π. to pass the guards, Hdt. :—metaph., κίνδυνον π. to pass through, i.e. overcome, a danger, Aesch.; π. ὅρκον, prob. to go through the words of the oath, Lat. jusjurandum peragere, Id. 3. rarely of Time, to pass through, complete, τοῦ βίου τέρμα Soph.; τὴν τελευταίαν ἡμέραν Eur. II. intr. to penetrate or pierce right through, of a weapon, Il.; of rain, Od. : to extend to a place, Xen. 2. to pass across, to pass, δι' Ὠκεανοῖο Od.; ἐπὶ πόντον Il.; διὰ

Κυανέας ἀκτάς through the Symplegades, Eur. 3. to pass to or from a place, εἰς Ἀΐδαο Theogn.; ἔξω δωμάτων Soph. :—c. acc. loci, π. Δελφούς Eur. 4. rarely of Time, διὰ γήρως π. Xen.; εὐδαίμων π. to live happy, Orac. ap. Xen. 5. to pass all bounds, to go too far, Soph.; so, π. ὀργῆς to pass all bounds in anger (or to cease from anger), Id. 6. with instrument of motion in acc., π. πόδα, ἴχνος Eur.

περάω (B), f. περάσω [ᾰ], Att. περῶ: aor. 1 ἐπέρασα, Ep. πέρασσα, ἐπέρασσα: pf. pass. πεπέρημαι: (πέρα) : —to carry beyond seas for the purpose of selling, to export for sale; then like πέρνημι, to sell men as slaves, Hom.; π. τινα Λῆμνον to sell one to Lemnos, Il.; or with a Prep., π. τινὰ ἐς Λῆμνον Ib.; π. τινὰ πρὸς δώματά τινος Od.

Πέργαμος, ἡ, Pergamus, the citadel of Troy, Il.; τὸ Πριάμου Πέργαμον Hdt.; τὰ Πέργαμα Soph., Eur., etc.: —then, any citadel, Aesch., Eur. 2. also Περγαμία, ἡ, Pind.

Περγασή, ἡ, a deme of the φυλὴ Ἐρεχθηΐς: Περγασῆσι at Pergasé, Ar.

περδικο-τρόφος, ον, (τρέφω) keeping partridges, Strab.

ΠΕ'ΡΔΙΞ, ῑκος, ὁ and ἡ, a partridge, Lat. perdix, Soph.

ΠΕ'ΡΔΟΜΑΙ, Dep. with aor. 2 act. ἔπαρδον, pf. πέπορδα; plqpf. πεπόρδειν :—to break wind, Lat. pedere, Ar.

πέρηθεν, πέρην, Ion. for πέραθεν, πέραν.

περητός, ή, όν, Ion. for περατός.

ΠΕ'ΡΘΩ, f. πέρσω: aor. 1 ἔπερσα: aor. 2 ἔπραθον, inf. πραθεῖν, Ep. πραθέειν :—Pass., with f. med. πέρσομαι: syncop. aor. 2 inf. πέρθαι, like δέχθαι from δέχομαι :— to waste, ravage, sack, destroy, a town, Hom. 2. of persons, to destroy, slay, Pind., Soph. :—metaph. of love, Eur. 3. of things, to destroy, Aesch., Soph. II. to get by plunder, Il., Eur.

ΠΕΡΙ', Prep. with gen., dat., and acc.: Radical sense, round about, all round, whereas ἀμφί properly means on both sides.

A. WITH GENITIVE: I. of Place, round about, around, Lat. circum, Od. 2. about, near, ἐσσόμεναι περὶ σεῖο Mosch. II. Causal, to denote the object about or for which one does something: 1. with Verbs of fighting or contending, μάχεσθαι περὶ πτόλιος Il.; περὶ Πατρόκλοιο θανόντος Ib.; so, τρέχειν περὶ ἑωυτοῦ, περὶ τῆς ψυχῆς Hdt. 2. about, for, on account of, μερμηρίζειν περὶ τινος Il.; φροντίζειν περὶ τινος Hdt. 3. with Verbs of hearing, knowing, speaking, about, concerning, Lat. circa, de, περὶ νόστου ἄκουσα Od., etc. 4. rather of the motive, than the object, περὶ ἔριδος μάρνασθαι to fight for very enmity, Il.; περὶ τῶνδε for these reasons, Ib. 5. about, as to, in reference to, οὕτως ἔσχε περὶ τοῦ πρήγματος τούτου Hdt.; so, τὰ περὶ τινος his circumstances, Thuc. :—also without the Art., ἀριθμοῦ πέρι as to number, Hdt. III. like Lat. prae, before, above, beyond, περὶ πάντων ἔμμεναι ἄλλων Il.; τετιμῆσθαι περὶ πάντων Ib.; κρατερὸς περὶ πάντων Hom. : in this sense, divided from its gen., περὶ φρένας ἔμμεναι ἄλλων in understanding to be beyond them, Il. IV. to denote value, περὶ πολλοῦ ἐστιν ἡμῖν it is worth much to us, Hdt.; περὶ πολλοῦ ποιεῖσθαί τι to reckon a thing for, i. e. worth, much, Lat. magni facere, Id.; περὶ πλείστου ἡγεῖσθαι Thuc.

B. WITH DATIVE: **I.** of Place, *round about, around,* of close-fitting dresses, armour, etc., ἔνδυνε περὶ στήθεσσι χιτῶνα ll.; κνημῖδας περὶ κνήμησιν ἔθηκεν lb.; περὶ δ' ἔγχεῖ .. καμεῖται will grow weary *by grasping the spear,* lb.; περὶ δουρὶ πεπαρμένος *spitted upon* it, *transfixed by* it, lb.; πεπτὼς περὶ ξίφει Soph.   **2.** of a warrior, *standing over* or *going round* a dead comrade so as to defend him (v. ἀμφιβαίνω, περιβαίνω); Αἴας περὶ Πατρόκλῳ βεβήκει ll.   **II.** Causal, much like περί c. gen., of an object *for* or *about* which one *struggles,* μαχήσασθαι περὶ δαιτί Od.; περὶ τοῖς φιλτάτοις κυβεύειν Plat.   **2.** so also with Verbs denoting fear, ἔδδεισεν δὲ περὶ ξανθῷ Μενελάῳ ll.; δεῖσαι περὶ τῷ χωρίῳ Thuc.   **3.** generally, of the cause or occasion, *for, on account of, by reason of,* Lat. *prae,* μὴ περὶ Μαρδονίῳ πταίσῃ ἡ Ἑλλάς Hdt.; περὶ σφίσιν αὐτοῖς πταίειν Thuc. :—in Poets also, περὶ δείματι *for* fear, Pind.; περὶ τάρβει, περὶ φόβῳ Aesch.   **C.** WITH ACCUSATIVE: **I.** of Place, properly referring to the object *round about* which motion takes place, περὶ βόθρον ἐφοίτων came flocking *round* the pit, Od.; ἄστυ πέρι διώκειν ll. :—hence, *near,* ἑστάμεναι περὶ τοῖχον ll.; οἳ περὶ Πηνειὸν ναίεσκον lb.; περὶ τὴν κρήνην *somewhere near* it, Plat.; ἡ περὶ Λέσβον ναυμαχία the sea-fight *off* Lesbos, Xen.   **2.** of persons *who are about one,* οἱ περί τινα a person's suite, attendants, associates, οἱ περὶ τὸν Πείσανδρον πρέσβεις Thuc.; οἱ περὶ Ἡράκλειτον his school, Plat.; οἱ περὶ Ἀρχίαν πολέμαρχοι Archias *and his colleagues,* Xen. :—later, οἱ περί τινα periphr. for the person himself, Plut.   **3.** of the object *about* which one is occupied or concerned, περὶ δόρπα πονεῖσθαι Hom.; εἶναι or γίγνεσθαι περί τι Thuc., etc.; ὁ περὶ τὸν ἵππον the groom, Xen.   **4.** denoting motion *about* or *in* a place, περὶ νῆσον ἀλώμενοι wandering *about* the island, Od.; χρονίζειν περὶ Αἴγυπτον Hdt.   **5.** *about, in the case of,* τὰ περὶ τὴν Αἴγυπτον γεγονότα Hdt.; εὐσεβεῖν περὶ θεούς Plat.: —also without a Verb, *about, in respect of, in regard to,* πονηρὸς περὶ τὸ σῶμα Plat.; ἀκόλαστος περὶ ταῦτα Aeschin.; τὰ περὶ τὰς ναῦς naval *affairs,* Thuc.; τὰ περὶ τοὺς θεούς Xen., etc.   **II.** of Time, περὶ λύχνων ἀφάς *about* the time of lamp-lighting, Hdt.; περὶ μέσας νύκτας *about* midnight, Xen.; περὶ ἡλίου δυσμάς Id.   Of numbers loosely given, περὶ ἑβδομήκοντα *about* seventy, Thuc.   **D.** POSITION : περί may follow its Subst., when it suffers anastrophé, ἥν πέρι, ἄστυ πέρι.   **E.** absol., as ADV., *around, about,* also *near, by,* Hom.   **II.** *before* or *above* others, in which case it commonly suffers anastrophé, Τυδείδη, πέρι μέν σε τίον Δαναοὶ ll.; πέρι κέρδεα οἶδεν Od.   **2.** περὶ κῆρι *very much* in heart, *right heartily,* περὶ κῆρι φιλεῖν lb.; περὶ κῆρι χολοῦσθαι lb.; so, περὶ σθένεῖ lb.   **3.** strengthd. περὶ πρό, where also περί recovers its accent, lb.   **F.** IN COMPOS. all its chief senses recur: **I.** *all round,* as in περιβάλλω, περιβλέπω, περιέχω.   **II.** of return to the same point, *about,* as in περιάγω, περιβαίνω, περιστρέφω.   **III.** *above, before,* as in περιγίγνομαι, περιτοξεύω: also *beyond measure, very, exceedingly,* as in περικαλλής, περιδείδω, like Lat. *per-* in *permultus, pergratus.*   **IV.** rarely = ἀμφί, as in περιδέξιος.

G. PROSODY :—though ι in περί is short, περί does not suffer elision. The exceptions to this rule are few.

περι-αγγέλλω, f. -αγγελῶ, *to announce by messages sent round,* Thuc.   **2.** absol. *to send* or *carry a message round,* Hdt.   **II.** c. dat. pers. et inf. *to send round orders for* people *to do something,* περιήγγελλον ταῖς πόλεσι στρατιὰν παρασκευάζεσθαι Thuc., etc.; with the inf. omitted, ναῦς περιήγγελλον, Lat. *imperabant naves,* Id.

περιαγείρω, *to go round and collect money :*—in Med. *to do so for oneself,* Plat.

περιαγής, ές, (περιάγνυμι) *broken in pieces,* Anth.   **II.** = περιηγής, *quite round,* Id.

περι-αγνίζω, f. σω, *to purify all round,* Luc.

περι-άγνυμι, f.-άξω, *to bend and break all round :* Pass., ὀψ̀ περιάγνυται the voice *is broken all round,* i. e. *spreads all round,* Il.

περι-άγω, f. ξω, *to lead* or *draw round,* Hdt.   **2.** *to lead about with one, have always by one,* Xen.; so in Med., Id.   **3.** *to turn round, turn about,* τὴν κεφαλήν Ar., etc. :—π. τὴν σκυταλίδα *to twist* it *round* in order to tighten a noose, Hdt.   **4.** *to put off,* Luc.   **5.** *to bring round to* a point, πρός τι Arist., etc.   **II.** c. acc. loci, *to go round,* περιάγουσι τὴν λίμνην κύκλῳ Hdt.; π. τὰς πόλεις N. T.   Hence

περιαγωγεύς, ὁ, *a windlass, capstan,* Luc.; and

περιαγωγή, ἡ, *a going round, a revolution,* Plat.

περι-ᾴδω, f. -ᾴσομαι, *to go about singing,* Luc.

περιαιρετός, ή, όν, *that may be taken off,* Thuc.

περι-αιρέω, f. ήσω : pf. -ῄρηκα : aor. 2 περι-εῖλον, inf. -ελεῖν :—*to take off something that surrounds, take off an outer coat, take away, strip off,* τὰ τείχη Hdt., Thuc. ; π. τὸν κέραμον *taking off* the earthen jar into which the gold had been run, Hdt. :—Med. *to take off from oneself,* π. τὴν κυνέην *to take off one's* helmet, Hdt.; βιβλίου περιαιρεόμενος *taking* [*the cover*] *off* the letter, i. e. *opening* it, Id. :—but Med. often just like Act. *to strip off, take away,* Xen., Plat. :—Pass. *to be taken off,* τοῦ ἄλλου περιῃρημένου *when* the rest *has been taken away,* Thuc.   **II.** Pass. also c. acc. rei, *to be stript of* a thing, περιῃρημένοι χρήματα καὶ συμμάχους Dem.; τοὺς στεφάνους περιῄρηνται Id.

περιακτέον, verb. Adj. of περιάγω, *one must bring round,* Plat.

περι-αλγέω, *to be greatly pained at,* τινί Thuc.

περι-αλγής, ές, (ἄλγος) *much pained, very sorrowful,* Plat.

περι-αλείφω, f. ψω, *to smear all over, anoint,* Ar.

περίαλλος, ον, *before all others ;* in Adv. περίαλλα, *before all,* h. Hom., Pind. : *exceedingly,* Soph.

περι-άλουργός, όν, *with purple all round,* κακοῖς π. *double-dyed* in villany, Ar.

περίαμμα, ατος, τό, (περιάπτω) *anything worn about one, an amulet,* Anth.

περι-αμπέχω, f. -αμφέξω : aor. 2 -ήμπεσχον :—also **περιαμπίσχω,** impf. -ήμπισχον :—*to put round about,* π. τινά τι *to put* a thing *round* or *over one,* Ar. :—Med. *to put round oneself, put on,* Plat.   **II.** *to cover all round,* Id.

περι-αμύνω [ῡ], *to defend* or *guard all round,* Plut.

περί-απτος, ον, *hung round one :* as Subst., περίαπτον, τό, = περίαμμα, Plat. : *an appendage,* Arist.

περι-άπτω, f. ψω, to tie, fasten, hang about or upon, apply to, γυίοις φάρμακα περάπτων (Aeol. form) Pind. : —Med. to put round oneself, put on to wear, Plat. 2. metaph., π. τιμάς, αἶσχός τινι to attach to one, Ar. ; ἀντὶ καλῆς [δόξης] αἰσχρὰν π. τῇ πόλει Dem. II. to light a fire all round or in the midst, N. T.

περι-αρμόζω, f. σω, to fit on all round, τί τινι Plut.

περι-αρτάω, f. ήσω, to hang round or on:—Pass. to be hung round, c. dat., Plut.

περι-αστράπτω, f. ψω, to flash around, c. acc., N. T.

περι-ασχολέω, f. ήσω, to be busy about a thing, Luc.

περι-αυχένιος, ον, (αὐχήν) put round the neck, Hdt.

περ-ίαχε, Ep. for περι-ίαχε, 3 sing. impf. of περιάχω.

περι-βαίνω, f. -βήσομαι: aor. 2 περι-έβην, Ep. περί-βην: —to go round, of one defending a fallen comrade, either to walk round and round him, or, like ἀμφιβαίνω, to bestride him, absol., Il. ; c. gen., περιβῆναι ἀδελφειοῦ κταμένοιο Ib. ; also, c. dat., Πατρόκλῳ περιβάς Ib. ; so, περὶ τρόπιος βεβαῶτα astride of the keel, Od. ; c. acc., π. ἵππον to bestride a horse, Plut. II. of sound, to come round one's ears, Plut.

περι-βάλλω, f. -βαλῶ: aor. 2 -έβαλον: — to throw round, περὶ χαῖρε βαλών having thrown his arms round him, Od. ; χέρας π. τινί Eur. ; περὶ δ᾽ ὠλέσας δέρᾳ βάλοιμι Id. ; π. τινὶ δεσμά Aesch. ; π. ναῦν περὶ ἕρμα to wreck it on a reef, Thuc.:—Med. to throw round oneself, put on, c. acc. rei, τεύχεα περιβαλλόμενοι putting on their arms, Od. ; π. ἔρυμα, ἕρκος, τείχεα to throw round oneself for defence, Il. c. dupl. acc., τεῖχος περιβάλλεσθαι πόλιν to build a wall round it, Id.:—in pf. pass. to have a thing put round one, Plat. ; περιβεβλημένος τὸ τεῖχος having his wall around him, Id. 2. metaph. to put round a person, i. e. invest him with it, π. τινὶ βασιληίην, τυραννίδα Id., Eur. ; δουλείαν Μυκήναις Eur. ; π. ἀνανδρίαν τινί, i. e. to make him faint-hearted, Id. II. reversely, c. dat. rei, to surround, encompass, enclose with, περιβάλλειν βρόχῳ τὸν αὐχένα Hdt. ; τινὰ πέπλοις Eur. ; π. τινὰ χερσί to embrace, Id. : — metaph., π. τινὰ συμφοραῖς, κακοῖς to involve one in calamities, evils, etc., Id. :—so in Med. to surround or enclose for oneself, Xen. 2. π. τινὰ χαλκεύματι to put him round the sword, i. e. stab him, Aesch. III. c. acc. only, to encompass, surround, περιβάλλει με σκότος Eur. ; π. τινά to embrace him, Xen. ; but also to clothe, N. T. :—Pass., τὸ περιβεβλημένον the space enclosed, enclosure, Hdt. :—Med., ἤλαυνον περιβαλλόμενοι [τὰ ὑποζύγια] surrounding them, Id. 2. to fetch a compass round, double, c. acc., ἵπποι περὶ τέρμα βαλοῦσαι Il. ; of ships, π. τὸν Ἄθων Hdt., etc. 3. to frequent, be fond of a place, Xen. IV. Med. to bring into one's power, and at, Lat. affectare, as we say ' to compass ' a thing, π. ἑωυτῷ κέρδεα Hdt. ; σωφροσύνης δόξαν π. Xen. :—pf. pass. to have come into possession of a thing, Hdt. 2. to cloke or veil in words, Plat. V. to throw beyond, and so, generally, to excel, surpass, μνηστῆρας δώροισι Od.; or, simply, π. ἀρετῇ to be superior in virtue, Il.

περί-βαρυς, υ, gen. εος, exceeding heavy, Aesch.

περιβάς, aor. 2 part. of περιβαίνω.

περιβέβλημαι, pf. pass. of περιβάλλω.

περί-βην, Ep. for περι-έβην, aor. 2 of περιβαίνω.

περιβῆναι, aor. 2 inf. of περιβαίνω.

περιβιόω, to survive, Plut.

περί-βλεπτος, ον, looked at from all sides, admired of all observers, Eur., Xen.

περι-βλέπω, f. ψω, intr. to look round about, gaze around, Xen., etc. II. trans. to look round at, πάντας Id. : so in Med., N. T. 2. to seek after, look about for, τινά or τι Luc. 3. to gaze on, admire, respect, Soph. ; π. βίαν to be jealous of, suspect force, or to covet it, Eur. :—Pass., περιβλέπεσθαι τίμιον, Lat. digito monstrari, Id.

περί-βλεψις, εως, ἡ, a looking about : close examination, Plut.

περι-βόητος, ον, poët. περί-βωτος, noised abroad, much talked of, famous, Thuc., Dem. 2. in bad sense, notorious, scandalous, Dem. :—Adv. -τως, notoriously, Aeschin., Dem. II. with or amid shouts, epith. of Ares, Soph.

περι-βόλαιον, τό, (περίβαλλω) that which is thrown round, a covering, θανάτου περιβόλαια corpse-clothes, Eur. ; π. σαρκὸς ἡβῶντα youthful incasements of flesh, i. e. youth, manhood, Id. : a chariot-cover, Plut.

περι-βολή, ἡ, (περιβάλλω) anything which is thrown round, a covering, Plat. ; χειρῶν περιβολαί embraces, Eur. ; so περιβολαί alone, Xen. ; βαλλειν χθονός, i. e. the grave, Eur. ; π. [ξίφεος] a scabbard, Id. : absol. of walls round a town, ἑπτάπυργοι π. Id. II. a space enclosed, compass, οἰκίης μεγάλης περιβολή a house of large compass, Hdt. 2. a circumference, circuit, Thuc. ; π. ποιεῖσθαι to make a circuit, Xen. III. metaph., 1. a compassing, endeavouring after, τῆς ἀρχῆς, Lat. affectatio imperii, Id. 2. ἡ π. τοῦ λόγου the whole compass of the matter, long and short of it, Isocr.

περί-βολος, ον, (περιβάλλω) going round, compassing, encircling, Eur. II. as Subst., περίβολος, ὁ, = περιβολή, ἐχίδνης περίβολοι the spires or coils of a serpent, Id. ; in pl. walls round a town, Hdt., Eur. ; so in sing., Thuc. 2. an enclosure, circuit, compass, π. νεωρίων Eur. ; of a temple, the precincts, Plut.

περι-βόσκω, to let feed around :—Pass., of cattle, to feed on all round, c. acc., Luc.

περι-βραχῑόνιος, α, ον, (βραχίων) round or on the arm, Plut. :—περιβραχιόνιον, τό, an armlet or piece of armour for the arm, Xen.

περι-βρύχιος [ῠ], α, ον, engulfed by the surge all round, οἴδματα π. waves swallowed up by one another, i. e. wave upon wave, Soph.

περι-βύω, f. -βύσω [ῠ], to stop up round about, to stuff in all round, τί τινι Luc.

περίβωτος, ον, poët. for περιβόητος, Anth.

περι-γίγνομαι, Ion. and later -γίνομαι -γίνομαι [ῑ]: f. -γενήσομαι: aor. 2 -εγενόμην: pf. -γέγονα:—to be superior to others, to prevail over, overcome, excel, c. gen., ἡνίοχος περιγίγνεται ἡνιόχοιο Il., etc. ; rarely c. acc., π. Ἕλληνας Hdt. :—absol. to be superior, prevail, Id., Thuc., etc. 2. of things, ἤν τι περιγένηται σφι τοῦ πολέμου if they gain any advantage in the war, Thuc. ; π. ὑμῖν πλῆθος νεῶν you have a superiority in number of ships, Id. II. to live over, get over, to survive, escape, Lat. salvus evadere, Hdt., Thuc., etc. ; οἱ περιγενόμενοι the survivors, Hdt. ; also

c. gen. rei, περιεγένετο τούτου τοῦ πάθεος *he survived this disaster*, Id. 2. of things, *to remain over and above*, Ar., Xen. 3. of things also, *to be a result or consequence*, ἐκ τῶν μεγίστων κινδύνων μέγισται τιμαὶ περιγίγνονται Thuc.; περιγίγνεταί τι *the upshot* of the matter *is so and so*, Dem.

περι-γλᾰγής, ές, (γλάγος) *full of milk*, Il.

περιγληνάομαι, Dep. (γλήνη) *to turn round the eye-balls, glare around*, of a lion, Theocr.

περί-γλωσσος, ον, (γλῶσσα) *ready of tongue*, Pind.

περι-γνάμπτω, f. ψω, *to double* a headland, Μάλειαν Od.

περίγραμμα, ατος, τό, *a line drawn round* a ring, Luc.

περιγραπτέον, verb. Adj. of περιγράφω, *one must trace out*, Plat.

περι-γραπτός, όν, *marked round*, ἐκ περιγραπτοῦ from *a circumscribed space*, Thuc.; and

περιγρᾰφή, ή, *a line drawn round, an outline, sketch*, Plat., Arist. 2. *a circumference, circuit*, Arist. 3. *that which is marked by an outline, a contour*, π. ποδοῖν Aesch. II. *dress*, Luc.

περι-γράφω [ᾰ], f. ψω, *to draw a line round, mark round*, Lat. *circumscribo*, Hdt.; π. κύκλον *to draw a* circle *round*, Id.:—absol. *to draw a circle*, Ar. 2. *to define, determine*, Xen.:—Pass., περιεγέγραπτο, limits had been drawn, Id. II. *to draw in outline, sketch out*, Lat. *delineare*, Arist. III. *to enclose* as it were *within brackets, to cancel*, Anth.; π. τινὰ ἐκ πολιτείας *to exclude* from civic privileges, Aeschin.

περιδέδρομα, pf. of περιτρέχω.

περι-δεής, ές, (δέος) *very timid* or *fearful*, Hdt.; τινος *of* or *for* a person or thing, Thuc.; π. μὴ . . , Id.:—Adv. -ῶς, *in great fear*, Id.

περι-δείδω, f. -δείσομαι: aor. 1 περιέδεισα, Ep. 3 pl. περίδδεισαν, part. περιδείσας: rf. περιδέδοικα, Ep. περιδείδια:—*to be in great fear about*, c. gen., Δαναῶν περιδείδια Ib.; c. dat. *to be in great fear* for, Αἴαντι περιδδείσαντες Ib.; ἐμῇ κεφαλῇ περιδείδια Ib.

περι-δέξιος, ον, = ἀμφιδέξιος, *with two right hands*, i.e. *using both hands alike*, Il. 2. *very dexterous*, Ar.

περι-δέραιος, ον, (δέρη) *passed round the neck*: as Subst., περιδέραιον, τό, *a necklace*, Arist., Plut.

περι-δέω, f. -δήσω, *to bind, tie round* or *on*, τί τινι Hdt.:—Med. *to bind round oneself, put on*, Id., Ar.

περι-δίδομαι, Med. of περιδίδωμι (which does not occur), *to stake* or *wager*, c. gen. rei (i. e. pretii), τρίποδος περιδώμεθον ἠὲ λέβητος *let us make a wager of* a tripod, i. e. *let us wager* a tripod (to be paid by the loser), Il.; ἐμέθεν περιδώσομαι αὐτῆς *I will wager for* myself, i. e. *pledge* myself, Od.; π. πότερον *to lay a wager* whether, Ar.; so, περιδίδομαι περὶ τῆς κεφαλῆς *I stake* my head, Id.; c. dat. pers. added, περίδου μοι περὶ θυματιδᾶν ἁλῶν *have a wager* with me for a little thyme-salt, Id.; περίδου νῦν ἐμοὶ Id.

περι-δῑνέω, f. ήσω, *to whirl* or *wheel round*, Aeschin.:—Pass. *to run circling round*, πόλιν περιδινηθήτην (3 dual aor. 1 pass.) Il.:—so in Med., Anth.; *to spin round* like a top, Xen. Hence

περι-δῑνής, ές, *whirled round*, Anth.; and

περιδίνησις, εως, ή, *a whirling round*, Plat.

περι-δίω, old form for περιδείδω, *to be in great fear for*, c. dat., only in 3 sing. impf., περὶ γὰρ δίε νηυσὶν Ἀχαιῶν Il., etc.

περι-διώκω, *to pursue on all sides*, Strab.

περίδου, aor. 2 imp. med. of περιδίδομαι.

περιδρᾰμεῖν, aor. 2 inf. of περιτρέχω.

περι-δράσσομαι, Att. -ττομαι, Dep. *to grasp* a thing *with the hand*, c. gen. rei, Plut.

περιδρομή, ή, (περιδρᾰμεῖν) *a running round*, Plut.; π. ποιεῖσθαι *to wheel about*, Xen. 2. *a revolution, orbit*, Eur.

περίδρομος, ον, (περιδρᾰμεῖν) *running round*, of a chariot-rail, of the nave of a wheel, Il.; of the rim of a shield, Eur. 2. *going about, roaming*, Theogn., Ar. II. pass. *that can be run round*, and so *standing apart, detached*, Hom.

περίδρομος, ὁ, (περιδρᾰμεῖν) as Subst. *that which surrounds*, as *the rim* of a shield, Eur.; *the string that runs round the top of a net* (cf. ἐπίδρομος), Xen.; *a gallery running round a building*, Id.

περι-δρύπτω, f. ψω, *to tear all round, to peel the bark off* a tree, Anth.:—Pass., ἀγκῶνας περιδρύφθη (Ep. aor. 1 pass.) *he had the skin all torn from off* his arms, Il.

περι-δύω, f. σω, *to pull off from round, strip off*, περίδυσε χιτῶνας Il.

περιδῶκα, Ep. for περι-έδωκα, aor. 1 of περιδίδωμι.

περιδώμεθον, 1 dual aor. 2 med. subj. of περιδίδωμι.

περιεῖδον, aor. 2 of περιοράω.

περι-ειλίσσω, Ion. for περι-ελίσσω.

περιεῖλον, aor. 2 of περιαιρέω.

περι-είλω, -ειλέω, or -ίλλω, *to fold* or *wrap round*, σακκία περὶ τοὺς πόδας Xen. 2. *to wrap up, swathe*:—Med. *to swathe oneself*, περιειλάμενος (aor. 1 part.), Ar.

περί-ειμι (εἰμί *sum*), inf. -εῖναι: part. περι-ών:—*to be around* a place, c. dat., Thuc.; τὰ περιόντα *circumstances*, Dem. II. *to be better than, superior to* another, *surpass, excel*, c. gen., Il., Hdt.; περίεσσι γυναικῶν εἶδός τε μέγεθός τε Od.; οἳ περὶ μὲν βουλὴν Δαναῶν περὶ δ' ἐστε μάχεσθαι (=μάχην) Il.; c. dat. rei, σοφίᾳ π. τῶν Ἑλλήνων Plat.: absol. *to be superior*, Hdt., etc.; ἐκ περιόντος at an advantage, Thuc. III. *to overlive, outlive*, τινι Hdt.: absol. *to survive, remain alive*, Il., Dem., etc.:—of things, *to be extant, to be in existence*, Hdt. 2. *to be over and above, to remain in hand*, of property, money, etc., Thuc.; οἰόμενοί περιεῖναι χρήματά τῳ imagining that any one has a *balance* in his hands, Dem. 3. *to be a result* or *consequence*, περίεστιν ὑμῖν ἐκ τούτων what you have got by all this is . . , Id.; τοσοῦτον ὑμῖν περίεστιν τοῦ πρὸς ἐμὲ μίσους you *have* so much hatred against me *left*, Philipp. ap. Dem.; c. inf., περίεστι ὑμῖν αὐτοῖς ἐρίζειν it remains for you to quarrel with them, Dem.

περίειμι (εἶμι *ibo*), inf. -ιέναι: part. περι-ιών:—*to go round fetch a compass*, Hdt.; π. κατὰ νώτου τινί *to get round* and take him in rear, Thuc.:—*to go about* with idle questions or stories, Dem. 2. c. acc. loci, *to go round, compass*, π. τὸν νηὸν κύκλῳ Hdt.; π. φυλακάς *to go round the guards, visit* them, Id.:—of sounds, αὐλῶν σε περίεισιν πνοή Ar. II. *to come round to* one, in succession or by inheritance, ἡ ἀρχή, βασιληίη περίεισι εἴς τινα Hdt. 2. of revolving periods, χρόνου περιιόντος as time *came round*, Id.; περιιόντι τῷ θέρει Thuc.

περιείργω, Att. for περιέργω.

περι-είρω, to insert or fix round, Hdt.

περιέκρυβον, aor. 2 of περικρύβω : v. περικρύπτω.

περιεκτικός, ή, όν, (περιέχω) grasping, Luc.

περιελάσις, εως, ή, a place for driving round, a road-way, Hdt. From

περι-ελαύνω, f. -ελῶ, to drive round, τὰς κύλικας π. to push the cups round, Xen. 2. to drive round, harass, Ar.:—Pass., Hdt. 3. to draw or build round, περὶ δ' ἕρκος ἔλασσε Il.:—Pass., περὶ δ' ἕρκος ἐλήλαται Od. II. seemingly intr. (sub. ἅρμα, ἵππον), to drive or ride round, Hdt., Att.

περι-ελίσσω, Att. -ττω, Ion. -ειλίσσω: f. ξω:—to roll or wind round, τι περί τι Hdt. :—Med., π. ἱμάντας to wind caestus straps round one's arms, Plat. :—Pass. to be wound round, περιελιχθέντα περὶ τὴν γῆν Id.

περι-έλκω, aor. 1 περιείλκυσα, to drag round, drag about, Xen. 2. to draw round another way, κύκλῳ π. τινά, Lat. huc illuc ducere, Plat. :—Pass., Id.

περι-έννυμι, Ep. aor. 1 περίεσσα, to put round, περὶ εἵματα ἕσσον Il.; περὶ τεύχεα ἕσσεν Ib.: Med., χλαῖναν περιέσσασθαι to put on one's cloak, Hes.

περι-έπω : impf. -εῖπον : f. -έψω : aor. 2 -έσπον, inf. -σπεῖν :—Med., f. -έψομαι:—Pass., aor. 1 inf. -εφθῆναι: —to treat with great care : 1. in good sense, εὖ π. τινά to treat him well, Hdt.; ὡς κάλιστα π. τινά Id.; π. τινὰ ὡς εὐεργέτην Xen.: alone also, to treat with respect or honour, to caress, Lat. colo, foveo, Id. 2. in bad sense, τρηχέως, κάρτα τρηχέως π. to treat, handle roughly, Hdt.; π. τινὰ ὡς πολέμιον Id.:—Pass., τρηχέως περιεφθῆναι ὑπό τινος !d.

περι-εργάζομαι : pf. -είργασμαι : Dep. : —to take more pains than enough about a thing, to waste one's labour on it, with a part., Σωκράτης περιεργάζεται ζητῶν Plat.; περιείργασμαι περὶ τούτων εἰπών Dem.:—c. dat. modi, τῷ θυλάκῳ περιεργάσθαι that they had overdone it with their 'sack' (i. e. need not have used the word), Hdt.:—pf. in pass. sense, οὐδὲ περιείργασται nor is there any superfluity, Luc. II. to be a busybody, meddle with other folk's affairs, Dem.

περιεργία, ή, over-exactness in doing anything, Luc. II. intermeddling, officiousness, Theophr., Luc. From

περί-εργος, ον, (*ἔργω) careful overmuch, Lys., etc. 2. busy about other folk's affairs, meddling, a busybody, Xen. II. pass. done with especial care, elaborate, Aeschin., etc. 2. superfluous, Plat., etc. 3. curious, superstitious, Plut.

περι-έργω, Att. -είργω :—to inclose all round, encompass, Hdt., Thuc.:—Pass., ἐν περιειργμένοις παραδείσοις in enclosed parks, Xen.

περι-έρχομαι : Dep. :—to go round, go about, Hdt., Att.:—to go about, like a beggar, Xen.; like a can-vasser, Lat. ambire, Dem. :—c. part. to go about doing a thing, Plat. :—c. acc. cogn., π. στάδια χίλια Ar. :—c. acc. loci, π. τὸν βωμόν to go round the altar, Dem.; τὴν ἀγοράν Dem. 2. c. acc. pers. to come round, en-compass, of sounds, περὶ κτύπος ἦλθε ποδοῖιν the sound of feet came round him, Od.; of the effect of wine, Κύκλωπα περὶ φρένας ἤλυθεν οἶνος Ib. 3. like Lat. circumvenire, to take in, to overreach, cheat, Hdt., Ar. II. to go round and return to a point, come

round, ἡ βασιληίη περιῆλθε ἔς τινα Hdt.; ἐς φθίσιν περιῆλθε ἡ νοῦσος the disease ended in . . , Id.; c. acc., ἡ τίσις περιῆλθε τὸν Πανιώνιον vengeance came at last upon him, Id. 2. of Time, to come round, Xen.

περι-ερρύην, aor. 2 pass. (in act. sense) of περιρρέω.

περι-εσθίω, f. -έδομαι: aor. 2 -έφαγον :—to eat all round, eat away, nibble at, Luc.

περιέσπᾶσα, aor. 1 of περισπάω.

περιεστώς, for -εστηκώς, pf. part. of περιΐστημι.

περι-έσχατα, τά, the surrounding extremities, Hdt.

περί-εφθος, ον, (ἕψω) thoroughly well cooked, Luc.

περι-έχω, also -ίσχω: f. -έξω and -σχήσω: aor. 2 -έσχον: aor. 2 med. -εσχόμην :—to encompass, em-brace, surround, Plat. 2. to surround so as to guard, Plut. 3. in Pass. to be shut in or be-leaguered, ὑπό τινος Hdt., Xen. 4. to embrace, comprise, comprehend, Plat., etc. II. to over-come, gain the victory, Thuc.: of an army, to outflank the enemy, Id. III. Med. to hold one's arms round another, take charge of, c. gen. pers., περίσχεο (Ion. aor. 2 med. imperat.) παιδὸς ἑῆς Il.: c. acc. to protect, Od. 2. to cling to, be fond of a person or thing, c. gen., Hdt. 3. c. inf., περιείχετο μὴ ἐκλιπεῖν he was urgent with them that they should not leave him, Id.

περι-ζαμενῶς, Adv. very violently, h. Hom.

περι-ζέω, to boil round, Luc.; poët. -ζείω, Anth.

περί-ζυγον, τό, a spare strap, Xen.

περί-ζωμα, τό, a girdle round the loins, apron, Plut.

περι-ζώννυμαι, Med. with pf. pass. -έζωσμαι, to gird round oneself, gird oneself with, ἐσθῆτα Plut.; τοῦ-τον τὸν ἄνδρα περιεζώσατο put him on as a defence, Ar.; περιεζῶσθαι τὴν φορβείαν to have their halter girded round them, Arist.

περι-ζώστρα, ή, an apron. II. a ribbon twined round a garland, Theocr.

περι-ηγέομαι, f. ήσομαι, Dep. to lead round, π. τινι τὸ οὖρος to shew one the way round the mountain, Hdt. 2. to explain, describe, Luc.

περι-ηγής, ές, =περιαγής II : of the arms, tied behind one, Anth.

περιήγησις, εως, ή, (περιηγέομαι) like περιγραφή, an outline, contour, Hdt. II. a leading round and explaining what is worth notice, a full descrip-tion, such as is given by guides and cicerones, Luc. :—geographical description, Strab.

περιηγητής, οῦ, ὁ, (περιηγέομαι) one who guides strangers round and shews what is worth notice, a cicerone, showman, Luc. :—a describer of geographi-cal details, Id.

περιήδη, Att. plqpf. of περίοιδα.

περι-ήκω, f. ξω, to have come round to one, τὰ σὲ περιήκοντα that which has fallen to thy lot, Hdt.; τοῦτον τὸν ἄνδρα φαμὲν περιήκειν τὰ πρῶτα we say that the greatest luck befel this man, Id. 2. of Time, to have come round, Plut.

περιήλθον, aor. 2 of περιέρχομαι.

περι-ήλυσις, ή, a coming round, encompassing, Plut. 2. a revolution, Hdt.

περι-ημεκτέω, f. ήσω, to be much aggrieved, to chafe greatly at, c. dat., Hdt.; c. gen. pers. to be aggrieved at or with him, Id. (Deriv. of -ημεκτέω uncertain.)

περιήνεικα, Ion. for -ήνεγκα, aor. 1 of περιφέρω, Hdt.
περι-ηχέω, f. ήσω, to ring all round, Il. :—so in Med., νῆσος περιηχουμένη τῷ κύματι Luc.
περιήχησις, εως, ἡ, a resounding, echoing, Plut.
περι-θαμβής, ές, (θάμβος) much alarmed, Plut.
περιθεῖναι, aor. 2 inf. of περιτίθημι :—περιθείς, part.
περί-θεσις, εως, ἡ, a putting on, N. T.
περί-θετος, ον, or περιθετός, ή, όν, put round, περιθεταὶ τρίχες false hair, Polyb.
περι-θέω, f. -θεύσομαι :—to run round, Hom., Hdt. ; c. acc. loci, Hdt., Xen.   II. to run about, Lat. discurro, Ar., Plat.   III. to rotate, revolve, ἀσπίδος αἰεὶ περιθεούσης, i. e. as he was always swaying his shield round and round, Hdt.
περι-θεωρέω, f. ήσω, to go round and observe, Luc.
περι-θρηνέομαι, Pass. to resound with wailing, Plut.
περι-θριγκόω, f. ώσω, to edge or fence all round, Plut.
περί-θῡμος, ον, very wrathful, Aesch. Adv. -μως, Id. ; περιθύμως ἔχειν to be very angry, Hdt.
περι-ιάπτω, to wound all round, περὶ θυμὸς ἰάφθη (3 sing. aor. 1 pass.) Theocr.
περι-ιάχω [ᾰ], to ring around, re-echo, Od. ; Ep. impf. περίαχε [ῐ], for περιίαχε, Hes.
περιϊδεῖν, aor. 2 inf. of περιοράω.
περιΐδμεναι, Ep. inf. of pf. περίοιδα.
περι-ίζομαι, Dep. to sit round about, Hdt. ; c. acc., Id.
περι-ιππεύω, f. σω, to ride round, Polyb.
περι-ίστημι,   A. in the trans. tenses, f. -στήσω, aor. 1 -έστησα, to place round, π. τί τινι Hdt. ; στρατὸν περὶ πόλιν Xen. :—metaph., π. τινὶ πλείω κακά Dem.   2. to bring round, π. πολιτείαν εἰς ἑαυτόν to bring it round to himself, Arist. :—esp. to bring into a worse state, Aeschin.   II. in aor. 1 med. to place round oneself, Xen.
B. Pass. and Med., with aor. 2 act. -έστην, pf. -έστηκα, plqpf. -ἑστήκειν, to stand round about, Il. ; κῦμα περιστάθη a wave rose around (Ep. aor. 1 pass.), Od.   2. c. acc. to stand round, encircle, surround, Hom. ; μήπως με περιστήωσ' ἕνα πολλοί (Ep. 3 pl. aor. 2 subj.), that their numbers surround me not, Il. ; metaph., τὸ περιεστὸς ἡμᾶς δεινόν Thuc.   II. to come round to one, νομίσαντες τὸ παρανόμημα ἐς τοὺς Ἀθηναίους περιεστάναι Thuc. :—c. dat. to come upon one, ἡμῖν ἀδοξία περιέστη Id. ; τοῦ πολέμου περιεστηκότος τοῖς Θηβαίοις Dem.   2. of events, to come round, turn out, esp. for the worse, ἐς τοῦτο περιέστη ἡ τύχη fortune was so completely reversed, Thuc. ; τοὐναντίον περιέστη αὐτῷ it turned out quite contrary for him, Id. ; c. inf., περιειστήκει τοῖς βοηθείας δεομένοις αὐτοὺς ἑτέροις βοηθεῖν it came round to those who required help to give help to others, Dem.   III. in late writers, to go round so as to avoid, Luc., N. T.
περιίσχω, = περιέχω.
περι-ιτέον, verb. Adj. of περίειμι (εἶμι ibo), one must make a circuit, Plat.
περιιών, part. of περίειμι (εἶμι ibo).
περικάδομαι, Dor. for -κήδομαι.
περι-καής, ές, (καίομαι) on fire all round : Adv., περικαῶς ἔχειν τινός to be hot with love for . . , Plut.
περι-καθάπτω, f. ψω, to fasten or hang on all round, ἀγγεῖον Plut.
περι-κάθαρμα, ατος, τό, an off-scouring, refuse, N. T.

περι-καθέζομαι, Dep. to sit down round, Luc. : c. acc. to sit down round a town, Dem.
περι-κάθημαι, Ion. -κάτημαι, inf. ἧσθαι : Ion. 3 pl. impf. περικατέατο (properly pf. of περικαθέζομαι) :— to be seated or to sit all round, Hdt. : of an army, to beleaguer, invest a town, Id. ; of ships, to blockade, Id : c. acc. pers. to sit down by one, Id.
περι-καίω, Att. -κάω, f. -καύσω, to burn round about : —Pass. to be all scorched, Hdt.
περι-κᾰκέω, (κακός) to be in extreme ill-luck, Polyb.
περικάκησις, εως, ἡ, extreme ill-luck, Polyb.
περι-καλλής, ές, (κάλλος) very beautiful, Hom.
περικᾰλυπτέα, verb. Adj. one must muffle or wrap oneself up, Ar.   From
περι-κᾰλύπτω, f. ψω, to cover all round, Il.   II. to put round as a covering, αὐτῷ περὶ κῶμ' ἐκάλυψα put sleep as a cloak round him, Ib. ; π. τοῖσι πράγμασι σκότον to throw a veil of darkness over . . , Eur.
περι-κάμπτω, f. ψω, to bend round : to drive round (sub. ἅρμα or ἵππους), Plat.
περι-καταρρέω, to fall in and go to ruin, Lys.
περι-καταρρήγνῡμι, f. -ρήξω, to tear off round about, strip off :—Med., περικατερρήξατο τὸν ἄνωθεν πέπλον she tore off and rent her outer garment, Xen.
περικάτημαι, Ion. for -κάθημαι.
περικάω, Att. for περικαίω.
περί-κειμαι, inf. -κεῖσθαι : f. -κείσομαι :—used as Pass. of περικατατίθημι, to lie round about, c. dat., εὗρε δὲ Πατρόκλῳ περικείμενον ὃν φίλον υἱόν she found her son lying with his arms round Patroclus, Il. ; γωρυτὸς τόξῳ περίκειτο there was a case round the bow, Od. : —absol. to lie or be round, Hes. ; τὰ περικείμενα χρυσία plates of gold laid on (an ivory statue), Thuc.   2. metaph., οὔ τι μοι περίκειται there is no advantage for me, it is nothing to me, Il.   II. c. acc. rei, to have round one, to wear, mostly in part., περικείμενοι [τελαμῶνας] περὶ τοῖσι αὐχέσι Hdt. ; π. δύναμιν invested with power, Plut. ; π. ἄλυσιν with a chain round one, N. T.
περι-κείρω, f. -κερῶ, to shear or clip all round, Hdt. ; Med., περικείρεσθαι τρίχας to have one's hair clipt, Id.
περι-κεφαλαία, ἡ, a covering for the head, a helmet, cap, Polyb. ; also περικεφάλαιον, τό, Id.
περι-κήδομαι, Dep. only in pres., to be very anxious about a person, c. gen., Od., Pind. :—π. τινι βιότου to take care of a living for him, Od.
περί-κηλος, ον, (κῆλον) exceeding dry, of timber, Od.
περι-κίων [ῑ], ον, surrounded with pillars, Eur.
περικλᾰσις, ἡ, ruggedness of ground, Polyb.
περι-κλάω, f. -κλάσω, to break one thing round or on another, τί τινι Plut. ; π. τὸν Τίβεριν to divert it, Id.
περι-κλειτός, ή, όν, famed all round, farfamed, Theocr.
περι-κλείω, Ion. -κληίω, old Att. -κλήω, f. -σω, to shut in all round, surround on all sides, Hdt., Thuc. ; so in Med., περικληήσασθαι τὰς ναῦς to get them surrounded, Thuc. ; and in Pass., ὑπὸ πλήθους περικληόμενοι closed in.
περι-κλινής, ές, (κλίνω) sloping on all sides, Plut.
περι-κλίνω, f. -κλινῶ, to decline, of the sun, Strab.
περι-κλύζομαι, Pass. to be washed all round by the sea, of an island, Thuc. ; of a strait, Plut.
περίκλυστος, η, ον, and ος, ον, washed all round by the sea, of islands, h. Hom., Aesch., etc.

περι-κλῡτός, ή, όν, heard of all round, famous, renowned, glorious, Lat. inclytus, Hom.

περι-κνημίς, ή, (κνήμη) a covering for the leg, Plut.

περι-κνίζω, f. σω, to scratch all round, keep nibbling; so in aor. 1 med. περικνίξασθε, of bees, Anth.

περι-κοκκάζω or -ύζω, aor. 1 -εκόκκασα or -υσα, to cry cuckoo all round, Ar.

περι-κομίζω, f. σω, to carry round, Thuc. :—Pass. to go round, Id.

περίκομμα, ατος, τό, (περικόπτω) that which is cut off all round, trimmings, mincemeat, Ar.

περίκομψος, ον, very elegant, exquisite, Ar.

περικοπή, ή, a cutting all round, mutilation, Thuc.; trepanning, Plut.　　II. the outline or general form of a person or thing, Polyb.　　III. a section or short passage in an author : a portion of scripture, as the Epistles and Gospels. From

περι-κόπτω, f. ψω, to cut all round, clip, mutilate, Dem.: Pass., περιεκόπησαν τὰ πρόσωπα had their faces mutilated, Thuc.　　2. π. χώραν to lay waste an enemy's country, from the practice of cutting down the fruit-trees, Dem.; hence, to plunder a person, Id. :—simply, to take away, intercept, Plut.

περι-κράνιος [ᾰ], ον, round the skull, πῖλος π. a skull-cap, Plut.

περι-κρᾰτής, ές, (κράτος) having full command over a thing, c. gen., N. T.

περικρεμάννῡμι, to hang round, τί τινι Anth. :—Pass. to hang round, to cling to, c. dat., Id.

περι-κρήμνος, ον, steep all round, Plut.

περι-κρούω, f. σω, to strike off all round : Pass., περικρουσθεῖσα πέτρας τε καὶ ὄστρεα having stones and shells knocked off, stript of them, Plat.

περι-κρύπτω, f. ψω: aor. 2 -έκρῠβον:—to conceal entirely, Luc., N. T.

περι-κτίονες, όνων, οἱ, Ep. dat. περικτιόνεσσι, (κτίζω) dwellers around, neighbours, Hom.; cf. ἀμφικτίονες.

περι-κτίται [τῐ], ῶν, οἱ, = foreg., Od.

περι-κυκλόω, f. ώσω, to encircle, encompass : mostly in Med. to surround an enemy, Hdt., Xen.　　II. intr. to go round, Luc.　Hence

περι-κύκλωσις, ή, an encircling, encompassing, Thuc.

περι-κυλινδέω, later -κυλίω [ῐ] : aor. 1 -εκύλισα :—to roll round, Ar.

περι-κύμων [ῡ], ον, (κῦμα) surrounded by waves, of islands, Eur.

περι-κωμάζω, f. σω, to carouse round, παλαίστρας Ar.

περι-κωνέω, f. ήσω, (κῶνος) to smear all over with pitch, π. τὰ ἐμβάδια to black shoes, Ar.

περι-λαμβάνω, f. -λήψομαι: aor. 2 -έλαβον :—to seize around, embrace, Xen.　　2. to encompass or surround an enemy, so as to intercept him, Hdt.; μετεώρους τὰς ναῦς π. to intercept them at sea, Thuc.; ἐπεὰν δὲ αὐτὸν περιλάβῃς when you get hold of him, catch him, Hdt. :—Pass. to be caught, οἴμοι, περιείλημμαι μόνος Ar.　　II. to comprehend, include, of a number of particulars, Isocr., Plat.

περι-λαμπής, ές, (λάμπω) very brilliant, Plut.

περι-λάμπω, f. ψω, to beam around, Plut.　　II. c. acc. to shine around, φῶς π. τινά N. T. :—Pass. to be illumined, Plut., Luc.

περι-λείπομαι, aor. 1 -ελείφθην, Pass. to be left remaining, remain over, survive, Il., Hdt., etc.

περι-λείχω, f. ξω, to lick all round, Ar.

περί-λεξις, ή, circumlocution, Ar.

περι-λέπω, f. ψω, to strip off all round, Il., Hdt.

περι-λεσχήνευτος, ον, talked of in every club (λέσχη), matter of common talk, Hdt.

περι-ληπτός, ή, όν, embraced or to be embraced, Plut.

περι-λιμνάζω, f. σω, to surround with water, insulate, τὴν πόλιν Thuc.

περι-λῑπής, ές, (περιλείπομαι) surviving, Plat.

περι-λιχμάομαι, Dep. to lick all round, Theocr., Luc.　　2. to lick up, Luc.

περίλοιπος, ον, = περιλιπής, Thuc.

περι-λούω, f. σω, to wash all over, Plut.

περί-λῡπος, ον, (λύπη) deeply grieved, Isocr., Arist.

περι-μαιμάω, to gaze or peep eagerly round, σκόπελον περιμαιμώωσα (Ep. part.), Od.

περι-μαίνομαι, Pass. to rush furiously about, Hes.

περι-μάκης [ᾰ], Dor. for περι-μήκης.

περι-μάσσω, Att. -ττω, f. ξω, to wipe all round, to purify by magic, disenchant by purification, Dem.

περι-μάχητος [ᾰ], ον, (μάχομαι) fought about, fought for or to be fought for, Ar., Thuc.; οὐ περιμαχητόν not a thing one would fight for, Xen.

περι-μένω, f. -μενῶ, to wait for, await, Hdt., Ar., etc.　　2. of events, to await, be in store for, Soph., Plat.　　II. c. inf. οὐ περιμένουσιν ἄλλους σφᾶς διολέσαι they do not wait for others to destroy them, Plat.; μηδ' ἐφ' ἑαυτὸν [ταῦτα] ἐλθεῖν π. Dem.　　III. absol. to wait, stand still, Hdt., Ar., etc.

περί-μεστος, ον, full all round, quite full of, τινός Xen.

περι-μετρέω, f. ήσω, to measure all round, Luc.

περίμετρον, τό, the circumference, Hdt.

περίμετρος, ον, (μέτρον) excessive, in size or beauty, very large or very beautiful, of Penelope's web, Od.　　II. περίμετρος (sc. γραμμή), ή, = περίμετρον, Polyb.

περιμήκετος, ον, poët. for sq. (cf. πάχετος), very tall or high, Hom.

περι-μήκης, ες, Dor. -μάκης [ᾰ], ες, (μῆκος) very tall or long, Od. :—very large, huge, Hdt.

περι-μηχᾰνάομαι, Ep. 3 pl. impf. -μηχανόωντο, Dep. to prepare very craftily, contrive cunningly, Od.

περι-μῡκάομαι, Dep. to roar round, τινα Plut.

περι-ναιετάω, to dwell round about or in the neighbourhood, Od.　　2. in pass. sense, to be inhabited, Ib.

περι-ναιέτης, ου, ὁ, (ναίω) one of those who dwell round, a neighbour, Il.

περι-νέω, f. -νήσω: aor. 1 inf. -νῆσαι, lengthd. -νηῆσαι: —to pile round, ὕλην (sc. περὶ τὸν πύργον) Hdt.　　2. π. τὴν οἰκίην ὕλῃ to pile it round with wood, Id.

περί-νεως, ὁ, gen. -νεω, nom. pl. -νεῳ: (ναῦς):—a supercargo or passenger, Thuc.

περινῆσαι, Ep. -νήησαι, aor. 1 inf. of περινέω.

περι-νίζω, f. -νίψω, to wash off all round :—Pass., περὶ δ' αἷμα νένιπται Il.

περι-νίσσομαι, Dep. to come round, of time, Eur.

περι-νοέω, f. ήσω, to contrive cunningly, Ar.　　II. to consider on all sides, consider well, Plut.　Hence

περίνοια, ή, quick intelligence : over-wiseness, Thuc.

περι-νοστέω, f. ήσω, to go round, to visit or inspect,

τὰς παλαίστρας Ar. 2. absol. *to go about, stalk about*, Id., Plat.

πέριξ, strengthd. for περί, **I.** as Prep. *round about, all round*, c. gen., Hdt., Xen. **2.** c. acc., Hdt., Aesch., Eur. **II.** as Adv. *round about, all round*, Hdt., Trag.: metaph., π. φρονεῖν *circuitously*, Eur.

περι-ξεστός, ή, όν, *polished round about*, πέτρη Od.

περι-ξέω, f. έσω, *to polish all round*, Theocr.

περι-ξῡράω, Ion. -έω, f. ήσω, *to shave all round*, Hdt.:—Pass., περιεξυρημένος τὸν πώγωνα *having one's beard clean shaven*, Luc.

περι-οδεία or -οδία, ή, (ὁδός) *a circuit*, Strab.

περιοδεύω, f. σω, *to go all round*, c. acc., Plut.

περιοδίζω, *to be periodical*, Strab. From

περί-οδος, ή, *a going round, a flank march*, Hdt., Thuc. **II.** *a way round, the circumference, circuit, compass*, τοῦ τείχεος, τῆς λίμνης Hdt.; absol., τὴν π. *in circumference*, Id. **III.** γῆς π. *a chart* or *map* of the earth (cf. πίναξ), Id., Ar. **IV.** *a going round in a circle, circuit*, Plut. **2.** of Time, *a cycle* or *period of time*, Pind., Plat., etc. **3.** *a prescribed course of life, system*, Plat. **4.** *a fit* of intermittent fever, Dem. **5.** περιφορά, *a course at dinner*, Xen.; π. λόγων *table-talk*, Id. **6.** *the orbit of a heavenly body*, Id. **V.** *a well-rounded sentence, period*, Arist.

περί-οιδα, **περι-ήδη**, pf. and plqpf. (in pres. and impf. sense), *to know well how to do*, c. inf., περίοιδε νοῆσαι Il.; c. dat., ἴχνεσι γὰρ περιήδη *for he was well skilled in the tracks*, Od.:—c. acc. rei et gen. pers., βουλῇ περιίδμεναι ἄλλων (Ep. inf.) *to be better skilled in counsel than others*, Il.

περιοικέω, f. ήσω, (περίοικος) *to dwell round* a person or place, c. acc., Hdt., Xen.

περιοικίς, ίδος, ή, fem. of περίοικος, *dwelling* or *lying round about, neighbouring*, Hdt., Thuc. **II.** as Subst. (sub. γῆ, χώρα), *the country round* a town, *the suburbs*, Thuc. **2.** *a town of* περίοικοι, *a dependent town*, Arist.

περι-οικοδομέω, f. ήσω, *to build round*, Dem. **II.** *to enclose by building round*, Id.:—Pass. *to be built up, walled in*, Thuc., Xen.; τὸ περιοικοδομημένον *the space built round, the enclosure*, Lat. *ovile*.

περί-οικος, ον, *dwelling round*, Hdt.:—οἱ π. *neighbours*, Id. **II.** in Laconia, οἱ περίοικοι were *the free inhabitants*, being remnants of the original population, who enjoyed civil but not political liberty, opp. on the one hand to the Spartans, and on the other to the Helots, Id., Thuc.

περι-ολισθάνω, aor. 2 -ώλισθον, *to slip away all round, slip off*, Plut. Hence

περιολίσθησις, ή, *a slipping away*, Plut.

περι-οπτέος, α, ον, verb. Adj. of περιοράω, *to be overlooked* or *suffered*, c. part., οὐ σφι περιοπτέα Ἑλλὰς ἀπολλυμένη Hdt.; c. inf., ἡμῖν τοῦτό ἐστι οὐ περιοπτέον, γένος τὸ Εὐρυσθένεος γενέσθαι ἐξίτηλον Id. **2.** *to be watched* or *guarded against*, Thuc. **II.** περιοπτέον *one must overlook* or *suffer*, Xen.

περί-οπτος, ον, (ὄψομαι) *to be seen all round, in a commanding position*, Plut. **2.** *conspicuous, admirable*, Id.:—Adv. -τως, *gloriously*, Id.

περι-οράω, impf. περιεώρων, Ion. περιώρεον: pf. περι-

εόρᾱκα: f. -όψομαι, pf. pass. -ῶμμαι, aor. 1 pass. -ώφθην: aor. 2 περιεῖδον: for pf. περίοιδα, v. sub voc.: —*to look over, overlook*, i. e. *to allow, suffer*: **1.** mostly c. part., οὐ περιεῖδον αὐτὸν ἁναρπασθέντα *they did not overlook his being carried off*, i. e. *did not suffer him to be* .., Hdt.; μὴ περιιδεῖν τὴν ἡγεμονίην αὖτις ἐς Μήδους περιελθοῦσαν Id., etc.; ταῦτα περιιδεῖν γιγνόμενα Dem.; but, εἰ ὑμᾶς τοὺς ἐναντιουμένους περιίδοιμεν *if we overlook your opposition*, Thuc. **2.** c. inf., περιιδόντες τοὺς Πέρσας ἐσελθεῖν *having suffered them to enter*, Hdt., etc.:—with the inf. omitted, οὐκ ἄν με περιείδες [ποιέειν] Id.; π. τὴν ὕβριν Xen. **II.** *to wait for*, τὸ μέλλον περιιδεῖν Thuc. **III.** Med. *to look about before doing a thing, to watch the turn of events, to watch and wait*, Id. **2.** c. gen. *to look round after, watch over*, Id.

περι-οργής, ές, (ὀργή) *very angry* or *wrathful*, Thuc. Adv. -γῶς, Aesch.

περί-ορθρος, ον, *towards morning*: τὸ π. *dawn*, Thuc.

περι-ορίζω, f. σω, *to mark by boundaries*, Plut. Hence

περιορισμός, ὁ, *a limitation*, Plut.

περι-ορμέω, f. ήσω, *to anchor round, to blockade*, Thuc.

περι-ορμίζω, f. ίσω, *to bring round* [a ship] *to anchor*, Dem.:—Med. *to come round*, Thuc.

περι-ορύσσω, Att. -ττω, f. ξω, *to dig round*, π. λίμνην *to dig a lake round*, Hdt. **2.** *to dig up around*, Plut. **3.** *to dig out around*, Id.

περι-ορχέομαι, f. ήσομαι, Dep. *to dance around*, Luc.

περιουσία, ή, (περί-ειμι, *supersum*) *that which is over and above* necessary expenses, *surplus, abundance, plenty*, Ar., Thuc., etc. **II.** absol. *abundance, plenty, wealth*, Plat., etc.: ἀπὸ περιουσίας *with plenty of other resources, ex abundanti*, Thuc., etc.; εἰς περιουσίαν *so as to bring advantage*, Dem.; ἐκ περιουσίας *at an advantage*, Id. **2.** *superiority* of numbers or force, Thuc. **3.** *a being saved, survival*, τίς οὖν ἡ ταύτης π.; *what is its chance of being saved?* Dem. Hence

περιούσιος, ον, *having more than enough: especial, peculiar*, N. T.

περιοχή, ή, (περιέχω) *compass, extent*:—*a mass, body*, Plut. **II.** *a portion circumscribed, a section* of a book, N. T.

περι-πᾰθής, ές, (παθεῖν) *in violent excitement, greatly distressed*, Polyb. **2.** absol. *passionate*, Luc.:—Adv. -θῶς, Id.

περι-παπταίνω, *to look timidly round*, Mosch.

περιπᾰτέω, f. ήσω, (περίπατος) *to walk up and down, to walk about*, Ar., Xen.: generally, *to walk*, Plat., etc. **2.** metaph. *to walk*, i. e. *live*, N. T. Hence

περιπᾰτητικός, ή, όν, *walking about while teaching*: hence Aristotle and his followers were called περιπατητικοί, *Peripatetics*, Cic., Luc.

περί-πᾰτος, ὁ, *a walking about, walking*, Plat., etc. **II.** *a place for walking, a covered walk*, Xen. **III.** *discourse during a walk, a philosophical discussion*, Ar. **2.** οἱ ἐκ τοῦ περιπάτου *the Peripatetics, school of Aristotle*, because he taught *walking in a περίπατος of the Lyceum* at Athens, Plut., etc.

περι-πείρω, *to pierce* as with a spit: metaph. *to pierce*, ἑαυτοὺς π. ὀδύναις N. T.

περι-πέλομαι, Dep. *to move round, be round about*,

only in Ep. syncop. part., of Place, c. acc., ἄστυ περιπλομένων δηίων while the enemy *are about* the town, Il. **2.** of Time, περιπλομένου δ' ἐνιαυτοῦ as the year *went round, passed*, Od., Hes.; περιπλομένων ἐνιαυτῶν Od.; πέντε π. ἐνιαυτούς during five *revolving* years, Il.

περίπεμπτος, ον, *sent round:* neut. pl. as Adv. *by sending round*, Aesch. From

περι-πέμπω, f. ψω, *to send round* from one place to another, *dispatch in all directions*, Hdt., Thuc.

περιπεσεῖν, aor. 2 inf. of περιπίπτω.

περι-πέσσω, Att. -ττω, f. -πέψω, of bread, *to bake all over*, Lat. *obcrustare:* metaph. *to crust* or *cover over, cook up*, Ar.; π. ἀβλαβῶς *to cover* the men without hurting them, Plut. :—Pass., ῥηματίοις περιπεφθείς (aor. 1 part.) *cajoled* by words, Ar.

περι-πετάννῦμι and -ύω: f. -πετάσω [ă]: pf. pass. -πέπταμαι:—*to spread* or *stretch around*, χέρα τινί Eur.; π. φοινικίδας *to spread* them *out*, Aeschin. :—Pass., περιπέπταται ὑγρὸς ἄκανθος *is spread round*, Theocr. Hence

περιπεταστός, ή, όν, *spread round* or *over*, Ar.

περιπέτεια, ἡ, *a turning right about*, i. e. *a sudden change* of fortune, such as that on which the plot in a Tragedy hinges, Arist. From

περιπετής, ές, (περιπεσεῖν) *falling round*, ἀμφὶ μέσση προσκείμενος π. lying *with his arms clasped round* her waist, Soph. **2.** *wrapt in*, πέπλοισι Aesch. **3.** ἔγχος π. the sword *round* which (i. e. *on which*) he has fallen, Soph. **II.** *falling in with* danger, etc., c. dat., Dem.; π. γενέσθαι τῇ αἰτίᾳ to become *liable* to . . , Plut. **III.** *changing suddenly*, περιπετέα πρήγματα a sudden reverse, Hdt.; π. τύχαι Eur.

περι-πέτομαι, f. -πτήσομαι: aor. -επτόμην: Dep. : —*to fly around*, Ar.

περιπέττω, Att. for περιπέσσω.

περι-πευκής, ές, (πεύκη) *very sharp, keen* or *painful*, Il.

περι-πήγνῦμι, f. -πήξω:—*to fix round*, to make a *fence round*, c. acc. loci, Pind. :—Pass., with pf. act. περιπέπηγα, *to be fixed around*, Plut. :—Pass., τὰ ὑποδήματα π. *are frozen on the feet*, Xen.

περι-πηδάω, f. ήσομαι, *to leap round* or *upon*, Luc.

περί-πηξις, ἡ, *a congealing round*, Strab.

περι-πίμπλαμαι, aor. 1 περιε-πλήσθην, Pass. *to be filled full*, Xen.

περι-πίμπρημι, *to set on fire round about;* impf. περιεπίμπρα Xen.; 3 pl. -επίμπρασαν Thuc.

περι-πίπτω, f. -πεσοῦμαι: aor. 2 -έπεσον :—*to fall around*, so as *to embrace*, τινί Xen. **2.** *to fall around*, i. e. *upon*, a weapon, τῷ ξίφει Ar. **II.** c. dat. *to fall in with*, Hdt., Xen.; of ships meeting by chance at sea, Hdt., Thuc. **2.** *to fall foul of* other ships, Hdt.; περὶ ἀλλήλας of one another, Id.; also, π. περὶ τόπον *to be wrecked* on a place, Id. **3.** metaph. *to fall in with, fall into*, c. dat., π. ἀδίκοισι γνώμῃσι *to encounter* unjust judgments, Id.; π. δουλοσύνῃ Id.; αἰσχρᾷ τύχῃ Eur.; but, ἑωυτῷ περιπίπτειν *to be caught in* one's own snare, Hdt.; so, τοῖς ἑαυτοῦ λόγοις περιπίπτειν Aeschin. **III.** *to change suddenly*, Polyb. **2.** *to fall on one side*, Plut.

περι-πίτνω, poët. for περιπίπτω: c. acc., καρδίαν π. *come over* or *upon* the heart, Aesch.

περι-πλανάομαι, Pass. *to wander about* a country,

c. acc., Hdt. : metaph. *to float round about* one, as the lion's skin round Hercules, Pind. **2.** absol. *to wander about*, ταῦτα π. *to be in* this state of *uncertainty*, Xen.

περι-πλάνιος [ă], ον, (πλάνη) Anth.

περι-πλάσσω, Att. -ττω: f. -πλάσω:—*to plaster* one thing *over* another, *form as a mould* or *cast round*, c. dat., Plat., etc.

περίπλεκτος, ον, *intertwining, crossing*, of the feet of dancers, Theocr. From

περι-πλέκω, f. ξω, *to twine* or *enfold round* :—Pass. *to fold oneself round*, c. dat.; ἱστῷ περιπλεχθείς Od.; absol., δίκτυον εὖ μάλα περιπλεκόμενον *close folding*, Xen. **II.** *to complicate, entangle*, Luc. **2.** *to wrap up in words*, Aeschin.

περιπλευμονία or -πνευμονία, Ion. -ίη, ἡ, (πλεύμων) *inflammation of the lungs*, Plat., Luc.

περί-πλευρος, ον, (πλευρά) *covering the side*, Eur.

περι-πλέχθην, Ep. aor. 1 pass. of περιπλέκω.

περι-πλέω, Ion. -πλώω:—*to sail* or *swim round*, absol., Hdt., etc.; ἀνὴρ πολλὰ περιπλευκώς a man of *many voyages*, Ar.; c. acc., π. Λιβύην, Πελοπόννησον, etc., Hdt., Thuc., etc.

περι-πλέως, ων, pl. -πλεω, neut. -πλεα, c. gen. *quite full of* a thing, Thuc., etc.: c. dat. *filled with* a thing, Anth. **II.** absol. *supernumerary, spare*, Xen.

περι-πληθής, ές, (πλῆθος) *very full of people*, Od. **2.** *very large*, Plut.; Comp. -έστερος, Luc.

περίπλικτος, ον, *crossed*, Luc. From

περι-πλίσσομαι, Dep. *to put the legs round* or *across*.

περιπλοκή, ἡ, (περιπλέκω) *a twining round, entanglement, intricacy*, Eur.

περίπλοκος, ον, (περιπλέκω) *entwined*, Anth.

περιπλόμενος, syncop. part. of περιπέλομαι.

περί-πλοος, ον, contr. -πλους, ουν, (πλέω) *sailing round*, Anth. **II.** pass. *that may be sailed round*, Thuc.

περί-πλοος, ὁ, contr. -πλους, gen. -πλου, nom. pl. -πλοι, (πλέω) *a sailing round* a place, c. gen., Hdt.; περὶ τόπον Thuc. **II.** *the account of a coasting voyage*, Luc.

περι-πλύνω [ῠ], *to wash clean, scour well*, Dem.

περιπλώω, Ion. and poët. for περιπλέω.

περιπνείω, Ep. for περιπνέω.

περιπνευμονία, v. περιπλευμονία.

περι-πνέω, f. -πνεύσομαι, *to breathe round* or *over* a place, c. acc., Pind.

περι-πόθητος, ον, *much-beloved*, Luc.

περι-ποιέω, f. ήσω, *to make to remain over and above, to keep safe, preserve*, Hdt., Thuc., etc. **2.** of money, *to save up, lay by*, Xen. **3.** *to put round* or *upon, procure*, τὴν δυναστείαν ἑαυτοῖς Aeschin.; π. τὰ πράγματα εἰς αὑτούς *to get* things into their own hands, Thuc. **II.** Med. *to keep* or *save for oneself*, Hdt., etc. :—*to compass, acquire, obtain*, Thuc., Xen.: —absol. *to make gain*, Xen. Hence

περιποίησις, ἡ, *a keeping safe, preservation*, N.T. **II.** (from Med.) *a gaining possession of, acquisition, obtaining*, Ib. **2.** *a possession*, Ib.

περι-ποίκιλος, ον, *variegated* or *spotted all over*, Xen.

περιπολ-άρχης or **-αρχος, ου, ὁ,** (περίπολος, ἄρχω) *a superintendent of police*, Thuc.

περι-πολέω, f. ήσω, *to go round* or *about, wander*

.

about, Soph., Eur.　II. c. acc. loci, to traverse, Plat.; π. στρατόν to prowl about it, Eur.　2. at Athens, περιπολεῖν τὴν χώραν to patrol the country (v. περίπολος), Xen.

περιπόλιον, τό, a station for περίπολοι, a guard-house, Thuc.

περιπόλιος, ον, lying round a place, c. gen., Strab.

περί-πολος, ον, (πολέω) going the rounds, patrolling: hence, as Subst.,　1. a watchman, patrol, Plut., etc. :—at Athens, the περίπολοι were young citizens between 18 and 20, who formed a sort of patrol to guard the frontier, Ar., Thuc.　2. generally, an attendant, follower, as fem., Soph.

περι-πόνηρος, ον, very rascally, as a pun on περιφόρητος, Ar.

περι-πορεύομαι, f. σομαι, Dep. to travel or go about a place, c. acc., Polyb.

περι-πόρφυρος, ον, (πορφύρα) edged with purple, π. ἐσθής a robe with a purple border, the Roman toga praetextata or laticlavia, Polyb., etc.:—hence περι-πορφυρό-σημος παῖς, ὁ, Lat. puer praetextatus, Anth.

περι-ποτάομαι, poët. for -πέτομαι, to hover about, Soph.

περι-πρό, Adv. very much, especially, Il.

περι-προχέομαι, Pass. to be poured all round, in aor. 1 part., ἔρος θυμὸν περιπροχυθείς love rushing in a flood over his heart, Il.

περι-πταίω, f. σω, to stumble upon, τινί Plut.

περι-πτίσσω, to strip off the husk:—pf. pass. part. περιεπτισμένοι free from the chaff, clean winnowed, Ar.

περίπτυγμα, ατος, τό, anything folded round, a covering, Eur.; and

περίπτυξις, ἡ, an embracing, Plut. From

περι-πτύσσω, f. ξω, to enfold, enwrap in a thing, τινά τινι Soph.; πέπλοι περιπτύσσοντες δέμας Eur.; π. γονύ, δέμας to clasp, embrace it, Id.　2. as military term, to outflank, Xen.　II. to fold round, π. χέρας to fold the arms round another, Eur.

περι-πτυχή, ἡ, something which enfolds, τειχέων περιπτυχαί enfolding walls, Eur.; δόμων Ar.; Ἀχαιῶν ναύλοχοι π. their naval cloak or fence, Eur.　II. an enfolding, embracing, Id.; ἐν ἡλίου περιπτυχαῖς in all that the sun embraces, i. e. all the world, Id.

περι-πτυχής, ές, (περιπτύσσω) folded round, Soph.　2. φασγάνῳ π. fallen around (i. e. upon) his sword, Id.

περί-πτωμα, ατος, τό, a calamity, Plat.

περι-πτώσσω, to fear greatly, Anth.

περί-πυστος, ον, known all round about, Anth.

περιρ-ράγης, ές, torn or broken all round, Anth.

περιρ-ραίνω, to besprinkle all round, esp. in sacred rites :—Med. to purify oneself, Theophr., Plut. Hence

περιρραντήριον, τό, an utensil for besprinkling, or a vessel for lustral water, Lat. aspergillum, Hdt.　II. περιρραντήρια ἀγορᾶς the parts of the forum sprinkled with lustral water, Lex ap. Aeschin.

περιρ-ρέω: f. -ρεύσομαι: pf. -ερρύηκα: aor. 2 pass. (in act. sense) -ερρύην:　I. c. acc. to flow round, τὸν δ' αἷμα περίρρεε Od.; νῆσον π. ὁ Νεῖλος Hdt., etc.:—Pass. to be surrounded by water, Xen.　II. to slip away on all sides, ἡ ἀσπὶς περιερρύη εἰς τὴν θάλασσαν slipped off his arm into the sea, Thuc.; [αἴ πέδαι] αὐτόμαται π. Xen.　2. to overflow on all sides, σοὶ περιρρείτω βίος may thy means of living abound, Soph.; οὐδενὸς

περιρρέοντος being superfluous, Plut. :—Pass. to be all dripping, ἱδρῶτι with sweat, Id.

περιρ-ρήγνυμι and -ύω, f. -ρήξω :—of clothes, to rend from round one, to rend and tear off, Dem. :—Med., περιερρήξατο τοὺς πέπλους tore off his own garments, Plut. :—Pass. to be torn off, Aesch.　II. to make a stream break or divide round a piece of land, [Βούσιρις] τὸν Νεῖλον περὶ τὴν χώραν περιέρρηξε Isocr. : Pass., κατὰ τὸ ὀξὺ τοῦ Δέλτα περιρρήγνυται ὁ Νεῖλος at the apex of the Delta the Nile is broken round it, i. e. breaks into several branches, Hdt.　III. to break a thing round or on another, to wreck, τὸ σκαφίδιον πρὸς πέτραν Luc.

περιρ-ρηδής, ές, doubled round or over a thing, c. dat., περιρρηδὴς τραπέζῃ Od. (The deriv. of -ρηδής is uncertain; perh. from ῥέω.)

περιρροή, ἡ, (περιρρέω) a flowing round, Plat.

περιρ-ρομβέω, f. ήσω, to make to spin round like a top, Plut.

περίρ-ροος, ον, contr. -ρους, ουν, = περίρρυτος, Hdt.

περίρ-ρῠτος, ον, and η, ον, like περίρροος, surrounded with water, sea-girt, of islands, Od., Hdt., etc.　2. act. flowing round, c. gen., περιρρύτων ὕπερ ἀκαρπίστων πεδίων Σικελίας over the barren plains that flow round Sicily, i. e. the sea, Eur.

περι-σαίνω, Ep. περισσαίνω, to wag the tail round, fawn upon, c. acc. or absol., Od.

περι-σείομαι, Pass. to be shaken all round, ἔθειραι περισσείοντο (Ep. for περιεσείοντο) the hair was floating round, Il.

περί-σεμνος, η, ον, very august, Ar.

περί-σεπτος, η, ον, much-revered, Aesch.

περί-σημος, Dor. -σᾱμος, ον, (σῆμα) very famous or notable, Lat. insignis, Eur., Mosch.

περισθενέω, to be exceeding strong, Ep. part. περισθενέων Od. From

περι-σθενής, ές, (σθένος) exceeding strong, Pind.

περι-σκελής, ές, (σκέλλω) dry and hard all round, exceeding hard, of iron, Soph. :—metaph. obstinate, stubborn, Id.

περι-σκελίς, ίδος, ἡ, (σκέλος) a leg-band, i. e. an anklet or bangle, Menand., Horat.

περι-σκέπτομαι, v. περισκοπέω. Hence

περί-σκεπτος, ον, to be seen on all sides, far-seen, conspicuous, Od.　2. admired, Anth.

περι-σκέπω, = περισκεπάζω, Polyb., Mosch.

περι-σκιρτάω, f. ήσω, to leap round, c. acc., Anth.

περι-σκοπέω, f. -σκέψομαι, -έσκεμμαι :—to look round, Soph.　II. to examine all round, observe carefully, consider well, Hdt., Thuc.: pf. part. περιεσκεμμένως, circumspect, Plut.

περι-σκῠλάκισμος, ὁ, (σκύλαξ) a sacrifice in which a puppy was sacrificed and carried about, Plut.

περι-σμᾰρᾰγέω, f. ήσω, to rattle all round, Luc.

περι-σοβέω, f. ήσω, to chase about, π. ποτήριον to push round the wine-cup, Menand.　II. to run bustling round, τὰς πόλεις Ar.

περι-σοφίζομαι, Dep. to overreach, cheat, Ar.

περισπασμός, ὁ, distraction, Polyb. From

περι-σπάω, f. -σπάσω, to draw off from around, to strip off :—Med. to strip oneself of, τὴν τιάραν Xen.　2. to strip bare, Eur.　II. to draw round, wheel

about, of an army, Polyb. : of a horse's bit, οὐ πάνυ π. *not pulling* it violently *round*, Luc. : — Med., περισπώμενος τὰς ὄψεις *turning about one's eyes*, Id.   III. *to draw off* or *away*, Arist. :—Pass. *to be distracted* or *engaged in business*, περί τι N. T.

περισπεῖν, aor. 2 inf. of περιέπω.

περι-σπειράω, f. άσω, *to wind round*, Plut. :—Med. *to surround* with soldiers, Id. :—Pass., of soldiers, *to form round* a leader, τινί Id. ; of serpents, *to twine round*, τινί Luc.

περισπερχέω, *to be much angered*, Hdt.   From

περι-σπερχής, ές, (σπέρχω) *very hasty*, π. πάθος a *rash, overhasty death*, Soph.

περί-σπλαγχνος, ον, (σπλάγχνον) *great-hearted*, Theocr.

περι-σπογγίζω, f. σω, *to sponge all round*, Theophr.

περι-σπούδαστος, ον, (σπουδάζω) *much sought after, much desired*, Luc.

περισσεία, ἡ, (περισσός) *surplus, abundance*, N. T.

περισσείομαι, Ep. for περισσείομαι.

περίσσευμα, Att. -ττευμα, ατος, τό, *that which remains over, abundance*, N. T.

περισσεύω, Att. -ττεύω, f. σω : impf. ἐπερίσσευον : (περισσός) :—*to be over and above* the number, c. gen., περιττεύσουσιν ἡμῶν οἱ πολέμιοι the enemy *will go beyond* us, *outflank* us, Xen.   II. absol. *to be more than enough, remain over*, Id., etc. ; τοσοῦτον τῷ Περικλεῖ ἐπερίσσευε such *abundance* of reason had Pericles, Thuc.   2. in bad sense, *to be superfluous*, Soph.   III. of persons, *to abound in* a thing, c. dat., N. T. :—also c. gen., π. ἄρτων *to have more than enough* of bread, Ib.   2. *to be superior, have the advantage*, Ib. : π. μᾶλλον *to abound* more and more, Ib.   IV. Causal, *to make to abound*, Ib. :—Pass. *to be made to abound*, Ib.

περισσολογία, ἡ, *over-talking, wordiness*, Isocr.   From

περισσο-λόγος, ον, (λέγω) *talking too much, wordy*, Soph.

περισσός, Att. περιττός, ή, όν, (περί) *beyond the regular number* or *size, prodigious*, Hes.   2. *out of the common way, extraordinary, uncommon, remarkable, signal, strange*, εἴ τι περισσὸν εἰδείη σοφίης if he has any *signal* gift of wisdom, Theogn. ; so, π. λόγος Soph. ; οὐ γὰρ περισσὸν οὐδὲν οὐδ' ἔξω λόγου πέπονθας Eur.   3. of persons, *extraordinary, eminent, remarkable*, esp. for learning, Id.   4. c. gen., περισσὸς ἄλλων πρός τι *beyond* others in a thing, Soph.; θύσει τοῦδε περισσότερα *greater things than* this, Anth. ; περιττότερα προφήτου *greater than* a prophet, N. T.   II. *more than sufficient, redundant, superfluous*, Xen. ; περιττὸν ἔχειν *to have a surplus*, Id. ; c. gen., τῶν ἀρκούντων περιττά *more than* sufficient, Id. :—often in military sense, οἱ π. ἱππεῖς the *reserve* horse, Id. ; π. σκηναί *spare* tents, Id. ; τὸ π. the *surplus, residue*, Id.   2. in bad sense, *superfluous*, Trag.   3. *excessive, extravagant*, περισσὰ μηχανᾶσθαι *to commit extravagancies*, Hdt.; περισσὰ δρᾶν, πράσσειν *to be overbusy*, Soph.   4. of persons, *extravagant, over-curious*, περισσὸς καὶ φρονῶν μέγα Eur. ; π. ἐν τοῖς λόγοις Δημοσθένης Aeschin.   III. in Arithmetic, ἀριθμὸς περιττός is an *odd, uneven* number, opp. to ἄρτιος, Plat., etc.

B. Adv. περισσῶς, *extraordinarily, exceedingly*, Hdt., Eur. ; π. παῖδας ἐκδιδάσκεσθαι to have them edu-

cated *overmuch*, Eur. ; also περισσά, Pind., Eur.   2. *in a peculiar manner, remarkably*, περισσότερον τῶν ἄλλων θάψαι τινά *more sumptuously*, Hdt.   3. often with a negat., οὐδὲν περισσότερον τῶν ἄλλων Plat.   4. τὰ περισσά *in vain*, Anth.   II. ἐκ περιττοῦ as Adv. *superfluously, uselessly*, Plat.   Hence

περισσότης, later Att. περιττ-, ητος, ἡ, *superfluity, excess*, Isocr.

περισσό-φρων, ὁ, ἡ, (φρήν) *over-wise*, Aesch.

περισσῶς, Adv. v. περισσός Β.

περιστᾰδόν, (περιστῆναι) Adv. *standing round about*, Il., Hdt., Att.

περι-στάζομαι, Pass. *to be bedewed all round*, Anth.

περιστάθη, Ep. 3 sing. aor. 1 pass. of περιίστημι.

περισταίην, aor. 2 opt. of περιίστημι :— -στάς, part.

περίστᾰσις, ἡ, (περιστῆναι) *a standing round, a crowd standing round*, Lat. *corona*, Theophr., etc.   II. *circumstances, a state of affairs*, Polyb. :—in bad sense, κατὰ τὰς π. in *critical times*, Id.   2. *outward pomp and circumstance*, Id.

περίστᾰτος, ον, (περιστῆναι) *surrounded and admired by the crowd*, Isocr.

περι-σταυρόω, f. ώσω, *to fence about with a palisade, to entrench*, Thuc. :—Med., περισταυρωσάμενοι *having entrenched themselves*, Xen.

περιστείλας, aor. 1 part. of περιστέλλω.

περι-στείχω, aor. 1 part. περίστειξας, *to go round about*, c. acc., Od.

περι-στέλλω, f. -στελῶ : aor. 1 -έστειλα :—*to dress, clothe, wrap up*, Pind., Plut. ; ἔπηξα δ' αὐτὸν εὖ περιστείλας I planted the sword *having wrapt* it well *with earth*, i. e. planted it *firmly*, Soph.   2. *to dress* or *lay out* a corpse, Lat. *componere*, Od., Hdt., Att. : simply, *to bury*, Plat.   II. metaph. *to wrap up, cloak, cover*, τἀδίκ' εὖ π. Eur. :—Med., τὰ σὰ περιστέλλου κακά Id.   2. *to take care of, protect, defend*, Soph. ; π. τοὺς νόμους *to maintain* the laws, Hdt.; τὰ πάτρια Dem.; π. ἀοιδὰν *to uphold* minstrelsy, Pind.

περι-στενάζομαι, Med. *to lament vehemently*, Plut.

περιστεναχίζομαι, Med. *to echo all round*, Od.

περι-στένω, *to make narrow, compress* : Pass., περιστένεται δέ τε γαστήρ, of wolves, Il.   II. *to sound round about*, c. acc., h. Hom.   2. *to bemoan*, Luc.

περιστερά, ἡ, *the common pigeon* or *dove*, Hdt., Soph., etc. (Deriv. unknown.)   Hence

περιστερεών, ῶνος, ὁ, *a dovecote*, Plat. : περιστερῶν, Aesop.

περι-στεφᾰνόω, f. ώσω, *to enwreathe, encircle*, Ar. :—Pass., πῖλοι πτεροῖσι περιεστεφανωμένοι Hdt. ; οὔρεσι περιεστεφάνωται Θεσσαλίη Id.

περι-στεφής, ές, (στέφω) *wreathed, crowned*, ἀνθέων π. *with a crown* of flowers, Soph.   II. act. *twining, encircling*, κισσός Eur.

περι-στέφω, f. ψω, *to enwreathe, surround*, νεφέεσσι περιστέφει οὐρανὸν Ζεὺς Od.

περιστῆναι, aor. 2 inf. of περιίστημι.

περι-στήωσι, Ep. 3 pl. aor. 2 subj. of περιίστημι.

περι-στίζω, f. ξω, *to prick* or *dot all round*, περιέστιξε τοῖς μαζοῖς τὸ τεῖχος she stuck the wall *all round* with breasts, Hdt. ; and so, περιστίξαντες κατὰ τὰ ἀγγήια τοὺς τυφλούς *having set* them *at equal distance round* the pails, Id.

περι-στῐχίζω, (στίχος) to put all round, Aesch.
περι-στοιχίζομαι, Med. to surround as with toils or nets, of a besieging army, Dem.
περί-στοιχος, ον, set round in rows, Dem.
περι-στονᾰχίζω, to groan all round, Hes.
περι-στρᾰτοπεδεύομαι, f. -εύσομαι, Dep. to encamp about, invest, absol. or c. acc., Xen. :—the Act. in later writers, Polyb., Plut., etc.
περι-στρέφω, f. ψω, to whirl round, of one preparing to throw, Hom.; π. ἵππον to wheel it round, Plut. :—Pass. to be turned round, spin round, Il.; π. εἰς τὰ ληθῆ to come round to it, Plat. 2. π. τὼ χεῖρε to tie his hands behind him, Lysias. Hence
περιστροφή, ἡ, a turning or spinning round, Plat.
περι-στρωφάομαι, Frequentat. of περιστρέφομαι, περιστρωφώμενος πάντα τὰ χρηστήρια going round to all the oracles, Hdt.
περί-στῡλος, ον, with pillars round the wall, surrounded with a colonnade, Hdt., Eur. II. as Subst., περίστυλον, τό, or περίστυλος, ὁ, a peristyle, colonnade round a temple or court-yard, Plut.
περι-σῡλάομαι, Pass., περισυλᾶσθαι τὴν οὐσίαν to be stripped of one's property, Plat.
περι-σύρω [ῡ], f. -σῠρῶ, to drag about, ἄνω καὶ κάτω Luc. II. to tear away from, τί τινος Polyb.
περισφύριος [ῠ], ον, (σφῡρόν) round the ankle, Anth. II. as Subst. περισφύριον, τό, a band for the ankle, anklet, Hdt., Anth.
περι-σχέμεν, Ep. for -σχεῖν, aor. 2 inf. of περιέχω.
περί-σχω, Ep. aor. 2 imperat. med. of περιέχω.
περι-σχίζω, f. ίσω, to slit and tear off, Plut., Luc. II. Pass., of a river, περισχίζεσθαι τὸν χῶρον to split round a piece of land, i. e. split into two branches so as to surround it, Hdt. ;—so, of a stream of men, to part and go different ways, Plat.
περι-σχοινίζω, f. σω, (σχοῖνος) to part off by a rope : —Med., of the Areopagitic Council, to part itself off by a rope from the audience, Dem.
περι-σώζω, f. σω, to save alive, to save from death or ruin, Xen. :—Pass. to escape with one's life, Id.
περιτάμνω, Ion. for περιτέμνω.
περι-ταφρεύω, to surround with a trench, Polyb.: Pass., ἐν περιτεταφρευμένῳ on entrenched ground, Xen.
περι-τείνω, f. -τενῶ, to stretch all round or over, Hdt.
περι-τειχίζω, f. σω, to wall all round, πλίνθοις Βαβυλῶνα Ar. 2. to surround with a wall, so as to beleaguer, Thuc. II. to build round, ὁ περιτετειχισμένος κύκλος Xen. Hence
περιτείχῐσις, ἡ, circumvallation, Thuc.
περιτείχισμα, a wall of circumvallation, Thuc.
περιτειχισμός, ὁ, = περιτείχισις, Thuc.
περι-τελέθω, to grow around, Hes.
περι-τελέω, f. έσω, to finish all round or completely : Pass., περὶ δ' ἤματα μακρὰ τελέσθη Od.
περι-τέλλομαι, only in part., Pass. to go or come round, ἂψ περιτελλομένου ἔτεος as the year came round again, Od.; περιτελλομέναις ἐνιαυτῶν as years go round, Il.; so, περιτελλομέναις ὥραις Soph.
περι-τέμνω, Ion. -τάμνω, f. -τεμῶ: pf. -τέτμηκα: aor. 2 -έτεμον :—to cut or clip round about, Lat. circumcidere, οἰνὰς περιταμνέμεν to prune them, Hes.; τὴν κεφαλὴν π. κύκλῳ περὶ τὰ ὦτα Hdt. :—Med., περι-

τάμνεσθαι βραχίονας to make incisions all round one's arms, Id. 2. of circumcision, Id. : and in Med., περιτάμνονται τὰ αἰδοῖα they practise circumcision, Id. 3. to cut off the extremities, τὰ ὦτα καὶ τὴν ῥῖνα Id. :—Pass., περιτάμνεσθαι γῆν to be curtailed of certain land, Id. II. to cut off and hem in all round, cut off, Lat. intercipere ; hence in Med., βοῦς περιταμνόμενος cutting off cattle for oneself, 'lifting' cattle, Od. :—Pass. to be cut off, intercepted, Xen.
περι-τέρμων, ον, (τέρμα) bounded all round, Anth.
περι-τέχνησις, ἡ, (τεχνάομαι) extraordinary art or cunning, Thuc.
περι-τίθημι, f. -θήσω: aor. 1 περιέθηκα: aor. 2 imperat. περίθες :—to place round, Od.; περιτιθέναι τί τινι Hdt. :—Med. to put round oneself, put on, Hom., Eur. II. metaph., like περιβάλλω, to bestow, confer upon, π. τινὶ βασιληίην, ἐλευθερίην Hdt., Thuc.; so, π. τὴν Μηδικὴν ἀρχὴν τοῖς Ἕλλησι to put the Median yoke round their necks, Thuc.
περι-τίλλω, f. -τῐλῶ: Pass., pf. -τέτιλμαι :—to pluck all round, περ. θρίδακα to strip the outside leaves off a lettuce, Hdt.; so, θρίδαξ περιτετιλμένη Id.
περι-τῑμήεις, εσσα, εν, much-honoured, h. Hom.
περι-τῐταίνω, aor. 1 part. -τιτήνας, to stretch round about, Il.
περίτμημα, ατος, τό, (περιτέμνω) a slice, shaving, Plat.
περιτομή, ἡ, (περιτέμνω) circumcision, N. T.
περίτομος, ον, (περιτέμνω) cut off all round, abrupt, steep, Lat. abruptus, Polyb.
περι-τοξεύω, f. σω, to overshoot, outshoot, τινά Ar.
περι-τρέπω, f. -τρέψω, to turn and bring round, Lys., N. T., etc. 2. to overturn, upset, Plat. II. intr. to turn or go round, Od.
περί-τρεσαν, Ep. 3 pl. aor. 1 of περιτρέω.
περι-τρέφομαι, Pass., περιτρέφεται κυκόωντι [the milk] forms curds as you mix it, Il.; σακέεσσι περιτρέφετο κρύσταλλος the ice froze hard upon the shields, Od.
περι-τρέχω, f. -θρέξομαι and -δρᾰμοῦμαι: aor. 2 -έδρᾰμον: pf. -δεδράμηκα :—to run round and round, run round, Theogn., Ar. 2. to run about, Plat. :—metaph. to be current, in vogue, Id. c. acc. to run round, Hdt., Ar. :—metaph. to circumvent, Ar.
περι-τρέω, f. -τρέσω, to tremble round about, λαοὶ περίτρεσαν the people stood trembling round, Il.
περί-τριμμα, τό, anything worn smooth by rubbing : metaph., π. δικῶν, of a pettifogger, Ar.; π. ἀγορᾶς Dem.
περι-τρομέω, = περιτρέμω :—Med., σάρκες περιτρομέοντο μέλεσσιν all the flesh crept on his limbs, Od.
περι-τροπέω, Ep. form of περιτρέπω : I. intr. περιτροπέων ἐνιαυτός a revolving year, Il. II. trans. to gather from all round, πολλὰ [μῆλα] περιτροπέοντες ἐλαύνοισι Od.; περιτροπέων φῦλ' ἀνθρώπων driving about, perplexing them, h. Hom.
περιτροπή, ἡ, (περιτρέπω) a turning round, revolution, circuit, Plat. 2. a turning about, changing, ἐν περιτροπῇ by turns, Hdt.
περι-τρόχᾰλος, ον, = περίτροχος: neut. pl. as Adv., περιτρόχαλα κείρεσθαι to have one's hair clipt all round, Hdt.
περι-τροχάω, collat. form of περιτρέχω, Anth.
περί-τροχος, ον, circular, round, Il.

περι-τρώγω, f. -τρώξομαι: aor. 2 -έτρᾰγον:—to gnaw round about, nibble off, purloin, Ar.:—metaph. to carp at, τινά Id.

περιττός, -εύω, -ωμα, v. περισσός, etc.

περι-τυγχάνω, f. -τεύξομαι: aor. 2 -έτῠχον: pf. -τετύχηκα:—to light upon, fall in with, meet with, a person or thing, c. dat., Thuc., etc.: absol., Id. II. of events, περιτυγχάνει μοι ἡ συμφορά the accident happens to, befals me, Id.

περι-τύμβιος, ον, (τύμβος) round or at the grave, Anth.

περι-υβρίζω, f. ίσω, to treat very ill, to insult wantonly, Hdt., Ar.:—Pass. to be so treated, Hdt.

περι-φαίνομαι, Pass. to be visible all round, of mountains, etc., ὄρεος κορυφῇ περιφαινομένοιο Il.; περιφαινομένῳ ἐνὶ χώρῳ h. Hom.; so, ἐν περιφαινομένῳ (without Subst.) Od.

περιφάνεια [φᾰ], ἡ, a being seen all round: conspicuousness, notoriety, πολλὴ π. τῆς χώρης ἐστί it is thoroughly known, Hdt.; διὰ τὴν π. τῶν ἀδικημάτων Dem. From

περιφᾰνής, ές, (περιφαίνομαι) seen all round, of a city, Thuc. 2. conspicuous, manifest, notable, notorious, Soph., Xen., etc.; Comp. and Sup., -φανέστερος, -έστατος, Ar., Xen.:—Adv. -νῶς, conspicuously, notably, manifestly, Soph., Ar., etc.; Comp. -έστερον, Dem.

περίφαντος, ον, =περιφανής, π. θανεῖται he will die in the sight of all, Soph. II. famous, renowned, Id.

περι-φείδομαι, Dep. to spare and save, c. gen., Theocr.

περιφέρεια, ἡ, the line round a circular body, a periphery, circumference, Arist. II. the outer surface, Plut. III. a round body, Id. From

περιφερής,ές,(περιφέρομαι) moving round,surrounding, c. gen., Eur. 2. surrounded by, c. dat., Id. II. round, circular, Plat.:—of bodies, spherical, globular, Id.:—of style, rounded, Arist.

περιφερό-γραμμος, ον, bounded by a circular line, Strab.

περι-φέρω, f. -οίσω: aor. 1 and 2 -ήνεγκα, -ήνεγκον:—to carry round, Hdt.: to carry about with one, Id., Eur.:—Pass., c. acc. loci, λέοντος περιενειχθέντος τὸ τεῖχος being carried round the wall, Hdt.; absol., περιφερόμενος swinging about (in a basket), Plat. 2. metaph., οὔτε μέμνημαι τὸ πρᾶγμα οὔτε με περιφέρει οὐδὲν εἰδέναι τούτων nor does [my mind] carry me back to the knowledge of any of these things, Hdt. 3. to move round, to hand round at table, Xen. 4. to turn round, τὴν κεφαλὴν Plut. 5. to carry round, publish:—Pass., περιεφέρετο τὸ ῥῆμα the saying was passed from mouth to mouth, Plat. 6. to carry to and fro, Plut. 7. to bring round, i. e. into one's own power, Id. II. intr. to survive, endure, hold out, Thuc. III. of periods of time, Hdt.; of argument, περιφέρεσθαι εἰς ταὐτό Plat. 2. to wander about, Xen.:—to be unsteady, wavering, Plut.

περι-φεύγω, f. -φεύξομαι, to flee from, escape from, c. acc., Il.; ψάμμος ἀριθμὸν π. the sand mocks thy numbering, Pind.:—absol. to escape from illness, Dem.

περιφλεγής, ές, very burning. Adv. -γῶς Plut. From

περι-φλέγω, f. ξω, to burn all round, Plut.

περι-φλεύω or -φλύω [ῠ], to scorch or char all round, of lightning, Ar.:—Pass., pf. -πέφλευσμαι, Hdt.

περί-φλοιος, ον, with bark all round, Xen.

περιφλύω, v. περιφλεύω.

περι-φοβέομαι, Pass. to fear greatly, Xen. From

περί-φοβος, ον, in great fear, exceeding fearful, Thuc., Xen.; τινος of a thing, Plat.

περι-φοίτησις, ἡ, (φοιτάω) a wandering about, Plut.

περί-φοιτος, ον, (φοιτάω) revolving, wandering, Anth.

περιφορά, ἡ, (περιφέρομαι) meats carried round, Xen. II. a going round, rotatory motion, circuit, revolution, Ar., Plat., etc. 2. the revolving vault of heaven, Plat. 3. metaph., ἐν ταῖς περιφοραῖς in society, Plut.

περιφόρητος, ον, able to be carried about, portable, Hdt. II. notorious, infamous, Plut.

περίφραγμα, ατος,τό, (περιφράσσω) an enclosure,Strab.

περι-φρᾰδής, ές, (φράζομαι) very thoughtful, very careful, h. Hom., Soph. Adv. -δέως, Hom.

περι-φράζομαι, Med. to think or consider about a thing, c. acc., Od.

περίφρακτος, ον, fenced round: περίφρακτον, τό, an inclosure, Plut. From

περι-φράσσω, Att. -ττω, f. ξω, to fence all round, Plat.

περι-φρονέω, f. ήσω, to compass in thought, speculate about, τὸν ἥλιον Ar. II. to overlook, to contemn, despise, Thuc. Hence

περιφρόνησις, ἡ, contempt, Plut.

περι-φρουρέω, f. ήσω, to guard all round, blockade closely:—Pass.,Thuc.

περί-φρων, ονος, ὁ, ἡ: voc. περίφρον: (φρήν):—very thoughtful, very careful, notable, of Penelopé, Hom. II. like ὑπέρφρων, haughty, over-weening, Aesch. 2. c. gen. despising a thing, Anth.

περι-φύομαι, Pass., with fut. med. -φύσομαι [ῠ]: pf. act. περιπέφῡκα, Ep. -πέφῡα: aor. 2 pass. περιέφῠν, inf. περιφῦναι, part. -φύς [ῠ], in late writers also with inf. and part. pass. περιφῦναι and -φῠείς:—to grow round about, Od. 2. of persons, to grow round, cling to, c. dat. or absol., Ib.; so of shoes, περιέφυσαν Περσικαί τινι Ar.

περι-φῠτεύω, f. σω, to plant round about, Il.

περι-φωνέω, f. ήσω, to sound round, re-echo, Plut.

περι-χᾰρᾰκόω, to surround with a stockade, Aeschin.

περι-χᾰρής, ές, (χαίρω) exceeding joyous or glad, Hdt., Soph., etc.; τινι at a thing, Hdt., Ar.:—τὸ π. excessive joy, Thuc.

περι-χειλόω, f. ώσω, to edge round, Xen.

περί-χειρον, τό, (χείρ) a bracelet, Polyb.

περι-χέω, f. -χεῶ: aor. 1 -έχεα:—Ep. περι-χεύω, aor. 1 περίχευα:—to pour round or over, τί τινι, properly of liquids, Hom.; of metal-workers, χρυσὸν κέρασιν περιχεύας having spread gold leaf round its horns, Il.; so in Med., ὡς δ' ὅτε τις χρυσὸν περιχεύεται ἀργύρῳ Od.:—Pass. to be poured around, περὶ δ' ἀμβρόσιος κέχυθ' ὕπνος Il.; τῶν ὀστέων περικεχυμένων heaped all round, Hdt.; of persons, περιχυθέντες crowding round, Id.

περι-χθών, ὁ, ἡ, round about the earth, Anth.

περι-χορεύω, f. σω, to dance round, Eur., Luc.

περι-χρίω [ῑ], f. σω, to smear or cover over, Luc.

περι-χώομαι, Ep. 3 sing. aor. 1 περιχώσατο: Med.:—to be exceeding angry about, c. gen., Il.

περι-χωρέω, f. ήσω, to go round, Ar. II. to

come round to, come to in succession, π. εἰς Δαρεῖον ἡ βασιληίη Hdt.

περί-χωρος, ον, round about a place : οἱ περίχωροι the people about, Dem., etc. :—ἡ π. (sc. γῆ) the country round about, N. T.

περι-ψάω, inf. -ψῆν : aor. 1 περιέψησα :—to wipe all round, to wipe clean, Ar. Hence

περίψημα, ατος, τό, anything wiped off, an offscouring, of a vile person, N. T.

περι-ψιλόομαι, aor. 1 -εψιλώθην, Pass. to be made bald or bare all round, περιψιλωθῆναι τὰς σάρκας to have one's flesh all stript off, Hdt.

περί-ψυκτος, ον, (ψύχω) very cold, Plut.

περιωδῦνία, ἡ, excessive pain, Plat. From

περι-ώδῦνος, ον, (ὀδύνη) exceeding painful, Aesch. II. suffering great pain, Dem.

περι-ωθέω, f. -ώσω, to push or shove about, Dem. 2. to push from its place :—Pass. pf. περιέωσμαι, to be pushed away, ἐκ πάντων περιεώσμεθα Thuc.; π. ἔν τινι to lose one's place in a person's favour, Id.

περι-ωπή, ἡ, (ὤψ) a place commanding a wide view, Hom.; ἐκ περιωπῆς by a bird's-eye view, Luc. II. circumspection, πολλὴν π. τινος ποιεῖσθαι to shew much caution in a thing, Thuc.

περι-ώσιος, ον, prob. Ion. for περι-ούσιος, immense, countless, Solon, Anth. :—neut. as Adv., περιώσιον, exceeding, beyond measure, Hom.; so pl. περιώσια, h. Hom. :—also c. gen., just like περί, περιώσιον ἄλλων far beyond the rest, Id., Pind.

πέρκη, ἡ, a river-fish so called from its dusky colour (v. sq.), the perch, Comici.

ΠΕΡΚΝΟ'Σ, ή, όν, darkcoloured, of grapes or olives beginning to ripen, Anth.; cf. ἐπί-περκνος. II. as Subst., name of an eagle, μόρφνον ὃν καὶ περκνὸν καλέουσι Il.

πέρνα, ης, ἡ, a ham, Lat. perna, Strab.

πέρνημι, part. περνάς : 3 sing. Ion. impf. πέρνασκε, like πιπράσκω, to export for sale, to sell as slaves (cf. περάω B), πέρνασχ' ὅντιν' ἕλεσκε πέρην ἁλὸς ἐς Σάμον Il.; περνάς νήσων ἐπὶ τηλεδαπάων Ib.; τοῖς ξένοις τὰ χρήματα περνάς Eur. :—Pass., κτήματα περνάμενα goods sold or for sale, Il.; πάντα πέρναται Ar.

πέρ-οδος, ἡ, Aeol. for περί-οδος.

περόνᾱμα, τό, Dor. for περόνημα.

περονάω, f. ήσω : Ep. aor. 1 περόνησα :—to pierce, pin, Il. :—Med., χλαῖναν περονήσασθαι to buckle on one's mantle, Ib. From

περόνη, ἡ, (πείρω) anything pointed for piercing or pinning, the tongue of a buckle or brooch, the buckle or brooch itself, Lat. fibula, Hom. : also a large pin used for fastening on the outer garment or cloak (ἱμάτιον), Hdt., Soph. II. the small bone of the leg, Lat. fibula, Xen.

περόνημα, Dor. -ᾱμα, ατος, τό, = πόρπαμα, a garment pinned or buckled on, Theocr.

περονητρίς, Dor. -ᾱτρίς, ίδος, ἡ, (περόνη) a robe fastened on the shoulder with a brooch, Theocr.

περονητίς, ίδος, fem. Adj. fastened with a brooch, Anth.

περονίς, ίδος, ἡ, = περόνη, Soph.

περπερεύομαι, Dep. to boast or vaunt oneself, N. T. From

ΠΕ'ΡΠΕΡΟΣ, ον, vainglorious, braggart, Polyb.

πέρσα, Ep. for ἔπερσα, aor. 1 of πέρθω.

περσέ-πολις, poët. also περσέ-πτολις, εως, ὁ, ἡ, (πέρθω) destroyer of cities, Aesch., etc. II. Persepolis, the ancient capital of Persia, Strab.

Περσεύς, gen. έως, Ion. έος, Ep. ῆος, ὁ, Perseus, son of Zeus and Danaé, Il., Hes., etc. :—Adj. Περσεῖος, α, ον, Eur.; Ep. Περσήιος, Theocr. :—Patron. Περσείδης, ου, ὁ, Ep. -ηιάδης, Il.

Περσεφόνη, ἡ, Ep. Περσεφόνεια ; also Φερσεφόνη, Περσέφασσα, Φερσέφασσα, Φερσέφαττα : — Persephoné, Proserpine, daughter of Zeus and Demeter, Il. : Hades carried her off, and as his consort she continued to reign in the lower world, see h. Hom. Cer. :— her temple is called Φερρεφάττιον, τό, Dem.

Περσηίς, ίδος, ἡ, sprung from Perseus, name of Alcmena, Eur. ; called Περσήιον αἷμα in Theocr.

Πέρσης, ου, ὁ : heterocl. acc. Πέρσεα : voc. Πέρσᾰ :—a Persian, inhabitant of Persis, Hdt., etc. Hence

Περσίζω, to imitate the Persians, speak Persian, Xen.

Περσικός, ή, όν, Persian, ἡ Περσική (sc. χώρα) Persia, Hdt., etc. 2. Περσικαί, αἱ, a sort of thin shoes or slippers, Ar. 3. Περσικός, ὁ, or Περσικόν, τό, the peach, Lat. malum Persicum. 4. Π. ὄρνις the common cock, Id. 5. τὰ Περσικά the Persian war, Plat., etc. ; in earlier writers called τὰ Μηδικά.

πέρσις, ἡ, (πέρθω) a sacking, sack, π. Ἰλίου, a poem by Arctinus, Arist.

Περσίς, ίδος, fem. of Περσικός, Persian, Aesch., etc. II. as Subst., 1. (sub. γῆ), Persis, Persia, now Farsistan, Hdt. 2. (sub. γυνή), a Persian woman, Xen. 3. (sub. χλαῖνα), a Persian cloak, Ar.

Περσιστί [ῐ], Adv., (Περσίζω) in the Persian tongue, Hdt., Xen., etc.

Περσο-διώκτης, ὁ, chaser of the Persians, Anth.

Περσονομέομαι, Pass. to be governed by the Persian laws or by Persians, Aesch. From

Περσο-νόμος, ον, (νέμω) ruling Persians, Aesch.

ΠΕ'ΡΥ͞ΣΙ, or before a vowel -σιν, Adv. a year ago, last year, Ar., etc. ; ἡ π. κωμῳδία our last year's comedy, Id. ; νῦν τε καὶ π. Xen. Hence

περυσῐνός, ή, όν, of last year, last year's, Ar., etc.

Περφερέες, οἱ, name of the five officers who escorted the Hyperborean maidens to Delos, Hdt.

πεσσᾷ, Dor. for πεζῇ.

πεσεῖν, Ep. -έειν, aor. 2 inf. of πίπτω :—πέσε, Ep. for ἔπεσε, 3 sing.

πέσημα, ατος, τό, a fall, Soph., Eur. ; τὸ οὐρανοῦ πές., i. e. the Palladium, Eur.; πεσήματα νεκρῶν dead corpses, (cf. πτῶμα) Id.

πέσος, τό, = πτῶμα II, pl. πέσεα Eur.

πεσοῦμαι, f. of πίπτω.

πεσσεία, Att. πεττ-, ἡ, a game at draughts, Plat.

πεσσευτής, οῦ, ὁ, (πεσσεύω) a draught-player, Plat.

πεσσευτικός, Att. πεττ-, ή, όν, fit for draught-playing (πεσσοί), skilled therein, Plat. : — πεττευτική (sc. τέχνη) = πεσσεία, Id.

πεσσεύω, Att. πεττ-, f. σω, to play at draughts (v. sub πεσσοί), Plat., Xen.

ΠΕΣΣΟ'Σ, Att. πεττός, ὁ, an oval-shaped stone for playing a game like our draughts, mostly in pl., Od., Hdt., etc. II. οἱ πεσσοί, the place in which the game was played, or the game itself, Eur.

ΠΕ'ΣΣΩ, Att. **πέττω**, later **πέπτω** (from which form come the tenses): f. **πέψω**: aor. 1 **ἔπεψα**:—Pass., f. **πεφθήσομαι**: aor. 1 **ἐπέφθην**: pf. pass. **πέπεμμαι**, inf. **πεπέφθαι**:—*to soften, ripen* or *change,* by means of heat : **I.** of the sun, *to ripen* fruit, Od.; cf. **πεπαίνω.** **II.** by the action of fire, *to cook, dress, bake,* Hdt., Ar. :—Pass., Hdt. :—Med., **πέσσεσθαι πέμματα** *to cook oneself* cakes, Id. **III.** of the stomach, *to digest,* like Lat. *concoquere,* Arist. **2.** metaph., **χόλον πέσσειν** *to cherish* or *nurse* one's wrath, Lat. *fovere,* Il.; **βέλος πέσσειν** *to have* a dart in one *to nurse,* Ib.; but in good sense, **γέρα πεσσέμεν** *to enjoy* them, Ib.; also, **ἀκίνδυνον αἰῶνα πέσσειν** *to lead a sodden* life of ease, Pind.

πεσών, aor. 2 part. of **πίπτω.**

πεταλισμός, ὁ, (as if from **πεταλίζω**) *petalism,* a mode of banishing too powerful citizens practised in Syracuse, like the **ὀστρακισμός** of Athens, except that the name was *written upon olive-leaves.*

πέτᾰλον, τό, (πετάννυμι) *a leaf,* mostly in pl., Hom.:—poët., **νεικέων πέταλα** contentious votes (cf. **πεταλισμός**), Pind. **II.** *a leaf of metal,* Luc.

πέτᾰλος, Ion. **πέτηλος, η, ον,** *broad, flat,* Anth.

πέτᾰμαι, = πέτομαι, q. v.

ΠΕΤΑΝΝΥ'ΜΙ and **-ύω,** later **πετάω:** f. **πετάσω,** Att. **πετῶ:** aor. 1 **ἐπέτᾰσα** Ar., Ep. **πέτᾰσα, πέτᾰσσα** :—Pass., aor. **ἐπετάσθην,** Ep. **πετ-:** pf. **πέπταμαι,** also **πεπέτασμαι:** 3 sing. plqpf. **πέπτατο,** Ep. **πέπτ-** :—*to spread out* sails or clothes, Od.; **χεῖρε πετάσσας** of one swimming, Ib.: metaph., **θυμὸν πετάσαι** *to open* one's heart, Ib. :—Pass., mostly in pf., *to be spread on all sides,* Hom.: part. *spread wide, opened wide,* of folding doors, **πύλαι πεπταμέναι** Il.; **πετάσθησαν** Od.

πέτασμα, ατος, τό, (πετάννυμι) *anything spread out :* in pl. *carpets,* Aesch.

πέτᾰσος, ὁ, (πετάννυμι) *a broad-brimmed felt hat,* chiefly used in Thessaly.

πέταυρον or **πέτευρον, τό,** *a perch* for fowls to roost at night, Theocr. (Deriv. uncertain.)

πετεηνός, ή, όν, Ep. for **πετεινός.**

πετεινός, ή, όν, Ep. **πετεηνός:** —*able to fly, full fledged,* of young birds, Od. :—of birds generally, *able to fly, winged,* Il. :—absol., **πετεηνά** *winged fowl,* Ib.; so, **τὰ πετεινά** *birds,* Hdt.

πέτευρον, τό, = πέταυρον, q. v.

πετοῖσα, Dor. for **πεσοῦσα,** aor. 2 part. fem. of **πίπτω.**

ΠΕ'ΤΟΜΑΙ, impf. **ἐπετόμην,** Ep. **πετ-:** f. **πετήσομαι,** syncop. **πτήσομαι:** aor. 2 syncop. **ἐπτόμην, πτέσθαι, πτόμενος,** also (as if from **ἵπταμαι**) **ἐπτάμην,** Ep. **πτάμην, πτάσθαι, πτάμενος,** Ep. subj. **πτῆται** for **πτᾶται:** also aor. 2 act. **ἔπτην,** inf. **πτῆναι,** part. **πτάς** (as if from **ἵπτημι**):—the pres. **πέτᾰμαι** is also used; and in late writers **ἵπταμαι** :—*to fly,* of birds, bees, gnats, etc., Hom., etc. :—then, of arrows, stones, javelins, etc., Il.: also of any quick motion, *to fly along, dart, rush,* of men, Ib., etc. **II.** metaph. *to be on the wing, flutter,* Lat. *volitare,* of uncertain hopes, Pind., Soph.; of fickle natures, Eur.; **ὄρνις πετόμενος** a bird *ever on the wing,* Ar.; **πετόμενόν τινα διώκεις** 'you are chasing a butterfly,' Plat.

πετόντεσσι, Aeol. aor. 2 part. dat. pl. of **πίπτω.**

ΠΕ'ΤΡΑ, Ion. and Ep. **πέτρη, ἡ,** *a rock, a ledge* or *shelf of rock,* Od. **2.** *a rock,* i. e. *a rocky peak* or *ridge,* Hom.; **π. σύνδρομοι, ξυμπληγάδες,** of the rocky islets of the Bosporus, Pind., Eur.; **π. δίλοφος,** of Parnassus, Soph.—Properly, **πέτρα** is *a fixed rock,* **πέτρος** *a stone :* in Od. 9, **πέτραι** are *masses of live rock* torn up by giants. **3. πέτρη γλαφυρή** *a hollow rock,* i. e. *a cave,* Il.; **δίστομος π.** *a cave in the rock* with a double entrance, Soph. **II.** proverbial usages :—on **οὐκ ἀπὸ δρυὸς οὐδ' ἀπὸ πέτρης,** v. **δρῦς** :—as a symbol of firmness, **ὁ δ' ἐστάθη ἠΰτε πέτρη** Od.; of hardheartedness, **ἐκ πέτρας εἰργασμένος** Aesch. Hence

πετραῖος, α, ον, *of a rock,* Hes.: *living on* or *among the rocks,* Od.; **Νύμφαι π.** *rock*-Nymphs, Eur. **2.** *of rock, rocky,* **τάφος π.** Soph.; **π. δειράς, λέπας, χθών, ἄντρα,** etc., Trag. **II. Πετραῖος,** epith. of Poseidon in Thessaly, who *clave the rocks of Tempé,* Pind.

πετρηδόν, (πέτρα) Adv. *like rock,* Luc.

πετρήεις, εσσα, εν, (πέτρα) *rocky,* Hom., Hes.

πετρ-ηρεφής, ές, (ἐρέφω) *o'er-arched with rock, rock-vaulted,* Aesch., Eur.

πετρ-ήρης, ες, (*ἄρω) *of rock, rocky,* Soph.

πετρίδιον, τό, Dim. of **πέτρα,** Anth.

πέτρῐνος, η, ον, (πέτρα) *of rock, rocky,* Hdt., Soph., Eur.

πετροβολία, ἡ, *a stoning,* Xen. From

πετρο-βόλος, ον, (βάλλω) *throwing stones,* Xen. **II.** as Subst., **πετροβόλος, ὁ,** *an engine for throwing stones,* Lat. *ballista,* Polyb., etc.

πετρό-κοιτος, ον, (κοίτη) *with bed of rock,* Anth.

πετρο-κυλιστής, οῦ, ὁ, *a roller of rocks,* Strab.

πετρορ-ρῐφής, ές, (ῥίπτω) *hurled from a rock,* Eur.

ΠΕ'ΤΡΟΣ, ὁ, *a stone,* distinguished from **πέτρα** (v. sub voce); in Hom., used by warriors, **λάζετο πέτρον μάρμαρον ὀκριόεντα** Il.; **βαλὼν μυλοειδέϊ πέτρῳ** Ib.: —proverb., **πάντα κινῆσαι πέτρον** Eur.

πετρο-τόμος, ον, (τέμνω) *cutting stones,* Anth.

πετρόω, f. ώσω, (πέτρος) *to turn into stone, petrify,* Anth. **II.** Pass. *to be stoned,* Eur.

πετρ-ώδης, ες, (εἶδος) *like rock* or *stone, rocky, stony,* like **πετραῖος, π. κατῶρυξ,** of a grave, Soph., Plat.

πεττεία, -ευμα, πεττός, Att. for **πεσσεία.**

πέττω, Att. for **πέσσω.**

πευθήν, ῆνος, ὁ, *an inquirer, spy,* Luc. From

πεύθομαι, poët. for **πυνθάνομαι,** Hom., Hes., Trag.; impf. **ἐπευθόμην** Il., Eur. Hence

πευθώ, οῦς, ἡ, (πυθέσθαι) *tidings, news,* Aesch.

πευκάεις, Dor. for **πευκήεις.**

πευκάλιμος [ᾰ], **η, ον,** prob. an Ep. lengthd. form of **πυκινός,** so that **ἐνὶ φρεσὶ πευκαλίμῃσι** (the only phrase used by Hom.) would mean *in wise, prudent, sagacious* mind : cf. **λευγάλεος** and **λυγρός.**

πευκεδανός, ή, όν, epith. of war, = **πευκήεις** II, Il.

ΠΕΥ'ΚΗ, ἡ, *the pine,* Il., Eur., etc. **II.** *anything made from its wood, a torch of pine-wood,* Trag. **2.** *a writing-tablet,* Eur. Hence

πευκήεις, Dor. **πευκάεις, εσσα, εν,** *of pine* or *pine-wood,* Eur.; **πευκᾶεν Ἥφαιστον** the fire *of pine-torches,* Soph. **II.** metaph. *sharp, piercing,* Aesch.

πεύκινος, η, ον, (πεύκη) *of* or *from pine* or *pine-wood,* Soph.; **π. δάκρυα** tears *of the pine,* i. e. the resinous drops that ooze from it, Eur.

πεύσομαι, f. of **πυνθάνομαι:** Dor. **πευσοῦμαι.**

πευστήριος, α, ον, of or for inquiry, πευστηρία (sc. θυσία) a sacrifice for learning the will of the gods, Eur.
πέφανται, 3 sing. pf. pass. of φαίνω. II. of *φένω.
πεφάσθαι, pf. pass. inf. of *φένω: πεφάσθω, 3 sing. pf. pass. imper. of φημί: πεφασμένος, pf. pass. part. both of φαίνω (cf. also φημί) and of *φένω.
πεφήσομαι, fut. 3 pass. both of φαίνω and *φένω.
πεφιδέσθαι, Ep. redupl. aor. 2 inf. of φείδομαι :—πεφιδοίμην, opt.
πεφιδήσομαι, Ep. redupl. f. of φείδομαι.
πεφιλαμένος, Dor. for –ημένος, pf. pass. part. of φιλέω.
πεφίμωσο [ῑ], pf. pass. imper. of φιμόω.
πέφνε, πεφνέμεν, πέφνων, v. sub *φένω.
πεφοβήατο, Ep. 3 pl. plqpf. pass. of φοβέω.
πεφοβημένος, η, ον, pf. pass. part. of φοβέω :—πεφοβημένως timorously, Xen.
πέφραδε, πεφραδέειν, πεφραδέμεν, v. sub φράζω.
πεφορτισμένος, pf. pass. part. of φορτίζω.
πέφραγμαι, pf. pass. of φράσσω.
πέφρικα, pf. of φρίσσω.
πεφροντισμένως, Adv. pf. pass. part. of φροντίζω, carefully, Strab.
πεφύᾱσι, Ep. for πεφύκᾱσι, 3 pl. pf. of φύομαι.
πεφυγμένος, pf. pass. part. of φεύγω.
πεφυζότες, Ep. for πεφευγότες, pf. part. pl. of φεύγω.
πέφυκα, pf. of φύω.
πεφυκότως, Adv. of πέφυκα, naturally, Arist.
πέφυκω [ῠ], Ep. pres. formed from πέφυκα, pf. of φύω ; impf. ἐπέφυκον Hes.
πεφυλαγμένος, Adv. pf. pass. part. of φυλάσσω, cautiously, Xen., Dem.   2. safely, Xen.
πεφυῖα, Ep. for πεφυκυῖα, pf. part. fem. of φύω :—pl. masc. πεφυῶτες, for πεφυκότες.
πη or πῃ, Ion. κη, Dor. πα : enclit. Particle :   I. of Manner, in some way, somehow, οὔ πη not in any way, not at all, Hom. ; οὐδέ τί πη Il. ; οὕτω πη in some such way, somehow so, Ib. ; τῇδέ πη Plat. ; ἄλλη γέ πη Id. ; εἴ πη if any way, Id.   II. of Space, by some way, to some place, to any place, Hom. :—c. gen., ἤ πῃ με πολιῶν ἄξεις ; wilt thou carry me to some city? Il.   2. in some place, somewhere, anywhere, Od., Att. ; πῇ μέν . . , πῇ δέ . . , on one side . . , on the other . . , Plut. ; partly . . , partly . . , Xen.
B. πῆ or πῇ; Ion. κῆ; Dor. πᾶ; interrog. Particle :   I. of Manner, in what way? how? Od., etc. ; πῇ δή; how tell me? Ib. ; πῇ μάλιστα; how exactly? Plat. :—also in indirect questions, ἐκαραδόκεον τὸν πόλεμον κῇ ἀποβήσεται Hdt., etc.   2. to what end? wherefore? Lat. quorsum? Hom.   II. of Space, which way? Lat. qua? πῇ ἔβη Ἀνδρομάχη ; Il., etc. ; πᾶ τις τράποιτ' ἄν ; Aesch.   2. more rarely like ποῦ; where? Il. ; πᾶ πᾶ κεῖται ; Soph. :—also in indirect questions, c. gen., ἐπειρώτα, κῆ γῆς . . , Hdt.
πηγάζω, f. άσω, (πηγή) to spring or gush forth, Anth.   2. c. acc. cogn. to gush forth with water, Id.
πηγαῖος, α, ον, and os, ον, (πηγή) of or from a well, π. ῥέος spring-water, Aesch. ; π. ἄχθος a weight of water, Eur. ; π. κόραι water Nymphs, Id.
πήγανον, τό, rue, Lat. ruta :—proverb., οὐδ' ἐν σελίνῳ οὐδ' ἐν πηγάνῳ, i. e. scarcely at the edge or beginning, because these herbs formed the borders of beds, Ar.

πηγάς, άδος, ή, (πήγνυμι III) anything congealed, hoarfrost, rime, Hes.
Πήγασος, ὁ, Pegasus, a horse sprung from the blood of Medusa, and named from the springs (πηγαί) of Ocean, near which she was killed, ridden by Bellerophon when he slew Chimaera, Hes. : later poets describe him as winged, Ar. : later still, he was the favourite of the Muses, under whose hoof the fountain Hippocrené (ἵππου κρήνη) sprang up on Helicon, Strab., etc. :—Adj. fem. Πηγασὶς κρήνη, Hippocrene, Mosch.
πηγεσί-μαλλος, ον, thick-fleeced, ἀρνειός Il.
ΠΗΓΗ', Dor. παγά, ή, mostly in pl. of running waters, streams, Hom., etc. ; distinct from κρουνός (the spring or well-head), κρουνὼ δ' ἵκανον καλλιρρόω, ἔνθα δὲ πηγαὶ δοιαὶ ἀναΐσσουσι Il. :—in sing., Aesch.   2. metaph. streams, of tears, πηγαὶ κλαυμάτων, δακρύων Id., Soph. ; so, πηγαὶ γάλακτος Soph. ; πόντου πηγαῖς with sea-water, Eur. ; παγαὶ πυρός Pind.   II. = κρήνη, a fount, source, πηγαὶ ἡλίου the fount of light, i. e. the East, Aesch. :—in sing., πηγὴ ἀργύρου, of the silver-mines at Laureion, Id. ; τῆς ἀκουούσης πηγῆς δι' ὤτων, i. e. the sense of hearing, Soph.   2. metaph. the fount, source, origin, πηγὴ κακῶν Aesch. ; ἡδονῶν, νοσημάτων Plat.
πήγμα, ατος, τό, (πήγνυμι) anything joined together, framework, of a ship, Anth. :—Lat. pegma, a moveable scaffold used in theatres, Juvenal.   2. metaph., π. γενναίως παγέν a bond in honour bound, Aesch.   II. π. τῆς χιόνος frozen snow, Polyb.
ΠΗ'ΓΝΥΜΙ and –ύω : f. πήξω, Dor. πάξω : aor. 1 ἔπηξα, Ep. πῆξα, Dor. part. πάξαις :—Med., f. πήξομαι : aor. 1 ἐπηξάμην :—Pass., f. παγήσομαι : aor. 1 ἐπήχθην, Ep. 3 pl. πήχθεν, Dor. subj. παχθῇ, part. πηχθείς : more commonly aor. 2 ἐπάγην [ἄ], Ep. πάγην, Ep. 3 pl. πάγεν, part. παγείς : pf. πέπηγμαι, πέπηγα is generally used as pf. pass. : plqpf. ἐπεπήγειν. Radic. sense, to make fast ; intr. and Pass. to be solid :   I. to stick or fix in any, ἐν δὲ μετώπῳ πῆξε (τὴν αἰχμὴν) Il. ; π. ἐπὶ τύμβῳ ἐρετμόν Od. :—to fix in the earth, plant, Soph. ; σκηνὴν π. to pitch a tent, Plat. ; (so Med., σκηνὰς πήξασθαι to pitch their tents, Hdt.) :—intr. pf. and Pass., δόρυ δ' ἐν κραδίῃ ἐπεπήγει the spear stuck fast in his heart, Il. ; ὀϊστοὶ πῆχθεν ἐν χροΐ Ib. ; [ξίφος] πέπηγεν ἐν γῇ Soph.   2. to stick or fix on, κεφαλὴν ἀνὰ σκολόπεσσι π. to stick the head on stakes, Il., etc. :—Pass., πηχθέντα μέλη ὀβελοῖσι having their limbs fixed on spits, Eur. ; παγέντες impaled, Aesch.   3. to fix the eyes upon an object, κατὰ χθονὸς ὄμματα π. Il. ; ὄμματα πέπηγε πρός τι Plat.   II. to fasten together, construct, build, νῆας πῆξαι Il. ; so Med., ἅμαξαν πήξασθαι to build oneself a wagon, Hes.   III. to make solid, stiff, hard, of liquids, to freeze, θεὸς πήγνυσι παν ῥέεθρον Aesch. ; ἔπηξε (sc. ὁ θεὸς) τοὺς ποταμούς Ar. :—intr. pf. and Pass. to become solid, stiff or hard, γοῦνα πήγνυται the limbs stiffen, Il. ; of liquids, to become congealed, freeze, Hdt. ; ἅλες πήγνυνται the salt crystallises, Id. ; κρύσταλλος ἐπεπήγει οὐ βέβαιος not frozen strong, Thuc.   IV. metaph. to fix, Lat. pangere foedus, intr. pf. and Pass. to be irrevocably fixed, established, εἷς ὅρος ἡμῖν παγήσεται Id. ; μὴ γὰρ ὡς θεῷ νομίζετ' ἐκείνῳ τὰ παρόντα πεπηγέναι πράγματα ἀθάνατα Dem.

πηγός, ή, όν, (πήγνυμι II) well put together, compact, strong, Il.; κύματι πηγῷ on the strong, big wave, Od.

πηγῡλίς, ίδος, fem. Adj. (πήγνυμι III) frozen, icy-cold, Od.; as Subst., =παγετός, πάχνη, Anth.

πηδάλιον, τό, (πηδός) a rudder or an oar used for steering, Od.; after Homer, a Greek ship commonly had two πηδάλια joined by cross-bars (ζεύγλαι) and worked by a handle or tiller (οἴαξ). 2. metaph. ἱππικὰ π. of reins, Aesch.; πηδαλίῳ δικαίῳ νωμᾶν στρατόν Pind.; τὰ π. τῆς διανοίας Plat.

ΠΗΔΑ΄Ω, f. Att. -ήσομαι: aor. 1 ἐπήδησα: pf. πεπήδηκα:—to leap, spring, bound, ὑψόσε ποσσὶν ἐπήδα Il.; π. ἐς σκάφος Soph.; c. acc. cogn., πήδημα πηδᾶν to take a leap, Eur.; c. acc. loci, πεδία πηδᾶν to bound over them, Soph.; π. πλάκα Eur. II. metaph. of an arrow, Il.; of the heart, to leap, throb, Ar., etc.; of sudden changes, τί πηδᾷς εἰς ἄλλους τρόπους; Eur.

πήδημα, ατος, τό, a leap, bound, Trag. II. a beating or throbbing of the heart, τὸ μέλλον καρδία πήδημ' ἔχει, i. e. beats with fearful presage, Eur.; and

πήδησις, ή, a leaping, Plut.; and

πηδητικός, ή, όν, springing, Arist., Luc.

ΠΗΔΟ΄Σ, ὁ, or πηδόν, τό, the blade of an oar, and generally an oar, ἀναρρίπτειν ἅλα πηδῷ Od.

πηκτή, Dor. πακτά, ή, (πηκτός) a net or cage set to catch birds, Ar. II. cream-cheese, Theocr.

πηκτίς, Aeol. and Dor. πακτίς, ίδος, ή, an ancient harp used by the Lydians, Hdt., etc. II. a sort of shepherd's pipe, joined of several reeds, like Pan's pipes (σύριγξ), Anth.

πηκτός, ή, όν, Dor. πακτός, ά, όν, (πήγνυμι) stuck in, fixed, Soph. II. well put together, constructed, built, of wood-work, Hom., Hes.; τὰ πακτὰ τῶν δωμάτων the barriers of the house, Eur. ap. Ar. III. congealed, curdled, γάλα Eur.

πῆλαι, aor. 1 inf. of πάλλω:—πήλας, part.

πῆλε, Ep. for ἔπηλε, 3 sing. aor. 1 of πάλλω.

Πηλεύς, ὁ: gen. έως Ep. ῆος: Att. acc. Πηλῆ:—Peleus, son of Aeacus, husband of Thetis, father of Achilles, prince of the Myrmidons in Thessaly, Hom.:—Adj. Πήλειος, α, ον, Ep. Πηλήιος, η, ον, of Peleus, Il.—Patron. Πηλείδης, ου, Ep. εω and αο, ὁ, son of Peleus, Ib.; Ep. also Πηληιάδης, Ib.; Aeol. Πηλεΐδας, Pind.:—also Πηλείων, ωνος, ὁ, Il.; Πηλείωνάδε to Peleus' son, Ib.

πήληξ, ηκος, ή, (πῆλαι) a helmet, casque, Il., Ar.

Πηλιακός, ή, όν, (Πήλιον) Pelian, of or from Mount Pelion, Anth.:—fem. Πηλιάς, άδος, Il.

πηλίκος [ἰ], η, ον, interrog. of τηλίκος, ἡλίκος, how great or large? Lat. quantus? Plat. II. of what age, of a certain age, Arist.

πήλινος, η, ον, (πηλός) of clay, Lat. fictilis, οἱ πήλινοι clay figures, Dem.

Πήλιον, Dor. Πάλιον, τό, Pelion, a mountain in Thessaly, Hom., Hes., Pind.; etc. Hence

Πηλιῶτις, ιδος, on or at the foot of Pelion, Eur.

πηλο-βάτης [ᾰ], ου, ὁ, mud-walker.

πηλοδομέω, f. ήσω, to build of clay, Anth. From

πηλό-δομος, ον, (δέμω) clay-built, τοῖχοι Anth.

πηλόομαι, Pass. to wallow in mire, Luc.

πηλο-πλάθος [ᾰ], ὁ, (πλάσσω) a potter, Luc.

ΠΗΛΟ΄Σ, ὁ, ή, clay, earth, such as was used by the potter and modeller, Lat. lutum, Hdt., Att. 2.

sometimes for βόρβορος or ἰλύς, mud, mire, as lutum for coenum, Hdt., Ar., etc.; proverb., ἔξω κομίζειν πηλοῦ πόδα, i. e. to keep out of difficulties, Aesch.; κάσις πηλοῦ ξύνουρος, cf. σύνορος.

πηλ-ουργός, όν, (*ἔργω) a worker in clay, Luc.

Πηλούσιον, τό, a town on the coast of Egypt bordering on Arabia, Hdt.:—Adj., τὸ Πηλούσιον στόμα the Eastern mouth of the Nile, Id.

πηλοφορέω, f. ήσω, to carry clay, Ar. From

πηλο-φόρος, ον, (φέρω) carrying clay.

πηλό-χῠτος, ον, moulded of clay, θάλαμοι π., of swallows' nests, Anth.

πηλ-ώδης, ες, (εἶδος) like clay, clayey, muddy, of places, Thuc.; of persons, Plat.

πῆμα, ατος, τό, (cf. πάσχω) suffering, misery, calamity, woe, bane, Hom., etc.; πήματα ἐπὶ πήμασι woe upon woe, Soph.; πῆμ' ἐπὶ πήματι κεῖται, the sword forged upon the anvil, Orac. ap. Hdt. II. of persons, a bane, calamity, Il., Soph. Hence

πημαίνω, f. ᾰνῶ, Ion. -ᾰνέω: aor. 1 ἐπήμηνα: Med., f. πημᾰνοῦμαι (also in pass. sense):—Pass., aor. 1 ἐπημάνθην, Ep. πημάνθην:—to bring into misery, plunge into ruin, undo, and, in milder sense, to grieve, distress, Hom., Trag.; π. τὴν γῆν to damage it, Hdt.:—absol. to do mischief, Il.:—Pass. to suffer hurt or harm, Od., Aesch., etc.; ἴσθι πημανούμενος wilt suffer woe, Soph. Hence

πημαντέος, α, ον, verb. Adj. to be injured, Theogn.

πημονή, ή, (πήμων) =πῆμα, Trag.

πημοσύνη, ή, =πημονή, πῆμα, Aesch.

Πηνελόπεια, ή, Penelope, wife of Ulysses, Od.; Πηνελόπη, Hdt., Ar.; Dor. Πάνελόπᾱ, Anth. (Her name is connected with the mythic tale of the web (πήνη, πηνίον), Spinster, v. Od.)

πηνέλοψ, Aeol. and Dor. πᾶν-, οπος, ὁ, a kind of duck with purple stripes, Ar.

ΠΗ΄ΝΗ, ή, the thread on the spool or shuttle, the woof, and in pl. the web, Eur. II. the bobbin or spool, like πηνίον, Anth.

πηνίζομαι, Dor. πᾱνίσδομαι, Dep., (πήνη) to wind thread off a reel, Theocr.

πηνίκα; interrog. Adv., correl. to τηνίκα and ἡνίκα, properly at what point of time? at what hour? Lat. quota hora? Luc.; πηνίκα μάλιστα; about what o'clock it is? Plat.; so, πηνίκ' ἄττα; Ar.; in full, πηνίκ' ἐστὶ τῆς ἡμέρας; Id. II. generally, for πότε; Dem.:—so, in an indirect question, Id.

πηνίον, Dor. πανίον [ᾱ], τό, (πήνη) the bobbin or spool on which the woof is wound, Il., Anth.

πήνισμα, ατος, τό, (πήνη) the woof on the spool, Anth.

πῆξαι, aor. 1 inf. of πήγνυμι.

πῆξε, Ep. for ἔπηξε, 3 sing. aor. 1 of πήγνυμι.

πῆξις, εως, ή, (πήγνυμι) a fixing, constructing, of wood-work, Plat. II. (from Pass.) congelation, Id.

ΠΗΟ΄Σ, Dor. πᾱός, οῦ, ὁ, a kinsman by marriage, Lat. affinis, Hom., Hes.

ΠΗ΄ΡΑ, Ion. πήρη, ή, a leathern pouch, a wallet, scrip, Lat. pera, Od., Ar. Hence

πηρίδιον [ἰ], τό, Dim., Ar.

πηρό-δετος, ον, binding a wallet, Anth.

ΠΗΡΟ΄Σ, ή, όν, disabled in a limb, maimed, Lat. mancus, Il., Anth.

πηρόω, f. ώσω, (πηρός) to lame, maim, mutilate, Ar. :
—Pass., πεπηρωμένος maimed, Dem. : metaph., πεπηρωμένος πρὸς ἀρετήν incapacitated for reaching virtue,
Arist. Hence
πήρωσις, ἡ, a being maimed, mutilation, imperfection, Plat., etc. : blindness, Luc.
πήσομαι, late form of πείσομαι, f. of πάσχω.
πηχυαῖος, α, ον, (πῆχυς) a cubit long, Hdt., Plat.
πηχύνομαι [ῠ], Med. to take into one's arms, Anth.
ΠΗ͂ΧΥΣ, εως, ὁ: gen. pl. πήχεων:—the fore-arm,
from the wrist to the elbow, Lat. ulna, Xen., etc. :—
generally, the arm, ἀμφὶ υἱὸν ἐχεύατο πήχεε λευκώ Il.,
etc. II. the centrepiece, which joined the two
horns of the bow, Hom. III. in pl., the horns or
sides of the lyre, opp. to ζυγόν the bridge, Hdt. IV.
as a measure of length, the distance from the point
of the elbow to the end of the little finger, Lat. cubitus or ulna, a cubit or ell, containing 24 δάκτυλοι
or 18¼ inches, Hdt. : the π. βασιλήιος was longer by
three δάκτυλοι = 27 δάκτυλοι or 20½ inches, Id. 2.
a cubit-rule, as we say 'a foot-rule,' Ar.
πιάζω, Dor. and late Att. for πιέζω : aor. 1 part. πιάξας.
πιαίνω, f. πιανῶ : aor. 1 ἐπίανα, poët. πίανα :—Pass.,
aor. 1 ἐπιάνθην : pf. πεπίασμαι : (πίων) :—to make
fat, fatten, Eur. ; π. χθόνα to fatten the soil, of a
dead man, Aesch. :—Pass. to be or become fat, Plat.,
etc. II. metaph., 1. to increase, enlarge,
πλοῦτον Pind. 2. to make wanton, excite, Aesch. :
—Pass. to wax fat and wanton, Id. ; ἔχθεσιν πιαίνεσθαι to batten on quarrels, Pind.
πιᾰλέος, α, ον, poët. for πίων, Anth.
πῖαρ, τό, indecl., (πίων) fat, Il. :—any fatty substance,
cream, Anth. :—metaph., πῖαρ ὕπ' οὖδας fatness is
beneath the ground, Od. 2. metaph., also, like Lat.
uber, the cream of a thing, the choicest, best, h.
Hom. ; π. χθονός, like οὖθαρ ἀρούρης, Anth.
πίασμα, ατος, τό, (πιαίνω) that which makes fat, of a
river, Aesch. ; π. χθονί bringing fatness to the soil, Aesch.
πίασμα, ατος, τό, Dor. and late Att. for πίεσμα.
πῑδᾰκόεις, εσσα, εν, (πῖδαξ) gushing, Eur.
πῑδᾰκ-ώδης, ες, (εἶδος) full of springs, Plut.
ΠΙ͂ΔΑΞ, ᾰκος, ἡ, a spring, fountain, Il., Hdt., Eur.
πῑδύω, to gush forth, Anth., Plut.
πιέζω, impf. ἐπίεζον Ep. πιέζον : f. πιέσω : aor. 1
ἐπίεσα :—Pass., aor. 1 ἐπιέσθην : pf. πεπίεσμαι or
πεπίεγμαι :—in Od. an impf. πιέζευν for πιέζον (from
πιεζέω) ; and part. πιεζεύμενος Hdt. :—another
Dor. and late Att. form is πιάζω :—aor. 1 ἐπίασα or
ἐπίαξα : aor. 1 pass. ἐπιάσθην :—to press, squeeze,
press tight, Hom., Att. II. to press or weigh
down, of a heavy weight, Pind., Ar. : metaph. to
oppress, straiten, distress, Hdt., Aesch., etc.—Pass.
to suffer greatly, Hdt., Att. 2. to press hard, of
a victorious army, Lat. premo, τοὺς ἐναντίους Hdt. :—
Pass., εἴ πη πιέζοιντο Thuc. 3. to repress, stifle,
Pind. III. later to lay hold of, ταῦρον πιάξας τᾶς
ὁπλᾶς by the hoof, Theocr. ; αὐτὸν τῆς χειρός N. T.
πιεῖν, aor. 2 inf. of πίνω.
πίειρα [ῐ], ἡ, fem. of πίων, fat, rich, of land, Hom.,
Pind., etc. ; δαὶς πίειρα a rich, plenteous meal, Il. ; of
wood, resinous, unctuous, Soph.
πιέμεν, Ep. for πιεῖν, aor. 2 inf. of πίνω.

Πιερία, Ion. -ίη, ἡ, Pieria, a district in the North of
Thessaly, Hom. : Πιερίηθεν, from Pieria, Hes.
Πιερίδες, αἱ, the Pierides, name of the Muses, as
haunting Pieria, Hes., Pind.
Πιερικός, ή, όν, of Pieria, Hdt.
πιέσαι, aor. 1 inf. of πιέζω. II. in late Gr., πιέσαι,
2 sing. fut. of πίνω.
πιεσθείς, aor. 1 part. of πιέζω.
πίεσμα, ατος, τό, (πιέζω) pressure, Anth.
πῖῄεις, εσσα, εν, poët. for πίων, Anth.
πίῃσθα, 2 sing. aor. 2 subj. of πίνω.
πιθάκνη, Att. φιδάκνη, ἡ, (πίθος) a wine-cask or jar,
Ar. ; used for storing figs in, Dem. : hence, οἰκεῖν ἐν
ταῖς πιθάκναις to live in casks, as Athenian immigrants
were forced to do during the Peloponn. war, Ar.
πίθακος, Dor. for πίθηκος.
πῑθᾰνολογέω, to use probable arguments, Arist.
πῑθᾰνολογία, ἡ, the use of probable arguments, as
opp. to demonstration (ἀπόδειξις) Plat. From
πῑθᾰνο-λόγος, ον, (λέγω) speaking so as to persuade.
πῑθᾰνός, ή, όν, (πείθω) calculated to persuade ; and
so, 1. of persons, having the power of persuasion,
persuasive, plausible, of popular speakers, Thuc.,
etc. :—c. inf., πιθανώτατος λέγειν Plat. 2. of arguments, Ar., Plat., etc. 3. of manners, persuasive,
winning, Xen. 4. of reports, plausible, specious,
probable, Hdt., Plat. 5. of works of art, producing
illusion, true to nature, Xen. II. pass. easy to
persuade, credulous, Aesch. 2. obedient, docile,
Xen. III. Adv. -νῶς, persuasively, Comp. -ώτερον,
Plat.
πῑθᾰνότης, ητος, ἡ, persuasiveness, Plat., Arist.
πῑθᾰνόω, f. ώσω, (πιθανός) to make probable, Arist.
πῐθεῖν, aor. 2 inf. of πείθω :—πιθέσθαι, med.
πῐθηκισμός, ὁ, a playing the ape, playing monkey's
tricks, Ar. From
πίθηκος [ῐ], Dor. πίθᾱκος, ὁ, an ape, monkey, Ar. ; as
fem., πίθηκος μήτηρ Babr. :—of persons, an ape, jackanapes, Ar., Dem. (Deriv. uncertain.)
πῐθηκο-φᾰγέω, f. ήσω, (φαγεῖν) to eat ape's flesh, Hdt.
πῐθηκο-φόρος, ον, (φέρω) carrying apes, Luc.
πιθήσας, as if from πιθέω, aor. 1 part. of πείθω.
πίθι, for πῖε, aor. 2 imper. of πίνω.
πῐθόμην, Ep. for ἐπιθόμην, aor. 2 med. of πείθω.
ΠΙ͂ΘΟΣ [ῐ], ὁ, a wine-jar of the largest kind (cf. ἀμφορεύς), Hom., etc. ; of earthenware, π. κεράμινος
Hdt. ; covered with a lid, Hes. 2. proverbs, εἰς
τὸν τετρημένον πίθον ἀντλεῖν, of the task of the
Danaïds, i.e. labour in vain, Xen. ; also ἐκ πίθω ἀντλεῖς,
i. e. you have plenty of wine, ' you are in clover,' Theocr.
πίθων, ὁ, a little ape, Babr. ; of a flatterer, Pind.
πίθων, ῶνος, ὁ, (πίθος) a cellar, Anth.
πῐθών, aor. 2 part. of πείθω.
πικραίνω, f. ᾰνῶ, (πικρός) to make sharp or bitter to
the taste, N. T. 2. metaph. in Pass. to be exasperated, foster bitter feelings, Plat., Theocr.
πικρία, ἡ, (πικρός) bitterness, of temper, Dem., Plut.
πικρίζω, f. ίσω, (πικρός) to be or taste bitter, Strab.
πικρό-γᾰμος, ον, miserably married, Od.
πικρό-γλωσσος, ον, of sharp or bitter tongue, Aesch.
πικρό-καρπος, ον, bearing bitter fruit, Aesch.
πικρός, ά, όν, and ός, όν:—properly (from πεύκη)

pointed, sharp, keen, ὀϊστός Il.; γλωχίς Soph.; metaph., γλώσσης πικροῖς κέντροισι Eur.   **II.** generally, sharp to the senses: 1. of taste, sharp, pungent, bitter, Hom., Hdt. :—so of smell, Od.   2. of feeling, sharp, keen, ὠδῖνες Il., Soph.   3. of sound, sharp, piercing, shrill, οἰμωγή, φθόγγος Soph.; γόοι Eur.   **III.** metaph., 1. of things, bitter, cruel, Od., Att.   2. of persons, bitter, malignant, Solon, Hdt., Att.; πικρὸς θεοῖς hateful to the gods, Soph.; πικρὸς πολίταις Eur.   3. embittered, sorrowing, Soph.   **B.** Comp. -ότερος, Sup. -ότατος Pind., etc.   **C.** Adv. πικρῶς, bitterly, cruelly, Aesch., Soph.; π. ἔχειν τινί, πρός τινα Dem.; π. φέρειν τι Eur.   Hence
πικρότης, ητος, ἡ, pungency, bitterness, of taste, Plat.   **II.** metaph. bitterness, cruelty, Hdt., Eur.
πικρό-χολος, ον, full of bitter bile, splenetic, Anth.
πικτίς, v. πυκτίς.
πῑλέω, f. ήσω, (πῖλος) to compress wool, πιληθεὶς πέτασος a felt hat, Anth.   **II.** Pass. to be close pressed, kneaded, Id.
πῑλίδιον, τό, Dim. of πῖλος, Lat. pileolus, Ar., Dem.
πῑλίον, τό, Dim. of πῖλος, Plut.
πῑ-λῑπής, ές, (λείπω) wanting the letter π, Anth.
πιλνάω, =πελάζω, to bring near, Hes. :—**πίλναμαι** (but with no act. form πίλνημι), to draw near to, approach, c. dat., ἅρματα χθονὶ πίλνατο the chariots went close to the ground, Il.; ἐπ' οὔδεϊ πίλναται Ib.; γαῖα καὶ οὐρανὸς πίλνατο earth and sky threatened to encounter (in the storm), Hes.
ΠΙ'ΛΟΣ, ὁ, wool or hair made into felt, used as a lining for helmets, Il.; for shoes, Hes.   **II.** anything made of felt, a felt skullcap, like the modern fez, Hes.; πίλους τιήρας φορέοντες wearing turbans for caps, Hdt.; ἀντὶ τῶν πίλων μιτρηφόροι ἔσαν Id.   2. a felt-cloth, Xen.   3. a felt-cuirass, Thuc.
πῑλοφορικός, ή, όν, accustomed to wear a πῖλος, Luc.
πῑλο-φόρος, ον, (πῖλος II, φέρω) wearing a cap, Anth.
πῑλωτός, ή, όν, (πιλόω) made of felt, Strab.
πῑμελή, ἡ, (πίων) soft fat, lard, Lat. adeps, Hdt., Soph.   Hence
πῑμελής, ές, fat, Luc., Babr.; Comp. -έστερος, Anth.
πιμπλάνομαι, Ep. for πίμπλαμαι, pass. of πίμπλημι, Il.
πίμπλαντο, Ep. 3 pl. impf. pass. of πίμπλημι.
Πίμπλεια, ἡ, a place in Pieria, sacred to the Muses, Strab. :—Adj., **Πιμπλήϊδες** Μοῦσαι Anth.
πιμπλέω, =sq.: Ion. part. pres. fem. πιμπλεῦσαι, Hes.
πίμπλημι, in pres. and impf. formed like ἵστημι; Ep. 3 sing. subj. πίμπλησι; imperat. πίμπλα or πίπλη: impf. 3 pl. ἐπίμπλασαν :—other tenses formed from πλήθω (which in the pres. and impf. is intr., v. πλήθω): f. πλήσω: aor. 1 ἔπλησα, Ep. πλῆσα: pf. πέπληκα: —Med., aor. 1 ἐπλησάμην :—Pass., f. πλησθήσομαι: aor. 1 ἐπλήσθην, Ep. 3 pl. πλῆσθεν: pf. πέπλησμαι: —besides these tenses, there was a poët. aor. 2 ἐπλήμην, Ep. 3 sing. and pl. πλῆτο, πλῆντο; cf. ἐμπίπλημι. (From Root ΠΛΕ or ΠΛΑ.)   To fill full of a thing, c. gen., Hom., etc.: c. dat. to fill with a thing, Eur. :—absol. to fill up, to fill, Il., Att.   2. to fill, discharge an office, Aesch.   **II.** Med. to fill for oneself, or what is one's own, πλήσασθαι δέπας οἴνοιο to fill oneself a cup of wine, Il.; πλ. νῆας to

get ships laden, Od.; θυμὸν πλήσασθαι ἐδητύος ἠδὲ ποτῆτος to satiate one's desire with meat and drink, Ib.; πεδία πίμπλασθ' ἁρμάτων fill the plain full of your chariots, Eur.   **III.** Pass. to be filled, become or be full of, c. gen., Hom., etc.   2. to have enough of a thing, πλησθῆναι αἱμάτων Soph.; ἡδονῶν Plat.; —rarely c. dat., δάκρυσι πλησθείς Thuc.
πίμπρημι, in pres. and impf., like ἵστημι; imper. πίμπρη, inf. πιμπράναι: impf. ἐπίμπρην :—the other tenses formed from πρήθω (which also takes a special sense, v. sub voce) :—f. πρήσω: aor. 1 ἔπρησα, Ep. πρῆσα, Ep. 3 sing. shortd. ἔπρεσε :—Pass., f. πεπρήσομαι or πρήσομαι: aor. 1 ἐπρήσθην: pf. πέπρησμαι. (From Root ΠΡΑ) :—to burn, burn up, πυρός with fire, Il.; πυρί Soph.; absol., Hes., Aesch.
πῑν, Comic abbrev. for πίκειν, Anth.
πῑνᾰκηδόν, Adv. (πίναξ) like planks, Ar.
πῑνᾰκιον, τό, Dim. of πίναξ, a small tablet, on which the δικασταί wrote their verdict, π. τιμητικόν, Lat. tabella damnatoria, Ar.;—on which a law was written, Id.; —on which the information in case of εἰσαγγελία was written, Dem.;—on which the rules for the δικασταί were written, Id. :—tablets, a memorandum book, Plat.   **II.** a tablet for painting upon, Luc.
πῑνᾰκίς, ίδος, ἡ, = πινάκιον: in pl., tablets, Plut.
πῑνᾰκίσκος, ὁ, = πινάκιον, Ar.
πῑνᾰκο-θήκη, ἡ, a picture-gallery, Strab.
πῑνᾰκο-πώλης, ου, ὁ, (πωλέομαι) one who sells small birds plucked and ranged upon a board, Ar.
ΠΙ'ΝΑΞ [ῐ], ᾰκος, ὁ, a board, plank, of a ship, Od.   2. a tablet for writing on, Il., Plat., etc.   3. a trencher, platter, Od.   4. a panel, picture, Lat. tabula, Simon.: generally, an engraved plate, of a map, Hdt.   5. a register, list, Lat. album, Dem., etc.
πῑνᾰρός, ά, όν, (πίνος) dirty, squalid, Eur.
Πινδάρειος, α, ον, of Pindar, Ar.
Πινδόθεν, Adv. from Mount Pindus, Pind.
ΠΙ'ΝΝΑ and **πίννη,** ἡ, the pinna, a bivalve, with a silky beard, Comici.
πιννο-τήρης, ου, ὁ, (τηρέω) the pinna-guard, a small crab that lives in the pinna's shell, like the hermitcrab: metaph. of a little parasitical fellow, Ar.
πῑνόεις, εσσα, εν, poët. for πιναρός, Anth.
πῑνόομαι, Pass. to be rusted, of statues, Plut.   From
ΠΙ'ΝΟΣ [ῐ], ὁ, dirt, filth, Lat. squalor, Soph., Eur.; metaph., σὺν πίνῳ χερῶν, i. e. by foul means, Aesch.
πῑνύσκω: Ep. aor. 1 ἐπίνυσσα, pass. ἐπινύσθην: (πνέω): to make prudent, admonish, correct, Il., Aesch.   Hence
πῑνύτη, ἡ, understanding, wisdom, Hom.
πῑνύτης, ητος, Dor. ᾱτος, ἡ, =foreg., Anth.
πῑνύτός, ή, όν, (πινύσσω) wise, prudent, discreet, understanding, Od., Solon.
πῑνύτό-φρων, ονος, ὁ, ἡ, (φρήν) of wise or understanding mind, Anth.
ΠΙ'ΝΩ [ῐ], Ep. inf. πιέμεναι and -έμεν: Ion. impf. πίνεσκον: f. πίομαι [ῑ], later πιοῦμαι: aor. 2 ἔπιον, Ep. πίον, 2 sing. subj. πίῃσθα, imper. πίε, Att. πῖθι, inf. πιεῖν, Ep. πιέμεν, πιεῖν, part. πιών, πιοῦσα :—Med., πίνομαι, also πίομαι :—Pass., Ep. impf. πίνετο. —Other tenses are formed from a Root ΠΟ, pf. πέπωκα :—Pass., f. ποθήσομαι: aor. 1 ἐπόθην: pf. inf. πεπόσθαι.   To drink, Hom., etc.; π. ὕδωρ Αἰσήποιο to drink its water,

i. c. live on its banks, Il. ;—or c. gen. partit. *to drink of* a thing, π. οἴνοιο (as Fr. *du vin*), Od. ; αἵματος ὄφρα πίω Ib. :—also, πίνειν κρητῆρας οἴνοιο *to drink* bowls of wine, Il. ; π. ἀπὸ κρήνης *to drink* of a spring, Theogn. ; δέπα, ἔνθεν ἔπινον Od.; π. ἐκ ταὐτοῦ ποτηρίου Ar. ; ἐξ ἀργύρου ἢ χρυσοῦ Plat. ; ἀπὸ τοῦ ποταμοῦ Xen. : —also, σκύφον ᾧπερ ἔπινον *with which* . . , Od. :— absol., Hom., etc.; πῖνε, πῖν᾽ ἐπὶ συμφοραῖς Ar. ; διδόναι πιεῖν *to give to drink,* Hdt.; πιεῖν αἰτεῖν Xen. :— in pf. πέπωκα, *to be drunk,* Eur.; but, πίνοντά τε καὶ πεπωκότα *drinking* and *having finished drinking,* Plat. : II. metaph. *to drink up,* as the earth does rain, Hdt. ; πιοῦσα κόνις μέλαν αἷμα Aesch., etc.

πῖν-ώδης, ες, (πίνος, εἶδος) *dirty, foul,* Eur.

πίομαι, f. of πίνω.

πῖος, α, ον, poët. form of πίων, *unctuous,* Hdt.

πῖπίσκω, f. πίσω [ῐ]: aor. 1 ἔπῖσα:—Causal of πίνω, *to give to drink,* πίσω σφε Δίρκας ὕδωρ *I will make* them *drink* the water of Dircé, Pind.

πιπράσκω, Ion. πιπρήσκω, shortd. from πι-περάσκω, redupl. form of περάω Β, pf. πέπρᾱκα: 3 sing. plqpf. ἐπεπράκει :—Pass., f. πρᾱθήσομαι and πεπρᾱσομαι [ᾰ] : aor. 1 ἐπρᾱθην [ᾰ], Ion. ἐπρήθην : pf. πέπρᾱμαι, Ion. πέπρημαι : 3 sing. plqpf. ἐπέπρᾱτο :—*to sell,* Dem. : II. *to be sold,* esp. for exportation, Hdt., Att. II. *to sell* for a bribe, of political leaders, Dem. : —metaph. in Pass., πέπρᾱμαι *I am bought and sold!* i. e. *betrayed, ruined, undone,* Soph.

πίπτω, shortd. from πι-πέτω (redupl. from Root ΠΕΤ): Ep. impf. πῖπτον : f. πεσοῦμαι, Ion. 3 sing. πεσέεται, pl. πεσέονται : aor. 2 ἔπεσον, Aeol. ἔπετον : pf. πέπτωκα, later also πέπτηκα, Ep. part. πεπτεώς, εῶτος, also πεπτηώς, ηυῖα, Att. poët. part. πεπτώς.

A. *To fall, fall down,* Hom., etc. ; πίπτειν ἐν κονίῃσιν *to fall in* the dust, i. e. *to fall and lie* there, Il. ; π. ἐν δεμνίοις Eur., etc. ; or without ἐν, πεδίῳ πίπτειν Il. ; π. δεμνίοις Eur. ; also, π. ἐπὶ χθονί Od. ; ἐπὶ γᾷ Soph. ; πρὸς πέδῳ Eur. ; with a Prep. of motion, π. ἐς πόντον Hes. ; ἐπὶ γᾶν Aesch. ; πρὸς οὖδας Eur.

B. Special usages : I. πίπτειν ἔν τισι *to fall violently upon, attack,* ἐνὶ νήεσσι πέσωμεν Il. ; πρὸς μῆλα καὶ ποίμνας Soph. 2. *to throw oneself down, fall down,* πρὸς βρέτη θεῶν Aesch. ; ἀμφὶ γόνυ τινός Eur. II. *to fall* in battle, πῖπτε δὲ λαὸς Il., etc.; οἱ πεπτωκότες *the fallen,* Xen.; π. δορί by the spear, Eur. ;—π. ὑπό τινος *to fall by* another's hand, Hdt. 2. *to fall, be ruined,* ὁ Ξέρξεω στρατὸς αὐτὸς ὑπ᾽ ἑωυτοῦ ἔπεσε, Lat. *mole sua corruit,* Id. 3. *to fall, sink,* ἄνεμος πέσε the wind *fell* (so Virg. *cadunt austri*), Od. 4. *to fall short, fail,* Plat. ; of a play, *to fail,* Ar. III. ἐκ θυμοῦ πίπτειν τινί *to fall out of* his favour, Il. ; so, π. ἐξ ἐλπίδων Eur. : —reversely, π. ἐς κακότητα Theogn.; εἰς νόσον Eur.; φόβον, ἀνάγκας Eur., Thuc., etc.; also, π. ἐν φόβῳ Eur. ; π. δυσπραξίαις Soph. 2. π. εἰς ὕπνον *to fall* asleep, Id. ; or simply ὕπνῳ Aesch. IV. πίπτειν μετὰ ποσσὶ γυναικός *to fall* between her feet, i. e. *to be born,* Il. V. of the dice, τὰ δεσποτῶν εὖ πεσόντα θήσομαι *I shall count* my master's throws *good or lucky,* Aesch. ; so of lots, ὁ κλῆρος π. τινί or παρά τινα Plat. ; ἐπί τινα N. T. 2. generally, *to*

fall, turn out, εὖ, καλῶς πίπτειν *to be lucky,* Eur., etc. VI. *to fall under, belong to* a class, Arist.

πί-ρωμις, an Egyptian word, = καλὸς κἀγαθός, Hdt. : in modern Coptic, *romi* is = Lat. *vir.*

Πῖσα or Πίση, Dor. Πίσα, ης, ἡ, (πῖσος) a fountain at Olympia, Hdt., Pind. :—Adv. Πίσηθεν, Anth. ; Adj. Πῖσαῖος, α, ον, *of* or *from Pisa,* Id. :—also Πῖσάτης [ᾱ], ου, ὁ, fem. Πῖσᾱτις, ιδος, Pind.

πίσῐνος [ῐ], η, ον, *made of peas,* ἔτνος π. *pea*-soup, Ar.

ΠΙΣΟΣ [ῐ], ὁ, *the pea,* Lat. *pisum,* Ar.

πῖσος, τό, (πίνω) only in pl. *meadows,* Hom.

ΠΙΣΣΑ´, Att. πίττᾰ, ἡ, *pitch,* Lat. *pix,* Il., Hdt., etc. : proverb., ἄρτι μῦς πίττης γεύεται, i. e. he has got the first taste of misery, Dem.

πισσ-ήρης, ες, (*ἄρω) = πισσήεις, Aesch.

πισσῖνος, Att. πιττῖνος, η, ον, *like pitch,* Luc.

πισσόομαι, Att. πιττ-, Med. (πίσσα) *to remove the hair by means of a pitch-plaster,* Luc.

πισσωτής, οῦ, ὁ, *one who pitches,* Luc.

πίστευμα, ατος, τό, = πίστωμα, Aesch.

πιστευτικός, ή, όν, *disposed to trust, confiding,* Arist.: —Adv., πιστευτικῶς ἔχειν τινί *to rely upon* one, Plat. II. *creating belief,* Id.

πιστεύω, f. εύσω : plqpf. ἐπεπιστεύκειν : (πίστις) :—*to trust, trust to* or *in, put faith in, rely on, believe in* a person or thing, c. dat. ; π. τινί Hdt., Att. ; with neut. Adj., λόγοις ἐμοῖσι πιστεύσον τάδε *believe* my words herein, Eur. ;—later, π. εἰς Θεόν *to believe on* or in God, N. T. ; π. ἐπὶ τὸν Κύριον Ib. :—absol. *to believe,* Hdt., Thuc. :—Pass. *to be trusted* or *believed,* Plat.; πιστεύ-εσθαι ὑπό τινος *to enjoy* his confidence, Xen. ; π. παρά τινι, πρός τινα Dem. ; ὡς πιστευθησόμενος as if *he would be believed,* Id. :—Med. *to believe mutually,* Id. 2. *to comply,* Soph. 3. c. inf. *to believe that, feel sure* or *confident that* a thing is, will be, has been, Eur., etc. ; π. ποιεῖν *to dare* to do a thing, Dem. :—Pass., πιστεύομαι ἀληθεύσειν *I am believed likely to speak truth,* Xen. 4. c. dat. et inf., τοῖσι ἐπίστευε σιγᾶν *to whom he trusted* that they would keep silence, in whose secresy he confided, Hdt. 5. *to believe, have faith,* N. T. II. π. τί τινι *to entrust* something to another, Xen., etc. :—Pass., πιστεύομαί τι *I am entrusted with* a thing, *have* it *committed* to me, Id.

πιστικός (Α), ή, όν, (πίνω) *liquid,* N. T. : others refer it to πίστις, in the sense of *genuine, pure.*

πιστικός (Β), ή, όν, (πίστις) *faithful* :—Adv., πιστικῶς ἔχειν τινί Plut. 2. *genuine,* v. foreg.

πίστις, ἡ, gen. εως : dat. πίστει, Ion. πίστῑ : Ion. nom. and acc. pl. πίστῑς : dat. πίστισι : (πείθομαι) :—*trust* in others, *faith,* Lat. *fides, fiducia,* Hes., Theogn., Att. ; c. gen. pers. *faith* or *belief in* one, Eur. :— generally, *persuasion* of a thing, *confidence, assurance,* Pind., Att. 2. *good faith, trustworthiness, faithfulness, honesty,* Lat. *fides,* Theogn., Hdt., Att. 3. in a commercial sense, *credit, trust,* πίστις τοσούτων χρημάτων ἐστί μοι παρά τινι I have *credit* for so much money with him, Dem.; εἰς πίστιν διδόναι τί τινι Id. 4. in Theol. *faith, belief,* as opp. to sight and knowledge, N. T. II. *that which gives confidence:* hence, 1. *an assurance, pledge of good faith, warrant, guarantee,* Soph., Eur. ; πίστιν καὶ ὅρκια ποιεῖσθαι to make a treaty by exchange of *assur-*

ances and oaths, Hdt.; οὔτε π. οὔθ' ὅρκος μένει Ar.; πίστιν διδόναι to give *assurances*, Hdt.; π. διδόναι καὶ λαμβάνειν to interchange *them*, Xen. :—of an oath, θεῶν πίστεις ὀμνύναι Thuc.; πίστιν ἐπιτιθέναι or προστιθέναι τινί Dem. :—φόβων π. *an assurance against* fears, Eur. **2.** *a means of persuasion, an argument, proof*, such as used by orators, Plat., etc.

πιστός (A), ή, όν, (πίνω) *liquid*; πιστά (sc. φάρμακα) *liquid medicines*, opp. to βρώσιμα, Aesch.

πιστός (B), ή, όν, (πείθω) : **A.** pass. *to be trusted* or *believed* : **I.** of persons, *faithful, trusty, true*, Il., Hes., Att. :—in Persia οἱ πιστοί were Privy-councillors, ' *trusty* and well-beloved,' Xen.; πιστὰ πιστῶν = πιστότατοι, Aesch. **2.** *trustworthy, worthy of credit*, Thuc., etc. **II.** of things, *trustworthy, sure*, of oaths, etc., Hom., etc.; οὐκέτι πιστὰ γυναιξίν no longer *can one trust* women, Od.; ἐλπὶς πιστὴ λόγῳ *warranted* by reason, Thuc. **2.** *deserving belief, credible, probable*, Hdt., Plat., etc. **III.** πιστόν, τό, as Subst., like πίστις II, *a pledge, security, warrant, certainty*, Soph., etc.; τὸ π. τῆς ἐλευθερίας Thuc.; τὸ π. ἔχοντες κἂν περιγενέσθαι feeling *confidence* that they should survive, Id. :—in pl., τὰ πιστὰ ποιεῖσθαι = πίστιν ποιεῖσθαι, Hdt.; πιστὰ θεῶν, of oaths, Xen.; πιστόν or πιστὰ δοῦναι καὶ λαβεῖν to give and receive *pledges*, to interchange *pledges*, Id., etc.

B. act. like πίσυνος, *believing, trusting in, relying on*, τινι Theogn., Aesch., etc. **2.** *obedient*, Xen. **3.** *faithful, believing*, N.T.

C. Adv. πιστῶς, *with good faith, persuasively*, Dem. **II.** *with disposition to believe*, Id.

πιστότης, ητος, ἡ, *good faith, honesty*, Hdt., Plat.

πιστόω, f. ώσω, (πιστός) *to make trustworthy*, πιστοῦν τινα ὅρκοις *to bind* him *by oaths*, Thuc. **II.** Pass. *to be made trustworthy, give a pledge* or *warrant*, ὅρκῳ πιστωθῆναί τινι *to bind oneself* to another by oath, Od. **2.** *to feel trust* or *confidence*, i. e. *to trust, to be persuaded*, πιστωθῆναι ἐνὶ θυμῷ Ib; πιστωθεὶς ὅτι . . , *feeling confidence that* . . , Soph. **III.** Med. *to give mutual pledges of fidelity, exchange troth*, χεῖράς τ' ἀλλήλων λαβέτην καὶ πιστώσαντο Il. :—πιστοῦσθαί τινα ὑφ' ὅρκου *to secure* his *good faith* by oaths, Soph. **2.** *to confirm, prove, make good, guarantee*, τι Polyb., Luc.

πίστρα, ἡ, (πι-πίσκω) *a drinking-trough* for cattle, Eur.

πίστωμα, ατος, τό, (πιστόω) *an assurance, warrant, guarantee, pledge*, Aesch., etc. **II.** of persons, γηραλᾶ πιστώματα, = πιστοὶ γέροντες, Id.

πιστώσαντο, Ep. 3 pl. aor. 1 med. of πιστόω.

πιστωτέος, α, ον, verb. Adj. *to be warranted*, Luc.

πίσυνος [ῐ], ον, (πείθω) *trusting in, relying* or *depending on, confiding in* another, c. dat., Il., Hdt.

πίσυρες [ῐ], πίσυρα, Aeol. for τέσσαρες, τέσσαρα.

πίσω [ῐ], f. of πιπίσκω.

Πιτάνη [ἄ], Dor. -να, ἡ, a place in Laconia, Hdt. :— ὁ Πιτανήτης λόχος, a corps of the Spartan army, Id.

πίτνημι, poët. form of πετάννυμι, *to spread out*, ἠέρα πίτνα (Ep. for ἐπίτνα) Il.; πιτνὰς εἰς ἐμὲ χεῖρας *stretching out* his arms to me, Od.; πίτναν τ' εἰς αἰθέρα χεῖρας (for ἐπίτναν) Pind. :—Pass., ἀμφὶ δὲ χαῖται πίτναντο Il.

πίτνω, = πετάννυμι, Hes.

πίτνω, poët. form of πίπτω, used by Pind. and Trag., when the penult is required to be short; cf. ἴσχω, μίμνω for ἔχω, μένω.

πίττα, ἡ, Att. for πίσσα.

πίττῖνος, πιττώδης, Att. for πίσσινος, πισσώδης.

πιτῠλεύω, f. σω, (πίτυλος) *to ply the plashing oar*, Ar.

ΠΙΤΥΛΟΣ [ῐ], ὁ, *the measured plash of oars*, Eur.; ἐνὶ πιτύλῳ with one *stroke*, all together, Aesch. **II.** *any quick repeated sound*, **1.** *the plash of falling drops*, π. δακρύων Eur.; π. σκύφου, of wine poured into a cup, Id. **2.** *the sound of repeated blows*, Aesch., Eur. :—metaph., πίτυλος Ἀργείου δορός Eur.; δὶς δυοῖν πιτύλοιν twice with two *strokes*, Id.; also *of violent frantic gestures, violence, passion*, Id.

πῐτῠο-κάμπτης, ου, ὁ, *pine-bender*, epith. of the robber Sinis, who killed travellers by tying them between two pine-trees bent down so as nearly to meet, and then let go again, Strab., Plut.

πῐτῠ-τρόφος, ον, (τρέφω) *growing pines*, Anth.

πίτυρον, τό, (πτίσσω) *the husks of corn, bran*, mostly in pl., Dem., Theocr.

ΠΙΤΥΣ [ῐ], υος, ἡ, Ep. dat. pl. πίτυσσιν, *the pine, stone pine*, Hom. :—proverb., πίτυος τρόπον ἐκτρίβεσθαι *to be destroyed like a pine*, i. e. *utterly*, because the pine when cut down never grows again, Hdt.

πῐτύ-στεπτος, ον, (στέφω) *pine-crowned*, Anth.

πῐτυ-ώδης, ες, (εἶδος) *abounding in pines*, Strab.

πι-φαύσκω, redupl. form of ΦΑ (Root of φαίνω), only in pres. and impf. : Ep. inf. πιφαυσκέμεν :—*to make manifest, declare, tell of*, Hom., Aesch. : absol., πιφαύσκων Διομήδεϊ *making signal* to him, Il. **2.** *to set forth* words, *utter*, μῦθον, ἔπεα Od. **3.** c. acc. et inf. *to tell* one to do, Aesch. **II.** Med. *to make manifest*, Il.; *to tell of, disclose*, Hom., Hes.

πίω, aor. 2 subj. of πίνω.

ΠΙΩΝ [ῐ], ὁ, ἡ, neut. πῖον, gen. πίονος, *fat, plump*, Lat. *pinguis*, Hom.; π. δημός *rich fat*, Il.; of oil, Hdt. **II.** of soil, *fat, rich*, Il.; also, πίονα ἔργα *pingues segetes*, Ib.; ὀπώρας πίων *ποτός*, of wine, Soph. **2.** of persons and places, *rich, wealthy*, Hom., Aesch.; πίονι μέτρῳ in *plenteous* measure, Theocr. **III.** The Comp. and Sup. are πῑότερος, πῑότατος, as if from πῖος.

πλᾱγά, Dor. for πληγή.

πλᾱγιάζω, f. άσω, (πλάγιος) *to turn sideways* or *aside*, πλ. πρὸς τοὺς ἀντίους ἀνέμους (sc. τὴν ναῦν) *to beat up against adverse winds*, Luc. : metaph., πλ. ἢ φωνήν ἢ πρᾶξιν *to adapt* them *to circumstances*, Plut.

πλᾱγί-αυλος, ὁ, *the cross-flute*, as opp. to the flute-à-bec, Theocr., Bion.

πλάγιος [ἄ], α, ον, and ος, ον, (πλάγος) *placed sideways, slanting, aslant*, Lat. *obliquus*, Thuc. **2.** πλάγια, τά, *the sides*, Hdt. :—in military sense, τοῖς πλαγίοις ἐπιέναι to attack *the flanks*, Thuc.; εἰς τὰ πλ. παράγειν or παραπέμπειν to make an army file off *right and left*, Xen.; πλαγίους λαβεῖν τοὺς πολεμίους to take the enemy *in flank*, Id. **3.** with Preps. in adverb. sense, εἰς πλάγιον *obliquely*, Id.; εἰς τὰ πλάγια, opp. to εἰς τὸ ἀντίον, Thuc.; ἐκ πλαγίου *in flank*, Id.; κατὰ πλάγια Xen. **II.** metaph. *not straightforward, crooked, treacherous*, φρένες Pind.; πλάγια φρονεῖν Eur.

πλᾰγιόω, = πλαγιάζω 1, Xen.

πλαγκτήρ, ῆρος, ὁ, (πλάζω) either (act.) *the beguiler*, (or pass.) *the roamer*, of Bacchus, Anth.

πλαγκτός, ή, όν, and ός, όν, (πλάζομαι) *wandering, roaming*, Aesch., Eur. 2. metaph. *wandering in mind, erring, distraught*, Od., Aesch. II. Πλαγκταὶ πέτραι are rocks beyond Scylla and Charybdis, affording so narrow a passage that even birds could scarcely get through, Od. ; transferred by later writers to the Symplegades, Hdt., etc.

πλαγκτοσύνη, ἡ, poët. for πλάνη, *roaming*, Od.

ΠΛΑΓΟΣ, τό, *the side*, old Dor. word.

πλάγξομαι, f. med. of πλάζω.

πλαγχθῆναι, aor. 1 pass. inf. of πλάζω.

ΠΛΑΔΑΡΟΣ, ά, όν, *wet, damp*, Anth.

ΠΛΑΖΩ, Ep. impf. πλάζον : aor. 1 ἔπλαγξα, Ep. πλάγξα :—Pass. and Med., Dor. πλάσδομαι, Ep. impf. πλαζόμην : f. πλάγξομαι : aor. 1 ἐπλάγχθην, Ep. πλάγχθην :—like πλανάω, *to make to wander* or *roam*, Hom. 2. *to lead astray, bewilder*, Id. II. Pass. *to wander, rove, roam about*, Od. ; ἀπὸ χαλκόφι χαλκὸς ἐπλάγχθη brass *glanced off from* brass, Il. ; c. gen. *to wander from*, ἀμαξιτοῦ Eur. ; so, τίς πλάγχθη πολύμοχθος ἔξω ; i. e. τίς ἐπλάγχθη ἔξω τοῦ πολύμοχθος εἶναι ; Soph. III. μέγα κῦμα πλάζ᾽ ὤμους the wave *drove* his shoulder *aside*, Il. : Pass., κύματι πλάζετο *was driven aside* by the wave, Od.

πλάθανον [ᾰ], τό, (πλατύς) *a mould* in which cakes were baked, Theocr.

πλάθω [ᾱ], poët. form of πελάζω, intr. *to approach, draw near*, c. dat., Soph. ; c. acc., Eur. ; absol., Id.

πλαίσιον, τό, *an oblong figure* or *body*, Ar. ; ἰσόπλευρον πλ. *a square*, Xen. ; of an army, ἐν πλαισίῳ τετάχθαι *to be drawn up* in *square*, Lat. *agmine quadrato*, as opp. to marching order, Lat. *agmine longo*, Thuc., Xen. (Prob. from same Root as πλατ-ύς.)

πλᾰκείς, aor. 2 pass. part. of πλέκω.

πλᾰκερός, ά, όν, (πλάξ) = πλατύς, *broad*, Theocr.

πλάκινος [ᾰ], η, ον, (πλάξ) *made of planks*, πλ. τρίπους *a tripod with a board on it*, Anth.

πλᾰκοῦς, οῦντος, ὁ, contr. from πλακόεις, (πλάξ) *a flat cake*, Lat. *placenta*, Ar.

πλάκτωρ, ορος, ὁ, Dor. for πλήκτωρ, Anth.

πλάν, Dor. for πλήν :—πλανάτας, Dor. for πλανήτης.

πλᾰνάω, f. ήσω :—Pass. and Med., f. -ήσομαι and -ηθήσομαι : aor. 1 ἐπλανήθην : pf. πεπλάνημαι : (πλάνη) :—like πλάζω, *to make to wander, lead wandering about*, Hdt., Aesch. :—*to lead from the subject*, in talking, Dem. 2. *to lead astray, mislead, deceive*, Soph., Plat. II. Pass. *to wander, roam about, stray*, Il., Aesch. ; c. acc. loci, *to wander over*, Lat. *oberrare*, Eur. ; but c. acc. cogn., πολλοὺς ἑλιγμοὺς πλανᾶσθαι *to wander* about as in a labyrinth, Xen. :— of reports, *to wander abroad*, Soph. 2. *to wander* in speaking, *digress*, Hdt. 3. c. gen., πλανηθεὶς καιροῦ *having missed* one's opportunity, Pind. 4. *to do a thing irregularly* or *at random*, Hdt. ; ἐνύπνια τὰ ἐς ἀνθρώπους πεπλανημέναθαὶ have visited them *irregularly*, Id. 5. *to wander in mind, to be at a loss*, Id., Aesch.

ΠΛΑΝΗ [ᾰ], ἡ, like ἄλη, *a wandering, roaming*, Hdt., Aesch. 2. *a digression*, Plat. II. metaph. *a going astray, error*, Id., etc.

πλάνημα [ᾰ], ατος, τό, *a wandering*, Aesch., Soph.

πλάνης [ᾰ], ητος, ὁ, *a wanderer, roamer, rover*, Soph., Eur. 2. πλάνητες ἀστέρες *the planets*, Xen. II. as Adj. *wandering*, Plut.

πλάνησις, εως, ἡ, (πλανάω) *a making to wander, a dispersing*, τῶν νεῶν Thuc.

πλᾰνητέον, verb. Adj. *one must wander*, Xen.

πλᾰνήτης, ου, Dor. πλανάτας, ὁ, = πλάνης, Soph., Plat. II. as Adj. *wandering, roaming*, Eur.

πλᾰνητικός, ή, όν, *disposed to wander*, Strab.

πλᾰνητός, ή, όν, (πλανάομαι) *wandering*, Plat.

πλαν-όδιος, α, ον, *going by bye-paths, wandering*, h. Hom. [ᾰ metri. grat.]

ΠΛΑΝΟΣ [ᾰ], ον, 1. act. *leading astray, cheating, deceiving*, Theocr., Mosch. II. πλάνος, ὁ, = πλάνη, *a wandering, roaming, straying*, Soph., Eur., etc. 2. metaph., φροντίδος πλάνοι *the wanderings* of thought, Soph. ; but, πλ. φρενῶν *wandering* of mind, madness, Eur. ; πλάνοις *in uncertain fits*, of a disease, Soph. ; κερκίδος πλάνοι, of the act of weaving, Eur. III. of persons, πλάνος, ὁ, *a deceiver, impostor*, N. T.

πλᾰνο-στῐβής, ές, *trodden by wanderers*, Aesch.

πλᾰνύττω, = πλανάομαι, *to wander about*, Ar.

ΠΛΑΞ, ἡ, gen. πλᾰκός, *a flat surface, flat land, a plain*, Aesch. ; πόντου πλάξ *the ocean-plain*, Pind. ; αἰθερία πλάξ Eur. : *the flat top of a hill, table-land*, Soph. 2. *a flat stone, tablet*, Luc., N. T.

πλάξεν, Dor. for πλῆξεν, 3 sing. aor. 1 of πλήσσω.

πλάξιππος, ον, Dor. for πλήξιππος.

πλάσμα, ατος, τό, (πλάσσω) *anything moulded, an image, figure*, Ar., etc. II. *anything imitated, a counterfeit, forgery*, Dem. III. *a formed style, affectation*, in orators or actors, Plut.

πλασμᾰτίας, ου, ὁ, *one addicted to lying*, Plut.

ΠΛΑΣΣΩ, Att. -ττω : f. πλάσω [ᾰ] : aor. 1 ἔπλᾰσα, poët. ἔπλασσα, Ep. πλάσσα :—Med., aor. 1 ἐπλασάμην :—Pass., aor. 1 ἐπλάσθην : pf. πέπλασμαι :—*to form, mould, shape*, Lat. *fingere*, properly of the artist who works in clay or wax, Hes., Hdt. ; τὴν ὑδρίαν πλάσαι *to mould* the water-jar, Ar. ; ἔπλαττεν οἰκίας *made clay* houses, Id. :—Pass. *to be moulded, made*, ὁ μὲν πλάσσεται one *is a-moulding*, Hdt. II. generally, *to mould and form* by education, training, Plat. III. *to form in the mind, form a notion* of a thing, Id. IV. *to put in a certain form* : Med., πλασάμενος τῇ ὄψει *having formed himself* in face, i. e. composed his countenance, Thuc. V. metaph. *to make up, fabricate, forge*, Soph., Dem. :— absol., πλάσας λέγειν *to speak from invention*, i. e. not the truth, Hdt. :—so in Med., Xen., etc. :—Pass., οὐ πεπλασμένος ὁ κόμπος not *fictitious*, Aesch.

πλάστειρα, fem. of πλάστης, Anth.

πλαστεύω, *to falsify*, Byz.

πλάστης, ου, ὁ, *a moulder, modeller*, Plat.

πλάστιγξ, Ion. πλήστιγξ, ιγγος, ἡ, *the scale of a balance*, Ar. : dual, *a pair of scales*, Id. II. *a collar for horses*, Eur. III. *a scourge*, Aesch. (In this last sense, at all events, from πλήσσω.)

πλαστικός, ή, όν, (πλάσσω) *fit for moulding, plastic*, αἱ πλ. τέχναι the *plastic arts*, Plat.

πλαστός, ή, όν, (πλάσσω) *formed, moulded* in clay or wax, Hes., Plat., etc. II. metaph. *fabricated, forged, counterfeit,* Hdt., Eur.; πλαστός a *supposititious* son, Soph.

πλάτα [ᾰ], Dor. for πλάτη.

πλᾰτᾰγέω, f. ήσω, *to clap, clap the hands,* Theocr.; *to clash, crack,* Id.:—so in Med., Anth. II. *to beat* the breasts, Bion; πλ. τύμπανα Anth.

πλᾰτᾰγή, ή, (πλατάσσω) *a rattle,* Arist.

πλᾰτᾰγημα, ατος, τό, (πλαταγέω) *a clapping,* Theocr.

πλᾰτᾰγώνιον, τό, (πλαταγέω) *the broad petal of the poppy* or *anemoné,* which lovers laid on the left hand, and struck with the right; it was a good omen if it burst *with a loud crack,* Theocr.

Πλάταια, ή, and in pl. **Πλαταιαί,** ῶν, αἰ, *Plataea* or *Plataeae* in Boeotia, Hdt., etc.:—Adv. **Πλαταιᾶσι,** before a vowel -σιν, *at Plataeae,* Thuc.: **Πλαταιεῖς,** έων, οἰ, Ion. -έες, Att. **Πλαταιῆς,** acc. -ᾶς, *Plataeans,* Hdt., etc.—Adj. **Πλαταιικός,** ή, όν, *of Pl.,* Id.; τὰ -κά *the events at Pl.,* Id.; fem. ἡ **Πλαταιὶς γῆ,** χώρα Id.

πλᾰτᾰμών, ῶνος, ὁ, (πλατύς) *a flat stone,* h. Hom.:—in pl. *ledges of rock,* Strab.

πλᾰτάνιστος, ή, =πλάτανος (q. v.), Il., Hdt.

πλᾰτανιστοῦς, οῦντος, ὁ, contr. for πλατανιστόεις, *a grove of plane-trees,* Lat. *platanetum,* Theogn.

πλάτᾰνος, ή, later form of πλατάνιστος, *the oriental plane,* Lat. *platanus,* Ar., Plat. (From πλατύς, because of its *broad leaves.*)

πλᾰτεῖα, ή, v. πλατύς.

πλᾰτειάζω, Dor. -άσδω, (πλατύς) *to speak* or *pronounce broadly,* like the Dorians, Theocr.

πλᾰτεῖον, τό, (πλατύς) *a tablet,* Polyb.

πλᾰτέως, Adv. of πλατύς.

πλάτη, Dor. **πλάτα,** ή, (πλᾰτύς) *a flat surface :* 1. *the blade of an oar, an oar,* Trag.; ναυτίλῳ πλάτη *by ship, by sea,* Soph.; οὐρίῳ πλάτη *with a fair voyage,* Id. 2. *a sheet of paper,* Anth.

πλατίον [ᾰ], Dor. for πλησίον.

πλᾰτίς, ιδος, ή, poët. for πελάτις, *a wife,* Ar.

πλᾰτόομαι, Pass. *to be made flat* like an oar-blade, Ar. From

πλάτος, εος, τό, (πλᾰτύς) *breadth, width,* Hdt., etc. :—absol., πλάτος or τὸ πλ., *in breadth,* Id., Xen.

πλᾰτός, ή, όν, shortd. for πελᾰτός, *approachable,* Aesch.

πλάττω, Att. for πλάσσω.

πλᾰτύγίζω, f. σω, (πλατύς) of a goose, *to beat the water with its wings, to splash about :*—metaph. *to make a splash, to swagger,* Ar.

πλᾰτύ-λέσχης, ου, ὁ, *a wide-mouthed babbler,* Anth.

πλατυντέον, verb. Adj. *one must extend,* Xen. From

πλᾰτύνω, f. ῠνῶ, (πλατύς) *to widen, make wide,* N. T. :—Med., πλατύνεσθαι γῆν *to widen one's territory,* Xen. :—Pass. *to grow broad, widen out,* Anth. : metaph., ἡ καρδία πεπλάτυνται *is opened, enlarged,* N. T.

πλᾰτύ-νωτος, ον, *broad-backed,* Batr.

πλᾰτύ-πῠγος, ον, (πυγή) *broad-bottomed,* πλοῖα Strab.

πλᾰτύρ-ρῑς, ῑνος, ὁ, ή, *broad-nosed,* Strab.

πλᾰτύρ-ροος, contr. -ρους, ουν, *broad-flowing,* Aesch.

ΠΛΑΤΥΣ, εῖα, ύ, Ion. fem. πλατέα :—*wide, broad,* Il.; αἰπόλια πλατέ' αἰγῶν *broad* herds, i. e. *large* or *widespread,* Hom.; π. πρόσοδοι Pind. 2. *flat, level,*

Hdt., Plat.; κάρυα τὰ πλατέα, i. e. chestnuts, Xen. 3. of a man, *broad-shouldered,* Soph. 4. metaph., πλατὺς κατάγελως *flat* (i. e. downright) mockery, Ar. : neut. as Adv., *flatly, merely,* Id. 5. πλατεῖα (sc. ὁδός), ή, *a street,* Lat. *platea,* Xen. :—(sub. χείρ), *the flat of the hand,* Ar. II. *salt, brackish,* Hdt.

πλᾰτύτης, ητος, ή, *breadth, bulk,* Xen.

Πλάτων [ᾰ], ωνος, ὁ, *Plato :* whence Adj. **Πλατωνικός,** ή, όν, *of Plato,* Anth.; Sup. -ώτατος, Luc. : Adv. -κῶς, *after the manner of Plato,* Strab.

πλέγδην, (πλέκω) Adv. *entwined, entangled,* Anth.

πλέγμα, ατος, τό, (πλέκω) *plaited work, wicker-work,* Plat., Xen. :—pl. *wreaths, braids,* Eur., N. T.

πλέες, acc. **πλέας,** v. πλείων sub fin.

πλεθριαῖος, α, ον, (πλέθρον) *broad* or *long,* Xen.

πλεθρίζω, f. σω, *to run* the πλέθρον; metaph. *to 'shoot with a long bow,'* Theophr.

πλέθρον, τό, as measure of length, *a plethron,* = 100 Greek or 101 English feet, ⅙ of a stade, Hdt., Xen. II. as a square measure, 10,000 square feet (Greek) = about 37 perches, Plat., Dem.;—used to translate the Rom. *jugerum,* though this was about 2 roods 19 perches, Plut. (Deriv. uncertain.)

Πλειάδες, Ion. **Πληιάδες,** αἰ, *the Pleiads,* seven daughters of Atlas, placed by Zeus among the stars, Hom., Hes.; only six are distinctly visible, whence the myth of the 'lost Pleiad,' Ovid. (Prob. from πλέω, *to sail,* because they rose at the beginning of *the sailing-season,* as Ὑάδες from ὕω, with reference to *the rainy season.* Poets, adopting the form Πελειάδες, represented them as *doves,* and the ὑάδες as *swine.*)

πλεῖν, Att. for πλέον, v. πλείων fin.

πλεῖος, πλειότερος, v. πλέως.

πλειστάκις [ᾰ], Adv. (πλεῖστος) *mostly, most often, very often,* Xen., etc.

πλειστ-ήρης, ες, (*ἄρω) *manifold,* ἅπας πλ. χρόνος all *the whole length of* time, Aesch. Hence

πλειστηρίζομαι, Dep. *to count as principal author,* Aesch.

πλειστο-βόλος, ον, *throwing the most,* of dicers, Anth.

πλειστόμ-βροτος, ον, *crowded with people,* Pind.

πλεῖστος, η, ον, Sup. of πολύς, *most, largest,* also *very much, very large,* both of number and size, Hom., etc.; πλεῖστός εἰμι τῇ γνώμῃ I incline *most* to the opinion, Hdt. 2. with the Art., οἱ πλεῖστοι, *much* like οἱ πολλοί, *the greatest number,* Thuc., etc.; τὸ πλεῖστον *τοῦ βίου the greatest part* of life, Plat.; also ἡ πλ. τῆς στρατιᾶς Thuc. II. Special usages : ὅσας ἂν πλείστας δύναιντο καταστρέφεσθαι *the greatest* number that they could *possibly* subdue, Hdt.; ὅτι πλ. Thuc., etc.;—εἷς ἀνὴρ πλεῖστον πόνον παρασχών the greatest of all men, Aesch. III. Adverb. usages :—πλεῖστον, = μάλιστα, *most,* Il., Att.; ὡς πλεῖστον, Lat. *quam maxime,* Xen.; sometimes added to a Sup., πλεῖστον ἐχθίστη, πλ. κάκιστος Soph. : so, πλεῖστα Id. :—*furthest,* Plat. 2. with the Art., τὸ πλ. *for the most part,* Ar. IV. with Preps. : 1. διὰ πλείστου *furthest off,* in point of space or time, Thuc. 2. εἰς πλεῖστον *most,* Soph. 3. ἐπὶ πλεῖστον *over the greatest distance, to the greatest extent,* in point of space or time, Hdt., Thuc.; ὡς ἐπὶ πλ. or ὡς ἐπὶ τὸ πλ. *for the most part.*

Plat.; περὶ πλείστου ποιεῖσθαι, v. περί A. IV.   4. ἐν τοῖς πλεῖστοι or πλεῖσται about the most, Thuc.

πλείω, poët. for πλέω, to sail.

πλείων and **πλέων**, ὁ, ἡ, neut. πλεῖον, πλέον, Att. also **πλεῖν**: pl. πλείονες, πλέονες, Att. πλείους, Att. neut. πλείω:—Ep. pl. πλέες, acc. πλέας, dat. πλεόνεσσι: Ion. and Dor. neut. πλεῦν, pl. πλεῦνες:—Comp. of πολύς, more, larger, both of number and size, Hom., etc.; τὸν πλείω λόγον all further speech, Soph.; πλείω τὸν πλοῦν the greater part of.., Thuc.:—of Time, longer, πλείων χρόνος Hdt.; πλείων νύξ the greater part of night, Il.   2. with the Art., οἱ πλέονες the greater number, like οἱ πολλοί, the mass or crowd, Hom.; οἱ πλεῦνες Hdt., etc.; c. gen., τὰς πλεῦνας τῶν γυναικῶν Id.:—the many, the people, opp. to the chief men, Thuc., etc.:—τὸ πλεῖον πολέμοιο the greater part of war, Hom.   II. pecul. usages of neut.: 1. as a Noun, more, πλεῖον ἔτι τούτου Hdt.; τὸ δὲ πλέον nay, what is more, Eur., Thuc.:—πλέον or τὸ πλέον a higher degree of a thing, Soph.; τὸ πλ. τοῦ χρόνου Thuc.:—πλέον ἔχειν to have the best of it, win, conquer, Id.; also, like πλεονεκτέω, c. gen., Hdt., etc.; also, πλέον ποιεῖν Plat.; ἐς πλ. ποιεῖν Soph.; οὐδὲν πλ. πράσσειν, etc., Eur.:—τί πλέον; what more, i. e. what good or use is it? Ar.; so, οὐδὲν ἦν πλέον Dem.:—ἐπὶ πλέον or ἐπίπλεον, as Adv., more, further, Hdt., Thuc., etc.; c. gen. beyond, ἐπὶ τὸ πλ. τινὸς ἱκέσθαι Theocr.; cf. περί A. III.   2. as Adv. more, rather, πλέον ἔφερέ οἱ ἡ γνώμη his opinion inclined rather, Hdt.:—also, τὸ πλέον, Ion. τὸ πλεῦν, for the most part, Id., etc.; τὸ πλ. = μᾶλλον, Thuc.   b. with Numerals, τοξόται πλ. ἢ εἴκοσι Xen.:—in this sense a contr. form πλεῖν is used by Att. writers, πλεῖν ἢ τριάκονθ᾽ ἡμέρας Ar.; πλεῖν ἢ χιλίας (sc. δραχμάς) Id., etc.;—but ἢ is often omitted, as in Lat. quam after plus, πλεῖν ἢ ἑξακοσίας Id.; so, ἔτη γεγονὼς πλείω ἑβδομήκοντα annos plus septuaginta natus, Plat.:—Comic phrase, πλεῖν ἢ μαίνομαι more than to madness, Ar.   c. the pl. πλείω is also used like πλέον, Thuc., Dem.

πλειών, ῶνος, ὁ, (πλέος) a full period, a year, Hes.

πλέκος, εος, τό, (πλέκω) wicker-work, Ar.

πλεκτάνάομαι, Pass. to be intertwined, πεπλεκτανημέναι δράκουσι, of the Erinyes, Aesch.   From

πλεκτάνη [ᾰ], ἡ, (πλέκω) anything twined or wreathed, a coil, wreath, spire, of serpents, Aesch.; πλ. καπνοῦ a wreath of smoke, Ar.   II. in pl. the meshes of a spider's web, Luc.; metaph., αἱ τῶν λόγων πλεκτάναι tortuous speeches, Id.

πλεκτή, ἡ, properly fem. of πλεκτός: 1. a coil, wreath, Aesch.   2. a twisted rope, cord, string, Eur.

πλεκτικός, ή, όν, (πλέκω) of plaiting, τέχναι Plat.

πλεκτός, ή, όν, (πλέκω) plaited, twisted, Hom., Hes., etc.; π. στέγαι wicker mansions, of the Scythian vans, Aesch.; πλεκτὴ Αἰγύπτου παιδεία the twisted task-work of Egypt, i. e. ropes of biblus, Eur.   2. wreathed, ἄνθη Aesch.; στέφανος Eur.

ΠΛΕ'ΚΩ: f. πλέξω: aor. 1 ἔπλεξα: pf. πέπλεχα:—Med., aor. 1 ἐπλεξάμην:—Pass., f. πλεχθήσομαι: aor. 1 ἐπλέχθην; but aor. 2 ἐπλάκην [ᾰ]: pf. πέπλεγμαι:—to plait, twine, twist, weave, braid, Il., etc.:—Med., πεῖσμα πλεξάμενος having twisted me a rope,

Od. :—Pass., κράνεα πεπλεγμένα of basket-work, Hdt.; σειραὶ πεπλεγμέναι ἐξ ἱμάντων Id.   II. metaph. to plan, devise, contrive, like ῥάπτειν, ὑφαίνειν, mostly of tortuous means, πλ. δόλον Aesch.; μηχανὰς Eur.; παντοίας παλάμας Ar.   2. of Poets, πλ. ὕμνον, ῥήματα Pind.; πλ. λόγους Eur.   3. in Pass. to twist oneself round, Aesch.

πλεονάζω, f. άσω: pf. pass. -ασμαι: (πλέον):—to be more, esp. to be more than enough, be superfluous, Arist.   II. of persons, to go beyond bounds, take or claim too much, Dem. :—c. dat. to presume upon, τῇ εὐτυχίᾳ Thuc.: of a writer, to be lengthy, tedious, Lat. multus sum, Strab.   2. πλεονάζειν τινός to have an excess of, abound in a thing, Arist.   III. c. acc. to state at a larger amount, Strab. :—Pass. to be exaggerated, Thuc.

πλεονάκις [ᾰ], Adv. (πλέων) more frequently, oftener, Plat.: several times, frequently, Arist.

πλεοναχῇ, (πλέων) Adv. in many points of view, Plat.

πλεοναχῶς, (πλέων) Adv. in various ways, Arist.

πλεονεκτέω, f. ήσω and ήσομαι: (πλεονέκτης):—to have or claim more than one's due, to get or have too much, to be greedy, grasping, arrogant, Hdt., Plat.: —also to gain or have some advantage, without any bad sense, Thuc., Xen.   2. c. gen. rei, to have or claim more of a thing, to have or claim a larger share, Thuc., etc.   II. c. gen. pers. to have or gain the advantage over, τῶν ἐχθρῶν Plat.   2. c. acc. pers. to overreach, defraud, Menand., N. T. :—Pass. to be overreached, Thuc., Xen. Hence

πλεονέκτημα, ατος, τό, an advantage, gain, privilege, Plat., Dem.: in pl. gains, successes, Xen.   II. an act of overreaching, selfish trick, Dem.

πλεον-έκτης, ου, ὁ, = ὁ πλέον ἔχων, one who has or claims more than his due, greedy, grasping, arrogant, Thuc., etc. :—as Adj., λόγος πλ. Hdt.; Sup. πλεονεκτίστατος, Xen.   2. πλεονέκτης τῶν πολεμίων making gain from their losses, Id.

πλεονεκτητέον, verb. Adj. of πλεονεκτέω, one must take more than one's share, Plat.

πλεονεκτικός, ή, όν, disposed to take too much, greedy, Dem., etc. Adv. -κῶς, Plat.; πλ. ἔχειν Dem.

πλεονεξία, Ion. -ίη, ἡ, the character and conduct of a πλεονέκτης, greediness, grasping, assumption, arrogance, Hdt., Thuc., etc.   II. gain, advantage, Xen., etc. ; ἐπὶ πλεονεξίᾳ with a view to one's own advantage, Thuc., Xen.   2. c. gen. pers. advantage over, Xen.   3. c. gen. rei, a larger share of a thing, Arist.; gain made from a thing, Dem.

πλέος, η, ον, Ion. for πλέως, full.

πλέτο, Ep. for ἔπλετο, 3 sing. impf. of πέλομαι.

πλεύμων, ονος, ὁ, later Att. form of πνεύμων.

πλεῦν, Ion. and Dor. for πλέον, neut. of πλέων: gen. πλεῦνος, pl. πλεῦνες.

πλεύνως, Adv. Ion. for πλεόνως (πλέων), Hdt.

ΠΛΕΥΡΑ', ᾶς, ἡ, = πλευρόν, a rib, Lat. costa, Hdt.: mostly in pl. the ribs, the side, Il., Hdt., Att. :—in sing., also, of one side, Soph.   II. the side of things and places, πλευραὶ νηός Theogn.; χωρίου, ποταμοῦ Plat.; of an army, αἱ πλ. τοῦ πλαισίου Xen.   III. the page of a book, Anth.

πλευρόθεν, Adv. from the side, Soph.

πλευρο-κοπέω, f. ήσω, (κόπτω) to smite the ribs, Soph.
πλευρόν, τό, = πλευρά, a rib : mostly in pl. the ribs, the side, Il., Hdt., etc. ;—also in sing., Soph. **II.** of places, πλευρὸν νεῶν the side of the bay where the ships lay, Id. ; τὸ δεξιὸν πλ. the right flank (of an army), Xen.
πλευρο-τῠπής, ές, striking the sides or ribs, Anth.
πλεύρωμα, τό, like πλευρόν, in pl. the side, Aesch.
πλευστέον, verb. Adj. from πλέω, one must sail, Dem.
πλευστικός, ή, όν, fit or favourable for sailing, Theocr.
ΠΛΕ'Ω, Ep. πλείω, Att. imper. πλεῖ : f. πλεύσομαι, Dor. πλευσοῦμαι, later πλεύσω : aor. 1 ἔπλευσα : pf. πέπλευκα :—Pass., aor. 1 ἐπλεύσθην : pf. πέπλευσμαι : besides πλώω, Ep. impf. πλῶον, Hom. has a syncop. aor. 2 ἔπλων, ως, ω, part. πλώς, compds. ἀπ-έπλω, etc. : Ion. inf. πλώειν, impf. ἔπλωον, f. πλώσομαι, aor. 1 ἔπλωσα, part. πλώσας, pf. πέπλωκα.—The Att. contracted only εε and εει, as in χέω :—to sail, go by sea, Hom., etc. ; c. acc. cogn., ὑγρὰ κέλευθα πλεῖν to sail the watery ways, Od. ; hence in Pass., τὸ πεπλευσμένον πέλαγος Xen.;—metaph., πλεῖν ὑφειμένη cf. ὑφίημι III. **II.** of ships, Il., Hdt., etc. **2.** of other things, to swim, float, Hom., etc. **3.** metaph., ταύτης ἔπι πλέοντες ὀρθῆς while we keep [the ship of] our country right, Soph. ; οὐδ' ὅπως ὀρθὴ πλεύσεται (sc. ἡ πόλις) προείδετο Dem.
πλέων, neut. πλέον, pl. πλέω, = πλείων, πλεῖον, πλείονα.
πλέως, πλέᾱ, πλέων, pl. πλέῳ, πλέᾱ, : Ion. πλέος, -έη, -έον : Ep. πλεῖος, ον : (πίμ-πλημι) :—full of a thing, c. gen., πλεῖαι οἴνου κλισίαι Il., etc. **2.** ῥάκη νοσηλείας πλέα rags infected with his sore, Soph. **II.** absol. full, Il., etc. **2.** of Time, full, complete, δέκα πλείους ἐνιαυτούς ten full years, Hes. **III.** Comp. πλειότερος Od.
πληγή, Dor. πλᾱγά, ή, (πλήσσω) a blow, stroke, Lat. plāga, Hom., etc. ; πληγὴν πέπληγμαι καιρίαν Aesch. ; in such phrases πληγὴν or πληγάς is often omitted, πολλὰς τυπτόμενος Ar., etc. :—the person struck is said πληγὰς λαβεῖν Id. ; the striker πληγὰς δοῦναι, ἐμβάλλειν, ἐντείνειν τινί Xen. **2.** a stroke by lightning, Hes. : a blow, stroke of calamity, Aesch. ; πλ. θεοῦ a blow from heaven, Soph.
πληγῆναι, aor. 2 pass. inf. of πλήσσω.
πλῆγμα, ατος, τό, = πληγή, Soph., Eur.
πλῆθος, εος, τό, Dor. πλᾶθος : (πίμ-πλημι) :—a great number, a throng, crowd, multitude, Il., Hdt., etc. **2.** τὸ πλῆθος, the greater number, the greater part, the mass, main body, Hdt., Xen., etc. :—the majority, the people, like δῆμος, Lat. plebs, Hdt., Att. —also the populace, mob, Xen. **II.** quantity or number, Hdt., Att. ; πλήθει παρόντες in force, Thuc. :—absol. in acc., κόσοι πλῆθος ἦσαν ; πλῆθος ἀνάριθμοι Aesch. **III.** magnitude, size or extent, ὅρος πλήθεῖ μέγιστον Hdt. ; πεδίον πλῆθος ἄπειρον Id., etc. **2.** quantity or amount, Thuc., Plat., etc. **IV.** of Time, length, Thuc., etc. **V.** with Preps., or with ὡς, in adv. sense, ἐς πλ. in great numbers, Id. :—ὡς πλήθει upon the whole, in general, Plat. ; so, ὡς ἐπὶ τὸ πλ. usually, mostly, Lat. ut plurimum, Id.
πληθύνω [ῠ], Causal of πληθύω, only in pres. and impf., to make full, increase, multiply, N. T., Hdt. **II.** Pass. to be in the majority, to prevail, Aesch. ; c.

inf., ἐπαινεῖν πληθύνομαι I am led by general opinion to approve, Id.
πληθύς [ῠ], ύος, ή, Ep. dat. πληθυῖ, fulness, a throng, a crowd, of people, Hom., Plut., etc. Hence
πληθύω, intr. form of πληθύνω, mostly in pres. and impf. to be or become full, τινός of a thing, Eur. :— absol. ἀγορῆς πληθυούσης, v. ἀγορά v :—of rivers, to swell, rise, Hdt. :—so in Med., Id. **2.** to increase in number, multiply, Aesch. **3.** to abound, τινί in a thing, Soph. **4.** to be general, prevail, Lat. invalescere, of reports, Aesch., Soph. ; ὁ πληθύων χρόνος increasing time, age, Soph.
πλήθω, Dor. πλάθω [ᾱ], poët. pf. (in pres. sense) πέπληθα, intr. form of πίμπλημι, mostly in pres : (πίμ-πλημι) :—to be or become full of a thing, c. gen., Il., Aesch. ; χεῖρας κρεῶν πλήθοντες having them full of flesh, Aesch. ; c. dat., Theocr. : absol. of rivers, to be full, brimming, Il. ; so, πλήθουσα Σελήνη at her full, Ib. ; ἀγορᾶς πληθυούσης, ἐν ἀγορᾷ πληθούσῃ, etc., v. sub ἀγορά v. **II.** trans., like πληθύνω, Anth.
πληθώρη, ή, Ion. word, fulness, πλ. ἀγορῆς, = ἀγορὰ πλήθουσα, Hdt. ; v. ἀγορά v. **II.** fulness, satiety, Id.
Πληιάς, -ϊάδες, Ep. for Πλειάς, -αδες.
πλήκτης, ου, ὁ, (πλήσσω) a striker, brawler, Plut.
πληκτίζομαι, Dep. only in pres. :—to bandy blows with one, c. dat., Il. **II.** to beat one's breast for grief, Lat. plangere, Anth. **III.** to indulge in dalliance, Strab.
πλῆκτρον, Dor. πλᾶκτρον, τό, (πλήσσω) anything to strike with : **1.** an instrument for striking the lyre, plectrum, h. Hom., Eur., etc. **2.** a spear-point, πλ. διόβολον, of lightning, Eur. **3.** a cock's spur, Lat. calcar, Ar. **4.** an oar or paddle, Hdt.
πλημμέλεια, ή, a mistake in music, false note : metaph. a fault, offence, error, Plat. ; and
πλημμελέω, f. ήσω, to make a false note in music : metaph. to go wrong, offend, err, τι in a thing, Eur., Plat., etc. ; εἴς τινα Aeschin. :—Pass., πλημμελεῖσθαι ὑπό τινος to be ill-treated by one, Plat., Dem. Hence
πλημμέλημα, ατος, τό, a fault, trespass, Aeschin.
πλημ-μελής, ές, (πλήν, μέλος) properly, out of tune, opp. to ἐμμελής. **II.** metaph. in discord, faulty, erring, Plat. **2.** of things, dissonant, discordant, unpleasant, πλημμελές τι δρᾶν παθεῖν Eur., etc.
πλήμμῡρα, ή, = πλημμυρίς, the flood-tide, Anth.
πλημμῡρέω, f. ήσω, to rise like the flood-tide, to over-flow, be redundant, Anth., Plut.
πλημμῡρίς [ῠ], ίδος, ή, a rise of the sea, πλημμυρὶς ἐκ πόντοιο of the wave caused by the rock thrown by the Cyclops, Od. : flood-tide (cf. ῥαχία), opp. to ἄμπωτις (ebb), Hdt. **2.** generally, a flood, deluge, Arist. ; of tears, Aesch., Eur. [ῠ in Hom., ῡ in Att.] (Deriv. uncertain : perh. from πλήθω, μύρω.)
πλήμνη, ή, the nave of a wheel, Il., Hes. (Perh. from πλήθω, the filled up or solid part of the wheel.)
πλήν, Dor. πλάν = πλέον : **A.** as Prep. with gen., more than, and so except, save, Od., Hdt. ; ὑπεγγύους πλὴν θανάτου liable to any punishment save, short of, death, Hdt. ; ἐπιτρέψαι περὶ σφῶν αὐτῶν πλὴν θανάτου save in respect of death, Thuc.
B. as Adv. : **I.** with single words and phrases, when a negat. precedes, οὐκ οἶδα πλὴν ἕν Soph.,

etc. :—after πᾶς, πάντες, ἕκαστος, and the like, παντὶ δῆλον πλὴν ἐμοί Plat. ; πᾶς is sometimes omitted, θνήσκουσι [πάντες] πλὴν εἷς τις Soph. ; after ἄλλος, τί ἄλλο πλὴν ψευδῆ what else but lies, Id. ; after a Comp., like ἤ, than, ταῦτ᾽ ἐστὶ κρείσσω, πλὴν ὑπ᾽ Ἀργείοις πεσεῖν Eur.   II. often joined with other Particles : 1. πλὴν εἰ, πλὴν ἐάν, Lat. nisi si, πλὴν εἴ τις κωμῳδοποιὸς τυγχάνει ὤν Plat. ; πλὴν ὅταν Aesch., etc. :—the Verb is often omitted, as with ὡσεί, ὡσπερεί, οὐδεὶς οἶδεν, πλὴν εἴ τις ὄρνις Ar.   2. πλὴν ἤ, much like πλὴν εἰ, οὐκ ἄλλως πλὴν ἢ Προδίκῳ Id.   3. πλὴν οὔ, only not, ἀπέπεμπε κήρυκας ἐς τὴν Ἑλλάδα, πλὴν οὐ ἐς᾽Αθήνας Hdt., πλὴν οὐ οἱ τύραννοι Xen.   4. πλὴν ὅτι except that . . , save that, καίτοι τί διαφέρουσιν ἡμῶν ἐκεῖνοι, πλὴν ὅτι ψηφίσματ᾽ οὐ γράφουσιν Ar. ; so, πλὴν ἢ ὅτι Hdt.   5. πλὴν ὅσον except or save so far as, Id. ; πλὴν καθόσον ἐτ Thuc. :—without a Verb, πάντων ἐρήμους, πλὴν ὅσον τὸ σὸν μέρος save so far as thou art concerned, Soph.

πλῆντο, 3 pl. Ep. aor. 2 pass. both of πίμπλημι and of πελάζω.

πλῆξα, Ep. for ἔπληξα, aor. 1 of πλήσσω.

πλήξ-ιππος, Dor. πλάξ-, ον, striking or driving horses, Il., Hes.

πλήρης, ες, gen. εος, contr. ους : Comp. -έστερος, Sup. -έστατος : (πλέος) :   I. c. gen. full of a thing, Hdt., Trag.   2. filled or infected by, πλήρης ὑπ᾽ οἰωνῶν τε καὶ κυνῶν βορᾶς polluted by birds and dogs with meat (torn from the body of Polynices), Soph.   3. satiated with a thing, Id. ; πλήρης ἐστὶ θηεύμενος he has gazed his fill, Hdt.   II. rarely c. dat. filled with, Eur.   III. absol. full, of a swoln stream, Hdt. ; of the moon, Id. ; of cups, Eur. :—esp. full of people, Ar.   2. full, complete, λαβεῖν τι πλῆρες Hdt., Eur. :—of number, τέσσερα ἔτεα πλήρεα four full years, Hdt.

πληρο-φορέω, f. ήσω, (φέρω) to fulfil, N. T.   II. in Pass., of persons, to have full satisfaction, to be fully assured, Ib. ; of things, to be fully believed, Ib.

πληροφορία, ἡ, fulness of assurance, certainty, N. T.

πληρόω, f. ώσω : pf. πεπλήρωκα : Med., f. πληρώσομαι : aor. 1 ἐπληρωσάμην :—Pass., f. -ωθήσομαι, also f. med. in pass. sense : (πλήρης) :—to make full :   I. c. gen. rei, to fill full of, Hdt., etc. :—Pass. to be filled full of, Aesch., etc. ; πλ. full of food, to gorge, satiate, βορᾶς ψυχὴν ἐπλήρουν Eur. ; metaph., πληροῦν θυμόν to glut one's rage, animum explere, Soph., etc.   I. c. dat. to fill with, Eur. : Pass., πνεύμασιν πληρούμενοι filled with breath, Aesch. ; πεπληρωμένος ἀδικίᾳ N. T.   III. πλ. ναῦν, τριήρη to man a ship, Hdt. ; πληροῦτε θωρακεῖα man the breast-works, Aesch. ; in Med., πληροῦσθαι τὴν ναῦν to man one's ship, Xen. :—Pass., of the ships, Thuc.   2. of number, to make full or complete, τοὺς δέκα μῆνας Hdt. ;—so in Med., N. T. :—Pass. to be completed, Hdt., N. T.   3. πλ. δικαστήριον to fill it, Dem.   4. to fulfil, pay in full, make up, Aesch., Thuc. :—Pass., νόμοι πληρούμενοι fully observed, Aesch.   5. ἐς ἄγγος βακχίου μέτρημα πληρώσαντες having poured wine into the vessel till it was full, Eur. :—Pass. to crowd in to a place, Id.   IV. intr., ἡ ὁδὸς πληροῖ ἐς τὸν ἀριθμὸν τοῦτο

the length of road comes in full to this number, Hdt. Hence

πλήρωμα, ατος, τό, a full measure, Eur.   2. πλ. δαιτός the satiety of the feast, Id. ; πλ. τυρῶν their fill of cheese, Id.   3. of ships, a full number, Hdt., Eur.; of single ships, their complement, Thuc., etc.   4. of number, the sum, total, Hdt., Ar.   5. a piece inserted to fill up, N. T.   6. fulness, full and perfect nature, Ib.   II. a filling up, completing, Soph. ; κυλίκων πλ. ἔχων to have the task of filling them, Eur.   2. fulfilment, N. T.

πλήρωσις, ἡ, (πληρόω) a filling up, filling, Plat. : often of eating and drinking, satiety, Id.   2. the completion of a number, Hdt.

πληρωτής, οῦ, ὁ, (πληρόω) one who completes, Dem.

πλῆσαι, aor. 1 part. of πίμπλημι.

πλησαίατο, Ep. 3 pl. aor. 1 med. opt. of πίμπλημι.

πλησιάζω, f. άσω : pf. πεπλησίακα : (πλησίος) :—to bring near, τινά τινι Xen. :—Pass. to come near, approach, τινι Eur.   II. intr., in sense of Pass., absol. to be near, Soph. :—to draw near to, approach, c. dat., Xen. ; rarely c. gen., Id.   2. c. dat. pers. to be always near, to consort or associate with, τῷ ἀνδρὶ Soph. ; γυναικί Dem.

πλῆσθεν, Ep. 3 pl. aor. 1 pass. of πίμπλημι.

πλησθήσομαι, f. pass. of πίμπλημι.

πλησιαίτερος, -αίτατος, irr.Comp. and Sup. of πλησίος.

πλησιασμός, ὁ, Dor. πλατιασμός, Dius in Stob. :—an approaching, approach, Arist.

πλησίος, α, ον, (πέλας) near, close to, c. gen. or dat., πλησίοι ἀλλήλων or ἀλλήλοισι Hom. :—absol. near, neighbouring, Il., Aesch., etc. :—as Subst. a neighbour, Ιδὼν ἐς τὸν ἄλλον Il., etc.   II.= Adv. πλησίον, Dor. πλατίον,= πέλας, near, nigh, hard by, c. gen., Hom., Hdt., etc. ; c. dat., Eur.   2. with the Art., ὁ πλησίον (sc. ὤν) one's neighbour, Theogn., Eur., etc. ; so in Dor., ὁ πλατίον Theocr. :—also, with Substs., ὁ πλ. παράδεισος Xen.   III. Comp. πλησιαίτερος, Sup. -αίτατος, Id.—Comp. Adv. πλησιαιτέρω, Hdt. ; -αίτερον, Xen. ; Sup. -αίτατα, Id.

πλησιό-χωρος, ον, near a country, bordering upon, τινι Hdt. ; absol., οἱ πλ. persons who live in the next country, next neighbours, Lat. finitimi, Id., Thuc.

πλησ-ίστιος, ον, (πίμ-πλημι) filling the sails, οὖρος Od., Eur.   II. pass. with full sails, Plut.

πλήσμιος, α, ον, (πίμ-πλημι) filling, satisfying, Plut. : τὸ πλήσμιον satiety, Id.

πλησμονή, ἡ, (πίμ-πλημι) a filling or being filled, satiety ; of food, repletion, satiety, surfeit, Eur., Xen. :—c. gen., τῶν ἄλλων ἐστὶ πλ. Ar.

πλήσσω, f. πλήξω : aor. 1 ἔπληξα, Ep. πλῆξα : pf. πέπληγα (used as pass. in late writers) : Ep. redupl. aor. 2 ἐπέπληγον or πεπλήγον, inf. πεπληγέμεν : Med. f. πληξόμαι : aor. 1 ἐπληξάμην : Ep. 3 sing. aor. 2 πεπλήγετο, 3 pl. πεπλήγοντο :—Pass., f. πληγήσομαι, and πεπλήξομαι : aor. 1 ἐπλήχθην : aor. 2 ἐπλήγην, later ἐπλάγην [ᾰ] : pf. πέπληγμαι : (the Root is ΠΛΑΓ, or ΠΛΗΓ). To strike, smite, Hom. ; of a direct blow, as opp. to βάλλω, Hom., etc. :—c. acc. dupl. pers. et partis, τὸν πλῆξε αὐχένα struck him on the neck, Il. ; πὺξ πεπληγέμεν, of boxers, Ib. :—c. acc. cogn., πλῆξ᾽ αὐτοσχεδίην (sc. πληγήν) Ib. ; πεπληγὼς πληγῇσιν having driven him

with blows, Ib.; πέπληγον χορὸν ποσίν, like Lat. *terram
pede pulsare*, Od.; ἵππους ἐς πόλεμον πεπληγμένοι to
whip on the horses to the fray, Il. ; of Zeus, *to strike
with lightning*, Hes. :—Med., μηρὼ πληξάμενος *having
smitten his thighs*, Il. ; πλήξασθαι τὴν κεφαλήν, in
sign of grief, Hdt. :—Pass. *to be struck, stricken,
smitten*, Hom., Trag.　　2. with acc. of the thing set
in motion, κονίσαλον ἐς οὐρανὸν ἐπίπληγον πόδες ἵππων
struck the dust up to heaven, Il.　　3. Pass. *to receive
a heavy blow, to be beaten*, Hdt., Thuc. :—*to be
stricken* by misfortune, Hdt.; στρατὸν τοσοῦτον πέπληγμαι, i. e. *I have lost* it *by this blow*, Aesch.　　II.
metaph. of violent emotions, *to strike* one *from* one's
senses, *amaze, confound*, Hom. :—Pass., συμφορῇ πε-
πληγμαι Hdt., etc.; δώροισι πληγείς *moved* by bribes, Id.

πλήστιγξ, Ion. for πλάστιγξ.

πλῆτο, 3 sing. Ep. aor. 2 pass. both of πίμπλημι and of
πελάζω.

πλινθεύω, f. σω, (πλίνθος) *to make into bricks, τὴν γῆν*
Hdt. :—absol. *to make bricks*, Ar.;—so in Med.,
Thuc.　　II. *to build of brick, τείχη* Id.　　III.
to make in the form of a plinth or *brick*, Ar.

πλινθηδόν, Adv. (πλίνθος) *brick-fashion*, i. e. in courses
with the joints alternating, Hdt.

πλίνθῐνος, η, ον, (πλίνθος) *of brick*, Hdt., Xen.

πλινθίον, τό, Dim. of πλίνθος, *a small brick*, Thuc.,
Xen.　　II.= πλαίσιον, *a rectangle* or *square*, Plut.

πλινθίς, ίδος, ἡ, Dim. of πλίνθος, *a whetstone*, Anth.

πλινθόομαι, Med. *to build as with bricks*, Anth.

πλινθο-ποιέω, f. ήσω, *to make bricks*, Ar.

ΠΛΙ'ΝΘΟΣ, ἡ, *a brick*, Hdt., Ar., etc. ; πλίνθους ἑλκύσαι, εἰρύσαι, Lat. *ducere lateres*, to make *bricks*, Hdt.;
ὀπτᾶν *to bake* them, Id.

πλινθουργέω, f. ήσω, *to make bricks*, Ar.　From

πλινθ-ουργός, ὁ, (*ἔργω*) *a brickmaker*, Plat.

πλινθοφορέω, f. ήσω, *to carry bricks*, Ar.　From

πλινθο-φόρος, ον, (φέρω) *carrying bricks*, Ar.

πλινθ-ὑφής, ές, (ὑφαίνω) *brick-built*, Aesch.

ΠΛΙ'ΣΣΟΜΑΙ, aor. 1 ἐπλιξάμην: pf. πέπλιγμαι :—*to
cross the legs*, as in *trotting*, πλίσσοντο πόδεσσιν they
trotted, Od. ; in comp., ἂν ἀπεπλίξατο would have
trotted off, Ar.

πλοη-τόκος, ον, (τεκεῖν) *producing navigation*, Anth.

πλοιάριον [ᾰ], τό, Dim. of πλοῖον, *a skiff, boat*, Ar., Xen.

πλόϊμος, v. πλώϊμος.

πλοῖον, τό, (πλέω) *a floating vessel, a ship, vessel*,
Hdt., Aesch., etc. ; πλοῖα λεπτά small *craft*, Hdt.,
Thuc. ; πλ. ἱππαγωγά transport-*vessels*, Hdt. ; πλ.
μακρὰ *ships* of war, Id. ; πλ. στρογγύλα or φορτηγικά
ships of burthen, merchantmen, Xen. :—when opp. to
ναῦς, *a merchant-ship* or *transport, τοῖς πλοίοις καὶ
ταῖς ναυσί* Thuc.

πλοκαμίς, ῖδος, ἡ, = πλόκαμος, *a lock* or *braid of hair*,
of women, Bion : in sing. *curling hair*, Theocr.

πλόκᾰμος, ὁ, (πλέκω) *a lock* or *braid of hair*, Aesch. :
in pl. *locks*, properly of women, Il. :—in sing. collectively, = κόμη, Hdt.; τριχὸς πλ. Aesch.

πλόκᾰνον, τό, (πλέκω) *a plaited rope*, Xen.

πλοκή, ἡ, (πλέκω) *a twining : anything woven, a web*,
Eur.　　II. metaph. *the complication* of a plot, opp.
to λύσις, Arist.

πλόκος, ὁ, (πλέκω) *a lock of hair, a braid, curl*,

Trag.　　II. *a wreath* or *chaplet*, πλόκοι σελίνων the
parsley-*wreath* at the Isthmian games, Pind.; μυρσίνης
πλόκοι Eur., etc.

πλόος, ὁ, Att. contr. πλοῦς ; pl. πλοῖ :—later, we have
a gen. sing. πλόος, as if of third declens. : (πλέω) :—*a
sailing, voyage*, Od., Hdt., Att. ; πλοῦν στέλλειν,
ποιεῖσθαι Soph. ; μῆκός ἐστι πλόος ἡμέραι τέσσερες its
length is four days' *sail*, Hdt.　　2. *time* or *tide for
sailing*, Hes., Soph., etc.; πλῷ χρῆσθαι to have a fair
wind, Thuc.　　3. proverb., δεύτερος πλοῦς, 'the next
best way ' (from those who use oars when the wind
fails), Plat.

πλουθ-ὑγίειᾰ, ἡ, (πλοῦτος) *health and wealth*, Ar. ;
parox. πλουθυγιεῖα (metri grat.) Id.

πλοῦς, Att. contr. for πλόος.

πλούσιος, α, ον, (πλοῦτος) *rich, wealthy, opulent*,
Hes., Theogn., Att.　　2. c. gen. rei, *rich* in a thing,
Lat. *dives opum*, Eur., Plat. :—also c. dat., Plut.　　II.
of things, *richly furnished, ample, abundant*, Soph.,
Eur.　　III. Adv. -ίως, Hdt., Eur.

Πλουτεύς, ὁ, collat. form of Πλούτων, gen. Πλουτέως,
-έος, Anth.; dat. Πλουτεῖ, -ῆι ; acc. Πλουτέα Id., etc.

πλουτέω, f. ήσω, (πλοῦτος) *to be rich, wealthy*, Hes.,
Theogn., Hdt., Att. ; πλ. ἀπὸ τῶν κοινῶν *to be rich*
from the public purse, Ar.　　2. c. gen. rei, *to be rich*
in a thing, Xen.　　3. c. dat. rei, πλ. ἐμπύροισιν Eur.,
Xen.　　4. c. acc. cogn., πλ. πλοῦτον Luc.　　Hence

πλουτηρός, ή, όν, *enriching*, ἔργον Xen. ; and

πλουτητέον, verb. Adj. *one must become rich*, Luc.

πλουτίζω, f. Att. -ιῶ, (πλοῦτος) *to make wealthy, enrich*,
Aesch., Xen.; ironic., πλ. τινὰ ἄταις Aesch. :—Pass.,
Ἅιδης γόοις πλουτίζεται Soph.; πλ. ἀπὸ βοσκημάτων,
ἐκ τῆς πόλεως *to gain* one's *wealth* from . . , Xen.

πλουτίνδην, (πλοῦτος) Adv. *according to wealth*, πλ.
αἱρεῖσθαι τοὺς ἄρχοντας Arist.

πλουτο-γᾰθής, ές, Dor. for -γηθής, (γηθέω) *rejoicing
in riches, wealthy*, Aesch.

πλουτο-δοτήρ, ῆρος, ὁ, = sq., Anth.

πλουτο-δότης, ου, ὁ, *giver of riches*, Hes.

πλουτο-κρᾰτία, ἡ, (κρατέω) *plutocracy*, Xen.

πλουτο-ποιός, όν, *wealth-creating*, Plut.

ΠΛΟΥ͂ΤΟΣ, ὁ, (perh. from πίμ-πλημι) *wealth, riches*,
Hom., etc. ; πλοῦτος χρυσοῦ, ἀργύρου *treasure* of gold,
silver, Hdt. :—metaph., γᾶς πλ. ἄβυσσος, of the whole
earth, Aesch. ; πλούτος εἵματος Id.　　II. as prop. n.
Plutus, god of riches, Hes.

πλοῦτος, εος, τό, = πλοῦτος, ὁ, N. T.

πλουτο-χθων, ονος, ὁ, ἡ, *rich in earthly treasures*, in
allusion perh. to the silver mines of Laureion, Aesch.

Πλούτων, ωνος, ὁ, *Pluto*, god of the nether world, Trag.:
(prob. from πλοῦτος) the *wealth-giver*, as spouse of
Demeter, who enriched men with the fruits of the earth.

πλοχμός, οῦ, ὁ, like πλόκαμος, mostly in pl. *locks,
braids of hair*, Il., Anth.　　II. *the tendrils* of the
polypus, Anth.

πλῦναν, Ep. for ἔπλυναν, 3 pl. aor. 1 of πλύνω.

πλῠνός, ὁ, (πλύνω) *a trough, tank*, or *pit, in which
dirty clothes were washed* by treading, Hom.　　II.
metaph. πλυνὸν ποιεῖν τινα, = πλύνω II, Ar.

πλυντήριος, ον, *of* or *for washing*: Πλυντήρια (sc.
ἱερά), τά, a festival at Athens, *in which the clothes of
Athena's statue were washed*, Xen., etc.

ΠΛΥ'ΝΩ [ῠ], Ion. impf. πλύνεσκον : f. πλῠνῶ, Ion. and Ep. πλῠνέω : aor. 1 ἔπλῡνα, Ep. πλῦνα :—Pass., f. πλῠνοῦμαι : pf. πέπλῠμαι :—to wash, clean, properly of linen and clothes, (opp. to λούομαι to bathe, νίζω to wash the hands or feet), Hom., Att.   2. to wash off dirt, Od.   II. as a slang term, πλύνειν τινά (as we say) ' to give him a dressing,' Ar., Dem.

πλύσις [ῠ], εως, ἡ, a washing, Plat.

πλωΐζω, Ion. impf. πλωΐζεσκον :—to sail on the sea, Hes.; οἱ Ἕλληνες μᾶλλον ἐπλώιζον began to use ships or practise navigation, Thuc. :—as Dep. πλωΐζομαι, Strab., Luc.

πλώϊμος or πλόϊμος, ον, (πλώω) fit for sailing :   1. of a ship, fit for sea, seaworthy, Thuc.   2. of navigation, πλωιμωτέρων γενομένων or ὄντων as navigation advanced, as circumstances became favourable for navigation, Id.

πλώσιμος, ον, (πλώω) navigable, πέλαγος Soph.

πλωτεύω, (πλώτης) to sail.   II. Pass. to be navigated, of the sea, to navigate, Polyb.

πλωτή, ἡ, v. πλωτός.

πλωτήρ, ῆρος, ὁ, (πλώω) a sailor, seaman, Ar., Plat.; including rowers and navigators, Arist.

πλωτικός, ή, όν, skilled in seamanship, a seaman, Plat., Plut.; also a shipowner, Plut.

πλωτός, ή, όν, (πλώω) floating, Od., Hdt.; πλωτοὶ swimmers, i. e. fish, Anth.   II. navigable, Hdt.   2. of seasons, fit for navigation, Polyb.

πλώω, Ion. for πλέω.

πνείω, Ep. for πνέω.

πνεῦμα, ατος, τό, (πνέω) a blowing, πνεύματα ἀνέμων Hdt., Aesch.: alone, a wind, blast, Trag., etc.   2. metaph., θαλερωτέρῳ πν. with more genial breeze or influence, Aesch.; λύσσης πν. μάργῳ Id.; πν. ταὐτὸν οὔποτ' ἐν ἀνδράσιν φίλοις βέβηκεν the wind is constantly changing even among friends, Soph.   II. like Lat. spiritus or anima, breathed air, breath, Aesch.; πν. βίου the breath of life, Id.; πν. ἀθροίζειν to collect breath, Eur.; πν. ἀφιέναι, ἀνιέναι, μεθιέναι to give up the ghost, Id.; πνεύματος διαρροαί the wind-pipe, Id.   2. that is breathed forth, odour, scent, Id.   III. spirit, Lat. afflatus, Anth.: inspiration, N. T.   IV. the spirit of man, Ib.   V. a spirit; in N. T. of the Holy Spirit, τὸ Πνεῦμα, Πν. ἅγιον :—also of angels, Ib.:—of evil spirits, Ib. Hence

πνευματικός, ή, όν, of spirit, spiritual, N. T.

πνεύμων, in later Att. πλεύμων, ονος, ὁ, (πνέω) the organ of breathing, the lungs, Lat. pulmo, Il., Plat.: mostly in pl., Trag.; πνεύμ' ἀνεὶς ἐκ πλευμόνων Eur.

πνεῖν, Dor. poët. for ἔπνεον, impf. of πνέω.

πνευστιάω, to breathe hard, pant, Arist.; Ep. part. πνευστιόων, Anth.

ΠΝΕ'Ω, Ep. πνείω, Ion. impf. πνείεσκον : f. πνεύσομαι, Dor. πνευσοῦμαι : aor. 1 ἔπνευσα : pf. πέπνευκα :—Like other dissyll. Verbs in -έω, this Verb only contracts εε, εει :—to blow, of wind and air, Od., Hdt., Att.; ἡ πνέουσα (sc. αὔρα) the breeze, N. T.   II. to breathe, send forth an odour, Od. :—c. gen. to breathe or smell of a thing, Anth.   III. of animals, to breathe hard, pant, gasp, Il., Aesch.   IV. generally, to draw breath, breathe, and so to live, Hom.; οἱ πνέοντες = οἱ ζῶντες, Soph.   V. metaph., c. acc.

cogn. to breathe forth, breathe, μένεα πνείοντες breathing spirit, of warriors, Il.; so, πῦρ πν. Hes.; φόνον, κότον Ἄρη Aesch.; so, πνέοντας δόρυ καὶ λόγχας Ar.; Ἀλφειὸν πνέων, of a swift runner, Id.   2. μέγα πνεῖν to be of a high spirit, give oneself airs, Eur.; τόσονδ' ἔπνευσας Id. :—also, with a nom., as if it were the wind, μέγας πνέων Id.; πολὺς ἔπνει καὶ λαμπρὸς ἦν Dem.

πνιγεύς, έως, ὁ, (πνίγω) an oven, heated by hot coals put inside it, like our brick ovens, Ar.

πνιγηρός, ά, όν, (πνίγω) choking, stifling, Ar.

πνιγίζω, = πνίγω, Anth.

πνιγμός, ὁ, (πνίγω) a choking or being choked, Xen.

πνιγόεις, εσσα, εν, = πνιγηρός, Anth.

πνῖγος, τό, (πνίγω) stifling heat, Ar., Thuc.

ΠΝΙ'ΓΩ [ῑ], f. πνίξω : aor. 1 ἔπνιξα :—Pass., f. πνιγήσομαι : aor. 1 ἐπνίχθην, aor. 2 ἐπνίγην [ῐ] : pf. πέπνιγμαι :—to choke, throttle, strangle, Plat. ; proverb., ὅταν τὸ ὕδωρ πνίγῃ, τί δεῖ ἐπιπίνειν; if water chokes, why should one drink more ? Arist. :—Pass. to be choked, stifled, Ar. : to be drowned, Xen.   2. metaph. to vex, torment, Luc.   II. to cook in a close-covered vessel, to stew, Hdt., Ar.   Hence

πνικτός, ή, όν, verb. Adj. strangled, N. T.

πνοή, Ep. πνοιή, ῆς, ἡ ; Dor. πνοά and πνοιά, ᾶς : (πνέω) :—a blowing, blast, breeze, Hom.; ἅμα πνοιῆς ἀνέμοιο along with, i. e. swift as, blasts of wind, Id.; μετὰ πνοιῆς ἀνέμοιο Id., etc. :—the blast of bellows, Thuc.   II. of animals, a breathing hard, of horses, Il., Soph.   2. generally, breath, ἔμπνους ἔτ' εἰμὶ καὶ πνοὰς πνέω Eur. :—metaph., πνοιὴ Ἡφαίστοιο the breath of Hephaestus, i. e. flame, Il.; θεοῦ πνοαῖσιν ἐμμανεῖς Eur.   III. a breathing odour, a vapour, exhalation, σποδὸς προπέμπει πλούτου πνοάς, of a burning city, Aesch.   IV. the breath of a wind-instrument, Pind., Eur.

πνοιή, Ep. for πνοή.

ΠΝΥ'Ξ, gen. πυκνός (not πνυκός), ἡ, the Pnyx, the place at Athens where the ἐκκλησίαι were held, Ar.; ἐν πυκνὶ ἐν τῇ ἐκκλησίᾳ Dem.   It was cut out of the side of a little hill west of the Acropolis, being of a semicircular form like a theatre.

ΠΟ'Α, ἡ, Ion. ποίη, Dor. ποία, grass, herb, Hom., etc.; ποία Μηδική, Lat. herba Medica, sainfoin or lucerne, Ar.   2. the grass, i. e. a grassy place, Plat., Xen.   II. in Poets, of Time, τέσσαρας πόας four grasses, i. e. summers, Anth.

ποάζω, of ground, to produce grass, Strab.

ποδ-αβρός, όν, tenderfooted, Orac. ap. Hdt.

ποδαγός, v. ποδηγός.

ποδ-άγρα, ἡ, a trap for the feet, Xen., Anth.   II. gout in the feet, opp. to χειράγρα.   Hence

ποδαγράω, to have gout in the feet, Ar.; and

ποδαγρικός, ή, όν, liable to gout, gouty, Plut.

ποδαγρός, όν, = foreg., Luc.

ποδᾰ-νιπτήρ, ῆρος, ὁ, (νίζω) a vessel for washing the feet in, a footpan, Hdt.

ποδά-νιπτρον [ᾰ], τό, (νίζω) water for washing the feet in, in pl., Od.

ποδαπός, ή, όν, from what country ? Lat. cujas ? generally, whence ? where born ? Hdt., Trag.; τίς καὶ π.; Plat.   2. generally, of what sort ? ποδαπός; οἷος μὴ δάκνειν . . , of what sort ? one that will not

bite, Dem.   (As in ἀλλοδαπός, ἡμεδαπός, ὑμεδαπός, τηλεδαπός, –δαπος is a termin. of uncertain origin.)

πόδ-αργος, ον, *swiftfooted* or *whitefooted*:—**Πόδαργος**, ὁ, *Swiftfoot* or *Whitefoot*, a horse, Il.; fem. **Ποδάργη**, a Harpy, Ib.

ποδ-άρκης, ες, (ἀρκέω) *sufficient with the feet, swiftfooted*, of Achilles, Il.; ποδάρκης ἀμέρα a day *of swiftness*, i.e. on which swift runners contended, Pind.; ποδάρκεων δρόμων τέμενος the field *of swift* courses, i.e. the Pythian racecourse, Id.

ποδ-ένδυτος, ον, (ἐνδύω) *drawn over the feet*, Aesch.

ποδεών, ῶνος, ὁ, (πούς) in pl., *the ragged ends* in the skins of animals, *formed by the feet and tail*, δέρμα λέοντος ἀφημμένον ἄκρων ἐκ ποδεώνων a lion's skin hung round one's neck by *the paws*, Theocr.   II. in sing. *the neck* or *mouth of a wineskin*, formed by one of these ends, the others being sewn up, Hdt.   2. generally *any narrow end, a strip of land*, Id.   3. *the lower corner of a sail, the sheet*, Luc.

ποδ-ηγός, Dor. and Trag. –αγός, ὁ, (ἡγέομαι) *a guide, attendant*, Soph., Eur.

ποδ-ηνεκής, ές, (ἐνέγκαι) *reaching to the feet*, Il., Hdt.

ποδ-ήνεμος, ον, *windswift*, of Iris, Il.

ποδ-ήρης, ες, (*ἄρω) *reaching to the feet*, πέπλος, χιτών π. a frock *that falls over the feet*, as in the archaïc Greek statues, Eur., Xen.; π. ἀσπίς the large shield *which covered the body quite down to the feet*, Xen.; στῦλος π. a *straight, firm pillar*, Aesch.   2. τὰ ποδήρη the parts about the feet, the feet, Id.

ποδιαῖος, α, ον, (πούς) *a foot long, broad*, or *high*, Xen.

ποδίζω, f. ίσω, (πούς) *to tie the feet*:—Pass. *to have the feet tied*, or *to be tied by the foot*, of horses, Xen.

ποδί-κροτος, ον, *welded to the feet*, Anth.

ποδιστήρ, ῆρος, ὁ, (ποδίζω) *foot-entangling*, of a long robe, Aesch. Hence

ποδίστρα, ή, *a foottrap*, Anth.

ποδοῖιν, Ep. gen. and dat. dual for ποδοῖν.

ποδο-κάκη, ή, also written **ποδοκάκκη**, properly, *footplague*, a kind of *stocks*, Dem., etc.

ποδο-κρουστία, ή, *a stamping with the feet*, Strab.

ποδορ-ράγής, ές, (ῥήγνυμι) *bursting forth at a stamp of the foot*, Anth.

ποδο-στράβη, ή, *a snare* or *trap to catch the feet*, Xen.

ποδό-ψηστρον, ὁ, (ψάω) *a footwiper, footcloth*, Aesch.

ποδώκεια, ή, *swiftness of foot*, Il., Eur. From

ποδ-ώκης, ες, (ὠκύς) *swiftfooted*, of Achilles, Il.; π. ἄνθρωπος Thuc.; λαγώς Xen.   2. generally, *swift, quick*, ὄμμα Aesch.; θεῶν π. βλάβαι Soph.

ποέω, v. ποιέω sub init.

ποηφάγέω, Ion. ποιηφαγέω, f. ήσω, *to eat grass*, Hdt.

ποη-φάγος [ἄ], ον, (φαγεῖν) *eating grass* or *herbs*.

ποθεινός, ή, όν, and ός, όν, (ποθέω) *longed for, desired, much desired*, esp. if absent or lost (v. πόθος), Trag.; ποθεινὸς ἦλθες Eur.; π. δάκρυα tears *of regret*, Id.; π. τοῖς φίλοις Ar.:—Adv., ποθεινοτέρως ἔχειν τινός *to long greatly for a thing*, Xen.

πόθεν; Ion. κόθεν;   I. interrog. Adv. *whence?* 1. of place, ἠρώτα, τίς εἴη καὶ π. ἔλθοι Od.; ποῖ δὴ καὶ πόθεν; Plat.;—c. gen., τίς πόθεν εἰς ἀνδρῶν; who and from what country art thou? Il.; πόθεν γῆς; Eur. 2. of origin, πόθεν γένος εὔχεται εἶναι; *from what source does he boast that his race is?* Od. 3. in speaking,

π. ἄρξωμαι; Aesch. 4. of the cause, *whence? wherefore?* Id.; alone, πόθεν; *how can it be? impossible!* Eur., Ar.   II. ποθεν, enclit. Adv. *from some place* or *other*, εἴ ποθεν Il.; εἰ καί π. ἄλλοθεν ἔλθοι Od.

ποθέρπω, Dor. for προσέρπω.

ποθέσπερος, ον, Dor. for προσέσπερος.

ποθέω, Ep. inf. ποθήμεναι (as if from πόθημι): Ep. impf. πόθεον, Ion. ποθέεσκον: f. ποθήσω and ποθέσομαι: aor. 1 ἐπόθεσα, Ep. πόθεσα, also ἐπόθησα: pf. πεπόθηκα: (πόθος):—*to long for, yearn after* what is absent, *to miss* or *regret* what is lost, Lat. *desiderare*, Hom., etc.; ποθεῖς τὸν οὐ παρόντα Ar.; π. τὰς ἐν τῇ νεότητι ἡδονάς Plat.:—Pass., ὦ ποθουμένη (sc. Εἰρήνη) Ar.   2. of things, *to require*, ποθεῖ ἡ ἀπόκρισις ἐρώτησιν τοιάνδε Plat.   II. c. inf. *to be anxious to do*, Eur.; τὸ νοσοῦν ποθεῖ σε ξυμπαραστάτην λαβεῖν my sickness *needs* to take thee as an assistant, Soph.   III. absol., τὸ ποθοῦν *one's desiring, one's longing*, Id.   2. as Dep., ποθουμένη φρήν the *longing* soul, Id.

ΠΟΘΗ', ή, = πόθος, *fond desire for* one, ἐμεῖο ποθὴν ἀπεόντος ἔχουσιν Il.; σῇ ποθῇ *from longing after* thee, Ib.   2. *want* of a thing, c. gen., Od.

πόθι; interrog. Adv., poët. for ποῦ; *where?* Od., Soph.;—c. gen., πόθι Νύσας; *in what part* of Nysa? Eur.   2. for ποῖ; *whither?* Anth.   B. ποθι, enclit. Adv., poët. for που, *anywhere* or *somewhere*, Il., Soph.   2. of Time, αἴ κέ ποθι Ζεὺς δῷσι if *ever* Zeus grant, Il.: *at length*, Od.   3. indefinite, *soever, haply, probably*, Hom.

ποθῖνός, ή, όν, poët. for ποθεινός, Anth.

ποθό-βλητος, ον, *love-stricken*, Anth.

πόθοδος, ή, Dor. for πρόσοδος.

ποθόρημι, Dor. for προσοράω.

ΠΟ'ΘΟΣ, ὁ, *a longing, yearning, fond desire* or *regret* (for something absent or lost), Lat. *desiderium*, Hom., etc.   2. c. gen. *desire* or *regret for* a person or thing, Id.; so, σὸς π. *yearning after* thee, Od.; τοὐμῷ πόθῳ Soph.   II. *love, desire*, Hes., etc.

ποῖ; interrog. Adv. (cf. ποῦ) *whither?* Lat. *quo?* Theogn., etc.   2. c. gen., ποῖ χθονός; ποῖ γῆς; *to what spot* of earth? Aesch.; ποῖ φροντίδος; ποῖ φρενῶν; ποῖ γνώμης; Soph.   II. *to what end?* in what point? ποῖ τελευτᾷ; Aesch.   B. ποι, enclit. Adv. *somewhither*, Soph., Ar., etc.

ποία, ποιάεις, contr. ποιᾶς, for ποίη, ποιήεις.

ΠΟΙΕ'Ω: Ep. impf. ποίεον, contr. ποίει, Ion. ποιέεσκον:—Med., 3 sing. Ion. impf. ποιήσκετο: f. ποιήσομαι (also used in pass. sense):—Pass., f. ποιηθήσομαι: aor. 1 ἐποιήθην: pf. πεποίημαι (also used in med. sense). [Att. Poets often use the penult. short, as ποιῶ, ποιεῖν, etc., which are often written ποῶ, ποεῖν, etc., as in Lat. *poëta, poësis*.]

  Used in two general senses, *to make* and *to do*.

  A. *to make, produce, create*, in Hom. often of building, π. δῶμα, τεῖχος, etc.; of smith's work, π. σάκος Il.; of works of art, Ib., etc.; ποιεῖν τι ἀπὸ ξύλου *to make* something of wood, Hdt.; π. πλοῖα ἐξ ἀκάνθης Id.; so, c. gen., π. νηὸν λίθου Id.; φοίνικος αἱ θύραι πεποιημέναι Xen.:—Med., οἰκία ποιήσασθαι *to build them* houses, Il.; also, *to have a thing made, get it made*, Hdt., Dem.   2. *to make, create*, ἕτερον Φίλιππον

ποιήσετε Dem. 3. of Poets, *to compose, write*, (old English *to make*), Lat. *carmina facere*, Hdt., Att. : —also, *to make* or *represent in poetry*, "Ομηρος 'Αχιλλέα πεποίηκε ἀμείνω 'Οδυσσέως Plat. : *to describe in verse*, Id. : *to put into verse*, Id. II. *to bring to pass, bring about, cause*, Hom., etc. : c. acc. et inf. *to cause* or *bring about* that . . , Od., etc. 2. of sacrifices, and the like, π. ἱρά, like ἔρδειν, Lat. *sacra facere*, Hdt., Xen., Thuc., etc. ; π. 'Ίσθμια *to hold* the Isthmian games, Xen. ; π. ἐκκλησίαν (as we say, *to make* a house), Thuc. :—Med. in same sense, but implying indirect action, ἀγορὴν ποιήσατο Il. 3. of war and peace, πόλεμον ποιεῖν *to cause* a war, but, π. ποιεῖσθαι *to make* war (on one's own part), Xen. ;—so, εἰρήνην π. *to bring about* a peace (for others) ; but, εἰρήνην ποιεῖσθαι *to make* peace (for oneself), etc. 4. the Med. is often used periphr. with Nouns, ποιεῖσθαι ὁδοιπορίην for ὁδοιπορεῖν, π. πλόον for πλέειν, θαῦμα π. for θαυμάζειν, ὀργὴν π. for ὀργίζεσθαι, Hdt. etc. :— π. λόγον τινός *to make* account of . . , Id. ; but, τοὺς λόγους π. *to hold* a conference, Thuc. III. with an Adj. as predic. *to make* so and so, ποιεῖν τινα ἄφρονα *to make* one senseless, Od. ; δῶρα ὄλβια ποιεῖν *to make* them blest, i. e. *to prosper them*, Ib. ; π. τοὺς Μήδους ἀσθενεῖς Xen. :—so with a Subst., ποιεῖσθαι τινα βασιλῆα Od. ; 'Αθηναῖον π. τινα Thuc. :—Med., ποιεῖσθαί τινα ἄλοχον or ἄκοιτιν *to take* her *to oneself* as wife, Il. ; ποιεῖσθαί τινα υἱόν *to make* him one's son, i. e. *to adopt* him as son (cf. εἰσποιέω), Hdt., Att. :—also, ἑωυτοῦ ποιεῖσθαί τι *to make* a thing one's own, Hdt. IV. *to put*, π. τι ἐνὶ φρεσί τινι Hom. ; π. τι ἐπὶ νόον τινί Hdt. 2. in war, π. τινας ὑπό τινι *to bring* under the power of . . , Dem. :—Med., ποιεῖσθαι ὑπ' ἑωυτῷ Hdt. ; ποιεῖσθαί τινας ἐς τὸ συμμαχικόν Id., etc. V. in Med. *to hold, deem, consider, reckon, esteem* a thing as . . , συμφορὴν ποιεῖσθαί τι *to take* it for a visitation, Id. ; δεινὸν ποιεῖσθαί τι, Lat. *aegre ferre*, Id. ; μέγα π., c. inf., *to deem* it a great matter that . . , Id. ; οὐκ ἀνάσχετον π. τι Thuc., etc. :—often with Preps., δι' οὐδενὸς π. τι *to hold* as naught, Soph. ;—ἐν ἐλαφρῷ, ἐν ὁμοίῳ π. Hdt. ; ἐν σμικρῷ, ἐν ὀργῇ Dem. ;—παρ' ὀλίγον, παρ' οὐδὲν π. τι Xen. ;—περὶ πολλοῦ, περὶ πλείονος, περὶ πλείστου ποιεῖσθαί τι Att. VI. *to put the case, assume* that . . , Hdt., Xen. :—Pass., οἱ φιλοσοφώτατοι ποιούμενοι *those who are reputed* . . , Plat. VII. of Time, οὐ π. χρόνον *to make* no long time, i. e. *not to delay*, Dem. ; τὴν νύκτα ἐφ' ὅπλοις ποιεῖσθαι *to spend* it under arms, Thuc.

B. *to do*, much like πράσσω, Hom., etc. ; οὐδὲν ἂν ὧν νυνὶ πεποίηκεν ἔπραξεν Dem. ; Σπαρτιητικὰ ποιέειν *to act* like a Spartan, Hdt. ; προσταχθὲν π. Soph., etc. 2. c. acc. dupl. *to do* something to another, κακά or ἀγαθὰ ποιεῖν τινά Hdt., etc. ; also εὖ, κακῶς π. τινά Xen., etc. :—also c. dat. pers., ἵππῳ τἀναντία π. Id. ; so in Med., φίλα ποιεῖσθαί τινι Hdt. 3. with an Adv., ὧδε ποίησον *do* thus, Id. ; ποίει ὅπως βούλει Xen. ;—so with a partic., εὖ ἐποίησας ἀπικόμενος Hdt., etc. :—καλῶς ποιῶν is sometimes almost Adverbial, καλῶς ποιοῦντες πράττετε Dem. ; εὖ ποιοῦν *fortunately*, Id. II. absol. *to be doing, to do* or *act*, ποιεῖν ἢ παθέειν *to do* or *have done to one*, Hdt. :—of medicine, *to work, operate*, Plat. ; so, ἡ εὔνοια

παρὰ πολὺ ἐποίει ἐς τοὺς Λακεδαιμονίους *good-will made greatly for the Lacedaemonians*, Thuc. ; so impers., ἐπὶ πολὺ ἐποίει τῆς δόξης τοῖς μὲν ἠπειρώταις εἶναι it was the general character of the one to be landsmen, etc., Id.

ποίη, Ion. for πόα, *grass*.

ποιήεις, Dor. -άεις, εσσα, εν, (ποίη) *grassy, rich in grass*, Hom., Soph. : neut. pl. contr. ποιᾶντα Pind.

ποίημα, ατος, τό, (ποιέω) *anything made* or *done*; hence, I. *a work*, Hdt., Plat. 2. *a poetical work, poem*, Plat. II. *a deed, act*, Id.

ποιημάτιον, τό, Dim. of ποίημα, Plut.

ποιηρός, ά, όν, = ποιήεις, Eur.

ποίησις, εως, ἡ, (ποιέω) *a making, fabrication, creation, production*, opp. to πρᾶξις (*action*), Hdt., Att. 2. of poetry, ἡ π. τῆς τραγῳδίας, etc., Plat.: absol. *poetic faculty, poesy, art of poetry*, Hdt., Ar., etc. b. *a poetic composition, poem*, Thuc., Plat. II. = εἰσποίησις, *adoption*, Dem. Hence

ποιητέος, α, ον, verb. Adj. *to be made* or *done*, Hdt., Att. ; τὸ ποιητέον *what must be done*, Thuc.

ποιητής, gen. οῦ, Ion. -έω, ὁ, *one who makes, a maker*, Xen., etc. II. *the maker of a poem, a poet*, Hdt., etc. 2. generally, *a writer*, Plat.

ποιητικός, ή, όν, (ποιέω) *capable of making, creative, productive*, Arist. II. *fitted for a poet, poetical*, Plat. ;—ἡ -κή (sc. τέχνη), *the art of poetry, poetry*, Id. :—Adv. -κῶς, Id.

ποιητός, ή, όν, (ποιέω) *made*, in the sense of εὖ ποιητός, *well-made*, δόμοις ἐνὶ ποιητοῖσι Hom. :—*made, created*, opp. to self-existent, Theogn. II. *made into something*, esp. *made into a son, adopted*, Plat. ; π. πολῖται *factitious* citizens, not so born, Arist. III. *made by oneself*, i. e. *invented, feigned*, Pind., Eur.

ποιήτρια, ἡ, fem. of ποιητής, *a poetess*, Luc.

ποιηφάγέω, ποιη-φάγος, = ποηφαγέω, -φάγος.

ποικιλ-άνιος, ον, Dor. for -ήνιος, *with broidered reins*, Pind.

ποικιλ-είμων, ον, gen. ονος, (εἷμα) *with spangled garb*, νὺξ π., in reference to the stars, Aesch.

ποικιλία, ἡ, (ποικίλλω) *a marking with various colours, embroidering, embroidery*, Plat.: in pl. *pieces of broidery*, Xen. II. *varied aspect, diversity*, Plat. 2. *versatility, subtlety, craft*, Plat.

ποικίλλω: aor. 1 inf. ποικῖλαι: pf. πεποίκιλκα, pass. πεποίκιλμαι: (ποικίλος) :—*to work in various colours, to broider, work in embroidery*, Eur. ; χορὸν ποίκιλλε *he wrought a χορός of cunning workmanship*, Il. 2. *to embroider* a robe, Pind., Plat., etc. II. generally, *to diversify, vary*, Eur., Plat. :—of style, *to embellish*, Pind. :—*to speak as in riddles*, Soph. Hence

ποίκιλμα, τό, *a broidered stuff, brocade*, Aesch. 2. *broidered work, broidery*, Hom. II. generally, *a variety, diversity*, Plat.

ποικιλό-βουλος, ον, (βουλή) *of changeful counsel, wily-minded*, Hes., Anth.

ποικιλό-γηρυς, Dor. -γᾶρυς, υος, ὁ, ἡ, *of varied voice, many-toned*, Pind.

ποικιλό-δειρος, ον, (δειρή) *with variegated neck*, Anth.

ποικιλό-δέρμων, ον, (δέρμα) *with pied skin*, Eur.

ποικιλό-θριξ, ὁ, ἡ, *with spotted hair, dappled*, Eur.

ποικιλό-θρονος, ον, *on rich-worked throne*, Sappho.

ποικῐλο-μήτης, ου, ὁ, voc. μῆτα, (μῆτις) *full of various wiles, wily-minded*, Hom.

ποικῐλο-μήχᾰνος, ον, *full of various devices*, Anth.

ποικῐλό-μορφος, ον, *of varied form, variegated*, Ar.

ποικῐλό-μῦθος, ον, *of various discourse*, Anth.

ποικῐλό-νωτος, ον, *with back of various hues*, Pind., Eur.

ποικῐλό-πτερος, ον, *with wings of changeful hue*, Eur.

ΠΟΙΚΙΛΟΣ [ῐ], η, ον, *many-coloured, spotted, mottled, pied, dappled*, of leopards, fawns, Hom., etc. II. of robes, *wrought in various colours, broidered*, Il., etc.; ἐν ποικίλοις κάλλεσιν, *of a rich carpet*, Aesch.; so, τὰ ποικίλα Id. 2. of metal work, τεύχεα π. χαλκῷ *in-wrought* with brass, Il., etc.: but, π. δεσμός *intricate*, Od. 3. ἡ στοὰ ἡ ποικίλη, *the Poecile* or *great hall at Athens adorned with paintings* of the battle of Marathon by Polygnotus, Aeschin. etc. III. metaph. *changeful, various, diversified, manifold*, Aesch., Plat.; —π. μῆνες the *changing* months, Pind. 2. of Art, π. ὕμνος a song *of changeful strain* or *full of diverse art*, Id.; so, ποικίλον κιθαρίζων Id. 3. *intricate, complex*, Hdt., Soph., etc.: —Adv., ποικίλως αὐδώμενος speaking *in double sense*, Soph. b. of abstruse knowledge, *intricate, subtle*, ποικίλον τι εἰδέναι Eur.; οὐδὲν π. nothing *abstruse* or *difficult*, Plat.:—so, of persons, *subtle, wily*, Aesch.; π. γὰρ ἀνήρ Ar. 4. *changeable, changeful, unstable*, Arist.:—ποικίλως ἔχειν to be *different*, Xen.

ποικῐλό-στολος, ον, (στόλος II) of a ship, *with variegated prow*, Soph.

ποικῐλο-τερπής, ές, (τέρπω) *delighting by variety*, Anth.

ποικῐλο-τευκτος, ον, (τεύχω) *manifold*, Anth.

ποικῐλο-τραυλος, ον, *twittering in various notes*, Theocr.

ποικῐλο-φόρμιγξ, ιγγος, ὁ, ἡ, *accompanied by the various notes of the lyre*, Pind.

ποικῐλό-φρων, ονος, ὁ, ἡ, = ποικιλομήτης, Eur.

ποίκῐλσις, εως, ἡ, (ποικίλλω) = ποικιλία, Plat.

ποικιλτέον, verb. Adj. of ποικίλλω, *one must work in embroidery*, Plat.

ποικιλτής, οῦ, ὁ, (ποικίλλω) *a broiderer*, Aeschin.

ποικῐλ-ῳδός, όν, (ᾠδή) *of perplexed and juggling song*, Soph.

ποιμαίνω, f. ᾰνῶ, (ποιμήν) *to be shepherd*, ἐπ' ὄεσσι over the sheep, Il. : c. acc. *to tend* a flock, Od., Eur., etc.; absol. Theocr. :—Pass., like νέμομαι, *to roam the pastures*, of flocks, Il., Eur. 2. in Aesch., πᾶς πεποίμανται τόπος every place *has been traversed* (as by a shepherd seeking after stray sheep). II. metaph. *to tend, cherish, mind*, Pind., Aesch. 2. like βουκολέω, *to beguile*, Theocr. : generally, *to deceive*, Eur.

ποιμάν, όν, Dor. for ποιμήν.

ποιμανόριον, τό, *a herd* : metaph. *an army*, Aesch.

ποιμ-άνωρ [ᾱ], ορος, ὁ, (ποιμαίνω) = ποιμήν II, Aesch.

ποιμενικός, ή, όν, (ποιμήν) *of* or *for a shepherd*, Theocr. :— ἡ -κή (sc. τέχνη), Plat.

ποιμένιος, α, ον, = ποιμενικός, Anth.

ποιμήν, ένος, ὁ, voc. ποιμήν, *a herdsman* or *shepherd*, Hom. : after Hom. always *a shepherd*, Eur., Plat., etc. II. metaph. *a shepherd* of the people, of Agamemnon, Hom., etc. : generally, *a captain, chief*, Soph., Eur. (Deriv. uncertain.)

ποίμνη, ἡ, *a flock*, Od. ; properly *of sheep* (cf. ποιμήν),

Hes., Hdt. ; of a ram, Eur. 2. metaph. of persons, Aesch. Hence

ποιμήιος, η, ον, *of a flock* or *herd*, Il., Hes.

ποίμνιον, τό, syncop. for ποιμένιον, = ποίμνη, *a flock*, Hdt., Soph., etc. II. metaph. of disciples, N. T.

ποιμνιο-τρόφος, and ποιμνοτρ-, ον, ὁ, = ποιμήν, Aquila V. T.

ποιμνίτης [ῐ], ου, ὁ, = ποιμενικός, ὑμέναιος π. a *shepherd's marriage song*, Eur.

ποιναῖος, α, ον, (ποινή) *punishing, avenging*, Anth.

ποινάτωρ [ᾱ], ορος, ὁ, ἡ, *an avenger, punisher*, Aesch.

ποινάω, *to avenge, punish* :—Med. *to avenge oneself on* another, c. acc., Eur.

ΠΟΙΝΗ', ἡ, *quit-money for blood spilt*, paid by the slayer to the kinsmen of the slain, (old Engl. *weregild*) ; c. gen. pers., δῶχ' υἷος ποινήν gave *ransom* or *were-gild for* the son, Il., etc. :—generally, *a price paid, satisfaction, retribution, requital, penalty*, Lat. *poena*, ἀπετίσατο ποινὴν ἑτάρων exacted *penalty* for his comrades, Od.; δυώδεκα κούρους, ποινὴν Πατρόκλοιο in *retribution* for the death of Patroclus, Il.; τῶν ποινὴν in *return* for these things, Ib. ; ποινὴν τῖσαι Ξέρξῃ τῶν κηρύκων ἀπολομένων to give Xerxes *satisfaction* for the death of his heralds, Hdt.; in Att. the pl. is more common; ποινὰς τῖσαι, δοῦναι to pay *penalties*, Lat. *dare poenas*, Aesch., etc. ; ποινὰς λαβεῖν to exact *them*, Lat. *sumere poenas*, Eur. 2. in good sense, *recompense, reward for* a thing, τινος Pind. 3. as the result of the quit-money, *redemption, release*, Id. II. personified, *the goddess of Vengeance*, Aesch., etc.

ποινῆτις, ιδος, ἡ, (ποινάω) *avenging*, Anth.

ποίνιμος, ον, (ποινή) *avenging, punishing*, Soph. 2. in good sense, *bringing return* or *recompense*, Pind.

ποιο-λογέω, f. ήσω, (ποία, λέγω) *to gather corn into sheaves*, Theocr.

ποιο-νόμος, ον, (νέμω) *feeding on grass* or *herbs*, Aesch.

ποῖος, α, ον, Ion. κοῖος, η, ον, *of what nature? of what sort?* Lat. *qualis?* used in questions :—in Hom. expressing surprise and anger, ποῖον τὸν μῦθον ἔειπες *what manner* of speech hast thou spoken! ποῖόν σε ἔπος φύγεν ἕρκος ὀδόντων! ποῖον ἔειπες! etc. 2. ποῖος οὐ; interrog. equiv. to ἕκαστος affirm., Hdt., Soph. 3. in Att. often with Art., τὸ ποῖον φάρμακον; Aesch. ; τὰ ποῖα τρύχη; Ar. ; τὸ ποῖον; Plat. etc. 4. ποῖός τις; makes the question less definite, κοῖόν μέ τινα νομίζουσιν εἶναι; Hdt. ; 'ποῖ' ἄττα; Plat.; τὰ τοῖ' ἄττα; Xen. 5. ποῖα, Ion. κοῖα, as Adv., = πῶς; Lat. *quomodo?* Hdt., Ar. II. like ὁποῖος, in indirect questions, διδάξω ποῖα χρὴ λέγειν Aesch. etc. (ποῖος, πόσος must be referred to a primitive *πός, as the correlat. Adjs. οἷος, ὅσος to ὅς.)

ποιός, ά, όν, Indef. Adj., *of a certain nature, kind* or *quality*, Plat.

ποιότης, ητος, ἡ, *quality*, Plat., Arist.

ποιπνύω : impf. ἐποίπνυον, Ep. ποίπνυον : aor. 1 part. ποιπνύσας [ῠ] : [υ of pres. long before a long syll., short before a short syll.] : (formed by redupl. from πνέω) :—*to be out of breath* from haste, *to puff* or *bustle about*, Lat. *satagere, exert oneself, be busy*, Hom.; aor. 1 part. with another Verb, δῶμα κορήσατε ποιπνύσασαι *make haste and sweep the house*, Od.

ποίφυγμα, ατος, τό, a blowing, snorting, Aesch. From
ποιφύσσω, (redupl. form from φυσάω) to blow, snort:
c. acc. to puff out, Anth.
ποι-ώδης, ες, (εἶδος) like grass, Hdt.
πόκα or ποκά [ᾰ], Dor. for πότε and ποτέ.
πόκες, αἱ, v. πόκος II.
ποκίζω, (πόκος) = πέκω, to shear wool: Med. to shear
for oneself, τρίχας ἐποκίξατο (Dor. aor. 1) Theocr.
ποκόομαι, Pass. to be clothed with wool, Anth. From
πόκος, ὁ, (πέκω) wool in its raw state, a fleece, Il., Eur.,
etc.: a lock or tuft of wool, Soph. II. proverb.
in heterocl. acc. of 3rd decl., εἰς ὄνου πόκας to an ass-
shearing, i. e. to no-place, Theocr.
πολέες, -έων, -έεσσι, -έας, Ep. for πολλοί, -ῶν, -έσι,
-ούς, from πολύς.
πολεμάρχειος, ον, of or belonging to the Polemarch;
—τὸ πολεμάρχειον his residence, Xen.; and
πολεμαρχέω, to be Polemarch, Hdt., Xen. From
πολέμ-αρχος, ὁ, one who begins or leads the war, a
leader, chieftain, Aesch. II. a Polemarch, 1. at
Athens, the third archon, who presided in the court in
which the causes of the μέτοικοι were tried, Ar.; —in
earlier times he was general-in-chief, as at Marathon,
Hdt. 2. at Sparta, a kind of brigadier, Id., Thuc.,
etc. 3. at Thebes officers of chief rank after the
Boeotarchs, Xen. 4. similarly at Mantineia, and
in other states, Thuc.
πολεμέω, f. ήσω: pf. πεπολέμηκα:—Pass., f. πολεμη-
θήσομαι, also πολεμήσομαι (in pass. sense): aor. 1
ἐπολεμήθην, pf. πεπολέμημαι: (πόλεμος):—to be at war
or go to war, make war, τινί with one, Hdt., etc.; ἐπί
τινα, πρός τινα Xen. 2. to fight, do battle, ἀπὸ τῶν
ἵππων Plat.: ἀπὸ καμήλων Xen. 3. generally, to
quarrel, wrangle, dispute with one, Soph., etc. II.
c. acc. to make war upon: Pass. to have war made
upon one, to be treated as enemies, Thuc., Xen. 2.
c. acc. cogn., πόλεμον πολ. Plat.:—Pass., ὁ πόλεμος
οὕτως ἐπολεμήθη Xen.; so, ὅσα ἐπολεμήθη whatever
hostilities passed, Id.
πολεμη-δόκος, Dor. πολεμᾱ-δόκος, ὁ, ἡ, (δέχομαι) war-
sustaining, Pind.
πολεμήιος, ον, Ion. Adj. (for no Att. form in -ειος
exists), warlike, πολεμήια ἔργα Il.; τεύχεα Ib.; πολεμήια = πολεμικά, τά, Hdt.
πολεμησείω, Desiderat. of πολεμέω, Thuc
πολεμητέον, verb. Adj. of πολεμέω, one must go to
war, Arist.:—pl. πολεμητέα, Thuc.
πολεμία, ἡ, v. πολέμιος III.
πολεμίζω, Ep. πτολεμίζω, f. ίξω, poët. form of πολεμέω, to wage war, make war, fight, τινί with one,
Hom.; ἄντα τινός, ἐναντίβιόν τινος Il.:—also in
Med., Pind. II. to fight with, absol. ῥηίτεροι
πολεμίζειν Il.
πολεμικός, ή, όν, (πόλεμος) of or for war, Thuc.;
ἄσπὶς πολεμικωτάτη most fit for service, Xen. 2.
ἡ -κή (sc. τέχνη), the art of war, war, Plat.:—τὰ
πολεμικά warlike exercises, Thuc., Xen. 3. τὸ
πολεμικόν the signal for battle, Xen. b. the
military class, opp. to the civilian, Arist. II. of
persons, skilled in war, warlike, Thuc., etc. III.
like an enemy, stirring up hostility, Xen.:—Adv.,
πολεμικῶς ἔχειν to be hostile, Id.

πολέμιος, α, ον, and ος, ον, (πόλεμος) of or belonging to
war, Pind., Aesch., etc.: —τὰ πολέμια whatever belongs
to war, war and its business, Hdt., Thuc., etc. II.
of or like an enemy, hostile, Pind., Trag., etc.:—π.
τινι hostile to one, Hdt., etc.:—as Subst. an enemy,
Hdt., Att.; οἱ π. the enemy, Thuc.:—τὸ π. hostility,
Id. 2. generally, opposed, adverse, Hdt.,
Plat. III. of or from the enemy, Aesch.,
Thuc.; πολέμια, τά, enemy's wares, contraband, Ar.:
—ἡ πολεμία (sc. γῆ, χώρα), the enemy's country,
Xen. IV. -ίως, in hostile manner, Plat.
πολεμιστήριος, α, ον, and ος, ον, of or for a warrior,
Hdt.; βοή, θώραξ π. Ar.; π. ἄρματα war-chariots,
Hdt.; ἐλᾶν τὰ πολεμιστήρια to drive the war-chariots,
a military game, Ar. II. τὰ πολεμιστήρια, =
τὰ πολεμικά, Xen.
πολεμιστής, Ep. πτολ-, οῦ, ὁ, (πολεμίζω) a warrior,
combatant, Il., Pind., etc. II. π. ἵππος a war-
horse, charger, Theocr.
πολεμό-κλονος, ον, raising the din of war, Batr.
πολεμό-κραντος, ον, (κραίνω) finishing war, Aesch.
πολεμο-λᾱμ-ᾰχαϊκός, ή, όν, a compd. of πόλεμος,
Λάμαχος, Ἀχαϊκός, a very Lamachus in war, Ar.
πολεμόνδε, Ep. πτόλ-, (πόλεμος) Adv. to the war,
into the fight, Il.
πολεμοποιέω, f. ήσω, to stir up war, Xen. From
πολεμο-ποιός, όν, (ποιέω) engaging in war, Arist.
ΠΟ'ΛΕΜΟΣ, Ep. πτόλεμος, ὁ, battle, fight, war, Hom.,
etc.; πόλεμον αἴρεσθαί τινι to levy war against another,
Aesch.; π. θέσθαι τινί Eur.; π. ἀναιρεῖσθαι, κινεῖν, ἐγείρειν, καθιστάναι, ἐπάγειν to begin a war; π. ποιεῖσθαι to
make war,—opp. to π. ἀναπαύειν, καταλύεσθαι to put
an end to it, make peace, all in Att.
πολεμο-φθόρος, ον, (φθείρω) wasting by war, Aesch.
πολεμόω, f. ώσω, (πόλεμος) to make hostile, make an
enemy of, τινά:—Med., πῶς οὐ πολεμώσεσθε αὐτούς;
surely you will make them your enemies, Thuc.:—
Pass. to be made an enemy of, become an enemy, Id.
πολεύω, like πολέω, only in pres., I. intr. to turn
about, Lat. versari, κατὰ ἄστυ π. to go about the city,
i. e. live therein, Od. II. trans. to turn up the
soil with the plough, Soph.
πολέω, (πέλω) like πολεύω, only in pres., I. to go
about, range over, νῆσον Αἴαντος πολεῖ Aesch.; τί σὺ
τῇδε πολεῖς; Eur.:—so in Med., Aesch. II. trans.
to turn up the earth with the plough, to plough, Hes.
πόλεων, gen. pl. of πόλις. II. πολέων, Ion. for
πολλῶν, gen. pl. of πολύς.
πόληος, πόληι, Ion. for πολλοῦ, πολλῷ, gen. and dat.
of πολύς:—πόληες, for πολλοί.
πολιά, ἡ, (πολιός) grayness of hair, Menand.
πολιαίνομαι, (πολιός) Pass. to grow white, Aesch.
πολιάοχος, ον, Dor. for πολιήοχος.
πολί-αρχος, ὁ, ruler of a city, Pind., Eur.
Πολιάς, άδος, ἡ, (πόλις) guardian of the city, epith.
of Athena in her oldest temple on the Acropolis of
Athens, as distinguished from Ἀθ. Παρθένος, Hdt.,
Soph.
πολιάτας, ὁ, Dor. for πολίτης, opp. to ξεῖνος, Pind.
πόλιες, -ίεσσι, Ep. for πόλεις, πόλεσι, nom. and dat.
pl. of πόλις.
πολίζω, Ep. aor. 1 πόλισσα, (πόλις) to build a city, to

build, Il. :—Pass., Ἴλιος πεπόλιστο (Ep. 3 sing. plqpf.) Ib.; so Hdt.   **II.** χωρίον πολίζειν *to colonise* a country *by building a city*, Xen.

πολιήοχος, ον, Ep. for πολιοῦχος.

πολιήτης, εω, ὁ, Ion. for πολίτης, *a citizen*, Il., Hdt., Aesch.; *a fellow-citizen, countryman*, Hdt.   **II.** as Adj., ψάμαθοι πολιήτιδος ἀκτᾶς sands on my *country's shore*, Eur.

πόλινδε, Adv. *into* or *to the city*, Il.

πολιό-θριξ, τρῐχος, ὁ, ἡ, *grayhaired*, Strab.

πολιο-κρόταφος, ον, *with gray hair on the temples*, i. e. *just beginning to be gray*, Il., Hes.

πολῐ-ορκέω, f. ήσω :—Pass., f. med. -ήσομαι (in pass. sense): aor. 1 ἐπολιορκήθην : pf. πεπολιόρκημαι : (πόλις, εἴργω, ἕρκος) :—*to hem in a city, blockade, beleaguer, besiege*, Hdt., Att. :—Pass. *to be besieged, in a state of siege*, Hdt.; of Scamander, *to be dammed back*, Plat.   **2.** metaph. *to be besieged, pestered*, Xen.

πολιορκητέος, α, ον, verb. Adj. *to be besieged*, Xen.

πολιορκητής, οῦ, ὁ, *taker of cities*, name of Demetrius son of Antigonus, Plut.

πολιορκητικός, ή, όν, *of* or *for besieging*, Polyb.

πολιορκία, Ion. -ίη, ἡ, *a besieging, siege*, Hdt., Thuc., etc.   **2.** metaph. *a besieging, pestering*, Plut.

ΠΟΛΙΟ͂Σ, ά, όν, and ός, όν, *gray, grizzled, grisly*, of wolves, of iron, of the sea, Il.   **2.** mostly of hair, *gray* or *hoary* from age, Hom.; π. πολιοί *gray-haired men*, Od., Soph., etc. :—absol., αἱ πολιαί (sc. τρίχες) Pind.; ἅμα ταῖς πολιαῖς κατιούσαις as the *gray hairs* come down (i. e. from the temples to the beard), Ar.; π. δάκρυον ἐμβαλών an *old man's* tear, Eur.   **b.** metaph. *hoary, venerable*, Id.   **II.** like λευκός, *bright, clear, serene*, Hes., Eur.

πολι-οῦχος, ον, Ep. -ήοχος, Dor. -άοχος, (ἔχω) *protecting a city*, Eur. :—mostly like Πολιεύς, Πολιάς, of the guardian deity of a city, Hdt., Aesch.

πολιό-χρως, ωτος, ὁ, ἡ, *white-coloured, white*, Eur.

ΠΟ'ΛΙΣ, ἡ : gen. πόλεως [dissyll. in Att. Poets], πόλεος, Ep. πόληος, Ion. and Dor. πόλιος [dissyll. in Il.]; also πόλευς :—dat. πόλει, Ep. πόληι, Ion. πόλι :—acc. πόλιν, Ep. also πόληα :—Pl. nom. πόλεις, Ep. πόλεες, Ion. πόλιες :—gen. πολίων :—dat. πόλισι, Ep. πολέεσσι, Dor. πολίεσι :—acc. πόλεις, πόλιας :—*a city*, Hom., Hes., etc.; πόλις ἄκρη and ἀκροτάτη, = ἀκρόπολις, *the citadel*, Il. : this at Athens was often called simply πόλις, while the rest of the city was called ἄστυ, Thuc., etc. :—the name of the city was often added in gen., Ἰλίου π., Ἄργους π. *the city of* . . , Aesch., etc.; also in appos., ἡ Μένδη π. Thuc.   **2.** *one's city* or *country*, Od., etc.   **II.** when πόλις and ἄστυ are joined, the former is the *body of citizens*, the latter *their dwellings*, Il.; ὧν πόλις ἀνάριθμος ὄλλυται, where πόλις = *a number of citizens*, Soph. :—hence, **2.** *the state* (πολιτεία), Hes., Pind., Att.: esp. *a free state, republic*, Soph., Xen., etc.   **3.** *the right of citizenship*, like Lat. *civitas*, Ar., Dem.

πόλισμα, τό, (πολίζω) *a city, town*, Hdt., Att.   **II.** *the community*, Soph.

πολισμάτιον, τό, Dim. of foreg., Polyb.

πολισσο-νόμος, ον, (πόλις, νέμω) *managing* or *ruling a city*, Aesch.; π. βιοτά a life *of social order*, Id.

πολισ-σόος, ον, (σώζω) *guarding cities*, h. Hom.

πολισ-σοῦχος, ον, poët. for πολιοῦχος, Aesch.   **II.** *dwelling in the city*, Id.

πολιτ-άρχης, ου, ὁ, *a civic magistrate*, at Thessalonica, N. T.

πολιτεία, Ion. -ηίη, ἡ, (πολιτεύω) *the condition and rights of a citizen, citizenship*, Lat. *civitas*, Hdt., Thuc., etc.; πολιτείαν δοῦναί τινι Xen.   **2.** *the life of a citizen, civic life*, Dem.   **3.** as a concrete, *the body of citizens*, Arist.   **II.** *the life and business of a statesman, government, administration*, Ar., Thuc., etc. :—in a collective sense, *the measures of a government*, Dem.   **III.** *civil polity, the condition* or *constitution of a state*, Thuc., etc. :—*a form of government*, Plat., etc.   **2.** *a republic, commonwealth*, Xen., etc.

πολίτευμα, ατος, τό, (πολιτεύω) *the business of government, an act of administration*, Dem.; ἕν τε τοῖς κατὰ τὴν πόλιν πολιτεύμασι καὶ ἐν τοῖς Ἑλληνικοῖς both in my home and foreign *policy*, Id.   **II.** *the government*, Arist.   **III.** = πολιτεία III, Id.

πολιτεύω, f. -σω, (πολίτης) *to live as a citizen* or *freeman, live in a free state*, Thuc., etc.   **2.** *to have a certain form of polity, conduct the government*, Id. :—Pass., of the state, *to be governed*, Plat., Xen., etc.; τὰ αὐτοῖς πεπολιτευμένα the *measures of* their *administration*, Dem.   **B.** commonly as Dep., f. πολιτεύσομαι : aor. 1 med. ἐπολιτευσάμην, and pass. ἐπολιτεύθην : pf. πεπολίτευμαι :—like the Act. *to be a free citizen, live as such*, Xen., etc.   **II.** *to take part in the government*, Thuc., Dem. : *to meddle with politics*, Plat.   **2.** c. acc. *to administer* or *govern*, Dem.; π. πόλεμον ἐκ πολέμου *to make* perpetual war *the principle of government*, Aeschin. : absol. *to conduct the government*, Ar., Dem.; οἱ πολιτευόμενοι *the ministers*, Dem.   **III.** *to have a certain form of government*, Plat., Aeschin.

πολιτηίη, ἡ, Ion. for πολιτεία.

πολίτης [ῐ], ου, ὁ, Ion. **πολιήτης**, *a member of a city* or *state* (πόλις), *a citizen, freeman*, Lat. *civis*, Hom., etc.   **2.** like Lat. *civis*, *a fellowcitizen*, Hdt., Aesch., etc.   **3.** θεοὶ πολῖται = πολιοῦχοι, Aesch.

πολιτικός, ή, όν, (πολίτης) *of, for*, or *relating to citizens*, Plat., etc.   **2.** *befitting a citizen*, Lat. *civilis*, *civic, civil*, Lat. *civilis*, Thuc.; πολιτικωτέρα ἐγένετο ἡ ὀλιγαρχία *more constitutional*, Arist. :—Adv., πολιτικῶς *like a citizen, in a constitutional manner*, Lat. *civiliter*, Dem.   **3.** *consisting of citizens*, τὸ πολιτικόν, = οἱ πολῖται, *the community*, Hdt., Thuc.: *the civic force*, opp. to οἱ σύμμαχοι, Xen., etc.   **4.** *living in a community*, Arist.   **II.** *of* or *befitting a statesman, statesmanlike*, Plat.   **III.** *belonging to the state* or *its administration, political*, Lat. *publicus*, Thuc. :—ἡ πολιτική (sub. τέχνη), *the art of government*, ἡ π. ἐπιστήμη or ἡ π. alone, *the science of politics*, Plat. :—τὰ πολιτικά, *state-affairs, public matters, government*, Thuc., etc.   **2.** *civil, municipal*, opp. to natural or general, Dem.   **IV.** generally, *of* or *for public life, public*, opp. to κατ' ἰδίας, Thuc., Xen.

πολῖτις, ιδος, fem. of πολίτης, Soph., Eur., etc.

πολῑτο-φύλαξ [ῠ], ἄκος, ὁ, *one who watches citizens*; οἱ π., in Larissa, the chief magistrates, Arist.

πολίχνη, ἡ, (πόλις) a small town, Plut.
πολίχνιον, τό, Dim. of foreg., Plat., etc.
πολι-ώδης, ες, (πολιός, εἶδος) grayish, whitish, Luc.
πολλάκις [ἄ] ; Ep. and Lyr. πολλάκι, (πολλός, πολύς) : Adv. : **I.** of Time, many times, often, oft, Il., etc. ; c. gen., π. τοῦ μηνός often in the month, Xen. **II.** of Degree and Number, π. μύριοι many tens of thousands, Plat. **2.** τὸ π. mostly, for the most part, Pind. : very much, altogether, Theocr. **III.** in Att., after εἰ, ἐάν, ἄν, perhaps, perchance, Lat. si forte, Ar., Plat. ; so, μὴ πολλάκις, Lat. ne forte, Thuc., etc.
πολλαπλάσιος [πλᾰ], α, ον, Ion. -πλήσιος, η, ον, (πολύς) :—many times as many, many times more or larger, Hdt. **2.** πολλ. ἤ. ., or ἤπερ. ., many times as many as. ., many times more or larger than. ., Id., Plat. ; so c. gen., Hdt., Thuc., etc. :— neut. pl. as Adv., Xen. Hence
πολλαπλᾰσιόω, f. ώσω, to multiply, Plat. Hence
πολλαπλᾰσίωσις, ἡ, multiplication, Plat.
πολλαπλήσιος, η, ον, Ion. for πολλαπλάσιος.
πολλαπλόος, η, ον, contr. -πλοῦς, ῆ, οῦν, manifold, many times as long, Plat. ; ὄνομα πολλαπλοῦν multi-compound, opp. to ἁπλοῦν, Arist. **II.** metaph., ἀνὴρ π. not simple and straightforward, Plat.
πολλᾰχῇ, Adv. many times, often, Hdt., Xen. **II.** in divers manners, Hdt., Soph., etc.
πολλᾰχόθεν, Adv. from many places or sides, Thuc., etc. **II.** from or for many reasons, Id.
πολλᾰχόθῐ, Adv. in many places, Xen.
πολλᾰχόσε, Adv. towards many sides, into many parts or quarters, Thuc. ; c. gen., π. τῆς Ἀρκαδίας Xen.
πολλᾰχοῦ, Adv. in many places, Eur., Plat. **2.** c. gen., π. τῆς γῆς Plat. **II.** = πολλαχῇ, many times, often, Hdt., etc.
πολλᾰχῶς, Adv. in many ways, Dem., etc.
πολλο-δεκάκις [ᾰ], Adv. many tens of times, Ar.
πολλός, πολλόν, Ion. masc. and neut. for πολύς, πολύ.
πολλοστη-μόριος, ον, many times smaller, Arist.
πολλοστός, ή, όν, (πολλός, πολύς) one of many, Lat. unus e multis, i. e. the smallest, least, Thuc., etc. :— Adv., δευτέρως καὶ πολλοστῶς in a very small degree, Arist. **2.** of Time, πολλοστῷ χρόνῳ after a very long time, Ar., Dem.
πόλος, ὁ, (πέλω) a pivot, hinge, axis : **1.** the axis of the globe, Plat., etc. **2.** the sphere which revolves on this axis, i. e. the vault of heaven, the sky or firmament, Lat. polus, Aesch., Eur. **3.** the orbit of a star, Anth. **II.** land turned up with the plough, Xen. **III.** a concave dial (called πόλος from being shaped like the vault of heaven), Hdt., Anth.
πολύ-αγρος, ον, (ἄγρα) catching much game, Anth.
πολύ-αθλος, ον, conquering in many contests, Luc.
πολύ-αιγος, ον, (αἴξ) abounding in goats, Anth.
πολυ-αίνετος, ον, = sq., Eur.
πολύ-αινος, ον, (αἰνέω) much-praised, or full of wise speech and lore, Hom.
πολυ-άϊξ [ᾰ], ῑκος, (ἀΐσσω) much-rushing, impetuous, furious, Hom. ; κάματος π. weariness caused by much fighting, Il.
πολυανδρέω, to be full of men, to be populous, Thuc.
πολύ-ανδρος, ον, (ἀνήρ) of places, with many men, full of men, Aesch. **2.** of persons, numerous, Id.

πολυ-ανθής, ές, much-blossoming, blooming, Od.
πολυανθρωπία, ἡ, a large population, multitude of people, Xen. From
πολυ-άνθρωπος, ον, full of people, populous, Thuc., etc. **II.** much-frequented, crowded, Luc. **III.** numerous, Polyb.
πολυ-άνωρ [ᾰ], opos, ὁ, ἡ, with many men, much-frequented, Eur., Ar. **II.** γυνὴ π. wife of many husbands, Aesch.
πολυ-άργυρος, ον, rich in silver, Hdt.
πολυ-άρητος [ᾱ], ον, (ἀράομαι) much-desired, Od.
πολυ-αρκής, ές, (ἀρκέω) much-helpful, supplying many wants, Hdt. :—τὸ π. durability, Luc.
πολυ-άρμᾰτος, ον, (ἅρμα) with many chariots, Soph.
πολυ-αρμόνιος, ον, (ἁρμονία) many-toned, Plat.
πολύ-αρνος, ον, with many lambs or sheep, rich in flocks, heterocl. dat. πολύαρνι, Il.
πολυ-αρχία, ἡ, the government of many, Thuc., Xen.
πολυ-αστράγᾰλος, ον, with many joints, Anth.
πολύ-αστρος, ον, with many stars, starry, Eur.
πολυ-αῦλαξ, ᾰκος, ὁ, ἡ, with many furrows, Anth.
πολυ-αύχενος, ον, (αὐχήν) with many necks, Anth.
πολυ-βᾰφής, ές, (βάπτω) much-dipped, Aesch.
πολυβενθής, ές, (βένθος) very deep, Hom.
πολύ-βοσκος, ον, (βόσκω) much-nourishing, Pind.
πολυβότειρα, fem. Adj. (βόσκω) much or all nourishing, Hom., Hes., in Ep. form πουλυβότειρα.
πολύ-βοτος, ον, (βόσκω) much-nourishing, Aesch.
πολύβοτρυς, vos, ὁ, ἡ, abounding in grapes, Eur.
πολύ-βουλος, ον, (βουλή) much-counselling, Hom.
πολυ-βούτης, ου, ὁ, (βοῦς) rich in oxen, Il.
πολύ-βροχος, ον, with many nooses, Eur.
πολυ-γᾰθής, ές, Dor. for πολυ-γηθής.
πολυ-γάλακτος, ον, with much milk ; poët. Sup. πουλυγαλακτοτάτη Anth.
πολυ-γηθής, ές, Dor. -γᾱθής, ές, (γηθέω) much-cheering, delightful, gladsome, Il., Hes.
πολύ-γλευκος, ον, abounding in new wine, Anth.
πολύ-γλωσσος, Att.-ττος, ον, (γλῶσσα) many-tongued, δρῦς π. the vocal (oracular) oak of Dodona, Soph. ; π. βοή an oft-repeated or loud-voiced cry, Id.
πολύ-γναμπτος, ον, much-bent, much-twisting, Pind. : curling, frizzled, σέλινον Theocr.
πολύ-γνώμων, ον, very sagacious, Plat.
πολύ-γνωτος, ον, well-known, Pind.
πολύ-γομφος, ον, well-bolted, νῆες Hes.
πολυγονέομαι, Pass. to multiply, Luc. ; and
πολυγονία, ἡ, fecundity, Plat. From
πολύ-γονος, ον, producing many at a birth, prolific, Hdt., etc.
πολυ-δαίδᾰλος, ον, much wrought, richly dight, of metal work, Hom. ; of embroidery, Hes. **II.** act. working with much art, very skilful, Il.
πολυ-δάκρυος, ον, = sq., Il., Eur.
πολύ-δακρυς, ὔος, ὁ, ἡ, (δάκρυ) of or with many tears : hence, **I.** much-wept, tearful, Il., Aesch. **II.** of persons, much-weeping, Eur., Ar.
πολυ-δάκρυτος, ον, much wept or lamented, Il. **2.** very lamentable, tearful, Od., Aesch. **II.** act. much-weeping, Eur.
πολυ-δάπᾰνος, ον, (δαπάνη) causing great expense, Hdt., Xen. **II.** of a person, extravagant, Xen.

πολυ-δέγμων, ον, gen. ονος, = πολυδέκτης, h. Hom.
πολυ-δειράς, άδος, ό, ή, (δειρή) with many ridges, Il.
πολυ-δέκτης, ου, ό, the Allreceiver, i. e. Hades, h. Hom.
πολυ-δένδρεος, ον, Ep. for sq., Od.
πολυ-δένδρος, ον, (δένδρον) with many trees, abounding in trees, heterocl. dat. pl. πολυδένδρεσσι Eur.
πολυ-δερκής, ές, (δέρκομαι) much-seeing, Hes.
πολύ-δεσμος, ον, fastened with many bonds, Od.
Πολυ-δεύκης, εος, ό, = ό πολλήν δόξαν ἔχων, Pollux, one of the Dioscuri, son of Leda, brother of Castor, Hom.
Πολυδεύκιον, τό, Com. Dim. of Πολυδεύκης, Luc.
πολύ-δικος, ον, having many lawsuits, litigious, Strab.
πολύ-δινής, ές, (δίνη) much-whirling, Anth.
πολύ-δίψιος, ον, very thirsty, Il.
πολύ-δονος, ον, (δονέω) much-driven, Aesch.
πολύ-δοξος, ον, (δόξα) having various opinions, Anth.
πολυδωρία, ή, open-handedness, Xen. From
πολύ-δωρος, ον, (δῶρον) richly dowered, Hom.
πολύ-εδρος, ον, (ἔδρα) polyhedral, Plut.
πολυ-ειδής, ές, (εἶδος) of many kinds, Thuc., Plat.
πολυειδία, ή, diversity of kind, Plat.
πολυ-έλαιος, ον, (ἔλαιον) yielding much oil, Xen.
πολυ-έλικτος, ον, much convoluted, πολ. ἀδονά the pleasure of the mazy dance, Eur.
πολυ-επαίνετος, ον, much-praised, Xen.
πολυ-επής, ές, (ἔπος) much-speaking, Aesch.
πολύ-εραστος, ον, much-loved, Xen.
πολυ-εργής, ές, = sq., Anth.
πολύ-εργος, ον, (*ἔργω) much-working, Theocr.
πολύ-ετής, ές, (ἔτος) of many years, full of years, Eur.
πολύ-ευκτος, ον, much-wished-for, much-desired, Orac. ap. Hdt., Aesch.
πολυ-εύχετος, ον, = πολυεύκτος, h. Hom.
πολύ-ζηλος, ον, full of jealousy and rivalry, Soph. II. much-desired, longed-for, loved, Id.
πολύ-ζήλωτος, ον, much envied, Eur.
πολύ-ζυγος, ον, (ζυγόν III) many-benched, νηῦς Il.
πολυ-ήγορος, ον, (ἀγορεύω) much-speaking, Anth.
πολυ-ήκοος, ον, (ἀκούω) having heard much, much-learned, Plat.
πολυ-ήμερος, ον, (ἡμέρα) of many days, Plut.
πολυ-ήρατος, ον, (ἐράω) much-loved, very lovely, Od.
πολυ-ηχής, ές, (ἦχος) many-toned, of the nightingale's voice, Od. : much or loud sounding, Il.
πολυ-ήχητος, Dor. -άχητος [ἄ], ον, loud-sounding, Eur.
πολυ-θάητος [ἄ], ον, poët. for πολυθέατος, Anth.
πολυ-θαρσής, ές, (θάρσος) much-confident, Hom.
πολυ-θέαμων [ἄ], ον, having seen much, c. gen., Plat.
πολύ-θεος, ον, of or belonging to many gods, Aesch.
πολύ-θερμος, ον, very warm or hot, Plut.
πολύ-θηρος, ον, (θήρ) abounding in wild beasts, Eur.
πολυ-θρέμμων, ον, (τρέφω) feeding many, Aesch.
πολύ-θρήνητος, ον, (θρηνέω) lamentable, Anth.
πολύ-θρηνος, ον, much-wailing, Aesch.
πολύ-θριξ, τρίχος, ό, ή, with much hair, Anth.
πολύ-θροος, ον, contr. -θρους, ουν, with much noise, clamorous, Aesch.
πολυ-θρύλητος [ῠ], ον, (θρυλέω) much-spoken-of, well-known, notorious, Plat.

πολύ-θυρος, ον, (θύρα) with many doors or openings, Luc. II. with many leaves, of tablets, Eur.
πολύ-θυτος, ον, abounding in sacrifices, Pind., etc.
πολυϊδρεία, ή, much knowledge or wisdom, in pl., νόου πολυϊδρείησι Od. From
πολύ-ϊδρις, Ion. gen. ιος, Att. εως, ό, ή, (εἰδέναι) of much knowledge, wisdom, shrewdness, Od., Ar.
πολύ-ιππος, ον, rich in horses, Il.
πολυ-ίστωρ, opos, ό, ή, very learned, Anth.
πολύ-ιχθυς, υος, ό, ή, abounding in fish, Strab. : also -ίχθυος, ον, h. Hom.
πολύ-καγκής, ές, (καίω) drying or parching exceedingly, δίψαι Il. II. very dry, Anth.
πολύ-κᾱής, ές, (καίω) much-burning, Anth.
πολυ-καισαρίη, ή, (Καῖσαρ) the government of many emperors at once, Plut.
πολύ-κάμμορος, ον, very miserable, Anth.
πολυ-καμπής, ές, (κάμπτω) much bent, Anth.
πολύ-κᾱνής, ές, (καίνω = κτείνω) much-slaughtering, θυσίαι π. βοτῶν slaughter of many beasts, Aesch.
πολύ-καπνος, ον, with much smoke, smoky, Eur.
πολυκάρηνος, Ep. πουλ-, ον, many-headed, Anth.
πολυκαρπία, ή, abundance of fruit, Xen. From
πολύ-καρπος, ον, rich in fruit, Od., Hdt., Att.
πολυκέρδεια, ή, great craft, πολυκερδείησιν Od. From
πολυ-κερδής, ές, (κέρδος) very crafty or wily, Od.
πολύ-κερως, ωτος, ό, ή, many-horned, π. φόνος the slaughter of much horned cattle, Soph.
πολύ-κεστος, ον, well-stitched, Il.
πολύ-κέφαλος, ον, (κεφαλή) many-headed, Plat.
πολύ-κηδής, ές, (κῆδος) full of care, grievous, Od.
πολύ-κηλος, ον, (κήρ) very deadly, Anth.
πολύ-κήτης, ες, (κῆτος) full of monsters, Theocr.
πολύ-κλαυστος or -κλαυτος, ον, and η, ον, much lamented, Aesch., Eur. II. act. much lamenting, Mosch.
πολύ-κλειτος, η, ον, far-famed, Pind.
πολύ-κλήεις, εσσα, εν, (κλέος) far-famed, Anth.
πολυκλήις, ιδος, ή, (κλείς IV) with many benches of rowers, in dat., νηὶ πολυκλήιδι, νηυσὶ πολυκλήισι Hom. ; acc. νῆα πολυκλήιδα Hes.
πολύ-κληρος, ον, of a large lot, with a large portion of land, Od., Theocr.
πολύ-κλητος, ον, called from many a land, of the Trojan allies, Il.
πολύ-κλυστος, ον, (κλύζω) much-dashing, Od. Hes. II. pass. washed by many a wave, Hes.
πολύ-κμητος, ον, (κάμνω) much-wrought, wrought with much toil, epith. of iron, as distinguished from copper, Il. ; π. θάλαμος Od. II. laborious, τέχνη Anth.
πολύ-κνημος, ον, (κνημός) with many mountain-spurs, mountainous, Il.
πολύ-κοινος, ον, common to many or to all, Pind., Soph.
πολύ-κοιρᾰνίη, ή, (κοίρανος) the rule of many, Il.
πολύ-κοιρανος, ον, wide-ruling, Aesch. ap. Ar.
πολύ-κόλυμβος, ον, (κολυμβάω) oft-diving, μέλη π., of the frogs, Ar.
πολύ-κρᾱνος, ον, (κρανίον) many-headed, Eur.
Πολυκράτειος, α, ον, of or belonging to Polycrates, Arist.
πολυ-κράτής, ές, (κράτος) very mighty, Aesch.
πολύ-κροτος, ον, and η, ον, loud-ringing, h. Hom.

πολύ-κρουνος, ον, with many springs, Anth.
πολυ-κτέανος, ον, (κτέανον) = πολυκτήμων, Pind.
πολυ-κτήμων, ον, gen. ονος, with many possessions, exceeding rich, Il., Soph.; c. gen., π. βίου Eur.
πολύ-κτητος, ον, of large possessions, wealthy, Eur.
πολυ-κτόνος, ον, (κτείνω) much-slaying, murderous, Aesch., Eur.
πολῠ-κῡδής, ές, (κῦδος) much-praised, very glorious, Anth.
πολῠ-κύμων, ον, gen. ονος, (κῦμα) swelling with many waves, Solon.
πολῠ-κώκῡτος, ον, much-lamenting, Theogn.
πολῠ-κωμος, ον, much-revelling, Anth.
πολύ-κωπος, ον, (κωπή) many-oared, Soph., Eur.
πολῠλήιος, ον, (λήιον) with many cornfields, Il.
πολύλ-λῐθος, ον, very stony, Anth.
πολύλ-λιστος, ον, (λίσσομαι) sought with many prayers, πολύλλιστον δέ σ' ἱκάνω, says Ulysses to the river which receives him from the sea (cf. τρίλλιστος), Od.
πολῠλογία, ἡ, much talk, loquacity, Xen. From
πολύ-λογος, ον, much-talking, talkative, loquacious, Xen., etc.
πολῠ-μᾰθής, ές, (μαθεῖν) having learnt or knowing much, Ar., Plat.
πολῠ-μᾰθία, ἡ, much-learning, Plat., etc.
πολῠ-μᾰνής, Ep. πουλυ-, ές, (μαίνομαι) very furious, Anth.
πολῠ-μάχητος, ον, (μάχομαι) much-fought-for, Luc.
πολῠ-μεθής, ές, (μέθυ) drinking much wine, Anth.
πολῠ-μελής, ές, (μέλος) with many members, Plat.
πολῠ-μερής, ές. (μέρος) consisting of many parts, manifold, of divers kinds, Arist.: Adv. -μερῶς, in many portions, N. T.
πολύ-μετρος, ον, (μέτρον) of many measures, hence copious, abundant, Eur. ap. Ar. II. consisting of many metres, h. Hom.
πολύ-μηκάς, άδος, ὁ, much bleating, Bacis ap. Hdt.
πολύ-μηλος, ον, (μῆλον) with many sheep or goats, rich in flocks, Il., Hes., Eur.
πολύ-μηνις, ιος, ὁ, ἡ, abounding in wrath, Anth.
πολύ-μητις, ιος, ὁ, ἡ, of many counsels, Hom.
πολῠμηχᾰνία, Ion. -ίη, ἡ, the having many resources, inventiveness, readiness, Od. From
πολῠ-μήχᾰνος, ον, (μηχανή) full of resources, inventive, ever-ready, of Ulysses, Il.
πολῠ-μῑγής, Ep. πουλυ-, ές, much-mixed, Anth.
πολῠ-μῑσής, ές, (μῖσος) much-hating, Luc.
πολυ-μνήστευτος, ον, (μνηστεύω) much-wooed, Plut.
πολυ-μνήστη, ἡ, (μνάομαι) much courted or wooed, wooed by many, Od.
πολυ-μνηστος, ον, (μνάομαι) much-remembering, mindful, Aesch. II. pass. much-remembered, Id.
Πολύμνια, ἡ, contr. for Πολυ-ύμνια, Polymnia or Polyhymnia, i. e. she of the many hymns, one of the nine Muses, Hes.
πολύ-μουσος, ον, (μοῦσα) rich in the Muses' gifts, Luc.
πολύ-μοχθος, ον, much-labouring, suffering many things, Soph., Eur. II. pass. won by much toil, Anth.: wrought with much toil, Theocr.
πολύ-μῡθος, ον, of many words, i. e. wordy, Hom. II. pass. much talked of, famous in story, Pind.

πολύ-νᾱος, ον, with many temples, Theocr.
πολῠ-ναύτης, ου, ὁ, with many sailors or ships, Aesch.
πολῠ-νεικής, ές, (νεῖκος) much-wrangling, Aesch.
πολῠ-νέφελας, Dor. gen. α, overcast with clouds, Pind.
πολῠ-νῐφής, ές, (νίφω) deep with snow, Eur.
πολύ-νοσος, ον, liable to many sicknesses, Strab.
πολύ-ξενος, Ion. -ξεινος, ον, and η, ον, of persons, entertaining many guests, very hospitable, Hes. II. visited by many guests, Pind., Eur.
πολύ-ξεστος, ον, (ξέω) much-polished, Soph.
πολυοινέω, f. ήσω, to be rich in wine, h. Hom. From
πολύ-οινος, ον, rich in wine, Thuc., Xen.
πολύ-ολβος, ον, very wealthy, Anth.: of things, very abundant, Id. II. act. rich in blessings, Id.
πολύ-όμμᾰτος, ον, (ὄμμα) many-eyed, Luc.
πολύ-όρνῑθος, ον, (ὄρνις) abounding in birds, Eur.
πολύ-οχλος, ον, much-peopled, populous, Polyb. II. very numerous, Arist.
πολυοψία, ἡ, abundance of meats or fish, Xen. From
πολύ-οψος, ον, abounding in fish, Strab. 2. luxurious, Luc.
πολῠ-πᾰθής, Ep. πουλυ-, ές, (παθεῖν) subject to many passions, much perturbed, Anth.
πολῠ-παίπᾰλος, ον, exceeding crafty, Od.
πολύ-παις, παιδος, ὁ, ἡ, with many children, Anth.
πολῠ-πάμ-φᾰος, ον, very bright-shining, Anth.
πολῠ-πάμων, ον, (πέ-παμαι) exceeding wealthy, Il.
πολῠ-πειρία, ἡ, (πεῖρα) great experience, Thuc.
πολῠ-πείρων, ον, (πεῖρας) with many boundaries, manifold, h. Hom.
πολῠ-πενθής, ές, (πένθος) much-mourning, exceeding mournful, Hom., Aesch.
πολῠ-πένθῑμος, ον, = foreg., Anth.
Πολυπημονίδης, ου, ὁ, son of Polypemon, with a play upon πολυπήμων, Od.
πολῠ-πήμων, ον, (πῆμα) causing manifold woe, baneful, h. Hom.: π. νόσοι diseases manifold, Pind.
πολύ-πηνος, ον, (πήνη) thick-woven, close-woven, Eur.
πολυ-πίδᾰκος [ῐ], ον, = sq., h. Hom.
πολῠπίδαξ, ᾰκος, ὁ, ἡ, with many springs, many-fountained, of Mt. Ida, Il.
πολύ-πικρος, ον, very keen or bitter; πολύπικρα as Adv., Od.
πολύ-πῐνής, ές, (πίνος) very squalid, Eur.
πολύ-πλαγκτος, ον, (πλάζω) much-wandering, wide-roaming, Od., Soph., Eur. II. act. leading far astray, driving far from one's course, ἄνεμος Il.—In Soph.Ant.615,π. ἐλπίς may be either wandering, uncertain hope, or misleading, deceitful; cf. πολυπλανής II.
πολυ-πλᾰνής, ές, (πλανάομαι) roaming far or long, Eur.; π. κισσός the straying ivy, Anth. II. much-erring, or, act., leading much astray, Id.
πολυ-πλάνητος [ᾰ], ον, = πολυπλανής, Hdt., Eur.; π. πόνοι the pains of wandering, Eur. II. of blows, falling in every direction, Aesch.
πολύ-πλᾰνος, ον, = πολυπλανής, Aesch., Eur.
πολυ-πλάσιος, α, ον, late for πολλα-πλάσιος, Anth.
πολύπλεθρος, ον, many πλέθρα in size, farstretching, Eur. II. of persons, rich in land, Luc.
πολυπλοκία, ἡ, cunning, craft, Theogn. From
πολύ-πλοκος,ον,(πλέκω) much-tangled,thick-wreathed, of a serpent's coils, Eur.; of the polypus, with tangled,

twisting arms, Theogn.   2. metaph. *much-twisting, complex, intricate*, Eur., Xen., Anth.

πολὔ-πόδης, ον, ὁ, poët. **πουλυ-,** = πολύπους, Anth.

πολυ-ποίκῖλος, ον, *much-variegated*, Eur.

πολύ-πονος, ον, of men, *much-labouring, much-suffering*, Pind., Eur.   2. of things, *full of pain and suffering, painful, toilsome*, Trag. Adv. -νως.

πολύπος, ον, ὁ, poët. for πολύπους.

πολὔ-πόταμος, ον, *with many* or *large rivers*, Eur.

πολὔ-πότης, Ep. **πουλυ-, ον, ὁ,** *a hard drinker*, Anth.

ʾπολὔ-πότνια, ἡ, strengthd. for πότνια, h. Hom.

πολύπους, ὁ, ἡ, neut. **πουν:** acc. masc. **πολύποδα:** pl. neut. **πολύποδα:**—*many-footed*, Soph., Plat.

πολύπους, or rather **πουλύπους, οδος, ὁ,** (for the form πολύπους is late).—Declension: nom. πουλύπους, acc. -πουν, gen. πουλύποδος:—pl., nom. πουλύποδες; acc. -ποδας; gen. πουλυποδῶν:—acc. also πουλύπους, gen. πουλύπου, pl. acc. πουλύπους:—later, **πολύπους,** acc. -πουν and -ποδα; pl. -ποδες, acc. -πους, -ποδας:—*the sea-polypus* or *octopus*, Lat. *pōlypus* (Horat.), Od., Theogn., etc.

πολυ-πραγμονέω, Ion. **-πρηγμονέω,** f. ήσω, *to be busy about many things*, in bad sense, *to be a meddlesome, inquisitive busybody*, Ar., Plat.: also, like νεωτερίζω, *to meddle in state affairs, intrigue*, Hdt., Xen.   2. c. acc. *to be curious after*, Menand.

πολυπραγμοσύνη, ἡ, *the character and conduct of the* πολυπράγμων, *curiosity, officiousness, meddlesomeness*, Ar., Thuc., etc.

πολυ-πράγμων, ʾον, gen. **ονος, (πρᾶγμα)** *busy after many things, over-busy*, mostly in bad sense, *meddlesome, officious, a busybody*, Lat. *curiosus*, an epith. often given to *the restless Athenians*, Ar., etc.

πολυπρηγμονέω, Ion. for πολυπραγμονέω.

πολυ-πρόβατος, ον, (πρόβατον) *rich in sheep* or *cattle,* πολυπροβατώτατοις Hdt.

πολυ-πρόσωπος, ον, (πρόσωπον) *many-faced, with many masks* or *characters*, Luc.

πολυ-πτόητος, Ion. **-πτοίητος, ον, (πτοέω)** *much-scared, much-agitated*, Luc.

πολύ-πτῠχος, ον, (πτύξ, πτυχή) *of* or *with many folds,* of mountains, Il., Hes., Eur.

πολύ-πυργος, ον, *with many towers*, h. Hom.

πολύ-πῡρος, ον, (πυρός) *rich in corn*, Hom.

πολύρ-ραπτος, ον, = sq., Theocr.

πολύρ-ράφος, ον, (ῥάπτω) *well-stitched*, Soph.

πολύρ-ρηνος, ον, (ῥήν) *rich in sheep*, Od.:—in pl. we have a heterocl. nom., ἄνδρες πολύρρηνες Il.

πολύρ-ριζος, ον, (ῥίζα) *with many roots*, Anth.

πολύρ-ροδος, ον, (ῥόδον) *abounding in roses*, Ar.

πολύρ-ροθος, ον, *much-roaring,* φροίμια π. the cries of *many voices*, Aesch.

πολυρ-ροίβδητος, ον, *much-whirring*, Anth.

πολύρ-ρῠτος, ον, *much* or *strong flowing*, Soph.

ΠΟΛΥΣ, πολλή, πολύ: gen. **πολλοῦ, ῆς, οῦ:** dat. **πολλῷ, ῇ, ῷ:** acc. **πολύν, πολλήν,** neut. —Ion. nom. **πολλός, ή, όν,** acc. **πολλόν, ήν, όν,** this Ion. declension being retained by the Att. in all cases, except the nom. and acc. masc. and neut. Hom. uses both Ion. and Att. forms. Special Ep. forms: **πουλύς, ύ,** gen. **πολέος,** pl. nom. **πολέες, πολεῖς,** gen. **πολέων,** dat. **πολέσι, πολέσσι, πολέεσσι,** acc. **πολέας.**

I. of Number, *many*, opp. to ὀλίγος, Hom., etc.;—with nouns of multitude, πουλὺς ὅμιλος Od.; πολλὸν πλῆθος Hdt., etc.:—also of anything often repeated, πολλὸν ἦν τοῦτο τὸ ἔπος Id.; πολλὸς αἰνεόμενος Id.; τούτῳ πολλῷ χρήσεται τῷ λόγῳ *often*, Dem.   2. of Size, Degree, Force, *much, mighty, great*, Il., etc.; π. ὕπνος *deep* sleep, Od.; π. ὑμέναιος a *loud* song, Il., etc.:—rarely of a single person, μέγας καὶ πολλὸς ἐγένεο Hdt.; ἢν πολλῇ ῥυῇ if she flow *with full stream*, metaph. from a river, Eur.; πολλῷ ῥέοντι Dem.; from the wind, πολὺς ἔπνει was blowing *strong*, Id.; often with a Partic., πολλὸς ἦν λισσόμενος he was *all* intreaties, Lat. *multus erat in precando*, Dem.; so, π. ἦν ἐν τοῖσι λόγοισι Id., etc.   3. of Value or Worth, πλέος or πολλοῦ ἄξιος Hom.; πολλοῦ and περὶ πολλοῦ ποιεῖσθαί τι, Lat. *magni facere*, cf. περί A. IV; ἐπὶ πολλῷ at a *high price*, Dem.   4. of Space, *large, wide, wide-stretched*, π. χώρη, πεδίον Il., Hes., etc.; πόντος, πέλαγος Hes., etc.;—πολλὸς ἔκειτο he lay *outstretched*, Il.;—π. κέλευθος a *far* way, Aesch., etc.   5. of Time, *long*, πολὺν χρόνον Hom., etc.; πολλοῦ χρόνου Ar.; ἐκ πολλοῦ Thuc.; ἔτι πολλῆς νυκτός, Lat. *multa nocte*, while still *quite* night, Id.   II. Special usages: 1. partitive c. gen., e.g. πολλοὶ Τρώων for πολλοὶ Τρῶες, Il.; πολλὸν σαρκός for πολλὴ σάρξ, Od.; in Prose, the Adj. generally takes the gender of the gen., τῆς γῆς οὐ πολλήν Thuc.   2. joined to another Adj. by καί, πολέες τε καὶ ἐσθλοί *many* men and good, Il.; π. καὶ πονηρά Xen.; μεγάλα καὶ π. Dem.   3. with the Art., of persons or things well known, Ἑλένα μία τὰς πολλὰς ψυχὰς ὀλέσασ' those *many* lives, Aesch.; ὡς ὁ πολλὸς λόγος *the common* report, Hdt.:—esp. οἱ πολλοί *the many*, i.e. *the greater number*, Thuc.; hence, like τὸ πλῆθος, *the people, the commonalty*, Id.; εἷς τῶν πολλῶν one of *the multitude*, Dem.   b. τὸ πολύ, c. gen., τῆς στρατιῆς τὸ πολλόν Hdt.; τῶν λογάδων τὸ πολύ Thuc.; but also, ὁ στρατὸς ὁ πολλὸς Hdt.   c. τὰ πολλά *the most*, Od., etc.   4. the pl. πολλά is used with Verbs in the sense of *very much, too much*, πολλὰ πράσσειν = πολυπραγμονεῖν, Eur., Ar.; π. ἔρξαι τινά to do one *much harm*, Aesch.   5. πολλάς with Verbs of beating, the Subst. πληγάς being omitted, v. πληγή I.   III. Adverbial usages: a. neut. πολύ (Ion. πολλόν), *much, very*, Hom., etc.; μάλα πολλά Ib.; πάνυ πολύ Plat.:—also of repetition, *many times, ofttimes, often, much*, Hom., etc.:—also with the Art., τὸ πολύ *for the most part*, Plat.; ὡς τὸ π. Xen.; so, τὰ πολλά, ὡς τὰ π. Thuc.   b. of Degree, *far, very much*, Hdt.; so absol. gen. πολλοῦ, *very*, θρασὺς εἶ πολλοῦ Ar.; πολλοῦ πολύς, πολλοῦ πολλή, πολλοῦ πολύ, *much too much*, Id.   c. of Space, *a great way, far*, οὗ πολλὸν π.   d. of Time, *long*, Id.   2. πολύ is often joined with Adjs. and Advs.,   a. with a Compar. to increase its compar. force, πολὺ κάλλιον, μεῖζον, πολλὸν ἀμείνων, ταυρότεροι *much, far* more beautiful, etc., Hom., etc.:—so dat. πολλῷ *by far*, Hdt., etc.   b. with a Sup., πολὺ πρῶτος, πολλὸν ἄριστος *far* the first, etc., Il., etc.:—also, πολλῷ πλεῖστοι Hdt.   c. in Att. with a Positive, ὦ πολλὰ μὲν τάλαινα, πολλὰ δ' αὖ σοφή Aesch.   IV. with Preps.,   1. διὰ πολλοῦ *at a great distance*, v. διά A. II. 2.   2. ἐκ πολλοῦ

from a great distance, Thuc.; for a long time, v. ἐκ II. 1. 3. ἐπὶ πολύ, a. over a great space, far, οὐκ ἐπὶ πολλόν Hdt. b. for a long time, long, Thuc. c. to a great extent, Plat.; so, ὡς ἐπὶ π. very generally, Thuc.; ὡς ἐπὶ τὸ π. for the most part, Id. 4. παρὰ πολύ, by far, v. παρά c. 1. 5. 5. περὶ πολλοῦ, v. supr. 1. 3. V. for Comp. πλείων, πλέων; Sup. πλεῖστος, v. sub vocc.

πολυσαρκία, ἡ, fleshiness, plumpness, Xen. From **πολύ-σαρκος**, ον, (σάρξ) very fleshy, Arist.

πολύ-σέβαστος, ον, the Lat. augustissimus, Anth.

πολύ-σεμνος, ον, exceeding venerable, Anth.

πολύ-σημάντωρ, ορος, ὁ, giving commands to many, h. Hom.

πολύ-σἰνής, ές, (σίνομαι) very hurtful, baneful, Aesch.

πολυσῖτία, ἡ, abundance of corn or food, Xen. From **πολύ-σῖτος**, ον, abounding in corn, Xen. II. high-fed, full of meat, Theocr.

πολύσκαλμος, ον, many-oared, Anth.

πολύ-σκαρθμος, ον, (σκαίρω) far-bounding, Il.

πολύ-σκηπτρος, ον, (σκῆπτρον) wide-ruling, Anth.

πολύ-σπᾰθής, ές, (σπάθη) thick-woven, Anth.

πολύσπαστος, ον, (σπάω) drawn by many cords:— πολύσπαστον, τό, a compound pulley, Plut.

πολύ-σπερής, ές, (σπείρω) wide-spread, Hom., Hes.

πολύ-σπλαγχνος, ον, of great mercy, N.T.

πολύ-σπορος, ον, (σπείρω) very fruitful, Eur.

πολυ-στάφῡλος [ᾰ], ον, rich in grapes, Il., Soph.

πολύ-στᾰχυς, υ, rich in ears of corn, Theocr.

πολύ-στεγος, ον, (στέγη) with many stories, Strab.

πολύ-στέλεχος, ον, with many stems, Anth.

πολυ-στένακτος, ον, causing many groans, Anth.

πολύ-στεφής, ές, (στέφω) decked with many a wreath, Aesch.; c. gen. wreathed with, δάφνης Soph.

πολυστῐχία, ἡ, a number of lines, Anth. From **πολύ-στῐχος**, ον, in many rows, Strab.

πολύ-στονος, ον, (στένω) much-sighing, mournful, Od., Aesch. 2. of things, causing many sighs, mournful, Il., Trag.

πολυστροφία, ἡ, convolution, Anth.

πολύ-στροφος, ον, (στρέφω) much-twisted, Anth.

πολύ-στῦλος, ον, with many columns, Strab., Plut.

πολυσύλλᾰβος, ον, (συλλαβή) polysyllabic, Luc.

πολυ-σχήμων, ον, (σχῆμα) of many shapes, varied in form, Strab.

πολύ-σχῐδής, ές, (σχίζω) = sq., Arist., Strab.

πολύ-σχιστος, ον, many-branching, κέλευθα Soph.

πολύ-σωρος, ον, rich in heaps of corn, Anth.

πολῠτάλαντος, ον, (τάλαντον) worth many talents, Luc. 2. possessing many talents, Id.

πολύ-ταρβής, ές, (τάρβος) much-frightened, Anth.

πολυτεκνία, ἡ, abundance of children, Arist. From **πολύ-τεκνος**, ον, with many children, prolific, Aesch.

πολυτέλεια, ἡ, extravagance, Hdt., Thuc. From **πολύ-τελής**, ές, (τέλος) very expensive, very costly, opp. to εὐτελής, Hdt., Thuc., etc. II. of persons, spending much, lavish, extravagant, Menand., etc.: —Adv. -λῶς, Xen.; Sup. -λέστατα, in the costliest manner, Hdt.

πολύ-τερπής, ές, (τέρπω) much-delighting, Anth.

πολῠ-τέχνης, ου, ὁ, skilled in divers arts, Solon.

πολυτεχνία, ἡ, skill in many arts, Plat. From

πολύτεχνος, ον, (τέχνη) skilled in many arts, Strab.

πολύτῑμητος [ῑ], ον, and η, ον, (τῑμάω) highly hon-oured, most honoured, Ar., Plat. II. very costly, Ar.

πολύ-τῑμος, ον, (τιμή) very costly, Anth., Babr.

πολύτῑτος, ον, (τίω) worthy of high honour, ap. Hdt.

πολύ-τλας, αντος, ὁ, (τλῆναι) having borne much, much-enduring, epith. of Ulysses, Hom., Soph.

πολυ-τλήμων, ονος, ὁ, ἡ, much-enduring, Hom., Ar.

πολύ-τλητος, ον, having borne much, miserable, Od.

πολύ-τμητος, ον, (τέμνω) much-lacerated, παρειά Anth.

πολύ-τρήρων, ωνος, ὁ, ἡ, abounding in doves, Il.

πολύ-τρητος, ον, much-pierced, full of holes, porous, Od.; of a flute, Anth.

πολύ-τρίπους [ῐ], ὁ, ἡ, abounding in tripods, Anth.

πολυτροπία, Ion. -ίη, ἡ, versatility, craft, Hdt. From **πολύ-τροπος**, ον, (τρέπω) much-turned, i.e. much-travelled, much-wandering, Lat. multum jactatus, of Ulysses, Od. II. turning many ways, of the polypus, Theogn. 2. metaph. shifty, versatile, wily, of Hermes, h. Hom., Plat.; τὸ π. τῆς γνώμης their versatility of mind, Thuc. III. various, mani-fold, Thuc.:—of diseases and war, changeful, compli-cated, Plut.:—Adv. -πως in many manners, N.T.

πολύ-τροφος, ον, (τρέφω) well-fed, Plut.

πολύ-ὑμνητος, ον, much-famed in song, Pind.

πολύ-ὑμνος, ον, much sung of, famous, Eur., Ar.

πολύφᾱμος, ον, Dor. for πολύφημος.

πολύ-φάρμᾰκος, ον, knowing many drugs or charms, Hom.

πολύ-φᾰτος, ον, (φημί) much-spoken-of, very famous, excellent, Pind.

πολύ-φημος, ον, Dor. -φᾱμος, ον, (φήμη) abounding in songs and legends, Od., Pind. II. many-voiced, wordy, Od.; ἐς πολύφημον ἐξενεῖκαι to bring it forth to the many-voiced, i.e. the agora (the 'parliament'), Orac. ap. Hdt.

πολυ-φθόρος, ον, (φθείρω) destroying many, deathful, rife with death or ruin, Pind., Aesch. II. pro-parox. πολύφθορος, ον, pass. utterly destroyed, Soph.

πολυφῐλία, ἡ, abundance of friends, Arist. From **πολύ-φῐλος**, ον, dear to many, Pind.

πολύ-φῐλτρος, ον, (φίλτρον) suffering from many love-charms, love-sick, Theocr.

πολύ-φλοισβος, ον, loud-roaring, θάλασσα Hom., etc.

πολύ-φονος, ον, murderous, Eur.

πολύφορβος, ον, and η, ον, (φορβή) feeding many, bountiful, Il., Hes.

πολυφορία, ἡ, productiveness, Xen. From **πολύ-φόρος**, ον, (φέρω) bearing much, Plat. II. that will bear much water, of strong wine: metaph., πολυφόρῳ δαίμονι συγκεκρᾶσθαι to have a fortune that wants tempering, Ar.

πολυ-φρᾰδής, ές, (φράζω) very eloquent or wise, Hes.

πολυφράδμων, ον, = πολυφραδής, Anth.

πολυφρόντιστος, ον, much-thinking, thoughtful, Anth.

πολυφροσύνη, ἡ, fulness of understanding, great shrewdness, Theogn., Hdt. From

πολύ-φρων, ονος, ὁ, ἡ, (φρήν) much-thinking, thought-ful, ingenious, inventive, Hom.

πολύ-φωνος, ον, (φωνή) much-talking, loquacious, Luc.

πολύ-χαλκος, ον, abounding in copper or brass, Hom. II. wrought of brass, all-brasen, Id.

πολῠ-χανδής, ές, (χανδάνω) wide-yawning, Theocr.

πολύ-χειρ, χειρος, ὁ, ἡ, with many hands, many-handed, Soph.   2. with many men, Aesch.

πολῠχειρία, ἡ, a multitude of hands, i. e. workmen or assistants, Thuc., Xen.

πολῠχορδία, ἡ, the use of many strings in the lyre, Plat.

πολύ-χορδος, ον, (χορδή) many-stringed, Theocr.: many-toned, of the flute, Plat.; also, π. ᾠδαί Eur.; π. γῆρυς the sound of many strings, Id.

πολυχρηματέω, f. ήσω, to abound in money, Strab.

πολυχρηματία, ἡ, greatness of wealth, Xen.

πολυ-χρήμᾰτος, ον, (χρῆμα) very wealthy.

πολυ-χρηστος, ον, useful for many purposes, Arist.

πολυ-χρόνιος, ον, long-existing, of olden time, ancient, h. Hom., Hdt., Xen.   II. lasting for long, Arist.:—Comp. -ώτερος, Plat.; Sup. -ώτατος, Xen.

πολύ-χρῦσος, ον, rich in gold, Hom.; of Aphrodité, Lat. aurea Venus, Hes.

πολυχρώμᾰτος, ον, = πολύχροος, Strab.

πολύ-χῠτος, ον, widely diffused, Plut.

πολύ-χωρος, ον, spacious, extensive, Luc.

πολύ-χωστος, ον, high-heaped, Aesch.

πολυψηφία, ἡ, number or diversity of votes, Thuc.

πολυ-ψήφῖς, ῖδος, ὁ, ἡ, with many pebbles, pebbly, of a river-bed, Orac. ap. Hdt.

πολύ-ψηφος, ον, = foreg., with many votes, Luc.

πολυ-ώδῠνος, ον, (ὀδύνη) very painful, Theocr.   II. pass. suffering great pain, Anth.

πολυ-ώνῠμος, ον, (ὄνομα) having many names, Plat.:—worshipped under many names, h. Hom., Soph.   II. of great name, famous, h. Hom., Hes.

πολυ-ωπής, ές, = sq., Anth.

πολυ-ωπός, όν, (ὠπή) with many meshes, δίκτυον Od.

πολυ-ωρέω, f. ήσω, (ὤρα) to be very careful, opp. to ὀλιγωρέω, Aeschin., Arist.

πολυ-ωφελής, ές, (ὄφελος) very useful, useful in many ways, Arist. Adv. -λῶς, Sup. -ωφελέστατα, Xen.

πολυώψ, ῶπος, ὁ, ἡ, = πολυωπός, Anth.

πομπαῖος, α, ον, (πομπή) escorting, conveying, Eur.; π. οὖρος a fair wind, Pind.   II. of Hermes, who escorted the souls of the dead, Aesch., Soph.

πομπεία, ἡ, (πομπεύω) a leading in procession, Polyb.   II. jeering, ribaldry, such as was allowed to those who took part in the processions at the festivals of Bacchus and Demeter, Dem.

πομπεῖον, τό, (πομπή) any vessel employed in solemn processions, Dem.   II. at Athens, a storehouse for such vessels, Id.

πομπεύς, gen. έως Ion. ῆος, ὁ, Att. pl. πομπῆς: (πομπός): —one who attends or escorts, a conductor, guide, Od.; of favourable winds, οὖροι πομπῆες νηῶν Ib.   2. one who attends a procession, Thuc.

πομπεύω, Ion. impf. πομπεύεσκον: (πομπή):—to conduct, escort, e. g. as a guide, Od.; Ἑρμοῦ τέχνην π. to use the escorting art of Hermes, Soph.   II. to lead a procession, π. πομπήν, Lat. pompam ducere, ap. Dem.:—Pass. to be led in triumph (at Rome), Plut.   2. absol. to march in a procession, Dem., Theocr.   III. to abuse with ribald jests (cf. πομπεία II), Dem.

πομπή, ἡ, (πέμπω) conduct, escort, guidance, Hom., etc.; οὐρία π. the conduct of a fair wind, Eur.   b.

concrete, an escort, Aesch., Eur.   2. a sending away, a sending home, Od.   3. a sending, mission, Hdt., Plat.: simply, a sending, ξύλων Thuc.   II. a solemn procession, Lat. pompa, ὑπὸ πομπῆς, σὺν πομπῇ in procession, Hdt.; μήλων κνισάεσσα πομπή the flesh of sheep for sacrifice carried in procession, Pind.; τὰς πομπὰς πέμπουσιν Dem.   2. τείνειν π. to lead a long procession, of a military expedition, Aesch., Eur. Hence

πομπικός, ή, όν, of or for a solemn procession, π. ἵππος a horse of state, Xen.:—metaph. pompous, showy, Plut.

πόμπῐμος, ον, and η, ον, (πομπή) conducting, escorting, guiding, Trag.:—c. gen., π. χώρα φίλων a land that lends escort to friends, Eur.; νόστου πόμπιμον τέλος the home-sending end of one's return, i. e. one's safe return, Pind.   II. pass. sent, conveyed, Soph., Eur.

πομπός, ὁ, (πέμπω) a conductor, escort, guide, Hom., Hdt.; of Hermes (cf. πομπαῖος), Soph.; πομποὶ attendants, guards, Id.: also πομπός, ἡ, a conductress, Od.   2. c. gen. rei, τῆσδε προστροπῆς π. conveyor, carrier of these suppliant offerings, Aesch.   3. a messenger, one who is sent for a person or thing, Soph.   II. as Adj., π. ἀρχαί the conducting chiefs, Aesch.; πῦρ πομπόν the missive fire, Id.

πομπο-στολέω, f. ήσω, to lead in procession, Strab.

πομφολῡγο-πάφλασμα, ατος, τό, the noise made by bubbles rising, Ar.

πομφολύζω, f. ξω, to bubble up, gush forth, Pind.

πομφόλυξ, ῠγος, ἡ, (πομφός) a bubble, Plat.

πονέω, πονέομαι, A. in early Greek only as Dep. πονέομαι, Ep. inf. -έεσθαι: impf. ἐπονεόμην, Ep. πονεῖτο: f. πονήσομαι: aor. 1 ἐπονησάμην, Ep. 3 sing. πονήσατο, also ἐπονήθην:—pf. πεπόνημαι, Ion. 3 pl. -έαται: 3 sing. plqpf. πεπόνητο: I. absol. to work hard, do work, suffer toil, Hom.; περὶ δόρπα πονέοντο were busied about their supper, Il.; so, πεπόνητο καθ' ἵππους was busy with the horses, of a charioteer, Ib.   2. metaph. to be in distress, to distress oneself, Ib.:—to suffer, be sick, Thuc.   II. c. acc. to work hard at, to make or do with pains or care, Hom., Hes.

B. after Hom., the act. form prevails: f. πονήσω: aor. ἐπόνησα, Dor. -ᾱσα:—pf. πεπόνηκα: 3 sing. plqpf. ἐπεπονήκει:—Pass., aor. 1 ἐπονήθην, Dor. subj. πονᾱθῇ (ᾱ): pf. πεπόνημαι: I. intr. to toil, labour, Theogn., Hdt., Att.; μάτην π. to labour in vain, Soph.; c. acc., τὰ μηδὲν ὠφελοῦντα μὴ πόνει do not labour at things that profit not, Aesch.   2. c. acc. cogn. π. πόνον, μόχθους to go through, suffer them, Trag.; also c. acc. partis, πονεῖν τὰ σκέλη Ar.   3. absol. to labour, be hard-pressed, suffer, Thuc., Xen.: to be worn out, spoilt, Dem.   4. Pass., impers., οὐκ ἄλλως αὐτοῖς πεπόνηται = πεπονήκασι, Plat.   II. trans., 1. c. acc. pers. to afflict, distress, Pind.:—Pass. to be worn out, to suffer greatly, Soph., Thuc.   b. Pass., also, to be trained or educated, Arist., Theocr.   2. c. acc. rei, like ἐκπονεῖν, to gain by toil or labour, χρήματα Xen.: Pass. to be won or achieved by toil, Pind. Hence

πόνημα, ατος, τό, that which is wrought out, work, Eur.: a work, book, Anth.

πονήρευμα, τό, a knavish trick, in pl., Dem. From

πονηρεύομαι, Dep. to be evil, act wickedly, play the rogue, Arist.; οἱ πεπονηρευμένοι Dem.

πονηρία, ἡ, (πονηρός) a bad state or condition, badness, Plat. II. in moral sense, wickedness, vice, knavery, Lat. pravitas, Id., Xen. : in pl. knavish tricks, rogueries, Dem. 2. baseness, cowardice, Eur.

πονηρο-διδάσκαλος, ον, teaching wickedness, Strab.

πονηρο-κράτέομαι, Pass. to be governed by the bad ; and πονηροκράτία, ἡ, government of the bad, Arist.

πονηρός, ά, όν, (πονέω) toilsome, painful, grievous, Theogn., Ar. II. in bad case, in sorry plight, useless, good-for-nothing, Ar., Plat., etc. :—Adv., πονηρῶς ἔχειν to be in bad case, Thuc. III. in moral sense, bad, worthless, knavish, Lat. pravus, improbus, Aesch., Eur. ; πονηρὸς κἀκ πονηρῶν rogue and son of rogues, Ar. ; πόνῳ πονηρός laboriously wicked, Id. :—ὁ π. the evil one, N. T. 2. base, cowardly, Soph. ; π. χρώματα the coward's hue, Xen.

πονηρό-φίλος, ον, fond of bad men, Arist.

πονητέον, verb. Adj. of πονέω, one must toil, Plat.

πόνος, ὁ, (πένομαι) work, esp. hard work, toil, Lat. labor, in Hom. mostly of war, μάχης π. the toil of battle, and π. alone = μάχη, πόνον ἔχειν, = μάχεσθαι, Il. ; ὁ Μηδικὸς π. battle with the Medes, Hdt. ; οἱ Τρωικοὶ πόνοι Id. 2. generally, toil, labour, Il., etc. 3. bodily exertion, exercise, Eur., Xen. ; ἐνάλιος π., i. e. fishing, Pind. 4. a work, task, business, ἐπεὶ π. ἄλλος ἔπειγεν Od., Soph. 5. implements for labour, stock in trade, Theocr. ; πόνος ἐντὶ θάλασσα the sea is their workshop, Mosch. II. the consequence of toil, distress, trouble, suffering, pain, Il., etc. III. anything produced by work, a work, τρητὸς μελισσᾶν π., of honey, Pind. ; τοὺς ἡμετέρους π. the fruits of our labour, Xen. IV. Πόνος a mythol. person, son of Eris, Hes.

ποντιάς, άδος, ἡ, poët. fem. of πόντιος, Pind., Eur.

ποντίζω, f. σω, (πόντος) to plunge in the sea, Aesch.

Ποντικός, ή, όν, from Pontus, Pontic, Π. δένδρεον, prob., the bird-cherry, Hdt.

πόντιος, α, ον, and ος, ον, (πόντος) of the sea, of Poseidon, h. Hom., Soph. ; π. δάκη sea monsters, Aesch. ; π. κύματα Id. ; ᾅδης πόντιος, i. e. death by drowning, Id. 2. by the sea, of places, Pind., Aesch. 3. in the sea, of islands, Pind. ; of ships, Aesch., etc. 4. of persons, δέχεσθαι ποντίους from the sea, Eur. ; ἀφιέναι πόντιον into the sea, Id. 5. brought by sea or from beyond sea, of iron, Aesch.

πόντισμα, ατος, τό, (ποντίζω) that which is cast into the sea, esp. as an offering, Eur.

ποντόθεν, Adv. from or out of the sea, Il.

ποντο-θήρης, ου, ὁ, one who fishes in the sea, Anth.

ποντο-μέδων, οντος, ὁ, lord of the sea, Pind., Aesch., etc.

πόντονδε, Adv. into the sea, Il.

Ποντο-πόρεια, ἡ, a Nereid, Sea-traverser, Hes.

ποντοπορέω, to pass over the sea, Ep. inf. -έμεναι Od. ; part. ποντοπορεύων sea-traversing, Ib.

ποντοπορεύω, f. ήσω, to pass the sea, νῆυς ποντοπορεύσα sea-sailing, Od. From

ποντο-πόρος, ον, (πορεύομαι) passing over the sea, seafaring, of ships, Hom., Soph.

Ποντο-ποσειδῶν, ῶνος, ὁ, Sea-Poseidon, Ar.

ΠΟ'ΝΤΟΣ, ου, ὁ: Ep. gen. ποντόφιν :—the sea, esp. the open sea, Hom., etc. II. of special seas, π. Ἰκάριος, Θρηίκιος Il. ; ὁ Αἰγαῖος π. Hdt. ; Ἰόνιος, Σαρω-

νικός, Σικελός, Eur. :—but most commonly, π. Εὔξεινος Id. ; ὁ Εὔξεινος π. Hdt. ; generally called simply ὁ Πόντος or Πόντος, Id., Att.

ποπάνευμα, ατος, τό, as if from ποπᾰνεύω, = sq., Anth.

πόπᾰνον, τό, (πέπτω) like πέμμα, a round cake, used at sacrifices, Ar.

πόπαξ, like πόποι, an exclamation, Aesch.

ποπάς, άδος, ἡ, = πόπανον, Anth.

πόποι, exclam. of surprise, anger or pain, ὢ πόποι oh strange! oh shame! Hom., Trag.

ποποποῖ, cry of the hoopoe, Ar.

ποππΰζω, Dor. -ύσδω : aor. 1 ἐπόππῠσα :—to whistle, cheep or chirp, Ar. II. of an inarticulate sound, commonly used by the Greeks in case of thunder, as a sort of charm, Id. III. in bad sense, to play ill on the flute, let the breath be heard in playing, Theocr.

ποππὕλιάζω, Dor. -άσδω, = foreg. 1, Theocr.

ποππυσμός, ὁ, (ποππύζω) a whistling, Xen.

πορεία, ἡ, (πορεύω) a walking, mode of walking or running, gait, Plat. II. a going, a journey, way, passage, Aesch., Plat. 2. a march, Thuc., Xen. 3. a crossing of water, passage, Aesch.

πορεῖν, aor. 2 inf., v. sub *πόρω.

πόρευμα, ατος, τό, a place in which one walks, βροτῶν πορεύματα their haunts, Aesch.

πορεύσιμος, ον, and η, ον, that may be crossed, passable, Xen. :—of a road, possible to pass, Eur.

πορευτέος, α, ον, verb. Adj. to be traversed, Soph., Xen. II. πορευτέον, one must go, Soph., Eur.

πορευτός, ή, όν, and ός, όν, gone over, passed, passable, Polyb. ; καιρὸς π. the season for travelling, Id. II. act. going, travelling, Aesch.

πορεύω, f. σω : aor. 1 ἐπόρευσα :—Med. and Pass., f. πορεύσομαι and πορευθήσομαι : aor. 1 ἐπορευσάμην and ἐπορεύθην : pf. πεπόρευμαι : (πόρος) : I. Act. to make to go, carry, convey, Pind., Soph. :—c. dupl. acc. to carry or ferry over, Νέσσος ποταμὸν βροτοὺς ἐπόρευσε Soph. ; γυναῖκ' λίμναν πορεύσας Eur. 2. of things, to bring, furnish, bestow, find, Id. II. Pass. and Med. to be driven or carried, Soph. 2. to go, walk, march, Hdt., Att. ; to go across, pass, Hdt., etc. ; c. acc. loci, to enter, π. στέγας Soph., etc. ; c. acc. cogn. μακρὰν ὁδὸν π. Xen. :—c. acc. loci, to go over, traverse, Id. 3. to walk, :—i. e. live, Soph.

πορθέω, f. ήσω, collat. form of πέρθω, to destroy, ravage, waste, plunder, Hom., Hdt., Trag. 2. in pres. and impf. to endeavour to destroy, to besiege a town, Hdt. : —to destroy, despoil, ruin, Aesch. :—in Pass. to be ruined, undone, Eur. Hence

πόρθημα, ατος, τό, = sq., Plut.

πόρθησις, ἡ, the sack of a town, Dem. ; and

πορθητής, οῦ, ὁ, a destroyer, ravager, Eur.

πορθήτωρ, ορος, ὁ, = πορθητής, Aesch.

πορθμεῖον, Ion. -ήιον, τό, (πορθμός) a place for crossing, a passage over, ferry, Hdt. II. a passage-boat, ferry-boat, Id., Xen. III. the fare of the ferry, ferryman's fee, Luc.

πόρθμευμα, ατος, τό, a passage, ferry, ὠκύπορον π. ἀχέων, of the river Acheron, Eur.

πορθμεύς, έως, Ion. ῆος, ὁ, a ferryman, Lat. portitor, Od., etc. ; π. νεκύων, of Charon, Eur. 2. generally, a boatman, seaman, Hdt., Theocr.

πορθμευτικός, ή, όν, engaged as a ferryman, Arist.

πορθμεύω, f. σω, (πορθμός) to carry or ferry over a strait, river, Lat. trajicere, Eur.; π. τινὰς εἰς Σαλαμῖνα Aeschin.: then, generally, to carry, bring, Trag.:—Pass. to be carried or ferried over, to pass from place to place, Hdt., Eur.; c. acc. loci, to pass through, Eur. II. the Act. is also used intr., like Lat. trajicere, to pass over, Anth.

πορθμήϊον, Ion. for πορθμεῖον.

πορθμίς, ίδος, ἡ, = πορθμεῖον II, a ship, boat, Eur.

πορθμός, ὁ, (περάω) a ferry or a place crossed by a ferry, a strait, firth, Od.; of the straits of Salamis, Hdt.; π. Ἕλλας the Hellespont, Aesch.; ὁ εἰς Ἅιδου π. the Styx, Eur. II. a crossing by a ferry, passage, Soph., Eur.; π. χθονός a passage to it, Eur.

πορίζω, f. Att. ποριῶ: aor. 1 ἐπόρισα: pf. πεπόρικα:—Med., f. Att. ποριοῦμαι: aor. 1 ἐπορισάμην:—Pass., f. πορισθήσομαι: aor. 1 ἐπορίσθην: pf. πεπόρισμαι: 3 sing. plqpf. ἐπεπόριστο: (πόρος). Properly, like πορεύω, to carry: to bring about, to furnish, provide, supply, procure, cause, Ar., Plat.; absol. θεοῦ ποριζόντος καλῶς Eur.:—often with a notion of contriving or inventing, Id., etc.:—Med. to furnish oneself with, to provide, procure, Lat. sibi comparare, Ar., Thuc.:—Pass. to be provided, Thuc., etc. 2. πορίζεταί τινι, impers., it is in one's power to do, c. inf., Xen.

πόριμος, ον, (πόρος) able to provide, full of resources, inventive, contriving, Ar.:—c. acc., ἄπορα πόριμος making possible the impossible, Aesch. II. pass. practicable, Luc. 2. well-provided, Thuc.

πόρις, ιος, ἡ, poët. for πόρτις, Od., Eur.

πορισμός, ὁ, (πορίζω) a providing, procuring, Polyb.: —a means of getting, Plut.: means of gain, N. T.

ποριστής, οῦ, ὁ, (πορίζω) one who supplies or provides, Thuc. 2. at Athens the πορισταί were a financial board appointed to raise extraordinary supplies, Procurators, Ar. 3. the name used by robbers of themselves, Conveyancers, Arist.

ποριστικός, ή, όν, (πορίζω) able to furnish, Xen.

ΠΟ´ΡΚΗΣ, ου, ὁ, a ring or hoop, passed round the joint of the spearhead and shaft, Il.

πορνεία, ἡ, fornication, prostitution, Dem.

πορνεῖον, τό, a house of ill-fame, brothel, Ar.

πορνεύω, to prostitute:—Pass., of a woman, to be or become a prostitute, Hdt., Dem., etc. II. intr. in Act.=Pass., Luc. From

πόρνη, ἡ, (πέρνημι) a harlot, prostitute, Ar.

πορνίδιον, τό, Dim. of πόρνη, Ar., etc.

πορνικός, ή, όν, (πόρνη) of or for harlots, π. τέλος the tax paid by brothel-keepers, Aeschin.

πορνοβοσκέω, f. ήσω, to keep a brothel, Ar.

πορνοβοσκία, ἡ, the trade of a brothel-keeper, Aeschin.

πορνο-βοσκός, ὁ, a brothel-keeper, Aeschin., Dem.

πορνο-φίλας, ὁ, (φιλέω) loving harlots, Anth.

πόρος, ὁ, (περάω) a means of passing a river, a ford, ferry, Lat. vadum, Il., Hdt., etc.; Πλούτωνος π. the Stygian ferry, Aesch. 2. a narrow sea, strait, firth, Lat. fretum, Hes., Aesch.; Ἰόνιος π. the Ionian sea which is the passage-way from Greece to Italy, Pind.:—ἐν πόρῳ in the passage-way (of ships), in the 'fair-way' Hdt. 3. periphr., πόροι ἁλός the paths of the sea, i.e. the sea, Od.; ἐνάλιοι π.

Aesch., etc.; so, of rivers, πόρος Ἀλφεοῦ, Σκαμάνδρου, i. e. the Alphëus, etc., Pind. 4. a way over a river, a bridge, Hdt. 5. generally a pathway, way, Aesch., Soph.; πόρος οἰωνῶν their pathway, Aesch. 6. a passage through the skin, οἱ πόροι the pores, Plat. II. c. gen. rei, a way or means of achieving, accomplishing, οὐκ ἐδύνατο π. οὐδένα ἀνευρεῖν Hdt.; π. ὁδοῦ a means of performing the journey, Ar.; π. κακῶν a means of averting evils, Eur.:—c. inf., πόρος τις τίσασθαι Id. 2. absol. a means of providing, contrivance, device, resource, Aesch., Ar. 3. at Athens, π. χρημάτων a way of getting or raising money, Xen., Dem.: in pl., 'ways and means,' resources, revenue, Dem. III. a going, journey, voyage, Aesch., Eur.

πόρπαμα, ατος, τό, (πορπάω) a garment fastened with a πόρπη, in pl., Eur.

πόρπαξ, ακος, ὁ, the handle of a shield, Soph., Eur., etc.; ἔχουσι πόρπακας [αἱ ἀσπίδες], i. e. they are ready for use, Ar. II. part of a horse's headgear, Eur.

πορπάω, Att. aor. 1 imper. πόρπασον (not -ησον) to fasten with a buckle, to buckle or pin down, Aesch.

πόρπη, ἡ, (πείρω) = περόνη, a buckle-pin, Eur.;—in pl. a buckle or brooch, Il., Eur.

πόρρω, -ωθεν, -ωτέρω, -ωθεν, v. sub πρόσω, πρόσωθεν.

πορσαίνω, v. πορσύνω.

πορσεῖον, πόρσιστα, v. sub πρόσω.

πορσύνω [ῡ]: f. -ῠνῶ, Ep. -ῠνέω: also πορσαίνω, Ep. f. -ανέω: (*πόρω):—to offer, present what one has prepared, in Hom. of the wife preparing her husband's bed. II. generally, to make ready, prepare, provide, Soph., Eur., etc.:—Med. to provide for oneself, get ready, Aesch. 2. of evils, ἐχθροῖς π. ἐχθρά Id.; π. τοῖς πολεμίοις κακά Xen.:—Pass., ἐπορσύνθη κακά 3. to arrange, adjust, manage, π. τὰ τοῦ θεοῦ Hdt.; τάδε Soph., etc. III. to treat with care, tend, Pind., etc.

πόρσω, v. sub πρόσω.

πόρταξ, ακος, ἡ, = πόρτις, a calf, Il.

πορτί, v. προτί.

ΠΟ´ΡΤΙΣ, ιος, ἡ, a calf, young heifer, Il., Soph.:—a young cow, Theocr., Mosch.

πορτι-τρόφος, ον, (τρέφω) nourishing calves, h. Hom.

πορφύρα [ῠ], Ion. -ρη, ἡ, (πορφύρω) the purple-fish, Lat. murex, Aesch. II. purple dye, purple, Hdt. III. = πορφυρίς, purple raiment, Aesch.

πορφύρεος, η, ον, Att. -οῦς, ᾶ, ον: I. Homeric usage (from πορφύρω), 1. of the swoln sea, dark-gleaming, dark; so, π. νεφέλη. 2. of blood, Il.; π. θάνατος, of death in battle, Ib. 3. of stuff, cloths, etc., dark, russet. 4. of the rainbow, prob. bright, lustrous; and of serpents glittering.—Hom. seems not to have known the πορφύρα, so that the word does not imply any definite colour. II. after Hom. (from πορφύρα) dark red, purple or crimson, Pind., Hdt., Trag. 2. purple-clad, in purple, Luc.

πορφυρεύς, έως, ὁ, a fisher for purple fish, Hdt.

πορφῠρευτικός, ή, όν, of or for a purple-dyer, Eur.

πορφῠρεύω, to catch purple fish.

πορφῠρίς, ίδος, ἡ, (πορφύρα) a purple garment or covering, Xen. II. a red-coloured bird, Ar.

πορφῠρίων, ωνος, ὁ, (πορφύρα) the water-hen, Ar.

πορφύρο-ειδής, ές, (εἶδος) purple-like, purply, Eur.
πορφύρο-πώλης, ου, ὁ, (πωλέω) a dealer in purple, fem.
πορφύρό-πωλις, ιδος, N. T.
πορφύρό-στρωτος, ον, spread with purple cloth, Aesch.
πορφύροῦς, ᾶ, οῦν, Att. contr. for πορφύρεος.
πορφύρω [ῡ], only in pres. and impf., properly of the sea, ὡς ὅτε πορφύρη πέλαγος μέγα κύματι κωφῷ as when the huge sea gleams darkly with dumb swell (i. e. with waves that do not break), Il. 2. metaph., πολλὰ δέ οἱ κραδίη πόρφυρε much was his heart troubled, Hom. II. after Hom., when the purple-fish (πορφύρα) and its dye became known, to grow purple or red, Bion, Anth. :—so in Med., εὔδια μέν Anth. (Prob. redupl. from φύρω.)
*ΠΟ΄ΡΩ, assumed as pres. to the aor. 2 ἔπορον and pf. pass. πέπρωμαι: I. aor. 2 ἔπορον, Ep. 3 sing. πόρε, inf. πορεῖν, part. πορών, to furnish, offer, present, give, Hom., Hes. ; εὖχος π. to fulfil a wish, Od. ; ὅρκον π. to offer to take an oath, Aesch. 2. to grant that . . , πόρε κούρησιν ἕπεσθαι τιμάς (for ὥστε ἕπεσθαι) Il. ; σοὶ θεοὶ πόροιεν, ὡς (= οἷα) ἐγὼ θέλω Soph. 2. = πορεύω, to bring, εἴ τις δεῦρο Θησέα πόροι Id. II. pf. only in 3 sing. πέπρωται, plqpf. πέπρωτο, it has or had been (is or was) fated, foredoomed, c. acc. pers. et inf., ἄμφω πέπρωται γαῖαν ἐρεῦσαι it is fated that both should redden earth, Il. ; τί γὰρ πέπρωται Ζηνὶ πλὴν ἀεὶ κρατεῖν; Aesch. ; so, πεπρωμένον ἐστί = πέπρωται, Id., Xen. 2. part. as Adj., πεπρωμένος, η, ον, allotted, fated to one, Il. ; of persons, destined to a thing, αἴσῃ Ib. :—absol. destined, Pind. ; πεπρ. βίος one's natural life (as in Lat. mors fatalis is a natural death), Id. ; so in Trag. and Xen. : ἡ πεπρωμένη (sc. μοῖρα), an appointed lot, Fate, Destiny, Hdt., Trag.
*πός; who? Pron., traced in the interrog. forms, πού, ποί, πῇ, πῶς, πω, πόθι, πόθεν, πότε, πότερος, πόσος, ποῖος, πόσος, to each of which there is a corresponding enclitic form, που, ποι, πη, πως, etc. ;—in these forms π in Ion. Gr. is represented by κ, as κού, κοῖ, etc.
ποσάκις [ᾰ], Adv. how many times? how often? Lat. quoties? Ep. Plat.
ποσα-πλάσιος, α, ον, how many times multiplied? how many fold? Lat. quotuplex? Plat. 2. c.gen. what multiple of . . ? Id.
ποσά-πους, ποδος, ὁ, ἡ, of how many feet? Plat.
ποσᾰχῶς, Adv. in how many ways? Arist.
πόσε, Adv. = ποῖ; whither? Hom.
Ποσειδάνιος, Dor. for Ποσειδώνιος.
Ποσειδεών, ῶνος, ὁ, the sixth month of the Athen. year, = latter half of December and former of January.
Ποσειδῶν, ὁ ; gen. ῶνος, acc. Ποσειδῶ, voc. Πόσειδον· Ep. Ποσειδάων [ᾰ], ἄωνος, acc. ἄωνα, voc. Ποσείδαον· Ion. Ποσειδέων, έωνος : Dor. Ποτῖδᾶν or Ποτειδᾶν, ᾶνος, acc. ᾶνα, voc. ᾶν :—Poseidon, Lat. Neptunus, son of Cronos and Rhea, brother of Zeus, god of the sea, husband of Amphitrité, Hom., etc. Hence
Ποσειδώνιος, α, ον, sacred to Poseidon, Eur. :—poët.
Ποσειδαώνιος and -ώνιος, Soph., Anth. : Dor. Ποσειδάνιος [ᾱ], Pind. II. Ποσειδώνιον (sc. ἱερόν), τό, the temple of Poseidon, Thuc. III. Ποσειδώνια, τά, his festival, Strab.
πόσθη, ἡ, (v. πέος) membrum virile, Ar.
πόσθων, ωνος, ὁ, comic word for a little boy, Ar.

ποσί, dat. pl. of πούς.
Ποσίδηιος, η, ον, Ion. for Ποσίδειος, sacred to Poseidon, Il. II. Ποσῐδήιον, τό, Ion. for Ποσίδειον, the temple of Poseidon, Od.
ποσίνδα, Adv. (πόσος) how many times? π. παίζειν = ἀρτιάζειν, Xen.
ΠΟ΄ΣΙΣ, ὁ, poët. πόσσις : gen. πόσιος, dat. πόσει, Ep. πόσεϊ : voc. πόσι or πόσις : pl. πόσεις : acc. πόσιας : a husband, spouse, mate, Hom., etc. ; κρυπτὸς π., of a paramour, Eur.
πόσῐς, ιος, Att. εως, ἡ : dat. πόσει, Ion. πόσι : (ΠΟ, Root of some tenses of πίνω) :—a drinking, drink, beverage, Hom. ; συγγίνεσθαι ἐς πόσιν to meet for a carousal, Hdt. ; παρὰ τὴν πόσιν, Lat. inter pocula, over their cups, Id. ; πόσιος ἐν βάθει Theocr. 2. a draught, Aesch.
πόσος; Ion. and Aeol. κόσος, η, ον ; interrog. Adj. corresponding to the relat. ὅσος and demonstr. τόσος, Lat. quantus? of what quantity? opp. to πηλίκος (which refers to bulk), often with τις added : 1. of Number, how many? Hdt., Att. : with sing. Nouns, how great? how much? π. τι πλῆθος; Aesch. 2. of Distance, how far? Xen. 3. of Time, how long? Soph., etc. 4. of Value, how much? Ar. ; πόσου; for how much? at what price? Lat. quanti? Id. ; so, ἐπὶ πόσῳ; Plat. II. ποσός, ή, όν, (oxyt.), indef. Adj. of a certain quantity or magnitude, Lat. aliquantus, Id., etc. Hence
ποσόω, to reckon up, count, τὰς ψήφους Theophr.
ποσσ-ῆμαρ, Adv. for how many days? Il.
ποσσί, ίν, Ep. for ποσί, ίν, dat. pl. of πούς.
ποσσί-κροτος, ον, struck with the foot in dancing, Orac. ap. Hdt.
ποσταῖος, α, ον, (πόστος) in how many days? Lat. quota die?
πόστος, η, ον, (πόσος) which of a number? Lat. quotus? πόστον δὴ ἔτος ἐστὶν ὅτε ξείνισσας ἐκεῖνον; how many years is it since . . ? Od. :—in indirect questions, πόστῳ μέρει with how small a part, Xen.
πότ, apocop. for ποτί, Dor. for πρός.
πότα, Aeol. for πότε.
πότ-ᾰγε, Dor. for πρόσ-αγε, Theocr.
ποτ-αείδω, Dor. for προσ-αείδω.
ποτ-αίνιος, α, ον, and ος, ον, (ποτί = πρός, αἶνος?) fresh, new, Lat. recens, Pind., Aesch. 2. metaph. new, unexpected, unheard of, Aesch., Soph.
ποτ-αμέλγω, f. ξω, Dor. for προσαμέλγω, Theocr.
ποτάμιος, α, ον, and ος, ον, (ποτᾰμός) of or from a river, Aesch., Eur. ; οἱ Ἵπποι οἱ π., v. ἱπποπόταμος.
ποτᾰμό-κλυστος, ον, (κλύζω) washed by a river, Strab.
ποτᾰμόν-δε, Adv. to or towards a river, Hom. From
ποτᾰμός, οῦ, ὁ, (ΠΟ, Root of some tenses of πίνω) a river, stream, Hom., etc. :—proverb., ἄνω ποταμῶν χωροῦσι παγαί, of extraordinary events, Eur. :—of rivers of fire or lava, Pind. II. as a person, Ποταμός, a river-god, Il.
ποτᾰμο-φόρητος, ον, carried away by a river, N. T.
ποτᾰμό-χωστος, ον, deposited by a river, Strab.
ποτᾰνής, ές, Dor. for προσηνής.
ποτᾰνός, ά, όν, Dor. for ποτηνός, winged, flying, furnished with wings, Pind., Eur. ; ἐν ποτανοῖς among

fowls, Pind. :—metaph., ποτανὸς ἐν Μοίσαισι, i. e. *soaring* in the arts of the Muses, Id.; ποτανᾷ μαχανᾷ by *soaring* art, i. e. by poesy, Id. From

ποτάομαι, Ep. -έομαι, Frequent. of πέτομαι; Dor. part. ποτήμενος: f. ποτήσομαι: aor. 1 ἐποτήθην, Dor. -άθην [ᾱ]: pf. πεπότημαι, Dor. -ᾱμαι, Ep. 3 pl. πεποτήαται: 3 sing. plqpf. πεπότητο:—*to fly about,* Hom.; κεραυνοὶ ποτέοντο Hes.: simply = πέτομαι, *to fly,* Aesch., Eur.; τὰ ποτήμενα συλλαβεῖν, of vain pursuits, Theocr. :—pf. (with pres. sense), *to be upon the wing,* Hom.   II. metaph. *to hover,* Aesch.   2. *to be on the wing, be fluttered,* Eur., Ar.

ποτ-αυλέω, Dor. for προσ-αυλέω.

ποτ-ᾱῷος, ῴα, ῷον, Dor. for προσ-ηῷος.

πότε, Ion. **κότε,** Dor. **πόκα,** (*πός) interrog. Particle used in direct and indirect questions, corresponding to the relat. ὅτε, ὁπότε and demonstr. τότε, *when? at what time?* Hom.; ποτ', εἰ μὴ νῦν Aesch.; also, ἐς πότε λήξει; Soph.   II. **ποτέ,** Ion. **κοτέ,** Dor. **ποκά,** enclit. Particle: 1. *at some time or other, at some time,* Hom., etc.   2. *at any time, ever,* Soph., etc.; often after relat. words, ὅστις ποτέ, ὅστις δήποτε, ὅστις δηποτοῦν, v. δήποτε; also after πω, v. πώποτε; and after negatives, when it often becomes one word with the negat., οὔποτε, μήποτε, οὐδέποτε, μηδέποτε.   3. in correl. clauses it stands first, with accent, ποτὲ μέν . . , ποτὲ δέ . . , *at one time . . , at another . . ,* Lat. *modo . . , modo . . ,* Plat.   III. of some unknown point of time, 1. the past, *once, erst,* Il., Trag.; in telling a story, *once upon a time,* Ar.   2. the future, *at some time,* Il., etc. :—with imperat., Lat. *tandem aliquando,* Soph.   3. in questions, τίς ποτε; Lat. *qui tandem? who in the world?* Aesch., etc.; v. τίποτε; τίπτε.

Ποτειδᾶν, Ποτείδαν, Dor. for Ποσειδῶν.

ποτέομαι, Ep. for ποτάομαι.

ποτεῖδον, ποτιδών, Dor. for προσεῖδον, προσιδών.

ποτένθης, Dor. for προσέλθης.

ποτέος, α, ον, verb. Adj. of πίνω, *drinkable.*   II. ποτέον, *one must drink,* Plat.

ποτ-ερίσδω, Dor. for προσ-ερίζω.

πότερος, α, ον; Ion. **κότερος,** η, ον; (*πός) :—*whether of the two?* Lat. *uter?* both in direct and indirect questions, ὁπότερος being the relat. form., Il., Hdt., Att.   II. neut. πότερον, πότερα, as Adv. at the beginning of an interrog. sentence containing two alternative propositions, πότερον . . , ἤ . . , Lat. *utrum . . , an . . , whether . . or . . ,* τίνες κατῆρξαν, πότερον Ἕλληνες ἢ παῖς ἐμός; Aesch.; πότερ' ἄκων ἢ ἑκών; Dem.   2. sometimes a third clause (with ἤ) is inaccurately added, πότερα παρὰ δήμου ἢ ὀλιγαρχίης ἢ μουνάρχου; Hdt.   3 the second alternative is sometimes left to be supplied, πότερα δὴ κερτομῶν λέγεις τάδε [ἢ μή . .]; Soph.   III. without interrog., like ἅτερος, *either of the two,* Lat. *alteruter,* Plat.

ποτ-έρχομαι, Dor. for προσ-έρχομαι.

ποτέρωθι; Adv. (πότερος) *on whether of the two sides? on which side* (of two)? Xen., etc.

ποτέρως, Adv. of πότερος, *in which of two ways?* Lat. *utro modo?* Xen., etc.   2. in indirect questions, διορίσαι π. λέγεις *to define which* you mean, Plat.

ποτ-έχω, Dor. for προσ-έχω.

ποτή, ἡ, = πτῆσις, *flight,* Od.

πότημα, ατος, τό, (ποτάομαι) *a flight,* Aesch.

ποτήρ, ῆρος, ὁ, (ΠΟ, Root of some tenses of πίνω) *a drinking-cup, wine-cup,* Eur.

ποτήριον, τό, (ΠΟ, Root of some tenses of πίνω) *a drinking-cup, wine-cup,* Hdt., Att.

ποτής, ῆτος, ἡ, (ΠΟ, Root of some tenses of πίνω) *a drinking, drink,* Hom.

πότης, ου, ὁ, fem. **πότις** (ΠΟ, Root of some tenses of πίνω) *a drinker, tippler, toper* :—metaph., πότης λύχνος *a tippling* lamp, i. e. that consumes much oil, Ar.: Comic Sup., ποτίστατος, Id.

ποτητός, ή, όν, (ποτάομαι) *flying, winged* : ποτητά, τά, *fowls, birds,* Od.

ποτί [ῐ], Dor. for πρός, also used by Hom. and Hes. and Trag.; in compds., as ποτινίσσομαι. Cf. προτί.

ποτι-βλέπω, Dor. for προσ-βλέπω.

Ποτῑδᾶς, Ποτῑδάν, Ποτῑδάων, Dor. for Ποσειδῶν, q. v.: hence the name of the Dor. city Ποτίδαια, ἡ, Ar., etc.:—**Ποτῑδαιάτης,** Ion. **-ήτης,** ὁ, *a Potidaean,* Hdt., etc.; **Ποτῑδαιατικός,** ή, όν, *Potidaean,* Thuc.

ποτῑδέγμενος, Dor. part. of προσδέχομαι, also in Hom.

ποτῑδεῖν, Dor. for προσιδεῖν.

ποτῑ-δέρκομαι, Dor. for προσ-δέρκομαι, also in Hom.

ποτι-δεύομαι, Dor. for προσ-δέομαι.

ποτι-δόρπιος, ον, Dor. form used by Hom. (the common form προσ-δόρπιος not in use), *of* or *serving for supper,* ὄβριμον ἄχθος ὕλης ἵνα οἱ ποτιδόρπιον εἴη that it might *serve to dress his supper,* Od.

ποτίζω, Dor. **ποτίσδω,** f. ίσω and ιῶ, (πότος) *to give to drink,* c. dupl. acc., τοὺς ἵππους νέκταρ ἐπότισε *gave* them nectar *to drink,* Plat.; ποτήριον π. τινά N. T.   2. *to water* the ground, Xen.; *to water* cattle, Theocr.

ποτί-θει, Dor. for πρός-θες.

ποτί-κλίνω, Dor. for προσ-κλίνω, Od.

ποτικός, ή, όν, (πότος) *fond of drinking,* Plut. : Adv., ποτικῶς ἔχειν *to be given to drinking,* Id.

ποτί-κρᾶνον, τό, Dor. for πρόσ-κρᾶνον, *a cushion,* Theocr.

ποτι-λέγω, ποτι-μάσσω, Dor. for προσ-.

πότιμος, ον, (πότος) *of water, drinkable, fresh,* Hdt., Xen., etc.   2. metaph. *fresh, sweet, pleasant,* Plat. :—of persons, *mild, gentle,* Theocr.

ποτι-μυθέομαι, Dor. for προσ-μυθέομαι.

ποτι-νίσσομαι, Dor. for προσ-νίσσομαι, Aesch.

ποτι-πίπτω, Dor. for προσ-πίπτω, Aesch.

ποτι-πτήσσω, Dor. for προσ-πτήσσω (not in use), *to crouch* or *cower towards,* c. gen., ἀκταὶ λιμένος ποτιπεπτηῦϊαι (Ep. pf. part. fem. for προσπεπτηκυῖαι) *verging towards* it, so as to shut it in, Od.

ποτι-πτύσσω, Dor. for προσ-πτύσσω, Od.

πότις, ιδος, fem. of πότης.

ποτι-στάζω, Dor. for προσ-στάζω.

ποτι-τέρπω, Dor. for προσ-τέρπω, Od.

ποτι-τρόπαιος, ον, Dor. for προσ-τροπαῖος, Aesch.

ποτι-φωνήεις, εσσα, εν, Dor. for προσ-φωνήεις, Od.

πότμος, ὁ, (ΠΕΤ, Root of πίπτω) *that which befals one, one's lot, destiny* : commonly of *evil destiny, death,* of the killer, πότμον ἐφείναι, or of the killed, πότμον ἐπισπεῖν, Hom.;—also in Pind. and Trag.   2. without a sense of *evil,* π. συγγενής *one's natural gifts,* Pind.; εὐτυχεῖ πότμῳ Aesch.; π. ξυνήθης πατρός *my*

father's customary *fortune*, Soph. [Penult. often short in Trag.]

πότνᾰ, ἡ, shorter form of πότνια, πότνα θεά Od. ; πότνα θεῶν h. Hom. ; πότνα θεῶν Eur.

πότνιᾰ, ἡ, (from same Root as πόσ-ις, δεσ-πότ-ης) a poët. title of honour, used chiefly in addressing goddesses or ladies : 1. = δέσποινα, *mistress, queen*, c. gen., πότνια θηρῶν (nom.) *queen* of wild beasts, Lat. *potens ferarum*, Il. ; πότνια βέλεων Pind. : absol., πότνι' Ἐρινύς Aesch. ; often in voc., ὦ πότνι' Ἥρα Id. ; ὦ πότνια (sc. Ἀθηναία) Ar. :—in pl. of the Eumenides, Hdt., Soph. ; also of Demeter and Proserpine, Soph., etc. 2. as Adj. *revered, august*, Hom.

Ποτνιαί, αἱ, an ancient Boeot. town, Strab. :—hence fem. Adj. Ποτνιάς, άδος, *Potnian*, Ποτνιάδες ἵπποι *Boeotian* mares, noted for their hot temper, hence *raging, furious*, Eur. Hence

ποτνιάομαι, Dep. *to cry* or *lament aloud, shriek, howl*, Plut., Luc.

ποτνιασμός, ὁ, *lamentation*, Strab.

ποτ-οπτάζω, Dor. verb, = προσ-οράω, Anth.

πότ-ορθρος, Dor. for πρόσ-ορθρος.

ποτός, ή, όν, verb. Adj. (ΠΟ, Root of some tenses of πίνω) *drunk, fit for drinking*, Aesch., Eur. II. as Subst., ποτόν, τό, *that which one drinks, drink*, esp. of wine, Hom., Hdt., Att. ; σῖτα καὶ ποτά *meat and drink*, Hdt. 2. πάτριον π. *drink* of my sires, Aesch. ; π. κρηναῖον Soph.

πότος, ὁ, (ΠΟ, Root of some tenses of πίνω) *drinking, a drinking-bout, carousal*, Xen. ; παρὰ πότον, Lat. *inter pocula*, Id. ; ἐν τοῖς πότοις Aeschin.

ποτ-όσδω, Dor. for προσ-όζω.

ποτ-τῶ, ποτ-τῷ, ποτ-τόν, ποτ-τώς, ποτ-τάν, Dor. for πρὸς τῶ, πρὸς τῷ, etc.

ποτ-ῴκειν, Dor. for προσ-εοίκειν.

ποῦ; Ion. κοῦ; interrog. Adv., in direct or indirect questions, corresponding to the relat. ὅπου, (properly a gen. of *πός; quis?*), *where?* Lat. *ubi?* Hom., etc. : —c. gen. loci, ποῦ γῆς; ποῦ χθονός; *where* in the world? Lat. *ubinam terrarum?* Aesch., etc. ; so, ποῦ ποτ' εἶ φρενῶν; Soph. ; ποῦ γνώμης εἶ; Id. ; ποῦ τύχης; *at what point of fortune?* Id. II. of manner, *how?* Eur. ; to express an inference very strongly, κοῦ γε δὴ . . οὐκ ἂν χωσθείη κόλπος . . ; *how* then would it not . . ? i. e. it certainly would . . , Hdt. ; also in Trag., in indignant questions, *how? by what right?* ποῦ σὺ μάντις εἶ σοφός; Soph.

πού, Ion. κού, enclit. Adv. *anywhere, somewhere*, Hom., etc. ; often with other Advs. of Place, οὐχ ἑκάς που *somewhere* not far off, Soph. ; πέλας που ; ἄλλοθι που Dem. :—c. gen., ἀλλά που αὐτοῦ ἀγρῶν in *some part* there of the fields, Od. ; εἴ που τῆς χώρας τοῦτο συνέβη Dem. II. also without reference to Place, *in some degree*, καί πού τι Thuc. :—often to qualify an expression, *anyway, possibly, perhaps, I suppose, I ween*, Hom., etc. ; εἴ που, ἐάν που, εἰ μή που Xen. ; τί που . . ; *what in the world?* Aesch. ; with numerals, δέκα κου *about* ten, Hdt. :—οὔ τί που denies with indignation or wonder, *surely it cannot be*, Soph., etc. ; whereas οὐ δήπου adds a suspicion that it is so, οὐ δήπου Στράτων; Ar.

πουλῠ-βότειρα, ἡ, Ion. for πολυ-βότειρα.

πουλύπους, ὁ, v. πολύπους.

πουλύς, πουλύ, Ep. for πολύς, πολύ.

ΠΟΥΣ, ὁ, ποδός, ποδί, πόδα : pl. dat. ποσί, Ep. ποσσί, πόδεσσι : dual gen. and dat. ποδοῖν, Ep. ποδοῖιν :—*a foot*, Lat. *pes, pedis*, Hom., etc. ; in pl., also, a bird's *talons*, Od. ; *the arms* of a polypus, Hes. ; ξύλινος π., of an artificial foot, Hdt. : phrases in respect to the footrace, περιγιγνόμεθ' ἄλλων πόδεσσιν, to be better than others in running, Od. ; ποσὶν ἐρίζειν to race *on foot*, Il. ; ποσὶ νικᾶν, ἀέθλια ποσσὶν ἄροντο Hom. :—the dat. ποσί is added to all kinds of Verbs denoting motion, ποσὶ βῆναι, δραμεῖν, ὀρχεῖσθαι, etc. ; for πόδα βαίνειν, v. βαίνω A. II. 3 :—metaph., νόστιμον ναῦς ἐκίνησεν πόδα started on its homeward way, Eur. 2. as a mark of close proximity, πρόσθεν ποδός or ποδῶν, προπάροιθε ποδῶν just before one, Hom. ; πὰρ ποδί *close at hand*, Pind. ; but, παρά or πὰρ ποδός *off-hand, at once*, Theogn. :—so, παρὰ πόδα *in a moment*, Soph. ; παρὰ πόδας Plut. :—πρὸ ποδῶν, like ἐμποδών, *close at hand*, Hdt., Att. ; τὰ πρὸς ποσί Soph. :—these phrases are opp. to ἐκ ποδῶν, out of *the way, far off*, Hdt. (cf. ἐκποδών). 3. to denote close pursuit, κατὰ πόδα on the track, Lat. *e vestigio*, Id., Att. ; c. gen. pers., κατὰ πόδας τινὸς ἔρχεσθαι, ἰέναι to come close *at his heels*, Hdt. 4. various phrases : ἐπὶ πόδα *backwards, facing the enemy*, ἐπὶ π. ἀναχωρεῖν, ἀνάγειν, ἀναχάζεσθαι to retire *leisurely*, Lat. *pedetentim*, Xen. b. περὶ πόδα, properly of a shoe, *round the foot*, i. e. *fitting exactly*, Theophr., Luc. c. ὡς ποδῶν ἔχει as he is off *for feet*, i. e. as quick as he can, Hdt. d. ἔξω τινὸς πόδα ἔχειν to have *one's foot* out of a thing, i. e. be clear of it, ἔξω κομίζου πηλοῦ πόδα Aesch. ; πημάτων ἔξω πόδα ἔχειν Id. :—opp. to εἰς ἄντλον ἐμβῆσαι πόδα, Eur. e. to denote energetic action, ἀμφοῖν ποδοῖν, Ar. ; βοηθεῖν ποδὶ καὶ χειρὶ καὶ πάσῃ δυνάμει Aeschin. ; for ὀρθῷ ποδί, v. ὀρθός II. 5. πούς τινος, periphr. for a person, σὺν πατρὸς μολὼν ποδί, i. e. σὺν πατρί, Eur. ; παρθένου δέχου πόδα Id. :—also, ἐξ ἑνὸς ποδός, i. e. μόνος ὤν, Soph. ; οἱ ἀφ' ἡσύχου π., i. e. οἱ ἡσύχως ζῶντες, Eur. II. metaph. of things, *the foot* or *lowest part*, esp. *the foot* of a hill, Lat. *pes montis*, Il., etc. 2. in a ship, are *the lower corners* of the sail or *the ropes fastened thereto, the sheets*, Od. ; χαλᾶν πόδα to slack away or ease off *the sheet*, Eur. ; τοῦ ποδὸς παριέναι to let go hold of it, Ar. ; ἐκπετάσαι πόδα (with reference to the sail), Eur. :—opp. to τείνειν πόδα, to haul *it* tight, Soph. ; ναῦς ἐνταθεῖσα ποδί a ship with her *sheet* close hauled, Eur. III. *a foot*, as a measure of length, 4 palms (παλασταί) or 6 fingers, about ⅓ of an inch longer than our foot, Hdt., etc. IV. *a foot* in Prosody, Ar., Plat.

ποῶ, = ποιῶ, ποιέω.

πο-ώδης, Ion. ποι-ώδης, ες, (πόα, εἶδος) *like grass, grassy*, Hdt., etc.

πρᾶγμα, Ion. πρῆγμα, τό, (πράσσω) *that which has been done, a deed, act*, Lat. *facinus*, Hdt., Att. ; τῶν πραγμάτων πλέον *more than facts*, Eur. ; τὸ σὸν τί ἐστι τὸ πρ. *what is your work in life?* Plat. ; γυναῖον πρ. ποιεῖν to do a woman's *work*, Dem. II. like Lat. *res, a thing, matter, affair*, Hdt., Att. ; σφισί τε καὶ Ἀθηναίοις εἶναι οὐδὲν πρ. they had no *thing* in common, Hdt. 2. *anything necessary* or *expedient*,

πρῆγμά ἐστι, c. inf., it is *necessary, expedient* to do, 'tis my *duty* or *business* to do, like Lat. *opus est*, Hdt.　**3.** *a thing of consequence* or *importance*, πρ. ποιεῖσθαί τι Id.; of a person, ἢν μέγιστον πρ. Δημοκήδης παρὰ βασιλέϊ he was made much of by the king, Id.; ἄμαχον πρ., of a woman, Xen.; ἀσταθμητότατον πρ. ὁ δῆμος Dem.　**4.** used of a battle, as we say *an action, affair*, Xen.　**5.** euphem. for something bad or disgraceful, *the thing, the business*, Thuc.; Εὐρυβάτου πρᾶγμα, οὐ πόλεως ἔργον his *job*, Dem.　**III.** in pl., πράγματα,　**1.** *circumstances, affairs*, Hdt., Att.; τοῖς πράγμασιν τέθνηκα τοῖς δ' ἔργοισι δ' οὔ by *circumstances*, not by acts, Eur.; ἀπηλλάχθαι πραγμάτων to be quit of the *business of life*, Plat.; ἀποτυγχάνειν τῶν πρ. to fail in success, Xen.　**2.** *state-affairs*, Eur., etc.; τὰ πολιτικὰ πρ. Plat.:—also, τὰ Περσικὰ πρ. the Persian *power*, Hdt.; ἐν ταῖς ναυσὶ τῶν Ἑλλήνων τὰ πρ. ἐγένετο Thuc.; καταλαμβάνειν τὰ πρ. to seize *the government*, Lat. *rerum potiri*, Id.; ἔχειν, κατέχειν τὰ πρ. Id.; οἱ ἐν τοῖς πράγμασι, like οἱ ἐν τέλει, those who are in *power* or *office*, the ministers, Id.; οἱ ἐπὶ τοῖς πρ. ὄντες, οἱ ἐπὶ τῶν πρ., Dem.:—νεώτερα πρ. *innovations*, Lat. *res novae*, Oratt.　**3.** one's *private affairs* or *circumstances*, Hdt., Att.　**4.** in bad sense, *troublesome business, trouble, annoyance*, Ar.; πράγματα ἔχειν, c. part., *to have trouble about* a thing, Hdt.; πρ. παρέχειν τινί to cause one *trouble*, Id.; c. inf., to cause one the *trouble* of doing, Plat.

πραγμᾰτεία, ἡ, *the careful prosecution of an affair, diligent study, hard work*, Plat., Dem., etc.　**II.** *occupation, business*, Plat., Aeschin.:—in pl. *affairs in general, dealings*, Plat., etc.　**III.** *the treatment* of a subject, Id.; *a treatise*, Arist.; *an historical work, systematic history*, Polyb., Luc.

πραγμᾰτεύομαι, Ion. **πρηγμ-:** aor. 1 ἐπραγματευσάμην and ἐπραγματεύθην: pf. πεπραγμάτευμαι: Dep.: (πρᾶγμα):—*to busy* or *exert oneself, take trouble*, Hdt., Xen., Plat.　**2.** *to be engaged in business, spend one's time* in business, Xen., etc.　**II.** c. acc. rei, *to take in hand, treat laboriously, undertake*, Plat.:—of authors, *to elaborate* a work, Ar., Plat.　**2.** of historians, *to treat systematically*, Polyb.; οἱ πραγματευόμενοι *systematic historians*, Id.　**III.** pf. πεπραγμάτευμαι also in pass. sense, *to be laboured at, worked out*, Plat., Aeschin. Hence

πραγματευτέος, α, ον, verb. Adj. *to be laboured at*, Arist.

πραγμᾰτικός, ή, όν, (πρᾶγμα) *fit for business, active, business-like;* οἱ πραγματικοί *men of action*, Polyb.　**2.** in Roman writers, *pragmaticus* was a kind of *attorney*, Cic.　**II.** of history, *systematic*, Polyb.: of a speech, conduct, etc., *able, prudent*, Id.:—Adv. -κῶς, Id.

πραγμάτιον, τό, Dim. of πρᾶγμα, *a trifling matter, petty lawsuit*, Ar.

πραγμᾰτο-δίφης [ῐ], ου, ὁ, (διφάω) *one who hunts after lawsuits, a pettifogger*, Ar.

πραγμᾰτ-ώδης, ες, (εἶδος) *laborious, troublesome:* Adv. -δῶς, Comp. -έστερον Dem.

πρᾶγος, εος, τό, poët. for πρᾶγμα, Pind., Aesch., Soph., Ar.　**2.** = πράγματα, *state-affairs*, Aesch.

πραθέειν, Ep. for πραθεῖν, aor. 2 inf. of πέρθω.

πραιτώριον, τό, = Lat. *Praetorium, the residence of* the Governor, *Government-house*, N. T.:—at Rome, the *Castra Praetoriana*, Ib.

πρακτέος, α, ον, verb. Adj. of πράσσω, *to be done*, Plat., etc.　**II.** πρακτέον, *one must do*, Soph., Plat.

πρακτήρ, Ion. **πρηκτήρ, ῆρος, ὁ,** (πράσσω) *one that does, a doer*, Il.　**II.** *a trader*, Lat. *negotiator*, Od.

πρακτικός, ή, όν, (πράσσω) *fit for action, fit for business, business-like, practical*, Xen., Plat.; αἱ πρ. ἀρχαί the principles *of action*, Arist.　**2.** *active, effective*, Polyb.; πρ. παρά τινος *carrying one's point* with another, Xen.　**3.** c. gen. *able to effect* a thing, etc., Arist.　**II.** of things, *active, vigorous*, Ar., Plat.

πρακτός, ή, όν, verb. Adj. of πράσσω: τὰ πρακτά *things to be done, points of moral action*, Arist.

πράκτωρ, ορος, ὁ, = πρακτήρ, *one who does* or *executes, an accomplisher*, Soph.; with a fem. Subst., Id.　**II.** *one who exacts payment, a taxgatherer*, Dem., etc.　**2.** in Poets also, *one who exacts punishment, a punisher, avenger*, Aesch., Soph.:—so as Adj., with a fem. Subst., *avenging*, Aesch.

Πράμνειος οἶνος, ὁ, *Pramnian wine*, Hom.; also **Πράμνιος,** Ar.:—so named from Pramné, prob. a hill in the island of Icaria.

πράν [ᾰ], Dor. Adv. = πρίν, *aforetime, erst*, Theocr.

πρᾱνής, Dor. and Att. for πρηνής.

πραξῐ-κοπέω, f. ήσω, (κόπτω) *to take by surprise* or *treachery*, Polyb.:—*to overreach, outwit*, τινά Id.

πρᾶξις, εως, Ion. **πρῆξις, ιος, ἡ,** (πράσσω) *a doing, transaction, business*, πλεῖν κατὰ πρῆξιν on a *trading voyage*, Od.; πρῆξις δ' ἥδ' ἰδίη, οὐ δήμιος a private, not a public *affair*, Ib.　**2.** *the result* or *issue* of a business, οὐ γάρ τις πρ. πέλεται γόοιο no good comes of weeping, Il.; so, οὔ τις πρ. ἐγίγνετο μυρομένοισιν Od.; πρ. οὐρίην θέλων Aesch.; χρησμῶν πρ. their *issue*, Id.　**II.** *an acting, transacting, doing,* κακότητος Theogn.; πρ. πολεμική, ποιητική, πολιτική Plat.:—*action*, opp. to πάθος, Id.; ἐν ταῖς πράξεσι *in actual life*, Id.　**2.** *action, exercise*, χειρῶν, σκελῶν Id.　**III.** *an action, act*, Soph., etc.　**IV.** like τὸ εὖ or κακῶς πράσσειν, *a doing* well or ill, *faring* so and so, one's *fortune, state, condition*, Hdt., Aesch., etc.　**V.** *practical ability, dexterity*, Polyb.:—also, *practice, trickery*, Id.　**VI.** *the exaction of money, recovery of outstanding debts* or *arrears*, πρ. συμβολαίων Plat., Dem.:—hence, *the exaction of vengeance, retribution*, Eur.　**VII.** in pl. *public* or *political life*, Dem.

πρᾱό-νως, Adv. of *πράων (= πρᾶος), *temperately*, Ar.

πρᾶος, ον, also **πραΰς,** Ion. **πρηΰς, εῖα, ΰ:**—the declension varies between the two forms:—the Att. sing. is from πρᾶος, except that the fem. is πραεῖα: poët. sing. from πραΰς, Ion. πρηΰς:—in pl., Att. nom. πρᾶοι; neut. πραέα, πρᾶα; gen. πραέων; dat. πραέσι; acc. πράους:—Comp. πραότερος; Ion. πρηΰτ-:—Sup. πραότατος, Ion. πρηΰτατος.　*Mild, soft, gentle, meek*, h. Hom., Pind., Plat.:—of a horse, *gentle*, Xen.; of other animals, *tame*, Id.　**2.** of actions, feelings, *mild*, Plat.　**II.** *making mild, taming*, Pind.　**III.** Adv. πράως (from πρᾶος), *mildly, gently*, Plat.; πράως ἔχειν πρός τι Id.; πράως λέγειν τὸ πάθος to speak *lightly* of it, Xen.; πράως διακεῖσθαι, opp. to ὀργίζεσθαι, Dem.;—Comp., Plat.;—Sup., πραότατα Id. Hence

πρᾱότης, ητος, ἡ, *mildness, gentleness*, Plat., etc.
πρᾱπίδες, αἱ, dat. πραπίσιν, Ep. πραπίδεσσι: — poët. word, 1. properly = φρένες, *the midriff, diaphragm*, Il.: then 2. like φρένες, *the wits, understanding, mind, heart*, Ib.:—sing. πραπίς, ίδος, Pind., Eur.
πρᾱσιά, Ion. -ιή, ἡ, (πράσον) properly *a bed of leeks*: generally, *a garden-plot*, Od.:—metaph., πρασιαὶ πρασιαί *in companies* or *groups*, N. T.
πράσῐμος, ον, (πρᾶσις) *for sale*, Lat. *venalis*, Xen.
πρᾶσις, εως, Ion. πρῆσις, ιος, ἡ, (πι-πράσκω) *a selling, sale*, ὠνῇ τε καὶ πρῆσι (Ion. dat.) χρέονται Hdt.; ἐπὶ πρῆσι *for sale*, Id.; πρᾶσιν ποιεῖσθαι Aeschin.
πρᾱσό-κουρον, τό, (κείρω) *a leek-slice*, Anth.
ΠΡΑ'ΣΟΝ [ᾰ], τό, *a leek*, Lat. *porrum*, Ar.
Πρασσαῖος, ὁ, poët. for πρασαῖος (= πράσινος), *Leek-green*, name of a frog, Batr.
Πρασσο-φάγος, ὁ, *Leek-eater*, name of a frog, Batr.
ΠΡΑ'ΣΣΩ, Ion. πρήσσω, Att. πράττω: f. πράξω, Ion. πρήξω:— aor. 1 ἔπραξα, Ion. ἔπρηξα: pf. πέπρᾱχα, Ion. πέπρηχα: 3 sing. plqpf.: pf. 2 πέπρᾱγα, Ion. πέπρηγα:—Med.; f. πράξομαι: aor. 1 ἐπραξάμην:—Pass., f. πραχθήσομαι, πεπράξομαι: aor. 1 ἐπράχθην: pf. πέπραγμαι. *To pass over*, ἅλα πρήσσοντες Od.; πρ. κέλευθον *to accomplish* a journey, Hom.; also c. gen., ἵνα πρήσσωμεν ὁδοῖο Il. II. *to achieve, bring about, effect, accomplish*, Ib.; οὔτι πρ. *to avail* naught, Ib.; πρ. δεσμόν *to cause* one's bondage, *bring* it on oneself, Pind.; πρ. ὥστε, Lat. *efficere ut*, Aesch.: —Pass., πέπρακται τοὔργον Id.; τὰ πεπραγμένα, Lat. *acta*, Pind., Att. 2. absol. *to effect an object, be successful*, Hom. 3. *to make* so and so (cf. ποιέω III.), Νηρηΐδων τινὰ πρ. ἄκοιτιν Pind. 4. *to have to do, be busy with*, τὰ ἑαυτοῦ πράττειν *to mind* one's own business, Soph., etc. 5. πράττειν τὰ πολιτικά, τὰ τῆς πόλεως *to manage* state-affairs, take part in the government, Plat.:—then, absol., without any addition, ἱκανὸς πράττειν, of a statesman, Xen. 6. generally, *to transact, negotiate, manage*, πρ. Θηβαίοις τὰ πράγματα *to manage* matters for their interest, Dem.; and in Pass., τῷ Ἱπποκράτει τὰ πράγματα ἐπράττετο matters were *negotiated* with him, Thuc.;—but τὰ πράγματα may be omitted, οἱ πράσσοντες αὐτῷ *those who were treating with* him, Id.; so, πράσσειν πρός τινα Id.; ἔς τινα Id.; also, πρ. περὶ εἰρήνης Xen.; οἱ πράσσοντες *the traitors*, Thuc.; also, πρ. ὅπως πόλεμος γένηται Id.; c. acc. et inf., τὴν ναῦν μὴ δεῦρο πλεῖν ἔπραττεν Dem.:—Pass., *of secret practices*, εἰ μή τι σὺν ἀργύρῳ ἐπράσσετο unless some bribery *was a-practising*, Soph.; ἐπράσσετο προδόσιος πέρι Thuc. III. *to practise*, Lat. *agere*, ἀρετάς Pind.; δίκαια ἢ ἄδικα Plat.: absol. *to act*, Id., etc. IV. intr. *to be in a certain state* or *condition, to do* or *fare so and so*, ὁ στόλος οὕτω ἔπρηξε Hdt., etc.; εὖ or κακῶς πράττειν *to do* or *fare* well or ill, Id., etc.; πρ. καλῶς Aesch.; εὐτυχῶς Soph.; πρ. ὡς ἄριστα καὶ κάλλιστα Thuc.; the pf. 2 πέπρᾱγα is mostly used in this sense, Hdt., Ar., etc. V. c. dupl. acc. pers. et rei, πράττειν τινά τι *to do* something to one, Eur., etc. 2. πράττειν τινὰ ἀργύριον *to exact* money from one, Hdt.: often in Att., of state-officers, who collected the taxes (cf. εἰσπράσσω, ἐκπράσσω III.), Plat., etc.; also, πρ. τι παρά τινος *to obtain* or *demand* from another, Hdt.:—metaph.,

φόνον πρ. *to exact punishment for* murder, *to avenge, punish*, Aesch.:—Pass., πεπραγμένος τὸν φόρον *called on to pay up* the tribute, Thuc.:—Med., πράξασθαί τινα ἀργύριον, χρήματα, μισθόν, τόκους *to exact for oneself*, Hdt., etc.; φόρους πράσσεσθαι ἀπό or ἐκ τῶν πόλεων Thuc.:—pf. and plqpf. pass. are used in med. sense, εἰ μὲν ἐπεπράγμην τοῦτον τὴν δίκην if *I had exacted* from him the full amount, Dem.
πρᾱτέος, α, ον, verb. Adj. of πιπράσκω, *to be sold, for sale*, Lat. *venalis*, Plat.
πρᾱτήρ, ῆρος, ὁ, (πι-πράσκω) *a dealer*, Plat., Dem.
πρᾱτήριον, Ion. πρητ-, τό, *a place for selling, a market*, Hdt.
πρᾱτός, ή, όν, verb. Adj. of πιπράσκω, *sold*, Soph.
πρᾶτος, α, ον, Dor. for πρῶτος (contr. from πρόατος), Ar., Theocr.; Sup. πράτιστος Theocr.
πράττω, Att. for πράσσω.
πρᾱΰ-γελως, Ion. πρηΰγ-, ὁ, ἡ, *softly-smiling*, Anth.
πρᾱΰ-μητις, ιος, ὁ, ἡ, *of gentle counsel, gracious*, Pind.
πρᾱΰνοος, Ion. πρηΰ- [ῠ], ον, *of gentle mind*, Pind.
πρᾱΰνσις, εως, ἡ, *a softening, appeasing*, Arist.; and
πρᾱΰντικός, ή, όν, *fit for appeasing*, Arist. From
πρᾱΰνω, Ion. πρηΰνω [ῠ]: f. ὔνῶ: aor. 1 ἐπρᾱϋνα:—Pass., aor. 1 ἐπρᾱΰνθην: (πραΰς):—*to make soft, mild* or *gentle, to soften, soothe, calm*, Hes., etc.; πρ. ἕλκος *to soothe* a raging sore, Soph.; πρ. τινὰ λόγοις Aesch.: —Pass. *to become soft* or *gentle, grow milder*, Hdt.; of passion, *to abate*, Id. 2. *to tame* wild animals, Hes., Xen.
πρᾱΰς, v. sub πρᾶος.
πρᾱΰ-τένων, Ion. πρηΰτ-, ὁ, *with tamed neck*, Anth.
πράως, v. sub πρᾶος III.
πρέμνοθεν, Adv. *from the stump*, i.e. *root and branch, utterly*, Aesch. From
ΠΡΕ'ΜΝΟΝ, τό, *the bottom of the trunk of a tree, the stump*: generally, *the stem, trunk*, Lat. *codex, caudex*, h. Hom., Xen., etc. II. *the root* or *bottom* of anything, πρέμνον πράγματος Ar.
πρέπον, οντος, τό, part. of πρέπω (III. 2).
πρεπόντως, Adv. part. of πρέπον, *in fit manner, meetly, beseemingly, gracefully*, Pind., Aesch. 2. c. dat. *in a manner befitting, suitably to*, Plat.; also c. gen., *like* ἀξίως, Id.
πρεπτός, ή, όν, *distinguished, renowned*, Aesch.
ΠΡΕ'ΠΩ, impf. ἔπρεπον: f. πρέψω: aor. 1 ἔπρεψα:—of impressions on the senses, 1. on the eye, *to be clearly seen, to be conspicuous*, ὁ δ᾽ ἔπρεπε καὶ διὰ πάντων Il.; c. dat. rei, *to be distinguished in* or *by* a thing, Aesch., Eur.:—absol. *to shine forth, shew itself, appear*, Pind., Aesch.; with a part., *to be clearly seen* as doing or being, Aesch. 2. on the ear, πρέπει the cry *sounds loud and clear*, Pind., Aesch. 3. on the smell, *to be strong* or *rank*, Aesch. II. *to be conspicuously like, to be like, to resemble*, c. dat., Pind., Eur. 2. c. inf., δράμημα φωτὸς Περσικὸν πρέπει μαθεῖν his running *is like* Persian to behold, i.e. one may see it is Persian, Aesch.; so, πρέπει ὡς τύραννος εἰσορᾶν Soph. III. *to be conspicuously fit, to become, beseem, suit*, c. dat. pers., θνατὰ θνατοῖσι πρέπει Pind., etc. 2. often in part., πρέπον ἐστί or ἦν for πρέπει or ἔπρεπε, Thuc., etc.; rarely c. gen., πρ. ἦν δαίμονος τοὐμοῦ τόδε Soph.:—part. neut. τὸ

πρέπον, οντος, *that which is seemly, fitness, propriety,* Lat. *decorum,* Plat. 3. rarely with a person as the subject, πρέπων ἔφυς φωνεῖν art *the fit person to speak,* Soph. 4. impers. πρέπει, Lat. *decet, it is fitting, it beseems, suits, becomes,* c. dat. pers. et inf., οὐ πρέπει ἄμμιν λύειν τείχη Theogn. ; ὡς πρέπει δούλοις λέγειν Eur. :—also c. acc. pers. et inf., τὸν πρέπει τυγχανέμεν ὕμνων Pind., etc. :—c. inf. only, πρέπει γαρνέμεν Id. :—when an acc. alone follows, an inf. must be supplied, τίσασθαι ὡς ἐκείνους πρέπει (sc. τίσασθαι) Hdt.

πρεπ-ώδης, ες, (εἶδος) *fit, becoming, suitable, proper,* Ar. ; c. dat., Xen., etc.

πρέσβᾰ, ης, ἡ, Ep. fem. of πρέσβυς, *the august, honoured,* mostly of Hera, Ἥρη, πρέσβα θεά Il.

πρεσβεία, ἡ, (πρεσβεύω) *age, seniority,* κατὰ πρεσβείαν Aesch. 2. *rank, dignity,* Plat. II. *an embassy, embassage,* Thuc., Plat. 2. *the body of ambassadors,* as we say, *the Embassy,* Ar., Thuc. :—*the ambassadors* of early times were *elders.*

πρεσβεῖον, Ion. -ήιον, τό, (πρέσβυς) *a gift of honour,* such as was offered to elders, Il. 2. *the privilege of age,* and generally, *a privilege,* Plat., etc. 3. *the right of the eldest, his share of the inheritance,* Dem.

πρέσβειρα, ἡ, fem. of πρέσβυς, = πρέσβα, h. Hom., Eur.

πρέσβευμα, τό, *an ambassador, embassy,* in pl., Eur.

πρέσβευσις, ἡ, *an embassage,* Thuc.

πρεσβευτής, οῦ, ὁ, (πρεσβεύω) *an ambassador,* Thuc., Plat., etc. II. *an agent or commissioner,* Dem.

πρεσβεύω, f. σω : pf. πεπρέσβευκα :—Med., aor. 1 ἐπρεσβευσάμην :—Pass., pf. πεπρέσβευμαι : (πρέσβυς): I. properly of age, 1. intr. *to be the elder or eldest,* Soph. ; τῶν προτέρων ἐπρέσβευε he was *the eldest* of the former children, Hdt. ; πρ. ἀπ᾽ αὐτοῦ *to be his eldest* son, Thuc. b. *to take the first place, be best,* Soph. :—c. gen. *to rank before, take precedence* of others, πρ. τῶν πολλῶν Plat. ; πρ. Ὀλύμπου πρ. Soph. 2. trans. *to place as eldest or first, to put first in rank, to pay honour or worship to,* Aesch., Soph. :—Pass. *to be put in the first rank, hold the first place,* Lat. *antiquior sum,* Aesch. ; c. gen., πρεσβεύεται κακῶν is *most notable* of mischiefs, Id. II. *to be an ambassador or go as one, serve or negociate as one,* Hdt., Eur., etc. ; v. πρεσβεία fin. 2. c. acc. objecti, πρ. τὴν εἰρήνην *to negotiate peace,* Dem. ; so, πρ. ὑπὲρ τουτωνί Id. 3. Med. *to send ambassadors,* Thuc. :—also *to go as ambassador,* Id. 4. Pass., τὰ ἑαυτῷ πεπρεσβευμένα his *negotiations,* Dem.

πρεσβηίον, Ion. for πρεσβεῖον.

πρεσβηίς, ίδος, ἡ, = πρέσβα, πρεσβηὶς τιμή the highest or most ancient honour, h. Hom.

πρέσβις, ἡ, poët. for πρεσβεία, *age,* κατὰ πρέσβιν according to age, h. Hom., Plat.

πρέσβιστος, η, ον, poët. Sup. of πρέσβυς, *eldest, most august, most honoured,* h. Hom., Aesch.

πρέσβος, τό, (πρεσβύς) *an object of reverence,* Aesch. ; πρ. Ἀργείων *august assembly* of Argives, Id.

πρεσβυγένεια, ἡ, *seniority of birth,* Hdt. From

πρεσβῡ-γενής, ές, (γίγνομαι) *eldest-born, first-born,* Il., Eur. II. οἱ πρεσβυγενεῖς *the senators,* Plut.

ΠΡΕ'ΣΒΥΣ, εως, ὁ, voc. πρέσβυ :—*an old man,* Lat. *senex,* (the prose form is πρεσβύτης), Soph., Eur. :—ὁ πρέσβυς is used much like ὁ πρεσβύτερος, *the elder,*

Aesch. :—pl. πρέσβεις, *elders,* always implying dignity, *chiefs, princes,* Id. ; Ep. πρέσβηες Hes. 2. Hom. uses only the Comp. and Sup., Comp. πρεσβύτερος, α, ον, *elder, older,* Il., Hdt., Pind., Att. ; ἐνιαυτῷ by a year, Ar. ; βουλαὶ πρεσβύτεραι *the wise councils of age,* Pind. ;—Sup. πρεσβύτατος, η, ον, *eldest,* Il., Hes., etc. : —the Comp. and Sup. were used of things, πρεσβύτερόν τι (or οὐδὲν) ἔχειν = Lat. *aliquid* (or *nihil*) *antiquius habere, to deem higher, more important,* τὰ τοῦ θεοῦ πρεσβύτερα ποιεῖσθαι ἢ τὰ τῶν ἀνδρῶν Hdt. ; πρεσβύτατον κρίνειν τι Thuc. ; πρεσβυτέρως γυμναστικὴν μουσικῆς τετιμηκέναι *more highly than* . . , Plat. : —hence, merely of magnitude, πρεσβύτερον κακὸν κακοῦ one evil *greater than* another, Soph. II. like πρεσβευτής, *an ambassador,* Aesch., Ar. ;—pl. πρέσβεις is more used than πρεσβευταί, Ar., Xen., etc. III. *a chief, president :* Comp. πρεσβύτερος, *an elder of the Jewish Council,* N. T., etc. : *an elder of the Church, presbyter,* Ib. Hence

πρεσβῠτέριον, τό, *a council of elders,* N. T.

πρεσβύτης [ῠ], ου, ὁ, = πρέσβυς I, Aesch., etc. :—fem. πρεσβῦτις, ιδος, *an aged woman,* Id. Hence

πρεσβῡτικός, ή, όν, *like an old man, elderly,* Lat. *senilis,* ὄχλος Ar. ; κακὰ πρ. the evils of age, Id. 2. *old-fashioned, antiquated,* Id. :—Adv. -κῶς, Plut.

πρευμένεια, ἡ, *gentleness of temper, graciousness,* Eur.

πρευμενής, ές, (πρᾶος, μένος) poët. Adj. *gentle of mood, friendly, gracious, favourable,* Aesch., Eur. :—Adv. -νῶς, Aesch. II. *propitiatory,* Id.

πρεών, όνος, ὁ, poët. for πρών, Anth.

πρῆγμα, πρηγμᾰτεύομαι, Ion. for πραγμ-.

πρηγορεών or πρηγορών, ῶνος, ὁ, *the crop of birds,* Ar. (From πρό, ἀγείρω, because birds *collect* their food there *before* it passes into the second stomach.)

πρηθῆναι, aor. 1 pass. inf. of πιπράσκω.

ΠΡΗ'ΘΩ, impf. ἔπρηθον : aor. 1 ἔπρησα : no pf. in use : —*to blow up, swell out by blowing,* ἔπρησεν δ᾽ ἄνεμος μέσον ἱστίον Od. 2. *to blow out, drive out by blowing,* τὸ δ᾽ [αἷμα] ἀνὰ στόμα πρῆσε he *blew* a shower of blood through his mouth, Il.

πρηκτήρ, πρηκτός, Ion. for πρακτήρ, πρακτός.

πρημαίνω, (πρήθω) *to blow hard,* Ar.

πρηνής, ές, Dor. and Att. πρᾱνής, gen. έος, contr. οὖς : (πρό) :—*with the face downwards, head-foremost,* Lat. *pronus,* opp. to ὕπτιος (Lat. *supinus*), Il., Hes. II. of the sides of hills, πρὸς κατὰ πρανοῦς *down hill,* Xen. ; κατὰ τὰ πρανῆ Id. Hence

πρηνίζω, *to throw headlong* :—Pass. *to fall headlong,* πρηνιχθείς Anth.

πρῆξαι, πρῆξις, Ion. for πρᾶξαι, πρᾶξις.

πρῆσεν, Ep. for ἔπρησεν, 3 sing. aor. 1 of πρήθω.

πρῆσις, ἡ, Ion. for πρᾶσις.

πρήσσω, Ion. for πράσσω.

πρηστήρ, ῆρος, ὁ, (πρήθω) *a hurricane,* Hes., Hdt.

πρήσω, f. both of πίπρημι *to burn,* and of πρήθω *to blow.*

πρητήριον, τό, Ion. for πρατήριον.

πρηύ-γελως, -νοος, πρηύνω, πρηύς, πρηυ-τένων, v. sub πραΰ-.

πρηών, ῶνος, ὁ, Ep. for πρών, Hes.

*πρίαμαι, defect. Dep., from which is formed ἐπριάμην (aor. 2 of ὠνέομαι) : 2 sing. ἐπρίω, Ep. 3 sing. πρίατο :

imperat. πρίασο, πρίω: subj. πρίωμαι, 2 sing. πρίῃ: opt. πριαίμην: inf. πρίασθαι (not πριάσθαι):— part. πριάμενος: (περάω):—to have a thing sold to one, to buy, purchase, Hom., Att.; c. dat. pretii, πρ. κτεάτεσσιν ἐοῖσιν to buy with one's money, Od.; c. gen., πρ. θανάτοιο to purchase by his death, Pind.; πρ. τι ταλάντου Xen.; π. πολλοῦ Id.; metaph., οὐδενὸς λόγου πρίασθαι to buy at no price, Soph.; πρ. τι παρά τινος Hdt.:—πρ. τίμιον τοὔλαιον to buy it dear, Ar. 2. to farm a tax, Xen.

Πρίᾰμος, ου, ὁ, Priam, Il., etc.; prob. a chief, king, (prob. from πρό), Patron. Πριαμίδης, ὁ, Ep. gen. -εω and -ao, Il.:—Adj. Πριαμικός, ή, όν, of or like Priam, Arist.; poët. fem. Πριαμίς, ίδος, Eur.

Πρίᾱπος, Ion. Πρίηπος, ὁ, Priāpus, the god of gardens and vineyards, and generally of country life, Luc. :— Adj. Πριάπειος, α, ον, Anth.

πρίν [ῐ], Adv., formed with a comparative force from πρό: A. Adv. of Time, before, I. of future time, before that time, sooner, with fut. Indic. or Subj. = fut., Hom.: with Opt. and κεν, Od. II. of past time, aforetime, formerly, once, erst, Hom.; so with the Art., τὸ πρίν γε . . , νῦν δὲ .; νῦν δὲ . τὸ πρίν γε Il.:—with the Art. the Part. ὤν is omitted, τὰ πρὶν πελώρια (sc. ὄντα) the giants of old, Aesch.; ἐν τῷ πρὶν χρόνῳ Soph.; ἐν τοῖς πρὶν λόγοις Thuc. B. πρὶν ἤ, as Conjunction, before that, before, ere, priusquam, Hom.; but ἤ is often omitted, so that πρίν becomes a Conjunction: the antecedent clause also has πρίν (or πρότερον, πρόσθεν, πάρος), so that πρίν the Conjunction is relat. to πρίν the Adv., especially after a negat.:—it is constructed with Inf., ναῖε δὲ Πήδαιον, πρὶν ἐλθεῖν υἷας Ἀχαιῶν Il.; οὐδὲ παύσεται χόλου, πρὶν κατασκήψαί τινα Eur. II. with a finite Verb: 1. with Ind., in which case Hom. uses πρίν γ' ὅτε, πρίν γ' ὅτε δή, until, μάχη τέτατο, πρίν γ' ὅτε δὴ Ζεὺς κῦδος Ἕκτορι δῶκε Il.; so, οὐκ ἦν ἀλέξημ' οὐδέν, πρίν γ' ἐγὼ σφίσιν ἔδειξα Aesch. 2. with Subj. only after negatives or equiv. of neg., οὐ καταδυσόμεθ', πρὶν μόρσιμον ἦμαρ ἐπέλθῃ we will not go down, till the day of death come on, Od.;—in Att. πρὶν ἄν is regular, οὐδὲν ἔστι τέρμα μοι μόχθων, πρὶν ἂν Ζεὺς ἐκπέσῃ τυραννίδος Aesch.; but ἄν is sometimes omitted, μὴ στέναζε, πρὶν μάθῃς Soph.; as always with πρὶν ἤ, πρὶν ἢ ἀνορθώσωσι Hdt. 3. with Opt., after historical tenses, οὐκ ἔθελεν φεύγειν πρὶν πειρήσαιτ' Ἀχιλῆος Il.; ἔδοξέ μοι μὴ ποιεῖσθαι, πρὶν φράσαιμί σοι Soph.

πρίνίδιον [ῑ], τό, Dim. of πρῖνος, Ar.

πρίνινος, η, ον, made from the πρῖνος, Lat. iligneus, Hes., Ar.:—metaph. oaken, i. e. tough, sturdy, Ar.

ΠΡΙ͂ΝΟΣ, ἡ, ὁ, the evergreen oak, ilex, or the scarlet oak, quercus coccifera, Hes., Ar., etc.

πρῖν-ώδης, ες, (εἶδος) tough as oak, Ar.

πρίονθ', i. e. πρίοντε, dual of the partic. πρίων, sawing.

πριον-ώδης, ες, (εἶδος) like a saw, Anth. [ῑ, metri grat.].

πριστήρ, ῆρος, ὁ, (πρίω) a saw: πριστῆρες ὀδόντες the incisors, Anth.

πριστός, ή, όν, verb. Adj. sawn, Od.

πρίω, imperat. of ἐπριάμην (v. *πρίαμαι), cf. πρίων.

ΠΡΙ͂Ω, imper. πρῖε: impf. ἔπριον: aor. 1 ἔπρισα:— Pass., aor. 1 ἐπρίσθην: pf. πέπρισμαι:—to saw, πρ. δίχα to saw asunder, Thuc.: Pass. to be cut in pieces,

Eur. II. πρίειν τοὺς ὀδόντας to grind or gnash the teeth, Ar.:—metaph. in Pass. to be irritated, Anth. III. to seize as with the teeth, bind fast, ζωστῆρι πρισθεὶς ἱππικῶν ἐξ ἀντύγων Soph.

πρίων (A), ὁ, gen. πρίονος and πρίωνος, a sawyer, Ar. II. a saw, Soph.; πρίων ὀδόντων a saw of teeth, i. e. a jagged row, Anth.; v. πρίων B. [ῑ, Att.; but ῑ in later Poets.]

πρίων (B), ὁ, a comic Noun, formed from πρίω, imperat. of ἐπριάμην, with a pun upon πρίων, a saw, ὁ πρ. ἀπῆν that rasping word 'buy' was unknown, Ar.

ΠΡΟ', before, Lat. prae:—
A. PREP. WITH GENIT.: I. of Place, before, in front of, πρὸ ἄστεος, πρὸ πυλάων Hom.; οὐρανόθι πρὸ Il.; χωρεῖν πρὸ δόμων to come out in front of, Soph. 2. before, in front of, for the purpose of shielding or guarding, στῆναι πρὸ Τρώων Il.:—in defence of, for, μάχεσθαι πρὸ γυναικῶν Ib.; ὀλέσθαι πρὸ πόληος, Lat. pro patria mori, Ib. 3. πρὸ ὁδοῦ further on the road, i. e. forwards, onward, Il.: (hence φροῦδος). II. of Time, before, πρὸ γάμοιο Od.; πρὶν ὁ τοῦ (= ὁ πρὸ τοῦ) ἐνόησεν one before the other, Il.; πρὸ τοῦ θανάτου Plat., etc.; πρὸ πολλοῦ long before, Hdt.; τὸ πρὸ τούτου before this, before, Thuc.; πρὸ τοῦ (often written προτοῦ) before, Hdt., Att. III. in other relations: 1. of Preference, before, sooner or rather than, κέρδος πρὸ δίκας αἰνῆσαι to praise sleight before right, Pind.; πᾶν πρὸ τῆς παρεούσης λύπης anything before, rather than, their actual grievance, Hdt.; πρὸ πολλοῦ ποιεῖσθαι to esteem above much, i. e. very highly, Isocr.; so, πρὸ πολλῶν χρημάτων τιμᾶσθαι Thuc.: redundant, after a Comp., ἡ τυραννὶς πρὸ ἐλευθερίης ἀσπαστότερον Hdt. 2. of Cause or Motive, Lat. prae, for, out of, from, πρὸ φόβοιο for fear, Il.; πρὸ τῶνδε therefore, Soph.
B. POSITION: never after its case, except after the Ep. gen. Ἰλιόθι πρό, οὐρανόθι πρό, ἠῶθι πρό.
C. πρό, absol. as Adv.: I. of Place, before, in front, forth, forward, Il. II. of Time, before, beforehand, Od.: before, earlier, Hes.: prematurely, Aesch. III. with other Preps. ἀποπρό, διαπρό, ἐπιπρό, περιπρό, προπρό, it strengthens the first Prep.
D. πρό IN COMPOS. I. with Substs., to denote 1. position before or in front, πρόθυρον, προπύλαια. 2. priority of rank, πρόεδρος; of order, προοίμιον. 3. standing in another's place, πρόμαντις, πρόξενος. II. with Adjs., to denote 1. proximity, readiness, πρόχειρος, πρόθυμος. 2. forth from, προθέλυμνος, πρόρριζος. 3. prematureness, πρόμοιρος, πρόωρος. III. with Verbs, 1. of Place, before, forwards, προβαίνω, προβάλλω: also before, in defence, προκινδυνεύω. 2. forth, προέλκω, προφέρω:—also publicly, προειπεῖν. 3. giving away, προδίδωμι. 4. before, in preference, προαιροῦμαι, προτιμάω. 5. before, beforehand, προαισθάνομαι, προοράω.

προ-αγγέλλω, f. -αγγελῶ, to announce beforehand, Xen.

προάγγελσις, ἡ, a forewarning, early intimation, Thuc.

προ-άγνυμι, aor. 1 -έαξα, to break before, Od.

προαγόρευσις, ἡ, a stating beforehand, Arist., Plut.

προ-αγορεύω, aor. 1 -ηγόρευσα: pf. -ηγόρευκα (but the

Att. fut. is προερῶ, aor. προεῖπον, pf. προείρηκα) :— Pass. -εύσομαι (in med. form) : pf. -ηγόρευμαι :—to tell beforehand, Thuc. : c. inf. to tell or declare beforehand that . . , Hdt., etc.; so, πρ. ὅτι . . , Xen.   2. to foretell, prophesy, τὸ μέλλον Id.   II. to speak before all, to state, declare or proclaim publicly, Hdt., Thuc.; to have a thing proclaimed by herald, Hdt.   2. c. inf. to order publicly, πρ. ὑμῖν παρεῖναι Id.; πρ. τοῖς πολίταις μὴ κινεῖν to forbid them to move, Plat. :—Pass., γυμνάζεσθαι προαγορεύεται ἅπασι Xen.; τὰ προηγορευμένα Id.   3. to give notice, notify, Plat.

προ-άγω [ἄ], f. άξω : pf. -ῆχα : aor. 2 -ήγαγον :—Pass., aor. 1 -ήχθην : pf. -ῆγμαι :—to lead forward, on, onward, Hdt., etc. : to escort on their way, Id., Xen.   2. to bring forward in public, Plat.   3. to lead on, induce, Hdt., Thuc.; c. inf., πρ. τινὰ κινδυνεύειν Thuc.; with Preps., πρ. θυμὸν ἐς ἀμπλακίην Theogn.; τινὰ εἰς φιλοποσίαν, εἰς μῖσος Xen.; ἐπ' ἀρετὴν Id. :—so in Med., ἐς γέλωτα προαγαγέσθαι τινά to move one to laughter, Hdt.; εἰς ἀνάγκην Dem.   4. to carry on or forward, πρ. τὴν πόλιν to lead it on to power, Thuc.; μέχρι πόρρω προήγαγον τὴν ἔχθραν carried it so far, Dem. :—Pass. to increase, wax, Id.   b. of persons, to promote or prefer to honour, Plut.   5. pf. pass. with med. sense, προῆκται παῖδας οὕτω ὥστε . . , has had them brought up in such a way that . . , Dem.; but also in pass. sense, τοῖς ἔθεσι προηγμένοι Arist.   II. intr. to lead the way, go before, advance, Plat., Xen., etc. :—an acc. added, to go before one, N. T.

προἄγωγεία, ἡ, the trade of a προαγωγός, pandering, Xen., Aeschin. From

προἄγωγεύω, f. σω, (προαγωγός) to prostitute, Lex ap. Aeschin.   2. metaph., πρ. ἑαυτὸν ὀφθαλμοῖς Ar.

προἄγωγή, ἡ, (προάγω) a leading on, promotion, rank, eminence, Polyb.

προἄγωγός, ὁ, (προάγω) one who leads on : a pander, pimp, procurer, Ar., Aeschin.   2. a negotiator, Xen.

προ-ἄγών, ῶνος, ὁ, a preliminary contest, prelude, Ar., Plat. :—the preparation for a festival, Aeschin.

προ-ἄγωνίζομαι, f. Att. -ιοῦμαι : pf. -ηγώνισμαι : Dep. :—to fight before, ἐξ ὧν προηγώνισθε=ἐξ ἀγώνων οὓς προηγωνίσθε, from the contests which you have before had, Thuc. :—pf. also in pass. sense, οἱ προηγωνισμένοι ἀγῶνες Plut.   II. to fight for or in defence of another, Id.

προἄγωνιστέον, verb. Adj. of προαγωνίζομαι, Plat.

προἄγωνιστής, οῦ, ὁ, one who fights for another, a champion, Plut.

προ-ἄδῐκέω, f. ήσω, to be the first in wronging :— Pass. to be wronged before or first, Dem., Aeschin.

προ-ᾴδω, f. -άσομαι, to sing before, prelude, Aeschin.

προ-αιδέομαι, Ion. -εῦμαι : Ion. 3 pl. plqpf. -ηδέατο : Dep. :—to owe one special respect, be under obligations to one, c. dat., Hdt.

προαίρεσις, εως, ἡ, (προαιρέομαι) a choosing one thing before another, an act of deliberate choice, a purpose, resolution, Plat., etc. :—κατὰ προαίρεσιν on purpose, as one will, Arist.   2. a purpose, plan, or scope of action, a course of life, principle of action, Dem.   3. in political language, a deliberate course of action, a

policy, Id. :—also, a mode of government, such as an oligarchy, Id.; in pl., τὰς κοινὰς πρ. your public principles, your general policy, Id.   4. a department of government, Id.   5. a political party, Id.

προαιρετέον, verb. Adj. one must choose, prefer, Plat.

προαιρετικός, ή, όν, (προαιρέομαι) inclined to prefer, deliberately choosing a thing, c. gen., Arist.   2. absol. purposing, intentional, Id.

προαιρετός, ή, όν, deliberately chosen, purposed, Arist.

προ-αιρέω, f. ήσω : pf. -ῄρηκα : aor. 2 προεῖλον :—to bring forth, produce from one's stores, Theophr.   2. to take away first, Babr.   II. mostly in Med., f. -αιρήσομαι : aor. 2 -ειλόμην : pf. pass. (in med. sense) -ῄρημαι :—to take away first for oneself, remove out of one's way, Plat.   2. to choose before or sooner than something else, prefer, τί τινος or τι πρό τινος Id.; τι ἀντί τινος Xen.   3. c. acc. only, to take by deliberate choice, choose deliberately, prefer, Plat., etc. :—absol., προαιρούμενος by preference, Arist.   4. c. inf. to prefer to do, Id. : to purpose or propose to do, Dem.

προ-αισθάνομαι, f. -αισθήσομαι : aor. 2 -ῃσθόμην :— Dep. to perceive or observe beforehand, Thuc., Xen.; πρ. τινος to become aware of a thing beforehand, Thuc.

προ-αιτιάομαι, Dep. to accuse beforehand, τινα εἶναι N. T.

προ-ἄκοντίζομαι, Pass. to be thrown like a javelin before, Luc.

προ-ἄκούω, f. -ακούσομαι : pf. -ακήκοα :—to hear beforehand, Hdt., Att.

προ-ἄλής, ές, (ἅλλομαι) springing forward, i. e. overhanging, abrupt, Il.   II. metaph.=προπετής :— Comp. Adv., προαλέστερον more eagerly, Strab.

προ-ἄλίσκομαι, Pass. : f. -ἀλώσομαι : aor. 2 -εάλων or -ήλων : pf. -εάλωκα or -ήλωκα :—to be convicted beforehand, Dem.

προ-ἄμαρτάνω, f. -ἁμαρτήσομαι : aor. 2 -ήμαρτον :—to fail or sin before, Hdt.

προ-ἄμύνομαι [ῠ], f. -αμὐνοῦμαι, Med. to defend oneself or take measures for defence beforehand, Thuc. : —c. acc. to take such measures against others, Id.

προ-αναβαίνω, f. -βήσομαι, to ascend before, so as to preoccupy, τὸν λόφον Thuc.

προ-αναβάλλομαι, aor. 2 -εβαλόμην, Med. to say or sing by way of prelude, Ar.

προ-ανάγω, to lead up before :—Pass. to put to sea before, Thuc.

προ-αναιρέω, f. ήσω : aor. 2 -ανεῖλον :—to take away before, Dem. : to refute by anticipation, Arist.

προ-ἄναισῐμόω, f. ώσω, to use up, spend before : Pass., pf. -ανησίμωμαι, Ion. -αναισίμωμαι, ἐν τῷ προαναισιμωμένῳ χρόνῳ πρότερον ἢ ἐμὲ γενέσθαι in times past before I was born, Hdt.

προ-ανακῑνέω, f. ήσω, to stir up before, Plut.   II. absol. to make previous movements, Arist.

προ-ανακρίνω [ῑ], f. -κρῐνῶ, to examine before, of the measures to be submitted to the vote of the people, Arist.

προ-αναλίσκω, f. ώσω : aor. 1 -ανάλωσα :—to use up or spend before, Thuc., Dem. :—Pass. to throw away one's life before, Thuc.

προ-αναρπάζω, f. σω and ξω, to carry off or arrest

beforehand, Dem.; πρ. τῆς παρασκευῆς = ἀναρπάζειν πρὸ τῆς παρασκευῆς, Plut.

προ-αναστέλλω, f. -στελῶ, *to check beforehand*, Plut.

προαναφωνέω, f. ήσω, *to say by way of preface*, Plut.

προ-αναχώρησις, ἡ, *a former departure*, Thuc.

προ-ανύτω, f. ύσω [ῠ], *to accomplish before*, Xen.

προ-απαγορεύω, (v. προ-απεῖπον) *to give in before*, Isocr.

προ-απαντάω, f. ήσω, *to go forth to meet*, Thuc. II. *to meet beforehand*, Id.

προ-άπειμι, (εἶμι ibo) *to go away first*, Luc.

προ-απεῖπον, aor. 2 of ἀπαγορεύω, *to give in* or *fail before*, Isocr.; pf. προαπείρηκα Id.

προ-απέρχομαι, f. -απελεύσομαι: aor. 2 -απῆλθον: Dep.: —*to go away before*, Thuc., Dem.

προ-απεχθάνομαι [ᾰ], Pass. *to begin hostilities before*, Dem.

προ-απηγέομαι, Ion. for προ-αφηγέομαι.

προ-αποδείκνυμι, f. -δείξω, *to prove before*, Isocr.

προ-αποθνήσκω, f. -θανοῦμαι: aor. 2 -έθανον:—*to die before* or *first*, Hdt., Plat.; *of a coward*, πρ. ἀπὸ τοῦ φόβου, i. e. *before his real death*, Xen.

προ-αποθρηνέω, f. ήσω, *to bewail beforehand*, Plut.

προ-αποκάμνω, f. -καμοῦμαι: aor. 2 -έκαμον: —*to grow tired before the end, give up the task* of doing, c. inf., Plat.; c. gen., Plut.

προ-αποκληρόομαι, *to be allotted beforehand*, Luc.

προ-αποκτείνω, f. -κτενῶ, *to kill beforehand*, Luc.

προ-απολαύω, f. -αύσομαι, *to enjoy beforehand*, Plut.

προ-απολείπω, f. ψω, intr. *to fail before*, i. e. *in comparison* of, c. gen., Antipho.

προ-απόλλυμι, f. -ολοῦμαι: pf. -όλωλα: Pass.:—*to be first destroyed, to perish before* or *first*, Thuc.; μὴ ἡ ψυχὴ προαπολλύηται (as if from -απολλύω) Plat.

προ-αποπέμπω, f. ψω, *to send away before*, Thuc. :— Med., Xen.

προ-αποστέλλω, f. -στελῶ, *to send away, dispatch beforehand* or *in advance*, Thuc. : —Pass. *to be sent in advance*, Id.; but, προαποσταληναί τινος = ἀποσταλῆναι πρό τινος, Id.

προ-αποσφάζω, f. ξω, *to slay before*, Luc.

προ-αποτρέπομαι, Med. *to turn aside before, leave off*, c. part., προαποτρέπομαι διώκων Xen.

προ-αποφαίνω, f. -φανῶ, *to declare before* :—Med., πρ. τὴν γνώμην *to declare one's opinion before*, Plat.

προ-αποχωρέω, f. ήσω, *to go away before*, Thuc.

προ-αρπάζω, f. σω and ξω, *to snatch away before*, Luc.; metaph., πρ. τὸ λεγόμενον *to snap at* a conclusion, *anticipate hastily*, Plat.

προ-ασκέω, f. ήσω, *to train* or *exercise before*, Isocr.

προ-άστειον, Ion. -ήιον, τό, *the space immediately in front* of or *round a town, a suburb*, Hdt., Thuc., etc.

προάστιον, τό, = προάστειον, Soph.

προ-αυδάω, f. ήσω, *to declare before* or *first*, Ar., in the contr. inf. πρωυδᾶν.

προ-αυλέω, f. ήσω, *to play a prelude on the flute*, Arist.

προ-αύλιον, τό, (αὐλός) *a prelude on the flute*, Arist.

προ-αφηγέομαι, Ion. **προ-απηγ-**, f. ήσομαι, Dep. *to relate before*, Hdt.

προ-αφικνέομαι, f. -ίξομαι, Dep. *to arrive first*, Thuc.

προ-αφίσταμαι, Pass., with pf. and aor. 2 act. :—*to fall off* or *revolt before*, Thuc. II. *to leave off* or *desist before*, Plat.

πρόβα, for προβῆθι, aor. 2 imper. of προβαίνω.

προβάδην [ᾰ], Adv. (προβαίνω) *as one walks*, Hes.; πρ. ἔξαγε *lead them out onward*, Ar.

προ-βαίνω, f. -βήσομαι: pf. -βέβηκα: Att. aor. 2 προύβην :—also Ep. part. προβιβάς (as if from βίβημι) :—*to step on, step forward, advance*, Hom., etc.:—*as a mark of Time*, ἄστρα προβέβηκε *they are far gone in heaven*, i. e. *it is past midnight*, Il.; ἡ νὺξ προβαίνει *the night is wearing fast*, Xen.; *then of Time itself*, τοῦ χρόνου προβαίνοντος *as time went on*, Hdt.; so, προβαίνοντος τοῦ ἔργου, τοῦ πολέμου Id.; *and of persons*, τοὺς προβεβηκότας τῇ ἡλικίᾳ *advanced in age*, Lys., etc. 2. *metaph. of narrative, argument, events*, προβήσομαι ἐς τὸ πρόσω τοῦ λόγου Hdt.; πρ. ἐπ' ἔσχατον θράσους Soph.; τὸ τῆς τύχης ἀφανὲς οἷ προβήσεται Eur.; πρ. πόρρω μοχθηρίας *to be far gone in knavery*, Xen.; πρ. εἰς τοῦτο ἔχθρας Dem. 3. *to advance, proceed*, προέβαινε τὸ ἔθνος ἄρχον *the nation kept making advances in dominion, kept extending its sway*, Hdt.; μὴ προβαίη μεῖζον ἢ τὸ νῦν κακόν *lest it creep on, increase*, Eur. II. *to go before*, i. e. *to be before* or *superior to* another, c. gen., προβέβηκας ἁπάντων Il.; Τρηχῖνος προβέβηκε *he was set over*, i. e. *ruled*, Trachis, Hes. III. c. acc. rei, *to overstep*, τέρμα προβάς (for ὑπερβάς) Pind. IV. *in Poets*, πόδα πρ. *to advance the foot*, Theogn.; τὸν πόδα Αr.; προβὰς κῶλον, ἀρβύλαν προβάς Eur.; v. βαίνω A. II. 3. V. *Causal, in fut. act., to put forward, advance*, τίς τρόπος ἄνδρα προβάσει [ᾰ]; Pind.

προ-βακχήιος, ὁ, Ion. for -ειος, *of Bacchus, leader of the Bacchanals*, Eur.

προ-βάλλω, f. -βαλῶ: pf. -βέβληκα: aor. 2 προέβαλον, Att. προύβαλον, Ion. προβάλεσκον :—*to throw before, throw* or *toss to*, Lat. *projicere*, Νότος Βορέῃ προβάλεσκε [σχεδίην] Od.; τοὺς μαζοὺς κυσὶ προέβαλε Hdt. II. *to put forward*, i. e. *to begin*, ἔριδα προβαλόντες Il. 2. *to put forward* as a *defence* or plea, Soph., Eur.:—Pass., Thuc. 3. *to propose for an office*, Andoc. 4. *to propose* a problem, riddle (cf. πρόβλημα IV), Ar., etc. 5. *to put forth beyond*, τί τινος Soph. III. πρ. ἑαυτόν *to give oneself up for lost*, Lat. *spem abjicere*, Hdt.; so, πρ. ἐμαυτὸν εἰς δεινὰς ἀράς Soph.

B. Med. with pf. pass. (which is used also in pass. sense) :—*to throw* or *toss before one*, οὐλοχύτας προβάλοντο Hom. : *to throw away, expose*, Soph. 2. *to lay before* or *first*, θεμειλία τε προβάλοντο Il. 3. *to set before oneself, propose to oneself*, ἔργον Hes. 4. *to propose for election*, Lat. *designare*, Hdt., Att. :— Pass. *to be so proposed*, Hdt. II. *to throw beyond, beat in throwing*; and so, *to surpass, excel*, c. gen. pers. et dat. rei, ἐγὼ δέ κε σεῖο νοήματί γε προβαλοίμην Il. III. *to hold before oneself*, τὼ χεῖρε Ar.; πρ. τὰ ὅπλα, i. e. *to present* arms, *whether for offensive or defensive purposes*, Xen.;—so, in pf. pass., κόντον προβεβλημένος *having* a pole *advanced*, with levelled pole, Luc.; also, προβεβλημένοι τοὺς θωρακοφόρους *having* them *to cover one in front*, Xen. :—absol. *to stand in front, stand on the defensive*, Id.; προαίρεσις προβεβλημένη *a defensive* system, Dem. :— c. gen., προβεβλῆσθαί τινος *to stand before, shield* him, Id. 2. *metaph. to put forward*, Id. :—*to bring*

forward or *cite in defence*, Plat. : *to cite as an example*, Hdt. :—*to use as an excuse* or *pretext*, Thuc. :—**προβέβληνται** (in med. sense), Id. **IV.** as Att. law-term, *to present* or *accuse* a person before the Ecclesia by the process called προβολή (v. προβολή IV) ; ὁ προβαλλόμενος *the prosecutor* in a προβολή, Dem. :—Pass. *to be accused*, Xen.

προ-βᾰσᾰνίζω, f. σω, *to torture before*, Luc.

προβάς, aor. 2 part. of προβαίνω.

πρόβᾰσις, ἡ, = προβατεία II, *property in cattle* (πρόβατα), *cattle*, Od.

προβᾶτε, 2 pl. aor. 1 imp. of προβαίνω.

προβᾰτεία, ἡ, (προβατεύω) *a keeping of sheep, a shepherd's life*, Plut. **II.** *property in cattle, a flock of sheep*, like the Homeric πρόβασις, Strab.

προβᾰτευτικός, ή, όν, *of* or *for cattle* :—ἡ -κή (sc. τέχνη) *the art of breeding* or *keeping sheep*, Lat. *pecuaria*, Xen. From

προβᾰτεύω, f. σω, (πρόβᾰτον) *to watch sheep, be a shepherd*, Anth.

προβᾰτικός, ή, όν, (πρόβᾰτον) *of sheep* or *goats* :—ἡ προβατικὴ (sc. πύλη) *the sheep-gate*, N. T.

προβάτιον, τό, Dim. of πρόβᾰτον, *a little sheep*, Lat. *ovicula*, Ar., Plat. ; cf. πρόβᾰτον.

προβᾰτο-γνώμων, ον, *a good judge of sheep* : metaph. *a good judge of character*, Aesch.

προβᾰτο-κάπηλος, ον, *a retailer of sheep*, Plut.

πρόβᾰτον, τό, mostly in pl. πρόβᾰτα, (προβαίνω) properly, *anything that walks forward ;* in Hom. generally of *cattle, flocks* and *herds ;* in Hdt. and Pind. also of *horses ;* τὰ λεπτὰ τῶν προβάτων *small cattle*, i. e. sheep and goats, Hdt. ; but in Att. always of *sheep*, Ar., Thuc. **2.** proverb. of stupid, lazy people, πρόβατ' ἄλλως *a set of sheep*, Ar. ; so, προβατίου βίος, i. e. *a lazy do-nothing life*, Id.

προβᾰτο-πώλης, ου, ὁ, (πωλέω) *a sheep-dealer*, Ar.

προβέβηκα, pf. of προβαίνω.

προβέβληκα, pf. of προβάλλω.

προ-βέβουλα, an isolated poët. pf. 2 (προ-βούλομαι does not occur), *to prefer* one to another, τινά τινος Il.

πρό-βημα, ατος, τό, (προβαίνω) *a step forward*, Ar.

προβήσομαι, f. of προβαίνω.

προ-βιάζομαι, Dep. *to force* a measure *through*, Aeschin.

προ-βῐβάζω, f. Att. -βιβῶ, Causal of προβαίνω, *to make step forward, lead forward, lead on*, τινά Soph., Ar., etc. :—*to lead on, induce*, λόγῳ τινὰ Xen. **2.** *to push forward, advance, to exalt*, τὴν πατρίδα Polyb. **3.** *to teach beforehand*, τινά τι Lxx. :—Pass., prob. in N. T.

προβῐβάς, part. (as if from -βίβημι) of προβαίνω.

προβλέπω, *to foresee :* so in Med., N. T.

πρόβλημα, ατος, τό, (προβάλλω) *anything projecting, a headland, promontory*, Soph. **II.** *anything put before one, a fence, barrier, screen*, Hdt., Att. ; πρ. σώματος, of *a shield*, Aesch. ; προβλήματα ἵππων χαλκᾶ *the brasen armour* of horses, Xen. **2.** c. gen. *a defence against* a thing, πέτρων Aesch. ; χείματος Eur. ; κακῶν Ar. **3.** πρ. φόβου ἢ αἰδοῦς ἔχειν *to have fear* or *shame as a defence*, Soph. **III.** *anything put forward* as *an excuse* or *screen*, Dem. ; so, πρ. λαβεῖν τινά (as we say) to make *a stalking horse* of him, Soph. **IV.** *that which is pro-*

posed, a task, business, Eur. **2.** *a problem* in Geometry, Plat.

προβλημᾰτ-ώδης, ες, (εἶδος) *problematical*, Plut.

προβλής, ῆτος, ὁ, ἡ, (προβάλλω) *forestretching, jutting*, Hom.: προβλῆτες, *without Subst., forelands, headlands*, Soph.

πρόβλητος, ον, (προβάλλω) *thrown forth, tossed away*, Lat. *projectus*, Soph.

προ-βλώσκω, Ep. inf. -βλωσκέμεν : aor. 2 inf. προμολεῖν :—*to go* or *come forth, to go out of the house*, Hom.

προ-βοάω, *to shout before, cry aloud*, Il., Soph.

προ-βοηθέω, Ion. -βωθέω, f. ήσω, *to hasten to aid before*, προβωθῆσαι ἐς τὴν Βοιωτίην Hdt.

προβόλαιος, ον, *held out before one, levelled, couched*, of a spear, Theocr. : ὁ πρ., alone, *a spear*, ap. Hdt.

προβολή, ἡ, (προβάλλω) *a putting forward*, esp. of a weapon for defence, τὰ δόρατα εἰς προβολὴν καθιέναι *to bring the spears to the rest*, Xen. ; ἐν προβολῇ θέσθαι ξίφος *to bring it to the guard*, Anth. ; ἐν προβολῇ ἑστάναι *to stand with spear in rest*, Plut. :—of a pugilist, *a lunging out with the fist*, Theocr. **II.** *a projection, a jutting rock, foreland* or *tongue of land*, Soph. ; Νειλόρυτος πρ. i. e. *the Delta of the Nile*, Anth. **III.** *a thing held before one as a defence, a fence, screen, bulwark*, Xen. : c. gen. *a defence against*, δείματος καὶ βελέων Soph. ; θανάτου Eur. **IV.** *a legal process in which the plaintiff appealed to the Ecclesia to support his suit before bringing it into court*, pl. προβολαί, Xen., Dem., etc.

προβόλιον, τό, Dim. of πρόβολος II, *a boar-spear*, Xen.

πρόβολος, ον, (προβάλλω) *anything that projects :* **I.** *a jutting rock, foreland*, Od. :—metaph. *a rock in the path, an obstacle*, Dem. ; λιμένας προβόλων ἐμπλῆσαι Id. ; πρόβολοι ξύλων *projecting barriers* of wood, Plut. **2.** *a defence, bulwark*, Xen. : of a person, *a shield, guardian*, Ar. **II.** *a hunting-spear*, Hdt. ; cf. προβόλαιος.

προβοσκίς, ίδος, ἡ, *a means of providing food : an elephant's proboscis*, Arist.

προ-βοσκός, ὁ, *an assistant herdsman*, Hdt.

προβούλευμα, ατος, τό, at Athens, *a preliminary order of the senate*, Dem., Aeschin.

προβουλευμάτιον, τό, Dim. of foreg., Luc.

προ-βουλεύω, f. σω, *to contrive* or *concert measures before*, Thuc. :—Med. *to debate* or *consider first*, Hdt., etc. **2.** of the Senate at Athens, *to frame* or *pass a προβούλευμα*, Xen., Dem. ; of magistrates, *to propose decrees*, Thuc. :—impers. in Pass., τῇ βουλῇ προβεβούλευται, c. acc. et inf., *it has been decreed that*, Xen. **3.** *to award by a decree of this kind*, Dem. **II.** *to have the chief voice in the senate and in passing decrees*, Xen. **III.** πρ. τινός *to deliberate for* one, *provide for* his interest, Ar., Xen.

προ-βουλή, ἡ, *forethought*, ἐκ προβουλῆς *of malice aforethought*, Antipho.

προβουλό-παις, ἡ, in Aesch., πρ. Ἄτης, = πρόβουλος παῖς Ἄτης, *the fore-counselling child of Até*.

πρό-βουλος, ον, (βουλή) *debating beforehand* :—pl. **πρόβουλοι, 1.** *commissioners to examine measures before they were proposed to the people*, Ar., etc. **2.** *deputies* of the Ionian states at the Panionium, Hdt. : also *the deputies* appointed by the Western Greeks to

consult on the mode of meeting Xerxes, Hdt. 3. at Athens, *a committee of Ten,* appointed before the constitution of the 400, Ar.

προ-βύω [ῦ], f. -βύσω :—πρ. λύχνον *to push up* the wick of a lamp, *to trim it,* Ar.

προβωθέω, Ion. for προβοηθέω.

προ-βώμιος, ον, *before the altar,* σφαγαί Eur. : **προβώμια, τά,** *a space in front of an altar,* Id.

προγαργαλίζω (sub. ἑαυτόν), f. σω, *to prepare oneself for tickling,* Arist.

προ-γαστρίδιον, τό, (γαστήρ) *a false paunch worn by actors,* Luc.

προ-γάστωρ, ορος, ὁ, ἡ, (γαστήρ) *fat-paunch,* Anth.

προ-γένειος, ον, (γένειον) *with prominent chin, long-chinned,* Theocr.

προ-γενής, ές, (γίγνομαι) *born before, primaeval,* Soph.: —Comp. **προγενέστερος, α, ον,** *earlier in birth,* i.e. *older,* Hom.; **οἱ πρ.** *our predecessors,* Arist.:—Sup. **προγενέστατος,** *eldest-born,* h. Hom.

προ-γεννήτωρ, ορος, ὁ, in pl. *forefathers,* Eur.

προ-γίγνομαι, Ion. and later -γίνομαι [ῑ]: f. -γενήσομαι: aor. 2 -προὐγενόμην: pf. προγέγονα and -γεγένημαι: Dep. :—*to come forwards,* τάχα προγένοντο *quickly they came in sight,* Il. II. *to be born before, exist before,* Hdt.; **οἱ προγεγονότες θεοί** Id.; **οἱ πρ. ἄνθρωποι** *former men,* and **οἱ προγεγενημένοι** Xen. 2. *of events and the like,* ταῦτά μοι προὐγεγόνει Plat. ; **τὰ προγεγενημένα** *things of old time,* Thuc.; **προγεγενημένοι πόλεμοι, καιροί** Id.

προ-γιγνώσκω, Ion. and later -γινώσκω: f. -γνώσομαι: aor. 2 -έγνων, Ep. inf. -γνώμεναι :—*to know, perceive, learn,* or *understand beforehand,* h. Hom., Plat., etc.; absol., Eur. 2. *to foreknow,* N. T. II. *to judge beforehand,* Thuc. ; *to provide,* Xen.

πρόγνωσις, ἡ, *a perceiving beforehand,* Luc. : in medicine, *prognosis of diseases,* Anth.

πρό-γονος, ὁ, *a forefather, ancestor,* Hdt., Att. ; **οἱ ἄνωθεν πρ.** Plat. ; **ἐκ προγόνων,** Lat. *antiquitus,* Id. :—also *of gods who are the authors* or *founders of a race* ; **Ζεῦ πρόγονε** Eur.; **θεοὶ πρόγονοι** Plat. :—metaph., **πόνοι πρόγονοι πόνων** *troubles parents of troubles,* Soph. II. *a child by a former marriage,* i.e. *one's step-son,* Lat. *privignus,* Eur. : fem. *a step-daughter,* Plut.

πρόγραμμα, ατος, τό, *a public proclamation* or *notice, programm,* Dem.; and

προγραφή, ἡ, *a public notice,* Xen. :—esp. *a sale of confiscated property,* Lat. *proscriptio,* Strab.

προ-γράφω [ᾰ], f. ψω, *to write before* or *first,* Thuc. II. *to give public notice of anything,* Ar., Dem. :—also *to summon by public notice,* ἐκκλησίαν Aeschin. :—Pass. *to be set forth publicly,* N. T. 2. = Lat. *proscribere,* Plut. III. *to write at the head of a list,* Id.

προ-γυμνάζω, f. σω, *to exercise* or *train beforehand,* Luc.

προ-δαῆναι, aor. 2 pass. inf. (with act. sense) from *προδάω, *to know beforehand,* part. προδαείς Od.

προ-δανείζω, f. σω, *to lend before* or *first,* Plut.

προ-δᾰπᾰνάω, f. ήσω, *to spend beforehand,* Luc.

προδέδωκα, pf. of προδίδωμι : pass. **προδέδομαι.**

προδείδω, f. σω, *to fear prematurely,* Soph.

προ-δείελος, ον, *before evening,* Theocr.

προ-δείκνυμι and -ύω : f. -δείξω, Ion. -δέξω :—*to shew* by way of example, Hdt. ; **τὸν ζωστῆρα προδέξας** *having pointed out* [the use of] *the girdle,* Id. 2. absol. *to tell first,* Aesch. II. *to foreshew* what is about to happen, Hdt., etc. :—c. acc. et inf. *to tell as known beforehand* that .., Thuc. III. *to point before* one, σκῆπτρῳ πρ. (sc. τὴν ὁδόν) *to feel one's way* with a stick, of a blind man, Soph. 2. pugilistic term, χερσὶ πρ. *to make feints* with the hands, *make as if one was going to strike,* Lat. *praeludere,* Theocr. :—in war, *to make a demonstration,* Xen.

προ-δειμαίνω, f. ᾰνῶ, *to fear beforehand,* Hdt.

προδείκτωρ, ορος, ὁ, Ion. for προδείκτωρ, (προδείκνυμι) *a foreshewer,* Hdt.

προ-δέρκομαι, Dep. *to see beforehand,* Aesch.

πρό-δηλος, ον, *clear* or *manifest beforehand,* Eur., etc. :—πρόδηλον ἤδη ἦν, ὅτι .. , Xen.; so, προδήλα γάρ [ἐστι], ὅτι μέλλουσι Hdt. :—ἐκ προδήλου *from a place in sight,* Soph. : Adv. -λως, Id. Hence

προδηλόω, f. ώσω, *to make clear beforehand, shew plainly,* Thuc. Hence

προδήλωσις, ἡ, *demonstration of the event,* Plut.

προ-διαβαίνω, *to go across before* others, τάφρον Xen.

προ-διαβάλλω, f. -βᾰλῶ, *to raise prejudices against* one *beforehand,* τινά Thuc. :—Pass. *to have prejudices raised against* one, Arist.

προ-διαγιγνώσκω, f. -γνώσομαι, *to perceive* or *understand beforehand,* Thuc. II. *to make a previous decree,* Id.

προ-διαίτησις, ἡ, *preparation by diet,* Luc.

προ-διαλέγομαι, Med., with aor. 1 pass., *to speak* or *converse beforehand,* Isocr.

προδιασύρω [ῡ], f. -σῠρῶ, *to pull in pieces* or *ridicule beforehand,* Arist.

προ-διαφθείρω, f. -φθερῶ, *to ruin beforehand,* Isocr. : *to bribe beforehand,* Dem. :—Pass., Thuc.

προ-διαχωρέω, *to have a previous difference* with another, Arist.

προ-διδάσκω, f. ἀξω, *to teach* one a thing *beforehand,* τινά τι Soph., Ar.; πρ. τινά Plat. :—c. acc. et inf., πρ. τινὰ σοφὸν εἶναι Soph. :—Med. *to have one taught beforehand,* Id. :—Pass. *to learn beforehand,* Thuc.

προ-δίδωμι, f. -δώσω, *to give beforehand, pay in advance,* Xen. II. *to give up to the enemy, deliver up, betray,* Lat. *prodere,* Hdt. :—c. inf., ὃν σὺ προὔδωκας θανεῖν Eur. :—Pass., Hdt., Soph. 2. *to forsake in distress, abandon,* Hdt., Att. : — Pass., Hdt. 3. absol. *to play false, desert,* Id., etc.; προδοῦσ᾽ ἁλίσκεται *is convicted of treachery,* Soph. ; πρ. πρὸς τοὺς κατιόντας *to treat treasonably with them,* Hdt. 4. with a thing as subject, *to betray* or *fail* one, Xen. :—intr. *to fail,* Lat. *deficere,* of a river that has run dry, Hdt.; of a tottering wall, Id. 5. with a thing as object, *to betray, give up,* Eur. ; χάριν πρ. *to be thankless,* Id. :—hence, *to give up as lost, bid adieu to,* ἡδονάς Soph. ; τὰς ἐλπίδας Ar.

προ-διεξέρχομαι, Dep. *to go out through before,* Xen. : —metaph. *to go through before,* τι Aeschin.

προ-διεργάζομαι, f. -άσομαι : pf. -δι-είργασμαι : Dep. : —*to work* or *mould beforehand,* Xen.

προ-διερευνάω, f. ήσω, *to discover by searching,* Xen.

προδιερευνητής, οῦ, ὁ, *one sent before to search,* Xen.

προ-διέρχομαι, Dep. *to go through before,* Xen.

προ-διηγέομαι, f. ήσομαι, Dep. *to relate beforehand, premise*, Hdt. Hence

προδιήγησις, ή, *a detailing beforehand*, Aeschin.

πρό-δῐκος, ὁ, (δίκη) *an advocate, defender, avenger*, Aesch. **2.** at Sparta, *a young king's guardian*, Xen.: *regent*, Plut.

προ-διοικέω, f. ήσω, *to regulate, order, govern, manage beforehand*, Dem.: Med. in act. sense, Aeschin.

προ-διομολογέομαι, f. ήσομαι, Dep. *to grant beforehand* :—Pass. *to be granted on both sides beforehand*, Arist.

προ-διώκω, f. -ώξομαι, *to pursue further* or *to a distance*, Thuc., Xen.

προ-δοθείς, aor. 1 pass. part. of προδίδωμι.

προ-δοκέω: only in pf. and plqpf. pass., ὥσπερ προεδέδοκτο αὐτοῖς as *had been before determined*, Thuc.; τὰ προδεδογμένα Id.; προὐδέδοκτο ταῦτά μοι *this was my former opinion*, Plat.

προ-δόκη, ή, (δοκεύω) *a place where one lies in wait, lurking-place*, Il.

πρό-δομος, ὁ, *the chamber entered immediately from the αὐλή*, serving as the guests' sleeping-room, Hom.

πρό-δομος, ον, *before the house*, Anth.

προ-δοξάζω, f. σω, *to judge beforehand*, Plat., Arist.

προδοσία, Ion. -ίη, ή, (προδίδωμι) *a giving up, betrayal, treason*, Hdt., Eur., Dem.

πρό-δοσις, ή, *payment beforehand, money advanced, earnest-money*, Dem.

προδότης, ου, ὁ, (προδίδωμι) *a betrayer, traitor*, Hdt., Att. **2.** *one who abandons in danger*, Aesch. Hence

προδοτικός, ή, όν, *traitorous*, Luc.

προδότις, ιδος, fem. of προδότης, *a traitress*, Eur.

πρόδοτος, ον, (προδίδωμι) *betrayed*, Soph., Eur.

πρό-δουλος, ον, *serving as a slave*, of a shoe, Aesch.

προδοῦναι, aor. 2 inf. of προδίδωμι:—προδούς, part.

προ-δράμων, aor. 2 inf. of προτρέχω. Hence

προδρομή, ή, *a running forward, a sally, sudden attack*, Xen.; and

πρό-δρομος, ον, *running forward, with headlong speed*, Trag. **2.** *going in advance*, Hdt., Dem.:—οἱ πρ. *the advanced guard,* 'the guides,' a corps in the Maced. army, Arr. **3.** metaph. *a precursor*, Plat.

προ-εγείρω, f. -εγερῶ, *to wake up before*, Arist.

προ-εγκάθημαι, Pass. *to be implanted before*, Polyb.

προεδρεύω, f. σω, (πρόεδρος) *to act as president*, Aeschin.; πρ. τῆς βουλῆς Dem.

προεδρία, Ion. -ίη, ή, *the privilege of the front seats* at public games, in theatres, in the public assemblies, given as an honour to ambassadors, etc., Hdt., Ar. **2.** in concrete sense, *the front seat*, ἐν προεδρίῃ κατήμενος *on a chair of state*, Hdt. **II.** *the office of πρόεδρος* (II), Arist.

πρό-εδρος, ὁ, (ἕδρα) *one who sits in the first place, a president*, Thuc., etc. **II.** in the Athenian ἐκκλησία, the πρυτάνεις *in office* were called πρόεδροι (v. πρύτανις). ap. Dem.

προ-εέργω, Ep. for -είργω, *to stop by standing before*, c. acc. et inf., προέεργε πάντας ὁδεύειν Il.

προ-εθίζω, f. σω, *to train beforehand* :—Pass. *to be so trained*, Xen., etc.

προέηκα, Ep. for -ῆκα, aor. 1 of προΐημι.

προ-εῖδον, aor. 2 with no pres. in use, προοράω being

used instead, part. προ-ϊδών, inf. -ἰδεῖν: cf. πρόοιδα :—*to see beforehand, catch sight of*, Hom., etc.; so in Med., προϊδέσθαι Od.: —absol. *to look forward*, Id. **2.** of Time, *to foresee, portend*, Orac. ap. Hdt., Pind.:—so in Med., Xen., etc. **II.** *to have a care for, provide against*, c. gen., ἡμέων οἰκοφθορημένων Hdt.; αὐτῶν (sc. τῶν ἀποβαινόντων) Thuc. :—so in Med., προϊδομένους αὐτῶν Id. :—*to make provision*, προϊδέσθαι ὑπέρ τινος Dem.

προ-εικάζω, f. σω, *to conjecture beforehand*, Arist.

πρό-ειμι, (εἶμι *ibo*) *to go forward, go on, advance*, Thuc., etc. **2.** of Time, προϊόντος τοῦ χρόνου as *time went on*, Hdt.; so, προϊόντος Xen.; προϊούσης τῆς νυκτός Id., etc. **3.** of persons reading, προϊὼν καὶ ἀναγιγνώσκων *going on* reading, Plat. **4.** *to go first, go in advance*, Xen. —c. gen. *to go before* or *in advance of*, τῆς στρατιῆς Hdt. **5.** *to go forth*, Xen. **6.** πρ. εἴς τι *to pass on to, begin* another thing, Id., Arist. **7.** of an action, *to go on well, succeed*, Xen.

πρό-ειμι, (εἰμί *sum*) *to be before*, Il.

προ-εῖπον, aor. 2 with no pres. in use, πρόφημι and προαγορεύω being used instead, part. προειπών, inf. -ειπεῖν: —v. προερέω:—*to tell* or *state before*, Plat.: *to premise*, Aeschin. **II.** *to proclaim* or *declare publicly*, Lat. *indicere*, πόλεμόν τινι Hdt., etc.:—πρ. τινι φόνου *to make proclamation* of murder against him, Dem. **III.** c. inf. *to order* or *command before*, Od., etc.; the inf. is sometimes omitted, πρ. Λυδοῖσι (sc. ποιέειν) τὰ ὁ Κροῖσος ὑπετίθετο Hdt.; πρ. ξεινίην τοῖσι Ἀκανθίοισι, like Lat. *imperare frumentum*, Id.

προείρηκα, pf. of προερέω:—προειρήσομαι, fut. pass.

προ-εισάγω [ἄ], Ion. προ-εσ-, f. ξω, *to bring in* or *introduce before*, Dem. :—Med. *to bring in beforehand for oneself, to bring in* from the country into the town, Hdt. **II.** intr., πρ. ἑαυτοῦ *to go on the stage before oneself*, Arist.

προ-εισενεγκεῖν, aor. 2 inf. of προεισφέρω.

προ-εισέρχομαι, Dep. *to come* or *go in before*, Dem.

προεισοίσω, fut. of προεισφέρω.

προ-εισπέμπω, f. ψω, *to send in before*, Xen.

προ-εισφέρω, f. -οίσω: aor. 2 -ήνεγκον:—*to advance money to pay the* εἰσφορά *for others*, Dem. Hence

προεισφορά, ή, *money advanced to pay the* εἰσφορά *for others*, Dem.

προεῖτο, 3 sing. plqpf. pass. of προΐημι.

προ-εκδέχομαι, Dep. *to intercept before*, Strab.

πρό-εκθεσις, ή, *an introduction, preface*, Polyb.

προ-εκθέω, f. -θεύσομαι, *to run out before, sally from the ranks, rush on*, Thuc.

προ-εκκομίζω, f. Att. ιῶ, *to carry out beforehand*, Hdt.

προ-εκλέγω, f. ξω, *to collect moneys not yet due*, Dem.

προ-εκπέμπω, f. ψω, *to send out before*, Plut.

προ-εκπλέω, f. -πλεύσομαι, *to sail out before*, Plut.

προ-εκπλήσσω, f. ξω, *to astound before*, Plut., Luc.

πρό-εκπτωσις, εως, ή, *a going beyond limits*, Strab.

προ-εκτίθεμαι, Med. *to set forth before* or *by way of preface*, Polyb.

προ-εκτρέχω, aor. 2 -εξέδραμον, *to run out before*, Plut.

προ-εκφοβέω, f. ήσω, *to scare away before*, Plut., Luc.

προεκφόβησις, εως, ή, *a previous panic*, Thuc.

προέλασις, ή, *a riding forward*, Xen. From

προ-ελαύνω, f. -ελάσω, seemingly intr. (sub. ἵππον), to ride on or forward, Xen.: c. gen. to ride before one, Id.:—Pass., of Time, ὡς πρόσω τῆς νυκτὸς προελήλατο (3 sing. plqpf. impers.) as the night was now far advanced, Hdt.

προελθεῖν, aor. 2 inf. of προέρχομαι.

προ-ελπίζω, f. σω, to hope for before, N.T.

προελών, aor. 2 part. of προαιρέω.

προ-εμβαίνω, f. -βήσομαι: aor. 2 -ενέβην:—to embark first or before, Plut.

προ-εμβάλλω, f. βαλῶ: pf. pass. -βέβλημαι:—to put in or insert before, Arist. II. absol., προεμβαλλόντων ἐς τὴν γῆν τῶν κερέων the horns first striking against the ground, of the βόες ὀπισθονόμοι, which by reason of their projecting horns were obliged to graze backwards, Hdt. 2. of ships, to make the charge (ἐμβολή) first, Thuc.

προ-εμβῐβάζω, f. -βιβῶ, to put in before, πρ. τινὰ εἰς ἀπέχθειαν to make one hated before, Polyb.

προεῖμεν, Ep. for προεῖναι, aor. 2 inf. of προΐημι.

προ-εν-άρχομαι, Dep. to begin before, N.T.

προενδείκνῡμαι, Dep. to exhibit oneself or make a demonstration before another, c. dat., Aeschin.

προενεγκεῖν, aor. 2 inf. of προφέρω.

προ-εννέπω, contr. προὐννέπω, only in pres. and impf., to proclaim, announce, Aesch., Eur.; πρ. τινὶ ὅτι.. Aesch.: c. inf., πρ. τινὰ χαίρειν I publicly bid him hail, Soph., Eur.

προενοίκησις, ἡ, a dwelling in a place before, Thuc.

προ-ενσείω, f. σω, to set at before, τινά τινι Plut.

προ-εντυγχάνω, f. -τεύξομαι, to converse with before, Plut., etc.; ὄψις πρ. τῆς φωνῆς his face begins to converse before he speaks, Id.

προ-εξαγγέλλω, to announce beforehand, Dem.

προ-εξαγκωνίζω, f. σω, of pugilists, to move the arms before beginning to fight: also of a speaker, Arist.

προ-εξάγω, f. ξω, to lead or carry out first, Hdt., Thuc. II. intr. to advance first, τῷ κέρᾳ with the wing, Thuc.:—so in Pass., Id.

προ-εξαιρέω, to take out before:—Pass. to be deprived of before, τι Luc.

προ-εξαΐσσω, Att. -ᾴσσω, f. ξω, to dart out before, as out of the ranks in battle, Hdt.; aor. 1 part. προεξᾴξαντες Thuc.

προ-εξαμαρτάνω, to do wrong before, Isocr.

προ-εξανίσταμαι, Pass., with aor. 2, pf., and plqpf. act. to rise and go out before or first, Hdt., Dem. 2. in a race, to start before the signal is given, Hdt.

προ-εξαπατάω, f. ήσω, to deceive before, Arist.

προ-εξαποστέλλω, f. -στελῶ, to send out before, Polyb.

προ-εξέδρα, Ion. -η, ἡ, a chair of state, Hdt.

προ-έξειμι (εἶμι ibo), to sally forth from, Thuc.

προεξελαύνω, f.-ελάσω [ᾰ], to ride out before, Plut. 2. π. πλοίῳ to run out in a ship before, Id.

προ-εξεπίσταμαι, contr. προὐξ-, Dep. to know well before, Aesch.

προ-εξερευνάω, contr. προὐξ-, f. ήσω, to investigate before, Eur. Hence

προεξερευνητής, contr. προὐξ-, οῦ, ὁ, an explorer sent before, Eur.

προ-εξέρχομαι, Dep. to go out before, τῷ πεζῷ with the infantry, Thuc.

προ-εξετάζω, f. σω, to examine before, Luc.

προ-εξεφίεμαι, contr. προὐξ-, Med. to enjoin beforehand, Soph.

προ-εξορμάω, f.ήσω, to set out or start beforehand, Xen.

προ-επαγγέλλομαι, Med. to promise before, N.T.

προ-επαινέω, f. ήσω, to praise before, Thuc.

προ-επανασείω, f. σω, to raise the hand against before: metaph. in Pass., ἡ παρασκευὴ προεπανεσείσθη it was in agitation before, Thuc.

προ-επαφίημι, to send forward against the enemy, Luc.

προ-επιβουλεύω, f. σω, to plot against one beforehand, τινί Thuc.:—Pass. to be the object of such plots, Id.

προ-επιξενόομαι, Pass. to be received as a guest before, Luc.

προ-επιπλήσσω, to be the first to blame, τινί Arist.

προ-επισκοπέω, with aor. 1 med. ἐσκεψάμην, pf. pass. -έσκεμμαι:—to inspect or consider before, Strab., Luc.

προ-επίσταμαι, Dep. to know or understand beforehand, Plat., Xen.

προ-επιχειρέω, f. ήσω, to be the first to attack, Thuc., Plut., etc. II. c. inf. to attempt beforehand, Plut.

προ-εποικέω, f. ήσω, to colonise before, Strab.

προ-εργάζομαι, Dep. with f. άσομαι, pf. -είργασμαι:— to do or work at beforehand, Hdt., Xen.:—pf. also in pass. sense, τὰ προειργασμένα former deeds, Thuc.; ἡ προειργασμένη δόξα glory won before, Xen.

προέργου, v. προὔργου.

προ-ερέσσω, aor. 2 -ήρεσα, Ep. -έρεσσα, to row forwards, Hom.

προερευνάομαι, Med. to search out first or before, οἱ προερευνώμενοι ἱππεῖς the videttes, Xen.

προ-ερέω, Att. contr. -ερῶ, serving as fut. to προεῖπον: hence pf. προείρηκα, pass. -ημαι: aor. 1 pass. προερρήθην, contr. προὐρρήθην :—to say beforehand, Plat. :—Pass., ἐκ τῶν προειρημένων Id.; τὰ προρρηθέντα Id.; ταῦτά μοι προειρήσθω be said by way of preface, Isocr. II. to order one to do a thing beforehand or publicly, τινί c. inf., Hdt.; also, πρ. τινί ὡς.. Id.:—Pass. impers., προείρητο αὐτοῖς ἐπιχειρεῖν orders had been given them not to attack, Thuc.; τὸ προειρημένον the prescribed implement, Hdt.; δεῖπνον πρ. ordered beforehand, Id.; πόλεμος προερρήθη, Lat. indictus est, Xen.

προ-ερύω, Ep. aor. 1 -έρυσσα, to draw on or forward, νῆα ἅλαδε προέρυσσεν drew the ship forward, by hauling her from the beach to the sea, Il. 2. of ships at sea, =προέρεσσω, Hom.

προ-έρχομαι: aor. 2 -ῆλθον: pf. -ελήλυθα, contr. προὐλήλυθα: Dep.:—like πρόειμι (which serves as the fut.), to go forward, go on, advance, Hdt., Thuc., etc.: —absol., προελθὼν ὁ κῆρυξ ἐκήρυττε Aeschin. 2. of Time, προελθόντος πολλοῦ χρόνου Thuc.; of persons, προεληλυθὼς τῇ ἡλικίᾳ far advanced in age, Xen. 3. to go on, in a story or argument, Plat. 4. metaph., τὰ Περσέων πρήγματα ἐς τοῦτο προελθόντα the power of the Persians having advanced to this height, Hdt.; εἰς πᾶν μοχθηρίας πρ. Dem.; εἰς τοῦτο προβέβηκεν ἔχθρας, ὥστε.. Id. 5. to go before or first, Xen.; πρ. τινος to go before him, Id.; later, πρ. τινα N.T. II. with instr. of motion, πρ. πόδα to advance the foot, Luc.

πρό-ες, -έστω, aor. 2 imper. of προΐημι.

προ-εσαξάμην, aor. 1 med. of προεισάγω.

προέσθαι, aor. 2 med. inf. of προΐημι.

πρόεσις, ἡ, (προΐημι) a throwing away, Arist.

προέστατε, Ion. for –εστήκατε, 2 pl. pf. of προΐστημι: –προεστώς, part.

προ-έσχον, aor. 2 of προέχω.

προετικός, ή, όν, (προΐημι) apt to throw away, giving lavishly, profuse, lavish, Xen., etc.; πρ. τινι giving lavishly to .., Arist. :—Adv. –κῶς, Id.

προετοιμάζω, to get ready before:—Med. to prepare for one's own use or purpose, Hdt.

προ-ευαγγελίζομαι, Dep. to preach the gospel beforehand, N.T.

προ-ευλᾰβέομαι, aor. 1 –ευλαβήθην: Dep.:—to take heed, be cautious beforehand, Dem.

προέφθᾰσα, aor. 1 of προφθάνω.

προ-εφοδεύομαι, Pass. to be traversed before, Strab.

προ-έχω, contr. προὔχω, f. –έξω: aor. 2 –έσχον, med. –εσχόμην, προυσχόμην: cf. προΐσχω:—to hold before, so as to protect another, Ar. Xen. :—Med. to hold before oneself, hold out before one, Hom., Ar. 2. metaph. in Med. to put forward, use as a pretext, Soph.; ὅπερ μάλιστα προὔχονται, μὴ ἂν γίγνεσθαι τὸν πόλεμον which is the chief reason they allege, to shew that the war would not arise, Thuc. b. to hold forth, offer, Id. II. to be possessed or informed of a thing beforehand, Hdt. 2. to have before others, τιμὴν προέξουσ᾽ τῶν ἐνδίκων shall have honour before the righteous, Soph.: absol., ὁ προέχων the first possessor, Arist.

B. intr. to jut out, project, of headlands, towers, hills, Hom., Hdt., etc. II. in running, to be the first, have the start, Il.; c. gen., προέχων τῶν ἄλλων getting before the rest, Hdt.; πρ. ἡμέρης ὁδῷ to keep ahead by a day's march, Id.; πρ. τῇ κεφαλῇ to beat by a head, in racing, Xen.;—of Time, προεῖχε [ἡ τριήρης] ἡμέρᾳ καὶ νυκτὶ started first by a day and night, Thuc. 2. of rank, c. gen., δήμου προὔχουσιν they are the first or chief of the people, h. Hom. :—absol. to be superior, to be eminent, Thuc.; τὸ προὔχον all that is eminent, Id.; οἱ προὔχοντες the chief men, Id. 3. to surpass, excel, c. gen., Hdt., Att.; πρ. τινὸς τιμήν to be preferred to him in honour, Soph. b. rarely c. acc. pers., Xen. :—Pass. to be excelled, N. T. III. impers., οὔ τι προέχει it naught avails, c. inf., Hdt.

προ-εώρᾱκα, pf. of προοράω.

προ-ηγεμών, όνος, ὁ, one who leads as a guide, Dem.

προ-ηγέομαι, f. ήσομαι, Dep. to go first and lead the way, to be the leader, Hdt., etc.; τινι for a person, i. e. to guide him, Ar., Xen.; πρ. τὴν ὁδόν Xen. 2. c. gen. to take the lead of, Id.;—later, c. acc., N. T. 3. of things, to go before, precede, Xen. 4. part. προηγούμενος, η, ον, going first, τὸ πρ. στράτευμα the van, Id. Hence

προηγητής, οῦ, ὁ, one who goes before to shew the way, a guide, Soph.; so προηγητήρ, ῆρος, ὁ, Eur.

προ-ηγορέω, f. ήσω, (προήγορος) to speak on the part of others, Xen.; πρ. τινί to speak for another, Plut.

προηγορία, ἡ, a speaking in behalf of others, Luc.

προ-ήγορος, ὁ, (ἀγορά) one who speaks in behalf of others, an advocate.

προηγουμένως, Adv. part. of προηγέομαι, beforehand, antecedently, Plut.

προῄδεον, Att. –ῄδη, plqpf. of πρόοιδα.

προ-ήδομαι, Pass. to be pleased before or first, Arist.

προήκα, aor. 1 of προΐημι.

προ-ήκης, ες, (ἀκή) pointed in front, Od.

προ-ήκω, f. –ήξω, to have gone before, be the first, Thuc., Xen. 2. to have advanced, πρ. ἐς βαθὺ τῆς ἡλικίας Ar.; εἰς τοῦτο προήκειν to have come to this pass, Dem.; of Time, τῆς ἡμέρας προηκούσας Plut. II. to reach beyond, τῆς ἄρκυος Xen.

προ-ησσάω, Att. –ηττάω, f. ήσω, to overpower beforehand, Polyb. :—pf. and plqpf. pass. to be beaten or worsted before, Id.

προθᾰλής, ές, (θάλλω) early growing, h. Hom.

προ-θέλυμνος, ον, (θέλυμνον) from the foundations or roots, προθελύμνην ἕλκετο χαίτας he tore his hair out by the roots, Il.; προθέλυμνα χαμαὶ βάλε δένδρεα he threw to earth trees uprooted, Ib.; ἐφόρει τὰς δρῦς προθελύμνους Ar. II. σάκος σάκεϊ προθελύμνῳ φράξαντες fixing shield on shield close-pressed,—where θέλυμνα are the several shields, each overlapping its neighbour, Hom.

προ-θερᾰπεύω, f. σω, to prepare beforehand, Plat. II. to court beforehand, Plut.

πρόθεσις, ἡ, (προτίθημι) a placing in public;—of a corpse, the laying it out (cf. προτίθημι II), Plat., Dem. 2. a public notice, Arist. 3. the statement of the case, Id. 4. οἱ ἄρτοι τῆς προθέσεως the loaves laid before, the shewbread, N. T. II. a purpose, end proposed, Philipp. ap. Dem. III. a supposition, calculation, Polyb.

προ-θέσμιος, α, ον, (θεσμός) fore-appointed, Luc. II. προθεσμία (sc. ἡμέρα), ἡ, in Att. law, a day appointed beforehand, within which money was to be paid, actions brought, claims made, elections held, Dem., Aeschin. :—generally, an appointed time, Plat.

προ-θεσπίζω, f. σω, to foretell, Aesch.

προθέω, f. θεύσομαι, to run before, Il.; πολὺ προθέεσκε (Ion. impf.) he was far ahead, Hom. 2. to run forward or forth, Xen. II. c. acc. to outrun, outstrip, Id.; c. gen., Plut.

προ-θέω, old form of προ-τίθημι, τούνεκά οἱ προθέουσιν ὀνείδεα μυθήσασθαι; do they therefore let him speak reproachful words? Il.

προ-θνήσκω, f. –θᾰνοῦμαι: aor. 2 –έθανον :—to die before, Thuc. II. to die for another, c. gen., Eur.

προθορών, aor. 2 part. of προθρώσκω.

πρό-θρονος, ὁ, a president, Anth.

προ-θρυλέω [ῠ], f. ήσω, to noise abroad beforehand, Luc.

προ-θρώσκω, to spring before, forth, forward, only in aor. 2 part. προθορών, Il.

πρόθῡμα, τό, (προθύω) a preparatory sacrifice, Ar.:—metaph., ἐμὸν θάνατον προθύμαT᾽ ἔλαβεν Ἄρτεμις Eur.

προ-θῡμέομαι: impf. προεθυμεόμην, contr. προὐθυμού-μην: f. med. –θυμήσομαι and pass. –θυμηθήσομαι: aor. 1 προὐθυμήθην: (πρόθυμος) :—to be ready, willing, eager, zealous to do a thing, c. inf., Hdt., Att.; also πρ. ὅπως Hdt., Att. 2. absol. to shew zeal, exert oneself, Hdt. :—to be of good cheer, Xen. 3. c. acc. rei, to be eager or zealous for, promote eagerly, desire ardently, Thuc., etc. Hence

προθῡμητέον, verb. Adj. *one must be eager*, Plat. ; and **προθῡμία**, Ion. -ίη, ἡ, *readiness, willingness, eagerness, zeal*, ᾗσι προθυμίῃσι [ῑ] πεποιθώς, i. e. πρόθυμος ὤν, Il. ; πάσῃ προθυμίᾳ with all *zeal*, Plat. ; ὑπὸ προθυμίας *zealously*, Id. **2.** c. gen. pers., ἐκ τῆς Κλεομένεος προθυμίης at his *desire*, Hdt. ; κατὰ τὴν τούτου προθυμίην as far as his *desire* goes, Id. ; τοῦ θεοῦ προθυμίᾳ by the *will* of the god, Eur. **3.** c. gen. rei, προθυμίη σωτηρίης *zeal* to save him, Hdt. ; πρ. ἔργου *readiness* for action, the *will* or *purpose* to act, Soph. **4.** πρ. ἔχειν, = προθυμεῖσθαι, Hdt. ; c. inf., Id., Att. **II.** *good-will, ready kindness*, Hdt. From

πρό-θῡμος, ον, *ready, willing, eager, zealous*, π. εἰμι, c. inf., = προθυμέομαι, Hdt., Att. **2.** c. gen. rei, *eager for*, Soph., Thuc. **3.** with Preps., πρ. εἴς τι Ar., Thuc., etc. ; ἐπί τι, πρός τι Xen. **4.** absol., Hdt., etc. :—τὸ πρόθυμον = προθυμία, Eur. **II.** *bearing good-will, wishing well*, Soph., Eur., etc. **III.** Adv. -μως, *readily, zealously, actively*, Hdt., etc. ; πρ. μᾶλλον ἢ φίλως with more *zeal* than *kindness*, Aesch. :—Comp. -ότερον, Thuc., etc. :—Sup. -ότατα, Hdt., etc.

προ-θύραιος [ῠ], α, ον, and ος, ον, (θύρα) *before the door* ; προθύραια, τά, the *space before a door*, h. Hom.

πρό-θῠρον, τό, (θύρα) the *front-door*, the *door leading from the* αὐλή, Hom. ; also in pl., Id. **2.** the *space before a door*, a kind of *porch* or *verandah*, Lat. *vestibulum*, Od., Hdt., Att. **3.** metaph. Κόρινθος πρόθυρον Ποτειδᾶνος Pind. ; πρόθυρα ἀρετῆς Plat.

προ-θύω, f. -θύσω and -θύσομαι :—*to sacrifice* or *offer before*, Plat. :—Med. *to have a person sacrificed* or *slaughtered before*, Luc. **II.** *to sacrifice for* or *in behalf of* another, c. gen., Eur. ; ὑπέρ τινος Id.

προΐ, **προΐος**, **πρόϊμος**, f. ll. for πρωΐ, πρώϊος, πρώϊμος.

προ-ΐάλλω, only in impf., *to send forth, dismiss*, Hom.

προ-ϊάπτω, f. ψω : aor. 1 -ίαψα :—*to send forward, to send untimely* to the nether world, Il., Aesch.

προϊδών, part. of προεῖδον.

προΐει, = προΐησι, 3 sing. of προΐημι :—**προΐειν**, Att. impf. :—**προϊείς**, part.

προ-ΐζομαι, Med. *to sit before, take the first seat*, Hdt.

προ-ΐημι, 3 pres. προΐει (as if from προΐω), 3 opt. προΐοι : Att. impf. προΐειν, εις, ει : f. προήσω : aor. 1 προῆκα, Ep. προέηκα : 3 pl. aor. 1 πρόεσαν, opt. προεῖεν : imperat. πρόες, 3 sing. προέτω ; inf. προέμεν for προεῖναι :—Med., aor. 1 προηκάμην : 3 pl. aor. 2 opt. πρόοιντο or πρόεοιντο :—Pass., pf. προεῖμαι, 3 sing. plqpf. προεῖτο :—*to send before, send on* or *forward*, Hom. : also, *to send* something *to* another, ἀγγελίας, φήμην Od. :—Hom. often with an inf. added, αἰετώ προέηκα πέτεσθαι, οὖρον προέηκεν ἀῆναι Od. **2.** *to send away, dismiss, let go*, Il. ; τήνδε θεῷ πρόες *let* her *go* to the god, i. e. in reverence to him, Ib. **3.** *to let loose, let fall*, esp. thoughtlessly, ἔπος προέηκε *let drop* a word, Od. ; πηδάλιον ἐκ χειρῶν προέηκε he *let* the helm *slip* from his hands, Ib. ; δάκρυα προῆκεν Eur. **4.** of missiles, *to send forth, shoot* or *dart forth*, Hom. **5.** of a river, ὕδωρ προΐει ἐς Πηνειόν it *pours* its water into the Peneius, Il. **6.** πρ. τινὶ ποιεῖν τι *to allow* one *to do*, Pind. **II.** *to give up, deliver over, betray* one to his enemy, Hdt., Thuc. :

—Pass. *to be given* or *thrown away*, εἰ προεῖτο ταῦτα Dem. **2.** ἐπὶ τὸ αὐτίκα ἡδὺ πρ. αὑτόν *to give up* or *devote* oneself to present delights, Xen. **B.** Med. *to send forward from oneself, drive forward*, Xen. :—of sounds, *to utter*, Aeschin., etc. **II.** *to give up, let go* : *to give up* to the enemy, Thuc., etc. ; πρ. σφᾶς αὐτούς gave themselves *up* as lost, Id. **2.** *to desert, abandon*, Id. ; οὐδαμῇ προΐεντο ἑαυτούς did not *lose* themselves (i. e. take bribes), Dem. **3.** *to give away, give freely*, Thuc., etc. ; προέσθαι ἀπὸ τῶν ἰδίων Dem. **4.** *to throw off* one's *clothes*, Id. : and, in bad sense, *to throw away*, τὸν καιρόν Id. ; τὰ πατρῷα Aeschin. : absol. *to be lavish*, Arist. **5.** a second predicate is sometimes added, ἡμᾶς προέσθαι ἀδικουμένους *to suffer* us to be wronged, Thuc. ; προέμενοι αὐτοὺς ἀπολέσθαι Xen. ; πρ. τινὶ ὑμᾶς ἐξαπατῆσαι Dem. **6.** *to suffer to escape*, Polyb. **7.** rarely in good sense, *to give over* to one, *confide to* one's *care*, Xen. **III.** *to neglect, disregard*, Arist. :—absol. *to neglect all advice*, *to be reckless*, Dem.

προῖκα, v. προίξ II.

προίκιος, ον, (προΐξ) *gratuitous*, Anth.

προίκτης, ου, ὁ, (προΐξ) *one who asks a gift, a beggar*, Od. ; ἀνὴρ π. *a beggar-man*, Ib.

ΠΡΟΙΞ, προικός, ἡ, *a gift, present*, προικὸς γεύσασθαι *to taste of a present*, Od. ; προικὸς χαρίσασθαι *to give away gratis* (προικός being gen. pretii), Ib. **2.** *a marriage-portion, dowry*, Plat., Dem. **II.** the Att. used acc. προῖκα as Adv., like δωρεάν, *as a free gift, freely, at one's own cost*, Lat. *gratis*, Ar., Plat. ; πρ. κρίνειν *without a gift, unbribed*, Dem.

προΐππεύω, f. σω, *to ride before others*, c. gen., Plut.

προ-ΐστημι, f. -στήσω : aor. 1 προὔστησα, part. προστήσας, inf. προστῆσαι : **A.** Causal in these tenses, as also in pres. and aor. 1 med., *to set before* or *in front*, προστήσας [σε] Τρωσὶ μάχεσθαι Il. **2.** *to set over* others, c. gen., Plat. **II.** Med., mostly in aor. 1, *to put* another *before oneself, choose* as one's *leader*, Hdt. : c. gen., προΐστασθαι τουτονὶ ἑαυτοῦ *to take* as one's *leader*, Plat. **2.** *to put before* one, *put in front*, Hdt., etc. **3.** metaph. *to put forward as a pretence, use as a screen*, τὰ τῶν Ἀμφικτυόνων δόγματα προστήσασθαι Dem. ; c. gen. *to use* one thing *as a pretext* for another, Id. **4.** *to prefer, value* one *above* another, τινά τινος Plat. **B.** Pass., with aor. 2 act. προὔστην : pf. προέστηκα, Ion. 2 pl. προέστατε, inf. προεστάναι, part. προεστώς : aor. 1 pass. προεστάθην :—*to put oneself forward, come forward*, Dem. **2.** c. acc. *to approach*, Soph. **3.** c. dat. *to stand before* or *face* another, Id. **II.** c. gen. *to be set over*, *be the chief power*, τῆς Ἑλλάδος, τῶν Ἀρκάδων Hdt. :—*to be at the head of* a party, *act as chief* or *leader*, τῶν παράλων, τῶν ἐκ τοῦ πεδίου Id. ; τοῦ δήμου Thuc. : hence absol., οἱ προεστῶτες, Ion. -εῶτες, *the leading men, chiefs, leaders*, Hdt., Thuc., etc. **2.** in various relations, *to govern, direct, manage*, οὐκ ὀρθῶς σεωυτοῦ προέστηκας *you do* not *manage* yourself well, Hdt. ; πρ. τοῦ ἑαυτοῦ βίου Xen. **3.** *to stand before* so as *to guard* him, Hdt. ; πρόστητε τύχης *be* our *defence against* fortune, Soph. ; ὁ προστὰς τῆς εἰρήνης the *champion* of peace, Aeschin. ;—also, προὐστήτην φόνου

were the authors of death, Soph. :—absol., βέλεα ἀρωγὰ προσταθέντα Id.

προ-ΐσχω, = προέχω, *to hold before, hold out,* of boys playing at ποσίνδα, Xen. :—mostly in Med. *to hold out before oneself, stretch forth,* χεῖρας Thuc. : c. gen. *to hold before,* τῶν ὄψεων τὰς χεῖρας Plut. II. metaph. in Med. *to put forward, use as a pretext, allege, plead,* Hdt., Thuc. 2. *to propose, offer,* Ib.

Προιτίδες (πύλαι), αἱ, one of the gates of Thebes, called from Proetus, Aesch.

προιών, part. of πρό-ειμι (εἶμι *ibo*).

προ-ίωξις [ῑ], ἡ, *pursuit of the foremost,* Hes.

πρόκἄ, Ion. Adv. (πρό) *forthwith, straightway, suddenly,* in Hdt., πρόκα τε or πρόκατε.

προ-καθεύδω, f. -ευδήσω, *to sleep before* or *first,* Ar.

προ-καθηγέομαι, Dep. *to go before and guide,* Polyb.; πρ. τῆς κρίσεως *to influence it beforehand,* Id.

προ-κάθημαι, Ion. -κάτημαι, properly pf. of προκαθέζομαι :—*to be seated before,* πρὸ τῆς ἄλλης Ἑλλάδος πρ. *to lie in front* of the rest of Greece, of the Thessalians, Hdt. 2. c. gen. *to be seated* or *lie before* a place, and so, *to protect, defend,* Id., Thuc.; στρατιᾶς πρ. Eur. II. *to preside over,* τῆς πόλεως Plat.

προ-καθίζω, Ion. -κατίζω, *to sit down* or *alight before,* Il. 2. *to sit in public, sit in state,* ἐς θρόνον Hdt. : —so in Med., Id. 3. *to settle before,* Id. II. trans. *to set over,* Polyb.

προ-καθίημι, f. -ήσω, *to let down beforehand :* metaph., πόλιν πρ. εἰς ταραχήν *to plunge* the city into confusion, Dem.; πρ. τινὰ ἐξαπατᾶν *to put* a person *forward* in order to deceive, Id.

προ-καθίστημι, f. -στήσω, *to set before ;* so in Med., Xen. II. Pass., with aor. 2 and pf. act., φυλακῆς μὴ προκαθεστηκυίας no guard *having been set beforehand,* Thuc.

προ-καθοράω, f. -κατόψομαι, *to examine beforehand, to reconnoitre,* Hdt.

προ-καίω, f. -καύσω, *to burn before :* Pass. *to be lighted before,* of fires, Xen.

πρόκακος, ον, *exceeding bad,* κακὰ πρόκακα evils *beyond* evils, Aesch.

προ-κἄλέω, f. -έσω, *to call forth :* mostly in Med., 3 sing. Ep. aor. 1 προκαλέσσατο, imper. προκάλεσσαι :— *to call out to fight, challenge, defy,* Lat. *provoco,* Hom.; so, πρ. εἰς ἀγῶνα Xen. 2. *to invite* or *summon beforehand,* τινὰ ἐς λόγους Hdt., Thuc. ; ἐς σπονδάς Thuc. ; ἐπὶ ξυμμαχίαν Id. 3. c. acc. et inf. *to invite* one *to do,* Id., etc. 4. absol., αὐτῶν προκαλεσαμένων *at* or *after* their invitation, Id. II. c. acc. rei, *to offer* or *propose,* δίκην Id. ; τὰς σπονδάς Ar. ; c. acc. pers. added, προκαλεῖσθαί τινα τὴν εἰρήνην *to offer* one peace, Id. 2. as Att. law-term, *to make an offer* or *challenge* to the opponent, such as to submit the case to arbitration, let slaves be put to the torture, Dem. ; cf. πρόκλησις :— Pass., πρ. ἐς κρίσιν περί τινος Thuc. III. *to call up* or *forth,* εὐγένειαν Eur.

προ-κἄλίζομαι, Dep., only in pres. imper. προκαλίζεο, Ep. 3 sing. impf. προκαλίζετο :—*to call forth* or *out, challenge, defy,* Hom.

προκἄλινδέομαι, Pass. *to fall prostrate before another,* Isocr., Dem.

προκάλυμμα, ατος, τό, *anything put before, a curtain,* such as was hung in doorways instead of doors, Aesch. 2. *a covering,* as a protection, Thuc. 3. metaph. *a screen* or *cloak,* Id., Luc. From

προ-κἄλύπτω, f. ψω, *to hang before as a covering :*— Med. *to put over oneself as a screen* or *cloak,* Eur. ; οὐ παρακαλυπτομένα παρηίδος *putting* no veil *over one's* face, Id. II. *to cover over,* ἥλιον νεφέλη πρ. Xen. : —Med., προὐκαλύψατο ὄμματα *veiled her eyes,* Eur.

προ-κάμνω, f. -καμοῦμαι : aor. 2 προέκαμον :—*to work* or *toil before,* Theogn. II. *to toil for* or *in defence of,* τινός Soph. III. *to grow weary, give up,* μὴ πρόκαμνε Aesch. ; μὴ προκάμητε πόδα Eur. IV. *to have a previous illness,* Thuc. ; — *to be distressed beforehand,* Id.

προ-κάρηνος [ἄ], ον, (κάρηνον) *head-foremost,* Anth.

προκάς, άδος, ἡ, = πρόξ, h. Hom.

προ-καταγγέλλω, f. -αγγελῶ, *to announce* or *declare beforehand,* N. T. Hence

προ-καταγιγνώσκω, f. -γνώσομαι, *to vote against beforehand, condemn by a prejudgment,* c. gen. pers., Dem., etc. ; absol., Ar. ; μὴ προκατεγνωκέναι μηδέν *not to prejudge* in any point, Dem. 2. c. inf., πρ. ἡμῶν ἥσσους εἶναι *to prejudge* us and say we are inferior, Thuc. 3. πρ. τί τινος, as, φόνον τινός, *to give a verdict of* murder *against* one *beforehand,* Oratt.

προ-κατάγομαι, Pass. *to get into harbour before,* τινος Luc. Hence

προκαταγωγή, ἡ, *a coming into port before,* Arr.

προ-καταθέω, *to run down before,* Xen.

προ-κατακαίω, f. -καύσω, *to burn all before one,* Xen.

προ-κατάκειμαι, Pass. *to lie down before,* Luc.

προ-κατακλίνω [ῑ], f. -κλῐνῶ, *to make to lie down before* others, Joseph. :—Pass., = προκατάκειμαι, Luc.

προ-καταλαμβάνω, f. -λήψομαι, *to seize beforehand, preoccupy,* Thuc., etc. :—Pass. *to be preoccupied,* Id. II. metaph. *to anticipate, frustrate,* Id., Aeschin. :—of persons, *to anticipate* or *surprise* them, Thuc. III. *to overpower* before, Id.

προ-καταλέγομαι, Pass. *to be described beforehand,* Hdt.

προ-καταλήγω, f. ξω, *to terminate beforehand,* Polyb.

προ-καταλύω, f. -λύσω [ῠ], *to break up* or *annul beforehand,* Thuc. ; τὸν βίον πρ. τοῦ ἔργου *to end his life before* finishing his work, Plut. :—Med., πρ. τὴν ἔχθρην *to end their mutual* enmity *before,* Hdt.

προ-καταπίπτω, *to fall down before :* λόγοι προκατέπιπτον εἰς τὴν Ῥώμην *rumours reached* Rome *beforehand,* Plut.

προ-καταπλέω, f. -πλεύσομαι, *to sail down before,* Polyb.

προ-καταρτίζω, f. σω, *to complete beforehand,* N. T.

προ-κατάρχω, f. ξομαι, *to begin a thing before* others, *to begin hostilities,* Polyb. II. προκατάρχεσθαί τινι τῶν ἱερῶν *to serve* one *with the first portion* of the victim (one of the privileges of the citizens of the mother-city in their colonies), Thuc.

προ-κατασκευάζω, f. σω, *to prepare beforehand,* Xen.

προ-κατασκευή, ἡ, *previous preparation, a preface, introduction,* Polyb.

προ-καταφεύγω, f. -φεύξομαι, *to escape to a place of safety before,* Thuc.

προ-καταχράομαι, pf. -κέχρημαι, Dep. *to use up beforehand,* Dem.

προ-κατελπίζω, f. σω, to hope beforehand, Polyb.
προ-κατεσθίω, f. -έδομαι, to eat up beforehand, Luc.
προ-κατέχω, f. -καθέξω, to hold or gain possession of beforehand, preoccupy, Thuc., Xen.:—Med. to hold down before oneself, h. Hom.
προ-κατηγορέω, to bring accusations beforehand, Dem.
προκατηγορία, ή, a previous accusation, Thuc.
προκατόψομαι, fut. of προκαθοράω.
πρόκειμαι, Ion. inf. -κέεσθαι: f. -κείσομαι:—used as Pass. of προτίθημι, to be set before one, of meats, Hom., Hdt. 2. to lie exposed, of a child, Hdt. :—to lie dead, Aesch., Soph.; ὁ προκείμενος the corpse laid out for burial, Soph., etc. 3. to be set before all, as the prize of a contest, Hes. :—metaph. to be set before all, be set forth, proposed, Lat. in medio poni, γνῶμαι τρεῖς προεκέατο three opinions were set forth, proposed, Hdt., etc. :—of contests, struggles, πόνος τε καὶ ἀγὼν πρόκειται Plat. :—in partic., ἄεθλος προκείμενος a task proposed, Hdt., etc.; τὰ προκείμενα, opp. to μέλλοντα, Soph.; τὸ προκείμενον πρῆγμα the matter in hand, Hdt. 4. to be set forth beforehand, to be prescribed, αἱ προκείμεναι ἡμέραι the prescribed days, Id.; so, ἐνιαυτοὶ πρόκεινται ἐς ὀγδώκοντα are set, fixed at, Id.; of laws, νόμοι οἱ προκείμενοι Soph.; of penalties, Thuc. II. to lie before, lie in front of, c. gen., Αἴγυπτος προκειμένη τῆς ἐχομένης γῆς Hdt.; τὰ προκείμενα τῆς χώρας ὄρη Xen. III. to precede, γράμμα πρ. an initial letter, Anth
προ-κέλευθος, ον, conducting, τινος Mosch.
προ-κενόω, f. ώσω, to empty beforehand, Luc.
προ-κήδομαι, Dep. only in pres. to take care of, take thought for, τινος Aesch., Soph.
προ-κηραίνω, f. ἀνῶ, to be anxious for, τινός Soph. : also, τί ποτ', ὦ τέκνον, τάδε κηραίνεις; why art thou thus anxious? Eur.
προ-κηρυκεύομαι, Dep. to negociate by herald, Aeschin.
προ-κηρύσσω, Att. -ττω, f. ξω, to proclaim by herald, prcclaim publicly, Soph.: c. acc. rei, Id.
προ-κινδῡνεύω, f. σω, to run risk before others, brave the first danger, bear the brunt of battle, Thuc., Dem.; τῷ βαρβάρῳ against the barbarians, Thuc.
προ-κῑνέω, to move forward, τὸν στρατόν Xen. : to urge on, ἵππον Id.:—Pass. with f. med. to advance, Id.
προ-κλαίω, Att. -κλάω: f. -κλαύσομαι:—to weep beforehand or openly, Soph., Eur. II. trans. to lament beforehand, Hdt., Eur.
προκληθείς, aor. 1 pass. part. of προκαλέω.
πρόκλησις, εως, Ion. ιος, ή, (προκαλέω) a calling forth, challenging, challenge, ἐκ προκλήσιος upon or by challenge, Hdt. II. an invitation, offer, proposal, Thuc., etc. III. as law-term, a challenge offered to the opponent, for the purpose of bringing disputed points to issue, somewhat like the Roman sponsio, Dem., etc.; πρ. προκαλεῖσθαι to make such a challenge, δέχεσθαι to accept it, Id.
προκλητικός, ή, όν, calling forth, challenging : προκλητικόν, τό, a challenge, Plut.
προ-κλίνω [ῑ], f. -κλινῶ, to lean forward, Soph.
πρό-κλῡτος, ον, (κλύω) heard formerly, of olden time, Il.
προ-κλύω, to hear beforehand, Aesch.
προ-κνημίς, ῖδος, ή, a covering for the leg, Polyb.

προκοιτία, ή, a watch kept before a place; in pl., like Lat. excubiae, Polyb. From
πρό-κοιτος, ὁ, (κοίτη) one who keeps watch before a place, Polyb.
προ-κολάζω, f. -άσομαι, to chastise beforehand, Arist.
προ-κολᾰκεύω, f. σω, to flatter beforehand, Plat.
προ-κόλπιον, τό, a robe falling over the breast, Theophr.
προ-κομίζω, f. σω, to bring forward, produce, Luc. II. Pass. to be carried before to a place of safety, Hdt.
προ-κόμιον, τό, (κόμη) the forelock of a horse, Xen.
προκοπή, ή, progress on a journey, generally, progress, advance, Polyb.; in pl., Plut., Luc. From
προ-κόπτω, f. ψω : Att. impf. προὔκοπτον :—to cut away in front : hence to forward a work (the metaph. being prob. taken from pioneers), Pass. to be forwarded, to advance, prosper, Hdt. II. with neut. Adjs., τὰ πολλὰ προκόψασ' having made most things ready, Eur.; τί ἂν προκόπτοις; what good would you get? Id.; οὐδὲν προὔκοπτον they were making no progress, Xen. 2. c. gen. rei, τοῦ ναυτικοῦ μέγα μέρος προκόψαντες having made improvements in their navy to a great extent, Thuc.; ἡμῶν προκοπτόντων τῆς ἀρχῆς ἐκείνοις since we promote the increase of their empire, Id.; ἐπὶ πλεῖον πρ. ἀσεβείας having advanced further in impiety, N. T. 3. absol. ἡ νὺξ προέκοψεν the night is far spent, Ib.; πρ. σοφίᾳ to advance in wisdom, Ib.
πρόκρῑμα, τό, prejudgment, prejudice, N. T. From
προ-κρίνω [ῑ], f. κρῑνῶ, to choose before others, choose by preference, prefer, select, Hdt., Att. :—Pass. to be preferred before others, τὰ προκεκριμένα the most eminent, Hdt.: c. inf., τοῦτο προκέκριται εἶναι κάλλιστον Xen.; inf., τὸ ἐμὲ προκριθῆναι ἄρχοντα Id. 2. c. gen. to prefer before others, Plat. :—Pass., τῶν ἄλλων προκεκρίσθαι Hdt. II. c. acc. et inf. to judge or decide beforehand that .., Xen. Hence
πρόκρῑτος, ον, chosen before others, select, Plat.
πρό-κροσσοι, αι or οι, α, ranged at regular intervals, like steps or battlements (v. κρόσσαι); of ships drawn up on the beach, ranged in a row, Il.; πρόκροσσαι ἐς πόντον ἐπὶ ὀκτὼ ranged in rows turned seawards eight deep, Hdt.; of a cup, πέριξ αὐτοῦ γρι- πῶν κεφαλαὶ οἱ πρόκροσσοι ἦσαν the heads of griffins were set at intervals round it, Id.
προ-κῠλινδέομαι, Pass. to roll at the feet of another, Lat. provolvi ad genua alicujus, τινι Ar. ; τινος Dem.
προ-κῠλίνδομαι, Pass. to roll forward, of a wave, Il.
προ-κύπτω, f. ψω, to stoop and bend forward, to peep out, Ar.
προ-κυρόομαι, Pass. to be confirmed before, N. T.
Προ-κύων, κυνός, ὁ, Procyon, a star which rises (about the middle of July) before the dog-star, Horat. II. πικροὶ Καλλιμάχου πρόκυνες, a nickname of the Grammarians, snappers and snarlers, Anth.
προ-κώμιον, τό, the prelude sung by a κῶμος, Pind.
πρό-κωπος, ον, (κώπη) of a sword, grasped by the hilt, drawn, Aesch., Eur. :—metaph. ready, Aesch.
προ-λάζῠμαι, Dep. to receive beforehand or by anticipation, τινος some of a thing, Eur.
προ-λᾰλέω, f. ήσω, to prate before, Anth.
προ-λαμβάνω, f. -λήψομαι : aor. 2 προὔλαβον : pf. -είλη- φα, pass. -είλημμαι :—to take or receive before, Eur., Dem., etc. 2. to take or seise beforehand, Dem.; πρ.

ὅπως .. *to provide* that .., Dem.; **προλαβὼν προεγνω-κότας ὑμᾶς** *first procured* your vote of condemnation, Id.   **3.** *to take before, take in preference*, τι πρό τινος Soph.   **4.** *to take away* or *off before*, **προύλα-βον μόγις πόδα** Eur.   **II.** *to be beforehand with, anticipate*, **1.** c. acc. pers. *to get the start of*, Xen., Dem. :—also c. gen. pers., Dem.   **2.** c. acc. rei, Eur.   **3.** c. gen. spatii, **πρ. τῆς ὁδοῦ** *to get a start* on the way, Hdt.; **πρ. τῆς φυγῆς** Thuc.   **4.** absol., **πολλῷ προύλαβε** *was far ahead*, Id. :—*to anticipate the event, prejudge*, Dem.; **προλαβόντες** *by anticipation*, Xen.   **III.** *to repeat from the origin*, Isocr.

προ-λέγω, f. ξω, *to choose before* others, *prefer* :— Pass., **Ἀθηναίων προλελεγμένοι** Il.; **πασᾶν ἐκ πολίων πρ.** Theocr.   **II.** *to foretell, announce beforehand*, of an oracle, Hdt., Att.   **2.** *to state publicly, proclaim*, c. acc. et inf., Aesch., etc.   **3.** **πρ. τινὶ ποιεῖν τι** *to order* him to do, Xen. —*to caution, warn*, Thuc.   **4.** *to denounce punishment*, **πρ. δεσμόν τινι** Dem.

προ-λείπω, f. ψω : pf. **-λέλοιπα** : aor. 2 **-προύλιπον** :— *to go forth and leave, to leave behind, forsake, abandon*, Hom., etc.; **μῆτίς σε προλέλοιπε** prudence *hath forsaken* thee, Od.; **χώραν πρ.** *to abandon* one's post, Thuc.   **2.** c. inf. *to omit* to do a thing, Theogn., Soph.   **3.** of things, *to desert, fail* one, Plat.   **II.** intr. *to cease* or *fail beforehand*, **Ἀτρείδαις οὐ προλείπει φόνος** Eur.; **εἰ τῳ προλείποι ἡ ῥώμη** Thuc.; of persons, *to faint, fall into a swoon*, Eur.

προ-λεσχηνεύομαι, Dep. *to hold conversations with* one *before*, c. dat. pers., Hdt.

προ-λεύσσω, *to see before oneself* or *in front*, Soph.

προλῐπεῖν, aor. 2 inf. of **προλείπω**.

πρόλογος, ὁ, (προλέγω) in Trag. and old Com. Poets, *the prologue, that portion of the play that comes before* the first chorus, Arist. ; but from the time of Eur., *a narrative of facts introductory to the plot*, Ar.

προ-λοχίζω, f. Att. ιῶ, *to lay an ambuscade beforehand* :—Pass., **αἱ προλελοχισμέναι ἐνέδραι** the ambush *that had before been laid*, Thuc.   **II.** *to beset with an ambuscade*, Id.

προ-λῡμαίνομαι, Dep. *to destroy beforehand*, Polyb.

προ-λῡπέομαι, Pass. *to feel pain before*, Plat. Hence **προλύπησις**, ἡ, *previous distress*, Plat.

προμᾱθεία, προμᾱθής, Dor. for **προμηθ-**.

προ-μᾰλάσσω, Att. -ττω, f. ξω, *to soften beforehand* : so in Med., Plut.

πρόμᾱλος, ἡ, a tree, prob. a kind of *willow*, Anth.

προ-μανθάνω, *to learn beforehand*, and (in aor. 2 **προύμαθον**) *to know beforehand*, Pind., Thuc., etc. :—c. acc. *to learn by rote*, Ar.: c. inf., **προύμαθον στέργειν τάδε** Soph.

προμαντεία, Ion. **-ηίη**, ἡ, *the right of consulting the Delphic Oracle first*, Hdt., Dem. From

προ-μαντεύομαι, f. σομαι, Dep. *to prophesy*, Hdt.: c. acc. *to foretell, predict*, Luc.

προμαντηίη, ἡ, Ion. for **προμαντεία**.

πρό-μαντις, εως, Ion. ιος, ὁ, ἡ, *a prophet* or *prophetess*, Eur.   **2.** the title of *the Pythia* or *Delphic priestess*, who gave out the answers of the oracle, Hdt., Thuc. ; so of the *priestess* at Dodona, Hdt.   **II.** as Adj. *prophetic*, **δίκη πρ.** justice *giving presage of the issue*, Soph.; **θυμὸς πρ.** 'my *prophetic* soul,' Eur. ; c. gen., **τούτων πρ. οὖσα** *prophetic, foreboding of* a thing, Aesch.

προ-μαρτύρομαι [ῠ], Dep. *to witness beforehand*, N. T.

προμάτωρ, Dor. for **προμήτωρ**.

προμᾰχέω, f. ήσω, (πρόμαχος) *to fight in front*, Xen.

προμᾰχεών, ῶνος, ὁ, *a bulwark, rampart*, Lat. *propugnaculum*, Hdt., Xen.; **πρ. τοῦ τείχεος** Hdt.

προμᾰχίζω, (πρόμαχος) *to fight before*, **Τρωσὶ** *in front* of the Trojans, as their champion, Il. ; also, *to fight as champion with* another, **Ἀχιλῆϊ** Ib.

προ-μάχομαι [ᾰ], Dep. *to fight before*, **ἁπάντων** *before* all, Il.   **II.** *to fight for* or *in defence of*, τινος Ar.

πρό-μᾰχος, ον, (μάχομαι) *fighting before* or *in front* : **πρόμαχοι**, οἱ, *the foremost fighters, champions*, Hom. ; **ἐν προμάχοισιν** *among the foremost*, Il. :—as Adj., **πρ. δόρυ** the *champion* spear, Soph.   **2.** *fighting for*, **πόλεως, δόμων** Aesch.

προ-μελετάω, f. ήσω, *to practise beforehand* : c. inf., Xen.

Προ-μένεια, ἡ, (μένος) name of a prophetess of Dodona, *Presage*, Hdt.

προ-μεριμνάω, f. ήσω, *to take thought before*, N. T.

προ-μετωπίδιος, α, ον, (μέτωπον) *before* or *on the forehead* :—**προμετωπίδιον**, τό, *the skin* or *hair of the forehead*, Hdt.   **2.** *a frontlet* for horses, Xen.

προμήθεια, Dor. **-μάθεια**, Ion. **προμηθίη**, in Att. Poets **προμηθία**: (προμηθής):—*foresight, forethought*, Hdt., Eur., etc. ; **ἐν προμηθίῃ ἔχειν τινά** *to hold in consideration*, Hdt. ; **προμηθίαν ἔχειν τινός** Eur., Plat.

Προμήθειος, α, ον, and ος, ον, (Προμηθεύς) *Promethean*, Anth.   **II. Προμήθεια**, τά, *the festival of Prometheus*, Xen.

προμηθέομαι, f. -ήσομαι: aor. 1 **προύμηθήθην** : Dep. : (προμηθής) :—*to take care beforehand, to provide for*, c. gen., Hdt. ; **ὑπέρ τινος, περί τι** Plat. ; absol., Aesch. : —generally, *to take heed*, Lat. *cavere*, **πρ. μή** .. Hdt. : —c. acc. *to shew regard* or *respect for*, Id., Plat.

Προμηθεύς, έως, Ion. έος, ὁ, Dor. **Προμᾱθεύς**, *Prometheus*, son of the Titan Iapetus and Themis, inventor of many arts: he is said to have made man from clay, and to have furnished him with the **ἔντεχνον πῦρ** stolen from Olympus : hence also his name (from προμηθής), opp. to his careless brother **Ἐπιμηθεύς**, —*Forethought* and *Afterthought*, Hes., Aesch., etc.   **II.** as appellat. *forethought*, Aesch.

προ-μηθής, Dor. **-μᾱθής**, ές, (μαθεῖν) *forethinking, provident, cautious*, Thuc. ; **τὸ προμηθές,** = προμήθεια, Id. : c. gen. *troubling oneself about* a thing, Soph.

προμηθία, -ίη, v. **προμήθεια**.

προμηθικῶς, Adv. *shrewdly, warily*, with allusion to the name Prometheus, Ar.

προ-μήκης, ες, (μῆκος) *prolonged, elongated*, Plut.

προ-μηνύω, f. ύσω [ῡ], *to denounce beforehand*, τινί τι Soph. : *to indicate before*, τι Plut.

προ-μήτωρ, Dor. **-μάτωρ** [ᾱ], opos, ἡ, *first mother* of a race, formed like **προπάτωρ**, Aesch., Eur.

προ-μηχᾰνάομαι, Dep. *to contrive beforehand*, Luc.

προ-μίγνῡμι, f. -μίξω, *to mingle beforehand* :—Pass., **παλλακίδι προμῐγῆναι** (aor. 2 inf.) *to have intercourse* with her *before*, Il.

προ-μισθόομαι, Pass. *to be hired beforehand*, Plut.

προ-μνάομαι, Dep. *to woo* or *court for* another, **ἡ προμνησαμένη** = προμνήστρια, Xen.   **2.** generally, *to solicit*, Id., Plut.   **II. προμνᾶταί τί μοι γνώμα** my mind *forebodeth* somewhat, Soph.

προ-μνηστεύομαι, = προμνάομαι, Luc.

προ-μνηστῖνοι, αι, one by one, one after the other, Od. (Perh. from μένω, for προμενετῖνοι—each waiting for the one before.)

προμνήστρια, ἡ, (προμνάομαι) a woman who woos or courts for another, a match-maker, Ar., Plat.; metaph., κακῶν πρ. of one who brings about evil, Eur.

πρό-μοιρος, ον, (μοῖρα) before the destined term, i. e. untimely, of death, Anth.

προμολεῖν, aor. 2 inf. of προβλώσκω.

προμολή, ἡ, an approach, of the foot of a mountain, Anth.; the mouth of a river, Id.

προμολών, aor. 2 part. of προβλώσκω.

πρόμος, ὁ, (πρό) the foremost man, = πρόμαχος, Hom.; πρ. τινί opposed to another in the front rank, Il.:—generally, a chief, Lat. primus, princeps, Trag.; πάντων θεῶν θεὸς πρόμος, of the Sun, Soph.

προ-μοχθέω, f. ήσω, to work beforehand, Eur.

πρό-ναος, or **πρό-ναιος, α, ον,** Ion. **προ-νήϊος, η, ον,** Att. **πρό-νεως:** (ναός):—before a temple, esp. of gods whose shrines or statues stood before the temple, as of Athena at Delphi, Hdt.; Παλλὰς προναία Aesch. II. as Subst., **πρόναος, ὁ,** = πρόδομος, the hall of a temple, through which one went to the ναός or cella, Hdt.

προ-ναυμαχέω, f. ήσω, to fight at sea for or in defence of, c. gen., Hdt.

προ-νέμω, f. -νεμῶ, to assign beforehand, τί τινι Pind.; καθαρὰς χεῖρας πρ. to present unspotted hands, Aesch. II. Med. to go forward in grazing: hence to gain ground, creep onward, of war, etc.

προ-νεύω, f. σω, to stoop or bend forward, Plat.; of a rider, Xen.; of rowers, Id.

πρόνεως, Att., and **προνήϊος,** Ion. for **πρόναος.**

προ-νηστεύω, f. σω, to fast before, Hdt.

προ-νικάω, f. ήσω, to gain a victory beforehand, Thuc.

προ-νοέω, f. ήσω, to perceive before, foresee, Il., Thuc., Arist.; προνοῶν ὅτι . . foreseeing that . . , Xen. II. to think of or plan beforehand, provide, Od.:—absol. to be provident, take measures of precaution, Eur., Thuc.:—πρ. ὅτι . . , to provide, take care that . . , Thuc.; ὅπως . . , Xen., etc. 2. c. gen. to provide for, take thought for, Id.

B. in same sense, Dep. **προ-νοοῦμαι:** f. ήσομαι: aor. 1 med. προὐνοησάμην and pass. προὐνοήθην: pf. προνενόημαι:—Act. to provide, Thuc., etc.:—c. inf. to take care to do, Eur. 2. c. gen. to provide for, Thuc., etc. Hence

προνοητέον, verb. Adj. one must provide, Xen.; and

προνοητικός, ή, όν, provident, cautious, wary, Xen. II. of things, shewing forethought or design, Id.: Adv. -κῶς, Id.

πρόνοια, Ion. -οίη, ἡ, (πρόνοος) foresight, foreknowledge, Aesch., Soph. II. foresight, forethought, forecast, Soph.; ἐκ προνοίας with forethought, purposely, Lat. consulto, Hdt.; ἀπὸ προνοίας τίνων by their precautions, Thuc.:—esp. of crimes committed with design or malice prepense, ἐκ προνοίας τραύματα Aeschin.; τὰ ἐκ πρ., opp. to ἀκούσια, Arist.:—πρόνοιαν ἔχειν (or ἴσχειν) τινός to take thought for . . , shew care for . . , Eur., etc.; περί τινος Soph.; c. inf., πολλὴν πρ. εἶχεν εὐσχήμως πεσεῖν Eur. 2. divine providence, Hdt., Att.

προνομαία, ἡ, = προνομή II, Plut.; of a fly, Luc.

προνομεύω, f. σω, to go out for foraging, Polyb.

προνομή, ἡ, (προνέμω) a foraging, a foraging expedition, foray, Xen.: in pl., foraging parties, Id. II. an elephant's trunk, Polyb. III. = sq., Luc.

προ-νομία, ἡ, (νόμος) a privilege, Strab., Luc.

προνόμιον, τό, (προνέμω) earnest-money, Luc.

πρό-νοος, ον, contr. -νους, ουν, = προμηθής, careful, Hdt.:—Comp. προνούστερος, Soph.

προ-νωπής, ές, (πρό, ὤψ, with ν inserted) stooping forwards, with head inclined, Lat. pronus, στείχει πρ., of one in deep grief, Eur.; πρ. ἐστι, of one dying, Id.; so, πρ. λαβεῖν to take her as she fell fainting forward, Aesch. 2. metaph. inclined, ready, πρ. ἐς τὸ λοιδορεῖν Eur. Hence

προνώπια, τά, the front of a house (cf. ἐνώπια), Eur.: metaph. in sing., χώρας Πελοπίας πρ., of Troezen, the outer portal of Peloponnesus, Id. II. as Adj. in front, before the door, Id.

πρόξ, gen. προκός, ἡ, the roe-deer, Od.: cf. προκάς.

πρόξεινος, ὁ, Ion. for **πρόξενος.**

προξενέω, f. ήσω: impf. προὐξένουν: f. -ήσω: pf. προὐξένηκα:—to be any one's πρόξενος, διὰ τὸ προξενεῖν ὑμῶν because he is your πρόξενος, Xen.; πρ. τῶν πρέσβεων to act as πρ. to the envoys of a friendly State, Dem.:—generally, to be one's protector, patron, Eur. II. from the duties of a πρόξενος (signf. II), 1. to manage or effect anything for another, Id.; πρ. θράσος to lend daring, Soph.; πρ. τιμήν τινι to procure it for him, Plut.:—also in bad sense, πρ. κίνδυνόν τινι to put danger upon one, Xen.:—also, c. dat. et inf., πρ. τινὶ δρᾶν to be the means of his seeing, Soph.; πρ. τινὶ καταλῦσαι βίον to grant one to die, Xen.:—also, πρ. τινὶ to be one's guide, Soph. 2. to introduce or recommend to another, Plat., Dem.

προξενία, ἡ, (πρόξενος) proxeny, i. e. a compact between a State and a foreigner, Lat. hospitium, Thuc., etc.; προξενίᾳ πέποιθα I trust my public friendship, Pind.; τινὰ πρ. ἐξευρήσεις; what protector wilt thou find? Eur. 2. the privileges of a πρόξενος Dem.

πρό-ξενος, Ion. **πρό-ξεινος, ὁ,** a public ξένος, public guest or friend, made so by an act of the State, such as was the King of Macedon to the Athenians, Hdt.;—the word expressed the same relation between a State and an individual of another State, that ξένος expressed between individuals of different States.—The πρόξενος enjoyed his privileges on the condition of entertaining and assisting the ambassadors and citizens of the State which he represented, so that the πρόξενοι answered to our Consuls, Agents, Residents, though the πρόξενος was always a member of the foreign State. II. generally, a patron, protector, Aesch.: as fem. a patroness, Soph.

προ-οδεύω, f. σω, to travel before, Luc.

προ-οδοιπορέω, f. ήσω, to travel before, Luc.

προ-οδοποιέω, f. ήσω: pf. προωδοπόίηκα:—to prepare the way before, prepare or pave the way, τινί for another, Arist. II. c. acc. to prepare beforehand, Plut.:—Pass. to be prepared before, Arist.: part. προωδοποιημένος, η, ον, prepared, ready, Id.

πρό-οδος, ον, going before: οἱ πρ. a party of soldiers in advance, Xen.

πρό-οδος, ἡ, a going on, advance, progress, Xen.

πρό-οιδα, pf. (cf. προεῖδον), inf. -ειδέναι, part. -ειδώς : plqpf. -οῄδη, -ῄδειν, f. -είσομαι :—to know beforehand, Hdt., Att.

προ-οικοδομέω, f. ἥσω, to build before :—Pass., Luc.

προοιμιάζομαι, Att. contr. φροιμιάζομαι : f. ἅσομαι : pf. πεφροιμίασμαι : Dep. :—to make a prelude, preamble or preface, Aesch., Xen.   II. c. acc. to say by way of preface, premise, φροιμιάζομαι θεούς begin by invoking them, Aesch. ; τί φροιμιάζει ; Eur. :—pf. in pass. sense, πεφροιμιάσθω τοσαῦτα let so much be said by way of preface, Arist. From

προ-οίμιον, τό, Att. contr. φροίμιον : (οἶμος) : — an opening or introduction to a thing ; in Music, a prelude, overture, Pind. ; in poems and speeches, a proëm, preface, preamble, introduction, Lat. exordium, Id., Xen.   2. metaph. of any prelude or beginning, φροίμιον χορεύσομαι Aesch. ; μηδέπω 'ν προοιμίοις only just beginning, Id. ; εἴ τι τοῦδε φρ. ματᾷ if any part of this presage be vain, Id.   II. generally, a hymn, Thuc., Plat.

προ-οίχομαι, Dep. to have gone on before, Xen.

προ-όμνυμι, Att. aor. 1 προύμοσα :—to swear before or beforehand, Dem.   2. to testify on oath before that . . , c. acc. et inf., Aesch., Dem.

προ-ομολογέω, f. ἥσω, to grant or concede beforehand, Plat. :—Pass., προωμολόγηταί τι εἶναι Id.

προοπτέον, verb. Adj. of προοράω, one must look to, be careful of, c. gen., Hdt.

πρό-οπτος, Att. contr. προῦπτος, ον, verb. Adj. of προοράω (f. -όψομαι) foreseen, manifest, Hdt., Att.

προ-ορατός, ή, όν, verb. Adj. to be foreseen, Xen.

προ-οράω, f. -όψομαι : pf. -εόρἀκα ; (cf. aor. 2 προεῖδον) :—to see before one, see what is just before the eyes, Thuc. : to look forward to, Xen. :—absol. to look before one or forward, Id.   2. to see before, foresee, τὸ μέλλον Hdt., Att. :—absol. τὸ προορᾶν σεν your foresight, Hdt.   3. c. gen. to provide or make provision for, Id.   II. in Att. also in Med., with pf. and plqpf. pass., to look before one, Xen.   2. to foresee, Thuc., Dem.   3. to provide for, Thuc., Dem.

προ-ορίζω, f. σω, to determine beforehand, to predetermine, pre-ordain, N. T.

προ-ορμάω, f. ἥσω, to drive forward :—Pass. to move forward, push on, Xen. ;—so intr. in Act., Id.

προ-ορχηστήρ, ῆρος, ὁ, one who leads the dance, Luc.

προ-οφείλω, Att. contr. προύφ-, f. ἥσω :—to owe beforehand : πρ. κακόν τινα to owe one an ill turn, i. e. to deserve evil at his hands, Eur. ; πρ. κακὸν ταῖς πλευραῖς to owe one's ribs a mischief, i. e. deserve a beating, Ar. :—Pass. to be due beforehand, of debts, ὁ προσφειλόμενος φόρος the arrears of tribute, Hdt. ; ἔχθρη προσφειλομένη εἴς τινα the hatred one has long had reason to feel, Id. ; εὐεργεσία προὔφειλομένη a kindness that has long remained as a debt, Thuc.   II. =ὀφείλω 1, to be due beforehand, Eur.

πρό-οψις, εως, ἡ, a foreseeing, Thuc. ; οὐκ οὔσης τῆς προόψεως since there was no seeing, Id.

προόψομαι, fut. of προοράω.

προ-παγής, ές, (πήγνυμι) prominent, Luc.

προπαθεῖν, aor. 2 inf. of προπάσχω.

προπαιδεία, ἡ, preparatory teaching, Plat. From

προ-παιδεύω, f. σω, to teach beforehand :—Pass., Plat.

πρό-πᾰλαι, Adv. very long ago, Ar.

πρόπαππος, ὁ, a great-grandfather, Oratt.

πρό-πᾰρ, (παρά) Prep. with gen. before, in front of, Hes., Eur.   II. Adv., before, sooner, Aesch.

προπαραβάλλω, to put beside beforehand :—Med. to do so for oneself, Thuc.

προ-παρασκευάζω, f. σω, to prepare beforehand, Thuc., etc. :—Med. to prepare for oneself, Id. :—Pass., ἐκ πολλοῦ προπαρεσκευασμένοι Id.

προ-παρέχω, f. -παρέξω, to offer before, Xen.   II. to supply before, Id.

προ-πάροιθε, before a vowel -θεν, Prep. with gen., before, in front of, Hom. ; πρ. ποδῶν at one's feet, i. e. close at hand, Id. ; ἠιόνος πρ. before, i. e. along the shore, Il. ; πρ. νεός before, i. e. beyond the ship, Od.   2. before the time of, Aesch.   II. as Adv., 1. of Place, in front, in advance, forward, before, Hom., Hes.   2. of Time, before, formerly, Hom., Aesch.

πρό-πᾱς, πᾶσα, πᾶν, strengthd. poët. form for πᾶς, πρόπαν ἦμαρ all day long, Hom. ; νῆας προπάσας all the ships together, Il. ; πρόπασα χώρα, γαῖα Aesch. ; πρόπαντος χρόνου Id. ; πρ. στόλος Soph. ; πρόπαντα κακὰ κακῶν Id. : neut. πρόπαν, as Adv., Eur.

προ-πάσχω, to suffer first or beforehand, Hdt., Thuc., etc. : to be ill-treated before, ὑπό τινος Thuc. :—also, ἀγαθὸν πρ. Xen.

προ-πάτωρ, ορος, ὁ, (πᾰτήρ) the first founder of a family, forefather, Hdt., Eur. :—in pl. ancestors, forefathers, Hdt., etc. ; ὦ Ζεῦ, προγόνων προπάτωρ Soph.

προ-πείθω, to persuade beforehand, Luc.

πρό-πειρα, ἡ, a previous trial or venture, πρόπειραν ποιεῖσθαι ἔν τινι, Lat. periculum facere in . . , Hdt. ; πρ. ποιεῖσθαι εἰ . . , Thuc.

πρό-πεμπτος, ον, only in neut. πρόπεμπτα as Adv. five days before, on the fifth day, Lex ap. Dem.

προ-πέμπω, f. ψω : aor. 1 προέπεμψα, contr. προὔπεμψα :—to send before, send on or forward, Hom., Hdt., Att. ; πρ. ἄχη to cause them, Soph.   2. of things, to send forth, Aesch. ; ἰοὺς πρ. to shoot forth arrows, Soph.   II. to conduct, attend, escort, Hdt., Att. : —to follow a corpse to the grave, Aesch. ; τιμὰς θεοῖς πρ. to carry offerings in procession, Id. ; jocosely, τὸν ἕνα ψωμὸν ἐνὶ ὄψῳ πρ. to let one piece of bread be attended by one condiment, Xen.   2. to pursue, Id.

προ-πέρυσι, Adv. two years ago, Plat., Dem., etc.

προ-πεσεῖν, aor. 2 inf. of προπίπτω.

προ-πετάννυμι and -ύω, f. -πετάσω, to spread out before, Xen.

προπέτεια, ἡ, reckless haste, vehemence, rashness, indiscretion, Dem., etc. From

προπετής, ές, (προπεσεῖν) falling forwards, inclined forward, Lat. proclivis, Xen.   2. thrown away, κεῖται προπετές [τὸ κάταγμα] Soph.   3. drooping, at the point of death, Id. ; cf. προνωπής.   II. metaph. 1. being upon the point of, πρ. ἐπὶ πολιὰς χαίτας Eur. ; τύμβου πρ. παρθένος Id.   2. ready for, prone to a thing, ἐπί or εἴς τι Xen. ; πρός τι Plat.   3. headlong, precipitate, rash, reckless, violent, Aeschin. ; ἡ πρ. ἀκρασία Arist. ; of a lot, drawn at random, Pind. :—of persons, οἱ θρασεῖς προπετεῖς

Arist. III. Adv. -τῶς, forwards, Xen. 2. headlong, hastily, Id., etc.; πρ. ἔχειν to be rash, Id.

προπέφανται, 3 sing. pf. pass. of προφαίνω.

προ-πηδάω, f. ήσομαι, to spring before, τῶν ἄλλων Luc. 2. to spring forward from, c. gen., Babr.

προ-πηλᾰκίζω, f. Att. ιῶ: (from πηλαξ = πηλός):—to bespatter with mud or to trample in the mire: metaph. to treat with contumely, to abuse foully, τινά Soph., Thuc., etc.:—Pass., ἰδὼν προπεπηλακισμένην [τὴν φιλοσοφίαν] Plat. II. c. acc. rei, to throw in one's teeth, Dem. Hence

προπηλάκῐσις, ἡ, contumelious treatment, Plat.; and

προπηλᾰκισμός, ὁ, = foreg., Hdt., Dem., etc.; and

προπηλᾰκιστικῶς, Adv. contumeliously, Dem.

προ-πίνω, impf. προὔπῑνον: f. -πίομαι: aor. 2 προὔπιον: pf. προπέπωκα:—to drink before another, c. gen., Luc. II. to drink to another, drink to his health, pledge him, Lat. propinare, because the custom was to drink first oneself and then pass the cup to the person pledged, προπίνω σοι Xen.; also, πρ. φιλοτησίας τινί (v. φιλοτήσιος II), Dem. 2. on festal occasions it was a custom to make a present of the cup to the person pledged, τὰ ἐκπώματα ἐμπίμπλας προὔπινε καὶ ἐδωρεῖτο Xen.: hence, simply, to give freely, make a present of, πρ. τὴν ἐλευθερίαν Φιλίππῳ to make liberty a drinking-present to Philip, give it carelessly to him, Dem.; Pass., c. gen. pretii, προπέποται τῆς αὐτίκα χάριτος τὰ τῆς πόλεως πράγματα the interests of the state have been sacrificed for mere present pleasure, Id.

προ-πίπτω, f. -πεσοῦμαι: aor. 2 προὔπεσον:—to fall or throw oneself forward, as in rowing, προπεσόντες ἔρεσσον, like Lat. incumbere remis, Od.:—of suppliants, to fall prostrate, Eur. II. to rush forward, rush headlong, Soph., Theocr. III. to move forwards, advance before the rest, Polyb.: to project, Id.

προ-πιστεύω, f. σω, to trust or believe beforehand, Xen., Dem.

προ-πίτνω, poët. for προπίπτω, to fall prostrate, ἐς γᾶν Aesch., Soph.

προ-πλέω, f. -πλεύσομαι, to sail before, Thuc.

πρό-πλοος, ον, contr. -πλους, ουν, sailing before or in advance, αἱ πρόπλοι νῆες the leading ships, Thuc.

προ-πλώω, Ion. for προπλέω, Hdt.

προ-ποδίζω, only in pres., (πούς) to advance the foot, Il.

προ-ποδών, Adv., better written divisim πρὸ ποδῶν.

προ-ποιέω, f. ήσω, to do before or beforehand, Hdt.; absol., προποιῆσαι to make the first move, Thuc. II. to prepare beforehand, plqpf. pass. προεπεποίητο Hdt.

προ-πολεμέω, f. ήσω, to make war for or in defence of another, τινός Isocr., etc.; ὑπέρ τινος Plat.: absol., οἱ προπολεμοῦντες the guards or defenders of a country, Id.; τὸ προπολεμῆσον the body intended to act as guards, Arist.

προπόλευμα, ατος, τό, service done, πρ. δάφνης its service or use, = πρόπολος δάφνη, Eur. From

προπολεύω, (πρόπολος) to minister.

πρό-πολος, ον, (πολέω) employing oneself before: 1. a servant that goes before one, an attendant, minister, Aesch., Eur., etc.: a rower, Pind. 2. one who serves a god, a minister, h. Hom., Ar.:—generally, a temple-servant, bedel, like νεωκόρος, Hdt., Ar.,

etc. II. as Adj. ministering to a thing, devoted to it, Pind.

προπομπεύω, f. σω, (προπομπός) to go before in a procession, τινός before him or it, Luc.

προπομπή, ἡ, (προπέμπω) an attending, escorting, Xen.:—a processional escort, Plut.

προπομπός, όν, (προπέμπω) escorting, esp. in a procession, Xen.: c. acc., πρ. χοάς carrying drink-offerings in procession, Aesch. II. as Subst. a conductor, escort, attendant, Id., Xen.

προ-πονέω, f. ήσω, to work or labour beforehand, Xen. 2. to work for or instead of another, τινός Id. 3. c. gen. rei, to work for, work so as to obtain, τῶν εὐφροσυνῶν Id. 4. c. acc. rei, to obtain by previous labour, Luc.:—Pass., τὰ προπεπονημένα the things so obtained, Xen. II. Med. to sink under affliction, Soph.

Προποντίς, ίδος, ἡ, the Fore-sea, i. e. the Sea of Marmora, that leads into the Pontus, Hdt., Aesch.

προπορεύομαι, Pass., with aor. 1 med., to go before or forward, Xen. 2. to come forward, Polyb. 3. to be promoted, advance, Id.

προ-πορίζομαι, Pass. to be provided beforehand, Luc.

πρόποσις, εως, ἡ, (προπίνω) a drinking to one, Polyb.

προπότης, ὁ, (προπίνω) one who drinks healths, προπόται θίασοι bands of revellers, Eur.

πρό-πους, ποδος, ὁ, the projecting foot of a mountain, its lowest part, Polyb., etc.

προ-πράσσω, Att. -ττω, f. ξω, to do before, Arist., Luc. II. to exact, Aesch.

προ-πρεών, ό, = sq.: metaph. friendly, kindly, Pind.

προ-πρηνής, ές, stronger form of πρηνής, with the face downwards, Lat. pronus, Il.; φασγάνῳ προπρηνεῖ with the edge of the sword, Od.:—neut. προπρηνές as Adv., forward, Il.

προπρο-κῠλίνδομαι, Pass. to keep rolling before another, roll at his feet, c. gen., προπροκυλινδόμενος πατρὸς Διός Il.; absol. roaming on for ever, Od.

πρό-πρυμνα, Adv. away from the stern, πρ. ἐκβολὰν φέρει, of throwing over the freight to save the vessel, metaph. in Aesch.

προ-πύλαιος [ῠ], α, ον, (πύλη) before the gate, of the statues of gods, Ar. II. προπύλαια, τά, the gateway of temples, Hdt., Ar., etc.:—in sing., Anth.

πρόπῠλον, τό, (πύλη) in pl., like προπύλαια, Hdt., Soph., etc.; in sing., Anth.

προ-πυνθάνομαι, f. -πεύσομαι: aor. 2 προὐπῠθόμην: Dep.:—to learn by inquiring before, hear beforehand, Hdt., Thuc.

πρό-πυργος, ον, offered for the towers, i. e. for the city, θυσίαι Aesch.

προ-ρέω, f. -ρεύσομαι, to flow forward, flow amain, of rivers, Hom.

προρρηθῆναι, aor. 1 pass. inf. of προερέω.

πρόρ-ρησις, ἡ, a foretelling, prediction, a previous instruction or warning, Thuc. II. public notice, a proclamation, πολεμεῖν ἐκ προρρήσεως Dem.

πρόρ-ρητος, ον, proclaimed, commanded, Soph.

πρόρ-ριζος, ον, (ρίζα) by the roots, root and branch, utterly, Lat. radicitus, Il.; πρόρριζόν τινα ἀνατρέπειν Hdt.; ἐκτρίβειν Eur.; πρόρριζος ἔφθαρται Soph.

ΠΡΟ΄Σ, Prep. with gen., implying motion from a place;

with dat., *abiding at* a place; with acc., *motion to* a place: Ep. also προτί, ποτί, Dor. ποτί.

A. WITH GEN., **I.** of Place, *from, from forth,* Hom., Soph. **2.** *on the side* or *quarter of,* νήσοισι πρὸς Ἤλιδος islands *looking (as it were) from* Elis, i. e. *towards* Elis, Od.; πρὸς τοῦ Ἑλλησπόντου ἵδρυται μᾶλλον ἢ τοῦ Στρύμονος lies more *towards* (i. e. nearer) the Hellespont than the Strymon, Hdt.; ἐστρατοπεδεύοντο πρὸς Ὀλύνθου Thuc., etc. :—often with words denoting the points of the compass, δύω θύραι εἰσίν, αἱ μὲν πρὸς βορέαο, αἱ δ' αὖ πρὸς νότου one looking *northwards*, the other *southwards*, Od.; so, οἰκέουσι πρὸς νότου ἀνέμου Hdt., etc. **3.** *before, in presence of, in the eyes of,* πρός τε θεῶν μακάρων πρός τε θνητῶν ἀνθρώπων Il.: ἄδικον οὔτε πρὸς θεῶν οὔτε πρὸς ἀνθρώπων Thuc. **4.** in supplication, adjuration, protestation, oaths, *before, by,* Lat. *per,* γουνάζομαί σε πρός τ' ἀλόχου καὶ πατρός Od.; ἐπιορκεῖν πρὸς δαίμονος to forswear oneself *by* the god, Il.; πρὸς θεῶν Att. :—the Trag. sometimes insert the pron. σε between the prep. and its case, as in Lat. *per te omnes deos oro,* πρός νύν σε πατρὸς πρός τε μητρὸς ἱκνοῦμαι Soph.; μὴ πρός σε γούνων Eur. **5.** of origin or descent, *from, on the side of,* τὰ πρὸς πατρὸς *by* the father's *side,* Hdt.; Ἀθηναῖον καὶ τὰ πρὸς πατρὸς καὶ τὰ πρὸς μητρός Dem.; πρὸς αἵματος blood-relations, Soph. **II.** *proceeding from* some cause, *from, at the hand of,* τιμὴν πρὸς Ζηνὸς ἔχοντες Od.; τυγχάνειν τινὸς πρὸς θεῶν Aesch. :—so with all Passive Verbs, προτὶ Ἀχιλλῆος δεδιδάχθαι to be taught *by* Achilles, Il.; τὸ ποιεύμενον πρὸς Λακεδαιμονίων Hdt., etc. :—*by means* or *agency of,* πρὸς ἀλλήλοιν θανεῖν Eur. :—also of things, πρὸς τίνος ποτ' αἰτίας τέθνηκεν; *from* or *by* what cause? Soph. **III.** of dependence or close connexion; and so, **1.** *dependent on* one, *under* one's *protection,* πρὸς Διός εἰσι ξεῖνοί Od.; πρὸς ἄλλης ἱστὸν ὑφαίνειν to weave a web *at the beck of* another woman, Il. **2.** *on* one's *side, in* one's *favour,* πρὸς σοῦ Soph.; πρὸς τῶν ἐχόντων τὸν νόμον τίθης Eur. **3.** *with, by,* μνήμην πρός τινος λείπεσθαι Hdt. **IV.** *fitting, suitable,* οὐ πρὸς τοῦ ἅπαντος ἀνδρός, not *befitting* every man, Id.; ἣ κάρτα πρὸς γυναικός ἐστιν 'tis very *like* a woman, Aesch.; οὐ πρὸς ἰατροῦ σοφοῦ θρηνεῖν Soph. :—also of qualities, πρὸς δίκης *agreeable to* justice, Id.; οὐ πρὸς τῆς ὑμετέρας δόξης Thuc.

B. WITH DAT., *hard by, near, at, on, in,* ποτὶ γαίῃ Od.; ποτὶ δρυσίν *among* the oaks, Il.; ἄγκυραν ποτὶ ναΐ κρημνάντων Ib.; πρὸς μέσῃ ἀγορᾷ Soph.; πρὸς τῇ γῇ ναυμαχεῖν Thuc.; αἱ πρὸς θαλάττῃ πόλεις Xen.; τὰ πρὸς ποσί that which is *close to* the feet, *before* one, Soph. **2.** *before, in the presence of,* πρὸς τοῖς θεσμοθέταις λέγειν Dem. **3.** with Verbs denoting *motion, followed by rest in* or *by* a place, *upon, against,* ποτὶ δὲ σκῆπτρον βάλε γαίῃ Hom.; βάλλειν τινὰ πρὸς πέτρῃ Od. **4.** with a notion of *clinging* closely, πρὸς ἀλλήλῃσιν ἔχεσθαι Ib.; προσπεπλασμένας πρὸς οὔρεσι Hdt.; so, to express close employment, *in, upon,* πρὸς αὐτῷ γ' εἰμὶ τῷ δεινῷ λέγειν Soph.; εἶναι or γίγνεσθαι πρός τινι to be *employed in* or *on* a thing, Plat.; ὅλον εἶναι πρός τινι Dem. **II.** *in addition to, besides,* πρὸς τοῖς παροῦσιν ἄλλα Aesch.; δέκα μῆνας πρὸς ἄλλοις

πέντε Soph.; πρὸς τῇ σκυτοτομίᾳ *in addition to* his trade of leather-cutter, Plat.; πρὸς τούτοις *besides this,* Lat. *praeterea,* Hdt., etc.; πρὸς τοῖς ἄλλοις *besides* all the rest, Thuc.

C. WITH ACCUS., **I.** of Place, *towards, to,* Lat. *versus,* ἰέναι πρὸς Ὄλυμπον Il.; πρὸς ἠῶ τ' ἠέλιόν τε, ποτὶ ζόφον Ib. **2.** with Verbs implying *previous* motion, *upon, against,* ἑστάναι πρὸς κίονα Od.; ποτὶ τοῖχον ἀρηρότες, ποτὶ βωμὸν ἵζεσθαι Ib.; ἑστάναι πρὸς σφαγάς to stand *ready for* slaughter, Aesch. **3.** with Verbs of seeing, etc., *towards,* ἰδεῖν πρός τινα Od.; so, στῆναι ποτὶ πνοίην to stand *so as to face* it, Il.; κλαίειν πρὸς οὐρανόν to cry *to* heaven, Ib. :—of points of the compass, πρὸς ζόφον κεῖσθαι to lie *towards* the West, Od.; ναίειν πρὸς Ἠῶ τ' Ἠέλιόν τε Ib.; πρὸς ἑσπέραν, ἄρκτον *towards* the West, etc. **4.** in hostile sense, *against,* πρὸς Τρῶας μάχεσθαι Il.; πρὸς θεὸν ἐρίζειν Pind.; χωρεῖν πρός τινα Soph.; —in speeches, πρός τινα *in reply to,* Lat. *adversus,* less strong than κατά τινος *against,* Dem. **5.** without any hostile sense, ἀγορεύειν, εἰπεῖν πρός τινα to address oneself *to* him, Il.; ἀμείβεσθαι πρός τινα Hdt.; also of communing *with* oneself, εἶπε πρὸς ὃν μεγαλήτορα θυμόν, προτὶ ὃν μυθήσατο θυμόν Il. :—of all sorts of intercourse, ὁμόσαι πρός τινα to take an oath *to* him, Od.; σπονδάς, συνθήκας ποιεῖσθαι πρός τινα Thuc.; ἡ πρός τινα ξυμμαχία Id.; ἡ πρός τινα φιλία, πίστις Xen., etc.; but also, πρός τινα ἔχθρα, ἀπιστία, μῖσος, πόλεμος Aesch., Xen., etc. **6.** of transactions, πρὸς Τυδείδην τεύχε' ἄμειβεν changed arms *with* Tydeides, Il.: of matters brought before a magistrate, λαγχάνειν πρὸς τὸν ἄρχοντα, γράφεσθαι πρὸς τοὺς θεσμοθέτας ap. Dem. **7.** εἶναι πρός τι to be *engaged in . . ,* Plut. **II.** of Time, *towards* or *near, at* or *about,* ποτὶ ἕσπερα *at even,* Od.; ἐπεὶ πρὸς ἑσπέραν ἦν Xen.; πρὸς ἠῶ Theocr.; πρὸς γήρας *for* or *in* old age, Eur. **III.** of Relation between two objects, **1.** *in reference to, in respect of, touching,* τὰ πρὸς τὸν πόλεμον, i. e. military matters, Thuc.; τὰ πρὸς βασιλέα our *relations to* the King, Dem.; τὰ πρὸς τοὺς θεούς our *duties to* the gods, Soph.; ὁ λόγος οὐδὲν πρὸς ἐμέ is nothing *to* me, concerns me not, Dem.; οὐδὲν αὐτῷ πρὸς τὴν πόλιν ἐστίν he has nothing to do *with* it, Id. :—often with Advs., ἀσφαλῶς ἔχειν πρός τι Xen. **2.** *in reference to, in consequence of,* πρὸς τοῦτο τὸ κήρυγμα Hdt.; ἀθύμως ἔχειν πρός τι Xen. :—often with neut. Pron., πρὸς τί; *wherefore?* *to what end?* Soph.; πρὸς οὐδέν *for* nothing, in vain, Id.; πρὸς ταῦτα *therefore, this being so,* Hdt., Att. **3.** *for* a purpose, ὡς πρός τι χρείας; Soph.; ἕτοιμος πρός τι Xen. **4.** *in proportion* or *relation to, in comparison of,* κοῖός τις ἀνὴρ δοκέοι εἶναι πρὸς τὸν πατέρα Hdt.; implying Superiority, πρὸς πάντας τοὺς ἄλλους, Lat. *prae aliis omnibus,* Id.; πρὸς τὰς μεγίστας καὶ ἐλαχίστας ναῦς τὸ μέσον σκοπεῖν the mean *between* the largest and smallest ships, Thuc. **5.** *in reference to, according to,* πρὸς τὸ παρεὸν βουλεύεσθαι Hdt.; πρὸς τὴν δύναμιν *according to* one's power, Dem.; πρὸς τὰς τύχας *agreeably to* one's fortunes, Eur. **6.** *in accompaniment to* musical instruments, πρὸς κάλαμον Pind.; πρὸς αὐλόν or τὸν αὐλόν Eur. **7.** often merely periphr. for Adv., as πρὸς βίαν = βιαίως, *by*

force, forcibly, Aesch.; **πρὸς τὸ καρτερόν** Id.; **πρὸς ἰσχύος κράτος** Soph.:—**πρὸς ἡδονὴν λέγειν, δημηγορεῖν** so as to please, Thuc.; **πρὸς τὸ τερπνόν** calculated to delight, Id.; **πρὸς χάριν** so as to gratify, Dem.;—and c. gen. rei, **πρὸς χάριν τινός**, like **χάριν** alone, Lat. gratia, for the sake of, **πρὸς χ. βορᾶς** Soph.; **πρὸς ἰσχύος χ.** by means of, Eur.; also, **πρὸς ὀργήν** with anger, angrily, Soph., etc.; **πρὸς τὸ λιπαρές** importunately, Id.; **πρὸς καιρόν** seasonably, Id.
    D. ABSOL. AS ADV.,=**πρός** B. II, besides, over and above, **πρὸς δέ** or **ποτὶ δέ** Il., Hdt., etc.; **πρὸς δὲ καί, πρὸς δὲ ἔτι, καὶ πρός** Hdt., etc.; **καὶ πρός γε** Eur.; **καὶ δὴ πρός** Hdt.
    E. IN COMPOS., it expresses   I. motion towards, **προσάγω, προσέρχομαι**.   II. addition, besides, **προσκτάομαι, προστίθημι**.   III. connexion and engagement with anything, as **πρόσειμι, προσγίγνομαι**.
προ-σάββατον, τό, the fore-sabbath, eve of the sabbath, N. T.
προσ-αγγέλλω, f. **-αγγελῶ**, to announce, **τινά τινι** Luc.   II. to denounce, **τῇ βουλῇ τινά** Plut.
προσἄγορευτέος, a, ον, verb. Adj. to be called or named, Plat.   II. **προσαγορευτέον**, one must call, **τινά τι** Arist. From
προσ-ἄγορεύω, f. **σω**: aor. 1 **-ηγόρευσα**: (but the Att. aor. is **προσεῖπον**), f. and pf. **προσερῶ, προσείρηκα**: aor. 1 pass. **προσηγορεύθην**:—to address, greet, accost, Lat. salutare, Hdt.: Pass., **δυστυχοῦντες οὐ προσαγορευόμεθα** in misfortune we are not spoken to, Thuc.   2. c. dupl. acc. to address or greet as so and so, **Δίκαν δέ νιν προσαγορεύομεν** Aesch.; **τὸν αὐτὸν πατέρα πρ.** Xen.: —c. inf., **πρ. τινὰ χαίρειν** to bid one hail or farewell, Ar.   3. to call by name, call so and so, **τὸν Ἀγαμέμνονα πρ. ποιμένα λαῶν** Xen.; **τί τὴν πόλιν προσαγορεύεις**; Plat.
προσ-άγω, f. **ξω**:—aor. 2 **προσήγαγον**, rarely aor. 1 **προσῆξα**: f. med. (in pass. sense), **προσάξομαι**:—to bring to or upon, **τίς δαίμων τόδε πῆμα προσήγαγε**; Od.; **θυσίας πρ. τινί** Hdt.; **πρ. πάντα** to furnish, supply, Xen.   2. to put to, add, **ἅμα ἠγόρευε καὶ ἔργον προσῆγε** Hdt.   3. to put to, bring to, move towards, apply, like Lat. applicare, **τὴν ἄνω γνάθον πρ. τῇ κάτω** Id.; **ὀφθαλμὸν πρ. κεγχρώμασι** to apply the eye closely to the eyelet-holes, Eur.   4. of meats, to set before, **βρώματά τινι** Xen.   5. metaph., **πρ. ὅρκον τινί** to put an oath to him, make him take it, Hdt.   6. in military sense, to bring up for the attack, move on towards, **τῇ Ποτιδαίᾳ τὸν στρατόν** Thuc.; **στρατιὰν πρ. πρὸς πολεμίους, πρ. μηχανὰς πόλει** Id.   7. metaph., **τὰς ἀνάγκας** Id.; **πρ. τόλμαν** to apply or put forth daring, Eur.   8. **πρ. φόρον** to bring in tribute, Thuc.   9. to bring to or before, **τῷ Κύρῳ τοὺς αἰχμαλώτους** Xen.: to introduce, **τινὰ πρὸς τὸν δῆμον, πρὸς τὴν βουλήν** Thuc.; **πρ. τοὺς πρέσβεις** Dem.   10. to bring hither, lead on, **ἐλπίς μ' ἀεὶ προσῆγε** Eur.:—Pass., **οἴκτῳ καὶ ἐπιεικείᾳ προσάγεσθαι** Thuc.   11. Pass. to attach oneself to, **τινι** Id.   II. seemingly intr. (sub. **ἑαυτόν, στρατόν**, etc.), to draw near, approach, esp. in a hostile sense, Xen.   2. (sub. **ναῦν**) to bring to, come to land, Polyb.
    B. Med. to bring or draw to oneself, attach to oneself, bring over to one's side, Lat. sibi conciliare,

Hdt., Thuc., etc.; **πάντων πρ. ὄμματα** to draw all eyes upon oneself, Xen.   2. absol. to draw to oneself, embrace, Eur., Ar.   3. c. inf. to induce one to do a thing, **ἡ Σφὶγξ σκοπεῖν ἡμᾶς προσήγετο** Soph.; **προσάξομαι δάμαρτ' ἐᾶν σε** will induce her to suffer thee, Eur.   II. to take to oneself, to take up, **ὀστᾶ** Id.; **τὰ ναυάγια** Thuc.:—to procure, import, Xen.; **τὰ προσαχθέντα** imports, Id.   Hence
προσᾰγωγεύς, έως, ὁ, one who brings to: **πρ. λημμάτων** one who hunts for another's profit, a jackal, Dem.
προσᾰγωγή, ἡ, a bringing to or up to, a bringing up, Polyb.   2. a bringing to, acquisition, **ξυμμάχων** Thuc.   II. (intr.) a solemn approach, as at festivals or in supplication, Hdt.   2. approach, access to a person, esp. to a king's presence, Xen., N. T.; and
προσᾰγωγός, όν, attractive, persuasive, Thuc., Luc.
προσ-ᾴδω, f. **-ᾴσομαι**, Dor. **ποτ-αείσομαι**:—to sing to, Theocr.   2. **πρ. τραγῳδίαν** to sing the songs in a Tragedy to music, Ar.   II. to harmonise, chime in, **τινί** with one, Soph.; absol., Plat.
προσ-αιθρίζω, to raise high in air, Aesch.
προσ-αιρέομαι, Med. to choose for oneself, **ἑαυτῷ πρ. τινα** to take for one's companion or ally, Lat. cooptare, Hdt.   2. generally, to choose in addition to, **τινά τινι** Thuc., Xen.
προσ-ᾴσσω, Att. **-ᾴσσω**, f. **ξω**, to rush to, Od.; **ὁμίχλη πρ. ὄσσοις** a cloud comes over my eyes, Aesch.
προσ-αιτέω, f. **ήσω**, to ask besides, **αἷμα πρ.** to demand more blood, Aesch.; **πρ. μισθὸν** to demand higher pay, Xen.   II. c. acc. pers. to importune, ask an alms of, Hdt.: c. acc. rei, to beg for a thing, Eur.: c. dupl. acc. to beg somewhat of one, Id., Xen.:—absol. to beg hard, to be importunate, Eur., Ar.   Hence
προσαίτης, ου, ὁ, a beggar, Luc.
προσ-αιτιάομαι, to accuse besides, **τινα** Plut.
προσ-ἀκοντίζω, f. **σω**, to shoot like a javelin, Luc.
προσ-ἀκούω, f. **-ἀκούσομαι**, to hear besides, Xen.
προσ-ἀκροβολίζομαι, Dep. to skirmish with besides, Polyb.
προσακτέον, verb. Adj. of **προσάγω**, one must bring to or near, Plat.   2. one must introduce, Arist.
προσ-ἀλείφω, f. **ψω**, to rub or smear upon, **τί τινι** Od.
προσ-ἀλλομαι, Dep. to jump up at one, like a dog, Xen.
προσ-ἀλπειος, ον, (Ἄλπεις) near the Alps, Strab.
προσ-άμβᾰσις, ἡ, poët. for **προσ-ανάβασις**.
προσ-ᾰμείβομαι, Dor. **ποτ-**, Med., to answer, **τινα** Theocr.
προσ-ᾰμέλγομαι, Dor. **ποτ-**, Pass. with fut. med. to yield milk besides, Theocr.
προσᾰμύνω [ῦ], f. **-ᾰμῠνῶ**, to come to aid, **τινί** Il.
προσ-ᾰμφιέννῡμι, Att. f. **-ᾰμφιῶ**, to put on over, **τί τινα** Ar.
προσ-αναβαίνω, f. **-βήσομαι**, to go up or mount besides, Xen.:—to rise higher, as a swollen river, Polyb.: metaph., **πρ. τῷ Ῥωμύλῳ** to go back to Romulus, Plut.
προσ-ανάβᾰσις, poët. **προσ-ἀμβ-**, ἡ, a going up, ascent, **κλίμακος προσαμβάσεις** ascent by means of ladders, i. e. scaling ladders, Aesch., Eur.; **πρ.** Eur.; **τειχέων** a place where they may be approached, Id.; **δωμάτων πρ.** i. e. the steps leading to the house, Id.
προσ-αναγιγνώσκω, f. **-γνώσομαι**, to read besides, Aeschin.

προσ-ανᾰγκάζω, f. σω: Ep. aor. 1 -ηνάγκασσα :—to force or constrain besides, Thuc. 2. to bring under command or discipline, Id. II. c. acc. et inf. to force one to do, h. Hom.; πρ. τινὰ παρεῖναι, ὁμολογεῖν Xen.; but inf. omitted, τοὺς μὴ δεχομένους τὰς σπονδὰς πρ. (sc. δέχεσθαι) Thuc.

προσ-αναγορεύω, to announce besides, Plat.

προσ-αναγράφω [ᾰ], to record besides, Luc.

προσ-ανάγω, f. ξω, seemingly intr. πρ. τῇ γῇ to put back to land, Plut.

προσ-αναιρέω, f. ήσω, to lift up besides : Med. to take upon oneself besides, πόλεμον Thuc. II. to destroy besides, τἀληθές Arist. III. of an oracle, to give an answer besides, Plat.; πρ. τινὶ ποιεῖν τι Dem.

προσ-ἀναισῑμόομαι, Pass. to be spent besides, Hdt.

προσ-ανακᾰλύπτω, f. ψω, to disclose besides, Strab.

προσ-ανάκλῐμα, τό, that on which one leans, Anth.

προσ-αναλαμβάνω, f. -λήψομαι, to take in besides, Dem. :—Pass., πλειόνων προσαναλαμβανομένων εἰς τὴν σύγκλητον, of a batch of new senators, Plut. II. to recal to strength : intr. to recover, Polyb.

προσ-ἀνᾱλίσκω, f. -ἀναλώσω, to lavish or consume besides, Plat., Dem.

προσ-αναπαύομαι, f. σω, Med. or Pass. to sleep beside, τινι Plut.

προσ-αναπληρόω, f. ώσω, to fill up or replenish besides, Arist., N. T. :—Med. to add so as to fill up, Plat.

προσ-αναρρήγνῡμι, f. -ρήξω, to break off besides, Plut.

προσ-ανασείω, f. σω, to shake up or about besides :— Pass. to be roused still further, Polyb.; δίκαι αὐτῷ προσανεσείοντο were being promoted against him, Plut.

προσ-αναστέλλω, to hold back besides, τὸν ἵππον Plut.

προσ-ανατέλλω, poët. προσ-αντ-, to rise up towards, Eur.

προσ-ανατίθεμαι, Med. to take an additional burthen on oneself, Xen.; but, πρ. τί τινι to contribute of oneself to another, N. T. II. προσανατίθεσθαί τινι to take counsel with one, Ib.

προσ-ανατρέχω, f. -δρᾰμοῦμαι, to run back, retrace past events, Polyb.

προσ-ανατρίβομαι [ῑ], Med. to rub oneself upon or against a thing, to frequent the gymnasium, Theophr.

προσ-άνειμι, (εἶμι ibo) to go up to, Thuc.

προσ-ανεῖπον, aor. 2 of προσαναγορεύω, to declare, publish, order besides, Xen.

προσ-ανέρπω, f. ψω, to creep up to, Plut.

προσ-ανερωτάω, f. ήσω, to ask or inquire further, Plat.

προσ-ανευρίσκω, f. -ευρήσω, to find out besides, Strab.

προσ-ανέχω, to -ανέξω, to wait patiently for a thing, c. dat., Polyb. :—also c. acc., Id.

προσ-ανής, ές, Dor. for προσ-ηνής.

προσ-άντης, ες, (ἄντην) rising up against, uphill, steep, Lat. adversus, Pind., Thuc. II. metaph. arduous, irksome, adverse, Hdt., Eur., etc. 2. of persons, adverse, hostile, τινί to one, Eur.; πρ. πρός τι setting oneself against it, Xen.

προσ-αντιλαμβάνομαι, Med. to take hold of one another, τῶν χειρῶν by the hands, Strab.

προσ-αξιόω, f. ώσω, to demand besides, Polyb.

προσ-απαγγέλλω, f. αγγελῶ, to announce besides, Xen.

προσ-απαιτέω, f. ήσω, to require from as a duty besides, Luc.

προσ-ᾰπᾰτάω, f. ήσω, to deceive besides, Strab.

προσ-απειλέω, f. ήσω, to threaten besides, ap. Dem.

προσ-απεῖπον, aor. 2 of προσαπαγορεύω, Aeschin.

προσ-απερείδομαι, Pass. to rely mainly upon, Polyb.

προσ-αποβάλλω, f. -βᾰλῶ, to throw away besides, Ar.

προσ-αποδείκνῡμι, f. -δείξω, to demonstrate besides, Plat. II. to declare besides, Strab.

προσ-αποδίδωμι, f. -δώσω, to pay as a debt besides, Dem. II. to add by way of completing, Strab.

προσ-αποκρίνομαι [ῑ], Dep. to answer with some addition, Plat.

προσ-αποκτείνω, f. -κτενῶ, to kill besides, Xen.

προσ-απόλλῡμι, and -ύω, f. -ολέσω, to destroy besides or also, Hdt., Eur. :—Med. aor. 2 -ωλόμην : pf. -όλωλα :—to perish besides or with others, Hdt.. Dem. II. to lose besides, τὴν ἀρχήν Hdt., Plat.

προσ-αποπέμπω, f. ψω, to send away or off besides, Ar.

προσ-απορέω, to propose a further difficulty, Arist.

προσ-αποστέλλω, f. -στελῶ, to despatch besides, Thuc.

προσ-αποστερέω, to defraud of besides, τῆς νίκης Dem.

προσ-αποτῑμάω, f. ήσω, to estimate besides, Dem.

προσ-αποτίνω [ῑ], f. -τίσω [ῑ], to pay besides, Plat.

προσ-αποφέρω, f. -αποίσω, to carry off besides :—Pass. to be returned besides as liable to taxation, Dem.

προσ-απτέον, verb. Adj. one must apply, τινί τι Plat. From

προσ-άπτω, Dor. προτι-άπτω, f. ψω, to fasten or attach to, attribute, τί τινι Il., Soph., etc. :—in bad sense, to fix upon, μή τι χρέος ἐμᾷ πόλει προσάψῃς Soph. 2. c. acc. only, to apply, Eur. 3. to deliver or confide to, ναυτικόν τινι Xen. II. intr. to be added, in oak κακοῖς κακὰ προσάψει Soph. III. Med. to fasten oneself upon, to lay hold of, reach, touch, Xen. 2. to meddle with, c. gen., Aeschin.

προσ-ᾰρᾰρίσκω, to fit to: pf. 2 προσάρᾱρα, Ion. -άρηρα :—intr., to be fitted to, ἐπίσσωτρα προσαρηρότα tires firmly fitted, Il. : an Ion. pf. pass. προσαρήρεται Hes.

προσ-αράσσω, Att. -ττω, f. ξω, to dash against, πρ. ναῦς σκοπέλοις Plut.

προσ-αρκέω, f. έσω, to yield needful aid, succour, assist, τινί Soph.; absol., Id., Eur.

προσ-άρκτιος, ον, (ἄρκτος) towards the north, Strab.

προσ-αρμόζω, new Att. -όττω, f. όσω :—to fit to, attach closely to, τί τινι Eur.; εἴς τι Plat. 2. metaph. to adapt, Id. 3. c. acc. only, πρ. τὴν χεῖρα to fit it on to the stump, Xen.; πρ. δῶρα to add fitting gifts, Soph. II. intr. to attach oneself : to suit or agree with a thing, τινί Plat.; πρός τι Xen.

προσ-αρτάω, f. ήσω, to fasten or attach to, τί τινι Babr. :—Pass. to be fastened or attached to, προσηρτημένον τῷ καλῷ τὸ ἀγαθόν Xen. : to accrue to one, λῆμμα προσήρτηται Dem.

προσ-ᾰτῑμόω, f. ώσω, to deprive of civil rights besides, Dem. : Pass., pf. part. προσητιμωμένος Id.

προσ-αυαίνομαι, Pass. to wither away upon, πέτραις Aesch.

προσ-αυδάω, f. ήσω, to speak to, address, accost, τινά Il., Trag. 2. c. acc. to address words to, Il. II. to speak of, τύχαν σθέν Eur. :—Pass., ἀδελφὴ προσηυδώμην was addressed as sister, Soph.

προσ-αύλειος, ον, *near a farm-yard, rustic*, Eur.

προσ-αύω, f. -αύσω, *to bring to*, πρὶν πυρὶ θερμῷ πόδα τις προσαύσῃ Soph. (The word αὔω seems to be = αἴρω.)

προσ-αφαιρέομαι, f. ἥσομαι, *to take away besides*, Dem.

προσ-αφικνέομαι, f. -αφίξομαι, Dep. *to arrive at a place or to arrive and join* a force, Thuc. II. *to approach*, τινα Anth.

προσ-αφίστημι, *to cause to revolt besides*, Thuc.

προσ-βαίνω, f. -βήσομαι : aor. 2 προσέβην : 3 sing. aor. 1 med. προσεβήσατο, Ep. -ετο :—*to step upon*, Hom., Il.; πρὸς τὸ κάτω τοῦ τόξου τῷ ἀριστερῷ ποδὶ πρ., so as *to get* a purchase in drawing it, Xen. 2. *to go to* or *towards, approach*, c. acc. loci, Hom., etc.; —c. dat., Plat. 3. *to mount, ascend*, Hdt., Soph. 4. absol. *to step on, advance*, Soph. 5. metaph. *to come upon*, τίς σε προσέβα μανία; Id.; ἄλλοις ἄλλα πρ. ὀδύνα Eur.

προσ-βάλλω, Dor. προτι-βάλλω, f. -βάλω :—*to strike* or *dash against*, τί τινι Il.; ἀψῖδα πέτρῳ πρ. *letting* it *dash against*, Eur.; τὸν πρὶν ὄλβον ἕρματι πρ. *to wreck* his happiness on a rock, Aesch.; πρ. θηρία τινί *to set* them *on* him, Dem.; πρ. δόρυ τινί Eur. :—without any notion of violence, *to put to, apply*, μαλακὰν χέρα πρ. [ἕλκει] of a surgeon, Pind.; πρ. παρειὰν παρηίδι Eur.; ὄμματα τέκνοις Id. 2. *to assign to, procure for*, κέρδος τινί Hdt.; πρ. Λακεδαιμονίοις Ὀλυμπιάδα *to give* them *the honour of* an Olympic victory, Id.; πρ. κακὸν τῇ πόλει Aesch.; εὔκλειαν σαυτῇ Soph.; πρ. δεῖμά τινι, Lat. *incutere timorem alicui*, Eur. 3. with acc. of the object struck, ἀρούρας προσβάλλειν, of the Sun, *to strike* the earth *with* his rays, Hom.; of smells, βροτοῦ [ὀσμὴ] με προσέβαλε Ar. 4. metaph. *to attend to* a thing or *to add*, Soph. 5. μή μ' ἀνάγκῃ προσβαλῇς τάδ' εἰκαθεῖν *do* not *drive* me by force to give way, Id. II. intr. *to strike against, to make an attack* or *assault upon*, τινί Aesch., etc.; πρὸς τὸ τεῖχος Hdt. :—absol. *to attack, charge*, Id.; προσβαλὼν αἱρεῖ τὴν πόλιν by assault, Xen. 2. *to put in* with a ship, ἐς τὸν λιμένα Thuc.; πρὸς Τάραντα Id.; c. dat., Σικελίᾳ Id. B. Med. *to throw oneself upon, attack*, τινα Il.

πρόσ-βασις, ἡ, (προσβαίνω) *a means of approach, access*, Hdt., Thuc.; προσβάσεις πύργων *means of approaching* the towers, Eur.

προσ-βατός, ή, όν, *accessible*, τινι Xen.; χωρίον ἔνθα οὐ προσβατὸν θανάτῳ *where was no point accessible* by death, Id.

προσ-βιάζομαι, f. άσομαι, Dep. *to compel, constrain*, τινα Ar. II. aor. 1 προσβιασθῆναι, in pass. sense, *to be forced* or *hard pressed*, Thuc.

προσ-βιβάζω, f. Att. -βιβῶ, Causal of προσβαίνω, *to make to approach, bring nearer*, τινά Plat. 2. metaph. *to bring over, persuade*, εὖ προσβιβάζεις με Ar., Xen.: of things, πρ. τι κατὰ τὸ εἰκός *to bring* it *into accordance with* probability, Plat.

προσ-βιόω, f. βιώσομαι, *to live longer*, Plut.

προσ-βλέπω, Dor. ποτι-βλέπω : f. -βλέψω and ψομαι : —*to look at* or *upon*, τινά Trag. :—rarely c. dat., Xen., Plut. 2. of things, *to regard*, Soph., Dem.

προσ-βοάομαι, Ion. aor. 1 -εβωσάμην, Med. *to call to oneself, call in*, Hdt.

προσ-βοηθέω, Ion. -βωθέω, f. ήσω, *to come to aid*,

come up with succour, προσβωθῆσαι ἐς τὴν Βοιωτίην Hdt. : absol., Thuc.

προσβολή, ἡ, (προσβάλλω) *a putting to, application*, e. g. of the touchstone (v. βάσανος), Aesch.; of the cupping-glass, Arist.; φίλαι πρ. προσώπων, of kisses, Eur.; absol. *a kiss* or *embrace*, Id. II. (from intr. sense) *a falling upon, an attack, assault*, Hdt., etc.; πρ. Ἀχαιῖς *an assault* of the Achaeans, Aesch. 2. generally, *attacks, assaults, visitations*, προσβολαὶ Ἐρινύων Id.; μιασμάτων Id. 3. without any hostile sense, *an approach, a means of approach*, προσβολὴν ἔχειν τῆς Σικελίας *to afford a means of entering* Sicily, Thuc. :—of ships, *a landing-place, place to touch at*, Id.; ἐν προσβολῇ εἶναι *to be* a place for ships to touch at, Id.

πρόσ-βορρος, ον, (βορρᾶς) *exposed to the north*, Eur.

προσ-βράχής, ές, (βράχος) *somewhat shallow*, Strab.

πρόσ-γειος, Dor. προτί-γειος, ον, (γῆ) *near the earth, near the ground*, Luc.

προσ-γελάω, f. άσομαι [ᾰ], *to look laughing at one*, τινά Hdt., Eur., etc.; c. acc. cogn., προσγελᾶτε τὸν πανύστατον γέλων *smile* your last smile *upon* me, Eur. 2. metaph., like Lat. *arrideo, to delight*, ὀσμὴ βροτείων αἱμάτων με προσγελᾷ Aesch.

προσ-γίγνομαι, Ion. and later -γίνομαι [ῐ] : f. -γενήσομαι : pf. -γεγένημαι : Dep. :—*to come* or *go to, to attach oneself to* another, τινι Hdt., etc.; τοῖς προσγιγνομένοις *by the reinforcements*, Thuc. 2. generally, *to be added, accrue*, Lat. *accedere*, Hdt., Eur., etc. 3. *to come to, happen to*, τινι Soph.

προσ-γράφω [ᾰ], f. ψω, *to write besides, add in writing*, Dem. :—Pass., τὰ προσγεγραμμένα *conditions added to a treaty*, Xen. :—Med. *to cause to be registered besides*, Dem.

προσ-γυμνάζω, f. σω, *to exercise at* or *in* a thing, Plat. :—Pass., προσγεγυμνασμένος πολέμῳ Plut.

προσ-δανείζω, f. σω, *to lend besides*: Med. *to have lent one*, i. e. *to borrow, besides*, Xen.

προσ-δᾰπᾰνάω, f. ήσω, *to spend besides*, Luc.

πρόσ-δεγμα, ατος, τό, (προσδέχομαι) *a reception*, Soph.

προσ-δεής, ές, (δέω B) *needing besides, yet lacking*, τινος Plat.

προσ-δεῖ, v. προσδέω B.

προσ-δέομαι, Dor. ποτι-δεύομαι : f. -δεήσομαι : aor. 1 -εδεήθην : Dep. :—*to be in want of, stand in need of, require besides*, τινος Thuc., etc.; ἢν τι προσδέωμαι *if I* be at all *in want*, Xen. : c. inf. *to desire also to do* a thing, Id. 2. rarely impers. = προσδεῖ, Id. II. *to beg* or *ask of* another, τί τινος Hdt. : —c. acc. pers. et inf. *to intreat* one *to* do, Id.; c. gen. pers. et inf. *to beg of* one *to* do, Id.

προσ-δέρκομαι, Dor. ποτι-δέρκομαι : f. -δέρξομαι : aor. 2 act. -έδρακον : aor. 1 pass. -εδέρχθην : pf. -δέδορκα : Dep. :—*to look at, behold*, Od., Aesch., etc. II. *to look closely upon*, Soph.

πρόσ-δετος, ον, *tied to* a thing, τινι Eur.

προσ-δέχομαι, Ion. -δέκομαι : f. -δέξομαι : Ep. aor. 2 part. sync. ποτιδέγμενος : Dep. :—*to receive favourably, accept*, Hdt. :—*to receive hospitably*, Soph., etc. : *to admit into* a place, Thuc. : *to admit to citizenship*, Plat. 2. *to admit* an argument, Id. II. Ep. part. ποτιδέγμενος, *waiting for* or *expecting*, Hom.;

so, **προσδεκομένους** τοιοῦτο οὐδέν Hdt.; τῷ Νικίᾳ προσδεχομένῳ ἦν was according to his *expectation*, Thuc.: —c. acc. et inf. fut. *to expect that* .., Hdt., etc. 2. absol. *to wait patiently*, Hom.

προσ-δέω (A), f. -δήσω, *to bind on* or *to attach*, Hdt.

προσ-δέω (B), f. -δεήσω, *to need besides*, c. gen., Eur. 2. impers. **προσδεῖ**, *there is still need of*, c. gen. rei, Thuc., Xen., etc.; c. inf., ἔτι προσδεῖ ἐρέσθαι Plat.

προσ-δηλέομαι, Dep. *to ruin* or *destroy besides*, Hdt.

προσ-διαβάλλω, f. βάλῶ, *to insinuate besides*, Plut. 2. *to slander besides*, Id.

προσδιαιρέομαι, Med. *to distinguish further*, Arist.

προσ-διαλέγομαι, Dep. *to answer in conversation* or *disputation*, Hdt.

προσ-διαμαρτύρέω, *to testify in addition*, Aeschin.

προσ-διανέμω, f. -νεμῶ, *to distribute besides*, Plut.: —Med., in pl., *to divide among themselves besides*, Dem.

προσ-διαπράσσω, f. ξω, *to accomplish besides*, Xen.

προσ-διασαφέω, f. ήσω, *to add by way of explanation*, Polyb.

προσ-διαφθείρω, f. -φθερῶ, *to destroy besides*, Soph.: —Pass. *to perish besides*, Isocr.

προσ-διδάσκω, f. άξω, *to teach besides*, Plat.

προσ-δίδωμι, f. -δώσω, *to give besides*, Soph., Eur., etc.

προσ-διηγέομαι, Dep. *to narrate besides*, Theophr.

προσδικάζομαι, Med. *to engage in a lawsuit*, Dem.

προσ-διορθόομαι, Med. *to correct besides*, Aeschin.

προσ-διορίζω, f. Att. ιῶ, *to define* or *specify besides*, Dem.: —so in Med., Arist.

προσ-δοκάω, Ion. -έω: f. ήσω: aor. 1 ἐδόκησα: —*to expect*: 1. c. inf. fut. *to expect that one will do* or *that a thing will be*, Hdt., etc.; so, c. inf. aor. and ἄν, *that one would do* or *that a thing would be*, Ar., etc.; without ἄν, Μενελέων προσδόκα μολεῖν expect his arrival, Aesch. 2. c. inf. praes. *to think, suppose* that one *is doing* or *that a thing is*, Eur. 3. c. acc. rei, *to expect, look for* a thing, Aesch., etc.; πρ. τινά *to expect, wait for* a person, Eur., etc. 4. Pass., τὸ προσδοκώμενον, opp. to τὸ ἄελπτον, Plat., etc.

προσ-δοκάω, aor. 1 -έδοξα, *to be thought besides*, c. inf., ἀπειρόκαλος προσέδοξεν εἶναι Dem.

προσδοκητός, ή, όν, (προσδοκάω) *expected*, Aesch.

προσδοκία, ή, (προσδοκάω) *a looking for, expectation*, μέλλοντος κακοῦ, θανάτου Plat.:—absol., Dem.:—foll. by a relat. word, προσδοκία ἦν μὴ .. or μὴ οὐ .., Thuc.; προσδοκίαν παρέχειν ὡς .., Id. 2. with Preps., πρὸς προσδοκίαν *according to expectation*, Id.

προσ-δόκιμος, ον, *expected, looked for*, or *to be expected*, Hdt. 2. often of persons, προσδόκιμος ἐς τὴν Κύπρον, ἐπὶ τὴν Μίλητον πρ. *expected to come to* Cyprus, *against* Miletus, Hdt.; τοῦ βαρβάρου προσδοκίμου ὄντος Thuc.

προσδρακεῖν, aor. 2 inf. of προσδέρκομαι.

προσδράμεῖν, aor. 2 inf. of προστρέχω.

προσ-εάω, f. -εάσω [ἆ], *to suffer to go further*, τινά N.T.

προσέβην, aor. 2 of προσβαίνω.

προσεβήσετο, Ep. for -ατο, 3 sing. aor. 1 med. of προσβαίνω.

προσ-εγγίζω, f. Att. ιῶ, *to approach*, τινί Anth.

προσ-εγγράφω [ἄ], f. ψω, *to inscribe besides upon a pillar*, Hdt.: *to add a limiting clause*, Aeschin.

προσ-εγγυάομαι, f. ήσομαι, Med. *to become surety besides*, πρ. τινα ὀφλήματος *to become his surety also for* the sum owed, Dem.

προσ-εγκελεύομαι, Med. *to exhort besides*, Plut.

προσ-εγχρίω [ῑ], *to besmear besides* or *once more*, Anth.

προσ-εδαφίζω, *to fasten to the ground*: Pass., pf., κύτος προσηδάφισται the shield is *made solid*, Aesch.

προσεδρεία, poët. -εδρία, ή, *a sitting by*: 1. *a besieging, blockade*, Lat. *obsessio*, Thuc. 2. *a sitting by a sick-bed*, Eur. From

προσεδρεύω, f. σω, (πρόσεδρος) *to sit near, be always at his side*, c. dat., Eur., Dem.; πρ. τῷ διδασκαλείῳ *to be in regular attendance* at the school, Id. 2. metaph. *to sit by and watch*, τοῖς πράγμασι Id.

προσεδρία, ή, v. προσεδρεία.

πρόσ-εδρος, ον, (ἕδρα) *sitting near*, πρ. λιγνύς smoke *hanging about*, Soph.

προσ-έειπον, Ep. for προσεῖπον.

προσ-εθίζω, *to accustom* or *inure* one *to* a thing, τινά τι Xen.; c. acc. et inf., Id.:—Pass. *to accustom oneself to* a thing, τινι Id.

προσειδέναι, inf. of πρόσοιδα.

προσ-εῖδον, inf. -ιδεῖν, part. -ιδών, aor. 2 without any pres. in use, προσοράω being used instead :—*to look at* or *upon*, Hdt., Aesch., etc. :—also in Med. προσϊδέσθαι, Pind., Aesch. II. Pass. προσείδομαι, *to be like*, Aesch.

προσείκα, Att. for προσέοικα.

προσ-εικάζω, f. άσω: aor. 1 -ήκασα :—*to make like, assimilate*, τί τινι Xen. :—Pass. *to be like, resemble*, τινι Aeschin. II. metaph. *to compare*, τί τινι Aesch., Eur.; κακῷ δέ τῳ προσεικάζω τόδε *I think this looks like mischief*, Aesch.: *to guess by comparison, conjecture*, Id.

προσ-είκελος, ον, *somewhat like*, c. dat., Hdt.

προσ-ειλέω, Dor. ποτι-ειλέω, f. ήσω, *to press* or *force towards*, Il.; μὴ προσείλει χεῖρα *press not your hand against me*, Eur.

προσειλόμην, aor. 2 of προσαιρέομαι.

πρόσ-ειλος, ον, (εἵλη) *towards the sun, sunny*, Aesch.

πρόσ-ειμι, inf. -εῖναι, (εἰμί *sum*) *to be added to, be attached to, belong to*, τινί Hdt., Soph., etc. 2. absol. *to be there, be at hand, be present*, Aesch., etc.; οὐδὲν ἄλλο προσῆν *there was nothing else in the world*, Dem.; τὰ προσόνθ᾽ ἑαυτῷ *one's own properties*, Id.; ταῦτα πρόσεσται *this too will be ours*, Xen.; τὸ προσόν *the surplus*, Dem.

πρόσ-ειμι, inf. -ιέναι, (εἶμι *ibo*) used in Att. as fut. of προσέρχομαι, and προσήειν as impf. :—*to go to* or *towards, approach*, absol., Hom., Att. :—c. dat. pers. *to go to, approach one*, Hdt., etc.; πρ. Σωκράτει *to visit him as teacher*, Xen. :—c. acc. loci, δῶμα, δόμους Aesch., Eur.; πρ. εἰς .., Soph., etc. 2. in hostile sense, *to go* or *come against, attack*, τῇ πόλει Xen.; πρός τινα Hdt.; ἐπί τινα Xen. 3. *to come over to the side of*, in war, Thuc. 4. *to come forward to speak*, πρ. τῷ δήμῳ Xen.; τῇ βουλῇ Dem.; πρὸς τὰς ἀρχάς Thuc. 5. of things, *to be added*, ἐλπὶς προσήει *hope alone was left*, Aesch. II. of Time, *to come on, be at hand*, ἐπεὰν προσίῃ ἡ ὥρη Hdt.; ἑσπέρα προσήει Xen. III. *to come in*, of revenue, Hdt., Thuc.; τὰ προσιόντα *the revenue*, Ar.

προσεῖπον, inf. -ειπεῖν, used as aor. 2 of προσαγορεύω:

Ep. **προσ-έειπον**, Dor., 3 sing. opt. **ποτιείποι**: Att. also aor. 1 **προσείπα** (cf. **προσερέω**):—to speak to one, to address, accost, Hom., etc.; πρ. ὀνόματί τινα Dem.:—c. dupl. acc., τί προσείπω σ᾽ ἔπος; Ar. 2. to address as so and so, πρ. τινὰ ὡς ἀλλότριον Plat.; πρ. τινὰ χαίρειν to bid him greeting, Eur. 3. to call so and so, to name, τί νιν προσείπω; Aesch.; τοῦτο γάρ σ᾽ ἔχω μόνον προσειπεῖν Soph.; ὅν μοι προσείπας πόσιν whom thou didst name my husband, Eur.

προσ-εισπράσσω, f. ξω, to exact besides, Plut.

προ-σείω, f. σω, to hold out and shake, πρ. χεῖρα to shake it threateningly, Eur.; προσείειν ἀνασείειν τε [τὸν πλόκαμον] to wave it up and down, Id.: metaph., πρ. φόβον to hold a thing out as a bugbear, Thuc.

προσ-εκβάλλω, f. -βαλῶ, to cast out besides, Dem. II. to draw out further, prolong, Strab.

προσ-εκπέμπω, f. ψω, to send away besides, Xen.

προσ-εκπυρόω, f. ώσω, to set on fire besides, Luc.

προσεκτέον, verb. Adj. of προσέχω, one must apply, Plat.: absol. one must attend, τινί to a thing, Aeschin.

προσεκτικός, ή, όν, (προσέχω) attentive, Xen.

προσ-εκτίλλω, f. -τιλῶ, to pluck out besides, τὰ πτερά Ar.

προσ-εκτίνω [ῐ], f. -τίσω [ῐ], to pay in addition, Plut.

προσ-έκυρσα, aor. 1 of προσκυρέω.

προσ-εκχλενάζω, f. σω, to ridicule besides, τινά Dem.

προσ-ελαύνω, f. -ελάσω, Att. -ελῶ: aor. 1 -ήλασα:— to drive or chase to a place, Thuc.:—Pass. to be driven or fixed to, πρός τι Plut. II. seemingly intr., 1. (sub. ἵππον), to ride towards, ride up, Hdt., Xen.; οἱ προσελαύνοντες the cavalry, Xen. 2. (sub. στρατόν), to march up, arrive, Id.

προσέλεκτο, 3 sing. Ep. aor. 2 pass. of προσλέγω.

προσελήλυθα, pf. of προσέρχομαι.

προσ-έλκω, f. -έλξω and -ελκύσω [ῠ]:—to draw towards, draw on, τινά:—Med. to draw towards oneself, attract, Theogn.; aor. 1 προσειλκυσάμην Eur.

προσ-ελλείπω, to be still wanting, Anth.

προσ-εμβαίνω, to step upon, trample on, τινί Soph.

προσ-εμβάλλω, to throw or put into besides, Plut.

προσ-εμβλέπω, f. ψω, to look into besides, Xen.

προσ-εμπικραίνομαι, Pass. to be yet more angry with, τινί Hdt.

προσ-εμφερής, ές, resembling, Hdt., Xen.

προσ-ενεχυράζω, f. σω, to seize as an additional pledge for payment, Dem.

προσ-εννέπω, to address, accost, Pind., Trag.; τάδε σ᾽ ἐγὼ πρ. I address these words to thee, Aesch. 2. c. inf. to intreat or command, τινὰ ποιεῖν τι Pind. 3. πρ. τινά τι to call by a name, Aesch.

προσ-εννοέω, f. ήσω, to think on, observe besides, Xen.

προσ-εντείνω, f. -τενῶ, to strain still more, πρ. πληγάς τινι to lay more blows on one, Dem.

προσ-εντέλλομαι, Dep. to enjoin besides, Xen.

προσ-εξαιρέομαι, Med. to choose besides, Hdt.

προσ-εξαμαρτάνω, f. -αμαρτήσομαι, to err besides or still more, Dem.

προσ-εξανδραποδίζομαι, Dep. to enslave besides, Dem.

προσ-εξανίσταμαι, Pass. with aor. 2 act. -ανέστην, to rise up to, Plut.

προσ-εξαπατάω, to deceive besides, Arist.

προσ-εξελίσσω, f. ξω, to unrol besides: of soldiers, to wheel them half-round, Polyb.

προσ-εξεργάζομαι, f. -άσομαι, Dep. to accomplish besides, Dem.; pf. -εξείργασμαι in pass. sense, Id.

προσ-εξερείδομαι, Pass. to support oneself by, ταῖς χερσί Polyb.

προσ-εξετάζω, f. σω, to search into besides, Dem.

προσ-εξευρίσκω, to find out or devise besides, Ar.

προσ-εξηπειρόω, f. ώσω, to turn still more into dry land, Strab.

πρόσεξις, ἡ, (προσέχω) attention, Plat.

προσ-έοικα, pf. with pres. sense (no pres. προσείκω being in use), Att. inf. προσεικέναι: Dor. plqpf. ποτῴκειν:—besides which we have a 2 sing. pf. pass. προσήιξαι in Eur.:—to be like, resemble, c. dat., Id., etc. II. to seem fit, τὰ μὴ προσεικότα things not fit and seemly, Soph.; so, οὐκ ἐμοὶ προσεικότα Id. III. to seem to do, c. inf., Dem.

προσ-επαινέω, f. -έσομαι, to praise besides, Aeschin.

προσ-επαιτιάομαι, Dep. to accuse besides, Plut.

προσ-επεῖπον, aor. 2, to say besides, Plut.

προσ-επεξευρίσκω, f. -ευρήσω, to invent for any purpose besides, Thuc.

προσ-επιβάλλω, to add over and above, Isocr.

προσ-επιγράφω [ᾰ], f. ψω, to write on besides, Theophr.

προσ-επίκειμαι, Pass. to be urgent besides, Dem.

προσ-επικοσμέω, to embellish besides, Polyb.

προσ-επικτάομαι, f. -κτήσομαι, Dep. to acquire besides, Arist.; πρ. Λυδοῖσί [τινας] to add them to the Lydian realm, Hdt.

προσ-επιλαμβάνομαι, f. -λήψομαι, Med. to take part with another in a thing, to help one in a thing besides, προσεπιλαβέσθαι τινὶ τοῦ πολέμου Hdt.

προσ-επιπλήσσω, Att. -ττω, f. ξω, to rebuke besides, τινί Arist.

προσ-επιπνέω, f. -πνεύσομαι, to blow favourably besides, Plut.

προσ-επιπονέω, f. ήσω, to work still more, προσεπιπονεῖν ἀκούοντας to take the additional trouble of listening, Aeschin.

προσ-επιρρίπτω, f. ψω, to throw to besides, Aesop.

προσ-επισιτίζομαι, Med. to provide oneself with further supplies of corn, Polyb.

προσ-επισκώπτω, f. ψω, to joke besides, Plut.

προσ-επίσταμαι, Dep. to know besides, Xen.

προσ-επιστέλλω, f. -στελῶ, to notify, enjoin, command besides, esp. by letter (v. ἐπιστολή), Thuc., Xen.

προσ-επισφραγίζομαι, Dep. to set one's seal to a thing besides, to testify besides, πρ. τι εἶναι Dem.

προσ-επιτάσσομαι, Med. to take one's post, Polyb.

προσ-επιτείνω, f. -τενῶ, to stretch still further, to lay more stress upon, τι Polyb. II. to torture or punish still more, τινά Id.

προσ-επιτέρπομαι, f. ψομαι, Pass. to enjoy oneself still more, Ar.

προσ-επιτίθημι, f. -θήσω, to add further, Arist.

προσ-επιτροπεύομαι, Pass. to be under guardianship, Dem.

προσ-επιφέρω, to bear or produce besides, Xen.

προσ-επιφωνέω, f. ήσω, to say besides, add, Plut.

προσ-επιχαρίζομαι, Dep. to gratify besides, τινι Xen.

προσεπτάμην [ᾰ], aor. 2 of προσπέτομαι.

προσ-εργάζομαι, f. -άσομαι, Dep. to work in addition to, τί τινι Eur., Plut.; ἀγαθὰ πρ. τινι to do good

service to one besides, Hdt.　2. to make or earn in addition, Xen.

πρόσ-εργον, τό, earnings, the interest of money, Dem.

προσ-ερείδω, f. σω, to thrust against, Polyb., Plut.　II. intr. to press against, Polyb.

προσερέσθαι, aor. 2 inf., with f. -ερήσομαι, Med. to ask besides, Plat.

προσ-ερεύγομαι, Dep. to belch at or against : metaph., of waves, to break foaming against, Hom.

προσ-ερέω, Att. contr. -ερῶ, as fut. of προσ-αγορεύω, προσεῖπον being aor. 2 : pf. προσείρηκα :—Pass., f. προσρηθήσομαι : aor. 1 προσερρήθην : pf. -είρημαι :—to speak to, address, accost, τινά Eur., etc.　2. c. dupl. acc. to call or name, πολίτας πρ. ἀλλήλους Plat.

προσ-ερίζω, Dor. **ποτ-ερίσδω**, f. σω, to strive with or against, Theocr.

προσ-έρπω, Dor. **ποθ-έρπω**, f. ψω : aor. 1 προσείρπῦσα : —to creep to :　1. absol. to creep or steal on, Soph., Ar. :—metaph., ὁ πρ. χρόνος, i. e. the time that's coming, Pind.; πᾶν τὸ πρ. every thing that approaches, Aesch.; τὸ πρ. what is coming, the coming event, Soph.; αἱ προσέρπουσαι τύχαι Aesch.　2. to come to or upon, c. acc. pers., Pind.; c. dat. pers., σοὶ πρόσερπον τοῦτ' ἐγὼ τὸ φάρμακον ὁρῶ, of punishment, Soph.

προσέρρηξα, aor. of προσρήσσω.

προσ-ερυγγάνω, aor. 2 -ήρῦγον, = προσερεύγομαι, Theophr.

προσ-έρχομαι : impf. -ηρχόμην : f. -ελεύσομαι (but the Att. impf. and fut. are προσήειν, πρόσειμι) : aor. 2 -ήλυθον, -ῆλθον : pf. -ελήλυθα : Dep. :—to come or go to, c. dat., Aesch., etc.; πρ. Σωκράτει to visit him as teacher, Xen. :—c. dat. loci, Aesch., Eur.; also c. acc. loci, Eur.; often also with Preps., ἐπί, εἰς, πρός : and with Advs., δεῦρο, πέλας :—absol. to approach, draw nigh, be nigh at hand, Hdt., Soph.　2. in hostile sense, πρ. πρός τινα Xen.　3. to come in, surrender, capitulate, Thuc.　4. to come forward to speak, πρ. τῷ δήμῳ Dem.; πρὸς τὸν δῆμον Aeschin.　5. to associate with one, πρός τινα Dem.　II. to come in, of revenue, Lat. redire, Hdt., Xen.

προσ-ερωτάω, f. ήσω, to question besides, τινά Plat.; Pass., Xen.　2. c. acc. rei, to ask besides, Arist.

προσ-εσπέριος, ον, towards the west, western, Polyb.

προσ-έσπερος, Dor. **ποθέσπερος**, ον, = foreg. : τὰ ποθέσπερα, as Adv. towards evening, Theocr.

προσ-εταιρέομαι, Med., = sq., Luc.

προσ-εταιρίζομαι, Med. to take to oneself as a friend, associate with oneself, τινα Hdt. Hence

προσεταιριστός, όν, joined with as a companion, attached to the same ἑταιρεία or club, Thuc.

προσ-έτι, Adv. over and above, besides, Hdt., Ar., etc.

προσ-ευθύνω, to bring to an account besides, Arist.

πρόσευξαι, aor. 1 imper. of προσεύχομαι.

προσ-ευπορέω, f. ήσω, to provide besides, Dem.

προσ-ευρίσκω, f. -ευρήσω, to find besides or also, Soph.

προσ-ευχή, ἡ, prayer, οἶκος προσευχῆς, of the Temple, N. T.　II. a place of prayer, an oratory or chapel, Ib., Juvenal.

προσ-εύχομαι, f. ξομαι, Dep. to offer prayers or vows, Aesch., Eur., etc.　2. c. acc., πρ. τὸν θεόν to address him in prayer, Ar.　3. absol. to offer prayers, to

worship, Hdt., Aesch., etc.　II. πρ. τι to pray for a thing, Xen.

προσ-εφέλκομαι, Med. to draw after one besides : metaph. to invite persons (to be citizens), Arist.

προσέφην, aor. 2 of πρόσφημι.

προσεχής, ές, (προσέχω) of Place, next to, πρ. ἑστάναι τινί in battle, Hdt. :—in geogr. sense, bordering upon, marching with, adjoining, c. dat., Id.; οἱ προσεχέες their next neighbours, Id.　2. exposed to the wind, Strab.

προσ-έχω and **προσ-ίσχω**, f. ξω : aor. 2 προσέσχον :— to hold to, offer, Aesch. : to bring to, τὴν ἀσπίδα προσίσχειν πρὸς τὸ δάπεδον Hdt.　2. πρ. ναῦν to bring a ship near a place, bring it to port, Hdt.; Μαλέᾳ προσίσχων πρῷραν Eur.; τίς σε προσέσχε χρεία; what need brought thee to land here ? Soph.; alone, to put in, touch at a place, προσσχεῖν ἐς τὴν Σάμον, πρὸς τὰς νήσους Hdt.;—also c. dat. loci, πρ. τῇ νήσῳ, etc., Id.; also c. acc. loci, προσέσχες τήνδε γῆν Soph. :— absol. to land, Hdt., etc.　3. to turn to or towards a thing, πρ. ὄμμα Eur.; πρ. τὸν νοῦν to turn one's mind to a thing, be intent on it, Lat. animadvertere, τινί or πρός τινι Ar., etc.; πρ. τὸν νοῦν πρός τινι Id. :—absol., πρόσεχε τὸν νοῦν take heed, Id.; so, πρ. τὴν γνώμην Thuc.　4. without τὸν νοῦν, πρ. ἑαυτῷ to give heed to oneself, Ar., Xen.; πρ. ἑαυτοῖς ἀπό τινος to be on one's guard against, N. T. :—absol., προσέχων ἀκουσάτω attentively, Dem.　b. to devote oneself to a thing, Lat. totus esse in illo, c. dat., Hdt., Thuc., etc.　c. c. inf. to expect to do, Hdt.　5. Med. to attach oneself to a thing, cleave to it, c. dat., Id., Ar.　6. Pass. to be held fast by a thing, ὑπό τινος Eur. :—metaph. to be implicated in a thing, c. dat., Thuc.　II. to have besides or in addition, Plat., Dem.

προσ-εῷος, ον, towards the east, Strab.

προσ-ζεύγνῦμαι, Pass. to be attached to, τινι Luc.

προσ-ζημιόω, f. ώσω, to punish besides, Plat.

πρόσ-ηβος, ον, (ἥβη) near manhood, Xen.

προσήγαγον, aor. 2 of προσάγω.

προσ-ηγορέω, f. ήσω, to address, Soph. : to console, Eur. Hence

προσηγόρημα, τό, the object of one's address, Eur.; and

προσηγορία, ἡ, an appellation, name, Isocr., Dem.; and

προσηγορικός, ή, όν, of or for addressing, πρ. ὄνομα the Roman praenomen or cognomen, Plut.

προσ-ήγορος, Dor. **ποτάγορος**, ον, (ἀγορεύω) addressing, accosting, αἱ πρ. δρύες the speaking oaks, Aesch.; τί ἐμοὶ προσήγορον; what word addressing me, i. e. addressed to me ? Soph.; c. dupl. gen., Παλλάδος εὐγμάτων προσήγορος addressing prayers to her, Id.　2. generally, conversable, mutually agreeable, Plat.　3. of things, agreeing, Id.　II. pass. τῷ προσήγορος; by whom accosted ? Soph.

προσήιξαι, 2 sing. pf. pass. of προσέοικα.

προσηκάμην, aor. 1 med. of προσίημι.

προσηκόντως, Adv. suitably, fitly, duly, πρ. τῇ πόλει as beseems the dignity of the state, Thuc.　From

προσ-ήκω, Dor. **ποθ-ήκω**, f. ξω :—to have arrived at a place, to have come, be near at hand, be present, Trag.; πρ. ἐπὶ τὸν ποταμόν to reach to the river, Xen.　II. metaph. to belong to, εἰ τῷ ξένῳ προσήκει Λαΐῳ τι

συγγενές if to the stranger *there belongs* any kin with Laius, Soph. ; τῷ γὰρ προσήκει τόδε; whom *does this concern?* Id. ; so οὐδὲν πρὸς τὸ Πέρσας πρ. τὸ πάθος Hdt. :—of persons, *to belong to, be related to,* τινί Eur. ; πρ. γένει Ar. :—c. inf., οὐ προσήκομεν κολάζειν τοῖσδε *we do* not *belong* to them to punish, i. e. it is not for them to punish us, Eur. **2.** impers. *it belongs to, concerns,* τί οὖν προσήκει ἐμοὶ Κορινθίων; what *have I to do with* the Corinthians? Ar., etc. **b.** c. dat. pers. et inf. *it belongs to, beseems,* οἷς προσῆκε πενθῆσαι Aesch. ; οὔ σοι προσήκει προσφωνεῖν Soph. : —also c. acc. pers., οὔ σε προσήκει λέγειν *'tis* not *meet* that thou should'st speak, Aesch. **III.** in Partic. *belonging* to one, αἰτία οὐδέν μοι προσήκουσα Dem. ; τὸ προσῆκον ἑκάστῳ ἀποδιδόναι, *suum cuique reddere,* Plat. :—absol., τὴν προσήκουσαν σωτηρίαν *one's own* safety, Thuc. ; τὰ μὴ προσήκοντα, = ἀλλότρια, Id. **2.** *befitting, beseeming, proper, meet,* Id. :—τὰ προσ-ήκοντα *what is fit, seemly, one's duties,* Xen. :— τὸ προσῆκον *fitness, propriety,* ἐκτὸς τοῦ προσήκοντος Eur. ; μᾶλλον τοῦ πρ., παρὰ τὸ πρ. Plat. **3.** of persons, *related, akin,* τοῖσι Κυψελίδαισι οὐδὲν ἦν προσή-κων Hdt. ; προσήκων βασιλεῖ Xen. ;—and as Subst., οἱ πρ. τινος *one's relations,* Aesch., Eur. ;—or οἱ πρ. alone, Hdt. :—hence, αἱ προσήκουσαι ἀρεταί *hereditary* fair fame, Thuc. **b.** οὐδὲν προσήκων *one who has* nothing *to do with* the matter, Plat. ; c. inf., οὐδὲν προσήκων ἐν γόοις παραστατεῖν *having* no *concern* with assisting one in sorrows, Aesch. **4.** absol. in neut. οὐ προσ-ῆκον *though* or *since it is* not *fitting,* Thuc., Plat.

προσ-ήλιος, ον, *towards the sun, exposed to the sun, sunny,* Xen.

προσ-ηλόω, f. ώσω, *to nail, pin,* or *fix to,* τί τινι, τι πρός τι Plat. **II.** *to nail up,* τὰ παρασκήνια Dem. :—Pass. *to be nailed to a plank,* Id.

προσήλῦτος, ον, (προσελήλυθα) *one that has arrived* at a place, *a sojourner,* Lat. *advena: one who has come over to Judaism, a convert, proselyte,* N. T.

πρόσ-ημαι, properly pf. of προσέζομαι, *to be seated upon* or *close to,* c. dat., Aesch., Soph. ; rarely c. acc., καρδίαν προσήμενος Aesch. :—generally *to be* or *lie near,* νᾶσοι τᾷδε γᾷ προσήμεναι Id. **II.** *to be-siege,* Lat. *obsidere,* Eur.

προ-σημαίνω, f. ἀνῶ, *to presignify, foretell, announce,* of the gods, Hdt., Eur., etc. **II.** *to declare be-forehand, proclaim,* τί τινι Eur. ; πρ. τινι ποιεῖν τι *to give them public notice to do* . . , Hdt.

προσημασία, ἡ, *a foretoken, prognostic,* Strab.

προσ-ήνεμος, ον, (ἄνεμος) *towards the wind, to wind-ward,* opp. to ὑπήνεμος, Xen.

προσ-ηνής, Dor. **προσ-ᾱνής** and **ποτ-ᾱνής, ές,** *soft, gentle, kindly,* Pind. ; προσηνές τι λέγειν Thuc. **2.** c. dat., λύχνῳ προσηνές, i. e. *suitable* for burning, Hdt. (For deriv., v. ἀπηνής). **II.** Adv. -νῶς, Theophr.

προσ-ηύδα, 3 sing. impf. of προσαυδάω :—**προσηυδή-την,** 3 dual.

προσ-ηχέω, f. ήσω, *to resound* or *re-echo,* Plut.

προσ-ηῷος, α, ον, Ion. for προσ-εῷος, Dor. **ποτ-αῷος,** *towards the East,* Theocr., Plut.

προσ-θᾱκέω, f. ήσω, *to sit beside* or *upon,* ἕδραν Soph.

πρόσθε, Ion. and poët. for πρόσθεν.

προσθεῖναι, aor. 2 inf. of προστίθημι :—**προσθείς,** part.

πρόσθεν, πρόσθε : Ion. and poët. Adv. : (πρό, πρός) :

A. Prep. with gen. : **I.** of Place, *before,* πρόσθ' ἵππων Il., etc. ; πρ. ποδῶν Od. ; πρ. πυλάων, πρ. πόλιος *before,* i. e. *outside,* Il. ;—in Att. with Art., ἐν τῷ πρ. τοῦ στρατεύματος *in front of* . ., Xen. ; εἰς τὸ πρ. τῶν ὅπλων καθέζεσθαι Id. **b.** with collat. notion of de-fence, στὰς πρόσθε νεκύων Il. ; πρόσθε φίλων τοκέων Ib. **2.** with Verbs of motion, πρ. ἔθεε φεύγοντα Ib., etc. **3.** metaph. *before, in preference to,* πρ. τιθέναι τί τινος Eur. **II.** of Time, *before,* πρόσθ' ἄλλων Il. ; τοῦ χρόνου πρ. θανοῦμαι Soph.

B. as Adv. : **I.** of Place, *before, in front,* πρόσθε λέων ὄπιθεν δὲ δράκων Il. :—οἱ πρ. the *front-rank* men, opp. to οἱ ὄπισθεν, Ib. :—Att., ὁ πρ. Xen. ; τὰ πρ. Id. **2.** with Verbs of motion, *on, forward,* πρ. ἡγεμονεύειν Od. ; πάριτε ἐς τὸ πρ. Ar. **II.** of Time, *before, formerly, erst,* Hom., etc. ; οἱ πρόσθεν ἄνδρες the men *of old,* Il. ; so, τοῦ πρ. Κάδμου Soph. ; ἡ πρ. the *elder,* Eur. ; so, οἱ πρ. πόνοι the *former, earlier* labours, Aesch. ; ἡ πρ. ἡμέρα Xen. :—also, τὸ πρ., as Adv., *formerly,* Hom. ; τὰ πρ., Aesch.

C. foll. by a Relat., πρόσθεν, πρίν . . , Lat. *prius-quam,* mostly with a negat., Od., Xen. :—also, πρόσθεν ἤ . . Soph. ; πρόσθεν πρίν ἤ Xen. **2.** like Lat. *potius,* πρ. ἀποθανεῖν ἤ . . *to die sooner than* . ., Xen.

προσθέοιτο, Ion. for -θεῖτο, 3 sing. aor. 2 opt. of προστίθημι.

πρόσθες, aor. 2 imper. of προστίθημι.

πρόσ-θεσις, ἡ, *a putting to, application* of ladders to a wall, Thuc. ; of the cupping-glass, Arist. **II.** *an adding, addition,* Plat.

προσθετέον, verb. Adj. *one must attribute,* τινί τι Xen.

πρόσθετος, ον, and η, ον, verb. Adj. of προστίθημι, *added, put on,* of false hair, Xen. **II.** Lat. *ad-dictus, given up* to the creditor, Plut.

προσ-θέω, f. -θεύσομαι, *to run towards* or *to* one, c. dat., τινί Thuc., Xen. ; absol., Xen.

προσθήκη, ἡ, (προστίθημι) *an addition, appendage, appendix,* Hdt., Aesch. ; ἐν προσθήκης μέρει *by way of appendage,* Dem. **2.** *something added, an accident,* Id. **II.** *assistance,* προσθήκη θεοῦ Soph.

πρόσθημα, ατος, τό, = προσθήκη I, Eur., Xen.

προσ-θιγγάνω, f. -θίξομαι : aor. 2 -έθιγον, *to touch,* τινός Soph., Eur. ; absol. προσθιγών *by his touch,* Aesch.

πρόσθιος, α, ον, (πρόσθεν) *the foremost,* opp. to ὀπίσ-θιος, οἱ πρ. πόδες the *fore-feet,* Hdt., etc. ;—οἱ πρ. ὀδόντες, Arist. ; χοροὶ οἱ πρ. the *front* rows of teeth, Ar.

προσθό-δομος, ὁ, *the former lord of a house,* Aesch.

προσ-θροέω, f. ήσω, *to address, call* by a name, τινα Aesch.

προσ-θύμιος, ον, (θυμός) *according to one's mind, wel-come,* τινί Anth.

προσ-ιζάνω, *to sit by* or *near,* c. acc., πρὸς ἄλλοτ' ἄλλον πημονὴ πρ. Aesch. :—metaph., c. dat., *to cleave to, cling to,* ἀρά μοι πρ. Id.

προσ-ίζω, f. -ιζήσω, *to sit by,* c. acc., Eur.

προσ-ίημι, f. προσήσω, med. -ήσομαι : aor. 1 προσῆκα, med. -ηκάμην :—*to send to* or *towards, let come to,* τινὰ πρός τινα Xen. : *to apply,* τί τινι Id. **II.** Med. προσίεμαι, *to let come to* or *near* one, *admit,* πρ. τινὰ εἰς τὴν ὁμιλίαν Plat. ; πρ. τοὺς βαρβάρους *to let* them *approach,* Xen. **2.** *to admit, allow, believe,*

τοῦτο μὲν οὐ προσίεμαι Hdt.; **προσηκάμην τὸ ῥηθέν**
Eur.　b. *to admit, accept, submit to,* ξεινικὰ νόμαια
Hdt.; πρ. τὰ προκεκηρυγμένα *to accept* the proposals,
Thuc.; **πρ. φάρμακον** *to take it,* Xen.　c. *to allow,
approve,* τὴν προδοσίην Hdt.; οὐδαμῇ πρ. οἱ θεοὶ τὸν
πόλεμον Xen.　3. c. inf. *to undertake* or *venture
to do,* Id.:—also, *to allow that,* Id.　4. c. acc.
pers. *to attach to oneself, attract, win, please,* οὐδὲν
προσιετό μιν nothing *moved* or *pleased* him, Hdt.; ἐν
δ' οὐ προσίεταί με one thing *pleases* me not, Ar.; τοῦτ'
οὐ δύναταί με προσέσθαι Id.

προσ-ικνέομαι, f. -ίξομαι, Dep. *to come to, reach,* c.
gen. *to reach so far as, come at,* Aesch., Ar.; also, πρ.
ἐφ' ἧπαρ Aesch.　2. *to approach as a suppliant,* c.
acc. loci, Id.　Hence

προσίκτωρ, ορος, ὁ, *one that comes to a god, a suppliant,* Aesch.　II. pass. *he to whom one comes as
a suppliant, a protector,* of a god, Id.

προσ-ιππεύω, f. σω, *to ride up to, charge,* Thuc., Plut.

προσ-ίστημι, f. -στήσω, *to place near, bring near,*
πρῷραν πρὸς κῦμα Eur.　II. Pass. προσίσταμαι,
with aor. 2 and pf. act., *to stand near to* or *by,* c.
dat., Hdt., Att.:—c. acc. with a notion of *approaching,*
βωμὸν προσέστην Aesch.:—with a Prep., πρ. πρὸς τῷ
δικαστηρίῳ Aeschin.:—c. gen., καρδίας προσίσταται is
in the region of the heart, Aesch.:—absol., Xen.,
etc.　2. metaph., προσίσταταί μοι *it comes into my
head, occurs to me,* ὅ σοι προσέστη Plat.; also c. acc.,
ὡς ἄρα μιν προσέστη τοῦτο Hdt.　3. *to set oneself
against, to give offence to,* τοῖς ἀκούουσιν Dem.

προσ-ιστορέω, *to narrate besides,* c. acc. et inf., Plut.

προσ-ίσχω, = προσέχω.

προσἴτέον, verb. Adj. of πρόσειμι (εἶμι *ibo*), *one must
go to* or *approach,* Xen.

προσ-καθέζομαι, f. -εδοῦμαι: aor. 2 -καθεζόμην:—*to
sit down before* a town, *besiege* it, Lat. *obsidere,* πόλιν
Thuc.; absol., Id.　2. *to sit by, watch,* τοῖς πράγμασιν Dem.

προσ-καθέλκω, aor. 1 -είλκῦσα, *to haul down besides,*
πλοῖα Plut.

προσκάθημαι, Ion. -κάτημαι, properly pf. of προσκαθέ-
ζομαι, *to be seated by* or *near, live with,* τινί Hdt.,
Theophr.　II. *to sit down against* a town, *besiege
it,* Lat. *obsidere,* Hdt., Thuc., etc.

προσ-καθίζω, *to sit down by* or *near,* c. acc., θᾶκον
οὐκ εὐδαίμονα Eur.; absol., Plat.:—Med. *to sit idle,*
Aeschin.　II. *to sit down before* a town, Polyb.

προσ-καθίστημι, f. -στήσω, *to appoint besides,* Plut.

πρόσ-καιρος, ον, *for a season, temporary,* N. T., Luc.

προσ-καίω, Att. -κάω: f. -καύσω:—*to set on fire* or
burn besides:—Pass., σκεύη προσκεκαυμένα pots *burnt
at the fire,* Ar.: metaph., προσκαίεσθαί τινι *to be in
love with* .., Xen.

προσ-κάλέω, f. έσω, *to call to, call on, summon,* Thuc.,
etc.　2. *to call on, invoke,* Soph.　II. Med.,
with pf. pass., *to call to oneself, call to one, call to
one's aid,* Hdt., Att.:—c. dupl. acc., ὃ προσκέκλημαι
αὐτούς *to which I have called* them, N. T.　2. in
Att., of an accuser, *to cite* or *summon into court,* Ar.,
etc.; ὕβρεως for an assault, Id.:—Pass. *to be summoned,* φόνου *on a charge of* murder, Dem., etc.;
προσκληθεὶς δίκην εἰς Ἄρειον πάγον *to have one's cause*

called before the Areopagus, Arist.; **ὁ προσκληθείς** *the
party summoned,* Dem.; so, ὁ προσκεκλημένος Ar.　3.
to cite as witness, Dem.

προσ-κάρδιος, Dor. **ποτι-κ-,** ον, *at the heart,* Bion.

προσ-καρτερέω, f. ήσω, *to persist obstinately in,* Xen.,
etc.　2. *to adhere firmly to* a man, *be faithful to*
him, τινί Dem.　Hence

προσκαρτέρησις, ἡ, *perseverance,* N. T.

προσ-καταβαίνω, f. -βήσομαι, *to descend besides,* Anth.

προσ-κατάβλημα, ατος, τό, (καταβάλλω) *that which is
paid besides :* in pl. *sums paid to make up a deficiency*
in the revenue, Dem.

προσ-καταγιγνώσκω, f. -γνώσομαι, *to condemn besides,* Antipho.　II. *to award to,* τί τινι Dem.

προσ-καταισχύνω, f. ὔνῶ, *to disgrace still further,*
Plut.

προσ-κατακλείω, *to shut up besides :* aor. 1 pass. -κα-
τεκλείσθην Aesop.

προσ-καταλέγω, f. ξω, *to enrol besides* or *in addition
to,* τινάς τισι Plut.:—Pass., Id.　II. *to reckon as
belonging to,* Strab.

προσ-καταλείπω, f. ψω, *to leave besides as a legacy,*
ἀρχήν τινι Thuc.　II. *to lose besides,* τὰ αὑτῶν Id.

προσ-καταλλάττομαι, Pass. with fut. med. -άξομαι, *to
become reconciled besides,* Arist.

προσ-κατανέμω, f. -νεμῶ, *to assign besides,* Plut.

προσ-κατ-ἀρϊθμέω, f. ήσω, *to count besides,* Plut.

προσ-κατασκευάζω, f. σω, *to furnish besides,* Dem.

προσ-κατασύρω [ῡ], *to pull down besides,* Anth.

προσ-κατατάσσω, f. ξω, *to append, subjoin,* Polyb.

προσ-κατατίθημι, f. -θήσω, *to pay down besides* or *as
a further deposit,* Ar.

προσ-κατηγορέω, f. ήσω, *to accuse besides,* ἐπίδειξιν
πρ. *to accuse* one *also* of making a display, Thuc.; πρ.
τινὸς ὅτι .. Xen.

πρόσ-κειμαι, f. -κείσομαι, (on the Ion. forms v. κεῖμαι),
serving as Pass. to προστίθημι, *to be placed* or *laid by*
or *upon, to lie by* or *upon,* οὔατα προσέκειτο handles
were upon it, Il.; τῇ θύρᾳ προσκεῖσθαι *to keep close to*
the door, Ar.; δοκοὶ τῷ τείχει προσκείμεναι *lying near*
the wall, Thuc.:—ὁ προσκείμενος ἵππος *the inside* horse
(turning a corner), Soph.　2. *to lie beside, cling to,*
Id.: of a woman, *to be given to wife,* τινί Hdt.　II.
generally, *to be involved in* or *bound up* with good or
evil, c. dat., Soph.　2. *to be attached* or *devoted to,*
τινί Hdt., Thuc., etc.; πρ. τῷ λεγομένῳ *to put faith
in* a story, Hdt.; πρ. οἴνῳ *to be addicted to* wine, Id.;
ἄγραις hunting, Soph., etc.　3. *to press upon, be
urgent with* a person, c. dat., Hdt., Xen.; προσκείμενος *with zeal,* Thuc.　b. in military sense, *to
press close* or *hard, pursue closely,* τινί Id.; absol.
to follow close, Ar.; τὸ προσκείμενον the enemy,
Hdt.　III. with a thing for the subject, *to fall to,
belong to,* τοῖσι θεῶν τιμὴ αὕτη προσκέεται Id.; πρ.
τινι δοῦλος Eur. :—*to be laid upon* as a charge, *to do*
something, c. inf., Hdt., Eur.　2. *to be added* or
attached to, Soph., Eur. :—absol. ἡ χάρις προσκείσεται
Soph.

προσ-κερδαίνω, f. ἄνῶ, *to gain besides,* Dem.

προσκεφάλαιον, τό, *a cushion for the head, pillow,*
Ar., etc. :—then, generally, *any cushion,* Theophr.

προσ-κηδής, ές, (κῆδος) *bringing into alliance* or *kin-*

dred, or, as others, *kind, affectionate*, Od.　**II.**
akin to, τινί Hdt. ; **προσκηδέες** *kinsfolk*, Anth.

προσ-κηρῡκεύομαι, Dep. *to send a herald to* one, Thuc.

προσ-κηρύσσω, Att. -ττω, f. ξω, *to summon* also, Luc.

προσ-κιγκλίζομαι, Pass. *to wag one's tail*, εὖ ποτεκιγκλίσθεν (Dor. for -ίζου) *how nimbly didst thou twist about!* Theocr.

προσ-κλάομαι, Pass. *to be shivered against*, Xen.

προσ-κληρόομαι, aor. 1 -εκληρώθην :—Pass. *to be attached to, keep company with*, N. T.

πρόσκλησις, ἡ, (προσκαλέω) *a judicial summons* or *citation*, Ar., Dem.

προσ-κλίνω [ῑ], f. -κλῐνῶ, *to make to lean against, put against*, Od. :—Pass., θρόνος ποτικέκλῐται (Dor. pf. pass.) *is leant against*, Ib. ; αὐτῇ [κίονι] *leans* or *stands against* the pillar, Ib. ; νῶτον ποτικεκλιμένον *his back thereon reclined*, Pind.　**II.** Pass. *to incline towards, to be attached to* one, N. T.　Hence

πρόσκλῐσις, ἡ, *inclination, proclivity*, Polyb. ; κατὰ πρόσκλισιν *with partiality*, N. T.

προσ-κλύζω, Dor. ποτι-, f. σω, *to wash with waves*, Xen. : c. dat. *to dash against*, Orac. ap. Aeschin.

προσ-κνάομαι, inf. -κνῆσθαι, Pass. or Med. *to rub oneself against*, τινί Xen.

προσ-κοιμίζομαι, Pass. *to lie down and sleep beside*, ταῖς κώπαις Xen.

προσ-κοινωνέω, f. ήσω, *to give* one *a share of* a thing, τινί ἀπό τινος Dem.

προσ-κολλάω, f. ήσω, *to glue on* or *to* :—Pass. *to stick* or *cleave to*, Plat., N. T. ; πρός τινα N. T.

προσ-κομίζω, f. Att. ῐῶ, *to carry* or *convey to* a place, πρὸς τόπον Thuc., Xen. ; πρ. τὴν μηχανὴν *to bring up* the engine to assault the wall, Thuc. :—Med. *to bring with* one, *bring home*, Id. : *to import*, Xen. :—Pass., *of ships, to be brought to* a place, Thuc.

πρόσκομμα, ατος, τό, (προσκόπτω) *a stumble, stumbling*, N. T. : *an occasion of stumbling*, Ib. : *an offence, obstacle*, Ib.

προ-σκοπέω, f. -κέψομαι : aor. 1 προὐσκεψάμην : 3 sing. plqpf. προὔσκεπτο :—*to see* or *consider beforehand, weigh well, look to, provide for*, προσκεψάμενος ἐπὶ σεωυτοῦ Hdt. ; πάντα προσκοπεῖν Soph. ; μὴ παθεῖν προεσκόπουν *were making provision* against suffering, Thuc. :—so in Med., τὸ σὸν προσκοπούμενος Eur.　**2.** *to watch* (like a πρόσκοπος or *spy*), τινά Ar. :—so in Med., προσκοπουμένη πόσιν Eur.　**3.** *to prefer before*, τί τινος Eur.　**II.** pf. and plqpf. in pass. sense, *to be considered* beforehand, Thuc., Plat.　Hence

προ-σκοπή, ἡ, *a looking out for*, Thuc.

προσ-κοπή, ἡ, (προσκόμμα) *an offence*, Polyb.

πρό-σκοπος, ον, *seeing beforehand* : as Subst. *an outpost, vidette*, Xen. ; in pl. *a reconnoitring party*, Id.

προσ-κόπτω, f. ψω, *to strike* one thing *against* another, τί πρός τι N. T. ; πρ. τὸν δακτυλόν που Arist.　**II.** intr. *to stumble* or *strike against*, τινί Xen. :—metaph. *to take offence at*, τινί Polyb.

προσ-κορής, ές, (κόρος) *satiating, palling*, Luc.

προσ-κοτόω, f. ώσω, *to darken* or *cloud over beforehand*, Polyb.

πρόσ-κρανον, v. ποτί-κρανον.

πρόσκρουσις, εως, ἡ, *a dashing against* a thing : *an offence*, Plut. ; and ·

πρόσκρουσμα, ατος, τό, *that against which one strikes, a stumblingblock, offence*, Dem.　From

προσ-κρούω, f. σω, *to strike against*, τινί Plat. : absol. *to stumble, fail*, Plut.　**II.** *to have a collision with* another, *give offence*, Dem. ; πρ. τινί Plut.　**2.** *to take offence at, be angry with*, τινί Dem., etc. : —absol. *to take offence*, Plat.

προσ-κτάομαι, f. ήσομαι, Dep. *to gain, get* or *win besides*, γῆν ἄλλην πρ. τῇ ἑωυτῶν Hdt. ; χώραν πρ. Thuc. ; πρ. πρὸς τὴν ἑωυτοῦ μοῖραν *to gain and add* to his own portion, Hdt ; βραχύ τι πρ. αὐτῇ [τῇ ἀρχῇ] *to make a small addition* to it, Thuc. ; pf. part. in pass. sense, τὰ προσκεκτημένα Id.　**2.** of persons, *to gain* or *win over*, πρ. τινα φίλον Hdt. ; πρ. τὸν Καλλίμαχον *to win over* Callimachus *to his side*, Id.

προσ-κτίζω, f. σω, *to build* or *found besides*, πόλιν Strab.

προσ-κυλίνδω, f. ίσω [ῑ], *to roll to, roll up*, Ar. : προσκυλίσας λίθον N. T.

προσ-κῠνέω, f. -ήσω :—aor. 1 -εκύνησα, poët. -έκῠσα, imper. πρόσκυσον, inf. -κύσαι, part. -κύσας : pf. -κεκύνηκα Plut. :—*to make obeisance* to the gods, *fall down and worship, to worship, adore*, c. acc., Hdt., Aesch., etc. :—proverb., οἱ προσκυνοῦντες τὴν Ἀδράστειαν σοφοί, of deprecating the wrath of Nemesis, Aesch. ; so, τὸν φθόνον δὲ πρόσκυσον Soph. :—also of sacred places, *to do reverence to*, ἔδη θεῶν Id. ; τὴν γῆν Id.　**2.** of the Oriental fashion of *making the salám* or *prostrating oneself before* kings and superiors, absol., Hdt. ; c. acc., πρ. τὸν Δαρεῖον ὡς βασιλέα *to make obeisance* to him as king, Id. ; πάντες σε προσκυνοῦμεν Soph., etc. :—later, c. dat., N. T.　Hence

προσκύνησις, ἡ, *adoration, obeisance, a salám*, Arist., Plut. ; and

προσκῠνητής, οῦ, ὁ, *a worshipper*, N. T.

προσ-κύπτω, f. ψω : pf. -κέκῠφα :—*to stoop to* or *over* one, Ar. ; πρ. τινὶ τὸ οὖς *to lean towards* one *and whisper in* his ear, Plat.

προσ-κῠρέω, with impf. -έκῠρον, f. -κύρσω, aor. 1 -έκυρσα (as if from -κύρω) :—*to reach, touch, arrive at*, c. dat., Hes.　**2.** *to meet with, fall upon*, τινί Theogn. ; also c. acc. rei, ὅσ᾽ ἐγὼ προσέκυρσα Soph. :—reversely, δόμοισι πῆμα προσκύρσαι *woe betides the house*, Aesch.

προσ-κύσαι [ᾰ], aor. 1 inf. of προσκυνέω.

πρόσ-κωπος, ον, (κώπη) *at the oar, a rower*, Thuc.

προσλᾰβεῖν, aor. 2 inf. of προσλαμβάνω.

προσ-λαγχάνω, f. -λήξομαι : pf. -είληχα :—*to obtain by lot besides*, δίκην πρ. *to obtain leave to bring* an action *also*, Dem.

προσ-λάζῠμαι, Dep. *to take hold of besides*, τινος Eur.

προσ-λᾰλέω, f. ήσω, *to talk to* or *with*, τινί Theophr.

προσ-λαμβάνω, f. -λήψομαι : aor. 2 -έλαβον :—*to take* or *receive besides, get over and above*, πρὸς τοῖς παροῦσιν ἄλλα [κακὰ] πρ. Aesch. ; πρ. αἰσχύνην Thuc., etc. :—so in Med., Eur., etc.　**2.** c. acc. pers. *to take to oneself, take as one's helper* or *partner*, Trag., Xen., etc. :—acc., πρ. τινὰ σύμμαχον Xen. :—also in Med., Polyb., etc.　**II.** like προσλαμβάνω, *to take hold of*, τινά Soph. :—Med. *to take hold of*, τινος Ar.　**2.** in Med., πρ. τινος *to take part in* a work, *be accessory to it*, Xen. ; προσελάβετο τοῦ πάθεος *he was partly the author of* the calamity, Hdt. ; πρ. τινι *to help, assist*, Ar.

προσ-λάμπω, f. ψω, *to shine with* or *upon*, Plat.
προσ-λέγομαι, Pass. *to lie beside*, προσέλεκτο (3 sing. aor. 2 syncop.) *she lay beside* or *by me*, Od.   **II.** Med. *to speak to, address, accost*, τινά Theocr. : metaph., κακὰ προσελέξατο θυμῷ *he took evil counsel with himself, meditated* evil, Hes.
προσ-λείπω, f. ψω, *to be lacking*, Arist.
προσ-λεύσσω, only in pres. *to look on* or *at*, c. acc., Soph. ; absol., Id.
προσληπτέον, verb. Adj. *one must add*, Strab.
προσ-λῑπᾰρέω, f. ήσω, *to persevere* or *persist in*, τοῖς χρήμασι in money-making, Plut. :—*to importune*, τινί Luc. : absol. *to be importunate*, Plut.   Hence
προσλῑπάρησις, εως, ἡ, *importunity*, Luc.
προσ-λογίζομαι, Dep. *to reckon* or *count in addition to*, τί τινι Hdt.   **2.** *to impute*, τί τινι Plut.   Hence
προσλογιστέον, verb. Adj., Hdt.
προσμᾰθητέον, verb. Adj. *one must learn besides*, Xen.
προσ-μανθάνω, f. -μᾰθήσομαι : aor. 2 -έμᾰθον :—*to learn besides*, Aesch., Ar.
προσ-μαρτῠρέω, f. ήσω, *to confirm by evidence*, Dem.   **II.** intr., πρ. τινί *to bear additional witness to* a thing, Polyb.
προσ-μάσσω, f. ξω, *to knead* one thing *to* or *with* another ; *to attach closely to*, πρ. τὸν Πειραιᾶ τῇ πόλει Ar. :—in Pass., πλευραῖσι προσμαχθέν *sticking close to his sides*, of the poisoned robe, Soph. : aor. 1 med. part., τηλέφιλον ποτιμαξάμενον *the leaf having attached itself closely to* [the hand], *sticking close*, Theocr.
προσ-μάχομαι [ᾰ], f. Att. -μαχοῦμαι, Dep. *to fight against*, τινι Plat. : *to assault* a town, Xen.
προσ-μειδιάω, f. άσω [ᾱ], *to smile upon*, with a sense of *approving*, Lat. *arrideo*, Luc.
προσ-μένω, f. -μενῶ, *to bide* or *wait still longer*, Hdt., Soph., etc.   **2.** c. dat. *to remain attached to, to cleave to*, τινί Aesch. ; πρ. ταῖς δεήσεσιν *to continue in* supplications, N. T.   **II.** trans. *to wait for, await*, c. acc., Theogn., Soph., etc. :—*to wait for* one in battle, i. e. *to stand one's ground against*, Pind. : —also c. acc. et inf. fut., Ὀρέστην προσμενοῦσ᾽ ἀεὶ ἐφήξειν Soph.
προσ-μεταπέμπομαι, Med. *to send for* or *send to fetch besides*, Thuc., Aeschin.
προσ-μηχᾰνάομαι, Pass. *to be cunningly fastened to* or *upon*, Aesch.   **II.** Med. *to contrive* or *procure for oneself*, αὐτοῖς ἀσφάλειαν Plat.
προσμίγνῡμι or -μίσγω : f. -μίξω : aor. 1 -έμιξα :—*to mingle* or *join to*, τί τινι Plut. :—metaph., πρ. δεσπόταν κράτει *to lead* him *to* sure victory, Pind. ; and reversely, πρ. κίνδυνόν τινι Aeschin.   **II.** intr. *to hold intercourse with, approach*, τινί Soph. :—of things, προσέμιξεν τοῦτος ἡμῖν *came suddenly upon* us, Id.   **2.** in hostile sense, *to go against, meet in battle, engage with*, τινί Hdt. ; πρός τινα Thuc. :—absol. *to engage*, Xen. ; ἄποροι προσμίσγειν difficult *to come to close quarters with*, Hdt.   **3.** *to come* or *go close up to*, προσέμιξαν τῷ τείχει Thuc. ; πρὸς τὰς ἐπάλξεις Id. ; but, πρὸς τὰς ἐντὸς [νέας] προσμίξαι *to form a junction with them*, Id. ; προσέμιξεν ἐγγὺς τοῦ στρατεύματος *came near* the army, Id. :—poët. c. acc., μέλαθρα πρ. Eur.   **4.** προσέμιξαν τῇ Νάξῳ, τῇ Πελοποννήσῳ

put to shore at, landed in, Hdt. ; τῷ Τάραντι προσμίσγει Thuc.   Hence
πρόσμιξις, ἡ, *a coming near to*, and (in hostile sense) *an attack, assault*, Thuc.
προσ-μίσγω, commoner form of προσ-μίγνυμι.
προσ-μισθόω, f. ώσω, *to let out for hire besides*, πρ. ἀφορμήν *to put* capital *out at interest*, Dem. :—Med. *to take into one's pay, to hire*, Thuc., Xen., etc.
προσ-μολεῖν, inf. aor. of pres. προσβλώσκω, which does not occur, *to come* or *to go, reach, arrive at*, c. acc., Soph. ; absol. *to approach*, Id.
πρόσ-μορος, ον, *doomed to woe*, Aesch.
προσ-μῡθέομαι, Dep. *to address, accost*, Od. : Ep. and Dor. aor. 1 inf. προτιμυθήσασθαι ; c. dat., Theocr.
προσ-μῡθεύω, f. σω, *to add further fictions*, Strab.
προσ-μῡθολογέω, f. ήσω, *to talk* or *prattle with* one, τινί Luc.
προσ-μῡθοποιέω, *to invent mythically besides*, Strab.
προσ-μύρομαι [ῡ], Dep. *to flow to* or *with*, Anth.
προσ-ναυπηγέω, f. ήσω, *to build in addition* : Pass., ἑτέρας [νέας] ἔδει ναυπηγέεσθαι Hdt.
προσ-νέμω, f. -νεμῶ, *to assign, attach* or *dedicate to*, ἑαυτόν τινι Dem. :—*to add*, Id. :—Pass. *to be assigned, attributed*, Id. :—Med. *to grant on one's own part*, πρόσνειμαι χάριν grant *a further* favour, Soph. ; προσνείμασθαί τινα θεῷ *to devote* him *to the god*, Ar.   **II.** πρ. ποίμνας *to drive* his *flocks to pasture*, Eur.
πρόσνευσις, ἡ, *a nodding to, decision*, Cic.   From
προσ-νεύω, f. σω, *to nod to, assent*, Plut.
προσ-νέω, f. -νεύσομαι, *to swim to* or *towards*, Thuc.
προσνήχομαι, Dep. *to swim towards*, τινί Plut.   **II.** intr. in Act. *to dash upon*, προσένᾰχε θάλασσα Theocr.
προσ-νίσσομαι, Dor. ποτι-νίσσομαι, only in pres., Dep. *to come* or *go to*, Il., Pind. ; θεοὺς θοίναις ποτινίσσ. *to approach* them with sacrifices, Aesch.   **II.** *to come against*, Soph.
προσ-νοέω, f. ήσω, *to perceive besides*, Xen.
προσ-νωμάω, f. ήσω, *to put to one's lips*, ὕδωρ (to be supplied), Soph.
προσ-ξυν-, for words so beginning, v. προσ-συν-.
προσ-οδεύομαι, Med. *to receive income* or *revenue*, Strab.
προσοδικός, ή, όν, (πρόσοδος II) *productive*, Strab.
προσόδιος, ον, *belonging to* or *used in processions, processional*, Plut. :—*a processional hymn, a thanksgiving*, Lat. *supplicatio*, Ar.
πρόσ-οδος, ἡ, *a going* or *coming to, an approach*, ἡ πρ. μάλιστα ταύτῃ ἐγένετο *the approach* was most feasible on this part, Hdt. ; ἀπείπατο τὴν πρ. rejected his *advances*, Id. ; πρ. μελάθρων *approach to the halls*, Eur.   **2.** *an onset*, πρόσοδοι τῆς μάχης onsets or attacks, Id.   **3.** like πομπή II, *a solemn procession* to a temple with singing and music, Ar., Xen.   **4.** *the coming forward* of a speaker in *a public assembly*, γράφεσθαι πρόσοδον *to petition for* a *hearing*, Dem. ; πρ. ποιεῖσθαι πρὸς τὸν δῆμον Aeschin.   **II.** *income, rent*, as opp. to principal, Dem. ; often in pl., Oratt.   **2.** of the public revenue, φόρων πρόσοδος Hdt. ; χρημάτων πρ. Thuc. ; mostly in pl. *the returns, revenue*, Lat. *reditus*, Hdt., Thuc., etc.
προσ-όζω, Dor. ποτι-όσδω, intr. *to smell of, be redolent of*, c. gen., Theocr.

πρόσ-οιδα, pf. without any pres. in use (v. *εἴδω B), to know besides; προσειδέναι χάριν to owe thanks besides, Ar., Plat.

προσ-οικειόω, f. ώσω, to assign to one as his own, τί τινι Strab. :—προσφκείου ἑαυτὸν 'Αντώνιος Ἡρακλεῖ associated himself with Hercules, Plut.

προσ-οικέω, f. ήσω, to dwell by or near, τινί Xen.: absol., οἱ προσοικοῦντες neighbouring tribes, Isocr. 2. c. acc. to dwell in or near, Ἐπίδαμνον Thuc.

προσ-οικοδομέω, f. ήσω, to build besides, πρ. [τεῖχος] to build another wall, Thuc.; τῷ μὲν ἐν τῇ ἀγορᾷ [βωμῷ] προσοικοδομήσας μεῖζον μῆκος having built an additional length to the altar in the agora, i. e. having added to its length, Id.

πρόσ-οικος, ον, dwelling near to, bordering on, neighbouring, Hdt., Thuc.; οἱ πρόσοικοι neighbours, Thuc.

προσ-οιστέος, α, ον, verb. Adj. of προσφέρω, to be added to, τινί Eur. II. προσοιστέον one must add, Plat., etc. 2. one must apply, use, γυμνάσια Arist.

προσ-οίχομαι, Dep. to have gone to a place, Pind.

προσ-οκέλλω, to run a ship on shore, Luc. 2. absol. of the ship, to run ashore, Id.

προσ-ολοφύρομαι [ῡ], Dep. to wail to, vent one's griefs to another, τινί Thuc.; πρ. ἀλλήλοις to wail to one another, Plut.

προσ-ομαρτέω, f. ήσω, to go along with, τινί Theogn., etc.

προσ-ομῑλέω, f. ήσω, to hold intercourse with, live or associate with, converse with, τινί Theogn., Eur., etc.; πρός τινα Xen.; τὰ ἴδια προσομιλοῦντες conducting our private intercourse, Thuc. II. to be attached, ποτὶ πέτρη Theogn. III. to be conversant with, πείρα Soph.; τῷ πολέμῳ Thuc.

προσ-όμνῡμι, f. -ομοῦμαι, to swear besides, Xen.

προσ-όμοιος, ον, and α, ον, much like, τινι Eur., Ar.

προσ-ομοιόω, f. ώσω, to be like, resemble, τὴν σύνεσιν ἀνθρώπῳ, τὴν ἀλκὴν δὲ δράκοντι Dem.

προσ-ομολογέω, f. ήσω, to concede or grant besides, τί τινι Plat.; to acknowledge a further debt, Dem.: —c. acc. et inf. to grant also that . . , Plat.:—Pass., παλαιὰ καὶ λίαν προσωμολογημένα Aeschin. 2. to promise further, c. inf. fut., Dem. 3. to come to terms, surrender, Xen. Hence

προσομολογία, ἡ, a further admission, Dem.

προσ-ομόργνῡμι, to wipe upon another, impart; so in Med., Plut.

προσ-όμουρος, ον, Ion. for προσόμορος (which does not occur), adjoining, adjacent, τινί Hdt.

προσ-ονομάζω, f. σω, to call by a name, πρ. θεούς to give them the name θεοί, Hdt.

προσ-οράω, f. -όψομαι: Dor. ποθ-όρημι, inf. -ορῆν: —to look at, behold, Mimnerm., Soph., etc.; cf. aor. 2 προσεῖδον :—so in Med., προσορωμένα Soph.

προσ-ορέγομαι, Med. to stretch oneself towards, to be urgent with, τινί Hdt.

πρόσ-ορθρος, ον, towards morning: Dor. τὸ πότορθρον, as Adv., Theocr.

προσ-ορίζω, f. Att. ιῶ, to include within the boundaries, add to a dominion, Strab. 2. to determine or fix besides, Plut. 3. in Med. as Att. law-term, προσωρίσατο τὴν οἰκίαν δισχιλίων he had the house marked with other stones (v. ὅρος II) to the amount

of 2000 drachmae, i. e. mortgaged it anew to that amount, Dem.

προσ-ορμάω, f. ήσω, intr. to rush on, Xen.

προσ-ορμίζομαι, f. Att. ιοῦμαι, Med. to come to anchor near a place, Hdt., Dem.; so in aor. 1 pass. προσωρμίσθην, N. T. Hence

προσόρμῐσις, ἡ, a coming to anchor or to land, Thuc.

πρόσ-ορμος, ὁ, a landing-place, Strab.

πρόσ-ορος, v. πρόσ-ουρος.

προσ-ορχέομαι, f. ήσομαι, Dep. to dance to or with, Luc.

προσ-ουδίζω, f. σω, (οὖδας) to dash to earth, Hdt., etc.

προσ-ουρέω, impf. -εούρουν: f. ήσω:—to make water upon, τινί Dem.; metaph., πρ. τῇ τραγῳδίᾳ, i. e. to trifle with it, Ar.

πρόσ-ουρος, ον, Ion. for πρόσορος, adjoining, bordering on, τῇ 'Αραβίῃ Hdt.: absol., τὰ πρόσορα the neighbouring parts, Xen. :—in Soph., ἵν' αὐτὸς ἦν πρόσουρος where he had no neighbour but himself, i. e. lived in solitude, Soph.

προσ-οφείλω, f. ήσω: aor. 2 -ώφελον :—to owe besides or still, Thuc., Xen.: absol., προσοφείλοντας ἡμᾶς ἐνέγραψεν Dem. :—Pass. to be still owing, be still due, Thuc.; so, ἡ ἔχθρη ἡ προσοφειλομένη ἐς 'Αθηναίους ἐκ τῶν Αἰγινητέων the hatred which was still due from the Aeginetans to the Athenians, i. e. their ancient feud, Hdt.

προσ-οφλισκάνω, f. -οφλήσω: aor. 2 -ώφλον, inf. -οφλεῖν :—to owe besides, Dem.: absol. to incur a debt, Arist. 2. as law-term, to lose one's suit and incur a penalty besides, Aeschin. 3. generally, to incur or deserve besides, αἰσχύνην Dem.

προσοχή, ἡ, (προσέχω) attention, Luc.

πρόσ-οψιος, ον, like ἐπ-όψιος, full in view, Soph.

πρόσ-οψις, ἡ, appearance, aspect, mien, Pind.; periphr., σὴ πρ. thy presence, i. e. thyself, Soph. II. a seeing, beholding, sight, view, Eur., Thuc.

προσ-παίζω, f. -παίξομαι: aor. 1 -έπαισα and -έπαιξα: —to play or sport with, τινί Xen., Plat. 2. absol. to sport, jest, Plat. II. c. acc., πρ. θεούς to sing to the gods, ὕμνον πρ. τὸν Ἔρωτα sang a hymn in praise of Eros, Id. 2. to banter, Id.

πρόσ-παιος, ον, (παίω) striking upon: hence, sudden, Aesch. :—ἐκ προσπαίου suddenly, Arist.

προσ-πᾰλαίω, f. σω, to wrestle or struggle with, τινί Pind., Plat.

Προσπαλτόθεν, Adv. from Prospalta, Dem.

προσ-παραγράφω, f. ψω, to write besides, add yet besides, Plat., Dem.

προσ-παρακαλέω, f. έσω, to call in besides, invite, Thuc. 2. to exhort besides, τινὰ εἶναι ἑτοῖμον Polyb.

προσ-παραμένω, f. -μενῶ, to remain by besides, Aesop.

προσ-παρασκευάζω, f. σω, to prepare besides, ἑτέραν δύναμιν Dem. :—Med. to prepare for oneself besides, Id.

προσ-παρατίθημι, to put before one besides, Polyb.

προσ-παρέχω, f. -έξω, to furnish or supply besides, τί τινι Thuc.; so in Med., Plat.

προσ-παροξύνω, f. ὑνῶ, to provoke besides, Strab.

προσ-παρτός, όν, (πείρω) fixed to (the rock), Aesch.

προσ-πασσαλεύω, Att. προσ-παττ-, f. σω, to nail fast to a place, τινά τινι Aesch.; πρός τι Ar. :—reversely, σανίδα προσπασσαλεύσαντες (sc. αὐτῷ) Hdt. II. to nail up or hang upon a peg, τὸν τρίποδα Id.

προσ-πάσχω, *to have an additional* or *special feeling,* Plat.; τινί *for* a thing, Luc., etc.   **II.** *to feel passionate love,* Isocr.

πρόσ-πεινος, ον, (πεῖνα) *hungry, a-hungered,* N. T.

προσ-πελάζω, f. άσω [ᾰ], *to make to approach, bring near to,* νέα ἄκρῃ προσπελάσας *having driven* the ship *against* the headland, Od. :—Pass. *to approach,* c. gen., Πανὸς προσπελασθεῖσα *having had intercourse with* Pan, Soph.   **II.** intr. *to draw nigh to, approach,* τινί Plat.

προσ-πέμπω, f. ψω, *to send to,* esp. of messengers or ambassadors, Ar., Thuc.; πρ. τινά τινι *to send* or *conduct* one person *to* another, Soph., Thuc.; simply, πρ. τινί *to send to* one (sc. ἄγγελον), Thuc., etc.; also, πρ. λόγους ἔς τινας Id.; absol., Hdt., Thuc.

προσ-περιβάλλω, f. -βᾰλῶ, *to put round besides,* περιτείχισμα τῇ πόλει Thuc. :—Med. *to throw* or *draw round oneself,* τείχη Isocr. :—Pass. *to be drawn round,* στρατοπέδῳ ἐρύματος προσπεριβαλλομένου Thuc.   **2.** Med. *to surround,* τὸν πεζὸν στρατὸν ταῖς ναυσὶ πρ. Plut.   **II.** Med., also, *to grasp at,* Dem.

προσ-περιγίγνομαι, Dep. *to remain over and above as surplus* or *net profit,* Dem., Plut.

προσ-περιλαμβάνω, *to embrace besides,* Dem.

προσ-περιοδεύω, f. σω, *to describe besides,* Strab.

προσ-περιποιέω, f. ήσω, *to lay by* or *save besides,* Dem.

προσ-περονάω, f. ήσω, *to fasten by means of a pin* (περόνη), and, generally, *to fasten on,* τι πρός τι Plat.; πρός τινι Xen.

προσπεσεῖν, aor. 2 inf. of προσπίπτω.

προσ-πέτομαι, f. -πτήσομαι : aor. 2 -επτάμην [ᾰ], but poët. also aor. 2 act. προσέπτην: Dep. :—*to fly to* or *towards,* Ar., Xen.   **II.** generally, *to come upon* one *suddenly, come over* one, διὰ προσέπτα με Aesch.; μέλος προσέπτα μο: or με *music stole over* my sense, Id.; τίς ἀρχὴ τοῦ κακοῦ προσέπτατο; Soph.

προσ-πεύθομαι, poët. for προσπυνθάνομαι, Soph.

προσ-πήγνυμι and -ύω, f. -πήξω: —*to fix to* or *on,* τί τινι Eur. :—absol. *to affix to the cross, crucify,* N. T.

προσ-πίλναμαι, Pass. *to approach quickly,* νήσῳ Od.

προσ-πίπτω, f. -πεσοῦμαι: (for ποτιπεπτηυῖαι, v. προσπτήσσω) :—*to fall upon, strike against,* ἔς τι Soph.; τινί Xen. :—*to fall against,* as a mound against a wall, Thuc.   **2.** *to fall upon, attack, assault,* τινί Id., Xen., etc.; absol., Thuc., Xen.   **3.** simply *to run to,* Hdt., Xen.   **4.** *to fall upon, embrace,* τινί Eur.; hence, πρ. τινί *to join the party of* another, Xen.   **5.** *to fall in with, light upon, meet with, encounter,* μὴ λάθῃ με προσπεσών Soph.; c. dat. rei, *to fall in with,* Eur., Xen.; —c. acc., μείζω βροτείας πρ. ὁμιλίας Eur.   **II.** of things,   **1.** of accidents, *to come suddenly upon, befal* one, τινί Hdt., Eur., etc. :— absol. *to occur,* Hdt., Thuc.; πρὸς τὰ προσπίπτοντα *according to circumstances,* Arist.   **2.** of expenses, *to fall upon,* Thuc.   **3.** *to come to one's ears, be told as news,* Aeschin.   **III.** *to fall down at* another's *feet, prostrate oneself,* Hdt., Soph. : c. dat., πρ. βωμοῖσι Soph.; γόνασί τινος Eur.; θεῶν πρὸς βρέτας Ar.   **2.** c. acc. *to fall down to, supplicate,* Eur.

προσ-πίτνω, poët. for προσ-πίπτω, *to fall upon* a person's *neck,* τινί Eur.; ἀμφὶ σὰν γενειάδα Id.   **2.** *to come in, come upon the scene,* Id.   **II.** of things,

to fall upon, of arrows, Aesch.; of anger, Eur.   **III.** *to fall down to* or *before, supplicate,* Soph.; c. dat., προσπίτνομέν σοι Id.; but more commonly c. acc., Aesch., etc.; προσπίτνω σε γόνασι Soph. :—c. inf., πρ. σε μὴ θανεῖν *I beseech* thee that I may not die, Id.

προσ-πλάζω, poët. shortd. for προσπελάζω (intr.), *to come near, approach,* Il.; c. dat., Od.

προσ-πλάσσω, Att. -ττω, f. άσω, *to form* or *mould upon* : Pass., pf. part., νεοσσιαὶ προσπεπλασμέναι ἐκ πηλοῦ πρὸς ἀποκρήμνοισι οὔρεσι nests *formed* of clay *and attached* to precipitous mountains, Hdt.

πρόσ-πλᾰτος, ον, (προσπλάζω) *approachable,* Aesch.

προσ-πλέκω, ξω, *to connect with* :—Pass. *to cling to, be implicated with,* τινι Strab.

προσ-πλέω, f. -πλεύσομαι : Ion. pres. -πλώω, aor. 1 προσέπλωσα:—*to sail towards* or *against,* Hdt., Thuc., etc.; τινί *against* one, Thuc.; of ships, Xen.

προσ-πληρόω, f. ώσω, *to fill up* or *complete* a number, ἱππέας πρ. εἰς δισχιλίους Xen.   **2.** *to equip* ships *besides, man still more* ships, Thuc.; so in Med., Xen.

προσ-πλωτός, ή, όν, *accessible from the sea,* i.e. *navigable,* Hdt.

προσ-πλώω, Ion. for προσπλέω.

προσ-πνέω, Ep. -πνείω: f. -πνεύσομαι :—*to breathe upon, inspire,* Theocr.   **II.** impers., c. gen., προσπνεῖ μοι κρεῶν *a smell of* meat *comes to* me, Ar.

προσ-ποιέω, f. ήσω, *to make over to,* Lat. *tradere alicui in manus,* πρ. τινὶ τὴν Κέρκυραν Thuc.; πρ. Λέσβον τῇ πόλει Xen.   **II.** Med., with aor. med. and pass., *to attach to oneself, win,* or *gain over,* τινά Hdt., Thuc., etc.; τὸν δῆμον Ar.; with a second acc. added, φίλους πρ. τοὺς Λακεδαιμονίους as friends, Hdt.; ὑπηκόους πρ. τὰς πόλεις Thuc.   **2.** *to take what does not belong to one, pretend to, lay claim to,* τὴν τῶν γεφυρῶν διάλυσιν Id.   **3.** *to pretend, feign, affect, simulate,* ὀργήν Hdt.; πρ. ἔχθραν *to use it as a pretence, allege,* Thuc.   **4.** c. inf. *to pretend to do* or *to be,* Hdt., etc.; πρ. μὲν εἰδέναι, εἰδότες δὲ οὐδέν Plat. :—c. inf. fut. *to make* as *if one* would, Xen.   **5.** with a negat., Lat. *dissimulare,* δεῖ δέ, εἰ καὶ ἠδίκησαν, μὴ προσποιεῖσθαι one must *make* as if it were not so, Thuc. Hence

προσποίημα, ατος, τό, *a pretence, assumption,* Arist.

προσποίησις, ή, *a taking something to oneself, acquisition,* Thuc.   **2.** *a pretension* or *claim* to a thing, c. gen., Id.   **3.** absol. *pretension,* Arist.

προσποιητικός, ή, όν, *making pretence to,* τινός Arist.

προσποιητός, όν, and **ή, όν,** *taken to oneself, assumed, affected, pretended,* Dem. :—Adv. -τῶς or -τως, opp. to τῷ ὄντι, Plat.; also προσποιητά as Adv., Babr.

προσ-πολεμέω, f. ήσω, *to carry on war against, be at war with* another, Thuc., Xen.

προσ-πολεμόομαι, Med. *to make one's enemy* or *go to war with* besides, Thuc.

προσπολέω, f. ήσω, (πρόσπολος) *to attend, serve,* τινί Eur.   **II.** Pass. *to be escorted by a train of attendants,* Soph.

πρόσ-πολος, ὁ, (πολέω) *a servant,* Soph., Eur.; *a ministering priest,* Trag.; πρ. φόνου *minister of death,* Aesch.   **2.** fem. *a handmaid,* Soph.

προσ-πορίζω, f. Att. ιῶ, *to procure* or *supply besides,* Xen., Dem.

προσ-πορπᾱτός, ή, όν, (πορπάω) fastened on with a πόρπη, pinned down, Aesch.

πρόσπταισμα, ατος, τό, a stumble against something, a stumble, Arist. From

προσ-πταίω, f. σω, to strike against a thing, to sprain, τὸ γόνυ Hdt.; πρ. τὸν πόδα to stumble along, halt, limp, Plut. :—absol. to stumble, limp, Ar., Xen. :—c. dat. to stumble upon, strike against, τινί Dem. :—of ships, to be wrecked, Hdt. II. metaph. to fail, esp. in war, to suffer a defeat, Id. III. πρ. τινί to offend, clash with, Plut.

προσπτῆναι, inf. of προσ-έπτην, aor. 2 of προσπέτομαι.

προσ-πτήσσω, f. ξω, to crouch or cower towards, ἀκταὶ λιμένος ποτικεπτηυῖαι (Ep. pf. part. for προσπεπτηκυῖαι) headlands, verging towards the harbour, i. e. shutting it in, Od.

προσπτῆται, 3 sing. aor. 2 med. subj. of προσπέτομαι.

πρόσ-πτυγμα, τό, the object of embraces, Eur. From

προσ-πτύσσω, f. ξω, to embrace, B. mostly as Dep. προσ-πτύσσομαι, Dor. ποτι-πτ-: f. -πτύξομαι: pf. προσ-έπτυγμαι :—of a garment, to fold itself close to, προσπτύσσετο πλευραῖσιν χιτών Soph. II. of persons, 1. to fold to one's bosom, clasp, embrace, Od., Eur., etc. ; στόμα γε σὸν προσπτύξομαι will press it to my lips, Eur. :— Pass., c. dat. to cling to, Soph. 2. metaph. to embrace, greet warmly, welcome, Od. ; c. dupl. acc., πρ. τινά τι to address a friendly greeting to one, Ib. ; προσπτύσσεσθαι μύθῳ to entreat warmly, importune, Ib.; θεῶν δαῖτας προσπτύσσεσθαι to welcome the feasts of the gods, Pind.

προσ-πτύω, f. -πτύσω and -πτύσομαι [ῠ] :—to spit upon, τινί Theophr., Luc. 2. metaph., πρ. τῷ καλῷ : absol., προσπτύσας Plut.

προσ-ραίνω, to sprinkle on one, τινί τι Strab.

προσραπτέον, verb. Adj. one must sew on, ap. Plut.

προσ-ράπτω, f. ψω, to stitch on : Pass., pf. part. τρίβωνες προσερραμμένοι patched coats, Plut.

προσ-ρέω, f. -ρεύσομαι : aor. 2 pass. -ερρύην :—to flow towards a point, to stream in, assemble, Hdt. 2. to rush up to, τινί Plut.

προσ-ρήγνῡμι and -ύω, f. -ρήξω, to dash or beat against (intr.), προσέρρηξεν ὁ ποταμὸς τῇ οἰκίᾳ N. T.

πρόσ-ρημα, ατος, τό, an address, salutation, Plat. II. that by which one is addressed, a name, designation, Id., Dem.

πρόσ-ρησις, ή, an addressing, accosting, πρόσρησιν διδόναι τινί to accost him, Eur. ; ἕνεκ' ἐμῆς προσρήσεως to enable me to address thee, Id.

προσ-ρητέος, α, ον, verb. Adj. to be addressed, called, Plat. II. προσρητέον, one must call, Id.

προσ-ριπτέω, = sq., Plut.

προσ-ρίπτω, f. ψω, to throw to, τί or τινά τινι Plut.

προσ-σαίνω, Dor. ποτι-σαίνω : aor. 1 -έσηνα :—to fawn upon, properly of dogs ; metaph., φῶτα προσσαίνειν κακόν Aesch. 2. of things, to please, like Lat. arridere, τινά Id., Eur.

προσ-σέβω, to worship or honour besides, Aesch.

προσ-σημαίνω, f. ἀνῶ, to connote, Arist.

πρόσσοθεν, Adv., Ep. for πρόσθεν, Il.

προσσοτέρω, Adv. poët. for προσωτέρω.

προσ-στάζω, Dor. ποτι-στ-, f. ξω, to drop on, shed

over, Pind. ; πραῢν ποτιστάζων ὕαρον letting fall mild words, Id.

προσ-σταυρόω, f. ώσω, to draw a stockade along or before a place, c. acc., Thuc.

προσ-στείχω, f. ξω : aor. 2 -έστιχον :—to go or come towards, Od. ; δεῦρο πρ. Soph.

προσ-στέλλω, f. -στελῶ, to lay upon : Med. to keep close to, τοῖς ὀρεινοῖς, of a general, Plut. II. in pf. pass. to be tight-drawn, close tucked in, ἰσχία προσεσταλμένα loins tucked up, of dogs, Xen.

προσ-στρατοπεδεύω, f. σω, to encamp near, τόπῳ Polyb.

προσ-σῡκοφαντέω, f. ήσω, to slander besides, Dem.

προσ-συμβάλλομαι, Med. to contribute to besides or at the same time, προσσυνεβάλετο τῆς ὁρμῆς contributed to their eagerness, Thuc.

προσ-συνοικέω, f. ήσω, to settle with others in a place, join with others in a settlement, c. dat. pers., Thuc.

προσ-σφάζω or -ττω, to slay at a place, c. dat., Plut.

πρόσσω, poët. for πρόσω.

προσ-σωρεύω, f. σω, to store up besides, Luc.

πρόσταγμα, ατος, τό, (προστάσσω) an ordinance, command, Plat., etc. ; ἐκ προστάγματος Dem.

προ-σταθείς, aor. 1 pass. part. of προ-ίστημι. II. **προσ-ταθείς**, of προσ-τείνω.

προσ-τακῆναι, aor. 2 pass. inf. of προστήκω.

προσ-τακτέον, verb. Adj. one must order, Plat.

προσ-τακτικός, ή, όν, of or for commanding, imperative, Plut.

προσ-τακτός, ή, όν, ordained, ordinary, Decr. ap. Dem.

προσ-ταλαιπωρέω, f. ήσω, to persist or persevere still further in a thing, c. dat., Thuc.

πρόσταξις, ή, (προστάσσω) an ordaining, an ordinance, command, Plat. II. an assessment, Thuc.

προ-στασία, Ion. -ίη, ή, (προστῆναι) a standing before, leadership, τοῦ δήμου, τοῦ πλήθους Thuc. :—absol. chieftainship, presidency, Id. II. a standing up for, patronage ; and in bad sense, partisanship, Dem. 2. = Roman patronatus, Plut. III. a place before a building, a court or area, Aeschin.

πρό-στασις, ή, (προστῆναι) outward dignity, pompous appearance, pomp, Plat.

προσ-τάσσω, Att. -ττω, f. ξω, I. c. acc. pers., 1. to place or post at a place, χωρεῖτε οἷ προστάσσομεν (sc. ὑμᾶς) Eur. :—Pass., προσταχθεὶς πύλαις Aesch., etc. 2. to attach to, assign to, Hdt. ; πρ. τινάς τινι to assign them to his command, Thuc. :—Pass., Ἰνδοὶ προσετετάχατο Φαρναζάθρῃ Hdt. 3. reversely, πρ. ἄρχοντα to appoint as commander over others, Id. II. c. acc. rei, to give as a command, prescribe, enjoin, ἔργον, πόνον πρ. τινί Id., etc. :—Pass., τοῖσι δὲ ἵππος προσετέτακτο to others orders had been given to supply cavalry, Id. ; τὰ προσταχθέντα orders given, Id.; τὸ προστεταγμένον Id. ; τὰ προσταχθησόμενα orders that will be given, Xen. :—absol., προσταχθέν μοι the order having been given me, Dem. 2. c. dat. pers. et inf. to command, order one to do, Hdt., etc. :—Pass., impers., προσετέτακτό τινι πρήσσειν Id. 3. c. acc. et inf., Eur. :—Pass. to be ordered to do, Hdt. : absol. to receive orders, Thuc.

προστατεία, ή, (προστάτης) = προστασία II, Xen.

προστᾰτεύω, = προστατέω, to be leader or ruler of, c.

gen., Xen.; absol. *to exercise authority*, Id.   **II.**
πρ. ὅπως .., *to provide* or *take care that* .., Id.

προστᾰτέω, f. ήσω, (προστάτης) *to stand before, be
ruler over, domineer over*, χθονός, δωμάτων Eur.; πρ.
τοῦ ἀγῶνος *to be steward* of the games, Xen.; absol.,
ὁ προστατῶν *he that acts as chief*, Id.   **II.** *to
stand before* as a defender, *to be guardian* or *protector
of*, πυλῶν Aesch.; ᾿Αργείων Eur.   **III.** ὁ προστατῶν χρόνος *the time that's close at hand*, Soph. Hence

προστᾰτήριος, α, ον, *standing before*, δεῖμα πρ. καρδίας
fear *hovering before*, or *domineering* over, my heart,
Aesch.   **II.** *standing before, protecting*, Id., Soph.

προστάτης, ου, ὁ, (προστῆναι) *one who stands before,
a front-rank-man*, Xen.   **II.** *a chief, leader* of a
party, Hdt.; ὁ πρ. τοῦ δήμου Thuc.   **2.** generally,
a president, ruler, Aesch., Eur., etc.; προστάται τῆς
εἰρήνης its *chief authors*, Xen.   **III.** *one who
stands before, a protector, guard, champion*, πυλω-
μάτων Aesch., Soph., etc.   **2.** at Athens, of *a citizen
who took care* of the μέτοικοι, as the Rom. *patronus*
took care of his *clientes*; προστάτην γράφεσθαί τινα *to
choose as one's patron*, Ar.; but, γράφεσθαι προστάτου
*to enter oneself by one's patron's name, attach oneself
to a patron*, Soph.   **IV.** προστάτης θεοῦ *one who
stands before a god to entreat him, a suppliant*, Soph.

προστᾰτικός, ή, όν, *of* or *for a προστάτης* (signf. 11)
Plat.   **2.** *of* or *for rank* or *honour*, Polyb.

προστάτις, ιδος, fem. of προστάτης, Luc.

προστάττω, Att. for προστάσσω.

προ-σταυρόω, f. ώσω, *to draw a stockade in front of*
or *along*, τὴν θάλασσαν Thuc.

προσ-τειχίζω, f. σω, *to add to a fortification, include
in the city-wall*, Thuc.

προσ-τεκταίνομαι, Med. *to add of oneself*, Plut.

προσ-τελέω, f. έσω, *to pay* or *spend besides*, Xen.

προσ-τέλλω, f. -στελῶ, *to guard* or *cover in front*,
Thuc.:—Med., προστέλλεσθαί τινα *to send armed into
the field*, Aesch.:—Pass., προϋστάλης ὁδόν *wast equipt
for, didst undertake, a journey*, Soph.

προ-στένω, *to sigh* or *grieve beforehand*, Aesch.

προ-στερνίδιον, τό, (στέρνον) *a covering for the breast*,
of horses, Xen.

πρό-στερνος, ον, (στέρνον) *before* or *on the breast*, Aesch.

προσ-τέρπω, Dor. **ποτι-τέρπω**, f. ψω, *to delight* or
please besides, Il.

προστεχνάομαι, f. ήσομαι, Dep. *to devise besides*, Plut.

προσ-τήκομαι, f. -τήξομαι, Pass., with pf. προστέτηκα,
to stick fast to, cling to, προστᾰκέντος ἰοῦ of the
poisoned robe *clinging* to Hercules, Soph.; and he is
said to be ὕδρας προστετακὼς φάσματι, Id.

προσ-τίθημι, Dor. ποτι-: imper. προστίθει: f. -θήσω:
aor. 1 -έθηκα: aor. 2 -έθην, subj. -θῶ:—Med., aor. 1
-εθηκάμην: aor. 2 -εθέμην, subj. -θῶμαι, 3 sing. opt.
-θεῖτο:—Pass., aor. 1 -ετέθην:—*to put to*, Lat. *apponere*, Od.; πρ. τὰς θύρας *to put to the door*, Hdt.;
πρ. κλίμακας τοῖς πύργοις Thuc.   **2.** *to hand over*
or *deliver to*, θεῶν γέρα ἐφημέροισι προστίθει Aesch.;
γυναῖκα πρ. τινί *to give* her to him as wife, Hdt.,
etc.   **3.** simply, *to give, bestow*, φερνάς Eur.; χρήματα Dem.   **II.** πρ. πρῆγμά τινι *to impose further
business on a man*, Hdt.; also c. inf., πρ. τινὶ πρήσσειν τι Id.:—then, πρ. τινὶ ἀτιμίην *to impose* disgrace

---

upon him, Id.; λύπην, πόνους Eur.; ζημίας τινί
Thuc.   **2.** *to attribute* or *impute to*, αἰτίαν τινί
Eur.; θράσος τινί Id.   **III.** *to add*, πρ. τι τῷ
νόμῳ Hdt.; ὅρκῳ πρ. (sc. τὸν λόγον), i. e. *to make oath
and then add* the statement, Soph. :—absol. *to make
additions, to augment*, Thuc.   **2.** esp. of adding
articles to documents, πρ. τι περὶ τῆς ξυμμαχίας Id.;
πρ. τῷ δικαίῳ *to add to* the definition of right, Plat.   **3.**
c. acc. pers., πρ. ἑαυτόν τινι *to join* his party, Thuc.

B. Med., προστίθεσθαι τὴν γνώμην τινί *to associate
one's* opinion to another, i. e. *agree with* him, Dem. :
absol. πρ. τις ἂν σὺ προσθῇ *to associate oneself to*, οἷς Soph.;
πρ. τῷ ἄστῳ *to be well-inclined to* him, Hdt. :—absol.
to come in, submit, ap. Dem.   **2.** *to give one's
assent, agree to* a thing, c. dat., Hdt., Thuc., etc.   **3.**
ψῆφον δ᾽ ᾿Ορέστῃ τήνδ᾽ ἐγὼ προσθήσομαι, literally, *will
deposit* this vote in favour of Orestes, Aesch.; so, μὴ
μιᾷ ψήφῳ προστίθεσθαι (sc. τὴν γνώμην), ἀλλὰ δυοῖν
Thuc.   **II.** c. acc. pers. *to associate with oneself*, i. e. *take to one as a friend* or ally, *win over*,
Hdt., Thuc.; φίλον πρ. τινά Hdt.; ταύτην πρόσθου
δάμαρτα *take* her to wife, Soph.   **2.** c. acc. rei, *to
add to oneself, gain*, πρ. πλέον *to be profited*, Id.;
πρ. χάριν=ἐπιχαρίζεσθαι, Id.; of evils, *to bring upon
oneself*, Trag., etc.   **b.** *to bring upon* others, προσ-
εθήκαντο πόλεμον *made* war, Hdt.; μῆνιν προσθέσθαι
τινί *to vent* wrath upon him, Id.

προσ-τῑλάω, f. ήσω, *to befoul with dung*, Ar.

προσ-τῑμάω, f. ήσω, *to award further penalty* besides
the regular one, Plat., Dem.; πρ. τῷ δημοσίῳ *to adjudge
to the treasury as a debt*, Dem. :—the Act. was used
of the Court, the Med. of the individual who proposed
the penalty, Lex ap. Dem.   Hence

προστίμημα [ῑ], ατος, τό, *that which is awarded over
and above the regular penalty, a fine*, Dem.

προσ-τραγῳδέω, *to exaggerate in tragic style*, Strab.

προσ-τρέπω, f. ψω, *to turn towards a god, to approach
with prayer, supplicate*, Soph.; c. acc. pers. et inf.
to entreat one to do, Id.; c. acc. rei et inf. *to pray
that*, Eur. :—so in Med., Aesch.   **2.** *to approach* (as
an enemy), Pind.

προσ-τρέφω, f. -θρέψω, *to bring up in* :—Pass., aor. 1
προσεθρέφθην, Aesch.

προσ-τρέχω, f. -δρᾰμοῦμαι : aor. 2 -έδρᾰμον :—*to run
to* or *towards, come to* one, πρός τινα Plat.; τινί Ar. :
absol. *to run up*, Xen., etc.   **2.** in hostile sense, *to
run at, make a sally*, πρός τινα Id.

προσ-τρίβω [ῑ], f. ψω, *to rub against* :—Pass., προσ-
τετριμμένος τισί *worn down by intercourse with*
others, Aesch. : Med., mostly in bad sense, *to inflict*
or *cause to be inflicted*, πληγάς τινι Ar. : Pass. *to be
inflicted upon*, τινί Aesch.   **2.** in good sense, πλούτου δόξαν προστρίβεσθαί τινι *to attach to* one the
reputation of wealth, Dem.   Hence

πρόστριμμα, ατος, τό, *that which is rubbed on* : metaph.
an affliction, Aesch.

προσ-τρόπαιος, Dor. **ποτι-τρόπαιος**, ον, (προστροπή) :   **I.** *turning oneself towards*, hence   **1.**
one who (having incurred pollution by sin or crime)
turns to a god for purification, a suppliant, Soph.,
etc.; as Adj. *suppliant*, πρ. λιταί Id.   **2.** of one
who has not yet been purified, *a polluted person*,

Lat. *homo piacularis*, Aesch., Eur. 3. *of the pollution incurred*, πρ. αἷμα *blood-guiltiness*, Eur. II. *a suppliant for vengeance*, Aesch. 2. pass. *to whom the murdered person turns* for vengeance, i.e. *an avenger*, Aeschin., etc.

προστροπή, ἡ, (προστρέπω) *a turning oneself towards a god for purification, the supplication* of a polluted person, Aesch.:—*any address to a god, prayers*, Id., Eur.; προστροπὴν θεᾶς *the duty of praying* to the goddess, *the priestly office*, Eur.; πόλεως προστροπὴν *a petition* to the city, Soph. 2. πρ. γυναικῶν *a suppliant band* of women, Aesch.

πρόστροπος, ον, (προστρέπω) like προστρόπαιος, *a suppliant*, τινος Soph.; absol., Id.

προσ-τυγχάνω, f. -τεύξομαι, *to obtain one's share of* a thing, c. gen., Soph.: c. dat. *to meet with, hit upon, light upon*, Plat.: ὁ προστυγχάνων, ὁ προστυχών *the first person one meets, the first that offers, any body*, Id.; τὰ προστυχόντα ξένια *the guests' fare* set before him, Eur.

προ-στῷον, τό, (στοά) *a portico*, Plat.

προσ-υβρίζω, f. -σω, *to maltreat besides*, Dem.

προ-συγγίγνομαι, old Att. προ-ξυγγ-, Dep. *to speak with* one *before*, τινι Thuc.

προ-συμμίσγω, *to intermix first*, τὸ ὕδωρ ἐς τὠυτό Hdt.

προ-συνοικέω, *to cohabit with before*, τινί Hdt.

προσ-υπάρχω, f. ξω, *to exist besides*, οὐδὲ ταφῆναι προσυπῆρχεν ἐμοί *and besides I could* not have been *buried*, Dem.

προσ-υπέχω (sc. λόγον), *to be answerable also for*, τῆς τύχης Dem.

προσ-φάγιον, τό, (φαγεῖν) *anything eaten with other food*: generally, *something to eat*, N. T.

πρόσφαγμα, ατος, τό, *a victim sacrificed for* others, Eur.; of the victim's blood, Id. II. *sacrifice, slaughter*, Aesch., Eur. From

προ-σφάζω, later Att. -σφάττω, f. ξω, *to sacrifice beforehand*, τινί Eur.

προσ-φαίνομαι, Pass. *to appear besides*, Xen.

προσφάσθαι, pres. or aor. 2 med. inf. of πρόσφημι.

πρόσ-φατος, ον, (πέφαμαι, pf. pass. of *φένω) *lately slain, fresh-slain*, Il., Hdt. II. generally, *fresh, recent*, Aesch., Dem. III. πρόσφατον as Adv. of Time, *recently, lately*, Pind.

προσφερής, ές, (προσφέρω) *brought near, approaching*: metaph. *resembling, similar*, τινι Hdt., Aesch., etc.; τὸ σῶμα προσφερὴς τῇ ψυχῇ Plat.:—rarely c. gen., πατρὸς προσφερεῖς ὀμμάτων Eur.; cf. ἐμφερής. II. = πρόσφορος, *serviceable*, τινι Hdt.

προσ-φέρω, Dor. ποτι-φέρω: f. προσοίσω: Ion. 1 aor. pass. -ενείχθην :—*to bring* to or *upon, apply to*, Lat. *applicare*, Hdt., Eur., etc.; but, πρ. χεῖρά τινι *to lay* hands *upon* one, Pind.; also *to offer* one's hand, as a friend, Xen.:—without dat. *to apply, exhibit, employ, use*, βίην Hdt.; πρ. πόλεμον *to bring war* it *to bear*, Pind.: also, πρ. πόλεμον Hdt. 2. *to add*, τί τινι Soph., Eur.; τι πρός τι Hdt. 3. *to present, offer, give*, λουτρὰ πατρί Soph.; δῶρα Thuc.; θυσίας N.T. b. esp. *of meat and drink, to offer, to set before* one, Xen.; πρ. τινι ἐμπιεῖν καὶ φαγεῖν Id. 4. *to bring forward, quote, cite*, Pind. 5. *to bring forward* proposals, *make an*

offer, πρ. λόγον or λόγους τινι Hdt., Thuc..: absol., πρ. περὶ ὁμολογίας Hdt., Thuc. II. *to contribute, bring in, yield*, ἑκατὸν τάλαντα Hdt., etc. III. *to bring one thing near* another, *make it like*, πρ. νόον ἀθανάτοις Pind.

B. Pass., with fut. med. προσοίσομαι, *to be borne towards*, of ships, *to put in*, Xen. 2. *to go against, attack, assault*, τινι or πρός τινα Hdt., etc.; absol. *to rush on, make an onset*, Id.; προσφέρεσθαι ἄποροι *difficult to engage*, Id. 3. simply, *to go to* or *towards*, ἐκ τοῦ Ἰκαρίου πελάγεος προσφερόμενοι *sailing*, Id. 4. *to deal with, behave oneself* in a certain way *towards* one, Id., Thuc.;—προσφέρεσθαι πρὸς λόγον *to answer* it, Xen. 5. προσφέρεσθαί τινι *to come near* one, *be like* him, Hdt. II. προσφέρεσθαί τινι *to be put* or *imposed upon* one, τὰ προσφερόμενα πρήγματα Id.

C. Med., προσφέρεσθαί τι *to take to oneself as meat* or *drink*, Xen.:—Pass., τὰ προσφερόμενα *meat* or *drink, food*, Id. 2. *to exhibit*, φιλοτιμίαν ὑμῖν N. T. 3. *to apply* or *cause to be applied*, Polyb.

προσ-φεύγω, f. -φεύξομαι, *to flee for refuge to*, τινί Plut. Hence

προσφευκτέον, verb. Adj. *one must be liable to a prosecution besides*, Dem.

πρόσ-φημι, mostly used in 3 sing. aor. 2 προσέφη, *to speak to, address*, τινά Hom., Hes.; absol., Hom.;— also inf. med. προσφάσθαι, Od.

προσ-φθέγγομαι, Dor. ποτι-φθ-, Dep. *to call to, address, accost, salute*, τινα Eur. 2. *to call by a name, call* so and so, Pind. Hence

προσ-φθεγκτός, Dor. ποτί-φθ-, ον, *addressed, saluted*, σοῦ φωνῆς *by thy voice*, Soph. II. act. *saluting*, Anth.; and

πρόσφθεγμα, ατος, τό, *an address, salutation*, Trag.

πρόσ-φθογγος, ον, *addressing, saluting*, μῦθοι πρ. *words of salutation*, Aesch.

προσ-φθονέω, f. ήσω, *to oppose through envy*, Plut.

προσφίλεια [ῐ], ἡ, *kindness, good-will*, Aesch. From

προσ-φῐλής, ές, (φιλέω) *dear, beloved*, τῶν ἡλίκων προσφιλεστάτῳ Hdt.; προσφιλέες τῷ βασιλέι *dear* or *friendly* to him, Id.;—of things, *pleasing, agreeable, grateful, dear*, Lat. *gratus*, Aesch., Soph. II. act., of persons, *kindly affectioned, grateful, well-disposed*, Soph., Thuc. :—Adv. -λῶς, *kindly*, Soph.; πρ. ἔχειν τινί *to be kindly affectioned* to one, Xen.

προσ-φῐλοκᾰλέω, f. ήσω, *to add from a love of splendour*, Strab.

προσ-φῐλονεικέω, f. ήσω, *to vie with* another *in* anything, τινι πρός τι Polyb.

προσ-φῐλοσοφέω, f. ήσω, *to speculate further upon*, τινί Luc. II. *to philosophise with* another, c. dat. pers., Id.

προσ-φοιτάω, f. ήσω, *to go* or *come to frequently, to resort* to a place, Dem., etc.; πρ. τινί *to visit constantly*, Strab.

προσφορά, ἡ, (προσφέρω) *a bringing to, applying, application*, Plat. II. (from Pass.) *that which is brought* to a person or thing, *an addition*, Soph. 2. *advantage, profit*, Id.:—*a bounty, gift*, Theophr.: *an offering*, N. T. Hence

προσφορέω, *to bring to, bring in*, Hdt., Xen.

προσφόρημα, ατος, τό, that which is set before one, victuals, Eur.

πρόσ-φορος, Dor. ποτί-, ον, (προσφέρω) serviceable, useful, profitable, Hdt., Soph.; absol., ἔχοντας τὰ πρ. Hdt., Thuc. 2. suitable, fitting, worthy, Pind.; c. dat., Id., Eur., etc. :—c. inf., οὐ πρόσφορον μολεῖν 'tis not fit or meet to go, Aesch. 3. πρόσφορον, τό, what is fitting or suitable, Arist. :—πρόσφορα, τά, fitting service, Aesch.; τὰ πρόσφορα all things meet or due, Eur.; τὰ πρ. as Adv., fitly, Id.

προσφυής, ές, (προσφύω) growing upon or from, attached to, ἔκ τινος Od. 2. πρ. τινι attached or devoted to, Plat. :—Adv. -ῶς, Ion. -έως, προσφυέως λέγειν to speak suitably, Hdt.

προσ-φύω, f. -φύσω [ῡ]: aor. 1 -έφυσα :—to make to grow to : metaph. to make sure, confirm, Aesch., Ar. II. Pass. or Med., f. -φύσομαι, with aor. 2 act. -έφυν, pf. -πέφυκα :—to grow to or upon, c. dat., Eur. :—metaph. to cling to, τῷ προσφὺς ἐχόμην Od.; and absol., προσφῦσα ll.; of a fish, τὠγκίστρῳ ποτεφύετο Theocr.

προσ-φωνέω, f. ήσω, to call or speak to, address, accost, τινά Hom., etc.; absol., Od.; τοῖσιν προσεφώνεε addressed [them] in these words, Ib.; (but c. dat. pers., N. T.) :—c. dupl. acc. to address words to a person, Il., Eur. 2. to call by name, Eur. II. c. acc. rei, to pronounce, utter, Soph. Hence

προσ-φωνήεις, εσσα, εν, addressing, capable of addressing, Od., in Dor. form ποτι-φωνήεις ; and

προσφώνημα, ατος, τό, that which is addressed to another, an address, Soph., Eur.; and

προσφώνησις, ἡ, an address : a dedication, Plut.

προσ-χαίρω, to rejoice at, τινί Plut.

προσ-χαρίζομαι, Dep. to gratify or satisfy besides, τινί Xen.; τινί τι to give freely besides, Strab.

προσ-χάσκω, aor. 2 -έχανον : pf. in pres. sense προσκέχηνα :—to gape or stare open-mouthed at one, μὴ χαμαιπετὲς βόαμα προσχάνῃς ἐμοί fall not prostrate before me with loud cries, Aesch.

προσχεθεῖν, aor. 2 inf. of προέχω (v. σχέθω), to hold before :—Med. to ward off from oneself, Theocr.

προσ-χέω, f. -χεῶ, to pour to or on, Luc.

πρόσχημα, ατος, τό, (προ-έχω) that which is held before : hence, I. a screen, cloak, Thuc. : a plea, pretence, pretext, ostensible cause, Soph.; so, πρ. τοῦ λόγου Hdt.; πρ. ποιεῖσθαι ὡς ἐπ' Ἀθήνας ἐλαύνει to make a pretence or show of marching against Athens, Id.; c. inf., πρ. ποιούμενοι μὴ προδώσειν to pretend that they will not betray, Thuc.; also, πρ. ποιεῖσθαί τι to put forward as a screen or disguise, Plat. :—πρόσχημα, acc. absol., by way of pretext, Hdt. II. outward show, ornament, as Miletus is called πρ. τῆς Ἰωνίης, Ionia's chief ornament, Id.; and the Pythian games τὸ κλεινὸν Ἑλλάδος πρ. ἀγῶνος, Soph.; πρ. τῆς τραγῳδίας the outward show of tragedy, Ar.

πρό-σχισμα, ατος, τό, the forepart of the shoe, from its being slit, Arist.

προσχόω, old pres. for προσχώννυμι.

προσ-χρῄζω, f. ήσω : Ion. -χρηίζω, f. -ήσω :—to require or desire besides, c. gen., Hdt., Soph. : c. gen. pers. et inf., προσχρηίζω ὑμέων πείθεσθαι I request you to obey, Hdt.; c. inf. only, τί προσχρηίζων

μαθεῖν ; Soph.; πᾶν ὅπερ προσχρῄζετε (sc. πυθέσθαι) Aesch.

προσ-χρίμπτω, Dor. ποτι-, f. ψω, to come near, Aesch.

πρόσχυσις, ἡ, (προσχέω) a sprinkling, N. T.

πρόσχωμα, ατος, τό, a deposit made by water, πρ. Νείλου, of the Delta of the Nile, Aesch. From

προσ-χώννῡμι and -ώω : aor. -έχωσα :—a pres. προσ-χόω also occurs in Thuc. :—to heap up besides : 1. πρ. ταῦτα τὰ χωρία to form these new lands by deposition, of rivers, Hdt. 2. to choke up with mud, silt up, τὸν ἀγκῶνα [τοῦ Νείλου] Id.; absol., ὁ ποταμὸς προσχοῖ ἀεί continually forms fresh deposits, Thuc. II. to throw earth against : Pass., ᾗ προσεχοῦτο [τὸ τεῖχος] where [the wall] had earth thrown against it, Id.

προσχωρέω, f. ήσω and -ήσομαι :—to go to, approach, c. dat., Hdt., Thuc.; absol., Xen. II. to come or go over to, come in, join, τινι or πρός τινα Hdt., Att.; absol., Thuc.; also, πρ. ἐς ὁμολογίαν or ὁμολογίᾳ Hdt., Thuc. 2. to accede to an opinion, Hdt.; πρ. λόγοις τινός Soph. : to make concessions, Eur. 3. to approach, i. e. to agree with, be like, τινί or πρός τινα Hdt. 4. to put faith in, believe, τινί Id. Hence

προσχώρησις, ἡ, a going towards, approach, Xen.

πρόσ-χωρος, ον, (χώρα) lying near, neighbouring, Aesch., Soph. II. as Subst., a neighbour, Hdt.

πρόσχωσις, ἡ, =πρόσχωμα, Thuc. II. a bank or mound raised against a place, Id.

προσ-ψαύω, Dor. ποτι-, f. σω, to touch upon, touch, τινί Pind.; absol., Soph.

προσ-ψηφίζομαι, f. Att. ιοῦμαι, Med. to vote besides, grant by a majority of votes, Plut.

προσ-ψύχω [ῡ], (ψυχή) to devote oneself heart and soul, Anth.

πρόσω, poët. πρόσσω ; Dor. and old Att. πόρσω ; later Att. πόρρω :—regul. Comp. and Sup. προσωτέρω, προσωτάτω, v. προσωτέρω ; poët. πόρσιον, πόρσιστα Pind. : (πρό).

A. absol. : I. of Place, forwards, onwards, further, Hom., etc.; μὴ πόρσω φωνεῖν to speak no further, Id.; μηκέτι πάπταινε πόρσιον Pind. :—also with the Art., πορεύεσθαι ἀεὶ τὸ πρόσω Hdt.; ἰέναι τοῦ πρ. Xen. II. of Distance, far off, far away, Pind.; ἐγγύς, οὐ πρόσω βεβηκώς Eur. 2. too far, Plat. III. of Time, forward, πρόσσω καὶ ὀπίσσω, v. sub ὀπίσω :—henceforth, hereafter, Aesch. ; ὡς πόρσιστα as late as possible, Pind.; ἤδη πόρρω τῆς ἡμέρας οὔσης far spent, Aeschin.

B. c. gen. : I. of Place, forwards to, further into, πρ. τοῦ ποταμοῦ Xen. :—metaph., πρ. ἀρετῆς ἀνήκειν to have reached a high point of virtue, Hdt.; πόρρω τῆς μοχθηρίας far in wickedness, Xen., etc. :—also with the Art., προβήσομαι ἐς τὸ πρ. τοῦ λόγου Hdt.; ἐς τὸ πρ. μεγάθεος τιμᾶσθαι to be honoured to a high point of greatness, i. e. very greatly, Id. II. of Distance, far from, οὐ πρ. τοῦ Ἑλλησπόντου Id. : metaph., πρ. δικαίων Aesch.; πόρρω εἶναι τοῦ οἴεσθαι Plat.; also foll. by ἀπό, πρ. ἀπὸ τῶν φορτίων Hdt.; ἀπὸ τοῦ τείχους Xen. III. of Time, πρόσω τῆς νυκτός far into the night, Hdt., Plat.; μέχρι π. τῆς ἡμέρας Xen.

προσῳδία, ἡ, (ᾠδή) a song sung to music. II. the tone or accent of a syllable, Plat.

προσ-ῳδός, όν, (ῳδή) in accord, in tune, harmonious, Eur.; c. dat., προσῳδὸς ἡ τύχη τῷμῷ πάθει Id.

πρόσωθεν, Att. πόρρωθεν, Ep. πρόσσοθεν, Adv. (πρόσω): —from afar, Il., Trag., etc.: —Comp. πορρωτέρωθεν, from a more distant point, Isocr. II. of Time, from long, long ago, Eur., Plat., etc.

προσ-ωνέομαι, Dep. to buy besides, Xen., Dem.

προσ-ωνυμία, ἡ, (ὄνομα) a surname, Plut.

προσώπατα, τά, old Ep. pl. of πρόσωπον.

προσωπεῖον, τό, (πρόσωπον) a mask, Luc.

προσωποληπτέω, to be a respecter of persons, N. T.

προσωπο-λήπτης, ου, ὁ, (λαμβάνω) a respecter of persons, N. T. Hence

προσωποληψία, ἡ, respect of persons, N. T.

πρόσ-ωπον, τό: pl. πρόσωπα, Ep. προσώπατα; dat. προσώπασι: (ὤψ):—the face, visage, countenance, mostly in pl., even of a single person, Hom., Soph., etc.; βλέπειν τινὰ εἰς πρ. Eur.; ἐς πρ. τινὸς ἀφικέσθαι to come before him, Id.:—κατὰ πρ. in front, facing, Thuc., etc.; ἡ κατὰ πρ. ἔντευξις a tête-à-tête, Plut.; also, πρὸς τὸ πρ. Xen.; λαμβάνειν πρ. τινος, = προσωποληπτεῖν τινα, N. T.:—metaph. ἀρχομένου πρ. ἔργου Pind. II. one's look, countenance, Lat. vultus, Aesch., etc.; οὗ τὸ σὸν δείσας πρ., cf. Hor. vultus instantis tyranni, Soph. III. = προσωπεῖον, a mask, Dem., Arist. 2. outward appearance, beauty, Pind. IV. a person, N. T., etc.; προσώπον in bodily presence, Ib.

προσωτέρω, Att. πορρωτέρω, Comp. of πρόσω, further on, further, Hdt.:—c. gen. further than, Id.; πορρ. τοῦ καιροῦ Xen.:—also with the Art., τὸ προσωτέρω Hdt. 2. further from, τῶν πυλῶν Plut. II. Sup. προσωτάτω, Att. πορρωτάτω, furthest, Xen.; τὰ προσωτάτω the furthest parts, Hdt.; also προσώτατα, Id.:—ὡς προσωτάτω as far as possible, Soph. 2. c. gen. furthest from, Plat.

προσ-ωφελέω, f. ήσω, to help or assist besides, contribute to assist, τινά Hdt., Eur.; also c. dat., like ἐπωφελέω, Hdt., Eur. Hence

προσωφέλημα, τό, help or aid in a thing, c. gen., Eur.

προσωφέλησις, ἡ, help, aid, advantage, Soph.

προσωφελητέον, verb. Adj. one must assist, Xen.

πρόταγμα, ατος, τό, (προτάσσω) the van, Plut.

προταινί [ῐ], Adv. (πρό) in front of, c. gen., Eur.

προτακτέον, verb. Adj. of προτάσσω, one must place in front, Xen. 2. one must prefer, τί τινος Aeschin.

πρότακτος, ον, posted in front, οἱ πρ. the van, Plut.

προ-ταμιεῖον, τό, a room before a storeroom, Xen.

προ-ταμιεύω, f. σω, to lay in beforehand, Luc.

προτάμνω, Ion. for προτέμνω.

προ-ταρβέω, f. ήσω, to fear beforehand, Aesch.; c. inf., Eur. II. to be anxious for one, τινος Soph.

πρό-τασις, ἡ, (προτείνομαι) a proposition, the premiss of a syllogism, Arist.

προ-τάσσω, Att. -ττω, f. ξω, to place or post in front, πρ. σφῶν αὐτῶν Ἀστύμαχον put him at their head, as speaker, Thuc.:—Med., προετάξατο τῆς φάλαγγος τοὺς ἱππέας he posted his horse in front of it, Xen.:—Pass. to stand before one, so as to protect, Aesch.; τὸ προταχθέν, οἱ προτεταγμένοι the front ranks, van, Xen. II. generally, to appoint or determine beforehand, χρόνον Soph.

προ-τέγιον, τό, (τέγος) the forepart of a roof, Plut.

προ-τείνω, f. -τενῶ, to stretch out before, hold before, Xen. 2. to expose to danger, Soph. 3. metaph. to hold out as a pretext or excuse, Hdt., Soph., etc. II. to stretch forth the hands, as a suppliant, Hdt., etc.; (so also in Med., Id.); πρ. τινί χεῖρα Soph.: —intr. to stretch forward, εἰς τὸ πέλαγος Plat. 2. πρ. δεξιάν to offer it as a pledge, Soph., etc.; so, πρ. πίστιν Dem. 3. to hold out, tender, shew at a distance, Lat. ostentare, Hdt., Aesch., etc.:—so in Med., Hdt., Plat. 4. to put forward as an objection, Dem.; so in Med., Plat. 5. in Med., μισθὸν προτείνεσθαι to demand as a reward, Hdt.

προ-τέλειος, ον, (τέλος) before consecration:—as Subst., προ-τέλεια (sc. ἱερά), τά, a sacrifice offered before any solemnity, προτέλεια νεῶν as an offering in behalf of the ships, Aesch.; προτέλεια παιδός a sacrifice before her marriage, Eur. II. generally, a beginning, ἐν προτελείοις κάμακος in the preliminary conflicts, Aesch.; ἐν βιότῳ πρ. Id.

προ-τελέω, f. έσω, to pay as toll or tribute, and generally to pay or expend beforehand, τί τινι Xen. II. to initiate or instruct beforehand, Luc.

προτελίζω, to present as an offering preliminary to marriage, Eur.

προ-τεμένισμα, ατος, τό, (τέμενος) the precincts or entrance of a τέμενος, Thuc.

προ-τέμνω, Ion. and Ep. -τάμνω: f. -τεμῶ: aor. 2 προὔταμον:—to cut up beforehand, Il. II. to cut off in front, cut short, Lat. praecidere, Od. III. Med. to cut forward or in front of one, εἰ ὦλκα διηνεκέα προταμοίμην if in ploughing I cut a long furrow before me, Ib.

προτενθεύω, to taste and take out the tid-bits; generally, to have the pick of a thing, Ar. From

προ-τένθης, ου, ὁ, one who picks out the tid-bits, a dainty fellow, gourmand, Ar. (Deriv. uncertain.)

προτεραῖος, α, ον, (πρότερος) on the day before, τῇ προτεραίᾳ ἡμέρᾳ Plat.; c. gen., τῇ πρ. ἡμέρᾳ τῆς μάχης Thuc.:—more commonly alone, τῇ προτεραίᾳ (sub. ἡμέρᾳ), Lat. pridie, Hdt., etc.

προτερέω, f. ήσω, (πρότερος) to be before, be in advance, Hdt.; πρ. τῆς ὁδοῦ to be forward on the way, Id. 2. to be beforehand, take the lead, Thuc. 3. to gain an advantage, Philipp. ap. Dem. Hence

προτέρημα, ατος, τό, an advantage, victory, Polyb.

πρότερος and πρῶτος, Comp. and Sup. formed from πρό, as Lat. prior, primus, from prae.

A. Comp. πρότερος, α, ον, I. of Place, before, in front, forward, Il.; πόδες πρ. the fore-feet, Od. II. of Time, before, former, sooner, Hom., etc.; οἱ πρότεροι men of former times, Il.; πρότερος γενεῇ Ib.; but, πρ. παῖδες children by the first or a former marriage, Od.; τῇ προτέρῃ (sc. ἡμέρᾳ) on the day before, Lat. pridie, Ib.; ὁ πρότερος Διονύσιος Dionysius the elder, Xen.:—the Adj. is often used where we use the Adv., ὅ με πρότερος κάκ' ἔοργεν Il., etc. 2. as a regular Comp., c. gen., Ib., Hdt., etc.; also foll. by ἤ, τῷ προτέρῳ ἔτει ἢ κρητῆρα [ἐλήϊσαντο] Hdt. III. of Rank, Worth, and generally of Precedence, before, above, superior, Dem.; πρ. τινος πρός τι superior to him in a thing, Plat. IV. after Hom., neut. πρότε-

ρον as Adv. *before, sooner, earlier*, Hdt., etc.; ὀλίγον πρ. Plat. :—c. gen., ὀλίγῳ τι πρ. τούτων Hdt., etc.; most commonly foll. by ἤ, Id., Att.; also by πρίν, πρὶν ἄν, πρὶν ἤ, Hdt., Att.; also used with the Art., τὸ πρ. τῶν ἀνδρῶν τούτων Hdt. : Adv. often between Art. and Subst., e. g. ὁ πρότερον βασιλεύς Id.

B. Sup. **πρῶτος**, η, ον, contr. from *πρόατος, Dor. **πρᾶτος: I.** Adj. *first*, serving as the ordinal to the cardinal εἷς, Hom. **2.** of Place, *first, foremost*, ἐνὶ πρώτοισι or μετὰ πρώτοισι *alone*, Il.; ἐν πρώτῳ ῥυμῷ *at the front* or *end of the pole*, Ib.; πρώτῃσι θύρῃσι *at the first* or *outermost doors*, Ib. **3.** of Time, πρὸς πρώτην ἔω *at first dawn*, Soph. **4.** of Order, πρῶτοι πάντων ἀνθρώπων Hdt.; τῇ πρώτῃ τῶν ἡμερῶν Id. :— ἐν πρώτοις, *among the first*, then like Lat. *imprimis*, *above all, especially, greatly*, Id.; in Att., ἐν τοῖς πρῶτοι (v. ὁ, ἡ, τό A. IV. 7) :—in late Greek it is even foll. by a gen., πρῶτός μου N. T. **5.** of Rank, μετὰ πρώτοισιν *among the first men* of the state, Od., etc. **II.** neut. pl. πρῶτα, τά, **1.** (sc. ἆθλα), *the first prize*, Il., Soph. **2.** *the first part, beginning*, τῆς Ἰλιάδος τὰ πρ. Plat., etc. **3.** *the first, highest*, in degree, τὰ πρ. τᾶς λιμῶ (Dor.) *the extremities* of famine, Ar.; ἐς τὰ πρῶτα τιμᾶσθαι Thuc. :—of persons, ἐὼν τῶν Ἐρετριέων τὰ πρῶτα Hdt.; τὰ πρῶτα τῆς ἐκεῖ μοχθηρίας *the chief* of the rascality down there, Ar. **III.** as Adv., **1.** τὴν πρώτην (sc. ὥραν, ὁδόν) *first, at present, just now*, Hdt., etc.; so, τὴν πρώτην εἶναι, like ἑκὼν εἶναι, *at first*, Id. **2.** with Preps., ἀπὸ πρώτης (sc. ἀρχῆς), Thuc. **3.** most commonly in neut. sing. and pl., πρῶτον, πρῶτα, **a.** *first, in the first place*, Lat. *primum*, Hom., etc. **b.** = πρότερον, *before*, Xen., Anth. **4.** *first, for the first time*, Soph., etc.; ἐπεὶ πρῶτον, Lat. *quum primum, as soon as*, Hom.; so, ὁππότε κε πρῶτον Od.; ὅτε or ὅταν πρ. Dem.; ἐὰν or ἢν πρ. Plat. **IV.** Adv. πρώτως, Arist., etc.

προτέρω, Adv. (from πρό, as ἀποτέρω from ἀπό), *further, forwards*, Hom.; καί νύ κε δὴ προτέρω ἔτ᾽ ἔρις γένετ᾽ the quarrel would have gone *further*, Il. Hence

προτέρωσε, Adv. *toward the front, forward*, h. Hom.

προ-τεύχω, *to do beforehand* :—pf. pass. inf. προτετύχθαι, *to have happened beforehand, to be past*, Il.

προτί [ῐ], Ep. form of πρός, Hom.

προτι-άπτω, -βάλλομαι, -ειλέω, -εῖπον, v. προσ-.

προ-τίθημι, 3 pl. προτιθεῖσι : f. -θήσω : aor. 1 προύθηκα :—Med., aor. 1 προεθηκάμην :—Pass., aor. 1 προύτέθην; the pres. and impf. pass. are supplied by πρόκειμαι :— *to place* or *set before, set out*, esp. of meals, τραπέζας πρότιθεν (Ep. for προυτίθεσαν) Od.; δαῖτά τινι προθεῖναι Hdt., etc. :—Med. *to have set before one*, δαῖτα Id. **2.** like Lat. *projicere*, πρ. τινὰ κυσὶν *to throw* him to the dogs, Il.; πρ. τινὰ θηρσὶν ἁρπαγήν Eur. **3.** generally *to hand over to, give over to*, τί τινι Soph. **4.** *to expose* a child, Hdt., etc. **5.** *to set up as a mark* or *prize, propose*, ἀέθλους Id.; ἄμιλλαν Eur. :—Pass., προὐτέθην ἆθλον δορός Id. **b.** *to propose as a penalty*, θάνατον πρ. ζημίαν Thuc., etc. **6.** *to set forth, fix, settle*, ἐς ἑβδομήκοντα ἔτεα οὖρον τῆς ζόης πρ. Hdt.; so in Med., οὖρον πρ. ἐνιαυτόν Id. **7.** *to propose* as a task, τί τινι Soph. :—Med. *to propose to oneself* as a task or object, Plat. **8.** Med. also,

to put forth on one's own part, display, shew, εὐλάβειαν Soph. **9.** προτίθεσθαί τινα ἐν οἴκτῳ *to set before oneself* in pity, i. e. *compassionate*, Aesch. **II.** πρ. νεκρόν *to lay out* a dead body, *let* it *lie in state*, Hdt.; so in Med., Eur., etc. **2.** *to set out* wares *for show* or *sale*, Luc. **3.** *to propose, bring forward* a thing to be debated, Lat. *in medium afferre*, προθεῖναι πρῆγμα, λόγον Hdt.; γνώμας Thuc. : —c. inf., προθεῖναι λέγειν *to propose* a discussion, Id. :—Med., πένθος προεθήκαντο *proposed to themselves, observed* mourning, Hdt. :—Pass., ψῆφος περὶ ἡμῶν προτεθεῖσα Dem. **4.** *to appoint, hold* a meeting, Luc. :—Med., προύθετο λέσχην *appointed* a council, Soph. **5.** Pass., οὐ προυτέθη σφίσι λόγος *speech was not allowed* them, Xen. **III.** *to put forward*, as one foot before the other, Eur. **2.** *to hold out* as a pretext, Soph. **IV.** *to put before* or *first*, τι Plat. :—Med. *to put in front*, τοὺς γροσφομάχους Polyb. **2.** *to put before* or *over*, πέπλον ὀμμάτων Eur. **3.** *to prefer* one to another, τί τινος Hdt., Eur.; ἡδονὴν ἀντὶ τοῦ καλοῦ Eur. :—Med., πάρος τοὐμοῦ πόθου προύθεντο τὴν τυραννίδα Soph.

προτι-μάσσω, Ep. for προσ-μάσσω.

προ-τῑμάω, f. ήσω, *to honour* one *before* or *above* another, *to prefer* one to another, τινά or τί τινος Plat., etc.; τινὰ ἀντί τινος or πρό τινος Id. **2.** c. acc. only, *to prefer in honour* or *esteem*, Aesch., etc. :—Pass. *to be so preferred*, Thuc., etc.; προτιμᾶσθαι ἀποθανεῖν *to be selected* as a victim to be put to death, Id. **3.** c. gen. only, *to care for, take heed of, reck of*, Aesch.; οὐδὲν πρ. τινός Eur., etc. **4.** c. inf. foll. by ἤ, *to wish rather, prefer*, προτιμῶντες καθαροὶ εἶναι ἢ εὐπρεπέστεροι Hdt. : c.inf. only, *to wish greatly, wish much* to do or be, Soph., Eur.; πρ. πολλοῦ ἐμοὶ ξεῖνος γενέσθαι *to value* at a great price the privilege of becoming my friend, Hdt. **5.** c. partic., πρ. τυπτόμενος *to care greatly* about being beaten, Ar. Hence

προτίμησις [ῐ], ἡ, *an honouring before* others, *preference*, Thuc.

προτι-μῡθέομαι, Ep. for προσ-μυθέομαι.

προ-τῑμωρέω, f. ήσω, *to help beforehand* or *first*, τινί Thuc. :—Med. *to revenge oneself before*, Id.

προτι-όσσομαι, Ep. Dep., only in pres. and impf., never in the common form προσ-όσσομαι :—*to look at* or *upon*, Od. **II.** of the mind, *to look on, look stedfastly on*, θάνατον Ib.; ἦ σ᾽ εὖ γιγνώσκων προτιόσσομαι from thorough knowledge of thee *I look on* my fate, Il.

προ-τίω, f. τίσω [ῑ], *to prefer in honour*, Aesch., Soph.

προ-τολμάομαι, aor. 2 -ετολμήθην, Pass. *to be first ventured* or *risked*, Thuc.

προτομή, ἡ, (προτέμνω) *the foremost* or *upper part of anything : a bust* or *half-figure*, Anth. **2.** *the forepart* of a ship, Id.

προτονίζω, *to haul up with* πρότονοι, Anth. From

πρότονοι, οἱ, (προτείνω) *two ropes from the masthead to the forepart of a ship, the forestays*, which kept the mast from falling back (opp. to ἐπίτονοι the backstays), Hom. :—in sing., σωτῆρα ναὸς πρότονον Aesch. **II.** in Eur., the πρότονοι are *sail-ropes, braces*.

προτοῦ, for πρὸ τοῦ, *ere this, aforetime, erst, formerly*, Hdt., Att.; ὁ προτοῦ (sc. χρόνος) Thuc.

προτρεπτικός, ή, όν, persuasive, ἡ πρ. σοφία skill in oratory, Plat. ; κήρυγμα προτρεπτικώτατον πρὸς ἀρετήν Aeschin. Adv. –κῶς, persuasively, Luc. From

προ-τρέπω, f. –τρέψω, to urge forwards : Med. to turn in headlong flight (cf. προτροπάδην), προτρέποντο μελαινάων ἐπὶ νηῶν Il. ; of the sun, ὅτ' ἂν ἂψ ἐπὶ γαῖαν ἀπ' οὐρανόθεν προτράπηται Od. ; metaph., ἄχεϊ προτραπέσθαι to give oneself up to grief, Il. II. to urge on, impel, Soph. ;—c. acc. pers. et inf. to urge on, impel, persuade one to do a thing, Hdt., Att. ; προτρ. τινὰ εἰς or ἐπὶ φιλοσοφίαν Plat. :—so in Med., c. acc. pers. et inf., Aesch., etc. ; τὰ κατὰ τὸν Τέλλον προετρέψατο ὁ Σόλων τὸν Κροῖσον Solon roused Croesus to enquire about Tellus, Hdt. ; προτρέψομαι I will exhort or urge thee, Soph. :—Pass. to be persuaded, Xen.

προ-τρέχω, f. –δρᾰμοῦμαι : aor. 2 προὔδρᾰμον :–to run forward, Xen. II. to run before, outrun, τινός Id.

πρό-τρῐτα, Adv. (τρίτος) three days before, or for three successive days, Thuc.

προτροπάδην [ᾰ], Dor. -δαν, Adv. (προτρέπω) head-foremost, with headlong speed, Il., Plat.

προτροπή, ἡ, (προτρέπω) exhortation, Arist.

προ-τυγχάνω, aor. 2 –έτυχον :–to come before one, τὸ προτῠχόν the first thing that came to hand, Pind.

προ-τῠπόω, f. ώσω, to mould beforehand : Med. to figure to oneself, conceive, Luc.

προ-τύπτω, f. ψω, intr. to press forwards, Τρῶες δὲ προὔτυψαν Il. ; ἀνὰ ῥῖνας προὔτυψε shot through his nostrils, Od. :—so in Pass., προτυπέν driven on (against Troy), or perh. stricken by an untimely blow, Aesch.

προὐβάλλον, προὔβην, contr. for προ-έβαλλον, προ-έβην.

προὐγράφον, contr. for προ-έγραφον.

προὐδῐδάξατο, προὔδωκα, contr. for προ-εδιδάξατο, προ-έδωκα.

προὔθετο, προὔθηκε, contr. for προ-έθετο, προ-έθηκε.

προὔκᾰμον, contr. for προ-έκαμον, aor. 2 of προκάμνω.

προὔκειτο, προὐκινδύνευσε, contr. for προ-έκειτο, προ-εκινδύνευσε.

προὐννέπω, v. sub προ-εννέπω.

προὐξένησε, προὐξεπίσταμαι, προὐξερευνάω and -ήτης, προὐξεφίεμαι, contr. for προ-εξ-.

προ-ϋπαρχή, ἡ, a previous service, Arist.

προ-ϋπάρχω, f. ξω, to be beforehand in a thing, to make a beginning of, c. gen., ἀδικίας Thuc. : c. dat. to begin with, πρ. τῷ ποιεῖν εὖ Dem. :—Pass., τὰ προϋπηργμένα benefits formerly received, Id. II. intr. to exist or be there before, Thuc., etc. ; προϋπάρξαντα what happened before, past events, Dem.

προὔπεμψα, contr. for προ-έπεμψα.

προ-ϋπεξορμάω, f. ήσω, to go out secretly before, Luc.

προ-ϋποβάλλω, f. –βαλῶ, to put under as a foundation :—Pass. to be prepared as materials, Luc.

προ-ϋπογράφω [ᾰ], to sketch out before : in Med., Plut.

προ-ϋπόκειμαι, Pass. to be mortgaged before, Plut.

προ-ϋπολαμβάνω, f. –λήψομαι, to assume beforehand, Arist.

προὔπτος, ον, contr. for πρόοπτος.

προὔργου, contr. for πρὸ ἔργου, serving for or towards a work, serviceable, profitable, useful, τι τῶν προὔργου something useful, Ar. ; πρ. ἐστὶ εἴς or πρός τι 'tis a step towards gaining one's end, Plat. ; οὐδὲν πρ. ἐστί, c. inf., Id. :—also as Adv. conveniently, opportunely,

προὔργου πεσεῖν Eur. II. Comp. προὐργιαίτερος, α, ον, more serviceable, πρ. ποιεῖσθαί τι to deem of more consequence, Thuc. ; πρ. γίγνεται, Plat.

προυσελέω, to maltreat, insult, only in two passages, ὁρῶν ἐμαυτὸν ὧδε προυσελούμενον Aesch. ; οὓς μὲν ἴσμεν εὐγενεῖς προυσελοῦμεν we insult those whom we know to be noble, Ar. (Deriv. uncertain.)

προὔσκεπτο, contr. for προ-έσκεπτο, 3 sing. plqpf. pass. of προσκοπέω.

προὐτίθει, προὐτρέπετο, προὔτυψα, contr. for προ-ετ-.

προὔφαινε, contr. for προ-έφαινε.

προ-υφαιρέω, f. ήσω, to filch beforehand, πρ. τὴν ἐκκλησίαν, i. e. get it held (without notice) before the expected time, Aeschin.

προὐφάνην, contr. for προ-εφάνην.

προὐφείλω, contr. for προ-οφείλω.

προὔχω, προὔχουσι, προὔχοντο, contr. for προ-έχ-.

προ-φαίνω, f. –φᾰνῶ : aor. 1 –έφηνα :–Pass., aor. 2 προὐφάνην, part. προφᾰνείς : 3 pl. pf. προπέφανται :— to bring forth, bring to light, shew forth, manifest, display, Soph. : metaph., Ἀχιλεὺς Αἴγιναν πρ. brought it into light, made it illustrious, Pind. :—Pass. to be shewn forth, come to light, appear, Hom., Soph. ; impers., οὐδὲ προὐφαίνετ' ἰδέσθαι nor was there light enough for us to see, Od. :—aor. 2 pass. part. προφᾰνείς, εἶσα, coming forward, appearing, Ib. 2. to indicate or declare before, Soph., Dem. 3. =προτίθημι I. 5, to propose, ἄθλα Xen. 4. Pass., metaph. of sound, to be plainly heard, προὐφάνη κτύπος Soph. II. to shew beforehand, foreshew, of oracles, Hdt., Soph. ; ὅκως στρατίην πέμψεις, οὐ προφαίνεις holdest out no hope that thou wilt send, Hdt. : —Pass. or Med. to shew itself or appear before, Xen. III. seemingly intr. (the cognate acc. φάος or φῶς being understood), to give forth light, shine forth, οὐδὲ σελήνη προὔφαινε Od. ; of a torch, Plut. ; ὁ προφαίνων a torch-bearer, Id. Hence

προφᾰνής, ές, shewing itself or seen beforehand, Arist. II. seen clearly or plainly, conspicuous, Xen. 2. metaph. quite plain or clear, Plat. ; ἀπὸ or ἐκ τοῦ προφανοῦς openly, Thuc. :—Adv. -νῶς, Polyb.

πρόφαντος, ον, (προφαίνω) far seen, hence far-famed, Pind. II. foreshewn, as by an oracle, Hdt., Soph. ; πρόφαντα δέ σφι ἐγίνετο oracles were delivered to them, Hdt.

προφᾰσίζομαι : impf. προὐφασιζόμην : f. Att. προφασιοῦμαι : aor. 1 προὐφασισάμην Dep. :–to set up as a pretext or excuse, allege by way of excuse, plead in excuse, c. acc., Theogn., Thuc., etc. ; c. inf. to allege as an excuse that , Dem. :—absol. to make excuses, Thuc. :—aor. 1 προφασισθῆναι in pass. sense, to be used as a pretext, Id. II. to allege (by way of accusation) that, Plat. From

πρόφᾰσις, ἡ, gen. εως, Ion. ιος: (προφαίνω or πρόφημι):— that which is alleged as the cause, an allegation, plea, καὶ ἐπὶ μεγάλῃ καὶ ἐπὶ βραχείᾳ ὁμοίως προφάσει to great or small plea alike, Thuc. ; πρ. ἀληθεστάτη Id. 2. mostly in bad sense, a mere pretext, a pretence, excuse, Hdt., etc. ; opp. to the true cause (αἰτία), Thuc. : c. gen. the pretext or pretence for a thing, Hdt., etc. :—absol. in acc., πρόφασιν in pretence, Il., Att. ; πρόφασιν μέν, opp.

to τὸ δ᾽ ἀληθές, Thuc.; so in dat., προφάσει Id. :—ἀπὸ προφάσιος τοιῆσδε from or on some such pretext as this, Hdt., etc. :—προφάσιος εἵνεκεν Id. :—ἐπὶ προφάσει by way of excuse, Theogn., Thuc.; so, ἐπὶ προφάσιος Hdt.; κατὰ πρόφασιν Id. :—foll. by an inf., αὕτη ἦν σοι πρ. ἐκβαλεῖν ἐμέ for casting me out, Soph.; πρόφασιν ἔχει τοῖς δειλαίοις μὴ ἰέναι gives them an excuse for not going, Plat. 3. phrases, πρόφασιν διδόναι, ἐνδιδόναι to give occasion, make an excuse, Dem.; πρ. ἐνδοῦναί τινι Thuc.; πρ. προτείνειν, προΐσχεσθαι to put forward an excuse, Hdt.; παρέχειν Ar.; προφάσιας ἕλκειν to keep making pretences, Hdt., etc.; elliptically, μή μοι πρόφασιν (sc. πάρεχε) no excuse, no shuffling, Ar. II. Pind. personifies Πρόφασις, as daughter of Epimetheus (Afterthought). III. in Soph. it must mean suggestion.

προφερής, ές, (προφέρω) poët. Adj. carried before, placed before, excelling, c. gen., Hes. :—Comp., more excellent, superior, surpassing, τῶν ἄλλων προφερέστερος Od.; c. inf., [ἡμίονοι] βοῶν προφερέστεραί εἰσιν ἑλκέμεναι are better than oxen in drawing, Il. :—Sup. προφερέστατος Ib., Hes. :—also Comp. and Sup., προφέρτερος, προφέρτατος Soph. II. looking older than one is, well-grown, precocious, Plat., Aeschin.

προ-φέρω, f. -οίσω: aor. 1 -ήνεγκα: aor. 2 -ήνεγκον: —-Ep. 3 sing. pres. subj. προφέρῃσι, as if from a form in μι:—to bring before one, bring to, present, offer, Il., Thuc. 2. of words, πρ. ὀνείδεά τινι to throw reproaches in his teeth, Il.: and so, πρ. τινί to throw in one's teeth, bring forward, allege, Lat. objicere, μή μοι δῶρα πρόφερε Ἀφροδίτης Ib. 3. simply, to utter, αὐδάν, μῦθον Eur.; πρ. Αἴγιναν πάτραν to proclaim it as their country, Pind. 4. to bring forward, cite, Thuc.; προφέρων Ἄρτεμιν pleading Artemis as authority, Aesch. 5. of an oracle, to propose as a task, Hdt. :—Pass., προὐνεχθέντος τινί (gen. absol.) if it were commanded one to do so, Aesch. II. to bring forward, display, Il.; ἔριδα πρ. to shew, i. e. engage in, rivalry, Od.; πόλεμόν τινι πρ. to declare war against one, Hdt. :—Med., ξεινοδόκῳ ἔριδα προφέρεσθαι to offer quarrel to one's host, Od. III. to bear on or away, to carry off, sweep away, of a storm, Hom. IV. to move forward, πόδα Eur. :—then, to promote, further, assist, ἠὼς προφέρει ὁδοῦ morning furthers one on the road, Hes.; πρ. εἴς τι to conduce, help towards gaining an object, Thuc. 2. intr. to surpass, excel another, c. gen., Hdt., Thuc.

προ-φεύγω, f. -φεύξομαι, aor. 2 προὔφῠγον :—to flee forwards, flee away, Il. II. c. acc. to flee from, shun, avoid, Hom.

προφητεία, ἡ, the gift of interpreting the will of the gods, Orac. ap. Luc. II. in N. T., the gift of expounding scripture, of speaking and preaching.

προφητεύω, Dor. προφᾱτ-: f. -εύσω: aor. 1 ἐπροφήτευσα:—to be an interpreter of the gods, μαντεύεο, Μοῖσα, προφατεύσω δ᾽ ἐγώ Pind.; τίς προφητεύει θεοῦ; who is his interpreter? Eur.; ὅστις σοι προφητεύσει τάδε who will give thee this oracular advice, Id. II. in N. T. to expound scripture, to speak and preach under the influence of the Holy Spirit.

προφήτης, Dor. προφάτης [ᾱ], ὁ, (πρόφημι) one who

speaks for a God and interprets his will to man, a prophet; so Teiresias is πρ. Διός, Jove's interpreter, Pind.; and of Apollo, Διὸς προφήτης ἐστὶ Λοξίας πατρός Aesch.; while the Pythia, in turn, became the προφῆτις of Apollo, Hdt.; so Poets are called οἱ τῶν Μουσῶν προφῆται interpreters of the Muses, Plat. 2. generally, an interpreter, declarer, ἐγὼ πρ. σοι λόγων γενήσομαι Eur.; so, the bowl is called κώμου προφάτης, Pind. II. in N. T., 1. one who possesses the gift of προφητεία, an inspired preacher and teacher. 2. the revealer of God's counsel for the future, a prophet (in the modern sense of the word), a predicter of future events. Hence

προφητικός, ή, όν, oracular, Luc.

προφῆτις, ιδος, fem. of προφήτης, of the Pythia, Eur.

προ-φθάνω [ᾰ], f. -φθάσω [ᾰ] and -φθήσομαι: aor. 1 -έφθᾰσα: aor. 2 προὔφθην (as if from a Verb in μι): —to outrun, anticipate, c. acc., Aesch., Plat. 2. absol. to be beforehand, Eur.

προ-φθίμενος [ῐ], η, ον, dead or killed before, Anth.

προ-φοβέομαι, f. ήσομαι, Pass. to fear beforehand, fear at the thought of, Xen. Hence

προφοβητικός, ή, όν, apt to fear beforehand, Arist.

προ-φορέομαι, Med., in weaving, to carry on the web by passing the weft across the warp: metaph., τὴν ὁδὸν προφορεῖσθαι to run to and fro, Ar.

προ-φράζω, f. σω, to foretell, Hdt.: pf. pass. part. προπεφραδμένα ἆθλα Hes.

πρόφρασσα, Ep. fem. of πρόφρων, kindly, gracious, Hom.

πρό-φρων, ονος, ὁ, ἡ, (φρήν) with forward mind, hence zealous, willing, ready, glad to do a thing, Hom., etc. 2. of acts, efforts, earnest, zealous, Id. II. Ep. Adv. προφρονέως, readily, earnestly, zealously, Il.; later προφρόνως Theogn., Att.

προφῠγεῖν, aor. 2 inf. of προφεύγω.

προφύγοισθα, Ep. 2 sing. aor. 2 opt. of προφεύγω.

προφῠλᾰκή, (προφυλάσσω) a guard in front; in pl. outposts, videttes, piquets, Xen.; in sing., ἡ πρ. αὐτοῦ his advanced guard, Id.; διὰ προφυλακῆς with an advanced guard, Thuc.

προφῠλᾰκὶς ναῦς, ἡ, a look-out ship, Thuc. From

προφύλαξ [ῠ], ᾰκος, ὁ, an advanced guard: οἱ προφύλακες = αἱ προφυλακαί, Thuc., Xen.

προ-φῠλάσσω, Att. -ττω, f. ξω, to keep guard before, to guard a place or house, c. acc., h. Hom. (in the Ep. 2 pl. imperat. προφύλαχθε, for προφυλάσσεσθε), Xen.; προφυλάσσειν ἐπί τινι to keep guard over a person or place, Hdt. :—absol. to be on guard, keep watch, ἡ προφυλάσσουσα (sc. ναῦς) = προφυλακίς, Id. : —Med. to guard oneself, to be on one's guard, take precautions, Id., Thuc. :—c. acc. to be on one's guard or take precautions against, Lat. cavere, Hdt., Xen.

προ-φῡράω, f. ήσω, to mix up or knead beforehand: metaph. in Pass., προπεφύραται λόγος the speech is all ready concocted or brewed, Ar.

προ-φῠτεύω, f. σω, to plant before: metaph. to engender, Soph.

προ-φωνέω, f. ήσω, to utter beforehand, Aesch.; προφωνεῖ τόνδε λόγον gives this order beforehand, Id. II. to order beforehand or publicly, c. dat. et inf., καί σοι προφωνῶ τόνδε μὴ θάπτειν Soph.; with inf. omitted, ὑμῖν προφωνῶ τάδε Id.

προ-χαίρω, to rejoice beforehand, Plat. **II.** in 3 sing. imperat. **προχαιρέτω**, far be it from me! away with it! Aesch.

προ-χαλκεύω, f. σω, to forge beforehand, Aesch.

πρό-χειλος, ον, with prominent lips, Strab.

προ-χειρίζω, f. Att. ιῶ, to put into the hand, have ready at hand, Polyb. :—Pass., in pf. part., taken in hand, undertaken, Plat., Dem.—**II.** as Dep. **προχειρίζομαι**, f. Att. : c. dat.,—**χειριοῦμαι**:—to take into one's hand, prepare for oneself, Dem. **2.** to choose, elect, Id. **3.** c. inf. to determine to do, Polyb.

πρό-χειρος, ον, (χείρ) at hand, ready, Aesch., Soph.; of a drawn sword or knife, Soph., Eur.; λίθοις καὶ . . ἀκοντίοις, ὡς ἕκαστός τι πρόχειρον εἶχε Thuc.; ὁ προχειρότατον ἔχω εἰπεῖν Dem. **2.** πρόχειρον [ἐστι] it is easy, c. inf., Plat., etc. **II.** of persons, ready to do, c. inf., Soph.; c. dat., πρ. τῇ φυγῇ ready for flight, Eur. **III.** Adv. -ρως, off-hand, readily, Plat.

προ-χειροτονέω, f. ήσω, to choose or elect before, Plat., Aeschin. **2.** to give a previous vote, Dem.

προ-χέω, f. -χεῶ : aor. 1 -έχεα:—to pour forth or forward, Il., Pind.; σπονδὰς προχέαι Hdt. :—metaph., ὄπα γλυκεῖαν Pind. :—Pass., metaph. of large bodies of men pouring over a plain, Il.

πρό-χνυ, Adv., (πρό, γόνυ) with the knees forward, i. e. kneeling, on one's knees, Il.; metaph., ὥς κεν ἀπόλωνται πρόχνυ that they may perish on their knees, i. e. may be brought low and perish, Ib.; so, πρόχνυ ὀλέσθαι Od.

προχοή, ἡ, (προχέω) mostly in pl., the outpouring, i.e. the mouth, of a river, Hom., Pind., etc.; sing. in Hes.

προχόη, ἡ, = πρόχοος, Anth.

προχοῖς, ίδος, ἡ, Dim. of πρόχοος, a chamberpot, Xen.

πρόχοος, Att. contr. **πρόχους**, ἡ: heterocl. dat. pl. πρόχουσι: acc. pl. πρόχους : (προχέω) :—a vessel for pouring out, a ewer for pouring water on the hands of guests, Hom., Soph.;—a wine-jug from which the cupbearer pours into the cups, Od.

προ-χορεύω, f. σω, to dance before in a chorus, πρ. κῶμον to lead a κῶμος or festive band, Eur.

προ-χρίω [ι], f. σω, to smear before, πρ. τί τινι to smear or rub with a thing, Soph.

πρό-χρονος, ον, of former time, Luc.

πρόχυσις, ἡ, (προχέω) a pouring out, πρ. τῆς γῆς a deposition of mud by a river, Lat. alluvies, Hdt. ; —in οὐλὰς κριθῶν πρόχυσιν ἐποιέετο (cf. sq.), πρόχυσιν ἐποιέετο must be taken as a simple Verb = προέχεε, Id.

προ-χύται [ῠ] (sc. κριθαί), αἱ = οὐλο-χύται, Eur.

προ-χύτης [ῠ], ου, ὁ, = πρόχοος, an urn for libations, Eur.

προχυτός, ή, όν, poured out in front :—Προχύτη νῆσος the island of Procida, formed by eruption from Vesuvius, Strab.

πρό-χωλος, ον, very lame or halt, Luc.

προ-χωρέω, f. ήσω, to go or come forward, advance, πρὸς ἐμὴν χεῖρα as my hand guides thee, Soph.; of troops, Thuc.:—of Time, to go on, Xen. **II.** metaph. of States, wars, enterprises, etc., to proceed, advance, go on, often with some word to denote a good or bad issue, εὖ προχωρῆσαι Eur.; προχωρησάντων ἐπὶ μέγα τῶν πραγμάτων Thuc.; τούτων προκεχωρηκότων ὡς ἐβούλοντο Xen. :—absol. to go on well, prosper, Hdt., etc. **2.** impers., **προχωρεῖ μοι** it goes

on well for me, I have success, ὡς οἱ δόλῳ οὐ προεχώρεε when he could not succeed by craft, Id.; c. inf., ἢν μὴ προχωρήσῃ ἀπελθεῖν if it be not possible to depart, Thuc. :—absol. in part., προκεχωρηκότων when things went on well, Xen. **3.** later, of persons, to advance, Luc.

προ-ωθέω, f. -ωθήσω and -ώσω : aor. 1 -έωσα, contr. part. **πρώσας** :—to push forward, push or urge on, Plat.; πρ. αὐτόν to rush on, Xen.

προ-ώλης, ες, (ὄλλυμι) ruined beforehand, Dem.

πρό-ωρος, ον, (ὥρα) before the time, untimely, Anth.

πρυλέες, έων, οἱ, men-at-arms, foot-soldiers, opp. to chiefs fighting from chariots, Il. (Deriv. uncertain.)

πρύμνα, ἡ, Ion. **πρύμνη**, fem. of πρυμνός (sub. ναῦς), the hindmost part of a ship, the stern, poop, Lat. puppis, Hom., etc.; he sometimes has it in full, νηΐ πάρα πρύμνῃ, ἐπὶ πρύμνῃ νηΐ, νηΐ ἐνὶ πρ., and in pl., νηυσὶν ἔπι πρύμνῃσι; though he also has πρύμνη νηός Od. :—ἐπὶ πρύμνην ἀνακρούεσθαι to back a ship (v. ἀνακρούω II); so, χωρεῖν πρύμναν to retire, draw back, Eur.; ἐπείγει κατὰ πρύμναν, of a fair wind, Soph.; κατὰ πρ. ἵσταται τὸ πνεῦμα Thuc. :—Ships were fastened or drawn up on land by the stern, Il. : hence, πρύμνας λῦσαι Eur.; cf. πρυμνήσιος. **2.** metaph. of the vessel of the State, Aesch. **II.** generally the bottom, πρ. Ὄσσας the foot of mount Ossa, Eur.

πρυμναῖος, α, ον, of a ship-stern, Anth.

Πρυμνεύς, ὁ, Steersman, name of a Phaeacian, Od.

πρύμνη, Ion. for πρύμνα.

πρύμνηθεν, Dor. -ᾶθεν, Adv. of πρύμνη, from the stern, Il., Aesch., Eur.

πρυμνήσιος, α, ον, (πρύμνα) of or from a ship's stern, κάλως Eur.:—neut. pl. πρυμνήσια (sc. δεσμά) sterncables, Lat. retinacula navis, Hom.

πρυμνήτης, ου, ὁ, (πρύμνα) the steersman :—metaph., χώρας πρ. ἄναξ 'the pilot' of the State, Aesch. **II.** as masc. Adj. = πρυμνήσιος, πρ. κάλως Eur.

πρυμνόθεν, (πρυμνόν) Adv. from the bottom, hence like Lat. funditus, utterly, root and branch, Aesch.

πρυμνός, τό, the lower part, end, Il.; πρυμνοῖς ἀγορᾶς ἔπι at the far end of the agora, Pind.

πρυμνός, ή, όν, Ep. Adj. the hindmost, undermost, end-most : in Hom. always of the end of the limb next the body, the root, πρυμνὸς βραχίων, πρυμνὴ γλῶσσα, etc.; so, πρυμνὴν ὕλην ἐκτάμνειν to cut off the wood at the root, Il.; δόρυ πρυμνόν the part of a spear-head where it joins the shaft, Ib.; λᾶας πρυμνὸς παχύς a stone broad at base, opp. to ὑπερθεν ὀξύς (which follows), Ib.; Sup. πρυμνότατος Od.:—for πρύμνη ναῦς, v. πρύμνα. (Deriv. uncertain.)

πρυμν-οῦχος, ον, (ἔχω) holding the ship's stern, Anth. **II.** detaining the ships (because they were anchored by the stern), Αὖλις Eur.

πρυμν-ώρεια, ἡ, (ὄρος) the foot of a mountain, Il.

πρυτανεία, Ion. -ηίη, ἡ, (πρυτανεύω) the prytany or presidency, at Athens a period of 35 or 36 days, about 1/10 of a year, during which the prytanes of each φυλή in turn presided in the βουλή and ἐκκλησία, Oratt.; ἑνδεκάτη τῆς πρυτανείας (sc. τῆς Πανδιονίδος) the 11th of the presidency of the Tribe Pandionis, Dem. **II.** any public office held by rotation, πρ.

τῆς ἡμέρης the chief command for the day, held by each general in turn, Hdt.

πρῠτᾰνεῖον, Ion. -ήιον, τό, (πρύτανις) the presidents' hall, town-hall, Lat. curia, Hdt., Thuc., etc.; consecrated to Hestia or Vesta, to whom a perpetual fire was kept burning in it, which in Colonies was brought from the Prytaneion of the mother-city: at Athens the Prytanes had their meals there, and there they entertained foreign ambassadors, Ar., Dem.: citizens also of high merit, and the children of those who had fallen in battle, were rewarded by a seat at this public table, ἐν πρυτανείῳ δειπνεῖν, σιτεῖσθαι Ar., Plat. II. a law-court at Athens, Dem., Plut. 2. πρυτανεῖα, τά, a sum of money deposited by each party to a lawsuit before the suit began, Ar., etc.; τιθέναι πρυτανεῖά τινι, i. e. bring an action against, Id.; ἵν' αἱ θέσεις γίγνοιντο τῇ νουμηνίᾳ (sc. τῶν πρυτανείων) Id.; δέχεσθαι τὰ πρ. to receive this deposit, i. e. to allow the action to be brought, Id.

πρῠτᾰνεύω, f. σω, to be πρύτανις or president, to hold sway, h. Hom. II. at Athens, to hold office as Prytanis, properly used of the presiding φύλη (v. πρύτανις II), ἔτυχεν ἡ φυλὴ Ἀκαμαντὶς πρυτανεύουσα Plat., etc. 2. πρ. περὶ εἰρήνης to put the question on a motion for peace, this being the duty of the Prytanes, Ar., etc. III. generally, to manage, regulate, Dem.:—Pass., πρυτανεύεσθαι παρά τινος to suffer oneself to be guided by one, Id.

πρυτανηίη, -ήιον, Ion. for πρυτανεία, -νεῖον.

πρύτᾰνις [ῠ], gen. εως, ὁ: pl. πρυτάνεις: (prob. from πρό):—a prince, ruler, lord, chief, of Hiero, Pind.; of Zeus, Id., Aesch. II. at Athens, a Prytanis or President: the πρυτάνεις were a committee of 50, chosen by lot from each of the 10 φυλαί, so that each set formed γₜₒ part of the βουλή or Council of 500: out of these 50 πρυτάνεις one was chosen by lot as chief-president (ἐπιστάτης); he chose 9 πρόεδροι; and the real business was in the hands of this smaller body, with a secretary (γραμματεύς) added.—The φυλή which first entered office every year was determined by lot; and their term of office (πρυτανεία) was about five weeks. During this time all treaties and public acts ran in their name, in this form: Ἀκαμαντὶς [φυλὴ] ἐπρυτάνευε, Φαίνιππος ἐγραμμάτευε, Νικιάδης ἐπεστάτει the Tribe Acamantis were the Presidency, Phaenippus the Secretary, Niciades the Chief-president, Thuc.

πρώ or πρῷ, πρῳαίτερον, πρῳαίτατα, v. πρωί.

πρῴζος, ον, Att. for πρώιζος.

πρώην, Dor. πρῴαν, (πρωί) lately, just now, Lat. nuper, Il., etc. II. the day before yesterday, οὐ χθές, ἀλλὰ πρ. Thuc.; πρώην τε καὶ χθές till yesterday or the day before, i. e. till very lately, Hdt.; so, χθές τε καὶ πρώην Ar.; πρώην καὶ χθές Dem.

πρωθ-ήβης, ου, ὁ, (πρῶτος) in the prime of youth, Hom.; fem. πρωθήβη Od.

πρωί [ῐ], Att. πρώ or πρῷ, Adv.: (πρό):—early in the day, early, at morn, Il.; c. gen., πρωὶ ἔτι τῆς ἡμέρης Hdt.; ἑκάστης ἡμέρας τὸ πρῷ Xen.; πρῷ τῇ ὑστεραίᾳ early next morning, Id.; ἅμα πρωί, ἀπὸ πρωί N. T. 2. generally, betimes, early, in good time, Lat. mature, tempestive, Hes., Ar., etc.; c. gen., πρῷ τῆς ὥρας Thuc. 3. = πρὸ καιροῦ, too soon, too

early, πρῷ γε στενάξεις Aesch.; πρῷ ἐσβαλόντες, καὶ τοῦ σίτου ἔτι χλωροῦ ὄντος Thuc.—πρωί takes its degrees of comparison from its deriv. Adj. πρώιος, Comp. πρωιαίτερον, Sup. πρωιαίτατα, Att. πρῳαίτερον, πρῳαίτατα, Thuc., etc.

πρωία, v. πρώιος.

πρωιζός, Att. πρῳζός, όν, = πρώιος: neut. pl. πρωιζά was used as Adv., just like πρώην, χθιζά τε καὶ πρωιζά yesterday or the day before, Il. II. οὕτω δὴ πρ. κατέδραθες so very early, Theocr.

πρώιμος [ῐ], ον, early, of fruits, Xen.

πρωινός [ῐ], ή, όν, later form of πρώιος, Babr.

πρώιος, Att. πρῷος, α, ον: (πρωί, πρῷ):—early, I. early in the day, at early morn, Il.; also, περὶ δείλην πρωίην (cf. δείλη) Hdt.:—πρωία used alone as Subst., ἦν δὲ πρωία, πρωίας γενομένης N. T. II. early in the year, πρώιος [ὁ στρατὸς] συνελέγετο Hdt.; πρῷα τῶν καρπίμων early fruits, Ar.

πρωκτός, ὁ, the anus, generally, the hinder parts, tail, Ar.

πρών, ὁ, gen. and dat. πρῶνος, not πρωνός, πρωνί (for it is contr. from πρεών): (πρό):—a foreland, head-land, Lat. promontorium, Il.; the pl. is πρώονες from the lengthd. form πρώων, Ib.:—in Aesch. Pers. 132, ἀμφοτέρας πρῶνα κοινὸν αἶας the foreland common to both continents is perh. the Chersonese; and Ib. 879, πρὼν ἅλιος the peninsula of Asia Minor.

πρώξ, ἡ, gen. πρωκός, a dewdrop, Theocr.

πρῷος, α, ον, Att. for πρώιος.

πρῷρα, ἡ, (not πρώρα, for it is contr. from πρώειρα): (πρό):—the forepart of a ship, a ship's head, prow, bow, Lat. prora, Od., etc.; πνεῦμα τοὐκ πρῴρας a contrary wind, opp. to κατὰ πρύμναν, Soph. 2. metaph., πρῷρα βιότου the prow of life's vessel, i. e. early youth, Eur.; πάροιθεν πρῴρας καρδίας before my heart's prow, in front of my heart, Aesch.

πρῴραθεν, Ion. -ηθεν, in Poets before a consonant -θε: Adv.: (πρῷρα):—from the ship's head, from the front, Pind., Thuc., etc.:—it is an old gen., and is so used ἐκ πρῴραθεν, by Theocr.

πρῳρατεύω, to be a πρῳράτης, Ar.

πρῳράτης [ᾱ], ὁ, = πρῳρεύς, Xen.

πρῳρεύς, έως, ἡ, (πρῷρα) the officer in command at the bow, the look-out man, Xen., etc.

πρῴρηθεν, Adv., Ion. for πρῴραθεν.

πρώσας, contr. from προώσας, aor. 1 part. of προωθέω.

πρωτ-άγγελος, ον, announcing first, c. gen., Anth.

πρωτ-άγριον, τό, (ἄγρα) the first fruits of the chase: mostly in pl., Anth.

πρωτᾰγωνιστέω, f. ήσω, to be πρωταγωνιστής, Plut.:—metaph. to play first fiddle, to take the lead, Arist.

πρωτ-ᾰγωνιστής, οῦ, ὁ, one who plays the first part, the chief actor, Lat. primarum partium actor, Arist.

πρώτ-αρχος, ὁ, first-beginning, primal, πρ. ἄτα Aesch.

πρωτεῖον, τό, (πρωτεύω) the chief rank, first place, Dem.:—mostly in pl. the first prize, first part or place, Plat., Dem.

Πρωτεσί-λαος, ὁ, Dor. -λας, α, Ion. and Att., -λεως, εω:—First-of-the-people, name of the hero who first leaped ashore at Troy, Il.:—Πρωτεσιλάειον, τό, his monument, Strab.

πρωτεύω, f. σω, (πρῶτος) to be the first, hold the first place, Plat., etc.:—to be first in a thing, καρτερίᾳ

Xen.; βδελυρίᾳ Aeschin.; περὶ κακίαν Id. 2. c. gen. pers. *to be first of* or *among, τῶν ῥητόρων* Id.

πρωτ-ηρότης, ου, ὁ, *the earliest plougher,* Hes.

πρώτιστος, η, ον, and *os, ον,* poët. Sup. of **πρῶτος,** *the very first, first of the first,* Hom.; *πολὺ πρώτιστος* Id.: neut. *πρώτιστον* as Adv. *first of all,* Od., Ar., etc.: —so *πρώτιστα,* Hom., Att.; —*τὸ πρώτιστον* Eur.; *τὰ πρώτιστα* Od.

πρωτό-βολος, ον, (*βάλλω*) *first struck,* Eur.

πρωτό-γονος, ον, (*γίγνομαι*) *first-born, firstling,* Il., Hes.; *φοῖνιξ πρ. first-created,* Eur. **2.** *of rank, πρ. οἶκοι high-born* houses, Soph. **3.** *first-ordained,* Luc.

πρωτό-ζυξ, ύγος, (*ζεύγνυμι*) *newly wedded,* Anth.

πρωτο-καθεδρία, ἡ, (*καθέδρα*) *the first seat,* N. T.

πρωτο-κλισία, ἡ, (*κλίνω*) *the first seat at table,* N. T.

πρωτο-κτόνος, ον, (*κτείνω*) *committing the first murder, the first homicide,* of Ixion, Aesch.

πρωτο-κύων, ὁ, *first dog,* i.e. *chief of the Cynics,* Anth.

πρωτόλεια, τά, (*λεία*) *the first spoils* in war, *the firstfruits; τῶν σῶν γονάτων πρωτόλεια* as *the first act* of my supplication, Eur.

πρωτό-μαντις, ὁ, ἡ, *the first prophet* or *seer,* Aesch.

πρωτό-μορος, ον, *dying* or *dead first,* Aesch.

πρωτο-πήμων, ονος, ὁ, ἡ, *first cause of ill,* Aesch.

πρωτό-πλοος, ον, Att. contr. *-πλους, ουν:*—*going to sea for the first time,* Od., Eur.; *πρ. πλάτα* the *first-plied* oar (of the ship Argo), Eur. **II.** *sailing first* or *foremost,* Xen.

πρωτο-πορεία, ἡ, *the advanced guard, vanguard,* Polyb.

πρῶτος, η, ον, v. **πρότερος B.**

πρωτο-στάτης [ἄ], *ου, ὁ,* (*στῆναι*) *one who stands first,* on *the right, the right-hand man,* Thuc.; but *οἱ πρ. the front-rank men,* Xen. **II.** metaph. *the leader of a party,* N. T.

πρωτοτόκια, τά, *the rights of the first-born, birthright,* N. T. From

πρωτο-τόκος, Dor. **πρᾱτο-, ον,** (*τίκτω*) *bearing her first-born,* Il., Theocr. **II.** proparox. **πρωτότοκος, ον,** pass. *first-born,* Anth., N. T.

πρωτό-τομος, ον, (*τέμνω*) *first cut,* Anth.

πρώτως, Adv. of **πρῶτος,** v. **πρότερος B. IV.**

πρωΰδᾶν, contr. for *προ-αυδᾶν,* Eur.

πρώων, ονος, ὁ, Ep. lengthd. form of **πρών.**

***ΠΤΑΙ'ΡΩ,** (the pres. in use was the Dep. **πτάρνυμαι**), aor. 2 *ἔπταρον:*—*to sneeze, μέγ᾽ ἔπταρε he sneezed aloud,* Od., Ar.; "*Ζεῦ σῶσον,*" *ἐὰν πτάρῃ,* as we say 'God bless you,' Anth.:—of a lamp, *to sputter,* Id.

πταῖσμα, τό, *a stumble, trip, false step,* Theogn. **II.** *a failure, misfortune, defeat,* Hdt., Dem., etc. From

ΠΤΑΙ'Ω: f. *πταίσω:* aor. 1 *ἔπταισα:* pf. *ἔπταικα:*— Pass., aor. 1 *ἐπταίσθην:* **I.** trans. *to make to stumble* or *fall, τινὰ πρός τινι* Pind.:—Pass., *τὰ πταισθέντα failures,* Luc. **II.** intr. *to stumble, trip, fall,* Soph., etc.; *πτ. πρός τινι to stumble against, fall over,* Aesch., Plat.; *πρός τι* Xen.; also, *μὴ περὶ Μαρδονίῳ πταίσῃ ἡ Ἑλλάς lest Hellas should get a fall* over him, i.e. *be defeated by him,* Hdt. **2.** metaph. *to make a false step, to fail,* Thuc., Dem.; so, *ἐλάχιστα, τὰ πλεῖστα πτ.* Thuc., etc.

πτάμενος, η, ον, aor. 2 part. of **πέταμαι.**

πτᾱνός, ά, όν, Dor. for **πτηνός.**

πτάξ, gen. πτᾱκός, ὁ, ἡ, (*πτήσσω*) = **πτώξ,** Aesch.

πταρμός, ὁ, (*πταίρω*) *a sneezing,* Ar., Thuc., etc.

πτάρνυμαι, *to sneeze,* (v. *πταίρω*), Xen.

πτάς, part. of ἔπτην, act. aor. 2 of **πέταμαι.**

πτάσθαι, aor. 2 inf. of **πέταμαι.**

πτάτο, Ep. for *ἔπτατο,* 3 sing. aor. 2 of **πέταμαι.**

ΠΤΕΛΕ'Α, Ion. *-έη, ἡ, the elm,* Lat. *ulmus,* Il.

πτερινος, η, ον, and *os, ον,* (*πτερόν*) *made of feathers, πτ. κύκλος a feather-fan,* Eur.; *πτ. ῥιπίς* Anth. **II.** *feathered, winged,* Ar.

πτερίσκος, ὁ, Dim. of **πτερόν,** Babr.

ΠΤΕ'ΡΝΑ, Ion. *πτέρνη, ἡ, the heel,* Il.: *the under part of the heel,* Aesch. **II.** *a ham,* Batr.

Πτερνο-γλύφος [ῠ], *ὁ,* (*γλύφω*) *Ham-scraper,* Batr.

Πτερνο-τρώκτης, ου, ὁ, (*τρώγω*) *Ham-nibbler,* Batr.

Πτερνο-φάγος, ὁ, (*φαγεῖν*) *Ham-eater,* Batr.

πτερο-δόνητος, ον, (*δονέω*) *moved by flapping wings:* metaph. *high-soaring,* Ar.

πτερόεις, εσσα, εν: contr. forms *πτερούσσα, πτεροῦντος, πτεροῦντα:*—*feathered, winged, ὀϊστοί, ἰοί* Il.; *πέδιλα* Hes., etc. **2.** *feather-like, light, λαίσηια* Il. **3.** metaph., *ἔπεα πτερόεντα winged words,* Hom., Hes.; so, *πτ. ὕμνος* Pind.; also, *φυγὴ πτερόεσσα* Eur.

πτερόν, τό, (*πτέσθαι*) mostly in pl. *feathers,* Od., Hdt., etc.; in sing. *a feather,* Ar. **2.** = *πτέρυξ, a bird's wing,* in pl. *wings,* Hom., Aesch.; *Παλλάδος ὑπὸ πτεροῖς ὄντας,* metaph. from chickens under the hen's wings, Aesch.:—*τῷ πτερὰ γίγνετο he got as it were wings,* i.e. *spirit, courage,* Il. **3.** *the wings of a bat* (v. *πτίλον* II), Hdt. **II.** *any winged creature,* as the Sphinx, Eur.; *a beetle,* Ar. **2.** like *οἰωνός,* Lat. *avis,* an *augury, omen,* Pind., Soph. **III.** *anything like wings:* as **1.** *a ship's wings,* i.e. *oars* (cf. *πτερόω*), *ἐρετμά, τά τε πτερὰ νηυσὶ πέλονται* Od.; *νηὸς πτερά* Hes., Eur.:—hence birds are said *πτεροῖς ἐρέσσειν,* Eur. **2.** *ἀέθλων πτερά,* i.e. *the wings* of victory, which lift the Poet to heaven, Pind. **3.** *a feathered arrow,* Eur. **4.** *τοῦ πώγωνος τὰ πτερά the points of the beard,* Luc. **5.** in Architecture, of *the rows of columns along the sides of Greek temples,* v. **ἄπτερος.**

πτερο-ποίκιλος, ον, *motley-feathered,* Ar.

πτερό-πους, ποδος, ὁ, *wing-footed,* of Hermes, Anth.

πτερορ-ρυέω, (*ῥέω*) *to shed the feathers, moult,* Ar.: metaph. *to be plucked, fleeced, plundered,* Id.

πτερο-φόρος, ον, (*φέρω*) *feathered, winged,* Aesch., Eur.; *πτ. φῦλα the feathered tribes,* Ar.:—metaph. *πτ. Διὸς βέλος the winged bolt of Zeus,* Id.

πτερο-φυέω, f. ήσω, (*φύω*) *to grow feathers,* Plat.

πτερο-φύτωρ [ῠ], *ορος, ὁ, ἡ, feather-producing,* Plat.

πτερόω, f. ώσω, (*πτερόν*) *to furnish with feathers* or *wings, feather, τινά* Ar.; *πτεροῦν βιβλίον to tie a paper to a feathered arrow,* Hdt.:—Pass. *to be* or *become feathered, to be fledged,* Ar., Plat. **2.** *to furnish a ship with oars:* metaph. in Pass. *σκάφος τάρσῳ ἐπτερωμένον winged with oars,* Eur. **II.** metaph. *to set on the wing, excite* (cf. *ἀναπτερόω*), Ar.:—Pass. *to be excited,* Luc.

πτερῠγίζω, f. ίσω, (*πτέρυξ*) *to flutter with the wings,* like young birds trying to fly, Ar.: *to flap the wings,* like a cock crowing, Id.:—in Ar. Eq. the word alludes to a play by Magnes called Ὄρνιθες.

πτερύγιον [ῠ], τό, Dim. of πτέρυξ, Arist.   II. the wing of a building, a turret or pinnacle, N. T.

πτερῠγωτός, ή, όν, (as if from πτερυγόω = πτερόω) having wings, winged, Ar.

πτέρυξ, ῠγος, ή: Ep. dat. pl. πτερύγεσσι: (πτερόν):— the wing of a bird, Il.; in pl. wings, Hom., etc.   2. a winged creature, a bird, Anth.   II. anything like a wing, the flap or skirt of a coat of armour, Xen.; also of the Dor. χιτών, Ar.   2. the broad edge of a knife or spear, Plut.   III. anything that covers or protects like wings, πτ. πέπλων Eur.; Εὐβοίης πτέρυξ, i. e. Aulis, Id.   IV. metaph., πτέρυγες γόων the wings, i. e. the flight or flow, of grief, Soph.; πτ. Πιερίδων Pind.

πτερύσσομαι, Att. -ττομαι, f. ξομαι, Dep. to clap the wings like a cock crowing, Babr., Luc.

πτέρωμα, ατος, τό, (πτερόω) that which is feathered, e.g. a feathered arrow, Aesch.   II. plumage, Plat.

πτέρωσις, ή, (πτερόω) plumage, Ar.

πτερωτός, ή, όν, and ός, όν, (πτερόω) feathered, Hdt., Eur., etc.   II. winged, Hdt., Trag.; so, πτ. φθόγγος, a sound as of wings, Ar.   2. πτερωτοί (sc. ὄρνιθες) feathered fowl, birds, Eur.

πτέσθαι, aor. 2 inf. of πέτομαι.

πτηναι, inf. of ἔπτην, act. aor. 2 of πέτομαι.

πτην-ολέτις, ιδος, ή, (ὄλλυμι) bird-killing, Anth.

πτηνός, ή, όν, and ός, όν, Dor. πτανός, ά, όν, (πτῆναι) feathered, winged, Trag., etc.; Διὸς κύνες, i. e. eagles, Aesch.   2. τὰ πτηνά winged creatures, fowls, birds, Id., Trag.; πτηνὸν ὀρνίθων γένος Ar.; πταναὶ θῆραι chase of winged game, Soph.   II. metaph., πτηνοὶ μῦθοι, like Homer's ἔπεα πτερόεντα, Eur.; πτ. ὄνειροι fleeting dreams, Id.

πτῆσις, ή, (πτῆναι) a flying, flight, Aesch.

πτήσομαι, fut. of πέτομαι.

ΠΤΗ´ΣΣΩ, f. πτήξω: aor. 1 ἔπτηξα, Dor. ἔπταξα, Ep. πτῆξα: (cf. κατα-πτήσσω): pf. ἔπτηχα, Ep. part. πεπτηώς, ῶτος: I. Causal, to frighten, scare, alarm, Lat. terrere, Il., Theogn.   II. intr. to crouch or cower down for fear (cf. πτώσσω), properly of animals, Soph.; of men, Pind., Att.; πτ. βωμὸν ὕπο Eur.; also c. acc. loci, πτ. βωμόν to flee cowering to the altar, Id.   2. to crouch like a wild beast ready to spring, Id.;—so of men in ambush, ὑπὸ τεύχεσι πεπτηῶτες Od.   3. c. acc. rei, to crouch for fear of, ἀπειλάς Aesch.

πτῆται, 3 sing. aor. 2 subj. of πέτομαι.

πτίλον [ῐ], τό, (πτέσθαι) used properly of the soft feathers or down under the true feathers, a piece of down, a plumelet, Ar.; cf. πτιλωτός.   II. a wing-like membrane in a kind of serpent, Hdt.

πτῐλό-νωτος, ον, with feathered back, Ar.

πτῑλωτός, ή, όν, (πτίλον) with membranous wings, opp. to πτερωτός, Arist.

πτῐσάνη [ᾰ], ή, (πτίσσω) peeled barley: a drink made thereof, barley-water, a ptisan, Ar.

ΠΤΙ´ΣΣΩ: aor. 1 ἔπτισα:—Pass., aor. 1 ἐπτίσθην: pf. ἔπτισμαι:—to winnow: to peel or to bray in a mortar, Hdt. Hence

πτιστής, οῦ, ὁ, one who shells or pounds, Anth.

πτόα or πτοία, ή, abject fear, terror, Polyb.

ΠΤΟΕ´Ω, Ep. πτοιέω: f. ήσω: Ep. aor. 1 ἐπτοίησα:—Pass., Ep. aor. 1 ἐπτοιήθην: pf. ἐπτόημαι, Ep. ἐπτοίη-

μαι:—to terrify, scare, Anth. :—Pass. to be scared, dismayed, φρένες ἐπτοίηθεν Od.; ἐπτοημένος Aesch., Eur.   II. metaph. to flutter, excite by any passion, τό μοι καρδίαν ἐπτόασεν Sappho:—Pass. to be in a flutter, be passionately excited, Theogn.; ἐπτοημένοι φρένας Aesch.; ὡς ἐπτόηται Eur. :—generally, μέθ᾽ ὁμήλικας ἐπτοίηται he gapes like one distraught after his fellows, Hes.; τὸ πτοηθέν distraction, Eur.

πτόησις, εως, ή, passionate excitement, Plat.

Πτολεμαϊκός, ή, όν, of or from Ptolemy, Strab.

Πτολεμαΐς, ΐδος, ή, name of several cities, esp. of one in Phoenicia, now Acre, Strab.

πτολεμίζω, πτολεμιστής, πτόλεμόνδε, Ep. for πολεμ-.

πτόλεμος, ό, Ep. for πόλεμος, as πτόλις for πόλις, Hom., Hes.

πτολίεθρον, τό, Ep. lengthd. from πτόλις, Hom.

πτολῐ-πόρθης, ου, ὁ, = πτολίπορθος, Aesch.

πτολῐ-πόρθιος, ον, = sq., of Ulysses, Od.

πτολί-πορθος [ῐ], ον, (πέρθω) sacking or wasting cities, Il., Pind.

πτόλις, ιος, ή, Ep. for πόλις, Hom., Aesch., Eur.

πτόρθος, ὁ, a young branch, shoot, sucker, sapling, Od., Eur., etc.; — πτ. μέγας, of Hercules' club, Anth.   II. a sprouting, budding, Hes.

πτύγμα, ατος, τό, (πτύσσω) anything folded, πέπλοιο πτύγμα a folded mantle, Il.

πτυκτός, ή, όν, (πτύσσω) folded, πτ. πίναξ folding tablets, Il.

πτύξ, ή, (not in nom., πτυχή being used instead), dat. πτῠχί, acc. πτύχα, pl. πτύχες, πτύχας: (πτύσσω): —a fold, leaf, plate, mostly in pl., πτύχες σάκεος plates of metal or leather used to form a shield, Il.: the folds of a garment, h. Hom., Eur.; of the entrails, Eur.:—of writing tablets (cf. πτυκτός), Trag.   II. in pl. of the sides of a hill (which viewed from a distance appears to be in folds), a cleft, glen, corrie, combe, Hom., etc.; also in sing., Il., Soph.:—so also of the sky with its cloud-clefts, Eur.:—metaph., ὕμνων πτυχαί varied turns of poesy, Pind.

πτύον, τό, (πτύω) a winnowing-shovel or fan, Lat. vannus, with which corn after threshing was thrown up against the wind to clear it of the chaff, Il. (in poët. gen. πτυόφιν), Theocr.

πτύρομαι [ῠ], aor. 2 ἐπτύρην [ῠ]: Pass.:—to be scared or frightened, properly of horses, Plut. Hence

πτυρτικός, ή, όν, timorous, Strab.

ΠΤΥ´ΣΣΩ, f. πτύξω: aor. 1 ἔπτυξα:—Med., f. πτύξομαι: aor. 1 ἐπτυξάμην:—Pass., aor. 1 ἐπτύχθην: aor. 2 ἐπτύγην [ῠ]: pf. ἔπτυγμαι: 3 sing. plqpf. ἔπτυκτο:— to fold, χιτῶνα, εἵματα πτύξαι to fold up garments, and put them by, Od.; χεῖρας πτύξαι ἐπί τινι to fold one's arms over or round another, Soph.; βιβλίον πτ. to fold up or close a book, N. T.:—Pass. to be folded, doubled up, Il.; Med. to fold round oneself, wrap round one, Eur.

πτυχή, ή, = πτύξ, Trag.

ΠΤΥ´Ω [ῠ]: f. πτύσω [ῠ] or πτύσομαι: aor. 1 ἔπτῠσα: pf. ἔπτῠκα:—Pass., aor. 1 ἐπτύσθην:—to spit out or up, Il.: absol. to spit, Hdt., Xen.   2. of the sea, to disgorge, Anth.:—absol., ἐπ᾽ ἀϊόνι πτύοντα, of waves, Theocr.; πτύσας with a splash, Anth.   3. metaph. πτύσας in token of abhorrence or loathing, Soph.;

πτύσας προσώπῳ with *loathing* in his face, Id.   4.

εἰς κόλπον πτύειν, Lat. *in sinum spuere*, done three times to avert a bad omen, Theocr.

πτωκάς, άδος, ἡ, (πτώσσω) *cowering, timorous*, Ep. Hom.: πτωκάδες in Soph. seem to be *timorous creatures, birds*.

πτῶμα, τό, (πίπτω, πέ-πτωκα) *a fall, pεσεῖν πτῶματ' οὐκ ἀνασχετά* Aesch.; *πίπτουσι πτώματ' αἰσχρά* Soph.   2. metaph. *a fall, calamity*, Lat. *casus*, Eur.   II. of persons, *a fallen body, corpse, carcase, πτῶμα Ἑλένης, Ἐτεοκλέους* Id.; also *πτώματα* alone, Aesch.

πτώξ, ὁ, gen. πτωκός, (πτώσσω) like πτάξ, *the cowering animal*, i.e. *the hare*, Il., Theocr.; also, *πτῶκα λαγωόν* (the two Subst. being joined, as in *ἱρηξ κίρκος, σῦς κάπρος*), Il.

πτώσιμος, ον, (πίπτω, πέ-πτωκα) *having fallen*, Aesch.

πτῶσις, εως, ἡ, (πίπτω, πέ-πτωκα) *a falling, fall*, Plat.   II. Lat. *casus*, the *case* of a noun, Arist.

πτωσκάζω, poët. for πτώσσω, Il.

πτώσσω, collat. form of πτήσσω, only in pres., to *crouch* or *cower from fear*, properly of animals (cf. πτάξ, πτώξ, πτωκάς), Od.; *πτώσσουσι καθ' ὕδωρ flee cowering* into the water, Ib.; of men, Ib.; *ττ. ὑφ' Ἕκτορι fly cowering* before Hector, Ib.; so, *εἰς ἐρημίαν ττ.* Eur.   2. *to go cowering* or *cringing about*, like a beggar, Od., Hes.   II. c. acc. pers., *οὐδ' ἔτι ἀλλήλους πτώσσοιμεν let us no longer flee from* one another, Il.; *ποῖ καί με φυγᾷ πτώσσουσι; whither have* they fled *for fear* of me? Eur.

πτωχεία, Ion. -ηίη, ἡ, *beggary, mendicity*, Hdt., Ar.

πτωχεύω, Ion. impf. πτωχεύεσκον: f. -εύσω :—to *be a beggar, go begging, beg*, Od., Ar., etc.   II. trans. *to get by begging, δαῖτα* Od.   2. c. acc. pers. *to beg* or *ask an alms of*, Theogn.

πτωχηΐη, Ion. for πτωχεία.

πτωχικός, ή, όν, (πτωχός) *of* or *fit for a beggar, beggarly*, Eur., Plat., etc.

πτωχίστερος, irreg. Comp. of πτωχός.

πτωχό-μουσος, ὁ, *a beggar-poet*, Gorg. ap. Arist.

πτωχο-ποιός, όν, *drawing beggarly characters*, of a poet, Ar.   2. *making poor*, Plut.

πτωχός, ή, όν, and ός, όν, (πτώσσω) one *who crouches* or *cringes, a beggar* (v. πτώσσω I. 2), Od., Hes., etc.; *πτωχὸς ἀνήρ a beggarman* Od., etc.; *πτωχή a beggar-woman*, Soph., N. T.   II. as Adj. *beggarly*, like πτωχικός, Soph., N. T.: c. gen., *poor in a thing*, Anth.   2. Comp. *πτωχότερος*, irreg. *πτωχίστερος*, Ar.: Sup. *πτωχότατος*, Anth.   3. Adv. -χῶς, *poorly, scantily*, Babr.

Πυαν-έψια (sc. ἱερά), τά, *the Pyanepsia*, an Athenian festival in the month Πυανεψιών, in honour of Apollo; said to be so called from the custom of cooking beans at the feast (*πύανον ἕψειν*), Plut.

Πυανεψιών, ῶνος, ὁ, *the fourth month of the Att. year*, so named from the festival Πυανέψια, = latter part of October and former of November, Theophr.

ΠΥΑ'ΝΟΣ, ὁ, *a kind of bean*.

πυγαῖος, α, ον, (πυγή) *of* or *on the rump*: τὸ πυγαῖον = ἡ πυγή, *the rump*, Hdt.

πύγ-αργος, ὁ, (πυγή) *white-rump*, the name of a kind of antelope, Hdt.   II. *the white-tailed eagle, the erne*, Soph., etc.

ΠΥ'ΓΗ', ῆς, ἡ, *the rump, buttocks*, Ar., etc.

πυγίδιον, τό, Dim. of πυγή, *a thin rump*, Ar.

πυγμαῖος, α, ον, (πυγμή II) *a πυγμή long* or *tall* : of men, *dwarfish*, Hdt. :—Πυγμαῖοι, οἱ, *the Pygmies*, a race of dwarfs on the upper Nile, said to have been warred on and destroyed by cranes, Il.

πυγμάχέω, f. ήσω, *to practise boxing, be a boxer*, Inscr. in Hdt., Anth.; and

πυγμαχία, ἡ, *boxing*, Lat. *pugilatus*, Il., Pind. From

πυγ-μάχος [ᾰ], ὁ, (πυγμή, μάχομαι) one *who fights with the fist, a boxer*, Lat. *pugil*, Od., Pind., etc.

πυγμή, ἡ, (πύξ) *a fist*, Lat. *pugnus*, *πυγμῇ νικήσαντα having conquered with the fist, in boxing*, Il.; later, *πυγμὴν νικᾶν* Eur.; *πυγμᾶς ἄεθλα* Pind.   2. *πυγμῇ νίψασθαι* in N. T., is interpr. = πύκα, *diligently*; or = πυκνά, *often, with*; cf. πυκνός B. II. and III.   II. a measure of length, *the distance from the elbow to the knuckles*, = 18 δάκτυλοι, about 13½ inches.

πῦγο-στόλος, ον, (στολή) *with sweeping train*, Hes.

πῡγούσιος, α, ον, poët. for πυγονιαῖος, *of the length of a πυγών*, Od.

ΠΥ'ΓΩ'Ν, όνος, ἡ, *the distance from the elbows to the first joint of the fingers*, = 20 δάκτυλοι or 5 παλαισταί, rather more than 15 inches, Hdt., Xen.

ΠΥ'ΕΛΟΣ, ἡ, *an oblong trough*, for feeding animals, Od.: *a bathing-tub*, Ar. :—*a vat, kitchen-boiler*, Id.

Πῡθαγόρας, ου Dor. α, ὁ, *the philosopher Pythagoras*, Hdt., etc. :—hence Πῡθᾱγόρειος, ον, Πῡθᾱγορικός, ή, όν, *of Pythagoras*, Arist. :—Πῡθᾱγορίζω, *to be a disciple of Pythagoras*, etc.

Πυθαεύς, έως, ὁ, *a name of Apollo* at Delphi :— Πυθαϊστής, οῦ, ὁ, one *who consults his oracle*, Strab.

Πῡθία (sc. ἱέρεια), ἡ, *the Pythia, priestess of Pythian Apollo* at Delphi, Hdt., etc.

Πύθια (sc. ἱερά), τά, *the Pythian games*, celebrated every four years (prob. in the 3rd Olympian year) at *Pytho* or Delphi in honour of *Pythian Apollo*, Pind., etc.

Πυθιάς, άδος, ἡ, pecul. fem. of Πύθιος : 1. (sub. ἱέρεια), = ἡ Πυθία, *the Pythian priestess*, Aesch.   2. (sub. ἑορτή), *the celebration of the Pythian games*, Pind.   3. (sub. πομπή), *a sacred mission* from Athens *to Pytho* or *Delphi*, Strab.

Πυθικός, ή, όν, *of* or *for Pytho, Pythian*, Trag., etc.

Πύθιον [ῠ], τό, (Πυθώ) *the temple of Pythian Apollo*, Thuc.

Πυθιο-νίκης [ῑ], ου, ὁ, (νικάω) *a conqueror in the Pythian games*, Pind.

Πυθιό-νῑκος, ον, (νίκη) *of* or *belonging to a Pythian victory*, Pind.

Πύθιος, α, ον, (Πυθώ) *Pythian*, i. e. *Delphian*, of Apollo, h. Hom., Pind., Att.; Π. alone, Eur.; *ἐν Πυθίου* in his *temple*, Thuc.   2. = Πυθικός, Pind., Soph., etc.   II. οἱ Πύθιοι, Lacon. Ποίθιοι, at Sparta, *four persons whose office it was to consult the Delphic oracle* on affairs of state, Hdt., Xen.

ΠΥΘΜΗ'Ν, ένος, ὁ, *the hollow bottom* or *stand of a cup*, Lat. *fundus*, Il., Hes., etc.   2. *of the sea, the bottom, depth*, Hes., Solon, etc.   3. *the bottom* or *foundation* of a thing, in pl., *χθόνα ἐκ πυθμένων κραδαίνειν* Aesch.; *ἐκ π. ἔκλινε κλῆθρα* Soph.; *δίκας π. the anvil-stand* on which is forged the sword of retribution, Id.   II. *the bottom, stock, root of a tree*,

Od., Solon :—metaph. *the stem* or *stock* of a family, Aesch. ; σμικροῦ γένοιτ' ἂν σπέρματος π. μέγας, i. e. great things might come from small, Id.

Πῦθοῖ, Adv. (Πυθώ) *at Pytho* or *Delphi,* Pind., Xen., etc.   2. *to Pytho* or *Delphi,* Plut.

Πῦθό-κραντος, ον, (κραίνω) *confirmed by the Pythian god :* τὰ Πυθόκραντα *the Pythian oracles,* Aesch.

Πῦθό-μαντις, εως, ὁ, ἡ, *the Pythian prophet,* Aesch. :—Π. ἑστία *the prophetic seat at Pytho,* Soph.

Πῦθό-νῖκος, ον, = Πυθιόνικος, Pind.

Πῦθο-χρήστης, Dor. -τας, ὁ, (χράω) *sent by the Pythian oracle,* Aesch.

Πῦθό-χρηστος, ον, (χράω) *delivered by the Pythian god,* Aesch., Xen.   II. = foreg., Eur.

ΠΥ'ΘΩ [ῠ] : f. πῡσω : aor. 1 ἔπῡσα, Ep. πῦσα :—*to make rot, to rot,* Il., Hes. :—Pass. *to become rotten, to decay,* Hom.

Πῦθώ, gen. οῦς, dat. οῖ, ἡ, *Pytho,* older name of that part of Phocis at the foot of Parnassus, in which lay the city of Delphi, Hom., etc.

Πῦθώδε, Adv. (Πυθώ) *to Pytho,* Od., Soph., Ar., etc.

Πῦθῶθεν, Adv. (Πυθώ) *from Pytho,* Pind.

Πύθων [ῠ], ωνος, ὁ, (cf. Πυθώ) *the serpent Python,* slain by Apollo.   II. πνεῦμα Πύθωνος *a spirit of divination,* N. T. : ventriloquists (ἐγγαστρίμυθοι) were called Πύθωνες, Plut.

Πῦθών, ῶνος, ἡ, = Πυθώ, Il., Pind., Soph., etc.

Πῦθωνάδε, Adv. = Πυθώδε, Pind.

Πῦθωνόθεν, Adv., = Πυθώθεν, Tyrtae., Pind.

πύκᾰ [ῠ], poët. Adv., v. πυκνός B. III.

πῦκᾰείς, έσσα, έν, (πύξ) = ἰσχυρός, *vehement,* Aesch.

πῦκάζω, Dor. **πυκάσδω** : Ep. aor. 1 πύκασα, πύκασσα : —Pass., aor. 1 ἐπυκάσθην : pf. πεπύκασμαι : (πύκα, πύξ) :—*to make close, cover* or *wrap up, enwrap,* Il. ; π. νῆα λίθοισι *to surround* a ship with stones, *so as to protect* it when laid up, Hes. :—*to cover thickly,* of a youth's chin, Od. ; πυκ. στεφάνοις *to cover thick* with crowns, Eur., Theocr. ; so in Med., στεφάνοις κεφαλὰς πυκασώμεθα Anth. ; also without στεφάνοις, to *crown, deck with garlands,* Eur. :—Pass., στέμμασι πυκασθείς Hdt. ; δάφνῃ πυκασθείς Eur. ; pf. part. πεπυκασμένος, *thickly covered,* ὄρος πεπυκασμένον a hill *well-clothed* with wood, Hes. :—Med., πυκάζου *cover thyself,* Eur.   2. metaph. Ἕκτορα ἄχος πύκασε φρένας *threw a shadow over* his heart, Il. :—Pass., νόον πεπυκασμένος, *close, cautious* of mind, Hes.   II. *to close, shut,* shut up, ἐντὸς πυκάζειν σφέας αὐτούς *to shut* themselves *close up* within, Od. ; πύκαζε (sc. τὸ δῶμα) shut it *close,* Soph.

πῦκῐ-μηδής, ές, (πύκα, μῆδος) *of close* or *cautious mind, shrewd,* Hom.

πῦκῐνά, neut. pl. used as Adv., v. πυκνός B.

πῦκῐνός, πυκνῶς, v. πυκνός.

πῦκῐνό-φρων, ὁ, ἡ, = πυκιμηδής, h. Hom.

πῦκνά, neut. used as Adv., v. πυκνός B. II.

πυκνίτης [ῐ], ου, ὁ, *assembled in the Pnyx,* Ar. ; cf. πνύξ.

πῦκνόν, neut. Adj. used as Adv., v. πυκνός B. II.

πῦκνό-πτερος, ον, (πτερόν) *thick-feathered,* π. ἀηδόνες, where it seems to be a poët. periphr. for πυκναί, *multitudinous,* Soph.

πυκνορράξ, ᾱγος, (ῥάξ) *thick with berries,* Anth.

πῦκνός, ή, όν, Ep. **πῦκῐνός,** ή, όν, (πύξ) *close, compact :*

and so,   I. of consistency, *close, firm, solid,* opp. to what is loose and porous (μανός, ἀραιός), Hom. ; πυκινὸν λέχος *a well-stuffed* bed, Id.   II. *close-packed, crowded, thick, close, dense,* Id. ; of the plumage of a sea-bird, Id. ; of foliage, Id. ; of *a shower of* darts or stones, Id., Hdt. ; of hair, Aesch., etc.   2. *frequent, many,* Lat. *creber,* Id., Eur., etc.   III. *well put together, compact, fast, strong,* Il.   IV. *close, concealed,* δόλος Ib.   V. generally, *strong* of its kind, *great, sore, excessive,* ἄτη Ib.   VI. metaph. of the mind, *sagacious, shrewd, wise,* Hom. ; πυκινοί *the wise,* Soph. ; of a fox, Ar.

B. Adv. **πυκινῶς,** and after Hom. **πυκνῶς,** θύραι or σανίδες πυκινῶς ἀραρυῖαι *close* or *fast shut,* Hom.   2. *very much, constantly, sorely, greatly,* Id.   3. *sagaciously, shrewdly, craftily,* Id.   II. Hom. also uses neuters **πυκινόν** and **πυκνά, πυκινόν** and **πυκινά** as Adv., *much, often ;* so also in Att. ; Comp. πυκνότερον, πυκνότερα ; Sup. πυκνότατα.   III. poët. Adv. **πύκα** [⌣⌣], as if from πύκος, *strongly,* Hom.   2. πύκα βάλλετο with *thick-falling* darts, Il.   3. *carefully, diligently,* Ib.

πυκνός, gen. of πνύξ.

πυκνό-στικτος, ον, *thick-spotted, dappled,* ἔλαφοι Soph.

πυκνότης, ητος, ἡ, (πυκνός) *closeness, thickness, denseness,* Ar., Thuc., etc.   II. *frequency,* Isocr., etc.   III. metaph. *sagacity, shrewdness, craft,* Ar.

πυκνόω, f. ώσω, (πυκνός) *to make close* or *solid, to pack close,* π. ἑαυτούς *to close* their ranks, Hdt. ; σαυτὸν στρόβει πυκνώσας spin yourself round *and concentrate your thoughts,* Ar. :—Pass. *to be compressed,* πυκνουμένῳ πνεύματι, i. e. without taking breath, Plut.   II. Pass. *to be thickly covered,* Xen.   Hence

πύκνωμα, ατος, τό, *close order* or *array,* Plut.   2. in pl. *combined notes,* or *recurrent notes,* in music, Plat.

πυκτεύω, f. σω, *to practise boxing, box, spar,* Xen., etc. ; εἰς κράτα π. *to strike with the fist* on the head, Eur.   From

πύκτης, ου, ὁ, (πύξ) *a boxer, pugilist,* Pind., Soph.

πυκτικός, ή, όν, *skilled in boxing,* Plat. :—ἡ -κή (sc. τέχνη) *the art of boxing,* Id.   2. *of* or *for boxers,* Id.

πυκτίς, ίδος, ἡ, = πυκτίον, *a writing tablet,* Anth.

πυκτίς, ίδος, prob. ἡ, an unknown animal, perh. *the beaver,* Ar.

Πῦλ-ᾱγόρας, ου, ὁ, (Πύλαι, ἀγείρω) one sent as a deputy *to Pylae,* where the Amphictyonic Council was held, *the deputy of a Greek State to that Council,* Dem., Aeschin.

Πῦλᾱγορέω, *to be* or *act as a* Πυλαγόρας, Dem.

Πύλαι, αἱ, v. πύλη II. 2.

Πῦλαία, Ion. -αίη (sc. σύνοδος), ἡ, fem. of πυλαῖος, *the autumn-meeting of the Amphictyons at Pylae,* Hdt. ; then, generally, *the Amphictyonic Council,* Id.   2. *the right of sending deputies to this Council,* Dem.   II. *a promiscuous crowd,* such as was found at these meetings, Plut. : then, *idle jesting, trifling,* Id.   Hence

πῦλᾱϊκός, ή, όν, *jesting, silly,* Plut.

πῦλαι-μάχος, ον, (μάχομαι) *fighting at the gates,* or *at Pylos,* Ar.

πῦλαῖος, α, ον, (Πύλαι) *at Pylae,* Anth.

πῠλ-άρτης, ου, ὁ, (ἄρω) gate-fastener, he that keeps the gates of hell, Hom.

πῠλᾶτις, ιδος, fem. Adj. at the gates, Soph.

πῠλᾰ-ωρός, ὁ, Ep. for πυλωρός, keeping the gate, a gate-keeper, Il. (Altered, to suit the Ep. metre, from πυλαορός, cf. τιμάορος, τιμωρός, and v. οὖρος custos.)

ΠΥ'ΛΗ [ῠ], ἡ, one wing of a pair of double gates, Hdt. : mostly in pl. the gates of a town, opp. to θύρα (a house-door), Il., Att. 2. in Trag., sometimes, of the house-door. 3. Ἀΐδαο πύλαι, periphr. for the nether world, hell, Hom., Aesch., etc. II. generally, an entrance, of the liver, π. καὶ δοχαὶ χολῆς the orifice and receptacle of gall, Eur. 2. an entrance into a country through mountains, a mountain-pass, Hdt. : esp. Πύλαι, αἱ, the common name for Θερμοπύλαι, the pass round the mountains from Thessaly to Locris, considered the Gates of Greece, Id. ; so, of the pass from Syria into Cilicia, Xen., etc. 3. also of narrow straits, by which one enters a broad sea, ἐπ' αὐταῖς λίμνης π. of the Thracian Bosporus, Aesch. ; ἐν πύλαις, of the Euripus, Eur.

Πυληγενής, = Πυλοιγενής.

Πυληγόρος, ὁ, Ion. for Πυλαγόρας, Hdt.

πῠλη-δόκος, ὁ, (δέχομαι) watching at the door, of Hermes, h. Hom.

πῠλίς, ίδος, ἡ, Dim. of πύλη, a postern, Hdt., Thuc.

Πῠλόθεν, Adv. from Pylos, Od.

Πῠλοι-γενής, ές, (γίγνομαι) sprung from Pylos, Il.

Πῠλόνδε, Adv. to or towards Pylos, Hom.

πῠλος [ῠ], ὁ, = πύλη, Il.

Πῠλος [ῠ], ὁ and ἡ, Pylos, a town and district of Triphylia in Peloponnesus, where Nestor ruled, Hom. Two towns of the same name, in Elis and Messenia, are often confounded with Triphylian Pylos.

πῠλ-ουρός, ὁ, (οὖρος custos) = πυλωρός, Hdt.

πῠλόω, f. ώσω, (πύλη) to furnish with gates, Xen. :— Pass. to be so furnished, Ar. Hence

πύλωμα [ῠ], ατος, τό, a gate, gateway, Aesch., Eur.

πῠλών, ῶνος, ὁ, (πύλη) a gateway, gate-house, Polyb., etc.

πῠλωρέω, to be a πυλωρός, keep the gate, Luc., etc.

πῠλ-ωρός, ὁ, a gate-keeper, warder, porter (v. πυλαωρός), Aesch., Eur. ; also as fem., ἡ π. δωμάτων γυνή Eur. :—metaph., τοῖον πυλωρὸν φύλακα τροφῆς such a watchful guardian of thy life, Soph.

πῠμᾰτ-ηγόρος, ον, (ἀγορεύω) last-speaking, ἠχώ Anth.

ΠΥ'ΜΑ'ΤΟΣ [ῠ], η, ον, hindmost, last, Il. :— also outermost, Ib. :—nethermost, φάρος Plat. ; π. Ταρτάρου βάθη Luc. 2. of Time, last, Hom. :—neut. πύματον and πύματα as Adv., at the last, for the last time, Hom. 3. of Degree, ὅ τι πύματον whatever is the last, worst fate, Soph.

πύνδαξ, ᾰκος, ὁ, (cf. πυθμήν) the bottom of a vessel, Theophr.

πῠνθάνομαι, lengthd. from Root ΠΥΘ (v. πεύθομαι) : Ep. impf. πυνθανόμην : f. πεύσομαι, Dor. πευσοῦμαι : aor. 2 ἐπῠθόμην ; imperat. πυθοῦ, Ion. πύθευ ; Ep. 3 sing. opt. πεπύθοιτο : pf. πέπυσμαι, 2 sing. πέπῠσαι, Ep. πέπῠσσαι, inf. πεπύσθαι : plqpf. ἐπεπύσμην, 3 sing. ἐπέπυστο, Ep. πέπυστο, 3 dual. πεπύσθην :—to learn by hearsay or by inquiry, Hdt. : 1. πυνθ. τί τινος to learn something from a person, Hom., etc. ; τι ἀπό τινος Aesch. ; ἔκ τινος Soph. ; παρά τινος Hdt. 2.

c. acc. rei only, to hear or learn a thing, Od., Att. 3. c. gen. to hear of, hear tell of, hear news of, Od., etc. 4. π. τινά τινος to inquire about one person of or from another, Ar. ; so, π. περί τινος Hdt.; Att. 5. c. part., πυθόμην ὁρμαίνοντα ὁδόν I heard that he was starting, Od. ; π. τὸ Πλημμύριον ἑαλωκός to hear that Plemmyrium had been taken, Thuc. :—so, οὔπω πυθέσθην Πατρόκλοιο θανόντος they had not yet heard of his being dead, Il. 6. c. inf. to hear or learn that, Soph., etc.

ΠΥ'Ξ, Adv. with clenched fist, πὺξ ἀγαθὸς Πολυδεύκης good at the fist, i. e. at boxing, Hom., etc. ; πὺξ μάχεσθαι with the fists, Il. ; πὺξ πατάσσειν, παίειν Ar.

πυξίνεος, α, ον, = sq., Anth.

πύξινος, η, ον, (πύξος) made of box-wood, Il., Theocr.

πυξίον, τό, a tablet of box-wood, Luc. From

πυξίς, ίδος, ἡ, a box of box-wood, Luc.

ΠΥ'ΞΟΣ, ἡ, the box-tree or box-wood, Lat. buxus.

ΠΥ'Ο'Σ, ὁ, the first milk after the birth, beestings, Lat. colostrum, Ar.

πύππαξ, an exclamation of surprise, bravo! Plat.

ΠΥ'Ρ, πυρός, τό, not used in pl. (v. πυρά) :—fire, Hom., etc. ; πῦρ καίειν or δαίειν to kindle fire, Id. ; πῦρ ἀνακαίειν, ἅπτειν, ἐξάπτειν, αἴθειν, ἐναύειν, v. sub vocc. ; πῦρ ἐμβάλλειν νηυσὶ Il. 2. the funeral-fire (cf. πυρά), Ib. 3. the fire of the hearth, πυρὶ δέχεσθαί τινα Eur. ; π. ἄσβεστον or ἀθάνατον the fire of Vesta in the Prytaneion, Plut. II. as a symbol of things irresistible or terrible, μάρναντο δέμας πυρὸς αἰθομένοιο they were fighting like burning fire, Il. ; κρεῖσσον ἀμαιμακέτου πυρός Soph. ; διὰ πυρὸς ἰέναι (as we say) to go through fire and water, Xen. ; but, διὰ πυρὸς ἦλθε ἑτέρῳ λέκτρῳ she raged furiously against the other partner of the bed, Eur. :—of persons, ὦ πῦρ σύ Soph. :—rarely as an image of warmth and comfort, Aesch.

πυρά, ῶν, τά, watch-fires, mostly in acc., καίωμεν πυρὰ πολλά Il. ; πυρὰ ἐκκαίειν Hdt. :—beacon-fires, Thuc. :—ἄτιμος ἐν πυροῖσι, of sacrificial fires, Aesch. (The accent, as well as the dat. πυροῖς, shews that it does not belong to πῦρ.)

πυρά, ᾶς, Ion. πυρή, ῆς, ἡ, any place where fire is kindled, 1. a funeral-pyre, Lat. bustum, Il., Hdt., etc. 2. a mound raised on the place of the pyre, Soph., Eur. 3. an altar for burnt sacrifice, Hdt., Eur. :—also the fire burning thereon, Hdt.

πῦρ-άγρα, ἡ, a pair of fire-tongs, Hom. Hence

πυραγρέτης, ου, ὁ, serving for tongues, Anth.

πῦρ-ακτέω, f. ήσω, (ἄγω) to turn in the fire, to harden in the fire, char, Od.

πῦρ-ακτόω, f. ώσω, = foreg., Strab., Luc.

πῦρᾰμίς, ίδος, ἡ, a pyramid, Hdt. (Prob. an Egypt. word.)

πῠρᾰμοῦς, οῦντος, ὁ, for πυραμόεις (πυρός), a cake of wheat and honey, given as a prize, Ar.

πῦρ-αυγής, ές, (αὐγή) fiery bright, h. Hom., Anth.

πυργηδόν, Adv. like a tower :—of soldiers, in columns, in close array, Il. ; v. πύργος II.

πυργηρέομαι, Pass. to be shut up as in a tower, to be beleaguered, Aesch., Eur. From

πυργ-ήρης, ές, (*ἄρω) of a place, fortified, ap. Paus.

πυργίδιον [ῐ], τό, Dim. of πύργος, Ar.

πύργῐνος, η, ον, (πύργος) tower-like, Aesch.

712   πυργοδάικτος — πυρπολέω.

πυργο-δάικτος, ον, (δαΐζω) destroying towers, Aesch.
πυργο-μάχέω, f. ήσω, (μάχομαι) to assault a tower, Xen.
ΠΥΡΓΟΣ, ὁ, a tower, Il., Hdt., etc. :—in pl. the city walls with towers, Il. ; so, collectively, in sing., Od., Eur.   b. a movable tower for storming towns, Xen.   2. metaph. a tower of defence, as Ajax is called πύργος Ἀχαιοῖς, Od.; παῖς ἄρσην πατέρ᾽ ἔχει πύργον μέγαν Eur.; θανάτων π. a tower of defence from deaths, Soph.   3. the highest part of any building, where the women lived, Il.   II. troops drawn up in close order, a column, Ib.; cf. πυργηδόν.
πυργοφορέω, f. ήσω, to bear a tower or towers, Luc. From
πυργο-φόρος, ον, bearing a tower, of Cybelé, Anth.
πυργο-φύλαξ [ῠ], ὁ, a tower-guard, warder, Aesch.
πυργόω, f. ώσω, (πύργος) to gird or fence with towers, Od., Eur. :—Med. to build towers, Xen. :—Pass., πυργωθείς furnished with a tower, of an elephant, Anth.   II. metaph. to raise up to a towering height, πυργῶσαι ῥήματα σεμνά 'to build the lofty rhyme,' Ar.; so, ἀοιδὰς ἐπύργωσε Eur. :—hence, to exalt, lift up, Id.; so, π. χάριν to exalt, exaggerate it, Id. :—Pass. to exalt oneself, Aesch.; πεπύργωσαι θράσει, λόγοις Eur.
πυργ-ώδης, ες, (εἶδος) like a tower, Soph.
πύργωμα, ατος, τό, (πυργόω) that which is furnished with towers, a fenced city, Orac. ap. Hdt., Eur. :—in pl. fenced walls, Aesch., Eur.
πυργῶτις, ιδος, fem. Adj. towering, Aesch.
πυρ-δαής, ές, (δαίω) burning with fire, incendiary, Aesch.
πυρεῖον, Ion. -ήιον, τό, mostly in pl. pieces of wood, rubbed one against another to produce fire, h. Hom., Soph., etc.
πυρέσσω, Att. -ττω, f. ξω: aor. 1 ἐπύρεξα: pf. πεπύρεχα: (πυρετός):—to be ill of a fever, Eur., Ar.
πυρετός, οῦ, ὁ, (πῦρ) burning heat, fiery heat, Il.   II. feverish heat, a fever, Ar., etc.
πυρέττω, Att. for πυρέσσω.
πυρεύς, έως, ὁ, (πῦρ) a fire-proof vessel, Anth.
πυρή, ῆς, ἡ, Ion. and Ep. for πυρά.
πυρήιον, τό, Ion. for πυρεῖον.
πυρήν, ῆνος, ὁ, the stone of stone-fruit, as of the olive, Hdt.
πυρή-νεμος, ον, (ἄνεμος) fanning fire, Anth.
πυρή-τοκος, ον, (πῦρ, τεκεῖν) producing fire, Anth.
πυρή-φατος, ον, (πυρός, πέφαται 3 sing. pf. pass. of *φένω) π. λάτρις Δήμητρος the wheat-slaying servant of Demeter, i. e. a millstone, Anth.
πυρη-φόρος, ον, (πυρός, φέρω) poët. for πυροφόρος, wheat-bearing, Od.
πυρία, Ion. -ίη, ἡ, (πῦρ) a vapour-bath, made by throwing scented substances on hot embers confined under a cloth, Hdt.
πυριάτη [ἄ], ἡ, (πυός) beestings-pudding, Ar.
πυριατήριον, τό, (πυριάω) a vapour-bath, heated by a furnace underneath, Plut.
πυρί-γενέτης, ου, ὁ, = sq., fire-wrought, Aesch.
πυρί-γενής, ές, (γίγνομαι) = foreg., born in fire : of instruments, wrought by fire, Eur.
πυρί-γονος, ον, producing fire, Plut.
πυρί-δαπτος, ον, (δάπτω) devoured by fire, Aesch.
πυρί-πηκής, ές, (ἀκή) with fiery point, Od.
πυρί-θαλπής, ές, (θάλπω) heated in the fire, Anth.

πυρί-κᾱής, ές, = πυρίκαυστος, Anth.
πυρί-καυστος, ον, or -καυτος, burnt in fire, Il.
πυρί-κοίτης, ες, (κοίτη) wherein fire lies asleep, νάρθηξ π., of the cane of Prometheus, Anth.
πυρί-λαμπής, ές, (λάμπω) bright with fire, Plut.
πυρί-ληπτος, ον, seized by fire, volcanic, Strab.
πυρί-μάνής, f. ήσω, (μαίνομαι) to break out into a furious blaze, Plut.
πύρῐνος [ῠ], η, ον, (πῦρ) of fire, fiery, hot, Anth.
πύρῐνος [ῠ], η, ον, (πυρός) of wheat, wheaten, Xen., etc.
πυρι-πνέων, ουσα, ον, part. with no Verb in use, fire-breathing, Eur.
πυρί-πνοος, ον, contr. -πνους, ουν, (πνέω) fire-breathing, fiery, Anth.
πυρι-σμάρᾰγος [ᾰ], ον, roaring with fire, Theocr.
πυρί-σπαρτος, ον, (σπείρω) sowing fire, inflaming, Anth.
πυρί-στακτος, ον, fire-streaming, Eur.
πυρίτης [ῑ], ου, ὁ, (πῦρ) of or in fire, Luc.
πυρί-τρόφος, ον, (τρέφω) cherishing fire, of billows.
πυρι-φλεγέθων, ουσα, ον, fire-blazing : as Subst., Pyriphlegethon, one of the rivers of hell, Od.
πυρι-φλεγής, ές, (φλέγω) flaming with fire, blazing, Xen.
πυρι-φλέγων, οντος, ὁ, = foreg., Eur.
πυρί-φλεκτος, ον, (φλέγω) blazing with fire, Eur.
πυρίχη [ῑ], ἡ, poët. for πυρρίχη, Anth.
πυρί-χρως, ωτος, ὁ, ἡ, fire-coloured, Alcidam. ap. Arist.
πυρ-καϊά, Ep. and Ion. -ιή, ἡ, (καίω) any place where fire is kindled, a funeral pyre, Il.   2. fire, conflagration, Hdt. : arson, Lex ap. Dem.   3. metaph. the flame of love, Anth.
πυρναῖος, α, ον, (πύρνον) fit for eating, Theocr.
πύρνον, τό, (πύρινος) wheaten bread, Od.
πυρο-βόλος, ον, (βάλλω) giving forth fire :—τὰ πυροβόλα bolts or arrows tipped with fire, Plut.
πῡρο-γενής, ές, (πυρός, γίγνομαι) made from wheat, Anth.
πυρόεις, εσσα, εν, (πῦρ) fiery, Anth.   2. ὁ Πυρόεις the Planet Mars, from his fiery colour, Arist.
πῡρο-κλοπία, ἡ, (κλοπή) a theft of fire, Anth.
πῡρο-λόγος, ον, (πυρός, λέγω) reaping wheat, Anth.
πῡροπωλέω, f. ήσω, to deal in wheat, Dem. From
πῡρο-πώλης, ου, ὁ, (πωλέω) a wheat-merchant.
πῡρορ-ρᾰγής, ές, (ῥήγνυμι) bursting in the fire, fire-flawed, cracked, Ar.
ΠΥΡΟΣ, ὁ, wheat, Hom.; also in pl., Od., etc.
πῡρο-φόρος, ον, (πυρός, φέρω) wheat-bearing, Il., Eur.
πῠρόω, f. ώσω, (πῦρ) to burn with fire, burn up, Hdt., Soph. : to burn as a burnt sacrifice, Aesch., Eur.; π. Κύκλωπος ὄψιν to burn out his eye, Eur. :—Med. παῖδα πυρωσαμένη having placed one's son on the pyre, Anth. :—Pass. to set on fire, to be burnt, Pind., Eur.   2. metaph. in Pass. to be inflamed or excited, Aesch.   II. Pass. also, of gold, to be proved or tested by fire, N. T.   III. to fumigate, Theocr.
πυρπαλαμάω, f. ήσω, to play tricks with fire, play mischievous tricks, h. Hom. From
πυρ-πάλαμος, η, ον, (παλάμη) wrought from fire, of a thunderbolt, Pind.
πύρ-πνοος, ον, contr. -πνους, ουν, = πυρίπνοος, fire-breathing, Τυφῶν Aesch., Eur.
πυρ-πολέω, f. ήσω, (πυρπόλος) to light and keep up a fire, watch a fire, Od., Xen.; π. τοὺς ἄνθρακας to stir up the fire, Ar.   II. to waste with fire, burn

and destroy, Id.;—Med., πυρπολέεσθαι πᾶσαν τὴν Ἀττικήν to cause it to be burnt with fire, Hdt. Hence

πυρπόλημα, ατος, τό, a watchfire, beacon, Eur.

πυρ-πόλος, ον, (πολέω) wasting with fire, burning, κεραυνός Eur.

πυρράζω, (πυρρός) to be fiery red, of the sky, N. T.

Πυρρικός, ή, όν, named after Pyrrhus, Theocr.

πυρρίχη [ῐ] (sc. ὄρχησις), ἡ, the pyrrhic dance, a kind of war-dance, Ar., Xen.;—attributed to one Πύρριχος the inventor.   2. generally, δειναὶ π. strange contortions, Eur.:—proverb., πυρρίχην βλέπειν 'to look daggers,' Ar.

πυρρῐχίζω, to dance the pyrrhic dance, Luc.

πυρρίχιος [ῐ], ὁ, of or belonging to the pyrrhic dance, Luc.   II. ποὺς π. a pyrrhic, i. e. a foot consisting of two short syllables, used in the πυρρίχη or war-song.

πυρρῐχιστής, οῦ, ὁ, a dancer of the πυρρίχη: οἱ π. the chorus of Pyrrhic dancers, Lys., Isae.

πύρρῐχος, η, ον, Dor. for πυρρός, red, Theocr.

πυρρο-γένειος, ον, (γένειον) red-bearded, Anth.

πυρρό-θριξ, ὁ, ἡ, red-haired, Solon.

πυρρο-κόραξ, ᾰκος, ὁ, a crow with a red beak, Plin.

πυρρόομαι, Pass. to become red, Arist.

πυρρ-οπίπης [ῐ], ου, ὁ, (ὀπιπτεύω) one that ogles young boys with a play upon πῡρο-πίπης, ogling wheat (i. e. dinner in the Prytaneium), Ar.

πυρρός, ά, όν, Ion. ή, όν; but in older Att. and Dor. **πυρσός**, ή, όν: (πῦρ):—flame-coloured, yellowish-red: of persons with red hair, like the Scythians, Lat. rufus, Hdt.; of the colour of the first beard, Aesch., Eur.   2. generally, red, tawny, Lat. fulvus, λέων Eur., Xen.   3. of persons also, red with blushes, Ar.; but, κύων πυρσ' ἔχουσα δέργματα glaring with red eyes, Eur.

πυρρό-τρῐχος, ον, = πυρρόθριξ, Theocr.

πυρσαίνω, (πυρσός) to make red, tinge with red, Eur.

πυρσεύω, f. σω, (πυρσός) to light up, kindle, πυρσεύσας σέλας Εὐβοίαν having lit up Euboea with beacon-fires (σέλας combining with the notion of the Verb), Eur.   II. to make signals by torches or beacon-fires, Xen.: metaph., πυρσεύετε κραυγὴν ἀγῶνος give a shout in signal of battle, Eur.:—Pass., δόξα ὥσπερ ἀπὸ σκοπῆς πυρσεύεται Plut.: impers., πυρσεύεται fire-signals are made, Luc.

πυρσο-βόλος, ον, (βάλλω) shooting forth fire, Anth.

πυρσό-νωτος, ον, red-backed, Eur.

πυρσός, οῦ, ὁ, heterog. pl. πυρσά, (πῦρ) a firebrand, torch, Il., Eur.:—in pl. fires, Anth.:—metaph., πυρσὸς ὕμνων Pind.; pl. the fires of love, Theocr.   II. a beacon or signal-fire, bale-fire, Hdt.   2. pl. πύρσα, watch-fires, Eur.

πυρσός, ή, όν, old Att. for πυρρός.

πυρσο-τόκος, ον, (τίκτω) fire-producing, π. λίθος a flint, Anth.

πυρσ-ώδης, ες, (εἶδος) like a firebrand, Eur.

πυρφορέω, f. ήσω, to be a πυρφόρος, to carry a torch, Eur.   II. to set on fire, Aesch.

πυρ-φόρος, ον, (φέρω) fire-bearing, Aesch.; of lightning, Pind., Aesch.:—πυρφόροι ὀϊστοί arrows with combustibles tied to them, Thuc.   II. in special senses,   1. epith. of Zeus in reference to his lightnings, Soph.; of Demeter, in reference to the torches

used by her worshippers, Eur.; of Artemis, Soph.; —but θεὸς πυρφόρος the fire-bearing god, the god who produces plague or fever, Id.   2. ὁ πυρφόρος, in the Lacedaemonian army, was the priest who kept the sacrificial fire, which was never allowed to go out, Xen.; hence proverb. of a total defeat, ἔδεε δὲ μηδὲ πυρφόρον περιγενέσθαι Hdt.

πῠρ-ώδης, ες, (εἶδος) like fire, fiery, Ar., etc.

πῠρ-ωπός, όν, (ὤψ) fiery-eyed, fiery, Aesch.

πύστις, εως, ἡ, (πυθέσθαι) rarer form of πεῦσις, enquiry, τὰς πύστεις ἐρωτῶντες, εἰ . . introducing the questions whether . . , Thuc.   II. that which is learnt by asking, tidings, Aesch., Eur.; κατὰ πύστιν ᾗ χωροίη according as they learnt which way he was gone, Thuc.; πύστει τῶν προγενομένων by hearing of what was done before, Id.

πῠτῐναῖος, α, ον, plaited with osier, πτερὰ πυτιναῖα are given to Diitrephes, because he had grown rich by his trade of a basket-maker, Ar.   From

πῠτίνη [ῐ], ἡ, a flask covered with plaited osier.

πῶ; Adv., Sicil. Dor. for ποῦ; where? Aesch.   II. πῶ μάλα; or πώμαλα; where in the world? how in the name of fortune? i. e. not a whit, Ar., Dem.

πω, Ion. **κω**, enclit. Particle, up to this time, yet, almost always with a negat. (like Lat. -dum in non-dum), with which it forms one word, οὔπω, μήπω.   II. after Hom., with questions which imply a negative, Soph., Thuc.

ΠΩΓΩΝ, ωνος, ὁ, the beard, Hdt., Ar., etc.:—metaph., πώγων πυρός a beard or tail of fire, Aesch.

πωγώνιον, τό, Dim. of πώγων, Luc., Anth.

πωγωνο-φόρος, ον, (φέρω) wearing a beard, Anth.

πώεα, τά, plur. of πῶυ.

πωλεία, ἡ, a breeding of foals, stud, breed, Xen.

πώλειος, α, ον, of a foal, χαίτη Suid.

πωλέομαι, Ion. **πωλεῦμαι**: Ep. impf. πωλεύμην, 2 sing. πωλέο, Ion. 3 sing. πωλέσκετο: f. πωλήσομαι, Ep. 2 sing. πωλήσεαι:—Frequent. of πολέομαι, to go up and down, go to and fro, Lat. versari in loco: hence, to go or come frequently, εἰς ἀγορὴν πωλέσκετο Il.; εἰς ἡμέτερον [δῶμα] πωλεύμενοι Od.

πώλευσις, ἡ, horsebreaking, Xen.   From

πωλεύω, f. σω, (πῶλος) to break in a young horse, Xen.

ΠΩΛΕ'Ω, Ion. 3 sing. impf. πωλέεσκε, f. -ήσω: aor. 1 ἐπώλησα:—to exchange or barter goods, to sell or offer for sale, Hdt., Att.; c. gen. pretii, ἐς Σάρδις χρημάτων μεγάλων π. to sell at a high price for exportation to Sardis, Hdt.; ἐπώλεε οὐδενὸς χρήματος refused to sell it at any price, Id.; ἐρέσθαι ὁπόσου πωλεῖ to ask what he wants for it, Xen.; absol., π. πρός τινα to deal with one, Xen.   2. π. τέλη to let out the taxes, Lat. locare, Aeschin.   3. to sell, i. e. give up, betray, Dem.:—of persons, to be bought and sold, Ar.   Hence

πώλης, ου, ὁ, a seller, dealer, Ar.; and

πώλησις, ἡ, a selling, sale, Xen.

πωλητήριον, τό, (πωλέω) a place where wares are sold, an auction-room, shop, Xen.   II. the office of the πωληταί, Dem.

πωλητής, οῦ, ὁ, one who sells; at Athens, the πωληταί were ten officers, who let out (locabant) the taxes and revenues to the highest bidders, Dem.

πωλικός, ή, όν, (πῶλος) of foals, fillies, or young horses, ἀπήνη π. a chariot drawn by horses, Soph., Eur.; π. διώγματα pursuit in chariot drawn by horses, Eur. 2. of any young animal, π. ἑδώλια the girls' apartments, Aesch.

πωλίον, τό, Dim. of πῶλος, a pony, Ar.

πωλοδαμνέω, f. ήσω, to break young horses, Eur., Xen. 2. metaph. to train up, Soph. From

πωλο-δάμνης, ου, ὁ, (δαμάω) a horsebreaker, Xen.

πωλο-μάχος [ᾰ], ον, (μάχομαι) fighting on horseback or in a chariot, Anth.

ΠΩ῀ΛΟΣ, ὁ and ἡ, a foal, young horse, whether colt or filly, Hom.: in Poets generally for ἵππος, Soph., etc. 2. a young animal, a puppy, Anth. 3. in Poets, in fem., a young girl, maiden, like δάμαλις, μόσχος, πόρτις, Lat. juvenca, Eur.:—more rarely masc., a young man, Aesch.

πωλο-τρόφος, ον, (τρέφω) rearing young horses, Anth.

πῶμα, ατος, τό, a lid, cover, Hom. (Of unknown origin.)

πῶμα, ατος, τό, (ΠΟ Root of some tenses of πίνω) a drink, a draught, Trag., Plat., etc.

πωμάζω, (πῶμα) to furnish with a lid, cover up, Babr.

πωμᾰλᾰ, v. πῶ.

πώ-ποτε, (πω, ποτέ) ever yet, mostly with negat., οὐ πώποτε, μὴ πώποτε, Hom., etc.

πώρῖνος, η, ον, v. πῶρος.

ΠΩ῀ΡΟΣ, ὁ, Lat. tophus, Ital. tufa, a porous stone; the πώρινος λίθος of Hdt. Hence

πωρόω, f. ώσω, to petrify, turn into stone: metaph. in Pass. to become hardened, of the heart, N. T. Hence

πώρωσις, εως, ἡ, petrifaction: metaph. hardness, N. T.

πῶς; Ion. κῶς; interrog. Adv. of manner, how? in what way or manner? Lat. qui? quomodo? in direct questions, as ὅπως in indirect, Hom., etc.:—with a second interrog. in the same clause, πῶς ἐκ τίνος νεὼς . . ἥκετε; how and by what ship came ye? Eur..:—c. gen., πῶς ἀγῶνος ἥκομεν; how are we come off in it? Id. 2. with Verbs of selling, how? at what price? πῶς ὁ σῖτος ὤνιος; Ar. 3. πῶς δοκεῖς; v. δοκέω I. 2. II. with other Particles, πῶς ἂν . .; Ep. πῶς κε or κεν . .; how possibly . .? Hom., Eur.: —in Trag., πῶς ἂν with opt. expresses a wish, O how might it be? i. e. would that it were . .! Lat. O si . .! O utinam . .! πῶς ἂν θάνοιμι; πῶς ἂν ὀλοίμην, etc. 2. πῶς ἄρα . ; in reply, how then . .? Hom. 3. πῶς γάρ . .; also in reply, as if something had gone before, [that cannot be], for how can . .? Id., Soph. 4. πῶς δή; how in the world? Il., etc. :—also, πῶς γὰρ δή; Od.; πῶς δῆτα . .; Aesch., etc. 5. καὶ πῶς . .; to introduce an objection, yet how can it be? Att. 6. πῶς οὐ . .; how not so . .? i. e. surely it is so . ., Thuc., etc. 7. πῶς οὖν . .; like πῶς ἄρα . .; Aesch., etc. 8. πῶς ποτε . .; how ever . .? Soph.

πως, Ion. κως, enclit. Adv. of manner, in any way, at all, by any means, Hom.; ὧδέ πως somehow so, Xen.; ἄλλως πως in some other way, Id.:—after hypothet. Particles, εἴπως, ἐάν or ἤν πως, Lat. si qua, si forte, Od., etc. II. πῶς, not enclitic, in a certain way, opp. to ἁπλῶς, Arist.

πωτάομαι, Ep. 3 pl. impf. πωτῶντο: aor. 1 ἐπωτήθην: —Ep. form of ποτάομαι, to fly about, Il., h. Apoll.

πότημα, ατος, τό, v. πότημα.

ΠΩ῀Υ, εος, τό, pl. πώεα, τά, (v. ποιμήν) a flock, of sheep, opp. to ἀγέλη (a herd of oxen), Hom., Hes.

P.

Ρ, ρ, ῥῶ, τό, indecl., seventeenth letter of Gr. Alphabet, as numeral ρ' = 100, but ͵ρ 100,000. Dialectic and other changes: 1. Aeol., at the end of words σ passed into ρ, as οὗτορ, ἵππορ for οὗτος, ἵππος; cf. Lat. arbor arbos, honor honos. 2. in Att., ρρ replaced the Ion. and old Att. ρσ, as ἄρρην, θάρρος for ἄρσην, θάρσος. 3. in some words ρ is transposed, as κάρτος Ep. for κράτος, ἀταρπός for ἀτραπός, κραδίη for καρδία: —mostly in Poets. II. ρ at the beginning of a word was pronounced so as to make a short vowel at the end of the word before long by position, as, ψυχρὴ ὑπὸ ῥιπῆς Il. 2. by reason of this pronunc., ρ was doubled after a Prep. or a privat., and after the augment, as ἀπορρίπτω, ἄρρωστος, ἔρριψα. 3. if ρ begins a word, it takes the rough breathing, except in Aeol.

ῥά [ᾰ], enclit. Particle, Ep. for ἄρα, Hom., and in lyric passages of Trag.

ῥαββί, ῥαββονί, ῥαββουνί, o my Master, Hebr. words in N. T.

ῥαβδίον, τό, Dim. of ῥάβδος, a little rod, a wand, Babr.

ῥαβδο-μᾰχία, ἡ, (μάχομαι) a fighting with a staff or foil, Plut.

ῥαβδονομέω, f. ήσω, to sit as umpire, Soph. From

ῥαβδο-νόμος, ον, (νέμω) holding a rod or wand; hence, like ῥαβδοῦχος, of the Rom. lictors, Plut.

ῬΑ῀ΒΔΟΣ, ἡ, a rod, wand, stick, switch, Lat. virga, Hom., Xen. 2. a magic wand, as that of Circé or Hermes, Hom. 3. a fishing-rod, Od.:—also a limed twig, for catching birds, Ar. 4. a spear-staff or shaft, Xen. 5. a staff of office, like the earlier σκῆπτρον, Pind. 6. the wand borne by the ῥαψῳδός: hence, κατὰ ῥάβδον ἐπέων according to the measure of his (Homer's) verses, Pind. 7. a rod for chastisement, Plat.; αἱ ῥάβδοι the fasces of the Roman lictors, Plut. II. a stripe or strip, Il.

ῥαβδουχέω, f. ήσω, to carry a rod or wand, as a badge of office:—Pass., at Rome, to have the fasces borne before one, Plut.; and

ῥαβδουχία, ἡ, at Rome, the fasces, Plut. From

ῥαβδ-οῦχος, ὁ, (ἔχω) one who carries a rod or staff of office: 1. a judge, umpire at a contest, Plat. 2. a magistrate's attendant, a beadle, Ar.:—so, at Rome, of the lictors who carried the fasces, Polyb., etc.

ῥαβδοφορέω, f. ήσω, to carry a wand or stick, Strab. From

ῥαβδο-φόρος, ον, (φέρω) = ῥαβδοῦχος 2, Polyb.

ῥάβδωσις, ἡ, (as if from ῥαβδόω) the fluting of columns, Arist.; cf.

ῥαβδωτός, ή, όν, (as if from ῥαβδόω, cf. ῥάβδος II) striped, Xen.

ῥᾰγάς, άδος, ἡ, (ῥαγῆναι) a rent, chink, Anth.

ῥαγδαῖος, α, ον, (ῥάγδην) tearing, furious, Plut., Luc.

ῥᾰγῆναι, aor. 2 pass. inf. of ῥήγνυμι.

ῥᾱγίζω, f. ίσω, (ῥάξ) to gather grapes, Theocr.

ῥᾱγο-λόγος, ον, (ῥάξ, λέγω) gathering berries, Anth.

ῥαδινάκη, ἡ, the Persian name for a black strong-smelling petroleum, Hdt.

ῬΑ῾ΔΙ῾ΝΟΣ, ή, όν, Aeol. βραδινός, ά, όν, slender, taper, Il., Theogn., etc. 2. of the limbs or body, taper, slim, Hes., Theogn. 3. generally, tender or mobile, ὄσσε Aesch.

ῥάδιος, α, ον, Att. also ος, ον; Ep. and Ion. ῥηίδιος, η, ον, [ῐ]: Comp. ῥᾴων, ῥᾷον (from the Root ῬΑ), Ion. ῥηίων, ῥηίον, Ep. ῥηίτερος, contr. ῥήτερος, Dor. ῥάτερος:—Sup. ῥᾷστος, η, ον, Ion. and Ep. ῥήιστος, Dor. ῥάϊστος, Ep. ῥηίτατος:—easy, ready, easy to make or do, opp. to χαλεπός, Hom., etc.; ῥηίδιόν τοι ἔπος a word easy for thee to understand, Od.:—c. inf., τάφρος ῥηιδίη περῆσαι easy to pass over, Il.; ῥηίτεροι πολεμίζειν easier to fight with, Ib. 2. ῥάδιόν ἐστι it is easy to do a thing, c. inf., Pind., Thuc.; c. acc. et inf., τύραννον εὐσεβεῖν οὐ ῥάδιον Soph.; also, ῥᾷστοί εἰσιν ἀμύνεσθαι = ῥάδιόν ἐστιν αὐτοὺς ἀμύνεσθαι, Thuc. b. also, ῥᾴδιόν ἐστι it is a light matter, you think little of doing, παρ' ὑμῖν ῥ. ξενοκτονεῖν Eur. II. of persons, easy, complaisant, Lat. facilis, commodus, Dem.:—in bad sense, reckless, Luc.

B. Adv. ῥαδίως, Ep. and Ion. ῥηιδίως, easily, lightly, readily, willingly, Hom., etc.; ῥαδίως φέρειν to bear lightly, make light of a thing, Eur., etc. 2. in bad sense, lightly, recklessly, rashly, Thuc.; ῥᾳδίως οὕτω in this easy, thoughtless way, Plat. II. Comp., ῥᾷον φέρειν Thuc. III. Sup. ῥᾷστα, esp. in phrases, ῥᾷστα φέρειν Soph.; ὡς ῥᾷστα φέρειν Aesch.

ῥᾳδιουργέω, f. ήσω, (ῥᾳδιουργός) to do things with ease or off-hand, Luc. II. to live an easy, lazy life, take things easily, Xen. 2. to act thoughtlessly or recklessly, to do wrong, misbehave, Id. Hence

ῥᾳδιούργημα, ατος, τό, a reckless act, crime, Plut.

ῥᾳδιουργία, ἡ, ease in doing, facility, Xen. II. easiness, laziness, sloth, Id. 2. recklessness, want of principle, wickedness, lewdness, Id.: fraud, Plut.

ῥᾳδι-ουργός, όν, (*ἔργω) properly, doing things easily; in bad sense, unscrupulous, reckless, Arist. 2. of things, impure, Xen.

ῥᾰθάμιγξ [θᾰ], ιγγος, ἡ, a drop, Il., Hes. II. of solids, a grain, bit, Il. (Deriv. uncertain.)

ῥᾰθᾰ-πῡγίζω, f. σω, (ῥάσσω, πυγή) to give one a slap on the buttocks, Ar.

ῥᾱθῡμέω, f. ήσω, to leave off work, to be remiss, Xen.

ῥᾱθῡμία, ἡ, easiness of temper, a taking things easily, Thuc. 2. recreation, relaxation, amusement, Eur. II. in bad sense, indifference, sluggishness, laziness, Xen., etc.; ῥ. κτήσασθαι to get a name for laziness, Eur. 2. heedlessness, rashness, Plat.

ῥᾱ-θῡμος, ον, taking things easy, indifferent, lazy, sluggish, Lat. socors, Soph., etc. II. of things, easy, Lat. securus, Isocr., Plat.:—Adv. -μως, Plat. 2. Adv. also, like ῥᾳδίως, lightly, with equanimity, Id.; Comp. -ότερον, Isocr.; -ότερα, Arist.

ῥαιβό-κρᾱνος, ον, (κράνιον) with crooked head, Anth.

ῬΑΙΒΟΣ, ή, όν, crooked, bent, Arist.

ῥαιβο-σκελής, ές, (σκέλος) crook-legged, Anth.

ῥᾱΐζω, Ion. ῥηΐζω, f. ίσω, (ῥάδιος) to grow easier, find relief, recover from illness, Plat., Dem.:—to take one's rest, Xen.

ῬΑΙ῾ΝΩ, f. ῥᾰνῶ: aor. 1 ἔρρᾱνα:—Pass., aor. 1 ἐρράνθην:

pf. ἔρραμμαι, 3 pl. ἔρρανται:—besides these are found two irreg. Ep. forms (as if from a pres. *ῥάζω), viz. 2 pl. aor. 1 imper. ῥάσσατε, 3 pl. pf. and plqpf. pass. ἐρράδαται, ἐρράδατο: I. to sprinkle, besprinkle, ῥάσσατε (sc. δῶμα ὕδατι) Od.; αἵματι βωμόν Eur.:—Pass., πύργοι αἵματι ἐρράδατ' Il.; αἵματι δ' ἐρράδαται τοῖχοι Od.:—of dust, ἵπποι ῥαίνοντο κονίῃ Il. 2. metaph., ῥ. τινὰ ὕμνῳ Pind. II. to sprinkle, with acc. of the thing sprinkled, ῥαίνειν ἐς τὰ βλέφαρα to sprinkle (vinegar) in their eyes, Ar. From

ῥαιστήρ, ῆρος, ὁ and ἡ, a hammer, Il., Aesch. From

ῬΑΙ῾Ω, poët. 3 sing. subj. ῥαίῃσι: f. ῥαίσω, Ep. inf. ῥαισέμεναι: aor. 1 ἔρραισα, subj. ῥαίσῃ:—Pass., aor. 1 ἐρραίσθην:—to break, shiver, shatter, wreck, Od.;—Pass., ῥαιόμενος one shipwrecked, Ib.; φάσγανον ἐρραίσθη was shivered, Il. II. to crush, destroy, in Pass., Aesch., Soph.

ῥακά, Hebr. word expressive of utter contempt, N. T.

ῥάκιον [ᾰ], τό, Dim. of ῥάκος, in pl. rags, Ar.

ῥάκιο-συρραπτάδης, ου, ὁ, a rag-stitcher, Ar.

ῥακό-δυτος, ον, (δύω) ragged, Eur.

ῥακόεις, εσσα, εν, ragged, torn, tattered, Anth. II. wrinkled, Id. From

ῬΑ῾ΚΟΣ [ᾰ], εος, τό, a ragged garment, a rag, Od., Ar.: in pl. ῥάκεα, Att. ῥάκη, rags, tatters, Od., Hdt., etc. 2. generally, a strip of cloth, Hdt.: a strip of flesh, Aesch. II. in pl. rents in the face, wrinkles, Ar. III. metaph. a rag, remnant, Anon. ap. Arist.; of an old seaman, ἁλίοιο βίου ῥάκος Anth. Hence

ῥακόω, f. ώσω, to tear in strips, Plut. Hence

ῥάκωμα, ατος, τό, in pl.,=ῥάκη, rags, Ar.

ῬΑ῾ΜΦΟΣ, εος, τό, a beak, bill, neb, Ar.

ῥᾱνίς, ίδος, ἡ, (ῥαίνω) a drop, Eur.; a rain-drop, Ar.

ῥαντήριος, α, ον, (ῥαίνω) of or for sprinkling:—in Aesch., it seems to be bedabbled, reeking.

ῥαντίζω, = ῥαίνω, N. T. II. to purify, Ib. Hence

ῥαντισμός, ὁ, a sprinkling, N. T.

ῬΑ῾Ξ, ῥᾱγός, ῥώξ, ῥωγός, ἡ, a grape, Lat. racemus, Plat.

ῥᾶον, neut. Adj. used as Adv.; v. ῥάδιος.

ῥᾱπίζω, f. ίσω, (ῥαπίς) to strike with a stick, to cudgel, flog, bastinado, Hdt., Dem. II. to slap in the face, N. T.

ῥᾱπίς, ίδος, ἡ, = ῥάβδος.

ῥάπισμα, τό, (ῥαπίζω) a stroke, a slap on the face, Luc.

ῥαπτός, ή, όν, (ῥάπτω) stitched, patched, Od. 2. metaph. strung together, continuous, of verses, Pind. II. worked with the needle: ῥαπτόν, τό, an embroidered carpet, Xen.; ῥαπτὴ σφαῖρα a stitched ball, of divers colours, Anth.

ῬΑ῾ΠΤΩ, f. ῥάψω: aor. 1 ἔρραψα, Ep. ῥάψα:—Med., aor. 1 ἐρραψάμην:—Pass., aor. 2 ἐρράφην [ᾰ]: pf. ἔρραμμαι:—to sew or stitch together, stitch, Il., Ar.:—Med., ῥάπτεσθαι ὀχετὸν δερμάτων to make oneself a pipe of leather, Hdt.; ῥαψάμενος τουτί (sc. τὸ προσκεφάλαιον) having got it stitched, Ar.; but also, to sew on or to one, Id.:—Pass., ἐρράφθαι τὸ χεῖλος to have one's lip sewed up, Dem. II. metaph. to devise, contrive, plot, Hom., etc.: proverb., τὸ ὑπόδημα ἔρραψας μὲν σύ, ὑπεδήσατο δὲ Ἀρισταγόρης you made the shoe, but Aristagoras put it on, Hdt.

Ῥᾶρος, ου, ὁ, Raros, father of Triptolemus:—hence τὸ

Ῥάριον (sc. πεδίον) the field of Rarus, sacred to Demeter, where tillage was first practised, h. Hom.
ῥάσσατε, irreg. 2 pl. aor. 1 of ῥαίνω.
ῥᾷστος, irreg. Sup. of ῥᾴδιος.
ῥᾳστωνεύω, = ῥαθυμέω, to be idle, listless, Xen. From
ῥᾳστώνη, Ion. ῥῃστώνη, ἡ, (ῥᾷστος) easiness or an easy way of doing anything, Plat.; ῥᾳστώνῃ or μετὰ ῥᾳστώνης with ease, easily, lightly, Id.; ῥᾳστώνην φυγῆς παρέχειν to provide an easy way of escape, Plut.   II. easiness of temper, good nature, kindness, Lat. facilitas, τινός to or towards a person, Hdt.   III. relief or recovery from, τῆς πόσεως from the effects of drinking, Plat.: absol. rest, leisure, ease, Id.; διὰ ῥᾳστώνην for the sake of resting, Xen.: —also luxurious ease, indolence, carelessness, Thuc., Dem.
ῥᾰφᾰνῑδόω, to thrust a radish up the fundament, a punishment of adulterers in Athens, Ar.   From
ῬΑ'ΦΑ'ΝΙΣ, ῖδος, ἡ, the radish, Lat. raphanus, Ar.
ῥᾰφεύς, έως, ὁ, (ῥάπτω) a stitcher, patcher: metaph., ῥ. φόνου a planner of murder, Aesch.
ῥᾰφή, ἡ, (ῥάπτω) a seam, Lat. sutura, Od.   2. the suture of the skull, Hdt.; so, ῥαφαὶ ὀστέων Eur.
ῥᾰφίς, Dor. ῥαπίς, ίδος, ἡ, (ῥάπτω) a needle, Anth.
ῥᾱχία, Ion. ῥηχίη, ἡ, (ῥήγνυμι, cf. ῥηγμῖν) the sea breaking on the shore, esp. the flood-tide, opp. to ἄμπωτις, Hdt.   II. a rocky shore or beach, Aesch., Thuc.
ῥᾱχίζω, f. ίσω, to cut through the spine, to cleave in twain, Aesch., Soph.   From
ῬΑ'ΧΙΣ [ᾰ], ιος Att. εως, ἡ, the lower part of the back, the chine, Il.: then, the spine or backbone, ὑπὸ ῥάχιν παγῆναι to be impaled, Aesch.   II. anything ridged like the backbone, a mountain-ridge, Hdt.
ῥᾱχι-ώδης, ες, (ῥαχία, εἶδος) with surf, Strab.
ῥᾱχός, Ion. ῥηχός, οῦ, ἡ, a thorn-bush, briar, Xen.: — collectively, a thorn-hedge, a wattled fence, Hdt.
ῥάψαι, aor. 1 inf. of ῥάπτω.
ῥαψῳδέω, f. ήσω, (ῥαψῳδός) to recite Epic poems, Plat.   2. in contemptuous sense, to repeat by heart or rote, to declaim, Dem., Luc.; c. inf. to keep saying that . . , Dem.
ῥαψῳδία, ἡ, (ῥαψῳδός) recitation of Epic poetry, Plat.   2. Epic composition, opp. to lyric (κιθαρῳδία), Id.   II. a portion of an Epic poem fit for recitation at one time, e. g. a book of the Iliad or Odyssey, a lay, canto, Plut., Luc.
ῥαψῳδικός, ή, όν, of or for a rhapsodist: ἡ -κή (with and without τέχνη), the rhapsodist's art, Plat.   From
ῥαψ-ῳδός, ὁ, (ῥάπτω, ᾠδή) properly one who stitches or strings songs together: esp. a person who recited Epic poems, a rhapsodist, applied to Homer, Plat.; but ῥαψῳδοὶ commonly meant a class of persons who got their living by reciting the poems of Homer, Plat.; v. ῥαψῳδία II.   II. Soph. calls the Sphinx ῥαψῳδὸς κύων, because she proposed her riddle publicly, as the rhapsodists did their lays.
ῥᾴων, irreg. Comp. of ῥᾴδιος.
ῥέα = ῥεῖα, easily, lightly, Il. [Sometimes used as one long syll.]
Ῥέα, Ep. Ῥείη, ἡ; also Ῥέη, Rhea, daughter of Uranus and Gaia, wife of Cronus, mother of the gods, Hom., etc.

ΡΈΓΚΩ, f. ῥέγξω, to snore, Lat. sterto, Aesch., Ar.; of horses, to snort, Eur.   (Formed from the sound.)
ῥέεθρον, Ion. and poët. for ῥεῖθρον.
ΡΈΖΩ, impf. ἔρεζον, Ep. ῥέζον, Ion. ῥέζεσκον: f. ῥέξω: aor. 1 ἔρρεξα, poët. ῥέξα, Dor. part. ῥέξαις:—Pass., aor. 1 part. ῥεχθείς:—to do, act, deal, Od.:—absol., Hom.:—c. acc. rei, to do, accomplish, make, Id., etc.: —Pass., μῆχος ῥεχθέντος κακοῦ a remedy for mischief once done, Il.   2. c. dupl. acc. pers. et rei, to do something to one, κακὸν ῥέξειν τινά Hom.; ἀγαθὰ ῥ. τινά Id.; also more rarely c. dat. pers., μηκέτι μοι κακὰ ῥέζετε do me no more mischiefs, Od.; ὅσα βροτοῖς ἔρεξας κακά Eur.   3. with strengthd. signf., εἴ τι ῥέξει if it shall avail aught, be of any service, Il.   II. in spec. sense, to perform sacrifices, Hom., Soph.; absol. to do sacrifice, Lat. operari, facere, ῥέζω θεῷ Hom.:—sometimes with the victim in acc., ῥέξω βοῦν ἧνιν will sacrifice it, Id.
ῥέθος, εος, τό, a limb, in pl. the limbs, body, Il.   II. in sing. the face, countenance, Soph., Eur.
ῥεῖα, Ep. for ῥέα, Adv. of ῥᾴδιος, easily, lightly, Hom.; θεοὶ ῥεῖα ζώοντες the gods who live at ease, Lat. securum agentes aevom, Id.; strengthd. ῥεῖα μάλ' Il.
ῥεῖθρον, τό, Att. contr. from Ion. ῥέεθρον, (ῥέω) that which flows, a river, stream, mostly in pl., ποταμοῖο ῥέεθρα Il.; Στυγὸς ὕδατος αἶπα ῥ. Ib.; streams of blood, Aesch.:—sing., Hdt., Aesch.   II. the bed or channel of a river, Il., Hdt.
ῥείω, Ep. for ῥέω.
ῥεκτήρ, ῆρος, ὁ, (ῥέζω) a worker, doer, Hes.
ῥέκτης, ου, ὁ, = ῥεκτήρ, active, Plut.
ῥέμβομαι, Dep. to roam, rove, roll about, Plut.: metaph. to be unsteady, act at random, Id.
ῥεμβ-ώδης, ες, (εἶδος) roving, rolling, Plut.
ῥέξαι, aor. 1 inf. of ῥέζω.
ῥέος, τό, (ῥέω) = ῥεῦμα, a stream, Aesch.
ΡΈΠΩ, f. ῥέψω: aor. 1 ἔρρεψα:—properly of the descending scale, to incline downwards, to sink, fall, Lat. vergere, inclinare, Il., Ar.:—of things, to incline one way or the other, to be always shifting, Pind.; ὕπνος ἐπὶ βλεφάροις ῥέπων sleep falling upon the eyes, Id.   2. of one of two contending parties, to preponderate, prevail, Hdt., Plat.   3. of persons, εὖ ῥέπει θεός is favourably inclined, Aesch.; ῥέπειν ἐπί τι to incline towards a thing, Dem.; εἴς or πρός τι Plat., Arist.; εἴς τινα Luc.   4. of duties, ῥ. εἴς τινα to fall or devolve upon one, Aesch., Soph.   5. of events, to fall, happen in a certain way, Soph.; ῥ. εἴς τι to turn or come to something, Aesch., Ar.
ῥερυπωμένος, pf. pass. part. of ῥυπόομαι.
ῥεῦμα, ατος, τό, (ῥέω) that which flows, a flow, stream, current, Aesch., Soph., etc.   2. the stream of a river, mostly in pl., Hdt., Eur.; a stream of lava, Thuc.: metaph. a stream or flood of men, Trag., Soph.   3. a flood, Thuc.   II. a discharge from the body, a flux, rheum, Luc.   Hence
ῥευμᾱτίζομαι, Pass. to flow as a current, Strab.
ῥευμάτιον, τό, Dim. of ῥεῦμα, a rivulet, Plut.
ῥεύσομαι, fut. of ῥέω.
ῥεχθείς, aor. 1 pass. part. of ῥέζω.
ῥευστικός, ή, όν, (ῥέω) flowing, liquid, Plut.
ΡΈΩ, Ep. ῥείω: 3 sing. impf. ἔρρει, Ep. ἔρρεε or

ῥέε :—f. ῥεύσομαι, Dor. ῥευσοῦμαι : aor. 1 ἔρρευσα :— Att. fut. and aor. 1 of pass. form, ῥυήσομαι, ἐρρύην : pf. ἐρρύηκα Plat.—This Verb, like πνέω, χέω, does not contr. εη, εο, εω. *To flow, run, stream, gush,* Hom., etc. :—with dat. of that which flows, πηγὴ ῥέει ὕδατι the fountain *runs with* water, Il. ; ῥέεν αἵματι γαῖα Ib. ; ῥεῖ γάλακτι πέδον Eur. ; of a river, μέγας ῥε᾿ *runs* with full stream, Hdt. ; so, πολὺς ῥεῖ, metaph. of men, Aesch. ; of a river, also, ῥ. ἀπὸ χιόνος *to derive its stream* from melted snow, Hdt. :—proverb., ἄνω ῥέειν *to flow* backwards, of impossibilities, Eur.　2. metaph. of things, ἐκ χειρῶν βέλεα ῥέον from their hands *rained* darts, Il. ; of a *flow* of words, ἀπὸ γλώσσης μέλιτος γλυκίων ῥέεν αὐδή Ib. ; absol., of the tongue, *to run glibly,* Aesch. (cf. Horat., *salso multoque fluenti*) : of words or sentiments, *to be current,* Soph.　3. *to fall, drop* off, e. g. of hair, Od., Theocr. : then, generally, *to flow* or *melt away, perish,* Soph., Plat.　4. of persons, ῥ. ἐπί or ἔς τι *to be inclined, given* to a thing, Isocr., Plat.　II. very rarely trans. *to let flow, pour,* ἔρρει χοάς Eur.　2. c. acc. cogn., ῥείτω γάλα, μέλι *let* the land *run* milk, honey, Theocr. ; οἶνον ῥέων Luc.

*ῥέω, *to say,* v. ἐρῶ.

ῥῆγμα, ατος, τό, (ῥήγνυμι) *a breakage, fracture,* Dem.

ῥηγμίν or -μίς, ῖνος, ὁ, *the sea breaking on the beach, the line of breakers, surf,* Hom. ; ἐπὶ or παρὰ ῥηγμῖνι θαλάσσης by *the edge of the sea,* Il.

ῥήγνυμι or -ύω (lengthd. from Root ΡΑΓ) : Ion. impf. ῥήγνυσκον : f. ῥήξω : aor. 1 ἔρρηξα :—Med., ῥήγνυμαι, f. ῥήξομαι : aor. 1 ἐρρηξάμην, Ep. ῥηξάμην :—Pass., f. ῥαγήσομαι : aor. 2 ἐρράγην [ᾰ] : pf. ἔρρηγμαι, for which the intr. ἔρρωγα is more used :—cf. also ῥήσσω, ῥάσσω.　*To break, break asunder* or *in pieces, rend, shiver, shatter,* Hom., etc. :—*to rend* garments, in sign of grief, Aesch. :—Med. *to break for oneself, get broken,* Il.　2. *to break* a line of battle or body of men, Ib., Hdt. ; in Med., ῥήξασθαι φάλαγγας, στίχας *to break oneself a way* through the lines, Il. ; absol., ῥήξασθαι *to break* or *force one's way,* Ib.　3. *to let break loose, let loose,* Ib.　4. ῥῆξαι φωνήν *to let loose* the voice, of children and persons who have been dumb *breaking into* speech, Hdt. : then *to speak freely, speak out* (like *rumpere vocem,* Virg.), Id., Ar., etc.　5. δακρύων ῥήξασα νάματα having *let loose* floods of tears, Soph. ; so, ῥ. κλαυθμόν Plut.　II. absol. in the form ῥήσσω, *to beat the ground, dance,* Il.　III. later, as a term of fighters, *to fell, knock down,* Dem.

B. Pass., mostly used in aor. 2 ἐρράγην [ᾰ], *to break, burst,* of waves, Il. ; of clouds, Ar.　2. *to break asunder, be rent,* of the earth in an earthquake, Plat. ; of garments, Xen.　3. *to burst forth,* like lightning, Ar.　4. of ships, *to be wrecked,* Dem. : metaph. of hopes, Aesch.

C. intr., like Pass., *to break forth,* of a river, *to break its bounds,* Hdt. :—metaph. of sudden misfortunes, bursts of passion, Soph.　II. in this intr. sense the pf. ἔρρωγα is commonly used of tears, Id. ; metaph., κακῶν πέλαγος ἔρρωγεν Aesch., etc.

ΡΗΓΟΣ, εος, τό, *a rug, blanket,* used as *the covering of a bed* or seat, Hom. ; or as *a garment,* Od.

ῥήδιος, Ion. contr. form for ῥηΐδιος.

ῥηθῆναι, aor. 1 pass. inf. of ἐρῶ : ῥηθήσομαι, fut.

ῥηΐδιος, Ion. for ῥάδιος :—ῥηΐζω, for ῥαΐζω.

ῥήϊστος, ῥήϊτατος, ῥηΐτερος, v. ῥάδιος.

ῥηκτός, ή, όν, (ῥήγνυμι) *that can be broken* or *rent, penetrable,* Il.

ῥῆμα, ατος, τό, (ῥέω, ἐρῶ) *that which is said* or *spoken, a word, saying,* Theogn., Hdt., etc. ; κατὰ ῥῆμα *word for word,* Aeschin.　2. *a phrase,* opp. to ὄνομα (a single word), Plat.　3. *the subject of speech, a thing,* N. T.　II. in Gramm., *a verb,* opp. to ὄνομα (a noun), ῥήματα καὶ ὀνόματα Plat.

ῥημάτιον, τό, Dim. of ῥῆμα, *a pet phrase, phrasicle,* Ar.

ῥήν, ῥηνός, ἡ, late word = *ἄρς, ἀρνός. Hence

ῥηνο-φορεύς, ὁ, (φέρω) *clad in sheepskin,* Anth.

ῥῆξαι, aor. 1 inf. of ῥήγνυμι.

ῥηξηνορία, ἡ, *might to break through armed ranks,* Od.　From

ῥηξ-ήνωρ, ορος, ὁ, (ῥήγνυμι, ἀνήρ) *breaking through armed ranks,* Hom.

ῥηξῐ-κέλευθος, ον, *opening a path,* of Apollo, Anth.

ῥηξί-νοος, ον, *breaking the spirit,* of Bacchus, Anth.

ῥῆξις, εως, ἡ, (ῥήγνυμαι) *a breaking, bursting,* ῥήξεις broken flames, a bad omen, Eur.

ῥῆσις, εως, Ion. ιος, ἡ, (*ῥέω, ἐρῶ) *a saying, speaking, speech,* Od., Hdt., etc. ; ἡ ἀπὸ Σκυθῶν ῥῆσις the Scythian *phrase,* Hdt.　2. *a resolution, declaration,* Id.　II. *a tale, legend,* Pind.　III. *a phrase* or *passage, a speech in a play,* Ar.

ῥήσσω, rarer collat. form of ῥήγνυμι.

ῥηστώνη, ἡ, Ion. for ῥαστώνη.

ῥητέον, verb. Adj. *one must mention,* Plat.

ῥήτερος, Ion. for ῥηΐτερος.

ῥητήρ, ῆρος, ὁ, (*ῥέω, ἐρῶ) *a speaker,* Il.

ῥητορεία, ἡ, *skill in public speaking, eloquence, oratory, rhetoric,* Plat.　II. *a piece of oratory, set speech,* Isocr.　From

ῥητορεύω, f. σω, (ῥήτωρ) *to speak in public, to use* or *practise oratory,* Plat. :—Pass., of the speech, *to be spoken,* Isocr.　II. *to teach oratory,* Strab.

ῥητορικός, ή, όν, (ῥήτωρ) *oratorical, rhetorical,* ἡ ῥητορική (sc. τέχνη) *rhetoric, the art of speaking,* Plat. ; ῥητορικὴ δειλία *an orator's* timidity, Aeschin. :— Adv. -κῶς, Plat.　2. of persons, *skilled in speaking, fit to be an orator,* Id., etc.

ῥητός, ή, όν, verb. Adj. of *ῥέω, ἐρῶ, *stated, specified,* Il. ; ἐς χρόνον ῥητόν at a set or stated time, Hdt. ; ἡμέραι ῥ. Thuc. ; ἐπὶ ῥητοῖς γέρασι with *fixed* prerogatives, Id. ; ῥ. ἀργυρίου a *stated* sum, Id. ; ἐπὶ ῥητοῖς on *stated* terms, on certain conditions, Hdt., Eur. :—Adv. ῥητῶς, *expressly, distinctly,* N. T.　2. *spoken of, known, famous,* Hes.　II. *that may be spoken* or *told,* Aesch., Soph. ; ῥητὸν ἄρρητόν τ' ἔπος, Lat. *fas nefasque,* Soph.　III. in Mathem., ῥητά are *rational quantities,* opp. to surds (ἄλογα), Plat.

ῥήτρα, ἡ, Ion. ῥήτρη, (*ῥέω, ἐρῶ) *a verbal agreement, bargain, covenant,* Od. ; παρὰ τὴν ῥήτραν Xen.　II. *the unwritten laws* of Lycurgus were called ῥῆτραι, Lex ap. Plut. : generally, *a decree, ordinance,* Tyrtae., Xen.　III. *speech, a word,* Luc.

ῥήτωρ, ορος, ὁ, (*ῥέω, ἐρῶ) *a public speaker, pleader,* Lat. *orator,* Eur., etc.

ῥηχίη, ῥηχός, Ion. for ῥαχία, ῥᾶχός.

ῥῑγεδᾰνός, ή, όν, making one shudder with cold, chilling: metaph., ῥιγεδανὴ Ἑλένη Helen at whose name one shudders, horrible, Il. From

ῥῑγέω, f. -ήσω: aor. ι ἐρρίγησα, Ep. ῥίγησα: pf. (with pres. sense) ἔρρῑγα, Dor. 3 pl. ἐρρίγαντι, Ep. 3 sing. subj. ἐρρίγῃσι; Ep. dat. part. ἐρρίγοντι (for ἐρριγότι): plqpf. ἐρρίγειν: (ῥῖγος):—to shiver or shudder with cold: metaph. to shudder with fear or horror, Il., Soph. :—c. inf. to shudder to do, shrink from doing, Il.; also, ῥ. μή .., Od. 2. to cool or slacken in zeal, Pind. 3. to bristle with arms, Theocr. II. trans. to shudder at anything, Il.

ῥῑγηλός, ή, όν, making to shiver, chilling, Hes.

ῥίγιον, neut. Comp. Adj. formed from ῥῖγος, more frosty, colder, Od. :—metaph. more horrible, Hom.

ῥίγιστος, η, ον, Sup. Adj. formed from ῥῖγος (as κύδιστος from κῦδος), coldest: most horrible, Il.

ῥῑγο-μάχης, or -χος, ου, ὁ, (μάχομαι) fighting with cold, Anth.

ῬΙ´ΓΟΣ, εος, τό, frost, cold, Lat. frigus, Od., etc.

ῥῑγόω, f. -ώσω, Ep. inf. -ωσέμεν:—aor. ι ἐρρίγωσα:—pf. ἐρρίγωκα:—this word, like ἱδρόω, has an irreg. contr. into ω, ῳ, for ου, οι, as 3 sing. subj. ῥιγῷ, opt. ῥιγῴη, inf. ῥιγῶν:—to be cold, shiver from cold, Od., Hdt.

ῬΙ´ΖΑ, ης, ή, a root, Od., Att.: in pl. the roots, Hom. 2. metaph. the roots of the eye, Od.; the roots or foundations of the earth, Hes., Aesch., etc. 3. ἐκ ῥιζῶν, Lat. radicitus, Plut. II. anything that grows like a root from one stem, whence Pindar calls Libya the τρίτη ῥίζα χθονός, considering the earth as divided into three continents. III. metaph. the root or stock from which a family springs, Lat. stirps, Pind., Aesch., etc.; and so a race, family, Aesch., Eur., etc.

ῥιζίον, τό, Dim. of ῥίζα, a little root, Ar.

ῥιζοβολέω, f. ήσω, to strike root, Anth. From

ῥιζο-βόλος, ον, (βάλλω) striking root.

ῥιζόθεν, (ῥίζα) Adv. by, from the roots, Luc.

ῥιζο-τόμος, ὁ, (τέμνω) one who cuts roots, Luc.

ῥιζοφᾰγέω, f. ήσω, to eat roots, Strab.; ῥ. τὰ σπέρματα to destroy them by nibbling the roots, Id. From

ῥιζο-φάγος [ᾰ], ον, (φαγεῖν) eating roots, Arist.

ῥιζόω, f. ώσω: aor. ι ἐρρίζωσα:—Pass., pf. ἐρρίζωμαι: (ῥίζα):—to make to strike root: metaph. to root in the ground, plant, Od.; ἐρρίζωσε τὴν τυραννίδα Hdt.:—Pass. to take root, strike root, Xen.: metaph. to be rooted, firmly fixed, Soph., N.T. II. Pass. also of land, to be planted with trees, Od. Hence

ῥίζωμα, ατος, τό, a root: metaph. a stem, race, Aesch.

ῥιζ-ωρύχος, ον, root-grubbing, of grammarians, Anth.

ῥίζωσις, εως, ή, a taking root, beginning life, Plut.

ῬΙΚΝΟ´Σ, ή, όν, shrivelled with cold: generally, shrivelled, crooked, h. Hom., Anth.

ῥιμφᾰ, (ῥίπτω) Adv. lightly, swiftly, fleetly, Il., Aesch.

ῥιμφ-άρμᾱτος, ον, (ἅρμα) of a swift chariot, Pind.; ῥ. ἀμίλλαις with the swift racing of chariots, Soph.

ῥίν, ή, later form for ῥίς.

ῥῑνάω, f. ήσω, (ῥίνη) to file, Anth.

ῥῑν-εγκατάπηξι-γένειος, ον, (ῥίς, ἐγκαταπήγνυμι) with a nose reaching to the chin, Anth.

ῬΙ´ΝΗ [ῑ], ή, a file or rasp, Xen.

ῥῑνηλᾰτέω, f. ήσω, to track by scent, Aesch. From

ῥῑν-ηλάτης, ου, ὁ, (ἐλαύνω) one who tracks by scent, of hounds.

ῥῑνό-βολος, ον, (βάλλω) emitted through the nose, of a snorting sound, Anth.

ῥῑνό-κερως, ωτος, ὁ, (ῥίς, κέρας) the Rhinoceros or Nose-horn, Strab.

ῥῑνόν, τό, = ῥινός II. 1, a hide, Il. 2. = ῥινός II. 2, a shield, Od.

ῥῑνός, οῦ, ή, the skin of a man, Hom. II. the hide of a beast, esp. an ox-hide, Id. 2. an ox-hide shield, Id.

ῥῑνό-σῑμος, ον, (ῥίς) snub-nosed, Luc.

ῥῑνο-τόρος, ον, (τείρω) shield-piercing, Il., Hes.

ῥῑν-οῦχος, ὁ, (ῥίς II) a sewer, Lat. cloaca, Strab.

ῬΙ´ΟΝ, τό, any jutting part of a mountain, 1. the peak, Hom. 2. a headland, foreland, Od., Thuc.

ῥίπεσσι, Ep. for ῥιψί, dat. pl. of ῥίψ.

ῥῑπή, ή, (ῥίπτω) the swing or force with which anything is thrown, Lat. impetus, αἰγανέης ῥιπή the flight of a javelin, Il.; ῥιπὴ Βορέαο the sweep or rush of the N. wind, Ib.; ῥιπὴ Διόθεν, of a storm, Aesch.; ἐννυχιᾶν ἀπὸ ῥιπᾶν prob. means from the quarter of the night storms, i.e. from the North, Soph.; ῥ. πυρός the rush of fire, Il. 2. ῥ. πτερύγων a flapping of wings, Aesch.; of the buzz of a gnat's wing, Id.; of quivering light, ῥιπαὶ ἄστρων Soph.; of any rapid movement, ῥ. ποδῶν Eur.; ἐν ῥιπῇ ὀφθαλμοῦ in the twinkling of an eye, N.T.

ῥιπίζω, f. ίσω, (ῥιπίς) to fan the flame, Lat. conflare, Ar. :—Pass. to be blown about, N.T.

ῥιπίς, ίδος, ή, (ῥίψ) a fan for raising the fire, Ar. II. a lady's fan, Anth.

ῥιπτάζω, f. άσω, Frequentative of ῥίπτω, to throw to and fro, toss about, Lat. jactare, Il.; ὀφρύσι ῥιπτάζειν to move the eyebrows up and down, h. Hom. :—Pass. to be tossed about, Plut.

ῥιπτέω, only in pres. and impf., a collat. form of ῥίπτω, Trag.; Ion. contr. 3 pl. ῥιπτεῦσι, Hdt.

ῥιπτός, ή, όν, verb. Adj. of ῥίπτω, thrown, ῥ. μόρος death by being thrown down (a precipice), Soph.

ῬΙ´ΠΤΩ, Ion. impf. ῥίπτασκον or -εσκον: f. ῥίψω: aor. ι ἔρριψα, Ep. ῥίψα: pf. ἔρριφα:—Pass., f. ι ῥιφθήσομαι, f. 2 ῥίφήσομαι, f. 3 ἐρρίψομαι: aor. ι ἐρρίφθην, aor. 2 ἐρρίφην [ῐ]: pf. ἔρριμμαι: 3 sing. plqpf. ἔρριπτο, Ep. ἐρέριπτο:—to throw, cast, hurl, Hom., etc.; ῥ. χθονί to throw on the ground, Soph. :—to cast a net, Pass., ἔρριπται ὁ βόλος the cast has been made, Orac. ap. Hdt. :—to throw or toss about, πλοκάμους Eur. II. to cast out of house or land, Soph. :—Pass., μὴ ῥιφθῶ κυσίν Id. III. to throw off or away, of arms, clothes, Eur., etc. IV. ῥ. λόγους to cast them forth, hurl them, Aesch., Eur. :—but also, to throw them away, waste them, Aesch., Eur.: Pass., οἴχεται ταῦτ' ἐρριμμένα Soph. V. to cast lots or dice, Eur., Plat. VI. ῥ. ἑαυτόν to throw or cast oneself down, Xen.;—then absol. to fling oneself, ἐς πόντον Theogn.; ἐς τάφρον Eur.

ῥιφθείς, ῥιπείς, aor. ι and 2 pass. part. of ῥίπτω.

ῬΙ´Σ, ή, gen. ῥινός, acc. ῥῖνα, pl. ῥῖνες:—the nose, Lat. nasus, Hom., Hdt., etc. 2. in pl. the nostrils, nose, Lat. nares, Il., etc. II. a pipe or conduit.

ΡΙΨ, ῥῑπός, dat. pl. ῥιψί, Ep. ῥίπεσσι :—plaited work, wicker-work, a mat, Lat. crates, Od., etc.

ῥίψ-ασπις, ιδος, ὁ, ἡ, throwing away his shield in battle, a recreant, Ar.

ῥῖψις, εως, ἡ, a throwing, casting, hurling, Plat. 2. a casting about of the eyes, Plut. II. a being thrown or hurled, Plat.

ῥιψο-κίνδυνος, ον, running needless risks, fool-hardy, reckless, Xen.

ῥίψ-οπλος, ον, throwing away one's arms, Aesch.

ῥόα, ἡ, Ion. and Ep. ῥοιή, a pomegranate-tree, Od. II. the fruit, a pomegranate, h. Hom., Ar. 2. a knob shaped like a pomegranate, Hdt.

ῥοά, ἡ, Dor. for ῥοή, a stream.

ῥοδάνη [ᾰ], ἡ, the woof or weft, Batr. From

ῥοδανός, ή, όν, waving, flickering, Il. (Deriv. uncertain.)

ῥόδεος, α, ον, (ῥόδον) of roses, Eur. II. like a rose, rosy, Anth.

ῥοδῆ, ἡ, contr. for ῥοδέα, a rose-tree, rose-bush, Archil.

Ῥοδιακός, ή, όν, (Ῥόδος) Rhodian, of Rhodes, Strab. :—also Ῥόδιος, α, ον, (Ῥόδος) Il., Xen.

ῥοδο-δάκτυλος, ον, rosy-fingered, of Aurora, Hom.

ῥοδο-ειδής, ές, (εἶδος) rose-like, rosy, Anth.

ῥοδόεις, εσσα, εν, (ῥόδον) of roses, Il., Eur. II. rose-coloured, Anth.

ῥοδό-μηλον, Dor. -μᾱλον, τό, a rose-apple : metaph. of a rosy cheek, Theocr.

ΡΟ´ΔΟΝ, τό, the rose, Lat. rosa, h. Hom., Theogn., etc. ; Aeol. βρόδον, Sappho :—metaph. ῥόδα μ' εἴρηκας you've spoken roses of me, have said all things sweet and lovely, Ar.

ῥοδό-πηχυς, Dor. -πᾱχυς, υ, gen. υος, rosy-armed, h. Hom., Hes., etc.

Ῥόδος, ου, ἡ, the isle of Rhodes, Il., etc.

ῥοδό-χρως, ωτος, ὁ, ἡ, = foreg., Theocr.

ῥοδωνιά, ἡ, (ῥόδον) a rose-bed, garden of roses, Lat. rosarium, Dem., etc.

ῥοή, ἡ, Dor. ῥοά, but in Att. ῥοή, Ep. gen. pl. ῥοάων [ᾰ] : (ῥέω) :—a river, stream, flood, Hom., etc. ; mostly in pl., ἐπ' Ὠκεανοῖο ῥοάων Il. ; ἀμπέλου ῥοαί the juice of the grape, Eur. :—metaph. the stream of song or poesy, Pind. ; also, ῥοαί the tide of affairs, Id.

ῥοθέω, f. ήσω, (ῥόθος) to make a rushing noise, to dash, of waves or the stroke of oars : hence, of any confused noise, ταῦτα ἐρρόθουν ἐμοί such clamours they raised against me, Soph. ; λόγοι ἐρρόθουν there was a noise of words, Id.

ῥοθιάζω, strengthd. form of foreg., of pigs, to make a guttling noise, Ar.

ῥοθιάς, άδος, ἡ, poët. fem. of ῥόθιος, dashing, Aesch.

ῥόθιος, ον, and α, ον, (ῥόθος) rushing, roaring, dashing, of waves, Od. ; of oars, Eur. II. as Subst. ῥόθια, τά, waves dashing on the beach, breakers, waves, Soph., etc. ;—collectively in sing. the surf, surge, Aesch., Eur. 2. a shout of applause, Ar. ; generally, a tumult, riot, Eur.

ΡΟ´ΘΟΣ, ὁ, a rushing noise, dash of waves or of oars, ἐξ ἑνὸς ῥόθου with one stroke, i. e. all at once, Aesch. 2. of any confused, inarticulate sound, Περσίδος γλώσσης ῥ. the noise of the Persian (i. e. barbarian) tongue, Id. (Formed from the sound.)

ῥοιά, ἡ, later Att. for ῥόα, mulberry.

ῥοιβδέω, f. ήσω, to swallow with a noise, suck down, of Charybdis, Od. ; cf. ἀναρροιβδέω. II. like ῥοιζέω, to move with a rustling sound, make to rustle, Aesch. Hence

ῥοίβδησις, ἡ, a whistling, piping, Eur.

ΡΟΙ˘ΒΔΟΣ, ὁ, any rushing noise, πτερῶν ῥ. the whirring of wings, Soph. ; ἀνέμου ῥ. whistling of the wind, Ar. (Formed from the sound.)

ῥοιζέω, Ion. impf. ῥοίζασκον or -εσκον : aor. 1 ἐρροίζησα, Ep. ῥοίζησα : (ῥοῖζος) :—to whistle, Lat. stridere, Il. ; of a snake, to hiss, Hes. :—Pass. to rush through the air, ἐρροίζητο (3 sing. plqpf.) Anth. Hence

ῥοίζημα, ατος, τό, a rushing, whirring noise or motion, as of birds, Ar. From

ΡΟΙ˘ΖΟΣ, ὁ, Ion. ἡ, the whistling or whizzing of an arrow, Il. :—any whistling or piping sound, as of a shepherd, Od. II. rushing motion, a rush, swing, Plut. (Formed from the sound.)

ῥοικός, ή, όν, crooked, Theocr.

ῥομβητός, ή, όν, spun round like a top, Anth.

ῥομβο-ειδής, ές, (εἶδος) rhomboïdal, Strab. ; ῥ. σχῆμα a rhomboïd, a four-sided figure with the opposite sides and angles equal.

ῥόμβος or ῥύμβος, ὁ, (ῥέμβω) a spinning-top or wheel, Lat. turbo, Eur., Anth. 2. a magic wheel, used by sorcerers to aid their spells, Theocr., Horat. II. a spinning, whirling motion, of a top or wheel, ἱέντα ῥόμβον ἀκόντων shooting forth whirling darts, Pind. ; ῥ. αἰετοῦ the eagle's swoop, Id. III. a rhomb, lozenge, i. e. a four-sided figure with all the sides, but only the opposite angles, equal, Euclid. 2. a fish, the turbot, brill.

ῥομβωτός, ή, όν, verb. Adj. (ῥόμβος III.), lozenge-shaped, Anth.

ῥομφαία, ἡ, a large sword, scymitar, used by the Thracians, Plut., N. T. (Foreign word.)

ῥόος, ου, ὁ, Att. contr. ῥοῦς, (ῥέω) a stream, flow, current, Hom., etc. ; ποταμοὺς ἔτρεψε νέεσθαι κὰρ ῥόον to flow in their own bed, Il. ; κατὰ ῥόον down stream, Od., Hdt., etc. ; πρὸς ῥόον against stream, Il. :—a current at sea, Thuc.

ῥόπαλον, τό, (ῥέπω) a club, cudgel, thicker at the buttend ; used to cudgel an ass, Il. ; to walk with, Od., etc. :—a war-club or mace, shod with metal, Ib., Hdt. II. = ῥόπτρον III., Xen.

ῥοπή, ἡ, (ῥέπω) inclination downwards, the sinking of the scale, Aesch. ; διαφέρειν τὴν ῥ. to disturb the balance, Plut. 2. metaph. the turn of the scale, the critical moment, Lat. momentum, ἔχεται ῥοπᾶς (sc. ἡ πόλις) is at a crisis of her fortunes, Alcae. ap. Ar. ; ῥ. Δίκας the balance or critical turn of Justice, Aesch. ; σμικρὰ παλαιὰ σώματ' εὐνάζει ῥοπή a slight turn of the scale lays aged bodies to rest, Soph. ; ἐπὶ σμικρᾶς ῥοπῆς dependent on a slight turn of the scale, of one dying, Eur. ; ἐπὶ ῥοπῆς μιᾶς ὄντες depending on a single turn of the scale, Thuc. ; ῥ. βίου the turning point of life, i. e. death, Soph. II. metaph. influence, Dem.

ῥόπτρον, τό, (ῥέπω) the wood in a mouse-trap which springs up when touched, Archil. ; metaph., δίκης ῥόπτρον Eur. II. a tambourine or kettle-

drum, Luc., Anth.　　**III.** *the knocker on a house-door*, Eur.

ῥοῦς, ὁ, Att. contr. for ῥόος.

ῥούσιος, ον, *reddish*, Lat. *russus*, Anth.

ῥοφέω, f. ήσω and ήσομαι: aor. 1 ἐρρόφησα:—*to sup greedily up, gulp down*, Aesch., Ar.　　2. *to drain dry, empty*, Ar.; so, ῥ. ἀρτηρίας, of the poison on the robe of Hercules, Soph.　　Hence

ῥοφητικός, ή, όν, *drawing in, absorbing*, Strab.; and

ῥοφητός, ή, όν, *that can be* or *is supped up*, Strab.

ῥοχθέω, f. ήσω: Ep. 3 sing. impf. ῥόχθει:—*to dash with a roaring sound*, of the sea, Od.　　From

ΡΟ'ΧΘΟΣ, ὁ, *a roaring of the sea*.

ῥο-ώδης, ες, (εἶδος) *with a strong stream*, of a sea *in which there are strong currents*, Thuc.: of rocks, *exposed to such seas*, Strab.

ῥύαξ, ἄκος, ὁ, (ῥέω) *a rushing stream, a torrent*, Thuc.; ὁ ῥ. τοῦ πυρός, *of a stream of lava*, Id.

ῥύατο, Ep. for ἐρύοντο, 3 pl. aor. 2 of ῥύομαι.

ῥυγχ-ελέφας, ὁ, *with an elephant's trunk*, Anth.

ῥυγχίον, τό, Dim. of ῥύγχος, Ar.

ῥύγχος, εος, τό, (ῥύζω) *a snout, muzzle*, of swine, Stesich.; of dogs, Theocr.: of birds, *a beak, neb*, Ar.

ῥύδην [ῡ], Adv. (ῥέω) *flowingly, abundantly*, Plut.

ῥύδόν, Adv., = foreg., *abundantly*, Od.

ΡΥ'ΖΩ, *to growl, snarl*, ῥύζει ἐπίκλαυτον νόμον *snarls its melancholy ditty*, Ar. (Formed from the sound.)

ῥυήσομαι, Att. fut. of ῥέω.

ῥυθμίζω, f. Att. ιῶ: Pass., pf. ἐρρύθμισμαι: (ῥυθμός):—*to bring into measure* or *proportion*: generally, *to order, to educate, train*, Xen., etc.:—metaph., ῥ. λύπην ὅπου *to define the place of grief*, Soph.:—metaph., ῥ. πλόκαμον *to arrange one's hair*, Eur.:—Pass., νηλεῶς ὧδ' ἐρρύθμισμαι *thus ruthlessly am I brought to order*, Aesch.

ῥυθμός, Ion. ῥυσμός, ὁ, (ῥέω) *measured motion, time, rhythm*, Lat. *numerus*, Ar., Plat., etc.:—ἐν ῥυθμῷ *in time*, Virgil's *in numerum*, Xen.; μετὰ ῥυθμοῦ Thuc.; θάττονα ῥυθμὸν ἐπάγειν *to play in quicker time*, Xen.　　**II.** *proportion* or *symmetry* of parts, Plat.　　**III.** generally, *arrangement, order*, Eur.　　**IV.** *the state* or *condition of the soul, temper, disposition*, Theogn., etc.　　**V.** *the form* or *shape of a thing*, Hdt.; of a breastplate, Xen.　　**VI.** *the wise, manner* or *fashion of a thing*, Eur.; τίς ῥ. φόνου; *what kind of slaughter?* Id.

ῥυκάνη [ᾰ], ἡ, *a plane*, Anth. (Deriv. uncertain.)

ῥῦμα, ατος, τό, (*ῥύω = ἐρύω) *that which is drawn*: 1. τόξου ῥῦμα, i. e. the Persian *archers*, opp. to λόγχης ἰσχύς, i. e. the Greek *spearmen*, Aesch.; ἐκ τόξου ῥύματος *from the distance of a bow-shot*, Xen.　　2. *a towing-line*, Polyb.　　**II.** (ῥύομαι) *a defence, protection*, Eur.; πύργου ῥ. *a tower of defence*, Soph.

ῥύμη, ἡ, (*ῥύω = ἐρύω) *the force, swing, rush* of a body in motion, Lat. *impetus*, ῥύμῃ *with a swing*, Thuc.; πτερύγων ῥύμῃ *the rush of wings*, Ar.; ἡ ῥ. τῶν ἵππων Xen.:—metaph., εὐτυχεῖ ῥύμῃ θεοῦ Eur.; ἡ ῥ. τῆς ὀργῆς *the vehemence of* passion, Dem.　　2. absol. *a rush, charge*, of soldiers, Thuc., Xen.　　**II.** *a street*, Lat. *vicus*, Polyb., N. T.

ῥύμμα, ατος, τό, (ῥύπτω) *anything for washing, soap*, Plat.

ῥυμός, οῦ, ὁ, (*ῥύω = ἐρύω) *the pole of a carriage*, Il., Hdt.; ἐν πρώτῳ ῥυμῷ *at the end of the pole*, Il.

ῥῡμ-ουλκέω, (ῥῦμα 1. 2, ἕλκω) *to tow*, Polyb., etc.

ῥύομαι, f. ῥύσομαι [ῡ]: aor. 1 ἐρρῡσάμην: Ep. 3 sing. aor. 2 ἔρῡτο, 3 pl. ἔρυντο, ῥύατο [ῡ], inf. ῥῦσθαι:—Dep.: but an aor. 1 ἐρρύσθην used in pass. sense also occurs:—*to draw to oneself*, i. e. *draw out of danger, to rescue, save, deliver*, Hom., Hes., etc.; ῥ. τινα ὑπὲκ θανάτου, ὑπὲκ κακοῦ *to save* from .., Hom.;—so c. gen., ῥ. τινα τοῦ μὴ κατακαυθῆναι Hdt.; or c. inf. alone, ῥ. τινα θανεῖν or μὴ κατθανεῖν Eur.: also, *to save from an illness, cure*, Hdt.: *to set free, redeem*, Il.; ἐκ δουλοσύνης Hdt.　　**II.** generally, *to shield, guard, protect*, of guardian gods, chiefs, etc., Il. etc.:—of defensive armour, Ib.　　2. Soph. has ῥῦσαι in a double sense, ῥῦσαι σεαυτὸν .., *deliver* thyself, and ῥῦσαι δὲ μίασμα τοῦ τεθνηκότος *deliver* us *from* the pollution; so, ῥ. τὰς αἰτίας *to remove the* charges, Thuc.　　**III.** *to draw back, to hold back, check*, Od., Pind.　　**IV.** *to keep off*, Pind.

ῥύπα [ῡ], τά, heterocl. plur. of ῥύπος, ὁ.

ῥῠπαίνω, f. ῥῠπᾰῶ, (ῥύπος) *to defile, disfigure, disparage*, Arist.:—Pass. *to be* or *become foul*, Xen.

ῥῠπαρία, ἡ, *dirt, filth: sordidness*, Critias, Plut.

ῥῠπᾰρός, ά, όν, (ῥύπος) *foul, filthy, dirty*:—metaph. *dirty, sordid*, Arist.:—Adv. -ρῶς, Anth.

ῥῠπάω, Ep. -όω, only in pres. and impf., (ῥύπος) *to be foul, filthy, dirty*, Od.; impf. ἐρρύπων, Ar.

ῥῠπόεις, εσσα, εν, = ῥυπαρός, Anth.

ῥῠπόομαι, Pass. *to be foul*, pf. part. ῥερῠπωμένος, Ep. for ἐρρυπωμένοι, *fouled, soiled*, Od.　　From

ΡΥ'ΠΟΣ [ῡ], ὁ, *dirt, filth, dirtiness, uncleanness*, heterocl. pl. ῥύπα, Od.; in sing., Plat., etc.

ῥῠπόω, ῥυπόωντα, Ep. for ῥυπάω, ῥυπάοντα.

ῥυππαπαί, *a cry of the Athenian rowers, like* ὦόπ, *yoho!* Ar.; hence, τὸ ῥυππαπαί *one's messmates*, Ar.

ῥύπτω, f. ψω, (ῥύπος) *to remove dirt from* garments, *to wash*, Arist.:—Pass. *to wash oneself*, ἐξ ὅτου ἐγὼ ῥύπτομαι *ever since I began to wash*, i. e. from childhood, Ar.

ῥυσαίνομαι, (ῥυσός) Pass. *to be wrinkled*, Anth.

ῥῦσθαι, Ep. aor. 2 inf. of ῥύομαι.

ῥῠσιάζω, f. άσω, (ῥύσιον) *to seize as a pledge, to drag away*, Eur.:—Pass. *to be so dragged away*, Id.

ῥῠσί-βωμος, ον, *defending altars*, Aesch.

ῥῠσί-διφρος, ον, *preserving the chariot*, Pind.

ῥύσιον [ῡ], τό, (ῥύομαι) *that which is dragged away*: I. *booty, prey*, ῥύσια ἐλαύνεσθαι, of cattle, Il.; τοῦ ῥυσίου θ' ἥμαρτε, i. e. Helen., Aesch.　　**II.** *that which is seized as a pledge, a pledge, surety*, ῥύσια δοῦναι Solon; ῥύσιον τιθέναι Soph.　　**III.** *that which is seized by way of reprisal*, φόνον φόνου ῥύσιον τῖσαι *to suffer death in reprisal for death*, Id.　　**IV.** in pl. *offerings for deliverance*, Anth.

ῥύσιος, ον, (ῥύομαι) *delivering, saving*, Aesch., Anth.

ῥῠσί-πολις, εως, ὁ, ἡ, *saving the city*, Aesch.

ῥῠσί-πονος, ον, *setting free from trouble*, Anth.

ῥύσις [ῡ], ἡ, (ῥέω) *a flowing, flow*, Plat.　　**II.** *the course of a river, stream*, Polyb.

ῥύσκομαι, = ῥύομαι: ῥύσκευ, Ep. 2 sing. impf., Il.

ῥυσμός, Ion. for ῥυθμός.

ῥῡσός, ή, όν, (*ῥύω, ἐρύω) *drawn up, shrivelled*,

wrinkled, Il., Eur., etc.; ῥ. ἐπισκύνιον, of a frown, Anth. Hence

ῥυσότης, ητος, ἡ, wrinkledness, wrinkles, Plut.

ῥυστάζω, Frequentat. of *ῥύω = ἐρύω, to drag about, πολλὰ ῥυστάζεσκεν (3 sing. Ion. impf.) περὶ σῆμα he dragged it many times round the grave of Patroclus, Il.; δμωὰς ῥυστάζειν κατὰ δώματα, Od. Hence

ῥυστακτύς, ύος, ἡ, a dragging about, maltreatment, Od.

ῥυτά, τά, v. ῥυτός 2.

ῥῡτ-ἄγωγεύς, έως, ὁ, the rope of a horse's halter, Xen.

ῥυτήρ, ῆρος, ὁ, (*ῥύω, ἐρύω) one who draws or stretches, ῥ. βιοῦ, ὀϊστῶν drawer of the bow, of arrows, Od. 2. like ἱμάς, the strap by which a horse draws, a trace, Il.:—also a rein, Ib.; ἀπὸ ῥυτῆρος with loose rein, Lat. immissis habenis, at full galop:—used as a strap to flog with, Dem., Aeschin. II. (ῥύομαι) a saver, guard, defender, Od.

ῥῡτῑδό-φλοιος, ον, with shrivelled rind, σῦκον Anth.

ῥῡτῑδόω, f. ώσω, (ῥυτίς) to make wrinkled:—Pass. to be so, pf. part. ἐρρυτιδωμένος Luc.

ῥῡτίς, ίδος, ἡ, (ῥύω, ἐρύω) a fold or pucker in the face, a wrinkle, Lat. ruga, Ar., Plat.

ῥῡτόν, τό, (*ῥύω, ἐρύω) = ῥυτήρ, a rein, Hes. II. (ῥέω) a drinking-cup, running to a point with a small hole, through which the wine ran, Dem.

ῥῡτός, ή, όν, (*ῥύω, ἐρύω) dragged along, ῥυτοὶ λάες stones dragged along, i. e. too large to carry, Od.

ῥῠτός, ή, όν, (ῥέω) flowing, running, fluid, liquid, Trag.

ῥύτωρ [ῠ], ορος, ὁ, (ῥύομαι) a saviour, deliverer, Aesch., Anth.; ῥυτόρ from a thing, Id.

***ῥύω**, whence ἐρύω, to draw; v. ῥύομαι.

ῥωγᾰλέος, α, ον, (ῥώξ) broken, cleft, rent, torn, Hom.

ῥωγάς, άδος, ὁ, ἡ, (ῥώξ) = foreg., ragged, Babr.; ῥ. πέτρα a cloven rock, Theocr.

ῥώθων, ωνος, ὁ, the nose: in pl. the nostrils, Strab.

Ῥωμαϊκός, ή, όν, and **Ῥωμαῖος**, α, ον, Roman, a Roman, Polyb., etc.; Adv. -κῶς, in Latin, Anth.

Ῥωμαϊστί, Adv. in Latin, Plut.

ῥωμᾰλέος, α, ον, (ῥώμη) strong of body, Plat. 2. of things, mighty, strong, Hdt.

ῥώμη, ἡ, (ῥώομαι) bodily strength, strength, might, Hdt., Trag., etc.; οὐ μιᾷ ῥώμῃ not single-handed, Soph. II. a force, i. e. army, Xen.

ῥώννῡμι, f. ῥώσω: aor. 1 ἔρρωσα:—Pass., ῥώννῠμαι, aor. 1 ἐρρώσθην: pf. ἔρρωμαι: (ῥώομαι):—to strengthen, make strong and mighty, Plut. II. mostly in pf. pass. (with pres. sense) ἔρρωμαι, and plqpf. ἐρρώμην (as impf.):—to put forth strength, have strength or might, Eur., Thuc.:—c. inf. to have strength to do, be eager to do, Thuc. 2. often in imperat., ἔρρωσο, farewell, Lat. vale, Xen.; also, φράζειν τινὶ ἐρρῶσθαι, Lat. valere jubere, Plat. 3. part. ἐρρωμένος, = ῥωμαλέος, v. sub voce.

ῥώξ, ῥωγός, ἡ, (ῥήγνυμι) a cleft: in Od., ῥῶγες μεγάροιο are narrow passages leading to the hall.

Ῥώομαι, 3 pl. impf. ἐρρώοντο, Ep. ῥώοντο: 3 pl. aor. ἐρρώσαντο:—to move with speed or violence: to dart, rush, rush on, Hom.; ῥ. περὶ πυρήν Od.; ἀμφ' Ἀχελώϊον ἐρρώσαντο danced about Acheloüs, Il.; χορὸν ἐρρώσαντο plied the lusty dance, h. Hom.; ὑπὸ ῥώοντο ἄνακτι lustily they moved under the king's weight, Il.; so,

γούνατα ἐρρώσαντο Od.; also of the hair, ἐρρώοντο μετὰ πνοιῇς ἀνέμοιο it waved streaming in the wind, Il.

ῥωπήιον, τό, (ῥώψ) Ion. for ῥωπεῖον (which is not found), only in pl. ῥωπήια, brushes, brushwood, Il.

ῥωπικός, ή, όν, (ῥῶπος) of or for petty wares, trumpery, worthless, Plut.; ῥωπικὰ γράψασθαι to paint poorly, coarsely, Anth.

ῬΩ͂ΠΟΣ, ὁ, petty wares, Aesch., Dem.

ῥωχμός, οῦ, ὁ, (ῥώξ) a cleft, ῥωχμὸς γαίης a gutter scooped out by heavy rains, Il.

ῬΩ͂Ψ, ῥωπός, ἡ, a shrub, bush: only pl. bushes, underwood, brushwood, Od.

Σ.

Σ, σ, σῖγμα, τό, indecl., a semi-vowel, eighteenth letter of the Gr. Alph.: as numeral σ' = 200, but ͵σ 200,000.

I. beside the form Σ, it was written as a semicircle Ϲ. In the written character, final σ became s: from which must be distinguished the character ϛ' = 6. There was also a Doric name σάν [ᾰ] (cf. σαμ-φόρας), which appeared at the end of the alphabet as σαμπί or σαμπῖ, ϡ, = 900.

II. dialectic and other changes: 1. Aeol. and Ion. into δ, as ὀδμή ἴδμεν for ὀσμή ἴσμεν. 2. Aeol. and Dor. into τ, τύ ἴττω Ποτίδαν ποτί φατί for σύ ἴστω Ποσειδῶν πρός φησί:—so in later Att., as μέταυλος τήμερον for μέσαυλος σήμερον:—in later Att., also σσ passed into ττ, πράττω τάττω for πράσσω τάσσω, θάλαττα ἥττων for θάλασσα ἥσσων. 3. in Aeol. and Dor., and in Poets, σ was often doubled, as ὄσσος μέσσος ὀπίσσω for ὅσος μέσος ὀπίσω, and in fut. and aor. 1 forms, as ὀλέσσω ὀλέσσω, etc. for δαμάσω ὀλέσω, etc. 4. σ sometimes passed into ππ or vice versa, as πέσσω and πέπτω, ὄψομαι (*ὄπτω) and ὕσσομαι, ἐνίσσω and ἐνίπτω. 5. into ξ, in fut. and aor. 1 of Verbs, with their deriv. Nouns, as ἐργάξομαι χείριξις for ἐργάσομαι χείρισις:—so in Ion., διξός τριξός for δισσός τρισσός; and in old Att., the Prep. σύν, with all its Compds., was written ξύν. 6. att. σ and σσ sometimes passed into ψ, cf. Ψ ψ III. 7. in Aeol., as in Lat., σ represents the aspirate, Σαλμυνσσός Ἁλμυδησσός, σῦς (Lat. sus) ὗς, ἅλς sal, ἕξ sex, ἑπτά septem, ἕρπω serpo, ὕλη sylva. 8. prefixed to words beginning with μ and τ, μύραινα σμύραινα, μικρός σμικρός, τέγος στέγω, Lat. tego; more rarely before κ and φ, σκίδναμαι κίδναμαι, σφάλλω fallo, σφενδόνη funda. 9. σ was inserted in the middle of words before θ, esp. by Poets in the 1 pers. pl. pass. and med., as τυπτόμεσθα for τυπτόμεθα; so ὄπισθεν for ὄπιθεν. 10. conversely, the Lacon. used to throw out σ between two vowels, writing Μῶα for Μοῦσα. 11. σ changed into ρ, Dor. and Att., when another ρ went before, as ἄρρην for ἄρσην, θάρρος for θάρσος. 12. Lacon., σ is substituted for θ, as σιός Ἀσάνα παρσένος for θεός Ἀθήνη παρθένος. 13. Dor., σσ for ζ, as μασδός τράπεσδα for μαζός τράπεζα. 14. s is appended to οὖτω ἄχρι μέχρι before a vowel.

σ', by apostr. for σέ; rarely for σοί. II. for σά, neut. pl. of σός.

σᾶ, fem. sing. and neut. pl. of σῶς.

σά μάν; Doric for τί μήν; Ar.

Σᾰβάζιος, ὁ, (Σαβός) a Phrygian deity, identified with Bacchus, Ar.:—τὰ Σαβάζια Bacchic orgies, Strab.

σᾰβᾰκός, ή, όν, shattered; metaph. enervated, Anth. (Deriv. unknown.)

σᾰβάκτης, ου, ὁ, a shatterer, destroyer, of a goblin who broke pots, Ep. Hom. (Deriv. uncertain.)

σαβαχθα-νί; a Chaldaean phrase, hast thou forsaken me? N.T.

σαβαώθ, Hebr. plur. hosts, armies, N.T.

Σαββᾰτίζω, f. σω, (Σάββατον) to keep the Sabbath, Lxx.

Σαββᾰτισμός, ὁ, a keeping of days of rest, N.T.

Σάββᾰτον, τό, the Hebrew Sabbath, i.e. Rest, N.T.; also in pl. of the single day, heterocl. dat. pl. σάββασι (as if from σάββας), Ib. 2. a period of seven days, a week, μία τῶν σαββάτων the first day of the week, Ib.

σᾰβοῖ, a cry at the feast of Sabazios, Dem.

σάγαρις, εως, Ion. ιος, ή, pl. σαγάρεις, Ion. -ῖς, a single-edged axe or bill, a weapon used by the Scythian tribes, Hdt., Xen. (Foreign word.)

σαγή [ᾰ], ή, (σάττω) a man's pack, baggage, αὐτόφορτος οἰκείᾳ σάγῃ, i.e. carrying his own baggage, Aesch.: generally, harness, equipment, Id., Eur. II. = σάγμα II, a pack-saddle, Babr.

σᾰγηναῖοι, α, ον, (σαγήνη) of or for a drag-net, Anth.

σᾰγηνεύς, έως, ή, = sq., Anth., Plut.

σᾰγηνευτής, ῆρος, ὁ, one who fishes with a drag-net, of a comb, τριχῶν σαγ. Anth.; and

σᾰγηνευτής, οῦ, ὁ, = foreg., Anth. From

σᾰγηνεύω, f. σω, to take fish with a drag-net (σαγήνη), Luc. II. metaph. to sweep as with a drag-net, i.e. to sweep the population off the face of a country by forming a line and marching over it, a Persian practice, Hdt., etc.: Pass., σαγηνευθεὶς ὑπ' ἔρωτι Anth.

σᾰγήνη, ή, a large drag-net for taking fish, a seine, Ital. sagena, Luc., N.T. (Deriv. unknown.)

σᾰγηνο-βόλος, ὁ, (βάλλω) one who casts a drag-net, a fisherman, Anth.

σᾰγηνό-δετος, ον, attached to a drag-net, Anth.

σᾰγη-φορέω, f. ήσω, (σάγος) to wear a cloak, Strab.

σάγμα, ατος, τό, (σάττω) mostly in pl. covering: the covering of a shield, Eur., Ar.: a large cloak, Ar. II. a pack-saddle, Strab., Plut. III. a pile, ὅπλων Plut.

ΣΑ΄ΓΟΣ [ᾰ], ὁ, a coarse cloak, used by the Gauls, Polyb. (Perh. a Gallic word.)

Σαδδουκαῖοι, οἱ, Sadducees, name of a Jewish sect, N.T.

σαθρός, ά, όν, rotten, decayed, unsound, cracked, Plat., Dem.—Adv., σαθρῶς ἱδρυμένος built on unsound foundations, Arist. 2. metaph., πρίν τι καὶ σαθρὸν ἐγγίνεσθαί σφι before any unsound thought comes into their heads, i.e. before they prove traitors, Hdt.; σ. λόγοι Eur. (Deriv. uncertain.)

ΣΑΙ΄ΝΩ, Ep. impf. σαῖνον: aor. 1 ἔσηνα, Dor. ἔσᾱνα: —of dogs, to wag the tail, fawn, Od.; οὐρῇ ἔσηνε, of the dog Argus, Ib. II. metaph. to fawn, cringe, Pind., Aesch. III. c. acc. pers. to fawn upon, Ar.: to pay court to, greet, Pind., Soph.; σ. μόρον to deprecate, shrink from death, Aesch.:—Pass., σαίνομαι ὑπ' ἐλπίδος Id. 2. to beguile, cozen, deceive, Id. 3. in N.T., σαίνεσθαι ἐν ταῖς θλίψεσι seems to mean to be moved, disturbed.

ΣΑΙ΄ΡΩ, aor. 1 ἔσηρα, part. σήρας: pf. with pres. sense σέσηρα: I. in pf. to draw back the lips and shew the teeth, to grin like a dog, Lat. ringi, σεσᾰρυῖα (Ep. for σεσηρυῖα) Hes.; σεσηρώς Ar.:—in good sense, smiling, Theocr.:—the neut. is used in Adv. sense, σεσᾱρὸς γελᾶν to laugh with open mouth, Theocr.; σεσηρὸς αἰκάλλειν, of a fox, Babr. II. in pres. and aor. 1, to sweep a floor, Eur. 2. c. acc. rei, to sweep up or away, Soph.

σᾰκεσ-πᾰλος, ον, (πάλλω) wielding a shield, Il.

σᾰκεσ-φόρος, ον, (φέρω) shield-bearing, Soph., Eur.

σᾰκίον, v. σακκίον.

σᾰκίτας, ὁ, Dor. for σηκίτης.

σακκίον, Att. σᾰκίον, τό, Dim. of σάκκος or σάκος, a small bag, Xen. 2. sackcloth, mourning, Menand.

σακκο-γενειο-τρόφος, ον, (σάκκος III, τρέφω) cherishing a huge beard, Anth.

σάκκος or σάκος [ᾰ], ὁ, a coarse hair-cloth, sack-cloth, Lat. cilicium, N.T. II. anything made of this cloth, a sack, bag, Hdt., Ar. III. a coarse beard, Ar. (Prob. a Phoenician word.)

σᾱκός, ὁ, Dor. for σηκός.

σάκος [ᾰ], τό, gen. εος, Ion. -ευς, (σάττω) a shield, Hom., etc. The earliest shields were of wicker-work or of wood, covered with ox-hides, and sometimes with metal-plates, (that of Ajax had seven hides and an eighth layer of metal); it was concave, so as to hold liquid, Aesch.

σάκτας, ου, ὁ, (σάττω) a sack, Ar.

σάκτωρ, ορος, ὁ, (σάττω) a packer, Ἄιδου σάκτωρ who crowds the nether world (with dead men), Aesch.

σακχ-ὑφάντης, ου, ὁ, (σάκκος, ὑφαίνω) one who weaves sackcloth, a sailmaker, Dem.

σᾰλάκων, ωνος, ὁ, a word of uncertain origin, denoting a swaggerer, Arist.

Σᾰλᾰμῖν-ᾰφέτης, ου, ὁ, betrayer of Salamis, Solon.

Σᾰλᾰμίνιος, α, ον, also ος, ον, Salaminian, of or from Salamis, Hdt. II. Σαλαμινία (sub. ναῦς), ή, one of the Athen. sacred ships, Ar., Thuc.; v. πάραλος III.

Σᾰλᾰμίς or Σᾰλᾰμίν [ῑ], gen. ῖνος, ή, Salamis, an island opposite Athens, Il., etc. II. a town of Cyprus founded by Teucer of Salamis, h. Hom., Hdt.

σάλασσα, Dor. for θάλασσα.

σᾰλάσσω, to overload, cram full, σεσαλαγμένος Anth.

σᾰλεύω, aor. 1 ἐσάλευσα:—Pass., f. σαλευθήσομαι: aor. 1 ἐσαλεύθην: pf. σεσάλευμαι: (σάλος):—to cause to rock, make to oscillate, shake to and fro, Eur., Anth.; σ. τοὺς ὄχλους to stir them up, N.T.:—Pass. to be shaken to and fro, totter, reel, χθὼν σεσάλευται Aesch. II. to move up and down, to roll, toss, as on the sea, Xen.:—metaph. to toss like a ship at sea, to be tempest-tost, be in sore distress, Soph., Eur. 2. of a ship also, to ride at anchor: metaph., σ. ἐπί τινι to ride at anchor on one's friend, depend upon him, Plut.

ΣΑ΄ΛΟΣ [ᾰ], ὁ, any unsteady, tossing motion, of an earthquake, Eur.: the tossing or rolling swell of the sea, Id.; so in pl., πόντιοι σάλοι Id. II. of ships or persons in them, a tossing on the sea, Soph.:—metaph. of the ship of the state, tempest-tossing, Id.; σάλον ἔχειν to be in distress, Plut.

σαλπιγγο-λογχ-ῠπηνάδαι, οἱ, (σάλπιγξ, λόγχη, ὑπήνη) lancer-whiskered-trumpeters, Ar.

σαλπιγκτής, οῦ, ὁ, a trumpeter, Thuc., Xen. From

σάλπιγξ, ιγγος, ἡ, a war-trumpet, trump, Il., Trag., etc. :—metaph., Πιερικὰ σ., of Pindar, Anth. II. a trumpet-call, ap. Arist. From

σαλπίζω, f. σω, aor. 1 ἐσάλπιγξα, Ep. σάλπιγξα, also ἐσάλπισα :—to sound the trumpet, give signal by trumpet, Xen. : c. acc. cogn., σ. ῥυθμούς Id.; cf. ἀνακλητικός : metaph., ἀμφὶ δὲ σάλπιγξεν οὐρανός heaven trumpeted around, of thunder as if a signal for battle, Il. :—impers., ἐπεὶ ἐσάλπιγξε (sc. ὁ σαλπιγκτής) when the trumpet sounded, Xen. (Deriv. uncertain.)

σᾶμα, ατος, τό, Dor. for σῆμα.

Σάμαινα, ἡ, (Σάμος) a ship of Samian build, Plut.

σᾱμαίνω, Dor. for σημαίνω.

Σᾰμάρεία, ἡ, Samaria, a city of Palestine :—Σᾰμαρείτης, ου, ὁ, a Samaritan, N. T., etc.; fem. -εῖτις, ιδος, Ib.

σάμβᾰλον, τό, Aeol. for σάνδαλον, Anth.

σαμβύκη [ῡ], ἡ, a triangular musical instrument with four strings, Lat. sambūca, Arist. II. an engine of like form used in sieges, Plut.

σαμβῡκιστής, οῦ, ὁ, a player on the sambūca :—fem. σαμβῡκίστρια, Plut.

σάμερον, Dor. for σήμερον.

Σάμη, ἡ, = Σάμος, Il.

Σᾱμο-θρᾴκη [ᾱ], Ion. -θρηίκη, ἡ, Samothrace, an island near Thrace, the seat of the mysteries of the Cabiri, Hdt. :—the inhabitants were Σαμοθρήικες, Id. ; Adj. Σᾱμοθράκιος, α, ον, Ion. -θρηίκιος, η, ον, Id.

Σάμος [ᾱ], ἡ, Samos, the name of several Greek islands: 1. an old name for Κεφαλληνία, Hom. 2. Σάμος Θρηικίη, = Σαμοθράκη, Il. 3. Samos, the large island over against Ephesus, h. Hom., etc. : hence Adj. Σάμιος, α, ον, Hdt.

σαμπῖ or σάμπι, v. Σ, σ I.

σαμ-φόρας, ου, ὁ, (φέρω) a horse branded with the letter σάν (v. sub Σ, σ), Ar.; cf. κοππατίας.

σάν, v. Σ, σ I.

σανδάλιον, τό, Dim. of σάνδαλον, Hdt.

σανδᾰλίσκος, ὁ, Dim. of σάνδαλον, Ar.

σάνδᾰλον, τό, a wooden sole, bound by straps round the instep and ankle, mostly in pl. sandals, h. Hom., etc. (Prob. a Persian word.)

σανδᾰράκη [ᾰ], ἡ, red or orange-coloured mineral, Arist. (Deriv. unknown.) Hence

σανδᾰράκῐνος, η, ον, of orange colour, Hdt.

σανδᾰράκ-ουργεῖον, τό, (*ἔργω) a pit whence σανδαράκη is dug, Strab.

σάνδιξ, ικος, ἡ, or σάνδιξ, ικος, ἡ, a bright red colour, also called ἀρμένιον, Strab.

σᾰνίδιον, τό, Dim. of σανίς, a small trencher, Ar. II. like πινάκιον, a tablet, Aeschin.

σᾰνιδόω, f. ώσω, to cover with planks.

σᾰνίδωμα, ατος, τό, a planking, framework, Polyb.

ΣᾰΝΙΣ, ίδος, ἡ, a board, plank, Anth., etc. II. anything made of planks : 1. a door, in pl. folding doors, Lat. fores, Hom. :—rare in sing., Eur. 2. a wooden platform, scaffold or stage, Od. : a ship's deck, Eur. 3. in pl. wooden tablets for writing on, Id. :—at Athens, tablets on which were written public

notices, Ar., etc. 4. a plank to which offenders were bound or nailed, Hdt. ; so perh. in Od. 22. 174.

σάος, as Posit., found only in the contr. form σῶς, σᾶ (v. σῶς) ; but Comp. σαώτερος Il., Xen., etc. : Comp. Adv. σαώτερον, Anth.

σαοφρονέω, σαοφροσύνη, σαόφρων, poët. for σωφρ-.

σάπεις, aor. 2 pass. part. of σήπω.

σάπῃ, Ep. for σάπῇ, 3 sing. aor. 2 pass. subj. of σήπω.

σᾰπῆναι, aor. 2 pass. inf. of σήπω.

σαπρία, ἡ, = σαπρότης, Anth.

σαπρός, ά, όν, (σαπῆναι) rotten, putrid, Theogn., Ar. ; of fish, stale, rancid, τάριχος Ar. II. generally, stale, worn out, Lat. obsoletus, Id. :—of persons, Id. 2. of wine, in good sense, mellow, Id. Hence

σαπρότης, ητος, ἡ, rottenness, putridity, Plat.

σάπφειρος, ἡ, a blue gem, the sapphire, or (as others think) lapis lazuli. (Prob. a Phoenician word.)

Σαπφώ, ἡ, gen. οῦς, acc. οῦν, voc. οῖ, Sappho.

σᾱπών, aor. 2 part. of σήπω.

σαργάνη [ᾰ], ἡ, a plait, braid, Aesch. 2. a basket, N. T. (Deriv. unknown.)

σαρδάνιος, α, ον, (σαίρω) used of bitter or scornful laughter, σαρδάνιον γελᾶν (sc. γέλωτα) ; μείδησε σαρδάνιον he laughed a bitter laugh, Od. ; so, ἀνεκάγχασε σαρδάνιον Plat. ; ridere γέλωτα σαρδάνιον Cic.—Others write Σαρδόνιον, deriving it from Σαρδώ, because such laughter resembled the effect produced by a Sardinian plant, which screwed up the face of the eater, Plut. : (hence our form sardonic.)

Σάρδεις, εων, αἱ, Sardes, the capital of Lydia, dat. Σάρδεσι, Aesch. :—Ion. Σάρδῑς· Hdt. ; gen. Σαρδίων, dat. Σάρδῑσι Hdt. :—Adj. Σαρδιᾱνός, Ion. -ηνός, ή, όν, Id. ; and Σαρδιᾱνικός, ή, όν, Ar.

σάρδιον, τό, the Sardian stone, carnelian, Plat.

σαρδόνιον, τό, the rope sustaining the upper-edge of a hunting-net, Xen.

σαρδόνιος, α, ον, v. Σαρδάνιος.

σαρδ-όνυξ, ῠχος, ὁ, (σάρδιον) the sardonyx, Anth.

Σαρδώ, ἡ, gen. όος contr. οῦς, dat. οῖ, Sardinia, Hdt., Ar. ; the obl. cases are sometimes Σαρδόνος, -όνι, -όνα (as if from Σαρδών), Polyb. :—Adj. Σαρδόνιος, α, ον, and Σαρδονικός, ή, όν, Hdt.

σάρῑσα or -ισσα, ἡ, the sarissa, a long pike used in the Macedonian phalanx, Polyb. (A foreign word.)

σαρκάζω, f. σω, (σάρξ) to tear flesh like dogs, Ar.

σαρκάω, = σαρκάζω, Ar.

σαρκίζω, f. ίσω, to strip off the flesh, scrape it out, Hdt.

σαρκῐκός, ή, όν, (σάρξ) fleshly, sensual, Anth.

σάρκῐνος, η, ον, (σάρξ) of flesh, in the flesh, Theocr. 2. = σαρκικός, opp. to πνευματικός, N. T. II. fleshy, corpulent, Plat.

σαρκο-λῐπής, ές, (λιπεῖν) forsaken by flesh, lean, Anth.

σαρκο-πᾱγής, ές, (παγῆναι) compact of flesh, Anth.

σαρκο-φάγος, ον, (φᾰγεῖν) eating flesh, carnivorous, Arist. II. λίθος σ. a limestone found at Assos in Troas, remarkable for consuming the flesh of corpses laid in it ; coffins were made of it, and such a coffin was called a σαρκοφάγος, Juven.

σαρκόω, f. ώσω, (σάρξ) to make to look like flesh, of a sculptor, Anth.

σαρκ-ώδης, ες, (εἶδος) fleshy, Xen., etc. : θεοὶ ἔναιμοι καὶ σαρκώδεες gods of flesh and blood, Hdt.

ΣΑ'ΡΞ, ἡ, (σαρκός) flesh, Lat. caro, Hom., etc. : in plur. the flesh or muscles of the body, ἔγκατά τε σάρκας τε καὶ ὀστέα Hom. ; so in Hes., Aesch., etc. :—so sometimes in sing., the flesh, the body, γέροντα τὸν νοῦν, σάρκα δ᾽ ἡβῶσαν φέρει Aesch.   II. the flesh, as opp. to the spirit, N. T. ; also for man's nature generally, Ib. ; πᾶσα σάρξ all human kind, Ib.

σάρον [ἄ], τό, (σαίρω II) a broom, besom, Anth. Hence

σᾰρόω, f. ώσω, = σαίρω II, to sweep clean, N. T. :— Pass., pf. part. σεσαρωμένος Ib.

Σαρπηδών, όνος and όντος, ὁ, voc. Σαρπῆδον, Il.

Σατάν or Σατᾶν, and Σατανᾶς, gen. ᾶ, ὁ, Satan, i. e. an adversary, enemy : name for the Devil, N. T. (Hebr. word.)

σατίνη [ῐ], ἡ, a war-chariot, chariot, car, h. Hom., Eur. (Deriv. unknown.)

σάτον, τό, a Hebrew measure, ¹⁄₃₀ of a κόρος, = about 1½ modii or 24 sextarii, N. T.

σάτρα, prob. for σάρ-τα, gold, Ar.   (Pers. word.)

σᾰτρᾰπεία, Ion. -ηίη, ἡ, a satrapy, the office or province of a satrap, Hdt., Xen. ; and

σατρᾰπεύω, f. σω, to be a satrap, exercise the authority of one, Xen.   2. c. gen. to rule as a satrap, σ. τῆς χώρας Id. ;—also c. acc., Id.   From

σᾰτράπης [ᾰ], ου, ὁ, a satrap, viceroy, Lat. satrăpa, Xen.   (Persian word.)

ΣΑ'ΤΤΩ : aor. 1 ἔσαξα : Pass., aor. 1 ἐσάχθην : pf. σέσαγμαι : Ion. 3 pl. plqpf. ἐσεσάχατο.   (The Root is ΣΑΓ, as in pf. pass., σάγμα, σάγος, σάγη.)   To pack or load, properly of putting the packsaddle on beasts of burthen : hence,   I. of warriors, in Pass. to be fully armed, Hdt. ; χαλκῷ σεσαγμένοι Theocr.   2. to furnish with all things needful, σάξαντες ὕδατι [τὴν ἐσβολήν] having furnished the entrance (into Egypt) with water, Hdt.   II. generally, to load heavily, fill quite full of a thing : Pass., c. gen., πημάτων σεσαγμένος laden with woes, Aesch. ; τριήρης σεσαγμένη ἀνθρώπων Xen. :—also c. dat. to fill full with a thing, Luc. ; χρυσῷ σαξάμενος πήρην Id. :—Pass., σεσαγμένος πλούτου τὴν ψυχὴν having his fill of riches, Xen.   III. to pack close, press down, Id.

Σᾰτῠρικός, ή, όν, (Σάτυρος) like a Satyr, Plut.   2. of or resembling the Satyric drama, Plat., Arist. :— σατυρικόν, τό, a Satyric drama, Xen.

Σᾰτῠρίσκος, ὁ, Dim. of Σάτυρος, Theocr.

Σάτῠρος, ὁ, Dor. Τίτυρος, a Satyr, companion of Bacchus, Hes., etc. : the Satyrs were represented with pointed ears, snub nose, goat's tail, and budding horns : later, goats' legs were added. They differed from Pan and Fauns by the want of real horns.   II. a play in which the Chorus consisted of Satyrs, the Satyric drama (not to be confounded with the Rom. Satura or Satira), Ar. It formed the fourth piece of a Tragic tetralogy : the only Satyric drama extant is the Cyclops of Eur.   (Deriv. uncertain.)

σαυλόομαι, Pass. (σαῦλος) to swagger, dance affectedly, Eur.

σαυλο-πρωκτιάω, to walk in a swaggering way, Ar.

σαῦλος, η, ον, swaggering, straddling, h. Hom., etc.

σαύνιον or σαυνίον, τό, a javelin, Menand., Strab. (Foreign word.)

σαύρα, Ion. σαύρη, ἡ, a lizard, Lat. lacerta, Hdt.

σαυρο-κτόνος, ον, (κτείνω) lizard-killer, epith. of Apollo, Plin.

Σαυρομάτης [ᾰ], ου, ὁ, a Sarmatian, Hdt. :—fem. Σαυρομάτις, Id.

σαῦρος, ὁ, = σαύρα, Lat. lacertus, Hdt.

σαυρωτήρ, ῆρος, ὁ, a spike at the butt-end of a spear, by which it was stuck into the ground, Il., Hdt.   (Deriv. uncertain.)

σαυτοῦ, σαυτῆς, v. σε-αυτοῦ.

σάφᾰ [σᾰ], poët. Adv. of σαφής, clearly, plainly, assuredly, of a surety, with Verbs of knowing, σάφα οἶδα, σάφα εἰδώς, Hom. ; also in Trag., σάφ᾽ οἶδα, σάφ᾽ ἴσθι, etc. ; σάφ᾽ ἴσθι, ὅτι .. Ar. ; also with Verbs of speaking, σάφα εἰπεῖν Hom., Pind.

σαφᾰνής, ές, Dor. for σαφηνής.

σαφέως, v. σαφής II.

σάφ-ηγορίς, ίδος, (ἀγορεύω) fem. Adj., speaking clearly or truly, Anth.

σάφήνεια, ἡ, distinctness, perspicuity, Plat., etc.

σᾰφηνέω, to tell distinctly, Aesch.   From

σᾰφηνής, Dor. -ᾱνής, ές, = σαφής, Aesch., Soph. : τὸ σαφανές the plain truth, Pind. Adv. -νῶς, Theogn., Aesch. ; Ion. -νέως, Hdt. Hence

σᾰφηνίζω, f. Att. ιῶ, to make clear or plain, point out clearly, explain, Aesch., Xen. Hence

σᾰφηνιστικός, ή, όν, explanatory, τινος of a thing, Luc.

ΣΑ'ΦΗ'Σ, ές, gen. έος contr. οῦς, clear, plain, distinct, manifest, h. Hom., Aesch., etc. ; τὸ σαφές the clear truth, Eur., etc.   2. of persons, Aesch., Eur. : of oracles and prophets, as in Virgil certus Apollo, sure, unerring, Soph.   II. Adv. σᾰφῶς, Ion. -έως, plainly, distinctly, well, σ. φράσαι, δεικνύναι, εἰδέναι, Hdt., Att. :—certainly, manifestly, Aesch., etc. ; ἦν σ. was manifest, Id. :—Comp. -έστερον, Sup. -έστατα, Id., etc.

ΣΑ'Ω, to sift, bolt, Hdt., in 3 pl. σῶσι.

σάω, pres. med. imperat. of σαόω.   II. Ep. 3 sing. impf. act.

σαώσω, fut. of σαόω : Ep. inf. σαωσέμεν.

σαώτερος, Comp. of σάος.

σαώτης, ου, ὁ, (σαόω) poët. for σωτήρ, Anth.

ΣΒΕ'ΝΝΥ-ΜΙ or -ύω : f. σβέσω, Ep. σβέσσω : aor. 1 ἔσβεσα, Ep. inf. σβέσσαι :—Med., f. σβήσομαι : aor. 1 ἐσβεσάμην :—Pass., aor. 1 ἐσβέσθην : pf. ἔσβεσμαι :— besides these, the aor. 2, pf. and plqpf. act. are used intr., ἔσβην, ἔσβηκα, ἐσβήκειν. To quench, put out, Lat. extinguere, Hdt., Pind.   2. generally, to quench, quell, check, σβ. χόλον, μένος Il. ; ὕβριν Simon. ; κύματα Ar., etc.   II. Pass. σβέννυμαι (with intr. tenses of Act., v. supr.), to be quenched, go out, Lat. extingui, of fire, Il. : metaph. of men, to become extinct, die, Anth.   2. generally, to be quelled or lulled, of wind, Od. Hence

σβεστήριος, α, ον, serving to quench fire, Thuc.

-σε, adverbial Suffix, denoting motion towards, e. g. ἄλλοσε to some other place.

σε-αυτοῦ, -ῆς, contr. σαυτοῦ, -ῆς, Ion. σεωυτοῦ, ῆς. reflexive Pron. of 2nd pers., of thyself, only in gen., dat. and acc. sing., masc. and fem., Hdt., Att. ; ἐν σαυτῷ γενοῦ contain thyself, Soph. :—in pl. separated,

ὑμῶν αὐτῶν, etc. : and orig. it was separated in sing., as in Hom., who always says σοὶ αὐτῷ, σ᾽ αὐτόν.

σεβάζομαι; Ep. 3 sing. aor. 1 σεβάσσατο: aor. 1 in pass. form ἐσεβάσθην:—to be afraid of, τι Il.

σέβας, τό, only in nom., acc., and voc. sing. : (σέβομαι):—reverential awe, a feeling of awe, Hom., etc. :—generally, reverence, worship, Trag.; c. gen. objecti, Διὸς σέβας reverence for Jove, Aesch. II. the object of awe, holiness, majesty, Eur. : periphr. for persons, σ. κηρύκων, i. e. Hermes, Aesch. 2. an object of wonder, a wonder, h. Hom., Soph. : an honour conferred on one, as the arms of Achilles on Ulysses, Soph.

σέβασμα, ατος, τό, an object of awe or worship, N. T.

Σεβαστιάς, ἡ, = Lat. Augusta, the Empress, Anth.

σεβαστός, ή, όν, (σεβάζομαι) reverenced, august : used to render the imperial name Augustus, Strab., N. T.

σεβίζω, f. Att. σεβιῶ: aor. 1 ἐσέβισα:—like σεβάζομαι, to worship, honour, Lat. revereor, Pind., Trag.; καινὰ λέχη σ. to devote oneself to a new wife, Eur.: —also in Med., οὐδὲν σεβίζει ἀράς standest not in awe of curses, Aesch.; aor. 1 pass. part., ἀγὼ σεβισθείς Soph.

ΣΕ'ΒΟΜΑΙ, mostly in pres.; aor. 1 ἐσέφθην: Dep. :— to feel awe or fear before God, to feel religious awe, feel shame, Il., Ar.; σεφθεῖσα awe-stricken, Plat.: c. inf. to dread or fear to do a thing, Aesch., Plat. 2. c. acc. pers. to honour with pious awe, to worship, Lat. veneror, Pind., Hdt., etc. :—then, to do homage to, pay honour or respect to, Trag.

σέβος, τό, = σέβας, in pl. σέβη, Aesch.

ΣΕ'ΒΩ, = the older form σέβομαι, used only in pres. and impf. to worship, honour, Pind., Att.; εὖ σέβειν τινά for εὐσεβεῖν εἴς τινα, Eur.:—c. inf., ὑβρίζειν οὐ σέβω, i. e. τὸ ὑβρίζειν, I do not respect, approve of insolence, Aesch.; τὸ μὴ ἀδικεῖν σέβοντες Id.—then, σέβομαι as Pass. to be reverenced, Soph. 2. absol. to worship, be religious, Aesch., Soph.

σέβεν, old poët. form of σοῦ, gen. of σύ.

Σειληνός, ὁ, Silenus, companion of Bacchus, Hdt.; father of the Satyrs, Eur.

Σειλην-ώδης, ες, (εἶδος) like Silenus, Plat

σεῖο, Ep. for σοῦ, gen. of σύ.

σεῖος, α, ον, Lacon. for θεῖος.

σειρά, Ion. σειρή, ἡ, (εἴρω, ἀείρω) a cord, rope, string, band, Hom.; σ. χρυσείη a cord or chain of gold, Il. 2. a cord with a noose, like the lasso, used by the Sagartians and Sarmatians to entangle and drag away their enemies, Hdt.

σειραῖος, α, ον, (σειρά) joined by a cord or band, ἵππος σ. = σειραφόρος, Soph. 2. of cord, twisted, βρόχοι Eur.

σειρα-φόρος, Ion. σειρη-, ον, (φέρω) led by a rope, Hdt. 2. σειραφόρος (sc. ἵππος), ὁ, a horse which draws by the trace only (being harnessed by the side of the yoke-horses, ζύγιοι), a trace-horse, outrigger : metaph., sometimes a yoke-mate, coadjutor, Aesch.; sometimes for one who has light work, Id.

Σειρήν, ῆνος, ἡ, a Siren : in pl. Σειρῆνες, αἱ, the Sirens, mythical sisters on the south coast of Italy, who enticed seamen by their songs, and then slew them, Od. Hom. only knows of two, whence Ep. dual. sign. Σειρήνοιιν. II. metaph. a Siren, deceitful woman, Eur. : the Siren charm of eloquence, Aeschin. (Deriv. unknown.)

σειρηφόρος, ον, Ion. for σειραφόρος.

σειριό-καυτος, ον, scorched by the sun or dog-star, Anth.

σείριος, ὁ, (σειρός) the scorcher, name of the dog-star, Lat. Sirius, which marks the season of greatest heat, i. e. Aug. 24 to Sept. 24, Hes., Eur.; called Σείριος κύων Aesch.; Σείριος ἀστήρ Hes.

σειρίς, ίδος, ἡ, Dim. of σειρά II, Xen.

σειρο-μάστιξ, ῑγος, ἡ, a knotted scourge, Eccl., Byz.

σειρο-φόρος, ον, = σειραφόρος 1, Eur.

σεισ-άχθεια, ἡ, (σείω, ἄχθος) a shaking off of burdens, Plut. : a name for the disburdening ordinance of Solon, by which all debts were lowered, Id.

σεισί-χθων, ονος, ὁ, (σείω) earth-shaker, epith. of Poseidon, Pind.

σεισμᾱτίας, ου, ὁ, of earthquakes, σεισμ. τάφος a burial in the ruins caused by an earthquake, Plut.

σεισμός, ὁ, (σείω) a shaking, shock, γῆς, χθονὸς σ. an earthquake, Eur.; absol., Hdt., Att. 2. generally, a shock, agitation, commotion, Plat., N. T.

σειστός, ή, όν, (σείω) shaken, Ar.

-σείω, ending of Verbs expressing desire, Desideratives, like Lat. -urio. They are formed from the fut., as δρασείω from δράσω, γελασείω from γελάσομαι.

ΣΕΙ'Ω, Ep. impf. σεῖον, f. σείσω: aor. 1 ἔσεισα: pf. σέσεικα:—Pass., aor. 1 ἐσείσθην: pf. σέσεισμαι:—to shake, move to and fro, Hom.; σ. ἔγχος, μελίην to shake the poised spear, Il.; κάρα σ., in sign of discontent, Soph. :—also, σείειν τῇ οὐρᾷ Xen. 2. of earthquakes, which were attributed to Poseidon, Hdt.; absol., σείσας by an earthquake, Ar.: impers., σείει there is an earthquake, Thuc., Xen. 3. metaph. to shake, agitate, disturb, Pind., Soph. 4. in Att., to accuse falsely or spitefully, so as to extort hushmoney, Ar.; cf. Lat. concutio. II. Pass. to shake, heave, quake, of the earth, Il., Hdt. :—metaph. to be shaken to its foundation, τὸ τερπνὸν πιτνεῖ σεσεισμένον Pind.; οἷς ἂν σεισθῇ θεόθεν δόμος Soph. 2. generally, to move to and fro : Pass., ὀδόντες ἐσείοντο his teeth were loosened, Hdt.; σεισθῆναι σάλῳ Eur. III. Med. to shake something of one's own, Theocr., Anth. 2. like Pass. to shake oneself, to shake, Il.

σελαγέω, (σέλας) to enlighten, illume :—Pass. to beam brightly, Ar.

σελαη-γενέτης, ου, ὁ, father of light, Anth.

σελάνα, -ναία, Dor. for σελήνη, σεληναία.

ΣΕ'ΛΑΣ, τό, gen. σέλαος, dat. σέλαϊ, contr. σέλα: pl. σέλᾱ:—a bright flame, blaze, light, σ. πυρός Il.; alone, Ib. :—lightning, a flash of lightning, Ib., Hdt., etc. :—a torch, h. Hom. :—the flash of an angry eye, Aesch. : metaph., φρῦκτος σ. Theocr.

σελασ-φόρος, ον, (φέρω) light-bringing, Aesch.

σελευκίς, ίδος, ἡ, a cup, named after Seleucus, Plut.

σεληναίη, ἡ, poët. for σελήνη, Ar.; Dor. σελαναία Eur.

σεληναῖος, α, ον, lighted by the moon, σ. νύξ a moonlight night, Orac. ap. Hdt., Anth. From

σελήνη, ἡ, Dor. σελάνα, (σέλας) the moon, Lat. luna, Hom.; σ. πλήθουσα the full-moon, Il.; νουμηνία κατὰ σελήνην, i. e. by the lunar month, Thuc.; πρὸς τὴν σελήνην by moonlight, Xen.; so, εἰς τὴν σ. Aeschin.:—τὴν σ. καθαιρεῖν, Horace's lunam deducere, of witches, Ar.; δεκάτῃ σελήνη in the tenth moon

(i. e. month), Eur.　　**II.** as fem. prop. n., *Selené, the goddess of the moon*, Hes., etc.　Hence

σεληνιάζομαι, Dep. *to be moonstruck,* i. e. *epileptic*, N.T.

σεληνιακός, ή, όν, *of* or *for the moon, lunar,* Plut.; and

σελῐδη-φάγος [ă], ον, (σελίς, φάγεῖν) *devouring leaves of books,* of a bookworm, Anth.

σέλῑνον, τό, *parsley,* Lat. *apium,* Hom., etc. :—with its leaves victors at the Isthmian and Nemean games were crowned, Pind. :—from its being planted in garden borders came the prov., οὐδ᾽ ἐν σελίνῳ οὐδ᾽ ἐν πηγάνῳ '*tis scarcely begun yet*,' Ar. (Deriv. unknown.)

ΣΕΛΙ´Σ, ίδος, ή, *a plank* : metaph. *a leaf of papyrus* :—generally, *the page of a book,* Anth.

Σελλοί, αἱ, *the Selli,* guardians of the oracle of Zeus at Dodona, bound to live a rough, austere life, Il., Soph.

σέλμα, ατος, τό, (σελίς?) *the deck of a ship,* h. Hom., Eur.　　**2.** in pl. σέλματα, *rowing-benches,* Lat. *transtra,* Trag.　　**3.** generally, *a seat, throne,* Aesch.　　**4.** σέλματα πύργων *scaffolds behind the parapet,* on which the defenders of the wall stood, Id.　　**5.** *logs of building timber,* Strab.

σεμίδᾰλις, ή, εως or **ιος,** *the finest wheaten flour,* Lat. *simila, similago,* Ar.

σεμνολογέω, f. ήσω, *to speak gravely* and *solemnly,* Aeschin. : —also as Dep. σεμνολογέομαι, *to talk in solemn phrases,* Dem.　From

σεμνο-λόγος, ὁ, (λέγω) *a grave* or *solemn talker,* Dem.

σεμνό-μαντις, εως, ὁ, *a grave and reverend seer,* Soph.

σεμνο-μῠθέω, f. ήσω, (μῦθος) = σεμνολογέω, Eur.

σεμνο-ποιέω, f. ήσω, *to make august, to magnify,* Strab.

σεμνο-προσωπέω, f. ήσω, (πρόσωπον) *to assume a grave, solemn countenance,* Ar.

σεμνός, ή, όν, (σέβομαι) *revered, august, holy, awful* :　　**I.** properly of certain gods ; at Athens esp. of the Furies, σεμναὶ θεαί or Σεμναί, Trag. ; σ. τέλη their rites, Id.　　**2.** then of things divine, h. Hom., Trag. ; σ. βίος a life *devoted to the gods,* Eur. ; σεμνὰ φθέγγεσθαι = εὔφημα, Aesch. ; τὸ σ. *holiness,* Dem.　　**II.** of human beings, *reverend, august, solemn, stately, majestic,* Hdt., Att.　　**2.** of things, Aesch., etc. ; οὐδὲν σ. nothing *very wonderful,* Arist. ; σεμνόν ἐστι, c. inf., 'tis a *noble, fine* thing to . . , Plat.　　**III.** in bad sense, *proud, haughty,* Trag. : —in contempt or irony, *solemn, pompous, grand,* Aesch., etc. ; σεμνὸν βλέπειν to look *grave and solemn,* Eur. ; ὡς σ. οὑπίτριπτος how *grand* the rascal is! Ar.; ὡς σ. ὁ κατάρατος Id.　　**IV.** Adv. -ῶς, Eur., etc. : Comp. -ότερον, Xen.

σεμνό-στομος, ον, (στόμα) *solemnly spoken,* Aesch.

σεμνότης, ητος, ή, (σεμνός) *gravity, solemnity, dignity, majesty,* Eur., Xen.　　**II.** in bad sense, *solemnity, pompousness,* Luc. ; of a girl, *prudery,* Eur.

σεμνό-τιμος, ον, (τιμή) *reverenced with awe,* Aesch.

σεμνόω, f. ώσω, *to make solemn* or *grand, to exalt, magnify, embellish,* Hdt.

σεμνύνω [ῠ], f. ῠνῶ, = foreg., *to exalt, magnify,* Hdt., Att. : —Pass. *to be in high repute,* Plat.　　**II.** Med. *to be grave, solemn, to affect a grave and solemn air,* Eur., Ar. ; σ. ἐπί τινι *to be proud* of a thing, *to pique oneself* on it, Dem. ; ἔν τινι Id.

σέο, Ep. for σοῦ, gen. of σύ.

σεπτός, ή, όν, verb. Adj. of σέβομαι, *august,* Aesch.

σέρῐς, ή, gen. -ιδος, a kind of *endive* or *chicory,* Anth.

σέρφος, ὁ, a kind of *gnat* or *winged ant,* Ar.

σέσαγμαι, pf. pass. of σάττω.

σεσαρωμένος, pf. pass. part. of σαρόω.

σεσαρώς, Dor. for σεσηρώς, Ep. fem. σεσᾰρυῖα.

σέσεισμαι, pf. pass. of σείω.

σέσηπα, pf. of σήπω.

σεσοφισμένως, Adv. part. pf. pass. *cunningly,* Xen.

σέσωσμαι, pf. pass. of σώζω.

σεῦ, enclit. σευ, Ion. for σοῦ, σου, gen. of σύ.

σεύα, Ep. aor. 1 of σεύω :—σεῦται for σεύεται.

σεῦτλον, τό, Ion. and late Att. for τεύτλον.

ΣΕΥ´Ω, Ep. aor. 1 ἔσσευα and σεῦα :—Med., Ep. 3 sing. aor. 1 σεύατο, pl. ἐσσεύαντο :—Pass., aor. 1 ἐσύθην [ῠ], ἐσσύθην [ῠ], poët. σύθην : pf. (with pres. sense) ἔσσυμαι, part. ἐσσύμενος (not -μένος) :—to these must be added poët. aor. 2 ἐσσύμην [ῠ], 2 sing. ἔσσυο, 3 sing. ἔσσυτο, Ep. σύτο, part. σύμενος :—besides these, σεύεται 3 sing. for σεύεται, σοῦνται 3 pl. for σεύονται, imperat. σοῦ, σούσθω, σοῦσθε.　*To put in quick motion* : *to drive, hunt, chase away,* Hom.; so in Med., Il.　　**2.** *to set on, let loose at,* κύνας σ. ἐπὶ συΐ Ib. : —c. inf. *to urge on,* Od.　　**3.** of things, *to throw, hurl,* Il.　　**II.** Pass. and Med. *to run, rush, dart* or *shoot along,* Hom., Trag. : —c. inf. *to hasten, speed to do* a thing, Il.　　**2.** metaph. *to be eager, have longings,* Od. ; v. ἐσσύμενος.

σεφθείς, aor. 1 part. of σέβομαι.

σέων, gen. pl. of σής.

σεωυτοῦ, fem. σεωυτῆς, Ion. for σεαυτοῦ, σεαυτῆς.

σηκάζω, f. σω, (σηκός) *to shut up in a pen* : Pass., σήκασθεν (for ἐσηκάσθησαν) κατὰ ῎Ιλιον were cooped up in Ilium, Il. ; ἐν αὐλίῳ σηκασθέντες Xen.

σηκίς, ίδος, ή, (σηκός) *a housekeeper, porteress,* Ar.

σηκίτης [ῑ], ου, Dor. **σᾱκίτας, ᾱ, ὁ,** (σηκός) *kept in the fold, sucking,* of a lamb, Theocr.

σηκο-κόρος, ὁ, ἡ, (κορέω) *cleaning a byre* or *pen, a herdsman,* Od.

ΣΗΚΟ´Σ, ὁ, Dor. **σᾱκός, ὁ,** *a pen, fold,* for lambs, kids, calves, Hom., Hes. ; σ. δράκοντος the dragon's *den,* Eur.　　**II.** *a sacred enclosure, chapel, shrine,* Soph., Eur.　　**2.** *a sepulchre, burial-place,* Simon.　　**III.** *the trunk of an old olive-tree,* Lys.

σηκόω, f. ώσω, *to weigh, balance,* Plut.　Hence

σήκωμα, Dor. **σάκωμα, ατος, τό,** *in the balance,* σμικρὸν τὸ σὸν σ. προστίθης slight is *the weight* that you throw into the scale, Eur.　　**II.** = σηκός II, *a sacred enclosure,* Id.

ΣΗˆΜΑ, Dor. **σᾶμα, ατος, τό,** *a sign, mark, token,* Hom., etc. ; the star on a horse's forehead, Il.　　**2.** *a sign from heaven, an omen, portent,* Hom., etc.　　**3.** generally, *a sign to do* or *begin something,* Od. ; *a watchword,* Eur. ; *a battle-sign, signal,* Id.　　**4.** *the sign by which a grave is known, a mound, cairn, barrow,* Lat. *tumulus,* Hom., etc. : —generally, *a grave, tomb,* Hdt., Att.　　**5.** *a token* by which any one's identity was certified : the σήματα λυγρά of Bellerophon were *pictorial,* not *written, tokens* (v. γράφω init.), Il. :—*the mark* on the lot of Ajax, Ib. : *the device* or *bearing on a shield,* Aesch. ; *the seal* impressed on a letter, Soph.　　**6.** *a constellation,* Il., Eur.

σημαία, ή, (σῆμα) a standard, Polyb. :- a band under one standard, the Roman manipulus, Id.

σημαίνω, f. σημᾰνῶ, Ion. -ᾰνέω : aor. 1 ἐσήμηνα and ἐσήμᾱνα :—Med., aor. 1 ἐσημηνάμην, ἐσημάνθην : pf. σεσήμασμαι, also 3 sing. σεσήμανται, inf. σεσημάνθαι : (σῆμα) :—to shew by a sign, indicate, make known, point out, Hom., etc. 2. absol. to give signs, make signals, Il., Trag. II. to give a sign or signal to do a thing, Il. ; c. inf., Hdt., etc. ; μὴ σημήναντός σου without any order from you, Plat. :— c. gen. to bear command over, τινός or ἐπί τισι Hom. : absol. to give orders, Id. ; σημαίνων = σημάντωρ, Soph. 2. in war, to give the signal of attack, Thuc. ; σ. τῇ σάλπιγγι Xen. ; σ. ἀναχώρησιν to make signal for retreat, Thuc. :—impers., σημαίνει (sc. ὁ σαλπιγκτής) signal is given, τοῖς Ἕλλησι ὡς ἐσήμηνε when signal was given for the Greeks to attack, Hdt. ; ἐσήμαινε πάντα παραρτέεσθαι signal was given to make all ready, Id. III. to signify, indicate, announce, declare, Eur., Hdt., Att. 2. generally, to signify, interpret, explain, Hdt., Aesch. ; absol., σήμαινε tell, Soph. IV. = σφραγίζω, to stamp with a sign or mark, to seal, Lat. obsignare, mostly in Med., Xen. :—Pass., εὖ σεσημάνθαι to be well sealed up, Ar. ; τὰ σεσημασμένα, opp. to τὰ ἀσήματα, Dem.

B. Med. σημαίνομαι, like τεκμαίρομαι, to give oneself a token, i. e. conclude from signs, conjecture, Soph. II. to mark for oneself, σημαίνεσθαι βύβλῳ (sc. βοῦν), i. e. by sealing a strip of byblus round his horn, Hdt.

σημαιο-φόρος, ον, (σημαία, φέρω) Lat. signifer, a standard-bearer, Polyb.

σημαντήριον, τό, a mark or seal upon anything to be kept, Aesch.

σημαντρίς γῆ, clay used for sealing, like our wax, Hdt.

σήμαντρον, τό, = σημαντήριον, a seal, Hdt., Eur. ; metaph., δεινοῖς σημάντροισιν ἐσφραγισμένοι, i. e. wounded, Eur.

σημάντωρ, ορος, ὁ, (σημαίνω II) one who gives a signal, a leader, commander, Hom. ; of a horse, a driver; of a herd, a herdsman, Il. : a subordinate officer, Hdt. 2. an informer, guide, indicator, Anth.

σημᾰτόεις, εσσα, εν, (σῆμα 4) full of tombs, Anth.

σημᾰτ-ουργός, ὁ, (*ἔργω) one who makes devices for shields, Aesch.

σημειο-γράφος [ᾰ], ον, a shorthand writer, Plut.

σημεῖον, τό, Ion. σημήιον, Dor. σαμᾶον, (σῆμα) a sign, a mark, token, Hdt., Att. 2. a sign from the gods, an omen, Soph., Plat. : esp. of the constellations, Eur. 3. a sign or signal to do a thing, made by flags, Hdt. ; αἴρειν, κατασπᾶν τὸ σ. to make or take down the signal for battle, Thuc. ; τὰ σημεῖα ᾔρθη the signals agreed upon were made, Id. 4. an ensign or flag, on the admiral's ship, Hdt. ; on the general's tent, Xen. :—then, generally, a standard, ensign, Eur. : hence, a boundary, limit, Dem. 5. a device upon a shield, Hdt., Eur. ; upon ships, a figure-head, Ar. 6. a signal, watchword, Thuc. II. in reasoning, a sign or proof, Ar., Thuc., etc. :—σημεῖον δέ· or σημεῖον γάρ· (to introduce an argument) this is a proof of it, Dem., etc.

σημειόω, f. ώσω, = σημαίνω, to mark (by milestones), Polyb. II. Med. to interpret as a sign, Strab.

σημει-ώδης, ες, (εἶδος) marked, remarkable, Strab.

σήμερον, Dor. σάμερον, (ἡμέρα with σ prefixed) Adv. to-day, Hom., Pind. :—the common Att. form was τήμερον, Ar., etc. ; εἰς τήμερον Plat. ; ἡ τ. ἡμέρα Dem.

σημήιον, τό, Ion. for σημεῖον.

σημικίνθιον or σιμικίνθιον, τό, the Lat. semicinctium, an apron or kerchief, N. T.

σημό-θετος, ον, having a mark set or affixed, Anth.

σηπεδών, όνος, ἡ, rottenness, putrefaction, Plat.

σηπία, ἡ, the cuttle-fish, which when pursued darkens the water by ejecting a liquid, Ar. (Deriv. unknown.)

ΣΗΠΩ, f. σήψω, to make rotten or putrid, make to fester, of a serpent's poison, Aesch. 2. metaph. to corrupt, waste, Plat. II. Pass., the pf. σέσηπα being used in pres. sense for σήπομαι: aor. 2 ἐσάπην [ᾰ] :—to be or become rotten, to rot, moulder, of dead bodies, Il. ; of timber, Hdt., Il. 2. of live flesh, to mortify, Hdt., Plat.

Σήρ, ὁ, gen. Σηρός, mostly in pl. Σῆρες, the Seres, an Indian people from whom the ancients got silk, Strab.

σῆραγξ, αγγος, ἡ, a hollow rock, cave, Plat. ; of a lion's den, Theocr. (Deriv. uncertain.)

σηρικός, ή, όν, (Σήρ) Seric, silken, Luc. :—Subst., σηρικόν or σιρικόν, τό, a silken robe, silk, N. T.

ΣΗΣ, ὁ, gen. σεός, pl. σέες, σέας, σέων ; later gen. σητός, etc.:—a moth which eats woollen stuff, Lat. tinea, Ar. :—metaph. for a bookworm, Anth.

σησάμαιος, η, ον, made of sesamé, Luc.

σησάμη [ᾰ], ἡ, sesamé, a plant, from the fruit of which (σήσαμον) an oil was pressed. (Deriv. unknown.)

σησάμη, ἡ, a sesame pudding, Ar.

σησάμινος [ᾰ], η, ον, made of sesamé, Xen.

σησαμόεις, εσσα, εν, of sesamé :—as Subst. (contr.) σησαμοῦς, ὁ, a sesamé-cake, Ar.

σήσαμον, τό, the seed or fruit of the sesamé-plant (σησάμη), Hdt., Ar. II. = σησάμη, Ar., Xen.

σησαμό-τυρον, τό, a mess of sesamé and cheese, Batr.

Σηστός, ή, or ὁ, Sestos, a town on the European side of the Hellespont, over against Abydos, Il.

σητό-βρωτος, ον, (σής, βι-βρώσκω) eaten by moths, N. T.

σητό-κοπος, ον, (κόπτω) = foreg., Anth.

-σθα, an ancient ending of 2 pers. sing. act., in Hom. and other Poets, mostly in subj., as ἐθέλῃσθα, ἔχῃσθα, εἴπῃσθα, rarely in opt. as κλαίοισθα. In Att. it was retained in some irreg. Verbs, ἦσθα, οἶσθα, ᾔδησθα.

σθεναρός, ά, όν, strong, mighty, Il., Eur. :—Comp. σθεναρώτερος Soph. From

ΣΘΕΝΟΣ, εος, τό, strength, might, Il., Pind. :—c. inf., σθ. πολεμίζειν strength to war, Il. ; σθ. καθελεῖν Eur. ; σθένει by force, Soph. ; λόγῳ τε καὶ σθένει both by right and might, Id. ; so, ὑπὸ σθένους Eur. ; παντὶ σθένει with all one's might, Thuc. 2. strength, might, of all kinds, moral as well as physical, σθένος τῆς ἀληθείας Soph. ; ἀγγέλων σθ. their might or authority, Aesch. II. a force of men, like δύναμις, Il., Soph. 2. metaph., like Lat. vis for copia, a quantity, profusion, Pind. III. periphr., like βίη, ἴς, μένος, as σθένος Ἰδομένηος, Ὠρίωνος, for Idomeneus, Orion, themselves, Il., Hes.

σθένω, only in pres. and impf., (σθένος) to have strength

or *might*, *be strong* or *mighty*, Soph., Eur. ; σθ. χερί, ποσί *to be strong in hand, in foot*, Soph., Eur. ; σθένοντος ἐν πλούτῳ Soph. ; τοσοῦτον σθένει Id. ; ὅσονπερ ἂν σθένῃ Id. ; οἱ κάτω σθένοντες *they who have power below*, Eur. **2.** c. inf. *to have strength* or *power to do, be able,* Soph., Eur.

σιᾰγών, Ion. σιηγών, όνος, ἡ, *the jawbone, jaw,* Soph. (Deriv. unknown.)

ΣΙ'ΑΛΟΝ or σίελον, τό, *spittle, saliva,* Xen., etc.

ΣΙ'ΑΛΟΣ, ὁ, *a fat hog,* with or without σῦς, Hom.

Σίβυλλα, ἡ, *a Sibyl, prophetess,* Ar., Plat. (Deriv. uncertain.) Hence

Σιβύλλειος, α, ον, *Sibylline,* Plut. ; and

Σιβυλλιάω, *to play the Sibyl* : metaph. *to be like an old Sibyl, old womanish,* Ar. ; and

Σιβυλλιστής, οῦ, ὁ, *a believer in the Sibyl, a seer, diviner,* Plut.

σῐβύνη, ἡ, and σῐβύνης [ῠ], ου, ὁ, *a hunting spear, a spear, pike,* Anth. :—Dim. σιβύνιον, τό, Polyb.

σῖγᾰ, Adv. (σιγή) *silently,* σῖγα ἔχειν *to be silent,* Soph. ; κάθησο σῖγα Ar. ; *alone,* σῖγα *hush ! be still !* Aesch. :—the public crier proclaiming *silence* said σῖγα πᾶς (sc. ἔστω) Ar. **2.** *under one's breath, in a whisper, secretly,* Aesch., Soph.

σῖγα, imperat. of σιγάω. **II.** σῐγά, Dor. for σιγή.

σῑγᾷ, 3 pers. sing. of σιγάω. **II.** Dor. dat. of σιγή.

σῑγάζω, (σιγή) *to bid one be silent,* τινά Xen.

σῑγαλέος, α, ον, (σιγή) *silent, still,* Anth.

σῑγαλόεις, εσσα, εν, *glossy, glittering, shining, splendid,* Hom. (From σίαλος, with γ inserted, and ι made long metri grat.)

σῑγᾶς, Dor. for σιγηλός.

σῑγάς, άδος, (σιγή) fem. Adj. *silent,* Aesch.

σῑγάω, f. ήσομαι, later ήσω : pf. σεσίγηκα :—Pass., f. σιγηθήσομαι : aor. 1 ἐσιγήθην : pf. σεσίγημαι :—*to be silent* or *still, to keep silence,* Hdt., Att. ; σῖγα, *hush ! be still !* Hom. :—Pass., τί σεσίγηται δόμος ; *why is the house hushed ?* Eur. **II.** trans. *to hold silent, to keep secret,* Hdt., Aesch., etc. :—Pass. *to be kept silent* or *secret,* Lat. *taceri,* Hdt., Eur., etc. ; ἐσιγήθη σιωπῇ *silence was kept,* Eur. From

ΣΙΓΗ', Dor. σιγά, ἡ, *silence,* σιγὴν ἔχειν *to keep silence,* Hdt. ; σιγὴν ποιεῖσθαι *to make silence,* Id. ; σιγὴν φυλάσσειν Eur. :—in pl., σιγαὶ ἀνέμων Id. **II.** σιγῇ, as Adv. *in silence,* Hom. ; also like σῖγα, as an exclam., σιγῇ νυν sc. ἔστε) *be silent now !* Od. ; also, *in an under tone, in a whisper,* Hdt. ; σιγῇ βουλεύεσθαι Xen. **2.** *secretly,* σιγῇ ἔχειν τι *to keep secret,* like σιωπᾶν, Hdt. ; σιγᾷ καλύψαι, στέγειν, κεύθειν Pind., Soph. **3.** c. gen., σιγῇ τινος *unknown to him,* Hdt., Eur.

σῑγηλός, ή, όν, Dor. σῑγᾱλός, όν, *disposed to silence, silent, mute,* Soph. ; τὰ σιγηλά *silence,* Eur.

σῑγηρός, ά, όν, later form for σιγηλός, Menand.

σιγῇς, Dor. 2 sing. of σιγάω.

σῑγητέον, verb. Adj. of σιγάω, *one must be silent,* Eur.

σίγλος or σίκλος, ὁ, the Hebr. *shekel,* a weight and coin, = 4 Att. δραχμαί, N. T. **2.** the Persian σ. was = 7½ Att. ὄβολοι, Xen.

σῖγμα, the letter *sigma,* v. sub Σ, σ.

σῑγύνης [ῠ], ου, ὁ, Cyprian word for *a spear,* Hdt. **II.** σιγύνης among the Ligyes near Marseilles was used for

κάπηλος, Id. **III.** the Σιγύναι were a people on the Middle Danube, Id.

σῑγῶντι, Dor. for σιγῶσι, 3 pl. of σιγάω.

σίδᾱρος, Aeol. and Dor. for σίδηρος :—for all forms in σιδαρ-, v. sub σιδηρ-.

ΣΙ'ΔΗ, ἡ, *a pomegranate.*

σιδηρεία, ἡ, (σίδηρος) *a working in iron,* Xen.

σιδηρεῖα, τά, *iron-works, iron-mines,* Arist.

σιδήρεος, α, Ion. η, ον, Ep. σιδήρειος, η, ον, Att. contr. σιδηροῦς, ᾶ, οῦν, Dor. σιδάρεος, -εος : (σίδηρος) :—*made of iron* or *steel, iron,* Lat. *ferreus,* Hom., etc. ; χεὶρ σιδηρᾶ *a grappling-iron,* Thuc. :—σιδήρειος ὀρυμαγδός, i. e. the clang of arms, Il. ; σιδήρεος οὐρανός *the iron sky,* i. e. the firmament, which the ancients held to be of metal, Od. **2.** metaph., σιδήρεος ἐν φρεσὶ θυμός *a soul of iron,* i. e. *hard as iron,* Hom. ; οἱ κραδίη σιδηρέη Od. ; σοί γε σιδήρεα πάντα τέτυκται *thou art iron all !* Ib. :—*of Hercules, the ironside,* Simon. ; ὦ σιδήρεοι *O ye ironhearted !* Aeschin. **II.** σιδάρεοι, οἱ, a Byzantine iron coin, always in Dor. form, Ar.

σιδηρεύς, έως, ὁ, *a worker in iron, a smith,* Xen.

σιδήριον, τό, (σίδηρος) *an implement* or *tool of iron,* σιδηρίων ἐπαΐειν *to feel iron,* not to be proof against it, Id. ; θερμὰ σιδήρια *hot irons,* Id.

σιδηρίτης [ῐ], ου, ὁ, fem. -ῖτις, ιδος : Dor. σιδᾱρίτας, α, ὁ :—*of iron,* σ. πόλεμος *iron war,* Pind. **2.** ἡ σιδηρῖτις λίθος *the loadstone,* Strab.

σίδηρο-βρώς, ῶτος, ὁ, ἡ, (βι-βρώσκω) *iron-eating,* Soph.

σιδηρο-δάκτῡλος, ον, *iron-fingered,* Anth.

σίδηρό-δετος, ον, *iron-bound,* ἐν ξύλῳ σιδηροδέτῳ, i. e. *in the stocks,* Hdt.

σίδηρο-κμής, ῆτος, ὁ, ἡ, (κάμνω) *slain by iron,* i. e. *by the sword,* used with the neut. dat. βοτοῖς, Soph.

σίδηρο-μήτωρ, ορος, ὁ, ἡ, (μήτηρ) *mother of iron,* Aesch.

σίδηρο-νόμος, ον, (νέμω) *distributing with iron,* i. e. *with the sword,* Aesch.

σίδηρό-νωτος, ον, *iron-backed,* Eur.

σίδηρό-πλαστος, ον, *moulded of iron,* Luc.

σίδηρό-πληκτος, Dor. -πλακτος, ον, *smitten by iron,* Aesch.

ΣΙ'ΔΗΡΟΣ, Dor. σίδᾱρος, ὁ, *iron,* Lat. *ferrum,* Hom., etc. : iron was the last of the metals brought into common use by the Greeks : hence it is πολύκμητος, *wrought with much toil,* Hom. : and was of high value, pieces of it being given as prizes, Il. It mostly came from the north and east of the Euxine, Σκύθης σ. Aesch. **II.** like Lat. *ferrum,* anything made of iron, an iron tool or weapon, *a sword* or *knife, an axe-head,* etc., Hom., etc. **III.** *a place for selling iron, a smithy, a cutler's shop,* Xen.

σίδηρό-σπαρτος, ον, *sown* or *produced by iron,* Luc.

σίδηρο-τέκτων, ονος, ὁ, *a worker in iron,* Aesch.

σίδηρο-τόκος, ον, (τίκτω) *producing iron,* Anth.

σίδηρο-τομέω, f. ήσω, (τέμνω) *to cut* or *cleave with iron,* Anth.

σίδηρ-ουργεῖον, τό, (*ἔργω) *iron-works,* Strab.

σιδηροῦς, ῆ, οῦν, Att. contr. for σιδήρεος, α, ον.

σιδηροφορέω, f. ήσω, *to bear iron, wear arms, go armed,* Thuc. :—Med., Id. **II.** Med. *to go with an armed escort,* Plut. From

σίδηρο-φόρος, ον, (φέρω) *bearing arms* or *tools,* Anth.

σίδηρό-φρων, ον, gen. ονος, *of iron heart,* Aesch., Eur.

σῐδηρό-χαλκος, ον, of iron and copper, τομή Luc.

σῐδηρο-χάρμης, ου, ὁ, fighting (or perhaps exulting) in iron, epith. of war-horses, Pind.

σῐδηρόω, f. ώσω, (σίδηρος) to overlay with iron, Luc.: —Pass., ἐσεσιδήρωτο ἐπὶ μέγα καὶ τοῦ ἄλλου ξύλου iron had been laid over a great part of the rest of the wood, Thuc.

σίδιον [σῐ], τό, (σίδη) pomegranate-peel, Ar.

Σῐδονίηθεν, (Σιδών) Adv. from Sidon, Il.

Σῐδών, ῶνος, ἡ, Sidon, one of the oldest cities of Phoenicia, Od., Hdt.: hence Adj. Σῐδόνιος, α, ον, Il., Aesch.; Σῐδώνιος, Hdt., Att.; fem. Σῐδωνιάς, άδος, Eur.:—Σῐδόνες, οἱ, men of Sidon, Il.; also Σῐδόνιοι Od.; Σῐδονίη (sc. γῆ) Ib.

ΣΙΖΩ, only in pres. and impf., to hiss, of hot metal plunged into water, to which is compared the hissing of the Cyclops' eye when the burnt stake was thrust into it, Od.; so, of a pot boiling, Ar.; of fish frying, Id. (Formed from the sound.)

Σῐθωνία, Ion. -ίη, Sithonia, a part of Thrace, Hdt.

Σῐκᾱνία, Ion. -ίη, ἡ, Sicania, i.e. the part of Sicily near Agrigentum: also=Σικελία, Od.:—Σικανός, ὁ, a Sicanian, Thuc.; Σικανικός, ή, όν, Id.

σικάριος, ὁ, the Lat. sicārius, an assassin, N.T.

Σικελία, ἡ, Sicily, Hdt., etc.: hence Σικελίδης, Dor. -δας, ὁ, Sicilian, Theocr. [Σῐ-, metri grat.]

Σικελικός, ή, όν, Sicilian, Ar., etc.; and Σικελιώτης, ου, ὁ, a Sicilian Greek, as distinguished from a native Σικελός, Thuc. From

Σικελός, ή, όν, Sicilian, of or from Sicily, Lat. Siculus, Od., Eur., etc. II. Σικελοί, οἱ, the Siceli, the old inhabitants of Sicily, Od., Hdt.

σίκερα, τό, a fermented liquor, N.T. (Hebr. word.)

σίκιννῐς [σῐ], or σίκῐνῐς, ιδος, ἡ, the Sicinnis, a dance of Satyrs used in the Satyrical drama, Eur., Luc. (Deriv. uncertain.)

σῐκύα, Ion. -ύη, ἡ, a fruit like the cucumber or gourd, perh. the melon, Arist. II. a cupping-glass, because it was shaped like the gourd, cucurbita, Id.

σίκυος or σικυός [ῐ], ὁ, a cucumber or gourd, Ar.

Σικυών, ῶνος, ἡ, Sicyon, Il; also ὁ, Xen.;—as Adj., γῆ Σ. Anth.:—regul. Adj. Σικυώνιος, α, ον, Sicyonian, Thuc.—Adv. Σικυώνοθε, of or from Sicyon, Pind.

Σικυώνια (sc. ὑποδήματα), τά, Sicyonians, a kind of women's shoes, Luc.

Σιληνός, ὁ, later form of Σειληνός.

σίλι, τό,=κρότων or κίκι, called in Hdt. σιλλικύπριον, τό.

σιλλαίνω, (σίλλος) to insult, mock, jeer, banter, Luc.

σιλλικύπριον, v. σίλι.

σίλλος, ὁ, squint-eyed, Luc. II. a satirical poem or lampoon in hexam. verse, such as those written by Timon of Phlius, who was called ὁ σιλλο-γράφος.

σίλλυβος, ὁ, a parchment-label (Lat. index) appended to the outside of a book, Cic. (Deriv. unknown.)

σίλουρος [ῐ], ὁ, a large river fish, Lat. silurus, perh. the sheat? Juvenal. (Deriv. unknown.)

ΣΙΛΦΗ, ἡ, an insect, blatta, Luc.: also=tinea, a book-worm, Id., Anth.

σίλφιον, τό, Lat. laserpitium, a plant, used in food and medicine, assafoetida, Solon, Hdt.

σιλφιο-φόρος, ον, (φέρω) bearing silphium, Strab.

σιμβλεύω, intr. to grow in a hive, of honey, Anth.

σιμβλήϊος, η, ον, of or from the hive: fem. σιμβληΐς, ΐδος, Anth.

ΣΙΜΒΛΟΣ, ὁ, a beehive, Hes., Theocr. 2. metaph. any store or hoard, Ar.

σιμικίνθιον, τό,=σημικίνθιον.

Σῐμόεις, εντος, ὁ, the river Simoïs, Il.; contr. Σῐμοῦς, οῦντος, Hes.; Adj. Σῐμοέντιος, contr. Σῐμούντιος, α, ον, or ος, ον, Eur.; poët. fem. Σῐμοεντίς, ΐδος, Id.; also Σῐμοείσιος, ον, Strab.

ΣῙΜΟΣ, ή, όν, snub-nosed, flat-nosed, like the Tartars (or Scythians, as the Ancients called them), Hdt., etc.: —of the nose, snub, flat, opp. to γρυπός, Xen.;—as this kind of nose gives a pert expression, σιμά as Adv. means sneeringly, Anth. II. metaph. bent upwards, up-hill, πρὸς τὸ σιμὸν διώκειν to pursue up-hill, Xen.:—generally, hollow, concave, Id.

Σῐμος, ὁ, masc. prop. n. Flat-nose, Anth.

σιμότης, ητος, ἡ, (σιμός) the shape of a snub nose, snubbiness, Xen. II. metaph., τὴν σ. τῶν ὀδόντων the upward curve of a boar's tusks, Id.

σιμοῦς, οῦντος, ὁ, contr. for Σιμόεις.

σῐμόω, f. ώσω, (σιμός) to turn up the nose, and generally, to bend upwards. Hence

σίμωμα [ῐ], ατος, τό, the upturned bow of a ship, Plut.

σῐνᾰμωρέω, f. ήσω, (σινάμωρος) to ravage or destroy wantonly, Hdt.:—Pass. to be treated wantonly, Ar.

σῐναμωρία, ἡ, mischievousness, Arist. From

σῐνά-μωρος [ᾰ], ον, mischievous, c. gen. rei, τῶν ἑωυτοῦ σ. ruining his own affairs, Hdt. (From σίνομαι, -μωρος, v. ἰό-μωροι.)

σίνᾱπῐ [σῐ], εως, τό,=Att. νᾶπυ, mustard, N.T.

σινδών, όνος, ἡ, sindon, a fine cloth, a kind of cambric or muslin, (prob. derived from Ἰνδός, Sind), Hdt.; σινδὼν βυσσίνη, used for mummy-cloth, Id.: generally, fine linen, Soph., Thuc. 2. a muslin garment, Luc.

σινέομαι, Ion. for σίνομαι.

σινιάζω, (σινίον)=σήθω, to sift, winnow, N.T. From

σινίον, τό, a sieve. (Deriv. unknown.)

σίνῐς [σῐ], ιδος, ὁ, acc. σίνιν, (σίνομαι) a ravager, plunderer, Aesch.:—as Adj. destroying, σ. ἀνήρ as an example of a γλῶσσα, Poëta ap. Arist. II. as prop. n., Σίνις, the Destroyer, a famous robber of the Isthmus of Corinth, called ὁ Πιτυοκάμπτης, Eur., Xen.

ΣῙΝΟΜΑΙ [ῐ], Ep. 2 sing. σίνηαι: Ion. impf. σινέσκετο, -οντο: f. σινήσομαι: 3 pl. aor. 1 ἐσίναντο, Ion. -έατο: I. to do no harm or mischief, to plunder, Od.; to destroy, Ib.; to pillage or waste a country, to waste or destroy the crops, Hdt. II. generally, to hurt, harm, damage, Hes., Hdt.: in war, to injure, harass, Hdt., Xen. Hence

σίνος [σῐ], εος, τό, hurt, harm, mischief, injury, Hdt. II. of things, a mischief, bane, plague, Aesch.

σίντης, ου, ὁ, (σίνομαι) destructive, ravenous, of wild beasts, Il.

Σίντιες, οἱ, (σίνομαι) the Sintians, early inhabitants of Lemnos, who were pirates, Hom.

σίντωρ, ορος, ὁ,=σίντης, Anth.

Σίνων, ωνος, ὁ, (σίνομαι) Sinon, i.e. the Mischievous, the Greek who persuaded the Trojans to receive the wooden horse, Soph.

Σῐνώπη, ἡ, Sinopé, a town of Paphlagonia on the Black Sea, Hdt.; Σῐνωπεύς, έως, ὁ, an inhabitant of it,

Xen., etc.; ἡ Σινωπίς or Σινωπῖτις, the country, Strab.

ΣΙ΄ΟΝ, τό, the water-parsnep or marsh-wort, Theocr.

σιός, Lacon. and Boeot. for θεός, Ar.

σίπυδνος, ἡ, = σιπύη, Poëta ap. Luc.

σίπύη (never σιπύα), ἡ, a meal-tub, meal-jar, flour bin, Ar. (Deriv. unknown.)

σίραιον [ῐ], τό, new wine boiled down, Lat. defrūtum, Ar. (Deriv. unknown.)

σίρῐκόν, τό, silk, v. σηρικός.

ΣΙΡΟ΄Σ [ῐ], ὁ, a pit or vessel for keeping corn, Dem.

σῐσύμβριον, τό, = sq., Ar.

σίσυμβρον [ῐ], τό, mint or thyme, Anth.

σίσῡρα [ῠ], ἡ, a cloak of goats-hair, which served as a garment by day and a coverlet by night, Ar.

σίσῠριγχίον, τό, a plant of the Iris kind, Theophr.

σίσυρνα, ἡ, = σισύρα, a garment of skin, Hdt. Hence

σίσυρνο-φόρος, ον, (φέρω) wearing a coat of skin, Hdt.

Σίσῠφος [ῐ], ου, ὁ, a king of Corinth, noted as the craftiest of men, punished in the shades below, Hom., etc. :—Adj. Σισύφειος, α, ον, Eur., etc.; fem. Σισυφίς, Theocr. (Prob. a redupl. form of σοφός (with Aeol. υ for ο), the Crafty.)

σῑτᾰγωγέω, f. ήσω, to convey corn, Luc.; and

σῑτᾰγωγία, ἡ, conveyance of corn, Luc. From

σῑτ-ᾰγωγός, όν, ῀conveying or transporting corn, σ. πλοῖα provision-ships, Hdt.; σ. ναῦς Thuc.

σῑτάθην [ᾱ], Dor. and poët. aor. 1 pass. of σιτέω.

σιτέομαι, Ion. 3 pl. impf. σιτέσκοντο : f. σιτήσομαι : aor. 1 ἐσιτήθην, Dor. poët. σιτάθην : (σῖτος) :—to take food, eat, Od., Hdt. 2. c. acc. to feed on, eat, Hdt. : metaph., σ. ἐλπίδας Aesch.; τὴν σοφίαν Ar.

σιτευτός, ή, όν, fed up, fatted, Xen., N.T. From

σιτεύω, f. σω : Ion. impf. σιτεύεσκον : (σῖτος) :—to feed, fatten, Hdt. :—Pass. to feed on, to eat, Plut.

σῑτηγέω, f. ήσω, = σιταγωγέω, to convey or transport corn, Dem. : to import corn, παρά τινος Id. ; and

σῑτηγία, ἡ, the conveyance or importation of corn, Dem. From

σῑτ-ηγός, όν, (ἄγω) = σιταγωγός, Dem.

σῑτηρέσιον, τό, provisions, victuals, esp. of soldiers' provision-money, Xen., Dem. :—at Rome, σιτ. ἔμμηνον a monthly allowance of grain to the poorer citizens, Lat. tessera frumentaria, Plut. From

σῑτηρός, ά, όν, of corn, μέτρα σ. corn-measures, Arist.

σίτησις, εως, ἡ, (σιτέω) an eating, feeding, ἐπὶ σιτήσει for home consumption, Hdt. ; σ. ἐν Πρυτανείῳ public maintenance in the Prytanēum, Ar., Plat. II. food, Hdt.

σιτίζω, aor. 1 ἐσίτισα :—Med., f. Att. -ιοῦμαι, Ion. -ιεῦμαι : aor. 1 ἐσιτισάμην : pf. σεσίτισμαι : (σῖτος) :—to feed, nourish, fatten, Hdt., Ar. :—Pass. = σιτέομαι, to eat, Theocr.

σιτικός, ή, όν, (σῖτος) of wheat or corn, σ. τροφή Strab. ; ὁ σ. νόμος lex frumentaria, Plut.

σιτίον, τό, (σῖτος) mostly in pl. σιτία : 1. grain, corn : food made from grain, bread, ποιεῖσθαι σιτία ἀπὸ ὀλυρῶν to feed off spelt, Hdt. 2. generally, food, victuals, provisions, σιτία ἡμερῶν τριῶν three days' provision, of soldiers, Ar.; σιτία καὶ ποτά meat and drink, Plat., Xen. 3. τὰν Πρυτανείῳ σιτία

public maintenance in the Prytanēum, Ar.; cf. σίτησις. 4. rarely food for dogs, Xen.

σῑτιστός, ή, όν, verb. Adj. of σιτίζω, = σιτευτός, N.T.

σῑτο-δεία, Ion. -δηίη, ἡ, (δέομαι) want of corn or food, Hdt., Thuc.

σῑτο-δόκος, ον, (δέχομαι) holding food, Anth.

σῑτοδοτέω, f. ήσω, to furnish with provisions :—Pass. to be provisioned or victualled, Thuc. From

σῑτο-δότης, ου, ὁ, (δί-δωμι) a furnisher of corn.

σῑτολογέω, f. ήσω, to collect corn, to forage, Polyb.

σῑτολογία, ἡ, a collecting of corn, a foraging, Plut.

σῑτο-λόγος, ὁ, (λέγω) a collector of corn or provisions.

σῑτο-μέτρης, ου, ὁ, (μετρέω) one who measures out corn : a magistrate who had to inspect the corn-measures, Arist. Hence

σῑτομετρία, ἡ, the office of σιτομέτρης, Plut. ; and

σῑτομέτριον, τό, a measured portion of corn, N.T.

σῑτο-νόμος, ον, (νέμω) dealing out corn or food, σ. ἐλπίς the hope of getting food, Soph.

σῑτοποιέω, f. ήσω, to prepare corn for food, to make bread, Eur. : σ. τινί to give victuals to any one, Xen. :—Med. to prepare food for oneself, take food, Id. ; and

σῑτοποιία, ἡ, breadmaking, the preparation of food, Xen. ; and

σῑτοποιικός, ή, όν, for breadmaking, Xen. From

σῑτο-ποιός, ὁ, ἡ, σ. ἀνάγκη the task of grinding and baking, Eur. II. as Subst. one that ground the corn in the handmill, Thuc. ; mostly fem. a baking-woman, Hdt. ; γυναῖκες σ. Id., Thuc.

σῑτο-πομπία, ἡ, (πέμπω) the conveyance or convoy of corn, Dem.

ΣΙ΄ΤΟΣ, ὁ, heterog. pl. σῖτα, τά, corn, grain, comprehending both wheat (πυρός) and barley (κριθή), Od., Thuc.; σ. ἀληλεσμένος ground corn, Hdt., Thuc. 2. food made from grain, bread, as opp. to flesh-meat, Od., Hdt.; σῖτον ἔδοντες, a general epith. of men as opp. to beasts, Od. ; hence of savages, who eat flesh only, οὐδέ τι σῖτον ἤσθιον Hes. 3. in wider sense, meat, as opp. to drink, σῖτος ἠδὲ ποτής Hom. ; σῖτα καὶ ποτά Hdt., etc. 4. rarely of beasts, food, fodder, Hes., Eur. II. in Att. Law, the public allowance of grain made to widows and orphans, Dem.

σῑτ-ουργός, όν, (*ἔργω) = σιτοποιός, Plat.

σῑτο-φάγος [ᾰ], ον, eating corn or bread, Od., Hdt.

σῑτο-φόρος, ον, (φέρω) carrying corn or provisions, Hdt.

σῑτο-φύλᾰκες, οἱ, corn-inspectors, Athenian officers, originally three in number, but afterwards ten in the City and five in Peiræus, who registered imports of corn, and saw that the corn-measures were right, Dem.

σίττᾰ, a cry of drovers to their flocks ; when ἀπό follows, to call them off ; sht! chit! when πρός, to lead them on, Theocr.

σῑτ-ώνης, ου, ὁ, (ὠνέομαι) a buyer of corn, a commissary for buying it, Dem.

σῑτωνία, ἡ, purchase of corn, the office of σιτώνης, Dem.

ΣΙΦΛΟ΄Σ, ή, όν, crippled, maimed, Lat. mancus. Hence

σιφλόω, f. ώσω, to maim, cripple, bring to misery, Il.

Σίφνος, ἡ, Siphnos, one of the Cyclades, Hdt. : Adj. Σίφνιος, α, ον, Siphnian, Id.

σίφων [ῐ], ωνος, ὁ, a tube, pipe, siphon, used for drawing

wine out of the cask, Hippon. :—*a service-pipe for water in houses*, Strab. (Deriv. unknown.)

σιωπάω, f. -ήσομαι, later -ήσω : aor. 1 ἐσιώπησα : pf. σεσιώπηκα :—Pass., f. σιωπηθήσομαι : aor. 1 ἐσιωπήθην : (σιωπή):—*to be silent* or *still, keep silence*, Hdt., Att.; φησὶν σιωπῶν, i. e. *his silence gives consent*, Eur. II. trans. *to hold silent, keep secret, not to speak of*, Xen. :—Pass. *to be kept silent* or *secret*, σιγῶσ᾽ ὧν σιωπᾶσθαι χρεών *keeping secret things which ought to be kept secret*, Eur.

σιωπή, ἡ, *silence*, Soph., Eur., etc.; σιωπὴν ποιεῖν Xen.; ἦν σ. *there was a hush* or *calm*, Soph. 2. *the habit of silence*, Dem. II. dat. σιωπῇ as Adv., *in silence*, Hom., Att. (Deriv. uncertain.)

σιωπηλός, ή, όν, (σιωπάω) *silent, still, quiet*, Eur.

σιωπηρός, ά, όν, = foreg., Xen.

σιωπητέος, α, ον, verb. Adj. *to be passed over in silence*, Luc. II. σιωπητέον, *one must pass over in silence*, Id.

ΣΚΑΖΩ, only in pres. and impf. *to limp, halt*, Il.; metaph., σκ. πρὸς τὴν θεραπείαν Luc. II. ὁ σκάζων, also χωλίαμβος, *the iambic verse of Hipponax*, being a regular senarius, with a spondee or trochee in the last place, Arist.

ΣΚΑΙΟΣ, ά, όν, Lat. *scaevus, left, on the left hand* or *side*, σκαιῇ (sc. χειρί) *with the left hand*, Il.; χειρὶ σκαιῇ Hes. II. *western, westward*, for the Greek *auspex* turned his face northward, and so *had the West on his left*; hence, Σκαιαὶ πύλαι *the West-gate* of Troy, Il.; σκαιὸν ῥίον *the western headland*, Od. 2. *unlucky, ill-omened, mischievous* (because birds of ill omen *appeared on the left* or *in the West*, birds of good omen on the right or in the East), Hdt., Soph. III. metaph. of persons, like French *gauche, lefthanded, awkward, clumsy*, Hdt., Eur., etc.

σκαιοσύνη, ἡ, = sq., Soph.

σκαιότης, ητος, ἡ, (σκαιός III) *lefthandedness, awkwardness*, Hdt., Soph., etc.

σκαι-ουργέω, f. ήσω, (*ἔργω) *to behave amiss*, Ar.

ΣΚΑΙΡΩ, only in pres. and impf., *to skip, frisk*, Hom.

σκάλάθυρμα, ατος, τό, *a quibble* :—hence Dim. **σκάλάθυρμάτιον**, τό, *a petty quibble*, Ar.

σκάλευς, έως, ὁ, (σκάλλω) *a hoer*, Xen.

σκάλεύω, pf. ἐσκάλευκα, = σκάλλω, *to stir, poke, ἄνθρακας* Ar., Luc.

σκάληνός, ή, όν, and ός, όν, *uneven, unequal, ἀριθμὸς σκ. an odd number*, Plat.; τρίγωνον σκ. *a triangle with unequal sides*, Arist.; of a path, *uneven*, Anth.

ΣΚΑΛΛΩ, only in pres. and impf. *to stir up, hoe*, Hdt.

σκαλμός, ὁ, *the pin* or *thole* to which the Greek oar was fastened by a thong (τροπωτήρ), Aesch., Ar.

σκάλοψ, οπος, ὁ, (σκάλλω) *the digger*, i. e. *the mole*, Ar.

Σκάμανδρος, ὁ, *the Scamander*, the famous river of Troy, ὃν Ξάνθον καλέουσι θεοί, ἄνδρες δὲ Σκάμανδρον Il.:—Adj.**Σκάμάνδριος**, ον,*Scamandrian*,Ib.,Soph.,etc.

σκᾶνά, Dor. for σκηνή.

σκανδάληθρον [ἄ], τό, *the stick in a trap* on which the bait is placed, and which, when touched by the animal, springs up and shuts the trap, *the trap-spring*: metaph., σκανδάληθρ᾽ ἱστὰς ἐπῶν *setting word-traps*, i. e. *words which one's adversary will catch at, and be* **caught** *himself*, Ar.

σκανδάλίζω, f. σω, *to make to stumble, give offence* to any one, τινά N. T. :—Pass. *to take offence*, Ib. From

σκάνδάλον, τό, *a trap* or *snare laid for an enemy*, N. T. :—metaph. *a stumbling-block, offence, scandal*, Ib. (Deriv. unknown.)

σκάνδιξ, ικος, ἡ, *chervil* (i. e. *Chaerophyllum*), Ar.

σκάπάνεύς, έως, ὁ, = σκαφεύς, Luc.

σκάπάνη [ᾰ], ἡ, (σκάπτω) *a digging tool, mattock*, Theocr., Anth. II. *the act of digging*, Anth.

σκάπτειρα, ἡ, fem. of σκαπτήρ, Anth.

σκαπτήρ, ῆρος, ὁ, *a digger, delver*, Hom. ap. Arist.

σκάπτον, τό, Dor. for σκῆπτρον.

σκαπτός, ή, όν, (σκάπτω) *dug: that may be dug*: —Σκαπτὴ ὕλη *a district in Thrace*, Hdt.

σκάπτω (Root ΣΚΑΦ), f. σκάψω : aor. 1 ἔσκαψα : pf. ἔσκαφα :—Pass., f. σκαφήσομαι : aor. 2 ἐσκάφην [ᾰ]: pf. ἔσκαμμαι :— *to dig, delve*, μοχθεῖν καὶ σκ. Ar.; proverb., σκάπτειν οὐκ ἐπίσταμαι Id. II. c. acc., 1. *to dig the ground*, Xen. 2. *to dig about*, φυτὰ σκ. (as we say *to hoe* turnips), h. Hom.: metaph. *to dig up*, Eur. 3. σκ. τάφρον *to dig* a trench, Thuc. :—Pass., τὰ ἐσκαμμένα *scores to mark* a leap, metaph., ὑπὲρ τὰ ἐσκαμμένα ἅλλεσθαι *to overleap the mark*, Plat.

σκαρδᾰμύσσω, Att. -ττω, f. ξω, *to blink, wink*, Eur., Xen. (Deriv. uncertain.)

σκᾰρίφισμός, ὁ, *a scratching up*, σκαριφισμοὶ λήρων *small criticisms, petty quibbles*, Ar.

σκατός, gen. of σκῶρ.

σκᾰτο-φάγος, ον, (φᾰγεῖν) *eating dirt*, Ar.

σκάφεύς, έως, ὁ, (σκάπτω) *a digger, delver, ditcher*,Eur.

σκάφη [ᾰ], ἡ, (σκάπτω) *anything dug* or *scooped out*, 1. *a trough* or *tub, basin* or *bowl*, Hdt. 2. *a light boat, skiff*, Ar. 3. proverb., τὴν σκάφην σκάφην λέγειν *to call a spade a spade*,' to call things by their right names, Luc.

σκάφῆναι, aor. 2 pass. inf. of σκάπτω.

σκᾰφίδιον, τό, Dim. of σκαφίς 1. 2, *a small skiff*, Strab.

σκᾰφίς, ίδος, ἡ, Dim. of σκάφη : esp., 1. *a bowl, milk-pail*, Od. :—*a pot* for honey, Theocr. 2. *a small boat, skiff, canoe*, Anth. II. *a shovel*, Id.

σκάφος [ᾰ], ἡ, (σκάπτω) *a digging, hoeing*, σκάφος οἰνέων *the time for hoeing vines*, Hes.

σκάφος [ᾰ], εος, τό, (σκάπτω) *the hull of a ship*, Lat. *alveus*, Hdt., Trag. :—generally, *a ship*, Aesch., Ar., etc. II. *a scattering* II, Anth.

ΣΚΕΔΑΝΝΥΜΙ, f. σκεδάσω [ᾰ], Att. σκεδῶ : aor. 1 ἐσκέδασα, Ep. σκέδασα :—Med., aor. 1 ἐσκεδασάμην : —Pass., f. σκεδασθήσομαι : aor. 1 ἐσκεδάσθην : pf. ἐσκέδασμαι :—*to scatter, disperse*, Hom. II. Pass. *to be scattered, to disperse*, of men, Hdt., Thuc.; of the rays of the sun, Aesch.; of a report, *to be spread abroad*, Hdt. Hence

σκέδασις, ἡ, *a scattering*, Od.

σκεδῶ, Att. fut. of σκεδάννυμι.

ΣΚΕΘΡΟΣ, ά, όν, *exact, careful* : Adv., -ῶς Aesch.

σκελετός, ή, όν, (σκέλλω) *dried up, withered* : as Subst. **σκελετός**, ὁ, *a dried body, mummy*, Anth., Plut.

σκελετ-ώδης, ες, (εἶδος) *like a mummy*, Luc.

ΣΚΕΛΛΩ, f. σκελῶ : aor. 1 ἔσκηλα, 3 sing. opt. σκήλειε :—*to dry, dry up, make dry, parch*, Il. II.

Pass., σκέλλομαι, with intr. pf. act. ἔσκληκα, to be parched, lean, dry, v. κατασκέλλομαι.

ΣΚΕΛΟΣ, εος, τό, the leg from the hip downwards, Hdt., etc.; πρυμνὸν σκέλος the ham or buttock, Il.: —as a military phrase, ἐπὶ σκέλος πάλιν χωρεῖν, ἀνάγειν to retreat with the face towards the enemy, Lat. pedetentim, Eur., Ar.   II. metaph., τὰ σκέλη the legs, i.e. the two long walls between Athens and Peiræeus, Strab.; τὰ μακρὰ σκ. Plut.

σκέμμα, ατος, τό, (σκέπτομαι) a subject for speculation, a question, Plat.   II. speculation, Id.

σκέπᾰ, nom. and acc. pl. of σκέπας.

σκεπάζω, f. άσω, (σκέπω) to cover, shelter, Xen.

σκέπανον, τό, (σκέπω) a covering, Anth.

σκεπανός, ή, όν, (σκέπω) sheltered or sheltering, Anth.

σκέπαρνον, τό, or σκέπαρνος, ὁ, a carpenter's axe or adze, used for smoothing the trunks of trees, different from the πέλεκυς, Od. (Deriv. uncertain.)

σκέπας, αος, τό, (σκέπω) a covering, shelter, ἐπὶ σκέπας in or under shelter, Od.; σκέπας ἀνέμοιο shelter from the wind, Ib.; nom. and acc. pl. σκέπᾰ, Hes.

σκέπασμα, ατος, τό, (σκεπάζω) a covering, shelter, Plat.

σκεπάω, only in pres., (σκέπω) to cover, shelter, ἀνέμων σκεπόωσι κῦμα (Ep. for σκεπάουσι) they ward off (provide shelter against) the sea raised by the wind, Od.; κόρυν σκεπάουσιν ἔθειραι Theocr.

σκέπη, ἡ, (σκέπω) a covering, shelter, protection, Xen.:—c. gen.; ἐν σκέπῃ τοῦ πολέμου under shelter from war, Hdt.; ὑπὸ τὴν Ῥωμαίων σκέπην under their protection, Polyb.

σκεπόωσι, Ep. 3 pl. of σκεπάω.

σκεπτέον, verb. Adj. of σκέπτομαι, one must reflect or consider, Ar., Thuc., etc.   2. σκεπτέος, α, ον, to be considered, examined, Antipho.

σκεπτικός, ή, όν, (σκέψις) reflective: οἱ σκεπτικοί, the Sceptics or philosophers who asserted nothing, but only opined, Cic. opinatores, Luc.

ΣΚΕΠΤΟΜΑΙ (in Att. σκοπῶ or σκοποῦμαι are used as the pres.): f. σκέψομαι: aor. 1 ἐσκεψάμην: pf. ἔσκεμμαι: I. to look about, look carefully, followed by Prep. εἰς, Od., Eur.:—c. acc. to look after, watch, Il., Hdt., Att.:—absol. to look out, reconnoitre, Hdt.; σκέψαι look, Aesch.; σκέψασθε look out, Ar.   II. of the mind, to look to, view, examine, consider, think on, Soph., Thuc., etc.:—σκέψασθε δέ· only consider, Thuc.   2. to think of beforehand, premeditate, Dem.   3. pf. also in pass. sense, ἐσκεμμένα things well-considered, Thuc.; σκοπεῖτε οὖν. Answ. ἔσκεπται Plat.; so 3 fut. pass. ἐσκέψεται Id.

σκέπω, = σκεπάζω, Luc.

σκερβόλλω, to scold, abuse, σκ. πονηρά to use foul abuse, Ar. (Deriv. unknown.)

σκευᾰγωγέω, f. ήσω, to carry away goods and chattels, Dem., Aeschin. From

σκευ-ᾰγωγός, όν, (σκεῦος) conveying goods:—τὰ σκ. baggage-wagons, Plut.; transport vessels, Strab.   II. as Subst. a baggage-master, Xen.

σκευάζω, f. άσω: aor. 1 ἐσκεύασα:—Med., aor. 1 ἐσκευασάμην:—Pass., f. σκευασθήσομαι: pf. ἐσκεύασμαι, Ion. 3 pl. ἐσκευάδαται: Ion. 3 pl. plqpf. -ατο: (σκεῦος): —to prepare, make ready, esp. to prepare or dress food, Hdt., Ar.; σκ. ἔκ τινος περικόμματα to make mince-meat of him, Ar.:—Med. to prepare for oneself, Eur., Plat.   2. generally to make ready, h. Hom.; σκ. ἡδονάς to provide, procure, Plat.:—Med., like μηχανάομαι, to contrive, bring about, Hdt.   II. of persons, to furnish, supply:—Pass., σιτίοισι εὖ ἐσκευασμένος Id.; ποταμοῖσι Σκύθαι ἐσκευάδαται Id.   2. to dress up, dress out, Id., Ar., etc.:— Pass., ἐσκευασμένοι fully accoutred, Thuc.; of things, τὰ προπύλαια τύποισι ἐσκευάδαται are decorated with figures, Hdt.

σκευάριον, τό, Dim. of σκεῦος, a small vessel or utensil, Ar.:—implements of gaming, Aeschin.

σκευᾰσία, ἡ, (σκευάζω) a preparing, dressing, Plat.

σκευαστέον, verb. Adj. of σκευάζω, one must prepare to do a thing, c. inf., Ar.

σκευαστός, ή, όν, verb. Adj. of σκευάζω, prepared by art, artificial, Plat.

σκευή, ἡ, (σκεῦος) equipment, attire, apparel, dress, Lat. apparatus, Hdt., Soph., etc.   2. a fashion, style of dress or equipment, Hdt., Thuc.   II. tackle, as of a net, Pind.

σκευο-θήκη, ἡ, a tool-chest, arms-chest, Aeschin.

σκευοποιέω, f. ήσω, (σκευοποιός) to fabricate, Plut.

σκευο-ποίημα, τό, in pl. the dress of a tragic actor, Plut.

σκευο-ποιός, ὁ, (ποιέω) a maker of masks and other stage-properties, Ar.

ΣΚΕΥΟΣ, εος, τό, a vessel or implement of any kind, Ar., Thuc., etc.:—pl. in collective sense, furniture, house-gear, utensils, chattels, Ar.:—esp. of military accoutrements, equipment, Thuc., Xen.: baggage, luggage, Lat. impedimenta, Ar., Xen.:—the tackling or gear of ships, Xen., N.T.   2. an inanimate object, a thing, Plat.   3. metaph., τὸ σκεῦος, the body, as the vessel of the soul, N.T.; σκεῦος ἐκλογῆς a chosen vessel, of St. Paul, Ib.

σκευοφορέω, f. ήσω, to carry baggage, Xen.:—Pass. to have one's baggage carried, Plut.

σκευοφορικός, ή, όν, of or for baggage-carrying, Xen.; βάρος σκ. the load for one animal, a beast's load, Id.

σκευο-φόρος, ον, (φέρω) carrying σκεύη, αἱ σκ. κάμηλοι the baggage-camels, Hdt.; τὰ σκ. (sc. κτήνη) the beasts of burden in an army, Thuc., etc.   II. as Subst., of persons, a baggage-carrier, porter, Ar.; οἱ σκ. the sutlers, camp-followers, Hdt., Thuc., etc.

σκευοφῠλᾰκέω, f. ήσω, to watch the baggage, Plut. From

σκευο-φύλαξ [ῠ], ᾰκος, ὁ, a storekeeper.

σκευωρέομαι, aor. 1 ἐσκευωρησάμην: pf. ἐσκευώρημαι: Dep.: (σκευωρός):—to look after the baggage (τὰ σκεύη): hence, generally, to examine throughly, ransack it, Plut.   II. to fabricate, make up, Dem.; with a sense of fraud or intrigue, Id.:—absol. to act knavishly, Id. Hence

σκευώρημα, ατος, τό, a fabrication, fraud, Dem.

σκευωρία, ἡ, attention to baggage: hence, generally, great care, excessive care, Arist.   II. fabrication, knavery, intrigue, Dem. From

σκευ-ωρός, όν, (ὤρα cura) = σκευοφύλαξ.

σκέψις, εως, ἡ, (σκέπτομαι) a viewing, perception by the senses, Plat.   II. speculation, consideration, Id.; νέμειν σκέψιν to take thought of a thing, Eur.; ἐνθεὶς τῇ τέχνῃ σκέψιν Ar.; σκ. περί τινος or τι inquiry

into, speculation on a thing, Plat.   **2.** *hesitation, doubt* (v. σκεπτικός), Anth.

σκῆλαι, aor. 1 inf. of σκέλλω.

σκηνάω, = sq., Xen.   **II.** σκηνάομαι Dep., with pf. and plqpf. pass., *to dwell, live,* Plat. ; ἐσκηνημένοι *in covered carriages* (v. σκηνή III), Ar. ; ἱερά, ἐν οἷς ἐσκήνηντο *in which they found harbourage,* Thuc.   **2.** c. acc., σκηνησάμενος καλύβην *having built him* a hut or cottage, Id.

σκηνέω, f. ήσω, (σκηνή) *to be* or *dwell in a tent, to be encamped,* Xen. : generally, *to be quartered* or *billeted,* ἐν οἰκίαις Thuc. ; ἐν κώμαις, κατὰ τὰς κώμας Xen. ; σκ. εἰς τὰς κώμας *to go* to the villages *and quarter themselves there,* Id.

ΣΚΗΝΗ΄, ἡ, *a covered place, a tent,* Hdt., Soph., etc. : — in pl. *a camp,* Lat. *castra,* Aesch., Xen.   **2.** generally, *a dwelling-place, house, temple,* Eur.   **II.** *a wooden stage* for actors, Plat. :—in the regular theatre, the σκηνή was a wall at the back of the stage, with doors for entrance and exit ; *the stage* (in our sense) was προσκήνιον or λογεῖον, the sides or wings παρασκήνια, and the wall under the stage, fronting the orchestra, ὑποσκήνια.   **2.** οἱ ἀπὸ σκηνῆς, *the actors, players,* Dem.   **3.** τὸ ἐπὶ σκηνῆς μέρος that which is *actually represented* on the stage, Arist. ; τὰ ἀπὸ τῆς σκηνῆς (sc. ᾄσματα), *odes sung on the stage,* Id.   **4.** metaph. *stage-effect, unreality,* σκηνὴ πᾶς ὁ βίος ' all the world's *a stage,*' Anth.   **III.** *the tented cover, tilt of a wagon,* Aesch., Xen. : also *a bed-tester,* Dem.   **IV.** *an entertainment given in tents, a banquet,* Xen.

σκήνημα, ατος, τό, (σκηνέω) = σκηνή, *a dwelling-place,* Xen. : in pl. *a nest,* Aesch.

σκηνίδιον, τό, Dim. of σκηνή, Thuc.

σκηνίς, ίδος, ἡ, = σκηνή, Plut.

σκηνίτης [ῑ], ου, ὁ, *a dweller in tents,* Strab. : metaph. *a low fellow,* Isocr.

σκηνο-βᾰτέω, f. ήσω, *to bring on the stage,* Strab.

σκηνογρᾰφία, ἡ, *scene-painting,* Arist. ; and

σκηνογρᾰφικός, ή, όν, *for* or *in the manner of scene-painting,* Strab. From

σκηνο-γράφος [ᾰ], ὁ, (γράφω) *a scene-painter.*

σκηνο-πηγία, ἡ, (πήγνυμι) *a setting up of tents : the Feast of Tents* or *Tabernacles,* N. T.

σκηνοποιία, ἡ, *a pitching of tents,* Polyb. From

σκηνο-ποιός, όν, (ποιέω) *tentmaking* :—as Subst. *a tentmaker,* N. T.

σκῆνος, Dor. σκᾶνος, εως, τό, = σκηνή :—metaph. *the body* (as the tabernacle of the soul), N. T.

σκηνο-φύλαξ [ῠ], ᾰκος, ὁ, ἡ, *a watcher in a tent,* Xen.

σκηνόω, f. ώσω, (σκηνή) *to pitch tents, encamp,* Xen.   = σκηνέω, *to dwell in a tent,* Plat. : generally, *to settle, take up one's abode,* Id. :—in pf. pass. *to live* or *be,* Plat.   **II.** *to occupy with tents,* Plut.

σκηνύδριον, τό, Dim. of σκηνή, Plut.

σκήνωμα, ατος, τό, = σκήνημα, Eur. ; soldiers' *quarters,* Xen.   **2.** metaph. *the body,* N. T.

σκῆπτον, τό, for σκῆπτρον, only in Dor. form σκᾶπτον, and compds. σκηπτ-οῦχος, σκηπτουχία.

σκηπτός, ὁ, (σκήπτω) *a thunder-bolt,* Soph., Xen. :— metaph. *of pestilence,* Aesch. ; *of war,* Eur., Dem.

σκηπτουχία, ἡ, *the bearing a staff* or *sceptre* as the *badge of command, military command,* Aesch. :— generally, *command, power,* Anth.

σκηπτ-οῦχος, Dor. σκαπτ-, ον, (σκῆπτον, ἔχω) *bearing a staff* or *sceptre* as the *badge of command,* σκ. βασιλεύς *a sceptred king,* Hom.   **2.** as Subst. *a wand-bearer,* an officer in the Persian court, Xen.

σκηπτο-φόρος, ον, (φέρω) = σκηπτροφόρος, Anth.

σκῆπτρον, τό, Dor. σκᾶπτον, later σκᾶπτρον : (σκήπτω) :—*a staff* or *stick to lean upon, a walking-stick,* Hom., Aesch. : metaph. of the daughters of Oedipus, σκῆπτρα φωτός his *staffs* or *supports,* Soph.   **II.** *a staff,* as the badge of command, *a sceptre :* in Hom. borne by chiefs, and transmitted from father to son, whence the passage in Il. 2 is called ἡ τοῦ σκήπτρου παράδοσις, Thuc. :—also borne by judges, by heralds, by speakers, who on rising to speak received it from the herald, Hom.   **2.** *the sceptre,* i. e. *royalty, kingly power, rule,* Il., Trag.

σκηπτροφορέω, f. ήσω, *to rule over,* c. gen., Anth. From

σκηπτρο-φόρος, ον, *bearing a sceptre, kingly,* Anth.

ΣΚΗ΄ΠΤΩ, f. σκήψω : aor. 1 ἔσκηψα :—Med., f. σκήψομαι : aor. 1 ἐσκηψάμην :—Pass., pf. ἔσκημμαι :   **I.** *to prop, stay* one thing *against* or *upon* another : Pass. and Med. *to lean upon a staff,* Hom. : metaph. *to lean upon* a person or thing, Dem.   **2.** c. acc. rei, *to put forward by way of support, allege* in excuse, Eur. :—in Med. *to allege on one's own behalf,* Hdt., Thuc. ; c. inf. *to pretend to be,* Ar., Dem.   **II.** *to hurl, dart,* Aesch. ; metaph., σκ. ἀλάστορα εἴς τινα Eur.   **2.** intr. *to fall heavily,* Aesch., Soph.

σκηρίπτομαι, Med., only in pres., *to support oneself,* Od. ; σκηριπτόμενος χερσίν τε ποσίν τε *pressing* with hands and feet, Ib.

σκῆψις, εως, ἡ, (σκήπτω) *a pretext, plea, excuse, pretence,* Trag. ; c. gen., κατὰ φόνου τινὰ σκῆψιν on some *pretence* of murder, Hdt. ; σκ. τοῦ μὴ ποιεῖν a *plea, excuse for* not doing, Dem.

ΣΚΙΑ΄, ᾶς, Ion. σκιή, ῆς, ἡ, *a shadow,* Od. ; σκιὰ ἀντίστοιχος ὥς like the *shadow* that is one's double, Eur.   **2.** *the shade* of one who is dead, *a phantom,* Od., Trag. ; so of *one worn to a shadow,* Aesch. :—in proverbs of man's mortal estate, σκιᾶς ὄναρ ἄνθρωπος Pind. ; εἴδωλον σκιᾶς Aesch., etc.   **II.** *the shade* of trees, etc., πετραίη σκιή *the shade* of a rock, Hes. ; ἐν σκιῇ Id. ; ὑπὸ σκιῇ Hdt. ; ὑπὸ σκιᾶς Eur. ; σκιὰν Σειρίου κυνός *shade* from it's heat, Aesch.

σκιᾱγρᾰφέω, f. ήσω, (σκιᾱγράφος) *to draw with gradations of light and shade : to sketch out,* Lat. *adumbrare* :—Pass., τὰ ἐσκιαγραφημένα Plat. Hence

σκιᾱγράφημα, ατος, τό, *a mere sketch,* Plat.

σκιᾱγρᾰφία, ἡ, (σκιαγράφος) *a sketch* or *rough painting,* such as to produce an effect at a distance, *scene-painting,* Plat. From

σκιᾱ-γράφος [ᾰ], ον, (γράφω) *drawing in light and shade, sketching.*

σκιάδειον [ᾰ], τό, (σκιά) *a sunshade, parasol,* Ar.

σκιάζω : f. Att. σκιῶ Soph. : aor. 1 ἐσκίασα :—Pass., aor. 1 ἐσκιάσθην : pf. ἐσκίασμαι : (σκιά) :—*to overshadow, shade,* Il., Eur.   **II.** generally, *to overshadow, cover,* Hes., Hdt. :—Pass., Eur.   **III.** *to shade in painting,* Luc.

σκιᾱ-μᾰχέω, f. ήσω, (μάχομαι) *to fight in the shade,*

i. e. *in the school* (for practice): *to fight with a shadow, to fight in vain*, Plat.

Σκιά-ποδες [ᾰ], οἱ, *Shade-footed*, a fabulous people in Libya, *with immense feet which they used as sunshades*, Ar.

σκιᾰρό-κομος, ον, (κόμη) *with shading leaves*, Eur.

σκιᾰρός, ά, όν, v. σκιερός.

σκιάς, άδος, ἡ, (σκιά) *any thing serving as a shade, a canopy, pavilion*, Theocr., Plut.

σκιᾰ-τρᾰφής, ές, (τρέφω) *brought up in the shade*.

σκιᾰτρᾰφία, ἡ, *a being brought up in the shade, a sedentary, effeminate life*, Plut.

σκιᾰτροφέω or **-τρᾰφέω**, Ion. **σκιητροφέω**, f. ήσω: (τρέφω):—*to rear in the shade*:—Pass. *to keep in the shade, shun heat and labour*, Hdt., Xen.   II. intr. in Act. *to wear a shade, cover one's head*, Hdt.; ἐσκιατροφηκώς, *of an effeminate man*, Plat.

σκιᾰτροφία, ἡ, = σκιατραφία.

σκιάω, = σκιάζω, *to overshadow*:—Pass. *to be shaded* or *become dark*, σκιόωντο ἀγυιαί (Ep. 3 pl. impf.) Od.

σκίδνημι, collat. form of σκεδάννυμι, *to disperse*:—Pass. σκίδναμαι, only in pres. and impf. *to be scattered, to disperse*, of a crowd, Hom.; of foam or spray, of a cloud of dust, Il.; σκιδναμένης Δημήτερος when the corn *is being scattered*, i. e. at seedtime, Orac. ap. Hdt.; ἅμα ἡλίῳ σκιδναμένῳ as the sun *begins to spread his light*, i. e. soon after sunrise, Hdt.

σκιερός or **σκιαρός**, ά, όν, (σκιά) *shady, giving shade*, Hom., Pind., etc.   2. *shady, shaded*, Hes., Pind.   3. *dark-coloured*, Anth.

σκιή, σκιητροφέω, ἡ, Ion. for σκιά, σκιατροφέω.

ΣΚΙ'ΛΛΑ, ης, ἡ, *a squill, sea-onion*, Theogn., Theocr.

σκιμᾰλίζω, f. Att. ιῶ, *to jeer at, flout*, τινά Ar. (Deriv. unknown.)

σκίμπους, ποδος, ὁ, *a small couch, low bed*, Ar., Xen. (Deriv. unknown.)

σκίμπτομαι, = σκήπτομαι, *to allege*, Pind.

σκινδάλαμος, Att. **σχινδάλαμος**, ὁ, *a splinter*, Lat. *scindula*:—metaph., λόγων σχινδάλαμοι *straw-splittings, quibbles*, Ar.

σκινδᾰλᾰμο-φράστης, ου, ὁ, *a straw-splitter*, Anth.

σκιο-ειδής, ές, (εἶδος) *fleeting like a shadow, shadowy*, Ar., Plat.

σκιόεις, εσσα, εν, (σκιά) *shady, shadowy*, οὔρεα σκιόεντα i. e. *thickly wooded*, Hom.; σκ. μέγαρα *dark chambers*, Od.   2. act., νέφεα σκ. *overshadowing clouds*, Hom.   II. *shadowy, unsubstantial*, Anth.

σκιόωντο, Ep. 3 pl. impf. of σκιάω.

σκίπων [ῑ], ωνος, ὁ, = σκῆπτρον, *a staff*, Hdt., Eur., etc.

Σκίρα [ῑ], τά, *the festival of Athena* Σκιράς, held in the month Pyanepsion, Ar.; different from the Σκιροφόρια, which fell in Scirophorion.

Σκιράς, άδος, ἡ, *name of Athena* (v. σκίρον), Strab.

σκιράφειον, τό, *a gambling-house*, Isocr.   From

σκίρᾰφος [ῑ], ὁ, *a dice-box*:—metaph. *trickery, cheating*, Hippon. (Deriv. uncertain.)

Σκιρῖται, οἱ, *the Scirites*, a division of the Spartan army, consisting of 600 foot: they fought on the left wing near the king, and were (originally at least) περίοικοι, from the Arcadian district Σκιρῖτις, Thuc., Xen.

σκίρον [ῑ], τό, *the white sunshade which was borne*

from the Acropolis, in the festivals of Athena **Σκιράς** (τὰ Σκίρα), Plut.

σκῖρον, τό, *the hard rind* of cheese, *cheese-parings*, Ar.

σκῖρος, ὁ, *stucco: any hard covering*, v. σκῖρον.

Σκῖρο-φορία, τά, v. Σκίρα, τά.

Σκιροφοριών, ῶνος, ὁ, *Scirophorion*, the 12th Attic month, the latter part of June and former of July, so called from the festival Σκιροφόρια, Antipho, etc.

σκιρτάω, f. ήσω, (σκαίρω) *to spring, leap, bound*, Il., Eur., etc.:—metaph. of gusts of wind, Aesch.   Hence

σκίρτημα, ατος, τό, *a bound, leap*, Aesch., Eur.; and

σκίρτησις, ἡ, *a bounding, leaping*, Plut.; and

σκιρτητής, οῦ, ὁ, *a leaper*, Mosch.

σκιρτο-πόδης, ου, ὁ, (σκιρτάω, πούς) *spring-footed*, Anth.

Σκίρτος, ὁ, (σκιρτάω) *Leaper*, name of a Satyr, Anth.

σκιρτῶεν, 3 pl. opt. of σκιρτάω.

Σκίρων [ῑ], ωνος, ὁ, *the wind which blew from the Scironian rocks* in the Isthmus, Strab.   II. *a robber who haunted the rocks between Attica and Megara, killed by Theseus*, Xen.; Σκείρωνος ἀκταί *the coast* near these rocks, Eur.; *the adjacent sea was* Σκιρωνικὸν οἶδμα θαλάσσης Simon. in Anth.; *the rocks themselves* Σκιρωνίδες πέτραι Eur.; Σκιρωνὶς ὁδός *the road from Athens to Megara*, Hdt.

Σκίταλοι [ῑ], οἱ, invoked as *the powers of impudence*, Ar. (Deriv. unknown.)

σκι-ώδης, ες, contr. from σκιο-είδης, *shady*, Eur.

σκληρᾱγωγέω, f. ήσω, (ἀγωγή) *to bring up hardy*, Luc.

σκληρο-καρδία, ἡ, *hardness of heart*, N.T.

σκληρός, ά, όν, (σκέλλω) *hard*, Lat. *durus*, Theogn., Aesch., etc.   2. of sound, *hard, harsh, crashing*, Lat. *aridus*, Hes., Hdt.   3. *hard, stiff, unyielding*, Lat. *rigidus*, Ar., Xen.:—of boys who look old for their age, *stiff, sturdy*, Plut., Luc.   II. metaph. of things, *hard, austere, severe*, Soph., Eur.; σκληρὰ μαλθακῶς λέγων Soph.   III. Adv. *σκληρῶς καθῆσθαι*, i. e. *on a hard seat*, Hence

σκληρότης, ητος, ἡ, *hardness*, Plat.   II. of persons, *hardness, harshness, austerity*, Id.

σκληρο-τράχηλος, ον, *stiffnecked*, N.T.

σκληρύνω [ῡ], f. ῠνῶ, (σκληρός) *to harden*:—metaph. *to harden the heart*, N.T.

σκληφρός, ά, όν, (σκέλλω) *slender, slight, thin*, Plat.

σκνῖπαῖος, α, ον, *dark*, σκν. ὁδίτης *a wanderer in the twilight*, Theocr.   From

σκνῑπός, ἡ, όν, *dim-sighted*. (Deriv. uncertain.)

σκολιό-θριξ, ὁ, ἡ, *with curled hair* or *leaves*, Anth.

σκόλιον, τό, neut. of σκολιός (sub. μέλος), *a song which went round at banquets*, sung to the lyre by the guests, Ar.; so called from its *zigzag course*—each guest who sung holding a myrtle-branch (μυρρίνη), which he passed across the table to any one he chose.

ΣΚΟΛΙΟ'Σ, ά, όν, *curved, winding, twisted, tangled*, Lat. *obliquus*, Hdt., Eur., etc.:—*bent sideways*, δουλείη κεφαλὴ σκολιή (Hor. *stat capite obstipo*) Theogn.: metaph. *crooked*, i. e. *unjust, unrighteous*, Il., Hes., etc.; σκολιὰ πράττειν, εἰπεῖν Plat.:—so Adv. σκολιῶς, Hes.   Hence

σκολιότης, ητος, ἡ, *crookedness*, Plut.: in pl. *the windings* of a stream, etc., Strab.

σκολίωμα, ατος, τό, (σκολιός) *a bend, curve*, Strab.

σκολοπίζω, (σκόλοψ) *to impale*.

ΣΚΟΛΟΨ, οπος, ὁ, *a pale, stake*, Il., Eur. :—in pl. σκόλοπες, *pales, a palisade*, Hom., etc.   2. *a thorn*, Babr., N. T.   II. *a tree*, Eur.

σκόλυμος, ὁ, *an eatable kind of thistle, an artichoke*, Hes. (Deriv. unknown.)

ΣΚΟΜΒΡΟΣ, ὁ, *a sea-fish, a kind of tunny*, Ar.

σκοπ-άρχης, ου, ὁ, (ἄρχω) *the chief scout, the leader of a reconnoitring party*, Xen.

σκοπελο-δρόμος, ον, *running over rocks*, Anth.

σκόπελος, ὁ, (σκοπέω) *a look-out place, a peak, headland* or *promontory*, Lat. *scopulus*, Hom., etc.

σκοπεύω, later form for σκοπέω, Strab., etc.

σκοπέω and σκοπέομαι, used by Att. writers only in pres. and impf., the other tenses being supplied by σκέπτομαι: (σκοπός) :—*to look at* or *after* a thing: *to behold, contemplate*, Pind., Soph., etc. :—absol. *to look out, watch*, Soph., etc.   2. metaph. *to look to, consider, examine*, Hdt., Att.; σκ. τι Thuc., etc.; σκ. περί τινος or τι Plat.: absol., ὀρθῶς σκοπεῖν Eur., etc.   3. *to look out for*, c. acc., Xen., etc.   II. Med., used just like Act., Soph., Eur.   III. Pass., σκοπῶν καὶ σκοπούμενος *considering* and *being considered*, Plat.

σκοπή, ή, = σκοπιά I, in pl., Aesch., Xen.

σκοπιά, Ion. -ιή, ή, (σκοπέω) *a lookout-place, a mountain-peak*, Hom.: of the Trojan acropolis, Eur.: cf. σκόπελος.   2. metaph. *the height* or *highest point* of anything, Pind.   II. *a watchtower*, Lat. *specula*, Hdt., Plat.   III. *a look-out, watch*, σκοπιὴν ἔχειν *to keep watch*, Od., Hdt.

σκοπιάζω, (σκοπιά) only in pres. and impf., *to look about one, spy from a high place* or *watchtower*, Il.: *to spy, explore*, Od.   II. trans. *to spy out, search out, discover*, c. acc., Il., Anth., etc. :—so in Med. *to look out for*, Theocr.

σκοπιήτης, ου, ὁ, (σκοπιά) *a highlander*, of Pan, Anth.

σκοπιωρέομαι, Dep. *to look out for, watch*, Ar.

σκοπι-ωρός, ὁ, (ὤρα, *cura*) *a watcher*.

σκοπός, ὁ and ή, (σκέπτομαι) *one that watches, one that looks after* things, Hom.; of gods and kings, *a guardian, protector*, Ὀλύμπου σκ. Pind.   2. *a look-out-man, watchman*, stationed on a σκοπιά, Lat. *speculator*, Hom., Xen.: *one who marks* game, Xen.   3. *a spy, scout*, Il., Trag.   II. *the object on which one fixes the eye, a mark*, Lat. *scopus*, Od.; ἀπὸ σκοποῦ *away from the mark*, Ib.; so, παρὰ σκοπόν *away from the mark*, Id.; σκοποῦ τυχεῖν *to hit the mark*, Id.; ἐπὶ σκοπὸν βάλλειν Xen.   2. metaph. *an aim, end, object*, Plat.

σκοράκίζω, f. Att. ιῶ, (ἐς κόρακας, v. κόραξ) *to dismiss contemptuously*, Luc. :—Pass. *to be treated contemptuously*, Dem.

σκορδίνάομαι, Ion. -έομαι, Dep. *to stretch one's limbs, yawn, gape*, Ar.   (Deriv. unknown.)

σκοροδ-άλμη, ή, *a sauce of brine and garlic*, Ar.

σκοροδίζω, f. ίσω, *to prime* game-cocks *with garlic* before fighting, Ar. :—Pass., ἐσκοροδισμένος *primed with garlic*, Id.

σκορόδιον, τό, Dim. of σκόροδον, Ar.

Σκοροδο-μάχοι, οἱ, (μάχομαι) *Garlic-fighters*, Luc.

ΣΚΟΡΟΔΟΝ, τό, *garlic*, Lat. *allium*, the root of which consists of several separate *cloves* (γελγῖθες), and is

thus distinguished from the onion (κρόμμυον), and leek (πράσον), Hdt.; in pl., Ar.

σκορπίζω, f. ίσω, *to scatter, disperse*, Strab., N. T. (Deriv. uncertain.)

σκορπίος, ὁ, *a scorpion*, Plat., Dem.   II. *an engine of war for discharging arrows*, Plut. (Deriv. uncertain.)

σκοταῖος, α, ον and ος, ον, (σκότος) *in the dark*, i. e. *before daybreak* or *after nightfall*, Xen.   II. of things, *dark, obscure*, Plut.

σκοτεινός, ή, όν, (σκότος) *dark*, Aesch., Eur., etc.; ἀνὰ τὸ σκοτεινόν *in the darkness*, Thuc.   2. of a person, *darkling, blind*, Soph., Eur.   II. metaph. *dark, obscure*, Eur., Plat. :—so Adv. -νῶς, Plat.

σκοτία, ή, (σκότος) *darkness, gloom*, Anth.

σκοτίζω, *to make dark* :—Pass. *to be darkened*, N. T.

σκότιος, α, ον and ος, ον, (σκότος) *dark*,   I. of persons, *in the dark, darkling*, σκότιον δέ ἑ γείνατο μήτηρ, i. e. *not in open wedlock*, Il.; so, σκότιοι παῖδες Eur.; σκ. εὐναί *clandestine loves*, Id., etc.   II. of things and places, *dark*, Id.   2. metaph. *like* σκοτεινός, *dark, obscure*, Ar.

σκοτο-δάσυ-πυκνό-θριξ, τρίχος, ὁ, ή, *dark with shaggy thick hair*, κυνῆ σκ., of a 'cap of darkness,' Ar.

σκοτο-δινιάω, (δίνη) only in pres. *to suffer from dizziness* or *vertigo*, Ar., Plat.

σκοτο-ειδής, ές, (εἶδος) *dark-looking*, Plat.

σκοτόεις, εσσα, εν, (σκότος) *dark*, Hes.

σκοτόμαινα, ή, = σκοτομήνη, Anth.

σκοτο-μήνη, ή, *a moonless night*. Hence

σκοτομήνιος, ον, *dark and moonless*, Od.

ΣΚΟΤΟΣ, ου, ὁ, *darkness, gloom*, Od., Att.   2. *the darkness of death*, Il., Eur.   3. *of blindness*, σκότον βλέπειν Soph.; σκότον δεδορκώς Eur.   4. metaph. σκότῳ κρύπτειν, like Horace's *nocte premere*, *to hide in darkness*, Soph.; so, διὰ σκότους ἐστί *it is dark and uncertain*, Xen.; κατὰ σκότος, ὑπὸ σκότου Soph., etc.

σκότος, εος, τό, = foreg., Plat., etc. Hence

σκοτόω, f. ώσω, *to make dark, to blind* :—Pass. *to be in darkness*: also *to suffer from vertigo*, Plat.

σκοτ-ώδης, ες, contr. for σκοτοειδής, dark, Plat.

σκύβαλον, τό, *dung, filth, refuse*, Anth. (Deriv. uncertain.)

σκυδμαίνω, only in pres., *to be angry*, τινί *with one*, Il. (in Ep. inf. σκυδμαινέμεν.)

ΣΚΥΖΟΜΑΙ, Ep. 3 sing. aor. 1 opt. σκύσσαιτο :—*to be angry* or *wroth with* one, τινί Hom.: absol.—*to be wroth*, Il.

Σκύθης [ῠ], ου, ὁ, voc. Σκύθα, *a Scythian*: proverb., Σκυθῶν ἐρημία, as we might say 'the desert of Africa,' Ar.: —fem. Σκύθαινα.   2. as Adj. *Scythian*, Aesch.   II. at Athens, *a policeman, one of the city-guard*, which was mostly composed of Scythian slaves, Ar.   Hence

Σκυθίζω, f. ίσω, *to behave like a Scythian* : hence, from the Scythian practice of scalping slain enemies, *to shave the head*, ἐσκυθισμένος ξυρῷ Eur.; and

Σκυθικός, ή, όν, *Scythian*, Aesch., etc.:—ἡ Σκυθική (sc. γῆ) Hdt., etc.:—fem. Σκυθίς, ίδος, acc. ίν, Aeschin.   II. Adv. -κῶς, Strab., Plut.

Σκυθιστί [τῑ], Adv. *in the Scythian tongue*, Hdt.

Σκύθο-τοξότης, ου, ὁ, *a Scythian bowman*, Xen.

σκυθράζω, *to be angry, peevish*, Eur. From

σκυθρός, ά, όν, (σκύζομαι) *angry, sullen*, Menand.

σκυθρωπάζω, f. σω: aor. 1 ἐσκυθρώπασα: pf. ἐσκυθρώπακα:—to look angry or sullen, be of a sad countenance, Ar., Xen., etc. From

σκυθρ-ωπός, όν, (σκυθρός, ὤψ) angry-looking, of sad countenance, sullen, Eur., Aesch., etc.:—τὸ σκυθρωπόν, = sq., Eur.—Adv., σκυθρωπῶς ἔχειν Xen. II. of things, gloomy, sad, melancholy, Eur.

σκυλάκαινα [ᾰ], ἡ, fem. of σκύλαξ, Anth.

σκυλάκεία, ἡ, a breeding of dogs, Plut.

σκυλάκευμα [ᾰ], ατος, τό, a whelp, cub, Anth.

σκυλάκεύω, f. σω, (σκύλαξ) to pair dogs for breeding, Xen. II. Pass. to be suckled, Strab.

σκυλάκιον [ᾰ], τό, Dim. of σκύλαξ, Plat., Xen.

σκυλᾰκ-ώδης, ες, (εἶδος) like a young dog: τὸ σκυλακῶδες the nature of puppies, Xen.

σκύλαξ [ῠ], ᾰκος, ὁ, and ἡ, (σκύλλω) a young dog, whelp, puppy, Lat. catulus, Od., Hes.:—generally, a dog, Soph., etc. 2. = σκυμνός, Eur.

σκύλευμα [ῠ], ατος, τό, mostly in pl. the arms stript off a slain enemy, spoils. Eur., Thuc. From

σκυλεύω, f. σω, (σκῦλον) to strip or despoil a slain enemy of his arms, Hes., Hdt.; c. acc. pers. et rei, Κύκνον σκυλεύσαντες ἀπ᾽ ὤμων τεύχεα having stript the arms of Cycnus from his shoulders, Hes. 2. c. acc. rei et gen. pers. to strip the arms off an enemy, Xen.; so, ἀπὸ τῶν νεκρῶν σκ. ψέλια Hdt.

σκύλη-φόρος, ον, poët. for σκυλοφόρος, Anth.

Σκύλλᾰ and Σκύλλη, ης, ἡ, (σκύλλω) Scylla, a monster barking like a dog, who inhabited a cavern in the Straits of Sicily, and rent unwary mariners, Od.

ΣΚΥ´ΛΛΩ, aor. 1 ἔσκύλα:—Pass., pf. ἔσκύλμαι:—to rend, mangle:—Pass., Aesch. 2. metaph.:—to trouble, annoy, Lat. vexare, N. T.:—Pass. or Med., μὴ σκύλλου trouble not thyself, Ib.; ἐσκυλμένοι troubled, distressed, Ib.

σκυλοδεψέω, f. ήσω, to tan hides, Ar. From

σκύλο-δέψης, ου, ὁ, (δέφω, f. δέψω) a tanner of hides, Ar.:—so σκύλό-δεψος, ὁ, Dem.

ΣΚΥ´ΛΟΝ, τό, mostly in pl. σκῦλα, the arms stript off a slain enemy, spoils, Soph., Thuc.; εἰς σκύλα γράφειν to write one's name on arms taken as spoil, Eur.: —rarely in sing., booty, spoil, prey, Id.

ΣΚΥ´ΛΟΣ [ῠ], εος, τό, a skin, hide, Theocr., Anth.

σκῦλο-φόρος, ον, (φέρω) receiving the spoil, Anth.

σκῦλο-χᾰρής, ές, (χαίρω) delighting in spoils, Anth.

ΣΚΥ´ΜΝΟΣ, ὁ, and ἡ, a cub, whelp, esp. a lion's whelp, Il., Hdt., Att.; of other animals, Eur., Plut.; in poets also of men, Ἀχίλλειος σκ. Eur.

Σκύρος, ἡ, the isle of Scyros, one of the Sporades, not far from Euboea, Hom.:—Adj. Σκύριος, ὁ, a Scyrian, Hdt.:—Adv. Σκύρόθεν from Scyros, Il.

σκυτάλη [ᾰ], ἡ, a staff, cudgel, club, Anth. II. at Sparta, a staff or baton, used as a cypher for writing dispatches:—a strip of leather was rolled slantwise round it, on which the dispatches were written lengthwise, so that when unrolled they were unintelligible: commanders abroad had a staff of like thickness, round which they rolled these papers, and so were able to read the dispatches—hence σκυτάλη came to mean a Spartan dispatch, Thuc., Xen.; and generally a message, Pind. (Deriv. uncertain.)

σκῦτᾰληφορέω, f. ήσω, to carry a club, Strab. From

σκῦτάλη-φόρος, ον, (φέρω) carrying a club, Strab.

σκῦτάλιον [ᾰ], τό, Dim. of σκύτάλον, Ar.

σκῦτᾰλίς, ίδος, ἡ, Dim. of σκυτάλη, a stick, Hdt.

σκύτᾰλον [ῠ], τό, = σκυτάλη 1, Pind., Hdt., Xen.

σκῦτεύς, έως, ὁ, (σκῦτος) = σκυτοτόμος, Ar., Plat., etc.

σκῦτεύω, f. σω, to be a shoemaker, Xen.

σκῦτικός, ή, όν, (σκῦτος) skilled in shoemaking:—ἡ -κή (sub. τέχνη) = σκυτοτομία, Plat.

σκύτινος, η, ον, (σκῦτος) leathern, made of leather, Hdt., Ar. 2. metaph. skinny, gaunt, Anth.

σκῦτο-δέψης, ου, ὁ, (δέφω, f. δέψω) a leather-dresser, currier, Theophr.: so, σκῦτόδεψος, ὁ, Plat., Luc.

ΣΚΥ˜ΤΟΣ, τό, like κύτος [ῠ], a skin, hide, esp. a dressed or tanned hide, Od., Ar., etc. II. a leather thong, a whip, Dem.; σκύτη βλέπειν to look whips, i. e. as if one was going to be whipt, Ar.

σκῦτοτομέω, f. ήσω, to cut leather for shoes, to be a shoemaker, Ar., Plat.; and

σκῦτοτομία, ἡ, shoemaking, Plat.; and

σκῦτοτομικός, ή, όν, of or for a shoemaker, Ar.; ὁ σκ. = ὁ σκυτοτόμος, Plat.: ἡ -κή (sc. τέχνη), = foreg., Id. From

σκῦτο-τόμος, ὁ, (τέμνω) a leather-cutter, a worker in leather, Il., Xen., etc.: esp. a shoemaker, cobbler, Ar.

σκῦτο-τράγέω, f. ήσω, (τραγεῖν) to gnaw leather, Luc.

ΣΚΥ´ΦΟΣ, ου, ὁ, or σκύφος, εος, τό, a cup, can, Od., Eur., etc.: a milk-pail, Theocr.

σκωληκό-βρωτος, ον, (βι-βρώσκω) eaten of worms, N. T.

σκώληξ, ηκος, ὁ, a worm, Lat. lumbricus, Il. 2. of the grubs, of insects, Ar., etc. (Deriv. uncertain.)

σκῶλος, ὁ, like σκόλοψ, a pointed stake, Il.

σκῶμμα, ατος, τό, (σκώπτω) a jest, joke, gibe, scoff, Ar.; ἐν σκώμματος μέρει by way of a joke, Aeschin.; σκ. παρὰ γράμμα a pun, Arist.

σκωμμάτιον [ᾰ], τό, Dim. of σκῶμμα, Ar.

σκωπτικός, ή, όν, mocking, jesting, Plut., Luc.; and

σκωπτόλης, ου, ὁ, a mocker, jester, Ar. From

ΣΚΩ´ΠΤΩ, f. σκώψομαι: aor. 1 ἔσκωψα:—Pass., aor. 1 ἐσκώφθην: pf. ἔσκωμμαι:—to hoot, mock, jeer, scoff at, τινά Ar.; also, σκ. εἰς τὰ ῥάκια to jest at his rags, Id.; εἴς τινα Aeschin. b. in good sense, to joke with, τινά Hdt. 2. absol. to jest, joke, be funny, Ar., Xen., etc.

ΣΚΩ˜Ρ, τό; gen. σκᾰτός:—dung, Ar. Hence

σκωρία, ἡ, the dross of metal, slag, scoria, Strab.

σκώψ, ὁ, gen. σκωπός, nom. pl. σκῶπες, (σκώπτω) a small kind of owl, Od., Theocr.

σμᾰράγδινος, η, ον, of smaragdus, N. T. From

σμάραγδος, ἡ, Lat. smaragdus, a precious stone of a green colour, a name given to the emerald and to malachite, Hdt. (Deriv. unknown.)

σμᾰρᾰγέω, f. ήσω, to crash, as thunder, Il.; of the sea, to roar, Ib.; of cranes, to scream, Ib. (Formed from the sound.)

ΣΜΑ´Ω, 3 sing. contr. σμῇ, inf. σμῆν, 3 sing. pass. σμῆται; but Ion. σμᾷ, σμᾶν, σμᾶται: impf. ἔσμων: aor. 1 ἔσμησα:—Med., part. σμώμενος: aor. 1 ἐσμησάμην:—to wipe or cleanse with soap or unguent; (but the Act. is mostly found in compds. δια-, ἐκ-, ἐπι-σμάω): —Med., σμᾶσθαι τὴν κεφαλήν to wash or anoint one's head, Hdt.

σμερδᾰλέος, α, Ion. η, ον, terrible to look on, fearful,

aweful, direful, Hom. 2. terrible to hear, in neut. as Adv., terribly, Id.; so in pl. σμερδαλέα, Il. (Deriv. uncertain.)

σμερδνός, ή, όν, = σμερδάλεος, Il., Aesch.:—as Adv., σμερδνόν Il.

σμήηγμα, ατος, τό, (σμήχω), soap or unguent, Plut.

σμηνο-δόκος, ον, (δέχομαι) holding a swarm of bees, Anth.

ΣΜΗ͂ΝΟΣ, Dor. σμᾶνος, εος, τό, a beehive, Hes., Plat. II. a swarm of bees, Aesch., etc.; of wasps, Ar.:—metaph., of clouds, Id., etc.

σμήχω: aor. 1 ἔσμηξα:—Pass., aor. 1 ἐσμήχθην:—longer form of σμάω, to wipe off by help of soap or unguent, to wash off, Od. II. to wipe clean, Babr.: proverb., Αἰθίοπα σμ. ' to wash a blackamoor white,' Luc.:—Med., σμηχομένα κρόταφον wiping her brow clean, Anth.

σμικρο-, for all words beginning thus, v. μικρο-.

σμικρός, ά, όν, Ion. and old Att. for μικρός.

σμῖλα, ή, = σμίλη, Anth.

σμῖλαξ, older Att. μῖλαξ, ἄκος, ἡ, Lat. taxus, the yew, Plat. II. the convolvulus, or perh. bryony, Trag., Ar.

σμίλευμα [ῐ], ατος, τό, a piece of carved work: metaph., σμιλεύματα ἔργων finely carved works, Ar.

σμιλευτός, ή, όν, cut, carved, Anth.

σμιλεύω, to carve finely. From

ΣΜΙ͂ΛΗ [ῐ], ἡ, a knife for cutting, carving or pruning, Plat., etc.: a graving tool, chisel, Anth.

σμιλίον, τό, Dim. of σμίλη, Lat. scalpellum, Luc.

Σμινθεύς, έως, ὁ, name of Apollo (from Σμίνθος or Σμίνθη a town in Troas), the Sminthian, Il.

σμίνθος, ὁ, a mouse (a Cretan word), Anth.

σμινύη, (not -ύα), ἡ, a two-pronged hoe or mattock, Lat. bidens, Ar., Plat.

σμογερός, poët. for μογερός, with pain, painful, Soph. Adv. -ρῶς, Id.

σμύρνα, Ion. σμύρνη, ἡ, like μύρρα, myrrh, the resinous gum of an Arabian tree, used for embalming the dead, Hdt.; called σμύρνης ἱδρώς by Eur.; also used for anointing, Ar.; and a salve, Hdt. (A foreign word.)

Σμύρνα, Ion. -νη, ἡ, Smyrna, in Ionia, Hdt., etc.

Σμυρναῖος, a, ον, of Smyrna, Pind.

σμυρναῖος, a, ον, (σμύρνα) of myrrh, Anth.

σμυρνίζω, f. σω, (σμύρνα) to flavour or drug with myrrh : Pass., οἶνος ἐσμυρνισμένος N. T.

σμυρνο-φόρος, ον, (φέρω) bearing myrrh, Strab.

ΣΜΥ͂ΧΩ [ῠ], aor. 1 ἔσμυξα:—Pass., aor. 1 ἐσμύχθην: aor. 2 ἐσμύγην [ῠ]:—to burn in a mouldering fire:—Pass. to smoulder away, Il., Mosch.

σμῶδιξ, ιγγος, ἡ, a weal, swollen bruise, caused by a blow, Il. (Deriv. unknown.)

σμώχω, f. ξω, (σμάω) to rub down, grind down, Ar.

σοβαρός, ά, όν, (σοβέω) properly, scaring birds away :—and so, I. rushing, rapid, Ar.:—Adv. -ρῶς, Id. II. swaggering, pompous, haughty, Id.; of a horse, Xen.:—Adv. -ρῶς, Plut.; also neut. as Adv., Theocr. 2. of things, Ar.

σοβέω, f. ήσω, (σοῦ, σοῦ):—to scare away birds, Ar., etc. 2. generally, to drive away, clear away, Xen. II. to move rapidly, πόδα σοβεῖν, of dancing, Ar.:—metaph. in Pass. to be much agitated, vehe-

mently excited, Anth., Plut. III. intr. to strut, swagger, bustle, Dem., Plut.; σόβει ἐς Ἄργος bustle off to Argos, Luc.

σοί and enclit. σοι, dat. of σύ.

σοῖο, Ion. for σοῦ, gen. of σός, σόν.

σολοικίζω, f. Att. ιῶ, (σόλοικος) to speak incorrectly, commit a solecism, φωνῇ Σκυθικῇ σολ. to speak bad Scythian, Hdt. Hence

σολοικισμός, ὁ, incorrectness in the use of language, a solecism, Luc.; and

σολοικιστής, οῦ, ὁ, one who speaks incorrectly, Luc.

σόλοικος, ον, speaking incorrectly, using provincialisms, Anacr., etc. II. metaph. erring against good manners, awkward, clumsy, Xen., Arist. (Said to come from the corruption of the Attic dialect by the Athenian colonists of Σόλοι in Cilicia.)

ΣΟ΄ΛΟΣ, ὁ, a mass or lump of iron, used in throwing, Il.; distinguished from the flat δίσκος or quoit.

σόος, η, ον, Ep. and Ion. form of σῶος, σῶς : v. σῶς.

σορο-πηγός, οῦ, ὁ, (πήγνυμι) a coffin-maker, Ar., Anth.

ΣΟΡΟ΄Σ, ἡ, a vessel for holding anything, esp. a cinerary urn, Il. :—a coffin, Hdt., Ar. II. as nickname of an old man or woman, Ar.

σός, ή, όν, possessive Adj. of pers. Pron. σύ, the earlier form being τεός, thy, thine, of thee, Lat. tuus, tua, tuum, Hom., etc.; Ep. gen. σοῖο;—in Att. often with the Art., δέμας τὸ σόν, τὸ σὸν κάρα :—σὸν ἔργον, c. inf., 'tis thy business to . . , Soph. ; so, σόν [ἐστι] alone, Aesch. :—οἱ σοί thy kinsfolk, people, Soph. :—τὸ σόν what concerns thee, thy interest, words, purpose, Id. :—τὰ σά thy property, Od. ; thy interests, Soph. 2. with a gen. added, τὰ σ᾽ αὐτῆς ἔργα Il.; σὸν μόνης δώρημα Soph. II. objective, for thee, σῇ ποθῇ Il.; σός τε πόθος σά τε μήδεα Od.; σῇ προμηθίᾳ Soph.

σοῦ, σοῦ, shoo! shoo !, a cry to scare away birds, Ar.

σουδάριον, τό, the Lat. sudarium, a kerchief, N. T.

σοῦμαι, contr. form of σεύομαι (σεύω).

σούνεκα, crasis for σοῦ ἕνεκα, Anth.

Σουνι-άρατος, ον, (Σούνιον) worshipped at Sunium, Ar.

Σουν-ιέρακος, ὁ, (ἱέραξ) Hawk-of-Sunium, Ar.

Σούνιον, τό, Sunium, the southern headland of Attica, Od., etc. :—Adj., Σουνιακός, ή, όν, Hdt. :—Σουνιεύς, έως, ὁ, pl. Σουνιεῖς, a man of Sunium, Decret. ap. Dem.

σουρίζει, crasis for σοι ὀρίζει, Aesch.

σοῦσθαι, med. inf. of σεύω : σούσθω, σοῦσθε, 3 sing. and 2 pl. imper.

Σουσί-γενής, ές, (γίγνομαι) born at Susa, Aesch.

σοῦσον, τό, the lily, a Phoen. word. II. Σοῦσα, τά, Susa, in the province of Susiana or Shushan, winter residence of the King of Persia, Hdt., Xen. :—Σούσιος, ὁ, a man of Susa, Xen.—Σουσίς, ίδος, ἡ, = Σοῦσα, Aesch. ; but Σ. γυνή a woman of Susa, Xen.

σουστί, crasis for σοι ἐστί.

σοφία, Ion. -ίη, ἡ, skill in handicraft and art, Il., Xen., etc. :—σ. τινός or περί τινος knowledge of, acquaintance with a thing, Plat. 2. sound judgment, intelligence, practical wisdom, such as was attributed to the Seven Wise men, Theogn., Hdt. ; in not so good a sense, cunning, shrewdness, craft, like δεινότης, Hdt. 3. wisdom, philosophy, Theogn., Att.

σοφίζω, f. σω, (σοφός) to make wise, instruct, N. T. 2.

Pass. *to be clever* or *skilled in* a thing, c. gen., ναυτιλίης σεσοφισμένος *skilled in* seamanship, Hes. :—absol. *to pursue wisdom, be well instructed,* Xen.   3. Med. *to teach oneself, learn,* τι Id.   II. σοφίζομαι, as Dep., with aor. 1 med. and pf. pass. *to play subtle tricks, deal subtly,* Theogn., Eur., etc. ; οὐδὲν σοφιζόμεσθα τοῖσι δαίμοσι *we argue* not *subtly about* the gods, Eur. :—in speaking, *to use sophistical arguments, to quibble,* περί τι Plat. ; καίπερ οὖτω τούτου σεσοφισμένου *though this man has dealt* thus *craftily,* Dem.   2. c. acc. rei, *to devise cleverly* or *skilfully,* Hdt., Ar. ; ἀλλότρια σ. *to meddle with* other men's *craft,* Ar. ; τὸ τοῦτο δεῖ σοφισθῆναι this one must *gain by craft,* Soph. :—pf. part. σεσοφισμένος in pass. sense, *craftily devised,* N. T.   3. c. acc. pers. *to deceive,* Anth.   Hence
σόφισμα, ατος, τό, *any skilful act, the skilful dressing of food,* Xen.   II. *a clever device, contrivance,* Hdt., Trag.   2. in less good sense, *a sly trick, artifice,* Eur., Thuc.; *a stage-trick, claptrap,* Ar.   3. *a captious argument, a quibble, fallacy, sophism,* Plat., etc.   Hence
σοφισμάτιον, τό, Luc. ; and
σοφιστέον, verb. Adj. *one must contrive,* Arist.
σοφιστεύω, f. σω, *to play the sophist, argue as one,* Dem.   2. *to give lectures,* of the Sophists, Plut.
σοφιστής, οῦ, ὁ, (σοφίζομαι) *a master of one's craft* or *art, an adept,* of a diviner, Hdt. ; of poets, Pind. ; of the Creator, Plat. ; metaph., σ. πημάτων *an adept in* misery, Eur.   2. like φρόνιμος, *one who is clever in matters of life, a wise man,* in which sense the seven Sages are called σοφισταί, Hdt. ; of Prometheus, Aesch.   II. at Athens, *a Sophist,* i. e. *a Professor* of grammar, rhetoric, politics, mathematics, such as Prodicus, Gorgias, Protagoras, Thuc., Plat., etc. At first the Sophists were held in honour ; but from their loose principles they fell into ill repute, and the word came to mean,   2. *a sophist* (in bad sense), *a quibbler, cheat,* Ar., Dem., etc.
σοφιστικός, ή, όν, (σοφιστής) *of* or *for a sophist,* Plat.   2. *like a sophist, sophistical,* Xen., etc. Adv. -κῶς, Plat.
σοφίστρια, ή, fem. of σοφιστής, Plat.
Σοφο-κλέης, contr. -κλῆς, ὁ ; gen. έους, later έος ; acc. έα :—*Sophocles,* Ar., etc.
σοφό-νοος, ον, contr. -νους, ουν, *wise-minded,* Luc.
ΣΟΦΟ'Σ, ή, όν, properly, *skilled in any handicraft* or *art, cunning in his craft,* Theogn., etc. ; of a charioteer, Pind. ; of poets and musicians, Id. ; of a soothsayer, Soph., etc.   2. *clever in matters of common life, wise, prudent, shrewd,* ἄνδρες Θεσσαλοί *shrewd* fellows, the Thessalians! Hdt. ; πολλὰ σοφός Aesch. ; μείζω σοφίαν σοφός Plat., etc. ; τῶν σοφῶν κρείσσω better *than all craft,* Soph. ; σοφόν [ἐστι] c. inf., Eur.   3. *skilled in the sciences, learned, profound, wise,* Id., Plat., etc. ; hence, ironically, *abstruse, obscure,* Ar., etc.   II. pass., of things, *cleverly devised, wise,* Hdt., etc.; σοφώτερ' ἢ κατ' ἄνδρα συμβαλεῖν things *too clever* for man to understand, Eur.   III. Adv. σοφῶς, *cleverly, wisely,* Soph., Eur., etc. :—Comp. -ώτερον, Eur. : Sup. -ώτατα, Id.

σόω, rare Ep. Verb for σαόω, σώζω, *to preserve, save, deliver,* 2 sing. subj. σόῃς, 3 sing. and pl. σόῃ, σόωσι, Il.
σπαδίζω, f. ξω, (σπάω) *to draw off,* Hdt.
σπάδων [ἄ], ὁ, (σπάω) *an eunuch,* Lat. *spado,* Plut.
σπαθάω, only in pres., in weaving, *to strike home the woof with the* σπάθη ; metaph., λίαν σπαθᾶν *to go too fast,* a cant phrase for throwing away money, Ar. ; so, σπ. τὰ χρήματα Plut. :—Pass., ἐσπαθᾶτο ταῦτα these *were the prodigalities indulged in,* Dem.
ΣΠΑ'ΘΗ [ἄ], ή, *a flat blade used by weavers* in the upright loom (instead of the comb (κτείς) used in the horizontal), for striking the threads of the woof home, so as to make the web close, Aesch.
σπαθίον, τό, Dim. of σπάθη, Anth.
ΣΠΑΙ'ΡΩ, *to gasp,* of dying fish, Anth. ; cf. ἀσπαίρω.
σπάκα, Median for κύνα, Hdt.
σπανίζω, f. Att. ιῶ, of things, *to be rare, scarce, scanty,* Pind., Ar.   2. of persons, *to lack* or *be in want of,* τινός Hdt., Aesch., etc. ;—so in Pass., ἐσπανίσμεθ' ἀρωγῶν Aesch. : absol. *to be in want,* Eur.
σπάνιος [ἄ], α, ον, (σπάνις) *rare, scarce, scanty,* Hdt., Eur. ; σπάνιον ἑαυτὸν παρέχειν, Lat. *difficiles aditus habere,* Plat. ; ὕδατι σπανίῳ χρώμενοι having a *scanty* supply of water, Thuc. ; c. inf., σπ. ἰδεῖν *rare* to behold, Xen. : of persons in an Adv. sense, σπάνιος ἐπιφοιτᾷ he *seldom* visits, Hdt. :—σπάνιόν ἐστι, c. inf., *it is seldom that . . ,* Xen. :—τὸ σπάνιον = σπάνις, Aeschin.   II. Comp. σπανιώτερος, Hdt., Thuc. : —Sup. -ώτατος, Att.   III. Adv. -ίως, *seldom,* Xen. ; so σπανίᾳ, Plat. : Comp. -ιώτερον, Thuc.
σπανιότης, ητος, ή, =sq., *lack* of a thing, Isocr.
ΣΠΑ'ΝΙΣ, ή, gen. εως, dat. ει, Ion. ι :—*scarcity, rareness, dearth, lack* of a thing, Eur., Dem. :—οὐ σπάνις [ἐστι] = οὐ σπάνιον, *there is no lack, no difficulty,* Eur.
σπανιστός, ή, όν, (σπανίζω) of things, *scanty,* Soph.
σπάνο-σίτία, ή, (σῖτος) *lack of corn* or *food,* Xen.
σπάραγμα, ατος, τό, *a piece torn off, a piece, shred, fragment,* ὅσων σπαράγματα all whose *mangled corpses,* Soph. ; σπάραγμα κόμας Eur.   II. = σπαραγμός, *a tearing, rending,* Id.
σπαραγμός, ὁ, *a tearing, rending, mangling,* Eur.   II. *a convulsion, spasm,* Soph.   From
σπαράσσω, Att. -ττω : f. ξω : aor. 1 ἐσπάραξα :—Pass., pf. ἐσπάραγμαι : (akin to σπαίρω) :—*to tear, rend in pieces, mangle,* Lat. *lacerare,* Eur., Ar. :—Med., σπαράσσεσθαι κόμας *to tear one's* hair, Eur.   2. *to rend asunder,* Aesch.   3. metaph. *to pull to pieces, attack,* Lat. *conviciis lacerare,* Ar., Plat.
σπαργανιώτης, ου, ὁ, *a child in swaddling-clothes,* h. Hom.   From
σπάργανον, τό, (σπάργω) *a swathing band,* and in pl. *swaddling-clothes,* h. Hom., Pind. ; παῖς ἔτ' ὢν ἐν σπαργάνοις Aesch. ; *tokens by which a person is identified,* Lat. *monumenta, crepundia,* Soph., Ar. Hence
σπαργανόω, f. ώσω, like σπάργω, *to wrap in swaddling-clothes, swathe,* Eur. :—Pass., pf. part. ἐσπαργανωμένος N. T.
σπαργάω, f. ήσω, *to be full to bursting, to swell, be ripe,* Eur.   II. metaph., like Lat. *turgere,* *to swell with passion,* Plat. :—absol. *to wax wanton, be insolent,* Plut. (Prob. from same Root as σφριγάω.)
ΣΠΑ'ΡΓΩ, Ep. aor. 1 σφάρξα, = σπαργανόω, h. Hom.

σπᾰρῆναι, aor. 2 pass. inf. of σπείρω :—σπᾰρείς, part.
σπαρνός, ή, όν, poët. for σπανός, σπάνιος, Aesch.
Σπαρτάκειος, α, ον, of Spartacus, Plut.
σπάρτη, ή, = σπάρτον, Ar. (with a play upon Sparta).
Σπάρτη, Dor. Σπάρτα, ή, Sparta, Hom., etc. :—hence Advs., Σπάρτηθεν, from Sparta, Od. ; Σπάρτηνδε, to Sparta, Ib. :—Σπαρτιάτης [ᾰ], ου, ὁ, a Spartan, Eur., Thuc. ; Ion. -ήτης, εω, Hdt. :—fem. -ᾶτις, ιδος, sub. γυνή) a Spartan woman, Eur., etc. ; (sub. χώρα) Laconia, Plut. ; also as Adj., Σπ. γυνή, χθών, γῆ Eur.
σπαρτίον, τό, Dim. of σπάρτον, a small cord, Ar.
σπάρτον, τό, a rope, cable, Il., etc. ; (prob. akin to σπείρα). II. a rope made from broom (σπάρτος).
σπαρτός, ή, όν, and ός, όν, (σπείρω) sown, grown from seed : metaph., σπαρτῶν γένος children of men, Aesch. II. at Thebes, Σπαρτοί, οἱ, the Sown-men, those who claimed descent from the dragon's teeth sown by Cadmus, the Cadmeans, Thebans, Pind., Eur. ; λόγχη σπαρτός the Theban spear, Eur. III. scattered, of the limbs of a corpse, Anth.
σπάρτος, ὁ and ή, Spanish broom, esparto, Xen., etc.
σπαρτο-φόρος, ον, (φέρω) bearing broom, Strab.
σπασθείς, aor. 1 pass. part. of σπάω.
σπάσμα, ατος, τό, (σπάω) a spasm, convulsion, τῶν ὑστερῶν Arist. II. a piece torn off, shred, Plut.
σπασμός, ὁ, (σπάω) a convulsion, spasm, Hdt., Soph.
σπάσσασθε, Ep. for σπάσασθε, 2 pl. aor. 1 med. of σπάω : so σπασσάμενος, part.
σπᾰτᾰλάω, to live lewdly, to run riot, N. T. From
σπᾰτάλη, ή, lewdness, wantonness, riot, luxury, Anth. (Deriv. unknown.)
σπᾰτάλημα, ατος, τό, (σπαταλάω) = foreg., Anth.
σπᾰτίλη [ῐ], ή, excrement, Ar. (Perh. akin to σκώρ, σκατός.)
ΣΠΑ'Ω, f. σπάσω [ᾰ] : aor. 1 ἔσπᾰσα, Ep. σπάσα : pf. ἔσπᾰκα :—Med., f. σπάσομαι : aor. 1 ἐσπᾰσάμην, Ep. σπᾰσάμην, 2 pl. Ep. σπάσσασθε, part. σπασσάμενος :—Pass., f. σπασθήσομαι : aor. 1 ἐσπάσθην :—pf. ἔσπᾰσμαι: 1. of a sword, to draw, Eur. ;—mostly in Med., Hom. :—Pass. to be drawn, Il. ; ἐσπασμένοι τὰ ξίφη having their swords drawn, Xen. 2. πάλιν σπᾶν to draw in tow (out of a helmet), Aesch. 3. absol., σπᾶτ' ἀνδρείως pull, hoist away, like men. II. of violent actions, to pluck off or out, κόμην Soph. 2. like σπαράσσω, to tear, rend, of beasts, Id. 3. to wrench, sprain :—Pass., τὸν μηρὸν σπασθῆναι Hdt. 4. to snatch, tear or drag away, Eur. 5. metaph. to carry away, draw aside, Soph., Plat. 6. Pass. to be convulsed, Soph. III. to draw in, suck in, quaff, Aesch., Eur. IV. to draw tight, pull the reins, Xen. 2. of angling : hence, proverb., οὐκ ἔσπασεν ταύτῃ γε ' he took nothing by his motion,' Ar. V. to adopt, appropriate, Anth.
σπεῖν, aor. 2 inf. of ἕπω.
σπεῖο, Ep. for σπέο, σπού, aor. 2 imper. of ἕπομαι.
σπεῖος, τό, Ep. for σπέος.
ΣΠΕΙ'ΡΑ, ή, Lat. spira, anything wound or coiled : in pl. the coils or spires of a serpent, Eur. ; also σπείραις δικτυοκλώστοις with the net's meshy folds, Soph. 2. σπείραι βόειαι thongs or straps of ox-hide bound round a boxer's fist, the caestus, Theocr. II. a body of

men-at-arms, the Roman manipulus, = two centuries, Polyb. :—also a cohort, N. T.
σπείρᾱμα, Ion. -ημα, ατος, τό, a coil, spire, convolution, Aesch. : αἰῶνος σπ. a period, cycle, Anth. From
σπειράομαι, (σπεῖρα) Pass. to be coiled or folded round.
σπειρηδόν, Adv. in coils or spires, spirally, Anth. II. (σπεῖρα II) of troops, in maniples, Polyb.
σπείρημα, Ion. for σπείραμα.
σπειρίον, τό, Dim. of σπεῖρον, a light, summer-gar-ment, Xen.
ΣΠΕΙ'ΡΟΝ, τό, a piece of cloth, εἴλυμα σπείρων a wrap-ping cloth, Od. ; κακὰ σπεῖρα sorry wraps, Ib. ; ἄτερ σπείρου without a shroud, Ib. ; also a sail, Ib.
σπειρ-οῦχος, ὁ, (ἔχω forming a circle, Anth.
ΣΠΕΙ'ΡΩ, Ion. impf. σπείρεσκον : f. σπερῶ : aor. 1 ἔσπειρα : pf. ἔσπαρκα :—Pass., aor. 2 ἐσπάρην [ᾰ] : pf. ἔσπαρμαι :—to sow : I. to sow seed, Hes., Att. 2. to sow children, to engender, beget them, Soph. :—Pass. to be born, Id., Eur. 3. to scatter like seed, strew, throw about, χρυσὸν καὶ ἄργυρον Hdt. ; δρόσον Eur. :—to spread abroad, as Virg. spargere voces, Soph. :—Pass. to be scattered, dispersed, Eur., Thuc. II. to sow a field, Hes., Hdt., etc. : Pass., ἡ σπειρομένη Αἴγυπτος the arable part of Egypt, Hdt. 2. proverb., πόντον σπείρειν, of lost labour, Theogn.
σπεῖσαι, aor. 1 inf. of σπένδω :—σπείσασκε, Ep. 3 sing.
σπεκουλάτωρ, ορος, ὁ, Latin speculator, one of the body-guard, N. T.
ΣΠΕ'ΝΔΩ, Ep. subj. 2 σπένδηισθα : Ion. impf. σπένδεσκον : f. σπείσω : aor. 1 ἔσπεισα, Ep. σπεῖσα, Ion. 3 sing. σπεί-σασκε : pf. ἔσπεικα :—Med., aor. 1 ἐσπεισάμην, Ep. 1 pl. subj. σπείσομεν, for —ωμεν :—Pass., aor. 1 ἐσπείσθην : pf. ἔσπεισμαι (used both in med. and pass. sense) :—to pour or make a drink-offering before drinking, Lat. libare, Hom. :—σπ. οἶνον to pour wine, Hom. ; λοιβάς Soph. ; σπονδάς, χοάς Eur. ; ellipt., σπ. ἀγαθοῦ δαίμο-νος (sc. σπονδήν) to pour a libation in honour of the good genius, Ar. :—rarely c. dat. rei, ὕδατι σπ. to make a drink-offering with water, Od. :—in N. T. the Pass. is used metaph. of a person, σπένδομαι ἐπὶ τῇ θυσίᾳ I am offered (as a drink-offering) over the sacrifice. 2. without any religious sense, to pour, Hdt., Xen., etc. II. Med. to pour libations one with another, and, as this was the custom in making treaties, to make a treaty, make peace, Hdt., Ar., etc. ; σπένδεσθαί τινι to make peace with one, Eur., etc. ; so, σπ. πρός τινα Thuc., etc. ; σπένδεσθαι τῇ πρεσβείᾳ to give it pledges of safe conduct, Aeschin. : c. acc., εἰρήνην σπεισάμενοι Λακεδαιμονίοισι having concluded a peace with them, Hdt. ; ἐσπεῖσθαι νεῖκος to make up a quarrel, Eur. ; σπ. ἀναίρεσιν τοῖς νεκροῖς to make a truce for taking up the dead, Thuc. :—Pass., of a treaty, to be con-cluded, Id.
ΣΠΕ'ΟΣ, Ep. σπεῖος, τό, a cave, cavern, grotto, Hom. : of the form σπέος, Hom. uses only nom. and acc. sing., with Ep. dat. σπῆι ; of the form σπεῖος, acc. sing., gen. σπείους, dat. pl. σπέσσι and σπήεσσι ; gen. pl. σπείων h. Hom.
σπέρμα, ατος, τό, (σπείρω) that which is sown : I. the seed of plants, Hes., Hdt., Att. :—also of animals, Pind., Eur. 2. metaph. of the germ, origin, element

of anything, σπ. πυρός Od.; φλογός Pind.; κακῶν Dem. II. seed, offspring, issue, Trag., etc. 2. race, origin, descent, Ib.

σπερμαίνω, f. ἄνῶ, to sow with seed: to beget, Hes.

σπερμολογία, ἡ, babbling, gossip, Plut. From

σπερμο-λόγος, ον, (λέγω) picking up seeds, of granivorous birds, Plut. II. metaph. one who picks up scraps of knowledge, a babbler, Dem., N. T.

σπερμο-φόρος, ον, (φέρω) bearing seed, Anth.

Σπερχειός, ὁ, the Spercheius, i. e. Rapid (from σπέρχω), a river of Thessaly, Il.

σπερχνός, ή, όν, hasty, rapid, hurried, Hes., Aesch.

ΣΠΕ'ΡΧΩ, the Act. only in pres. and impf.: Pass., aor. 1 part. σπερχθείς:—to set in rapid motion; σπ. to be in haste to do a thing, c. inf., Il.; σπ. ἐρετμοῖς to hasten with oars, to ply them rapidly, Od.: part. σπερχόμενος as Adv., in haste, hastily, hurriedly, Hom., Eur. 2. metaph. to be hasty and angry, Il., Hdt.; μὴ σπέρχου be not hasty, Eur. II. intr. = Pass., ὅτε σπέρχωσιν ἄελλαι when storms are driven rapidly, Hom.

σπές, σπέτε, 2 sing. and pl. aor. 2 imperat. of εἶπον.

σπέσθαι, aor. 2 inf. of ἕπομαι.

σπέσσι, dat. pl. of σπέος.

ΣΠΕΥ'ΔΩ, Ep. inf. σπευδέμεν: f. σπεύσω: aor. 1 ἔσπευσα, Ep. σπεῦσα, Ep. 1 pl. subj. σπεύσομεν for —ωμεν: pf. ἔσπευκα:—Med., f. σπεύσομαι:—Pass., pf. ἔσπευσμαι: I. trans. to set a-going, to urge on, hasten, quicken, Hom., etc.:—also, to seek eagerly, strive after, Theogn.; promote zealously, to press or urge on, Soph., etc.; so in Med., Aesch.:—Pass., to be urged on, Hdt. 2. c. acc. et inf., σπεύσατε Τεῦκρον μολεῖν urge him to come, Soph. II. intr. to press on, hasten, to exert oneself, strive eagerly or anxiously, Il., Att.; ὡς σὺ σπεύδεις as you urge, contend, Plat.: part. σπεύδων as Adv. in haste, eagerly, Il., Aesch. 2. c. inf. to be eager to do a thing, Hes., Hdt., etc.; so in Med., σπευδόμεναι ἀφελεῖν Aesch. 3. c. acc. rei et inf. to be anxious that . ., Hdt., Xen.

σπῆι, Ep. dat. of σπέος:—σπήεσσι, pl.

σπήλαιον, τό, (σπέος) a grotto, cave, cavern, Plat.

σπηλαι-ώδης, ες, (εἶδος) cavern-like, Plat.

σπιδής, ές, gen. έος, wide, broad, διὰ σπιδέος πεδίοιο Il. (Found nowhere else: deriv. unknown.)

σπῐθᾰμή, ἡ, the space one can span with the thumb and little finger, a span, Lat. dodrans, about 7½ inches, Hdt., Plat. (Deriv. uncertain.)

σπῐλᾰδ-ώδης, ες, (εἶδος) rock-like: rocky, Strab.

ΣΠΙ'ΛΑ'Σ, άδος, ἡ, a rock over which the sea dashes, a ledge of rock, Od.:—generally, a slab, Soph.

ΣΠΙ'ΛΟΣ [ῐ], ὁ, a spot, stain, blemish, N. T. Hence

σπῑλόω, f. ώσω, to stain, soil, N. T.:—Pass., pf. part. ἐσπιλωμένος Ib.

σπινθᾰρίς, ίδος, ἡ, = σπινθήρ, a spark, h. Hom.

ΣΠΙΝΘΗ'Ρ, ῆρος, ὁ, a spark, Lat. scintilla, Il., Ar.

ΣΠΙ'ΝΟΣ, ὁ, a bird of the finch kind, the siskin, Ar.

σπλαγχνεύω, f. σω, to eat the inwards (σπλάγχνα) of a victim after a sacrifice, Ar. II. to prophesy from the inwards, Strab.

σπλαγχνίζομαι, Dep. to feel compassion, mercy, N. T.

σπλάγχνον, τό,—mostly in pl. σπλάγχνα, the inward parts, esp. the viscera thoracis, i. e. heart, lungs, liver, kidneys, which in sacrifices were reserved to be eaten by the sacrificers, Hom., etc. :—hence the sacrificial feast, Lat. visceratio, Ar. :—also as used in divination, Aesch., etc. 2. any part of the inwards, the womb, Pind., Soph. : so in sing., Aesch. II. metaph. like our heart, the seat of the feelings and affections, Id., Eur., etc. :—so in sing., Soph., Eur.; ἀνδρὸς σπλάγχνον ἐκμαθεῖν to learn a man's inward nature, Eur. (Deriv. uncertain.)

ΣΠΛΗ'Ν, ὁ, gen. σπληνός, the milt, spleen, Hdt.

σπογγιά, ἡ, = σπόγγος, a sponge, Ar.

σπογγίζω, f. ίσω, (σπόγγος) to wipe with a sponge, Dem.

σπογγίον, τό, Dim. of σπόγγος, Ar.

ΣΠΟ'ΓΓΟΣ and σφόγγος, ὁ, a sponge, Hom., etc.

σποδ-εύνης, ου, ὁ, (εὐνή) lying on ashes, Anth.

σποδέω, f. ήσω, to pound, smite, crush, Ar.:—Pass., σποδούμενος νιφάδι pelted by the storm, Eur.; πρὸς πέτρας σπ. dashed against the rocks, Id.; absol., στρατὸς κακῶς σπ. handled roughly, in sorry plight, Aesch. (Deriv. uncertain.)

σποδιά, Ion. -ιή, ἡ, (σποδός) a heap of ashes, ashes, Od., Eur. II. metaph., = σποδός III, Anth.

σποδίζω, f. Att. ιῶ, (σποδός) to roast or bake in the ashes, burn to ashes, Ar., Plat.

σποδόομαι, Pass. to be burnt to ashes, Anth.

ΣΠΟΔΟ'Σ, ἡ, wood-ashes, embers, and generally, ashes, Od., Hdt., Att. : the ashes of the dead, Aesch., Soph., etc. II. dust, Hdt. III. metaph. σπ. κυλίκων, of a bibulous old woman, 'a sponge,' Anth.

στολάς, άδος, ἡ, Aeol. for στολή, a leathern garment, buff-jerkin, Ar., Xen.

σπόμενος, aor. 2 med. part. of ἕπομαι.

σπονδαρχία, ἡ, the beginning of the libation, the right of beginning it, Hdt. From

σπονδ-αρχος, ον, (ἄρχω) beginning the drink-offering.

σπονδεῖος, α, ον, used at a libation:—σπονδεῖος (sc. πούς), ὁ, in metre, a spondee, a foot consisting of two long syllables, being the metre proper to the slow melodies used at σπονδαί (a treaty).

σπονδή, ἡ, (σπένδω) a drink-offering, i. e. the wine poured out to the gods before drinking, Lat. libatio, Hes., Hdt.; σπονδὰς θεοῖς λείβειν, σπένδειν Aesch., Eur. II. in pl. σπονδαί was a solemn treaty or truce, (because solemn drink-offerings were made on concluding them); σπονδαὶ ἄκρητοι the truce made by pouring unmixed wine, Il.; αἱ Λακεδαιμονίων σπ. the truce with them, Thuc.; σπονδὰς παραδιδόναι Ar.; δέχεσθαι Thuc.; τυχεῖν Xen.; σπ. ποιεῖσθαί τινι to make a truce with one, Hdt.; πρός τινα Ar.; σπ. τέμνειν (like ὅρκια τέμνειν) Eur.; σπ. ἄγειν πρός τινας Thuc. 2. αἱ Ὀλυμπιακαὶ σπ. the solemn truce or armistice during the Olympic games, Id. 3. the treaty itself, εἴρηται ἐν ταῖς σπ. Id.

σπονδῖτις, ιδος, fem. Adj. making a σπονδή, Anth.

σπονδο-φόρος, ὁ, (φέρω) one who brings proposals for a truce or treaty of peace (σπονδαί), Ar. II. a herald or officer who published the sacred σπονδαί of the Olympic and other games, Pind., etc.

σπονδύλη, σπόνδυλος, v. sub σφονδ-.

σπορά, ἡ, (σπείρω) a sowing of seed, Plat.: of children, origin, birth, Aesch., Soph. 2. seed-time, Eur. II. the seed sown, Id.:—of persons, seed, offspring, Soph: generally, θῆλυς σπ. the female race, Eur. Hence

σποράδην [ἄ], Adv. *scatteredly, here and there*, Lat. *sparsim*, Thuc., Plat.: *casually*, Anth.

σποράδικός, ή, όν, *scattered*, τὰ σπ. ζῷα, opp. to τὰ ἀγελαῖα (*gregarious*), Arist.

σποραῖος, α, ον, = σπόριμος :—σποραῖα, τά, *seeds*, Babr.

σποράς, άδος, ὁ, ἡ, (σπείρω) mostly in pl. *scattered, dispersed*, Hdt., Thuc.; of men, σποράδες ᾤκουν, i.e. *not in communities*, Arist.; αἱ Σποράδες (sc. νῆσοι) the islands off the west coast of Asia Minor, opp. to αἱ Κυκλάδες, Strab.

σπορητός, οῦ, ὁ, (σπορά) *sown corn, growing corn*, Aesch. 2. *a sowing of corn*, Xen.

σπόριμος, ον, (σπείρω) *sown, to be sown, fit for sowing*, Xen., Theocr.; τὰ σπόριμα *the corn-fields*, N.T.; μέτρον σπ. *a measure of seed-corn*, Anth.

σπόρος, ὁ, (σπείρω) *a sowing*, Hdt., Xen., etc. 2. *seed-time*, Xen., Theocr. II. *seed*, Theocr. 2. *produce, fruit, harvest, crop*, Hdt., Soph.

σπόρῳ, Dor. gen. of σπόρος.

σποῦ, in Scythian, *an eye*, Hdt.

σπουδάζω, f. άσομαι: aor. 1 ἐσπούδασα: pf. ἐσπούδακα:—Pass., aor. 1 ἐσπουδάσθην: pf. ἐσπούδασμαι: I. intr. *to make haste*, 1. of things, *to be busy, eager, zealous, earnest* to do a thing, c. inf., Soph., etc.; also, σπ. περί τινος or τι Xen., Plat.; εἴς or πρός τι Dem.; ἐπί τινι Xen. 2. of persons, σπ. πρός τινα *to be busy* with him, Plat.; σπ. περί τινα *to be anxious* for his success, *canvass* for him, Xen.; ὑπέρ τινος Dem. 3. absol. *to be serious or earnest*, Ar., etc.; ἐσπουδακότι προσώπῳ with a *grave* face, Xen. II. trans., 1. c. acc. rei, *to do* anything *hastily* or *earnestly*, Eur., Plat., etc.:—Pass. *to be zealously pursued*, Eur., etc.:—esp. in pf. part., *serious*, Plat., etc. 2. Pass., also, of persons, *to be treated with respect, to be courted*, Arist., etc.

σπουδαιο-λογέω, f. ήσω, (λέγω) *to speak seriously, talk on serious subjects*, Xen.; so in Med., Id.:—Pass., *to be treated seriously*, Id.

σπουδαῖος, α, ον, (σπουδή) of persons, *earnest, serious*, Xen.; *active, zealous*, Plut. 2. *good, excellent*, Hdt., Plat.; σπουδαῖος τὴν τέχνην Xen. 3. of men of character and importance, Id. 4. in moral sense, *good*, opp. to πονηρός, Id. II. of things, *worth one's serious attention, serious, weighty*, Theogn., Hdt., Att. 2. *good of its kind, excellent*, Hdt., etc. III. Adv. σπουδαίως, *seriously, earnestly, well*, Xen., etc.:—Comp., -ότερον, Id.; Sup. -ότατα, *most carefully, in the best way*, Hdt.—There are also irreg. Comp. and Sup. σπουδαι-έστερος, -έστατος.

σπουδ-άρχης, ου, ὁ, (ἄρχω) *one who canvasses for office, a place-man*, Xen. Hence

σπουδαρχία, ἡ, *canvassing for office*, Lat. *ambitus*, Plut.; and

σπουδαρχιάω, *to canvass for office*, Arist.

σπουδαρχίδης, ου, ὁ, comic Patronymic of σπουδάρχης, *Son of Placeman*, Ar.

σπούδασμα, ατος, τό, (σπουδάζω) *a thing* or *work done with zeal, a pursuit*, Plat.

σπουδαστέος, α, ον, verb. Adj. of σπουδάζω, *to be sought for zealously*, Xen. II. σπουδαστέον, *one must bestir oneself, be earnest or anxious*, Eur., etc.

σπουδαστής, οῦ, ὁ, (σπουδάζω) *one who wishes well to another, a supporter, partisan*, Lat. *fautor*, Plut. Hence

σπουδαστικός, ή, όν, *zealous, earnest, serious*, Plat.

σπουδαστός, ή, όν, (σπουδάζω) *that deserves to be sought* or *tried zealously*, Plat.

σπουδή, ἡ, (σπεύδω) *haste, speed*, Hdt., etc.; ὅκως σπουδῆς ἔχει τις *according as one makes speed*, Id. II. *zeal, pains, exertion, trouble*, Od., Att.: —σπουδὴν ποιεῖσθαι, c. inf., *to take pains* to do a thing, Hdt.; c. gen., σπουδήν τινος ποιήσασθαι *to make much ado about* a thing, Id.; so, σπ. ἔχειν τινός or εἴς τι Eur.; σπουδῇ ὅπλων *with great attention to* the arms, Thuc.:—in pl. *zealous exertions*, Hdt., Eur.; also *party feelings, rivalries*, Hdt., Ar. III. *zeal, earnestness, seriousness*, Eur., etc. 2. *an object of attention, a serious engagement*, Eur. IV. σπουδῇ, as Adv. *in haste, hastily*, Od., Hdt., Att. 2. *with great exertion, with difficulty, hardly, scarcely*, Hom. 3. *earnestly, seriously, urgently*, Eur., etc.; πολλῇ σπ. *very busily*, Plat., etc.; so with Preps., ἀπὸ σπουδῆς *in earnest, seriously*, Il.; μετὰ σπουδῆς Xen.

σπυράς, Att. σφυράς, άδος, ἡ, *a ball of dung*, as that of sheep or goats: pl. *sheeps'* or *goats' dung*, Ar.

σπυρίδιον [ῐ], τό, Dim. of σπυρίς, Ar.

σπυρίς, ίδος, ἡ, *a large basket, a creel* (v. κόφινος), Hdt., Ar., etc. (Deriv. uncertain.)

Στάγειρος, ή, *a city in Macedonia*, Hdt., etc. :—Σταγειρείτης, ὁ, *a Stagyrite*, of Aristotle.

στάγμα, ατος, τό, (στάζω) *a drop, distilment*, Aesch.

σταγών, όνος, ἡ, (στάζω) *a drop*, Trag.

στάδαιος, α, ον, (στάδην) *standing erect* or *upright*, Aesch.; στ. ἔγχη pikes for *close fight*, opp. to missiles (cf. στάδιος 1), Id.

σταδιασμός, οῦ, ὁ, *a measuring by stades*, Strab.

σταδιεύς, έως, ὁ, = σταδιοδρόμος, Anth.

σταδίη, ἡ, v. στάδιος.

σταδιοδρομέω, f. ήσω, *to run in the stadium*, Dem. From

στᾰδιο-δρόμος, ὁ, *one who runs the stadium, one who runs for a prize*, Simon., Aeschin.

στάδιον [ᾰ], τό: pl. στάδια and στάδιοι, but never στάδιος in sing.: (στῆναι) :—*a fixed standard of length, a stade*, = 100 ὄργυιαι or 6 πλέθρα, i.e. 600 Greek or 606¾ English feet, about ⅛ of a *Roman mile*, Polyb.: —ἑκατὸν σταδίοισιν ἄριστος ' *best by a hundred miles*,' Ar.; πλεῖν ἢ σταδίῳ λαλίστερος *more loquacious than a mile and more*, Id. II. *a race-course* (that of Olympia being a stade long), Pind., etc.; ἀγωνίζεσθαι στ. *to run a race*, Hdt.; στ. νικᾶν *to win one*, Xen.

στάδιος [ᾰ], α, ον, (στῆναι) *standing firm*, στᾰδίη ὑσμίνη *close fight*, Lat. *pugna stataria*, Il.; ἐν σταδίῃ (sc. ὑσμίνῃ) Ib. 2. *firm, strong*, Pind.

ΣΤΑ'ΖΩ, f. στάξω, Dor. 1 pl. σταξεῦμες: aor. 1 ἔσταξα, Ep. στάξα: I. of persons, 1. c. acc. rei, *to drop, let fall* or *shed drop by drop*, Il., Aesch., etc. 2. c. dat. rei, αἵματι στ. *to drip with blood*, Aesch.; στάζων ἱδρῶτι Soph.;—rarely c. gen., Id. II. intr. of things, *to drop, fall in drops, drip, trickle*, Hdt., Soph., Eur.; metaph., στάζει ἐν ὕπνῳ πόνος Aesch.

στάθεν, poët. for ἐστάθησαν, 3 pl. aor. 1 pass. of ἵστημι: but II. σταθέν, part. neut.

σταθερός, ά, Ion. ή, όν, (στῆναι) *standing fast, stead-*

fast, ἡ σταθερή (sc. γῆ), *terra firma*, Anth.;—of the sea, *calm*, *still*, Id. **2.** στ. μεσημβρία *high noon*, when the sun seems to *stand still* in the meridian, Plat. **3.** metaph. *steady*, *deliberate*, Anth.

σταθευτός, ή, όν, *scorched*, *burnt*, Aesch. From

σταθεύω, f. σω, *to scorch*, *roast*, *fry*, Ar.

σταθήσομαι, f. pass. of ἵστημι.

στάθι, Dor. for στῆθι, aor. 2 imperat. of ἵστημι.

σταθμάω, f. ήσω, (στάθμη) *to measure by rule*, Eur.: —Pass., with f. med. -ήσομαι, *to be measured*, *estimated*, Ar. **II.** as Dep. (v. σταθμόω), *to estimate distance or size*, *without actual measurement*, Hdt., Plat.: metaph. *to estimate one thing by another*, τί τινι Plat.; absol. *to conjecture*, Soph. **2.** *to attach weight to* a thing, *value it*, Plat.

στάθμη, ἡ, (στῆναι) *a carpenter's line*, Hom., Theogn.; —properly *a line rubbed with chalk*, distinguished from the rule (κανών) Xen., etc.:—proverb., παρὰ στάθμην *by the rule*, Lat. *ad amussim*, Theogn.; but in Aesch., παρὰ στ. *beside the line*, *beyond measure*; κατὰ στ. *noeîn to guess aright*, Theocr. **II.** *the plummet* or *the plumbline*, Anth. **III.** *the line which bounds the racecourse*, *the goal*, Lat. *meta*, Pind., Eur. **IV.** metaph. *a law*, *rule*, Ὑλλίδος στάθμας ἐν νόμοις, i.e. *according to laws of Dorian rule*, Pind.

σταθμητός, ή, όν, (σταθμάω) *to be measured*, Plat.

σταθμόνδε, Adv. *to the stall*, *homewards*, Od.

σταθμός, ό, pl. σταθμοί, but in Att. also σταθμά: (στῆναι):—*a standing place* for animals, Lat. *stabulum*, *a stable*, *fold*, Il.: *a stye*, Od.: of men, *a dwelling*, *abode*, Hes., Soph. **2.** *quarters*, *lodgings* for travellers or soldiers, Lat. *statio*, Xen. **3.** in Persia, σταθμοί were *stations* on the royal road, where the king rested, Hdt.: hence *a day's journey*, *day's march*, averaging about 5 parasangs or 15 miles, Id., Xen. **4.** like Lat. *statio*, *a station* for ships, Eur. **II.** *an upright post*, *the bearing pillar* of the roof, Od.: *a door-post*, esp. in pl., Hom., Att. **III.** *the balance*, Ar., Il.; ἱστᾶν σταθμῷ τι πρός τι *to weigh one thing against another*, Hdt. **2.** *weight*, σταθμὸν ἔχειν τάλαντον *to weigh a talent*, Id.; absol. in acc., ἴσα σταθμόν *equal in weight*, Id.; ἡμιπλίνθια σταθμὸν διτάλαντα *two talents in or by weight*, Id.:—in pl. *weights*, Eur., etc.

σταθμόω:—the aor. 1 med. σταθμώσασθαι is = σταθμήσασθαι (v. σταθμάω II), *to form an estimate*, *to judge* or *conclude by or from* a thing, Hdt.

σταίην, aor. 2 opt. of ἵστημι.

σταῖμεν, **σταῖτε**, **σταῖεν**, Att. for σταίημεν, σταίητε, σταίησαν, aor. 2 opt. pl. of ἵστημι.

ΣΤΑΙΣ or **σταίς**, τό, gen. σταιτός, *flour of spelt mixed and made into dough*, Hdt. Hence

σταίτινος, η, ον, *of flour* or *dough of spelt*, Hdt., Plut.

στακτός, ή, όν, (στάζω) *oozing out in drops*, *trickling*, *dropping*, *distilling*, Ar.

στάλα, Dor. for στήλη.

στάλαγμα, τό, *that which drops*, *a drop*, Aesch., Soph.

σταλαγμός, ό, (σταλάσσω) *a dropping*, *dripping*, Aesch., Eur.; στ. εἰρήνης *the least drop* of peace, Ar.

σταλάσσω, f. ξω, *to let drop*, δάκρυ Eur. **II.** intr.

of things, *to drop*, *drip*, Id.; c. acc. cogn., στ. φόνον *to drop* blood, Id. (Akin to στάζω.)

σταλάω, = σταλάσσω, *to drop*, *let fall*, δάκρυ Anth.

σταλῆναι, aor. 2 inf. of στέλλω.

στάλιξ, ίκος, ή, (σταλῆναι) *a stake to which nets are fastened*, Xen., Theocr.

σταλῖτις, Dor. for στηλῖτις.

σταλ-ουργός, όν, Dor. for στηλ-, (*ἔργω) *furnished with a στήλη* or *gravestone*, Anth.

στάμεν, Dor. for στῆναι, aor. 2 inf. of ἵστημι.

στάμῖνες, οἱ, Ep. dat. pl. σταμίνεσσι: (στῆναι):—*the ribs* of a ship, *which stand up* from the keel, Lat. *statumina*, Od.

σταμνίον, τό, Dim. of στάμνος, *a wine-jar*, Ar.

στάμνος, ό, and ἡ, (στῆναι) *an earthen jar for racking off wine*, Ar.: cf. ἀμφορεύς.

στάν, Aeol. 3 pl. aor. 2 of ἵστημι. **2.** neut. of part.

σταξεῦμες, Dor. for στάξομεν, 1 pl. f. of στάζω.

στάς, **στᾶσα**, **στάν**, aor. 2 part. of ἵστημι.

στασιάζω, f. άσω, (στάσις): **I.** intr. *to rebel*, *revolt*, *rise in rebellion*, τινί *against* one, Hdt., Xen., etc.; πρός τινα Xen. **2.** in the Greek states, *to form a party* or *faction*, *be at odds*, *quarrel*, Hdt., etc. **3.** of the states themselves, *to be at discord*, *be distracted by factions*, Ar., Thuc., etc. **II.** trans. *to revolutionise*, *throw into confusion*, τὴν πόλιν Lys., etc. Hence

στασιαστικός, ή, όν, *seditious*, *factious*, Plat., etc.: Adv., στασιαστικῶς ἔχειν *to be factious*, Dem.

στάσιμος, ον, (στάσις) *standing*, *stationary*; of water, *stagnant*, Xen. **2.** *stable*, *steadfast*, *steady*, *firm*, Plat.:—of men, *steadfast*, *steady*, *solid*, Lat. *constans*, Id.:—of music, Arist. **II.** στάσιμον (with or without μέλος), in Tragedy, *a regular song of the Chorus*, prob. so named because it was not sung till the chorus had taken its stand in the orchestra.

στάσις [ἄ], εως, ἡ, (στῆναι) *a standing*, *the posture of standing*, Aesch., Plat. **2.** *a position*, *posture*, *post*, *station*, Hdt., Eur.; τῆς στάσεως παρασύρων τὰς δρῦς *tearing the oaks from their ground*, Ar. **3.** *a point of the compass*, ἡ στ. τῆς μεσαμβρίης Hdt. **4.** *the position*, *state* or *condition* of a person, Lat. *status*, Plat. **II.** *a party*, *company*, *band*, Aesch.: *a sect* of philosophers, Plut. **III.** esp. *a party formed for seditious purposes*, *a faction*, Solon, Hdt., Att. **2.** *sedition*, *discord*, Hdt., Att.; στάσιν ποιεῖσθαι Isocr.; πόλιν εἰς στάσιν ἐμβάλλειν Xen.

στάσι-ώδης, ες, *factious*, Arist.: *quarrelsome*, Xen.

στάσι-ωρός, ό, (ὥρα) *watcher of the station* or *fold*, Eur.

στάσιωτεία, ἡ, *a state of faction*, Plat. From

στάσιώτης, ου, ό, (στάσις) mostly in pl. *the members of a party* or *faction*, *partisans*, Hdt., Att. Hence

στάσιωτικός, ή, όν, *factious*, *seditious*, Thuc.

στάσκε, Ion. 3 sing. aor. 2 of ἵστημι.

στάσω, Dor. for στήσω, fut. of ἵστημι.

στατέον, verb. Adj. of ἵστημι, *one must appoint*, Plat.

στατήρ, ῆρος, ό, (στῆναι) *a weight* = λίτρα: then a *coin of various values*: **1.** the *gold stater* best known at Athens was the Persian, called στατὴρ Δαρεικός or simply Δαρεικός, *Daric*, from Darius Hystaspes, worth about 1*l*. 2*s*., Hdt., Thuc. **2.** later a *silver stater* was in use, = τετράδραχμον, N.T., Xen.

στᾰτίζω, poët. for ἵστημι, to place : Pass. =ἵσταμαι, to stand, Eur. :—so also intr. in Act., Id.

στᾰτός, ή, όν, verb. Adj. of ἵστημι, placed, standing, στατὸς ἵππος a stalled horse, Il., Soph. :—στατὸς χιτών a tunic reaching to the feet, Plut.

σταυρός, ὁ, (στῆναι) an upright pale or stake, Hom., etc. : of piles driven in to serve as a foundation, Hdt., Thuc. II. the Cross, N. T. : its form was represented by the Greek letter T, Luc.

σταυρο-φόρος, ον, (φέρω) bearing the cross, Anth.

σταυρόω, f. ώσω, (σταυρός) to fence with pales, impalisade, Thuc. II. to crucify, Polyb., N. T.

σταύρωμα, ατος, τό, a palisade or stockade, Lat. vallum, Thuc., Xen. ; and

σταύρωσις, ή, = ἀσταφίς, Thuc.

στᾰφίς, ίδος, ή, = ἀσταφίς, Theocr.

στᾰφῠλή, ή, a bunch of grapes, Hom., Theocr. II. parox. σταφύλη, the plummet of a level, ἵπποι σταφύλῃ ἐπὶ νῶτον ἔϊσαι horses matched in height by the level, matched to a nicety, Il. (Deriv. uncertain.)

στᾰφῠλίς, ίδος, ή, σταφυλή, a bunch of grapes, Theocr.

στᾰφῠλο-κλοπίδης, ὁ, (κλέπτω) a grape-stealer, Anth.

στᾰχυη-τόμος, ον, (τέμνω) cutting ears of corn, Anth.

στᾰχυη-τρόφος, ον, nourishing ears of corn, Anth.

στᾰχυ-μήτωρ, ορος, ή, mother of ears of corn, Anth.

στᾰχυο-στέφᾰνος, ον, crowned with ears of corn, Anth.

ΣΤΑ'ΧΥ'Σ [ᾰ], υος, ὁ: Ep. dat. pl. σταχύεσσι: Att. acc. στάχῠς:—an ear of corn, Lat. spica, Il., Hes., etc. :—metaph., στ. ἄτης Aesch.; of the Theban Σπαρτοί, Eur. 2. generally, a scion, child, progeny, Anth.

στέαρ, τό, gen. στέατος [as trochee]: (prob. from ΣΤΑ, Root of ἵ-στη-μι) :—stiff fat, tallow, suet, Lat. sebum, opp. to πιμελή (Lat. adeps, soft fat), Od., Xen.

στεγάζω, f. άσω, = στέγω, to cover, Xen. : metaph., ὕπνος στ. τινά covers, embraces one, Soph. :—Pass., πλοῖον ἐστεγασμένον a decked vessel, Antipho.

στεγάνη [ᾰ], ή, (στέγω) a covering, Anth.

στεγᾰνός, ή, όν, (στέγω) covering so as to keep out water, water-tight, waterproof, Xen., Anth. 2. generally, covering, enclosing, confining, of a net, Aesch. II. closely covered, λευκῆς χιόνος πτέρυγι στεγανός, of Polynices, represented as an eagle, covered by his white Argive shield (v. λεύκασπις), Soph. ; of a building, roofed, Thuc. 2. metaph., τὸ οὐ στεγανόν leakiness, Plat. III. Adv. -νῶς, confinedly, through a tube, Thuc.

στέγ-αρχος, ὁ, (στέγη) master of the house, Hdt.

στέγασμα, ατος, τό, (στεγάζω) anything which covers, a covering, Xen. :—a roof, Lat. tectum, Plat.

στεγαστέον, verb. Adj. one must cover, Xen.

στεγαστός, ή, όν, (στεγάζω) covered, sheltered, Strab.

στεγαστρίς, ή, (στεγάζω) that serves for covering, Hdt.

στέγαστρον, τό, (στεγάζω) a covering, cover, wrapper, Aesch., Plut.

στέγη, ή, (στέγω) a roof, Lat. tectum, Hdt., Aesch., Xen., etc. II. a roofed place, a chamber, room, Hdt., Xen., etc.; ἔρκειος στ., of a tent, Soph.; ἐκ κατώρυχος στέγη, of the grave, Id. 2. often in pl., like Lat. tecta, a house, dwelling, Aesch.; κατὰ στέγας at home, Soph.

στεγνός, ή, όν, contr. from στεγανός, waterproof, Hdt.;

στεγνὰ οἰκήματα, of a cave, Eur. 2. as Subst., στεγνόν, τό, a covered dwelling, Xen.

στεγνο-φυής, ές, (φυή) of thick nature, Anth.

στέγος, εος, τό, a roof: then, like στέγη, a house, mansion, Aesch., Soph., etc. :—of an urn containing ashes, Soph.

ΣΤΕ'ΓΩ, f. ξω, to cover closely, so as to keep water either out or in : A. to keep water out, νῆες οὐδὲν στέγουσαι not watertight, Thuc. :—so in Med., στέγεσθαι ὄμβρους to keep off rain from oneself, Pind.; ναῦς οὐκ ἐστέξατο κῦμα Anth. 2. generally, to keep off, fend off weapons, etc., δόρυ στέγειν Aesch.; στ. τὰς πληγάς Ar. 3. later, to bear up against, endure, Polyb., N. T. :—absol. to contain oneself, hold out, N. T. II. with acc. of the thing covered, to cover, shelter, protect, Soph., Xen. 2. to cover, conceal, keep hidden, Soph., Eur. :—Pass. to be kept secret, Thuc. ; παρ' ὑμῶν εὖ στεγοίμεθ' let my counsel be kept secret by you, Soph.

B. to keep water in, hold water, keep in, Eur., Plat. II. generally, to contain, hold, Soph., Eur.

ΣΤΕΙ'ΒΩ, Ep. impf. στεῖβον, f. ψω : aor. 1 ἔστειψα :—to tread on, tread under foot, Hom. : c. acc. cogn. to tread or walk on a path, Eur. ; also, χορούς στείβειν to tread measures, Id. 3. absol. to tread, Id. II. to stamp down, in Pass., Theocr. ; αἱ στειβόμεναι ὁδοί the beaten roads, Eur.

στεῖλα, Ep. for ἔστειλα, aor. 1 of στέλλω.

στειλειή, ή, the hole for the handle of an axe, Od. (Deriv. unknown.) Hence

στειλειόν, τό, the handle or helve of an axe, Od.

στειν-αύχην, ενος, ὁ, ή, narrow-necked, Anth.

στεινό-πορος, στεινός, στεινότης, Ion. for στεν-.

στεῖνος, εος, τό, (στείνω) a narrow, strait, confined space, Hom. ; στεῖνος ὁδοῦ Il. II. generally, pressure, straits, distress, h. Hom. ; σωφρονεῖν ὑπὸ στένει to learn wisdom by suffering, Aesch.

στείνω, only in pres. and impf., (στενός) to straiten : Pass. to become strait, to be narrowed, Od.; of persons, to be straitened for room, Il. 2. to be or become full, be thronged, c. gen., στείνοντο δὲ σηκοὶ ἀρνῶν the folds were crowded with lambs, Od.; c. dat., ποταμὸς στεινόμενος νεκύεσσι Il. :—metaph., ἀρνειὸς λαχνῷ στεινόμενος burdened with its wool, Od.

στεινωπός, Ion. for στενωπός.

στείομεν, Ep. for στῶμεν, 1 pl. aor. 2 subj. of ἵστημι.

στεῖρα (Α), ή, (στερεός) a ship's keel, esp. the curved part of it, cutwater, Lat. carina, Hom.

στεῖρα (Β), ή, a cow that has not calved, Od. : of a woman, barren, N. T., Anth. From

στεῖρος, ον, = στερρός II, barren, Lat. sterilis, Eur.

ΣΤΕΙ'ΧΩ : aor. 1 ἔστειξα : aor. 2 ἔστιχον :—to walk, march, go or come, Od., Hdt., Trag. :—c. acc. loci, to go to, approach, Trag. 2. to go after one another, go in line or order (whence στίχος, στίχες, στοῖχος), Il., Hdt. 3. c. acc. cogn., στ. ὁδόν Aesch., Soph.

στελεόν, τό, = στειλειόν, a handle, Babr., Anth. Hence

στελεόω, f. ώσω, to furnish with a handle, Anth.

στελεχη-τόμος, ον, (τέμνω) cutting stems, Anth.

στελεχόομαι, Pass. to grow into a stem, Strab.

στέλεχος, τό, (στέλλω) the crown of the root, stump, whence the trunk springs, Lat. codex, Pind., Dem.

στελίδιον [ῐ], τό, Dim. of στελεόν, Babr.

ΣΤΕΛΛΩ, f. στελῶ, Ep. στελέω: aor. 1 ἔστειλα, Ep. στεῖλα: pf. ἔσταλκα:— Med., aor. 1 ἐστειλάμην: Pass., f. σταλήσομαι: pf. ἔσταλμαι: plqpf. ἐστάλμην, Ep. 3 pl. ἐστάλατο, Ion. ἐσταλάδατο:—to set in order, to arrange, array, equip, make ready, Hom., Hdt., Att.:—also, στέλλειν τινὰ ἐσθῆτι to furnish with a garment, Hdt.; so c. dupl. acc., στολὴν στ. τινὰ Eur.:—Med., στείλασθαι πέπλους to put on robes, Id.; metaph., ἐπὶ θήρας πόθον ἐστέλλου didst set thy heart upon the chase, Id.:—Pass. to fit oneself out, get ready, Il., Hdt.; στολὴν ἐσταλμένος equipt in a dress, Hdt.; ἐστ. ἐπὶ πόλεμον Xen.; metaph., ἐπὶ τυραννίδ' ἐστάλης Ar.   II. to despatch on an expedition, and, generally, to despatch, send, Aesch., Soph.:—Pass. to get ready for an expedition, to start, set out, Hdt.; and in aor. 2 pass. to have set out, to be on one's way, Id.; c. acc. cogn., ὁδὸν στέλλεσθαι Soph.; στέλλου begone! Aesch.   2. in Att. the Act. has sometimes the intr. sense of the Pass., like Lat. trajicere, to prepare to go, start, set forth, where στόλον may be supplied, ἔστειλε ἐς ἀποικίην Hdt., etc.:—reversely, ἡ ὁδὸς εἰς Κόρινθον στέλλει leads to Corinth, Luc.   III. Med. in sense of μεταπέμπομαι, to send for one, Soph.: also to fetch, bring a person to a place, Id.   IV. to bring together, gather up, ἱστία στείλαν took in, furled the sails, Od.: and in Med., ἱστία μὲν στείλαντο they furled their sails, Il.; χιτῶνας ἐστάλατο they girded up their clothes to work, Hes.   2. in Med. also to check, repress, λόγον στέλλεσθαι to draw in one's words, i.e. not speak out the whole truth, Eur.   3. also in Med. to shrink from a thing, avoid it, N.T.

στελμονίαι, αἱ, broad belts put round dogs when used to hunt wild beasts, Xen.

ΣΤΕΜΒΩ, to shake, agitate, Aesch.

στέμμα, ατος, τό, (στέφω) a wreath, garland, wound by suppliants round a staff or olive branch, Il., Soph.; sometimes worn on the head, Hdt.

στέμφυλον, τό, (στέμβω) a mass of olives from which the oil has been pressed, olive-cake, Ar.

στέναγμα, ατος, τό, a sigh, groan, moan, Soph., Eur.

στεναγμός, ὁ, a sighing, groaning, moaning, Trag.

στενάζω, f. -άξω: aor. 1 ἐστέναξα: (στένω):—to sigh often, sigh deeply, generally, to sigh, groan, moan, Trag.; τί ἐστέναξας τοῦτο; why utterdst thou this moan? Eur.; c. acc. cogn.. παιᾶνα στ. Id.   2. trans. to bemoan, bewail, Soph., etc.

στενακτέον, verb. Adj. one must bewail, Eur.; and στενακτός, ή, όν, to be mourned, giving cause for grief, Soph., Eur.   2. mournful, Eur.

στεναχίζω or στοναχίζω, Ep. lengthd. form of στενάχω, only in pres. and impf. to sigh, groan, wail, Hom.:—so in Med., Il.   II. trans. to bewail, lament, Od.

στενάχω [ᾰ], lengthd. form of στένω, only in pres. and impf. to sigh, groan, wail, Hom.: so in Med., Il., Aesch., Soph.:—metaph. of the roar of torrents, Il.; the loud breathing of horses galloping, Ib.; στοὰς στεναχούσης groaning from being overcrowded,

Ar.   II. trans. to bewail, lament, Il., Aesch.; so in Med., Od.

στενολεσχέω, f. ήσω, to talk subtly, quibble, Ar. From στενο-λέσχης, ου, ὁ, a quibbler.

στενό-πορθμος, ον, at or on a strait, Eur.

στενο-πορία, ἡ, a narrow way or pass, Xen. From στενό-πορος, Ion. στειν-, ον, with a narrow pass or outlet, Hdt., Aesch., Eur.   2. as Subst. στενόπορα, Ion. στειν-, τά, narrow passes, defiles, Hdt., Thuc.:—in sing. στενόπορον, τό, a strait, narrow, Xen.

στενός, Ion. στεινός, ή, όν, (στένω) narrow, strait, Hdt., Eur., etc.; ἐν στενῷ, Ion. στεινῷ, in a narrow compass, Hdt., Aesch.   2. as Subst., τὰ στενά the straits, of a pass, Hdt.; of a sea, Thuc.; also, ἡ στενή a narrow strip of land, Id.   II. metaph. narrow, close, confined, ἀπειληθῆναι ἐς στεινόν to be driven into a corner, Hdt.; εἰς στ. καταστῆναι Dem.   2. scanty, little, petty, Plat.—From old Ion. forms στεινότερος, ·ότατος, come irr. Att. στενότερος, -ότατος: but reg. στενώτερος also occurs.

στένος, εος, τό, cf. Ion. στεῖνος.

στενό-στομος, ον, (στόμα) narrow-mouthed, Strab.

στενότης, Ion. στειν-, ητος, ἡ, (στένος) narrowness, straitness, Hdt., Thuc.

στενοχωρέω, f. ήσω, to straiten for room, Luc.:—Pass. to be crowded together: metaph. to be straitened, N.T.

στενοχωρία, ἡ, narrowness of space: want of room, Thuc., etc.:—metaph., ἡ στ. τοῦ ποταμοῦ the difficulty of passing the river, Xen. From στενό-χωρος, ον, of narrow space, strait.

στενόω, Ion. στεινόω, to straiten:—in Pass., Anth.

Στέντωρ, ορος, ὁ, Stentor, a Greek at Troy, famous for his loud voice, Il.:—Adj. Στεντόρειος, ον, Stentorian, with a voice like Stentor's, Arist.

ΣΤΕΝΩ, only in pres. and impf., Ep. impf. στένον:— to moan, sigh, groan, Hom., Trag.; so in Med., Aesch., Eur.   2. c. gen. to moan or sigh for, Eur.; ὑπέρ τινος Aesch.; τινι or ἐπί τινι Eur.; c. acc. cogn., πένθος οἰκεῖον στ. Soph.:—Med., Aesch.   3. c. acc. to bewail, lament, Id., etc.; στένειν τινὰ τῆς τύχης to pity him for his ill fortune, Id.: so in Med., στένεσθαί τινα Eur.

στεν-ωπός, Ion. στειν-ωπός, όν, (στενός, ὤψ) narrow-looking, narrow, strait, confined, Il.   II. as Subst., στεινωπός (sc. ὁδός), ἡ, a narrow passage or way, strait, Od., etc.

στεπτός, ή, όν, (στέφω) crowned, Anth.

στέργηθρον, τό, (στέργω) a lovecharm, love, affection, in sing. and pl., Aesch., Eur.

στέργημα, ατος, τό, a love-charm, τινος to influence him, Soph. From

ΣΤΕΡΓΩ, f. στέρξω: aor. 1 ἔστερξα: pf. ἔστοργα:— Pass., aor. 1 ἐστέρχθην: pf. ἐστέργμαι:—to love, of the mutual love of parents and children, Soph., Eur., etc.; of king and people, Hdt., Soph.; of a country and her colonies, Thuc.; of brothers and sisters, Eur.; of friends, Soph.; of husband and wife, Hdt., Soph.   II. generally, to be fond of, shew liking for, Theogn., Soph., etc.:—also of things, to accept gladly, Hdt., etc.   III. to be content or satisfied, acquiesce, Soph., Dem.; στέρξον oblige me, do me the favour, Soph.   2. c. acc. to be

content with, acquiesce in, submit to, bear with, Hdt.; στ. τὴν τυραννίδα bear with it, Aesch.; στ. κακά Soph. :—also c. dat., στ. τοῖσι σοῖς Eur.; τῇ ἐμῇ τύχῃ Plat. :—c. part., πῶς ἂν στέρξαιμι κακὸν τόδε λεύσσων Soph.; στ. ξυμφορᾷ νικώμενοι Eur. :—rarely c. inf., οὐκ ἔστεργέ σοι ὅμοιος εἶναι Id.   IV. to entreat one to do, Ἀπόλλω στέργω μολεῖν Soph.

ΣΤΕΡΕΟΣ, ά, όν, stiff, stark, firm, solid, Hom., etc.; αἰχμὴ στερεὴ πᾶσα χρυσέη all of solid gold, Hdt. :—Adv. -εῶς, firmly, fast, Hom.   2. metaph. stiff, stubborn, harsh, Id., etc.: so in Adv., Id.   II. στ. ἀριθμός a cubic number, Arist.

στερεό-φρων, ονος, ὁ, ἡ, (φρήν) stubborn-hearted, Soph.

στερεόω, f. ώσω, to make firm or solid, Xen. :—to strengthen, N. T. :—Pass. to be made strong, Xen.

ΣΤΕΡΕΩ, f. στερήσω and στερῶ: aor. 1 ἐστέρησα, Ep. inf. στερέσαι: pf. ἐστέρηκα :—Pass., with f. med. στερήσομαι: aor. 1 ἐστερήθην: in aor. 2 part. στερείς: pf. ἐστέρημαι: 3 sing. plqpf. ἐστέρητο :—to deprive, bereave, rob of anything, c. acc. pers. et gen. rei, Od., Trag., etc. :—Pass. to be deprived, bereaved or robbed of anything, c. gen., Hdt., Att.   II. c. acc. rei, to take away, Anth. :—Pass. to have taken from one, βίον στερείς Eur.

στερέωμα, ατος, τό, (στερεόω) a solid body, foundation: metaph. steadfastness, N. T.

στέρησις, ἡ, (στερέω) deprivation, privation, of a thing, Thuc.: absol. negation, privation, Arist.

στερίσκω, = στερέω, only in pres., to deprive of a thing, Thuc. :—Pass. to be deprived of a thing, Hdt., Att.

στερῖφος, η, ον, = στερεός, στερρός, firm, solid, Thuc.   II. = στεῖρος, Lat. sterilis, barren, Plat.

στερκτός, ή, όν, verb. Adj. of στέργω, to be loved, amiable, loved, Soph.

ΣΤΕΡΝΟΝ, τό, the breast, chest, both in sing. and pl., Hom., Trag.   2. the breast as the seat of the affections, the heart, Trag.

στερνο-τυπής, ές, (τύπτω) of or from beaten breasts, Eur., Anth. Hence

στερνοτυπία, ἡ, a beating of the breast for grief, Luc.

στερν-οῦχος, ον, (ἔχω) broad-swelling, of a plain, Soph.

ΣΤΕΡΟΜΑΙ, only in pres. and impf., = στερέομαι, to be wanting in, to lack, want, Lat. carere, c. gen., Hes., Hdt., Att. :—absol. to suffer loss, Soph., Xen.

ΣΤΕΡΟΠΗ, ἡ, = like ἀστεροπή, ἀστραπή, a flash of lightning, Il., Hes., etc. :—generally flash, gleam, sheen, Hom.

στεροπ-ηγερέτα, ὁ, Ep. for στεροπηγερέτης, either (from ἀγείρω, cf. νεφεληγερέτα), he who gathers the lightning, or (from ἐγείρω) who rouses the lightning, Il.

Στερόπης, ου, ὁ, Lightner, name of one of the three Cyclopes, Hes.

στεροψ, οπος, ὁ, ἡ, (στεροπή) flashing, Soph.

στερρό-γυιος, ον, (γυῖον) with strong limbs, Anth.

ΣΤΕΡΡΟΣ, ά, όν, and ός, όν, = στερεός, stiff, firm, solid, strong, Eur. :. stiff with age, Ar.   2. hard, rugged, uneasy, λέκτρα Eur.   3. metaph. stubborn, obdurate, hard, Aesch., Eur., etc. :—Adv., στερρῶς, stiffly, obstinately, Xen.

ΣΤΕΡΩ, not used in Act., v. στέρομαι.

στεῦμαι, Dep., used by Hom. only in 3 sing. pres. and impf. στεῦται, στεῦτο, and once by Aesch. in 3 pl.

στεῦνται :—c. fut. inf. to make as if one would, to promise or threaten that one will, Il.; also with aor. inf., στεῦται ἀκοῦσαι Od.; so, στεῦνται ἀμφιβαλεῖν Aesch. : —absol., στεῦτο he made eager efforts, Od. (Deriv. uncertain.)

στεφάνη [ᾰ], ἡ, (στέφω) anything that encircles the head, for defence or ornament :   I. the brim of the helmet, projecting behind as well as before, Il.   2. part of a woman's head-dress, a diadem, coronal, Il., Hes., etc. :—metaph., of a city, ἀπὸ στεφάναν κέκαρσαι πύργων thou hast been shorn of thy coronal of towers, Eur.   II. the brim or edge of anything, the brow of a hill, edge of a cliff, Il.; of a basket, Mosch.

στεφανηπλόκια, τά, a place where wreaths are plaited or sold, Anth. From

στεφάνη-πλόκος, ον, (πλέκω) plaiting wreaths, Plut.

στεφἄνηφορέω, Dor. στεφᾰνᾱφ-, f. ήσω, to wear a wreath, Eur., Dem.; and

στεφἄνηφορία, Dor. στεφᾰνᾱφ-, ἡ, the wearing a wreath, esp. of victory, Pind., Eur.   II. the right of wearing a crown, Dem. From

στεφάνη-φόρος, ον, (φέρω) wearing a crown or wreath, crowned, Eur.; στ. ἀγών = στεφανίτης ἀγών, Hdt.   II. the title of certain magistrates who had the right of wearing crowns, as the Archons, Aeschin.

στεφανίζω, Dor. aor. 1 ἐστεφάνιξα, to crown, Ar.

στεφανίτης [ῑ], ου, ὁ, of a crown: στ. ἀγών a contest in which the prize was a crown, Xen., Dem. From

στέφανος, ὁ, (στέφω) properly, that which surrounds, στ. πολέμοιο the circling crowd of fight, Il.; of the wall round a town, Pind.; καλλίπαις στ. a circle of fair children, Eur.   II. a crown, wreath, garland, chaplet, Hes., etc.: esp. at the public games, a crown of victory, Pind., Hdt., etc. :—these prize-crowns were mostly of leaves, of κότινος at the Olympic games, δάφνη at the Pythian, σέλινον at the Nemean, κισσός or πίτυς at the Isthmian.   2. generally, the meed of victory, the prize, victory, like Lat. palma, Soph.; στέφανον προτιθέναι to propose a prize, Thuc.   3. generally, a crown of glory, an honour, Inscr. ap. Hdt. :—a crown as a badge of office or distinction, Dem. Hence

στεφανόω, f. ώσω: (στέφανος):   I. used by Hom. only in 3 sing. pf. and plqpf. of Pass., ἐστεφάνωται, -ωτο: —to be put round, Lat. circumdari, ἣν περὶ μὲν φόβος ἐστεφάνωται round about which (the shield) is Terror wreathed, Il.; ἀμφὶ δέ μιν νέφος ἐστεφάνωτο all round about him was a cloud, Ib.; περὶ νῆσον πόντος ἐστεφάνωται the sea lies round about the island, Od.   2. to be surrounded, Lat. cingi, ἐστεφανωμένος τιήρην μυρσίνῃ having his tiara wreathed with myrtle, Hdt.   II. Act. to crown, wreathe, χαίτην Pind.; στ. τινά Eur. etc.: c. dupl. acc., εὐαγγέλια στεφανοῦν τινά to crown one for good tidings, Ar. :—Pass. to be crowned or rewarded with a crown, Pind. :—Med. to crown oneself, στεφανοῦσθε κισσῷ Eur., Ar.   2. in Med. to win a crown, of the victor at the games, Pind.   3. to crown as an honour or reward, Eur., Lys. :—to crown or honour with libations, Eur.   4. Pass. to wear a crown as a badge of office, Xen., Dem.

στεφἄν-ώδης, ες, (εἶδος) like a wreath, wreathed, Eur.

στεφάνωμα [ἄ], ατος, τό, that which surrounds, a crown or wreath, Theogn., Pind.; στ. πύργων [the city's] coronal of towers, Soph.　2. a crown as the prize of victory, Pind.　3. an honour, glory, Id.

στεφάνως, Dor. acc. pl. of στέφανος.

στέφος, εος, τό, (στέφω) a crown, wreath, garland, Eur.; pl. στέφη, = στέμματα, Aesch., Soph.　2. of libations, Aesch.

ΣΤΕ'ΦΩ, f. στέψω: aor. 1 ἔστεψα:—Pass., aor. 1 ἐστέφθην: pf. ἔστεμμαι:—to put round, Lat. circumdare, ἀμφὶ κεφαλῇ νέφος ἔστεφε δῖα θεάων Il.; θεὸς μορφὴν ἔπεσι στέφει Od.:—Med. to put round one's head, Anth.　II. to surround, crown, wreath, τινὰ ἄνθεσι Hes.; μυρσίνης κλάδοις Eur.:—Med., στέφου κάρα crown thy head, Id.:—Pass. to be crowned, Aesch.　2. to crown with libations, Soph.

στέωμεν, Ion. 1 pl. aor. 2 subj. of ἵστημι.

στῆ, Ep. 3 sing. aor. 2 of ἵστημι.

στήδην, Adv., = στάδην II, by weight.

στήῃς, στήῃ, Ep. 2 and 3 sing. aor. 2 subj. of ἵστημι.

στήθεσφι, Ep. gen. pl. of στῆθος.

στῆθι, aor. 1 imper. of ἵστημι.

ΣΤΗ'ΘΟΣ, εος, τό, the breast, Lat. pectus, Hom., Xen.　II. metaph. the breast as the seat of feeling, the heart, Hom. (always in pl.), Aesch.

στήκω, late pres. formed from ἔστηκα (pf. of ἵστημι), to stand, N. T.

στήλη, Dor. στάλα, ἡ, (στέλλω?) a block of stone used as a prop or buttress to a wall, Il.: a block of rock-crystal, in which the Egyptian mummies were cased, Hdt.　II. a block or slab, bearing an inscription; and so, 1. a gravestone, Hom., Att.　2. a block or slab, inscribed with record of victories, dedications, treaties, decrees, etc., Hdt., Att.; γράφειν τινὰ εἰς στήλην, ἀναγράφειν ἐν στήλῃ, whether for honour, or for infamy, Hdt., Dem.:—also the record itself, a contract, agreement, κατὰ τὴν στήλην according to agreement, Ar.; στῆλαι αἱ πρὸς Θηβαίους Dem.　3. a boundary post, Xen.:—the turning-post at the end of the racecourse, Lat. meta, Soph., Xen.　4. for Στῆλαι Ἡρακλήϊαι, v. Ἡράκλειος.

στηλίδιον, τό, Dim. of στήλη, Theophr.

στηλίς, ίδος, ἡ, Dim. of στήλη, Strab.

στηλίτης [ῑ], Dor. στᾱλ-, ου, ὁ, fem. -ῖτις, ιδος, of or like a στήλη, Luc., Anth.　II. inscribed on a στήλη, posted or placarded as infamous, στηλίτην τινὰ ἀναγράφειν, ποιεῖν Isocr., Dem.

στηλόω, f. ώσω, to set up as a monument, Anth.

στήμεν, στήμεναι, Ep. aor. 2 inf. of ἵστημι.

στημόνιον, τό, Dim. of στήμων (signf. 1), Arist.

στημορράγέω, intr. to be torn to shreds, Aesch.

στήμων, ονος, ὁ, (στῆναι) the warp in the ancient upright loom, Hes., Plat.　II. a thread, Plat.

στήρ, στήτος, τό, contr. for στέαρ, as κῆρ for κέαρ.

στήριγμα, τό, a support, Eur.　2. = στήριγξ 2, Plut.

στηριγμός, ὁ, a propping, supporting; and (in pass. sense) fixedness, steadfastness, N. T.

στήριγξ, ιγγος, ἡ, a support, prop, stay, Xen.　2. the fork with which the pole of a two-wheeled chariot was propped, Lat. furca, Lys.

στηρίζω, aor. 1 ἐστήριξα, Ep. στήριξα, later ἐστήρισα:—Med., aor. 1 ἐστηριξάμην:—Pass., aor. 1 ἐστηρίχ-

θην: pf. ἐστήριγμαι: 3 sing. plqpf. ἐστήρικτο: (στῆναι):—to make fast, prop, fix, set, Il.; λίθον κατὰ χθονὸς ἐστ. he set the stone fast in the ground, Hes.: —Med. to fix for oneself, Anth.　2. metaph. to confirm, establish, N. T.　II. intr. = Pass., στηρίξαι ποσὶν ἔμπεδον Od.; κῦμα οὐρανῷ στηρίζον a wave rising up to heaven, Eur.; and metaph., κλέος οὐρανῷ στηρίζον Id.　2. of diseases, to fix, settle, determine to a particular part, ὁπότε εἰς τὴν καρδίαν στηρίξαι (sc. ἡ νόσος) Thuc.

B. Pass. and Med. to be firmly set or fixed, to stand fast or steady, στηρίξασθαι to get a firm footing, Il.; δώματα πρὸς οὐρανὸν ἐστήρικται the house is lifted up to heaven, Hes.; so, ὀρθὴ δ' ἐς ὀρθὴν αἰθέρ' ἐστηρίξατο Eur.　2. metaph., ὅπου στηρίζει ποτέ wheresoever thou art tarrying, art settled, Soph.

στῆσα, Ep. aor. 1 of ἵστημι.

στήσιος, ὁ, (στῆναι) Ζεὺς Στ. Jupiter Stator, Plut.

στησί-χορος [ῐ], ον, establishing χοροί:—hence as n. pr., Στησίχορος, Dor. Στᾱσ-, ὁ, the Lyric poet Stesichorus, whose real name was Tisias, Simon.

στήσομαι, f. med. of ἵστημι.

στήτη or στήτα, ἡ, rare Dor. word for γυνή, Anth.

στήωσι, Ep. 3 pl. aor. 2 subj. of ἵστημι.

στιβάδιον, τό, Dim. of στιβάς, Plut., Luc.

στιβάδο-κοιτέω, f. ήσω, (κοίτη) to sleep on litter, Polyb.

στιβᾰρός, ά, όν, (στείβω) compact, strong, stout, sturdy, Hom., Hes.

στιβάς, άδος, ἡ, (στείβω) a bed of straw, rushes, or leaves, Eur., Theocr.　2. a mattress, pallet, Hdt., Ar.

στιβεῖν, aor. 2 inf. of στείβω.

στιβέω, (στίβος) to tread, traverse: Pass., πᾶν ἐστίβηται πλεῦρον every side has been traversed, Soph.

στίβη [ῐ], ἡ, (στείβω?) frozen dew, rime, hoar frost, Od.

στίβι, τό, Lat. stibium, = στίμμι.

στιβίζομαι, Med. or Pass. to paint one's eyelids and eyebrows with black paint (στίβι), Strab.

στίβος [ῐ], ὁ, (στείβω) a trodden way, track, path, h. Hom., Soph., etc.　II. a track, footstep, Hdt., Aesch., etc.; κατὰ στίβον on the track or trail, Hdt.; στίβοι φιλάνορες traces of her who had lain in the bed, Aesch.　III. a going, gait, Soph.

στίγεύς, έως, ὁ, (στίζω) one who tattooes, a tattooer, Hdt.

στίγμα, ατος, τό, (στίζω) the mark of a pointed instrument, a tattoo-mark, brand, Hdt., N. T.

στιγμάτηφορέω, f. ήσω, to bear tattoo-marks, Luc. From

στιγμάτη-φόρος, ον, (φέρω) bearing tattoo-marks.

στιγμᾰτίας, ου, Ion. -ίης, εω, ὁ, one who bears tattoo-marks, a branded culprit, runaway slave, Xen., etc.

στιγμή, ἡ, (στίζω) = στίγμα, a spot, point, Arist.:— metaph. a jot, tittle, Dem.; ἐν στ. χρόνου in a moment, N. T.

στίζω, f. στίξω: aor. 1 ἔστιξα:—Pass., pf. ἔστιγμαι: (the Root is ΣΤΙΓ, cf. ἔ-στιγ-μαι, στιγ-μή, etc.):— to mark with a pointed instrument, to tattoo, Hdt., Xen.　2. to brand, as a mark of disgrace, Hdt., Ar.; ἔστιζον στίγματα βασιλήϊα branded them with the royal brand-marks, Hdt.; esp. of runaways, δραπέτης ἐστιγμένος Ar.　3. c. dupl. acc., στίγματα στίζειν τινά to brand one with a mark, Hdt.　4. metaph., βακτηρίᾳ στ. to beat black and

blue, Ar.   5. *to mark with a full stop*, Lat. *inter-pungere*, Anth.

στικτός, ή, όν, verb. Adj. of στίζω, *punctured*, Anth. :—generally, *spotted, dappled*, Soph., Eur. ; στικτὰ ὄμματα, of the hundred eyes of Argus, Eur.

ΣΤΙ'ΛΒΩ, chiefly in pres. and impf., *to glisten*, Hom., Eur. ; c. acc. cogn., στ. ἀστραπάs *to flash* lightning, Eur. :—metaph. *to shine, be bright*, Id.

στίλη [ῐ], ή, *a drop*, Lat. *stilla* : metaph. *a little bit, a moment*, Ar.

στιλπνός, ή, όν, (στίλβω) *glittering, glistening*, Il.

***στίξ**, ή, only in gen. στιχός, acc. στίχα, and in nom. and acc. pl. στίχες, στίχας : (στείχω) :—the other cases being taken from στίχος, *a row, line, rank* or *file*, esp. of soldiers, Il., Aesch., etc.:—metaph., ἐπέων στίχες *verses, lays*, Pind.

στιπτός, ή, όν, (στείβω) *trodden down, close-pressed*, Lat. *stipatus*, Soph. ; στιπτοὶ γέροντες *tough, sturdy old fellows*, Ar.

στῖφος, εος, τό, (στείβω) *a close-pressed* or *compact body* : *a body of men in close array, a column, mass*, Hdt., Aesch. ; νεῶν στῖφος *the close array* of ships, Aesch.

στιφρός, ά, όν, like στιβαρός, *firm, solid*, Xen.

στίχ-αοιδός, ὁ, *one who sings verses, a poet*, Anth.

στιχάομαι, Dep., Ep. 3 pl. impf. ἐστιχόωντο : (*στίξ) *to march in rows* or *ranks*, esp. of soldiers, Il. ; of ships in line, Ib. ; of shepherds with their herds, Ib. : later, we have Ep. 3 pl. στιχόωσι in same sense, Mosch.

στίχες, στίχας, nom. and acc. pl. of *στίξ.

στιχεῖν, aor. 2 inf. of στείχω.

στίχῖνος, η, ον, (στίχος) *of lines* or *verses*, στ. θάνατος of one *who was rhymed to death*, Anth.

στιχο-γράφος [ᾰ], ον, (γράφω) *writing verse*, Anth.

στίχος [ῐ], ὁ, (στείχω) *a row* or *file* of soldiers, Xen.   II. *a line of poetry, a verse*, Ar.

στλεγγίς, ίδος, ή, *a scraper, to remove the oil and dirt* (γλοιός) *from the skin in the bath*, Plat., etc.   II. *a tiara*, Xen. (Deriv. uncertain.)

ΣΤΟΑ' or **στοιά**, ᾶς, ή, *a roofed colonnade, piazza, cloister*, Lat. *porticus*, Hdt., Xen.   II. at Athens this name was given to various public buildings : 1. *a storehouse, magazine, warehouse* for corn, Ar. 2. ή βασίλειος or ή τοῦ βασιλέως στοά *the court* where the ἄρχων βασιλεύς sat, Id., Plat. 3. *the Poecilé* or *Painted Chamber*, in which Zeno of Citium taught, and so his school was called οἱ ἐκ τῆς στοᾶς or Στωικοί, Luc.   III. *a shed to protect besiegers*, Polyb.

στοιβάζω, f. σω, *to pile up, pack together*, Luc.

στοιβή, ή, (στείβω) *a plant used for stuffing* or *padding ;* and metaph. '*padding*,' *an expletive*, Ar.

Στοϊκός, ή, όν, poët. for Στωικός, Anth.

στοιχάς, άδος, ή, (στοῖχος) *in rows :—*αἱ Στοιχάδες (sc. νῆσοι) *a row of islands* off Marseilles, now *les Isles d'Hières*, Strab.

στοιχεῖον, τό, (στοῖχος) properly, *one of a row :* hence, I. in the sun-dial, *the shadow of the gnomon*, Ar. II. generally, *one of a series, an elementary sound* of the voice, *a letter*, Plat. :—κατὰ στοιχεῖον *in the order of the letters, alphabetically*, Anth. 2. in pl. *the elements*, Plat., etc. 3. *the elements of knowledge, rudiments*, ἀρξάμενοι ἀπὸ τῶν στ. Xen.

στοιχέω, f. ήσω, (στοῖχος) *to go in a line* or *row : to go in battle-order*, Xen. II. c. dat. *to be in line with, walk by* rule or principle, c. dat., N. T.

στοιχ-ηγορέω, f. ήσω, *to tell in regular order*, Aesch.

στοιχίζω, f. σω, *to set a row of poles with nets* to drive the game into, Xen. II. *to order* or *arrange in system*, Aesch.

στοῖχος, ὁ, (στείχω) *a row*, στοῖχοι τῶν ἀναβαθμῶν, of *a flight of steps*, Hdt. ; κατὰ στοῖχον *in a row*, Thuc.: of ships, *a column*, ἐν στοίχοις τρισί Aesch. ; of soldiers, *a file*, Thuc.   II. *a line of poles supporting hunting-nets*, Xen.

στολάς, άδος, ή, (στόλος) *moving in close array*, Eur.

στολή, ή, (στέλλω) *an equipment, armament*, Aesch. II. *equipment, raiment, apparel*, Hdt., Trag. 2. *a piece of dress, a garment, robe*, Soph., Eur., etc. ; στ. θηρός, of the lion's skin which Hercules wore, Eur.

στολιδόομαι, Med. *to dress oneself in* a garment, c. acc., Eur.

στολιδωτός, ή, όν, verb. Adj. of στολιδόομαι, στ. χιτών *a tunic hanging in folds*, Xen.

στολίζω, f. ίσω, (στολίς) *to put in trim*, στολίσας νηὸς πτερά *having trimmed* the sails, Hes. 2. *to equip, dress :*—Pass., ἐστολισμένος δορί *armed* with spear, Eur. 3. metaph. *to deck, adorn*, Anth.

στόλιον, τό, Dim. of στολή II, *a scanty garment*, Anth.

στολίς, ίδος, ή, = στολή II, *a garment, robe*, Eur., etc. ; νεβρῶν στολίδες, i. e. *fawnskins worn as garments*, Id. 2. νηῶν στολίδες *sails*, Anth. II. in pl. *folds in* a garment, Eur.

στόλισμα, ατος, τό, (στολίζω) *a garment, mantle*, Eur.

στολμός, ὁ, = στολή II, Aesch., Eur.

στόλος, ὁ, (στέλλω) *an equipment* for warlike purposes, *an expedition* by land or sea, Hdt., Trag., etc. ; τεθριπποβάμων στ. *an equipage with four horses*, Eur. 2. generally, *a journey* or *voyage*, Soph., etc. ; ἰδίῳ στόλῳ *in a journey* on one's own account, opp. to δημοσίῳ or κοινῷ στ. (on behalf of the state), Hdt., Thuc. 3. *the purpose* or *cause of a journey, a mission, errand*, Soph., Ar. 4. *an armament, army*, or, *a sea-force, fleet*, Att. ; οὐ πολλῷ στόλῳ, i. e. *in one ship*, Soph. ; πρόπας στόλος *all the host*, Id. 5. παγκρατίον στ., periphr. for παγκράτιον, Pind. II. = ἔμβολον, *a ship's beak*, Id., Aesch.

ΣΤΟ'ΜΑ, Dor. στύμα, ατος, τό, *the mouth*, Lat. *os*, Hom., etc. 2. *the mouth as the organ of speech*, δέκα μὲν γλῶσσαι, δέκα δὲ στόματ' Il. ; στ. τὸ δῖον *the mouth* of Jove, Aesch. ; Μοισᾶν στόμα *their mouthpiece*, Theocr. ;—with Preps. ἀνὰ στόμα ἔχειν *to have always in one's mouth*, Eur. ; ἀπὸ στόματος *by word of mouth*, Xen., etc. : διὰ στόμα *in every one's mouth*, Aesch. ; πᾶσι διὰ στόματος 'tis the common *talk*, Theocr. : ἐξ ἑνὸς στ. *with one voice*, Ar. ; κατὰ στόμα *face to face*, Hdt., Att. II. στ. ποταμοῦ *the mouth* of a river, Lat. *ostia*, Hom., etc. ; so, ἠϊόνος στ. *the wide mouth* of the bay, Il. ; στ. τοῦ Πόντου, Lat. *fauces Ponti*, Hdt. :—also, *a chasm* or *cleft* in the earth with a stream gushing out, Id. ; τὸ ἄνω, τὸ κάτω στόμα τοῦ ὀρύγματος *the opening* or *width* of the trench at top, at bottom, Id. 2. *any outlet* or *entrance*, Od., Xen. III. *the foremost part, face, front :* 1. of weapons, *the point*, Il. ; *the edge* of

a sword, N. T. :—also like Lat. *acies, the front*, στόμα πολέμοιο, ὑσμίνης Il.; so alone, Xen. **2.** generally, ἄκρον στ. πύργων *the top* of the towers, Eur.; τὸ στόμα τοῦ βίου *the verge of life*, Xen.

στομᾰ-λίμνη, ἡ, *a salt-water lake, estuary*, Strab.: so, **στομάλιμνον**, τό, Theocr.

στόμ-αργος, ον, *busy with the tongue, loud-tongued*, Aesch., Soph.; στ. γλωσσαλγία *wearisome wordiness*, Eur.

στομᾰτ-ουργός, όν, (*ἔργω) *wordmaking*, Ar.

στόμᾰχος, ὁ, (στόμα) properly, *a mouth, opening:* hence, **1.** *the throat, gullet*, Il. · **2.** in late Gr. *the orifice of the stomach, the stomach.*

στόμιον, τό, Dim. of στόμα: *the mouth of a cave*, Soph.: *a cave, vault*, Aesch.: *the socket of a bolt*, Anth. **II.** *a bridle-bit, bit*, Hdt., Trag.; metaph., στ. Τροίας *a bit* or *curb* for Troy, i. e. the Greek army, Aesch.

στομόω, f. ώσω, (στόμα) *to muzzle* or *gag*, Hdt. **II.** (στόμα II) *to furnish with an edge:* metaph. *to steel, harden, train* for anything, Ar. :—Pass., Plut. **III.** *to fringe, fence*, Id.; Pass., [δράκαινα] ἐχίδναις ἐστομωμένη Eur.

στομφάζω, f. άσω, (στόμφος) *to mouth, rant, vaunt*, Ar.
στόμφαξ, ᾰκος, ὁ, ἡ, (στόμφος) *a mouther, ranter*, Ar.
στόμφος, ὁ, (στόμα) *mouthing, bombast, rant.*
στόμωμα, ατος, τό, (στομόω) *a mouth, entrance*, Aesch.
στόμωσις, εως, ἡ, (στομόω) *a furnishing with a sharp edge:* metaph., πολλὴν στόμωσιν ἔχειν *to have a sharp edge*, Soph.

στονᾰχέω, Dor. 3 pl. -εῦντι: f. ήσω: aor. 1 ἐστονάχησα, like στενάχω, *to groan, sigh*, Il. **II.** trans. *to sigh, groan over* or *for*, τινά Soph., Mosch. From

στονᾰχή, ἡ, (στενάχω) *a groaning, wailing*, Hom., Eur.; in pl. *groans, sighs*, Il., Soph.

στονόεις, εσσα, εν, (στόνος) *causing groans* or *sighs*, Hom., Aesch., etc. **2.** generally, *mournful, sad, wretched*, Hom., Soph.; neut. as Adv., Aesch.

στόνος, ὁ, (στένω) *a sighing, groaning, lamentation*, Hom.; *of the sea*, Soph.

στόνυξ, ῠχος, ὁ, *any sharp point*, as of a rock, Eur.: *a pen-knife*, Anth. (Deriv. unknown.)

στοργή, ἡ, (στέργω) *love, affection*, of parents and children, Antipho.

στορέννυμι, shortened **στόρνῡμι**, imper. στόρνυ: by metath., **στρώννῡμι**, impf. ἐστρώννυον: f. στορέσω, Att. στορῶ, also στρώσω: aor. 1 ἐστόρεσα, Ep. στόρεσα, also ἔστρωσα: plqpf. ἐστρώκειν:—Med., aor. 1 ἐστορεσάμην, Ep. στ-, also ἐστρωσάμην:—Pass., pf. ἐστρωμαι: 3 sing. plqpf. ἔστρωτο. (The Root is ΣΤΟΡ.) *To spread the clothes over a bed*, λέχος στορέσαι, Lat. *lectum sternere, to make up a bed*, Il.; κλίνην ἔστρωσαν Hdt.; absol. *to make a bed*, χαμάδις στορέσας Od. **b.** generally *to spread, strew*, ἀνθρακιήν στ. Il.; στιβάδας N. T. **2.** *to spread smooth, level*, πόντον στ., Lat. *sternere aequor*, Od. :—metaph. *to calm, soothe*, στορέσας ὀργήν Aesch. **b.** *to level, lay low* a tree, Anth.: metaph., λῆμα στ., Eur.; φρόνημα Thuc. **3.** ὁδὸν στ. *to pave* a road, Lat. *viam sternere* :—Pass., ἐστρωμένη ὁδός Hdt. **II.** *to strew* or *spread with* a thing, μυρσίνησι τὴν ὁδόν Id. :—Pass., of a room, *to be ready-furnished*, N. T.; cf. στρῶμα.

στόρθυγξ, υγγος, ὁ or ἡ, *a point, the tyne* of a deer's horn, Anth.

στόρνυμι, = στορέννυμι, q. v.

στοχάζομαι, f. -άσομαι: aor. 1 ἐστοχασάμην: pf. ἐστόχασμαι: (στόχος) :—*to aim* or *shoot at*, c. gen., τοῦ σκοποῦ Plat., etc. **2.** metaph. *to aim at, endeavour after*, Id.; στ. φίλων κριτῶν *to aim at having* friends as judges, Xen. **II.** *to endeavour to make out, to guess* at a thing, c. gen., Isocr. :—absol. *to make guesses, conjecture*, Soph., Xen.

στόχασμα, ατος, τό, *the thing aimed, a javelin*, Eur.

στοχαστέον, verb. Adj. *one must aim at*, τοῦ μέσου Arist.

στοχαστικός, ή, όν, *skilful in aiming at, able to hit*, c. gen., Arist. **2.** *able to guess, sagacious*, Plat.: Adv., στοχαστικῶς ἔχειν *to be sagacious*, Arist.

ΣΤΟ´ΧΟΣ, ὁ, *an aim, shot*, Eur.

στραγγᾰλίζω, f. σω, (στράγξ) *to strangle*, Strab.

στραγγεύομαι, Med. (στράγξ) *to squeeze oneself up, twist oneself*, metaph. *to keep loitering about*, Ar.

στραγγ-ουρία, ἡ, (στράγξ, οὐρέω) *retention of the urine, strangury*, Ar.

ΣΤΡΑ´ΓΞ, ἡ, gen. στραγγός, *that which is squeezed out, a drop*, Anth.

στράπτω, f. ψω, = ἀστράπτω, *to lighten*, Soph.

στρᾰτ-άρχης, ου, ὁ, *the general of an army*, Hdt.

στρᾰτ-αρχος, ὁ, = στρατάρχης, Pind.

*στρᾰτάω, assumed as pres. of the Ep. 3 pl. impf. ἐστρατόωντο, *they were encamped*, Il.

στρᾰτεία, Ion. -ηίη, ἡ, (στρατεύω) *an expedition, campaign*, στρατηίην or -είαν ποιεῖσθαι Hdt., Thuc.; ἀπὸ στρατείας *coming from war*, after *service done*, Aesch.; κατὰ τὴν Σιτάλκου στρατείαν *about the time* of his *expedition*, Thuc.; ἐπὶ στρατείας or ἐν στρατείᾳ εἶναι *to be on foreign service*, Plat., Xen.: pl. *military service, warfare*, Plat. **2.** στρ. ἡ ἐν τοῖς μέρεσιν, *an expedition* for special service, to train the young soldiers next after serving as περίπολοι, Aeschin.

στράτευμα, ατος, τό, (στρατεύω) *an expedition, campaign*, Hdt., Att. **II.** *an armament, army*, Hdt., Att. :—also *a naval armament*, Soph., Thuc. **2.** = στρατεύσιμος 2, *the host, people*, Eur.

στρατεύσιμος, ον, *fit for service, serviceable*, Xen.

στράτευσις, ἡ, (στρατεύω) *an expedition*, Hdt.

στρατευτέον, verb. Adj. *one must make an expedition*, Xen. From

στρᾰτεύω, f. σω, (στρατός) *to serve in war, serve as a soldier, do military service, take the field, march*, Hdt., Att.; c. acc. cogn., στρ. στρατείαν Eur. **II.** Dep. **στρατεύομαι**, f. -εύσομαι: aor. 1 ἐστρατευσάμην and ἐστρατεύθην: pf. ἐστράτευμαι :—*to serve, take the field*, Lat. *militari*, Hdt.; ἐστρατευμένος *having been a soldier*, Ar. **2.** *to lead an army, march*, Hdt., Att.

στρᾰτηγέω, f. ήσω, (στρατηγός) *to be general*, Hdt., Att. :—c. gen. *to be general of* an army, Hdt., Att.:— *to lead as general*, c. dat., ἐστρατήγησε Λακεδαιμονίοισι Hdt.; c. acc. cogn., στρ. πόλεμον *to conduct* war, Dem.: with neut. Adj., *to do* a thing *as general*, τοῦτο Xen.; πάντα Dem. :—Pass. *to be conducted*, Plat., Dem. **2.** metaph., ποῦ σὺ στρατηγεῖς τοῦδε; how claim'st thou *to command* this man? Soph. Hence

στρᾰτήγημα, ατος, τό, the act of a general, esp. a piece of generalship, a stratagem, Xen., etc.

στρᾰτηγία, Ion. -ίη, ἡ, (στρατηγός) the office, dignity, or post of general, command, Hdt., Att.; of naval command, Xen. 2. the office of στρατηγός at Athens, a sort of War-minister, Ar., Plat. :—at Rome the Praetorship, Plut. 3. a period of command, campaign, Xen. II. the qualities or skill of a general, generalship, Id.

στρᾰτηγιάω, Desiderat. of στρατηγέω, to wish to be a general, wish to make war, Xen., Dem.

στρᾰτηγικός, ή, όν, (στρατηγός) of or for a general, Plat. :—ἡ -κή (sc. τέχνη) = στρατηγία II, Id.; so, τὰ στρ. Xen. II. of persons, fitted for command, versed in generalship, Id., etc. :—Adv. -κῶς, εὖ καὶ στρ. Ar. 2. at Rome, praetorian, Strab.

στρᾰτήγιον, τό, the general's tent, Lat. praetorium, Soph., Dem. 2. at Athens, the place where the στρατηγοί held their sittings, Aeschin.

στρᾰτηγίς, ίδος, fem. Adj. of the general, πύλαι στρ. the entrance of the general s tent, Soph.; ναῦς στρ. the admiral's ship, flag-ship, Thuc.; so, ἡ στρ. alone, Hdt. : at Rome, σπεῖρα στρ. the praetorian cohort, Plut.

στρᾰτηγός, Dor. στρατᾱγός, ὁ, the leader or commander of an army, a general, Hdt., Att. : generally, a commander, governor, Soph. II. at Athens, the title of 10 officers elected yearly to command the army and navy, and conduct the war-department, with the Polemarch at their head, Hdt., Thuc., etc.; when distinguished from ναύαρχος and ἵππαρχος the στρατηγός is commander of the infantry, Dem. 2. one of the chief magistrates of several Greek cities, Hdt., Polyb. 3. στρ. ὕπατος, or στρατηγός alone, the Roman Consul, Polyb.; στρ. ἐξαπέλεκυς the Praetor, Id. :—also one of the duumviri or chief magistrates of Roman colonies, N.T. 4. an officer who had the custody of the Temple at Jerusalem, Ib.

στρατιή, ἡ, Ion. for στρατεία.

στρᾰτηλᾰσία, Ion. -ίη, ἡ, an expedition, campaign, Hdt. II. the army itself, Id. From

στρᾰτηλᾰτέω, f. ήσω, to lead an army into the field, Hdt., Aesch., etc. II. c. gen. to be commander of, to command, Eur.; c. dat., Id. From

στρᾰτ-ηλάτης [ᾰ], ου, ὁ, (ἐλαύνω) a leader of an army, a general, commander, Soph., Eur., etc.; of an admiral, στρ. νεῶν Aesch.

στρᾰτία, Ion. -ιή, ἡ, = στρατός, an army, Aesch., Thuc., etc. : absol. a land force, as distinguished from a fleet, Hdt. 2. generally, a host, company, band, Pind. II. = στρατεία, an expedition, Ar., Thuc.

στρᾰτί-αρχος, ὁ, = στράταρχος, Hdt.

στράτιος [ᾰ], α, ον, (στρατός) warlike, Hdt.

στρᾰτιώτης, ου, ὁ, (στρατιά) a citizen bound to military service; generally, a soldier, Hdt., Att.; collectively, ὁ στρατιώτης the soldiers, Thuc. Hence

στρᾰτιωτικός, ή, όν, of or for soldiers, Xen., etc. :—τὸ στρ. (sc. ἀργύριον) the pay of the forces, Dem.; but, τὸ στρ. (sc. πλῆθος) the soldiery, Thuc.; τὰ στρατιωτικά (sc. πράγματα) military affairs, Xen. 2. fit for a soldier, military, στρ. ἡλικία the military age, Id. 3. warlike, soldierlike, γένη Arist. II.

Adv. like a soldier, Isocr. :—of ships, στρατιωτικώτερον παρεσκευασμένοι equipped rather as troop-ships than for battle, Thuc.

στρᾰτιῶτις, ιδος, fem. of στρατιώτης; as Adj., στρ. ἀρωγά the martial aid, Aesch. 2. στρ. (sc. ναῦς), a troop-ship, transport, Thuc., Xen.

στρᾰτο-λογέω, (λέγω) to levy soldiers : Pass., Plut.

στρᾰτο-μάντις, εως, ὁ, prophet to the army, Aesch.

στρᾰτοπεδ-άρχης, ου, ὁ, a military commander, Lat. tribunus legionis, Luc.

στρᾰτοπεδεία, ἡ, = στρατοπέδευσις, Xen.

στρᾰτοπέδευσις, ἡ, an encamping, Xen. 2. an encampment, the position of an army, Id.; and

στρᾰτοπεδευτικός, ή, όν, of an encampment, Polyb.

στρᾰτοπεδεύω, f. σω, to encamp, bivouac, take up a position, Xen., etc. : also as Dep. στρατοπεδεύομαι, Hdt., Thuc., etc.; pf. ἐστρατοπεδεῦσθαι to be in camp, Xen. : of a fleet, to be stationed, Hdt. From

στρᾰτό-πεδον, τό, the ground on which soldiers are encamped, a camp, encampment, Hdt., Aesch. :—hence, a camp, encamped army, Hdt., Thuc. II. generally, an army, Hdt.; also, a squadron of ships, Id., Thuc. 2. the Roman legion, Polyb.

ΣΤΡΑ·ΤΟ·Σ, ὁ, an encamped army, generally, an army, host, ἀνὰ στρατόν or κατὰ στρ. throughout the army, Hom.; Ep. gen. στρατόφι Il.; of a naval force, Aesch., etc. 2. the soldiery, people, exclusive of the chiefs, Hom. : so, the commons, people, Pind., Aesch. 3. any band or body of men, Pind.

στρᾰτο-φύλαξ [ῠ], ᾰκος, ὁ, a commanding officer, Strab.

στρᾰτόω, to lead to war; only found in aor. 1 pass. part. στρατωθέν (sc. στόμιον) the curb formed by the army, Aesch. : v. στρατάω.

Στρᾱτωνίδης, ου, ὁ, Comic patronymic, Son of the army, Ar.

στρεβλός, ή, όν, (στρέφω) twisted, crooked, Arist.; of the brows, knit, wrinkled, Anth.: metaph., στρεβλοῖσι παλαίσμασι by cunning dodges in wrestling, Ar.

στρεβλότης, ητος, ἡ, crookedness, Plut.

στρεβλόω, f. ώσω : aor. 1 ἐστρέβλωσα : (στρεβλός) :—to twist or strain tight, στρ. τὰ ὅπλα ὄνοισι to draw the cables taut with windlasses, Hdt.: to screw up the strings of an instrument, Plat. II. to twist or wrench a dislocated limb, with a view to setting it, Hdt. 2. to stretch on the wheel or rack, to rack, torture, Ar. :—Pass., στρεβλοῦσθαι ἐπὶ τροχοῦ Id. 3. metaph. to pervert or distort words, N.T.

στρέμμα, τό, (στρέφω) a wrench, strain, sprain, Dem.

στρεπτ-αιγλος, α, ον, (αἴγλη) whirling-bright, Ar.

στρεπτός, ή, όν, verb. Adj. of στρέφω, flexible, pliant : στρεπτὸς χιτών a shirt of chain-armour, Lat. lorica annulata, Il.; στρεπταὶ λύγοι pliant withs, Eur.: twined, wreathed, Anth. 2. στρεπτός, ὁ, a collar of twisted or linked metal, Lat. torques, Hdt., Xen., etc. 3. of pastry, a twist or roll, Dem. II. metaph. to be bent or turned, στρεπτοὶ καὶ θεοὶ αὐτοί the gods themselves may be turned (by prayer), Il.; στρ. γλῶσσα a glib, pliant tongue, Ib. III. bent, curved, of a pick-axe, Eur. : of a bow, Theocr.

στρεπτο-φόρος, ον, (στρεπτός I. 2, φέρω) wearing a collar, Lat. torquatus, Hdt.

στρεύγομαι, Pass. to be squeezed out in drops:

metaph. *to be drained of one's strength, exhausted,* Hom.

στρεφε-δῖνέω, f. *ήσω, to spin* or *whirl* something *round:* Pass., ὅσσε οἱ στρεφεδίνηθεν (for –νήθησαν) his eyes *span round,* of one stunned by a blow on the nape of the neck, Il.

ΣΤΡΕ'ΦΩ, Ep. impf. στρέψασκον: f. στρέψω: aor. 1 ἔστρεψα, Ep. στρέψα: pf. ἔστροφα:—Med., f. στρέψομαι: aor. 1 ἐστρεψάμην: pf. pass. ἔστραμμαι (in med. sense):—Pass., f. στραφήσομαι: aor. 1 ἐστρέφθην, Ion. and Dor. ἐστράφθην: aor. 2 ἐστράφην:—*to turn about* or *aside, turn,* Hom., etc.; στρ. ἵππους *to turn* or *guide* horses, Il.; στρ. σάκος *to sway* the shield, Soph. **II.** ἄνω καὶ κάτω στρ. *to turn* upside down, Aesch., Plat.; so, κάτω στρ. Soph.; so, στρέφειν alone, *to overturn, upset,* Eur. **III.** *to twist* a rope, Xen. **2.** metaph. of pain, *to twist, torture,* Ar., Plat. **IV.** *to twist, plait,* ἐστραμμένα Xen.: *to spin,* Luc. **V.** metaph. *to turn* a thing *over* in one's mind, τί στρέφω τάδε; Eur., Dem. **VI.** *to turn from the right course, divert, embezzle,* Lys.

B. Pass. and Med. *to turn oneself, to turn round* or *about, turn to and fro,* Il.; ἔνθα καὶ ἔνθα στρέφεσθαι, of one *tossing* in bed, Ib. **2.** *to turn to* or *from* an object, *to turn back, return,* Ib., Soph.; στραφέντες ἔφευγον Xen. **3.** of the heavenly bodies, *to revolve,* Od.; of the distaff, Plat. **II.** *to twist about,* like a wrestler trying to elude his adversary; so, in argument, *to twist and turn, shuffle,* τί ταῦτα στρέφει; why d'ye shuffle so? Ar.; τί δῆτα ἔχων στρέφει; why then *do you* keep shuffling, Plat.; πάσας στροφὰς στρέφεσθαι *to twist* every way, Id. **2.** *to turn and change,* Soph.; τοῦ δὲ σοῦ ψόφου οὐκ ἂν στραφείην I would not *turn* for any noise of thine, Id. **III.** *to twist oneself up* with a thing, *stick close* to it, Od.:—then, like Lat. *versari, to be always engaged,* Plat. **2.** generally, *to be at large, go about,* Soph. **3.** ἐστραμμένος, η, ον, of places, ἐστρ. ἐπὶ τόπον turned towards, Polyb.

C. in strict Med. sense, *to turn about with oneself, take back,* Soph.

D. intr. in Act., like Pass. *to turn about,* Il.; of soldiers, *to wheel about,* Xen.

στρέψασκον, Ep. impf. of στρέφω.

στρεψο-δῐκέω, f. *ήσω, (δίκη) to twist* justice, Ar.

στρεψο-δῐκο-πᾰνουργία, ἡ, *cunning in the perversion of justice,* Ar.

στρηνής, ές, *strong, hard, rough, harsh:* neut. as Adv., Anth. (Deriv. uncertain.) Hence

στρηνιάω, f. άσω, *to run riot, wax wanton,* N. T.

στρῆνος, ὁ, εος, τό, (στρηνής) *wantonness,* N. T.

στρῐβῑλῐκίγξ, Comic word, οὐδ' ἂν στριβιλικίγξ not the *least,* not *a fraction,* Ar.

στροβέω, f. *ήσω, (στρόβος) to twist, twirl* or *whirl about,* Ar.:—metaph. *to make dizzy, distract,* Aesch.: —Pass. *to whirl about,* Id.

στροβιλίζω, f. σω, *to twist about,* Anth.

στροβῐλο-ειδής, ές, (εἶδος) *conical,* Strab.

στρόβῐλος, ὁ, (στρόβος) *anything twisted* or *whirled: a top,* Plat. **2.** *a whirlpool, whirlwind,* Luc. **3.** *a whirling dance, pirouette,* Ar.

στροβῑλός, ή, όν, (στρόβος) *spinning, whirling,* Anth.

στροβῑλ-ώδης, ες, contr. for στροβιλοειδής, Plut.

στρόβος, ὁ, (στρέφω) *a twisting* or *whirling round,* of the effect of a whirlwind, Aesch.

στρογγύλλω, f. ὑλῶ, *to twirl, spin,* Anth. From

στρογγύλος [ῠ], η, ον, (στράγγω) *round, spherical,* Hdt., Ar., etc.; λίθοι στρ. *pebbles,* Xen. **2.** *circular,* Plat. **3.** *round, compactly formed,* Xen. **4.** of ships, στρ. ναῦς, στρ. πλοῖον, a merchant-*ship, from its round shape,* as opp. to the long narrow ship-of-war (μακρὰ ναῦς), Hdt., Thuc.; etc. **II.** metaph. of phrases, *well-rounded, compact, pithy, terse,* Ar., Plat. :—Adv., στρογγυλώτατα *as tersely as possible,* Arist. Hence

στρογγῠλότης, ητος, ἡ, *roundness,* Plat.

στρομβηδόν, Adv. *like a top, whirling,* Anth. From

στρόμβος, ὁ, (στρέφω) *a body rounded* or *spun round:* hence, **1.** *a top,* Lat. *turbo,* Il. **2.** *a whirlwind,* Aesch. **3.** *a snail,* Theocr.

στρούθειον μῆλον, τό, a kind of *quince,* Anth.

στρουθο-κάμηλος [ᾰ], ὁ, also ἡ, *an ostrich,* from its *camel-like* neck, Strab.

ΣΤΡΟΥΘΟ'Σ, ὁ and ἡ, *the sparrow,* Il., etc. **2.** ὁ μέγας στρ. *the large bird,* i. e. *the ostrich, Struthio,* Xen.: also called στρουθὸς κατάγαιος (i. e. the bird *that runs on the ground,* does not fly), Hdt.; also simply στρουθός, like στρουθοκάμηλος, Ar.

στρουθο-φάγος, ον, *feeding on birds,* Strab.

στροφαῖος, α, ον, (στροφεύς), epith. of Hermes, *standing as porter at the door-hinges,* with a play on the sense of *twisty, shifty,* Ar.

στροφάλιγξ [ᾰ], ιγγος, ἡ, (στροφαλίζω) *a whirl, eddy,* Hom.:—metaph., στρ. μάχης Anth.

στροφᾰλίζω, Frequent. of στρέφω, ἠλάκατα στρ. *to turn* the spindle, Od.

στροφάς, άδος, ὁ, ἡ, (στρέφω) *turning round,* Ἄρκτου στροφάδες κέλευθοι the Bear's *revolving* path, Soph. **II.** Στροφάδες (sc. νῆσοι), αἱ, *the Drifting Isles,* a group not far from Zacynthus, supposed to have been once floating.

στροφεῖον, τό, (στρέφω) *a twisted noose, cord,* Xen. **2.** *a windlass, capstan,* on which a cable runs, Luc.

στροφεύς, έως, ὁ, (στρέφω) *the socket* in which the pivot of a door (ὁ στρόφιγξ) moved, Ar.

στροφέω, f. *ήσω, to have the colic* (v. στρόφος II), Ar.

στροφή, ἡ, (στρέφω) *a turning, e. g.* of a horse, Xen.; ἐν στροφαῖσιν ὀμμάτων with *rolling* of the eyes, Eur. **2.** *a twist,* such as wrestlers make to elude their adversary, Plat. :—metaph. *a trick, dodge,* Ar. **II.** *the turning of the* Chorus *as they danced from right to left of the* ὀρχήστρα: *the strain sung during this evolution, the strophé,* to which the ἀντιστροφή answers.

στρόφιγξ, ιγγος, ὁ, (στρέφω) *the pivot, axle* or *pin on which a body turns,* Eur. **2.** στρόφιγγες were *pivots working in sockets,* at top and bottom of a door, which served instead of hinges, Plut. **3.** metaph., στρ. γλώττης, of a *well-hung* tongue, Ar.

στρόφιον, τό, Dim. of στρόφος, *a band worn by women round the breast,* Ar. **II.** *a headband worn by priests,* Plut.

στρόφις, ιος, ὁ, (στρέφω) *a twisting, slippery fellow,* Ar.

στροφίς, ίδος, ἡ, = στρόφιον, Eur.

στροφο-δῑνέομαι, (δινέω) Pass. *to wheel eddying round*, of vultures wheeling round their nest, Aesch.

στρόφος, ὁ, (στρέφω) *a twisted band* or *cord*, used as a sword-belt, Od.: generally, *a cord, rope*, Hdt. 2. = στρόφιον, *a maiden-zone*, Aesch. 3. *a swathing-cloth, swaddling-band*, h. Hom. II. *a twisting of the bowels, colic*, Lat. *tormina*, Ar.

Στρῡμονίας, Ion. -ίης (sc. ἄνεμος), ὁ, *a wind blowing from the Strymon*, i. e. *a NNE. wind*, Hdt.

Στρῡμών, όνος, ὁ, *the Strymon*, a river of Thrace, Hes., Hdt.:—Adj. Στρυμόνιος, α, ον, *of the Strymon*, Aesch., Eur.; and Στρυμονικός, ή, όν, Strab.

στρυφνός, ή, όν, (στύφω) *of a taste which draws up the mouth, rough, harsh, astringent*, Xen., Anth. II. metaph. *of temper* or *manner, harsh, austere*, Ar., Xen.

στρυφνότης, ητος, ἡ, *a rough, harsh taste*: metaph. *harshness of temper*, Plut.

στρῶμα, ατος, τό, (στρώννυμι) *anything spread* or *laid out for lying* or *sitting upon, a mattress, bed*, Lat. *stragulum, vestis stragula*, Theogn.:—in pl. *the bed-clothes, the coverings of a dinner-couch*, Ar., etc. 2. *a horsecloth, horse-trappings*, Xen.

στρωμᾰτό-δεσμον, τό, *a leathern* or *linen sack in which slaves had to tie up the bedclothes* (στρώματα), Xen., Aeschin.

στρωμᾰτο-φύλαξ [ῠ], ᾰκος, ὁ, ἡ, *one who has the care of the bedding*, Plut.

στρωμνή, ἡ, *a bed spread* or *prepared; generally, a bed, couch*, Pind., Aesch., etc.: *a mattress, bedding*, Xen.; στρ. ἄφθιτος, of the golden fleece, Pind. From

στρώννῡμι and -ύω, v. στορέννυμι.

στρώσον, aor. 1 imper. of στρώννυμι.

στρώτης, ου, ὁ, *one that gets couches ready*, Plut.

στρωτός, ή, όν, *spread, laid, covered*, Hes., Eur.; στρωτὰ φάρη *bed clothes*, Soph.

στρωφάω, Frequent. of στρέφω, as τρωπάω of τρέπω, *to turn constantly*, στρ. ἠλάκατα *to keep turning the spindle*, i. e. *spin*, Od.:—Pass. *to keep turning*, so as *to face the enemy*, Il.: *to roam about, wander*, Ib.; στρ. ἀνὰ τὴν πόλιν Hdt.; hence, like Lat. *versari in loco, to move freely in a place, live* there, Il.; ἐν λέχει στρωφώμενος, i. e. claiming a husband's rights, Aesch.

στύγ-άνωρ [ᾰ], ορος, ὁ, ἡ, (στυγέω, ἀνήρ) *hating a man* or *the male sex*, Aesch.

στύγερός, ά, όν, (στυγέω) poët. Adj. *hated, abominated, loathed*, or *hateful, abominable, loathsome*, Hom., Trag.:—c. dat. *bearing hatred* or *malice towards one*, στυγερὸς δέ οἱ ἔπλετο θυμῷ Il. 2. *hateful, wretched, miserable*, Soph., Ar. II. Adv. -ρῶς, *to one's sorrow, miserably*, Hom., Soph.

στύγερ-ώπης, ες, (ὤψ) *of hateful look, horrible*, Hes.

στύγερ-ωπός, όν, = foreg., Anth.

ΣΤΎΓΕΏ: aor. 1 ἐστύγησα and ἔστυξα: pf. ἐστύγηκα: aor. 2 ἔστυγον:—Pass., f. στυγήσομαι in pass. sense: aor. 1 ἐστυγήθην:—*to hate, abominate, abhor*, stronger than μισέω, Hom., Trag.:—c. inf. *to hate* or *fear* to do a thing, Il., Soph.:—Pass. *to be abhorred, detested*, Aesch.; τί δ' ἐστι πρός γ' ἐμοῦ στυγούμενον; what is *the horrid thing* that I have done? Soph. II. in aor. 1, *to make hateful*, Od. Hence

στύγημα [ῠ], ατος, τό, *an abomination*, Eur.; and

στύγητός, όν, *hated, abominated, hateful*, Aesch., N. T.

Στύγιος [ῠ], α, ον, and ος, ον, (Στύξ) *Stygian*, Aesch., Soph. II. = στυγητός, *hateful, abominable*, Eur.

στυγνάζω, f. άσω, *to look gloomy, be sorrowful*, N. T.; of weather, *to be gloomy, lowering*, Ib.

στυγνός, ή, όν, (στυγέω) *hated, abhorred, hateful*, Aesch., Soph.:—c. dat. *hateful* or *hostile to one*, Aesch., Soph. II. *gloomy, sullen*, Lat. *tristis*, Aesch., Eur.; ὁρᾶν στυγνός *gloomy to behold*, Xen.;—στυγνὸς εἴκων *yielding sullenly, with an ill grace*, Soph.; neut. as Adv., Id.

στυγνότης, ητος, ἡ, *gloominess, sullenness*, Plut.

στυγνόω, *to make gloomy*:—Pass. *to be gloomy*, Anth.

στυγό-δεμνος, ον, (δέμνιον) *hating marriage*, Anth.

στύγος [ῠ], εος, τό, (στυγέω) *hatred*, as expressed in looks, *sullenness, gloom*, Aesch. II. *an object of hatred, an abomination*, Id.; of persons, δεσπότου στ. *thy hated lord*, Id.; στύγη θεῶν, of the Erinyes, Id.:—*a deed of horror*, Id.

στῡλίς, ίδος, ἡ, Dim. of στῦλος: like στηλίς, *a mast to carry a sail at the stern*, as in a yawl, Plut.

στῡλίσκος, ὁ, Dim. of στῦλος, *a staff* or *rod*, Strab.

στῡλο-πῑνάκιον, τό, *a pillar with figures on it*, Anth.

ΣΤΎΛΟΣ, ὁ, *a pillar*, as *a support* or *bearing*, Hdt., etc.

στῡλόω, f. ώσω, *to prop with pillars*; metaph. in Med., ζωὴν στυλώσασθαι *to support one's life* (by means of children), Anth.

στύμα, ατος, τό, Aeol. for στόμα.

Στύμφᾱλος, Ion. -ηλος, ἡ, *a city and mountain of Arcadia*, Il.:—Adj. Στυμφάλιος, α, ον, Ion. -ήλιος, η, ον, Hdt., etc.; fem. Στυμφᾱλίς, ίδος, Strab.

Στύξ, ἡ, gen. Στυγός, (στυγέω) *the Styx*, i. e. *the Hateful*, a river of the nether world, by which the gods in Homer swore their most sacred oaths, Il.

στύξαιμι, aor. 1 opt. of στυγέω.

στυππεῖον, τό, *the coarse fibre of flax* or *hemp, tow, oakum*, Lat. *stuppa*, Hdt., Xen., etc.

στυππειο-πώλης, ου, ὁ, (πωλέω) *a dealer in oakum*, Ar.

στυπτηρία, Ion. -ίη (στύφω), ἡ, *an astringent earth, alum* or *vitriol*, Hdt.

στυράκῐνος [ᾰ], η, ον, (στύραξ) *made of the wood of the tree στύραξ*, Strab.

στυράκιον [ᾰ], τό, Dim. of στύραξ (Β), ἀκοντίου Thuc.

στύραξ (A), ᾰκος, ὁ, *storax*, a fragrant gum, Arist. II. ἡ, *the tree producing this gum*, Hdt.

στύραξ (Β), ᾰκος, ὁ, *the spike at the lower end of a spear-shaft*, Xen., Plat.

στυφελιγμός, ὁ, *ill-usage, abuse*, Ar. From

στυφελίζω, f. ξω, (στυφελός) *to strike hard, smite*, Il.; of the wind, *to drive away* clouds, Ib.; ἐξ ἑδέων στυφελίξαι *to thrust* him from his seat, Ib. 2. generally, *to treat roughly, misuse, maltreat*, Hom.

ΣΤΥΦΕΛΟΣ, ή, όν, and ος, όν, (στύφω) *hard, rough*, Aesch. II. metaph. *harsh, severe, cruel*, Id.

στυφλός, όν, = foreg., Trag.

στυφο-κόπος, ον, (στύπος, κόπτω) *striking with a stick*; used, like ὀρτυγοκόπος, of a game, in which they put quails in a ring, and hit them with little sticks; if a quail ran out of the ring, it was beaten, Ar.

ΣΤΥΦΩ [ῠ], f. ψω, *to draw together*: Pass., χείλεα στυφθείς *having his lips drawn up by the taste*, Anth.

στωικός, ή, όν, (στοά) *of a colonnade* or *piazza*:—

hence, *Stoïc, of* or *belonging to the Stoïcs* (because Zeno taught in the στοὰ Ποικίλη), N. T. ; cf. **Στοϊκός.**

στωμυλία, ἡ, *wordiness,* Ar. : *small talk,* Anth.

στωμῠλιο-συλλεκτάδης, ου, ὁ, *a gossip-gleaner,* Ar.

στωμύλλω, (from στωμύλος, as στρογγύλλω from στρογγύλος) :—*to be talkative, to chatter, babble,* Ar. :—so as Dep. **στωμύλλομαι,** f. **στωμυλοῦμαι,** aor. 1 ἐστωμυλάμην, Id.   Hence

στώμυλμα, ατος, τό, = στωμυλία, Ar.

στωμύλος [ῠ], *ον,* and **η, ον** : (στόμα) :—*mouthy, wordy, talkative, chattering, glib,* Ar., Theocr. ; τὰ στ. ταῦτα this *nonsense,* Anth.

ΣΥ' [ῠ], subst. Pron. of the second pers., *thou* : Ep. **τύνη** [ῠ], Aeol. and Dor. **τύ,** Lat. *tu,* Engl. *thou.*—Gen. **σοῦ,** enclit. **σου,** Ep. **σεῦ, σέο, σεῖο, σέθεν,** and as enclit. **σευ, σεο,** Ion. **σεο, σεῦ,** Dor. **τεῦ, τευ,** lengthd. **τεοῦ,** Ep. **τεοῖο** :—Dat. **σοί,** Ion. and Dor. **τοί,** enclit. **τοι,** Dor. **τεΐν, τίν** :—Acc. **σέ,** enclit. **σε,** Dor. **τέ,** or (enclit.) **τυ.**   2. strengthd. by compos. with the enclit. **γε, σύγε** (like ἔγωγε), *thou at least, for thy part,* in Hom., etc., Dor. **τύγα** Theocr.   II. Dual nom. and acc. **σφῶι,** *you two, both of you,* Hom. ; also **σφώ** Il., Att. : —Gen. and Dat. **σφῶιν** Hom. ; contr. **σφῷν** Od., Att.   III. Plur., nom. **ὑμεῖς, ye,** *you,* Hom., etc., Aeol. and Ep. **ὕμμες,** Dor. **ὑμές** :—Genit. **ὑμῶν,** Ep. **ὑμέων** (dissyll.) and **ὑμείων,** Hom :—Dat. **ὑμῖν,** Id., etc., Trag. also **ὑμίν** [ῑ] :—Aeol. and Ep. **ὕμμι, ὕμμιν** :— Acc. **ὑμᾶς,** Dor. **ὑμέας** (dissyll.), Aeol. and Ep. **ὕμμε.**

συ-αγρεσία, ἡ, (σῦς, ἄγρα) *a boar-hunt,* Anth.

Σῠβᾰρίζω, f. *ίσω, to live like a Sybarite,* Ar.

Σύβᾰρις [ῠ], **ἡ,** gen. **εως,** Ion. **-ιος,** *Sybaris,* a city of Magna Graecia, on a river of the same name, noted for luxury, Hdt., etc.   Hence

Σῠβᾰρίτης [ῑ], *ου, ὁ, a Sybarite,* Hdt., Ar. :—fem. **Συβᾰρῖτις, ιδος,** Ar. ; and as Adj., Theocr. ; and

Σῠβᾰριτικός, ή, όν, *of Sybaris : λόγοι* Σ. a class of fables among the Greeks, Ar.

σῠ-βόσιον, τό, (σῦς, βόσκω) *a herd of swine,* Hom.

Σύ-βοτα, τά, (σῦς, βόσκω) *swine-pastures,* name of some islets near Corcyra, Thuc.

σῠβότης, ου, ὁ, = συβώτης, Arist.

σῠ-βώτης, ου, ὁ, (σῦς, βόσκω) *a swineherd,* Od., Hdt.

σύγ-γᾰμος, ον, *united in wedlock, married,* ἄλλῳ to another, Eur. :—generally, *connected by marriage,* Id.   2. ξύγγαμός σοι Ζεύς *sharing* thy *marriage-bed,* of Amphitryon, Id. : pl. *the rival wives of one man,* Id.

συγ-γείτων, ονος, ὁ, ἡ, *bordering, neighbouring,* Eur.

συγγένεια, ἡ, (συγγενής) *sameness of descent* or *family, relationship, kin,* Eur., etc. : c. gen. *kin, relationship with* or *to* another, ἡ ξ. τοῦ θεοῦ Plat. ; also, ἡ πρὸς τοὺς παῖδας σ. Isocr.   2. *ties of kindred, family connexion, influence,* Plat.   II. *one's kin, kinsfolk, kinsmen,* Eur. ; in pl. *families,* Dem.

συγ-γενής, ές, (γίγνομαι) *born with, congenital, natural, in-born,* Pind., Aesch. ; συγγενεῖς μῆνες the months *of my natural life,* Soph. :—so in Adv., συγγενῶς δύστηνος *miserable from my birth,* Eur.   II. *of the same kin, descent* or *family with* another, *akin to* him, τινι Hdt., Att. :—absol. *akin, cognate,* Trag., etc. :—as Subst. *a kinsman, relative, τινος* of another, Ar., Plat. :—in pl., οἱ συγγενεῖς *kinsfolk, kinsmen,* Hdt., etc. :—τὸ συγγενές, = συγγένεια, Aesch., etc. ;

εἰ τούτῳ προσήκει Λαΐῳ τι σ. if this man had any *connexion* with Laius, Soph.   2. metaph. *akin, cognate, of like kind,* Ar., Plat.   III. at the Persian court, συγγενής was a title bestowed by the king as a mark of honour (like *Cousin*), Xen.   Hence

συγγενικός, ή, όν, *congenital, hereditary,* Plut.   II. *of* or *for kinsmen, σ. φιλία between kinsfolk,* Arist. : —Adv. **-κῶς,** *like kinsfolk,* Dem.

συγ-γέρων, οντος, ὁ, *a co-mate in old age,* Babr.

συγγεωργέω, f. **ήσω,** *to be a fellow-labourer,* Isae.   From

συγ-γέωργος, ὁ, *a fellow-labourer,* Ar.

συγ-γηθέω, pf. **-γέγηθα,** *to rejoice with,* τινί Eur.

συγ-γηράσκω, f. **-γηράσομαι,** aor. 1 **-εγήρασα** :—*to grow old together with,* τινί Hdt. ; absol., Aesch.

σύγ-γηρος, ον, (γῆρας) *growing old together,* Anth.

συγ-γίγνομαι, Ion. **συγγίν-** [ῑ] : f. **-γενήσομαι,** aor. 2 **-εγενόμην,** pf. **-γέγονα** : Dep. :—*to be with* any one, *hold converse* or *communication with, associate* or *keep company with,* τινί Hdt., Att. ; so, also, σ. ἐς λόγους τινί Ar.   2. *of disciples* or *pupils, to hold converse with* a master, *consult* him, Id., etc.   3. *to come to assist,* τινί or πρός τινα Aesch. ; absol., Soph.   4. *to come together, meet,* Hdt., etc. ; οἱ συγγιγνόμενοι *comrades,* Xen.

συγ-γιγνώσκω, Ion. **συγγιν-** : f. **-γνώσομαι** : aor. 2 **-έγνων** : pf. **-έγνωκα** :—*to think with, agree with,* τινί Xen. ; c. acc., τὴν ἁμαρτίαν ξυνέγνωσαν *shared* the error, Thuc. :—absol. *to consent, agree,* Hdt., Thuc. ; so in Med., Hdt.   II. σ. ἑαυτῷ *to be conscious,* καὶ αὑτοὶ ξυνέγνωσαν σφίσιν ὡς ἠδικηκότες Lys. :—so in Med., συνεγινώσκετο ἑωυτῷ οὐκέτι εἶναι δυνατός Hdt.   2. *to allow, acknowledge, own, confess,* τι Id., Att. ; c. acc. et inf., Hdt. ; c. part., ξυγγνοίμεν ἂν ἡμαρτηκότες Soph. :—absol. *to confess one's error,* in Act. and Med., Id.   III. *to have a fellow-feeling with* another : and so, *to make allowance for* him, *excuse, pardon, forgive,* τινί Id., etc. ; σ. τινὶ τὴν ἁμαρτίαν, Lat. *ignoscere alicui culpam,* Eur. ; also c. gen. rei, Plut.

σύγγνοια, ἡ, = συγγνώμη II. 2, Soph.

συγ-γνώμη, ἡ, *acknowledgment, confession,* συγγνώμην ἔχειν, ὅτι . . *to acknowledge that . . ,* Hdt.   II. *a fellow-feeling with* another, *a lenient judgment, allowance,* Ar., N. T.   2. *pardon, forgiveness,* συγγνώμην ἔχειν *to pardon,* τινί Hdt., Att. ; *τινός* for a thing, Hdt., Att. :—opp. *to* συγγνώμης τυγχάνειν, *to obtain forgiveness,* Xen., etc. ; ξυγγνώμην λήψονται, *will be pardoned,* Thuc.   3. *of acts,* συγγνώμην ἔχει *admit of excuse, are excusable,* Soph. ; ἔχειν τι ξυγγνώμης Thuc.

συγγνωμονικός, ή, όν, *inclined to pardon, indulgent,* Arist.   II. *of things, pardonable,* Id. ; and

συγγνωμοσύνη, ἡ, = συγγνώμη, Soph.   From

συγ-γνώμων, Att. **ξυγγν-, ον,** gen. **ονος,** (συγγιγνώσκω III) *disposed to pardon, indulgent,* Xen. ; σ. εἶναί τινος *to be disposed to forgive* a thing, Eur.   2. pass. *pardoned, deserving pardon* or *indulgence, allowable,* Thuc.

συγγνωστέον or **-έα,** verb. Adj. of συγγιγνώσκω, *one must pardon, indulge,* τινί Plat.

συγ-γνωστός, όν, verb. Adj. *to be pardoned, pardonable, allowable,* Eur., etc. :—συγγνωστόν or συγγνωστά ἐστι, c. inf., Id.

συγγομφόω — συγκαταθάπτω. **753**

συγγομφόω, f. ώσω, *to fasten together with nails,* Plut.
σύγ-γονος, ον, poët. Adj.=συγγενής, *born with, congenital, inborn, natural,* Pind., Aesch.   II. *connected by blood, akin,* Lat. *cognatus,* Pind., Eur.:—as Subst. *a brother, sister,* Eur.; *σύγγονοι kinsfolk, cousins,* Pind.
σύγγραμμα, ατος, τό, (συγγράφω) *a writing, a written paper,* Hdt., Plat., etc.:—*a written composition, book, work,* Xen., etc.; esp. *a prose work, treatise, a written speech,* Id., Isocr.   II. *a clause* of a law, Aeschin.   2. *a physician's prescription,* Xen.
συγγράφεύς, έως, ό, (συγγράφω) *one who collects and writes down historic facts, an historian,* Xen.: generally, *an author, a prose-writer,* Ar., Plat.   II. συγγραφεῖς, οἱ, at Athens (in the 21st year of Pelop. war) *commissioners appointed to draw up measures* for altering the constitution, Thuc.
συγγράφή, ή, (συγγράφω) *a writing* or *noting down,* Hdt.   II. *that which is written, a writing, book: a history, narrative,* Thuc., etc.   2. *a written contract, a covenant, bond,* Lat. *syngrapha,* Id.; συγγ. *ναυτικαί a bond to secure money* lent on bottomry, Dem.; ἀνδριάντα ἐκδεδωκὼς κατὰ συγγραφήν *having contracted for its execution,* Id.   Hence
συγγράφικός, ή, όν, *given to writing,* esp. *in prose,* Luc.   Adv., συγγραφικῶς ἐρεῖν *to speak like a book,* i. e. *with great precision,* Plat.
συγ-γράφω [ᾰ], f. ψω, *to write* or *note down,* Lat. *conscribere,* Xen.;—so in Med. *to have a thing written down, take care that* it *is written down,* Hdt.   2. *to describe,* Id.   II. *to compose a writing* or *a work in writing,* Lat. *conscribere,* πόλεμον ξ. *to write the history of* the war, Thuc.:—esp. *to write in prose,* Plat.   2. *to compose a speech* to be delivered by another, Isocr., Plat.:—Med. *to get speeches composed,* Plat.   III. *to compile, draw up,* τοὺς πατρίους νόμους Xen.:—Med., συγγράφεσθαί τι *to draw up a contract* or *bond,* Id.; συγγράφεσθαι εἰρήνην πρός τινα *to make a treaty* of peace with another, Isocr.; absol. *to sign a treaty,* Thuc.:—πατέρες συγγεγραμμένοι= the Rom. *Patres conscripti,* Plut.   2. *to draw up a form of motion* to be submitted to vote, Xen.: so in Med., Plat.   IV. *to paint by contract,* Ar.
συγ-γυμνάζω, f. σω, *to exercise together:*—Pass. *to exercise oneself with* or *together,* Plat.   Hence
συγγυμναστής, οῦ, ό, *a companion in bodily exercises,* Plat., Xen.
σύ-γε, v. σύ.
συγ-καθᾰγίζω, f. Att. ιῶ, *to burn up together,* Plut.
συγ-καθαιρέω, Ion. συγκατ-: f. ήσω: aor. 1 συγ-καθεῖλον:—*to put down together, to join in putting down,* τὸν βάρβαρον Thuc.   II. *to accomplish a thing with* any one, τί τινι Hdt.
συγ-καθαρμόζω, f. σω, *to join in composing the limbs* of a dead man, *to join in preparing for burial,* Soph.
συγ-καθέζομαι, f. -εδοῦμαι, *to sit down together,* Plat.
συγ-καθείργω, Att. for -κατείργω, *to shut up with* another, τινά τινι Xen., etc.:—Pass. *to be shut up with,* τινί Aeschin.
συγ-καθέλκω, f. ξω: aor. 1 -είλκῦσα:—*to drag down together:*—fut. pass. συγκαθελκυσθήσεται Aesch.

συγ-καθεύδω, f. -ευδήσω, *to sleep with,* τινί Aesch.
συγκάθημαι, properly pf. of συγκαθέζομαι, *to be seated* or *sit with* or *by the side of,* Hdt., Eur.: *of a number of persons, to sit together, sit in conclave,* Ar., Thuc.
συγ-καθιερόω, f. ώσω, *to join in dedicating,* Plut.
συγ-καθίζω, f. -ιζήσω, *to make to sit together:*—Med. or Pass. *to sit in conclave, meet for deliberation,* Xen.   II. intr., *to sit with* one, Luc.
συγ-καθίημι, f. -καθήσω, *to let down with* or *together, to deposit together,* Eur.:—σ. *ἑαυτόν to let* oneself *down, lower* oneself, εἴς τι Plat.; and absol. (sub. ἑαυτόν) *to stoop, condescend, accommodate oneself to* others, c. dat., Id.
συγ-καθίστημι, f. -καταστήσω: aor. 1 -κατέστησα:—*to bring into place together,* ap. Dem.   2. *to join in setting up,* Lat. *constituere,* τὴν τυραννίδα Aesch., etc.:—*of settling* disturbed countries, Thuc.:—*to help in arranging, managing, treating,* Eur.
συγ-καίω, Att. -κάω [ᾰ], f. -καύσω, *set on fire with* or *at once, burn up,* Lat. *comburere,* Plat.
συγ-κᾰκοπᾰθέω, f. ήσω, *to partake in sufferings,* N. T.
συγκᾰκουχέομαι, Pass. *to endure adversity with* another, τινί N. T.
συγ-κᾰλέω, f. -καλέσω, Att. -καλῶ: 1. *to call to council, convoke, convene,* Il., Hdt., Att.:—so in Med., Hdt., N. T.   2. *to invite with others to* a feast, Xen.
συγκᾰλυπτέος, α, ον, *to be veiled, concealed,* Aesch.; and
συγκᾰλυπτός, ή, όν, *wrapped up,* Aesch.   From
συγ-κᾰλύπτω, f. ψω, *to cover* or *veil completely,* Od., Eur.: Pass., συγκεκαλυμμένη *muffled up,* Plut.:—Med. *to wrap oneself up, cover one's face,* Xen.
συγ-κάμνω, f. -καμοῦμαι: aor. 2 συνέκᾰμον:—*to labour* or *suffer with, sympathise with,* τινί Aesch., Eur.   2. *to work, toil* or *travail with* another, τινί Soph., Eur.: absol. *to join in labour,* Soph.
συγ-καμπή, ή, *a bight, joint,* Xen.
συγ-κάμπτω, f. ψω, *to bend together, bend the knee,* Plat.: Pass., συγκεκαμμένῳ τῷ σκέλει, of a person mounting a horse, Xen.: *of the action of sitting down,* ξυγκαμφθεὶς κάθημαι Plat.
συγ-κᾰσιγνήτη, ή, *an own sister,* Eur.
σύγ-κᾰσις, ό and ή, *an own brother* or *sister,* Eur.
συγ-καταβαίνω, f. -βήσομαι: aor. 2 -έβην:—*to go* or *come down with,* τινί Eur.   2. *to go down together,* esp. *to the sea-side,* Thuc.   3. *to come down to one's aid,* Aesch.   4. *to come down to, agree to,* Polyb.
συγ-καταβάλλω, f. -βᾰλῶ, *to throw down along with,* ἑαυτόν τινι Plut.
συγ-καταγηράσκω, f. -γηράσομαι: aor. 1 -εγήρᾱσα:—*to grow old together with,* τινί Hdt.
συγ-κατάγω, f. ξω, *to join in bringing back,* τὸν δῆμον Aeschin.
συγ-καταδιώκω, f. ξω, *to pursue with* or *together,* Thuc.
συγ-καταδουλόω, f. ώσω, *to join in enslaving,* τινά τινι Thuc.; so in Med., Id.
συγ-καταδύνω [ῡ] and -δύω: aor. 2 -κατέδυν:—*to sink* or *set together with,* Theocr.   Hence
συγκατάδῦσις, εως, ό, *a sinking together,* Strab.
συγκατᾰζεύγνῡμι, f. -ζεύξω, *to yoke together, join in marriage,* τινά τινι Plut.:—Pass., ἄτη συγκατέζευκται *has become a yoke-fellow* with misery, Soph.
συγ-καταθάπτω, f. ψω, *to bury along with,* Hdt.

συγκατάθεσις, ἡ, (συγκατατίθημι) approval, agreement, concord, N. T.   II. submission, Plut.

συγ-καταθέω, to make an inroad with another, Xen.

συγ-καταθνήσκω, to die along with, τινί Mosch.

συγ-καταίθω, to burn together, Soph.

συγ-καταινέω, f. έσω, to agree with, favour, τινί Xen.   II. c. acc. rei, to sanction, approve, Plut.

συγκαταιρέω, Ion. for συγκαθαιρέω.

συγ-καταίρω, to come to land together, Plut.

συγ-κατακαίω, Att. -κάω [ᾰ], f. -καύσω:—to burn together or also, τὰς σκηνάς Xen. :—Pass. to be burnt with, τινί Hdt.

συγ-κατάκειμαι, Pass. to lie with or together, Plat.

συγ-κατακλείω, Ion. -κληίω, f. -κλείσω, to shut in or enclose with or together, Hdt.

συγ-κατακλίνω [ῑ], f. -κλῑνῶ, to make to lie with : —Pass. to lie together, Ar.   2. Pass., also, to lie on the same couch with another at table, Id.

συγ-κατακόπτω, to cut up together :—Pass., Plut.

συγ-κατακτάομαι, Dep. to join with another in acquiring, σ. Φιλίππῳ τὴν ἀρχήν Dem.

συγ-κατακτείνω, aor. 2 -κατέκτανον, irr. part. -κατακτάς :—to slay together, Soph., Eur.

συγ-καταλαμβάνω, f. -λήψομαι, to seize, take possession of together, Xen. : to occupy at the same time, in a military sense, Thuc.

συγ-καταλείπω, f. ψω, to leave together, σ. φρουράν to leave a joint garrison in a place, Thuc.

συγ-καταλύω, f. σω, to join or help in undoing or putting down, τὸν δῆμον Thuc., etc.

συγ-καταμίγνῡμι, and -ύω, f. -μίξω, to mix in with, mingle, blend with, Χάριτας Μούσαις συγκαταμιγνύς Eur. :—Pass. to be absorbed in a thing, Xen.

συγ-καταμύω, f. σω, to be quite closed up, Anth.

συγ-καταναυμαχέω, f. ήσω, to assist in conquering by sea, τινά Aeschin.

συγ-κατανέμω, f. -νεμῶ, to assign also :—Med. to divide jointly among themselves, τὴν γῆν Thuc.

συγ-κατανεύω, f. σω, to consent to a thing, τινί Polyb.

συγ-καταπίμπλημι, f. -πλήσω, to infect likewise, Antipho.

συγκαταπράσσω, Att. -ττω, f. ξω, to join in accomplishing, Act. and Med., Dem.

συγ-καταρρίπτω, f. ψω, to throw down together, Luc.

συγ-κατασκάπτω, f. ψω, to demolish with another or altogether, Eur.

συγ-κατασκεδάννῡμαι, Med. to pour over at the same time, Xen.

συγ-κατασκευάζω, f. σω, to help in establishing or framing, Thuc., etc. ; σ. τὸν πόλεμον to join in promoting the war, Dem.

συγ-κατασκηνόω, f. ώσω, to bring into one dwelling with others, Xen.

συγ-κατασκήπτω, f. ψω, to dart down together, Plut.

συγ-κατασπάω, f. άσω [ᾰ], to pull down with oneself, Luc. :—Pass., τὰ φρούρια τὰ εἰς τὴν Σύρων ἐπικράτειαν συγκατασπασθέντα which were at the same time brought under their dominion, Xen.   II. to gulp down together, Luc.

συγ-καταστᾰσιάζω, f. σω, to help in stirring up, Plut.

συγ-καταστρέφω, f. ψω, to bring to an end together, Plut.   II. Med. to conquer together or at the same time, Thuc., etc.

συγ-κατατάσσω, Att. -ττω, f. ξω, to arrange or draw up together, Xen.

συγ-κατατίθημι, f. -θήσω, to deposit together or at the same time : Med., σ. τινι τὴν αὐτὴν δόξαν to deliver the same opinion with another, Plat. :—then, with dat. only, to agree with, assent to, Philipp. ap. Dem.

συγ-κατατρώγω, to eat at the same time, Plut.

συγ-καταφᾰγεῖν, aor. 2 inf. of συγκατεσθίω.

συγ-καταφλέγω, f. ξω, to burn with or together, Luc.

συγ-καταψεύδομαι, f. -ψεύσομαι, Dep. to join in a lie against, τινός Aeschin.

συγ-καταψηφίζομαι, f. Att. -ιοῦμαι, Dep. to condemn with or together, Plut.   II. Pass. to be reckoned along with others, N. T.

συγκατέδομαι, fut. of συγκατεσθίω.

συγ-κάτειμι, (εἶμι ibo) to go down with, τινι Luc.

συγ-κατείργω, Ion. for συγκαθείργω.

συγ-κατεργάζομαι, f. -άσομαι : pf. pass. -είργασμαι : Dep. :—to help or assist any one in accomplishing a work, τί τινι Hdt., Eur.: c. dat. only, to cooperate with, Hdt.   2. to help to conquer a country, Plut.   3. to join in murdering, Eur.

συγ-κατέρχομαι, Dep. with aor. and pf. act., to come back together, return from exile together, Lys., etc.

συγ-κατεσθίω, f. -έδομαι : pf. -εδήδοκα : aor. 1 κατέφαγον :—to eat up, devour with or together, Plut.

συγ-κατεύχομαι, f. -εύξομαι, Dep. to join in praying for a thing, Soph.

συγ-κατηγορέω, to join in accusing, τινός Dem.

συγ-κάτημαι, Ion. for συγκάθημαι.

συγ-κατοικέω, f. ήσω, to dwell with one, τινι Soph.

συγ-κατοικίζω, f. σω, to colonise jointly, join in colonising, Hdt., Thuc.   II. to plant in a place along with others, Eur.   III. metaph. to establish jointly, Thuc.

συγ-κατοικτίζομαι, f. Att. -ιοῦμαι, Med. to lament with or together, Soph.

συγ-κατορθόω, f. ώσω, to help in righting, Isocr.

συγ-κατορύσσω, Att. -ττω, to bury with, τί τινι Plut.

συγ-καττύω, to patch up, cobble, of leather-workers : Pass., θώραξ ἐκ δερμάτων συγκεκαττυμένος Luc.

συγκέας, aor. 1 part. of συγκαίω.

σύγ-κειμαι, Pass. to lie together, Soph.   II. as Pass. of συντίθημι, to be composed or compounded, ἔκ τινων of certain parts, Plat., etc.   2. of written works, to be composed, Thuc., Plat., etc.   3. to be contrived, concocted, Eur., etc.   III. to be agreed on by two parties, Thuc. : in part. agreed on, arranged, αἱ συγκείμεναι ἡμέραι Hdt. ; κατὰ τὰ συγκείμενα according to the terms agreed on, Id. ; ἐκ τῶν ξυγκειμένων Thuc.   2. impers. σύγκειται, it has been or is agreed on, Hdt., Thuc., etc. ; so, συγκειμένου σφι, c. inf., since they had agreed to . . , Hdt.

συγκεκάλυμμαι, pf. pass. of συγκαλύπτω.

συγκέκομμαι, pf. pass. of συγκόπτω.

συγκέκρᾱμαι, pf. pass. of συγκεράννῡμι.

συγκεκροτημένως, Adv. pf. pass. part. of συγκροτέω, in a finished way, Luc.

συγ-κελεύω, f. σω, *to join in ordering,* Eur., Thuc.
συγ-κεντέω, f. ήσω, *to pierce together, to stab at once,* Lat. *telis confodere,* Hdt. :—Pass., έμελλε συγκεντηθήσεσθαι Id.
συγ-κεράννῦμι or -ύω, f. -κεράσω [ᾰ]: pf. -κέκρᾱκα : —Pass., f. -κρᾱθήσομαι : aor. 1 -εκράθην [ᾱ], Ion. -εκρήθην : pf. -κέκρᾱμαι :— *to mix up with, commingle* or *blend with, temper by mixing with,* τί τινι Plat. **2.** *to mix together, commingle,* πολλά Id. ; έξ αμφοτέρων ξ. *to make a mixture* of both, Id. **3.** *to attemper, compose,* N.T. **II.** Pass. *to be commingled, blended together,* Aesch., Eur., etc. **2.** of friendships, *to be formed by close union,* Hdt. :—Med., συγκεράσασθαι φιλίαν *to form a close friendship,* Id. **3.** of persons, *to be closely attached to,* τινι Xen. : *to become involved in misfortune,* Soph., etc. ; οίκτῳ συγκεκραμένη *deeply affected* by . . , Id.
συγ-κεραυνόω, f. ώσω, *to strike with* or *as with a thunderbolt, shiver in pieces,* Eur.
συγ-κεφᾰλαιόω, f. ώσω, *to bring together under one head, to sum up,* Xen. :—Pass. *to be brought under one head, summed up,* Aeschin. ; of business, *to be summarily done,* Xen.
συγκεχῠμένως, Adv. pf. pass. part. of συγχέω, *confusedly, indiscriminately,* Arist.
συγ-κινδῡνεύω, f. σω, *to incur danger along with,* τινι Thuc., etc. ;—absol. *to be partners in danger,* Xen., Dem., etc.
συγ-κῑνέω, f. ήσω, *to stir up together,* N.T.
συγ-κλαίω, f. -κλαύσομαι, *to weep with,* τινί Anth.
συγ-κλάω, f. -κλάσω, *to break off* :—Pass. *to be cramped,* Plat.
σύγκλεισις, old Att. ξύγκλησις, εως, ή : (συγκλείω) : —*a shutting up, closing up* (of a line of battle), Thuc. **II.** *a narrow pass, defile,* Plut.
συγ-κλείω, f.-κλείσω : Ion. -κληίω, f.-κλήσω :— old Att. ξυγ-κλήω, f.-κλήσω :—Pass., aor. 1 συνεκλείσθην, old Att. ξυνεκλήσθην : pf. συγκέκλειμαι or -εισμαι, old Att. ξυνκέκλημαι, Ion. συνκεκλήιμαι :—*to shut* or *coop up, hem in, enclose,* Hdt. ; ές τόπον Thuc. ; ξυνέκλῃε διὰ μέσου *shut off and intercepted* them, Id. :— Pass., λίμνη συγκεκλημένη ούρεσι Hdt. ; συγκεκλημένη *muffled,* Eur. **2.** *to set together to fight as in the lists,* Id. **II.** *to shut close, to close,* όμμα Id. ; τὰς πύλας Thuc. : absol., σύγκλειε *shut the doors,* Ar. **III.** σ. τὰς ασπίδας *to lock* their shields, Xen. : absol. *to close up* the ranks of an army, Thuc. : Pass., τὸ οὐ ξυγκλησθέν *the part that was not closed up,* of a gap in the line, Id. **2.** Pass. *to be well linked,* Eur.
συγ-κλέπτω, f. ψω, *to steal along with,* Antipho.
συγ-κληρονόμος, ον, *a joint-heir with,* τινός N.T.
σύγ-κληρος, ον, *having portions that join, bordering, neighbouring,* Eur.
συγ-κληρόω, f. ώσω, *to embrace in one lot, choose by lot,* Plut. **II.** *to assign by the same lot,* τί τινι Dem. : *to couple with one,* τινά τινι Aeschin.
σύγκλησις, συγκλήω, v. σύγκλεισις, συγκλείω.
συγκλητικός, ή, όν, *of senatorial rank,* Lat. *senatorius,* Plut. From
σύγ-κλητος, ον, *called together, summoned,* Soph. **II.** σ. εκκλησία at Athens, an assembly *specially summoned* by the στρατηγός (opp. to the ordinary meetings, αἱ

κύριαι), Decret. ap. Dem. :—generally, σύγκλητος (sc. εκκλησία), ή, *a legislative body,* Arist.
συγ-κλῖναι, αἱ, *the meeting-line at the foot of two mountain slopes,* Plut. From
συγ-κλίνω [ῑ], f. -κλῑνῶ, *to lay together* :—Pass. *to lie with* another, c. dat., Hdt., Eur.
συγ-κλονέω, *to dash together, confound utterly,* Il.
σύγ-κλῠς, ὕδος, ὁ, ή, (κλύζω) *washed together* by the waves ; metaph., άνθρωποι σύγκλυδες *a promiscuous crowd, a mob, rabble,* Lat. *colluvies hominum,* Thuc. ; so σύγκλυδες alone, Plat.
συγκοιμάομαι, Pass., with f. -ήσομαι, pf. -κεκοίμημαι : —*to sleep with, lie with* another, c. dat., Hdt., Trag.
συγκοίμημα, τό, *partner of one's bed,* in pl., Eur. ; and
συγκοίμησις, ή, *a sleeping together,* Plat.
συγ-κοιμίζω, f. σω, *to join in wedlock,* τινά τινι Ar.
συγ-κοινόομαι, f. ώσομαι, Med. *to communicate, impart,* τί τινι Thuc.
συγ-κοινωνέω, f. ήσω, *to have a joint share of* a thing, c. gen., Dem. **2.** c. dat. *to take part in, have fellowship with,* N.T.
συγ-κοινωνός, ή, όν, *partaking jointly of* a thing, c. gen., N.T.
σύγ-κοιτος, ὁ, ή, (κοίτη) *a bedfellow, partner,* Pind.
συγ-κολλάω, *to glue* or *cement together,* Ar., Plat.
συγκολλητής, οῦ, ὁ, *one who glues together, a fabricator,* Ar.
σύγ-κολλος, ον, (κόλλα) *glued together* : Adv., συγκόλλως έχειν *to fit exactly,* Aesch.
συγ-κομϊδή, ή, *a gathering in* of harvest, Thuc., Xen. **2.** in pass. sense, *a being gathered together, crowding* into a place, Thuc.
συγ-κομίζω, f. Att. -ιῶ, *to carry* or *bring together, collect,* Hdt. :—Med., with pf. pass., *to bring together to oneself, collect,* Id., Xen. ; σ. πρὸς έαυτόν *to claim as one's own,* Xen. :—Pass. *to be heaped together,* Hdt. ; metaph. ταῦτα συγκομίζεται *are gained both at once,* Soph. **2.** of the harvest, *to gather in, store up, house* it, in Act. and Med., Xen. :—Pass., of the harvest, όργᾳ συγκομίζεσθαι it is ripe *for carrying,* Hdt. **II.** *to help in burying,* Soph.
συγκοπή, ή, *a cutting short* : in Gramm. *syncopé,* i.e. *a cutting* a word *short by striking out one* or *more letters,* Plut. From
συγ-κόπτω, f. ψω : pf. -κέκοφα :—*to break up, cut up,* Hdt., Xen. **2.** *to thrash soundly, pound well,* Xen. ;—Pass., pf. inf. συγκεκόφθαι Ar. ; part. συγκεκομμένος Eur.
συγ-κοσμέω, f. ήσω, *to confer honour on, to be an ornament to,* Xen.
συγ-κουφίζω, f. Att. ιῶ, *to help to lighten, help to keep above water,* Luc.
σύγ-κρᾶσις, εως, ή, *a mixing together, commixture, blending, tempering,* Thuc., Plat., etc.
συγ-κρᾰτέω, f. ήσω, *to keep* troops *together,* Plut.
σύγ-κρᾰτος, ον, (κεράννῦμι) *mixed together, closely united,* Eur.
συγ-κρίνω [ῑ], f. -κρῐνῶ, *to compound,* Plat. **II.** *to compare,* τι πρός τι Arist., etc. : *to measure, estimate,* Anth. Hence
σύγκρϊσις, ή, *a compounding,* Plat., etc. **II.** *a comparing, comparison,* Arist., etc. ; and

συγκρῐτέον, verb. Adj. *one must compare*, Arist.

συγ-κροτέω, f. ήσω, *to strike together; σ. τὼ χεῖρε to clap* the hands for joy, Xen.; but also *to smite* them *together* in grief, Luc.:—Pass. *to be applauded*, Xen.　　　II. *to hammer* or *weld together*, Ar.: hence, *to weld* a number of men *into one body*, i. e. *organise* them, Dem., etc.:—pf. pass. part. συγκεκροτημένοs *well-trained, in good discipline*, Xen., Dem.

σύγκρουσιs, ή, *collision: a conflict*, Plut.; and συγκρουσμόs, ό, =foreg., Plut.　From

συγ-κρούω, f. σω, *to strike together*, Lat. *collido*, σ. τὼ χεῖρε *to clap* the hands, Ar.　　2. *to bring into collision*, Dem.; σ. τινὰs ἀλλήλοιs *to wear out by collision*, Thuc.　　3. intr. *to clash together, come into collision*, Id., etc.

συγ-κρύπτω, f. ψω, *to cover up* or *completely*, Eur.:—*to conceal utterly*, Id., Xen., etc.

συγ-κτάομαι, f. ήσομαι, Dep. *to win* or *gain along with* another, c. dat., Thuc.; τὴν ὅλην χώραν συγκτήσασθαι *to have gained joint possession* of it, Arist.

συγ-κτίζω, f. ίσω: pf. -έκτῐκα:—*to join with* another *in founding* or *colonising*, Hdt., Thuc.　　II. Pass., pf. part. συνεκτισμένοs *well-cultivated*. Hence

συγκτίστηs, ου, ό, *a joint-founder* or *coloniser*, Hdt.

συγκῠβευτήs, οῦ, ό, *a fellow-gamester*, Aeschin. From

συγ-κῠβεύω, f. σω, *to play at dice with*, τινί Hdt.

συγ-κῠκάω, f. ήσω, *to confound utterly*, Ar.

συγ-κῠλινδέομαι, Pass. *to roll about* or *wallow together*, Xen.

συγ-κῠνηγέτηs, ου, ό, =συγκυνηγόs, Xen., Aeschin.

συγκῠνηγέω, f. ήσω, =συγκυνηγετέω, Arist.　From

συγ-κῠνηγόs, Dor. and Att. -κῠνᾱγόs, ό, ή, *a fellow-hunter*, Eur.; fem. *a fellow-huntress*, Id.

συγ-κύπτω, f. ψω, *to bend forwards, stoop and lay heads together*, Ar.:—metaph., συγκύψαντεs ποιοῦσι they do it *in concert, in conspiracy*, Ar.: ἐs ἓν συγκεκυφέναι *to be acting in concert*, Ar.:—generally, *to draw together*, of the wings of an army, Xen.

συγ-κῠρέω: aor. 1 -εκύρησα and -έκυρσα:—*to come together by chance*, Il., Hdt.: *to meet with* an accident, συγκύρσαι τύχῃ Soph.; εἰs ἓν μοίραs ξυνέκυρσαs art *involved* in one and the same fate, Eur.　　2. c. part., like τυγχάνω, συνεκύρησε παραπεσοῦσα νηῦs fell in the way *by chance*, Hdt.　　II. of events and accidents, like συμβαίνω, *to happen, occur*, Id., Eur.: —impers., c. inf., συνεκύρησε γενέσθαι *it came to pass that* .., Thuc.:—so, in Pass., τὸ ἐs Λακεδαιμονίουs συγκεκυρημένον Id.　　III. of places, *to be contiguous to*, τινί Polyb.　Hence

συγκῠρία, ή, *coincidence*, κατὰ συγκυρίαν *by chance*, N. T.

συγκύρσειαν, 3 pl. aor. 1 opt. of συγκυρέω.

σύγ-κωλοs, ον, (κῶλον) *with limbs close together*, Xen.

συγ-κωμάζω, f. άσω, Dor. άξω, *to march together in a κῶμοs* or *band of revellers*, Pind.

σύγ-κωμοs, ό, ή, *a fellow-reveller*, Eur., Ar.

συγ-κωμῳδέω, *to satirise as in a comedy*, Luc.

συγ-χαίρω, f. -χαρήσομαι, *to rejoice with, take part in joy*, Aesch., Ar.; τινί *with* another, Arist.　　II. *to wish* one *joy, congratulate*, σ. τινί τῶν γεγενημένων *to wish* one *joy* of the events, Dem.

συγχάρητε, 2 pl. aor. 2 subj. of συγχαίρω.

συγ-χειμάζομαι, Med. *to go through the winters with* one, Ar.

συγ-χειρουργέω, f. ήσω, *to put hand to* a thing *together, to accomplish*, Isae.

συγ-χέω: f. -χεῶ, εῖs, εῖ: aor. 1 -έχεα, Ep. -έχευα, inf. -χεῦαι:—Pass., aor. 1 -εχύθην [ῠ]: Ep. 3 sing. aor. 2 σύγχῠτο:—*to pour together, commingle, confound*, Il., Dem., etc.:—Pass. *to be in confusion*, Il.　　2. like συγχώννυμι, *to make ruinous, destroy, obliterate, demolish*, Hdt., Eur.　　II. of the mind, *to confound, trouble*, Hom., Hdt., etc.:—Pass., Eur.　　2. *to confound, make of none effect, frustrate*, Il., Hdt., Att.

συγ-χορευτήs, οῦ, ό, *a companion in a dance*, Xen.

συγ-χορεύω, f. σω, *to join in the dance*, Ar.:—*to be of the same chorus*, Arist.

συγ-χορηγέω, f. ήσω, *to furnish as supplies*, Plut.　　II. *to contribute towards* a thing, c. dat., Id.

συγ-χορηγόs, όν, *a fellow-choragus*: generally, *sharing with* a partner *in the expense*, Dem.

σύγχορτοs, ον, *with the grass joining*, i. e. *bordering upon*, c. gen., Eur.; Φαρσαλίαs σύγχορτα πεδία i. e. *the marches* or *boundaries of Pharsalia*, Id.

συγχόω, v. συγχώννυμι.

συγ-χράομαι, f. ήσομαι, Dep. *to make joint use of, avail oneself of*, c. dat., Polyb.: generally *to have dealings with*, τινί N. T.　　II. *to borrow jointly*, τί τινοs something *from* another, Polyb.

σύγ-χροοs, ον, contr. -χρουs, ουν (χρόα) *of like colour* or *look*, Polyb.

συγ-χύνω, only in pres., =συγχέω, *to confound*, N. T.

σύγχῠσιs, εωs, ή, (συγχέω) *a commixture, confusion*, Eur.; σ. ἔχειν *to be confounded*, Id.　　II. of contracts and treaties, *a violation*, Thuc., etc.

συγ-χωνεύω, f. σω, *to melt down*, Dem.

συγ-χώννῡμι and -ύω, in earlier writers συγχόω, inf. συγχοῦν: f. -χώσω: pf. pass. -κέχωσμαι:—*to heap all together, to heap with earth, cover with a mound, bank up*, Hdt.　　II. *to make into ruinous heaps, demolish*, Id.　　2. generally, *to confound*, Aesch.

συγ-χωρέω, f. ήσω and -ήσομαι:—*to come together, meet*, πέτραι συγχωροῦσαι the Symplegades, Eur.; συγχωρεῖν λόγοιs *to meet* in argument, Id.　　II. *to make way, give place, yield* or *defer to*, Lat. *concedere*, τινί Ar., etc.; Συρηκοσίοισι τῆs ἡγεμονίηs συγχ. *to make concessions to* them *about* the command, Hdt.; in bad sense, *to be in collusion with, connive at*, τοῖs πονηροῖs Dem.; ξ. πρόs τινας *to come to terms with* them, Thuc.　　2. *to accede* or *agree, assent to, acquiesce in* another's opinion, Hdt., Att.:—absol. *to agree, acquiesce, consent, assent*, Soph.; τὸ συγκεχωρηκὸs τῆs εὐσεβείαs *a yielding, unexacting temper of piety*, Dem.　　3. c. acc. rei, *to concede, give up, yield*, Hdt., Att.:—Pass., τὰ συγχωρηθέντα χρήματα Dem.　　4. *to concede* or *grant* in argument, Plat.; c. acc. et inf. *to grant that*, Id.　　5. impers. συγχωρεῖ, *it is agreed, it may be done*, ὅπῃ ἂν ξυγχωρῇ *as may be agreed*, Thuc.　Hence

συγχώρημα, ατοs, τό, *a concession*, Plut.; and

συγχωρητέοs, α, ον, verb. Adj. *to be conceded*, Luc.　　2. neut., συγχωρητέον *one must concede*, Plat.: so in pl. συγχωρητέα, Soph.

σύδην [ῠ], Adv. (σεύω) impetuously, hurriedly, Aesch.

σύειος, α, ον, (σῦς) of swine, Lat. suillus, Xen., Luc.

συ-ζάω, f. -ζήσω, to live with another, c. dat., Dem., etc.; c. dat. rei, σ. φιλοπραγμοσύνῃ to pass one's life in meddling, Id. :—absol. to live together, Arist.

συ-ζεύγνυμι, f. -ζεύξω, to yoke together, couple or pair together, Hdt., Xen. : esp. in marriage, Eur., etc. :— Med. to yoke for oneself, Xen. :—Pass. to be yoked or coupled with, τινί Eur. : absol., συζυγέντες ὁμιλοῦσι they live in close familiarity, Xen. Hence

σύζευξις, εως, ἡ, a being yoked together, esp. of wedded union, Plat. :—of things, close union, combination, Id.

συ-ζητέω, f. ήσω, to search or examine together with another, c. dat., Plat. II. σ. τινί or πρός τινα to dispute with a person, N. T. Hence

συζητητής, οῦ, ὁ, a joint inquirer : a disputer, N. T.

συ-ζοφόω, f. ώσω, to darken utterly, Anth.

συζυγία, ἡ, = σύζευξις, Eur. II. a yoke of animals, a pair, Id., Plat.

σύζυγιος, α, ον, poët. for σύζυγος, joined, united, Eur.

σύζυγος, ον, (συζεύγνυμι) yoked together, paired, σ. ὁμαυλίαι wedded union, Aesch. 2. as fem. Subst. a wife, Eur. ; masc. a yoke-fellow, comrade, Id., Ar.

σύζυξ, ῠγος, ὁ, ἡ, = σύζυγος, of a wedded pair, Eur.

συ-ζωοποιέω, to quicken together with, τινά τινι N. T.

σύθην, poët. aor. 1 pass. of σεύω :—συθείς, part.

συκάζω, f. σω, (συκῆ) to pluck ripe figs, Ar., Xen.

συκάμινον [ᾰ], τό, the fruit of the συκάμινος, a mulberry, Lat. morum, Arist.

συκάμινος [ᾰ], ἡ and ὁ, the mulberry-tree, Lat. morus, Theophr. II. = συκόμορος, N. T.

συκῆ, ἡ, Ion. and Ep. συκέη : Ion. gen. pl. συκέων or συκεέων : (σῦκον) :—the fig-tree, Lat. ficus (the fruit being σῦκον), Od. 2. = σῦκον 1, a fig, Ar.

συκίδιον [κῐ], τό, Dim. of σῦκον, Ar.

συκίζω, f. ίσω, (σῦκον) to fatten with figs, Anth.

σύκινος, η, ον, (συκῆ) of the fig-tree, σ. ξύλον fig-wood, Ar. :—the wood of the fig was spongy and useless (Horace's inutile lignum), Plat. :—hence, 2. metaph., σύκινοι ἄνδρες worthless, good-for-nothing fellows, Theocr.; σ. σύζυγος a false, treacherous comrade, with a play on συκοφαντικός, Ar.

συκίς, ίδος, ἡ, (συκέη) a slip or cutting from a fig-tree, a young fig-tree, Ar.

συκολογέω, f. ήσω, to gather figs, Ar. From

συκο-λόγος, ον, (λέγω) gathering figs.

συκομορέα or -αία, ἡ, = συκόμορος, N. T.

συκό-μορον, τό, the fruit of the συκόμορος, Strab.

συκό-μορος, ἡ, (μόρον) the fig-mulberry, an Egyptian kind that bears its fruit on the branches, called also συκάμινος ἡ Αἰγυπτία, Theophr.

συκο-μωραία, ἡ, = συκόμορος, N. T.

ΣΥΚΟΝ, τό, the fruit of the συκῆ, a fig, Lat. ficus, Od., etc. : proverb., σῦκα αἰτεῖν, i. e. to be dainty, Ar. II. a wart on the eyelid, Id. Hence

συκόομαι, Pass. to be fed with figs, Anth.

συκο-τράγ̔ω, ας, ἡ, (τραγεῖν) to eat figs, Theophr.

συκοφαντέω, f. ήσω, (συκοφάντης) :— 1. c. acc. pers. to accuse falsely, slander, calumniate, Ar., Plat. :— Pass. to be falsely accused, Xen., etc. 2. c. acc. rei, to misrepresent, Dem. :—but also, to extort by false accusations, Lys., N. T. 3. absol. to deal

in false accusations, Ar., Plat. : generally, to deal falsely, to give false counsel, Dem. Hence

συκοφάντημα, ατος, τό, a sycophant's trick, false accusation, calumny, Aeschin.

συκο-φάντης, ου, ὁ, (φαίνω) a false accuser, slanderer, Ar., etc.; (never used in the modern sense of sycophant, i. e. κόλαξ) :—generally, a false adviser, Dem. (Commonly derived from σῦκον, φαίνω, one who informed against persons exporting figs from Attica : better perh. a fig-shewer, i. e. one who brings figs to light by shaking the tree (the figs having been hidden in the thick foliage) ; and then, metaph., one who makes rich men yield up their fruit by false accusations). Hence

συκοφαντιά, ἡ, false accusation, slander, calumny, Xen., etc. II. a sophism, Arist.; and

συκοφαντίας, ου, ὁ, the Sycophant-wind (cf. καικίας) Ar.; and

συκοφαντικός, ή, όν, slanderous, calumnious, Dem. : Adv. -κῶς, Isocr.

συκοφάντρια, ἡ, fem. of συκοφάντης, Ar.

συκόφασις, ἡ, used metri grat. for συκοφαντία, Anth.

συκοφορέω, f. ήσω, to carry figs, Anth. From

συκο-φόρος, ον, (φέρω) fig-bearing, Strab.

σύλα, Ep. for ἐσύλα, 3 sing. impf. of συλάω.

σύλα, τά, v. σύλη.

συλ-αγωγέω, (σῦλα, ἀγωγός) to carry off as booty, lead captive, N. T.

συλάω, 3 sing. impf. ἐσύλα, Ep. σύλα, Ion. σύλασκε :— Pass., f. συληθήσομαι : (σύλη) :—to strip off, esp. to strip off the arms of a slain enemy : c. acc. pers. et rei, to strip off from another, strip him of his arms, Il., Eur. :—Pass., c. acc. rei, to be stript, robbed, deprived of a thing, Trag. II. c. acc. pers. only, to strip a man of his arms, to strip bare, pillage, plunder, Il., Hdt., etc. III. c. acc. rei only, to strip off, τεύχεα ἐσύλα Il. :—also to take off or out, ἐσύλα τόξον took out the bow [from its case], Ib.; σύλα πῶμα φαρέτρης took the lid off the quiver, Ib. 2. to carry off, seize as spoil or booty, Hdt., Att. :—Pass. to be carried off as spoil, Hdt.; to be taken away, Eur. ; c. gen. rei, τίς σε συλᾷ πάτρας; who carries thee away from this country? Id.

συλεύω, Ep. for foreg., used in pres. and impf. to despoil of arms, Il. : also, to despoil secretly, to trick, cheat, Ib.

συλέω, = συλάω :—Med. to steal for oneself, κηρίον ἐκ σίμβλων συλεύμενος (Dor. for -ούμενος) Theocr.

ΣΥΛΗ, ἡ, or **ΣΥΛΟΝ**, τό, the right of seizing the ship or cargo of a foreign merchant, to cover losses received through him : generally, the right of seizure, right of reprisal, mostly in pl. σύλαι or σύλα; σύλας διδόναι τινί κατά τινος Dem.; ὅπου σύλαι μὴ ὦσιν Ἀθηναίοις where the Athenians have [to fear] no right of seizure, ap. Dem.; σῦλα ποιεῖσθαι to exercise this right, Lys.

συλήτειρα, ἡ, fem. as if from συλητήρ, a robber, Eur.

συλλᾰβεῖν, aor. 2 inf. of συλλαμβάνω :—συλλαβέσθαι, inf. med. Hence

συλλᾰβή, ἡ, that which holds together, Aesch. 2. Pass. that which is held together, of several letters taken together, so as to form one sound, a syllable, Id., Plat., etc. Hence

συλλᾰβίζω, f. σω, to join letters into syllables, to pronounce letters together, Luc.

συλ-λαγχάνω, f. -λήξομαι: pf. -είληχα:—to be chosen by lot with others, Plut.

συλ-λᾰλέω, f. ήσω, to talk or converse with another, N.T.

συλ-λαμβάνω, f. -λήψομαι: pf. συνείληφα, pass. -είλημμαι: aor. 1 συνέλαβον, inf. συλλᾰβεῖν:—Pass., f. -ληφθήσομαι:—to collect, gather together, esp. to rally scattered troops, Hdt., Xen., etc.   2. simply, to take with one, take up and carry off, Soph., Ar.: to buy up, Ar.   3. to put together, close the mouth of a corpse, Plat.; σ. αὐτοῦ τὸ στόμα to shut his mouth, Ar.   4. in speaking, to comprehend, comprise, Hdt., Plat.   II. to lay hold of, seize, grasp, c. acc., Hdt., Soph.; c. gen., σ. τῶν σχοινίων to lay hold of them, Ar.; absol. in part., ξυλλαβών quickly, in a hurry, Id.:—also in Med., c. gen., ξυλλαβέσθαι τοῦ ξύλου Id.   2. to apprehend, arrest, Hdt., Att.:—Pass., πρὶν ξυλληφθῆναι before they were arrested, Thuc.   3. of the mind, to comprehend, understand, Hdt., Pind.   III. to receive at the same time, enjoy together, Hdt.   IV. of females, to conceive, Luc.   V. c. dat. pers. to take part with, assist, Hdt., Att.:—absol. to assist, Aesch., etc.   2. c. dat. pers. et c. gen. rei, to take part with one in a thing, Eur., Ar.:—so in Med., συνελάβετο τοῦ στρατεύματος Hdt.; νόσου συλλαβέσθαι Soph.: to contribute towards a thing, Thuc.

συλ-λέγω, f. -λέξω: aor. 1 συνέλεξα: pf. -είλοχα:—Med., f. -λέξομαι, aor. 1 -ελεξάμην:—Pass., f. -λεγήσομαι: aor. 1 -ελέχθην, aor. 2 -ελέγην: pf. -είλεγμαι (also used in med. sense), and λέλεγμαι:—to collect, gather, Il., Hdt., Att.:—σ. μέλη to compile, scrape together tunes, Ar.; σ. ὕβρεις αὐτοῦ to compile a list of them, Dem.:—Med. to collect for oneself, for one's own use, Il., etc.   2. σ. σθένος to collect one's powers, make a rally, Eur.:—Pass. to be collected, of the mind, Plat.   II. of persons, to call together, Eur.:—so in Med., Od., etc.:—Pass. to come together, assemble, Hdt., Att.   2. to collect, get together, στασιώτας Hdt.; σ. στρατόν to levy an army, Lat. conscribere, Thuc.

σύλ-λεκτρος, ον, (λέκτρον) partner of the bed, Eur.

συλλήβδην, (συλλαμβάνω) Adv. collectively, in sum, in short, Theogn., Aesch., etc.

συλ-λήγω, f. ξω, to finish together with, c. dat., Anth.

συλληπτέον, verb. Adj. of συλλαμβάνω, one must seize together, Eur.   2. συλληπτέος, α, ον, to be seized, Luc.

συλλήπτρια, ἡ, fem. of sq., Xen.

συλλήπτωρ, ορος, ὁ, a partner, accomplice, assistant, Aesch.; τινός in a thing, Eur., etc.

συλληφθῆναι, aor. 1 inf. pass. of συλλαμβάνω.

σύλ-ληψις, εως, ἡ, a taking together: a seizing, arresting, ποιεῖσθαι ξύλληψιν to arrest, Thuc.   II. conception, Plut.

συλλογή, ἡ, (συλλέγω) a gathering, collecting, Thuc.: metaph., ἐν γενείου ξυλλογῇ τριχώματος in the first harvest of a beard, i. e. in early manhood, Aesch.   2. a levying of soldiers, Lat. conscriptio, Xen.   3.

a summary, recapitulation, Dem.   II. (from Pass.) an assembly, meeting, Hdt., Lys.   Hence

συλ-λογίζομαι: aor. 1 συνελογισάμην and -ελογίσθην: pf. -λελόγισμαι: Dep.:—to collect and bring at once before the mind, to compute fully, sum up, Hdt., Dem.   II. to collect or conclude from premisses, Lat. colligere, Plat., Dem.   2. to conclude by way of syllogism, Arist.:—pf. in pass. sense, συλλελογισμένα logically concluded, Id.

συλλογϊμαῖος, α, ον, collected from divers places, Luc.

συλλογισμός, ὁ, (συλλογίζομαι) computation, Plat.   II. a conclusion, inference from premisses, Id.

συλλογιστέος, α, ον, verb. Adj. of συλλογίζομαι, to be concluded, Plat.   II. neut. συλλογιστέον one must compute or conclude, Arist.

συλλογιστικός, ή, όν, (συλλογίζομαι) of or for concluding, syllogistic, Arist.:—Adv. -κῶς, Id.

σύλ-λογος, ὁ, (λέγω) an assembly, Hdt., Att.; σύλλογον ποιεῖσθαι to convene an assembly, opp. to διαλύειν, Hdt., etc.:—a muster of forces, Xen.   II. metaph. collectedness, presence of mind, Eur.

συλ-λούομαι, Med. or Pass. to bathe together, Plut.

συλ-λοχίζω, f. σω, to incorporate soldiers, Plut.

συλ-λοχίτης [ῐ], ου, ὁ, a soldier of the same λόχος, Hdt.

συλ-λυπέω, f. ήσω, to hurt or mortify together, σ. τινα αὐτῷ to make him share one's grief, Arist.   II. Pass., f. -λυπηθήσομαι and in med. form -λυπήσομαι:—to sympathise or condole with, τινί Hdt., Att.

συλ-λυσσάομαι, Pass. to go mad with, τινι, Anth.

συλ-λύω, f. ύσω, to help in loosing, Eur.:—to help to solve a difficulty or end a quarrel, Soph.   II. to rest under the same roof, Aesch.; cf. καταλύω.

σῦλ-όνυξ, ὔχος, ὁ, ἡ, (συλάω) paring the nails, Anth.

σῦμα, Lacon. for θῦμα.

συμ-βαίνω, f. -βήσομαι: pf. -βέβηκα, 3 pl. sync. -βεβᾶσι, Ion. inf. -βεβάναι: aor. 2 συνέβην, inf. συμβῆναι:—Pass., 3 sing. aor. 1 subj. ξυμβᾰθῇ: pf. inf. βεβᾶσθαι:—to stand with the feet together, opp. to διαβαίνειν, Xen.   2. to stand with, so as to assist, Soph.; σ. κακοῖς, i. e. increase them, Eur.   3. to meet, τινί Xen.; συμβέβηκεν οὐδαμοῦ has never come in my way, has had naught to do with me, Eur.   II. metaph. to come together, come to an agreement, come to terms, Lat. convenire, τινί with another, Hdt., Att.; c. inf., σ. ὑπήκοοι εἶναι Thuc.; Pass., of the terms, to be agreed on, Id.   2. of things, to coincide or correspond with, c. dat., Hdt., Att.:—absol., Trag., etc.   3. to fall to one's lot, c. dat. pers., Eur., Dem.   III. of events, to come to pass, happen, Lat. contingere, Aesch., Plat., etc.:—impers., συνέβη μοι, c. inf., it happened to me to do a thing, Hdt., etc.; also c. acc. it happened that I did, Id., Thuc., etc.: ξυμβαίνει c. inf. it happens to be, i. e. it is so and so, Plat.:—τὸ συμβεβηκός a chance event, contingency, Dem.; so, τὰ συμβαίνοντα Xen.; τὰ συμβάντα Id.   2. joined with Adverbs or Adjectives, to turn out in a certain way, ὀρθῶς συνέβαινε Hdt.; κακῶς, καλῶς ξυμβῆναι Xen., etc.   3. of consequences, to result, follow, Thuc.: so, of logical conclusions, Plat.

συμ-βακχεύω, f. σω, to join in the feast of Bacchus or Bacchic revelry, Eur., Plat.

σύμ-βακχος, ὁ and ἡ, *joining in Bacchic revelry*, Eur.
συμ-βάλλω : f. -βᾰλῶ : aor. 2 -ἐβᾰλον, inf. -βᾰλεῖν :
pf. -βέβληκα:—Pass., aor. 1 -εβλήθην :—Hom. has an
intr. aor. 2 συμβλήτην, -βλήμεναι, Med. σύμβλητο,
-βλήηντο, -βληται, -βλήμενος, with f. συμβλήσομαι,
2 sing. συμβλήσεαι:—*to throw together, dash together*,
Il., Eur., etc.: *to unite* their streams, of rivers, Il. :
—so in Med., Hdt. **2.** *to throw together, collect*, Xen. **3.** intr. *to come together, meet*, Aesch.,
Soph., Xen. **4.** *to close* the eyes, in sleep or
death, Aesch. ; but, ποῖον ὄμμα συμβαλῶ; how shall
I *meet* her eyes *with mine?* Eur. **5.** generally, *to join, unite*, σ. σχοινία *to twist* ropes, Ar. ;
ξ. δεξιάς *to join* hands, Eur. ; σ. λόγους Id. :—Pass.,
κριθὰς ἵπποις συμβεβλημένας barley *thrown* in heaps
before them, Xen. **6.** σ. συμβόλαιά τινι or πρός
τινα *to make a contract* with a person, *to lend* him
money *on bond*, Dem.; συμβόλαιον εἰς τἀνδράποδα
συμβεβλημένον money *lent* on the security of the
slaves, Id. ; absol., in same sense, Plat. **7.** *to
contribute, lend*, Xen.:—so in Med., Hdt., etc. ;
τὸ μὴ ἀγανακτεῖν ἄλλα πολλὰ συμβάλλεται many circumstances *contribute* to my feeling no vexation,
Plat. ; συμβάλλεσθαι εἰς or πρός τι *to contribute*
towards, Hdt., Att. ; c. gen. partit., ξυμβάλλεται
πολλὰ τοῦδε δείματος many things *contribute* [*their
share*] *of* this fear, i. e. join in causing it, Eur. **8.**
συμβάλλεσθαι γνώμας *to add* one's *opinion* to that of
others, Hdt. **9.** συμβάλλειν λόγους *to converse*,
and συμβάλλειν, absol., like Lat. *conferre* for *conferre
sermonem*, σ. πρός τινα N. T. :—so in Med., συμβάλλεσθαι λόγους Xen. ; συμβάλλεσθαί τι *to have something to say*, Plat., etc. **II.** *to bring* men
together in hostile sense, *to set* them *together, match*
them, Il., etc. :—Med. *to join in fight.* **2.** intr.
to come together, engage, Il. : *to come* to blows, τινί
with another, Hdt., Aesch. **3.** σ. μάχην, Lat.
committere pugnam, Eur. ; ἔχθραν σ. τινί Id. ;—
metaph., συμβαλεῖν ἔπη κακά *to bandy* reproaches,
Soph. **4.** Med. *to fall in with* one, *meet* him *by
chance*, c. dat., Hom., who uses Ep. aor. 2 ξύμβλητο
and f. συμβλήσομαι solely in this sense. **III.**
to put together, and in Pass. *to correspond, tally*,
Aesch. **2.** *to compare*, τί τινι Hdt. ; ἐν πρὸς ἕν
Id. ; τι πρός τι Plat. :—Pass., τὸ Βαβυλώνιον τάλαντον
συμβαλλόμενον πρὸς τὸ Εὐβοεικόν the Babyl. talent
being compared with, reduced to, the Euboïc,
Hdt. **3.** in Med. *to put together, reckon, compute*,
Id. **4.** *to compare* one's own opinion *with facts*,
and so *to conclude, infer, conjecture, interpret*,
Pind., Soph., etc. :—so in Med. *to make out, understand*, Hdt. **IV.** in Med. *to agree upon, fix,
settle*, Xen.
σύμβαμα, τό, (συμβαίνω III) *a chance, casualty*, Luc.
συμβάς, aor. 2 part. of συμβαίνω.
συμ-βᾰσείω, Desiderat. of συμβαίνω II, *to wish to make
a league* or *covenant* with another, τινί Thuc.
συμ-βᾰσῐλεύω, f. σω, *to rule* or *reign together with*,
τινί Luc.
σύμβᾰσις, εως Ion. ιος, ἡ, (συμβαίνω II) *an agreement,
arrangement, treaty*, Hdt., Eur. ; δὸς ξύμβασιν τέκνοις
make them friends, Eur.

συμβᾰτήριος, ον, = sq., Thuc.
συμβᾰτικός, ή, όν, (συμβαίνω II) *tending to agreement,
conciliatory*, ξυμβ. λόγοι Thuc. ; ̯οὐδὲν πράξαντες ξυμ-
βατικόν having effected nothing *towards an agreement*,
Id.:—Adv.,—κῶς ἔχειν to be inclined *to agreement*,Plut.
συμβεβάναι [ᾰ], for -βεβηκέναι, pf. inf. of συμβαίνω.
συμ-βελής, ές, *hit by several arrows at once*, Polyb.
συμβῆναι, aor. 2 inf. of συμβαίνω.
συμ-βιάζομαι, pf. -βεβίασμαι, Pass. *to be forced together, to be reduced* or *extorted by force*, Dem.
συμ-βῐβάζω, Causal of συμβαίνω, *to bring together* :
Pass. *to be joined* or *knit together, framed*, N.T. **2.**
metaph. *to bring together, reconcile*, Hdt. ; σ. τινά
τινι *to reconcile* one to another, Thuc. **II.** *to put
together, compare, examine*, Plat. **III.** *to prove
logically*, Arist., N. T. **2.** *to teach, instruct*, N. T.
Hence
συμβῐβαστικός, ή, όν, *leading to reconciliation*, Plut.
σύμ-βιος, ον, ὁ and ἡ, *a companion, partner*, Arist. :
a husband or *wife*, Anth.
συμ-βιόω, f. -βιώσομαι : pf. -βεβίωκα : aor. 2 -εβίων,
inf. -βιῶναι :—*to live with* another, c. dat., Dem. ;
in pl. *to live together*, ὡς κοινῇ συμβιωσόμενοι Plat.
συμβιωτέον, verb. Adj. *one must live with*, τινί Arist.
συμβλήμενος, Ep. aor. 2 med. part. of συμβάλλω (II. 4).
συμβλήσομαι, Ep. fut. med. of συμβάλλω (II. 4).
συμβλητός, ή, όν, verb. Adj. of συμβάλλω, *comparable,
capable of being compared*, absol. or c. dat., Arist.
συμ-βοάω, f. ήσομαι, *to shout together, with*, τινί
Xen. **II.** c. acc. *to call on* others *at once*, Id.
συμβοηθεία, ἡ, *joint aid* or *assistance*, Thuc. From
συμ-βοηθέω, f. ήσω, *to render joint aid, join in assisting*, Thuc., Xen.
συμβόλαιον, τό, like σύμβολον, *a mark* or *sign to conclude from, a token*, Hdt. : *a symptom*, Soph. **II.**
at Athens, *a contract, covenant, bond*, in acknowledgment of a loan, Oratt. ; in pl., of *a single contract*,
Plat., etc. ; τὰ Ἀθήναζε καὶ τὰ Ἀθήνηθεν συμβ. *a
bond for money lent* on freights to and from Athens,
Dem. **2.** generally, *an engagement*, Eur. **III.**
intercourse, Plut. Hence
συμβόλαιος, α, ον, *of* or *concerning contracts*, Thuc.
συμβολέω, *to meet* or *fall in with*, τινί Aesch. From
συμβολή, ἡ, (συμβάλλομαι) *a coming together, meeting, joining*, Xen. : *the juncture* of two parts, *the
end*, Lat. *commissura*, Hdt., Plat. **II.** in hostile
sense, *an encounter, engagement, battle*, Hdt.,
Aesch. **III.** = συμβόλαιον II, *a contract, covenant*,
Arist. ; in Ar. Ach. there is a play on signfs. II and III,
encounter and *accounts, charge* and *charges*. **IV.**
in pl., συμβολαί were *contributions* for a common
meal, πίνειν ἀπὸ συμβολῶν, like *de symbolis esse* in
Terent., Att. ; *the entertainment* itself, *a picnic*, Xen.
συμβολικός, ή, όν, (σύμβολον) *signifying by a sign* or
symbol, symbolical, figurative, Luc. From
σύμβολον, τό, (συμβάλλω III) *a sign* or *token by which
one infers* a thing, Trag. ; λαμπάδος τὸ σύμβολον
the token of the beacon-fire, Aesch. :—often in pl., of
marks on the body, Eur. ; of *omens*, Aesch. **2.**
a pledge or *pawn*, on which money was advanced,
Lys. **3.** in pl. *tallies*, Lat. *tesserae hospitales*, i. e.
the halves of a bone or coin, which two persons broke

between them, each keeping one piece, Hdt., Eur., etc. **4.** at Athens, *a ticket, counter*, Lat. *tessera*, such as were given to the dicasts, on presenting which they received their fee, Dem. **5.** *a permit* or *licence* to reside, given to aliens, Ar.; *a ticket* given by each person who·joined in a picnic, to be presented for payment at the end (cf. συμβολή IV), Id. **6.** in Eccl. *the distinctive mark* of Christians, *a confession of faith, a creed*, Lat. *symbolum.* **II.** in legal phrase, σύμβολα were *covenants between two states for protection of commerce*, Dem., etc.; σύμβολα ποιεῖσθαι πρὸς πόλιν to make *a commercial treaty* with a state, τὰ σ. συγχέειν to violate *such treaty*, Id.

σύμβολος, ὁ, = σύμβολον I. I, *an augury, omen*, Aesch., Xen.

συμβούλευμα, ατος, τό, *advice given*, Xen., Arist.; and **συμβουλευτέος,** α, ον, verb. Adj. *to be given as advice*, Thuc. **II.** -τέον, *one must advise*, τινί Isocr.

συμβουλευτικός, ή, όν, *of* or *for advising, deliberative*, of orators, Arist. From

συμ-βουλεύω, f. σω, *to advise, counsel*, Lat. *consulere alicui*, c. dat. pers. et inf., *to advise* one to do a thing, Hdt., Thuc., etc. **2.** without the inf., σ. τινί τι Hdt., Plat.; σ. τι *to recommend* a measure, Hdt., Att. :—Pass., τὰ συμβουλευόμενα *the advice given*, Xen. **3.** absol. *to advise, give advice*, Soph.; ὁ συμβουλεύων or -εύσας, *an adviser*, Lat. *auctor sententiae*, Arist. **II.** Med. *to consult with* a person, i. e. *ask* his *advice*, Lat. *consulere aliquem*, c. dat., Hdt., etc. : absol. *to consult, deliberate*, Xen.

συμβουλή, ή, = συμβουλία, Hdt., Xen., etc. **II.** *counsel, consultation, deliberation, debate*, Plat.

συμ-βουλία, Ion. -ίη, ἡ, (βουλή) *advice* or *counsel given*, Hdt., Xen.; in pl. *counsels*, Xen.

συμ-βούλιον, τό, (βουλή) *counsel*, N. T. **II.** *a council*, Plut.

συμ-βούλομαι, f. ήσομαι: pf. -βεβούλημαι :—Dep. *to will* or *to wish with·another*, c. dat., Eur. **2.** *to agree with*, τινί Plat. :—absol. *to consent*, Id.

σύμ-βουλος, ὁ, (βουλή) *an adviser, counsellor*, Hdt., Soph., etc.; as fem., Xen. :—c. gen. pers. one's *adviser*, Aesch., etc.; also, σ. τινι Ar., etc. :—but c. gen. rei, σ. λόγου τοῦδέ μοι γένεσθε be my *counsellors in* this matter, Aesch.; also, περὶ or ὑπέρ τινος Id., Isocr. :—ξύμβουλός εἰμι = συμβουλεύω, *to advise*, c. inf., Aesch.

συμ-βύω, f. ύσω, *to cram* or *huddle together*, Ar.

σύμ-βωμος, ον, *worshipped on a common altar*, Strab.

συμμαθεῖν, aor. 2 inf. of συμμανθάνω.

συμ-μαθητής, οῦ, ὁ, *a fellow-disciple*, Plat.

συμμαίνομαι, aor. 2 συνεμάνην [ἄ] :—Pass., with intr. pf. act. συμμέμηνα :—*to be mad together, join in madness*, τινι with one, Luc.

συμ-μανθάνω, f. -μαθήσομαι : aor. 2 συνέμαθον :—*to learn along with* another, c. dat., Xen.: absol. *to share in the knowledge* of a thing, Soph.; ὁ συμμαθών one that is accustomed *to* a thing, Xen.

συμ-μάρπτω, f. ψω, *to seize* or *grasp together*, Hom.

συμ-μαρτύρέω, f. ήσω, *to bear witness with* or *in support* of another, c. dat., Soph., Thuc.; τι to a fact, Solon, Xen.; also, σ. τινι πάντα ὡς ἀληθῆ λέγει Xen.

συμ-μαρτύρομαι [ῡ], Dep. = συμμαρτυρέω, N. T.

συμ-μάρτῦς, ῠρος, ὁ, ἡ, *a fellow-witness*, Soph.

συμ-μαστῑγόω, f. ώσω, *to whip* or *lash along with* or *together*, Luc.

συμμᾰχέω, f. ήσω, (σύμμαχος) *to be an ally, to be in alliance*, Aesch., Thuc. :—generally, *to help, aid, succour*, τινί Soph., etc. :—Pass. *to be assisted*, Luc.

συμμᾰχία, Ion. -ίη, ἡ, *an alliance offensive and defensive* (opp. to an ἐπιμαχία, *defensive*), Hdt., etc.; συμμαχίαν ποιεῖσθαι πρός τινα Id.; τινί Thuc. **2.** generally, *the duty of an ally*, Aesch. **II.** = τὸ συμμαχικόν, *the body of allies*, Hdt., Thuc.: also, *the country of one's allies*, Thuc. **2.** *an allied* or *auxiliary force*, Id., Xen.

συμμᾰχικός, ή, όν, (σύμμαχος) *of* or *for alliance*, θεοὶ ξ. the gods *invoked at the making of an alliance*, Thuc. **II.** τὸ συμμαχικόν, *the auxiliaries, allied forces*, Hdt., Thuc. **2.** *a treaty of alliance*, Thuc.: τὰ -κά *matters respecting alliances*, Xen. **III.** Adv. -κῶς, *like an ally*, Isocr.

συμμᾰχίς, ίδος, fem. of σύμμαχος, *allied*, Thuc., Xen.; ξ. πόλις an *allied state*, Thuc.; also ἡ σ. (without πόλις) Id. **II.** = τὸ ξυμμαχικόν, *the body of allies*, Id.

συμ-μάχομαι [ἄ], f. οῦμαι : aor. 1 συνεμαχεσάμην : pf. συμμεμάχημαι : Dep. :—*to fight along with* others, *to be an ally, auxiliary*, Xen. : generally, *to help, succour*, τινι Id.; τὸ οἰκὸς ἐμοὶ συμμάχεται probability *is on my side*, Hdt.

σύμ-μᾰχος, ον, (μάχη) *fighting along with, allied with*, τινι Hdt., Att. : as Subst. *an ally*, and in pl. *allies*, Hdt., Att. **2.** of things, συμμάχῳ δορί Aesch.; νόμος σύμμαχος τῷ θέλοντι Hdt.; c. gen. rei, ἀρετὴ τῶν ἔργων σύμμαχος Xen.

συμ-μεθέπω, *to sway jointly*, Anth.

συμ-μεθίστημι, *to help in changing*, 3 sing. συμμεθιστᾷ (from -ιστάω) Strab. **II.** Pass., with aor. 2 et pf. act., *to change places along with* another, Plut.

συμ-μελετάω, f. ήσω, *to exercise* or *practise with* or *together*, Anth.

συμ-μένω, f. μενῶ, *to hold together, keep together*, Thuc., etc.: of treaties or agreements, *to hold, continue*, Hdt., Thuc.

συμ-μερίζω, f. σω, *to distribute in shares* : Med. *to take share in* or *with*, c. dat., N. T.

συμ-μεσουράνησις, ἡ, (οὐρανός) *a being in the same meridian*, Strab.

συμ-μεταβάλλω, f. -βᾰλῶ, *to change along with* other things, τί τινι Anth., Plut. :—Pass. *to change sides and take part with*, τινι Aeschin. **II.** intr. in Act. *to change with* or *together*, Arist.

συμ-μετα-κοσμέομαι, Pass. *to change one's habits along with* another, c. dat., Plut.

συμ-μεταπίπτω, f. -πεσοῦμαι, *to change along with* others, c. dat., Aeschin.

συμ-μεταφέρομαι, Pass. *to be borne off together*, Plut.

συμ-μεταχειρίζομαι, Dep. *to take charge of* a thing *with* others, Isae.

συμ-μετέχω, f. -μεθέξω, *to partake of* a thing *with* others, *take part in* a thing *with* others, c. dat. pers. et gen. rei, Eur.; with gen. rei only, Id., Xen.

συμ-μετεωρίζομαι, Pass. *to be raised together*, Strab.

συμμετίσχω, = συμμετέχω, Soph.

συμ-μετοικέω, f. ήσω, to emigrate along with another, c. dat., Plut.

συμμέτοχος, ον, partaking with another in a thing, the partner of another, N. T.

συμμετρέω, f. ήσω, (σύμμετρος) to measure by comparison with another thing:—Pass., 1. ἦμαρ συμμετρούμενον χρόνῳ this day measured by calculation of time, Soph. 2. absol. to be commensurate with, Id. 3. οἶς ὁ βίος ξυνεμετρήθη who had their life measured out, Thuc. II. Med. to measure for oneself, compute exactly, Hdt.; ξυνεμετρήσαντο [τὸ τεῖχος] ταῖς ἐπιβολαῖς τῶν πλίνθων calculated its height by counting the courses of bricks, Thuc. Hence

συμμέτρησις, ἡ, commeasurement, Thuc.; and

συμμετρία, ἡ, commensurability, Arist. II. symmetry, due proportion, Plat., etc.

σύμ-μετρος, ον, (μέτρον) commensurate with another thing, Eur.: exactly fitting, Aesch.; τῷδε τἀνδρὶ ξ. being of like age with, Soph.; ποίᾳ σύμμετρος τύχῃ; coincident with what chance? i. e. in the very nick of time, Id.; v. infr. III. 2. 2. commensurable, Arist. II. in measure with, proportionable, exactly suitable, Isocr., etc. 2. absol. in right measure, in due proportion, symmetrical, opp. to ὑπερβάλλων and ἐλλείπων, Plat., etc. 3. generally, fitting, meet, due, Aesch.; σύμμετρος ὡς κλύειν within fit distance for hearing, Soph. III. Adv. -τρως, Isocr., etc. 2. in due time, Eur.

συμ-μητιάομαι, Dep. to take counsel with or together, Il.

συμ-μηχανάομαι, f. ήσομαι, Dep. to help to provide or procure, Xen. 2. to form plans with another, c. dat., Plut.

σύμμιγα, Adv. promiscuously with others, c. dat., Hdt.

συμ-μιγής, ές, (μίγνυμι) commingled, promiscuous, Soph., Eur., etc. 2. c. dat. commingled with, Aesch.

συμ-μίγνῡμι and -ύω; 3 sing. imper. συμμίγνυ: Ep. and Ion., pres. συμμίσγω: f. -μίξω:—Med., f. -μίξομαι (also in pass. sense):—to mix together, commingle, h. Hom.; to mix one thing with another, τί τινι Hdt., Att.; c. acc. only, συμμίξαντες τὰ στρατόπεδα having combined them, Hdt.:—Pass., of a river, to be mingled with another river, c. dat., Il.: to join forces, of two armies, Thuc.:—metaph., οὐδείς [ἐστι] τῷ κακῷ οὐ συνεμίχθη there is none who has not misery as an ingredient in his nature, Hdt.; συμμιγέντων τούτων πάντων when all these things happened together, Id. 2. to unite, θεοὺς γυναιξὶ h. Hom.:—Pass. to have intercourse with, c. dat., Hdt., Aesch. 3. metaph., σ. τινὰ τύχᾳ to make him acquainted with fortune, Pind.; πρῆγμα συμμῖξαί τινι to communicate a matter to another, Hdt. II. intr. in Act. to have intercourse with, to associate or communicate with others, c. dat., Theogn., Hdt., etc.; σ. πρός τινα to join him, Xen.:—generally, to meet for conversation or traffic, Hdt.; σ. τινί to converse with, Id., Eur. 2. in hostile sense, to meet in close fight, come to blows, engage, τινί with one, Hdt., etc. 3. generally, to meet, Xen.

σύμ-μικτος, ον, commingled, promiscuous, Hes., Soph.: esp. of troops, irregular, Hdt., Thuc. Adv. -τως, Strab.

συμ-μιμητής, οῦ, ὁ, a joint-imitator, N. T.

συμ-μιμνήσκομαι, Pass. to bear in mind with, Dem.

συμμῖξαι, aor. 1 inf. of συμμίγνυμι.

σύμ-μιξις, εως, ἡ, commixture, τινος πρός τι Plat. II. intercourse, Plut.

συμ-μῑσέω, f. ήσω, to join with in hating, Polyb.

συμ-μίσγω, = συμμίγνυμι, Hom., etc.

σύμ-μολπος, ον, (μολπή) = συνῳδός, Eur.

συμ-μορία, ἡ, (μέρος) a co-partnership or company: at Athens, after 377 B.C., the 1200 wealthiest citizens were divided into 20 συμμορίαι or companies, 2 in each tribe (φυλή); each being called on in its turn to discharge extraordinary expenses, Xen., Dem.

σύμ-μορος, ον, united for purposes of taxation, Thuc.

σύμ-μορφόομαι, Pass. to be conformed to, τινι N. T.

σύμ-μορφος, ον, (μορφή) conformed to, c. gen., N. T.

συμ-μοχθέω, f. ήσω, to share in toil with, τινί Eur.

συμ-μνέω, f. ήσω, to initiate together, Plut.

σύμ-μνω, f. -μύσω, to be shut up, to close, be closed, of wounds, Il.; συμμεμυκώς with closed eyes, Plat.

συμπάθεια, ἡ, fellow-feeling, sympathy, Arist.

συμ-παθεῖν, aor. 2 inf. of συμπάσχω.

συμ-παθέω, f. ήσω, to sympathise, Isocr., etc.

συμ-πᾰθής, ές, (παθεῖν) sympathising with, τινί Arist.: absol. sympathetic, Id.

συμ-πᾰθία, Ion. -ίη, ἡ, poët. for συμπάθεια, Anth.

συμ-παιᾱνίζω, f. σω, to sing paeans with, τινί Dem.

συμ-παιδεύω, f. σω, to teach together, educate at the same time, Xen.: Pass. to be educated with others, Isocr.

συμ-παίζω, f. ξομαι, to play or sport with another, c. dat., Soph.; absol., Hdt.; c. acc. cogn., μετ᾽ ἐμοῦ σύμπαιζε τὴν ἑορτήν keep the feast together with me, Ar.

συμ-παίκτωρ, ορος, ὁ, = συμπαιστής, Xen., Anth.

συμπαίσδεν, Dor. inf. of συμπαίζω.

συμπαιστής, οῦ, ὁ, a playmate, playfellow, Plat.:—fem. συμπαίστρια, ἡ, Ar.

συμ-παίκτωρ, ορος, ὁ, = foreg., Xen.

συμ-παίω, f. -παιήσω, to dash against, τί τινι Soph. II. intr. to dash together, Eur.

συμ-πᾰνηγυρίζω, f. σω, to attend a solemn assembly with another, c. dat., Plut.

συμ-παραβύω, to cram in along with, τινά τινι Luc.

συμ-παραγγέλλω, f. ελῶ, to help in canvassing for an office, c. dat., Plut.

συμ-παραγίγνομαι, f. -γενήσομαι, Dep. to be ready at the same time, of fruit ripening, Hdt. II. to stand by another, to come in to assist, Thuc.

συμ-παραδηλόω, f. ώσω, to shew incidentally at the same time, Strab.

συμ-παραθέω, f. -θεύσομαι, to run along together, Dem.

συμ-παραινέω, f. έσω, to join in recommending, τί τινι Ar.: to join in approving, τι Id.

συμ-παρακαθίζω, to make to sit beside: so in Med., Dem. II. Med. also to sit close beside, Plat.

συμ-παρακᾰλέω, f. έσω, to invite together or at the same time, Xen., Plat. II. to ask for at the same time, τι ἀπό τινος Xen.

συμ-παρακελεύομαι, Dep. to join in exciting, Isocr.

συμ-παρ-ᾰκολουθέω, f. ήσω, to follow in a parallel line with, keep up with, τινί Isocr., etc.: absol., Xen.

συμ-παρακομίζω, f. Att. -κομιῶ, to carry along the

coast *with* one, of a commander, Thuc.; Pass. *of the ships*, Id.

συμ-παρακύπτω, f. ψω, *to bend oneself along with*, Luc.

συμ-παραλαμβάνω, f. -λήψομαι, *to take along with* one, *take in as an adjunct*, Plat.

συμ-παραμένω, f. μενῶ, *to stay along with* or *among* others, c. dat., Thuc.

συμ-παραμιγνύω, *to mix in together*, Ar.

συμ-παρανεύω, f. σω, *to express assent also*, Arist.

συμπαρανήχομαι, Dep. *to swim beside together*, Luc.

συμ-παραπέμπω, f. ψω, *to escort along with* others, τὴν παραπομπήν Aeschin.; τὴν ὄψιν σ. τινί *to follow* him *with one's eyes*, Plut.

συμ-παρ-απόλλῠμαι, Pass., with pf. -όλωλα, *to perish along with* or *besides*, Dem.

συμ-παρασκευάζω, f. σω, *to assist in getting ready* or *bringing about*, Xen., Dem.

συμπαραστᾰτέω, f. ήσω, *to stand by so as to assist*, c. dat., Aesch.; absol., Ar.　From

συμ-παραστᾰτης, ου, ὁ, *one who stands by to aid, a joint helper* or *assistant*, Soph., Ar.

συμ-παρατάσσομαι, Att. -ττομαι, Pass. *to be set in array with* others, *fight along with* them, c. dat., Isocr.

συμ-παρατηρέω, *to keep watch together*, Plat.

συμ-παρατίθημι, *to place alongside of* others, Polyb.

συμ-παρατρέφω, f. -θρέψω, *to bring up* or *keep at the same time*, of dogs and other animals, Xen.

συμ-παρατρέχω, f. -δρᾰμοῦμαι, *to run along with*, Plut.

συμ-παραφέρω, f. -παροίσω, *to carry along together* :—Pass. *to rush along together*, Xen.

συμ-πάρειμι, (εἰμί *sum*) *to be present also* or *at the same time*, Xen., etc.　2. *to stand by, to come to help*, τινί Id., Dem.

συμπάρειμι, (εἶμι *ibo*) *to go beside also* or *together*, 3 sing. impf. συμπαρῄει, Xen., Aeschin.

συμ-παρεισέρχομαι, Dep. *to go in along with*, Luc.

συμ-παρέπομαι, f. -έψομαι, Dep. *to go along with, accompany*, c. dat., Xen., etc.

συμ-παρέχω, f. -παρέξω, *to assist in causing*, φόβον τινί Xen.; *in procuring*, ἀσφάλειάν τινι Id.

συμ-παρίπταμαι, Dep. *to fly along with*, Luc.

συμ-παρίστημι, *to place beside one also*, Pind.　II. Pass., c. aor. 2 et pf. act., *to stand beside, assist*, τινι Soph.

συμ-παρομαρτέω, f. ήσω, =συμπαρέπομαι, Xen.

συμ-παροξύνω, f. ῠνῶ, *to provoke with* or *together*, Xen.

συμ-παρορμάω, f. ήσω, *to urge on with* or *together*, Plut.

σύμ-πᾶς, Att. ξύμπας, -πᾶσα, -πᾶν, *all together, all at once, all in a body*, Hom., Hdt., Att.; in Att., the Art. is often added in the case of Numerals, πέντ' ἦσαν οἱ ξύμπαντες Soph.　II. with collective nouns, *the whole*, ὁ σ. στρατός Hdt.; στρατὸς σ. Soph.; ξύμπασα πόλις the state *as a whole*, Thuc.; ξ. γνώμη the *general scope* (of a speech), Id.　2. τὸ σύμπαν *the whole together, the sum* of the matter, Hdt.; τὸ ξύμπαν εἰπεῖν Thuc.　III. τὸ σύμπαν, as Adv. *altogether, on the whole, in general*, Id., etc.

συμ-πάσχω, f. -πείσομαι : pf. -πέπονθα : aor. 2 συνέπαθον :—*to suffer together, be affected by the same thing*, Plat.　II. *to have a fellow-feeling, sympathise, feel sympathy*, Id.

συμ-πᾰτάσσω, f. ξω, *to strike with* or *together*, Eur.

συμ-πᾰτέω, f. ήσω, *to tread together, trample under foot*, Babr.:—Pass. *to be trampled under foot*, Aeschin.

συμ-πεδάω, f. ήσω, *to bind together* :—metaph. of frost, *to benumb*, Xen.

συμ-πείθω, f. σω, *to join* or *assist in persuading*, Xen.;—also, σ. τοῦ μὴ ἀθυμεῖν *to help in persuading against despair*, Thuc.:—Pass. *to allow oneself to be persuaded at the same time*, Aeschin.

σύμ-πειρος, ον, (πεῖρα) *acquainted with*, τινι Pind.

συμ-πείρω, *to pierce through together*, Plut.

συμ-πέμπω, f. ψω, *to send with* or *at the same time*, Hdt., Att.　2. *to help in conducting*, Lys.

συμ-πενθέω, f. ήσω, *to join in mourning for a thing*, τι Isocr.　II. intr. *to mourn together with*, τινί Aesch.; absol., Eur.

συμ-πένομαι, Dep. *to be poor along with* another *in a thing*, τινί τινος Plat.

συμ-περαίνω, f. ᾰνῶ, *to join* or *assist in accomplishing*, Eur.:—Med., συμπεραίνεσθαί τινι ἔχθραν *to join fully in enmity with* another, Dem.　II. *to decide* or *conclude absolutely*, σ. φροντίδα *to make up one's mind*, Eur.; κλῆθρα μοχλοῖς σ. *to make the doors doubly sure* by bars, Id.:—Pass. *to be quite finished*, Xen.　Hence

συμπέρασμα, ατος, τό, *a conclusion*, Arist.　Hence

συμπερασματικός, ή, όν, *conclusive* : Adv. -κῶς, Arist.

συμ-πέρθω, f. σω, *to destroy with* or *together*, Eur.

συμ-περιάγω, f. ξω, *to carry about with* or *together*, Xen.:—Pass. *to go round with* or *together*, Id.:—Med. *to lead about with oneself*, Id.

συμ-περιᾰγωγός, ὁ, ἡ, *an assistant in converting* others, Plat.

συμ-περίειμι, *to go round with* another, c. dat., Xen.

συμ-περιθέω, f. -θεύσομαι, *to run about together*, Luc.

συμ-περιλαμβάνω, f. -λήψομαι, *to comprehend* in a treaty *with* others, Philipp. ap. Dem.　II. Med. *to take part together* in a thing, c. gen., Luc.

συμ-περινοστέω, f. ήσω, *to go round together with, follow along with*, τινί Luc.

συμ-περιπᾰτέω, f. ήσω, *to walk round* or *about with*, τινί Plat.: absol., οἱ συμπεριπατοῦντες *their companions in walking round*, Arist.

συμ-περιπλοκή, ἡ, (περιπλέκω) *inter-connexion*, Luc.

συμ-περιποιέω, f. ήσω, *to help in procuring*, Polyb.

συμ-περιτρέχω, f. -δρᾰμοῦμαι, *to run round together*, Luc.

συμ-περιφέρω, f. -οίσω, *to carry round along with* or *together*, Plat.　II. Pass. *to be carried round together*, Id.　2. συμπεριφέρεσθαί τινι *to have inter-course with* one, Polyb.: *to adapt oneself to* circum-stances, c. dat., Aeschin.　3. *to be well acquainted with* things, Polyb.

συμ-περιφθείρομαι, Pass. *to go about with* any one *to one's own ruin*, Luc.

συμ-περονάω, f. ήσω, *to pin together*, Plut.

συμ-πέτομαι, Dep. *to fly with* or *together*, Luc.

συμ-πήγνῡμι and -ύω, f. -πήξω, *to put together, con-struct, frame*, Pind., Eur., etc.:—Med. *to construct for oneself*, Luc.　II. *to make solid, congeal, condense*, Il.

σύμ-πηκτος, ον, *put together, constructed, framed*, Hdt., Ar.

συμ-πιέζω, f. σω, to press or squeeze together, to grasp closely, Plat. :—Pass. to be squeezed up, Xen.

συμ-πίνω [ῑ], f. -πίομαι: aor. 2 συνέπιον:—to drink together, join in a drinking bout, Hdt., Ar., etc.

συμ-πίπτω, f. -πεσοῦμαι : pf. -πέπτωκα : aor. 2 συνέπεσον : — to fall together, meet in battle, come to blows, Lat. concurrere, Hom., Hdt.: σ. ἐς νείκεα Hdt. : to encounter, κλύδωνι Eur. ; νηί Thuc. 2. generally, to fall in with, meet with accidents, misfortunes, c. dat., Hdt., Soph. II. of ailments, events, to fall upon, happen to, c. dat. pers., Aesch., Isocr. ; also ἔς τινα Hdt. 2. absol. to happen or fall out at the same time, concur, Id. 3. c. part., like τυγχάνω, τόδε συνέπεσε γενόμενον Id. 4. impers., συνέπεσε, it happened, fell out, came to pass, c. inf., Id. ; ξυνέπεσεν εἰς τοῦτο ἀνάγκης . . matters came to such a pass that . . , Thuc. ; or c. acc. et inf., Id. III. to coincide, agree or be in accordance with, τινί Hdt. : absol. to agree exactly, Id. ; ἐμοὶ σὺ συμπέπτωκας ἐς ταὐτὸν λόγου have come to exactly the same point with me, Eur. IV. to fall together, i. e. fall in, collapse, of a house, Lat. concidere, Id., Thuc. ; σῶμα συμπεσόν a frame having collapsed from disease, Plat.

συμ-πίτνω, poët. for συμ-πίπτω, when the penult. is to be short, to fall or dash together, of waves, Aesch. II. to concur, Id. ; c. dat., Eur.

συμ-πλανάομαι, Pass. to wander about with, Polyb.

συμ-πλάσσω, Att. -ττω : aor. 1 συνέπλάσα :—to mould or fashion together, γαίης of clay, Hes. : — Pass., Ar. 2. of speakers and writers, ξυνομολογοῦντες καὶ ξ. by agreeing on an hypothesis and a fiction, Plat. 3. metaph. to feign or fabricate together, Dem.

συμ-πλατάγέω, f. ήσω, to sound by striking together, σ. χερσί to clap with the hands, Il.

συμ-πλείονες, neut. -ονα, several together, Lat. complures, Arist.

συμ-πλέκω, f. ξω, to twine or plait together, Plat. ; τινί with a thing, Theocr. ; συμπλέκοντες τὼ χεῖρε εἰς τοὐπίσω joining their hands behind them, Thuc. II. Pass. to be twined together, entwined, entangled, Eur.; ἴχνη συμπεπλεγμένα tracks entangled, crossing in different directions, Xen. 2. of persons wrestling, to be locked together with another, c. dat., Hdt.: generally, to be engaged in close fight, Dem. : of a ship, to be entangled with her opponent, Hdt. :—then, metaph. to be entangled in, τῇ Σκυθῶν ἐρημίᾳ συμπλακῆναι Ar. ; συμπεπλέγμεθα ξένῳ we are entangled or engaged with him, Eur. ; of war, to be entangled in, Dem. III. intr. in Act., = Pass., Eur.

σύμ-πλεος, Att. -πλεως, α, ον, quite full, Xen.

συμ-πλέω, f. -πλεύσομαι : Ion. -πλώω, -πλώσομαι : to sail in company with, τινί Hdt., etc. ; absol., Thuc.

συμπληγάς, άδος, ἡ, (συμπλήσσω) striking or dashing together, ξυμπληγάδες πέτραι the justling rocks, i. e. the Κυάνεαι νῆσοι, which were supposed to close in on all who sailed between them, Eur. ; also Ξυμπληγάδες (without πέτραι) Id. ; also in sing., Id.

συμ-πληγδην, (πλήσσω) Adv. with clapping of hands, Theocr.

συμ-πληθύνω [ῡ], to multiply or increase together, Xen.

συμ-πληθύω, to help to fill or increase, Hdt.

συμ-πληρόω, f. ώσω, to help to fill, σ. τοῖσι Ἀθηναίοισι τὰς νέας to help them in manning the ships, Hdt. II. to fill up, ξ. ἑξήκοντα ναῦς to man them fully, Thuc.

συμπλοϊκός, ή, όν, (σύμπλοος) sailing with or together, συμπλ. φιλία friendship of shipmates, Arist.

συμπλοκή, ἡ, (συμπλέκω) an intertwining, complication, Plat. 2. a close struggle or engagement, Id.

σύμπλοος, ον, contr. -πλους, ουν, (συμπλέω) sailing with one in a ship, a shipmate, Hdt. ; c. dat. pers., Eur. :—poët. of ships, Anth. 2. metaph. a partner or comrade in a thing, c. gen., Soph.

συμπλώω, Ion. for συμπλέω.

συμ-πνέω, f. -πνεύσομαι, to breathe together with, τινί Anth. : metaph., ἐμπαίοις τύχαισι σ. to go along with the sudden blasts of fortune, to yield or bow to them, Aesch. 2. absol. to agree together, conspire, Dem.

συμ-πνίγω [ῑ], f. -πνίξομαι, to throttle, choke, press closely, N. T.

σύμπνοος, ον, contr. -πνους, ουν, (συμπνέω) animated by one breath, in accord with, τινι Anth.

συμ-ποδίζω, f. σω, to tie the feet together, bind hand and foot, Ar. :—Pass. to be entangled in a net, Xen. II. metaph. to entangle, Lat. impedire, Plat.

συμ-ποιέω, f. ήσω, to help in doing a thing, Isae.

συμ-ποιμαίνομαι, Pass. to feed together, Eur.

συμ-πολεμέω, f. ήσω, to join in war, Thuc., Xen., etc. ; τινί with one, Xen.

συμπολίζω, to unite into one city:—Pass., Strab.

συμ-πολιορκέω, f. ήσω, to join in besieging, to besiege jointly, Hdt., Thuc., etc.

συμ-πολῑτεία, ἡ, a federal union of states, a confederacy, league, Polyb.

συμ-πολῑτεύω, f. σω, to live as fellow-citizens or members of one state, τισί with others, Thuc. :—Med., οἱ συμπολιτευόμενοι one's fellow-citizens, Isocr.

συμ-πολίτης [ῑ], ου, ὁ, a fellow-citizen, Eur.

σύμ-πολλοι, αι, α, many together, Plat.

συμ-πομπεύω, f. σω, to accompany in a procession, to escort, Aeschin.

συμ-πονέω, f. ήσω, to work with or together, to take part in labouring, τινί with one, Aesch., Soph., etc. : also, σ. κακοῖς to take part in evils, Eur. :—absol. to labour or suffer together, Soph., etc.

συμ-πονηρεύομαι, Dep. to join others in villainy, c. dat. pers., Isocr.

συμ-πορεύομαι, f. -εύσομαι : aor. 1 συνεπορεύθην : Dep.: —to go or journey together, Eur. ; τινι with one, Xen., etc. II. to come together, of the Senate, Polyb.

συμ-πορθέω, f. ήσω, to help to destroy, c. dat. pers., Eur. ; οἱ συμπεπορθημένοι involved in like ruin, Strab.

συμ-πορίζω, f. σω, to help in procuring, Thuc. :— Med. to do so for oneself, Id.

συμ-ποσία, ἡ, (πόσις) a drinking together, Pind.

συμποσιαρχέω, ήσω, to be a συμποσίαρχος, Arist.

συμποσί-αρχος, ὁ, the president of a drinking-party, toastmaster, Lat. magister bibendi, Xen., etc.

συμπόσιον, τό, (συμπίνω) a drinking-party, symposium, Theogn., Hdt., etc. II. the room in which such parties were given, drinking-room, Luc.

συμπότης, ου, ὁ, (συμπίνω) a fellow-drinker, booncompanion, Hdt., Eur. Hence

συμποτικός, ή, όν, of or for a συμπόσιον, convivial, jolly, Ar. ; σ. ἁρμονίαι airs suited for drinking songs, Plat.:—συμποτικός a jolly fellow, Ar.:—Comp. -ώτερος, Sup. -ώτατος, Luc.

συμ-πραγμᾰτεύομαι, f. -εύσομαι, Dep. to assist in transacting business, c. dat. pers., Plut.

συμπράκτωρ, Ion. -πρήκτωρ, ορος, ὁ, a helper, assistant, Hdt., Xen.: c. gen. rei, σ. ὁδοῦ a companion in travel, Soph.

συμ-πράσσω, Att. -ττω, Ion. -πρήσσω, f. ξω, to join or help in doing, τί τινι Aesch., Eur., etc. ; σ. τινὶ τἀγαθά to assist one in procuring what is good, Arist.: —c. acc. rei only, Soph. ; σ. εἰρήνην to help in negotiating peace, Xen.; c. dat. pers. only, to act with, cooperate with, τινί Thuc., etc. 2. absol. to lend aid, cooperate, Soph., Xen., etc. ; οἱ ξυμπράσσοντες the confederates, Thuc. II. intr., σὺν κακῶς πράσσοντι συμπράσσειν κακῶς to share in another's woe, Eur. III. Med. to assist in avenging, συνεπρήξαντο Μενέλεῳ τῆς Ἑλένης ἁρπαγάς Hdt.

συμ-πρεπής, ές, (πρέπω) befitting, Aesch.

συμ-πρέπω, to befit, beseem, Pind.

συμ-πρεσβευτής, οῦ, ὁ, a fellow-ambassador, Aeschin.

συμ-πρεσβεύω, f. σω, to be a fellow-ambassador, be joined or associated with on an embassy, Dem., Aeschin.: Med. to join in sending an embassy, Thuc.

σύμ-πρεσβυς, εως, ὁ, = συμπρεσβευτής, but only in pl., Thuc., Dem., etc.

συμ-πρεσβύτερος [ῠ], ὁ, a fellow-presbyter, N. T.

συμ-πρήκτωρ, -πρήσσω, Ion. for -πράκτωρ, -πράσσω.

συμ-πρίασθαι, aor. 2 inf. (no pres. in use, cf. *πρίαμαι), to buy together, buy up, Arist.

συμ-προάγω [ᾰ], f. ξω, to lead forward together: intr. to move forward with or together, Plut.

συμ-πρόεδρος, ὁ, a joint-president, Aeschin.

συμ-προθῡμέομαι, Dep. to have equal desire with, share in eagerness with, τινί Thuc.: absol., Xen. 2. c. acc. rei, to join zealously in promoting, Id. 3. c. dat. rei, to take zealous part in, Xen. 4. c. inf. to share in the desire that . . , Thuc., Xen., etc.

συμ-προξενέω, f. ήσω, to help in furnishing with means, Eur.

συμ-προπέμπω, f. ψω, to join in escorting, Hdt., Ar., etc. ; σ. τινὰ ναυσίν Thuc.

συμ-προσψαύω, f. σω, to clash against, τινί Aesop.

συμ-πτύσσω, f. ξω, to fold together, fold up and lay by, Soph.

σύμπτωμα, ατος, τό, (συμπίπτω) a chance, casualty, Arist.: in bad sense, a mishap, mischance, Thuc.

σύμπτωσις, ή, (συμπίπτω) a collapsing, Strab. II. a meeting, Polyb. : in hostile sense, an attack, Id.

σύμ-πυκνος, ον, pressed together, compressed, Xen.

συμ-πυνθάνομαι, aor. 2 συνεπυθόμην, Dep. to inquire about with another, τί τινι Xen.

συμ-πῠρόω, to burn up with or together, Eur.

συμφᾰγεῖν, aor. 2 inf. of συνεσθίω.

συμ-φᾰνής, ές, (φανῆναι) manifest at the same time, quite manifest, Arist.

συμφερόντως, Adv. part. pres. profitably, Isocr.

συμ-φερτός, ή, όν, united, banded together, Il.

συμ-φέρω, f. συνοίσω: aor. 1 συνήνεγκα, Ion. -ήνεικα: aor. 2 -ήνεγκον: pf. -ενήνοχα: Δ. Act., I.

to bring together, gather, collect, Hdt., Thuc., etc. 2. to contribute, Aesch., Eur. 3. to bring into conflict, Aesch. 4. to bear along with or together, Xen.:—of sufferings and labours, to bear jointly, help to bear, Soph., Eur.: to bear with, excuse, Aesch. II. intr. to confer a benefit, be useful or profitable, Hdt., Att. 2. impers. it is of use, is profitable, expedient, c. inf., Aesch., etc. 3. part. συμφέρων, ουσα, ον, useful, expedient, fitting, Soph., etc.:—in neut. as Subst., συμφέρον, οντος, τό, use, profit, advantage, expediency, Lat. utile, Id., Thuc., etc.:—also in pl., τὰ συμφέροντα Soph., etc.; also in aor. part., τὸ τῷ ξυνενεγκόν Thuc. III. intr., also, 1. to work with, agree with, assist, τινί Soph., Eur., etc.: —to bear with, give way, τινί Soph. 2. to fit, suit, τινί Ar., Xen. 3. of events, to happen, take place, turn out, c. inf., Hdt.
 B. Pass. συμφέρομαι, f. συνοίσομαι: aor. 1 -ηνέχθην, Ion. -είχθην: pf. -ενήνεγμαι:—to come together, to meet in battle, engage, Lat. congredi, Il., Thuc.: simply, to meet, Plat. II. to come to terms, be of one mind or to agree with, τινί Hdt.: —absol. to agree together, be of one mind, concur, come to terms, Id., Soph., etc. 2. c. dat. rei, to adapt oneself to, acquiesce in, Plat. ;—also, συμφέρεται ὠυτὸς εἶναι is found to be one and the same, Hdt. ; οὐ συμφέρεται περὶ τινος does not agree with their story, Id. III. of events, to happen, turn out, occur, come to pass, Id., Ar., etc. 2. impers. it happens, falls out, Hdt.

συμ-φεύγω, f. -φεύξομαι, to flee along with, τινί Hdt., Eur., etc.; σὺν φεύγουσι συμφεύγειν Eur. 2. to be banished along with or together, ξυνέφυγε τὴν φυγὴν ταύτην shared in this banishment, Plat.

σύμ-φημι, f. -φήσω: aor. 1 συνέφησα: aor. 2 συνέφην: —to assent, approve, or agree fully, Aesch., etc. 2. c. acc. rei, to concede, agree to, grant, Plat., Xen.; absol., ξύμφημί σοι I grant you, Plat. ; ξύμφαθι ἢ ἄπειπε say yes or no, Id. 3. c. acc. et inf. to agree that . . , Soph., Plat. 4. c. inf. fut. to promise, Xen.

συμ-φθέγγομαι, Dep. to sound with, accord with, τινι Plut.

συμ-φθείρω, to destroy together or altogether, Eur., Luc.

συμφθίνω [ῑ], to decay along with, poët. aor. 2 pass. συνέφθῑτο, Anth.

σύμ-φθογγος, ον, sounding together, in concert, Aesch.

συμ-φῐλέω, f. ήσω, to love mutually, Soph.

συμ-φῐλοκᾰλέω, f. ήσω, to be candidate for an honour along with another, Plut.

συμ-φῐλονεικέω, f. ήσω, to take part in a dispute with, side with, τινί Plat., etc. 2. absol. to join in a disputation, Plut.

συμ-φῐλοσοφέω, to join in philosophic study, Arist.

συμ-φῐλοτῑμέομαι, f. ήσομαι, Dep. to join in zealous efforts, Plut.

συμ-φλέγω, f. ξω, to burn to cinders, Eur., Theocr.

συμ-φοβέω, f. ήσω, to frighten at the same time : —Pass. to be afraid at the same time, Thuc.

συμ-φοιτάω, Ion. -έω, f. ήσω, to go regularly to a place together, Hdt.: esp. to go to school together, Ar., Dem., etc. ; τινι with one, Luc. Hence

συμφοίτησις, ή, a going to school together, Aeschin.; and

συμφοιτητής, οὗ, ὁ, a schoolfellow, Plat., Xen.
συμ-φονεύω, f. σω, to join another in killing, c. dat., Eur.
συμφορά, Ion. -ή, ἡ, (συμφέρω III), an event, circumstance, chance, hap, Hdt., Att.; αἱ ξ. τῶν βουλευμάτων the results, issues of the counsels, Soph.; ξυμφορᾶς ἵν' ἕσταμεν in what a hazardous state we are, Id. 2. esp. a mishap, mischance, misfortune, Hdt., Att.; συμφορῇ χρῆσθαι to be unfortunate, Hdt. 3. in good sense, good luck, a happy issue, Trag.
συμφορεύς, ὁ, (συμφέρω) a Lacedaemonian officer, a sort of aide-de-camp, Xen.
συμ-φορέω, f. ήσω, to bring together, to gather, collect, heap up, Hdt., Thuc., etc.:—Pass. to be collected, Plat. Hence
συμφόρησις, ἡ, a bringing together, Plut.; and
συμφορητός, ή, όν, brought together, collected, σ. δεῖπνον, σ. ἑστίασις a meal to which each guest contributes, Lat. coena collatitia, Arist.
σύμφορος, ον, (συμφέρω III) happening with, accompanying, λιμὸς ἀεργῷ σύμφορος ἀνδρί hunger is the sluggard's companion, Hes.; c. gen., πενίης σύμφορα Id. II. useful, profitable, expedient, suitable, good, c. dat., Id., Thuc.: —σύμφορόν ἐστι = συμφέρει, c. inf., Hdt.; Πλούτῳ συμφορώτατον Ar.:—τὰ σύμφορα what is expedient, Soph., Thuc., etc.; τὸ ὑμέτερον ξ. your plea of expediency, Thuc.:—Adv. συμφόρως ἔχειν to be expedient, Xen.; Comp. συμφορώτερον, Thuc.; Sup. -ώτατα, Eur., etc. 2. rarely of persons, ξυμφορώτατοι προσπολεμῆσαι most convenient to make war upon, Thuc.
συμφράδμων, ονος, ὁ, ἡ, one who joins in considering, a counsellor, Il. II. in accord with, c. gen., Anth.
συμ-φράζομαι, f. -άσομαι, Ep. -άσσομαι: pf. -πέφρασμαι: Med.:—to join in considering, to take counsel with, c. dat., Od. 2. τίς τοι συμφράσσατο βουλάς; who imparted his counsels to thee? Ib. 3. to contrive, Hes., Soph. II. Act. συμφράζω, to mention at the same time, Strab.
συμ-φράσσω, Att. -ττω, f. ξω, to press or pack closely together, Hdt., Xen. 2. absol. of troops, to close their ranks, form in close order, Xen. II. to block up, close, Id.
συμφρονέω, f. ήσω, (σύμφρων) to be of one mind with, to agree, Polyb. II. to consider well, ἃ δέον ἦν ποιεῖν Plut. 2. to collect oneself, Id.
συμφρόνησις, Dor. -ᾱσις, ἡ, agreement, union.
συμ-φροντίζω, f. σω, to have a joint care for, τινός Luc.
σύμ-φρουρος, ον, (φρουρά) watching with, μέλαθρον σύμφρουρον ἐμοί the chamber that keeps watch with me, i. e. in which I lie sleepless, Soph.
σύμ-φρων, ονος, ὁ, ἡ, (φρήν) of one mind, brotherly, Aesch.:—favouring, propitious, Id.
συμ-φυγάς, άδος, ὁ, ἡ, a fellow-exile, Eur., Thuc.
συμ-φυής, ές, (φύομαι) born with one, congenital, natural, Plat., etc. 2. adapted by nature, Plut. II. attached, adhering, τινί to a thing, Anth.
συμ-φύλαξ [ῠ], ᾰκος, ὁ, a fellow-watchman or guard, Thuc., Plat., Xen., etc.
συμ-φυλάσσω: f. ξω, to keep guard along with others, Hdt.: to guard with others, τι Xen.
συμ-φυλέτης, ου, ὁ, of the same φυλή, Lat. contribūlis: generally, a fellow-countryman, N. T.

σύμ-φῡλος, ον, (φῦλον) of the same stock or race, οἱ σύμφυλοι his congeners, Babr.
σύμ-φυρτος, ον, commingled, confounded, Eur. From
συμ-φύρω [ῠ]: pf. pass. -πέφυρμαι:—to knead together: beat black and blue, Theocr. :—Pass., Eur.; ψυχὴ συμπέφυρται μετὰ τοῦ κακοῦ Plat.
συμ-φῡσάω, f. ήσω, to blow together:—hence, like Lat. conflare, to beat up, contrive, Ar. II. Pass., of the wind, to blow at the same time, Plut.
συμ-φῡτεύω, f. σω, to plant along with or together: metaph. to have a hand in contriving, Soph. :—Pass. to be implanted also, Xen.
σύμφῡτος, ον, (συμφύομαι) born with one, congenital, innate, natural, inborn, inbred, Pind., Plat.; σ. αἰών our natural age, i. e. old age, Aesch.; νεικέων σ. τέκτων the natural author of strife, i. e. cause of strife natural to the race, Id.; ἐς τὸ σ. according to one's nature, Eur. 2. c. dat. natural to, Lys.
συμ-φύω, f. -φύσω, to make to grow together, Plat. II. Pass., with pf. act. συμπέφυκα, aor. 2 συνέφῡν: — to grow together, Id., Xen. 2. to grow to or into, σ. ἀλλήλοις Plat. 3. to grow up with one, to become natural, Arist.
συμ-φωνέω, f. ήσω, to agree in sound, be in harmony, Plat. II. metaph. to agree with, hold the same opinions with, τινί Id. 2. to make an agreement or bargain with any one, πρός τινα Xen.; σ. τινὶ δηναρίου to agree with one for a denarius, N. T.: Pass., συνεφωνήθη ὑμῖν it was agreed between you, Ib. 3. to conspire, Arist. Hence
συμφωνία, ἡ, concord or unison of sound, Plat. II. metaph. harmony, agreement, Id.
σύμ-φωνος, ον, (φωνή) agreeing in sound, in unison, h. Hom., Ar.: generally, echoing to cries, Soph. 2. metaph. harmonious, friendly, Pind., Soph.; σ. τινι in harmony or agreement with, Plat.
συμ-ψαύω, f. σω, to touch one another, Xen.
συμ-ψάω, f. ήσω, to sweep away, of a rapid river, Hdt.
συμ-ψηφίζω, f. σω, to reckon together, count up, N. T.
σύμ-ψηφος, ον, voting with, τινι Plat., etc.; σ. τινί τινος voting with one for a thing, Id.:—absol. voting together, of the same opinion, Dem.
συμ-ψοφέω, f. ήσω, to make a noise together, Polyb.
σύμ-ψῡχος, ον, (ψυχή) of one mind, at unity, N. T.
ΣΥΝ [ῠ], old Att. ξύν, Prep. with dat., Lat. cum: I. along with, in company with, together with, δεῦρ' ἦλθε σὺν Μενελάῳ Il. 2. with collat. notion of help, σὺν θεῷ with God's help or blessing, (the God being conceived as standing with one), Hom., etc.; σὺν θεῷ εἰρημένον spoken as by inspiration, Hdt.: so, σὺν δαίμονι, σὺν Διί, σὺν Ἀθήνῃ Il.; so also, σύν τινι εἶναι or γίγνεσθαι to be with another, i. e. on his side, of his party, Xen.; οἱ σύν τινι any one's friends, followers, Id. 3. endued with, ἄκοιτις σὺν μεγάλῃ ἀρετῇ Od.: of things that belong or are attached to a person, στῆ σὺν δουρί Il.; σκῆπτρον, σὺν τῷ ἔβη Ib.; αὐτῇ σὺν φόρμιγγι Ib. (here, in Att., the σύν is often omitted). 4. of two or more things taken together, θύελλαι σὺν βορέῃ, ἄνεμος σὺν λαίλαπι Il.; also of coincidence in point of time, ἄκρᾳ σὺν ἑσπέρᾳ Pind. 5. of connexion or consequence, σὺν μεγάλῳ ἀποτῖσαι to pay with a great loss, i. e. suffer greatly, Il.; σὺν τῷ

σῷ ἀγαθῷ to your advantage, Lat. *tuo cum commodo*, Xen. ; σὺν μιάσματι *attended with* pollution, Soph. :— and, generally, *in accordance with ; σὺν δίκᾳ* Pind., σὺν κόσμῳ, σὺν τάχει, etc., nearly = Advs. δικαίως, κοσμίως, ταχέως, Att.   6. *with, by means of,* σὺν νεφέεσσι κάλυψεν γαῖαν Od., Pind. ; πλοῦτον ἐκτήσω σὺν αἰχμῇ Aesch.   7. *with* Ordin. Numerals, ἐμοὶ σὺν ἑβδόμῳ, i. e. *myself with* six others, Id.   **B.** σύν AS ADV. *together,* Aesch., Soph.   2. *besides, also, likewise,* Od., Trag.

C. IN COMPOS.   1. *with, along with, together,* Lat. *con-* :—in Compos. with a trans. Verb, as κτείνω, σύν may refer to two things, *to kill one person as well as another,* or, *to join with another in killing.*   2. *of the completion of an action, altogether, completely,* as in συμπληρόω, συντέμνω.   3. *joined with numerals,* σύνδυο *two together* or *by twos, two and two ;* so σύντρεις, σύμπεντε, etc., like Lat. *bini, terni,* etc.   **II.** συν- *before* β μ π φ ψ, *becomes* συμ- ; *before* γ κ ξ χ, συγ- ; *before* λ, συλ- ; *before* σ, συσ-, *but before* στ, συ-, *as* συστῆναι.

συνᾰγᾰγεῖν, aor. 2 inf. of συνάγω.

συν-ᾰγᾰνακτέω, *to be vexed along with,* τινί Polyb.

συν-ᾰγᾰπάω, f. ήσω, *to love along with,* τινί Polyb.

συν-άγγελος, ὁ, *a fellow messenger* or *ambassador,* Hdt.

συν-αγγία, ἡ, (ἄγγος) *a confined space,* Babr.

συν-ᾰγείρω, f. -αγερῶ : aor. 1 συνήγειρα, Ep. ξυνάγειρα :—Pass., 3 pl. aor. 1 συνήγερθεν (for ησαν) :—*to gather together, assemble,* Il., Hdt. :—esp. *to collect an army,* Hdt. :—Pass. *to gather together, come together, assemble,* Il. ; συναγρόμενοι, Ep. syncop. aor. 2 pass. part., *those assembled, an assembly,* Ib.   2. *to collect* the means of living, Od. ; and in Med. *to collect for oneself,* Ib.   3. metaph., σ. ἑαυτόν *to collect* oneself, Plat. :—so in Pass., Id.

συνάγκεια, ἡ, = μισγάγκεια, Anth.

συν-άγνῡμι, aor. 1 συνέαξα, *to break together, break to pieces, shiver, shatter,* Hom.

συν-ᾰγορεύω, (the fut. in use is συνερῶ, aor. 2 συνεῖπον, pf. συνείρηκα) :—*to join in advocating, advocate the same thing with,* τί τινι Thuc., Xen.   2. *to join in advising* another, τινί Lys.   3. σ. τινί *to speak with* or *in behalf of* a person, *support* him, *advocate* his *cause,* Thuc. : so, c. dat. rei, σ. τινὸς σωτηρίᾳ Dem.

συν-αγρεύω, *to join in the chase,* Anth.

συναγρόμενος, Ep. aor. 2 part. pass. of συναγείρω.

συν-άγω : impf. -ῆγον, Dor. -ᾱγον, Ep. -άγον : f. συνάξω : aor. 2 συνήγαγον : pf. συνῆχα and συναγήοχα, Pass. συνῆγμαι :—*to bring together, gather together, collect, convene,* Hom., Hdt., Att.   2. *in hostile sense, to join battle, begin* the battle-strife, Il. :—also like συμβάλλω, *to match* two warriors *one against the other,* Aesch. :—hence intr., σ. εἰς μέσσον *to engage* in fight, Theocr.   3. *to bring together, join in one, unite,* h. Merc., Aesch. ; σ. γάμους *to contract* a marriage, Xen.   4. *to receive into one's house,* N. T.   **II.** *to gather together* stores, crops, etc., Xen., etc.   **III.** *to draw together,* so as to make the extremities meet, Hdt., Thuc. : also *to draw together, narrow, contract,* Hdt.   2. *to contract* the brows, Ar. ; σ. τὰ ὦτα *to prick* the ears, of dogs, Xen.   **IV.** *to*

collect from premises, i. e. *to conclude, infer,* Lat. *colligere,* Arist. Hence

συνᾰγωγεύς, ὁ, *one who brings together, a convener,* Lys.   **II.** *one who unites,* Plat. ; and

συνᾰγωγή, ἡ, *a bringing together, uniting,* Plat.   2. *a place of assembly, synagogue,* N. T.   **II.** σ. πολέμου *a levying* of war, Thuc.   2. *a gathering in* of harvest, Polyb.   3. *a drawing together, contracting,* σ. στρατιᾶς *a forming* an army *in column,* Plat. ; σ. τοῦ προσώπου *a pursing up* or *wrinkling* of the face, Isocr.   4. *a collection* of writings, Lat.   **III.** *a conclusion, inference,* Id.

συν-ᾰγωγός, όν, *bringing together, uniting,* Plat.

συν-ᾰγωνιάω, *to share in the anxiety,* Polyb.

συν-ᾰγωνίζομαι, f. Att. ιοῦμαι, Dep. *to contend along with, to share in a contest,* τινί *with* one, Thuc., etc. :—generally, ξ. τινι *to share in the fortunes of* another, Id.   2. *to help, succour,* τινί Dem.   3. absol. *to fight on the same side,* Thuc.

συν-ᾰγωνιστής, οῦ, ὁ, *one who shares with* another *in a contest, a fellow-combatant, coadjutor,* Plat., etc. ; τινός *for* a thing, Aeschin., Dem.

συν-άδελφος, ον, *one that has a brother* or *sister,* Xen.

συν-ᾰδῐκέω, f. ήσω, *to join in wrong* or *injury,* τινί *with* another, Thuc., Xen. ; absol., Thuc., Xen. :— Pass. *to be wronged alike,* Dem.

συν-ᾴδω, f. -ᾴσομαι, *to sing with* or *together,* Aeschin. ; σ. ᾠδάν Eur.   2. generally, *to be in accord with,* τινί Soph., Plat.   **II.** trans. *to celebrate together,* τινά Theocr.

συν-ᾰείδω, poët. for συνᾴδω, Theocr.

συν-ᾰείρω : aor. 1 -ήειρα : = συναίρω, *to raise up together,* Il.   **II.** *to bind* or *yoke together,* Ib. : —Med., συναείρεται ἵππους Ib.

συν-ᾱθλέω, f. ήσω, *to strive together,* τινί *for* a thing, N. T.   2. *to strive* or *labour with* others, τισί Ib.

συν-ᾰθροίζω, f. σω, *to gather together, assemble,* of soldiers, Xen., Plat., etc.   2. of things, in Pass., τὸ κεφάλαιον τούτων συνηθροισμένον the sum of these *collected amounts,* Plat.   3. of a single person, οὐ ξυνήθροισται στρατῷ *has not joined* the main army, Eur.

συναθροισμός, ὁ, *a collection, union,* Babr.

συν-ᾰθύρω [ῡ], *to play with,* τινί Mosch.

συν-ᾰΐγδην, (ἀΐσσω) Adv. *pressing violently together,* Hes.

σύν-αιμος, ον, (αἷμα) *of common blood, kindred,* Soph., Eur.   2. as Subst. *a kinsman, kinswoman,* esp. *a brother, sister,* Soph.   3. Ζεὺς ξ. *as presiding over kindred,* Id. ; νεῖκος ξ. *strife between kinsmen,* Id.

συν-αινέω, f. έσω, *to join in praising,* Aesch.   **II.** *to consent,* absol., Id., Soph., etc. ; σ. τινί *to agree with* a person, Hdt.   2. c. acc. rei, *to agree to, promise,* Soph., Xen., etc. : *to grant at once,* Xen.   3. c. inf. *to agree* or *consent* to do, Id.

συν-αίνῠμαι, Dep. *to take up,* Il.

συν-αιρέω, f. ήσω, f. 2 συνελῶ : aor. 2 συνεῖλον, Ep. σύνελον :—*to grasp* or *seize together, to seize at once,* Od., Thuc.   2. *to bring together, bring into small compass ;* in speaking, ξυνελὼν λέγω *briefly, in a word,* Thuc. ; ὡς συνελόντι εἰπεῖν Xen. ; so, συνελόντι alone, Dem.   **II.** *to make away with, crush,* ὀφρῦς σύνελεν λίθος Il. :—metaph. *to make an end of,* τὸν

πόλεμον Plut. :—Pass., Thuc. 2. *to help to take* or *conquer*, Hdt., Thuc.

συν-αίρω, poët. **συναείρω** (q. v.) : aor. 1 συνῆρα :—*to take up together*, Arist., Plut. ; σ. λόγον μετά τινος *to balance accounts with another*, N. T. **II.** Med. *to take part in* a thing, c. gen., Thuc. 2. c. acc. rei, *to help in bearing*, Id., Dem. ; also *to engage in* a thing, *undertake* it, Aesch., Eur. 3. τῶν σκελῶν σ. *to catch by both legs*, Plut. **III.** Pass., συναίρεσθαι εἰς τὸ αὐτό *to be joined together*, *unite*, Xen. 2. *to contribute, assist*, Dem.

συν-αισθάνομαι, aor. 2 -ησθόμην, Dep. *to perceive also* or *at the same time*, Dem.

συν-αιτιάομαι, f. άσομαι [ᾱ], Dep. *to accuse along with*, Plut.

συν-αίτιος, ον, and α, ον : 1. c. gen. rei et dat. pers. *being the cause of* a thing *jointly with* another, σ. τινι ἀθανασίας *helping* him *towards* immortality, Isocr. ; σ. τινος γενέσθαι τινί *to share in the guilt of* a thing *with* another, Id. 2. c. gen. rei only, *being joint-cause of, accessory to, contributing to*, Dem., etc. :—as Subst., ἡ ξυναιτία φόνου *accomplice in murder*, Aesch. :—absol., οὐκ αἴτιων, ἀλλ' ἴσως ξυναιτίων Plut.

συν-αιχμάζω, f. σω, *to fight with* or *together*, Anth.

συν-αιχμάλωτος, ον, *a fellow-prisoner*, N. T.

συν-αιωρέομαι, Pass. *to be held suspended together with*, c. dat., Plut.

συν-ακμάζω, f. σω, *to bloom at the same time*, Anth.

συν-ακολασταίνω, *to live dissolutely with* another, Plut.

συν-ακολουθέω, f. ήσω, *to follow closely, to accompany*, τινί Ar., Thuc. 2. σ. λόγῳ *to follow* an argument *completely*, Plat.

συν-ακοντίζω, f. σω, *to throw a javelin along with* or *at once*, Antipho. **II.** *to shoot down*, τινά Polyb.

συν-ακούω, f. ούσομαι, *to hear along with* or *at the same time*, Xen. ; σ. ἀλλήλων *to hear each other*, Id.

συν-ακροάομαι, f. άσομαι [ᾱ], Dep. *to be a fellow-hearer*, Plat.

συνακτέον, verb. Adj. of συνάγω, *one must bring together*, Plat. **II.** *one must conclude*, Arist.

συνακτικός, ή, όν, *able to bring together*, τὸ σ. *power of accumulation* in oratory, Luc.

συν-ἀλἄλάζω, *to cry aloud together*, Polyb. **II.** c. acc. *to greet aloud*, Eur.

συν-αλγέω, f. ήσω, *to share in suffering, sympathise*, Soph. :—absol., οἱ ξυναλγοῦντες *those who are partners in sorrow*, Id. 2. c. dat. rei, *to sympathise, shew sympathy* at or *in*, Aesch., Eur. Hence

συναλγηδών, όνος, ἡ, *joint grief* :—in pl., = αἱ συναλγοῦσαι, *partners in pain*, Eur.

συν-ἀλείφω, f. ψω, *to smear* or *gloss over*, Arist.

συν-αλίζω, aor. 2 συνήλισα, *to bring together, collect*, Hdt. :—Pass. *to come together, assemble*, Id., Xen., etc. ; of a single person, *to associate with* others, N. T.

συναλλαγή, ἡ, *an interchange* of words for purposes of *conciliation*, Soph., Eur. : absol. *a reconciliation, making of peace*, Thuc. : pl. *a treaty of peace*, Xen. 2. generally, *commerce, intercourse*, Eur. **II.** *intervention*, δαιμονίων ξυναλλαγαῖς *by special interventions* of the deities, Soph. ; νόσου ξυναλλαγῇ *by intervention* of disease, Id. : generally, *the issue of*

intervention, a contingency, incident, Id. ; ὀλεθρίαισι συναλλ. *with destructive issues*, Id.

συνάλλαγμα, ατος, τό, *a mutual agreement, covenant, contract*, Dem., etc. : in pl. *dealings between men*, Arist. ; and

συνάλλαξις, ἡ, *exchange*, Plat. From

συν-αλλάσσω, Att. -ττω, f. ξω, *to bring into intercourse with, associate with*, τινά τινι Aesch. :—Pass. *to have intercourse with*, τινί Soph., Eur. 2. *to reconcile*, τινά τινι Thuc. :—Pass. and Med. *to be reconciled, to make a league* or *alliance with*, πρός τινα Id., Xen. ; absol. *to make peace*, Thuc., Xen. **II.** intr. *to have dealings with* another, Soph., Eur. 2. *to enter into engagements* or *contracts*, Dem., Arist.

συν-άλλομαι, Dep. *to leap together*, Luc.

συν-αλοάω, aor. 1 -ηλόησα, *to thresh out together, to grind to powder, crush, shiver*, Theocr.

συν-ἀλύω, *to wander about with* another, c. dat., Plut.

συν-άμἄ, Adv. for σὺν ἅμα, *together*, Anth., Luc. ; τινί *with* one, Theocr.

συν-ἁμιλλάομαι, f. ήσομαι, Dep. *to contend* or *struggle together*, Eur.

συν-αμπέχω and -αμπίσχω, *to cover up closely, to wrap up*, Aesch. :—Med., τί συναμπίσχει κόρας ; *why dost veil thine* eyes ? Eur.

συν-αμφότεροι, αι, α, *both together*, Theogn., Hdt., Att. :—sing. in collective sense, τὸ ξ. = συναμφότεροι, Plat. ; τοῦτο συναμφότερον *this united power*, Dem.

συν-άμφω, οἱ, αἱ, *both together*, Plat., etc.

συν-αναβαίνω, *to go up with* or *together* into central Asia, Hdt., Xen. ; τινί *with* one, Xen.

συν-αναβοάω, f. βοήσομαι, *to cry out together*, Xen.

συν-αναγκάζω, f. σω, *to join* or *assist in compelling*, Isocr., Dem. :—Pass. *to be compelled at the same time*, Dem. **II.** *to execute by force also*, Isocr. :— Pass., ὅρκοι συνηναγκασμένοι *extorted* oaths, Eur.

συν-αναγράφω, f. ψω, *to register* or *record together* :— Pass., συναναγραφῆναι ἐν τοῖς συμμάχοις Aeschin.

συν-ανάγω, f. ξω, *to carry back together* :—Pass. *to retire together*, Polyb. **II.** Pass. also, *to go to sea together*, Dem.

συν-αναδίδωμι, f. -δώσω, *to give back along with*, Luc.

συν-αναζεύγνῡμι, f. -ζεύξω, *to set out along with*, Plut.

συν-αναιρέω, f. -ήσω : aor. 2 -ανεῖλον :—*to destroy together with*, τινά τινι Polyb. 2. *to destroy altogether* or *utterly*, Isocr. :—Pass., Thuc. **II.** *to give the same answer*, Plat.

συν-ανάκειμαι, Pass. *to recline together at table*, N. T.

συν-ανακεράννῡμαι, aor. 1 -εκράθην [ᾱ], Pass. *to be mixed up with*, τινί Luc.

συν-ἀνἁλίσκω, f. -αναλώσω, *to expend together* or in *company*, Dem. **II.** *to help by spending money*, Xen.

συν-αναμίγνῡμι, -μίξω, *to mix up together* : Pass. *to be associated with* others, c. dat., Luc.

συν-αναπαύομαι, Pass. *to take rest with* others, N. T.

συν-αναπείθω, f. σω, *to assist in persuading*, τινά ποιεῖν τι Thuc., etc.

συν-αναπέμπω, f. ψω, *to send up together*, Plut.

συν-αναπλέκω, *to entwine together with*, τί τινι Luc.

συν-αναπράσσω, Att. -ττω, f. ξω, *to join in exacting* payment, Xen.

συν-αναρριπτέω, *to throw up together*, Luc.

συν-ανασκάπτω, f. ψω, *to dig up besides*, Strab.

συν-ανασπάω, f. -σπάσω, *to draw up together*, Luc.

συν-ανάσσω, f. ξω, *to rule with*, Anth.

συν-αναστρέφω, f. ψω, *to turn back together*, intr., Plut.   **II.** Pass. and Med. *to live along with* or *among* others, c. dat., Id.

συν-ανατήκω, f. ξω, *to melt with* or *together*, Plut.

συν-ανατίθημι, f. -θήσω, *to dedicate along with*, Luc.

συν-ανατολή, ή, *a rising together*, Strab.

συν-ανατρέχω, f. -δραμοῦμαι, *to run up with*, Plut.

συν-αναφθέγγομαι, f. ξομαι, Dep. *to cry out* or *speak together*, Plut.

συν-αναφύρω [ῡ], *to knead up together* :—Pass., aor. 2 -εφύρην [ῠ], *to wallow together*, Luc.

συν-αναχρέμπτομαι, Dep. *to cough up together*, Luc.

συν-ανίστημι, f. -στήσω, *to make to stand up* or *rise together*, Xen. : *to assist in restoring*, Id.   **II.** Pass. with aor. 2 act., *to rise at the same time*, Id. ; τινι *with one*, Id.

συν-αντάω, Ep. 3 dual impf. -αντήτην : f. -ήσω : aor. 1 -ήντησα : pf. -ήντηκα :—*to meet face to face*, of two persons, Od. ; of many persons, *to meet together, assemble*, Philipp. ap. Dem.   **II.** like ἀντάω, *to meet with, meet*, τινί Eur., Ar. ; so in Med., Il. :—c. acc. cogn., συναντᾶν συνάντησιν Eur.   **2.** c. dat. rei, *to come in contact with*, φόνῳ Id.   **III.** *to befal*, of accidents, etc., τινί Plut., N. T. Hence

συνάντησις, ή, *a meeting*, Eur.

συν-αντιάζω, =συναντάω, τινί, Soph.

συν-αντλέω, f. ήσω, *to drain along with*, σ. πόνους τινί *to join* him *in bearing* all his sufferings, Lat. *una exhaurire labores*, Eur.

συν-άντομαι, Dep. only in pres. and impf. *to fall in with, meet*, absol. or c. dat., Hom., etc. ; in hostile sense, *to meet* in battle, Il. : metaph., φόρμιγγι σ. *to approach* (i. e. *use*) the lyre, Pind.

συν-άνύτω [ῠ], *to come to an end with*, c. dat., Aesch.

συνανύω, f. σω, *to arrive together*, Plut.

συν-αξιόω, f. ώσω, *to join in requiring*, Xen.

συναοιδός, ὁ, =συνῳδός, Eur.

συνάορος, ον, Dor. and Att. for συνήορος.

συν-απάγω, f. ξω, *to lead away with* another, c. dat., Xen. ; absol., Id.   **II.** Pass. *to be led away likewise*, N. T.   **2.** *to accommodate oneself to* a thing, c. dat., Id.

συν-απαίρω, intr. *to sail* or *march away together*, Luc.

συν-απαρτίζω, f. σω, *to correspond exactly with, lie over against*, τινί Strab.

συν-άπας, ἄσα, ἄν, like σύμπας, strengthd. for πᾶς, πᾶσα, πᾶν, *all together*, mostly in pl., Hdt., etc. :—in sing., with collective Nouns, τὸ συνάπαν στράτευμα Id.

συν-απειλέω, f. ήσω, *to threaten at the same time*, Luc.

συν-απεργάζομαι, Dep. *to help in completing*, Plat.

συναπεχθάνομαι, Dep. *to become an enemy together*, Plut.

συναπίσταμαι, Ion. for συναφίσταμαι.

συν-αποβαίνω, f. -βήσομαι, *to disembark together with*, τινί Hdt.

συν-απογράφομαι, Med. *to enter one's name together with* others, as a candidate, Plat.

συν-αποδημέω, f. ήσω, *to be abroad together*, Arist.

συν-απόδημοι, οἱ, *those who live abroad together*, Arist.

συν-αποδιδράσκω, *to run away along with*, ξυναποδρᾶναί τινι (aor. 2 inf.), Ar.

συν-αποδοκιμάζω, f. σω, *to join in reprobating*, τι Xen.

συναποθανεῖν, aor. 2 inf. of συναποθνήσκω.

συν-αποθνήσκω, f. -θανοῦμαι, *to die together with* another, c. dat., Hdt. : absol. *to die with* one, Plat.

συν-αποικίζω, f. Att. ιῶ, *to go as* colonists *together*, Luc.

συν-αποκάμνω, f. -κᾰμοῦμαι, *to cease from weariness together*, Eur.

συν-αποκτείνω, f. -κτενῶ, *to kill together*, Aeschin.

συν-απολαμβάνω, f. -λήψομαι, *to receive in common* or *at once*, Xen.

συν-απολάμπω, f. ψω, *to shine forth together*, Luc.

συν-απόλλῡμι, f. -ολέσω, *to destroy together*, σ. τοὺς φίλους *to destroy one's* friends *as well as* oneself, Thuc.; σ. τὰ χρήματα *to lose* the money *also*, Dem. :—Pass. *to perish together*, Thuc. ; τινι *with one*, Hdt.

συν-απολογέομαι, Dep. *to join in defending*, Dem.

συν-απομᾰραίνομαι, Pass. *to fade away and die together*, Xen.

συν-απονεύω, f. σω, *to bend away together*, τοῖς σώμασιν αὐτοῖς ἴσα τῇ δόξῃ ξυναπονεύοντες *swerving* with their bodies *in sympathy with* their thought, Thuc.

συν-αποπέμπω, f. ψω, *to send off together*, Xen.

συν-αποῤῥήγνῡμι, f. -ρήξω, *to break together*, Plut.

συν-αποσβέννῡμι, f. -σβέσω, *to put out with* or *together*, τί τινι Anth. :—Pass., with aor. 2 act. -έσβην, pf. -έσβηκα, *to be put out together*, Plut.

συν-αποστέλλω, f. -στελῶ, *to despatch together with* another, c. dat., Thuc., Xen.

συν-αποστερέω, f. ήσω, *to help to strip* or *cheat*, τινά τινος one of a thing, Dem.

συν-αποφαίνομαι, f. -φανοῦμαι, Med. *to assert likewise* or *together, to agree in asserting*, Isocr., etc.

συν-άπτω, f. -άψω, *to tie* or *bind together, to join together, unite*, σ. χέρα, in sign of friendship, Eur.; ἰδού, ξυνάψω (sc. τὴν χέρα) Id. ; but, σ. χεῖρά τινος ἐν βρόχοις *to bind it fast*, Id. :—σ. πόδα or ἴχνος τινί *to meet* him, Id. ; σ. κῶλον τάφῳ *to approach* the grave, Id. ; so, φόνος σ. τινὰ ξίφ Id. :—ξ. βλέφαρα *to close* the eyes, Id. ; σ. στόμα *to kiss* one, Id. :—σ. κακὰ κακοῖς *to link* misery with misery, Id. ; but, σ. κακόν τινι *to link* him *with misery*, Id. : σ. τινὶ δαῖτα *to give* one a meal, Id. : proverb., σ. λίνον λίνῳ *to join* thread to thread, i. e. to compare things of the same sort, Plat.   **2.** *to connect in thought, to combine*, Id. : σ. μηχανήν *to frame* a plan, Aesch.; σ. ὕναρ εἴς τινα *to connect* it with him, *refer* it to him, Eur. ; ξυνῆψε πάντας ἐς μίαν βλάβην *involved* them in one loss, Id.   **II.** in hostile sense, σ. εἰς μάχην *to bring* into action, Hdt. ; ἐλπὶς πόλεις ξυνῆψε *engaged* them *in conflict*, Eur.   **2.** σ. μάχην *to join* battle, Hdt. ; τινί *with* one, Aesch. ; πρός τινα Thuc. : also (without μάχην) *to engage*, Hdt., Ar. :—Pass., νεῖκος συνῆπταί τινι πρός τινα Hdt.   **III.** in friendly sense, *to unite*, Xen. :—Pass., συνάπτεσθαί τινι *to have intercourse with*, Anth.   **2.** c. acc. rei, σ. μῦθον, ὅρκους Eur.; σ. τινὶ γάμους, λέκτρα, κῆδος *to form an alliance by* marriage, Id. : ξυνάπτεσθαι κῆδος τῆς θυγατρός *to get one's* daughter married, Thuc.

    B. intr. :   **I.** in local sense, *to border on, lie next to*, Hdt. ; Τήνῳ συνάπτει Ἄνδρος Aesch.   **2.**

of Time, *to be nigh at hand*, Pind. ; so of events, λύπη σ. τινί Eur. 3. metaph. of thoughts, *to meet together*, Arist. : — *to be connected with*, πρός τι Id. II. of persons, σ. λόγοισι *to enter into con-versation*, Soph. ; so, ἐς λόγους ξ. τινί Eur. ; also, σ. εἰς χορεύματα *to join* in the dance, Id. ; σ. ἐς χεῖρα γῆ, i. e. *to come close* to land, Id. 2. τύχα ποδὸς ξυνάπτει μοι, i. e. I have come in good time, Id. C. Med. *to be next to, connected with*, τινι Xen. 2. *to take part with* one, *to assist*, τινι Eur. ; absol., Aesch. 3. *to bring upon* oneself, πληγάς Dem.

συν-απωθέω, f. ήσω, *to push away together*, Luc.

συνᾶραι, aor. 1 inf. of συναίρω.

συν-ἀρᾰρίσκω, *to join together*. II. intr. in pf. συνάρηρα, *to hang together*, h. Hom.

συν-ἀράσσω, Att. -ττω, f. ξω, *to dash together, dash in pieces, shiver, shatter*, Hom. ; σ. οἶκον, πόλιν Eur. : —Pass. *to be shattered*, Od.; Hdt. ; συναράσσεσθαι κε-φαλὰς *to have their heads dashed together*, Hdt.

συν-ἀρέσκω, f. -αρέσω, *to please* or *satisfy together*, c. dat., Dem. 2. impers., like Lat. *placet*, συναρέσκει μοι I am content also, Xen.

συνάρηρα, pf. intr. of συναραρίσκω.

σύν-αρθρος, ον, (ἄρθρον) *linked together with*, Aesch.

σύν-ἀρῐθμέω, f. ήσω, *to reckon in, to take into the account, enumerate*, Isae. ; so in Med., Aeschin. :—Pass. *to be counted with* others, *to be taken into account*, Arist.

συν-ἀριστάω, f. ήσω, *to take breakfast* or *luncheon with*, τινί Ar., Aeschin.

συν-ἀριστεύω, f. σω, *to do brave deeds together*, Eur.

συν-αρκέομαι, Dep. *to acquiesce along with*, τινι Theophr.

συν-αρμόζω, Att. -όττω : Dor. f. -όξω :—Pass., pf. -ήρμοσμαι, aor. 1 -ηρμόσθην : 1. in physical sense, *to fit together*, Thuc. ; συναρμόζειν βλέφαρα *to close* them, Eur. :—Pass., λίθοι εὖ συνηρμοσμένοι Hdt. 2. *to put together*, so as to make a whole, σκάφος, ἵππον Eur. :—Pass., εὖ καλῶς συνηρμοσμένα Dem. 3. *to combine in* act or *thought*, Solon, Plat. 4. metaph. *to adapt* one thing to another, εὐχερείᾳ σ. βροτούς, i. e. to make them indifferent to crime, Aesch. :—Pass., πρὸς παρόντα συνηρμοσμένος Xen. II. intr. *to fit together, agree*, Plat., Xen.

συν-αρμολογέομαι, Pass. *to be fitted* or *framed to-gether*, N. T.

συν-αρμοστής, οῦ, ὁ, one who fits together, λίθων Luc. II. a joint-governor, Id.

συναρμόττω, Att. for συναρμόζω.

συν-αρπάζω, f. -άσω and -άσομαι : aor. 1 -ήρπασα and αξα :—*to seize and carry clean away*, Trag., etc. :— Pass., Soph. 2. ξ. χεῖρας *to seize and pin* them *together*, Eur. 3. metaph., σ. φρενί *to seize with* the mind, *grasp*, Soph., Ar.

συν-αρτάω, f. ήσω, *to knit* or *join together*, Eur., Luc. :—Pass. *to be closely engaged* or *entangled*, Thuc. : *to be attached to, combined with*, τινι Arist. : *to hang close on* an enemy's rear, Plut.

συν-αρχία, ή, (ἀρχή) joint administration, Strab. II. in pl., αἱ συναρχίαι, *the collective magistracy*, Arist.

σύν-αρχος, ον, a partner in office, colleague, Arist.

συν-άρχω, f. ξω, *to rule jointly with*, τινί Hdt. 2.

absol. *to be a colleague in office*, Thuc. : ὁ συνάρχων a colleague, Id.

συν-ασκέω, f. ήσω, *to join in practising*, Isocr., Dem.

συν-ασπῐδόω, f. ώσω, *to keep the shields close together, stand in close order*, Xen.

συν-ασπίζω, f. Att. ιῶ, *to be a shield-fellow* or *com-rade*, Eur. II. = συνασπιδόω, Luc.

συν-ασπιστής, οῦ, ὁ, *a shield-fellow, comrade*, Soph.

συν-ασχάλάω, only in pres. *to sympathise indignantly with* a thing, c. dat., Aesch.

συν-ασχάλλω, f. -ἄλῶ, = foreg., Aesch.

συν-ασχολέομαι, Pass. *to do business with*, τινι Plut.

συν-ἄτῑμάζομαι, Pass. *to be disgraced with*, τινι Plut.

συνᾰτῑμόομαι, = foreg., Plut.

συν-αυαίνω, f. ἄνῶ, *to dry quite up*, Eur. :—Pass. *to be dried up* also, Plat.

συν-αυδάω, f. ήσω, *to speak together : to agree, con-fess, allow*, Soph.

συν-αυλέω, f. ήσω, *to accompany on the flute*, Luc.

συναυλία, ή, *a concert of flutes*; Ar. 2. metaph., δύσορνις ἄδε ξ. δορός this ill-omened *concert* of battle of the single combat of the brothers, Aesch. II. (from αὐλή) *a dwelling together*, Arist.

συν-αυλίζομαι, Pass. *to congregate*, Babr.

σύν-αυλος, ον, (αὐλός) *in concert with the flute* : generally, *sounding in unison*, Ar. : generally, *in har-mony with*, τινι Eur.

σύναυλος, ον, (αὐλή) *dwelling with, living in the folds with* (sc. ταῖς ποίμναις), Soph. : metaph. θείᾳ μανίᾳ ξ., i. e. *afflicted with madness*, Id.

συν-αυξάνω and -αύξω, f. -αυξήσω, *to increase* or *enlarge along with* or *together*, Xen. :—Pass. *to in-crease* or *wax larger together with* a thing, c. dat., Hdt., Eur. 2. *to join* or *assist in increasing*, Xen., Arist. Hence

συναύξησις, εως, ή, *common growth*, Polyb.

συν-αφαιρέω, f. ήσω, *to take away together* :—Med. *to assist in rescuing*, Thuc.

συνᾰφᾰνίζομαι, Pass. *to perish with*, τινι Strab.

συν-αφίστημι, Ion. συν-απ- : aor. 1 συναπέστησα :— *to draw into revolt together*, Thuc. :—Pass., Ion. συναπίσταμαι, with aor. 2 and pf. act., *to fall off* or *revolt along with* others, c. dat., or absol., Hdt., Thuc.

συναχθῆναι, aor. 1 inf. of συνάγω.

συν-άχθομαι, f. -αχθέσομαι and -αχθεσθήσομαι : aor. 1 opt. -αχθεσθείην : Dep. *to be grieved with* or *to-gether, to condole with*, τινι Hdt., Dem., etc. ; c. dat. rei, *at* a thing, Xen.

συν-δαΐζω, f. ξω, *to kill with the rest, kill also*, Soph.

συν-δαίνυμι, f. -δαίσω, *to entertain together*, σ. γάμους τινί *to share* a marriage *feast with* one, Eur.

συν-δαίτης, ου, ὁ, = συνδαίτωρ, Luc.

συν-δαίτωρ, ορος, ὁ, *a companion at table*, Aesch.

συν-δάκνω, f. -δήξομαι, *to bite together*, συνδ. τὸ στό-μιον of a horse, *to take* the bit *in his teeth*, Xen.

συνδακρύω [ῡ], f. σω, *to weep with* or *together*, Eur. II. c. acc. *to lament together*, Plut.

συν-δᾰνείζω, Med. *to collect by borrowing*, Plut.

συν-δειπνέω, f. ήσω, *to dine* or *sup with* another, c. dat., Xen. ; μετά τινων Dem. :—absol. *to dine* or *sup with* others, Xen., etc. ; οἱ ξυνδειπνοῦντες *the members of a picnic party*, Id.

σύν-δειπνον, τό, a common meal or banquet, Lat. convivium, Plat.

σύν-δειπνος, ὁ, ἡ, (δεῖπνον) a companion at table, Lat. conviva, Eur., Xen.

συν-δεκάζω, f. σω, to bribe all together, Xen., Aeschin.

σύν-δενδρος, ον, (δένδρον) thickly-wooded, Babr.

συν-δέομαι, Dep. to join in begging, τί τινος something of a person, Dem.

σύν-δεσμος, ὁ, heterog. pl. σύνδεσμα, a bond of union, bond, fastening, Eur., Thuc.: metaph., good men are called ὁ ξ. τῆς πόλεως the bond that keeps the state together, Plat.   2. in Grammar, a conjunction, Arist.

συν-δεσμώτης, ου, ὁ, a fellow-prisoner, Thuc., Plat.

σύν-δετος, ον, bound hand and foot, Soph.   II. as Subst. σύνδετον, τό, a band, Eur.

συν-δέω, Att. ξυν-δέω, f. -δήσω:—to bind or tie together, of two or more things, συνέδησα πόδας Od.; τοὺς πόδας καὶ τὰς χεῖρας Plat.; δέλτον σ. to fasten up the tablets, Eur.:—Pass., ἰσχία μὴ συνδεδεμένα flanks not drawn up, of dogs, Xen.   2. of persons, to bind hand and foot, Il., Hdt., etc.   3. to bind up a wound, Il.   4. generally, to bind together, unite, Eur., Plat.   II. Med., σύνδησαι πέπλους gird up thy robes, Eur.

σύν-δηλος, ον, quite clear or manifest, Arist.

συν-δηλόω, f. ώσω, to make altogether clear, Arist.

συν-δημᾰγωγέω, to join in seeking popularity, Plut.

συν-διαβαίνω, f. -βήσομαι, to go through or cross over together, Thuc., Xen.

συν-διαβάλλω, f. -βαλῶ, to convey over together: absol., Lat. una trajicere, συνδ. τὸν κόλπον to cross the gulf together, Thuc.   II. to accuse along with, Dem.:—Pass. to be accused together, Thuc.

συν-διαβιβάζω, Causal of συνδιαβαίνω, to carry through or over together, Xen.

συν-διαγιγνώσκω, f. -γνώσομαι, to join with others in determining or decreeing, Thuc.

συν-διάγω [ἄ], f. ἄξω, to go through together: absol. (sc. τὸν βίον) to live together, Arist.

συν-διαιτάομαι, Pass. to dwell with or together, Thuc., Isocr. Hence

συνδιαίτησις, ἡ, a living together, intercourse, Plut.

συν-διαιτητής, οῦ, ὁ, a joint arbitrator, Dem.   II. one who lives with another, a companion, Luc.

συν-διακινδῡνεύω, f. σω, to share in danger, Hdt., Plat.

συν-διακομίζομαι, Pass. to cross over together, Plut.

συν-διακοσμέω, to set in order together, Plat., Plut.

συνδιάκτορος, ὁ, a fellow-διάκτορος, i.e. a mate of Hermes, Luc.

συν-διαλλάσσω, Att. -ττω, f. ξω, to help in reconciling, τινὰ πρός τινα Dem.

συν-διαλύω, f. -λύσω [ῠ], to help in putting an end to, Isocr.   2. to help in reconciling, Dem.   3. Med. to help to pay, Luc.

συν-διαμένω, to stand one's ground with others, Xen.

συν-διαμνημονεύω, f. σω, to call to remembrance along with or together, Dem., Aeschin.

συν-διανεύω, f. σω, to turn every way together, Polyb.

συν-διανοέομαι, Dep. to deliberate with, τινι Polyb.

συν-διαπλέω, to sail through together, Luc.

συν-διαπολεμέω, f. ήσω, to carry on a war along with,

νῆες αἱ ξυνδιαπολεμήσασαι ships which remained with him throughout the war, Thuc.

συν-δι-ἀπορέω, f. ήσω, to start doubts or questions together, Plut.

συν-διαπράσσω, Att. -ττω, f. ξω, to accomplish together or besides, Isocr., Luc., etc.   II. Med. to negotiate at the same time, Xen.

συν-διασκοπέω, f. -σκέψομαι, to look through or examine along with, τί τινι or μετά τινος Plat. :—so in pres. med., Id.

συν-διαστρέφω, f. ψω, to distort together :—Pass. to be twisted together with, τινί Plut.

συν-διασώζω, to assist in preserving, Thuc., Dem.

συν-διατᾰλαιπωρέω, f. ήσω, to endure hardship with or together, Plat.

συν-διατελέω, f. Att. -τελῶ, to continue with to the end, Plat.

συν-διατηρέω, f. ήσω, to assist in maintaining, Polyb.

συν-διατρίβω [ῑ], f. ψω, to pass or spend time with or together, Aeschin.   2. absol. (sub. βίον) to live constantly with, οἱ τῷ Σωκράτει συνδιατρίβοντες his disciples, Xen.   II. to occupy oneself with a thing, c. dat., Isocr.

συν-διαφέρω, f. -διοίσω, to bear along with one, Luc.   II. to bear to the end along with, help in maintaining, Hdt., Ar.

συν-διαφθείρομαι, Pass. to perish along with, τινι Isocr.

συν-διαχειμάζω, f. σω, to be in winter quarters along with or together, Plut.

συν-διαχειρίζω, f. σω, to assist in accomplishing, Hdt.

συν-διεκπίπτω, f. -πεσοῦμαι, to rush out through together, Plut.

συν-διέξειμι, (εἶμι ibo) to go through together with, Xen.

συν-διημερεύω, f. σω, to spend the day with, τινί Xen.

συν-δικάζω, f. σω, to be assessor to a judge, Lys.

συν-δικαστής, οῦ, ὁ, a fellow-dicast or juryman, Ar.

συν-δικέω, f. ήσω, to act as one's advocate, Aesch., Xen., etc.; σ. τινί Plat.; Ζεύς σοι τόδε συνδικήσει Zeus will be thy advocate herein, Eur.   2. to be one of the public advocates, Dem. From

σύν-δῐκος, ὁ, ἡ, (δίκη) one who helps in a court of justice, an advocate, Lat. patronus, Aesch., Dem.   2. at Athens, the σύνδικοι were public advocates appointed to represent the state, Dem.   3. after the 30 Tyrants, the σύνδικοι were judges to determine disputes about confiscated property, Lys.   II. belonging jointly to, σ. Ἀπόλλωνος καὶ Μοισᾶν κτέανον their joint possession, Pind. :—Adv. συνδίκως, with joint sentence, jointly, Aesch.

συν-διοικέω, f. ήσω, to administer together with another, c. dat., Dem.

συν-διοράω, to examine together, Isocr.

συν-διορίζομαι, Pass. to be determined also, Strab.

συν-δισκεύω, f. σω, to play at quoits with, τινι Luc.

συν-διώκω, f. Att. -διώξομαι, to chase away together, join in the chase, Thuc.   II. as law-term, to join in the prosecution, Lex ap. Dem.

συν-δοκέω, f. -δόξω and -δοκήσω :—to seem good also, ταῦτα κἀμοὶ συνδοκεῖ Ar.; ταῦτα ξυνέδοξε τοῖς ἄλλοις Thuc. :—absol., in answers, ξυνεδόκει ἡμῖν ταῦτα; were we agreed on these points? i.e. we were agreed, Plat.   2. impers. it seems good also, Eur., Ar.,

etc. :—so, absol., in part., **συνδοκοῦν ἄπασιν ὑμῖν** since you all agree, Xen. ; **συνδόξαν τῷ πατρί** since the father approved, Id. II. so in pf. pass. part., **λόγος τοῖς ἐπιεικεστάτοις συνδεδογμένος** in which they also agree, Plat.

συν-δοκιμάζω, f. σω, to examine together, Isocr.

συν-δοξάζω, f. σω, to join in approving, Arist. 2. to agree with, **τῷ σώματι** Porph. in Stob. II. Pass. to be glorified together, N. T.

σύνδοξαν, aor. 1 part. neut. of **συνδοκέω**.

συν-δουλεύω, f. σω, to be a fellow-slave with, **τινί** Eur.

σύν-δουλος, ὁ, ἡ, a fellow-slave, Hdt., Eur., etc. : a special fem. **συνδούλη** in Babr.

συν-δράω, f. δσω [ᾱ], to do together, help in doing, Soph., Thuc. ; σ. **τί τινι** Eur. ; ξ. **αἷμα καὶ φόνον** to help in bloodshed and murder, Id. ; **τὸ συνδρῶν χρέος** the joint necessity, Id.

συνδρομάς, άδος, fem. of **σύνδρομος**, αἱ σ. **πέτραι**, = **συμπληγάδες**, Eur. ; σ. **Κυάνεαι** Theocr.

συν-δρομή, ἡ, (δρόμος) a tumultuous concourse of people, ap. Arist. 2. of things, ἡ σ. **τοῦ λόγου** its conclusion, moral, Anth.

σύν-δρομος, ον, running together, meeting, σ. **πέτραι**, = **συνδρομάδες**, Pind. 2. as Subst. a place where several roads meet, Strab. II. running along with, close-following, Anth. :—Adv. **συνδρόμως** Aesch.

συν-δυάζω, f. άσω, to join two and two, couple, Arist. : —Pass. to be coupled with something else, Id. 2. in Pass. to be coupled, to pair, Xen.

συν-δυάς, άδος, ἡ, (δύο) paired, σ. **ἄλοχος** one's wedded wife, Eur.

συνδυασμός, ὁ, (συνδυάζομαι) a being taken two together, Arist. 2. a coupling, pairing, Id.

συνδυαστικός, ή, όν, disposed to live in pairs, Arist.

σύν-δυο, οἱ, αἱ, τά, two together, two and two, in pairs, Lat. bini, h. Hom., Hdt., Plat.

συν-δυστῠχέω, f. ήσω, to share in misfortune, Eur.

συν-δώδεκα, οἱ, αἱ, τά, twelve in all, Eur.

συν-εγγίζω, f. σω, to draw near together, Polyb. Hence

συνεγγισμός, ὁ, a drawing near together, of constellations, Strab.

συν-εγγυάω, f. ήσω, to join in betrothing, Plut.

σύν-εγγυς, Adv. : 1. of Place, near together, Thuc., etc. ; σ. **ἀλλήλων** or **ἀλλήλοις** Arist. :—**τὸ** σ. nearness, proximity, Id. 2. of Time, Id. 3. of Quality, οἱ σ. persons of similar rank, Id. ; ἡ σ. **αἰτία** the proximate cause, Id.

συν-εγείρω, f. -εγερῶ, to help in raising, N. T. :—Pass. to rise together, Ib.

συνεδρεία, ἡ, = **συνεδρία**, Arist.

συν-εδρεύω, f. σω, (σύνεδρος) to sit together, sit in council, Aeschin.; οἱ **συνεδρεύοντες** members of council, Dem. 2. to hold a council, deliberate, Id.

συνεδρία, ἡ, a sitting together, a circle of friends, Xen. :—gregariousness, which in birds was a favourable omen, Aesch. II. a council, Aeschin. ; and

συνέδριον, τό, a body of men assembled in council, a council-board, council, Xen., etc. ; of the Roman Senate, Polyb. ; the Jewish Sanhedrim, N. T. :—esp. of a congress of Allies or Confederates, Hdt., Dem., etc. 2. a council-chamber, Hdt., Xen. From

σύν-εδρος, ον, (ἕδρα) sitting with in council, of persons,

Hdt. ; **ἐκ ξυνέδρου καὶ τυραννικοῦ κύκλου**, = **ἐκ κύκλου τῶν συνεδρευόντων τυράννων**, Soph. II. as Subst. one who sits with others, a councillor, Id. ; **σύνεδροι** select commissioners, Thuc., etc.

συν-είκοσι, Ep. for **συν-είκοσι**, twenty together, by twenties, Lat. viceni, Od.

συν-εργω, Ep. for **συνέργω** :—**συν-εργάθον**, Ep. impf.

συνέζευξα, aor. 1 of **συ-ζεύγνυμι**.

συν-εθέλω, to have the same wish, to consent, Xen. : —in Poets **συνθέλω**, Soph., Eur.

συνέθεντο, 3 pl. aor. 2 med. of **συν-τίθημι**.

συν-εθίζω, f. Att. ιῶ, to accustom, σ. **τινὰ ποιεῖν τι** to accustom him to do . . , Dem., Aeschin. :—Pass. to become used or habituated, and in aor. to be so, Thuc., Plat. ; c. inf., **συνειθίσθην ποιεῖν τι** Xen. :—also impers., **συνειθισμένον ἦν** it had become the custom, Lys. Hence

συνεθιστέον, verb. Adj. one must accustom oneself, Plat.

συνειδέναι, inf. of **σύνοιδα**. Hence

συνείδησις, ἡ, self-consciousness : conscience, N. T.

συνεῖδον, aor. 2 of **συνοράω**.

συνειδώς, part. of **σύνοιδα**.

συνειλεγμένος, pf. pass. part. of **συλ-λέγω**.

συν-ειλέω, f. ήσω, to crowd together, Hdt. ; of things, to bind tight together, Id. :—Pass. to be crowded or pressed together, Xen., etc.

συνείληφα, -είλημμαι, pf. of **συλλαμβάνω**.

συνείληχα, pf. of **συλλαγχάνω**.

σύν-ειμι, f. ἔσομαι, (εἰμί sum) to be with, be joined or linked with a thing, c. dat., Od. ; periphr. for a simple Verb, σ. **ὀνείρασιν** to dream, Aesch. ; σ. **νόσῳ** = **νοσεῖν**, Soph.; **κακοῖς πολλοῖς** ξ. to be acquainted with miseries, Id. ; σ. **πράγμασι** to be engaged in business, Ar. ; σ. **ἡδοναῖς, λύπαις, δείμασι** Plat. ; —reversely, **ἐμοὶ ξύνεστιν ἐλπίς** Eur. ; and absol., **ἄται ἀεὶ ξυνοῦσαι** Soph. ; ὁ **χρόνος ξυνὼν μακρός** Id. II. to have intercourse with a person, live with, **τινι** Id., Eur., etc. ; **μετά τινος** Ar. 2. to live with a husband, = **συνοικέω**, Hdt. 3. to attend, as to a pupil attends a master, Xen., etc. ; of the teacher, Id. :—οἱ **συνόντες** associates, disciples, partisans, Plat. 4. to have dealings with, **τινι** Thuc. ; σ. **ἵπποις** to have to do with them, Plat. 5. to take part with, **τινι** Aesch., etc.

σύνειμι, (εἶμι ibo) to go or come together, to assemble, Il., Hdt., Thuc. 2. in hostile sense, to meet in battle, Il., etc. : of states, to engage in war, Thuc. 3. in peaceable sense, to come together, meet to deliberate, Id. II. of revenue, to come in, Hdt.

συν-εῖπον, aor. 2 of **συναγορεύω** or **σύμφημι** :—to speak with any one, confirm what another says, Isocr. : to agree with, **τινι** Xen. 2. to advocate another's cause, Dem. ; generally, to help, further, Isocr. 3. to help to tell, Eur.

συν-είργνῡμι, = **συνέργω**, Plut.

συνείργω, Att. for **συνέργω**.

συνείρηκα, used as pf. of **σύμφημι**.

συν-είρω, only in pres. and impf. to string together, Lat. connectere, Ar., Plat. II. to string words together, Dem., etc. : then, seemingly intr. (sub. **λόγους**) to speak on and on, go on without pausing, Xen.

συνείς, aor. 2 part. of **συνίημι**.

συν-εισάγω, f. ξω, to bring in together, Xen.

συν-εισβαίνω, f. -βήσομαι, to embark in a ship with others, σ. πλοῖον ναύταισι Aesch.; σ. ταὐτὸν σκάφος Eur.

συν-εισβάλλω, f. -βᾰλῶ, intr. to make an inroad into a country together, join in an inroad, Hdt., Thuc.

συν-εισέρχομαι, Dep. to enter along with or together, δόμους Eur.; ἐς οἴκους Id., etc.

συνείσομαι, used as fut. of σύνοιδα.

συν-εισπίπτω, f. -πεσοῦμαι, to fall or be thrown into with others, Xen.   II. to rush in together, of soldiers pursuing the besieged to the gates and getting in with them, Hdt., Thuc.

συν-εισπλέω, f. -πλεύσομαι, to sail into together, Xen.

συν-εισπράσσω, Att. -ττω, f. ξω, to help one (τινί) in exacting money from another (τινά), Dem.

συν-εισφέρω, f. -εισοίσω, to join in paying the war-tax (εἰσφορά), Dem.

συν-εκβαίνω, f. -βήσομαι, to go out together, Xen.

συν-εκβάλλω, f. -βᾰλῶ, to cast out along with, τί τινι Hdt.   2. to assist in casting out or expelling, Xen.

συν-εκβῐβάζω, f. -βῐβῶ, Causal of συνεκβαίνω, to help in bringing out, Xen.

συν-εκδημέω, f. ήσω, to be abroad with, τινί Plut.

συν-έκδημος, ὁ, a fellow-traveller, N. T.

συν-εκδίδωμι, f. -δώσω, to give out or give up together, Plut.   2. to help a poor man in portioning out his daughter, Dem.

συν-εκδύομαι, f. -δύσομαι [ῠ], Med. to put off at the same time, Hdt.

συν-εκθνήσκω, f. -θᾰνοῦμαι, to faint along with, σ. τῷ πώματι, i. e. to drink till wine and drinker fail together, Eur.

συν-εκκαίδεκα, sixteen together, by sixteens, Dem.

συν-εκκαίω, f. -καύσω, to set on fire together, Plut.

συν-εκκλέπτω, f. ψω, to help to steal away, Eur.; σ. γάμους to help in concealing the marriage, Id.

συν-εκκλησιάζω, f. σω, to frequent the ἐκκλησία together, Plut.

συν-εκκομίζω, f. Att. ιῶ, to carry out along with, Plut.   II. to help in carrying out, help in achieving, Eur.; σ. τινὶ κακά to help one in bearing evils, Id.

συν-εκκόπτω, f. ψω, to help to cut away, Xen.

συν-εκκρούομαι, Pass. to be driven from one's purpose together, Plut.

συν-εκλεκτός, ή, όν, chosen along with, τισί N. T.

συνεκλύομαι, Pass. to be dissolved together, Anth.

συν-εκπέμπω, f. ψω, to send out together, Xen.

συνεκπεράω, f. άσω [ᾱ], to come out together, Xen.

συν-εκπίνω [ῑ], f. -πίομαι, to drink off together, Xen.

συν-εκπίπτω, f. -πεσοῦμαι, to rush out together with others, c. dat., Plut.   2. to be driven out or banished together, Id.   3. to disappear together, Luc.   II. of voting tablets, to come out in agreement, to happen to agree, Hdt.; αἱ πλεῖσται γνῶμαι συνέπιπτον ναυσιμαχέειν agreed in advising to fight, Id.; then of persons, οἱ πολλοὶ Θεμιστοκλέα κρίνοντες συνέπιπτον agreed in choosing, Id.   2. c. dat. to come out equal to another, run a dead heat with him, συνεξέπιπτε τῷ πρώτῳ Id.   III. to be thrown out together, to be rejected, Luc.

συν-εκπλέω, Ion. -πλώω, f. -πλεύσομαι, to sail out along with, τινί Hdt.; Thuc.

συν-εκπνέω, f. -πνεύσομαι, to breathe one's last along with another, c. dat., Eur.

συν-εκπονέω, f. ήσω, to help in working out, Eur.: to help in achieving or effecting, Id.   2. without acc., σ. τινί to assist to the utmost, Id.   II. to assist in supporting, συνεκπονοῦσα κῶλον Id.

συν-εκπορίζω, f. Att. ιῶ, to help in procuring or supplying, τί τινι Xen.

συνεκποτέα, verb. Adj. of συνεκπίνω, one must drink off at the same time, Ar.

συν-εκπράσσω, Ion. -πρήσσομαι, Med. to assist in avenging, Hdt.

συν-εκσώζω, f. σω, to help in delivering, Soph.

συν-εκτάσσω, Att. -ττω, to arrange in line with, Xen.

συνεκτέον, verb. Adj., one must keep together, Xen.

συν-εκτίκτω, to bring forth together, Arist.

συνεκτίνω, f. -τίσω [ῑ], to pay along with or together, to help in paying, Dem.

συν-εκτρᾰχύνομαι, Pass. to be furious together, Plut.

συν-εκτρέφω, f. -θρέψω, to rear up along with or together, Plat.: —Pass. to grow up with, τινί Eur.

συν-εκτρέχω, f. -δρᾰμοῦμαι, to sally out together, Xen.

συν-εκφέρω, f. -εξοίσω, to carry out together, esp. to burial, to attend a funeral, Thuc.

συν-εκχέω, f. -χεῶ, to pour out together, Anth.

συνέλᾰβον, aor. 2 of συλλαμβάνω.

συνελάουν, impf. of συνελαλάω.

συν-ελαύνω, f. -ελάσω [ᾰ]: aor. 1 -ήλᾰσα, Ep. -έλασσα:—to drive together, Il., Xen.; σὺν δ᾽ ἤλασ᾽ ὀδόντας gnashed his teeth together, Od.   II. to match in combat, set to fight, Hom. :—intr., ἔριδι ξυνελαυνέμεν to meet in quarrel, Il.

συνελεῖν, aor. 2 inf. of συναιρέω.

συν-ελευθερόω, f. ώσω, to join in freeing from another, c. gen., Hdt. :—absol. to join in freeing, Id., Thuc.

συνελήλῠθα, pf. of συνέρχομαι.

συνελθεῖν, aor. 2 inf. of συνέρχομαι.

συν-ελίσσω, Ion. συν-ειλ-, Att. -ττω, f. ξω, to roll together :—Pass. to involve oneself in a thing, c. dat., Soph.   2. intr. to coil itself up, of a serpent, Eur.

συνελκυστέον, verb. Adj. one must draw together, Xen. From

συν-έλκω, f. ξω : aor. 1 -είλκῠσα:—to draw together, to draw up, contract, Ar.   II. to draw out along with, to help to draw out, Id., Xen.

συνελών, aor. 2 part. of συναιρέω.

συν-εμβαίνω, f. -βήσομαι, to embark together, τινί with one, Luc.

συν-εμβάλλω, f. -βᾰλῶ, to help in applying, Ar.   II. intr. to fall upon also, to join in attacking, Xen.; to make a joint inroad, Dem.

συν-εμβολή, ἡ, a throwing in together, σ. κώπης the regular dip of all the oars together, to the sound of the κέλευσμα, Aesch.   II. a junction, fastening, Id.

συνέμεν, for συνεῖναι, aor. 2 inf. of συνίημι.

συνέμιχθεν, for -ησαν, 3 pl. aor. 1 pass. of συμμίγνυμι.

συν-εμπίπρημι, f. -πρήσω, to burn together, Eur.

συν-εμπίπτω, f. -πεσοῦμαι, to fall in or upon together, Luc.   2. to fall on or attack together, Plut.

συν-έμπορος, ὁ, ἡ, a fellow-traveller, companion, attendant, Trag., Plat. :—metaph., λύπη δ᾽ ἄμισθος ἐστί σοι ξ. Aesch.; c. gen. rei, σ. χορείας partner in the dance, Ar.

συν-ενδίδωμι, f. -δώσω, to give in together, Plat.

συνενέγκαι, aor. 1 inf. of συμφέρω.

συν-ενείκομαι, Ep. for συμφέρομαι, to strike or dash against a thing, c. dat., Hes.

συν-εξάγω, f. ξω, to lead out together, Hdt. : Pass. to be carried away together, Anth.

συν-εξαιρέω, f. ήσω : aor. 2 -εξείλον, Ion. inf. -εξελέειν : —to take out together, to help in removing, Hdt. :— Med., Eur. : to take away also, Xen. 2. to help in taking, Eur., Xen.

συν-εξαίρω, to assist in raising : Pass., aor. 1 part. συνεξαρθείς being lifted up at once, Plut. ; being excited at the same time, Luc.

συν-εξἄκολουθέω, f. ήσω, to follow constantly, to attend everywhere, Polyb.

συν-εξἄκούω, f. ούσομαι, to hear all together, Soph.

συν-εξαλείφω, f. ψω, to abolish together, Plut.

συν-εξἄμαρτάνω, f. -αμαρτήσομαι, to have part in a fault, Thuc., etc. ; τινί with one, Dem., etc.

συν-εξἄμείβω, f. ψω, to remove together, Babr.

συν-εξανίστημι, f. -αναστήσω, to stir up together, Plut. II. Pass., with aor. 2 and pf. act., to rise up at the same time, rise and come forth with, Id. 2. to rise in rebellion, revolt together, Id.

συν-εξἄπἄτάω, f. ήσω, to cheat together or also, Dem.

συν-έξειμι, (εἶμι ibo) to go out along with or together, Thuc. ; c. dat., Xen.

συν-εξελαύνω, f. Att. -ελῶ, to drive out along with or together, Aesch.

συν-εξερύω, f. σω, to draw out together, Anth.

συν-εξέρχομαι : aor. 2 -εξῆλθον : Dep. :—to go or come out with, τινί Hdt., Eur.

συν-εξετάζω, f. σω, to search out and examine along with or together, Plat. :—Pass., οἱ συνεξεταζόμενοι μετά τινος or τινι his party or adherents, Dem.

συν-εξευρίσκω, to assist in finding out, Eur., Isocr.

συν-εξημερόομαι, Pass. to be civilised together, Plut.

συν-εξιχνεύω, f. σω, to trace out along with, τί τινι Plut.

συν-εξορμάω, f. ήσω, to help to urge on, Isocr. II. intr. to rush forth or sally out together, Xen.

συν-εξωθέω, f. ήσω, to thrust out together, Strab.

συν-εοχμός, ὁ, poët. for συν-οχμός, = συνοχή, a joining, joint, Il.

συν-επάγω, f. ξω, to lead together against, Thuc. 2. to join in bringing in a foreign force to aid, Id.

συν-επἄγωνίζομαι, f. -ιοῦμαι, Dep. to join in stirring up a contest besides, Polyb.

συν-επἄδω, poët. -αείδω, f. -άσομαι, to join in celebrating, Eur.

συν-επαινέω, f. έσω, Ep. ήσω, to approve together, give joint assent, consent, Aesch., Xen. ;—c. inf., σ. μάχεσθαι to join in the recommendation to fight, Thuc. ;—σ. τι to consent or agree to, Id. II. to join in praising, τινα Xen., Plat.

συν-έπαινος, ον, joining in approbation of a thing, συν. εἶναι to give one's consent to a thing, τινι or absol., Hdt. ; c. acc. et inf. to consent that . . , Id.

συν-επαίρω, f. -ἄρῶ, to raise or lift at the same time, Xen. :—Pass. to be elevated together with, τινί Luc. II. to urge on together or also, Xen. :— Pass. to rise together with others, c. dat., Plut.

συν-επαιτιάομαι, f. -σομαι, Dep. to accuse also of a thing, τινά τινος Thuc.

συν-επαιωρέομαι, Pass. to continue soaring over, Plut.

συν-επἄκολουθέω, f. ήσω, to follow closely, Plat.

συν-επἄμύνω [ῠ], f. -ῠνῶ, to join in repelling, τινά Thuc.

συν-επανίστημι, to make to rise up against together. II. Pass., with aor. 2 act., to join in a revolt, Hdt., Thuc. ; τινι or ἅμα τινι Hdt.

συνέπαξα, Dor. for -έπηξα, aor. 1 of συμπήγνυμι.

συν-επανορθόω, aor. 1 συνεπηνώρθωσα (v. ἀνορθόω) to join in reestablishing, Dem.

συν-επάπτομαι, Ion. for συν-εφάπτομαι.

συνεπήδησα, aor. 1 of συμπεδάω.

συν-έπειμι, (εἶμι ibo) to join in attacking, τινι Thuc.

συν-επεισπίπτω, to rush in upon together, Plut.

συν-επεισφέρομαι, Med. to help to bring in, Xen.

συν-επεκπίνω, f. -πίομαι, to drink off together, Anth.

συν-επελαφρύνω [ῠ], f. -ῠνῶ, to help to make light, i. e. to assist in bearing, Hdt.

συν-επερείδω, f. σω, to help in inflicting, πληγήν Plut. ; σ. ὑπόνοιάν τινι to help to fix a suspicion on him, Id. II. c. acc. pers. to transfix, συνεπερείσας τῇ ῥύμῃ τοῦ ἵππου charging him with all the force of his horse, Id.

συν-επερίζω, f. σω, to contend also with, τινί Anth.

συνέπεσον, aor. 2 of συμπίπτω.

συνεπεσπόμην, Ion. aor. 2 of συνεφέπομαι.

συνεπέστην, aor. 2 of συνεφίστημι.

συν-επευθύνω, f. ῠνῶ, to help to direct or guide, τι Plut.

συν-επεύχομαι, f. ξομαι, Dep. to join in prayer, Thuc. ; but c. inf. fut. to make a vow also to do a thing, Xen.

συν-επηχέω, f. ήσω, to join in a chant or chorus, Xen. II. to resound with a thing, Luc.

συν-επιβαίνω, f. -βήσομαι, to mount together, τοῦ τείχους on the wall, Plut.

συν-επιβάλλω, f. -βἄλῶ, to apply one's mind also, to consider a thing together, Polyb. II. to coincide with, καιροῖς Id.

συν-επιβλάπτομαι, Pass. to be damaged together with, τινι Arist.

συν-επιβουλεύω, f. σω, to join in plotting against another, Xen.

συν-επιγρἄφεύς, ὁ, a fellow-registrar, fellow-clerk, Isocr.

συν-επιδείκνῡμι or -ύω, to point out together, Polyb.

συν-επιθειάζω, to ascribe to divine interposition, Plut.

συν-επιθῡμέω, f. ήσω, to desire along with, τινί τινος Xen.

συν-επίκειμαι, Pass. to join in attacking, Ar.

συν-επικλάω, to break down at once, Plut.

συν-επικοσμέω, f. ήσω, to help to adorn, Xen., Arist.

συν-επικουρέω, f. ήσω, to join as an ally, help to relieve, Xen.

συν-επικουφίζω, f. σω, to lighten at the same time, Plut. II. to help in relieving, Id.

συν-επικρἄδαίνω, to move backwards and forwards together with, Xen.

συν-επικρύπτω, f. ψω, to help to conceal, Plut.

συν-επιλαμβάνομαι, Med. to take part in together, have a share in, partake in, c. gen. rei, Hdt., Thuc. : σ. τινι τινος to take part with or assist one in a thing, Luc. ; σ. τινι τοῦ φόβου to contribute towards increasing their fear, Thuc. 2. c. gen. pers. to take the part of, Plut. II. Act. in same sense, λόγῳ καὶ ἔργῳ συνεπιλαμβάνειν τινί to take part with him in word and deed, Thuc.

συν-επιμελέομαι, Dep. (μέλομαι) *to join in taking care of* or *attending to*, τινος Thuc., Xen.; σ. τῆς στρατιᾶς *to have joint charge of* the army, Xen.; absol., Id.

συν-επιμελητής, οῦ, ὁ, *a coadjutor*, Xen.

συν-επιρρέπω, f. ψω, *to incline towards together*, Plut.

συν-επιρρώννῡμι, *to help to strengthen*, Plut.

συν-επισκοπέω, f. -σκέψομαι, *to examine together with*, τί τινι Xen.

συν-επισπάω, f. σπάσω [ᾰ], *to draw on together*, Plut.   II. Med. *to draw on along with one*, esp. *to ruin*, Plat., Dem., etc.

συν-επισπεύδω, f. σω, *to join in forcing onward*, Xen.

συν-επίσταμαι, Dep. *to be privy to*, Xen., Luc.

συν-επιστατέω, f. ήσω, *to act as a common patron*, Plat.

συν-επιστέλλω, *to send with* or *together*, Luc.

συν-επιστρατεύω, f. σω, *to join in making war*, τινί *with* another, Thuc., Dem.

συν-επιστρέφω, f. ψω, *to turn at the same time*, Plat.   2. *to help to make attentive*, Plat.

συν-επισχύω, f. ύσω [ῠ], *to join in supporting*, Xen.

συν-επιτείνω, f. -τενῶ, *to help to aggravate*, Polyb.

συν-επιτελέω, f. έσω, *to help to accomplish*, Plut.   2. *to join in performing*, παιᾶνα θεῷ Xen.

συν-επιτίθημι, f. -θήσω, *to help in putting on*, Plut.   II. Med. *to join in attacking*, τινι Thuc.; ξ. τῷ ἔργῳ *to fall to the work together*, Id.

συν-επιτῑμάω, f. ήσω, *to join in chiding*, Plut.

συν-επιτρίβω [ῐ], f. ψω, *to destroy at once*, Xen.

συν-επίτροπος, ὁ, *a joint guardian*, Dem.

συν-επιφέρω, f. -επoίσω, *to join in applying*, Plut.

συν-επιχειρέω, *to attack together*, Polyb.

συν-επιψεύδομαι, Dep. *to join in lying*, Luc.

συν-επιψηφίζω, *to join in ratifying* a law, Arist.

συνέπνιξα, aor. 1 of συμπνίγω.

συν-έπομαι, aor. 2 -εσπόμην: Dep.:—*to follow along with*, *follow closely*, absol., Od., Thuc., etc.; c. dat., Hdt., etc.; οὔ σοι τῷ βίῳ ξυνέσπετο (thy fortunes) *remained* not *constant* to thy life, Soph.   2. σ. τῷ λόγῳ *to follow* the argument *to its consequences*, Plat.: —absol., ξυνέπομαι *I follow*, i.e. *understand*, Id.

συν-επόμνῡμι, f. -ομόσω, *to swear besides*, Xen.

συν-ερανίζω, f. σω, *to join in contributing*, *to collect*, Luc.:—Med. *to receive contributions*, Plut.

συν-εραστής, οῦ, ὁ, *a joint lover*, Xen.

συνεράω (A), f. άσω [ᾱ], *to pour together*, *gather together*, συνεράσαι τοὺς λόγους Isocr.

συν-εράω (B), impf. -ήρων, *to love together with*, τινί Eur.; so in Ep. med. inf. συνέρασθαι, Bion.

συν-εργάζομαι, f. -άσομαι: Dep.:—*to work with*, *coöperate*, Soph.; σ. πρός τι *to contribute towards* or *to* a thing, Xen.   II. aor. 1 -ειργάσθην, pf. -είργασμαι in pass. sense, λίθοι ξυνειργασμένοι stones *wrought so as to fit together*, i.e. in ashlar-work, Thuc.; συνειργάσθη ἔργον *it was wrought*, Anth.

συν-εργάτης [ᾰ], ου, ὁ, *a fellow-workman*, *helpmate*, *coadjutor*, Soph., Eur.; c. gen. *an accomplice* or *assistant in* a thing, Eur.

συνεργάτινης [ῐ], ου, ὁ, poët. for συνεργάτης, Anth.

συν-εργάτις [ᾰ], ιδος, ὁ, fem. of συνεργάτης.

συνεργέω, impf. -ήργουν, (συνεργός) *to work together with*, *help in work*, *coöperate*, Eur., Xen., etc.;— generally, *to coöperate with*, *assist*, τινί Dem.   Hence

συνέργημα, ατος, τό, *assistance*, *support*, Polyb.

συνεργήτης, ου, ὁ, poët. for συνεργάτης, Anth.

συνεργία, ἡ, (συνεργέω) *joint working*, *coöperation*, Arist.; in bad sense, *conspiracy*, *collusion*, Dem.

συν-εργός, όν, (*ἔργω) *working together*, *joining* or *helping in work*, and as Subst. *a fellow-workman*, *helpmate*, *coadjutor*, *accomplice*, Eur., Thuc., etc.; c. dat. pers., Eur., Thuc. :—c. gen. rei, σ. τείχεος *helping to make* it, Pind.; σ. ἀδίκων ἔργων, ἀρετᾶς *helping towards* them, Eur.; σ. τινί τινος *helping* a person *in* a thing, Xen.; εἶς or πρός τι Id.   II. *of the same trade as* another, *a fellow-workman*, *colleague*, Dem.

συν-έργω, old form of Att. συνείργω, f. συνείρξω: Ep. συνέεργω, impf. συνέεργον or συνεέργαθον:—*to shut up* or *enclose together*, Hom., Soph.   II. *to fasten together*, Od. :—*to unite*, Plat.

συν-έρδω, f. ξω, *to join in a work*, *help*, τινί Soph.

συν-ερείδω, f. σω, *to set firmly together*, Od. : *to bind together*, *bind fast*, Eur. :—Pass., συνερεισθεὶς χέρας δεσμοῖς *with* one's *hands tight bound*, Id.   2. σ. τὸν λογισμόν *to reason closely*, Plut.   II. intr. *to meet in close conflict*, Id.

συν-ερέω, Att. -ερῶ, fut. without pres. in use (v. συναγορεύω): pf. -είρηκα :—*to speak with* or *together*, *advocate*, *support* in a speech, c. dat., Xen., Dem.

συν-έριθος, ἡ, *a helpmate*, Od., Ar.; σ. τέχναι *assistant arts*, Plat.; σ. ἄτρακτος Anth.

συν-ερκτικός, ή, όν, (συνέργω) of a speaker, *driving his opponent into a corner*, *cogent*, Ar.

σύνερξις, ἡ, (συνέργω) *close union*, *wedlock*, Plat.

συν-έρρηγμαι, pf. pass. of συρρήγνυμι.

συν-έρχομαι, f. -ελεύσομαι, but the Att. fut. is σύνειμι (εἶμι ibo): Dep. with aor. 2 and pf. act.:—*to go together* or *in company*, Il.   II. *to come together*, *assemble*, Hdt., Eur., etc.; σ. ἐς τωὐτό Hdt.; σ. ἐς λόγους τινί Id.; simply, σ. τινι *to have dealings* or *intercourse with*, Soph.   2. in hostile sense, *to meet in battle*, Hdt.; also of the battle, μάχη ὑπό τινων ξυνελθοῦσα *engaged in*, *contested* by them, Thuc.   3. *to come together*, *be bonded together*, Eur., Plat. : *to form a league*, Dem.   4. c. acc. cogn., ταύτην τὴν στρατείαν ξυνῆλθον *joined* in this expedition, Thuc.; so, τὸ σὸν λέχος ξυνῆλθον *shared* thy bed, Soph.   III. of things, *to be joined in one*, Id., Eur.; of numbers, *to make up* a sum, Hdt.   2. of events, *to concur*, *happen together*, Id.

συν-ερωτάω, f. ήσω, *to ask with* or *at the same time*, Luc.   II. *to establish* a point *by means of question and answer*, Id.

σύνες, aor. 2 imper. of συνίημι.

σύνεσις, Att. ξύνεσις, ἡ, (σύν-ειμι (εἶμι ibo) *a coming together*, *union*, ξύνεσις δύω ποταμῶν Od.   II. (συνίημι) *quick comprehension*, *mother-wit*, *intelligence*, *sagacity*, Thuc.; of animals, Plat.   2. c. gen. rei, *intelligence in* a thing, *sagacity in respect to* it, Id.; περί τινος Thuc.   III. *conscience*, = συνείδησις, Eur.   IV. *a branch of art* or *science*, Arist.

συνεσπάραξα, aor. 1 of συνσπαράσσω.

συνεσπόμην, aor. 1 of συνέπομαι.

συνεσταλμένος, pf. pass. part. of συστέλλω.

συνεσταώς, for -εστηκώς, pf. part. of συνίστημι.

συνεσταυρωμένος, pf. pass. part. of συσταυρόω.

συνεστέον, verb. Adj. of σύνειμι (εἰμί sum), one must associate with, τινί Plat.

συνέστειλα, aor. 1 of συστέλλω.

συνεστηκότως, Adv. pf. part. of συνίστημι, steadfastly, gravely, Arist.

συνέστην, aor. 2 of συνίστημι.

συν-εστιάω, f. άσω [ᾰ], to entertain in one's house, Anth. :—Pass. to feast along with or together, Dem.

συν-έστιος, ον, (ἑστία) sharing one's hearth or house, a fellow-lodger, guest, Lat. contubernalis, Soph., Eur.; —ξυνέστιοι πόλεος his fellow-citizens, Aesch. :—c. dat. pers., σ. σοι καὶ ὁμοτράπεζος Plat. ; c. dat. rei, ξ. ἐμοὶ θοίνῃ associates with me in the feast, Eur. 2. of Zeus, guardian of the hearth, Aesch.

συνεστραμμένως, Adv. part. pf. pass. of συστρέφω, in a close packed manner, tersely, Arist.

συνεστώ, οῦς, ἡ, (σύνειμι) = συνουσία II, a party, banquet, Hdt.

συνεστώς, for -εστηκώς, pf. part. of συνίστημι.

σύνεσχον, aor. 2 of συνέχω.

συν-έταιρος, ὁ, a companion, partner, comrade, Hdt.

συνετάφην [ᾰ], aor. 2 pass. of συνθάπτω.

συνέτλην, aor. 2 of συντολμάω.

συνετός, ή, όν, (συνίημι) intelligent, sagacious, wise, Lat. prudens, Hdt., Pind., etc. ; τὸ συνετόν = σύνεσις, Eur., Thuc. :—c. gen. rei, intelligent in a thing, ξυνετὸς πολέμου Eur. ; also c. acc., τὰ οἰκτρὰ ξ. Id. II. pass. intelligible, Theogn., Hdt., etc. ; act. and pass. senses conjoined, εὐξύνετος ξυνετοῖσι βοά Eur. III. Adv. -τῶς, intelligently, Id. 2. intelligibly, Plut.

συν-ευδαιμονέω, f. ήσω, to share in happiness, Xen.

συν-ευδοκέω, f. ήσω, to consent to a thing, c. dat., N. T. 2. to sympathise with, τινί Ib.

συν-εύδω, f. -ευδήσω, to sleep with, Hdt., Soph. II. τοῦ ξυνεύδοντος χρόνου in the time coincident with sleep, Aesch.

συνευημερέω, f. ήσω, to enjoy the day or be happy together, Dem.

συν-ευνάζομαι, Pass. to lie with, Pind., Soph.

συν-ευνάομαι, Pass., = συνευνάζω, Hdt., Luc.

συν-ευνέτης, ου, ὁ, a bed-fellow, husband, consort, Eur. :—fem. συνευνέτις, ιδος, a wife or concubine, Id.

σύν-ευνος, ὁ, ἡ, (εὐνή) a consort, Pind., Trag.

συν-ευπάσχω, to derive profit together, Dem.

συν-ευπορέω, f. ήσω, to help to contribute, Dem. 2. c. gen. rei, to assist by contributing towards, Id. 3. to help in contriving, Plut.

συν-ευτυχέω, f. ήσω, to be fortunate together, Eur.

συν-εύχομαι, f. ξομαι, Dep. to pray with or together, Eur.; ταῦτα δὴ ξ. I join in the same prayer, Id.

συν-ευωχέομαι, Pass. to fare sumptuously or feast together, τινί with one, Luc.

συν-εφάπτομαι, Ion. συνεπ-, f. -άψομαι, Dep.: 1. c. gen. rei, to take part in, ἔργου Pind. ; τοὺς συνεφαπτομένους those who take part in [the war], Aeschin. 2. c. gen. pers. to join one in attacking, Hdt.

συν-εφεδρεύω, f. σω, to wait to fight the conqueror, Polyb. :—σ. τινί to watch closely, Id.

συν-εφέλκω, aor. 1 -είλκυσα (cf. ἕλκω) :—to draw after or along with one together, Plat.

συν-εφέπομαι, aor. 2 -εφεσπόμην, Ion. -επεσπόμην, Dep. :— to follow together, Hdt. ; τινι with one, Xen.

συν-έφηβος, ὁ, at the age of youth together, a young comrade, Aeschin.

συν-εφίστημι, f. -επιστήσω: aor. 1 -επέστησα :—to set on the watch together, make attentive, Polyb. :—then (sub. τὸν νοῦν), to attend to, observe along with, Id. II. Pass. συνεφίστᾰμαι, with aor. 2 act. to stand over, superintend along with or together, Thuc. 2. to rise up together, κατά τινος against one, N. T.

συνέχεια, ἡ, (συνεχής) continuity, Arist. 2. connexion or sequence of words or arguments, Luc. II. continued attention, perseverance, Dem.

συνέχεα, Ep. for -έχεα, aor. 1 of συγχέω.

συνεχής, ές, (συνέχω) holding together : I. of space, continuous, contiguous, Thuc., Plat. :—c. dat. continuous with or contiguous to, in a line with, Hdt., Eur. II. of Time, continuous, unintermitting, Xen. ; τὸ ξυνεχές = συνέχεια, Thuc. III. of persons, constant, persevering, Xen. B. Adv. συνεχῶς, Ion. -έως : 1. of Time, continually, Hes.; Sup. -έστατα Xen. 2. with Numbers, continuously, Ar., Thuc. II. in Ep. συνεχές as Adv., Il.; συνεχὲς αἰεί unceasing ever, Od. [σῠνεχές Hom., and σῠνεχέως Hes., the first syll. being lengthd.]

συν-εχθαίρω, f. ἀρῶ, to join in hating, Anth.

συνέχθω, poët. for συνεχθαίρω, Soph.

συν-έχω, f. ξω: aor. 2 συνέσχον :—fut. med. in pass. sense, Dem. :—to hold or keep together, Il. : to enclose, encompass, embrace, Hes., Plat. 2. to keep together, keep from dispersing, of soldiers, Xen., Dem. : —then, σ. πόλιν to keep the state together, keep it from falling to pieces, Eur. ; καὶ θεοὺς καὶ ἀνθρώπους ἡ κοινωνία ξ. Plat. ; σ. τὴν πολιτείαν Dem. ; so, ξ. τὴν εἰρεσίαν to keep the rowers together, make them pull in time, Thuc. 3. to constrain or force one to a thing, N. T. 4. to compress, oppress, Ib. : Pass. to be constrained, oppressed, afflicted, Hdt., Att. II. intr. to meet, εἰς ἓν Arist.

συν-ηβολέω, (βᾰλεῖν, with η inserted) to fall in with, c. dat., Babr.

σύν-ηβος, ὁ, ἡ, (ἥβη) a young friend, Eur.

συνηγορέω, f. ήσω, (συνήγορος) to be an advocate, σ. τινί to be his advocate, plead his cause, Ar., Aeschin. ; also σ. ὑπέρ τινος Dem. ; περί τινος Arist. II. σ. τῷ κατηγόρῳ to second the accuser, Soph. Hence συνηγορία, ἡ, advocacy of another's cause, a speech in his behalf, Aeschin. ; and συνηγορικός, ή, όν, of or for a συνήγορος :—τὸ συνηγορικόν the advocate's fee, being a drachma per diem paid to the public συνήγοροι, Ar.

συν-ήγορος, ον, (ἀγορά) speaking with, of the same tenor with, Soph. II. as Subst. one who speaks with another, an advocate, Aesch. :—at Athens the συνήγοροι were of two kinds, 1. public advocates, ten being appointed annually to represent the state, Ar., Dem., etc. 2. private advocates, counsel, who were not allowed to take a fee, Dem.

συν-ηδέᾱτε, Ion. for -ᾔδειτε, 2 pl. plqpf. of σύνοιδα.

συν-ήδομαι, f. -ησθήσομαι : aor. 1 -ήσθην : Dep. :—to rejoice together, Plat., Xen., etc. :—σ. τινι to rejoice with, sympathise with, Hdt., Att. 2. c. dat. rei,

to rejoice at a thing, *be pleased, gratified*, Arist. ; ἐπί τινι Xen.　3. c. dat. pers. et rei, Soph.

συν-ηδύνω, f. ὑνῶ, *to make pleasant to the taste* :— generally, *to help in cheering*, Arist.

συνήθεια, ἡ, (συνήθης) *habitual intercourse, acquaintance, society, intimacy*, Lat. *consuetudo*, Aeschin., etc.　II. *habit, custom, habituation*, h. Hom., Plat.: c. gen., ἔργου *habituation* to a thing, Dem.　2. *the customary use* of a phrase, Aeschin.

συν-ήθης, ες, gen. εος, contr. ους, (ἦθος) *dwelling* or *living together, accustomed* or *used to each other*, Hes. : *like each other in habits*, Thuc., Plat. :—σ. τινί *intimate with* one, Plat.　II. *habituated, accustomed*, τινί *to* a thing, Id.　2. of things, *habitual, customary, usual, ordinary*, Soph., Thuc. ; τὸ ξύνηθες ἥσυχον your *habitual* quietness, Thuc. ; τὸ σύνηθες *custom*, Xen.　III. Adv. -θως, *habitually, as is usual*, Aeschin.

συνήθροισμαι, pf. pass. of συναθροίζω.

συνῆκα, aor. 1 of συνίημι.

συν-ήκω, f. ξω, *to have come together, to be assembled, to meet*, Thuc.　II. σ. εἰς ἕν *to meet* in a point, Xen.

συνῆλθον, aor. 2 of συνέρχομαι.

συν-ῆλιξ, ικος, ὁ, ἡ, *of like* or *equal age*, Lat. *aequalis, a playmate, comrade*, Aesch., Anth.

συν-ηλυσίη and -ήλυσις, εως, ἡ, (ἤλυθον, aor. 2 of ἔρχομαι) *a meeting, assembly*, Anth.

συνημερευτής, οῦ, ὁ, *a daily companion*, Arist. From

συν-ημερεύω, f. σω, *to pass the day together* or *with*, τινί Xen., etc.

συνημοσύνη, ἡ, used in pl., like συνθῆκαι, *agreements, covenants, solemn promises*, Il. From

συνήμων, ον, (συνίημι) *united*.

συνήορος, Dor. and Att. συνάορος, ον, (συναείρω) *linked with, accompanying*, c. dat., Od., Pind.　2. absol. *joined in wedlock*, and as Subst. *a consort*, Eur.

συν-ηρετέω, f. ήσω, (ἐρέτης) *to assist in rowing* : generally, *to assist, befriend*, τινί Soph.

συν-ηρεφής, ές, (ἐρέφω) *thickly covered*, Hdt., Plut. :— metaph., ξυνηρεφὲς πρόσωπον her *clouded* face, Eur.

συνήρμοσμαι, pf. pass. of συναρμόζω.

συνήρπασα, -άσθην, aor. 1 act. and pass. of συναρπάζω.

συν-ησσάομαι, Att. -ττάομαι, Pass. *to be conquered together*, Xen.

συν-ηχέω, f. ήσω, *to sound together* or *in unison*, Plut.　II. *to ring with, echo to*, c. dat., Theophr.

συνήχθην, aor. 1 pass. of συνάγω.

συνῆψα, aor. 1 of συνάπτω.

συνθᾱκέω, f. ήσω, *to sit with*, σ. νυκτί *to take counsel with* the night, Eur.　From

σύν-θᾱκος, ον, *sitting with* or *together* with, Ζηνὶ σύνθακος θρόνων *partner* with Zeus of his throne, Soph. :— generally, *a partner*, Eur.

συν-θάλπω, f. ψω, *to warm together* : — metaph. *to warm* or *soothe by flattery besides*, Aesch.

συν-θάπτω, f. ψω, *to bury together, join in burying*, Aesch., Trag., Plat., etc. ; τινά τινι one *with* another, Eur. :—Pass. *to be buried with*, τινί Hdt., Thuc., etc.

συν-θεάομαι, Dep. : *to view together*, of spectators at games, Plat., Xen.　2. *to examine together*, Xen.

συν-θεᾱτής, οῦ, ὁ, *a fellow-spectator*, Plat.

συνθέμενος, aor. 2 med. part. of συντίθημι.

σύνθεο, Ep. for -θοῦ, aor. 2 med. imper. of συντίθημι.

συν-θερίζω, *to reap together*, Ar.

συνθεσία, ἡ, (συντίθημι) mostly in pl., like συνθῆκαι, *a covenant, treaty*, Il. ; Ep. gen. pl. συνθεσιάων Ib.

σύνθεσις, ἡ, (συντίθημι) *a putting together, composition, combination*, Plat. ; γραμμάτων συνθέσεις, i. e. syllables and words, Aesch. :—also, of an author's *composition*, Isocr.　II. metaph., like συνθεσία, *an agreement, treaty*, Pind., Plut.　III. Lat. *synthesis* was *a suit of clothes*, Mart. ; esp. *a loose gown*, worn at dinner-parties, Id.

συνθετέον, verb. Adj. *one must compound*, Plat.

συνθετικός, ή, όν, (συντίθημι) *skilled in putting together, constructive*, Plat., Luc.

σύν-θετος, ον, *put together, composite, compound*, Plat., Xen. : *complex*, Arist.　II. *put together, fictitious*, Aesch.　III. metaph. *agreed upon*, ἐκ συνθέτου *by agreement*, Lat. *ex composito*, Hdt.

συν-θέω, f. -θεύσομαι, *to run together with* : metaph., οὐχ ἡμῖν συνθεύσεται ἥδε γε βουλή this counsel *will* not *run smoothly, will* not *succeed*, for us, Od.　II. *to run together, meet in one point*, Xen.

συν-θεωρέω, f. ήσω, *to act* as θεωρός or *go to a festival together*, Lys. ; τινί *with* one, Ar.

συνθήκη, ἡ, (συντίθημι) *a composition*, of words and sentences, Luc.　II. *a conventional agreement, convention, compact*, Plat., Arist. ; ἐκ συνθήκης, *ex composito, by agreement*, Plat., Arist.　2. *the article of a compact* or *treaty*, Thuc. :—mostly in pl. *the articles of agreement*, and collectively, *a contract, compact, covenant, treaty*, Hdt., Att. ; συνθήκας ποιέεσθαί τινι Hdt., Ar. ; ἐκ τῶν συνθηκῶν *according to the covenant*, Isocr. ; κατὰ τὰς σ. Thuc.

σύνθημα, ατος, τό, (συντίθημι) *anything agreed upon, a preconcerted signal*, Hdt., Thuc. ; so, δέλτον ἐγγεγραμμένην ξυνθήματα *having symbols inscribed upon it*, Soph.　2. *a watchword*, Hdt., Thuc., etc. ; σ. παρέρχεται *the word* is passed round, Xen. ; σ. παραδιδόναι, παραγγέλλειν *to pass it*, Id.　3. *any token* or *sign*, Soph.　4. = συνθῆκαι, *an agreement, covenant*, Plat. ; σ. ποιεῖσθαι Xen. ; ἀπὸ συνθήματος *by agreement*, Lat. *ex composito*, Hdt., Thuc. ; so, ἐκ σ. Hdt.

συνθηρᾱτής, οῦ, ὁ, *one who joins in quest of*, τινός Xen. From

συν-θηράω, f. άσω [ᾱ], *to hunt together, join in the chase*, τινί *with* one, Id.　2. *to catch* or *find together*, in Med., Soph. :—Pass., χεῖρες συνθηρώμεναι hands *caught and bound together*, Id.

συνθηρευτής, οῦ, ὁ, = συνθηρατής, Xen. From

συν-θηρεύω, f. σω, = συν-θηράω, Plat.

σύν-θηρος, ον, (θήρα) *hunting with*, τινί Xen. : absol. *hunting in company*, Anth.　2. c. gen. *joining in quest of*, Xen.

συν-θιᾱσώτης, ου, ὁ, *a partner in the* θίασος : generally, *a fellow, comrade*, Ar.

συν-θλάω, f. άσω [ᾰ], *to crush together* :—Pass. *to be broken in pieces*, N. T.

συν-θλίβω [ῑ], f. ψω, *to press together, compress*, Arist.

συν-θνήσκω, f. -θανοῦμαι, *to die with* or *together*, Aesch., Soph., etc. ; c. dat., θανόντι συνθανεῖν Soph. :—of things, συνθνήσκουσα σποδός embers *expiring with* (the

flames), Aesch.; ἡ γὰρ εὐσέβεια σ. βροτοῖς accompanies them even in death, Soph.

συν-θοινάτωρ [ᾰ], ορος, ὁ, a partaker in a feast, Eur.

συν-θραύομαι, Pass. to be broken in pieces, shivered, Eur. (Deriv. uncertain.)

συν-θραύω, f. ώσω, to break in pieces, shiver, Eur.

σύν-θρηνος, ον, mourning with, τινι Anth.: a partner in mourning, Arist.

συν-θριαμβεύω, f. σω, to share in a triumph, Plut.

σύν-θρονος, ον, enthroned with, τινι Anth.

σύν-θροος, ον, sounding together with, accompanying, c. dat., Anth.

συν-θρύπτω, f. ψω, to break in pieces: to crush, N. T.

συν-θύω, f. -θύσω, to offer sacrifice together, join in sacrifice, Aeschin.; τινί with one, Eur.

συνϊδεῖν, aor. 2 inf. of συνοράω.

συνιεῖ, 3 sing. of συνίημι (as if from συνιέω).

συνιέμεν, Ep. for συνεῖναι, inf. of συνίημι.

συν-ιερεύς, έως, ὁ, a fellow-priest, Plut.

συν-ιζάνω, only in pres. and impf. to sink in, collapse, Theocr., Plut.　2. to sink, of the wind, Luc.

συνίζησις, ἡ, a settlement, collapse, Plut.

συν-ίζω, f.-ιζήσω, to sit together, to hold a sitting, Hdt.

συν-ίημι, Att. ξυν-, 2 pers. -ίης; 3 sing. and pl. -ιεῖ, -ιοῦσι; imperat. ξυνίει; 3 sing. subj.-ίῃ; inf. -ιέναι, Ep. -ιέμεν; part. -ιείς:—impf. συνίην or -ιειν; 3 pl. ξυνίεσαν, Ep. ξυνίεν:—f. συνήσω:—aor. 1 συνῆκα, Ep. ξυνέηκα: aor. 2 imper. συνές, part. συνείς:—Med., 3 sing. aor. 2 ξύνετο, 1 pl. subj. συνώμεθα.　I. to bring or set together, in hostile sense, like Lat. committere, ἔριδι ξυνέηκε μάχεσθαι Il.　2. Med. to come together, come to an agreement, Ib.　II. metaph. to perceive, hear, c. acc. rei, Hom., etc.; c. gen. pers., Il.; rarely c. gen. rei, Ib.　2. to understand, ξ. ἀλλήλων to understand one another's language, Hdt.; mostly c. acc. rei, Id., Att.:—absol., τοῖς ξυνιεῖσι to the intelligent, Theogn.

συν-ικνέομαι, f. -ίξομαι: aor. 2 -ῖκόμην:—to pertain to, interest, Arist.

συνιμέν, Ep. for συνιέναι, inf. of σύνειμι (εἶμι ibo).

συνιοῦσι, 3 pl. of συνίημι (as if from συνιέω).

συν-ίππαρχος, ὁ, a joint commander of horse, Hdt.

συν-ιππεύς, έως, ὁ, a comrade in cavalry service, Dem.

σύνϊσαν, Ep. 3 pl. impf. of σύνειμι (εἶμι ibo) went together.　II. Ep. 3 pl. plqpf. of σύνοιδα, shared in the knowledge.

συν-ιστάω, = συν-ίστημι III, N. T.

συν-ίστημι, impf. -ίστην: f. συστήσω: aor. 1 συνέστησα:—to set together, combine, associate, unite, band together, Hdt., Thuc.; μαντικὴν ἑαυτῷ συστῆσαι to bring prophetic art into union with himself, i. e. to win, acquire it, Hdt.　II. to put together, organise, frame, Thuc., Dem.:—to contrive, σ. θάνατον ἐπί τινι Hdt.; σ. τιμάς to settle prices, Dem.; so in aor. 1 med., Isocr.　III. to bring together as friends, introduce or recommend one to another, τινά τινι Plat., etc.: Pass., συνεστάθη Κύρῳ Xen.　2. of a debtor, to offer another as a guarantee, τινά τινι Isocr.　B. Pass., with aor. 2 act. συνέστην: pf. συνέστηκα, part. συνεστηκώς, contr. συνεστώς, ῶσα, ώς or ός, Ion. συνεστεώς, εῶσα, εώς: also f. med. συστήσομαι:—to stand together, Hdt., Xen.; of soldiers, to form in

order of battle, Xen.　II. in hostile sense, πολέμοιο συνεσταότος when battle is joined, Il.:—so, of persons, συνίστασθαί τινι to meet him in fight, be engaged with, Hdt., Att.:—absol., συνεστηκότων τῶν στρατηγῶν when the generals were at issue, Hdt.　2. to be involved in a thing, λίμῷ καὶ καμάτῳ Id.; συνεστῶτες ἀγῶνι Thuc.　III. to form a league or union, Id.; τὸ ξυνιστάμενον the conspirators, Ar.; so, οἱ ξυνεστῶτες, τὸ συνεστηκός Thuc., Aeschin.　2. generally, to be connected or allied, as by marriage, c. acc. cogn., λέχος Ἡρακλεῖ ξυστᾶσα Soph.　IV. to be put together, organised, framed, Xen.　2. to arise, become, take place, Dem.　3. to hold together, endure, continue, Hdt.: in military sense, ξυνεστὼς στρατός a well-disciplined army, Eur.; στράτευμα συνεστηκός a standing army, Dem.　V. to be compact, solid, firm, Xen.　VI. to be contracted, ξυνεστὸς φρενῶν = σύστασις B. II. 2, Eur.

συν-ίστωρ, ορος, ὁ, ἡ, knowing along with another, conscious, ὡς θεοὶ ξυνίστορες as the gods are witnesses, Soph., etc.　2. c. acc. (with the verbal constr.), πολλὰ συνίστορα κακά conscious of many evils, Aesch.

συνισχαίνω, f. ἀνῶ, to help to dry up:—metaph. to join with in reducing, Eur.

συν-ισχυρίζω, f. ίσω, to help to strengthen, Xen.

συν-ίσχω, = συνέχω:—Pass. to be afflicted, Plat.

συν-ναίω, to dwell with others, c. dat., Aesch., Soph.

συν-νάσσω, f. ξω, to pack tight together, Hdt.

συν-ναυβάτης [ᾰ], ου, ὁ, a shipmate, Soph.

συν-ναυμαχέω, f. ήσω, to engage in a sea-fight along with others, c. dat., Hdt., Ar.

συν-ναύτης, ου, ὁ, a shipmate, Soph., Eur.

συν-νέμω, f. -νεμῶ, to tend together, of the shepherd: generally, to make one's associate, Plut.

συννενέαται, Ion. 3 pl. pf. pass. of συννέω.

συν-νεύω, f. σω, to incline to a point, converge, Plut.　II. to consent, agree, Soph.

σύν-νεφος, ον, (νεφέλη) cloudy, overcast, Thuc.

συν-νεφέω, pf. -νένοφα, to collect clouds, Ar.:—impers. συννεφεῖ it is cloudy (cf. ὕει), Arist.　II. metaph. of persons, συννεφοῦσα ὄμματα wearing a clouded look, Eur. From

συν-νεφής, ές, (νέφος) clouded over, cloudy:—of persons, gloomy, Eur.

συν-νέω, f. -νήσω, to pile or heap together, heap up, Hdt.:—Pass., pf. part. ξυννενημένος Thuc.; Ion. 3 pl. pf. pass. συννενέαται Hdt.

συν-νέω, f. -νεύσομαι, to swim together or with, Luc.

συν-νήχομαι, f. -ξομαι, Dep. to swim with, τινι Luc.

συν-νικάω, to have part in a victory with, τινί Eur.

συν-νοέω, f. ήσω, to meditate or reflect upon a thing, Soph.:—so in Med., Eur.　II. to perceive by thinking, comprehend, understand, Plat., etc.:—so in Med., Ar.　Hence

σύννοια, Ion. -ίη, ἡ, meditation, deep thought, Soph., etc.; συννοίῃ ἐχόμενος wrapt in thought, Hdt.　2. anxious thought, anxiety, Aesch., Eur.; συννοίᾳ οἷον δέδρακε by remorse for the deed, Eur.

σύν-νομος, ον, (νέμομαι) feeding together, gregarious, Ar., etc.: metaph. ἄταισι σύννομοι associated with miseries, Aesch.　2. σ. τινί τινος partner with one in a thing, λέκτρων ξύννομε partner of the bed, Id.:

metaph., θαλάσσης σύννομοι πέτραι, of the Symplegades which *lie between* two seas, Eur.　3. absol. as Subst., σύννομος, ὁ, ἡ, *a partner, mate,* of soldiers, Aesch., Soph.; of a wife, Soph.

σύν-νοος, ον, Att. contr. **-νους, ουν,** *in deep thought, thoughtful,* Isocr.　2. *thoughtful, circumspect,* Arist.

συν-νοσέω, f. ήσω, *to be sick* or *ill together,* Eur.; τινί *with* one, Id.

συν-νυμφοκόμος, ον, *helping to deck a bride,* Eur.

συν-οδεύω, f. σω, *to travel in company,* Plut.

συνοδία, ἡ, *a journey in company,* Cic.　II. *a party of travellers, caravan,* Strab., N. T.

συν-οδίτης [ῑ], ου, ὁ, *the member of a σύνοδος,* Anth.

συν-οδοιπορέω, f. ήσω, *to travel together,* τινί *with* one, Luc.; and

συνοδοιπορία, ἡ, *a travelling together,* Babr. From

συν-οδοίπορος, ὁ, *a fellow-traveller,* Xen., Luc.

σύν-οδος, ὁ, ἡ, = συνοδοιπόρος, Anth.

σύν-οδος, ἡ, *an assembly, meeting,* Hdt., Att.; ξύνοδοι *political unions,* Ar., Thuc.　2. *a national meeting,* like πανήγυρις, Thuc., Arist.　3. in hostile sense, *a meeting* of two armies, Ar., Thuc., etc.　II. of things, *a coming together, in-coming,* χρημάτων σύνοδοι Hdt.: *a meeting, junction,* κυάνεαι σύνοδοι θαλάσσης, of the *straits* of the Hellespont, Eur.; ἡ ξ. τοῦ πλησίον ἀλλήλων τεθῆναι the *junction* resulting from approximation, Plat.

σύν-οιδα, pf. with pres. sense (there being no pres. συνείδω), 1 pl. ξύνισμεν, 3 pl. -ίσασι; imper. ξύνισθι: inf. -ειδέναι:—plqpf. with impf. sense, συνῄδειν, Att. -ῄδη, dual -ῄστην, pl. -ῆσμεν, -ῆστε, -ῆσαν, Ion. 2 pl. -ῄδεᾰτε: f. συνείσομαι, rarely συνειδήσω:—*to share in knowledge,* be *cognisant* of a thing, *be privy* to it, Lat. *conscius esse,* Hdt., Att.　2. ἑαυτῷ συνειδέναι τι *to be conscious* of a thing, Ar., Plat., etc.:—with part., which may be　**a.** in nom., ξ. ἐμαυτῷ σοφὸς ὤν Plat.; without the reflex. Pron. *to be conscious that,* ξυνισθά γ' εἰς ἔμ' οὐκ εὔορκος ὤν Eur.　**b.** in dat., ξ. ἐμαυτῷ οὐδὲν ἐπισταμένῳ *I am conscious that* I know nothing, Plat.　**c.** in acc., ξύνοιδ' Ὀρέστην ἐκπαγλουμένην *I know well that* thou *admirest* him, Aesch.　3. absol. ξυνειδώς, *an accomplice,* ξ. τις Thuc.; also, ὁ ξ. τινι Id.　**b.** neut. τὸ συνειδός = συνείδησις, *joint knowledge, consciousness,* Dem.

συν-οικειόω, f. ώσω, *to bind together as friends* or *kinsmen, to associate* or *combine with,* τινά τινι Plut., etc.: Pass. *to be closely united,* Arist.

συν-οικέω, f. ήσω, *to dwell together,* Plat., etc.; σ. τινι *to live with,* Aesch., etc.　2. *to live together* in wedlock, *cohabit,* Hdt., Eur., etc.; τούτων συνοικησάντων γίνεται Κλεισθένης from their *marriage* sprang Cleisthenes, Hdt.　3. metaph., ἄχθος ᾧ ξυνοικεῖ the grief with which *he is associated,* Soph.; so, σ. φόβῳ Eur.; ἡδοναῖς, ἀμαθίᾳ Plat.; ἱππικοῖς ἐν ἤθεσι ξ. *being versed* in the ways of horses, Eur.　**b.** reversely, with the thing as subject, γῆρας ἵνα πάντα κακὰ κακῶν ξυνοικεῖ old age with which all evils *are associated,* Soph.; of the poisoned robe of Hercules, *to cling closely,* Id.　II. c. acc. loci, *to colonise jointly with,* Κυρηναίοισι σ. Λιβύην Hdt.:—Pass., of a country, *to be thickly peopled,* Xen. Hence

συνοίκημα, ατος, τό, *that with which one lives, a housefellow,* Hdt.; and

συνοίκησις, ἡ, *cohabitation,* πωλέεσθαι ἐπὶ συνοικήσι (Ion. for -ήσει), Hdt.; and

συνοικήτωρ, ορος, ὁ, *a house-fellow,* Aesch.

συνοικία, ἡ, = συνοίκησις, Παλλάδος δέξομαι ξυνοικίαν will accept the offer of *living with her,* Aesch.　II. *a body of people living together, a settlement, community,* Plat.　III. *a house in which several families live, a house divided into flats,* Lat. *insula,* opp. to οἰκία (a dwelling occupied by one family), Thuc., Xen., etc.　2. *a back-room, outhouse,* Ar.

συν-οικίζω, f. Att. ιῶ: pf. -ῴκικα:—*to make to live with,* Isocr.; σ. τινί τὴν θυγατέρα *to give* him one's daughter *in marriage,* Hdt.　II. *to combine in one city, unite under a capital* or *metropolis,* ξ. πάντας (sc. ἐς τὰς Ἀθήνας) Thuc.:—Pass., ξυνοικισθείσης πόλεως the city having *been regularly formed,* opp. to κατὰ κώμας οἰκίζεσθαι, Id.　III. *to join in peopling* or *colonising* a country, Eur., Thuc.　IV. generally *to unite, associate,* Plat.

συνοίκιον, τό, (σύνοικος) *a joint lodging:* pl. συνοίκια (sc. ἱερά), τά, *a public feast in memory of Theseus' uniting all Attica under* Athens, celebrated on the 17th Boëdromion, Thuc.

συνοίκισις, ἡ, *union with the capital,* Thuc.; and

συνοικισμός, ὁ, *a living together, marriage,* Plut.　II. = συνοίκισις, Id.; and

συνοικιστήρ, ῆρος, ὁ, *a fellow-colonist,* Pind.

συν-οικοδομέω, f. ήσω, *to build together,* Plut.:—metaph. in Pass. *to be edified together,* of believers, N. T.　2. Pass. *to be built in with other materials,* λίθοι ξυνῳκοδομημένοι Thuc.

σύν-οικος, ον, *dwelling in the same house with* others, c. dat., Aesch.; ξ. εἰσιέναι to enter the house *as an inmate,* Soph.:—of persons *living in the same country, a fellow-inhabitant, denizen,* Hdt., Thuc., etc.　2. metaph. *associated with, wedded to, used to,* of persons, ξ. ἀλλαγᾷ βίου Soph.; κακῷ Plat.:—of things, *associated with,* σκότῳ λιμὸς ξύνοικος Aesch., etc.

συν-οικουρός, όν, *living at home together:* c. gen., σ. κακῶν *a partner* in mischief, Eur.

συν-οικτίζω, f. σω, *to have compassion on,* τινά Xen.

συν-οίομαι, aor. 1 -ῴθην, Dep. *to hold the same opinion with* others, *to assent,* Plat.

συνοίσω, fut. of συμφέρω.

συν-ολισθαίνω or **-άνω,** f. -ολισθήσω, *to slip and fall together,* Plut., etc.

συν-όλλυμι, *to destroy together,* Bion:—Med., aor. 2 -ωλόμην, *to perish along with,* τινι Eur.

συν-ολολύζω, f. ξω, *to raise a loud cry together,* Xen.

σύνολος, ον, and **η, ον,** *all together,* Plat., etc.　II. τὸ σύνολον, as Adv. *on the whole, in general, altogether,* Id., etc.:—reg. Adv. συνόλως, Isocr.

συν-οτμαίμων, ὁ, ἡ, *one of the same blood, a brother* or *sister,* Aesch., Eur.

συν-ομαλύνω, f. ῠνῶ, *to make quite level,* Plut.

συν-ομαρτέω, f. ήσω, *to follow along with, attend on,* τινί Solon; absol., Eur.

συν-ομήθης, ες, = συνήθης, Anth.

συν-ομῆλιξ, Dor. **-ᾶλιξ, ικος, ὁ, ἡ,** *a comrade,* Theocr.

συν-ομῑλέω, f. ήσω, to converse with, τινί N.T.

συν-όμνῡμι or -ύω, f. -ομόσω, to swear together, Xen., Plut. 2. to promise by oath, τί τινι Soph. ; ξυνώμοσαν θάνατον πατρί joined in swearing death against him, Aesch. II. to join in a league or confederacy, Id., Thuc. 2. to form a confederacy with others, c. dat., Thuc. : in bad sense, to conspire, Hdt., Ar., etc.

συν-ομοιοπαθέω, f. ήσω, to be similarly affected with, τινί Arist.

συν-ομολογέω, f. ήσω, to say the same thing with, to agree with, τινί Hdt., Xen., etc. :—to confess together, confess, concede, αὐτὰ ταῦτα Thuc. :—of disputants, to agree upon certain points, c. acc., Xen., Plat. ;—so in Med., Plat. : — Pass., τὰ ἄλλα συνωμόλογηται Xen., etc. II. to agree to do, promise, τί τινι Id. III. to come to terms with, make a covenant with, Id.

συν-ομορέω, f. ήσω, to abut upon a place, c. dat., N.T.

συν-ομώνῠμος, ον, having the same name with, c. gen., Anth.

συν-οπᾱδός, ὁ, a companion, Plat.

σύν-οπλος, ον, (ὅπλον) under arms together, allied, Eur.

συν-οπτικός, ή, όν, (ὄψομαι) seeing the whole together, taking a comprehensive view, Plat. ; and

σύν-οπτος, ον, (ὄψομαι) that can be seen at a glance, in full view, Arist. From

συν-οράω, f. -όψομαι : aor. 2 -εῖδον, inf. -ιδεῖν : cf. σύνοιδα :—to see together or at the same time, Xen. II. to see in one view, see at a glance, whether with the eyes or mind, Plat., Dem. :—in speaking, to take a general view, Isocr., etc.

συν-οργίζομαι, aor. 1 -ωργίσθην : Dep. :—to be angry together with, τινί Isocr., Dem., etc.

συνορέω, f. ήσω, (σύνορος) to be conterminous, Polyb.

σύν-ορθρος, ον, dawning along with, σύνορθρον αὐγαῖς dawning with the first beams of day, Aesch.

συν-ορίνω [ῐ], only in pres., to rouse or stir up together, Il. :—Pass., συνορινόμεναι φάλαγγες the lines with one impulse, Ib.

σύν-ορκος, ον, bound together by oath, Xen.

συν-ορμίζω, f. ίσω, to bring to anchor together, Xen.

συν-όρνυμαι, Pass.=συνορίνομαι, to start or set forth together, (in poët. aor. 2 part. συνόρμενος), Aesch.

σύν-ορος, Ion. -ουρος, ον, conterminous with, τῇ Ἀττίκῃ or τῆς Ἀττικῆς Plut.: metaph., κόνις πηλοῦ κάσις ξύνουρος dust twin-sister of mud, Aesch.

σύν-ουρος, Ion. for σύν-ορος.

συνουσία, Ion. -ίη, ἡ, (συνών, συνοῦσα, part. of σύνειμι) a being with, social intercourse, society, conversation, communion, Hdt., Att. ; ἡ τοῦ θείου σ. communion with the divinity, Plat. ; so, τῆς νόσου ξυνουσίᾳ by long intercourse with the disease, Soph. ; ἡ πρὸς Σωκράτην σ. αὐτοῖν their intercourse with him, Xen. ; in pl., ξυνουσίαι θηρῶν, = οἱ ξυνόντες θῆρες, Soph. 2. intercourse with a teacher, attendance on his lectures, Xen. 3. cohabitation, Plat., Xen. II. a society, company, party, Hdt., Plat., etc. Hence

συνουσιαστής, οῦ, ὁ, a companion, disciple, Xen.

συνουσιαστικός, ή, όν, suited for society, sociable, Ar.

συν-οφρυόομαι, f. -οφρύομαι, (ὀφρύς) Pass. to have the brow knitted, ξυνωφρυμένη with knitted brow,

Soph. ; ξυνωφρυωμένῳ προσώπῳ with frowning countenance, Eur.

σύν-οφρυς, υ, gen. υος, with meeting eyebrows, Theocr.

συν-οχέομαι, Pass. to travel together in a chariot, Plut.

συνοχή, Att. ξυν-, ἡ, (συνέχομαι) a being held together, ἐν ξυνοχῇσιν ὁδοῦ at a narrow part of the road, Il. II. constraint, affliction, anguish, N.T.

συνοχηδόν, Adv. (συνέχω) holding together, Anth.

σύνοχος, ον, (συνέχω) joined together : metaph. agreeing with, suiting, Eur.

συνόχωκα, Ep. intr. pf. of συνέχω (for συνόκωχα), to be held together, ὤμω ἐπὶ στῆθος συνοχωκότε shoulders contracted upon the chest, Il.

σύν-οψις, εως, ἡ, a general view, Plat.

συνόψομαι, fut. of συνοράω.

σύνταγμα, τό, that which is put together in order : 1. a body of troops, squadron, contingent, Xen. 2. the constitution of a state, σ. πολιτείας a form of constitution, Isocr. 3. an arrangement of musical notes, Arist. 4. a regular collection of writings, a work, book, doctrine, Plut. 5. = σύνταξις II. 3, Aeschin.

συνταγμάτ-άρχης, ου, ὁ, the leader of a σύνταγμα (1), Luc.

συντᾰκείς, aor. 2 pass. part. of συντήκω.

συν-τᾰλαιπωρέω, f. ήσω, to endure hardships together, share in misery, Soph.

συντάμνω, Ion. for συντέμνω.

συντανύω, f. ύσω [ῠ], =συντείνω, to stretch together, πολλῶν πείρατα συντανύσαις (Dor. for -ύσας) bringing together the issues of many events, Pind.

σύνταξις, εως, ἡ, (συντάσσω) a putting together, arranging, arrangement, organisation, order, Thuc., Xen. : rule, Dem. 2. a systematic treatise, Arist. : a narrative, Polyb. 3. grammatical construction, syntax, Luc. II. a body of troops, ἡ εἰς μυρίους σ. their contingent towards 10,000, Xen. 2. a covenant, contract, Dem. 3. an assigned impost, contribution, Id., Aeschin. 4. a payment, allowance, pension, Dem.

συν-τᾰράσσω, Att. -ττω, f. ξω, to throw all together into confusion, to confound, disturb, trouble, Lat. conturbare, Il., Hdt., Att. :—Pass., αἰθὴρ πόντῳ ξυντετάρακται air is confounded with sea, Aesch. : to be thrown into confusion, of soldiers, Thuc. ; of social order, Soph., Thuc. ; metaph. of persons, to be confounded, greatly troubled, much distressed, Hdt.

συν-τάσσω, Att. -ττω, f. ξω, to put in order together, esp. of soldiers, to draw up, put in array, Hdt., Thuc., etc. ; σ. πεζοὺς τῷ ἱππικῷ to draw up the foot in line with the horse, Xen. :—Pass., συντεταγμένοι παντὸς τοῦ στρατοῦ in the best order of all the army, Thuc. : —so in Med. to form in line, συνταξάμενοι τισι or μετά τινων with others, Xen. ;—but the Med. is also trans., συνταξάμενος τὴν φάλαγγα having drawn up his phalanx, Id. 2. in Pass., of single persons, to be collected, resolute, steady, Thuc., Xen. II. to arrange, organise, Plat. :—in bad sense, to concoct, Aeschin. :—Pass. to be organised, Arist. ; οἱ συντεταγμένοι the conspirators, Xen. 2. of taxation, to fix or assess a payment, Aeschin. :—Pass. to be organised

for paying contributions, Dem. :—Med. *to agree to such assessment,* Id.   3. c. inf. *to ordain, prescribe,* τινὰ ποιεῖν τι Xen., Aeschin. ; of a physician, θεράπειαν σ. τινί Plut. :—Pass. *to be prescribed,* ταῦτα τῷ ναυάρχῳ συνετάχθη Dem.   III. Med. *to agree together,* Id.   IV. Med. also, σ. τινι *to take leave of one, bid him farewell,* Anth.

συν-ταχύνω [ῠ], f. ῠνῶ, *to hurry on,* τι Hdt.   II. intr., ὁ βίος συνταχύνει *life hastens to an end,* Id.

συντέθλασμαι, pf. pass. of συνθλάω.

συντέθραμμαι, pf. pass. of συντρέφω.

συν-τείνω, f. -τενῶ, *to stretch together, strain, draw tight, brace up,* Eur., Plat.   2. *to strain to the uttermost, urge on, exert,* Eur. ; γνώμῃ συντεταμένῃ *with earnest* purpose, Xen.   3. intr. in Act. *to exert oneself, strive, hasten,* Lat. *contendere,* Plat., Plut.   II. *to direct earnestly to one* point, Plat.   2. intr. *to direct all one's powers to one* object, *to be bent upon* doing a thing, c. inf., Eur. ; σ. εἴς τι Dem. ; πρός τι Isocr., etc.

συν-τειχίζω, f. Att. ιῶ, *to help to build a wall* or *fortification,* Thuc., Xen.

συν-τεκμαίρομαι, Dep. *to conjecture from signs* or *symptoms, to calculate,* Thuc., Xen.

συν-τεκνοποιέω, *to breed children with,* ἀνδρί Xen.

συν-τελέθω, = συντελέω III, *to belong to,* Pind.

συντέλεια, ἡ, (συντελέω II), *a joint payment, joint contribution for public burdens,* Dem.; εἰς σ. ἄγειν τὰς χορηγίας, i. e. to leave the choregia to be *defrayed by subscription,* Id.   II. at Athens, *a partnership for bearing public burdens,* Decret. ap. Dem.   2. generally, *a company,* of the gods, who separately were called τέλειοι, Aesch.   III. *combination of efforts, the consummation* of a scheme, Polyb.

συν-τελέω, f. έσω, *to bring quite to an end, complete, accomplish,* Dem.; σ. τὴν δαπάνην *to make up the whole* expense, Dem.; σ. εἰς τὰ ἑκατὸν ἅρματα *to make up the number* of 100 chariots, Xen. : — so in Med., Polyb.   II. *to pay towards common expenses, contribute,* Aeschin., Dem.   III. since at Athens all citizens were classed acc. to the *contributions* to which they were liable, σ. εἰς . . meant *to belong to* a class, *be counted in* it, σ. εἰς τοὺς νόθους Dem. :—hence σ. εἰς Ἀθήνας, εἰς τὸ Ἀρκαδικόν, used of a number of small states *tributary* or *subject* to a larger, Thuc.; c. dat., σ. Θηβαίοις Isocr.

συν-τελής, ὁ, ἡ, (τέλος) *joining in payment, a contributor,* Dem.   2. *belonging to the same* συντέλεια (II) or *company,* Id. :—metaph., [οὔτε] Πάρις, οὔτε σ. πόλις *neither Paris nor his associate* city, Aesch.   II. *tributary,* Dem.   Hence

συν-τέμνω, Ion. -τάμνω ; f. -τεμῶ : aor. 2 -έτεμον, inf. -τεμεῖν :—*to cut in pieces : to cut down, cut short,* Lat. *concīdere,* Thuc. : — metaph. *to curtail, abridge,* Aesch., Ar. :—esp. of expenses, Thuc., Xen. : of persons, *to cut off,* Soph.   2. σ. χιτῶνας *to cut out, shape* them, Xen.   II. seemingly intr. (sub. ὁδόν) *to cut the road short, cut across,* Hdt. :—so, of speech, *to cut the matter short, speak briefly,* Eur.   III. really intr., τοῦ χρόνου συντάμνοντος as the time *became short,* Hdt.

συν-τερετίζω, *to whistle an accompaniment,* Theophr.

συν-τερμονέω, f. ήσω, *to border on,* τινί Polyb. From

συν-τέρμων, ον, *bordering on, close together,* Anth.

συν-τεταγμένως, Adv. part. pf. pass. of συντάσσω, in *set terms,* Plat.

συν-τεταμένως, Adv. part. pf. pass. of συντείνω, *earnestly, eagerly, vigorously,* Ar., Plat.

συν-τετραίνω, f. -τρήσω : aor. 2 -έτρησα : pf. pass. -τέτρημαι :—*to bore through so as to meet,* σ. τοὺς μυχοὺς ἀλλήλοις *carrying* their creeks *through so as to meet* one another, Hdt. ; ἕτερον [μέταλλον] συντρῆσαι εἰς τὰ τῶν πλησίον *to run* another gallery into one's neighbour's mines, Dem. :—Pass. *to be carried by a connecting channel* or duct, Plat., Arist.   II. metaph., δι' ὤτων συντέτραινε μῦθον *let* the word *pierce through thy ears,* Aesch.

συν-τέτριμμαι, pf. pass. of συν-τρίβω : συν-τετρίφθαι, inf.

συν-τεχνάζω, f. σω, *to join in plots with,* τινί Plut.

σύν-τεχνος, ὁ, ἡ, (τέχνη) *practising the same art,* c. gen. one's *mate* or *fellow-workman,* Ar.

συν-τήκω, f. ξω, *to fuse into one mass, to weld together,* Lat. *conflare,* Plat.   2. *to melt down, dissolve :* metaph. *to make to waste* or *pine away,* Eur.   II. Pass. συντήκομαι, aor. 1 -ετήχθην, aor. 2 -ετάκην [ᾰ] : and in same sense intr. pf. act. συντέτηκα :—*to be fused into one mass :* metaph., σ. τινι *to become absolutely one with* another, c. dat., Eur., Plat.   2. *to melt away, disappear,* Xen. :— metaph. *to waste* or *fall away,* Eur.

συν-τηρέω, f. ήσω, *to preserve together :* Pass., N. T.   2. *to watch one's opportunity,* Plut.

συν-τίθημι, f. -θήσω, *to put together,* Hdt., Xen., etc. ; σ. ἄρθρα στόματος *to close the lips,* Eur.   2. in Arith. *to add together,* Hdt., Eur., etc. : also συντιθεὶς γέλων *adding* laughter, Soph.   II. *to put together,* of builders, Thuc., Xen.   2. *to construct, frame, build,* Hdt. :—σ. τι ἀπό or ἔκ τινος *compose* or *make* one thing *of* another, Id.   3. *to construct* or *frame* a story, Eur., Ar., etc. :—of an author, *to compose,* Thuc.   4. *to frame, devise, contrive,* ὁ συνθεὶς τάδε *the framer* of this plot, Soph. ; σ. ψευδεῖς αἰτίας Dem.   5. *to put together, take in, comprise,* Eur. ; ἐν βραχεῖ ξυνθεὶς λόγῳ *putting* things *shortly together,* Soph.

B. Med. συντίθεμαι, *to put together for oneself,* i. e. *to observe, take heed to,* σύνθετο βουλήν, ἀοιδήν Hom. ; and, simply, *to perceive, hear,* ὅπα σύνθετο Od. : absol., σύνθεο *take heed,* Hom.   2. *to set in order, organise,* Xen.   II. *to conclude, form,* ἄνδρεσσι κακοῖς συνθέμενοι φιλίην Theogn. ; συντίθεσθαι συμμαχίην Hdt. ; σ. ναῦλον *to agree upon the fare,* Xen. :—Pass., τοῦ συντεθέντος χρόνου *at the time agreed upon,* Plat.   2. c. inf. *to covenant* or *agree to do,* Hdt., Thuc.   3. absol. *to make a covenant,* Hdt., Xen.

συν-τιμάω, f. ήσω, *to honour together* or *alike,* Lys.   II. *to estimate together :*—Med., συνετιμήσαντο ὑπὲρ ἐμοῦ ταύτην τὴν εἰσφορὰν *they fixed this as the estimate of* my contribution, Dem.

συν-τῑνάσσω, f. ξω, *to shake to the foundations,* σὺν δὲ μάχαν ἐτίναξε, i. e. *closed with him,* Theocr.

συν-τιτρώσκω, f. -τρώσω, *to wound in many places,* Xen.

συν-τολμάω, f. ήσω, *to venture together* :—Dor. 2 sing. aor. 2 συν-έτλας, Eur.

συντομία, ή, *conciseness*, Plat., Arist. From

σύντομος, ον, (συντέμνω) Lat. *concisus, cut short, abridged, shortened*, esp. of a road, σ. ἄτραπος *a short cut*, Ar. ; συντομώτατον *the shortest cut*, Hdt. ; τὰ ξυντομώτατα Thuc. ; ἡ σύντομος (sub. ὁδός) Hdt. **2.** of language, *concise, brief, curt, short*, Aesch., Eur., etc. **II.** Adv. -μως, *concisely, shortly, briefly*, Aesch., etc. :—so also neut. pl. σύντομα Soph. : Comp. and Sup. -ώτερον, -ώτατα, Isocr. ; also -ωτάτως, Soph. **2.** of Time, *shortly, immediately*, Id., Xen., etc.

συντονία, ή, *intense application* or *exertion*, Arist.

σύντονος, ον, (συντείνω) *strained tight*, ἔχειν τὸ σ. *to be strained tight*, Xen. **2.** *intense, impetuous, violent*, Soph. **2.** of persons, *earnest, serious, severe, vehement*, Plat., etc. : so of Music, *severe*, Arist. :—Adv. -νῶς, *intensely, eagerly, severely*, Plat. ; so neut. pl., σύντονα Eur. :—Comp. -ώτερον, Arist.

συν-τραγῳδέω, f. ήσω, *to act tragedy together*, Luc.

συν-τράπεζος [ᾰ], ον, (τράπεζα) *a messmate*, Xen. ; βίον σ. ἔχειν *to live with one*, Eur.

σύν-τρεις, οἱ, αἱ, -τρια, τά, *three together, by threes*, Od.

συν-τρέφω, f. -θρέψω, *to feed together* or *besides*, Xen. **II.** Pass. *to grow up together*, Id. ; τινι *with one*, Eur. **2.** of feelings or sentiments, *to grow up with*, Arist., Plut. : *to be organised*, of bodies, Plat. **3.** *to come together, concur, agree*, Hdt., Xen. **4.** *to concur, coincide*, of time, Eur., Dem. ; σ. τινι *to concur* or *coincide with*, Soph. **II.** *to run alongside*, Xen.

συν-τριαινόω, f. ώσω, *to shatter as with a trident*, Eur.

συν-τρίβω [ῑ], f. ψω :—Pass., -τρίβήσομαι : aor. 2 -ετρίβην [ῐ] :—*to rub together*, f. σ. τὰ πυρεία *to rub dry sticks together to procure a light*, Luc. **II.** *to shiver to atoms*, Ar., etc. ; σ. τὰς ναῦς *to stave them in*, by running them aground, Thuc. **2.** of persons, *to beat to a jelly, crush*, Lat. *contundere*, Eur. :—c. gen. partis, συντρίβειν τῆς κεφαλῆς Isocr. ; and in Pass., συντριβῆναι τῆς κεφαλῆς *to have one's head broken*, Ar.

συν-τριήραρχος, ὁ, *a partner in the equipment of a trireme*, Dem. :—συντριηραρχέω, *to be a συντριήραρχος*, Lys.

συντροφία, ή, *a being reared together, common nurture*, Plut. **II.** *a brood*, Anth. From

σύντροφος, ον, (συντρέφω) *brought up together with* another, c. dat., Hdt., Ar. :—often of domestic animals, Hdt., Xen. :—absol., τὸ σ. γένος *the people bred up with* me, Soph. **2.** generally, *living with*, Id. ; σ. ὄμμα *the eye or presence of a companion*, Id. ; σ. ὢν (sc. ἀνάγκαις) *being born to difficulties*, Eur. **3.** of things, *having grown up with one, congenital, natural*, Soph. ; τὰ ξύντροφα *every-day evils*, Thuc. :—σ. τινι *natural* or *habitual to*, τῇ Ἑλλάδι πενίη σύντροφος

Hdt. **II.** act. *a helping in the preservation*, τινος *of* a thing, Xen.

συν-τροχάζω, like συντρέχω, *to run together*, Plut.

συν-τυγχάνω, f. -τεύξομαι : aor. 2 -έτυχον :—*to meet with, fall in with*, τινί Hdt., Soph., etc. : οἱ συντυχόντες, of two persons *meeting*, Hdt. ; but, ὁ συντυχών, like ὁ τυχών, *the first that meets one, any one*, Eur. ; ὁ ἀεὶ ξυντυχών Id. ; so of things, τὸ συντυχόν *what first comes to hand, anything common, mean, bad*, Hdt., Xen. **2.** rarely, like τυγχάνω, c. gen., which is governed by σύν, συντυχὼν κακῶν ἀνδρῶν *having like others met with* evil men, Soph. **II.** of accidents, *to happen to, befall*, τὰ συντυχόντα σφι Hdt. :—absol. *to happen, fall out*, εὖ ξυντυχόντων *if things go well*, Aesch. ; ὁ ξ. κίνδυνος Thuc. :—impers., συνετύγχανε, συνέτυχε *it happened that . . .*, c. inf., Id.

συν-τῠραννοκτονέω, *to join in slaying tyrants*, Luc.

συν-τῠρόω, f. ώσω, *to make into cheese together* : hence, comically, τὰκ Βοιωτῶν συντυρούμενα *the troubles that are being concocted* on the part of the Boeotians, Ar.

συντῠχία, Ion. -ίη, ή, (συντυγχάνω) *an occurrence, a hap, chance, event, incident*, Solon, Hdt., Att. ; ὡς ἑκάστοις τῆς ξυντυχίας ἔσχεν *according to the circumstances of each party*, Thuc. ; κατὰ συντυχίην *by chance*, Hdt. :—in pl. *the chances of life, circumstances*, Thuc. **2.** sometimes *a happy chance, success*, Pind., Hdt. ;—or *a mishap, misfortune*, Eur.

συν-ύπατος, ὁ, *a colleague in the consulship.* Hence

συν-υποδείκνῡμι and -ύω, f. -δείξω, *to indicate together*, τί τινι Polyb.

συν-υποδύομαι, Med. *to undergo together*, Plut.

συν-υποκρίνομαι [ῑ], Dep. *to play a part along with* others : *to help* another *in maintaining* a thing, Plut.

συν-υποτίθεμαι [ῐ], Med. *to help in composing*, Plut.

συν-υπουργέω, f. ήσω, *to coöperate with*, τινί N.T., Luc.

συν-ὑφαίνω, pf. -ύφηνα :—*to weave together* : metaph. *to frame with art, devise cunningly*, Od., Luc. :—Pass., ὥστε ταῦτα συνυφανθῆναι *so that* this *web was woven*, i. e. this business undertaken, Hdt.

συν-ωδίνω [ῑ], *to be in travail together*, Eur.

συν-ῳδός, όν, (ᾠδή) *singing* or *sounding in unison with, responsive*, Eur. **2.** absol. *in harmony, accordant*, Plat. **II.** metaph. *according with, in harmony with*, τινί Hdt., Eur., etc.

συν-ωθέω, f. -ωθήσω and -ώσω, *to force together, compress forcibly*, Xen.

συνώμεθα, 1 pl. aor. 2 med. subj. of συνίημι.

συνωμοσία, ή, (συνόμνυμι) *a being leagued by oath, conspiracy*, Ar., Thuc., etc. ; ξ. δήμου καταλύσεως *for putting down the democracy*, Thuc. **2.** *a confederacy*, Id. **II.** *a body of men leagued by oath, a political union* or *club*, Id., Plat.

συνωμότης, ου, ὁ, (συνόμνυμι) *a fellow-conspirator, confederate*, Hdt., Att.

συνώμοτος, ον, (συνόμνυμι) *leagued by oath* : ξυνώμοτον, τό, *a confederacy*, Thuc.

συν-ωνέομαι, f. ήσομαι, Dep. *to collect by offering money*, σ. ἵππον *to hire a body of* cavalry, Hdt. **II.** *to buy up*, Lat. *coëmere*, Xen., etc. :—the pf. συνεώνημαι is pass., ὁ συνεωνημένος σῖτος *corn bought up*, Lys. ; but act. in Dem.

συνωνῠμία, ἡ, *a synonym*, Arist. From
συν-ώνῠμος, ον, (ὄνομα) *of like name*, Eur., Arist.
συνωριαστής, οῦ, ὁ, *one who drives a συνωρίς*, Luc. From
συν-ωρίζω, f. σω, *to yoke together* :—Med., ξυνωρίζου χέρα *join* thy hand *with mine*, Eur. ; and
συνωρῐκεύομαι, Dep. *to drive a pair*, Ar. From
συνωρίς, ίδος, ἡ, (συνήορος) *a pair of horses*, Lat. *biga*, Eur., Ar.   **2.** generally, *a pair* or *couple of* anything, Trag. ; ποδοῖν ξυνωρίς *a coupling fetter* for the feet, Aesch.
συν-ωφελέω, f. ήσω, *to join in aiding* or *relieving*, τινά Xen. ; rarely τινί, Soph.
συνωχᾰδόν, Adv. (συνέχω) poët. for συνοχηδόν, *of Time, perpetually, continually*, Hes.
συο-κτᾰσία, ἡ, (σῦς, κτείνω) *slaughter of swine*, Anth.
συο-φόντης, ου, ὁ, (σῦς, *φένω) *swine-slayer* ; fem. συοφόντις, Anth.
Σύρα, ἡ, fem. of Σύρας, *a Syrian woman*, Ar.
Σῠράκουσαι [ᾰ], αἱ, Ion. Συρήκουσαι, Dor. Συράκοσαι and Συράκοσσαι, *Syracuse*, Hdt., etc.:—Adj. Σῠράκό-σιος, α, ον, *Syracusan*, and as Subst. *a Syracusan*, Ion. Συρηκούσιος, Id. ; poët. Συρηκόσιος, Anth. : — ἡ Συρακοσία [χώρα] *the territory of* S., Thuc.
σύρ-γαστρος, ὁ, properly συρόγαστρος, (σύρω, γαστήρ) *trailing the belly*, as a worm, Anth.
σύρδην, Adv. (σύρω) *dragging, in a long line*, Aesch.
Σῠρία, Ion. -ίη, (sc. γῆ) ἡ, *Syria*, Hdt., etc. : Σ. ἡ Παλαιστίνη *Palestine*, Id.; Κοίλη Σ. *the district between Libanus and Anti-libanus*, Strab.
σύριγμα [ῠ], τό, (συρίζω) *the sound of a pipe*, Eur., Ar.
σῠριγμός, ὁ, (συρίζω) *a whistling, hissing*, Xen.
σῦριγξ, ιγγος, ἡ, *a pipe* :   **I.** *a musical pipe, a shepherd's pipe, Panspipe*, Il., Hes., Att.   **II.** *anything like a pipe :*   **1.** *a spear-case*, = δορατοθήκη, Il.   **2.** *the hole in the nave of a wheel*, Trag.   **3.** *a duct* or *channel in the body*, in pl. *the nostrils*, Soph.
ΣΥΡΙΖΩ, later Att. συρίττω, Dor. συρίσδω· f. συρίξομαι : aor. 1 ἐσύριξα, later ἐσύρισα :—*to play the σῦριγξ, to pipe*, Eur., Theocr. ; c. acc. cogn., συρίζων ὑμεναίους Eur.   **II.** *to whistle, hiss*, Aesch., Ar. : —c. acc. cogn., συρίζων φόνον *hissing forth murder*, Aesch.   **2.** *to hiss* an actor, Lat. *explodere*, Dem.
Σῠρίζω, f. σω, (Σύρος) *to speak like a Syrian*, Luc.
Σῠρῐη-γενής, ές, (γενέσθαι) *Syrian-born*, Orac. ap. Hdt.
σῠρικτήρ, ῆρος, ὁ, = συριστής, Anth.
σῠρικτής, οῦ, Dor. -τάς, ᾶ, ὁ, = συριστής, Theocr.
Σύριος [ῠ], α, ον, *of* or *from Syria*, Hdt., Aesch., etc.
σῠρίσδω, for συρίζω, Theocr.
σῠρισμός, ὁ, = συριγμός, Luc.
σῠριστής, οῦ, ὁ, (συρίζω) *a piper*, Luc.
Σῠριστί, (Σύρος) Adv. *in the Syrian language*, Σ. ἐπίστασθαι *to understand Syrian*, Xen.
σῠρίττω, late Att. for συρίζω.
σύρμα, τό, (σύρω) *anything trailed* or *dragged :*   **1.** *a theatric robe with a long train, syrma* in Juven. :—periphr., σ. τερηδόνος *a long woodworm*, Anth.   **2.** *sweepings, refuse, litter*, Heraclit. ap. Arist.
σῠρμαία, Ion. -αίη, ἡ, (συρμός) *purge-plant*, a name given to *the radish*, as used by the Egyptians (v. μελανοσυρμαῖος), Hdt., Ar.   Hence
συρμαΐζω, f. σω, *to take a purge*, Hdt.
σῠρμός, ὁ, (σύρω) *any lengthened sweeping motion*,

Lat. *tractus, the track* of meteors, Plat. ; of storms, Anth. ; *the trail* of a serpent, Plut.
Σῦρος, ὁ, *Syros*, one of the Cyclades, Strab. ; called Σῠριή in Od.
Σύρος [ῠ], ὁ, *a Syrian*, Hdt., Att.
Σῠρο-φοῖνιξ, ῐκος, ὁ, *a Syro-phoenician*, Luc. : fem. Συροφοίνισσα, N. T.
σύρραξις, ἡ, (συρράσσω) *a dashing together*, Plut.
συρ-ράπτω, f. ψω, *to sew* or *stitch together, sew up*, Lat. *consuo*, Hes., Hdt.
συρ-ράσσω, Att. -ττω, = συρρήγνυμι II, *to dash together, fight with* others, c. dat., Thuc., Xen.
συρ-ρέζω, f. ξω, *to do sacrifice together*, Anth.
συρ-ρέω, f. -ρεύσομαι : pf. -έρρηκα : aor. 2 pass. -ερρύην (in act. sense) :—*to flow together* or *in one stream*, Plat. :—metaph. of men, *to flow* or *stream together*, Hdt., Xen.   **II.** *to float together with*, Luc.
συρ-ρήγνῡμι or -ύω : f. -ρήξω :—Pass., pf. -έρρηγμαι : aor. 2 -ερράγην [ᾰ] : intr. pf. 2 -έρρωγα :—*to break in pieces*, Plut. :—Pass., κακοῖσι συνέρρηκται *he is broken down by sufferings*, Od.   **2.** *to dash together* :—Pass., of war, *to break out*, Plut.   **II.** intr. *to break out together, break forth*, of rivers, συρρηγνῦσι ἐς τὸν Ἕρμον *break into the Hermus, join it*, Hdt. : so pf. συνέρρωγα (in pres. signf.) and plqpf. (in impf.), ὁ πόλεμος ξυνερρώγει *the war broke out*, Thuc.   **2.** like συρράσσω, *to meet in battle, engage*, Plut.
συρ-ριζόομαι, Pass. *to have the roots united*, Luc.
Σύρτις, gen. εως, Ion. ιος, (σύρω) *the Syrtis*, name of two large sand-banks (Major and Minor) on the coast of Libya, Hdt., etc.
σύρφαξ, ᾰκος, ὁ = συρφετός 1. 1, Ar.
συρφετός, ὁ, (σύρω) *anything swept together, sweepings, refuse, rubbish, litter*, Lat. *quisquiliae*, Hes.   **2.** metaph. *a mixed crowd, mob, rabble*, Plat. : of a single person, *one of the mob* (cf. Hor. *plebs eris*), Id.
συρφετ-ώδης, ες, (συρφετός, εἶδος) *jumbled together, promiscuous*, Luc.
ΣΥΡΩ [ῠ], f. σῠρῶ : aor. 1 ἔσῡρα : pf. σέσυρκα :—Pass., aor. 2 ἐσύρην [ῠ] : pf. σέσυρμαι :—*to draw, drag*, or *trail along*, Theocr. :—Pass. *to trail along*, Anth.   **2.** *to drag by force, hale*, Theocr. :—of rivers, *to sweep* or *carry down* with them, Anth. :—Pass. *to be swept away*, Plut.
σῦς, acc. σῦν, v. ὗς.
συ-σκεδάννῡμι, f. -σκεδῶ, *to help in scattering, to toss about*, Ar.
συσκέψομαι, fut. of συσκοπέω.
συ-σκευάζω, f. άσω, *to make ready by putting together, to pack up* baggage for another, Xen.   **2.** *to help in preparing*, τὸ δεῖπνόν τινι Ar. :—in bad sense, *to contrive, concert, get up*, Dem.   **II.** Med., with pf. pass. συσκεύασμαι, *to pack up one's baggage, to pack up*, Lat. *convasare, vasa colligere*, Thuc., Xen., etc. : part. aor. 1 med. and pf. pass. *all packed up, in marching order, ready for a start*, Xen. ; aor. 2 acc., συνεσκευασμένος τὰ ἑαυτοῦ ἐνθάδε *with all his goods packed up and brought hither*, Lys.   **2.** *to contrive, get up, organise*, Dem.   **3.** *to bring together, scrape up for one's own use* or *advantage*, σ. χρήματα Lycurg.   **4.** *to arrange for one's own interests, band together*, Dem.   Hence

συσκευᾰσία, ἡ, a packing up, getting ready, for a journey or march, Xen.

συ-σκευωρέομαι, Dep. to contrive, organise, Dem.

συ-σκηνέω, f. ήσω, to live in the same tent with another, to mess together, Xen. ; τινί with one, Id.

συσκηνία, ἡ, a dwelling in one tent : of soldiers, a messing together, Xen.

συσκήνια, τά, = the Spartan φιλίτια, Xen.

σύ-σκηνος, ὁ, (σκηνή) one who lives in the same tent, a messmate, Lat. contubernalis, Thuc., Xen.

συ-σκηνόω, f. ώσω, = συσκηνέω, Xen.

συ-σκιάζω, f. άσω, to shade quite over, throw a shade over, shade closely or thickly, Hes. ; γένυν σ., i. e. to get a beard, Eur. : metaph., συσκηνῶσαι τὰς ἁμαρτίας Dem.   II. intr. to be thick-shaded, Eur.

σύ-σκιος, ον, (σκιά) closely shaded, thickly shaded, Xen.; σύσκιόν τι a closely-shaded place, Luc.

συ-σκοπέω, f. -σκέψομαι, to contemplate along with or together, Plat.

συ-σκοτάζω, f. σω, to grow quite dark : impers., συσκοτάζει it grows dark, Thuc., Xen.

συ-σκυθρωπάζω [ᾰ], f. σω, to look gloomy together, Xen.

συ-σπᾰράσσω, Att. -ττω, f. ξω, to tear in pieces, N. T.

σύσπαστος, ον, or συσπαστός, όν, drawn together, closed by drawing together, Plat. From

συ-σπάω, f. -σπάσω [ᾰ], to draw together, draw up, contract, Plat., Luc.   II. to draw together by stitching, sew together, Xen.   III. in Med. to draw along with one, Plut.

συ-σπειράομαι : pf. -εσπείραμαι : Pass., of soldiers, to be formed in close order (v. σπεῖρα II), Xen.; σ. ἐπὶ τόπον to march in such order to a place, Id.   2. to be coiled up, Luc.

συ-σπείρω, f. ερῶ, to sow together, Luc.

συ-σπένδω, f. -σπείσω, to join in making a libation, Dem., Aeschin.

συ-σπεύδω, f. σω, to assist zealously, τινὶ ποιεῖν τι Hdt.

συ-σπλαγχνεύω, f. σω, to join in eating the sacrificial meat (τὰ σπλάγχνα), Ar.

σύ-σπονδος, ον, (σπονδή) = ὁμόσπονδος, Aeschin.

συ-σπουδάζω, f. άσω, to make haste together, to join in zealous exertion, Ar., Xen. : c. acc. rei, to pursue or execute zealously together with, τί τινι Xen.

συσ-σαίνομαι, Pass. to feel flattered by a thing, Polyb.

συσ-σεβίζω, to join in celebrating, θυσίας θεῷ Eur.

συσσεύω, to urge on together, βοῶν κάρηνα h. Hom.

συσ-σημαίνομαι, Med. to join in signing, Dem.

σύσ-σημον, τό, (σῆμα) a fixed sign or signal, N. T.   2. a pledge, Anth.

συσ-σιτέω, f. ήσω, to mess with, τινί Ar. :—absol. in pl. to mess together, Plat., Dem.   Hence

συσσίτησις, ἡ, = sq., Plut. : and

συσσιτία, ἡ, a messing together, a public mess, Xen.

συσσίτιον [ῑ], τό, mostly in pl. συσσίτια, τά, a common meal, public mess, such as were used in Crete and Lacedaemon, Hdt., Plat., etc.   II. a mess-room, common-hall, Eur., Plat.

σύσ-σιτος, ὁ, one who eats together, a messmate, Theogn., Hdt., Att.

συσ-σώζω, f. σω, to help to save or preserve, Eur., Thuc.

σύσ-σωμος, ον, (σῶμα) united in one body, N. T.

συσ-σωφρονέω, f. ήσω, to be a partner in temperance, Eur.

συστᾰδόν, Adv. (συστῆναι) standing close together, hand to hand, Thuc.

συστάς, άδος [ᾰ], ἡ, (συστῆναι) standing together, planted closely, Arist.

συ-στασιάζω, f. σω, to join in faction or sedition, take part therein, Thuc.

συ-στασιαστής, ὁ, a fellow-rioter, N. T.

σύστᾰσις, ἡ, (συνίστημι) a putting together, composition, Arist.; σ. προσώπου a studied expression of countenance, of Pericles, Plut.   II. a bringing together, introduction, recommendation, Polyb., Plut.
    B. (συνίσταμαι) a standing together, meeting : in hostile sense, close combat, conflict, Hdt. , metaph., σ. γνώμης a conflict of mind, intense anxiety, Thuc.   2. a meeting, a knot of men, Eur.; κατὰ ξυστάσεις γιγνόμενοι forming into knots, Thuc. : a political union, Dem.   3. friendship or alliance, Polyb. : a conspiracy, Plut.   II. construction, structure, constitution, Plat., Arist. : absol. a political constitution, Plat.   2. metaph. of the mind, σ. φρενῶν contraction, sternness, sullenness, Eur.

συ-στασιώτης, ὁ, ὁ, a member of the same faction, a partisan, Hdt.

συστᾰτικός, ή, όν, (συνίστημι III) introductory, σ. ἐπιστολή a letter of introduction, N. T.

συ-σταυρόομαι, Pass. to be crucified with, τινί N. T.

συ-στεγάζω, f. σω, to cover entirely, τινί with a thing, Plat. :—Pass., Xen.

συ-στέλλω, f. -στελῶ : pf. -έσταλκα :—to draw together, draw in : to shorten sail (sub. τὰ ἱστία), Ar. : to draw soldiers into a fort, Plut.   2. to contract, reduce, Plat., Dem. :—Pass. to cower together, Eur. ; ξυστέλλεσθαι ἐς εὐτέλειαν to retrench, Thuc.   3. metaph. to lower, humble, abase, Isocr. :—Pass., Eur.   II. Pass., also, to be wrapped up, shrouded, Id. ; aor. 2 part. συσταλείς, tucked up, ready for action, Ar.

συ-στενάζω, to lament with, τινί Eur. ; absol., N. T.

συ-στένω, = συστενάζω, Arist.

συ-στεφᾰνόομαι, Pass. to wear a crown with, τινί Dem.

σύστημα, τό, (συστῆναι) a whole compounded of parts, a system, Plat. :—a composition, Arist.   2. an organised government, constitution, Id.   3. a body of soldiers, a corps, Polyb.   4. of the Roman Senate, Plut.

συστοιχέω, to correspond to, τινί N. T. ; and

συστοιχία, ἡ, a coördinate series, Arist.   From

σύ-στοιχος, ον, standing in the same row, coördinate, correspondent, opp. to ἀντίστοιχος (standing in opposite rows), Arist.

συστολή, ἡ, (συστέλλω) a drawing together, contraction, limitation, Plut.

συστολίζω, = συστέλλω, to put together, fabricate, Eur.   II. to unite, τινά τινι Anth.

συ-στρᾰτεία, ἡ, a common campaign, Xen.

συ-στρᾰτεύω, f. -εύσω, and as Dep. συστρατεύομαι, f. -εύσομαι :—to make a campaign or serve together, to join or share in an expedition, absol., Hdt., Thuc., etc. ; τινί with another, Hdt., Thuc.

συστρᾰτηγέω, to be the fellow-general of, τινός Dem.

συ-στράτηγος, ὁ, a joint-commander, Eur., Thuc., etc.

συ-στρᾰτιώτης, ου, ὁ, a fellow-soldier, Lat. commilito, Xen., etc.

συ-στρᾰτοπεδεύομαι, Dep. to encamp along with, τινι or σύν τινι Xen.

σύστρεμμα, ατος, τό, anything twisted up together : a body of men, a crowd, concourse, Polyb. From

συ-στρέφω, f. ψω, to twist up into a ball, Lat. conglobare : of animals, to gather themselves together, in preparing to spring, Plat. : of soldiers, σ. ἑωυτούς to collect themselves, rally, Hdt. : Pass., συστραφέντες in a body, Id. ; ἐπὶ πεντήκοντα ἀσπίδων συνεστραμμένοι ἦσαν they were formed in a mass 50 deep, Xen. II. of soldiers, also, συστρέφειν ἐπὶ δόρυ to wheel them to the right, Id. ; σ. τὸν ἵππον to turn him sharply, Plut. III. to form into an organised whole, unite, Hdt. :—Pass. to unite, club together, conspire, Thuc., Aeschin. IV. of sentences, narratives, and the like, to compress, Arist. : absol., συστρέψας γράφει writes briefly, curtly, Aeschin. :—Pass., ῥῆμα βραχὺ καὶ συνεστραμμένον a short and pithy saying, Plat. Hence

συστροφή, ἡ, a dense mass of men, a gathering of people, Hdt. 2. a sudden storm, Polyb.

συ-σφάζω, to slay along with : Pass., aor. 2 inf. συσφαγῆναι to be slain with another, τινι Eur.

συ-σφίγγω, to condense :—Pass., Anth.

συ-σχημᾰτίζω, to conform one thing to another, τι πρός τι Arist. :—Pass. to form oneself after another, to be conformed to his example, N. T.

συ-σχολάζω, f. σω, to be a fellow-pupil or companion in philosophy, to pass one's-time with or together, Plut.

σύτο [ῠ], Ep. 3 sing. aor. 2 pass. of σεύω.

σῠφεός and σῠφειός, ὁ, (σῦς) a hog-sty, Od. ; συφεόνδε to the sty, Ib.

σῠ-φόρβιον, τό, (σῦς, φέρβω) a herd of swine, Anth.

σῠ-φορβός, ὁ, (σῦς, φέρβω) a swineherd, Hom.

ΣΥΧΝΟ'Σ, ή, όν, of Time, long, Hdt., etc. ; σ. λόγος a long speech, Plat. II. of Number, many, Hdt., Ar., etc. ; many days together, Ar. :—c. gen., συχναὶ τῶν νήσων Hdt. :—absol., συχνοὶ many people together, Ar., etc. :—with sing. nouns, much, great, Id., Plat., etc. ; τὸ πολίχνιον συχνὸν ποιεῖν to make the small town large, Plat. :—c. gen., τῆς μαρίλης συχνήν Ar. B. the Adv. συχνῶς (Antipho) is rare, the neut. συχνόν, συχνά being used instead, often, much, Plat. : far, Xen. II. dat. συχνῷ with Comp. Adj., νεώτερος ἐμοῦ καὶ συχνῷ younger by a good deal, Dem.

σφᾰγεῖον, τό, (σφάζω) a bowl for catching the blood of the victim in sacrifices, Eur. II. = σφάγιον, the victim, Id.

σφᾰγεύς, έως, ὁ, (σφάζω) a slayer, butcher, Eur.: a murderer, cut-throat, Dem. :—in Soph., ὁ σφαγεὺς ἕστηκε the slayer is set, i. e. the sword on which Ajax is about to throw himself :—a sacrificial knife, Eur.

σφᾰγή, ἡ, (σφάζω) slaughter, butchery, in sing. and pl., Trag., Plat., etc. ; αἵματος σφαγή the blood gushing from the wound, Aesch. ; καθάρμοσον σφαγάς close the gaping wound, Eur. II. the throat, the spot where the victim is struck (cf. Lat. jugulum, jugulari), in pl., Id., Thuc.

σφᾰγῆναι, aor. 2 pass. inf. of σφάζω.

σφᾰγιάζομαι, f. άσομαι, Dep. (σφάγιον) to slay a victim, sacrifice, Hdt., Xen. II. in Act. σφαγιάζω, Ar.,

Plut. :—hence aor. 1 pass. part. σφαγιασθείς, slain, sacrificed, Hdt., Xen. Hence

σφᾰγιασμός, ὁ, a slaying, sacrificing, Eur., Plut.

σφάγιον [ᾰ], τό, (σφάζω) a victim, offering, Soph., Eur. : —mostly in pl., Hdt., Aesch., etc. 2. slaughter, sacrifice, in pl., Eur.

σφάγιος, α, ον, (σφάζω) slaying, slaughtering, σφ. μόρος slaughter, Soph.

σφᾰγίς, ίδος, ἡ, (σφάζω) a sacrificial knife, Eur.

ΣΦΑ'ΔΑ'ΖΩ or σφαδάζω, only in pres. and impf. to struggle, plunge, of horses, Aesch., Xen. ; cf. ἀσφάδαστος. 2. to struggle, shew impatience, Plut. Hence

σφᾰδασμός, ὁ, a spasm, convulsion, Plat.

σφάζω (Root ΣΦΑΓ), later Att. σφάττω : f. σφάξω : aor. 1 ἔσφαξα :—Pass., f. 2 σφαγήσομαι : aor. 2 ἐσφάγην [ᾰ], more rarely aor. 1 ἐσφάχθην : pf. ἔσφαγμαι :—to slay, slaughter, properly by cutting the throat (v. σφαγή II.), Hom. II. esp. to slaughter victims for sacrifice, Il., Eur. 2. generally to slay, kill, first applied to human victims, Pind., Trag. ; σφ. τινὰ ἐς τὸν κρητῆρα so that the blood run into the bowl, Hdt.

ΣΦΑΙ'ΡΑ', ας, ἡ, a ball, playing-ball, Od., Plat. 2. any ball : the terrestrial globe, the earth, Strab.

σφαιρηδόν, Adv. like a globe or ball, ἧκε δέ μιν σφαιρηδὸν ἑλιξάμενος Il. ; and

σφαιρίζω, f. Att. ιῶ, to play at ball, Plat. ; and

σφαιρικός, ή, όν, globular, spherical : τὰ σφαιρικά the doctrine of the spheres, astronomy, Anth.

σφαίρισις, ἡ, (σφαιρίζω) a playing at ball, Arist.

σφαιριστήριον, τό, (σφαιρίζω) a ball-court, Theophr.

σφαιρο-ειδής, ές, (εἶδος) ball-like, spherical, Plat. ; σφαιροειδές, τό, a rounded end (cf. σφαιρόω II.), Xen

σφαιρο-ποιέω, f. ήσω, to make spherical, Strab.

σφαιρόω, f. ώσω, (σφαῖρα) to make spherical :—Pass. to be rounded, στήθεα ἐσφαίρωτο his chest was round and arched, Theocr. II. Pass., also, ἀκόντια ἐσφαιρωμένα spears with buttons at the point, like our foils, Xen., Arist. Hence

σφαιρωτός, ή, όν, with a button at the end, Xen.

σφᾰκελίζω, to be gangrened, ἐσφακέλισε τὸ ὀστέον Hdt.

ΣΦΑ'ΚΕΛΟΣ [ᾰ], ὁ, gangrene :—generally, a spasm, convulsion, Aesch., Eur. : metaph., σφ. ἀνέμων the convulsive fury of winds, Aesch.

σφᾰλερός, ά, όν, (σφάλλω) likely to make one stumble or trip : metaph. slippery, perilous, dangerous, Lat. lubricus, Hdt., Eur., etc. :—σφαλερόν [ἐστι], c. inf., it is dangerous to . . , Plat., etc. II. (σφάλλομαι) ready to fall, tottering, reeling, staggering, Aesch., Soph. ; σφ. σύμμαχοι Dem.

σφάλλω (Root ΣΦΑΛ) : f. σφᾰλῶ : aor. 1 ἔσφηλα, Ep. σφῆλα : pf. ἔσφαλκα :—Pass., f. 2 σφᾰλήσομαι, in med. form σφᾰλοῦμαι : aor. 2 ἐσφάλην [ᾰ] : pf. ἔσφαλμαι : 3 sing. plqpf. ἔσφαλτο : Lat. fall-o (the σ being lost) : —to make to fall, throw down, overthrow, properly by tripping up, to trip up in wrestling, Hom., Pind., Eur. ; σφ. ναῦς to throw her on her beam-ends, Plut. ; ἵππος σφ. τὸν ἀναβάτην throws him, Xen. :—Pass. to be tripped up, Ar. ; of a drunken man, σφαλλόμενος reeling, staggering, Id. II. generally to cause to fall, overthrow, defeat, Hdt., Soph., Thuc. :—Pass. to be overthrown, to fall, fail, be undone, become helpless, Hdt., Att. ;

τόδ' ἐσφάλη this *mishap took place*, Soph. ; οὔ τι μὴ σφαλῶ γ' ἐν σοί *I shall* not *fail in thy business*, Id. **III.** *to baffle, foil, balk, disappoint*, Hdt., Soph. :—Pass. *to err, go wrong, be mistaken*, Hdt., Soph. 2. the Pass. is also used c. gen. rei, *to be balked of* or *foiled in* a thing, ἢ καὶ πατήρ τι σφάλλεται βουλευμάτων; Aesch. ; σφάλλεσθαι γάμου Eur. ; τῆς δόξης Thuc. Hence

σφάλμα, ατος, τό, *a trip, stumble, false step*, Anth. **II.** metaph., 1. *a fall, failure, defeat*, Hdt., Thuc., Eur., etc. 2. *a fault, failing, error*, Hdt.

σφἄρἄγέομαι, Dep. only in pres. and impf., *to burst with a noise, to crackle, sputter*, ῥίζαι σφαραγεῦντο *the roots of his eye crackled* or *hissed* (when Ulysses burnt them with the hot stake), Od. **II.** *to be full even to bursting*, Ib. ; and

σφἄρἄγίζω, only in Ep. impf. σφαράγιζον *to stir up with noise and bustle*, Hes.

ΣΦΑ'ΡΑΓΟΣ, ὁ, *a bursting with a noise*.

σφᾶς and **σφάς**, acc. of σφεῖς. **II.** **σφάς** [ᾰ], acc. pl. fem. of σφός.

σφάττω, later Att. for σφάζω, impf. ἔσφαττον.

σφε, acc. masc. and fem. of σφεῖς, = αὐτούς, αὐτάς, *them*, Il., Aesch., Soph. 2. as acc. dual, = αὐτώ, αὐτά, Hom. 3. neut. acc. pl., = αὐτά, Theocr. **II.** as acc. sing. of ἵ, = αὐτόν, αὐτήν, *him, her*, Hdt., Trag.

σφἄ̆ᾶ, σφἄ̆έᾱς, v. σφεῖς.

σφεδᾰνός, ή, όν, = σφοδρός, *furious*, Anth. **II.** in Hom. only as Adv. *vehemently, eagerly*.

ΣΦΕΙ'Σ, masc. and fem. pl. of the Pron. of 3rd person, *they*, = αὐτοί, Hdt., Att. :—Gen. σφέων, in Hom. of a monosyll. ; Ep. also σφείων : Att. σφῶν :—Dat. σφισι (-ιν), Hom., Aesch. ; more common in the apoc. forms σφι, σφιν, Hom., Hdt., Att. : the use of σφι, σφιν as dat. sing. for οἷ is rare, h. Hom., Aesch., Soph.:—Acc. σφέᾱς, mostly enclit. pronounced as a *long* syllable, Hom., Hdt. ; also σφᾶς and σφείας (or σφεῖας) Od. ; σφας (enclit.) or σφᾶς, Trag. ; cf. σφε. **II.** in Hom. this Pron. is always personal, and therefore he uses no neut. ; but Hdt. has neut. pl. σφέα. 2. this Pron. is used both for the demonstr. αὐτοί, *they*, and for the reflex. αὐτῶν, etc., *themselves* ;—in the latter case often strengthd. σφῶν αὐτῶν, σφέας αὐτούς, σφᾶς αὐτούς, Hes. ; sometimes for ἀλλήλους, Id. **III.** rarely for 2nd pers. pl., μετὰ σφίσιν for μεθ' ὑμῖν, Il. ; σφέας for ὑμᾶς, Hdt.

ΣΦΕ'ΛΑΣ, τό, *a footstool*, Od. : Ep. pl. σφέλα Ib.

σφενδάμνῐνος, η, ον, *of maple wood* : metaph. of persons, 'hearts of oak,' Ar. From

σφένδαμνος, ή, *the maple*, Lat. *acer*, Theophr.

σφενδονάω, f. ήσω, *to sling, to use the sling*, Thuc., Xen. 2. *to strike by slinging*, Babr. **II.** *to throw as from a sling* :—Pass., Eur. 2. *to move like a swing, to swing to and fro*, Id. From

ΣΦΕΝΔΟ'ΝΗ, Lat. *funda* (the σ being lost), *a sling*, Il. : metaph., σφενδόνας ἀπ' εὐμέτρου *with well-measured throw, as from a sling*, Aesch. 2. *the hoop* of a ring *in which the stone was set* as in a sling, esp. *the broader part round the stone*, as in Lat. *funda* for *pala annuli*, Eur., Plat. **II.** *the stone* or *bullet of the sling*, Xen. ; τοιαύταις σφ., *of hailstones*, Ar.

σφενδονήτης, ου, ὁ, (σφενδονάω) *a slinger*, Hdt., Thuc.

σφενδονητικός, ή, όν, *of* or *for slinging* :– ἡ -κή (sc. τέχνη), *the art of slinging*, Plat.

σφετερίζω, f. σω or ξω, (σφέτερος) *to make one's own, appropriate, usurp*, Plat. :—so, as Dep. **σφετερίζομαι**, Xen., Dem. Hence

σφετερισμός, ὁ, *appropriation*, ἐπὶ σφετερισμῷ ἑαυτοῦ *for one's own use and advantage*, Arist. ; and

σφετεριστής, ὁ, *an appropriator*, Arist.

σφέτερος, α, ον, possessive Adj. of 3rd pers. pl. (σφεῖς), *their own, their*, Lat. *suus*, Hom., etc. ; strengthd., αὐτῶν σφετέρῃσιν ἀτασθαλίῃσιν Od. ;—in Prose, the gen. ἑαυτῶν is more common, but σφέτερος occurs in Thuc., etc. ; τὸ σφέτερον *their own feelings, their own business*, Id., Plat. ; οἱ σφέτεροι *their own people*, Thuc. 2. also of 3rd sing., *his* or *her own, his, her*, for ἑός, ὅς, Hes., Pind., Aesch. **II.** in Poets sometimes of other persons : 1. of 2nd pl., = ὑμέτερος, *your own*, Il., Hes. , etc. 2. of 2nd sing., = σός, *thine own*, *tuus*, Theocr. 3. of 1st sing., = ἐμός, *mine own, meus*, Id. 4. of the 1st pl., = ἡμέτερος, *our own, noster*, Xen.

σφέων, Ep. and Ion. for σφῶν, gen. of σφεῖς.

σφῇ, dat. fem. of σφός.

σφηκιά, ἡ, (σφήξ) *a wasps' nest*, Eur., Ar.

σφηκίσκος, ὁ, (σφήξ) *a piece of wood pointed like a wasp's tail, a pointed stick* or *stake*, Ar.

σφηκόω, f. ώσω, (σφήξ) *to make like a wasp*, i. e. *to pinch in at the waist* : generally, *to bind tightly*, Anth. **II.** Pass., πλοχμοί, οἱ χρυσῷ τε καὶ ἀργύρῳ ἐσφήκωντο (3 pl. plqpf.) *braids of hair, which were bound tightly with gold and silver*, Il.

σφηκ-ώδης, ες, *wasp-like, pinched in at the waist like a wasp*, Ar.

σφήκωμα, ατος, τό, *the point of a helmet* where the plume is fixed in, Ar.

σφῆλαι, aor. 1 inf. of σφάλλω.

σφῆλεν, Ep. 3 sing. aor. 1 of σφάλλω.

ΣΦΗ'Ν, σφηνός, ὁ, *a wedge*, Ar., etc. ;—used as an instrument of torture, Aesch.

σφηνο-κέφαλος, ον, (κεφαλή) *with peaked head*, Strab.

σφηνο-πώγων, ωνος, ὁ, *with peaked beard*, Luc.

ΣΦΗ'Ξ, σφηκός, Dor. **σφάξ, σφακός**, ὁ, *a wasp*, Lat. *vespa*, Il., Hdt., Att.

Σφηττός, ὁ, *a deme of the Acamantian* φυλή *in Attica*, Strab. ; Σφηττοῖ *in* or *at Sphettos*, Aeschin. ; Σφηττόθεν *from Sph.*, Plut. :—**Σφήττιος**, ὁ, *a Sphettian*, Ar., Aeschin.

σφί, σφίν, dat. of σφεῖς.

σφιγγίον, τό, *a bracelet, necklace*, Luc. From

ΣΦΙ'ΓΓΩ, f. σφίγξω : aor. 2 ἔσφιγξα :—Pass., aor. 1 ἐσφίγχθην : pf. ἔσφιγμαι :—*to bind tight, bind fast*, Aesch., Theocr. :—Pass., Theocr. Hence

σφιγκτήρ, ῆρος, ὁ, *a band, lace*, Od.

σφιγκτός, ή, όν, verb. Adj. of σφίγγω, *tight-bound* : neut. pl. σφιγκτά as Adv., Anth.

σφίγκτωρ, ορος, ὁ, poët. for σφιγκτήρ, Anth.

Σφίγξ, Σφιγγός, ἡ, *Sphinx, a she-monster*, Hes. ; in Trag. represented as proposing a riddle to the Thebans, and murdering all who failed to guess it ; Oedipus guessed it, and she thereupon killed herself. (Prob. from σφίγγω, *the Throttler*.)

σφίν, σφίσι, σφίσιν, dat. of σφεῖς.

σφογγίον, σφόγγος, Att. for σπόγγος.

σφόδρᾰ, Adv., *very, very much, exceedingly, violently,* Hdt., Soph., etc.: with Adjs., σφ. ὑπέρτεροι *far* superior, Pind.; σφ. ἄδικος Plat. :—with a Subst., τὴν σφόδρα φιλίαν Id.   II. σφόδρα γε, καὶ σφ. γε, in answers, *most certainly,* Id.   From

ΣΦΟΔΡΟ'Σ, ά, όν, and also ός, όν, *vehement, violent, excessive,* Thuc., etc.   2. of men, *violent, impetuous,* Plat. : also *strong, robust,* Xen.   Hence

σφοδρότης, ητος, ἡ, *vehemence, violence,* Xen.; and

σφοδρύνομαι, Pass. *to be* or *become vehement,* σφοδρύνεσθαι τινι *to put unbounded trust* in a thing, Aesch.

σφονδύλη [ῠ], ἡ, *a kind of beetle,* Ar.

σφονδύλιος [ῠ], ὁ, like σφόνδυλος, *a vertebra,* Il.

σφονδῡλο-δίνητος [ῐ], ον, *twirled on a spindle,* Anth.

σφόνδῡλος, ὁ, *a vertebra,* Ar. :—in pl. *the backbone, spine,* or *the neck,* Eur.   II. Lat. *verticillus, the round weight* attached to a spindle, Plat.

σφός, σφή, σφόν, (σφεῖς) poët. for σφέτερος, *their, their own, belonging to them,* Il., etc.   2. in sing. *his* or *her, his own* or *her own,* Theogn.

σφρᾱγῑδ-ονῠχ-αργο-κομήτης, ου, ὁ, (σφραγίς, ὄνυξ, ἀργός) Comic name for a coxcomb, *a long-haired fop with rings and natty nails,* Ar.

σφρᾱγίζω, Ion. σφρηγίζω, f. ίσω, Att. ιῶ :—*to seal,* Eur. :—Med. *to seal for oneself, have sealed,* Plut.: —Pass., pf. part. ἐσφραγισμένος *sealed up, kept under seal,* Aesch.   II. *to mark as with a seal, to mark,* Anth.; δεινοῖς σημάντροισιν ἐσφραγισμένοι, of wounded persons, Eur.   III. metaph. *to set a seal on, confirm, stamp with approval,* N. T., Anth.: Med. *to assure of* a thing, c. acc. rei, N. T.: *to limit,* Anth.   2. *to seal* or *accredit* as a faithful servant, as a believer, τινά N. T.   From

ΣΦΡΑ'ΓΙ'Σ, Ion. σφρηγίς, ῖδος, ἡ, *a seal, signet, seal-ring,* Hdt., Ar., etc.   2. *the gem* or *stone for a ring,* Hdt., Luc.   II. *the impression of a signet-ring, a seal,* Soph., Thuc. :—metaph. σφρηγὶς ἐπικείσθω τοῖσδε, as a warrant, Theogn.; γλώσσῃ σφρ. ἐπικείσθω Anth.

σφράγισμα, ατος, τό, (σφραγίζω) *an impression of a signet-ring, a seal,* Eur., Xen.

σφρῑγάω, (σπαργάω) only in pres. *to be full to bursting :* of young persons, high-fed horses, etc., *to be plump, fresh, vigorous, to be in full health and strength,* Lat. *vigere,* Eur., Ar., etc.   2. metaph., σφριγῶν μῦθος *a vigorous, violent speech,* Eur.

σφυγμός, ὁ, (σφύζω) *a throbbing of parts, pulsation, vibration,* Plut.

σφυγμ-ώδης, ες, (εἶδος) *like the pulse,* Arist.

σφυδάω, only in pres., = σφύζω: metaph. *to be in full vigour,* Aesch.

σφύζω, Dor. σφύσδω (Root ΣΦΥΓ), only in pres. and impf., *to throb, beat,* of the pulse, Plat.: *to be feverish,* Theocr.

ΣΦΥ'ΡΑ', ἡ, *a hammer,* Od., Hdt.   2. *a beetle, mallet,* for breaking clods of earth, Hes., Ar.

σφῡρ-ήλᾰτος, ον, (ἐλαύνω) *wrought with the hammer, beaten out,* as opp. to *cast* metal (χωνευτός), Hdt., Aesch., etc.   II. metaph. *wrought as of iron, rigid,* Luc.

ΣΦΥ'ΡΟ'Ν, τό, *the ankle,* Il., Att.   II. metaph. *the foot* of a mountain, Pind., Anth.; also, Λιβύας ἄκρον σφυρόν *the very furthest part* of Libya, Theocr.

σφύσδην, Dor. for σφύζειν, inf. of σφύζω.

σφώ, shortened nom. and acc. for σφῶϊ, v. σύ II.

σφωέ, dual nom. and acc. of Pron. of 3rd pers. ; dat. σφωῒν :—*they two, both of them,* only masc. and fem., and always enclit., Hom.

σφῶϊ, σφῶϊν, dual masc. and fem. of Pron. of 2nd pers., *ye two* ; v. σύ II.

σφωΐτερος [ῐ], α, ον, possess. Adj. of σφῶϊ, Pron. of 2nd pers. dual, *of you two,* σφωΐτερον ἔπος *the word of you two,* Il.; for 2nd pers. sing., *thine own, thine, thy,* Theocr.   2. of 3rd pers. sing., *his* or *her own,* Lat. *suus,* Id.

σφῶν, contr. for σφῶϊν, gen. and dat. of σφώ.

ΣΧΑ῀ΔΩ'Ν, όνος, ἡ, *a honey-cell,* and in pl. *a honeycomb,* Lat. *favus,* Ar., Theocr.

ΣΧΑ'ΖΩ, impf. ἔσχων (as if from *σχάω): f. σχάσω [ᾰ]: aor. 1 ἔσχᾰσα :—properly *to let loose :* hence *to slit, open,* Ar.; σχ. φλέβα *to open a vein,* Xen., etc. :—of flowers, σχ. κάλυκας Anth.   II. *to let fall, drop,* Xen.   2. *to let go,* σχάσας τὴν φροντίδα *having let* the mind *go, given* it *play,* Ar.; σχ. τὰς μηχανὰς *to let off* the engines, Plut.   3. *to check, stop, stay,* Lat. *inhibere,* κώπαν σχάσον, i. e. *cease* rowing, Pind.; σχάσον ὄμμα *lower* thine eyes, Eur.: —Med., σχασάμενος τὴν ἱππικήν *having dropt* one's horsemanship, 'given up the turf,' Ar.

ΣΧΑ'ΛΙ'Σ, ίδος, ἡ, *a forked stick used to prop* nets, Xen.

*σχάω, v. σχάζω.

σχέ, aor. 2 imper. of ἔχω.

σχέδην, Adv. (σχεῖν, aor. 2 of ἔχω) *gently, thoughtfully,* Xen.

σχεδία, Ion. -ίη, ἡ, *a raft, float* (such as was *made off-hand,* cf. σχέδιος II), Od., Thuc.; generally, *a boat, ship,* Eur., Theocr.   2. *a bridge of boats,* of the bridge of Xerxes, Hdt., Aesch.

σχεδιάζω, f. άσω, (σχέδιος) *to do a thing off-hand,* Plat.

σχεδίην, Ep. Adv. (acc. fem. of σχέδιος), of Place, *near, close at hand,* Lat. *cominus,* Il.   II. of Time, *straightway, at once,* Babr.

σχέδιος, α, ον, (σχεδόν) :   I. of Place, *hand to hand,* in or *for close combat,* Aesch.   II. of Time, *on the spur of the moment, off-hand,* Anth.

σχεδόθεν, Adv. properly, *from nigh at hand, nigh at hand, near,* Lat. *cominus,* Hom.; c. gen., Od.   From

σχεδόν, Adv. (σχεῖν, aor. 2 of σχέδιος) :   I. of Place, *close, near, hard by, nigh,* Lat. *cominus,* Hom., Hes.; σχεδὸν οὔτασε Il.; c. gen., γαίης σχ. Od.; c. dat., νῆσοι σχεδὸν ἀλλήλῃσι Il.   2. with Verbs of motion, σχ. ἐλθεῖν, ἰέναι Hom.   II. metaph. of relationship, σχ.   III. of Time, [θάνατος] δή τοι σχ. ἐστιν Il.; σοὶ δὲ γάμος σχ. ἐστι Od.   IV. of Degree, *nearly, all but, almost, just,* σχ. ταὐτά Hdt.; σχ. πάντες Id., etc.   2. with Verbs, esp. of saying or knowing, σχ. ἐπίσταμαι *satis scio,* Soph.; σχ. οἶδα Eur.

*σχέθω, assumed as a pres. = ἔχω, *to hold :* but only found in forms which belong to an aor. 2 ἔσχεθον, poët. for ἔσχον, viz. 3 sing. and pl. σχέθε, σχέθον, Ep. for ἔσχεθεν, ἔσχεθον, imper. σχέθετω, inf. σχεθέμεν, part. σχεθών :—*to hold,* Hom.   2. simply *to have,* Pind.,

Aesch. **II.** *to hold back, keep away* or *off*, Hom. ; αἷμα ἔσχεθον *staunched* the blood, Il.

σχεῖν, aor. 2 inf. of ἔχω.

ΣΧΕΛΙ′Σ, ἰδος, ἡ, mostly in pl. σχελίδες, *ribs of beef*, Ar.

σχέμεν, σχέμεναι, Ep. for σχεῖν, aor. 2 inf. of ἔχω.

σχένδυλα, ἡ, (σχεῖν) *a pair of pincers* or *tongs*, Anth.

σχέο, Ep. for σχοῦ, aor. 2 med. imp. of ἔχω.

Σχερία, ἡ, *Scheria*, the island of the Phaeacians, Od. : supposed to be the same as *Corcyra, Corfu*.

σχερός, ὁ, (σχεῖν) found only in dat., ἐν σχερῷ *in a line, one after another, uninterruptedly, successively*, Pind. ; cf. ἐπισχερώ.

σχές, aor. 2 imp. of ἔχω.

σχέσθαι, aor. 2 med. inf. of ἔχω.

σχέσις, εως, ἡ, (σχεῖν) *a state, condition*, Luc. **2.** generally, *the nature quality, fashion* of a thing, Aesch., Xen., etc.

σχετήριον, τό, (σχεῖν) *a check, remedy*, λιμοῦ against hunger, Eur.

σχετλιάζω, f. άσω, *to complain of hardship, to complain angrily, inveigh bitterly*, Ar., Oratt. Hence

σχετλιασμός, ὁ, *passionate complaint*, Thuc., Arist.

σχέτλιος, α (Ion. η), ον, also ος, ον, (σχεῖν) : **I.** of persons, properly, *unwearying*, σχέτλιος ἐσσι Il. **2.** in bad sense, *unflinching, cruel, merciless*, Hom. : —so in Att., *wicked*, Dem., etc. :—of beasts, *savage*, Hdt. **3.** like τλήμων, *miserable, wretched, unhappy*, Aesch., Eur. ; often with a notion of contempt, ὦ σχετλιώτατε ἀνδρῶν *O most wretched fool !* Hdt. ; ὦ σχέτλιε Soph.; c. gen., ὦ σχετλία τῶν πόνων *O wretched for thy sufferings*, Eur. **II.** of things, σχ. ὕπνος *cruel* sleep, during which Odysseus was abandoned by his companions, Od. ; σχέτλια ἔργα *cruel, shocking* doings, Ib. ; σχέτλια παθεῖν Eur., etc. ; σχ. καὶ δεινά Ar. : also, σχέτλια [ἐστί], c. acc. et inf., Soph. **III.** Adv. –ίως, Isocr.

σχέτο, 3 sing. aor. 2 med. of ἔχω.

σχῆμα, ατος, τό, (σχεῖν) like Lat. *habitus, form, shape, figure*, Eur., Ar., etc. ; as a periphr., σχῆμα πέτρας = πέτρα, Soph. ; σχ. δόμων Eur. **2.** *form, figure, appearance*, as opp. to the reality : *a show, pretence*, Thuc.; ἔχει τι σχῆμα Eur. **3.** *the bearing, look, air, mien* of a person, Hdt., Soph. : in pl. *gestures*, Xen. **4.** *the fashion, manner, way* of a thing, σχ. στολῆς *fashion* of dress, Soph. ; σχ. βίου, μάχης Eur. : absol. *dress, equipment*, Ar., Plat. **5.** *the form, character, characteristic property* of a thing, Thuc.; βασιλείας σχ. *the form* of monarchy, Arist. **6.** *a figure* in dancing, Ar. : in pl. *pantomimic gestures, postures*, Id., Eur. Hence

σχηματίζω, f. Att. ιῶ :—Pass., pf. ἐσχημάτισμαι Arist., v. infr. II. 1; but in sense of Med., v. 1. 2 : **I.** intr. *to assume a certain form, figure, posture* or *position*, Plat. : absol. *to gesticulate, dance figures*, Ar. :—Med., προστάσεως ἣν σχηματίζονται of the pompous appearance which *they assume*, Plat. **2.** in Med. also, *to demean oneself* in a certain way, *make a show of* being or doing, εἰδὼς ἐσχημάτισται he made *as if* he knew him, Id. ; c. inf., σχηματίζονται ἀμαθεῖς εἶναι *they pretend* to be ignorant, Id. **II.** trans. *to give* a certain *form to* a thing, *to form, fashion*, Plut. :—Med., σχηματίζεσθαι κόμην *to ar-*

range one's hair, Eur. :—Pass. *to be fashioned*, Aesch.; also *to deck out, dress up, embellish*, Luc.; *to gesticulate*, Xen.

σχημάτιον [ᾰ], τό, Dim. of σχῆμα : in pl. *the figures of a dance*, Hdt.

σχημᾰτισμός, ὁ, *the assumption of a certain form* or *appearance, deportment*, Plat. **2.** in bad sense, *assumption of manner, pretence*, Id.

σχημᾰτο-ποιέω, f. ήσω, *to bring into a certain form* : Pass. *to take a certain shape* or *posture*, Xen.

σχήσω, fut. of ἔχω.

σχίδαξ, ακος, ὁ, = σχίζα, Anth.

σχίζα, Ion. σχίζη, ης, ἡ, (σχίζω) *a piece of wood cleft off, a lath, splinter*, Lat. *scindula*, Od., Ar. : in pl. *cleft wood, fire-wood*, Hom. **2.** *an arrow*, Anth.

σχίζω (Root ΣΧΙΔ), f. ίσω [ῐ] : aor. 1 ἔσχῐσα : Ep. σχίσσα :—Pass., aor. 1 ἐσχίσθην : pf. ἔσχισμαι :—*to split, cleave*, Hes. ; ἔσχισε δώδεκα μοίρας, i. e. *divided* them *into* twelve parts, h. Hom. ; σχ. κάρα πελέκει Soph. **2.** generally, *to part, separate*, Νεῖλος μέσην Αἴγυπτον σχίζων Hdt. :—Pass., ἐσχίσθη ὁ ποταμός Id. ; Νεῖλος σχίζεται τριφασίας ὁδοὺς *branches* into three channels, Id. ; ἐσχίζοντό σφεων αἱ γνῶμαι their opinions *were divided*, Id.

σχῐνο-κέφαλος, ον, (σχῖνος II) *with a squill-shaped* (i. e. *peaked*) *head*, epith. of Pericles, Plut.

σχῖνος, ἡ, *the mastich-tree*, Lat. *lentiscus*, Theocr. **2.** *its fruit*, Hdt. **II.** *a squill*, = σκίλλα, Ar.

σχισθῆναι, aor. 1 pass. inf. of σχίζω.

σχίσις [ῐ], εως, ἡ, (σχίζω) *a cleaving, cleavage, parting, division*, Plat.

σχίσμα, ατος, τό, (σχίζω) *a cleft, a rent* in a garment, N. T. **II.** *division* of opinion, *schism*, Ib.

σχισμός, ὁ, (σχίζω) *a cleaving*, Aesch.

σχιστός, ή, όν, (σχίζω) *parted, divided*, Soph., Eur.

σχοίατο, for σχοῖντο, 3 pl. aor. 2 med. of ἔχω.

σχοίην, aor. 2 opt. of ἔχω.

σχοίνινος, η, ον, (σχοῖνος) *made of rushes*, Eur.

σχοινίον, τό, Dim. of σχοῖνος II, *a cord*, Hdt., etc.

σχοινίς, ίδος, ἡ, = σχοινίον, Theocr.

σχοινισμός, ὁ, (σχοῖνος) *a fencing with ropes* : in pl. *roping, rope-fences*, Plut.

σχοινῖτις, ιδος, ἡ, (σχοῖνος) *made of rushes*, Anth.

σχοινίων, ωνος, ὁ, *the sedge-bird*, Arist. **II.** *an effeminate air on the flute*, Plut.

σχοινο-βάτης [ᾰ], ου, ὁ, (βαίνω) *a rope-dancer, schoenobates* in Juven.

ΣΧΟΙΝΟΣ, ὁ, *a rush*, Lat. *juncus, scirpus*, Hdt., Ar., etc. **2.** *a reed*, used as *an arrow* or *javelin*, Batr., Ar. **II.** *a place where rushes grow, a rush-bed*, Od., Pind. **III.** *a rush-rope*, and generally, *a rope, cord*, Orac. ap. Hdt. **2.** *a fence* round a garden, Anth. **IV.** *a land-measure*, = 2 Persian parasangs, = 60 stades, Hdt.

σχοινο-τενής, ές, (σχοῖνος IV, τείνω) *stretched out like a measuring line, drawn in a straight line*, Hdt.; σχοινοτενὲς ποιήσασθαι *to draw a straight line*, Id.

σχολάζω, f. άσω, (σχολή) *to have leisure* or *spare time, to be at leisure*, Thuc., etc. :—c. inf. *to have leisure* or *time to do* a thing, Xen. **2.** *to loiter, linger, delay*, Eur., Dem. **II.** σχ. ἀπό τινος, Lat. *vacare a re, to have rest* or *respite from* a thing, *cease from doing*,

Xen.   **III.** σχολάζειν τινί, Lat. *vacare rei, to have leisure* or *opportunity for* a thing, *to devote one's time to* it, Dem.; πρός τι Xen.   **2.** also c. dat. pers. *to devote himself to*, τοῖς φίλοις Id.: esp. of scholars, σχ. τινί *to devote oneself to* a master, *attend his lectures*, Id.; and absol. *to give lectures*, Plut.   **IV.** of a place, *to be vacant* or *unoccupied*, Id.

σχολαῖος, α, ον, (σχολή) *at one's leisure, leisurely, tardy*, Thuc., Xen. :—Adv. -ως, Id.; Comp. σχολαίτερα Hdt.; or -αίτερον, Thuc.; Sup. -αίτατα, Xen.

σχολαιότης, ητος, ἡ, *leisureliness, laziness*, Thuc.

σχολαστήριον, τό, *a place for passing leisure in*, Plut.

σχολαστής, οῦ, ὁ, (σχολάζω) *one who lives at ease*, Plut.   **II.** as Adj. *leisurely, idle*, βίος Id.

σχολαστικός, ή, όν, (σχολάζω) *enjoying leisure*, Lat. *otiosus*, Arist.; τὸ σχολαστικόν *leisure*, Id.   **II.** *devoting one's leisure to learning, a scholar*, Plut. : —in bad sense, *a pedant, simpleton*, Luc.

ΣΧΟΛΗ', ἡ, *spare time, leisure, rest, ease*, Lat. *otium*, Hdt., etc.; σχολὴν ἄγειν and ἔχειν to be at *leisure*, keep *quiet*, Eur., etc.; σχ. ποιεῖσθαι to find *leisure*, Xen.; σχ. λαβεῖν Eur.; σχολή [ἐστί] μοι I have *time*, Ar., etc. :—with a Prep., ἐπὶ σχολῆς *at leisure*, at a *fit time*, Eur.; κατὰ σχολήν Id.   **2.** c. gen. *rest from* a thing, σχολῇ κακοῦ Soph.; so, σχ. ἀπό τινος Plat.   **3.** *idleness*, Eur.   **II.** *that in which leisure is employed*, esp. *a learned discussion, lecture*, Plat., etc.   **2.** *a place for lectures, a school*, Arist., etc.

B. σχολῇ as Adv. *in a leisurely way, tardily*, like σχολαίως, Soph., Thuc., etc.   **2.** *at one's leisure*, i. e. *scarcely, hardly, not at all*, Soph., etc.; σχολῇ γε Id. :—to introduce an à fortiori argument, εἰ αὗται μὴ ἀκριβεῖς εἰσί, σχολῇ αἱ ἄλλαι *if these are not exact, hardly can the rest be so*, Plat.

σχόλιον, τό, (σχολή II) *a short note, scholium*, Luc.

σχόμενος, aor. 2 med. part. of ἔχω : imper. σχοῦ.

σχῶ, aor. 2 subj. of ἔχω : 1 pl. σχῶμεν : part. σχών.

σῶ, v. σάω, σήθω.

σῷ, Att. contr. for σῶοι.

σώζω (σῶς), pf. σέσωκα :—Med., f. σώσομαι : aor. 1 ἐσωσάμην :—Pass., f. σωθήσομαι : aor. 1 ἐσώθην : pf. σέσωσμαι, 3 sing. σέσωσται and σέσωται : —besides these forms, we have   **1.** (from σόω) subj. σόης, -η, -ωσι ;   **2.** (from σαόω) 3 sing. σαοῖ, 3 pl. σαοῦσι ; imperat. σάω or σάον ; 3 sing. impf. σάω ; f. σαώσω, aor. 1 ἐσάωσα :—Pass., aor. 1 inf. σαωθῆναι, imperat. σαωθήτω, Ep. 3 pl. ἐσάωθεν : fut. med. σαώσομαι.   **3.** (from contr. pres. σώω) part. σώοντες, Ion. impf. σώεσκον.   *To save, keep* :   **1.** of persons, *to save from death, keep alive, preserve*, Hom., Att.   **2.** of things, *to keep safe, preserve*, Hom. :—Med. *to keep* or *preserve for oneself*, Soph., etc.   **3.** *to keep, observe, maintain* laws, etc., Trag. :—Pass., Thuc.   **4.** *to keep in mind, remember*, Eur., Plat. :—so in Med., Soph., Plat.   **II.** with a sense of motion to a place, *to bring one safe to*, τὸν δ' ἐσάωσεν ἐς ποταμοῦ προχοὰς Od.; σ. τινὰ πρὸς ἤπειρον Aesch. :—in Pass. *to come safe, escape to* a place, ἐς οἶκον Hdt.; ἐπὶ θάλατταν Xen.   **2.** *to carry off safe, rescue from* danger, ἐκ πολέμοιο Il.; ἐκ θανάτοιο Od.; ἀπὸ στρατείας Aesch.: —c. gen., ἐχθρῶν σῶσαι χθόνα *to rescue* the land from enemies, Soph.; Pass., σωθῆναι κακῶν Eur.   **3.** c.

inf., αἵ σε σώζουσιν θανεῖν *who save* thee *from* dying, Id.   **4.** absol. τὰ σώσοντα *what is likely to save*, Dem.

σωκέω, only in pres. *to have strength*, Aesch.   **2.** c. inf. *to be in a condition to* do, Soph.   From

ΣΩ͂ΚΟΣ, ὁ, *the stout, strong one*, of Hermes, Il.

Σωκρατέω, f. ήσω, *to do like Socrates, to Socratise*, Ar.

Σω-κράτης [ᾰ], ὁ, (σῶς, κράτος) *Socrates* : gen. Σωκράτους : acc. Σωκράτην Xen., but also (as if of 3rd decl.) Σωκράτη Ar., Plat.   Hence

Σωκρατίδιον, τό, Dim. *dear little Socrates*, Ar.

Σωκρατικός, ή, όν, *Socratic, of Socrates*, Arist., etc.; οἱ Σωκρ. *the philosophers of his school*, Luc. Adv. -κῶς, *more Socratico*, Cic.

ΣΩΛΗ'Ν, ῆνος, ὁ, *a channel, gutter, pipe*, Hdt.

σῶμα, ατος, τό, (deriv. uncertain), *the body* of a man : in Hom. always *the dead body, corpse, carcase*, whereas *the living body* is δέμας.   **2.** *the living body*, Hes., Hdt., Att. ; τὸ σ. σώζειν or -εσθαι *to save* one's *life*, Dem., Thuc. ; ἔχειν τὸ σ. κακῶς, ὡς βέλτιστα, to be in a bad, a good state of body, Xen.   **3.** *body*, as opp. to the *soul* (ψυχή), Plat., etc. ; τὰ τοῦ σ. ἔργα *bodily labours*, Xen. ; τὰ εἰς τὸ σ. τιμήματα *bodily punishments*, Aeschin.   **II.** periphr., ἀνθρώπου σῶμα = ἄνθρωπος, Hdt. ; esp. in Trag., σῶμα θηρός = ὁ θήρ, Soph., etc. :—often of slaves, σ. αἰχμάλωτα Dem., etc.   **III.** generally, *a body*, i. e. *any material substance*, Plat., etc.   **IV.** *the whole body* or *mass* of a thing, ὑπὸ σώματι γῆς Aesch. ; τὸ σ. τῆς πίστεως *the body* of the proof, Arist.

σωμ-ασκέω, f. ήσω, *to exercise the body*, Xen. :— metaph., σ. τὸν πόλεμον *to train oneself* for war, Plut.

σωμασκία, ἡ, *bodily exercise, training of the body*, esp. of an *athletic* kind, Xen., etc.

σωμᾰτικός, ή, όν, (σῶμα) *of* or *for the body, bodily*, Lat. *corporeus*, Arist. :—Adv. -κῶς, N. T.   **2.** *bodily, corporeal, material*, Arist.

σωμάτιον [ᾰ], τό, Dim. of σῶμα, *a poor body*, Isocr.

σωμᾰτο-ειδής, ές, (εἶδος) *of the nature of a body, bodily, material*, Plat.

σωμᾰτο-ποιέω, f. ήσω, *to make into a body, to consolidate, organise*, Polyb.   **II.** *to provide with bodily strength, to recruit*, Id.

σωμᾰτο-φθορέω, (φθείρω) *to corrupt the body*, Aesch.

σωμᾰτο-φὔλάκιον, τό, (φυλακή) *a place where a body is kept, a sepulchre*, Luc.

σῶν, Att. acc. sing. for σῶον.

σῶος, α, ον, contr. σῶς, q. v.

σωπάω, Dor. and poët. for σιωπάω.

σώρᾰκος, ὁ, (σωρός) *a basket* or *box*, Babr.

σωρείτης, ου, ὁ, (σωρός) masc. Adj. *heaped up* : ὁ σωρείτης [συλλογισμός] *a sorites* or *heap of syllogisms*, the conclusion of one forming the premiss of the next, Luc.

σώρευμα, ατος, τό, *a heap, pile*, Xen.   From

σωρεύω, f. εύσω, (σωρός) *to heap* one thing *on* another, Lat. *coacervare*, Arist., N. T.   **II.** *to heap with* something, c. dat., Anth.

σωρηδόν, Adv. *by heaps, in heaps*, Anth.   From

σωρός, ὁ, (σορός) *a heap*, Lat. *acervus*, Hes., etc.   **2.** generally, *a heap, quantity*, Ar.

ΣΩ͂Σ, ὁ, ἡ, only found in nom. σῶς, acc. σῶν, pl. σῶς ; neut. σᾶ :—the Ion. σόος is used by Hom. in all cases except the nom. sing. σῶς :—the form σῶος used by

Att. writers only in pl. σῶοι, σῶαι, σῶα:—the radic. form σάος occurs in the Comp. σαώτερος, v. sub σάος:—radic. sense *safe and sound, alive and well, in good case*, Lat. *salvus*, Hom., Hdt., Thuc. II. of things, *sound, whole, safe*, Hom. 2. of events, *safe, sure, certain*, νῦν σῶς αἰπὺς ὄλεθρος Il.

σωσί-πολις [ῐ], ιδος, ὁ, ἡ, *saving the city*, Ar.

σωστέον, verb. Adj. of σώζω, *one must save*, Eur.

σῶστρα, τά, (σώζω) *a reward for saving one's life, a thankoffering for deliverance*, σῶστρα τοῦ παιδὸς θύειν Hdt.; σ. τίνειν Luc. 2. *a reward for bringing back* lost cattle or slaves, Hdt., Xen.

σώτειρα, ἡ, fem. of σωτήρ, Hdt., Eur., etc. 2. epith. of goddesses (cf. *Juno Sospita*), Pind., Ar.

σωτήρ, ῆρος, ὁ, voc. σῶτερ: (σώζω):—*a saviour, deliverer, preserver*, c. gen. subjecti, τῆς Ἑλλάδος *saviour* of Greece, Hdt.; also c. gen. objecti, σ. νόσου, κακῶν *a preserver from* disease, ills, Soph., Eur. 2. epith. of *protecting* gods, esp. of Ζεὺς Σωτήρ, Pind., Trag.: to him *the third cup* of wine was dedicated, τρίτον Σωτῆρι σπένδειν Pind., etc.; proverb., τὸ τρίτον τῷ σωτῆρι the third (i. e. the lucky) time, Plat.; of other gods, as of Apollo, Hermes, Aesch.; even with fem. deities, Τύχη σωτήρ, for σώτειρα, Id. 3. in N. T. *the Saviour*. II. in Poets, as an Adj., *saving*, Aesch.; with fem. Subst., σωτῆρες τιμαί the office or prerogative of *saving*, of the Dioscuri, Eur.

σωτηρία, Ion. -ίη, ἡ, *a saving, deliverance, preservation, safety*, Lat. *salus*, Hdt., Att.; σ. τινὶ διδόναι, φέρειν Eur.; σωτηρίαν ἔχειν Soph., etc. 2. *a way* or *means of safety*, Aesch., Eur., etc. 3. *a safe return*, ἡ ἐς τὴν πατρίδα σ. Thuc.; ἡ οἴκαδε σωτηρία Dem.; also, νόστιμος σ. Aesch. II. of things, *a keeping safe, preservation*, τινός of anything, Hdt., Aesch., etc. 2. *security, guarantee for safety*, ἔστω τινὸς guarantee *for the safe keeping* of a thing, ap. Dem.; σωτηρίαι τῆς πολιτείας *ways of preserving* it, Arist. 3. *security, safety*, Thuc.

σωτήριος, ον, (σωτήρ) *saving, delivering*, Thuc., Plat., etc.; ἐλπὶς σπέρματος σωτηρίου hope of seed *to preserve* the race, Aesch.:—c. dat. *bringing safety* or *deliverance to* one, Id., Eur.:—Comp. -ιώτερος, α, ον, *more likely to bring safety*, Xen. II. of persons, much like σωτήρ, Soph., Eur. II. as Subst. σωτήρια, τά, like σωτηρία, ἡ, *deliverance, safety*, Aesch., Soph.; so in sing., πόλεως σ. Aesch. 2. σωτήρια (sc. ἱερά), τά, *a thankoffering for deliverance*, Xen.

σωφρονέω, f. ήσω, (σώφρων) *to be sound of mind*, Hdt. 2. *to be temperate, discreet, shew self-control*, Aesch., Ar., etc.; σ. περὶ τοὺς θεούς Xen. 3. *to come to one's senses, learn self-control*, Hdt., etc. 4. Pass., τὰ σεσωφρονημένα μοι *things I had done with discretion*, Aeschin. Hence

σωφρόνημα, τό, *an instance of temperance*, Xen.; and

σωφρονητέον, verb. Adj. *one must be temperate*, Luc.

σωφρονητικός, ή, όν, = σωφρονικός, Xen.

σωφρονίζω, f. Att. ιῶ, (σώφρων) *to recal* a person *to his senses, to chasten*, Eur., Xen., etc.:—Pass. *to be chastened, to learn self-control*, Thuc., etc. 2. of passions, *to correct, moderate*, Xen.; so, σ. ἄμπνοας to pant less violently, Eur.; ἐς εὐτέλειαν σ. to reduce expenses, Thuc.

σωφρονικός, ή, όν, (σώφρων) *naturally temperate, moderate, sober*, Xen., etc.:—Adv. -κῶς, Ar.

σωφρονιστήρ, ῆρος, ὁ, = σωφρονιστής, Plat.

σωφρονιστής, οῦ, ὁ, (σωφρονίζω) *one that makes temperate, a chastener, chastiser*, Thuc., Plat., etc.

σωφροσύνη, Dor. -ύνα, Ep. σαοφροσύνη, ἡ, *soundness of mind, moderation, discretion*, Od., Theogn., Att. 2. *moderation in desires, self-control, temperance, chastity, sobriety*, Lat. *temperantia, modestia*, Ar., Plat., etc. From

σώ-φρων, Ep. σαό-φρων, ονος, ὁ, ἡ: neut. σῶφρον, (σῶς, φρήν) *of sound mind*, Lat. *sanae mentis*:—hence *sensible, discreet, wise*, Hom., Hdt., Xen. 2. of things, σώφρονα εἰπεῖν Eur.; ἄλλο τι σωφρονέστερον γιγνώσκειν Thuc.:—σῶφρόν ἐστι, c. inf., Id. II. *having control over the sensual desires, temperate, self-controlled, moderate, chaste, sober*, Trag., Plat., etc.:—so, σ.γνώμη Aesch.; σ. ἀριστοκρατία Thuc. 2. τὸ σῶφρον = σωφροσύνη, Eur., Thuc., etc. III. Adv. -όνως, Hdt.—Comp. σωφρονέστερον, Thuc.; so, ἐπὶ τὸ σωφρονέστερον Hdt.:—but -εστέρως, Eur.:—Sup. -έστατα, Isocr.

ΣΩ'ΧΩ, Ion. for ψώχω, *to rub*: cf. κατα-σώχω.

σώω, Ep. for σώζω.

T.

Τ, τ, ταῦ, τό, indecl., nineteenth letter of the Gr. alphabet: as numeral τ' = 300, but ‚τ = 300,000.

I. τ is the tenuis dental mute, related to the medial δ and the aspirate θ. II. Changes of τ: 1. Aeol. and Dor., τ for σ, as τύ (Lat. *tu, thou*) for σύ; τοί τέ τῦκον φατί for σοί σέ σῦκον φησί. 2. in new Att., as in Dor. and Boeot., ττ for σσ, mostly in Verbs, πράττω for πράσσω, etc. 3. in Ion. the tenuis τ for its aspirate θ, as αὖτις for αὖθις; so, the tenuis remains unchanged before an aspirate, as κατεῖλον, κατ' ἡσυχίην. 4. the Poets, metri grat., insert τ after π at the beginning of some words, e. g. πτόλις, πτόλεμος.

τ', apostroph. for τε, *and*. 2. the Particle τοι is not elided before ἄν and ἄρα, τ' ἄν, τ' ἄρα, μέντ' ἄν, but joined with them by crasis, τἄν, τἄρα, μεντἄν. 3. so, τό, τά are never elided, but form crasis, as τἀγαθόν, τἀγαθά.

τά, neut. pl. of ὁ, ὅ, and ὅς.

τάβλα or τάβλη, ἡ, = Lat. *tabula, a dice-table*, Anth.

ταβλιόπη, ἡ, comic word, formed after Καλλιόπη, *a game at dice*, Anth.

τἀγαθά, crasis for τὰ ἀγαθά:—τἀγαθόν for τὸ ἀγαθόν.

τἀγαμέμνονος, crasis for τοῦ Ἀγαμέμνονος.

ταγεία, ἡ, *the office* or *rank of* ταγός, Xen.

τάγεις, aor. 2 pass. part. of τάσσω.

ταγεύω, f. σω, (ταγός) *to be Chief* of Thessaly, Xen.:—Pass. *to be united under one* ταγός, Id. II. Med. *to let* soldiers *be posted* or *stationed*, Aesch.

ταγέω, f. ήσω, (ταγός) *to be ruler*, ἁπάσης Ἀσίδος τ. Aesch.

ταγή, Dor. ταγά, ἡ, (ταγός) *an array, command*:—collectively, ξύμφρων ταγά *the chiefs* of one mind, Aesch.

τάγηνον [ᾰ], τό, a frying-pan, saucepan, Ar., Luc.; often in form τήγᾰνον.

τάγης [ᾰ], ου, ὁ, = τάγος, Xen.

τάγμα, ατος, τό, (τάσσω) that which has been ordered or arranged : esp., I. an ordinance, ἐκ δύοιν τ. from a combination of two constitutions, Arist. II. a body of soldiers, a regiment or brigade, Xen., etc.: —the Roman manipulus, Polyb.

τᾱγός, ὁ, (τάσσω) a commander, chief, Aesch., Eur. II. esp. the Chief of Thessaly, Xen.

τᾰγ-οῦχος, ὁ, (ἔχω) holding command, Aesch.

τᾰγχέλεια, crasis for τὰ ἐγχέλεια.

τᾰδελφοῦ, crasis for τὸ or τὰ ἀδελφοῦ.

τᾰδικεῖν, crasis for τὰ ἀδικεῖν :—τἄδικον, for τὸ ἄδικον.

τάθη, Ep. for ἐτάθη [ᾰ], 3 sing. aor. 1 pass. of τείνω.

Ταίναρος, ἡ, Taenarus, the southern point of Laconia, Pind., etc.: neut. Ταίναρον, τό, Strab.

ταινία, ἡ, (τανύω, τείνω) a band, riband, fillet, esp. a head-band, worn in sign of victory, Xen., Plat., etc. II. a strip or tongue of land, Plut., etc.

ταινιό-πωλις, ἡ, a dealer in ταινίαι, Dem.

ταινιόω, f. ώσω, (ταινία) to bind with a head-band, as a conqueror, Thuc., Xen.: Pass. to be crowned, Ar.

ταῖτιον, = τᾴτιον.

τᾰκεῖ, τᾰκείνων, crasis for τὰ ἐκεῖ, τὰ ἐκείνων.

τᾰκερός, ά, όν, (τήκω) melting in the mouth, tender, Com.: of eyes, melting, languishing, Anth.

τακτικός, ή, όν, (τάσσω) fit for ordering or arranging, esp. in war, τ. ἀνήρ a tactician, Xen.; τακτικὸν ἡγεῖσθαί τι to think it a good piece of tactics, Id.; οἱ τ. ἀριθμοὶ the regular battalions, Id.: τὰ τακτικά the art of drawing up soldiers in array, tactics, Id.

τακτός, ή, όν, verb. Adj. of τάσσω, ordered, prescribed, τ. ἀργύριον a stated sum, Thuc.; σῖτος τ. a fixed quantity of corn, Id.; τ. ὁδός a prescribed way, Dem.

τάκω [ᾰ], Dor. for τήκω.

τᾰλᾰ-εργός, όν, (*τλάω, ϝέργον) enduring labour, drudging, of mules, Hom., Hes.; of Hercules, Theocr.

τᾰλαιπωρέω : pf. τεταλαιπώρηκα :—Pass., aor. 1 ἐταλαιπωρήθην :—to go through hard labour, to suffer hardship or distress, Eur., Thuc., etc. II. trans. to weary, wear out, Isocr. :—in Pass. to be worn out, be sore distressed, Ar., etc.; and

τᾰλαιπωρία, Ion. -ίη, ἡ, hard work, hardship, suffering, distress, Thuc.; in pl. hardships, Hdt. 2. bodily suffering or pain, caused by disease, Thuc. From

τᾰλαί-πωρος, ον, prob. a form of ταλαπείριος, suffering, miserable, Aesch., etc. :—Adv. -ρως, Thuc. 2. of things, τ. βίος Soph.; πράγματα Ar.

τᾰλαί-φρων, ονος, ὁ, ἡ, (*τλάω, φρήν) suffering in mind, wretched, Soph., Eur.: daring, Soph. :—voc. ταλαίφρον, Id.

τᾰλᾰ-κάρδιος, ον, (*τλάω) patient of heart, stout-hearted, of Hercules, Hes.: of Oedipus, much-enduring, miserable, Soph.

τᾰλαντεύω, f. σω, to weigh or measure out, Anth.

τᾰλαντιαῖος, ον, α, or, worth α talent, Dem. From

τάλαντον, τό, (*τλάω) a balance, Theogn., Ar. :—in pl. a pair of scales, Il., etc. II. anything weighed, 1. a definite weight, a talent, in Hom. of gold; but the weight of the Homeric talent is unknown. 2. in later times the τάλαντον was both a weight and a sum

of money represented by that weight of silver :—the Attic talent weighed about 57.75 lbs. avoird., and its value in our money was about 200l. There was, of course, no such coin as a talent. For purposes of coinage, a talent of silver was coined into 6000 drachmae.

τᾰλαντ-οῦχος, ον, (ἔχω) holding the balance : metaph., Ἄρης τ. who turns the scale in battle, Aesch.

τᾰλαός, ή, όν, (*τλάω) = τλήμων, Ar.

τᾰλᾰ-πείριος, ον, (*τλάω, πεῖρα) subject to many trials, much-suffering, of Ulysses, Od. :—hence, vagrant, vagabond, Anth.

τᾰλᾰ-πενθής, ές, (*τλάω, πένθος) patient in woe, Od.

τᾰλᾰρίσκος, ὁ, Dim. of sq., quasillus, Theocr., Anth.

ΤΑ'ΛΑΡΟΣ [τᾰ], ὁ, a basket, Lat. qualus, Od.; πλεκτὸς τάλ. a basket of wicker-work, in which new-made cheeses were placed so as to let the whey run off, Hom.

τᾰλᾶς, τάλαινα (also τάλας), τάλαν (like μέλας) : gen. ἄνος, αίνης, ανος : voc., τάλας or -αν, v. infra : (*τλάω) : — suffering, wretched, Lat. miser, Od., Trag.; ὦ τάλας ἐγώ Soph.; ὦ τάλαιν᾽ ἐγώ Aesch.; ὦ τάλαν Soph. :—c. gen. causae, τάλαν᾽ ἐγὼ τῆς ὕβρεως wretched that I am for this insolence, Ar. :—in bad sense, τάλαν wretch! Od.—Comp. τᾰλάντερος, α, ον : Sup. τᾰλάντατος, η, ον, Ar. [τᾰλᾶς ; Dor. also τᾰλᾶς : voc. τάλᾰν.]

τᾰλᾰσία, ἡ, wool-spinning, Xen., etc. Hence

τᾰλάσιος, ον, (*τλάω) of or for wool-spinning, Xen.

τᾰλᾰσι-ουργέω, f. ήσω, to spin wool, Xen., Luc.; and

τᾰλᾰσιουργικός, ή, όν, of or for wool-spinning, Xen.

τᾰλᾰσι-ουργός, ὁ, ἡ, (*ἔργω) a wool-spinner, Plat.

τᾰλᾰσί-φρων, ονος, ὁ, ἡ, (*τλάω, φρήν) patient of mind, stout-hearted, Il.: epith. of Ulysses, Hom.

τᾰλάσσῃς, -σῃ, 2 and 3 sing. Ep. aor. 1 of *τλάω.

τᾰλαύ-ρινος, ον, (*τλάω, ῥινός) with shield of tough bull's-hide, Il.: τ. χρώς a thick tough hide, Anth. :— neut. as Adv., ταλαύρινον πολεμίζειν to fight toughly, stoutly, Il.

τᾰλᾰ-φρων, ὁ, ἡ, shortd. for ταλασί-φρων, Il.

τᾰληθές, crasis for τὸ ἀληθές.

τᾱλίκος, ον, Dor. for τηλίκος.

τᾱλις, ιδος, ἡ, a marriageable maiden, Soph. (Deriv. uncertain.)

τἄλλα, crasis for τὰ ἄλλα :—τἀμά, for τὰ ἐμά.

τάμε, Ep. 3 sing. aor. 2 of τέμνω :—ταμέειν, Ep. inf.

ταμεῖον, τό, = ταμιεῖον, Babr.

τᾰμέσθαι, aor. 2 med. inf. of τέμνω.

τᾰμεσί-χρως, ὁ, ἡ, (τέμνω) cutting the skin, wounding, Il.

τᾰμία, Ion. -ίη, ἡ, a housekeeper, housewife, Hom., Xen.

τᾰμίας, Ion. -ίης, ου, ὁ, (τέμνω) one who carves and distributes, a dispenser, Il., Pind., Ar. :—of Zeus, as the dispenser of all things to men, Il.; so Aeolus is τ. ἀνέμων Od. :—of kings or rulers, a controller, director, Pind.; τ. κώμων master of the revels, Id.; τ. Διός the priest of Zeus, Id. : τ. Μοισᾶν, i. e. a poet, Id.; οἶκος τ. στεφάνων that hath store of crowns, Id.; τῆς τε ἐπιθυμίας καὶ τῆς τύχης τ. controller both of his desire and of fortune, Thuc.; τ. τριαίνης, of Poseidon, Ar. II. in Prose, a controller of payments, treasurer, Hdt.; τ. τοῦ ἱροῦ the controller of the sacred treasure in the citadel of Athens, Id. 2. at Rome, the quaestor, Plut.

τᾰμιεία, ἡ, (ταμιεύω) stewardship, management, eco-

nomy, Xen.   II. *the office of paymaster*, as a polit. term, Arist.   2. at Rome, *the quaestorship*, Plut.

ταμιεῖον, τό, (ταμιεύω) *a treasury*, Thuc., etc.   2. *a magazine*, Xen.

ταμίευμα, ατος, τό, = ταμιεία, Xen.

ταμιευτικός, ή, όν, *of* or *for stewardship* :—at Rome, *belonging to the quaestorship*, Plut.

ταμιεύω, f. σω :—Pass., pf. τεταμίευμαι: (ταμίας) : —*to be controller* of receipts and expenditure, *to be treasurer, paymaster*, Ar., Dem. :—c. gen., τ. τῆς Παράλου *to be paymaster of* the Paralus, Dem.   2. at Rome, *to be quaestor*, Plut.   II. trans. *to deal out, dispense*, Plat., etc. :—Pass., τοὺς νόμους τετα-μιεύμεθα *we have* the laws *dealt out*, Lysias :—Med., ταμιεύεσθαι εἰς ὅσον βουλόμεθα ἄρχειν *to control* the limits to which we mean to extend our sway, Thuc.   2. of keeping house, *to regulate, manage*, Ar., Xen. :— Pass., χώρα ταμιευομένα τινί *governed* or *possessed* by one, Pind.   3. *to store up*, Dem. ; Ζηνὸς ταμιεύεσκε γονὰς *she was the depository of* it, Soph.

ταμίη, ταμίης, Ion. for ταμία, ταμίας.

τάμῑσος [ᾰ], ἡ, *rennet*, Theocr.

τάμμέσῳ, crasis for τὰ ἐν μέσῳ.

τάμνω, Ion. for τέμνω.

τάμπᾰλιν, crasis for τὰ ἔμπαλιν.

τᾰμών, Ion. aor. 2 part. of τέμνω.

τᾶν, crasis for τοι ἄν :—but **τὰν**, for τὰ ἐν.

τᾶν or **τάν**, indecl., only in phrase, ὦ τᾶν or ὦ τάν, *sir, my good friend*, Soph., Eur., Plat., etc. ; used in addressing several persons, ὦ τᾶν, ἀπαλλαχθῆτον Ar. (Origin uncertain.)

Τάναγρα, ἡ, a town of Boeotia, Hdt., etc. :—Adj. **Ταναγρικός**, ή, όν, *of Tanagra*, Id. :—**Ταναγραῖος**, ὁ, a man of *Tanagra*, Xen. :—ἡ **Ταναγραϊκή** *the district of T.*, Plut.

τᾰνα-ήκης, ες, (ἀκή) *with long point* or *edge*, Il.

τᾰναί-μῡκος, ον, *far-bellowing*, Anth.

τἀναντία, crasis for τὰ ἐναντία.

τᾰναό-δειρος, ον, (δείρη) *long-necked*, Ar.

τᾰναός, ή, όν, and ός, όν, (τείνω) *stretched, out-stretched, tall, long, taper*, Il. ; πλόκαμος τ. *long flow-ing* locks, Eur. ; τ. αἰθήρ *outspread* ether, Id. ; τ. γῆρας *long old age*, Anth.

τᾰναύ-πους (i. e. τανάϝπους), ποδος, ὁ, ἡ, old Ep. form for τανύπους, *stretching the feet, long-striding, long-shanked*, h. Hom., Od.

τᾰνδον, crasis for τὰ ἔνδον.

τἀνδρί, τἀνδρός, crasis for τῷ ἀνδρί, τοῦ ἀνδρός.

τἀνέκᾰθεν, crasis for τὸ ἀνέκαθεν.

τᾰνη-λεγής, ές, (ταναός, λέγω) *laying one out at length*, epith. of death, Hom.

τᾱνίκα, Dor. for τηνίκα.

Τάνις, εως or ιος, ἡ, a town in lower *Egypt*, the Hebrew *Zoan*, Strab. :—ὁ **Τανίτης** νόμος the *Tanite* nome, Hdt.

τἀνταῖα, crasis for τὰ ἀνταῖα.

τανταλόομαι, for ταλαντόομαι, (τάλαντον) Pass. *to be balanced* or *swung*, ἐπὶ γᾷ πέσε τανταλωθείς fell *with a swing* upon earth, Soph.

Τάνταλος [τᾰ], ὁ, *Tantalus*, king of Phrygia, ancestor of the Pelopidae, Od. :—Adj. **Ταντάλειος**, α, ον, *of* or *belonging to T.*, Eur. :—**Τανταλίδης**, ου, ὁ, *son of*

T., Aesch. :—**Τανταλίς**, ίδος, *daughter of T.*, i. e. Niobé, Anth.   (From *τλάω, prob. in relation to his *long endurance* of torment.)

τἀνταῦθα, crasis for τὰ ἐνταῦθα :—**τἀντεῦθεν**, for τὰ ἐν-τεῦθεν.

τἀντός, crasis for τὰ ἐντός.

τἀντίπᾰλον, crasis for τὸ ἀντίπαλον.

τᾰνύ-γλωσσος, ον, (τανύω, γλῶσσα) *long-tongued, chattering*, Od.

τᾰνύ-γλώχῑς, ῖνος, ὁ, ἡ, (τανύω) *with long point*, Il.

τᾰνύ-δρομος, ον, *running at full stretch*, Aesch.

τᾰνύ-έθειρα, ἡ, (τανύω) *with flowing hair*, Pind.

τᾰνύ-ήκης, ες, (τανύω, ἀκή) like ταναήκης, *with long point* or *edge*, Hom.   II. *tapering*, Il.

τᾰνύ-ηλιξ, ῑκος, ὁ, ἡ, (τανύω) *of extended age*, Anth.

τᾰνύ-θριξ, τρῐχος, ὁ, ἡ, (τανύω) *long-haired, shaggy*, Hes.

τάνῡμαι, Pass., = τανύομαι, *to be stretched*, Il.

τᾰνῡ-μήκης, ες, (τανύω, μῆκος) *long-stretched, tall*, ἰτέαι Anth.

τανῦν, Adv. for νῦν, *now, at present*, v. νῦν 1.

τᾰνύ-πεπλος [ῠ], ον, (τανύω) *with flowing peplos*, Hom.

τᾰνύ-πλεκτος [ῠ], ον, (τανύω) *in long plaits*, Anth.

τᾰνύ-πλευρος [ῠ], ον, (τανύω, πλευρά) *long-sided, enor-mous*, Anth.

τᾰνύ-πους [ῠ], ὁ, ἡ, = ταναύπους, Soph.

τᾰνύ-πτερος, ον, shorter form of τανυσίπτερος, Hes., Pind.

τᾰνυ-πτέρυξ, ῠγος, ὁ, ἡ, = τανύπτερος, Il.

τᾰνύρ-ριζος, ον, (τανύω, ῥίζα) *with far-stretching roots*, Hes.

τᾰνῠσί-πτερος, ον, (τανύω, πτερόν) *with extended wings, long-winged*, Od., Hes., Ar.

τᾰνυστύς, ύος, ἡ, (τανύω) *a stretching, stringing*, Od.

τᾰνύ-σφυρος, ον, (τανύω, σφυρόν) *with taper ancles*, Hes.

τᾰνύ-φλοιος, ον, (τανύω) *of trees, with long-stretched bark*, i. e. *of tall* or *slender growth*, Il.

τᾰνύ-φυλλος [ῠ], ον, (τανύω, φύλλον) *with long-pointed leaves*, of the olive, Il.   II. *with thick foliage, leafy*, Theocr.

τᾰνύω, f. ύσω, Ep. -ύω : aor. 1 ἐτάνυσα, Ep. ἐτάνυσσα, τάνυσσα :—Med., Ep. aor. 1 part. τανυσσάμενος :—Pass., aor. 1 ἐτανύσθην, Ep. 3 pl. τάνυσθεν : 3 sing. pf. τετά-νυσμαι: (τείνω) :—*to stretch, strain, stretch out*, Il. ; τ. βιόν *to string* a bow, Od. ; and in Med., τόξον τανυσ-σάμενος *having strung* his bow, Il. :—of putting the strings to a harp, ἐτάνυσσε χορδήν Od. ; τ. κανόνα *to push* the weaving-bar tight, i. e. *to weave*, Il. ; ὅπως τανύσῃ when *he reins in* [the horses], Ib. ; ἐπὶ Ἀκρά-γαντι τανύσσας *having aimed* them, Pind. :—Pass., γναθμοὶ τάνυσθεν (for ἐτανύσθησαν) the hollow cheeks *filled out*, Od. ; *to run at full stretch*, of horses galloping, Hom.   2. metaph. *to strain, make more intense*, μάχην Il. ; ἔριδα πολέμοιο πεῖραρ τάνυσσαν *strained* the tug of war, Ib.   II. *to stretch out, lay along, lay*, Hom. ; τ. τινὰ ἐν κονίης, ἐπὶ γαίῃ *to lay* one in the dust, *stretch* him *at his length*, Id. :—Pass. *to lie stretched out*, Id. : *to extend*, Od. ; ἐπὶ χθονὶ κεῖτο τανυσθείς Il. :—also, τρίβος τετάνυστο the path *stretched away*, Theocr.

ταξιαρχέω, f. ήσω, *to be a taxiarch*, Ar., Thuc., etc. From

ταξί-αρχος, ου, ὁ, = ταξίαρχος, Hdt. (in gen. pl. ταξι-αρχέων).

ταξιαρχία, ἡ, *the office of taxiarch*, Arist.   From

ταξί-αρχος, ὁ, *the commander of a squadron*, Hdt.   **II.** at Athens, *the commander of a* τάξις (1. 4), *the corresponding cavalry-*officers *being* φύλαρχοι, Ar. : *generally an officer*, Xen.

ταξί-λοχος, ον, *commanding a* λόχος *or division*, Anth.

ταξιόομαι, Pass. *to engage in battle*, Pind.

τάξις, εως, Ion. ιος, ἡ, (τάσσω) *an arranging* :   **I.** in *military sense* :   1. *a drawing up, the order or disposition of an army*, Thuc., Xen., etc. ; τὰ ἀμφὶ τάξεις *tactics*, Xen.   2. *battle array, order of battle*, Lat. *acies*, κατὰ τάξιν Hdt. ; ἐν τάξει Thuc., etc.   3. *a single rank* or *line* of soldiers, Lat. *ordo*, ἐπὶ τάξεις ὀλίγας γίγνεσθαι to be drawn up a few *lines* deep, Id.   4. *a body of soldiers, a squadron*, Aesch., Soph. : at Athens, *the quota of infantry furnished by each* φυλή (cf. ταξίαρχος 11), Lys. : of smaller bodies, *a company, cohort*, Xen. ; so of ships, *a squadron*, Aesch. :—generally, *a band, company*, Id.   5. *a post* or *place in the line* of battle, Lat. *statio*, Hdt. ; μένειν ἐν τῇ ἑωυτοῦ τάξει, opp. to ἐκλείπειν τὴν τ., Id.   **II.** generally, *an arrangement, order*, Plat., etc.   2. *order, regularity*, Id.   3. τ. τοῦ φόρου *an assessment* of tribute, Xen. : *an arrangement with creditors*, Lex ap. Dem.   4. *a political order, a constitution*, Arist.   **III.** metaph. from 1. 5, *the post* or *position* one holds, Aesch., etc. ; ἐν Θετταλῶν τάξει, ἐν ἐχθροῦ τ. *viewed as* Thessalians, *as* an enemy, Dem. ; ἐν ἐπηρείας τάξει *by way of* insult, Id.   2. *one's duty towards* another, ἡ ὑπέρ τινος τ. Id. ; ἡ εὐνοίας τ. *the duty* of good-will, Id.   **IV.** *a class* of men, as of magistrates, Xen., Dem.

ΤΑ'ΞΟΣ, ὁ, *the yew-tree*, Lat. *taxus*.

ΤΑΠΕΙΝΟ'Σ, ή, όν, *low* :   1. of Place, *lying low*, Hdt. ; ταπεινὰ νέμεσθαι to live *in low regions*, Pind. ; of stature or size, *low*, Xen.   2. of the condition of persons, *brought down, humbled, submissive*, Hdt., Aesch., etc. : *of low rank, lowly, mean*, Lat. *vilis*, Eur., etc. : *small, poor, weak*, Id., Dem. : — Adv. ταπεινῶς πράττειν to be *poorly off*, Isocr.   3. of the spirits, *humbled, dejected*, Thuc., Xen.   4. in moral sense, *partly bad, mean, base, abject*, Xen., etc. ; partly good, *lowly, humble*, Id., N. T.   5. of things, *mean, low, poor*, τ. σχῆμα mean apparel, Xen. : of style, *low, poor*, Arist. ; Adv., ταπεινῶς λέγειν Id.   Hence

ταπεινότης, ητος, ἡ, *lowness* of stature, Hdt.   2. of condition, *low estate, abasement*, Thuc., Isocr.   3. *lowness of spirits, dejection*, Xen.   4. in moral sense, *baseness, vileness*, Plat.

ταπεινοφροσύνη, ἡ, *lowliness, humility*, N. T.   From

ταπεινό-φρων, ονος, ὁ, ἡ, (φρήν) *lowly in mind*, Plut.

ταπεινόω, f. ώσω, (ταπεινός) *to lower* :—Pass., πᾶν ὅρος ταπεινωθήσεται N. T.   **II.** metaph. *to lessen, to humble* φθόνον Plut. : *to disparage*, Polyb.   2. *to humble, abase*, Xen., Aeschin. :—Pass., Plat., Xen.   3. in moral sense, *to make lowly, to humble*, N. T. :—Pass. *to humble oneself*, Ib.   Hence

ταπείνωσις, ἡ, *humiliation, abasement, defeat*, Plat.   2. *low estate, low condition*, N. T.

ταπέκεινα, crasis for τὰ ἀπέκεινα.

ΤΑ'ΠΗΣ [ἄ], ητος, ὁ, *a carpet, rug*, Lat. *tapes*, Hom., Ar.

ταπί, crasis for τὰ ἐπί :—**ταπιεικῆ**, for τὰ ἐπιεικῆ :—**ταπιτίμια**, for τὰ ἐπιτίμια :—**ταπίχειρα**, for τὰ ἐπίχειρα.

τάπις [ἄ], ιδος, ἡ, = δάπις, τάπης, Xen.

ταπό, crasis for τὰ ἀπό :—**ταποβαῖνον**, for τὸ ἀποβαῖνον.

ταπόρρητα, crasis for τὰ ἀπόρρητα.

ταπρῶτα, for τὰ πρῶτα, *at first*, Il.

τάρα, crasis for τοι ἄρα.

τάραγμα [ἄ], ατος, τό, (ταράσσω) *disquietude*, Eur.

τάραγμός, ὁ, *disturbance, confusion*, Aesch., Eur.

ταρακτικός, ή, όν, (ταράσσω) *disturbing*, c. gen., τῆς ψυχῆς Plut.

τάρακτρον, τό, (ταράσσω) *a tool for stirring with*, Ar.

τάράκτωρ, ὁ, poët. for ταράκτης, Aesch.

Ταραντῖνον, τό, *a fine Tarentine woman's garment* : Dim. **Ταραντινίδιον**, τό, Luc.

τάραξί-καρδιος, ον, (καρδία) *heart-troubling*, Ar.

τάραξ-ιππό-στρατος, ον, *troubling the horse-array*, of Cleon as a foe to the 'Ιππεῖς, Ar.

Τάρας, αντος, ὁ, *Tarentum*, a town of Magna Graecia, Hdt., Thuc. :—Adj. **Τάράντινος**, η, ον, *Tarentine*, Strab. ; **Τ.**, ὁ, *a Tarentine*, Hdt.

τάράσσω, Att. -ττω, in Att. also shortd. **θράσσω**, (Root **ΤΑΡΑΧ**) f. ταράξω : aor. 1 ἐτάραξα : pf. τετάραχα, Ep. τέτρηχα (infr. 111) :— Pass., f. ταραχθήσομαι, med. ταράξομαι in pass. sense: aor. 1 ἐταράχθην : pf. τετάραγμαι.   *To stir, stir up, trouble*, in a physical sense, ἐτάραξε πόντον Od. ; σύν τ. τήν τε γῆν καὶ τὴν θάλατταν Ar. ; βροντήμασι κυκάτω πάντα Aesch. ; πάντα τ., of a speaker, *to jumble up*, Dem. ; δεινὰ τ. makes ' confusion worse confounded,' Soph.   2. *to trouble the mind, confound, agitate, disturb, disquiet*, Trag., Plat., etc. : absol. *to cause confusion*, Plat.   3. of an army, *to throw into disorder*, Hdt., Xen., etc. :—Pass. *to be in disorder*, Hdt., Thuc.   4. of political matters, *to agitate, distract*, Ar. :—Pass. *to be in a state of disorder* or *anarchy*, Thuc., Dem.   5. ταράττεσθαι ἐπὶ τῶν ἵππων *to be shaken in one's seat* on horseback, Xen.   **II.** *to stir up* mud, *raise by stirring up*, Ar. : metaph., τ. νεῖκος, πόλεμον Soph., Plat. ; Pass., πόλεμος ἐταράχθη Dem.   **III.** intr. pf. τέτρηχα, *to be in disorder* or *confusion, to be in an uproar*, τετρήχει δ' ἀγορή Il. ; ἀγορὴ τετρηχυῖα Ib.   Hence

τάραχή, ἡ, *trouble, disorder, confusion*, Pind., Thuc., etc.   2. of an army or fleet, Thuc., etc. ; ἐν τῇ ταραχῇ *in the confusion*, Hdt.   3. *political confusion, tumult*, and in pl. *tumults, troubles*, Id., Att. ; τ. γίγνεται τῶν ξυμμάχων πρὸς τοὺς Λακεδαιμονίους Thuc.

τάραχος [ἄ], ὁ, = ταραχή, Xen.

τάράχ-ώδης, ες, (εἶδος) *troublous, turbulent*, Hdt. ; ἴχνη τ. *uncertain, baffling*, Xen.   **II.** *troubled, disordered*, Arist.   2. of an army, Thuc., Xen.   **III.** Adv., ταραχωδῶς ζῆν to live *in a state of confusion*, Isocr. ; τ. ἔχειν πρός τινα to be *rebelliously disposed*, Dem. ; Sup. -έστατα Isocr.

ταρβάλεος, α, ον, *frighted, fearful*, h. Hom., Soph.

ταρβέω, f. ήσω, (τάρβος) *to be frightened, alarmed, terrified*, Hom. ; τ. φόβῳ Soph., Eur. :— absol. *to shew fear*, Il., Aesch. ; τὸ ταρβεῖν *a state of fear*, Eur. ; μή με ταρβήσας προδῷς *from fear*, Soph. ; τεταρβηκώς *fear-stricken*, Eur.   **II.** c. acc. *to fear, dread*, Il., Aesch., etc.   2. *to stand in awe of, revere*, Aesch.

ΤΑ΄ΡΒΟΣ, εος, τό, *fright, alarm, terror,* Il., Trag., etc.   2. *awe, reverence,* τινός *for* one, Aesch.   II. *an object of alarm, a fear, alarm,* Soph., Eur.

ταρβοσύνη, ή, Ep. for τάρβος, Od.

ταρβόσυνος, η, ον, *affrighted* or *affrighting,* Aesch.

τἀργύριον, crasis for τὸ ἀργύριον; τἀργυρίου for τοῦ ἀργ-:—τἄρια, for τὰ ἔρια.

τἄρῑχεία, Ion. -ηΐη, ή, *a preserving, pickling :* in pl., αἱ Ταρῑχεῖαι *factories for salting fish,* Hdt., Strab.

τἄρῑχευσις, ή, *embalming,* of mummies, Hdt.   2. *pickling, salting,* of fish, Id.; and

τἄρῑχευτής, οῦ, ὁ, *an embalmer,* of mummies, Hdt. From

τἄρῑχεύω, f. εύσω, (τάριχος) *to preserve the body by artificial means, to embalm,* of the Egyptian mummies, Hdt., Plat.   II. *to preserve* meat or fish *by salting, pickling,* or *smoking,* Plat. :—Pass., [ἰχθύας] ἐξ ἅλμης τεταριχευμένους Hdt.; τεμάχη τεταριχευμένα *preserved* meat, Xen.   III. metaph. in Pass. *to shrivel up,* Aesch.; τεταριχευμένος *stale,* Dem.

τἄρῑχιον, τό, Dim. of τάριχος, Ar.

τἄρῑχοπωλεῖον, τό, *the salt-fish market,* Theophr.

τἄρῑχοπωλέω, *to sell salt fish,* Plat.   II. *to be engaged with the embalming of corpses,* Luc. From

τἄρῑχο-πώλης, ου, ὁ, (πωλέω) *a dealer in salt fish,* Plut., etc.

τάρῑχος [ἄ], ου, ὁ, *a dead body preserved by embalming, a mummy,* Hdt.   II. *meat* or *fish preserved by salting, pickling,* or *smoking,* Id.

τάρῑχος, ους, τό, =foreg. II, Ar., etc.

ταρπῆναι, Ep. ταρπήμεναι, aor. 2 pass. inf. of τέρπω.

ταρσός, Att. ταρρός, ὁ, (τέρσομαι) *a stand* or *frame* of wicker-work, *a crate,* Lat. *cratis,* Od., Thuc. :—generally, *a basket,* Ar.   2. *a mat of reeds,* built into brickwork to bind it together, Hdt.   II. *any broad flat surface,* as,   1. τ. ποδός *the flat* of the foot, *the part between the toes and the heel,* Il., Hdt.   2. τ. κωπέως *the flat* or *blade* of an oar, Lat. *palmula,* Hdt. : absol. *an oar,* Eur. :—in collective sense, *the oars* on one side of a ship, Thuc.   3. τ. πτέρυγος *the flat* of the wing, *a wing,* Ar.'h. : of a peacock's *tail,* Mosch.

Ταρτάρειος [ἄ], α, ον, *Tartarean, horrible,* Eur., Luc.

Τάρταρος [ἄ], ὁ and ἡ : heterog. pl. Τάρταρα, τά, *Tartarus,* a dark abyss, as deep below Hades as earth below heaven, the prison of the Titans, Il., Hes., etc. :—later, *the nether world,* like Ἅιδης, Hes., Aesch. (Deriv. uncertain.) Hence

Ταρτᾱρόω, *to cast into Tartarus* or *hell,* N. T.

Τάρτησσος, ὁ and ἡ, a city of Spain at the mouth of the Baetis, the *Tarshish* of Scripture, Hdt., Strab. :—Ταρτήσσιος, α, ον, *Tartessian,* Hdt., Ar.

ταρφέες, οἱ, ταρφέα, τά, plur. of ταρφύς.

ταρφειός, ά, όν, v. ταρφύς.

τάρφθη, -θεν, Ep. 3 sing. and pl. aor. 1 pass. of τέρπω.

τάρφος, εος, ὁ, *a thicket,* Il. (From τρέφω *to thicken.*)

ταρφύς, εῖα (or ύς), ύ, (τρέφω) *thick, close,* Aesch.; pl. masc. and neut., like Lat. *frequentes,* ταρφέες ἰοί *thick-flying* arrows, Il.; ταρφέα δρώματα Ib. :—neut. pl. ταρφέα as Adv. *ofttimes, often,* Hom. :—ταρφειαί in Il. must belong to a nom. ταρφειός, unless we write ταρφεῖαι, from ταρφύς.

τἀρχαῖον, crasis for τὸ ἀρχαῖον.

ταρχύω, f. ύσω : Pass., Ep. aor. 1 ταρχύθην [ῡ] Anth. : —*to bury solemnly,* Il.

τάσις [ἄ], εως, ή, (τείνω) *tension, intensity, force,* Plut.; Ὀφρύων τ. *a raising* of the eye-brows, Anth.

τάσσω (Root ΤΑΓ), Att. -ττω : f. τάξω : aor. 1 ἔταξα : pf. τέταχα :—Pass., f. ταχθήσομαι and τάξομαι : aor. 1 ἐτάχθην, rarely aor. 2 ἐτάγην [ἄ] : pf. τέταγμαι, 3 pl. τετάχαται : 3 pl. plqpf. τετάχατο.   *To arrange, put in order,* Hdt., etc. : esp. *to draw up in order of battle, to form, array, marshal,* both of troops and ships, Hdt., Thuc., etc. :—Pass. *to be drawn up,* Hdt.; ἐπὶ τεττάρων ταχθῆναι *in four lines,* Xen.; κατὰ μίαν τεταγμένοι *in single column,* Thuc.: absol., τεταγμένοι *in rank and file,* opp. to ἄτακτοι, Id., etc. :—Med. *to fall in, form in order* of battle, Id.   2. *to post, station,* Hdt., Aesch., etc. :—Pass., Hdt., etc.; ἐς τὸ πεζόν or ἐς π. τετάχθαι or ταχθῆναι *to serve among the infantry,* Id.; c. acc. cogn., τάξιν τινὰ ταχθῆναι Plat.   II. *to appoint* to any service, military or civil, τ. τινὰ ἐπί τινος *one over* a thing, *to a service or task,* Dem., etc.; ἐπί τινι Aesch., etc.; ἐπί τι Ar., etc.; πρός τι Xen. :—Pass., τετάχθαι ἐπί τινι *to be appointed* to a service, Hdt., etc.; ἐπὶ τι Ar.   2. c. acc. et inf. *to appoint one to do* a thing, Xen.; and in Pass. *to be appointed* to do, Aesch., etc. :—also (sine inf.), οἱ τεταγμένοι βραβεῖς Soph.; πρέσβεις ταχθέντες Dem.   3. c. acc. et inf. also, *to order* one to do a thing, Hdt., Soph., etc.; also, τ. τινὶ ποιεῖν τι Hdt., etc. :—Pass., ἐτάχθην or τέταγμαι ποιεῖν τι Id. :—also impers., ἰῷμεν, ἵν' ἡμῖν τέτακται (sc. ἰέναι) Soph.; οἷς ἐτέτακτο βοηθεῖν Thuc.   4. *to assign to* a class, τ. εἰς τάξιν τινά Xen.; τ. ἑαυτόν τινων *to act as one of* a *set,* Dem. :—Pass., πρὸς τὴν ξυμμαχίαν ταχθῆναι *to join* it, Thuc.   III. c. acc. rei, *to place in a certain order,* χωρὶς τ. τι Hdt.; πρῶτον τ. τι Xen.   2. *to appoint, ordain, order, prescribe,* Soph., Plat. :—Pass., τὸ ταχθέν Soph.; τὰ τεταγμένα Xen.   3. of taxes or payments, *to appoint* or *fix* a *certain* payment, τ. τινὶ φόρον Aeschin., etc.; with an inf. added, χρήματα τάξαντες φέρειν Thuc.; τάσσεσθαι ἀργυρίου *to fix* the price, Id. :—Pass., τὸ ταχθὲν τίμημα Plat. : —Med. *to take a payment on oneself,* i. e. *agree to pay* it, φόρον τάξασθαι Hdt.; χρήματα ἀποδοῦναι ταξάμενοι Thuc.   4. in Med., also, generally, *to agree upon, settle,* Plat.   5. *to impose* punishments, τ. δίκην Ar.; τιμωρίαν Dem. :—so in Med., Hdt.   6. in pf. part. pass. *fixed, prescribed,* ὁ τεταγμένος χρόνος Id., etc.; ἡ τετ. ἡμέρα, ἔτος Xen., etc.; ἡ τετ. χώρα Id.

τάτα, =τέττα, Anth.

τᾱτάω, Dor. for τητάω.

τᾄτιον, crasis for τὸ αἴτιον.

τάττω, Att. for τάσσω.

ταῦ, τό, the letter τ, Plat.

Ταΰγετον, Ion. Τηΰγετον, τό, *Mount Taÿgetus,* between Laconia and Messenia, Od., Hdt., etc.

ταύρειος, α, ον, and ος, ον, (ταῦρος) *of bulls, oxen,* or *cows,* Lat. *taurinus,* Trag.   II. *of bull's-hide,* Il.

ταυρ-ελάτης [ἄ], ου, ὁ, (ἐλαύνω) *a bull-driver* :—a Thessalian *bull-fighter, tauridor,* Anth.

ταύρεος, α, ον, =ταύρειος; epith. of Poseidon in Boeotia, because bulls were offered to him, Hes.

ταυρηδόν, Adv. *like a bull, savagely*, Ar., Plat.

ταυρο-βόλος, ον, (βάλλω) *slaughtering bulls*, τελετὴ τ. a *sacrifice of a bull*, Anth.

ταυρο-βόρος, ον, (βι-βρώσκω) *devouring bulls*, Anth.

ταυρο-γάστωρ, ορος, ὁ, (γαστήρ) *with bull's paunch*: metaph. *enormous*, Anth.

ταυρο-δέτης, ου, ὁ, (δέω) *bull-binder*, in fem. -δέτις, ιδος, Anth.

ταυρό-κερως, ωτος, ὁ, ἡ, (κέρας) *bull-horned*, Eur.

ταυρό-κρᾱνος, ον, (κράνιον) = ταυροκέφαλος, Eur.

ταυρο-κτονέω, f. ήσω, *to slaughter bulls*, Aesch. From

ταυρο-κτόνος, ον, (κτείνω) *slaughtering bulls*, Soph.

ταυρό-μορφος, ον, (μορφή) *bull-formed*, Eur.

ταυρόομαι, Pass., only in pres. *to become savage as a bull*, Aesch., Eur.; ταυροῦσθαι ὄμμα τινί *to cast savage glances on one*, Eur.

ταυρο-πάτωρ [ᾰ], ορος, ὁ, ἡ, (πατήρ) *sprung from a bull*, of bees, Theocr.

ταυρο-πόλος, ἡ, (πολέω) a name of Artemis, *worshipped at Tauris*, or *hunting bulls*, Eur. ;—so ταυροπόλα (Dor. for -πόλη), Soph.

ταυρό-πους, ὁ, ἡ, πουν, τό, *bull-footed*, Eur.

ΤΑΥ͂ΡΟΣ, ὁ, a *bull*, Hom., etc.: also ταῦρος βοῦς, like σῦς κάπρος, κίρκος ἴρηξ, Il.:—ἄπεχε τῆς βοὸς τὸν ταῦρον, oracularly of Agamemnon and his wife, Aesch.

ταυροσφαγέω, f. ήσω, *to cut a bull's throat*, τ. ἐς σάκος *to cut its throat* (so that the blood runs) *into a hollow shield*, Aesch. From

ταυρο-σφάγος, ον, (σφάττω) *bull-slaughtering, sacrificial*, Soph.

ταυρο-φάγος, ον, (φάγεῖν) *bull-eating*, Ar.

ταυρο-φόνος, ον, = ταυροσφάγος, Pind., Theocr., etc.

ταῦτα, neut. pl. of οὗτος.   II. ταὐτά, crasis for τὰ αὐτά.

ταυτάζω, v. τευτάζω.

ταύτῃ, dat. fem. dat. of οὗτος, *in this way*.

ταυτί, strengthd. Att. for ταῦτα, neut. pl. of οὗτος.

ταυτό, Att. —τόν, Ion. τωυτό, crasis for τὸ αὐτό, τὸ αὐτόν.

ταυτο-κλίνής, ές, (κλίνω) *under the same climate*, Strab.

ταυτο-λόγος, ον, *tautologous*, Anth.

ταὐτόματον, crasis for τὸ αὐτόματον, a *chance*, ἀπὸ ταὐτομάτου *spontaneously, by chance*, Thuc., Plat.

ταὐτο-ποιέω, f. ήσω, *to do the same with*, τινί Arist.

ταὐτότης, ητος, ἡ, (τὸ αὐτό) *identity*, Arist.

ταφᾰνῆ, crasis for τὰ ἀφανῆ.

τάφε, poët. for ἔταφε: v. τέθηπα.

ταφέσει, crasis for τῇ ἀφέσει.

ταφεύς, έως, ὁ, (θάπτω) a *burier*, Lat. *vespillo*, Soph.

τᾰφή, ἡ, (θάπτω) *burial*, Lat. *sepultura*, Hdt.: *mode of burial*, Id.   2. in pl. also, a *burial-place*, Hdt., Soph. ;—in sing., σῆς εἰ στερήσομαι ταφῆς, of *the urn* supposed to contain the ashes of Orestes, Soph.   3. *payment for burial, a burial-fee*, Dem.

τᾰφήϊος, η, ον, Ion. for ταφεῖος (not used), *of* or *for a burial*, τ. φάρος a *winding-sheet, shroud*, Od.

τάφιος, α, ον, = foreg., τ. λίθος a *gravestone*, Anth.

ταφόδια, crasis for τὰ ἐφόδια.

τάφος [ᾰ], ὁ, (θάπτω) a *burial, funeral*, Lat. *funus*, Hom., Soph., etc. ; δαίνυναι τάφον *to give a funeral-feast*, Hom.   2. *the act of burying*, Soph.   II. *the grave* itself, *tomb*, Hes., Hdt., etc. ;—in pl. of a *single grave*, Hdt., Soph. ; ὄντες ἐν τάφοις *though dead*

and buried, Aesch. ; οἱ πατρὸς τάφοι *his being buried*, Soph.   2. ἔμψυχός τις τ. a 'living skeleton,' Luc.

τάφος [ᾰ], εος, τό, (τέθηπα) *astonishment, amazement*, Od.

ταφρεία, ἡ, a *making of ditches* or *trenches*, Dem. From

ταφρεύω, f. σω, (τάφρος) *to make a ditch*, Xen., Aeschin.

τάφρη, ἡ, Ion. for τάφρος, Hdt.

τάφρος, ἡ, (θάπτω) a *ditch, trench*, Hom., etc. ; τάφρον ὀρύσσειν Il., etc. ; τ. ἐλαύνειν *to draw a trench*, Ib.

τάφων, aor. 2 part. ; v. τέθηπα.

τᾰχᾰ, Adv. (τᾰχύς) *quickly, presently, forthwith*, Lat. *statim*, Hom., etc.   II. *perhaps*, Plat., etc.:—so also τάχ' ἄν *probably, perhaps, may be*, with optat., Hdt., Att.:—τάχ' ἄν alone, in answers, Plat., etc.:— strengthd., ἴσως τάχα Xen. ; τάχα τοίνυν ἴσως Dem. ; τάχ' ἄν ἴσως Soph., etc.   III. for Comp. τάχιον, Sup. τάχιστα, v. τᾰχύς C.

τᾰχέως, Adv. of τᾰχύς.

τᾰχῑνός, ή, όν, poët. for τᾰχύς, Theocr.:—neut. pl. τᾰχινά, = τάχα, Id.

τᾰχίων [ῑ], τάχιστος, v. τᾰχύς C.

τάχος, εος, τό, (τᾰχύς) *swiftness, speed, fleetness, velocity*, Il., Plat.   2. τ. φρενῶν *quickness* of temper, *hastiness*, Eur.   II. τάχος is often used in Adverbial phrases for τᾰχέως, absol. in acc., Aesch., etc.: —with Preps., ἀπὸ τάχους Xen. ; διὰ τάχους Soph., etc. ; ἐν τάχει Aesch., etc. ; εἰς τάχος Xen., etc. ; κατὰ τάχος Hdt., Thuc. ; μετὰ τάχους Plat. ; σὺν τάχει Soph. :—also with relatives, ὡς τάχος, like ὡς τάχιστα, Hdt., Aesch. ; so, ὅ τι τάχος Hdt., Soph. ; ὅσον τάχος Soph. :—also, ὡς τάχεος εἶχεν ἕκαστος as each was off *for speed*, i. e. as quickly as they could, Hdt. ; ὡς εἶχον τάχους Thuc.

τᾰχὔ-άλωτος, ον, *conquered quickly* or *easily*, Hdt.

τᾰχὔ-βάτης [ᾰ], ου, ὁ, (βαίνω) *fast-walking*, Eur.

τᾰχὔ-βουλος, ον, (βουλή) *hasty in counsel*, Ar.

τᾰχὔ-δακρυς, υ, gen. υος, *soon moved to tears*, Luc.

τᾰχνεργία, ἡ, *quickness in working*, Xen. From

τᾰχὔ-εργός, όν, (*ἔργω) *working quickly*.

τᾰχὔ-μηνις, εως, ὁ, ἡ, *swift to anger*, Anth.

τᾰχὔ-μορος, ον, *quickly dying, shortlived*, Aesch.

τᾰχὔ-ναυτέω, f. ήσω, (ναύτης) *to sail fast*, Thuc.

τᾰχύνω [ῡ], f. ὔνῶ: aor. 1 ἐτάχῦνα: (τᾰχύς) :—*to make quickly*, Soph. ; τοῖα σπερχόμενος ταχύνει *such are the words which in his eager haste he speaks*, Eur.   II. intr. *to be quick, to make haste, speed, hurry*, Aesch., Soph., Xen.

τᾰχὔ-πειθής, ές, *soon persuaded, credulous*, Theocr.

τᾰχὔ-πορος, ον, *quick of motion*, Aesch., Eur.

τᾰχὔ-ποτμος, ον, = ταχύμορος, Pind.

τᾰχὔ-πους, ποδος, ὁ, ἡ, πουν, τό, *swift-footed*, Eur., Ar.

τᾰχὔ-πτερνος, ον, (πτέρνα) *swift-footed*, Theogn.

τᾰχὔ-πτερος, ον, (πτερόν) *swift-winged*, Aesch.

τᾰχὔ-πωλος [ῠ], ον, *with fleet, swift horses*, Il.

τᾰχὔρ-ροθος, ον, *swift-rushing*, Aesch.

τᾰχὔρ-ρωστος, ον, (ῥώομαι) *swift-rushing*, Soph.

ΤΑΧΥΣ [ῠ], εῖα, ύ: I. of motion, *quick, swift, fleet*, opp. to βραδύς, Hom., etc. ; ταχὺς πόδας Il. ; ταχὺς θείειν Hom.   II. of thought and purpose, *quick, rapid, hasty*, φρονεῖν γὰρ οἱ ταχεῖς οὐκ ἀσφαλεῖς Soph. ; c. inf., βλάπτειν τ. Ar. ; τὸ ταχύ *speed, haste*, Eur.   2. so of actions, events, *quick, rapid, sudden*,

πήδημα Soph.; πόλεμος Thuc.; τ. ἐλπίδες *fleeting hopes*, Pind.

B. Adv., 1. regul. form τᾰχέως, *quickly*, Il., Att. 2. the Adv. is also expressed by periphr., διὰ ταχέων *in haste*, Thuc., etc.; ἐκ ταχείας Soph.; cf. τάχος II. 3. neut. ταχύ as Adv., Id., etc.; more often τάχα (q. v.).

C. Degrees of Comparison: **I.** Comp.: 1. regul. form τᾰχύτερος, α, ον, Hdt. 2. θάσσων, neut. θᾶσσον, gen. ονος, new Att. θάττων, neut. θᾶττον, Hom., Att.:—neut. as Adv., Hom., etc.; θᾶσσον ἂν κλύοιμι *sooner*, i. e. *rather*, would I hear, Soph.; θᾶσσον also, like Lat. *ocius*, often stands for the Positive, οὐ θᾶσσον οἴσεις; i. e. make haste and bring, Id.; ὅ τι θᾶσσον, like ὅ τι τάχιστα, Theocr.; ἐπειδὰν θ. Plat. 3. the form ταχίων [ῑ], neut. ιον, is rare in good Att. **II.** the regular Sup. ταχύτατος, is rare, Pind.; ταχύτατα as Adv., Xen. 2. the usual form is τάχιστος, η, ον, mostly in neut. pl. τάχιστα as Adv., ὅττι τάχιστα *as soon as possible*, Lat. *quam celerrime*, Il.; Att. ὅ τι τάχιστα Soph., etc.:—so, ὅσον τ. Aesch.; ὡς τ. Hdt., Att.; ὅπως τ. Aesch., etc.:—these are ellipt. phrases, for ὡς δυνατὸν τ. Hdt.; ὡς or ᾗ ἂν δύνωμαι τ. Xen., etc.:—also after Particles of Time, like Lat. *quum primum*, ἐπεί (Ion. ἐπεί τε) τάχιστα Hdt., Att.; ἐπειδὴ τ. Plat., etc.; ἐπεάν or ἐπήν, ἐπειδὰν τ. Hdt., etc.; ὅταν τ. Xen. 3. often also in Prose, τὴν ταχίστην (sc. ὁδόν), as Adv. *by the quickest way*, i. e. *most quickly*, Hdt., etc. Hence

τᾰχῠτής, ῆτος, Dor. -τάς, ᾶτος, ἡ, *quickness, swiftness*, Hom., Hdt., Plat.

τάων [ᾱ], Dor. and Aeol. gen. pl. fem. of ὁ, ἡ, τό.

τᾰώνιος or -ειος, ον, *of a peacock*, Luc. From

ΤΑΩ΄Σ or ταῶς (sometimes written ταῶς), ὁ; gen. ταώ or ταῶ; acc. ταών or ταῶν: pl., nom. ταῴ or ταῷ; gen. ταών; acc. ταώς or ταῶς:—but also (as if from a nom. ταών) pl. dat. ταῶσι, acc. ταῶνας:—*a peacock*, Lat. *pavo*, Ar., etc.: metaph. of *coxcombs*, Id.

τε, enclitic Particle, *and*, answering to Lat. *que*, as καί to *et*. It may simply join clauses, as ὃς Χρύσην ἀμφιβέβηκας Κίλλαν τε ζαθέην, Τενέδοιό τε ἶφι ἀνάσσεις Il.; or it may be repeated as τε . . τε . ., *both . . and . .*, as πατὴρ ἀνδρῶν τε θεῶν τε Hom. So also τε . ., καί . ., as διαστήτην Ἀτρείδης τε καὶ δῖος Ἀχιλλεύς Il., etc.:—used to show coincidence of Time, μεσαμβρίη τέ ἐστι καὶ τὸ κάρτα γίγνεται ψυχρὸν Hdt., etc. 2. the combination καί τε is peculiar to Ep., *and also*, Hom. **II.** in Ep. Poetry, τε is attached to many relative Pronouns or Particles, without altering their sense, as ὅσσος τε, γάρ τε, δέ τε, μέν τε, ἔνθα τε, ἵνα τε, etc.: in Att., this τε was dropped, except in a few words, as ἅτε, ὥστε, ἐφ᾽ ᾧτε, οἷός τε, ἔστε.

τέ, Dor. for σέ, acc. sing. of σύ.

τέ, apostroph. for τεά, neut. pl. of τεός.

ΤΕ΄ΓΓΩ, f. τέγξω: aor. 1 ἔτεγξα:—Pass., aor. 1 ἐτέγχθην:—*to wet, moisten*, Pind., etc.; of tears, Trag.: —Pass. τέγγομαι, *I weep*, Aesch.; τ.βλέφαρα Eur. 2. c. acc. cogn., τ. δάκρυα *to shed* tears, Pind.; τέγγει δακρύων ἄχναν Soph.:—Pass., ὄμβρος ἐτέγγετο a shower *fell*, Id. **II.** *to soften* (properly, *by soaking* or *bathing*), Pind.:—metaph. in Pass., τέγγει γὰρ οὐδέν thou art no whit *softened*, Aesch.; οὔτε

λόγοις ἐτέγγεθ᾽ ἥδε Eur. **III.** *to dye, stain*, Lat. *tingere*; metaph., like Lat. *imbuere*, Pind.

Τεγέα, ας, Ion. -έη, ης, ἡ, *Tegea* in Arcadia, Il., Pind., etc. :—Τεγεάτης [ᾰ], Ion. -ήτης, ὁ, *of Tegea*, Hdt., etc.:—fem. Τεγεᾶτις, ιδος, *the Tegeate country*, Thuc.: —Adv. -ατικός, Ion. -ητικός, ἡ, όν, Hdt.

τέγεος, ον, (τέγος) *at* or *near the roof*, τ. θάλαμοι, of the women's chambers, = ὑπερῷον, Il.

ΤΕ΄ΓΟΣ, εος, τό, like στέγος, *a roof*, Lat. *tectum*, Od., Ar., etc.; οὐπὶ τοῦ τέγους you on the *roof!* Od.; Ar. **II.** *any covered part of a house, a hall, room, chamber*, Od., Pind.

τεθᾰλώς, τεθάλυῖα, pf. part. of θάλλω.

τεθαρρηκότως, Adv. of θαρρέω, *boldly*, Polyb.

τεθάφᾰται, Ion. 3 pl. pf. pass. of θάπτω.

τέθηπα (Root ΘΑΠ), pf. with pres. sense (no pres. is found), Ep. plqpf. ἐτεθήπεα as impf. : **I.** intr. *to be astonished, astounded, amazed*, Od., Hdt.; mostly in part. τεθηπώς *amazed, astonied*, Il.:—to this belongs also aor. 2 ἔταφον, used by Hom. only in part. ταφών, in the phrases ταφὼν ἀνόρουσε, στῆ δὲ ταφών; but 3 sing. τάφε (for ἔταφε) occurs in Pind.; and 1 sing. ἔταφον in Aesch. 2. c. acc. *to be amazed at*, Luc.

τέθμιος, ον, or α, ον, Dor. for θέσμιος, *settled, regular*, Lat. *solennis*, Id.:—τέθμιον, τό, = sq., Id.

τεθμός, ὁ, Dor. for θεσμός, *a law, custom*, Pind.

τεθορεῖν, redupl. for θορεῖν, aor. 2 inf. of θρώσκω.

τεθορῠβημένως, Adv. part. pf. pass. of θορυβέω, *tumultuously*, Xen.

τεθριππο-βάμων [ᾰ], ὁ: τ. στόλος, = τέθριππον, Eur.

τεθριππο-βάτης [ᾰ], ου, ὁ, *driver of a four-horse chariot*, Hdt.

τέθριππος, ον, (τέτταρες, ἵππος) *with four horses abreast, four-horsed*, Pind., Eur.; ἅμιλλαι τ. the chariot-race, Eur. **II.** τέθριππον (sc. ἅρμα), τό, *a four-horse chariot*, Hdt., Eur.; τ. ἵππων *a team of four abreast*, Il.

τεθριπποτροφέω, *to keep a team of four horses*, Hdt.

τεθριππο-τρόφος, ον, (τρέφω) *keeping a team of four horses*, τ. οἰκία, i. e. a wealthy family *that could support this contest* in the games, Hdt.

τεθυωμένως, pf. pass. part. of θυόω.

τεῖδε, Dor. for τῇδε.

τεΐν [ῑ], Dor. and Ep. dat. sing. of σύ.

τείνω (Root ΤΑΝ, cf. τανύω): f. τενῶ: aor. 1 ἔτεινα, Ep. τεῖνα : pf. τέτᾰκα :—Pass., f. τᾰθήσομαι: aor. 1 ἐτάθην [ᾰ], Ep. τάθην: pf. τέτᾰμαι: plqpf. 3 sing. and pl., τέτατο, τέταντο, 3 dual τετάσθην. *To stretch* by main force, *to stretch to the uttermost*, τόξον ἔτεινεν *stretched* it *to its full*, Il.; ἐξ ἄντυγος ἡνία τείνας *having tied* the reins *tight* to the chariot-rail, Ib. :—Pass., [ἱμὰς] τέτατο the strap *was made tight*, Il.; ἱστία τέτατο the sails *were stretched*, Od.:—absol., μὴ τείνειν ἄγαν not *to strain* the cord too tight, Soph. 2. metaph., ἴσον τείνειν πολέμου τέλος *to strain* the even tug of war, Il. :—Pass., ἐπὶ ξυροῦ μάχη τέταται Il.; ἵπποισι τάθη δρόμος their pace *was strained* to the utmost, Ib.: also, *to exert oneself, be anxious*, Pind. 3. *to stretch out, spread*, Ζεὺς λαίλαπα τείνει Il.; νὺξ τέταται βροτοῖσιν night *is spread* over mankind, Od.; so, of light, τέτατο φάος Soph.; of sound,

ἀμφὶ νῶτ' ἐτάθη πάταγος Soph.   4. to aim at, direct towards a point, properly from the bow, τείνειν βέλη Id. : then, metaph., τ. φόνον εἴς τινα to aim death to one, design it for him, Eur. ; τ. λόγον εἴς τινα Plat.   II. to stretch out in length, Hdt. :—Pass. to lie out at length, lie stretched, ταθεὶς ἐπὶ γαίη Il. ; ταθεὶς ἐνὶ δεσμῷ lying stretched in chains, Od.   2. to stretch or hold out, present, τινὰ ἐπὶ σφαγάν Eur. :—Med., τείνεσθαι χέρε to stretch out one's hands, etc., Theocr.   3. to extend, lengthen, of Time, Aesch., Eur. ; τείνειν λόγον Aesch.
B. intr., of geographical position, to stretch out or extend, Hdt., Xen. :—of Time, τείνοντα χρόνον lengthening time, Aesch.   II. to exert oneself, struggle, ἐναντία τινί Plat. : to hurry on, hasten, Eur., Xen.   III. to extend to, reach, Lat. pertinere, ἐπὶ τὴν ψυχήν Plat.   2. to tend, refer, belong to, Lat. spectare ad, τείνει ἐς σέ it refers to, concerns you, Hdt., Eur., etc. ; ποῖ τείνει; to what tends it ? Plat. ; ἐγγύς τι τείνειν τοῦ θανάτου Id.
τεῖρος, εος, τό, Ep. form of τέρας, found only in pl., the heavenly constellations, signs, only once in Hom., τὰ τείρεα πάντα, τά τ' οὐρανὸς ἐστεφάνωται Il. ; ἐνὶ τείρεσιν αἰθέρος h. Hom.
τείρω (Root ΤΕΡ), impf. ἔτειρον, only in pres. and impf. act. and pass. :—to rub hard : of the effects of pain, sorrow, to wear away, wear out, distress, Hom., Aesch. :—Pass. τείροντο καμάτῳ τε καὶ ἱδρῷ Il. ; τείρετο δ' αἰνῶς she was sore distressed, Ib., etc.   II. intr. to suffer distress, ἦ μάλα δὴ τείρουσι υἷες Ἀχαιῶν Ib.
τειχεσι-πλήτης, ου, ὁ, (πελάζω) approacher of walls, i. e. stormer of cities, Il.
τειχέω, f. ήσω, = τειχίζω, to build walls, Hdt. ; τεῖχος τ. Id.   II. trans. to fortify, τὸν Ἰσθμόν Id.
τειχήεις, εσσα, εν, = τειχίεις, Strab.
τειχ-ήρης, ες, (ἀραρίσκω) enclosed by walls, beleaguered, besieged, Hdt., Thuc., etc.
τειχίζω, f. Att. ιῶ : aor. 1 ἐτείχισα : pf. τετείχικα : (τεῖχος) :—to build a wall, Ar., etc. : c. acc. cogn., τ. τεῖχος to build it, Thuc. ; so in Med., τεῖχος ἐτειχίσαντο they built them a wall, Il. :—Pass. to be built, Pind. : 3 sing. plqpf. τετείχιστο, impers., buildings had been erected, there were buildings, Hdt.   II. trans. to wall or fortify, τὸ οὖρος Id. ; τὴν πόλιν Thuc., Dem. : in Med., τειχίζεσθαι τὸ χωρίον Thuc. : —Pass. to be walled or fenced with walls, Id. ; τὰ τετειχισμένα the fortified parts, Id.
τειχιόεις, εσσα, εν, (τεῖχος) walled, high-walled, Il.
τειχίον, τό, (τεῖχος) a wall, Od. :—any dimin. sense it has consists in its being commonly limited to private buildings, as opp. to city-walls.
τείχισις, ἡ, (τειχίζω) the work of walling, wall-building, Thuc., Xen.
τείχισμα, ατος, τό, (τειχίζω) a wall or fort, fortification, Eur., Thuc.
τειχισμός, ὁ, = τείχισις, Thuc.
τειχοδομέω, f. ήσω, to build a wall, Anth. ; and
τειχοδομία, ἡ, a building of walls, Plut. From
τειχο-δόμος, ον, (δέμω) building walls.
τειχ-ολέτις, ιδος, ἡ, destroyer of walls, ap. Plut.
τειχομαχέω, f. ήσω, to fight the walls, i. e. to besiege, Hdt., Thuc., etc. ; τ. τινί Ar. ; πρός τινα Plut. From

τειχο-μάχης [ᾰ], ου, ὁ, (μάχομαι) storming walls, an engineer, Ar. Hence
τειχομᾰχία, Ion. -ίη, ἡ, a battle with walls, i. e. a siege, Hdt. : the 12th Iliad was so called, Plat.
τειχο-μελής, ές, (μέλος) walling by music, of Amphion's lyre, Anth.
τειχο-ποιός, όν, (ποιέω) building walls or forts, Luc.   II. οἱ τειχοποιοί, at Athens, officers chosen to repair the city-walls, Dem., Aeschin.
τεῖχος, εος, τό, a wall, esp. a wall round a city, town-wall, in sing. and pl., Hom. ; τειχέων κιθῶνες coats of walls, i. e. walls one within the other, Hdt. ; τεῖχος ἐλαύνειν, δέμειν Il., etc. ; οἰκοδομεῖν Hdt. ; τ. περιβάλλεσθαι moenia sibi circumdare, Id. ; also, τ. περιβάλλεσθαι τὴν πόλιν Id. ; τ. ῥήξασθαι to breach the wall, Il. ; so in Prose, τ. καθαιρεῖν, κατασκάπτειν Hdt., etc.   2. τὰ μακρὰ τείχη at Athens were lines of wall connecting the city-wall with the harbours, called respectively τὸ βόρειον or Peiraïc, and τὸ νότιον or Phaleric wall.—τεῖχος, τείχη differ from τοῖχος, as Lat. murus, moenia from paries, city-walls from a house-wall ; cf. τειχίον.   II. any fortification, a castle, fort, Hdt. : pl. of a single fort, fortifications, Id.   III. a fortified town, Id., Xen., etc. ; so in pl. (Deriv. uncertain.)
τειχοφὔλᾰκέω, f. ήσω, to guard the walls, Plut. From
τειχο-φύλαξ [ῠ], ᾰκος, ὁ, a guard of the walls, Hdt.
τειχύδριον, τό, Dim. of τεῖχος, Xen.
τείως, Adv., Ep. and Ion. for τέως.
τέκε, Ep. 3 sing. aor. 2 of τίκτω :—τεκεῖν, inf.
τεκμαίρομαι, f. τεκμᾰροῦμαι : aor. 1 ἐτεκμηράμην, Ep. τεκμηράμην : Dep. : (τέκμαρ) :—to fix by a mark or boundary, to ordain, decree, Hom. : to lay a task upon a person, enjoin, appoint, Od. :—c. inf. to design, purpose to do, h. Hom.   II. to judge from signs and tokens, to form a judgment respecting a thing, calculate, Eur. : absol. to conjecture, Xen. :—the reason is added in the dat., ἐμπύροις τεκμαίρεσθαι to judge by the burnt-offering, Pind. ; τεκμ. ἔργῳ κοὔ λόγῳ τ. Aesch. ; τὰ καινὰ τοῖς πάλαι Soph., etc. :—c. inf., τ. τοῦτο οὕτω ἕξειν Xen.
B. an Act. τεκμαίρω occurs in Poets, to shew by a sign or token, τεκμαίρει χρῆμ' ἕκαστον circumstance proves the man, Pind. ; τεκμαίρει ἰδεῖν gives signs [for men] to see, Id. ; τέκμηρον, ὅ τι μ' ἐπαμμένει παθεῖν shew me what it awaits me to suffer, Aesch.
ΤΕΚΜΑΡ, Ep. τέκμωρ, τό, indecl. a fixed mark or boundary, goal, end, Il. ; τέκμωρ Ἰλίου the end of Ilium, Ib.   2. an end, object, purpose, Pind.   II. like τεκμήριον, a fixed sign, sure sign or token, as Zeus says that his nod is μέγιστον τέκμωρ ἐξ ἐμέθεν the highest, surest pledge I can give, Il. ; ἣν δ' οὐδὲν αὐτοῖς οὔτε χειμῶνος τ. οὔτ' ἦρος Aesch., etc.
τέκμαρσις, ἡ, (τεκμαίρομαι) a judging from sure signs.
τεκμήραντο, Ep. 3 pl. aor. 1 of τεκμαίρομαι.
τεκμήριον, τό, (τεκμαίρομαι) like τέκμαρ II, a sure sign or token, Hdt., Att.   II. a positive proof, Aesch., Plat., etc. :—in Att. Prose τεκμήριον δέ as an independent clause, now the proof of it is this (which follows), Thuc., etc. Hence
τεκμηριόω, f. ώσω, to prove positively, Thuc. ; εἰ τῳ ἱκανὸς τεκμηριῶσαι if he seem a sufficient voucher.

Id.; τοσαῦτα ἐτεκμηρίωσε ὅτι . . thus much *evidence he gave* to the fact that . . , Id.

τεκμηρι-ώδης, ες, *of the nature of a* τεκμήριον, Arist.

τέκμωρ, τό, Ep. form of τέκμαρ.

τεκνίον, τό, Dim. of τέκνον, *a little child*, Anth., N. T.

τεκνογονέω, *to bear young, bear children*, Anth., N.T.; and

τεκνογονία, ἡ, *child-bearing*, N. T. From

τεκνο-γόνος, ον, *begetting* or *bearing children*, Aesch.

τεκνο-κτόνος, ον, (κτείνω) *murdering children*, Eur.

τεκν-ολέτειρα, ἡ, *having lost one's young*, of the nightingale, Soph.

τέκνον, ου, τό, (τίκτω) *that which is borne* or *born, a child* (cf. Scottish *bairn*, from Anglo-S. *beran, to bear*), Hom., etc.; *my son, my child*, sometimes with masc. Adj., φίλε τέκνον Id.; the relat. Pron. or Participle often follows in masc. or fem. **2.** of animals, *the young*, Id., etc. **3.** metaph., flowers are γαίας τέκνα Aesch.; birds αἰθέρος τέκνα Eur. [The penult. is long in Hom., in Trag. more often short.]

τεκνοποιέω, f. ήσω, (τεκνοποιός) in Act., of the woman, *to bear children*, in Med., of the man, *to beget them*, Xen.: in Med. of both parents, *to breed children*, Id.

τεκνοποιητικός, ή, όν, *of* or *for the production of children:* ἡ -κή (sc. τέχνη) Arist.

τεκνοποιΐα, ἡ, *production of children*, Xen.,

τεκνό-ποινος, ον, (ποινή) *child-avenging*, Aesch.

τεκνο-ποιός, όν, (ποιέω) of the wife, *child-bearing*, Hdt.; of the husband, *child-begetting*, Eur.

τεκνο-σπορία, ἡ, *a begetting of children*, Anth.

τεκνοῦσσα, οὖσσα, οὖν, contr. for τεκνόεις, εσσα, εν, *having borne children*, Soph.

τεκνο-φάγος, ον, (φαγεῖν) *eating children:*—hence **-φᾱγία**, ἡ, *a devouring of children*, Luc.

τεκνο-φονέω, *to murder children*, Anth. From

τεκνο-φόνος, ον, (*φένω) *child-murdering*.

τέκον, Ep. for ἔτεκον, aor. 2 of τίκτω:—τέκοιεν, 3 pl. opt.

τεκνόω, f. ώσω, *to furnish* or *stock with children*, Eur.:—Pass. *to be furnished with children*, i. e. *to have them*, Id. **II.** Act., of the man, *to beget* children, Id.;—Med., of the female, *to bear* them: metaph., ὄλβος τεκνοῦται it has offspring, Aesch.; χθὼν ἐτεκνώσατο φάσματα Eur.:—Pass. *to be born*, Trag.; γάμον τεκνοῦντα καὶ τεκνούμενον, i. e. *a marriage where husband and son are one*, Soph. Hence

τέκνωσις, εως, ἡ, *a begetting, bearing*, τέκνωσιν ποιεῖσθαι *to have children*, Thuc.

τέκος, εος, τό, Ep. dat. pl. τέκεσσι, τεκέεσσι, (τίκτω) poët. for τέκνον, Hom., etc. **2.** of animals, Il., etc.; in pl. *the young*, Ib.

τεκταίνομαι, f. τεκτανοῦμαι: aor. 1 ἐτεκτηνάμην, Ep. 3 sing. τεκτήνατο: Dep.:—of a carpenter, *to make, work, frame*, Il.:—absol. *to do joiners' work*, opp. to smiths' work, Ar., Xen. **2.** of other artificers, h. Hom., Plat. **3.** metaph. *to devise, plan, contrive*, esp. by craft, Lat. *machinari*, ἐτεκτήναντ' ἀπόφθεγκτόν μ' they kept me from speech of them, Eur.; πᾶν ἐπ' ἐμοὶ τεκταινέσθω (sc. Cleon) Ar. **II.** later, Act. τεκταίνω in same sense, Anth., Luc.; hence partic. pass. τεκταινόμενος, Ar., Dem.

τεκτονεῖον, τό, *workshop of a carpenter*, Aeschin.

τεκτονία, ἡ, (τέκτων) *carpentry*, Anth.

τεκτονικός, ή, όν, (τέκτων) *practised* or *skilled in building*, Plat. : as Subst. *a good carpenter* or *builder*, opp. to a smith, Xen. :—ἡ -κή (sc. τέχνη) *joiners' work, carpentry*, Plat., etc.

τεκτοσύνη, ἡ, *the art of a joiner, carpentry*, ἀνὴρ εὖ εἰδὼς τεκτοσυνάων Od.; ἄτιμον χέρα τεκτοσύνας *hand unhonoured in its art*, Eur. From

τέκτων, ονος, ὁ, (τίκτω) *any worker in wood*, esp. *a carpenter, joiner*, Hom., etc.; opp. to *a smith* (χαλκεύς), Plat., Xen.; to *a mason* (λιθολόγος), Thuc., etc. **2.** generally, *any craftsman* or *workman*, τ. κεραοξόος *a worker* in horn, Il.; of a *metal-worker*, Eur.; *a sculptor*, Soph., Eur. **3.** *a master in any art*, Pind.; τ. νωδυνιᾶν, i. e. *a physician*, Id. **4.** *a maker, author*, νεικέων Aesch.; κακῶν Eur.

τεκών, aor. 2 part. of τίκτω.

τελᾰμών, ῶνος, ὁ, *a broad strap for bearing* anything (from Root ΤΛΑ, *τλάω, whence also the hero Telamon took his name, cf. Ἄτλας): **1.** *a leathern strap* or *belt*, for bearing both shield or sword, Hom. **2.** *a broad linen bandage* for wounds, Il., Hdt., Eur.; for swathing mummies, Hdt.

ΤΕΛΕΘΩ, 3 sing. Ion. impf. τελέθεσκε, *to come into being, to be quite* or *fully so and so*, νὺξ τελέθει Il.: —then simply *to be so and so*, ἀριπρεπέες τελέθουσι, μινυνθάδιοι τελ. Hom., Trag.

τέλειος and **τέλεος**, α (Ion. η), ον, in Att. also ος, ον: (τέλος):—*having reached its end, finished, complete*, Il., etc.: of victims, *perfect, without spot* or *blemish*, Ib.; τὰ τέλεα τῶν προβάτων Hdt.; of sacrifices, ἱερὰ τέλεια *of full tale* or *number*, or *performed with all rites*, Thuc.; so, ἀετὸς τελειότατος πετεηνῶν is prob. *the surest bird of augury*, Il. **2.** of animals, *full-grown*, Xen., etc. **3.** of persons, *absolute, complete, accomplished, perfect in his* or *its kind*, Plat., etc.:—so of things, φάρμακον τελεώτατον Id.; τ. ἀρετή, φιλία, etc., Arist. **4.** of prayers, vows, etc., *fulfilled, accomplished*, Pind., Aesch.; ὄψις οὐ τελέη *a vision which imported* nothing, Hdt.; τ. ψῆφος *a fixed resolve*, Soph. **5.** in Arith., those numbers are τέλειοι, which are equal to the sum of their divisors, as 6 = 3 + 2 + 1, Plat. **II.** of the gods, *fulfilling prayer*, Ζεὺς τ. Zeus *the fulfiller*, Pind., Aesch.; of Hera ζυγία, Lat. *Juno pronuba*, the presiding goddess of marriage, Pind., Aesch., etc.:—so, τέλειος ἀνήρ = Lat. *paterfamilias, the lord* of the house, Aesch. **III.** = τελευταῖος, *last*, Soph. **IV.** τέλειον (not τέλεον), τό, *a royal banquet*, as a transl. of the Pers. *tycta*, Hdt. **V.** Adv. τελέως, *at last*, Aesch., Plat., etc. **2.** *perfectly, absolutely, thoroughly*, Hdt. **3.** the neut. τέλεον is also used as Adv., Luc. **VI.** Comp. and Sup.: Hom. uses τελεώτερος, -εώτατος or τελειότερος, -είότατος, as his metre requires: in Att. τελεώτερος, -ώτατος prevail. Hence

τελειόω and **τελεόω**, f. ώσω, *to make perfect, complete:* **I.** of things, *to make* it *perfect, complete, accomplish*, Hdt., Thuc., etc. :—Pass. *to be accomplished*, Hdt., Soph.; τελεωθέντων ἀμφοτέροισι when both parties *had their wishes accomplished*, Hdt. :— of prophecies, *to be fulfilled*, N. T. **II.** of persons, *to bring* one *to perfection*, Hdt.; τελειῶσαι λόχον

to make the ambush *successful*, Soph. :—Pass. *to attain perfection, come to the end of one's labours*, Id. : *to reach maturity*, Plat.

τελείω, Ep. for τελέω.

τελείωσις or **τελέωσις**, εως, ἡ, (τελειόω) *accomplishment, fulfilment*, N. T.

τελειωτής, οῦ, ὁ, *an accomplisher, finisher*, N. T.

τελεό-μηνος, ον, (μήν) *with full complement of months*, τ. ἄροτος, i. e. *a full twelvemonth*, Soph.

Τελέοντες, οἱ, one of the four old Attic Tribes, prob. (from τελέω III), *the Consecrators, Priests*; or (from τελέω II) the *Payers, Farmers*, Hdt.

τέλεος, **τελεόω**, v. τέλειος, τελειόω.

τελέσειας, 2 sing. aor. 1 opt. of τελέω.

τελεσθείς, aor. 1 pass. part. of τελέω.

τελεσιούργημα, τό, *an accomplished purpose*, Polyb.

τελεσι-υργός, όν, *working out its end, effective*, Plat.

τέλεσμα, ατος, τό, (τελέω) *money paid* or *to be paid, a payment, outlay*, Luc.

τελεσσι-δώτειρα, poët. for τελεσιδ-, *she that gives completeness* or *accomplishment*, Eur.

τελεσσί-φρων, ονος, ὁ, ἡ, (φρήν) poët. for τελεσίφρων, *working its will*, Aesch.

τελεστήριον, τό, (τελέω III) *a place for initiation*, as the temple of Eleusis, Plut. II. **τελεστήρια**, τά, *a thank-offering for success*, Xen.

τελεστικός, ή, όν, (τελέω III) *initiatory, mystical*, Plat.

τελέστωρ, ορος, ὁ, (τελέω III) *a priest*, Anth.

τελεσφορέω, f. ήσω, *to bring fruit to perfection*, N. T. II. *to pay toll* or *custom*, Xen.

τελεσ-φόρος, ον, (τέλος, φέρω) *bringing to an end*, τελεσφόρον εἰς ἐνιαυτόν *for a year completing its round, for a complete year*, Hom.; τελεσφόροι ἀραί, εὐχαί *tending to accomplishment*, Aesch., Eur.; φάσματα ὃ̀ς τελεσφόρα *grant accomplishment to the visions*, Soph.; τ. χάριν δοῦναι *to grant the favour of fulfilment*, Id. II. *accomplishing one's purpose*, Μοῖρα Aesch.; Δίκη Soph.; πεσεῖν ἐς τὸ μὴ τελεσφόρον *to fall powerless to the ground*, Aesch. 2. *bringing fruit to perfection*, δένδρον Plut.: *having the ordering of a thing*, c. gen., Aesch.

τελετή, ῆς, ἡ, (τελέω) *initiation in the mysteries*, Hdt., Plat., etc.; ἐς χεῖρας ἄγεσθαι τὴν τελετήν *to take in hand the matter of initiation*, Hdt. :—in pl. *mystic rites at initiation*, Eur., Ar., etc. II. *a festival accompanied by such rites*, in pl., Pind.; in sing., Eur. Hence

τελεῦντι, Dor. for τελοῦσι, 3 pl. of τελέω.

τελευταῖος, α, ον, (τελευτή) *last*, Lat. *ultimus*, Hdt.; τὰ τ. *the endings* or *terminations*, Id.; τελευταίους στῆσαι *to station in the rear ranks*, Xen. 2. of Time, ἡ τελευταία, with or without ἡμέρα, *the last day allowed for payment*, Dem.; *one's last day*, Soph. 3. *last, uttermost*, ὕβρις Id. II. τὸ τελευταῖον, as Adv. *the last time, last of all*, Hdt., Xen., etc.; or τελευταῖον Plat., etc.; and τὰ τελευταῖα Thuc. 2. *at last, in the last place*, Ar., etc.: but, 3. the Adj. is often used with Verbs, where we should use the Adv., ὁ τελευταῖος δραμών Aesch.; παρελθόντες τελευταῖοι Thuc.

τελευτάω, Ion. -έω, f. ήσω :—Pass., with med. τελευτήσομαι: aor. 1 ἐτελευτήθην :—*to complete, finish, ac-*complish, Lat. *perficere*, Hom. : *to fulfil an oath* or *promise*, Id.; τελευτᾶν τινι κακὸν ἦμαρ *to bring about an evil day for one*, Od. :—so in Att., ποῖ τελευτῆσαί με χρή; *to what end must I bring it?* Soph.; Ζεὺς ὅ τι νεύσῃ, τοῦτο τελευτᾷ Eur., etc. :—Pass. *to be fulfilled, to come to pass, happen*, Hom., Eur. 2. *to bring to an end*, esp., τ. τὸν αἰῶνα *to finish life*, i. e. *to die*, Hdt.; τ. βίον Aesch. :—also, c. gen., τελευτᾶν βίου *to make an end of life*, Xen.; so, λόγου τ. Thuc.: —also without βίου, *to end life, to die*, Hdt., Att.; τ. ὑπό τινος *to die* by another's hand or means, Hdt. II. intr. 1. *to be accomplished*, Id. 2. *to come to an end, to end*, Lat. *finire*, Id., Att. :— foll. by a Prep., τ. ἔς τι *to come to a certain end, issue in*, Hdt., Att.; ποῖ (= ἐς τί) τελευτᾷ; *in what does it end?* Aesch. 3. *to die*, v. supr. 4. the part. τελευτῶν, ῶσα, ῶν, was used as Adv., *at the end, at last*, τελευτῶν ἔλεγε Hdt.; κἂν ἐγίγνετο πληγὴ τελευτῶσα *there would have been a fray to finish with*, Soph.; τὰς ὀλοφύρσεις τελευτῶντες ἐξέκαμνον *at last they got tired of mourning*, Thuc. 5. of a country, *to come to an end*, Hdt. From

τελευτή, ἡ, (τελέω) *a finishing, completion, accomplishment*, Od. 2. *a termination, end*, Il., Att.; τῆς ὁδοῦ Ar.; ἡ τ. τοῦ πολέμου Thuc. 3. esp. *an end of life*, βιότοιο τ. Il.; βίου Hdt., etc :—also periphr., θανάτοιο τ. *the end that death brings*, Lat. *mortis exitus*, Hes. 4. *the end, event, issue*, Pind., Aesch. 5. with Preps., in adv. sense, ἐς τελευτήν, *at the end, at last*, Hes., Soph.; ἐπὶ τελευτῆς Plat.; ἐν τελευτῇ Aesch. II. *the end, extremity of any thing*, τελευταὶ Λιβύης *the extremities* of Libya, Hdt. 2. *the end* of a sentence, Arist.

τελέω, Ep. also **τελείω**: Ep. impf. τέλεον: f. τελέω, Ep. τελέσσω, Ion. τελέω, Att. τελῶ: aor. 1 ἐτέλεσα, Ep. ἐτέλεσσα: pf. τετέλεκα :—Pass., Ep. pres. τελέομαι: f. τελεσθήσομαι, and f. med. in pass. sense, 3 sing. τελεῖται, inf. τελέεσθαι, τελεῖσθαι, part. τελεύμενος: aor. 1 ἐτελέσθην: pf. τετέλεσμαι, 3 sing. plqpf. ἐτετέλεστο: (τέλος) :—*to complete, fulfil, accomplish*, and, generally, *to execute, perform*, Lat. *perficere*, Hom. : —Pass., Id.; ἅμα μῦθος ἔην, τετέλεστο δὲ ἔργον 'no sooner said than done,' Il. 2. *to fulfil* one's *word*, Hom. : *to grant* one *the fulfilment* of anything, τί τινι Id.; τ. νόον τινί *to fulfil* his *wish*, Il.; τελέσαι κότον, χόλον *to glut* his *fury, wrath*, Ib.: c. inf., οὐδ' ἐτέλεσσε φέρων *he succeeded* not in bringing, Ib.; ὅρκια τελεῖν, like ὅρκον τελευτᾶν, *to complete* or *confirm an oath*, Ib. 3. *to make perfect*, ἀρετάν Pind.; τ. τινα *to bless* him *with perfect happiness*, Ib.; so, τελεσθεὶς ὄλβος Aesch. :—also, *to bring a child to maturity, bring* it *to the birth*, Eur. 4. *to bring to an end, finish, end*, ὁδόν Il., etc.; without ὁδόν, *to finish one's course to a place, arrive at it*, Thuc. 5. of Time, Od., etc. :— Pass., ἤματα μακρὰ τελέσθη Ib.: of men, *to come to one's end*, Aesch. 6. intr. like Pass. *to be fulfilled, turn out* so and so, Il., Soph. II. *to pay* what one owes, *pay* one's *dues*, Il.: generally, *to pay, present*, Hom., Att.: absol. *to pay tax*, Hdt. :—Pass., of money, *to be paid*, Id.; of persons, *to be subject to tax* or *tribute*, Dem. 2. *to lay out, spend*, Hdt. :—Pass.

to be spent or *expended*, Id. ; ἐs τὸ δεῖπνον τετρακόσια τάλαντα τετελεσμένα laid *out* upon the supper, Id. **3.** since, in many Greek cities, the citizens were distributed into classes acc. to their taxable property, τ. εἴs τινas meant *to be rated as belonging to* a class, Lat. *censeri inter,* τ. ἐs Ἕλληνas, ἐs Βοιωτούs *to belong to* the Greeks, the Boeotians, Id. ; εἰs ἀστοὺs τ. *to become* a citizen, Soph. ; εἰs γυναῖκas ἐξ ἀνδρῶν τ. *to become* a woman instead of a man, Eur. : hence, πρὸs τὸν πατέρα τελέσαι *to compare* with his father, Hdt. **III.** like τελειόω II, *to make perfect,* i. e. *to initiate* in the mysteries, Plat., Dem. :—Pass. *to have oneself initiated,* Lat. *initiari,* Ar., Plat., etc. ; Διονύσῳ τελεσθῆναι *to be consecrated* to Dionysus, *initiated in* his *mysteries,* Hdt. :—c. acc., τελεσθῆναι Βακχεία Ar. **2.** metaph., στρατηγὸs τελεσθῆναι *to be formally appointed* general, Dem. ; τετελεσμένos σωφροσύνῃ *a votary of* temperance, Xen. **3.** also of sacred rites, *to perform,* Eur., Anth.

τελέως, Adv., v. τέλεos.

τελήεις, εσσα, εν, (τελέω) = τέλειos, *perfect, complete,* of victims, ἔρδειν or ῥέζειν τεληέσσas ἑκατόμβas to offer hecatombs, either *of full tale* or *number,* or *of full grown beasts,* or *of beasts without blemish,* Il. ; τελήεντεs οἰωνοί birds *of sure augury,* h. Hom. **II.** τελήειs ποταμόs, of Ocean, the river *in which all others end,* or *ever-circling,* Hes.

ΤΕ′ΛΛΩ, aor. I ἔτειλα : pf. τέταλκα :—*to make to arise, accomplish,* Pind. :—Pass. *to come forth, arise,* Id. **II.** intr. in Act., ἡλίου τέλλοντos at sunrise, Soph.

τέλμα, ατos, τό, *standing water, a pool, pond, marsh, swamp,* Ar., Plat.: in pl. *low land subject to inundation, water-meads,* Hdt. **II.** *the mud of a pool, mud for building with, mortar,* Id. (Deriv. uncertain.)

τελμᾰτ-ώδης, εs, (εἶδos) *marshy, muddy,* ὕδωρ Plut.

ΤΕ′ΛΟΣ, εos, τό, *the fulfilment* or *completion* of anything, Lat. *effectus,* i. e. its *consummation, issue, result, end,* Hom., etc. ; τ. πολέμου its *issue,* Il. ; τ. ἐπιτιθέναι τινί *to put a finish* to a thing, i. e. *give* it effect, Ib. ; τ. ἐπιγίγνεται ἀρῇσι one's prayers are *accomplished,* Od. :—τέλος ἔχειν *to have reached the end, to be finished* or *ready,* Il. ; τ. ἔχει δαίμων ὅπα θέλει the deity keeps *the result* in his own power, Eur. :—τ. λαβεῖν *to be completed,* Plat. **2.** esp. of *the end* of life, τὸ τ. βίου, Soph., Eur. ; and without βίου, *the end, death,* Hdt. **3.** periphr. in various phrases, τέλos θανάτου *the point* or *term* of death, Lat. *exitus mortis,* Hom. ; so, τ. γάμοιο = γάμος, Od., etc. **4.** Adverbial usages : **a.** τέλos *at last,* Hdt., Thuc. : so, εἰs or ἐs τέλos Hdt. :—διὰ τέλous *throughout, for ever, completely,* Trag. :—τέλει, Lat. *omnino, at all,* Soph. **II.** *the end proposed, chief matter,* μύθου τ. Il. **2.** *the end of action,* Plat. :—hence = τὸ ἀγαθόν, *the chief good,* Cicero's *finis bonorum,* Arist. **3.** *perfection, full age,* ἀνδρὸs τ. man's *full age,* manhood, Plat. ; τέλos ἔχειν or λαμβάνειν *to be grown up,* Id. **4.** *a final decision, determination,* Aesch. **5.** *the prize* at games, Pind. **III.** *supreme authority,* Eur., etc. **2.** *a magistracy, office,* οἱ ἐν τέλει men *in office, magistrates,* Soph., Thuc., etc. ; οἱ ἐν τέλει βεβῶτεs Soph. :—then, τὸ τέλos *the government,* Aesch. ; τὰ

τέλη *the magistrates,* Thuc., Xen., etc. **3.** generally, *a task, office,* Aesch. ; ὀμμάτων τέλη the *duties* of the eyes, Eur. **IV.** *a body of soldiers,* Il. ; ἐν τελέεσσιν in squadrons, Il. ; so, κατὰ τέλεα Hdt. : —δίρρυμα τέλη troops of chariots, Aesch. ; and of ships, τρία τέλη τῶν νεῶν Thuc. **V.** *that which is paid for state purposes, a toll, tax, duty,* Ar., Plat., etc. ; ἀγορᾶs τ. *a market-due,* Ar. ; τέλος πρίασθαι, πωλεῖν to farm *a tax,* or let *it,* Dem., Aeschin. ; for λύειν τέλη, v. λύω v. 2 :—generally, *outlay, expense,* Thuc. :— hence, at Athens, *the property at which a citizen was rated for taxation,* Lat. *census* ; and then, *a class, order,* of citizens, Dem., etc. **VI.** in pl. *offerings* or *sacred rites* due to the gods, Trag. :—esp. of the Eleusinian mysteries, Soph., Eur., etc. **2.** of marriage, *as the consummation of life,* Aesch., Soph.

τέλοσδε, Adv. *towards the end* or *term,* Il.

τέλσον, τό, *a boundary, limit,* τέλσον ἀρούρηs Il. (Deriv. uncertain.)

Τελχίν, ῖνos, ὁ, *one of the Telchines,* the first inhabitants of Crete, and the first workers in metal, Aesch. **II.** as appellat. τελχίν, *a mischievous elf,* Anth.

τελωνέω, f. ήσω, *to be a tax-gatherer,* Luc. From

τελ-ώνης, ου, ὁ, (τέλos v) *a farmer* or *collector of the taxes,* Ar., Aeschin. : in N. T. = Lat. *publicanus.*

τελωνία, ἡ, *the office of* τελώνηs, Dem.

τελωνιάς, άδos, ἡ, *of tolls* or *customs,* μᾶζα τ. the good fare *of the tax-gatherers,* Anth.

τελωνικός, ή, όν, *of* or *for* τελωνία, τ. νόμοι the *excise and custom* laws, Dem.

τελώνιον, τό, (τελώνηs) *a custom-house,* N. T.

τεμάχιον, τό, Dim. of τέμαχos, Plat.

τέμαχος, εos, τό, (τέμνω) *a slice of salt-fish,* Ar., Xen. etc. : generally, *a slice of meat,* Luc.

τεμενίζω, f. Att. ιῶ, *to make a sacred grove* (τέμενos), *to consecrate,* Plat.

τεμεῖν, aor. 2 inf. of τέμνω.

τεμένιos, a, ον, *of* or *in the sacred precincts,* Soph.

τεμενίτης [ῑ], ου, ὁ, = τεμένιos : at Syracuse, *Apollo of the Temenos,* Thuc. :—fem., ἡ ἄκρα ἡ Τεμενῖτιs the height *on which was the Temenos of Apollo,* Id.

τέμενος, εos, τό, (τέμνω III. 2) *a piece of land cut off,* assigned as *a domain* to kings and chiefs, Hom. **II.** *a piece of land dedicated* to a god, *the sacred precincts,* Id. : in it stood the temple, Hdt. :—metaph., the *sacred valley* of the Nile is the τέμ. Νείλοιο, Pind. ; the Acropolis is the ἱερὸν τ. of Pallas, Ar.

τέμνω (Root **TEM,** cf. τέμω), Ion., Dor. and Ep. τάμνω : f. τεμῶ, Ion. τεμέω : aor. 2 ἔτεμον, Ion. and Dor. ἔταμον, Ep. τάμον, Ep. inf. ταμέειν : pf. τέτμηκα :—Med., f. τεμοῦμαι : aor. 2 ἐταμόμην, inf. ταμέσθαι :—Pass., f. τμηθήσομαι : aor. I ἐτμήθην : pf. τέτμημαι :—*to cut, hew,* Hom., etc. ; ὀδόντas οἵous τέμνειν teeth fit for *cutting,* Xen. **2.** *to cut, wound, maim,* Il. ; πρὸs δέρην τ. *to wound* her in the neck, Aesch. **3.** of a surgeon, *to cut,* Il. : absol. *to use the knife,* as opp. to cautery (κάειν), Aesch., Xen., etc. :—Pass. *to be operated upon,* Plat. **II.** *to cut up, cut to pieces,* Hom., etc. :—*to slaughter, sacrifice,* Il., Eur. **2.** ὅρκια τάμνειν *to sacrifice* in attestation of an oath, and so *to take solemn oaths,* Hom. ; θάνατόν νύ τοι ὅρκι᾽ ἔταμνον *I made* a truce

which was death to thee, Il.:—Med., of two parties, ὅρκια τάμνεσθαι Hdt.:—cf. Lat. foedus ferire.　3. φάρμακον τέμνειν to cut or chop up a plant for purposes of medicine or witchcraft, Aesch., etc.; ἄκος τέμνειν to contrive a means or remedy, Eur.　4. to divide, of a river, μέσην τ. Λιβύην to cut it in twain, Hdt.; δίχα τ. to cut in two, bisect, Plat.　III. to cut asunder, cut off, sever, κεφαλὴν ἀπὸ δειρῆς Il., etc.; with double acc., ἐρινεὸν τάμνε ὄρπηκας cut the branches off the fig-tree, Ib.; and in Pass., τρίχας ἐτμήθην had them cut off, Eur.　2. to part off, mark off, τέμενος Il.　IV. to cut down, fell trees, Ib., etc.:—Med., δοῦρα τάμνεσθαι to fell oneself timber, Od., Hdt.　2. λίθον τ. to hew stone, Plat.: Med., λίθους τάμνεσθαι to have them wrought or hewn, Hdt.　3. to cut down for purposes of destruction, Eur., etc.; τ. τὴν γῆν to ravage the country by felling the trees and cutting the corn, Hdt., Thuc.; with partit. gen., τῆς γῆς τ. to waste part of it, Thuc.　V. to cut or hew into shape, δούρατα Od., etc.　VI. to cut lengthwise, to plough, Solon.　2. τ. ὁδόν to cut or make a road, Thuc.:—Pass., τέτμηνται κέλευθοι Pind.　3. also to make one's way, advance, τ. ὁδόν Eur.; τὴν μεσόγαιαν τ. τῆς ὁδοῦ to take the middle road, strike through the interior, Hdt.; μέσον τέμνειν to hold a middle course, Plat.　4. of ships, to cut through the waves, plough the sea, Od.:—so of birds, to cleave the air, Ar.　VII. to bring to a decision, Lat. decidere, Pind., Eur.

Τέμπεα, contr. Τέμπη, τά, Tempé, the valley between Olympus and Ossa, through which the Peneius escapes into the sea, Hdt.

ΤΕ'ΜΩ, radical form of τέμνω, Il.

τεναγίζω, f. σω, (τέναγος) to be covered with shoal water, stand in pools, Plut.

τεναγῖτις, ιδος, fem. Adj. shallow, Anth.　From

τέναγος, εος, τό, (τείνω) shoal-water, a shoal, shallow, lagoon, Lat. vadum, Hdt., Thuc.

τεναγ-ώδης, ες, (εἶδος) covered with shoal-water, standing in pools, Polyb.

ΤΕ'ΝΔΩ, to gnaw, gnaw at, Hes.

τενθεία, ἡ, lickerishness, gluttony, Ar.　From

τένθης, ου, ὁ, (τένθω) a dainty feeder, gourmand, Ar.

τένων, οντος, ὁ, (τείνω) any tight-stretched band, a sinew, tendon, Hom.; τ. ποδός the outstretched foot, Eur.:—absol. the foot, Aesch., Eur.

τέο, Ion. and Dor. gen. of interrog. τίς, Il.　II. τεο, Ion. and Dor. gen. of enclit. τις, Od., Hdt.

τέο, Dor. gen. of σύ (τύ), Ep. τεοῖο, Il.

τέοισι; Ion. for τισί; dat. pl. of τίς; who? Hdt.

τεός, ή, όν, Lat. tuus, Ep. and Ion. for σός, Hom., Hes., Hdt.: Dor. τεός, ά, όν, Pind., and Trag. Chorus.

τεράζω or τεράζω, only in pres., (τέρας) to interpret portents or prodigies, Aesch.

τέραμνον or -εμνον, τό, in pl., chambers, a house, Eur.

ΤΕ'ΡΑΣ, τό: gen. ατος, Ep. αος, Ion. εος: pl., nom. τέρᾰτᾰ, Ep. τέραα, Ion. τέρεα: gen. τερῶν, Ep. τεράων: dat. τέρασι, Ep. τεράεσσι:—a sign, wonder, marvel, Lat. portentum, prodigium, Hom.; esp. of signs in heaven, Il. (cf. τεῖρος).　II. in concrete sense, a monster, Διὸς τ. αἰγιόχοιο, of the Gorgon's head, Ib.; of a serpent, Ib.; of Typhoëus, Aesch.; of Cerberus, Soph.

τερα-σκόπος, ον, poët. for τερατοσκόπος, Aesch., Soph.; καρδία τ. 'my prophetic soul,' Aesch.

τεράστιος, ον, (τέρας) monstrous, Theophr., Luc.

τερᾰτεία, ἡ, a talking marvels, jugglery, Ar.　From

τερᾰτεύομαι, (τέρας) Dep. to talk marvels, Lat. portenta loqui, Ar., Aeschin.; τ. τῷ σχήματι to indulge in marvellous gesticulation, Aeschin.

τερᾰτολογέω, f. ήσω, to tell of marvels, Luc.; and

τερᾰτολογία, ἡ, a telling of marvels, marvellous tales, Isocr., Luc.　From

τερᾰτο-λόγος, ὁ, (λέγω) of which marvellous things are told, portentous, Plat.

τερᾰτουργία, ἡ, love of the marvellous, Luc.　From

τερᾰτ-ουργός, ὁ, (*ἔργω) a wonder-worker, Luc.

τερᾰτ-ώδης, ες, (εἶδος) portentous, Ar., Plat.

τερᾰτ-ωπός, όν, (ὤψ) marvellous-looking, h. Hom.

τερέβινθος, v. τέρμινθος.

τερεβινθ-ώδης, ες, (εἶδος) full of terebinth-trees, Anth.

τέρεμνον, v. τέραμνον.

τερετίζω, f. Att. ιῶ, to whistle, Babr.　(Formed from the sound.)　Hence

τερέτισμα, ατος, τό, a whistling, trilling, Anth.

τέρετρον, τό, (τείρω) a borer, gimlet, Lat. terebra, Od.

τερηδών, όνος, ἡ, (τείρω) the wood-worm, Lat. teredo, Ar.

τέρην, εινᾰ, εν, gen. τέρενος, είνης (poët. -ένης), ενος: (τείρω):—properly rubbed smooth, and so smooth, soft, delicate, Lat. tener, Hom., etc.; ὄψις τέρεινα a tender sight, i. e. one that causes tender feelings, Eur.:—Comp. τερεινότερος, Sappho.

τερθρεύομαι, Dep. to use claptraps, Dem.　(Prob. contr. from τερατεύομαι.)

τέρθριος, ὁ, the rope from the end of a sail-yard (τέρθρον), the brace, Ar.

ΤΕ'ΡΘΡΟΝ, τό, the end of the sail-yard, cornu antennae: generally, an extremity, summit, h. Hom.

ΤΕ'ΡΜΑ, ατος, τό, an end, boundary, Lat. terminus:　1. the goal round which chariots had to turn at races, Lat. meta, Il.; δρόμου τέρματα Soph.　2. the mark set to shew how far a quoit was thrown, Od.　3. metaph. an end, issue, event, Aesch.　II. generally, an end, limit, Id.; so in pl. boundaries, Hdt.　2. an end, πρὸς τέρμα εἶναι, ἐπὶ τέρμ' ἀφικέσθαι to have reached the limit, be at the end, Aesch., Soph.; τ. βίου the term or end of life, death, Soph., Eur., etc.; ἐπὶ τέρματι at last, Aesch.　3. the end or highest point, κακῶν Eur.; πρὸς τέρμασιν ὥρας Ar.　4. periphr., τέρμα ὑγιείας = ὑγιεία, Aesch.; τ. τῆς σωτηρίας Soph.　5. the highest power, supremacy, τ. Κορίνθου ἔχειν to be sovereign of Corinth, Simon.; θεοὶ ἁπάντων τέρμ' ἔχοντες Eur.

Τερμέρειον or Τερμέριον κακόν, τ., proverb. of a misfortune one brings on oneself, said to be derived from one Τέρμερος a highwayman, Plut.

τερμίνθινος or τερεβίνθιος, α, ον, of the terebinth-tree, Xen.

τέρμινθος, later τερέβινθος, ἡ, the terebinth or turpentine tree, Theophr., Anth.

τερμιόεις, εσσα, εν, (τέρμα) going even to the end, ἀσπὶς τερμιόεσσα a shield that reaches from head to foot, Il.; so, χιτὼν τ. Od.

τέρμιος, α, ον, (τέρμα) at the end, last, always of Time,

τ. ἡμέραι the day *of death*, Soph. ; τερμία χώρα the spot *where one is destined to end life*, Id.

τερμόνιος, α, ον, *at the world's end*, Aesch. From τέρμων, ονος, ὁ, = τέρμα, *a boundary*, Eur. ; and in pl., Id. **2.** = Lat. *Terminus*, Plut. **II.** *an end*, βίου Eur.

Τερπιάδης, ου, ὁ, (τέρπω) *Son of Delight*, name of the minstrel Phemius, Od.

τερπι-κέραυνος, ον, *delighting in thunder*, Il., Hes.

τερπνός, ή, όν, (τέρπω) *delightsome, delightful, pleasant, agreeable, glad*, Theogn., Aesch., etc.; τὸ τερπνόν *delight, pleasure*, Thuc. ; τὰ τερπνά *delights, pleasures*, Xen. **2.** of persons, αὐτῷ τερπνός *with joy* to himself, Soph. :—Comp. and Sup. τερπνότερος, -ότατος, Theogn. ; later, -ιστος :— Adv. τερπνῶς, Id.

ΤΕ´ΡΠΩ, Ep. 3 sing. subj. τέρπησι : Ion. impf. τέρπεσκον : f. τέρψω : aor. 1 ἔτερψα :—Pass. and Med. have a fourfold aor., 1. aor. 1 ἐτέρφθην, Ep. ἐτάρφθην, τάρφθην, 3 pl. τάρφθεν, 2. Ep. aor. 2 ἐτάρπην, τάρπην, inf. ταρπῆναι, ταρπήμεναι, 1 pl. subj. τράπείομεν (for ταρπῶμεν), 3. aor. 1 ἐτερψάμην, Ep. subj. τέρψομαι, 4. Ep. aor. 2 ἐταρπόμην ; also redupl. through all moods, τεταρπόμην, τετάρπετο, τεταρπώμεσθα, τεταρπόμενος. *To satisfy, delight, gladden, cheer*, Hom., Hdt., Att. :—absol. *to give delight*, Od. ; τὰ τέρποντα *delights*, Soph. **II.** Pass. and Med., 1. c. gen. rei, *to have full enjoyment of* a thing, *have enough of it*, Hom.; metaph., τεταρπώμεσθα γόοιο *let us take our fill* of lamentation, Id. **2.** *to enjoy oneself, make merry*, c. dat. modi, φόρμιγγι, μύθοισι, etc., Id., etc.; so, τ. ἐν θαλίης Od., etc. :— also c. part., τέρψει κλύων Soph. ; τέρπεται τιμώμενος Eur. :—absol., πῖνε καὶ τέρπου *drink* and *be merry*, Hdt. **3.** c. acc. cogn. *to enjoy*, τ. ὄνησιν Eur.

τερπωλή, ή, poët. for τέρψις, Od., Theogn.

τερσαίνω, *to dry up, wipe up*, Il. From ΤΕ´ΡΣΟΜΑΙ, Pass. with Ep. aor. 2 inf. τερσῆναι, τερσή-μεναι, as if from ἐτέρσην :—*to be* or *become dry, to dry up*, ἕλκος ἐτέρσετο the wound *dried up*, Il. ; θειλόπεδον τέρσεται ἠελίῳ the plain is *baked* by the sun, Od. ; c. gen., ὄσσε δακρυόφιν τέρσοντο eyes *became dry of* tears, Ib. **II.** Act. intr. in 3 sing. f. τέρσει (as if from τέρρω), Theocr.

τερφθείην, aor. 1 pass. opt. of τέρπω.

τερψί-μβροτος, ον, *gladdening the heart of man*, Ἥλιος Od.

τερψί-νοος [ῐ], ον, *heart-gladdening*, Anth.

τέρψις, εως and ιος, ἡ, (τέρπω) *enjoyment, delight*, τινός *from* or *in* a thing, Hes., Trag.; τέρψις ἐστί μοι, c. inf., it is my *pleasure* to do, Soph. :—absol. *gladness, joy, delight, pleasure*, Theogn., Aesch.

Τερψι-χόρη, Dor. -χόρα, ἡ, *Terpsichore, Dance-enjoying*, one of the nine Muses, Hes.

τερψί-χορος, ον, also α, ον, *enjoying the dance*, Anth.

τεσσαρά-βοιος, ον, (βοῦς) *worth four steers*, Il.

τεσσᾰρᾰ-καί-δεκα, v. τεσσαρεσκαίδεκα.

τεσσαρακαιδεκά-δωρος, ον, *fourteen hand-breadths long*, Anth.

τεσσαράκοντα [ᾰ], Att. τεττᾰράκοντα, Ion. τεσσεράκοντα, οἱ, αἱ, τά, indecl. : (τέσσαρες) :—*forty*, Hom., etc. **II.** οἱ τ. *the Forty*, a body of justices who went round the Attic demes to hear causes, Dem.

τεσσαρακοντα-ετής, ές, (ἔτος) *forty years old*, Hes. :— Att. fem. τετταρακονταετίς, ίδος, Plat.

τεσσᾰράκοντ-όργυιος, ον, *forty fathoms high*, Hdt.

τεσσᾰράκοντούτης, ον, ὁ, = τεσσαρακονταετής, Luc.

τεσσᾰράκοστός, ή, όν, *fortieth*, Lat. *quadragesimus*, Thuc. **II.** τεσσαρακοστή [μοῖρα], ή, *a fortieth*, a coin of Chios, Id.

ΤΕ´ΣΣΑ˘ΡΕΣ, οἱ, αἱ, τέσσαρα, τά, gen. ων : dat. τέσσαρσι, poët. τέτρᾰσι :—new Att. τέττᾰρες, τέτταρα :—in Ion. Prose, τέσσερες, τέσσερα, dat. τέσσερσι ;—Dor. τέτορες, τέτορα ;—Aeol. and Ep. πίσυρες, πίσυρα ;— Boeot. πέττᾰρες :—*four*, Lat. *quatuor*, Hom., etc.

τεσσᾰρεσ-καί-δεκα, Ion. τεσσερ-, οἱ, αἱ, τά, *fourteen*, Lat. *quatuordecim*, the first part remaining unaltered with a neut. Subst., as, τεσσερεσκαίδεκα ἔτη Hdt.

τεσσᾰρεσκαιδέκᾰτος, Ion. τεσσερ-, η, ον, *fourteenth*, Hdt., etc.

τεσσᾰρεσκαιδεκ-έτης, ου, ὁ, *fourteen years old*, Plut.

τεσσεράκοντα, τέσσερες, Ion. for τεσσαρ-.

τεταγμένως, Adv. part. pf. pass. of τάσσω, *in orderly manner*, Xen.

τετᾰγών, όντος, ὁ, Ep. redupl. aor. 2 part., with no pres. in use, ῥῖψε ποδὸς τεταγών *having seized* him *by the foot*, Il. ; ῥίπτασκον τεταγών Ib. (From Root ΤΑΓ, cf. Lat. *tango*, *te-tig-i*.)

τέτᾰκα, pf. of τείνω.

τέταλμαι, pf. pass. of τέλλω :—τέταλτο, 3 sing. plqpf.

τέτᾰμαι, pf. pass. of τείνω.

τετᾰνό-θριξ, ὁ, ἡ, *with long straight hair*, Plat.

τετᾰνός, ή, όν, (τείνω) *straightened, smooth*, Anth.

τετάνυστο, 3 sing. plqpf. pass. of τανύω.

τεταραγμένως, Adv. part. pass. pf., *confusedly*, Isocr.

τετάρπετο, 3 sing. redupl. aor. 2 pass. of τέρπω :— τεταρπώμεσθα, 1 pl. subj. :—τεταρπόμενος, part.

τεταρταῖος, α, ον, *on the fourth day*, τ. γενέσθαι *to be four days dead*, Hdt.; ἀφικνεῖσθαι τεταρταίους Plat. **2.** τ. πυρετός *a quartan fever*, Id.

τεταρτη-μόριον, τό, *a fourth part, quadrans*, Hdt.

τέταρτος, Ep. also τέτρᾰτος, η, ον, *fourth*, Lat. *quartus*, Hom. **II.** τὸ τέταρτον, as Adv. *the fourth time*, Id. : as Adv., without Art., *fourthly*, Plat. **III.** ἡ τετάρτη : **1.** (sub. ἡμέρα), *the fourth day*, Hes., Xen. **2.** (sub. μοῖρα), *a liquid measure* (cf. our *quart*), Hdt.

τετάσθην, Ep. 3 dual plqpf. pass. of τείνω :—τέτατο, Ep. 3 sing.

τετάχᾰται, Ion. 3 pl. pf. pass. of τάσσω.

τέτευχα, pf. of τυγχάνω. **II.** pf. of τεύχω.

τετεύχᾰται, -το, 3 pl. pf. and plqpf. pass. of τεύχω.

τετεύχετον, 3 dual pf. of τεύχω.

τετεύχησθαι, pf. pass. inf. with pres. sense, formed from the Subst. τεύχεα, without any pres. in use, *to be armed*, Od.

τέτηκα, pf. of τήκω.

τετίημαι, pf. formed as if from τιέω, but with no pres. in use, *to be sorrowful, to sorrow, mourn*, τετίησθον Il. ; τετιημένος (τετιημένη) ἦτορ *sorrowful* at heart, Hom. **II.** so also in act. pf. part., τετιηότι θυμῷ *with sorrowing* heart, Il. ; δὴν δ' ἀνέῳ ἦσαν τετιηότες they were long silent *from grief*, Ib.

τετιμένος, pf. pass. part. of τίω.

τετῑμῆσθαι, pf. pass. inf. of τιμάω.

τέτλᾰθι, τετλάτω, Ep. pf. imper. of *τλάω :—τετλαίην, opt. :—τετλάμεν, -άμεναι, inf.

γέτληκα, pf. of *τλάω : Ep. part. τετληώς.

τέτμηκα, τέτμημαι, pf. act. and pass. of τέμνω :—Ep. part. τετμηώς.

τέτμον, and ἔτετμον, an Ep. aor. 2 without any pres. in use, with and without augm. :—to overtake, reach, come up to, find, Hom.; of old age, to come upon one, Od. 2. c. gen. to partake of, Hes.

τέτοκα, pf. of τίκτω.

τετολμηκότως, Adv. pf. part. of τολμάω, Polyb.

τέτορες, οἱ, αἱ, τέτορα, τά, Dor. for τέσσαρες.

τετορήσω, Ep. redupl. fut. of τορέω.

τέτρᾰ-, for τέτορα, τέσσαρα in compd. words.

τετρᾰ-βάμων [ᾰ], ον, gen. ονος (βαίνω) four-footed, Eur.; τ. χηλαί, ψάλια of the hoofs, trappings of horses, Id.; τετραβάμοσι γυίοις in the shape of a quadruped, Id.

τετρα-γλώχῑς, ῑνος, ὁ, ἡ, with four angles, square, Anth.

τετρά-γυος, ον, (γύα) containing four measures of land, Od.

τετρᾰγωνίζω, f. Att. ιῶ, to make square, Plat.

τετρᾰγωνο-πρόσωπος, ον, square-faced, Hdt.

τετρά-γωνος [ᾰ], ον, (γωνία) with four equal angles, rectangular or square, Lat. quadratus, Hdt.; δόκοι τ. squared beams, Thuc. :—τετράγωνον, τό, a square, Plat.: a body of men drawn up in square, Lat. agmen quadratum, Xen. 2. τ. ἀριθμός a square number, i. e. a number multiplied into itself, Plat. II. metaph. square, i. e. perfect, Simon. ap. Plat.

τετρᾰδεῖον, τό, (τετράς) a number of four, a quarternion, N. T.

τετρά-δραχμον, τό, a coin of four drachms, a tedradrachm, worth about 3s. 2d., Plut.

τετρα-έλικτος, ον, four times wound round, Anth.

τετρα-ένης, ες, (ἔνος) of four years, four years old, Lat. quadrimus, Theocr.

τετρα-ετής, ές, or -έτης, ες, (ἔτος) four years old, Hdt. II. of four years, χρόνος Id. Hence

τετραετία, ἡ, a term of four years, Plat.

τετρά-ζυγος, ον, (ζυγόν) four-yoked, Eur.

τετρᾰ-θέλυμνος, ον, (θέλυμνον) of four layers, τ. σάκος a shield of four ox-hides, Hom.

τετραίνω, Ion. f. τετρᾰνέω : Ep. aor. 1 τέτρηνα :—other tenses are formed from *τράω, f. τρήσω : aor. 1 ἔτρησα :—Pass., pf. τέτρημαι :—to bore through, pierce, perforate, Hom. :—Pass., λίθος τετρημένος Hdt.; ὁ οὐρανὸς τέτρηται the sky has holes in it, Id.; χάσμα τῆς γῆς τετρημένον a chasm formed by perforating the earth, Plat.

τετρακαιδεκα-έτης, ες, of fourteen years : fem. τετρᾰκαιδεκέτις, ιδος, fourteen years old, Isocr.

τετρά-κερως, ων, (κέρας) four-horned, Anth.

τετράκις [ᾰ], Adv. four times, Lat. quater, Od., Hdt., Att. :—τετράκι, Pind.

τετρᾰκισ-μύριοι [ῠ], αι, α, four times ten thousand, forty thousand, Xen.

τετρᾰκισ-χίλιοι [ῑ], αι, α, four thousand, Hdt., Att.

τετρά-κλῑνος, ον, (κλίνη) with four couches, Luc.

τετρά-κνᾱμος, ον, Dor. for -κνημος, four-spoked, of a wheel, Pind.

τετρᾰ-κόρυμβος, ον, with four clusters, i. e. thick-clustering, Anth.

τετρᾰκόσιοι, αι, α, (τέσσαρες) four hundred, Hdt., etc.; in sing., τετρακοσία ἀσπίς Xen. II. οἱ τ., at Athens, the oligarchy established in 411 B.C., Thuc.

τετρά-κυκλος, ον, four-wheeled, Hom., Hdt.

τετρᾰ-κωμία, ἡ, (κώμη) a union of four villages, Strab.

τετρᾰ-λογία, ἡ, (λόγος) a series of four dramas, three Tragedies and one Satyric play, exhibited at the festivals of Dionysus : the three Tragedies were called τριλογία, as the Oresteia of Aesch.

τετρά-μετρος [ᾰ], ον, (μέτρον) consisting of four metres, i. e. in iambic or trochaic verse, consisting of four double feet or syzygies : τὸ τετράμετρον is generally the trochaic tetrameter, Ar., Xen.

τετρά-μηνος [ᾰ], ον, (μήν) of four months, lasting four months, Thuc.

τέτραμμαι, pf. pass. of τρέπω.

τετρᾰμοιρία, ἡ, a fourfold portion, Xen. From

τετρά-μοιρος [ᾰ], ον, (μοῖρα) fourfold, Eur.

ΤΕ'ΤΡΑΞ, αγος, and ἄκος, ὁ, perh. the pheasant, Ar.

τετρᾱορία, ἡ, a four-horsed chariot, Pind.

τετρ-άορος, contr. τέτρ-ωρος, ον, (ἀείρω) yoked four together, Od.; τ. ἄρμα a four-horsed chariot, Pind. II. four-legged, Soph.

τετρᾰ-πάλαστος, ον, four spans long or broad, Hdt.

τετρά-πηχυς [ᾰ], υ, gen. εως, four cubits (six feet) long, Hdt., Plat.; of men, six feet high, Ar.

τετραπλάσιος [ᾰ], α, ον, fourfold, four times as much, Lat. quadruplex, Plat.

τετρά-πλεθρος [ᾰ], ον, consisting of four plethra, Polyb.

τετρά-πλευρος [ᾰ], ον, (πλευρόν) four-sided, Anth.

τετράπλῇ, Adv. in a fourfold manner, fourfold, Il.

τετρα-πλόος, η, ον, contr. -πλοῦς, ῆ, οῦν, fourfold, Lat. quadruplus, Plut.; τὸ τ.,=τετραμοιρία, Xen.

τετρᾰ-ποδηδόν, Adv. (πούς) on four feet, Ar.

τετρᾰ-ποδιστί, Adv. (πούς) on all fours, Luc.

τετρά-πολις [ᾰ], εως, ἡ, of or with four cities, λαὸς τ., of the northern part of Attica, Eur.

τετρά-πολος [ᾰ], ον, (πολέω) turned up or ploughed four times, Theocr.

τετρά-πορος [ᾰ], ον, with four passages or openings, Anth. II. coming four ways, Id.

τετρά-πους [ᾰ], ὁ, ἡ, -πουν, τό, four-footed, Lat. quadrupes, Hdt.:—τετράπουν, τό, a quadruped, pl. τετράποδα Id., Ar., etc. II. of things, four feet in length, Plat.

τετρα-πτερυλλίς, ίδος, ἡ, (πτερόν) a four-wing, i. e. a grasshopper or locust, Ar.

τετρά-πτῑλος [ᾰ], ον, (πτίλον) four-winged, Ar.

τέτραπτο, Ep. 3 sing. plqpf. pass. of τρέπω.

τετράρ-ρυμος, ον, with four poles, i. e. eight-horsed, Xen.

τετραρχέω, f. ήσω, to be tetrarch, τῆς Γαλιλαίας N. T.

τετράρχης, ου, ὁ, a tetrarch, i. e. a ruler of one of four provinces, Strab., etc.

τετραρχία, ἡ, a tetrarchy, the province of a tetrarch, esp. in Thessaly, the four provinces being Thessaliotis, Phthiotis, Pelasgiotis, Hestiaeotis, Eur., Dem. 2. under the Romans the name tetrarchy was given to any division of a country, as to Palestine, which after Herod was divided into three tetrarchies, Plut., etc.

τετράς, άδος, ἡ, the fourth day of the month, Hes., Ar.

τετρα-σκελής, ές, (σκέλος) four-legged, four-footed, τ.

οἰωνός, of a kind of griffin, Aesch.; τ. ὕβρισμα the wanton violence of Centaurs, Eur.

τετρα-στάδιος, ον, (στάδιον) four stades in length, Strab.: τετραστάδιον, τό, a length of four stades, Id.

τετρά-σχοινος, ον, four σχοῖνοι long, Strab.

τέτρᾰτος, η, ον, poët. for τέταρτος, fourth, Hom., etc.; τὸ τέτρατον the fourth time, Il., Hes.

τετρά-τρῠφος, ον, (θρύπτω) broken into four pieces, Hes.

τέτρᾰφα, pf. both of τρέπω and of τρέφω.

τετρᾰ-φάληρος [ᾰ], ον, epith. of a helmet, prob. with four crests or plumes, Il.

τετρᾰ-φάλος, ον, = foreg., Il.

τετράφᾰται, -το, Ep. 3 pl. pf. and plqpf. pass. of τρέφω.

τετράφθω, 3 sing. pf. pass. imper. of τρέπω.

τετρά-φῠλος, ον, (φυλή) divided into four tribes, Hdt.

τέτρᾰχᾰ [ᾰ], (τέσσαρες) Adv. in four parts, Plat.

τετραχῇ, Adv. = foreg., Xen., Luc.

τετραχθά [ᾰ], Adv., poët. for τέτραχα, Hom.

τετρά-χοος, ον, holding four χόες, Anth.

τετρά-χυτρος, ον, (χύτρα) made of four pots, Batr.

τετρεμαίνω, redupl. form of τρέμω, Ar.

τέτρημαι, pf. pass. of τετραίνω.

τετρ-ήμερος, ον, of four days : μετὰ τὴν τετρήμερον (sc. ἡμέραν) after the fourth day, Arist.

τέτρηνα, Ep. aor. 1 of τετραίνω.

τετρ-ήρης (sc. ναῦς), ἡ, a quadrireme, Polyb.

τέτρηχα, pf. intr. of ταράσσω : part. fem. τετρηχυῖα : 3 sing. plqpf. τετρήχει.

τετρίγει [ῑ], Ep. 3 sing. plqpf. of τρίζω :—τετρῑγώς, υἶα, pf. part.; τετρῑγῶτας, Ep. for -ότας, acc. pl.

τετρ-όργυιος, ον, (ὄργυια) of four fathoms, Anth.

τέτροφα, pf. of τρέφω.

τετρ-ώβολος, ον, (ὄβολος) of four obols :—τετρώβολον, τό, a four-obol piece, a soldier's daily pay, Ar.

τέτρωμαι, pf. pass. of τιτρώσκω.

τέτρ-ωρος, ον, contr. for τετρ-άορος.

τετρ-ώροφος, ον, (ὀροφή) of four stories, Hdt.

τετρ-ώρυγος, ον, = τετρόργυιος, Xen.

τέττᾰ, a friendly or respectful address of youths to their elders, Father, Il.

τεττᾰράκοντα, τέτταρες, etc., Att. for τεσσαρ-.

τεττῑγο-φόρας, ου, ὁ, (φέρω) wearing a τέττιξ : epith. of the Athenians (cf. τέττιξ 1. 2), Ar.

τεττῑγ-ώδης, ες, (εἶδος) like a τέττιξ, Luc.

τέττιξ, ῑγος, ὁ, a kind of grasshopper, the cicala, Lat. cicada, an insect fond of basking on bushes, when the male makes a chirping noise by striking the wing against the breast, Il., etc. 2. χρύσεος τ. a golden cicada, worn by the Athenians before Solon's time, as an emblem of their claim to being αὐτόχθονες (for such was the supposed origin of the insect), Ar., Thuc.

τέτυγμαι, pf. pass. of τεύχω :—τετύγμην, Ep. plqpf.

τετῠκεῖν, Ep. redupl. aor. 2 inf. of. τεύχω.

τέτυμμαι, pf. pass. of τύπτω.

τέτυξα, 2 sing. pf. pass. of τεύχω :—τέτυξο, Ep. 2 sing. plqpf. :—τετύχθαι, pf. inf. ; τετύχθω, 3 sing. imper.

τετυφωμένως, Adv. pass. pf. part. of τυφόω, stupidly, Dem.

τετύχηκα, pf. of τυγχάνω.

τεῦ, Dor. gen. of σύ. II. τεῦ, Ion., Ep., Dor. gen. of τίς ; who ?, but τευ enclit. of τις, some one.

τεῦγμα, τό, (τεύχω) that which is made, a work, Anth.

ΤΕΥΘΙΣ, ίδος [ῐ], ἡ, a cuttle-fish, Ar.

τευκτικός, ή, όν, (τυγχάνω) able to gain, τινός Arist.

τεύξεια, Ep. aor. 1 opt. of τεύχω.

τεῦξις, εως, ἡ, attainment : also = ἔντευξις, Anth.

τεύξομαι, fut. of τυγχάνω. II. fut. med. of τεύχω.

τεῦς, Aeol. and Dor. gen. of σύ.—

τευτάζω, f. άσω : pf. τετεύτακα :—for ταυτάζω, to say or do the same thing, τ. περί τι to dwell upon a thing, be wholly engaged in it, Plat.

τευτλίον, τό, Dim. of τεῦτλον, Ar.

τευτλόεις, εσσα, εν, contr. οὖς, οῦσσα, οῦν, of or full of beet : hence Τεύτλουσσα, Beet-island, Thuc.

ΤΕΥ῾ΤΛΟΝ, τό, Ion. and in later Att. σεῦτλον, beet, Lat. beta, Batr., Ar., etc.

τευχεσ-φόρος, ον, (φέρω) wearing armour, Aesch., Eur.

τευχηστήρ, ῆρος, ὁ, (τεῦχος) an armed man, warrior, Aesch. : also τευχηστής, οῦ, ὁ, Id.

τεύχοισα, Dor. for -ουσα, part. fem. of τεύχω.

τεῦχος, εος, τό, (τεύχω) a tool, implement :—mostly in pl. τεύχεα, 1. implements of war, armour, arms, harness, Hom., Hes. ;—so τεύχη in Trag. 2. in pl., also, the gear of a ship, tackle, Od. II. in sing. a vessel of any kind, a bathing-tub, Aesch. ; a cinerary urn, Id., Soph. ; a balloting-urn, Aesch. ; a vase for libations, Id. ; a vase or ewer for water, Eur. ; a pot or jar, Xen. ; ξύλινα τ. chests, Id. III. the human frame, body, Arist. IV. a book, Anth. ; hence πεντάτευχ ος, ἡ, the Pentateuch.

τευχο-φόρος, ον, (φέρω) bearing arms, armed, Eur.

ΤΕΥ῾ΧΩ, f. τεύξω : aor. 1 ἔτευξα, Ep. τεῦξα : pf. τέτευχα : Ep. redupl. aor. τετυκεῖν :—Med., f. τεύξομαι : Ep. redupl. aor. 2 inf. τετυκέσθαι :—Pass., 3 f. τετεύξομαι : aor. 1 ἐτύχθην : pf. τέτυγμαι, plqpf. ἐτετύγμην, Ep. 3 pl. τετεύχαται, ἐτετεύχατο, τετεύχατο. To make ready, make, build, work, Hom., Hes., Trag. ;—of a cook, δεῖπνον τευκεῖν to dress or prepare a meal, Od. ; and in Med., δεῖπνον τετυκέσθαι to have a meal prepared, Hom. :—Pass., δώματα τετεύχαται ἐτεύχατο βωμοί Ib. ; c. gen., χρυσοῖο τετεύχαται are wrought of gold, Ib. ; also, τετυγμένα δώματα λάεσσιν built with stones, Od. ; but, δόμος αἰθούσησι τετυγμένος built or furnished with vestibules, Il. 2. the pf. part. τετυγμένος often passes into the sense of an Adj., = τυκτός, well-made, well-wrought, Hom. ; ἀγρὸς καλὸν τετ. well wrought, well tilled, Od. ;—metaph. νόος τετυγμένος a ready, constant mind, Ib. 3. pf. act. part. once in pass. sense, ῥινοῖο τετευχὼς made of hide, Ib. II. of events, to cause, make, bring to pass, bring about, ὄμβρον ἠὲ χάλαζαν Il. ; τ. βοήν to make a cry, Il. ; τ. to bring it about, Ib. :—Pass., esp. in pf., to be caused, and so to arise, occur, happen, exist, Hom., etc. III. c. acc. pers. to make so and so, ἄγνωστον τ. τινά Od. ; τ. τινὰ μέγαν, εὐδαίμονα Aesch., Eur. ; c. dupl. acc., τί σε τεύξω ; what shall I make of thee ? Soph. ;—hence in pf. pass. simply for γίγνεσθαι or εἶναι, Ζεὺς ταμίης πολέμοιο τέτυκται Il. ; γυναικὸς ἄφ᾽ ἀντὶ τεύξω thou wast like a woman, Ib.

ΤΕ῾ΦΡΑ, Ion. τέφρη, ἡ, ashes, Il., Ar. : also a kind of pungent dust or snuff. Hence

τεφρός, ά, όν, ash-coloured, Babr.

τεφρ-ώδης, ες, (εἶδος) Babr., Plut.

τεχθείς, aor. 1 part. pass. of τίκτω.

τεχνάζω, f. άσω, (τέχνη) to employ art, Arist.   **II.** to use art or cunning, deal subtly, use shifts or subterfuges, Hdt., Ar., etc.;—c. inf. to contrive cunningly that, Arist.: so aor. 1 med. ἐτεχνασάμην, Hdt.

τεχνάομαι, f. ήσομαι: aor. 1 ἐτεχνησάμην, Ep. τεχν-: pf. τετέχνημαι: (τέχνη): Dep.:—to make by art, to execute skilfully, Od.   2. also as Pass. to be made by art, Xen.   **II.** to contrive or execute cunningly, Il., Soph.:—absol., θεοῦ τεχνωμένου if God contrives, Soph.:—c. inf. to contrive how to do, Thuc.

τέχνασμα, ατος, τό, (τεχνάζω) anything made or done by art, a handiwork, κέδρου τεχνάσματα, of a cedar-coffin, Eur.   **II.** an artifice, trick, Id., Xen.

τέχνη, ἡ, (τίκτω) art, skill, craft in work, cunning of hand, esp. of metal-working, Od.; of a shipwright, Il.; of a soothsayer, Aesch., Soph.   2. art, craft, cunning, in bad sense, δολίη τ. Od.; in pl. arts, wiles, cunning devices, Ib., etc.   3. the way, manner or means whereby a thing is gained, without any sense of art or craft, μηδεμιῇ τέχνῃ in no wise, Hdt.; πάσῃ τέχνῃ by all means, Ar.; παντοίῃ τ. Soph.   **II.** an art, craft, trade, ἐπίστασθαι τὴν τ. to know his craft, Hdt.; ἐν τῇ τέχνῃ εἶναι to practise it, Soph.; ἐπὶ τέχνῃ μανθάνειν τι to learn a thing professionally, Plat.; τέχνην ποιεῖσθαί τι to make a trade of it, Dem.   **III.** an art, i. e. a system or method of making or doing, Plat., Arist.; ἢ φύσει ἢ τέχνῃ Plat.; μετὰ τέχνης, ἄνευ τέχνης Id.   **IV.** = τέχνημα, a work of art, handiwork, Soph.   Hence

τεχνήεις, εσσα, εν, poët. Adj. cunningly wrought, Od.; —Adv. τεχνηέντως, artfully, skilfully, Ib.   **II.** of persons, γυναῖκες ἱστὸν τεχνῆσσαι (contr. from –ήεσσαι) skilful at the loom, Ib.

τέχνημα, ατος, τό, (τεχνάομαι) = τέχνασμα, Soph.   2. of a man, the abstr. for the concr., πανουργίας τέχνημα a masterpiece of villainy, Id.   **II.** an artful device, trick, artifice, Eur.:—generally a device, invention, Plat.

τεχνήμων, ον, (τέχνη) cunningly wrought, αὐλοί Anth.

τεχνητός, ή, όν, (τεχνάομαι) artificial, Plut.

τεχνικός, ή, όν, (τέχνη) of persons, artistic, skilful, workmanlike, Plat., etc.   **II.** of things, made or done by art, artistic, systematic, Id.   **III.** Adv. -κῶς, by rules of art, in a workmanlike manner, Id.

τεχνίον, τό, Dim. of τέχνη, Plat.

τεχνίτης [ῑ], ου, ὁ, (τέχνη) an artificer, artisan, craftsman, skilled workman, Plat., etc.:—c. gen. rei, skilled in a thing, Xen.; also τι or περί τι Id.   **II.** a trickster, intriguer, Luc.

τεχνῖτις, ιδος, fem. of τεχνίτης, Anth.

τεχνολογέω, f. ήσω, to bring under rules of art, to systematize, Arist.   From

τεχνο-λόγος, ον, treating by rules of art.

τεχνοσύνη, ἡ, poët. for τέχνη, Anth.

τεχνύδριον, τό, Dim. of τέχνη, Plat.

τέῳ; Ion. for τίνι; dat. of τίς; who? Hdt.   **II.** τεῳ, Ion. dat. of τις, any one, Od.

τέων; Ion. for τίνων; gen. pl. of τίς; who? Od.   2. of τις, any one, Hdt.

τέως, Ep. τείως, Adv. of Time, so long, meanwhile, the while, correlat. to ἕως, ἕως ἐγὼ ἡλώμην, τείως . . while

I was wandering, meantime . . Od.; ἐσθίων τέως, ἕως . . Ar.   **II.** for a time, a while, τείως μὲν . . , αὐτὰρ νῦν Od.; τέως μὲν . . , εἶτα δὲ . . Ar., etc.   **III.** up to this time, hitherto, Hdt., Ar.

τῆ, old Ep. imperat. = λάβε, take, in Hom. always followed by a second imperat., τῆ, σπεῖσον Διΐ Il.; τῆ, πίε οἶνον Od.; τῆ νῦν, καί σοι τοῦτο κειμήλιον ἔστω Il. (Perh. akin to τε-ταγ-ών.)

τῇ, dat. fem. of ὁ, like ταύτῃ, here, there, Hom.

τήγανον, v. τάγηνον.

τῇδε, dat. fem. of ὅδε, as Adv. here, thus, Hom.

τήθη, ἡ, a grandmother, Ar., Plat., etc.

τηθίς, ίδος, ἡ, a father's or mother's sister, aunt, Dem.

ΤΗ͂ΘΟΣ, εος, τό, an oyster, τήθεα διφῶν diving for oysters, Il.

Τηθύς [ῠ], ύος [ῠ], ἡ, Tethys, wife of Oceanus, Il.; daughter of Uranus and Gaia, mother of the river-gods and Oceanides, Hes.   **II.** in Virgil, Tethys is the sea itself. (Prob. from τήθη, the all-mother.)

τηκεδών, όνος, ἡ, (τήκομαι) a melting away: a wasting away, consumption, decline, Od.

τηκτός, ή, όν, verb. Adj. of τήκομαι, melted, molten, Eur.   **II.** soluble, Plat.

τήκω (Root. ΤΑΚ), Dor. τάκω [ᾱ]: f. τήξω, Dor. ταξῶ: aor. 1 ἔτηξα: pf. τέτηκα:—Pass., aor. 2 ἐτάκην [ᾰ]; rarely aor. 1 ἐτήχθην:—but in classic Gr. the pf. and plqpf. pass. are supplied by the intr. act. pf. τέτηκα, ἐτετήκειν :—   **I.** Act. to melt, melt down (trans.), of metals, Hdt., etc.: to dissipate clouds, Id.   2. metaph. to cause to waste or pine away, Od., Eur.   **II.** Pass., with intr. pf. act. τέτηκα, to be dissolved, melt away, of snow, to thaw, Od., Hdt., Att.; of metals, Hes.; ἄλφιτα πυρὶ τ. is consumed, Theocr.; of a corpse, to fall away, Soph.; πῦρ τετακὸς a dead fire, Eur.   2. metaph. to melt or waste away, pine, Hom., Hdt., Att.; βλέμμα τηκόμενον a languishing look, Plut.

τηλ-αυγής, ές, (τῆλε, αὐγή) far-shining, far-beaming, h. Hom., Ar.   **II.** of distant objects, far-seen, conspicuous, Theogn., Soph.   **III.** Adv. -γῶς, clearly, distinctly, N. T.

ΤΗ͂ΛΕ, Adv., like τηλοῦ, at a distance, far off, far away, Hom., Hes. :—c. gen. far from, Hom.

τηλε-βόλος, ον, (βάλλω) striking from afar, Pind.

τηλέ-γονος, ον, (γίγνομαι) born far from one's father or fatherland, Od.

τηλεδᾰπός, ή, όν, (τῆλε, –δαπος being a termin.) from a far country, Od.: of places, far off, distant, Il.

τηλεθάω, lengthd. for θάλλω (cf. τέθηλα), mostly in pres. part., luxuriant-growing, blooming, flourishing, ὕλη τηλεθόωσα Il.; ἐλαῖαι τηλεθόωσαι Od.; χαίτη τηλεθόωσα luxuriant hair, Il.

τηλε-κλειτός, όν, far-famed, Hom.

τηλε-κλητός, όν, summoned from afar, Il.

τηλε-κλῠτός, όν, = τηλεκλειτός, Hom.

τηλε-μάχος [ᾰ], ον, (μάχομαι) fighting from afar.   **II.** as prop. n. proparox., Τηλέμαχος, ὁ, son of Ulysses, Od.

τηλε-πλάνος, ον, far-wandering, devious, Aesch.

τηλέ-πομπος, ον, far-sent, far-journeying, Aesch.

τηλέ-πορος, ον, far-travelling, far-reaching, Ep. Ar.   2. far-distant, Soph.

τηλέ-πῠλος, ον, (πύλη) with gates far apart, Od.

τηλε-σκόπος, ον, (σκοπέω) far-seeing, Ar.   II. proparox. τηλέσκοπος, ον, pass. far-seen, conspicuous, Hes., Anth.

τηλε-φανής, ές, (φαίνομαι) appearing afar, far-seen, conspicuous, Od., Ar.   2. of sound, heard plainly from afar, Soph.

τηλέ-φιλον, τό, faraway-love, love-in-absence, a plant used by lovers to try whether their love was returned; the leaf being laid on the hand was struck smartly, and a loud crack was a favourable omen, Theocr.

τηλία, ἡ, a board or table with a raised edge, a baker's board, ap. Arist.   2. a table or stage whereon gamecocks and quails were set to fight, Aeschin.   3. a chimney-board, Ar.   4. the hoop of a corn-sieve, Id.

τηλίκος [ῐ], η, ον, of such an age, so old or so young, antecedent to the relat. ἡλίκος, Hom. :—c. inf., οὐ ἐπὶ σταθμοῖσι μένειν τηλίκος not so young as to stay at home, Od.   II. so great, Lat. tantus, Anth.

τηλικόσδε, ήδε, όνδε, and **τηλικοῦτος**, αύτη, οῦτον, (also τηλικοῦτος as fem.), strengthd. forms of τηλίκος (as ὅδε, οὗτος of ὁ):   I. of persons, of such an age, τηλικόσδ' ὤν Soph., etc.; old as I am, Eur.; νοῦς τηλικοῦτος the mind of one so old as he is, Soph.:—of extreme youth, so young, τηλικάσδ' ὁρῶν πάντων ἐρήμους girls of so tender age, Id., etc.:—repeated in opp. senses, οἱ τηλικοίδε καὶ διδαξόμεσθα δὴ φρονεῖν ὑπ' ἀνδρὸς τηλικοῦδε we old as we are shall take lessons forsooth from one so young, Id.   II. of things, so great, so large, Lat. tantus, Plat., etc.

τηλόθεν, Adv. (τηλοῦ) from afar, from a foreign land, Il., Soph.;—τηλόθε in Pind.   2. sometimes = τῆλε, τηλοῦ, Hom.; c. gen., τηλόθεν Πελειάδων far from them, Pind.

τηλόθῐ, Adv. = τῆλε, τηλοῦ, Hom.:—c. gen., τηλόθι πάτρης Il.

τηλο-πέτης, ες, (πέτομαι) far-flying, Anth.

τηλ-ορός, όν, = τηλουρός, Eur.

τηλόσε, (τηλοῦ) Adv. to a distance, far away, Il., Eur.

τηλοτάτω, Adv., Sup. of τηλοῦ, farthest away, Od. :—hence Adj., **τηλότερος**, Anth.

ΤΗΛΟΥ´, Adv., like τῆλε, afar, far off or away, in a far country, Hom., Hes.; τηλοῦ ἀγρῶν in a far corner of the country, Ar.   2. c. gen., mostly, far from, Od.; τ. σέθεν far from thee, Eur.

τηλ-ουρός, όν, (ὅρος) with distant boundaries; hence far-away, distant, remote, Aesch., Eur.

τηλύγετος [ῠ], η, ον, an only child, a darling child, Hom.; once of two sons, perhaps twins, Il.:—in Eur., τηλύγετος χθονὸς ἀπὸ πατρίδος, it means born far away, living away from, as if a compd. of τηλυ (= τῆλε), γενέσθαι: but the Homeric sense is opposed to this; and the deriv. remains uncertain.

τηλ-ωπός, όν, (ὤψ) seen from afar, far away, Soph.   2. metaph. of sound, heard from afar, Id.

τημελέω, f. ήσω, to protect, look after, c. acc., Eur.; c. gen. to take care of, Id. (Deriv. uncertain.)

τήμερον, v. σήμερον.

τημῆ, crasis for τῇ ἐμῇ.

τῆμος, Dor. **τᾶμος**, Adv. then, thereupon, of past time, answering to the relat. ἦμος, Il., Soph., Theocr.

τημόσδε, Dor. **ταμόσδε**, Adv., = τῆμος, Theocr.

τημοῦτος, = τημόσδε, τῆμος, Hes.

την-άλλως or **τὴν ἄλλως**, Adv., elliptic for τὴν ἄλλως ἄγουσαν ὁδόν in the way leading differently, i.e. in no particular way, Plat.   2. to no purpose, in vain, Dem.

τηνεῖ, Adv., Dor. for ἐκεῖ, there, Theocr. :—also = ὧδε, here, Id.

τήνελλα, a word formed by Archilochus to imitate the twang of a guitar-string: from his hymn beginning with τήνελλα καλλίνικε, these words became the mode of saluting conquerors, Ar.   II. so in Adj. form, ἐὰν νικᾷς, τήνελλος εῖ you will be greeted with huzzas, Id.

τηνίκα [ῐ], Dor. **τᾱνίκα**, Adv., (τῆνος) antec. to Relat. ἡνίκα, at that time, then; also with the Art. (often written τοτηνίκα), Soph.   2. absol. at that time [of day], Theocr.

τηνῐκάδε, Adv., at this time of day, so early, Plat.

τηνῐκαῦτα, commoner form for τηνίκα, at that time, then, Hdt., Soph., Xen.; c. gen., τ. τοῦ θέρους at this time of summer, Ar.   II. under these circumstances, in this case, Id., Xen.

τηνόθι, Adv. of τῆνος, in that case, then, Theocr.

τῆνος, τήνα, τῆνο, Dor. for κεῖνος, ἐκεῖνος, he, she, it, Theocr.   2. like Lat. ille, iste, the famous, or the notorious, Id.

τηνῶ, Adv., Dor. for ἐκεῖ, there, Theocr.

τηνῶθεν, Adv. of τῆνος, Dor. for ἐκεῖθεν, Ar.; also **τηνῶθε**, Theocr.

τηξί-μελής, ές, wasting the limbs, νοῦσος Anth.

τηρέω, f. ήσω, (τηρός) :—to watch over, protect, guard, Pind., Ar. :—Pass. to be constantly guarded, Thuc.; f. med. τηρήσομαι in pass. sense, Id.   2. to take care that . . , Arist., Ar., Plat.   II. to give heed to, watch narrowly, observe, Ar.; τὰς ἁμαρτίας Thuc.   2. to watch for, c. acc., Soph., Ar.; παραστείχοντα τηρήσας having watched for him as he was passing by, Soph.   3. absol. to watch, keep watch, Arist. :—c. inf. to watch or look out, so as to . . , Thuc.   III. to observe or keep an engagement, Isocr., etc.; τ. εἰρήνην Dem. Hence

τήρησις, εως, ἡ, a watching, keeping, guarding, Arist.   2. vigilance, Thuc.   II. a means of keeping, a place of custody, Id.

τηρητέον, verb. Adj. of τηρέω, one must watch, Plat.

ΤΗΡΟ´Σ, ὁ, a warden, guard, Aesch.

τητάομαι, Dor. **τᾱτ-**, (τήτη) Pass. only used in pres., to be in want, suffer want, Hes.; τὸ τητᾶσθαι privation, Soph.   2. c. gen. to be in want of, be deprived or bereft of, Id., Eur.

τῆτες, Adv. this year, of or in this year, Ar. (τῆτες is related to σῆτες, ἔτος, as τήμερον to σήμερον, ἡμέρα.)

τηύσιος, α (Ion. η), ον, idle, vain, undertaken to no purpose, Od. :—Adv. τηυσίως, Theocr.

τιάρᾱ [ᾰρ], ἡ, and **τιάρας**, ου, Ion. **τιήρης**, εω, ὁ :—a tiara, the Persian head-dress, Hdt.; worn by the great king, Aesch., Xen.

τιαρο-ειδής, ές, shaped like or like a tiara, Xen.

ΤΙ´ΓΡΙΣ, ἡ, gen. τίγριος and τιγρίδος; acc. τίγριν: pl., nom. τίγρεις and τιγρίδες :—a tiger, unknown in Greece till after Alexander's time.

τίεσκον, Ion. impf. of τίω.

τίη, Att. **τιή**, strengthd. form of τί; why? wherefore? Hom., Hes. and Att. Comedy; cf. ὁτιή.

τιήρης, ου, ό, Ion. for τιάρας.

τῑθαιβώσσω, of bees, to store up honey, Od. (Akin to τιθήνη?)

τῑθὰς ὄρνις, άδος, ἡ, barn-door fowl, hen, Anth.

τῑθᾰσευτής, οῦ, ὁ, one who tames, Ar. From

τῑθᾰσεύω, only in pres., to tame, domesticate, Plat., Xen. 2. of trees, to reclaim, cultivate, Plut.

τῑθᾰσός, όν, of animals, tame, domestic, Lat. cicur, Plat.; of plants, cultivated, Plut. 2. metaph. domestic, intestine, Ἄρης Aesch. (Deriv. uncertain.)

τιθέασι, 3 pl. of τίθημι.

τῑθείς, part. of τίθημι : but II. τῑθεῖς, 2 sing.

τῑθέμεναι, -έμεν, Ion. for τιθέναι, inf. of τίθημι.

τίθεν, Dor. for ἐτίθεσαν, 3 pl. impf. of τίθημι.

τίθεσκον, Ion. impf. of τίθημι.

τῑθέω, = τίθημι : hence 2 and 3 sing. τιθεῖς, τιθεῖ.

τιθήμεναι, Ep. for τιθέναι, inf. of τίθημι.

τιθήμενος, Ep. for τιθέμενος, part. med. of τίθημι.

τίθημι [ῐ], (from Root ΘΕ), τίθης Ep. τίθησθα ; τίθησι Dor. τίθητι ; 3 pl. τιθέασι, Ion. τιθεῖσι; also 2 and 3 sing. τιθεῖς, τιθεῖ (as if from τιθέω) :—Impf. ἐτίθην, ἐτίθης, ἐτίθη, Ep. τίθη; also 2nd and 3rd ἐτίθεις, ἐτίθει, Ep. 3 pl. τίθεσαν, τίθεν, late ἐτίθουν; Ion. impf. ἐτίθεα :—imperat. τίθει :—inf. τιθέναι, Ep. also τιθήμεναι, τιθέμεν :—F. θήσω, Ep. inf. θησέμεναι, θησέμεν :—Aor. 1 ἔθηκα, only in indic. ; Ep. 3 pl. θῆκαν :—Aor. 2 ἔθην, not used in indic. sing., pl. ἔθεμεν, ἔθετε, ἔθεσαν Ep. θέσαν ; imperat."θές ; subj. θῶ, Ion. θέω, Ep. θείω, Ep. 2 and 3 sing. θείῃς, θείῃ, 1 pl. θέωμεν, θείομεν for θείωμεν : opt. θείην, 1 pl. θείημεν and θεῖμεν, 3 pl. θεῖεν : inf. θεῖναι Ep. θέμεναι, θέμεν : part. θείς :—Pf. τέθεικα :—Med. τίθεμαι, 2 sing. τίθεσαι : imperat. τίθεσο, τιθοῦ, Ep. τίθεσσο ; Ep. part. τιθήμενος :—F. θήσομαι :—Aor. 1 ἐθηκάμην, only in indic. and partic. ; 2 sing. ἐθήκαο, Ep. 3 sing. θήκατο ; part. θηκάμενος :—Aor. 2 ἐθέμην ; imper. θέο, θοῦ : subj. θῶμαι : opt. θείμην :—Pass. τίθεμαι, F. τεθήσομαι : Aor. 1 ἐτέθην : Pf. τέθειμαι.

A. in local sense, to set, put, place, Hom., etc. :— in Att., πόδα τ. to plant the foot, i. e. walk, run, Aesch. ; τετράποδος βάσιν θηρὸς τίθεσθαι, i. e. to go on all fours, Eur. : θεῖναί τινί τι ἐν χερσίν to put it in his hands, Il.; ἐς χεῖρά τινος into his hand, Soph. 2. θέσθαι τὴν ψῆφον to lay one's voting-pebble on the altar, put it into the urn, Aesch. ; so, τίθεσθαι τὴν γνώμην to give one's opinion, Hdt. ; and τίθεσθαι absol. to vote, Soph. 3. θεῖναί τινί τι ἐν φρεσί, ἐν στήθεσσι to put or plant it in his heart, Hom. ; ἐν στήθεσσι τιθεῖ νόον Il., etc. : Med., θέσθαι θυμὸν ἐν στήθεσσι to lay up wrath in one's heart, Ib. ; θέσθαι τινὶ κότον to harbour enmity against him, Ib. 4. to deposit, as in a bank, Hdt., Xen.; also, ἐγγύην θέσθαι Aesch. :— Pass., τὰ τεθέντα the deposits, Dem. :—metaph., χάριν or χάριτα θέσθαι τινί to deposit a claim for favour with one, to lay an obligation on one, Hdt., etc. 5. to pay down, pay, Dem. 6. to place to account, put down, reckon, in rationes referre, Id. 7. in military language, τίθεσθαι τὰ ὅπλα has three senses, a. to pile arms, as in a camp, to bivouac, Thuc. :—hence, to take up a position, draw up in order of battle, Hdt., etc. b. to lay down one's arms, surrender, Xen. ; so, πόλεμον θέσθαι to settle, end it, Thuc. c. εὖ θέσθαι ὅπλα to

keep one's arms in good order, Xen. ; like εὖ ἀσπίδα θέσθω, Il. 8. to lay in the grave, bury, Ib., Aesch., etc. 9. τιθέναι τὰ γόνατα to kneel down, N.T. II. to set up prizes in games, Lat. proponere, Il., etc. :— Pass., τὰ τιθέμενα the prizes, Dem. 2. θεῖναι ἐς μέσον, Lat. in medio ponere, to lay before people, Hdt. ; so, τ. εἰς τὸ κοινόν Xen. 3. to set up in a temple, to devote, dedicate, Hom., Eur. III. to assign, award, τιμήν τινι Il. :—Med., ὄνομα θέσθαι to give a name, Od., Hdt., etc. IV. τιθέναι νόμον to lay down or give a law, of a legislator, Soph., etc. : Med., of republican legislators, to give oneself a law, make a law, Hdt., etc. :—so, θεῖναι θεσμόν Aesch. ; σκῆψιν θεῖναι to allege an excuse, Soph. V. to establish, institute, ἀγῶνα Aesch., Xen. VI. to ordain, command, c. acc. et inf., Xen. ; γυναικὶ σωφρονεῖν θήσει Eur. ; so, with Advs., οὕτω νῦν Ζεὺς θείη so may he ordain, Od.; ὡς ἄρ' ἔμελλον θησέμεναι Il.

B. to put in a certain state, to make so and so, θεῖναί τινα αἰχμητήν, μάντιν Hom. ; θεῖναί τινα ἄλοχόν τινος to make her another's wife, Il. ; τοῖόν με ἔθηκε ὅπως ἐθέλει has made me such as she will, Od. ; σῦς ἔθηκας ἑταίρους thou didst make my comrades swine, Ib. ; ναῦν λᾶαν ἔθηκε Ib. :—so, with an Adj., θεῖναί τινα ἀθάνατον to make him immortal, Ib. ; also of things, ὄλεθρον ἀπευθέα θῆκε left it unknown, Ib. :—often in Med., γυναῖκα or ἄκοιτιν θέσθαι τινά to make her one's wife, Od. ; παῖδα or υἱὸν τίθεσθαί τινα, like ποιεῖσθαι, to make her one's child, adopt him, Plat. 2. c. inf. to make one do so and so, τιθέναι τινὰ νικῆσαι to make him conquer, Pind., etc. II. in reference to mental action, mostly in Med., to lay down, assume, hold, reckon or regard as so and so, τί δ' ἐλέγχεα ταῦτα τίθεσθε; Od.; εὐεργέτημα τ. τι Dem. 2. foll. by Advs., ποῦ χρὴ τίθεσθαι ταῦτα ; in what light must we regard these things? Soph. ; οὐδαμοῦ τιθέναι τι to hold of no account, nullo in numero habere, Eur. 3. foll. by Preps., τ. τινὰ ἐν τοῖς φίλοις Xen. ; τίθεσθαί τινα ἐν τιμῇ Hdt. ; θέσθαι παρ' οὐδέν to set at naught, Aesch., etc. 4. with an infin., οὐ τίθημ' ἐγὼ ζῆν τοῦτον I hold not that he lives, count him not as living, Soph. 5. to lay down, assume, Plat., etc. III. to make, work, execute, Lat. ponere, of an artist, ἐν δ' ἐτίθει νεῖον Il. 2. to make, cause, bring to pass, ἔργα Ib.; ὀρυμαγδόν Od., etc. 3. in Med. to make for oneself, θέσθαι κέλευθον to make oneself a road, Il. ; μεγάλην ἐπιγουνίδα θέσθαι to get a large thigh, Od. ; θέσθαι πόνον to work oneself annoy, Aesch. 4. periphr. for a single Verb, σκέδασιν θεῖναι = σκεδάσαι, to make a scattering, Od. ; so in Med., θέσθαι μάχην for μάχεσθαι, Il. ; σπουδὴν, πρόνοιαν θέσθαι Soph. IV. εὖ θέσθαι to settle, arrange, or manage well, τὰ σεωυτοῦ Hdt. ; τὸ παρόν Thuc. :—also, καλῶς θεῖναι or θέσθαι Soph., Eur. ; εὖ θέσθαι Soph.

τῑθηνέομαι, Med. to nurse, suckle, tend as nurse, Theogn., Xen. 2. to keep up, maintain, Soph.

τῑθήνη, ἡ, (*θάω, with redupl.) a nurse, Il., Soph.

τῑθηνητήρ, ῆρος, ὁ, = τιθηνός, Anth. :—fem. -τειρα = τιθήνη, Id. Hence

τῑθηνητήριος, α, ον, nursing, Anth.

τῑθηνός, όν, (*θάω, with redupl.) nursing, πόνων τιθηνοὺς

ἀποδιδοῦσά σοι τροφάς repaying thee *nursing* tendance for *nursing* labours, Eur.

τίθησθα, Ep. 2 sing. of τίθημι.

τίθητι, Dor. 3 sing. of τίθημι.

τίθυμᾰλος [ῠ], ὁ, *spurge, euphorbia ;* heterocl. pl. τιθύμαλα, Anth. (Deriv. unknown.)

Τιθωνός, ὁ, *Tithonus,* brother of Priam, husband of Eos (Aurora), and father of Memnon, Hom. :—metaph. of a decrepit old man, because Aurora begged Zeus to grant immortality to Tithonus, but forgot to ask for eternal youth, Ar. ; ὑπὲρ τὸν Τιθωνὸν ζῆν Luc.

τίκτω (Root **ΤΕΚ**): f. τέξω and τέξομαι, poët. inf. also τεκεῖσθαι : aor. 2 ἔτεκον, Ep. τέκον : pf. τέτοκα :—Med., aor. 2 ἐτεκόμην, Ep. τεκόμην :—*to bring into the world ;* of the father, *to beget,* of the mother, *to bring forth,* Hom., Att. ; so also in Med., Il. ; οἱ τεκόμενοι of the mother, Aesch. **2.** the 3 pl. aor. 2 τέκον, ἔτεκον is used of both parents, Hom. : hence οἱ τεκόντες *the parents,* Aesch., Soph. **3.** separately, ὁ τεκών *the father,* Aesch. ; ἡ τεκοῦσα *the mother,* Id. ; and as Subst., c. gen., ἡ κείνου τεκών Eur. **II.** of female animals, *to bear young, breed,* Hom. ; ᾠὰ τ. *to lay* eggs, Hdt. **III.** of vegetable produce, *to bear, produce,* [γαῖα] τίκτει ἔμπεδα μῆλα Od. :—so in Med., γαῖαν ἣ τὰ πάντα τίκτεται Aesch. **IV.** metaph. *to generate, produce,* τὸ δυσσεβὲς ἔργον πλείονα τίκτει Id. ; of Night as the mother of Day, τῆς τεκούσης φῶς τόδ' εὐφρόνης Id. ; τ. ἀοιδάς Eur. ; πόλεμον Plat.

τίλλοισα, Dor. part. fem. of sq.

ΤΙΛΛΩ, f. τῐλῶ : aor. 1 ἔτῑλα :—Pass., aor. 1 ἐτίλθην : pf. τέτιλμαι :—*to pluck* or *pull out* hair, Lat. vello, Il. ; so in Med., χαίτας τίλλεσθαι *to pluck out one's* hair, Od. **2.** with acc. of that *from which* the hair or feathers *are plucked,* τίλλειν πέλειαν Ib. ; κάρα τ. Aesch. ; τ. πλάτανον *to pluck* its leaves *off,* Plut. :—Pass. *to have one's* hair *plucked out,* Ar. **II.** Med., τίλλεσθαί τινα *to tear one's* hair *in sorrow for* any one, Il. **III.** metaph. *to pluck, vex, annoy,* Lat. vellicare, Pass., Ar.

τίλσις, εως, ἡ, *a plucking out,* Arist.

τίλων, ὁ, a fish of the Thracian lake Prasias, Hdt.

τῑμαλφέω, f. ήσω, *to do honour to,* Aesch.

τῑμ-αλφής, ές, (τιμή, ἀλφεῖν) *fetching a prize, costly, precious,* Plat.

τιμᾶντα, Dor. for τιμῆντα, acc. of τιμῆς.

τῑμάορος, ον, Dor. for τιμωρός.

τῑμά-οχος, ον, (ἔχω) *having honour,* h. Hom.

τῑμασεῦντι, Dor. for τιμήσουσι, 3 pl. fut. of sq.

τῑμάω, f. ήσω : aor. 1 ἐτίμησα : pf. τετίμηκα :—Med., f. τιμήσομαι in pass. sense : aor. 1 ἐτιμησάμην :—Pass., f. τιμηθήσομαι and τετιμήσομαι : aor. 1 ἐτιμήθην : pf. τετίμημαι : (τιμή) :—*to pay honour to, hold in honour, to honour, revere, reverence,* Hom., Hdt., Att. :—absol. *to bestow honours,* Dem. :—hence, simply, *to reward,* Hdt., Xen. :—Pass. *to be honoured, held in honour,* Id. ; c. gen. rei, τιμῆς τετιμῆσθαι *to be held worthy* of honour, Il. **II.** of things, *to hold in honour, value, prize,* Pind., Eur. :—also = προτιμάω, *to prefer,* Aesch. **2.** c. gen. pretii, *to estimate, value* or *assess* at a certain price, Thuc. :—so in Med., Xen., etc. **3.** rarely, *to give as an honour,* Pind., Soph. **III.**

as Att. law-term : **1.** in Act., of the judge, *to estimate the amount of punishment due* to the criminals, *award the penalty,* Lat. litem aestimare, Plat. ; τ. τὴν μακράν τινι *to award* him the long line, i. e. sentence of death, Ar. ; absol., τιμᾶν βλέπω I carry *penalty* in my eyes, Id. :—the sentence awarded in gen., τ. τινί θανάτου (sc. δίκην) *to give sentence* of death *against* a man, i. e. *to condemn* him to death, Plat., Dem. ; τίνος τιμήσειν αὐτῷ προσδοκᾷς τὸ δικαστήριον ; at what do you expect the court *to fix* his *penalty ?* Dem. :—Pass., τιμᾶσθαι ἀργυρίου *to be condemned* to a fine, τινος *for* a thing, Lex ap. Dem., etc. **2.** Med., of the parties before the court (cf. τίμημα 2), **a.** of the accuser, τιμᾶταί μοι ὁ ἀνὴρ θανάτου (sc. τὴν δίκην) he *estimates* the penalty due to me *at* death (gen. pretii), Plat., etc. **b.** of the person accused, τιμήσεσθαι τοιούτου τινὸς ἐμαυτῷ *to estimate* the penalty due to me at so high a rate, Id. **c.** with acc. of the penalty or offence, πέντε μυριάδων τιμησάμενος τὴν δίκην Plut., etc.

τῑμή, ἡ, (τίω) *that which is paid in token of worth* or *value* : **1.** *worship, esteem, honour,* and in pl. *honours,* Hom., etc. ; ἐν τ. ἄγεσθαι, τίθεσθαι τινά Hdt. ; ἀπονέμειν, ἀποδοῦναι Soph., Plat. :—c. gen., ἡ τ. θεῶν *the honour due* to them, Aesch. **2.** *honour, dignity, lordship,* Hom. :—*the prerogative* of a king, and in pl. *prerogatives,* Od., Trag. **3.** *a dignity, office, magistracy,* and in pl., like Lat. honores, *civil honours,* Hdt., Att. ; οἱ ἐν τιμαῖς men *in office,* Eur. ; τιμὴ ἄχαρις *a thankless office,* Hdt. **4.** *an authority, magistracy,* τ. δίσκηπτρος, of the Atridae, Aesch., Soph. **5.** *a present of honour, offering,* Hes., Aesch. : *a reward, present,* Lat. honorarium, Soph. **II.** of things, *worth, value,* or *price,* Lat. pretium, ἐξευρίσκειν τιμῆς τι *to get a thing at a price* (i. e. a high price), Hdt. ; ἐμοὶ δὲ τιμὰ τᾶσδε πᾶ γενήσεται ; how shall I get *payment* for this ? Ar. **III.** *an estimate* of damages, *compensation,* ἄρνυσθαί τινι τιμήν *to get* one *compensation,* Il. ; τίνειν or ἀποτίνειν τιμήν τινι *to pay* or *make* it, Ib. ; οὐ σὴ ἡ τιμή *not yours* the *penalty,* Plat. **2.** *a valuation, estimate,* for purposes of assessment, τοῦ κλήρου Id. Hence

τῑμήεις, εσσα, εν ; contr. τιμῆς, acc. τιμῆντα : Dor. **τιμάεις** :—*honoured, esteemed,* Hom. :—Comp., τιμηέστερος Od. **2.** of things, *prized, costly,* Hom. : Sup. τιμήεστατος Od.

τίμημα, ατος, τό, (τιμάω) *an estimate, valuation,* Eur., Dem. **2.** *an estimate of damages, a penalty,* Lat. litis aestimatio, Ar., Plat. :—generally *a payment,* τύμβου for neglect of his tomb, Aesch. **3.** *estimate of property* for taxation, *rateable property,* Lat. census, Plat., etc. ; ἡ ἀπὸ τιμημάτων πολιτεία, = τιμοκρατία, Xen.

τῑμῆντα, contr. for τιμήεντα, acc. of τιμηείς.

τῑμήορος, ον, Ion. for τιμάορος, τιμωρός.

τῑμῆς, contr. for τιμήεις.

τίμησις, εως, ἡ, (τιμάω) *a valuation* of property, *value,* Plat. **2.** *an assessment* of damages, Aeschin., etc. ; *a rating* or *assessment,* Arist.

τῑμητεία or -ία, (τιμητής II) ἡ, *the censorship,* Lat. censura, Plut.

τιμητέος, α, ον, verb. Adj. of τιμάω, *to be honoured, valued,* Eur., Plat., etc. **II.** τιμητέον, *one must honour, esteem, estimate,* Xen., etc.

τῑμητεύω, to be censor, Plut. From
τῑμητής, οῦ, ὁ, (τιμάω) a valuer, estimater, Plat. II.
at Rome, the censor, who assessed the property of the
citizens, Polyb.
τῑμητικός, ή, όν, forming an estimate, 1. for determining the amount of punishment, πινάκιον τ.
Ar. 2. for determining the amount of property, ἡ
τιμητικὴ ἀρχή=τιμητεία, Plut.: τιμητικός, ὁ, = Lat. vir
censorius, one who has been censor (τιμητής), Id.
τῑμητός, ή, όν, verb. Adj. of τιμάω, rateable, v. ἀτίμητος.
τίμιος, α, ον, and ος, ον, (τῑμή) valued: I. of
persons, held in honour, honoured, worthy, Od., Hdt.,
Att. II. of things, costly, prized, Trag.: also
costly, dear, Hdt. 2. conferring honour, honourable, Aesch., Xen. :—τὰ τιμιώτατα=τὰ φίλτατα, Dem.
τῑμιότης, ητος, ἡ, worth, value, preciousness, Arist.
τῑμο-κρᾰτία, ἡ, (κρατέω) a state in which the love of
honour is the ruling principle, Plat. II. a state
in which honours are distributed according to property, timocracy, Arist. Hence
τῑμοκρᾰτικός, ή, όν, of or for a τιμοκρατία I, Plat. II.
ἡ τ. πολιτεία, =τιμοκρατία II, Arist.
τῖμος, ὁ, poët. form of τιμή II, Aesch.
τῑμωρέω, f. ήσω :—Med., f. ήσομαι: aor. 1 ἐτιμωρησά-
μην :—Pass., pf. τετῑμώρημαι, also used in med. sense :
(τιμωρός) :—to help, aid, succour, τινί Hdt., Soph.,
etc. :—absol. to lend aid, give succour, Hdt. II.
to assist one who has suffered wrong, to avenge him,
c. dat., Id. :—so in Med., Soph., Eur. :—in full construction the person avenged is in dat., the person on
whom vengeance is taken in acc., and the crime
avenged in gen.; τιμωρεῖν τινι τοῦ παιδὸς τὸν φονέα to
avenge him on the murderer for [the murder of] his
son, Xen. :—also, c. acc. rei, τ. τὸν φόνον to avenge
his slaughter, Plat. :—Pass. to be visited with vengeance, Id., etc.; impers., τετιμώρηται τῷ Λεωνίδῃ
vengeance has been taken for him, he has been avenged,
Hdt. 2. τιμωρεῖν τινά to take vengeance on him,
Soph. :—in Med. to exact vengeance from, visit with
punishment, τινά Hdt., Att.; Ἑαυτὸν τιμωρούμενος
Self-tormentor, name of a play by Menander :—c. gen.
rei, τιμωρεῖσθαί τινά τινος to take vengeance on one for
a thing, Hdt., Att. :—so, also, τ. τινὰ ἀντί τινος Hdt. :
—c. acc. rei, σ᾽ ἀδελφῆς αἷμα τιμωρήσεται will visit
thy sister's blood on thee, Eur. 3. in Med. also
absol. to avenge oneself, seek vengeance, Hdt., Xen.,
etc.; τὸ τιμωρησόμενον the probability of vengeance,
Dem.; ἐς Λεωνίδεα τετιμώρησαι thou wilt have vengeance taken in respect to Leonidas, Hdt. Hence
τῑμώρημα, ατος, τό, help, aid, succour given, c. dat.,
Hdt. II. an act of vengeance : a penalty, Plat.
τῑμωρητέον, verb. Adj. one must assist, Hdt.; so in
pl. τιμωρητέα, Thuc. II. one must visit with
vengeance, punish, τινά Isocr. III. τιμωρητέος,
α, ον, that ought to be punished, Dem.; and
τῑμωρητήρ, ῆρος, ὁ, an avenger, Hdt.; and
τῑμωρητικός, ή, όν, revengeful, Arist.; τὰ τιμωρητικά
acts of revenge, Id.
τῑμωρία, Ion. -ίη, ἡ, help, aid, assistance, succour,
Hdt., Thuc. II. assistance to one who has
suffered wrong, retribution, vengeance, punishment,
Hdt., etc.; πατρὸς τ. vengeance taken for him, Eur.;

ἐπὶ τῇ ἡμετέρᾳ τ. for the purpose of punishing us,
Thuc.; ποιεῖσθαι τιμωρίαν to execute vengeance, Dem.;
τ. εὑρεῖν τινος to find vengeance at his hand, Aesch.;
τιμωρίαν λαμβάνειν, τιμωρίας τυγχάνειν are used both
of the avenger and the sufferer, Plat., Thuc. :—in pl.,
penalties, Plat. From
τῑμ-ωρός, όν, contr. from τιμ-άορος: (τιμή, ἀείρω):—
upholding honour; and so, I. helping, aiding,
succouring, and as Subst. a helper, aider, Hdt., Thuc.;
τὸν ἐμὸν τιμάορον my tutelary god, Aesch. II.
assisting one who has suffered wrong, avenging, and
as Subst. an avenger, Id., Soph., etc.; c. gen. rei,
helping one to vengeance for a thing, Soph. :—λόγος
τ. a plea or argument for vengeance, Hdt.
τίν [ῐ], like τεΐν, Dor. dat. of σύ. II. Dor. for σέ.
τίναγμα [ῐ], ατος, τό, a shake, quake, Anth.
τῐνάκτειρα, ἡ, (τινάκτηρ not being in use) a shaker,
τῆς τινάκτειρα νόσος, of Poseidon's trident, Aesch.
τῐνάκτωρ, ορος, ὁ, a shaker, τ. γαίας, of Poseidon, Soph.
ΤΙΝΑ'ΣΣΩ, f. ξω: Pass., aor. 1 ἐτινάχθην, Ep. 3 pl.
τίναχθεν :—to shake or brandish a weapon or shield,
Il., Aesch., etc. 2. generally, to shake, τ. γαῖαν, of
Poseidon, Il.; θρόνον ἐτίναξε upset the seat, Od. : of
wind, to scatter, Ib. :—Med., τιναξάσθην πτερά they
shook their wings, Ib. :—Pass., ἐτινάσσετο Ὄλυμπος
shook or quaked, Hes.
τίνυμαι [ῐ], inf. τίνυσθαι, poët. for τίνομαι (v. τίνω
II), to punish, chastise, c. acc. rei, λώβην τινύμενος
chastising insolence, Od. : absol. to avenge oneself,
Hdt. 2. to avenge, take vengeance for a thing,
c. acc., Hes., Eur. 3. to exact as penalty, δὶς
τόσα Hes.
ΤΙ'ΝΩ (with tenses formed from τίω), [ῑ Ep., ῐ Att.]:
f. τίσω [ῑ]: aor. 1 ἔτῑσα :—Med., f. τίσομαι: aor. 1
ἐτῑσάμην :—Pass., aor. 1 ἐτίσθην : I. Act. to pay
a price by way of return, to pay a penalty (whereas
τίω means to pay, honour), Hom., Soph., etc. :—also to
pay a debt, acquit oneself of an obligation, τίσειν
αἴσιμα πάντα Od.; τ. χάριν τινί to render one thanks,
Aesch.; τ. ἰατροῖς μισθὸν Xen. :—also to pay for, repay,
εὐαγγέλιον Od.; τροφάς τινι Eur. :—with gen. of the
thing for which one pays, τ. ἀμοιβὴν βοῶν τινί to pay
compensation for the oxen, Od.; also, τ. πληγὴν ἀντὶ
πληγῆς Aesch. :—but also with acc. of the thing for
which one pays, the price being omitted, to pay or
atone for a thing, τίνειν ὕβριν Hom.; τ. μητρὸς δίκας
for thy mother, Eur. :—more rarely c. acc. pers., τίσεις
γνωτὸν τὸν ἔπεφνες thou shalt make atonement for
the son thou hast slain, Il. 2. absol. to make return
or requital, Solon, Soph. II. Med. to have a
price paid one, make another pay for a thing,
avenge oneself on him, to chastise, punish, Lat.
poenas sumere de aliquo, c. acc. pers., Hom., Trag.,
etc. 2. c. gen. criminis, τίσεσθαι Ἀλέξανδρον κακότητος to punish him for his wickedness, Hom.,
Hdt. 3. c. acc. rei, to take vengeance for a thing,
Hom. 4. c. dupl. acc. pers. et rei, ἐτίσατο ἔργον
ἀεικὲς ἀντίθεον Νηλῆα he made Neleus pay for the
misdeed, visited it on his head, Od.; also, τίσασθαί τινα
δίκην to exact retribution from a person, Eur. 5.
absol. to repay oneself, take vengeance, Hom.
τιό τιό, imitation of a bird's note, Ar.

τίποτε; or τί ποτε; *what* or *why, tell me?* Lat. *quid tandem?* Soph.

ιίπτε; Ep. syncop. form for τίποτε; Hom., Aesch. :—before an aspirate, τίφθ' Il.

ΤΙΣ, τι, Indef. Pron. *any one, any thing,* enclitic through all cases;—but τίς; τί; Interrog. Pron. *who? what?* oxyt. in nom., parox. in other cases.

A. Indef. Pron. τις, τι :—gen. τινος, Ion. τεο, τευ, Att. του :—dat. τινι, Ion. τεῳ, Att. τῳ :—acc. τινα, τι :—dual τινε :—pl. τινες, neut. τινα :—gen. τινων, Ion. τεων :—dat. τισι, τισιν :—acc. τινας, neut. τινα. *Any one, any thing, some one, some thing;* and as Adj. *any, some,* and serving as the Indef. Art. *a, an:* in the latter case it agrees with its Subst., φίλος τις a friend, θεός τις a god, i. e. not a man; in the former it is followed by gen. pl., φίλων τις one of thy friends, θεῶν τις one of the gods. II. special usages : 1. *some one* (of many), i. e. *many a one,* ὧδε δέ τις εἴπεσκεν so men said, Hom. 2. *any one concerned, each one,* Il.; τοὺς ξυμμάχους αὐτόν τινα κολάζειν that *every man* should himself chastise his own allies, Thuc.; ἄμεινόν τινος better than *any* others, Dem. :—this is more fully expressed by adding other pronominal words, τις ἕκαστος Od., etc.; πᾶς τις Hdt., etc.; οὐδείς or μηδείς τις Eur., Xen. 3. in reference to a person, whom one avoids naming, δώσει τις δίκην *some one* I know will suffer, Ar.; so euphem. for something bad, ἤν τι ποιῶμεν, ἤν τι πάθωμεν Thuc. 4. indefinitely, where we say *they,* French *on,* μισεῖ τις ἐκεῖνον *they* hate him, Dem. 5. τις, τι, emphat. of a person or thing, *some great one, some great thing,* ηὔχεις τις εἶναι you boasted that you were *somebody,* Eur.; δοκοῦσι τινὲς εἶναι Dem.; κἠγών τις φαίνομαι ἦμες I too seem to be *somebody,* Theocr.; so in neut., οἴονταί τι εἶναι Plat.; λέγειν τι to be near the mark, opp. to οὐδὲν λέγειν, Id. 6. emphat. *a man,* opp. to *a brute,* τις ἢ κύων Ar.: reversely, with sense of contempt, Θερσίτης τις ἦν there was *one* Thersites, Soph. 7. with prop. names τις commonly signifies *one of the same sort,* as, ἤ τις Ἀπόλλων ἢ Πάν either *an* Apollo or *a* Pan, Aesch.; Ἀφροδίτη τις Eur. 8. with Adjs. τις takes a restrictive sense, ὥς τις θαρσαλέος ἐσσι a bold *kind of* fellow, i. e. *very* bold, Od.; δυσμαθής τις a *dull sort* of person, Plat. 9. with numerals, ἑπτά τινες *some seven,* seven or so, Thuc.; ἐς διακοσίους τινάς Id.; so without numeral, ἡμέρας τινάς *some days,* i. e. *several,* Id.; ἐνιαυτόν τινα a year *or so,* Id.; so, οὐ πολλοί τινες, τινες οὐ πολλοί, ὀλίγοι τινές Id. :—so also ὅσος τις χρυσός what a store of gold, Od. 10. with Pronominal words, οἶός τις what sort of *a* man, Il.; ποῖός τις and ὁποῖός τις Soph., Xen., etc.; τις τοιόσδε Hdt.; τοιοῦτός τις Xen. :—ὅταν δ' ὁ κύριος παρῇ τις when the lord, *whoever* he be, is here, Soph. :—in opposed clauses, ὁ μέν τις . . , ὁ δὲ . . Eur., Plat., etc. 11. the neut. τι is used as Adv. *somewhat, in any degree, at all,* Il., etc. 12. ἤ τις ἢ οὐδείς few or none, *next to none,* Hdt.; ἤ τι ἢ οὐδέν *little* or *nothing,* Plat.

B. Interrog. Pron. τίς, τί ;—gen. τίνος, Ion. τέο, τεῦ, Att. τοῦ : dat. τίνι, Ion. τέῳ : acc. τίνα, neut. τί :—Pl. τίνες, τίνα : gen. τίνων, Ion. τέων : dat. τίσι, Ion. τέοισι, Att. τοῖσι : acc. τίνας, τίνα : I. in direct questions, *who? which?* neut. *what? which?* Lat. *quis,*

quae, quid?, Hom., etc. : relating to other words in the same case, τίς δ' οὗτος ἔρχεαι; *who* art thou *that* comest?* Il.; τίν' ὄψιν σὴν προσδέρκομαι; *what* face is this I see of thine? Eur. :—τίς ἄν or κεν, with the opt., expresses doubt, *who could, who would* do so? Hom. : —in double questions, τί λαβόντα τί δεῖ ποιεῖν; *what* has one received and *what* must one do? Dem.; so, τίς πόθεν εἶς ἀνδρῶν; *who* and *whence* art thou? Od. 2. τίς with Particles : τίς γάρ; Lat. *quisnam? why who? who possibly?* Il., etc.; τίς δή; *who then?* Theogn.; τίς δῆτα; Soph.; τίς ποτε; *who in the world? who ever?* Xen. 3. neut. τί; as a simple question, *what?* Aesch.; also, *why?* Il. b. τί μοι; τί σοι; *what* is it to me? to thee? Soph., etc.; c. gen., τί μοι ἔριδος; *what* have I to do with the quarrel? Il.; τί ἐμοὶ καὶ σοί; *what* is there (in common) to me and thee? *what* have I to do with thee? N. T. c. τί with Particles :—τί γάρ; *why not? how else?* Lat. *quid enim? quidni?* i. e. *of course, no doubt,* Aesch., etc.; τί δέ; Lat. *quid vero?* Plat.; τί δέ, εἰ . .; but *what,* if . .? Eur.; τί δή; τί δήποτε; *why ever? why in the world?* Plat. :—τί μή; *why not?* Lat. *quidni?* Trag. :—τί μήν; i. e. *yes certainly,* Plat., etc. II. τίς is sometimes used for ὅστις in indirect questions, ἠρώτα δὴ ἔπειτα, τίς εἴη καὶ πόθεν ἔλθοι Od.; οὐκ ἔχω τί φῶ Aesch. 2. τίς; τί; with part., followed by a verbal clause, forms one sentence in Greek where we use two, εἴρετο τίνες ἐόντες προαγορεύουσι; *who* they *were* that *proclaim?* Hdt.; καταμεμάθηκας τοὺς τί ποιοῦντας τοῦνομα τοῦτ' ἀποκαλοῦσιν; have you learnt *what they do whom* men call so and so? Xen. III. τίς; = ποῖος; Soph. IV. τί was never elided; but the hiatus is allowed in Att., τί οὖν; Ar.; τί ἔστιν; Soph.; τί εἶπας; Id.

τῖσαι, aor. 1 inf. of τίνω.

τῖσαίατο, Ion. for τίσαιντο, 3 pl. aor. 1 opt. of τίνω.

τίσις [ῐ], εως, ἡ, (τίνω) *payment by way of return* or *recompense, retribution, vengeance,* Hom., etc.; τίσιν δοῦναί τινος to suffer *punishment* for an act, Lat. *poenas dare,* Hdt.; κασιγνήτου τίσις *for* him, Soph.; in pl., Ὀροίτεα τίσιες μετῆλθον (where it may be personified, *avengers,* like Ἐρίνυες), Hdt. 2. *power to repay* or *requite,* both in bad and good sense, Theogn.

τῖσον, aor. 1 imper. of τίνω.

τιταίνω, aor. 1 ἐτίτηνα, Ep. τίτηνα, Ep. redupl. for τείνω, τανύω, *to stretch,* τόξα τιταίνων *bending* his bow, Il.; so in Med., ἐτιταίνετο τόξα was *bending* his bow, Hom. 2. *to stretch out,* ἐτίταινε τάλαντα was *holding* them *out,* Il.; ἐτίταινε τραπέζας was *laying* them *out,* Od. 3. *to draw at full stretch,* of horses, etc., ἅρμα τιταίνειν Il.; ἄροτρον τιταίνετον Ib.; absol., τιταίνετον *haste along,* Ib. 4. Pass. *to strain* or *exert oneself,* chiefly in part., τιταινόμενος *with vehement effort,* Od.; of a horse galloping, τιταινόμενος πεδίοιο *stretching* over the plain (*ventre à terre*), Il.; so of birds, τιταινομένω πτερύγεσσιν Od.

Τιτάν, ᾶνος, ὁ, mostly in pl. Τῖτᾶνες, Ion. Τιτῆνες, οἱ, dat. Τίτησι, Ep. Τιτήνεσσι :—*the Titans,* a race of gods placed beneath Tartarus, Il. (where two are named—Iapetus and Cronus), acc. to Hes., six sons and six daughters of Uranus and Gaia; hurled from Olympus into nether darkness, Hes. : other names are given by later Poets, as Atlas, Aesch.; Prometheus,

Soph.; Θέμις Aesch.; and in Lat. Poets *Titan* is the Sun-god. (The oldest deriv. of the name is given in Hes., *the Stretchers, Strivers;* others connect it with τίτας (from τίνω), *Avengers.*)

Τῑτᾱνίς, Ion. Τιτηνίς, ίδος, ή, fem. of Τιτάν, Aesch.

Τῑτᾱνο-κράτωρ, ορος, ό, (κρατέω) *conqueror of the Titans,* Luc.

Τῑτᾱνο-κτόνος, ον, (κτείνω) *slaying Titans,* Batr.

τίτᾰνος [ῐ], ή, a white earth, *chalk* or *gypsum,* Hes.

Τῑτᾱν-ώδης, ες, (εἶδος) *Titan-like, Titanic,* Τιτανῶδες βλέπειν Luc.

τίτᾱς [ῐ], ου, ό, Dor. for τίτης, = τιμωρός, *avenger,* Aesch.

Τῑτῆνες, οἱ, Ion. for Τιτᾶνες.

τιτθεία, ή, *an acting as a nurse, nursing,* Dem. From

τιτθεύω, f. σω, *to be a nurse, act as a nurse,* Dem. II. trans. *to suckle, nurse,* Id. From

τίτθη, ή, (*θάω) *a nurse,* Ar.

τιτθίον, τό, Dim. of τιτθός, Ar.

τιτθός, ό, (*θάω) *a teat, nipple,* Lysias.

τίτλος, ό, the Lat. *titulus, a title, inscription,* N. T.

τιτρώσκω (Root ΤΡΩ, whence the tenses are formed), f. τρώσω: aor. 1 ἔτρωσα:—Pass., f. τρωθήσομαι, also in med. form τρώσομαι, 3 f. τετρώσομαι:—aor. 1 ἐτρώθην: pf. τέτρωμαι:—*to wound,* Hom.:—τετρῶσθαι τὸν μηρόν *to have a wound* in the thigh, Hdt.: —c. acc. cogn., τιτρώσκειν φόνον *to inflict* a death-wound, Eur. 2. generally, *to damage, cripple,* of ships, Hdt., Thuc. 3. metaph., of wine, *to do one a mischief,* Eur., Xen.

Τίτυο-κτόνος, ον, (κτείνω) *slaying Tityus,* Anth.

Τίτυός, ό, *Tityus,* son of Gaia, a giant, Od.

Τίτυρος [ῐ], ό, Dor. for Σάτυρος, *an ape,* Theophr.

τῑτύσκομαι, only in pres. and impf., combining the senses of τεύχω, τυγχάνω: I. like τεύχω, *to make, make ready, prepare,* τιτύσκετο πῦρ Il.; ὑπ' ὄχεσφι τιτύσκετο ἵππω *he put* two horses to the chariot, Ib. II. like τυγχάνω, *to aim, shoot,* τινός *at* a person, Ib.:—absol., βάλλε τιτυσκόμενος Od.; ἄντα τιτύσκεσθαι *to aim at* a mark right opposite, Ib.; so, of one putting a key into a lock, ἄντα τιτυσκομένη Ib. 2. metaph., φρεσὶ τιτύσκεσθαι *to aim at doing* a thing, i.e. *to purpose, design,* c. inf., Hom.

ΤΙ'ΦΗ, ή, an insect, perh. *the water-spider,* that runs on the top of smooth water, Lat. *tipula,* Ar.

τίφθ', for τίπτε, before an aspirate.

τῖφος, εος, τό, *standing water, a pond, pool, marsh,* Theocr. (Deriv. uncertain.)

ΤΙ'Ω [ῑ Ep., ῐ Att.], impf. ἔτιον, Ep. τῖον, Ion. τίεσκον, Ep. inf. τιέμεν:—Med., f. τίσω [ῐ]: Ion. 3 sing. impf. τιέσκετο: pf. τέτιμαι, part. τετιμένος:—*to pay honour to* a person (whereas τίνω means *to pay a price),* *to honour,* Hom., Aesch., Eur.:—Pass., pf. pass. part. τετιμένος *honoured,* Hom. II. = τιμάω II, τὸν δὲ [τρίποδα] *to value,* τρίποδα δωδεκάβοιον τῖον they valued the tripod at twelve steers' worth, Il.; τῖον δέ ἑ τεσσάραβοιον valued her at four steers' worth, Ib. III. for fut. and aor. 1 τίσω, ἔτισα, v. τίνω.

τλάθῡμος, ον, Dor. for τληθυμος.

τλαίην, aor. opt. of *τλάω.

τλάμων, Dor. for τλήμων.

*ΤΛΑ'Ω, a radical form not used in pres. (which is supplied by the pf. τέτληκα, or the Verb τολμάω): f.

τλήσομαι, Dor. τλάσομαι: Ep. aor. 1 ἐτάλασσα, subj. ταλάσσω: more commonly aor. 2 ἔτλην (as if from a pres. *τλῆμι), Ep. τλῆν, Dor. ἔτλᾱν, 3 pl. ἔτλησαν, Ep. ἔτλᾰν; imperat. τλῆθι, Dor. τλᾶθι; 2 sing. subj. τλῇς; opt. τλαίην, 3 pl. τλαῖεν; inf. τλῆναι, Ep. τλήμεναι; part. τλάς, τλᾶσα:—pf. (with pres. sense) τέτληκα, Ep. 1 pl. τέτλαμεν, imperat. τέτλᾰθι, τετλάτω; opt. τετλαίην; inf. τετλάμεναι, τετλάμεν, part. τετληώς, fem. τετληυῖα, τετληότος: I. *to take upon oneself, to bear, suffer, undergo:* c. acc. rei, ἔτλην οἷ' οὔπω καὶ ἄλλος Il.; ἔτλην ἀνέρος εὐνήν I submitted *to be wedded to a man,* Ib.; τλῇ ὀϊστόν submitted *to be wounded by* it, Ib.; ἔτλα πένθος Pind., etc. 2. absol. *to hold out, endure, be patient, submit,* Hom.; esp. in imperat., τέτλαθι, μῆτερ ἐμή Il.; τλῆτε, φίλοι Od.; in part., τετληότι θυμῷ *with patient* soul, Ib.; κραδίη τετληυῖα Ib. II. c. inf. *to dare* or *venture* to do, Ib., Pind., etc.:—in Att. Poets, *to dare to do* a thing good or bad, hence either *to have the courage, hardihood, effrontery, cruelty,* or *to have the grace, patience,* to do anything, ἔς τι δὴ ἔτλην γεγωνεῖν till I *took courage* to tell, Aesch.; ἔτλα ἀλλάξαι submitted *to exchange,* Soph.; οὐδ' ἔτλης ἐφυβρίσαι *nor hadst thou the cruelty to* insult, Id.; οὐ γὰρ ἂν τλαίην ἰδεῖν I could not *bear* to see, Ar. II. 2. c. acc. rei, *to dare* a thing, i.e. *dare to do* it, ἄτλητα τλᾶσα Aesch.; εἰ καὶ τοῦτ' ἔτλη Soph. 3. c. part., τάδε τέτλαμεν εἰσορόωντες Od.

τλῆθι, aor. 2 imper. of *τλάω.

τλή-θυμος, Dor. τλά-, ον, *stout-hearted,* Anth.

τλήμεναι, Ep. for τλῆναι, aor. 2 inf. of *τλάω.

*τλῆμι, v. *τλάω.

τλημόνως, Adv. of τλήμων.

τλημοσύνη, ή, *that which is to be endured, misery, distress,* in pl., h. Hom. II. *endurance,* Plut.

τλήμων, Dor. τλάμων, ονος, ό, ή: voc. τλῆμον and τλήμων: (*τλάω):—*suffering, enduring, patient, stout-hearted,* of Ulysses, Il.; so Pind., etc. 2. *bold, daring, hardy, reckless,* Il., Trag. II. *suffering, wretched, miserable,* Trag., Xen. III. Adv. τλημόνως, *patiently,* Aesch., Eur., etc.

τλῆν, Ep. for ἔτλην, aor. 2 of *τλάω.

τλησι-κάρδιος, ον, (καρδία) *hard-hearted,* Aesch. II. *miserable,* Aesch.

τλήσομαι, f. of *τλάω.

τλητός, ή, όν, Dor. τλᾱτός, ά, όν, verb. Adj. of *τλάω: I. act. *suffering, enduring, patient, steadfast,* Il. II. pass., with a negat., οὐ τλ. not *to be endured, intolerable,* Trag.

τμάγεν [ᾰ], Ep. 3 pl. aor. 2 pass. of τμήγω.

τμήγω, f. τμήξω: aor. 1 ἔτμηξα: aor. 2 ἔτμᾰγον:—Pass., aor. 2 ἐτμάγην, Ep. 3 pl. τμάγεν (from τέμνω), *to cut, cleave:* Med., ὁδὸν ἐτμήξαντο cut their way, Anth. 2. metaph. in aor. 2 pass. *to be divided* or *dispersed, to part,* Il.

τμήδην, Adv. (τέμνω) *by cutting, so as to cut,* Il.

τμηθείς, aor. 1 pass. part. of τέμνω.

τμῆμα, ατος, τό, (τέμνω, τμήγω) *a part cut off, a section, piece,* Plat. 2. *a cut, incision, wound,* Id.

τμῆσις, εως, ή, (τέμνω) *a cutting:* ἡ τμ. τῆς γῆς *the ravaging* of a country, Plat. II. = τμῆμα, a section, Id.

τμητέον, verb. Adj. of τέμνω, one must cut, Plat.

τμητός, ή, όν, (τέμνω) cut, shaped by cutting, Soph., Eur. 2. that can be cut or severed, Theocr.

τμητο-σίδηρος [ῐ], ον, cut down with iron, Anth.

Τμῶλος, ὁ, Mt. Tmolus in Lydia, Il., etc.

τοδί [ῐ], neut. of ὁδί.

τόθεν, poët. Adv., antecedent to relat. ὅθεν (being an old gen. of ὁ):—hence, thence, Hes. 2. for relat. ὅθεν, Aesch. II. thereafter, thereupon, Id.

τόθῐ, poët. Adv., antecedent to relat. ὅθι (being an old locat. case of ὁ):—there, in that place, Od., Pind. 2. also for relat. ὅθι, where, Pind.

τοι, enclit. Particle, serving to express belief in an assertion, let me tell you, surely, verily, used to express an inference, then, consequently, Hom.; and in Trag., to introduce a general sentiment. II. to strengthen other Particles, γάρ τοι, ἤτοι, καίτοι, μέντοι, τοιγάρτοι, etc.: cf. τἆρα, τἂν, μεντἂν.

τοι, Dor., Ion. and Ep. for σοί, dat. sing. of σύ: always enclitic.

τοί, ταί, Ep. and Ion. for οἱ or οἵ, αἱ or αἵ, nom. pl. of ὁ and ὅς, Hom.

τοι-γάρ, = τοί γε ἄρα, so then, wherefore, therefore, accordingly, Hom., Att. 2. strengthd. τοιγαροῦν, Ion. τοιγαρῶν, so for example, Xen.: also in Poets, Soph. 3. τοιγάρτοι, Plat.

τοῖιν, Ep. for τοῖν, gen. and dat. dual of ὁ.

τοί-νυν, (νυν) therefore, accordingly, Hdt., Trag. 2. to resume or continue a speech, moreover, Soph., Xen.

τοῖο, Ion. and Ep. for τοῦ, gen. sing. of ὁ.

τοῖος, τοία (Ion. τοίη), τοῖον, demonstr. Pron., antecedent to relat. οἷος, Lat. talis, of such kind or quality, such, such-like, τοῖος ἐών, οἷος οὗτις Ἀχαιῶν (sc. ἐστίν) Il., etc.:—τοῖος in Hom. mostly refers to something gone before, such as is said, Ib. 2. with qualifying words, τοῖος χείρας such in his hands, Od.; τεύχεσι τοῖος Il.; τοῖος, c. inf., such as to do, i. e. fit or able to do, Od. II. with an Adj. of the same gender and case, it increases the sense of the Adj., ἐπιεικὴς τοῖος just of moderate size, Il.; πέλαγος μέγα τοῖον a sea so large, Od.; κερδαλέος τοῖος so very crafty, Ib. III. neut. τοῖον as Adv. so, thus, so very, so much, Hom.; —so, τοίως, Theocr.

τοιόσ-δε (Ion. ἥδε), -άδε (Ion. ἥδε), -όνδε, stronger form of τοῖος, anteced. to οἷος, as ἀοιδοῦ τοιοῦδ' οἷος ὅδ' ἐστί of such a minstrel as is this one, Od.; absol., ἀλλ' ὅδ' ἐγὼ τοιόσδε here am I such as you see, Ib.:—also, so great, so noble, so bad, τοιάδε λαίφη such clothes, i. e. so bad, Ib.; τοσόσδε καὶ τοιόσδε Hdt.:—also with a qualifying word, τοιόσδ' ἠμὲν δέμας ἠδὲ καὶ ἔργα such both in form and works, Od.:—with the Art., ὁ τ. ἀνήρ Aesch., etc.; οἱ τοιοίδε Soph.; ἐν τῷ τοιῷδε in such circumstances, Hdt.:—the sense is made more indef. in τοιόσδε τις such a one, Thuc.:—neut. pl. τοιάδε as follows, τοιαῦτα as aforesaid, Hdt.

τοιοσδί, αδί, ονδί, Att. strengthd. form of τοιόσδε, Ar.

τοι-οῦτος, -αύτη, -οῦτο (Ion. -ον), stronger form of τοῖος, such as this, anteced. to οἷος, Od., etc.; to ὅσος, Il.: absol., with an intensive sense, so great, so noble, so bad, etc., Ib., Att.; τοιοῦτος ὤν being such a wretch, Soph.:—c. gen., τοιοῦτος Ἀχαιῶν such a man among them, Il.:—τοιοῦτός ἐστι or γίγνεται εἴς or περί τινα he is

so disposed towards any one, Xen., etc. :—strengthd., τ. ἕτερος just such another, Hdt.; ἄλλους τοσούτους Id. : —with the Art., οἱ τοιοῦτοι Aesch., etc. 2. the sense is made more indef. in τοιοῦτός τις or τις τοιοῦτος such a one, Pind., Thuc., etc.; τοιαῦτ' ἄττα Plat. 3. τοιοῦτον or τὸ τ. such a proceeding, Thuc.; διὰ τὸ τ. for such a reason, Id., etc. 4. in narrative, τοιαῦτα properly refers to what goes before, Aesch., etc. :—after a question, τοιαῦτα affirms like ταῦτα, just so, even so, Eur. 5. τοιαῦτα absol., τὰ πλοῖα, τὰ τοιαῦτα ships and such-like, Dem. 6. τοιαῦτα as an Adv., in such wise, Soph.

τοιουτοσί, -αυτηΐ, -ουτοΐ or -ουτονί, Att. strengthd. form of τοιοῦτος, Ar., etc.

τοιουτό-τροπος, ον, of such kind, such like, Hdt., Thuc.

τοιουτ-ώδης, ες, (εἶδος) of such kind, Luc.

τοῖσδεσι, -εσσι, -εσσιν, Ep. forms for τοῖσι δέ, Hom.

τοῖχος, ὁ, (τεῖχος) the wall of a house or court, Lat. paries, Hom., Att. :—in pl. the sides of a ship, Od., Eur., etc. :—of the human body, Eur. 2. proverb., ὁ εὖ πράττων τοῖχος = 'the right side of the hedge,' Ar.

τοιχωρῠχέω, f. ήσω, to dig through a wall like a thief, to be a housebreaker, Ar., Xen. 2. metaph., οἷα ἐτοιχωρύχησαν περὶ τὸ δάνειον what thievish tricks they played with their loan, Dem. From

τοιχ-ωρύχος [ῠ], ὁ, (ὀρύσσω) one who digs through the wall, i. e. a housebreaker, burglar, robber, Ar.

τοκά, Dor. for τότε.

τοκάς, άδος, ἡ, (τίκτω) of or for breeding, Od. 2. having just brought forth, Lat. feta, τ. λέαινα a lioness with cubs, Eur.; also of women, Id.:—τοκάδα τὴν κεφαλὴν ἔχειν, of Zeus in labour at Athena, Luc.

τοκετός, οῦ, ὁ, = τοκός, birth, delivery, Anth.

τοκεύς, έως, ὁ, (τίκτω) one who begets, a father, Hes.; generally, a parent, Aesch. :—mostly, in pl. τοκεῖς, Ep. τοκῆες, parents, Hom., Hdt., Trag.; —in dual, τοκῆε δύω Od.

τοκίζω, (τόκος II. 2) to lend on interest, Lat. faenerari, Dem.; τ. τόκον to practise usury, Anth. Hence

τοκισμός, ὁ, the practice of usury, Xen.; and

τοκιστής, οῦ, ὁ, an usurer, Plat., Arist.

τοκογλῠφέω, f. ήσω, to practise sordid usury, Luc.

τοκο-γλύφος [ῠ], ὁ, (γλύφω) one who carves out interest, a sordid usurer, Luc.

τόκος, ὁ, (τίκτω) a bringing forth, childbirth, parturition, Il.; in pl., Soph., Eur. 2. the time of parturition, Hdt. II. the offspring, young, a child, son, Hom., Aesch., etc. 2. metaph. the produce of money lent out, interest, Lat. usura, Ar., etc.; ἐπὶ τόκῳ or ἐπὶ τόκον δανείζεσθαι to borrow at interest, Dem.; τόκοι τόκων compound interest, Ar. 3. the produce of land, Xen.

τοκο-φορέω, f. ήσω, to bring in interest, Dem.

τόλμᾰ, ης, ἡ, (*τλάω) courage, to undertake or venture a thing, boldness, daring, hardihood, courage, Pind., Hdt., Att.; τῶνδε τόλμαν σχεθεῖν to have courage for this business, Aesch. 2. in bad sense, over-boldness, recklessness, Lat. audacia, Trag., etc. II. a bold or daring act, Ib. Hence

τολμάω, Ion. -έω, Dor. 2 sing. τολμῇς: f. τολμήσω, Dor. ἀσῶ: pf. τετόλμηκα, Dor. ἄκα:—to undertake, take heart either to do or bear anything terrible or

difficult, Hom., etc. :—absol. *to hold out, endure, be patient, submit*, Id., Att. :—c. acc. rei, *to endure, undergo*, Theogn., Eur.   II. c. inf. *to have the courage, hardihood, effrontery, cruelty*, or *the grace, patience, to do* a thing in spite of any natural feeling, *to venture, dare to do*, Hom., Att.   2. sometimes c. part., ἐτόλμα βαλλόμενος *he submitted to be* struck, Od. ; τόλμα ἐρῶσα Eur.   3. c. acc., τολμᾶν πόλεμον *to undertake, venture on* it, Od. ; τοιαῦτα, πάντα τ. Trag. ; also, τ. τὰ βέλτιστα Thuc. : Pass., οἷ᾽ ἐτολμήθη πατήρ such things as my father *had dared* (or *done*) against him, Eur.

τολμήεις, Dor. -άεις [ᾰ], εσσα, εν, *enduring, stouthearted*, Od. : *daring, bold, adventurous*, Il :—contr. **τολμῆς**, ῆσσα, ῆν, whence Sup. τολμήστατε Soph.

τόλμημα, ατος, τό, (τολμάω) *an adventure, enterprise, deed of daring*, Eur., etc.

τολμηρός, ά, όν, (τολμάω) = τολμήεις, Thuc. ; τὸ τολμηρόν τινος his *hardihood*, Id. ; Adv. -ρῶς, Id. ; Comp. -ότερον, Id.

τολμῆς, contr. for τολμήεις.

τολμητέον, verb. Adj. of τολμάω, *one must venture*, Eur.

τολμητής, οῦ, ὁ, (τολμάω) *a bold, venturous man*, Thuc.

τολμητός, ή, όν, verb. Adj. of τολμάω, *to be ventured* ; ἔστ᾽ ἐκείνῳ πάντα τολμητά all things are *within the compass of his daring*, Soph. ; ἐλπὶς τ. Eur.

τολοιπόν, Adv. *for the rest, for the future* :—better divisim τὸ λοιπόν.

τολῠπεύω, f. σω, properly, *to wind off* wool *into a clew* for spinning : metaph. *to wind off, achieve, accomplish*, ἐγὼ δὲ δόλους τολυπεύω, of Penelope's web (where there is a play on the literal sense), Od. ; τ. πόλεμον Hom.   From

τολύπη [ῠ], ἡ, *a clew* or *ball of wool*, Lat. *glomus*, Ar., Anth.   (Deriv. uncertain.)

τομαῖος, α, ον, and ος, ον, (τομή) *cut, cut off*, Aesch., Eur.   II. *cut in pieces, cut* or *shredded ready for use*, Aesch.

τομάω, (τομή) only in part., *to need cutting*, πρὸς τομῶντι πήματι for a disease *that needs the knife*, Soph.

τομεύς, έως, ὁ, (τεμ-εῖν) *one that cuts, a shoemaker's knife*, Plat. : *the edge of a knife*, Xen.

τομή, ἡ, (τέμνω) *the end left after cutting, the stump* of a tree, Il. ; δοκοῦ τ. *the end of a beam*, Thuc. ; λίθοι ἐν τομῇ ἐγγώνιοι stones cut square, Id. ; so, τομῇ προσθεῖσα βόστρυχον having fitted the lock *to the place from which it was cut*, Aesch.   II. *a cutting, hewing, cleaving*, ἐν τομᾷ σιδήρου by stroke of iron, Soph. ; φασγάνου τομαί Eur. :—as a surgical operation, τομῇ χρῆσθαι Plat. ; διὰ καύσεών τε καὶ τομῶν by cautery *and the knife*, Id.

τόμιον, τό, (τομή) *a victim cut up* for sacrifice ; τὰ τόμια the parts of the victim, Dem.

τομός, ή, όν, verb. Adj. of τέμνω, *cutting*, ἔστηκεν ἢ τομώτατος is placed as it will *cut sharpest*, Soph.

τόμος, ὁ, (τέμνω) *a cut, slice*, Batr., Ar.   II. *part of a book, a tome, volume*.

τονάριον [ᾰ], τό, (τόνος) *a pitch-pipe*, Plut.

τονθορύζω, only in pres., *to speak inarticulately, mutter, babble*, Ar.   (Formed from the sound.)

τόνος, ὁ, (τείνω) *that by which a thing is stretched, a rope, cord, brace*, οἱ τόνοι τῶν κλινέων the cords

of beds, Hdt. ; ἐκ τριῶν τόνων of three *plies* or *strands*, of ropes, Xen. :—in machines, *strainingcords*, Plut.   II. *a stretching, tightening, straining, strain, tension*, Hdt.   2. of sounds, *a straining, raising* of the voice, Aeschin., Dem. :—*the pitch* of the voice, Plat., etc.   3. *measure, metre*, Hdt.   b. in Music, τόνοι were *modes* or *keys differing in pitch*, of which in early Greek music there were three, *the Dorian, Lydian*, and *Phrygian*.   III. *exertion of force, mental exertion, energy*, Luc. :—generally, *force, strength, intensity*, Plut.   IV. metaph. *the tenour of one's way, a course*, Pind., Plut.

τονῦν, = τὸ νῦν, *for the present*, v. νῦν I.

τοξάζομαι, f. άσομαι, (τόξον) Dep. *to shoot with a bow*, Od. ; c. gen. *to shoot at*, Ib.

τοξ-αλκέτης, ου, ὁ, (ἀλκή) *mighty with the bow*, Anth.

τοξάριον [ᾰ], τό, Dim. of τόξον, Luc.

τόξ-αρχος, ὁ, *lord of the bow, bowman, archer*, Aesch.   II. *captain of the archers*, Thuc.

τόξευμα, ατος, τό, *that which is shot, an arrow*, Hdt., Eur., etc. ; ὅσον τ. ἐξικνέεται the distance of a *bowshot*, Hdt. ; πρὶν τ. ἐξικνεῖσθαι before *an arrow* reached them, Xen. ; ἐντὸς τοξεύματος within *bow-shot*, Id. ; ἔξω τοξεύματος Thuc. :—metaph., καρδίας τοξεύματα Soph.   II. collective in pl. for οἱ τοξόται, *the archery*, Hdt.

τοξευτός, ή, όν, *struck by an arrow*, Soph.   From

τοξεύω, f. σω, *to shoot with the bow*, τινὸς at a mark, Il., Soph. ; εἴς τινα Hdt. :—metaph. *to aim at*, c. gen., Eur. :—absol. *to use the bow*, Hdt., Thuc., etc. ; καθ᾽ ὑπερβολὰν τοξεύσας having shot *too high*, Soph.   II. c. acc. *to shoot* or *hit with an arrow*, τινά Eur., Xen. :—Pass. *to be struck by an arrow*, Thuc.   2. c. acc. rei, *to shoot from a bow* : metaph., *to discharge, send forth*, ὕμνους Pind. ; ταῦτα ἐτόξευσεν μάτην hath shot *these arrows in vain*, Eur. : —Pass., πᾶν τετόξευται βέλος Aesch.

τοξ-ήρης, ες, (ἀραρίσκω) *furnished with the bow*, Eur.   2. = τοξικός, Id. ; τ. ψαλμός the twang *of the bowstring*, Id.

τοξικός, ή, όν, (τόξον) *of* or *for the bow*, Aesch. :—ἡ τοξική (sc. τέχνη) *archery*, Plat.   II. of persons, *skilled in the use of the bow*, τοξικώτατος Xen.

τοξο-βόλος, ον, (βάλλω) *shooting with the bow*, Anth.

τοξο-δάμᾱς [δᾰ], αντος, ὁ, (δαμάω) = sq., Aesch.

τοξό-δαμνος, ον, *subduing with the bow*, τ. Ἄρης *the war of archers*, i. e. the Persians, Aesch. ; τ. Ἄρτεμις Eur.

τόξον, τό, (τυγ-χάνω) *a bow*, Hom. ; often in pl., because the ancient bow was of two pieces of horn joined by the πῆχυς in the middle ; τόξα τιταίνειν or ἕλκειν *to draw the bow*, Il. :—as *the bow* was specially the Oriental weapon, τόξου ῥῦμα meant the Persians, opp. to λόγχης ἰσχύς (the Greek *spearmen*), Aesch. :—metaph., τόξῳ *by guess*, Id.   II. in pl. also, *bow and arrows*, Hom., Hdt., etc.   III. metaph., τόξα ἡλίου its *rays*, Eur.   Hence

τοξο-ποιέω, *to make like a bow, to arch*, τ. τὰς ὀφρῦς, of a supercilious person, Ar.

τοξοσύνη, ἡ, *bowmanship, archery*, Il., Eur.

τοξότης, ου, Dor. -τας, α, ὁ, (τόξον) *a bowman, archer*, Il., Hdt., Trag., etc.   2. *the Archer, Sagittarius*, a sign in the Zodiac, Luc.   II. *at Athens*,

οἱ τοξόται were the city-guard, also called Σκύθαι, because they were slaves bought from the parts north of Greece, Ar., etc.

τοξ-ουλκός, όν, (ἕλκω) drawing the bow, Aesch.　II. αἰχμὴ τ. the bowstretching arrow, Id.

τοξοφορέω, f. ήσω, to bear a bow, of Eros, Anth.

τοξο-φόρος, ὁ, ἡ, (φέρω) bow-bearing, Il., Eur., etc.: —ὁ τοξοφόρος = τοξότης, Hdt.

τόπαζος, ὁ, the topaz, Anth.

τοπάζω, f. άσω, (τόπος) to aim at, guess, Aesch., Ar.

τοπάλαι, τοπάλαιόν, τόπαν, τοπαράπαν, τοπαραντίκα, τοπάροιθε, τοπάρος, better written divisim τὸ πάλαι, τὸ παλαιόν, etc.

τόπ-αρχος, ὁ, ἡ, ruling over a place, γυνὴ τ. the mistress, Aesch.

τοπικός, ή, όν, concerning τόποι or common-places, Arist.

τοπογράφέω, f. ήσω, to determine the site, Strab. From

τοπο-γράφος [ᾰ], ὁ, (γράφω) a topographer.

τοπο-θετέω, f. ήσω, (τί-θημι) to mark the site of a place, Strab.

τοπο-μᾰχέω, f. ήσω, (μάχομαι) to wage war by holding strong positions, Plut.

ΤΟ'ΠΟΣ, ὁ, a place, Lat. locus, Aesch., etc.; periphr., χθονὸς πᾶς τόπος, i. e. the whole earth, Id.; Πέλοπος ἐν τόποις in Peloponnesus, Id., etc.; ὁ τόπος τῆς χώρας the local circumstances of the district, Dem.　2. place, position, Aeschin.　3. a place or passage in an author, N. T., etc.　II. a topic, Aeschin.: a common-place in Rhetoric, Arist.　III. metaph. a place, occasion, opportunity, Thuc.

τοπρίν, τοπρόσθεν, τοπρότερον, τοπρῶτον, better written divisim τὸ πρίν, etc.

τορεία, ἡ, (τορεύω) a carving in relief, Plut.

τορεύς, έως, ὁ, (τείρω) a borer, piercer, Anth.

τορευτός, ή, όν, worked in relief: metaph. elaborate, Anth. From

τορεύω, f. σω, (τόρος) to work in relief, Strab.:—c. acc. to represent in this manner, Anth.

τορέω, f. ήσω: aor. 1 part. τορήσας: aor. 2 ἔτορον: (τόρος):—to bore through, pierce, Il.　2. metaph. to proclaim in shrill piercing tones, in redupl. fut. τετορήσω, Ar.: cf. τορός.　II. like τορνεύω, to work, shape, Anth.

τόρμος, ὁ, any hole or socket, in which a pin or peg is stuck, Hdt. (Deriv. uncertain.)

τορνευτο-λῠρ-ασπῐδο-πηγός, ὁ, (τορνεύω, λύρα, ἀσπίς, πήγνυμι) lyre-turner and shield-maker, Ar.

τορνεύω, f. σω, (τόρνος) to work with a lathe-chisel: metaph. of verses, to turn neatly, to round off, Ar.　II. to turn round, as an auger, Eur.

τορνόομαι, Dep. to mark off with the τόρνος, to make round, τορνώσαντο σῆμα they rounded off the barrow, Il.; ὅσσον τίς τ' ἔδαφος νηὸς τορνώσεται large as the bottom of a ship which a man shall round off, with allusion to the round shape of a merchant-vessel (cf. γαυλός), Od.

τόρνος, ὁ, (τείρω) a carpenter's tool for drawing a circle, compasses, Theogn., Hdt., Eur.

τορός, ά, όν, (τείρω) piercing:　1. of the voice, piercing, thrilling, Luc.; so in Adv., τορῶς γεγωνεῖν Eur.:—metaph., τ. φόβος thrilling fear, Aesch.　2. metaph. clear, distinct, plain, Id.:—so in Adv., το-

ρῶς τεκμαίρειν, λέγειν Id., etc.　II. of persons, sharp, ready, smart, Xen.:—so in Adv., ἐπερείδεσθαι τορῶς Ar.

τοροτίξ, imitation of a bird's note, Ar.

τορύνη [ῠ], ἡ, (τόρος) a stirrer, ladle, Ar. From

τορύνω [ῠ], (τορός) to stir, stir up or about, Ar.

τοσάκῑς [ᾰ], Ep. τοσσάκῐ, Adv. (τόσος) so many times, so often, Il.

τοσαυτάκις [ᾰ], Adv., = τοσάκις, Plat.

το-σήμερον, Adv., = σήμερον, to-day, Bion.

τόσος, poët. τόσσος, η, ον, antecedent to relat. ὅσος; —Lat. tantus: of Size, Space, Quantity, so great, so vast: of Time, so long: of Number, in pl., so many: of Sound, so loud: of Degree, so much, so very:— often in Hom. and Hes., οὔτι τόσος γε ὅσος Αἴας not so huge as Ajax, Il.: absol. just so much or just so many, Od.; τρὶς τόσσα δῶρα thrice as many gifts, Il.; δὶς τόσα κακά Soph.　2. used for ὅσος, Lat. quantus, Pind.　II. τόσον and τόσσον as Adv., so much, so far, so very, Lat. tantum, τ. πλέες so many more, Il., etc.　2. ἐκ τόσου so long since, Hdt.　3. τόσῳ with a Comp., and by so much more, Thuc.　III. regul. Adv., δὶς τόσως Eur.

τοσόσ-δε, Ep. τοσσόσ-δε, ἥδε, όνδε, = τόσος in all senses, Hom.:—c. inf. so strong, so able, to do a thing, Od.　II. neut. τοσόνδε, Ep. τοσσόνδε, as Adv. so very, so much, Hom., etc.; of Time, so long, Aesch.　2. as Subst., τοσόνδ' ἔχεις τόλμης Soph.

τοσοσδί, τοσηδί, τοσονδί, = τοσουτοσί, Plat.

τοσουτ-άριθμος, ον, of so large a number, Aesch.

τοσ-οῦτος, -αύτη, -οῦτο or -οῦτον: Ep. τοσσοῦτος, etc.:—Pron.:= τόσος in all senses, but with a stronger demonstr. force, Hom., etc.; of persons, so large, so tall, καί σε τοσοῦτον ἔθηκα Il.; so great in rank, skill, or character, Soph., etc.:—in pl. so many, Hom., etc.:—also τοσοῦτος μέγαθος so large, Hdt.; τοσοῦτος τὸ βάθος so deep, Xen.:—with numeral Advs., δὶς τ., πολλάκις τ., etc., Thuc., etc.; ἕτερον τοσοῦτο as large again, Hdt.　II. neut. as Subst., so much, thus much, τοσοῦτον ὀνήσιος Od.; τοσαῦτ' ἔλεξε Aesch.; —with Preps., διὰ τοσούτου at so small a distance, Thuc.; ἐς τοσοῦτο so far, Lat. hactenus, eatenus, Hdt., etc.; ἐκ τ. from so far, so off, Xen.; ἐν τοσούτῳ in the meantime, Ar.; ἐπὶ τοσοῦτο so far, Hdt.; κατὰ τοσοῦτον so far, Plat.; μέχρι τοσούτου so far, so long, Thuc.; παρὰ τοσοῦτον κινδύνου into such imminent danger, Id.　III. neut. also as Adv., so much, so far, Od., Soph., etc.　2. so much, Hom., Thuc., etc.:—but τοσούτῳ is more common with Comparatives, Hdt., etc.

τοσ-ουτοσί, -αυτηί, -ουτονί, later Att. for τοσοῦτος, with a stronger demonstr. force, Ar., Plat., etc.

τόσσαις, Dor. for τόσσας, aor. 1 part. of an unknown pres. = τυγχάνω, to happen to be, Pind.

τοσσάκι, Ep. for τοσάκις.

τοσσάτιος [ᾰ], η, ον, Ep. for τόσος, so great, much, Anth.: in pl. so many, Id.

τοσσῆνος, Dor. for τοσοῦτος, Theocr.

τοσσόσδε, Ep. for τοσόσδε.

τοσσοῦτος, αὕτη, οῦτον, Ep. for τοσοῦτος.

τότε, Dor. τόκᾰ, Adv. at that time, then, Lat. tunc, Antec. to Relat. ὅτε or ὁπότε, opp. to νῦν, Il., Hom.,

etc. :—also in indef. sense, *in those times, formerly,* Soph., etc. ; τότ' ἢ τότε *at one time* or *other,* Aesch., Eur.   **2.** joined with other Particles, καὶ τότε δή Hom. ; καὶ τότ' ἔπειτα Il. ; τότε δή ῥα Od., etc. ; τότ' ἤδη *then* at length, Hes.   **3.** with the Article, οἱ τότε the men *of that time,* Il., etc. ; οἱ τότε ἄνθρωποι Hdt. ; τῇ τόθ' ἡμέρᾳ Soph. ; ἐν τῷ τότε (sc. χρόνῳ) Thuc.   **4.** εἰς τότε until *then,* Dem. ; ἐκ τότε or ἐκτότε since *then,* Plut.

τοτέ (with changed accent), Adv. *at times, now and then,* τοτὲ μὲν . . , τοτὲ δὲ . . , *at one time* . . , *at another* . . , Od., Aesch., etc. ; τοτ' ἄλλος, ἄλλοθ' ἄτερος Soph. ; τοτὲ μὲν . . , αὖθις δὲ . . , Plat.

τοτελευταῖον, τοτέταρτον, τοτηνίκᾰ, τοτηνίκαδε, τοτηνίκαῦτα, better written divisim τὸ τελευταῖον, etc.

τοτοβρίξ, imitation of *a bird's note,* Ar.

τοτοῖ, an exclam., Aesch. ; τοτοτοῖ, Soph.

τοτρίτον, better written divisim τὸ τρίτον.

τού, Boeot. for σύ, the Lat. *tu, thou.*

τοὔβολοῦ, crasis for τοῦ ὀβολοῦ.

τοὔγκυκλον, crasis for τὸ ἔγκυκλον.

τοὔκ, crasis for τὸ ἐκ.

τοὔκειθεν, crasis for τὸ ἐκεῖθεν.

τοὔλασσον, crasis for τὸ ἔλασσον : τοὐλάχιστον, for τὸ ἐλάχιστον.

τοὐμόν, τοὔμπᾰλιν, τοὔμποδῶν, τοὔμπροσθεν, τοὔμφῦλον, Att. crasis for τὸ ἐμόν, τὸ ἔμπαλιν, etc.

τοὐναντίον, crasis for τὸ ἐναντίον.

τοὔναρ, crasis for τὸ ὄναρ.

τοὔνδικον, crasis for τὸ ἔνδικον.

τοὔνεκα, crasis for τοῦ ἕνεκα, *for that reason, therefore,* Hom., etc.   **II.** interrog., for τίνος ἕνεκα; *wherefore?* Anth.

τοὔνθενδε, crasis for τὸ ἔνθενδε.

τοὔνομα, crasis for τὸ ὄνομα.

τοὐντεύθεν, crasis for τὸ ἐντεῦθεν, *henceforth.*

τοὐξειργασμένον, crasis for τὸ ἐξειργασμένον.

τοὐξημβλωμένον, crasis for τὸ ἐξημβλωμένον.

τοὐξύθῦμον, crasis for τὸ ὀξύθυμον.

τοὐπέκεινα, crasis for τὸ ἐπέκεινα.

τοὐπί, crasis for τὸ ἐπί.

τοὐπιεικές, crasis for τὸ ἐπιεικές.

τοὐπιόν, crasis for τὸ ἐπιόν.

τοὐπίσαγμα, crasis for τὸ ἐπίσαγμα.

τοὐπίσημα, crasis for τὸ ἐπίσημα.

τοὔπισθεν, crasis for τὸ or τοῦ ὄπισθεν.

τοὐπίσω, crasis for τὸ ὀπίσω, Thuc.

τοὐπιχώριον, crasis for τὸ ἐπιχώριον.

τοὖπος, crasis for τὸ ἔπος.

τοὐπτάνιον, crasis for τὸ ὀπτάνιον.

τοὐρανοῦ, crasis for τοῦ οὐρανοῦ.

τοὔργον, crasis for τὸ ἔργον.

τουτάκῐς [ᾰ], poët. Adv. for τότε, antec. to ὁπόταν, Theogn. ; absol., Pind. ; also τουτάκι, Id.   **2.** = οὔτως, relative to ὡς (*as*), Ar.

τουτεί, Adv., Dor. for ταύτῃ, Theocr.

τούτερον, Ion. crasis for τὸ ἕτερον.

τουτί, τουτογί, τουτοδί, Att. forms for τοῦτο, τοῦτό γ', τοῦτο δ' ; v. οὗτος.

τουτόθεν and -θε, Adv. *hence, thence,* Theocr. : so, τουτῶθεν, Adv., Id.

τοὔφ', crasis for τὸ ἐπί.

τόφρᾰ, demonstr. Adv. of Time, *up to* or *during that time, so long,* antecedent to relat. ὄφρα, Il.   **2.** absol. *meanwhile,* Hom.

Τρᾰγᾰσαῖος, α, ον, *of* or *from the Epirotic city* Τραγασαί, Strab. :—of swine, Τραγασαῖα *in Tragasaean fashion,* with a play on τραγεῖν, Ar. ; Τραγασαίου πατρός, with a play on τράγος, Id.

τρᾰγεῖν, aor. 2 inf. of τρώγω.

τράγειος, α, ον, (τράγος) *of* or *from a he-goat :* ἡ τραγείη (sc. δορά) *a goat's skin,* Theocr.

τρᾰγ-έλᾰφος, ὁ, *the goat-stag,* as the Greeks called a fantastic animal, represented on Eastern carpets and the like, Ar.

τράγεος, α, ον, =τράγειος, Anth.

τράγημα [ᾰ], ατος, τό, properly *that which is eaten for eating's sake,* mostly in pl., *dried fruits* or *sweetmeats,* eaten as *dessert,* Lat. *bellaria,* Ar., Xen.   Hence τρᾰγημᾰτίζω, *to eat sweetmeats,* Arist. : so Med., τραγηματίζομαι, Theophr.

τρᾰγῐκός, ή, όν, (τράγος) *of* or *like a goat, goatish,* Plut., etc.   **II.** *of* or *for tragedy, tragic* (cf. τραγῳδία), Hdt., Xen., etc. ; τρ. λῆρος *tragic trumpery,* Ar.   **2.** generally, *tragic, stately, majestic,* Id., Plat.   **3.** in bad sense, *in tragic style, plaintive,* Dem.   **III.** Adv. -κῶς, *in tragic style* or *fashion,* Plat.   **2.** οἰκεῖν τρ. *to live in splendour,* Plut.

τράγῐνος, η, ον, *like* τράγειος, *of a he-goat,* Anth.

τρᾰγίσκος, ὁ, Dim. of τράγος, *a young he-goat,* Theocr., Anth.

τρᾰγο-κουρικός, ή, όν, (κουρά) *for shearing he-goats,* Luc.

τρᾰγό-κτονος, ον, (κτείνω) *of slaughtered goats,* Eur.

τρᾰγο-μάσχᾰλος, ον, (μασχάλη) *with armpits smelling like a he-goat,* Ar.

τρᾰγό-πους, ποδος, ὁ, ἡ, *goat-footed,* Anth.

τράγος [ᾰ], ὁ, (τρᾰγεῖν) *a he-goat,* Lat. *hircus,* Od., etc.

τρᾰγο-σκελής, ές, (σκέλος) *goat-shanked,* Hdt., Luc.

τρᾰγο-φάγέω, f. ήσω, (φᾰγεῖν) *to eat he-goats,* Strab.

τράγω, Dor. for τρώγω.

τρᾰγῳδέω, f. ήσω, (τραγῳδός) *to act a tragedy,* Ar.   **2.** c. acc. objecti, *to represent in tragedy,* Luc. :—Pass. *to be the subject of a tragedy,* Isocr., etc.   **II.** metaph. *to tell in tragic phrase, to declaim,* Dem.

τρᾰγῳδία, ἡ, (τραγῳδός) *a tragedy,* invented by the Dorians, and at first of lyric character (τραγικοὶ χοροί Hdt.) ; then transplanted to Athens, where it assumed its dramatic form, Ar., etc.   Its proper sense is *goat-song,* because in early times a goat was the prize, or because the actors were clothed in goat-skins.   **II.** generally, *any grave, serious poetry,* Plat.

τρᾰγῳδικός, ή, όν, *befitting tragedy,* χοροί Hdt., Ar. ; τραγῳδικὸν βλέπειν *to look tragic,* Ar. ; ὠδυνήθην τραγῳδικόν *suffered a tragic woe,* Id.

τρᾰγῳδιο-γράφος, ον, (γράφω) *writing tragedies,* Polyb.

τρᾰγῳδο-διδάσκαλος, ὁ, *a tragic poet,* who trained his own chorus and actors, Ar.

τρᾰγῳδο-ποιός, ὁ, (ποιέω) *a maker of tragedies, a tragic poet, tragedian,* Ar., Plat., etc.

τρᾰγ-ῳδός, ὁ, (ἀοιδός, ᾠδός) properly, *a goat-singer* (v. τραγῳδία), i. e. *a tragic poet and singer,* these characters being orig. one, Ar. :—later, when the poets ceased to *act,* the term meant *a tragedian* or *tragic actor,* the tragic poet being called τραγῳδοποιός or

τραγῳδοδιδάσκαλος. 2. of *members of the tragic chorus*, Ar. II. the pl. is often used = τραγῳδία, ἐν τοῖσι τραγῳδοῖς *in tragedy*, Id., Dem., etc.

Τράλλεις or Τραλλεῖς, οἱ, *Trallians*, Thracian barbarians, Plut.

τρᾰνής, ές, (τε-τραίνω) *piercing* : metaph. *clear, distinct* :—Adv., τρανῶς εἰδέναι, μανθάνειν Aesch., Eur. ; Comp. τρανότερον, Anth. Hence

τρᾰνόω, f. ώσω, *to make clear, plain, distinct*, Anth.

τρά-πεζα [ᾰ¹, ης, ἡ, (prob. for τετρά-πεζα, *four-legged*), *a table*, esp. *a dining-table*, Hom., Hdt., etc. ; ξενίη τρ. *the hospitable board*, Od. ; τραπέζῃ καὶ κοίτῃ δέκεσθαι *to entertain at bed and board*, Hdt. ; Περσικὴν τράπεζαν παρετίθετο *he kept a table in the Persian fashion*, Thuc. ; εἰς ἀλλοτρίαν τράπεζαν βλέπειν *to live at other men's table*, Xen. 2. *a table*, as implying what is upon it, *a dinner, meal*, Hdt., etc. ; Συρακοσία τρ., *proverb. of luxurious living*, Hor. *Siculae dapes*, Plat. II. *a money-changer's table, a bank*, Lat. *mensa argentaria*, Id., etc. ; ἡ ἐγγύη ἡ ἐπὶ τὴν τρ. *security given to the bank*, Dem. ; οἱ ἐπὶ ταῖς τραπέζαις *bankers*, Isocr. Hence

τρᾰπεζεύς, έως, ὁ, *at, of a table*, κύνες τραπεζῆες (Ion. for τραπεζεῖς) *dogs fed from their master's table*, Hom.

τρᾰπεζῑτεύω, f. σω, *to be engaged in banking*, Dem.

τρᾰπεζίτης [ῑ], ου, ὁ, (τράπεζα II) *one who keeps a bank, a banker*, Lat. *argentarius*, Dem. Hence

τρᾰπεζῑτικός, ή, όν, *of or for the banker*, Isocr.

τρᾰπεζο-ποιΐα, ἡ, *table-making*, Strab.

τράπείομεν, Ep. for τραπῶμεν, 1 pl. aor. 2 pass. of τρέπω.

τράπέσθαι, aor. 2 med. inf. of τρέπω.

τρᾰπέω, only in pres. *to tread grapes*, Od., Hes. (Deriv. uncertain : cf. Lat. *trapetum*.)

τρᾰπῆναι, aor. 2 pass. inf. of τρέπω.

τρᾰπητέον, verb. Adj. of τρέπω, *one must turn*, Luc.

τράπω, Ion. for τρέπω.

τρᾰσιά, ἡ, (ταρσός) *a crate*, whereon to dry figs, Ar.

τραυλίζω, f. Att. ιῶ, (τραυλός) *to lisp*, Lat. *balbutire*, as Alcibiades made *r* into *l*, Ar. ; of children, Id.

ΤΡΑΥΛΟ'Σ, ή, όν, *lisping*, Lat. *balbus*, esp. of children, Hdt. II. of *the swallow, twittering*, Anth. (Prob. from the sound.) Hence

τραυλότης, ητος, ἡ, *a lisping*, Plut.

τραῦμα, Ion. and Dor. τρῶμα, ατος, τό, (τείρω) *a wound, hurt*, Hdt., Att. ; τραῦμα λαβεῖν ὑπό τινος Dem. ; λαβεῖν καὶ δοῦναι Plut. II. of things, *a hurt, damage*, as of ships, Hdt. III. in war, *a blow, defeat*, Id. IV. ἡ τραύματος γραφή *an indictment for wounding* (with intent to murder), Aeschin.

τραυμᾰτίας, ου, ὁ, Ion. τρωμ-, *a wounded man*, οἱ τρ. *the wounded of an army*, Hdt., Thuc. ; and

τραυμᾰτίζω, Ion. τρωμ- : pf. τετραυμάτικα, pass. -ισμαι: aor. 1 pass. ἐτραυματίσθην :—*to wound*, Hdt., Att.

τράφεν, Aeol. and Ep. for ἐτράφησαν, 3 pl. aor. 2 pass. of τρέφω. II. Dor. for τρέφειν, inf. of τρέφω.

τρᾰφερός, ά, όν, (τρέφω) properly, *well-fed*, οἱ τραφεροί or τὰ τραφερά *the fat ones*, i.e. fishes, Theocr. II. τραφερή (sub. γῆ), ἡ, as Subst. *the dry land, land*, ἐπὶ τραφερήν τε καὶ ὑγρήν Hom.

τράφην [ᾰ], Ep. aor. 2 pass. of τρέφω.

τραφθῆναι, aor. 1 pass. inf. of τρέπω.

τράφω, Aeol. and Dor. for τρέφω.

τράχέως, Adv. of τραχύς.

τράχήλια, τά, (τράχηλος) *scraps of meat and gristle about the neck, scraps, offal*, Ar.

τράχηλιαῖος, α, ον, *of, on*, or *from the neck*, Strab.

τράχηλίζω, f. ίσω, (τράχηλος) of wrestlers, *to bend the neck back*, and so *to overpower*, Theophr. :—Pass. *to have one's neck bent back so that the throat gapes when cut* : hence, *to be laid open*, N. T.

τράχηλο-δεσμότης, ου, ὁ, *chaining the neck*, Anth.

τράχηλος [ᾰ], ὁ, *the neck, throat*, Hdt., Eur., etc. (Deriv. uncertain.)

Τρᾰχίς, Ion. Τρηχίς, ῖνος, ἡ, *Trachis*, in Thessaly, named from the *ruggedness* (τραχύτης) of the district, Il., etc. :—Adj. Τρᾱχίνιος [ῑ], α, ον, Ion. Τρηχ-, Hdt., etc. ; also ος, ον, Theocr. :—οἱ Τραχίνιοι *the people of Tr.*, Hdt., etc. :—ἡ Τραχινία *the country*, Id., Soph., etc. ; also called Τραχίς, Thuc.

τράχύνω [ῡ], Ion. τρηχ- : pf. τετράχῠκα :—Pass., aor. 1 ἐτράχύνθην : pf. τετράχυσμαι, inf. -υνθαι : (τραχύς) :— *to make rough, rugged, uneven*, Plat. :—Pass. *to become rough*, Id. ; τρ. τῇ φωνῇ *to use rough harsh tones*, Plut. 2. in Aesch. Theb., τράχυνε refers to τραχύς γε μέντοι δῆμος (just before) *call them rough*, I care not. 3. metaph. in Pass. *to be exasperated*, Plat. II. intr. *to be rough*, Plut.

ΤΡΑ'ΧΥ'Σ, εῖα, ύ : Ion. τρηχύς, fem. τρηχέα ; poët. fem. also τρηχύς :—*rugged, rough*, Lat. *asper*, Hom., etc. ; as epith. of Ithaca, Od. ; cf. Τραχίς :—also, *rough, shaggy*, Xen. :—of a bit, *rough, sharp*, Id. : of the voice of boys, when it breaks, Plut. 2. *rough, harsh, savage*, Pind., Aesch., etc. II. Adv. τράχέως, Ion. τρηχέως, *roughly*, Hdt. ; τραχέως ἔχειν *to be rough*, Isocr. ; τρ. φέρειν, Lat. *aegre ferre*, Plut.

τράχύ-στομος, ον, (στόμα) *of rough speech* or *pronunciation*, Strab.

τράχύτης, ητος, ἡ, (τραχύς) *roughness, ruggedness*, Xen. ; *sharpness*, of a bit, Id. 2. of persons, *roughness, harshness*, ὀργῆς Aesch.

τράχω [ᾰ], Dor. for τρέχω.

τράχών, ῶνος, ὁ, *a rugged, stony tract*, Luc. :—so Τρᾰχωνῖτις, ιδος, ἡ, N. T., etc.

ΤΡΕΙ'Σ, οἱ, αἱ, τρία, τά : gen. τριῶν : dat. τρισί : acc. τρεῖς, τρία :—Lat. *tres, tria, three*, Hom., etc.

τρεισ-καί-δεκα, οἱ, αἱ, τρια-καί-δεκα, τά, *thirteen*, Hdt., Att. ; also written divisim, gen. τριῶν καὶ δέκα, dat. τρισὶ καὶ δέκα, etc. :—an indecl. form τρισκαίδεκα occurs, in all genders and cases, Hom., Ar., etc.

ΤΡΕ'ΜΩ, only in pres. and impf., 3 sing. Ep. impf. τρέμε :—Lat. *tremo, to tremble, quake, quiver*, Il., Eur. :—c. inf. *to tremble* or *fear to do*, Aesch., Soph. : —c. acc. *to tremble at, fear*, Soph., Eur., etc.

τρεπτέον, verb. Adj. of τρέπω, *one must turn*, Ar.

ΤΡΕ'ΠΩ, f. τρέψω : aor. 1 ἔτρεψα : aor. 2 ἔτρᾰπον : pf. τέτροφα, later τέτράφα :—Pass., f. τράπήσομαι : aor. 1 ἐτρέφθην, Ion. inf. τραφθῆναι : aor. 2 ἐτράπην [ᾰ], Ep. subj. τραπείομεν for τραπῶμεν : pf. τέτράμμαι, 3 pl. ἐτράφαται ; 3 sing. imperat. τετράφθω : 3 sing. plqpf. τέτράπτο, 3 pl. τετράφατο. *To turn* or *direct towards a thing*, Hom., etc. ; mostly followed by a Prep., τρ. τινὰ εἰς εὐνήν *to shew* him to bed, Il. ; τρ. πόλεις εἰς ὕβριν Thuc. ; τρ. κεφαλὴν πρὸς ἥλιον Od. 2. Pass. *to turn one's steps, turn in a certain direction*, τραφθῆ-

ναι ἀν' Ἑλλάδα to roam up and down Greece, Od.; c. acc. cogn., τρέπεσθαι ὁδόν to take a course, Hdt.　3. Pass. also to turn or betake oneself, εἰς ἀοιδήν Od.; ἐπὶ ἔργα Il.; ἐφ' ἁρπαγήν Thuc.; πρὸς λῃστείαν Id.　4. Pass. and Med., of places, to be turned or look in a certain direction, πρὸς ζόφον Od.; πρὸς ἄρκτον, πρὸς νότον Hdt., etc.　II. to turn, i.e. turn about, τρέπειν ἵππους Il.; τὰ καλὰ τρ. ἔξω to turn the best side outmost, Pind.:—Pass., αἰχμὴ τράπετο the point bent back, Il.; of the solstice, ἐπειδὰν ἐν χειμῶνι τράπηται ἥλιος (v. τροπή 1) Xen.　2. τρ. τὴν αἰτίαν, τὴν ὀργὴν εἴς τινα to divert the blame, the anger upon another, Isae., Dem.:—Pass., in imprecations, ἐς κεφαλὴν τρέποιτο ἐμοί on my head be it! Ar.　3. to turn another way, to alter, change, νόον, φρένας Hom., etc.; ἐς γέλων τρ. τὸ πρᾶγμα Ar.:—Pass. to be changed, change, Hom., etc.; c. acc. cogn., τρεπόμενος τροπὰς undergoing changes, Aeschin.　III. to turn or put to flight, rout, defeat, Il., Hdt., etc.; τρ. φύγαδε, Lat. convertere in fugam, Il.; τρ. ἐς φυγήν Eur.;—so, in aor. 1 med., to put an enemy to flight, Xen.:—Pass. to be put to flight, turn and flee, Aesch., Xen., etc.; so in Med., ἐς φυγὴν τραπέσθαι Hdt., Thuc.:—also intr. in Act., φύγαδ' ἔτραπε Il.　IV. to turn away, keep off, hinder, τρ. τινὰ ἀπὸ τείχεος Ib.; βέλος ἔτραπεν ἄλλῃ Ib.　V. to overturn, like ἀνατρέπω, Aesch.　VI. to turn, apply, τρ. τι ἐς ἄλλο τι Hdt.; ποῦ τέτροφας τὰς ἐμβάδας; what have you made of your shoes? Ar.:—Pass., ποῖ τρέπεται τὰ χρήματα; Id.

τρέσσα, Ep. for ἔτρεσα, aor. 1 of τρέω.

ΤΡΕ'ΦΩ, Dor. τράφω: f. θρέψω: aor. 1 ἔθρεψα, Ep. θρέψα: aor. 2 ἔτραφον: pf. τέτροφα, Pass., f. τράφήσομαι, but mostly in med. form θρέψομαι: aor. 1 ἐθρέφθην: aor. 2 ἐτράφην [ᾰ], Ep. τράφην, and 3 pl. ἔτραφεν: pf. τέθραμμαι, inf. τεθράφθαι:　I. to thicken or congeal a liquid, γάλα θρέψαι to curdle it, Od.; τυρὸν τρέφειν Theocr.:—Pass., with intr. pf. act. τέτροφα, to become firm, περὶ χροῒ τέτροφεν ἄλκη Od.　II. to make to grow or increase, to bring up, breed, rear, Hom., etc.; c. acc. cogn., τρ. τινὰ τροφήν τινα to bring up in a certain way, Hdt.:—Med. to rear for oneself, Od., etc.:—Pass. to be reared, grow up, Hom.; κάρτιστοι τράφεν ἄνδρες grew up the strongest men, Il.; ἐξ ὅτου 'τράφην ἐγώ from the time when I left the nursery, Ar.; μιᾶς τρέφει πρὸς νυκτός, i.e. art a child of night, Soph.　2. of slaves, horses, dogs and the like, to rear and keep them, Hom., etc.; τρ. παιδαγωγούς Aeschin.; τρ. γυναῖκα Eur.:—metaph., αἰγιαλὸν ἔνδον τρέφει he keeps quite a sea-beach in the house, Ar.:—Pass. to be bred, reared, Soph.　3. to let grow, cherish, foster, χαίτην τρέφε Il.; τὴν ὑπήνην τρ., κόμην τρ. = κομάω, Hdt.;—also, τάδ' ὕεσσι τρέφει ἀλοιφήν this is what puts fat on swine, Od.　4. of earth and sea, to produce, teem with, χθὼν τρέφει φάρμακα Ib.; θάλασσα τρέφουσα πορφύραν Aesch.　5. to have within oneself, to contain, keep, have, ὅ τι πόλις τέτροφεν ἄφιλον Soph.; τρέφειν τὴν γλῶσσαν ἡσυχωτέραν to keep his tongue more quiet, Id.; νόσον τρ. Id.; οἵας λατρείας τρέφει what services she constantly performs, Id.　III. to maintain, support, τρ. Ἥλιος χθονὸς φύσιν Aesch.; τρ. τὸν πατέρα Aeschin.: esp. to maintain an army or navy, Thuc.,

Xen.　IV. aor. 2 act. in intr. sense, ἔτραφον = pass. ἐτράφην, ὃς ἔτραφ' ἄριστος Il.; τραφέμεν (Ion. for τραφεῖν) Hom.　2. so pf. τέτροφα, v. supr. 1.

τρέχνος, εος, τό, a twig, Anth. (Deriv. unknown.)

ΤΡΕ'ΧΩ, Dor. τράχω, f. θρέξομαι: aor. 1 ἔθρεξα, Ion. θρέξασκον: also (from Root ΔΡΕΜ or ΔΡΑΜ) f. δράμοῦμαι, Ion. -έομαι: aor. 2 ἔδραμον: pf. δεδράμηκα [ᾰ], poët. pf. δέδρομα:—Pass., pf. δεδράμημαι:—to run, Lat. curro, Hom., etc.; of horses, Il.:—of things, to run, move quickly, Hom., etc.　II. c. acc. loci, to run over, Eur., Xen.　III. c. acc. cogn., τρ. δρόμον, ἀγῶνα to run a course, a heat, Eur., etc.: often metaph., ἀγῶνα δρ. to run a risk, Id.; πολλοὺς ἀγῶνας δραμεῖν περὶ σφέων αὐτέων to run many risks for their lives, Hdt.:—sometimes the acc. is omitted, τρ. περὶ ἑωυτοῦ to run the risk of his life, Id.; τρ. περὶ τῆς νίκης Xen.　2. παρ' ἐν πάλαισμα νικᾶν he was within one bout of carrying off the victory, Hdt.

ΤΡΕ'Ω, inf. τρεῖν: aor. 1 ἔτρεσα, Ep. τρέσσα:—this Verb is never contracted, except when the contraction is into ει:—to flee from fear, flee away, Il.; μὴ τρέσας without fear, Aesch.; οὐδὲν τρέσας Plat.:—τρέσας is used like a Subst., a runaway, coward, Il.; Ἀριστόδημος ὁ τρέσας Hdt.　II. trans. to flee from, fear, dread, be afraid of, c. acc., Il., Trag., Xen.

τρῆμα, ατος, τό, (τε-τραίνω) a perforation, hole, aperture, orifice, Lat. foramen, Ar., Plat.　Hence

τρημάτόεις, εσσα, εν, porous, Anth.

τρήρων, ωνος, ὁ, ἡ, (τρέω) timorous, shy, Hom.

τρητός, ή, όν, verb. Adj. of τε-τραίνω, perforated, with a hole in it, Od.; τρητὰ λέχεα, prob. inlaid bedsteads, or having holes through which the cords that supported the bedding were drawn—τρητὸς μελισσῶν πόνος, i.e. the honeycomb, Pind.; τρ. λίθαξ pumice-stone, Anth.

τρηχάλεος, η, ον, poët. for τρηχύς, Anth.

τρηχύνω [ῠ], τρηχύς, Ion. for τραχ-.

τρῑ-, Prefix, from τρίς or τριά, in compds. three times, thrice, Lat. ter.

τρία, neut. of τρεῖς.

τριάζω, f. ξω, (τρία) to vanquish, of a wrestler, who did not win until he had conquered in three bouts (παλαίσματα).

τρίαινα, ἡ, a trident, the badge of Poseidon, Hom.

τριαινόω, f. ώσω, to heave with the trident: generally, to heave or prise up, overthrow, Eur.　II. τρ. τὴν γῆν δικέλλῃ to break it up with a mattock, Ar.

τριᾶκάς, Ion. τριηκάς, άδος, ἡ, contr. for obsol. τριακοντάς: (τρεῖς, τρία):—the number thirty, Aesch.　II. the thirtieth day of the month, Hes.: hence, a month, containing 30 days, Luc.　III. a political division, containing thirty families.

τριᾱκονθ-άμμᾰτος, ον, (ἅμμα) with or of thirty knots, Xen.

τριᾱκονθ-ήμερος, Ion. τριηκοντ-, ον, of thirty days, Hdt.

τριᾱκοντα [ᾰ], Ion. τριηκ-, οἱ, αἱ, τά, indecl., with a gen. τριηκόντων in Hes.; dat. τριηκόντεσσι Anth.:—thirty, Lat. triginta, Hom., etc.　II. οἱ τριάκοντα, 1. at Sparta, the council of thirty, assigned to the kings, Xen.　2. at Athens, the Thirty, commonly called the thirty tyrants, appointed on the taking of Athens (B.C. 404), Plat., etc.

τριᾱκοντα-ετής, Ion. τριηκ-, ές, thirty years old, Plat.; in contr. form, οἱ τριακοντοῦται the men of

thirty years, Id.; fem. τριακοντοῦτις Isae. II.
τριακονταέτης, ες, of or for thirty years, Thuc.;—in
fem. form, σπονδαὶ τριηκοντουτίδες Hdt.; αἱ τριακοντού-
τιδες σπονδαί Ar.
τριᾱκοντά-ζυγος, ον, with thirty benches, Theocr.
τριᾱκοντάκῑς [ᾰ], Adv. thirty times, Plut.
τριᾱκοντ-αρχία, ἡ, the rule of the Thirty, at Athens, Xen.
τριᾱκοντά-χους, ουν, producing thirtyfold, Strab.
τριᾱκόντορος (sc. ναῦς), ἡ, a thirty-oared ship, Thuc.,
Xen.; in Hdt. written τριηκόντερος.
τριᾱκοντ-ούτης, -ούτις, v. τριακοντα-ετής.
τριᾱκοντ-ώρυγος, ον, (ὀργυιά) of thirty fathoms, Xen.
τριᾱκόσιοι, Ion. τριηκ-, αι, α, three hundred, Hom.,
Hdt., etc.; also with collective noun in sing., ἵππος τρ.
Xen. II. οἱ τρ. at Athens, the richest members
of the συμμορίαι, who managed their affairs, Dem. 2.
the Three Hundred, who fell at Thermopylae, Hdt.
τριᾱκοσιο-μέδιμνοι, οἱ, those whose property produced
300 medimni, i. e. the Ἱππεῖς.
τριᾱκοσιό-χους, ουν, producing three hundredfold, Strab.
τριᾱκοστός, Ion. τριηκ-, ή, όν, the thirtieth, Hdt.,
etc. II. τριακοστή, ἡ, a duty of one-thirtieth, Dem.
τριᾱκτήρ, ῆρος, ὁ, (τριάζω) a victor, Aesch.
τρι-άρμενος, ον, with three sails or masts, Luc.
τριάς, άδος, ἡ, (τρεῖς) the number three, a triad, Plat.
τρῑβᾰκός, ή, όν, (τρίβω) rubbed, worn, Anth., Luc.
Τρῐβαλλοί, οἱ, the Triballi, a people on the borders
of Thrace; as a Comic name for barbarian gods, Ar.:
—Adj. Τρῐβαλλικός, ή, όν, Hdt.
τρῐ-βελής, ές, (βέλος) three-pointed, Anth.
τρῐβή, ἡ, (τρίβω) a rubbing or wearing away, wasting,
Aesch. II. practice, as opp. to theory, Xen.:
also mere practice, routine, as opp. to true art,
Plat. III. that about which ne is busied, an
object of care, Lat. cura, Aesch. IV. of Time, a
spending, Soph., Plat.; ἀξίαν τρῐβὴν ἔχει 'tis time well
spent, Aesch.; βίος οὐκ ἄχαρις ἐς τὴν τρῐβήν a life
pleasant enough in the spending, Ar. 2. delay,
putting off, ἐς τρῐβὰς ἐλᾶν to seek delays, Soph.; τρῐβὰς
πορίζειν Ar.; and with the Verb omitted, μὴ τρῐβὰς ἔτι
no more delays, Soph.
τρῐβολ-εκτράπελος [ᾰ], ον; in Ar. τριβολεκτράπελα
στωμύλλειν to deal in coarse rude jests.
τρῐ-βολος [ῐ], ον, = τρῐ-βελής: as Subst. a caltrop, i. e. a
three-spiked implement, formed so that one of the spikes
must point upwards, used to lame the enemy's horses,
Plut. 2. a prickly plant, a burr, thistle, N.T. II.
τρίβολοι, οἱ, a threshing-machine, boards with sharp
stones fixed in the bottom, Anth.
τρίβος [ῐ], ἡ, and ὁ, a worn or beaten track, the high
road, highway, Hdt., Eur.: a footpath, Xen. II.
rubbing, attrition, Aesch. III. metaph. delay, Id.
ΤΡΙ'ΒΩ, f. τρίψω: aor. 1 ἔτριψα, inf. τρίψαι: pf. τέ-
τρίφα:—Pass., f. τρῐβήσομαι and τετρίψομαι: aor. 1
ἐτρίφθην: aor. 2 ἐτρίβην [ῐ]: pf. τέτριμμαι, Ion. 3 pl.
τετρίφαται:—to rub: to rub or thresh corn, Il.; μοχλὸν
τρίψαι ἐν ὀφθαλμῷ to work round the stake in his eye,
Od.; χρυσὸν βασάνῳ τρ. to rub it on a touchstone, so as
to test its purity (cf. παρατρίβω), Theogn.:—Med., χρη-
στηρίοις ἐν τοῖσδε τρίβεσθαι μύσος to rub one's pollution upon these shrines, pollute them with it,
Aesch. 2. to rub down, grind, pound, Ar.,

etc. 3. to crush, βότρυν Id. II. to wear out
by rubbing: Pass., of a road, to wear or tread it
smooth, ἀτραπὸς τετριμμένη Id. 2. of Time, to
wear away, spend, Lat. terere vitam, Soph., Eur.:—
absol. to waste time, tarry, Aesch. 3. to waste or
ravage a country, Eur. III. metaph., 1. of
persons, to wear out, Hes.: Pass. to be worn out, Il.,
Thuc.:—Med., τρίψεσθαι αὐτὴν περὶ αὑτήν to wear itself
out by internal struggles, Id.:—Pass., τριβόμενος ληός
an oppressed people, Hdt. 2. of money and property,
to waste, squander it, Id. 3. to use constantly,
Ar. 4. Pass. to be much busied or engrossed with
a thing, Hdt. Hence
τρίβων [ῐ], ωνος, ὁ, a worn garment, threadbare cloak,
Ar., Plat., etc.; and
τρίβων, ὁ, ἡ, as Adj. practised or skilled in a thing,
c. gen., Hdt., Eur., etc. 2. absol., a hackneyed,
crafty fellow, rogue, Ar.
τρῐβωνικῶς, Adv. like a τρίβων, cloak-wise, Ar.
τρῐβώνιον, τό, Dim. of τρίβων, Ar.
τρῑ-γένεια, ἡ, a third generation, Strab. Hence
τρῑ-γέρων, οντος, ὁ, ἡ, triply old, τρ. μῦθος τάδε φωνεῖ
'tis a thrice-told tale, Aesch.
τρῑ-γίγας [γῐ], ὁ, a triple (i. e. huge) giant, Orph.
ΤΡΙ'ΓΛΗ, ἡ, the red mullet: also τρίγλᾰ, Anth.
τρί-γληνος, ον, (γλήνη) with three pupils: then, of
earrings, with three bright drops, Hom.
τριγλο-φόρος, ον, (φέρω) bearing mullets, τρ. χιτών
a net for catching them, Anth.
τρί-γλυφος, ον, (γλύφω) thrice-cloven: as Subst.,
τρίγλυφος, ἡ, in Doric architecture, the triglyph, a
three-grooved tablet placed at equal distances along
the frieze, Eur.:—also τρίγλυφον, τό, Arist.
τρι-γλώχῑς, ῖνος, ὁ, ἡ, three-barbed, Il.
τριγμός or τρισμός, ὁ, (τρίζω) a scream, squeak, Plut.
τρῑγονία, ἡ, the third generation, Dem. From
τρί-γονος, ον, (γίγνομαι) thrice-born: in pl. simply =
τρεῖς, three, Eur.
τρίγωνο-ειδής, ές, (εἶδος) triangular-shaped, Polyb.
τρί-γωνος, ον, (γωνία) three-cornered, triangular,
Aesch. II. as Subst., τρίγωνον, τό, a triangle,
Plat.: name of a musical instrument, Id.
τρί-δουλος, ον, a slave through three generations,
thrice a slave, Soph.
τρί-δραχμος, ον, worth or weighing three drachms, Ar.
τρι-έλικτος, ον, thrice coiled, Orac. ap. Hdt., Anth.
τρι-έμβολος, ον, (ἐμβολή) like three ships' beaks, Ar.
τρι-ετηρίς (sc. ἑορτή), ίδος, ἡ, a triennial festival,
Hdt., Eur. 2. (sub. περίοδος), a period of three
years, h. Hom., Arist.
τρι-έτης, ον, or τρι-ετής, ές, ὁ, (ἔτος) of or for three
years, Hdt., Theocr.: neut. τριέτες as Adv. for three
years, Od.
τρι-ζυγής, ές, τρί-ζυγος, ον, and τρί-ζυξ, ὁ, ἡ, three-
yoked, three in union, of the Graces, Eur., Anth.
τρίζω (Root ΤΡΙΓ): pf. τέτρῑγα (used as a pres.), Ep.
part. τετρῑγῶτες, for τετρῑγότες:—of animals, to utter
a shrill cry, to scream, cry, of young birds, Il.;
of bats, etc.; of ghosts (which, in Shaksp., 'squeak
and gibber'), Hom., etc. 2. of other sounds, νῶτα
τετρίγει (Ep. plqpf.) the wrestlers' backs cracked, Il.;
τρ. τοὺς ὀδόντας to gnash the teeth, N. T.; of a

musical string, *to twang*, Anth. (Formed from the sound.)

τριηκάς, άδος, ή, Ion. for τριακάς.

τριήκοντα, τριηκόσιοι, etc., Ion. for τριακ-.

τριηκοντήμερος, Ion. for τριακονθήμερος.

τρι-ημι-πόδιον, τό, (πούς) *a length of three half-feet, a foot and a-half*, Xen.

τριηραρχέω, f. ήσω : pf. τετριηράρχηκα :—*to be a τριήραρχος, to command a trireme*, Hdt., Thuc. : c. gen., τρ. νηός Hdt. **II.** *at Athens, to be trierarch*, i. e. *fit out a trireme for the public service*, Ar. ; Pass., τριηραρχοῦσιν οἱ πλούσιοι, ὁ δὲ δῆμος τριηραρχεῖται the rich *find trierarchs*, the people *has trierarchs found* it, Xen. Hence

τριηράρχημα, ατος, τό, *the trierarch's crew*, Dem. ; and

τριηραρχία, ή, *the command of a trireme*, Arist. **II.** at Athens, *the fitting out of a trireme for the public service, a trierarchy*, Xen. Hence

τριηραρχικός, ή, όν, *of or for the trierarchy*, Dem.

τριήρ-αρχος, ὁ, *the captain of a trireme*, Hdt., Att. **II.** *at Athens, a trierarch, who had to fit out a trireme for the public service*, Ar., Thuc.

τριηρ-αύλης, ου, ὁ, (αὐλός) *the flute-player*, who gave the time to the rowers in the trireme, Dem.

τρι-ήρης (sub. ναῦς), ή, gen. εος, ους, Ion. ευς ; acc. εα, η : nom. pl. εες, εις : gen. τριηρέων, -ρῶν ; gen. dual τριήροιν : (τρίς, -ήρης) :—Lat. *triremis, a galley with three banks of oars*, the common form of the Greek ship-of-war, Hdt., etc. : first built by the Corinthians, Thuc. :—cf. θαλάμιος, ζυγίτης, θρανίτης. Hence

τριηρικός, ή, όν, *of or for a trireme*, Dem.

τριηρίτης [ῑ], ου, ὁ, *a trireme-man*, Hdt., Thuc.

τριηρο-ποιός, όν, (ποιέω) *building triremes*, Dem.

τρι-θάλασσος, Att. -ττος, ον, *touching on* or *connected with three seas*, Strab.

Τρι-κάρανος, ὁ, *the Three-headed*, a satirical attack on *three* cities, Sparta, Athens, Thebes, Luc. From

τρι-κάρηνος [ᾰ], ον, (κάρηνον) *three-headed*, Hes., Hdt.

τρί-κέφαλος, ον, (κεφαλή) *three-headed*, Luc.

τρί-κλινος, ον, (κλίνη) *with three couches*: as Subst., τρίκλινος (sub. οἶκος), ὁ, *a dining-room with three couches*, the Roman *triclinium*.

τρί-κλωστος, ον, *thrice-spun, three-twisted*, Anth.

τρί-κόλωνος, ον, (κολώνη) *three-hilled*, Orac. in Strab.

τρί-κόρυθος, ον ; and

τρί-κορυς, ῠθος, ὁ, *with triple plume*, Eur.

τρί-κόρυφος, ον, (κορυφή) *three-topped*, Strab.

τρί-κόρωνος, ον, (κορώνη) *thrice a crow's age*, Anth.

τρί-κρανος, ον, *three-headed*, of Cerberus, Soph., Eur.

τρί-κῡμία, ή, (κῦμα) *the third wave, a huge wave*, for the third was supposed to be the largest (as in Lat. the *fluctus decumanus*), Plat. :—metaph., τρ. κακῶν Aesch.

τρίλ-λιστος, ον, poët. for τρί-λιστος, (λίσσομαι) *thrice* (i. e. *often* or *earnestly*) *prayed for*, Il.

τρῑλογία, ή, *a trilogy*, v. τετραλογία.

τρί-λοφία, ή, *a triple crest*, Ar.

τρί-μάκαιρα, fem. as if from τρίμακαρ, *thrice-blest*, Anth.

τρί-μετρος, ον, (μέτρον) *of verses, consisting of three metres*; i. e. *in iambics, trochaics, and anapaestics, of three syzygies* (of two feet each) ; but *in dactylics of three single feet* : τρ. ἴαμβος an iambic verse *of*

three metres or *six feet, versus senarius*, Hdt. ; so τόνος τρίμετρος *trimeter verse*, Id. ; τρίμετρον, τό, Ar.

τρί-μηνος, ον, (μήν) *of three months*, Soph. ; so, ή τρίμηνος *a period of three months*, Hdt.

τρίμμα, ατος, τό, (τρίβω) *that which is rubbed*: metaph., like τρίβων II. 2, *a practised knave*, Ar.

τριμμός, ὁ, (τρίβω) *a beaten road*, Xen.

τρί-μοιρία, ή, (μοῖρα) *a triple portion, triple pay*, Xen.

τρί-μοιρος, ον, (μοῖρα) *threefold, triple*, Aesch.

τρί-μορφος, ον, (μορφή) *three-formed* :—in pl. = τρεῖς, Μοῖραι τρ. *the three* fates, Aesch.

Τρῑνακρία, ή, *Sicily*, a later form of Θρινακίη, Thuc.

τρίναξ [ῐ], ᾰκος, ή, (ἀκή) *a trident* or *three-pronged mattock*, Anth.

τριξός, ή, όν, Ion. for τρισσός.

τρί-οδος, ή, *a meeting of three roads*, Lat. *trivium*, Theogn., Eur., etc. **2.** Hecaté, Lat. *Trivia*, ἁ θεὸς ἐν τριόδοισι Theocr. ; οἷος ἐκ τριόδου i. e. *vulgar*, Luc.

τριόδους, όδοντος, ὁ, ή, *with three teeth, three-pronged* : as Subst., *a trident*, Pind.

Τριόπιον, τό, *a headland of Caria*, on which was a temple consecrated to Apollo, τὸ Τριοπικὸν ἱρόν, ὁ Τριόπιος ᾿Απόλλων Hdt.

τρι-όρχης, ου, ὁ, (ὄρχις) *a kind of hawk*, perh. *the buzzard*, Ar.

τριοτό, *a sound* imitative of a bird's voice, Ar.

τρί-παις, παιδος, ὁ, ή, *having three children*, Plut.

τρί-πᾰλαι, Adv. *long long ago*, Ar.

τρί-πάλαιστος or -αστος, ον, *three hands broad, long*, etc., Hdt.

τρί-παλτος, ον, (πάλλω) *thrice-brandished* ; metaph. *threefold, manifold*, Aesch.

τρί-πάνουργος [ᾰ], ον, *triply-base, an arch-rogue*, Anth.

τρί-πάχυιος [ᾰ], ον, (παχύς) or **τρι-πάχυντος**, ον, (πάχυνω) *thrice-fattened, thrice-gorged*, Aesch.

τρί-πέτηλος, ον, (πέτηλον) *three-leafed*, h. Hom.

τρί-πηχυς, υ, gen. εος, *three cubits long* or *tall*, Hdt., Att.

τρί-πίθηκίνος, η, ον, *thrice* or *thoroughly apish*, Anth.

τρίπλαξ, ᾰκος, ὁ, ή, (τρίς) *triple, threefold*, Lat. *triplex*, Il.

τριπλασιάζω, f. σω, *to triple, take three times*, Plut.

τρῑπλάσιος [ᾰ], α, ον, *thrice as many, thrice as much, thrice as great* as, c. gen., Ar., Plat., etc. : —absol., τριπλασίαν δύναμιν εἶχε (sc. τῆς προτέρας) Xen. **II.** τριπλάσιον as Adv., τριπλάσιον *thrice as much*, Ar.

τρί-πλεθρος, ον, (πλέθρον) *three πλέθρα wide*, Xen.

τρί-πλευρος, ον, (πλευρά) *three-sided*.

τριπλῇ, dat. fem. of τριπλόος.

τρί-πλόος, η, ον, contr. -πλοῦς, ῆ, οῦν, (τρεῖς) *triple, threefold*, ἐν τριπλαῖς ἀμαξιτοῖς = ἐν τριόδῳ, Soph. ; ὄνομα τρ. *compounded of three*, Arist. :—Att. neut. pl. τριπλᾶ, Aesch. :—dat. fem. τριπλῇ as Adv., Il., Luc.

τριπόδεσσι, Ep. for τρίποσι, dat. pl. of τρίπους.

τρί-πόδης, ου, ὁ, (πούς) *three feet long*, Hes.

τρίποδη-φορέω, f. ήσω, *to bring a tripod, offer it as a sign of victory*, Strab.

τρῑπόθητος, Dor. -ᾱτος, ον, *thrice* (i. e. *much*) *longed for*, Bion, Mosch.

τρί-πολις, εως, Ion. -ιος, ὁ, ή, *with three cities*, Pind.

τρί-πόλιστος, ον, (πολίζω) *thrice-repeated*, Soph.

τρί-πολος, ον, (πολέω) *thrice ploughed*, Hom., Hes.

τρῐπόνητος ἔρις, ἡ, a contest between three labouring women, Anth.

τρί-πορθος, ον, (πέρθω) thrice-wasted, Anth.

τρίπος [ῐ], ου, ὁ, poët. for sq., Il., Hes.

τρί-πους [ῐ], ποδος, ὁ, ἡ, -πουν, τό, three-footed, of or with three feet: and so I. measuring three feet, Hdt., Plat. II. going on three feet, of an old man who leans on a staff, Hes.; so, τρίποδας ὁδοὺς στείχει Aesch. III. with three feet, three-legged: 1. a tripod, a three-footed brass kettle or caldron, Hom.: —from a tripod of this kind (Lat. cortina) the Delphic Priestess delivered her oracles, Eur., Ar. 2. a three-legged table, Xen.

τριπτήρ, ῆρος, ὁ, (τρίβω) = sq.:—the vat into which the oil runs when pressed out: metaph., τρ. δικῶν a vat to receive the juice of law-suits, Ar.

τρίπτης, ου, ὁ, (τρίβω) a rubber, shampooer, Plut.

τρί-πτυχος, ον, (πτυχή) threefold, Lat. triplex, Il., Eur.

τρί-πωλος, ον, of or with three horses: τρ. ἅρμα δαιμόνων, of the three goddesses on Mount Ida, Eur.

τρίρ-ρῡμος, ον, with three poles, i. e. with four horses abreast, Aesch.

τρίς [ῐ], Adv. of τρεῖς, thrice, three times, Lat. ter, Hom., etc.; τρὶς τόσος thrice as much or many, Il., etc.; ἐς τρίς up to three times, even thrice, Hdt., Att.: —used to add force to a word in compds., such as τρισάθλιος, τρίσμακαρ, like Lat. ter beatus, thrice blest: —proverb., τρὶς ἓξ βάλλειν to throw thrice six, i. e. the highest throw (there being three dice), Aesch.

τρισ-άθλιος, α, ον, thrice-unhappy, Soph., etc.

τρισ-άλαστος, ον, thrice-tormented, Anth.

τρί-σᾱμος, ον, Dor. for τρίσημος.

τρισ-άριθμος, ον, thrice-numbered, Orac. ap. Luc.

τρισ-άσμενος, η, ον, thrice-pleased, most willing, Xen.

τρισ-άωρος, ον, thrice-untimely, Anth.

τρισ-δείλαιος, ον, = τρισάθλιος, Anth.

τρισ-δύστηνος, ον, = foreg., Anth.

τρισ-εινάς (sc. ἡμέρα), άδος, ἡ, the third ninth day in a month; i. e. the ninth day (ἡ ἐννεάς) of the third decad, the.29th, Hes.

τρισ-έπαρχος, ὁ, thrice an ἔπαρχος, i. e. Praetor, Anth.

τρισ-ευδαίμων, ον, thrice-happy, Luc.

τρισ-καίδεκα, v. τρεισ-καίδεκα.

τρισκαιδεκά-πηχυς, υ, thirteen cubits high, ἀνὴρ τρ., of a long lazy loom, Theocr.

τρισκαιδεκα-στάσιος [στᾰ], ον, (ἵστημι) of thirteen times the value of silver, Hdt.

τρισ-και-δέκατος, η, ον, thirteenth, Hom., etc.; ἡ τρισκαιδεκάτη (sc. ἡμέρα) the 13th day, Od.

τρισκαιδεκᾰ-φόρος, ον, fruiting thirteen times, Luc.

τρισκαιδεκ-έτης, ου, ὁ, (ἔτος) thirteen years old, Lys.

τρισ-κᾰκοδαίμων, ον, thrice unlucky, Ar.

τρί-σκαλμος, ον, with three oarpins; but νᾶες αἱ τρ. are simply = τριήρεις, Aesch.

τρισ-κατάρᾱτος, ον, thrice-accursed, Dem.

τρι-σκελής, ές, three-legged, ξόανον Theocr.

τρισ-κοπάνιστος [ᾰ], ον, thrice-kneaded, Batr.

τρίσ-μᾰκαρ, ᾰρος, ὁ, ἡ, thrice-blest, Od., Ar., etc.

τρισ-μᾰκάριος, α, ον, = foreg., Ar.

τρισ-μᾰκάριστος, η, ον, = τρίσμακαρ, Luc.

τρισ-μύριοι [ῠ], αι, α, thrice ten thousand, 30,000,

Hdt., Ar., etc.:—in sing. with a collective Subst., τρισμυρία ἵππος thirty thousand horse, Aesch.

τρισμῡριό-πᾰλαι, Adv. 30,000-times long-ago, Ar.

τρίσ-όλβιος, ον, thrice happy or fortunate, Anth.

τρίσ-ολυμπιο-νίκης [ῐ], ου, ὁ, (νικάω) thrice victorious at Olympia, Pind.

τρι-σπίθᾱμος, ον, (σπιθαμή) three spans long, Hes., Xen.

τρί-σπονδος, ον, (σπονδή) thrice-poured, τρ. χοαί a triple drink-offering, of honey, milk, and wine, Soph.

τρισσάτιος [ᾰ], α, ον, poët. for τρισσός, Anth.

τρισσόθεν, Adv. from three sides, Anth. From

τρισσός, Ion. τριξός, ή, όν, (τρίς) threefold, Lat. triplex, Eur., etc.:—Adv. -ῶς, Anth. II. in pl., = τρεῖς, Pind., Soph., etc.

τρί-στεγος, ον, (στέγη) of or with three stories: τὸ τρ. (sc. οἴκημα) the third story, N. T.

τριστοιχί, Adv. in three rows, Il., Hes. From

τρί-στοιχος, ον, in three rows, Od.:—threefold, Anth.

τρί-στομος, ον, (στόμα) three-edged or -pointed, Anth.

τρί-σύλλᾰβος, ον, (συλλαβή) trisyllabic, Luc.

τρισ-χίλιοι [χῑ], αι, α, three thousand, Il., etc.

τρισχῑλιοστός, ή, όν, the three-thousandth, Plat.

τρί-σώμᾰτος, ή, όν, three-bodied, Lat. tricorpor, Aesch.

τρῑτᾰγωνιστέω, f. ήσω, to be a τριταγωνιστής, Dem. From

τρῑτ-ᾰγωνιστής, οῦ, ὁ, on the stage, the player who took the third part, a third-rate actor, Dem.

τρῑταῖος, α, ον, (τρίτος) on the third day, used with Verbs so as to agree with the subject, τριταῖοι ἐγένοντο ἐν τῇ Ἀττικῇ Hdt.; ἐσβεβληκὼς τριταῖος ἐς Μηλιέας having invaded Melis three days before, Id.; τρ. γενόμενος after being three days dead, Id.:—τριταῖος (sc. πυρετός), ὁ, a tertian fever, Plat. II. of events, lasting three days, Eur. III. generally for τρίτος, Id.

τρῐ-τᾰλαντιαῖος, α, ον, = sq., Plut.

τρῐτάλαντος [τᾰ], ον, (τάλαντον) of three talents, Ar. 2. worth three talents, Isae.

τρί-τάλᾱς, αινα, ᾰν, thrice-wretched, Eur., Anth.

τρί-τάνυστος [ᾰ], ον, thrice-stretched, very long, Anth.

τρίτᾰτος [ῐ], α, ον, poët. lengthd. for τρίτος, Il.

τρῐτη-μόριος, α, ον, (μόριον) forming a third part of, c. gen., Hdt. II. as Subst., τριτημόριον, τό, a third part, a third, Id., Thuc., etc.

τρῐτημορίς, ίδος, ἡ, = τριτημόριον, Hdt.

τρῐτο-βάμων [ᾰ], ον, (βαίνω) forming a third foot, Eur.

Τρῑτο-γένεια, ἡ, (γίγνομαι) Trito-born, a name of Athena, Hom., Hes. (From the Lake Τριτωνίς in Libya, near which the goddess was born, Eur. Others interpret τριτογένεια born on the third day of the month, or the third child after Apollo and Artemis.)

Τρῑτο-γενής, έος, ὁ, = foreg., h. Hom., Orac. ap. Hdt.

τρί-τοκος, ον, (τίκτω) bearing three times or three at a time, Anth.

τρίτος [ῐ], η, ον, (τρεῖς) the third, Lat. tertius, Hom., etc.; τρίτος ἦλθε he came himself the third, i. e. with two others, Od.; so, τρίτος αὐτός, Att.:—the third often appears as completing the tale, τρίτην ἐπενδίδωμι (sub. πληγήν) the third and finishing stroke, Aesch.; cf. σωτήρ I. 2. II. τρίτη, with or without ἡμέρα, the day after to-morrow, ἐς τρίτην ἡμέραν Ar.; τῇ τρίτῃ Xen.;—but, χθὲς καὶ τρ. ἡμέραν yesterday and the day before, Id. III. τρίτον as Adv., thirdly, Soph., Eur., etc.; also, τὸ τρίτον Hom., Att. IV.

τρίτα, τά, 1. (sub. ἱερά) *a sacrifice to the dead, offered the third day after the funeral,* Isae. 2. **τὰ τρίτα λέγειν τινί** to play *the third part* to any one, Dem.

τρῑτό-σπονδος, ον, (σπονδή) **τρ.** αἰών *a life in which one has poured the third libation* (to Ζεὺς Σωτήρ), i. e. *complete* felicity, Aesch.

τρῑτό-σπορος, ον, (σπείρω) *sown for the third time,* **τρ.** γονή *the third generation,* Aesch.

τριττύς, ύος, ἡ, *the number three,* Lat. *ternio*: esp. *a sacrifice of three animals,* a boar, goat, and ram, Ar. II. at Athens, *a third of the* φυλή, Dem., Aeschin.

Τρῑτώ, οῦς, ἡ, = Τριτογένεια, Anth.

Τρίτων [ῐ], ωνος, ὁ, *Triton,* a sea-god, son of Poseidon and Amphitrité, Hes. :—pl. **Τρίτωνες,** *Tritons,* a lower race of sea-gods, Mosch. 2. *the god of the Libyan lake Tritonis,* Hdt. II. *a river in Libya,* joining the lake Tritonis with the sea, Id., Aesch.

Τρῑτωνιὰς λίμνη, ἡ, *the Libyan lake Tritonis,* Eur.

Τρῑτωνίς, ίδος, ἡ, *Tritonis,* a lake in Libya famous for old Greek legends, Pind., Hdt.; cf. Τριτογένεια.

τρῐφάσιος [ᾰ], α, ον, (τρεῖς) *threefold,* Lat. *triplex,* Hdt. :—in pl., much the same as τρεῖς, Id.

τρῐφίλητος [ῐ], Dor. **-ᾱτος, ον,** *thrice-beloved,* Theocr.

τρί-φυλλον, τό, *a plant, tre-foil, clover,* Hdt.

τρί-φῡλος, ον, (φυλή) *of three tribes,* τριφύλους ποιέειν to divide *into three tribes,* Hdt.

τρίχᾰ [ῐ], Adv., (τρίς) *threefold, in three parts,* Lat. *trifariam,* Hom.; c. gen., **τρ.** νυκτὸς ἔην 'twas in the *third watch* of the night, Od.; τρίχα σχίζειν τι Hdt.

τρῐχ-άϊκες [-ᾱϊ-], οἱ, *the threefold people,* i. e. the Dorians, so called from their three tribes, Od. (Deriv. uncertain.)

τρῐ-χάλεπτος, ον, (χαλέπτω) *very angry,* Anth.

τρί-χαλκον, τό, *a coin worth three* χαλκοῖ, Theophr.

τρί-χᾱλος, ον, Dor. for τρίχηλος, (χηλή) *cloven in three,* Aesch.

τρῐχῇ, Adv., common Prose form of τρίχα, *in* or *into three parts,* Hdt., Xen. II. *in three ways, triply,* Plat.

τρῐχθά, Adv., Ep. lengthd. form of τρίχα, *in* or *into three parts,* Hom.

τρίχινος, η, ον, (θρίξ, τριχ-ός) *of hair,* Xen.

τρῑχίς, ίδος, ἡ, (θρίξ) *a kind of anchovy full of small hair-like bones,* Ar.

τρῑχό-βρως, ωτος, ὁ, ἡ, *eating hair*: hence τριχόβρωτες, = σῆτες or θρῖπες, *moths,* Ar.

τρῐ-χοίνῑκος, ον, (χοῖνιξ) *holding* or *measuring three* χοίνικες, Xen.: Comic phrase, **τρ.** ἔπος *a most capacious* word, Ar.

τρῐ-χόλωτος, ον, *thrice-detested,* Anth.

τρί-χο-μαλλος, ον, *hair-fleeced,* Anth.

τρῐχόομαι, (θρίξ, τριχός) Pass. *to be furnished with hair,* Arist.

τρῐχορρυέω, f. ήσω, *to shed the hair,* Ar. From

τρῐχορ-ρυής, ές, (ῥέω) *shedding the hair.*

τρῐχοῦ, (τρίχα) Adv. *in three places,* Hdt.

τρῐχό-φοιτος ἴουλος, *the first down of youth just passing into hair,* Anth.

τρίχωμα, ατος, τό, (τριχόομαι) *a growth of hair, hair,* Hdt., Xen.; ἐν γενείῳ συλλογὴ τριχώματος, i. e. just at the age of manhood, Aesch.

τρῖψαι, aor. 1 inf. of τρίβω.

τριψ-ημερέω, (τρῖψαι, ἡμέρα) *to waste the day,* Lat. *terere tempus,* Ar.

τρῖψις, εως, ἡ, (τρίβω) *rubbing, friction,* Plat., etc. II. *resistance to the touch when rubbed, firmness,* Hdt. III. τρίψεις *potted meats,* Anth.

τρι-ώβολον, τό, (ὀβολός) *a three-obol-piece, a half-drachma,* at Athens, *the pay of the dicasts* for a day's sitting, first given by Pericles, Ar. 2. *the pay of the marine soldiery* (ἐπιβάται), Thuc.

τρι-ώροφος, ον, (ὄροφος) *of three stories* or *floors,* Hdt.

τρι-ώρυγος [ῠ], ον, (ὀργυιά) *of three fathoms,* Xen.

Τροία, Ion. **Τροίη, ἡ,** *Troy,* whether of the city, 'Troy-town,' Hom., etc.; or the country, *the Troad,* Il. :—also **Τροία** as trisyll., Soph.; Dor. **Τρωία** Pind., Aesch.; contr. **Τρῴα** Pind. :—hence **Τροίαθεν,** Ion. **-ηθεν,** *from Troy,* Od.; ἀπὸ Τροίηθε Il.; Dor. **Τρωΐαθεν** Pind. :—**Τροίανδε,** Ion. **-ηνδε,** *to Troy,* Il., etc.; Dor. **Τρῴανδε** Pind.

Τροιζήν, ῆνος, ἡ, *Troezen* in Argolis, Il., Hdt., etc. :—Adj. **Τροιζήνιος, α, ον,** Eur.; fem. **Τροιζηνίς, ίδος,** Thuc.: οἱ Τροιζήνιοι *the people,* Hdt.

τρομερός, ά, όν, (τρέμω) *trembling,* Eur.: *trembling for fear, quaking,* Id. II. *fearful,* Id.

τρομέω, f. ήσω, (τρόμος) *to tremble, quake, quiver,* esp. *from fear,* Il. :—c. inf. *to fear to do,* Theocr. II. c. acc. *to tremble before* or *at a person, to stand in awe of,* Hom.—In each sense Hom. uses both Act. and Med., but only in pres. and impf.; Ep. and Ion. **τρομέοιτο** for τρομέοιντο, Il.; Ion. part. **τρομεύμενος** Solon.

τρόμος, ὁ, (τρέμω) *a trembling, quaking, quivering,* esp. *from fear,* Il., Aesch. 2. *from cold,* Plat.

τροπαία (sc. πνοή), ἡ, *an alternating wind* :—metaph., λήματος, φρενὸς τροπαία *a change in the spirit* of one's mind, Aesch.; **τρ.** κακῶν *a release from evils,* Id.

τρόπαιον, τό, *a trophy,* Lat. *tropaeum,* Trag., etc.; i. e. *a monument* of the enemy's *defeat* (τροπή II), consisting of arms taken from the enemy, hung on trees or posts; the common phrase was στῆσαι or στήσασθαι **τρ.** to set up *trophies,* Eur., Thuc.; ἱδρῦσαι Eur.; c. gen. pers., τροπαῖα τῶν πολεμίων *a trophy* won from the enemy, Id.; so, τροπαῖ' ἔστησε τῶν ἐμῶν χερῶν Soph.; and, στῆσαι τροπαῖα κατὰ or ἀπὸ τῶν πολεμίων, Lat. *triumphare de aliquo,* Oratt.

τροπαῖος, α, ον, *of* or *for defeat* (τροπή II), ἐχθρῶν θύειν τροπαῖα (sc. ἱερά) *a sacrifice for their defeat,* Eur.; Ζεὺς Τρ., as *giver of victory,* Soph. 2. *causing rout,* Ἕκτορος ὄμμασι τροπαῖοι, i. e. *terrible to the eyes* of Hector, Eur. II. like ἀποτρόπαιος, *averting,* Lat. *averruncus,* Ζεύς Soph.

τροπαιο-φόρος, ον, (φέρω) *bearing trophies,* Plut.

τρόπᾱλις, ιδος, ἡ, *a bundle, bunch,* σκορόδων τρ. *a bunch* of garlic, Ar. (Deriv. unknown.)

τροπέω, poët. form for τρέπω *to turn,* Il.

τροπή, ἡ, (τρέπω) *a turn, turning*: 1. τροπαὶ ἠελίοιο *the tropics* or *solstices,* i. e. *midsummer* and *midwinter,* Lat. *solstitium* and *bruma,* when the sun *appears to turn his course* and cross the ecliptic. Hom. speaks of τροπαὶ ἠελίοιο as denoting a point in the heavens, prob. to the westward, Od.; τροπαὶ θεριναί and χειμεριναί, Hdt., Att. :—when τροπαί is used alone, it mostly refers to *the winter solstice,* περὶ ἡλ᾽ου τροπάς

(sc. χειμερινάς) Thuc. 2. *a turn, change,* = μεταβολή, Aeschin., Plut. 3. τροπαὶ λέξεως *a change of speech by figures or tropes* (τρόποι), Luc. II. *the turning of the enemy, putting* him *to flight, a rout,* τροπήν (or τροπάς) τινος ποιεῖν or ποιεῖσθαι *to put* one *to flight,* Hdt., Ar., etc.; τροπὴ γίγνεται Hdt.; ἐν τροπῇ δορός *in the rout* caused by the spear, Soph.

τροπικός, ή, όν, (τροπή) *of the solstice,* ὁ τροπικός (sc. κύκλος) *the tropic* or *solstice,* Arist.; αἱ τρ. ἡμέραι Id. II. *in Rhetoric, tropical, figurative.*

τρόπις, ἡ, τρόπιος, acc. τρόπιν, (τρέπω) *a ship's keel,* Od., Hdt.; τρόπεις θέσθαι *to lay* the *keel,* Plut.; and metaph., λέγε τὴν τρόπιν τοῦ πράγματος.

τροπός, ὁ, (τρέπω) *a twisted leathern thong,* with which the oar was fastened to the thole, Od.

τρόπος, ὁ, (τρέπω) *a turn, direction, course, way,* Hdt. II. *a way, manner, fashion,* τρόπῳ τοιῷδε *in such wise,* Hdt.; τίνι τρόπῳ; Lat. *quomodo? how?* Aesch., etc.; ποίῳ τρ.; Id.; ἑνί γε τῷ τρ. *in one way or other,* Ar.; παντὶ τρόπῳ *by all means,* Aesch.; οὐδενί τρ., μηδενί τρ. *in no wise, by no means, on no account,* Hdt., etc. :—so in pl., τρόποισι ποίοις; Soph.; ναυκλήρου τρόποις Id. 2. absol. in acc., τίνα τρόπον; *how?* Ar.; τρ. τινά *in a manner,* Eur.; οὐδένα, μηδένα τρ. Xen.; πίτυος τρόπον *after the manner* of a pine, Hdt.; in pl., κεχώρισται τοὺς τρόπους *in its ways,* Id.; πάντας τρόπους *in all ways,* Plat. 3. with Preps., γυναικὸς ἐν τρόποις, ἐν τρ. Ἰξίονος Aesch. :—ὄρνιθος τρ. Luc.; κατὰ πάντα τρ. Ar., etc.; κατὰ πάντας τρόπους Id. :—κατὰ τρόπον, absol., *fitly, duly,* Lat. *rite,* Isocr. III. *of persons, a way of life, habit, custom,* Pind.; μῶν ἡλιαστά τρ.; Answ. μάλλα θατέρου τρ. are you a Heliast?—No, but of the other *sort,* Ar. :—a man's *character, temper,* τρόπου ἡσυχίου *of a quiet temper,* Hdt.; οὐ τοὐμοῦ τρόπου *not* to my *taste,* Ar.; πρὸς τοῦ Κύρου τρόπου Xen.; so in pl. *ways, habits,* σκληρὸς τοὺς τρόπους Ar.; ὑπηρετεῖν τοῖς τρόποις τινός Id. IV. *in Music,* τρ. Λύδιος Pind.; ᾠδῆς τρόπος Plat. V. *in speaking or writing, manner, style,* Isocr. :—but in Rhetoric, *tropes, figures,* Cic.

τροπο-φορέω, f. ήσω, *to bear with,* τινά N. T.

τροπόω, f. ώσω, (τροπός) *to furnish the oar with its thong:* Med., τροποῦτο κώπην ἀμφὶ σκαλμόν *fastened* his oar *by its thong* round the thole, Aesch. :—Pass., of the oar, *to be furnished with its thong,* Ar. Hence

τροπωτήρ, ῆρος, ὁ, = τροπός, Ar., Thuc.

τροφᾱλίς, ίδος, ἡ, (τρέφω 1) *a piece* of cheese, Ar.

τροφεῖα, τά, (τροφεύω) *pay for bringing up, the wages of a nurse* or *rearer,* Aesch., etc. II. βίου τροφεῖα one's *living, food,* Soph.; τροφεῖα μητρός *mother's milk,* Eur.

τροφεύς, έως, ὁ, (τροφή) *one who rears* or *brings up, a foster-father,* Soph., Eur.; of a woman, *a nurse,* Aesch. :—metaph. of the plains and fountains of Troy, χαίρετ' ὦ τροφῆς ἐμοί *ye who reared* me, Soph.; πάσης κακίας τρ. *one who fosters* all wickedness, Plat.

τροφή, ἡ, (τρέφω) *nourishment, food, victuals,* Hdt., Soph., etc.; ἡ καθ' ἡμέραν τρ. one's *daily bread,* Thuc.; τροφὴν παρέχειν *to furnish provisions, forage,* Id. 2. βίου τροφή or τροφαί *a way of life, livelihood, living,* Soph.; so, τροφή alone, δουλίαν ἕξειν τροφήν Id.; then,

simply, *a mode of life, life,* Plat. 3. *that which provides sustenance,* as the bow of Philoctetes, Soph. II. *nurture, rearing, bringing up,* Hdt., Trag.; in pl., ἐν τροφαῖσιν *while in the nursery,* Aesch., etc. 2. *education,* Eur., etc. III. sometimes, in Poets, *a brood,* νέα τροφή, of young people, Soph.; ἀρνῶν τροφαί, i. e. *young lambs,* Eur.

τροφίας, ου, ὁ, (τρέφω) *brought up in the house, stall-fed,* Plut.

τρόφῐμος, ον, and η, ον, (τροφή) *nourishing:* c. gen., γᾶ τρόφιμε τῶν ἐμῶν τέκνων Eur. 2. as Subst., τρόφιμος, ὁ, *the master of the house,* ἡ τροφίμη *the mistress,* Anth. II. pass. *nourished and reared up, a nursling, foster-child,* Eur.; οἱ τρόφιμοι *our nurslings, pupils,* Plat., Xen.

τρόφις, ὁ, ἡ, τρόφι, τό, gen. ιος, (τρέφω) *well-fed, stout, large,* τρόφι κῦμα *a huge, swollen wave,* Il.; of men, ἐπεὰν γένωνται τρόφιες οἱ παῖδες *when the children grow big,* Hdt.

τροφόεις, εσσα, εν, (τρέφω) *well-fed:* hence *large, big,* of waves, Hom.

τροφός, ὁ and ἡ, (τρέφω) *a feeder, rearer, nurse,* Od., Hdt., Att.: metaph., of a city, Pind., Aesch.

τροφοφορέω, f. ήσω, *to bring* one *nourishment, maintain, sustain,* N. T.

Τροφώνιος, ὁ, the builder of the temple of Apollo at Delphi, h. Hom., Hdt.; καταβαίνων ὥσπερ ἐς Τροφωνίου (sc. ἄντρον) Ar.

τροχάζω, f. σω, (τροχός) *to run like a wheel, to run along, run quickly,* Hdt., Xen., etc.; τρ. ἵπποις, of a charioteer, Eur.

τροχαῖος, α, ον, *running, tripping,* Anth. II. τροχαῖος (sc. πούς), ὁ, *a trochee* or *foot consisting of a long and short syllable,* used in quick time, Plat., Arist.

τροχᾰλός, ή, όν, (τρέχω) *running,* τροχαλόν τινα τιθέναι *to make* one *run quick,* Hes.; τρ. ὄχοι *swift-rolling,* Eur.

τροχερός, ά, όν, (τροχός) *running, tripping,* Arist.

τροχηλᾰτέω, f. ήσω, *to drive a chariot: to drive about, drive round and round,* Eur.

τροχ-ηλάτης [ᾰ], ου, ὁ, (ἐλαύνω) *one who guides wheels,* i. e. *a charioteer,* Soph., Eur.

τροχ-ήλᾰτος, ον, (ἐλαύνω) *driven on wheels, wheel-drawn,* Aesch., Soph. 2. *dragged by* or *at the wheels,* Eur. 3. metaph. *hurried along like a wheel* or *chariot,* Id.; μανία τρ. *whirling madness,* Id.

τροχιά, ἡ, (τροχός) *the round of a wheel,* Anth.

τροχίζω, f. Att. ιῶ, (τροχός) *to turn round on the wheel, torture,* Arist.

τροχιλία, ἡ, *the sheaf of a pulley, roller of a windlass,* and the like, Lat. *trochlea,* Ar.

τροχίλος [ῐ], ὁ, (τρέχω) *a small bird, the sandpiper,* said to pick leeches out of the crocodile's throat, Hdt.

τροχιός, ά, όν, = τροχόεις, *round,* Anth.

τρόχις, ὁ, (τρέχω) *a runner, messenger,* Aesch.

τροχο-δῑνέομαι, Pass. *to whirl* or *roll round,* Aesch.

τροχο-ειδής, ές, (εἶδος) *round as a wheel, circular,* Theogn., Hdt.

τροχόεις, εσσα, εν, *round as a wheel, round,* Anth.

τροχο-ποιέω, f. ήσω, *to make wheels,* Ar.

τροχός, ὁ, (τρέχω) *anything that runs round:* I. *a round cake,* Od. II. *a wheel,* Il., Soph.;

τροχοὺς μιμεῖσθαι to imitate *wheels*, of one who bends back so as to form a wheel, Xen. **2.** *a potter's wheel*, Il. **3.** *the wheel of a stage-machine*, Ar. **4.** *the wheel of torture*, ἐπὶ τοῦ τροχοῦ στρεβλοῦσθαι Id., etc.; τῷ τροχῷ τινα προσδεῖν Luc. **III.** a boy's *hoop*, the Graecus trochus of Horat. **IV.** τροχοὶ γῆς, θαλάσσης *circles* or *zones* of land, sea, Plat. **V.** *a ring* on the bit of a bridle, Xen.

B. τρόχος, ὁ, *a running, course*, μὴ πολλοὺς τρόχους ἁμιλλητῆρας ἠλίου not many racing *courses* of the sun, i. e. not many days, Soph.; παῖδες ἐκ τρόχων πεπαυμένοι Eur. **2.** *a race-course*, Id.

τρύβλιον, τό, *a cup, bowl*, Ar.

τρυγάω, f. ήσω, (τρύγη):   **I.** with acc. of the fruit or crop, *to gather in*, Lat. *vindemiare*, ἑτέρας [σταφυλὰς] τρυγόωσιν Od.; καρπόν Hdt. :—metaph., τρυγήσομεν αὐτήν (sc. Εἰρήνην) Ar. :—Pass., τετρυγημένοι καθ᾽ ὥραν gathered in due season, Luc. **2.** absol., Ar.   **II.** with acc. of the trees or ground, ὅτε τρυγόωεν ἀλωήν (Ep. opt. for τρυγῷεν) when they *gathered fruit off* the vineyard, Il. **2.** proverb., ἐρήμας τρυγᾶν (sc. ἀμπέλους) *to strip* unwatched vines, i. e. to be bold where there is nothing to fear, Ar.

ΤΡΥ'ΓΗ [ῠ], ἡ, *ripe fruit, a grain-crop, corn*, οὐδὲ τρύγην οἴσεις h. Hom. **2.** *the vintage*, Anth.

τρυγητήρ, ῆρος, ὁ, *one who gathers grapes*, Lat. *vindemiator*, Hes. [with ῡ.]

τρύγητος, ὁ, (τρύγάω) *a vintage, harvest*, Plut., Luc. **2.** *the time thereof, the harvest* or *vintage*, Thuc.

τρύγη-φόρος, ον, (φέρω) *bearing fruits*, esp. wine, h. Hom.

τρυγικός, ή, όν, *of lees*, = κωμῳδικός, Ar.

τρυγο-δαίμων, ονος, ὁ, Com. word for τρυγῳδός, with a play on κακοδαίμων, *a poor-devil poet*, Ar.

τρύγ-οιπος [ῠ], ὁ, (τρύξ, ἷπος) *a straining-cloth* for wine, Ar.

τρυγόνιον, τό, Dim. of τρυγών I, Anth.

τρυγόωεν, Ep. for τρυγῷεν, 3 pl. opt. of τρυγάω.

τρυγῳδία, ἡ, = κωμῳδία, Ar.; and

τρυγῳδικός, ή, όν, = κωμῳδικός, Ar.   From

τρυγ-ῳδός, ὁ, (τρύξ, ᾠδή) *a lees-singer*, = κωμῳδός, because the singers *smeared their faces with lees* (peruncti faecibus ora, Hor.), Ar.

τρυγών, όνος, ἡ, *the turtle-dove*, Ar.   From

τρύζω, (Root ΤΡΥΓ), Ep. impf. τρύζεσκον: aor. 1 ἔτρυξα: mostly in pres. and impf. :—*to make a low murmuring sound, to coo*, of the note of the ὀλολυγών, Theocr. :—metaph. of men, *to mutter, murmur*, Il. (Formed from the sound.)

τρυμαλιά, ἡ, (τρύω) = τρύμη, *a hole*, ἡ τρ. τῆς ῥαφίδος *the eye* of the needle, N. T.

τρύμη [ῠ], ἡ, (τρύω) *a hole*: metaph. *a sharp fellow, sly knave*, Ar.

τρύξ, ἡ, gen. τρυγός, (akin to τρύγη) *new wine not yet fermented, wine with the lees in it, must*, Lat. *mustum*, Hdt., Ar.   **II.** *the lees of wine*, Lat. *faex*, Hdt., Ar.:—metaph. of *an old man* or *woman*, Ar.

τρύπᾰνον [ῠ], τό, *a carpenter's tool, a borer, auger*, Lat. *terebra*, worked by a thong, Od., Eur.

τρυπάω, f. ήσω: Pass., pf. τετρύπημαι: (τρύω) :—*to bore, pierce through*, Od. :—Pass., τὰ ὦτα τετρυπημένος *having* one's ears *pierced for earrings*, Xen.;

ψῆφος τετρυπημένη *the pebble* of condemnation *which had a hole in it*, Aeschin. **2.** τρ. τῷ ποδὶ τὴν βελόνην *to force* the point *through* the foot, Anth.

τρύπη, ἡ, (τρύω) *a hole*, Anth.

τρύπημα [ῠ], ατος, τό, (τρυπάω) *a hole*, τρ. νεώς, i. e. one of the holes through which the oars worked, Ar. : like τρυμαλιά, *the eye* of a needle, N. T.

τρυπῶ, 3 sing. opt. of τρυπάω.

τρυσ-άνωρ, ορος, ὁ, ἡ, (τρύω) *wearying a man*, Soph.

τρῡσί-βιος, ον, (τρύω) *wearing out life*, Ar.

τρῠτάνη [ᾰ], ἡ, *the tongue of a balance*, and generally, *a balance, pair of scales*, Lat. *trutina*, Ar., Dem. (Deriv. uncertain.)

τρυφάλεια, ἡ, *a helmet*, Il. (Deriv. uncertain.)

τρῠφάω, f. ήσω, (τρυφή) *to live softly, delicately, luxuriously, to fare sumptuously*, Eur. :—part. τρυφῶν as Adj. *delicate, effeminate, luxurious, voluptuous*, Ar., Plat.; τὸ τρυφῶν, as Subst., *effeminacy*, Ar. **II.** *to be licentious, revel, run riot, wax wanton*, Eur., etc.; *to be extravagant*, Arist. **III.** *to give oneself airs, be fastidious*, Eur., Plat.

τρῠφεραίνομαι, Pass. *to be fastidious*, τρυφερανθείς *with a coxcomb's airs*, Ar.

τρῠφερός, ά, όν, (τρυφή) *delicate, dainty*, Eur., Anth. **II.** of persons, *effeminate, luxurious, voluptuous*, Ar., etc. :—τὸ τρυφερόν *effeminacy*, ἐς τὸ τρυφερώτερον *to more effeminate habits*, Thuc. :—neut. as Adv., τρυφερῶς *voluptuously*, Ar.; τρ. λαλεῖν *to speak softly*, Theocr.

τρῠφή, ἡ, (θρύπτω) *softness, delicacy, daintiness*, Eur., Plat., etc. :—in pl. *luxuries, daintinesses*, Lat. *deliciae*, Eur. **II.** *luxuriousness, wantonness*, Plat. **III.** *daintiness, insolence, fastidiousness*, Id.

τρῠφηλός, ή, όν, rare poët. form of τρυφερός, Anth.

τρῠφημα, ατος, τό, *that in which one takes pride, a pride*, Eur.

τρῠφος, εος, τό, (θρύπτω) *that which is broken off, a piece, morsel, lump*, Od., Hdt.

τρῠχηρός, ά, όν, (τρῦχος) *ragged, tattered*, Eur.

τρύχνος, ἡ, *nightshade*, used as a symbol of *sweet forgetfulness*, Theocr.

τρῠχόομαι, Pass. *to be worn out*, pf. part. τετρυχωμένος Thuc.

τρῦχος, εος, τό, (τρύω) *a worn out garment, a rag, shred*, Eur.;—in pl. *rags, tatters*, Id.

τρύχω [ῠ], f. τρύξω, (τρύω) *to wear out, waste, consume*, Od., Hes.; πτωχὸν τρύξοντά τε αὐτόν a beggar *to eat him out of house and home*, Od.; τρύχει ψυχὰν *distresses, afflicts* the soul, Soph.; τρ. στρατείαις τὴν πόλιν Xen. :—Pass. *to be worn out*, Od., Soph., etc. :—τρύχεσθαί τινος *to pine away for* some one, Eur.

ΤΡΥ'Ω, f. τρύσω [ῠ]: Pass., pf. τέτρῡμαι :—*to rub down, wear out*, Aesch. :—Pass. *to be worn out*, τετρῦσθαι ἐς τὸ ἔσχατον κακοῦ Hdt.; τετρυμένος ταλαιπωρίῃσι Id.

Τρῳάς, άδος, ἡ, contr. for Τρωιάς.

τρωγάλια, τά, (τρώγω) *fruits eaten at dessert, figs, nuts, sweetmeats*, Ar.

τρώγλη, ἡ, (τρώγω) *a hole formed by gnawing, a mouse's hole*, Batr., Babr.

τρωγλο-δύτης [ῠ], ου, ὁ, (δύω) *one who creeps into holes* :—Τρωγλοδύται, οἱ, *Troglodytes, Cave-men*, an Aethiopian tribe, Hdt.

τρωγλο-δύων, part. with no indic. in use, *creeping into a hole*, of a mouse, Batr.

ΤΡΩ'ΓΩ : f. τρώξομαι : aor. 1 ἔτρωξα : aor. 2 ἔτρᾰγον : —Pass., pf. τέτρωγμαι :—*to gnaw, nibble, munch*, of herbivorous animals, as mules, Od.; of swine, Ar.; of cattle, Theocr. II. of men, *to eat* vegetables or fruit, Hdt., Ar.

Τρωίαθεν, Adv. *from Troy*, Pind.

Τρωιάς, contr. Τρῳάς, άδος, fem. of Τρώιος, *Trojan*, Od.; Τρωιάδες γυναῖκες, or alone, Τρωιάδες Il. II. γῆ Τρῳάς *the Troad*, Soph.; so ἡ Τρωάς Hdt.

Τρωικός, ή, όν, (Τρώς) *Trojan*, Il., Soph., etc.; τὰ Τρωικά *the times of Troy*, Hdt.

Τρώιος, η, ον, contr. Τρῳός, *of Tros*, Il. II. *Trojan*, Ib.

τρωκτά, τά, v. τρωκτός.

τρώκτης, ου, ὁ, (τρώγω) *a gnawer, nibbler* : Phoenician traffickers are called τρῶκται, *greedy knaves*, Od.; so, τρῶκται χεῖρες *greedy* hands, Anth.

τρωκτός, ή, όν, verb. Adj. of τρώγω, *to be eaten raw : eatable*, Hdt. II. τρωκτά, τά, = τρωγάλια, Id.

τρῶμα, τρωματίζω, τρωματίης, Ion. for τραυμ-.

τρώμᾱ, ἡ, Dor. for *τραύμη = τραῦμα, Pind.

Τρωξ-άρτης, ου, ὁ, (ἄρτος) *Bread-gnawer*, Batr.

τρώξιμος, ον, = τρωκτός, Theocr.

τρῶξις, εως, ἡ, (τρώγω) *a biting*, τῶν ὀνύχων Arist.

Τρῳός, v. Τρώιος.

Τρωο-φθόρος, ον, (φθείρω) *destructive to the Trojans* or *to Troy*, Anth.

τρωπάω, Frequent. of τρέπω, *to turn constantly, change* its *notes*, of the nightingale, Od. :—Med. *to turn oneself, turn about*, Hom.

Τρώς, Τρωός, ὁ, *Tros*, the mythic founder of Troy, Il. II. pl. Τρῶες, Τρώων, οἱ, *Trojans*, Hom., etc.

τρωτός, ή, όν, verb. Adj. of τιτρώσκω, *to be wounded, vulnerable*, Il., Att.

τρωχάω, Frequent. of τρέχω, *to run fast, gallop*, Hom.

τύ, Dor. nom. for σύ. II. Dor. acc. for σέ.

τυβί, τό, an Egypt. winter month, Hdt.

τυγχάνω (Root ΤΥΚ) Ep. impf. τύγχανον : f. τεύξομαι : aor. 2 ἔτυχον, Ep. τύχον, Ep. subj. τύχωμι, -ῃσι : Ep. also aor. 1 ἐτύχησα : pf. τετύχηκα, later τέτευχα : 3 sing. Ion. plqpf. ἐτετεύχεε :—Pass., aor. 1 ἐτεύχθην : pf. τέτευγμαι.

A. *to hit*, esp. *to hit a mark* with an arrow, Hom., etc. : he mostly constructs it with acc., when the object hit is alive, with gen. when it is lifeless ; so, τ. τοῦ σκοποῦ Xen. ;—a prep. is sometimes added, κατὰ κληῖδα, κατὰ ζωστῆρα τυχήσας [τινά] Il. ;—absol., ἤμβροτες οὐδ' ἔτυχες Ib.; the part. τυχών is often joined with βάλλειν, οὐτᾶν, etc., Ib. II. *to hit upon, light upon* : 1. *to meet by chance, meet with, fall in with* a person, absol., Od.; c. gen., Aesch., etc. :—aor. 2 part. ὁ τυχών, *the first one meets, any one*, Lat. *quivis*, Hes., Plat., etc.; οἱ τυχόντες *every-day men, the vulgar*, Xen.; so, τὸ τυχόν *any chance thing*, Plat. 2. *to meet with, hit, reach, gain, get, obtain* a thing, and in the past tenses (like κέκτημαι), *to be in possession of*, have, c. gen., Od.; c. acc. :—after Hom. also c. acc., τ. μισθόν Hdt. ; τὰ πρόσφορα Aesch., etc. :—gen. pers. added, *to obtain* a thing *from* a person, τ. τί τινος Soph.; τινὸς παρά τινος Od. 3. also in bad sense, βίης

τυχεῖν *to meet with, suffer* violence, Hdt.; τ. κακῶν Eur. 4. absol. *to hit the mark, to make a hit*, Il., Att. ; so, τυχόντες καλῶς Aesch. 5. *to have the lot* or *fate*, ὅς κε τύχῃ *whoever draws the lot* (to die), Il.

B. intr. *to happen to be at* a place, εἴπερ τύχῃσι μάλα σχεδόν *if by chance she be* quite near, Il., etc. 2. of events, and things generally, *to happen to* one, *befal* one, *fall to* one's *lot*, c. dat. pers., Ib., Att. ; also *to turn out well*, Od. 3. impers., ὅπως ἐτύγχανεν *as it chanced*, i. e. *without any rule, indefinitely*, Eur. ; ὡς or ὥσπερ ἔτυχεν Xen. ; ὁπότε τύχοι *when it chanced, sometimes*, Plat. II. joined with a part., τὰ νοέων τυγχάνω *which I have just now in* my mind, Hdt. ; ὃ τυγχάνω μαθών *which I have just learnt*, Soph. ; ἔτυχον στρατευόμενοι *they were just then engaged* in an expedition, Thuc. ;—in phrase τυγχάνω ὤν, simply = εἰμί, Aesch., Soph., etc. 2. the part. is often omitted, ἔνδον γὰρ ἀρτὶ τυγχάνει (sc. ὤν) Soph. ; εἰ σὺ τυγχάνεις ἐπιστήμων Plat. :—sometimes indeed τυγχάνειν is used very much like εἶναι, τ. ἐν ἐμπύροις *to be engaged* in sacrifice, Eur. ; ὡς ἕκαστοι ἐτύγχανον *just as they all were*, Xen. 3. in many phrases it is easy to supply a part., ὅ τι ἂν τύχωσι, τοῦτο λέγουσι *they say whatever comes uppermost* (i. e. ὅ τι ἂν τύχωσι λέγοντες), Plat. III. neut. part. τυχόν, absol. like παρόν, *since it is so befel*, Luc. 2. as Adv. *perchance, perhaps*, Xen., Plat.

Τυδεύς, ὁ, gen. Τυδέως, Ep. ἔος or ῆος : acc. Τυδέα, Ep. ῆα and ῆ :—the hero *Tydeus*, one of the Seven against Thebes, Hom.

τυῖδε or τυΐδε, Dor. for τῇδε, *here*, Theocr. 2. for δεῦρο, with Verbs of motion, Id.

τύκη, ἡ, (τύκος) *mason's work*, Eur.

τυκίζω, f. Att. ιῶ, (τύκος) *to work stones*, Ar.

τύκισμα, ατος, τό, *a working of stones :* in pl., κανόνων τυκίσματα, i. e. *walls of stone worked* by rule, opp. to the rude Cyclopean building, Eur.

τύκον, τό, Boeot. for σῦκον.

τύκος [ῠ], ὁ, (τεύχω) *an instrument for working stones with, a mason's hammer* or *pick*, Eur. II. *a battle-axe*, Hdt.

τυκτά, a Persian word (*tacht*), which Hdt. translates by τέλειον δεῖπνον βασιλήιον.

τυκτός, ή, όν, verb. Adj. of τεύχω, τυκτὸν κακόν *created to be an evil*, a *born plague*, Il. ; τυκτὴ κρήνη *a fountain made by man's hand*, Od. : then, like εὔτυκτος, *well-made, well-wrought*, Hom.

ΤΥ'ΛΗ [ῠ], ἡ, like τύλος, *any callous lump :* a porter's *shoulder*, which has grown *callous* from carrying weights, Ar. 2. *a cushion, bolster*, Anth.

τυλίσσω, Att. -ττω, *to twist up :* *to bend :* aor. 1 pass. ἐτυλίχθη Theocr.

τύλος [ῠ], ὁ, = τύλη 1, *a knot* or *callus*, Xen. ; esp. inside the hands, Luc. II. *a knob* or *knot ; a knobbed bolt, a ship-bolt, trenail*, Ar.

τυλόω, f. ώσω, (τύλος) *to make knobby :*—Pass., ῥόπαλα σιδήρῳ τετυλωμένα *clubs knobbed* with iron, Hdt. II. *to make callous*, Xen. :—Pass. *to be callous*, Theocr.

τυλωτός, ή, όν, verb. Adj. ῥόπαλα τυλωτά *knobbed clubs*, like τετυλωμένα, Hdt.

τύμβευμα, ατος, τό, *a tomb, grave*, Soph. II. *that which is* or *is to be buried, a body*, Eur. From

τυμβεύω, f. σω, (τύμβος) to bury, entomb, Soph., Eur.   2. χοὰς τυμβεῦσαί τινι to pour libations on one's grave, Soph.   II. intr. to dwell entombed, Id.

τυμβ-ήρης, ες, entombed, Soph.   II. grave-like, sepulchral, Id.

τυμβίτης [ῑ], ου, ὁ, (τύμβος) in or at the grave, Anth.

τυμβ-ολέτης, ου, ὁ, = τυμβώρυχος, Anth.; fem. τυμβολέτις, ιδος, Id.

ΤΥ'ΜΒΟΣ, ὁ, a sepulchral mound, cairn, barrow, Lat. tumulus, Hom., Hdt., Att.   2. generally, a tomb, grave, Aesch.; ὥσπερ ἀπὸ τύμβου πεσών like an old grave-man, Ar.   3. also the tombstone with the figure of the dead, Eur.   II. of an old man, Eur., Ar.

τυμβ-οῦχος, ον, (ἔχω) sepulchral, Anth.

τυμβο-φόνος, ον, grave-murdering, disturbing the dead, Anth.

τυμβοχοέω, f. ήσω, to throw up a cairn or barrow, Hdt.; and

τυμβοχόη, ἡ, the throwing up a cairn, Il. From

τυμβο-χόος, ον, (χέω) throwing up a cairn or barrow, Anth.   II. τ. χειρώματα cairns thrown up by work of hand, Aesch.

τυμβό-χωστος, ον, (χώννυμι) heaped up into a cairn, high-heaped, Soph.

τυμβωρῠχία, ἡ, grave-robbing, Anth. From

τυμβ-ωρῠχος [ῠ], ὁ, (ὀρύσσω) one who digs up graves, a grave-robber, Ar.

τύμμα, ατος, τό, (τύπτω) a blow, Aesch., Theocr.

τυμπανίζω, f. ίσω, (τύμπανον) to beat a drum :—Pass., τυμπανίζεσθαι κατὰ τὰς ἐξόδους to march out to the sound of drums, Strab.   II. Pass. to be beaten to death, bastinadoed, N. T.

τυμπάνιον [ᾰ], τό, Dim. of τύμπανον, Strab.

τυμπᾰνιστής, οῦ, ὁ, (τυμπανίζω) fem. τυμπανίστρια, of a priestess of Cybelé, Dem.

τύμπᾰνον, τό, (τύπτω) a kettledrum, such as was used esp. in the worship of Cybelé, Hdt., Eur.   II. a drum-stick : generally, a staff, cudgel, Ar.   III. in Virg. tympana are wheels of solid wood.

Τυνδάρεος, ὁ, Tyndareos or Tyndarus, husband of Leda, Od., Eur. : Att. Τυνδάρεως, εω, ὁ, Aesch., etc. : patron. Τυνδᾰρίδης [ῑ], ου, ὁ, Pind. ; pl. οἱ Τυνδαρίδαι, Castor and Pollux, Hdt., etc.—Adj. Τυνδάρειος, α, ον, and ος, ον, Eur.:—fem. patron. Τυνδαρίς, ίδος, ἡ, Id.

τύνη [ῡ], Ep. and Dor. for τύ, σύ, thou.

τυννός, ή, όν, Dor. for μικρός, so small, so little, Lat. tantillus, Theocr.

τυννοῦτος, ον and ο, lengthd. form of τυννός, Lat. tantillus, Ar. ; with ι demonstr., τυννουτοσί, -ονί, Id. ; gen. and dat. τυννουτουί, -φί, Id.

τυντλάζω, to work in the mud : hence, to grub round the roots of a vine, Ar.

τύπᾰνον [ῠ], τό, (τύπτω) poët. for τύμπανον, a drum, h. Hom., Eur.

τῠπείην, aor. 2 pass. opt. of τύπτω :—τῠπείς, part.

τῠπή, ἡ, (τύπτω) a blow, wound, in pl., Il.

τύπος [ῠ], ὁ, (τύπτω) a blow, Orac. ap. Hdt.   II. the effect of a blow, the print or impress of a seal, Eur.; στίβου τύπος the print of a footstep, Soph. :—τύποι marks, letters, Plat. :—ὁ τ. τῶν ἵππων the sound of their tread, Xen.   2. anything wrought of metal or stone, in pl. figures worked in relief, Hdt., Eur. :—then, simply,

a figure, image, statue, Hdt., Eur.   3. τύπος τινός a man's form, i. e. himself, Ἱππομέδοντος τ. Aesch. ; βραχιόνων τ. = βραχίονες, Eur.   4. general form or character, the type or model of a thing, Plat. :—an example, N. T.   5. an outline, sketch, draught, Plat. ; so, τύπῳ, ἐν τύπῳ in outline, in general, Id.

τυπόω, f. ώσω, to form, mould, model, Plat. : so in Med., Anth.

τύπτω (Root ΤΥ'Π) Ep. impf. τύπτον : f. τύψω, Att. τυπτήσω : aor. 1 ἔτυψα, later ἐτύπτησα :—Pass., aor. 1 ἐτύφθην : aor. 2 ἐτύπην [ῠ] : f. τῠπήσομαι : pf. inf. τετύφθαι.   To beat, strike, smite, Il., etc. ; ἅλα τύπτον ἐρετμοῖς Od. ; ἴχνια τύπτειν to tread in his very track, Il. :—absol. Ζέφυρος λαίλαπι τύπτων the west wind beating, lashing with fury, Ib.   2. metaph., ἄχος κατὰ φρένα τύψε sharp grief smote him to the heart, Ib. ; ἡ ἀληθηίη ἔτυψε Καμβύσεα Hdt., etc.   II. Med., like κόπτομαι, Lat. plangor, to beat one's breast for grief, Id. ; c. acc. pers. to mourn for a person, Id.   III. Pass. to be beaten, struck or wounded, Hom., etc. : to be stung, Xen.   2. c. acc. cogn. to receive blows or wounds, ἕλκεα, ὅσσ' ἐτύπη Il. ; τύπτομαι πολλάς (sc. πληγάς) I get many blows, Ar. ; so c. dat., καιρίη (sc. πληγῇ) τετύφθαι Hdt.

τῠπώδης, ες, (τύπος II., εἶδος) like an outline :—Adv. -δῶς, summarily, Strab.

τύπωμα [ῠ], τό, (τυπόω) that which is moulded, τ. χαλκόπλευρον of a brazen urn, Soph. : a figure, outline, Eur.

τύπωσις [ῠ], ἡ, (τυπόω) a mould, model, Plut.

τυραννεύω, f. εύσω, and τυραννέω, f. ήσω, the former always in Hdt. ; both in Att. Poets, as the metre required : aor. 1 ἐτυράννευσα, -ησα : pf. τετυράννευκα, -ηκα :—Pass., f. med. τυραννήσομαι in pass. sense :— aor. 1 ἐτυραννεύθην :—to be a τύραννος, an absolute sovereign or despot, and in aor. to become such, Hdt., etc. : to be a prince or princess, Eur.   2. c. gen. to be despotic ruler of a people or place, Solon, Hdt., Att.   3. c. acc. to govern, Luc. :—Pass. to be governed despotically, Hdt., Thuc.   II. to be tyrannical, imperious, Plat.

τυραννίζω, to take the part of tyrants, Dem.

τυραννικός, ή, όν, (τύραννος) of or for a despotic ruler, royal, princely, Trag. ; κύκλος τ. the circle or assembly of kings, Soph.   2. befitting a tyrant, despotic, imperious, τυραννικὰ φρονεῖν Ar. ; τ. ξυνωμοσία in favour of tyranny, Thuc. ; τὰ τυραννικά the times of despotic government, Arist. :—Adv. -κῶς, Plat. ; Comp. -ώτερον, Arist.

τυραννίς, ίδος, ἡ, voc. τυραννί, (τύραννος) kingly power, sovereignty, Pind., Trag.   II. absolute power, despotic rule, Hdt., Att. ; τ. ὑμῶν lordship over you, Dem.   2. pl., αἱ τυραννίδες, = οἱ τύραννοι, Hdt.

τυραννοκτονέω, f. ήσω, to slay a tyrant, Luc. :—Pass. to be slain as a tyrant, Id. ; and

τυραννοκτονία, ἡ, the slaying of a tyrant, Luc. From

τυραννο-κτόνος, ὁ, ἡ, (κτείνω) slayer of a tyrant, Luc.

τυραννο-ποιός, ὁ, (ποιέω) a maker of tyrants, Plat.

τύραννος [ῠ], ὁ, an absolute sovereign, unlimited by law or constitution, Hdt., Aesch., etc. : not applied to old hereditary sovereignties (βασιλεῖαι) such as those of Hom. or of Sparta ; for the term rather regards the irregular way in which the power was gained,

than the way in which it was *exercised*, being applied to the mild Pisistratus, but not to the despotic kings of Persia. However, the word soon came to imply reproach, like our *tyrant*, Plat., etc. **2.** in a wider sense, *the tyrant's son*, or *any member of his family*, Soph. :—so, ἡ τύραννος was both *the queen* herself or *a princess*, Eur. **II.** τύραννος, ον, as Adj. *kingly, royal*, Trag. **2.** *imperious, despotic*, Thuc.; τύραννα δρᾶν Soph. (τύρ-αννος is prob. from same Root as κύρ-ιος, κοίρ-ανος.)

τῠραννο-φόνος, ον, (*φένω) *slaying tyrants*, Anth.

τυρβάζω, f. άσω, *to trouble, stir up*, Lat. *turbare*, Ar. :—Pass., τ. περί τι *to be troubled* about a thing, Id.

ΤΎΡΒΗ, ἡ, *disorder, tumult*, Lat. *turba*, Xen.

τύρευμα [ῠ], ατος, τό, *that which is curdled, cheese*, Eur.

τῠρευτήρ, ῆρος, ὁ, *one who makes cheese*, of Hermes as god of goatherds, Anth. From

τῠρεύω, f. εύσω, (τυρός) *to make cheese* :—metaph. *to make a mess* of anything, Dem.

Τύριος, α, ον, (Τύρος) *of Tyre, Tyrian*, Hdt., etc.

τῠρίσδω, Dor. for συρίζω.

Τῦρο-γλύφος [ῠ], ὁ, *Cheese-scooper*, a mouse, Batr.

τῠρόεις, εσσα, εν, contr. τῠροῦς, οῦσα, οῦν : (τυρός) :—*like cheese* : τυρόεις (sc. πλακοῦς), *a cheese*, Theocr.

τῠρό-κνηστις, ἡ, *a cheese-scraper, cheese-grater*, Ar.

τῠρό-νωτος, ον, *cheese-backed, spread with cheese*, Ar.

τῠρο-ποιέω, f. ήσω, *to make cheese*, Strab.

τυροπωλέω, f. ήσω, *to sell like cheese*, Ar.

τῠρο-πώλης, ου, ὁ, (πωλέω) *a cheesemonger*, Ar.

ΤΥ'ΡΟ'Σ, οῦ, ὁ, *cheese*, Hom., Ar., etc.

Τύρος, ἡ, *Tyre*, in Phoenicia, Hdt., etc.

Τῠρο-φάγος, ὁ, (φάγεῖν) *Cheese-eater*, name of a mouse in Batr.

τῠρο-φόρος, ον, (φέρω) *with cheese on it*, Anth.

τῠροῦς, οῦσσα, οῦν, contr. for τυρόεις.

Τῠρρην-ολέτης, ου, ὁ, (ὄλλυμι) *destroyer of Tyrrhenians*, Anth.

Τυρρηνός, v. Τυρσηνός.

Τυρσηνός, ή, όν, Ion. and old Att. for Τυρρηνός, *Tyrrhenian, Etruscan*, Hes., Hdt., Trag. :—also, Τυρσηνικός, ή, όν, Aesch.

ΤΎΡΣΙΣ, ἡ, gen. ιος, acc. τύρσιν ; but nom. and acc. pl. τύρσεις, gen. έων, dat. εσι :—*a tower*, Lat. *turris*, Pind., Xen.

ΤΥΤΘΟ'Σ, όν, later also ή, όν, *little, small*, of children, Hom., Aesch.; τ. θηρίον of a bee, Theocr., etc. **II.** τυτθόν, as Adv. *a little, a bit*, Hom. ; τ. ἔτι ζώων breathing yet *a little*, Il. ; τ. ἐδείησεν it wanted *a little*, Od. :—of the voice, *softly, gently*, Il. **2.** *by a little, scarcely, hardly*, Lat. *vix*, Ib. ; so neut. pl., Aesch. **III.** τυτθὰ διατμῆξαι, κεάσσαι *to cut small*, Od.

τῠφεδᾰνός, ὁ, (τύφω) *one with cloudy wits, a stupid fellow, dullard*, Ar.

τύφη, ἡ, *a plant used for stuffing beds*. Hence

τῠφ-ήρης, ες, *made from τύφη*, Anth.

τυφλό-πους, ὁ, ἡ, *with blind foot*, of Oedipus, Eur.

τῠφλός, ή, όν, (τύφω) *blind*, Il., etc. :—c. gen., τ. τινος *blind* to a thing, Xen. :—τὰ τυφλὰ τοῦ σώματος, i.e. one's *back*, Id. :—of the limbs of the blind, τ. πούς, χείρ Eur. ; cf. τυφλόπους. **II.** of things, *blind, dark, obscure*, Aesch., Soph. ; τ. σπιλάδες *blind* rocks,

Anth. **2.** of channels, *blind*, i.e. *closed, choked with mud*, Plut. **III.** Adv., τυφλῶς ἔχειν πρός τι *to be blind* to it, Plat.

τυφλό-στομος, ον, *with blind mouth*, of rivers, Strab.

τυφλότης, ἡ, (τυφλός) *blindness*, Plat.

τῠφλόω, f. ώσω, *to blind, make blind*, Hdt., Eur. :—Pass. *to be* or *become blind*, Hdt., Eur. **2.** metaph. in Pass., μόχθος τετύφλωται *is baffled*, Pind. ; τῶν μελλόντων τετύφλωνται φραδαί *wisdom is blind* as to the future, Id. Hence

τύφλωσις, ἡ, (τυφλόω) *a making blind, blinding*, Isocr.

τυφλώττω, (τυφλός) *to be blind*, Luc.

τῦφο-γέρων, οντος, ὁ, (τύφω) *an old man dim and dull with age, a dullard, dotard*, Ar.

τῦφος, ὁ, (τύφω) *smoke, vapour*, Anth. :—metaph. *conceit, vanity*, Plut.

τῠφόω, f. ώσω, (τῦφος) *to wrap in smoke ;* metaph. in pf. pass. τετύφωμαι, *to be in the clouds, to be crazed, demented*, Plat., Dem.

τύφω [ῠ]: aor. 1 ἔθυψα: pf. τέθῠφα :—Pass., f. τῠφήσομαι : aor. 2 ἐτύφην [ῠ]: pf. τέθυμμαι :—*to raise a smoke, καπνὸν τ.* Hdt. :—absol. *to smoke*, Soph. **II.** *trans. to smoke out*, τοὺς σφῆκας Ar. **2.** metaph., καπνῷ τ. πόλιν *to fill the town with smoke*, Id. **3.** *to consume in smoke, to burn slowly*, Eur. :—Pass. *to smoulder*, Id. :—metaph. τυφόμενος πόλεμος *smouldering*, but not yet broken out, Plut. ; so of *concealed* love, Anth.

Τῠφωεύς, έως, Ep. έος, ὁ: contr. Τῠφώς, gen. Τυφῶ, acc. Τυφῶ :—*Typhoëus* or *Typhos*, a giant buried by Zeus in Cilicia, Il., Pind.

Τῠφῶν, ῶνος, ὁ, Ep. Τῠφάων, ονος, *Typhon*, son of Typhoëus and father of the Winds, Hes. Hence

Τῠφωνικός, ή, όν, *tempestuous*, N. T.

τυφωνο-ειδῶς, (Τυφῶν) Adv. *like a whirlwind*, Strab.

Τῠφώς, ῶ, ὁ, contr. for Τυφωεύς, q. v. **II.** as appellat. τυφώς, gen. τυφῶ, dat. τυφῷ, *a whirlwind, typhoon*, Aesch., etc.

τύχαιος, α, ον, (τύχη) *accidental, chance*, Plut.

τύχε [ῠ], Ep. 3 sing. aor. 2 of τυγχάνω.

ΤΥ'ΧΗ [ῠ], ἡ, (cf. τυγχάνω) *the good which man obtains* (τυγχάνει) *by the favour of the gods, good fortune, luck, success*, Theogn., Hdt., etc. ; σὺν τύχῃ Soph. ; θείᾳ τύχῃ, Lat. *divinitus*, Hdt., etc. :—hence Τύχη was deified, like Lat. *Fortuna*, Τύχη Σώτειρα Pind. ; Τ. Σωτήρ Aesch. **II.** generally, *fortune, chance*, good or bad, in sing. and pl., Hdt., Att. **2.** rarely of positive *ill fortune*, ἢν χρήσωνται τύχῃ, i. e. if they are killed, Eur. ; τύχῃ *by ill-luck*, Antipho. **3.** esp., ἀγαθὴ τ. Aesch., etc. ; in dat. ἀγαθῇ τύχῃ *'in God's name,'* Dem., etc. ; by crasis, τἀγαθῇ Ar. ;—this formula was also introduced into treaties, like Lat. *quod felix faustumque sit*, Λάχης εἶπε, τύχῃ ἀγαθῇ τῶν Ἀθηναίων ποιεῖσθαι τὴν ἐκεχειρίαν Decr. in Thuc. :—so ἐπ' ἀγαθῇ τύχῃ Ar., etc. **4.** Adverbial usages, τύχῃ *by chance*, Lat. *forte, forte fortuna*, Soph., etc. ; ἀπὸ τύχης Arist. ; ἐκ τύχης Plat. ; διὰ τύχην Isocr., etc. ; κατὰ τύχην Thuc., etc. **III.** *a chance, hap, accident*, Aesch., Soph., etc. ; τῆς τύχης, τὸ ἐμὲ τυχεῖν . . ! *what a piece of ill-luck, that . .* ! Xen. ; mostly of *mishaps, misfortunes*, Aesch., etc. Hence

τῠχηρός, ά, όν, lucky, fortunate, Aesch.:—Adv. -ρῶς, Ar.
τῠχήσας, aor. 1 part. of τυγχάνω.
τῠχθείς, aor. 1 pass. part. of τεύχω.
τῠχοιμι, aor. 2 opt. of τυγχάνω.
τῠχόν, Adv., v. τυγχάνω B. III. 2.
τῠχόντως, Adv. aor. 2 part., by chance, Arist.
τύχος, ὁ, (τεύχω) = τύκος, Theogn.
τῠχών, aor. 2 part. of τυγχάνω.
τύψασκον, Ion. and Ep. aor. 1 of τύπτω.
τῷ, dat. sing. neut. of ὁ, ἡ, τό, used absol. therefore,
in this wise, thereupon, Hom.　　II. τῷ; for τίνι;
dat. sing. of τίς; who? 　　2. τῳ, enclit. for τινί, dat.
sing. of τις, some one.
τὥγαλμα, Ion. crasis for τὸ ἄγαλμα.
τωθάζω, Dor. -σδω: f. τωθάσομαι: aor. 1 ἐτώθασα, subj.
τωθάσω :—to mock, scoff or jeer at, flout, Hdt., Ar.:
—Pass. to be jeered, Plat.　　2. absol. to jeer, Ar.
τωθασμός, ὁ, scoffing, jeering, Arist.
τὠληθές, Ion. crasis for τὸ ἀληθές.
τὠπό, τὠποβαῖνον, Ion. crasis for τὸ ἀπό, τὸ ἀποβαῖνον.
τὠργείου, Dor. crasis for τοῦ Ἀργείου.
τὠρχαῖον, Ion. crasis for τὸ ἀρχαῖον.
τώς, demonstr. Adv., = ὥς, οὕτως, so, in this wise, Hom.,
Hes., Aesch.　　II. Dor. = οὗ, where, Theocr.
τὠτρεκές, crasis for τὸ ἀτρεκές, Anth.
τωὔλιον, Dor. crasis for τὸ αὔλιον, Theocr.
τωὐτό (not τωῦτό or τὠυτό), gen. τωὐτοῦ, dat. τωὐτῷ,
Ion. crasis for τὸ αὐτό, etc.

Υ.

Υ, υ, τό, indecl., twentieth letter of Gr. alphabet : as
numeral υʹ = 400, but ͵υ = 400,000. Called ὕψιλόν, because
the orig. sound was broad, like ου, and afterwards like thin
like French u. The Gr. υ, like Lat. v, was originally both
a vowel (u) and a semi-vowel (v), v. infr. II.　　I.
Interchanges of υ with other vowels, 　　1. Aeol. for ο,
as ὄνυμα στύμα ὕρνις for ὄνομα στόμα ὄρνις; also πίσυρες for πέτορες (τέσσαρες), cf. νύξ, Lat. nox.　　2.
Aeol., the diphth. ου became οι, Μοῖσα for Μοῦσα,
λέγοισα for λέγουσα.　　3. υ sometimes replaces οι,
as κοινός ξυνός, κοίρανος κύριος.　　4. Boeot. ῠ for ω,
as χελύνη for χελώνη.　　II. υ as a semivowel represented vau (Ϝ), the digamma, sometimes it formed the
diphth. αυ, as αὐέρυσαν for ἀνϝέρυσαν (v. αὐέρύω),
αὐίαχοι for ἀνϝίαχοι, ἀυάτα for ἀϝάτα (ἄτη), καλαύροψ
for καλάϝροψ, ταλαύρινος for ταλάϝρινος, ταναύποδες
for ταναϝόποδες; sometimes the dipth. ευ, as εὔαδεν
for ἔϝαδεν.
ὒ ὔ, a sound to imitate a person snuffing a feast, Ar.
Ὑάδες, ων, αἱ, (ὕω) the Hyades, seven stars in the head
of the bull, which threatened rain when they rose
with the sun, Il., Hes. (Commonly deriv. from ὕω,
cf. Lat. Pluviae: but the genuine Lat. name was
suculae, piglings, as if ῦς were the root; and this
agrees with the quantity, υ being short in ὑάδες, long
in ὕω: Eur. however has ὑάδες with ῠ.)
ὕαινα, ἡ, the hyaena, an animal of the dog kind, with a
bristly mane like a hog (whence the name), Hdt.
Ὑακίνθια (sc. ἱερά), τά, a Lacedaemonian festival in

honour of Hyacinthus, held in the month Hecatombaeon, Hdt., Thuc., etc.
ὑακινθῖνο-βᾰφής, ές, (βάπτω) dyed hyacinth-colour,
Xen.
ὑακίνθῐνος, η, ον, hyacinthine, Od., Eur.
Ὑάκινθος [ᾰ], ὁ, Hyacinthus, a Laconian youth, beloved
by Apollo, who killed him by a cast of the discus, Eur.
ὑάκινθος, ὁ and ἡ, the hyacinth, Il., etc.;—a flower
said to have sprung up from the blood of Hyacinthus
or of Ajax; and the petals were thought to bear the
letters ΑΙ, or ΑΙΑΙ, Mosch.; hence the epithet γραπτά
in Theocr. The hyacinth seems to have comprehended
several dark blue flowers: Hom. speaks of dark
hair as ὑακινθίνῳ ἄνθει ὁμοῖαι, and Theocr. calls it
black.　　II. a precious stone, of blue colour, not
(prob.) our jacinth, but the sapphire, N. T.
ὑάλεος [ᾰ], α, ον, (ὕαλος) = ὑάλινος, of glass, Anth. :
—contr. ὑαλοῦς, ᾶ, οῦν, of glass, Strab., Luc.
ὑάλῐνος, η, ον, (ὕαλος) of crystal or glass, Ar. : also
ὑέλινος, η, ον, Anth.
ὕαλος or ὕελος, ὁ and ἡ, a clear, transparent stone,
used by the Egyptians to enclose their mummies in,
oriental alabaster, Hdt.　　2. a convex lens of crystal,
used as a burning-glass, Ar.　　II. glass, Lat.
vitrum, Plat. : glass itself existed in the time of Hdt.,
but was not called ὕαλος till Plato's time. (The word
is said to be Egyptian. Others refer it to ὕω, as if
the orig. sense were rain-drop.)
ὑαλοῦς, ᾶ, οῦν, contr. for ὑαλέος.
ὑᾰλό-χρους, ουν, (χρόα) glass-coloured, Anth.
ὑββάλλω, Ep. syncop. for ὑποβάλλω.
ΥΒΟΣ [ῠ], ή, όν, hump-backed, Theocr.
ὑβρίζω [ῠ], Dor. -ίσδω : f. Att. ιῶ : aor. 1 ὕβρισα,
pf. ὕβρικα : plqpf. ὑβρίκειν :—Med., f. ὑβριοῦμαι :—
Pass., f. ὑβρισθήσομαι : aor. 1 ὑβρίσθην : pf. ὕβρισμαι,
(ὕβρις) :—to wax wanton, run riot, Od., Aesch., etc. ;
opp. to σωφρονεῖν, Xen.　　2. of over-fed horses or
asses, to neigh or bray and prance about, Lat. las-
civire, Hdt., Xen.　　3. metaph. of a rapid rushing
river, Hdt.　　II. in dealing with other persons,
ὕβρ. τινά to treat him despitefully, to outrage, insult,
affront, maltreat, Il., Aesch.; more commonly, ὕβρ.
εἴς τινα to commit an outrage upon or towards him,
Eur., Plat.; ὕβρ. ἐπί τινα to exult over a fallen foe,
Eur.　　2. c. acc. cogn., ὕβρ. ὕβριν Aesch., Eur., etc. :
—with a neut. Adj., ὕβρ. τάδε to commit these outrages,
Hdt.; so, τῶν ἀδικημάτων τῶν ἐς Ἀθηναίους ὕβρισμαι
Id.; and with double acc., ὕβριν ὑβρίζειν τινά Eur. :—
hence in Pass., ὕβριν ὑβρισθῆναι Id., Dem.　　3. at
Athens in legal sense, to do one a personal outrage, to
maltreat, assault, Oratt. :—Pass., γυναῖκες καὶ παῖδες
ὑβρίζονται Thuc.; ὑβριζόμενος ἀποθνήσκει he dies of
ill-treatment, Xen. ;—and of acts, τὰ ὑβρισμένα outrages, Lys.　　4. pf. pass. part., of things, arrogant,
ostentatious, σημεῖ᾽ ἔχων ὑβρισμένα Eur.; στολὴ ὑβρισ-
μένη Xen.
ΥΒΡΙΣ [ῠ], gen. εως and εος, Ep. ιος :—wantonness, wanton violence or insolence, Od., Hdt.,
etc. ; of actions, ἆρ᾽ οὐχ ὕβρις τάδ᾽; Soph.; ταῦτ᾽ οὐχ
ὕβρις ἐστί; Ar. :—Adv. usages, ὕβρει in wantonness or insolence, Soph.; ἐφ᾽ ὕβρει Eur.; δι᾽ ὕβριν
Dem.　　2. of lewdness, opp. to σωφροσύνη, Theogn.,

Xen. 3. of over-fed horses, *riotousness, restiveness*, Hdt., Pind. II. = ὕβρισμα, Hom. ; sometimes like ὑβρίζω, foll. by a Prep.,῞Ηρας μητέρ᾽ εἰς ἐμὴν ὕβρις her *outrage* towards . . , Eur. ; ἡ κατ᾽ Ἀργείους ὕ. Soph. ; ἡ πρὸς τοὺς δημότας ὕ. Hdt. ; also c. gen. objecti, ὕ. τινός towards him, Id., etc. :—in pl. *wanton acts, outrages*, Hes., Eur., etc. 2. *an outrage on the person, violation*, Pind., Att. 3. in Att. law, ὕβρις comprehended all *the more serious injuries done to the person, grievous assault*, the slighter kind being αἰκία [ῑ] : hence ὕβρις was remedied by *public indictment* (γραφή), αἰκία by *private action* (δίκη). III. *a loss, damage*, N. T. B. as masc. = ὑβριστής, *a violent, overbearing man*, ὕβριν ἀνέρα Hes.

ὑβρίσδω, Dor. for ὑβρίζω.

ὕβρισμα, ατος, τό, (ὑβρίζω) *a wanton* or *insolent act, an outrage*, Hdt., Eur., etc. ; τόδ᾽ ὕβρισμ᾽ ἐς ἡμᾶς ἠξίωσεν ὑβρίσαι Eur., Xen. ; τὰ τούτων ὑβρίσματα εἰς ἐμέ Dem. II. *an object of insolence*, ὕβρισμα θέσθαι τινά = ὑβρίζειν, Eur. III. = ὑβριστής, Id.

ὑβριστέος, α, ον, verb. Adj. *that may be insulted*, Dem.

ὑβριστήρ, ῆρος, ὁ, poët. for sq., Anth.

ὑβριστής, οῦ, ὁ, (ὑβρίζω) *a violent, overbearing person, a wanton, insolent man*, Hom., Hdt., Att. 2. opp. to σώφρων, *lustful, lewd*, Ar., Xen. 3. of animals, *wanton, restive, unruly*, Eur., Xen. 4. of natural forces, ὑβριστὴς ἄνεμος Hes. ; ὑβριστὴς ποταμός Aesch. Hence

ὑβριστικός, ή, όν, *given to wantonness, wanton, insolent, outrageous*, Plat., etc. :—τὸ ὑβριστικόν an *insolent disposition*, Xen. :—Adv. -κῶς, Plat. ; Comp. -ώτερον, Dem.

ὕβριστος, η, ον, (ὑβρίζω) *wanton, insolent, outrageous* : —hence Comp. ὑβριστότερος, Hdt., Xen. ; Sup. ὑβριστότατος, Ar., Xen.

ὑγεία, ἡ, late form for ὑγίεια, Plut. ; Ion. ὑγείη, Anth.

ὑγιάζομαι, Pass. *to become healthy, get well*, Arist.

ὑγιαίνω [ῠ], f. ἀνῶ : aor. 1 ὑγίᾱνα, Ion. ὑγίηνα :—Pass., aor. 1 ὑγιάνθην : (ὑγιής) :—*to be sound, healthy* or *in health*, Lat. *bene valere*, Hdt., Ar., etc. 2. *to be sound of mind*, Theogn., Ar., etc. ; τὰς φρένας ὑγ. Hdt. 3. of *soundness* in political or religious opinion, τὸ ὑγιαῖνον τῆς Ἑλλάδος Id.

ὑγίεια [ῠ], ἡ, and sometimes ὑγιεία, (ὑγιής) *health, soundness* of body, Lat. *salus*, Hdt., Att. :—pl. ὑγίειαι, *healthy states* or *conditions*, Plat. 2. of the mind, ὑ. φρενῶν *soundness of mind*, Aesch.

ὑγιεινός [ῠ], ή, όν, (ὑγιής) *good for the health, wholesome, sound, healthy*, Xen., etc. 2. of persons, *healthy, sound*, Lat. *sanus*, Plat. ; τὸ ὑγ. *health*, Arist. II. Adv., ὑγιεινῶς ἔχειν, = ὑγιαίνειν, Plat : —Comp. ὑγιεινοτέρως and -ρον, Sup. -ότατα, Xen.

ὑγιής [ῠ], εσσα, εν, Boeot. for ὑγιής, Pind.

ὑγιηρός [ῠ], ά, όν, (ὑγιής) *good for the health, wholesome*, Pind. II. of persons, *healthy, hearty, sound*, Lat. *sanus*, Id.

ΥΓΙΗ῾Σ [ῠ], ές, gen. έος : dat. ὑγιεῖ : acc. ὑγιᾶ, Ion. ὑγιέα :—dual ὑγιῆ :—neut. pl. ὑγιῆ : gen. ὑγιῶν :— Comp. and Sup. ὑγιέστερος, -ατος :—*sound, healthy, hearty, sound in body*, Lat. *sanus*, ὑγιέα ἀποδέξαι or ποιεῖν τινα *to restore him to health, make him sound*,

Hdt. ; ὑγιὴς τὸ δῆγμα *cured* of the bite, Xen. 2. of condition, σῶς καὶ ὑγιής *safe and sound, in good case*, Hdt., Thuc. II. *sound in mind, sound-minded*, Eur., Plat. 2. of words, opinions, and the like, *sound, wholesome, wise*, Il., Thuc., Plat. : often with a negat., λόγος οὐχ ὑγ. Hdt. ; μηδὲν ὑγιὲς φρονῶν Soph. ; οὐδὲν ὑγ. λέγειν Eur., etc. III. Adv. ὑγιῶς, *healthily, soundly*, κρίνειν, Plat., Dem.

ὑγρά, ἡ, v. ὑγρός 1. 2.

ὑγραίνω, f. ἀνῶ, (ὑγρός) *to wet, moisten*, Eur., Xen. : of a river, *to water* a country, Eur.

ὑγρο-μελής, ές, (μέλος) *with supple, soft limbs*, Xen.

ὑγρο-πορέω, f. ήσω, *to go through the water*, Anth.

ΥΓΡΟ῾Σ, ά, όν, *wet, moist, running, fluid*, Hom., etc. ; ὑγρὸν ἔλαιον, i. e. olive-oil, as opp. to fat, Id. ; ὑγρὸν ὕδωρ *running* water, Od. ; ἄνεμοι ὑγρὸν ἀέντες *winds blowing moist* or *rainy*, as opp. to *dry, parching*, Ib. 2. ἡ ὑγρά, Ion. ὑγρή, *the moist*, i. e. *the sea*, Hom. ; so, ὑγρὰ κέλευθα *the watery ways*, i. e. *the sea*, Id. ; and ὑγρά alone, opp. to ἀπείρων γαῖα, Id. 3. τὸ ὑγρόν and τὰ ὑγρά *wet, moisture, water*, Hdt. 4. μέτρα ὑγρὰ καὶ ξηρά *liquid* and *dry measure*, Plat. 5. θῆρες ὑγροί *water-animals*, opp. to πεζοί, Anth. II. *soft, pliant, supple, lithe*, Lat. *mollis*, of the eagle's back, Pind. ; of youthful limbs, Plat. ; ὑγρὰ ἔχειν τὰ σκέλη of a horse, Xen. ; so of colts, γόνατα ὑγρῶς κάμπτειν, ὑγρῶς τοῖς σκέλεσι χρῆσθαι (cf. Virgil's *mollia crura reponit*), Id. ; so, ὑ. ἄκανθος (Virg. *mollis acanthus*), Theocr. 2. *languid, feeble*, of one dying, Soph., Eur. 3. of the eyes, *swimming, melting, languishing*, ὄμμασιν ὑγρὰ δεδορκώς Anth., etc. 4. metaph. of persons, *facile, soft-tempered, pliant, easy*, Plut. : *luxurious*, ὑ. πρὸς τὴν δίαιταν Id.

ὑγρότης, ητος, Dor. -ότας, ᾱτος, ἡ, (ὑγρός) *wetness, moisture*, Plat. II. *pliancy, suppleness*, Xen. : of a flame, *flickering motion, lambency*, Eur. 2. *languor*, Plut.

ὑγρό-φθογγος, ον, *making a gurgling sound*, Anth.

ὑγρώσσω, (ὑγρός) *to make wet, moisten*, Aesch.

ὑδαρής, ές, gen. έος, (ὕδωρ) of wine, *mixed with too much water, watery, washy*, Xen. :—metaph. *washy, feeble, languid*, Aesch., Arist.

ὑδᾰσι-στεγής, ές, *water-proof*, Anth.

ὑδᾰτῖνος, η, ον, and os, ον, (ὕδωρ) *of water, watery*, ὑδ. νάρκισσος *that loves the water*, Anth. II. like ὑγρός II, *pliant, supple*, Id.

ὑδάτιον, τό, Dim. of ὕδωρ, *a rivulet*, Plat.

ὑδᾰτόεις, όεσσα, όεν, (ὕδωρ) *watery, like water*, Anth. II. *transparent as water, thin, fine*, Id.

ὕδᾰτος, gen. of ὕδωρ.

ὑδᾰτοποσία, ἡ, *a drinking of water*, Luc. ; and

ὑδᾰτοποτέω, *to drink water*, Luc. From

ὑδᾰτο-πότης, ὁ, *a water-drinker*.

ὑδᾰτο-τρεφής, ές, (τρέφομαι) *growing in* or *by the water*, Od.

ὑδᾰτόω, f. ώσω, (ὕδωρ) *to make watery* :—Pass. *to be liquid, watery*, Anth.

ὕδει, Ep. for ὕδατι, dat. of ὕδωρ.

ὕδερος, ὁ, (ὕδωρ) like ὕδρωψ, *dropsy*, Arist.

ὑδνέω, *to nourish*.

ὕδρα, Ion. ὕδρη, ἡ, (ὕδωρ) *a hydra, water-serpent*, or

the Lernaean hydra, Hes., Soph. ; ὕδραν τέμνειν, proverb. of labour in vain, because two heads sprang up for every one which was cut off, Plat.

ὑδραίνω, f. ἀνῶ : aor. 1 ὕδρηνα : (ὕδωρ) :—to water the earth, of a river, Eur. ; ὕδρ. τινά to wash, sprinkle with water, Id. :—Med. to wash oneself, bathe, ὑδρηναμένη Od. ; λουτρὰ ὑδράνασθαι χροΐ to pour water over one's body, Eur.   II. ὑδραίνειν χοάς τινι to pour libations to one, Id.

ὑδρεία, ἡ, (ὑδρεύω) a drawing water, fetching water, Thuc., etc.   II. a watering-place, Plut.

ὑδρεῖον, Ion. ὑδρήιον, τό, (ὑδρεύω) a water-bucket, well-bucket, Hdt.   II. a water-tank, Strab.

ὑδρεύω, f. σω, (ὕδωρ) to draw, fetch or carry water, Od., Theogn. :—Med. to draw water for oneself, fetch water, πολῖται Od., Hdt., Att.

ὑδρήιον, Ion. for ὑδρεῖον.

ὑδρηλός, ή, όν, (ὕδωρ) watery, wet, Od., Aesch. ; κρωσσοὶ ὕδρ. water pots, Eur.

ὑδρηνάμην, aor. 1 med. of ὑδραίνω.

ὑδρία, ἡ, (ὕδωρ) a water-pot, pitcher, urn, Ar. :— proverb. ἐπὶ θύραις τὴν ὑδρίαν to break the pitcher at the door, = 'there's many a slip 'twixt cup and lip,' Arist.   II. a vessel of any kind, a pot of money, Ar.   2. the balloting urn in the law-courts, Isocr., Dem.   3. a cinerary urn, Ar., Luc.

ὑδριάς, ή, (ὑδρία) of the water, Anth.

ὑδρο-ειδής, ές, (εἶδος) like water, watery, Eur.

ὑδρόεις, εσσα, εν, (ὕδωρ) fond of the water, Eur.

Ὑδρο-μέδουσα, ἡ, Water-ruler, name of a frog in Batr.

ὑδροποσία, Ion. -ίη, ἡ, water-drinking, Xen., etc.; and

ὑδροποτέω, f. ήσω, to drink water, Hdt., Xen., etc. From

ὑδρο-πότης, ου, ὁ, a water-drinker, Xen. : in Comic phrase, a thin-blooded, mean-spirited fellow, Anth.

ὑδρορρόα, ἡ, but in Att. also -ρόη, a water-course, whether on the ground, a conduit, canal, sluice, Ar. ; or on the roof, a gutter, spout, Id.

ὕδρος, ὁ, (ὕδωρ) like ὕδρα, a water-snake, Il., Hdt.

ὑδροφορέω, f. ήσω, to carry water, Xen. ; and

ὑδροφορία, ἡ, a water-carrying, a festival of Apollo, Luc. From

ὑδρο-φόρος, ον, (φέρω) carrying water, Plut.   II. as Subst., ὕδρ., ὁ and ἡ a water-carrier, Hdt., Xen.

ὑδρο-χόος, ὁ, (χέω) the water-pourer, name of the constellation Aquarius, Anth.

ὑδρο-χύτος, ον, (χέω) gushing with water, Eur.

ὑδρωπικός, ή, όν, dropsical : metaph., ναῦς ὑδρ. Anth.

ὕδρωψ, ωπος, ὁ, (ὕδωρ) dropsy.   II. a dropsical person.

ΫΔΩΡ [ῠ], τό, gen. ὕδατος [ῠ Ep.], dat. ὕδατι, Ep. also ὕδει (as if from ὕδος) :—water, of any kind, but in Hom. rarely of sea-water (which he calls ἁλμυρὸν ὕδωρ) ;—also in pl., ὕδατ' αἰενάοντα Od. ; ὕδατα Καφίσια the waters of Cephisos, Pind :—ὕδωρ κατὰ χειρός water for washing the hands, Ar. ; ὕ. ἐπὶ χεῖρας ἔχευαν Hom.—Proverbs. γράφειν τι εἰς ὕδωρ of anything untrustworthy, Soph. ; ἐν ὕδατι γρ. Plat. ; ὅταν τὸ ὕδωρ πνίγῃ, τί δεῖ ἐπιπίνειν ; if water chokes, what more can be done ? of a desperate case, Arist.   2. rain-water, rain, Il., Hdt., Att. ;—more definitely, ὕδωρ ἐξ οὐρανοῦ Thuc., etc. ; Ζεὺς ὕδωρ ὕει, ὁ θεὸς ὕδωρ ποιεῖ Ar.   3. for the phrase ἐν ὕδατι βρέχεσθαι,

Hdt., v. βρέχω.   4. in Att. law-phrase, τὸ ὕδωρ was the water of the water-clock (κλεψύδρα), Dem. ; ἐν τῷ ἐμῷ ὕδατι, ἐπὶ τοῦ ἐμοῦ ὕδατος in the time allowed me, Id. ; οὐκ ἐνδέχεται πρὸς τὸ αὐτὸ ὕ. εἰπεῖν one cannot say (all) in one speech, Id. ; ἐπίλαβε τὸ ὕ. stop the water (which was done while the speech was interrupted by the calling of evidence and reading of documents), Id. ; ἀποδιδόναι τινὶ τὸ ὕ. to give him the turn of speaking, Aeschin.

ὕειος, α, ον, (ὗς) of or belonging to swine, ὑεία κοιλία pig's tripe, Ar. :—θηρίον ὕ., as a type of brutish ignorance, Plat.

Ὑέλη, ἡ, Velia in Lower Italy, Hdt.

ὑέλινος, ὑελίτης, ὕελος, Ion. and late forms of ὑαλ-.

ὕεσσι, Ep. for ὑσί, dat. pl. of ὗς.

ὑετόεις [ῠ], εσσα, εν, rainy, Anth.   From

ὑετός [ῠ], ὁ, (ὕω) rain, Lat. pluvius, Il., Hes., Ar. :— esp. a heavy shower, Lat. nimbus, whereas ὄμβρος, Lat. imber, is a lasting rain, and ψεκάς or ψακάς a drizzling rain, Xen., etc.   II. as Adj. in Sup. ἄνεμοι ὑετώτατοι the rainiest winds, Hdt.

ὑηνία, ἡ, swinishness, swinish stupidity, Ar.   From

ὑηνός, ή, όν, (ὗς) swinish, Plat.

Ὕης [ῠ], ου, ὁ, (ὕω) epith. of Ζεὺς ὄμβριος, and of Bacchus :—to which of these the cry of Ὕης ἄττης in Dem. should be referred, is doubtful.

ὑθλέω, f. ήσω, to talk nonsense, trifle, prate, Lat. nugari, Ar.   From

ΫΘΛΟΣ, ὁ, idle talk, nonsense, Plat., Dem. ; in pl., ὕθλους λέγειν, like Lat. nugae, Plat.

υἷα, υἷας, Ep. acc. sing. and pl. of υἱός.

υἱάσι, poët. dat. pl. of υἱός.

υἴδιον, τό, Dim. of ὗς, Xen.   II. υἱδιον, τό, Dim. of υἱός, Ar.

υἰδοῦς, οῦ, ὁ, (υἱός) like υἱδεύς, a grandson, Xen., Dem.

υἱιδεύς, έως, ὁ, = υἱδοῦς, Isocr.

ὑικός, ή, όν, (ὗς) of or for swine, ὑικόν τι πάσχειν to have something of the swine's nature, Xen.

υἱο-θεσία, ἡ, (τίθημι Β. 1) adoption as a son, N. T.

ΥΙΟΣ, ὁ, regul. υἱόν, υἱοῦ, υἱῷ, υἱόν :—also declined as if there were a nom. *υἱεύς, gen. υἱέος, dat. υἱεῖ, Ep. υἱέϊ, acc. υἱέα : dual υἱέε, υἱέοιν : pl. υἱεῖς, Ep. υἱέες, υἱέϊ, υἱεῖς, Ep. υἱέας : Hom. also has (as if from a nom. *υἷς) gen. υἷος, dat. υἷι, acc. υἷα, dual υἷε (distinguished from the voc. sing. υἱέ by the accent), pl. υἷες, υἱάσι, υἷας :—in late Ep. we have gen. υἱῆος, υἱῆϊ, etc.   A son, Lat. filius, Hom., etc. ; υἱὸν ποιεῖσθαί τινα to adopt him as a son, Aeschin. ; υἱεῖς ἄνδρες grown up sons, Dem. :—rarely of animals, N. T.   2. periphr., υἷες Ἀχαιῶν, for Ἀχαιοί, Il. ; cf. παῖς. [Hom. sometimes makes the 1st syll. short, as if it were υός.]

υἱωνός, οῦ, ὁ, (υἱός) a grandson, Hom., Plut.

ὕλαγμα [ῠ], ατος, τό, (ὑλάω) the bark of a dog, Eur. : metaph., νηπίοις ὑλάγμασιν with idle snarlings, Aesch.

ὑλαγμός [ῠ], ὁ, (ὑλάω) a barking, baying, Il., Xen.

ὑλ-αγωγεύς [ῠ], f. ήσω, (ἀγωγός) to carry wood, Dem.

ὑλαῖος, α, ον, (ὕλη) of the forest, savage, Theocr.

ὑλακή, ἡ, (ὑλάω) a barking, howling, Anth., Plut.

ὑλακό-μωρος, ον, always barking, still howling or yelling, Od.

ὑλακτέω [ῠ] : aor. 1 ὑλάκτησα : (ὑλάω) :—to bark, bay, howl, of dogs, Il., Ar. ; of hounds, to give tongue,

Xen. 2. metaph., κραδίη ὑλακτεῖ *howls for rage*, Od.; c. acc. cogn. *to yell forth bold and shameless words*, Soph.; ἄμουσ᾽ ὑλακτῶν *howling* his uncouth songs, Eur. II. trans. *to bark at*, τινά Ar., Isocr. Hence

ὑλακτητής, οῦ, ὁ, *a barker*, Anth.
ὑλᾱ-τόμος, Dor. for ὑλη-τόμος.
ΥΛΑ΄Ω [ῠ], only in pres. and impf. *to howl, bark, bay*, of dogs, Od.: so in Med., κύνες οὐχ ὑλάοντο Ib. II. trans. *to bark* or *bay at*, τινά Od., Theocr. (Formed from the sound.)
ὑλειώτης, ου, ὁ, (ὕλη) *a forester*, Anth.
ΥΛΗ [ῡ], ἡ, Lat. *sylva, a wood, forest, woodland*, Hom., Hdt., etc.; τὰ δένδρα καὶ ὕλη *fruit-trees* and *forest-trees*, Thuc.: *copse, brushwood*, opp. to timber-trees, Xen. II. *wood cut down, firewood, fuel*, Hom., etc. III. like Lat. *materia, stuff* of which a thing is made, *the raw material, wood, timber*, Od., Hdt. 2. in Philosophy, *matter*, Arist. 3. *subject matter*, Id.
ὑλήεις, εσσα, εν, also ὑλήεις as fem.: Dor. ὑλάεις, contr. neut. pl. ὑλᾶντα: (ὕλη):—*woody, wooded*, Hom., Soph., Eur.; ἄταρπος ὑλ. a path *through the wood*, Anth. 2. *dwelling in the woods*, Id.
ὑλη-κοίτης, ου, ὁ, *one who lodges in the wood*, Hes.
ὑλη-τόμος, ον, Dor. ὑλᾱτόμος, = ὑλοτόμος, Theocr.
ὑλη-φόρος, ον, = ὑλο-φόρος, Ar.
ὑλη-ωρός, όν, (οὖρος) *watching the wood*, Anth.
ὑλίζω, f. ίσω, *to filter, strain*: v. δι-υλίζω. (Deriv. uncertain.)
ὑλο-βάτης, ου, ὁ, *one who haunts the woods*, Anth.
ὑλό-κομος, ον, (κόμη) *thick grown with wood*, Eur.
ὑλο-σκόπος, ον, *watching over woods*, Anth.
ὑλοτομέω, *to cut* or *fell wood*, Hes.; and
ὑλοτομία, ἡ, *the cutting* or *felling of wood*, Arist. From
ὑλο-τόμος, ον, (τέμνω) *cutting* or *felling wood*, Il.:—as Subst. ὑλοτόμος, ὁ, *a wood-cutter, woodman*, Ib., Soph. II. proparox. ὑλότομος, ον, pass. *cut in the wood*: τὸ ὑλότομον *a plant* used as a charm, h. Hom.
ὑλ-ουργός, όν, (*ἔργω) *working wood*: as Subst. ὑλουργός, ὁ, *a carpenter* or *woodman*, Eur.
ὑλο-φάγος [ᾰ], ον, (φαγεῖν) *feeding in the woods*, Hes.
ὑλο-φορβός, όν, (φέρβομαι) *feeding in the woods*, Eur.
ὑλο-φόρος, ον, (φέρω) *a wood-carrier*, Anth.
ὑλ-ώδης, ες, (εἶδος) *woody, wooded*, Thuc.; τὰ ὑλώδη *wooded ground*, Xen. II. *turbid, muddy*, Plut.
ὑλωρός, ὁ, (οὖρος) = ἀγρονόμος, *a forester*, Arist.
Ὑμάν, Dor. for Ὑμήν.
ὑμέες, ὑμεῖς, nom. pl. of σύ.
ὑμέναιος [ῠ], ὁ, (Ὑμήν) *hymenaeus, the wedding* or *bridal song*, sung by the bride's attendants as they led her to the bridegroom's house, Il., Trag. 2. *a wedding*, Soph., Eur.; and in pl., Soph., Eur. II. = Ὑμήν, *Hymen*, the god of marriage, addressed in wedding-songs, Ὑμὴν ὦ Ὑμέναι᾽ ἄναξ Eur.; Dor. Ὑμὰν ὦ Ὑμέναιε Theocr. Hence
ὑμεναιόω [ῠ], f. ώσω, *to sing the wedding-song*, Aesch. 2. *to wed, take to wife*, Theocr.; proverb., πρίν κεν λύκος οἶν ὑμεναιοῖ Ar.
ὑμενήιος, ὁ, (Ὑμήν) epith. of Bacchus, Anth.
ὑμενό-πτερος [ῠ], ον, (πτερόν) *membrane-winged*, Luc.
ὑμές [ῠ], Dor. for ὑμεῖς.
ὑμέτερος [ῠ], α, ον, (ὑμεῖς) *your, yours*, Lat. *vester*,

Hom., etc.; with a Pron. added in gen., ὑμέτερος ἑκάστου θυμός the courage of each of *you*, Il.; ὑμέτερος αὐτῶν θυμός *your* own mind, Od.;—ὑμέτερόνδε *to your house*, Il.:—τὸ ὑμέτερον *your part, your business*, Hdt.; τὸ δ᾽ ὑμ. πρᾶξαι *your character* is to do so and so, Thuc.:—with the Article, αἱ ὑμέτεραι ἐλπίδες hopes *raised by you*, Id.; τῇ ὑμ. παρακελεύσει for the purpose of advising *you*, Plat.
ΥΜΗ΄Ν, ένος, ὁ, *a thin skin, membrane*, Arist.
ΥΜΗ΄Ν, ένος, ὁ, *Hymen*, the god of marriages, v. Ὑμέναιος. [ῠ, whereas in Ὑμέναιος, υ is short.]
ὕμμες, ὕμμι and –ιν, ὕμμε, Aeol. for ὑμεῖς, ὑμῖν, ὑμᾶς.
ὑμν-ἀγόρας, ου, ὁ, (ἀγορεύω) *a singer of hymns*, Anth.
ὑμνέω, Ep. –είω, Dor. 3 pl. ὑμνεῦσι, fem. part. ὑμνεῦσα: f. ήσω: (ὕμνος): I. with acc. *to sing, laud, sing of*, Lat. *canere*, c. acc., Hes., Trag.:—also in Prose, *to celebrate, commemorate*, Hdt., Xen.;—c. dupl. acc., ἃ τὴν πόλιν ὕμνησα the points wherein *I praised* our city, Thuc.:—Pass., Ἀργεῖοι ὑμνέαται (Ion. for –ηνται) have been praised, Hdt.; ὑμνηθήσεται πόλις Eur.; αἱ ὑμνούμεναι φιλίαι the *famous* friendships, Arist. 2. c. acc. cogn. *to sing*, Aesch., Eur. II. *to tell over and over again, to repeat, recite, rehearse*, Lat. *decantare*, Plat.; ὑμνήσεις κακά wilt *sing continually* of thy ills, Soph.; τὰν ἐμὰν ὑμνεῦσαι (Ion. for –ούσαι) ἀπιστοσύναν ever singing of my want of faith, Eur.:—Pass., βαῖ, ἀεὶ δ᾽ ὑμνούμενα few words, but *such as oft repeated*, Soph. III. intr. *to sing, chant*, Thuc., Xen. 2. in a pass. sense, φῆμαι ὑμνήσουσι περὶ τὰ ὦτα will *ring* in their ears, Plat. [In Eur. sometimes ῠ.]
ὑμνητέον, verb. Adj. *one must praise*, Plat., Luc.
ὑμνητήρ, ῆρος, ὁ, = ὑμνητής, Anth.; fem., ὑμνήτειρα Id.
ὑμνητής, οῦ, ὁ, (ὑμνέω) *a singer, praiser*, Plat.
ὑμνητός, ή, όν, verb. Adj. of ὑμνέω, *sung of, praised, lauded*, Pind.
ὑμνο-θέτης, ου, ὁ, *a composer of hymns, a lyric poet*, Theocr., Anth.
ὑμνο-ποιός, όν, (ποιέω) *making hymns*: as Subst., ὑμν., ὁ, *a minstrel*, Eur.
ὑμνο-πόλος, ον, (πολέω) *busied with songs of praise*: as Subst., ὑμν., ὁ, *a poet, minstrel*, Anth.
ΥΜΝΟΣ, ὁ, *a hymn, festive song* or *ode, in praise* of gods or heroes, Od.; ὕμνος θεῶν *to* or *in honour of* the gods, Aesch.; τιμῶν θεὸν ὕμνοισιν Eur.:—in Trag. also of *mournful songs*, Aesch., etc.
ὑμνῳδέω, f. ήσω, *to sing a hymn* or *song of praise*: generally, *to sing*, ὑμν. θρῆνον Aesch. II. = χρησμῳδέω, Eur. [ῠ in Aesch.]
ὑμνῳδία, ἡ, *the singing of a hymn, hymning*, Eur. II. = χρησμῳδία, *a prophetic strain*, Id.
ὑμν-ῳδός, όν, (ῳδή) *singing hymns*, ὑμν. κόραι the *minstrel* maids, Eur.
ὅμοιος, α, ον, Aeol. for ὅμοιος.
ὑμός [ῠ], ά and ή, όν, Dor. and Ep. for ὑμέτερος, *your*, Hom., Hes. II. in Pind. also for σός.
ὗν, acc. of ὗς.
ΥΝΙΣ [ῠ], ἡ, *a ploughshare*, Babr., Plut.
ὑο-μουσία, ἡ, *swine's music, swinish taste in music*, Ar.
ὑό-πρῳρος, ον, of a ship, *having a beak turned up like a swine's snout*, Plut.
ὑός, gen. of ὗς.

ὑοσ-κύᾰμος, ὁ, (ὗς) hen-bane, Hyoscyamus, Xen.

ὑο-φόρβιον, τό, = συο-φόρβιον, a herd of swine, Strab.

ὑπ-άγγελος, ον, summoned by messenger, Aesch.

ὑπ-αγκᾰλίζω, f. ίσω and ιῶ, to clasp in the arms, embrace, Eur. :—Pass., γένος ὑπηγκαλισμένη having them clasped in her arms, Id. Hence

ὑπαγκάλισμα [ᾰ], ατος, τό, that which is clasped in the arms, a beloved one, Soph., Eur.

ὑπᾰγορεύω, the aor. in Att. is ὑπεῖπον, the pf. ὑπείρηκα: —to dictate, Lat. praeire verbis, Xen., Dem.   II. to suggest, Plut.

ὑπ-άγω, f. ὑπάξω: aor. 2 ὑπήγαγον: A. trans. to lead or bring under, ὕπαγε ζυγὸν ἵππους bring them under the yoke, Il.; simply, ὑπάγειν ἡμιόνους Od.   2. metaph. to bring under one's power, Hdt., Luc.:—Med. to bring under one's own power, reduce, Thuc.   II. to bring a person before the judgment-seat (the ὑπό refers to his being set beneath the judge's seat), Hdt.; ὑπ. τινὰ εἰς δίκην Thuc.; ὑπ. τινὰ θανάτου on a capital charge, Xen.   III. to lead slowly on, to lead on by degrees, τὰς κύνας Id. :—to lead on by art or deceit, Hdt., Xen.; ὑπ. τινὰ εἰς ἐλπίδα Eur.:—so in Med., Xen.; ὑπ. τοὺς Θηβαίους to win them, Dem. :—in Med. also to suggest a thing so as to lead a person on, Eur., Xen.   IV. to take away from under, withdraw, Il. : Pass., ὑπαγομένου τοῦ χώματος Thuc.   2. to draw off, τὸ στράτευμα Id.
B. intr., of an army, to draw off or retire slowly, Hdt., Thuc.   II. to go slowly forwards, draw on, ὕπαγ' ὦ, ὕπαγ' ὦ on with you! Eur.; ὕπαγε, τί μέλλεις ; Ar. :—of an army, to come gradually on, Xen.

ὑπᾰγωγή, ἡ, a leading on gradually, Xen.   II. (from ὑπάγω intr.) a retreat, withdrawal, Thuc.

ὑπ-αείδω, contr. -ᾴδω: aor. 1 ὑπ-ᾆσα:—to sing by way of accompaniment, in tmesi, Λίνον δ' ὑπὸ καλὸν ἄειδεν Il.; ὑπ. μέλος Ar.; ὑπ. τινί to accompany with the voice, Id.

ὑπαί, Ep. for ὑπό.

ὑπαι-δείδοικα, Ep. for ὑποδέδοικα, pf. of ὑποδείδω.

ὑπ-αιδέομαι, to shew some respect for, τινα Xen.

ὑπαιθᾱ, Adv.(ὑπαί) out under, slipping away, Il.   II. Prep. with gen. under, at the side of, Ib.

ὑπ-αίθριος, ον, and α, ον, (αἰθήρ) under the sky, in the open air, a-field, ὑπ. κατακοιμηθῆναι, of an army, Hdt., Thuc.; ὑπ. δρόσοι Aesch.

ὕπ-αιθρος, ον, = foreg.: ὕπαιθρον, τό, as Subst., ἐν ὑπαίθρῳ, sub Dio, in the open air, Xen.   2. τὰ ὕπαιθρα, the field, the open country, Polyb.

ὑπ-αίθω, to set on fire below or secretly, Soph.

ὑπ-αινίσσομαι, Att. -ττομαι, Dep. to intimate darkly, hint at, Dem., Plut.

ὑπ-αιρέω, Ion. for ὑφ-αιρέω.

ὑπ-αΐσσω, Att. -ᾴσσω, f. ξω, to dart beneath, c. acc., Il.   II. to dart from under, c. gen., Ib. :—also, ὑπᾴξας διὰ θυρῶν Soph.

ὑπ-αισχύνομαι [ῡ], Pass. to be somewhat ashamed, τινά τι of a thing before a person, Plat.

ὑπ-αίτιος, ον, under accusation, called to account, responsible, τινος or ὑπέρ τινος for a thing, Antipho; τινι to a· person, Xen.; ὑπαίτιόν ἐστί τί τινι a charge is made against one, Id.

ὑπᾰκοή, ἡ, (ὑπακούω) obedience, N. T.

ὑπ-ᾰκούω, f. -ακούσομαι: I. absol. to listen, hearken, give ear, Hom., Eur.   2. to make answer when called, Od., Theocr.   3. foll. by a case, to listen or hearken to, give ear to, attend to, τινός Ar., etc.; also, ὑπ. τινί Thuc., etc.   II. Special senses :   1. of porters, to answer a knock at the door, ὑπ. τινί Plat., Theophr.; ὁ ὑπακούσας the porter, Xen.   2. of a judge, to listen to a complainant, τινί Id. :—but of accused persons, to answer to a charge, Dem.   3. of dependents and subjects, to submit to, τινός Hdt., Xen.; τινί Ar., Thuc. : also to yield to, comply with, τινί Plat. :—c. gen. rei, to give ear to, Xen.; ὑπ. τῷ ξυμφόρῳ τινός to comply with his interest, Thuc.:—absol. to give way, submit, comply, Hdt.   4. to answer one's expectations, to succeed, Luc.   5. metaph., αὐγαῖς ἡλίου ὑπ. to be subject to the sun's rays, Pind.

ὑπ-ᾰλείφω, f. ψω, to lay thinly on, to spread like salve ; in Med., ὑπαλείφεσθαι φάρμακον Plat.   II. to anoint, τὼ ὀφθαλμώ Ar. :—in Med. to anoint oneself, Id.; ὑπ. τοὺς ὀφθαλμούς to anoint one's eyes, Xen. :— Pass. of the eyes, ὑπαληλιμμένοι Id.

ὑπ-ᾰλεύομαι, (ἀλεύω) Ep. Dep., = ὑπαλύσκω, ὑπαλευάμενος θάνατον (aor. 1 part.) Od.; ὑπαλεύεο φήμην (imper.) Hes.

ὑπ-αλλᾰγή, ἡ, an interchange, exchange, change, Eur.

ὑπάλλαγμα, ατος, τό, that which is exchanged, νόμισμα ὑπάλλαγμα τῆς χρείας money is the exchangeable representative of demand, Arist.   From

ὑπ-αλλάσσω, Att. -ττω, f. ξω, to exchange, Luc.

ὑπ-άλπειος, α, ον, ("Αλπεις) under the Alps ;—ἡ ὑπαλπεία (sc. χώρα) sub-Alpine Italy, Plut.

ὑπάλυξις, εως, ἡ, a shunning, escape, Hom. From

ὑπ-ᾰλύσκω, Ep. aor. 1 ὑπ-άλυξα, = ὑπαλεύομαι, to avoid, shun, flee from, escape, Hom.

ὑπ-αναγιγνώσκω, f. -γνώσομαι, to read by way of preface, premise by reading, Aeschin.

ὑπ-ανᾱλίσκω, aor. 1 ὑπ-ανάλωσα, to waste away, spend or consume gradually, Thuc., Plut., etc.

ὑπανάστᾱσις, ἡ, a rising up from one's seat, Plat.

ὑπαναστᾱτέον, verb. Adj. of ὑπανίσταμαι, one must rise up, Xen.

ὑπαναχωρέω, f. ήσομαι, to retire slowly, Thuc.

ὕπ-ανδρος, ον, (ἀνήρ) under a man, subject to him, married, N. T., Plut.

ὑπ-άνειμι, (εἶμι ibo) to come on, creep on, Luc.

ὑπ-ανέμιος, Dor. for ὑπ-ηνέμιος.

ὑπ-ανῑάομαι, Pass. to be somewhat distressed, opt. -ιῷτο Ar.

ὑπανίημι, to remit or relax a little, Plut. :—intr., τοῦ φόβου ὑπανέντος (aor. 2 part.) Id.

ὑπ-ανίσταμαι, Pass. with aor. 2 and pf. act. to rise, stand up, Theogn.; of game, to start up, to be sprung, Xen.   2. ὑπ. τῆς ἕδρης to rise up from one's seat to make room or shew respect to another, Lat. assurgere alicui, Hdt., Ar., etc.

ὑπ-ανοίγω or -γνυμι, f. ξω: pf. ὑπανέῳγα:—to open from below : to open underhand or secretly, Dem.

ὑπ-αντάω, Ion. -έω : f. -ήσομαι, aor. 1 -ήντησα :—to come or go to meet, either as a friend or in arms, τινί Xen., etc. :—also c. gen., Soph.   II. metaph. to meet, reply or object to, τινί Eur.

ὑ-παντιάζω, f. άσω [ᾰ], to come or go to meet, step forth to meet, encounter, absol., Il., Aesch., etc. : c. dat., Aesch., Xen., etc. ; also c. acc., Hdt., Plut.

ὕπ-αντρος, ον, with caverns underneath, Strab.

ὑπ-ᾰπειλέω, f. ήσω, to threaten underhand, τινί Xen.

ὑπ-άπειμι, (εἶμι ibo) to depart stealthily or slowly, to withdraw, retreat, Thuc.

ὑπ-αποκῑνέω, f. ήσω, intr. to move off secretly, sneak away from, c. gen., Ar.

ὑπ-άπτω, Ion. for ὑφ-άπτω.

Υ̓ΠΑΡ, τό, indecl., a waking vision, opp. to ὄναρ (a dream), οὐκ ὄναρ, ἀλλ' ὕπαρ no illusive dream, but a reality, Od. ; so Pind., Aesch. II. the acc. is used as Adv., in a waking state, awake, Plat. ; ὄναρ ἢ ὕπαρ ζῆν to pass life asleep or awake, Id. 2. ὕπαρ in reality, actually, Id.

ὑπ-άργῠρος, ον, having silver underneath; hence, 1. containing silver, veined with silver, πέτρα, χθών Eur. :—containing a proportion of silver, metaph. of men, Plat. II. sold or hired for silver, mercenary, venal, Pind.

ὑπαρκτέον, verb. Adj. of ὑπάρχω, one must begin, Plat.

ὑπ-άρκτιος, ον, (ἄρκτος) towards the north, Plut.

ὕπ-αρνος, ον, with a lamb under it, i. e. suckling a lamb or (metaph.) a babe, Eur.

ὑπ-αρπάζω, Ion. for ὑφ-αρπάζω.

ὑπαρχή, the beginning : ἐξ ὑπαρχῆς, from the beginning, afresh, anew, Lat. denuo, Soph., Dem.

ὕπ-αρχος, ὁ, commanding under another, a lieutenant, lieutenant-governor, viceroy, Hdt., etc.

ὑπ-άρχω, f. ξω: aor. 1 ὑπῆρξα :—Pass., pf. ὑπηργμαι, Ion. -αργμαι :—to begin, make a beginning, absol., Od., Eur., etc. 2. c. gen. to make a beginning of, ἀδικίης Hdt. ; πολλῶν κακῶν Eur., etc. 3. c. part to begin doing, ὑπῆρξαν ἄδικα ποιεῦντες Hdt. ; ὑπάρχει εὖ ποιῶν τινα Xen. 4. c. acc., ὑπ. εὐεργεσίας εἴς τινα or τινι to begin [doing] kindnesses to one, Dem., Aeschin. :—Pass. to be begun, τὰ ἔκ τινος ὑπαργμένα (Ion. for ὑπηργ-) Hdt. :—impers., ὑπῆρκτο αὐτοῦ a beginning of it had been made, Thuc.

B. to begin to be, come into being, arise, spring up, Aesch., etc. 2. to be in existence, to be there, to be ready, Hdt., Att. ;—c. gen., ὑπάρχει τῶνδε there is store of these things, Aesch. :—oft. in part., ἡ ὑπάρχουσα οὐσία the existing property, Isocr. ; τὰ ὑπάρχοντα ἁμαρτήματα Thuc. ; τῆς ὑπ. τιμῆς for the current price, Dem. 3. simply to be, Trag., Thuc., etc. 4. sometimes with a part., much like τυγχάνω, τοιαῦτα [αὐτῷ] ὑπῆρχε ἐόντα Hdt. ; ὑπ. ἐχθρὸς ὤν Dem. II. like ὑπόκειμαι II. 2, to be laid down, to be taken for granted, Plat. ; τούτων ὑπαρχόντων = quae cum ita sint, Id. III. to belong to, fall to one, accrue, ὑπάρχει τινί τι one has, Hdt., Thuc. ; ἡ ὑπάρχουσα φύσις your own proper nature, its normal condition, Thuc. 2. of persons, ὑπ. τινί to be devoted to one, Xen., Dem. ; καθ' ὑμῶν ὑπάρξει ἐκείνῳ he will be on his side against you, Dem. IV. often in neut. pl. part., τὰ ὑπάρχοντα, 1. existing circumstances, present advantages, Thuc., Xen., etc. 2. what belongs to one, one's possessions, means, Thuc., etc. V. impers., ὑπάρχει, the fact is that . ., c. acc. et inf., Soph. 2. it is allowed, it is possible,

c. dat. et inf., ὑπ. μοι εἶναι or ποιεῖν τι Thuc., Plat. :—absol., ὥσπερ ὑπῆρχε as well as was possible, Thuc. 3. in neut. part., like ἐξόν, παρόν, etc., ὑπάρχον ὑμῖν πολεμεῖν since it is allowed you to make war, Id.

ὑπ-ασπίδιος [πῐ], ον, (ἀσπίς) under shield, covered with a shield, τὸν ὑπ. κόσμον the arms of Ajax, Soph.; ὑπ. κοῖτον ἰαύειν to sleep an armed sleep, sleep in arms, Eur. : neut. pl. ὑπασπίδια as Adv., Il.

ὑπ-ασπίζω, to serve as shield-bearer, τινί Pind., Eur.

ὑπ-ασπιστής, οῦ, ὁ, a shield-bearer, armour-bearer, esquire, Hdt., Eur., etc.

ὑπ-ᾁσσω, Att. for ὑπ-αῐσσω.

ὑπᾰτεύω, f. σω, (ὕπατος) to be consul, Plut.

ὑπάτη (sc. χορδή), ἡ, the lowest note of the three which formed the Gr. scale (v. μέση, νεάτη), Plat.

ὑπᾰτικός, ή, όν, of consular rank, Lat. consularis, Plut.

ὕπᾰτος, η, ον, for ὑπέρτατος, like Lat. summus for supremus, the highest, uppermost, of Zeus, ὕπατος κρειόντων, θεῶν ὕπ., Hom. ; οἱ ὕπατοι the gods above, Lat. superi, opp. to οἱ χθόνιοι, Lat. inferi, Aesch.; ὕπατός τις some god above, Id. 2. simply of Place, ἐν πυρῇ ὑπάτη on the very top of the funeral pile, Il. 3. of Time, last, Lat. supremus, Soph., Anth. 4. of Quality, highest, best, Pind. II. c. gen., like the Prep. ὑπό, ὕπατος χώρας supreme over the land, Aesch. ; ὕπατοι λέχεων high above the nest, Id. III. as Subst., ὕπατος, ὁ, the Roman consul, Polyb., etc.

ὑπ-αυλέω, f. ήσω, to play on the flute in accompaniment, Luc.

ὕπ-αυλος, ον, (αὐλή) under or in the court, c. gen., σκηνῆς ὕπαυλος under shelter of the tent, Soph.

ὑπαυχένιος, α, ον, under the neck, Anth. : as Subst., ὑπαυχένιον, τό, a cushion for the neck, Luc.

ὑπ-αφίσταμαι, Pass., with aor. 2 and pf. act., to step back slowly, to withdraw, Antipho.

ὕπ-αφρος, ον, somewhat frothy, ὄμμα ὑπ. an eye dim with tears, Eur.

ὑπ-άφρων, ονος, ὁ, ἡ, somewhat stupid, Hdt.

ὑπ-έᾱσι, Ion. for ὑπ-εισι, 3 pl. of ὕπειμι (εἰμί sum).

ὑπ-έγγυος, ον, having given surety, liable to be called to account or punished, responsible, Aesch. ; ὑπ. πλὴν θανάτου liable to any punishment short of death, Hdt. : c. dat., τὸ γὰρ ὑπέγγυον δίκα καὶ θεοῖσιν liability to human and divine justice, Eur.

ὑπ-εγχέω, f. -χεῶ, to pour in yet more, Plut.

ὑπ-έδδεισαν, Ep. for -έδεισαν, 3 pl. aor. 1 of ὑποδείδω.

ὑπ-εδείδισαν, 3 pl. plqpf. of ὑποδείδω.

ὑπ-έδεκτο, Ep. 3 sing. aor. 2 of ὑποδέχομαι.

ὑπ-έδρᾰμον, aor. 2 of ὑποτρέχω.

ὑπ-έδῡν, aor. 2 of ὑποδύομαι.

ὑπ-εθερμάνθην, aor. 1 pass. of ὑποθερμαίνω.

ὑπ-ειδόμην, aor. 2 med., inf. -ιδέσθαι, to view from below, to behold, Eur. II. metaph. to mistrust, suspect, Id. :—ὑφοράω is used as pres.

ὑπ-εικάθεῖν, aor. 2 inf. of ὑπείκω, opt. ὑπεικάθοιμι Soph., Plat.

ὑπεικτέον, verb. Adj. one must yield, Soph., Plat.

ὑπ-είκω, Ep. ὑπο-είκω, with impf. ὑπόεικον : f. ὑπείξω, Ep. ὑπείξομαι, ὑποείξομαι : aor. 1 ὑπεῖξα, Ep. ὑπόειξα : cf. ὑπεικαθεῖν :—to retire, withdraw, depart, νεῶν ἄπο from the ships, Il. ; ὑπ. τινὶ ἕδρης to retire from one's seat for another (cf. ὑπανίσταμαι), Od. ; ὑπ. τινὶ λόγων, i. e. to allow him to speak first, Xen. 2. to

yield, give way, τιμαῖς ὑπ. *to give way to authority*, Soph.; ὑπ. τινί Xen.: absol. *to give way, comply*, Hom., etc.; τὸ ὑπεῖκον, = οἱ ὑπείκοντες, Eur.:—c. inf. νῶν ὑπεῖκε τὸν κασίγνητον μολεῖν *concede to us that he may come*, Soph. 3. c. acc., χεῖρας ἐμὰς ὑπόειξε *he scaped my hands*, Il.

ὕπ-ειμι (εἰμί *sum*) *to be under*, Lat. *subesse*, c. dat., Il.; πολλῆσι [ἵπποις] πῶλοι ὑπῆσαν *under many mares were sucking foals*, Ib.; *of horses, to be under the yoke, to be yoked in the chariot*, Hdt. II. *to be or lie underneath*, Id., Aesch. 2. *to be laid down*, ὑπόντος τοῦδε *this being granted*, Eur. 3. *to remain concealed, lurk*, Xen. 4. *of things, to be left remaining, remain, be at command*, Hdt., Att. III. *to be subjected or subject*, Eur.

ὕπ-ειμι, (εἶμι *ibo*) used as fut. of ὑπέρχομαι, *to steal secretly upon one*, Lat. *subire*, c. acc., Ar. II. *to depart gradually or secretly*, Hdt.

ὑπείξω, fut. of ὑπείκω.

ὑπ-εῖπε, aor. 2 with no pres. in use (ὑπαγορεύω being used instead): f. ὑπ-ερῶ: pf. ὑπ-είρηκα:—*to say as a foundation or preface, to premise, suggest*, Eur., Thuc., etc. 2. *to subjoin, add*, Ar., Dem. 3. *to suggest an explanation, explain, interpret*, Soph., Plat.

ὑπείρ, Ep. for ὑπέρ, used when a long syll. is needed before a vowel, e. g. ὑπεὶρ ἅλα Hom.

ὑπειρ-έβαλον, Ep. aor. 2 of ὑπερβάλλω.

ὑπειρ-έχω, Ep. for ὑπερ-έχω.

ὑπείρ-οχος, ον, Ep. and Ion. for ὑπέρ-οχος.

ὑπ-είσας, Ion. aor. 1 part. of ὑφ-εῖσα.

ὑπ-εισδύνομαι, Med. with aor. 2 act. -εισέδυν, *to get in secretly, to slip or steal in*, Hdt.

ὑπ-εισέρχομαι, aor. 2 -εισῆλθον, Dep. *to enter secretly, to come into one's mind*, Luc.

ὑπ-έκ, before a vowel ὑπ-έξ, (ὑπό, ἐκ) poët. Prep. with gen. *out from under, from beneath, away from*, Il.

ὑπ-εκδέχομαι, Dep. *to have under one*, of a cow, πόρτιν μαστῷ ὑπ. *to have a calf under her udder*, Anth.

ὑπ-εκδράμω, aor. 2 inf. of ὑπεκτρέχω.

ὑπ-εκδύομαι, Med., with aor. 2 act., *to slip out of, escape*, c. acc., Eur.; c. gen., Plut.; absol., ὑπεκδύς *having slipped out*, Hdt.

ὑπ-εκέχῦτο, 3 sing. plqpf. of ὑπεκχέω.

ὑπεκθέω, *to run off secretly or gradually*, Plut.

ὑπ-εκκαλύπτω, f. ψω, *to uncover below or a little*, Anth.

ὑπέκκαυμα, ατος, τό, (ἐκκαίω) *combustible matter, fuel*, Xen.:—metaph. *an incentive*, Lat. *fomes, fomes of love* Id.

ὑπ-έκκειμαι, f. -εκκείσομαι, Pass. *to be carried out to a place of safety, to be stowed safe away*, Hdt., Thuc.

ὑπ-εκκλίνω [ῑ], -εκκλῐνῶ, *to bend aside, escape*, Ar.: c. acc. *to shun, avoid*, Plut.

ὑπ-εκκομίζω, f. Att. ιῶ, *to carry out or away secretly*, Thuc., etc.:—Med., ὑπεκκομίσασθαι πάντα *to get all one's goods carried secretly out*, Plut.

ὑπ-εκλαμβάνω, f. -λήψομαι, *to carry off underhand*, Eur.

ὑπ-εκλίνθην, aor. 1 pass. of ὑποκλίνω.

ὑπ-εκλύω, f. -λύσω, *to loosen or weaken gradually*, Plut.

ὑπ-εκπέμπω, f. ψω, *to send out secretly*, Thuc., Eur.: —Pass., c. acc. loci, τὸ Φωκέων πέδον ὑπεξεπέμφθην *I was sent out secretly* to Phocis, Soph.

ὑπ-εκπλέω, -πλεύσομαι, *to sail out secretly*, Plut.

ὑπ-εκπροθέω, f. -θεύσομαι, *to run forth from under, outstrip*, Il.:—absol. *to run on before*, Hom.

ὑπ-εκπρολύω, f. -λύσω, *to loose from under*, ἡμιόνους μὲν ὑπεκπροέλυσαν ἀπήνης *loosed* the mules *from under* the carriage-yoke, Od.

ὑπ-εκπρορέω, f. -ρεύσομαι, *to flow forth from under*, Od.

ὑπ-εκπροφεύγω, f. -φεύξομαι: aor. 2 -έφῠγον:—*to flee away secretly, escape and flee*, Hom.

ὑπ-εκρέω, f. -ρυήσομαι: aor. 2 ὑπεξερρύην:—*to flow out under*:—metaph. *to pass away gradually*, Plat.: *to slip out*, Plut.

ὑπ-εκρήγνῦμαι, Pass. *to be gradually broken away*, Plut.

ὑπ-εκρίπτω, f. ψω, *to cast down out of*, Plut.

ὑπ-εκρύφθην, aor. 1 pass. of ὑπο-κρύπτω.

ὑπ-εκσώζω, f. σω, *to save by drawing away from*, Aesch.: absol., αὑτὸν ὑπεξεσάωσεν (Ep. for -έσωσεν) Il.

ὑπεκτίθεμαι, aor. 2 -εκθέμην, Med. *to bring one's goods to a place of safety, carry safely away*, ἔστ' ἂν τέκνα ὑπεκθέωνται (3 pl. aor. 2 subj.) Hdt.; so in Att.:— Pass. *to be carried out to a place of safety*, Hdt.

ὑπ-εκτρέπω, f. ψω, *to turn gradually or secretly from a thing*, τί τινος Soph.:—Med. *to turn aside from*, c. acc., Plat.; c. inf., ὑπεκτραπέσθαι μὴ οὐ ξυνεκσώζειν *to decline the task* of helping to save, Soph.

ὑπ-εκτρέχω, f. -δρᾰμοῦμαι: aor. 2 ὑπεξέδρᾰμον:—*to run out from under, escape from*, c. acc., Hdt., Soph., etc.; c. inf., ἢν ἐγὼ μὴ θανεῖν ὑπεκδράμω Eur. II. *to run out beyond*, Soph.

ὑπ-εκφέρω, f. -εξοίσω, *to carry out a little*, ὑπεξέφερεν σάκος *lifted it a little outwards*, so that Teucer could take shelter under it, Il. II. *to carry out from under*, υἱὸν ὑπεξέφερε πολέμοιο Ib.: *to carry away, bear onward*, Od. III. intr., ὑπ. ἡμέρης ὁδῷ *to get the start* by a day's journey, Hdt.

ὑπ-εκφεύγω, f. -φεύξομαι: aor. 2 -εξέφῠγον:—*to flee away or escape secretly*, Hom., Soph. II. mostly c. acc. *to escape from*, Il., Thuc.

ὑπ-εκχᾰλάω, f. άσω, *to slacken gradually*, Anth.

ὑπ-εκχωρέω, f. ήσω, *to withdraw or retire slowly or unnoticed*, Hdt.:—c. dat. pers. *to retire and give place to* another, Plat.; ὑπ. τῷ θανάτῳ *to make way for death*, i. e. *to escape it*, Id.

ὑπ-έλαβον, aor. 2 of ὑπο-λαμβάνω.

ὑπ-ελαύνω, f. -εξελῶ, (sub. τὸν ἵππον), *to ride up* so as to meet, Xen.

ὑπ-ελθεῖν, aor. 2 inf. of ὑπέρχομαι.

ὑπ-έλοντο, Ep. for ὑφ-είλοντο, 3 pl. aor. 2 med. of ὑφ-αιρέω.

ὑπ-έλῠντο, 3 pl. Ep. aor. 2 pass. of ὑπολύω.

ὑπ-ελύσαο, Ep. 2 sing. aor. 1 med. of ὑπολύω.

ὑπ-εμείναο, Ep. 2 pl. of ὑπομένω.

ὑπ-εμνάασθε, Ep. 2 pl. of ὑπομνάομαι.

ὑπ-εμνήμῠκε, Ep. pf. of ὑπ-ημύω, *he hangs down his head, stands with head hung down*, Il.

ὑπ-εναντιόομαι, Dep. *to oppose secretly*, Plut.

ὑπ-εναντίος, α, ον, *set over against, meeting*, ἀλλήλοισιν Hes. 2. *set against, opposite*, of enemies in battle, Thuc. ὑπ. *the enemy*, Xen. 3. *opposed, opposite*: c. dat. *opposite or contrary to*, Hdt., Xen.: —as Subst., τὸ ὑπεναντίον τούτου πέφυκε *the contrary hereto generally happens*, Hdt.; τὰ ὑπ. τούτων *on the*

contrary, Id.　II. Adv. -ίως, in a manner contrary to, τῷ νόμῳ Aeschin.

ὑπ-ενδίδωμι, f. -ενδώσω, to give way a little, Thuc.

ὑπ-ένδυμα, ατος, τό, an undergarment, Anth. From

ὑπενδύομαι, Pass., ὑπενδεδυμένοι χιτῶνας having tunics on under their arms, Plut.

ὑπ-ένερθε, and before a vowel -θεν, Adv. underneath, beneath, Hom., Ar.　2. under the earth, in the nether world, Lat. apud inferos, Od.　II. as Prep., c. gen., under, beneath, Hom., Pind.

ὑπ-εξάγω [ᾰ], f. ξω : aor. 2 ὑπεξήγαγον :—to carry out from under, esp. out of danger, Hom., Hdt.　II. ὑπ. πόδα to withdraw gradually, retire slowly, Eur.; and so, without πόδα, Hdt., Xen.

ὑπ-εξαιρέω, f. ήσω : aor. 2 -εξεῖλον :—to take away from below, αἷμα ὑπ. to drain away blood, Soph.　2. to make away with, to destroy gradually, Eur.; τοὐπίκλημ' ὑπεξελών having done away with the charge, Soph. :—Pass., Hdt., Thuc.　II. Med. to take out privily for oneself, steal away, Il.　2. to put aside, except, exclude, Plat., Dem.

ὑπ-εξακρίζω, f. σω, to ascend to the summit, Eur.

ὑπ-εξαλέασθαι, inf. aor. 1 of ὑπεξαλέομαι, Dep. to flee out from under, avoid, c. acc., Il.

ὑπ-εξαλύσκω, f. ύξω, =foreg., c. acc., Hes.

ὑπ-εξαναβαίνω, to step suddenly back, Theocr.

ὑπ-εξανάγομαι, Pass. to put out to sea secretly, Thuc.

ὑπ-εξαναδύομαι, Med., with aor. 2 act. -έδυν, to come up from under, emerge, ὑπεξαναδὺς ἁλός Il.; ὑπ. κεφαλῇ to duck or stoop so as to avoid a blow, Theocr.

ὑπ-εξανίσταμαι, =ὑπανίσταμαι, Plut., Luc.; ὑπ. τινι to rise and make room for him, Plut., Luc.

ὑπ-εξαντλέω, to drain out from below, exhaust, Eur.

ὑπέξειμι, (εἶμι ibo) to go away secretly, withdraw gradually, Hdt.; ὑπ. τινι to make way for one, give way to him, Dem. :—of fire or snow, to disappear gradually, Plat.

ὑπεξειρύω, Ion. for ὑπεξερύω.

ὑπ-εξελαύνω, f. -ελῶ, to drive away gradually, Hdt.

ὑπ-εξελών, aor. 2 part. of ὑπεξαιρέω.

ὑπ-εξερύω, Ion. -ειρύω, f. σω, to draw out from under, draw away underhand, Hdt.

ὑπ-εξέρχομαι, Dep. with aor. 2 act. -εξῆλθον, pf. -εξελήλυθα :—to go out from under : to go out secretly, withdraw, retire, Thuc., Dem. :—rarely c. acc. pers. to withdraw from, escape from, Thuc.　2. to rise up and quit one's settlements, to emigrate, Hdt.　II. to go out to meet, Id.

ὑπ-εξεσάωσα, Ep. for -έσωσα, aor. 1 of ὑπεκσώζω.

ὑπ-εξέφυγον, aor. 2 of ὑπεκφεύγω.

ὑπ-εξέχω, intr. to withdraw or retire secretly, Hdt.

ὑπ-εξίσταμαι, Pass., with aor. 2 and pf. act., to depart secretly, ὑπ. τῆς ἀρχῆς to give up all claim to it, like Lat. abdicare se magistratu, Hdt.; so c. inf., ὑπ. ἄρχειν Luc.　2. c. acc. to go out of the way of, to give place to, make way for, Xen. : c. dat. to yield to, give way to, Plut.

ὑπ-έπλευσα, aor. 1 of ὑποπλέω.

ὑπ-έπτατο, 3 sing. aor. 2 of ὑπο-πέταμαι.

ὑπέρ [ῠ], Ep. also ὑπείρ, Lat. super :—hence are formed Comp. and Sup. ὑπέρτερος, -τατος.
　A. WITH GENIT.,　I. of Place, over, above :　1.

in a state of rest, στέρνον ὑπὲρ μαζοῖο Il.; ὑπὲρ κεφαλῆς στῆναί τινι to stand over his head, Hom. : of countries, above, further inland, οἰκέοντες ὑπὲρ Ἁλικαρνησσοῦ μεσόγαιαν Hdt.　2. in a state of motion, over, across, ὑπὲρ θαλάσσης καὶ χθονὸς ποτωμένοις Aesch.　3. over, beyond, ὑπὲρ πόντου Od.　II. metaph., from the notion of standing over to protect, for, for defence of, in behalf of, ἐκατόμβην ῥέξαι ὑπὲρ Δαναῶν Il.; θύειν ὑπὲρ τῆς πόλεως Xen.; ὑπὲρ τῆς πατρίδος ἀμύνειν to fight for one's country, etc.　2. for the sake of a person or thing, λίσσεσθαι ὑπὲρ τοκέων, ὑ. πατρὸς καὶ μητρός Il.　3. c. inf. for the purpose of, ὑπὲρ τοῦ μηδένα ἀποθνήσκειν to prevent any one from dying, Xen.　4. for, instead of, in the name of, ὑπὲρ ἑαυτοῦ Thuc.; στρατηγῶν ὑπὲρ ὑμῶν acting as general by commission from you, Dem.　III. like περί, on, of, concerning, Lat. de, ὑπὲρ σέθεν αἴσχεα ἀκούω Il.; τὰ λεγόμενα ὑπέρ τινος Hdt.
　B. WITH ACC., expressing that over and beyond which a thing goes,　I. of Place, over, beyond, Hom., Plat.　II. of Measure, over, above, exceeding, beyond, ὑπὲρ τὸ βέλτιστον Aesch.; ὑπὲρ ἐλπίδα Soph., etc.　2. of transgression, beyond, contrary to, ὑπὲρ αἶσαν, ὑπὲρ μοῖραν, ὑπὲρ ὅρκια Il.　III. of Number, above, upwards of, ὑπὲρ τεσσεράκοντα Hdt., Xen.; ὑπὲρ τὸ ἥμισυ more than half, Xen.　IV. of Time, beyond, i. e. before, earlier than, ὁ ὑπὲρ τὰ Μηδικὰ πόλεμος Thuc.
　C. POSITION : ὑπέρ may follow its Subst., but then by anastrophé becomes ὕπερ, Hom., Trag.
　D. AS ADV. over much, above measure, ὑπὲρ μὲν ἄγαν Eur.; written ὑπεράγαν, Strab., etc.
　E. IN COMPOS.,　1. of Place, over, beyond, in ὑπερ-βαίνω, ὑπερ-πόντιος.　2. for, in defence of, in ὑπερ-ασπίζω, ὑπερ-αγέω.　3. above measure, in ὑπερ-ήφανος, ὑπερ-φίαλος.

ὑπέρα [ῠ], ἡ, (ὑπέρ) an upper rope : pl. ὑπέραι, the braces attached to the ends of the sailyards (ἐπίκρια), by means of which the sails are shifted fore and aft, to catch the wind, Od.

ὑπερ-άβέλτερος, ον, above measure simple or silly, Dem.

ὑπερ-άγαμαι, Dep. to be exceedingly pleased, Plat.　II. to admire above measure, τινος for a thing, Luc.

ὑπερ-αγανακτέω, f. ήσω, to be exceeding angry or vexed at a thing, c. gen., Plat.; c. dat., Aeschin.

ὑπερ-αγάπάω, to love exceedingly, make much of, Dem.

ὑπερ-αγωνιάω, to be in great distress, Plat., Dem.

ὑπερ-αής, ές, gen. έος, (ἄημι) blowing hard, Il.

ὑπερ-αιμόω, f. ώσω, (αἷμα) to have over-much blood, Xen.

ὑπερ-αίρω, f. -ἀρῶ, to lift or raise up over, Plat. :—Med. or Pass. to lift oneself above, to exalt oneself, be exalted, N.T.　II. intr.,　1. c. acc. to climb or get over, pass over, Lat. transcendere, Xen.; ὑπ. τὴν ἄκραν to double the cape, Id. :—as military term, to outflank, Id.　2. to transcend, excel, outdo, τινά τινι one in a thing, Dem.　3. to overshoot, go beyond, exceed, καιρόν Aesch.　III. to overflow, Dem.

ὑπερ-αισχρος, ον, exceeding foul or ugly, Xen.

ὑπερ-αισχύνομαι, Pass. to feel much ashamed, Aeschin.

ὑπερ-αιωρέομαι, Pass. to hang or be suspended over, project over, τινος Hdt.　2. in nautical language,

c. gen. loci, *to lie off* a place, τῇσι νηυσὶ ὑπεραιωρηθέντες Φαληροῦ Hdt.

ὑπέρ-ακμος, ον, (ἀκμή) *past the bloom of youth*, N. T.

ὑπερ-ἀκοντίζω, f. Att. ιῶ, *to overshoot*, i. e. *to outdo*, c. acc., Ar.; *ὑπ. τινὰ κλέπτων to outdo* one in stealing, Id.

ὑπερ-ακρῑβής, ές, *exceedingly exact*, Luc.

ὑπερ-ακρίζω, f. σω, *to mount and climb over*, c. acc., Xen.   II. *to project, beetle over*, c. gen., Eur.

ὑπερ-άκριος, ον, (ἄκρα) *over* or *upon the heights*, οἱ Ὑπεράκριοι, = οἱ Διάκριοι, *the highlanders* or *inhabitants of the Attic uplands*, opp. to the richer classes of the plains and coasts, Hdt.   2. τὰ ὑπ. *the heights above* the plain, *the uplands*, Id.

ὑπέρ-ακρος, ον, *over* or *on the top:* Adv., ὑπεράκρως ζῆν *to carry everything to excess*, Dem.

ὑπερ-αλγέω, f. ήσω, *to feel pain for* or *because of*, τινός Soph., Eur.   2. *to grieve exceedingly*, τινί *at* a thing, Hdt., Arist.:—absol., Eur.

ὑπερ-αλγής, ές, gen. έος, *exceeding grievous*, Soph.

ὑπερ-αλκής, ές, (ἀλκή) gen. έος, *exceeding strong*, Plut.

ὑπερ-άλλομαι, aor. 1 —ηλάμην: syncop. 3 sing. aor. 2 ὑπέρ-αλτο, part. -άλμενος: Dep. :—*to leap over* or *beyond*, c. gen., Il.; also c. acc., Ib.; so Xen.

ὑπερ-αλλος, ον, *above others, exceeding great*, Pind.

ὑπερ-άλπειος, ον, (Ἄλπεις) *transalpine*, Strab.

ὑπερ-αναιδεύομαι, Pass. *to be surpassed in impudence*, Ar.

ὑπερ-αναίσχυντος, ον, *exceeding impudent*, Dem.

ὑπερ-ανατείνομαι, Pass. *to exert oneself excessively*, Luc.

ὑπερ-άνθρωπος, ον, *superhuman*, Luc.

ὑπερ-ανίσταμαι, Pass., with aor. 2 and pf. act. *to stand up* or *project beyond*, Luc.

ὑπερ-αντλέομαι, Pass. *to be very leaky*, ὑπ. ἄλμῃ *to be* water-logged, Luc. From

ὑπέρ-αντλος, ον, of a ship, *quite full of water* (ἄντλος), *water-logged*, Plut. :—metaph. *overcharged*, ὑπέραντλος συμφορᾷ Eur.; ταῖς φροντίσιν Plut.

ὑπερ-άνω [ᾰ], Adv. *over, above*, Luc.

ὑπερ-ἀπατάομαι, Pass. *to be deceived excessively*, Anth.

ὑπερ-αποθνήσκω, f. -θανοῦμαι: aor. 2 -έθανον :—*to die for*, τινός Xen.; ὑπέρ τινος Plat.

ὑπερ-αποκρίνομαι [ῑ], Med. *to answer for* one, *defend* him, τινος Ar.

ὑπερ-απολογέομαι, Dep., with fut. and aor. 1 med. *to speak in behalf of, defend*, τινος Hdt., Xen.

ὑπερ-αρρωδέω, Ion. for ὑπερορρωδέω, *to be exceeding afraid*, τῇ Ἑλλάδι for Hellas, Hdt.

ὑπερ-ασθενής, ές, *exceeding weak*, Arist.

ὑπέρ-ασθμος, ον, (ἄσθμα) *panting exceedingly*, Xen.

ὑπερ-ασπάζομαι, Dep. *to be exceeding fond of*, τινα Xen.

ὑπερ-άτοπος, ον, *beyond measure, absurd*, Dem.

ὑπερ-αττικός, ή, όν, *carrying the use of the Attic dialect to excess*, Luc. : Adv. -κῶς, Id.

ὑπερ-αυγής, ές, gen. έος, *shining exceedingly*, Luc.

ὑπερ-αυξάνω and -αύξω, f. -αυξήσω, *to increase above measure* :—Pass. *to be so increased*, Andoc.   II. intr. *to increase exceedingly*, N. T.

ὑπέρ-αυχος, ον, *over-boastful, overproud*, Thuc.

ὑπέρ-αυχος, ον, (αὐχή) *over-boastful, overproud*, Soph., Xen.; ὑπέραυχα βάζειν Aesch.

ὑπερ-άφανος, ον, Dor. for ὑπερ-ήφανος.

ὑπερ-αχθής, ές, (ἄχθος) *overburdened*, Theocr.

ὑπερ-άχθομαι, Pass. *to be exceedingly grieved at* a thing, c. dat., Hdt., Soph.

ὑπερβαίνω, f. -βήσομαι: aor. 2 ὑπερ-έβην, Ep. ὑπέρ-βην, Ep. 3 pl. ὑπέρβᾰσαν :—*to step over, mount, scale*, c. acc., ὑπ. τεῖχος Il., etc.; ὑπ. δόμους *to step over* the threshold of the house, Eur.; ὑπ. τοὺς οὔρους *to cross* the boundaries, Hdt. :—of rivers, *to go over their banks, overflow*, Id.   2. *to overstep, transgress*, τοὺς νόμους Id., Soph.: τοὺς ὅρκους Dem.: absol. *to transgress, trespass, sin*, ὅτε κέν τις ὑπερβήῃ (Ep. aor. 2 subj.) Il.   3. *to pass over, pass by, leave out, omit*, τινά, Dem.   II. *to go beyond, to surpass, outdo*, c. acc., Plat.; absol., Theogn.

B. Causal in aor. 1, *to put over*, Xen.

ὑπερβαλλόντως, Adv. of sq., *exceedingly*, Plat.

ὑπερβάλλω, f. -βαλῶ, Ion. -βαλέω: aor. 2 ὑπειρ-έβαλον :—*to throw over* or *beyond a mark, to overshoot*, c. acc., Il.   2. ὅτε μέλλοι ἄκρον [λόφον] ὑπερβαλέειν when he was just about *to force the stone over the top*, Od.   3. intr. *to run beyond, overrun* the scent, of hounds, Xen.   4. *to outstrip* or *pass*, τινάς Soph.   II. metaph. :   1. *to overshoot, outdo, surpass, prevail over*, c. gen., βροντῆς ὑπερβάλλοντα κτύπον Aesch.; also c. acc., ὑπ. τινι *to outdo* one in a thing, Eur.   2. *to go beyond, exceed*, c. acc., Hes., etc.; ὑπ. ἑκατὸν ἔτεα *to exceed* 100 years, in age, Hdt.; ὑπ. τὸν χρόνον, i. e. be too late, Xen. :—also c. gen., Plat.   3. absol. *to exceed all bounds*, Aesch., Eur., etc.; οὐχ ὑπερβαλών keeping within bounds, Pind. : *to be in excess*, Arist. :—often in part., ὑπερβάλλων, ουσα, ον, *exceeding, excessive*, Aesch., Plat.; τὰ ὑπ. ὑπερβάλλοντα *an over-high estate*, Eur.; τὸ ὑπ. αὐτῶν *such part* of them *as is extraordinary*, Thuc.   4. *to go on further and further*, προέβαινε ὑπερβάλλων *he went on bidding more and more*, Hdt.; ᾔει τοσαῦτα ὑπερβάλλων Thuc.   III. *to pass over, cross* mountains, rivers, etc., c. acc., Aesch., Eur.; also c. gen., Eur. :—of ships, *to double* a headland, c. acc., Hdt., Thuc. :—absol. *to cross over*, Hdt., Xen.   2. of water, *to run over, overflow*, c. acc., Hdt.   3. of the Sun, *to be at its height* or its *utmost heat*, Id.

B. Med., with pf. pass. = A. II, *to outdo, overcome, conquer*, τινα Hdt., Soph., etc. :—absol. *to be conqueror, to conquer*, Hdt.   2. *to exceed, surpass*, τινα Id., Ar., etc. :—absol. *to exceed*, Hdt. :—pf. pass. part., ὑπερβεβλημένη γυνή *an excellent, surpassing* woman, Eur.   3. *to overbid, outbid*, τινα Xen.   II. *to put off, postpone*, Hdt. ;—but, ἢν ὑπερβάλωνται κείνην τὴν ἡμέραν συμβολὴν μὴ ποιεύμενοι *if they let that day pass without fighting*, Id. :—absol. *to delay, linger*, Id., Plat.

ὑπερ-βάρης, ες, (βάρος) *exceeding heavy*, Aesch.

ὑπερβασία, Ion. -ίη, ἡ, (ὑπερβαίνω) *a transgression of law, trespass*, Hom., Soph. : also in pl., Il.

ὑπέρβᾰσις, εως, ἡ, = sq., *transgression*, Theogn.

ὑπερ-βᾰτός, ή, όν, verb. Adj. of ὑπερβαίνω, *to be passed* or *crossed, scaleable*, of a wall, Thuc.   2. *transposed*, of words, Plat.   II. act. *going beyond*, τῶνδ' ὑπερβατώτερα *going far beyond* these, Aesch.

ὑπερβεβλημένως, Adv. of ὑπερβάλλω, *beyond all measure, immoderately*, Arist.

ὑπερ-βήη, Ep. 3 sing. aor. 2 subj. of ὑπερβαίνω.

ὑπερ-βιάζομαι, Dep. to press exceeding heavily, of the plague, Thuc.

ὑπερ-βιβάζω, f. -βιβῶ, Causal of ὑπερβαίνω, to carry over, c. dupl. acc., Luc.

ὑπέρ-βιος, ον, (βία) of overwhelming strength or might, Pind. II. in bad sense, overweening, lawless, wanton, Hom. :—neut. ὑπέρβιον as Adv., Il.

ὑπερ-βολάδην [ἄ], Adv. immoderately, excessively, Theogn. From

ὑπερβολή, ἡ, (ὑπερβάλλω) a throwing beyond others: an overshooting, superiority, Thuc. 2. excess, over-great degree of a thing, Plat.; in various phrases, χρημάτων ὑπερβολῇ πρίασθαι to buy at an extravagant price, Eur.; οὐκ ἔχει ὑπερβολήν it can go no further, Dem.; εἴ τις ὑπ. τούτου if there's aught beyond (worse than) this, Id.; ὑπερβολὴν ποιεῖσθαι to go to all extremities, to put an extreme case, Id.; foll. by a gen., ὑπ. ποιεῖσθαι ἐκείνων τῆς αὑτοῦ βδελυρίας to carry his own rascality beyond theirs, Id.; ἐπέφερον τὴν ὑπ. τοῦ καινοῦσθαι pushed on their extravagance in revolutionising, Thuc. 3. with a Prep. in Adverbial sense, = ὑπερβαλλόντως, εἰς ὑπερβολὴν in excess, exceedingly; c. gen. far beyond, τοῦ πρόσθεν εἰς ὑπ. πανοῦργος, i. e. far more wicked, Eur.:—καθ' ὑπερβολὴν τοξεύσας with surpassing aim, Soph.; καθ' ὑπ. extravagantly, Isocr., etc. 4. overstrained phrase, hyperbolé, Id., Arist. II. a crossing over mountains, Xen. III. (from Med.) a deferring, delay, Hdt., Dem.

Ὑπερ-βόρεοι, οἱ, (Βορέας) the Hyperboreans, an imaginary people in the extreme north, distinguished for piety and happiness, Pind., Hdt.; τύχη ὑπερβόρεος, proverb. of more than mortal fortune, Aesch.

ὑπερ-βράζω, to boil or foam over, in aor. pass., Anth.

ὑπερ-βρῐθής, ές, (βρῖθος) gen. έος, = ὑπερβαρής, Soph.

ὑπερ-βρύω, to be overfull, Luc.

ὑπ-εργάζομαι, f. άσομαι, Dep. to work under, plough up, prepare for sowing, Xen. II. to subdue, reduce : pf. in pass. sense, to be subdued, Eur. III. to do underhand or secretly, Plut. IV. = ὑπηρετέω, to do a service: pf. in pass. sense, πόλλ' ὑπείργασται φιλά many kind acts have been done, Eur.

ὑπερ-γέλοιος, ον, above measure ridiculous, Dem.

ὑπερ-γεμίζω, f. ίσω, to overfill, overload, Xen.

ὑπέρ-γηρως, ων, exceeding old, of extreme age, Luc. : τὸ ὑπέργηρων extreme old age, Aesch.

ὑπέρ-δᾰσυς, υ, very hairy, Xen.

ὑπερ-δεής, ές, Ep. acc. ὑπερδέᾰ, for ὑπερδεέα: (δέος) :—above all fear, undaunted, Il.

ὑπερ-δείδω, f. -δείσω, to fear for one, c. gen., Aesch., Soph. : absol. to be in exceeding fear, Hdt.

ὑπερ-δειμαίνω, to be much afraid of, τινά Hdt.

ὑπέρ-δεινος, ον, exceeding alarming, Dem., Luc.

ὑπερ-δέξιος, ον, lying above one on the right hand, Xen. :—simply, lying above, ὑπ. χωρίον higher ground, Id.; τὰ ὑπερδέξια Id.; ἐξ ὑπερδεξίου from above, Id. : —c. gen. commanding from above, Polyb. 2. metaph. having the advantage in a thing, Id. : victorious over, τινος Plut.

ὑπερ-δέω, to bind over, τί τινι Anth.

ὑπερ-διατείνομαι, Pass. to exert oneself above measure, Dem., Luc.

ὑπερδικέω, to plead for, act as advocate for, τινός Plat.; ὑπ. τὸ φεύγειν τινός to advocate his acquittal, Aesch.

ὑπέρ-δῐκος, ον, (δίκη) more than just, severely just, Pind.; κἂν ὑπέρδικ' ᾖ be they never so just, Soph.; Adv. -κως, Aesch.

ὑπ-ερεθίζω, f. σω, to stimulate a little, Babr.

ὑπερ-εῖδον, inf. ὑπερῑδεῖν, used as aor. 2 of ὑπεροράω.

ὑπ-ερείδω, f. σω, to put under as a support, Pind., Plat. II. to under-prop, support, Plut.

Ὑπερείη, ἡ, High-land, of the Phaeacians, Od.

ὑπ-ερείπω, to subvert :—Pass., Plut. II. intr. in aor. 2 ὑπήριπον, to tumble, fall down, Il.

ὑπερ-έκεινα, Adv. on yon side, beyond, c. gen., N. T.

ὑπ-ερεκθερᾰπεύω, f. σω, to seek to win by excessive attention, Aeschin.

ὑπερεκπερισσοῦ, Adv., = ὑπὲρ ἐκ περισσοῦ, super-abundantly, N. T.

ὑπερ-εκπίπτω, f. -πεσοῦμαι, to go beyond all bounds, Luc.

ὑπερ-εκπλήσσω, f. ξω, to frighten beyond measure :— Pass. to be in amazement, Xen.; ὑπερεκπεπληγμένος Φίλιππον admiring him exceedingly, Dem.

ὑπερ-εκτείνω, to stretch beyond measure, ἑαυτόν N. T.

ὑπερ-εκτίνω [ῐ], to pay for any one, τινός Luc.

ὑπερ-εκχύνομαι, (ἐκχέω) Pass. to run over, N. T.

ὑπερ-ελαφρος, ον, exceeding light or nimble, Xen.

ὑπερ-εμπίπλημι, to fill over-full :—Pass. to be over-full, τινος of a thing, Xen., Luc.

ὑπερ-εμφορέομαι, Pass. to be filled quite full, Luc.

ὑπερ-εντυγχάνω, to intercede, ὑπέρ τινος for one, N. T.

ὑπερ-εξακισχίλιοι [ῑ], α, α, above 6000, Dem.

ὑπερ-επαινέω, to praise above measure, Hdt., Ar.

ὑπερ-επιθυμέω, f. ήσω, to desire exceedingly, Xen.

ὑπερέπτη, 3 sing. aor. 2 act. of ὑπερπέτομαι.

ὑπ-ερέπτω, (ἐρέπτομαι) to eat away from under, κονίην ὑπέρεπτε ποδοῖιν Il.

ὑπερ-έρχομαι, Dep. with aor. 2 and pf. act. :—to pass over a river, c. acc., Xen. II. to surpass, excel, Pind.

ὑπερ-εσθίω, f. -έδομαι, to eat immoderately, Xen.

ὑπερ-έσχεθον, poët. aor. 2 of ὑπερέχω.

ὑπέρ-ευ, Adv. exceeding well, excellently, Xen., Dem.

ὑπερ-ευγενής, ές, exceeding noble, Arist.

ὑπερ-ευδαιμονέω, f. ήσω, to be exceeding happy, Arist.

ὑπερ-ευφραίνομαι, Pass. to rejoice exceedingly, Luc.

ὑπερ-εχθαίρω, to hate exceedingly, Soph.

ὑπερ-έχω, Ep. ὑπειρ-έχω: Ep. impf. ὑπείρ-εχον: aor. 2 ὑπερ-έσχον, poët. -έσχεθον :—to hold one thing over another, τί τινος Il.; ὑπ. χεῖρά τινος to hold the hand over him, so as to protect, Il., Theogn.; also c. dat. pers., Hom. 2. to have or hold above, ὑπείρεχεν εὐρέας ὤμους he had his broad shoulders above the rest, i. e. over-topped them by the head and shoulders, Il. II. intr. to be above, rise above the horizon, Od. : to be above water or the ground, Hdt.; c. gen., ὑπερέσχεθε γαίης rose above, overlooked the earth, Il.; [σταυροὺς] οὐχ ὑπερέχοντας τῆς θαλάσσης Thuc., etc. 2. in military phrase, to outflank, c. gen., Xen. 3. metaph. to overtop, exceed, outdo, c. acc., Aesch., Eur. :—also c. gen., Plat., etc. 4. absol. to overtop the rest, be prominent, Hdt., Xen. :

to prevail, οἱ ὑπερσχόντες the more powerful, Aesch.; ἐὰν ἡ θάλαττα ὑπέρσχῃ to be too powerful, Dem. **III.** c. gen. rei, to rise above, Ar. **IV.** c. acc. to get over, cross, Thuc.

ὑπερ-ζέω, f. -ζέσω, to boil over : metaph., of a man, Ar.

ὑπερ-ήδομαι, Pass. to be overjoyed at, τινι Hdt. ; c. part., ὑπερήδετο ἀκούων he rejoiced much at hearing, Id.

ὑπερ-ηδύς, υ, exceeding sweet, Luc. Adv. -έως, Xen. ; Sup. -ήδιστα, Luc.

ὑπερημερία, ἡ, a being over the day : as law-term, the latest day for payment, Dem. **2.** forfeiture of recognisances, a distress, Id. From

ὑπερ-ήμερος, ον, (ἡμέρα) over the day for payment, after which the debtor became liable to have his goods seized, Dem. ; ὑπερήμερον λαμβάνων τινά, i. e. having a right to distrain upon him, Id. **II.** metaph., ὑπ. τῆς ζώης past the term of life, Luc. ; ὑπ. τοῦ βίου beyond the term of human life, Id.

ὑπερ-ημίσυς, υ, above half, more than half, Hdt. ; τινος of a thing, Xen.

ὑπ-έρημος, ον, somewhat desolate, Plut.

ὑπερ-ηνόρεος, ον, = sq., Theocr.

ὑπερ-ηνορέων, οντος, ὁ, part. with no pres. in use, exceedingly manly :—but always in bad sense, overbearing, overweening, Hom. **II.** in Com. phrase, excelling men, thinking oneself more than man, Ar. From

ὑπερ-ήνωρ, Dor. -άνωρ, ορος, ὁ, ἡ, (ἀνήρ) overbearing, overweening, Hes., Eur.

ὑπερ-ήσει, 3 sing. fut. of ὑπερίημι.

ὑπερ-ηφανέω, used by Hom. only in part., much like ὑπερηνορέων, overweening, arrogant, Il. **II.** trans. to treat disdainfully, Luc. ; and

ὑπερηφανία, ἡ, arrogance, disdain, Xen., Dem. :—c. gen. objecti, contempt towards or for another, Plat., Dem. From

ὑπερ-ήφανος, ον, prob. for ὑπερ-φανής, η being inserted : **1.** in bad sense, overweening, arrogant, haughty, Hes., Aesch., Dem. ; οἰκίαι ὑπερηφανώτεραι Dem.—so in Adv., ὑπερηφάνως ἔχειν to bear oneself haughtily, Plat. ; ὑπ. ζῆν to live prodigally, Isocr. **2.** in good sense, magnificent, splendid, Plat.

ὑπερ-θαλασσίδιος, ον, above the coast-land, Hdt.

ὑπερ-θαυμάζω, Ion. -θωμάζω, f. -άσομαι, to wonder exceedingly, Hdt., Luc.

ὑπερ-θαύμαστος, ον, most admirable, Anth.

ὑπέρθεν, and metri grat. -θε, (ὑπέρ) from above or merely above, Il. : of the body, above, in the upper parts, opp. to ἔνερθε, Ib. **2.** from heaven above, i. e. from the gods, Hom. **3.** of Degree, yet more, Soph. **II.** c. gen. above, over, Pind., Aesch., etc. ; ὑπ. γίγνεσθαί τινος to get the better of one, Eur. ; also, ὑπερθεν εἶναι ἤ . . , to be above or beyond, i. e. worse than . . , Id.

ὑπέρθεσις, εως, ἡ, (ὑπερτίθημι) postponement, Polyb.

ὑπερ-θέω, f. -θεύσομαι, to run beyond, ὑπ. ἄκραν to double the headland, proverb. of escaping from danger, Aesch. **2.** to outstrip, outdo, c. acc., Eur.

ὑπερ-θνήσκω, to die for another, c. gen. or absol., Eur.

ὑπερ-θρώσκω, f. -θοροῦμαι, Ep. -θορέομαι: aor. 2 -έθορον, Ep. ὑπέρ-θορον, inf. -θορεῖν, Ion. -θορέειν :—to overleap, leap or spring over, c. acc., Il., etc. ;—also c. gen., Eur.

ὑπέρ-θυμος, ον, high-spirited, high-minded, daring, Hom., Hes., etc. **II.** in bad sense, overdaring, overweening, Hes. :—overspirited, of a horse, Xen. **III.** vehemently angry :—Adv., ὑπερθύμως ἄγαν in over-vehement wrath, Aesch.

ὑπέρ-θυρον [ῠ], τό, (θύρα) the lintel of a door or gate, Lat. superliminare, Od., Hes.

ὑπέρ-θυρον, τό, = foreg., Hdt.

ὑπερθωμάζω, Ion. for -θαυμάζω.

ὑπερ-ιάχω [ᾰ], to shout above, out-shout, c. gen., Anth.

ὑπερ-ἰδεῖν, inf. of ὑπερ-εῖδον.

ὑπερ-ἴημι, f. -ήσω, to outdo, Od.

ὑπερ-ικταίνομαι, Pass., in the phrase, πόδες ὑπερικταίνοντο the feet went exceeding swiftly, Od. (Deriv. unknown.)

Ὑπεριονίδης, ου, ὁ, patronym. of Ὑπερίων, Hyperion's son, i. e. Ἥλιος, Od., Hes.

ὑπερ-ἴπταμαι, later form for ὑπερπέτομαι, Plut., Luc.

ὑπερ-ἴσταμαι, Pass., with aor. 2 and pf. act. :—to stand over another, c. gen., Hdt. : esp. to stand over one for protection, protect, τινος Soph.

ὑπερ-ίστωρ, ορος, ὁ, ἡ, knowing too well, c. gen., Soph.

ὑπερ-ἴσχυρος, ον, exceeding strong, Xen.

ὑπερ-ἴσχω, = ὑπερέχω, intr. to be above, to prevail over, c. gen., Hes. **II.** to protect, τινός Anth.

Ὑπερίων [ῑ], ονος, ὁ, Hyperion, the Sun-god, joined with Ἥλιος, or alone for Ἥλιος, Hom. Some derive it from ὑπὲρ ἰών, he that walks on high : others simply bring Ὑπερίων from ὑπέρ, the God above.

ὑπερ-κάθημαι, properly pf. pass. of -έζομαι, to sit over or upon, ἐπί τινος Xen. :—metaph. to sit over and watch, keep an eye on, τινος Id.

ὑπέρ-καλος, ον, exceeding beautiful, Arist.

ὑπερ-κάμνω, to suffer or labour for, τινός Eur.

ὑπερ-καταβαίνω, f. -βήσομαι, to get down over, get quite over, c. acc., Il. ; c. gen., Anth.

ὑπερ-καταγέλαστος, ον, exceedingly absurd, Aeschin.

ὑπερκατάκειμαι, Pass. to lie or sit above, at table, c. gen., Plut., Luc.

ὑπερ-κατηφής, ές, very distressing, Luc.

ὑπερ-καχλάζω, f. σω, to run bubbling over, Luc.

ὑπέρ-κειμαι, Pass. to lie or be situate above, Isocr. **II.** to be postponed.

ὑπερ-κενόομαι, Pass. to be quite empty, Galen.

ὑπερ-κέρασις, ἡ, an outflanking on one wing, Polyb.

ὑπερ-κλύζω, f. σω, to overflow, Strab.

ὑπερ-κολάκεύω, f. σω, to flatter immoderately, Dem.

ὑπερ-κομίζω, f. ιῶ, to carry over, Strab.

ὑπέρ-κομπος, ον, overweening, arrogant, Aesch.

ὑπέρ-κοπος, ον, (κόπτω) overstepping all bounds, extravagant, arrogant, Aesch., Soph. :—Adv. -πως, excessively, Aesch.

ὑπερ-κορέννυμι, f. -κορέσω, to over-fill or glut, τινά τινος one with a thing, Theogn.

ὑπέρ-κοτος, ον, exceeding angry, cruel, Aesch. :—Adv. -τως, Eur.

ὑπερ-κρεμάννυμι, f. -κρεμάσω [ᾰ], to hang up over, ὑπ. ἄτην τινί Pind. :—Pass. to impend, Theogn.

ὑπερ-κτάομαι, f. -κτήσομαι, Dep. to acquire over and above, Soph.

ὑπερ-κύδας [ῠ], αντος, ὁ, (κῦδος) exceeding famous or

renowned, only in acc., ὑπερκύδαντας Ἀχαιούς Il.; ὑπερκύδαντα Μενοίτιον Hes.

ὑπερ-κύπτω, f. ψω, *to stretch and peep over*, Plat.; c. gen., Luc. II. *to step beyond, overstep*, c. acc., Anth.

ὑπέρ-λαμπρος, ον, *exceeding bright*, Ar. II. of sound, *very clear* or *loud*, Dem.

ὑπερ-λαμπρύνομαι [ῡ], Pass. *to make a splendid show : to shew great eagerness*, Xen.

ὑπερ-λίαν [ῑ], Adv. *exceedingly, beyond all doubt*, N. T.

ὑπερ-λῡπέομαι, Pass. *to be vexed beyond measure*, Hdt.

ὑπερ-μαζάω, *to be overfull of barley bread* (μᾶζα), *to be wanton from high feeding*, Luc.

ὑπερ-μαίνομαι, f. -μανοῦμαι, aor. -εμάνην [ᾰ], Pass. *to be* or *go stark mad*, Ar.

ὑπερ-μάκης [ᾱ], ες, Dor. for ὑπερ-μήκης.

ὑπερ-μάχέω, f. ήσω, *to fight for* or *on behalf of*, τινός Soph., Eur.; σὺ ταῦτα τοῦδ' ὑπερμαχεῖς ἐμοί; *dost thou fight thus for him against me?* Soph.

ὑπερμάχητικός, ή, όν, *inclined to fight for*, Plut. From

ὑπερ-μάχομαι, Dep. = ὑπερμαχέω, Plut.; τᾆδ' πατρὸς ὑπερμαχοῦμαι *will fight this battle for* him, Soph.

ὑπέρ-μάχος, ον, *a champion, defender*, Anth.

ὑπερ-μεγάθης [ᾰ], ες, Ion. for ὑπερ-μεγέθης.

ὑπερ-μεγας, ἀλη, α, *immensely great*, Ar.

ὑπερ-μεγέθης, Ion. -άθης, ες, gen. εος, = ὑπέρμεγας, Hdt., Dem.

ὑπερ-μεθύσκομαι, aor. 1 -εμεθύσθην : Pass. :—*to get* (and in aor. *to be*) *excessively drunk*, Hdt.

ὑπερ-μενέτης, ου, ὁ, poët. for ὑπερμενής, h. Hom.

ὑπερ-μενέων, οντος, ὁ, part. with no pres. in use, *exceeding mighty*, Od. From

ὑπερ-μενής, ές, (μένος) *exceeding mighty, exceeding strong*, Hom., Hes.

ὑπέρ-μετρος, ον, *beyond all measure, excessive*, Plat.

ὑπερ-μήκης, ες, gen. -εος, (μῆκος) *exceeding long*, Aesch.; ἡ βασιλέος χείρ ὑπ. *the king's arm is very long, reaches very far*, Hdt. 2. *exceeding high*, of mountains, Id. 3. ὑπερμάκης βοά *a cry exceeding loud*, Pind.

ὑπέρμορον, ὑπέρμορα, v. μόρος.

ὑπερ-νέφελος, ον, (νεφέλη) *above the clouds*, Luc.

ὑπερ-νεωλκέω, f. ήσω, *to haul ships over land*, Strab.

ὑπερ-νῑκάω, f. ήσω, *to be more than conqueror*, N. T.

ὑπερ-νότιος, ον, (Νότος) *beyond the south wind*, i.e. *at the extreme south*, Hdt.

ὑπερ-ογκος, ον, *of excessive bulk, swollen to a great size*, Xen., Dem. 2. *immoderate, excessive*, Plat.

ὑπεροιδαίνω, *to be much swollen*, of a river, Anth.

ὑπερ-οικέω, f. ήσω, *to dwell above* or *beyond*, c. gen., Hdt.; also c. acc., Id.

ὑπέρ-οικος, ον, *dwelling above* or *beyond*, c. gen., Hdt.

ὑπεροπλία, ἡ, (ὑπέροπλος) *overweening confidence in arms, proud defiance, presumptuousness*, ὑπεροπλίησι [Ep. dat. pl., with ῑ], Il.

ὑπερ-οπλίζομαι, f. ίσομαι : -οπλίσσαιτο 3 sing. Ep. aor. 1 opt. : Dep. : (ὁπλίζω) :—*to vanquish by force of arms*, or (from ὑπέροπλος) *to treat scornfully*, Od.

ὑπέρ-οπλος, ον, (ὅπλον) *proudly trusting in force of arms, defiant, presumptuous*, ὑπέροπλον εἰπεῖν (as Adv.) *to speak defiantly, presumptuously*, Il.; ἠνορέη,

βίη ὑπέροπλος Hes. II. *of conditions, excessive, overwhelming*, Pind.

ὑπερόπτης, poët. -όπτᾱ, gen. ου, ὁ, (ὑπερόψομαι) *a contemner, disdainer of* a thing, c. gen., Soph., Thuc. : absol. *disdainful, haughty*, Theocr., Arist. Hence

ὑπεροπτικός, ή, όν, *disposed to despise others, contemptuous, disdainful*, Isocr., Dem.:—Adv.-κῶς, Xen.

ὑπέροπτος, ον, (ὑπερόψομαι) *disdainful*, Anth.; neut. pl. as Adv., Soph.

ὑπερ-οράω, Ion. -έω : f. -όψομαι : aor. 2 -εῖδον, inf. -ιδεῖν : aor. 1 pass. ὑπερώφθην :—*to look over, look down upon*, c. acc., Hdt. II. *to overlook, slight, despise*, Id., Thuc., etc. :—also c. gen. *to shew contempt for*, Xen.

ὑπεροπία, ἡ, v. ὑπερόριος.

ὑπερ-ορίζω, f. σω, *to drive beyond the frontier, banish*, Plat. ; in Pass., Aeschin.

ὑπερ-όριος, ον, and α, ον, poët. -ούριος : (ὅρος) :— *over the boundaries* or *confines, living abroad*, Dem., Theocr.; ὑπ. ἀσχολία occupation *in foreign parts*, Thuc.; τὰ ὑπ. *foreign affairs*, Arist. 2. ἡ ὑπερορία (sc. γῆ), *the country beyond one's own frontiers, a foreign country*, Plat., Xen. II. *foreign to the purpose, outlandish, out-of-the-way*, Aeschin.

ὑπερ-όρνυμαι, Pass. *to rise and hang over*, c. dat., Soph.

ὑπερ-ορρωδέω, *to be much afraid*, τινός *for* one, Eur.

ὙΠΕΡΟΣ, ὁ, or ὕπερον, τό, *a pestle to bray and pound with*, Hes., Hdt. II. *anything shaped like a pestle, a club, cudgel*, Plut., Luc.

ὑπερ-ουράνιος, ον, *above the heavens*, Plat.

ὑπερούριος, ον, Ion. and poët. for ὑπερόριος.

ὑπεροχή, ἡ, (ὑπερέχω II) *a projection, an eminence*, Polyb. II. metaph. *preëminence, superiority*, ἡ δὲ νίκη ὑπεροχή τις Arist.

ὑπέροχος, Ion. ὑπείρ-, ον, (ὑπερέχω II) *prominent, eminent, distinguished above* others, c. gen., Il.; absol., Hdt.; ὑπέροχος βία *overbearing* force, Soph.

ὑπεροψία, ἡ, *contempt, disdain for* a person or thing, c. gen., Thuc., etc.: absol. *haughtiness, arrogance*, Isocr.

ὑπερ-όψομαι, fut. of ὑπεροράω.

ὑπερ-πἄγής, ές, (πάγος) *very frosty* : τὸ ὑπ. *excessive frost*, Xen.

ὑπερπάθέω, f. ήσω, *to be grievously distressed*, ὑπερπαθήσας' Eur. From

ὑπερ-πἄθής, ές, (πάθος) *grievously afflicted*.

ὑπερ-παίω, mostly in pf. -πέπαικα, *to overstrike*, i.e. *to surpass, exceed*, c. gen., Ar.; c. acc., Dem.

ὑπερ-πἄλύνω, *to strew* or *scatter over*, Anth.

ὑπερ-περισσεύομαι, f. σω, Med. *to abound more and more*, N. T.

ὑπερ-περίσσως, Adv. *beyond all measure*, N. T.

ὑπερ-πέταμαι, aor. 2 -επτάμην [ᾰ], and in act. form -έπτην, Dor. -έπτᾶν, ὑπερπέτομαι, Soph.

ὑπερ-πετάννυμι, f. -πετάσω, *to stretch over*, Luc.

ὑπερ-πετής, ές, *flying over* or *above*, Strab. :—metaph. *high-flying*, Luc.

ὑπερ-πέτομαι, aor. 2 -επτόμην :—*to fly over*, of a spear, Hom. 2. c. acc. *to fly over* or *beyond*, Od.; also c. gen., Plut.

ὑπερ-πηδάω, f. -ήσομαι, *to leap over*, c. acc., Ar. II. metaph. *to overleap, transgress*, Dem., Aeschin.

ὑπέρ-πικρος, ον, *exceeding sharp in temper*, Aesch.

ὑπερ-πίμπλημι, f. -πλήσω, to overfill : Pass., aor. 1 ὑπερεπλήσθην, to be overfull, Arist.;—c. gen., ὑπερπλησθείς μέθης Soph.

ὑπερτίνω [ῑ], to drink overmuch, Xen.

ὑπερπίπτω, f. -πεσοῦμαι, to fall over, run over, project, Strab.   II. of Time, to be past, gone by, Hdt.

ὑπερ-πλεονάζω, f. σω, to abound exceedingly, N. T.

ὑπερ-πλήθης, ες, superabundant, ὑπερπλήθη ἐξημαρτηκώς having done more misdeeds than enough, Dem.

ὑπερ-πληρόω, f. ώσω, to fill overfull, Xen. :—Pass. to be overfull, to be gorged, Id.

ὑπερ-πλησθῆναι, aor. 1 inf. pass. of -πίμπλημι.

ὑπερ-πλούσιος, ον, over-wealthy, exceeding rich, Arist.

ὑπερπλουτέω, f. ήσω, to be exceeding rich, Ar. From

ὑπέρ-πλουτος, ον, = ὑπερπλούσιος, Aesch., Plat.

ὑπερ-πολάζω, (πέλω) to overflow, Strab.

ὑπέρ-πολυς, -πόλλη, -πολυ, Ion. ὑπέρπολλος, η, ον, overmuch, in pl. over many, Aesch., Xen.

ὑπερ-πονέω, f. ήσω, to labour beyond measure, take further trouble, Xen.   II. to bear or endure for others, Soph.   2. in Med. c. gen. pers., Id.

ὑπέρ-πονος, ον, quite worn out, Plut.

ὑπέρ-πόντιος, ον, and α, ον, over the sea, Aesch.; φοιτᾷς ὑπερπόντιος Soph.   2. from beyond the sea, i. e. foreign, strange, Pind.

ὑπέρ-πτἄτο, poët. 3 sing. aor. 2 of ὑπερ-πέταμαι.

ὑπέρ-πτωχος, ον, exceeding poor, Arist.

ὑπερ-πυππάζω, (πύππαξ) to make very much of one, to fondle and caress him, Ar.

ὑπερ-πυρριάω, f. άσω [ᾱ], to blush scarlet for another, c. gen., Ar.

ὑπερ-πωτάομαι, poët. for ὑπερπέτομαι.

ὑπερ-ράγην [ᾱ], aor. 2 pass. of ὑπορ-ρήγνυμι.

ὑπερ-σεμνύνομαι [ῠ], Med. to be exceeding solemn or pompous, Xen.

ὑπέρ-σοφος, ον, exceeding wise or clever, Ar., Plat.

ὑπερ-σπουδάζω, to take exceeding great pains, Luc.

ὑπερ-σχεθεῖν, poët. for -σχεῖν, aor. 2 inf. of ὑπερέχω.

ὑπέρ-σχῃ, -σχοι, 3 sing. subj. and opt. aor. 2 of ὑπερέχω.

ὑπέρτᾶτος, η, ον, poët. Sup. of ὑπέρ, uppermost, highest, supreme, Il., etc.   II. of age, eldest, Pind.

ὑπερ-τείνω, f. -τενῶ :   I. trans. to stretch or lay over, Hdt.: to hold out over to, τί τινι Eur.; ὑπ. σκιὰν σειρίου κυνὸς to stretch over [the house] a shade from the sun, Aesch.; ὑπ. χεῖρά τινος to stretch the hand over one for protection, Eur.; ὑπ. πόδα ἀκτῆς to stretch one's foot over the beach, i. e. pass over it, Id.   2. to strain to the uttermost, Plut.   II. intr. to stretch or jut out over, Thuc. :—also c. acc., ὑπ. τὸ κέρας to outflank the enemy's wing, Xen.   2. metaph. to exceed the measure or number of, c. gen., Dem.; c. acc. to exceed, τὴν ἀνθρωπίνην φύσιν Arist.

ὑπερ-τελέω, f. έσω, to overleap, c. acc., Aesch.

ὑπερ-τελής, ές, gen. έος, (τέλος) leaping over the strait, Aesch.   2. c. gen. rising or appearing above, Aesch.; ἄθλων ὑπερτελής having reached the end of labours, Soph.

ὑπερ-τέλλω, f. -τελῶ, to appear above, ὑπερτείλας ὁ ἥλιος the sun when he is well above the horizon, Hdt.; ὑπ. ἐκ γαίας to start from the ground, Eur.; c. gen., φαρέων μαστὸς ὑπερτέλλων appearing above her dress,

Id. ; κορυφῆς ὑπερτέλλων πέτρος hanging over the head [of Tantalus], Id.

ὑπερ-τενής, ές, stretching over, laid over, Aesch.

ὑπερτερία, Ion. -ίη, ἡ, the upper part or body of a carriage, Od. From

ὑπέρτερος, α, ον, poët. Comp. from ὑπέρ, over or above, upper, κρέα ὑπέρτερα flesh from the outer parts of a victim, opp. to the σπλάγχνα or inwards, Od.   2. metaph. higher, nobler, more excellent, Il. : stronger, mightier, Soph.   3. c. gen. victorious or triumphant over, Pind., Eur.; οὐδὲν οἶδ' ὑπέρτερον I know nothing further, more certain, Soph.   II. neut. as Adv., better than, c. gen., Id.

ὑπερ-τήκω, to melt exceedingly, Strab.

ὑπερ-τίθημι, f. -θήσω, to set higher, erect, Anth.   2. to set on the other side, carry over, Plut.   3. in Med. to hold over, so as to protect, Anth.   II. metaph., παντὶ θεὸν ὑπερτιθέμεν to set God over all, Pind.   2. to communicate a thing to another, ὑπερετίθεα (Ion. impf. for -ετίθην) τὰ ἔμελλον ποιήσειν Hdt. :—so in Med., esp. in order to ask advice, Id.

ὑπερ-τῑμάω, f. ήσω, to honour exceedingly, τινά Soph.

ὑπέρ-τονος, ον, overstrained, strained to the utmost, at full pitch, exceeding loud, Aesch., Ar.

ὑπερ-τρέχω, f. -δρᾰμοῦμαι: aor. 2 -έδρᾰμον :—to run over or beyond, outrun, escape, c. acc., Theogn., Eur.   2. to excel, surpass, τινά Eur. : absol. to prevail, Id.   II. to overstep, transgress a law, Soph.

ὑπ-ερυθριάω, f. άσω [ᾱ], to blush a little, Ar.

ὑπ-έρυθρος, ον, somewhat red, reddish, Thuc., Plat.

ὑπερ-ύψηλος, ον, exceeding high, Xen.

ὑπερ-υψόω, f. ώσω, to exalt exceedingly, τινά N. T.

ὑπερ-φαίνομαι, Pass. to shew oneself over or above a place, c. gen., Thuc.

ὑπερ-φᾰλαγγέω, f. ήσω, to extend the phalanx so as to outflank the enemy : generally, to outflank, Xen.; c. gen., ὑπ. τοῦ στρατεύματος Id.

ὑπερφᾰνής, ές, gen. έος, (φαίνομαι) appearing over or above, outtopping others, Xen.

ὑπερ-φᾰτος, ον, (φατός, φημί) above speech, unspeakable, Pind.

ὑπερ-φέρω, f. -οίσω : aor. 1 -ήνεγκα, aor. 2 -ήνεγκον :—to bear or carry over a place, ὑπ. τὸν ἰσθμὸν τὰς ναῦς Thuc.:—Pass., [αἱ ναῦς] αἱ ὑπερενεχθεῖσαι τὸν ἰσθμόν Id.   II. intr. to rise above, to surpass, excel, have the advantage over, τινός τινι one in a thing, Hdt., Ar.; also c. acc. pro gen., ὑπερφέρεις τόλμῃ τόλμαν Eur. : absol. to excel, have preëminence, Hdt., Soph.

ὑπέρφευ, Adv., = ὑπερφυῶς, Aesch., Eur.

ὑπερφθέγγομαι, Dep. to sound above, τὰ ἔργα ὑπ. τοὺς λόγους Luc.

ὑπερφθίνομαι [ῐ], Pass. to die for or in behalf of, ὑπερέφθιτο (poët. aor. 2) πατρός Pind.

ὑπερ-φίαλος, ον, overbearing, overweening, arrogant, Hom. :—Adv. -λως, exceedingly, Id. : arrogantly, Od. (Deriv. uncertain : perh. an Ep. form either of ὑπέρβιος or of ὑπερ-φυής.)

ὑπερ-φῐλέω, f. ήσω, to love beyond measure, Ar., Xen.

ὑπερ-φοβέομαι, Pass. with fut. med., to be overfrightened, fear exceedingly, Aesch., Xen.

ὑπέρ-φοβος, ον, very fearful, timid, Xen.

ὑπερ-φορέω, to carry over, Xen.

ὑπερ-φρονέω, f. ήσω, to be over-proud, to have high thoughts, Aesch.; ὑπ. τινί to be proud in or of a thing, Hdt., Plat. 2. c. acc. to look down upon, despise, Aesch., Ar.:—Pass. to be despised, Thuc. 3. c. gen. to think slightly of, Eur., Ar.

ὑπέρφρων, ονος, ὁ, ἡ, (φρήν) over-proud, haughty, disdainful, arrogant, Aesch., Eur.: neut. pl. ὑπέρφρονα as Adv., Soph. 2. in good sense, ἐκ τοῦ ὑπέρφρονος from a sense of superiority, Thuc.

ὑπερ-φυής, ές: Att. acc. sing. -φυᾶ, neut. pl. -φυῆ or -φυᾶ: (φύομαι): 1. overgrown, enormous, Hdt., Ar. 2. monstrous, marvellous, extraordinary, Hdt., Ar.:—joined with a relat., ὑπερφυὴς ὅσος extraordinary how great, i. e. extraordinarily great, Ar., Plat. II. Adv. -ῶς, over-much, marvellously, strangely, exceedingly, Ar., Plat.; in affirm. answers, ὑπερφυῶς μὲν οὖν Plat.

ὑπερ-φύομαι, Pass., with aor. 2 and pf. act., to surpass, excel, c. acc., Hdt.

ὑπερ-φυσάομαι, Pass. to be inflated excessively, Luc.

ὑπερ-φωνέω, f. ήσω, to outbawl, τινά Luc.

ὑπερ-χαίρω, f. ήσω, to rejoice exceedingly at a thing, c. dat., Eur.; c. part., μανθάνων ὑπ. Xen.

ὑπερ-χλίω or -χλιδάω, to be over-wanton or arrogant, Soph.

ὑπ-έρχομαι, f. -ελεύσομαι: Dep. with aor. 2 and pf. act.:—to go or come under, enter, Lat. subire, c. acc., Od., Aesch. II. of involuntary feelings, to come upon, steal over one, c. acc., Τρῶας τρόμος ὑπήλυθε Il.; ὑπῆλθέ με φόβος Soph., etc. III. of persons, to creep into another's good graces, to fawn on, cringe to, c. acc., Ar., Plat. 2. to undermine, beguile, Soph., Eur. IV. to advance slowly, of an army, Xen.

ὑπέρ-χρεως, ων, over head and ears in debt, Dem.

ὑπέρ-ψυχρος, ον, very frigid, Luc.

ὑπ-ερωέω, f. ήσω, to start back, recoil, Il.

ὑπερῴη, ἡ, the upper part of the mouth, the palate, Il. (From ὑπέρ, v. ὑπερῷος.)

ὑπερωιόθεν, Adv. from an upper room, Od. From

ὑπερῷον, Ep. -ώιον, τό, the upper part of the house, the upper story or upper rooms, where the women resided, Hom.:—in Att., an attic, garret, Ar. (v. sq.).

ὑπερῷος, α, ον, being above, Plut. (From ὑπέρ; -φος being a term., as πατρῷος, μητρῷος from πατήρ, μήτηρ.)

ὑπερώτατος, η, ον, poët. for ὑπέρτατος, Pind.

ὑπ-ερωτάω, f. ήσω, to reply by a question, Plat.

ὑπ-εσσεῖται, Dor. 3 sing. fut. of ὕπειμι (εἰμί sum).

ὑπ-εστᾶν, Dor. for -έστην, aor. 2 of ὑφ-ίστημι.

ὑπ-έστειλα, aor. 1 of ὑπο-στέλλω.

ὑπ-έστρεψα, aor. 1 of ὑπο-στρέφω.

ὑπ-έσχεθον, poët. aor. 2 of pf. pass. of ὑπισχνέομαι.

ὑπ-εσχέτο, 3 sing. aor. 1 of ὑπ-ισχνέομαι.

ὑπ-έτρεσα, aor. 1 of ὑπο-τρέω.

ὑπ-εύθυνος, ον, liable to give account for one's administration of an office, accountable, responsible, Hdt., Aesch., etc.:—ὑπεύθυνοι, οἱ, at Athens, magistrates who had to submit their accounts to public auditors (λογισταί), Ar., etc. 2. c. gen. responsible for, ὑπ. ἀρχῆς ἑτέρας ap. Dem.; of slaves, σῶμα ὑπ. ἀδικημάτων their body is liable for their misdeeds, i. e. they must pay for them with their body, Id. 3.

c. dat. responsible to another, dependent on them, Lat. obnoxius, Id., Aeschin.

ὑπ-έφηνα, aor. 1 of ὑπο-φαίνω.

ὑπ-έφράδα, Ep. aor. 2 of ὑπο-φράζω.

ὑπ-έχευα, aor. 1 of ὑπο-χέω.

ὑπ-έχω, f. ὑφ-έξω: aor. 2 ὑπέσχον, poët. ὑπέσχεθον:—to hold or put under, ὑποσχὼν θηλέας ἵππους (cf. Virg. supposita de matre), Il.: to hold out the hand to receive something, Ib., Dem.: to hold a cup under another vessel, while something is poured into it, Hdt., Ar.; ὑπ. μαστόν, of the mother giving suck, Eur. 2. to supply, afford, furnish, Pind.; ὑπ. τινί [φόβον] to occasion him fear, Thuc.:—ὑπ. ἑαυτόν submit oneself to another, Xen., Plat. II. to uphold, support, c. acc., Hdt. 2. Lat. sustinere, to undergo, be subject to, suffer, Soph., Eur.; ὑπ. δίκην τινός to have to give an account of a thing, Hdt., Att.; ὑπ. δίκην to undergo a trial, Thuc.; ὑπ. λόγον τινί to render account to another, Plat., Xen., etc. 3. to sustain, maintain, λόγον an argument, Arist.

ὑπ-ήκοος, ον, (ἀκοή) giving ear, listening to, τινι Anth. II. obedient, subject to another, c. gen., Hdt., Aesch., etc.; so, c. dat., Eur., Xen. 2. c. dat. rei, ναυσὶν ὑπ. liable to furnish ships, Thuc. III. absol. as Subst., ὑπήκοοι, οἱ, subjects, Id., etc.; ἡ ὑπήκοος (sc. χώρα) τὸ ὑπήκοον=οἱ ὑπ., Id.

ὑπ-ῆλθον, aor. 2 of ὑπ-έρχομαι.

ὑπημύω, v. sub ὑπεμνήμυκε.

ὑπ-ηνέμιος, Dor. -ἀνέμιος, ον, (ἄνεμος) lifted or wafted by the wind, Theocr. II. full of wind, ᾠόν a wind-egg, which produces no chicken, Ar.:—metaph. vain, idle, empty, Luc.; of men, braggart, Plut.

ὑπ-ήνεμος, ον, (ἄνεμος) under the wind, under shelter from it, Soph., Theocr.; ἐκ τοῦ ὑπηνέμου on the lee-side, Xen.: metaph. gentle, Eur. II. swift as the wind, Anth.

ὑπήνη, ἡ, (ὑπό) the hair on the under part of the face, the beard, Ar.

ὑπηνήτης, ου, ὁ, one that is just getting a beard, with one's first beard, Hom., Plat.:—generally bearded, Anth.

ὑπ-ηοῖος, η, ον, (ἠώς) about dawn, towards morning, early, Hom.; στίβη ὑπηοίη morning frost, Od.

ὑπ-ήργμαι, pf. pass. of ὑπ-άρχω.

ὑπηρεσία, ἡ, (ὑπηρέτης) the body of rowers and sailors, the ship's crew, Thuc., etc. II. service, Ar., etc.

ὑπηρέσιον, τό, (ὑπηρέτης) the cushion on a rower's bench, Thuc. II. = ὑπηρετικὸν πλοῖον, Strab.

ὑπηρετέω, f. ήσω: plqpf. ὑπηρετήκειν: (ὑπηρέτης) to do service on board ship, to do rower's service:— hence to be a servant, do service, serve, Soph., Ar. 2. c. dat. to minister to, serve, Lat. inservire, Hdt., Att.; ὑπ. τοῖς τρόποις to comply with, humour his ways, Ar.; ὑπ. τῷ λόγῳ to second, support it, Eur.; —ὑπ. τινί to help one in a thing, Soph., Ar., etc. 3. absol. to serve, lend aid, Soph.:—Pass. to be done as service, Hdt., Isocr. Hence

ὑπηρέτημα, ατος, τό, service rendered, service, Plat.; ποδῶν ὑπ. feet that serve one, Soph.

ὑπ-ηρέτης, ου, ὁ, (ἐρέτης) properly an under-rower, under-seaman, v. ὑπηρεσία. II. generally an underling, servant, attendant, assistant, Lat. apparitor, Hdt., Att.:—c. gen. objecti, ὑπ. ἔργου a helper in a

work, Xen.   2. at Athens,   a. *the servant who attended each man-at-arms* (ὁπλίτης) *to carry his baggage and shield*, Thuc.   b. ὁ τῶν ἔνδεκα ὑπ. *the assistant* of the Eleven, employed in executions, Plat.

ὑπηρέτησις, ἡ, (ὑπηρετέω) *service*, Arist.

ὑπηρετητέον, verb. Adj. *one must serve*, τινί Arist.

ὑπηρετικός, ή, όν, *of* or *for the* ὑπηρέται, *menial*, Plat.; ὅπλα ὑπ. *the arms of the hired soldiery*, Xen.   2. *of* or *for service, doing service*, Plat., etc.   3. *subordinate*, Arist.   4. κέλης ὑπ. a cock-boat, *attending on* a larger vessel, Xen.; τὸ ὑπ. (sc. πλοῖον) *an attendant vessel, despatch-boat, tender*, Dem.

ὑπηρέτις, ιδος, fem. of ὑπηρέτης II, Eur.

ὑπ-ήριπον, Ep. aor. 2 of ὑπ-ερείπω.

ὑπ-ήσω, Ion. for ὑφ-ήσω, fut. of ὑφ-ίημι.

ὑπ-ηχέω, f. ήσω, *to sound under* or *in answer, to echo, respond*, Hes.

ὑπ-ίημι, Ion. for ὑφ-ίημι.

ὑπ-ίλλω, aor. 1 ὑπῖλα, *to force underneath*, properly of a dog *putting its tail between* the legs: metaph., σοὶ ὑπίλλουσι στόμα *keep down* their tongue before thee, i. e. *fawn and cringe* before thee, Soph.

ὑπ-ίστημι, Ion. for ὑφ-ίστημι.

ὑπ-ισχνέομαι, contr. -οῦμαι, poët. also ὑπίσχομαι :—f. ὑποσχήσομαι : aor. 2 ὑπεσχόμην : pf. ὑπέσχημαι : 3 sing. plqpf. ὑπέσχητο :—a collat. form of ὑπέχομαι, *to promise* or *engage* to do a thing, Il., Att. :—in Att. also, sometimes, *to take upon oneself*, i. e. *to undertake to do, to promise* a thing, c. acc., Hom.; with inf. aor., Xen.   2. absol. *to promise, make promises*, Hdt.   3. with inf. pres. *to profess that* one is, *profess* to be, Id., Plat. : also *to profess* to do a thing, Plat., Xen.

ὑπνίδιος, α, ον, (ὕπνος) *drowsy*, Anth.

ὑπνο-δότης, ου, ὁ, *giver of sleep*, Aesch. :—fem. ὑπνο-δότειρα, *she that gives sleep*, Eur.

ὑπνο-μάχεω, f. ήσω, (μάχομαι) *to fight with sleep, withstand sleep*, Xen.

ὝΠΝΟΣ [ῠ], ὁ, *sleep, slumber*, Hom., etc.; χάλκεος ὕπνος, i. e. *the sleep of death*, Il. :—ὕπνος τινὰ ἐπέρχεται, ἐπορούει, ἱκάνει, αἱρεῖ, λαμβάνει Hom., etc.; εἰς ὕπνον πεσεῖν Soph. :—ἐν ὕπνῳ *in sleep*, Eur. ;—καθ' ὕπνον Soph. ;—περὶ πρῶτον ὕπνον *about one's first sleep*, Ar.   II. *Sleep*, twin-brother of Death, Il.

ὑπνο-φόβης, ου, ὁ, (φοβέω) *scaring in sleep*, Anth.

ὑπνόω, f. ώσω :—Pass., pf. part. ὑπνωμένος : (ὕπνος) :—*to put to sleep* :—Pass. *to fall asleep, sleep*, Hdt.

ὕπνω, Dor. for ὕπνου, gen. of ὕπνος.

ὑπν-ώδης, ες, (εἶδος) *sleepy, drowsy*, Eur., Plat.

ὑπνώσσω, Att. -ττω, (ὕπνος) *to be sleepy* or *drowsy*, Aesch., Plat. : simply, *to sleep*, Eur.

ὑπνώω, for ὑπνάω = ὑπνώσσω, *to sleep*, Hom.

ὙΠΟ΄ [ῠ], Lat. *sub*, Prep. with gen., dat. and acc. : Ep. ὑπαί before δ, π.

A. WITH GEN.,   I. of Place, *from under*, ῥέει κρήνη ὑπὸ σπείους Od. : of rescuing *from under* another's power, after the Verbs ἐρύεσθαι, ἁρπάζειν, Il.; ἵππους λῦσαν ὑπὸ ζυγοῦ they loosed the horses *from under* the yoke, Hom.   2. *under, beneath*, μοχλὸν ὑπὸ σποδοῦ ἤλασα thrust the bar *in under* the embers, Od.; ὑπὸ στέρνοιο τυχήσας having hit him *under* the breast, Il.; ὑπὸ χθονός Hom., etc.   II. of the Agent, with pass. Verbs, *by*, Lat. *a* or *ab*, ὑπό

τινος δαμῆναι Il.; ὑφ' ἑαυτοῦ *by* one's own action, i. e. *of oneself*, Thuc.; so also, with neut. verbs, φεύγειν ὑπό τινος, i. e. to flee *before* him, Il. ; ἔπαινον ἔχειν ὑπό τινος Hdt.   2. of things as well as persons, ὡς διάκεινται ὑπὸ τῆς νόσου Thuc.; ἐνδακρύειν χαρᾶς ὕπο Aesch.; μαίνεται ὑφ' ἡδονῆς Soph. ; ὀρύσσειν ὑπὸ μαστίγων to dig *under fear* of scourges, Hdt.   3. of *accompanying* music, *to the sound of*, κωμάζειν ὑπ' αὐλοῦ Hes.; πίνειν ὑπὸ σάλπιγγος Ar.: then, of anything *attendant*, δαΐδων ὑπὸ λαμπομενάων ἡγίνεον *by* torchlight, Il. ; ὑπ' εὐφήμου βοῆς θῦσαι *to offer* a sacrifice *accompanied by* it, Soph. ; ὑπὸ πομπῆς *in* or *with* solemn procession, Hdt.

B. WITH DAT. of Place or Position, ὑπὸ ποσσί Il. ; ὑπὸ πλατανίστῳ Ib.; ὑπ' Ἰλίῳ *under* its walls, Eur. ; ὑφ' ἅρμασι *under*, i. e. *yoked to*, the chariot, Il.   2. ὑπὸ χερσί τινος δαμῆναι to be subdued *under*, i. e. *by force* of his arms, Ib.; ὑπὸ δουρὶ δαμῆναι Ib.   II. of the person *under* whose *power* or *influence* a thing is done, φέβεσθαι ὑπό τινι to flee *before* him, Ib. ; ὑπὸ πομπῇ τινος βῆναι to go *under* his convoy, Ib.   2. expressing *subjection*, ὑπό τινι *under* one's *power*, Od. ; εἶναι ὑπό τινι to be *subject* to him, Thuc.; ἔχειν ὑφ' ἑαυτῷ to have *under* one, Xen.   3. of things coming *under* a class, ἐργασίαι ὑπὸ ταῖς τέχναις Plat.   4. as in A. II. 3, ὑπ' αὐλητῆρι προσθ' ἔκιον advanced *to the music* of the flute-player, Hes. : generally, of attendant circumstances, ἐξ ἁλὸς εἶσι πνοιῇ ὕπο Ζεφύροιο Od. ; ὑπὸ σκότῳ, νυκτί Aesch.

C. WITH ACCUS. of Place, *towards and under*, ὑπὸ σπέος ἤλασε μῆλα drove them *under*, i. e. *into*, the cave, Il.; ὑπὸ ζυγὸν ἤγαγεν Od. ; ὑπὸ δικαστήριον ἄγειν to bring *under* or *before* the tribunal, Hdt.   2. like ὑπό c. dat. *without* sense of motion, ὑπ' ἠῶ τ' ἠέλιόν τε everywhere *under* the sun, Il. ; ὑπὸ τὴν ἄρκτον Hdt. ; τὸ ὑπὸ τὴν ἀκρόπολιν Thuc.   II. of *subjection*, ποιεῖσθαι ὑπὸ σφᾶς Id., etc.   III. of Time, like Lat. *sub*, *just after, just about*, ὑπὸ νύκτα *towards* night, Il.; ὑπὸ ταῦτα *about that* time, Hdt.; ὑπὸ τὸν νηὸν κατακαέντα *about* the time of its burning, Il.; ὑπὸ τὸν σεισμόν *about the time* of the earthquake, Thuc.   IV. of accompaniment, ὑπὸ αὐλὸν διαλέγεσθαι Xen.   V. ὑπό τι, as Adv. *to a certain degree, in some measure*, Lat. *aliquatenus*, Plat.

D. POSITION : ὑπό can always follow its Subst., becoming by anastrophe ὕπο.

E. AS ADV., *under, below, beneath*, Hom.   2. *behind*, Hdt.   II. *secretly, unnoticed*, Il.

F. IN COMPOSITION :   I. *under*, both of rest and motion, ὕπ-ειμι, ὑπο-βαίνω.   2. of the *casing* or *covering* of one thing with another, as ὑπό-χρυσος.   3. to express *subjection*, ὑπο-δαμνάω, ὑφ-ηνίοχος.   II. *somewhat, a little*, ὑπο-κινέω, ὑπό-λευκος : *underhand, secretly*, ὑπο-θωπεύω.

ὑπο-άμουσος, ον, *somewhat estranged from the Muses*, Plat.

ὑπό-βαθρον, τό, *anything put under* : *a framework* to support a couch, *a rocking apparatus*, Xen.

ὑπο-βαίνω, f. -βήσομαι, *to go* or *stand under* : metaph., τεσσαράκοντα πόδας ὑποβὰς τῆς ἑτέρης [πυραμίδος] τωὐτὸ μέγαθος *having gone* 40 feet *below* the like size of the other pyramid, i. e. building it 40 feet

lower, Hdt.; μικρὸν ὑποβάς, a little below (in the book), Strab.

ὑπο-βάλλω, Ep. **ὑβ-βάλλω**: f. -βαλῶ: pf. -βέβληκα: —to throw, put or lay under, Od.; τί τινι Eur.   2. to lay under, as a foundation, Aeschin.   3. to subject, submit, ἐχθροῖς ἐμαυτόν Eur.   II. Med. to substitute another's child for one's own, Lat. supponere, Hdt., Plat., etc.   III. to suggest, whisper, as a prompter does, Il., Plat., etc.: Med. to make false suggestions, Soph.   IV. in Med. to appropriate, Plut.

ὑπο-βαρβᾱρίζω, to speak a little like a foreigner, speak rather broken, Plat.

ὑπόβασις, εως, ἡ, (ὑποβαίνω) a going down: a crouching down, esp. of a horse that lowers itself to take up the rider, Xen.

ὑπο-βένθιος, ον, (βένθος) under the depths, Anth.

ὑποβήσσω, Att. -ττω, to have a slight cough, Luc.

ὑπο-βῐβάζω, f. Att. -βιβῶ, Causal of ὑποβαίνω, to bring down: Med. to crouch down, of a horse that stoops to take up the rider, Lat. subsidere, Xen.

ὑπο-βλέπω, f. ψομαι, to look up from under the brows at, glance at, to look askance at, eye suspiciously or angrily, Lat. limis oculis suspicere, Plat.; also ὑπ. ἐλεεινά to cast piteous glances, Anth.:—Pass. to be looked at with suspicion, Eur.

ὑποβλήδην, (ὑποβάλλω) Adv. throwing in covertly, i. e. by way of caution or reproof, or by way of interruption, Il.   II. askance, h. Hom.

ὑποβλητέος, α, ον, verb. Adj. to be put under, Xen.

ὑπό-βλητος, ον, (ὑποβάλλω) put in another's place, counterfeit, suborned, false, Soph.

ὑποβολή, ἡ, (ὑποβάλλω):   I. actively, a throwing or laying under, Plat.   2. a substitution by stealth, esp. of supposititious children, Id.   3. a suggesting, ἐξ ὑποβολῆς by admonition, Xen.   II. the subject-matter of a speech, Luc.

ὑποβολιμαῖος, α, ον, (ὑποβολή I. 2) substituted by stealth, supposititious, of children, Hdt., Plat.

ὑπο-βρέμω, to roar or rumble beneath, Aesch.

ὑπο-βρέχω, to wet or moisten a little:—Pass., pf. part. ὑποβεβρεγμένος somewhat drunk, Luc.

ὑπόβρυχα, v. ὑπόβρυχος.

ὑπό-βρυχιος [ῠ], α (Ion. η), ον, under water, Hdt.

ὑπό-βρυχος, ον, = foreg.: neut. pl. ὑπόβρυχα as Adv., under water, Od., Hdt.

ὑπό-γαιος, ον, v. ὑπό-γειος.

ὑπο-γάστριον, τό, (γαστήρ) the paunch, Lat. abdomen: the paunch of the tunny, a favourite dish at Athens, Ar.

ὑπό-γειος, Ion. and late Att. -γαιος, ον, (γῆ) under the earth, subterraneous, Hdt., etc.

ὑπο-γελάω, f. -γελάσομαι, to laugh slily, Lat. subridere, Plat.

ὑπο-γενειάζω, to entreat by touching the chin, Aeschin.

ὑπο-γίγνομαι, Ion. and in late Gr. -γίνομαι: f. -γενήσομαι: Dep.:—to grow up after or in succession, Lat. subnasci, Il., Hdt.

ὑπό-γλαυκος, ον, somewhat gray, Xen.

ὑπο-γλαύσσω, to glance furtively, Mosch.

ὑπο-γλῠκαίνω, to sweeten a little: metaph. to coax and smooth down, τινά Ar.

ὑπο-γνάμπτω, f. ψω, to bend gradually, h. Hom.

ὑπο-γραμμᾰτεύς, έως, ὁ, an under-secretary, Ar., etc.

ὑπο-γραμμᾰτεύω, f. σω, to serve as under-secretary, τινί Oratt.

ὑπογρᾰφεύς, έως, ὁ, one who writes under another's orders, a secretary, amanuensis, Plut., Luc.

ὑπο-γρᾰφή, ἡ, a signed bill of indictment, Plut.   II. an outline, τενόντων ὑπογραφαί traces of feet, Aesch.: —an outline, sketch, Lat. adumbratio, Plat., etc.   III. a painting under of the eyelids, Xen.

ὑπο-γράφω [ᾰ], f. ψω, to write under an inscription, subjoin or add to it, Thuc.; ὑπογράψας ἐπιβουλεῦσαί με having added (to the accusation) that . . , Dem.:— Med. to bring an additional accusation against him, Eur.   2. to sign, subscribe:—Med., ὑπ. τὰς καταβολάς to sign and so make oneself liable, Dem.   3. to write from dictation, Plut.   II. to write under, i. e. to trace letters for children to write over, Plat.: metaph., νόμους ὑπ. to trace out laws as guides of action, Id.   2. to trace in outline, sketch out, Lat. adumbrare, Id., etc.   III. ὑπογράφειν or -γράφεσθαι τοὺς ὀφθαλμούς to paint under the eyelids, Luc.

ὑπό-γυιος or **ὑπό-γυος**, ον, (γυῖον) under one's hand, nigh at hand, Isocr., Dem.   II. just out of hand, fresh, new, Lat. recens, Isocr., Dem.; ὑπόγυιόν ἐστι ἐξ οὗ . . , it is a very short time since . . , Isocr.   III. sudden, Arist.:—ἐξ ὑπογύου off hand, on the spur of the moment, Xen., Plat.   2. of persons, ὑπ. τῇ ὀργῇ in the first burst of anger, Arist.

ὑπο-δαίω, to light, kindle under, Il.

ὑπο-δακρύω, f. σω, to weep a little or secretly, Luc.

ὑπο-δαμνάω, to master or weaken beneath one, Il.:— Pass., ὑποδάμναμαι (as if from ὑποδάμνημι) to be overcome, let oneself be overpowered or overcome, Od.; aor. 1 part. ὑποδμηθεῖσα (v. δαμάζω), of a woman, subdued by a man, yielding to him, h. Hom., Hes.: —Med., ἔρως φρένας ὑποδάμναται Theocr.

ὑποδεδιώς, ὁ, Comic name of a bird in Ar., Fear-ling.

ὑπο-δέδρομα, pf. of ὑποτρέχω.

ὑπο-δεής, ές, gen. έος, (δέομαι) somewhat deficient, inferior; mostly in Comp. ὑποδεέστερος, Hdt., Plat.; ἐκ πολλῷ ὑποδεεστέρων with resources much inferior, Thuc.:—Adv. -εστέρως, Id.

ὑπό-δειγμα, τό, a token, mark, Xen.:—a pattern, Polyb.

ὑπο-δείδω, f. σω: aor. 1 ὑπέδεισα, Ep. -έδδεισα: Ep. pf. ὑπαιδείδοικα: pf. 2 ὑπο-δείδια: 3 pl. plqpf. ὑπεδείδισαν: I. trans. to cower under or before, or to fear secretly, c. acc., Hom.:—so of birds, to cower beneath, αἰγυπιὸν ὑποδείσαντες Soph.   II. absol., Od.; cf. ὑποδεδιώς.

ὑπο-δείκνυμι and -ύω: f. -δείξω, Ion. -δέξω:—to shew secretly, Hdt.; ὑποδέξας ὄλβον having given a glimpse of happiness, Id.; ὑπ. ἀρετήν to make a shew of virtue, Thuc.   2. absol. to indicate one's will, Xen.   II. to shew by tracing out, mark out, Hdt.: absol. to set a pattern, Xen.   2. generally, to teach indirectly or by indication, Isocr.; c. inf., N. T. Hence

ὑποδεικτέος, α, ον, verb. Adj. to be traced out, Polyb.

ὑπο-δειλιάω, to be somewhat cowardly, Aeschin.

ὑπο-δειμαίνω, to stand in secret awe of, τινά Hdt.

ὑπο-δέκομαι, Ion. for ὑπο-δέχομαι.

ὑπο-δέμω, to lay as a foundation, Hdt.

ὑποδεξίη, ἡ, like ὑποδοχή, the reception of a guest,

means of entertainment, πασά τοι ἔσθ᾽ ὑποδεξίη [ῑ, metri grat.], Il.

ὑπο-δέξιος, α, ον, (ὑποδέχομαι) capacious, Hdt.

ὑπόδεσις, εως, ἡ, (ὑποδέομαι) a putting on one's shoes, Arist., Luc. 2. as concrete, = τὰ ὑποδήματα, footgear, boots and shoes, Plat., Xen.

ὑποδέχνυμαι, poët. for sq., Anth.

ὑπο-δέχομαι, Ion. -δέκομαι: f. -δέξομαι: aor. 1 -εδεξάμην and in pass. form -εδέχθην: 3 sing. Ep. aor. 2 ὑπέδεκτο, 2 pl. imper. ὑπόδεχθε, inf. ὑποδέχθαι, part. ὑποδέγμενος: Dep.:—to receive beneath the surface, Il. 2. to receive into one's house, receive hospitably, Hom., etc.; ὁ ὑποδεξάμενος one's host, Isocr. 3. to give ear to, hearken to, εὐχάς Hes.; τοὺς λόγους Hdt. 4. to take in charge as a nurse, h. Hom., Plat. 5. metaph., πῆμα ὑπέδεκτό με sorrow was my host, Od.; στυγερὸς ὑπεδέξατο κοῖτος a hateful nest awaited them, of ensnared birds, Ib. II. to take upon oneself, undertake a task, promise, Hom.; with inf. fut., Hdt., etc.; less often with inf. aor., Id.; ὑπ. μεγάλα τινί to make him great promises, Id. 2. to admit, allow a charge, Id.; οὐκ ὑπ. to refuse to admit, deny, Id. III. to submit to, bear patiently, Od. IV. like Lat. excipere, 1. to wait for, abide the attack of, Hes., Xen.:—of hunters, to lie in wait for game, Xen. 2. to come next to, border upon, Hdt. V. of a woman, to conceive, Xen.

ὑπο-δέω, f. -δήσω, to bind or fasten under, Hdt. II. esp. to underbind, i. e. to shoe, because the sandals or shoes were bound on with straps, Plat.:—Med. to bind under one's feet, put on shoes, Ar., Xen., etc.; also c. acc., ὑποδησάμενος κοθόρνους Hdt.:—so in pf. pass., ὑποδήματα ὑποδεδεμένος with shoes on one's feet, Plat.; and absol., ὑποδεδεμένοι with their shoes on, Xen.; so, ὑποδεδεμένοι τὸν ἀριστερὸν πόδα with shoes on the left foot, Thuc.

ὑπο-δηλόω, f. ώσω, to shew privately, Plut.

ὑπόδημα, ατος, τό, (ὑποδέω) a sole bound under the foot with straps, a sandal, ποσὶν ὑποδήματα δοῦσα (i. e. δέουσα) Od.; ποσὶν ὑποδήματα δοίην (i. e. δεοίην) Ib., etc.; ὑπόδημα κοῖλον, or ὑπόδημα alone, = Lat. calceus, a shoe or half-boot, Ar., etc.

ὑπο-δῆσαι, aor. 1 inf. of ὑπο-δέω.

ὑπο-διδάσκαλος, ὁ, an under-teacher, of a chorus, Plat.

ὑπο-δίδωμι, f. -δώσω, to give way, Plat.

ὑπό-δικος, ον, (δίκη) brought to trial or liable to be tried, Lys., etc.:—τινος for a thing, Aesch., Oratt.; ὑπόδικός τινι liable to action from a person, Dem., etc.

ὑπο-δίφθερος, ον, (διφθέρα) clothed in skins, Luc.

ὑπο-δμηθείς, aor. 1 pass. part. of ὑπο-δαμάω.

ὑπο-δμώς, ῶος, ὁ, an under-servant, Od.

ὑπόδοσις, εως, ὁ, (ὑποδίδωμι) a remission, Aesch.

ὑποδοχή, ἡ, (ὑποδέχομαι) a reception, entertainment, Hdt., Eur., etc.; εἰς ὑποδοχὴν τοῦ στρατεύματος for the reception of the army (in hostile sense), Thuc. 2. a harbouring of runaway slaves, Id. 3. means for entertaining, Plut. II. acceptance, support, Aeschin. III. a supposition, assumption, Dem. IV. a receptacle, reservoir, Arist.

ὑπόδρᾰ, (ὑπό) Adv. only in phrase ὑπόδρα ἰδών, looking from under the brows, looking askance, grimly, Il.

ὑπο-δρᾰμεῖν, aor. 2 inf. of ὑπο-τρέχω.

ὑποδρηστήρ, ῆρος, ὁ, (ὑποδράω) an under-servant, attendant, assistant, Od.

ὑποδρομή, ἡ, (ὑποδραμεῖν) a running under or into the way of a thing, Antipho.

ὑπόδρομος, ον, (ὑποδραμεῖν) running under, πέτρος ὑπ. ἴχνους a stone in the way of his foot, Eur.

ὑπό-δροσος, ον, somewhat moistened or dewy, Theocr.

ὑπο-δρώω, Ep. for ὑπο-δράω, to serve, be serviceable to, τινί Od.

ὑποδύνω, v. ὑποδύω.

ὑπο-δύς, aor. 2 part. of ὑπο-δύω.

ὑποδύτης [ῠ], ου, ὁ, a garment under a coat of mail, Plut.

ὑπο-δύω and -δύνω, to put on under, κιθῶνας ὑποδύνειν τοῖσι εἵμασι Hdt. 2. to slip in under, Id.:—also to assume secretly, slip into, c. acc., Id.:—also to slip from under, Xen. 3. metaph. to undergo danger, Hdt. II. Med. ὑποδύομαι, f. -δύσομαι: aor. 1 -εδυσάμην, Ep. 3 sing. -εδύσετο: so also aor. 2 act. -έδυν, pf. -δέδῠκα:—to go under, get under, sink beneath, Lat. subire, c. acc., Od.; ὑπ. ὑπὸ τὴν ζεύγλην Hdt.:—so, ὑπ. ὑπὸ τῶν κεραμίδων to creep under, Ar.; φέρει τινὰ ὑποδεδυκότα underneath it, Id. 2. to put one's feet under a shoe, to put it on, Id. 3. metaph. to put on a character (because the actor's face was put under a mask), Plat., Arist. 4. c. gen. to come from under, come forth from, Od. III. to go under so as to bear, to bear on one's shoulders, Il. 2. to enter into war, Hdt. 3. metaph. to undergo danger, c. acc., Xen.; ὑπ. αἰτίαν to make oneself subject to.., Dem. 4. c. inf. to undertake to do, Hdt. 5. of feelings, to steal over one, c. acc., Aesch.:—c. dat., πᾶσιν ὑπέδυ γόος sorrow stole upon all, Od. 6. absol. to slip or slink away, Dem. 7. absol., ὀφθαλμοὶ ὑποδεδυκότες sunken eyes, Luc.

ὑπο-είκω, v. ὑπ-είκω.

ὑπο-ζάκορος, ὁ or ἡ, an under-priest or priestess, Hdt.

ὑπο-ζεύγνυμι and -ύω: f. -ζεύξω:—Pass., aor. 2 ὑπ-εζύγην [ῠ]: pf. -έζευγμαι:—to yoke under, put under the yoke, ὑπ. ἵππους ἡμιόνους Od.:—Pass. to be yoked under, submit to, ἀνάγκαις Aesch.; πόνῳ Soph.

ὑπο-ζύγιον [ῠ], τό, (ζυγόν) a beast for the yoke, a beast of burden, Lat. jumentum, Theogn., Hdt., etc.

ὑπόζωμα, ατος, τό, the diaphragm, midriff, Arist. II. in pl. braces passed under the hull of a vessel, so as to undergird her (cf. ὑποζώννυμι II), Plat.

ὑπο-ζώννυμι and -ύω, f. -ζώσω:—Pass., pf. ὑπ-έζωσμαι:—to undergird, Plut.; ζειρὰς ὑπεζωσμένοι girt with ζειραί, Hdt. II. to undergird or frap a ship (v. ὑπόζωμα II), Polyb., N. T.

ὑπόζωσμα, ατος, τό, less Att. form for ὑπόζωμα (II), Plut.

ὑπο-θάλπω, f. ψω, to heat inwardly, Aesch.:—Pass. to glow under a thing, c. dat., Anth.

ὑπο-θείς, aor. 2 part. of ὑπο-θέω.

ὑπο-θερμαίνω: Pass., aor. 1 ὑπ-εθερμάνθην:—to heat a little:—Pass. to grow somewhat hot, be heated, Il.

ὑπό-θερμος, ον, somewhat hot or passionate, Hdt.

ὑπο-θέσθαι, aor. 2 med. inf. of ὑπο-τίθημι.

ὑπόθεσις, εως, ἡ, (ὑποτίθημι) that which is placed under, a foundation, hypothesis, supposition, Lat. assumptio, Plat. 2. the subject under discussion, the

question, Xen., Dem., etc. **II.** *that which is laid down as a rule of action, a principle,* Dem. : generally, *a purpose, plan, design,* Plat. **III.** *a cause, pretext,* Plut.

ὑποθετέον, verb. Adj. *one must assume,* Arist.

ὑπο-θέω, f. -θεύσομαι, *to run in under, make a secret attack,* Pind. **2.** *to run in before, to supplant,* Ar. **II.** of dogs, *to run in too hastily,* Xen.

ὑποθήκη, ἡ, (ὑποτίθημι) *a suggestion, counsel, warning, piece of advice,* Hdt., Arist. **II.** *a pledge, a mortgage,* Dem.

ὑποθημοσύνη, ἡ, *a suggestion, hint, warning,* ὑποθημοσύνησιν Ἀθήνης (Ep. dat. pl.) Hom. ; Ἑρμοῦ ὑποθημοσύνῃ Xen. From

ὑποθήμων, ονος, ὁ, ἡ, (ὑποτίθημι) *suggesting advice.*

ὑπο-θήσω, fut. of ὑπο-τίθημι.

ὑπο-θλίβω [ῑ], f. ψω, *to press under* or *gently,* Luc.

ὑπο-θορυβέω, f. ήσω, *to begin to make a clamour,* Thuc.

ὑπο-θράττω, Att. for ὑπο-ταράσσω, Plut.

ὑπο-θρύπτομαι, Pass., *to be delicate* or *remiss,* Plut.

ὑπο-θῡμίς, ίδος, ἡ, (θυμός) *a garland worn on the neck,* Sappho.

ὑπο-θῡμίς, ἡ (?), *an unknown bird,* Ar.

ὑπο-θωπεύω, f. σω, *to flatter a little, win by flattery,* Ar. :—absol. *to use flattery,* Hdt.

ὑπο-θωρήσσομαι, Med. *to arm oneself in secret,* Il.

ὑπ-οιάχω [ᾱ], *to sound forth in answer,* Anth.

ὑπ-οικέω, f. ήσω, *to dwell under :* *to lie hidden,* Anth.

ὑπ-οικίζομαι, Pass. with aor. 1 med., = foreg., Anth.

ὑπ-οικοδομέω, *to build under* a place, c. gen., Luc.

ὑπ-οικουρέω, f. ήσω, *to keep the house, stay at home :* —metaph. *to lurk, lie hidden,* Luc. **II.** trans. *to engage in* or *plot underhand,* Plut. **2.** c. acc. pers. *to work secretly upon,* Id. ; νόσος ὑπ. αὐτούς *crept in among* them, Id.

ὑπ-οιμώζω, f. -οιμώξομαι, *to wail softly, to whimper,* Luc.

ὑπο-κάθημαι, Ion. -κάτημαι, Dep. *to be seated in* a place, *station oneself,* Hdt. **II.** *to sit in* ambush, Xen. **2.** c. acc. pers. *to lie in wait for,* Hdt.

ὑπο-καθίζω, f. Att. ιῶ, *to place in ambush :*—Med. *to lie in ambush,* Xen.

ὑπο-καίω, Att. -κάω, f. -καύσω, *to burn by applying fire below,* Hdt. ; *to offer secret sacrifices,* Aesch. **2.** *to light under,* Luc.

ὑπο-κάμπτω, f. ψω, *to bend short back, turn in under,* Il. **II.** intr. *to turn short back, double* as a hare, Xen. :—metaph., c. acc., *to fall short of,* καιρόν Aesch.

ὑπο-κάρδιος, ον, (καρδία) *in the heart,* Theocr.

ὑπο-καταβαίνω, f. -βήσομαι, *to descend by degrees* or *stealthily,* Plat., Thuc. : *to come down a little,* Xen.

ὑπο-κατακλίνομαι [ῑ], Pass. *to lie down under, to submit, yield,* τινι to one, Plat. :—absol. *to give in,* Dem.

ὑπο-κάτω [ᾰ], Adv. *below, under,* c. gen., Plat.

ὑπόκειμαι, used as Pass. of ὑποτίθημι, with f. ὑποκείσομαι, but aor. 1 ὑπετέθην :—*to lie under* or *beneath,* Il., Thuc. ; c. dat., Plat. **II.** in various metaph. senses, **1.** *to be put under* the eyes or mind, i. e. *to be submitted* or *proposed to one,* Pind. ; αἱ ὑποκείμεναι ἐλπίδες one's *present* hopes, Dem. ; ὑπόκειταί μοι ὅτι . . *I have laid down the rule,* that . . , Hdt. **2.** *to be laid down* or *assumed as an hypothesis,* Plat., etc. ; τούτων ὑποκειμένων = Lat. *his*

positis, Id. ; impers., ὑπόκειται *a rule is laid down,* Dem. ; ὑποκείσθω ὅτι . . *let it be granted that . . ,* Arist. **3.** *to be suggested,* Hdt. **4.** *to be left at bottom, left remaining,* Thuc., Dem. **5.** *to be subject to, submit to,* τινι Plat. : absol. *to be submissive,* Id. **6.** *to be left behind in pledge, to be pledged* or *mortgaged,* τινος *for* a certain sum, Dem., etc. ; ὑποκείμενοι, of persons, *bound for payment* of a sum of money, Id. **7.** *to underlie,* as a substratum, Plat., etc. **8.** *to be subordinate,* Id.

ὑπο-κηρύσσομαι, Att. -ττομαι, Med. *to make known by voice of herald* or *crier, to have* a thing *proclaimed* or *cried,* esp. for sale, Aeschin. ; σεαυτὸν ὑπ. *to advertise* yourself, Plat.

ὑπο-κῑνέω, f. ήσω, *to move lightly,* Ζεφύρου ὑποκινήσαντος (sc. τὸ κῦμα) Il. **2.** metaph. *to urge gently on,* Plat. **II.** intr. *to move a little, stir a finger,* Hdt., Ar. **2.** metaph. *to be deranged,* Plat.

ὑπο-κλαίω, Att. -κλάω, *to shed secret tears,* Aesch.

ὑπο-κλέπτω, f. ψω, *to steal underhand, filch,* Babr. : —Pass. *to be stolen away,* Pind. **2.** ὑποκλέπτεσθαί τι *to be defrauded of* a thing, Soph.

ὑπο-κλίνομαι [ῑ], Pass. *to recline* or *lie down under,* c. dat., σχοίνῳ ὑπεκλίνθη Od.

ὑπο-κλονέομαι, Pass. *to be driven in confusion before* one, τινι Il.

ὑπο-κλοπέομαι, Pass. *to lurk in secret places,* Od.

ὑπο-κλύζω, f. ύσω, *to wash from below,* Anth.

ὑπο-κνίζω, f. σω, *to tickle* or *excite a little,* Pind. :— Pass. *to be somewhat excited,* Anth.

ὑπο-κόλπιος, ον, *under the folds of the robe,* Anth.

ὑπό-κοπος, ον, *somewhat tired,* Xen.

ὑπο-κόπτω, f. ψω, *to cut beneath, to hamstring,* Plut.

ὑπο-κορίζομαι, f. ίσομαι : Dep. :—*to talk child's language,* **1.** trans. *to call by endearing names,* Ar. **2.** *to call by a fair name, gloss over* or *palliate,* Plat., Dem. **3.** reversely, *to call something good by a bad name, to nickname,* Xen. **II.** intr. *to use diminutives,* Arist. Hence

ὑποκόρισμα, ατος, τό, *a coaxing* or *endearing name,* Aeschin.

ὑποκορισμός, ὁ, = foreg., Plut. **II.** *the use of diminutives,* Arist.

ὑπο-κουρίζομαι, Ion. for -κορίζομαι, *to soothe with soft names,* Pind.

ὑπό-κουφος, ον, *somewhat light* or *fickle,* Plut.

ὑπο-κρᾱτηρίδιον, Ion. ὑποκρητ-, τό, *the stand of a* κρατήρ, Hdt.

ὑπο-κρέκω, f. ξω, of stringed instruments, *to answer in sound,* i. e. *to sound in harmony with,* τινι Pind.

ὑπο-κρητηρίδιον, Ion. for ὑπο-κρατ-.

ὑπο-κρίνομαι [ῑ], f. -κρῐνοῦμαι, Ion. -έομαι : aor. 1 ὑπεκρῐνάμην : later also aor. 1 and pf. pass. in med. sense, ὑπεκρίθην [ῑ], ὑποκέκριμαι :—*to reply, make answer, answer,* Hom., Hdt. **2.** *to expound, interpret, explain,* Od., Ar. :—the Att. word in this sense is ἀπο-κρίνομαι. **II.** of actors, *to answer on the stage :* hence *to play a part,* τὴν Ἀντιγόνην ὑποκέκριται Dem. ; ὑπ. τὸ βασιλικόν *to take* the king's *part,* Arist. ; ὑποκρ. τραγῳδίαν, κωμῳδίαν *to play* a tragedy, a comedy, Id. ; absol. *to play a part, be an actor,* Id. **2.** *to represent dramatically :* hence *to*

exaggerate, Dem. 3. metaph. *to play a part, to feign, pretend*, c. inf., Id.

ὑποκρίσια, ἡ, rarer form for ὑπόκρισις II, Anth.

ὑπόκρῐσις, εως, ἡ, (ὑποκρίνομαι): **I.** in Ion. *a reply, answer*, Hdt. **II.** in Att. *the playing a part* on the stage, *the actor's art*, Arist. 2. *an orator's delivery, declamation*, Id. 3. metaph. *the playing a part, hypocrisy*, Phocyl.

ὑποκρῐτής, οῦ, ὁ, (ὑποκρίνομαι) *an interpreter* or *expounder*, Plat., Luc. **II.** *one who plays a part* on the stage, *a player, actor*, Ar., Plat., etc. 2. metaph. *a pretender, dissembler, hypocrite*, N. T.

ὑποκρῐτικός, ή, όν, *belonging to* ὑπόκρισις (II), *having a good delivery*, Arist. 2. *suited for speaking* or *delivery*, ὑποκριτικωτάτη λέξις Id.: ἡ -κή (sc. τέχνη), *the art of delivery*, Id. 3. metaph. *pretending to* a thing, c. gen., Luc.

ὑπο-κρούω, f. σω, *to strike gently*, Anth.: *to beat time, give the time*, Plut. **II.** metaph. *to break in upon, interrupt*, c. acc., Ar. **III.** in Med. *to find fault with, attack*, Id.

ὑπο-κρύπτω, f. ψω, *to hide under* or *beneath*, ἄχνῃ ὑπεκρύφθη [the ship] *was hidden beneath* the spray, Il.

ὑπό-κρώζω, f. ξω, *to croak faintly*, as a sick person, Luc.

ὑπό-κυκλος, ον, *running on wheels*, Od.

ὑπο-κύομαι, Med. *to conceive, become pregnant*, ὑποκῡσαμένη (not -κυσσαμένη), Hom., Hes.

ὑπο-κύπτω, f. ψω, *to stoop under a yoke*, οἱ Μῆδοι ὑπέκυψαν Πέρσῃσι *bowed to* the Persian *yoke*, Hdt.: absol., of suppliants, *to bow down*, Ar., Xen. **II.** c. acc., ὑπ. τὰν τύλαν *to stoop* the shoulder so as to let a load be put on, Ar.

ὑπό-κῡφος, ον, *somewhat humped*, Strab.

ὑπό-κωλιον, τό, (κῶλον) *the thigh* of an animal, Xen.

ὑπο-κωμῳδέω, f. ήσω, *to ridicule a little*, Luc.

ὑπό-κωφος, ον, *somewhat deaf*, Ar., Plat.

ὑπο-λαμβάνω, f. -λήψομαι: aor. 2 ὑπ-έλαβον: pf. -είληφα:—*to take up by getting under*, as the dolphin did Arion, Hdt.: *to receive into its bosom*, N. T. **b.** *to bear up, support*, Hdt. **c.** *to take by the hand*, Plat. 2. *to seize* or *come suddenly upon*, of fear, Hom.; of a fit of madness, a pestilence, Hdt.; δυσχωρία ὑπελάμβανεν αὐτούς, i. e. they came suddenly into difficult ground, Xen.; then, of events, *to follow next, come next*, Hdt. 3. *to take up* the discourse *and answer, to reply, rejoin, retort*, Thuc., Plat., etc.:—absol., in dialogue, ἔφη ὑπολαβών, ὑπ. ἔφη, ὑπ. εἶπεν *he said in answer*, Hdt., Thuc., etc. **b.** *to take up, interrupt*, Xen. 4. *to take up* the conqueror, *fight with* him, Lat. *excipere*, Thuc. 5. *to take up a charge*, Id. **II.** = ὑποδέχομαι, *to receive and protect*, Xen. 2. *to accept* or *entertain* a proposal, Hdt., Dem. **III.** *to take up* a notion, *assume, suppose*, c. inf., Hdt., Plat.:—the inf. omitted, *to conceive of* a thing as being so and so, Plat.; καίπερ ὑπειληφὼς ταῦτα though *I assume* this to be so, Dem.:—Pass., τοιοῦτος ὑπολαμβάνομαι Isocr. 2. *to apprehend* a thing, Eur., Plat. 3. *to suspect, disbelieve*, Xen. **IV.** *to take secretly*, Thuc. 2. *to draw off from duty, seduce*, Id. **V.** ὑπ. ἵππον, as a term of horsemanship, *to hold up* or *to check* the horse, Xen.

ὑπο-λαμπής, ές, *shining with inferior lustre*, Hes.

ὑπο-λάμπω, f. ψω, *to shine under, shine in under*, Xen.:—so in Med., Anth. **II.** *to shine a little, begin to shine, just appear*, τὸ ἔαρ ὑπέλαμπε Hdt.; ὑπ. ἡ ἡμέρα Plut.

ὑπο-λείβω, *to pour secret libations*, Aesch.

ὑπο-λείπω, f. ψω, *to leave remaining*, Od., Thuc., etc. 2. of things, *to fail* one, ὑπολείψει ὑμᾶς ἡ μισθοφορά Lys. **II.** Pass., c. fut. med., *to be left remaining*, Hom., Hdt. 2. of things, *to remain in force*, Thuc. 3. *to stay behind*, Od.: c. gen., ὑπολείπεσθαι τοῦ στόλου *to stay behind* the expedition, i. e. not to go upon it, Hdt. 4. *to be left behind* in a race, Ar.: of stragglers in an army, *to lag behind*, Xen.; ὑπ. μικρὸν τοῦ στόματος *to fall behind* the front rank, Id. 5. metaph. *to be inferior to*, τινός Arist. 6. absol. *to fail, come to an end*, Soph.:—ὑπ. τινά ὁ λόγος *fails* him, Arist. **III.** Med. *to leave behind one*, Thuc.; ὑπολείπεσθαι αἰτίαν *to leave* cause for reproach *against oneself*, Thuc.

ὑπό-λεπτος, ον, *somewhat fine*, Luc.

ὑπο-λευκαίνομαι, Pass. *to become white underneath* or *somewhat white*, Il.

ὑπο-λήνιον, τό, (ληνός) *the vessel under a press* to receive the wine or oil, *a vat*, Lat. *lacus*, N. T.

ὑποληπτέον, verb. Adj. of ὑπολαμβάνω, *one must suppose, understand, think of*, Plat.

ὑπόληψις, εως, (ὑπολαμβάνω) *a taking up*, esp. *a taking up the word, taking up the matter* where another leaves off, Plat.:—*a rejoinder, reply*, Isocr. **II.** *a taking in a certain sense, an assumption, conception*, Dem. 2. *a hasty judgment, suspicion*, Luc.

ὑπ-ολίζων, ον, *somewhat less* or *fewer*, Il.

ὑπό-λιθος, ον, *somewhat stony*, Luc.

ὑπο-λιμπάνω, later for ὑπολείπω, *to leave behind*, N. T.

ὑπ-ολισθάνω, f. -ολισθήσω, *to slip* or *slide gradually*, Luc.

ὑπό-λισπος, Att. -λισφος, ον, *somewhat smooth, worn smooth*, Ar.

ὑπό-λιχνος, ον, *somewhat lickerish* or *dainty*, Luc.

ὑπο-λογέω, f. ήσω, *to take account of*, τινός Arist.

ὑπο-λογίζομαι, f. ίσομαι, Att. ιοῦμαι: Dep.:—*to take into account, take account of*, Plat., Dem. Hence

ὑπολογιστέον, verb. Adj. *one must take into account*, Plat.

ὑπό-λογος, ον, *held accountable* or *liable*, Dem.; ὑπόλογον ποιεῖσθαι *to hold responsible*, Plat.; οὐδέν σοι ὑπόλογον τίθεμαι I put down nothing *to your account*, Id.

ὑπό-λογος, ὁ, *a taking into account, a reckoning, account*, ὑπόλογον ποιεῖσθαί τι Lat. *rationem habere rei*, Dem.; ἐν ὑπολόγῳ ποιεῖσθαί τι Lys.

ὑπό-λοιπος, ον, *left behind, staying behind*, Hdt.; οἱ ὑπ. *those who remained alive*, Id. 2. of things, ὑπ. τὸ βάραθρον γίγνεται *the pit still remains*, Ar.; ὅσα ἦν ὑπ. all that *remained to be done*, Thuc.

ὑπο-λόχαγος, ὁ, *an under-λοχαγός, a lieutenant*, Xen.

ὑπο-λύριος [ῠ], ον, (λύρα) *under the lyre*; δόναξ ὑπ. *a reed to which the lower ends of the strings were attached*, Ar.

ὑπο-λύω, f. σω [ῡ]: aor. 1 ὑπ-έλῡσα: pf. ὑπο-λέλῠκα:—Pass., pf. -λέλῠμαι: 3 pl. Ep. aor. 2 ὑπ-έλῠντο:—*to loosen beneath* or *below*, ὑπέλυσε γυῖα *made* his limbs

give way under him, Il. :—Pass., γυῖα ὑπέλυντο Ib. **II.** to loose from under the yoke, Hom., Thuc. :—to loose from bonds, Od. ; in Med., τὸν ὑπελύσαο δεσμῶν thou didst free him from bonds by stealth, Il. **2.** to untie a person's sandals from under his feet, take off his shoes, Aesch., Ar. :—Med. to take off one's sandals or shoes, or to have them taken off, Ar. **b.** c. acc. pers. to unshoe him, take off his shoes, Plat.

ὑπόμαζοι, οἱ, the parts under the breast, Bion.

ὑπό-μακρος, ον, somewhat long, longish, Ar.

ὑπο-μᾰλᾰκίζομαι, Pass. to grow cowardly by degrees, Xen.

ὑπό-μαργος, ον, somewhat mad, in Comp. ὑπομαργότερος, Hdt.

ὑπο-μάσσω, Att. -ττω, f. ξω, to smear or rub underneath, Theocr.

ὕπ-ομβρος, ον, mixed with rain, θέρος ὑπ. a rainy summer, Plut.

ὑπο-μειδιάω, to smile a little or gently, Anacreon.

ὑπο-μεῖναι, aor. 1 inf. of ὑπο-μένω.

ὑπο-μείων, ον, gen. ονος, somewhat less :—ὑπομείονες, subordinate citizens, opp. to ὅμοιοι, Xen.

ὑπο-μέμφομαι, Dep. to blame a little or secretly, Plut.

ὑπο-μεμψίμοιρος, ον, somewhat discontented with his lot, Cic.

ὑπομενετέον, verb. Adj. of ὑπομένω, one must sustain, abide, endure, Thuc., etc.

ὑπομενετικός, ή, όν, patient of, τῶν δεινῶν Arist.

ὑπο-μένω, f. -μενῶ : aor. 1 ὑπ-έμεινα :—to stay behind, survive, Od., Hdt., Att. **II.** trans., **1.** c. acc. pers. to await another, to await his attack, bide the onset, Il., Hdt. ; ὑπ. τὰς Σειρῆνας to abide their presence, Xen. **2.** c. acc. rei, to be patient under, abide patiently, submit to, Hdt., Thuc., etc. ; ὑπ. τὴν κρίσιν to await one's trial, Aeschin. ; to wait for, τὴν ἑορτήν Thuc. **3.** absol. to stand one's ground, stand firm, Il., Hdt., etc. ; ὑπομένων καρτερεῖν to endure patiently, Plat. **4.** c. inf. to submit or dare to do a thing, wait to do, persist in doing, like Lat. sustinere, Od., Xen. **5.** so with part. relating to the subject, εἰ ὑπομενέουσι χεῖρας ἀνταειρόμενοι if they shall dare to lift their hands, Hdt. ; ὑπομένει ὠφελούμενος he submits to be helped, Plat. :—with part. relating to the object, ὑπ. Ξέρξεα ἐπιόντα to await his attack, Hdt., etc.

ὑπο-μίγνῡμι, f. -μίξω, to add by mixing, Lat. admisceo, τί τινι Plat. **II.** intr. to run close under a place, c. dat., Thuc.

ὑπο-μιμνήσκω, f. -μνήσω: aor. 1 ὑπ-έμνησα: **I.** Act., **1.** to remind one of a person or thing, τινά τινος Od., Thuc. ; ὑπ. τινά τι Thuc., Xen. : ὑπ. τινά τι put him in mind, Plat. **2.** c. acc. rei, to bring back to one's mind, mention, suggest, τι Hdt., Soph., etc. ; τινί τι Aesch. **3.** c. gen. rei, to remind one of, to make mention of, Thuc., etc. **II.** Pass. or Med. to call to mind, remember, Xen. **2.** to make mentiòn, περί τινος Aesch.

ὑπό-μισθος, ον, serving for pay, hired, Luc.

ὑπομνάομαι [ᾰ], Dep. to court clandestinely, ὑπεμνάασθε (Ep. 2 pl. impf.) γυναῖκα Od.

ὑπό-μνημα, ατος, τό, a remembrance, memorial, Thuc.,

etc. **2.** a note, memorandum, Dem. :—in pl. memoranda, notes, minutes, Lat. commentarii, Plat.

ὑπόμνησις, εως, ἡ, a reminding, Thuc., etc. **2.** a mentioning, ὑπ. ποιεῖσθαί τινος to make mention of a thing, Id. ; ὑπ. κακῶν a tale of woe, Eur.

ὑπο-μνηστεύομαι, Med. to betroth, Arist. :—Pass., ὑπομνηστευθείς one betrothed, Id.

ὑπ-όμνυμαι, f. -ομοῦμαι : Med. :—to make oath that a person cannot appear in court : to apply for a postponement of the trial, Dem. :—Pass., ὑπομοσθέντος τούτου this affidavit being put in by way of excuse, Id. **2.** to bar proceedings by an affidavit in a γραφὴ παρανόμων, Xen.

ὑπομονή, ἡ, (ὑπομένω) a remaining behind, Arist. **II.** a holding out, patient endurance, Id. :—the enduring to do, αἰσχρῶν ἔργων Theophr.

ὑπό-μωρος, ον, rather stupid or silly, Luc.

ὑπο-ναίω, to dwell under a place, c. acc., Anth.

ὑπονέμομαι, Med. to eat away beneath or secretly, Anth.

ὑπό-νέφελος, ον, (νεφέλη) under the clouds, Luc.

ὑπο-νήιος, ον, under the promontory Νεῖον, lying at its base, Od.

ὑπο-νήχομαι, Dep. to swim under water, dive, Plut.

ὑπο-νίφω [ῑ], to snow a little : impers., ὑπένιφε it was snowing a little, Thuc. :—Pass., νὺξ ὑπονιφομένη a snowy night, Id.

ὑπο-νοέω, f. ήσω, to think secretly, suspect, Hdt., Eur., etc. :—c. acc. pers. et inf. to suspect that . . , Hdt. ; τῶν λεγόντων ὑπενοεῖτε you feel suspicious of the speakers, Thuc. **II.** generally, to suspect, conjecture, form guesses about, Ar. : absol., ὑπονοοῦντες by conjecture, Plat.

ὑπόνοια, ἡ, (ὑπονοέω) a hidden thought : hence, **I.** a suspicion, conjecture, guess, supposition, Ar., etc. ; ὑπόνοιαι τῶν μελλόντων notions formed of future events, Thuc. **II.** the real meaning of a thing, the true intent, deeper sense, Xen., Plat., etc.

ὑπονομηδόν, Adv. by means of pipes, Thuc. From

ὑπό-νομος, ον, underground, Strab. **II.** ὑπόνομος, ὁ, as Subst. an underground passage, mine, Thuc. **2.** a water-pipe, Xen.

ὑπο-νοσέω, f. ήσω, to be rather sickly, Luc.

ὑπο-νοστέω, f. ήσω, to go back, retire, Hdt. :—to go down, sink, settle, Id. Hence

ὑπονόστησις, εως, ἡ, subsidence, of the sea, Plut.

ὑπο-νύσσω, f. ξω, to prick or sting underneath : generally, to sting, Theocr.

ὑπο-νυστάζω, f. ξω, to fall asleep gradually, Plat.

ὑπό-ξῠλος, ον, (ξύλον) wooden underneath, i.e. of wood covered with a coat of metal, Luc.

ὑπο-ξῠράω or -έω, to shave or cut off some of the hair : —Pass., pf. part. ὑπεξυρημένος shorn or shaven, Luc.

ὑπο-ξύριος [ῠ], α, ον, (ξυρόν) under the rasor, Anth.

ὑπο-ξύω [ῠ], f. σω, to scrape slightly, Anth.

ὑπο-πᾰλαίω, f. σω, to go down voluntarily in wrestling, Luc.

ὑπο-πάσσω, f. -πάσω [ᾰ], to strew under, Hdt.

ὑπο-πεινάω, f. ήσω, to be rather hungry, to begin to be hungry, Ar.

ὑπό-πεμπτος, ον, sent covertly, as a spy, Xen.

ὑπο-πέμπω, f. ψω, to send under : Pass. to be sent

beneath, σκότον Eur.   II. *to send secretly : to send as a spy, send in a false character*, Thuc., Xen.

ὑπο-πεπτηῶτες, Ep. pf. part. pl. of ὑπο-πτήσσω.

ὑπο-πέρδομαι, Dep., with aor. 2 act. ὑπέπαρδον, *to break wind a little*, Ar.

ὑπο-περκάζω, only in pres., *to begin to turn colour*, of grapes, Od.

ὑπο-πετάννῡμι, f. -πετάσω, *to spread out under*, Od.

ὑπό-πετρος, ον, *somewhat rocky*, Hdt.

ὑπο-πῐθηκίζω, f. σω, *to play the ape a little*, Ar.

ὑπο-πίμπλημι, f. -πλήσω :—Pass., aor. 1 ὑπ-επλήσθην : —*to fill by degrees* :—Pass., πώγωνος ἤδη ὑποπιμπλάμενος now *beginning to have a thick beard*, Plat. ; ὑπο-πίμπλαμαι τοὺς ὀφθαλμοὺς δακρύων *have my* eyes *filling with tears*, Luc.   II. in Pass. of women, τέκνων ὑποπλησθῆναι *to become mothers of many children*, Hdt.

ὑπο-πίμπρημι, f. -πρήσω : aor. 1 -έπρησα :—*to set on fire below*, τὴν ὕλην Hdt.   2. *to burn as on a funeral-pyre*, τινάς Id.

ὑπο-πίνω [ῐ], f. -πίομαι : aor. 2 ὑπ-έπιον : pf. ὑπο-πέπωκα :—*to drink a little, drink moderately*, Plat.   2. *to drink slowly, go on drinking*, Ar., Xen.   3. ὑπο-πεπωκώς *rather tipsy*, Ar., Xen.

ὑπο-πίπτω, f. -πεσοῦμαι : aor. 2 ὑπ-έπεσον : pf. ὑπο-πέπτωκα :—*to fall under* or *down, to sink in*, Plut.   2. *to fall down before* any one, c. acc., Plat. : —hence, *to be subject* to him, *fall under his power*, Isocr. ; of a flatterer, *to cringe to*, τινί Dem. ; c. acc. ὑποπεσὼν τὸν δεσπότην Ar.   3. *to fall behind* another, Dem.   II. *to get in under* or *among*, Thuc.   III. of accidents, *to happen, fall out*, Isocr.   2. of persons, *to fall under a punishment*, c. dat., Plut.   IV. of places, *to lie under* or *below*, c. dat., Polyb.

ὑπο-πλάκιος [ᾰ], α, ον, *under mount Placus*, in the Troad, Il.

ὑπό-πλεος, ον, Att. -πλέως, ων, *pretty full*, c. gen., δείματός εἰμι ὑπ. am *somewhat afraid*, Hdt.

ὑπο-πλέω, f. -πλεύσομαι, *to sail under*, ὑπ. τὴν Κύπρον, i. e. *under the lee* of Cyprus, N. T.

ὑποπλώω, Ion. for ὑποπλέω, Anth.

ὑπο-πνέω, f. -πνεύσω, *to blow gently*, N. T.

ὑπο-πόδιον, τό, (πούς) *a footstool*, Luc.

ὑποποιέω, *to put under* :—Med. *to subject to oneself*, Luc.   2. *to produce gradually*, Plut.   3. in Med. *to gain by underhand tricks, to win over*, τινά Dem.   II. in Med. *to assume, affect*, Plut.

ὑπο-πόλιος, ον, *somewhat gray*, Luc.

ὑπο-πορεύομαι, Dep. *to go beneath the ground*, Plut.

ὑπό-πορτις, ιος, ἡ, *with a calf under her*, of a cow :— metaph. of a woman, Hes.

ὑπο-πρίᾱμαι, Dep. *to buy under the price*, Theophr.

ὑπο-πρίω [ῑ], *to gnash the teeth secretly*, Luc.

ὑπό-πτερος, ον, (πτερόν) *winged*, Hdt., Soph., etc. ; of a ship, Pind.   2. metaph. *swift-flying, soaring*, Id. ; ὑπ. φροντίς *flighty, giddy thought*, Aesch.

ὑπ-οπτεύω, f. σω, *to be suspicious*, Xen. ; also, ὑπ. εἴς τινα *to have suspicions of him*, Thuc.   2. *to suspect, guess, suppose*, Xen.   II. trans. *to suspect, hold in suspicion*, Soph., Thuc. ; ὑπ. τινὰ εἴς τι of something, Hdt., etc. :—Pass. *to be suspected, mistrusted*, Thuc. ; impers., ὡς ὑπωπτεύετο as was generally *suspected*, Xen.   2. c. acc. pers. et inf.

to suspect that, Hdt., Thuc., etc.   3. c. acc. rei, *to look suspiciously on*, Thuc. :—but also, ὑπ. τι *to suspect something*, Eur., Xen. From

ὑπόπτης, ου, ὁ, (ὑπόψομαι) *suspicious, jealous*, Soph., Thuc. : of a horse, *shy*, Xen.

ὑπο-πτήσσω, f. ξω, *to crouch* or *cower beneath*, like hares or birds, πετάλοις ὑποπεπτηῶτες (Ep. part. pf. for ὑποπεπτηκότες), Il. ; ὑποπτήξας τάφῳ Eur.   II. metaph. *to crouch before* another, *bow down to*, τινί Xen. ; also, ὑπ. τινά Aesch., Xen. :—absol. *to be modest* or *shy*, Xen.

ὑπόπτος, ον, (ὑπόψομαι) *looked at from beneath* the brows, i. e. *viewed with suspicion* or *jealousy*, Lat. *suspectus*, Aesch., Thuc. ; c. inf., ὑπ. αὐτοῖς μὴ πέμψαι *suspected* by them of not having sent, Thuc.   2. of things, τάδ' ἦν ὕποπτα Eur. ; ὕποπτον καθεστήκει it was *a matter of jealousy*, Thuc.   3. Adv., ὑπόπτως διακεῖσθαι or ἔχειν *to lie under suspicion*, Id., Xen.   II. act. *suspecting, suspicious* of a thing, c. gen. ; τὸ ὕποπτον *suspicion, jealousy*, Thuc. ; τῷ ὑπ. μου *from suspicion of me*, Id. :—Adv. *with suspicion*, Id. ; ὑπ. ἔχειν πρός τινα Dem.

ὑπο-πτῠχίς, ίδος, ἡ, (πτυχή) *a joint*, τοῦ θώρακος Plut.

ὑπο-πυθμίδιος, ον, (πυθμήν) *under the bottom*, Anth.

ὑπό-πωλος, ον, *with a foal under her*, Strab.

ὑπο-ρῑπίζω, *to fan from below* or *gently*, Anth.

ὑπ-όρνῡμι, f. -όρσω : aor. 1 -ῶρσα :—*to rouse secretly* or *gradually*, Hom. ; τοῖον γὰρ ὑπόρορε Μοῦσα such *was the Muse's power to move*, Od. :—Pass. *to rise secretly* or *gradually*, Ib.

ὑπ-όροφος, ον, (ὄροφος, a reed), ὑπ. βοά the soft note *of the pipe*, Eur.

ὑπορ-ράπτω, f. ψω, *to stitch underneath* : metaph., ὑπ. λόγον *to make up a story*, Eur.

ὑπορ-ρέω, f. -ρυήσομαι, *to flow under* or *beneath*, Plut.   2. *to flow gradually away*, Id. : metaph. *to stream gradually* to a place, Luc.   II. metaph. also, *to slip* or *glide into unperceived*, Lat. *subrepere*, Plat., Dem.   2. *to slip away*, of time, Ar. ; of flowers, *to perish*, Theocr. ; of the hair, *to fall off*, Luc. ; and of friends, Id.

ὑπορ-ρήγνῡμι or -ύω, *to make to burst downwards* : —Pass., οὐρανόθεν ὑπερράγη (aor. 2) αἰθήρ ether *was cleft from beneath the sky*, Il.

ὑπόρ-ρηνος, ον, (ῥήν, ἀρήν) *with a lamb under it*, Il.

ὑπορ-ρῑπίζω, f. σω, *to fan from below* or *gently*, Anth.

ὑπορ-ρίπτω, f. ψω, *to throw under*, ὑπ. τινὰ τοῖς θηρίοις *to throw* him *to the wild beasts*, Plut.

ὑπ-ορύσσω, Att. -ττω, f. ξω, *to dig under, undermine*, Hdt.

ὑπ-ορχέομαι, f. ήσομαι, Dep. *to dance with* or *to music*, Aesch. :—c. acc. cogn., ὄρχησιν ὑπ. Plut.   II. *to sing and dance* a character, of a pantomimic actor, Luc. Hence

ὑπόρχημα, ατος, τό, *a hyporcheme* or *choral hymn to Apollo*, mostly in Cretic verses, Plat.

ὑπό-σαθρος, ον, *somewhat rotten*, Luc.

ὑπο-σαλπίζω, f. ξω, *to prelude on the trumpet*, Anth.

ὑπο-σείραιος, ον, *dragged alongside*, Eur.

ὑπο-σείω, Ep. ὑποσ-σείω, f. σω, *to shake below* : ὑποσ-σείουσιν ἱμάντι *they set* it *in motion below* by the thong by which an auger is turned, Od.

ὑπο-σημαίνω, f. ᾰνῶ, to give secret signs of, to indicate or intimate, Thuc. 2. in military sense, σάλπιγγι ὑπ. to make signal by sound of trumpet, Id.

ὑπο-σῑγάω, f. -ήσομαι, to be silent during, Aeschin.

ὑπο-σίδηρος, ον, having a mixture or proportion of iron in it, Plat.

ὑπο-σιωπάω, f. -ήσομαι, to pass over in silence, Aeschin.

ὑπο-σκάζω, f. άσω, to halt a little, Luc.

ὑπο-σκᾰλεύω, to stir underneath, poke up, τὸ πῦρ Ar.

ὑπο-σκάπτω, f. ψω, to dig under, ὑπ. μακρὰ ἅλματα to mark a long leap by a line, Pind.

ὑπο-σκελίζω, to trip up one's heels, upset, Lat. supplantare, Dem., Luc. 2. metaph., ὑπ. καὶ ἀνατρέπων Plat., Dem.

ὑπό-σκιος, ον, (σκιά) under shade, Plut.

ὑπο-σόλοικος, ον, guilty of a slight solecism, Cic.

ὑπο-σπᾰνίζομαι, Pass., pf. part. ὑπεσπανισμένος, to be scant or stinted of a thing, c. gen., Aesch. 2. of things, to be lacking, left undone, Soph.

ὑπο-σπάω, f. άσω [ᾰ], to draw away from under, Plat., Dem. 2. to withdraw secretly, ὑπέσπασε φυγῇ πόδα withdrew his foot secretly, stole away, Eur.

ὑπο-σπείρω, to sow secretly, Anth.

ὑπό-σπονδος, ον, (σπονδή) under a treaty, bound or secured by treaty, Hdt., Xen.:—esp. of taking up the dead from a field of battle, τοὺς νεκροὺς ὑποσπόνδους ἀποδιδόναι to allow a truce for taking up the dead, Thuc.; τοὺς νεκροὺς ὑπ. κομίζεσθαι, ἀναιρεῖσθαι to demand a truce for so doing, in acknowledgment of defeat, Hdt., Xen., etc.

ὑποσ-σαίνω, ὑποσ-σείω, Ep. for ὑπο-σαίνω, ὑπο-σείω.

ὑπο-στάθμη, ἡ, = ὑπόστασις, sediment, Plat.; ἐν τῇ Ῥωμύλου ὑποστάθμῃ, in faece Romuli, Plut.

ὑπο-σταίην, aor. 2 opt. of ὑφ-ίστημι:—ὑπο-στάς, part.

ὑπόστᾰσις, εως, ἡ, (ὑφίσταμαι) that which settles at the bottom, sediment, Arist. II. anything set under, subject-matter of a speech or poem, Polyb., etc. 2. the foundation or ground of hope, confidence, assurance, N. T. III. substance, the real nature of a thing, essence, Ib.

ὑποστάτης [ᾰ], ου, ὁ, (ὑφίσταμαι) that which stands under, a support, prop, Plut.

ὑποστᾰτός, όν, verb. Adj. of ὑφίσταμαι, to be borne or endured, Eur.

ὑπο-στᾰχύομαι, (στάχυς) Pass. to grow up or wax gradually like ears of corn, Od.

ὑπο-στεγάζω, to support from underneath, Aesch.

ὑπό-στεγος, ον, (στέγη) under the roof, in or into the house, Soph.

ὑπο-στέγω, to hide under, Xen.

ὑπο-στέλλω, f. -στελῶ: aor. 1 -έστειλα: pf. -έσταλκα:—to draw in, ἱστίον ὑπέστειλε made him furl his sail, Pind. 2. to draw back for shelter, Plut.; ὑπ. ἑαυτόν to shelter oneself behind, τινί Id.; also to withdraw himself, N. T. II. Med., ὑποστέλλεσθαί τι to cloak a thing through fear, to prevaricate, dissemble, Eur., Plat., etc.; μηδὲν ὑποστειλάμενος without dissimulation, Dem.

ὑπο-στενάζω, to moan in an undertone, Soph. II. to groan under the weight of, τι Aesch.

ὑπο-στενᾰχίζω or -στονᾰχίζω, to groan beneath one, c. dat., Il., Hes.

ὑπο-στένω, to moan in a low tone, begin to moan, Soph.: to grumble, Ar.

ὑπο-στῆναι, aor. 2 inf. of ὑφ-ίστημι.

ὑπο-στηρίζω, to underprop, sustain, Luc.

ὑπο-στήτω, 3 sing. aor. 2 imper. of ὑφ-ίστημι.

ὑποστολή, ἡ, a shrinking back, evasion, N. T.

ὑπο-στονᾰχίζω, = ὑποστεναχίζω.

ὑπο-στορέννῡμι or rather -στόρνῡμι, also -στρώννυμι or -ύω: f. -στορέσω, aor. 1 -εστόρεσα; also -στρώσω, aor. 1 -έστρωσα: pf. ὑπέστρωκα: pass. ὑπέστρωμαι:—to spread, lay or strew under, esp. of bed-clothes, δέμνια ὑποστορέσαι Od.; λέκτρα ὑποστρῶσαί τινι to make his bed for a man, i. e. serve him as a wife, Eur.:—Pass., αἱ εὐναὶ ὑποστόρνυνται Xen.; ᾗ χαλκὸς ὑπέστρωται which has copper laid under it, ap. Hdt.

ὑποστρᾰτηγέω, to serve as lieutenant under another, c. dat., Xen. From

ὑπο-στράτηγος, ὁ, a lieutenant-general, Xen.

ὑπο-στρέφω, f. ψω, to turn round about, turn back, ἵππους Il.; Βακχίαν ὑποστρέφων ἅμιλλαν bringing back the Bacchic struggle, i. e. changing sorrow into tumultuous joy, Soph. II. intr. to turn about, turn short round, Il., Hdt., Att.:—so in Pass., αὖτις ὑποστρεφθείς Il. 2. generally, to return, Od., Hdt.; so in fut. med., Od. 3. to turn away, and so elude an attack, Eur., Xen. 4. part. ὑποστρέψας as Adv. reversely, Ar.

ὑπο-στροβέω, to agitate inwardly, Aesch.

ὑποστροφή, ἡ, a turning about, wheeling round, Hdt.: ἐξ ὑποστροφῆς, of the chariot, after turning round the meta at the end of the δίαυλος, i. e. turning sharply round, Soph.:—on the contrary, ap. Dem.

ὑπόστρωμα, ατος, τό, that which is spread under, a bed, litter, Xen.

ὑπο-στρώννῡμι, = ὑπο-στορέννυμι.

ὑπο-στύφω [ῡ], f. ψω, to be somewhat astringent, Plut.

ὑπο-συγχέω, f. -χεῶ, to confuse a little:—Pass. to be somewhat confused, Luc.

ὑπο-συρίζω, Att. -ίττω, f. ξω, to whistle gently, rustle, Aesch.

ὑπο-σύρω [ῡ], to drag down, Plut., Luc.

ὑπο-σφίγγω, to bind tight below, Anth.

ὑπο-σχεθεῖν, poët. for ὑπο-σχεῖν, aor. 2 inf. of ὑπ-έχω.

ὑπό-σχεο, Ep. aor. 2 imper. of ὑπ-ισχνέομαι.

ὑπο-σχές, aor. 2 imper. of ὑπ-έχω.

ὑπο-σχέσθαι, aor. 2 inf. of ὑπ-ισχνέομαι.

ὑποσχεσίη, ἡ, Ep. for ὑπόσχεσις, Il.

ὑποσχέσιον, τό, = sq., Anth.

ὑπόσχεσις, εως, ἡ, (ὑπισχνέομαι) an undertaking, engagement, promise, Hom., Hdt., Att.; ὑπ. ἀπολαβεῖν to receive the fulfilment of a promise, Xen.; ἀπαιτεῖν τὰς ὑπ. to demand their fulfilment, Arist.; ὑπ. ψεύδεσθαι to fail in its performance, Aeschin. II. a profession (as a mode of life), Luc.

ὑπο-σχόμενος, aor. 2 part. of ὑπισχνέομαι:—ὑπό-σχωμαι, subj.

ὑπο-σχών, aor. 2 part. of ὑπ-έχω.

ὑποτᾰγή, ἡ, subordination, subjection, submission, N. T.

ὑπο-τάμνω, Ion. for ὑπο-τέμνω.

ὑπο-τᾰνύω, = ὑποτείνω, Il.

ὑπο-τᾰράσσω, contr. -θράσσω, Att. -ττω: f. ξω:—to

stir up, trouble from below or a little, Ar. :—Pass. to be somewhat troubled, Luc.

ὑπο-ταρβέω, f. ήσω, to shrink before, τινά Il.

ὑπο-ταρτάριος [ἄ], ον, under Tartarus, of the Titans, Il., Hes.

ὑπότᾰσις, εως, ή, (ὑποτείνω) extension, πεδίων ὑποτάσεις the plains that stretch below, Eur.

ὑπο-τάσσω, Att. -ττω, f. ξω:—to place or arrange under, τί τινι Plut. II. to post under, to subject, ἑαυτόν τινι Id.; ἑαυτῷ τὰ πάντα N. T. :—Pass. to be obedient, τινι Ib.

ὑπο-τείνω, f. -τενῶ, to stretch under, put under, ἀντήριδας ὑπ. πρὸς τοὺς τοίχους to fix stay-beams so as to strengthen the ship's sides, Thuc. 2. to strain tight, Ar.: metaph. to intensify, Soph. II. to hold out hopes, to offer to do a thing, c. inf., Hdt., Thuc. :—also, ὑπ. τινὶ μισθούς Ar.; ἐλπίδας Dem. 2. to suggest, ὑπ. τινὶ λέγειν Eur.

ὑπο-τειχίζω, f. Att. ιῶ, to build a wall under or across, build a cross-wall, Thuc. Hence

ὑποτείχῐσις, εως, ή, the building of a cross-wall, Thuc.; and

ὑποτείχισμα, ατος, τό, a cross-wall, Thuc.

ὑπο-τελέω, f. έσω, to pay off, discharge a payment, Hdt., Xen., etc.; absol. to pay tribute, Thuc.

ὑπο-τελής, ές, gen. έος, (τέλος IV) subject to pay taxes, taxable, tributary, Lat. vectigalis, Thuc.; in full, ὑποτελὴς φόρου Id. II. act. receiving as payment, c. gen., Luc.

ὑπο-τέμνω, Ion. -τάμνω: f. -τεμῶ and -τεμοῦμαι: aor. 2 ὑπ-έταμον, Ep. inf. -ταμέειν: pf. -τέτμηκα:—Pass., aor. 1 -ετμήθην: pf. -τέτμημαι:—to cut away under, cut away, Hom.: Pass., Aeschin. 2. to cut underhand or unfairly, of a leather-seller, Ar. II. to cut off, intercept, Xen.: so in Hdt.; ὑποτέμνεσθαι τὰς ὁδούς to cut off one's way, stop one short, Ar.; ὑποτέμνεσθαί τινα to intercept him, Xen.

ὑπο-τίθημι, f. -θήσω: aor. 1 ὑπ-έθηκα:—to place under, τί τινι Il.:—Med. to place under one's feet, Xen. 2. to place under as a foundation or beginning, Id., Dem.:—Pass. to be laid down, assumed, Plat.:—Med. to lay down as a principle, take for granted, assume, Id., Dem.; c. acc. et inf. to assume or suppose that.., Plat. II. to hold out under, present, Luc.: metaph. to suggest, Eur., etc.:—so in Med. to suggest, hint a thing to one, ὑποθέσθαι τινὶ βουλήν Il.; ἔπος, ἔργον ὑποθέσθαι τινί to suggest a speech, an action, to any one, advise or counsel him thereto, Hom., Hdt., etc. 2. c. dat. pers. only, ὑποθέσθαι τινί to advise, admonish one, Od., Ar., etc.: c. inf. to advise one to do a thing, Hdt., Thuc. 3. to propose, σκοπόν as a mark or aim, Arist.:—Med. to propose to oneself, Isocr. III. to put down as a deposit or stake, to pawn, pledge, mortgage, Hdt., Aeschin., etc.:—in Med., of the mortgagee, to lend money on pledge, Dem. 2. to stake, hazard, venture, Plat.; ὑποθεὶς τὸν ἴδιον κίνδυνον at his own risk, Dem.

ὑπο-τῑμάομαι, Med. as law-term, much like ἀντιτιμάομαι, to propose a less penalty for oneself, Xen.

ὑπ-οτοβέω, to sound in answer, echo, Aesch.

ὑπο-τονθορύζω, to murmur in an under-tone, Luc.

ὑποτοπεύω, =sq., τινά Thuc.; c. acc. et inf., Id.

ὑποτοπέω, aor. 1 -ετόπησα:—to suspect, surmise, Thuc.; c. acc. et inf., Id. 2. c. acc. pers. to suspect him, Id. II. so as Dep. ὑποτοπέομαι, aor. 1 ὑπετοπήθην:—to suspect a thing, Hdt., Ar.; c. acc. et inf. to suspect that.., Hdt., Ar.

ὑπο-τραυλίζω, f. σω, to lisp a little, Luc.

ὑπο-τρέμω, to tremble a little, Plat.

ὑπο-τρέφω, f. -θρέψω, to bring up secretly :—Med. to cherish secretly, Xen., Luc.:—Pass. to grow up in succession, Lat. subnasci, Plat.

ὑπο-τρέχω, f. -θρέξομαι and -δρᾰμοῦμαι : aor. 2 -έδρᾰμον: poët. pf. -δέδρομα:—to run in under, ὑπέδραμε καὶ λάβε γούνων she ran in under the sword and clasped his knees, Od.; ὑπὸ τοὺς πόδας τοῦ ἵππου ὑπέδραμε κύων Hdt.: hence to trip up, Ar. II. to run or stretch away under, h. Hom. III. to run in between, intercept, Ar., Xen. 2. to insinuate oneself into any one's good graces, flatter or deceive, Eur., Plat.

ὑπο-τρέω, f. -τρέσω, to tremble a little, to shrink back, give ground, Il.: c. acc. to flee before, Ib.

ὑπο-τρηχύνω, ὑπό-τρηχυς, Ion. for ὑπο-τράχ-.

ὑπο-τρίβω [ῑ], f. ψω, to rub down the ingredients of a dish, Cratin. Hence

ὑπότριμμα, ατος, τό, a dish compounded of various ingredients pounded up together, Lat. moretum, Com.

ὑπο-τρομέω, = ὑποτρέμω, to tremble under one, of a man's limbs, Il. From

ὑπότρομος, ον, somewhat afraid or timid, Aeschin., Luc.

ὑποτροπή, ή, (ὑποτρέπω) a turning back, repulse, Plut. II. a relapse, recurrence, Id.

ὑπότροπος, ον, (ὑποτρέπω) returning, Hom., Eur. 2. rallying from the effect of a blow, Theocr.

ὑπο-τροχάω, poët. for ὑποτρέχω, Mosch.

ὑπο-τρύζω, to murmur, hum in an undertone, Anth.

ὑπο-τρώγω, f. ξομαι: aor. 2 ὑπ-έτρᾰγον :—to eat by way of preparation, Xen.

ὑπο-τῠπόω, to sketch out, Lat. adumbrare, Arist.

ὑπο-τύπτω, f. ψω, to strike or push down, κοντῷ ὑπ. ἐς λίμνην to poke down into the lake with a pole, Hdt.; ὑποτύπτουσα φιάλη ἐς τὴν θήκην dipping with a cup into the chest, Id.; ὑποτύψας τούτῳ (sc. τῷ κηλωνηίῳ) ἀντλέει he draws it dipping with the bucket into the water, Id.; ὑπ. τοῖν ποδοῖν Ar. Hence

ὑποτύπωσις [ῠ], εως, ή, an outline, pattern, N. T.

ὑπο-τύφομαι [ῠ], Pass. to burn with a smouldering fire, burn secretly, Plut., Luc.

ὑπό-τῡφος, ον, somewhat arrogant, Plut.

ὑπ-ουθάτιος [ἄ], α, ον, under the udder, sucking, Anth.

ὑπ-ουλος, ον, (οὐλή) of wounds, festering under the scar: metaph. with festering sores underneath, unsound beneath, Plat., etc.; ὑπ. αὐτονομία a hollow independence, Thuc.; κάλλος κακῶν ὕπουλον a fair outside skinning over ills below, Soph.:—Adv., ὑπούλως ἀκροᾶσθαι to render a hollow obedience, Plut.

ὑπ-ουράνιος, ον, under heaven, under the sky, Il. II. reaching up to heaven, Hom.

ὑπουργέω, f. ήσω, (ὑπουργός) to render service or help to one, to serve, assist, succour, τινί Hdt., etc.; χρηστὰ ὑπ. (sc. τοῖς Ἀθηναίοισι) to do them good service, Hdt., etc.; ὑπ. χάριν τινί Aesch. :—Pass., τὰ ὑπουργημένα services done or rendered, Hdt.

ὑπούργημα, ατος, τό, a service done or rendered, Hdt., Xen.; and
ὑπουργητέον, verb. Adj. one must be kind to, Luc.
ὑπουργία, ἡ, service rendered, Soph., Arist. From
ὑπ-ουργός, όν, (ἔργον) rendering service, serviceable, promoting, conducive to a thing, c. dat., Xen.
ὑπο-φαίνω, f. -φᾰνῶ, to bring to light from under, θρῆνυν ὑπέφηνε τραπέζης he drew the stool from under the table, Od. 2. to shew a little, just shew, Dem. II. Pass. to be seen under, ὑπὸ τὰς πύλας πόδες ὑποφαίνονται Thuc. 2. to just shew oneself, be half seen, Xen. III. Act. used intr. of the dawn of day, ὑποφαίνει ἡμέρα day just begins to break, Id.; so, ὑποφαίνει ἔαρ Id.:—metaph., τὰ νῦν ὑποφαίνοντα the difficulties now dawning upon us, Plat.
ὑποφᾶτις, Dor. for ὑποφήτις.
ὑπό-φανσις, ἡ, (φαίνω) a light shewing through a small hole : a narrow opening, Hdt.
ὑπο-φείδομαι, f. σομαι, Dep. to spare a little, Xen.
ὑποφειδομένως, Adv. somewhat sparingly, rarely, Plut.
ὑπο-φέρω, f. ὑπ-οίσω : aor. 1 ὑπήνεγκα (Ion.) or aor. 2 ὑπήνεγκον :—to carry away under, esp. to bear out of danger, Il. II. to bear or carry by being under, to bear a burden, Xen.: metaph. to support, bear, endure, submit to, πόνους καὶ κινδύνους Isocr.; γῆρας καὶ πενίαν Aeschin., etc. III. to hold out, suggest, proffer, Soph.; to pretend, allege, Xen. IV. to carry down :—Pass. to be borne down by a stream, Plut.: metaph. to slip or sink down, decay, Id.
ὑπο-φεύγω, f. ξομαι, to flee from under, shun, Il., Eur.: to withdraw from, endeavour to evade, Thuc. II. absol. to retire a little, withdraw, Hdt., Thuc.
ὑποφητεύω, to hold the office of ὑποφήτης, Luc.
ὑπο-φήτης, ου, ὁ, (φημί) a suggester, interpreter, a priest who declares an oracle, Il.; Μουσάων ὑποφῆται, i. e. poets, Theocr.
ὑπο-φῆτις, Dor. -φᾶτις, ἡ, fem. of ὑποφήτης, Pind., Anth.
ὑπο-φήτωρ, οροs, ὁ, ἡ, = ὑποφήτης, Anth.
ὑπο-φθάνω [ᾰ]: aor. 2 ὑπ-έφθην, inf. ὑπο-φθῆναι, part. -φθάς, also in med. part. -φθάμενος :—to haste before, be or get beforehand, Il.; ὑποφθάμενος κτεῖνεν Od. II. c. acc. to be beforehand with one, Plut.; Med., τὸν ὑποφθαμένη φάτο μῦθον Od.
ὑπο-φθέγγομαι, f. ξομαι, Dep. to speak in an undertone, of a ventriloquist, Plat. 2. to reply, Plut.
ὑπο-φθονέω, f. ήσω, to feel secret envy at, τινι Xen.
ὑπό-φθονος, ον, somewhat jealous : Adv., ὑποφθόνως ἔχειν to behave somewhat jealously, Xen.
ὑπο-φλέγω, f. ξω, to heat from below, Anth.
ὑπό-φόνιος, ον, murdering secretly, Soph.
ὑπο-φορά, ἡ, (ὑποφέρω) a holding under, putting forward, by way of excuse, Xen.
ὑπο-φραδμοσύνη, ἡ, (φράδμων) suggestion, counsel, Hes.
ὑπο-φρίσσω, Att. -ττω, f. ξω, to shudder slightly, Luc.
ὑπο-φύγειν, aor. 2 inf. of ὑπο-φεύγω.
ὑπο-φύω, to make to grow up, Il.
ὑπο-φωλεύω, to lie hidden under, τινι Anth.
ὑπο-φωνέω, f. ήσω, to call out in answer, Plut.: to sing in answer, Mosch.
ὑπο-χάζομαι, Ep. aor. 2 -κεκαδόμην : Dep.:—to give way gradually or a little, Il.

ὑπο-χᾰλῑνίδιος, α, ον, (χαλινός) under the bridle :— ἡ ὑποχαλινιδία (sc. ἡνία), a chin-strap attached to the bit, Xen.
ὑπό-χαλκος, ον, containing a mixture of copper, Plat.
ὑπο-χᾰράσσω, Att. -ττω, f. ξω, to engrave under, Plut.
ὑπο-χᾰροπός, όν, somewhat bright-eyed, Xen.
ὑπο-χάσκω, aor. 2 ὑπ-έχᾰνον, pf. ὑποκέχηνα :—to gape a little, Ar., Xen.
ὑπό-χειρ, ὁ, ἡ, = sq., Soph.
ὑποχείριος, ον, and α, ον, (χείρ) under the hand, in hand, Od. 2. of persons, under any one's hand, under command, subject, τινι Hdt., etc. ; λαβεῖν τινα ὑποχείριον to get into one's power, Eur. ; ἔχειν τινὰ ὑπ. Thuc.
ὑπο-χέω, f. -χέω : aor. 1 ὑπ-έχεα, Ep. -έχευα :—Pass., pf. ὑπο-κέχυμαι, —to pour into a cup placed under, to pour out ; of dry things, to strew or spread under, Hom. : Pass., φύλλα ὑποκεχυμένα ὑπὸ τοῖς ποσί leaves scattered under the feet, Hdt. :—metaph., ἀπιστίη ὑπεκέχυτο αὐτῷ distrust was poured secretly into him, i. e. stole over him, Id.
ὑπο-χθόνιος, ίη, ον, (χθών) under the earth, subterranean, Hes., Eur.
ὑπό-χθων, ονος, ὁ, ἡ, = foreg., Anth.
ὑπ-οχλέομαι, Pass. to be rolled beneath, Il.
ὑπο-χορηγέω, f. ήσω, to supply, Strab. Hence
ὑποχορηγία, ἡ, a supplying, succour, Strab.
ὑπ-οχος, ον, (ὑπέχω) subject, τινι Xen. ; βασιλῆς βασιλέως ὑποχοι king's subjects or officers, of the great king, Aesch. 2. = ἔνοχος, liable to, τινος Dem.
ὑπό-χρεως, ων, gen. ω, (χρέος) indebted, in debt, Ar. ; ὑπ. τινος his debtor, Plut. 3. of property, involved, Lat. obaeratus, Dem. 3. c. gen., ὑπ. φιλίας bound by ties of friendship, Plut.
ὑπο-χρίω [ῐ], to smear under or upon, τί τινι Hdt. ; ὑπ. τινι to paint his face under the eyes, Xen. :—Med., ὑποχρίεσθαι τοὺς ὀφθαλμούς to paint one's own eyes underneath, Id.
ὑπό-χρῡσος, ον, containing a mixture or proportion of gold : metaph. of persons, Plat.
ὑπο-χωρέω, f. ήσομαι, to go back, retire, recoil, Il., Thuc. ; often in part., ὑποχωρήσας φεύγει Dem. 2. c. gen. to retire from a place, Xen. ; ὑπ. τινι τοῦ θρόνου to withdraw from one's seat in honour of another, give it up to him, Ar.; and, ὑπ. τινι to give way to another, Thuc. 3. c. acc. to avoid, shun, Id., Plat. II. to go on in succession, Pind.
ὑποχώρημα, ατος, τό, a downward evacuation, Theophr.
ὑποχώρησις, εως, ἡ, a going back, retirement, retreat, Polyb. 2. a retiring-place, retreat, Luc.
ὑπό-ψαμμος, ον, having sand under, γῆ ὑποψαμμοτέρη somewhat sandy, Hdt.
ὑπό-ψᾱρος, ον, somewhat dappled, ἵππος Strab.
ὑπ-οψία, Ion. -ίη, ἡ, (ὑπόψομαι) suspicion, jealousy, ὑποψίην ἔχειν ἔς τινα Hdt., Att. ; πρός τινα Dem. ; ἐν ὑπ. ποιεῖσθαι Aeschin. 2. of the object, ἔχειν ὑπ. to admit of suspicion, Plat. ; ὑπ. παρέχειν Thuc.
ὑπ-όψιος, ον, (ὑπόψομαι) viewed from beneath the brows ; ὑπόψιος ἄλλων viewed with suspicion among others, Il.
ὑπ-οψωνέω, f. ήσω, to underbid in the purchase of victuals or to buy up underhand, Ar.

ὑπτιάζω, f. άσω, (ὕπτιος) to bend oneself back, to carry one's head high, Aeschin. :—Pass., κάρα ὑπτιάζεται his head lies supine, Soph.   Hence

ὑπτίασμα, ατος, τό, that which is laid back, ὑπτιάσματα χερῶν supplication with hands upstretched, Lat. supinis manibus, Aesch.; ὑπτίασμα κειμένου πατρός his father's body as it lies supine, Id.; and

ὑπτιασμός, ὁ, a laying oneself backwards, Luc.

ὑπτιαστέον, verb. Adj. of ὑπτιάζω, one must throw back, ἑαυτόν Xen.

ὑπτιόομαι, Pass. to be upset, Aesch.

ὕπτιος, α, ον, (from ὑπό, as Lat. supinus from sub):— laid back, laid on one's back, πέσεν ὕπτιος he fell backwards, opp. to πρηνής, Il.; of a quadruped, ὀρθοῦ ἑστεῶτος καὶ ὑπτίου rearing upright and falling backwards, Hdt.   II. generally with the under side uppermost, χείρ ὑπτία the hollow of the hand, Plut.; ἐξ ὑπτίου κράνους from the upturned helmet, with the hollow uppermost, Aesch.; so, παράθες ὑπτίαν (τὴν ἀσπίδα) Ar.; ἀψὶς ὑπτία a half-wheel with the concave side uppermost, Hdt.; ὑπτίοις σέλμασιν ναυτίλλεται he sails with the bottom uppermost, i. e. suffers shipwreck, Soph.; ἐξ ὑπτίας νεῖν to swim on the back (in metaph. sense), Plat.   III. of land, sloping evenly, of Egypt, Hdt.   Hence

ὑπ-ωθέω, f. -ώσω, to push or thrust away, Il.

ὑπ-ωλένιος, ον, and α, ον, under the elbow, Theocr.

ὑπωμοσία, ἡ, an oath taken to delay proceedings (v. ὑπόμνυμι II), an application for postponement of a trial, Dem.   2. an oath taken by the prosecutor in a γραφὴ παρανόμων (v. παράνομος II), with the effect of suspending the proposed decree, Id.

ὑπωπιάζω, f. άσω, to strike one under the eye :—Pass. to have a black eye, ὑπωπιασμένος Ar.   II. metaph. to bruise, mortify, N. T.: also, to annoy greatly, wear out, Ib.   From

ὑπ-ώπιον, τό, (ὤψ) the part of the face under the eyes: generally the face, countenance, Il.   II. a blow in the face, a black eye, Ar.

ὑπώρεια, ἡ, the foot of a mountain, the skirts of a mountain range, Il., Hdt.

ὑπ-ώροφε, 3 sing. pf. intr. of ὑπ-όρνυμι.

ὑπ-ωρόφιος, ον, and α, ον, (ὄροφος) under the roof, in the house, Il., Pind., Ar.

ὑπ-ώροφος, ον, = foreg., Eur.: of a swallow's nest, under the eaves, Anth.

ὑπ-ωχρος, ον, pale yellow, sallow, Luc.

ΥΡΧΑ, ἡ, a jar, for pickles, Ar.

ΥΣ, ὗν, gen. ὑός [ῠ], or σῦς, σῦν, gen. σὑός, ὁ and ἡ: pl., nom. ὕες (Att. ὗς), σύες, acc. ὗας, σύας (Att. σῦς); gen. σὑῶν; dat. ὑσί, συσί, Ep. also ὕεσσι, σύεσσι :— the wild swine, whether boar (hog) or sow, Hom., etc.; σῦς ἄγριος Il.; also σῦς κάπριος or κάπρος, v. sub vocc.   2. the domestic pig, Hom., etc.

ΥΣΓΗ, ἡ, a shrub from which the dye ὕσγινον is derived.

ὑσγῖνο-βαφής, ές, dyed scarlet, Xen., Luc.

ὕσγινον, τό, a dye from the shrub ὕσγη, scarlet, Anth.

ὑσθῆναι, aor. 1 pass. inf. of ὕω.

ΥΣΜΙΝΗ [ῑ], ἡ, a fight, battle, combat, Il.; metaplast. Ep. dat. ὑσμῖνι as if from ὑσμίν or ὑσμίς, Ib.

ὕσπληγξ or ὕσπληξ, ἡ, gen. ηγγος and ηγος; Dor. ὕσπλαγξ, αγγος, a rope drawn across the racecourse,

let down when the runners were to start, the starting-line, Plat., Anth.   II. the snare or gin of a bird-catcher, Theocr. (Deriv. uncertain.)

ΥΣΣΟΣ, ὁ, a javelin, the Roman pilum, Polyb., etc.

ὕσσωπος, ἡ, hyssop, prob. the caper-plant, N. T.

ὑστάτιος [ᾰ], α, ον, poët. for ὕστατος, as μεσσάτιος for μέσσος, Hom. :—neut. as Adv. at last, Il.

ὕστατος, η, ον, v. ὕστερος B.

ὑστέρα, Ion. ὑστέρη, ἡ, the womb, mostly in pl. ὑστέραι, Ion. gen. -εων, Hdt., etc. (Deriv. uncertain.)

ὑστεραῖος, α, ον, (ὕστερος) on the day after, the next day (cf. προτεραῖος); τῇ ὑστεραίᾳ (Ion. -αίη) ἡμέρᾳ on the following day, next day, Lat. postridie, Hdt.; often without ἡμέρᾳ, Id., Att.; also, ἐς τὴν ὑστεραίην Hdt.; ἐν τῇ ὑστ. Plat. :—c. gen., τῇ ὑστεραίᾳ τῆς μάχης on the day after the battle, Id.   II. = ὕστερος, later, subsequent, Hdt., Xen.

ὑστερέω, f. ήσω: pf. ὑστέρηκα: plqpf. ὑστερήκειν :— Pass., aor. 1 ὑστερήθην: (ὕστερος):—to be behind or later, come late, Hdt., Att.   II. c. gen. rei, to come later than, come too late for, ὑστέρησαν ἡμέρῃ μιῇ τῆς συγκειμένης came one day after the appointed day, Hdt.; τῆς Μυτιλήνης ὑστερήκει had come too late to save Mytilené, Thuc.; ὑστ. τῆς πατρίδος to fail to assist it, Xen.   2. c. gen. pers. to come after him, Id.; also c. dat. to come too late for him, Thuc.   III. metaph. to come short of, be inferior to, τινός Plat., etc.   IV. to come short of, fail to obtain :—so in Med., ὑστερεῖσθαί τινος N. T.   2. absol. to be in want, Ib.   V. of things, to fail, be wanting, Lat. deficere, Ib.

ὑστέρημα, ατος, τό, deficiency, need, want, N. T.

ὑστέρησις, ἡ, = foreg., N. T.

ὑστερίζω, f. Att. ἰῶ: aor. 1 ὑστέρισα: (ὕστερος) :—to come after, come later or too late, Thuc., Xen.   II. c. gen. rei, to come short of, come too late for, Dem.; to lag behind, Xen.   III. metaph. to come short of, be inferior to any one, c. gen., Id. :—absol., ὑστ. τὸ εἰδέναι he falls short in knowledge, Id.

ὑστερό-ποινος, ον, (ποινή) avenging after the act, late-avenging, Aesch.

ὑστερό-πους, ὁ, ἡ, neut. -πουν, coming late, Anth.

ὕστερος, ὕστατος, latter, last, Comp. and Sup. without any Posit. Adj. in use.

A. ὕστερος, α, ον, latter,   I. of Place, latter, coming after, following, Eur., Xen. :—c. gen., ὕστεροι ἡμῶν behind us, Plat.; ὑστέρα νεὼς behind (slower than) a ship, Aesch.   II. of Time, next, Il.; τῷ ὑστέρῳ ἔτει in the next year, Xen.; ὑστέρῳ χρόνῳ in after time, Aesch., etc. :—c. gen., ὕστερος than, after, Il., Plat.; also ὑστέρῳ χρόνῳ τούτων Hdt.   2. later, too late, Il., Soph.   3. c. gen. rei, too late for, Hdt., Ar.   4. as Subst. οἱ ὕστεροι = Lat. posteri, Eur.   III. of inferiority in Age, Worth, or Quality, γένει ὕστερος, i. e. younger, Il. :— c. gen., οὐδενὸς ὕστ. second to none, Soph., Thuc.; ὕστερος τῶν νόμων below the laws, Aeschin.   IV. neut. ὕστερον as Adv. behind, c. gen., Xen.   2. of Time, later, afterwards, Hom., etc.; also ὕστερα Od.: —c. gen., ὕστερον τούτων later than these things, after them, Hdt.; πολλῷ ὕστ. τῶν Τρωικῶν Thuc.   B.

in Adv. sense with Preps., ἐς ὕστερον Od., Hdt., etc. :—ἐν ὑστέρῳ Thuc. :—ἐξ ὑστέρης Hdt. **B.** ὕστατος, η, ον, *last*, **I.** of Place, πρῶτοί τε καὶ ὕστατοι Il. **II.** of Time, τίνα πρῶτον, τίνα δ' ὕστατον ἐξεναρίξω; Ib. ; πρὸς ὕστ. φῶς Aesch. : ἡ ὑστάτη (sc. ἡμέρα) τῆς ὀρτῆς *the last day* of the feast, Hdt. ; οὐκ ἐν ὑστάτοις *not among the last*, Eur. ; οἱ ὕστατοι εἰπόντες Dem., etc. :—c. gen., ὕστατος ἀλώσιος *all too late for . .* , Pind. **III.** the neut. sing. and pl. as Adv., πύματόν τε καὶ ὕστατον Od. ; ὕστατα καὶ πύματα Il. ; νῦν ὕστατα Ib. ; ὕστατα Hdt., etc. **2.** in Adv. sense with Preps., ἐν ὑστάτοις *at last*, Plat.

ὑστερο-φθόρος, ον, (φθείρω) *late-destroying*, Soph.

ὑστερό-φωνος, ον, *sounding after, echoing*, Anth.

ὕστριξ, ἴχος, ὁ and ἡ, *the porcupine*, Hdt. (Deriv. uncertain.) Hence

ὑστρῖχίς, ίδος, ἡ, *a whip for punishing slaves*, Ar.

ὑφ-άγεο or -εῦ, Dor. for ὑφηγοῦ, imper. of ὑφηγέομαι.

ὕφαιμος, ον, (αἷμα) *suffused with blood, blood-shot*, Dem. **II.** of temperament, *sanguine*, Plat.

ΎΦΑΙ'ΝΩ [ῠ], Ion. impf. ὑφαίνεσκον : f. ὑφᾰνῶ : aor. 1 ὕφηνα, later, ὕφᾱνα : pf. ὕφαγκα :—Pass., aor. 1 ὑφάνθην : pf. ὕφασμαι :—*to weave*, ἱστὸν ὑφαίνειν *to weave a web*, Hom. ; ἱμάτιον Plat., etc. :—absol. *to weave, ply the loom*, Hdt.:—Med., ἱμάτιον ὑφαίνεσθαι *to weave oneself a cloak*, Plat. **II.** *to contrive, plan, invent*, Lat. *texere*, δόλον ὑφαίνειν Il. ; μῆτιν ὑφ. Od. **III.** generally, *to create, construct*, Pind.

ὑφαίρεσις, εως, ἡ, *a taking away from under, a purloining*, ap. Dem. From

ὑφ-αιρέω, f. ήσω : aor. 2 ὑφεῖλον : Ion. ὑπ-αιρέω, etc. :—*to seize underneath* or *inwardly*, Hom. **II.** *to draw* or *take away from under* a thing, c. gen., Il., Plat. :—also τὴν χεῖρα ὑφῄρει *tried to draw it away*, Ar. **2.** *to take away underhand, filch away*, Thuc. ; ὑφ. τῆς ὑποψίας *gradually to take away part of . .* , Id. :—Pass., ὑπαραιρημένος (Ion. pf. part.) *put secretly away, made away with*, Hdt. :—so in Med. *to take away underhand, filch away, purloin*, Id., Ar., etc. **3.** in Med. also c. acc. pers., ὑφ. τινά τινος *to rob* him of a thing, Aeschin.

ὕφ-αλος, ον, (ἅλς) *under the sea*, ὑφ. Ἔρεβος the *darkness of the deep*, Soph. ; τὸ ὕφαλον *the lower waters*, Strab.

ὑφάντης, ου, ὁ, (ὑφαίνω) *a weaver*, Plat.

ὑφαντικός, ή, όν, (ὑφαίνω) *skilled in weaving*, Plat. : Adv. -κῶς, *in weaver-like fashion*, Id. **II.** ἡ ὑφαντική (sc. τέχνη), *the art of weaving*, Id.

ὑφαντο-δόνητος, ον, (δονέω) *woven by the flight of the shuttle*, Ar.

ὑφαντός, ή, όν, verb. Adj. of ὑφαίνω, *woven*, Od., Trag. ; ὅσα ὑφαντά τε καὶ λεῖα *brocaded* and plain stuffs, Thuc.

ὑφ-άπτω, Ion. ὑπ-άπτω, f. ψω, *to set on fire from underneath*, Hdt., Eur., etc. **2.** metaph. *to inflame unperceived*, Xen.

ὑφ-αρπάζω, Ion. ὑπ-αρπάζω : f. -άσομαι :—*to snatch away from under*, Xen. **2.** *to take away underhand, filch away*, Lat. *surripere*, Ar. **3.** ὑφ. λόγον *to snatch away* a word just when one is going to speak it, *take the word out of one's mouth*, Hdt. : *to snap up*, Ar.

ὑφαρπάμενος, poët. for ὑφαρπασάμενος.

ὕφασμα [ῠ], ατος, τό, (ὑφαίνω) *a woven robe, web*, Od.

ὑφαστρίς, ίδος, ἡ, = ὑφάντρια, Hesych.

ὑφάω, poët. for ὑφαίνω, Ep. 3 pl. ὑφόωσι, Od.

ὑφ-ειμένως, Adv. part. pf. pass. of ὑφίημι, *remissly, less violently*, Lat. *submisse*, Xen.

ὑφ-εῖσα, Ion. ὑπ-εῖσα (v. ἵζω I), *I placed under* or *secretly*, ὑπείσας ἄνδρας *having set* them *in ambush*, Hdt.

ὑφεκτέον, verb. Adj. of ὑπέχω, *one must submit to*, Plat.

ὑφελκτέον, verb. Adj. of ὑφέλκω, *one must draw away*, τῶν δαδίων *some of* the torches, Ar.

ὑφ-έλκω, f. -ελκύσω : (v. ἕλκω) :—*to draw away gently*, ὑφ. τινὰ ποδοῖιν *to draw one away* by the two feet, Il. : —*to draw away by undermining*, Thuc.

ὑφ-ελοίατο, Ion. 3 pl. aor. 2 med. opt. of ὑφ-αιρέω.

ὑφ-έντες, aor. 2 part. pl. of ὑφ-ίημι.

ὑφ-έρπω, f. -ερπύσω [ῠ] : (v. ἕρπω) :—*to creep on secretly*, Lat. *subrepere*, ὑφεῖρπε γὰρ πολύ the report *was spreading* far, Soph. **II.** like ὑπέρχομαι II, of involuntary feelings, *to steal upon, come over*, Lat. *subire animum*, χαρά μ' ὑφέρπει, τρόμος μ' ὑφ. Aesch.

ὑφή, ἡ, (ὑφαίνω) *a web*, in pl., Aesch., Eur.

ὑφ-ηγέομαι, f. ήσομαι : Dep. :—*to go just before, to guide, lead*, τινι Eur., Plat., etc. :—absol. *to go first, lead the way*, Soph., Thuc., Plat. ; κατὰ τὸν ὑφηγημένον τρόπον *according to the normal plan*, Arist. **II.** c. acc. cogn., ὑφ. τὴν ὁδόν *to shew the way*, Plut. **2.** c. acc. rei, *to shew the way to, instruct in*, Xen., Plat. **III.** *to lead to* a thing, *indicate* that it is so, Aesch. Hence

ὑφήγησις, εως, ἡ, *a guiding, guidance*, Dem.

ὑφηγητήρ, ῆρος, ὁ, = sq., Soph., Anth.

ὑφηγητής, οῦ, ὁ, (ὑφηγέομαι) *one who leads the way, a guide, leader*, Soph. ; ὡς ὑφηγητοῦ τινος (sc. ὄντος) *as if led by* some (invisible) *guide*, Id. **2.** *a teacher, master*, Plut.

ὑφηνιοχέω, f. ήσω, *to be a* ὑφηνίοχος, Luc. :—Pass. *to drive after* or *behind*, of chariots, Dem.

ὑφ-ηνίοχος, ὁ, *the charioteer, as subordinate to the warrior in his chariot*, Il.

ὑφ-ήσσων, ον, gen. ονος, *somewhat less* or *smaller*, Hes.

ὑφ-ιζάνω, = ὑφίζω, *to crouch beneath*, c. dat., Eur.

ὑφίζησις, εως, ἡ, *a settling* or *sinking*, Strab. From

ὑφ-ίζω, *to sit down, crouch*, Eur.

ὑφ-ίημι, Ion. ὑπ-ίημι : f. ὑφ-ήσω : (v. ἵημι) :—*to let down*, ὑφ. ἱστόν *to lower* the mast, Il. ; ὑφ. ἱστία, Lat. *submittere vela*, h. Hom. **2.** *to put under*, τί τινι Hom. ; τι ὑπό τι Xen. :—*to put a young one under its dam, put it to suck*, Od., Theocr. ; in Med., of the mother, ὑφίεσθαι μαστοῖς *to put it to* her breast, *to suckle it*, Eur. **3.** ὑφ. τινά *to engage* any one *secretly, to prepare* him *to play a part, to suborn*, Soph. : Pass., ὡς ἔχιδν' ὑφειμένη like a snake *secretly introduced, slipped in*, Id. **4.** *to give up, surrender*, Xen. **II.** intr. *to slacken, relax* or *abate from* a thing, e. gen., ὑπεὶς τῆς ὀργῆς Hdt. ; absol. *to give in, abate*, οὐδὲν ὑπιέντες Id. :—so too in Med., Id. ; so of things, τὸ ὕδωρ ὑπίεται τοῦ ψυχροῦ *abates from* its chill, Id. ; τοῦ στόματός γε ὑφ. *I give way as to it*, Xen. ; c. dat. *to yield, give way to* any one, τοῖς πολεμίοις Id. **III.** in Med. and Pass. *to lower*

one's sails, Ar.; mostly in part. pf., πλεῖν ὑφειμένῃ δοκεῖ μοι methinks I should run *with lowered sails*, i. e. *to lower* my tone, Soph.　　2. σώζω νεοσσοὺς ὄρνις ὡς ὑφειμένη, like a *cowering hen*,—or perhaps *with my* nestlings *under me*, Eur.　　3. generally, *to submit*, Xen.; c. inf., κατθανεῖν ὑφειμένη *submissively prepared* to die, Eur.

ὑφ-ικάνω [ᾱ], = ὑπέρχομαι II, *to steal over* one, Il.

ὑφ-ίστημι, f. ὑποστήσω: aor. 1 ὑπέστησα:—in these tenses Causal, *to place* or *set under*, τί τινι Hdt., Pind.; τρεῖς σταυροὺς ὑπίστησι *plants* three piles in the lake *to support* a house, Hdt.:—metaph., γνώμας ὑποστήσας σοφάς *having laid* them *as a foundation*, Soph.　　2. *to post secretly* or *in ambush*, Hdt., Xen.　　II. Causal also in fut. and aor. 1 med. *to substitute*, τί τινι one thing *for* another, Xen.
　　B. Pass., with aor. 2 act. ὑπ-έστην, pf. ὑφ-έστηκα, Ion. part. ὑπ-εστεώς:—*to stand under* as *a support*, c. dat., Hdt.　　2. *to sink to the bottom, settle*, τὸ ὑφιστάμενον the milk, opp. to τὸ ἐφιστάμενον (the cream), Id.　　II. *to place oneself under* an *engagement, engage* or *promise* to do, c. inf. fut., ὅσσ᾽ Ἀχιλῆι ὑπέστημεν δώσειν Il., etc.; c. inf. aor., οὔ τίς με ὑπέστη σαῶσαι Ib.; c. inf. pres., Hdt.:—absol., *after promise given*, Od.; ὥσπερ ὑπέστη as *he promised*, Thuc.:—when foll. by acc., an inf. may be supplied, τρίποδας οὕς οἱ ὑπέστη (sc. δώσειν) Il.; ἐκτελέουσιν ὑπόσχεσιν ἥνπερ ὑπέσταν Ib.　　2. *to submit* to any one, τινι Ib.　　3. c. acc. rei, *to submit to, consent to*, ὁ τὸ ἐλάχιστον ὑπιστάμενος *who offers to take* the least, Hdt.; ὑφ. τὸν πλοῦν *to undertake* it *unwillingly*, Thuc.; so, ὑφ. τὸν κίνδυνον Id.:—rarely c. dat., ὑφ. ξυμφοραῖς ταῖς μεγίσταις Id.　　b. *to undertake* an office, Xen.　　III. *to lie concealed* or *in ambush*, Hdt., Eur., etc.　　IV. *to support* an *attack, to resist, withstand*, c. dat., Aesch.; c. acc., Eur., Thuc.:—absol. *to stand one's ground, face the enemy*, Lat. *subsistere*, Eur., Thuc.

ὑφ-οράω, f. ὑπ-όψομαι: aor. 2 ὑπ-εῖδον and med. -ειδόμην:—*to look at from below, view with suspicion* or *jealousy, suspect*, τινά Thuc., etc.

ὑ-φορβός, ὁ, = συφορβός, Od.

ὑφ-ορμέω, f. ἥσω, *to lie secretly at anchor*, Polyb.

ὑφορμίζομαι, Pass. and Med., *to come to anchor secretly* or *under* a place, Thuc., Plut. Hence

ὑφόρμισις, ἡ, = sq., Anth.

ὕφορμος, ὁ, (ὅρμος II) *an anchorage*, Strab.

ὑφόωσι, Ep. for ὑφῶσι, 3 pl. of ὑφάω.

ὕφ-υδρος, ον, (ὕδωρ) *under water*, of a diver, Thuc.

ὑψ-αγόρας, Ion. -ης, ου, ὁ, (ἀγορεύω) *a big talker, boaster, braggart*, Od.

ὑψ-αυχενίζω, f. σω, *to carry the neck high, shew off*, Anth. From

ὑψ-αύχην, ενος, ὁ, ἡ, *carrying the neck high*, ἵππος Plat.:—metaph. *stately, towering*, Eur.

ὑψ-ερεφής, ές, (ἐρέφω) *high-roofed, high-vaulted*, Hom., Ar.

ὑψ-ηγόρος, ον, (ἀγορεύω) *talking big, grandiloquent, vaunting*, Aesch.

ὑψήεις, ήεσσα, ῆεν, poët. for ὑψηλός, Anth.

ὑψηλ-αυχενία, ἡ, (αὐχήν) *a carrying the neck high*, Xen.

ὑψηλό-κρημνος, ον, *with lofty cliffs*, Aesch.

ὑψηλολογέομαι, Dep. *to talk high, speak proudly*, Plat.

ὑψηλό-λογος, ον, *talking high, vaunting*.

ὑψηλό-νοος, ον, contr. -νους, ουν, *high-minded*: τὸ ὑψηλόνουν Plat.

ὑψηλός, ή, όν, (ὕψι) *high, lofty, high-raised*, Lat. *altus, sublimis*, Hom., Hdt., Trag., etc.; of a *highland* country, χώρη ὀρεινὴ καὶ ὑψηλή Hdt.; ὑψηλὰ χωρία Thuc.　　II. metaph. *high, lofty, stately*, Pind., Plat.; ὑψηλὰ κομπεῖν *to talk loftily*, Soph.; πνεῦμα ὑψηλὸν αἴρειν Eur.

ὑψηλοφρονέω, *to be highminded*, N. T. From

ὑψηλό-φρων, ονος, ὁ, ἡ, (φρήν) *high-minded, high-spirited, haughty*, Eur., Plat.

ὑψ-ηρεφής, ές, = ὑψερεφής, Il.

ὑψ-ηχής, ές, gen. έος, (ἠχος) *high-sounding*, ἵπποι ὑψηχέες *loud-neighing*, Il.

ὝΨΙ, Adv. *on high, aloft*, Hom.: *on the high sea, out at sea*, Od. (Hence ὑψίων, ὑψίτερος, ὑψίστος.)

ὑψί-βατος, ον, *set on high, high-placed*, Pind., Soph.

ὑψί-βόας, ου, ὁ, *loud-shouter*, name of a frog, Batr.

ὑψί-βρεμέτης, ου, ὁ, (βρέμω) *high-thundering*, Hom.

ὑψί-γέννητος, ον, *born on high*, ἐλαίας ὑψιγέννητος κλάδος its *topmost* shoot, Aesch.

ὑψί-γυιος, ον, *with high limbs, high-stemmed*, Pind.

ὑψί-ζυγος, ον, (ζυγόν) of a rower, *sitting high on the benches*; of Zeus, *high-throned*, Il., Hes.

ὑψί-θρονος, ον, *high-throned*, Pind.

ὑψί-κάρηνος, ον, (κάρηνον) *high-topped*, h. Hom.

ὑψί-κέλευθος, ον, *wandering on high*, Anth.

ὑψί-κερως, ων, gen. ω, (κέρας) *high-horned*, Od., Soph.:—also metapl. acc. ὑψικέρᾱτα πέτραν *a high-peaked rock*, Pind. ap. Ar.

ὑψί-κομος, ον, (κόμη) *with lofty foliage, towering*, Hom., Hes., Eur.

ὑψί-κομπος, ον, *high boasting, arrogant*: Adv., Soph.

ὑψί-κρημνος, ον, *with high crags*, of a mountain, Ep. Hom.　　II. of towns, *built on a high crag*, Aesch.

ὑψί-λοφος, ον, *high-crested*, Pind.

ὑψί-μέδων, οντος, ὁ, *ruling on high*, Hes., Ar.　　II. metaph. *towering*, Pind.

ὑψί-μέλαθρος, ον, (μέλαθρον) *high-built*, h. Hom.

ὑψί-νεφής, ές, (νέφος) *dwelling high in the clouds*, Pind.

ὑψί-πᾱγής, ές, (πᾱγῆναι) *high-built, towering*, Anth.

ὑψί-πεδος, ον, *with high ground, high-placed*, Pind.

ὑψί-πετήεις, εσσα, εν, = ὑψιπέτης, Hom.

ὑψί-πέτηλος, ον, Ep. for ὑψιπέτᾱλος, *with high foliage, towering*, Hom.

ὑψι-πέτης, ου, Dor. -πέτας, α, ὁ, (πέτομαι) *high-flying, soaring*, Hom., Ar.: generally *lofty*, Eur.

ὑψί-πολις, ἡ, *high* or *honoured in one's city*, Soph.

ὑψί-πους, ὁ, ἡ, *high-footed, lofty*, Soph.

ὑψί-πρυμνος, ον, (πρύμνα) *with high stern*, Strab.

ὑψί-πρωρος, ον, (πρῷρα) *with high prow*, Strab.

ὑψί-πῡλος, ον, (πύλη) *with high gates*, Il., Eur.

ὑψί-πυργος, ον, *high-towered*, Aesch., Soph.

ὕψιστος, η, ον, Sup. without any Posit. in use, (ὕψι) *highest, loftiest*, Aesch., Soph., etc.; ἐν τοῖς ὑψίστοις, i. e. *in heaven above*, N. T.

ὑψίτερος, α, ον, Comp. of Adv. ὕψι, *loftier*, Theocr.

ὑψι-φᾱνής, ές, (φαίνομαι) = sq., Anth.

ὑψι-φαής, ές, (φάος) *high-shining, far-seen*, Anth.

ὑψί-φρων, ονος, ὁ, ἡ, (φρήν) *high-minded, haughty*, Pind.

ὑψῐ-χαίτης, ου, ὁ, (χαίτη) long-haired, Pind.
ὑψόθεν, Adv., (ὕψος) from on high, from aloft, from above, Lat. desuper, Il., Hes. II. like ὕψου, high, aloft, on high, Anth. 2. c. gen. above, over, Pind.
ὑψόθῐ, Adv. (ὕψος) like ὕψου, aloft, on high, Il.
ὑψ-όροφος, ον; high-roofed, high-ceiled, Hom.
ὕψος, εος, τό, (ὕψι) height, Hdt., Att.; ὕ. ἔχειν, λαμβάνειν to rise to some height, Thuc. :—absl. ὕψος, in height, opp. to μῆκος or εὖρος, Hdt. II. metaph. the top, summit, crown, Plat.
ὑψόσε, Adv. of motion, aloft, on high, up high, Hom.; ὑψόσ' ἔχοντες high reaching, Il.
ὕψου, Adv., (ὕψος) aloft, on high, Hom.; τῆς πόλιος ἐκκεχωσμένης ὕψου having the soil raised to a great height, Hdt. :—metaph., ὕψου ἐξᾶραί τι to praise it highly, Id.; ὕψου αἴρειν θυμόν Soph.
ὑψόω, f. ώσω, (ὕψος) to lift high, raise up, Batr., Anth.: Med. to raise for oneself, Anth. II. metaph. to elevate, exalt, N. T.
ὝΩ [ῠ], f. ὕσω [ῠ]: aor. 1 ὗσα :—Pass., aor. 1 ὕσθην : pf. ὕσμαι :—to send rain, to rain, Ζεὺς ὕε Hom., etc.; ὁ θεὸς ὕει Hdt. :—then, the nom. being omitted, ὕει used impers., Lat. pluit, it rains, Hes., Hdt.; ὕοντος when it is raining, Ar.; ὕοντος πολλῷ ἐπὶ it was raining heavily, Xen. 2. c. acc. loci, ἑπτὰ ἐτέων οὐκ ὗε τὴν Θήρην for seven years it did not rain on Thera, Hdt. :—hence in Pass., with fut. med. to be rained on, Od.; ὕσθησαν αἱ Θῆβαι Thebes was rained upon, i. e. it rained there, Hdt.; ἡ χώρη ὕεται, i. e. it rains in the country, Id. 3. c. acc. cogn., ὕσε χρυσόν it rained gold, Pind.; καινὸν ἀεὶ Ζεὺς ὕει ὕδωρ Ar.

Φ.

Φ, φ, φῖ, τό, indecl., twenty-first letter of the Gr. alphabet: as a numeral φ' = 500, but ͵φ = 500,000.
The consonant Φ arose from the labial Π followed by the aspirate, and was anciently written ΠΗ.
I. changes of Φ: 1. in Aeol., Dor. and Ion. the aspirate was often dropped, and φ became π, as in ἀσπάραγος σπόγγος σπυράς for ἀσφάραγος σφόγγος σφυράς, whereas the Att. sometimes used φ for π, as φανός φάτρα for πανός πάτρα. 2. in Aeol., Dor., and Ion. φ is sometimes put for θ, as φήρ φλάω for θήρ θλάω.
II. older Poets sometimes treated φ as a double consonant, so that a short vowel before it becomes long by position, as in ὄφις, Ζεφύριος quasi ὔπφις, Ζεππύριος.
φᾶ, Dor. and Ion. for ἔφη, 3 sing. aor. 2 of φημί.
φάανθεν, lengthd. for φάνθεν, Ep. for ἐφάνθησαν, 3 pl. aor. 1 pass. of φαίνω.
φαάντερος, α, ον, Ep. Comp. of φαεινός, brighter, Anth.; Sup. φαάντατος, η, ον, brightest, Od.
φᾰγέειν and φᾰγέμεν, Ep. for φαγεῖν.
ΦΑΓΕΙΝ, inf. of ἔφαγον, with no pres. in use, used as aor. 2 of ἐσθίω :—to eat, devour, φαγέμεν καὶ πιέμεν Od.; φαγεῖν τε καὶ πιεῖν Ar., etc.; c. gen. to eat of a thing, Od. 2. to eat up, devour, squander, Ib. II. in N. T. occurs a f. φάγομαι, 2 sing. φάγεσαι. Hence

φάγες, Ep. 2 sing. of φαγεῖν :—φάγῃσι, Ep. 3 sing. subj.
φᾰγός, ὁ, a glutton, N. T.
φάγωντι, Dor. for φάγωσι, 3 pl. subj. of φαγεῖν.
φάε, Ep. for ἔφαε, 3 sing. impf. of φάω.
φαεθοντίς, ίδος, poët. fem. of φαέθων, shining, Anth.
φαέθω, (φάω) to shine, only found in part. φαέθων, beaming, radiant, Hom., Soph., Eur.; absol., πάννυχα καὶ φαέθοντα nights and days, Soph. II. as a prop. n. 1. Φαέθων, ὁ, Shiner, one of the steeds of Eôs, Od. 2. son of Helios or Apollo, famous for his unlucky driving of the sun-chariot, Eur. 3. the planet Jupiter, Cic.
φαεινός, Dor. and Att. φαεννός, η, ον, (φάω) shining, beaming, radiant, Hom., Pind., Trag. 2. of the voice, clear, distinct, far-sounding, Pind. 3. generally, splendid, brilliant, Id.
φαείνω, Ep. collat. form of φαίνω, to shine, give light, of the sun, Od., Hes.
φαεννός, ή, όν, collat. form of φαεινός.
φαεσί-μβροτος, ον: (φάος, βροτός, with μ inserted) :—bringing light to mortals, Hom., Eur.
φαεσ-φόρος, ον, (φάος, φέρω) light-bringing, Aesch., Eur.
φάθι [ᾰ], imper. of φημί.
Φαίαξ, ᾱκος, Ion. Φαίηξ, ηκος, ὁ, a Phaeacian: they were the Homeric inhabitants of the island of Scheria (i. e. Corcyra, now Corfu), Od.
φαιδῐμόεις, εσσα, εν, collat. form of sq., Il.
φαίδιμος, ον and η, ον, (φάω) shining, of men's limbs, prob. in reference to the common use of oil, Od., Hes., Pind. 2. of heroes, famous, glorious, Hom., Aesch.
φαιδρό-νους, ουν, with bright, joyous mind, Aesch.
φαιδρόομαι, Pass. to beam with joy, Xen. From
φαιδρός, ά, όν, (φάω) bright, beaming, Aesch.: sparkling, of water, Anth. 2. metaph. beaming with joy, bright, joyous, jocund, Solon, Trag., Xen. :—Adv. -δρῶς, joyously, cheerily, Xen.; neut. pl. φαιδρά as Adv., Soph. Hence
φαιδρότης, ητος, ἡ, brightness: joyousness, Isocr.
φαιδρυντής, οῦ, ὁ, a cleanser, washer :—fem. φαιδρύντρια, ἡ, Aesch.
φαιδρύνω [ῡ], (φαιδρός) to make bright, to cleanse, Aesch.; θεαὶ μορφὰν ἐφαίδρυναν gave me a bright form, Eur.: —in Med., χρόα φαιδρύνεσθαι to wash one's skin clean, Hes. II. metaph. to cheer, Aesch. :—Pass. to beam or brighten up with joy, Xen.
φαιδρ-ωπός, όν, with bright, joyous look, Aesch., Eur.
φαίην, pres. and aor. 2 opt. of φημί.
φαικάς, άδος, ἡ, a white shoe, Anth.
φαικάσιον, τό, Dim. of φαικάς, Plut.
φαινόλης, ου, ὁ, formed from the Lat. paenula, a thick upper garment, a cloak, N. T.
φαινόλις, ἡ, (φαίνω) light-bringing, h. Hom.
φαίνω, f. φᾰνῶ, Ion. φᾰνέω: opt. φᾰνοίην: aor. 1 ἔφηνα, Dor. ἔφᾱνα: Ep. 3 sing. aor. 2 φάνεσκε: pf. πέφαγκα :—intr. pf. πέφηνα :—Med., f. φᾰνοῦμαι, Ion. φᾰνέομαι: aor. 1 ἐφηνάμην :—Pass., Ion. impf. φαινέσκετο: f. 2 φᾰνήσομαι (never φανθήσομαι): Ep. 3 sing. 3 f. πεφήσεται: aor. 1 ἐφάνθην, Ep. ἐφάανθην, 3 pl. φάανθεν: aor. 2 ἐφάνην [ᾰ], Ep. 3 pl. φάνεν, Ep. subj. φανήῃ, inf. φανήμεναι :—pf.

πέφασμαι, 3 sing. πέφανται, inf. πεφάνθαι, part. πεφασμένος, 3 pl. plqpf. ἐπέφαντο : (φάω).

A. Act. *to bring to light, make to appear*, Hom., etc. :—Med. *to exhibit as one's own*, Soph.   **b.** *to shew forth, make known, reveal, disclose, shew*, Od., Soph. etc. : γόνον Ἑλένῃ φ. *to shew* her a child, i. e. grant her to bear one, Od.   **2.** *of sound, to make* it *clear* to the ear, *make it ring clear*, Ib., Aesch.   **3.** *to make clear, explain, expound*, Hdt.   **4.** in Att. *to inform against one, to indict, impeach*, Ar. :—*to inform of* a thing *as contraband*, Id. : Pass., τὰ φανθέντα articles *informed against* as contraband, Dem.   **b.** absol. *to give information*, Xen.   **5.** φαίνειν φρουράν at Sparta, *to proclaim* a levy, *call out* the array, Id.   **II.** absol. *to give light*, Od. ; so of the sun, moon, etc., φ. τινί Ar. ; Theocr. ; so of the Dioscuri *shining* in mid-air, Eur. ; ἀγανὴ φαίνουσ' ἐλπίς soft *shining* hope, Aesch.   **III.** Hom. uses the Ion. aor. φάνεσκε really intr., *appeared* : —also pf. 2 πέφηνα is intr., Hdt., Soph., Dem.

B. Pass. *to come to light, be seen, appear*, Hom. ; of fire, *to shine brightly*, Id. :—often of the *rising* of heavenly bodies, Il., Hes. ; of daybreak, φάνη ῥοδοδάκτυλος Ἠώς Hom.   **2.** of persons, *to come into being*, φανεὶς δύστηνος born to misery, Soph. ; δοῦλος φανεὶς shewn to be, *having become*, a slave, Id. :—also of events, τέλος πέφανται Il. ; τὸ φανθέν *what has once come to light*, Soph., etc.   **II.** *to appear to be* so and so, c. inf., ἥτις ἀρίστη φαίνεται εἶναι Od. ; τοῦτό μοι θειότατον φαίνεται γενέσθαι Od.:—inf. omitted, ὅστις φαίνηται ἄριστος Od., etc. :—also c. part., but φαίνεσθαι c. inf. indicates that *a thing appears to be* so and so, φαίνεσθαι c. part. states the fact *that it manifestly is* so and so, ἐμοὶ σὺ πλουτέειν φαίνεαι you *appear* to me to be rich, Hdt. ; but, εὔνους ἐφαίνετο ἐών he was *manifestly* well-inclined, Id. ; φαίνεται ὁ νόμος βλάπτων the law *manifestly harms*, but, φαίνεται ὁ νόμος ἡμᾶς βλάψειν *it appears* likely to *harm* us, Dem. :—with the part. omitted, Κᾶρες ἐφάνησαν (sc. ὄντες) *they were manifest* Carians, Thuc. ; τί φαίνομαι (sc. ὤν) ; *what do I look like?* Eur.   **2.** in dialogue, φαίνεταί σοι ταῦτα; *does this appear* so? *is not this so?* Answ. φαίνεται, *yes*, Plat. ; [τοῦτο] φῂς εἶναι; Answ. φαίνομαι (sc. λέγειν) Xen.   **3.** οὐδαμοῦ φανῆναι *nullo in loco haberi*, Plat. Hence

Φαίνων, ὁ, a planet, *Shiner*, our Saturn, Cic.

ΦΑΙΟ'Σ, ά, όν, *dusky, dun, gray*, Lat. *fuscus*, Plat.

φαιο-χίτων [ῐ], ωνος, ὁ, ἡ, *dark-robed*, Aesch., [second syll. long, quasi φαιοκχίτων ; v. Χ χ fin.].

ΦΑ'ΚΕΛΟΣ, ὁ, *a bundle, fagot*, Lat. *fasciculus*, Hdt., Eur. ; ὕλης φάκελοι *fascines*, Thuc.

φἀκῆ, ῆς, ἡ, *a dish of lentils* (φακοί), *lentil-soup*, Ar.

ΦΑ'ΚΟΣ, ὁ, *lentil*, and *its fruit*, Hdt., etc.

φἀλαγγηδόν, Adv. (φάλαγξ) *in phalanxes*, Il., Polyb.

φἀλάγγιον, τό, = φάλαγξ III, Plat., Xen.

φἀλαγγομάχέω, f. ήσω, *to fight in a phalanx;* generally, *to fight in the ranks*, Xen. From

φἀλαγγο-μάχης, ου, ὁ, (μάχομαι) *one who fights in the phalanx*, Anth.

φάλαγξ [ἄ], αγγος, ἡ, *a line of battle, battle-array*, Il. ; mostly in pl. *the ranks*, Ib., Hes.   **2.** *the phalanx*, i. e. *the heavy infantry* (ὁπλῖται) *in battle-order*, Xen.,

etc. : *the formation of the phalanx* differed ; the Spartan line at Tegea was eight deep, Thuc. ; the Theban at Delium twenty-five, Id. ; the phalanx was brought to perfection by Philip of Macedon.   **b.** for *the main body, centre*, as opp. to the wings (κέρατα), Xen.   **c.** *a camp*, Id.   **II.** *a round piece of wood, a trunk, log*, Hdt.   **III.** *a venomous spider* (cf. φαλάγγιον), Ar. (Deriv. uncertain.)

φάλαινα, v. φάλλαινα.

φἄλακρόομαι, Pass. *to become bald*, Hdt. From

φἄλακρός, ά, όν, (φαλός) *baldheaded, bald*, Hdt., Plat., etc. ; πρόσωπον φαλακρόν Eur.

φάλανθος, ον, (φαλός) *bald in front*, Anth. Hence

φἄλαντίας, ου, ὁ, *a bald man*, Luc.

φάλἄρα [ἄ], τά, (φαλός) *bosses* on the sides of the helmet, to which the chin-straps were attached, Il. : —the sing., φάλαρον τιάρας, part of the headdress of the old Persian kings, Aesch.   **II.** *bosses* or *discs of metal*, used to adorn the head-gear of horses, Lat. *phalĕrae*, Hdt., Soph., etc.

φἄλἄρίς, ίδος, ἡ, (φαλαρός) *the coot*, so called from its *bald white head*, Ar.

φάλἄρον, τό, v. φάλαρα, τά.

φάλἄρος, α, ον, (φαλός) *having a patch of white*, ὁ κύων ὁ φάλαρος *the dog with a white spot*, Theocr.

φἄληριάω, (φάλαρος) *to be patched with white*, κύματα φαληριόωντα *waves crested with white foam*, Il.

Φάληρον [ἄ], τό, *Phalerum*, the western harbour of Athens :—**Φαληροῖ**, *at Phalerum*, Xen. ; **Φαληρόθεν** from Ph., Plat.; **Φαληρόνδε**, *to Ph.*, Thuc. :—**Φαληρεύς**, έως, ὁ, *a Phalerian*, Hdt. :—Adj. **Φαληρικός**, ή, όν, Ar.

φάλῆς, ῆτος, ὁ, = φαλλός :—as a divinity, *Phales*, associated with the worship of Bacchus, Ar.

φάλλαινα (not φάλαινα), ἡ, *a whale*, Lat. *bālaena*, Babr. :—hence *of any monster*, Lat. *bellua*, Ar.

φαλλικός, ή, όν, *of or for the* φαλλός :—τὸ φαλλικόν (sc. μέλος) *the phallic song*, Ar.

φαλλός, ὁ, *membrum virile, phallus*, a figure borne in procession in the Bacchic orgies, as an emblem of the generative power in nature, Hdt., Ar.

φἄλός, ή, όν, (φάω) *shining, white*.

ΦΑ'ΛΟΣ [ἄ], ὁ, *a part of the helmet* worn by the Homeric heroes, either *a metal ridge in which the plume* (λόφος) *was fixed*, or (rather) *the peak of the helmet* : then, an ἀμφίφαλος κυνέη would be one that had a peak behind as well as before.

φάμα, Dor. for φήμη.

φἄμέν, (enclit.) 1 pl. pres. of φημί.   **II. φάμεν**, Ep. for ἔφαμεν, 1 pl. aor. 2.

φάμενος, aor. 2 med. part. of φημί.

φάν, poët. for ἔφησαν, 3 pl. aor. 2 of φημί.

φάναι [ἄ], inf. of φημί.   **II. φᾶναι**, aor. 1 inf. of φαίνω.

φἄναῖος, α, ον, (φανή) *giving* or *bringing light*, Eur.

φἄνείην, aor. 2 pass. opt. of φαίνω.

φἄνεῖμεν, poët. for —είημεν, 1 pl. aor. 2 pass. of φαίνω.

φἄνείς, aor. 2 pass. part. of φαίνω.

φάνεν, Ep. 3 pl. aor. 2 pass. of φαίνω.   **II. φάνέν**, neut. part.

φἄνερό-μῑσος, ον, *openly hating*, Arist.

φἄνερός, ά, όν, and ός, όν, (φαίνω) *open to sight, visible, manifest, evident*, Hdt., Att. :—φανερός εἰμι, c. part.,

φανεροί εἰσι ἀπικόμενοι they are *known* to have come, Hdt.; so, φανεροὶ γιγνόμενοι ὅτι ποιοῦσιν Xen. **2.** *open,* of a road, Hdt. **3.** φ. οὐσία *real* property, opp. to money (ἀφανής ὅ), Dem., etc. **4.** of votes, φ. ψήφῳ by *open* vote, opp. to κρύβδην (ballot), Thuc., etc. **5.** Adv. -ρῶς, *openly, manifestly,* Hdt., Att.: Comp. φανερώτερον Thuc.:—τὸ φανερόν is often joined with Preps. in adverb. sense, ἐκ τοῦ φανεροῦ *openly,* Hdt., etc.; so, ἐν τῷ φανερῷ Xen.; ἐς τὸ φανερόν Thuc. **II.** of gods, *known, acknowledged,* Hdt.; of persons, *conspicuous,* Soph., Thuc.

φανερό-φῐλος, ον, *openly loving, an open friend,* Arist.

φανερόω, f. ώσω, (φανερός) *to make manifest,* N.T. **II.** *to make known* or *famous :*—Pass. *to become so,* Hdt.

φᾰνή, ἡ, (v. φάω) *a torch :—a torch-procession,* such as took place in the Bacchic orgies, Eur.

φᾰνήῃ, Ep. for φανῇ, aor. 2 pass. of. φαίνω:—φάνηθι, imper.:—φανήμεναι, Ep. for inf. φανῆναι.

φᾰνίον, τό, Dim. of φανός, Anth.

φᾰνοίην, f. opt. of φαίνω.

φᾰνός, ή, όν, (φαίνω) *light, bright,* Xen.:—τὸ φανόν *brightness, light,* Plat. **2.** of garments, *washed clean,* Ar. **II.** metaph. *bright, joyous,* Aesch., Plat. **2.** *conspicuous,* Plat. **3.** Adv. -νῶς *perspicuously ;* Sup. φανότατα, Luc.

φᾱνός, ὁ, (φάω) *a torch* of vine-twigs, Xen.; cf. **πᾶνός.**

φαντάζομαι, Pass., f. φαντασθήσομαι: aor. 1 ἐφαντάσθην:—like φαίνομαι, *to become visible, appear, shew oneself,* Hdt., Eur. **2.** *to make a show, exalt oneself,* Lat. *se ostentare,* Hdt. **3.** φαντάζεσθαί τινι *to make oneself like* some one, Aesch. **4.** in Ar., = συκοφαντεῖσθαι, *to be informed against.* Hence

φαντᾱσία, ἡ, *imagination, the power by which an object is presented* (φαίνεται) *to the mind* (the object presented being φάντασμα), Plat., Arist.

φάντασμα, ατος, τό, (φαντάζω) = φάσμα, *an appearance, phantasm, phantom,* Aesch., Eur.:—*a vision, dream,* Theocr. **II.** in Philosophy, v. φαντασία. **2.** *a mere image, unreality,* Plat.

φάντες, nom. pl. aor. 2 part. of φημί.

φαντί, Dor. for φασί, 3 pl. of φημί.

φάο, Ep. for φάσο, pres. med. imperat. of φημί.

ΦΑ'ΟΣ, τό, gen. φάεος (φάους) ; dat. φάει ; resolved Ep. nom. and acc. pl. φάεα [ᾱ metri grat.]: Att. contr. φῶς, φωτός, etc.:—*light, daylight,* Hom., etc.:—in Poets, of life, ζώειν καὶ ὁρᾶν φάος ἠελίοιο Id.; λείπειν φάος ἠελίοιο Hes.; πέμπειν τινὰ ἐς φάος Aesch.; πρὸς φῶς ἀνελθεῖν Soph. **2.** of *day-light,* ἐν φάει Od.; φῶς γίγνεται it is becoming *light,* i. e. day is breaking, Plat.; ἕως ἔτι φῶς ἐστι while there is still *light,* Id. **3.** *the light* of a torch, lamp, fire, Od., Aesch. **4.** *the light* of the eyes, Pind.; pl. φάεα the eyes, Lat. *lumina,* Od. **II.** *light,* as a metaph. for deliverance, happiness, victory, Il.: also in addressing persons, γλυκερὸν φάος dear *light of my life,* Od.; ὦ φίλτατον φῶς Soph.

᾽φ-άπτουσα, = ἐφ-άπτουσα, ε being absorbed.

φάραγξ [ᾰ], αγγος, ἡ, *a cleft* or *chasm* in a mountain, *a ravine, gully,* Aesch., Eur. (Deriv. uncertain.)

φᾰρέτρα, Ion. -τρη, ἡ, (prob. from φέρω) *a quiver* for arrows, Lat. *pharetra,* Hom.

φᾰρετρεών, ῶνος, ὁ, = φαρέτρα, Hdt.

φᾰρέτριον, τό, Dim. of φαρέτρα, Mosch.

Φᾰρισαῖος, ου, ὁ, *a Pharisee, Separatist* (from *phârash, to distinguish*), one of a sect who *separated themselves* from other Jews as affecting superior holiness.

φαρμᾰκάω, (φάρμακον) *to suffer from the effect of poison, to be ill* or *distraught,* Dem.

φαρμᾰκείᾱ, ἡ, (φάρμακον) *the use of drugs, potions, spells,* Plat. **2.** *poisoning, witchcraft,* Lat. *veneficium,* Dem. **II.** *remedy, cure,* Arist.

φαρμᾰκεύς, έως, ὁ, (φάρμακον) *a poisoner, sorcerer,* Soph.

φαρμᾰκεύω, f. σω, (φάρμακον) *to administer a drug,* Plat. **2.** *to use enchantments,* φαρμακεύειν τι ἐς τὸν ποταμόν *to use* it *as a charm to calm* the river, Hdt. **II.** c. acc. pers. *to drug, give* him *a poisonous* or *stupefying drug,* Eur.

φαρμᾰκίς, ίδος, fem. of φαρμακεύς, *a sorceress, witch,* Lat. *venefica,* Ar., Dem.

φάρμᾰκον, τό, *a drug, medicine,* Hom., etc.: the φάρμακα *applied outwardly* were χριστά, ἔγχριστα, ἐπίχριστα (*ointments*), and παστά, ἐπίπαστα, καταπλαστά (*plasters*), Theocr., Ar.; *those taken inwardly* βρώσιμα, and πότιμα, ποτά, πιστά, Aesch., Eur., etc. :—c. gen., φ. νόσου *a medicine for* it, *remedy against* it, Aesch.; φ. κεφαλῆς *for* a head-ache, Plat. **2.** in bad sense, *an enchanted potion, philtre,* so *a charm, spell, enchantment,* Od., Theocr. :—also *a drug, poison,* Soph., Eur. **II.** *a remedy, cure,* Hes.; φ. πραΰ, of a bridle, Pind.; c. gen. *a remedy against,* βλάβης Aesch.; πόνων, λύπης Eur. **2.** c. gen., also, *a means of producing, σωτηρίας* Id.; *σοφίας* Plat. **III.** *a dye, paint, colour,* Hdt., etc.

φαρμᾰκοποσία, ἡ, *a drinking of medicine,* Xen., Plat. **2.** *a drinking of poison,* Luc.

φαρμᾰκο-πώλης, ου, ὁ, *a dealer in drugs,* Ar.

φαρμᾰκός, ὁ, *a poisoner, sorcerer, magician,* N. T. **II.** *one who is sacrificed as an atonement* for others, *a scape-goat,* Ar.; and, since worthless fellows were reserved for this fate, φαρμακός became a general name of reproach, Id., Dem.

φαρμᾰκο-τρίβης [ῐ], ου, ὁ, (τρίβω) *one who grinds drugs* or *colours,* Dem.

φαρμᾰκόω, f. ώσω, *to endue with healing power,* Pind.

φαρμᾰκ-ώδης, ες, (εἶδος) *of the nature of a φάρμακον, medicinal,* Arist. **2.** *poisonous,* Plut.

φαρμάσσω, Att. -ττω, f. ξω, *to treat by using φάρμακα,* of a metal-worker, who *hardens* iron by plunging it in water, Od. **II.** *to heal* or *relieve by medicine,* Plat. **2.** *to bewitch by potions* or *philtres :* hence *to bewitch by flattery,* Id.: metaph. in Pass. of a lamp, as φαρμασσομένη χρίματος παρηγορίαις Aesch.

φᾶρος, later also φάρος [ᾰ], εος, τό, Ep. dat. pl. φάρεσσι : (φέρω) :—*a large piece of cloth, a web,* Hom., Eur. **II.** like χλαῖνα, *a cloak* or *mantle,* worn over the χιτών, Hom., etc.:—used as *a shroud* or *pall,* Id., Soph.; also as *a coverlet,* Soph.

Φάρος [ᾰ], ου, ἡ, *Pharos,* an island in the bay of Alexandria, Od., Thuc., etc.; famous for its lighthouse, Strab.: then, as appell., φάρος, ὁ, *a lighthouse,* Anth.

φάρσος, εος, τό, *a part, portion,* φάρσεα πόλιος *the quarters* of a city, Hdt. (Deriv. uncertain.)

φάρυγξ [ᾰ], ἡ, more rarely ὁ, gen. φάρυγος:—*the throat, gullet,* Od., Eur., etc.

φάς, φᾶσα, φάν, aor. 2 part. of φημί.
φαγγᾰνίς, ίδος, ή, Dim. of sq., Anth.
φάσγανον, τό, a sword, Hom., Soph. (Deriv. uncertain.)
φασγᾰν-ουργός, όν, (*ἔργω) forging swords, Aesch.
φάσηλος [ᾰ], ὁ, a sort of bean, Ar. II. hence Lat. phasēlus, a light boat, skiff, from its likeness in shape to a bean-pod, Catull., Horat.
φάσθαι, pres. med. inf. of φημί; φάσθε, 2 pl. imper.; φάσθω, 3 sing.
φᾱσί, 3 pl. of φημί.
Φᾱσιᾱνός, όν, from the river Phasis (v. Φᾶσις) :— ὁ φ. (sc. ὄρνις), the Phasian bird, pheasant, Ar. :—so Φασιᾱνικὸς ὄρνις, with a play on συκοφάντης, Id.
φάσις [ᾰ], (A), εως, ή, (φαίνω) an accusation, Dem.
φάσις [ᾰ], (B), εως, ή, (φημί) an assertion, Arist.
Φᾶσις, ιος, ὁ, the river Phasis in Colchis, being the boundary of Europe and Asia, Hes., Hdt., etc.
φάσκω, impf. ἔφασκον, Ep. φάσκον (used as impf. of φημί) the inf. and part. pres. of φημί are also supplied by φάσκω: besides this we find Att., imper. φάσκε :—to say, affirm, assert, often with a notion of alleging or pretending, Od., Hdt., Att.; ὡς ἔφασκεν as he said, as he alleged, Soph. 2. to think, deem, expect, Hom., Soph. 3. to promise, c. inf. fut., Od., Thuc.
φάσμα, ατος, τό, (φαίνομαι) an apparition, phantom, Hdt., Aesch., etc.; φ. ἀνδρός the spectral appearance of a man, Hdt. :—a vision in a dream, Aesch., etc. 2. a sign from heaven, portent, omen, Hdt., Trag. 3. a monster, prodigy, Hdt.; periphr., φάσμα ταύρου a monster of a bull, Soph.
ΦΑ΄ΣΣΑ, Att. φάττα, ή, a wild pigeon, ringdove, Ar.
φασσο-φόνος, ον, (*φένω) dove-killing, Il.
φᾱσῶ, Dor. for φήσω, fut. of φημί.
φᾰτέ, 2 pl. of φημί.
φᾰτειός, ά, όν, Ep. for φατέος, οὔτι φατειός un-utterable, un-speakable, Hes.
φᾰτέον, verb. Adj. of φημί, one must say, Plat.
φᾰτί, Dor. for φησί, 3 sing. of φημί.
φᾰτίζω, f. ίσω, Dor. ίζω: aor. ἐφάτισα :—Pass., aor. 1 ἐφατίσθην : pf. πεφάτισμαι :—to say, speak, report, ἐφάτισαν [τὰ γρᾰμματα] Φοινίκηια κεκλῆσθαι they spoke of them by the name of Phoenician, Hdt. :— Pass., τὸ φατιζόμενον as the saying is, Soph. II. to promise, engage, betroth, τὴν παῖδά τινι Eur. :— Pass., ἐμὴ φατισθεῖσα my promised bride, Id.
φάτις [ᾰ], ή: acc. φάτιν: voc. φάτι or φάτις : contr. acc. pl. φάτῑς: (φημί). 1. like φήμη, a voice from heaven, the voice of an oracle, an oracle, Aesch., Soph. 2. a saying among men, common talk, rumour, report, Lat. fama, Od., Trag.; κατὰ φάτιν as report goes, Hdt.; ὡς φ. κρατεῖ Aesch.; ὥσπερ ἡ φ. Soph.; φ. [ἐστί] 'tis said that . . , Pind.; ἡ φ. μιν ἔχει the report goes of him, Hdt. 3. the subject of a saying, a theme, Soph. II. speech, words, of a single person, Soph.: speech, language, Aesch.
φάτνη, ή, a manger, crib, feeding-trough, Hom., Hdt., Att. (Prob. from Root ΠΑΤ, πατέομαι.)
φάτο, Ep. for ἔφᾰτο, 3 sing. aor. 2 med. of φημί.
φᾰτός, ή, όν, verb. Adj. of φημί, that may be spoken, οὐ φατός un-speakable, un-utterable, in-effable, Hes., Pind. 2. metaph. named, famous, notable, Hes.
φάττα, ή, Att. for φάσσα, Ar.: Dim. φάττιον, τό, Id.

φαυλ- επί-φαυλος, ον, bad upon bad, bad as bad can be, Anth.
φαυλίζω, f. Att. ιῶ, (φαῦλος) to hold cheap, to depreciate, disparage, Xen.
ΦΑΥ΄ΛΟΣ, η, ον, and ος, ον, like φλαῦρος, of things, easy, slight, Eur., Ar., etc. : Adv., φαύλως κρίνειν to estimate lightly, Aesch.; φ. ἀποδιδράσκειν to get off easily, Ar.; Sup., φαυλότατα καὶ ῥᾷστα Id. 2. trivial, paltry, petty, sorry, poor, Thuc., etc.; φαῦλα ἐπιφέρειν to bring paltry charges, Hdt.: Adv., οὔτι φαύλως with no trivial force, Eur. II. of persons, low in rank, mean, common, οἱ φαυλότατοι the commonest sort (of soldiers), Thuc., etc.: also in point of education opp. to σοφός, Eur., etc.; c. inf., φαῦλος μάχεσθαι Id.; φ. λέγειν Plat. 2. careless, thoughtless, indifferent, Lat. securus, Eur.:—Adv., φαύλως εὕδειν Id.; φ. λογίσασθαι to estimate off-hand, roughly, Ar.; φ. εἰπεῖν, Lat. strictim dicere, carelessly, roughly, Plat. 3. in good sense, simple, unaffected, Id. : Adv., φαύλως παιδεύειν τινα Xen. Hence
φαυλότης, ητος, ή, meanness, paltriness, pettiness, badness, of persons and things, Xen., etc.; ἡ φ. τῶν στρατηγῶν their want of skill, Dem.; lack of judgment, Xen. 2. in good sense, plainness, simplicity, Id.
φαυσ-ίμβροτος, ον, = φαεσ-ίμβροτος, Pind.
ΦΑ΄Ω, 3 sing. Ep. impf. φάε, to give light, shine (like φαίνω II), Od.
ΦΕ΄ΒΟΜΑΙ, Pass., only in pres. and impf., = φοβέομαι, to be put to flight, flee affrighted, Hom.
ΦΕ΄ΓΓΟΣ, εος, τό, light, splendour, lustre, h. Hom., Pind., Trag.: esp. like φάος, φῶς, daylight, Trag.; δεκάτῳ φέγγει ἔτους in the tenth year's light, i. e. in the tenth year, Aesch. :—also moonlight, Xen. 2. of men, φ. ἰδεῖν to see the light, come into the world, Pind.; λιπεῖν φ. Eur. 3. the light of torches or fire, Aesch. :—a light, torch, Ar.; pl. φέγγη watch-fires, Plut. 4. the light of the eyes, Eur., Theocr.; τυφλὸν φ., i. e. blindness, Eur. 5. light, as a metaph. for glory, pride, joy, Pind., Aesch., etc.
φέγγω, to make bright :—Pass. to shine, gleam, Ar.
φείδεο, Ep. imper. of sq.
φειδίτια, τά, v. sub φιλίτια.
ΦΕΙ΄ΔΟΜΑΙ, 3 pl. poët. impf. φείδοντο: f. φείσομαι, Ep. πεφῑδήσομαι: aor. 1 ἐφεισάμην, Ep. 3 sing. φείσατο :—Ep. redupl. aor. 2 πεφίδόμην, opt. πεφιδοίμην, inf. πεφιδέσθαι: Dep. :—to spare, Lat. parcere : I. to spare persons and things in war, i.e. not destroy them, c. gen., Hom., Att. :—absol. to spare, be merciful, Thuc. II. to spare in using, to refrain from using, use sparingly, ἵππων φειδόμενος, i. e. taking care of them, Il.; μὴ φείδεο σίτου Hes.; φείδεο τῶν νηῶν Hdt.; τι φειδόμεσθα τῶν λίθων; why refrain from using them ? Ar.; φ. μήτε χρημάτων μήτε πόνων Plat. 2. absol. to be sparing, be thrifty, live thriftily, Theogn.; οἱ γεωργοῦντες καὶ φειδόμενοι Dem. :—this part is used as Adj. = φειδωλός, Ar. :— Adv. φειδομένως sparingly, N. T., Plut. III. to draw back from, τοῦ κινδύνου Xen.; φείδου μηδὲν ὧνπερ ἐννοεῖς shrink not at all from that thou hast in mind, Soph. :—also c. inf. to spare or cease to do, forbear from doing, Eur.
φειδώ, όος, contr. οῦς, ή, (φείδομαι) a sparing, νεκύων

II.   II. absol. *thrift, parsimony,* Od., Hes. : *thrift* in exposing oneself to danger, Thuc.

φειδωλή, ή, = φειδώ, Il., Solon.

φειδωλία, ή, = φειδώ, Ar., Plat.

φειδωλός, ή, όν, and ός, όν, *sparing, thrifty,* and as Subst. *a niggard, miser,* Ar., Plat. ; φ. γλῶσσα *a niggard* tongue, Hes. : —c. gen., φ. χρημάτων Plat. ; τὸ φειδωλόν = φειδώ, Id. : —Adv. -λῶς, Id.

φείδων, ωνος, ὁ, *an oil-can with a narrow neck, that lets only a little run out,* Theophr.   II. as pr. n. **Φείδων,** name of an old man in Com. Poets, *Thrifty :* —hence patron. **Φειδωνίδης,** ου, ὁ, *Thrifty-son,* Ar.

φείσασθαι, aor. 1 inf. of φείδομαι : **φείσατο,** Ep. 3 sing.

φειστέον, verb. Adj. of φείδομαι, *one must spare,* Isocr.

φελλεύς, έως, ὁ, *stony ground :* as pr. n., Ar.

φελλΐνος, η, ον, *made of cork,* Luc.

φελλίον, τό, = φελλεύς, Xen.

φελλό-πους, ὁ, ή, πουν, τό, *cork-footed,* Luc.

ΦΕΛΛΟ΄Σ, ὁ, *the cork-tree,* Lat. *quercus suber :* —its *bark, cork,* Lat. *cortex,* Pind., Aesch. Hence

Φελλώ, οῦς, ή, *Cork-land,* Luc.

φενάκη [ᾰ], ή, (φέναξ) *false hair, a wig,* Luc.

φενᾰκίζω, f. σω, *to play the* φέναξ, *cheat, lie,* Ar., Dem.   2. trans. *to cheat, trick,* τινά Ar., Dem. : —Pass. *to be cheated,* Ar., Dem. Hence

φενᾰκισμός, *cheatery, quackery, imposition,* Ar., Dem.

ΦΕ΄ΝΑΞ, ᾰκος, ὁ, *a cheat, quack, impostor,* Ar.

ΦΕ΄ΝΩ, only found in Ep. aor. 2 ἔπεφνον, πέφνον, (sync. from redupl. form πέ-φενον), subj. πέφνῃς, ῃ, inf. πεφνέμεν, part. πέφνων (parox. as if from a pres. πέφνω) : —*to slay,* Hom., Soph.   II. besides this aor., from a Root **ΦΑ,** come pf. pass. 3 sing. and pl. πέφαται, πέφανται, inf. πεφάσθαι ; and 2 sing. fut. pass. πεφήσεαι, Hom.

φερ-ανθής, ές, (ἄνθος) *flower-bringing,* Anth.

φερ-ασπις, ιδος, ὁ, ή, *shield-bearing,* h. Hom., Aesch.

ΦΕ΄ΡΒΩ, only in pres. and impf., with plqpf. ἐπεφόρβειν, *to feed, nourish,* Pind., Eur. ; c. gen. *to feed* oxen on a thing, h. Hom.   2. = σώζω, *to preserve,* Hes.   II. Pass. *to be fed, feed upon* a thing, Lat. *pasci, vesci,* παρέξω δαῖθ᾽ ὑφ᾽ ὧν ἐφερβόμην *I shall make food for those by whom I feed myself,* Soph.   2. *to eat, feed on,* c. acc., Lat. *depasci,* Eur.   3. *to enjoy, have,* νόον Pind.

φέρε, imper. of φέρω, v. φέρω IX.

φερε-αυγής, ές, (αὐγή) *bringing light,* Anth.

φερ-έγγυος, ον, (ἐγγύη) *giving surety :* —generally, *to be depended upon, trusty, sure,* Aesch. : —c. inf. *capable, sufficient,* οὐ φ. εἰμι παρασχεῖν Hdt. ; λιμὴν φ. διασῶσαι τὰς νέας Id. : —c. gen. rei, *warrant for* a thing, *able to answer for,* Soph. ; so, φερεγγυώτατος πρὸς τὰ δεινά Thuc.

φερέ-κακος, ον, (κακόν) *inured to toil* or *hardship,* Polyb.

φερέ-καρπος, ον, *yielding fruit,* Anth.

φερέμεν, Ep. for φέρειν, inf. of φέρω.

φερέ-νῑκος, ον, (νίκη) *carrying off victory,* Pind.

φερέ-οικος, ον, *carrying one's house with one,* of the Scythians, Hdt. : —as Subst. *the house-carrier,* i. e. *snail,* Hes.

φερέ-πονος, ον, *bringing toil and trouble,* Pind.

φερέσ-βιος, ον, *life-giving,* γαῖα h. Hom., Hes.

φέρεσκε, 3 sing. Ion. impf. of φέρω.

φερεσ-σᾰκής, ές, gen. έος, (σάκος) *shield-bearing,* Hes.

φερε-στάφῠλος, ον, (σταφυλή) *yielding bunches of grapes,* Anth.

φερετρεύομαι, Pass. *to be carried on a litter,* Plut. From

φέρετρον, τό, (φέρω) *a bier, litter,* Polyb. :—contr. φέρτρον Il.

φέρην, Aeol. for φέρειν, inf. of φέρω.

φέριστος, η, ον, v. φέρτατος.

φέρμα, ατος, τό, (φέρω) *that which is borne, the fruit of the womb* (cf. *bairn* from *bear*), Aesch.

φερνή, ή, (φέρω) *that which is brought by the wife* (cf. ἕδνον), *a dowry, portion,* Lat. *dos,* Hdt., Eur. ; also in pl. of *a dower,* as consisting of divers presents, Eur. ; but, φερναὶ πολέμου, of a wife won in battle, Id. : —in pl., also, *bridal gifts,* Id.

φέροισα, Dor. for φέρουσα, part. fem. of φέρω.

φέροντι, Dor. for φέρουσι, 3 pl. of φέρω.

Φερρέφαττιον, τό, *a temple of Persephoné,* Dem.

Φερρέφασσα, ή, = Περσέφασσα, Περσεφόνη, Soph., Eur. ; **Φερσέφαττα** Ar. ; **Φερρέφαττα** Plat.

Φερσεφόνη, poët. for Περσεφόνη, Pind.

φέρτατος, η, ον, *bravest, best,* Hom. : —of things, κακῶν φέρτατον *the best,* i. e. *least bad,* of two evils, Il.   2. in form **φέριστος,** Ib. ; mostly in voc. φέριστε, Ib., Aesch., Soph.   II. Comp., **φέρτερος,** α, ον, *braver, better,* Hom. : —πολὺ φέρτερόν ἐστιν 'tis much *better,* Id. ; —τέττιγος φέρτερον ἄδεις, as Adv., Theocr. (The posit. occurs in προ-φερής : perh. the Root is φέρ-εσθαι, so that the orig. sense would be *quick in action, vigorous.*)

φερτός, ή, όν, verb. Adj. of φέρω, *endurable,* Eur.

φέρτρον, contr. for φέρετρον, Il.

ΦΕ΄ΡΩ, a Root only used in pres. and impf. ; Ep. 2 pl. imper. φέρτε, 3 sing. subj. φέρῃσι, inf. φερέμεν : impf. φέρον, Ion. φέρεσκον.   II. from Root **ΟΙ** come f. οἴσω, Dor. οἰσῶ, 1 pl. οἰσεῦμες : Ep. imper. οἶσε, οἰσέτω ; inf. Ep. οἰσέμεν, οἰσέμεναι : fut. med. οἴσομαι (also used in pass. sense) ; pass. οἰσθήσομαι.   III. from Root **ΕΝΕΚ** or **ΕΝΕΓΚ** come aor. 1 ἤνεγκα, Ep. ἔνεικα, and aor. 2 ἤνεγκον, in pl. always ἠνέγκαμεν, -ατε, -αν : imperat., ἔνεγκε, ἐνεγκάτω : optat., ἐνέγκαιμι and -οιμι : inf. ἐνεγκεῖν, Ep. -έμεν : part. ἐνεγκών, later ἐνέγκας : —in Med., aor. 1 is almost solely used : —from same Root come pf. ἐνήνοχα, aor. 1 pass. ἠνέχθην, Ion. ἠνείχθην, pf. ἐνήνεγμαι, 3 sing. plqpf. ἐνήνεκτο.

Radic. sense, *to bear,* Lat. *fero :*   **A.** *to bear* or *carry* a load, Hom., Att. ; of a woman with child, Aesch., Soph.   II. *to bear, bear along,* implying motion, πόδες φέρον Il. ; horses are said ἅρμα φέρειν Ib. ; of a wind, Hom. ἢ βορέας εἰς τὴν Ἑλλάδα φέρει *is fair* for Greece, Xen.   III. *to bear, endure, suffer,* Od., etc. ; of wine, τὰ τρία φέρων *bearing* three parts of water, instead of ἴσον ἴσῳ, Ar. : —often with Advs., βαρέως, δεινῶς, χαλεπῶς φέρειν τι, like Lat. *aegre, graviter ferre, to bear* impatiently, *take* ill or *amiss,* opp. to κούφως, ῥᾳδίως φέρειν, Lat. *leviter ferre, to bear* patiently, *take* easily, Hdt., Att. : —such phrases are constructed mostly c. acc. rei ; sometimes, c. dat. only, βαρέως φέρειν τοῖς παροῦσι Xen.   IV. *to bring, fetch,* Hom., Att. :—Med. *to bring with one,* or *for one's own use,* Od., etc.   2. *to bring, offer, present,*

δῶρα Ib.; χάριν τινὶ φ. to grant any one a favour, do him a kindness, Hom., Att. 3. to bring, produce, work, cause, Hom.; φ. κακόν, πῆμα, ἄλγεα to work one woe, Id.:—to produce, bring forward, cite, Dem. 4. to bring one word, to tell, announce, Aesch., etc. :—so in Med., λόγους φ. Eur.; but also, ἔπος φέρεσθαι to have word brought one, receive, Id. 5. to pay something due or owing, φόρον φέρειν to pay as tax or tribute, Thuc.; μισθὸν φ. Xen. (but also to receive pay, Ar., Thuc.):—of property, to bring in, yield as rent, Isae. 6. ψῆφον φ. to give one's vote, Lat. ferre suffragium, Aesch.; ψῆφος καθ' ἡμῶν οἴσεται (as Pass.) Eur. :—hence φέρειν τινά, to appoint to an office, Dem. V. to bear, bring forth, produce, of the earth or of trees, Od., Hdt., etc. :—absol. to bear, bear fruit, be fruitful, Hdt. VI. to carry off or away, Il. : of stormy winds, Od.; of a river, Hdt. :—Med. to carry off with one, Od., Xen., etc. 2. to carry off as booty or plunder, Il., etc. :—often in the phrase φέρειν καὶ ἄγειν, v. ἄγω I. 3 :—φέρειν alone, to rob, plunder, θεῶν ἱερά Eur.; ἀλλήλους Thuc. :—Med. in same sense, Hom. 3. to carry off, gain, win, achieve, Il., Soph., etc.; μισθὸν φέρειν (v. supr. IV. 5) :—so in Med. to win for oneself, Il., Att. :—metaph., τὰ πρῶτα, τὰ δεύτερα φέρεσθαι to win and hold the first, the second rank, Hdt.; πλέον or πλεῖον φέρεσθαι to gain the advantage over any one, τινος Id., etc. ;—the Med. being used of that which one gets for one's own use, esp. to take home, Id. VII. absol., of roads, to lead to a place, ἡ ὁδὸς φέρει εἰς .., like Lat. via fert or ducit ad .., Id., Thuc., etc. 2. of a tract of country, to stretch, extend to or towards, like Lat. vergere or spectare ad .., φέρειν ἐπί or ἐς θάλασσαν Hdt., etc. 3. metaph. to lead to, be conducive to, ἐς αἰσχύνην φέρει Id.; ἐς βλάβην φέρον Soph. b. to aim at a thing, hint or point at, refer to it, εἰς or πρός τι Hdt., Plat.; so, τοῦ δήμου φέρει γνώμη, ὡς .., the people's opinion inclines to this, that .., Hdt.; τῶν ἡ γνώμη ἔφερε συμβάλλειν their opinion inclined to giving battle, Id. c. impers. much like συμφέρει, it tends (to one's interest), is conducive, φέρει σοι ταῦτα ποιεῖν; Id. d. intr., v. B. I. 2. VIII. to carry in the mouth, i. e. to speak much of, Aeschin. : Pass., εὖ, πονηρῶς φέρεσθαι to be well or ill spoken of, Xen. : also absol. φέρεται, like Lat. fertur, [the report] is carried about, i. e. it is said, τοιόνδε φέρεται πρῆγμα γίγνεσθαι Hdt. IX. imper. φέρε, like ἄγε, used as Adv. come, now, well, φέρ' εἰπὲ δή μοι Soph.; so, before 1 pers. sing. or pl. subj. used imperatively, φέρε ἀκούσω Hdt.; φ. δὴ ἴδωμεν, φ. δὴ σκεψώμεθα Plat. 2. before a question, φέρε τροπαῖα πῶς ἄρα στήσεις; well then, how wilt thou erect trophies? Eur. X. part. neut. τὸ φέρον, as Subst. fortune, fate, τὸ φέρον ἐκ θεοῦ φέρειν χρή ye must bear what heaven bears to you, awards you, Soph.

B. Pass. is used in most of the above senses, esp., I. to be borne along by waves or winds, to be swept away, Od.; ἧκε φέρεσθαι he sent him flying, Il.; ἧκα πόδας καὶ χεῖρε φέρεσθαι I let go my hands and feet, let them swing free [in the leap], Od. 2. often in part. with another Verb of motion, φερόμενοι ἐσέπιπτον they fell on them with a rush, Hdt.; ᾠχόμην

φερόμενος Plat. ;—so, in part. act. used intr., φέρουσα ἐνέβαλε νηΐ she bore down upon the ship and struck it, Hdt.; φέρων hurriedly, in haste, Aeschin. II. of voluntary motion, ἰθὺς φέρεται Il.; ὁμόσε τινὶ φέρεσθαι to come to blows with him, Xen., etc. III. metaph., εὖ, κακῶς φέρεσθαι to turn out well or ill, succeed or fail, νόμοι οὐ καλῶς φέρονται Soph.; τὰ πράγματα κακῶς φέρεται Xen.; ἐὰν ταῦτα φέρεσθαι to let these things take their course, Dem. :—of persons, εὖ φερόμενος ἐν στρατηγίαις being successful in his commands, Thuc.

φεῦ, exclamation of grief or anger, ah! alas! woe! like Lat. vah, vae, Trag.; φεῦ τάλας Soph., etc.: c. gen., φεῦ τοῦ ὄρνιθος alas for the omen! Aesch. 2. of astonishment or admiration, ah! oh! Eur., etc.; c. gen., φεῦ τοῦ ἀνδρός oh what a man! Xen.: c. acc., φεῦ τὸ καὶ λαβεῖν πρόσφθεγμα τοιοῦδ' ἀνδρός oh but to get speech of such a man! Soph.

φεύγω, (Root ΦΥΓ): Ion. impf. φεύγεσκον :—f. φεύξομαι, Dor. φευξοῦμαι (also in Att., metri grat.): aor. 2 ἔφυγον, Ion. φύγεσκον :—pf. πέφευγα; Ep. part. pass. πεφυγμένος in act. sense, and πεφυζότες (cf. φύζα).

I. to flee, take flight, run away, Il. ;—with Preps., φ. ἀπό or ἔκ τινος Hom., etc.; rarely c. gen. only, πεφυγμένος ἦεν ἀέθλων Od. :—c. acc. cogn., φεύγειν φυγήν Eur.; (so, φυγῇ φ. Plat.); φ. τὴν παρὰ θάλασσαν (sc. ὁδόν) to flee toward the sea, Hdt. 2. the pres. and impf. properly express the endeavour to flee: hence the part. φεύγων is added to the compd. Verbs ἀποφεύγω, ἐκφεύγω, προφεύγω, to distinguish the attempt from the accomplishment, βέλτερον, ὡς φεύγων προφύγῃ κακὸν ἠὲ ἁλῴη it is better that one should flee and escape than stay and be caught, Il.; φεύγων ἐκφ. Hdt., etc. 3. φ. εἰς .. to have recourse to .., take refuge in .., Eur. 4. c. inf. to be shy of doing, shrink from doing, Hdt., Plat.; and with the inf. omitted, to shrink back, Soph. II. c. acc. to flee from, to shun, avoid, Hom., etc.; φ. φόνον to flee the consequences of the murder, Eur. :—the part. pf. pass. also retains the acc. in Hom., who joins it with εἶναι or γενέσθαι = πεφευγέναι, e. g. μοῖραν δ' οὔτινά φημι πεφυγμένον ἔμμεναι I say that no man can escape his doom, Il.; πεφυγμένον ἄμμε γενέσθαι Ib. 2. of things, ἡνίοχον φύγον ἡνία the reins escaped from his hands, Ib. III. to flee one's country for a crime, Hom.; οἱ φεύγοντες the exiles, Thuc.; φ. πατρίδα Od. 2. φ. ὑπό τινος to be banished by him, Hdt., Xen. :—absol. to go into exile, be an exile, Lat. exulare, Hdt. IV. as Att. law-term, to be accused or prosecuted: ὁ φεύγων the accused, defendant, Lat. reus, opp. to ὁ διώκων the accuser, prosecutor, Ar., Oratt. : c. acc., φ. γραφήν or δίκην to be put on one's trial for something, Ar., Plat.; the crime being added in gen., φ. φόνου (sub. δίκην) to be charged with murder, Lys., etc.; φ. ἀσεβείας ὑπό τινος is accused of impiety by some one, Plat.

φεύξω, f. ξω, to cry φεῦ, cry woe, only found once, τί τοῦτ' ἔφευξας; Aesch.

φευκτέον, verb. Adj. of φεύγω, one must flee, Eur.

φευκτός, ή, όν, verb. Adj. of φεύγω, to be shunned or avoided, Arist. 2. that can be avoided, Soph.

φευξείω, to wish to escape, Eur.

φεῦξις, εως, ἡ, = φύξις, Soph.

φεύξομαι, -οῦμαι, f. of φεύγω.

φεψαλόομαι, Pass. *to be burnt to ashes*, Aesch. From

ΦΕ'ΨΑ'ΛΟΣ, ου, ὁ, *a spark, piece of the embers*, Ar.; ἀσπὶς ἐν τῷ φεψάλῳ κρεμήσεται, i. e. will be hung in the chimney, of things laid by and unused, Id.

φή, enclit. for φησί, 3 sing. of φημί. II. **φῆ**, Dor. **φᾶ**, poët. for ἔφη, 3 sing. aor. 2.

φηγίνεος, α, ον, = sq., Anth.

φηγίνος, η, ον, *oaken*, Il. From

φηγός, ἡ, (φάγεῖν) *a kind of oak*, bearing an esculent acorn, Lat. *fagus*, our *beech*, though the names are not identical), sacred to Ζεύς, Il., Soph. II. *the acorn of the same tree*, Ar.

φήῃ, Ep. for φῇ, 3 sing. pres. subj. of φημί.

φηλήξ, ηκος, ἡ, *a wild fig* (prob. from φηλός, *deceitful*, because it seems ripe when it is not really so), Ar.

φηλητεύω, *to cheat, deceive*, h. Hom. From

φηλητής, οῦ, ὁ, (φῆλος) *a knave, thief*, Hes., etc.

φῆλος, ον, *deceitful*. Hence

φηλόω, f. ώσω, *to cheat, deceive*, Aesch.: Pass., φηλούμενοι Eur.

φήμη, ἡ, Dor. **φάμα**, Lat. *fama*: (φημί):—*a voice from heaven, a prophetic voice*, Od.; so, when Ulysses prays to Zeus, φήμην τίς μοι φάσθω, he is answered by thunder, Ib.; hence *an oracle, divination, omen*, Hdt., Soph., etc. 2. *saying or report* spread among men, *rumour*, Hes., Aeschin.; ὑποδεεστέρα τῆς φήμης inferior *to the report* of them, i.e. exaggerated, Thuc. 3. *the talk or report* of a man's character, Hes., etc.:—esp. *good report, fame*, Hdt., Pind.; also, φ. πονηραί Aesch., etc. 4. φᾶμαι *songs of praise*, Pind. II. *any voice or words, a speech, saying*, Aesch.:—esp. *a common saying, a tradition, legend*, Eur., Plat. 2. *a message*, Trag.

φημί (Root ΦΑ, cf. φάω), φής, φησί, pl. φαμέν, φατέ, φασί; Dor. φαμί, φασί or φατί, 3 pl. φαντί:—aor. 2 ἔφην (Ep. φῆν), ἔφησθα rarely ἔφης (Ep. φῆσθα, φῆς), ἔφη (Ep. φῆ, Dor. φᾶ); 3 pl. ἔφασαν or ἔφαν, Ep. φάν; imper. φάθί: subj. φῶ, φῇς, φῇ (Ep. φῆσιν, φήῃ); opt. φαίην, 1 pl. φαῖμεν, 3 pl. φαῖεν, φαίησαν; inf. φάναι, poët. φάμεν; part. φάς, φᾶσα, φάν:—f. φήσω, Dor. φάσω: aor. 1 ἔφησα, Dor. 3 sing. φᾶσε, part. φήσας:—Med., aor. 2 ἐφάμην, ἔφατο (Ep. φάτο), ἔφαντο (Ep. φάντο); imper. φάο, φάσθω, φάσθε; inf. φάσθαι; part. φάμενος: fut. Dor. φάσομαι [ᾰ]:—Pass., 3 sing. imper. pf. πεφάσθω, part. πεφασμένος. II. the impf. act. should be ἔφην, like the aor. 2, but ἔφασκον was generally used instead.

Radical sense: *to declare, make known*; and so, *to say, affirm, assert*, either absol., or foll. by inf. or by acc.; the inf. is often omitted, σὲ κακὸν καὶ ἀναλκίδα φήσει (sc. εἶναι) Il.; but also, Κορινθίους τί φῶμεν; what *shall we say* of them? Xen.:—then, since *what one says* commonly expresses a belief or opinion, *to think, deem, suppose*, Il.; φαίης κε ζάκοτόν τέ τιν' ἔμμεναι ἄφρονά τε *you would say, would think*, he was . . , Ib.; μὴ φαθὶ λεύσσειν *think* not that you see, Theocr. II. Special Phrases: 1. φασί, *they say, it is said*, Hom., Att.; but in Prose also φησί, like French *on dit*, Dem.; (so Lat. *inquit, ait*). 2. φημί is sometimes joined with a synon. Verb, e. g. ἔφη

λέγων, ἔφησε λέγων Hdt.; λέγει οὐδὲν φαμένη Id. 3. in repeating dialogues, the Verb commonly goes before its subject, ἔφην ἐγώ, ἔφη ὁ Σωκράτης said I, said Socrates; but the order is sometimes inverted, ἐγὼ ἔφην, ὁ Σωκράτης ἔφη I said, Socrates said. III. in a more definite sense, like κατάφημι, *to say yes, affirm*, Hom., Att.; καὶ τοὺς φάναι and they *said yes*, Hdt.; καὶ φημὶ κἀπόφημι Soph.; whereas οὔ φημι means *to say no, deny, refuse*, ἡ Πυθίη οὐκ ἔφη χρήσειν said she would *not* answer, Hdt.; ἐὰν μὴ φῇ if he say no, Ar.; φάθι ἢ μή say yes or no, Plat.

φημίζω, Ep. f. -ίξω: aor. 1 ἐφήμισα, Dor. ἐφάμιξα: (φήμη):—*to utter a voice*, φήμην φημίζειν Aesch. 2. *to spread a report*, Hes.: *to prophesy*, Aesch.:—Med. *to express in words*, Id. II. in Med. also *to promise*, τί τινι Eur.

φῆμις, ιος, ἡ, poët. for φήμη, *speech, talk*, Hom.; δήμου φ. *the voice or judgment* of the people, Od.;—but δήμοιο φῆμις (Od. 15. 468) seems to be *the place where the people talk, the place of assembly* (ἀγορά). 2. *fame, reputation*, Ib.

φῆν, Ion. for ἔφην, aor. 2 of φημί.

φῆναι, aor. 1 of φαίνω:—**φήνειε**, 3 sing. opt.

ΦΗ'ΝΗ, ἡ, prob. = ἁλιαίετος, the *sea-eagle*, Od., Ar.

ΦΗ'Ρ, ὁ, gen. φηρός, Aeol. for θήρ, Lat. *fera*, Pind.: pl. **φῆρες**, *of the Centaurs*, Il.

φηρο-μανής, ές, (μαίνομαι) *game-mad, madly fond of wild animals*, epith. of Bacchus, Anth.

φῆς, 2 sing. of φημί. II. **φῆς, φῆσθα**, Ep. for ἔφης, 2 sing. aor. 2.

φθάν, Ep. for ἔφθασαν, 3 pl. aor. 2 of φθάνω.

ΦΘΑ'ΝΩ [ᾰ]: f. φθήσομαι, also φθάσω [ᾰ]: aor. 1 ἔφθᾰσα, Dor. ἔφθαξα: aor. 2 ἔφθην, Ep. 3 sing. φθῆ, 3 pl. φθάν; subj. φθῶ, φθῇς, 3 sing. φθήῃ, φθῇσιν, 1 pl. φθέωμεν, φθέωσιν: Ep. opt. 3 sing. φθαίησι; inf. φθῆναι; part. φθάς; Ep. also part. med. φθάμενος:—pf. ἔφθᾰκα. [φθᾱνω always in Att.; φθᾰνω twice in Il.] *To come* or *do first* or *before* others: I. c. acc. pers. *to be beforehand with, overtake, outstrip, anticipate*, Il., Hdt., Att.: so, ἔφθησαν τὸν χειμῶνα Hdt.:—Pass. *to be overtaken*, Anth. II. absol. *to come first*, Eur., etc.; τοῦ φθάσαντος ἁρπαγή the prey of *the first comer*, Aesch.:—with Preps. *to come* or *arrive first*, ἐς τὸν Ἑλλήσποντον Thuc., etc. III. the action *in which* one outstrips another is expressed by the part. agreeing with the subject, [Ἄτη] φθάνει βλάπτουσα *is beforehand* in doing mischief, Il.; φθῆ μιν Τηλέμαχος βαλών Telemachus *was beforehand with* him *in* striking, Od.:—in translation, the part. often becomes the chief Verb and φθάνειν is rendered by an Adv., *quicker, sooner, first, before, beforehand*, ἔφθησαν ἀπικόμενοι arrived *first*, Hdt.; so with part. pass. εἰ κε φθήῃ τυπείς should he be wounded *first*, Il.; so φθάνω εὐεργετῶν I am *the first* to shew a kindness, Xen.:—these clauses, being compar. in sense, are sometimes foll. by a gen., φθᾶν ἱππήων κοσμηθέντες they were marshalled *before* the horsemen, Il.; or by πρὶν . . , πρὶν ἤ, ἔφθη ὀρεξάμενος, πρὶν οὐτάσαι Id.; ἔφθησαν ἀναβάντες πρὶν ἤ . . Hdt. 2. part. φθάς or φθάσας, Ep. φθάμενος, used like an Adv., ὅς μ' ἔβαλε φθάμενος, for ὅς μ' ἔφθη βαλών, Il.; οὐκ ἄλλος φθὰς ἐμεῦ κατήγορος ἔσται no other shall be an accuser *before* me,

Hdt.; ἀνέῳξάς με φθάσας you opened the door *before* me, Ar.   3. rarely with the inf., like Lat. *occupo*, μόλις φθάνει θρόνοισιν ἐμπεσοῦσα μὴ χαμαὶ πεσεῖν hardly *escapes* falling on the ground by falling *first* on the seat, Eur.; φθάνει ἐλθεῖν he is *first* to come, Ar.   IV. φθάνω with οὐ and part., followed by καί, like Lat. *simul ac*, denotes two actions following close on each other, οὐ φθάνειν χρὴ συσκιάζοντας γένυν, καὶ ὁρμᾶν you must *no sooner* get your beard, than you march, Id.; οὐκ ἔφθη μοι συμβᾶσα ἡ ἀτυχία καὶ εὐθὺς ἐπεχείρησαν no *sooner* had misfortune befallen me, *when* they attempted, Dem.   2. οὐκ ἂν φθάνοις, οὐκ ἂν φθάνοιτε, with part. pres., denote impatience, οὐκ ἂν φθάνοιτε ἀπαλλασσόμενοι you could *not be too quick* in departing, i. e. *make haste and* be off, Hdt.; οὐκ ἂν φθάνοιτον τοῦτο πράττοντε Ar.; οὐκ ἂν φθάνοις λέγων Plat.:—so, the part. φθάσας is used with imper., λέγε φθάσας speak *quickly*, τρέχε φθάσας, etc.   3. in answers, οὐκ ἂν φθάνοιμι I could not *be too quick*, i. e. I will begin directly, Plat.

φθαξῶ, Dor. fut. of φθάνω.

φθαρτικός, ή, όν, *destructive of*, τινος Arist.

φθαρτός, ή, όν, verb. Adj. of φθείρω, *perishable*, Arist.

ΦΘΕ'ΓΓΟΜΑΙ, f. φθέγξομαι: aor. 1 ἐφθεγξάμην: pf. ἔφθεγμαι:—to *utter a sound or voice*, esp. *to speak loud and clear, speak*, Hom., etc.   2. of animals, as a horse, *to neigh, whinny*, Hdt.; of an eagle, *to scream*, Xen.; of a fawn, *to cry*, Theocr.   3. of inanimate things, of a door, *to creak*, Ar.; of thunder, *to sound*, Xen.; of musical instruments, Il.   II. = ὀνομάζω, *to name, call by name*, Plat.   III. c. acc. pers. *to celebrate* one *aloud, extol*, Pind. Hence

φθέγμα, ατος, τό, *the sound of the voice, a voice*, Pind., Aesch., etc.: of a person, ὦ φθέγμ' ἀναιδές, for ὦ φθεγξάμενε ἀναιδῆ, Soph.   2. *language, speech*, Id.   3. *a saying, word*, Id.   II. of other sounds, as of birds, *cries*, Id., Eur.; of a bull, *roaring*, Eur.; φθ. θυείας the *grinding* of the mortar, Ar.; of the nightingale's song, Id.

ΦΘΕΙ'Ρ, ὁ: gen. φθειρός: dat. pl. φθειρσί:—*a louse*, Lat. *pediculus*, Hdt., Ar.   2. *a worm* in vegetables, Luc.   3. *a fir-cone*.

φθειρίασις, εως, ἡ, the *morbus pedicularis*, Plut. From

φθειριάω, f. άσω, *to have morbus pedicularis*, Plut.

φθειροτραγέω, (φθείρ 3, τρώγω) *to eat fir-cones*, Hdt.

φθείρω (Root ΦΘΕΡ, ΦΘΑΡ): f. φθερῶ, Ion. φθερέω, Ep. φθέρσω: aor. 1 ἔφθειρα: pf. ἔφθαρκα:—Med., f. φθεροῦμαι (in pass. sense):—Pass., f. φθαρήσομαι: aor. 2 ἐφθάρην [ᾰ], poët. 3 pl. ἔφθαρεν: pf. ἔφθαρμαι, 3 pl. ἐφθάραται:—*to ruin, waste, spoil, destroy*, Lat. *perdere*, Od., Hdt., etc.:—Pass. *to go to ruin, perish*, Trag., etc.   II. Pass.,   1. φθείρεσθε (as a curse) *may ye perish! ruin seize ye!* Il.; φθείρου plague take thee! *away with thee!* Lat. *abi in malam rem!* Ar.; so, εἰ μὴ φθερεῖ if *thou depart* not . . , Eur.; c. gen., φθείρεσθε τῆσδε *off from* her! i. e. unhand her, let her go, Id.; φθείρεσθαι πρός . . *to run headlong to* . ., Dem.   2. *to have suffered loss from shipwreck*, Eur.   3. of women, χερσοὺς φθαρῆναι *to pine away* in barrenness, Soph.

φθερσι-γενής, ές, (γένος) *destroying the race*, Aesch.

φθέωμεν, φθέωσιν, Ep. for φθῶμεν, φθῶσιν, 1 and 3 pl. aor. 2 subj. of φθάνω.

φθῇ, Ep. for ἔφθη, 3 sing. aor. 2 of φθάνω.

φθήῃ, **φθήσιν**, Ep. 3 sing. aor. 2 subj. of φθάνω.

φθήσομαι, fut. med. of φθάνω.

Φθία [ῐ], ας, Ion. **Φθίη**, ης, ἡ, *Phthia* in Thessaly, the home of Achilles, Hom.; **Φθίηνδε** *to Phthia*, **Φθίηφι** at *Phthia*, Il.:—hence **Φθιώτης**, ου, ὁ, *a man of Phthia*, Hdt., etc.:—**Φθιῶτις γῆ** *the land of Phthia*, Eur., etc.; so **Φθιάς**, άδος, ἡ, Id.

φθινάς, άδος, ἡ, (φθίνω) intr. *waning*, Eur.   II. act. *causing to decline, wasting*, Soph.

φθίνασμα [ῐ], ατος, τό, as if from φθινάζω, *a declining, sinking*, Aesch.

φθινάω or –έω, f. ήσω, collat. form of φθίνω, Luc.

φθινό-καρπος, ον, *having lost fruitfulness*, Pind.

φθῐν-οπωρίς, ίδος, fem. Adj. *autumnal*, Pind.

φθῐν-όπωρον, τό, (ὀπώρα) *late autumn, the fall of the year*, Hdt., Thuc.

φθινύθω [ῠ], poët. for φθίνω, only in pres. and impf.; 3 sing. Ep. impf. φθινύθεσκε: 1. trans. *to waste, consume*, Od.; φθ. κῆρ cause it *to pine away*, Ib.   2. intr. *to waste or pine away, decay*, of men, Hom.

φθινύλλα [ῐ], ἡ, (φθίνω) nickname for a thin or delicate woman, *starveling*, Ar.

φθίνω, v. φθίω.

φθίος, α, ον, v. Φθία.

φθῐσ-ήνωρ, ορος, ὁ, ἡ, (φθίω, φθίσω) *destroying* or *killing men*, Il., Hes.

φθῖσθαι, Ep. aor. 2 pass. inf. of φθίω.

φθῐσίμ-βροτος, ον, (φθίω, φθίσω) for φθισίβροτος, *destroying men*, Il., Od.

φθίσις [ῐ], εως, ἡ, (φθίω, φθίσω) *a perishing, decay*, Pind. :—of the moon, *a waning*, Arist.

φθῖτο, Ep. 3 sing. aor. 2 med. of φθίω.

φθῐτός, ή, όν, verb. Adj. of φθίω, Trag. word, only used in pl. φθιτοί (always without the Art.) *the dead*, Aesch., Eur.   II. *liable to perish*, Arist.

ΦΘΙ'Ω [ῐ], impf. ἔφθιον, more commonly **φθίνω** [ῐ], impf. ἔφθῐνον: for fut. and aor. 1, v. inf. II:—Med., f. φθίσομαι [ῑ]:—Pass., 3 pl. aor. pass. ἐφθίθεν: pf. ἔφθῐμαι, ἔφθῐται: plqpf. ἐφθίμην [ῐ], also used as aor. 2 ἔφθῐσο, ἔφθῐτο, Ep. 3 pl. ἐφθίατο: imper. 3 sing. φθίσθω, Ep. subj. φθίεται (for –ηται), φθιόμεσθα (for –ώμεθα), opt. φθίμην, φθῖτο, inf. φθῖσθαι, part. φθίμενος: there is no diff. of sense in Act. and Pass.:   1. *to decay, wane, dwindle*, of Time, πρίν κεν νὺξ φθῖτο (aor. 2 pass. opt.) first would the night *be come to an end*, Od.; so, τῆς νῦν φθιμένης νυκτός Soph.; φθίνουσιν νύκτες τε καὶ ἤματα they wane or *pass away*, Od.; μηδέ σοι αἰὼν φθινέτω let not thy life *be wasted*, Ib.:—so, in the monthly reckoning, μηνῶν φθινόντων in the moon's *wane*, i. e. towards the month's end, Ib. :—μὴν φθίνων the *ending* of the month, v. Ἵστημι B. III. 3.   2. of the stars, *to decline, set*, Aesch.   3. of men, *to waste away, pine, perish*, Hom., Eur.;—of things, *to fade away, disappear*, Soph. :—so in Pass. αὐτὸς φθίεται Il.; ἤδη φθίονται Hom.:—often in part. φθίμενος, *slain, dead*, Id.; φθίμενοι *the dead*, φθιμένοισι μετείην Od., Trag.   II. Causal, in f. φθίσω [ῑ], aor. 1 ἔφθῐσα, *to make to decay or pine away, to consume, destroy*, Hom.; once in Aesch. φθίσας [ῐ].

Φθιώτης, –ῶτις, v. Φθία.

φθογγάζομαι, Dep., = φθέγγομαι, Anth.

φθογγή, ἡ, = φθόγγος, Hom., etc.

φθόγγος, ὁ, *any clear, distinct sound,* esp. *the voice* of men, Hom., Att. ; also of animals, Soph., Eur. II. generally, *a sound,* as distinguished from *a voice* (φωνή), Plat. : —of musical sounds, Eur.

φθοῖς, ἰος, ὁ : nom. et acc. pl. φθοῖς, *a kind of cake,* Ar.

φθονερός, ά, όν, (φθόνος) *envious, jealous, grudging,* of persons, Theogn., Att. : —Adv., φθονερῶς ἔχειν to be *enviously* disposed, Plat., Xen., etc.

φθονέω, f. ήσω : aor. 1 ἐφθόνησα : — Med., fut. in pass. sense φθονήσομαι : —Pass., f. φθονηθήσομαι : aor. 1 ἐφθονήθην : (φθόνος) : —*to bear ill-will* or *malice, bear a grudge, be envious* or *jealous,* Il., Xen., etc. : —c. dat. pers., πτωχὸς πτωχῷ φθονέει Hes. ; φθ. τινὶ εὖ πρήσσοντι *to envy* him for his good fortune, Hdt. ; also c. dat. rei, *to feel envy* at a thing, Isocr. ; ἐπί τινι Xen. : — c. dat. pers. et gen. rei, οὔ τοι ἡμιόνων φθονέω I *bear* thee no *grudge for* the mules, Od. ; μή μοι φθονήσῃς τοῦ μαθήματος Plat. : —c. gen. rei only, *to be grudging of* a thing, ἀλλοτρίων φθονέειν Od. II. *to refuse* to do a thing *from envy* or *ill-will, to grudge* doing, c. inf., Ib., Eur., etc. ; μὴ φθονήσῃς *do not refuse,* Lat. *ne graveris,* μὴ φθο. διδάξαι Plat. : —also c. acc. et inf., ἐφθόνησαν [οἱ θεοὶ] ἕνα ἄνδρα βασιλεῦσαι Hdt. ; —also c. dat. et inf., τῇ δ' οὐκ ἂν φθονέοιμι ἄψασθαι ; Od. III. Pass. *to be envied* or *begrudged,* Lat. *invideor,* Hdt., Eur., etc.

φθόνησις, εως, ἡ, *a jealous refusal,* Soph.

ΦΘΟ'ΝΟΣ, ὁ, *ill-will, envy, jealousy,* Lat. *invidia,* Hdt., etc. ; φθόνον ἔχειν to feel *envy* or *jealousy,* Aesch. ; but, also, to incur *envy* or *dislike,* Plat. ; so, φθόνον ἀλφάνειν Eur., etc. : —c. gen. objecti, *envy for, jealousy of,* τῶν Ἑλλήνων φθόνῳ Hdt., etc. ; but c. gen. subjecti, *envy* or *jealousy felt by* another, Eur., etc. : — in pl. *envyings, jealousies, heartburnings,* Isocr. 2. *jealousy* was ascribed to the gods, τὸν φθόνον πρόσκυσον *deprecate* their jealousy, Soph. II. *refusal from ill-will* or *envy,* οὐδεὶς φθόνος, c. inf., said when you grant a request willingly, Plat. ; so, ἀποκτείνειν φθόνος [ἐστὶ] 'tis *invidious,* I dare not tell, Eur.

φθορά, Ion. **φθορή**, ἡ, (φθείρω) *destruction, ruin, perdition,* Hdt., Trag., etc. ; and of men, *mortality, death,* esp. by pestilence, Thuc. 2. *the decay* of matter, Plat. 3. *the seduction,* Lex ap. Aeschin.

φθόρος, ὁ, = φθορά, Theogn., Thuc. ; ἴτ' ἐς φθόρον = φθείρεσθε (v. φθείρω II. 1), a common form of cursing, Aesch. ; οὐκ ἐς φθόρον; Id. II. like ὄλεθρος, *a pestilent fellow,* Ar., Dem.

-φι, -φιν, an old term. of dat. for -ῃ, as, ἧφι βίηφι πεποιθώς ; for -ῳ, as θεόφιν ἀτάλαντος ; also pl., as, ναῦφι for ναυσί. 2. of gen. for -ης, as, ἐξ εὐνῆφι ; for -ου, as, ἐκ θεόφιν, for -ος, κράτεσφι for κρατός, *of the head.*

φιαλεῖς, 2 sing. fut. of φιάλλω.

φιάλη [ἄ], ἡ, *a broad, flat vessel, a bowl,* used to boil liquids in, Il. ; used as *a cinerary urn,* Ib. 2. after Hom. *a broad, flat bowl* for drinking or pouring libations, Lat. *patera,* Hdt., Att. (Deriv. uncertain.)

φιάλλω, f. φιαλῶ, *to undertake, set about* a thing, Ar. (Deriv. uncertain.)

φιαρός, ά, όν, *shining, bright,* Theocr. (Akin to πίων, *pinguis ?*)

φιβάλεως [ἄ], ω, ἡ, *a kind of early fig,* called from Φίβαλις, a district of Attica or Megaris :—pl., nom. φιβάλεῳ, acc. φιβάλεως Ar.

φιδίτια, τά, v. φιλίτια.

φιλ-άβουλος, ον, *wilfully unadvised,* Anth.

φιλ-άγλαος, ον, *loving splendour,* Pind., Anth.

φιλ-άγραυλος, ον, *fond of the country,* Anth.

φιλ-αγρευτής, οῦ, ὁ, *fond of the chase,* a hunter, Babr. : —fem. φιλ-αγρέτις, ιδος, Anth.

φιλ-άγρυπνος, ον, *fond of waking, wakeful,* Anth.

φιλ-άγων [ἄ], ωνος, ὁ, ἡ, *loving the games,* Anth.

φιλαδελφία, ἡ, *brotherly love,* N. T. From

φιλ-άδελφος [ἄ], ον, *loving one's brother* or *sister, brotherly, sisterly,* Soph., Xen.

φιλ-άεθλος, ον, *fond of the games,* Anth.

φιλ-αθήναιος, ον, *fond of the Athenians,* Ar.

φίλαι, Ep. 2 sing. aor. 1 med. imperat. of φιλέω.

φιλ-αιδήμων, ον, gen. ονος, *loving modesty,* Anth.

φιλ-αίματος, ον, (αἷμα) *bloodthirsty,* Aesch., Eur.

φιλαίτερος, φιλαίτατος, irreg. Comp. and Sup. of φίλος.

φιλ-αίτιος, ον, (αἰτία) *fond of accusing, censorious,* Xen., Dem. : —τὸ φ. *censoriousness,* Plut. II. *liable to blame* or *attack,* Dem.

φιλ-ακόλουθος, ον, *readily following,* Ar.

φιλ-άκρατος, Ion. -ητος, ον, *fond of sheer wine,* Anth.

φιλ-αλέξανδρος, ον, *a friend of Alexander,* Strab.

φιλ-αλήθης, ες, gen. εος, *loving truth,* Arist.

φιλ-άμπελος, ον, *loving the vine,* Ar.

φιλαμπελόω, *to love the vine,* Tzetz.

φιλ-αναγνώστης, ου, ὁ, *fond of reading,* Plut.

φιλ-ανάλωτής, οῦ, ὁ, *fond of spending, prodigal of,* c. gen. rei, Plat.

φιλανδρία, ἡ, *love for the male sex,* Eur. 2. *love for a husband,* Luc., Anth. From

φίλ-ανδρος, ον, (ἀνήρ) *loving men,* Aesch. 2. *loving one's husband,* N. T.

φιλ-ανθρακεύς, έως, ὁ, *friend of colliers,* Ar.

φιλανθρώπευμα, ατος, τό, *a humane act,* Plut. From

φιλανθρωπεύομαι, Dep. *to act humanely,* πρός τινα Dem. ; and

φιλανθρωπέω, f. ήσω, *to treat humanely,* Polyb. ; and

φιλανθρωπία, ἡ, *humanity, benevolence, kindliness,* Plat., Xen., etc. :—in pl. *acts of humanity, kindnesses, courtesies,* Dem. 2. of God, *love to man,* N. T. II. of things, ἡ τοῦ ὀνόματος φιλ. its *humanity, kindliness, mildness,* Dem. ; ἡ φ. τῆς τέχνης, speaking of agriculture, Xen. From

φίλ-άνθρωπος, ον, *loving mankind, humane, benevolent, kindly,* Aesch., Xen., etc. : —of dogs and horses *loving men, gentle,* Xen. II. of things, *humane, humanising,* Id., etc. III. Adv., φιλανθρώπως τινὶ χρῆσθαι Dem.

φίλ-άνωρ [ά], ορος, ὁ, ἡ, (ἀνήρ) Dor. for φιλήνωρ, *fond of one's husband, conjugal,* Aesch.

φιλάοιδος, ον, *fond of singing,* Theocr., Anth.

φιλἄπεχθημοσύνη, ἡ, *fondness for making enemies, quarrelsomeness,* Isocr., Dem. From

φιλ-απεχθήμων, ον, gen. ονος, (ἀπεχθάνομαι) *fond of making enemies, quarrelsome,* Isocr., Dem. Adv., φιλαπεχθημόνως ἔχειν to be *quarrelsome,* Plat.

φιλ-απλοϊκός, ή, όν, (ἁπλοῦς) *fond of simplicity,* Luc.

φίλ-απόδημος, ον, *fond of travelling,* Xen.

φῑλαργῠρία, ἡ, love of money, covetousness, Isocr., etc.

φῑλ-άργῠρος, ον, fond of money, covetous, Soph., Xen., etc.; Sup. φιλαργυρώτατος, Xen. :—τὸ φιλάργυρον = φιλαργυρία, Plat.

φῑλ-άρετος [ᾰ], ον, (ἀρετή) fond of virtue, Arist.

φῑλ-ἀριστείδης, ον, ὁ, a friend of Aristides, Anth.

φῑλάρμᾰτος, ον, fond of the chariot-race, Pind., Eur.

φῑλαρχία, ἡ, love of rule, lust of power, Theophr., Plut.

φίλ-αρχος, ον, (ἀρχή) fond of power, ambitious, Plat.

φίλᾱσε, Dor. and poët. 3 sing. aor. 1 of φιλέω.

φῑλ-αστράγᾰλος, ον, fond of playing at ἀστράγαλοι, Anth.

φίλᾰτο [ῐ], Ep. 3 sing. aor. 1 med. of φιλέω.

φίλ-αυλος, ον, fond of the flute, Soph., Eur., etc.

φίλ-αυτος, ον, (αὑτοῦ) loving oneself, Arist.

φίλ-έγγυος, ον, (ἐγγύη) readily giving security or bail, Strab.

φιλέεσκε, Ep. 3 sing. impf. of φιλέω.

φίλ-έθειρος, ον, (ἔθειρα) attached to the hair, Anth.

φίλ-ειδήμων, ον, (εἰδέναι) fond of learning, Strab.

φίλ-έκδημος, ον, = φιλαπόδημος, Strab.

φίλ-έλλην, ηνος, ὁ, ἡ, fond of the Hellenes, Hdt., Plat.

φιλέοισα, Dor. part. fem. of φιλέω.

φιλέοντι, Dor. 3 pl. of φιλέω.

φίλ-επιτῑμητής, οῦ, ὁ, a censorious person, Isocr.

φίλ-εραστής, οῦ, ὁ, fond of a lover, or fond of having lovers, Plat., Arist. Hence

φιλεραστία, ἡ, devotion to a lover, Plat.

φιλεργία, ἡ, love of labour, industry, Xen., Dem.

φίλ-εργός, όν, (ἔργον) loving work, industrious, Dem.

φίλ-έρῑθος, ον, fond of wool-spinning, Theocr., Anth.

φίλερως, ωτος, ὁ, ἡ, prone to love, full of love, Anth.

φίλ-έσπερος, ον, fond of evening, Anth.

φίλεταιρία, ἡ, attachment to one's comrades, Xen.

φίλ-έταιρος, ον, fond of one's comrades or partisans, true to them, Thuc., Xen., etc. :—Adv. -ρως, Aeschin.

φίλ-εύιος, ον, loving the cry of εὐοῖ, of Bacchus, Anth.

φίλεχθής, ές, gen. έος, = φίλεχθρος, Theocr.

φιλέω, Ep. inf. φιλήμεναι : Ion. and Ep. 3 sing. impf. φιλέεσκε : f. φιλήσω, Ep. inf. φιλησέμεν : aor. 1 ἐφίλησα : pf. πεφίληκα :—Med., Ep. aor. 1 ἐφιλάμην (as if from φίλλω), 3 sing. ἐφίλατο, φίλατο, imperat. φῖλαι :—Pass., f. med. φιλήσομαι in pass. sense (for φιληθήσομαι) : aor. 1 ἐφιλήθην, Ep. 3 pl. ἐφίληθεν : pf. πεφίλημαι : (φίλος) :—to love, regard with affection, Lat. diligere, Hom., etc.; φ. τινὰ φιλότητα to feel affection for him, Od.; to love and cherish as one's wife, Hom. :—the Ep. aor. 1 med. in act. sense, Il. 2. to treat affectionately or kindly, to welcome a guest, Hom. :—Pass., παρ' ἄμμι φιλήσεαι welcome shalt thou be in our house, Od. 3. to kiss, Aesch., etc.; c. dupl. acc., τὸ φίλαμα, τὸ τὸν Ἄδωνιν φίλασεν the kiss wherewith she kissed him, Mosch. :—Med. to kiss one another, Hdt. 4. of things, to love, like, approve, Od., Soph. II. c. inf. to love to do, be fond of doing, and so to be wont or used to do, Hdt., Trag. 2. of things, events, αὖρα φιλέει πνέειν Hdt.; φιλεῖ μεγάλα στρατόπεδα ἐκπλήγνυσθαι great armies are apt to be seized with panic, Thuc.; πάντα ἀνθρώποισι φιλέει γίγνεσθαι everything comes to man by experience, Hdt.; and without γίγνεσθαι, οἷα δὴ

φιλεῖ as is wont, Plat.; also impers., ὡς δὴ φιλεῖ as it is usual, Lat. ut solet, Plut.

φίλη, ἡ, v. φίλος 1. 1.

φίληδέω, f. ήσω, to find pleasure in, take delight in a thing, c. dat., Ar. From

φίλ-ηδής, ές, (ἧδος) fond of pleasure, Arist. Hence

φιληδία, ἡ, delight, Ar.

φίλ-ήδονος, ον, (ἡδονή) fond of pleasure, Luc., etc. 2. wont to bring delight, Anth.

φίληκοέω, f. ήσω, to be attentive, Polyb.; and

φίληκοΐα, ἡ, fondness for hearing or listening to, c. gen., Isocr. From

φίλ-ήκοος, ον, (ἀκοή) fond of hearing discussions, Plat.

φίλ-ηλάκᾰτος, ον, (ἠλακάτη) fond of the spindle, Anth.

φίλ-ηλιάς, άδος, ἡ, fond of the sun, Telesilla.

φίλ-ηλιαστής, οῦ, ὁ, one who delights in the trials of the court Heliaea, Ar.

φίλημα, Dor. φίλᾱμα, ατος, τό, a kiss, Eur., Xen., etc.

φιλήμεναι, Ep. inf. of φιλέω.

φίλημοσύνη, ἡ, (φιλέω) friendliness, affection, Theogn.

φίλ-ήνεμος, ον, (ἄνεμος) loving wind : of a flute, played by the breath, Anth.

φίλ-ήνιος, ον, (ἡνία) following the rein, tractable, Aesch.

φίλ-ήρετμος, ον, (ἐρετμός) loving the oar, Od.

φίλησα, Ep. aor. 1 of φιλέω :—φιλησέμεν, Ep. fut. inf.

φίλησί-μολπος, ον, (μολπή) = φιλόμολπος, Pind.

φίλησις, εως, ἡ, (φιλέω) a feeling of affection, Arist.

φιλητέον, verb. Adj. of φιλέω, one must love, Soph.

φιλητικός, ή, όν, (φιλέω) disposed to love, τινος Arist. : absol. loving, affectionate, Id.

φιλητός, ή, όν, verb. Adj. of φιλέω, to be loved, worthy of love, Arist.; τὸ φ. the object of love, Id.

φιλήτωρ, ορος, ὁ, (φιλέω) a lover, Aesch.

φιλία, Ion. -ίη, ἡ, (φιλέω) friendly love, affection, friendship, distinct from ἔρως, as Lat. amicitia from amor, Hdt., Eur., etc.; φ. ποιεῖσθαι πρός τινα Xen.; with gen., διὰ φιλίαν αὑτοῦ through friendship for him, Thuc.; ἡμετέρη φ. friendship with us, Theogn.; φιλία ἡ ἐμή Xen., etc. 2. fondness for a thing, Plat.

φιλῐκός, ή, όν, (φίλος) of or for a friend, befitting a friend, friendly, Xen., etc. :—φιλικά proofs or marks of friendship, Id. Adv. -κῶς, in a friendly way, Plat., etc.; φ. ἔχειν to be kindly disposed, Xen.

Φίλιννα, ἡ, (φίλος) prop. n. used as a term of affection, Darling, Ar.

φίλιος, α, ον, and ος, ον : (φίλος) : I. act. of or from a friend, friendly, Hdt., Trag., etc.; φ. τριήρης a friendly ship, Thuc.; ἡ φιλία (sc. γῆ, χώρα) a friendly country, opp. to ἡ πολεμία, Xen. 2. Ζεὺς φίλιος Zeus as god of friendship, Plat.; ναὶ τὸν φίλιον (sub. Δία) Ar.; πρὸς φιλίου Plat. II. pass. beloved, dear, Trag. III. Adv. -ίως, Thuc., etc.

Φιλιππίζω, f. Att. ιῶ, to be on Philip's side or party, to Philippize, Dem., Aeschin.

Φιλιππικός, ή, όν, (Φίλιππος) of or against Philip, Dem.

φίλ-ιππος, ον, fond of horses, horse-loving, Pind., Eur., etc. :—Sup. φιλιππότατος, Xen.

φιλίτια, τά, (φίλος) = συσσίτια, the common meals or public tables at Sparta, Arist. :—φιλίτιον, τό, the common hall in which the public table was kept, Xen., Plut. :—others read φιδίτιον or φειδίτιον -ια, (as if from φείδομαι) a frugal table, cheap dinner.

φῐλό-βακχος, ον, loving Bacchus or wine, Anth.
φῐλο-βᾰσίλειος, ον, loving monarchy, Plut.
φῐλο-βᾰσιλεύς, έως, ὁ, a friend to the king, Plut.
φῐλο-γᾱθής, ές, Dor. for φιλο-γηθής.
φῐλό-γαιος, ον, (γαῖα) loving the earth, Anth.
φῐλό-γᾰμος, ον, longing for marriage, Eur.
φῐλο-γαστορίδης, ου, ὁ, (γαστήρ) one who loves his belly, a glutton, Anth.
φῐλο-γέλοιος, ον, fond of the ludicrous, Arist.
φῐλό-γελως, ὁ, ἡ, laughter-loving, Plat., Arist.
φῐλογεωργία, ἡ, fondness for a country life, Xen. From
φῐλο-γέωργος, ον, fond of a country life, Xen.
φῐλο-γηθής, ές, only in Dor. form -γᾱθής, (γηθέω) loving mirth, mirthful, Aesch.
φῐλογραμμᾰτέω, to love books, Plut. From
φῐλο-γράμμᾰτος, ον, (γράμματα) loving books, Plut., etc.
φῐλογυμναστέω, to love gymnastic exercises, Plat.
φῐλο-γυμναστής, οῦ, ὁ, fond of gymnastic exercises; and φῐλογυμναστία, ἡ, fondness for gymnastic exercises, Plat.
φῐλογυμναστικός, ή, όν, of or for a φιλογυμναστής, Plat.
φῐλογύνης [ῠ], ου, ὁ, fond of women, pl. φιλογύναικες Plat.
φῐλό-δενδρος, ον, fond of trees or the wood, Anth.
φῐλο-δέσποτος, ον, loving one's lord or master, ἀνδράποδα φ. slaves that hug their chains, Hdt.; δῆμος φ. Theogn.
φῐλό-δημος, ον, a friend of the δῆμος, the commons' friend, Ar.:—φ. ἔργον a popular act, Id.
φῐλό-δικαιος, ον, loving the right, loving justice, Arist.
φῐλό-δῐκος, ον, fond of lawsuits, litigious, Lys., Dem.
φῐλοδῐκέω, f. ήσω, to be fond of litigation, Thuc.
φῐλ-οδίτης [ῑ], ου, ὁ, a friend of travellers, Anth.
φῐλοδοξέω, f. ήσω, to love fame, seek honour, ἐπί τινι for or in a thing, Arist.; and
φῐλοδοξία, ἡ, love of honour or glory, Polyb. From
φῐλό-δοξος, ον, (δόξα) loving honour or glory, Plat.: τὸ φιλόδοξον, = foreg., Luc.
φῐλό-δουπος, ον, loving noise, Anth.
φῐλοδωρία, ἡ, fondness for giving, bounteousness, Luc.
φῐλό-δωρος, ον, (δῶρον) fond of giving, bountiful, Xen.   II. of things, munificent, Dem.
φῐλο-εργός, όν, (ἔργον) fond of work, industrious, Anth.
φῐλό-ζέφυρος, ον, loving the west wind, Anth.
φῐλό-ζωος, ον, (ζωή) fond of one's life, Arist.   II. φιλόζωος, ον, (ζῷον) fond of animals, Xen.
φῐλο-θεάμων [ᾰ], ον, fond of seeing, fond of shows, plays or spectacles, Plat.; c. gen., φ. τῆς ἀληθείας Id.
φῐλό-θεος, ον, loving God, pious, Arist., etc.
φῐλό-θεωρος, ον, = φιλοθεάμων, Arist.
φῐλοθηρία, ἡ, love of hunting, love of the chase, Xen.
φῐλό-θηρος, ον, (θήρα) fond of hunting, Xen., etc.: Sup. φιλοθηρότατος, Id.
φῐλο-θουκυδίδης, ου, ὁ, fond of Thucydides, Anth. [with ῡ].
φῐλοθύτης [ῠ], ου, ὁ, fond of sacrifices, Ar.   II. pass., ὄργια φιλόθυτα rites offered by zealous worshippers, Aesch.
φῐλοϊερεύς, έως, ὁ, a friend of priests, Io. Damasc.
φῐλ-οίκειος, ον, loving one's relations, Arist.
φῐλ-οικοδόμος, ον, fond of building, Xen.
φῐλ-οικτίρμων, ον, prone to pity, Eur., Plat.

φῐλ-οίκτιστος, ον, = φιλοικτίρμων, Soph.
φῐλ-οικτος, ον, moving pity, ἀπ' ὄμματος βέλει φιλοίκτῳ with piteous glance shot from her eyes, Aesch.
φῐλοινία, Ion. -ίη, ἡ, love of wine, Hdt.   From
φῐλ-οινος, ον, fond of wine, Plat., etc.
φῐλό-καινος, ον, loving novelty or innovation: τὸ φιλόκαινον love of novelty, Luc.
φῐλοκᾰλέω, f. ήσω, to cultivate a taste for the beautiful, Thuc.   2. to be eager, c. inf., Plut.   From
φῐλό-κᾰλος, ον, loving the beautiful, Plat., Xen., etc.: —fond of effect and elegance, Xen.   II. fond of honour, seeking honour, Id.
φῐλο-καμπής, ές, gen. έος, (κάμπτω) easily bending, lithe, Anth.
φῐλο-καρποφόρος, ον, bearing fruit abundantly, Anth.
φῐλοκέρδεια, ἡ, love of gain, greed, Xen.; and
φῐλοκερδέω, to be greedy of gain, Xen.   From
φῐλο-κερδής, ές, (κέρδος) greedy of gain, Theogn., etc.
φῐλο-κέρτομος, ον, fond of jeering, Od., Theocr.
φῐλο-κηδεμών, όνος, ὁ, ἡ, fond of one's relatives, Xen.
φῐλο-κίνδῡνος, ον, fond of danger, adventurous, Xen., Dem.; πρὸς τὰ θηρία φιλοκινδυνότατος Xen.:—Adv. -νως, eagerly, Id.   2. in bad sense, fool-hardy, Dem.
φῐλο-κισσοφόρος, ον, fond of wearing ivy, Eur.
φῐλό-κνῑσος, ον, (κνίζω) fond of pinching, prurient, Anth.
φῐλό-κοινος, ον, fond of society, Anth.
φῐλό-κόλαξ, ὁ, ἡ, fond of flatterers, Arist.
φῐλοκοσμία, ἡ, love of ornament or show, Plut.   From
φῐλό-κοσμος, ον, loving ornament, Plut.
φῐλό-κρημνος, ον, loving steep rocks, Anth.
φῐλό-κρότᾰλος, ον, (κρόταλον) loving rattles, Anth.
φῐλό-κροτος, ον, loving noise, h. Hom.
φῐλο-κτέανος, ον, (κτέανον) loving possessions, greedy of gain, covetous, Sup. φιλοκτεανώτατος, Il.
φῐλό-κῠβος, ον, fond of dice, Ar.
φῐλο-κῠδής, ές, (κῦδος) loving glory, h. Hom.
φῐλο-κῠνηγέτης, ου, ὁ, = φιλοκύνηγος, Xen.
φῐλο-κύνηγος [ῠ], ον, loving the chase, Plut.
φῐλο-κύων, -κύνος, ὁ, fond of dogs, Plat.
φῐλο-λάκων [ᾰ], ωνος, ὁ, ἡ, fond of the Laconians, Plut.
φῐλο-λήιος, ον, (ληίη) loving booty, h. Hom.
φῐλολογέω, f. ήσω, to love learning, to study, Plut.
φῐλολογία, ἡ, love of learning, studiousness, Isocr.
φῐλό-λογος, ον, fond of speaking, Plat.   2. fond of learning, literary, Lat. studiosus, Arist.
φῐλό-λοίδορος, ον, fond of reviling, abusive, Dem.
φῐλομάθεια, ἡ, love of learning, Plat.; and
φῐλο-μᾰθέω, f. ήσω, to be fond of learning, Plat.   From
φῐλο-μᾰθής, ές, (μαθεῖν) fond of learning, eager after knowledge, Plat.; Sup. φιλομαθέστατος, Xen.; τὸ φιλομαθές = φιλομάθεια, Plat.   2. c. gen. rei, eager after a thing, Id., Xen.
φῐλό-μαντις, εως, ὁ, ἡ, one who takes note of divinations or omens, Luc.
φῐλό-μαστος, ον, loving the breast, Aesch.
φῐλομᾱχέω, f. ήσω, to be eager to fight, Plut.   From
φῐλό-μᾱχος, ον, loving the fight, warlike, Aesch.
φῐλ-όμβρος, ον, (ὄμβρος) rain-loving, Anth.
φῐλο-μήλᾱ, Ion. -λη, ἡ, the nightingale, because, acc. to the legend, Philomela was changed into this bird, Dem. (Deriv. uncertain.)

φῑλ-όμηρος, ον, *fond of Homer*, Strab.

φίλο-μήτωρ, ορος, ὁ, ἡ, (μήτηρ) *loving one's mother*, Plut.

φῑλομ-μειδής, ές, poët. for φιλο-μειδής, (μειδάω) *laughter-loving*, epith. of Aphroditè, Hom., Hes.

φῑλό-μολπος, ον, (μολπή) *loving dance and song*, Pind.

φῑλομουσία, ἡ, *love of the Muses*, Luc. From

φῑλό-μουσος, ον, (μοῦσα) *loving the Muses*, generally, *loving music and the arts*, Ar., Plat., etc.

φῑλομῡθέω, *to be fond of fables*, Strab. ; and

φῑλομῡθία, ἡ, *a love of fables*, Strab. From

φῑλό-μῡθος, ον, *fond of legends* or *fables*, Arist.   II. *fond of talking*, Id.

φῑλο-ναύτης, ου, ὁ, *loving sailors*, Anth.

φῑλονεικέω, f. ήσω, (φιλόνεικος) *to be fond of strife, engage in eager rivalry, be contentious*, φιλονεικῶν *out of contentiousness* or *party spirit*, Thuc., Plat. ; φ. πρός τινα Lys. :—c. acc., φ. τὸ ἐμὲ εἶναι τὸν ἀποκρινόμενον *to be eager* that I should be the answerer, Plat. ; τὰ χείρω φ. *to be so obstinate as to choose* the worst, Thuc.   2. in good sense, *to struggle emulously*, φ. περὶ τῶν καλλίστων Isocr.

φῑλονεικητέον, verb. Adj. of foreg., Isocr.

φῑλονεικία, ἡ, *love of strife, eager rivalry, contentiousness, party-spirit*, Thuc., etc.   2. in good sense, *emulation*, Xen. ; διὰ φιλονεικίαν *eagerly*, Id.

φῑλό-νεικος, ον, *fond of strife, eager for strife, contentious*, Pind., Plat.   2. in good sense, *emulous*, of spirited horses, Xen. : τὸ φιλόνεικον = φιλονεικία, Id. :—Adv. -κως, *in eager rivalry*, Id., Plat., etc.

φῑλο-νύμφιος, ον, *loving the bridegroom or bride*, Anth.

φῑλόξεινος, ον, poët. for φιλόξενος.

φῑλοξενία, Ion. -ίη, ἡ, *hospitality*, Theogn. From

φῑλό-ξενος, poët. -ξεινος, ον, *loving strangers, hospitable*, Od., Aesch. ; παθεῖν φιλόξενον ἔργον *to meet with an act of hospitality*, Pind.

φῑλο-παίγμων, ον, (παίζω) *fond of play, playful, sportive*, Od., Ar.

φῑλό-παις, παιδος, ὁ, ἡ, *loving its young*, χελιδών Anth.

φῑλο-παίσμων, ον, = φιλοπαίγμων, Plat.

φῑλο-παράβολος, ον, *fond of daring, venturous*, Plut.

φῑλό-πατρία, ἡ, *love of one's country, patriotism*, Ar.

φῑλό-πατρις, ιδος, ὁ, ἡ, acc. φιλόπατριν, *loving one's country*, Polyb., Luc.

φῑλο-πάτωρ [ᾰ], ορος, ὁ, ἡ, *loving one's father*, Eur.

φῑλοπευστέω, f. ήσω, *to be fond of inquiry*, Polyb.

φῑλο-πεύστης, ου, ὁ, *fond of enquiring, curious*.

φῑλό-πλεκτος, ον, *usually braided*, Anth.

φῑλό-πλοος, ον, contr. -πλους, ουν, *fond of sailing*, Anth.

φῑλ-οπλος, ον, (ὅπλα) *loving arms*, Anth.

φῑλοπλουτία, ἡ, *love of riches*, Plut. From

φῑλό-πλουτος, ον, *loving riches*, φ. ἅμιλλα *eager pursuit of wealth*, the race *for riches*, Eur.

φῑλοποιέομαι, Med. (φιλοποιός) *to make one's friend, attach to oneself*, τινα Polyb.

φῑλο-ποιητής, οῦ, ὁ, *a friend of poets*, Plat.

φῑλό-ποιμνιος, ον, (ποίμνη) *loving the flock*, Theocr.

φῑλο-ποιός, όν, (ποιέω) *making friends*, Plut.

φῑλό-πολεμος, ον, Ep. φιλο-πτ-, *fond of war, warlike*, Il., Plut. : Adv. -μως, Isocr.

φῑλό-πολις, ὁ, ἡ, poët. φῑλό-πτολις: acc. -πολιν ; pl. -πόλεις ; but also gen. -πόλιδος, pl. -πόλιδες,

-πόλιδας :   I. *loving the city*, Aesch.   II. *loving one's city, patriotic*, Ar., Thuc. ; τὸ φιλόπολι *patriotism*, Thuc.

φῑλο-πολίτης [ῑ], ου, ὁ, *loving one's fellow-citizens*, Plut.

φῑλοπονέω, f. ήσω, (φιλόπονος) *to love labour, work hard, be laborious* or *industrious*, Xen., Plat.

φῑλοπονηρία, ἡ, *a love of bad men and actions*, Theophr.

φῑλο-πόνηρος, ον, *a friend to bad men*, Plut.

φῑλοπονία, ἡ, *love of labour, laboriousness, industry*, Plat. ; φ. τινός *laborious practice* of a thing, Dem.

φῑλό-πονος, ον, *loving labour, laborious, industrious, diligent*, Soph., Plat. :—Sup. -ώτατος, Isocr. :—Adv., φιλοπόνως ἔχειν *to be diligent*, Xen.   2. of things, *toilsome, laborious*, πόλεμος Id.

φῑλοποσία, ἡ, *love of drinking*, Xen., Plat. From

φῑλο-πότης, ου, ὁ, *a lover of drinking, fond of wine*, Hdt., Ar.

φῑλοπραγμοσύνη, ἡ, *a busy disposition, meddlesomeness, restless habits of life*, Plat., Dem. From

φῑλο-πράγμων, gen. ονος, ὁ, ἡ, *fond of business :* in bad sense, *a meddlesome fellow, busybody*, Isae.

φῑλοπροσηγορία, ἡ, *easiness of address*, Isocr. From

φῑλο-προσήγορος, ον, *easy of address, affable*, Isocr.

φῑλο-πρωτεύω, *to strive to be first*, N. T.

φῑλό-πρωτος, ον, *fond of being first :* τὸ φιλόπρωτον *eagerness to be first*, Plut.

φῑλό-πτολεμος, φῑλό-πτολις, poët. for φιλο-πόλεμος, φιλό-πολις.

φῑλό-πῡρος, ον, *loving wheat*, Anth.

φῑλ-οπωριστής, οῦ, ὁ, *loving autumn-fruits*, Anth.

φῑλ-όργιος, ον, (ὄργια) *fond of orgies*, Anth.

φῑλ-όρθιος, ον, *loving what is straight* or *right*, Anth.

φῑλ-ορμίστειρα, ἡ, *she who loves the harbour*, Anth.

φῑλορνῑθία, ἡ, *fondness for birds*, Ar. From

φῑλ-όρνις, ῑθος, ὁ, ἡ, *fond of birds*, Plut.   II. *loved* or *haunted by birds*, Aesch.

φῑλορ-ρώθων, ωνος, ὁ, ἡ, *attached to the nose*, Anth.

φῑλορ-ρώξ, ὁ, ἡ, (ῥάξ) *loving grapes*, Anth.

φῑλ-όρτυξ, ῠγος, ὁ, ἡ, *fond of quails*, Anth.

ΦΙ'ΛΟΣ, η, ον, [ῑ: but voc. φίλε with ῑ in Hom.]:   I. pass. *loved, beloved, dear*, Lat. *amicus, carus*, Hom., etc. ; c. dat. *dear to one*, Id. ; voc. φίλε may be used with neut. nouns, φίλε τέκνον Od. ; a gen. was sometimes added to the voc., φίλ' ἀνδρῶν Theocr. ; ὦ φίλα γυναικῶν Eur. :—often as Subst., φίλος, ὁ, *a friend*, Hom. :—proverb., ἔστιν ὁ φ. ἄλλος αὐτός *a friend* is another self, Arist. ; κοινὰ τὰ τῶν φίλων Plat. :—so in fem. φίλη, ἡ, *a dear one, friend*, Lat. *amica*, Hom., Att. :—φίλον, τό, *an object of love*, Soph. ; τὰ φίλτατα *one's nearest and dearest*, such as wife and children, Trag.   2. of things, *dear, pleasant, welcome*, Hom. :—as predic., φίλον ἐστί or γίγνεταί μοι 'tis *dear* to me, *pleases* me, Lat. *cordi est*, Id., Hdt., etc. ; εἰ τόδ' αὐτῷ φίλον κεκλημένῳ if it *please* him to be so called, Aesch.   3. in Poets, φίλος is used of *one's own* limbs, life, etc., φίλον δ' ἐξαίνυτο θυμόν he took away *dear* life, Il. ; φίλον ἦτορ, φίλα γούνατα, πατὴρ φίλος, φίλη ἄλοχος Hom. ; φίλην ἄγεσθαι *to take as his own* wife, Il.   II. in act. sense, like φίλιος, *loving, friendly*, Hom. ; c. gen., φίλαν ξένων ἄρουραν *friendly* to strangers, Pind. ;

φίλα φρονέειν τινί to feel kindly, Il.; φ. ποιεῖσθαί τινι to make friends with one, Hdt. **III.** Adv. φίλως, φίλως χ' ὁρόῳτε ye would fain see it, Il.; φ. ἐμοί in a manner dear or pleasing to me, Aesch.; φ. δέχεσθαί τινα Xen. **IV.** φίλος has several forms of comparison: 1. Comp. φιλίων [ῐ], ον, Od. 2. Comp. φίλτερος, Sup. φίλτατος, v. sub vocc. 3. Comp. φιλαίτερος, Sup. φιλαίτατος, Xen., Theocr. 4. in Att. μᾶλλον φίλος Aesch., etc.; Sup. μάλιστα φ. Xen.

φῐλό-σῑτος, ον, fond of corn, occupied about it, Xen. **II.** fond of food, fond of eating, Plat.

φῐλό-σκηπτρος, ον, (σκῆπτρον) sceptred, Anth.

φῐλό-σκηπων, ωνος, ὁ, ἡ, loving a staff, of Pan, Anth.

φῐλό-σκόπελος, ον, loving rocks, Anth.

φῐλό-σκώμμων, ον, fond of scoffing or jesting, Hdt.

φῐλοσοφέω, pf. πεφιλοσόφηκα, (φιλόσοφος) to love knowledge, pursue it, philosophise, Lat. philosophari, Hdt., Thuc., etc.; φιλοσοφοῦντά με δεῖ ζῆν, says Socrates, Plat. 2. to teach philosophy, Isocr. **II.** c. acc. to discuss philosophically, to investigate, study, Lat. meditari, Isocr.; φιλοσοφίαν φιλοσοφεῖν to pursue philosophy, Xen. 2. generally, to study a thing, Isocr. Hence

φῐλοσοφητέον, verb. Adj. one must pursue wisdom, Plat., etc.

φῐλοσοφία, ἡ, love of knowledge and wisdom, pursuit thereof, speculation, study, Plat., etc. 2. the systematic treatment of a subject, investigation, Isocr. 3. philosophy, the investigation of truth and nature, Plat., etc. From

φῐλό-σοφος, ὁ, a lover of wisdom, first used by Pythagoras, who called himself φιλόσοφος a lover of wisdom, not σοφός, a sage, Cic.: then in a wide sense of scientific men, learned men, Plat., etc. 2. a philosopher, i. e. one who speculates on the nature of things and truth, Ar., etc.; defined as ὁ τῆς ἀληθείας φιλοθεάμων, Plat. **II.** as Adj. loving knowledge, philosophic, Id.: of arguments, etc., scientific, philosophic, Id.; τὸ φιλόσοφον = φιλοσοφία, Id. **III.** Adv., φιλοσόφως διακεῖσθαι Isocr.; φ. ἔχειν Plat.

φῐλο-σπήλυγξ, υγγος, ὁ, ἡ, fond of grottoes, Anth.

φῐλό-σπονδος, ον, used in drink-offerings, Aesch.

φῐλό-στέφανος, ον, loving crowns, garlanded, h. Hom.

φῐλό-στονος, ον, loving sighs, piteous: Adv. -νως, Aesch.

φῐλοστοργία, ἡ, tender love, affectionateness, Xen.

φῐλό-στοργος, ον, (στέργω) loving tenderly, affectionate, of the love of parents and children, brothers and sisters, Xen., Theocr., etc.; τὸ φιλόστοργον = φιλοστοργία, Xen.:—Adv. φιλοστόργως, Plut.

φῐλο-στρᾰτιώτης, ου, ὁ, the soldier's friend, Xen.

φῐλό-σώματος, ον, (σῶμα) loving the body, Plat.

φῐλό-τεκνος, ον, loving one's children or offspring, Hdt., Eur.

φῐλοτεχνέω, f. ήσω, to love art, practise an art, Plat.

φῐλό-τεχνος, ον, (τέχνη) fond of art, artistic, Plat.: τὸ φιλότεχνον ingenuity, Plut.

φῐλότης, ητος, ἡ, (φίλος) friendship, love, affection, Hom., etc.; φ. τινός friendship with, affection for, Od.; διὰ τὴν λίαν φιλότητα βροτῶν by his over great love for men, Aesch.; ὦ φιλότης = ὦ φίλε, my friend, Plat. Hence

φῐλοτήσιος, α, ον, and ος, ον, Dor. φιλοτάσιος [ᾱ], of

friendship or love, promoting it, Od., Soph. **II.** ἡ φιλοτησία or -ῆσιος (with or without κύλιξ), the cup sacred to friendship, the loving-cup, Theogn., Ar.; φιλοτησίας προπίνειν (where φιλοτησίας is prob. acc. pl.), to drink healths, Dem.

φῐλοτῑμέομαι, f. ήσομαι: aor. 1 ἐφιλοτιμήθην: pf. πεφιλοτίμημαι: (φιλότιμος):—Dep. to love or seek after honour, to be ambitious, emulous, jealous, Ar., etc.; φ. ὅτι .. to be jealous because .., Xen.:—the object of ambition is added with a Prep., φιλ. ἐπί τινι to pride oneself upon it, Id., etc.; ἔν τινι Plat.;—with neut. Adj., ἀεί τι φιλοτιμούμενος pursuing some object of ambition, Xen. 2. c. inf. to strive eagerly and emulously to do a thing, endeavour earnestly, aspire, Id.:—c. acc. et inf. to be anxious that .., Id. Hence

φῐλοτίμημα, ατος, τό, an act of ambition or magnificence, Plut. **II.** rivalry, Luc.; and

φῐλοτῑμία, Ion. -ίη, ἡ, the character of the φιλότιμος, love of distinction, ambition, Eur., Thuc., etc.:—in good sense, Xen.: c. gen. objecti, φ. τινός emulous desire for a thing, Plat., etc.; φ. πρός τινα ambitious rivalry with him, Isocr. 2. ambitious pertinacity, obstinacy, Hdt. 3. ambitious display, prodigality, Dem., Aeschin. **II.** the object coveted, honour, distinction, credit, Dem.

φῐλό-τῑμος, ον, (τιμή) loving honour, covetous of honour, ambitious, emulous, Eur., Plat., etc.; in good sense, Xen., Isocr.:—with abstr. Nouns (in both senses), εὐχά Aesch.; ἦθος Eur.; σοφίαι Ar.; φ. ἐπί τινι eager to be honoured for a thing, covetous of distinction in .., ἐπὶ σοφίᾳ, ἐπ' ἀρετῇ Plat. 2. emulously prodigal, lavish, Dem. 3. in pass. sense, = πολυτίμητος, august, Aesch. **II.** Adv. -μως, ambitiously, emulously, φ. ἔχειν to vie emulously, Plat.; φ. ἔχειν πρός τι to strive, exert oneself eagerly after a thing, Xen.

φῐλο-τοιοῦτος, ὁ, fond of such and such things, Arist.

φῐλό-τύραννος, ον, friend of tyranny, Plut.

φῐλό-φθογγος, ον, loving noise, noisy, Anth.

φῐλό-φιλος, ον, loving one's friends, Arist.

φῐλοφρονέομαι, f. ήσομαι: aor. 1 ἐφιλοφρονησάμην and -φρονήθην: Dep. (φιλόφρων):—to treat affectionately, to shew kindness to, τινα Hdt., Plat.; φ. τινα τῇ δικέλλῃ to entertain him with a blow of the mattock, Luc. 2. c. dat., φιλοφρονήσασθαί τινι to shew a favour to one, Xen.:—aor. 1 pass. φιλοφρονηθῆναι, in a reciprocal sense, to shew kindness one to another, to greet one another, Id.; so φιλοφρονήσασθαι ἀλλήλους Id. 3. absol. to be of a kindly, cheerful temper, Id.

φῐλοφροσύνη, ἡ, (φιλόφρων) friendliness, kindliness, Il.; τινός towards one, Hdt.; πρός τινα Plat.: pl. friendly greetings, Pind. **II.** cheerfulness, Xen.

φῐλοφρόσυνος, ον, = sq., Anth.

φῐλό-φρων, ονος, ὁ, ἡ, (φρήν) kindly minded, kindly, friendly, affable, Pind., Aesch., etc.: Adv., φιλοφρόνως ἀσπάζεσθαι to greet kindly, Hdt.; φ. ἔχειν πρός τινα to be kindly minded towards one, Xen.

φῐλο-χορευτής, οῦ, ὁ, friend of the choral dance, Ar.

φῐλό-χορος, ον, loving the choir or choral dance, Aesch.

φῐλοχρηματέω, f. ήσω, to love money, Plat. Hence

φῐλοχρημᾰτία, ἡ, *love of money*, Plat.

φῐλο-χρημᾰτιστής, οῦ, ὁ, *fond of money-making*, Plat.

φῐλό-χρήμᾰτος, ον, (χρῆμα) *loving money, fond of money*, Plat., etc. : τὸ φιλοχρήματον = φιλοχρηματία, Id.; Sup. -ώτατος, Diod. Adv., φιλοχρημάτως ἔχειν = φιλοχρηματεῖν, Isocr.

φῐλοχρημοσύνη, ἡ, = φιλοχρηματία, Plat., Anth.

φῐλό-χρηστος, ον, *loving goodness or honesty*, Xen.

φῐλό-χρῡσος, ον, *fond of gold*, Luc., Anth.

φῐλοχωρέω, f. ήσω, (φιλόχωρος) *to be fond of a place, to abide there always, haunt it*, Hdt. Hence

φῐλοχωρία, ἡ, *fondness for a place, love of one's haunts, local attachment*, Ar.

φῐλό-χωρος, ον, (χώρα) *fond of a place.*

φῐλό-ψευδής, ές, gen. έος, *fond of lies or lying*, Il., Plat.

φῐλό-ψογος, ον, *fond of blame, censorious*, Eur., Plat.

φῐλοψῡχέω, f. ήσω, (φιλόψυχος) *to love one's life: to be cowardly or faint-hearted*, Tyrtae., Eur. Hence

φῐλοψῡχητέον, verb. Adj. *one must love life*, Plat.; and

φῐλοψῡχία, Ion. -ίη, ἡ, *love of life*, Hdt., Plat.

φῐλό-ψῡχος, ον, (ψυχή) *loving one's life, cowardly, dastardly, faint-hearted*, Eur.

φίλτατος, η, ον, irreg. Sup. of φίλος, Hom., Trag.

φίλτερος, α, ον, irreg. Comp. of φίλος, Hom., Hes.

φιλτραῖος, ὁ, *Charmer*, name of a mouse, Batr. From

φίλτρον (properly φίλητρον, from φιλέω), τό, *a love-charm*, (cf. Shakspeare's 'medicines to make me love him'), ἐστὶν φίλτρα μοι θελκτήρια ἔρωτος Eur.; of the robe of Nessus by which Deïanira hoped to win back the love of Hercules, Soph. 2. generally, *a charm, spell*, as a means of winning or influencing others, hence the bit is called φ. ἵππειον, Pind.; Apollo's oracles are φίλτρα τόλμης *spells to produce* boldness, Aesch.; children are a φίλτρον *of love* to their parents, Eur., etc. 3. in pl. *love, affection*, Id.

φῐλ-ύδρηλος, ον, *loving moisture*, Anth.

φῐλύρα [ῠ], Ion. -ρη, ἡ, *the lime or linden tree*, Lat. tilia, Hdt.

φῐλύρῐνος [ῠ], η, ον, *of the lime or linden tree, light as linden wood*, Ar.

φῐλ-ωρείτης, ου, ὁ, (ὄρος) *a lover of mountains*, Anth.

ΦΙ͂ΜΟ͂Σ, ὁ, with heterog. pl. φῑμά, τά, *a muzzle*, Lat. capistrum, Luc. II. *the nose-band* of a horse's bridle, fitted with pipes through which the horses' breath made a whistling sound, Aesch. III. *a kind of cup*, used as *a dice-box*, Lat. fritillus, Aeschin.

φῑμόω, f. ώσω, *to muzzle, shut up* as with a muzzle, φ. τῷ ξύλῳ τὸν αὐχένα *to make fast* his neck in the pillory, Ar. : metaph. *to muzzle, put to silence*, N. T.: Pass., aor. 1 imper. φιμώθητι *be thou silenced*, Ib. -φιν, v. sub -φι.

ΦΙΤΡΟ͂Σ, ὁ, *a block of wood, log*, Hom.

φῑτυ, τό, poët. for φίτυμα, Ar.

φίτῡμα, ατος, τό, (φιτύω) *a shoot, scion*, of a son, Aesch.

φῑτῡ-ποίμην, ενος, ὁ, *a tender of plants, gardener*, Aesch.

φῑτύω, f. ύσω [ῡ]: aor. 1 ἐφίτῡσα:—poët. for φυτεύω when the 1st syll. is to be long, *to sow, plant, beget, call into being*, Trag.:—Med. of the woman, *to produce, bear*, Hes.; Ep. 2 sing. f. φιτύσεαι Mosch.

*φλάζω, intr. form of φλάω, only in aor. 2 ἔφλᾰδον, *to be rent with a noise*, Aesch.

φλαττόθρατ and φλαττοθραττοφλαττόθρατ, Comic

words in Ar., meant to ridicule a bombastic style—'sound without sense.'

φλαυρίζω, f. ίσω, Att. for φαυλίζω, Plut. From

φλαῦρος, α, ον, collat. form of φαῦλος, *petty, paltry, trivial*, Solon, Pind., Hdt. 2. *paltry, sorry, indifferent, bad*, Aesch., Soph.; φλαῦρον ἐργάζεσθαί τινα *to do one a mischief*, Ar.; φλαῦρον εἰπεῖν τινα *to speak disparagingly* of him, Id. 3. *useless*, Soph. II. of persons, οὐ φλαυροτάτους τιμωρούς *not the meanest* or *weakest* avengers, Hdt.; τῆς στρατιῆς τὸ φλαυρότατον *the least serviceable part*, Id. 2. *shabby, plain*, of personal appearance, Id. 3. *bad*, opp. to χρηστός, Eur. III. Adv., φλαύρως ἔχειν *to be ill*, Hdt.; φλ. ἔχειν τινός *to be ill off* for a thing, Thuc.; but, φλαύρως ἔχειν τὴν τέχνην *to know an art badly*, Id.; φλ. ἀκούειν, like Lat. male audire, *to be ill spoken of*, Id.

φλαυρότης, ητος, ἡ, = φαυλότης, Plut.

φλαυρ-ουργός, όν, (*ἔργω) *working badly*, ἀνὴρ φλ. *a sorry workman*, Soph.

ΦΛΑ'Ω, impf. 3 sing. ἔφλα: f. φλάσω [ᾰ]: aor. 1 ἔφλᾰσα:—like θλάω, *to crush, pound*, Pind. 2. *to bruise with the teeth, eat up, eat greedily*, Id.

φλεγέθω, poët. form of φλέγω, only in pres. : I. trans. *to burn, scorch, burn up*, Il. :—Pass., ὄφρα πυρὶ φλεγεθοίατο νεκροί Ib. II. intr. *to blaze, flare up*, of fire, Ib.; of the sun, Soph., Eur.

φλέγμα, ατος, τό, (φλέγω) *flame, fire, heat*, Il. II. *inflammation, heat*: also *phlegm, a morbid humour*, Lat. pituita, Hdt.:—in Poets, like χολή, *gall, bile*, Anth.

φλεγμαίνω, aor. 1 ἐφλέγμᾱνα and -ηνα: (φλέγμα):—*to be heated, inflamed, to fester*, φλεγμαίνουσα πόλις, opp. to ὑγιής, Plat.

φλεγμᾰτ-ώδης, ες, (εἶδος) *inflammatory*, Plat.

Φλέγρα, ας, ἡ, *Phlegra*, an ancient name for Pallené in Thrace, Hdt.; Φλέγρας πεδίον, in which the giants are said to have been conquered by the gods, Pind., Ar.; Φλεγραία πλάξ Aesch.; also Φλέγραι, Pind.

φλεγύας, ου, ὁ, (φλέγω) *fiery red, red-brown*, of the eagle (μόρφνος), Hes.

φλεγυρός, ά, όν, (φλέγω) *burning*: metaph. *ardent*, Ar.

ΦΛΕ'ΓΩ, f. φλέξω : aor. 1 ἔφλεξα:—Pass., aor. 1 ἐφλέχθην: aor. 2 ἐφλέγην.

A. trans. *to burn, burn up*, Il., Aesch. :—Pass. *to take fire, blaze up*, Il. 2. metaph. *to kindle, inflame* with passion, Soph., Eur. :—Pass., like Lat. uri, *to burn with passion, be inflamed*, Soph., Ar. II. *to light up*, Ζεὺς βέλος φλέγων *making it blaze or flash*, Aesch.; metaph., ἄταν οὐρανίαν φλέγων *letting the flame of mischief blaze up* to heaven, Soph.:—Pass. *to blaze up, be a-light*, Aesch. 2. metaph. *to make illustrious* or *famous*, Lat. illustrare, Pind.:—Pass. *to be or become so*, Id.

B. intr. *to burn, flame, blaze*, Aesch., Soph.; of armour, *to flash*, Eur. 2. metaph. *to break forth*, of passion, Aesch. 3. *to shine forth, become famous*, Pind.

φλέδων, ονος, ὁ, ἡ, (φλέω) *a babbler;* of a woman, Aesch.

φλέξις, ιδος, ἡ, *an unknown bird*, Arist.

ΦΛΕ'Ψ, ἡ, gen. φλεβός, (φλέω?) *a vein*, Il., etc.; φλέβα σχάζειν *to open a vein*, Xen. 2. *a vein* of metal, Id.

ΦΛΕ´Ω, only in pres., *to teem with abundance, abound,* Aesch.

ΦΛΕ´ΩΣ, ω, ὁ, a kind of *flowering rush* or *reed,* Ar.

φληνάφάω, *to chatter, babble,* Ar. From

φλήνάφος, ὁ, (φλέω) *idle talk, nonsense,* Luc.

φλῑά, ἡ, in pl. φλιαί, = σταθμοί, *the doorposts, jambs,* Od., Bion.; in sing., Theocr.

Φλιάσιος, α, ον, (Φλιοῦς) *Phliasian,* Hdt., etc.

φλίβω [ῑ], dialectic form of θλίβω, Theocr.

Φλιοῦς, οῦντος, ὁ, *Phliûs,* in the North of Peloponnesus, Hdt., Thuc.

φλόγεος, α, ον, (φλόξ) *burning, flaming,* Il., Eur.

φλογερός, ά, όν, (φλόξ) *flaming, fiery-red,* Eur.

φλογίζω, f. Att. ιῶ, (φλόξ) *to set on fire, burn, burn up,* Soph.:—Pass. *to be set on fire, to blaze, flame,* Id.: metaph., *of the tongue,* N. T. Hence

φλογιστός, ή, όν, verb. Adj. *burnt up,* Soph.

φλογμός, ὁ, (φλέγω) *flame, blaze,* as of lightning, Eur.; *fiery heat,* Aesch.; *feverish heat,* Luc.

φλογόεις, εσσα, εν, = φλόγεος, Anth.

φλογόομαι, (φλόξ) Pass. *to blaze,* Theophr.

φλογ-ωπός, όν, (ὤψ) *fiery-looking, flaming,* Aesch.; φλ. σήματα *omens by fire* (not *lightning*), Id.

φλόγωσις, εως, ἡ, (φλογόομαι) *burning heat, inflammation,* Thuc.

φλογ-ώψ, ὁ, ἡ, = φλογωπός, Aesch.

φλόϊνος, η, ον, *of* or *from the water-plant* φλέως (Ion. φλοῦς), ἐσθῆτες φλόϊναι *mat-*garments, Hdt.

φλοιός, ὁ, (φλέω) *the bark* of trees, *bast* or *bass, smooth bark,* Il., Hdt., etc.

φλοῖσβος, ὁ, (φλέω) *any confused noise, the noise of battle, the battle-din,* Il.; *the roar* of the sea, Aesch.

φλόξ, ἡ, gen. φλογός, (φλέγω) *a flame* of fire, Hom.; φλόγα δαίειν *to kindle a flame,* Il.; ἐγείρειν Xen.; σβέσαι *to put* it *out,* Thuc.; also of lightning, Aesch., Eur.; *of the heat of the sun,* Aesch.; *the flame* or *flash* of a bright helmet, Il.;—φλ. οἴνου *the fiery strength* of wine, Eur.

φλόος, ὁ, (φλέω) rarer form of φλοιός, Anth.   II. φλοῦς, Ion. for φλέως, Hdt.

φλυᾱρέω, Ion. φλυηρέω, f. ήσω, (φλύᾱρος) *to talk nonsense, play the fool,* Lat. *nugari,* Hdt., Ar.:— c. acc. cogn., φλυαρίαν φλυαρεῖν Plat. Hence

φλυᾱρία, ἡ, *silly talk, nonsense, foolery,* Ar., Plat., etc.; often in pl. *fooleries,* Lat. *nugae,* Plat.

φλύᾱρος, ὁ, (φλύω) *silly talk, foolery, nonsense,* Ar.   II. *a silly talker, tatler, babbler,* Plat., N. T.

φλυᾱρ-ώδης, ες, (εἶδος) *fooling,* Plut.

φλύζω, v. φλύω.

φλυηρέω, Ion. for φλυᾱρέω.

φλύκταινα, ἡ, (φλύω) *a blister* caused by rowing, Ar.: of *pustules* caused by plague, Thuc.   2. *a blister* on bread, Luc.

φλύω, f. σω: aor. 1 ἔφλῡσα, as if from φλύζω, (φλέω): *to boil over, bubble up:* metaph. *to overflow with words, talk idly, babble, brag,* Aesch.

φοβερός, ά, όν, (φόβος) *fearful,* whether act. or pass.:   I. act. *causing fear, dreadful, terrible, formidable,* Hdt., Aesch., etc.; πλήθει φ. *formidable* only from numbers, Thuc.; c. inf., φ. ἰδεῖν, φ. προσιδέσθαι *fearful* to behold, Aesch., Eur.: τὸ ξύνηθες τοῖς πολίταις φοβερόν the *terror* habitual to the people, Thuc.   2. *matter*

for *fear, regarded with fear,* οὐδὲ ὅρκος φ. Id.; φοβεροὶ ἦσαν μὴ ποιήσειαν they *gave cause for fear* lest . . , Xen.; τὸ φ. *terror, danger,* Id.; φοβερόν [ἐστι] μή . . there is *reason to dread* that . . , Id.   II. pass. *feeling fear, afraid, timid,* Soph., Thuc., etc.   2. *caused by fear, panic,* Thuc.; φ. φροντίδες *anxious* thoughts, Plat.   III. Adv. -ρῶς, in both senses, Xen., etc.; Comp., φοβερώτερον, Sup., -ώτατα, Id. Hence

φοβερότης, ητος, ἡ, *terribleness,* Arist.

φοβεσι-στράτη [ᾰ], ἡ, *scarer of hosts,* Ar.

φοβέω (φόβος): 3 pl. imper. φοβεόντων: Ion. impf. φοβέεσκον:—f. -ήσω: aor. 1 ἐφόβησα:—Pass. and Med., Ion. 2 sing. φόβεαι; Ion. impf. φοβέο or φοβεῦ, Ep. 3 pl. impf. φοβέοντο:—f. φοβήσομαι, later φοβηθήσομαι: aor. 1 ἐφοβήθην, Ep. 3 pl. ἐφόβηθεν or φόβηθεν:—pf. πεφόβημαι: plqpf. ἐφοβήμην, Ep. 3 pl. -ήατο.

A. Act. *to put to flight,* Lat. *fugo,* Il.   II. *to strike with fear, to terrify, frighten, alarm,* Lat. *terreo,* Hdt., Att.; πόνος ὁ μὴ φοβῶν *free from alarm,* Soph.; φοβήσαντες κατεστήσαντο τὴν πολιτείαν they *established* it *by terror,* Plat.

B. Pass. and Med. *to be put to flight, to flee affrighted, flee,* Hom.; φοβηθείς *in flight,* Il.; ὑπό τινος φοβέεσθαι *to flee* before him, Ib.   II. *to be seized with fear, be affrighted, fear,* Hdt., Att.; φοβεῖσθαι εἴς or πρός τι *to be alarmed at a thing,* Soph.; ἀμφί τινι *to fear about a thing,* Hdt.; περί τινος Xen.; περί τινι Thuc., etc.:—φοβεῖσθαι μή *to fear lest a thing will be,* Lat. *vereri ne . . ,* Eur., etc.; so, φ. ὅπως μή . . Thuc.; so, φοβ. ὅτι . . , ὡς . . *to fear that . . ,* not like Lat. *vereri ut . . ,* Id., etc.:—φοβ. c. inf. *to fear to do, be afraid of doing,* Aesch., Trag.   2. c. acc. pers. *to stand in awe of, dread, fear,* Soph., etc.: c. acc. rei, *to fear* or *fear about* a thing, Id.

ΦΟ´ΒΗ, ἡ, *a lock* or *curl of hair,* Aesch., Soph.   2. *the mane* of a horse, Eur.   II. metaph., like κόμη, *the tresses* of trees, *foliage,* Soph., Eur.

φόβηθεν, Ep. 3 pl. aor. 1 pass. of φοβέω.

φόβημα, ατος, τό, (φοβέω) *a terror,* τινος to one, Soph.

φοβητέον, verb. Adj. of φοβέομαι, *one must fear,* Plat.   2. φοβητέος, α, ον, *to be feared,* Id.

φοβητικός, ή, όν, (φοβέομαι) *liable to fear, fearful, timid,* Arist.

φοβητός, ή, όν, (φοβέομαι) *to be feared,* τινι Soph.

φόβητρον, τό, (φοβέω) *a scarecrow, terror,* in pl. *terrors,* Plat., N. T.

φόβος, ὁ, (φέβομαι) *flight,* Lat. *fuga,* the only sense in Hom.; φόβονδε = φύγαδε, μή τι φόβονδ᾽ ἀγόρευε *counsel* not *to flight,* Il., etc.:—Φόβος is personified as son of Ares, Ib., Hes.   II. *panic fear,* such as *causes flight,* στρατῷ φ. ἐμβάλλειν Hdt.:—then generally, *fear, terror,* properly of *the outward show of fear,* and so distinguished from δέος (*the sensation of fear*), Aesch., etc.: the Object of fear is in gen., *fear* of another, Id., etc.; so φ. ἀπό τινος Xen.; ἔκ τινος Aesch.; πρός τινος Soph.;—but, φ. περί or ὑπέρ τινος *fear for* or *concerning . . ,* Thuc.:—with Verbs, ποιεῖν or παρέχειν τινί Xen.; φόβον ἐμβάλλειν, ἐντιθέναι τινί *to strike terror* into one, Lat. *metum incutere*

alicui, Xen., etc. ;—of the person who feels fear, φόβον λαμβάνειν Eur. ; φόβος ἔχει με Aesch. ; φ. ἐμπίπτει μοι Xen. ; διὰ φόβου ἔρχομαι Eur.:—also in pl., Aesch., etc.   **2.** *an object of terror, a terror*; φόβος ἀκοῦσαι *a terror* to hear, Hdt. :—pl., ἣν φόβους λέγῃ Soph.

φοιβάζω, f. άσω, (Φοῖβος) *to prophesy*, Anth.

φοιβάς, άδος, ἡ, *a priestess of Phoebus:* generally, *a prophetess*, Eur.

φοιβαστικός, ή, όν, (φοιβάζω) *prophetic:* c. gen., φ. χρησμῶν *uttering* oracles, Plut.

φοιβάω, f. ήσω (φοῖβος) *to cleanse, purify*, Theocr.

Φοίβειος, α, ον, and ος, ον, Ion. **Φοιβήιος**, η, ον :— *of Phoebus, sacred to him*, Hdt., Eur.

Φοίβη, ἡ, Lat. *Phoebe*, one of the daughters of Uranus and Gaia, Hes. ; mother of Phoebus, Aesch.

Φοιβηίς, ίδος, poët. fem. of Φοίβειος, Anth.

Φοιβό-ληπτος, ον, *possessed by Phoebus*, Plut.:—Ion. **Φοιβό-λαμπτος**, Hdt.

φοῖβος, η, ον, (prob. from φάος) *bright, radiant*, Aesch.   **II.** as prop. n., **Φοῖβος**, ὁ, *Phoebus*, i.e. *the Bright* or *Pure:* Hom. commonly joins Φοῖβος Ἀπόλλων, but also has Φοῖβος alone.

φοινήεις, εσσα, εν, (φοινός) *blood-red*, Il., Mosch.

φοινίκ-άνθεμος, ον, (ἄνθεμον) *with purple flowers*, Pind.

φοινίκεος [ῐ], έα, εον, (φοῖνιξ B) *purple-red, purple* or *crimson*, and (generally) *red*, Lat. *puniceus*, Hdt., Pind.:—Att. contr. **φοινίκοῦς**, ᾶ, οῦν, Xen.

Φοινίκη [ῐ], ἡ, *Phoenicia*, Od., etc.; cf. Φοῖνιξ.   **II.** *the country of Carthage*, Eur.

φοινίκήϊος, η, ον, Ion. for φοινίκειος, *of the date-palm*, ἐσθὴς φοινικηΐη a garment *of palm leaves*, Hdt. ; φ. οἶνος *palm-wine*, Id.   **II.** *Phoenician*, Id. ; Φοινικήϊα γράμματα, of the ancient Ionic alphabet, Id.

Φοινικικός, ή, όν, *Phoenician*, Hdt., etc. ; sometimes to express great antiquity, Plat. :—later, *Punic*, to express treachery, Polyb.   **II.** φοινικικός = φοινίκεος : metaph., κακὰ φοινικικά ' of deep dye,' Ar.

φοινικιοῦς, οῦσσα, οῦν, = φοινίκεος, Ar.

φοινικίς, ίδος, ἡ, (φοῖνιξ) *a red* or *purple cloth*, Ar., Xen.   **2.** *a red cloak*, Ar. ; φοινικίδ᾽ ὀξεῖαν πάνυ *a red cloak* as bright as bright can be, Id.   **3.** *a red curtain* or *carpet*, Aeschin.   **4.** *a red flag*, Lys., Polyb.

φοινικιστής, οῦ, ὁ, (φοῖνιξ B) *with the Persians, a wearer of purple*, i. e. *one of the highest rank*, Lat. *purpuratus*, Xen.

Φοινικιστί, Adv. *in the Phoenician tongue*, Polyb.

φοινικό-βαπτος, ον, *purple-dyed*, ἐσθήματα Aesch.

φοινικο-βατέω, *to climb palms*, Luc.

φοινικο-δάκτυλος, ον, *crimson-fingered*, Arist.

φοινικόεις, εσσα, εν, (φοῖνιξ), = φοινίκεος, *dark-red, purple* or *crimson*, Hom., Hes. [In hexam., φοινικόεσ- σαν, -όεντα, are pronounced as if contracted.]

φοινικό-κροκος, ον, (κρόκη) *of purple woof*, Pind.

φοινικό-λοφος, ον, *purple* or *crimson-crested*, Eur.

φοινικό-πάρῃος [ᾰ], ον, Ion. for -πάρειος, *red-cheeked*, epith. of ships, the bows of which were painted red, Od.

φοινικό-πεζα, ἡ, *ruddy-footed*, epith. of Demeter : prob. from the colour of ripe corn, Virgil's *rubicunda Ceres*, Pind.

φοινικό-πτερος, ον, *red-feathered:* name of a water-bird, perh. *the flamingo*, Ar.

φοινικο-σκελής, ές, (σκέλος) *red-legged*, Eur.

φοινικο-στερόπας, α, ὁ, Dor. for -στερόπης, *hurler of red lightnings*, Ζεύς Pind.

φοινικό-στολος, ον, *sent by Phoenicians*, Φοιν. ἔγχεα, i. e. ἔγχεα τοῦ τῶν Φοινίκων στόλου, Pind.

φοινίκοῦς, ῆ, οῦν, v. sub φοινίκεος.

φοινικο-φαής, ές, (φάος) *ruddy-glancing*, πούς Eur.

Φοῖνιξ, ῖκος, ὁ, ἡ, *a Phoenician*, Hom.   **2.** fem., Φοίνισσα γυνή Od., Eur. ; χθών, νῆσος Eur.

φοῖνιξ, ῖκος, ὁ, appellat. *a purple-red, purple* or *crimson*, because the discovery and earliest use of this colour was ascribed to the Phoenicians, Hom.   **2.** as Adj., ὁ, ἡ, (also φοίνισσα as fem. in Pind.), *red, dark red*, of a *bay* horse, Il. ; of *red* cattle, Pind. ; of fire, Id., Eur. :—φοῖνιξ and its derivs. included all *dark reds*, from crimson to purple, while the *brighter shades* were denoted by πορφύρεος, ἁλουργής, κόκκινος.   **II.** *the date-palm, palm*, Od., Eur., etc.   **III.** the fabulous bird *phoenix*, which came from Arabia to Egypt every 500 years, Hdt. :—proverb., φοίνικος ἔτη βιοῦν Luc.

φοίνιος, α, ον, and ος, ον, (φοινός) poët. for φόνιος, when the first syll. is to be long, *of* or *like blood, blood-red, red*, Od., Aesch., Soph.   **II.** *bloody, blood-stained, murderous*, Pind., Aesch., etc.

Φοίνισσα, φοίνισσα, fem. of Φοῖνιξ, φοῖνιξ.

φοινίσσω, f. ξω, (φοινός) *to redden, make red*, Orac. ap. Hdt., Eur. :—Pass. *to be* or *become red*, Soph., Eur.

φοινός, ή, όν, (φόνος) *blood-red*, Il. : *blood-stained, murderous*, h. Hom.

φοιτάλεος, α, ον, and ος, ον, (φοιτάω) *roaming wildly about*, Mosch.   **II.** act. *driving madly about, maddening*, Aesch. ; Eur.

φοιταλιώτης, ου, ὁ, of Bacchus, *the roamer*, Anth.

φοιτάς, άδος, (φοιτάω) fem. Adj. *roaming madly*, of Cassandra, Aesch. ; of the Bacchantes, Eur. ; φ. νόσος *madness, frenzy*, Soph. ; φ. ἐμπορίη, of commerce *by sea*, Anth. ;—also used with a neut. Subst., φοιτάσι πτεροῖς on *wandering wings*, Eur.

φοιτάω, Ion. -έω: impf., Ep. 3 dual φοιτήτην for ἐφοιτάτην : (φοῖτος) :—*to go to and fro, up and down, to stalk* or *roam about*, Hom., etc. ; διὰ νηὸς φ. *to keep going* about the ship, Od. ; horses *at pasture*, Hdt. ; of hounds *casting about* for the scent, Xen.   **2.** *to roam wildly about*, Hom., Soph. ; of the priests of Cybelé, Anth.   **3.** *to resort* to a person as a friend, φ. παρά τινα *to visit* him, Plat. ; *to resort constantly* to a person or place for any purpose, ἐφοίτεον παρὰ Δηιόκεα δικασόμενοι Hdt. ; φ. ἔς τε ἀγορὴν καὶ ἐξ ἀγορῆς Id. ; φ. πρὸς τοὺς Ἀθηναίους, of embassies, Thuc. ; φοιτᾶν ἐπὶ τὰς θύρας τινός *to frequent, wait* at a great man's door, Hdt. :—so, of a dream, *to haunt* one, ἐν ὀνείρασι Eur., Plat.   **4.** *to resort to* a person as a teacher, παρὰ τὸν Σωκράτη Plat. ; παῖς ὢν ἐφοίτας ἐς τίνος διδασκάλου [οἶκον] ; Ar. ; absol. *to go to school*, Plat., Dem.   **II.** of things, *to come in regularly, be imported*, ἐξ ἐσχάτης [γῆς] ὅτε κασσίτερος ἡμῖν φοιτᾷ καὶ τὸ ἤλεκτρον Hdt. ; σῖτός σφισι πολλὸς ἐφοίτα corn *came in* to them in plenty, Id. : —also, of *the coming in of tribute* or *taxes*, Lat. *redire*, τάλαντον ἀργυρίου Ἀλεξάνδρῳ ἡμέρης ἑκάστης ἐφοίτα a talent of silver *came in* to Alexander every

day, Id. **2.** of *fits* of pain, ἥδε [νόσος] ὀξεῖα φοιτᾷ καὶ ταχεῖ' ἀπέρχεται Soph.

φοίτησις, εως, ἡ, *a constant going,* mostly in pl., Xen.: esp. *a going to school,* Plat.

φοιτητής, οῦ, ὁ, (φοιτάω I. 4) *a scholar, pupil,* Plat.

ΦΟΙ῀ΤΟΣ, ὁ, *a constant going* or *coming:*—metaph. *wandering of mind,* Aesch.

φολκός, ὁ, found only in Il., as epith. of Thersites, prob. *bandy-legged,* Lat. *valgus.* (Deriv. uncertain.)

φόλλις, εως, ὁ, the Lat. *follis, bellows,* Anth.

φόναξ, ακος, ὁ, (φόνος) *eager for blood,* Xen.

φονάω, Desiderative, *to be athirst for blood, to be murderous,* Soph.; part. pl. dat. fem. φονώσαις Id.

φόνευμα, ατος, τό, (φονεύω) *that which is destined for slaughter,* Eur.

φονεύς, ὁ, gen. έως Ep. ῆος; acc. φονέᾶ or φονέᾰ: nom. pl. φονέες, contr. φονεῖς; acc. φονέας; contr. φονεῖς: (*φένω):—*a murderer, slayer, homicide,* Hom., Hdt., Att.; of the sword on which Ajax had thrown himself, Soph.:—also as fem., *a murderess,* Eur.; as Adj., φονέα χεῖρα *murdering* hand, Id. Hence

φονεύω, f. σω, *to murder, kill, slay,* Hdt., Aesch., etc.:—Pass. *to be slain,* Eur., Thuc.

φονή, ἡ, (*φένω) *slaughter, murder,* always in pl., Il.; ἐν τῇσι φονῇσιν εἶναι to be in *the act of slaying,* Hdt.; ἐν φοναῖς πεσών Aesch.; σπᾶν φοναῖς to rend *murderously,* Soph.; ἄπεστιν ἐν φοναῖς θηροκτόνοις he is absent *a-killing* game, Eur.

φονικός, ή, όν, (φόνος) *inclined to slay, murderous, bloody, sanguinary,* Thuc., Plat. **II.** *of murder* or *homicide,* φ. δίκαι trials *for homicide,* Arist.; φ. νόμοι laws *respecting homicide,* Dem.; τὰ φ. *murderous acts, murder, homicide,* Isocr.

φόνιος, ον, and ος, α, ον, (φόνος) poët. form of φονικός, *of blood, bloody,* Aesch., Eur. **II.** *bloody, blood-stained, blood-reeking, murderous,* Trag.:—neut. pl. as Adv., φόνια δερκόμενος Ar. **2.** of actions, etc., *bloody, murderous, deadly,* Eur. Cf. φοίνιος.

φονο-λῐβής, ές, (λίβος) *blood-dripping, blood-reeking,* Aesch.

φονό-ρῡτος, ον, metri grat. for φονόρ-ρυτος, *blood-reeking,* Aesch.

φόνος, ὁ, (*φένω) *murder, homicide, slaughter,* Hom., Hes., etc.; φ. Ἑλληνικός *a slaughter* of Greeks, Hdt.: in pl., φόνοι τ' ἀνδροκτασίαι τε Od.; φόνοι, στάσεις, ἔρις, μάχαι Soph. **2.** in law, *murder, homicide,* φόνου διώκειν τινά to prosecute one *for* murder, Antipho; φ. ἑκούσιος and ἀκούσιος *murder and manslaughter,* Dem. **3.** *blood shed in murder, gore,* ἀμ φόνον, ἀν νέκυας Il.; also, ἐρυγόμενοι φόνον αἵματος = φόνιον αἷμα, Ib.; ἐμοῦσα θρόμβους φόνου vomiting clots *of blood,* Aesch., etc. **4.** *a corpse,* τὸν Ἑλένας φόνον Eur. **II.** of the agent of slaughter, φόνον ἔμμεναι ἡρώεσσι to be *a death* to heroes, Il.; φόνος γενέσθαι τινί Od.

φοξός, ή, όν, *pointed,* epith. of Thersites, φοξὸς κεφαλήν *peaked* in head, having a *sugar-loaf* head, Il. (Deriv. uncertain.)

φορά, ἡ, (φέρω) *a carrying,* Soph.; ψήφου φ. *the giving* one's vote, voting, Eur. **2.** *a bringing in* of money, *payment,* Thuc., Xen. **3.** *a bringing forth, productiveness,* Plat. **II.** (from Pass. φέρομαι) *a being borne* or *carried along, motion, movement,* ἡ τῶν ἄστρων φορά Id. **2.** *rapid motion, a rush,* Lat. *impetus,* Dem. **III.** (also from Pass.) *that which is borne, a load, freight, burden,* Plut. **2.** *that which is brought in* or *paid as rent* or *tribute,* Thuc., Xen., etc. **3.** *that which is brought forth, fruit, produce, a crop,* Arist.:—metaph., φορὰ προδοτῶν *a large crop* of traitors, Dem.

φοράδην [ᾰ], (φέρομαι) Adv. *borne along, borne* or *carried in a litter,* or the like, as a sick person, Eur., Dem. **2.** *with rushing motion, violently,* Soph.

φορβάς, άδος, ὁ, ἡ, (φέρβω) *giving pasture* or *food, feeding,* Soph. **II.** *in the pasture, out at grass, grazing with the herd,* Eur.

φορβεία, ἡ, (φορβή) *a feeding-string,* i. e. *the halter by which a horse is tied to the manger,* Xen. **II.** *a mouthband* of leather *put like a halter* round the lips of pipers, to assist them in blowing, Ar.

φορβή, ἡ, (φέρβω) *pasture, food, fodder, forage,* Il., Hdt.; of birds of prey, Soph.

φορεῖον, τό, (φέρω) *a litter,* Lat. *lectīca,* Dinarch.

φορεύς, gen. έως, Ion. ῆος, ὁ, (φέρω) *a bearer, carrier,* Il.: ἵππος φορεύς a *pack*-horse, Plut.

φορέω, Ep. 3 sing. subj. φορέῃσι, Ep. inf. φορῆναι, φορήμεναι (as if from φόρημι):—impf. ἐφόρεον, Ion. ἐφόρευν, φορέεσκον: f. φορήσω: aor. 1 ἐφόρησα, Ep. φόρησα:—Frequent. of φέρω, *to bear* or *carry constantly, to be used to carry,* ἵπποι οἳ φορέεσκον Πηλείωνα Il.; of a slave, ὕδωρ ἐφόρει Od.; so, ἀγγελίας φορέειν *to serve as a messenger* (ἀγγελίην φέρειν simply *to carry* a message), Hdt.; φ. θρεπτήρια, of Oedipus *carrying about* food in a wallet, Soph. **2.** commonly of clothes and armour, *to bear constantly, wear,* Lat. *gesto,* Hom., etc. **3.** *to have, possess,* ἀγλαΐας φορέειν to be splendid, Od.; ἰσχυρὰς φ. τὰς κεφαλάς Hdt.; ὑπόπτερον δέμας φ. Eur. **II.** Pass. *to be borne violently along, be hurried along,* Trag.; *to be storm-tost,* Ar.; *to be carried away,* Thuc. **III.** Med. *to fetch for oneself, fetch regularly,* Eur. Hence

φορηδόν, Adv. *bearing like a bundle,* Luc.; and

φόρημα, ατος, τό, *that which is carried, a load, freight,* Lat. *gestamen,* Soph., Xen. **2.** *that which is worn, an ornament,* Plut., etc. **3.** as translation of Lat. *ferculum,* Id.

φορήμεναι, φορῆναι, Ep. inf. of φορέω.

φορητός, ή, όν, and ός, όν, verb. Adj. *borne, carried,* Pind. **II.** *to be borne, endurable,* Aesch., Eur.

φόρῐμος, ον, (φέρω) *bearing, fruitful,* Anth.

Φορκίδες [ῐ], ίδων, αἱ, *the daughters of Phorcys,* the three Gorgons, *Stheino, Euryălē, Medūsa,* Pind., Aesch.

Φόρκῡς, ῡος, ὁ, *Phorcys,* a sea-god, father of the Graiae and Gorgons, Hes.: gen. also Φόρκῡνος (as if from Φόρκυν), Od.

φορμηδόν, Adv. (φορμός) *like mat-work, cross-wise, athwart,* Thuc.

φόρμιγξ, ιγγος, ἡ, *the phorminx,* a kind of *lyre* or *harp,* the oldest stringed instrument of the Greeks, esp. as the instrument of Apollo, Hom.; with seven strings (after Terpander's time), Pind. (Commonly referred to φέρω, as if it were *the portable lyre:* better perh. from Root **ΦΡΕΜ,** Lat. *fremo, to sound.*) Hence

φορμίζω, f. ίσω, Dor. ίξω, *to play the* φόρμιγξ, Hom.

φορμικτής, Dor. **-τάς**, ὁ, *a harper*, Pind., Ar.
φορμίς, ίδος, ἡ, Dim. of φορμός, Ar. Hence
φορμίσκος, ὁ, = foreg., Plat.
φορμορ-ράφέομαι, (ῥάπτω) Pass. *to be stitched like a mat, to be hampered*, a word of Demosth. ridiculed by Aeschin.
φορμός, ὁ, (φέρω) *a basket for carrying* corn, Hes., Hdt. 2. *a mat*, Lat. *storea*, Hdt., Ar. 3. *a seaman's cloak, of coarse plaited stuff*, Theocr. II. *a corn measure*, Lys.
φορολογέω, f. ήσω, *to levy tribute from*, Polyb., Plut.
φορο-λόγος, ον, (λέγω) *levying tribute*, Plut.
φορός, όν, (φέρω) *bringing on one's way, forwarding*, of a wind, *favourable*, Polyb., etc. II. *bringing in, productive*, Theophr.
φόρος, ὁ, (φέρω) *that which is brought in, tribute*, such as is paid *by subjects to a ruling state*, as by the Asiatic Greeks to Athens, Thuc.; φόρου ὑποτελεῖς subject to pay *tribute*, Id.; φόρον ὑποτελέειν to pay *tribute*, Hdt.; ἀπάγειν, φέρειν Ar.; φ. τάξασθαι to agree to pay *it*, Hdt.; τάξαι to impose it, Dem. 2. *any payment*, Xen., Plut.
φορτηγέω, f. ήσω, (φορτηγός) *to carry freights* or *loads* in ships, Hdt. Hence
φορτηγία, ἡ, *a carrying of loads, carrying trade*, Arist.
φορτηγικός, ή, όν, *of* or *for carrying loads*, πλοῖον φ. a ship *of burden*, Thuc., Xen. From
φορτ-ηγός, ὁ, (ἄγω) *one who carries burdens, a carrier, trafficker, merchant*, Theogn., Polyb.
φορτίζω, f. ίσω, (φόρτος) *to load*, Babr.; φορτίον φ. τινά *to load* one with a burden, N.T.:—Med., τὰ μείονα φορτίζεσθαι *to ship* the smaller part *of one's wealth*, Hes.—Pass. *to be heavy laden*, pf. part. πεφορτισμένος N.T., Luc.
φορτίκός, ή, όν, (φόρτος) *of the nature of a burden*: metaph. (cf. φόρτος II) *burdensome, wearisome*, Dem., Luc. 2. *coarse, vulgar, common*, Ar., Plat.; of arguments, *low, vulgar, ad captandum vulgus*, Plat.; τοῦ φορτικοῦ ἕνεκα *out of vulgar arrogance*, Aeschin.: —Adv. φορτικῶς, *coarsely, vulgarly, like a clown*, Plat., etc.
φορτίον, τό, (φόρτος) *a load, burden*, Ar., Xen. 2. *a ship's freight* or *lading*, Lycurg.: in pl. *wares, merchandise*, Hes., Hdt., Att. 3. *of a child in the womb*, Xen. 4. metaph. φ. ἄρασθαι to take *a heavy burden* upon one, Dem. (Dim. only in form.)
φορτίς, ίδος, ἡ, like ναῦς φορτηγός, *a ship of burden, merchantman*, Od. From
φόρτος, ὁ, (φέρω) *a load, a ship's freight* or *cargo*, Od., Hes., etc. 2. metaph. *a heavy load* or *burden*, φ. χρείας, κακῶν Eur. II. in Att. *tiresome stuff, something common, low, coarse, vulgar*, Ar.
φορύνω [ῠ], only in impf. pass. *to be spoiled, defiled*, Od. (Deriv. uncertain.)
φορύσσω, aor. 1 part. φορύξας, *to defile*, Od. (Deriv. uncertain.)
φορῠτός, ὁ, (φέρομαι) *whatever is swept along by the wind*, and so (like συρφετός, from σύρω), *rubbish, sweepings, chaff*, Ar.
φόως, τό, Ep. lengthd. from φῶς, which is itself contr. from φάος, *light*, Hom., only in nom. and acc. sing.; cf. **φόωσδε**, *to the light, to the light of day*, Il.

φράγδην, (φράσσω) Adv. *fenced, armed*, Batr.
φράγέλλιον, τό, Lat. *flagellum, a scourge*, N.T. Hence
φράγελλόω, f. ώσω, Lat. *flagello, to scourge*, N.T.
φράγμα, ατος, τό, (φράσσω) *a fence, breast-work, screen*, Hdt., Plat. 2. generally *a defence*, φρ. μετώπων of a stag's horns, Anth.
φραγμός, ὁ, (φράσσω) *a fencing in, blocking up*, Soph. II. like φράγμα, *a fence, paling, palisade*, Hdt. 2. *a place fenced off, an enclosure*, Anth. 3. metaph. *a partition*, N.T.
φράγνῦμι, = φράσσω, Anth., Plut.
φράδάζω, *to make known*, γᾶν φράδασσε (poët. aor. 1) Pind. From
φράδή, ἡ, (φράζω) *understanding, knowledge*, Pind. II. *a hint, warning*, Aesch., Eur.
φράδής, ές, gen. έος, (φράζω) *understanding, wise, shrewd*, opp. to ἀφραδής, Il.
φραδμοσύνη, ἡ, poët. Noun, *understanding, shrewdness, cunning*, in dat. pl. φραδμοσύνησιν h. Hom., Hes.
φράδμων, ον, gen. ονος, = φραδής, Il., Orac. ap. Hdt.
φράζω, (Root ΦΡΑΔ): poët. impf. φράζον: f. φράσω: aor. 1 ἔφρᾰσα, Ep. φράσα, poët. also φράσσα: pf. πέφρᾰκα: Ep. aor. 2 πέφρᾰδον, ἐπέφρᾰδον, imper. πέφρᾰδε, 3 sing. opt. πεφράδοι, inf. πεφραδέειν, πεφραδέμεν:— Med., Ep. imper. φράζεο, φράζευ: Ep. 3 sing. impf. φράζετο, φραζέσκετο: f. φράσομαι, Ep. φρασσόμαι: —aor. 1 ἐφρασάμην, Ep. φρασάμην, 3 sing. and pl. ἐφράσατο, φράσαντο; Ep. 3 sing. subj. φράσσεται; Ep. inf. φράσσασθαι:—Pass. (in same sense as Med.), aor. 1 ἐφράσθην: pf. πέφρασμαι. *To point out, shew, indicate*, Hom.; μῦθον πέφραδε πᾶσιν *make known* the word to all, Od.; ἔφρασε τὴν ἀτραπόν Hdt.; φωνῆσαι μὲν οὐκ εἶχε, τῇ δὲ χειρὶ ἔφραζε Id. 2. *to shew forth, tell, declare*, Hdt., Att.: c. gen. *to tell of*, Soph., etc.:—it differs from λέγω, as *telling, declaring* from simply *speaking*. 3. c. dat. pers. et inf. *to tell* one to do so and so, Hom., Thuc. 4. absol. *to give counsel, advise*, Soph., Aeschin. II. Med. and Pass. *to indicate to oneself*, i.e. *to think* or *muse upon, consider, ponder, debate*, Hom., etc.; ἐνὶ φρεσὶ μῆτιν ἀμείνω Il.; ἀμφὶς φρ. *to think differently*, Ib. 2. *to think of, purpose, contrive, devise, design*, φ. τινι θάνατον Hom.; φράσσεται ὥς κε νέηται *will contrive* how . . , Od. 3. c. acc. et inf. *to think, suppose, believe, imagine* that . . , Ib., Hdt. 4. *to remark, perceive, observe*, Hom.; c. gen., like αἰσθάνομαι Theocr. 5. *to watch, guard*, Od.:—*to beware of*, Orac. ap. Hdt.; φράζευ κύνα *cave canem*, Ar.;—c. inf., φράζου μὴ φωνεῖν *take heed* not to speak, Soph.:—so absol. *to take heed*, Aesch., Soph.
φράξαντο, Ep. 3 pl. aor. 1 med. of φράσσω.
φράσδω, Dor. for φράζω.
φρασίν, Dor. for φρεσίν, dat. pl. of φρήν.
φράσις [ᾰ], εως, ἡ, *speech; enunciation*, Plut.
φράσσαντο, Ep. 3 pl. aor. 1 med. of φράζω.
φράσσεται, Ep. 3 sing. aor. 1 subj. of φράζω.
φράσσω, Att. -ττω, (Root ΦΡΑΓ): aor. 1 ἔφραξα:— Med., f. φράξομαι:—Pass., f. φραγήσομαι: aor. 1 ἐφράχθην: aor. 2 ἐφράγην [ᾰ]: pf. πέφραγμαι: 3 plqpf. ἐπέφρακτο:—in Att. the letters are sometimes transposed, e.g. φάρξασθαι for φράξασθαι, πέφαργμαι for πέφραγμαι, φαρκτός for φρακτός. *To fence in, hedge*

round, esp. for protection or defence, to fence, secure, fortify, φράξε [τὴν σχεδίην] ῥίπεσσι he fenced the raft with mats, Od. : —Med., φράξαντο νῆας they fenced in their ships, Il. ; φραξάμενοι τὴν ἀκρόπολιν Hdt. ; but, ἐφράξαντο τὸ τεῖχος they strengthened it, Id. ; absol. to strengthen one's fortifications, Thuc. : — Pass., φραχθέντες σάκεσιν fenced with shields, Il. ; absol., πεφραγμένοι fenced, fortified, prepared for defence, Hdt., Thuc.　　II. to put up as a fence, φράξαντες δόρυ δουρί, σάκος σάκεϊ joining spear close to spear, shield to shield (so as to make a fence), Il. ; φράξαντες τὰ γέρρα having put up the shields as a fence, Hdt.　2. in Xen., of dogs, to put down the tail.　　III. to stop up, block, τὴν ὁδόν Hdt. ; τοὺς ἔσπλους Thuc.　2. metaph. to bar, stop : Pass., ἵνα πᾶν στόμα φραγῇ N. T.

φραστήρ, ῆρος, ὁ, (φράζω) a teller, expounder, informer, τινος of or about a thing, Xen. ; φραστὴρ ὁδῶν a guide, Id. ; φραστῆρες ὀδόντες the teeth that tell the age.

φράτηρ [ᾰ], gen. φράτερος, or φράτωρ, φράτορος, ὁ, (φράτρα) a member of a φράτρα : in pl. those of the same φράτρα, clansmen, Aesch., Ar. ; εἰσάγειν τὸν υἱὸν εἰς τοὺς φράτερας (which was done when the boy came of age) Ar. ; ἐγγράφειν τινὰ εἰς τοὺς φρ. Isae. ; οὐκ ἔφυσε φράτερας (v. φραστήρ), he has not cut his citizenteeth, is no true citizen, Ar. ; φράτερες τριωβόλου clansmen of the dicast's fee, Id.　Hence

φρᾱτορικός, ή, όν, = φράτριος, Dem.

φράτρα, ή, Ion. φρήτρη, Dor. πάτρα, Att. φρατρία : —a brotherhood : in Hom. a people of kindred race, a tribe, clan, κρῖν᾽ ἄνδρας κατὰ φρήτρας, ὡς φρήτρη φρήτρηφιν ἀρήγῃ choose men by clans, that clan may stand by clan, Il.　II. at Athens the φρατρία was a subdivision of the φυλή, as at Rome the curia of the tribus, Isocr., etc. : every φυλή consisted of three φρατρίαι, whose members were called φράτερες or φράτορες (as those of a φυλή were φυλέται) : every φρατρία contained 30 γένη, so that by Solon's constitution Athens had 12 φρατρίαι, and 360 γένη or old patrician houses. (From the same Root as Lat. fräter.)　Hence

φρᾱτριάζω, f. άσω, to be in the same φρατρία, Dem.

φρᾱτρί-αρχος, ὁ, president of a φρατρία, Dem.

φράτριος [ᾱ], α, ον, Ion. φρήτριος, ίη, ιον, of or belonging to a φράτρα : at Athens, epith. of Zeus and Athena, as tutelary deities of the phratriae, Plat., Dem.

φράττω, Att. for φράσσω.

φράτωρ, ορος, v. φράτηρ.

ΦΡΕ'ΑΡ, τό, gen. φρέατος, Ep. pl. φρείατα, a well (distinguished from κρήνη, a spring), Il., Hdt.　2. a tank, cistern, reservoir, Lat. puteus, Hdt., Thuc. : an oiljar, Ar.　Hence

φρεᾱτία, ή, a tank or reservoir, Xen. ; and

φρεᾱτίας, ὁ, leading to a tank or reservoir, Xen.

Φρεαττώ or Φρεᾱτώ, οῦς, ή, a court in Peiræeus, where homicides used to present themselves for trial, only in dat., ἐν Φρεαττοῖ Dem., Arist.

φρενᾰπᾰτάω, f. ήσω, to deceive, N. T.　From

φρεν-ᾰπᾰτης, ου, ὁ, (ἀπάτη) a soul-deceiver, N. T.

φρεν-ήρης, ες, gen. εος, (ἀραρίσκω) master of his mind, sound of mind, Lat. compos mentis, Hdt., Eur.

φρενῑτιάω, to have a violent fever, be delirious or frantic, Plut.　From

φρενῖτις, ιδος, ή, (φρήν) inflammation of the brain, phrenitis.

φρενοβλάβεια, ή, damage of the understanding, madness, folly, Luc.　From

φρενοβλᾰβής, ές, (βλάπτω) damaged in the understanding, deranged, Lat. mente captus, Hdt.

φρενο-γηθής, ές, (γηθέω) heart-gladdening, Anth.

φρενο-δᾱλής, ές, (δηλέομαι) ruining the mind, Aesch.

φρενόθεν, Adv. of or from one's own mind, Soph.

φρενο-κλόπος, ον, (κλέπ-τω) stealing the understanding, deceiving, Anth.

φρενο-ληστής, οῦ, ὁ, a robber of the understanding, a deceiver, Anth.

φρενο-μᾰνής, ές, (μαίνομαι) distracting the mind, maddening, Aesch.

φρενο-μόρως, Adv. (μόρος) so as to destroy the mind, Soph.

φρενο-πληγής, ές, (πλήσσω) striking the mind, i. e. driving mad, maddening, Aesch.

φρενό-πληκτος, ον, (πλήσσω) stricken in mind, frenzy-stricken, Aesch.

φρενο-πλήξ, ῆγος, ὁ, ή, = φρενόπληκτος, Anth.

φρενο-τέκτων, ον, building with the mind, ingenious, Ar.

φρενόω, f. ώσω, (φρήν) to make wise, instruct, inform, teach, τινά Trag., Xen. ; φρενώσω δ᾽ οὐκέτ᾽ ἐξ αἰνιγμάτων, i. e. will teach plainly, Aesch.　　II. in Pass. to be elated, Babr.

φρεν-ώλης, ες, (ὄλλυμι) distraught in mind, frenzied, Aesch.

ΦΡΕ'Ω, f. φρήσω, akin to φέρω, but found only in the compds. διαφρέω, ἐκφρέω, εἰσφρέω, ἐπεισφρέω.

ΦΡΗ'Ν, ή, gen. φρενός, pl. φρένες, gen. φρενῶν, dat. φρεσί, Dor. φρασί : I. properly = διάφραγμα, the midriff or muscle which parts the heart and lungs (viscera thoracis) from the lower viscera (abdominis), Aesch. ; usually in pl., Arist., etc.　II. in Hom., φρήν or φρένες = the parts about the heart, the breast, Lat. praecordia, Il. ; φρένες ἀμφιμέλαιναι Ib.　2. the heart, as the seat of the passions, Hom., etc. ; ἐκ φρενός from one's very heart, Aesch. ; φῦσαι φρένας to produce a haughty spirit, Soph.　3. the heart or mind, as the seat of thought, φρενὶ νοεῖν, ἐπίστασθαι Il., etc. ; μετὰ φρεσὶ μερμηρίζειν Od. ; κατὰ φρένα εἰδέναι, γνῶναι Il., etc. ; κατὰ φρένα καὶ κατὰ θυμόν, as in Lat. mens animusque, Ib. ;—hence men lose their φρένες, i. e. their wits, Od. ; πλήγη φρένας ἃς πάρος εἶχεν Il. ;—so, in Att., φρενῶν ἀφεστάναι, ἐκστῆναι to be out of one's wits, Soph., Eur. ; ποῦ ποτ᾽ εἶ φρενῶν ; satisne sanus es ? Soph. ; φρενῶν ἐπήβολος in possession of one's senses, Id. ; ἔνδον φρενῶν Eur. ; ἐξ ἄκρας φρενός, i. e. superficially, Aesch.　4. of beasts, Il.　5. will, purpose, Soph.

φρήτρη, ή, Ion. for φράτρα : Ep. dat. φρήτρηφιν.

φρήτριος, η, ον, Ion. for φράτριος.

φρῑκᾰλέος, α, ον, shivering with cold : horrid, Anth.　From

φρίκη [ῑ], ή, (φρίσσω) a shuddering, shivering, Plat.　2. shuddering, esp. from religious awe, Hdt., Soph.

φρικτός, ή, όν, verb. Adj. of φρίσσω, to be shuddered at, horrible, Plut.

φρῑκ-ώδης, ες, (εἶδος) that causes shuddering, horrible,

Eur., Ar. :—neut. φρικῶδες, as Adv. *horribly*, Eur. :— Adv. -δῶς, Sup., φρικωδέστατα ἔχειν *to be in utter horror*, Dem.

φρῑμάσσομαι, Att. -ττομαι, f. ξομαι, Dep. *to snort and leap about, to neigh and prance*, of horses, Hdt. ; of goats, Theocr. (Perh. formed from the sound.)

φρίξ, ή, gen. φρῑκός, (φρίσσω) *the ruffling* of a smooth surface : *the ripple* caused by a gust of wind over the smooth sea, Lat. *horror*, Od. **II.** *a bristling up*, of the hair, Babr.

φρῖξαι, aor. 1 inf. of φρίσσω.

φριξο-κόμης, ου, ὁ, (κόμη) *with bristling hair*, Anth.

φρίσσω, Att. **φρίττω**, (Root **ΦΡΙ-Κ**) : f. φρίξω : aor. 1 ἔφριξα : pf. πέφρῑκα ; with poët. part. πεφρίκοντες Pind. :—*to be rough* or *uneven on the surface, to bristle*, Lat. *horrere*, of a corn-field, Il., Eur. ; of a line of battle, Il. ; of hair or bristles, *to bristle up, stand on end*, Hes., Theocr. ;—c. acc. cogn., φρίσσειν λοφιήν *to set up his bristly* mane, Od. ; φρ. νῶτον Il. ; χαίτην Ar. **2.** φρίσσοντες ὄμβροι, like Virgil's *horrida grando*, Pind. **3.** ἄσθματι φρίσσων πνοὰς *ruckling* in his throat, of one just dying, Id. **II.** of a feeling of chill, when one's skin contracts and forms what we call *goose-skin*, or when the hair stands up on end : **1.** of the effect of cold, *to shiver*, Hes. **2.** of the effect of fear, *to shiver, shudder*, Aesch., Soph. : c. acc. *to shudder at* one, Il., Soph. ; πέφρικα Ἐρινὺν τελέσαι *I tremble* at the thought of her accomplishing, Aesch. ;—so c. dat., ἐρετμοῖς φρίξουσιν *they shall shudder* at the oars, Orac. ap. Hdt. :—also c. part., πέφρικα λεύσσων *I shudder at seeing*, Aesch. ; and c. inf. *to fear to do*, Dem. **3.** *to thrill* with passionate joy, Soph.

φροιμιάζομαι, -αστέον, v. sub προοιμ-.

φροίμιον, τό, contr. for προ-οίμιον, as φροῦδος for πρὸ ὁδοῦ.

φρονέω, Ep. 3 sing. subj. φρονέῃσι : Ep. impf. φρόνεον : f. -ήσω, aor. 1 ἐφρόνησα : (φρήν) :—*to think, to have understanding, to be sage, wise, prudent*, ἄριστοι μάχεσθαί τε φρονέειν τε *best both in battle and counsel*, Il. ; τὸ μὴ φρονοῦν, of an infant, Aesch. ; οἱ φρονοῦντες *the wise*, Soph. ; τὸ φρονεῖν = φρόνησις, *wisdom, understanding*, Id. :—with Advs., εὖ φρονεῖν Hdt., Trag. ; καλῶς φρ. Od., etc. **II.** *to be minded* in a certain way, *to mean, intend, purpose*, c. inf., Il. ; φρόνεον [ἰέναι] *were minded to go*, Ib. :—absol., φρονῶν ἔπρασσον *prudens faciebam, purposely*, Soph. ; τοῦτο φρονεῖ ἡ ἀγωγὴ ἡμῶν *this is what your bringing us here means*, Thuc. **2.** with a neut. Adj., φρ. τινί τι *to be so* and *so minded towards* him, πατρὶ φίλα φρονέων *kindly minded towards* him, Hom. ; so, κακὰ φρονέουσι ἀλλήλοισιν Il. ; so with Advs., εὖ φρονεῖν τινι (v. supr.) Od., etc. **3.** without a dat., ἀγαθά or κακά φρ. Hom. ; πυκνά or πυκινά φρ. *to have wise thoughts, be cunningly minded*, Od. ; ἐφημέρια φρ. *to think* only of the passing day, Ib. ; θνητὰ φρ. Eur. ; τυραννικὰ φρ. *to have tyranny in mind*, Ar. ; ἀρχαῖα φρ. *to have old-fashioned notions*, Id. ; esp., μέγα φρονεῖν *to be high-minded*, Il., Soph., etc. ; in bad sense, *to be presumptuous, conceited, pride oneself*, ἐπί τινι on a thing, Plat., etc. ; ἐφ' ἑαυτῷ μέγα φρ. Thuc. ; φρ. μεῖζον ἢ κατ' ἄνδρα *to have thoughts* too high for man, Soph. ; σμικρὸν φρ. *to be low-minded, poor-spirited*, Id. ;

ἧσσον, ἔλασσον φρ. Eur., etc. ; οὐ σμικρὸν φρ. ἔς τινα Id. **4.** τά τινος φρονεῖν *to be of* his *mind*, *of* his *party, side with* him, Hdt., etc. ; φρ. τὰ Βρασίδου Ar. ; —so ἴσον ἐμοὶ φρονέουσα *thinking* like me, Il. ; τὰ αὐτά, κατὰ τωὐτὸ φρ. *to be* like-*minded*, Hdt. **III.** *to have a thing in one's mind, mind, take heed to* a thing, Od., Aeschin., etc. **IV.** *to be in possession of one's senses, to be sensible, be alive*, ἔτι φρονέοντα, for ἔτι ζῶντα, Il. ; ἐν τῷ φρονεῖν γὰρ μηδὲν ἥδιστος βίος Soph. :—also *to be in one's senses*, Id. ; φρονῶν οὐδὲν φρονεῖς *though in thy wits thou'rt* nothing wise, Eur. Hence

φρόνημα, ατος, τό, *one's mind, spirit*, Lat. *animus*, Aesch., Plat., etc. **2.** *thought, purpose, will*, Soph. ; pl. *thoughts*, Trag. **II.** either in good or bad sense, **1.** *high feeling, highmindedness, high spirit, resolution, pride*, Hdt., Aesch., etc. : pl. *high thoughts, proud designs*, Hdt., Plat. **2.** in bad sense, *presumption, arrogance*, Aesch., Eur., etc. ; and in pl., Isocr., Plut., etc. **III.** pl. = φρένες, *the heart, breast*, Aesch. Hence

φρονημᾰτίας, ου, ὁ, *self-confident, high-spirited*, or (in bad sense) *presumptuous, arrogant*, Xen., Arist. ; and

φρονηματίζομαι, Pass. *to become presumptuous*, Arist.

φρόνησις, εως, ή, (φρονέω) *a minding* to do so and so, *purpose, intention*, Soph. **2.** *arrogance*, Eur. **II.** *thoughtfulness, prudence*, Plat., etc.

φρονητέον, verb. Adj. of φρονέω, *one must think* : μέγα φρ. *one must pride oneself*, Xen.

φρόνῐμος, ον, *in one's right mind, in one's senses*, Soph. **II.** *staid, unmoved, discreet*, Xen. ; τὸ φρ. *presence of mind*, Id. **III.** *wise, sensible, prudent*, Lat. *prudens*, Plat., etc. :—τὸ φρόνιμον *prudence*, Id. ; and in pl., ἄπορος ἐπὶ φρόνιμα *devoid of wisdom*, Soph. ; φρονιμώτατα λέγειν Xen. **2.** Adv. -μως, Ar., Plat., etc. ; φρ. ἔχειν Xen. ; Comp. φρονιμώτερον, Isocr.

φρόνις, εως, ή, (φρήν) *prudence, wisdom*, περιοιδε δίκας ἠδὲ φρόνιν ἄλλων [Nestor] *knows well the customs and wisdom of other men*, Od. ; κατὰ φρόνιν ἤγαγε πολλήν *he brought back much wisdom from Troy*, Ib.

φρονούντως, Adv. pres. act. part. of φρονέω, *wisely, prudently*, Soph.

φροντίζω, f. Att. ῶ : aor. 1 ἐφρόντισα : pf. πεφρόντικα : **I.** absol. *to think, consider, reflect, take thought, have a care, give heed*, Theogn., Hdt., Att. : *to be thoughtful* or *anxious*, πεφροντικὸς βλέπειν *to look thoughtful*, Eur. **II.** with an object, **1.** c. acc. rei, *to think of, consider, to think out, devise, contrive*, Hdt., Att. ; foll. by relat. clause, the Verb being in fut., φ. τοῦτο, ὅκως μὴ λείψομαι Hdt. ; φρ. πρὸς ἑαυτὸν ὡς δώσει Id. ; φρ. ὅπως .. *to take thought* or *consider* how a thing shall be done, Plat. **2.** c. gen. *to take thought for, give heed to* a thing, *care about* it, *regard* it, mostly with a negat., Περσέων οὐδὲν φρ. Hdt. ; Πενθέως οὐ φροντίσας Eur. ; οὐδὲ τῶν νόμων φροντίζουσι Plat. ;—so with Advs. implying a negat., σμικρὸν φρ. Σωκράτους Id. :—so also, with a Prep., φρ. περί τινος *to be concerned* or *anxious about* a thing, Hdt., Xen. :—μὴ φροντίσῃς *heed it not*, Ar. ; οὐ, μὰ Δί', οὐδ' ἐφρόντισα Id. From

φροντίς, ίδος, ή, (φρονέω) *thought, care, heed, attention* bestowed upon a person or thing, c. gen., φροντίδ' ἔχειν τινός Eur. ; ἐν φροντίδι εἶναι περί τινος Hdt. **2.**

absol. *thought, meditation,* Aesch., Soph. ; ἐν φροντίδι μοι ἐγένετο [τὸ πρῆγμα] Hdt. ; ἐμβῆσαί τινα ἐς φροντίδα to set one *a thinking,* Id., etc. :—in pl. *thoughts,* αἱ δεύτεραί πως φροντίδες σοφώτεραι Eur. 3. *deep thought, care, concern,* Aesch. ; οὐ φροντὶς Ἱπποκλείδῃ no *matter* to Hippocleides! Hdt.

φρόντισμα, ατος, τό, (φροντίζω) *that which is thought out, a thought, invention,* Ar.

φροντιστέον, verb. Adj. of φροντίζω, one must take heed, Eur., Plat.

φροντιστήριον, τό, *a place for meditation, a thinking-shop, school,* Ar., Luc. From

φροντιστής, οῦ, ὁ, (φροντίζω) *a deep, hard thinker,* as Socrates is called in derision by Ar. ; so, φρ. τῶν μετεώρων, τῶν οὐρανίων *a thinker on* supra-terrestrial things, Xen. ; μετέωρα φρ. Plat. Hence

φροντιστικός, ή, όν, *thoughtful,* Luc. :—Adv. -κῶς, Xen.

φροῦδος, η, ον, and ος, ον, (contr. from πρὸ ὁδοῦ, as φροίμιον from προοίμιον) :—*gone away, clean gone,* (as Hom. says πρὸ ὁδοῦ ἐγένοντο) : 1. of persons, *gone, fled, departed,* Soph., etc. ; c. part., φροῦδοί [εἰσι] διώκοντές σε they are *gone* in pursuit, Id. ; of the dead, φρ. αὐτὸς εἶ θανών thou art dead *and gone,* Id., Eur. 2. *undone, ruined, helpless,* Eur. II. of things, *gone, vanished,* Soph., Eur. ; φροῦδη μὲν αὐδή, φροῦδα δ᾽ ἄρθρα they are *gone,* i. e. refuse their office, Eur.

φρουρά, Ion. -ρή, ἡ, (v. φρουρός) *a looking out, watch, guard,* as a duty, Hdt., Aesch. ; φρουρὰν ἄζηλον ὀχήσω shall keep unenviable *watch,* Aesch. ; φρουρὰ ὄμματος my watchful eye, Soph. ; φρουρᾶς ᾁδειν to sing *while on guard,* Ar. 2. *a prison,* Plat. II. of persons, *a watch, guard, garrison,* Hdt., Aesch., etc. ; esp. of *frontier-posts,* which were guarded in Attica by the περίπολοι, Xen. 2. at Sparta, *a body of men destined for service,* φρουρὰν φαίνειν (v. φαίνω A. I. 5).

φρουραρχία, ἡ, *the office* or *post of φρούραρχος, place of commandant,* Xen. From

φρούρ-αρχος, ὁ, *commander of a watch* or *fortress,* Xen.

φρουρέω, aor. 1 ἐφρούρησα :—Med., f. -ήσομαι in pass. sense :—Pass., aor. 1 ἐφρουρήθην : (φροῦρος) :—*to keep watch* or *guard,* Hdt., Thuc. II. trans. *to watch, guard,* Hdt., Trag., etc. ; στόμα φρουρεῖν εὔφημον, i. e. *to keep silent,* Eur. :—Pass. *to be watched* or *guarded,* Hdt., Trag. 2. *to watch for,* Eur. ; φρ. τὸ χρέος to *observe* one's duty, Soph. III. Med., like φυλάσσομαι, to be on one's guard against, beware of, c. acc., Eur. :—Act. in same sense, Soph., Eur.

φρούρημα, ατος, τό, *that which is watched* or *guarded,* λείας βουκόλων φρουρήματα the herdsmen's *charge* of cattle, Soph. II. *a guard,* Aesch. ; of a single man, Id. III. *watch, ward,* φρούρημα ἔχειν Eur.

φρουρητός, ή, όν, verb. Adj. of φρουρέω, *watched, guarded,* Anth.

φρουρήτωρ, ορος, ὁ, (φρουρέω) *a watcher,* Anth.

φρούριον, τό, (φρουρός) *a watch-post, garrisoned fort, citadel,* Aesch., Thuc., etc. II. *the guard, garrison,* of a place, Aesch., Thuc.

φρουρίς, ίδος, ἡ, (φρουρός) *a guard-ship,* Thuc., Xen.

φρουρο-δόμος, ὁ, *watching the house,* Anth.

φρουρός, ὁ, *a watcher, guard,* Eur., Thuc., etc. (Contr. for προ-ουρός, as φροῦδος from πρὸ ὁδοῦ.)

φρύαγμα, ατος, τό, (φρυάσσομαι) *a violent snorting, neighing,* Aesch., Soph. II. metaph. *wanton behaviour, insolence,* Anth.

φρυαγμάτίας, ου, ὁ, *a hot-tempered horse* : metaph. as Adj. *arrogant, wanton,* Plut.

φρυαγμο-σέμνᾰκος, ον, *wanton and haughty,* Ar.

φρυάσσομαι, Att. -ττομαι : f. ξομαι : Dep. :—of spirited horses, *to neigh and prance,* Anth. ; φρ. πρὸς τοὺς ἀγῶνας *to neigh eagerly* for the race, Plut. 2. metaph. of men, *to be wanton, unruly,* Anth. :—so in aor. 1 act. ἐφρύαξα, N. T.

φρῡγᾰνίζομαι, *to gather sticks for fuel.* Hence

φρῡγᾰνισμός, ὁ, *a gathering of dry sticks for fuel, a collecting firewood,* Thuc.

φρύγᾰνον [ῠ], τό, (φρύγω) mostly in pl. *dry sticks, firewood,* Lat. *sarmenta,* Hdt., Ar., etc. :—the sing. only in collective sense = τὰ φρύγανα, Ar.

φρύγῐλος [ῐ], ὁ, a bird, perh. *a finch,* Lat. *fringilla,* Ar.

Φρύγιος [ῠ], α, ον, and ος, ον, (Φρύξ) *Phrygian, of, from Phrygia,* Eur. 2. Φρ. νόμοι, μέλη *Phrygian music,* i. e. *music played on the flute, wilder than the music for the lyre,* Id. Hence

Φρῠγιστί, Adv. of music, *in the Phrygian mode,* Plat.

ΦΡΥΓΩ [ῡ], f. φρύξω, Dor. ξῶ : aor. 1 ἔφρυξα :—Pass., aor. 1 ἐφρύχθην, aor. 2 ἐφρύγην [ῠ] : pf. πέφρυγμαι. *To roast* or *fry,* Ar. ; ἐρετμοῖσι φρύξουσι they shall cook with the [wood of] the oars, Orac. ap. Hdt. :—Pass., πεφρυγμέναι κριθαί *roasted* barley, Thuc. 2. of the sun, *to parch,* Lat. *torrere,* Theocr. Hence

φρυκτός, ή, όν, verb. Adj. *roasted,* Ar. II. as Subst., φρυκτός, ὁ, *a signal-fire, bale-fire, beacon,* Aesch. ; φρυκτοὶ πολέμιοι αἴρονται ἐς τόπον *fire-signals* of an enemy's approach are made to a place, Thuc.

φρυκτωρέω, f. ήσω, *to give signals by fire* :—Pass., ἐφρυκτωρήθησαν νῆες προσπλέουσαι the approach of ships *was* signalled by beacon-fires, Thuc. ; and

φρυκτωρία, ἡ, *a giving signals by beacons* or *alarm-fires, telegraphing,* Aesch., Ar. ; and

φρυκτώρ.ον, τό, *a beacon-tower, light-house,* Plut. From

φρυκτ-ωρός, ὁ, (φρυκτὸς II, οὖρος (B)) *a fire-watch,* i. e. *one who watches to give signals by beacon-fires,* Aesch., Thuc.

ΦΡΥΝΗ [ῠ], ἡ, *a toad,* Arist.

Φρῠνίχειος, α, ον, *of* or *like Phrynichus* (the Com. Poet), τὸ Φρ. ἐκλακτίζειν Ar.

φρῦνος, ὁ, like φρύνη, *a toad,* Arist.

φρύξω, fut. of φρύγω.

Φρύξ, ξ, gen. φρῠγός, *a Phrygian,* Il. :—as the name of a slave, Ar. : cf. *Davus, Geta.*

φῦ, *fie! faugh!* an exclamation of disgust, Ar. II. Ep. 3 sing. aor. 2 of φύω.

φύγᾰδε, Adv. (φυγή) like φόβονδε, *to flight, to flee,* φύγαδ᾽ ἔτραπεν ἵππους turned his horses *to flight,* Il.

φῠγᾰδεύω, f. σω, (φυγάς) *to drive from a country, banish,* Xen., Dem.

φῠγᾰδικός, ή, όν, *of* or *for an exile,* φ. προθυμία the reckless zeal *of an exile,* Thuc. Adv. -κῶς, Plut.

φῠγᾰδο-θήρας, ου, ὁ, (θηράω) *one who hunts after runaways* or *exiles,* Plut.

φῠγ-αίχμης, ου, ὁ, (αἰχμή) *fleeing from the spear, un-warlike, cowardly,* Aesch.

φῠγάς, άδος, ὁ, ἡ, (φεύγω) *one who flees* from his

country, *a runaway, fugitive, a banished man, exile, refugee*, Lat. *exul, profugus*, Hdt., Att. ; φυγάδα ποιεῖν τινα Xen. ; κατάγειν φυγάδας to recall them ; etc.   **II.** of an army, *put to flight*, Soph.

φυγγάνω, collat. form of φεύγω, Aesch., Soph.

φύγε [ῠ], Ep. 3 sing. aor. 2 of φεύγω.

φυγεῖν, aor. 2 inf. of φεύγω.

φῠγή, ἡ, (φεύγω) *flight in battle*, Lat. *fuga*, Od., Hdt., Trag. ; dat. φυγῇ adverbially, *in hasty flight*, Soph., Eur. ; φυγῇ φεύγειν Plat.   **2.** *flight or escape* from a thing, *avoidance* of it, c. gen., νόσων φυγαί Soph. ; φυγαὶ λέκτρων Eur.   **II.** *banishment, exile*, Lat. *exilium*, Trag., Soph. ; φυγὴν φεύγειν to go into banishment, Plat. ; ζημιοῦν φυγῇ Eur. ; φυγῆς τιμᾶσθαι (sc. δίκην), to be awarded the penalty *of exile*, Plat.   **2.** as a collective Noun, = φυγάδες, *a body of exiles or refugees*, Thuc., Aeschin.

φῠγο-δέμνιος, ον, *shunning the marriage-bed*, Anth.

φῠγο-δῐκέω, f. ήσω, (δίκη) *to shun, shirk a trial*, Dem.

φῠγομᾰχέω, f. ήσω, *to shun battle or war*, Polyb. From

φῠγό-μᾰχος, ον, (μάχομαι) *shunning battle*, Simon.

φῠγό-ξενος, ον, *shunning strangers, inhospitable*, Pind.

φῠγοπονία, ἡ, *aversion to work*, Polyb. From

φῠγό-πονος, ον, *shunning work or hardship*, Polyb.

φῠγό-πτόλεμος, ον, poët. for φυγοπόλεμος, *shunning war, cowardly*, Od.

φῠγών, aor. 2 part. of φεύγω.

φύζα, ἡ, *headlong flight, rout*, Hom.   Hence

φυζᾰκῑνός, ή, όν, *flying, runaway, shy*, Il.

φυζᾰλέος, α, ον, = foreg., Anth.

φυή, Dor. φυά, ἡ, (φύω) *growth, stature*, esp. *fine growth, noble stature*, Hom. ; Νέστορι εἰδός τε μέγεθός τε φυήν τ' ἄγχιστα ἐῴκει he was like Nestor both in shape and size and *stature* (or *growth*), Il.   **II.** poët. for φύσις, *one's natural powers, nature, genius*, Pind.   **III.** *the flower or prime of age*, Id.

φύη or φυίη, 3 sing. aor. 2 opt. of φύω.

φυῆναι, aor. 2 pass. inf. of φύω.

φῠκιόεις, εσσα, εν, *full of sea-weed, weedy*, Il., Theocr.

φύκίον or φύκιον, τό, = φῦκος I, mostly used in pl., Plat., Theocr.   **II.** = φῦκος II, *rouge*, Luc.

φῦκο-γείτων, ονος, ὁ, ἡ, *near the sea-weed, dwelling by the sea*, Anth.

ΦΥ͂ΚΟΣ, εος, τό, Lat. *fucus*, *sea-weed, sea-wrack, tangle*, Il.   **II.** *a red colour prepared from it, rouge*, Lat. *fucus*, Ar., Theocr.

φυκτός, ή, όν, older form of φευκτός, *to be shunned or escaped, avoidable*, Hom.

φῡλάζω, f. άξω, *to divide into tribes*, Plut.

φῠλάκεσσι, Ep. for φύλαξι, dat. pl. of φύλαξ.

φῠλᾰκή, ἡ, (φυλάσσω) *a watching or guarding, watch, guard, ward*, esp. *by night*, φυλακῆς μνήσασθε keep *watch and ward*, Il. ; so, φυλακὰς ἔχειν Ib. ; ὅπως ἀφανὴς εἴη ἡ φ. that there might be nothing visible *to watch*, Thuc. ; φυλακὴν φυλάττειν to keep *watch*, Xen. ; τὰς φ. ποιεῖσθαι Id. ; φυλακὰς καταστήσασθαι to set *watches*, Ar.   **2.** *a watch or guard*, of persons, Plat., Xen., etc. ; ἡ τοῦ σώματος φ. a body *guard*, Dem. :—*a guard or garrison*, Hdt. ; ἡ ἐν τῇ Ναυπάκτῳ φ., of a squadron of ships, Thuc.   **3.** of place, *a watch, station, post*, Il., Xen.   **4.** of time, *a watch of the night*, Hdt., Eur., etc.   **5.** *a*

place for keeping others in, *a ward, prison*, Anth., N. T.   **II.** *a watching, guarding, keeping, preserving*, whether for security or custody, ἔχειν ἐν φυλακῇ τινά to keep *guarded or occupied*, Hdt. ; τὸν τῆς γλώσσης χαρακτῆρα ἐν φυλακῇ ἔχειν to preserve the same character of language, Id. ; so, διὰ φυλακῆς ἔχειν or ποιεῖσθαί τι, Thuc. :—also, φυλακὴν ἔχειν, = φυλάττεσθαι, to keep *guard, be on the watch, περί τινα* Hdt. ; ἦσαν ἐν φυλακῇσι were *on their guard*, Id.   **2.** *guardianship*, Arist.   **3.** *a safe-guard*, Isocr.   **III.** (from Med.) *precaution*, Plat.   Hence

φῠλᾰκικός, ή, όν, *fitted for watching or guarding, watchful, careful*, Plat.

φῠλᾰκίς, ίδος, fem. of φύλαξ, Plat.

φῠλᾰκός [ῠ], ὁ, Ep. and Ion. for φύλαξ, Il., Hdt.

φῠλακτέος, α, ον, verb. Adj. of φυλάσσω, *to be watched or kept*, Soph., Eur.   **II.** φυλακτέον *one must observe, obey*, Plat.   **2.** (from Med.) *one must guard against, τι* Aesch., Plat.

φῠλακτήρ, ῆρος, ὁ, poët. for φύλαξ, Il.

φῠλακτήριον, τό, (φυλάσσω) *a guarded post, a fort or castle*, Hdt. : *an outpost*, Lat. *statio*, Thuc., Xen.   **2.** *a safe-guard, preservative*, Dem. ; among the Jews φυλακτήρια were strips of parchment with texts from the Law written on them, used as *amulets*, N. T.

φῠλακτικός, ή, όν, *preservative*, c. gen., Arist.   **II.** of persons, *vigilant, observant*, Xen. ; φ. ἐγκλημάτων *cherishing the recollection of* them, Arist.   **2.** (from Med.) *cautious*, Id.

φύλαξ [ῠ], ᾰκος, ὁ, (φυλάσσω) *a watcher, guard, sentinel*, Lat. *excubitor*, Hom., Att. ; οἱ φ. *the garrison*, Thuc., Xen., etc. ; φύλακες τοῦ σώματος *body-guards*, Plat. :—also as fem., κλῂς ἐπὶ γλώσσῃ φ. Soph., Eur., etc.   **II.** *a guardian, keeper, protector*, Hes., etc. ; —c. gen. objecti, φ. δορός *a protector against* it, the spear, Eur.   **2.** *an observer, τοῦ δόγματος* Plat. ; τοῦ ἐπιταττομένου Xen.   **3.** of things, φύλακες ἐπὶ τοῖς ὠνίοις, of the ἀγορανόμοι, Lys.

φύλαξις, εως, ἡ, (φυλάσσω) *a security*, Eur.

φῠλαρχέω, f. ήσω, *to be or act as φύλαρχος*, Xen. ; and

φῠλαρχία, ἡ, *the office of φύλαρχος*, Arist.   From

φύλ-αρχος, ὁ, *the chief of a φυλή, a phylarch*, Hdt., Xen. :—used to transl. the Rom. *tribunus*, Plut.   **II.** at Athens, *the commander of the cavalry furnished by each tribe*, v. ἵππαρχος.

φῠλάσιος [ᾱ], ὁ, *a man of Phylé* (in Attica), Ar.

φῠλάσσω, Att. -ττω, (Root ΦΥΛΑΚ), Ep. inf. φυλασσέμεναι : f. φυλάξω : aor. 1 ἐφύλαξα, Ep. φύλ- : pf. πεφύλαχα :—Med., f. -άξομαι, also in pass. sense : aor. 1 ἐφυλαξάμην :—Pass., aor. 1 ἐφυλάχθην : pf. πεφύλαγμαι, imper. πεφύλαξο.

A. absol. *to keep watch and ward, keep guard*, Hom., Il. ; σὺν κυσὶ φυλάσσοντες περὶ μῆλα Il.

B. trans. *to watch, guard, keep, defend*, Hom., etc. ; φυλάττειν τινὰ ἀπό τινος *to guard* one from a person or thing, Xen. :—also φ. τινὰ μὴ πάσχειν *to guard* one against suffering, Soph. :—Pass. *to be watched, kept under guard*, Hdt.   **2.** *to watch for, lie in wait or ambush for*, Hom., Thuc. ; φ. τὸ σύμβολον *to look out for* the signal-fire, Aesch. : *to watch, to wait for, observe* an appointed time or a fixed event, Hdt., Thuc. ; φ. νύκτα *to wait for* night, Thuc.   **3.**

metaph. *to keep, maintain, cherish,* χόλον, ὅρκια Il.; φ. ἔπος *to observe* a command, Ib.; νόμον Soph.; φ. σκαιοσύναν *to cling to* it, *foster* it, Id.:—Pass., φυλάττεσθαι παρά τινι *to be fostered in* or *by* .., Id. **4.** *to keep* or *continue in* a place, τόδε δῶμα φυλάσσοις Od. **C.** Med., with pf. pass., **I.** absol. *to be on one's guard, keep watch,* νύκτα φυλασσομένοισι Il.; πεφυλαγμένος εἶναι *to be cautious, prudent,* Ib.; so, φυλασσομένους πορεύεσθαι *with caution,* Xen. **2.** c. acc. *to keep* a thing *by* one, *bear* it *in* mind, Hes., Soph. **3.** *to guard, keep safe,* καὶ κεφαλὴν πεφύλαξο Orac. ap. Hdt. **4.** c. inf. *to take care* to do, Hdt. **5.** c. gen., φυλάσσεσθαι τῶν νεῶν *to take care for* the ships, *be chary of* them, Thuc. **II.** φυλάσσεσθαί τι or τινα *to beware of, be on one's guard against, shun, avoid,* Hdt., Aesch.; also φ. πρός τι Thuc.; ἀπό τινος Xen.; c. part., εἰσορῶν φυλάξομαι *I will take care* to look on, Soph.;—c. inf., φ. μὴ ποιεῖν *to take care* not to do, *guard against* doing, Hdt.; φ. τὸ μὴ γενέσθαι τι Dem.; so, φ. μή or φ. ὅπως μή .., with subj., *to take care* lest a thing happen, Eur., Xen.: rarely c. gen., τῶν εὖ φύλαξαι Soph. **III.** sometimes Act. has sense of Med., Eur., Plat.

φῠλετεύω, f. σω, *to adopt into a tribe,* Arist.

φῠλέτης, ου, ὁ, (φυλή) *one of the same tribe, a tribesman,* Lat. *tribulis,* ὦ φυλέτα Ar.

φῠλετικός, ή, όν, *of* or *for a* φυλέτης, *tribal,* Arist.

φῡλή, ἡ, (φύω) like φῦλον, *a race* or *tribe* of men, κατὰ φυλάς Xen. **II.** *a body* of men *united by ties of blood and descent, a clan,* such as those among the Dorians (φ. γενική), Pind.; of the four old Attic Tribes, Hdt., Eur.; of the Jewish, N. T. **2.** *a tribe* connected *by local habitation,* like our *hundred* or *county,* such as the ten local tribes at Athens formed by Cleisthenes (φ. τοπική), Hdt., etc.—The subdivisions of the φυλαὶ γενικαί were φρατρίαι, those of the φυλαὶ τοπικαί were δῆμοι. **III.** *the contingent* of soldiers *furnished* by a tribe, Hdt., Thuc., etc.:—later, *a brigade* of cavalry, Xen.; cf. φύλαρχος II.

φῠλία, ἡ, a tree mentioned with the olive in Od.; either *the wild olive,* or *the buck-thorn.*

φῠλλάς, άδος, ἡ, (φύλλον) *a heap of leaves, bed* or *litter of leaves,* Hdt., Soph. **2.** *the leaves* or *foliage* of a tree, Aesch.:—*a branch* or *bough,* Eur., Ar. **3.** poët. for *a tree* or *plant,* φ. Παρνησία, i. e. the laurel, Eur.; φ. μυριόκαρπος, of a thick grove, Soph.

φυλλεῖον, τό, mostly in pl. *green-stuff, small herbs,* such as mint and parsley, Ar.

φύλλῐνος, η, ον, (φύλλον) *of* or *from leaves, made of leaves,* Theocr., Luc.

φυλλοβολέω, f. ήσω, *to shed the leaves,* Ar. From

φυλλο-βόλος, ον, (βάλλω) *shedding leaves,* Theophr.

φυλλό-κομος, ον, (κόμη) *thick-leaved,* Ar.

φύλλον, τό, (φλέω) *a leaf;* in pl. *leaves,* or collectively *the leaves, foliage* of a tree, Hom., Hdt., etc.; οἵη περ φύλλων γενεή, τοίη δὲ καὶ ἀνδρῶν *the generation of leaves, such is that of men,* Il.; φύλλοις βάλλειν Eur.; in sing., φύλλον ἐλάας, poët. for ἐλάα, Soph.:—metaph. of choral songs, φύλλ' ἀοιδᾶν Pind. **2.** of flowers, *a petal,* Hdt., Theocr. **II.** *a medicinal herb,* Soph.

φυλλορ-ρόος, ον, (ῥέω) *leaf-shedding.* Hence

φυλλορροέω, f. ήσω, *to shed the leaves,* in Com. phrase, φ. ἀσπίδα *to shed* or *let drop* one's shield, Ar.

φυλλό-στρωτος, ον, *strewed* or *covered with leaves,* Eur.:—also dat. φυλλοστρῶτι (as if from φυλλο-στρώς), Theocr.

φυλλο-φόρος, ον, (φέρω) *bearing leaves,* φ. ἀγών a contest *in which the prize is a crown of leaves,* Pind.

φυλλο-χοέω, *to shed leaves* or *hair,* Anth. From

φυλλο-χόος, ον, (χέω) *shedding the leaves.*

φῡλο-κρῑνέω, *to make distinctions of race,* Thuc.

φῦλον, τό, (φύω) *a race, tribe, class* of men, Hom., etc.; oft. in pl. *hosts, swarms,* also of other animals, *swarms of gnats,* Il.; φῦλον ὀρνίθων *the race of birds,* Soph. **2.** *a sex,* Hes.; τὸ θῆλυ, τὸ ἄρρεν φ. Xen. **II.** in closer sense, *a race of people, a nation,* φῦλα Πελασγῶν Il.; κελαινὸν φ., of the Aethiopians, Aesch., etc. **III.** more closely still, =φυλή II. **1.**, *a clan* or *tribe* of men acc. to blood or descent, κατὰ φῦλα Il.

φύλοπις [ῠ], ιδος, acc. ιδα and ιν, ἡ, *the battle-cry, din of battle, battle,* Hom. (Deriv. uncertain.)

φῦμα, ατος, τό, (φύω) like φυτόν, *a growth:* esp. *a tumour,* Hdt.

φύμεναι [ῠ], Ep. for φῦναι, aor. 2 inf. of φύω.

φύξῐμος, ον, (φεύγω) *offering a chance of escape:* neut. φύξιμον *a place of escape, a place of refuge,* Od.; ἱερὸν φ. *an asylum,* Plut. **II.** c. acc., φύξιμός τινα *able to flee from* or *escape* one, Soph.

φύξιον, τό, like φύξιμον, *a place of refuge,* Plut.

φύξις, εως, ἡ, =φυγή, Il.

φύραμα, ατος, τό, *that which is mixed* and *kneaded, dough,* N. T. From

φῡράω [ῠ], f. -άσω [ᾱ]: aor. 1 ἐφύρασα:—Pass., aor. 1 ἐφυράθην [ᾱ], Ion. -ήθην: pf. πεφύρημαι: (φύρω):—*to mix* flour or meal *so as to make* it *into dough, to knead,* Hdt., Xen.; γῆν φυράσειν φόνῳ *to make* earth *into* a bloody *paste,* Aesch.:—Pass., οἴνῳ καὶ ἐλαίῳ πεφυραμένα ἄλφιτα Thuc. **2.** metaph., μαλακὴν φωνὴν φυράσασθαι *to make up* a soft voice, Ar.

φύρδην, Adv. (φύρω) *mixedly, in utter confusion,* Aesch., Xen.; Dor. φύρδαν, Anth.

φύρσω, aor. 1 subj. of sq.

ΦΥ΄ΡΩ [ῠ], impf. ἔφῡρον: aor. 1 ἔφυρσα, later ἔφῡρα:—Pass., f. πεφύρσομαι: aor. 1 ἐφύρθην; later aor. 2 ἐφύρην:—*to mix* something *dry* with something *wet,* mostly with a sense of *mixing so as to soil* or *defile,* δάκρυσιν εἵματ' ἔφυρον *they wetted, sullied* their garments with tears, Il.; also c. gen., χείλεα φύρσω αἵματος Od.:—Pass., δάκρυσι πεφυρμένη Ib.; αἵματι οἶκος ἐφύρθη Aesch. **2.** of dry things, κόνει φύρουσα κάρα Eur.; γαίᾳ πεφύρσεσθαι κόμαν *to be doomed to have* one's hair *defiled* with earth, Pind. **II.** metaph. *to mingle together, confuse,* ἔφυρον εἰκῇ πάντα *they mixed* all things up together, did all at random, Aesch., etc.:—Pass. *to be mixed up,* ἐκ πεφυρμένου καὶ θηριώδους from a *confused* and savage state, Eur. **2.** in Pass. also *to mix with others, have dealings with* him, Plat.

φύς, aor. 2 part. of φύω: ὁ φύς *a son;* cf. φύσας.

ΦΥ΄ΣΑ, ης, ἡ, *a pair of bellows, bellows,* mostly in pl., Il., Thuc.; in sing., Hdt. **II.** *a wind, blast, wind in the stomach,* in pl., Plat. **2.** of fire, *a stream* or *jet,* h. Hom. **3.** *an air-bubble,* Luc.

φυσᾶντες, Aeol. for –ῶντες, part. nom. pl. of φυσάω.

φύσας, aor. 1 part. of φύω : ὁ φύσας a father ; cf. φύς.

φῡσάω, Ion. –έω : f. ήσω : (φῦσα) :   I. absol. to blow, puff, of bellows, Il. ; of the wind, δεινὰ φυσᾶν to snort furiously, Eur. ; μέγα φυσᾶν, Lat. magnum spirare, to be indignant, Id. ; φ. τὸ αἷμα to breathe blood and murder, Soph.   II. trans. to puff or blow up, distend, Ar., Xen. ; of bag-pipers, Ar. ; φ. τὰς γνάθους to puff them out, Dem. : — Pass. to be inflated, ἡ γαστὴρ ἐπεφύσητό μοι Ar.   2. metaph. to puff one up, make him vain, and so to cheat, Dem. : — Pass. to be puffed up, ἐπί τινι at a thing, Xen.   3. to blow up, kindle a fire :   but also   4. to blow out, extinguish, τὴν λαμπάδα Ar.   5. to blow out, spurt out, Soph.   6. to blow a wind-instrument, Eur., Ar., Theocr.

φυσέω, Ion. for φυσάω.

φύσημα, ατος, τό, (φῦσάω) that which is blown or produced by blowing, φ. δύστλητον a hard-drawn breath, Eur. ; ὀνοφῶδη αἰθέρος φυσήματα, of stormy blasts, Id. ; πόντιον φ. the roaring or raging of the sea, Id. ; μέλανος αἵματος φυσήματα black blood blown from the nostrils, of newly slaughtered cattle, Id.   II. a bubble, Luc.   III. a blowing, puffing, snorting, of a horse, Xen. : metaph. conceit, Plat.

φυσητήρ, ῆρος, ὁ, (φυσάω) an instrument for blowing, blowpipe or tube, Hdt.

φῡσίᾱμα, τό, a breathing hard, blowing, Aesch. From

φῡσιάω, Ep. part. φῡσιόων, intr. to blow, puff, breathe hard, pant, Il., Aesch., Soph.

φυσιγγόομαι, Pass. (φῦσιγξ) to be excited by eating garlic, properly of fighting cocks : hence the Megarians (who were large growers of garlic) are said to be ὀδύναις πεφυσιγγωμένοι infuriated by vexations, Ar.

Φῡσί-γναθος, ὁ, Puff-cheek, name of a frog, Batr.

φῡσι-γνώμων, ον, = φυσιογνώμων, Theocr.

φῡσιγξ, ιγγος, ἡ, the stalk of garlic, or the outer coat of a clove of garlic. (Deriv. uncertain.)

φῡσί-ζοος, ον, (φύω, ζωή) life-producing, Hom.

φῡσικός, ή, όν, (φύσις) natural, native, opp. to διδακτός, Xen., Arist.   II. of or in the order of nature, natural, physical, opp. to ἠθικός, Arist.

φῡσιογνωμονέω, to study features, judge a man's character by his features, Dem.   From

φῡσιο-γνώμων, ον, gen. ονος, judging of a man's character by his features, Arist.

φῡσιόω, (φῦσα) to puff up, N.T. : (for Ep. part. φυσιόων, v. φυσιάω).

φύσις [ῠ], ἡ, gen. φύσεως, poët. φύσεος, Ion. φύσιος : Att. dual φύσει or φύση : (φύω) :—the nature, natural qualities, powers, constitution, condition, of a person or thing, Od., Hdt., Att.   2. like φυή, form, stature, ἢ νόον ἤ τοι φύσιν either in mind or outward form, Pind. ; τὸν δὲ Λάιον, φύσιν τίν' εἶχε, φράζε Soph. ; τὴν ἐμὴν ἰδὼν φύσιν Ar.   3. of the mind, one's nature, natural bent, powers, character, Soph., etc.   4. often periphr., πέτρου φύσιν σύ γ' ὀργάνειας, i. e. would'st provoke a stone, Id. ; ἡ φ. αὐτοῦ for αὐτός, Plat.   II. nature, i. e. the order or law of nature, κατὰ φύσιν πεφυκέναι to be made so by nature, naturally, Hdt., etc. ;—opp. to παρὰ φύσιν, Eur., Thuc. ; so, προδότης ἐκ φύσεως a traitor by nature,

Aeschin. :—so, in dat. φύσει, by nature, naturally, Ar., etc. :—φύσιν ἔχει, c. inf., it is natural that .. , Hdt., Plat.   2. origin, birth, φύσει γεγονότες εὖ Hdt. ; φ. νεώτερος Soph. ; so, τὴν φύσιν Xen.   III. nature, universe, Plat., Arist.   IV. as a concrete term, creatures, animals (cf. φύστις), θνητὴ φ. mankind, Soph. ; πόντου εἰναλία φ. the creatures of the sea, Id. ; θήλεια φ. woman-kind, Xen. ; οἱ τοιαῦται φύσεις such creatures as these, Isocr.   V. a nature, kind, sort, βιοτῆς φύσις Soph. : species, Xen.   VI. sex, Soph., Thuc.

φῡσίωσις, εως, ἡ, (φυσιόομαι) a being puffed up, inflation, N.T.

φύσκη, ἡ, (φῡσάω) a sausage or black-pudding, Ar.

φυστή (sc. μᾶζα), ἡ, a kind of barley-cake, the dough being lightly mixed, not kneaded firmly, Anth. ; φ. μᾶζα Ar.   (Deriv. uncertain.)

φύστις, εως, ἡ, (φύω) a progeny, race, Aesch.

φῡτᾱλία, Ion. –ίη, ἡ, (φυτόν) a planted place, an orchard or vineyard, opp. to corn-land (ἄρουρα), Il.   II. a plant, Anth.   [υ is made long in dactylic verses.]

φῡτάλμιος, ον, (φύω) producing, nourishing, fostering, φυτάλμιοι γέροντες fostering sires or aged parents, Aesch. ; λέκτρα φ. the marriage bed, Eur.   II. natural, by nature ; Soph. O.C. 150 should be pointed thus : ἐ ἐ ἀλαῶν ὀμμάτων ! ἆρα καὶ ἦσθα φυτάλμιος δυσαίων ; woe for thy blind eyes ! say wast thou thus miserable by nature, from thy birth ?

φῡτεία, ἡ, (φυτεύω) a planting, Xen.   II. the growth of a plant, Id.   III. a plant, N.T.

φύτευμα, ατος, τό, a plant, Pind., Soph. ; and

φυτευτήριον, τό, a plant grown in a nursery, Xen.   II. a nursery or plantation, Dem. ; and

φυτευτός, ή, όν, verb. Adj. planted, produced, Plat.

φῡτεύω, f. σω : aor. 1 ἐφύτευσα :—Pass., aor. 1 ἐφυτεύθην, poët. 3 pl. φύτευθεν : pf. πεφύτευμαι : (φυτόν) :   I. to plant trees, Od., Hdt., etc. :—absol., Hes., Xen. :—Med. to plant for oneself, Pind.   2. metaph. to beget children, Hes., Hdt., etc. ; ὁ φυτεύσας alone, the father, Soph., Eur., etc. ; οἱ φυτεύσαντες the parents, Soph. : metaph., ὕβρις φυτεύει τύραννον Id. :—Pass. to spring from parents, τινος, ἔκ or ἀπό τινος Pind., Soph.   3. generally, to produce, bring about, cause, κακόν or κακὰ φ. Hom. ; φ. πῆμα Soph. :—Pass., ὄλβος σὺν θεῷ φυτευθείς Id.   II. to plant ground with fruit-trees, φ. γῆν Thuc. ; φ. ἄγρον Xen. :—Pass., γῆ πεφυτευμένη, opp. to ψιλή, Hdt., Dem.

φῡτικός, ή, όν, (φυτόν) of or belonging to plants, τὸ φ. the principle of vegetable life, Arist.

φύτλη, ἡ, (φύω) a stock, generation, Pind., Anth.

φῡτο-εργός, όν, poët. for φυτουργός, Anth.

φῡτόν, τό, (φύω) that which has grown, a plant, tree, Il., Hes., etc.   II. generally a creature, of men, Eur., Plat.   2. like ἔρνος, of men, a descendant, child, Eur., Theocr.

φῡτός, ή, όν, verb. Adj. of φύω, shaped by nature, without art, Pind.

φῡτοσκᾰφία, ἡ, gardening, Anth. From

φῡτο-σκάφος [ᾰ], ον, (σκάπτω) digging round plants, φ. ἀνήρ a delver, gardener, Theocr.

φῠτο-σπόρος, ον, planting:—metaph., ὁ φυτ. a father, Soph.

φῠτ-ουργός, όν, (*ἔργω) working at plants ; as Subst. a gardener, vinedresser, Anth. II. metaph. begetting, Soph., Eur. : the author of a thing, Plat.

φῠτ-ώνῠμος, ον, named from a plant or tree, Anth.

ΦΥ′Ω : impf. ἔφυον, Ep. 3 sing. φύεν : f. φύσω [ῠ] : aor. 1 ἔφῡσα :—Med., f. φύσομαι:—intr. tenses of Act., pf. πέφῡκα, Ep. 3 pl. πεφύᾱσι, Ep. part. fem. πεφυυῖα, acc. pl. πεφυῶτας : plqpf. ἐπεφύκειν, Ep. πεφύκειν, Ep. 3 pl. ἐπέφῡκον : aor. 2 ἔφῠν (as if from φῦμι), Ep. 3 sing. φῦ, 3 pl. ἔφυν (for ἔφῡσαν, which is also 3 pl. of aor. 1), 3 sing. opt. φύη or φύιη, inf. φῦναι, Ep. φύμεναι, part. φύς.—Later we have an aor. 2 pass. ἐφύην, subj. φυῶ, -ῇ, -ῶσι.

A. trans., in pres., fut., and aor. 1 act., to bring forth, produce, put forth leaves, etc., Hom., etc. ; so, τρίχας ἔφυσεν made the hair grow, Od. : of a country, φύειν καρπόν τε καὶ ἄνδρας Hdt. 2. of men, to beget, engender, generate, Lat. procreare, Eur., etc. ;—ὁ φύσας the begetter, father (opp. to ὁ φύς, the son, v. infr. B. 1. 2), Soph. ; and of both parents, οἱ φύσαντες Eur. : metaph., ἥδ’ ἡμέρα φύσει σε will bring to light thy birth, Soph. ; χρόνος φύει ἄδηλα Id. 3. of persons in regard to themselves, φ. πώγωνα to grow or get a beard, Hdt. ; φ. πτερά Ar. : hence the joke in φύειν φράτερας, v. φράτηρ. 4. metaph., φρένας φύειν to get understanding, Soph. ; δόξαν φύειν to form a high opinion of oneself, Hdt. II. absol. to put forth shoots, ἀνδρῶν γενεὴ ἡ μὲν φύει ἡ δ’ ἀπολήγει one generation is putting forth scions, the other is ceasing to do so, Il. ; δρύες φύοντι Theocr.

B. Pass., with the intr. tenses of Act., viz. aor. 2, pf. and plqpf., to grow, wax, spring up, arise, Od. ; φύεται αὐτόματα ῥόδα Hdt. ; so, τοῦ κέρα ἐκ κεφαλῆς ἐκκαιδεκάδωρα πεφύκει from his head grew sixteen palms long, Il., Plat. ; τῶν φύντων αἴτιος the cause of the things produced, Dem. 2. of men, to be begotten or born, most often in aor. 2 and pf., ὁ λωφήσων οὐ πέφυκέ πω he that shall abate it is not yet born, Aesch. ; μὴ φῦναι νικᾷ not to have been born were best, Soph. :—c. gen., φῦναι or πεφυκέναι τινός to be born or descended from any one, Aesch., etc. ; ἀπό τινος Soph., etc. II. the pf. and sometimes the aor. 2 take a pres. sense, to be so and so by nature, πέφυκε κακός, σοφός Trag., etc. ; so, οἱ καλῶς πεφυκότες Soph. :—then, simply, to be so and so, ἔφυς μητὴρ θεῶν Aesch. ; ἁπλοῦς ὁ μῦθος τῆς ἀληθείας ἔφυ Eur. 2. c. inf. to be by nature disposed to do so and so, ἔφυ πράσσειν Soph. ; φύσει μὴ πεφυκότα τοιαῦτα φωνεῖν not formed by nature so to speak, Id. ; πεφύκασιν ἁμαρτάνειν Thuc. 3. with Preps., φῦναι ἐπὶ δακρύοις to be by nature prone to tears, Eur. ; πεφυκὼς πρὸς ἀρετήν Xen. 4. c. dat. to fall to one by nature, be one’s natural lot, πᾶσι θνατοῖς ἔφυ μόρος Soph., etc. 5. impers., c. inf., it is natural to do, Arist. :—absol., ὡς πέφυκε as is natural, Xen.

Φώκαια, ἡ, a city in Ionia, h. Hom., Hdt., etc. :—hence Φωκαιεύς, Att. Φωκᾱεύς, έως, ὁ, a Phocaean, Hdt., Thuc.

Φωκεύς, έως, ὁ, a Phocian, Il. (in Ep. gen. pl. Φωκήων), nom. pl. Φωκέες Hdt., Φωκεῖς Thuc., Φωκῆς Soph.,

gen. Φωκέων Aesch. II. Φωκίς (sc. γῆ), ἡ, Phocis, on the Corinthian gulf, W. of Boeotia, Xen.; as Adj., Phocian, Trag. III. Adj. Φωκικός, ή, όν, Phocian, Dem.

ΦΩ′ΚΗ, ἡ, a seal, Od., Hdt.

φωλάς, άδος, ἡ, - φωλεύουσα, lurking in a hole, Anth. ; of the bear, lying torpid in its cave, Theocr. II. full of lurking places, Babr.

φωλεός, ὁ, a hole, den, of lions, Babr. ; of foxes, N. T. (Deriv. unknown.) Hence

φωλεύω, to lurk in a hole or den, Theocr., Babr.

φωνάεις, Dor. for φωνήεις.

φωνασκέω, f. ήσω, to practise one’s voice, learn to sing or declaim, Dem.

φωνασκία, ἡ, practice of the voice, declamation, Dem.

φωνασκικός, ή, όν, of or for exercising the voice, φ. ὄργανον a pitch-pipe, Plut. From

φων-ασκός, ὁ, (ἀσκέω) one who exercises the voice, a singing-master, declaiming-master, Sueton.

φωνέω, f. ήσω, (φωνή) to produce a sound or tone : 1. properly of men, to speak loud or clearly, or simply to speak, Hom., etc. ;—c. acc. cogn., ὄπα φωνήσασα making the voice sound, Od. ; so, βέκος φ. to utter the sound βέκος, Hdt. ; so with neut. Adj., μέγιστα φωνέειν to have the loudest voice, Il. ; μέγα φ. Aesch. :—absol. to cry aloud, Soph. ; to sing, Theocr. 2. of animals, to utter their cries, Arist. ; of the cock, to crow, N. T. 3. of a musical instrument, to sound, Eur. ; but βροντὴ φ. it has a voice, is significant, Xen. II. c. acc. pers. to speak to, call to, Il. ; c. dat. to cry to, Ζεῦ ἄνα, σοὶ φωνῶ Soph. 2. to call by name, call, Id., N. T. 3. φ. τινα, c. inf., to command one to do, σὲ φωνῶ μὴ συγκομίζειν Soph. III. c. acc. rei, to speak or tell of, Aesch., Soph.

φωνή, ἡ, (φάω) a sound, tone, properly the sound of the voice, mostly of men, Lat. vox, Hom., etc. ; of a battle-cry, Xen. ; φωνὴν ῥηγνύναι, Virgil’s rumpere vocem, to utter an articulate sound, Hdt., Ar. ; φ. ἱέναι, Lat. vocem edere, Hdt., etc. : pl. αἱ φ. the tones of the voice, Plat. :—proverb., φωνῇ ὁρᾶν, of a blind man, Soph. 2. the voice or cry of animals, Od., Hdt., etc. 3. any articulate sound, as opp. to inarticulate (ψόφος), Soph., etc. 4. of sounds from inanimate objects, φ. συρίγγων Eur. ; ὀργάνων Plat. II. the faculty of speech, discourse, Lat. sermo, Soph. 2. language, Lat. lingua, Hdt. 3. a kind of language, dialect, Aesch., Thuc., etc. III. a phrase, saying, τὴν Σιμωνίδου φ. Plat. Hence

φωνήεις, Dor. -άεις [ᾱ], εσσα, εν : neut. pl. contr. φωνᾶντα :—uttering a voice or speech, endowed with speech, vocal, Hes., Eur. ; βέλη (i. e. ἔπη) φωνᾶντα συνετοῖσι speaking to the wise, Pind. : of animals, endowed with speech, Xen. 2. of a song, sounding, Pind. 3. τὰ φωνήεντα (with and without γράμματα) vowels.

φώνημα, τό, (φωνέω) a sound made, voice, Soph. 2. a thing spoken, speech, language, Id.

φωνητός, ή, όν, (φωνέω) to be spoken, Anth.

ΦΩ′Ρ, ὁ, gen. φωρός, a thief, Lat. fur, Hdt., etc. II. φωρῶν λιμήν, a harbour near Athens, a little westward of Peiraeus, used by smugglers, Dem. Hence

φωρά, Ion. φωρή, ἡ, a theft, Bion. Hence

φωράω, f. άσω [ᾰ], *to search after a thief* or *theft, search a house*, Ar.   **2.** in Pass. *to be detected*, Dem. ; with part., κλέπτης ὢν φωρᾶσθαι Dem. ; so, κακὸς [ὢν] ἐφωράθη φίλοις Eur. :—also of things, ἀργύριον ἐφωράθη ἐξαγόμενον money *was discovered* to be in course of exportation, Xen.

φωριᾰμός, ή, *a chest, trunk, coffer*, esp. for clothes and linen, Hom. (Derivation unknown.)

φωρίδιος, α, ον, poët. for φώριος, *stolen*, Anth.

φώριος, ον, (φώρ) *stolen* : τὰ φ. *stolen goods*, Luc.   **II.** metaph. *secret, clandestine*, Theocr.

ΦΩ'Σ, gen. φωτός, ὁ : dual φῶτε, φωτοῖν : pl. φῶτες, φωτῶν, φωσί : used by Poets, just like ἀνήρ, *a man*, Hom., Trag.   **II.** *a man*, as opp. to a woman, Od., Soph. ; δὔ οἰκτρὼ φῶτε, of a man and his wife, Eur.   **III.** *a man*, opp. to a god, Il., Aesch.

φῶς, τό, contr. for φάος, *light*, q. v.

φψ̂ς, ή, pl. φῷδες, contr. from φωίς, q. v.

φωστήρ, ῆρος, ὁ, (φῶς) *that which gives light, an illuminator*, Anth. :—οἱ φωστῆρες *the lights of heaven, stars*, Id., N. T.

φωσ-φόρος, ον, (φέρω) *bringing* or *giving light*, Eur., Ar. :—as Subst., ὁ φωσφόρος (sc. ἀστήρ), *the light-bringer*, Lat. *Lucifer*, i. e. *the morning-star*, a name specially given to the planet Venus, Cic.   **2.** of the eye, Eur., Plat.   **II.** *torch-bearing*, epith. of certain deities, esp. of Hecaté, Eur.

φωτ-ᾰγωγός, όν, *guiding with a light* : φωταγωγός (sc. θύρα), ή, *an opening for light, a window*, Luc.

φωτεινός, ή, ον, (φῶς) *shining, bright*, Xen.

φωτίζω, f. Att. ιῶ, *to enlighten, illuminate* : *to instruct, teach*, N. T.   **2.** *to bring to light, publish*, Ib.   **3.** *to enlighten spiritually*, and then *to baptize*, Ib.   Hence

φωτισμός, ὁ, *illumination, light*, N. T.

X.

Χ, χ, χῖ, τό, indecl., twenty-second letter of Gr. alphabet : as numeral, χ' = 600, ͵χ = 600,000 : but in Inscrr., Χ is the first letter of χίλιοι, αι, α, = 1000.—Changes of χ, in the dialects :   **1.** Dor. for θ, as ὄρνιχος for ὄρνιθος.   **2.** Ion. represented by κ, as δέκομαι κιθών for δέχομαι χιτών.   **3.** put before λ to strengthen the sound, as χλαῖνα for λαῖνα, χλιαρός for λιαρός.

The Poets in some words treated χ as a double consonant, so that a short vowel before it becomes long, as in βρόχος, ἰᾱχή, ἰᾱχέω (qq.v.), φαιοχίτων.

χάδε, Ep. 3 sing. aor. 2 of χανδάνω :—χαδέειν, Ep. inf.

ΧΑ'ΖΩ, *to cause to retire*, the Act. only in Ep. redupl. aor. 2 κέκᾰδον, f. κεκᾰδήσω :—*to force to retire from, deprive of*, τοὺς ψυχῆς κεκαδών Il. ; ἀριστῆας κεκαδήσει θυμοῦ καὶ ψυχῆς Od.   **B.** Med. **χάζομαι**, Ep. impf. χάζετο, Ep. imper. χάζεο : f. χάσομαι, Ep. χάσσομαι : aor. 1 ἐχᾰσάμην, Ep. 3 sing. χάσσατο, inf. χάσασθαι, part. χασσά-μενος :—also κεκάδοντο (for κεχάδοντο) 3 pl. of a redupl. aor. 2 κεκαδόμην :—*to give way, draw* or *shrink back, retire*, Il.   **2.** c. gen. *to draw back* or *retire from*, χάζεσθε μάχης Ib., etc. ; so, χ. ἐκ βελέων, ὑπ' ἔγχεος Ib. ; οὐδὲ δὴν χάζετο ἀνδρός nor in truth was he

(or *it*, the stone) *far from* the man, i. e. nearly hit him, Ib.

χαίνω, v. χάσκω.

ΧΑ'Ϊ'ΟΣ [ᾱ], α, ον, *genuine, true, good*, Lacon. word in Ar. ; so, χαός, όν, χαοὶ οἱ ἐπάνωθεν *the good men* of olden time, Theocr.

χαιρηδών, όνος, ή, *delectation*, Com. word in Ar., formed after ἀλγηδών.

χαίρην, Dor. for χαίρειν.

χαίρω, (Root ΧΑΡ), 3 pl. imper. χαιρόντων : impf. Ep. χαῖρον, Ion. χαίρεσκον : f. χαιρήσω, Ep. redupl. inf. κεχᾰρησέμεν, later also χαρῶ : aor. 1 ἐχάρησα : pf. κεχάρηκα, Ep. part. acc. κεχαρηότα :—Med. (in same sense), f. χᾰρήσομαι, Ep. κεχᾰρήσομαι :—Ep. 3 sing. aor. 1 χήρατο : Ep. redupl. 3 pl. aor. 2 κεχάροντο ; opt. 3 sing. and pl. κεχάροιτο, -οίατο :—Pass. (in same sense), aor. 2 ἐχάρην [ᾰ], Ep. χάρην, part. χαρείς : pf. κεχάρημαι, part. κεχαρμένος : plqpf. 3 sing. and pl. κεχάρητο, -ηντο.   *To rejoice, be glad, be delighted* Hom., etc. ; χ. θυμῷ or ἐν θυμῷ, χ. φρεσὶν ᾗσι Id. :—c. dat. rei, *to rejoice at, be delighted with, take delight in* a thing, Id., etc. ; so, χαίρειν ἐπί τινι Soph., Xen. :—c. part., χαίρω τὸν μῦθον ἀκούσας I rejoice at having heard, Il. ; χαίρεις ὁρῶν Eur. ; χαίρω φειδόμενος Ar. ;—with part. pres. χαίρω sometimes takes the sense of φιλέω, *to be wont to do*, χαίρουσι χρεώμενοι Hdt., etc.   **II.** with negat., οὐ χαιρήσεις thou wilt or *shalt not rejoice*, i. e. *thou shalt* not *go unpunished, shalt repent it*, Ar. ; so in Hom., οὐδέ τιν' οἴω Τρώων χαιρήσειν Il. ; so with an interrog., σὺ χαιρήσειν νομίζεις ; Plut. : v. inf. IV. 2.   **III.** imperat. χαῖρε, dual χαίρετον, pl. χαίρετε, is a common form of greeting,   **1.** at meeting, *hail, welcome*, Lat. *salve*, Hom., Att. ; κῆρυξ Ἀχαιῶν, χαῖρε.   Answ. χαίρω I *accept the greeting*, Aesch.   **2.** at taking leave and parting, *fare-thee-well, farewell, good-bye*, Lat. *vale*, Od., Att.   **3.** the notion of *taking leave* or *parting* appears also in the 3 pers. sing. χαιρέτω, *have done with* it, *away with* it, εἴτε ἐγένετο ἄνθρωπος εἴτε ἐστι δαίμων, χαιρέτω as to the question whether he was born a man or is a divinity, *let it be put aside*, Hdt. ; χαιρέτω βουλεύματα Eur.   **IV.** χαίρων, *glad, joyful, delighted*, Hom. ; so, κεχαρηκώς Hdt.   **2.** joined with another Verb, in the sense of *safe, with impunity*, Lat. *impune*, χαίρων ἀπαλλάττει Id. ; with a negat., οὐ χαίρων, Lat. *haud impune*, to one's *cost*, οὐ χαίροντες ἐμὲ γέλωτα θήσεσθε Id. ; οὔ τι χαίρων ἐρεῖς Soph. : v. supr. II.   **3.** in same sense as imper. (supr. III), σὺ δέ μοι χαίρων ἀφίκοιο may'st thou *fare well* and arrive, Od. ; ἀλλ' ἐρπέτω χαίρουσα let her go *with a benison*, Soph.   **V.** the inf. is used to refer to the word χαῖρε as used in greeting (supr. III. 1), χαίρειν δὲ τὸν κήρυκα προὐννέπω I bid the herald *welcome*, Id. :—at the beginning of letters the inf. stood alone (λέγει or κελεύει being omitted, as in Lat. S. = salutem, for S. D. = salutem dicit), Κῦρος Κυαξάρῃ χαίρειν Xen.   **2.** in bad sense, like χαίρετω, ἐᾶν χαίρειν τινά or τι *to dismiss from one's mind, put away from one, renounce*, Hdt., Ar., etc. ; πολλὰ χ. κελεύειν τινά Ar. ; so c. dat. pers., πολλὰ χαίρειν ξυμφοραῖς καταξιῶ Aesch. ; φράσαι χαίρειν Ἀθηναίοισι Ar.

ΧΑΙ'ΤΗ, ή, *long, flowing hair*, Hom. ; and in pl. of a

single person, χαίτας πεξαμένη Il. 2. of a horse's mane, Ib. ; of a lion's mane, Lat. juba, Eur., Ar. 3. metaph. of trees, leaves, foliage, in pl., Theocr.

χαιτήεις, Dor. χαιτάεις, εσσα, εν, with long flowing hair, Pind., Anth.

χαίτωμα, ατος, τό, (as if from χαιτόω), a plume, Aesch.

χᾰλά, ή, Dor. for χηλή.

ΧΑΛΑΖΑ, ης, ή, hail, Lat. grando, Il. ; pl. a hail-shower, hailstorm, Xen., Plat. ; χ. στρογγύλαι hail-stones, Ar. :—metaph. any pelting shower, ὀμβρία χ. Soph. ; χ. αἵματος Pind. Hence

χᾰλαζάω, to hail, Luc. II. to have pimples or tubercles, Ar.

χᾰλαζ-επής, ές, hurling abuse as thick as hail, Anth.

χᾰλαζήεις, Dor. -άεις, εσσα, εν, (χάλαζα) like hail, φόνος χ. murder thick as hail, Pind.

χᾰλαίνω, poët. for χαλάω 1. 4, Hes.

χᾰλαργός, όν, Dor. for χηλαργός.

χᾰλᾰρός, ά, όν, (χαλάω) slack, loose, Thuc., Xen. ; χ. κοτυληδών a loose, supple joint, Ar. ; χ. ἁρμονίαι loose, languid, effeminate music, Plat. Hence

χᾰλᾰρότης, ητος, ή, slackness, looseness, Xen.

χάλᾰσις, εως, ή, (χαλάω) a slackening, loosening, Plat.

χάλασμα, ατος, τό, (χαλάω) a slackened condition : a gap in the line of battle, σύμμετρον ἔχειν χ. to be placed at fitting intervals, Plut. From

Χᾰλαστραῖος, α, ον, of or from Chalastra on the Thermaïc gulf :—τὸ Χαλαστραῖον (sc. νίτρον), soda, found there, and used for purposes of cleansing, Plat.

ΧΑΛΑΩ, f. χᾰλάσω [ᾰ] : aor. 1 ἐχάλασα, Ep. χάλασσα, Dor. part. χαλάξαις :—Pass., aor. 1 ἐχαλάσθην : pf. κεχάλασμαι :— I. trans. to slacken, loosen, χ. βιόν, τόξα to unstring the bow, h. Hom., Plat. : metaph., χ. τὴν ὀργήν Ar. 2. to let down, let sink, fall or droop, πτέρυγα χαλάξαις Pind. ; χαλάσας τὸ μέτωπον having unbent the brow, Ar. ; δίκτυα χ. N. T. 3. to let loose, loose, release, Aesch. :—absol. to let go, slacken one's hold, Id. 4. ἡνίας χ. to slack the reins, Plat. 5. κλῆθρα or κλῇδας χ. to loose the bars or bolts, i. e. undo or open the door, Soph., Eur. ; also, πύλας μοχλοῖς χαλᾶτε Aesch. 6. to loosen or undo things drawn tightly together, Soph., Eur. :—Pass., πρὶν ἂν χαλασθῇ δεσμά Aesch. II. intr. to become slack or loose, Eur. ; πύλαι χαλῶσι the gates stand open, Xen. :—metaph. c. gen., to have a remission of, μανιῶν, κακῶν Aesch. ; τῆς ὀργῆς Ar. 2. c. dat., χ. τινί to yield to any one, to be indulgent to him, Aesch. 3. absol. to remit, to grow slack, Plat.

Χαλδαῖος, ὁ, a Chaldaean, Hdt., etc. II. an astrologer, caster of nativities, Cic., etc.

χαλεπαίνω, f. -ᾰνῶ : aor. 1 ἐχαλέπηνα :—Pass., aor. 1 ἐχαλεπάνθην :—to be severe, sore, grievous, like Lat. ingravescere, of storms, Hom. 2. mostly of persons, to be violent, sorely angry, savage, Il., Att. :—c. dat. to be angry with others, Hom., etc. ; so, χ. ἐπί τινι Od. ; πρός τινα Xen. :—also c. dat. pers. et rei, χ. τινὶ τοῖς εἰρημένοις to be angry with him for his words, Id. II. to provoke to anger, Arist. :—Pass. to be provoked, Xen. III. in Pass. also, to be treated harshly, Plat.

ΧΑΛΕΠΟΣ, ή, όν, Lat. difficilis : 1. hard to bear, painful, sore, grievous, Hom., Hdt., Att. ; [θώρακες]

δύσφοροι καὶ χ., of ill-fitting cuirasses, Xen. : τὸ χαλεπὸν τοῦ πνεύματος the severity of the wind, Id. ; τὰ χαλεπά hardships, sufferings, Id. 2. hard to do or deal with, difficult, Ar., Thuc., etc. ; χαλεπὸς ὁ βίος life is a hard thing, Xen. :—c. inf., χαλεπή τοι ἐγὼ ἀντιφέρεσθαι = χαλεπόν ἐστί μοι ἀντιφέρεσθαί σοι, Il. ; so, χαλεπὸν δέ τ' ὀρύσσειν [τὸ μῶλυ] Od. ; χ. προσπολεμεῖν ὁ βασιλεύς Isocr. :—χαλεπόν [ἐστι], c. inf., 'tis hard, difficult to do, Hom. 3. dangerous, Od., Thuc. 4. of ground, difficult, rugged, Thuc., Xen. ; χ. χωρίον a place difficult to take, Xen. II. of persons, hard to deal with, harsh, severe, stern, strict, Od. ; χαλεπώτερος a more bitter enemy, Thuc. ; χαλεπώτατοι most difficult to deal with, most dangerous or troublesome, Id. :—of judges, severe, Hdt., Dem. 2. of savage animals, Xen. 3. ill-tempered, angry, testy, Ar. ; ὀργὴν χαλεπός Hdt.

B. Adv. χαλεπῶς, hardly, with difficulty, Lat. aegre, διαγνῶναι χ. ἦν ἄνδρα ἕκαστον 'twas difficult to distinguish, Il. ; χ. εὑρίσκειν, opp. to ῥᾳδίως μανθάνειν, Isocr. ; οὐ or μὴ χαλ. without much ado, Thuc. 2. hardly, scarcely, δοκέω χ. ἂν Ἕλληνας Πέρσηρι μάχεσθαι Hdt. ; χ. ἂν πεῖσαιμι Plat. 3. χ. ἔχει = χαλεπόν ἐστι, Thuc., Xen. 4. painfully, miserably, χαλεπώτερον, -ώτατα ζῆν Plat. ; ἐν τοῖς χαλεπώτατα διάγειν to live in the utmost misery, Thuc. II. of persons, harshly, severely, Eur., Thuc., etc. :—χ. φέρειν τι, like Lat. aegre ferre, Thuc. : often in the phrase χ. ἔχειν, to be angry, Xen. ; χ. ἔχειν τινὶ ἐπί τινι to be angry with a person for a thing, Dem. ; χ. διακεῖσθαι πρός τινα Plat. 2. χ. ἔχειν, also, = Lat. male se habere, Id.

χαλεπότης, ητος, ή, (χαλεπός) difficulty, ruggedness, Thuc. II. of persons, difficulty, harshness, rigour, severity, Id., etc. 2. ill-temper, vice, of a horse, Xen.

χᾰλέπτω, f. ψω, Causal of χαλεπαίνω, to oppress, depress, crush, Od., Hes. II. Pass., χαλεφθείς τινι enraged at one, Theogn. III. intr. to be angry, vexed at, τινί Bion.

χᾰλί-κρητος, ον, poët. for ἄκρατος, unmixed, Archil.

χᾰλῐνᾰγωγέω, to guide with or as with a bridle, to bridle, Luc., N. T. From

χᾰλῐν-ᾰγωγός, όν, guiding as with a bridle.

χᾰλῐνο-ποιική (sc. τέχνη), ή, bridle-making, Arist.

ΧΑΛΙΝΟΣ, ὁ, a bridle, bit, Il. ; χαλινὸν ἐμβαλεῖν γναθοῖς Eur. :—of the horse, χαλινὸν οὐκ ἐπίσταται φέρειν Aesch. ; χ. δέχεσθαι Xen. ; χ. ἐνδακεῖν to champ the bit, Plat. :—of the rider, τὸν χ. διδόναι to give a horse the rein, Xen. ; ὀπίσω σπᾶν Plat. 2. metaph. of anything which curbs or restrains, of an anchor, Pind. ; χαλινοῖς ἐν πετρίνοισι, of Prometheus bound to the rock, Aesch. II. generally, a strap or thong, Eur. Hence

χᾰλῐνόω, f. ώσω, to bridle or bit a horse, Xen. Hence

χᾰλίνωσις, εως, ή, a bridling, Xen.

χᾰλῐνωτήρια (sc. ὅπλα), τά, cables or ropes to moor ships to the shore, Eur.

ΧΑΛΙΞ [ᾰ], ῐκος, ὁ and ή, a small stone, pebble, in pl., Luc., etc. 2. as collect. in sing., gravel, rubble, used in building, Thuc. ; so also in pl., Ar.

ΧΑΛΙΣ [ᾰ], ιος, ὁ, sheer wine, Lat. merum, Hippon.

χᾰλιφρονέω, f. ήσω, to be lightminded, Od. ; and χᾰλιφροσύνη, ή, levity, thoughtlessness, Od. From χᾰλί-φρων, ονος, ὁ, ή, (χάλις) light-minded, thoughtless, Od.

χαλκ-άρμᾰτος, ον, (ἅρμα) with brasen chariot, Pind.

χάλκ-ασπις, ιδος, ὁ, ή, with brasen shield, Pind., Soph.:—of one who ran the armed footrace, Pind.

χαλκ-έγχης, ες, (ἔγχος) with brasen lance, Eur.

χαλκεία, ή, smith's work, opp. to τεκτονική (joiner's work), Plat.

χαλκεῖον, Ion. -ήιον, τό, a smith's shop, forge, smithy, Hdt., Plat.   II. = χαλκίον, a copper, caldron, Hdt., Plat.   2. a metal reflector in a lamp, Xen.

χάλκειος and χαλκήιος, η, ον, Ep. for χάλκεος, of copper or bronze, brasen, Hom. ; χαλκήιος δόμος, = χαλκεῖον, a forge, Od. ; χάλκειον γένος, of the Age of brass, Hes.

χαλκ-έλᾰτος, ον, poët. for χαλκήλατος, Pind.

χαλκ-εμβολάς, άδος, poët. fem. of sq., Eur.

χαλκ-έμβολος, ον, (ἔμβολος) with brasen beak : as the name of a special kind of ship, Plut.

χαλκ-εντής, ές, (ἔντεα) brass-armed, Pind.

χαλκεο-θώραξ, Ion. -θώρηξ, ηκος, ὁ, ή, with brasen breastplate, Il.

χαλκεο-κάρδιος, ον, with heart of brass, Theocr.

χαλκεο-μήστωρ, ὁ, skilled in arms, Eur.

χαλκεό-πεζος, ον, (πέζα) brass-footed, Anth.

χαλκέ-οπλος, ον, (ὅπλον) with arms of brass, Eur.

χάλκεος, έα, Ion. -έη, εον, also χάλκεος, ον : Att. χαλκοῦς, ῆ, οῦν : (χαλκός) :—of copper or bronze, brasen, Lat. aeneus, aheneus, Hom., etc. ; χ. Ζεύς a bronze statue of Zeus, Hdt. ; ἡ χαλκῆ Ἀθηνᾶ Dem. ; χάλκεον ἱστάναι τινά (v. ἵστημι Α. III).   b. χ. ἀγών a contest for a shield of brass, Pind.   2. metaph. brasen, i. e. stout, strong, χάλκεον ἦτορ, a heart of brass, Il. ; δψ χ. Ib. ; χ. ὕπνος, i. e. the sleep of death, Virg. ferreus somnus, Ib.   II. as Subst., v. χαλκοῦς.

χαλκεο-τευχής, ές, (τεῦχος) armed in brass, Eur.

χαλκεό-φωνος, ον, (φωνή) with voice of brass, i. e. strong and clear, Il., Hes.

χάλκευμα, ατος, τό, (χαλκεύω) anything made of brass, e. g. an axe or sword, Aesch.

χαλκεύς, έως, ὁ : pl. χαλκεῖς, Att. -ῆς, Ep. -ῆες, acc. χαλκέας :—a worker in copper, a smith, opp. to τέκτων (a joiner), Il.   2. generally, a worker in metal, a smith, Od., Hdt., etc.

χαλκευτής, οῦ, ὁ, = χαλκεύς, Anth.

χαλκευτικός, ή, όν, (χαλκεύς) of or for the smith's art, Xen.   II. of persons, skilled in metal-working, Id. :—ἡ -κή (sc. τέχνη), the smith's art or trade, Id.

χαλκευτός, ή, όν, verb. Adj. wrought of metal, wrought, Anth.   From

χαλκεύω, f. σω, (χαλκός) to make of copper or (generally) of metal, to forge, Il., Soph., etc. :—Med. to forge for oneself, Theogn., Ar. :—Pass. to be wrought or forged, Ar.   II. absol. to be a smith, work as a smith, ply the hammer, Id., Thuc. ; τὸ χαλκεύειν the smith's art, Xen.

χαλκέων, ῶνος, ὁ, Ep. for χαλκεῖον, a forge, smithy, Od.

χαλκηδών, όνος, ή, a precious stone, chalcedony, N. T. (Deriv. unknown.)

χαλκήιον, χαλκήιος, v. χαλκεῖον, χάλκειος.

χαλκ-ήλᾰτος, ον, (ἐλαύνω) of beaten brass, Aesch., Eur.

χαλ-κήρης, ες, gen. εος, (ἀραρίσκω) fitted with brass, tipped with brass, of arms, Il.

Χαλκῐδεῖς, οἱ, v. Χαλκίς.

Χαλκῐδικός, ή, όν, of or from Chalcis, Hdt., Ar.

χαλκί-οικος, ον, dwelling in a brasen house, epith. of Athena at Sparta, from the brasen shrine in which her statue stood, Eur., Thuc.

χαλκίον, τό, a copper vessel, a copper, caldron, kettle, pot, Ar., Xen.   2. a cymbal, Theocr.   3. a copper ticket given to the dicasts, Dem.   4. a piece of copper money, a copper, Ar.

χαλκίς, ίδος, ή, = κύμινδις, Il.

Χαλκίς, ίδος, ή, Chalcis in Euboea, said to have its name from neighbouring copper-mines, Il., Hes. :—the people were Χαλκιδεῖς, Ion. -έες, acc. -έας, Hdt., Ar.

χαλκο-άρης [ᾰ], ες, gen. εος, poët. form of χαλκ-ήρης, brass-armed, Pind.

χαλκο-βᾰρής, ές, gen. έος, (βάρος) heavy or loaded with brass, Hom. :—also fem. χαλκοβάρεια (as if from χαλκόβαρυς), Id.

χαλκο-βᾰτής, ές, gen. έος, (βαίνω) standing on brass, with brasen base, or with floor of brass, χαλκοβατὲς δῶ, of the house of Zeus, Hom.

χαλκο-βόας, ου, ὁ, = χαλκεόφωνος, Soph.

χαλκο-γένειος, ον, (γένειον) = sq., Anth.

χαλκό-γενυς, v, with teeth of brass, Pind.

χαλκο-γλώχιν, ἵνος, ὁ, ή, with point or barb of brass, Il.

χαλκο-δαίδαλος, ον, working in brass, Anth.

χαλκο-δάμᾱς, αντος, ὁ, ή, subduing, i. e. sharpening, brass, Pind.

χαλκό-δετος, ον, brass-bound, Trag.

χαλκο-θώραξ, ᾱκος, ὁ, ή, = χαλκεοθώραξ, Soph.

χαλκο-κνήμῑς, ιδος, ὁ, ή, brass-greaved, Il.

χαλκο-κορυστής, οῦ, ὁ, armed or equipt with brass, Il.

χαλκό-κροτος, ον, sounding with brass, i. e. with brasen cymbals, Pind. : of horses, brasen-hoofed, Ar.   II. = χαλκήλατος, Eur.

χαλκο-λίβανον, τό, an uncertain word in N. T. commonly taken to mean fine brass.

χαλκο-μίτρας, ον, with girdle of brass, Pind.

χαλκό-νωτος, ον, brass-backed, Eur.

χαλκο-πᾰγής, ές, (πήγνυμι) made of brass, Anth.

χαλκο-πάρῃος, Dor. -πάρᾱος, ον, with cheeks or sides of brass, of helmets, Hom. ; of a javelin, Pind.

χαλκό-πεδος, ον, (πέδον) with floor of brass, Pind.

χαλκό-πλευρος, ον, (πλευρά) with sides of brass, τύπωμα χαλκ., of a cinerary urn, Soph.

χαλκό-πληθής, ές, gen. έος, armed all in brass, Eur.

χαλκό-πληκτος, Dor. -πλακτος, ον, (πλήσσω) smiting with brasen edge or = χαλκήλατος, Soph.

χαλκό-πους, ὁ, ή, to express the solid strength of their hoofs, brass-hoofed, Il. ; χ. Ἐρινύς, to express her untiring pursuit, Soph. ; χαλκόπους ὁδός, simply, the threshold of brass, Id.

χαλκό-πῠλος, ὁ, ή, (πύλη) with gates of bronze, Hdt. ; χαλκ. θεά, epith. of Athena, Eur.

χαλκο-πώγων, ωνος, ὁ, = Lat. Ahenobarbus, Plut.

ΧΑΛΚΟΣ, οῦ, ὁ, copper, Lat. aes, Hom., etc. ; called in reference to its colour, ἐρυθρός, Il. :—copper was the first metal wrought for use, τοῖς δ᾽ ἦν χάλκεα μὲν τεύχη χάλκεοι δέ τε οἶκοι, χαλκῷ δ᾽ εἰργάζοντο, μέλας

δ' οὐκ ἔσκε σίδηρος Hes. :—hence χαλκός came to be used for *metal* in general; and, when men learnt to work iron, χαλκός was used for σίδηρος, and χαλκεύς came to mean *a blacksmith*. χαλκός also meant *bronze* (i. e. *copper alloyed with tin*), not *brass* (i. e. *copper alloyed with zinc*, which was a later invention), and this was its sense when applied to arms. **II.** *anything made of brass* or *metal*, as a spear, sword, knife, etc., Il. ; χαλκὸν ζώννυσθαι of a warrior girding on his armour, Ib., etc. **2.** of vessels, *a copper, caldron, urn*, Hom., etc. **3.** of *a brasen mirror*, Anth. **4.** *a copper coin*, like χαλκοῦς II, Id.

χαλκο-στέφανος, ον, *brass-crowned*, τέμενος Anth.

χαλκό-στομος, ον, (στόμα) *with brasen mouth*, χ. κώδων Τυρσηνική, i. e. *a trumpet*, Soph. **II.** *with edge* or *point of brass*, Aesch.

χαλκό-τευκτος, ον, *made of brass*, Eur.

χαλκό-τοξος, ον, (τόξον) *armed with brasen bow*, Pind.

χαλκοτορέω, *to work* or *form of brass*, Anth. From

χαλκό-τορος, ον, (τείρω) *wrought of brass*, Pind.

χαλκο-τύπος [ῠ], ὁ, (τύπτω) *a worker in copper, coppersmith*, Xen. ; *a smith*, Dem. **II.** proparox. as Adj. χαλκότυπος, ον, pass. *struck with brass, inflicted with brasen arms*, Il.

χαλκουργικός, ή, όν, *of* or *for a coppersmith* : ἡ -κή (sc. τέχνη) *the art of working in brass* or *bronze*, Arist.

χαλκ-ουργός, όν, ὁ, (*ἔργω), *a coppersmith*, Luc.

χαλκοῦς, ῆ, οῦν, Att. contr. from χάλκεος, Soph., etc. **II.** as Subst. χαλκοῦς, ὁ, *a copper coin*, ⅛ an obol, somewhat less than a farthing, Dem., etc.

χαλκο-φάλαρος, ον, (φάλαρα) *adorned with brass*, Ar.

χαλκόφι, Ep. gen. of χαλκός.

χαλκο-χάρμης, ου, ὁ, (χάρμη) *fighting in brass*, i. e. *in brasen armour*, Pind.

χαλκο-χίτων [ῐ], ωνος, ὁ, ἡ, *brass-clad*, Il.

χαλκό-χυτος, ον, *cast in bronze*, Anth.

χαλκόω, f. ώσω, (χαλκός) *to make in bronze*, Anth. :— Pass., χαλκωθείς *clad in brass*, Pind. Hence

χάλκωμα, ατος, τό, *anything made of bronze* or *copper, a brass utensil, vessel, instrument*, Ar., Xen.: *the brasen beak of a ship*, Plut.

Χἄλυβδικός, ή, όν, *Chalybian* : Χαλυβδικόν, τό, *steel*, Eur. From

χάλυβος, ὁ, = χάλυψ, Aesch., Eur.

Χάλυψ [ᾰ], ῠβος, ὁ, one of the nation of the *Chalybes* in Pontus, famous for the preparation of steel, Hdt., etc. ; οἱ σιδηροτέκτονες Χάλυβες Aesch. **II.** as appellat., χάλυψ, *hardened iron, steel*, Id., Soph.

χᾰμάδῐς, Adv. Ep. for χαμᾶζε (as οἴκαδις for οἴκαδε), *to the ground, on the ground*, Il., Aesch.

χᾰμᾶζε, Adv. (χαμαί) *to the ground, on the ground*, Lat. *humi*, Hom., Eur., Ar.

χᾰμᾶθεν, Adv. (χαμαί) *from the ground*, Hdt., Ar.

ΧΑΜΑΙ [ᾰ], Adv. *on the earth, on the ground*, Lat. *HUMI*, Hom., Hdt., Att. **2.** metaph., χ. καλύπτειν *to bury underground*, Pind. ; χ. ἔρπεσθαι *to be humble, modest*, Luc. **II.** = χαμᾶζε, χαμάδις, Il., Eur.

χᾰμαι-γενής, ές, gen. έος, (γίγνομαι) *earth-born*, Hes., Pind.

χᾰμαι-εύνης, ου, ὁ, (εὐνή) *lying, sleeping on the ground*, Il. :—fem. χᾰμαῐ-ευνάς, άδος, Od.

χᾰμαί-ζηλος, ον, *seeking the ground, low-growing*,

dwarf, χ. φυτά Arist. :—χᾰμαίζηλος (sc. δίφρος), ὁ, *a low seat, stool*, Plat. **II.** metaph. *of low estate*, Luc.

χᾰμαικοιτέω, f. ήσω, *to lie on the ground*, Luc. From

χᾰμαι-κοίτης, ου, ὁ, (κοίτη) = χαμαιεύνης, Soph.

χᾰμαι-λεχής, ές, gen. έος, (λέχος) = χαμαιευνής, Anth.

χᾰμαι-λέων, οντος, ὁ, *the chameleon*, a kind of lizard known for changing its colour, Arist., Plut.

χᾰμαι-πετής, ές, (πίπτω) *falling to the ground*, Eur. ; χ. φόνος *blood that has fallen on the earth*, Id. ; χαμαιπετεῖς ἔκεισθε ye were lying *prostrate*, Aesch. **2.** *lying on the ground*, Plat. **3.** *on the ground*, εὐνή Eur. **4.** Adv. -τῶς, *along the ground*, like a goose's flight, Luc. **II.** metaph. *falling to the ground*, i. e. *coming to naught*, Pind. **2.** *grovelling, low*, of style, Luc.

χᾰμαιτῠπεῖον, τό, *a brothel*, Luc. From

χᾰμαι-τύπη [ῠ], ἡ, (τύπτω) *a harlot*.

χάμ-ερπής, ές, gen. έος, (ἕρπω) *creeping on the ground, grovelling*, Anth.

χᾰμ-εύνη, ἡ, *a bed on the ground, pallet-bed*, Aesch., Eur. : generally, *a bedstead*, Ar. From

χᾰμεύνιον, τό, Dim. of χαμεύνη, Plat.

χᾰμευνίς, ίδος, ἡ, = foreg., Theocr.

χᾰμηλός, ή, όν, (χαμαί) *on the ground, creeping*, Anth. : of a horse's hoofs, Xen. **2.** *diminutive, trifling*, Anth. ; χαμηλὰ πνέων one of a *low* spirit, Pind.

χᾱμίν, Dor. crasis for καὶ ἡμίν.

χᾱμόθεν, Adv. = χαμᾶθεν, Xen.

χάμψαι, οἱ, Egyptian name for κροκόδειλοι, Hdt.

χάν, ἡ, Dor. for χήν, *a goose*.

χᾱν, crasis for καὶ ἃ ἄν.

Χαναναῖος, α, ον, *a Canaanite* or (more correctly) *Chanaanite*, N. T.

χᾶνας, Dor. for χῆνας, acc. pl. of χήν.

χανδάνω (Root ΧΑΔ) : f. χείσομαι :—aor. 2 ἔχαδον, Ep. χάδον, inf. χαδέειν : pf. with pres. sense, κέχανδα : 3 sing. plqpf. κεχάνδει :—*to take in, hold, comprise, contain*, λέβης τέσσαρα μέτρα κεχανδώς a caldron *containing* four measures, Il. ; οὐκ ἐδυνήσατο πάσας αἰγιαλὸς νῆας χαδέειν the beach could not *hold* all the ships, Ib. ; Ἥρῃ δ' οὐκ ἔχαδε στῆθος χόλον the breast of Hera could not *contain* her rage, Ib. ; ὡς οἱ χεῖρες ἐχάνδανον as much as his hands could *hold*, Od. **II.** metaph. *to be capable*, ἤυσεν ὅσον κεφαλὴ χάδε Il. ; κεκραξόμεσθά γ' ὁπόσον ἡ φάρυγξ ἂν χανδάνῃ Ar. Hence

χανδόν, Adv. *with mouth wide open, greedily*, Od., Luc.

χᾰνεῖν, aor. 2 inf. of χάσκω :—χάνοι, 3 sing. opt.

ΧΑ'ΟΣ, εος, Att. ους, τό, *chaos*, the first state of the universe, Hes., etc. **2.** *infinite space, the expanse*, Ar. **3.** *the nether abyss, infinite darkness*, Anth.

χάος, όν, v. χάϊος.

χαρά, ἡ, (χαίρω) *joy, delight*, Trag., etc. ;—but c. gen. objecti, *joy in* or *at a thing*, Eur. ; κέρτομος θεοῦ χ. *a joy* sent by some god to grieve my heart, Id. :—χαρᾷ *with joy*, Aesch. ; so, χαρᾶς ὕπο Id. ; σὺν χαρᾷ Soph. **II.** *a joy*, of persons, N. T.

χάραγμα, ατος, τό, (χαράσσω) *any mark engraven* or *imprinted*, χ. ἐχίδνης the serpent's *mark*, i. e. its *bite*, Soph. ; τὸ χ. τοῦ θηρίου the mark of the beast, N. T. ; χ. τέχνης *carved work*, Ib. ; τὸ χ. τοῦ νομίσματος *the impress* on the coin, Plut. : absol. *an inscription*, Anth.

χᾰράδρα, Ion. χαράδρη, ἡ, (χαράσσω) a mountain-stream, a torrent, which cuts itself (χαράσσει) a way down the mountain-side, Il. :—hence, a loud, brawling voice is compared to the φωνὴ χαράδρας, Ar.　II. the bed of a torrent, a gully, ravine, Il., etc.　2. a conduit for carrying rain-water off a road, Dem.

χαραδραία, ης, ἡ, = χαράδρα, Anth.

χᾰραδριός, ὁ, a yellowish bird dwelling in clefts (χαράδραι), perh. the curlew, Ar.: χαραδριοῦ βίον ζῆν, of a glutton, Plat.

χᾰραδρόομαι, pf. κεχαράδρωμαι: aor. 1 ἐχαραδρώθην: (χαράδρα): Pass. :—to be broken into clefts by mountain-streams, to be intersected by ravines, Hdt.

χάρᾰκο-ποιία, ἡ, the making of a vallum, Polyb.

χᾰρᾰκόω, f. ώσω, to fence by a palisade, fortify, Aeschin., Plut.

χᾰρακτήρ, ῆρος, ὁ, (χαράσσω) a mark engraved or impressed, the impress or stamp on coins and seals, Eur.; εὐδοξίας χαρακτῆρα τοῖς ἔργοις ἐπέβαλεν set a stamp of good repute upon them, Isocr.　2. metaph. the mark impressed (as it were) on a person or thing, a distinctive mark, characteristic, character, χ. γλώσσης of a particular language or dialect, Hdt.; of persons, ὁ χ. τοῦ προσώπου Id.; ἀνδρῶν οὐδεὶς χ. ἐμπέφυκε σώματι no outward mark has been set by nature on the person of men, Eur.; φανερὸς χ. ἀρετᾶς Id.

χᾰρακτός, ή, όν, verb. Adj. of χαράσσω, notched, toothed, like a saw or file, Anth.

χᾰράκωμα, ατος, τό, (χαρακόω) a place paled round, an entrenched camp, Xen., Plut.　II. a palisade, rampart, Lat. vallum, Xen., Dem.

χᾰράκωσις, ἡ, a palisading, Lycurg., Plut.

χάραξ, ᾰκος, ὁ, also ἡ, (χαράσσω) a pointed stake: esp., I. a vine-prop or pole, Ar., Thuc.　II. a pale, used in entrenchments, Ar., Dem.　2. collectively, = χαράκωμα II, Dem., Polyb.

χᾰράσσω, Att. -ττω (Root ΧΑΡΑΚ) f. ξω :—to make sharp or pointed, sharpen, whet, Hes.　2. to furnish with notches or teeth, like a saw, Arist. :—Pass., σκύταλον κεχ. ὄζοις a staff jagged or rugged with branches, Theocr.: metaph., [ὄμμα] ἠλεμάτοις ἀκτῖσι χαράσσεται sparkles with false lights, of the effect produced by painting the eye-lids, Anth.　3. metaph. in Pass., κεχαραγμένος τινί exasperated at any one, Hdt.; κείνῳ τόδε μὴ χαράσσου be not angry at him for this, Eur.　II. to cut into furrows, cut, scratch, Pind. :—Pass., κέκοπται καὶ χαράσσεται πέδον Aesch.　III. to engrave, inscribe, Theocr., Anth.

χᾰρῆναι, aor. 2 pass. inf. of χαίρω.

χᾰρῐ-δότης, ου, ὁ, = sq., of Bacchus, Plut.

χᾰρῐ-δώτης, ου, ὁ, Joy-giver, h. Hom.

χᾰρίεις, χαρίεσσα, χαρίεν (not χάριεν, v. inf. IV): gen. χαρίεντος, dat. -εντι: (χάρις) :—graceful, beautiful, lovely, Hom.　II. in Att. graceful, elegant, accomplished, οἱ χαρίεντες men of taste and refinement, men of education, Isocr., Plat.　2. so of things, graceful, elegant, neat, pretty, Ar., Plat.; —iron. χαρίεν γάρ, εἰ . . it would be a pretty thing, if . . ! Xen.　III. Adv. χαριέντως, gracefully, elegantly, neatly, daintily, cleverly, Plat.　2. kindly, courteously, Isocr.　IV. the neut. as Adv., when it was written proparox. χάριεν, Ar., Plat.

χᾰριεντίζομαι, f. Att. ιοῦμαι : Dep. :—to be witty, to jest, Lat. festive loqui, σπουδῇ χαριεντίζεσθαι to jest in earnest, Plat.　Hence

χᾰριεντισμός, ὁ, wittiness, wit, Plat.

χᾰρι-εργός, όν, elegantly working, artistic, Anth.

χᾰρίζομαι, f. ίσομαι, Att. ιοῦμαι: aor. 1 ἐχαρισάμην :—Pass., f. χαρισθήσομαι, and aor. 1 ἐχαρίσθην, in pass. sense: pf. κεχάρισμαι in act. and in pass. sense: (χάρις) :—to say or do something agreeable to a person, shew him favour or kindness, to oblige, gratify, favour, humour, Lat. gratificari, c. dat. pers., Hom., Hdt., Att. :—absol. to make oneself agreeable, court favour, comply, Aesch., Dem.; c. dat. modi, μή μοι ψεύδεσσι χαρίζεο do not court favour with me by lies, Od.; τῷ αὐτῷ by the same arts, Thuc.　2. in Att. to gratify or indulge a humour or passion, like Lat. indulgere, θυμῷ Soph.; γλώσσῃ Eur.; etc.　3. to humour another in argument, i. e. let him have the best of it, Plat.　II. c. acc. rei, to offer willingly, give cheerfully, give freely, Hom., Hdt., Att.　2. c. gen. partit. to give freely of a thing, ἀλλοτρίων Od.; χαριζομένη παρεόντων giving freely of such things as were ready, Ib.　3. c. acc. pers. to give up as a favour, i. e. not after lawful trial, N. T., Plut.　4. to forgive, Lat. condonare, N. T.　III. Pass. to be pleasing, agreeable, τοῖσι Εὐβοέεσσι ἐκεχάριστο it was done to please the Euboeans, Hdt.; ταῦτα μὲν οὖν μνήμῃ κεχαρίσθω Plat. :—Adv. κεχαρισμένως, Ar.

χάριν, v. χάρις VI. 1.

χᾰριξῇ, Dor. for χαρίσει, 2 sing. fut. of χαρίζομαι.

ΧΑΡΙΣ [ᾰ], ἡ, gen. χάρῐτος: acc. χάριν and χάριτα: pl. χάριτες: dat. χάρισσι, poët. χάρισσι or χαρίτεσσι: (χαίρω): Grace, Lat. gratia: I. outward grace or favour (as we say well or ill favoured), grace, loveliness, Hom., etc.; τῷγε καὶ Ἀθήνη κατέχευεν Ἀθήνη over him Athena shed grace, Od.; of persons, pl. graces, charms, Ib., etc. :—more rarely of things, ἔργοισι χάριν καὶ κῦδος ὀπάζειν Ib.; ἡ τῶν λόγων χ. Dem.　II. grace or favour felt, whether on the part of the Doer or the Receiver :　1. on the part of the Doer, grace, graciousness, kindness, goodwill, τινός for or towards one, Hes., Thuc., etc.　2. on the part of the Receiver, the sense of favour received, thankfulness, thanks, gratitude, Il.; τινός for a thing, οὐδέ τίς ἐστι χάρις μετόπισθ' εὐεργέων Od.; c. inf., οὔ τις χάρις ἦεν μάρνασθαι one has no thanks for fighting, Il.; χάριν εἰδέναι τινί to acknowledge a sense of favour, feel grateful, Ib., Hdt., Att. :—χ. ἔχειν τινί τινος to feel gratitude to one for a thing, Hdt., Att.; χ. ὀφείλειν to owe gratitude, be beholden, Soph.; χάριν κατατίθεσθαί τινι to lay up a store of gratitude with a person, i. e. earn his thanks, Hdt., etc.; χάριν λαμβάνειν τινός to receive thanks from one, Soph.; so, κτᾶσθαι χάριν Id.; χ. κομίσασθαι Thuc.　3. favour, influence, as opp. to force, χάριτι πλείον ἢ φόβῳ Id.　III. a favour done or returned, a grace, kindness, boon, χάριν φέρειν τινί to confer a favour on one, to please him, do a thing to oblige him, Hom.; χάριν θέσθαι τινί Hdt., Att.; so, ὑπουργεῖν τινι Aesch.; παρασχεῖν Soph.; νέμειν Id.; δοῦναι Aesch.; —χ. τίνειν to return a favour, Id.; ἀντιδιδόναι Thuc.; ἀποδιδόναι Plat.:

—χ. ἀποστερεῖν to withhold *a return* for what one has received, Plat. **IV.** *a gratification, delight,* τινός *in* or *from* a thing, Pind., Eur., etc. **V.** δαιμόνων χάρις *homage due to them, their worship, majesty,* Aesch. ; so, ὅρκων χ. Eur. ; εὐκταία χ. *an offering* in consequence of a vow, Aesch. **VI.** Special usages : 1. acc. sing. as Adv., χ. τινός *in any one's favour, for his pleasure, for his sake,* χάριν Ἕκτορος Il. ; γλώσσης χάριν *for* one's *tongue's pleasure,* i. e. *for* talking's *sake,* Hes. :—then much like a Prep., Lat. *gratiâ, causâ, for the sake of, on account of,* τοῦ χάριν ; *for what reason?* Ar. ; so, ἐμὴν χάριν, σὴν χάριν *for my, thy pleasure* or *sake,* Lat. *mea, tua gratia,* Aesch., Eur. :—also, χάριν τινός *as far as regards, as to,* ἔπους σμικροῦ χ. Soph. 2. with Preps., εἰς χάριν τινός *to do* one *a pleasure,* Thuc. ; οὐδὲν εἰς χ. πράσσειν Soph. :—πρὸς χάριν πράσσειν τι Id. ; πρὸς χάριν λέγειν Eur., etc. ; πρὸς χάριν βορᾶς *for the sake of my flesh, for the pleasure of devouring it,* Soph. :—πρὸς χάριν alone, *as a favour, freely,* to their *heart's content,* Id. :—ἐν χάριτι *for* one's *gratification, pleasure,* ἐν χάριτι διδόναι or ποιεῖν τινί τι Xen., Plat. :—διὰ χαρίτων εἶναι or γίγνεσθαί τινι *to be on terms of friendship* or *mutual favour* with one, Xen. **B. Χάρις, ἡ,** as a mythological pr. n., *Charis,* wife of Hephaestus, Il. 2. mostly in pl. **Χάριτες, αἱ,** *the Charites* or *Graces,* Lat. *Gratiae,* who confer all grace, even the favour of Victory in the games, Pind. :—in Hom. their number is undefined ; Hes. first reduced them to three, *Aglaïa, Euphrosyné, Thalia.*

χάρισμα, ατος, τό, (χαρίζομαι) *a grace, favour : a free gift, gift of God's grace,* N. T.

χαρίσσασθαι, Ep. aor. 1 inf. of χαρίζομαι.

χαριστέον, verb. Adj. of χαρίζομαι, *one must gratify,* τινί Plat. **II.** *one must give freely,* Arist.

χᾰριστήριος, ον, *of* or *for thanksgiving,* Plut. **II.** as Subst., **χαριστήριον, τό,** *a thank-offering :* in pl. χαριστήρια, τά, *thank-offerings,* Xen.

χαρῐτία, ἡ, *a jest, joke,* Xen.

χαρῐτο-βλέφᾰρος, ον, (βλέφαρον) *with eyelids* or *eyes like the Charites,* Anth.

χαρῐτο-γλωσσέω, (γλῶσσα) *to speak to please, gloze with the tongue,* Aesch.

χαρῐτόω, f. ώσω, (χάρις) *to shew grace to* any one, τινά N. T. :—Pass. *to have grace shewn one, to be highly favoured,* Ib.

χαρῐτ-ώπης, ον, ὁ, fem. χαριτῶπις, ιδος, (ὤψ) *graceful of aspect,* Anth.

χάρμα, ατος, τό, (χαίρω): **I.** in concrete sense, *a source of joy, a joy, delight,* τινί to any one, Il. ; also, χ. τινός one's *delight,* Eur. ; oft. in pl. *joys, delights,* Od., etc. 2. *a source of malignant joy,* Il. ; χάρματα ἐχθροῖς Aesch. **II.** *joy, delight,* Od., Hes.

χάρμη, ἡ, (χαίρω) *the joy of battle, lust of battle,* Hom. : hence it passed into the sense of *battle,* Il.

χαρμονή, ἡ, = χάρμα I, *a joy,* Eur. ; pl. *joys, delights,* Id. **II.** = χάρμα II, *joy, delight,* Soph., Xen.

χαρμόσυνος, η, ον, (χαίρω) *joyful, glad :* χαρμόσυνα ποιεῖν *to make rejoicings,* Hdt.

χαρμό-φρων, ονος, ὁ, ἡ, (φρήν) *heart-delighting,* or *of joyous heart,* h. Hom.

χᾰρ-οπός, ή, όν, (χαρά, ὤψ) *glad-eyed, bright-eyed,*

χαροποὶ λέοντες Od., Hes. ; θῆρες Soph. :—later, it denoted *light-blue* or *grayish colour,* ὄμματά μοι γλαυκᾶς χαροπώτερα πολλὸν Ἀθάνας Theocr. ; also of the Germans, v. χαροπότης. 2. of the eyes of youths, *sparkling with joy, joyous, gladsome,* Theocr., Anth. Hence

χᾰροπότης, ητος, ἡ, *brightness of eye : a light-blue colour,* Plut.

χαρτάριον, τό, Dim. of χάρτης, Anth.

χάρτη, ἡ, = sq., *a sheet of paper,* to which the Stoics compared the soul at birth, dub. in Plut.

χάρτης, ου, ὁ, Lat. *charta, a leaf of paper,* made from the separated layers of the papyrus, Anth.

χαρτός, ή, όν, verb. Adj. of χαίρω, *that is matter of delight, causing delight, welcome,* Lat. *gratus,* Soph., Plat. :—χαρτά *delights,* Eur. ; τὸ χαρτόν Plut. 2. of persons, εἰ χαρτὸς ἀνέλθοι Anth.

Χάρυβδις, εως, Ion. ιος, ἡ, *Charybdis,* a dangerous whirlpool on the coast of Sicily, opposite the Italian rock Scylla, Od., Eur., etc. 2. generally, *a whirlpool, gulf,* Eur. 3. metaph. of a rapacious person, Lat. *barathrum,* χ. ἁρπαγῆς Ar. (Deriv. unknown.)

χάρων, ωνος, ὁ, ἡ, poët. for χαροπός : hence as prop. n. *Charon,* the ferryman of the Styx, *from his bright fierce eyes,* Eur., Ar.

Χᾱρωνῖται, οἱ, Lat. *Orcini, Senators brought up from the nether world* (i. e. from the lower ranks), such as were created by the will of Caesar, Plut.

χασκάζω, f. άσω, Frequentat. of χάσκω, *to keep gaping at* or *after* one, Ar.

χάσκω (Root **ΧΑ** or **ΧΑΝ**) : later pres. **χαίνω** : f. χανοῦμαι :—aor. 2 ἔχανον : pf. κέχηνα : plqpf. ἐκεχήνειν, Dor. and old Att. ἐκεχήνη. Lat. *hio, to yawn, gape,* τότε μοι χάνοι εὐρεῖα χθών then *may earth yawn for me,* i. e. *to swallow me,* Il. ; πρὸς κῦμα χανών, of one *drowning,* Od. 2. *to gape* (in eager expectation), χάσκοντες κούφαις ἐλπίσι τερπόμεθα Solon ; ὅτε δὴ Ἐκεχήνη when *I was all agape,* Ar. ; so, πρὸς ταῦτα κεχήνετε Id. ; κεχηνότες *gaping fools,* Id. 3. *to yawn* (from weariness, ennui, or inattention), Id. **II.** more rarely, *to speak with open mouth, to utter,* Lat. *hisco,* c. acc. τὰ δεινὰ ῥήματα χανεῖν ; Soph. ; τοῦτ' ἐτόλμησεν χανεῖν ; Ar. Hence

χάσμα, ατος, τό, *a yawning hollow, chasm, gulf,* Hdt., etc. ; of Tartarus, Hes., Eur., Hdt. **II.** = χάσμημα, Eur. **III.** generally, *any wide expanse,* χάσμα πελάγεος τὸ δὴ Αἰγαῖον καλέεται Hdt. Hence

χασμάω, *to yawn, gape wide,* Ar. **II.** as Dep. **χασμάομαι,** Plat.

χασμέομαι, = χασμάομαι, part. χασμεύμενος, Theocr.

χάσμη, ἡ, (χάσμα) *a yawning, gaping,* Plat.

χάσμημα, τό, *a wide yawn* or *gape,* Lat. *rictus,* Ar.

ΧΑΤΕΩ, only in pres. : **I.** c. inf. *to crave, long to do* a thing, Od. ; absol. χατέοντί περ ἔμπης Il. ; μάλα περ χατέουσι Od. **II.** c. gen. *to crave, have need of,* Ib. Hence

χᾰτίζω, only in pres., *to have need of, crave,* c. gen., Hom. : absol. ὅσσον χατίζει nor *in want* [of anything], Id. ; χατίζων *a needy, poor person,* Hes. 2. *to lack, be without,* χ. ἔργοιο, i. e. *to be idle,* Id. :— Med. *to fail, be wanting,* Aesch.

χαυλι-όδους, -όδοντος, ὁ, ἡ, neut. -όδουν, *with out-*

standing teeth or *tusks*, Hes.   **II.** of the teeth, *outstanding, tusky,* ὀδόντες χαυλιόδοντες of the crocodile's teeth, Hdt.; also without ὀδόντας, τετράπουν χαυλιόδοντας φαῖνον of the hippopotamus, Id. (Deriv. of χαυλι- unknown.)

χαυνο-πολίτης, ου, ὁ, *a gaping cit,* who *swallows openmouthed* all that's told him (cf. Κεχηναῖοι), Ar.

χαυνό-πρωκτος, ον, *wide-breeched,* Ar.

χαῦνος, η, ον, and ος, ον, (χαίνω) :—*gaping :* hence, *porous, spongy, loose,* Plat.   **II.** metaph. *unsubstantial, empty, frivolous,* Solon, Pind., Ar. Hence

χαυνότης, ητος, ἡ, *porousness, sponginess,* Xen., Plut.   **II.** metaph. *empty vanity,* Plat., Arist.; and

χαυνόω, f. ώσω, *to make porous* or *flaccid.*   **II.** metaph. *to puff up, fill with conceit,* Eur., Plat. Hence

χαύνωμα, ατος, τό, *loosened earth,* Plut.; and

χαύνωσις, εως, ἡ, *a making slack* or *loose,* metaph. *the making a thing light, weakening its force and weight* (like Lat. *elevatio*), Ar.

χέε, Ep. for ἔχεε, 3 sing. aor. 1 of χέω.

χεζητιάω, Desiderat. of χέζω, Ar.

χέζω (Root ΧΕΔ) : f. χεσοῦμαι : aor. 1 ἔχεσα : aor. 2 ἔχεσον : pf. κέχοδα, pass. κέχεσμαι :—*to ease oneself, do one's need,* Ar. :—Pass., σπέλεθος ἀρτίως κεχεσμένος *dung just dropt,* Id.

χειά, Ion. **χειή,** ἡ, *a hole,* esp. of serpents, Il., Pind. (From Root ΧΑ, χάσκω.)

χειλο-ποτέω, f. ήσω, *to drink with the lips, sip,* Anth.

χεῖλος, εος, τό: pl., gen. χειλῶν, poët. dat. χείλεσσι : *a lip,* Lat. *labrum,* Hom., etc.; proverb., χείλεσι γελᾶν *to laugh with the lips* only, Il.; χείλεα μέν τ' ἐδίην', ὑπερῴην δ' οὐκ ἐδίηνεν *wetted the lips,* but not the palate, i. e. *drank sparingly,* Ib.; ἀπὸ χειλέων, opp. to ἀπὸ καρδίας, with 'lip-service,' Plut.   **2.** of birds, *a bill, beak,* Eur.   **II.** metaph. of things, *the edge, brink, brim, rim,* of a bowl, Od., Hdt., etc.; of a ditch, Il., Hdt.; of rivers, Hdt. Hence

χειλόω, f. ώσω, *to surround with a lip* or *rim,* Xen.

χεῖμα, ατος, τό, (v. χιών) *winter-weather, cold, frost,* Lat. *hiems,* Hom.   **2.** *winter* as a season of the year, opp. to θέρος, Od., Att.; χεῖμα (acc. absol.) *in winter,* Od., Hes.; so dat. χείματι, Soph.   **II.** *a storm,* Aesch., Eur. Hence

χειμάδιον, τό, *a winter-dwelling, winter-quarters,* χειμαδίῳ χρῆσθαι Λήμνῳ Dem. :—mostly in pl., χειμάδια πήγνυσθαι *to fix one's winter-quarters,* Plut.; and

χειμάζω, f. άσω, *to pass the winter,* opp. to θερίζω, Ar., Xen., etc. :—of armies, *to go into winter-quarters, to winter,* Lat. *hiemare,* Hdt., Xen.   **II.** *to raise a storm* or *tempest,* θεοῦ τοιαῦτα χειμάζοντος Soph.; ὅταν χειμάζῃ ὁ θεὸς ἐν τῇ θαλάσσῃ Xen. :—then,   **2.** impers., like ὕει, νίφει, ἐχείμαζε ἡμέρας τρεῖς (in impf. sense) *the storm continued* for three days, Hdt.   **III.** c. acc. *to agitate* or *distress like a storm,* Soph. :—Pass. *to be driven by a storm, suffer from it,* Thuc.; χειμασθεὶς ἀνέμῳ Id.: metaph. *to be tempest-tost, distressed,* esp. of the state considered as a ship, Eur., Ar.; also of single persons, Trag., Plat.

χειμαίνω, f. ἀνῶ, (χεῖμα) *to drive by a storm* :—Pass. *to be driven by a storm, be tempest-tost,* of a ship, Hdt.; metaph., φόβῳ κεχείμανται φρένες Pind.   **II.**

intr. *to be stormy,* θάλασσα ἄγρια χειμήνασα Anth. : —impers., χειμαίνοντος *when it is stormy,* Theocr.

χείμαρος, ὁ, (χεῖμα) *a plug in a ship's bottom,* drawn out when the ship was brought on land, to let out the bilge-water, Hes.

χείμάρ-ροος, ον, Att. contr. **-ρους,** ουν, and shortened **χείμαρ-ρος,** ον : (ῥέω) :—*winter-flowing, swollen by rain* and *melted snow,* ποταμὸς χ. Il., Hdt.; παρὰ ῥείθροισι χειμάρροις Soph.; φάραγγες ὕδατι χειμάρρῳ ῥέουσαι Eur.   **II.** as Subst. (without ποταμός), *a torrent,* Xen., Dem.   **2.** like χαράδρα II. 2, *a conduit,* Dem.

χειμαρ-ρώδης, ες, (εἶδος) *like a torrent,* Strab.

χειμασία, Ion. -ίη, ἡ, *a passing the winter, wintering,* Hdt.

χειμ-ασκέω, f. ήσω, *to exercise oneself in winter,* Polyb.

χειμερίζω, f. σω, = χειμάζω I, Hdt.

χειμερινός, ή, όν, (χεῖμα) *of* or *in winter, of* or *in winter-time,* opp. to θερινός, χ. τροπαί (v. τροπή I), Hdt., Thuc., etc.; τὴν χ. (sc. ὥρην) *during the winter-season,* Hdt.   **2.** *wintry,* Thuc. : v. χειμέριος.

χειμέριος, α, ον, and ος, ον, (χεῖμα) *wintry, stormy,* Il., Hes., Soph.; ὥρη χειμερίη *the wintry* or *stormy season,* Od., Hes.; ἥμαρ χ. Il.; οἱ χειμεριώτατοι μῆνες *the most wintry, stormy* months, Hdt.; χ. νύξ *a stormy* night (in *summer* time), Thuc.; ἀκτὰ χειμερία κυματοπλήξ *a shore stricken by the wintry waves,* Soph.   **2.** metaph., χ. λύπη *raging* pain, Id.— χειμέριος generally means *wintry, stormy,* χειμερινός *in the winter season.*

χειμο-φῠγέω, (φεύγω) *to shun the winter* or *wintry weather,* Strab.

χειμών, ῶνος, ὁ, (v. χιών) *winter,* opp. to θέρος, Il., Att.; χειμῶνος *in winter-time,* Xen.; τοῦ χ. *in the course of the winter,* Thuc.; χειμῶνα *during winter,* Soph.; τὸν χ. *during the winter,* Hdt., Xen.   **2.** *the wintry quarter* of the heavens, *the north,* Βορέας καὶ χ. Hdt.   **II.** *wintry weather, a winter-storm,* and generally *a storm,* Hom., Hdt., Att.; χ. κατερράγη Hdt.; ἐπέπεσέ σφι χ. μέγας Id.; ὥρσε θεὸς χειμῶνα Aesch.; χ. νοτερός *a storm* of rain, Thuc. :— in pl., ὑπὸ τῶν χ. *by means of the winter-storms,* Hdt.   **2.** metaph. θεόσσυτος χ. *a storm of calamity* sent by the gods, Aesch.; δορὸς ἐν χειμῶνι in the *storm* of battle, Soph.; θολερῷ χ. νοσήσας, of the madness of Ajax, Id.

ΧΕΙ'Ρ, ἡ, χειρός, χειρί, χεῖρα, dual χεῖρε, χεροῖν, pl. χεῖρες, χερῶν, χερσί, χεῖρας ;—the penult. being regularly short, when the ult. is long :—but Poets used the penult. long or short, as the verse required, χερός, χερί, χέρα, χέρε, χέρι, χέρας, poët. forms, dat. pl. χείρεσι, χείρεσσι, χέρεσσι : acc. pl. χέρρας. *The hand,* Hom., etc.: also *the hand and arm, the arm,* χεῖρα μέσην ἀγκῶνος ἔνερθεν Il.; χεῖρες ἀπ' ὤμων ἀίσσοντο Hes.; so, ἐν χερσὶ πεσεῖν *into the arms,* Il., etc.; ἄκρη χείρ, to denote *the hand* as distinct from *the arm,* Ib.   **II.** Special usages: **1.** to denote position, ἐπ' ἀριστερὰ χειρός Od.; ἐπὶ δεξιὰ χειρός Pind.; λαιᾶς χειρός *on the left hand,* Aesch.; ποτέρας τῆς χειρός; *on which hand?* Eur.   **2.** the dat. is common with Verbs which imply the use of hands, χειρὶ λαβεῖν, χερσὶν ἑλέσθαι, etc., Hom., etc.   **3.**

the gen. is used when *one takes a person by the hand*, χειρὸς ἔχειν τινά Il.; χειρὸς ἑλών Ib. **4.** the acc. is used when *one takes the hand of a person*, χεῖρα γέροντος ἑλών Ib.; χεῖράς τ᾽ ἀλλήλων λαβέτην, in pledge of good faith, Ib. **5.** other uses of the acc.: **a.** of suppliants, χεῖρας ἀνασχεῖν θεοῖς, in prayer, Ib.; χεῖρας ἀμφιβάλλειν γούνασι or δείρῃ Od.; also, χεῖρας αἴρειν is to hold up *hands* in voting, Xen., etc.:—χεῖρα ὑπερέχειν τινός or τινί to hold *the hand* over him as a protector, Il. **b.** in hostile sense, χεῖρας or χεῖρα ἐπιφέρειν τινί, ἐφιέναι τινί Hom. **c.** χεῖρας ἀπέχειν τινός to keep *hands* off a person or thing, Lat. *abstinere manus ab aliquo*, Id. **6.** with Preps., ἀπὸ χειρὸς λογίζεσθαι to reckon *off hand*, *roughly*, Ar.:—διὰ χερῶν λαβεῖν, literally, to take *between the hands*, Soph.; διὰ χειρὸς ἔχειν to have *in hand*, i. e. *under control*, Thuc.; and so, to have a work *in hand*, Id.: —so, εἰς χεῖρας λαμβάνειν to take *in hand*, undertake, Eur.; ἄγεσθαί τι ἐς χεῖρας Hdt.; ἐς χεῖρας ἱκέσθαι τινός to fall into his *hands*, Il.; ἐς χεῖρας ἐλθεῖν, ἰέναι τινί to come to *blows* or *close quarters* with, Lat. *manum conserere cum aliquo*, Aesch., Soph.; Hdt. expresses this by ἐς χειρῶν νόμον ἀπικέσθαι:—also, εἰς χεῖρας δέχεσθαι or ὑπομένειν to await their charge, Xen., Thuc.: —ἐκ χειρός *from near at hand*, *close*, Lat. *cominus*, Xen.:—ἐν χερσίν or ἐν χειρὶ ἔχειν, like διὰ χειρὸς ἔχειν, to have *in hand*, *be engaged in*, Hdt., Plat.; ἐν χερσὶ *to hand*, Lat. *cominus*, Thuc.:—κατὰ χειρός, of washing the hands before meals, ὕδωρ κατὰ χειρός or κατὰ χειρὸς ὕδωρ (sc. φερέτω τις), Ar.:—μετὰ χερσὶν ἔχειν *between*, i. e. *in*, *the hands*, Il.; but, μετὰ χεῖρας ἔχειν to have *in hand*, *be engaged in*, Hdt., Thuc.:—πρὸ χειρῶν *close before one*, Soph., Eur.:—πρὸς χεῖρα at a sign *given by hand*, Soph.:—ὑπὸ χεῖρα ποιεῖσθαι to bring *under one's power*, Xen.; cf. ὑποχείριος. **III.** to denote *act* or *deed*, as opp. to mere words, in pl., ἔπεσιν καὶ χερσὶν ἀρήξειν Il.; χερσίν τε ποσίν τε Ib.; χερσὶν ἢ λόγῳ Soph.; μιᾷ χειρί single-handed, Dem.; χειρὶ καὶ ποδὶ καὶ πάσῃ δυνάμει Aeschin.:—esp. of deeds of violence, πρὶν χειρῶν γεύσασθαι before we try *force*, Od.; ἀδίκων χειρῶν ἄρχειν to give the first *blow*, Xen. **IV.** like Lat. *manus*, a body of men, a *band*, *number*, Hdt., Thuc.; πολλῇ χ. Eur.; οἰκεία χείρ, for χεὶρ οἰκετῶν, Id. **V.** one's *hand*, i. e. *handwriting*, N. T.: also *a handiwork*, *a work of art*, σοφαὶ χέρες Anth. **VI.** of any implement resembling a hand: **1.** a kind of *gauntlet* or *target*, Xen. **2.** χ. σιδηρᾶ a *grappling-iron*, *grapnel*, Thuc.

χειρᾰγωγέω, f. ήσω, to lead by the hand, absol., Luc.
χειρ-ᾰγωγός, ὁ, one that leads by the hand, a leader, guide, N. T.
χειρ-απτάζω, f. άσω, (ἅπτω) to touch with the hand, take in hand, handle, Hdt.
χείρεσσι, Ep. dat. pl. of χείρ.
χειριδωτός, όν, having sleeves, sleeved, κιθὼν χειριδωτός, worn by Asiatics, Hdt.; cf. ἐξωμίς.
χείριος, α, ον, = ὑποχείριος, in the hands, in the power or control, Eur.; mostly with a Verb, χειρίαν ἐφείς τινι having left me as a captive to another, Soph.; χείριον λαβεῖν τινα to get him *into one's power*, Eur.
χειρίς, ίδος, ἡ, (χείρ) a covering for the hand, a glove,

Od., Xen.: also a covering for the arm, a loose sleeve, such as the Persians wore, Lat. *manica*, Hdt.
χειρο-δάϊκτος, ον, (δαΐζω) slain by hand, Soph.
χειρο-δεικτος, ον, (δείκνυμι) Lat. *digito monstratus*, manifest, Soph.
χειρο-δίκης [ῑ], ου, ὁ, (δίκη) one who asserts his right by hand, uses the right of might, Hes.
χειρο-δράκων [ᾰ], οντος, ὁ, with serpent arms, Eur.
χειρο-ήθης, ες, (ἦθος) accustomed to the hand, manageable; of animals, submissive, tame, Lat. *mansuetus*, Hdt., Xen. **2.** of things, tolerable, Plut.
χειρό-μακτρον, τό, a cloth for wiping the hands, a towel, napkin, Lat. *mantile*, Hdt., Xen.
χειρο-μύλη, ἡ, a hand-mill, Xen.
χειρο-νομέω, f. ήσω, to move the hands in pantomimic gestures, to gesticulate, Xen.; τοῖς σκέλεσι χειρονομεῖν, of one standing on his head, Hdt.
χειρονομία, ἡ, gesticulation, Luc.
χειρο-πληθής, ές, (πλῆθος) filling the hand, as large as can be held in the hand, λίθος Xen.; κορύνη Theocr.
χειρο-ποιέω, to make by hand:—Med., χειροποιεῖται τάδε perpetrates these acts, Soph. Hence
χειροποίητος, ον, made by hand, artificial, opp. to αὐτοφυής (natural), Hdt.; φλὸξ χ. a fire kindled by the hand of man, Thuc.
χειρο-τένων, οντος, ὁ, ἡ, with outstretched arms, of the crab, Batr.
χειρότερος, α, ον, Ep. for χείρων, Il., Hes.
χειροτέχνημα, ατος, τό, a work of art, Babr. From
χειρο-τέχνης, ου, ὁ, a handicraftsman, artisan, Hdt., Ar., etc.; τίς ὁ χ. ἰατορίας; who is the skilled surgeon? Soph. Hence
χειροτεχνία, ἡ, handicraft, Plat.; and
χειροτεχνικός, ή, όν, of or for handicraft, skilful, χειροτεχνικώτατος Ar. **2.** of artisans, Plat.
χειροτονέω, f. ήσω, (χειρότονος) to stretch out the hand, for the purpose of voting, Plut., Luc. **II.** c. acc. pers. to vote for, elect, properly by show of hands, Ar., Dem.:—Pass. to be elected, Ar., etc.; χειροτονηθῆναι, election, was opp. to λαχεῖν, appointment by lot, Plat., etc. **2.** c. acc. rei, to vote for a thing, Dem.; so c. inf. to vote that .., Aeschin.:— Pass., κεχειροτόνηται ὕβρις εἶναι it is voted, ruled to be violence, Dem. Hence
χειροτονητός, ή, όν, verb. Adj. elected by show of hands, Aeschin.; ἀρχὴ χ. an elective magistracy, opp. to κληρωτῇ, Id.
χειροτονία, ἡ, a voting or electing by show of hands, Thuc. **2.** a vote, Lat. *suffragium*, in pl., Aeschin.
χειρό-τονος, ον, (τείνω) stretching out the hands, λιταὶ χ. offered with outstretched hands, Aesch.
χειρουργέω, (χειρουργός) to do with the hand, execute, esp. of acts of violence, Thuc., Aeschin. **2.** to have in hand, pursue practically, Arist. Hence
χειρούργημα, ατος, τό, handiwork, Plat.; and
χειρουργία, ἡ, a working by hand, practice of a handicraft or art, skill herein, Plat., etc. **II.** a handicraft, Id.:—esp. the practice of chirurgery, surgery.
χειρουργικός, ή, όν, of or for handiwork, Arist.
χειρ-ουργός, όν, (*ἔργω) doing by hand, Plut. **II.** χειρουργός, ὁ, a chirurgeon, surgeon, Id., Anth.
χειρόω, f. ώσω, (χείρ) to bring into hand, to manage,

master, subdue, Ar. **II.** mostly in Med., f. -ώσομαι : aor. 1 ἐχειρωσάμην : pf. κεχείρωμαι :—*to conquer, overpower, subdue,* Hdt., Trag., etc. : *to take prisoner,* Eur. ; so, τήνδ' ἐχειρούμην ἄγραν *became master of* this booty, Soph. **2.** *without any sense of violence, to master, subdue,* Xen., etc. **III.** χειροῦμαι is also Pass. *to be subdued,* Trag. ; f. χειρωθήσομαι Dem. ; aor. 1 ἐχειρώθην Hdt., Soph. ; pf. κεχείρωμαι Aesch., Thuc. Hence

χείρωμα, ατος, τό, *that which is conquered, a conquest,* Aesch. **2.** *a deed of violence, assault,* Soph. **II.** *a work wrought by the hand,* τυμβοχόα χ., *of earth thrown up,* Aesch.

χείρων, ὁ, ἡ, neut. χεῖρον, gen. ονος, acc. ονα : nom. and acc. pl. χείρονες, -ας, χείρονα, contr. in Att. Prose χείρους, χείρω ; dat. χείροσι, poët. χειρόνεσσι (for the Ep. and Dor. forms χερείων, χερήων, poët. χειρότερος, χερειότερος, v. sub vocc.) :—irreg. Comp. of κακός : (from Root ΧΕΡ, v. χερείων II) : **I.** *of persons, worse, meaner, inferior,* Hom., etc. ; σὺ μὲν ἐσθλός, ἐγὼ δὲ σέθεν πολὺ χείρων Il. : in moral sense, *worse than others, a knave,* Soph., Thuc., etc. **2.** *worse in quality, inferior,* Il. ; χ. εἰς τὴν ἀρετήν Plat. ; χ. τὰ πολεμικά Xen. ; c. inf., χ. ποιεῖν Id. **II.** *of things, inferior,* Il., Xen. **2.** *worse, more severe, νόσος* Eur. ; *μοῖρα* Plat. **III.** the neut. is used, **1.** as a Subst., τὰ χερείονα *the worse advice, ill counsels,* Il. :—ἐπὶ τὸ χεῖρον τρέπεσθαι, κλίνειν *to fall off, get worse,* Xen. **2.** χεῖρόν τινι (sc. ἔστι or ἔσται) *it is* or *will be worse for one,* Od., Xen. ; οὐ χεῖρον, in an answer, *'tis well,* Ar. **3.** as Adv., like Lat. *pejus, worse,* χεῖρον βουλεύεσθαι Thuc. ; βιῶναι, ζῆν Plat. **b.** *in inferior degree, less,* Xen., etc.

B. Sup. **χείριστος, η, ον,** *worst,* Lat. *pessimus,* Plat., etc. : esp. οἱ χείριστοι *men of lowest degree,* Xen.

Χείρων, ωνος, ὁ (χείρ) *Cheiron,* one of the Centaurs, a famous *chirurgeon* (cf. χειρουργός 11), teacher of Achilles, Il.

χειρ-ῶναξ, ακτος, ὁ, *one who is master of his hands* (ἄναξ τῶν χερῶν), i. e. *a handicraftsman, artisan, mechanic,* Hdt. Hence

χειρωναξία, Ion. -ίη, ἡ, *handicraft, work,* Hdt., Aesch.

Χειρωνίς (sc. βίβλος), ίδος, ἡ, *a book on surgery,* Anth.

χείσομαι, fut. of χανδάνω.

χείω, Ep. for χέω, *to pour.*

χελεύς, έως, ὁ, = χέλυς, Hesych.

χελιδόνειος, ον, v. χελιδόνιος.

χελιδόνιον, τό, *swallow-wort, celandine,* Theocr., Anth.

χελιδόνιος or -ειος, α, ον, (χελιδών) *of the swallow, like the swallow,* esp. *coloured like the swallow's throat, reddish-brown, russet,* Ar.

χελιδονίς, ίδος, ἡ, poët. for χελιδών, Anth.

χελιδόνισμα, ατος, τό, *the swallow-song,* an old song sung at the return of the swallows, cf. Ar. Av. 1410 sq.

ΧΕΛΙ-ΔΩ'Ν, όνος, ἡ, voc. χελιδόν, also χελιδοῖ (as if from a nom. χελιδώ) :—*the swallow,* Od., etc. :— the twittering of the swallow was proverbially used of barbarous tongues by the Greeks, Aesch. ; χελιδόνων μουσεῖα (v. μουσεῖον) : proverbs also, μία χελιδὼν ἔαρ οὐ ποιεῖ Arist. **II.** *the frog in a horse's foot,* so called from its being *forked like the swallow's tail,* Xen.

χελύνη [ῠ], ἡ, = χεῖλος, *the lip,* Ar.

ΧΕ'ΛΥΣ, υος, ἡ, *a tortoise,* Lat. *testudo* :—then, since Hermes made *the lyre* by stretching strings on its shell, which acted as a sounding-board, χέλυς came to mean *the lyre,* h. Hom. Merc., Eur. **II.** *the arched breast, the chest,* from its likeness of shape to the back of a tortoise, Eur. Hence

χελώνη, ἡ, *a tortoise,* h. Hom., Hdt. ; prov. of insensibility, ἰὼ χελῶναι μακάριαι τοῦ δέρματος oh ye tortoises, *happy in your thick skins!* Ar. **II.** like Roman *testudo,* a pent-house formed of shields overlapping each other like the scales on a tortoise's back, used by storming parties in approaching a city's walls : then, generally, *a pent-house* for protecting besiegers, Xen.

χέννιον, τό, *a kind of quail,* Anth.

χέραδος, τό, *the mud, sand, gravel, and rubbish, silt,* brought down by torrents, Il. (Deriv. uncertain.)

χερειότερος, α, ον, Ep. for sq., Il.

χερείων, Dor. **χερήων, ὁ, ἡ,** Ep. for χείρων, *meaner, inferior,* in rank, worth or wealth, Hom. **2.** *of things,* οὔ τι χέρειον *'tis not the worse part,* i. e. *'tis the better part,* Od. **II.** besides this, we have several irreg. forms (as if from a nom. χέρης), dat. χέρηι, acc. χέρηα, nom. pl. χέρηες, acc. neut. χέρηα, all used in compar. sense, χώσεται ἀνδρὶ χέρηι shall be wroth with a man *of meaner rank,* Il. ; ἐσθλὰ μὲν ἐσθλὸς ἔδυνε, χέρηα δὲ χείρονι δόσκεν, where ἐσθλά ἐσθλός and χέρηα χείρονι are evidently correlative, Ib. ; with a gen., εἷο χέρηα *inferior to* himself, Ib. ; χέρηα πατρός Od.

χέρεσσι, Ep. dat. pl. of χείρ.

χερι-άρης [ἄ], ον, ὁ, (ἀραρίσκω) *skilled in fitting with the hand, dexterous,* Pind.

χερί-φυρής, ές, (φύρω) *mixed* or *kneaded by hand,* Anth.

χερμάδιον [ἄ], τό, *a large stone, a boulder,* used as a missile, Hom. (Deriv. uncertain.)

χερμάς, άδος, ἡ, = Homer's χερμάδιον, Pind., Aesch.

χερμαστήρ, ῆρος, ὁ, *a slinger,* χ. ῥινός the leather *of a sling,* out of which the stone was thrown, Anth.

χερνής, ῆτος, Dor. **χερνάς, ᾶτος, ὁ,** *one who lives by his hands, a day-labourer, a poor man,* Anth. **2.** as Adj. *poor, needy,* ἐν δόμοις χερνῆσι Eur. (Deriv. uncertain.)

χερνήτης, ου, ὁ, = χερνής, Aesch. Hence

χερνητικός, ή, όν, of or for a day-labourer : τὸ χ., *the proletariate,* Arist.

χερνῆτις, ιδος, fem. of χερνήτης, *a woman that spins for daily hire,* Il.

χέρ-νῖβον, τό, *a vessel for water to wash the hands, a basin,* Il. From

χερνίπτομαι, f. ψομαι, (χείρ, νίζω) : Med. :—*to wash one's hands,* esp. before sacrifice, Il., Ar., etc. **2.** *to sprinkle with holy water, purify* or *dedicate thereby,* Eur. Hence

χέρνιψ, ιβος, ἡ, *water for washing the hands,* before meals, or before sacrifices and religious services, Od., Ar. **2.** pl. χέρνιβες, *purifications with holy water,* Eur. ; εἴργεσθαι χερνίβων *to be excluded from the use thereof,* as were those defiled by bloodshed, Dem. ; χέρνιβας νέμειν *to allow the use of it,* Soph. ; χερνίβων κοινωνός *a partaker therein,* i. e. *a member of* the

household, Aesch. **3.** rarely of *libations* to the dead, Id., Soph.

χερο-μῦσής, ές, (μύσος) *defiling the hand,* Aesch.

χερό-πληκτος, ον, *stricken by the hand,* χερόπληκτοι δοῦποι the sound *of beating with the hand,* Soph.

χερός, poët. for χειρός, gen. of χείρ.

χερρό-νησος, ή, Att. for χερσόνησος.

χερρός, Aeol. for χειρός, gen. of χείρ.

χερσαῖος, α, ον, (χέρσος) *on* or *of dry land,* ὄρνιθες χ. land-birds, opp. to λιμναῖοι, Hdt.; χ. κροκόδειλος a lizard, Id. :—also of *landsmen,* as opp. to seamen, Eur., Thuc.; κῦμα χερσαῖον στρατοῦ, an army, opp. to a fleet, Aesch.

χερσεύω, *to be dry land, to lie waste* or *barren,* Xen.

χερσόθεν, Adv. (χέρσος) *from dry land,* Eur. **II.** *from the ground,* Pind. Hence

χερσόθῖ, Adv. *on dry land,* Anth.

χέρσονδε, Adv. (χέρσος) *to* or *on dry land,* Il., Theocr.

χερσονησίζω, Att. **χερρ-,** f. ίσω, *to form a* χερσόνησος or *peninsula,* Polyb.

χερσονήσιος, later Att. **χερρ-, α, ον,** *of* or *like a peninsula :* of the Thracian Chersonese, Eur.

χερσονησίτης [ῑ], later Att. **χερρ-, ου, ὁ,** *a dweller in the Thracian Chersonese,* Eur., Dem.

χερσονησο-ειδής, later Att. **χερρ-, ές,** (εἶδος) *like a peninsula, peninsular,* of Mount Athos, Hdt.

χερσό-νησος, later Att. **χερρό-, ή,** *a land-island,* i. e. *a peninsula,* Hdt. **II.** as pr. n. *the Chersonese,* i. e. the peninsula of Thrace that runs along the Hellespont, Id. :—also *the Tauric Chersonese, Crimea,* Id.; the peninsula between Epidaurus and Troezen, Thuc.

χέρσος, later Att. **χέρρος, ή,** *dry land, land,* ἐπὶ χέρσου, opp. to ἐν πόντῳ, Od.; κύματα κυλινδόμενα προτὶ χέρσον Ib.; κῦμα χέρσῳ ῥηγνύμενον Il.; χέρσῳ *on* or *by land,* Aesch., Eur. **II.** as Adj., **χέρσος, ον,** *dry, firm,* of land, Hdt.; ἐν κονίᾳ χέρσῳ, opp. to πόντῳ, Pind. **2.** *dry, hard, barren,* Hdt., Soph.; χ. λιμήν a harbour *left dry,* Anth. **3.** metaph. *barren, without children,* of women, Soph. : c. gen. *barren of,* πυρὰ χέρσος ἀγλαϊσμάτων Eur. (Prob. from same Root as ξηρός.)

χερύδριον, τό, Dim. of χείρ, Mosch.

χεσείω, Desiderat. of χέζω, Lat. *cacaturio,* Ar.

χεῦαι, Ep. for χέαι, aor. 1 inf. of χέω:—**χεῦε, χεῦαν,** Ep. 3 sing. and pl.

χεῦμα, ατος, τό, (χέω) *that which is poured, a stream,* Il., Trag. **II.** *that into which water is poured, a bowl,* Hdt.

χεύομεν, Ep. 1 pl. aor. 1 of sq. :—also, **χεύω,** Ep. fut.

χέω (Root ΧΥ), f. **χεῶ,** Ep. **χεύω:** aor. 1 **ἔχεα,** Ep. ἔχευα, Ep. subj. χεύομεν : pf. κέχυκα :—Med., f. χέομαι : aor. 1 ἐχεάμην, Ep. ἐχευάμην, χευάμην :—Pass., f. χυθήσομαι : aor. 1 ἐχύθην [ῠ] : Ep. 3 sing. and pl. aor. 2 χύτο [ῠ], ἔχυντο, χύντο, part. χύμενος : pf. κέχυμαι : Ep. 3 sing. plqpf. κέχυτο. Radic. sense, *to pour :* **I.** properly of liquids, *to pour out, pour,* Hom., etc.; Zeus χέει ὕδωρ, i. e. he makes it rain, Il.; χέει χιόνα βορέας Eur.; absol., χέει *it snows,* Il. :—Med. *to pour for oneself,* esp. of drink-offerings, χοὰς χεόμην νεκύεσσι Od., etc. :—Pass. χέονται κρῆναι they *gush forth,* Eur.;

χυθέντος ποτοῦ ἐς γῆν Soph. **2.** χ. δάκρυα *to shed* tears, Il., Eur. :—Pass., of tears, *to pour* or *gush forth,* Hom.; so of blood, *to be shed,* Aesch. **3.** in Pass. *to become liquid, melt, thaw,* Xen. **II.** of solids, *to shed, scatter,* φύλλα Il.; πτερά Od.; χ. κόνιν κὰκ κεφαλῆς Hom.; χ. καλάμην χθονί, of a mower or reaper (v. καλάμη), Il. **2.** like χώννυμι, *to throw out* earth, so as to form a mound, σῆμα, τύμβον χ. Hom. **3.** χ. δοῦρα *to pour* or *shower* spears, Il.; Med., βέλεα χέοντο they *showered* their arrows, Ib. **4.** *to let fall* or *drop,* ἠνία Ib.; so, χέειν κρόκου βαφὰς (v. βαφή II) Aesch.; but, καρπὸν χ., of trees, *to produce* fruit *abundantly,* Od. **5.** in Pass. *to be thrown* or *heaped up together,* Hom., Hdt. **6.** in Pass. also of living beings, *to pour* or *stream in a dense mass* or *throng,* Hom. **III.** metaph. of sounds, *to pour forth,* φωνήν, αὐδήν Od.; φθόγγον Aesch. **2.** of things that obscure the sight, κατ' ὀφθαλμῶν χέεν ἀχλύν *shed* a dark cloud over the eyes, Il.; πολλὴν ἠέρα χεῦε *shed* a mist abroad, Od. :—Pass., ἀμφὶ δέ οἱ θάνατος χύτο *was shed* around him, Il.; νόσος κέχυται Soph.; φρὶξ ἐπὶ πόντον ἐχεύατο (Med. in pass. sense), Il. **3.** of persons, ἀμφ' αὐτῷ χυμένη *throwing herself* around him, Hom.; so in Med., ἀμφὶ υἱὸν ἐχεύατο πήχεε Il. **4.** pf. pass. κέχυμαι, *to be wholly engaged in,* Δᾶλος, ἐν ᾇ κέχυμαι Pind.

χή, crasis for καὶ ἡ.

χήλ-αργος, Dor. **χᾱλ-, ον,** (χηλή) *with fleet hoofs,* χ. ἄμιλλαι the racing *of fleet horses,* Soph.

χηλευτός, ή, όν, verb. Adj. *netted, plaited,* Hdt. From

χηλεύω, (χηλή III) *to net, plait,* Eupol.

ΧΗΛΗ', ῆς, *a horse's hoof,* Hes., Eur. :—also, *a cloven hoof,* Eur. **2.** in pl., of *the talons* of a bird, Trag.; of a wolf's *claws,* Theocr. **II.** *a sea-bank, break-water,* formed of stones laid at the base of a sea-wall, to break the force of the waves (so called because it projected *like a hoof*), Lat. *crepido,* Thuc., Xen. **2.** *the spur of a mountain* or *ridge of rocks* answering a like purpose, Thuc. **III.** *a cloven implement,* such as a *netting-needle ;*—cf. χηλεύω.

χηλός, οῦ, ή, *a large chest* or *coffer,* Hom., Theocr.

ΧΗ'Ν, ὁ and **ή,** gen. χηνός : gen. pl. χηνῶν ; irreg. acc. pl. χένας :—Lat. *anser,* the wild goose, Il. : *the tame goose,* Od., etc. :—νὴ or μὰ τὸν χῆνα was Socrates' form of oath, instead of Ζῆνα.

χην-ἀλώπηξ, εκος, ὁ, *the fox-goose, vulpanser,* an Egyptian species, living in holes, Hdt., Ar.

χήνειος, α, ον, Ion. **χήνεος, η, ον,** *of* or *belonging to a goose,* Lat. *anserinus,* Hdt.

χηνίσκος, ὁ, Dim. of χήν :—*a ship's stern turned up like a goose's neck,* Luc.

χήρα, Ion. **χήρη, ή,** *bereft of a husband, a widow,* Lat. *vidua,* c. gen., χήρη σευ ἔσομαι, says Andromaché to Hector, Il.; χῆραι γυναῖκες *widow* women, Ib.; so Eur., etc. **2.** from χῆρα was formed the masc. χῆρος (as *widower* from *widow*), Anth. **II.** **χῆρος, α, ον,** as Adj., in metaph. sense, *widowed, bereaved,* χῆρα μέλαθρα Eur.; c. gen., φάρσος στελεοῦ χῆρον *a piece torn from the stem,* Anth. (Deriv. uncertain.)

χηραμός, ὁ, ή, = χειά, *a hole, cleft, hollow,* Il.; of a mouse's *hole,* Babr.

χήρατο, 3 sing. Ep. aor. 1 of χαίρω.

χηρεία, ἡ, (χηρεύω) widowhood, Thuc.

χήρειος, α, ον, (χήρα) widowed, Anth.

χηρεύω, f. σω, (χήρα) intr. to be bereaved of a person or thing, c. gen., Od., Theogn. 2. absol. to be bereaved of a husband, to be widowed, live in widowhood, Dem., etc.;—of a man, to be a widower, Plut.; so, χηρεύσει λέχος Eur. 3. to live in solitude, of an exile, Soph. II. trans. to bereave, Eur.

χῆρος, α, ον, v. χήρα II. II. χῆρος, ὁ, v. χήρα I.

χηρόω, f. ώσω, trans. to make desolate, χήρωσε δ᾽ ἀγυιάς Il.; χήρωσας γυναῖκα thou did'st widow her, Ib. 2. c. gen. to bereave of a thing, Anth. :—Pass., Ἄργος ἀνδρῶν ἐχηρώθη Hdt. II. intr., like χηρεύω, to be bereft of, τινός Theogn.

χηρωσταί, ῶν, οἱ, (χηρόω) kinsmen, who divide the property of one who dies without heirs (χῆρος) Il.

χήσεῖτε, Dor. crasis for καὶ ἥσετε (fut. of ἵημι).

χῆτις, ἡ, = χῆτος, χήτι συμμάχων (Ion. dat.), Hdt.; χήτεϊ οἰκείων Plat.

χῆτος, εος, τό, (χάτέω) want, need, c. gen. pers., χητεῖ τοιοῦδ᾽ ἀνδρός from want or need of such a man, Il.; χήτεϊ τοιοῦδ᾽ υἷος Ib. Hence

χητοσύνη, ἡ, need, destitution, loneliness, Anth.

χθἄμᾰλός, ή, όν, (χαμαί, with θ inserted) near the ground, on the ground, flat, Hom., Theocr.

ΧΘΕ΄Σ, Adv., (lengthd. ἐχθές, q. v.) yesterday, h. Hom., Plat., etc.; οἱ χθὲς λόγοι Plat.; πρώην τε καὶ χθές or χθὲς καὶ πρώην (v. πρώην).

χθεσῖνός, ή, όν, = χθιζός, Luc.

χθιζῖνός, ή, όν, = χθιζός, Ar.

χθιζός, ή, όν, (χθές) of yesterday, τὸ χθιζὸν χρεῖος their yesterday's debt, Il.; ὁ χθ. πόνος yesterday's labour, Hdt.; in adverb. sense, with Verbs, χθιζὸς ἔβη he went yesterday, Il.; χθ. ἤλυθες Od., etc. :—neut. χθιζόν as Adv. = χθές, Hom.; so pl. χθιζά, v. πρώϊζος.

χθόνιος, α, ον, and ος, ον, (χθών) in, under or beneath the earth, Hes., Soph.; of subterranean noises, κτυπεῖ Ζεὺς χθ. Soph.; χθ. βροντήματα Aesch. :—also, χθόνιοι θεοί the gods of the nether world, Lat. Inferi, Id.; and χθόνιοι alone, Pind., Aesch.; χθόνιαι θεαί, i. e. Demeter and Persephoné, Hdt.; of the Erinyes, Soph.; χθ. Ἑρμῆς, as conductor of the dead, Aesch., Soph.; χάρις ἡ χθονία grace with the gods below, Soph. II. of or from the earth, of the Titans, as sons of Gaia, Hes., Aesch. 2. like ἐγχώριος, of persons, in or of the country, native, Soph. III. of things, of the earth, χθ. κόνις Aesch.

χθονο-στῐβής, ές, (στείβω) treading the earth, Soph.

χθονο-τρεφής, ές, (τρέφω) bred from earth, Aesch.

ΧΘΩ΄Ν, ἡ, gen. χθονός, the earth, ground, Hom., Trag.;—to denote life upon the earth, ζῶντος καὶ ἐπὶ χθονὶ δερκομένοιο Il.; χθόνα δῦναι to go beneath the earth, i. e. to die, Ib.; κατὰ χθονὸς κρύπτειν τινά Soph.; κοῦφά σοι χθὼν ἐπάνω πέσειε Eur. 2. of the nether world, οἱ ὑπὸ χθονός, i. e. those in the shades below, Lat. inferi, Aesch.; κατὰ χθονὸς θεαί, i. e. the Erinyes, Id. 3. earth, i. e. the whole earth, the world, Id., Soph. 4. Earth, as a goddess, Aesch. II. a particular land or country, of Ithaca, Od.; of Libya, Pind.; χθὼν Ἀσιᾶτις, Δωρίς, Ἀργεία, Ἑλλάς, Ἰδαία, etc., Trag.

χῖδρον, τό, mostly in pl. χῖδρα, τά, unripe wheaten-groats, as ἄλφιτα are barley-groats, Ar.

χῑλῑαρχέω, f. ήσω, to be a χιλίαρχος, Plut.

χῑλῐ-άρχης, ου, ὁ, = χῑλίαρχος, Hdt.

χῑλῐαρχία, ἡ, the office or post of χιλίαρχος, Xen. 2. the office of the tribuni militares, Id.

χῑλῐ-αρχος, ὁ, the commander of a thousand men, a chiliarch, Aesch., Xen. II. used to translate the Roman tribunus militum, Polyb., etc.;—also of the tribuni militares consulari potestate, Plut.

χῑλῐάς, άδος, ἡ, the number one thousand, a thousand, Hdt., Aesch.; c. gen., πολλαὶ χιλιάδες ταλάντων Hdt. : —generally, a very large number, Theocr.

χῑλῐ-έτης, ου, ὁ, or χιλι-ετής, έος, ὁ, ἡ, (ἔτος) lasting a thousand years, Plat.

ΧΙ΄ΛΙΟΙ [ῐ], αι, α, a thousand, Lat. mille, Il. : it commonly agrees with its Subst., but is also a Subst. foll. by a gen., χίλιοι Πελοποννησίων Thuc. :—to express a thousand drachmae, χίλιαι is often used alone, περὶ χιλιῶν κινδυνεύειν Dem. : in military language in sing. with collective nouns, ἵππος χιλίη a thousand horse, Hdt.

χῑλῐό-ναυς, εως, ὁ, ἡ, of a thousand ships, Eur.

χῑλῐο-ναύτης, ου, Dor. -ναύτας, α, ὁ, ἡ, with or of a thousand ships, Aesch., Eur.

χῑλῐό-πᾰλαι, Adv. a thousand times long ago, long long ago, Eur.

χίλιος, α, ον, v. χίλιοι.

χῑλῐοστός, ή, όν, (χίλιοι) the thousandth, Plat., Xen.

χῑλῐοστύς, ύος, ἡ, (χίλιοι) a body of a thousand, Xen.

χῑλῐο-τάλαντος [ᾰ], ον, (τάλαντον) weighing or worth a thousand talents, Plut.

ΧΙΛΟ΄Σ, οῦ, ὁ, green fodder for cattle, forage, provender, Hdt., Xen.; προέρχεσθαι ἐπὶ χιλόν to go on to forage, Xen. :—χ. ξηρός hay, Id. Hence

χῑλόω, f. ώσω, to feed horses in stall, Xen.

Χῑλώνειος, α, ον, of or from Χίλων: τὸ Χ. the saying of Chilon, Arist.

χίμαιρα [ῐ], fem. of χίμαρος, a she-goat, Lat. capra, Il., Hes., Att. II. Χίμαιρα, ἡ, Chimaera, a fire-spouting-monster, with lion's head, serpent's tail, and goat's body, killed by Bellerophon, Il.

χἴμαιρο-θύτης [ῠ], ου, ὁ, goat-sacrificer, Anth.

χἴμαιρο-φόνος, ον, (*φένω) goat-slaying, Anth.

χῑμάρ-αρχος, ὁ, goat-leader, τράγος χ. the he-goat that leads the flock, Anth.

ΧΙ΄ΜΑ΄ΡΟΣ [ῐ], ὁ, a he-goat, Lat. caper, = τράγος, Ar., Theocr. II. also fem. = χίμαιρα, Theocr., Anth.

χῑμάρο-σφακτήρ, ῆρος, ὁ, (σφάζω) a goat-slayer, Anth.

χίμετλον, τό, (χεῖμα) a chilblain, kibe, Lat. pernio, Ar.

Χῑο-γενής, ές, (γίγνομαι) of Chian growth, Anth.

χιόνεος, α, ον, (χιών) snowy, snow-white, Bion, Anth. [ῑ in hexam. verse].

χιονίζω, f. ίσω, to snow upon, cover with snow : impers., ἐχιόνιζε τὴν χώρην it was snowing over the country, Hdt. : εἰ ἐχιόνιζε if it was snowing, Id.

χιονό-βλητος, ον, snow-beaten, Ar.

χιονο-θρέμμων, ον, gen. ονος, (τρέφω) fostering snow, snow-clad, Eur.

χιονό-κτῠπος, ον, (τύπτω with κ inserted) snow-beaten, Soph.

χιονο-τρόφος, ον, = χιονοθρέμμων, Eur.

χιονό-χρως, ωτος, ὁ, ἡ, with snow-white skin: snow-white, of a swan, Eur.

χιον-ώδης, ες, (εἶδος) like snow, snowy, Eur.

Χίος, ἡ, Chios, in the Aegean, an island, famed for its wine, Od.: also the town of Chios, Hdt., Thuc. Hence Χῖος, α, ον, (contr. from Χίιος), Chian, of or from Chios, Χ. ἀοιδός, i. e. Homer, Theocr.; Χῖος οἶνος Ar.; so Χῖος alone, Anth. 2. as Subst., Χῖοι, οἱ, the Chians, Hdt., Thuc. II. ὁ Χῖος (sc. βόλος), the worst throw on the dice, the side with the ace-dot being called Χῖος, the opp. side with the size-point being Κῷος:—for οὐ Χῖος ἀλλὰ Κεῖος, v. Κέως.

ΧΙΤΩ´Ν, Ion. κιθών, ῶνος, ὁ, the garment worn next the skin, a frock, Lat. tunica: 1. in early times, a man's frock, Hom.; sometimes with a girdle, and reaching to the feet (τερμιόεις), Od.; of linen, Ib.; over it was worn a mantle (φᾶρος, χλαῖνα), which was laid aside in the house. 2. in later times we hear of two sorts of χιτών, the Ionian and the Dorian;—the Ionian like the Homeric, but worn by women, as well as men, Hdt.; disused by the men about the time of Pericles, Thuc.;—Dorian adopted at Athens when the Ionian was laid aside. The Dorian χιτών was also worn by Spartan women, being open at the side (σχιστός), and fastened with περόναι, Hdt.—Over this χιτών was worn the ἱμάτιον. II. of soldiers, a coat of mail, of leather covered with scales or rings, Il., Hdt. III. the upper leather of a shoe, in pl., Xen. IV. metaph. any coat, case, or covering, λάϊνος χιτών (v. λάϊνος); τειχέων κιθῶνες, i. e. walls, Hdt.; of a serpent's skin, Eur. (Probably an Oriental word.)

χιτωνάριον, τό, Dim. of χιτών, Anth.

χιτώνιον, τό, Dim. of χιτών, properly a woman's frock or shift, Ar.;—also of men, Luc.

χιτωνίσκος, ὁ, Dim. of χιτών, a short frock, worn by men, Ar., Xen., etc.; of women, a shift, Dem.

χιών, όνος, ἡ, snow, Hom., etc.; νιφάδες χιόνος snow-flakes, Il.; χιὼν πίπτουσα Hdt.; χιόνι κατανίφει Ar. II. snow-water, ice-cold water, Eur. (From Root ΧΙ, cf. χεῖ-μα, Lat. hi-ems.)

*χλάδω, assumed as pres. of κέχλᾱδα, to exult, a pf. form in Pind.; καλλίνικος κεχλᾱδώς, of a triumphal hymn, κεχλάδοντας ἥβᾳ, of young heroes.

χλαῖνα, Ion. χλαίνη, ης, ἡ, Lat. laena, a large square upper-garment, a cloak, mantle, Hom.; it was made of wool, and worn over the χιτών, thrown over the shoulders, fastened with a pin or brooch (περόνη).—It is also called φᾶρος by Hom., and in later Greek ἱμάτιον, Latin pallium. (Deriv. uncertain.)

χλαινίον, τό, Dim. of χλαῖνα, Anth.

χλαινόω, to cover with a cloak, to clothe, Anth.

χλαίνωμα, ατος, τό, clothing, χλ. λέοντος a lion's skin cloak, Anth.

χλαμύδη-φόρος, ὁ, one who wears a χλαμύς, a horse-man, cavalier, of the ephebi, Theocr.

χλαμύδιον [ῠ], τό, Dim. of χλαμύς, Plut. 2. a shabby cloak, Id.

χλαμυδο-ειδής, ές, (εἶδος) like a χλαμύς, Strab.

χλαμυδουργία, ἡ, the making of χλαμύδες, the trade of a χλαμυδουργός, Xen. From

χλαμυδουργός, ὁ, (*ἔργω) a maker of χλαμύδες.

ΧΛΑΜΥ´Σ [ῠ], ύδος, ἡ: acc. χλαμύδα, χλάμυν:—a short mantle, worn by horsemen, Xen.; and by the Athen. ἔφηβοι, Anth. 2. generally, a military cloak, Plut.:—also the general's cloak, Lat. paludamentum, Id.

χλᾱνίδιον [ῐ], τό, Dim. of χλανίς, mostly a woman's mantle, Hdt., Soph., Eur.

χλᾱνιδο-ποιΐα, ἡ, the art of a χλανιδοποιός, Xen.

χλᾱνιδο-ποιός, όν, (ποιέω) making χλανίδες.

ΧΛΑΝΙ´Σ, ίδος, ἡ, an upper-garment of wool, a shawl, finer than the χλαῖνα, mostly worn by women, Hdt.; χλανίδα φορεῖν, as a mark of effeminacy, Dem.

χλᾱνίσκιον, τό, Dim. of χλανίς, a cloaklet, Ar., Aeschin.: so χλανισκίδιον, τό, Ar.

χλᾱρός, ά, όν, exultant, χλαρὸν γελᾶν Pind.

χλευάζω, f. άσω, (χλεύη) to joke, jest, scoff, jeer, Ar., Dem.:—so in Med., Plut. 2. c. acc. to mock, scoff at, Dem. Hence

χλευασία, ἡ, mockery, scoffing, Dem.

χλευασμός, ὁ, – χλευασία, Dem. 2. a joke, Plut.

χλευαστής, οῦ, ὁ, a mocker, scoffer, Arist.

ΧΛΕΥΗ´, ἡ, a joke, jest, h. Hom.; χλεύην ποιεῖσθαί τινα to make a jest of one, Anth.

χλῆδος, ὁ, slime, mud, rubbish, Dem.

χλιαίνω, f. ἀνῶ: aor. 1 ἐχλίηνα:—Pass., aor. 1 ἐχλιάνθην: (χλίω):—to warm, Ar., Anth. 2. to heat with passion:—Pass. to be so heated, Anth.

χλιαρός, ά, όν, Ion. χλιερός, ή, όν, (χλίω) warm, luke-warm, Lat. tepidus, Hdt., Ar. 2. of persons, luke-warm, N. T.

χλιδαίνομαι, Pass. (χλιδή) to be luxurious, revel, Xen.

χλιδᾱνός, ή, όν, (χλιδή) luxurious, delicate, voluptuous, Aesch., Eur.

χλιδάω, f. ήσω, (χλιδή) to be soft or delicate, χλιδῶσα μολπή Pind.:—to live delicately, to revel, luxuriate, τινί in a thing, Aesch.; χλ. ἐπί τινι to pride oneself upon a thing, Soph.

χλιδή, ἡ, (χλίω) delicacy, daintiness, luxury, effeminacy, Hdt., Aesch., Plat. 2. wantonness, insolence, arrogance, Aesch., Soph. 3. luxuries, fine raiment, costly ornaments, Lat. deliciae, Eur.;—so in pl., Id.; κατάτομοι χλιδαί luxuriant hair cut from the head, Soph.; παρθένιον χλιδάν a maiden's pride, Eur.

χλίδημα, τό, = χλιδή, Eur.

ΧΛΙ´Ω [ῑ], only in pres. to be or become warm: hence to luxuriate, revel, ἐν τοῖσι σοῖς πόνοισι Aesch.

χλο-αυγής, ές, (αὐγή) with a greenish lustre, Luc.

χλοερός, poët. for χλωρός.

χλοερο-τρόφος, ον, (τρέφω) producing green grass, Eur.

ΧΛΟΗ´, ης, Dor. χλόα, ας, the first shoot of plants in spring, the green blade of corn or grass, Hdt., Eur., etc. 2. the young verdure of trees, foliage, Eur.

χλοη-κομέω, to be green as a young leaf, Anth.

χλοηρός, ά, όν, = χλοερός, χλωρός, Eur.

χλοη-φόρος, ον, bearing green grass or leaves, Eur.

χλούνης, ου, ὁ, Epic epith. of the wild boar, of unknown sense and deriv., perh. for χλο-εύνης, couching in the greenwood, χλ. σῦς ἄγριος Il.; χλούναι σύες Hes.

χλοῦνις, ἡ, a word of unknown sense (like χλούνης), perh. freshness, youthful vigour, Aesch.

χλωρηΐς, ΐδος, poët. fem. of χλωρός, pale-green, brown-green, of the nightingale, Od.

χλωρό-κομος, ον, (κόμη) green-leaved, Eur.

χλωρός, poët. χλοερός, ά, όν, (χλόη) greenish-yellow (like young grass or leaves), pale-green, light-green, green, grassy, Od., Soph., Eur.; σίτου ἔτι χλωροῦ ὄντος Thuc. 2. yellow, of honey, Hom.; ἀμφὶ χλωρὰν ψάμαθον on the yellow sand, Soph. II. generally, pale, pallid, bleached, χλωρὸς ὑπαὶ δείους Il.;—then, as an epith. of fear, χλωρὸν δέος Hom. :— yellow, pallid, of persons affected by the plague, Thuc. III. without regard to colour, green, i. e. fresh, Od., Ar. 2. metaph. fresh, living, χλωρὸν αἷμα Soph., Eur.; χλωρὸν δάκρυ, like θαλερὸν δάκρυ, the fresh, bursting tear, Eur.; χλ. μέλεα fresh, young limbs, Theocr.

χλωρότης, ητος, ἡ, greenness, Plut.

χνάνω, properly = κνάω, to gnaw, nibble, Eur.

χνοάζω, f. άσω, of youths, to get the first down on the chin: metaph., χνοάζων ἄρτι λευκανθὲς κάρα just sprinkling his hair with white (cf. Shakspeare's 'sable silvered'), Soph.

χνοάω, like χνοάζω (only in pres.), of youths, Theocr., Luc.: of the down on the cheeks, to appear, Anth.

ΧΝΟΉ, Ion. χνοίη, ἡ, the box of a wheel in which the axle turns, the nave, Lat. modiolus, Aesch., Soph. 2. metaph., χνόαι ποδῶν the joints on which the feet play, as the wheels on the axle, Aesch.

ΧΝΟ͂ΟΣ, ὁ, Att. contr. χνοῦς, gen. χνοῦ :—any light porous substance, ἁλὸς χνόος the foam that gathers at the edge of the sea, Od.; πωλικὸς χν. horse's foam, Anth. II. the first down on the chin of youths, Lat. lanugo, Ar.: the bloom on fruit, Anth.

χόα, heterocl. acc. of χοῦς.

χοανεύω, contr. χωνεύω, to cast into a mould (χόανος), Ar. II. to cast metal :—Pass., κεχωνευμένος Plut. From

χοάνη [ἄ], contr. χώνη, (χέω) a funnel, Lat. infundibulum, Plat. II. = χόανος, Anth.

χόανος, ὁ, (χέω) a melting-pot, from which the metal was run into the mould, Il., Hes. II. the mould for casting metal in, Anth.

χόες, heterocl. pl. of χοῦς.

χοή, ἡ, (χέω) a drink-offering, Lat. libatio, such especially as were made to the dead (λοιβή or σπονδή being that made to the gods), Od.; often in pl., Trag. 2. rarely of any other than funeral libations, Soph.

χο-ήρης, ες, (ἀραρίσκω) fitted for the Pitcher-feast at Athens (v. χοῦς Α. ΙΙ), Eur.

χοη-φόρος, ον, (φέρω) offering χοαί to the dead ; Χοηφόροι, a Tragedy by Aesch., in which the Chorus pours libations to the shade of Agamemnon.

χόϊ, heterocl. dat. of χοῦς.

χοϊκός, ή, όν, (χοῦς Β) of earth or dust, N. T.

χοινικίς, ίδος, ἡ, (χοῖνιξ) the circle of a crown, Dem.

χοῖνιξ, ικος, ἡ, a choenix, a dry measure, = four κοτύλαι or two sextarii, about a quart Engl., Hdt.; the choenix of corn was one man's daily allowance, Id.; hence, ὅς κεν ἐμῆς γε χοίνικος ἅπτηται i. e. whoever eats of my bread, Od. II. a kind of shackle or stocks for fastening the legs in, Ar., Dem.

χοιραδ-ώδης, ες, (εἶδος) full of χοιράδες, rocky, Strab.

χοιράς, άδος, ἡ, of a hog, χ. πέτραι rocks (rising just above the sea) like a hog's back (cf. Virgil's dorsum immane maris), Pind., Anth. :—hence χοιράς as Subst., a sunken rock, Hdt., Aesch.; so, χ. Δηλία the Delian rock, the rocky isle of Delos, Aesch. II. in pl. scrofulous swellings in the glands of the neck, Anth.

χοίρειος, α, ον, Ep. χοίρεος, η, ον, (χοῖρος) of a swine, Ar., Xen.; χοίρεα (sc. κρέα) pig's-flesh, Od.

χοιρίνη [ῑ], ἡ, a small sea-muscle : its shell was used by the Athenian dicasts in voting, Ar.

χοίρινος, η, ον, = χοίρειος, of hog's skin, Luc.

χοιρίον, τό, Dim. of χοῖρος, a pigling, porker, Ar.

χοιρο-κομεῖον, τό, (κομέω) a pigsty, Ar.

χοιρο-κτόνος, ον, (κτείνω) : χοιρόκτονοι καθαρμοί purification by the sacrifice of swine, Aesch.

χοιρο-πώλης, Dor. -ας, α, ὁ, (πωλέομαι) a pig-jobber, Ar.

ΧΟΙ͂ΡΟΣ, ὁ and ἡ, a young pig, porker, Od., etc.

Χολαργεύς, έως, ὁ, a man of the deme Χόλαργος, Ar.

χολάς, άδος, ἡ, commonly in pl. χολάδες, the bowels, intestines, guts, Il.; made into harp-strings, Anth. (Deriv. uncertain.)

χολάω, (χολή) to be full of black bile, to be melancholy mad, Ar. II. = χολόομαι, to be angry, Mosch.; so in Pass., Theogn.

ΧΟΛΉ, ἡ, gall, bile, Aesch., Eur., Thuc., etc. 2. pl. χολαί, the gall-bladder, Soph.; called δοχαὶ χολῆς in Eur. ;—so in sing., Aesch. II. metaph., like χόλος, Lat. bilis, bile, gall, i. e. bitter anger, wrath, Id., Ar., etc.; πάνυ ἐστί μοι χολή stirs my bile, makes me sick, Ar.; χολὴν κινεῖν τινι Id.

χολίκιον, τό, Dim. of χόλιξ, Theophr.

χόλιξ, ικος, ἡ, mostly in pl. χόλικες, like χολάδες, the guts or bowels of oxen, Ar.; in sing., Id.

χόλιος, α, ον, and ος, ον, (χόλος) raging, angry, Anth.

Χολλείδης, ου, ὁ, a man of the deme Cholleidae, Ar.

ΧΌΛΟΣ, ὁ, like χόλη, gall, bile, Il. II. generally metaph. bile, gall, bitter anger, wrath, Hom., Hdt., Att.; χόλος ἔδυ τινά Il.; χόλος ἔμπεσε θυμῷ Ib.; χόλον πέσσειν, καταπέσσειν (v. sub vocc.); χ. σβέσσαι παῦσαι Ib.; χόλου παύεσθαι Hes. :—c. gen. objecti, anger towards or because of another, Il.; c. gen. rei, anger for, because of a thing, Soph. 2. an object of anger, Anth. Hence

χολόω, f. ώσω, Ep. inf. χολωσέμεν : aor. 1 ἐχόλωσα :— to make angry, provoke, anger, Hom., Soph. II. Med. and Pass. χολόομαι : 3 sing. opt. χολῷτο contr. from χολοῖτο: f. χολώσομαι and κεχολώσομαι: aor. 1 med. and pass. ἐχολωσάμην, ἐχολώθην: pf. κεχόλωμαι, part. κεχολωμένος : plqpf. Ep. 3 pl. κεχολώατο :— to be angered or provoked to anger, Hom.; βασιλῆϊ χολωθείς angry with the king, Il.; c. gen., κεχολωμένος τινὸς angry because of a person or thing, Hom.

χολ-ώδης, ες, (εἶδος) like bile or gall, bilious, Plat. II. bilious, angry, Luc.

χολώθην, Ep. aor. 1 pass. of χολόω.

χολώσεαι, Ep. 2 sing. aor. med. subj. of χολόω.

χολωσέμεν, Ep. inf. fut. of χολόω.

χολωτός, ή, όν, verb. Adj. of χολόω, angry, wrathful, Hom.

χόνδρος, ὁ, a grain or lump of salt, ἁλὸς τρύφεα κατὰ χόνδρους μεγάλους pieces of salt in large grains, Hdt. :—χόνδρος absol. for salt, Anth. II. in pl. groats of wheat or spelt : gruel made therefrom, Ar.

χονδρός, ά, όν, granular, coarse, χονδροὶ ἅλες rock-salt, Ar.

χόος, heterocl. gen. of χοῦς.

χοραγός, Dor. and Att. for χορηγός.

χορ-αύλης, ου, ὁ, (αὐλός) one who accompanies a chorus on the flute, Anth., Plut.

χόρδευμα, τό, a sausage or black-pudding, Ar. From

χορδεύω, f. σω, to make into sausages: metaph., χ. τὰ πράγματα to make mince-meat of state-affairs, Ar.

χορδή, ἡ, gut-string, the string of a lyre, Lat. chorda, Od., Eur. II. tripe, Batr.: also = χόρδευμα, Ar.

χορεία, ἡ, (χορεύω) a dance, esp. the choral or round dance with its music, Eur., Ar. II. a dance-tune, Ar.

χόρευμα, ατος, τό, (χορεύω) a choral dance, Eur.

χορευτέον, verb. Adj. of χορεύω, one must dance, Eur.

χορευτής, οῦ, ὁ, (χορεύω) a choral dancer, Pind., Ar.: —metaph., θεοῦ χ. the follower of a god, Plat.

χορευτικός, ή, όν, of or for the dance, Luc. From

χορεύω, f. -σω: aor. 1 ἐχόρευσα: pf. κεχόρευκα:— Med., f. -εύσομαι: aor. 1 ἐχορευσάμην:—Pass., aor. 1 ἐχορεύθην: pf. κεχόρευμαι: (χορός):—to dance a round or choral dance, Soph., etc.; esp. of the Bacchic chorus, Eur.:—to take part in the chorus, regarded as a matter of religion, Soph.: to be one of a chorus, Ar.: —c. dat. pers. to dance to him, in his honour, Eur. 2. generally, to dance, esp. from joy, Soph., Eur. 3. metaph. to practise a thing, be versed in it, Plat. c. acc. cogn., φροίμιον χορεύσομαι I will dance a prelude (to festivities), Aesch.; χ. γάμους to celebrate them, Eur.; ὄργια Μουσῶν Ar.:—Med., χορεύεσθαι δίνας to ply the eddying dance, Eur.:—Pass., κεχόρευται ἡμῖν (sings the Chorus) our part is played, Ar. 2. trans. to celebrate in choral dance, Ἴακχον Soph.:—Pass. to be celebrated in choral dance, Id. III. Causal, to set one a dancing, to rouse, wake to the dance, τινά Eur.; so, πόδα χορεύειν Anth.

χορηγεῖον, τό, the place in which a chorus was trained, their dancing-school, Dem. II. in pl. χορηγεῖα or χορήγια, τά, supplies for an army, Lat. commeatus, Polyb.; cf. χορηγία II. 2.

χορηγέω, f. ήσω, (χορηγός) to lead a chorus, Plat.: metaph. to take the lead in a matter, c. gen., τούτου τοῦ λόγου Id. II. in Att. χορηγεῖν, to defray the cost of bringing out a chorus at the public feasts, to act as choragus, Oratt.; c. dat., χ. χορῷ Plat.; χ. ἀνδράσι ἐς Διονύσια Lys.; χ. κωμῳδοῖς Id.; also with the feast in acc., χορ. Λήναια Ar.; Διονύσια Dem.:—Pass. to have choragi found for one, χορηγοῦσιν μὲν οἱ πλούσιοι, χορηγεῖται δὲ ὁ δῆμος Dem. 2. metaph. to minister to, χ. ταῖς σεαυτοῦ ἡδοναῖς Aeschin. 3. metaph. also, a. c. acc. pers. to furnish abundantly with a thing, esp. with supplies for war, Polyb.:—Pass. to be well supplied, Arist. b. c. acc. rei, to supply, furnish, Dem.

χορηγία, ἡ, the office of a χορηγός at Athens, the defraying of the cost of the public choruses, being the chief of the λειτουργίαι, Thuc., etc. II. means for providing χοροί: abundance of means, fortune, Arist. 2. metaph. supplies for war, Polyb.

χορηγικός, ή, όν, of or for a χορηγός, χ. ἀγῶνες rivalry in bringing out choruses, Xen.

χορήγιον, v. χορηγεῖον II.

χορ-ηγός, Dor. χοραγός, ὁ, (χορός, ἡγέομαι) a chorus-leader, Plat.:—the leader of a train or band, Soph., Eur. II. at Athens, one who defrayed the costs for bringing out a chorus, Dem., Aeschin. 2. one who supplies the costs for any purpose, Dem., Aeschin.

χορικός, ή, όν, (χορός) of or for a choral dance, choral, Plat., Arist.

ΧΟΡΙΟΝ, τό, the membrane that encloses the fetus, the afterbirth, Lat. secundae: pl. χόρια, τά, a dish made by stuffing it with honey and milk, a kind of haggis, Ar.: proverb., χαλεπὸν χορίῳ (Dor. gen.) κύνα γεῦσαι 'don't let a dog taste blood,' Theocr. (cf. Horace, canis a corio nunquam absterrebitur uncto).

χοροδιδασκαλία, ἡ, the office of χοροδιδάσκαλος, Plat.

χοροδιδασκαλικός, ή, όν, of or for the χοροδιδάσκαλος: ἡ -κή (sc. τέχνη), = foreg., Plat.

χορο-διδάσκαλος, ὁ, the person who trained the chorus to dance and sing, the chorus-master, Ar., Dem.:— this was originally the Poet himself, v. διδάσκω II.

χορο-ήθης, ες, (ἦθος) accustomed to the choral dance, h. Hom.

χορο-θαλής, ές, (θάλλω) flourishing in the dance, Anth.

χοροι-μανία, ἡ, furious dancing, Anth.

χοροιτυπία, ἡ, choral dancing, Il., Anth. From

χοροι-τύπος [ῠ], ον, Ep. for χορο-τύπος, beating the ground in the dance, dancing, Pind. II. proparox. χοροίτυπος, ον, pass. played to the choral dance, h. Hom.

χορόν-δε, Adv. to the festive dance, Il.

χορο-παίκτης, ου, ὁ, dancing merrily, Anth.

χορο-ποιός, όν, (ποιέω) instituting or arranging a chorus, Xen. II. leading the dance, Soph., Eur.

ΧΟΡΟΣ, οῦ, ὁ, a round dance, used at banquets and festive occasions, Hom., Hes.:—at Athens, the χορὸς κύκλιος performed round the altar of Dionysus, Hdt., Eur., etc. 2. from the Dionysiac Chorus arose the Attic Drama, which consisted at first of tales inserted in the intervals of the Dance (ἐπεισόδια), recited by a single actor: this dramatic chorus was either τραγικός consisting usually of 15 persons, and κωμικός of 24. When a Poet wished to bring out a piece, he asked a Chorus from the Archon, and the expenses, being great, were defrayed by some rich citizen (the χορηγός): it was furnished by the Tribe and trained originally by the Poet himself (hence called χοροδιδάσκαλος). II. a chorus, choir, i.e. a band of dancers and singers, h. Hom., Pind. 2. generally, a choir or troop, τέκνων Eur.; also of things, χ. σκευῶν a row of dishes, Xen.; χ. ὀδόντων a row of teeth, whence the joke of οἱ πρόσθιοι χοροί, for the front teeth, Ar. III. a place for dancing, λείηναν χορόν Od., etc.

χορο-στασία, ἡ, (ἵστημι) institution of choruses: generally, a chorus, dance, Anth.

χορτάζω, f. άσω, to feed, fatten cattle, Hes., Ar.:—Pass. to eat their fill, Plat. Hence

χορτασία, ἡ, a being fed, feasting, Anth.

χόρτασμα, ατος, τό, fodder, forage: food for men, N.T.

ΧΟΡΤΟΣ, ὁ, an inclosed place, a feeding-place, αὐλῆς ἐν χόρτῳ Il. 2. generally, any feeding-ground, in pl., χόρτοι λέοντος Pind.; χόρτοι εὔδενδροι Eur. II. food, fodder, provender, esp. for cattle, Hes., etc.; grass, N.T.; χόρτος κοῦφος hay, Xen.: opp. to σῖτος (food for man), Hdt., Xen.: food generally, Eur., Anth.

χοῦς (A), ὁ, (χέω) Lat. *congius*, a liquid measure = 12 κοτύλαι, nearly 3 quarts, Ar., etc. :—the Att. decl. is χοῦς, χοός, χοῖ, χόα [ᾰ]: pl., χόες, χοῶν, χουσί, χόας. 2. proverb. of attempts to measure the immeasurable, οἱ τῆς θαλάττης λεγόμενοι χόες Plat.　II. Χόες, οἱ, *the Pitcher-feast*, the second day of the Anthesteria at Athens, Ar., Dem.

χοῦς (B), χοῦ, ὁ, (χέω) *earth thrown down* or *heaped up*, like χῶμα, Hdt. 2. = κονιορτός, *dust*, N. T.

χοὖτω, crasis for καὶ οὖτω, Theocr.

ΧΟ΄Ω, inf. χοῦν, part. χῶν: impf. ἔχουν; later, χώννυμι, -ύω (qq. v.): f. χώσω: aor. 1 ἔχωσα: pf. κέχωκα :— Pass., f. χωσθήσομαι: aor. 1 ἐχώσθην: pf. κέχωσμαι: (χέω) :—*to throw* or *heap up*, of earth, χοῦσι χῶμα μέγα Hdt.; χώματα χῶν πρὸς τὰ τείχεα *throwing up banks against* . . , Id.; χῶμα ἔχουν πρὸς τὴν πόλιν Thuc.; νῆσον χώσας σποδῷ *having formed an island with heaped up* ashes, Hdt. 2. *to block up by throwing earth in*, χ. τοὺς λιμένας Dem., Aeschin.: —Pass. of bays in the sea, *to be silted up*, Hdt.; of cities, *to be raised on mounds*, Id. 3. *to cover with earth, to bury*, χῶσαί τινα τάφῳ Eur. :—Pass. *to be covered with a heap of earth*, i. e. *to have a sepulchral mound raised over one*, Anth.

χραίνω, f. χρανῶ: aor. 1 ἔχρανα = χράω (A), *to touch slightly*, ὀλιγάκις ἄστυ χραίνων, i. e. *keeping aloof from it*, Eur. 2. *to stain, spot, defile*, Aesch. :— esp. of moral pollution, Soph., Eur. :—Med., χεῖρα χραίνεσθαι φόνῳ Soph. :—Pass. *to be defiled*, Id.

χραισμέω, f. ἤσω, Ep. inf. -ησέμεν :—aor. 1 Ep. 3 sing. χραίσμησε: also 3 sing. Ep. aor. 2 χραῖσμε, subj. χραίσμῃ, χραίσμῃσι: (χράω C, χράομαι) :—*to ward off from one*, c. acc. rei et dat. pers., ὄλεθρόν τινι χρ. Il. 2. c. dat. pers. only, *to defend* any one, *help, aid, succour, avail* him, Ib.; χραισμεῖν τι *to assist, avail* at all, Ib.

χράομαι, *to use*, v. χράω C.

ΧΡΑ΄Ω (A), or χραύω, f. χραύσω :—*to scrape, graze, wound slightly*, ὅν ῥά τε ποιμὴν χραύσῃ Il.; cf. ἐγχραύω, ἐπιχράω.

ΧΡΑ΄Ω (B) only in impf., c. dat. pers. *to fall upon, attack, assail*, στυγερὸς δέ οἱ ἔχραε δαίμων Od. II. c. inf. *to be bent on doing, to be eager to do*, τίπτε ἐμὸν ῥόον ἔχραε κήδειν; *why was he so eager to vex my stream?* Il.; μνηστῆρες, οἳ ἐχράετε ἐσθιέμεν καὶ πινέμεν ye suitors, who were *so eager to eat and drink*, Od. 2. to this must also be referred the forms χρῇς, χρῇ, (formed like λῇς, λῇ from λάω, διψῇς, -ῇ, πεινῇς, -ῇ from διψάω, πεινάω) = χρῄζω, *to desire*, εἴτε χρῇ θανεῖν whether *she desires to die*, Soph.; δρᾶν ἃ χρῇς Id.; εἴτε χρῇς (sc. κηρύσσειν με) Id.; οὐ χρῆσθα (sc. φωνεῖν); Ar.

ΧΡΑ΄Ω (C), *to furnish what is needful* :—Att. χράω, χρῇς, χρῇ, Ion. χρᾷς, χρᾷ, Ion. part. χρέων, χρείων, Ep. χρείων :—impf. ἔχραον, 3 sing. ἔχρη: f. χρήσω: aor. 1 ἔχρησα :—Pass., aor. 1 ἐχρήσθην: pf. κέχρημαι: 3 sing. plqpf. ἐκέχρηστο :—Med., Ion. χρέομαι, inf. χρέεσθαι, part. χρεόμενος or χρεώμενος :—impf. 3 pl. ἐχρέοντο or -έωντο: f. χρήσομαι. 1. Act. of gods and oracles, *to furnish the needful answer, to declare, pronounce, proclaim*, χρήσω βουλὴν Διός h. Hom.; ἡ Πυθίη οἱ χρᾷ τάδε Hdt., etc.: c. inf. *to warn* or *direct by oracle*, χρήσαντ' ἐμοὶ ἐκτὸς αἰτίας εἶναι *that I should be*,

Aesch.; τοῦ θεοῦ χρήσαντος Thuc. 2. Pass. *to be declared, proclaimed* by an oracle, τίς οὖν ἐχρήσθη; Eur.; of the *oracle*, τὰ χρηστήρια ταῦτά σφι ἐχρήσθη Hdt.; πείθου τὰ χρησθέντ' Soph.: impers., c. inf., καί σφι ἐχρήσθη ἀνέμοισι εὔχεσθαι Hdt. 3. Med. *to consult a god* or *oracle, to inquire of* a god or oracle, *consult* him or it, c. dat., ψυχῇ χρησόμενος Τειρεσίαο Od.; χρ. θεῷ, Lat. *uti oraculo*, Hdt., etc. —From the sense of *using an oracle* comes the general sense of χράομαι *to use* (infr. III) :—absol. *to consult the oracle*, Od., Hdt.; οἱ χρώμενοι *the consulters*, Eur. :—pf. part., κεχρημένος *one who has received an oracular response*, Arist.

II. *to furnish with* a thing, in which sense κίχρημι was the pres. in use, with f. χρήσω: aor. 1 ἔχρησα: pf. κέχρηκα :—Med., pres. in use κίχράμαι, aor. 1 ἐχρησάμην: —*to furnish the use of* a thing, i. e. *to lend*, Hdt., Ar., etc.—Med. *to have furnished one, borrow*, Eur.; πόδας χρήσας, ὄμματα χρησάμενος *having lent* feet and *borrowed* eyes, of a blind man carrying a lame one, Anth.

III. Dep. χράομαι, Att. χρῶμαι, χρῇ, χρῆται, χρῆσθε, χρῶνται, Ion. χρᾶται or χρέεται, χρέονται: imper., Att. χρῶ, Ion. χρέω or χρέο, 3 pl. χρήσθων: inf. Att. χρῆσθαι, Ion. χρᾶσθαι or χρέεσθαι; part. Att. χρώμενος, Ion. χρεόμενος or χρεώμενος :—impf. Att. ἐχρῶμην, ἐχρῶντο, Ion. ἐχρᾶτο, ἐχρέοντο (or -έωντο) :— f. χρήσομαι, also κεχρήσομαι: aor. 1 ἐχρησάμην: pf. κέχρημαι. From the sense of *consulting* or *using an oracle* (v. χράω (C). 3) comes the common sense *to use*, Lat. *uti*, Il., etc.; φρεσὶ κέχρητ' ἀγαθῇσι he was *endowed with a good heart*, Od.: c. dat., χρῆσθαι ἀργυρίῳ *to have* money *to use* for a purpose, *use it thereon*, Plat.; χρ. ναυτιλίῃσι, θαλάσσῃ Hdt., Thuc. 2. in various relations, ὀργῇ or θυμῷ χρῆσθαι *to indulge one's* anger, give vent to it, Hdt. b. of external things, *to experience, suffer, be subject to*, νιφετῷ Id.; χρ. γαληνείᾳ *to have* fair weather, Eur.; ὁμολογίᾳ χρ. *to come to an agreement*, Hdt.; ζυγῷ χρ. δουλίῳ *to become a slave*, Aesch.; συμφορᾷ, συντυχίῃ, εὐτυχίῃ χρ., Lat. *uti fortuna mala, prospera*, Hdt., etc.; νόμοις χρ. *to live under laws*, Eur.; χρ. ἀνομίᾳ Xen., etc. :—in many cases, χρῆσθαι merely paraphrases the Verb cognate to its dat., μόρῳ χρ. i. e. *to die*, Hdt.; ὠνῇ καὶ πράσει χρ. = ὠνεῖσθαι καὶ πιπράσκειν, *to buy and sell*, Id.; χρ. δρασμῷ = διδράσκειν, Aeschin.; χρ. φωνῇ = φωνεῖν, διαβολῇ χρ. = διαβάλλεσθαι etc., Plat. c. χρῆσθαί τινι εἴς τι *to use* for an end or purpose, Hdt., Xen., etc.; ἐπί τι or πρός τι Xen. ;—also with neut. Adj. as Adv., χρ. τινι ὅ τι βούλεταί τις *to make* what *use one likes* of him, Hdt.; ἀπορέων ὅ τι χρήσεται *not knowing what to make of* it, Id.; τί χρήσομαι τούτῳ; *what use shall I make* of him? Ar.; οὐκ ἂν ἔχοις ὅ τι χρῷο σαυτῷ Plat. 3. of persons, χρῆσθαί τινι, with an Adv. of manner, *to treat* him so and so, χρῆσθαί τινι ὡς ἀνδρὶ ψεύστῃ Hdt.; χρῆσθαί τινι ὡς φίλῳ Thuc.; also, φιλικῶς χρῆσθαί τινι Xen.; but ὡς is often omitted, φίλῳ χρώμενος διδασκάλῳ Aesch., etc.—also, χρῆσθαί τινι (without φίλῳ) like Lat. *uti* for *uti familiariter, to be intimate with* a man, Xen. :—absol., οἱ χρώμενοι *friends*, Id. 4. χρῆσθαι ἑαυτῷ *to make use of* one's powers, Plat.; also, παρέχειν ἑαυτόν τινι χρῆσθαι *to place oneself at the disposal*

of another, Xen. **5.** absol., or with an Adv., οὕτω χρῶνται οἱ Πέρσαι so the Persians are wont to do, such is their custom, Id. **6.** pf. κέχρημαι (in pres. sense), to be in need or want of, to yearn after, c. gen., Hom., Soph., Eur. :—part. κεχρημένος used as an Adj., needy, in need, poor, Od., Hes., Eur. **7.** the pf. appears as a strengthd. pres., to have in use, and so to have, possess, φρεσὶ γὰρ κέχρητ' ἀγαθῇσι Od. **8.** aor. 1 pass. χρησθῆναι, to be used, αἱ νέες οὐκ ἐχρήσθησαν Hdt. ; ἕως ἂν χρησθῇ so long as it be in use, Dem. **IV.** for χρή, v. sub voc.

χρέᾱ, Ep. for χρέεα, pl. of χρέος.

χρεία, Ion. **χρείη**, ἡ, (χράομαι, χρέος) use, advantage, service, Theogn., Plat. ; τὰ οὐδὲν εἰς χρείαν things of no use or service, Dem. ; χρείαν ἐρευνᾶν, v. ἐρευνάω 1 : —pl. services, Pind., Dem. **2.** as an action, using, use, κτῆσις καὶ χρ. having and using, Xen., Plat. ; πρὸς τὴν ἀνθρωπίνην χρ. Xen. **3.** of persons, familiarity, intimacy, intercourse, πρός τινα with one, Plat. **II.** like Lat. opus, need, want, necessity, Aesch., etc. ; ἵν' ἔσταμεν χρείας considering in what great need we are, Soph. ; χρείᾳ πολεμεῖν to war with necessity, Id. :—c. gen. want or lack of a thing, Aesch., etc. ; ἐν χρείᾳ δορός in the need or stress of war, Soph. ; χρεία ἐστὶ [γίγνεταί] μοι τινός, Lat. opus est mihi aliqua re, Plat. ; ἔτι μου χρείαν ἕξει will have need of my help, Aesch. ; ἐν χρείᾳ εἶναι or γίγνεσθαί τινος Plat. ; pl., αἱ τοῦ σώματος χρ. Xen. ; αἱ ἀναγκαῖαι χρ. Dem. **2.** the result of need, want, poverty, Soph., Plut. **3.** a request of necessity, opp. to ἀξίωσις (a claim of merit), Thuc. : generally, a request, Aesch. **4.** a needful business, a need, requirement, ὡς πρὸς τί χρείας ; for what purpose? Soph. ; ἡ πολεμικὴ χρ. καὶ ἡ εἰρηνικὴ the requirements of war and of peace, Arist. **5.** generally, a business, employment, Polyb., N. T.

χρείη, 3 sing. opt. of χρή.

χρεῖος, -ά, Ep. for χρέος.

χρεῖος, ον, (χρή) needing, being in want of, c.gen., Eur.

χρειώ, όος, contr. οῦς, ἡ, Ep. for χρεώ.

χρεμετίζω, f. σω, to neigh, whinny, Lat. hinnire, of horses, Il., Hdt., etc. (Formed from the sound.) Hence

χρεμετισμός, ὁ, a neighing, whinnying, Ar.

χρεμίζω, =χρεμετίζω, Ep. 3 pl. aor. 1 χρέμισαν, Hes.

χρέμπτομαι, f. ψομαι, Dep. to clear one's throat, to hawk and spit, cough, Eur. (Formed from the sound.)

χρέομαι, Ion. for χράομαι.

χρέος and **χρέως**, Ep. **χρεῖος**, τό ; gen. χρέους :—pl., nom. and acc. χρέα, Att. χρέᾱ ; gen. χρεῶν, Ep. χρειῶν : (χράομαι, χράω) : **I.** that which needs must pay, an obligation, debt, Od. ; a debt for stolen cattle, Il. ; χρεῖος ἀποστήσασθαι to pay a debt in full, Ib. ; ἀρᾶς τίνει χρ. pays the debt demanded by the curse, Aesch. ; χρέος πόλει προσάπτειν to attach a further debt, i. e. guilt to the city, Soph. ; χρέος ἀποδιδόναι to repay a debt, Hdt., Ar. :—in pl. debts, χρειῶν λύσις Hes. ; τὴν οὐσίαν ἅπασαν χρέα κατέλιπε left all the property in outstanding debts, Dem. **II.** a needful business, an affair, matter, ἑὸν αὐτοῦ χρεῖος Od. : a requirement, a purpose, Soph. : c. gen., like χάριν, for the sake of, σὸν οὐκ ἔλασσον ἢ κείνης χρέος Eur. **2.**

like χρῆμα, a thing, τί χρέος ;=τί χρῆμα ; wherefore? Aesch. ; ἐφ' ὅ τι χρ. ἐμόλετε ; Eur. **III.** in Od., ἦλθον Τειρεσίαο κατὰ χρέος seems to be = Τειρεσίᾳ χρησόμενος, I came to consult him :—but, κατὰ χρέος according to what is due, as is meet, h. Hom. **IV.** a duty, task, charge, office, Pind., Trag. **V.** = χρεία, want, need, τί δὲ τοῦδ' ἔχει πλέκους χρέος ; Ar.

χρεώ, Ion. for χράω (C), to deliver an oracle, h. Hom.

χρεώ, Ep. **χρείω**, gen. οῦς, ἡ : (χρέος, χρεία) :—want, need ; hence desire, longing, urgent wish, Hom. ; ἦ τι μάλα χρεώ of a truth something is much needed, Il. ; χρειοῖ ἀναγκαίῃ by dire necessity, Ib. ; c. gen., χρειὼ ἐμεῖο want, need of me, Hom. **2.** χρειὼ ἱκάνεται want, necessity arises, Id. ; so, χρειὼ γίγνεται Il. ; τίπτε δέ σε χρειὼ δεῦρ' ἤγαγε ; Od. **3.** χρ. ἱκάνει τινά comes upon him, ἐμὲ δὲ χρεὼ γίγνεται αὐτῆς (sc. τῆς νηός) need of the ship comes upon me, Il. ; οὐδέ τί μιν χρεὼ ἔσται τυμβοχόης nor will need of a grave be felt by him, Ib. **4.** hence the elliptical use of χρεώ c. acc. pers., τίπτε δέ σε χρεώ (sc. ἱκάνει) ; Hom. ; c. gen. rei, οὔτι με ταύτης χρεὼ τιμῆς need of it touches me not, Il. ; χρεὼ βουλῆς ἐμὲ καὶ σέ Ib. ;—also c. inf., τὸν χρεὼ ἐστάμεναι κρατερῶς he needs must stand firm, Ib. ; οὐδέ τί μιν χρεὼ νηῶν ἐπιβαινέμεν Od. [χρεώ in Hom. is a monosyll.]

χρεω-κοπίδης, ου, ὁ, (κόπτω) one who cancels his debts, an insolvent, Plut.

χρεώμενος, Ion. part. of χράομαι.

χρεών, τό, indecl., properly a part. neut. of χρή, that which must be, τὸ χρεὼν γίνεσθαι Hdt. ; τὸ χρεὼν τοῦ χρησμοῦ Plut. **II.** need, necessity, fate, Eur., Plat. **2.** χρεών (sc. ἐστι), much like χρή, 'tis fated, necessary, Lat. oportet, c. inf., Theogn., Aesch., etc. **3.** sometimes as a neut. part. (like ἐξόν, etc.), it being necessary, since it was necessary, Hdt. **III.** more rarely that which is expedient or right, Soph., Ar., etc. **IV.** absol., οὐ χρεὼν ἄρχετε ye rule unrightfully, Thuc.

χρέως, τό, v. sub χρέος.

χρεώστης, ου, ὁ, (χρέος) a debtor, Luc.

χρε-ωφειλέτης, ου, ὁ, (ὀφείλω) a debtor, one in debt, N. T., Plut.

χρή, v. χράω (B). II.

χρή, ἡ, = χρεών II, need, necessity, χρὴ 'σται, which serves as a fut. to χρή, it will be needful, c. inf., Soph.

χρή, impers. : subj. χρῇ : opt. χρείη : inf. χρῆναι, poët. also χρῆν :—impf. ἐχρῆν, also without the augm. χρῆν even in Att. : (χράω (C)) :—it is fated, necessary, Aesch., etc. ; οὐδὲ ἐν ἴαμα ὅ τι χρῆν προσφέροντας ὠφελεῖν no one remedy which one was sure to do good by administering, Thuc. :—c. inf. it must, must needs, one must or ought to do, Hom., Att. ; more often, like Lat. oportet, c. acc. pers. et inf. one must, one must needs, it behoves, befits one to . . , οὐδέ τί σε χρὴ νηλεὲς ἦτορ ἔχειν Il., etc. ; often the inf. must be supplied from the context, τίπτε μάχης ἀποπαύεαι ; οὐδέ τί σε χρή (sc. ἀποπαύεσθαι), why cease from battle ? for it behoves thee not, Il. ; so, ὅθι χρὴ πεζὸν ἐόντα (sc. μάρνασθαι) ; ἐπιπλεύσεώς σε χρή (sc. ἐπιπλεῦσαι) Thuc. :—absol., ἐρεῖ τις, οὐ χρῆν [sc. τοῦτο ποιεῖν], ἀλλὰ τί χρῆν εἴπατε Eur. ap. Ar. **2.** c. acc. pers. et gen. rei, οὐδέ τί σε χρὴ ἀφροσύνης thou

hast no *need of* imprudence, i. e. it does not *befit* thee, Il. ; μυθήσεαι ὅττεό (i. e. ὅτου) σε χρή thou wilt say what thou *hast need* of, Od. **II.** sometimes in a less strong sense, πῶς χρὴ τοῦτο περᾶσαι; how *is one to* get through this? Theocr. **III.** τὸ χρῆν (infin.) =χρεών, *fate, destiny*, Eur.

χρήζω, Ion. χρηίζω : Dor. χρήσδω, Megar. χρήσδω :— f. χρήσω : Ion. aor. 1 inf. χρηίσαι : used by Att. writers only in pres. and impf. : (χράω (B). II) :—*to need, want, lack, have need of,* c. gen., Hom., Aesch. :—absol. in part. χρηίζων *lacking, needy, poor*, Od., Hes. **2.** *to desire, long for, ask for*, c. gen., Hdt., Aesch. :— rarely c. acc. rei, Hdt., Soph. ;—often an inf. must be supplied, φράζε ὅ τι χρήζεις (sc. φράζειν) Ar., etc. **b.** c. acc. pers. et inf. *to ask* or *desire* that one should do a thing, Hdt. ; so also c. gen. pers. et inf. *to desire of* one to do, Id. ; c. inf. only, *to desire* to do a thing, Trag. c. dupl. gen. pers., τῶνδε ἐγὼ ὑμέων χρηίζων συνέλεξα Hdt. **3.** μὴ θανεῖν ἔχρηζες (Soph. O. C. 1713) is explained, *O that thou hadst not desired* to die,—a very unusual construction ; cf. ἐπωφέλησα ἐτ rei, τῶνδε for ὄφελον (supr. 541). **4.** the part. χρήζων is used absol. for εἰ χρήζει, *if one will, if one chooses*, Theogn., Aesch. :—also, τὸ χρῆζον *your solicitation*, Eur.

χρήζω, = χράω (c), *to deliver an oracle, foretell*, Eur.
χρηίζω, Ion. for χρήζω.
χρηίσκομαι, Ion. Frequent. of χρηίζω, *to be much in want of*, τινι Hdt.

χρῆμα, ατος, τό, (χράομαι) *a thing that one uses* or *needs*: in pl. *goods, property, money, gear, chattels*, Od., Hes., etc. ; πρόβατα καὶ ἄλλα χρ. Xen. ; κρείσσων χρημάτων superior *to money*, i. e. incorruptible, Thuc. ; χρημάτων ἀδωρότατος Id.—rare in sing. in this sense, ἐπὶ κόσῳ χρήματι; for how much *money ?* Answ. ἐπ’ οὐδένι, Hdt. **II.** generally, *a thing, matter, affair, event*, Hes., Hdt. ; κινεῖν πᾶν χρῆμα ‘ to leave no stone unturned,’ Hdt. :—of a battle, *an affair*, Plut. **2.** χρῆμα is often expressed where it might be omitted, δεινὸν χρ. ἐποιεῦντο Hdt. ; ἐς ἀφανὲς χρ. ἀποστέλλειν ἀποικίαν to send out a colony without any certain destination, Id. ; τί χρῆμα; like τί; *what ?* τί χρῆμα δρᾷς; Soph. ; τί χρῆμα πάσχω; τί δ’ ἐστὶ χρῆμα; what is *the matter ?* Aesch., etc. **3.** used in periphrases to express something strange or extraordinary, μέγα σῦς χρῆμα *a monster* of a boar, Hdt. ; τὸ χρ. τῶν νυκτῶν ὅσον what a terrible length the nights are, Ar. : λιπαρὸν τὸ χρ. τῆς πόλεως what a grand city ! Id. ; κλέπτον τὸ χρ. τἀνδρός a thievish *sort* of fellow, Id. ; σοφόν τοι χρῆμ’ ἄνθρωπος truly a clever *creature* is he ! Theocr. :—so, to express a great number, as we say, *a lot, a deal, a heap*, πολλόν τι χρ. τῶν ὀφίων, χρ. πολλὸν νεῶν Hdt. ; ὅσον τὸ χρ. παρνόπων what a *lot* of locusts ! Ar. ; ὅσον τὸ χρ. πλακοῦντος Id. ; τὸ χρ. τῶν κόπων ὅσον what a lot of them ! Id. ; —also of persons, χρῆμα θηλειῶν womankind, Eur. ; μέγα χρ. Λακαινᾶν Theocr.

χρημᾰτίζω, f. ίσω, Att. ιῶ : pf. κεχρημάτικα : (χρῆμα) : —*to negotiate, transact business, have dealings*, esp. in money matters (though this sense is mostly confined to the Med.), Thuc., Isocr. **2.** *to consult, deliberate*, Dem., Aeschin. **3.** *to give audience to, to*

answer after deliberation, τινί Xen. ; τινὶ περί τινος Thuc. **4.** of an oracle, *to give a response* to those who consult it, Plut. :—Pass. *to receive an answer* or *warning*, N. T. ; ἢν αὐτῷ κεχρηματισμένον *a warning had been given* him, Ib. **II.** Med. χρηματίζομαι, f. Att. –ιοῦμαι : pf. κεχρημάτισμαι :— *to negotiate* or *transact business for oneself, to make money*, Thuc., Plat. ; χρ. χρήματα Xen. **2.** generally, *to transact business, have dealings, hold conference with*, τινι Hdt. **3.** c. acc. rei, χρηματίζεσθαι τὸ νόμισμα *to traffic in* money, Arist. **III.** in later writers, the Act. means *to take and bear a title* or *name, to be called* or *styled* so and so, χρηματίζει βασιλεύς Polyb. ; Ἴσις ἐχρημάτισε Plut. ; χρηματίσαι Χριστιανούς N. T. ; generally, *to be called*, Ib.

χρημᾰτικός, ή, όν, (χρῆμα) *of* or *for money*, χρ. ζημία a *money* fine, Plut. ; χρ. συμβόλαια *money* contracts, Id. ; οἱ χρηματικοί *the moneyed men*, Id.

χρημᾰτισμός, ὁ, (χρηματίζω) *an oracular response, divine warning*, N. T. **II.** (from Med.) *money-making*, Plat. : *gain, profit*, Dem.

χρημᾰτιστέον, verb. Adj. of χρηματίζω, *one must make money*, Xen.

χρημᾰτιστήριον, τό, (χρηματίζω) *a place for transacting business, a counting-house*, Plut.

χρημᾰτιστής, οῦ, ὁ, (χρηματίζω) *a man in business, money-getter, trafficker*, Plat., Xen. **2.** as Adj.,= sq., Arist. Hence

χρημᾰτιστικός, ή, όν, *of* or *for money-making*, ὁ χρ. *a man of business*, Plat. ; χρ. οἰωνός an omen *portending gain*, Xen. ; τὸ χρηματιστικόν *the commercial class*, Arist. :—ἡ –κή (sc. τέχνη), *the art of money-making, traffic*, Plat.

χρημᾰτο-δαίτης, ου, ὁ, (δαίω) *a divider of wealth*, Aesch.

χρημᾰτο-ποιός, όν, (ποιέω) *money-making*, Xen.

χρημοσύνη, ἡ, like χρεία, *need, want, lack*, Tyrtae., Theogn.

χρῆς, χρῆσθα, v. sub χράω (B). II. 2.
χρῆσδω, Dor. for χρήζω.

χρησῐμεύω, *to be useful* or *serviceable*, τινί to one, Luc.

χρήσῐμος, η, ον, and ος, ον, (χράομαι) *useful, serviceable, good for use, good, apt* or *fit* in its kind, Hdt., Att. ; τὸ αὐτίκα χρ. present *advantage*, Thuc. ;—χρ. εἴς τι useful for something, Att. ; ἐπί τι Plat. ; πρός τι Eur. ; *useful for* doing, Ar. **2.** *serviceable, useful*, Soph., Eur., etc. ; χρησίμους ἑαυτοὺς παρέχειν τῇ πόλει to shew themselves *serviceable* to the state, Dem. **3.** *much-used*, Hdt. **4.** νόμισμα οὐ χρήσιμον ἔξω *money that will not pass* abroad, Xen. **II.** Adv., χρησίμως ἔχειν *to be serviceable*, Thuc. ; χρ. τινι *with advantage* to him, Id.

χρῆσις, εως, ἡ, (χράομαι) *a using, employment, use made* of a thing, Pind. ; in pl. *uses, advantages*, Id., Xen. :—opp. to κτῆσις (possession), Plat., etc. **2.** *means of using, usefulness*, Thuc., Plat. ; ἔχειν χρῆσιν *to be useful*, Dem. **3.** *intimacy, acquaintance*, Lat. *usus*, Isocr. ; ἡ χρ. ἡ πρὸς ἀλλήλους Arist. **II.** (χράω (c. I), *the response of an oracle*, Pind. **III.** (χράω (c). II), *a lending, loan*, Arist.

χρησμ-αγόρης, ου, ὁ, (ἀγορεύω) *an utterer of oracles, a prophet*, Anth. Hence

χρησμηγορέω, to utter oracles, Luc.
χρησμολογέω, to utter oracles, divine, Ar. From
χρησμο-λόγος, ον, (λέγω) uttering oracles, divining,
χ. ἀνήρ a soothsayer, diviner, Hdt.   II. an expounder of oracles, an oracle-monger, Id., Ar.
χρησμο-ποιός, όν, (ποιέω) making oracles in verse,
Luc.
χρησμός, ὁ, (χράω (c). 1) the answer of an oracle,
oracular response, oracle, Solon, Hdt., Att.
χρησμοσύνη, ἡ, (χράομαι) need, want, poverty,
Tyrtae.   II. importunity, Hdt.
χρησμο-φύλαξ [ῠ], ἄκος, ὁ, a keeper of oracles, Luc.
χρησμῳδέω, f. ήσω, to chant oracles: generally, to
deliver oracles, prophesy, Hdt., Ar., etc.; and
χρησμῳδία, ἡ, the answer of an oracle, a prophecy,
Aesch., Plat.; and
χρησμῳδικός, ή, όν, oracular, Luc. From
χρησμ-ῳδός, όν, (ᾠδή) chanting oracles, or delivering
them in verse; generally prophesying, prophetic, χρ.
παρθένος, of the Sphinx, Soph.   II. as Subst. a
soothsayer, oracle-monger, Plat.
χρῆσται or χρῆ 'σται, v. χρῆ.
χρηστέον, verb. Adj. one must use, c. dat. rei, Xen.
χρηστεύομαι, Dep. to be good and kind, N. T.
χρηστηριάζω, f. άσω, like χράω (c). 1, to give oracles,
prophesy, Strab.   II. Med., like χράομαι, to have
an oracle given one, consult an oracle, Hdt.; χρ.
θεῷ to consult a god, like χρήσασθαι θεῷ, Id. From
χρηστήριον, τό, (χράω (c). 1) an oracle, i. e., 1. the
seat of an oracle, such as Delphi, h. Hom., Hdt., Eur.:
—in pl. for sing., Aesch.   2. the answer of an
oracle, oracular response, Hdt., Trag.   II. an
offering for the oracle, made by those consulting it;
generally, a sacrificial victim, χρ. θέσθαι Pind., Aesch.;
—and a victim, sacrifice, Soph.
χρηστήριος, α, ον, and os, ον, (χράω (c). 1), of or from
an oracle, oracular, prophetic, Aesch., Eur.; Ἀπόλλον
χρηστήριε author of oracles, Hdt.
χρήστης, ου, ὁ: gen. pl. χρήστων (not χρηστῶν, to
distinguish it from the gen. pl. of χρηστός): (χράω (c).
II):—a creditor, usurer, dun, Ar.   2. (from the
Med.) a debtor, Dem.
χρηστικός, ή, όν, (χράομαι) knowing how to use, understanding the use of a thing, c. gen., Arist.   2. of
things, useful, serviceable, Plut.
χρηστο-ήθης, ες, (ἦθος) well-disposed, Arist.
χρηστολογία, ἡ, fair speaking, smooth speech, N. T.
χρηστο-λόγος, ον, (λέγω) speaking plausibly, N. T.
χρηστός, ή, όν, verb. Adj. of χράομαι, like χρήσιμος,
useful, good of its kind, serviceable, τινι Hdt., Eur.;
of victims and omens, boding good, auspicious, Hdt.;
τελευτή χρηστή a happy end or issue, Id.:—τὰ χρηστά,
as Subst., good services, benefits, kindnesses, Id.;
χρηστὰ συμβουλεύειν Ar.   2. in moral sense, good,
opp. to μοχθηρός, Plat.; τὸ χρηστόν, opp. to τὸ αἰσχρόν, Soph.   II. of men, good, a good man and
true; generally, good, honest, worthy, trusty, Hdt.,
Soph., etc.;—also like χρήσιμος, of good citizens,
useful, deserving, Ar., Thuc., etc.   2. οἱ χρηστοί,
like οἱ ἀγαθοί, Lat. optimates, Xen.   3. of the
gods, kind, propitious, Hdt.   4. good, mild, kind,
kindly, N. T.:—in bad sense, simple, silly, like εὐήθης,

Ar., Plat.; ὦ χρηστέ Dem.   III. Adv. -τῶς, well,
properly, Hdt.   Hence
χρηστότης, ητος, ἡ, of persons, goodness, honesty,
Eur.   2. goodness of heart, kindness, Isae., N. T.
χρηστοφίλία, ἡ, the having good friends, the friendship of good men, Arist.   From
χρηστό-φίλος, ον, possessed of good friends, Arist.
χρῖμα, τό, older form of χρῖσμα, unguent, oil, Aesch.
χρίμπτω, f. ψω, (χρίω) to bring near, (so used by Hom.
only in compd. ἐγχρίμπτω, q. v.); πόδα χρίμπτουσα ῥα-
χίαισι keeping one's steps close along the shore, Aesch.;
ὑπὸ στήλην ἔχριμπτε ἀεὶ σύριγγα kept the wheel ever
close to the post, Soph.; h. Hom., Eur., Theocr.:—
Pass. to touch the surface of a body, to graze, scratch,
wound, Lat. radere, stringere, χριμφθεὶς πέλας close
even to touching, Od.: generally, to come nigh, draw
near, approach, c. dat., δόμοισι χρίμπτεσθαι Aesch.;
τείχεσι Eur.; so in aor. 1 med. χρίμψασθαι, h.
Hom.   II. intr. in Act., = Pass., Eur.
χρῖσα, Ep. aor. 1 of χρίω.
χρῖσμα, ατος, τό, (χρίω) later form for χρῖμα, anything
smeared on, esp. a scented unguent, thicker than
μύρον, Xen.   II. whitewash, stucco, Luc.
Χριστιᾱνός, ὁ, a Christian, first in Act. Ap. 11. 26.
χριστός, ή, όν, verb. Adj. of χρίω, to be rubbed on,
φάρμακα χριστά salves, Aesch., Eur.   II. of persons,
anointed: ΧΡΙΣΤΟΣ, ὁ, the Anointed One, the
CHRIST, as a transl. of the Hebr. Messiah, N. T.
ΧΡΙΩ [ῑ], Ep. impf. χρῖον: f. χρίσω: aor. 1 ἔχρῖσα,
Ep. χρῖσα:—Pass., aor. 1 ἐχρίσθην: pf. κέχρισμαι or
κέχρῖμαι: 3 sing. plqpf. ἐκέχρῑστο ⲟⲣ -ῖτο:—to touch
on the surface: to rub or anoint with scented unguents, Hom.; λόεον καὶ χρῖον ἐλαίῳ Od.; πέπλον χρ.
to infect with poison, Soph.; metaph., ἱμέρῳ χρῖσασ'
οἰστόν Eur.:—Med. to anoint oneself, Od., Hes.: c.
acc. rei, χρίεσθαι ἰούς to anoint (i. e. poison) one's
arrows, Od.:—Pass., χρίεσθαι ὑπὸ τοῦ ἡλίου of a dead
body left exposed to the sun, Hdt.   II. to rub over
with colour: Pass. to be coloured, Id.: — Med.,
χρίεσθαι τὰ σώματα to smear their bodies, Xen.   III.
to wound on the surface, prick, sting, Aesch.:—Pass.,
ὀξυστόμῳ μύωπι χρισθεῖσ' Id.
χρόα, ἡ, Att. and later form for χροιά.
χρόα, χροί, heterocl. acc. and dat. of χρώς.
χροιά, Ion. χροιή, later Att. χρόα, (χρώς) the surface
of a body, the skin; the body itself, Il., Theogn.,
Ar.   II. the superficial appearance of a thing,
its colour, Aesch., Eur., etc.:—esp. the colour of the
skin, the complexion, Aesch., Eur.
χροΐζω, f. ίσω, poët. form of χρώζω, to touch on the surface; generally, to touch, Eur.
χρόμαδος, ὁ, a crashing sound, χρ. γενύων, of a pugilistic contest, Il.   (Formed from the sound.)
χρονίζω, f. Att. ιῶ, (χρόνος) intr. to spend time, Hdt.:
to take time, tarry, linger, delay, be slow, Aesch.,
Thuc.; c. inf. to delay to do, N. T.   2. of things,
χρονίζον μένειν to remain long, Aesch.   II. Pass.
to be prolonged or protracted, Id.   2. to grow up,
χρονισθείς Id.
χρονικός, ή, όν, (χρόνος) of or concerning time, κανόνες
Plut.:—τὰ χρονικά (sc. βιβλία) chronology, Id.
χρόνιος, α, ον, and os, ον, (χρόνος) of persons, after ⲋ

long time, late, χρόνιος ἐλθών Od. ; χρ. φανείς Soph. 2.
for a long time, χρόνιόν τινα ἐκβάλλειν, ἐλαύνειν Id. ;
χρόνιός εἰμ᾽ ἀπὸ βορᾶς I have been long without food,
Eur. 3. long-delaying, lingering, Aesch. ; χρόνιοι
μέλλετε πράσσειν Soph.; χρόνια τὰ τῶν θεῶν Eur. II.
of things, long, lasting long, long-continued, χρόνια
λέκτρ᾽ ἔχων having been long married, Id. ; χρ. πόλεμοι Thuc. III. Adv. -ίως, Arist.: neut. pl.
χρόνια as Adv., Eur. :—Comp. -ώτερον, Pind.
χρονιστέον, verb. Adj. one must spend time, Arist.
χρονο-γράφος [ᾰ], ον, (γράφω) recording times and
events: as Subst. a chronicler, annalist, Strab.
ΧΡΟ´ΝΟΣ, ὁ, time, Hom., etc. 2. a definite time, a
while, period, season, δεκέτης, τρίμηνος χρ. Soph. ; χρ.
βίου, ἥβης Eur. :—pl. periods of time, τοῖς χρόνοις ἀκριβῶς with chronological accuracy, Thuc.; τοῖς χρόνοις
by the dates, Isocr. 3. Special phrases: a. acc.,
χρόνον for a while, Od., etc.; so, πολὺν χρόνον for a
long time, Ib.; τὸν ἀεὶ χρ. for ever, Eur., etc.; ἕνα
χρ. at once, once for all, Il. b. gen., ὀλίγου χρόνου
in a short time, Hdt.; πολλοῦ χρόνου Ar.; πόσου χρ.;
for how long? Id. c. dat., χρόνῳ in time, at last,
Hdt., Trag.; so, χρόνῳ ποτέ Hdt., etc.; also with the
Art., τῷ χρόνῳ Ar. 4. with Prepositions:—ἀνὰ χρόνον in course of time, after a time, Hdt. :—ἀφ᾽ οὗ
χρόνου from such time as . . , Xen. :—διὰ χρόνου after
an interval of time, Soph., Thuc.; διὰ πολλοῦ χρόνου
Hdt., Ar. :—ἐκ πολλοῦ χρόνου a long time since, long
ago, Hdt. :—ἐν χρόνῳ in time, at length, Aesch. :—
ἐντὸς χρόνου within a certain time, Hdt. :—ἐπὶ χρόνον
for a while, Hom.; πολλὸν ἐπὶ χρ. Od. :—ἐς χρόνον
hereafter, Hdt. :—σὺν χρόνῳ, like χρόνῳ or διὰ χρόνου,
Aesch. :—ὑπὸ χρόνου by lapse of time, Thuc. II.
lifetime, an age, Soph.; χρόνῳ βραδύς Id. III. a
season, portion of the year, Xen. IV. delay, loss,
of time, Dem.; χρόνους ἐμποιεῖν to interpose delays, Id.
χρονο-τρῑβέω, f. ήσω, (τρίβω) to waste time, loiter,
Arist., N. T. II. c. acc., χρ. τὸν πόλεμον to protract the war, Plut.
χροός, heterocl. gen. of χρώς : no nom. χροῦς occurs.
χρῡσ-ἄμοιβός, ὁ, (ἀμείβω) exchanging for gold :—
metaph. Ἄρης σωμάτων χρυσαμοιβός War, who traffics
in men's bodies, Aesch.
χρῡσ-άμπυξ, ῡκος, ὁ, ἡ, with fillet or frontlet of gold,
of horses, Il.; of goddesses, h. Hom., Hes.
χρῡσ-ανθής, ές, (ἄνθος) with golden flower, Anth.
χρῡσ-άνιος, Dor. for χρυσήνιος.
χρῡσ-ανταυγής, ές, reflecting golden light, Eur.
χρῡσ-άορος [ᾱ], ον, (ἄορ) like χρυσάωρ, with sword of
gold, epith. of Apollo and other gods, Il., h. Hom., Pind.
χρῡσ-άρμᾰτος, ον, (ἅρμα) with or in car of gold, Pind.
χρῡσ-ασπις [ῠ], ιδος, ὁ, ἡ, with shield of gold, Pind.,
Eur.
χρῡσ-αυγής, ές, gen. έος, gold-gleaming, Soph., Ar.
χρῡσάωρ [ᾱ], ορος, ὁ, ἡ, (ἄορ) = χρυσάορος, Hes., Pind.
χρῡσεῖον, τό, (χρυσός) a goldsmith's shop, Strab. II.
a gold-mine : in pl. χρυσεῖα, gold-mines, Xen.
χρῦσειος [ῠ], η, ον, Ep. for χρύσεος (q. v.), Hom., Hes.
χρῡσ-ελεφαντ-ήλεκτρος, ον, of gold, ivory, and elec-
trum, overlaid therewith, Epigr. ap. Plut.
χρῡσεο-βόστρῠχος, ον, = χρυσοβόστρυχος, Eur.
χρῡσεό-δμητος, ον, formed of gold, Aesch.

χρῡσεό-κυκλος, ον, with disk of gold, of the sun, Eur.
χρῡσεό-μαλλος, ον, = χρυσόμαλλος, Eur.
χρῡσεο-μίτρης, ου, ὁ, (μίτρα) = χρυσομίτρης, Anth.
χρῡσεο-πήληξ, ηκος, ὁ, ἡ, = χρυσοπήληξ, h. Hom.
χρῡσεο-πήνητος, ον, (πήνη) with woof of gold, gold-
inwoven, Eur.
χρῡσεος, η, ον, Att. contr. χρυσοῦς, ῆ, οῦν (so ἀργύρεος,
-οῦς, χάλκεος, -οῦς), Ep. χρύσειος, η, ον : (χρυσός) :—
golden, of gold, decked or inlaid with gold, Hom.,
etc. : sometimes, = ἐπίχρυσος, gilded, gilt, Hdt.; cf.
ἵστημι A. III. 2. χρύσεια μέταλλα gold mines, Thuc.;
v. χρυσεῖον II. II. gold-coloured, golden-yellow,
Il. metaph. golden, χρυσέη Ἀφροδίτη Hom.;
χρ. ὑγίεια Pind.; χρ. ἐλπίς Soph.; the first age of man
was the golden, Hes. [χρυσέη, χρυσέην, χρυσέου,
χρυσέῳ etc., in Hom. must be pronounced as disyll.]
χρῡσεο-σάνδᾰλος, ον, with sandals of gold, Eur.
χρῡσεό-στολμος, ον, decked, dight with gold, Aesch.
χρῡσεό-στολος, ον, (στέλλω) = foreg., Eur.
Χρῡσηίς, ίδος, ἡ, patronym. of Χρύσης, ου, ὁ, daughter
of Chryses, Il.
χρῡσ-ηλάκᾰτος, ον, with spindle of gold, Il., Soph.
χρῡσ-ήλᾰτος, ον, (ἐλαύνω III) of beaten gold, gold-
wrought, Trag.
χρῡσ-ήνιος, Dor. -άνιος, ον, (ἡνία) with reins of gold,
Hom., Soph.
χρῡσ-ήρης, ες, gen. εος, (ἀραρίσκω) furnished or decked
with gold, golden, Eur.
χρῡσίδιον [σῐ], τό, Dim. of χρυσίον, a small piece of
gold, Isocr., Dem.
χρῡσίον, τό, Dim. of χρῦσος, a piece of gold, generally,
gold, Hdt., Thuc., etc.; pl., Dem. 2. gold coin,
money, Eur., Ar., Plat., etc.; χρυσία pieces of gold,
Plat. II. as a term of endearment, my golden
one! my little treasure! Ar., Anth.
χρῡσίς, ίδος, ἡ, a vessel of gold, piece of gold plate,
Ar. II. a gold-broidered dress or shoes, Luc.
χρῡσίτης [ῑ], ου, ὁ, fem. χρυσῖτις, ιδος, like gold, containing gold, ψάμμος χρυσῖτις Hdt.
χρῡσο-βᾰφής, ές, (βάπτω) gilded, gold-embroidered,
Plut., Anth.
χρῡσο-βέλεμνος, ον, with arrows of gold, Anth.
χρῡσό-βωλος, ον, (βῶλον) with soil of gold, Eur.
χρῡσό-γονος, ον, (γίγνομαι) born or begotten of gold,
χρ. γενεά, i. e. the Persians, because (by the legend)
they were descended from Perseus, who was begotten
of Zeus in the form of a shower of gold, Aesch.
χρῡσο-δακτύλιος, ον, with ring of gold, N. T.
χρῡσό-δετος, ον, bound with gold, set in gold, σφρηγίς
Hdt. :—enriched with gold, Soph., Eur.
χρῡσοειδής, ές, (εἶδος) like gold, Plat., Xen.
χρῡσό-ζῠγος, ον, (ζυγόν) with yoke of gold, Xen.
χρῡσό-θρονος, ον, gold-enthroned, Il., Pind.
χρῡσο-κάρηνος [ᾰ], ον, Dor. -ᾱνος, with head of gold,
Eur.
χρῡσό-κερως, ωτος, ὁ, ἡ, and -ρως, ων, gen. ω: (κέρας) :
—with horns of gold, Pind., Eur. II. with gilded
horns, of a victim ready for sacrifice, Aeschin.
χρῡσο-κόλλητος, ον, soldered or inlaid with gold, Eur.
χρῡσο-κόμης, ου, Dor. -κόμας, α, ὁ, (κόμη) the golden-
haired, Hes., Eur.; ὁ Χρ. absol. for Apollo, Pind.,
Eur. II. with golden ornaments in the hair, Luc.

χρῡσό-κομος, ον, = foreg., Anth.; with golden plumage, of birds, Hdt.

χρῡσολογέω, f. ήσω, to speak of gold, Luc. From

χρῡσο-λόγος, ον, (λέγω) speaking of gold.

χρῡσό-λογχος, ον, (λόγχη) with spear of gold, Eur.

χρῡσο-λύρης [ῠ], ον, Dor. -λύρας, α, ὁ, (λύρα) with lyre of gold, Ar., Anth.

χρῡσό-μαλλος, ον, with golden wool or fleece, Eur.

χρῡσο-μηλολόνθιον, τό, Dim. as if from χρυσομηλολόνθη, little golden beetle, as a term of endearment, Ar.

χρῡσο-μίτρης, ου, Dor. -μίτρας, α, ὁ, (μίτρα) with girdle or headband of gold, Soph.

χρῡσό-νωτος, ον, with golden back or surface; χρ. ἡνία a rein studded with gold, Soph.

χρῡσό-παστος, ον, sprinkled gold, gold-spangled, of gold tissue, Aesch.

χρῡσο-πέδῑλος, ον, (πέδιλον) gold-sandalled, Od., Hes.

χρῡσο-πήληξ, ηκος, ὁ, ἡ, with helm of gold, Aesch., Eur.

χρῡσο-πλόκᾰμος, ον, golden-haired, h. Hom.

χρῡσο-πλύσιον, τό, (πλύνω) a gold-wash, placer, where gold is washed from the river sand, Strab.

χρῡσοποιός, ὁ, (ποιέω) a goldsmith, Luc.

χρῡσό-πρᾰσος, ὁ, the chrysoprase, a precious stone of golden-green colour, N. T.

χρῡσό-πρυμνος, ον, (πρύμνα) with gilded poop, Plut.

χρῡσό-πτερος, ον, (πτερόν) with wings of gold, Il.

χρῡσόρᾱπις, ὁ, poët. for χρυσόρραπις, Pind.

χρῡσο-ρόης, ον, ὁ, (ῥέω) poët. for χρυσορρόης, with streams of gold, Eur.

χρῡσόρ-ρᾱπις, ιδος, ὁ, ἡ, with wand of gold, Od.

χρῡσόρ-ρυτος, ον, gold-streaming, Aesch. :—poët. χρῡσόρῠτος, ον, γοναὶ χρ., of Perseus the son of Danaë, Soph.

ΧΡΥΣΟ'Σ [ῠ], οῦ, ὁ, gold, Lat. aurum, Hom., etc.; χρυσὸν ἔδυνε put on golden armour, Il.; χρ. ἄπυρος unsmelted, opp. to χρ. ἄπεφθος (pure refined gold), Hdt.; λευκὸς χρυσός white gold, i. e. alloyed with silver, Id.; χρυσὸς κοῖλος gold wrought into vessels, gold plate, Luc.

χρῡσο-στέφανος, ον, gold-crowned, Hes., Eur., etc.; χρ. ἄεθλα in which the prize was a crown of gold, Pind.

χρῡσο-τέκτων, ονος, ὁ, a goldsmith, Anth.

χρῡσότερος, α, ον, a Compar. formed from χρυσός, more golden, Anth.

χρῡσό-τευκτος, ον, wrought of gold, Aesch., Eur.

χρῡσο-τευχής, ές, (τεῦχος) with golden armour, Eur.

χρῡσό-τοξος, ον, (τόξον) with bow of gold, Pind.

χρῡσο-τρίαινος, ον, (τρίαινα) with trident of gold, Ar.

χρῡσό-τῠπος, ον, (τύπτω) wrought of gold, Eur.

χρῡσ-ουργεῖον, τό, (*ἔργω) a gold mine, Strab.

χρῡσοῦς, ῆ, οῦν, Att. contr. for χρύσεος.

χρῡσο-φαής, ές, (φάος) with golden light, Eur.

χρῡσο-φάλαρος, ον, with trappings of gold, Eur.

χρῡσο-φεγγής, ές, (φέγγος) gold-beaming, Aesch.

χρῡσό-φῑλος, ον, gold-loving, Anth.

χρῡσοφορέω, f. ήσω, to wear golden ornaments or apparel, Hdt. : with golden scales, Luc. From

χρῡσο-φόρος, ον, (φέρω) wearing gold, i. e. golden ornaments, Hdt., Eur.

χρῡσο-φύλαξ [ῠ], ᾰκος, ὁ, ἡ, keeping gold, χρ. θύλακος a money bag, Plut. :—as Subst. a gold-keeper, Hdt., Eur.

χρῡσο-χαίτης, poët. -χαίτᾱ, ὁ, golden-haired, Pind.

χρῡσο-χάλῑνος [ᾰ], ον, with gold-studded bridle, Hdt., Xen.

χρῡσό-χειρ, χειρος, ὁ, ἡ, with gold rings, Luc.

χρῡσο-χίτων [ῐ], ωνος, ὁ, ἡ, with coat of gold, Anth.

χρῡσοχοεῖον, τό, the shop of a χρυσοχόος, ap. Dem.

χρῡσοχοέω, f. ήσω, to work in gold, work as a goldsmith, Ar., Xen. II. to smelt ore in order to get gold from it; whence χρυσοχοεῖν was used proverb. of those who fail in any tempting speculation, Plat.; and

χρῡσοχοϊκός, ή, όν, of or for a gold-smith, χρ. τέχνην ἐργάζεσθαι to follow the trade of a goldsmith, ap. Dem. From

χρῡσο-χόος, ὁ, (χέω) one who melts gold, of one who gilds the horns of a victim, Od. 2. a goldsmith, Dem.

χρῡσό-χροος, ον, contr. -χρους, ουν, gold-coloured, Anth.

χρῡσόω, f. ώσω, to make golden, gild, Luc. :—Pass. to be gilded, Hdt., Ar. Hence

χρῡσῶ, Dor. for χρυσοῦ, gen. of χρυσός.

χρῡσωμα, ατος, τό, (χρυσόω) wrought gold, Eur.

χρῡσ-ωνέω, f. ήσω, (ὠνέομαι) to change gold, Isocr.

χρῡσ-ωπός, όν, (ὤψ) with golden face, beaming like gold, Eur. II. gold-coloured, Plut.

χρῡσωρυχεῖον, τό, a gold-mine, Strab. From

χρῡσ-ωρύχος [ῠ], ον, (ὀρύσσω) digging for gold, Strab.

χρύσωσις [ῠ], εως, ἡ, (χρυσόω) a gilding, Plut.

χρῡσ-ώψ, ῶπος, ὁ, ἡ, = χρυσωπός, Eur.

χρῶ, Att. imper. of χράομαι.

χρῷ, heterocl. dat. of χρώς.

χρώζω, later χρώννῡμι (q.v.): f. χρώσω: aor. 1 ἔχρωσα: —Pass., aor. 1 ἐχρώσθην: pf. κέχρωσμαι: (χράω Α): —to touch the surface of a body, and generally, to touch, γόνατα μὴ χρώζειν ἐμά Eur. II. to tinge, stain, χρωσθεὶς ὑπὸ τοῦ ἡλίου Luc. 2. to defile, Anth. : metaph. in Pass., κεχρώσμεθα κακοῦ πρὸς ἀνδρός Eur.

χρῶμα, ατος, τό, the surface, skin : the colour of the skin, the complexion, Hdt.; χρῶμα ἀλλάσσειν Eur.; μεθιστάναι τοῦ χρώματος Ar. 2. generally, colour, Plat., Xen. :—metaph. in pl. ornaments, embellishments, Plat. ; embellishments in Music, Id.

χρωμάτιον, τό, Dim. of foreg., a colour, paint, Anth.

χρώννῡμι, = χρώζω, Luc.

χρώς, ὁ, gen. χρωτός, dat. χρωτί (Att. also χρῷ), acc. χρῶτα : Ion. gen. χροός, dat. χροΐ, acc. χρόα : (χράω Α): —like χροά (χροιά), the surface of the body, the skin, Hom. : also the flesh, opp. to the bone, Id. :—generally, the body, frame, Pind., Trag. 2. ἐν χροΐ, Att. ἐν χρῷ, close to the skin, ἐν χροῒ κείρειν to shave close, Hdt. ; ἐν χρῷ κεκαρμένος Xen. :—metaph., ξυρεῖ γὰρ ἐν χρῷ τοῦτο it touches one nearly, comes home, Soph.; ἐν χρῷ παραπλέειν to sail past so as to shave or graze, Lat. radere, Thuc. :—absol. ἐν χρῷ (also written ἐγχρῷ or ἐγχρῷ), near at hand, hard by, Luc. II. the colour of the skin, complexion, Hom., Eur. 2. generally, colour, Aesch.

χρωτίζω, f. ίσω, like χρώζω, to colour :—Med., χρωτίζεσθαι τὴν φύσιν to tinge one's nature, Ar.

χύδην [ῠ], Adv. (χέω) in floods or heaps; hence, I. without order, at random, promiscuously, Plat., Anth. II. in flowing language, i. e. in prose, Arist. III. abundantly, wholly, utterly, Anth.

χῠθείην, aor. 1 opt. pass. of χέω.

χῡλός, οῦ, ὁ, (χέω) juice, esp. juice produced by decoction or digestion :—metaph., χυλὸν διδοὺς στωμυλμάτων administering a decoction of small talk, Ar.; χ. φιλίας Id.

χῡμεῖς, crasis for καὶ ὑμεῖς.

χύμενος [ῠ], η, ον, Ep. aor. 2 pass. part. of χέω.

χῡμός, οῦ, ὁ, (χέω) like χυλός, juice, Plat.

χύντο, 3 pl. Ep. aor. 2 pass. of χέω.

χύσις [ῠ], εως, ἡ, (χέω) a flood, stream, Aesch. 2. of dry things, a heap, φύλλων χ. Od.: a quantity, σαρκῶν Anth. 3. metaph. of the lapse of time, Id.

χυτλάζω, f. άσω, to pour out: metaph. to throw carelessly down, χύτλασον σεαυτὸν ἐν τοῖς στρώμασιν Ar.

χύτλον, τό, (χέω) anything that can be poured: water and oil for the bath. Hence

χυτλόω, f. ώσω, to wash :—Med. to anoint oneself after bathing, Od.

χύτο [ῠ], 3 sing. Ep. aor. 2 pass. of χέω.

χῠτός, ή, όν, verb. Adj. of χέω, poured, shed, αἷμα χυτόν blood shed, Aesch. 2. of dry things, shot out, heaped up, χυτὴ γαῖα a mound of earth, a sepulchral mound, Hom. :—as Subst., χυτός, ὁ, = χῶμα, a mound, bank, dike, Hdt. II. melted, ἀρτήματα λίθινα χυτά pendants of melted stone, Id. III. generally, liquid, flowing, Pind., Anth.

χύτρα, ἡ, (χέω) an earthen pot, a pot for boiling, pipkin, Lat. olla, Ar., Xen. 2. χύτραι, pots of pulse offered to inferior deities, Ar.

χυτρεοῦς, οῦν, (χύτρα) of earthenware, Ar.

χυτρεύς, έως, ὁ, (χύτρα) a potter, Lat. figulus, Plat.

χυτρίδιον [ῐ], τό, Dim. of χύτρα, a small pot, cup, Ar.

χυτρίς, ἡ, Dim. of χύτρα, Hdt.

χυτρό-πους, ποδος, ὁ, pl. χυτρόποδες, a pot with feet, or a portable stove for putting a pot upon, Hes.

χύτρος, ὁ, = χύτρα. II. οἱ Χύτροι was the name given to the hot baths at Thermopylae, Hdt. 2. the pot-feast, the 3rd day of the Anthesteria, and 13th of the month Anthesterion, Ar.

χώ, for καὶ ὁ.

χὤδωνις, crasis for καὶ Ἄδωνις.

χώεο, Ep. imper. of χώομαι.

χὠκ, crasis for καὶ ὁ ἐκ.

χωλαίνω, f. ἀνῶ, (χωλός) to be or go lame, Plat.

χωλεία, ἡ, lameness, Plat., Luc. From

χωλεύω, to be or become lame, to halt, limp, Il., Xen. II. trans. to make lame :—Pass. to be lame, Luc.: generally, to be maimed or imperfect, Plat.

χωλ-ίαμβος, ὁ, a lame iambic, i. e. one that has a spondee for an iambus in the last place, said to be invented by Hipponax.

χωλο-ποιός, όν, (ποιέω) making lame, of Euripides, as being fond of introducing lame men upon the stage, Ar.

ΧΩΛΟ'Σ, ή, όν, lame in the feet, halting, limping, χωλὸς πόδα Hom.; χωλὸς ἀμφοτέροις (sc. ποσί) Luc. II. metaph. maimed, imperfect, defective, Lat. mancus, Plat., Xen.

χῶμα, ατος, τό, (χόω) earth thrown up, a bank, mound, thrown up against the walls of cities to take them, Hdt., Thuc. :—a dike to hinder a river from overflowing, Hdt. :—a dam, Id. :—a mole or pier, carried out into the sea, Lat. moles, Id., Dem. II. like Lat. tumulus, a sepulchral mound, Hdt., Trag.

χωνεύω, χώνη, contr. from χοανεύω, χοάνη.

χὠνήρ, crasis for καὶ ὁ ἀνήρ.

χώννῡμι, -ύω, later form of χόω, Polyb., etc.

ΧΩ'ΟΜΑΙ, Ep. imper. χώεο : 3 sing. Ep. impf. χώετο : f. χώσομαι : aor. 1 ἐχωσάμην, Ep. 3 sing. subj. χώσεται : Dep. :—to be angry, wroth, indignant, Hom. ; χωόμενος κῆρ, θυμόν Il. ; κηρόθι Od. 1. c. dat. pers. to be angry at one, ὅτε χώσεται ἀνδρί Il. 2. c. gen. pers. vel rei, χωόμενος γυναικός about or because of her, Ib. ; χώσατο δ᾽ αἰνῶς νίκης τε καὶ ἔγχεος Ib. 3. c. acc. rei, only in the phrase μή μοι τόδε χώεο be not angry with me for this, Od.

χώπη, crasis for καὶ ὅπη.

χωπόταν, crasis for καὶ ὁπόταν.

χὤπως, crasis for καὶ ὅπως.

χώρα, Ion. χώρη, ἡ, = χῶρος, the space in which a thing is, Lat. locus, οὐδέ τι πολλὴ χώρη μεσσηγύς Il. ; ὀλίγῃ ἐνὶ χώρῃ Ib. 2. generally, a place, Hom. 3. one's place, position, ἐν χώρῃ ἔσεσθαι Il. ; esp. a soldier's post, χώραν λείπειν Thuc. ; χώραν λαβεῖν to find one's place, ἕως ἂν χώραν λάβῃ τὰ πράγματα till they are brought into position, into order, Xen. 4. metaph. one's place in life, station, place, position, Ἄρης δ᾽ οὐκ ἐνὶ χώρᾳ the spirit of war is not there, Aesch. ; ἐν ἀνδραπόδων or μισθοφόρων χώρᾳ εἶναι to be in the position of slaves or mercenaries, Xen. ; ἐν οὐδεμιᾷ χώρᾳ εἶναι to be in no esteem, nullo loco haberi, Id. :—also, κατὰ χώραν (χώρην) εἶναι, ἔχειν to be in one's place, to keep a thing in its place, Hdt., Ar. ; κατὰ χ. μένειν to stand one's ground, Hdt., Att. II. land, viz., 1. a land, country, Lat. regio, Od., Hdt., Trag. 2. a piece of land, an estate, farm, Lat. ager, Xen. 3. the country, opp. to the town, Lat. rus, τὰ ἐκ τῆς χώρας, ὁ ἐκ τῆς χώρας σῖτος Thuc., Xen.

χωρέω, f. χωρήσω, Att. generally in med. form, χωρήσομαι : aor. 1 ἐχώρησα : pf. κεχώρηκα : (χῶρος) :—to make room for another, give way, draw back, retire, withdraw, Il. ; γαῖα ἔνερθεν χώρησεν the earth gave way from beneath, i. e. opened, h. Hom. ;—πρύμναν χ. = κρούεσθαι πρύμναν, to put back, retire, Eur. ;—χωρεῖτε begone! Aesch. :—Construction : 1. c. gen. loci, χώρησεν ἐπάλξιος he retired from the rampart, Il. ; also, ἀπὸ ὑσμίνης χωρήσαντες Ib. ; ἐκ πυλῶν Aesch. 2. c. dat. pers. to give way to one, retire before him, οὐδ᾽ ἂν Ἀχιλλῆι χωρήσειεν Il. II. to go forward, move on or along, Lat. incedere, and then simply to go or come, Hdt., etc. : to go on one's journey, travel, Soph. ; χ. πρὸς ἔργον to come to action, come on, begin, Id. ; χ. πρὸς ἧπαρ to go to one's heart, Id. ; διὰ φόνου χ. Eur. ; κάτω χώρει go downwards, i. e. beginning from the upper parts of the body, Aesch. :—absol., χ. ὁ ποταμός Plat. ; ὁμόσε χ. to join battle, Thuc. ; of Time, νὺξ ἐχώρει the night was passing, near an end, Aesch. : —also c. acc. loci, Κεκροπίαν χθόνα χ. Eur. 2. to go on, advance, Lat. procedere, οὐ χωρεῖ τοὔργον Ar. ; τόκοι χωροῦσιν Id. 3. to come to an issue, turn out in a certain manner, παρὰ σμικρὰ κεχώρηκε have come to little, of oracles, Hdt. ; εὐτυχέως χ., Lat. bene cedere, Id. :—absol., like προχωρέω, to go on well, succeed, Id. 4. to spread abroad, Id. ; διὰ πάντων χωρεῖν to spread among all, Xen. III. trans. = χανδάνω, to have room for a thing, to hold, contain, esp. of measures, ὁ κρητὴρ χωρέει ἀμφορέας ἑξακοσίους Hdt. ;

ἡ πόλις οὐκ ἐχώρησεν αὐτούς Thuc.; χωρήσατε ἡμᾶς take us into your hearts, N. T.

χωρίδιον [ῐ], τό, Dim. of χωρίον, Lys., Plut.

χωρίζω, f. Att. ιῶ: pf. pass. κεχώρισμαι, 3 pl. Ion. κεχωρίδαται: (χωρίς):   I. in local sense, to separate, part, sever, divide one thing from another, τί τινος Eur., Plat.; τι ἀπό τινος Plat.:—χ. πάντα κατὰ φυλάς Xen.;—οἱ χωρίζοντες the Separaters, a name given to those Grammarians who ascribed the Iliad and Odyssey to different authors:—Pass. to be separated, severed, divided, Hdt., Eur.   II. to separate in thought, to distinguish, τὸ ἡδύ τε καὶ δίκαιον Plat., etc.:—Pass. to differ, to be different, κεχωρίδαται πολλὸν τῶν ἄλλων ἀνθρώπων Hdt.; more rarely, χωρίζεσθαί τινι Id.; νόμοι κεχωρισμένοι τῶν ἄλλων ἀνθρώπων laws apart from the others, far different, Id.

χωρίον, τό, Dim. (only in form) of χῶρος and χώρα: 1. a particular place, a place, spot, district, Hdt., Thuc., etc.; ἐκ τοῦ αὐτοῦ χ. this same spot, Hdt.   2. a place, post, esp. a fortified post, Id., Thuc., etc.   3. landed property, an estate, Thuc., Xen.   4. a place of business, office, Dem.   5. in Geometry, a space enclosed by lines, Ar., Plat.   6.=τόπος 1. 3, a place, passage in a book, Luc.: a part or period of history, Thuc.

χωρίς, Adv., separately, asunder, apart, by oneself or by themselves, Hom.; κεῖται χ. ὁ νεκρός Hdt.; χ. θέσθαι to set apart, keep in reserve, Thuc.; χ. οἰκεῖν to live apart, Dem.; μή με χ. αἰτιῶ accuse me not without evidence, Soph.; χ. ποιεῖν to distinguish, Isocr.; χωρὶς δέ . . , and separately, besides, Thuc.: —separately, one by one, Lys.; χωρὶς ἤ except, χ. ἤ ὅτι except that, Hdt.; χ. ἤ ὅκοσοι except so many as, Id.   2. metaph. of different nature, kind, or quality, Soph., Eur.   II. as Prep. c. gen. without, Aesch., Soph., etc.; χ. Ζηνός without his help or will, Lat. sine Diis, Soph.   2. separate from, apart or aloof from, far from, χ. ἀνθρώπων στίβου Id.; ἡ ψυχὴ χ. τοῦ σώματος Plat.   3. independent of, without reckoning, not to mention, besides, Hdt., Aesch.   4. differently from, otherwise than, Plat., Dem.

χωρισμός, ὁ, (χωρίζω) separation, Plat.

χωριστέον, verb. Adj. of χωρίζω, one must separate, τι ἀπό τινος Plat.

χωριστός, ή, όν, (χωρίζω) verb. Adj.:   I. in local sense, separated, separable, Arist.   II. separate or separable in thought, Id.

χωρίτης [ῐ], ου, ὁ, (χώρα) a countryman, rustic, boor, Xen., Anth.:—fem. -ῖτις, ιδος, a country girl, Luc.   2. one dwelling in a spot or country, a native, Aesch. Hence

χωρῑτικός, ή, όν, of or like a countryman, rustic, rural, Plut.: Adv. -κῶς, in rustic fashion, Xen.

χωρογραφέω, f. ήσω, to describe countries, Strab.; and

χωρογραφικός, ή, όν, of or for the description of countries, Strab. From

χωρο-γράφος [ᾰ], ον, describing countries, Strab.

χῶρος, ὁ, a piece of ground, ground, place, Hom., etc.   II. a land, country, Hdt.; in pl. lands, places, Id., Soph.   2. land, an estate, Xen.   3. the country, Lat. rus, Id. (Deriv. uncertain.)

Χῶρος, ὁ, the North-west wind, Lat. Caurus, N. T.

χωρο-φῐλέω, =φιλοχωρέω, to haunt a place, Antipho.

χῶς, crasis for καὶ ὡς.

χώσεται, Ep. for χώσηται, 3 sing. aor. 1 subj. of χώομαι.

χωσθῆναι, aor. 1 pass. inf. of χόω.

χῶσις, εως, ἡ, (χόω) a heaping up, esp. of earth, raising a mound or bank, esp. against a city, Thuc.   2. a filling in, blocking up by earth thrown in, Id.

χώσους, crasis for καὶ ὅσους.

χωστός, ή, όν, verb. Adj. made by earth thrown up, Eur.

χὥταν, crasis for καὶ ὅταν.

χὥτι, crasis for καὶ ὅτι.

Ψ.

Ψ ψ, ψῖ, τό, indecl., twenty-third letter of the Gr. alphabet: as a numeral, ψ´ = 700, but ͵ψ = 700,000.— The letter ψ is a double Consonant, compounded of the labial π or φ with σ, = πσ, φσ: the character ψ, ascribed to Simonides, was adopted at Athens in the archonship of Euclides (Ol. 94. 2) at the same time with η, ω, ξ.

ψαίρω, only in pres., (ψάω):   I. trans. to graze, scrape, touch gently, οἶμον αἰθέρος ψαίρει is ready to skim the path of ether, Aesch.   II. intr. to move lightly, flutter, rustle, murmur, Luc.

ψαιστός, ή, όν, verb. Adj. of ψάω: τὰ ψαιστά (sc. πόπανα) cakes of ground barley, used at sacrifices, Ar.

ψαίστωρ, ορος, ὁ, (ψάω) one that wipes off, Anth.

ψακάζω, f. άσω, (ψακάς) to rain in small drops, drizzle, drip, Ar.: impers., ψακάζει it drizzles. From

ψακάς, later ψεκάς, άδος, ἡ, (ψάω) any small piece broken off, a grain, morsel, bit, ἀργυρίου μηδὲ ψακάς, i. e. not even a silver penny, Ar.; collectively, ψάμμου ψεκάς grains of sand, Anth.   II. a drop of rain; and collectively, drizzling rain, ὕσθησαν αἱ Θῆβαι ψακάδι Hdt.; ψακὰς δὲ λήγει drops are ceasing, i. e. a storm is coming, Aesch.:—generally, rain, Eur.; ψακάδι φοινίας δρόσου with a sprinkling of bloody dew, Aesch.   2. Comic name for a sputterer, Ar.

ψαλιδό-στομος, ον, nipper-mouthed, of a crab, Batr.

ψαλίζω, (ψαλίς) to clip with scissors, Babr.

ψάλιον [ᾰ], τό, part of the bridle, a kind of curb-chain, Xen.; ψαλίοις ἐδάμασε πώλους Eur.   2. generally, a chain, bond, Aesch.; metaph., of a person, ψ. οἰκετῶν a curb upon the household, Id. (Deriv. unknown.)

ψαλίς, ίδος, ἡ, a pair of scissors, Lat. forfex, Anth.   II. a building with a pointed stone roof, a vault, Lat. fornix, Soph. (Deriv. unknown.)

ψάλλω, f. ψαλῶ: aor. 1 ἔψηλα: pf. ἔψαλκα: (ψάω):— to touch sharply, to pluck, pull, twitch, Aesch.; τόξου νευρὰν ψ. to twang the bow-string, Eur.; βέλος ἐκ κέραος ψ. to send a shaft twanging from the bow, Anth.; so, σχοῖνος μιλτοφυρὴς ψαλλομένη a carpenter's red line, which is twitched and then suddenly let go, so as to leave a mark, Ib.   II. to play a stringed instrument with the fingers, not with the plectron, Hdt., Ar., Plat.   2. later, to sing to a harp, sing, N. T.

ψάλμα, τό, a tune for a stringed instrument, Anth.

ψαλμός, ὁ, a twitching or twanging with the fingers, of a bow, Eur.   II. mostly of musical strings: the

sound of the harp, Pind., Aesch.   **2.** later, a song sung to the harp, a psalm, N. T.

ψαλμο-χᾰρής, ές, delighting in harp-playing, Anth.

ψάλτρια, ἡ, (ψάλλω) a female harper, Plat., etc.

ψάμᾰθος [ψᾰ], ἡ, poët. form of ψάμμος, sand, sea-sand, Hom., Soph., etc.; in pl., νῆα ἐπὶ ψαμάθοις on the sands, Hom.   **2.** proverb. of a countless multitude, ὅσα ψάμαθός τε κόνις τε Il.; in pl. grains of sand, Ib.

ψᾰμᾰθ-ώδης, ες, (εἶδος) = ψαμμώδης, sandy, h. Hom.

ψαμμᾰκόσιοι (not ψαμμοκ-), αι, α, sand-hundred, a Comic word formed from ψάμμος, ἑκάτον, after the analogy of the cardinal numbers διακόσιοι, τριακόσιοι (from δὶς ἑκατόν, τρὶς ἑκατόν), to denote a countless multitude, Eupol.:—so also the exaggerated form **ψαμμᾱκοσιο-γάργαροι,** αι, α, in sand-hundred heaps, Ar.

ψάμμη, Dor. ψάμμα, ἡ, = ψάμμος, Hdt., Aesch.

ψάμμῐνος, η, ον, (ψάμμος) of sand, sandy, Hdt.

ψάμμιος, α, ον, (ψάμμος) on the sand, Aesch.

ψαμμίτης [ῑ], ου, ὁ, sand, sandy, Anth.

ψάμμος, ἡ, sand, so called from its loose, crumbling nature (from ψάω), Od., etc.:—proverb., ψάμμος ἀριθμὸν περιπέφευγεν Pind.   **II.** ἡ ψ. the sandy desert of Libya, Hdt. (Both ψάμμος and ψάμαθος sometimes drop ψ and become ἄμμος, ἄμαθος.)

ψαμμ-ώδης, ες, (εἶδος) like sand, sandy, Hdt.

ΨΑ'Ρ, ὁ, gen. ψᾱρός: Ion. ψήρ, ψηρός:—a starling, mentioned as flying in a cloud, ψηρῶν νέφος Il.

ψᾱρός, ά, όν, (ψάρ) like a starling, i. e. speckled, dappled, ψ. ἵππος a dapple-gray horse, Ar.

ψαῦσις, εως, ἡ, a touching, Plut.

ΨΑΥ'Ω, f. ψαύσω: aor. 1 ἔψαυσα: pf. ἔψαυκα:—Pass., aor. 1 ἐψαύσθην: pf. ἔψαυσμαι: (akin to ψάω):—to touch, c. gen., Il., etc.; c. dat. instrumenti, Ib.; χεροῖν ἔψαυσα πηγῆς Aesch.: but ψαύειν τινι to touch a thing, Pind.: —in Soph. it seems to be used c. acc., κεῖνος ψαύων τὸν θεόν assailing the god, Antig. 961; but Ib. 857, ἔψαυσας μερίμνας, πατρὸς οἶτον thou didst touch on a theme of grief,—my father's fate,—μερίμνας is gen., and οἶτον acc. in apposition.   **2.** to touch as an enemy, lay hands upon, τινός Eur.   **3.** to touch, reach, affect, ἄκρας καρδίας ἔψαυσέ μου Id.:—Med. also, to reach, gain, Pind.

ψᾰφᾰρίτης, ου, ὁ, fem. -ῖτις, ιδος, = ψαφαρός, Anth.

ψᾰφᾰρό-θριξ, -τρῐχος, ὁ, ἡ, with rough coat, h. Hom.

ψᾰφᾰρός, ά, όν, (ψάω) easily reduced to powder, friable, crumbling, Aesch., Anth.; ἡ ψαφαρή the sandy shore, Anth.   **2.** of liquids, thin, watery, Id.

ψᾰφᾰρό-χροος, ον, contr. -χρους, ουν, rough on the surface, squalid, Eur.

ΨΑ'Ω [ᾱ], ψῇς, ψῇ (not ψᾷς, ψᾷ), inf. ψῆν: impf. contr. ἔψην: f. ψήσω: aor. 1 ἔψησα:—to touch lightly, rub; cf. καταψάω.   **II.** intr. to crumble away, vanish, disappear, Soph.

ψέ, Dor. for σφέ, σφέας, like ψίν for σφίν, Theocr.

ΨΕ'ΓΩ, f. ψέξω: aor. 1 ἔψεξα:—to blame, censure, τινά Theogn., etc.;—ψ. τινὰ περί τινος to blame one for a thing, Plat.; διά τι Id.; ἐπί τινι Xen.:—also, c. dupl. acc., Soph.; ἃ ψέγομεν τὸν Ἔρωτα Plat.:—Pass., ἡ ἐπιείκεια οὐ ψέγεται there is no objection to it, we find no fault with it, Thuc.

ΨΕΔΝΟ'Σ, ή, όν, thin, spare, scanty, of hair, Il., Anth.; of a person, bald-headed, Luc.

ψεκάζω, ψεκάς, later forms for ψακάζω, ψακάς.

ψέκτης, ου, ὁ, (ψέγω) a censurer, disparager, Plat.

ψεκτός, ή, όν, verb. Adj. blamed, blameable, Plat.

ψέλιον or **ψέλλιον,** τό, an armlet or anklet, Lat. armilla, Hdt., Xen.

ψελιο-φόρος, ον, (φέρω) wearing bracelets, Hdt.

ψελιόω (ψέλιον) to twine, ψ. αὐχένα στεφάνοις Anth.

ψελλίζω, f. ίσω, (ψελλός) to falter in speech, speak inarticulately:—so in Med., Plat., Arist.

ψέλλιον, τό, = ψέλιον.

ψελλισμός, ὁ, a pronouncing indistinctly: metaph., ποδάγρας ψ. unpronounced (i. e. suppressed) gout, Plut.

ΨΕΛΛΟ'Σ, ή, όν, unable to pronounce certain letters, Arist.   **II.** pass. of words, inarticulate, obscure, Aesch.

ψευδαγγελέω, f. ήσω, to bring false news, Ar.; and **ψευδαγγελία,** ἡ, a false report, Xen. From

ψευδ-άγγελος, ὁ, a false or lying messenger, Il.

ψευδ-άδελφος, ὁ, a false brother, N. T.

ψευδ-ἄμάμαξῠς, νος, ὁ, a bastard vine, Ar.

ψευδ-ἀπόστολος, ὁ, a false apostle, N. T.

ψευδ-αρτάβας [ᾰ], (ἀρτάβη) Comic name of a mock-Persian, False-measure, Ar.

ψευδ-ατράφαξυς, νος, ἡ, false orach, Comic name of a plant, Ar.

ψευδ-αττικός, ή, όν, false Attic, Luc.

ψευδ-αυτόμολος, ὁ, ἡ, a sham deserter, Xen.

ψευδ-ενέδρα, ἡ, a feigned ambuscade, Xen.

ψευδέσσι or **ψεύδεσσι,** Ep. dat. pl., v. ψευδής I. 2.

ψευδηγορέω, f. ήσω, to speak falsely, Aesch. From

ψευδ-ηγόρος, ον, (ἀγορεύω) speaking falsely, Anth.

ψευδη-λογέω, = ψευδο-λογέω, Luc.

ψευδήμων, ον, poët. for ψευδής, Anth.

ψευδής, ές, gen. έος, (ψεύδομαι) lying, false, Lat. mendax, Hes., etc.; ἐπὶ ψευδῆ ὁδὸν τρέπεσθαι to betake oneself to lying ways, Hdt.   **2.** of persons, lying, and as Subst. a liar, οὐ γὰρ ἐπὶ ψευδέσσι πατὴρ Ζεὺς ἔσσετ' ἀρωγός Zeus will not assist lying men (others read ἐπὶ ψεύδεσσι from ψεῦδος, will not assist lies); ψ. φαίνεσθαι to be detected in falsehood, Thuc.   **3.** τὰ ψευδῆ falsehoods, lies, ψευδῆ λέγειν Aesch., Ar.   **II.** pass. belied, beguiled, deceived, Eur.   **III.** Adv. falsely, Id., Thuc.

ψεῦδις, ιος, ὁ, ἡ, poët. for ψευδής, Pind.

ψευδο-βοήθεια, ἡ, pretended help, Xen.

ψευδο-δῐδάσκαλος, ὁ, a false teacher, N. T.

ψευδο-κῆρυξ, ῠκος, ὁ, a lying herald, Soph.

ψευδοκλητεία or -ία, ἡ, (κλητήρ) a prosecution against one who has falsely subscribed his name as witness, γραφὴ ψευδοκλητείας a prosecution for such false subscription, Dem.

ψευδο-κύων, κύνος, ὁ, a sham Cynic, Plut.

ψευδό-λιτρος, ον, Att. for ψευδό-νιτρος: ψ. κονία lie or soap made from adulterated soda, Ar.

ψευδολογέω, f. ήσω, to speak falsely, spread false reports, Isocr., Aeschin.

ψευδολογία, ἡ, a false speech, falsehood, Isocr., Dem.

ψευδο-λόγος, ον, (λέγω) speaking falsely, Ar., Anth.

ψεύδομαι, v. ψεύδω B.

ψευδό-μαντις, εως, ὁ, ἡ, a false prophet, Hdt., Trag.

ψευδομαρτῠρέω, f. ήσω, to be a false witness, bear false witness, Plat., Xen.

ψευδομαρτῠρία, ἡ, false witness, Dem.: mostly in gen. pl., ψευδομαρτυριῶν δίκη a prosecution for false witness, Isae., etc.; ψευδομαρτυριῶν ἐπισκήπτεσθαί τινι to make allegation of perjury against one, Dem. From

ψευδο-μάρτυς, ῠρος, ὁ, a false witness, Plat.

ψευδο-νέρων, ὁ, a false-Nero, Luc.

ψευδό-νιτρος, ον, v. ψευδό-λιτρος.

ψευδο-νύμφευτος γάμος, ὁ, (νυμφεύω) a false, feigned marriage, Eur.

ψευδο-πάρθενος, ἡ, a pretended maid or virgin, Hdt.

ψευδ-όρκιος, ον, (ὅρκος) perjured, forsworn, Hdt.

ψεύδ-ορκος, ον, = foreg., Eur.

ψεῦδος, εος, τό, (ψεύδω) a falsehood, untruth, lie, Hom., etc.; εἴτε ψεῦδος ὑπόσχεσις ἢ καὶ οὐχί whether the promise be a lie or no, Il. II. pl., ψεύδεα spots, pimples on the nose, Theocr.

ψευδο-στομέω, f. ήσω, (στόμα) to speak falsely, Soph.

ψευδό-φημος, ον, (φήμη) of false divination, Soph.

ψευδό-φίλιππος, ὁ, a false Philip, Luc.

ψευδό-χριστος, ὁ, a false Christ, N.T.

ψεύδω (Root ΨΥΔ), f. ψεύσω: aor. 1 ἔψευσα:—Pass., f. ψευσθήσομαι: aor. 1 ἐψεύσθην: pf. ἔψευσμαι, 3 sing. imperat. ἐψεύσθω:—to cheat by lies, beguile, Soph., etc.:—Pass. to be cheated, deceived, Aesch., etc. 2. ψ. τινά τινος to cheat, balk, disappoint one of a thing, Id., Soph.; also c. acc. rei, ἐλπίδας ψ. τινά Xen.: —Pass. to be cheated, balked, disappointed of a thing, ψευσθῆναι ἐλπίδος, γάμου Hdt.; δείπνου Ar. 3. Pass., also, to be deceived, mistaken in or about a thing, ἐψευσμένοι γνώμης mistaken in opinion, Hdt.; ἐψευσμένοι τῆς τῶν Ἀθηναίων δυνάμεως deceived in their notions of the Athenian power, Thuc.; ἐψεύσθαι ἑαυτῶν, opp. to εἰδέναι ἑαυτούς, Xen.:—also, ψευσθῆναι ἔν τινι Hdt.; περί τινος Xen.: also c. acc., αὐτοὺς ἐψευσμένη Ἑλλάς deceived in its estimate of them, Thuc. 4. of statements, to be untrue, ἡ τρίτη τῶν ὁδῶν μάλιστα ἔψευσται Hdt. II. c. acc. rei, like ψευδοποιέω, to represent a thing as a lie, to falsify, Soph.:—Pass., ἡ ψευσθεῖσα ὑπόσχεσις the promise broken, Thuc.

B. earlier and more common is the Dep. ψεύδομαι, Ep. imper. ψεύδεο: f. ψεύσομαι: aor. 1 ἐψευσάμην: pf. ἔψευσμαι:— I. absol. to lie, speak false, play false, Hom., etc. 2. c. acc. rei, to say that which is untrue, ὅτι τοῦτο ψεύδομαι Plat.; ἅπερ αὐτὸν οὐ ψεύδομαι which I do not speak falsely about him, Andoc. 3. to be false, perjured or forsworn, Hes. II. like Act. II, to belie, falsify, ὅρκια ψεύσασθαι to break them, Il.; so, ψ. γάμους Eur.; so in plqpf. pass., ἔψευστο τὴν ξυμμαχίαν Thuc.; τὰ χρήματα ἐψευσμένοι ἦσαν had broken their word about the money, Xen. III. like Act. I, to deceive by lies, cheat, Aesch., Eur.; ψ. τινά τι to deceive one in a thing, Soph., Eur.

ψευδ-ώνυμος, ον, (ὄνομα) under a false name, falsely called, Aesch. Adv. -μως, by a false name, Id.

ψευσί-στυξ, ῠγος, ὁ, ἡ, (στυγέω) hating falsehood, Anth.

ψεῦσμα, ατος, τό, (ψεύδω) a lie, untruth, Plat.

ψευστέω, f. ήσω, to be a liar, lie, cheat, Il. From

ψεύστης, ου, ὁ, (ψεύδω) a liar, cheat, Il., etc. 2. as Adj., like ψευδής, lying, false, Pind., Anth.

ψεφ-αυγής, ές, gen. έος, (αὐγή) dark-gleaming, i.e. glimmering, gloomy, Eur.

ψεφηνός, ή, όν, dark, obscure, of a person, Pind.

ΨΕ'ΦΟΣ, εος, τό, darkness, Alcae.

ψῆ, 3 sing. of ψάω. II. ψῆ, for ἔψη, 3 sing. impf.

ψῆγμα, ατος, (ψήχω) that which is rubbed or scraped off, shavings, scrapings, chips, Lat. ramentum, ψ. (with or without χρυσοῦ) gold dust, Hdt.; ψ. πυρωθέν, i. e. dust and ashes, Aesch.

ψήκτρα, ἡ, (ψήχω) an instrument used by bathers, a scraper, like στλεγγίς, Eur., Anth.

ψῆλαι, aor. 1 inf. of ψάλλω.

ψηλᾰφάω, mostly in pres., (ψάω) to feel or grope about like a blind man or one in the dark, χερσὶ ψηλαφόων (Ep. for -άων), of the blinded Cyclops, Od.; ψηλαφῶντες ὥσπερ ἐν σκότῳ Plat. 2. c. acc. rei, to feel about for, search after, Ar., N.T. II. to feel, touch, stroke, Xen., N.T.

ψηλάφημα, ατος, τό, a touch, a caress, Xen.

ΨΗ'Ν, ὁ, gen. ψηνός, the gall-insect, which lives in the fruit of the wild fig and male palm, Hdt., Ar. Hence

Ψηνίζω, to Psenize, alluding to the Ψῆνες, a Comedy by Magnes, Ar.

ψῆξις, εως, ἡ, (ψήχω) a rubbing down, currying, Xen.

ψήρ, ὁ, gen. ψηρός, Ion. for ψάρ.

ΨΗ'ΤΤΑ, ἡ, a flat-fish such as a plaice, sole, turbot, Lat. rhombus, Plat., etc.

ψηττό-ποδες, οἱ, (πούς) turbot-footed, name of a fabulous people, Luc.

ψηφῑδο-φόρος, ον, (φέρω) = ψηφοφόρος, Hdt.

ψηφίζω, f. Att. ιῶ: aor. 1 ἐψήφισα: pf. ἐψήφικα:—to count or reckon, properly with pebbles (ψῆφοι, cf. Lat. calculare from calculus), Anth. II. more freq. as Dep. ψηφίζομαι, f. Att. ψηφιοῦμαι: aor. 1 ἐψηφισάμην: pf. ἐψήφισμαι:—properly, to give one's vote with a pebble, which was thrown into the voting urn, absol., ψηφίζεσθαι ἐς ὑδρίαν Xen.: generally, to vote, Hdt.; τινι for any one, Dem. 2. c. acc. rei, to vote for, carry by vote, πόλεμον Thuc.; ψ. παρασκευήν Id., etc. 3. c. inf. to vote, give one's vote to do a thing, Hdt., Aesch., etc.:—c. acc. et inf. to vote that, ψ. τὰς σπονδὰς λελύσθαι Thuc. 4. ψ. περί, ὑπέρ τινος Plat., Aeschin. III. Act. in same sense as Med., only in Soph. Aj. (δίκην ἐψήφισαν), and in late writers:—but the aor. 1 pass. ψηφισθῆναι is used in pass. sense, to be voted, Thuc., Xen., etc.; so pf. part. ἐψηφισμένοι θανεῖν condemned by vote, die, Eur.

ψηφίς, ῖδος, ἡ, Dim. of ψῆφος, a small pebble, Il., Luc. 2. a pebble for reckoning, Anth.

ψήφισμα, ατος, τό, (ψηφίζομαι) a proposition carried by vote: esp. a measure passed in the ἐκκλησία, a decree, Ar.; τὸ Μεγαρέων ψ. the decree concerning them, Thuc.; so, περὶ Μεγαρέων ψ. Id.; ψ. γράφειν to bring in a decree, Ar., Dem.; ψ. ἐπιψηφίζειν, of the πρόεδροι, to put it to the vote, Aeschin.; ψ. νικᾶν to carry it, Id.; ψ. καθαιρεῖν to rescind it, Lat. abrogare, Thuc.

ψηφισμάτο-πώλης, ου, ὁ, a decree-monger, Ar.

ψηφισμᾰτ-ώδης, ες, of the nature of a decree, Arist.

ψηφο-ποιός, όν, (ψῆφος II, ποιέω) making votes or tampering with them, Soph.

ΨΗ'ΦΟΣ, Dor. ψᾶφος, ἡ, (ψάω) a small stone, a pebble, rubbed and rounded in river-beds or on the sea-shore,

Lat. *calculus*, Pind., Hdt.　　**II.** *a pebble used for reckoning, a counter,* ψήφοις λογίζεσθαι *to calculate by arithmetic, to cipher,* Hdt. ; hence *to reckon exactly* or *accurately,* Ar. ; ἐν ψήφῳ λέγειν Aesch. :—in pl. *accounts,* καθαραὶ ψῆφοι *an exact balance,* Dem.　**2.** *a pebble used for playing at draughts,* Plat.　**3.** *a pebble used in voting,* which was thrown into the voting-urn (ὑδρία), Hdt., Att. ; ψῆφον φέρειν *to give one's vote,* Lat. *suffragium ferre,* Aesch., etc.; so, ψῆφον τίθεσθαι Hdt. :—ψήφῳ κρίνειν, διακρίνειν *to determine by vote,* Thuc., etc. :—in collective sense, ψ. γίγνεταί περί τινος *a vote is taken,* Antipho ; ἡ σώζουσα, ἡ καθαιροῦσα ψῆφος *the vote* of acquittal, of condemnation, Lys., Dem. :—τὴν ψῆφον ἐπάγειν *to put the vote* or *question,* like ἐπιψηφίζειν, Thuc.　**b.** *that which is carried by vote,* ψ. καταγνώσεως *a vote* of condemnation, Thuc. ; ψῆφος περὶ φυγῆς *a vote* of banishment, Xen.　**c.** *any resolve* or *decree,* e. g. of a king, Soph. ; λιθίνα ψᾶφος *a decree* written on stone, Pind. ; δίδοῖ ψᾶφον παρ' αὑτᾶς [the oak] *gives judgment* of itself, Id.　**d.** ψῆφος Ἀθηνᾶς, *Calculus Minervae,* a proverb. phrase to express *acquittal.*—*The vote by* ψῆφος, *ballot,* must be distinguished from that by κύαμος, *lot ;* the former being used in *trials,* the latter in *elections.*　**4.** *the place of voting* (as πεσσοί for the place of play), Eur.

ψηφοφορέω, f. ήσω, *to give one's vote, vote,* Luc.

ψηφοφορία, ἡ, *vote by ballot,* Arist. : generally, *voting,* Plut. From

ψηφο-φόρος, ον, (φέρω) *giving one's vote.*

ψήχω, f. ψήξω, (ψάω) *to rub down, curry* a horse, Xen. : —*to stroke, pat,* Lat. *mulcere,* Eur.　**II.** *to rub down, wear away,* Anth.

ψίαθος, ἡ, *a rush mat,* Ar. ; Dor. pl. acc. ψιάθως, Id. (Deriv. unknown.)

ψιάς, άδος, ἡ, = ψακάς, *a drop,* Il.

ΨΙΖΩ : pf. pass. ἔψισμαι :—*to feed on pap* :—Pass. *to be so fed,* Anth.

ψιθυρίζω, Dor. -σδω : f. Att. ιῶ : (ψίθυρος) :—*to whisper, say into the ear,* Plat., Theocr. :—metaph., ὅταν πλάτανος πτελέᾳ ψιθυρίζῃ when the plane *whispers* to the elm, Ar.　Hence

ψιθύρισμα, ατος, τό, *a whispering,* Anth. : of trees *rustling,* Theocr. ; and

ψιθυρισμός, ὁ, *a whispering,* Luc.　**2.** *whispering, slandering,* N. T. ; and

ψιθυριστής, οῦ, ὁ, *a whisperer : a slanderer,* N. T.

ΨΙΘΥΡΟΣ [ῐ], ον, *whispering : slanderous,* Soph.　**II.** as Subst., ψίθυρος, ὁ, = ψιθυριστής, *a whisperer, slanderer,* Pind.　**2.** *twittering,* of birds, Anth. (Perh. formed from the present.)

ψιλικός, ή, όν, *of* or *for a light-armed soldier* (ψιλός) : τὰ ψιλικά, = οἱ ψιλοί, *the light troops,* Luc.

ψιλο-μετρία, ἡ, *heroic poetry,* as not being accompanied *by music* (v. ψιλός IV. 2), Arist.

ΨΙΛΟΣ, ή, όν, *bare,*　**I.** of land, ψιλὴ ἄροσις *a bare corn-field,* Il. ; πεδίον μέγα τε καὶ ψιλόν Hdt. : c. gen., γῇ ψιλὴ δενδρέων *land bare of trees,* Id. :—ψιλὴ γεωργία *the tillage of land for corn,* opp. to γ. πεφυτευμένη (*for vines* and *olives*), Arist.　**II.** of animals, *stript of hair* or *feathers, bare, smooth,* δέρμα Od. ; ἶβις ψιλὴ κεφαλήν *bald on the head,* Hdt.　**2.** generally, *bare,*

uncovered, ψιλὸν ὡς ὁρᾷ νέκυν Soph. :—c. gen. *bare of, separated from,* ψιλὴ σώματος οὖσα [ἡ ψυχή] Plat.　**b.** *bare, stript of appendages,* ψιλὴ τρόπις *the bare keel* with the planks torn from it, Od. ; ψ. θρίδαξ *a lettuce with the side-leaves pulled off,* Hdt. ; ψ. μάχαιραι *swords without other arms,* Xen.　**III.** οἱ ψιλοί (sc. τῶν ὅπλων) *soldiers without heavy armour, light troops,* such as archers and slingers, opp. to ὁπλῖται, Hdt., Thuc., etc. ; τὸ ψιλόν, opp. to τὸ ὁπλιτικόν, Xen. ; ψ. ἔχων τὴν κεφαλήν *bare-headed, without helmet,* Id.　**IV.** ψιλὸς λόγος *bare language,* i. e. *prose,* as opp. to poetry which is clothed in metre, Plat. ; also, ψ. λόγος is a *mere speech,* a speech *unsupported by evidence,* Dem.　**2.** ψιλὴ ποίησις *mere poetry, without music,* i. e. *Epic poetry,* as opp. to *Lyric,* Plat. :—but, ψιλὴ μουσική *instrumental music unaccompanied by the voice,* Arist.　**3.** Oedipus seems to call Antigoné his ψιλὸν ὄμμα, as being *the one poor eye* left him, Soph.　**V.** Adv. ψιλῶς, *merely, only,* Plut.　Hence

ψιλότης, ητος, ἡ, *nakedness,* of a plain, Plut.　**2.** *baldness,* Id.

ψιλόω, f. ώσω, (ψιλός) *to strip bare* of hair, Hdt. :—Pass. *to become bald,* Hes. : generally, *to be laid bare,* Xen.　**II.** c. gen. *to strip bare of, to strip of* a thing, Hdt.　**2.** generally, *to leave naked, unarmed* or *defenceless,* Thuc.　**III.** Pass. also of things, *to be stripped off* something, τὰ κρέα ἐψιλωμένα τῶν ὀστέων Hdt.

ψιμύθιον or **ψιμμύθιον,** τό, (ψίμυθος) *white lead,* used to whiten the face, Ar., Xen.

ψιμυθιόω, f. ώσω, *to paint with white lead,* τὸ πρόσωπον Plut. :—Pass., pf. inf. ἐψιμυθιῶσθαι Lys.

ψίμυθος [ῐ], ὁ, radic. form of ψιμύθιον, Anth. (Prob. a foreign word.)

ψίν, Dor. for σφίν, dat. of σφεῖς.

ΨΙΞ, ἡ, gen. ψιχός, ὁ, ἡ, *a crumb, morsel.*

ψιττακός, ὁ, *a parrot,* Plut. ; also ψιττάκη, ἡ, Arist. (A foreign word.)

ψιχ-άρπαξ, αγος, ὁ, (ψίξ) *Crumb-filcher,* name of a mouse in Batr.

ψιχίον, τό, Dim. of ψίξ, *a crumb of bread,* N. T.

ψογερός, ά, όν, *fond of blaming, censorious,* Pind. From

ψόγος, ὁ, (ψέγω) *a blamable fault, a blemish, flaw,* Simon.　**II.** *blame, censure,* Pind., Trag., etc. ; ψόγον τινὶ ἐπενεγκεῖν Thuc.

ψολόεις, εσσα, εν, (ψόλος) *sooty, smoky :* as epith. of κεραυνός, *smouldering, lurid,* Od.

ψολο-κομπία, ἡ, *smoky* (i. e. empty) *talk,* Ar.

ΨΟΛΟΣ, ὁ, *soot, smoke,* Aesch.

ψοφέω, f. ήσω : pf. ἐψόφηκα : (ψόφος) :—*to make an inarticulate noise, to sound, make a noise,* Eur. ; ψοφεῖ λάλον τι *sounds chatter-like,* as if it were tested like a pot, to see if it were cracked, Ar. ; ὥσπερ κύμβαλον ψοφεῖ Xen.　**II.** c. acc., ψοφεῖν τὰς θύρας *to knock at the door inside,* to shew that some one was coming out, Menand. :—also of the door (intr.), εἰ αἱ θύραι νύκτωρ ψοφοῖεν, i. e. if they *were heard to open,* Lys.

ψοφο-δεής, ές, gen. έος, (δέος) *frightened at every noise, shy, timid,* Plat. :—τὸ ψοφοδεές *timidity,* Plut.

ψοφο-μήδης, ες, gen. εος, (μήδομαι) meditating noise, uproarious, epith. of Bacchus, Anth.

ΨΟ'ΦΟΣ, ὁ, any inarticulate sound, a sound, noise, Hom., Eur., etc.; of musical instruments, ψ. λωτοῦ, κιθάρας Eur.　2. a mere sound, empty sound, noise, Soph., Eur.; ψόφου πλέως, of Aeschylus, Ar.

ψοφ-ώδης, ες, (εἶδος) noisy, Arist.

ψυγῆναι, aor. 2 inf. of ψύχω:—ψυγήσομαι, fut. 2 pass.

ψυδνός, ή, όν, or ψυδρός, ά, όν, (ψεύδομαι) false, Theogn.

ψύθος [ῠ], εος, τό, poët. collat. form of ψεῦδος, a lie, untruth, Aesch.

ψυκτήρ, ῆρος, ὁ, (ψύχω) a wine-cooler, a vessel holding from 2 to 6 μετρηταί, Plat.

ΨΥ'ΛΛΑ, ης, ἡ, a flea, Lat. pulex, Ar., Xen.

ψυλλο-τοξότης, ου, ὁ, a flea-archer, Comic word in Luc. formed like ἱππο-τοξότης.

ψῦξα, aor. 1 inf. of ψύχω.

ψῡχᾰγωγέω, f. ήσω, (ψυχαγωγός) to lead departed souls to the nether world, of Hermes, Luc.　II. metaph. to attract the souls of the living, to win over, persuade, allure, Xen., etc.: in bad sense, to inveigle, delude, Isocr. Hence

ψῡχᾰγωγία, ἡ, a winning of souls, persuasion, Plat.

ψῡχᾰγωγικός, ή, όν, attractive, persuasive, Plat.

ψῡχ-ᾰγωγός, όν, leading souls to the nether world, of Hermes.　II. evoking souls to question them, evoking the dead, Aesch.:—as Subst. a necromancer, psychagogue, Eur.

ψῡχ-ᾰπάτης [ᾰ], ου, ὁ, beguiling the soul, Anth.

ψῡχάριον [ᾰ], τό, Dim. of ψυχή, Luc.

ψύχεινός, ή, όν, (ψύχω) cooling, cool, fresh, Xen.

ψῡχή, ἡ, (ψύχω) breath, Lat. anima, esp. as the sign of life, the life, spirit, Hom., etc.; ψυχή τε μένος τε ψυχή τε καὶ αἰών, ψυχὴ καὶ θυμός Hom.; τὸν δ' ἔλιπε ψυχή, of one swooning, Il.; ψυχὴν παρθέμενος staking or risking one's life, Od.; so, ἐμὴν ψυχὴν παραβαλλόμενος Il.; μάχεσθαι περὶ ψυχῆς for one's life, i. e. to save it, Od.; τρέχειν περὶ ψυχῆς Hdt.; ὁ περὶ τῆς ψυχῆς ἀγὼν the struggle is for life and death, Soph.; ποινὴν τῆς Αἰσώπου ψυχῆς ἀνελέσθαι to take revenge for the life of Aesop, Hdt.; ψυχὴν ἀφιέναι to give up the ghost, Eur.　2. metaph. of things dear as life, χρήματα γὰρ ψυχὴ βροτοῖσι Hes.; πᾶσι δ' ἀνθρώποις ψυχὴ τέκν' [ἐστί] Eur.　II. the departed soul, spirit, ghost, Hom.　2. the soul or spirit of man, Lat. anima, opp. to σῶμα, Plat., Xen.:—ψυχή τινος, periphr. for the man himself, Soph.; also ψυχαί, souls, = ἄνθρωποι, Aesch., Ar.:—hence in addressing persons, ὦ μελέα ψυχή Soph.; ὦ ἀγαθὴ καὶ πιστὴ ψ. Xen.; πᾶσα ψυχὴ ὑποτασσέσθω let every soul be subject, N. T.　3. the soul, heart, ψυχὴν ἄριστε Ar.; ἐκ τῆς ψυχῆς with all the heart, Xen.　4. appetite, δοῦναί τι τῇ ψυχῇ, like Lat. indulgere animo, Aesch.　III. the soul, mind, understanding, ψυχὴν οὐκ ἄκρος Hdt.

ψύχιος, η, ον, (ψυχή) alive, living, Pythag. ap. Luc.

ψῡχίδιον, τό, Dim. of ψυχή, Lat. animula, Luc.

ψῡχικός, ή, όν, (ψυχή) of the soul or life, spiritual, opp. to σωματικός, Arist., Anth.　2. concerned with the life only, animal, ὁ ψ. ἄνθρωπος the natural man, opp. to ὁ πνευματικός, N. T.

ψῡχο-δαΐκτης, ου, ὁ, killing the soul, Anth.

ψῡχο-δοτήρ, ῆρος, ὁ, giver of the soul or life, Anth.

ψῡχο-λῐπής, ές, (λείπω) lifeless, Anth.

ψῡχο-μᾰχέω, f. ήσω, (μάχομαι) to fight to the last gasp, fight desperately, Polyb. Hence

ψῡχομᾰχία, ἡ, desperate fighting, Polyb.

ψῡχο-πλᾰνής, ές, making the soul wander, Anth.

ψῡχο-πομπός, όν, conductor of souls, of Charon, Eur.

ψῡχορρᾰγέω, f. ήσω, to let the soul break loose, i. e. to lie at the last gasp, Lat. animam agere, Eur.

ψῡχορ-ρᾰγής, ές, gen. έος, (ῥήγνυμι) letting the soul break loose, hence lying at the last gasp, Eur.

ψῦχος, εος, τό, (ψύχω) cold, ἐν ψύχει in winter-time, Soph.; ἐν τῷ ψύχει καθηῦδον in the cold, Plat.;— pl. ψύχεα, Att. ψύχη, Lat. frigora, frosts, cold weather, Hdt., Xen.　2. coolness, cool, ψύχεος ἱμείρων Od.; metaph., ψ. ἐν δόμοις πέλει Aesch.

ψῡχοσ-σόος, ον, saving the soul, Anth.

ψῡχο-τᾰκής, ές, (τήκω) melting the soul, Anth.

ψῡχόω, f. ώσω, (ψυχή) to give life to, λίθον Anth.

ψυχρο-δόχος, ον, (δέχομαι) receiving what is cold, οἶκος ψ. the cold-bath room, Luc.

ψυχρολογέω, f. ήσω, to use frigid phrases, Luc.; and

ψυχρολογία, ἡ, frigid phraseology, Luc. From

ψυχρο-λόγος, ον, (λέγω) using frigid phrases.

ψῡχρόομαι, Pass. to grow cold, be cool, Anth.

ψῡχρός, ά, όν, (ψύχω) cold, chill, Il.; so we say 'cold steel') Ib.; of water, ψ. ὕδωρ Od., Thuc.; and ψυχρόν alone, ψυχρῷ λοῦνται Hdt.; of dead things, νέκυς Soph.; also τὸ ψυχρόν=ψῦχος, cold, Id.:—Comp. -ότερος, Hdt., Plat.　II. metaph., Lat. frigidus,　1. of things and events, cold, unreal, ψ. ἐπικουρίη Hdt.; ἐπαρθεὶς ψυχρῇ νίκῃ Id.; ψ. παραγκάλισμα Soph.; ψυχρὰ τέρψις, ἐλπίς Eur.　2. of persons, cold-hearted, heartless, spiritless, Plat., Xen.　3. of language; cold, frigid, Plat., Dem.

ψυχρότης, ητος, ἡ, coldness, cold, Plat.　II. metaph. of persons, coldness of heart, Dem.: sluggishness, Plut.

ΨΥ'ΧΩ [ῠ], f. ψύξω: aor. 1 ἔψυξα:—Pass., f. 1 ψυχθήσομαι, f. 2 ψυγήσομαι: aor. 1 ἐψύχθην: aor. 2 ἐψύχην [ῠ]: pf. ἔψυγμαι:—to breathe, blow, ἦκα μάλα ψύξασα Il.　II. commonly, to make cold, cool, refrigerate, Hdt., Plat.:—Pass. to grow cold or cool, Hdt., Ar., etc.　III. to dry, make dry:—Pass., Xen.

ψωλός, ὁ, one circumcised, lewd, Ar.

ψωμίζω, f. Att. ιῶ, to feed with sops or tid-bits, Ar.:— Pass., οἷς ψωμίζεται with what tid-bits he is fed, Id.　II. to employ in feeding others, τὰ ὑπάρχοντα ψ.

ψωμίον, τό, Dim. of ψωμός, N. T.

ψώμισμα, ατος, τό, = ψωμός, Arist., Plut.

ψωμός, οῦ, ὁ, (ψάω) a morsel, bit, ψωμοὶ ἀνδρόμεοι gobbets of man's flesh, Virgil's sanies ac frusta, Od.; also in Xen.

ψώρα, Ion. ψώρη, ἡ, (ψάω) the itch, scurvy, scab, mange, Lat. scabies, impetigo, Hdt., Plat. Hence

ψωραλέος, α, ον, scabby, mangy, Xen.

ψωράω, or ψωριάω, to have the itch, scab, or mange, Plat.

ψώχω, (ψάω) to rub out, ψ. τὰς στάχυας N. T.

Ω.

Ω, ω, ὦ μέγα, twenty-fourth letter of the Gr. alphabet:
—as a numeral ω´ = 800, but ͵ω = 800,000. The name
of ὦ μέγα, great or long o, was given at a later period
to distinguish it from ὃ μικρόν little or short o : but
the form Ω was not adopted at Athens till the Archonship of Euclides (B.C. 403) ; v. sub E, H.

Changes of ω, esp. in the dialects : 1. Ion.
sometimes for α, as ὤνθρωπος ὤριστος for ἄνθρωπος
ἄριστος. 2. Ion. also for αυ, as θῶμα τρῶμα for
θαῦμα τραῦμα:—this is also Dor., ὦλαξ for αὔλαξ. 3.
Aeol. and Dor. ω for ου, as ὠρανός Μῶσα κῶρος
λιπῶσα for οὐρανός Μοῦσα κοῦρος λιποῦσα ; so, ου
and ους in gen. sing. and acc. pl. of 2nd decl. pass
into ω and ως. 4. Dor., ω becomes ᾱ, as πρῶτος
πρώτιστος θεωρός become πρᾶτος πράτιστος θεᾱρός ;
so gen. pl. of 1st decl. -ων becomes -ᾶν. 5. Aeol.
sometimes also υ, as χελύνη for χελώνη.

ὦ and ὤ, Exclamation, expressing surprise, but also joy
and pain, like our O! oh! with nom., ὦ τάλας ἐγώ
Soph., etc. ; with gen., ὦ χρυσῷ Theocr. 2. with
vocat. it is a mere address, ὦ θεοί, ὦ Ζεῦ, etc. ; with
imperat., ὦ χαῖρε Aesch.—In the first sense it is usually
written ὤ, in the second ὦ.

ὤ, Dor. for οὗ, gen. of ὅς, qui.

Ὠαρίων, Ὠαρίωνειος, Dor. for Ὠρίων, Ὠρίωνειος.

ὤας, τό, Dor. for οὖας, οὖς, the ear.

ὠβά, ἡ, in Laconia, a subdivision of the Spartan φυλαί
(clans), Plut. Hence

ὠβάζω, f. ξω, to divide the people into ὠβαί, Plut.

ὠγαθέ, crasis for ὦ ἀγαθέ.

ὠγινόμοι, crasis for οἱ αἰγινόμοι, Anth.

ὠγμός, ὁ, (ὤζω) a crying oh! Aesch.

Ὠγυγία, ἡ, Ogygia, a mythical island in the Mediterranean, the abode of Calypso, Od.

Ὠγύγιος [ῠ], α, ον, and ος, ον, Ogygian, of or from
Ogyges, an Attic king of mythical times ; hence generally primeval, primal, Hes., Pind. ; τὰς ὠγ. Θήβας,
τὰς ὠγ. Ἀθήνας Aesch.

ὤδας, Dor. gen. of ᾠδή.

ὧδε, demonstr. Adv. of ὅδε : I. of Manner, in this
wise, so, thus, and (more strongly) so very, so exceedingly, Hom., etc. :—ὧδε is answered by ὥς, so . . , as
. . , Id. ; followed by a relat., τίς ὧδε τλησικάρδιος,
ὅτῳ . . ; Aesch. ; ὧδέ πως somehow so, Xen., etc. 2.
of Condition, πρόμολ᾽ ὧδε come forth just as thou art,
at once, Hom. 3. of something following, thus, as
follows, Id. ; ὧδ᾽ ἡμείψατο Soph. 4. c. gen., ὧδε
γένους thus off for family, Eur. II. of Place,
hither, here, Soph., Theocr.

ᾤδεον, impf. of οἰδέω.

Ὠδεῖον, τό, the Odeüm, a public building, erected by
Pericles for musical performances, also used as a law-
court, Ar., Plut. From

ᾠδή, ἡ, contr. for ἀοιδή (as ᾄδω for ἀείδω), a song, lay,
ode, h. Hom., Soph., Eur. ; pl. lyric poetry, Plat. II.
song, singing, Plut.

ὡδί [ῑ], Att. stronger form of ὧδε, Ar., Plat.

ᾠδικός, ή, όν, fond of singing, vocal, musical, Luc.
Adv. -κῶς, Ar.

ὠδίν, ἡ, later form of ὠδίς, N. T.

ὠδίνω [ῑ], mostly in pres., to have the pains or throes
of childbirth, to be in travail or labour, Il., Plat.,
etc. 2. c. acc. to be in travail of a child, to bring
forth, Eur. II. metaph. of any great pain, to be
in travail or anguish, Od., Eur. : to work hard, to
travail, of bees, Anth. :—of the mind, ὥστε μ᾽ ὠδίνειν
τί φῄς so that I am in an agony as to what you mean,
Soph. 2. c. acc. to be in travail with a thing, c.
acc., Id., Anth.

ὠδίς, ῖνος, ἡ : Ep. dat. pl. ὠδίνεσσι :—mostly in pl. the
pangs or throes of labour, travail-pains, Il. ; ἐν μόναις
ὠδῖσιν at a single birth, Pind. ; ἐν ὠδίνων ἀνάγκαις
Eur. ; in sing. travail-pain, anguish, Pind., Soph. 2.
in sing. also, the fruit of travail or labour, a birth,
child, Aesch., Eur. ; ἄπτερον ὠδῖνα τέκνων, of young
birds, Eur. II. metaph. any travail, anguish,
Aesch. ; also in pl., of love, pangs, Soph., Plat.

ᾠδο-ποιός, όν, (ποιέω) making songs or odes, Theocr.

ᾠδός, ὁ, contr. for ἀοιδός, a singer, Eur., Plat.

ὠδώδει, poët. for ὀδώδει, 3 sing. plqpf. of ὄζω.

ὤεον, τό, poët. for ᾠόν, an egg, Simon.

ὤζησα, aor. 1 of ὄζω.

ὤζυρέ, ὤζυρά, crasis for ὦ οἰζυρέ, ὦ οἰζυρά.

ὤζω, (ᾦ) to cry oh! Aesch.

ὠή, a cry or call, oh there! Lat. heus, Aesch., etc.

ὨΘΕΩ : Att. impf. ἐώθουν, but 3 sing. also ὤθει, Ion.
ὤθεσκε : f. ὠθήσω and ὤσω : aor. 1 ἔωσα ; Ion. and Ep.
ὦσα, Ep. 3 sing. ὤσασκε :—Med., aor. 1 ἐωσά-
μην, Ion. and Ep. ὠσάμην :—Pass., f. ὠσθήσομαι : aor. 1
ἐώσθην : pf. ἔωσμαι, Ion. part. ὠσμένος :—to thrust,
push, shove, force onwards or away, λᾶαν ἄνω ὤθεσκε
he kept pushing it upwards, Od. ; ἀπ᾽ ὀφθαλμῶν νέφος
ὦσεν Ἀθήνη Il. ; ἐκ μηροῦ δόρυ ὦσε he forced the spear
from the thigh, Ib. ; ὦσαί τινα ἀφ᾽ ἵππων Ib. ; ὦσαι
ἑαυτὸν ἐς τὸ πῦρ to rush into the fire, Hdt. ; so, ὠθ. τινὰ
ἐπὶ κεφαλήν to throw him headlong down, Plat. ; κατὰ
πετρῶν Eur. ; ὦσαι τὴν θύραν to force the door, Ar. 2.
to push or force back in battle, Il. 3. to thrust out,
banish, Trag. ; ὦσαί τινα φυγάδα Plat. ; ὠθ. τινα ἄθαπτον
Soph. 4. metaph., ὠθ. τὰ πρήγματα to hurry matters
on, hurry them, Hdt. 5. absol., ὦσα παρὲξ pushed
off from land, Od. ; ὤθει βιαίως Eur. II. Med.,
mostly in aor. 1, to thrust or push from oneself, push
or force back, repulse, esp. in battle, τείχεος ἂψ ὤσασθαι Il. ; ὤσασθαι προτὶ Ἴλιον, προτὶ ἄστυ Ib. ; ὤσασθαι
τὴν ἵππον Hdt. ; ὠσαμένων τὸ κέρας Thuc. III.
Pass. to be thrust on, to fall violently, ἐπὶ κεφαλήν
Hdt. ; πρὸς βίαν Eur. 2. to force one's way, Xen.,
Plat. : to crowd on, throng, like ὠστίζομαι, Xen. Hence

ὠθίζομαι, Pass., like ὠστίζομαι, to push against one
another, justle, struggle, Luc. :—metaph. to wrangle,
Hdt. Hence

ὠθισμός, ὁ, a thrusting, pushing, ὠθ. ἀσπίδων, of shield
against shield, Thuc. II. (from Pass.) a justling,
struggling, of combatants in a mêlée, Hdt., Xen. :—
metaph., ὠθισμὸς λόγων a hot dispute, Hdt.

ᾤετο [ῑ], 3 sing. impf. of οἴομαι.

ὦϊξ, aor. 1 of οἴγνυμι.

ὡίσθην, aor. 1 of οἴομαι.
ὠκ, Dor. crasis for ὁ ἐκ.
ὦκα, poët. Adv. of ὠκύς, *quickly, swiftly, fast*, Hom.; strengthd., μάλ' ὦκα, ὦκα μάλ' Id.   2. of Time, ὦκα ἔπειτα *immediately thereafter*, Id.
ὠκέᾰ, Ep. for ὠκεῖα, fem. of ὠκύς.
Ὠκεᾰνίνη [ῑ], ἡ, *daughter of Ocean*, Hes.
ὠκεᾰνίς, ίδος, fem. Adj. *of or from ocean*, αὖραι Pind.
Ὠκεᾰνῖτις, ιδος, = foreg., Anth.   2. ἡ ὠκ. (sub. γῆ) *the shore of ocean*, Strab.
Ὠκεᾰνόνδε, Adv. *to Ocean*, h. Hom.   From
Ὠκεᾰνός, οῦ, ὁ, *Oceanus*, son of Uranus and Gaia, Hes.: wedded to Tethys, sire of Thetis, Il.—Homer's Oceanus is *a great River* (ὠκεανὸς ποταμός), which compasses the earth's disc, returning into itself (ἀψόρροος).   II. in later times, *Ocean* remained as the name of *the great Outward Sea*, opp. to the Inward or Mediterranean (θάλασσα, πόντος), Hdt., Pind., etc.
ὠκειάων [ᾰ], Ep. for ὠκειῶν, gen. pl. fem. of ὠκύς.
ὠκέως, Adv. of ὠκύς, Pind.
ὠκήεις, εσσα, εν, poët. form of ὠκύς, Anth.
ὤκιστα, Sup. Adv. of ὠκύς, *most swiftly*, Od.
ὤκιστος, ὠκίων, irreg. Sup. and Comp. of ὠκύς.
ὤκνεον, impf. of ὀκνέω.
ᾠκτείρα, aor. 1 of οἰκτείρω.
ὠκύ-ᾰλος, ον, (ἅλς) *sea-swift, speeding o'er the sea*, of a ship, Hom., Soph.
ὠκύ-βολος, ον, (βάλλω) *quick-shooting, quick-striking*, of the bow, Soph.; of arrows, Anth.
ὠκύ-δήκτωρ, ορος, ὁ, (δάκνω) *sharp-biting*, Anth.
ὠκύ-δίδακτος, ον, *quickly taught*, Anth.
ὠκύ-δίνητος, Dor. -ᾱτος, ον, *quick-whirling*, Pind.
ὠκυ-δρόμας, ου, ὁ, = sq., Anth.
ὠκύ-δρομος, ον, *swift-running*, Eur.
ὠκυ-επής, ές, gen. έος, (ἔπος) *quick-speaking*, Anth.
ὠκύ-θοος, α, ον, (θέω) *swift-running*, Eur.
ὠκύ-μάχος, ον, (μάχομαι) *quick to fight*, Anth.
ὠκύ-μορος, ον, *quickly-dying, dying early*, of Achilles, Il.; ὠκυμορώτατος ἄλλων Ib.   II. act. *bringing a quick or early death*, Hom.
ὠκύ-πέτης, ου, ὁ, (πέτομαι) *swift-flying, swift-running*, Il., Hes.; metaph. ὠκ. μόρος Soph.
ὠκύ-ποινος, ον, (ποινή) *quickly-avenged*, Aesch.
ὠκύ-πομπος, ον, *quick-sending, conveying rapidly*, Eur.
ὠκύ-πορος, ον, *quick-going*, of ships, Il.: of streams, *swift-flowing*, Aesch.
ὠκύ-πος, ον, rare poët. collat. form of sq., Anth.
ὠκύ-πους, ποδος, ὁ, ἡ: acc. masc. ὠκύπουν: Ep. dat. pl. -πόδεσσι, etc.:—*swift-footed*, of horses, Hom.; ἱππικῶν ὠκύπους ἀγών Soph.; κύνες Eur., etc.
ὠκύ-πτερος, ον, (πτερόν) *swift-winged*, Il.   II. ὠκύπτερα, τά, *the long quill-feathers in a wing*, Ar.
ὠκύ-ρόης, Dor. -ρόας, ὁ, = sq., Eur., Anth.
ὠκύ-ροος, ον, poët. Adj. *swift-flowing*, Il.
ὠκύς [ῠ], ὠκεῖα, ὠκύ, gen. έος, είας, έος: Ep. fem. ὠκέᾰ: pl., fem. ὠκέαι, Ep. acc. ὠκέας: dat. ὠκειάων: (akin to ὀξύς):—*quick, swift, fleet*, Od.; πόδας ὠκύς, of Achilles, Il.; πόδας ὠκέα, of Iris, Ib., etc.   2. = ὀξύς, *sharp*, Anth.   II. Adv. -έως, Pind.; but in form ὦκα, formed like τάχα, often in Hom.   III. degrees of Comparison, regul. ὠκύτερος, ὠκύτατος Od.: irreg. Sup., ὤκιστος Il., Aesch.

ὠκύ-σκοπος, ον, *quick-aiming*, Ἀπόλλων Anth.
ὠκύτης, ητος, ἡ, *quickness, swiftness, fleetness, speed*, Pind., Eur.
ὠκύ-τόκος, ον, *causing quick and easy birth*: metaph. of a river, *with quickening, fertilising power*, Soph.   II. proparox. ὠκύ-τοκος, *quickly born*:— as Subst., ὠκύτοκον, τό, *quick birth, easy delivery*, Hdt.
ὦλαξ, ακος, ἡ, Dor. for αὖλαξ.
ὤλαφος, crasis for ὁ ἔλαφος.
ὠλέ-κρᾱνον, τό, *the point of the elbow*, Arist.
ἸΩΛΕΝΗ, ἡ, Lat. ULNA, *the elbow*, or rather *the arm from the elbow downwards*, h. Hom., Trag., etc.; περὶ ὠλέναις δέρᾳ βάλλειν Eur.; ὠλ. ἄκραι *the hands*, Id.; ψήφους διηρίθμησε ὠλένῃ *with the hand*, Id.
Ὤλενος, ἡ, *Olenos*, a city of Achaia, Il.; prob. named from its lying *in the bend* (ὠλένη) *of a hill*.
ὤλεσα, aor. 1 of ὄλλυμι.
ὠλεσί-βωλος, ον, *clod-crushing*, Anth.
ὠλεσί-καρπος, ον, *losing its fruit*, ἰτέαι ὠλ., because these trees *shed their fruits* before ripening, Od.
ὠλεσί-οικος, ον, *destroying the house*, Aesch.
ὤλετο, 3 sing. aor. 2 med. of ὄλλυμι.
ὠλιγώρημαι, pf. pass. of ὀλιγωρέω.
ὠλίσθησα, ὤλισθον, aor. 1 and 2 of ὀλισθαίνω.
ὦλλος, ὦλλοι, Ion. crasis for ὁ ἄλλος, οἱ ἄλλοι.
ὠλόμην, aor. 2 med. of ὄλλυμι.
ὦλξ, ἡ, syncop. for ὦλαξ, αὖλαξ, *a furrow*, only in acc. ὦλκα, ὦλκας, Il., Mosch.
ὠμ-αχθής, ές, (ἄχθος) *heavy to the shoulders*, Anth.
ὦμες, Dor. for ὦμεν, 1 pl. subj. of εἰμί.
ὠμ-ηστής, οῦ, ὁ, (ὠμός, ἐσθίω) *eating raw flesh*, Il., Aesch., Soph., etc.; with a fem., Ἔχιδνα ὠμηστής Hes.:—as a mark of *savageness, brutality*, ὠμ. καὶ ἄπιστος ἀνήρ Il.
ὤμιον, Dim. of ὦμος, Anth.
ὤμμαι, pf. pass. of ὁράω.
ὠμμάτωμαι, pf. pass. of ὀμματόω.
ὠμο-βόειος, Ion. -βόεος, or ὠμοβόϊνος, α, ον, *of raw, untanned ox-hide*, Hdt., Xen.:—ἡ ὠμοβοέη (sc. δορά) *a raw ox-hide*, Hdt.
ὠμο-βρώς, ῶτος, ὁ, ἡ, (βιβρώσκω) *eating raw flesh*, Eur.
ὠμο-γέρων, οντος, ὁ, ἡ, *a fresh, active old man*, Il.
ὠμο-δᾰκής, ές, (δάκνω) *fiercely gnawing*, Aesch.
ὠμό-δροπος, ον, (δρέπω) *plucked unripe*, νόμιμα ὠμ., properly, the right of *plucking the fresh fruit*, Aesch.
ὠμο-θετέω, f. ήσω, (τίθημι) in sacrificing, *to place the raw slices* duly on the altar (v. μηρία), Hom.:—so in Med., ὠμοθετεῖτο Od.
ὤμοι or ὤμοι, = ὦ μοι, Lat. hei mihi, *woe's me*, Soph.
ὠμοίωσα, aor. 1 of ὁμοιόω.
ὠμο-κρᾰτής, ές, gen. έος, (ὠμός) *of rude untamed might*, or (ὦμος) *strong-shouldered*, Soph.
ὠμο-πλάτη [ᾰ], ἡ, (ὦμος) *the shoulder-blade*, Theocr.; mostly in pl. ὠμοπλάται, Lat. scapulae, Xen., etc.
ἸΩΜΟΣ, ὁ, Lat. HUMERUS, *the shoulder with the upper arm* (ὠλένη, ulna, being the lower), ἐπ' ὤμου φέρειν Od.; ὤμοισι φορέειν Il.; ἔχειν ἀνὰ ὤμῳ Od.; ὤμοισι τοῖς ἐμοῖσι 'by the strength of mine arms,' Hdt.; ἀποστρέφειν τὸν ὦ. to dislocate *it*, Ar.   2. also of animals, as of a horse, Lat. armus, Il., Xen.
ἸΩΜΟΣ, ή, όν, *raw, undressed*, Lat. crudus, of flesh, Hom.; ὠμὸν καταφαγεῖν τινά to eat one *raw*, proverb.

of savage cruelty, Xen.; so, ὠμὸν βεβρώθοις Πρίαμον Il.   **2.** of fruit, *unripe*, Ar., Xen.   **II.** metaph. *savage, fierce, cruel*, Trag., Thuc., etc. :—neut. pl. ὠμά, as Adv., *savagely*, Il.; Adv. ὠμῶς, Thuc., etc.; Sup., ὠμότατα διακεῖσθαι πρός τινα Isocr.   **2.** *rude, rough*, Soph.; ὠμότερος συκοφάντης *a more coarse, more unmitigated* sycophant, Dem.:—Adv. *rudely, coarsely*, Id.   **3.** (from 1.2) ὠμὸν γῆρας *an unripe, untimely, premature* old age, Od., Hes.

ὤμοσα, aor. 1 of ὄμνυμι.

ὠμό-σῑτος, ον, of the Sphinx, *eating men raw*, Aesch.; χηλαῖσιν ὠμοσίτοις, also of the Sphinx, Eur.

ὠμο-σπάρακτος [ᾰ], ον, (σπαράσσω) *torn in pieces raw*, Ar.

ὠμότης, ητος, ἡ, (ὠμός) *rawness* : metaph. *savageness, fierceness, cruelty*, Eur., Xen., etc.

ὠμο-τόκος, ον, *bringing forth untimely offspring* :— metaph. of a vine, Anth.

ὠμο-φάγος [ᾰ], ον, (ὠμός, φαγεῖν) *eating raw flesh, carnivorous*, Il., Thuc.

ὠμό-φρων, ονος, ὁ, ἡ, (φρήν) *savage-minded, savage*, Trag.   Adv. ὠμοφρόνως, Aesch.

ὦν, Ion. and Dor. for οὖν.

ὦνα, ὦναξ, crasis for ὦ ἄνα, ὦ ἄναξ.

ὠνάμην [ᾰ], aor. 1 med. of ὀνίνημι.

ὤνατο, 3 sing. aor. 1 of ὄνομαι.

ὤνεμος, Dor. crasis for ὁ ἄνεμος.

ὠνέομαι, f. ἤσομαι :—in Att. with syllabic augment, impf. ἐωνούμην (but ὠνέετο, ὠνέοντο in Hdt.) :—aor. 1 is very dub. (for the Att. aor. is ἐπριάμην): pf. ἐώνημαι: (ὦνος): Dep. :—*to buy, purchase*, opp. to πωλέω, πιπράσκω, as Lat. *emere* to *vendere* ; but in pres. and impf. *to offer to buy, deal for, bargain* or *bid* for a thing, Hes.; ὠνέεσθαι τῶν φορτίων *wished to buy* some of their wares, *began to bargain* for them, Hdt.; Κροῖσός σφι ὠνεομένοισι ἔδωκε gave it them *when they offered to buy*, Id.; ὤν. τι παρά τινος *from* another, Id.; ὤν. ἐκ Κορίνθου *to buy goods* from Corinth, Xen.:—c. gen. pretii, *to buy for* so much, Hdt., Att.:—absol. in partic., ὠνούμενος *by purchase*, Xen.; ὁ ὠνούμενος *the purchaser*, Id.; ὁ ἐωνημένος *the owner by purchase* (of a slave), Ar.   **2.** *to farm public taxes* or *tolls*, or rather *to bid for* them, ὠν. μέταλλα Dem., etc.   **3.** *to buy off, avert by giving hush-money*, Id.; ὠν. τινα *to buy* a person, of one who bribes, Id.   **II.** sometimes used as Pass. *to be bought*, as ὠνούμενά τε καὶ πιπρασκόμενα Plat.; pf. part. ἐωνημένος Id., Dem.; 3 sing. plqpf. ἐώνητο Ar.; in aor. 1 ἐωνήθην Xen.

ὠνή, ἡ, (ὦνος) *a buying, purchasing*, Lat. *emptio*, ὠνὴ καὶ πρᾶσις *buying* and *selling*, Hdt., Plat.   **2.** *a purchase, a bargain*, Eur.   **II.** *a contract for the farming of taxes*, Andoc., Plut.   **III.** *the purchase-money, price*, Lys., Plut.

ὠνήμην, Ep. aor. 2 med. of ὀνίνημι :—ὠνήθην, aor. 1.

ὠνήρ, Ion. and Dor. crasis for ὁ ἀνήρ.

ὤνησα, aor. 1 of ὀνίνημι.

ὠνητέος, α, ον, verb. Adj. of ὠνέομαι, *to be bought*, Plat.   **2.** ὠνητέον, *one must buy*, Luc.

ὠνητής, οῦ, ὁ, *a buyer, purchaser*, Xen., Aeschin.

ὠνητός, ή, όν, and ός, όν, verb. Adj. *bought*, of slaves, Od., Soph., etc.; ὠνητὴ δύναμις *a mercenary* force, opp. to οἰκεία, Thuc.   **II.** *to be bought, that may*

be bought, Lat. *venalis*, ἐλπίς Eur.; c. gen. pretii, δόξα χρημάτων οὐκ ὠνητή *not to be bought for* money, Isocr.; but, χρήμασιν *with* money, Thuc.

ὤνθρωπε, Att. crasis for ὦ ἄνθρωπε :—ὤνθρωπος, ὤνθρωποι, Ion. crasis for ὁ ἄνθρωπος, οἱ ἄνθρωποι.

ὤνιος, α, ον, and ος, ον, (ὦνος) *to be bought, for sale*, Lat. *venalis*, πῶς ὁ σῖτος ὤνιος; how's corn *selling?* Ar.; ἐς ὤνιον ἐλθεῖν *to come to market*, Theogn.; ὤνιον εἶναι *to be on sale*, Plat. :—τὰ ὤνια *goods for sale, market-wares*, Xen., etc.:—c. gen. pretii, αἵματος ἡ ἀρετὴ ὠνία Aeschin.   **2.** *venal*, of a magistrate, Arist.

ὤνητε, crasis for ὦ ἀνόητε.

ὤνομα, τό, Aeol. for ὄνομα.

ὠνομασμένως, Adv. part. pf. pass. of ὀνομάζω, *by giving names*, Arist.

ὤνοντο, 3 pl. impf. of ὄνομαι.

῏ΩΝΟΣ, ὁ, Lat. *venum, purchase-money, a price, sum paid* for a thing, Hom.; c. gen. rei, Λυκάονος ὦνον ἔδωκεν *for* Lycaon, Il.   **II.** *purchase*, Od.

ὠνοσάμην, aor. 1 med. of ὄνομαι.

ᾠνοχόουν, impf. of οἰνοχοέω.

ᾤνωμαι, pf. pass. of οἰνόω.

ὦξ, Dor. crasis for ὁ ἐξ.

ᾦξε, 3 sing. aor. 1 of οἴγνυμι.

῏ΩΟΝ, τό, Lat. *OVUM, an egg*, Att.   **2.** of the *eggs* or *spawn* of fish, Hdt.

ὠόπ, also ὠὸπ ὄπ, a cry of the κελευστής to make the rowers stop pulling, *avast !* Ar.

ὤπασα, aor. 1 of ὀπάζω.

ὤπερ, Dor. for οὗπερ, *where*, Theocr.

ὤπλεον, impf. of ὀπλέω.

ὠπλίσσατο, Ep. 3 sing. aor. 1 med. of ὁπλίζω.

ὤπολλον, crasis for ὦ Ἄπολλον.

ὠπόλλων, crasis for ὁ Ἀπόλλων.

ὠπολοί, crasis for οἱ αἰπολοί.

ὦπται, 3 sing. pf. pass. of ὁράω.

ὤπτησα, aor. 1 of ὀπτάω.

ὤρ, ἡ, Ep. dat. pl. ὤρεσσιν, contr. for ὄαρ.

῏ΩΡΑ, Ion. ὤρη, ἡ, (akin to οὖρος B) *care, concern, heed, regard* for a person or thing, c. gen., Hes., Soph.; μηδεμίαν ὤρην ἔχειν γυναικῶν Hdt.

῏ΩΡΑ, Ion. ὤρη, ἡ : Ep. gen. pl. ὡράων, Ion. ὡρέων : poët. dat. pl. ὥραισι :—Lat. *hora* : *any time* or *period*, whether of the year, month, or day (νυκτός τε ὥραν καὶ μηνὸς καὶ ἐνιαυτοῦ Xen.): hence   **I.** *a part of the year, a season* ; in pl. *the seasons*, Od., Hes., etc.; περιτελλομέναις ὥραις Soph.; τῆς ὥρας τοῦ ἐνιαυτοῦ Thuc. :—at first three seasons were distinguished, —*spring*, ἔαρος ὥρη, ὥρη εἰαρινή Hom.; —*summer*, θέρεος ὥρη Hes.; ὥρα θερίνη Xen. ;—*winter*, χείματος ὥρη Hes.; ὥρη χειμερίη Od. ;—a fourth, ὀπώρα, first in Alcman.   **2.** absol. *the prime of the year, spring-time*, ὅσα φύλλα γίγνεται ὥρῃ Hom. :—in historians, *the part of the year available for war, the summer-season*, or (as we say) *the season*, Thuc., etc.   **3.** *the year* generally, Hdt.; ἐν τῇ πέρυσιν ὥρᾳ *last year*, Dem., etc.   **4.** in pl. *the quarters of the heavens*, the summer being taken as south, winter as north, Hdt.   **II.** *a part of the day*, αἱ ὧραι τῆς ἡμέρας *the times* of day, i.e. morning, noon, evening, night, Xen.; also, νυκτὸς ἐν ὥρῃ in night *time*, h. Hom.; ὕψε τῆς ὥρας *late in the day*, Dem.   **2. day and night**

were prob. first divided into *twenty-four hours* by Hipparchus (about 150 B.C.): but the division of the natural day (from sunrise to sunset) into *twelve parts* is mentioned by Hdt. (2. 109).　　**III.** *the time* or *season* for a thing, ὅταν ὥ. ἥκῃ Xen., etc.　　**2.** c. gen. rei, ὥρη κοίτοιο, ὕπνου *the time for* sleep, bed-*time*, Od.; ὥρη δόρποιο Ib.; καρπῶν ὧραι Ar.　　**3.** ὥρα [ἐστίν], c. inf., *'tis time* to do a thing, ἀλλὰ καὶ ὥρη εὕδειν Od.; δοκεῖ οὐχ ὥρα εἶναι καθεύδειν Xen., etc.　　**4.** in adverb. usages, τὴν ὥρην *at the right time*, Hdt., Xen.; but, τὴν ὥ. *at that* hour, Hes.:—ἐν ὥρῃ *in due time*, in *good time*, Od., Ar.:—also, αἰεὶ ἐς ὥρας *in successive seasons*, Od.;—καθ’ ὥραν Theocr.;—πρὸ τῆς ὥρας Xen.　　**IV.** metaph. *the prime of life, youth, early manhood*, ὥραν ἔχειν Aesch.; πάντες οἱ ἐν ὥρᾳ Plat., etc.; φεῦ φεῦ τῆς ὥρας! τοῦ κάλλους! ah! *what youth!* what beauty! Ar., etc.　　**V.**=τὰ ὡραῖα, *the fruits of the year*, Xen.

B. in mythol. sense, αἱ Ὧραι, *the Hours*, keepers of heaven’s gate, Il.; and ministers of the gods, Ib.; three in number, daughters of Zeus and Themis, Hes.; often therefore joined with the Χάριτες, h. Hom., Hes.

ὡραῖος, α, ον, *produced at the right season* (ὥρα), *seasonable, timely*: esp. of fruits, like Lat. *hornus* (from *hora*), βίος or βίοτος ὡρ. *store of fruits gathered in due season*, Hes.; ὡρ. καρποί *the fruits of the season*, Hdt.; so ὡραῖα, τά, Thuc., Xen.:—also of animals, ὡρ. ἄρνες *yearling lambs*, Anth.　　**2.** ἡ ὡραία, like ὥρα **1. 2**, *the summer season*, esp. the months during which the troops kept the field, Dem.; —but also, τὴν μὲν ὡραίην οὐχ ὕει it does not rain in *the season* (sc. of rain), Hdt.　　**II.** *happening* or *done in season, in due season, seasonable*, ἄροτος, ἔργον Hes.; ὡραῖόν ἐστι the weather is *fair*, Plut.　　**2.** metaph. *seasonable, due, proper*, ὡραῖα ἱερά Plat.　　**III.** of persons, *seasonable* or *ripe* for a thing, c. gen., γάμων or γάμου ὡραίη Hdt.; ἐς ἥβην ὡρ. γάμων Eur.: —of old persons, *ripe for death*, πατήρ γε μὴν ὡραῖος Id.; ὡραίῳ ἕσταμεν βίῳ Id.　　**2.** *in the bloom of youth, blooming*, Hes., Xen.:—generally, *beautiful*, N.T. Hence

ὡραιότης, ητος, ἡ, *ripeness of fruits*, Arist.　　**II.** *the bloom of youth*, Xen.

ὡρᾰκιάω, f. άσω [ᾰ], *to faint, swoon away*, Ar. (Deriv. uncertain.)

ὡρᾰνός, Aeol. for οὐρανός.

ὥρᾱσι, -ιν, Adv. (ὥρα) *in season, in good time*, Ar.

ὡρεί-τροφος, ον, poët. for ὀρεί-τροφος, of Bacchus, Anth.

ὠρέξαμην, aor. 1 med. of ὀρέγω.

ὠρεσί-δουπος, ον, poët. for ὀρεσί-δουπος, *making a din on the mountains*, Anth.

ὠρεσῐ-δώτης, ου, ὁ, (ὥρεα=ὡραῖα) *one who gives ripe fruits in their season*, Anth.

ὥρεσσιν, Ep. dat. pl. of ὥρ.

ὥρετο, 3 sing. aor. 2 med. of ὄρνυμι.

ὡρεύω, (ὥρα) *to attend to, mind*, c. acc., Hes.

ὥρη, ὥρη, ἡ, Ἰόν. for ὥρα, ὥρα.

ὡρη-φόρος, ον, (φέρω) *leading on the seasons*, or *bringing on the fruits in season*, h. Hom.

ὡρίζεσκον, Ion. impf. of ὡρίζω.

ὡρῐκός, ή, όν, (ὥρα) *in one’s prime, youthful, bloom-*

ing, Ar.: Adv., ὡρικῶς πυνθάνει you ask *so maidenly, so prettily*, Id.

ὥρῐμος, ον, poët. for ὡραῖος, *ripe*, Anth.

ὡρίνθην, aor. 1 pass. of ὀρίνω.

ὥριος, α, ον, and ος, ον, poët. for ὡραῖος, *produced in season*, ὥρια *the fruits of the season*, Od., Theocr.　　**II.** generally, *in due season, seasonable*, Hes., Anth.　　**III.** ὥρια, τά, *the season*, νόσον ὥρια τίκτει Bion.

ὡρισμένος, pf. pass. part. of ὁρίζω.

ὥριστος, Ion. crasis for ὁ ἄριστος.

Ὠρίων. ωνος, ὁ, *Orion*, one of the giants, a mighty hunter, loved by Aurora, slain by Artemis, Od.　　**II.** *a bright constellation* named after him, which rose just after the summer solstice, and was usually followed by storms, Hom. [ῑ in Hom., ῐ Att.]

ὡρμάθην [ᾰ], Dor. for ὡρμήθην, aor. 1 pass. of ὁρμάω.

ὡρμᾶτο, 3 sing. impf. pass. of ὁρμάω.

ὡρμέᾱται, -έᾱτο, Ion. for ὥρμηνται, -ηντο, 3 pl. pf. and plqpf. pass. of ὁρμάω.

ὥρνυεν, ὥρνῡτο, 3 sing. impf. act. and med. of ὄρνυμι.

ὡροθετέω, f. ήσω, *to take note* of a thing *in casting a nativity*, Anth.　　**II.** *to be in the ascendant at the natal hour*, of one’s ruling planet, Id.　　From

ὡρο-θέτης, ου, ὁ, (τίθημι) *one who takes note of times.*

ὡρό-μαντις, εως, ὁ, *the hour-prophet*, of the cock, Babr.

ὡρονομέω, f. ήσω, *to rule the hour* of birth, of planets, Anth.　　From

ὥροπε, 3 sing. redupl. aor. 2 of ὄρνυμι.

ὥρος, εος, τό, Dor. for ὄρος, *a mountain*, Theocr.

ὥρος, ὁ, *a year*:—in pl. *annals*, Luc.

ὥρσα, aor. 1 of ὄρνυμι:—ὥρτο, 3 sing. aor. 2 med.

ὡρύγή, ἡ, = ὡρυθμός, Plut.

ὥρυγμα, ατος, τό, = sq., Anth.

ὡρυθμός, ὁ, *a howling, roaring*, Theocr.

ὥρυξα, aor. 1 of ὀρύσσω.

ὡρύομαι [ῡ]: aor. 1 ὠρῡσάμην: Dep.:—Ion. and poët. Verb, *to howl*, properly of wolves and dogs, Theocr., etc.:—of men, ὄρθιον ὠρύσαι Pind.; of savages, either in mourning or joy, Hdt.　　**II.** trans. *to howl over*, τήνον μὲν θῶες, τήνον λύκοι ὠρύσαντο Theocr.; so, ὠρ. ἐπί τινι Luc.; περί τινα Bion. (Formed from the sound.)

ὡρχαῖος, Ion. crasis for ὁ ἀρχαῖος.

ὡρχεόμην, Ion. 3 dual impf. of ὀρχέομαι.

ὠρχεῦντο, Dor. 3 pl. impf. of ὀρχέομαι.

ὠρώρει, 3 sing. plqpf. of ὄρνυμι.

ὠρωρέχᾰται, Ion. 3 pl. pf. pass. of ὀρέγω.

ὠρώρυκτο, Ion. 3 pl. pf. pass. of ὀρύσσω.

ὡς: **A.** ADVERB of Manner, either ὥς (with accent) Demonstr. *so, thus*, Lat. *sic*;—or ὡς (without accent) Relat., as, Lat. *ut*.　　**B.** ὡς, as CONJUNCTION. **C, D.** various usages.

A. of Manner:　　**I.** ὥς, Demonstr. =οὕτως, *so, thus*, Lat. *sic*, Hom., Hdt.; rare in Att.:—καὶ ὥς, *even so, nevertheless*, μηδ’ ὥς, *not even so, in no wise*, Hom., Soph.　　**2.** in Comparisons, ὥς.., ὡς.., *so.. as.*., Lat. *sic.. ut.*., Il., Plat.　　**3.** *thus, for instance*, Od.　　**II.** ὡς, Relat., *as*, Lat. *ut*, first in Hom.; οὕτως ὡς, Lat. *sic ut*; but the antec. is often omitted: similés are commonly introduced by ὡς ὅτε, ὡς δ’ ὅτε, where ὅτε often seems superfluous, ἤριπε δ’, ὡς ὅτε πύργος [ἤριπε] Il.:—this

ὡς takes the accent at the end of a clause or when it follows the word dependent on it; θεὸς δ᾽ ὡς τίετο δήμῳ Il.; οἱ δὲ φέβοντο, βόες ὥς Od. **2.** *according as*, where the relat. Pron. ὅσος might stand, as ἐλὼν κρέας ὥς (i. e. ὅσον) οἱ χεῖρες ἐχάνδανον Ib.; σοὶ θεοὶ πόροιεν ὡς ἐγὼ θέλω Soph. **3.** parenthetically, to qualify a general statement, ὡς ἐμοὶ δοκεῖ, ὡς ἔοικε, etc., *as it seems*; often with γε or γοῦν added, ὡς γοῦν *as at any rate*:—these phrases become elliptical, ὡς ἐμοί or ὥς γ᾽ ἐμοί (sc. δοκεῖ); ὡς ἀπ᾽ ὀμμάτων (sc. εἰκάσαι) *to judge by eyesight*, Soph.;—also, ὡς Λακεδαιμόνιος (sc. ὤν) *considering* he was a Lacedaemonian, Thuc.; ὡς γυνή *as* a woman, *like* a very woman, Soph.:—so ὡς is attached to the Object of the Verb, συμπέμψας αὐτὸν ὡς φύλακα (sc. εἶναι) having sent him with them *as* a guard, Hdt.; ὡς ἐπὶ φρυγανισμόν *as if* for collecting fuel, Thuc. **III.** to limit or augment the force of Adverbs: ὡς ἀληθῶς *as* of a truth, i. e. *in very truth*, Plat.; also after Adverbs expressing anything extraordinary, θαυμαστῶς or θαυμασίως ὡς, ὑπερφυῶς ὡς, v. sub vocc.:—also with the Sup., like ὅ τι and ὅπως, ὡς μάλιστα, = Lat. *quam maxime*, ὡς ῥᾷστα, = *quam facillime*; ὡς τάχιστα, = *quam celerrime*, Hdt., etc.:—in the phrases ὡς τὸ πολύ, ὡς ἐπὶ τὸ πολύ Plat.; ὡς ἐπὶ τὸ πλῆθος Id. **2.** so also with Adjs., ὅπως ὡς βέλτισται ἔσονται Id.; ὡς ἐς ἐλάχιστον Thuc.

B. ὡς as CONJUNCTION: **I.** with Substantive Clauses, for ὅτι, Lat. *quod*, *that*, expressing a fact, μηκέτ᾽ ἐκφοβοῦ, ὥς σε ἀτιμάσει Soph., etc. **II.** ὡς with Final Clauses, *that, in order that*, Lat. *ut*; ὡς, and ὡς ἄν, Ep. ὥς κεν, being used, like other Final Conjunctions, with the subj. after the principal tenses of the indic., and with the opt. after the past tenses: cf. ἵνα B, ὅπως B. **2.** with past tenses of the indic. to express an event that is past, and therefore impossible, τί μ᾽ οὐκ ἔκτεινας, ὡς ἔδειξα μήποτε . .; *so that I never should* . ., Soph. **3.** ὡς c. inf., to limit an assertion, ὡς εἰπεῖν *so to say*, Lat. *ut ita dicam*, Hdt.; ὡς ἔπος εἰπεῖν, etc.; ὡς εἰκάσαι to make a guess, i. e. *probably*, Id. **III.** just like ὥστε c. inf., *so that*, Lat. *adeo ut, ita ut*, εὗρος ὡς δύο τριήρεας πλέειν ὁμοῦ in breadth *such that* two triremes could sail abreast, Id. **2.** ἢ ὡς after a Comp., μάσσον᾽ ἢ ὡς ἰδέμεν Pind.; μαλακώτεροι, ἢ ὡς κάλλιον Plat. **IV.** Causal, like ὅτι or ἐπεί, *as, inasmuch, as, since*, Lat. *quia, quandoquidem*, τί ποτε λέγεις; ὡς οὐ μανθάνω Soph. **V.** Temporal, like ἐπεί, *when*, Lat. *ut*, ἐνῶρτο γέλως, ὡς ἴδον laughter arose among them, *when* they saw, Il.; with optat., to express a repeated action, *whenever*, ὡς ἀπίκοιτο Hdt. **2.** ὡς seems to be used for ἕως or ἔστε, *so long as, while*, ὡς ἂν αὐτὸς ἥλιος αἴρῃ Soph.:—in later Gr. = ἕως, *while*, N. T. **VI.** = ὅπως, *how*, like Lat. *ut* for *quomodo*, μερμήριζε, ὡς Ἀχιλῆα τιμήσειε Il.;—so, οὐκ ἔσθ᾽ ὡς *nowise can it be that*, Soph.; οἶσθ᾽ ὡς ποίησον, by a mixture of constructions for ὡς χρὴ ποιῆσαι, Id.; v. *εἴδω B. 5. **2.** ὡς ἂν ποιήσῃς *however* thou may'st act, Id. **VII.** Local, for ὅπου, *where*, Theocr.

C. some special usages: **I.** with Participles, to give the reason or motive of the action expressed by the Verb, *if, as*, διαβαίνει, ὡς ἀμήσων τὸν σῖτον Hdt. **2.**

with Participles in the case of the Object, λέγουσιν ἡμᾶς ὡς ὀλωλότας they speak of us *as* dead, Aesch. **3.** with Participles put absolutely, ἐρώτα ὅ τι βούλει, ὡς τἀληθῆ ἐροῦντος (i. e. πιστεύων με ἐρεῖν) Xen., etc. **II.** so also before Prepositions, ἀνήγοντο ὡς ἐπὶ ναυμαχίαν (i. e. ὡς ναυμαχήσοντες) Thuc.; πλεῖς ὡς πρὸς οἶκον Soph.; ὡς ἐκ κακῶν ἐχάρη Hdt. **III.** the Preps. εἰς, ἐπί, came to be omitted, and ὡς itself appears to be used as a Prep. c. acc., but only c. acc. pers., τὸν ὅμοιον ἄγει θεὸς ὡς τὸν ὅμοιον god brings like *to* like, Od.; ὡς Ἄγιν ἐπρεσβεύσαντο Thuc.

D. ὡς before independent sentences:— **I.** ὡς as an emphatic exclamation, *how*, as Lat. *ut* for *quam*, ὡς ἄνοον κραδίην ἔχες *how* silly a heart hadst thou! Il.; ὡς ἀγαθόν Od.; ὡς ἀστεῖος ὁ ἄνθρωπος *how* charming he is! Plat. **2.** when it is joined to a Verb, its force extends to the whole sentence, ὥς ὑπερδέδοικά σου *how greatly* do I fear for thee, Soph. **3.** it also denotes a quick succession of events, ὡς ἴδεν, ὥς μιν Ἔρως φρένας ἀμφεκάλυψεν *how* he saw, *how* did Love encompass his heart, i. e. he saw *and straightway* Love . ., Il.; ὡς ἴδον, ὡς ἐμάνην, ὥς μευ περὶ θυμὸς ἰάφθη Theocr.; (so Virg. *ut vidi, ut perii, ut me malus abstulit error*). **II.** ὡς to express a wish, like εἴθε, Lat. *utinam, oh that!* with the opt. ὡς ἀπόλοιτο καὶ ἄλλος Od.; ὡς μὴ θάνοι *oh that* he might not die! Ib. **2.** ὡς joined with other words of wishing, ὡς ὤφελες αὐτόθ᾽ ὀλέσθαι Il.; ὡς δὴ μὴ ὄφελον νικᾶν Od.

E. ὡς with Numerals marks that they are to be taken only as a round number, *as it were, about, nearly*, σὺν ἀνθρώποις ὡς εἴκοσι Xen.; παῖς ὡς ἑπταετής *some* seven years old, Plat.

F. ὡς in some Elliptical Phrases: **1.** ὡς τί (sc. γένηται); *to what end?* Eur. **2.** ὡς ἕκαστος *each separately*, Lat. *pro se quisque*, Hdt., Thuc.

G. Etymology: ὡς is an Adv. form of the relat. ὅς, as τώς of ὁ, οὕτως of οὗτος.

ὥς, τό, Dor. for οὖς, *ear*.

ὦσα, Ep. and Ion. for ἔωσα, aor. 1 act. of ὠθέω:— ὥσαιμεν, 1 pl. opt.

ὡσ-άν, or ὡς ἄν, Ep. ὥς κε or ὥς κεν, being ὡς with a conditional force added. **2.** *as if, as it were*, Dem., N. T.

ὥσασκε, Ep. for ὦσε, 3 sing. aor. 1 act. of ὠθέω.

ὡσ-αύτως, Adv. (ὥς, αὕτως) *in like manner, just so*, ὡς δ᾽ αὕτως Il.; ὡσαύτως καί . . *in like manner* as . ., Hdt.; so c. dat., ὡς δ᾽ αὕτως τῇσι κυσὶ θάπτονται Id.; ὡσ. ἔχειν Plat.

ὥσδε, Dor. for ὄζε, 3 sing. impf. of ὄζω.

ὡσ-εί, or ὡς εἰ, Ep. ὡς εἴ τε, Adv. *just as if, as though*, ἐφίλησ᾽ ὡς εἴ τε πατὴρ ὃν παῖδα φιλήσῃ Il. **II.** like ὡς E, with Numerals, *about*, Hdt., Xen.

ὡσθήσομαι, fut. pass. of ὠθέω.

ὡσίν, dat. pl. of οὖς.

ὥς κε and ὥς κεν, Ep. for ὡς ἄν.

ὥς περ, or ὥσπερ, Adv. of Manner, *like as, even as, just as*, ἀλώμενος ὥσπερ Ὀδύσσευς Od., etc.;—Hom. often puts a word between ὡς and περ, e. g. ὥς σύ περ αὐτή, ὡς τοπάρος περ, ὡς ἔσται περ; ὥσπερ εἶχον *just as they were, then and there*, Hdt.; εὐθὺς ὥσπερ

εἶχεν Xen. ;—strengthd., ὥσπερ γε exactly as, Ar. ; ὁμοίως, ὥσπερ Thuc.   II. to limit or modify an assertion, like ὡσπερεί, as it were, Lat. tanquam, ὥσπερ ἐγγελῶσα Soph.   III. of Time, as soon as, Ar.

ὥσπερ εἰ or ὡσπερεί, Adv., just as if, even as, Lat. quasi, tanquam, ὥσπερ εἰ παρεστάτεις Aesch., ὥσπερ τις μηδὲν διδοίη Soph.   II. ὥσπερ ἂν εἰ or ὡσπερανεί (which properly is elliptical for ὥσπερ ἂν ἦν, εἰ . .), Plat.

ὥσπερ οὖν or ὡσπεροῦν, Adv. even as, just as, ὥσπερ οὖν ἀπώλετο Aesch.   II. as indeed, as no doubt, εἰ δ' ἔστιν (ὥσπερ οὖν ἐστι) θεός Plat.

ὥσ-τε,   A. as Adv., bearing the same relation to ὡς, as ὥστε to ὅς, and used by Hom. more frequently than ὡς in similes ; rare in Att. Poets, κατώρυχες δ' ἔναιον ὥστ' ἀήσυροι μύρμηκες Aesch., etc.   II. as, as being, like ἅτε, Lat. utpote, ῥεῖα μάλ', ὥστε θεός very easily, as being a goddess, Il. ; ὥστε περὶ ψυχῆς since it was for life, Od. ; ὥστε ταῦτα νομίζων Hdt.   B. as Conjunction, to express the result or effect of the action in the principal clause :   I. with Inf. so as to do a thing, εἰ δέ σοι θυμὸς ἐπέσσυται, ὥστε νέεσθαι if thy heart is bent upon returning, Il. ; οὐ τηλίκος, ὥστε πιθέσθαι not of such age as to obey, Od. ; freq. in Att.   2. after Comparatives with ἤ, when the possibility of the consequence is denied, μέζω κακὰ ἢ ὥστε ἀνακλαίειν greater woes than that one is wont to weep for, i. e. too great for tears, Hdt. ; μεῖζον ἢ ὥστε φέρειν δύνασθαι κακόν Xen. :—the Posit. is sometimes put for the Comp., ψυχρὸν ὥστε λούσασθαι (for ψυχρότερον ἢ ὥστε . .) too cold to bathe in, Id.   3. on the condition that . ., like ἐφ' ᾧτε, παραδοῦναι σφᾶς αὐτοὺς Ἀθηναίοις, ὥστε βουλεῦσαι ὅ τι ἂν ἐκείνοις δοκῇ Thuc.   II with the Indic., to express the result with emphasis, οὐχ οὕτω φρενοβλαβέες, ὥστε ἐβούλοντο not so insane, as to wish, Hdt. ; βέβηκεν, ὥστε πᾶν ἔξεστι φωνεῖν Soph., etc.   2. at the beginning of a sentence, to mark a strong conclusion, and so, therefore, consequently, ὥστ' ὄλωλα καί σε προσδιαφθερῶ Id. ; with the Imper., ὥστε μὴ λίαν στένε Soph. ; ὥστε θάρρει Xen.   III. with part., for inf., by attraction to a participle in the principal clause, τοσοῦτον διενεγκόντες, ὥσθ' ἐπιτάττοντες differing so much as to impose commands, Isocr.

ὡστίζομαι, f. Att. ὡστιοῦμαι : Med. :—Frequentat. of ὠθέομαι, to push and be pushed about, mostly c. dat. pers., ὡστιεῖ Κλεονύμῳ you will justle with Cleonymus, Ar. ; ὡστιοῦνται ἀλλήλοισι περὶ πρώτου ξύλου Id. ; absol., εἰς τὴν προεδρίαν πᾶς ἀνὴρ ὡστίζεται justles for the first seat, Id.

ὥστοργος, Dor. crasis for ὁ ἄστοργος.

ὠσφρόμην, aor. 2 of ὀσφραίνομαι.

ὤσω, fut. of ὠθέω.

ὠτἀκουστέω, f. ήσω, to hearken to, listen, watch covertly, Hdt., Xen., etc. From

ὠτ-ἀκουστής, οῦ, ὁ, (ἀκούω) a listener, spy, Arist.

ὠτάν or ὠτάν, ὦ τᾶν or ὦ τάν, v. τάν, τᾶν.

ὠτάριον [ᾰ], τό, Dim. of οὖς, a little ear, Anth.

ὦτε, Dor. for ὅτε (Α), Pind.

ὠτειλή, ἡ, a wound just inflicted, δεῖξεν αἷμα κατάρρεον ἐξ ὠτειλῆς Il. ; αἷμ' ἔτι θερμὸν ἀνήνοθεν ἐξ ὠτ. Ib.   II.

the mark of a wound, a scar, Xen., Plut. (Deriv. uncertain.)

ὠτίον, τό, Dim. of οὖς, but often = οὖς, Anth., N. T.

ὠτίς, ίδος, ἡ, (οὖς) a kind of bustard with long ear-feathers, prob. the great bustard, Xen.

ὠτρύνα, aor. of ὀτρύνω.

ὠτώεις, εσσα, εν, (οὖς, ὠτός) poët. Adj. with ears or handles, Il., Hes.

ωὑτός, Ion. and Dor. for ὁ αὐτός.

ὤφειλα, aor. 1 of ὀφέλλω.

ὠφέλεια and ὠφελία, Ion. ὠφελίη, ἡ : (ὠφελέω) :—help, aid, succour, assistance, esp. in war, Thuc. ; τὴν ὠφ. παρέχειν τινί Id. ; ὠφελίας τυγχάνειν Id. ; οὐ μετὰ τῶν κειμένων νόμων ὠφελίας not for such assistance as is consistent with the laws (ὠφελίας being = ὠφελίας ἕνεκα) Id.   II. utility, use, profit, advantage, benefit, Hdt., Soph. ; c. gen. objecti, ἐπ' ὠφελείᾳ τῶν φίλων for service to them, for their benefit, Plat.   2. a source of gain or profit, a benefit, service, Id., etc.   3. spoil, booty, game, Xen., Plut.

ὠφελές, ε, 2 and 3 sing. aor. 2 of ὀφέλλω II.

ὠφελέω, f. ήσω : aor. 1 ὠφέλησα : pf. -ηκα : plqpf. ὠφελήκη :—Pass., f. ὠφεληθήσομαι, and fut. med. in pass. sense, ὠφελήσομαι : aor. 1 ὠφελήθην : pf. ὠφέλημαι : 3 sing. plqpf. ὠφέλητο : (ὄφελος) :—to help, aid, assist, succour, to be of use or service to any one :   1. absol. to be of use or service, τὰ μηδὲν ὠφελοῦντα Aesch. ; οὐδὲν ὠφελεῖ Thuc.   2. mostly c. acc. pers., like Lat. juvare, to be of service to, to benefit, Hdt., Aesch., etc. ; ὠφ. τινα ἔς τι to be of use to one towards a thing, Thuc.   3. more rarely c. dat. pers., like Lat. prodesse, Trag., Antipho.   4. once c. gen., οὐδεὶς ἔρωτος τοῦδ' ἐφαίνετ' ὠφελῶν no one appeared to help towards this desire, Soph.   5. c. acc. cogn., ὠφέλειαν ὠφ. τινα to render him a service, Plat. ; so with a neut. Adj., οὐδὲν τινα ὠφ. to do one no service, Hdt. (v. supr. 1) ; πολλά, πλέον, πλεῖστον, ὡς πλεῖστα ὠφ. Eur., etc.   II. Pass. to be helped, i. e. to receive help, aid, or succour, to derive profit or advantage, πρός τινος from a person or thing, Hdt. ; ἔκ τινος Aesch. ; ἀπό τινος Thuc. ; ὑπό or παρά τινος Plat. ; c. part., ὠφελεῖσθαι ἰδών to be profited by the sight of a thing, Thuc. ; c. adj. neut., οὐδὲν ὠφελουμένη Soph.

ὠφέλημα, ατος, τό, a useful or serviceable thing, a service, benefit, Aesch., Eur.   II. generally, use, advantage, profit, Soph., Xen. ; and

ὠφέλησις, εως, ἡ, a helping, aiding ; and so (generally) like ὠφέλεια, use, service, advantage, Soph. ; and

ὠφελητέος, α, ον, verb. Adj. necessary or proper to be assisted, Xen.   II. ὠφελητέον, one must assist, τὴν πόλιν Id.

ὠφελία, Ion. -ίη, v. sub ὠφέλεια.

ὠφέλιμος, ον and η, ον, helping, useful, serviceable, profitable, advantageous, beneficial, of persons and things, Thuc., Plat., etc. ; τινι to one, Eur., etc. ; ἔς τι for a purpose, Thuc. ; πρός τι Plat. ;—τὸ ὠφ. as Subst., Id. :—Adv. -μως, Xen. ; Sup. -ώτατα, Id.

ὤφελλον, Ep. for ὤφελον, aor. 2 of ὀφέλλω.

ὠφήμερε, crasis for ὦ ἐφήμερε.

ὤφθην, aor. 1 pass. of ὁράω.

ὤφληκα, pf. of ὀφλισκάνω.

ὦφλον, aor. 2 of ὀφλισκάνω.

ὦχα, pf. of οἴγνυμι :—ὦχατο, Ion. for ῳγμένοι ἦσαν, 3 pl. plqpf. pass.

ῴχετο, 3 sing. impf. of οἴχομαι.

ὠχράω, f. ήσω, to turn pale or wan, ὠχρᾶν χρόα to be wan of countenance, Od. ; and

ὠχριάω, = ὠχράω, to be pallid, Ar., Arist.

ΩΧΡΟ΄Σ, ά, όν, pale, wan, sallow, of complexion, Eur., Ar. ; of a frog, Batr. :—τὸ ὠχρόν the colour yellow, Plat.　Hence

ὦχρος, ου, ὁ, paleness, wanness, esp. the pale hue of fear, ὦχρος δέ μιν εἷλε παρειάς Il. ; and

ὠχρότης, ητος, ἡ, paleness, Plat.

ῴχωκα, Ion. pf. of οἴχομαι.

ὤψ, ἡ, (ὄψομαι, fut. of ὁράω) the eye, face, countenance, Hom., Hes. ; εἰς ὦπα ἰδέσθαι τινί to look one in the face, Il. ; and absol., εἰς ὦπα ἰδέσθαι Od. ; but, θεῆς εἰς ὦπα ἔοικεν in face she is like the goddesses, Il.

ὦψαι, 2 sing. pf. pass. of ὁράω.

NOTES

NOTES

NOTES

NOTES

NOTES

NOTES

NOTES

NOTES

NOTES

NOTES

NOTES

NOTES

NOTES

NOTES